RECORD COLLECTOR

RARE RECORD PRICE GUIDE 2006

PUBLISHED BY
RECORD COLLECTOR MAGAZINE
THE WORLD'S LEADING PUBLICATION FOR
COLLECTORS OF RARE RECORDS AND MEMORABILIA

EDITOR
Jack Kane

EDITOR IN CHIEF
Alan Lewis

ADDITIONAL RESEARCH
Jake Kennedy
Tim Jones
Joel McIver

ART DIRECTOR
Ian Gray

PRODUCTION MANAGER
Val Cutts

Published in the United Kingdom 2004 by
Diamond Publishing Ltd. Room 101, 140 Wales Farm Road, London W3 6UG

Founded by Sean O'Mahony in 1987.

Printed in England ISBN No. 0 9532601 4 3

CONTENTS

THE ULTIMATE COLLECTOR'S GUIDE 4

HOW TO USE THE GUIDE 6

HISTORY OF THE GUIDE 10

STATE OF THE MARKET 12

USING THE GUIDE: A brief summary 16

ACKNOWLEDGEMENTS 17

IMPORTANT TERMS used in the guide 18

ADVERTISEMENT SECTION:
Record Fairs, Specialist Shops and Services 20

RARE RECORD PRICE GUIDE 32

VARIOUS ARTISTS COMPILATIONS 1417

FILM & TV SOUNDTRACKS 1447

ORIGINAL CAST RECORDINGS 1457

SPOKEN WORD RECORDINGS 1460

MUSIC LIBRARY LPs 1460

ADDENDA 1462

RECORD COLLECTOR'S
BACK ISSUES INDEX 1476

PAGES FOR YOUR NOTES 1494

RECORD COLLECTOR'S
GRADING SYSTEM 1502

RECORD COLLECTOR'S
GRADING READY RECKONER 1503

ABBREVIATIONS used in the guide 1504

THE ULTIMATE COLLECTOR'S GUIDE

Welcome to the seventh edition of the *Rare Record Price Guide*, the largest and most comprehensive book of its kind. Like its predecessors, this volume has been compiled by the expert research team of *Record Collector*, the world's leading magazine in the field.

The goal of this book is simple: to list and value every collectable pop and rock record issued in the UK since 1950. As regular readers will already know, the *Rare Record Price Guide* doesn't just include vinyl singles, EPs and LPs, although they are still very heavily featured. It also provides information about every other way in which recorded music has been sold to the public over the last 50 years or more, from the brittle 78rpm shellac singles of the 1950s, to the latest permutations of digital sound on compact discs and beyond. We certainly haven't forgotten tape, either, in all its various forms, from old reel-to-reels through the heyday of the 8-track cartridge and the cassette to the digital audio tapes (DATs) of more recent years, though they are becoming less collectable.

Musically, the coverage is equally diverse and thorough. Although the majority of items listed in this book could be at least vaguely described as 'rock' or 'pop', every aspect of music-making outside the specialist classical field is featured in these pages. For nearly 30 years, record collecting itself has expanded enormously, both in terms of the number of people taking part and the types of music that they are interested in.

THE BEATLES

Rest assured that no matter how obscure your tastes, you'll find the most sought-after items here — whether your particular obsession is 50s rockabilly or 60s MOR, 70s jazz-funk or 80s post-punk, 90s Acid Jazz or today's nu-blues. If it's collectable, and it was released in the UK, then you'll find it in the *Rare Record Price Guide*.

WHO SAYS HOW MUCH IT'S WORTH?

The question we're always asked about the prices listed in this book is how we calculate them. The answer is a mix of our 25 years of experience in the field; our ongoing research into the latest prices at record fairs and shops, and in sales both via mail order and online; and the invaluable help of a dedicated and extremely knowledgeable team of consultants and experts, who themselves regularly buy and sell items in their specialist areas.

ELVIS PRESLEY

As we always say, however, there is no fixed price for a second-hand record, no matter how rare it is. There are still bargains to be found out there, while in other situations — like a feverishly competitive auction — particularly sought-after items can fetch prices way above their 'book' value. The price of a rare record is purely determined by what people are prepared to pay for it.

That said, our close scrutiny of the collecting market since the start of the 1980s allows us to make the best possible judgement about the records in this book. Prices may vary from one part of the country to another, or depending whether a disc is being sold in a shop, via an advert in *Record Collector*, at a major international fair, or on the net. But we believe that the values we list are the most accurate and realistic you'll find anywhere.

The other important point, which can't be repeated often enough, is that anyone selling records to a professional dealer can't expect to raise more than 50% of the prices listed here, except in very unusual cases. It doesn't matter whether you're selling rock'n'roll or jewellery, the same basic mark-up applies right across the collecting field, to cover the dealer's costs and profit margin. If you're selling directly to another collector, however, you can obviously hope to obtain the prices we list — though please remember that all the values in this book are for records in absolutely perfect (or 'Mint') condition. To find out what you should be paying, or charging, for a record in less than perfect condition, check the Ready Reckoner printed at the back of this book.

ACROSS THE AGES

Although many of the most valuable items listed in the *Rare Record Price Guide* date back to the 1950s and 1960s, don't be fooled into thinking that record collecting is all about the distant past. As you turn the pages, you'll find plenty of releases from the 21st century as well as the 20th — the latest promos by major artists, for example, alongside limited edition singles by cult indie bands, and other rarities which were on sale one day and then became fiendishly hard to track down the next.

Check the details of those brand-new collectables, and you'll get some idea which of tomorrow's releases are likely to be sought-after in the future. But there are some things you can't predict — like the identity of the next rock band to emerge from obscurity, and become international superstars. Don't forget that virtually every record listed in this book, even the ones worth several thousand pounds, was once available for a few pounds, or even pence. For all those thousands of releases which have already become collector's items, however, the *Rare Record Price Guide* tells you what they are, what they look like, and how much they're going to cost.

HOW TO USE THE GUIDE

PRICING YOUR RECORDS

Although the *Rare Record Price Guide 2006* contains a comprehensive listing of collectable UK releases, it does NOT list all the recordings made by the artists we've included. More detailed discographies of important artists can be found every month in *Record Collector* magazine.

MINIMUM VALUES FOR INCLUSION

ONLY THOSE RELEASES WHICH ARE CURRENTLY SOLD AT THE MINIMUM VALUES LISTED BELOW HAVE BEEN INCLUDED.

Any other releases obviously sell for less than these prices.

7" SINGLES, MAXI-SINGLES, CASSETTE SINGLES, DOUBLE PACKS & FLEXIDISCS	£5
78s	£6
10" SINGLES	£7
EPs, 12" SINGLES, CASSETTE EPs AND CD SINGLES	£8
LPs	£12
DOUBLE-LPs	£15
CD ALBUMS	£18

NOTE: EPs from the 1950s and 1960s usually sold at around twice the retail price of a 7" single. But most so-called EPs released since 1976 actually retailed at the same price as 7" singles. These records have been included in the Guide if they are worth £5 or more.

CURRENT MINT VALUES

The prices listed in this book are for the original issues of records, cassettes and CDs in MINT condition. Bear in mind that most records which turn up from the 1950s, 60s and even the early 1970s are NOT in Mint condition and their value will be affected accordingly. To find out the value of any item which is in less than Mint condition, consult our Grading System on page 1502 and the Ready Reckoner on page 1503.

ALPHABETICAL ORDER

The artists in this Guide are listed in alphabetical order, from A to Z. After the alphabetical listings, there is a section of Various Artists compilation releases, divided into several sections covering singles and 50s & 60s EPs, 70s, 80s & 90s EPs, LPs, film soundtrack LPs and original cast recordings from theatrical shows.

The alphabetical order within the Guide has been determined by the first letter of a group name or an artist's surname. The word 'The' has not been taken into account when placing artists in alphabetical order; for instance, 'The Beatles' are listed under 'B', rather than 'T'.

The order follows the usual alphabetical principle of 'reading through' an artist's name or title, so that (for example) 'Peter Gabriel' is listed before 'Gabriel's Angels', and 'Generation X' is listed before 'Gen X'. Names and titles which include numbers appear as if the number was spelt out in full; e.g. the band '2.3' are listed as if their name was 'Two.Three'.

CHRONOLOGICAL ORDER

Within each artist entry, records are listed in chronological order of release. Singles (including 7", 10", 12", CD, cassette, and double packs) are listed first; then EPs; and finally LPs (including cassette and CD albums).

In the case of long entries, different formats of releases have also been grouped together under separate headers to make them easier to find.

PACKAGING AND INSERTS

All prices refer to records with all their original packaging and inserts (where applicable) intact. Wherever possible, we have provided details of inserts and special items of packaging for each entry — pointing out gatefold sleeves, lyric sheets and other bonus items like posters, for example.

Any record with some or all of these additional items missing will obviously be worth less than the values listed here. The level of depreciation depends on the missing items: in some cases, the value of an album can be dramatically reduced without its collectable insert (as in the case of the Who's *The Who Sell Out* LP, for example), while in others, it is the record itself that is desirable, and the insert is only of secondary importance (as with the Picadilly Line LP, *The Huge World Of Emily Small*).

DOUBLE PRICES: PICTURE SLEEVES

Since 1978, all U.K. 7", 10" and 12" singles have usually been issued in picture sleeves. Before 1978, however, picture covers were definitely the exception rather than the rule.

All those singles which originally appeared in a picture sleeve are listed with the abbreviation '(p/s)'. Where the picture sleeve was only available with the first batch of singles, there are two prices listed: the first refers to the record with its picture sleeve, the second without. If only one price is listed, then the single has to have its picture sleeve intact and in Mint condition to qualify for this value.

Most singles from the 1950s, 1960s and early 1970s were issued in 'company' sleeves, carrying the name and logo of the label which issued the record. Unless a picture sleeve is indicated, the prices listed in this guide are for singles with their company sleeves intact and, like the records themselves, in Mint condition. Most collectors are not too concerned about company sleeves — although in isolated cases (like the cult 60s label Planet), the company sleeves can be harder to find than the records themselves.

Company sleeves don't usually have much effect on a record's value. For example, an original Creation single from 1966, valued at £40, may only be worth £30 without its Planet company sleeve. At the other extreme, no doo-wop collector is going to be bothered if a copy of a rarity like The Penguins' Earth Angel, valued at £1,800+, comes in a plain sleeve, or indeed, no sleeve at all — what matters here is that the record is in Mint condition.

DOUBLE PRICES: FREEBIES & INSERTS

Two prices have been listed for those items which were available in more than one form. 'Freebie' singles given away with newspapers and magazines have two values: the first for the record with the publication, the second for the disc itself. Records which were issued only briefly with an insert, like a poster or lyric sheet, are often priced both with and without the extra packaging.

DOUBLE PRICES: CHANGES IN DESIGN

Two or more prices have been given for records which were released more than once with the same catalogue number, but in slightly different form — with a change of label colour or sleeve design (for instance, the substitution of triangular centres by round centres on late 1950s singles), or the manufacture of more recent singles in a variety of different coloured vinyls.

These variations of packaging and presentation can make an enormous difference to the value of a record, which is why we have documented them here. They help collectors identify the first pressing or edition of each release, which is almost always more sought-after than later issues of the same record. One notable example is the first edition of the Beatles' *Please Please Me* LP, which featured the black-and-gold Parlophone label for a few weeks, before the introduction of the more modern-looking yellow-and-black label. Black-and-gold copies of the stereo version of this LP are worth £3000, as against £180 for the first yellow-and-black edition issued a few weeks later.

Occasionally, second pressings can be worth more than the originals, as is the case with early Shadows and Cliff Richard singles. Green label copies of these 45s sold in their millions, while later re-pressings on black labels are much scarcer. So always check which pressing of any record you are buying before parting with your money.

MONO AND STEREO

In the case of EPs and LPs from the 1950s and 1960s, mono and stereo releases often have different values — and different catalogue numbers. Both prices are listed, together with the separate catalogue numbers for the two versions of each release (mono first, then stereo). Where the mono and stereo editions are worth the same amount, only one price has been listed.

The last few years have seen a polarisation in the prices between mono and stereo pressings — increasingly so for those late mono releases from 1968 to 1970, when the single-channelled format was being phased out in favour of the twin-tracked stereo. Similarly, early stereo copies should prove to be sound investments.

UK RELEASES AND EXPORT ISSUES

Only U.K. releases are included in the *Rare Record Price Guide*, not overseas issues. The exceptions to this rule are a handful of folk releases and U2 singles, all from the Irish Republic, which were heavily imported into Britain, but not officially issued here. The other exceptions are 'Export Releases'. These were manufactured in the UK in the 1950s and 1960s by companies like EMI and Decca for distribution to countries which didn't have their own pressing plants. Because they were pressed in very small quantities, and then distributed to the furthest corners of the globe, export records by artists like the Beatles and the Rolling Stones are often worth many times the values of similar items pressed for the UK.

UK RELEASES PRESSED OVERSEAS

Although the great majority of the records we've listed were manufactured in the UK, not all UK releases were made in this country — or vice versa. For example, a large proportion of the Rolling Stones' US singles on the London label in the 1960s were actually manufactured in Britain. More recently, many British releases by major labels — notably Warners —

have been made in Europe, and sent in identical form to Britain and many other countries. In these cases, the record sleeves often carry many different catalogue numbers, to cater for every country where the records are being distributed.

The problem of identifying the country where a particular record has been issued has grown more difficult with the advent of CDs. In these cases, it is the packaging that helps you identify the origin of a particular CD, rather than the disc itself.

78rpm RELEASES

The market for 78rpm singles has slowed somewhat since the last RRPG. The common misconception about 78s is that they are more valuable than 7" singles. In fact, the opposite is true in most cases, as far more 78s were sold in the 1950s than 45rpm 7" singles.

The last batches of 78s issued from 1958 to 1960 are the main exception to this rule (see Elvis Presley's entry, for example). As these were often only available in small quantities (as the public switched to 45s), or even by special order, they can prove to be much harder to find than their 45rpm equivalents.

All these collectable 78s from the 1950s are included in this edition of the *Rare Record Price Guide*, although we've removed those titles issued prior to 1950 because these represent a very different era of popular music. The vast majority of 78s, it should be added, are worth less than £6.

COMMERCIAL RELEASES, NOT PROMOS

In general, this Guide only includes records which were manufactured for commercial release, or for distribution in some way to the public — as a freebie with a magazine, for example.

Promotional records, demos, acetates and test pressings have not usually been included, apart from exceptional cases where these items actually reached the public, or where (as with artists like the pre-Iron Maiden act, Urchin) one promo single has become so famous among collectors that it would have been misleading for it not to be mentioned. The major exceptions to this rule are artists like the Beatles, and modern artists like The Pet Shop Boys and Robbie Williams, whose promos are often more valuable than their commercial releases.

Full details of the values of non-commercial rarities like promos, demos, acetates and test pressings can be found in the articles and discographies in *Record Collector* every month.

IMPORTANT NOTE

Every effort has been taken to ensure that the information contained in this Price Guide is as accurate and up-to-date as possible. However, the publishers cannot take any responsibility for any errors or omissions; nor can they be held responsible or liable for any loss or damage to any person acting on the information in this Guide. The publishers welcome any corrections or additions to the Guide, which will be considered for future editions.

Email: rrpg@metropolis.co.uk

THE HISTORY OF THE RARE RECORD PRICE GUIDE

RECORD COLLECTOR MAGAZINE

Record Collector was first published in 1979, and the magazine quickly established itself as the bible of pop and rock history. When the magazine was born, record collecting was a small, rather disorganised business, which wasn't making much effort to encourage new people to get involved.

From the start, *Record Collector* set out to provide the information that collectors needed, whether they'd been buying and selling records for years, or were just starting to build up a collection. There were two vital things they wanted to know: what records had been released by their favourite artists, and how much were they worth?

Every issue of *Record Collector* has provided complete discographies (lists of record releases, complete with full catalogue numbers, release dates and current Mint values) for an amazing variety of performers, from pre-rock stars like Frank Sinatra to the latest chart-bound arrivals and cult indie bands, via every imaginable style and genre along the way. Our in-depth features have provided the essential information to help readers get the most out of their music — by explaining the history of the artists and the records.

THE CHANGING FACE OF THE RARE RECORD PRICE GUIDE

In 1987, we published our first price guide — a slim volume which was designed as a quick and easy reference source to records by around 2000 important artists.

That was only the beginning, though. We soon began work on the first edition of the book you're holding. Published in late 1992, the first *Rare Record Price Guide* filled 960 pages and listed 60,000 rare and collectable records.

The response to that book was tremendous, but we quickly realised that the collecting market was changing so fast that we couldn't rest on our laurels. Every year, thousands of new records reach the shops, in a bewildering variety of formats — everything from 7" singles and cassettes to expensive multi-CD boxed sets.

A small but sizeable proportion of these new releases became instant collector's items. Over the last 20 years, it's been common for record companies to issue special limited editions — anything from a few hundred to a few thousand copies — which sell out in a few days. The most sought-after of these records can triple or quadruple their value within a few months.

At the same time, interest in vinyl from the past continues to grow. As collectors track down all the records they want in a particular genre, they start to broaden their horizons. As a result, obscure items from the 50s, 60s, 70s and 80s become much-wanted treasures on the collectors' market — and their prices rise to reflect the new demand.

That's why we published a second edition, a year later, which grew to 1152 pages, with 70,000 records listed. And this was expanded again for the 1995 edition (over 75,000 entries and 1252 pages) and 1997/98 edition

(85,000 entries and 1440 pages), to take in all the latest collectable release The Millennium Edition ran to 1504 pages; another two years on, the *Rare Record Price Guide 2002* was bigger than ever, the RRPG 2004 was bigger still. Now you're holding the latest edition, covering more than 50 years of popular music in enormous detail.

THE BIRTH OF COLLECTING

When the collecting scene was in its infancy in the 1970s, the market was focused on particular artists or genres. All the early attention was concentrated on 1950s rock'n'roll, and 1960s beat music. In addition, major artists like the Beatles, the Rolling Stones, Elvis Presley and David Bowie began to attract specialist collectors. But the whole collecting scene blossomed during the 1980s and it's now true to say that there aren't any musical styles which *aren't* collectable. Folk, jazz, techno, rap, blues, heavy metal, punk, psychedelia, progressive rock, film soundtracks, soul, funk, reggae, disco, mainstream rock and pop, even classical — each genre boasts its share of in-demand rarities.

LIMITED EDITIONS

In the late 1970s, the arrival of punk spawned scores of new, independent record labels, which had fresh views about the way to market their releases. It became common for singles to appear in picture sleeves, as they had done overseas since the 1960s.

Records also began to appear on coloured vinyl or as picture discs, in an attempt to attract more buyers. Never slow to cash in on a marketing trend, the major record companies soon joined in. By the early 1980s, they were issuing a bewildering variety of editions of the same record in slightly different formats.

This sudden change in marketing techniques helped to trigger an entirely new development on the collecting scene. For the first time, records were becoming instant collector's items. A limited-edition single could be released one week, and sell for twice its retail price a fortnight later.

That opened the floodgates. No longer were 1950s and 1960s records the only things you'd find in the collector's shops. Now, it was open season, for anything and everything from Tubby Hayes to U2.

COMPACT DISCS

The arrival of CDs in the mid-1980s was greeted with doom and gloom in some quarters. But some CDs — notably compilations of old, obscure 45s — have actually helped to increase the market for old vinyl releases. So many vintage recordings are available on CD that record-buyers today have a wider musical choice than ever before.

If you grew up in the 1960s, you probably remember that it was difficult to find the records that had been hits only a few years earlier. Now, you can go into most record stores and buy compilations of music from every era of pop and rock history. For thousands of collectors, however, owning the music on a new CD isn't enough — and they track down the original releases of music made before they were born.

Fifteen years later, the CD is well established as a collectable format — particularly for promotional items, limited edition singles, and CD issues by 80s artists which have yet to be reissued.

STATE OF THE MARKET

Since the last edition of the *Rare Record Price Guide*, there have been the changes in the market which collectors have come to expect — very rare items have increased in value, while many low-grade collectables, especially from the 1980s and 90s, have dipped below the collecting radar. However, there have also been some unexpected developments: who'd have thought that with the explosion in downloading — legitimate and otherwise — and the apparent dominance of the CD, there would have been a resurgence in sales of the humble 7" single? In fact, that's just what has happened. Figures for the first quarter of 2004 show that sales of 7" singles grew by an incredible 48 per cent in the UK. Many of these sales have occurred outside the mainstream — former Blur guitarist and indie stalwart Graham Coxon released his single Freakin' Out *only* on vinyl, for example. However, even mainstream artists have been bitten by the vinyl bug. You'll find that most of Robbie Williams' collectables in the new *RRPG* are CDs, but even he has an eye for nostalgia — witness his promo 78, a new entry at £40.

12" singles are also looking healthier than they have for some time, largely due to the fact that they are favoured by the dance and hip hop scene. This area is reflected better than ever before in the new edition of the *RRPG*, with artists such as Brit-rappers Blade and Hijack represented for the first time.

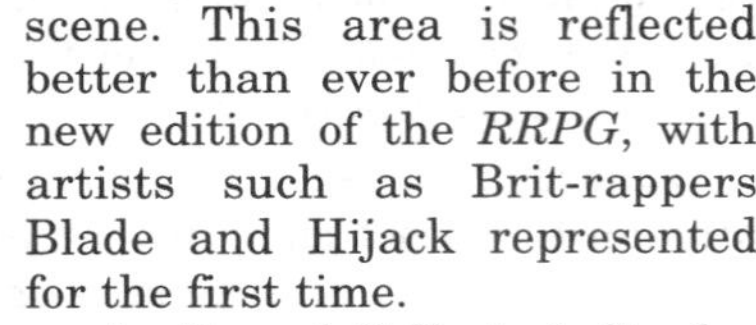

ROBBIE WILLIAMS

As *Record Collector's* Singles page demonstrates every month, the vinyl single is still the format of choice for many new acts. As well as being an unmatched promotional tool, the 7" is an ideal way to capture the attention of 'real' music lovers and the young fans who are essential for a band's success. They are also an economical way of getting the music 'out there'. Often, the fact that indie 7"s have a limited run can make them very collectable in a short space of time — the Australian band The Vines' first British single, Factory, was pressed up in a quantity of 500 only a few years ago, and is now worth £35. Also, bands such as the White Stripes have an overt fondness for old music and records, making all their releases available on vinyl — the double LP of their *Elephant* album is worth a substantial £125.

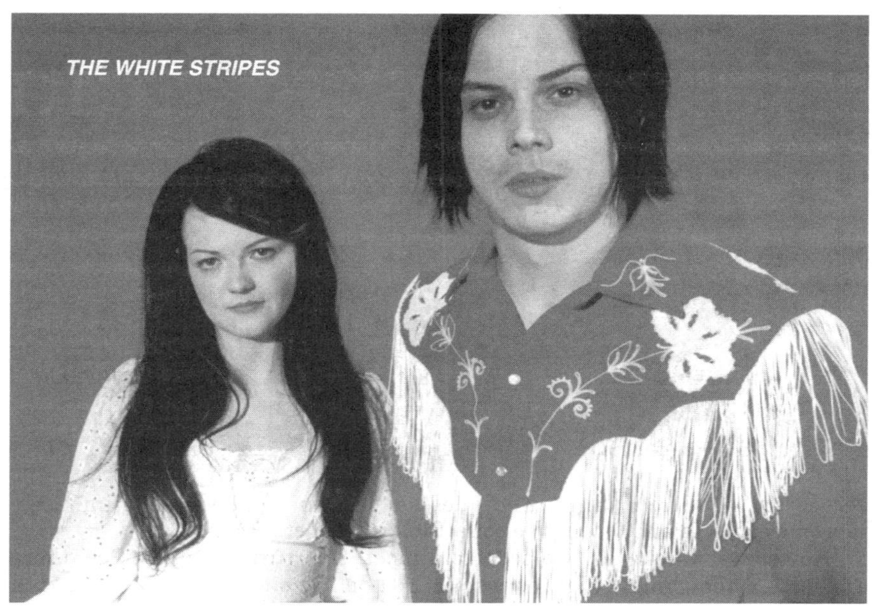

As well as having collector appeal, it now seems like vinyl may be the most *durable* format we have for recorded music — according to the giant collectors' shop Beano's, the CD has not proved itself as a long-term storage medium. New research shows that the aluminium foil in a CD can corrode, rendering the disc unplayable — such a thing has happened to many late-80s discs on the Phonogram label, which infamously turned brown. A scratch on a vinyl record only makes a certain part of the disc useless, whereas a flaw in a CD can mean that it is entirely unplayable.

New developments in music storage threaten to render the CD as obsolete as the cassette. In the last *RRPG* we discussed the possible effects which the new SACD and DVDA formats would have on the market. Millions of Britons now have DVD players, and should therefore favour the latter format, but it remains to be seen if both SACD and DVDA will become as collectable as their predecessors.

Even these novel formats could be rendered obsolete by digital downloading of music files. The hope of the music industry is that legal downloads will revive the market, but the threat of illegal file-sharing still looms large. Also, collectors do not appear to be well-served by the legal download sites — a common complaint lodged against the iTunes download service is that it does not make a catalogue available, so that you can't find out what's available before signing up. Even if you do decide to sign up, there's no guarantee that what you want will be available. Despite boasting over 700,000 songs, iTunes has been criticised by *Record Collector* readers for its paucity. One thing we do know is that much of the indie and underground music which we cover in *Record Collector* will not be available online — indie labels are boycotting iTunes, as they have deduced that it will be bad business to use it. Consequently, there will be music out there that will only be available on record — something that will no doubt increase its collectability.

There are also legitimate concerns regarding the format of digital downloads; mp3s, when created at 128kbs, have inferior sound quality compared to the newer download formats FLAC and SHN, and indeed, to CDs themselves. And all this is supplemental to the perennial bugbear of collectors, digital

LED ZEPPELIN

versus analogue recordings. The question is, can a collection of infinitely reproduceable 1s and 0s ever be collectable? Instinct says not.

Nowadays, whenever two collectors meet, talk turns to eBay. Yes, there are some astonishingly high prices reached on the site, but many items fall far short of their true value, disappointing the vendor and failing to reach their reserve price. The *RRPG* takes eBay prices into account, but is cautious when it comes to assessing the value of a record on the basis of what might be a one-off sale. For example, a Mint mono copy of the Rolling Stones album *Let It Bleed* was seen to go on eBay for the incredible sum of £1,040. This cannot, however, be taken as a serious price, as there are many Mint copies of it around, and if they were all put up for auction the price would soon drop. It should be seen for what it is — a freakish one-off. There are a number of problems with buying on eBay that one should be aware of. One of these is grading. *RC* has heard of many instances where a buyer has purchased a record listed as Mint or Ex, only to find that it is merely VG or even Good. The only thing one can do in this situation — if the vendor refuses a refund — is to leave negative feedback on the eBay website, which is not much comfort when you've shelled out £500 for a sub-par item. A more serious problem is that of rigged bidding: a vendor can enlist a crony to continually drive up bidding by small increments, therefore leading a serious bidder to end up paying very substantial sums.

Another serious problem is that of mis-selling. *RC* knows of one collector who was thrilled to purchase the A&M pressing of God Save The Queen by the Sex Pistols. He won this for what seemed to be the bargain price of £1,900, only to find out when it arrived that it was a Japanese reissue worth only £40. eBay were of little help in the affair, leaving the buyer with very little possibility of getting his money back. Collectors should be very wary of buying top-of-the- range items from eBay, unless they are being sold by reputable shops or dealers.

God Save The Queen is a good example of how tip-top collectables are increasing in value — in the brown envelope and with the press release, the A&M copy is worth a massive £5,500 as we go to press. Another 7" that hits the high-value mark is a new entry in this edition of the *RRPG*: one of the most collectable bands around, Led Zeppelin now have a prime item added to their list in the form of a small-centre-holed version of their classic Whole Lotta Love. There's only one copy known of this, hence accounting for its sky-high price of £1,500.

Long-established dealer Bill Allerton says that collectable mint LPs and singles are now being treated as investments by money men, and that Mint and Rare usually means premium prices. This edition of the *RRPG* reflects this development in the market; many low-range items have been deleted — even ones from as long ago as the 50s, as it is no longer enough for a record to be old to make it collectable. The collecting market is becoming rationalised and streamlined. Trends are still important — skinhead reggae is realising high prices: for example the various artists LP *Loch Ness Monster* has doubled in price to £100. But outside of areas such as rock'n'roll, psych, new wave, reggae, hard rock and prog, much of pop is losing interest for collectors. The Beatles remain the most collectable band around, and this is reflected in their new contract pressings section, in which there are some records worth many thousands. Scarcity means high prices even in genres, like indie, which are traditionally associated with low values. The Smiths test pressing EPs of *Meat Is Murder* have doubled in price to £1,000, and mid-to-late period NWOBHM is now attracting high prices, with bands like China Doll and Cynic achieving values in the hundreds.

Soundtracks are still of great interest, and this edition of the *RRPG* reflects that, with new entries such as Christopher Komeda's *Cul De Sac* EP (£300), and Witch Hunt (Theme From *Psychomania*) by Frog (£100). As stated above, dance/electronic music — especially from the 90s and the present — is becoming notable; there are expanded entries for acts such as the Sabres Of Paradise, and new entries for bands such as Lemon Jelly. But it's not just new music that is better represented — vintage vinyl by avant-garde artists such as Derek Bailey is covered better than in previous editions, with many LPs on which he appears valued at £100.

In the past, collectors who couldn't make it to London or other major cities were limited to mail order listings in magazines such as *Record Collector*. However, nowadays access to the internet has expanded collecting as never before — websites such as Gemm, Netsounds and the British Viny Network give music fans unprecedented opportunities to find what they're looking for — and at competitive prices, too. With the *RRPG* in your hands, you should be able to find out what's out there, and decide whether an asking price is fair or not. Using a wider range of consultants and dealers and covering genres such as Acid Jazz and Electronica in more detail than ever before, we think that this edition of the *RRPG* is an essential guide for anyone interested in adding 'that record' to their collections.

MORRISSEY of THE SMITHS

USING THE GUIDE
A BRIEF SUMMARY

ALL PRICES REFER TO RECORDS AND PACKAGING IN MINT CONDITION

(See pages 1502/1503 for Grading System and Ready Reckoner)

ARTISTS AND GROUPS are listed in alphabetical order. Numerical names (e.g. 2.3) are listed as if the numbers are spelt in full (i.e. Two.Three).

ALL RECORDS LISTED ARE U.K. COMMERCIAL RELEASES

with the following exceptions:

(1) Records pressed in the U.K. for export overseas.

(2) Important demo or promo releases.

(3) Records or flexidiscs included as freebies with magazines, books and other records.

In general, promo and demo editions are not included, except when these records contain unique material and/or packaging, or are by major collectable artists.

EACH ENTRY includes:

SINGLES (7" 45s & cassettes) valued at £5 or more

78s and 10" singles valued at £6 or more

EPs, 12" singles & CD singles valued at £8 or more

LPs valued at £12 or more

DOUBLE-LPs valued at £15 or more

CD ALBUMS valued at £18 or more

Records worth less than these prices have not been included.

WITHIN EACH ENTRY, records are listed in chronological order of release, within each of the following categories (where applicable):

78s, SINGLES, EPs, LPs, CDs, PROMOS. The exceptions are major artists like the Beatles, the Rolling Stones and Elvis Presley, where the entry is further divided into originals, reissues and label variations.

Where TWO PRICES are listed for a single item, they refer to

(a) the record with and without a special insert or piece of packaging

(b) mono and stereo editions of EPs and LPs

(c) versions of the same record with different artwork, vinyl colour, etc.

ACKNOWLEDGEMENTS

CONSULTANTS

Kingsley Abbott, Tim Abbot, Keith Bainton, Mark Barry (Reckless), Stuart Budd, Mike Cambridge (Esprit), Jeremy Collingwood, John Dalton (Little Pot Stove Records), Lee 'n' Paul (Energy Mail Order), John Fisher (Recent & Rare Records, Joe Geesin, Kevin Golding, Paul Green (Sounds Original), Les Hare, Mark Hosken (Hedonizm), Vince Oldham, Polo O'Maoileoin, Eddie Piller & Dizzy Holmes, Chris Savory, Eddie Shaw, Bob Solly, Neil Thompson, Jonny Trunk, Deke Wheeler, Eric White (Out Of Time), Dave Wilson

THANKS ALSO TO:

Bill Allerton, Andy Bean (Intoxica), Jerry Bloom, Bob Brooks, Jason Draper, Roger Cudby, Chris Eborn, John Esplen, Fat Barry (Norman Records), Stephen Forrest, Walter Geertsen, Brian Hawkins, Jason Hodgson, Rob Hooch, Jon Jemmett, Dave Lewis, Steven Lippert, Marco, Luca & Roberto @ Rock Bottom, Mark @ Sound 323, Des McMahon, Terry McLoughlin, Pete Nash, Andy Neill, Alan Ould, Dale Palmer, Alan Parker, Mike Richards, Phil Smee, Alan Trench, Jack Trevellion, David Wells, Jason Weir

SPECIAL THANKS TO

J.R. "Bob" Dobbs — for inspiration.

AND AN EXPRESSION OF GRATITUDE FOR THE WORK OF:

Terry Hounsome, Vernon Joynson, Paul Pelletier, Martin Popoff, Martin C. Strong, Michael Turner and Robert Schoenfeld.

THANKS ALSO TO THE FOLLOWING FANZINES, WEBZINES AND FAN CLUBS (PAST AND PRESENT) FOR THEIR ASSISTANCE:

Agnetha, Benny, Bjorn, Frida Fanclub (Abba), A-Ha Fanclub, www.alfie-uk.com (Alfie), Banglemania (Bangles), Chapter 24 (Syd Barrett), www.thebees.info (The Bees), More Black Than Purple (Ritchie Blackmore), Oasis (Blondie/Debbie Harry), Photograph (Colin Blunstone), A Thousand Marc Feld Charms (Marc Bolan), Bucketfull Of Brains (psych), Late For The Real World (Buzzcocks), Full Circle (Byrds), Open House (John Cale), The Man In Black (Johnny Cash), Petula (Petula Clark), Petula & Company (Petula Clark), The Eddie Cochran Connection, Crickets File (The Crickets), So Far . . . (Crosby, Stills & Nash), Get Thy Bearings (Donovan), Donovan's Friends, Pink Moon (Nick Drake), Natural Progressions (The Eagles), The Duane Eddy Circle, The Biggest Library Yet (The Fall), Lonely Is . . . (4AD), Official International Billy Fury Appreciation Society, Kontakt (Peter Gabriel), The Waiting Room (Genesis), Airwaves (Gordon Giltrap), Rebels Without Applause (Sid Griffin), Hors d'Oeuvres (Roy Harper), Jimpress (Jimi Hendrix), Univibes (Jimi Hendrix), Carousel Newsletter (Hollies), Pipeline (instrumental music), Man In The Mirror (Michael Jackson), Start! (Jam), Spirit (Brian Jones), Kiss Kollector, Fire-Ball Mail (Jerry Lee Lewis), Love Is In The Air (Lindisfarne), The Castle (Love), Nut Inc. (Madness), Terrible Beauty (Manic Street Preachers), Aspire For Life (Manic Street Preachers), Stay Beautiful (Manic Street Preachers), 4-Real (Manic Street Preachers), Guy Mitchell Appreciation Society, Wavelength (Van Morrison), Razamanewz (Nazareth), Now Dig This (R'n'R), Only Olivia (Olivia Newton-John), In Bloom (Nirvana), Asylum (Gary Numan), World Storm (Gary Numan), Headshrinker (Oasis), Dark Star (Mike Oldfield), The Organ (Pronk), Shire News (Steve Peregrine Took Appreciation Society), Fanatically (Pet Shop Boys), Brain Damage (Pink Floyd), Interstellar Overdrive (Pink Floyd), The Amazing Pudding (Pink Floyd), Suzi & Other Four Letter Words (Suzi Quatro), Princes Of The Universe (Queen), The Days Of Our Lives (Queen), Official Queen International Fan Club (Queen), Radiohead World Service, www.atease.com (Radiohead), www.followmearound.com (Radiohead), Ramones Ramones, Destiny (Johnnie Ray), Cliff United (Cliff Richard), Constantly Cliff (Cliff Richard), Tumbling Dice (Rolling Stones), Shadsfax (Shadows), The Darlings Of Wapping Wharf Launderette (The Small Faces), On The Level (Status Quo), Smiler (Rod Stewart), Strangled (Stranglers), The Official Magazine Of The Suede Information Service (Suede), Simply The Best (Tina Turner), Misty Green & Blue (UFO Appreciation Society), Official Uriah Heep Appreciation Society, Pilgrims (Van Der Graaf Generator), Walkerpeople (Walker Brothers), The Walkers (Walker Brothers), Waves (Clifford T. Ward), All Mod Icon (Paul Weller/TSC/Jam), Boys About Town (Paul Weller/TSC/Jam), www.whitestripes.com (The White Stripes), (Generations (The Who), Coloured Rain (Stevie Winwood/Traffic), Hot Ash (Wishbone Ash), The Revealing (Yes), Broken Arrow (Neil Young).

IMPORTANT TERMS
USED IN THIS GUIDE

acetate	one-off disc cut by hand in a mastering studio, used for demonstration purposes
adaptor	plastic outer disc clipped onto 3" CDs to make them compatible with 5" CD players
art sleeve	pictorial cover using graphics rather than photographs or drawings
artwork	original design for sleeves or labels
audiophile pressing	high quality pressing for hi-fi enthusiasts
blister pack	shaped outer PVC packaging, usually for 3" CDs
bonus disc	disc given away free with another disc
bootleg	illegal pressing of material
box set	records or CDs in presentation case
budget release	pressing which retailed below full-price
catalogue number	manufacturer's reference number on record labels and sleeves
CD-R	one-off CD, digital equivalent of acetate
CD-ROM	audio/visual computer-compatible CD
CD Video	5" CD containing several audio tracks and (usually) one video track; now obsolete
company sleeve	standard non-picture sleeve for singles, printed with name or logo of label
counterfeit	illegal reproduction of official release (a.k.a. pirates)
DAT	digital audio tape
deleted	no longer commercially available
demo	record issued for demonstration purposes; not commercially available
die-cut sleeve	sleeve with circular hole cut into the centre
digipak	gatefold CD sleeve with plastic inner tray
DJ-only	record issued for radio airplay only
double groove	record with two grooves pressed concentrically on same side
double pack	two singles issued together as one package
DVDAC	digital versatile disc Audio
DVD	digital versatile disc
8-track cartridge	1970s tape format, popular for in-car entertainment; now obsolete
EP	extended play disc, with four or more tracks, usually in a picture sleeve
EPK	electronic press kit; i.e. short promo-only documentary available on video
envelope p/s	large mailing-type cover with envelope-style foldover flap
etched disc	one-sided vinyl record with laser-etched graphics (e.g. group's signatures) on other side
export issue	record or CD pressed in the UK for sale exclusively overseas
factory custom pressing	unofficial record pressed after hours (usually on coloured vinyl) at official pressing plant
flexidisc	thin, flexible record, usually issued free with magazine, etc.
flipback sleeve	LP or EP cover glued together with card flaps from the front folded over onto the back
foldaround/foldout/ foldover sleeve	sleeve which opens out as a poster, etc.
freebie	record given away free of charge
gatefold sleeve	double-size sleeve opening out like a book
import	record or CD pressed abroad but sold in the UK
inlay	printed paper booklet with CD packaging
inner sleeve	protective sleeve inside main cover
insert	loose item included as part of a record's packaging, e.g. postcard, poster, lyric sheet, etc.
interview album	spoken word record, often used as promo

jewel case	standard clear plastic case for cassettes and CDs
jukebox centre	plastic centre inserted into record with large centre hole
jukebox issue	record issued exclusively to jukebox franchise holders
laminated sleeve	cover with high-gloss plastic coating
large centre hole	1.5 inch (3.8 cm) hole in singles
long box	tall, rectangular outer card packaging for CDs
LP	long playing vinyl record; standard album format superseded by CDs
matrix number	master tape number, scratched into the 'land' or run-off groove area; sometimes also found on the record label
maxi-single	early 70s term for an EP, featuring more than two tracks, often in a picture sleeve
megamix	medley of different tracks, often linked by dance beats
mid-price release	record which retails at a discount
mispressing	record or CD pressed with incorrect material
mono	one-channelled playback system
numbered (no'd)	individually numbered, limited edition release
obi	sealed paper strip wrapped around sleeve of disc; originated in Japan where obis were printed with Japanese translations of foreign titles
one-sided	vinyl record which plays on one side only
picture disc	novelty record made by sealing a picture within clear vinyl
picture sleeve	pictorial paper or card sleeve, used specifically for one particular record
plain sleeve	single sleeve without special printing or artwork
premium	record available via a special offer with another product — e.g. food or drink
press kit	information pack with photos and biography, used by record companies to promote new releases
private pressing	record issued and distributed by private individuals rather than a company
promo	promotional record or item sent out to the media for publicity purposes
push-out centre	centre of a single connected to the rest of the disc at 3 or 4 points, so it can be pushed out for use on jukeboxes, etc.
quadrophonic	1970s four-channelled playback system, now obsolete
reel-to-reel tape	1960s tape format, superseded by cassette
reissue	re-release of a deleted disc
remix	different version of existing track created by rearranging its component parts
removeable/ replaceable centre	centre which can be removed from a record without damage and later replaced (not to be confused with jukebox or 'spider' centres)
re-pressing	a second run of a record or CD which hasn't been deleted
run-off groove	groove between end of playing surface and record label
sampler	compilation showcasing an artist or label
sealed/shrinkwrapped	machine-wrapped in cellophane
shaped disc	any non-circular record
shellac	brittle material used for 78s
slipcase	small card cover used for some CDs and cassette singles
solid centre	centre of record which cannot be removed, as on LPs
stickered sleeve	sleeve with sticker as an integral part of its packaging
stereo	two-channelled playback system
test pressing	manufacturer's sample record, pressed for quality control
tri-centre	push-out triangular centre on some 1950s singles/EPs
tri-fold	triple fold-out sleeve
uncut picture disc	shaped disc not yet trimmed to proper shape
unissued/unreleased	disc not made commercially available; may or may not have been pressed
vinyl	material from which records are made
warp	buckle in vinyl caused by heat
white label	usually blank, perhaps printed or handwritten labels, often for promo purposes; term also used for demo, promo or test pressing
withdrawn	record deliberately removed from sale by its manufacturer

Kingbee Records

519 Wilbraham Road,
Chorlton-cum-Hardy,
Manchester M21 0UF.

The Collector's Choice

Specialists in indie, punk,
funk, sixties, reggae
and all types of soul

Collections bought 0161 860 4762

Kellys Records

Est. 1969.
Rare Collectables.
CDs. Records. Tapes.
Videos. DVDs

www.kellysrecords.com

Tel: 029 20377355

The Balcony Central Market
Cardiff CF10 2AU

Collectors Record & CD Fairs

Bristol, Portsmouth, Cambridge, Bournemouth Milton Keynes, Reading, Southampton, Oxford

Rare Pop, Rock, Oldies, Punk, Psych, Prog, Jazz, Glam, Indie, Soul, etc

Vinyl, 45s, 12"s, LPs, CDs
BUY • SELL • EXCHANGE
50% vinyl to be found at all fairs
Tel: 0207 642 3762
www.tvfairs.co.uk

Sounds Original

COLLECTORS
RECORD SHOP

50s and 60s Specialist

169 SOUTH EALING ROAD,
EALING, LONDON W5
(nr South Ealing Tube Station, Piccadilly Line)
TEL. 020 8560 1155
www.soundsoriginal.co.uk
E-mail: mail@soundsoriginal.co.uk
OPEN WED-SAT 11.00-5.30

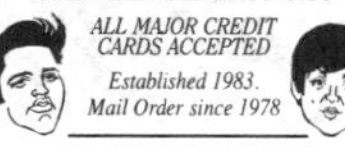

ALL MAJOR CREDIT CARDS ACCEPTED
Established 1983.
Mail Order since 1978

DISC COVERY RECORDS LTD.

3 KINGSWAY, HUNCOAT, ACCRINGTON
LANCS BB5 6LA
TEL: 01254 231387/07739 526262

www.disc-coveryrecords.com
Email us: sales@disc-coveryrecords.com

WE SPECIALISE IN SELLING/ BUYING AND TRADING RARE RECORDS, CD's AND ALL MUSIC MEMORABILIA FROM THE UK/EUROPE AND R.O.W.

TRY US FIRST FOR ROCK/POP/INDIE/METAL/ PUNK/60's →NOW!!

OVER 20,000 IN STOCK!!

MORE THAN MUSIC

MORE THAN MUSIC - Worldwide QUALITY MAIL ORDER
PO Box 2809, Eastbourne, East Sussex, BN21 2EA, UK

Specialising in 'THE BEATLES'

Visit us On-Line for an extensive selection of Beatles rarities!!

www.mtmglobal.com

Phone: (+44) 01323 649 778
Fax: (+44) 01323 649 779
Email: morethnmus@aol.com

CALL US NOW!! We are always looking to BUY any BEATLES Original items - EXCELLENT PRICES PAID!!

Record & CD Fairs

Busy South Midlands Events

Fair information and Webshop
www.vinylbank.co.uk
or phone 01926 400472

B.B.S.

http://www.zyworld.com/SIGN4

MEMORABILIA, AUTOGRAPHS, COLLECTIBLES
(U.A.C.C. member)
ROCK, POP, METAL, MOVIE
Tel: 01723 372432
ring or e-mail
clay145@hotmail.com
for catalogue...
QUALITY ITEMS ALWAYS SOUGHT

For the biggest selection of original & re-issue U.S. issue 45's in the country!

Beatin' Rhythm Records

42 TIB ST, MANCHESTER, M4 1LA
Phone: 0161 834 7783
Fax: 0161 834 9835

Specialists in: northern soul, funk, doo-wop, rock'n'roll & pop classics from the 50's to the 90's.

First class worldwide mail order anytime.

OPEN 7 DAYS
Check our 45's online
www.beatinrhythm.com

COB RECORDS

Specialists In Quality Second Hand LPs, Cassettes, CDs, Videos & DVDs

See a selection of our rarer LPs on
www.cobrecords.com

Thousands of other LPs, CDs, Cassettes & Videos in stock. Enquiries welcome. ALL ITEMS GUARANTEED A1 PERFECT.

We buy or part-exchange most LPs, CDs, Videos and DVDs. All items must be in A1 condition. Send list + s.a.e. for our offer.

Free 12,000 titled catalogue available.

Cob Records, Mailroom 4, Porthmadog, Gwynedd, North Wales. LL49 9NA. U.K.
Tel: 01766-512170.
Fax 01766-513185
www.cobrecords.com
e-mail rcb@cobrecords.com

Worldwide Service. Established 1969

BACKTRACK SOUNDTRACKS

For the largest selection of Original Soundtracks In the U.K on LP & CD.
For Free catalogue: Tel: 01797 222777
www.backtrackrye.com

GRAMMAR SCHOOL RECORDS

The Old Grammar School,
High Street, Rye, E. Sussex, TN31 7JF.

Open 7 days a week 10 – 5.30pm
40,000 LPs and 45s in stock + CDs, Tapes, 78s, 8-tracks, DVDs & Videos.
All music styles. Tel: 01797 222752
www.grammarschoolrecords.com

✶ Premier Music Fairs

RECORD & CD FAIRS

Held throughout the North-west, Yorkshire and the North Midlands. Bringing together the regions top specialist dealers. For details of upcoming fairs see the current edition of Record Collector magazine.

SPECIAL INTRODUCTORY RATES FOR NEW TRADERS

01457 854851
www.premierfairs.co.uk

GOATS RECORDS

RECORDS AND CD'S OF ALL GENRES, INCLUDING MANY IMPORTS AND PROMOS

WWW.GOATSRECORDS.COM
TEL: 01902 787498
MOBILE: 07745197242

RECOLLECT

ALL TYPES OF RECORDS, CDS, TAPES, VIDEOS, DVDS, MEMORABILIA, RARITIES AND BARGAINS

GRAHAM SAGE
10 NORTH STREET
STROOD, ROCHESTER
KENT ME2 4SH
(Just off the High Street)

SHOP: 01634 711257
MOBILE: 07715 635152
E-MAIL ADDRESS:
Recollect123@hotmail.com

Listen To The Music - Get a Jukebox!
You don't have to take centres out your records to play them on a jukebox.
Second-hand prices from £800! Records, Neons & brand-new jukeboxes.
01252 819321.
www.selectrecordsandjukeboxes.com.

TRACKBACK Audio Accessories

We supply from stock top quality:

- CD, Video, DVD, DVD Audio & Cassette cases in all sizes
- Masterbags and Sleeves for Record, Tape & Disc in Card, Paper, Polypropylene & PVC
- Mailing Envelopes and Packaging

For prices and availability, please ring or fax.

TEL: 01803 853181 FAX: 01803 853191
PO Box 53, Brixham, TQ5 8XW

ALICE COOPER PINK FLOYD/ LED ZEPPELIN

Leading specialists on Alice Cooper Worldwide. 1000s of rare albums. Send for giant list and which artist you require to

SR Records
73 Pine Road,
Brentry, Bristol
BS10 6RU
England
Tel 0117 9501646

COLLECTORS VINYL

Established 1976, bi-monthly auction lists of 1500+ collectable singles, EP's, LP's and print, plus great bargain set sales. Many customers have been with us since we started. Why not you?

Send s.a.e to
18 Grange Road,
Camberley,
GU15 2DH,
or on the web at
www.collectorsvinyl.co.uk

---

soundbite fairs

Regular fairs within the M25 area
A wide range of music on vinyl and CD

FREE ADMISSION

Check out Record Collector and our web page for dates
http://freespace.virgin.net/infora.spin

"8 years of customer satisfaction"

---

www.popsych.co.uk

Popsych Records,
PO BOX 3632,
Weymouth DT3 5YJ

e-mail: adrian@popsych.co.uk
Garage/Psych/Punk etc
Tel/Fax: 01305 816822
(24 hours)

SKA, REGGAE, ROOTS

Send SAE for latest list of Ska, Rock Steady, Reggae, Roots, Dub 1960-1983. 45s, 12", LP's.

S.H.M. Records,
PO Box 3759,
London SE27 SDO.
Phone 020 8473 9864

E-mail: records@shmrec.fsnet.co.uk
Website: www.shmrec.fsnet.co.uk

PERFECT FOR SMALL TRADERS

Contact Ibex Distribution, 23 Percy St., Hanley, Stoke-On-Trent ST1 1NA. Tel: (01782) 281777.
E-mail:
becky@ibexdistribution.co.uk
See us at
www.ibexdistribution.co.uk
Call Becky Hall. Same day service. We accept all major credit cards and ship worldwide. Northern Soul, Psych, Reggae, 60s, Punk, overstocks etc. We carry all the major and many specialist labels.

Second Spin

71 HINTON ROAD
KINGSTHORPE
NORTHAMPTON
NN2 8NU

SPECIALISING IN BUYING AND SELLING RARE DELETED COLLECTABLE VINYL LPs PROGRESSIVE FUSION BLUES PSYCHEDELIC FOLK

SEND FOR OUR CATALOGUE (SAE 47P)

secondspin@cwcom.net
www.secondspin.cwc.net

FOR MUSIC AND POP MEMORABILIA
log on to www.carlgresham.co.uk

Quality Records, CD's & Memorabilia Bought & Sold

Phone: (01327) 311568
Email:
Andy@visual-vinyl.co.uk

VISUAL VINYL,
22 SPENCER CRESCENT,
DAVENTRY,
NORTHANTS,
NN11 5DX

www.visual-vinyl.co.uk

---

blackvinyl records.com

for re-issues and rare rock, folk, jazz and blues LPs.

Other stock available.
Or telephone
+44 0141 334 0389

IAN EDWARDS

MAKERS OF FINE HAND MADE FURNITURE
Elegant Storage solutions for Hi-Fis, Books, LPs, CDs, DVDs and Mini-Discs
Special orders welcome

1120 CD 7-drawer Georgian style Drawer Chest

Established since 1970

Adjustable shelf rotary unit can hold 2296 CDs, etc.

The Old Chapel, 282 Skipton Road
Harrogate • N. Yorks HG1 3HE
Tel: 01423 500442
Fax: 01423 705200
www.iansbespokefurniture.co.uk
Call for free brochure

MINT VALUE £

A

90s	Tycoon TY 1	5 In The Morning/8 Fingers (p/s)	12
90s	Tycoon TY 2	House Under The Ground/40 (p/s)	12
90s	Tycoon TYCD 3	Bad Idea/Look What You Made Me Do/40 (CD, card sleeve)	10
90s	Tycoon TYCD 4	Number One (Radio Edit)/Alright/Ouch/No. 1 (CD)	8
90s	Tycoon COUP 006	House Under The Ground/GLITTERBOX: Take Me To Bed (CD)	10
90s	Tycoon TY 6	Number One/Good Idea (stickered p/s)	8
90s	Tycoon TY 10	Lake Tahoe/Monkey Kong Jr. (picture disc)	12

AARDVARK

70	Deram Nova SDN 17	AARDVARK (LP)	70

A—AUSTR

70	Holy Ground HG 113	A—AUSTR — MUSICS FROM HOLY GROUND (LP, with booklet, 99 only)	325
89	Magic Mixture MM 1	A—AUSTR (LP, reissue, 425 only)	35
95	Holyground 010101LP	A—AUSTR (LP, second reissue, foldover gatefold sleeve)	20

(see also Bill Nelson)

ABACUS

74	York YR 207	Indian Dancer/Be That Way	6
72	Polydor 2371 215	ABACUS (LP)	40

A BAND CALLED DORIS

(see under Doris)

ABBA

73	Epic EPC 1793	Ring Ring/Rock'N'Roll Band (yellow label)	50
74	Epic EPC 2452	Ring Ring (second version)/Rock'N'Roll Band (yellow label)	8
74	Epic EPC 2848	So Long/I've Been Waiting For You (yellow label)	18
75	Epic EPC 3229	I Do I Do I Do I Do I Do/Rock Me (yellow label)	8
79	Epic EPC 7499	Voulez Vous/Angel Eyes (p/s)	8
79	Epic EPC 7499	Voulez Vous/Angel Eyes (red or yellow vinyl, p/s)	600
79	Epic EPC 8088	I Have A Dream/Take A Chance On Me (live) (gatefold p/s)	15
80	Epic EPC 8835	The Winner Takes It All/Elaine (p/s)	10
80	Epic EPC 12-8835	The Winner Takes It All/Elaine (12", gatefold pop-up p/s)	45
81	Epic EPCA 13-1456	Lay All Your Love On Me/On & On & On (12" p/s)	12
81	Epic EPCA 11-1740	One Of Us/Should I Laugh Or Cry (picture disc)	15
82	Epic EPCA 11-2971	Under Attack/You Owe Me One (picture disc)	30
82	Lyntone LYN 11763	Konica Pop Flexi (1-sided flexidisc, p/s, featuring edits of Abba's "Lay All Your Love On Me" & tracks by Stars On 45 & Nolan Sisters)	8
82	Lyntone LYN 12570/1	Happy Xmas From The Stars (with other artists, flexidisc, some with *Smash Hits* magazine)	12/8
82	Epic EPCA 2618	GREATEST ORIGINAL HITS (EP)	12
82	Epic EPCA 2618	GREATEST ORIGINAL HITS (EP, cassette)	10
83	Epic A 3894	Thank You For The Music/Our Last Summer (poster p/s)	18
83	Epic WA 3894	Thank You For The Music/Our Last Summer (shaped picture disc)	25
84	Kelloggs KELL 1	I Have A Dream/SHAKIN' STEVENS: Oh Julie ('Rice Krispies' premium)	8
84	Epic ABBA 26	ANNIVERSARY BOXED SET (26 x blue vinyl 7", numbered, 2,000 only)	375
84	Epic ABBA 26	ANNIVERSARY BOXED SET (26 x black vinyl 7")	110
86	Readers Digest (no cat. no.)	The Best Of Abba (flexidisc sampler)	8
93	Polydor 859 085-2	MORE ABBA GOLD (4-track CD, promo only)	50
93	Polydor ABBA 1DJ	Summer Night City/Eagle/Ring Ring (12", 1-sided sampler, promo only)	30
94	Polydor 853 891-2	DREAM WORLD (CD, 4-track sampler, promo only)	75
99	No label ABBA 1	MAMMA MIA (4-track CD)	15
99	Polydor 563 213-2	Waterloo (CD, 1 track, promo-only)	35
99	Polydor 563 286-2	ABBA Singles Collection 1974-1982 (29 CD singles in card sleeves & 1-track CD picture disc, with booklet, in silver tin, 20,000 only)	80
74	Epic EPC 80179	WATERLOO (LP, yellow label)	18
75	Epic EPC 80835	ABBA (LP, yellow label)	18
76	Epic EPC 69218	GREATEST HITS (LP, gatefold sleeve, yellow label, some with "Fernando" sticker)	16
78	Epic EPC 86052	THE ALBUM (LP, gatefold sleeve, some with sticker)	15/12
79	Epic EPC 11-86086	VOULEZ VOUS (LP, picture disc)	70
80	Epic EPC 86123	GRACIAS POR LA MUSICA (LP)	18
80	Epic ABBOX 1	SUPER TROUPER (LP, box set with book & poster)	60
83	Epic ABBOX 11-2/ ABBA-11-10	THE SINGLES — THE FIRST TEN YEARS (2-LP, picture discs, with poster, ticket & booklet in box)	60
83	Epic EPC 10043	THANK YOU FOR THE MUSIC — A COLLECTION OF LOVE SONGS (LP)	20
83	Epic CDEPC 10022	SUPER TROUPER (CD, original issue)	20
83	Epic CDEPC 10032	THE VISITORS (CD, original issue)	20
84	St. Michael 1361/5704	THE HIT COLLECTION (cassette, with 64-page book *Their Story*, available via Marks & Spencer)	40
86	R. Digest GABA-A-112	THE BEST OF ABBA (5-LP box set)	30
86	R. Digest GABC-C-112	THE BEST OF ABBA (5-cassette box set)	40
99	Polar Music Int. ABBA.INT	THE INTERVIEW ... (CD, 12-page booklet with unique artwork)	50

(see also Hep Stars, Hootenanny Singers, Agnetha Faltskog, Frida, Northern Lights)

BILLY ABBOTT & JEWELS

63	Cameo Parkway P 874	Groovy Baby/Come On And Dance With Me	25

A.B.H.

78 Music Bank BECK 694 Geoffrey/Colt 45 Rock (no p/s) . . . 20

SHIRLEY ABICAIR

56 Parlophone MSP 6224 Willie Can/Happy Trails . . . 10
57 Parlophone R 4347 Bimini/Where The Sun Always Shines (with Humphrey Lyttleton) . . . 5
64 Piccadilly 7N 35364 I Will Be There/Am I Losing You . . . 5
66 Pye 7N 17119 Flowers Never Bend With The Rainfall/I Know . . . 5
67 Pye 7N 17389 So Goes Love/Carnival . . . 5
67 Piccadilly 7N 35383 This Girl/You Can't Hide (A Broken Heart) . . . 5
57 Parlophone GEP 8612 FAIR DINKUM (EP) . . . 10

MICK ABRAHAMS (BAND)

71 Chrysalis ILPS 9147 (A MUSICAL EVENING WITH) THE MICK ABRAHAMS BAND (LP, g/fold sleeve) . . 25
72 Chrysalis CHR 1005 AT LAST (LP, circular foldout sleeve) . . . 35
75 SRT SRTM 73313 HAVE FUN LEARNING THE GUITAR WITH MICK ABRAHAMS (LP, solo, initally with typed insert) . . . 20/16
(see also Blodwyn Pig, Jethro Tull, Mighty Flyers)

ABRASIVE WHEELS

81 Abrasive ABW 1 Army Song/Juvenile/So Low (p/s) . . . 20
82 Riot City RIOT 4 VICIOUS CIRCLE (EP, p/s) . . . 15
82 Riot City RIOT 9 Army Song/Juvenile/So Slow (p/s, reissue, red vinyl) . . . 8
82 Riot City RIOT 16 Burn The Schools/Urban Rebels/Burn 'Em Down (p/s) . . . 8
82 Riot City CITY 001 WHEN THE PUNKS GO MARCHING IN (LP) . . . 25

MIKE ABSALOM

60s Sportsdisc ILP 1081 THE MIGHTY ABSALOM SINGS BATHROOM BLUES (LP) . . . 15
69 Saydisc SDL 162 SAVE THE LAST GHERKIN FOR ME (LP) . . . 50
71 Vertigo 6360 053 MIKE ABSALOM (LP, swirl label, poster sleeve) . . . 60
72 Philips 6308 131 HECTOR AND OTHER PECCADILLOS (LP) . . . 18

ABSOLUTE

85 Reset 7REST 5 TV Glare/At The Third Stroke (p/s) . . . 15
85 Reset 12 REST 5 TV Glare/At The Third Stroke (12", p/s) . . . 25
87 Reset 7REST 8 Can't You See/Love In My Heart (release cancelled) . . . 85
(see also Erasure)

ABSOLUTE ELSEWHERE

76 Warner Bros K 16697 Earthbound/Gold Of The Gods (p/s) . . . 5
76 Warner Bros K 56192 IN SEARCH OF THE ANCIENT GODS (LP, with booklet) . . . 12

ABSOLUTELY FABULOUS

94 Parlophone CDR 6332 Absolutely Fabulous (7" Mix)/(Our Tribe Tongue-In-Cheek Mix)/ Absolutely Dubious/This Wheel's On Fire (CD, withdrawn) . . . 20
(see also Pet Shop Boys)

ABYSSINIAN BAPTIST CHOIR

63 Philips 847095 BY ABYSSINIAN BAPTIST CHOIR (LP) . . . 30

ABYSSINIANS

73 Harry J. HJ 6652 Yim Mas Gan/JOHN CROW GENERATION: Crank Shaft . . . 15
75 Grounation GR 2029 Love Comes And Goes/(Version) . . . 6
76 Soundtrack TST 109 African Race/Satta A Massagana . . . 5
77 Klik KL 631 Forward On To Zion/Satta A Massagana . . . 5
79 Different HAVE 18 Declaration Of Rights/African Race . . . 5
77 Different GETL 100 FORWARD TO ZION (LP) . . . 20

ACADEMY

69 Morgan Bluetown BTS 2 Rachel's Dream/Munching The Candy (as Academy featuring Polly Perkins) 15
69 Morgan Bluetown BT 001 POP-LORE ACCORDING TO THE ACADEMY (LP) . . . 100
(see also Polly Perkins)

ACCELERA DECK

90s Endorphin ENDORLP 0001 NARCOTIC BEATS (2-LP, green vinyl) . . . 20

ACCELERATORS

81 Spiv ACCEL EP POPGUNS AND GREEN LANTERNS (12" EP) . . . 10

ACCENT

67 Decca F 12679 Red Sky At Night/Wind Of Change . . . 200
(see also Rick Hayward)

ACCENTS

59 Coral Q 72351 Wiggle, Wiggle/Dreamin' And Schemin' . . . 40
59 Coral Q 72351 Wiggle, Wiggle/Dreamin' And Schemin' (78) . . . 15

ACCIDENT

84 Flicknife SHARP 016 A CLOCKWORK LEGION (LP) . . . 20
(see also Major Accident)

ACCIDENTS

80 H. Line 'n' Sinker HOOK 1 Blood Spattered With Guitars/Curtains For You (p/s) . . . 25
80 Hook Line 'n' Sinker KISS ME ON THE APOCALYPSE (LP, unreleased; 6 test pressings only, some supposedly with proof sleeves) . . . 100/50

ACCIDENTS ON EAST LANCS.

81 Roach RR 1 The Back End Of Nowhere/Rat Race (p/s) . . . 100
81 Roach SPLIFF 001 Tell Me What You Want/We Want It Legalised (no p/s) . . . 70

ACCOLADE

70 Columbia DB 8688 Natural Day/Prelude To A Dawn . . . 8
70 Columbia SCX 6405 ACCOLADE (LP) . . . 25
72 Regal Zono. SLRZ 1024 ACCOLADE 2 (LP) . . . 30
(see also Gordon Giltrap, Wizz Jones, Pauline Filby, Don Partridge)

MINT VALUE £

ACCURSED

80s	Wrek 'Em ACC 3	Going Down (p/s)	8
83	Wrek 'Em ACC 1	AGGRESSIVE PUNK (LP)	20

AC/DC

76	Atlantic K 10745	It's A Long Way To The Top (If You Wanna Rock'N'Roll)/ Can I Sit Next To You, Girl? (no p/s)	15
76	Atlantic K 10805	Jailbreak/Fling Thing (original issue with running times on label, dark label, heavy print, no p/s)	20
76	Atlantic K 10860	High Voltage/Live Wire (some in p/s)	80/15
77	Atlantic K 10899	Dirty Deeds Done Dirt Cheap/Big Balls/The Jack (maxi-single, 'schoolboy' p/s)	45
77	Atlantic K 11018	Let There Be Rock (edit)/Problem Child (initially with small label lettering & 3.06 timing, no p/s)	10/5
78	Atlantic K 11142	Rock'N'Roll Damnation/Sin City (initially with small label lettering & 3.05 timing, no p/s)	7
78	Atlantic K 11142T	Rock'N'Roll Damnation/Sin City (12", p/s)	20
78	Atlantic K 11207	Whole Lotta Rosie (live)/Hell Ain't A Bad Place To Be (live) (dark labels; later reissued with lighter labels; no p/s)	8/6
78	Atlantic K 11207T	Whole Lotta Rosie (live)/Hell Ain't A Bad Place To Be (live) (12", no p/s)	20
79	Atlantic K 11321	Highway To Hell/If You Want Blood (You've Got It) ('1979' on p/s)	8
79	Atlantic K 11406	Girl's Got Rhythm/Get It Hot (p/s, initially without 'Elephant Head' motif)	12/8
79	Atlantic K 11406E	Girl's Got Rhythm/If You Want Blood (You've Got It)/Hell Ain't A Bad Place To Be (live)/Rock'N'Roll Damnation (EP, gatefold envelope p/s)	10
80	Atlantic K 11435	Touch Too Much/Live Wire (live)/Shot Down In Flames (live) (p/s)	7
80	Atlantic K 11435	Touch Too Much/Live Wire (live)/Shot Down In Flames (live) (p/s, misprinted back-to-front)	10
80	Atlantic K 10805	Jailbreak/Fling Thing (reissue, light label, fine print; initially without 'Elephant Head' motif on p/s)	18/12
80	Atlantic K 11018	Let There Be Rock (edit)/Problem Child (reissue, no p/s, large label lettering)	6
80	Atlantic K 11142	Rock'N'Roll Damnation/Sin City (reissue, initially without 'Elephant Head' motif on p/s)	10
80	Atlantic K 11321	Highway To Hell/If You Want Blood (You've Got It) (reissue, '1980' on p/s)	6
80	Atlantic HM 1	High Voltage/Live Wire (reissue, p/s)	5
80	Atlantic HM 2	Dirty Deeds Done Dirt Cheap/Big Balls/The Jack (reissue, p/s)	5
80	Atlantic HM 3	It's A Long Way To The Top (If You Wanna Rock'N'Roll)/ Can I Sit Next To You? (p/s, reissue)	5
80	Atlantic HM 4	Whole Lotta Rosie (live)/Hell Ain't A Bad Place To Be (live) (p/s, reissue)	5
80	Atlantic K 11600	You Shook Me All Night Long/Have A Drink With Me (p/s)	7
80	Atlantic K 11600	You Shook Me All Night Long/Have A Drink With Me (p/s, mispressing, A-side plays "Shake A Leg")	100
80	Atlantic K 11630	Rock'N'Roll Ain't Noise Pollution/Hell's Bells (some with large production credit on p/s)	each 5
80	Atlantic K 11630T	Rock'N'Roll Ain't Noise Pollution/Hell's Bells (12", p/s, with badge)	12/8
82	Atlantic K 11706	Let's Get It Up/Back In Black (live) (p/s)	5
82	Atlantic K 11706T	Let's Get It Up/Back In Black (live)/TNT (live) (12", p/s)	10
82	Atlantic K 11721	For Those About To Rock (We Salute You)/Let There Be Rock (live) (p/s)	5
82	Atlantic K 11721	For Those About To Rock (We Salute You)/Let There Be Rock (live) (p/s, mispressing, B-side actually has 'Gloria' by Laura Branigan)	5
82	Atlantic K 11721T	For Those About To Rock (We Salute You)/Let There Be Rock (ext'd live) (12", p/s)	10
82	Atlantic SAM 143	For Those About To Rock (We Salute You)/C.O.D. (12", p/s, promo only)	65
83	Atlantic A 9774	Guns For Hire/Landslide (p/s)	5
83	Atlantic A 9774P	Guns For Hire/Landslide (logo-shaped picture disc)	20
84	Atlantic A 9651	Nervous Shakedown/Rock'N'Roll Ain't Noise Pollution (live) (p/s; some with silver labels)	each 5
84	Atlantic A 9651C	Nervous Shakedown/Rock'N'Roll Ain't Noise Pollution (live)/ Sin City (live)/This House Is On Fire (live) (cassette)	7
84	Atlantic A 9651P	Nervous Shakedown/Rock'N'Roll Ain't Noise Pollution (live) (shaped picture disc)	20
84	Atlantic A 9651T	Nervous Shakedown/Rock'N'Roll Ain't Noise Pollution (live)/ Sin City (live)/This House Is On Fire (live) (12", p/s)	8
85	Atlantic A 9532W	Danger/Back In Business (poster p/s)	6
85	Atlantic A 9532P	Danger/Back In Business (fly-shaped picture disc)	20
85	Atlantic A 9532T	Danger/Back In Business (12", p/s)	8
86	Atlantic A 9474	Shake Your Foundations/Stand Up (p/s)	5
86	Atlantic A 9474C	Shake Your Foundations/Stand Up ('calendar' poster p/s)	7
86	Atlantic A 9474P	Shake Your Foundations/Stand Up (Angus-shaped picture disc)	15
86	Atlantic A 9474T	Shake Your Foundations/Stand Up/Jailbreak (live) (12", p/s)	10
86	Atlantic A 9425P	Who Made Who/Guns For Hire (live) (shaped picture disc)	18
86	Atlantic A 9425TW	Who Made Who (remix)/Guns For Hire (live) (12", some with stickered p/s & poster)	15/8
86	Atlantic A 9377P	You Shook Me All Night Long/She's Got Balls (live) (shaped picture disc)	15
88	Atlantic A 9136TP	Heatseeker/Go Zone/Snake Eye (12", picture disc)	12
88	Atlantic A 9136TW	Heatseeker/Go Zone/Snake Eye (12", gatefold p/s)	8
88	Atlantic A 9136CD	Heatseeker/Go Zone/Snake Eye (3" CD)	10
88	Atlantic A 9098TP	That's The Way I Wanna Rock'N'Roll/Kissin' Dynamite/Borrowed Time (12", picture disc)	10
88	Atlantic A 9098CD	That's The Way I Wanna Rock'N'Roll/Kissin' Dynamite/Shoot To Thrill/ Whole Lotta Rosie (3" CD with adaptor, 5" case)	10
90	Atco B 8907P	Thunderstruck/Fire Your Guns (10", picture disc)	8
90	Atco SAM 693	Thunderstruck/Mistress For Christmas/Moneytalks/ Fire Your Guns (12", red vinyl with insert, promo only)	18
90	Atco B 8886P	Moneytalks/Mistress For Christmas/Borrowed Time (12", picture disc w/ insert)	8
91	Atco 8830X	Are You Ready/Got You By The Balls (numbered p/s, with patch)	5
91	Atco 8830W	Are You Ready/Got You By The Balls (numbered 'satchel' p/s)	5
92	Atco SAM 1089	Highway To Hell (live) (4.57)/Highway To Hell (live) (3.58) (12", with insert, no p/s, promo only)	10

92	Atco SAM 1127	Dirty Deeds Done Cheap (live)/Shoot To Thrill (live) (12", with 2 tracks by Screaming Jets; no p/s, promo only)	12
95	East West 3BALLCD	Hail Caesar/Hard As A Rock/Ballbreaker (CD, no'd hologram p/s, promo only)	25
95	East West A 4368X	Hard As A Rock/Caught With Your Pants Down (yellow vinyl, numbered p/s)	5
76	Atlantic K 50257	HIGH VOLTAGE (LP, 'cartoon' sleeve)	12
77	Atlantic K 50366	LET THERE BE ROCK (LP, with Shorewood Packaging-printed sleeve)	12
77	Atlantic K 50366	LET THERE BE ROCK (LP, mispressing, both sides play Side 1)	200
79	Atlantic K 50628	HIGHWAY TO HELL (LP, test pressing in alternative "live" proof sleeve)	300+
81	Atlantic SAM 155	JAPAN TOUR ' 81 (LP, picture disc, promo only, clear or black rim)	120/100
81	Atlantic 60149	BOX SET (3-LP, including "High Voltage", "Dirty Deeds Done Cheap" & "Powerage", promo 7" & poster; export issue)	25
91	Atco WX 364P	THE RAZOR'S EDGE (LP, picture disc with inlay card)	15
95	East West SAM 1693	BALLBREAKERS (CD, promo only compilation)	30

(see also Geordie, A II Z, Home)

BUDDY ACE

68	Action ACT 4504	Got To Get Myself Together/Darling Depend On Me	15
64	Vocalion VEP 1-70164	BUDDY ACE (EP)	100

CHARLIE ACE

70	High Note HS 051	Creation (Version)/GAYTONES: Creation (Version Three)	15
70	Punch PH 49	Silver And Gold/PHILL PRATT ALLSTARS: Bump And Bore	15
70	Punch PH 53	Book Of Books/WINSTON HARRIS: Musical Dove	12
70	Punch PH 62	Love (You) I Madly/Especially For You	12
70	Punch PH 67	Do Something/MAYTONES: Run Babylon	10
71	G.G. GG 4507	Ontarius Version/G.G. ALL STARS: Ontarius Version 2	10
71	G.G. GG 4518	Do Something/MAYTONES: Groove Me	18
71	Upsetter US 359	The Creeper/UPSETTERS: The Creeper (Version)	18
71	Smash SMA 2325	Need No Whip/Grine Grine	18

(see also Charles, Paulette & Gee, Gaytones, Phil Pratt Allstars, Maytones, G.G. Allstars, Upsetters, Gaby Wilton & Charlie Ace)

JOHNNY ACE

61	Vogue V 9180	Pledging My Love/Anymore	75
61	Vocalion V 9180	Pledging My Love/Anymore (reissue)	25
62	Vogue VE 1-70150	JOHNNY ACE (EP)	100
61	Vocalion VA 160177	THE MEMORIAL ALBUM (LP)	150

RICHARD ACE (& SOUND DIMENSIONS)

67	Coxsone CS 7031	Don't Let The Sun Catch You Crying/VICEROYS: Magadown	40
67	Studio One SO 2022	I Need You/SOUL VENDORS: Cool Shade	30
69	Studio One SO 2072	More Reggae (with Sound Dimensions)/GLADIATORS: Hello Carol	30
69	Trojan TR 654	Hang 'Em High (with Sound Dimensions)/ BLACK & GEORGE: Candy Lady	15
70	Sugar SU 104	Sound Of The Reggae/Got To Build A Wall	10

(see also Viceroys, Soul Vendors, Gladiators, Ken Boothe)

A CERTAIN RATIO

79	Factory FAC 5	All Night Party/The Thin Boys (p/s, 5,000 only, 1,000 with sticker stating "ltd. edition on poor quality vinyl")	10/8
80	Factory FAC 22	Blown Away/Flight/And Then Again (12", p/s, with inner sleeve)	8
81	Factory FAC 52	Waterline/Funaezekea (12", p/s)	8
82	Factory FAC 62-7	Knife Slits Water/Tumba Rumba (p/s)	5
82	Factory FAC 62T	Knife Slits Water/Kether — Hot Knives Mix-In Special (12", p/s)	8
83	Factory FAC 72-7	I Need Someone Tonite (edit)/Don't You Worry 'Bout A Thing (edit) (promo)	8
84	Factory FAC 112P	Life's A Scream (edit)/There's Only This (edit) (promo pack including 7", photo & biography in custom ACR envelope)	10
79	Factory FAC 16C	THE GRAVEYARD AND THE BALLROOM (cassette, 4 different coloured plastic wallets, with insert)	10
85	private label	A CERTAIN RATIO LIVE IN AMERICA (cassette, sold at gigs)	15

(see also Sir Horatio)

ACES

63	Parlophone R 5094	Wait Until Tomorrow/The Last One	15
64	Parlophone R 5108	I Count The Tears/But Say It Isn't So	15

ACES

81	Etc ETC 01	One Way Street/Why Should It Be Mine (p/s)	20

(see also Menace)

ACHES & PAINS

66	Page One POF 008	There's No Other Like Your Mother/Again And Again	15

ACHILLES & HIS HEELS

61	Fontana H 340	Brigitte Bardot/Acapulco	10

ACHOR

76	Cedar CEDAR 1	END OF MY DAY (LP)	60
78	Dove Tail DOVE 54	HOSANNA TO THE SON OF DAVID (LP)	30

(see also Wine Of Lebanon, Valley Of Achor)

ACID GALLERY

69	CBS 4608	Dance Around The Maypole/Right Toe Blues	50

(see also Christie, Epics, Carl Wayne & Vikings, Roy Wood, Outer Limits)

ACID MOTHERS TEMPLE

00	Staticresonance 2	MONSTER OF THE UNIVERSE (Monster Of The Universe/Wholly Weary Flashback//Surfin' Paris-Texas/Midnight Mountain Dew (EP, 2 x 7", p/s, sold on tour, 500 only)	30
01	Staticresonance 1	ABSOLUTELY FREAKOUT, ZAP YOUR MIND (LP, 1000 only)	20

MINT VALUE £

DAVID ACKLES

68 Elektra EKSN 45039 La Route A Chicago/Down River . . . 8
69 Elektra EKSN 45054 Laissez Faire/Blue Ribbons . . . 7
70 Elektra EKSN 45079 Subway To The Country/That's No Reason To Cry . . . 7
68 Elektra EKL 4022 DAVID ACKLES (LP, orange label, also stereo EKS 74022) . . . 30
70 Elektra EKS 74060 SUBWAY TO THE COUNTRY (LP, orange label) . . . 22
72 Elektra K 42112 AMERICAN GOTHIC (LP) . . . 15
73 CBS 32466 FIVE AND DIME (LP) . . . 18

BARBARA ACKLIN

68 MCA MU 1038 Love Makes A Woman/Come And See Me Baby . . . 10
69 MCA MU 1071 Am I The Same Girl/Be By My Side . . . 5
69 MCA MU 1102 Love Makes A Woman/Come And See Me Baby (reissue) . . . 5
69 MCA MU 1103 Am I The Same Girl/Be By My Side (reissue) . . . 5
75 Brunswick BR 26 Love Makes A Woman/Am I The Same Girl . . . 5
69 MCA MUP(S) 366 LOVE MAKES A WOMAN (LP) . . . 30
71 MCA MUPS 410 SEVEN DAYS OF NIGHT (LP) . . . 30
71 MCA MUPS 416 SOMEBODY ELSE'S ARMS (LP) . . . 25
75 Capitol E-ST 11377 A PLACE IN THE SUN (LP) . . . 15
(see also Gene Chandler & Barbara Acklin)

ACME ATTRACTIONS

81 Orchid OR1 Eve Of Destruction/It's OK (p/s, with Bonnie Parker) . . . 50

SEPH ACRE & PETS

58 Pye International 7N 25001 You Are My Love/Rock And Roll Cha Cha . . . 15
58 Pye International N 25001 You Are My Love/Rock And Roll Cha Cha (78) . . . 10
(see also Pets)

ACT

67 Columbia DB 8179 Cobbled Streets/One Heart . . . 30
67 Columbia DB 8261 Here Come Those Tears Again/Without You . . . 25
68 Columbia DB 8331 Just A Little Bit/The Remedies Of Doctor Brohnicoy . . . 40

ACT

87 ZTT 12 ZTAS 28 Snobbery And Decay (That's Entertainment)/Poison/ I'd Be Surprisingly Good For You (12", p/s) . . . 8
87 ZTT 12 ZACT 28 Snobbery And Decay (That's Entertainment)/Poison/I'd Be Surprisingly Good For You (12", gatefold p/s) . . . 8
87 ZTT 12 XACT 28 Snobbery And Decay (Naked Civil Remix)/Strong Poison/Theme From Snobbery And Decay (12", gatefold p/s, some with poster) . . . 18/10
87 ZTT CID 28 Emotional Highlights From Snobbery And Decay: Snobbery And Decay (Extended For Stephanie Beecham)/I'd Be Surprisingly Good For You/Poison/ (Theme From) Snobbery And Decay (CD, gatefold card sleeve) . . . 30
87 ZTT CT 01 Snobbery And Decay (Moonlighting Mix)/Instant 1/Instant 2 (12" promo, plain black die-cut sleeve) . . . 30
87 ZTT VIMM 1 Absolutely Immune 2/Bloodrush/States Of Logic (12", p/s) . . . 40
88 ZTT CD IMM 2 I Can't Escape From You (Love And Hate)/Heaven Knows I'm Miserable Now/ Dear Life/I Can't Escape From You (CD) . . . 30
88 ZTT BET 1 Chance/Winner '88 (p/s, withdrawn) . . . 60
88 ZTT BETT 1 Chance (12 To 1 Mix)/Winner '88/Chance (We Give You Another Chance) (12", p/s, withdrawn) . . . 120
88 ZTT BETCD 1 Chance (12 To 1 Mix)/Winner '88/Chance (We Give You Another Chance) (CD, existence unconfirmed)
88 ZTT ZQCD 1 LAUGHTER, TEARS AND RAGE (CD) . . . 45
(see also Propaganda, Claudia Brücken, Glenn Gregory & Claudia Brücken, Thomas Leer)

ACTION

65 Parlophone R 5354 Land Of 1000 Dances/In My Lonely Room . . . 70
66 Parlophone R 5410 I'll Keep On Holding On/Hey Sah-Lo-Ney . . . 75
66 Parlophone R 5474 Baby You've Got It/Since I Lost My Baby . . . 75
67 Parlophone R 5572 Never Ever/Twenty Fourth Hour . . . 75
67 Parlophone R 5610 Shadows And Reflections/Something Has Hit Me . . . 80
81 Edsel E 5001 I'll Keep On Holding On/Wasn't It You? (p/s) . . . 10
81 Edsel E 5002 Since I Lost My Baby/Never Ever/Wasn't It You (p/s) . . . 10
82 Edsel E 5003 Shadows And Reflections/Something Has Hit Me (p/s) . . . 10
84 Edsel E 5008 Hey Sah-Lo-Ney/Come On, Come With Me (p/s) . . . 10
80 Edsel ED 101 THE ULTIMATE ACTION (LP, with inner sleeve) . . . 20
85 Dojo DOJO LP 3 ACTION SPEAK LOUDER THAN. . . (mini-LP) . . . 15
(see also Boys, Sandra Barry & Boys, Mighty Baby, Reg King, Stone's Masonry)

ACTION PACT

81 Subversive ANARCHO 1 HEATHROW TOUCHDOWN (EP, 1 side by Dead Man's Shadow) . . . 20
82 Fallout FALL 003 Suicide Bag/Stanwell/Blue Blood (p/s) . . . 10
83 Fallout FALL 010 People/Times Must Change/Sixties Flix (p/s) . . . 10
83 Fallout FALL 019 Question Of Choice/Hook Line & Sinker (p/s) . . . 10

ACTRESS

69 CBS 4016 It's What You Give/Good Job With Prospects . . . 60

ROY ACUFF & SMOKY MOUNTAIN BOYS

57 Brunswick 05635 I Like Mountain Music/It's Hard To Love (And Not To Be In Love) . . . 10
57 Brunswick 05635 I Like Mountain Music/It's Hard To Love (And Not To Be In Love) (78) . . . 10
65 Capitol T 2276 THE VOICE OF COUNTRY MUSIC (LP) . . . 15
65 Hickory LPM 101 ONCE MORE (LP) . . . 15
65 Hickory LPM 117 HAND CLAPPING GOSPEL SONGS (LP) . . . 15
66 Hickory LPM 125 GREAT TRAIN SONGS (LP) . . . 15
68 London HAB 8361 SINGS FAMOUS OPRY FAVOURITES (LP) . . . 15

ADAM & THE ANTS

78 Decca F 13803 Young Parisians/Lady (p/s, original with paper labels) . . . 6
79 Do It DUN 8 Xerox/Whip In My Valise (p/s, mispressed b-side 'Physical') . . . 5

MINT VALUE £

80	CBS SCBS 8877	Kings Of The Wild Frontier/Press Darlings (p/s)	5
80	CBS SCBS 9039	Dog Eat Dog/Physical (p/s)	5
81	Lyntone LYN 9285	A.N.T.S. (1-sided blue flexidisc with *Flexipop* magazine issue 4)	6/4
82	Do It DUNX 20	Friends/Kick/Physical (picture disc)	5
89	Damaged Goods FNARR 7	Young Parisians/Lady/(interview) (12", white vinyl, p/s, 2,000 with no'd fanzine)	10
89	Damaged Goods FNARR 7	Young Parisians/Lady/(interview) (12", picture disc, with postcard	
79	Do It RIDE 3	DIRK WEARS WHITE SOX (LP)	20

(see also Adam Ant, Maneaters, Models)

ADAM, MIKE & TIM

64	Decca F 12040	Little Baby/You're The Reason Why	7
65	Decca F 12112	That's How I Feel/It's All Too True	6
65	Decca F 12221	Little Pictures/Summer's Here Again	7
66	Columbia DB 7836	Flowers On The Wall/Give That Girl A Break	8
66	Columbia DB 7902	A Most Peculiar Man/Wedding Day	8

(see also Mike Sedgewick)

ADAMO

64	Columbia DB 7273	Another Love Affair/Make Tonite Last Forever	5
65	Columbia DB 7329	She Was An Angel/The Stars Will Shine (Vous Permettez Monsiuer)	5
66	HMV POP 1499	Nobody Ever Told Sandy/Tears Come (The Hurt Has Begun)	5
67	HMV POP 1601	Inch Allah (God Willing)/The Tramp With A Beard	5
67	HMV POP 1609	Let's Stop The World From Turning/Hitch Hiker	5
63	HMV 7EG 8860	BELGIUM'S TOP RECORDING STAR ADAMO (EP)	10

ALICIA ADAMS

61	Capitol CL 15195	Love Bandit/Oom Dooby Doom Lovey Dovey Sh' Boom	15

ARTHUR K. ADAMS

68	Blue Horizon 57-3136	She Drives Me Out Of My Mind/Gimme Some Of Your Lovin'	20

BILLY ADAMS

60	Capitol CL 15107	Count Every Star/Peggy's Party	30

BILLY ADAMS

69	London HL 10258	I Need Your Love/Why Don't You Believe Me	8

CLIFF ADAMS ORCHESTRA

60	Pye International 7N 25056	The Lonely Man Theme/Trigger Happy	12

DANNY ADAMS & CHALLENGERS

64	Philips BF 1346	Bye Bye Baby, Bye Bye/I'm So Proud Of You	8

DERROLL ADAMS

72	Village Thing VTS 17	FEELIN' FINE (LP, with inner sleeve)	22

EDITH ADAMS

55	Brunswick 05406	Ohio (with Rosalind Russell)/A Little Bit In Love	5

EVE ADAMS

61	Qualition PSP 7131	Kookie Talk/My Love Dear	5

FAYE ADAMS

56	London HLU 8339	I'll Be True/Happiness To My Soul	500
56	London HLU 8339	I'll Be True/Happiness To My Soul (78)	30

GAYLE ADAMS

82	Epic A 2167	Baby I Need Your Loving/Don't Jump To Conclusions	10

GLADSTON ADAMS

69	Trojan TR 659	Dollars And Cents/TOMMY McCOOK: Popcorn Reggay	25

(see also Gladstone Anderson)

GLEN ADAMS

67	Island WI 3072	Silent Lover/I Remember	22
67	Island WI 3083	She (actually titled "I'm Shocking")/SONNY BURKE: Some Other Time	22
67	Island WI 3099	Grab A Girl/DELROY WILSON: This Heart Of Mine	22
67	Island WI 3100	Hold Down Miss Winey/VINCENT GORDON: Sounds And Soul	35
67	Island WI 3106	That New Girl/UNIQUES: Speak No Evil	20
67	Island WI 3120	She's So Fine/ROY SHIRLEY: Girlie	22
68	Blue Cat BS 126	She Is Leaving/UNIQUES: Girls Like Dirt	18
68	Trojan TR 621	Rent Too High/Every Time	8
68	Collins Downbeat CR 006	Cool Cool Rocksteady (act. D. Tony Lee)/OWEN GRAY: Girl I Will Be Leaving	40
68	Duke DU 58	My Girl/GLADIATORS: You Were To Be	10
68	Bullet BU 414	Cat Woman/PETER TOUCH: Selassie Serenade (B-side actually by Peter Tosh)	15
68	Collins Downbeat CR 010	King Sized/I'm Gonna Take You Back (B-side actually by Owen Gray)	35
68	Giant GN 33	Lonely Girl/ROY SHIRLEY: Warming Up The Scene	12
69	Amalgamated AMG 837	She's So Fine/ERNEST WILSON: Private Number	10
70	Gas GAS 141	Leaving On A Jet Plane/REGGAE BOYS: Phrases	8
71	Big BG 321	Weary Version 3/TONY BREVETT: Hills And Valleys	14
71	Explosion EX 2048	Never Fall In Love/JET SCENE: Jet 747	10

(see also Glen Amams, Reggae Boys, Roy Shirley, Maxie & Glen, Delroy Wilson, Derrick Morgan, Ernest Wilson, Owen Gray)

JOHNNY ADAMS (& GONDOLIERS)

59	Top Rank JAR 192	Come On/Nowhere To Go (as Johnny Adams & Gondoliers)	10
69	Polydor 56775	Reconsider Me/If I Could See You One More Time	5
72	Atlantic K 10245	I Wish It Would Rain/You're A Lady	5

JUNE ADAMS

66	King KG 1038	River Keep Movin'/Heavenly Father	18

MARIE ADAMS

59	Capitol CL 14963	A Fool In Love/What Do You Want To Make Those Eyes At Me For	40

(see also Johnny Otis)

MINT VALUE £

PAUL & LINDA ADAMS
75 S. Folk & Country SFA 27 FAR OVER THE FELL (LP) 18

RAY ADAMS
61 Pye International 7N 25099 You Belong To My Heart/Hear My Song, Violetta 5
61 Pye International 7N 25117 Soria Moria/Little Rosemarie 5
62 Pye International 7N 25129 Walk Hand In Hand/Crying Cloud 5
62 Decca F 11507 Venus In Blue Jeans/He's Got My Sympathy 10
62 Pye 7N 15481 Gypsy/Brother Bill 5

RITCHIE ADAMS
60 London HLU 9200 Back To School/Don't Go My Love, Don't Go 25

RUSH ADAMS
54 Parlophone MSP 6101 I'm Sorry Dear/No One To Cry To 10
55 Parlophone CMSP 33 Then I'll Be Happy/Arizona (with Ace Dooley & Son) (export issue) 10
56 MGM SP 1162 Love Plays The Strings Of My Banjo/Kiss! Kiss! Kiss! 10
56 MGM SP 1176 The Birds And The Bees (with Loulie Jean Norman)/My Buddy's Girl 10
(see also David Rose)

RYAN ADAMS
90s Lost Highway LC 00268 172 259-7 Nuclear/Song For Keith (limited edition, numbered p/s) 8

WOODROW ADAMS
65 Blue Horizon BH 1001 Baby You Just Don't Know/Wine Head Woman (99 copies only) 175

ADAM'S APPLES
77 Brunswick BR 42 Don't Take It Out On This World/Don't You Want To Take Me Home 20

AD CONSPIRACY
79 Diamond AD CONSPIRACY (LP) 20

CANNONBALL ADDERLEY
67 Capitol CL 15489 Mercy Mercy Mercy/Games 7
67 Capitol CL 15500 Why (Am I Treated So Bad)/I'm On My Way 5
62 Riverside RLP 12-311 THE CANNONBALL ADDERLEY QUINTET IN SAN FRANCISCO (LP) 25
62 Riverside RLP 12-318 WORK SONG (LP, actually by Nat Adderley) 25
65 Fontana FJL 107 WOW! (LP) 15
65 Fontana FJL 117 WHAM! (LP) 15
68 Capitol ST 2987 ACCENT ON AFRICA (LP) 15
(see also Nancy Wilson, Miles Davis, John Coltrane)

ADDICTS
64 Decca F 11902 That's My Girl/Here She Comes 40

JOHN ADDISON
64 United Artists UP 1053 The Girl With Green Eyes/Love Theme From "Tom Jones" 6

ADDIX
79 Zig Zag ZZ 22002 Too Blind To See/(No Such Thing As A) Bad Boy (p/s) 15

ADDRISSI BROTHERS
59 London HL 8922 Cherrystone/Lilies Grow High (some copies have tri-centre) 25
59 London HL 8922 Cherrystone/Lilies Grow High (78) 15
59 London HL 8973 Un Jarro/Saving My Kisses 15
59 London HL 8973 Un Jarro/Saving My Kisses (78) 10
59 Columbia DB 4370 Back To The Old Salt Mine/It's Love 25

BOBBY ADENO
66 Vocalion V 9279 The Hands Of Time/It's A Sad World 25

ADICTS
81 Dining Out TUX 1 LUNCH WITH THE ADICTS (EP, with insert & screen-printed p/s) 30
82 Fall Out FALL 002 Viva La Revolution/Steamroller (p/s) 10
82 Razor RZS 101 Chinese Takeaway/You'll Never Walk Alone (p/s) 7
83 Razor RZS 104 Bad Boy/Shake, Rattle, Bang Your Head (p/s) 5
83 Razor RZLP 104 Bad Boy/Shake, Rattle, Bang Your Head (shaped picture disc) 7
81 Dwed SMT 008 SONGS OF PRAISE (LP) 14
81 Fall Out FALL LP 006 SONGS OF PRAISE (LP, reissue, yellow vinyl, 2,000 only) 14
81 Fall Out FALL LP 006P SONGS OF PRAISE (LP, reissue, picture disc) 14
82 Razor RAZ 2 SOUND OF MUSIC (LP) 14

BETH ADLAM with BUZZ & BOYS
60 Starlite ST45 024 Seventeen/I'll Walk Into The Sea 15

LARRY ADLER
56 Columbia SCM 5217 Rififi/Malaguena 10
57 HMV POP 405 Weeping Willows/Theme On Four Notes 12

ADLIBS (U.K.)
65 Fontana TF 584 Neighbour Neighbour/Lovely Ladies 45

AD-LIBS (U.S.)
66 Red Bird RB 10-102 The Boy From New York City/Kicked Around 40
69 Deep Soul DS 9102 Giving Up/Appreciation 22
75 Contempo CS 9029 The Boy From New York City/Johnny My Boy 10
79 Inferno HEAT 1 New York In The Dark/The Boy From New York City (p/s, coloured vinyl) 5

ADMIRALS
65 Fontana TF 597 Promised Land/Palisades Park 40

AD NAUSEUM
83 Flicknife FLS 12 BRAINSTORM (EP, p/s) 12

A.D. 1984

Year	Label/Cat. No.	Title	£
79	Voyage VOY 005	The Russians Are Coming/New Moon Falling (p/s)	12
81	Grand Prix GP 003	The Clockwork Generation/Melody In The Key Of Time (p/s)	10

DALE ADRIATICO

Year	Label/Cat. No.	Title	£
67	Parlophone R 5583	I Hurt Too Easy/All (Una Moglie Americana)	12

ADVENTURES

Year	Label/Cat. No.	Title	£
61	Philips BBL 7548	CAN'T STOP TWISTIN' (LP)	30

ADVENTURERS

Year	Label/Cat. No.	Title	£
60	Capitol CL 15108	Trail Blazer/Rip Van Winkle	40

ADVERTISING

Year	Label/Cat. No.	Title	£
77	EMI EMI 2710	Lipstick/Lonely Guys (p/s)	10
77	EMI EMI 2754	Stolen Love/Suspender Fun (p/s)	12
78	EMI EMC 3253	ADVERTISING JINGLES (LP, with inner sleeve)	20

(see also Secret Affair, Innocents, Simon Boswell)

ADVERTS

Year	Label/Cat. No.	Title	£
77	Stiff BUY 13	One Chord Wonders/Quickstep (p/s, 1st pressing with push-out centre)	15
77	Stiff BUY 13	One Chord Wonders/Quickstep (p/s, re-pressing with solid centre)	6
77	Anchor ANC 1043	Gary Gilmore's Eyes/Bored Teenagers (p/s, some with blanked-out eyes on label, white or pink lettering on p/s, push-out or solid centre)	6/5
77	Anchor ANC 1047	Safety In Numbers/We Who Wait (p/s)	5
78	Bright BR 1	No Time To Be 21/New Day Dawning (p/s)	8
78	RCA PB 5128	Television's Over/Back From The Dead (p/s)	6
79	RCA 5160	My Place/New Church (p/s)	8
83	Bright BULB 1	Gary Gilmore's Eyes/We Who Wait/New Day Dawning (p/s)	10
78	Bright BRL 201	CROSSING THE RED SEA WITH THE ADVERTS (LP, red vinyl, 5,000 only)	12

(see also TV Smith's Explorers)

AEROSMITH

Year	Label/Cat. No.	Title	£
73	CBS 1898	Dream On/Somebody	12
76	CBS 4000	Dream On/Somebody (reissue)	5
76	CBS 4452	Last Child/Combination	5
77	CBS 4878	Walk This Way/Uncle Salty	5
77	CBS S AR 2	Draw The Line/Bright, Light, Fright (p/s)	8
78	CBS 6584	Come Together/Kings And Queens	5
80	CBS 8220	Remember (Walking In The Sand)/Bone To Bone (p/s)	5
87	Geffen GEF 29TP	Dude (Looks Like A Lady)/Simoriah/Once Is Enough (12", picture disc)	12
88	Geffen GEF 34TP	Angel/Girl Keeps Coming Apart (12", picture disc)	10
88	Geffen GEF 34CD	Angel (A.O.R. Remix)/Angel/Girl Keeps Coming Apart/ Dude (Looks Like A Lady) (3" CD, with adaptor in 5" case)	8
89	Geffen GEF 63TP	Love In An Elevator/Young Lust/Ain't Enough (10", picture disc)	8
89	Geffen GEF 63CD	Love In An Elevator (Edit)/Ain't Enough/Young Lust (3" CD, gatefold p/s)	8
89	Geffen GEF 68P	Janie's Got A Gun/Voodoo Medicine Man (shaped picture disc)	12
89	Geffen GEF 68CD	Janie's Got A Gun/Rag Doll (Live!)/Voodoo Medicine Man (3" CD, gatefold p/s)	8
90	Geffen GEF 72P	Dude (Looks Like A Lady)/Monkey On My Back (shaped picture disc)	12
90	Geffen GEF 72CD	Dude (Looks Like A Lady) (Extended Rockin' Dude)/ Love In An Elevator (live)/Walk This Way (live) (CD)	8
90	Geffen GEF 76CD	Rag Doll/Mama Kin (live)/Dream On (live) (CD)	8
93	Geffen GFST 56	Cryin'/Walk On Down/I'm Down (12", white vinyl)	8
97	Columbia 664075 7	Falling In Love/Fall Together (picture disc, numbered sleeve)	5
89	CBS 4607038	GREATEST HITS (LP, 'European Tour' picture disc)	12

(see also Run DMC, Flame)

AEROVONS

Year	Label/Cat. No.	Title	£
69	Parlophone R 5790	The Train/A Song For Jane	40
69	Parlophone R 5804	World Of You/Say Georgia	60

A FAIR SET

Year	Label/Cat. No.	Title	£
65	Decca F 12168	Honey And Wine/Runaround	12

AFEX

Year	Label/Cat. No.	Title	£
67	King KG 1058	She Got The Time/I Never Knew Love Was Like This	90

AFFINITY

Year	Label/Cat. No.	Title	£
70	Vertigo 6059 007	I Wonder If I Care As Much/Three Sisters	15
70	Vertigo 6360 004	AFFINITY (LP, gatefold sleeve, swirl label)	70

(see also Linda Hoyle, Ice)

AFFLICTED

Year	Label/Cat. No.	Title	£
81	Bonk AFF 1	I'm Afflicted/Be Aware (rubber-stamped white labels, plain sleeve, some with insert)	12/10
82	Bonk AFF 2	All Right Boy/Who Can Tell (p/s, stamped white labels)	10
82	Bonk AFF 4	Afflicted (untitled single in stamped striped bag)	10
82	Bonk AFF 3	THE AFFLICTED MAN'S MUSICAL BAG (LP, stamped white label in stamped bag sleeve)	15
82	Bonk AFF 6	HIGH SPEED AND THE AFFLICTED MAN — GET STONED (LP)	12

AFGHAN WHIGS

Year	Label/Cat. No.	Title	£
93	Blast First BFF P89	Gentlemen/Mr Superlove	10
93	Blast First BFF P95	Debonair/My Curse/Ready (gatefold p/s)	10
93	Blast First BFF P96	What Jail Is Like/Revenge	10
94	Blast First BFFP 95T	Debonair/My Curse/Little Girl Blue/Ready (12", some with poster)	10/8

A FLOCK OF SEAGULLS

Year	Label/Cat. No.	Title	£
85	Jive AFOS 1	COLLECTION (10 x 7" pack)	18
85	Jive AFLOCK 1	COLLECTION (10 x 12" pack)	20
83	Jive HOPX 201	A FLOCK OF SEAGULLS (LP, picture disc)	12
83	Jive HIPX 4	LISTEN (LP, picture disc)	12

MINT VALUE £

AFRICAN
72 Sioux SI 006 — Cock Mouth Kill Cock/ERROL T.: I Need To Know ... 8

AFRICAN BEAVERS
65 RCA RCA 1447 — Find My Baby/Jungle Fever ... 8

AFRICAN MUSIC MACHINE
72 Mojo 2092 046 — Black Water Gold (Pearl)/Making Nassau Fruit Drink ... 12
73 Contempo CR 13 — Tropical/The Girl In France ... 12
73 Contempo CR 25 — Never Name A Baby/Dapp ... 10
74 Contempo CS 2025 — Mr Brown/Camel Time ... 8

AFRIQUE
73 Pye International 7N 25616 — Soul Makossa/Hot Mud ... 8
74 Mainstream MSL 1018 — SOUL MAKOSSA (LP) ... 15

AFRO
71 Punch PH 89 — Lonely World/ALTON ELLIS ALL STARS: Put It On ... 15

AFRO ENCHANTERS
63 Island WI 071 — Peace And Love/Wayward African ... 18

AFTERMATH
87 Moshroom MOSH 2001 — DON'T CHEER ME UP (LP) ... 12

AFROTONES
69 Trojan TR 655 — Things I Love/ERIC FATTER: Since You've Been Gone ... 10
69 Duke DU 19 — Freedom Sound/BOYS: Easy Sound ... 12
69 High Note HS 023 — All For One/BELTONES: Broken Heart ... 10
(see also Delroy Wilson)

AFTER DARK
81 After Dark AD 001 — Evil Woman/Johnny/Lucy (p/s) ... 120
83 Lazer PROMO 1 — Deathbringer/Call Of The Wild (picture disc, promo only) ... 90
83 Lazer PROMO 1 — Deathbringer/Call Of The Wild (white label test pressing) ... 100

AFTER TEA
68 Ace Of Clubs SCL-R 1251 — AFTER TEA (LP) ... 35
(see also Ray Fenwick)

AFTER THE FIRE
80 Epic EPC 8394 — Love Will Always Make You Cry/Every Mother's Son (p/s, withdrawn) ... 7
75 Rapid RR 001 — SIGNS OF CHANGE (LP, with insert) ... 100
80 Epic EPC 84545 — 80-F (LP, with original mix, unreleased, only on cassette with white labels) ... 15
82 Epic EPC 85135 — BATTERIES NOT INCLUDED (LP, withdrawn version with different sleeve) ... 12
(see also Narnia, Waiting For The Sun)

AFX
(see under Aphex Twin)

AGENTS
79 Grapevine GRP 142 — Trouble/The Love I Hold ... 15

AGGROVATORS
70 Jackpot JP 751 — Sex Machine/You Left Me And Gone (both act. by Dave Barker & Aggrovators) .. 20
70 Smash SMA 2302 — Big Red Ball Parts 1 & 2 (A-side actually "Big Red Bumble" by Lloyd Tyrell; B-side actually "Big Bumble Version" by Lloyd & Devon) ... 15
71 Smash SMA 2312 — One More Bottle Of Beer/Beer Version ... 12
73 Smash SMA 2339 — Straight To Jackson Head/You Are My Angel ... 12
73 Downtown DT 500 — Dreadlocks Man/Rasta Wants Peace (both actually by Rasta Twins) ... 12
(see also Dave Barker, Dennis Alcapone, Jerry Lewis [Jamaica], Delroy Wilson, John Holt, Alton Ellis, Cornell Campbell)

AGINCOURT
70 Merlin HF 3 — FLY AWAY (LP, with insert) ... 450
(see also Friends, Ithaca, Alice Through The Looking Glass, Tomorrow Come Someday, BBC Radiophonic Workshop/Peter Howell)

AGNES STRANGE
75 Birdsnest BN 1 — Give Yourself A Chance/Clever Fool ... 8
77 Baal BDN 38048 — Can't Make Up My Mind/Johnny B. Goode ... 8
75 Birdsnest BRL 9000 — STRANGE FLAVOUR (LP) ... 70

AGONY BAG
80 Monza MON 2 — Rabies Is A Killer/Never Never Never (p/s) ... 10
(see also Pesky Gee, Black Widow)

AGORA
94 Z Records ZEDD 010 — LATIN CONNECTION EP (12") ... 10

AGROS
71 Punch PH 56 — What Do You Fall In Love For/SLICKERS: Too Much ... 15

A GUY CALLED GERALD
88 Rham RX 8804 — Voodoo Ray/Escape/Rhapsody In Acid/Blow Your House Down (12", p/s) ... 15

A-HA
84 Warner Bros W 9146 — Take On Me/And You Tell Me (silver/blue p/s) ... 40
84 Warner Bros W 9146T — Take On Me (Extended)/And You Tell Me/Stop And Make Your Mind Up (12", silver/blue p/s, some with poster & stickers) ... 130/90
85 Warner Bros W 9006T — Take On Me/Love Is The Reason (12", black & white p/s) ... 10
85 Warner Bros W 9006 — Take On Me/Love Is The Reason (reissue, colour p/s with gatefold booklet) ... 6
86 Warner Bros W 8846P — The Sun Always Shines On T.V./Driftwood (shaped picture disc) ... 15
86 Lyntone — The Sun Always Shines On T.V. (U.S. Remix) (square picture flexidisc with *No. 1* magazine) ... 8/5
86 Warner Bros W 8736P — Train Of Thought (Remix)/And You Tell Me (train-shaped picture disc) ... 10
86 Warner Bros W 8663TP — Hunting High And Low (Extended)/Hunting High And Low (Remix)/ The Blue Sky (Demo) (12", picture disc) ... 8

86	Warner Bros W 8663T	Hunting High And Low (Extended)/Hunting High And Low (Remix)/ The Blue Sky (Demo) (12", p/s with 'Morten', 'Pal' or 'Mags' poster)	each 8
86	Warner Bros W 8500TP	Cry Wolf (Extended)/Cry Wolf (7" Version)/Maybe Maybe (12", picture disc)	8
87	Warner Bros W 8405TP	Manhattan Skyline (Extended Remix)/Manhattan Skyline (LP Version)/ We're Looking For The Whales (12", picture disc)	8
87	Warner Bros W 8305TP	The Living Daylights (Extended)/(7" Remix)/(Instrumental) (12", picture disc)	10
88	Warner Bros W 7936TP	Stay On These Roads (Extended Remix)/Soft Rains Of April (Original Mix) (12", picture disc)	10
88	Warner Bros W 7936CD	Stay On These Roads (Extended Remix)/Soft Rains Of April (Original Mix)/ Take On Me/Cry Wolf (3" CD with adaptor in 5" case)	8
88	Warner Bros W 7840TP	The Blood That Moves The Body (Extended)/The Blood That Moves The Body (LP Version)/There's Never A Forever Thing (12", picture disc)	10
88	Warner Bros W 7749WW	Touchy!/Hurry Home ('liquid' poster p/s)	8
88	Warner Bros W 7749CD	Touchy! (Go-Go Mix)/Hurry Home/Hunting High And Low (3" CD, 5" case)	8
88	Warner Bros W 7636TP	You're The One (12" Remix)/You're The One (Instrumental)/ Out Of The Blue Comes Green (12", picture disc)	8

(see also Phenomena)

AHAB

82	Chicken Jazz JAZZ 5	Party Girl/Don't Give Up On Us (p/s)	6

(see also Another Pretty Face, Waterboys)

AHAB & WAILERS

63	Pye 7N 15553	Cleopatra's Needle/Neb's Tune	15

AIM

94	Detour DR 018	Call Your Name/Out On The Streets (p/s,1,000 only, 100 on blue vinyl)	8/5

ALYN AINSWORTH

59	Parlophone R 4533	Bedtime For Drums/The Cobbler's Song (with His Orchestra)	7
59	Parlophone R 4533	Bedtime For Drums/The Cobbler's Song (with His Orchestra) (78)	15
59	Parlophone R 4594	18th-Century Rock/Hell's Bells (with Rock-A-Fellas)	8
62	Parlophone R 4882	Niagara Theme/On The Seine	5

AIR

95	Mo' Wax MW 047CD	MODULAR MIX EP (CD)	18
00	Virgin (no cat. no.)	PLAYGROUND LOVE EP (CD-R, paper title sleeve)	20
01	Virgin (no cat. no.)	RADIO NO. 1 EP (CD-R, paper title sleeve)	20
98	Source V 2848	MOON SAFARI (LP)	12

AIRBRIDGE

82	Carve Up CU 3	PARADISE MOVES (LP)	15

AIR LIQUIDE

94	Smile/Profile SM 9008	ROBOT WARS EP (10", picture disc)	12

AIRTO

71	Buddah 2318 040	SEEDS TO THE GROUND — THE NATURAL SOUNDS OF AIRTO (LP)	15
73	CTI CTI 18	FINGERS (LP)	15
74	CTI CTI 21	IN CONCERT (LP, with Deodato)	15
74	CTI CTI 23	VIRGIN LAND (LP)	15

(see also Deodato)

BOBBY AITKEN (& CARIBBEATS)

62	Island WI 028	Baby Baby (actually with Patsy)/Lonely Boy	25
62	Blue Beat BB 93	Never Never (South Virginia)/Isabella (as Bobby Aitken & Buster's Group)	20
63	Blue Beat BB 146	Don't Leave Me/Mom And Dad (as Bobby Aitken & Tinse)	20
63	Rio R 14	I've Told You/Please Go Back	20
63	Rio R 15	It Takes A Friend/LAUREL AITKEN: Sunshine	20
64	Rio R 34	Rolling Stone/LESTER STERLING'S GROUP: Man About Town	20
64	Rio R 40	Garden Of Eden/Whiplash	20
64	Rio R 50	Little Girl/Together	20
65	Rio R 52	Rain Came Tumbling Down/SHENLEY & LUNAN: Something Is On Your Mind	20
65	Rio R 64	Mr Judge/BINZ: Times Have Changed	20
65	Black Swan WI 441	Jerico/LESTER STERLING: Lunch Time	25
66	Ska Beat JB 252	Thunderball/ORIGINATORS: Chelip Chelip	35
67	Doctor Bird DB 1071	Keep On Pushing/You Won't Regret It	30
67	Doctor Bird DB 1072	Let Them Have A Home/Temptation (with Caribbeats)	30
67	Doctor Bird DB 1077	Sweets For My Sweet/How Sweet It Is (with Caribbeats)	20
67	Island WI 3028	Kiss Bam Bam/CYNTHIA RICHARDS: How Could I	100
67	Giant GN 11	What A Fool/Curfew (with Caribbeats)	25

(see also Caribbeats, Laurel Aitken, Frank Cosmo, Lloyd & Glen)

LAUREL AITKEN (& BLUE BEATS)

59	Kalypso XX 15	Sweet Chariot/Nebuchnezer	20
59	Kalypso XX 16	Aitken's Boogie/Cherrie	20
60	Kalypso XX 19	Baba Kill Me Goat/Tribute To Collie Smith	20
60	Starlite ST45 011	Boogie In My Bones/Little Sheila	30
60	Starlite ST45 014	Honey Girl (with Caribs)/Drinkin' Whisky (with Bluebeats)	30
60	Melodisc M 1570	Mary Lee/Lonesome Lover (with Bluebeats)	22
60	Blue Beat B 1	Boogie Rock/Heavenly Angel (white label)	60
60	Blue Beat BB 1	Boogie Rock/Heavenly Angel (blue label)	25
60	Blue Beat BB 10	Jeannie Is Back/If It's Money You Need	22
60	Blue Beat BB 14	Judgment Day/Yea Yea Baby	25
60	Blue Beat BB 22	Railroad Track/Tell Me Darling	25
60	Blue Beat BB 25	More Whisky/LLOYD CLARKE: Parapinto Boogie	25
61	Starlite ST45 034	Love Me Baby/Stars Were Made	25
61	Blue Beat BB 40	Bartender/Mash Potato Boogie	20
61	Blue Beat BB 52	Bouncing Woman/Nursery Rhyme Boogie (with Blue Beats)	20
61	Blue Beat BB 70	Mighty Redeemer/Please Don't Leave Me	20
62	Blue Beat BB 84	Brother David/Back To New Orleans (with Blue Beats)	25
62	Blue Beat BB 109	Lucille/I Love You More Everyday	25

			MINT VALUE £
62	Blue Beat BB 120	Sixty Days And Sixty Nights/Going To Kansas City	30
62	Blue Beat BB 142	Jenny Jenny/Weary Wanderer (with Bandits and Ruddy & Sketto)	25
62	Dice CC 1	Mabel/You Got Me Rocking (with Hyacinth)	15
63	Dice CC 13	Sweet Jamaica/Bossa Nova Hop	15
63	Blue Beat BB 164	Zion/Swing Low Sweet Chariot	25
63	Blue Beat BB 194	Little Girl/Daniel Saw The Stone	25
63	Duke DK 1002	Low Down Dirty Girl/Pink Lane Shuffle	25
63	Island WI 092	I Shall Remove/We Got To Move	20
63	Island WI 095	What A Weeping/Zion City Wall	20
63	Island WI 099	In My Soul/One More River To Cross	20
63	Rio R 11	Adam & Eve/BOBBY AITKEN: Devil Woman	15
63	Rio R 12	Mary/Hometown	15
63	Rio R 13	Bad Minded Woman/Life	15
63	Rio R 17	Devil Or Angel/Fire	15
63	Rio R 18	Freedom Train/Peace Perfect Peace	15
64	Rio R 35	Rock Of Ages/The Mule	15
64	Rio R 36	Leave Me Standing/Bagaboo (Bug-A-Boo)	15
64	Rio R 37	John Saw Them Coming/Jericho	15
64	R&B JB 167	Yes Indeed/You Can't Stop Me From Loving You	15
64	R&B JB 170	Pick Up Your Bundle And Go/Let My People Go	15
64	R&B JB 171	Bachelor Life/You Was Up	15
64	Columbia DB 7280	Be Mine/Don't Stay Out Late	10
64	Blue Beat BB 249	This Great Day/I May Never See My Baby	20
64	J.N.A.C. 1	West Indian Cricket Test/3 Cheers For Worrell	10
64	Black Swan WI 401	Lion Of Judah/Remember My Darling (B-side with Cynthia Richards)	15
64	Black Swan WI 411	The Saint/Go Gal Go	15
64	Dice CC 28	Jamaica/I Don't Want No More	10
65	Dice CC 31	We Shall Overcome/You Left Me Standing	10
65	Rio R 53	Mary Don't You Weep/I Believe	25
65	Rio R 54	Mary Lou/Jump And Shout	25
65	Rio R 56	One More Time/Ring Don't Mean A Thing	25
65	Rio R 65	Let's Be Lovers/I Need You	25
65	Island WI 198	Boogie In My Bones/Little Sheila	10
65	Island WI 252	How Can I Forget You/Weeping And Crying (white label, existence unconfirmed)	
66	Blue Beat BB 340	Clementine/Bongo Jerk	30
66	Blue Beat BB 369	Shame And Scandal/Coconut Woman	20
66	Ska Beat JB 232	Jumbie Jamboree/Looking For My Baby	30
66	Ska Beat JB 236	Propaganda/Shake	30
66	Ska Beat JB 239	Green Banana/Darling	35
66	Rio R 91	How Can I Forget You/I've Been Weeping And Crying	20
66	Rio R 92	Baby Don't Do It/That Girl	20
66	Rio R 97	We Shall Overcome/Street Of Glory	20
66	Rio R 99	Clap Your Hands/Revival	20
66	Rainbow RAI 101	Don't Break Your Promises/Last Night (with Soulmen)	15
66	Rainbow RAI 106	Voodoo Woman/Bewildered And Blue (B-side with Carols)	15
67	Rainbow RAI 111	Sweet Precious Love/I Want To Love You Forever (with Carols)	15
67	Columbia Blue Beat DB 102	Rock Steady/Blowin' In The Wind	12
67	Columbia Blue Beat DB 106	I'm Still In Love With You Girl/Blue Rhythm	12
67	Fab FAB 5	Never You Hurt/I Need You (as Laurel Aitken & Soulmen)	10
68	Fab FAB 45	For Sentimental Reasons/Last Waltz (as Laurel Aitken & Rainbows)	8
68	Doctor Bird DB 1160	Mr Lee/Birmingham Girl	20
68	Doctor Bird DB 1161	La La La (Means I Love You)/DETOURS: Sunnyside	20
69	Doctor Bird DB 1187	Fire In Your Wire/Quando Quando	20
69	Doctor Bird DB 1190	Rice And Peas/CLASSICS: Worried Over Me	20
69	Doctor Bird DB 1196	Reggae Prayer/Deliverance Will Come	20
69	Doctor Bird/J.J. DB 1197	The Rise And Fall (Of Laurel)/If You're Not Black	25
69	Doctor Bird DB 1202	Haile Haile (The Lion)/SEVEN LETTERS: Call Collect	25
69	Doctor Bird DB 1203	Carolina/Kingston Town	25
69	Junior JR 105	Think Me No Know/RECO: Trombone Man	15
69	Nu Beat NB 024	Woppi King/Mr Soul	10
69	Nu Beat NB 025	Suffering Still (with Girlie)/Reggae '69	10
69	Nu Beat NB 032	Haile Selassie/Blues Dance	10
69	Nu Beat NB 033	Lawd Doctor (with Girlie)/Big Fight In Hell Stadium	10
69	Nu Beat NB 035	Run Powell Run/RICO RODRIGUEZ: A Message To You	15
69	Nu Beat NB 039	Save The Last Dance/Walk Right Back	10
69	Nu Beat NB 040	Don't Be Cruel/John B.	10
69	Nu Beat NB 043	Shoo Be Doo/Babylon Gone	12
69	Nu Beat NB 044	Landlords And Tenants/Everybody Sufferin'	10
69	Nu Beat NB 045	Jesse James/Freedom	10
69	Nu Beat NB 046	Pussy Price Gone Up/Gimme Back Me Dollar	10
69	Nu Beat NB 047	Skinhead Train/Kent People	15
70	Nu Beat NB 048	Skinhead Invasion/Benwood Dick (unissued, blank white label demos only)	18
70	Nu Beat NB 048	Mr Popcorn/GRUVY BEATS: Share Your Popcorn	8
70	Nu Beat NB 049	I've Got Your Love/GRUVY BEATS: Blue Mink	8
70	Nu Beat NB 050	Scandal In Brixton Market/Soul Grinder (both sides with Girlie)	10
70	New Beat NB 054	Nobody But Me/Baby Please Don't Go	8
70	New Beat NB 056	I'll Never Love Any Girl/The Best I Can	8
70	New Beat NB 057	Reggae Popcorn/Take Me Back	8
70	New Beat NB 063	Baby I Need Your Loving/Think It Over	8
70	New Beat NB 065	Sex Machine/Since You Left	8
70	New Beat NB 072	Pachanga/Version	8
70	Ackee ACK 104	Pussy Got Thirteen Life/Single Man	10
70	Ackee ACK 106	Sin Pon You/Everynight	10
70	Bamboo BAM 16	Moon Rock/Cut Up Munno	12
70	Pama PM 818	Mary's Boy Child/RUPIE EDWARDS ALLSTARS: Version	6

70	Pama Supreme PS 300	Why Can't I Touch You/Can't Turn Your Back On Me	6
71	Trojan TR 7826	It's Too Late/AITKEN'S BAND: Slow Rock	7
71	New Beat NB 078	True Love/The Best I Can	6
71	New Beat NB 089	I Can't Stop Loving You/El Paso	12
71	Black Swan BW 1408	If It's Hell Below/Just A Little Bit Of Love	6
72	Big Shot BI 605	Take Me In Your Arms/Two-Timing Woman	6
72	Camel CA 90	Africa Arise/GI GINGRI: Holy Mount Zion	6
72	Columbia DB 8914	Pretty Face In The Market Place/Come Back To My Lonely World	6
75	Camel CA 2007	La Vien Rose/Spanish Eyes	6
80	I-Spy SEE 4	Big Fat Man/It's Too Late (as Laurel Aitken & Unitone)	6
66	Rio LR 1	SKA WITH LAUREL (LP)	150
67	Doctor Bird DLM 5012	SAYS FIRE (LP)	110
69	Pama PSP 1012	THE HIGH PRIEST OF REGGAE (LP)	80
69	Pama ECO 8	SCANDAL IN BRIXTON MARKET (LP, with Girlie)	65
69	J.J.	RISE AND FALL (LP)	90

(see also Laurel & Owen, Girlie, King Horror, Lorenzo, Ruts, Bobby Aitken, Classics, Beresford Ricketts, Duke Reid, Tommy McCook)

A-JAES

64	Oak RGJ 132	I'm Leaving You/Kansas City	1,000

AKA & CHARLATANS

78	Vanity VANE 1	Heroes Are Losers/Lady Of The Night/Perhaps One Day (12", various screen-printed die-cut p/s)	12

JEWEL AKENS

65	London HLN 9954	The Birds And The Bees/Tic Tac Toe	10
65	London HLN 9969	Georgie Porgie/Around The Corner	8
66	Ember EMB S 219	Dancin' Jenny/A Wee Bit More of Your Lovin'	12
65	London HA-N 8234	THE BIRDS AND THE BEES (LP)	25

AK 47

81	Output ORR 202	Stop! Dance!/Autobiography/Hilversum-Ao (p/s)	5

(see also AK Process, File Under Pop)

JAN AKKERMAN

73	Harvest HAR 5069	Blue Boy/Minstrel-Farmers Dance	6
74	Atlantic K 10427	House Of The King/Javeh	5
78	Atlantic K 11014	Crackers/Wings Of Strings (no p/s)	5
73	Harvest SHSP 4026	PROFILE (LP)	12
74	Atlantic K 40522	TABERNAKEL (LP)	12
78	CBS 81843	ARANJUEZ (LP)	12
78	Atlantic K 50420	JAN AKKERMAN (LP)	12
78	Atlantic K 11131	Crackers/Angel Watch (no p/s)	5

(see also Hunters [Holland], Brainbox, Focus)

AK PROCESS

79	Output OPQ 101	Electronic Music: After All Love/Post Town (p/s, white labels)	6

(see also AK 47)

AKRYLYKZ

80	Double R RED 2	Spyderman/Smart Boy (p/s)	7
80	Polydor POSP 128	Spyderman/Smart Boy (reissue, p/s)	5
80	Polydor 2059 253	J.D./Ska'd For Life (p/s)	6

ROLANDO AL

(see under Roland Alphonso)

AL & VIBRATORS

67	Doctor Bird DB 1085	Move Up/Lone Lover	20
69	High Note HS 005	Check Up/I'll Come Back	12
69	High Note HS 007	Move Up Calypso/PATSY: Fire In Your Wire	10

(see also Vibrators, Patsy Todd, Lord Power)

ALABAMA JUG BAND

55	Brunswick OE 9161	ALABAMA JUG BAND (EP)	15
67	Ace Of Hearts AH 163	JUGS AND WASHBOARDS (LP)	12

STEVE ALAIMO

62	Pye International 7N 25161	My Friends/Going Back To Marty	10
63	Pye International 7N 25174	Little Girl/Every Day I Have To Cry	25
63	Pye International 7N 25199	It's A Long Long Way To Happiness/A Lifetime Of Loneliness	10
66	HMV POP 1531	So Much Love/Truer Than True	15
68	Atlantic 588 227	Watching The Trains Go By/Thank You For The Sunshine Days	5

ALARM

81	White Cross W 3/4	Unsafe Buildings/Up For Murder (gatefold p/s)	50
82	Illegal ILS 0032	Marching On/Across The Border/Lie Of The Land (p/s)	8
83	I.R.S. PFPC 1023	68 Guns Parts 1 & 2 (p/s, with free cassette: "The Stand"/"Across The Border"/ "Marching On"/"Lie Of The Land"/"For Freedom" (all live) [CS 70504])	6
84	I.R.S. IRS 103	The Deceiver/Reason 41 (p/s, clear vinyl)	5
84	I.R.S. IRS 103	The Deceiver/Reason 41 (p/s, mispress on mustard vinyl)	30
84	I.R.S. IRSD 103/103A	The Deceiver/Reason 41//Lie Of The Land/Legal Matter (double pack, g/fold p/s)	6
		Eye Of The Hurricane (CD, promo only)	8
80s	Lyntone	Twp/Swnllyd (red vinyl flexidisc, with tour magazine)	8

(see also Seventeen)

ALBA

77	Rubber RUB 021	ALBA (LP)	12

BILLY ALBERT "THE KID"

56	Vogue Coral Q 72214	Black Jack/The Golden Touch	15

MINT VALUE £

EDDIE ALBERT

55	London HL 8136	I'm In Favour Of Friendship/Come Pretty Little Girl	30
55	London HL 8136	I'm In Favour Of Friendship/Come Pretty Little Girl (78)	10
56	London HLU 8241	Little Child (Daddy Dear) (with Sondra Lee)/Jenny Kissed Me	30
56	London HLU 8241	Little Child (Daddy Dear) (with Sondra Lee)/Jenny Kissed Me (78)	10

MEL ALBERT

59	Top Rank JAR 178	Sugar Plum/Never Let Me Go	15
59	Top Rank JAR 178	Sugar Plum/Never Let Me Go (78)	10

ALBERTO & RICARDO

64	RCA RCA 1376	Love's Made A Fool Of You/I'll Do It To You	6

ALBERTO Y LOST TRIOS PARANOIAS

76	Big T BIG 541	Dread Jaws/De Version	6
77	Stiff LAST 2	SNUFF ROCK (EP, p/s)	5
78	Logo GO(D) 323	DEAD MEAT EP (double pack, gatefold p/s)	5
82	New Hormones ORG 30	Cruisin' With Santa/Unfunny Art-School Parody Band (p/s)	7
76	Transatlantic TRA 316	ALBERTO Y LOST TRIOS PARANOIAS (LP)	12
77	Transatlantic TRA 349	ITALIANS FROM OUTER SPACE (LP)	12
78	Logo LOGO 1009	SKITE (LP)	12

(see also Mothmen, Charlie Parkas)

AL ALBERTS

58	Coral Q 72344	Things I Didn't Say/God's Greatest Gift (78)	10

(see also Four Aces [U.K.])

ALBION BAND

76	Harvest HAR 5113	Hopping Down In Kent/Merry Sherwood Rangers (as Albion Dance Band)	5
77	Harvest HAR 5128	The Postman's Knock/La Sexte Estample Real (as Albion Dance Band)	5
78	Harvest HAR 5156	Poor Old Horse/Ragged Heroes (p/s)	5
79	Harvest HAR 5175	Pain And Paradise/Lay Me Low (p/s)	6
76	Island HELP 25	BATTLE OF THE FIELD (LP, as Albion Country Band)	12
76	Harvest SHSP 4059	THE PROSPECT BEFORE US (LP, as Albion Dance Band)	12
78	Harvest SHSP 4092	RISE UP LIKE THE SUN (LP)	12

(see also Shirley Collins, Fairport Convention, Keith Dewhurst & Albion Band)

MICHAEL ALBUQUERQUE

69	United Artists UP 35037	Better Men Than Me/Burn Burn Burn	7
70	United Artists UP 35098	Roll Him Over/Blind Man	7

(see also Michael D'Albuquerque, E.L.O.)

ALCO

(see under Threads Of Life)

DENNIS ALCAPONE

70	Explosion EX 2039	Revelation Version/Marka Version	15
70	Supreme SUP 214	You Must Believe Me (with Niney)/ RUPIE EDWARDS ALLSTARS: Funk The Funk	12
70	Big Shot BI 565	Shades Of Hudson/Spanish Amigo	18
71	Treasure Isle TI 7069	The Great Woggie/TOMMY McCOOK & SUPERSONICS: Buttercup Version	25
71	Banana BA 328	Duppy Serenade (as Innkeeper)/Sunshine Version	15
71	Banana BA 341	(Love Me) Forever Version/I Don't Want To See You Cry	15
71	Upsetter US 373	Well Dread/UPSETTERS: Dread Version	10
71	Upsetter US 377	Alpha And Omega/JUNIOR BYLES: Beat Down Babylon	15
71	Duke DU 125	Medley Version/Version Two	10
71	Prince Buster PB 8	Sons Of Zion/ANSELL COLLINS: Short Circuit	10
71	Prince Buster PB 12	Let It Roll (with Max Romeo)/ANSELL COLLINS: Clear Blue (w/l demos only)	20
71	Jackpot JP 773	Jumping Jack (with John Holt)/AGGROVATORS: King Of The Track	20
71	Jackpot JP 775	Togetherness (Black & White) (with John Holt)/DELROY WILSON: Live Good	10
71	Jackpot JP 776	Tell It Like It Is/Come Along	10
71	Dynamic DYN 421	Horse And Buggy/ROLAND ALPHONSO & DENZIL LAING: Buggy And Horse	15
71	Dynamic DYN 422	Ripe Cherry/INNER CIRCLE: Red Cherry	10
71	Dynamic DYN 427	Alcapones Guns Don't Bark/Alcapones Guns Don't Bark Version	20
71	Camel CA 74	This A Butter/PHIL PRATT ALLSTARS: Version	12
71	Tropical AL 003	False Prophet/MAX ROMEO: Rude Medley	12
72	Tropical AL 019	Worldwide Love (with Twinkle Brothers)/CARL MASTERS: Gable Up	12
72	Ackee ACK 146	Power Version/BLUESBLASTERS: Martie (B-side actually titled "Margie")	18
72	Prince Buster PB 24	Giant/PRINCE BUSTER: Science	20
72	Upsetter US 381	Wonderman (with Dave Barker, actually by Dave Barker)/ Place Called Africa (with Dave Barker & Junior Byles)	20
72	Upsetter US 388	Master Key/UPSETTERS: Keyhole	20
72	Grape GR 3035	Rasta Dub/UPSETTERS: Rasta Version	20
72	Attack ATT 8027	Fine Style/WINSTON SCOTLAND: On The Track	15
72	Duke DU 131	The Sky's The Limit/HUDSON'S ALLSTARS: Limit Version	12
72	Duke DU 147	Get In The Groove (with Dennis Brown)/DYNAMITES: Version	12
72	Techniques TE 918	Look Into Yourself/TECHNIQUES ALLSTARS: Yourself Version	15
72	Green Door GD 4041	Rub Up A Daughter/TONY'S ALLSTARS: Daughter Version	20
72	Bullet BU 509	Dub Up A Daughter/PRINCE TONY'S ALL STARS: Version	20
73	Downtown DT 508	You Don't Say/TONY'S ALLSTARS: Version	15
73	Treasure Isle TI 7074	Wake Up Jamaica/Version (with Tommy McCook)	18
73	Jackpot JP 808	Cassius Clay/SLIM SMITH: Love And Affection	15
73	Bread BR 1121	Musical Liquidator/Lorna Banana (B-side with Prince Jazzbo)	15
73	G.G. GG 4538	Musical Alphabet/BUCKLEY ALLSTARS: Things Gonna Change (B-side actually by Maytones)	15
73	Pyramid PYR 7008	Belch It Off/Jack Horner	12
71	Trojan TBL 187	GUNS DON'T ARGUE (LP)	30
73	Magnet MGT 001	KING OF THE TRACK (LP)	30
74	Attack ATLP 1005	BELCH IT OFF (LP)	20
75	Live And Love LALP 104	DREAD CAPONE (LP)	25

MINT VALUE £

77 Third World TWS 801 SIX MILLION DOLLAR MAN (LP) 16
77 Third World TWS 911 INVESTIGATOR ROCK (LP) 16
(see also El Paso, Dennis & Lizzy, Mad Roy, D. Smith, Wailing Souls, Innkeepers, GG Allstars, Stranger Cole, Lizzy & Dennis, Lee)

CRAIG ALDEN

60 London HLW 9224 Crazy Little Horn/Goggle-Eye'd 8

STEVE ALDO (& CHALLENGERS)

64 Decca F 12041 Can I Get A Witness/Baby What You Want Me To Do (with Challengers) 100
66 Parlophone R 5432 Everybody Has To Cry/You're Absolutely Right (solo) 140

RONNIE ALDRICH

54 Decca F 10248 Coach Call Boogie/Donegal Cradle Song 10
54 Decca F 10274 Wolf On The Prowl/Mudhopper 10
55 Decca F 10494 Ko Ko Mo (I Love You So)/Rock Love (with Squads). 10
55 Decca F 10544 Rock Candy/Boom, Boom Boomerang (with Squads) 10
55 Decca F 10564 Rhythm 'N Blues/Where Ya Gone, Baby? (with Squads). 10
57 Columbia DB 3882 Right Now, Right Now/Rock And Roll Boogie (with Squadronaires) 20
57 Columbia DB 3945 Crazy Bear/The Big Band Beat (with Squadronaires). 10
60 Decca F 11283 Friendly Persuasion/Our Concerto (with Dreamers). 5
60 Decca F 11310 The Singer Not The Song/Pepe (with Dreamers). 5
69 Decca F 12909 Ride My See-Saw/Romance On The North Sea (with London Festival Orch.) 5
(see also Squadronaires, Joan Regan)

URIE ALDRIDGE

71 Harry J. HJ 6634 Set Me Free/LLOYD WILLIS: Free Version 8
(see also John Holt)

ALEANNA

78 Inchrecronin INC 7421 ALEANNA (LP) 30

AKI ALEONG (& HIS LICORICE TWISTERS)

61 Reprise R 20021 Trade Winds, Trade Winds/Without Your Love 8
61 Reprise R 6011 TWISTIN' THE HITS (LP). 22

DON ALESSI

66 Salvo SLO 5521 LP GUITAR SPECTACULAR! (LP) 30

ALETHIONS

70s Myrrh Gold MYR 1002 R.S.V.P. (LP) 25

ARTHUR ALEXANDER

62 London HLD 9523 You Better Move On/A Shot Of Rhythm And Blues 40
63 London HLD 9566 Where Have You Been/Soldier Of Love 30
63 London HLD 9641 Anna/I Hang My Head And Cry 30
63 London HLD 9667 Go Home Girl/You're The Reason 30
64 London HLD 9899 Black Night/Ole John Amos. 20
66 London HLU 10023 (Baby) For You/The Other Woman 20
76 Buddah BDS 439 Everyday I Have To Cry/Everybody Needs Somebody To Love 10
63 London RE-D 1364 ALEXANDER THE GREAT (EP) 75
63 London RE-D 1401 ARTHUR ALEXANDER (EP). 75
62 London HA-D 2457 YOU BETTER MOVE ON (LP). 150

DAVID ALEXANDER

74 Rare Earth RES 112 Love Love Love/Missy 5

JEFF ALEXANDER & HIS ORCHESTRA

58 London HA-P 2130 ALFRED HITCHCOCK PRESENTS — MUSIC TO BE MURDERED BY (LP, also stereo SH-P 6012). 45/35

TEXAS ALEXANDER

61 Fontana 467 136TE TREASURES OF NORTH AMERICAN NEGRO MUSIC VOLUME 7 (EP) 15

LLOYD ALEXANDER REAL ESTATE

68 President PT 157 Gonna Live Again/Watcha Gonna Do 40

LOREZ ALEXANDRIA

60 Parlophone PMD 1062 LOREZ SINGS PREZ (LP). 35

ALFALFA

77 EMI EMC 3213 ALFALFA (LP, with inner sleeve) 12

ALFI & HARRY

56 London HLU 8242 Trouble With Harry/A Little Beauty (triangular centre, gold lettering on label) . . . 40
57 London HLU 8494 Closing Time/Safari 10
(see also David Seville)

ALFIE

01 Regal (no cat. no.) Zoom (p/s, 1-track square coloured vinyl, 300 only). 45
01 Twisted Nerve TN 033 You Make No Bones/Don't Be Blue (p/s). 5
00 Twisted Nerve TN 011 ALFIE EP: Sure And Simple Time/Ooze A Lullaby/Check The Weight (10") 25
00 Twisted Nerve TN 016 BOOKENDS: James's Dream (Parts 1 & 2)/Talking Song (gatefold p/s). 10
00 Twisted Nerve BOOKENDS EP (10") 20

CLEM ALFORD

74 Columbia SCX 6571 MIRROR IMAGE — THE ELECTRONIC SITAR OF CLEM ALFORD (LP) 40
75 KPM KPM 1183 INDIA (LP, music library issue, side 2 only) 45
(see also Sagram, Magic Carpet)

SANDRA ALFRED

58 Oriole CB 1408 Rocket And Roll/Six Day Rock 75
58 Oriole CB 1408 Rocket And Roll/Six Day Rock (78) 20
(see also Sandra Barry, Slack Alice)

ALFRED & MELMOTH

68 Island WI 3130 I Want Someone/ALFRED BROWN: One Scotch One Bourbon One Beer 15

MINT VALUE £

LYNN ALICE

76	K&B KB 5520	(You Keep Me) Hanging On/(You Keep Me) Hanging On	7

ALICE IN CHAINS

92	Columbia 658 888-7	Would?/Man In The Box (picture disc, numbered, PVC sleeve)	10
92	Columbia 658 888-6	Would?/Man In The Box/Brother/Right Turn (12", green vinyl, no'd die-cut slv.)	12
93	Columbia 659 090-6	Them Bones/We Die Young/Got Me Wrong/Am I Inside (12", no'd, blue vinyl)	15
93	Columbia 659 365-7	Angry Chair/I Know Somethin' About You (snakeskin wallet sleeve)	10
93	Columbia 659 751-7	Down In A Hole/Rooster (picture disc)	10
93	Columbia 659 751-6	Down In A Hole/A Little Bitter/Rooster/Love Hate Love (12", die cut p/s)	8
93	Columbia 659 751-2	Down In A Hole/Version/What The Hell Have I/Rooster (CD)	8
95	Columbia 662 623-7	Grind (green vinyl, numbered card)	10

ALICE ISLAND BAND

74	Warren WAR 341	SPLENDID ISOLATION (LP, with insert)	190

ALICE THROUGH THE LOOKING GLASS

69	H&F Recording/SNP (no cat. no.)	ALICE THROUGH THE LOOKING GLASS (LP, private pressing, handmade sleeve, actually by Peter Howell & John Ferdinando)	450
97	Tenth Planet TP 032	ALICE THROUGH THE LOOKING GLASS (LP, reissue, no'd, 1,000 only)	12

(see also Ithaca, Friends, Agincourt, Tomorrow Come Someday, BBC Radiophonic Workshop/Peter Howell)

ALIEN KULTURE

81	RAR LRAR 1	Asian Youth/Culture Crossover (p/s)	40

ALIEN SEX FIEND

83	Anagram ANA 11	Ignore The Machine/The Gurl At The End Of My Gun (p/s)	5
84	Anagram ANA 18	R.I.P./New Christian Music (cream & black p/s & red vinyl or b&w poster p/s)	6/7
84	Anagram 10 ANA 18	R.I.P./New Christian Music/Crazee (10", p/s)	7
84	Anagram 11 ANA 25	E.S.T. (Trip To The Moon)/Boneshaker Baby/I Am A Product (live) (11", PVC sleeve with insert)	8
85	Anagram PANA 11	Ignore The Machine/The Gurl At The End Of My Gun (picture disc)	5
90	Windsong 02	ASF BOX (box set, export issue, 4,000 only, with 3 coloured vinyl singles [12", 11" & 10"], poster, T-shirt & imitation dog turd)	25

(see also Demon Preacher, Demons)

(Dr.) ALIMANTADO

70s	Sun & Star ST 003	Best Dress Chicken/She Wreng-Ep	8

ALIVE 'N KICKING

70	Roulette RO 517	Tighter, Tighter/Sunday Morning	6

ALKATRAZ

76	Rockfield UAS 30001	DOING A MOONLIGHT (LP)	12

ALL ABOUT EVE

85	Eden EDEN 1	D For Desire/Don't Follow Me (12", p/s)	15
86	Eden EDEN 2	In The Clouds/End Of The Day/Love Leads Nowhere (12", p/s, some with poster)	12/10
87	Eden EVEN 3	Our Summer/Lady Moonlight (p/s)	5
87	Eden EVENX 3	Our Summer (extended)/Lady Moonlight/Shelter From The Rain (12", p/s)	8
91	Mercury EVCX 13	In The Clouds/Never Promise/Scarlet/More Than The Blues/Road To Your Soul (live fan club cassette, some including "She Moves Through The Fair")	12/7
80s	fan club	LIVE AT THE BRIXTON ACADEMY (live cassette)	15

(see also Ghost Dance, Gene Loves Jezebel)

ALLAM

73	Fab FAB 190	Hide & Seek/Version (actually by Allen & Mr. Lonely)	12

JOHNNIE ALLAN

74	Oval 1001	Promised Land/SHELTON DUNAWAY: Betty And Dupree	8

RICHARD ALLAN/ALLEN

60	Parlophone R 4634	As Time Goes By/Only Love	18
60	Parlophone R 4673	Everyday/Doctor In Love (as Richard Allen)	6
60	Parlophone R 4711	Don't Ever Say You're Gonna Leave Me/Poetry In Motion	6

STEVE ALLAN

79	Creole CR 164	Together We Are Beautiful/All Mine	5

(see also Alan Carvell, Carvells, Five Sapphires, Al Southern)

ALL DAY

73	private pressing	YORK POP MUSIC PROJECT (LP)	200

ANNISTEEN ALLEN

55	Capitol CL 14264	Fujiyama Mama/Wheels Of Love	200
55	Capitol CL 14264	Fujiyama Mama/Wheels Of Love (78)	25
57	Brunswick 05639	Don't Nobody Move/The Money Tree	40
57	Brunswick 05639	Don't Nobody Move/The Money Tree (78)	10

BARBARA ALLEN

59	Felsted AF 115	Tommy's Song/Never Let Me Go	10
59	Felsted AF 115	Tommy's Song/Never Let Me Go (78)	15

BOBBY ALLEN (& COMMANCHES)

62	Fontana 267252 TF	I'll Forget About You/Your Cheatin' Heart	10
63	Fontana TF 401	Here Comes The Bride/Nothing's Impossible	10
64	Fontana TF 429	Half As Much As You/So In Love With You (with Commanches)	10

(see also Commanches)

CLAY ALLEN

62	Starlite ST45 086	This Time It's Really Goodbye/Broken Home	12
63	Starlite ST45 096	I Can't Stop The Blues From Moving/You've Got The Cleanest Mind	12
63	Starlite ST45 106	Crazy Crazy World/Just A Stone's Throw Away	12

MINT VALUE £

DAEVID ALLEN

75 Virgin VS 123 Fred The Fish/It's The Time Of Your Life (p/s, promo only) 10
79 Charly CY 51056 Much Too Old/I Am A Freud (with New York Gong, p/s with insert) 6
83 Charly CY 2101 ALIEN IN NEW YORK (12" EP) 8
75 Caroline C 1512 BANANA MOON (LP) 30
76 Virgin V 5024 GOOD MORNING! (LP, by Daevid Allen & Euterpe) 12
81 Shanghai HAI 201 THE DEATH OF ROCK AND OTHER ENTRANCES (mini-LP, with poster) 12
(see also Gong, Planet Gong, Soft Machine)

DAVE ALLEN

69 Philips BF 1748 The Good Earth/A Way Of Life 6

DEAN ALLEN

58 London HLM 8698 Rock Me To Sleep/Ooh-Ooh Baby Baby 40
58 London HLM 8698 Rock Me To Sleep/Ooh-Ooh Baby Baby (78) 20

HENRY 'RED' ALLEN

66 CBS BPG 62400 FEELING GOOD (LP) 15

JEFF ALLEN

57 HMV JO 477 That'll Be The Day/Guilty Mind (export issue) 30

JERRY ALLEN & HIS TRIO

54 Decca F 10248 S'Posin'/When I Needed You Most 7
55 Decca F 10443 Kind/Delaunay's Dilemma 7

LEE ALLEN (& HIS BAND)

58 HMV POP 452 Walkin' With Mr. Lee/Promenade 40
58 HMV POP 452 Walkin' With Mr. Lee/Promenade (78) 20
59 Top Rank JAR 265 Cat Walk/Creole Alley 15
59 Top Rank JKR 8020 WALKIN' WITH MR LEE (EP) 40
62 Ember ELR 3312 MOOD MUSIC LIBRARY (LP, uncredited library issue, generic sleeve) 50
(see also Huey 'Piano' Smith & Clowns)

MAURICE ALLEN

58 Pye 7N 15128 Ooh Baby/Rockhearted 25
58 Pye N 15128 Ooh Baby/Rockhearted (78) 10

RAY ALLEN TRIO

54 Parlophone MSP 6134 Love My Love/Why Should I Love You 6
55 Parlophone MSP 6163 Amapola/Love In Rhyme 5

RED ALLEN

62 Longhorn BLH 0005 Trouble Round My Door/Beautiful Brown Eyes 10

REX ALLEN

54 Brunswick 05341 This Ole House/They Were Doin' The Mambo (with Tex Williams) 15
57 Brunswick 05675 The Little White Horses/Drango 10
57 Brunswick 05677 Wringle Wrangle/Westward Ho The Wagons 10
57 Brunswick 05699 Flower Of San Antone/Money, Marbles And Chalk 10
59 Top Rank JAR 188 One More Sunrise (Morgen)/The Little Old Church In The Valley 5
62 Mercury AMT 1191 Don't Go Near The Indians/Touched So Deeply 5
57 Brunswick OE 9317 WESTWARD HO THE WAGONS (EP) 15
64 Mercury 10011MCE COUNTRY AND WESTERN ACES (EP) 15
(see also Tex Williams, Patti Page)

STEVE ALLEN (& HIS ORCHESTRA)

56 Vogue Coral Q 72118 The Ballad Of Davy Crockett/Very Square Dance 10
58 Vogue Coral Q 72310 Pretend You Don't See Her/But I Haven't Got Him 5
58 London HL 8742 Almost In Your Arms (Love Song From "Houseboat")/Hula Hoop 5
(see also George Cates)

TONY ALLEN

62 Philips BBE 12522 Time To Swing (EP) 10

VERNON ALLEN

64 R&B JB 169 Fari Come/Babylon 15

(Vernon) ALLEN & (Milton) HAMILTON

66 Blue Beat BB 348 It Is I/Baby What's More 15
66 Blue Beat BB 353 You're The Angel/Someone Like You 15

WOODY ALLEN

64 Colpix PX 775 Spot Floyd/The Bullet 5
65 Colpix PXL 488 WOODY ALLEN VOLUME 2 (LP) 25
65 Colpix PXL 518 WOODY ALLEN (LP) 25

ALLENS

75 Mowest MW 3029 High Tide/California Music 6

ALLEY CATS

59 Vogue V 9155 Last Night/Snap-Crackle And Pop 25
59 Vogue V 9155 Last Night/Snap-Crackle And Pop (78) 10

BOB ALLISON

64 Solar SRP 103 You've Got Everything/Change Your Mind 15

GENE ALLISON

58 London HLU 8605 Hey, Hey, I Love You/You Can Make It If You Try 100
58 London HLU 8605 Hey, Hey, I Love You/You Can Make It If You Try (78) 25

JERRY ALLISON & CRICKETS

65 Liberty LIB 10196 Now Hear This/Everybody's Got A Little Problem 15
(see also Crickets, Ivan)

LUTHER ALLISON

71 Delmark DS 625 LOVE ME MAMA (LP, blue label) 15

MINT VALUE £

LYNN ALLISON

57 Columbia DB 3867 Mama From The Train (A Kiss, A Kiss)/Song Of The Sparrow . . . 10
57 Columbia DB 3906 If Only/The Sky . . . 10

MOSE ALLISON

61 Fontana H 292 Baby Please Don't Go/Deed I Do . . . 25
64 Columbia DB 7330 I Love The Life I Live/Life Is Suicide . . . 10
59 Esquire EP 214 PARCHMAN FARM (EP) . . . 20
59 Esquire EP 221 BACK COUNTRY SUITE (EP) . . . 20
60 Esquire EP 224 BLUEBERRY HILL (EP) . . . 20
61 Esquire EP 231 THAT MAN MOSE AGAIN (EP) . . . 20
64 Columbia SEG 8353 ALLISON SINGS THE BLUES (EP) . . . 20
59 Esquire 32-051 BACK COUNTRY SUITE (LP) . . . 20
59 Esquire 32-071 LOCAL COLOUR (LP) . . . 20
59 Esquire 32-083 YOUNG MAN MOSE (LP) . . . 20
60 Esquire 32-094 CREEK BANK (LP) . . . 20
61 Esquire 32-131 AUTUMN SONG (LP) . . . 20
62 Esquire 32-171 RAMBLIN' WITH MOSE (LP) . . . 20
63 London HA-K 8083 SWINGIN' MACHINE (LP, as Mose Allison Jazz Group) . . . 20
64 Columbia SX 6058 V-8 FORD (LP) . . . 20
64 Stateside SL 10106 MOSE ALLISON SINGS (LP) . . . 15
66 Atlantic 587/588 007 MOSE ALIVE (LP) . . . 15
66 CBS Realm RM(S) 52318 I LOVE THE LIFE I LIVE (LP) . . . 20
66 Atlantic 587/588 031 WILD MAN ON THE LOOSE (LP) . . . 10
67 Transatlantic PR 7189 AUTUMN SONG (LP) . . . 10
68 Transatlantic PR 7279 MOSE ALLISON (LP) . . . 10
72 Atlantic 2400 205 WESTERN MAN (LP) . . . 15
72 Prestige PR 24002 MOSE ALLISON (2-LP) . . . 18
73 Atlantic K 40460 MOSE IN YOUR EAR (LP) . . . 15

ALLISONS (U.K.)

61 Fontana H 294 Are You Sure/There's One Thing More (as Allisons [Bob & John], m/s) . . . 8/35
61 Fontana H 304 Words/Blue Tears . . . 10
61 Fontana H 336 What A Mess!/Lorraine (some in p/s) . . . 15/5
61 Fontana H 362 Lesson In Love/Oh, My Love . . . 10
62 Fontana 267 231TF Sweet And Lovely/Sugar Love . . . 5
62 Fontana 267 255TF I'll Cross My Fingers/You Should Be Sorry . . . 5
69 Fontana TF 1021 Are You Sure/There's One Thing More (p/s) . . . 5
61 Fontana TFE 17339 THE ALLISONS (EP) . . . 20
61 Fontana TFL 5135 ARE YOU SURE (LP, also stereo STFL 558) . . . 25/30

ALLISONS (U.S.)

64 Stateside SS 289 Surfer Street/Money (vocal: Darlene Love) . . . 25
(see also Blossoms, Darlene Love)

ALLMAN BROTHERS BAND

73 Capricorn/Sound For Industry SFI 165 Ramblin' Man/MARSHALL TUCKER BAND: Take The Highway (flexidisc free with *Rolling Stone* magazine) . . . 8/5
70 Atco 228 033 THE ALLMAN BROTHERS BAND (LP) . . . 18
71 Atco 2400 032 IDLEWILD SOUTH (LP) . . . 15
(see also Duane Allman, Gregg Allman, Duane & Gregg Allman, Allman Joys, Hourglass)

DUANE ALLMAN

72 Capricorn K 67502 AN ANTHOLOGY (2-LP) . . . 20
(see also Allman Brothers, Duane & Gregg Allman)

DUANE & GREGG ALLMAN

73 Polydor 2310 235 DUANE & GREGG ALLMAN (LP) . . . 15
(see also Allman Brothers, Duane Allman, Gregg Allman)

GREGG ALLMAN

73 Capricorn K 47508/CP0116 LAID BACK (LP) . . . 15
(see also Allman Brothers, Duane & Gregg Allman)

ALLMAN JOYS

73 Mercury 6398 005 ALLMAN JOYS (LP) . . . 16

ALL NIGHT BAND

79 Contact CON 5 Lovely Ladies/It's My Life . . . 8

ALL SAINTS (1.9.7.5.)

94 ZTT SAM 1372 Silver Shadow (Shadow '94)/(UK Swing One)/(Club Sax)/(B-Bop)/(UK Swing Two)/(Jungle)/(Rap Dub)/(Underground Mix)/(Rare Groove)/(Bogle Dub) (12", as All Saints 1.9.7.5., double-pack, stickered title sleeve, promo only) . . . 15
95 ZTT ZANG 53 Silver Shadow/(UK Swing One) (p/s, as All Saints 1.9.7.5.) . . . 6
95 ZTT ZANG 53C Silver Shadow/(UK Swing One) (cassette, as All Saints 1.9.7.5.) . . . 5
95 ZTT ZANG 53T SILVER SHADOW (12" EP, as All Saints 1.9.7.5., remixes) . . . 8
95 ZTT ZANG 53CD SILVER SHADOW (CD EP, as All Saints 1.9.7.5., remixes) . . . 12
(see also Drive)

TOMMY ALLSUP

65 London HA-U 8218 BUDDY HOLLY SONG BOOK (LP) . . . 30

TONY ALMERICO'S DIXIELAND JAMBOREE ALLSTARS

55 London RE-P 1019 DIXIELAND (EP, reissued as RE-D 1019) . . . 15/12

ALMIGHTY

90 Polydor PZP 75 WILD AND WONDERFUL EP (12" picture disc, numbered die-cut sleeve) . . . 8
91 Polydorj PZP 144 DEVIL'S TOY EP (12", numbered poster sleeve) . . . 8

JOHNNY ALMOND MUSIC MACHINE

69 Deram DM 266 Solar Level/To R.K. . . . 20
69 Deram DML/SML 1043 PATENT PENDING (LP) . . . 25
70 Deram SML 1057 HOLLYWOOD BLUES (LP) . . . 40
(see also Alan Price Set, Zoot Money, Paul Williams Set, John Mayall & Bluesbreakers, Mark-Almond, Jon Mark)

MINT VALUE £

MARC ALMOND

SINGLES

84	Some Bizzare BZS 2310	The Boy Who Came Back (Extended)/Joey Demento (Extended) (10", p/s)	15
84	Some Bizzare BZS 2312	The Boy Who Came Back (Loud Cut)/Joey Demento (Extended) (12", p/s)	8
84	Some Bizzare BZS 2410	You Have (Ext.)/Black Mountain Blues/Split Lip (Ext.) (10", p/s, with lyric sheet)	12
84	Some Bizzare BZS 2412	You Have (Long Version)/Joey Demento/Split Lip (Long Version) (12", p/s)	10
84	Some Bizzare BZS 2510	Tenderness Is A Weakness (Extended)/Love For Sale/Pink Shack Blues (live)/ The Heel (live) (10", p/s, with lyric insert)	15
86	Some Bizzare GLOWY 2-10	A Woman's Story/The Heel/A Salty Dog/The Plague/ The Little White Cloud That Cried/For One Moment/ Just Good Friends (10", picture disc, stickered PVC sl.)	8
86	Some Bizzare GLOW 3-13	Ruby Red (Re-recorded Extended Dance Mix)/(Instrumental)/ I'm Sick Of You Tasting Of Somebody Else (12", stickered p/s; some mispressed with same track repeated on Side 1)	20/15
87	Some Bizzare GLOWD 4	Melancholy Rose/Gyp The Blood//Pirate Jenny/Surabaya Johnny (double pack, gatefold p/s)	7
87	Some Bizzare GLOW 4-12	Melancholy Rose/Gyp The Blood/A World Full Of People/Black Lullaby (12", p/s with postcard)	8
88	Parlophone RX 6186	Tears Run Rings/Everything I Wanted Love To Be (box set with booklet, cards & badge)	5
88	Parlophone CDR 6186	Tears Run Rings (Extended)/Everything I Wanted Love To Be/ Tears Run Rings (7" Version) (CD)	10
89	Parlophone RX 6201	Something's Gotten Hold Of My Heart (with "Special Guest Star Gene Pitney")/ Something's Gotten Hold Of My Heart (numbered box set with booklet, 2 cards & badge & sticker)	8
89	Parlophone PSR 500	Kept Boy (etched B-side, no p/s, cancelled freebie intended for "The Stars We Are" LP)	25
90	Parlophone 12RPD 6252	The Desperate Hours/The Gambler (12", picture disc)	10
91	WEA Y 2633TP	My Hand Over My Heart/Deadly Serenade (12", picture disc)	10
91	Mercury SOFCP 1	Say Hello Wave Goodbye '91/Numbers (Original Version)/Torch (Original Extended Version) (CD, picture disc)	10
91	Mercury SOFCD 2	Tainted Love (Original 7" Version)/Where The Heart Is (Remix)/Tainted Love (Remixed By Mendelsohn) (CD in leather wallet, various colours)	12
92	WEA YZ 638T	Extract From "Trois Chanson De Bilitis"/The Days Of Pearly Spencer/ Dancing In A Golden Cage/Dancing In A Golden Cage (Reflection In A Golden Eye) (12", withdrawn, 300 only)	15
92	WEA YZ 638CDX	Extract From "Trois Chanson De Bilitis"/The Days Of Pearly Spencer/ Dancing In A Golden Cage (CD, no'd holographic disc in metallic card p/s)	8

FLEXIDISCS & FREEBIES

82	Lyntone LYN 12505	Discipline (as 'Marc Almond & Friends', flexidisc with *Flexipop* issue 23)	12/7
84	Gutter Hearts LYN 14210	My Death (fan club flexidisc)	12
86	MM Vinyl Conflict 1	Oily Black Limousine (col. vinyl, b/w 3 songs by others, free with *Melody Maker*)	6
86	(no label or cat. no.)	Your Aura (live) (fan club flexidisc)	10
89	Offbeat 1	Tears Run Rings (La Magia Dance Mix) (3" CD, with *Offbeat* magazine)	10
92	(no label or cat. no.)	Christmas In Vegas (fan club flexidisc)	5
95	(no label or cat. no.)	When I Was A Young Man (fan club cassette)	10

PROMOS

88	Parlophone PSR 500	Kept Boy (1-sided, B-side etched)	25
90	Parlophone RDJ 6263	Waifs & Strays (12" Grid Mix)/Waifs & Strays (The Grid Twilight Mix) (12")	8
91	Mercury SOFT DJ 112	Say Hello Wave Goodbye '91 (The Long Goodbye Ext. Mendelsohn Remix)/ Memorabilia '91 (Extended Grid Remix) (12", p/s)	8
91	Mercury SOFT DJ 212	Tainted Love (Mendelsohn Remix)/Tainted Love (The Grid Remix) (12", p/s)	8
91	Mercury SOFT DJ 3	Bedsitter (Grid Remix)/Torch (Original) (p/s)	15
91	Mercury SOFT DJ 312	Tainted Love (MegaMix '91)/Bedsitter (Original 12" Version) (12", p/s)	15
92	WEA YZ 633 CDDJ	The Days Of Pearly Spencer/Bruises/Dancing In A Golden Cage (CD)	12
95	Mercury MRXDJ 431	Adored And Explored (Andy Meecham Big Long Club Mix)/(X-Press 2 Supervox Mix)/(X-Press 2 Extreme Excess Mix)/(Kung-Fu Mix)/(Kung-Fu Instrumental Mix)/(Beatmasters Master Dub) (12", double pack, red vinyl)	10
95	Mercury MRRDJ 431	Adored And Explored (Andy Meecham Slow Fat Dub) (12", 1-sided white label)	25
95	Mercury MRXDJ 437	The Idol (Tin Tin Out Mix)/(Idolised)/(Teenage Dream Mix)/(Mad Dog Mix) (12", double pack, white vinyl)	10
96	Mercury MXDJ 444	Out There (Non Eric Remix)/(B-Flats Northern Soul Mix)/(House Of Usher Remix)/(DA Clubheroes Remix)/(DA Clubheroes Rework) (12")	10
96	Mercury MERDJ 444	Out There (Tony De Vit Mix Parts 1 & 2)/(Space Cat Mix)/(F*** TheCustomsMix)/ (Sticky Black Plastic Mix)/(Valerie Singleton Mix)/ (Cabaret Mix) (12" double pack)	10
96	EMI PJDJ 25	Yesterday Has Gone (Balearico Mix)/Yesterday Has Gone (with P.J. Proby) (12")	8
96	EMI MARC PJDJ 25	Yesterday Has Gone (with My Life Story Orchestra & P.J. Proby) (12")	8

LPs

84	Gutter Hearts GH 1	BITE BACK + BLUES (fan club-only LP, credited to "Raoul & The Ruined")	30
95	EMI CDMATBOX 1	TREASURE BOX 1 (2-CD, box set)	20
97	Some Bizzare SBZCD 022	VIOLENT SILENCE/FLESH VOLCANO (CD, withdrawn)	20

(see also Soft Cell, Marc & Mambas, Burmoe Brothers, Vicious Pink Phenomena, Flesh Volcano, Annie Hogan, Sally Timms, Gene Pitney)

ALMOND LETTUCE

68	Columbia DB 8442	The Tree Dog Song/To Henry With Hope	6
69	Philips BF 1764	Magic Circle/Twenty Weary Miles	15

ALMOND MARZIPAN

70	Trend TNT 53	Open Up Your Heart/Summer Love	12
70	Trend TNT 55	Marie Take A Chance/I'll Forget You	6

MINT VALUE £

HERB ALPERT (& TIJUANA BRASS)

64	Stateside SS 286	Mexican Drummer Man/The Great Manolette	10
67	Pye International 7N 25419	Casino Royale (From The Film)/The Wall Street Rag (unissued)	
68	A&M AMS 700	Casino Royale (From The Film)/The Wall Street Rag (p/s)	5
69	A&M AMS 755	Without Her/Sandbox (p/s)	5

ALPHASTONE

90s	Enraptured RAPTLP 18	ELASTICATED WAVEBAND (LP, clear vinyl, 100 only)	15
90s	Enraptured RAPTLP 33	LIFE IS A MOTORWAY EP (2 x 12", gatefold sleeve, limited issue)	10

CARLTON ALPHONSO

67	Pama PM 700	Where In This World/Peace Makers	25
69	Grape GR 3000	Belittle Me/Keep Your Love	12

CLYDE ALPHONSO

69	Studio One SO 2076	Good Enough/Let The Music Play	25

ORVILLE ALPHONSO

65	Caribou CRC 1	Belly Lick/Inspiration	10

ROLAND ALPHONSO (alias ROLAND AL)

61	Blue Beat BB 58	Blackberry Brandy/ALVIN & CECIL: Marjorie	60
62	Blue Beat BB 112	Four Corners Of The World (with Alley Cats)/SHINERS: Romantic Shuffle	50
64	R&B JB 164	Crime Wave/MAYTALS: Hello Honey	40
65	Island WI 217	El Pussy Cat/LORD BRYNNER: Tiger In Your Tank	30
65	Ska Beat JB 210	Nimble Foot/ANDY & JOEY: Love Is Stronger	50
65	Ska Beat JB 216	Nuclear Weapon (with Baba Brooks)/STRANGER COLE: Love Thy Neighbour	50
65	Rio R 5804	Jazz Ska/HYACINTH: Oh Gee	50
66	Blue Beat BB 356	Just A Closer Walk/Jericho Train	70
66	Island WI 259	James Bond/LEE PERRY: Just Keep It Up	60
66	Doctor Bird DB 1010	From Russia With Love/Cleopatra (with Soul Brothers)	50
66	Doctor Bird DB 1011	Sufferer's Choice (with Soul Brothers)/SOULETTES: I Want To Be	50
66	Doctor Bird DB 1013	WAILERS: Rude Boy/ROLANDO AL & SOUL BROTHERS: Ringo's Theme (This Boy)	80-100
66	Doctor Bird DB 1017	Sugar And Spice/Get Out Of My Life (with Soul Brothers)	50
66	Doctor Bird DB 1020	Phoenix City (with Soul Brothers)/DEACONS: Men Alone	35
66	Doctor Bird DB 1023	Doctor Ring-A-Ding/FREDDIE & HEARTACHES: Here Is My Heart	60
66	Doctor Bird DB 1039	WAILERS: Rasta Put It On/ROLAND AL & SOUL BROTHERS: Ska With Ringo	100
66	Ska Beat JB 231	Rinky Dink (So Good) (with Studio One Orchestra)/ SCRATCH & DYNAMITES: Deacon Johnson	50
67	Pyramid PYR 6003	Middle East/Wise Man	40
67	Pyramid PYR 6004	El Torro/007 (Shanty Town)	10
67	Pyramid PYR 6005	Women Of The World (& Beverley's Allstars)/SPANISHTONIANS: Kisses	20
67	Pyramid PYR 6006	On The Move (& Beverley's Allstars)/ DESMOND DEKKER & ACES: It's A Shame	12
67	Pyramid PYR 6007	Jungle Bit (& Beverley's Allstars)/ NORMAN GRANT: Somebody Please Help Me	20
67	Pyramid PYR 6008	The Cat/DESMOND DEKKER & ACES: Rudy Got Soul	20
67	Pyramid PYR 6009	Guantanamera Ska (& Beverley's Allstars)/SPANISHTONIANS: Suffer Me Not	40
67	Pyramid PYR 6011	Nothing For Nothing/DESMOND DEKKER & ACES: Rude Boy Train	25
67	Pyramid PYR 6018	Sock It To Me (& Beverley's Allstars)/SPANISHTONIANS: Rudie Gets Plenty	30
68	Pyramid PYR 6022	Whiter Shade Of Pale/On The Move	10
68	Pyramid PYR 6030	Dreamland/MAYTALS: 54-46, Was My Number	30
68	Pyramid PYR 6043	Stream Of Life/MAYTALS: Struggle	12
68	Coxsone CS 7077	Reggae In The Grass/ROY RICHARDS: Get Smart	45
69	Gas GAS 112	A Thousand Tons Of Megaton (actually by Derrick Morgan)/Musical Resurrection	20
69	Jackpot JP 704	Zapatoo The Tiger/Music House	7
70	Punch PH 39	Roll On (& Upsetters)/CARL DAWKINS: True Love	6
71	Banana BA 340	Mellow Mood (Way To My Heart)/MAYTALS: Marching On	22

(see also Eric Morris, Bob Marley/Wailers, Prince Buster, Hopeton Lewis, Joe White, Johnny Melody; Monty & Roy; Derrick Morgan, Niney, Jackie Opel; Owen & Leon; Kentrick Patrick, Duke Reid; Roy & Millie; Slickers, Lou Sparkles, Jack Sparrow, Austin Faithful, Clancy Eccles, Charmers, Denny & Wilson, Dennis Alcapone, Ken Boothe, Larry Marshall)

ALPINES

68	Double D DD 110	Get Ready/CARIBBEATS: Come Back Charlie	20

ALQUIN

73	Polydor 2480 152	MARKS (LP)	15

RITA ALSTON

70	Trojan TR 7751	Popcorn Funky Reggae/NAT COLE: My Love	5
70	Trojan TR 7752	All Kinds Of Everything/CARL LEVEY: Instrumental Version	5

(see also Rita, Nat Cole)

SHIRLEY ALSTON

75	London SHA 8491	WITH A LITTLE HELP FROM MY FRIENDS (LP)	20

(see also Shirelles)

ALTECS

61	London HLU 9387	Easy/Recess	12

(see also The Black Dog)

ALTERNATIVE TV

77	Sniffing Glue SG 75 RPS	Love Lies Limp (1-sided flexidisc with *Sniffing Glue* fanzine issue 12)	20/5
77	Deptford Fun City DFC 02	How Much Longer/You Bastard (p/s)	8
77	Deptford Fun City DFC 02	How Much Longer/You Bastard (p/s, labelled 'alternate versions')	7
78	Deptford Fun City DFC 04	Life After Life/Life After Dub (p/s)	5
78	Deptford Fun City DFC 06	Life/Love Lies Limp (p/s)	5
78	Deptford Fun City DFC 07	Action Time Vision/Another Coke (live) (p/s)	6
79	Deptford Fun City DFC 10	The Force Is Blind/Lost In Room (Vibing Up The Senile Man) (p/s, last track uncredited)	5

MINT VALUE £

78 Deptford Fun City DLP 01 THE IMAGE HAS CRACKED (LP) . . . 12
78 Deptford Fun City DLP 02 WHAT YOU SEE IS ... WHAT YOU ARE (LP, 1 side by Here & Now) . . . 12
78 Deptford Fun City DLP 03 VIBING UP THE SENILE MAN (PART ONE) (LP) . . . 12
79 Crystal CLP 01 LIVE AT THE RAT CLUB '77 (authorised bootleg) (LP) . . . 12
80 Deptford Fun City DLP 05 ACTION TIME VISION (LP, with inner sleeve) . . . 12
80 Weird Noise WEIRD 001 SCARS ON SUNDAY (shared C60 cassette, 1 side by Good Missionaries) . . . 15
80 Conventional CON 14 AN YE AS WELL (cassette, shared with Good Missionaries) . . . 15
(see also Mark Perry, Good Missionaries, The Door & The Window, Jools Holland, Alex Fergusson, Rat & Whale)

ALTERNATORS
78 Energy NRG 001 No Answers/The Kid Don't Know (no p/s) . . . 40

ALTERNOMEN UNLIMITED
79 Object OM 06 Facade/Connections (p/s) . . . 5
(see also Spherical Objects)

ALTON (Ellis) & EDDY
60 Blue Beat BB 17 Muriel/CLUE J. & HIS BLUES BLASTERS: Silky . . . 40
62 Island WI 009 My Love Divine/Let Me Dream . . . 30
(see also Alton Ellis)

ALTON & FLAMES
(see under Alton Ellis)

ALVARO
77 Squeaky Shoes SSRM 1 DRINKING MY OWN SPERM (LP) . . . 15
(see also 101'ers)

ALVYN
69 Morgan Bluetown MR 18S You've Gotta Have An Image/Mind The Gap . . . 7

AMALGAM
69 Transatlantic TRA 196 A PRAYER FOR PEACE (LP) . . . 35
73 A Records A 002 PLAY BLACKWELL & HIGGINS (LP) . . . 18

GLEN AMAMS
69 Escort ES 804 Rich In Love/WOODPECKERS: Zumbelly . . . 15
(see also Glen Adams)

A MAN CALLED ADAM
90s Acid Jazz JAZID 4T A.P.B. (12", company sleeve) . . . 12
90s Acid Jazz JAZID 15T Earthly Powers/Techno Powers (12", p/s) . . . 15
(see also Leftfield)

AMAZIAH
74 Sunrise SR 001 STRAIGHT TALKER (LP, private pressing with insert) . . . 165

AMAZING BLONDEL
72 Island WIP 6153 Alleluia (Cantus Firmus To Counterpoint)/Safety In God Alone . . . 7
75 DJM DJS 407 Be So Happy/Queen . . . 6
76 DJM DJS 661 I'll Go The Way I Came/Liberty Belle . . . 6
76 DJM DJX 503 Mulgrave Street/Sad To See You Go/Hole In The Head . . . 6
70 Bell SBLL 131 THE AMAZING BLONDEL AND A FEW FACES (LP) . . . 70
70 Island ILPS 9136 EVENSONG (LP, gatefold sleeve) . . . 18
71 Island ILPS 9156 FANTASIA LINDUM (LP, with inner lyric sleeve) . . . 18
72 Island ILPS 9205 ENGLAND (LP, gatefold sleeve) . . . 15
73 Island ILPS 9257 BLONDEL (LP, gatefold sleeve) . . . 15
75 DJM DJLPS 443 MULGRAVE STREET (LP) . . . 14
76 DJM DJLPS 446 INSPIRATION (LP) . . . 14
76 DJM DJLPS 472 BAD DREAMS (LP) . . . 12
77 DJM DJF 20203 LIVE IN TOKYO (LP) . . . 12
(see also Dimples, Gospel Garden)

AMAZING DANCING BAND
68 Verve VS 567 Deep Blue Train/Simon Smith & His Amazing Dancing Bear . . . 20
67 Verve SVLP 9214 AMAZING DANCING BAND (LP) . . . 30

AMAZING FRIENDLY APPLE
69 Decca F 12887 Water Woman/Magician . . . 75

AMAZING SPACE FROGS
79 Ribbett RIB 1 THE DIRTY HABITS EP . . . 25

AMBERGRIS
70 Paramount SPFL 262 AMBERGRIS (LP) . . . 15

AMBER SQUAD
80 Sound Of Leicester ST 1 (I Can't) Put My Finger On You/Tell You A Lie (p/s) . . . 60
80 Dead Good DEAD 17 Can We Go Dancing?/You Should See (What I Do To You In My Dreams) (p/s) . . . 40

AMBOY DUKES (U.K.)
66 Polydor 56149 Turn Back To Me/I Never Complain About You . . . 7
67 Polydor 56172 All I Need/Doing The Best I Can . . . 8
67 Polydor 56190 High Life In Whitley Wood (Parts 1 & 2) . . . 7
68 Polydor 56228 Judy In Disguise/Who's Foolin' Who . . . 7
68 Polydor 56243 Simon Says/The Marquis . . . 7
68 Polydor 56281 He Came To See Me Yesterday/Easy Going Me . . . 6

(AMERICAN) AMBOY DUKES
68 Fontana TF 971 Let's Go Get Stoned/It's Not True . . . 18
67 Fontana (S)TL 5468 THE AMBOY DUKES (LP) . . . 75
69 London HA-T/SH-T 8378 JOURNEY TO THE CENTER OF THE MIND (LP, as American Amboy Dukes) . . . 35
69 London HA-T/SH-T 8392 MIGRATION (LP, as American Amboy Dukes) . . . 30
74 Discreet DS 2203 TOOTH, FANG AND CLAW (LP) . . . 25
(see also Ted Nugent)

MINT VALUE £

AMBROSE & HIS ORCHESTRA
55 MGM SPC 2 Chelsea/My Guy's Come Back (export issue) . . . 5
55 MGM SPC 3 Chee Chee-oo Chee (Sang The Little Bird) (export issue) . . . 5
55 MGM SPC 4 Whistling Willie/Get Happy (export issue) . . . 5
55 MGM SPC 9 Slide Rule/Tango Capriccioso (export issue) . . . 5
56 MGM SP 1151 Lilacs In The Rain/Deep Purple . . . 5

AMANDA AMBROSE
63 RCA Victor RD 7605 THE AMAZING AMANDA AMBROSE (LP) . . . 15

SAMMY AMBROSE
65 Stateside SS 385 This Diamond Ring/Bad Night . . . 80
65 Stateside SS 399 Monkey See Monkey Do/Welcome To Dreamsville . . . 90

AMBROSE SLADE
69 Fontana TF 1015 Genesis/Roach Daddy . . . 200
69 Fontana STL 5492 BEGINNINGS (LP, laminated sleeve, black label with silver print; beware of counterfeits with matt sleeve & black & white label) . . . 230
75 Contour 6870 678 BEGINNINGS OF SLADE (LP, reissue, different cover & running order, withdrawn) . . . 55
(see also Slade, 'N Betweens)

AMBROSIA
75 20th Century BT 434 AMBROSIA (LP) . . . 15
76 20th Century BT 519 SOMEWHERE I'VE NEVER TRAVELLED (LP, with inner sleeve) . . . 15
78 Warner Bros K 56252 LIFE BEYOND L.A. (LP) . . . 12
80 Warner Bros K 56811 ONE EIGHTY (LP) . . . 12

AMEBIX
82 Spiderleg SDL 6 Who's The Enemy/Carnage/No Gods No Masters (p/s) . . . 20
83 Spiderleg SDL 10 Winter/Beginning Of The End (p/s) . . . 18

LOLA AMECHE
53 Oriole CB 1143 Rock The Joint/Don't Let The Stars Get In Your Eyes (78) . . . 15
53 Oriole CB 1172 The Knockin' Song/So Far So Good (78) . . . 10

AMEN
99 Road Runner RR 21315 COMA AMERICA EP . . . 6

AMEN CORNER
67 Deram DM 136 Gin House Blues/I Know (early copies entitled "Gin House" on label) . . . 10
67 Deram DM 151 The World Of Broken Hearts/Nema . . . 6
68 Deram DM 172 Bend Me Shape Me/Satisnek The Job's Worth . . . 5
68 Deram DM 197 High In The Sky/Run, Run, Run . . . 5
69 Deram DM 228 The World Of Broken Hearts/Gin House Blues . . . 5
69 Immediate IM 073 (If Paradise Is) Half As Nice/Hey Hey Girl . . . 5
69 Immediate IM 081 Hello Susie/Evil Man's Gonna Win . . . 5
69 Immediate IM 084 Get Back/Farewell To The Real Magnificent Seven . . . 5
69 Immediate AS 3 So Fine (promo only 'single sampler' for IMSP 023) . . . 20
76 Immediate SV 104 (If Paradise Is) Half As Nice/Bend Me Shape Me/ Hello Susie/High In The Sky (double pack, gatefold p/s) . . . 6
80 Virgin SV 104 THE IMMEDIATE CATALOGUE (doublepack, p/s) . . . 8
68 Deram DML/SML 1021 ROUND AMEN CORNER (LP) . . . 25
69 Immediate IMSP 023 THE NATIONAL WELSH COAST LIVE EXPLOSION COMPANY (LP, g/fold sl.) . . . 20
69 Immediate IMSP 028 FAREWELL TO THE REAL MAGNIFICENT SEVEN (LP, gatefold sleeve) . . . 18
(see also Andy Fairweather-Low, Fairweather, Mayfield's Mule, Judas Jump)

AMERICAN BREED
67 CBS 2888 Step Out Of Your Mind/The Same Old Thing . . . 10
67 CBS 2972 Step Out Of Your Mind/The Same Old Thing (reissue) . . . 5
68 Stateside SS 2078 Bend Me Shape Me/Mindrocker . . . 5
68 Dot DOT 101 Green Light/Don't It Make You Cry . . . 5
68 Dot DOT 106 Ready, Willing And Able/Take Me If You Want Me . . . 5
67 Dot DOLP 255 AMERICAN BREED (LP) . . . 20
68 Dot (S)LPD 502 BEND ME, SHAPE ME (LP) . . . 20
68 Dot (S)LPD 507 NO WAY TO TREAT A LADY (LP, soundtrack) . . . 30
68 Dot (S)LPD 518 PUMPKIN, POWDER, SCARLET AND GREEN (LP) . . . 15
69 Dot (S)LPD 526 THE LONELY SIDE OF THE CITY (LP) . . . 12

AMERICAN GYPSY
71 CBS 7027 Gypsy Queen Pt 1/Dead & Gone . . . 6
75 BTM SBT 101 Angel Eyes/Lady Eleanor . . . 5
75 BTM BTM 1001 AMERICAN GYPSY (LP) . . . 25

(AMERICAN) POETS
66 London HLC 10037 She Blew A Good Thing/Out To Lunch (as American Poets) . . . 110
71 United Artists UP 35308 She Blew A Good Thing/Out To Lunch (reissue, as Poets) . . . 12

AMERICAN SPRING
72 United Artists UP 35376 Good Time/Sweet Mountain . . . 8
72 United Artists UP 35421 Mama Said/Tennessee Waltz . . . 8
73 CBS CBS 1590 Shyin' Away/Falling In Love . . . 12
72 United Artists UAG 29363 AMERICAN SPRING (LP) . . . 35
(see also Beach Boys, Honeys)

AMERICAN YOUTH CHOIR
71 Polydor 2066 013 Together We Can Make It/Keep Your Fine Self Near Me . . . 50

EDDIE AMES
57 HMV POP 311 The Bean Song/I'd Give You The World . . . 10

NANCY AMES
66 Columbia DB 7809 Friends And Lovers Forever/I've Got A Lot Of Love . . . 20
66 Columbia DB 8039 Cry Softly/I Don't Want To Talk About It . . . 40

MINT VALUE £

AMES BROTHERS

Year	Label/Cat. No.	Title	Value
53	HMV 7M 153	You, You, You/My Life, My Love, My Happiness	15
54	HMV 7M 179	I Can't Believe That You're In Love/Boogie Woogie Maxine	25
54	HMV 7M 209	The Man With The Banjo/Man, Man, Is For The Woman Made	10
54	HMV 7M 253	Hopelessly/One More Time	10
55	HMV 7M 281	The Naughty Lady Of Shady Lane/Addio	10
55	HMV 7M 310	Sweet Brown-Eyed Baby/Sympathetic Eyes	10
55	HMV 7M 322	Wrong Again/Merci Beaucoup	10
55	HMV 7M 331	So Will I/My Bonnie Lassie	10
56	HMV 7M 410	My Love, Your Love/If You Wanna See Mamie Tonight	10
56	HMV 7MC 46	If You Wanna See Mamie Tonight/It Only Hurts For A Little While (export issue)	10
56	HMV POP 242	I'm Gonna Love You/It Only Hurts For A little While	5
56	HMV POP 264	49 Shades Of Green/Summer Sweetheart	5
57	RCA RCA 1015	Rocking Shoes/Tammy	10
57	RCA RCA 1021	So Little Time/Melodie D'Amour	10
58	RCA RCA 1049	In Love/A Very Precious Love	10
58	RCA RCA 1091	No One But You (In My Heart)/Pussy Cat	10
59	RCA RCA 1104	Red River Rose/When The Summer Comes	10
59	RCA RCA 1118	(Yes, I Need) Only Your Love/Dancin' In The Streets	10
59	RCA RCA 1135	Someone To Come To/Mason-Dixon Line	10
57	HMV 7EG 8237	EXACTLY LIKE YOU (EP)	10
59	RCA RCX 1047	BEST OF THE AMES BROTHERS (EP)	10
56	Coral LVA 9071	THE SOUNDS OF CHRISTMAS HARMONY (LP)	10

AMITY

Year	Label/Cat. No.	Title	Value
76	Red Rag RRR 001	AMITY (LP)	100

AMM

Year	Label/Cat. No.	Title	Value
66	Incus EP 1	AT THE ROUNDHOUSE (EP)	165
67	Elektra EUKS 7256	AMM MUSIC (LP)	110

(see also Eddie Provost Band)

ALBERT AMMONS

Year	Label/Cat. No.	Title	Value
52	Vogue V 2109	Boogie Woogie Stomp/Boogie Woogie Blues (78)	10
54	Vogue V 2201	Chicago In Mind (with Meade 'Lux' Lewis)/Two And Few (78)	10
54	Vogue V 2213	Bass Goin' Crazy/Suitcase Blues (78)	10
55	Vogue EPV 1071	ALBERT AMMONS (EP)	40
57	Brunswick OE 9325	BOOGIE WOOGIE STOMP (EP)	40
54	Mercury MG 25012	ALBERT AMMONS (10" LP)	40
62	Storyville SLP 184	BOOGIE WOOGIE TRIO (LP)	25

(see also [Big] Joe Turner)

ALBERT AMMONS & PETE JOHNSON

Year	Label/Cat. No.	Title	Value
55	HMV DLP 1011	EIGHT TO THE BAR (10" LP)	30

ALBERT AMMONS, PETE JOHNSON & MEADE 'LUX' LEWIS

Year	Label/Cat. No.	Title	Value
55	Columbia SEG 7528	SHOUT FOR JOY (EP)	25
63	Riverside RLP 12-106	GIANTS OF BOOGIE WOOGIE (LP)	25

(see also Pete Johnson, Meade 'Lux' Lewis)

GENE AMMONS (BAND)

Year	Label/Cat. No.	Title	Value
60	Starlite ST45 017	Echo Chamber Blues/Ammons' Boogie	55
63	Starlite ST45 097	Anna/Cae' Cae'	12
62	Esquire EP 249	BOSSA NOVA BY THE BOSS (EP)	12
59	Esquire 32-047	HI FI JAM SESSION (LP)	25
59	Esquire 32-077	FUNKY (LP)	25
60	Esquire 32-097	JAMMIN' WITH GENE (LP)	25
62	Esquire 32-147	BLUE GENE (LP)	25
63	Esquire 32-177	BOSS TENOR (LP)	25
63	Esquire 32-178	BAD! BOSSA NOVA (LP)	40
72	Prestige PR 24021	JUG & DODO (LP, with Dodo Marmarosa)	15
73	Prestige PR 10019	YOU TALK THAT TALK (LP)	15
73	Prestige PR 10021	BROTHER JUG (LP)	15
74	Prestige PR 24036	JUGANTHOLOGY VOL. 1 (LP)	15

AMON DÜÜL II

Year	Label/Cat. No.	Title	Value
70	Liberty LBF 15355	Archangel's Thunderbird/Burning Sister	30
69	Liberty LBS 83279	PHALLUS DEI (LP)	50
70	Liberty LSP 101/LBS 83359	YETI (2-LP, gatefold sleeve)	40
71	United Artists UAD 60003/4	DANCE OF THE LEMMINGS (2-LP, gatefold sleeve)	30
72	Sunset SLS 50257	PHALLUS DEI (LP, reissue)	12
72	United Artists UAG 23927	CARNIVAL IN BABYLON (LP, gatefold sleeve)	30
72	United Artists UAG 29406	WOLF CITY (LP, gatefold sleeve)	25
73	United Artists USP 102	LIVE IN LONDON (LP)	14
73	United Artists UAS 29504	VIVE LA TRANCE (LP, with inner sleeve)	14

(see also Utopia)

AMORPHOUS ANDROGYNOUS

Year	Label/Cat. No.	Title	Value
93	Quigley LPEBV 1	TALES OF EPHIDRINA (LP)	18
93	Quigley CDEBV 1	TALES OF EPHIDRINA (CD)	18

(see also Future Sound Of London)

ADAM AMOS & NOEL ROCKS

Year	Label/Cat. No.	Title	Value
60s	Celtic Music CM 011	CASUAL ON THE BALCONY (LP)	15
60s	Celtic Music CM 026	ADAM AMOS & NOEL ROCKS (LP)	15

TORI AMOS

Year	Label/Cat. No.	Title	Value
91	East West YZ 618T	ME AND A GUN EP (12")	22
91	East West YZ 618CD	ME AND A GUN EP (CD)	22
91	East West YZ 618	Silent All These Years/Me And A Gun (p/s)	8
91	East West YZ 618T	Silent All These Years/Upside Down/Me And A Gun/Thoughts (12", p/s)	10

		MINT VALUE £
91	East West YZ 618CD	Silent All These Years/Upside Down/Me And A Gun/Thoughts (CD) 8
92	East West A 7531T	China/Sugar/Flying Dutchman/Humpty Dumpty (12", p/s) 10
92	East West A 7531CD	China/Sugar/Flying Dutchman/Humpty Dumpty (CD) 12
92	East West A 7504	Winter/The Pool (p/s) 5
92	East West A 7504CDX	Winter/Angie/Smells Like Teen Spirit/Thank You (CD, digipak) 22
92	East West A 7479CD	Crucify (Remix)/Here In My Head/Mary/Crucify (LP version) (CD) 8
92	East West A 7479CDX	CRUCIFY LIVE EP (CD, box set, with art prints, some sealed) 40/30
92	East West A 7433	Silent All These Years/Ode To The Banana King Part 1 (p/s) 5
92	East West A 7433CD	Silent All These Years/Upside Down/Me And A Gun/Thoughts (CD) 8
92	East West A 7433CDX	Silent All These Years/Ode To The Banana King Part 1/Song For Eric/ Happy Phantom (CD, digipak) 20
94	East West A 7281CDX	Cornflake Girl/A Case Of You/If 6 Were 9/Strange Fruit (CD, digipak) 18
94	East West A 7263CDX	Pretty Good Year/Home On The Range (with Cherokee addition)/ Daisy Dead Petals (CD, digipak) 8
94	East West A 7257CDX	PAST THE MISSION EP: Upside Down (live)/Past The Mission (live)/ Icicle (live)/Flying Dutchman (live) 8
98	East West AT 0045C	Raspberry Swirl (Lip Gloss Version)/(Sticky Extended Vocal Mix)/ (Scarlet Spectrum Feels) (CD, withdrawn) 12
99	Atlantic AT 0077CD2	GLORY OF THE 80s EP (CD, part 2 of 2-CD set, mispressing, plays CD-1 tracks) 12
97	East West PROP 100	BOYS FOR PELE (CD, promo, card sleeve) 30

AMOS & SARA

81	(private release)	THE PRIVATE WORLD OF AMOS (cassette) 10
82	It's War Boys £9	Go Home Soldier/Enough Is Enough/Surveillance O.H.M.S. (12", screenprint p/s) 10

(see also Homosexuals)

AMPS

90s	Enraptured RAPTLP 16	PASSÉ*PRÉSENT (2-LP, 1 disc audiophile vinyl, 1 blue vinyl, numbered) 20

ANAL FLEAS

82	Rectal FLEA 45	Psych/Over the Edge/Landlord/Go Down (p/s, with insert) 80

ANAN

68	Pye 7N 17571	Haze Woman/I Wonder Where My Sister's Gone 35
68	Pye 7N 17642	Madena/Standing Still 25

ANATHEMA

94	Peaceville CC 6	We Are The Bible (purple vinyl) 20

ANCIENT GREASE

71	Mercury 6338 033	WOMAN AND CHILDREN FIRST (LP) 35

(see also Eyes Of Blue, Big Sleep, Man, Gary Pickford-Hopkins)

AND ALSO THE TREES

83	Reflex (no cat. no.)	AND ALSO THE TREES (EP, cassette only) 20
84	Reflex RE 3	The Secret Sea/Secrecy (p/s) 8
84	Reflex 12 RE 6	The Secret Sea/Secrecy/There Were No Bounds/The Tease The Tear/ Midnight Garden/Wallpaper Dying (12", p/s) 10
84	Reflex FS 9	Shantell/Wallpaper Dying (p/s) 8
84	Reflex LEX 1	AND ALSO THE TREES (LP) 20

ERIC ANDERSEN

65	Fontana TFL 6061	TODAY IS THE HIGHWAY (LP) 18
68	Fontana STFL 6068	'BOUT CHANGES AND THINGS TAKE 2 (LP) 16

CARLEEN ANDERSON

90s	Circa YR12	DUSKY SAPPHO EP (12", p/s) 15

CAROL ANDERSON

79	Grapevine GRP 133	Sad Girl/I'll Get Off At the Next Stop 8

ERNESTINE ANDERSON

59	Mercury AMT 1035	Be Mine/I Don't See Me In Your Eyes Any More 5
59	Mercury AMT 1073	My Love Will Last/Call Me Darling 5
60	Mercury AMT 1082	There Are Such Times/You, You, You 5
60	Mercury AMT 1103	A Kiss To Build A Dream On/Come On, Baby, Let's Go 10
61	Mercury AMT 1137	A Lover's Question/That's All I Want From You 15
64	Sue WI 309	Keep An Eye On Love/Continental Mind 50
65	Stateside SS 455	Somebody Told You/How Many Times 10
65	Mercury MF 912	Jerk & Twine/You Can't Buy Love 10
60	Mercury ZEP 10057	RUNNING WILD (EP) 10
60	Mercury ZEP 10089	WELCOME TO THE CLUB (EP) 10
61	Mercury ZEP 10105	AZURE-TE (EP) 10
61	Mercury ZEP 10124	JUST A SWINGIN' (EP) 10
64	Mercury 10007 MCE	ERNESTINE ANDERSON (EP) 10
58	Pye Nixa NPT 19025	BY SPECIAL REQUEST (LP) 10
59	Mercury MMC 14016	RUNNIN' WILD (LP) 20
60	Mercury MMC 14037	THE FASCINATING ERNESTINE (LP) 15
61	Mercury MMC 14062	MOANIN' (LP) 20
64	Sue ILP 911	THE NEW SOUND OF ERNESTINE ANDERSON (LP, unissued) 50
67	Columbia S(C)X 6145	ERNESTINE ANDERSON (LP) 15

GLADSTONE ANDERSON (& FOLLOWERS)

69	Blue Cat BS 172	Judas/The World Come To An End (with Followers) 12
74	Ashanti ASH 413	It May Sound Silly/Gladdy's Workshop 6
73	Ashanti SHAN 103	IT MAY SOUND SILLY (LP) 15

(see also Stranger & Gladdy, Tommy McCook)

IAN (A.) ANDERSON

71	Village Thing VTSX 1002	One More Chance/Policeman's Ball 12
69	Saydisc EP SD 134	ALMOST THE COUNTRY BLUES (EP, with Elliot Jackson) 30
68	Saydisc Matchbox SDM 159	THE INVERTED WORLD (LP, with Mike Cooper) 45

MINT VALUE £

69	Liberty LBS 83242E	STEREO DEATH BREAKDOWN (LP, as Ian Anderson Country Blues Band)	35
70	Fontana STL 5542	BOOK OF CHANGES (LP)	25
70	Village Thing VTS 3	ROYAL YORK CRESCENT (LP)	12
72	Village Thing VTS 9	A VULTURE IS NOT A BIRD YOU CAN TRUST (LP)	12
72	Village Thing VTS 18	SINGER SLEEPS ON AS BLAZE RAGES (LP)	12

(see also Mike Cooper, Anderson Jones Jackson)

JON ANDERSON

76	Atlantic K 10840	Flight Of The Moorglade/To The Runner	5
80	Atlantic K 11619	Some Are Born/Days (p/s)	5

(see also Hans Christian, Warriors, Yes, Mike Oldfield, Jon & Vangelis)

KIP ANDERSON

67	President PT 163	You'll Lose A Good Thing/I'm Out Of Love	6

MILLER ANDERSON

71	Deram DM 337	Bright City/Another Time, Another Place	7
71	Deram SDL 3	BRIGHT CITY (LP)	25

(see also Voice, At Last The 1958 Rock'n'Roll Show, Keef Hartley Band, Hemlock, Dog Soldier, Lyn Dobson)

REUBEN ANDERSON

66	Doctor Bird DB 1045	Christmas Time Again/DESMOND TUCKER: Oh Holy Night	10

SONNY ANDERSON

60	London HLP 9036	Lonely Lonely Train/Yes, I'm Gonna Love You	75

UDELL T. ANDERSON

69	Direction 58-4212	Love Ain't Love/Funky Walk	6

VICKI ANDERSON

71	Polydor 2001 150	Super Good/Super Good (Version)	15
73	Mojo 2093 005	I'm Too Tough For Mr Big Stuff/Sound Funky	10
74	Mojo 2093 028	Don't Throw Your Love In The Garbage Can/Land Of Milk And Honey/ BOBBY BYRD: Sayin' It And Doin' It Are Two Different Things	8

(see also Bobby Byrd, James Brown)

ANDERSON, HARLEY & BATT

88	Epic PEEPS 1	Whatever You Believe/Whatever You Believe (live) (p/s)	10
88	Epic PEEPS 12P 1	Whatever You Believe (live)/Whatever You Believe/ Deep Is My Yearning (12", p/s)	10

(see also Steve Harley, Mike Batt)

ANDERSON, JONES, JACKSON

68	Saydisc 33 SD 125	ANDERSON, JONES, JACKSON (EP)	25

(see also Ian A. Anderson, Al Jones)

ANDERSON'S ALLSTARS

68	Blue Cat BS 133	Intensified Girls/Jump And Shout	35

BARBARA ANDREWS

70	Escort ERT 838	Lonesome Feeling/RAINY BOP: Hop Scotch	15

BARRY ANDREWS

80	Virgin VS 378	Rossmore Road (NW1)/Win A Night Out With A Well Known Paranoiac (p/s)	5

(see also XTC, Shriekback, Robert Fripp)

CATHERINE ANDREWS

80	Cat Tracks PURR LP 2	FRUITS (LP, with lyric sheet & poster sleeve)	55

(see also Gordon Giltrap, Inner City Unit)

CHRIS ANDREWS

65	Decca F 12236	Yesterday Man/Too Bad You Don't Want Me	5
65	Decca F 22285	To Whom It Concerns/It's All Up To You Now	5
66	Decca F 22365	Something On My Mind/I'll Do The Best I Can	5
66	Decca F 22404	Whatcha Gonna Do Now?/Lady Oh Lady	5
66	Decca F 22472	Stop That Girl/I'd Be Far Better Off Without You	5
66	Decca F 22521	That's What She Said/Write It Down	5
67	Decca F 22597	I'll Walk To You/They've All Got Their Eyes On You	5
67	Decca F 22668	Hold On/Easy	25
68	Pye 7N 17617	The Man With The Red Balloon/Keep Your Mind On The Right Side	5
69	Pye 7N 17727	Pretty Belinda/Maker Of Mistakes	5
70	Pye 7N 17958	Yo Yo/Hey Babe	5

(see also Chris Ravel & Ravers)

DAVE ANDREWS & SUGAR

68	Jewel JL 04	I'm On My Way/Beatin' Of My Heart	50

EAMONN ANDREWS

56	Parlophone R 4234	High Wind/The Legend Of Wyatt Earp	5
57	Parlophone R 4318	The Ship That Never Sailed/The Magic Tree	5

ERNIE ANDREWS

60	Vogue V 9166	'Round Midnight/Lover Come Back To Me	15
65	Capitol CL 15407	Where Were You/What Do I See In The Girl	15
76	Capitol CL 15873	Fine Young Girl/Then I'll Know	5

HARVEY ANDREWS

72	Cube BUG 20	In The Darkness/Soldier	5
72	Cube BUG 26	Learning The Game/Don't Know The Time	5
65	Transatlantic TRAEP 133	HARVEY ANDREWS (EP)	20
70	Decca Nova SDN 9	PLACES AND FACES (LP)	30
72	Cube HIFLY 10	WRITER OF SONGS (LP, with lyric insert)	12
73	Fly HIFLY 15	FRIENDS OF MINE (LP, gatefold sleeve)	12
75	Transatlantic TRA 298	FANTASIES FROM A CORNER SEAT (LP)	12
75	Transatlantic BIG 525	(I'm Resigning) From Today/Darby And Joan (with Graham Cooper)	5
76	Transatlantic TRA 329	SOME DAY (LP)	12

MINT VALUE £

INEZ ANDREWS & ANDREWETTES
65 Vogue EDVP 1283 — INEZ ANDREWS & ANDREWETTES (EP) 40

JOHN ANDREWS & LONELY ONES
66 Parlophone R 5455 — A Rose Growing In The Ruins/It's Just Love 30

LEE ANDREWS (& HEARTS)
57 London HL 7031 — Teardrops/Girl Around The Corner (solo, export issue) 300
58 London HLM 8546 — Teardrops/Girl Around The Corner (solo) 300
58 London HLM 8546 — Teardrops/Girl Around The Corner (solo) (78) 50
58 London HLU 8661 — Try The Impossible/Nobody's Home (as Lee Andrews & Hearts) 500
58 London HLU 8661 — Try The Impossible/Nobody's Home (as Lee Andrews & Hearts) (78) 50

PATTY ANDREWS
55 Capitol CL 14324 — Without Love/Where To My Love? 12
55 Capitol CL 14374 — Suddenly There's A Valley/Booga Da Woog 12
(see also Bing Crosby, Jimmy Durante)

TIM ANDREWS
67 Parlophone R 5656 — Sad Simon Lives Again/You Won't Be Seeing Me Anymore 5
68 Parlophone R 5695 — Your Tea Is Strong/(Something About) Suburbia 5
70 Parlophone R 5824 — Tiny Goddess/Josephine 5
(see also Fleur De Lys, Rupert's People)

TIM ANDREWS & PAUL KORDA
68 Parlophone R 5714 — Smile If You Want To/Makin' Love To Him 5
68 Parlophone R 5746 — Angel Face/Waiter Get Me A Drink 5
69 Parlophone R 5769 — How Many Hearts Must Be Broken/Discovery 5
(see also Paul Korda)

ANDREWS SISTERS
57 Capitol CL 14705 — Rum And Coca-Cola/No, Baby 10
57 Capitol CL 14807 — I'm Goin' Home/By His Word 10
58 Capitol CL 14826 — One Mistake/Melancholy Moon 5
58 Capitol CL 14878 — Torero/Sunshine 5
59 Brunswick 05782 — I'll Be With You In Apple Blossom Time/Oh! Johnny 5
59 Capitol CL 14998 — I've Got An Invitation To A Dance/My Love Is A Kitten 5
60 Capitol CL 15170 — Rum And Coca-Cola/I'll Be With You In Apple Blossom Time 5
61 Ace Of Hearts AH 21 — BY POPULAR DEMAND (LP) 10

ANDROIDS OF MU
80 Fuck Off FLP 001 — BLOOD ROBOTS (LP) 12

ANDROMEDA
69 RCA RCA 1854 — Go Your Way/Keep Out 'Cos I'm Dying 20
69 RCA SF 8031 — ANDROMEDA (LP) 170
90 Reflection MM 06 — SEVEN, LONELY STREET (LP, numbered & signed, 500 only) 15
95 Kissing Spell KSLP 9497 — LIVE 1967 (LP) 12
(see Attack, Five Day Week Straw People, Hard Stuff, Atomic Rooster, John Du Cann, Fuzzy Duck)

AND THE NATIVE HIPSTERS
79 Heater Volume HVR 003 — There Goes Concorde Again.../Stands, Still The Building.../ I Wanna Be Around (several different coloured photocopied foldaround sleeves with insert in polythene bag) . . . . each 8
82 Illuminated/Glass HIP 1 — TENDERLY HURT ME (Poor Prince/Hang Ten/Tenderly Hurt Me/Stuck) (12" EP, p/s) 12

ANDWELLA('S DREAM)
69 CBS 4301 — Sunday/Midday Sun (as Andwella's Dream) 50
69 CBS 4469 — Mrs. Man/Felix (as Andwella's Dream) 80
69 CBS 4634 — Mr. Sunshine/Shades Of Grey (as Andwella's Dream) 40
70 Reflection RS 1 — Every Little Minute/Michael Fitzhenry (as Andwella) 5
70 Reflection RS 3 — Hold Onto Your Mind/Shadow Of The Night (as Andwella) 8
71 Reflection RS 6 — People's People/Are You Ready (as Andwella) 7
69 CBS 63673 — LOVE AND POETRY (LP, as Andwella's Dream) 325
70 Reflection REFL 10 — WORLD'S END (LP, as Andwella, with poster) 25
71 Reflection REF 1010 — PEOPLE'S PEOPLE (LP, as Andwella) 25
(see also David Lewis, David Baxter)

BOB ANDY
67 Island WI 3040 — I've Got To Get Back Home/SONNY BURKE: Rudy Girl 40
68 Studio One SO 2063 — Too Experienced/Let Them Stay 35
68 Coxsone CS 7074 — Born A Man/MARCIA GRIFFITHS: Mark My Word 40
69 Doctor Bird DB 1183 — The Way I Feel/ETHIOPIANS: Long Time Now 40
69 Studio One SO 2075 — I'm Going Home/SOUND DIMENSION: Straight Flush 40
70 Harry J. HJ 6612 — Peace Of Mine/Weep 10
71 Trojan TR 7809 — Green Green Valley/Peace Of Mind 6
71 Trojan TR 7821 — One Woman/You Don't Know (B-side actually "Save Me Version" by Bob Andy Band) 6
71 Trojan TR 7840 — One Woman/You Don't Know 6
71 London HLJ 7127 — Games People Play/GAYLETTES: Son Of A Preacher Man (export issue) 10
72 Sioux SI 019 — Baby I Need Your Loving/CIRCLES: Mammy Blue 6
72 Sioux SI 020 — Everyday People/HONG GANG: Smoking Wild 6
72 Green Door GD 4047 — Life/HARRY J. ALL STARS: Version 10
73 Green Door GD 4059 — You Don't Know/The Border Song 18
73 Horse HOSS 31 — One Woman/Second Hand Love 6
75 Fab FAB 241 — Feeling Soul/SOUND DIMENSION: Part 2 10
(see also Bob & Marcia, Larry & Alvin)

HORACE ANDY
72 Attack ATT 8026 — Feel Good All Over/PHIL PRATT ALLSTARS: Feel Good (Version) 6
73 Bread BR 1170 — Don't Try To Use Me/Goddess Of Love 6
73 Randy's RAN 533 — Don't Think About Me (with Earl Flute)/DINO PERKINS: Skin Him Alive 18

MINT VALUE £

74 Ackee ACK 530 — Til/IMPACT ALLSTARS: Version . . . 6
75 Fab FAB 260 — Oh Lord Why Lord/SOUND DIMENSION: Part 2 . . . 10
72 Trojan TBL 197 — YOU ARE MY ANGEL (LP) . . . 20
(see also Jon Cuno, Big Youth)

ANDY & BEY SISTERS
59 Fontana H 174 — Pretty Baby/Sweeter Than Sweet . . . 10
59 Fontana H 197 — Scoubidou/Don't Get Around Much Anymore . . . 10

ANDY & CLYDE
65 Rio R 62 — Never Be A Slave/Magic Is Love . . . 15
65 Rio R 69 — I'm So Lonesome/WINSTON STEWART: Day After Day . . . 15
65 Rio R 71 — We All Have To Part/UPSETTERS: Scandalizing . . . 15

ANDY & JOEY
62 Island WI 056 — Have You Ever/Cross My Heart . . . 20
64 Port-O-Jam PJ 4009 — I Want To Know/My Love Has Gone . . . 15
64 Ska Beat JB 162 — You're Wondering Now/You'll Never (copies also exist on R&B label) . . . 15
(see also Roland Alphonso)

ANGEL
74 Cube BUG 41 — Good Time Fanny/Who D'Ya Think You're Foolin' . . . 5
74 Cube BUG 51 — Little Boy Blue/Tragedy Queen . . . 10

ANGEL
76 Casablanca CBC 4007 — ANGEL (LP, with insert) . . . 22
76 Casablanca CBC 4010 — HELLUVA BAND (LP) . . . 18

JOHNNY ANGEL
60 Parlophone R 4642 — Chinese Butterfly/My Very Good Friend The Milkman . . . 12
60 Parlophone R 4679 — Too Young To Go Steady/You're Thrilling . . . 12
61 Parlophone R 4750 — What Happens To Love/Luna Luna Luna Lu . . . 12
61 Parlophone R 4795 — Trocadero-Double-Nine-One-O/Web Of Love . . . 12
62 Parlophone R 4874 — Look, Look Little Angel/Jenny From Missouri . . . 12
62 Parlophone R 4948 — Better Luck Next Time/The Power Of You . . . 12
63 Parlophone R 5026 — A Touch Of Venus/The Two Together . . . 12

MARIAN ANGEL
65 Columbia DB 7537 — It's Gonna Be Alright/Tomorrow's Fool . . . 10
65 Columbia DB 7705 — You Can't Buy My Love/One Way Only . . . 10
66 CBS 202391 — Little Bit Of Sunshine/All The Time In The World . . . 5

ANGELA & HER FANS
66 Pye 7N 17108 — Love Ya Illya/I Know You . . . 20
(see also Alma Cogan)

ANGELIC UPSTARTS
78 Dead IS/AU/1024 — Murder Of Liddle Towers/Police Oppression (p/s, 1,000 only) . . . 30
78 Rough Trade RT/SW 001 — Murder Of Liddle Towers/Police Oppression (reissue, p/s) . . . 5
79 Warner Bros K 17354 — I'm An Upstart/Leave Me Alone (green vinyl, no p/s) . . . 5
79 Warner Bros K 17354T — I'm An Upstart/Leave Me Alone (12", p/s) . . . 8
79 Warner Bros K 17426C — Teenage Warning/The Young Ones (red vinyl, no p/s) . . . 5
80 Warner Bros SPZ 2 — I'm An Upstart/Never 'Ad Nothin' (cassette single) . . . 6
80 Zonophone Z 7 — Last Night Another Soldier/The Man Who Came In From The Beano (p/s) . . . 5
81 Zonophone Z 12 — England/Stick's Diary (p/s) . . . 10
83 Anagram ANA 12 — The Burglar (p/s, unissued)
85 Gas GM 3010 — Brighton Bomb/Thin Red Line/Soldier (12", banned 'Maggie Thatcher' p/s) . . . 15
79 Warner Bros K 56717 — TEENAGE WARNING (LP) . . . 12
80 Warner Bros K 56806 — WE GOTTA GET OUT OF THIS PLACE (LP) . . . 12
81 Zonophone ZEM 102 — LIVE (LP, some with free live flexidisc: "We're Gonna Take The World"/"Leave Me Alone"/"The Young Ones"/"White Riot" [no cat. no.]) . . . 15/12
85 Gas GLP 4012 — THE POWER OF THE PRESS (LP) . . . 12

ANGELINA
65 Fontana TF 648 — I Just Don't Know How/Wishing My Life Away . . . 5

BOBBY ANGELO & TUXEDOS
61 HMV POP 892 — Baby Sitting/Skinny Lizzie . . . 30
61 HMV POP 982 — Don't Stop/I Gotta Have You . . . 40
(see also Innocents [UK], End)

JERRY ANGELO
59 Parlophone R 4548 — Crush Me/Mary Lou . . . 15
59 Parlophone R 4561 — If You Change Your Mind/I Love You My Love . . . 15
60 Parlophone R 4656 — Maria Elena/Old Man River . . . 10
62 Palette PG 9031 — Lonely Hill/Make Her Mine . . . 10
62 Palette PG 9034 — Innocent Angel/The Boy Who Walks Alone . . . 10

MICHAEL ANGELO & HIS ORCHESTRA
61 Columbia DB 4705 — Rocco's Theme/Spinneree . . . 12
62 Columbia DB 4800 — Tears/The Roman Spring Of Mrs Stone . . . 15
(see also John Barry)

MAYA ANGELOU
57 London HA-U 2062 — MISS CALYPSO (LP) . . . 20

ANGEL PAVEMENT
69 Fontana TF 1059 — Baby You've Gotta Stay/Green Mello Hill . . . 10
70 Fontana TF 1072 — Tell Me What I've Got To Do/When Will I See June Again . . . 10
(see also Fortes Mentum, Pussy)

ANGELS
62 Pye International 7N 25150 — Everybody Loves A Lover/Blow Joe . . . 15
63 Mercury AMT 1211 — My Boyfriend's Back/Now . . . 15
63 Mercury AMT 1215 — I Adore Him/Thank You And Goodnight . . . 15
64 Philips BF 1312 — Wow Wow Wee/Snowflakes And Teardrops . . . 10
(see also Beach-Nuts)

MINT VALUE £

ANGELWITCH

80	EMI EMI 5064	Sweet Danger/Flight Nineteen (p/s)	10
80	EMI 12EMI 5064	Sweet Danger/Flight Nineteen/Hades Paradise (12", p/s)	25
80	Bronze BRO 108	Angel Witch/Gorgon (p/s)	8
81	Bronze BRO 121	Loser/Suffer/Dr Phibes (p/s)	10
85	Killerwatt KIL 3001	Goodbye/Reawakening (no p/s)	6
80	Bronze BRON 532	ANGELWITCH (LP)	15
85	Killerwatt KILP 4001	SCREAMIN' N' BLEEDIN' (LP)	20

ANGIE

79	Stiff BUY 51	Peppermint Lump/ANGIE'S ORCHESTRA: Breakfast In Naples (p/s)	6

(see also Pete Townshend)

ANGLIANS

67	CBS 202489	A Friend Of Mine/Daytime Lover	20

(see also Moving Finger)

ANGLOS

65	Fontana TF 561	Incense/You're Fooling Me (unissued)	
65	Brit WI 004	Incense/You're Fooling Me	40
65	Fontana TF 589	Incense/You're Fooling Me (reissue)	25
67	Sue WI 4033	Incense/You're Fooling Me (unissued)	
69	Island WIP 6061	Incense/You're Fooling Me (2nd reissue)	5

(see also Spencer Davis Group, Stevie Winwood)

ANGRY YOUNG MEN

59	Fontana H 187	Big Daddy/Ciribiribin	10
59	Fontana H 187	Big Daddy/Ciribiribin (78)	10

ANIMAL MAGNET

81	EMI 12 EMI 5240	Welcome To The Monkey House/Game Over Player 1 (12")	8

ANIMALS

64	Columbia DB 7247	Baby Let Me Take You Home/Gonna Send You Back To Walker	10
64	Columbia DB 7301	The House Of The Rising Sun/Talkin' 'Bout You	5
64	Columbia DB 7354	I'm Crying/Take It Easy	5
65	Columbia DB 7445	Don't Let Me Be Misunderstood/Club-A-Go Go (standard issue, matrix: '2N')	5
65	Columbia DB 7445	Don't Let Me Be Misunderstood/Club-A-Go Go (mispressing, with 'demo' version of A-side, matrix: '1N')	15
65	Columbia DB 7539	Bring It On Home To Me/For Miss Caulker	10
65	Columbia DB 7639	We've Gotta Get Out Of This Place/I Can't Believe It	5
65	Columbia DB 7741	It's My Life/I'm Going To Change The World	5
66	Decca F 12332	Inside Looking Out/Outcast	10
66	Decca F 12407	Don't Bring Me Down/Cheating	10
82	Rak RRP 1	The House Of The Rising Sun/Don't Let Me Be Misunderstood/I'm Crying (picture disc)	5
63	Graphic Sound ALO 10867	I JUST WANNA MAKE LOVE TO YOU (12" EP, 1-sided, 99 only, as Alan Price Rhythm & Blues Group or as Animals, private pressing, blank white cover, typed label)	450
64	Columbia SEG 8374	THE ANIMALS IS HERE (EP)	25
65	Columbia SEG 8400	THE ANIMALS (EP)	30
65	Columbia SEG 8439	THE ANIMALS NO. 2 (EP)	35
65	Columbia SEG 8452	THE ANIMALS ARE BACK (EP)	30
65	Decca DFE 8643	IN THE BEGINNING THERE WAS EARLY ANIMALS (EP, reissue of Graphic Sound EP)	30
66	Columbia SEG 8499	ANIMAL TRACKS (EP)	35
64	Columbia 33SX 1669	THE ANIMALS (LP)	60
64	EMI Regal SREG 1104	THE ANIMALS (LP, export issue)	30
65	Columbia 33SX 1708	ANIMAL TRACKS (LP)	50
65	Columbia TA-SX 1708	ANIMAL TRACKS (reel-to-reel tape)	20
66	Columbia SX 6035	THE MOST OF THE ANIMALS (LP)	20
66	Columbia TA-SX 6035	THE MOST OF THE ANIMALS (reel-to-reel tape)	15
66	Decca LK 4797	ANIMALISMS (LP)	40
76	DJM DJSL 069	IN CONCERT FROM NEWCASTLE (LP)	12

(see also Eric Burdon & Animals, Alan Price, Danny McCullough)

ANIMALS & MEN

80	Strange Days DAYS 1	The Terraplane Fixation/Shell Shock (p/s)	5
80	TW HIT 101	Don't Misbehave In The New Age/Machines (p/s)	5

ANIMATED EGG

69	Marble Arch MAL 890	ANIMATED EGG (LP)	30

ANITA & TH' SO AND SO'S

62	RCA RCA 1278	Joey Baby/Rinky Tinky Rhythm	5

PAUL ANKA

78s

60	Columbia DB 4390	It's Time To Cry/Something Has Changed Me (78)	10

SINGLES

57	Columbia DB 3980	Diana/Don't Gamble With Love (mauve label)	15
57	Columbia DB 3980	Diana/Don't Gamble With Love (re-pressings on green or black label)	15
57	Columbia DB 4022	I Love You, Baby/Tell Me That You Love Me (mauve or green label)	10
58	Columbia DB 4063	You Are My Destiny/When I Stop Loving You (mauve or green label)	10
58	Columbia DB 4110	Crazy Love/Let The Bells Keep Ringing (mauve or green label)	10
58	Columbia DB 4172	Midnight/Verboten! (Forbidden)	10
58	Columbia DB 4199	Just Young/So It's Goodbye	10
59	Columbia DB 4241	(All Of A Sudden) My Heart Sings/That's Love	5
59	Columbia DB 4286	I Miss You So/Late Last Night	5
59	Columbia DB 4324	Lonely Boy/Your Love	5
59	Columbia DB 4355	Put Your Head On My Shoulder/Don't Ever Leave Me	5

MINT VALUE £

60 Columbia DB 4390 It's Time To Cry/Something Has Changed Me . . . 5
60 Columbia DB 4434 Puppy Love/Adam And Eve . . . 5
60 Columbia DB 4472 My Home Town/Waiting For You . . . 5
60 Columbia DB 4504 Hello Young Lovers/I Love You In The Same Old Way . . . 5
60 Columbia DB 4524 Summer's Gone/I'd Have To Share . . . 5
61 Columbia DB 4582 The Story Of My Love/Don't Say You're Sorry . . . 5
61 Columbia DB 4629 Tonight My Love, Tonight/I'm Just A Fool Anyway . . . 5
61 Columbia DB 4669 I Talked To You (On The Telephone)/Dance On Little Girl . . . 5
61 Columbia DB 4702 Cinderella/Kissin' On The Phone . . . 5
62 Columbia DB 4772 The Bells At My Wedding/Loveland . . . 5
62 RCA RCA 1276 Love Me Warm And Tender/I'd Like To Know . . . 5
62 RCA RCA 1318 Eso Beso/Give Me Back My Heart . . . 5
63 RCA RCA 1340 Remember Diana/At Night (p/s) . . . 6
65 RCA RCA 1434 To Wait For Love/Behind My Smile (some in p/s) . . . 5
67 RCA RCA 1567 I Don't Wanna Catch Him Round You Anymore/Sunrise, Sunset . . . 5
68 RCA RCA 1676 Can't Get You Out Of My Mind/When We Get There . . . 40

EPs

57 Columbia SEG 7747 DIANA (EP) . . . 20
58 Columbia SEG 7801 ANKA AGAIN (EP) . . . 20
59 Columbia SEG 7890 SING SING SING (EP) . . . 20
60 Columbia SEG 7985 SINGS SONGS FROM 'GIRLS' TOWN' AND OTHER SUCCESSES (EP) . . . 25
64 RCA RCX 7127 FLY ME TO THE MOON (EP) . . . 10
64 RCA RCX 7152 FOUR GOLDEN HITS (EP) . . . 10
64 RCA RCX 7170 SYLVIE (EP) . . . 10

LPs

58 Columbia 33SX 1092 PAUL ANKA (LP, green label) . . . 50
59 Columbia 33SX 1196 MY HEART SINGS (LP) . . . 30
60 Columbia 33SX 1268 ANKA SWINGS FOR YOUNG LOVERS (LP) . . . 30
60 Columbia 33SX 1282 PAUL ANKA SINGS HIS BIG 15 (LP) . . . 20
60 Columbia 33SX 1287 IT'S CHRISTMAS EVERYWHERE (LP) . . . 40
61 Columbia 33SX 1395 PAUL ANKA SINGS HIS BIG 15 VOL. 2 (LP) . . . 22
62 Columbia 33SX 1432 PAUL ANKA SINGS HIS BIG 15 VOL. 3 (LP) . . . 22
62 RCA RD 27257/SF 5129 YOUNG ALIVE AND IN LOVE (LP, mono/stereo; add £5 with photo insert) . . . 18/22
62 RCA RD/SF 7533 LET'S SIT THIS ONE OUT (LP, mono/stereo) . . . 18/22
63 RCA RD/SF 7547 OUR MAN AROUND THE WORLD (LP, mono/stereo) . . . 18/22
63 RCA RD/SF 7573 ANKA'S 21 GOLDEN HITS (LP, mono/stereo) . . . 18/22
63 RCA RD/SF 7613 SONGS I WISH I'D WRITTEN (LP, mono/stereo) . . . 18/22
64 RCA RD 7700 EXCITEMENT ON PARK AVENUE — LIVE AT THE WALDORF ASTORIA (LP) . . . 120
68 RCA RD/SF 7956 TIMELESS (LP) . . . 18

(see also Micki Marlo & Paul Anka, Neil Sedaka)

ANNALISE

99 Boss Tunage BOSTAGE 701 Signposts And Alleyways/Empire Builder (p/s, 1-sided green vinyl with free CD, numbered, 250 copies only) . . . 10

ANNETTE (& AFTERBEATS)

59 Top Rank JAR 137 Lonely Guitar/Wild Willie . . . 20
59 Top Rank JAR 137 Lonely Guitar/Wild Willie (78) . . . 10
59 Top Rank JAR 233 First Name Initial/My Heart Became Of Age (with Afterbeats) . . . 10
60 Top Rank JAR 343 It Took Dreams/O Dio Mio . . . 10
60 Pye International 7N 25061 Pineapple Princess/Luan Cha Cha Cha (with Afterbeats) . . . 10
64 HMV POP 1270 Muscle Beach Party/I Dream About Frankie . . . 30
64 HMV POP 1322 Scrambled Egghead/Merlin Jones . . . 10
65 HMV POP 1447 The Monkey's Uncle (with The Beach Boys)/How Will I Know My Love . . . 30
59 Gala 45XP 1046 TALL PAUL (EP) . . . 20
64 HMV CLP 1782 ANNETTE'S BEACH PARTY (LP) . . . 50
60s Buena Vista BV 3305 DANCE ANNETTE (LP) . . . 30

ANNETTE & KEYMEN

64 King KG 1006 Look Who's Blue/How Can I Tell Him . . . 5

ANNIS

79 GTO GT 266 Don't Play Your Games/After Me . . . 8

ANNIVERSARY

78 Aerco AERE 102 GIVE ME A SMILE (EP) . . . 20

ANN-MARGRET

61 RCA RCA 1245 I Just Don't Understand/I Don't Hurt Anymore . . . 10
61 RCA RCA 1267 It Do Me So Good/Gimme Love . . . 5
64 RCA RCA 1396 Man's Favourite Sport/Hey Little Star . . . 5
64 RCA RCX 7148 THE VIVACIOUS ONE (EP) . . . 25
62 RCA RD 27239/SF 5116 AND HERE SHE IS (LP, mono/stereo) . . . 30/40
62 RCA Victor RD/SF 7503 ON THE WAY UP (LP, mono/stereo) . . . 25/35
63 RCA Victor RD/SF 7580 BYE BYE BIRDIE (LP, mono/stereo) . . . 25/35
64 RCA Victor RD/SF 7632 BEAUTY AND THE BEARD (LP, mono/stereo, with Al Hirt) . . . 20/30
64 RCA Victor RD/SF 7649 BACHELORS' PARADISE (LP, mono/stereo) . . . 30/40
64 RCA Victor RD/SF 7591 "ANNE MARGRET" (LP, mono/stereo) . . . 30/40

(see also Al Hirt)

ANNO DOMINI

71 Deram SML-R 1085 ON THIS NEW DAY (LP) . . . 100

ANONYMOUSLY YOURS

69 Trojan TR 680 Get Back/ERNIE SMITH: Not For Sale . . . 12
69 Trojan TR 681 It's Your Thing/'69 (B-side actually by Wallace Wilson) . . . 30
69 Duke DU 40 Organism/Itch . . . 15

ANOREXIA

80 Slim SJP 812 Rapist In The Park/I'm A Square/Pets . . . 35

MINT VALUE £

ANOTHER PRETTY FACE

79 New Pleasures Z1 All The Boys Love Carrie/That's Not Enough (green & white foldout p/s) 10
79 New Pleasures Z1 All The Boys Love Carrie/That's Not Enough (red & white p/s) 7
80 Virgin VS 320 Whatever Happened To The West?/Goodbye 1970's (p/s) 6
80 Chicken Jazz JAZZ 1 Only Heroes Live Forever/Heaven Gets Closer Everyday (poster p/s) 10
81 Chicken Jazz JAZZ 2 I'M SORRY THAT I BEAT YOU, I'M SORRY THAT I SCREAMED, FOR A MOMENT THERE I REALLY LOST CONTROL (8-track cassette, some with fanzine; add £5 if also with badge) 40/25
(Some copies of the above cassette exist with tracks from the DNV single taped onto the end; see under DNV)
81 Chicken Jazz JAZZ 3 Soul To Soul/A Woman's Place/God On The Screen (foldout p/s) 12
(see also DNV, Funhouse, Waterboys, Ahab)

ANOTHER SUNNY DAY

88 Sarah SARAH 003 Anorak City (5¾" flexidisc free with *Are You Scared To Get Happy* fanzine [SARAH 004], 1,500 only) 30/15
88 Sarah SARAH 007 I'm In Love With A Girl Who Doesn't Know I Exist/Things Will Be Nice/ The Centre Of My Little World (14" x 10" foldout poster p/s) 25
89 Caff CAFF 7 Genetic Engineering/Kilburn Towers (p/s, with inner) 30

BRETT ANSELL

62 Oriole CB 1701 That's Where Lonesome Lives/The Door Is Open 12
62 Oriole CB 1725 The Outsider/Rosalita 15

ANSELL (Collins) & ELAINE

72 Camel CA 98 Presenting Cheater/RON WILSON: Official Trombone 20

ANSWERS

66 Columbia DB 7847 It's Just A Fear/You've Gotta Believe Me 110
66 Columbia DB 7953 That's What You're Doing To Me/Got A Letter From My Baby 40
(see also Misunderstood, High Tide)

ADAM ANT

82 CBS A 2367 Goody Two Shoes/Red Scab (p/s, credited to 'Adam & the Ants') 6
82 CBS A 2892 Desperate But Not Serious/Why Do Girls Love Horses? (non-gatefold p/s, existence unconfirmed)
82 CBS CBSA 2892 Desperate But Not Serious/Why Do Girls Love Horses? (gatefold p/s) 5
83 CBS A 3614 Puss 'N' Boots/Kiss The Drummer (p/s) 5
83 CBS KELL 3 Puss 'N' Boots/BONNIE TYLER: Total Eclipse Of The Heart (Kellogg's Rice Crispies freebie) 5
83 CBS WA 3614 Puss In Boots/Kiss The Drummer (picture disc) 5
84 CBS A 3589 Strip/Yours, Yours, Yours (standard or 'calendar' poster p/s) . . . . each 5
84 CBS WA 3589 Strip/Yours, Yours, Yours (picture disc) 5
84 CBS TA 4719 Apollo 9 (Splashdown Remix)/Instrumental Splashdown (12", p/s) 10
85 CBS A 6367 Vive Le Rock/Greta X (p/s, mispressing, both sides play "Vive Le Rock") 6
90 MCA DMCAX 1387 Room At The Top (7" Version)/(House Vocal)/Bruce Lee (CD in numbered tin) 8
89 MCA MCA 1387 Room At The Top/Bruce Lee (p/s) 6
89 MCA DMCAT 1387 Room At The Top/(House Vocal Version)/Bruce Lee (CD, card sleeve) 8
04 NV CDEP 10 SAVE THE GORILLA EP: Save The Gorilla/Jungle Rock/Monkey Man/Monkey Man/Stranded In The Jungle (CD, batch destroyed, 2 copies only) 50
85 CBS CD 26583 VIVE LE ROCK (CD, with extra track "Human Bondage Den") 75
94 Arcade ARC 310 000-2 THE VERY BEST OF ADAM ANT (CD, with free live CD) 18
(see also Adam & The Ants, Maneaters)

ANTEEEKS

66 Philips BF 1471 I Don't Want You/Ball And Chain 200

PAUL ANTELL

65 Pye International 7N 25329 The Times They Are A-Changin'/Yesterday And Tomorrow 12

BILLIE ANTHONY

54 Columbia SCM 5143 This Ole House/Oh, What A Dream 10
54 Columbia SCM 5155 Teach Me Tonight/Don't Let The Kiddygeddin 15
55 Columbia SCM 5164 Butterscotch Hop/No More 15
55 Columbia SCM 5174 Tweedlee Dee/Shake The Hand Of A Stranger 25
55 Columbia SCM 5184 Something's Gotta Give/Boom Boom Boomerang 10
55 Columbia SCM 5191 The Banjo's Back In Town (with Big Ben Banjo Band)/Ten Little Kisses 10
55 Columbia SCM 5210 Bring Me A Bluebird/The Old Pi-anna Rag 10
56 Columbia SCM 5286 A Sweet Old Fashioned Girl/The Treasure Of Love 5
56 Columbia DB 3818 Lay Down Your Arms/One Finger Piano 5
57 Columbia DB 3874 I Dreamed/The Charge Of The Light Brigade (B-side with ex-R.S.M. Brittain) 10
57 Columbia DB 3935 Rock-A-Billy/A Needle And Thread 20
57 Columbia DB 3970 One/It's Fun Finding Out About London (with Big Ben Banjo Band) 8
57 Columbia DB 4021 Love And Kisses/Everybody's Buddy 8
58 Columbia DB 4141 You/Careful, Careful (Handle Me With Care) 8
59 Columbia DB 4279 Too Late Now/Yes, We Have No Bananas 8
60 Columbia DB 4394 Sure Fire Love/A Handful Of Gold 8
(see also Big Ben Banjo Band)

DAVE ANTHONY'S MOODS

66 Parlophone R 5438 New Directions/Give It A Chance 40
(see also David Anthony)

DAVID ANTHONY

68 Island WI 3148 All Night/Out Of My Mind 30
(see also Dave Anthony's Moods)

LITTLE JOHN ANTHONY

60 Ember EMB 3302 TEENAGE DANCE PARTY (LP) 15

MARC ANTHONY

63 Stateside SS 210 Let's All Cheer Again/Why Do I Love You 12

MINT VALUE £

MARK ANTHONY & JETS

70	Unity UN 565	More Balls/TONY KING: Bum Ball (Chapter II)	7

RAY ANTHONY

55	Capitol CL 14205	I Don't Hurt Anymore/Woman's World	5
55	Capitol CL 14243	Juke Box Special/Heat Wave	10
55	Capitol CL 14275	Baby You/Happy Hornblowers (with Dick Stabile Orchestra)	5
55	Capitol CL 14306	Sluefoot/Something's Gotta Give	5
55	Capitol CL 14321	Learnin' The Blues/Mmmm Mamie	5
55	Capitol CL 14345	Pete Kelly's Blues/DC-7	5
55	Capitol CL 14354	Hernando's Hideaway/The Bunny Hop	10
56	Capitol CL 14525	Flip-Flop/Hurricane Anthony	10
56	Capitol CL 14553	Cry Me A River/Bullfighter's Lament	5
56	Capitol CL 14567	Rockin' Through Dixie/Madeira	5
56	Capitol CL 14588	The Sleep Walker/Braziliera (Mexican Storm Song)	5
56	Capitol CL 14648	I Love You, Samantha/I Am In Love	5
56	Capitol CL 14670	Love Is Just Around The Corner/Dancing Lovers	5
57	Capitol CL 14689	Rock Around The Rock Pile/The Girl Can't Help It	40
57	Capitol CL 14689	Rock Around The Rock Pile/The Girl Can't Help It (78)	20
57	Capitol CL 14703	Plymouth Rock/Calypso Dance	10
57	Capitol CL 14740	The Incredible Shrinking Man/This Could Be The Night	5
57	Capitol CL 14752	The Lonely Trumpet/Cello-phane	5
57	Capitol CL 14769	The Bunny Hop/The Hokey Pokey	10
57	Capitol CL 14775	Drive-In/Show Me The Way To Go Home	5
58	Capitol CL 14929	Peter Gunn/Tango For Two (Mmm Shall We Dance?)	12
59	Capitol CL 15019	The Bunny Hop Rock/Walkin' To Mother's	10
57	Capitol EAP 1-823	THE GIRL CAN'T HELP IT (EP)	40
57	Capitol EAP 1-958	ROCK AND ROLL WITH RAY ANTHONY (EP)	30
57	Capitol EAP 1008	THE LONGEST WALK (EP)	10
53	Capitol LC 6570	RAY ANTHONY'S ORCHESTRA (10" LP)	15
53	Capitol LC 6615	SWEET AND LOVELY (10" LP)	15
53	Capitol LC 6617	HOUSE PARTY (10" LP)	15
54	Capitol LC 6653	I REMEMBER GLENN MILLER (10" LP)	15
55	Capitol LC 6692	ARTHUR MURRAY SWING FOXTROTS (10" LP)	15

(see also Gordon MacRae & Ray Anthony)

RAYBURN ANTHONY

60	London HLS 9167	Who's Gonna Shoe Your Pretty Little Feet/There's No Tomorrow	30

VAL ANTHONY

53	Columbia SCM 5079	Walk With The Wind/No Tears, No Regrets	5
54	Columbia SCM 5103	The Heart Of A Fool/The Portuguese Fishermen	5

ANTHONY & IMPERIALS

(see under Little Anthony & Imperials)

ANTHRAX (U.K.)

83	Small Wonder SMALL 27	THEY'VE GOT IT ALL WRONG (EP, p/s)	6
83	Crass 221984/9	CAPITALISM IS CANNIBALISM (EP, foldout p/s)	5

ANTHRAX (U.S.)

86	Island 12ISP 285	Madhouse/Air/God Save The Queen (12", picture disc)	15
86	Island 12IS 285	Madhouse/Air/God Save The Queen (12", p/s with patch)	10
87	Megaforce MRS 05(P)	Armed And Dangerous (12" EP, import, some as picture disc)	15/10
87	Island LAWP 1	I Am The Law/Bud E. Luvbomb And Satan's Lounge Band (picture disc)	8
87	Island ISX 316	I Am The Law (live)/Bud E. Luvbomb And Satan's Lounge Band/ Madhouse (live) (red vinyl, p/s)	8
87	Island 12IS 316	I Am The Law/Bud E. Luvbomb And Satan's Lounge Band (12", poster p/s)	15
87	Island ISP 325	Indians/Sabbath Bloody Sabbath (picture disc with sticker)	6
87	Island IS 325	Indians/Sabbath Bloody Sabbath (p/s, orange vinyl)	5
87	Island IS 325	Indians/Sabbath Bloody Sabbath (p/s, orange vinyl, mispress)	6
87	Island 12IS 325	Indians/Sabbath Bloody Sabbath/Taint (12", poster p/s)	8
87	Island 12ISP 325	Indians/Sabbath Bloody Sabbath/Taint (12", picture disc)	8
87	Island ISP 338	I'm The Man/Caught In A Mosh (logo-shaped picture disc)	5
88	Island CIDP 379	Make Me Laugh/Friggin' In The Riggin'/Anti-Social (live) (CD, 7" 'pyramid' card pack)	8
89	Island CIDX 409	Anti-Social/Parasite/Le Sects (3" CD)	8
90	Island ISP 476	Got The Time/Who Put This Together (picture disc)	5
86	Music For Nations MFN62P	SPREADING THE DISEASE (LP, picture disc)	15
87	Music For Nations MFN14P	FISTFUL OF METAL (LP, picture disc)	15
87	Island PILPS 9865	AMONG THE LIVING (LP, picture disc)	15
88	Island PILPS 9916	STATE OF EUPHORIA (LP, picture disc, die-cut sleeve)	12

ANTI ESTABLISHMENT

80	Charnel House CADAV 1	1980/Mechanical Man (p/s)	10
82	Glass GLASS 022	Future Girl/No Trust (p/s)	5
83	Glass GLASS 023	Anti Men/Misunderstood (p/s)	5

ANTI NOWHERE LEAGUE

82	WXYZ ABCD 1	So What/Streets Of London (p/s, withdrawn)	8
82	WXYZ ABCD 1T	So What/Streets Of London (12", p/s, withdrawn)	10
82	WXYZ ABCD 2	I Hate ... People/Let's Break The Law (p/s)	6
82	WXYZ ABCD 4	Woman/Rocker (picture disc)	6

ANTI PASTI

80	Rondelet ROUND 2	FORE SORE POINTS (EP)	15

ANTI SOCIAL

77	Dynamite DRO 1	Traffic Lights/Teacher Teacher (no p/s)	500

MINT VALUE £

ANTI SOCIAL
82 Lightbeat SOCIAL 1 MADE IN ENGLAND (EP) . . . 20
82 Beat The System BTS 2 Battle Scarred Skinheads/Sewer Rat/Official Hooligan (p/s) . . . 12
82 Beat The System FIT 2 Too Many People/Let's Have Some (p/s) . . . 5
82 Lightbeat (no cat. no.) THE NEW PUNKS EP (cassette) . . . 12

ANTI SYSTEM
83 Paragon/Pax PAX 11 DEFENCE OF THE REALM (EP) . . . 10

ANTOINE
66 Vogue VRS 7009 Les Elucubrations D'Antoine/J'ai Oublié La Nuit . . . 10
66 Vogue VRS 7017 Before The Good Thing/Elephants Looking At Me . . . 6
66 Vogue VRS 7022 Ma Fete Forraine/Only These Few Snowflakes . . . 6
68 Vogue VRS 7028 La Tramontana/lo Voglie Andaré In Guerra . . . 6
69 Vogue VRS 7031 The Football Match/Where Did Everyone Go To . . . 6
68 Vogue VRL 3032 ANTOINE (LP) . . . 30

ANTOINETTE
64 Decca F 11820 Jenny Let Him Go/Please Don't Hurt Me Anymore . . . 15
64 Piccadilly 7N 35201 There He Goes (The Boy I Love)/Little Things Mean A Lot . . . 15
65 Piccadilly 7N 35223 Thank You For Loving Me/If You Really Love Me . . . 15
65 Piccadilly 7N 35252 Our House/What's A-Happening To Me . . . 5
66 Piccadilly 7N 35293 Why Don't I Run Away From You/There's No-One In The Whole Wide World . . . 15
66 Piccadilly 7N 35310 Lullaby Of Love/I'm For You . . . 10
(see also Toni Daly)

REY ANTON
62 Oriole CB 1771 Hey Good Looking/Mary Lou . . . 12
63 Oriole CB 1811 Peppermint Man/Can't Say More Than That (with Batons) . . . 12
63 Oriole CB 1843 How Long Can This Last/If You Don't Want Me Now . . . 18
64 Parlophone R 5132 You Can't Judge A Book By The Cover/It's Cold Outside (with Peppermint Men) . . . 25
64 Parlophone R 5172 Heard It All Before/I Want You (with Peppermint Men) . . . 15
65 Parlophone R 5245 Wishbone/Kingsway (with Peppermint Men) . . . 15
65 Parlophone R 5274 Girl You Don't Know Me/Don't Treat Me Bad (with Peppermint Men) . . . 15
65 Parlophone R 5310 Nothing Comes Easy/Breakout (with Peppermint Men) . . . 15
65 Parlophone R 5358 Premeditation/Now That It's Over (with Pro Form) . . . 30
66 Parlophone R 5420 Don't You Worry Boy/Hold It Babe (with Pro Formula) . . . 15
66 Parlophone R 5487 Things Get Better/Newsboy (with Pro Form) . . . 15

TERRY ANTON
65 Pye 7N 15857 Leave A Little Love/Don't Say Goodbye . . . 8

DAVE ANTONY
68 Mercury MF 1031 Race With The Wind/Hide And Seek . . . 22
(see also Dave Anthony['s Moods])

RAY ANTHONY
57 Capitol LC 6809 STANDARDS (LP) . . . 12

MARK ANTONY & AVENGERS
60s Malconi MCD LP 17 MARK ANTONY & THE AVENGERS (LP, private pressing, plain sleeve) . . . 100

ANTS
63 Parlophone R 5082 Christmas Star/Wandering . . . 15

ANVIL FLUTES & CAPRICORN VOICES
68 Deram DM 208 April Showers/Jolie Gendarme . . . 6
68 Deram DML/SML 1026 SOMETHING NEW IS COMING (LP) . . . 15

ANY TROUBLE
84 EMI AMLS 2401203 WRONG SIDE OF THE RACE (2-LP) . . . 18

APARTMENT
80 Heartbeat PULSE 7 The Car/Winter (p/s) . . . 20

APEX RHYTHM & BLUES ALLSTARS
59 John Lever AP 100 Yorkshire Relish/Caravan . . . 60
60s John Lever JLEP 1 APEX RHYTHM & BLUES ALLSTARS (EP, no p/s) . . . 350
(see also Ian Hunter)

APHEX TWIN
91 Mighty Force 01 ANALOGUE BUBBLEBATH VOL. 1 (12", with Schizophrenia, 4-track, label on 1 side only) . . . 40
91 Rabbit City CUT 001 ANALOGUE BUBBLEBATH VOL. 1 (12" EP) . . . 60
91 Rabbit City CUT 009 Analogue Bubblebath Vol. 2 (Didgeridoo 'Aboriginal' Mix) (12", 1-sided, white label, 500 only) . . . 60
92 Outer Rhythm/R+S RSUK DIDGERIDOO (12", 4-track in stickered sleeve) . . . 25
92 Outer Rhythm/R+S RSUK DIDGERIDOO (CD EP) . . . 100
92 R&S/Apollo AMBLP 39 SELECTED AMBIENT WORKS 85-92 (2-LP) . . . 25
93 Rabbit City CUT 002 ANALOGUE BUBBLEBATH VOL. 2 (12" EP, 1-sided, 500 only) . . . 60
93 Rephlex CAT 008 ANALOGUE BUBBLEBATH VOL. 3 (12" EP, paper bag sleeve) . . . 25
93 Rephlex CAT 008 ANALOGUE BUBBLEBATH VOL. 3 (CD EP, bubble wrap sleeve) . . . 20
94 Warp WARPLP 21 SELECTED AMBIENT WORKS VOL. 2 (3-LP, brown vinyl, gatefold sleeve, numbered limited edition) . . . 30
94 Rephlex CAT 019 ANALOGUE BUBBLEBATH VOL. 4 (12", 4-track, p/s) . . . 12
95 Warp WAP 67 HANGABLE AUTOBULB I EP (12" EP, plain sleeve, 1,000 only) . . . 50
95 Warp WAP 69 HANGABLE AUTOBULB II EP (12" EP, plain sleeve, 1,000 only) . . . 40
97 Rephlex CAT 00897 ANALOGUE BUBBLEBATH VOL 3.1 (12" only, 4 different tracks) . . . 10
(see also Caustic Window, Polygon Window, Q-Chastic, Kosmic Kommando)

APHRODITE'S CHILD
68 Mercury MF 1039 Rain & Tears/Don't Try To Catch A River . . . 15
69 Mercury MF 1079 End Of The World/You Always Stand In My Way . . . 10

MINT VALUE £

69	Polydor 56769	I Want To Live/Magic Mirror	10
69	Polydor 56785	Let Me Love, Let Me Live/Marie Jolie	5
70	Polydor 56791	It's Five O'Clock/Funky Mary	5
72	Vertigo 6032 900	Break/Babylon	5
68	Mercury SMCL 20140	END OF THE WORLD/RAIN AND TEARS (LP)	20
69	Mercury 138 351	IT'S FIVE O'CLOCK	15
72	Vertigo 6673 001	666 — THE APOCALYPSE OF JOHN (2-LP, swirl labels, red cover)	30
77	Vertigo 6641 581	666 (2-LP, reissue, as Aphrodite's Child with Demis Roussos & Vangelis, different sleeve, 'spaceship' labels)	15

(see also Vangelis, Forminx)

APOLLOS

60	Mercury AMT 1096	Rockin' Horses/Just Dreaming	10

APOLLO XI

91	Wau! Mr. Modo APOLLO 11	Peace (In The Middle East) (7" Mix 2)/Peace (Sea Of Tranquility Mix)/ Peace (Is This Really The Orb? Mix) (12")	12

(see also Orb)

APOSTOLIC INTERVENTION

67	Immediate IM 043	(Tell Me) Have You Ever Seen Me/Madame Garcia	190

(see also Small Faces, Humble Pie)

APPALACHIANS

63	HMV POP 1158	Bony Moronie/It Takes A Man	10
65	Mercury MF 930	Look Away/My Broken Heart	5

DAVE APPELL (& APPLEJACKS)

55	Brunswick 05396	Smarter/My Heart Will Wait For You (as Dave Appell & Applejacks)	20
57	Columbia DB 3894	Country Dance/Applejack (as Dave Appell & Applejacks)	20
62	Columbia DB 4763	Happy Jose/Noivous (as Dave Appell & Orchestra)	5

(see also Applejacks [U.S.], John Zacherle)

APPLE

68	Page One POF 101	Let's Take A Trip Down The Rhine/Buffalo Billy Can	70
68	Page One POF 110	Doctor Rock/The Other Side	100
69	Page One POLS 016	AN APPLE A DAY (LP, some with 'apple' insert)	550/450

APPLEJACKS (U.K.)

64	Decca F 11833	Tell Me When/Baby Jane	5
64	Decca F 11916	Like Dreamers Do/Everybody Fall Down	5
64	Decca F 11981	Three Little Words/You're The One For Me	5
65	Decca F 12050	Chim Chim Chiree/It's Not A Game Anymore (export, unissued)	10
65	Decca F 12106	It's Not A Game Anymore/Bye Bye Girl	5
65	Decca F 12216	I Go To Sleep/Make Up Or Break Up	20
65	Decca F 12301	I'm Through/We Gotta Get Together	5
67	CBS 202615	You've Been Cheating/Love Was In My Eyes	10
64	Decca LK 4635	THE APPLEJACKS (LP)	100

APPLEJACKS (U.S.)

58	London HLU 8753	Mexican Hat Rock/Stop, Stop Red Light	10
58	London HL 7063	Mexican Hat Rock/Stop, Stop Red Light (export issue)	10
59	London HLU 8806	Rocka-Conga/Am I Blue	10
60	Top Rank JAR 273	Circle Dance/Love Scene	5

(see also Dave Appell)

APPLETREE THEATRE

68	Verve (S)VLP 6018	PLAYBACK (LP)	30
72	MGM 2353 051	PLAYBACK (LP, reissue)	12

CHARLIE APPLEWHITE

54	Brunswick 05358	No One But You/Parade	6
55	Brunswick 05411	Prize Of Gold/Mister Publisher (Have I Got A Song For You)	6
55	Brunswick 05416	Blue Star — The Medic Theme/A Prayer Was Born	20

APPLIANCE

90s	Enraptured RAPT 1020	TIME AND SPACE EP: Number Three Channel Is Clear/King Of The Flight Simulator/In The Event Of Just Looking/Ursa Major (10", p/s)	7

APRIL WINE

72	Pye 7N 45163	Bad Side Of The Moon/Believe In Me	6
73	Pye 7N 45624	Weeping Widow/Just Like That	6

AQUARIAN AGE

68	Parlophone R 5700	10,000 Words In A Cardboard Box/Good Wizard Meets Naughty Wizard	112

(see also Twink, Tomorrow, Clem Cattini Ork, Nicky Hopkins)

AQUARIANS

71	Ackee ACK 135	Circy Cap/Circy Version	12
71	Ackee ACK 137	Rebel/Invasion Version	12

(see also Augustus Pablo, Herman)

AQUATONES

58	London HLO 8631	You/She's The One For Me	50
58	London HLO 8631	You/She's The One For Me (78)	10

AQUILA

70	RCA SF 8126	THE AQUILA SUITE (LP, gatefold sleeve)	55

(see also Patrick Campbell-Lyons)

ARABIS

69	Doctor Bird DB 1204	Jump High Jump Low/TONY SHABAZZ: Stool Pigeon	15

ARABS

78	Hit Run APLP 9002	CRY TUFF — DUB ENCOUNTER CHAPTER 1	20

MINT VALUE £

ARAB STRAP

Year	Label / Cat. No.	Title	Value
96	Chemikal Underground CHEM 007	The First Big Weekend/Gilded (700 only)	15
97	Chemikal Underground CHEM 017	Hey! Fever/Girls Of Summer (p/s)	10
98	Too Many Cooks BROTH 001	Live: Packs Of Three/Blood	15
99	Go! Beat STRAP PRO	Sampler (CD, promo, 4-track, card sleeve)	12
98	Chemikal U'nd CHEM 021	PHILOPHOBIA (2-LP)	18
99	Go! Beat 547387	MAD FOR SADNESS (LP, 1000 only)	12
99	Go! Beat 547387 2	MAD FOR SADNESS (CD, 3000 only)	18

ARANBEE POP SYMPHONY ORCHESTRA

Year	Label / Cat. No.	Title	Value
66	Immediate IMLP/IMSP 003	TODAY'S POP SYMPHONY (LP)	150

(see also Andrew Oldham Orchestra, Keith Richard[s])

ARBORS

Year	Label / Cat. No.	Title	Value
66	CBS 202410	Symphony For Susan/Love Is The Light	7
68	CBS 3221	Valley Of The Dolls/You Are The Music	6
69	CBS 4137	The Letter/Most Of All	6
69	CBS 4379	I Can't Quit Her/Lovin' Tonight	6
69	CBS 4640	Motet Overture/Touch Me	7

ARC

Year	Label / Cat. No.	Title	Value
71	Decca SKL-R 5077	ARC . . . AT THIS (LP)	40

(see also Heavy Jelly, Skip Bifferty, Bell & Arc)

ARC

Year	Label / Cat. No.	Title	Value
80	Orchrist ORC 1	Tribute (To Mike Hailwood) (p/s)	60

ARCADIA

Year	Label / Cat. No.	Title	Value
85	EMI 12 NSR 1	Election Day (Consensus Mix)/Election Day (7" Version)/ She's Moody And Grey She's Mean And She's Restless (12", promo in foil sleeve, some sealed)	20/15
85	EMI 12 NSRA 1	Election Day (Cryptic Cut No Voice Mix)/Election Day (7" Mix)/ Election Day (Consensus Mix) (12", p/s)	10
85	EMI 12 NSRX 1	Election Day (The Fact And Story Mix) (12", 1-sided, white label, plain black black sleeve, promo only)	40

(see also Duran Duran)

ARCADIUM

Year	Label / Cat. No.	Title	Value
69	Middle Earth MDS 102	Sing My Song/Riding Alone	30
69	Middle Earth MDLS 302	BREATHE AWHILE (LP)	165

(see also 'Middle Earth Sampler' in Various Artists)

ARCHIES

Year	Label / Cat. No.	Title	Value
69	RCA RD/SF 8073	SUGAR SUGAR (LP)	15

TONI ARDEN

Year	Label / Cat. No.	Title	Value
55	HMV 7M 314	Beware/I'll Step Aside	5
57	Brunswick 05645	Little By Little/Without Love (There Is Nothing)	15
57	Brunswick 05679	My Empty Heart/Like A Baby	15
58	Brunswick 05745	Padre/All At Once	5

NEIL ARDLEY

Year	Label / Cat. No.	Title	Value
65	Decca SKL 4690	WESTERN UNION (LP)	150
69	Verve SVLP 9236	DEJEUNER SUR L'HERBE (LP)	200
70	Columbia SCX 6414	GREEK VARIATIONS (LP, with Ian Carr & Don Rendell)	200
72	Regal Zono. SLRZ 1028	A SYMPHONY OF AMARANTHS (LP)	200
74	Argo ZDA 164/5	WILL POWER (2-LP, with Ian Carr, Stan Tracey & Mike Gibbs)	125
75	Gull GULP 1018	KALEIDOSCOPE OF RAINBOWS (LP)	50
78	Decca TXS-R 133	HARMONY OF THE SPHERES (LP, featuring John Martyn)	25

(see also Ian Carr, Don Rendell, New Jazz Orchestra, Michael Gibbs)

AREA CODE 615

Year	Label / Cat. No.	Title	Value
70	Polydor 2066 249	Stone Fox Chase/Always The Same	5

COLIN AREETY

Year	Label / Cat. No.	Title	Value
73	Deram DM 383	I Don't Want To Be Right/One Night Affair	5

ARENA TWINS

Year	Label / Cat. No.	Title	Value
59	London HL 7071	Mama, Care Mama/Little Pig (export issue)	20

ARGENT

Year	Label / Cat. No.	Title	Value
71	Epic S EPC 5423	Celebration/Kingdom	5
71	Epic S EPC 9135	Hold Your Head Up/Closer To Heaven/Keep On Rollin' (p/s)	5
72	Epic S EPC 8115	Tragedy/Rejoice	5
73	Epic S EPC 1628	It's Only Money (Part 2)/Candle On The River	5
73	Epic S EPC 1243	God Gave Rock'N'Roll To You/Christmas For The Free	5
70	CBS 63781	ARGENT (LP)	15
71	Epic EPC 64190	RING OF HANDS (LP)	12
72	Epic EPC 64962	ALL TOGETHER NOW (LP, with booklet)	12
74	Epic EQ 32195/Q 65475	IN DEEP (LP, quadrophonic)	15
74	Epic EPC 88063	ENCORE (2-LP)	18

(see also Zombies, Unit 4 + 2, Roulettes, John Verity Band, Phoenix)

ARGONAUTS

Year	Label / Cat. No.	Title	Value
85	Lyntone LYN 18249/50	Apeman/Under My Thumb (signed white label, no p/s)	10

(see also Madness)

ARGOSY

Year	Label / Cat. No.	Title	Value
69	DJM DJS 214	Mr. Boyd/Imagine	10

ARGUS

Year	Label / Cat. No.	Title	Value
84	ABS SRT 4KS258	Holocaust/The Widow (title sleeve)	250

(see also People Like Us)

MINT VALUE £

ARISTOCRATS
64 Oriole CB 1928 — Girl With The Laughing Eyes/I Picked You . . . 8

ARIZONA BOYS' CHOIR
56 Columbia SCM 5215 — Ballad Of Davy Crockett/Blue Shadows On The Trail . . . 8

ARIZONA SWAMP COMPANY
70 Parlophone R 5841 — Train Keeps Rollin'/Tennessee Woman . . . 25
(see also Nashville Teens)

ARKADE
70 Stateside SS 8053 — Sing Out The Love/Susan . . . 5
71 Probe PRO 521 — Morning Of Our Lives/Rhythm Of The People . . . 5

DEE ARLEN
59 Philips PB 950 — Stay/Why Should We Wait Any Longer . . . 10
59 Philips PB 950 — Stay/Why Should We Wait Any Longer (78) . . . 10

STEVE ARLEN
58 Melodisc M 1458 — That's Love/Easy 'N' Free . . . 10
60 HMV POP 835 — Suddenly I'm In Love/Happy Days . . . 5

DEKE ARLON (& OFFBEATS)
64 HMV POP 1340 — I Need You/I Must Go And Tell Her . . . 20
64 Columbia DB 7194 — I'm Just A Boy/Can't Make Up My Mind . . . 30
65 Columbia DB 7487 — If I Didn't Have A Dime/Gotta Little Girl . . . 10
65 Columbia DB 7753 — Little Piece Of Paper/I've Been Away (solo) . . . 10
66 Columbia DB 7841 — Hard Times For Young Lovers/Little Boy (solo) . . . 15

ARMAGEDDON
75 A&M AMLH 64513 — ARMAGEDDON (LP, with inner sleeve) . . . 22
(see also Keith Relf, Steamhammer)

KAY ARMEN
55 MGM SP 1146 — He/Suddenly There's A Valley . . . 5
58 Brunswick 05729 — Ha! Ha! Ha! (Chella Lla!)/Till . . . 5

ARMENIAN JAZZ QUARTET
57 London HLR 8454 — Pretty Girl/Harem Dance . . . 15

RUSSELL ARMS
57 London HLB 8406 — Cinco Robles (Five Oaks)/The World Is Made Of Lisa (gold/silver label) . . . 22/14
57 London HL 7018 — Cinco Robles (Five Oaks)/The World Is Made Of Lisa (export issue) . . . 12

ARMS & LEGS
76 MAM MAM 140 — Janice/She'll Surprise You . . . 8
76 MAM MAM 147 — Heat Of The Night/Good Times . . . 8
77 MAM MAM 156 — Is There Any More Wine/She'll Surprise You . . . 8
(see also Joe Jackson)

FRANKIE ARMSTRONG (& FRIENDS)
79 Action Against Corrie RRFA 001 — We Must Choose/RED RINSE: A Woman's Right To Choose (private pressing) . . 30
72 Topic 12TS 216 — LOVELY ON THE WATER (LP) . . . 18
75 Topic 12TS 273 — SONGS AND BALLADS (LP) . . . 15
(see also A.L. Lloyd)

JACK ARMSTRONG
57 Beltona SEP 43 — NORTHUMBRIAN PIPE MUSIC (EP) . . . 12
74 Saydisc SDL 252 — CELEBRATED MINSTREL (LP) . . . 15

LOUIS ARMSTRONG

SINGLES
53 Columbia SCM 5061 — King Of The Zulus/Lonesome Blues . . . 15
54 Columbia SCM 5118 — Chicago Breakdown/Twelfth Street Rag . . . 15
54 Columbia SCM 5142 — I'm Not Rough/Put 'Em Down Blues . . . 15
54 Brunswick 05303 — Basin Street Blues (Parts 1 & 2) . . . 15
54 Brunswick 05332 — Skokiaan (Parts 1 & 2) . . . 10
54 Brunswick 05347 — Muskrat Ramble/Someday You'll Be Sorry (B-side with Commanders) . . . 10
55 Brunswick 05364 — Trees/Spooks . . . 5
55 Brunswick 05400 — Ko Ko Mo (I Love You So)/Struttin' With Some Barbecue (with Gary Crosby) . . . 10
55 Brunswick 05460 — Pretty Little Missy/Bye And Bye . . . 5
55 Brunswick 05505 — Christmas Night In Harlem/Christmas In New Orleans . . . 5
56 Brunswick 05574 — Easy Street/Lazybones (with Gary Crosby) . . . 5
56 Capitol CL 14643 — Now You Has Jazz (with Bing Crosby)/High Society Calypso . . . 5
57 Brunswick 05649 — This Younger Generation/In Pursuit Of Happiness . . . 5
58 Brunswick 05772 — The Mardi Gras March/I Love Jazz . . . 5
59 MGM MGM 1035 — The Beat Generation/Someday You'll Be Sorry . . . 7
59 Philips PB 967 — Mack The Knife/The Faithful Hussar . . . 5
59 Pye International 7N 25043 — The Formula For Love (with Nina & Frederick)/Struttin' With Some Barbecue (with Velma Middleton) . . . 5
60 Philips JAZ 108 — Mahogany Hall Blues Stomp/On The Sunny Side Of The Street (p/s) . . . 5
60 Philips JAZ 112 — Way Down Yonder In New Orleans/Do You Know What It Means To Miss (p/s) . . . 5
60 MGM MGM 1107 — Muskrat Ramble/Dardanella . . . 5
61 HMV POP 954 — Battle Royal Parts 1 & 2 . . . 5
68 Stateside SS 2116 — The Sunshine Of Love/Hellzapoppin' . . . 5
69 United Artists UP 35059 — We Have All The Time In The World/Pretty Little Missy . . . 30
69 United Artists UA 3172 — We Have All The Time In The World/Pretty Little Missy (reissue, p/s) . . . 35

EPs
55 Brunswick OE 9035 — PRESENTING LOUIS ARMSTRONG AND THE MILLS BROTHERS . . . 10

MINT VALUE £

LPs

51 Brunswick LA 8528 LOUIS ARMSTRONG CLASSICS (10") . . . 20
51 Brunswick LA 8534 JAZZ CONCERT (10") . . . 20
52 Brunswick LA 8537 NEW ORLEANS DAYS (10") . . . 20
52 Brunswick LAT 8017 SATCHMO AT SYMPHONY HALL . . . 15
52 Brunswick LAT 8018 SATCHMO AT SYMPHONY HALL . . . 15
52 Brunswick LAT 8019 SATCHMO AT PASADENA . . . 15
53 Brunswick LA 8597 LOUIS ARMSTRONG JAZZ — CLASSICS (10") . . . 18
53 London AL 3501 PLAYS THE BLUES (10") . . . 25
53 Columbia 33S 1007 JAZZIN' WITH ARMSTRONG (10") . . . 18
53 HMV DLP 1015 NEW YORK TOWN HALL CONCERT 1947 (10") . . . 18
54 Columbia 33SX 1029 LOUIS ARMSTRONG AND HIS HOT FIVE . . . 15
54 HMV DLP 1036 LAUGHIN' LOUIS (10") . . . 18
54 Columbia 33S 1041 LOUIS ARMSTRONG AND HIS HOT SEVEN (10") . . . 18
54 Brunswick LA 8679 SATCHMO SERENADES (10") . . . 18
54 Brunswick LA 8681 LOUIS ARMSTRONG AND THE MILLS BROTHERS (10") . . . 18
54 Brunswick LA 8691 BASIN STREET BLUES (10") . . . 18
55 Columbia 33S 1058 RENDEZVOUS AT THE SUNSET CAFE (10") . . . 18
55 Columbia 33S 1069 LOUIS ARMSTRONG (10") . . . 18
55 HMV DLP 1105 SATCHMO SESSION (10") . . . 18
55 Philips BBL 7017 SATCHMO PLAYS W.C. HANDY . . . 12
55 Philips BBL 7046 LOUIS ARMSTRONG AND EARL HINES . . . 12
55 Brunswick LA 8698 LOUIS' HOT FIVES AND SEVENS (10") . . . 18
55 Brunswick LA 8700 BLUEBERRY HILL (10") . . . 18
56 Philips BBL 7064 SATCH PLAYS FATS . . . 12
56 Philips BBL 7091 AMBASSADOR SATCH . . . 12
56 Brunswick LAT 8084 LOUIS ARMSTRONG AT THE CRESCENDO VOL. 1 . . . 12
56 Brunswick LAT 8085 LOUIS ARMSTRONG AT THE CRESCENDO VOL. 2 . . . 12
57 Philips BBL 7134 LOUIS ARMSTRONG STORY VOL. 1 . . . 12
57 Philips BBL 7189 LOUIS ARMSTRONG STORY VOL. 2 . . . 12
57 Brunswick LAT 8210 LOUIS AND THE ANGELS . . . 12
57 Brunswick LAT 8211 SATCHMO — A MUSICAL AUTOBIOGRAPHY . . . 12
57 Brunswick LAT 8212 SATCHMO — A MUSICAL AUTOBIOGRAPHY . . . 12
57 Brunswick LAT 8213 SATCHMO — A MUSICAL AUTOBIOGRAPHY . . . 12
57 Brunswick LAT 8214 SATCHMO — A MUSICAL AUTOBIOGRAPHY . . . 12
58 Philips BBL 7202 LOUIS ARMSTRONG STORY VOL. 3 (with Earl Hines) . . . 12
58 Fontana TFR 6003 LOUIS ARMSTRONG AND HIS HOT FIVE (10") . . . 15

(see also Danny Kaye, Ella Fitzgerald & Louis Armstrong, Nina & Frederik, Bing Crosby, Earl 'Fatha' Hines, Red Onion Jazz Babies)

B.J. ARNAU

72 Mojo 2092 028 I Want To Go Back There Again/I Love You . . . 5
72 Polydor 2058 238 The Big Hurt/Hey Brenda . . . 10
73 RCA RCA 2365 Live And Let Die/In One Night . . . 5

(see also Brenda Arnau)

BRENDA ARNAU

68 United Artists UP 2244 Gonna Spread Love/Christian . . . 5
68 United Artists UP 2265 Yesterday I Heard The Rain/Where Do You Go . . . 5

GINNY ARNELL

60 Brunswick 05836 Carnival/We . . . 15
63 MGM MGM 1217 Dumb Head/How Many Times Can One Heart Break . . . 25
63 MGM MGM 1243 I Wish I Knew What Dress To Wear/He's My Little Devil . . . 20
65 MGM MGM 1270 Just Like A Boy/Portrait Of A Fool . . . 20
65 MGM MGM 1283 Little Bit Of Love/B-I-I-I-Why . . . 20

CHICO ARNEZ (& HIS LATIN AMERICAN ORCHESTRA)

71 Gemini GMS 019 Leg Box/Reggae Deck . . . 5

(see also Jackie Davies)

CALVIN ARNOLD

68 MGM MGM 1378 Funky Way/Snatchin' Back . . . 10
68 MGM MGM 1449 Mama In Law/Mini Skirt . . . 10

EDDY ARNOLD

53 HMV MH 178 Moonlight And Roses/I'm Gonna Lock My Heart (& Throw Away The Key) (78, export issue) . . . 7
54 HMV 7MC 10 Prayer/Robe Of Calvary (export issue) . . . 35
54 HMV 7MC 16 Free Home Demonstrations/If I Never Get To Heaven (export issue) . . . 15
54 HMV 7MC 19 Second Fling/My Everything (export issue) . . . 15
54 HMV 7MC 22 Hep Cat Baby/This Is The Thanks I Get (For Loving You) (export issue) . . . 25
55 HMV 7MC 32 In Time/Two Kinds Of Love (export issue) . . . 15
55 HMV 7M 339 I Walked Alone Last Night/The Richest Man (In The World) . . . 10
55 HMV B 10918 The Kentuckian Song/The Cattle Call (78) . . . 8
57 RCA RCA 1008 Gonna Find Me A Bluebird/Little Bit . . . 10
57 RCA RCA 1017 Scarlet Ribbons/Bayou Baby (A Cajun Lullaby) . . . 10
58 RCA RCA 1057 Little Miss Sunbeam/My Darling, My Darling . . . 10
59 RCA RCA 1138 Tennessee Stud/What's The Good (Of All This Love) . . . 10
60 RCA RCA 1212 Just Out Of Reach/Before This Day Ends . . . 5
54 HMV 7EG 8020 EDDY ARNOLD (EP) . . . 15
55 HMV 7EG 8080 CHAPEL ON THE HILL (EP) . . . 15
59 RCA Camden CDN 133 EDDY ARNOLD (LP) . . . 15

KOKOMO ARNOLD

69 Saydisc Matchbox SDR 163 KOKOMO ARNOLD (LP) . . . 20

MALCOLM ARNOLD

58 Philips BBE 12194 BRIDGE ON THE RIVER KWAI (EP) . . . 12
62 Decca DFE 8507 THE LION (EP) . . . 12

MINT VALUE £

PAUL ARNOLD

67 Pye 7N 17317 Somewhere In A Rainbow/Got A Feeling . . . 7
68 Pye 7N 17473 Bon Soir Dame/Don't Leave. . . . 6
(see also Overlanders)

P.P. ARNOLD

66 Immediate IM 040 Everything's Gonna Be Alright/Life Is But Nothin' . . . 115
67 Immediate IM 047 The First Cut Is The Deepest/Speak To Me . . . 20
67 Immediate IM 055 The Time Has Come/If You See What I Mean . . . 10
68 Immediate IM 061 (If You Think You're) Groovy/Though It Hurts Me Badly . . . 15
68 Immediate IM 067 Angel Of The Morning/Life Is But Nothin' . . . 5
69 Immediate IM 079 The First Cut Is The Deepest/The Time Has Come . . . 5
69 Polydor 56350 Bury Me Down The River/Give A Hand, Take A Hand . . . 5
70 Polydor 2058 061 Likely Piece Of Work/May The Winds Blow . . . 5
80 Virgin/NEMS SV 103 Angel Of The Morning/Everything's Gonna Be Alright/The First Cut Is The Deepest/Groovy/The Time Has Come (doublepack, gatefold p/s) . . . 5
67 Immediate IMLP/IMSP 011 THE FIRST LADY OF IMMEDIATE (LP, withdrawn) . . . 200
68 Immediate IMSP 017 KAFUNTA (LP, gatefold sleeve) . . . 60
(see also Ikettes, Nice, Small Faces, Spectrum, P.P. & Primes)

ARRIVAL

70 Decca SKL 5055 ARRIVAL (LP). . . . 15

ARRIVALS

69 Pye 7N 17761 Scooby Doo/She's About A Mover . . . 20

ARROWS (U.K.)

69 Pye 7N 17756 Mercy/See Saw. . . . 10

ARROWS (U.S.)

65 Capitol CL 15386 Apache '65/Blue Guitar . . . 10

ARS NOVA

68 Elektra EKSN 45029 Zoroaster/Pavan For My Lady . . . 12
68 Elektra EKSN 45034 Fields Of People/Song To The City . . . 12
68 Elektra EKS 74020 ARS NOVA (LP, orange label, gatefold sleeve) . . . 30
69 Atlantic 588 196 SUNSHINE AND SHADOWS (LP). . . . 20

ART

67 Island WIP 6019 What's That Sound (For What It's Worth)/Rome Take Away Three . . . 20
69 Island WIP 6048 Room With A View/SPOOKY TOOTH: Nobody There At All (promo only). . . . 40
75 Island WIP 6224 What's That Sound (For What It's Worth)/Flying Anchors. . . . 6
67 Island ILP 967 SUPERNATURAL FAIRY TALES (LP, pink label, laminated sleeve). . . . 100
75 Island ILP 967 SUPERNATURAL FAIRY TALES (LP, reissue, matt sleeve, 'palm tree' label) . . . 30
(see also V.I.P.'s, Baron With His Pounding Piano, Spooky Tooth, Luther Grosvenor, Hapshash & Coloured Coat)

ART ATTACKS

78 Albatross TIT 1 I'm A Dalek/Neutron Bomb (p/s) . . . 20
79 Fresh FRESH 3 First And Last: Punk Rock Stars/Rat City/First And Last (p/s). . . . 18
(see also Monochrome Set, Tagmemics, Kray Cherubs)

ART BEARS

81 Recommended RE 6622 CODA TO "MAN AND BOY" (EP, live, 1-sided clear vinyl, silk-screened p/s, 1,750 only, 500 signed & numbered for subscribers). . . . 12/10
78 Recommended REC 2188 HOPES AND FEARS (LP, gatefold sleeve with poster & booklet). . . . 12
79 Recommended REC 0618 WINTER SONGS (LP, with booklet) . . . 12
81 Recommended RE 6622 THE WORLD AS IT IS TODAY (LP, 45rpm, with booklet) . . . 12
(see also Henry Cow, Slapp Happy)

ARTERY

79 Limited Edition TAKE 1 Mother Moon/Pretends/Heinz (p/s) . . . 10
80 Aardvark STEAL 3 Unbalanced/The Slide (p/s, some with EP [Perhaps/Turtle/Toytown/Heinz]). . . . 8/6
81 Aardvark AARD 5 Cars In Motion/Life And Death (p/s) . . . 6
81 Armageddon AS 026 Afterwards/Into The Garden (p/s). . . . 6
82 Red Flame RFM 4 OCEANS (LP, with insert). . . . 12
(see also Mission)

DAVE & TONI ARTHUR

70 Trailer LER 1 Bushes And Briars/Lazio Feher. . . . 6
67 Transatlantic TRA 154 MORNING STANDS ON TIPTOE (LP) . . . 30
69 Topic 12T 190 THE LARK IN THE MORNING (LP, blue label) . . . 30
71 Trailer LER 2017 HEARKEN TO THE WITCHES' RUNE (LP, red label). . . . 35
(see also Strollers)

ANDY ARTHURS

77 EMI EMI 2618 Listen To My Brain (Kapounding)/Come To The Party (p/s) . . . 7
78 Radar ADA 7 I Can Detect You For 1,000,000 Miles/I Am A Machine (p/s, withdrawn). . . . 10

ARTISTICS

66 Coral Q 72488 I'm Gonna Miss You/Hope We Have. . . . 30
67 Coral Q 72492 Girl I Need You/I'm Glad I Met You . . . 25
70 MCA MU 1117 I'm Gonna Miss You/Hope We Have (reissue) . . . 6
76 Brunswick BR 39 I'm Gonna Miss You/GENE CHANDLER: There Was A Time . . . 15
66 Columbia GET MY HANDS ON SOME LOVIN' (LP) . . . 175

ART MOVEMENT

68 Decca F 12768 I Love Being In Love With You/The Game Of Love . . . 8
68 Decca F 12836 Loving Touch/Happy Song. . . . 7
69 Columbia DB 8602 Yes Sir . . . No Sir/Sally Goes Round The Moon . . . 6
70 Columbia DB 8651 For As Long As You Need Me/Nice 'n' Easy . . . 6
70 Columbia DB 8697 The Sooner I Get To You/Morning Girl. . . . 6

ART NOUVEAUX

64 Fontana TF 483 Extra Terrestrial Visitations/The Way To Play It . . . 18

MINT VALUE £

ART OBJECTS

80	Heartbeat PULSE 10	Showing Off To Impress The Girls/Our Silver Sister (live) (p/s)	15
81	Fried Egg EGG 007	Hard Objects/Bibliotheque/Fit Of Pique (p/s)	12
81	Heartbeat HB 5	BAGPIPE MUSIC (LP)	20

ART SCIENCE TECHNOLOGY

90	Debut DEBTX 3100	A.S.T./Esus Flow (2 mixes) (12", p/s)	15

(see also Future Sound Of London, Stakker)

ARTWOODS

64	Decca F 12015	Sweet Mary/If I Ever Get My Hands On You	50
65	Decca F 12091	Oh My Love/Big City	30
65	Decca F 12206	Goodbye Sisters/She Knows What To Do	30
66	Decca F 12384	I Take What I Want/I'm Looking For A Saxophonist Doubling French Horn Wearing Size 37 Boots	50
66	Decca F 12465	I Feel Good/Molly Anderson's Cookery Book	60
67	Parlophone R 5590	What Shall I Do/In The Deep End	160
66	Decca DFE 8654	JAZZ IN JEANS (EP)	300
66	Decca LK 4830	ART GALLERY (LP)	250
70	Decca Eclipse ECM 2025	ART GALLERY (LP, reissue in different sleeve, also stereo [ECS 2025])	15
73	Spark SRLM 2006	THE ARTWOODS (LP)	30
83	Edsel ED 107	100 OXFORD STREET (LP, with foldout insert)	15

(see also St. Valentine's Day Massacre, Keef Hartley Band, Jon Lord, Dog Soldier, Lucas & Mike Cotton Sound)

ARZACHEL

69	Evolution Z 1003	ARZACHEL (LP)	250

(see also Egg, Steve Hillage, Khan, Hatfield & the North, National Health, Gong)

A.S.A.P.

(see under Adrian Smith & Project)

ASGARD

72	Threshold TH 10	Friends/Children Of A New Born Age	6
73	Threshold TH 15	In The Realm Of Asgard/Town Cryer	6
72	Threshold THS 6	IN THE REALM OF ASGARD (LP, gatefold sleeve)	30

ASH

94	La La Land LA LA 001	Jack Names The Planets/Don't Know (wraparound p/s in poly bag, 5,000 only)	15
94	Infectious INFECT 13S	Petrol/The Little Pond/A Message From Oscar Wilde And Patrick The Brewer (p/s, 500 only)	12
94	Infectious INFECT 16S	Uncle Pat/Different Today (p/s, 1,000 only)	12
95	Infectious INFECT 21J	Kung Fu/Day Of The Triffids (p/s, 'Japanese' wraparound no'd p/s in poly bag)	8
95	Infectious INFECT 21S	Kung Fu (mispressed, 1-sided only, p/s)	6
95	Infectious INFECT 21C	Kung Fu/Kung Fu (red vinyl promo)	8
95	Infectious INFECT 27C	Angel Interceptor/Angel Interceptor (blue vinyl, promo only, hand-stamped p/s)	7
95	Infectious INFECT 27J	Angel Interceptor/Girl From Mars (jukebox issue)	7
95	Fantastic Plastic FP 004	Get Ready/Zero Zero Zero (red vinyl, 1,000 only)	7
95	Infectious INFECT 24S	Girl From Mars/Astral (Conversations With Toulouse Lautrec)/ Cantina Band (p/s)	10
95	Infectious INFECT 27S	Angel Interceptor/5 A.M. Eternal/Give Me Some Truth (ltd. Ed., numbered p/s)	6
96	Infectious INFECT 41S	Oh Yeah/T Rex/Everywhere Is All Around/Oh Yeah (Quartet Version) (yellow vinyl, p/s, 5000 only)	6
96	Infectious INFECT 40LP	1977 (LP, gatefold, stickered sleeve)	12
94	Infectious INFECT 14LP	TRAILER (LP, with yellow vinyl 7", "Silver Surfer"/"Jazz '59" [INFECT 14S])	25
98	Infectious INFECT 60LP	NU-CLEAR SOUNDS (LP, clear vinyl, limited edition, gatefold sleeve)	12

IRVING ASHBY & HIS COMBO

58	London HLP 8578	Big Guitar/Motatin'	35
58	London HLP 8578	Big Guitar/Motatin' (78)	22

JOHNNY ASHCROFT

59	Felsted AF 118	A Pub With No Beer/Bouquet For The Bride	5
60	HMV POP 759	Little Boy Lost/My Love Is A River	10

ASHFORD & SIMPSON

78	Warner Brothers 12K 17096	Don't Cost You Nothing/Let Love Use Me (12")	15
78	Warner Brothers 12K 17237	It Seems To Hang On (12")	12

(see also Valerie Simpson)

ASHKAN

70	Decca Nova (S)DN-R 1	IN FROM THE COLD (LP)	45

TYRONE ASHLEY

76	Pye 7N 25704	Feet Start Moving/Moving On	5
76	Tomorrow 10	Nothing Short Of A Miracle/(Instrumental Version)	10

MICKEY ASHMAN

60	Pye Jazz NJL 25	TAKING THE MICKEY (LP)	25
61	Pye Jazz NJL 29	THROUGH DARKEST ASHMAN (LP)	45

VIC ASH QUARTET

56	Tempo A 135	Blue Lou/Doxy	7
56	Tempo A 137	Early Morning/Just One Of Those Things	7
55	Jazz Today JTE 100	SESSION FOR FOUR (EP)	35
56	Nixa NJE 1002	HOAGY (EP)	15
56	Nixa NJE 1032	VIC ASH & FOUR (EP)	25
56	Columbia SEG 7634	CLARINET VIRTUOSO (EP)	15
56	Tempo EXA 44	MODERN JAZZ SCENE (EP)	15

(see also Maxine Sullivan, Jazz Five)

MINT VALUE £

BUD ASHTON (& HIS GROUP)

60	Embassy WB 409	Because They're Young/Apache	5
61	Embassy WEP 1058	SWINGING GUITARS (EP)	10
63	Embassy WEP 1088	MORE SWINGING GUITARS (EP)	10

(see also Typhoons, Jaybirds, Paul Rich)

GARY ASHTON

68	Pye 7N 17494	Springtime Of Our Years/His Lordship	5

TONY ASHTON

72	Purple PUR 109	Celebration/Sloeback	5

(see also Green Bullfrog)

(TONY) ASHTON & (JON) LORD

74	Purple PUR 121	We're Gonna Make It/Band Of The Salvation Army Band	7
74	Oyster OYR 101	TONY ASHTON: The Resurrection Shuffle/Ballad Of Mr Giver	6
74	Purple TPS 3507	FIRST OF THE BIG BANDS (LP)	12

(see also Tony Ashton, Ashton Gardner & Dyke, Paice Ashton & Lord, Jon Lord, Deep Purple)

ASHTON, GARDNER & DYKE

69	Polydor 56306	Maiden Voyage/See The Sun In My Eyes	40
70	Polydor 583 081	ASHTON, GARDNER & DYKE (LP)	15
71	Capitol E-ST 563	THE WORST OF ASHTON, GARDNER AND DYKE (LP)	12
72	Capitol EA-ST 22862	WHAT A BLOODY LONG DAY IT'S BEEN (LP)	12

(see also Ashton & Lord, Remo Four, Creation, Birds, Mike Hurst & Method, Badger, Medicine Head, Family)

ASIA

82	Geffen GEFA 2228	Only Time Will Tell/Ride Easy (picture disc)	10
82	Geffen WA 3580	Don't Cry/True Colours (blue or green logo-shaped picture disc)	12/10

(see also Yes, Emerson Lake & Palmer, Steve Howe)

ASLAN

76	Profile GMOR 006	PAWS FOR THOUGHT (LP)	140
77	Profile GMOR 144	SECOND HELPINGS (LP)	165

SVEND ASMUSSEN

54	Philips PB 343	Sh-Boom/Do, Do, Do, Do, Do, Do It Again (78)	12

MONICA ASPELUND

77	RCA PB 9044	Lapponia/La-La, Sing A Song	8

GARY & VERA ASPEY

70s	Topic 12 TS 299	A TASTE OF HOT POT (LP)	15

ASPHALT RIBBONS

88	Lily LILY 002	PASSION, COOLNESS, INDIFFERENCE (12", p/s)	15
89	In Tape IT 063	THE ORCHARD EP (p/s)	12
89	In Tape ITTI 063	THE ORCHARD EP (12", p/s)	15
89	In Tape IT 068	Good Love/Long Lost Uncle/The Day I Turned Bad (p/s)	12
89	In Tape ITTI 068	Good Love/Long Lost Uncle/The Day I Turned Bad (12", p/s)	15
89	In Tape IT 6545 1	Over Again/EVA: Unquenchable (p/s, promo only)	15

(see also Tindersticks)

MARY ASQUITH

78	Mother Earth MUM 1204	CLOSING TIME (LP)	30

ASSAGAI

71	Vertigo 6059 034	Telephone Girl/I'll Wait For You	7
71	Vertigo 6360 030	ASSAGAI (LP, gatefold sleeve, swirl label)	25
72	Philips 6308 079	ZIMBABWE (LP)	15
70s	Sounds Superb SPR 90054	AFRO ROCK (LP)	15

LYS ASSIA

54	Decca F 10097	O Mein Papa/Ponylied	6
57	Decca DFE 6383	A CONTINENTAL STAR PRESENTS FOUR CONTINENTAL HITS (EP)	15

ASSOCIATES

79	Double Hip DHR 1	Boys Keep Swinging/Mona Property Girl (no p/s, 500 only)	60
79	MCA MCA 537	Boys Keep Swinging/Mona Property Girl (no p/s, demos more common, £25)	30
80	Fiction FICS 11	The Affectionate Punch/You Were Young (p/s)	8
81	Fiction FICSX 13	A/Would I ... Bounce Back (p/s)	6
81	RSO RSO 78	Kites/A Girl Named Property (p/s, band on A-side credited as "39 Lyon St.")	5
81	RSO RSOX 78	Kites/A Girl Named Property (12", p/s, A-side credited as "39 Lyon St.")	8
81	Situation Two SIT 10	Message Oblique/Blue Soap (p/s)	8
82	Lyntone LYN 11649	Even Dogs In The Wild (clear 1-sided flexi free with *Flexipop* mag, issue 20)	8/5
82	Lyntone LYN 11649	Even Dogs In The Wild (one-sided hard vinyl test pressing)	30
82	Beggars Banquet BEG 86	Tell Me Easter's On Friday/Straw Towels (unreleased, white labels only)	25
84	WEA YZ 16T	Waiting For The Loveboat (Extended Version)/(John Peel Session Version)/ Schampout (Extended Version) (12", stickered p/s)	8
85	WEA YZ 28P	Breakfast/Breakfast Alone (picture disc, stickered PVC sleeve)	5
85	Sounds/WEA CRACKER 1	CHRISTMAS CRACKER 45 (cassette, includes "Breakfast [live at Ronnie Scott's]", free with *Sounds*)	5
85	WEA YX 47TE	Take Me To The Girl/Perhaps/God Bless The Child (live)/Even Dogs In The Wild (live)/The Boy That Santa Claus Forgot (live) (10", p/s)	10
88	WEA YZ 310 TX	Heart Of Glass (The Temperament Mix)/Heart Of Glass/Her Only Wish/ Heaven's Blue (12", 3-D p/s, shrinkwrapped with 3-D glasses)	10
88	WEA YZ 310CD	Heart Of Glass/Her Only Wish/Breakfast/Those First Impressions (3" CD in 5" case, with adaptor)	15
88	WEA YZ 329B	Country Boy/Just Can't Say Goodbye (12" Mix)/Take Me To The Girl/ Heart Of Glass (Dub Mix) (33rpm, p/s, unissued)	
88	WEA YZ 329T	Country Boy/Heart Of Glass (Dub Mix)/Just Can't Say Goodbye (12" Mix) (12", p/s, unissued, white labels only)	100
88	WEA YZ 329CD	Country Boy/Just Can't Say Goodbye (12" Mix)/Take Me To The Girl/ Heart Of Glass (Dub Mix) (3" CD with adaptor in jewel case, unissued)	100

MINT VALUE £

89	Strange Fruit SFPSC 075	PEEL SESSIONS: It's Better This Way/Nude Spoons/Me, Myself And The Tragic Story/A Matter Of Gender/Ulcragyceptemol (cassette)	5
90	Circa YRTB 46	Fever (Album Version)/Green Tambourine/Groovin' With Mr. Bloe (12", p/s, with 2 prints)	8
90	Circa YRTB 46	Fever (Single Version)/Green Tambourine/Groovin' With Mr. Bloe (12", p/s, with different B-sides, unreleased, handwritten white label, test pressings only)	15
90	Circa YRCDT 46	Fever (Single Version)/Groovin' With Mr. Bloe/Fever In The Shadows (CD)	15
90	Circa YRTX 49	Fire To Ice/The Glamour Chase/Green Tambourine/Groovin' With Mr. Bloe (10", p/s)	7
90	Circa YRCD 49	FIRE TO ICE EP (CD, card p/s, with inner sleeve)	18
90	Circa YRCD 56	JUST CAN'T SAY GOODBYE EP (CD, slimline jewel case)	18
90	WEA YZ 534	POPERETTA EP: Waiting For The Loveboat (Slight Return)/ Club Country Club (p/s)	5
90	WEA YZ 534C	POPERETTA EP: Waiting For The Loveboat (Slight Return)/ Club Country Club (cassette)	5
90	WEA YZ 534T	POPERETTA EP: Waiting For The Loveboat (Extended Voyage)/ Club Country Club/Club Country Club (Time Unlimited)/ Waiting For The Loveboat (Slight Return) (12", p/s)	10
90	WEA YZ 534CD	POPERETTA EP: Waiting For The Loveboat (Slight Return)/Club Country Club/ Waiting For The Loveboat (Extended Voyage)/Club Country Club (Time Unlimited) (CD)	10
91	Circa YRTPR 56	Just Can't Say Goodbye (Extended Mix)/(Club Mix) (12", unreleased, white label test pressing, label credits "I Never Can Say Goodbye")	10
90	Circa BILLY 1	WILD AND LONELY (12" sampler, p/s)	8
90	Circa BILLYC 1	WILD AND LONELY (cassette sampler, card sleeve)	10
90	Circa BILLYCD 1	WILD AND LONELY (CD sampler, printed PVC sleeve)	12
93	Amnesty Intl. DSAPC 71	Amnesty International (picture disc, PVC sleeve, Billy MacKenzie features on photograph but not on recording, promo only)	15
90	Circa CIRCD 11	WILD AND LONELY (CD)	30
82	Beggars Banquet BEGA 43	FOURTH DRAWER DOWN (LP, gatefold sleeve with poster, label also credits SITU 2)	15
82	WEA 240 005-4 (WX 24C)	SULK (cassette, includes U.S. edition, U.K. edition, extra tracks & exclusive remixes)	12
88	WEA WX 222C	THE GLAMOUR CHASE (unreleased, advance cassette only; with extra track "Take Me To The Girl")	40
88	WEA 244 619-2	THE GLAMOUR CHASE (CD, with extra track "Take Me To The Girl", unissued)	
88	WEA K 240 005-2	SULK (CD)	18

(see also Billy MacKenzie, Jih)

ASSOCIATION

66	London HLT 10054	Along Comes Mary/Your Own Love	8
66	London HLT 10074	Cherish/Don't Blame It On Me	7
66	London HLT 10098	Pandora's Golden Heebie Jeebies/Standing Still	10
67	London HLT 10118	No Fair At All/Looking Glass	8
67	London HLT 10140	Windy/Sometime	8
67	London HLT 10157	Never My Love/Requiem For The Masses	8
68	Warner Bros WB 7163	Everything That Touches You/We Love Us	6
68	Warner Bros WB 7195	Time For Livin'/Birthday Morning	6
68	Warner Bros WB 7229	Six Man Band/Like Always	6
69	Warner Bros WB 7267	Goodbye Columbus/The Time It Is Today	8
70	Warner Bros WB 7372	Just About The Same/Look At Me, Look At You	6
67	London HA-T 8305	AND THEN . . . ALONG COMES THE ASSOCIATION (LP)	30
67	London HA-T 8313	RENAISSANCE (LP)	25
67	London HA-T/SH-T 8342	INSIGHT OUT (LP)	25
68	Warner Bros W(S) 1733	BIRTHDAY (LP)	25
69	Warner Bros W(S) 1767	GREATEST HITS (LP)	20
69	Warner Bros W(S) 1786	GOODBYE COLUMBUS (LP, soundtrack)	20
69	Warner Bros W(S) 1800	THE ASSOCIATION (LP)	20

FRED ASTAIRE

57	HMV POP 337	Funny Face/AUDREY HEPBURN: How Long Has This Been Going On	5
57	MGM MGM 963	Paris Loves Lovers (with Cyd Charisse & Carol Richards)/All Of You	5
57	MGM MGM 964	The Ritz Roll And Rock/JANIS PAIGE: Satin And Silk	10
57	MGM EP 601	SHOES WITH WINGS ON (EP)	10
56	Philips BBL 7052	THE BEST OF FRED ASTAIRE (LP)	22

(see also Judy Garland, Bing Crosby)

ASTERIX

70	Decca F 13075	Everybody/If I Could Fly	15

EDWIN/TED ASTLEY (ORCHESTRA)

63	Oriole CB 1880	The World Ten Times Over/Soho	25
65	RCA RCA 1492	Danger Man Theme/Saint Theme	65
66	Decca F 12389	The Baron/Drop Head (as Ted Astley)	55

ANN ASTON

74	Pye 7N 45403	I Can't Stop Myself From Loving You Babe/Freedom Train	6

ASTON & YEN

66	Doctor Bird DB 1064	Skillamy/BABA BROOKS & BAND: Party Time	18

ASTON HALL

80	Tamebeat TAME 001	The Daily Sun/Popular People (p/s)	8

ASTORS

65	Atlantic AT 4037	Candy/I Found Out	40
69	Atlantic 584 245	Candy/I Found Out (reissue)	10

ASTRAL NAVIGATIONS

71 Holyground HG 114/ NSR 172 — ASTRAL NAVIGATIONS (LP, actually by Lightyears Away & Thundermother, poster cover & booklet, 250 copies only, some numbered) ... 250
89 Magic Mixture MM 2 — ASTRAL NAVIGATIONS (LP, reissue with booklet, 425 copies only) ... 35
90s Holyground HBG 122/1 CD — ASTRAL NAVIGATIONS (CD) ... 18
(see also Bill Nelson, David John & Mood)

ASTRONAUTS (U.K.)

79 Bugle BLAST 1 — THE ASTRONAUTS EP (All Night Party/Back Soon/ Everything Stops The Baby/Survivors) (p/s) ... 12
80 Bugle BLAST 5 — PRANKSTERS IN REVOLT (EP) ... 10
81 Bugle GENIUS 001 — PETER PAN HITS THE SUBURBS (LP) ... 40
82 Bugle GENIUS 002 — IT'S ALL DONE BY MIRRORS (LP) ... 30
86 All The Madmen MAD 5 — IT'S ALL DONE BY MIRRORS (LP, reissue) ... 12
(see also Restricted Hours, Syndicate)

ASTRONAUTS

63 RCA Victor RCA 1349 — Baja/Kuk ... 15
63 RCA Victor RD 7662 — ORBIT KAMPUS (LP) ... 45

ASTRONAUTS

66 Hala Gala HG 9 — Before You Leave/Syncopate ... 5
67 Island WI 3065 — Before You Leave/Syncopate (reissue) ... 5

A SUDDEN SWAY

(see under Sudden Sway)

ASYLUM CHOIR

68 Mercury SMCL 21041 — A LOOK INSIDE THE ASYLUM CHOIR (LP) ... 18
(see also Leon Russell)

ATACAMA

71 Charisma CAS 1039 — ATACAMA (LP) ... 18
72 Charisma CAS 1060 — THE SUN BURNS UP ABOVE (LP) ... 18

ATHENIANS

64 ESC ESC 1 — You Tell Me/Little Queenie (custom sleeve) ... 45
64 Waverley SLP 532 — I've Got Love If You Want It/I'm A Lover Not A Fighter (some in p/s) ... 120/65
65 Waverley SLP 533 — Thinking Of Your Love/Mercy Mercy (some in custom sleeve) ... 60/40

GLENN ATHENS & TROJANS

65 Spot 7E 1018 — GLENN ATHENS & TROJANS (EP) ... 350

ATHLETE

00s Regal REG 72 — Westside/Dungeness/One Of Those Days (p/s, with stencil, 1,000 only) ... 12
00s Regal REG 72CD — Westside/Dungeness/One Of Those Days (CD, card sleeve, 1,000 only) ... 12

PETE ATKIN

70 Philips 6006 050 — Be Careful When They Offer You The Moon/Master Of The Revels ... 5
70 Fontana 6309 011 — BEWARE THE BEAUTIFUL STRANGER (LP) ... 15
71 Philips 6308 070 — DRIVING THROUGH MYTHICAL AMERICA (LP) ... 12
73 RCA SF 8336 — A KING AT NIGHTFALL (LP) ... 12
74 RCA LPLI 5014 — THE ROAD OF SILK (LP) ... 12

BENNY ATKINS

60 Mercury AMT 1113 — Lipstick On Your Lips/I'm Following You ... 15

CHET ATKINS

59 RCA Victor RCA 1153 — Boo Boo Stick Beat/Django's Castle ... 10
60 RCA Victor RCA 1174 — Teensville/One Mint Julep ... 10
60 RCA Victor RCA 1209 — "The Dark At The Top Of The Stairs" Theme/Hocus Pocus ... 5
64 RCA Victor RCA 1382 — Susie Q/Windy & Warm ... 5
65 RCA Victor RCA 1441 — Cloudy And Cool/Travelin' ... 5
65 RCA Victor RCA 1464 — Yakety Axe/Letter Edged In Black ... 6
66 RCA Victor RCA 1515 — From Nashville With Love/Rhythm Guitar ... 5
68 RCA Victor RCA 1773 — Light My Fire/Mrs Robinson ... 5
69 RCA Victor RCA 1797 — Those Were The Days/"Zorba The Greek" Theme ... 5
63 RCA Victor RCX 7118 — GUITAR GENIUS (EP) ... 20
60 RCA Victor RD 27168 — TEENSVILLE (LP) ... 20
60 RCA Victor RD 27194 — THE OTHER CHET ATKINS (LP) ... 16
60 RCA Victor RD 27214 — CHET ATKINS' WORKSHOP (LP) ... 16
62 RCA Victor RD 7507 — GENIUS WITH CHET ATKINS (LP) ... 15
62 RCA Victor RD 7519 — CARIBBEAN GUITAR (LP) ... 15
62 RCA Camden CDN 160 — CHET ATKINS AND HIS GUITAR (LP) ... 15
62 RCA Camden CDN 165 — DOWN HOME (LP) ... 15
63 RCA Victor RD/SF 7529 — OUR MAN IN NASHVILLE (LP, mono/stereo) ... 15/20
63 RCA Victor RD 7557 — TRAVELIN' (LP) ... 15
63 RCA Victor RD/SF 7602 — TEENSCENE (LP, mono/stereo) ... 15/20
63 RCA Victor RD/SF 7647 — PROGRESSIVE PICKING (LP, mono/stereo) ... 15/20
63 RCA Victor RD 7664 — BEST OF CHET ATKINS (LP) ... 15
64 RCA Victor RD 7691 — REMINISCING (LP, with Hank Snow) ... 15
65 RCA Victor RD 7710 — MY FAVOURITE GUITARS (LP) ... 15
65 RCA Victor RD 7763 — MORE OF THAT GUITAR COUNTRY (LP) ... 15
66 RCA Victor RD 7805 — POPS GO COUNTRY (LP, with Boston Pops Orchestra) ... 12
66 RCA Victor RD/SF 7813 — CHET ATKINS PICKS ON THE BEATLES (LP, mono/stereo) ... 15/20
67 RCA Victor RD 7838 — FROM NASHVILLE WITH LOVE (LP) ... 15
67 RCA Victor RD 7882 — IT'S A GUITAR WORLD (LP) ... 15
68 RCA Victor RD/SF 7934 — SOLO FLIGHTS (LP) ... 15
69 RCA Victor SF 8064 — PICKS ON THE POPS (LP) ... 12
60s RCA Camden CDN 5110 — GUITAR GENIUS (LP) ... 12
70 RCA Victor SF 8092 — SOLD GOLD 70 (LP) ... 12
70 RCA Victor SF 8130 — YESTERGROOVIN' (LP) ... 12
(see also Country Hams, Hank Snow, Mark Knopfler)

MINT VALUE £

CHET ATKINS & MARK KNOPFLER
90 CBS 656373 7 — Poor Boy Blues/So Soft Your Goodbye (p/s) — 5

ATLANTIC BRIDGE
71 Dawn DNX 2507 — I Can't Lie To You/Hilary Dickson/Childhood Room (p/s) — 7
70 Dawn DNLS 3014 — ATLANTIC BRIDGE (LP, gatefold sleeve) — 15

ATLANTICS
64 Windsor WPS 129 — Don't Say No/Send Him To Me — 15

ATLANTIS
73 Vertigo 6360 609 — ATLANTIS (LP, swirl label, German-made sleeve) — 12

ATLAS
78 Emerging WIL 001 — AGAINST ALL THE ODDS (LP, private pressing) — 25

AT LAST THE 1958 ROCK & ROLL SHOW
68 CBS 3349 — I Can't Drive/Working On The Railroad — 25
(see also Ian Hunter, Mott The Hoople, Freddie 'Fingers' Lee, Miller Anderson, Charles Woolfe)

ATMOSFEAR
79 Elite DAZZ 1 — Dancing In Outer Space/Dancing In Outer Space (Version) (12") — 15
79 MCA 12 MCA 543 — Dancing In Outer Space/Dancing In Outer Space (Version) (12", co. sleeve) — 12
80 Elite DAZZ 2 — Motivation/Extract (12", p/s) — 10
79 Elite DAZZ 4 — Journey To The Powerline (Remix)/LEVEL 42: Sandstorm (12", w/l promo) — 100
83 Elite DAZZ 23 — What Do We Do? (Club Mix)/What Do We Do?/Xtra Special (12", p/s) — 8
84 Elite DAZZ 31 — When Tonight Is Over/(versions) (12") — 10
84 Elite DAZZ 35 — Telepathy/(versions) (12") — 10
81 MCA MCF 3110 — ENTRANCE (LP) — 15
84 Elite ATM 33-1 — FIRST/FOURMOST (mini-LP) — 15
(see also Level 42)

ATMOSPHERES
59 London HLW 8977 — Kabalo/The Fickle Chicken — 25
59 London HLW 8977 — Kabalo/The Fickle Chicken (78) — 10
60 London HLW 9091 — Telegraph/Caravan — 25

ATOMIC ROOSTER
70 B&C CB 121 — Friday The 13th/Banstead (initial copies in p/s) — 15/8
70 B&C CB 131 — Tomorrow Night/Play The Game — 7
71 B&C CB 157 — Devil's Answer/Rock — 7
72 Dawn DNS 1027 — Stand By Me/Never To Lose — 6
72 Dawn DNS 1029 — Save Me/Close Your Eyes — 6
74 Decca FR 13503 — Tell Your Story (Sing Your Song)/O.D. (as Vincent Crane's Atomic Rooster) — 8
80 EMI EMI 5084 — Do You Know Who's Looking For You/Throw Your Life Away (p/s) — 6
80 EMI 12EMI 5084 — Do You Know Who's Looking For You (Ext.)/Throw Your Life Away (12", p/s) — 10
81 Polydor POSP 334 — Play It Again/Start To Live (p/s) — 5
81 Polydor POSPX 334 — Play It Again/Start To Live/Devil's Answer (live) (12", p/s) — 8
82 Polydor POSP 408 — End Of The Day/Living Underground (p/s) — 5
82 Polydor POSPX 408 — End Of The Day/Living Underground/Tomorrow Night (live) (12", p/s) — 8
70 B&C CAS 1010 — ATOMIC ROOSTER (LP) — 30
70 B&C CAS 1026 — DEATH WALKS BEHIND YOU (LP, gatefold sleeve) — 25
71 Pegasus PEG 1 — IN HEARING OF ATOMIC ROOSTER (LP, gatefold sleeve) — 18
72 Dawn DNLS 3038 — MADE IN ENGLAND (LP, limited 'denim' cover) — 30
73 Dawn DNLS 3038 — MADE IN ENGLAND (LP, re-pressing, standard cover) — 15
73 Dawn DNLS 3049 — NICE'N'GREASY (LP) — 30
83 Towerbell TOWLP 004 — HEADLINE NEWS (LP) — 12
(see also Crane/Farlowe, Chris Farlowe, Crazy World Of Arthur Brown, Hard Stuff, Leaf Hound, Andromeda, John Du Cann)

ATOMS
79 Rinka R 23 — Max Bygraves Killed My Mother/Beatles Jacket (colour silk-screened p/s in poly bag with inserts) — 10

A II Z
81 Polydor POSP 243 — No Fun After Midnight/Treason (no p/s) — 12
81 Polydor POSPX 243 — No Fun After Midnight/Treason/Valhalla's Force (12", p/s, red vinyl) — 18
81 Polydor POSP 314 — I'm The One Who Loves You/Ringside Seat (p/s) — 15
80 Polydor 2383 587 — THE WITCH OF BERKELEY — LIVE (LP, initially sealed with sew-on patch) — 25/20
(see also AC/DC)

ATTACK (U.K.)
67 Decca F 12550 — Try It/We Don't Know — 140
67 Decca F 12578 — Any More Than I Do/Hi-Ho Silver Lining — 35
67 Decca F 12631 — Created By Clive/Colour Of My Mind — 60
68 Decca F 12725 — Neville Thumbcatch/Lady Orange Peel — 75
72 Decca F 13353 — Hi-Ho Silver Lining/Any More Than I Do (reissue, unissued)
90 Reflection MM 08 — MAGIC IN THE AIR (LP) — 20
(see also Andromeda, Five Day Week Straw People, Nice)

ATTACK (U.S.)
67 Philips BF 1585 — Washington Square/Please Phil Spector — 20

ATTAK
82 No Future OI 17 — Today's Generation: Murder In The Subway/Future Dreams (p/s) — 8
83 No Future PUNK 6 — ZOMBIES (LP) — 15

ATTEMPTED MOUSTACHE
78 Skeleton SKL 003 — Superman/No Way Out (folded p/s) — 8

AT THE GATES
94 Peaceville CC7 — Gardens Of Grief (yellow vinyl) — 15

ATTICA BLUES

97	Mo' Wax MW 38	Blueprint/Until Next Time/Lonesome Child (12")	8
97	Mo' Wax MWCD 38	Blueprint/Until Next Time/Lonesome Child (CD, card sleeve)	10
97	Mo' Wax MW 38R	Blueprint/(Mixes) (12")	15

ATTRACTION

66	Columbia DB 7936	Stupid Girl/Please Tell Me	45
66	Columbia DB 8010	Party Line/She's A Girl	95

ATTRITION

81	Sound For Industry SFI 671/A.R.R. 002	Fear/Devoid (flexidisc, p/s, some with *Adventures In Reality* fanzine, issue 5)	10/5
85	Third Mind TMS 04	Shrinkwrap/Pendulum Turns (12", p/s with insert)	10
84	Uniton Recordings 1984-1	MONKEY IN A BIN (12" EP, poster p/s, split with tracks by Schamanen Circel)	12
87	Hamster HAM 18	DEATH HOUSE (mini-LP)	12
87	Hamster HAM 18	DEATH HOUSE (cassette)	12

ATTRIX

78	Attrix RB 01	Lost Lenore/Hard Times (p/s, stamped white labels)	15
81	Scoff DT 011	Procession/11th Hour (p/s)	10

WINIFRED ATWELL

55	Decca F 10448	Song Of The Sea/The Black Mask Waltz	10
55	Decca F 10476	Big Ben Boogie/Winnie's Waltzing Rag	10
55	Decca F 10496	17th Century Boogie/Stranger In Paradise	10
55	Decca F 10634	"Let's Have A Ding-Dong" Medley	10
56	Decca F 10681	Poor People Of Paris (Poor John)/Piano Tuners Boogie	15
56	Decca F 10727	Port-Au-Prince/Startime	8
56	Decca F 10762	Left Bank (C'est A Hambourg)/Rampart Street Rock	8
56	Decca F 10785	Bumble Boogie/St. Louis Blues	7
56	Decca F 10796	Make It A Party (medley, both sides)	7
57	Decca F 10852	Let's Rock 'N' Roll (medley, both sides)	8
57	Decca F 10886	Spaceship Boogie/Jane Street	8
55	Decca DFE 6099	BOOGIE WITH WINIFRED ATWELL (EP)	10
50s	Decca	10" LPs	each 12

AUBREY SMALL

72	Polydor 2058 204	Loser/Oh What A Day It's Been	8
71	Polydor 2383 048	AUBREY SMALL (LP, with insert)	60

(see also Sons Of Man)

AUDIENCE

71	Charisma CB 126	Belladonna Moonshine/The Big Spell	6
71	Charisma CB 141	Indian Summer/It Brings A Tear/Priestess (some in p/s)	8/5
71	Charisma CB 156	You're Not Smiling/Eye To Eye	5
72	Charisma CB 185	Stand By The Door/Thunder And Lightnin'	5
72	Charisma CB 196	Raviole/Hard Cruel World	5
69	Polydor 583 065	AUDIENCE (LP)	80
70	Charisma CAS 1012	FRIEND'S FRIEND'S FRIEND (LP)	15
71	Charisma CAS 1032	THE HOUSE ON THE HILL (LP, gatefold sleeve with lyric inner sleeve)	15
72	Charisma CAS 1054	LUNCH (LP, gatefold sleeve)	12

(see also Howard Werth & Moonbeams)

AUDREY

69	Downtown DT 414	Love Me Tonight/BROTHER DAN ALLSTARS: Show Them Amigo	12
69	Downtown DT 418	Lover's Concerto/BROTHER DAN ALLSTARS: Along Came Roy	12
69	Downtown DT 436	You'll Lose A Good Thing/DESMOND RILEY: If I Had Wings	12
70	Downtown DT 452	Sweeter Than Sugar/The Way You Move	12
70	Downtown DT 454	Oh I Was Wrong/Let's Try It Again (B-side with Dandy)	12
70	Downtown DT 457	Someday We'll Be Together/MUSIC DOCTORS: Sunset Rock	12
70	Downtown DT 463	How Glad I Am/DANDY & AUDREY: I'm So Glad	12
70	Trend 6099 006	Getting Ready For A Heartache/M Y O B: Leave Me Alone	10

(see also Dandy)

BRIAN AUGER (&) TRINITY

65	Columbia DB 7590	Fool Killer/Let's Do It Tonight (as Brian Auger Trinity)	60
65	Columbia DB 7715	Green Onions '65/Kiko (as Brian Auger Trinity)	50
67	Columbia DB 8163	Tiger/Oh Baby, Won't You Come Back Home To Croydon, Where Everybody Beedle's And Bo's (solo)	35
67	Marmalade 598 003	Red Beans And Rice Pts 1 & 2	35
68	Marmalade 598 006	I Don't Know Where You Are/A Kind Of Love In (with Julie Driscoll, unissued in favour of "This Wheel's On Fire")	
69	Marmalade 598 015	What You Gonna Do/Bumpin' On Sunset	15
70	RCA RCA 1947	I Want To Take You Higher/Just Me Just You	7
71	Polydor 2058 119	This Wheel's On Fire/Road To Cairo (as Brian Auger & Julie Driscoll)	6
71	Polydor 2058 133	Marie's Wedding/Tomorrow City (as Brian Auger's Oblivion Express)	6
73	CBS 1444	Inner City Blues/Light Of The Path (as Brian Auger's Oblivion Express)	6
74	CBS 2309	Straight Ahead/Change	6
68	Marmalade 608 004	DON'T SEND ME NO FLOWERS (LP, with Jimmy Page & Sonny Boy Williamson)	50
69	Marmalade 607/608 003	DEFINITELY WHAT! (LP)	35
69	Polydor 2334 004	THE BEST OF BRIAN AUGER, JULIE DRISCOLL & THE TRINITY (LP)	18
70	RCA SF 8101	BEFOUR (LP)	20
71	RCA SF 8170	OBLIVION EXPRESS (LP)	18
71	Polydor 2383 062	BETTER LAND (LP)	15
72	Polydor 2383 104	SECOND WIND (LP, as Brian Auger's Oblivion Express)	15
73	CBS 65625	CLOSER TO IT (LP)	12
74	CBS 80058	STRAIGHT AHEAD (LP)	12

(see also Julie Driscoll Brian Auger & Trinity, Shotgun Express, Jimmy Page, Sonny Boy Williamson)

MINT VALUE £

AU GO-GO SINGERS

65 Columbia DB 7493 San Francisco Bay Blues/Pink Polemoniums ... 10
64 Columbia 33SX 1696 THEY CALL US AU GO-GO SINGERS (LP) ... 50
(see also Buffalo Springfield, Stephen Stills, Poco)

GEORGIE AULD

54 Vogue Coral Q 2002 Manhattan/Solitaire ... 5
60 Top Rank JAR 281 Hawaiian War Chant/Sleepy Lagoon ... 5
(see also Lancers, Modernaires)

AUM

69 London HA-K/SH-K 8401 BLUESVIBES (LP) ... 30

CLIFF AUNGIER

68 Polydor 56250 Time/Fisherboy ... 6
68 RCA RCA 1730 My Love And I/Abigail ... 6
69 Pye 7N 17753 Lady From Baltimore/Back On The Road Again ... 6
69 Pye NSPL 18294 LADY FROM BALTIMORE (LP) ... 15
(see also Royd Rivers & Cliff Aungier)

AUNTIEPUS

79 Septic AUNT 1 Half-Way To Venezuela/Marmalade Freak (p/s) ... 6
(see also Damned)

AU PAIRS

81 Human HUMAN 1 PLAYING WITH A DIFFERENT SEX (LP) ... 12
82 Kamera KAM 010 SENSE AND SENSUALITY (LP, with insert) ... 12
83 AKA AKA 6 LIVE IN BERLIN (LP) ... 12

AURORA

83 Aurora RAM 9 I'll Be Your Fantasy/If I Really Knew Her (no p/s) ... 150

BURNER-LEE AUSTIN

73 Mojo 2093 027 Gimme Your Hand/Real Woman ... 6

PATTI AUSTIN

69 United Artists UP 35018 The Family Tree/Magical Boy ... 5
70 United Artists UP 35097 Your Love Made The Difference In Me/It's Easier To Laugh Than Cry ... 5
71 CBS 7180 Are We Ready For Love/Now That I Know What Loneliness Is ... 10
74 Probe PRO 608 Music To My Heart/Love 'Em And Leave 'Em Kind Of Love ... 5

PETER AUSTIN

68 Caltone TONE 125 Your Love/Time Is Getting Harder ... 12
(see also Little Freddy, Mr. Foundation)

REG AUSTIN

65 Pye 7N 15885 My Saddest Day/I'll Find Her ... 50

SIL AUSTIN

57 Mercury MT 132 Slow Walk/Wildwood (78) ... 10
58 Mercury MT 189 Fall Out/Green Blazer (78) ... 10
58 Mercury 7MT 220 Don't You Just Know It/Rainstorm ... 15
58 Mercury 7MT 225 Hey, Eula/The Last Time ... 10
58 Mercury MEP 9540 THE BAND WITH THE BEAT (EP) ... 40
58 Mercury MEP 9541 GO SIL GO (EP) ... 40
58 Mercury MPL 6534 SLOW WALK ROCK (LP) ... 50

AUSTRALIAN PLAYBOYS

67 Immediate IM 054 Black Sheep R.I.P./Sad ... 500
(see also Procession)

AUTECHRE

91 Hardcore HARD 003 Cavity Job/Accelera 1 + 2 (12", 1,000 only) ... 80
94 Warp 10WAP 11 BASSCADET REMIXES (3 x 10" p/s in box) ... 25
93 Warp LP 17LTD INCUNABULA (2-LP set, silver vinyl) ... 50
(see also Gescom)

AUTOGRAPHS

78 RAK RAK 281 While I'm Still Young/Fabulous (p/s) ... 15

AUTOMATIC DLAMINI

87 D For Drum DLAM 2 I Don't Know You But... /I've Never Seen That Colour Anywhere Before (p/s, with insert) ... 5
87 Idea IDEA 009 Me And My Conscience (p/s) ... 5
87 Idea IDEAT 009 Me And My Conscience (12", p/s) ... 8
87 Idea IDEALP 001 THE D IS FOR DRUM (LP) ... 12
92 Big Intl. BOT 04 FROM A DIVA TO A DIVER (LP, also CD BOT 04CD) ... 12/20
(see also P.J. Harvey)

AUTOMATICS

78 Island WIP 6433 Wakin' With The Radio On/Watch Her Now (unissued)
78 Island WIP 6439 When Tanks Roll Over Poland Again/Watch Her Now (p/s) ... 10

AUTOPSY

89 Peaceville VILE 12 SEVERED SURVIVAL (LP, picture disc) ... 20
91 Peaceville VILE 25 MENTAL FUNERAL (LP, picture disc) ... 20

GENE AUTRY

59 London HLU 9001 Nine Little Reindeer/Buon Natale ... 5
66 Realm RM 52319 THE BEST OF GENE AUTRY (LP) ... 10
67 RCA Victor RD 7839 GOLDEN HITS (LP) ... 10

AUTUMN VINE

70 Evolution E 2447 He Ain't No Superman/Maxi Baby ... 6

MINT VALUE £

AVALANCHE

71	Parlophone R 5890	Finding My Way Home/Rabbits	35

(see also Norman Haines Band)

FRANKIE AVALON

58	HMV POP 453	Dede Dinah/Ooh-La-La	25
58	HMV POP 453	Dede Dinah/Ooh-La-La (78)	10
58	London HL 8636	You Excite Me/Darlin'	40
58	London HL 8636	You Excite Me/Darlin' (78)	10
58	HMV POP 517	Ginger Bread/Blue Betty	25
58	HMV POP 517	Ginger Bread/Blue Betty (78)	10
59	HMV POP 569	I'll Wait For You/What Little Girl?	25
59	HMV POP 569	I'll Wait For You/What Little Girl? (78)	10
59	HMV POP 603	Venus/I'm Broke	12
59	HMV POP 603	Venus/I'm Broke (78)	10
59	HMV POP 636	Bobby Sox To Stockings/A Boy Without A Girl	15
59	HMV POP 636	Bobby Sox To Stockings/A Boy Without A Girl (78)	10
59	HMV POP 658	Just Ask Your Heart/Two Fools	15
59	HMV POP 658	Just Ask Your Heart/Two Fools (78)	10
60	HMV POP 688	Why/Swinging On A Rainbow	5
60	HMV POP 727	Don't Throw Away All Those Teardrops/Talk, Talk, Talk	5
60	HMV POP 742	The Faithful Kind/Gee Whizz — Whilikins — Golly Gee	10
60	HMV POP 766	Where Are You/Tuxedo Junction	10
60	HMV POP 794	Togetherness/Don't Let Love Pass Me By	5
60	HMV POP 816	Green Leaves Of Summer/Here's To The Ladies	5
58	HMV 7EG 8471	FRANKIE AVALON (EP)	35
58	HMV 7EG 8482	FRANKIE AVALON NO. 2 (EP)	35
58	HMV 7EG 8507	FRANKIE AVALON NO. 3 (EP)	35
60	HMV 7EG 8632	SONGS OF THE ALAMO (EP)	18
59	HMV CLP 1346	SWINGIN' ON A RAINBOW (LP)	35
60	HMV CLP 1423	SUMMER SCENE (LP)	35
60	HMV CLP 1440/CSD 1358	YOUNG AND IN LOVE (LP, mono/stereo)	30/40
64	United Artists ULP 1078	MUSCLE BEACH PARTY (LP)	50

AVALONS

66	Island WI 263	Everyday/I Love You	15

AVANT-GARDE

68	CBS 3704	Naturally Stoned/Honey And Gall	7

AVANT GARDENER(S)

77	Virgin VEP 1003	GOTTA TURN BACK (EP)	6
80	Appaloosa AP 013	DIG IT (LP)	12

AVAVA

91	A5 AVA 5555	AVAVA (LP, 500 only)	12

AVENGER

83	Neat NEAT 31	Too Wild To Tame/On The Rocks (p/s)	5
85	Neat NEAT 1026	KILLER ELITE (LP, with lyric insert)	15

AVENGERS

68	Parlophone R 5661	Everyone's Gonna Wonder/Take My Hand	10

(see also Vanity Fair)

HARVEY AVERNE BARRIO BAND

90s	Acid Jazz JAZID 93	THE HARVEY AVERNE BARRIO BAND (LP)	15

AVO-8

80	Stroppo STROP 1	Gone Wrong/Target One/No Hesitation (p/s)	10

ALAN AVON & TOY SHOP

70	Concord CON 005	These Are The Reasons/Night To Remember	150

(see also Hedgehoppers Anonymous)

VALERIE AVON

67	Columbia DB 8201	He Knows I Love Him Too Much/To Be Let	15

(see also Avons)

AVON CITIES' JAZZ BAND

56	Tempo A 151	Shim-Me Sha-Me Wabble/Hawaiian War Chant	10
60	Tempo A 169	Upper Set/American Patrol	8
56	Tempo LAP 10	AVON CITIES JAZZ BAND (LP)	50
58	Tempo TAP 18	AVON CITIES JAZZ (LP, with Ray Bush)	40
60s	Eclipse ECS 2175	BRISTOL FASHION (LP)	15

(see also Ray Bush)

AVONS

59	Columbia DB 4363	Seven Little Girls Sitting In The Back Seat/Alone At Eight	5
60	Columbia DB 4413	Pickin' Petals/We Fell In Love	5
60	Columbia DB 4461	We're Only Young Once/I Keep Dreaming	5
60	Columbia DB 4522	Four Little Heels/This Was Meant To Be	5
61	Columbia DB 4569	Rubber Ball/Cool And Cosy	5
61	Columbia DB 4700	Skin Divin'/Little Bo Peep	5
62	Columbia DB 4280	Tonight I Cannot Sleep/Gotta Go	5
62	Columbia DB 4899	A Wonderful Dream/Tonight You Belong To Me	5
63	Decca F 11588	Hey Paula/I Wanna Do It	5
63	Decca F 11641	Love Should Be True/All About You	5
64	Fontana TF 442	I Am The Girl/Once Upon A Summer's Day	5

(see also Valerie Avon, Avon Sisters)

AVON SISTERS

59	Columbia DB 4236	Jerri-Lee (I Love Him So)/Baby-O	15
59	Columbia DB 4236	Jerri-Lee (I Love Him So)/Baby-O (78)	10

MINT VALUE £

AWAY FROM THE SAND
70s Beaujangle DB 0003 AWAY FROM THE SAND (LP) . . . 30
(see also Bev Pegg, Dave Cartwright, Brindley Brae)

AXEGRINDER
89 Peaceville VILE 7 RISE OF THE SERPENT MEN (LP) . . . 20

DAVID AXELROD
68 Capitol ST 2982 SONGS OF INNOCENCE (LP) . . . 55
73 MCA MCF 2664 THE AUCTION (LP) . . . 50

AXIS
80 Metal Minded ISAX 1047 Lady/Messiah (p/s) . . . 6
81 Axis When You Hold Me . . . 8
81 Neat NEAT 13 You Got It/One Step Ahead (p/s) . . . 5

HOYT AXTON
64 Stateside SL 10082 GREENBACK DOLLAR (LP) . . . 22
64 Stateside SL 10096 THUNDER 'N' LIGHTNIN' (LP) . . . 22
66 London HA-F/SH-F 8276 THE BEST OF HOYT AXTON (LP) . . . 22

KEVIN AYERS (& WHOLE WORLD)
70 Harvest HAR 5011 Singing A Song In The Morning/Eleanor's Cake Which Ate Her . . . 10
70 Harvest HAR 5027 Butterfly Dance/Puis-Je? (with Whole World) . . . 12
71 Harvest HAR 5042 Stranger In Blue Suede Shoes/Stars (with Whole World) . . . 10
72 Harvest HAR 5064 Oh! Wot A Dream/Connie On A Rubber Band . . . 10
73 Harvest HAR 5071 Caribbean Moon/Take Me To Tahiti (some in p/s) . . . 20/5
74 Island WIP 6194 The Up Song/Everybody's Sometimes & Some People's All The Time Blues . . . 6
74 Island WIP 6201 After The Show/Thank You Very Much . . . 6
75 Harvest HAR 5100 Caribbean Moon/Take Me To Tahiti . . . 6
76 Island WIP 6271 Falling In Love Again/Everyone Knows The Song . . . 6
76 Harvest HAR 5107 Stranger In Blue Suede Shoes/Fake Mexican Tourist Blues (possibly some in p/s) . . . 20/5
76 Harvest HAR 5109 Caribbean Moon/Take Me To Tahiti (reissue, some in different p/s) . . . 20/5
77 Harvest HAR 5124 Star/The Owl . . . 6
80 Harvest HAR 5198 Money, Money, Money/Stranger In Blue Suede Shoes (p/s) . . . 6
83 Charly/Celluloid CYZ 7107 My Speeding Heart/Champagne & Valium (p/s) . . . 10
86 Illuminated LEV 71 Stepping Out/Only Heaven Knows (no p/s) . . . 15
70 Harvest SHVL 763 JOY OF A TOY (LP, gatefold sleeve) . . . 35
70 Harvest SHSP 4005 SHOOTING AT THE MOON (LP, with Whole World) . . . 30
72 Harvest SHVL 800 WHATEVERSHEBRINGSWESING (LP, gatefold sleeve) . . . 20
73 Harvest SHVL 807 BANANAMOUR (LP, gatefold sleeve, some with booklet) . . . 30/15
74 Island ILPS 9263 THE CONFESSIONS OF DR. DREAM AND OTHER STORIES (LP, with inner) . . . 15
75 Island ILPS 9322 SWEET DECEIVER (LP, with inner sleeve) . . . 12
75 Harvest SHDW 407 JOY OF A TOY/SHOOTING AT THE MOON (2-LP, reissue, gatefold sleeve) . . . 15
76 Harvest SHSP 2005 ODD DITTIES (LP) . . . 12
76 Harvest SHSP 4057 YES WE HAVE NO MAÑANAS (LP, with inner sleeve) . . . 12
78 Harvest SHSP 4085 RAINBOW TAKEAWAY (LP) . . . 12
80 Harvest SHSP 4106 THAT'S WHAT YOU GET BABE (LP, with inner sleeve) . . . 12
83 Charly CR 30224 DIAMOND JACK AND THE QUEEN OF PAIN (LP) . . . 15
86 Illuminated AMA 25 AS CLOSE AS YOU THINK (LP) . . . 25
92 Permanent PERM LP 5 STILL LIFE WITH GUITAR (LP) . . . 15
(see also Soft Machine, Lady June, Lol Coxhill, David Bedford, Mike Oldfield, Bridget St. John)

AYERS, CALE, NICO & ENO
74 Island ILPS 9291 JUNE 1ST, 1974 (LP) . . . 18
(see also Kevin Ayers, John Cale, Nico, Brian Eno)

ROY AYERS (UBIQUITY)
76 Polydor 2066 671 Evolution/Mystique Voyage (as Roy Ayers' Ubiquity) . . . 8
77 Polydor 2066 842 Running Away/Cincinnati Growl (as Roy Ayers' Ubiquity) . . . 8
78 Polydor 2066 896 Freaky Dee Jay/You Came Into My Life . . . 5
78 Polydor AYERS 12 Get On Up Get On Down/And Don't Say No (12") . . . 10
79 Polydor POSP 53 Fever/Is It Too Late To Try . . . 5
79 Polydor POSPX 53 Fever/Is It Too Late To Try (12") . . . 10
80 Polydor STEPX 9 Don't Stop The Feeling (12") . . . 10
80 Polydor POSP 135 Running Away/Can't You See Me . . . 5
80 Polydor POSPX 135 Running Away/Can't You See Me (12") . . . 12
80 Polydor POSPX 186 Sometimes, Believe In Yourself (12") . . . 8
83 Polydor UM 1T Silver Vibrations/Fast Money (12") . . . 8
87 Urban URBX 6 Can't You See Me/Love Will Bring Us Back Together/Sweet Tears (12", p/s) . . . 8
83 Uno Melodic UMLP 2 DRIVIN' ON UP (LP) . . . 15
(see also Jack Wilson Quartet)

AYRSHIRE FOLK
74 Deroy AYRSHIRE FOLK (LP, private pressing) . . . 60

AYSHEA
65 Fontana TF 627 Eeny Meeny/Peep My Love . . . 8
68 Polydor 56276 Celebration Of The Year/Only Love Can Save Me Now . . . 30
69 Polydor 56302 Another Night/Taking The Sun From My Eyes . . . 7
70 Polydor 2001 029 Mr White's White Flying Machine/Ship Of The Line . . . 6
70 Polydor 2058 074 Who's Gonna Rescue Jesus/The Flowers Are Mine . . . 6
71 MAM MAM 59 Old Fashioned Love Song/Family Of A Man . . . 6
73 Harvest HAR 5073 Farewell/The Best Years Of My Life . . . 6
74 DJM DJS 339 Another Without You Day/Moonbeam . . . 5
70 Polydor 2384 026 AYSHEA (LP) . . . 30
74 DJM DJLPS 445 LIFT OFF WITH AYSHEA (LP) . . . 15
(see also Ayshea Brough)

MINT VALUE £

AZTEC CAMERA

81	Postcard 81-3	Just Like Gold/We Could Send Letters (die-cut sleeve, some with card)	18/10
81	Postcard 81-8	Mattress Of Wire/Lost Outside The Tunnel (p/s)	15
82	Rough Trade RT 112	Pillar To Post/Queen's Tattoos (p/s)	5
82	Rough Trade RT 112P	Pillar To Post/Queen's Tattoos (picture disc)	8
83	Rainhill ACFC 1	Oblivious (Langer/Winstanley Remix)/Oblivious (Colin Fairley Remix) (fan club issue, no p/s)	20
87	WEA YZ 154 CD	Deep & Wide & Tall (Breakdown Mix)/Bad Education (3" CD, card sleeve)	10

(see also French Impressionists)

AZUSA PLANE

96	Enraptured RAPT 4506	untitled/GRIMBLE GRUMBLE: untitled (some on blue vinyl)	10/6

AZYMUTH

79	Milestone MRC 101	Jazz Carnival/Fly Over The Horizon (12")	15
78	ECM ECM 1130	THE TOUCHSTONE (LP)	12
80	ECM ECM 1163	DEPART (LP, with Ralph Towner)	12
80	Milestone M 9097	OUTUBRO (LP)	12

BOB AZZAM & HIS ORCHESTRA

60	Decca F 21235	Mustapha/Tintarella Di Luna	10
61	Oriole CB 1599	Couscous/Abuglubu	7

IKE B & CRYSTALS

68	Island WI 3151	Try A Little Merriness/Patricia	25

B's

70s	private pressing	IN YOUR BONNET (LP)	35

MEHER BABA

70	Univ. Spiritual League 1	HAPPY BIRTHDAY (LP, with inserts, 6 Pete Townshend tracks, 100 only)	110
70	Univ. Spiritual League 2	I AM (LP, with inserts, features 5 Pete Townshend tracks)	65
76	Univ. Spiritual League 3	WITH LOVE (LP, features 3 Pete Townshend tracks)	55
70s	MBO MBO 1	STAR OF THE SILENT SCREEN . . . MEHER BABA (LP, reissue of "Happy Birthday" without inserts)	20
70s	MBO MBO 2	I AM (LP, reissue, without inserts)	20

(see also Pete Townshend)

BABE RUTH

71	Capitol CL 15869	Elusive/Say No More	6
72	Harvest HAR 5087	Wells Fargo/Theme From A Few Dollars More	5
75	Harvest HAR 5090	Private Number/Somebody's Nobody	5
72	Harvest SHSP 4022	FIRST BASE (LP)	15
73	Harvest SHVL 812	AMAR CABALLERO (LP)	15
75	Harvest SHSP 4038	BABE RUTH (LP)	12

(see also Jenny Haan, Bernie Marsden, Wild Turkey)

BABES IN TOYLAND

92	Strange Fruit SFPMA 211	PEEL SESSIONS EP (10", numbered, 4000 copies)	7
95	WEA WO 291TEX	Sweet 69/SFW (numbered p/s)	5

ALICE BABS

63	Fontana TF 409	After You've Gone/St. Louis Blues Twist	12

MONTY BABSON

59	London HLJ 8877	All Night Long/The Things Money Cannot Buy	10
59	London HLJ 8877	All Night Long/The Things Money Cannot Buy (78)	25
60	London HAJ 2212	ALL NIGHT LONG (LP)	15

BABY BIRD

96	Echo ECS 026	You're Gorgeous/Bebe Limonade (p/s, gold vinyl)	6
96	Echo ECSCX 026	You're Gorgeous/Bebe Limonade/Ooh Yeah/Car Crash (CD, mirrored silver digipak)	8
96	Echo ECS 031	Candy Girl/Farmer (picture disc)	5
97	Echo ECS 033	Cornershop/Death Of A Neighbourhood (picture disc)	5
95	Baby Bird LP 1	IF I WAS BORN A MAN (LP, 500 only)	12
95	Baby Bird LP 2	BAD SHAVE (LP, 500 only)	12

BABY DOLLS

60	Warner Bros WB 16	Quiet!/Hey, Baby!	10

BABY HUEY

71	Buddah 2365 001	LIVING LEGEND — THE BABY HUEY STORY (LP)	45

BABY JANE & ROCKABYES

63	United Artists UP 1010	How Much Is That Doggie In The Window/My Boy John	25

BABY LEMONADE

87	Sha La La 003	The Jiffy Neckware Creation/BACHELOR PAD: Girl Of Your Dreams (flexidisc, p/s, with *Are You Scared To Be Happy* fanzine)	10/6
87	Narodnik NRK 004	The Secret Goldfish/Real World (p/s)	8

MINT VALUE £

BABYLON
69 Polydor 56356 — Into The Promised Land/Nobody's Fault But Mine (some in p/s) 35/20
(see also Carole Grimes)

BABY RUTH
71 Decca F 13234 — Rupert's Magic Feather/Flood 8

BABY SUNSHINE
75 Deroy DER 1301 — BABY SUNSHINE (LP, with insert) 75
(see also Fairy's Moke)

BACCA
73 Grape GR 3048 — George Foreman/Version 6

BURT BACHARACH
65 London HLR 9968 — Trains And Boats And Planes/Wives And Lovers 10
65 London HLR 9983 — What's New Pussycat/My Little Red Book (B-side with Tony Middleton) 30
69 A&M AMS 702 — Bond Street/Alfie 15
65 London HAR/SHR 8233 — HIT MAKER! (LP, 1st pressing, plum/blue label, mono/stereo) 12
67 RCA Victor RD/SF 7874 — CASINO ROYALE (LP, soundtrack, mono/stereo) 60/70
67 A&M AMLS 908 — REACH OUT (LP, initial copies with flipback sleeve) 15/12
68 A&M AMLS 938 — MAKE IT EASY ON YOURSELF (LP) 12
68 London HAR/SHR 8233 — HIT MAKER! (LP, 2nd pressing, black/plum label, mono/stereo) 12
(see also Tony Middleton, Breakaways)

BACHDENKEL
77 Initial IRL 001 — LEMMINGS (LP, some with bonus EP) 25/15
77 Initial IRL 002 — STALINGRAD (LP, numbered) 15

JOHNNY BACHELOR
60 London HLN 9074 — Mumbles/Arabella Jean 100

BACHELORS (U.K.)
58 Parlophone R 4454 — Platter Party/Love Is A Two Way Street 30
58 Parlophone R 4454 — Platter Party/Love Is A Two Way Street (78) 10
59 Parlophone R 4547 — Please Don't Touch/Ding Dong 30
60 Decca F 11300 — Lovin' Babe/Why Can't It Be Me 25

BACHELORS (Ireland)
72 Decca F 13248 — Diamonds Are Forever/Where There's A Heartache 5

BACH TWO BACH
71 Mushroom 100 MR 10 — BACH TWO BACH (LP) 18

BACK ALLEY CHOIR
72 York SYK 517 — Smile Born Of Courtesy/Why Are You Here 40
73 York FYK 406 — BACK ALLEY CHOIR (LP, 500 only) 260

BACKBEAT PHILHARMONIC
61 Top Rank JAR 576 — Rock And Roll Symphony Parts 1 & 2 10

BACK DOOR
72 Blakey BLP 5989 — BACK DOOR (LP, sold at gigs) 40
73 Warner Bros K 46231 — BACK DOOR (LP) 12
76 Warner Bros K 56243 — ACTIVATE (LP) 12

MIRIAM BACKHOUSE
77 Mother Earth MUM 1203 — GYPSY WITHOUT A ROAD (LP) 110

BACK PORCH MAJORITY
65 Columbia DB 7627 — Ramblin' Man/Good Time Joe 6

BACKSEAT ROMEOS
80 Future Earth FER 007 — Zero Ambition/In The Night (p/s) 35

BACK TO ZERO
79 Fiction FICS 004 — Your Side Of Heaven/Back To Back (p/s) 12

BACKWORLD
01 World Serpent H7 004 — A Vagrant Thought/The Tide (picture disc, no p/s) 5
02 World Serpent H7 006 — Hands Of Ash/Melody (p/s) 5

BACKYARD HEAVIES
73 Action ACT 4616 — Just Keep On Truckin'/Never Can Say Goodbye 25

GAR BACON
58 Felsted AF 107 — Mary Jane/Chains Of Love 30
58 Felsted AF 107 — Mary Jane/Chains Of Love (78) 10
59 Fontana H 196 — Marshal, Marshal/Too Young To Love 30
59 Fontana H 196 — Marshal, Marshal/Too Young To Love (78) 10

BACON FAT
70 Blue Horizon 57-3171 — Nobody But You/Small's On 53rd 18
70 Blue Horizon 57-3181 — Evil/Blues Feeling 18
70 Blue Horizon 7-63858 — GREASE ONE FOR ME (LP) 55
71 Blue Horizon 2431 001 — TOUGH DUDE (LP) 55
(see also Dirty Blues Band, George 'Harmonica' Smith)

BAD ACTORS
80 Sophist. Noise SONO 1 — Strange Love/Energy Society (p/s) 6
80 Plastic Speech — Love Song/Are They Hostile (p/s) 5

BAD BOYS
64 Piccadilly 7N 35208 — The Owl And The Pussycat/That's What'll Do 20

BAD BRAINS
82 Alt. Tentacles VIRUS 13 — I Luv Jah/Sailin' On/Big Takeover (12", p/s) 8
83 Food For Thought YUMT101 — I And I Survive (An' T'ing)/Destroy Babylon (12", p/s) 12

BADFINGER

70	Apple APPLE 20	Come And Get It/Rock Of All Ages (p/s)	12
70	Apple APPLE 31	No Matter What/Better Days (p/s)	20
71	Apple APPLE 35	Name Of The Game/Suitcase (unreleased)	
72	Apple APPLE 40	Day After Day/Sweet Tuesday Morning (p/s)	18
72	Apple APPLE 42	Baby Blue/Flying (unreleased in U.K.)	
73	Warner Bros K 16323	Love Is Easy/My Heart Goes Out	5
74	Apple APPLE 49	Apple Of My Eye/Blind Owl	25
79	Elektra K 12345	Lost Inside Your Love/Come Down Hard	6
79	Elektra K 12369	Love Is Gonna Come At Last/Sail Away	7
70	Apple SAPCOR 12	MAGIC CHRISTIAN MUSIC (LP)	60
70	Apple SAPCOR 16	NO DICE (LP, gatefold sleeve)	55
72	Apple SAPCOR 19	STRAIGHT UP (LP)	60
73	Warner Bros K 56023	BADFINGER (LP, with insert)	20
74	Apple SAPCOR 27	ASS (LP, with inner sleeve)	45
74	Warner Bros K 56076	WISH YOU WERE HERE (LP, withdrawn)	70+
89	Edsel ED 302	SHINE ON (LP)	15
91	Apple SAPCOR 12	MAGIC CHRISTIAN MUSIC (LP, reissue, gatefold sleeve with bonus 12" [SAPCOR 121])	25
92	Apple SAPCOR 16	NO DICE (LP, reissue, gatefold sleeve with bonus 12" [SAPCOR 161])	25
93	Apple SAPCOR 19	STRAIGHT UP (LP, reissue, gatefold sleeve with bonus 12" [SAPCOR 191])	25
95	Apple SAPCOR 28	COME AND GET IT — THE BEST OF BADFINGER (2-LP, gatefold sleeve)	30

(see also Iveys, Masterminds, Gary Walker & Rain, Natural Gas, Blue Goose)

BADGE

81	Metal Minded MM 2	Silver Woman/Something I've Lost (p/s)	25

BADGER

74	Epic EPC 2326	White Lady/Don't Pull The Trigger	5
73	Atlantic K 40473	ONE LIVE BADGER (LP, gatefold pop-up sleeve)	18
74	Epic EPC 80009	WHITE LADY (LP)	12

(see also Ashton Gardner & Dyke, Jackie Lomax)

BADLY DRAWN BOY

98	Twisted Nerve TNXL001	Roadmovie/My Friend Cubilas (feat. Doves) (die-cut sleeve, with insert)	40
99	Twisted Nerve TNXL 003R	Once Around The Block/Another Pearl (p/s)	7
90s	Twisted Nerve (no cat. no.)	I Love You All (one-track musical box, 150 only)	150
01	Twisted Nerve TNXL 011	Donna And Blitzen (p/s, one-sided, 800 only)	12
97	Twisted Nerve TN 001	EP1 (EP, 500 only)	250
98	Twisted Nerve TN 002	EP2: I Love You All/The Treeclimber/I Love You All (I Loop You All Andy Votel Mix)/Thinking Of You (EP, 1,000 only)	90
98	Twisted Nerve XL TN 001T	EP3 (EP, 1,000 only)	12
98	Twisted Nerve XL TN 001CD	EP3 (CD EP, gatefold card sleeve, 1,000 only)	8
99	Twisted Nerve TNXL 002R	IT CAME FROM THE GROUND (10" EP, orange vinyl, card sleeve, 500 only)	15
00	Twisted Nerve TNXLCD 133	THE HOUR OF THE BEWILDERBEAST (LP, 1st pressing, withdrawn, with version of 'Magic In The Air' with the line "Love Is Contagious", and Woody Allen on sleeve)	25
00	Twisted Nerve TNXLCD 133	THE HOUR OF THE BEWILDERBEAST (CD, 1st pressing, withdrawn, with version of 'Magic In The Air' with the line "Love Is Contagious", and Woody Allen on sleeve)	20

(see also Doves)

BAD NEWS

87	EMI EM 24X	Bohemian Rhapsody/Life With Brian (scratch'n'sniff p/s)	5
87	EMI EMP 24	Bohemian Rhapsody/Life With Brian (p/s, with sew-on patch)	7
87	EMI 12EM 24	Bohemian Rhapsody/Pretty Woman/Life With Brian (12", standard p/s)	8
87	EMI 12EM 24X	Bohemian Rhapsody/Pretty Woman/Life With Brian (12", scratch'n'sniff p/s)	10
87	EMI EM 36	Cashing In On Christmas/Bad News (p/s)	5
87	EMI EMG 36	Cashing In On Christmas/Bad News (Christmas card poster pack)	7
87	EMI 12EM 36	Cashing In On Christmas (Let's Bank Mix)/Bad News/Cashing In On Christmas (12", p/s)	8

(see also Brian May)

BAD TASTE

88	Newgate SRT8KS 1554	Rockin' Girl (p/s, some with insert)	30/10

JOAN BAEZ

65	Fontana TF 564	We Shall Overcome/Don't Think Twice It's All Right	5
65	Fontana TF 587	There But For Fortune/Plaisir D'Amour	5
66	Fontana TF 727	Pack Up Your Sorrows/Swallow Song	5
65	Fontana TF 604	It's All Over Now Baby Blue/Daddy You've Been On My Mind	6
65	Fontana TF 639	Farewell Angelina/Queen Of Hearts	6
66	Vanguard VA 2	Love Minus Zero/Love Is Just A Four-Letter Word	5
60	Fontana TFE 18005	JOAN BAEZ SINGS SILVER DAGGER & OTHER SONGS (EP)	8
63	Fontana TE 18012	WITH GOD ON OUR SIDE (EP)	10
60	Fontana (S)TFL 6002	JOAN BAEZ (LP)	12
61	Fontana (S)TFL 6025	JOAN BAEZ 2 (LP)	12
62	Fontana (S)TFL 6035	IN CONCERT 2 (LP)	12
64	Fontana (S)TFL 6043	JOAN BAEZ 5 (LP)	12
65	Fontana (S)TFL 6058	FAREWELL ANGELINA (LP)	12

(see also Earl Scruggs)

DOC BAGBY

58	Fontana H 106	Dumplin's/Sylvia's Calling (78)	10

BURR BAILEY (& SIX SHOOTERS)

63	Decca F 11686	San Francisco Bay/Like A Bird Without Feathers (with Six Shooters)	30
64	Decca F 11846	Chahawki/You Made Me Cry	50

CLIVE BAILEY & RICO'S GROUP

62	Blue Beat BB 92	Evening Train/Going Home	18

MINT VALUE £

DEREK BAILEY
70s Incus INCUS 2 — SOLO GUITAR (LP) 100
70s Incus INCUS 2R — SOLO GUITAR (LP) 100
74 Incus INCUS 12 — LOT 74 (LP) 80
80 Incus INCUS 40 — AIDA (LP) 50
85 Incus INCUS 48 — NOTES (LP) 50
04 Organ Of Corti — TAPS (LP, 220gm vinyl, limited issue) 15
(see also Tony Oxley, Springboard, Steve Lacy & Derek Bailey, Anthony Braxton & Derek Bailey, Jamie Muir & Derek Bailey, David Sylvian)

DEREK BAILEY & EVAN PARKER
75 Incus INCUS 16 — THE LONDON CONCERT (LP) 60
85 Incus INCUS 50 — COMPATIBLES (LP) 50
(see also Evan Parker)

DEREK BAILEY & HAN BENNINK
72 Incus INCUS 9 — SELECTIONS FROM LIVE PERFORMANCES AT VERITY'S PLACE (LP) 100
76 Incus INCUS 25 — COMPANY 3 (LP) 50

DEREK BAILEY & TONY COE
79 Incus INCUS 34 — TIME (LP) 50

DEREK BAILEY & TRISTAN HONSINGER
76 Incus INCUS 20 — DUO (LP) 50

DEREK BAILEY, ANTHONY BRAXTON & EVAN PARKER
76 Incus INCUS 23 — COMPANY 2 (LP) 50

DEREK BAILEY, BARRY GUY & PAUL RUTHERFORD
70 Incus INCUS 3/4 — ISKRA 1903 (LP) 100
(see also Barry Guy)

DEREK BAILEY, EVAN PARKER & HAN BENNINK
70 Incus INCUS 1 — THE TOPOGRAPHY OF THE LUNGS (LP) 100

DEREK BAILEY, HUGH DAVIES, JAMIE MUIR, EVAN PARKER
70s Incus INCUS 17 — THE MUSIC IMPROVISATION COMPANY 1968-1971 (LP) 50

MILDRED BAILEY
57 Parlophone GEP 8600 — MILDRED BAILEY AND HER ALLEY CATS (EP) 10
54 Brunswick LA 8692 — THE ROCKIN' CHAIR LADY (10" LP) 20

PEARL BAILEY
54 Vogue Coral Q 2026 — She's Something Spanish/What Happened To The Hair 5
56 HMV POP 244 — Tired/Go Back Where You Stayed Last Night 5
56 London HLN 8354 — That Certain Feeling/Hit The Road To Dreamland 10
56 London REU 1104 — THAT CERTAIN FEELING (EP) 10
62 Columbia SX 1447 — HAPPY SOUNDS (LP, with Louis Bellson) 12

ROY BAILEY (U.K.)
71 Trailer LER 3021 — ROY BAILEY (LP) 15
76 Fuse AC 262 — NEW BELL AWAKE (LP) 12
82 Fuse CF 382 — HARD TIMES (LP, with insert) 12
(see also Leon Rosselson)

ROY BAILEY (Jamaica)
72 Duke DU 146 — Run Away Child/Wedding March 6

ZEDDIE BAILEY
73 Grape GR 3037 — Babylon Gone/TONY KING: Speak No Evil 7

ALY BAIN & MIKE WHELLANS
70s Trailer LER 2022 — ALY BAIN & MIKE WHELLANS (LP) 15

BOB BAIN & HIS MUSIC
58 Capitol CL 14912 — Wagon Wheels/Strollin' Home 6
58 Capitol T965 — Rockin' rollin' and Strollin' (LP) 40

ARTHUR BAIRD SKIFFLE GROUP
56 Beltona BL 2669 — Union Train/Union Maid 30
56 Beltona BL 2669 — Union Train/Union Maid (78) 20

BAJA MARIMBA BAND
63 London HL 9828 — Comin' In The Back Door/December Child 7

CHET BAKER (QUARTET)
56 Vogue V 2377 — My Funny Valentine/But Not For Me 5
56 Vogue V 2381 — Just Friends/Daybreak 5
56 Vogue V 2232 — Winter Wonderland/This Time The Dream's On Me 5
56 Vogue V 2309 — Long Ago And Far Away/Bea's Flat 5
54 Vogue LDE 045 — CHET BAKER QUARTET (10" LP) 20
55 Philips BBL 7022 — CHET BAKER AND STRINGS (LP) 10
55 Vogue LDE 116 — CHET BAKER QUARTET (10" LP) 20
56 Vogue LAE 12018 — CHET BAKER SINGS (LP) 20
56 Vogue LDE 159 — CHET BAKER SEXTET (10" LP) 20
56 Vogue LDE 163 — CHET BAKER ENSEMBLE (10" LP) 20
56 Vogue LDE 182 — CHET BAKER SINGS (10" LP) 20
56 Felsted PDL 85008 — CHET BAKER QUARTET VOL. 1 (LP) 20
56 Felsted PDL 85013 — CHET BAKER QUARTET VOL. 2 (LP) 20
57 Felsted PDL 85036 — I GET CHET (LP, as Chet Baker & His Combo) 20
57 Vogue LAE 12044 — CHET BAKER QUARTET AT ANN ARBOR (LP) 20
57 Vogue LAE 12076 — CHET BAKER AND HIS CREW (LP, mono) 20
58 Vogue LAE 12109 — CHET BAKER — PHIL'S BLUES (LP) 20
59 Vogue SEA 5005 — CHET BAKER AND HIS CREW (LP, stereo) 15
59 Vogue LAE 12164 — CHET BAKER SINGS (LP) 10
59 Vogue LAE 12183 — CHET BAKER AND ART PEPPER SEXTET — PLAYBOYS! (LP) 15
(see also Art Pepper, Russ Freeman & Chet Baker Quartet, Gerry Mulligan)

MINT VALUE £

DESMOND BAKER & CLAREDONIANS
66 Island WI 295 — Rude Boy Gonna Jail/SHARKS: Don't Fool Me 30
(see also Claredonians)

DOROTHY BAKER
63 Parlophone R 5040 — A Little Like Lovin'/Try Being Nice To Me 5

ERNEST BAKER
00 Grapevine 2000 110 — Alone Again/Do It With Feeling 10

GINGER BAKER('S AIRFORCE)
70 Polydor 56380 — Man Of Constant Sorrow/Doin' It 5
71 Polydor 2058 107 — Atunde! (We Are Here)/Part 2 (as Ginger Baker Drum Choir) 5
70 Polydor 2662 001 — GINGER BAKER'S AIRFORCE (2-LP, gatefold sleeve) 20
70 Polydor 2383 029 — AIRFORCE II (LP, gatefold sleeve, with insert) 15
72 Polydor 2383 133 — STRATAVARIOUS (LP) 15
(see also Graham Bond Organisation, Cream, Blind Faith, Fela Ransome-Kuti [& Africa '70], Harold McNair, Griffin, Denny Laine)

GLEN BAKER
85 The Stand THE STAND 3 — BRIEF ENCOUNTER (LP) 20
(see also Enid)

JEANETTE BAKER
59 Vogue Pop V 9143 — Everything Reminds Me Of You/JEANETTE & DECKY: Crazy With You 250
59 Vogue Pop V 9143 — Everything Reminds Me Of You/JEANETTE & DECKY: Crazy With You (78) 25

JOE BAKER
65 Parlophone PMC 1251 — Dial Joe Baker (LP) 12

KENNY BAKER
53 Parlophone MSP 6019 — Round About Midnight/Afternoon In Paris 6
53 Parlophone MSP 6057 — Hayfoot, Strawfoot/The Continental 6
54 Parlophone MSP 6062 — Trumpet Fantasy/Melancholy Baby 6
54 Parlophone MSP 6082 — That's My Desire/Stompin' At The Savoy 6
54 Parlophone MSP 6114 — I Speak To The Stars/Wanted 6
54 Parlophone MSP 6121 — Peg O' My Heart/The Other Side 6
56 Pye Nixa N 15059 — Blues I Love To Sing/Baker's Dozen (as Kenny Baker Dozen) (78) 8
55 Jazz Today JTL 1 — OPERATION JAM SESSION (10" LP, with The Jazz Today Unit) 55
55 Jazz Today JTL 4 — KENNY BAKER QUARTET/AFTER HOURS GROUP (10" LP) 30
55 Jazz Today JTL 5 — TRIBUTE TO BENNY CARTER (10" LP, with The Jazz Today Unit, one side by Bertie King Jazz Group) 22
56 Pye Nixa NPT 19003 — BAKER'S DOZEN VOL. 1 (LP) 15
57 Pye Nixa NPT 19020 — DATE WITH THE DOZEN (LP) 18
57 Pye Nixa NJL 10 — PRESENTS THE HALF DOZEN (LP) 40
57 Pye Nixa NJT 517 — BAKER PLAYS McHUGH (LP) 25
59 Columbia 33S1140 — BLOWIN' UP A STORM (LP) 50
75 77 77S56 — BAKER'S JAM (LP) 25

LAVERN BAKER (& GLIDERS)
55 Columbia SCM 5172 — Tweedle Dee/Tomorrow Night (with Gliders) 450
55 Columbia DB 3591 — Tweedle Dee/Tomorrow Night (with Gliders) (78) 20
55 London HLA 8199 — Play It Fair/That Old Lucky Sun (with Gliders) 325
55 London HLA 8199 — Play It Fair (with Gliders)/That Old Lucky Sun (78) 20
56 London HLE 8260 — My Happiness Forever (with Gliders)/Get Up! Get Up! (You Sleepy Head) 300
56 London HLE 8260 — My Happiness Forever (with Gliders)/Get Up! Get Up! (You Sleepy Head) (78) 20
57 Columbia DB 3879 — Jim Dandy/Tra La La (with Gliders) 400
57 Columbia DB 3879 — Jim Dandy/Tra La La (with Gliders) (78) 20
57 London HLE 8396 — I Can't Love You Enough/Still 150
57 London HLE 8396 — I Can't Love You Enough/Still (78) 20
57 London HLE 8442 — Game Of Love/Jim Dandy Got Married 250
57 London HLE 8442 — Game Of Love/Jim Dandy Got Married (78) 20
57 London HLE 8524 — Humpty Dumpty Heart/Love Me Right 150
57 London HLE 8524 — Humpty Dumpty Heart/Love Me Right (78) 20
58 London HLE 8638 — Learning To Love/Substitute 100
58 London HLE 8638 — Learning To Love/Substitute (78) 20
58 London HLE 8672 — Whipper Snapper/Harbour Lights 100
58 London HLE 8672 — Whipper Snapper/Harbour Lights (78) 20
59 London HLE 8790 — I Cried A Tear/St. Louis Blues 50
59 London HLE 8790 — I Cried A Tear/St. Louis Blues (78) 15
59 London HLE 8871 — I Waited Too Long/You're Teasing Me 30
59 London HLE 8871 — I Waited Too Long/You're Teasing Me (78) 15
59 London HLE 8945 — So High So Low/If You Love Me (I Won't Care) 30
59 London HLE 8945 — So High So Low/If You Love Me (I Won't Care) (78) 15
60 London HLE 9023 — Tiny Tim/For Love Of You 40
60 London HLE 9252 — Bumble Bee/My Turn Will Come 25
61 London HLE 9300 — You're The Boss/I'll Never Be Free (with Jimmy Ricks) 25
61 London HLK 9343 — Saved/Don Juan 25
61 London HLK 9468 — Hey, Memphis/Voodoo Voodoo 55
63 London HLK 9649 — See See Rider/The Story Of My Love (I Had A Dream) 25
65 Atlantic AET 6009 — THE BEST OF LAVERN BAKER (EP) 75
58 London HA-E 2107 — ROCK 'N' ROLL WITH LAVERN BAKER (LP) 300
58 London Jazz LTZK 15139 — SINGS BESSIE SMITH (LP) 50
61 London HA-K 2422 — SAVED (LP) 75
63 London HA-K 8074 — SEE SEE RIDER (LP) 50
64 Atlantic ATL 5002 — THE BEST OF LAVERN BAKER (LP, plum label) 50
68 Atlantic 587/588 133 — SEE SEE RIDER (LP, reissue) 20

MICKEY BAKER
70 Major Minor SMLP 67 — IN BLUNDERLAND (LP) 20
(see also Mighty Flea)

MINT VALUE £

SALLY BAKER
70s Old Dog PUP 1 IN THE SPOTLIGHT (LP) . . . 30

SAM BAKER
68 Monument MON 1009 I Believe In You/I'm Number One . . . 10

TWO-TON BAKER
55 London HL 8121 Clink, Clank (In My Piggy Bank)/Mr. Froggie (Went A Courtin') . . . 55
55 London HL 8121 Clink, Clank (In My Piggy Bank)/Mr. Froggie (Went A Courtin') (78) . . . 15

VICKY BAKER
64 London HLU 9856 No More Foolish Stories/Darling Say The Word . . . 15

YVONNE BAKER
77 London HLU 10553 You Didn't Say A Word/BOBBY PARIS: Night Owl . . . 30
(see also Sensations, Bobby Paris)

BAKER-GURVITZ ARMY
75 Mountain TOP 4 The Gambler/Time . . . 5
74 Vertigo 9103 201 BAKER-GURVITZ ARMY (LP) . . . 15
75 Mountain TOPS 101 ELYSIAN ENCOUNTER (LP) . . . 12
76 Mountain TOPS 111 HEARTS ON FIRE (LP, with inner sleeve) . . . 12
(see also Ginger Baker, Three Man Army, Parrish & Gurvitz, Gun)

BAKERLOO
69 Harvest HAR 5004 Driving Backwards/Once Upon A Time . . . 25
69 Harvest SHVL 762 BAKERLOO (LP) . . . 80
(see also May Blitz)

BAKER STREET PHILHARMONIC
71 Pye International 7N 25540 The Last One/Theme From 'Love Story' . . . 6
70 Pye Intl. NSPL 28131 BY THE LIGHT OF THE MOON (LP) . . . 20
(see also Mike Vickers)

BAKER TWINS
64 Pye 7N 15628 He's No Good/Words Written On Water . . . 15

BALAAM & THE ANGEL
86 Virgin CDV 2377 THE GREATEST STORY EVER TOLD (CD) . . . 8

BALANCE
81 Portrait PRTA 1477 Breaking Away/It's So Strange . . . 8
73 Incus INCUS 11 BALANCE (LP) . . . 70
73 private pressing IN FOR THE COUNT (LP) . . . 22
81 Portrait BALANCE (LP, reissue) . . . 15
82 Portrait IN FOR THE COUNT (LP, reissue) . . . 12

BALDHEAD GROWLER
67 Jump Up JU 531 Sausage/Bingo Woman . . . 8

CHRIS BALDO
68 Vogue VRS 7029 Living For Your Love/Arretez – Vous A Saint Michel . . . 15

LONG JOHN BALDRY
64 United Artists UP 1056 Up Above My Head (I Hear Music In The Air)/You'll Be Mine (with Rod Stewart) . . . 45
65 United Artists UP 1078 I'm On To You Baby/Goodbye Baby . . . 12
65 United Artists UP 1107 How Long Will It Last/House Next Door . . . 40
66 United Artists UP 1124 Unseen Hands/Turn On Your Lovelight . . . 12
66 United Artists UP 1136 The Drifter/Only A Fool Breaks His Own Heart . . . 45
66 United Artists UP 1158 Cuckoo/Bring My Baby Back To Me . . . 8
67 United Artists UP 1204 Only A Fool Breaks His Own Heart/Let Him Go (And Let Me Love You) . . . 15
67 Pye 7N 17385 Let The Heartaches Begin/Annabella (Who Flies To Me When She's Lonely) . . . 5
68 Pye 7N 17455 Hold Back The Daybreak/Since I Lost You Baby . . . 6
68 Pye 7N 17563 Mexico (Underneath The Sun In)/We're Together . . . 6
68 Pye 7N 17593 When The Sun Comes Shining Thru'/Wise To The Ways Of The World . . . 6
69 Pye 7N 17664 It's Too Late Now/Long And Lonely Nights . . . 6
69 Pye 7N 17815 Wait For Me/Don't Pity Me . . . 6
70 Pye 7N 17921 Setting The Tail Of A Fox On Fire/Well I Did . . . 7
70 Pye 7N 45007 When The World Is Over/Where Are My Eyes? . . . 6
71 Warner Bros K 16105 Rock Me When He's Gone/Flying (as John Baldry) . . . 6
72 Warner Bros K 16175 Iko Iko/Mother Ain't Dead (with Rod Stewart) . . . 7
72 Warner Bros K 16217 Everything Stops For Tea/Hambone . . . 5
65 United Artists UEP 1013 LONG JOHN'S BLUES (EP, with Hoochie Coochie Men) . . . 75
64 United Artists ULP 1081 LONG JOHN'S BLUES (LP, with Hoochie Coochie Men) . . . 100
66 United Artists (S)ULP 1146 LOOKING AT LONG JOHN (LP) . . . 45
67 Pye N(S)PL 18208 LET THE HEARTACHES BEGIN (LP) . . . 25
68 Pye N(S)PL 18228 LET THERE BE LONG JOHN (LP, unissued)
69 Hallmark HM 560 LONG JOHN BALDRY & THE HOOCHIE COOCHIE MEN (LP) . . . 15
69 Pye N(S)PL 18306 WAIT FOR ME (LP) . . . 22
71 Warner Bros K 46088 IT AIN'T EASY (LP) . . . 15
72 Warner Bros K 46160 EVERYTHING STOPS FOR TEA (LP, Rod Stewart duets on 1 track) . . . 15
(see also Rod Stewart, Alexis Korner, Bluesology)

BALIL
92 Rhythmic Tech. ART 1 NORT ROUTE (12") . . . 20

KEITH BALFOUR
69 Studio One SO 2079 Dreaming/Tired Of Waiting . . . 18

CANNON BALL (Carl Bryan) & JOHNNY MELODY (Moore)
69 Big Shot BI 518 Parapinto/Cool Hand Luke . . . 20

MINT VALUE £

KENNY BALL & HIS (JAZZ) BAND

59 Collector JDN 101 — Waterloo/Wabash Cannonball 10
60 Pye 7N 15272 — Teddy Bears' Picnic/Waltzing Matilda 10
67 Pye 7N 17348 — When I'm Sixty Four/Goodnight Irene 5
59 Jazz Collector JEN 2 — KENNY BALL & HIS BAND (EP) 20
59 Tempo EXA 83 — KENNY BALL JAZZ BAND (EP) 20
60 Pye NJE 1086 — KENNY BALL PLAYS (EP) 12
60 Pye Jazz NJL 24 — INVITATION TO THE BALL (LP) 25
61 Pye Jazz NJL 28 — KENNY BALL AND HIS JAZZMEN (LP) 18
62 Pye Jazz NJL 42 — THE KENNY BALL SHOW (LP, as Kenny Ball & His Jazzmen) 18
64 Pye Jazz NJL 54 — TRIBUTE TO TOKYO (LP) 25
70 Fontana 6438 032 — FLEET STREET LIGHTNING (LP) 12
72 Pye NSPL 18306 — HAVE A DRINK ON ME (LP) 12
72 Pye NSPL 18379 — MY VERY GOOD FRIEND FATS WALLER (LP) 12
73 Pye NSPL 18415 — LET'S ALL SING A HAPPY TUNE (LP) 12
77 Spiral SPJ 9000 — SATURDAY NIGHT AT THE MILL (LP) 12
(see also Gary Miller)

BALLADEERS

59 Columbia DB 4364 — Tom Gets The Last Laugh/Morning Star 5

DAVE BALLANTYNE

66 Columbia DB 7807 — I Can't Express It/Ginger Eyes 7
66 Columbia DB 7896 — Love Around The World/Wonder Full Of Women 7
(see also Just Plain Jones, Esprit De Corps)

FLORENCE BALLARD

68 Stateside SS 2113 — It Doesn't Matter How I Say It (It's What I Say That Matters)/ Goin' Out Of My Head 40
(see also Supremes)

HANK BALLARD (& MIDNIGHTERS)

59 Parlophone R 4558 — The Twist/Kansas City 50
60 Parlophone R 4682 — Finger Poppin' Time/I Love You, I Love You So-o-o 40
60 Parlophone R 4688 — The Twist/Teardrops On Your Letter 35
60 Parlophone R 4707 — Let's Go, Let's Go, Let's Go/If You'd Forgive Me 40
61 Parlophone R 4728 — The Hoochie Coochie Coo/LITTLE WILLIE JOHN: Walk Slow 40
61 Parlophone R 4762 — Let's Go Again/Deep Blue Sea 50
61 Parlophone R 4771 — The Continental Walk/What Is This I See 30
72 Mojo 2093 010 — Annie Had A Baby/Teardrops On Your Letter 10
80s Urban — From The Loveside/FOSTER SYLVERS: Misdemeanor 10
61 Parlophone PMC 1158 — SPOTLIGHT ON HANK BALLARD (LP) 120
63 London HA 8101 — THE JUMPIN' HANK BALLARD (LP) 100
(see also Midnighters)

KAYE BALLARD

55 Brunswick 05376 — Triumph Of Love/Where Were You Last Night? 10
55 Brunswick 05436 — Don't You Tell Pa/In Love And Out Again 10

RUSS BALLARD

74 Epic S EPC 3122 — Loose Women/Danger Zone Part 1 10
78 Epic S EPC 6316 — Treat Her Right/What Does It Take 6
85 EMI EA 185 — Voices/Living Without You (p/s) 7
(see also Argent, Roulettes)

BALLISTIC BROTHERS

93 Delancey St DST 001 — Volume 1 (Versus The Eccentric Afro's) (12" EP) 8
94 Delancey St DST 005 — Volume 2 (Versus The Eccentric Afro's) (12" EP, double pack) 12
(see also Black Science Orchestra, X-Press 2)

BALLOON BUSTERS

69 Pye 7N 17748 — Alcock And Brown/Bluer Than Blue 5

BALLOON FARM

68 London HLP 10185 — A Question Of Temperature/Hurtin' For Your Love 150

BALLS

71 Wizard WIZ 101 — Fight For My Country/Janie Slow Down 12
(see also Denny Laine, Lemon Tree, Trevor Burton, Uglys, Wizzard)

LORI BALMER

68 Polydor 56293 — Treacle Brown/Four Faces West 12

BALTIMORE & OHIO MARCHING BAND

67 Stateside SS 2065 — Lapland/Condition Red 100
68 Stateside (S)SL 10231 — LAPLAND (LP) 30

BAMA WINDS

69 Island ILPS 9096 — WINDY (LP) 20

BAMBIS

64 Oriole CB 1965 — Not Wrong/Handle With Care 40
65 CBS 201778 — Baby Blue/If This Is Love 40

BAMBOO SHOOT

68 Columbia DB 8370 — The Fox Has Gone To Ground/There And Back Again Lane 300

BAMBOOS OF JAMAICA

70 Pye Intl. 7N 25515 — Reggae Man/Candy 5

BANANA BUNCH

71 DJM DJS 252 — Tra-La-La Song/Season Of The Rain 5
(see also Nite People)

BANANAMEN

83 Big Beat NS 88 — The Crusher/Love Me/Surfin' Bird (p/s) 5

MINT VALUE £

BANANARAMA

81	Demon D 1010	Aie A Mwana/Dubwana (p/s)	5
81	Deram DMX 446	Aie A Mwana (Extended)/Dubwana (Extended) (12", p/s)	8
83	London NANX 6	Robert De Niro's Waiting/Push (3 x 12", coloured vinyl with different labels)	8
84	London NANAJ 8	Hotline To Heaven/State I'm In (p/s, with jigsaw)	5
86	London NANDP 11	More Than Physical (Alternate Mix)/Scarlett//Venus/White Train (double pack, gatefold p/s)	5
87	London NANCD 15	I Can't Help It (Extended Club Mix)/Ecstasy (Chicago House Stylee) (CD)	8
88	London NANCD 16	I Want You Back/Bad For Me/Amnesia (Extended 12" Version)/ (The Theme From The Roxy)/Love In The First Degree (House Remix) (CD)	8
88	London NANCD 17	Love, Truth And Honesty (Dance Hall Version)/Strike It Rich (Full Length Club Mix)/I Want You Back/Love, Truth And Honesty (CD)	8
85	London NANPD 9	Do Not Disturb (Keren, Sarah or Siobhan-shaped picture disc, with plinth)	each 12
86	London NANPD 10	Venus/White Train (picture disc)	8
86	London NANXR 10	Venus (The Hellfire Mix)/Venus (Dub)/White Train (12", p/s)	12
86	London NANXRR 10	Venus (The Fire & Brimstone Mix)/Venus (Dub)/White Train (12", p/s)	12
86	London NANA 11	More Than Physical/Scarlet (poster p/s)	5
86	London NANE 12	TRICK OF THE NIGHT EP (gatefold p/s)	8
88	London NANXR 14	Love In The First Degree (Eurobeat Style)/Mr. Sleaze (Rare Groove Remix) (12", p/s)	10
88	London NANB 17	Love, Truth & Honesty/Strike It Rich (box set with 4 postcards & poster)	15
88	London NANCD 18	Nathan Jones (Extended Version)/Venus (Extended Version)/Once In A Lifetime (CD)	18

BANBARRA

76	United Artists UP 36113	Shack Up Parts 1 & 2	8
85	Stateside 12STATES 1	Shack Up (Extended)/Shack Up (Part 1)/Shack Up (Part II) (12" p/s)	10

THE BAND

68	Capitol CL 15559	The Weight/I Shall Be Released	10
69	Capitol CL 15613	Up On Cripple Creek/The Night They Drove Old Dixie Down	10
72	Capitol CL 15737	Don't Do It/Rag Mama Rag	5
73	Capitol CL 15767	Ain't Got No Home/Get Up Jake	5
78	Warner Bros K 17187	Theme From The Last Waltz/Out Of The Blue	5
68	Capitol (S)T 2955	MUSIC FROM BIG PINK (LP, black/rainbow label)	15

(see also Levon & The Hawks, Bob Dylan, Ronnie Hawkins, Robbie Robertson)

BAND AID

85	Mercury FEEDP 1	Do They Know It's Christmas?/Feed The World (shaped picture disc)	5

BANDITS

02	Centro Del Banco 7176-47	The Warning/Free Me Rain (stickered die-cut sleeve, 500 only)	20
02	Centro Del Banco 7176-4	The Warning/Free Me Rain (CD, stickered die-cut sleeve, 500 only)	20
02	Centro Del Banco 7176-6	Once Upon A Time/On My Way (stickered die-cut sleeve, 750)	12
02	Centro Del Banco 7176-67	Once Upon A Time/On My Way (CD, stickered die-cut sleeve, 2000 only)	10
00s	Centro Del Banco (no cat. no.)	The Warning Dub/Guns Of Brixton (Live [The Bandits V The Mad Professor]) (12", p/s, 1000 only)	20

BAND OF ANGELS

64	United Artists UP 1049	Not True As Yet/Me	22
64	United Artists UP 1066	Gonna Make A Woman Of You/She'll Never Be You	22
66	Piccadilly 7N 35279	Leave It To Me/Too Late My Love	22
66	Piccadilly 7N 35292	Invitation/Cheat And Lie	22

(see also Mike D'Abo)

BAND OF THE IRISH GUARDS

66	Studio Two TWO 125	MARCHING WITH THE BEATLES (LP)	12

BAND OF MERCY & SALVATION

69	Duke DU 20	Suffering Stink/BOB MELODY: The Break (B-side actually by Winston Francis)	10

BANDOGGS

78	Transatlantic LTRA 504	BANDOGGS (LP)	12

(see also Peter & Chris Coe)

BANDWAGON

(see under Johnny Johnson & Bandwagon)

BANDY LEGS

74	WWW WWS 01	Ride Ride/Don't Play Games	20
76	Jet JET 783	Bet You Can't Dance/Circles	20

(see also Quartz)

JAYASRI BANERJEE

67	Polydor 583 010	CLASSICAL INDIAN RAGAS (LP)	12

ED BANGER

78	Rabid TOSH 106	Kinnel Tommy/Baby Was A Baby (p/s)	7
78	EMI International INT 570	Kinnel Tommy/Baby Was A Baby (reissue, numbered p/s)	7
81	Spiv DIV 1	I've Just Had My Car Nicked/P.C. Plod/Sponge (p/s, with photo insert)	8
83	Cloud Nine CNS 01	Poor People/Vicars In The Dark (p/s)	7

(see also Nosebleeds, Slaughter & The Dogs)

BANGOR FLYING CIRCUS

70	Stateside-Dunhill SSL 5022	BANGOR FLYING CIRCUS (LP)	15

BESSIE BANKS

64	Red Bird BC 106	Go Now/Sounds Like My Baby	50
67	Verve VS 563	I Can't Make It (Without You Baby)/Need You	50
68	Soul City SC 105	Go Now/Sounds Like My Baby (reissue)	15
75	Contempo CS 2070	Baby You Sure Know How To Get To Me/Try To Leave Me If You Can	10

MINT VALUE £

DARRELL BANKS

66	London HL 10070	Open The Door To Your Heart/Our Love (Is In The Pocket) (demo only)	600
66	Stateside SS 536	Open The Door To Your Heart/Our Love (Is In The Pocket)	45
67	Atlantic 5841 120	Angel Baby (Don't You Ever Leave Me)/Look Into The Eyes Of A Fool	50
69	Stax STAX 124	Just Because Your Love Is Gone/I'm The One Who Loves You	45
77	Atlantic K 10879	Angel Baby (Don't You Ever Leave Me)/ Look Into The Eyes Of A Fool (reissue)	10
78	Contempo CS 8005	Open The Door To Your Heart/Angel Baby (Don't You Ever Leave Me)	5
69	Stax SXATS 1011	HERE TO STAY (LP)	40

HOMER BANKS

66	Liberty LIB 12028	A Lot Of Love/Fighting To Win	25
67	Liberty LIB 12047	60 Minutes Of Your Love/Do You Know What	30
67	Liberty LIB 12060	Hooked By Love/Lady Of Stone	30
68	Minit MLF 11004	Round The Clock Lover Man/Foolish Hearts Break Fast	15
68	Minit MLF 11007	60 Minutes Of Your Love/A Lot Of Love	15
69	Minit MLF 11015	Me Or Your Mama/I Know You Know I Know You Know	15
70	Liberty LBF 15392	60 Minutes Of Your Love/I Know You Know I Know You Know	10
72	United Artists UP 35360	Hooked By Love/Lady Of Stone (reissue)	5

LARRY BANKS

67	Stateside SS 579	I Don't Wanna Do It/I'm Coming Home	22

LLOYD BANKS

66	Reaction 591 008	We'll Meet Again/Look Out Girl	12

PETER BANKS

73	Sovereign SNVA 7256	PETER BANKS (LP, gatefold sleeve)	18

(see also Syndicats, Syn, Neat Change, Yes, Flash, Jan Akkerman, Phil Collins, Steve Hackett)

ROSIE BANKS

76	Tamla Motown TMG 1037	Darling Baby/Whole New Thing	10

(see also Sly & Family Stone)

BANNED

77	Can't Eat EAT 1 UP	Little Girl/CPGJ's (stamped white labels, some in handmade p/s)	50/12
77	Harvest HAR 5145	Little Girl/CPGJ's (p/s, reissue)	10

BANSHEES

64	Columbia DB 7361	I Got A Woman/Don't Say Goodnight And Mean Goodbye	45
65	Columbia DB 7530	Big Buildin'/Mockingbird	30
65	Columbia DB 7752	I'm Gonna Keep On Loving You/Yes Indeed	25

(NB: this group does not include Bryan Ferry)

BARBARA & BRENDA

68	Direction 58-3799	Never Love A Robin/Sally's Party	15

BARBARA & WINSTON

64	Island WI 418	The Dream/I Love You	18

BARBARA ANN

65	Piccadilly 7N 35221	You've Lost That Loving Feeling/Till The Summer Time	10
65	Piccadilly 7N 35244	Black Is The Colour Of My True Love's Hair/Since You've Loved Me	5

BARBARIANS

65	Stateside SS 449	Are You A Boy Or Are You A Girl/Take It Or Leave It	35
66	Stateside SS 497	Moulty/I'll Keep On Seeing You	30

BARBECUE BOB

67	Kokomo K 1002	GEORGIA BLUES NO. 1 (LP, 99 copies only)	100

JOHN HENRY BARBEE

65	Storyville 670 171	PORTRAITS IN BLUES VOLUME 9 (LP)	20

CHRIS BARBER('S JAZZ BAND)

78s

59	Pye Jazz NJ 2026	Petite Fleur/Bugle Boy March	10

SINGLES

54	Decca F 10417	Chimes Blues/Merrydown Rag	10
54	Columbia SCMC 10	White Christmas/On A Christmas Day (with Lonnie Donegan, export issue)	35
55	Decca F 10492	Bobby Shafto/The Martinique	5
55	Decca F 10666	It's Tight Like That/All The Girls Go Crazy About The Way I Walk	5
56	Decca FJ 10724	The World Is Waiting For The Sunrise/St. Louis Blues	5
56	Decca FJ 10790	I Never Knew Just What A Girl Could Do/Storyville Blues	5
56	Tempo A 116	Precious Lord, Lead Me On (with Lonnie Donegan)/Tiger Rag	15
56	Tempo A 132	Saratoga Swing/Ice Cream	5
57	Tempo A 160	Ice Cream/Down By The Riverside	5
58	Pye Jazz 7NJ 2011	Whistlin' Rufus/Hushabye	5
58	Pye Jazz 7NJ 2004	Tuxedo Rag/Brown Skin Mama	5
58	Pye Jazz 7NJ 2007	High Society/Papa De-Da-Da	5
58	Pye Jazz 7NJ 2023	When The Saints Go Marching In (both sides)	5
59	Pye Jazz 7NJ 2026	Petite Fleur/Bugle Boy March	5
59	Columbia DB 4333	Lonesome (with Monty Sunshine)/There'll Be A Hot Time In The Old Town Tonight (with Ottilie Patterson)	5
60	Pye Jazz 7NJ 2030	Bill Bailey Won't You Please Come Home/Wild Cat Blues	5
60	Columbia DB 4501	Bohemia Rag/Swanee River	5
60	Columbia DB 4531	The Mountains Of Mourne/Real Old Mountain Dew (with Ottilie Patterson)	5
61	Columbia SCD 2156	Mama He Treats Your Daughter Mean/Swipsy Cakewalk (with Ottilie Patterson)	5

EPs

55	Columbia SEG 7568	PLAYS SPIRITUALS	10
55	Columbia SEG 7586	BARBER GOES TO TOWN WITH ELLINGTON	10
55	Tempo EXA 6	CHRIS BARBER'S NEW ORLEANS JAZZ BAND	10
55	Tempo EXA 22	CHRIS BARBER'S JAZZ BAND	10

			MINT VALUE £
55	Decca DFE 6238	JAZZ AT THE ROYAL FESTIVAL HALL	10
55	Decca DFE 6252	CHRIS BARBER AT THE ROYAL FESTIVAL HALL	10
56	Decca DFE 6344	CHRIS BARBER AT THE ROYAL FESTIVAL HALL NO. 2	10
56	Decca DFE 6382	BARBER'S BEST	10
56	Jazz Today JTE 103	PLUS/MINUS 1	15
56	Pye Jazz NJE 1013	PLUS/MINUS 1 (reissue)	10
56	Pye Jazz NJE 1007	CHRIS BARBER SPECIAL	8
57	Pye Jazz NJE 1039	CHRIS BARBER IN CONCERT PT. 1	8
57	Pye Jazz NJE 1040	CHRIS BARBER IN CONCERT PT. 2	8
57	Decca DFE 6463	NEW ORLEANS BLUES	20
58	Pye Jazz NJE 1068	CHRIS BARBER JAZZ PARADE VOL. 1	8
58	Pye Jazz NJE 1073	CHRIS BARBER JAZZ PARADE VOL. 2	8
59	Esquire EP 206	CHRIS BARBER NOT IN HI FI (with Washboard Wonders)	20
59	Columbia SEG 7980	BANDBOX VOL. 1 (also stereo ESG 7789)	8/12
59	Pye Jazz NJE 1075	CHRIS BARBER JAZZ PARADE VOL. 3	8
59	Pye Jazz NJE 1076	CHRIS BARBER JAZZ PARADE VOL. 4	8
59	Pye Jazz NJE 1077	CHRIS BARBER JAZZ PARADE VOL. 5	8
59	Pye Jazz NJE 1078	CHRIS BARBER JAZZ PARADE VOL. 6	8
50s	Storyville SEP 300	TIGER RAG	10
50s	Storyville SEP 306	MAKING WHOOPEE	8
50s	Storyville SEP 310	DOWN HOME RAG	8
50s	Storyville SEP 314	TRAD JAZZ SCENE IN EUROPE NO. 3	8
50s	Storyville SEP 340	MARYLAND	8
50s	Storyville SEP 360	LORD, YOU'VE SURE BEEN GOOD TO ME	8
50s	Storyville SEP 412	WILDCAT BLUES	8
60	Pye Jazz NJE 1084	CHRIS BARBER JAZZ PARADE VOL. 8	10
60	Pye Jazz NJE 1088	CHRIS BARBER JAZZ PARADE VOL. 9	8
60	Columbia SEG 7994	BANDBOX VOL. 1 No. 2 (also stereo ESG 7801)	8/12
60	Columbia SEG 8030	EXTRACTS FROM BARBER IN BERLIN (with Ottilie Patterson, also stereo ESG 7821)	8/12
61	Columbia SEG 8075	BARBER IN BERLIN VOL. 2	8
61	Columbia SEG 8081	PAT (with Pat Halcox, also stereo ESG 7846)	8/12
61	Columbia SEG 8110	INTRODUCING IAN (with Ian Wheeler)	12
62	Columbia SEG 8182	INTERNATIONAL VOL. 2 PT. 1 — BARBER IN COPENHAGEN	10
62	Columbia SEG 8214	BARBER'S BLUES BOOK VOL. 1	10
63	Columbia SEG 8224	IN BARBER'S CHAIR	12
LPs			
54	Decca LF 1198	NEW ORLEANS JOYS (10", with Lonnie Donegan's Skiffle Group)	30
55	Nixa Jazz Today NJL 1	ECHOES OF HARLEM (with Ottilie Patterson)	30
55	Jazz Today JTL 3	CHRIS BARBER PLAYS VOL. 1 (10")	30
56	Nixa Jazz Today NJT 500	CHRIS BARBER PLAYS VOL. 1 (10", reissue)	20
56	Nixa Jazz Today NJT 502	CHRIS BARBER PLAYS VOL. 2 (10")	20
57	Nixa Jazz Today NJT 505	CHRIS BARBER PLAYS VOL. 3 (10")	20
57	Nixa Jazz Today NJT 508	CHRIS BARBER PLAYS VOL. 4 (10")	20
57	Columbia 33S 1112	JAZZ SACRED AND SECULAR (10", with Lonnie Donegan)	50
57	Nixa Jazz Today NJL 6	CHRIS BARBER IN CONCERT (with Ottilie Patterson)	35
58	Pye Nixa Jazz NJL 15	CHRIS BARBER IN CONCERT VOL. 2 (with Ottilie Patterson)	20
58	Pye Nixa Jazz NJL 17	CHRIS BARBER IN CONCERT VOL. 3 (with Ottilie Patterson)	20
58	Decca LK 4246	BARBER'S BEST	20
59	Columbia 33SX 1158	BAND BOX VOL. 1	25
59	Columbia 33SX 1189	BARBER IN BERLIN VOL. 1 (with Ottilie Patterson)	40
59	Columbia 33SX	BARBER IN BERLIN VOL. 2 (with Ottilie Patterson)	30
60	Columbia 33SX 1245	BAND BOX VOL. 2 — ELITE SYNCOPATIONS (stereo SCX 3319)	30/35
60	Ace Of Clubs ACL 1037	THE BEST OF CHRIS BARBER (with Ottilie Patterson & Lonnie Donegan)	15
61	Columbia 33SX 1274	BARBER IN COPENHAGEN (also stereo SCX 3342)	each 35
61	Columbia 33SX 1321	CHRIS BARBER'S AMERICAN JAZZ BAND (also stereo SCX 3376)	each 40
61	Columbia 33SX 1333	BLUES BOOK (with Ottilie Patterson, also stereo SCX 3384)	each 40
61	Columbia 33SX 1346	AT THE LONDON PALLADIUM (also stereo [SCX 3392])	50/100
61	Columbia 33SX 1401	BEST YET!	35
65	Columbia 33SX 1657	GOOD MORNIN' BLUES	45
65	Decca LK 4742	FOLK BARBER STYLE (mono)	30
65	Phase 4 Stereo PFS 4070	FOLK BARBER STYLE (as Chris Barber & His Jazz Band)	20
71	Polydor 2683 001	GET ROLLING	15
78	Black Lion BLP 12172	SIDEWAYS	25
78	Black Lion BLM 51003	STORY — VOLUME 1: IN THE BEGINNING	20
78	Black Lion BLM 51004	STORY — VOLUME 2: VISITING INFLUENCES	20
78	Black Lion BLM 51005	STORY — VOLUME 3: THE SEVENTIES	20
79	Black Lion BLP 12182	SWING IS HERE	18
82	Black Lion BLM 51008	COME FRIDAY	12
82	Black Lion 61003/4	BARBICAN BLUES	15

(see also Ottilie Patterson, Lonnie Donegan, Sonny Terry & Brownie McGhee, Kenneth Washington & Chris Barber, Dickie Bishop & Sidekicks)

CHRIS BARBER'S SKIFFLE GROUP

51	Esquire 10-180	Everybody Loves My Baby/Whoop It Up (with Washboard Wonders) (78)	20
58	Pye Jazz 7NJ 2014	Doin' My Time/Where Could I Go? (with Johnny Duncan)	8
58	Pye Jazz 7NJ 2017	Can't You Line 'Em/Gipsy Dave (with Dickie Bishop)	10
57	Pye Jazz NJE 1025	CHRIS BARBER SKIFFLE GROUP (EP)	15

(see also Lonnie Donegan, Johnny Duncan & Blue Grass Boys)

CHRIS BARBER'S BAND

67	Marmalade 598 005	Catcall/Mercy Mercy Mercy	50
69	Marmalade 558 013	Battersea Rain Dance/Sleepy Joe	12
69	Marmalade 608 009	BATTERSEA RAIN DANCE (LP, as Chris Barber & His Band)	35

CHRIS BARBER SOUL BAND

65	Columbia DB 7461	Finishing Straight/Morning Train	22

(see also Louis Jordan & Chris Barber)

FRANK BARBER FIVE

62 Ember JBS 709 Flyover/Golden Shadows . . . 6
(see also Frank & Barbarians)

DAVE BARBOUR & HIS ORCHESTRA

59 Oriole CB 1507 Tough/Bu Bam . . . 8
59 Oriole CB 1507 Tough/Bu Bam (78) . . . 15

EDDIE BARCLAY & HIS ORCHESTRA

57 Felsted ESD 3041 JAMES DEAN — MUSIC FROM HIS FILMS (EP) . . . 30

EDDIE BARCLAY & QUINCY JONES

58 Felsted PDL 85056 EDDIE AND QUINCY (LP) . . . 20

RUE BARCLAY & PEGGY DUNCAN

54 London HL 8033 Tongue Tied Boy/River Of Tears . . . 35

BARCLAY JAMES HARVEST

68 Parlophone R 5693 Early Morning/Mr. Sunshine . . . 25
69 Harvest HAR 5003 Brother Thrush/Poor Wages . . . 15
70 Harvest HAR 5025 Taking Some Time On/The Iron Maiden . . . 15
71 Harvest HAR 5034 Mocking Bird/Vanessa Simmons . . . 10
72 Harvest HAR 5051 I'm Over You/Child Of Man . . . 10
72 Harvest HAR 5058 Thank You/Medicine Man . . . 10
73 Harvest HAR 5068 Rock And Roll Woman/The Joker (BJH logo p/s) . . . 12
74 Polydor 2058 474 Poor Boy Blues/Crazy City . . . 7
74 Polydor (matrix: SH 1041/2) Negative Earth/RARE BIRD: Diamonds (33rpm flexidisc free with *Sounds*) . . . 10/6
75 Harvest HAR 5094 Mocking Bird/Galadriel . . . 5
75 Polydor 2058 660 Titles/Song For You . . . 5
77 Polydor 2229 198 LIVE (Rock'n'Roll Star/Medicine Man Part 1/Medicine Man Part 2) (EP, p/s) . . . 6
77 Polydor 2058 904 Hymn/Our Kid's Kid (p/s) . . . 5
78 Polydor 2059 002 Friend Of Mine/Suicide? (live) . . . 5
78 Polydor POSP 012 Loving Is Easy/Polk Street Rag (blue or black vinyl) . . . 5/7
79 Polydor POSP 097 Love On The Line/Alright Down Get Boogie (Mu Ala Rusic) (p/s) . . . 5
80 Polydor POSP 140 Capricorn/Berlin (no p/s) . . . 5
80 Polydor POSP 195 Life Is For Living/Shades Of B Hill (p/s) . . . 5
81 Polydor BARC 1 Life Is For Living (jukebox version)/Hymn (no p/s, jukebox issue) . . . 8
83 Polydor POPPX 585 Just A Day Away/Looking From The Outside (shaped picture disc) . . . 8
83 Polydor POSP 640 Waiting For The Right Time/Blow Me Down . . . 5
83 Polydor POSPX 640 Waiting For The Right Time (LP)/Waiting For The Right Time (edit)/ Blow Me Down (12", p/s) . . . 8
84 Polydor POSP 674 Victims Of Circumstance/Victims Of Circumstance (instrumental) (p/s) . . . 5
84 Polydor POSPP 674 Victims Of Circumstance/Victims Of Circumstance (instrumental) (shaped picture disc) . . . 8
84 Polydor POSPX 674 Victims Of Circumstance/Victims Of Circumstance (instrumental) (12", p/s) . . . 8
84 Polydor POSPX 674 Victims Of Circumstance/Victims Of Circumstance (instrumental)/Love On The Line (12", white label test pressing) . . . 12
84 Polydor POSP 705 I've Got A Feeling/Rebel Woman (p/s) . . . 5
86 Polydor POSP 834 He Said Love/On The Wings Of Love (p/s) . . . 5
90 Polydor PO 67 Cheap The Bullet/Shadows On The Sky (p/s) . . . 5
90 Polydor PZCD 67 Cheap The Bullet/Shadows On The Sky/Alone In The Night (live)/ Hold On (live) (CD) . . . 8
91 Swallowtail SWALLOW 2 Too Much On Your Plate (fan club flexi) . . . 10
70 Harvest SHVL 770 BARCLAY JAMES HARVEST (LP) . . . 18
71 Harvest SHVL 788 ONCE AGAIN (LP) . . . 18
71 Harvest SHVL 794 BARCLAY JAMES HARVEST AND OTHER SHORT STORIES (LP) . . . 18
72 Harvest Q4SHVL 788 ONCE AGAIN (LP, quadraphonic) . . . 22
(see also Bombadil, John Lees, Woolly Wolstenholme)

PETER BARDENS

70 Transatlantic TRA 222 THE ANSWER (LP) . . . 25
71 Transatlantic TRA 243 PETER BARDENS (LP, gatefold sleeve) . . . 22
76 Transatlantic TRASAM 36 VINTAGE '69 (LP, featuring Peter Green, some on clear vinyl) . . . 15
(see also Cheynes, Peter B's, Shotgun Express, Them, Village, Camel, Steve Tilston)

BRIGITTE BARDOT

66 Vogue VRS 7018 Mister Sun/Gang Gang (some in p/s) . . . 150+/50
68 Pye International 7N 25450 Harley-Davidson/Contact (some in p/s) . . . 100/30
63 Philips BL 7561 BRIGITTE BARDOT (LP) . . . 125

BOBBY BARE

60 Top Rank JAR 310 I'm Hanging Up My Rifle/That's Where I Want To Be . . . 12
63 RCA RCA 1352 Detroit City/Heart Of Ice . . . 6
63 RCA RCA 1366 500 Miles Away From Home/It All Depends On Linda . . . 6
64 RCA RCX 7139 DETROIT CITY (EP) . . . 20
66 RCA RD 7783 CONSTANT SORROW (LP) . . . 18
68 RCA RD 7918 THE ENGLISH COUNTRYSIDE (LP, with Hillsiders) . . . 12
(see also Bill Parsons, Skeeter Davis & Bobby Bare)

BAREFOOT BLUES BAND

70 Beacon BEA 163 Can't You See/Sunday Morning Barefoot Blues . . . 15
72 Deram DM 353 The Spirit Of Joe Hill/I Believe In Music . . . 8
73 Deram DM 372 Getting Better All The Time/Half Of Me . . . 6

MINOUCHE BARELLI

67 CBS 2806 Boum Badaboum/Let Me Take You . . . 20

MARK BARKAN

67 Stateside SS 2064 A Great Day For The Clown/Pity The Woman . . . 10

BAR-KAYS

67 Stax 601 014 Soul Finger/Knucklehead . . . 15
68 Stax 601 036 A Hard Day's Night/I Want Someone . . . 10

MINT VALUE £

69	Atlantic 584 244	Soul Finger/Knucklehead (reissue)	5
69	Stax STAX 135	Midnight Cowboy/A.J. The House Fly	5
70	Stax STAX 146	Sing And Dance/I Thank You	5
69	Atco 228 030	SOUL FINGER (LP)	30
69	Stax SXATS 1009	GOTTA GROOVE (LP)	25
71	Stax 2362 003	BLACK ROCK (LP)	20
73	Stax 2325 087	DO YOU SEE WHAT I SEE? (LP)	15
76	Stax STX 1033	COLD BLOODED (LP)	20

(see also Otis Redding)

BUTCH BARKER

75	Creole CR 113	The Joker/Juicie Brucie	8

DAVE BARKER

70	Duke DU 74	Funkey Reggae/TOMMY McCOOK & SUPERSONICS: I Love You My Baby (B-side actually by Versatiles)	30
70	Punch PH 20	Prisoner Of Love/BUSTY & UPSETTERS: Soul Juice	30
70	Punch PH 22	You Betray Me/Will You Still Love Me Tomorrow?	20
70	Punch PH 25	Shocks Of Mighty Parts 1 & 2	25
70	Punch PH 42	Reggae Meeting/MARTIN ALL STARS: Soul Bone	20
70	Jackpot JP 736	The Fastest Man Alive/NORMAN GRANT: Bloodshot Eyes	15
70	Jackpot JP 742	Wet Version/I Got To Get Away	15
70	Jackpot JP 745	Girl Of My Dreams/On Broadway	15
70	High Note HS 049	She Want It/FIRST GENERATION: Give Him Up	15
70	Randy's RAN 503	October/RANDY'S ALLSTARS: Time Out	15
70	Unity UN 567	Blessed Are The Meek (with Slim Smith)/JEFF BARNES & UNIQUES: The People's Voice	15
70	Upsetter US 331	Shocks Of Mighty/Set Me Free (with Upsetters)	20
70	Upsetter US 344	Some Sympathy/UNTOUCHABLES: Tender Love	20
70	Upsetter US 347	Sound Underground/Don't Let The Sun Catch You Crying	20
71	Upsetter US 358	Shocks '71/HURRICANES: You've Got To Be Mine	20
71	Upsetter US 362	Groove Me/UPSETTERS: Screwdriver	20
71	Upsetter US 364	What A Confusion/UPSETTERS: Confusion — Version 2	18
71	Ackee ACK 113	Johnny Dollar/Version	15
71	Ackee ACK 119	Life Of A Millionaire/Version	12
71	Trojan TR 7851	Sex Machine/You Left Me And Gone (both sides with Aggrovators)	20
71	Punch PH 69	What A Confusion/BOB MARLEY: Small Axe	35
71	Supreme SUP 228	Double Heavy/Johnny Dollar	15
71	Downtown DT 482	Only The Strong Survive/Only The Strong — Version	15
72	Jackpot JP 803	You'll Be Sorry/Green Grow The Lilacs	15
72	Big Shot BI 614	Are You Sure/I Don't Know Why (B-side actually by Sensations)	12
72	Fab FAB 25	Green Grow The Lilacs/JIMMY RILEY: Keep An Eye (On Your Closest Friend) (white label)	15
76	Trojan TRL 127	PRISONER OF LOVE (LP)	40

(see also Glen & Dave, Dave & Ansell Collins, Bobby & Dave, Aggrovators, David Crooks, Dennis Alcapone, Don Drummond, Owen Gary, Lizzy & Dennis, Bob Marley, Lester Sterling, Busty Brown)

RONNIE BARKER

78	EMI EMI 2768	Going Straight/String Bean Queen	6

BARLEY BREE

67	Piccadilly 7N 35393	Sometime In The Morning/Save Your Love	12

BARNABY RUDGE

68	CBS 3262	Joe, Organ & Co./Railway Jim	6

(see also Will Malone)

BARNEY J. BARNES & INTRO.

67	Decca F 12662	It Must Be Love/Can't Stand The Pain	10

BENNY BARNES

60	Mercury AMT 1094	Token Of Love/That-A-Boy Willie	20

DENA BARNES

80	Grapevine GRP 141	If You Ever Walked Out Of My Life/Who Am I	20

JEFF BARNES

70	Jackpot JP 735	Get In The Groove/JOHN HOLT: A Little Tear	20
70	Unity UN 568	1,000 Tons Of Version/Wake The Nation (B-side with Hugh Roy)	20
70	Pama PM 802	Jeff Barnes Thing/LENNOX BROWN: Lover's Mood	12
71	Smash SMA 2313	Wake The Nation (with Hugh Roy)/1,000 Tons Of Version	15

(see also Hugh Roy, Dave Barker, Darker Shade Of Blue, Delroy Wilson)

J.J. BARNES

67	Polydor 56722	Day Tripper/Deeper In Love	25
69	Stax STAX 130	Baby Please Come Back Home/Easy Living	20
73	Tamla Motown TMG 870	Real Humdinger/Please Let Me In/I Ain't Gonna Do It	10
74	Contempo CS 2009	To An Early Grave/To An Early Grave (Instrumental Version)	5
75	Contempo CLP 520	THE GROOVESVILLE MASTERS (LP)	15
77	Contempo CLP 604	SARA SMILE (LP)	10

J.J. BARNES/STEVE MANCHA

69	Stax SXATS 1012	RARE STAMPS (LP)	45

LLOYD BARNES

64	Blue Beat BB 235	Time Is Hard/BUSTER'S ALLSTARS: Reincarnation	30

RICHARD BARNES

68	Columbia DB 8436	Woman, Woman/The Princess And The Soldier	5
68	Columbia DB 8507	Look Away/Mr In Between	5
70	Philips BF 1840	Take To The Mountains/But It's Now I Need Your Love	5
70	Philips 630 8027	RICHARD BARNES (LP)	20

(see also Quiet Five)

MINT VALUE £

SIDNEY BARNES

76 Charly CYS 1007 — I Hurt On The Other Side/Good Lovin' . . . 12

ERIC BARNET(T)

68 Gas GAS 100 — The Horse (actually by Theo Beckford & Group)/Action Line (actually by Versatiles) . . . 12
69 Gas GAS 106 — Te Ta Toe (act. by Theo Beckford & Group)/ MILTON BOOTHE: Lonely And Blue . . . 10
69 Crab CRAB 37 — Quaker City/Double Up (both actually by Theo Beckford & Group) . . . 10
70 Gas GAS 130 — Pink Shark/Swing Free (both actually by Theo Beckford & Group) . . . 10
70 Gas GAS 147 — Bumper To Bumper/Fat Turkey (both actually by Theo Beckford & Group) . . . 10
(see also Theo[philus] Beckford)

BARRY BARNETT

58 HMV POP 487 — The Book Of Love/All I Have To Do Is Dream . . . 10
58 HMV POP 511 — When/Secretly . . . 10
58 HMV POP 521 — My Lucky Love/Too Young To Love . . . 10
58 HMV POP 532 — Susie Darlin'/Just A Dream . . . 10
59 HMV POP 579 — The Diary/Only A Memory . . . 10
59 HMV POP 627 — Cuckoo Girl/I'll String Along With You . . . 10

BARNSTORMERS SPASM BAND

58 Parlophone R 4416 — Whistling Rufus/Won't You Come Home, Bill Bailey? . . . 10
58 Parlophone R 4416 — Whistling Rufus/Won't You Come Home, Bill Bailey? (78) . . . 10
59 Tempo A 168 — Stormin' The Barn/That's All There Is (There Ain't No More) . . . 10
59 Tempo A 168 — Stormin' The Barn/That's All There Is (There Ain't No More) (78) . . . 10
(see also Original Barnstormers Spasm Band)

H.B. BARNUM

61 Fontana H 299 — Lost Love/Hallelujah . . . 15
65 Capitol CL 15391 — The Record (Baby I Love You)/I'm A Man . . . 50
76 Capitol CL 15851 — Heartbreaker/Searchin' For My Soul . . . 5
79 Capitol CL 16067 — Heartbreaker/BOBBY PARIS: I Walked Away . . . 5
64 RCA Victor RCX 7147 — THE GREAT H.B. BARNUM (EP) . . . 150
62 RCA Victor RD/SF 7500 — THE BIG VOICE OF BARNUM . . . H.B., THAT IS (LP, mono/stereo) . . . 10
63 RCA Victor RD/SF 7543 — EVERYBODY LOVES H.B. (LP, mono/stereo) . . . 10
(see also Robins)

CARL BARON & CHEETAHS

63 Columbia DB 7162 — This Is Only The Beginning/Beg Borrow Or Steal . . . 15

RIKKY BARON

60 Parlophone R 4706 — Angry Young Man/My Lonely Heart . . . 12

BARON WITH HIS POUNDING PIANO

65 Sue WI 398 — Is A Blue Bird Blue/In The Mood . . . 35
(see also V.I.P.'s)

BARONS (U.S.)

57 London HLP 8391 — Don't Walk Out/Once In A Lifetime . . . 1,500
57 London HLP 8391 — Don't Walk Out/Once In A Lifetime (78) . . . 100
71 Jay Boy BOY 45 — No More Baby Love/Society Don't Let Us Down . . . 10

BARONS (U.K.)

61 Oriole CB 1608 — Cossack/Summertime . . . 18
61 Oriole CB 1620 — Samurai/Whirlwind . . . 15

BARRABAS

76 Atlantic K 10716 — Checkmate/Four Seasons Woman . . . 5

BARRACUDAS

79 Cells CELLOUT 1 — I Want My Woody Back/Subway Surfin' (p/s) . . . 35
80 Zonophone Z 5 — Summer Fun/Chevy Baby (p/s, with/without stickers) . . . 15/6
80 Zonophone Z 8 — His Last Summer/Barracuda Waver/Surfers Are Back (p/s) . . . 8
80 Zonophone Z 11 — (I Wish It Could Be) 1965 Again/Rendezvous (p/s) . . . 6
81 Zonophone Z 17 — I Can't Pretend/The KGB (Made A Man Out Of Me) (p/s) . . . 6
83 Lyntone BOB 7 — Very Last Day/There's A World Out There (flexi with *Bucketfull Of Brains*) . . . 8/5
80 Zonophone ZONO 103 — DROP OUT WITH THE BARRACUDAS (LP) . . . 20

DICKIE BARRETT

58 MGM MGM 976 — Smoke Gets In Your Eyes/Remember Me . . . 50
58 MGM MGM 976 — Smoke Gets In Your Eyes/Remember Me (78) . . . 10

JOE BARRETT

55 Brunswick 05432 — I'm Sincere/Why Did You Break My Heart? . . . 10

RICHARD BARRETT & CHANTELS

59 HMV POP 609 — Come Softly To Me/Walking Through Dreamland . . . 25
(see also Chantels)

RITCHIE BARRETT

62 London HLK 9552 — Some Other Guy/Tricky Dicky . . . 60

'SWEET EMMA' BARRETT

60s Riverside RLP 364 — THE BELL GAL AND HER DIXIELAND BOYS (LP) . . . 15

SYD BARRETT

69 Harvest HAR 5009 — Octopus/Golden Hair . . . 120
88 Strange Fruit SFPS 043 — THE PEEL SESSIONS (12", EP, initially with metallic sleeve) . . . 15/12
88 Strange Fruit SFPSCD 043 — THE PEEL SESSIONS (CD EP) . . . 10
70 Harvest SHVL 765 — THE MADCAP LAUGHS (LP, laminated or matt gatefold sleeve) . . . 40/25
70 Harvest SHSP 4007 — BARRETT (LP, laminated or textured flipback sleeve) . . . 40/25
70s Harvest SHSP 4007 — BARRETT (LP, textured non-flipback sleeve) . . . 15
74 Harvest SHDW 404 — SYD BARRETT (2-LP, reissue of "Madcap" & "Barrett", gatefold sleeve) . . . 18
88 Harvest SHSP 4126 — OPEL (LP, gatefold sleeve) . . . 12
93 EMI SYD BOX 1 — CRAZY DIAMOND (3-CD box set, with booklet) . . . 20
97 Harvest 7423 855663 18 — THE MADCAP LAUGHS (LP, 180gm reissue, heavy quality sleeve) . . . 15
97 Harvest 7423 821450 11 — BARRETT (LP, 180gm reissue, heavy quality sleeve) . . . 15

99	Harvest SVLP 153	OPEL (2-LP, 180gm reissue, heavy quality sleeve)	18
99	Simply Vinyl SVLP 153	OPEL (LP 180gm reissue, heavy quality gatefold sleeve)	18
00	Simply Vinyl SVLP 281	BARRETT (LP, 180gm reissue, heavy quality gatefold sleeve)	18
00	Simply Vinyl SVLP 289	THE MADCAP LAUGHS (LP, 180gm reissue, heavy quality gatefold sleeve)	18

(see also Pink Floyd)

WILD WILLY BARRETT

77	Logo GO 105	Return Of Kong/Nice To Know You're My Friend (p/s)	5
79	Polydor 2059 067	Let's Play Schools/I Did It Otway (p/s)	5
86	Galvanised DIP 1	ORGANIC BONDAGE (LP, with Stephen Two Names; in wooden sleeve)	15

(see also John Otway/Wild Willy Barrett)

RAY BARRETT

69	Fontana STF 5487	NO TROUBLE NOW (LP)	12

RAY BARRETTO

63	Columbia DB 7051	El Watusi/Ritmo Sabroso	10
65	Columbia DB 7684	El Watusi/Swingin' Shepherd Blues	10
69	London HL 10262	Acid/Mercy Mercy Baby	50
67	Island ILP 946	EL WATUSI (LP)	30
69	London HA/SH 8383	ACID (LP)	40

BARRIER

68	Eyemark EMS 1013	Georgie Brown/Dawn Breaks Through (some in handmade p/s)	130/110
68	Philips BF 1692	The Tide Is Turning/Place In Your Heart	8
68	Philips BF 1731	Spot The Lights/Uh	45

BARRINO BROTHERS

72	Invictus INV 523	I Shall Not Be Moved/When Love Was A Child	8

BARRON KNIGHTS

62	Fontana H 368	Let's Face It/Never Miss A Chance	5
63	Columbia DB 7108	Jo-Anne/That's My Girl	5
64	Columbia DB 7188	Comin' Home Baby/Peanut Butter	5
64	Columbia DB 7317	Call Up The Groups Medley (both sides)	5
64	Columbia DB 7375	Come To The Dance/Choose Me Tonight	5
64	Columbia DB 7427	The House Of Johann Strauss/She's The One	5
65	Columbia DB 7525	Pop Goes The Workers Medley (both sides)	5
65	Columbia DB 7698	It Was A Very Good Year/Worry And Wonder	5
65	Columbia DB 7780	Merry Gentle Pops Medley (both sides)	5
66	Columbia DB 7884	Round The World Rhythm & Blues/Where There's A Will	5
66	Columbia DB 7933	Doing What She's Not Supposed To Do/Every Night	5
66	Columbia DB 8071	Under New Management Medley (both sides)	5
67	Columbia DB 8161	Lazy Fat People/In The Night	5
67	Columbia DB 8280	Here Come The Bees/It's A Sin	5
68	Columbia DB 8423	I Never Will Marry/Cold In My Nose	5
68	Columbia DB 8485	An Olympic Record/An Olympic Record	5
69	Columbia DB 8612	Love And The World Loves With You/Along Come Those Summer Days	5
69	Columbia DB 8679	Traces/Awake	5

BARROW POETS

68	Fontana TF 939	Letter In A Bottle (Music "Sleepy Lagoon")/Dynamite Barbee (Music "Barbee Song")	7
67	Barrow BR 1	AT THE PRINTER'S DEVIL (EP, private pressing)	30
63	Argo PLP 1072	PRESENT AN ENTERTAINMENT OF POETRY AND MUSIC (LP)	30
68	Fontana 6857 003	FINEST FOLK (LP)	20
70	RCA SF 8110	JOKER (LP)	20
72	Argo ZSW 508	OUTPATIENTS (LP)	25
72	Argo ZSW 511	MAGIC EGG (LP)	25

AL BARRY

70	Duke DU 81	Ooh Wee/Hold It Baby	5
70	Doctor Bird DB 1502	Morning Sun/MARKONIANS: Over And Over	5

(see also Desmond Dekker & Aces)

DAVE BARRY & SARA BERNER

56	London HLU 8324	Out Of This World With Flying Saucers Parts 1 & 2	40
56	London HLU 8324	Out Of This World With Flying Saucers Parts 1 & 2 (78)	10

GENE BARRY

65	Pye 7N 15873	I'll Remember You/I've Got Your Number)	8
65	RCA RD 7715	SINGS OF LOVE AND THINGS (LP)	15

JOE BARRY

61	Mercury AMT 1149	I'm A Fool To Care/I Got A Feeling	22
68	Stateside SS 2127	I Started Loving You Again/California Bound	18
62	Mercury ZEP 10130	A FOOL TO CARE (EP)	150

JOHN BARRY (SEVEN)

78s

57	Parlophone R 4363	Zip Zip/Three Little Fishes (as John Barry & The Seven)	10
58	Parlophone R 4394	Every Which Way/You've Gotta Way (as John Barry Seven)	10
58	Parlophone R 4418	Big Guitar/Rodeo (as John Barry Seven)	8
58	Parlophone R 4453	Pancho/Hideaway (as John Barry Seven)	8
58	Parlophone R 4488	Farrago/Bee's Knees (as John Barry Seven)	8
59	Parlophone R 4530	Long John/Snap 'n' Whistle (as John Barry Seven)	8
59	Parlophone R 4560	Little John/For Pete's Sake (as John Barry Seven)	8

SINGLES

57	Parlophone R 4363	Zip Zip/Three Little Fishes (as John Barry & The Seven)	80
58	Parlophone R 4394	Every Which Way/You've Gotta Way (as John Barry Seven)	50
58	Parlophone R 4418	Big Guitar/Rodeo (as John Barry Seven)	35

			MINT VALUE £
58	Parlophone R 4453	Pancho/Hideaway (as John Barry Seven)	15
58	Parlophone R 4488	Farrago/Bee's Knees (as John Barry Seven)	15
59	Parlophone R 4530	Long John/Snap 'n' Whistle (as John Barry Seven)	15
59	Parlophone R 4560	Little John/For Pete's Sake (as John Barry Seven)	15
59	Parlophone R 4582	Twelfth Street Rag/Christella (as John Barry Seven)	15
60	Columbia DB 4414	Hit And Miss/Rockin' Already (as John Barry Seven)	12
60	Columbia DB 4446	Beat For Beatniks/Big Fella (as John Barry Orchestra)	10
60	Columbia DB 4480	Blueberry Hill/Never Let Go (as John Barry Orchestra)	10
60	Columbia DB 4505	Walk Don't Run/I'm Movin' On (as John Barry Seven)	5
60	Columbia DB 4554	Black Stockings/Get Lost Jack Frost (as John Barry Seven)	5
61	Columbia DB 4598	The Magnificent Seven/Skid Row (as John Barry Seven)	5
61	Columbia DB 4659	The Menace/Rodeo (as John Barry Orchestra)	5
61	Columbia DB 4699	Starfire/A Matter Of Who (as John Barry Seven)	5
61	Columbia DB 4746	Watch Your Step/Twist It (as John Barry Seven)	5
62	Columbia DB 4806	Cutty Sark/Lost Patrol (as John Barry Seven & Orchestra)	5
62	Columbia DB 4898	The James Bond Theme/The Blacksmith Blues (with Orchestra) (green or black labels)	5
62	Columbia DB 4941	The Lolly Theme/March Of The Mandarins (as John Barry Seven & Orchestra)	5
63	Columbia DB 7003	The Human Jungle/Onward, Christian Spacemen (some in p/s)	18/5
63	Ember EMB S 178	Kinky/Fancy Dance	5
63	Ember EMB S 181	007/From Russia With Love (some in p/s)	18/5
63	Ember EMB S 183	Elizabeth/The London Theme	5
63	Ember EMB S 185	Zulu Stamp/Monkey Feathers (mauve/grey or red/yellow label; some in p/s)	25/5
63	Lyntone LYN 378	Theme Music From The Ingersoll Trendsetters T.V. Commercial (flexidisc; some with 8-page A4 promo booklet)	35/18
64	Columbia DB 7414	Twenty-Four Hours Ago/Seven Faces	10
64	United Artists UP 1060	Seance On A Wet Afternoon/Oublie Ça	10
64	United Artists UP 1068	Goldfinger/Troubador	10
64	Stateside SS 296	Barney's Blues/Theme From The Film "Man In The Middle" (No More)	10
65	CBS 201747	A Man Alone (Ipcress File Theme)/Barbara's Theme	10
65	CBS 201822	The Syndicate/What A Question	10
66	CBS 202390	Vendetta/The Danny Scipio Theme	5
66	CBS Special WB 730	James Bond Theme/RAY CONNIFF: Love Is Blue (p/s)	7
67	CBS 202451	Wednesday's Child (Quiller Memorandum)/Sleep Well My Darling	10
67	CBS 2825	You Only Live Twice/The Girl With The Sun In Her Hair	10
67	Ember EMB S 243	007/The Loneliness Of Autumn (some in p/s)	15/5
69	CBS 3935	The Lion In Winter Parts 1 & 2	10
69	CBS 4468	Midnight Cowboy/Fun City	10
69	CBS 4680	On Her Majesty's Secret Service/We Have All The Time In The World	10
70	Probe PRO 518	The Last Valley/Main Title Theme	5
71	CBS 7469	Theme From "The Persuaders"/The Girl With The Sun In Her Hair	5
72	Polydor 2058 216	This Way Mary/Diamonds Are Forever	10
72	Polydor 2058 275	The Adventurer/Follow Follow	10
77	Casablanca CAN 111	Theme From "The Deep"/DONNA SUMMER: Down Deep Inside	5
80	United Artists UP 634	Midnight Cowboy/Fun City (p/s)	6
83	Cherry Red CHERRY 67	Cutty Sark/The Lolly Theme (p/s)	5
86	MCA MCA 1195	Somewhere In Time/Rhapsody On A Theme By Paganini	5
90	Epic 6567 96 7	John Dunbar Theme/Dances With Wolves (p/s)	7

EPs

58	Parlophone GEP 8737	THE BIG BEAT (as John Barry Seven)	40
61	Columbia SEG 8069	THE JOHN BARRY SOUND (as John Barry Seven)	20
62	Columbia SEG 8138	BEAT GIRL (as John Barry Seven, with Adam Faith)	40
63	Columbia SEG 8255	JOHN BARRY THEME SUCCESSES	20
63	United Artists UEP 1011	FROM RUSSIA WITH LOVE (soundtrack)	25
64	Ember EMB EP 4544	LONELINESS OF AUTUMN	22
64	United Artists UEP 1012	GOLDFINGER (soundtrack)	25
65	Ember EMB EP 4551	JAMES BOND IS BACK	25
65	United Artists UEP 1015	THUNDERBALL: Thunderball/Death Of Fiona/Bond Below Disco Volante/ Mr Kiss Kiss Bang Bang (soundtrack)	22
67	CBS WEP 1126	THEMES FROM JAMES BOND FILMS (mail order via Carr's Sport biscuits)	10
67	CBS WEP 1129	BIG THEMES FROM THE BIG SCREEN (mail order via Wall's)	10
67	CBS WEP 1131	GREAT SCREEN THEMES (mail order via Lyon's Bakery)	10

LPs

60	Columbia 33SX 1225	BEAT GIRL (soundtrack, with Adam Faith)	50
61	Columbia 33SX 1358	STRINGBEAT (also stereo SCX 3401)	30/40
63	United Artists (S)ULP 1052	FROM RUSSIA WITH LOVE (soundtrack, mono/stereo)	25/35
63	Colpix PXL 459	ELIZABETH TAYLOR IN LONDON (mono/stereo)	40/50
64	Ember NR 5012	ZULU (soundtrack, yellow/orange label, flipback sleeve)	25
64	Stateside S(S)L 10087	MAN IN THE MIDDLE (soundtrack, with Lionel Bart)	55
64	United Artists (S)ULP 1076	GOLDFINGER (soundtrack, mono/stereo)	22/25
65	Ember NR 5025	JOHN BARRY PLAYS 007	30
65	Ember NR 56088	FOUR IN THE MORNING (soundtrack, mono/stereo)	35/45
65	CBS BPG 62598	PASSION FLOWER HOTEL (original cast, mono only)	30
65	CBS BPG 62530	THE IPCRESS FILE (soundtrack, mono only)	50
65	United Artists ULP 1104	THE KNACK (AND HOW TO GET IT) (soundtrack)	40
65	United Artists (S)ULP 1110	THUNDERBALL (soundtrack, mono/stereo)	18/20
65	Fontana (S)TL 55021	KING RAT (soundtrack)	30
66	Fontana STL 5387	THE WRONG BOX (soundtrack, release cancelled)	
66	CBS (S)BPG 62402	THE GREAT MOVIE SOUNDS OF JOHN BARRY	15
66	Ember NR 5032	JOHN BARRY MEETS CHAD & JEREMY	20
66	CBS (S)BPG 62665	THE CHASE (soundtrack, mono/stereo)	30/40
66	CBS (S)BPG 62869	THE QUILLER MEMORANDUM (soundtrack, mono/stereo)	20/30
66	MGM MGM-C 8010	BORN FREE (soundtrack, featuring Matt Monro, 1st pressing)	18
67	CBS 63038	JOHN BARRY CONDUCTS HIS GREATEST MOVIE HITS	15
67	United Artists (S)ULP 1168	THE WHISPERERS (soundtrack)	30
67	United Artists (S)ULP 1171	YOU ONLY LIVE TWICE (soundtrack)	20

MINT VALUE £

67	United Artists LAS 29021	THE BEST OF BOND (mono)	15
68	Stateside S(S)L 10263	DEADFALL (soundtrack, Shirley Bassey on 1 track)	45
69	United Artists UAS 29020	ON HER MAJESTY'S SECRET SERVICE (soundtrack, foldout sleeve)	20
69	United Artists UAS 29021	THE BEST OF BOND (stereo reissue)	15
69	CBS 70049	THE LION IN WINTER (soundtrack)	20
69	MCA MUPS 360	BOOM! (soundtrack, with Georgie Fame)	50
70	CBS 63952	READY WHEN YOU ARE, JB	15
71	CBS 64816	THE PERSUADERS (TV soundtrack)	15
71	United Artists UAS 29216	DIAMONDS ARE FOREVER (soundtrack)	20
71	Probe SPB 1027	THE LAST VALLEY (soundtrack, some with insert)	40/35
71	MCA MUPS 441	MARY QUEEN OF SCOTS (soundtrack)	30
72	Ember SE 8008	JOHN BARRY REVISITED (foldout sleeve, initially in 'nude' gatefold sleeve)	30/25
72	Warner Bros K 56009	ALICE'S ADVENTURES IN WONDERLAND (soundtrack, gatefold sleeve)	15
72	CBS 64816	FILM THEMES FROM JOHN BARRY	15
72	United Artists UAD 60027/8	THE JAMES BOND COLLECTION (2-LP, with booklet)	30
73	Polydor 2383 156	THE CONCERT JOHN BARRY	18
74	United Artists UAS 29671	THE MAN WITH THE GOLDEN GUN (soundtrack)	15
74	Polydor 2383 300	PLAY IT AGAIN	18
74	Phase 4 Stereo PFS 4339	THE DAY OF THE LOCUST (soundtrack)	20
76	CBS 22014	THE MUSIC OF JOHN BARRY (2-LP)	22
76	Polydor 2383 405	AMERICANS	22
76	Reprise K 54090	KING KONG (soundtrack, with poster)	15
77	Polydor 2383 461	THE VERY BEST OF JOHN BARRY	12
79	EMI MUTM 21	THE BEST OF JOHN BARRY 7 & ORCHESTRA	12
79	United Artists UAG 30247	MOONRAKER (soundtrack)	15
79	Pickwick SHM 3017	THE BLACK HOLE (soundtrack)	12
80	CBS 31862	THE BIG SCREEN MUSIC OF JOHN BARRY	12
83	A&R FILM 001	HIGH ROAD TO CHINA (soundtrack)	18
83	A&M AMLX 64967	OCTOPUSSY (soundtrack)	12
83	A&M 394 967-2	OCTOPUSSY (CD, soundtrack, withdrawn)	75
84	CBS CBS 31862	THE BIG SCREEN HITS OF JOHN BARRY	12
85	Parlophone BOND 1	A VIEW TO A KILL (soundtrack)	12
87	Warner Bros 925 616-1	THE LIVING DAYLIGHTS	12
92	EMI CD BOND 007	THE BEST OF JAMES BOND 30th ANNIVERSARY COLLECTION (2-CD, limited ed.)	40

(see also Alan Bown, Chad & Jeremy, Adam Faith, Elizabeth Taylor, Desmond Lane, Johnny Pearson, Tony Bennett, Jim Lowe, Lyn Paul, Russ Conway, Lance Fortune, Alan Haven, Countdowns, Johnny De Little, Marion Ryan, Dick Kallman)

KAY BARRY

62	Embassy WB 534	Bobby's Girl/James (Hold The Ladder Steady)	5
63	Embassy WB 599	Be My Baby/Bye Bye Birdie	5
65	Embassy WB 674	Terry/Girl Don't Come	5

(see also Bud Ashton)

LEN BARRY

65	Cameo Parkway P 969	Hearts Are Trump/Little White House	20
65	Brunswick 05942	1-2-3/Bullseye	10
66	Brunswick 05949	Like A Baby/Happiness	10
66	Brunswick 05955	Somewhere/It's A Crying Shame	10
66	Brunswick 05962	It's That Time Of The Year/Happily Ever After	10
66	Brunswick 05966	I Struck It Rich/Love Is	10
67	RCA RCA 1588	The Moving Finger Writes/Our Love	15
68	Bell BLL 1022	4-5-6 Now I'm Alone/Funky Night	5
71	Now! NOW 1003	Now I'm Alone/Funky Night	5
72	MCA MU 1172	1-2-3/You Baby	5
73	Paramount PARA 3031	Heaven And Earth/I'm Marching To The Music	6
73	Paramount PARA 3039	It's Time To Fall In Love/Touching, Holding, Feeling	6
66	Cameo Parkway CPE 556	HAVIN' A GOOD TIME (EP)	25
65	Brunswick LAT 8637	1-2-3 (LP)	25
66	Cameo Parkway C 1082	LEN BARRY AND THE DOVELLS (LP)	25
69	Bulldog BDL 1013	MORE FROM THE 1-2-3 MAN (LP)	18
69	RCA Intl. INTS 1027	MY KIND OF SOUL (LP)	15

(see also Dovells, Electric Indian)

MARGARET BARRY (& MICHAEL GORMAN)

58	Topic 10T 6	STREET SONGS AND FIDDLE TUNES OF IRELAND (10" LP, mid-blue label, later buff/black or dark blue/silver labels)	20/15
60	Top Rank Intl. 25/020	IRELAND'S QUEEN OF THE TINKERS SONG (LP, Margaret Barry solo)	20
65	Topic 12T 123	HER MANTLE SO GREEN (LP, dark blue/silver label, or reissue in diff. sl.)	15/12
67	Xtra XTRA 5037	THE BLARNEY STONE (LP)	12
68	Emerald GEM 1003	COME BACK PADDY REILLY (LP)	15

SANDRA BARRY (& THE BOYS)

64	Decca F 11851	Really Gonna Shake/When We Get Married (as Sandra Barry & Boys)	35
65	Pye 7N 15753	The End Of The Line/We Were Lovers	15
65	Pye 7N 15840	Question/You Can Take It From Me	15
66	Pye 7N 17102	Stop! Thief/I Won't Try To Change Your Mind	15

(see also Boys, Sandra Alfred, Slack Alice)

BARRY & THE TAMERLANES

63	Warner Bros WB 116	I Wonder What She's Doing Tonight/Don't Go	40
64	Warner Bros WB 124	Roberta/Butterfly	15
64	Warner Bros WM 8145	I WONDER WHAT SHE'S DOING TONIGHT (LP)	75

(see also Barry De Vorzon)

BARRY & TONY

65	Decca F 12224	Lost Love/Make It Or Break It	10

(see also Brothers Grimm)

MINT VALUE £

BARRY SISTERS (U.S.)

56 London HLA 8248 Cha Cha Joe/Baby Come A Little Closer 50
56 London HLA 8248 Cha Cha Joe/Baby Come A Little Closer (78) 10
56 London HLA 8304 Till You Come Back To Me/Intrigue 50
56 London HLA 8304 Till You Come Back To Me/Intrigue (78) 10
56 Columbia DB 3843 Sing Me A Sentimental Love Song/The Italian Theme 12
58 Columbia DB 4215 I Hear Bells/I Get Up Ev'ry Morning 10
60 Columbia DB 4562 Misty/Why Don't You Do Right? 10
60 Columbia 33SX 1309 SIDE BY SIDE (LP) 25
(see also Three Barry Sisters)

CHRIS BARTLEY

67 Cameo Parkway P 101 The Sweetest Thing This Side Of Heaven/Love Me Baby 60
68 Bell BLL 1031 I Found A Goodie/Be Mine Forever 25
75 Right On RO 105 I See Your Name/I See Your Name (Instrumental) 8
86 Move MIS 4 Baby I'm For Real/I've Found A Goodie/Truer Words Were Never Spoken/ The Sweetest Thing This Side Of Heaven (12", p/s) 15

BARTOK

82 On ON 1 Insanity/I Am The Bomb (p/s) 8
(see also Jah Wobble)

EVA BARTOK

67 Philips BF 1589 Broken Blossoms/Wait For Summer 5

RIA BARTOK

64 Columbia DB 7362 See If I Care/I Don't Wanna Leave You 5

EILEEN BARTON

55 Vogue Coral Q 72060 The Year We Fell In Love/I Don't Want To Mambo Polka 15
55 Vogue Coral Q 72075 Fujiyama Mama/I'd've Baked A Cake 100
56 Vogue Coral Q 72122 Cry Me A River/Come Home 25
56 Vogue Coral Q 72148 Teenage Heart/My Social Hot Dog 15
56 Vogue Coral Q 72205 Spring It Was/I Have To Tell You 10
57 Vogue Coral Q 72250 Too Close For Comfort/Here I Am In Love Again 10
57 Vogue Coral Q 72270 Without Love/The Scene Of The Crime 10

ROD BARTON (& THE LINCOLNAIRES)

62 Salvo SLO 1812 Dear Old San Francisco/Does A Chinese Chicken Have A Pigtail 25

BASEMENT

03 Deltasonic DLT 009 Medicine Day/Stuck On The Street (At Minus Ten) (numbered p/s, 1000 only) 10

BASHERS

76 Virgin VS 154 The Womble Bashers/Womble Bashers Wock 20
(see also Mike McGear)

BASHFUL ALLEY

82 Ellie Jay BA 001 Running Blind/My, My, My (p/s, black-and-white or black-and-yellow sleeve) 50
82 Graffiti BA 001 Running Blind/My, My, My (p/s, reissue) 35

COUNT BASIE & HIS ORCHESTRA

67 Coral Q 72497 Green Onions/Hang On Sloopy 10
68 MCA MCA 1014 For Your Precious Love/Uptight (with Jackie Wilson) 10
68 Decca AD 1008 For Your Precious Love/Uptight (with Jackie Wilson, export issue) 22
53 Brunswick LA 8589 BASIE'S BEST (10" LP) 15
53 Mercury MG 25015 KANSAS CITY 7/LESTER YOUNG QUARTET (LP, 1 side each) 15
54 Oriole/Mercury MG 25015 COUNT BASIE/LESTER YOUNG (10" LP, 1 side each) 15
55 Columbia 33S 1054 THE COUNT (10" LP) 12
55 Philips BBR 8036 THE OLD AND THE NEW COUNT (10" LP) 12
55 Columbia Clef 33C 9010 THE COUNT BASIE SEXTET (10" LP) 12
61 Columbia SX 1332 STRING ALONG WITH BASIE (LP) 12
65 Verve VLP/SVLP 9082 BASIELAND (LP) 12
66 United Artists (S)ULP 1127 BASIE MEETS BOND (LP) 20
(see also Joe Williams, Jackie Wilson, Tony Bennett, Lester Young, Ella Fitzgerald)

BASIES

67 Coxsone CS 7030 River Jordan/SOUL VENDORS: Swing Easy 30

BASKIN & COPPERFIELD

70 Decca F 13053 The Long And Winding Road/Beautiful Blue Eyes 5
(see also Rubettes)

ALFIE BASS

60 Pye 7N 15286 Villikens And His Dinah/Rat Catcher's Daughter 5

BILLY BASS

69 Pama PM 761 I Need Your Love So Bad/I'm Coming To 15

FONTELLA BASS

65 Chess CRS 8007 Don't Mess Up A Good Thing (with Bobby McClure)/OLIVER SAIN: Jerk Loose 30
65 Chess CRS 8007 Don't Mess Up A Good Thing/Baby What You Want Me To Do (different B-side, existence unconfirmed)
65 Chess CRS 8023 Rescue Me/Soul Of The Man 15
66 Chess CRS 8027 Recovery/Leave It In The Hands Of Love 18
66 Chess CRS 8032 I Can't Rest/Surrender 18
66 Chess CRS 8042 Safe And Sound/You'll Never Know 15
69 Chess CRS 8090 Rescue Me/I Can't Rest 10
69 Chess CRS 8023 Rescue Me/Soul Of The Man (reissue) 5
72 Mojo 2092 032 Who You Gonna Blame/Hold On This Time 5
72 Mojo 2092 045 I Want Everyone To Know/I Need To Be Loved 5

MINT VALUE £

66 Chess CRE 6015 FONTELLA'S HITS (EP) 40
66 Chess CRE 6020 I CAN'T REST (EP) 30
66 Chess CRE 6025 FONTELLA BASS AND BOBBY McCLURE (EP) 30
66 Chess CRL 4517 THE NEW LOOK (LP) 30
72 Mojo 2916 018 FREE (LP) 20
(see also Bobby McClure)

SHIRLEY BASSEY

SINGLES

57 Philips JK 1006 The Banana Boat Song/Tra La La (jukebox issue) 15
57 Philips JK 1018 If I Had A Needle And Thread/Tonight My Heart She Is Crying (jukebox issue) 15
57 Philips JK 1034 Puh-leeze! Mister Brown/Take My Love, Take My Love (jukebox issue) 15
58 Philips PB 845 As I Love You/Hands Across The Sea 5
58 Philips PB 860 Kiss Me, Honey Honey, Kiss Me/There's Never Been A Night 5
59 Philips PB 917 Love For Sale/Crazy Rhythm 5
59 Philips PB 919 My Funny Valentine/How About You? 5
59 Philips PB 975 Night And Day/The Gypsy In My Soul 5
61 Philips BF 1091 Birth Of The Blues/The Careless Love Blues 5
64 Columbia DB 7360 Goldfinger/Strange How Love Can Be 5
66 United Artists UP 1134 Don't Take The Lovers From The World/Takeaway 5
67 United Artists UP 1192 Big Spender/Dangerous Game 5
68 United Artists UP 2254 To Give/My Love Has Two Faces 5
71 United Artists UP 35293 Diamonds Are Forever/Pieces Of Dreams 5
77 United Artists UP 36247 I Let You Let Me Down/Razzle Dazzle (withdrawn) 5

LPs

58 Philips BBR 8130 BORN TO SING THE BLUES (10") 10
60 Columbia 33SX 1286 SHIRLEY (also stereo SCX 3352) 15/5
62 Columbia 33SX 1454 LET'S FACE THE MUSIC (also stereo SCX 3454) 12/5
(see also Yello, Nelson Riddle Orchestra, John Barry)

BASSIX

90 Champion CHAMP 12 CLOSE ENCOUNTERS (12", p/s) 8

BAS-SHEVA

55 Capitol CL 14218 Flame Of Love/I Just Wanna Be Your Loving Baby 10

JOE BATAAN

75 RCA RCA 2457 Latin Strut/Peace, Friendship And Solidarity 20
75 RCA RCA 2553 The Bottle/When You're Down 15
69 London HA/SH 8386 RIOT! (LP) 40

JUNE BATEMAN

64 Sue WI 347 I Don't Wanna/NOBLE 'THIN MAN' WATTS & HIS BAND: Noble's Theme 45

COLLIN BATES TRIO

68 Fontana SFJL 913 BREW (LP) 75

JON BATES

65 CBS 202818 Where Were You Last Night/If Anything Goes Wrong 5

MARTYN BATES

82 Cherry Red TRED 38 LETTERS WRITTEN (10" EP) 10
80s Ambivalent Scale IMAGINATION FEELS LIKE POISON (CD, with book, 500 only) 20
(see also Eyeless In Gaza)

BATMAN THEME

88 Bam Caruso NRIC 107 Batman Theme/Batman Theme (Instrumental Mix) (p/s) 8
(see also Jan & Dean)

STIV BATORS

79 London/Bomp HLZ 10575 It's Cold Outside/The Last Year (p/s) 15
(see also Dead Boys, Lords Of The New Church, Wanderers)

BATS

64 Columbia DB 7429 Accept It/Lovers Lie Sleeping 20
66 Decca F 22534 Listen To My Heart/Stop Don't Do It 10
67 Decca F 22568 You Will Now, Won't You?/You Look Good Together 20
67 Decca F 22616 Hard To Get Up In The Morning/Take Me As I Am 20

MIKE BATT

68 Liberty LBF 15093 Mister Poem/Fading Yellow 10
68 Liberty LBF 15122 I See Wonderful Things In You/Mary Goes Round 6
69 Liberty LBF 15210 Your Mother Should Know/Suddenly 8
(see also Hapshash & Coloured Coat, Anderson Harley & Batt)

BATTERED ORNAMENTS

70 Harvest HAR 5013 Goodbye We Loved You (Madly)/CHRIS SPEDDING: Rock'n'Roll Band 20
69 Harvest SHVL 758 MANTLE-PIECE (LP) 200
(see also Pete Brown & His Battered Ornaments, Chris Spedding, People Band)

SKIP BATTIN

72 Signpost SGP 756 Central Park/St. Louis Browns 6
72 Signpost SG 4255 SKIP (LP) 18
(see also Skip & Flip, Byrds, Flying Burrito Brothers, Evergreen Blueshoes)

JEAN BATTLE

72 Mojo 2027 010 Love Making/When A Woman Loves A Man 8

BATTLEAXE

82 Guardian GRC 132 Burn This Town/Battleaxe (no p/s) 22

BAUHAUS

79 Small Wonder TEENY 2 Bela Lugosi's Dead/Boys/Dark Entries (12", p/s, white vinyl) 15
88 Small Wonder TEENY 2P Bela Lugosi's Dead/Boys/Dark Entries (12", reissue, picture disc) 10

			MINT VALUE £
88	Small Wonder TEENY 2CD	Bela Lugosi's Dead/Boys/Dark Entries (CD, no'd reissue, 2,000 only)	10
89	Small Wonder TEENY 2	Bela Lugosi's Dead/Boys/Dark Entries (12", reissue, green or blue vinyl, p/s)	12/10
91	Small Wonder TEENY 2	Bela Lugosi's Dead/Boys/Dark Entries (12", reissue, pink, clear or purple vinyl, in corresponding coloured p/s)	each 10
80	Axis AXIS 3	Dark Entries/Untitled (brown label, p/s)	18
80	Axis AD 3	Dark Entries/Untitled (blue label, p/s)	8
80	4AD BEG 37	Dark Entries/Untitled (p/s, blue 4AD labels, lists BEG 37 on sleeve)	10
80	Beggars Banquet BEG 37	Dark Entries/Untitled (p/s, red Beggars Banquet labels)	10
82	Beggars Banquet AD 3	Dark Entries/Untitled (reissue, 'nudes' label, no contact address on p/s)	7
80	4AD AD 7	Terror Couple Kill Colonel/Scopes/Terror Couple Kill Colonel II (p/s)	5
80	4AD AD 7	Terror Couple Kill Colonel/Scopes/Terror Couple Kill Colonel II (version) (mispressed with 'rejected' version of third track, p/s)	25
80	4AD AD 17	Telegram Sam/Crowds (p/s)	5
81	Beggars Banquet BEG 54	Kick In The Eye/Satori (p/s)	5
81	Beggars Banquet BEG 54T	Kick In The Eye/Satori (12", white label in stamped plain sleeve)	8
81	Beggars Banquet BEG 59	The Passion Of Lovers/David J: Peter Murphy: Kevin Haskins: Daniel Ash (p/s, with lyric insert)	5
82	Beggars Banquet BEG 74	Kick In The Eye/Harry/Earwax (p/s)	5
82	Beggars Banquet BEG 74T	Kick In The Eye/Poison Pen/Harry/Earwax (12" mispressing, p/s, matrix: A1)	30
82	Beggars Banquet BEG 79	Spirit/Terror Couple Kill Colonel (live) (p/s, with Beggars labels)	5
82	Beggars Banquet BEG 79	Spirit/Terror Couple Kill Colonel (live) (p/s, mispressed, A-side plays Gary Numan's "We Take Mystery [To Bed]")	10
82	Beggars Banquet BEG 79P	Spirit/Terror Couple Kill Colonel (live) (picture disc in printed PVC sleeve)	8
82	Beggars Banquet BEG 83	Ziggy Stardust/Third Uncle ('Bauhaus' label with p/s, or Beggars label, no p/s)	5
82	Beggars Banquet BEG 83T	Ziggy Stardust/Party Of The First Part/Third Uncle/Waiting For The Man (12", p/s, with stickered poster p/s)	10
82	Lyntone LYN 12106	A God In An Alcove (Early Version) (blue flexidisc with *Flexipop*, issue 23)	12/7
82	Lyntone LYN 12106	A God In An Alcove (Early Version) (hard vinyl test pressing)	30
83	Lyntone LYN 13777/8	The Sanity Assassin/Spirit In The Sky (fan club freebie, 320 only)	175
84	Beggars Banquet BEG 91P	She's In Parties/Departure (picture disc in PVC sleeve)	8
88	Beggars Banquet BBP 4CD	THE SINGLES 1981-1983 (CD EP)	10
82	Beggars Banquet BEGA 38	PRESS THE EJECT AND GIVE ME THE TAPE (LP, with bonus 45 "Satori In Paris" [BH 1] & poster)	12
82	Beggars Banquet BEGA 42	THE SKY'S GONE OUT (LP, with bonus LP "Press The Eject And Give Me The Tape" [BEGA 38] & inner sleeves)	12
83	B. Banquet BEGA 45P	BURNING FROM THE INSIDE (LP, picture disc)	12
85	Beggars Banquet BEGA 64	1979-1983 (LP, with numbered inserts)	12
88	B. Banquet BAUCD BOX 1	1979-1983 (2-CD, boxed set with book & badge, numbered, 2,000 only, export issue)	30

(see also Sinister Ducks, Tones On Tail, David J., Love & Rockets)

ART BAXTER

56	Philips PB 652	Jingle Rock/Rock And Roll Rag (78)	10
57	Philips PB 666	Don't Knock The Rock/Rock Rock Rock (78)	10
57	Philips BBR 8107	ROCK YOU SINNERS (10" LP)	250

DAVID BAXTER

70	Reflection REFL 9	GOODBYE DAVE (LP)	30

(see also David Lewis)

LES BAXTER & HIS ORCHESTRA

54	Capitol CL 14166	I Love Paris/Manhattan	12
55	Capitol CL 14217	When You're In Love/Romantic Rio	12
55	Capitol CL 14237	Cherry Pink And Apple Blossom White/Play Me Hearts And Flowers	12
55	Capitol CL 14239	Earth Angel/Happy Baby (as Les Baxter & Bombers)	20
55	Capitol CL 14249	I Ain't Mad At You (with Bombers)/Blue Mirage	12
55	Capitol CL 14257	Unchained Melody/Blue Star (The Medic Theme)	15
55	Capitol CL 14344	Wake The Town And Tell The World/I'll Never Stop Loving You	10
56	Capitol CL 14533	Poor John/"Helen Of Troy" Theme	6
56	Capitol CL 14546	The Trouble With Harry/Havana	5
57	Capitol CL 14677	Giant/There's Never Been Anyone Else But You	5
59	Capitol CL 15055	Sabre Dance/Milord	5
60	Capitol CL 15140	Ooch-I-Baba/Boomada (as Les Baxter Drums)	5
66	Pye International 7N 25351	Michelle/Little Girl Lonely	5
59	Capitol T/ST 1248	WILD GUITARS (LP)	15
60	Capitol (S)T 1355	TEEN DRUMS (LP)	18

(see also Leonard Pennario)

RONNIE BAXTER

60	Top Rank JAR 293	I Finally Found You/Is It Because?	7

B.B. BLUNDER

71	United Artists UP 35203	Sticky Living/Rocky Yagbatee Yagbag	6
71	United Artists UP 35204	Little Boy/10,000 Miles	6
71	United Artists UAG 29156	WORKERS' PLAYTIME (LP)	15

(see also Reg King & B.B. Blunder, Action, Julie Driscoll Brian Auger & Trinity, Kevin Westlake, Mark Charig)

BBC RADIOPHONIC WORKSHOP/PETER HOWELL

64	Decca F 11837	Doctor Who/BRENDA & JOHNNY: This Can't Be Love (unboxed Decca logo)	20
72	Decca F 11837	Doctor Who/BRENDA & JOHNNY: This Can't Be Love (reissue, boxed logo)	8
73	BBC RESL 11	Doctor Who/Reg (blue/white label, credits 'Delia Derbyshire', 'TARDIS' p/s)	10/6
76	BBC RESL 11	Doctor Who/Reg (reissue, no p/s, silver label)	6
78	BBC RESL 11	Doctor Who/Reg (2nd reissue, in 'TARDIS' p/s, blue label, white rim)	6
80	PRT RESL 80	Doctor Who/The Astronauts ('Tom Baker' p/s, as 'Peter Howell & BBC Radiophonic Workshop')	10
82	PRT RESL 80	Doctor Who/The Astronauts (reissue, 'Peter Davison' p/s)	10
84	PRT RESL 80	Doctor Who/The Astronauts (2nd reissue, 'Colin Baker' p/s)	7
72	BBC REC 93S	TEST CARD MUSIC (LP)	12
78	BBC REC 316	DOCTOR WHO SOUND EFFECTS No. 19 (LP)	12

(see also Dr. Who, Jon Pertwee, Ray Cathode, Radiophonic Workshop, Ithaca, Alice Through The Looking Glass, Agincourt, Blossom Toes)

MINT VALUE £

BEA & DEE

59 Capitol CL 15066 Jerry/Wishing Time . . . 10

BEACH BOYS

SINGLES

62 Capitol CL 15273 Surfin' Safari/409 . . . 30
63 Capitol CL 15285 Ten Little Indians/County Fair . . . 75
63 Capitol CL 15305 Surfin' USA/Shut Down . . . 20
64 Capitol CL 15339 Fun, Fun, Fun/Why Do Fools Fall In Love . . . 30
64 Capitol CL 15350 I Get Around/Don't Worry Baby . . . 8
64 Capitol CL 15361 When I Grow Up (To Be A Man)/She Knows Me Too Well . . . 8
65 Capitol CL 15370 Dance, Dance, Dance/The Warmth Of The Sun . . . 8
65 Capitol CL 15384 All Summer Long/Do You Wanna Dance . . . 8
65 Capitol CL 15392 Help Me Rhonda/Kiss Me Baby . . . 7
65 Capitol CL 15409 California Girls/Let Him Run Wild . . . 7
65 Capitol CL 15425 The Little Girl I Once Knew/There's No Other (Like My Baby) . . . 10
66 Capitol CL 15432 Barbara Ann/Girl Don't Tell Me . . . 6
66 Capitol CL 15441 Sloop John B/You're So Good To Me . . . 6
66 Capitol CL 15459 God Only Knows/Wouldn't It Be Nice . . . 7
66 Capitol CL 15475 Good Vibrations/Wendy . . . 7
67 Capitol CL 15502 Then I Kissed Her/Mountain Of Love . . . 6
67 Capitol CL 15510 Heroes And Villains/You're Welcome . . . 6
67 Capitol CL 15521 Wild Honey/Wind Chimes . . . 6
68 Capitol CL 15527 Darlin'/Country Air . . . 6
68 Capitol CL 15545 Friends/Little Bird . . . 6
68 Capitol CL 15554 Do It Again/Wake The World . . . 6
68 Capitol CL 15572 Bluebirds Over The Mountain/Never Learn Not To Love . . . 6
69 Capitol CL 15598 Break Away/Celebrate The News . . . 6
70 Capitol CL 15640 Cottonfields/The Nearest Faraway Place (black label) . . . 6
70 Stateside SS 2181 Tears In The Morning/It's About Time . . . 6
71 Stateside SS 2190 Long Promised Road/Deirdre . . . 6
71 Stateside SS 2194 Don't Go Near The Water/Student Demonstration Time (demos in p/s £20) . . . 6
72 Reprise K 14173 You Need A Mess Of Help To Stand Alone/Cuddle Up (p/s) . . . 10
72 Capitol CMS 1 Wouldn't It Be Nice/Fun Fun Fun/California Girls (printed sleeve) . . . 6
72 Capitol CMS 2 Barbara Ann/Dance Dance Dance/You're So Good To Me (printed sleeve) . . . 6
74 Reprise K 14346 California Saga: California/Sail On Sailor/Marcella/I'm The Pied Piper (printed sleeve) . . . 5
76 Reprise K 14411 Child Of Winter/Susie Cincinnati (withdrawn) . . . 100+
76 Reprise K 14440 Rock And Roll Music/The T.M. Song (p/s) . . . 5
76 Capitol PSR 402 Good Vibrations/Interview With Carl Wilson (promo only) . . . 10
77 Reprise K 14481 Mona/Rock And Roll Music/Sail On Sailor/Marcella (p/s) . . . 5
78 Capitol CL 15969 Little Deuce Coupe/SUNRAYS: I Live For The Sun/SUPERSTOCKS: Hot Rod High (p/s) . . . 5
79 Caribou 12-7204 Here Comes The Night/(Disco Version)/Baby Blue (12", p/s, blue vinyl) . . . 8
79 Capitol BBP 26 SINGLES COLLECTION (26 x 7" box set) . . . 50

EPs

63 Capitol EAP 1-20540 SURFIN' USA . . . 25
64 Capitol EAP 1-20603 FUN, FUN, FUN . . . 25
64 Capitol EAP 5267 FOUR BY THE BEACH BOYS . . . 20
64 Capitol EAP 4-2198 BEACH BOYS CONCERT . . . 22
64 Capitol EAP 1-20781 THE BEACH BOYS HITS . . . 18
67 Capitol EAP 6-2458 GOD ONLY KNOWS . . . 20
77 EMI PSR 402 20 GOLDEN GREATS ALL YOU NEED TO KNOW (promo, white sleeve) . . . 20

LPs

62 Capitol T 1808 SURFIN' SAFARI (mono only) . . . 40
63 Capitol (S)T 1890 SURFIN' USA (mono/stereo) . . . 30/40
63 Capitol (S)T 1981 SURFER GIRL (mono/stereo) . . . 25/35
63 Capitol (S)T 1998 LITTLE DEUCE COUPE (mono/stereo) . . . 22/30
63 Capitol (S)T 2027 SHUT DOWN VOLUME 2 (mono/stereo) . . . 22/30
64 Capitol (S)T 2164 THE BEACH BOYS' CHRISTMAS ALBUM (mono/stereo) . . . 30/25
64 Capitol (S)T 2198 BEACH BOYS CONCERT (mono/stereo) . . . 20/25
64 Capitol (S)T 2110 ALL SUMMER LONG (mono/stereo) . . . 20/25
65 Capitol (S)T 2398 BEACH BOYS' PARTY! (mono/stereo) . . . 20/25
65 Capitol (S)T 2269 BEACH BOYS TODAY! (mono/stereo) . . . 20/25
65 Capitol (S)T 2354 SUMMER DAYS (AND SUMMER NIGHTS!!) (mono/stereo) . . . 18/22
66 Capitol (S)T 2458 PET SOUNDS . . . 35
66 Capitol (S)T 20856 THE BEST OF THE BEACH BOYS . . . 12
67 Capitol (S)T 1981 SURFER GIRL (reissue, non-flipback sleeve) . . . 12
67 Capitol (S)T 20956 THE BEST OF THE BEACH BOYS VOL. 2 . . . 12
67 Capitol (S)T 9001 SMILEY SMILE . . . 20
68 Capitol (S)T 2859 WILD HONEY (mono/stereo) . . . 25/18
68 Capitol (S)T 2895 FRIENDS (mono/stereo) . . . 30/18
69 Capitol (S)T 21142 THE BEST OF THE BEACH BOYS VOL. 3 (mono/stereo) . . . 15/12
69 Capitol E-T/E-ST 133 20/20 (mono/stereo, gatefold sleeve) . . . 22/18

(The above LPs were originally issued with flipback sleeves & rainbow-rim black labels; later orange or yellow label copies are worth half-to-two-thirds the value.)

70 Stateside SSLA 8251 SUNFLOWER (gatefold sleeve) . . . 18
71 Stateside SSL 10313 SURF'S UP (textured sleeve, some with gatefold insert) . . . 20/15
73 Reprise/Brother K 54008 HOLLAND (with insert & bonus EP "Mount Vernon And Fairway" [K 54008/7] in p/s) . . . 25
73 Reprise/Brother K 54008 HOLLAND . . . 12
77 EMI EMTV 1 20 GOLDEN GREATS (blue vinyl) . . . 12
78 Brother K 54102 M.I.U. ALBUM (with inner sleeve) . . . 12
79 Caribou CRB 11-86081 L.A. (LIGHT ALBUM) (picture disc) . . . 15
70s Capitol ST 2458 PET SOUNDS (reissue, green or orange label) . . . 12
81 WRC SM 651-657 THE CAPITOL YEARS (7-LP box set) . . . 35
86 EMI ENS 1179 PET SOUNDS (remastered reissue) . . . 12

(see also Brian Wilson, Dennis Wilson, Bruce Johnston, Legendary Masked Surfers, American Spring, Annette, Flame, Flames, California Music, Rutles, Moon, Murry Wilson, Mike Love)

BEACHCOMBER
70 Parlophone R 5850 — Surfin' Soul/Nothing To Say — 7

BEACHCOMBERS
63 Columbia DB 7124 — Mad Goose/You Can't Sit Down — 35
64 Columbia DB 7200 — Night Train/The Keel Row — 35
(the above singles do not feature Keith Moon)

BEACH-NUTS
65 London HL 9988 — Out In The Sun (Hey-O)/Someday Soon — 22
(see also Angels, Strangeloves)

BEACON STREET UNION
68 MGM MGM 1416 — Blue Suede Shoes/Four Hundred And Five — 25
68 MGM MGM-C(S) 8069 — THE EYES OF THE BEACON STREET UNION (LP) — 40

GEORGE BEAN
63 Decca F 11762 — Secret Love/Lonely Weekends — 22
64 Decca F 11808 — Will You Be My Lover Tonight?/It Should Be You — 10
64 Decca F 11922 — A Sad Story/Er Um Er — 10
65 Decca F 12228 — She Belongs To Me/Why Must They Criticise? (as George Bean & Runners) — 15
67 CBS 2801 — The Candy Shop Is Closed/Smile From Sequin — 10
68 CBS 3374 — Bring Back Lovin'/Floatin' — 22
(see also Trifle, Bean & Loopy's Lot)

BEAN & LOOPY'S LOT
66 Parlophone R 5458 — A Stitch In Time/Haywire — 20
(see also Alan Bown Set)

BEANO
74 Deram DM 424 — Candy Baby/Rock And Roll (Gonna Save Your Soul) — 6
75 Deram DM 427 — Little Cinderella/Bye And Bye — 5

BEANS
62 Starlite ST45 071 — Jumping Beans/Salute To Fitz — 12
62 Starlite ST45 076 — Hey Janey/Crazy Dog — 12

BEAR
68 Verve FTS 3059 — GREETINGS CHILDREN OF PARADISE (LP) — 35

DEAN BEARD & CREW CATS
57 London HLE 8463 — Rakin' And Scrapin'/On My Mind Again — 300
57 London HLE 8463 — Rakin' And Scrapin'/On My Mind Again (78) — 25

BEARS
79 Good Vibrations Intl. GVI 1 — Insane/Decisions (p/s) — 25
79 Waldo's JS 001 — On Me/Wot's Up Mate (p/s, various designs, with insert) — 18

BEARZ
80 Axis AXIS 2 — She's My Girl/Girls Will Do (p/s) — 20
84 Occult OCC 1 — Darwin/Julie (p/s) — 12

BEAS
68 Pama PM 744 — Dr. Goldfoot And His Bikini Machine/Where Do I Go From You — 25

BEASTIE BOYS
86 Def Jam A 7055 — Hold It, Now Hit It/Acapulco (p/s) — 5
86 Def Jam TA 7055 — Hold It, Now Hit It/Acapulco (12", p/s) — 8
86 Def Jam 650 114 7 — She's On It/Slow'n'Low (p/s) — 5
86 Def Jam 650 114 6 — She's On It/Slow'n'Low/Hold On, Now Hit It (12", p/s) — 8
87 Def Jam 650 169 7 — It's The New Style/Paul Revere (p/s) — 5
87 Def Jam 650 169 6 — It's The New Style/It's The New Style (Instrumental)/Paul Revere/Paul Revere (Instrumental) (12", p/s) — 8
87 Def Jam 650 418 7 — (You Gotta) Fight For Your Right (To Party)/Time To Get Ill (p/s) — 5
87 Def Jam 650 418 6 — (You Gotta) Fight For Your Right (To Party)/Time To Get Ill (12", p/s) — 8
87 Def Jam BEASTP 1 — No Sleep Till Brooklyn/Posse In Effect (plane-shaped picture disc) — 8
87 Def Jam BEASTT 1 — No Sleep Till Brooklyn/Posse In Effect (12", p/s) — 8
87 Def Jam BEASTP 3 — Girls/She's Crafty (poster p/s) — 5
87 Def Jam BEASTQ 3 — Girls/She's Crafty (logo shaped picture disc) — 8
92 Capitol CDCL 665 — Jimmy James (Single Version)/The Blue Nun/Jimmy James (Original Original Version)/Drinkin' Wine (CD, slimline jewel case) — 15
92 Capitol 12CLS 665 — Frozen Metal Head/Jimmy James (Single Version)/So What'cha Want (All The Way Live Freestyle Version)/Jimmy James (Original Original Version)/Drinkin' Wine (12", white p/s) — 8
92 Capitol CDCLS 665 — Frozen Metal Head/Jimmy James (Single Version)/So What'cha Want (All The Way Live Freestyle Version)/Jimmy James (Original Original Version)/Drinkin' Wine (CD) — 15
94 Capitol CL 716 — Get It Together/Sabotage/Dope Little Song (green vinyl, p/s) — 8
94 Capitol 7243 8 8173476 — Sure Shot/Mullet Head/Sure Shot (Caldato Mix) (red vinyl, p/s) — 7
98 (no cat. no.) — Intergalactic (Prisoners Of Technology Mix)/Robot Wars (10" acetate, 1 copy only) — 50+
82 Rat Cage MOTR 21 — POLLY WOG STEW (EP) — 10
82 Rat Cage MOTR 21 — POLLY WOG STEW (12" EP) — 12
86 Rat Cage MOR 26 — COOKY PUSS EP: Cooky Puss/Bonus Batter/Beastie Revolution/Cookie Puss (Censored Version) (p/s) — 5
86 Rat Cage MOTR 26CD — COOKY PUSS EP: Cooky Puss/Bonus Batter/Beastie Revolution/Cooky Puss (Censored Version) (CD) — 8
88 Rat Cage MOTR 21T — POLLY WOG STEW (12" EP, reissue) — 10
92 Capitol CDCL 653 — PASS THE MIC (Netty's Girl/Something's Got To Give/Pass The Mic [Pt. 2, Skills To Pay The Bills]) (CD, slimline jewel case) — 12
95 Grand Royal GR 026 — AGLIO E OLIO (CD EP, card sleeve) — 10
87 Def Jam 450 062 1 — LICENSED TO ILL (LP, with poster) — 12
(see also Money Mark)

MINT VALUE £

BEAT

79 2-Tone TT 6 — **Tears Of A Clown/Ranking Full Stop (paper label, company sleeve)** 5
(see also Fine Young Cannibals)

NICKY BEAT & THE BEATNICKS

78 Rigid IS BEAT 1033 — **I Can Hear Voices/Split Second Love/Starstruck (p/s)** 10

BEAT BOYS

63 Decca F 11730 — **That's My Plan/Third Time Lucky** 30
(see also Rats)

BEAT BROTHERS

63 Polydor NH 52185 — **Nick Nack Hully Gully/Lantern Hully Gully** 40
(see also Tony Sheridan & Beat Brothers, Bobby Patrick Big Six)

BEAT CHICS

64 Decca F 12016 — **Skinny Minnie/Now I Know** 20

BEATHOVEN

88 CBS 651 626-7 — **Socrates/Socrates (withdrawn)** 30

THE BEATLES

SINGLES

(Original Parlophone Beatles singles came in a variety of company sleeves, which are referred to here as "Type X", etc., and are depicted in the illustrations accompanying this text. When a sleeve is not specified, details are unknown.)

1962

(with "The Parlophone Co. Ltd." in upper-lower case & "Recording first published 1962" label text, without "Sold in UK ..."; all issues before 1967 have push-out centres)

FIRST PRESSING

Parlophone 45-R 4949 — **Love Me Do/P.S. I Love You** (red label, 'Ringo on drums & no tambourine' version; with or without "Made In Great Britain" credit; in sleeve Type A, B, or C) 100
(note: the 1982 red label re-pressing of "Love Me Do" includes the word "mono" & "Produced by George Martin" on the label)

1963

(with "The Parlophone Co. Ltd." in either upper-lower or upper case & "Recording first published 1963" label text, without "Sold in UK ...")

FIRST PRESSINGS

Parlophone 45-R 4983 — **Please Please Me/Ask Me Why** (red label; with or without "Made In Great Britain" credit; in sleeve Type A, B or C) 140
Parlophone R 5015 — **From Me To You/Thank You Girl** (in Type 1 sleeve) 10
Parlophone R 5055 — **She Loves You/I'll Get You** (in Type 1 sleeve) 10
Parlophone R 5084 — **I Want To Hold Your Hand/This Boy** (with "The Parlophone Co. Ltd" in upper-case only; in Type 1 sleeve) 10

KNOWN SECOND PRESSINGS

Parlophone R 4949 — **Love Me Do/P.S. I Love You** (black label, with "The Parlophone Co. Ltd" in upper-lower case, matrix suffixed with '1N' indicating 'Ringo on drums & no tambourine' version) 120
Parlophone 45-R 4983 — **Please Please Me/Ask Me Why** (black label, with "The Parlophone Co. Ltd" in upper-lower case, with "45" prefix) 15

KNOWN THIRD PRESSING

Parlophone R 4983 — **Please Please Me/Ask Me Why** (black label, with "The Parlophone Co. Ltd" in upper-lower case, without "45" prefix) 30

1964

FIRST PRESSINGS

(with "The Parlophone Co. Ltd." in either upper-lower, or upper case, "Recording first published 1964" & "Sold in UK ..." label text)

Parlophone R 5114 — **Can't Buy Me Love/You Can't Do That** (with "The Parlophone Co. Ltd" in upper case; in Type 1 sleeve**)** 10
Parlophone R 5160 — **A Hard Day's Night/Things We Said Today** (Type 1B sleeve) 10
Parlophone R 5200 — **I Feel Fine/She's A Woman** (with "The Parlophone Co. Ltd" in upper case; in Type 1B sleeve) 10

KNOWN THIRD PRESSING

Parlophone R 4949 — **Love Me Do/P.S. I Love You** (black label, with "The Parlophone Co. Ltd" in upper case, matrix suffixed with 1N' indicating 'Ringo on drums & no tambourine' version) 80

KNOWN FOURTH PRESSING

Parlophone R 4983 — **Please Please Me/Ask Me Why** (with "The Parlophone Co. Ltd" in upper case) 20

1965

FIRST PRESSINGS

(with "The Parlophone Co. Ltd." in upper case, & "Sold in UK ..." label text)

Parlophone DP 562 — **If I Fell/Tell Me Why** (domestic pressing of export issue; in Type 1B sleeve) 50
Parlophone R 5265 — **Ticket To Ride/Yes It Is** (in Type 2 sleeve) 10
Parlophone R 5305 — **Help!/I'm Down** (in Type 2 sleeve) 10
Parlophone R 5389 — **We Can Work It Out/Day Tripper** (in Type 3 sleeve) 12

KNOWN SECOND PRESSINGS

(with "The Gramophone Co. Ltd" in upper case, & "Sold in UK ..." label text)

Parlophone R 5305 — **Help!/I'm Down** 10
Parlophone R 5389 — **We Can Work It Out/Day Tripper** 10

1966

(with "The Gramophone Co. Ltd" in upper case, & "Sold in UK ..." label text)

FIRST PRESSINGS

Parlophone R 5452 — **Paperback Writer/Rain** (in Type 4 or 5 sleeve) 12
Parlophone R 5493 — **Yellow Submarine/Eleanor Rigby** (in Type 5 or 6 sleeve) 10

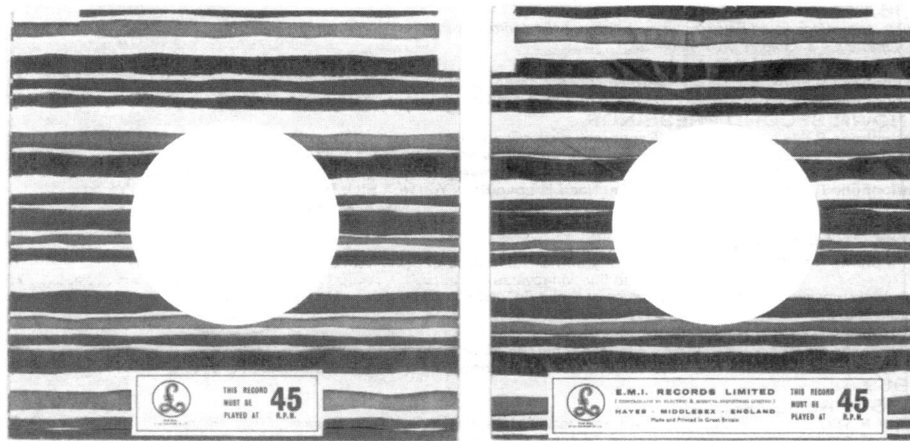

Sleeve Type A: coloured wavy lines with small box on front (left), large box on reverse (right).

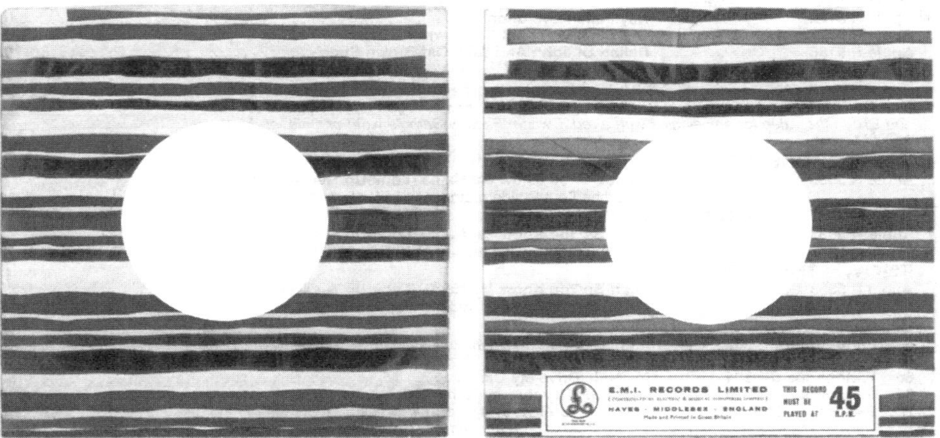

Sleeve Type B: coloured wavy lines without box on front (left), with large box on reverse (right).

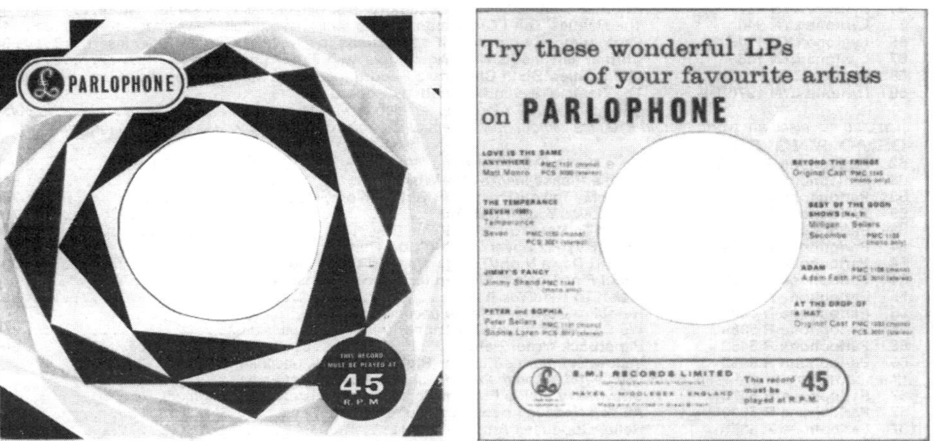

Sleeve Type C: multicoloured shapes on front (left) and LP details on reverse (right).

MINT VALUE £

1967

(all the pressings listed below have push-out or solid centres, with "The Gramophone Co. Ltd" in upper case & "Sold in UK ..." label text)

FIRST PRESSINGS

Parlophone R 5570	**Strawberry Fields Forever/Penny Lane** (250,000 only in p/s)	80
Parlophone R 5655	**Hello, Goodbye/I Am The Walrus** (company sleeve, with "7/- to 50/- " on reverse)	10

KNOWN SECOND PRESSINGS

Parlophone R 5452	**Paperback Writer/Rain** (solid centre only)	10
Parlophone R 5493	**Yellow Submarine/Eleanor Rigby** (solid centre only)	10
Parlophone R 5570	**Strawberry Fields Forever/Penny Lane** (in Type 5, 6 or 7 sleeve)	10
Parlophone R 5620	**All You Need Is Love/Baby You're A Rich Man** (with reference to "Live World Television Transmission"; most in Type 8 sleeve)	10

1968

FIRST PRESSINGS

Parlophone R 5675	**Lady Madonna/The Inner Light** (with Fan Club insert; sleeve with "7/- to 50/-" on reverse)	75

(all Apple pressings except for early issues of "Let It Be" come in black, glossy "Apple" sleeves)

Apple R 5722	**Hey Jude/Revolution**	15

KNOWN SECOND PRESSINGS

Parlophone R 5675	**Lady Madonna/The Inner Light** (no insert)	10
Parlophone R 5084	**I Want To Hold Your Hand/This Boy** (solid centre)	30

1969

FIRST PRESSINGS

Apple R 5777	**Get Back/Don't Let Me Down** (as "The Beatles with Billy Preston")	12
Apple R 5786	**Ballad Of John And Yoko/Old Brown Shoe**	12
Apple R 5814	**Something/Come Together** (without "Sold in UK..." label text)	20

KNOWN SECOND PRESSINGS

(without "Sold in UK ..." label text)

Apple R 5722	**Hey Jude/Revolution**	10
Apple R 5777	**Get Back/Don't Let Me Down** (as "The Beatles with Billy Preston")	10
Apple R 5786	**Ballad Of John And Yoko/Old Brown Shoe**	10

KNOWN THIRD PRESSING

Parlophone R 5305	**Help!/I'm Down** (with "The Parlophone Co. Ltd" label text)	15

*(later 1970s Parlophone copies of Beatles singles with **EMI boxed logos** are of nominal value. add £10 to the value for any singles with a red & white "Factory Sample Not For Sale" sticker)*

1970

FIRST PRESSING

Apple R 5833	**Let It Be/You Know My Name (Look Up The Number)** (scratched-out B-side matrix: APPLES 1002, p/s)	35

KNOWN SECOND PRESSING

Apple R 5833	**Let It Be/You Know My Name (Look Up The Number)** (scratched-out B-side matrix: APPLES 1002, no p/s)	10

KNOWN THIRD PRESSING

Apple R 5833	**Let It Be/You Know My Name (Look Up The Number)** B-side matrix: 7YCE 21408, no p/s)	6

EXPORT SINGLES

64	**Parlophone DP 562**	**If I Fell/Tell Me Why** (without "Sold in UK..." label text)	40
65	**Parlophone DP 563**	**Yesterday/Dizzy Miss Lizzy**	75
66	**Parlophone DP 564**	**Michelle/Drive My Car**	150
68	**Parlophone DP 570**	**Hey Jude/Revolution** (with or without Swedish p/s)	60/50
70	**Parlophone P-R 5833**	**Let It Be/You Know My Name (Look Up The Number)** (no p/s)	80

("Let It Be" was pressed with "Parlophone" label text on one side & "Gramophone" on the other)

70	**Apple P-R 5833**	**Let It Be/You Know My Name (Look Up The Number)** (no p/s)	100

FAN CLUB FLEXIDISCS

63	**Lyntone LYN 492**	**The Beatles' Christmas Record** (gatefold p/s)	80
64	**Lyntone LYN 757**	**Another Beatles Christmas Record** (p/s, with gatefold newsletter insert)	40
65	**Lyntone LYN 948**	**The Beatles' Third Christmas Record** (p/s, with gatefold newsletter insert)	40
66	**Lyntone LYN 1145**	**Pantomime: Everywhere It's Christmas** (p/s, with 7" x 7" newsletter insert)	55
67	**Lyntone LYN 1360**	**Christmas Time (Is Here Again)** (p/s, with 7" x 7" newsletter insert)	65
68	**Lyntone LYN 1743/4**	**The Beatles' Sixth Christmas Record** (p/s, some with 'Superpix' sales insert)	60/50
69	**Lyntone LYN 1970/1-IL**	**The Beatles' Seventh Christmas Record** (p/s, some with 2 x foolscap fan club newsletters)	60/50

(fan club flexidiscs are worth around £10 less without newsletters, and a third of the listed values without picture sleeves)

DEMO SINGLES

62	**Parlophone 45-R 4949**	**Love Me Do/P.S. I Love You** (McCartney misspelt "McArtney", 250 only)	3,000
63	**Parlophone 45-R 4983**	**Please Please Me/Ask Me Why**	1,500
63	**Parlophone (45-)R 5015**	**From Me To You/Thank You Girl** (with or without '45-' prefix)	each 700
63	**Parlophone R 5055**	**She Loves You/I'll Get You**	700
63	**Parlophone R 5084**	**I Want To Hold Your Hand/This Boy**	700
64	**Parlophone R 5114**	**Can't Buy Me Love/You Can't Do That**	700
64	**Parlophone R 5160**	**A Hard Day's Night/Things We Said Today** (red "A" on both sides)	700
64	**Parlophone R 5200**	**I Feel Fine/She's A Woman** (existence unconfirmed)	
65	**Parlophone R 5265**	**Ticket To Ride/Yes It Is**	600
65	**Parlophone R 5305**	**Help!/I'm Down** (existence unconfirmed)	
65	**Parlophone R 5389**	**We Can Work It Out/Day Tripper** (red "A" on both sides)	600
66	**Parlophone R 5452**	**Paperback Writer/Rain**	600
66	**Parlophone R 5493**	**Yellow Submarine/Eleanor Rigby** (existence unconfirmed)	

(the above demos have white labels with a red "A" on the A-side, unless otherwise stated)

67	**Parlophone R 5570**	**Strawberry Fields Forever/Penny Lane** (existence unconfirmed)	
67	**Parlophone R 5620**	**All You Need Is Love/Baby You're A Rich Man**	500
67	**Parlophone R 5655**	**Hello, Goodbye/I Am The Walrus**	500
68	**Parlophone R 5675**	**Lady Madonna/The Inner Light**	500
69	**Parlophone R 5814**	**Something/Come Together**	1,000

(the above 5 demos have green labels with a white "A" on the A-side. Demos with centres missing are worth half the listed values)

Green sleeve Type 1: straight cut at top (left) and "6/- to 50/- record tokens" on reverse (right).

Green sleeve Type 1B: wavy cut at top (left) and "6/- to 50/- record tokens" on reverse (right).

Green sleeve Type 2: rectangular box on front (left),"6/- to 50/- record tokens" on reverse (right).

			MINT VALUE £
68	**Apple (no cat. no.)**	**Hey Jude/Revolution** (green & white Apple 'custom' label, handwritten details)	500
69	**Apple R 5777**	**Get Back/Don't Let Me Down** (green and white Apple 'custom' label test pressing, typed details)	500
69	**Parlophone R 5786**	**Ballad Of John And Yoko/Old Brown Shoe** (existence unconfirmed)	
70	**Parlophone R 5833**	**Let It Be/You Know My Name (Look Up The Number)** (existence unconfirmed)	
76	**Parlophone R 6013**	**Yesterday/I Should Have Known Better** (green generic p/s)	40
76	**Parlophone R 6016**	**Back In The U.S.S.R./Twist And Shout** (green generic p/s)	40
78	**Parlophone R 6022**	**Sgt. Pepper's Lonely Hearts Club Band/With A Little Help From My Friends/ A Day In The Life** (p/s)	40

(the last three demos listed above have silver/black paper labels with a silver "A")

UNIQUE PROMO SINGLES

68	**Apple (no cat. no.)**	**OUR FIRST FOUR** (4 x 7" in presentation pack, including "Hey Jude" [R 5722] & "Those Were The Days" by Mary Hopkin [APPLE 2], "Sour Milk Sea" by Jackie Lomax [APPLE 3] & "Thingumybob" by Black Dyke Mills Band [APPLE 4]; each mounted in PVC pocket on printed dayglo card insert, in 10" x 12" card or scarcer plastic outer box)	750/1,000
76	**EMI SPSR 401**	**Medley Of Songs For "Rock'n'Roll Music"** (excerpts)	250
77	**Sound For Industry SFI 291**	**The Beatles' Collection (Singles 1962-1970)** (flexidisc "audition disc" sampler for box set [BS 24], with foldout p/s & "Dear Customer" letter)	10

80s & 90s SINGLES: REISSUES & PICTURE DISCS

82	**Parlophone R 6055**	**The Beatles Movie Medley/I'm Happy Just To Dance With You** (p/s)	5
82	**Parlophone R 4949**	**Love Me Do/P.S. I Love You** (p/s, red label reissue, with "mono" notice & publishing miscredited to "Ardmore & Beechwood")	10
82	**Parlophone RP 4949**	**Love Me Do/P.S. I Love You** (picture disc, with/without publishing miscredit)	15/10
82	**Parlophone 12R 4949**	**Love Me Do/P.S. I Love You/Love Me Do** (Original Single Version) (12", p/s)	15
83	**Parlophone RP 4983**	**Please Please Me/Ask Me Why** (picture disc)	10
83	**Parlophone RP 5015**	**From Me To You/Thank You Girl** (picture disc, some with "Souvenir From Abbey Road Studios" sticker on sleeve)	25/10
83	**Parlophone RP 5055**	**She Loves You/I'll Get You** (picture disc)	25
83	**Parlophone RP 5084**	**I Want To Hold Your Hand/This Boy** (picture disc)	10
84	**Parlophone RP 5114**	**Can't Buy Me Love/You Can't Do That** (picture disc)	10
84	**Parlophone RP 5160**	**A Hard Day's Night/Things We Said Today** (picture disc)	25
84	**Parlophone RP 5200**	**I Feel Fine/She's A Woman** (picture disc)	10
85	**Parlophone RP 5265**	**Ticket To Ride/Yes It Is** (picture disc)	10
85	**Parlophone RP 5305**	**Help!/I'm Down** (picture disc)	10
85	**Parlophone RP 5389**	**We Can Work It Out/Day Tripper** (picture disc)	10
86	**Parlophone RP 5452**	**Paperback Writer/Rain** (picture disc)	15
86	**Parlophone RP 5493**	**Yellow Submarine/Eleanor Rigby** (picture disc)	15
87	**Parlophone RP 5570**	**Strawberry Fields Forever/Penny Lane** (picture disc, later with slightly larger picture on disc)	each 15
87	**Parlophone RP 5620**	**All You Need Is Love/Baby You're A Rich Man** (picture disc)	15
87	**Parlophone 12R 5620**	**All You Need Is Love/Baby You're A Rich Man** (12", p/s)	15
87	**Parlophone RP 5655**	**Hello, Goodbye/I Am The Walrus** (picture disc)	10
88	**Parlophone RP 5675**	**Lady Madonna/The Inner Light** (picture disc, with "Past Masters" insert)	10
88	**Apple RP 5722**	**Hey Jude/Revolution** (picture disc, with "Apple" insert)	10
88	**Apple 12R 5722**	**Hey Jude/Revolution** (12", p/s)	15
88	**Apple 12RP 5722**	**Hey Jude/Revolution** (12", picture disc with "Apple" insert)	15
89	**Apple RP 5777**	**Get Back/Don't Let Me Down** (with Billy Preston, picture disc, with "20th Anniversary" insert)	10
89	**Apple RP 5786**	**Ballad Of John And Yoko/Old Brown Shoe** (picture disc, with "20th Anniversary" insert)	10
89	**Apple RP 5814**	**Something/Come Together** (picture disc, with "20th Anniversary" insert)	10
90	**Apple RP 5833**	**Let It Be/You Know My Name (Look Up The Number)** (picture disc, with "20th Anniversary" insert)	10

(all the picture discs listed above were issued in PVC sleeves)

SINGLES BOX SETS

76	**Parlophone/Apple BS 24**	**THE BEATLES' SINGLES COLLECTION 1962-1970** (24 x 7", each in green p/s, green & white stickered box set)	25
76	**Parlophone/Apple/ World Record Club**	**THE BEATLES' COLLECTION** (24 x 7", mail-order black box set; later copies with "Sgt. Pepper's Lonely Hearts Club Band" [R 6022])	25
78	**Parlophone/Apple BSC 1**	**THE BEATLES' SINGLES COLLECTION** (26 x 7" blue box set, with insert; some copies include mispressing of "Get Back" [Apple R 5777])	40
82	**Parlophone/Apple BSCP 1**	**THE BEATLES' SINGLES COLLECTION** (27 x 7" blue box set, with bonus picture disc "Love Me Do" [RP 4949], export issue)	50
82	**Parlophone/Apple BSCP 1**	**THE BEATLES' SINGLES COLLECTION** (27 x 7" blue box set, with mispressed picture disc "Love Me Do"/"Love Me Do" [RP 4949], export issue)	50
89	**Parlophone/Apple CDBSC 1**	**THE BEATLES' SINGLES COLLECTION** (22 x 3" CD single box set)	50

EPs: 1963

(unless otherwise indicated, all 60s EPs have push-out centres & laminated, flipback sleeves, with "The Parlophone Co. Ltd." & "Recording first published 1963" label text, but without "Sold in UK ...")

FIRST PRESSINGS

Parlophone GEP 8882	**TWIST AND SHOUT**	18
Parlophone GEP 8880	**THE BEATLES' HITS** (without "Recording first published 1963" label text)	18
Parlophone GEP 8883	**THE BEATLES (No. 1)**	20

KNOWN SECOND PRESSING

Parlophone GEP 8880	**THE BEATLES' HITS**	18

EPs: 1964

(with "The Parlophone Co. Ltd.", "Recording first published 1964" & "Sold in UK ..." label text)

FIRST PRESSINGS

Parlophone GEP 8891	**ALL MY LOVING** (*without* "Sold in UK..." label text)	20
Parlophone GEP 8899	**GOLDEN DISCS** (unreleased, 2 x 1-sided test pressings [matrices: 7TCE-1N & 7TCE-1N] & 1 set of label proofs only; price does not include labels)	2,000

Green sleeve Type 3: wavy cut at top (left) and "Fran The Fan" advert on reverse (right).

Green sleeve Type 4: wavy cut at top (left) and "Morphy-Richards offer" advert on reverse (right).

Green sleeve Type 5: straight cut at top (left), "Fran The Fan, Dear Miss Brown" ad. on reverse (right).

MINT VALUE £

Parlophone GEP 8913 LONG TALL SALLY ... 18
Parlophone GEP 8920 EXTRACTS FROM THE FILM "A HARD DAY'S NIGHT" ... 25
Parlophone GEP 8924 EXTRACTS FROM THE ALBUM "A HARD DAY'S NIGHT" ... 40

KNOWN SECOND PRESSING

Parlophone GEP 8882 TWIST AND SHOUT ... 18
Parlophone GEP 8891 ALL MY LOVING ... 18

EPs: 1965

(with "The Parlophone Co. Ltd.", & "Sold in UK ..." label text)

FIRST PRESSINGS

Parlophone GEP 8931 BEATLES FOR SALE ... 25
Parlophone GEP 8938 BEATLES FOR SALE (No. 2) ... 50

(with "The Gramophone Co. Ltd.", & "Sold in UK ..." label text)

KNOWN SECOND PRESSING

(with "The Gramophone Co. Ltd.", & "Sold in UK ..." label text)

Parlophone GEP 8883 THE BEATLES (No. 1) ... 18

KNOWN THIRD PRESSING

Parlophone GEP 8880 THE BEATLES' HITS ... 18
Parlophone GEP 8882 TWIST AND SHOUT ... 18

EPs: 1966

(with "The Gramophone Co. Ltd.", & "Sold in UK ..." label text)

FIRST PRESSINGS

Parlophone GEP 8948 YESTERDAY ... 80
Parlophone GEP 8952 NOWHERE MAN ... 100

KNOWN SECOND PRESSING

Parlophone GEP 8946 THE BEATLES' MILLION SELLERS (with "Million Sellers" label text) ... 35

EPs: 1967

(with "The Gramophone Co. Ltd.", & "Sold in UK ..." label text)

FIRST PRESSING

Parlophone MMT-1 MAGICAL MYSTERY TOUR (2-EP, gatefold sleeve, with booklet & blue lyric sheet; push-out or solid centre; mono) ... 50
Parlophone SMMT-1 MAGICAL MYSTERY TOUR (2-EP, gatefold sleeve, with booklet & blue lyric sheet; stereo) ... 60

KNOWN SECOND PRESSINGS

Parlophone GEP 8931 BEATLES FOR SALE (with "The Parlophone Co. Ltd" label text; solid centre) ... 20
Parlophone GEP 8952 NOWHERE MAN (solid centre) ... 45

(the above titles with "The Gramophone Co. Ltd.", & label text, but without "Sold in UK..." are 70s re-pressings, and are worth half the listed values. Later copies with "EMI" label text & varnished sleeves are worth approximately one-third the listed values)

EPs: REISSUES & BOX SET

73 Parlophone SMMT-1 MAGICAL MYSTERY TOUR (2-EP, gatefold sleeve, stereo only, with booklet & yellow lyric sheet) ... 20
81 Parlophone BEP 14 THE BEATLES EP COLLECTION (14-EP box set, with bonus stereo EP [SGE 1]) ... 50

LPs: 1963

(with "The Parlophone Co. Ltd." label text but without "Sold in UK ...")

FIRST PRESSINGS

Parlophone PMC 1202 PLEASE PLEASE ME (black & gold label, with "Dick James Mus. Co." publishing credit for "Please Please Me", "I Saw Her Standing There", "Misery", "Do You Want To Know A Secret" & "There's A Place"; E. J. Day sleeve; mono) ... 750
Parlophone PCS 3042 PLEASE PLEASE ME (black & gold label, with "Dick James Mus. Co." publishing credit for "Please Please Me", "I Saw Her Standing There", "Misery", "Do You Want To Know A Secret" & "There's A Place"; E. J. Day sleeve; stereo) ... 3,000
Parlophone PMC 1206 WITH THE BEATLES (black & yellow label, with "Recording first published", & "Jobete" publishing credit for "Money"; G & L or E. J. Day sleeve, with large "mono" on front cover; mono) ... 90
Parlophone PCS 3045 WITH THE BEATLES (black & yellow label, with "Recording first published", & "Jobete" publishing credit for "Money"; G & L or E. J. Day sleeve, with large "stereo" on front cover; stereo) ... 180

(above pressings have polythene-lined "Use Emitex" die-cut inner sleeves)

SECOND PRESSINGS

(with "The Parlophone Co. Ltd." label text but without "Sold in UK ...")

Parlophone PMC 1202 PLEASE PLEASE ME (black & gold label, with "Northern Songs" publishing credit for "Please Please Me", "I Saw Her Standing There", "Misery", "Do You Want To Know A Secret" & "There's A Place"; E. J. Day sleeve; mono) ... 750
Parlophone PCS 3042 PLEASE PLEASE ME (black & gold label, with "Northern Songs" publishing credit for "Please Please Me", "I Saw Her Standing There", "Misery", "Do You Want To Know A Secret" & "There's A Place"; E. J. Day sleeve; stereo) ... 3,000
Parlophone PMC 1206 WITH THE BEATLES (black & yellow label, with "Recording first published", & "Dominion, Belinda" publishing credit for "Money"; G & L or E. J. Day sleeve, with large "mono" on front cover; mono) ... 40
Parlophone PCS 3045 WITH THE BEATLES (black & yellow label, with "Recording first published", & "Dominion, Belinda" publishing credit for "Money"; G & L or E. J. Day sleeve, with large "stereo" on front cover; stereo) ... 120

THIRD PRESSINGS

(with "The Parlophone Co. Ltd." label text but without "Recording first published 1963" & "Sold in UK ...")

Parlophone PMC 1202 PLEASE PLEASE ME (with large "mono" on front cover; E. J. Day sleeve; mono) ... 150
Parlophone PCS 3042 PLEASE PLEASE ME (with large "stereo" on front cover; E. J. Day sleeve; stereo) ... 400

FOURTH PRESSINGS

(with "The Parlophone Co. Ltd." & "Recording first published 1963", label text but without "Sold in UK ...")

Parlophone PMC 1202 PLEASE PLEASE ME (G & L or E. J. Day sleeve, with large "mono" on front cover; mono) ... 60
Parlophone PCS 3042 PLEASE PLEASE ME (G & L or E. J. Day sleeve, with large "stereo" on front cover; stereo) ... 180

Green sleeve Type 6: top wavy cut, front rectangular box (left), "6/- to 50/-" on reverse (right).

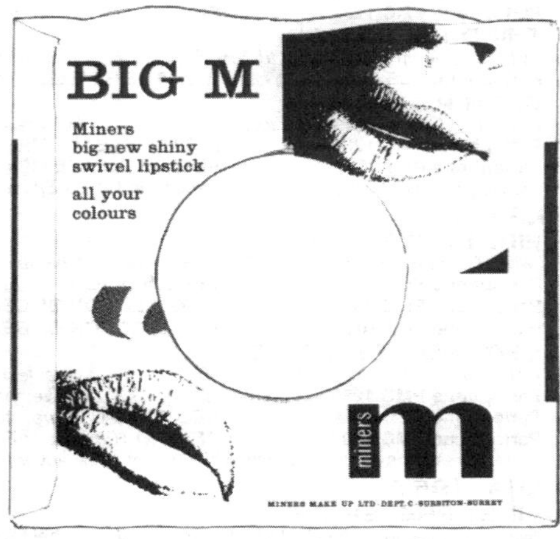

Green sleeve Type 7: wavy cut at top (left) and "Big M" advert on reverse (right).

Green sleeve Type 8: wavy cut at top (left) and "Hit make-up" advert on revesre (right).

MINT VALUE £

LPs: 1964

FIRST PRESSINGS

(with "The Parlophone Co. Ltd.", "Recording first published 1964" & "Sold in UK ..." label text)

Parlophone PMC 1230	**A HARD DAY'S NIGHT** (G & L or E. J. Day sleeve, mid-sized "mono" on front cover; mono)	50
Parlophone PCS 3058	**A HARD DAY'S NIGHT** (G & L sleeve, mid-sized "stereo" on front cover; stereo)	120
Parlophone PMC 1240	**BEATLES FOR SALE** (G & L gatefold sleeve, with outline "mono" on front cover; mono)	40
Parlophone PCS 3062	**BEATLES FOR SALE** (G & L gatefold sleeve, with outline "stereo" on front cover; stereo)	80

FIFTH PRESSINGS

(with "The Parlophone Co. Ltd.", "Recording first published 1963" & "Sold in UK ..." label text)

Parlophone PMC 1202	**PLEASE PLEASE ME** (G & L sleeve, with large "mono" on front cover; mono)	30
Parlophone PCS 3042	**PLEASE PLEASE ME** (G & L sleeve, with large "stereo" on front cover; stereo)	60

LPs: 1965

FIRST PRESSINGS

(with "The Gramophone Co. Ltd.", & "Sold in UK ..." label text)

Parlophone PMC 1255	**HELP!** (G & L sleeve, with outline "mono" on front cover; mono)	40
Parlophone PCS 3071	**HELP!** (G & L sleeve, with outline "stereo" on front cover; stereo)	70
Parlophone PMC 1267	**RUBBER SOUL** ('loud' cut matrix: [XEX 579-1], G & L or E. J. Day sleeve; mono)	80
Parlophone PCS 3075	**RUBBER SOUL** (G & L or E. J. Day sleeve; stereo)	75

SECOND PRESSINGS

(with "The Gramophone Co. Ltd.", & "Sold in UK ..." label text)

Parlophone PMC 1230	**A HARD DAY'S NIGHT** (small "mono" on front cover; mono)	30
Parlophone PCS 3058	**A HARD DAY'S NIGHT** (small "stereo" on front cover; stereo)	40
Parlophone PCS 3062	**BEATLES FOR SALE** (outline "stereo" on front gatefold sleeve; stereo)	40
Parlophone PMC 1267	**RUBBER SOUL** (matrix: [XEX 579-4 or 5]; mono)	45

THIRD PRESSINGS

(with "The Gramophone Co. Ltd..", & "Sold in UK ..." label text)

Parlophone PCS 3045	**WITH THE BEATLES** (small "stereo" on front cover; stereo)	40

SIXTH PRESSINGS

(with "The Gramophone Co. Ltd.", & "Sold in UK ..." label text)

Parlophone PMC 1202	**PLEASE PLEASE ME** (mono, with small "mono" on front cover)	30
Parlophone PCS 3042	**PLEASE PLEASE ME** (stereo, with small "stereo" on front cover)	40

(above pressings come with tracing-paper-lined ,"Use Emitex" die-cut inner sleeves)

LPs: 1966

FIRST PRESSINGS

(with "The Gramophone Co. Ltd.", & "Sold in UK ..." label text)

Parlophone PCS 7009	**REVOLVER** (G & L or E. J. Day sleeve; stereo)	80
Parlophone PMC 7016	**A COLLECTION OF BEATLES OLDIES** (G & L or E. J. Day sleeve; mono)	60
Parlophone PCS 7016	**A COLLECTION OF BEATLES OLDIES** (G & L or E. J. Day sleeve; stereo)	70

SECOND PRESSINGS

(with "The Gramophone Co. Ltd.", & "Sold in UK ..." label text)

Parlophone PMC 1255	**HELP!** (G & L sleeve; mono, with small solid black "mono" on front cover)	30
Parlophone PCS 3071	**HELP!** (G & L sleeve; stereo, with small solid black "stereo" on front cover)	45
Parlophone PMC 7009	**REVOLVER** (G & L or E. J. Day sleeve; mono)	60

(above pressings come with plain white or sepia "LP advertising" inner sleeves)

LPs: 1967

FIRST PRESSINGS

(with "The Gramophone Co. Ltd.", & " Sold in UK ..." label text)

Parlophone PMC 7027	**SGT. PEPPER'S LONELY HEARTS CLUB BAND** (G & L laminated gatefold sleeve, with red & white inner & cut-out insert; mono)	80
Parlophone PCS 7027	**SGT. PEPPER'S LONELY HEARTS CLUB BAND** (G & L laminated gatefold sleeve, with red & white inner & cut-out insert; stereo)	90

LPs: 1968

FIRST PRESSINGS

(with top-opening G & L gatefold sleeve, black inners, poster & 4 colour prints. Dark green label with "Sold in UK ..." text)

Apple PMC/PCS 7067/8	**THE BEATLES** (mono or stereo, numbered below 0000010)	8,000-10,000+
Apple PMC/PCS 7067/8	**THE BEATLES** (mono or stereo, numbered between 0000011 & 0001000)	1,000+
Apple PMC/PCS 7067/8	**THE BEATLES** (mono or stereo, numbered between 0001001 & 0010000)	500
Apple PMC 7067/8	**THE BEATLES** (mono, numbered above 0010000)	200
Apple PCS 7067/8	**THE BEATLES** (stereo, numbered above 0010000)	150

1969

FIRST PRESSINGS

(with G & L sleeve & black inners. Dark green label with& "Sold in UK ..." text)

Apple PMC 7070	**YELLOW SUBMARINE** (with red lines above & below rear sleevenote; mono)	250
Apple PCS 7070	**YELLOW SUBMARINE** (with red lines above & below rear sleevenote; stereo)	75
Apple PCS 7080	**GET BACK** (LP, unreleased, acetates only)	
Apple PCS 7088	**ABBEY ROAD** (black or plain white inner sleeve, with Apple logo aligned to Side 1 track listing on rear sleeve; with "Her Majesty" credit on label)	30

SECOND PRESSINGS

(with G & L sleeve. Label text with "The Gramophone Co. Ltd." but without "Sold in UK ...")

Parlophone PCS 3075	**RUBBER SOUL** (some with E. J. Day sleeve; stereo)	50
Parlophone PCS 7009	**REVOLVER** (stereo)	50
Parlophone PMC 7016	**A COLLECTION OF BEATLES OLDIES** (mono)	40
Parlophone PCS 7016	**A COLLECTION OF BEATLES OLDIES** (stereo)	50
Parlophone PCS 7027	**SGT. PEPPER'S LONELY HEARTS CLUB BAND** (gatefold sleeve, with white inner & cut-out insert; stereo)	50

(above pressings come with plain white or sepia "LP advertising" inner sleeves with G & L sleeve, black inners. Label text without "Sold in UK ...")

		MINT VALUE £
Apple PCS 7067/8	**THE BEATLES** (top-opening, numbered g/fold sl., poster & 4 colour prints; stereo)	60
Apple PCS 7070	**YELLOW SUBMARINE** (with red lines above & below rear sleevenote; stereo)	60

THIRD PRESSINGS

(with G & L sleeve. Label text with "The Gramophone Co. Ltd." but without "Sold in UK ...")

Parlophone PMC 1230	**A HARD DAY'S NIGHT** (small "mono" on front cover; mono)	35
Parlophone PCS 3058	**A HARD DAY'S NIGHT** (small "stereo" on front cover; stereo)	40
Parlophone PCS 3062	**BEATLES FOR SALE** (gatefold sleeve; stereo)	40
Parlophone PMC 1255	**HELP!** (small solid black "mono" on front cover; mono)	35
Parlophone PCS 3071	**HELP!** (small solid black "stereo" on front cover; stereo)	40
Parlophone PMC 1267	**RUBBER SOUL** (mono)	50
Parlophone PMC 7009	**REVOLVER** (mono)	50
Parlophone PMC 7027	**SGT. PEPPER'S LONELY HEARTS CLUB BAND** (laminated gatefold sleeve, & cut-out insert; mono)	60

(above pressings come with plain white or sepia "LP advertising" inner sleeves)

FOURTH PRESSINGS

(with G & L sleeve. Label text with "The Gramophone Co. Ltd." but without "Sold in UK ...")

Parlophone PCS 3045	**WITH THE BEATLES** (small "stereo" on front cover; stereo)	40

(above pressings have plain white or sepia "LP advertising" inner sleeves)

SEVENTH PRESSINGS

(with G & L sleeve & sepia "LP advertising" inner. Label has "The Gramophone Co. Ltd." but no "Sold in UK ...")

Parlophone PMC 1202	**PLEASE PLEASE ME** (small "mono" on front cover; mono)	50
Parlophone PCS 3042	**PLEASE PLEASE ME** (small "stereo" on front cover; stereo)	40

(Please Please Me, With The Beatles, A Hard Day's Night, Help!, Rubber Soul, Revolver, A Collection Of Beatles Oldies & Yellow Submarine were originally issued with ***flipback*** *sleeves. Beatles For Sale, Sgt. Pepper's Lonely Hearts Club Band & The Beatles have visible flaps inside gatefold sleeves. Abbey Road has internal flaps)*

LPs: 1970

FIRST PRESSINGS

(with G & L sleeve & dark green label)

Apple PXS 1	**LET IT BE** (box set, dark green label red Apple logo on rear sleeve & white inner, with *Get Back* book housed in black card tray ['PXS 1' not listed on package])	250
Apple/Lyntone LYN 2154	**FROM THEN TO YOU (The Beatles' Christmas Album)** (fan club issue, some with labels reversed)	260

SECOND PRESSING

Apple PCS 7096	**LET IT BE** (green Apple logo on rear sleeve, plain white inner)	15

EXPORT LPs: ORIGINALS

(with yellow/black labels, unless otherwise stated)

65	Parlophone CPCS 101	**SOMETHING NEW** (1st pressing, with "Parlophone Co. Ltd." label text)	600
65	Parlophone CPCS 101	**SOMETHING NEW** (2nd pressing, with "Gramophone Co. Ltd." label text)	400
66	Parlophone CPCS 103	**THE BEATLES' SECOND ALBUM**	500
66	Parlophone CPCS 104	**BEATLES VI**	500
68	Parlophone P-PCS 7067/8	**THE BEATLES** (2-LP, numbered, top opening 'mono' gatefold sleeve with "stereo" sticker & black inners, poster & 4 colour prints)	1,200
69	Odeon PPCS 7070	**YELLOW SUBMARINE** (Odeon sticker on rear of Apple sleeve)	2,000
69	Parlophone P-PCS 7088	**ABBEY ROAD** (Parlophone sticker on rear of Apple sleeve)	1,200
70	Parlophone P-PCS 7096	**LET IT BE**	1,200
70	Parlophone CPCS 106	**HEY JUDE** (silver/black label, one EMI boxed logo, laminated sleeve)	600

EXPORT LPs: REISSUES

(with silver/black labels, unless otherwise stated)

69	Parlophone CPCS 101	**SOMETHING NEW** (one EMI boxed logo)	250
69	Parlophone CPCS 103	**THE BEATLES' SECOND ALBUM** (one EMI boxed logo)	250
69	Parlophone CPCS 104	**BEATLES VI** (one EMI boxed logo)	250
69	Parlophone P-PCS 7088	**ABBEY ROAD** (Parlophone sticker on rear of Apple sleeve; one EMI boxed logo)	300
69	Apple CPCS 106	**HEY JUDE** (2nd reissue, dark green label)	150
70	Parlophone P-PCS 7096	**LET IT BE** (one EMI boxed logo)	400
70	Parl./Apple (P-)PCS 7096	**LET IT BE** (2nd reissue, Apple label [PCS 7096] in Parlophone sleeve)	50
70	Parlophone CPCS 103	**THE BEATLES' SECOND ALBUM** (2nd reissue, two EMI boxed logos)	250
70s	Parl./Apple (P-)CPCS 106	**HEY JUDE** (Apple label [CPCS 106] in Parlophone sleeve [P-CPSC 106])	75
73	Apple CPCS 106	**HEY JUDE** (3rd reissue, light green label)	35
78	Parlophone PCTC 255	**MAGICAL MYSTERY TOUR** (transparent yellow vinyl)	50
78	Apple PCS 7067/8	**THE BEATLES** (2-LP, white vinyl, gatefold sleeve)	70
78	Apple PCS 7088	**ABBEY ROAD** (green vinyl)	50
78	Apple PCS 7096	**LET IT BE** (white vinyl)	50

LPs: 1969 RE-PRESSINGS

(with laminated flipback sleeves & silver/black labels with ***one*** *boxed EMI logo)*

69	Parlophone PMC 1202	**PLEASE PLEASE ME** (mono)	50
69	Parlophone PCS 3042	**PLEASE PLEASE ME** (stereo)	20
69	Parlophone PCS 3045	**WITH THE BEATLES** (stereo only)	20
69	Parlophone PCS 3058	**A HARD DAY'S NIGHT** (stereo only)	20
69	Parlophone PCS 3062	**BEATLES FOR SALE** (gatefold sleeve, stereo only)	20
69	Parlophone PMC 1255	**HELP!** (mono)	50
69	Parlophone PCS 3071	**HELP!** (stereo)	20
69	Parlophone PCS 3075	**RUBBER SOUL** (stereo only)	20
69	Parlophone PCS 7009	**REVOLVER** (stereo only)	20
69	Parlophone PCS 7016	**A COLLECTION OF BEATLES OLDIES** (stereo only)	20
69	Parlophone PMC 7027	**SGT. PEPPER'S LONELY HEARTS CLUB BAND** (laminated gatefold sleeve, with cut-out insert, mono)	40
69	Parlophone PCS 7027	**SGT. PEPPER'S LONELY HEARTS CLUB BAND** (laminated gatefold sleeve, with cut-out insert, stereo)	20
73	Apple PCS 7067/8	**THE BEATLES** (2-LP, un-numbered, laminated, side-opening gatefold sleeve, with poster & 4 soft card colour prints, stereo only)	20
79	Parlophone PHO 7027	**SGT. PEPPER'S LONELY HEARTS CLUB BAND** (picture disc, die-cut sleeve)	15

LPs: 1980s RE-PRESSINGS

(lightweight vinyl with yellow/black labels listing "mono", unless otherwise stated)

MINT VALUE £

82	Parlophone PMC 1202	**PLEASE PLEASE ME** (mono)	15
82	Parlophone PMC 1206	**WITH THE BEATLES** (mono)	15
82	Parlophone PMC 1230	**A HARD DAY'S NIGHT** (mono)	15
82	Parlophone PMC 1240	**BEATLES FOR SALE** (gatefold sleeve, mono)	15
82	Parlophone PMC 1255	**HELP!** (mono)	15
82	Parlophone PMC 1267	**RUBBER SOUL** (mono)	15
82	Parlophone PMC 7009	**REVOLVER** (mono)	15
82	Parlophone PMC 7027	**SGT. PEPPER'S LONELY HEARTS CLUB BAND** (gatefold sleeve with cut-out inserts, mono)	15
82	Apple PMC 7067/8	**THE BEATLES** (2-LP, un-numbered, side-opening gatefold sleeve, with poster & 4 prints, light green Apple label; mono)	25
82	Apple PMC 7070	**YELLOW SUBMARINE** (light green Apple label; mono)	15

LPs: RETROSPECTIVES

76	Parlophone PCTC 255	**MAGICAL MYSTERY TOUR** (gatefold sleeve with 24-page stapled insert)	25
77	EMI EMTV 4	**THE BEATLES AT THE HOLLYWOOD BOWL** (gatefold sleeve with inner)	15
77	Parlophone PCSP 721	**LOVE SONGS** (2-LP, gatefold sleeve)	15
78	Apple PCSPR 717	**THE BEATLES 1962-1966** (2-LP, red vinyl, gatefold stickered sleeve with lyric inners; without sticker £15)	20
78	Apple PCSPB 718	**THE BEATLES 1967-1970** (2-LP, blue vinyl, gatefold stickered sleeve with lyric inners; without sticker £15)	20
79	Parlophone PCS 7184	**HEY JUDE** (black/silver label with two boxed EMI logos)	20
79	Parlophone PSLP 261	**RARITIES**	15
80	Parlophone PCS 7214	**THE BEATLES' BALLADS**	12
82	Parlophone EMTVS 34	**THE BEATLES' GREATEST HITS** (2-LP, unreleased)	
82	Parlophone PCS 7218	**REEL MUSIC** (with inner & 12-page insert)	15
80s	MFP MFP 50506	**ROCK 'N' ROLL MUSIC VOL. 1** (with George Martin's 1976 mixes)	12
80s	MFP MFP 50502	**ROCK 'N' ROLL MUSIC VOL. 2** (with George Martin's 1976 mixes)	12
80s	MFP MFP 41 5676	**THE BEATLES AT THE HOLLYWOOD BOWL**	15
88	HMV BPM 1	**PAST MASTERS VOLUME 1 & 2** (2-LP, gatefold sleeve)	25
94	Apple PCSP 726	**LIVE AT THE BBC** (2-LP, gatefold sleeve, with inners)	15
95	Apple PCSP 727	**ANTHOLOGY 1** (3-LP, gatefold sleeve, with inners)	15
96	Apple PCSP 728	**ANTHOLOGY 2** (3-LP, gatefold stickered sleeve, with inners)	15
96	Apple PCSP 729	**ANTHOLOGY 3** (3-LP, gatefold stickered sleeve, with inners)	15
99	Apple 521 4811	**YELLOW SUBMARINE SONGTRACK** (gatefold stickered sleeve)	20
99	Apple 521 4811	**YELLOW SUBMARINE SONGTRACK** (yellow vinyl, gatefold stickered sleeve)	15

REEL-TO-REEL TAPES: ORIGINALS

69	Apple DTA-PMC 7067/8	**THE BEATLES** (5" spool, mono)	50
69	Apple DTD-PCS 7067/8	**THE BEATLES** (5" spool, stereo)	40
70	Apple TA-PMC 7088	**ABBEY ROAD** (mono)	80
70	Apple TD-PCS 7088	**ABBEY ROAD** (stereo)	40
70	Apple TA-PMC 7096	**LET IT BE** (mono)	100
70	Apple TD-PCS 7096	**LET IT BE** (stereo)	40

(unless otherwise stated, the above issues were on 4" spools with printed leaders, and were housed in jewel cases with inlays)

REEL-TO-REEL TAPES: REISSUES

(issued on 4" spools with printed leaders, and housed in jewel cases with inlays)

68	Parlophone TA-PMC 1202	**PLEASE PLEASE ME** (mono)	15
68	Parlophone TD-PCS 3042	**PLEASE PLEASE ME** (stereo)	15
68	Parlophone TA-PMC 1206	**WITH THE BEATLES** (mono)	15
68	Parlophone TD-PCS 3045	**WITH THE BEATLES** (stereo)	15
68	Parlophone TA-PMC 1230	**A HARD DAY'S NIGHT** (mono)	15
68	Parlophone TD-PCS 3058	**A HARD DAY'S NIGHT** (stereo)	15
68	Parlophone TA-PMC 1240	**BEATLES FOR SALE** (mono)	15
68	Parlophone TD-PCS 3062	**BEATLES FOR SALE** (stereo)	15
68	Parlophone TA-PMC 1255	**HELP!** (mono)	15
68	Parlophone TD-PCS 3071	**HELP!** (stereo)	15
68	Parlophone TA-PMC 1267	**RUBBER SOUL** (mono)	15
68	Parlophone TD-PCS 3075	**RUBBER SOUL** (stereo)	15
68	Parlophone TA-PMC 7009	**REVOLVER** (mono)	15
68	Parlophone TD-PCS 7009	**REVOLVER** (stereo)	15
68	Parlophone TA-PMC 7016	**A COLLECTION OF BEATLES OLDIES** (mono)	15
68	Parlophone TD-PCS 7016	**A COLLECTION OF BEATLES OLDIES** (stereo)	15
68	Parlophone TA-PMC 7027	**SGT. PEPPER'S LONELY HEARTS CLUB BAND** (mono)	15
68	Parlophone TD-PCS 7027	**SGT. PEPPER'S LONELY HEARTS CLUB BAND** (stereo)	15

ALBUM BOX SETS

78	Parlophone BC 13	**THE BEATLES COLLECTION** (13 x LP, stereo, some with poster)	80
82	Parlophone BMC 10	**THE BEATLES MONO COLLECTION** (10 x LP, red box)	350

CD ALBUMS & BOX SETS

87	HMV BEACD 25/1	**PLEASE PLEASE ME/WITH THE BEATLES/A HARD DAY'S NIGHT/ BEATLES FOR SALE** (4 x CD, numbered 12" black box set with *Book Of Beatles Lists* paperback book)	100
87	HMV BEACD 25/2	**HELP!/RUBBER SOUL/REVOLVER** (3 x CD, numbered 12" red box set with insert & reprint of *Beatles Book Monthly*, issue 12)	50
87	HMV BEACD 25/3	**SGT. PEPPER'S LONELY HEARTS CLUB BAND** (CD, numbered 12" box set with booklet, cut-outs & badge)	25
87	HMV BEACD 25/4	**THE BEATLES** (2-CD, numbered 12" box set with booklet & badge)	30
87	HMV BEACD 25/5	**YELLOW SUBMARINE** (CD, numbered 12" box set with insert, cut-outs & badge)	35
87	HMV BEACD 25/6	**MAGICAL MYSTERY TOUR** (CD, numbered 12" box set with booklet, poster & badge)	35
87	HMV BEACD 25/7	**ABBEY ROAD** (CD, numbered 12" box set with 2 posters, booklet & badge)	20
87	HMV BEACD 25/8	**LET IT BE** (CD, numbered 12" box set with booklet & badge)	20
88	HMV BEACD 25/9	**PAST MASTERS VOL. 1** (CD, numbered 12" box set with booklet & badge)	15
88	HMV BEACD 25/10	**PAST MASTERS VOL. 2** (CD, numbered 12" box set with booklet & badge)	15

MINT VALUE £

POLYDOR RECORDINGS

SINGLES

(with push-out centres & orange labels, unless otherwise stated)

Year	Label	Title	£
62	**Polydor NH 66833**	**My Bonnie/The Saints (When The Saints Go Marching In)** (as Tony Sheridan & The Beatles; 1st pressing, 'broad' title & "Made In England" label text)	75
63	**Polydor NH 66833**	**My Bonnie/The Saints (When The Saints Go Marching In)** (as Tony Sheridan & The Beatles; 2nd pressing, push-out or solid centre, 'narrow' title & "Made In England" label text)	60
64	**Polydor NH 52906**	**Sweet Georgia Brown/Nobody's Child** (German import only, unissued in U.K.)	
64	**Polydor NH 52275**	**Cry For A Shadow** (A-side credited to 'Beatles')/ **TONY SHERIDAN & THE BEATLES: Why (Can't You Love Me Again)** ('scroll' label, with "Made In England" text)	50
64	**Polydor NH 52317**	**Ain't She Sweet** (A-side as 'The Beatles, vocal: John Lennon')**/If You Love Me, Baby** (B-side credited to 'The Beatles with Tony Sheridan, vocal'; 1st pressing, 'scroll' label with "Made In England" text)	60
64	**Polydor NH 52317**	**Ain't She Sweet/If You Love Me, Baby** (2nd pressing, red label, with "Made In England" text)	25

EPs

Year	Label	Title	£
64	**Polydor EPH 21 610**	**TONY SHERIDAN WITH THE BEATLES** (1st pressing, German import in U.K. p/s, orange 'scroll' label; "Why" songwriting credit as 'Sheridan' or 'Sheridan-Crompton')	50
64	**Polydor EPH 21 610**	**TONY SHERIDAN WITH THE BEATLES** (2nd pressing, German import in U.K. p/s, red label; "Why" songwriting credit as 'Sheridan' or 'Sheridan-Crompton')	25

LPs

Year	Label	Title	£
64	**Polydor Hi-Fi 46 432**	**THE BEATLES' FIRST** (purple/black sleeve, Germany only, unissued in U.K.)	
67	**Polydor Special 236 201**	**THE BEATLES' FIRST** (as Tony Sheridan & The Beatles, 1st pressing, without 'stereo' on label or sleeve, 'pop art' sleeve)	60
67	**Polydor Special 236 201**	**THE BEATLES' FIRST** (later pressings with 'stereo' on label & sleeve, minor label variations, 'pop art' sleeve)	40

CONTRACT PRESSINGS

(Records pressed by non-EMI companies on contract, owing to overwhelming demand; Decca contract pressings have no stamper letters (G or D) positioned at 3 o'clock to the matrix number; the centre has a ridge 3mm from the perimeter. Pye pressings have no stamper letters (G or D) at 3 o'clock to the matrix number; the centre has no ridge, and is finished with rough edges. Pye pressings are thicker and heavier than EMI and Decca pressings.)

SINGLES

Year	Label	Title	£
63	**Parlophone R 5055**	**She Loves You/I'll Get You** (Decca pressing)	50
63	**Parlophone R 5084**	**I Want To Hold Your Hand/This Boy** (Decca pressing)	50
63	**Parlophone R 5084**	**I Want To Hold Your Hand/This Boy** (Pye pressing)	50
64	**Parlophone R 5114**	**Can't Buy Me Love/You Can't Do That** (Pye pressing)	50
64	**Parlophone R 5200**	**I Feel Fine/She's A Woman** (Decca pressing)	50
64	**Parlophone R 5200**	**I Feel Fine/She's A Woman** (Pye pressing)	50
65	**Parlophone R 5305**	**Help!/I'm Down** (Decca pressing)	75
67	**Parlophone R 5655**	**Hello Goodbye/I Am The Walrus** (Decca pressing)	60
68	**Apple R 5722**	**Hey Jude/Revolution** (Decca pressing)	75
68	**Apple R 5722**	**Hey Jude/Revolution** (Philips pressing, three-pronged push-out centre)	150
68	**Apple R 5722**	**Hey Jude/Revolution** (Pye pressing)	75

LPs

(Decca contract pressings have no stamper letters (G or D) positioned at 3 o'clock to the matrix number; the label has a circular impression 15mm from the outer edge. Pye pressings are a dark, translucent red when held up to a strong light.)

Year	Label	Title	£
63	**Parlophone PMC 1202**	**PLEASE PLEASE ME** (Decca pressing)	300
63	**Parlophone PMC 1206**	**WITH THE BEATLES** (Decca pressing)	250
63	**Parlophone PMC 1206**	**WITH THE BEATLES** (Pye pressing)	500
68	**Parlophone P-PCS 7067/8**	**THE BEATLES** (export issue, yellow & black labels, Decca pressing)	4,000
69	**Parlophone P-PCS 7088**	**ABBEY ROAD** (export issue, yellow & black labels, Decca pressing)	3,000
69	**Parlophone P-PCS 7099**	**ABBEY ROAD** (export issue, silver & black labels, Decca pressing)	1,000
70s	**Apple PCSP 717**	**THE BEATLES 1962-1966** (2-LP, gatefold sleeve with lyric inners, Pye pressing)	150
84	**Parlophone/ Nimbus PCS 7027**	**SGT. PEPPER'S LONELY HEARTS CLUB BAND** (mail-order only, from *Practical Hi-Fi Magazine*, Nimbus pressing)	600

FRENCH PRESSINGS

SINGLE

Year	Label	Title	£
67	**Parlophone R 5655**	**Hello Goodbye/I Am The Walrus** (Pathé Marconi pressing)	50

LPs

(Parlophone label LPs have 'Made in France' on EMI rim copy. Apple label LPs have 'Made in France by Pathé Marconi EMI' rim copy. All discs are in British-printed sleeves bearing 'Made in France' stickers.)

Year	Label	Title	£
73	**Parlophone PCS 3042**	**PLEASE PLEASE ME**	20
73	**Parlophone PCS 3045**	**WITH THE BEATLES**	20
73	**Parlophone PCS 3058**	**A HARD DAY'S NIGHT**	20
73	**Parlophone PCS 3062**	**BEATLES FOR SALE** (gatefold sleeve)	20
73	**Parlophone PCS 3071**	**HELP!**	15
73	**Parlophone PCS 3075**	**RUBBER SOUL**	15
73	**Parlophone PCS 7009**	**REVOLVER**	15
73	**Parlophone PCS 7016**	**A COLLECTION OF BEATLES OLDIES**	15
73	**Parlophone PCS 7027**	**SGT. PEPPER'S LONELY HEARTS CLUB BAND** (gatefold sleeve with cut-out insert, some copies with banded vinyl)	15
73	**Apple PCS 7067/8**	**THE BEATLES** (2-LP, un-numbered, laminated, side-opening gatefold sleeve, with four colour prints & poster)	25
73	**Apple PCS 7070**	**YELLOW SUBMARINE**	15
73	**Apple PCS 7088**	**ABBEY ROAD** (some copies with banded vinyl)	15
73	**Apple PCS 7096**	**LET IT BE**	15
73	**Apple PCSP 717**	**THE BEATLES 1962-1966** (2-LP, gatefold sleeve with lyric inners)	25
73	**Apple PCSP 718**	**THE BEATLES 1967-1970** (2-LP, gatefold sleeve with lyric inners)	25

MINT VALUE £

MISPRINTS & MISPRESSINGS

SINGLES

63 Parlophone R 4983 **Please Please Me/Ask Me Why** (A-side actually plays 'Quiet Morning' by the Brian Fahey Orchestra) . . . 100
67 Parlophone R 5620 **All You Need Is Love/Baby You're A Rich Man** (with no reference to "Live World Television Transmission") . . . 100

EPs

64 Parlophone GEP 8882 **TWIST AND SHOUT** (label error: "Do You Want A Know A Secret") . . . 80
65 Parlophone GEP 8946 **THE BEATLES' MILLION SELLERS** (label error: "Beatles Golden Discs") . . . 35

LPs

64 Parlophone PCS 3062 **BEATLES FOR SALE** (label error: "I'm A Losser") . . . 400
65 Parlophone CPCS 101 **SOMETHING NEW** (export issue, label error: "Sold in UK") . . . 700
65 Parlophone PCS 3075 **RUBBER SOUL** (label error: "Norweigian Wood") . . . 400
66 Parlophone CPCS 106 **BEATLES VI** (export issue, label error: "Sold in UK") . . . 700
66 Parlophone PMC 7009 **REVOLVER** (copies with side 2 matrix no.: XEX 606-1 have 'Remix 11' of "Tomorrow Never Knows", G & L or E. J. Day sleeve; mono only) . . . 500
67 Parlophone PMC 7027 **SGT. PEPPER'S LONELY HEARTS CLUB BAND** (label omits "A Day In The Life" credit; G & L laminated gatefold sleeve, with plain white inner & insert; mono only) . . . 500
68 Apple PCS 7067/8 **THE BEATLES** (label error: "Rocky Racoon") . . . 350
69 Parlophone PMC 7027 **SGT. PEPPER'S LONELY HEARTS CLUB BAND** (mono; matrix YEX 637/8; plays stereo) . . . 600
69 Apple CPCS 106 **HEY JUDE** (label error: "Revolutions") . . . 500
69 Apple PCS 7088 **ABBEY ROAD** (Apple logo misaligned to Side 1 track listing on rear sleeve; with or without "Her Majesty" credit on label; black or plain white inner sleeve) . . . 120
69 Apple PCS 7088 **ABBEY ROAD** (label omits "Her Majesty") . . . 75
99 Parlophone PCS 3075 **RUBBER SOUL** (label error: pressed on Apple) . . . 200

(see also John Lennon, Paul McCartney/Wings, George Harrison, Ringo Starr, Pete Best Four, Quarry Men, Tony Sheridan, George Martin, Billy Preston, Yoko Ono)

BEATMEN

64 Pye 7N 15659 **You Can't Sit Down/Come On Pretty Baby** . . . 15
65 Pye 7N 15792 **Now The Sun Has Gone/Please Believe** . . . 10

BEAT MERCHANTS

64 Columbia DB 7367 **Pretty Face/Messin' With The Man** . . . 45
65 Columbia DB 7492 **So Fine/She Said Yeah** . . . 50

BEATS INTERNATIONAL

90 Go! Discs 8421961 **LET THEM EAT BINGO (LP, with free LP 'Bingo Beats')** . . . 12

BEAT SIX

64 Decca F 12011 **Bernadine/The River And I** . . . 15

(see also Guys)

BEATSTALKERS

65 Decca F 12259 **Ev'rybody's Talking 'Bout My Baby/Mr. Disappointed** . . . 40
66 Decca F 12352 **Left Right Left/You'd Better Get A Better Hold On** . . . 40
66 Decca F 12460 **A Love Like Yours/Base Line** . . . 25
67 CBS 2732 **My One Chance To Make It/Ain't No Soul (Left In These Old Shoes)** . . . 35
67 CBS 3105 **Silver Treetop School For Boys/Sugar Coated Man** . . . 35
68 CBS 3557 **Rain Coloured Roses/Everything Is For You** . . . 35
69 CBS 3936 **When I'm Five/Little Boy** . . . 35

PAUL BEATTIE

57 Parlophone R 4385 **I'm Comin' Home/Nothing So Strange** . . . 40
58 Parlophone R 4429 **Me, Please Me/Wanderlust** . . . 10
58 Parlophone R 4468 **A House, A Car, And A Wedding Ring/Banana** . . . 20

E.C. BEATTY

59 Felsted AF 127 **Ski King/I'm A Lucky Man** . . . 30
59 Felsted AF 127 **Ski King/I'm A Lucky Man (78)** . . . 10

BEAU

69 Dandelion S 4403 **1917 Revolution/Sleeping Town** . . . 7
69 Dandelion S 63751 **BEAU (LP)** . . . 25
71 Dandelion DAN 8006 **CREATION (LP, with The Way We Live)** . . . 25

(see also Way We Live)

BEAU BRUMMELS

65 Pye International 7N 25293 **Laugh, Laugh/Still In Love With You Baby** . . . 12
65 Pye International 7N 25306 **Just A Little/They'll Make You Cry** . . . 12
65 Pye International 7N 25318 **You Tell Me Why/I Want You** . . . 12
65 Pye International 7N 25333 **Don't Talk To Strangers/In Good Time** . . . 12
66 Pye International 7N 25342 **Good Time Music/Sad Little Girl (unissued)**
65 Pye International NPL 28062 **INTRODUCING THE BEAU BRUMMELS (LP, mono only)** . . . 45

BEAU-MARKS

60 Top Rank JAR 377 **Clap Your Hands/Daddy Said** . . . 40

(see also Del-Tones, Milton De Lugg Orchestra)

JIMMY BEAUMONT

66 London HLZ 10059 **You Got Too Much Going For You/I Never Loved Her Anyway** . . . 50

BEAUMONT HANNANT

93 GPR GENP(X) 14 **TASTES AND TEXTURES VOLUME 1 EP (12", p/s)** . . . 8
93 GPR GPRLP 2 **BASIC DATA MANIPULATION: TASTES & TEXTURES VOL. 2 (12" EP, double pack)** . . . 15
93 GPR GENP(X) 21 **TASTES AND TEXTURES VOL. 3 (12" EP, p/s)** . . . 8
94 GPR GENP(X) 33 **ORMEAU EP (12", custom sleeve)** . . . 8
94 GPR GENP(R) 33 **ORMEAU EP (with Joseph Johnson) (12", custom sleeve)** . . . 8
94 GPR GENP(CD) 33 **ORMEAU EP (with Lisa Husik) (CD)** . . . 8

MINT VALUE £

95 GPR GENP(X) 37 PSI - ONYX EP (12", double pack, custom sleeve) . . . 8
95 GPR GENP(CD) 37 PSI - ONYX CONCEPT EP (CD) . . . 8
95 GPR GENP(X) 39 NOTIONS OF TONALITY VOL. 1 (12" EP, custom sleeve) . . . 8
95 GPR GENP(R) 39 NOTIONS OF TONALITY VOL. 1 (12" EP, custom sleeve) . . . 8
95 GPR GENP(CD) 39 NOTIONS OF TONALITY VOL. 1 (CD EP, compilation of above 12"s) . . . 8
96 GPR GENP(X) 40 NOTIONS OF TONALITY VOL. 2 (12" EP, custom sleeve) . . . 8
96 GRP GENP(R) 40 NOTIONS OF TONALITY VOL. 2 (12" EP, custom sleeve) . . . 8
96 GPR GENP(CD) 40 NOTIONS OF TONALITY VOL. 2 (CD EP, compilation of above 12"s) . . . 8

BEAVER & KRAUSE

72 Warner Bros K 46130 GANDHARVA (LP) . . . 15
72 Warner Bros K 46184 ALL GOOD MEN (LP) . . . 15

BEAVERS

58 Capitol CL 14909 Road To Happiness/Low As I Can Be . . . 10

JACKIE BEAVERS

75 Buddah BDS 423 Mr Bump Man/Somebody Help The Bigger Man . . . 10
76 Jay Boy BOY 102 Trying To Get Back To You Girl/Trying To Get Back To You Girl (Version) . . . 8

BEAZERS

64 Decca F 11827 The Blue Beat/I Wanna Shout . . . 35
(see also Chris Farlowe, Little Joe Cook)

BE-BOP DELUXE

73 Smile LAFS 001 Teenage Archangel/Jets At Dawn (mono, 1,000 only) . . . 25
74 Harvest HAR 5081 Jet Silver (And The Dolls Of Venus)/Third Floor Heaven . . . 8
75 Harvest HAR 5091 Between The Worlds/Lights (withdrawn) . . . 40+
75 Harvest HAR 5098 Maid In Heaven/Lights . . . 5
76 Harvest HAR 5110 Kiss Of The Light/FUNKY PHASER & HIS UNEARTHLY MERCHANDISE: Shine . . . 5
77 Harvest HAR 5135 Japan/Futuristic Manifesto . . . 5
78 Harvest HAR 5147 Panic In The World/Blue As A Jewel . . . 5
78 Harvest HAR 5158 Electrical Language/Surreal Estate (p/s) . . . 5
77 Harvest SHVL 816 LIVE! IN THE AIR AGE (LP, with bonus EP "Live! In The Air Age" [PSR 412]) . . . 12
(see also Bill Nelson)

BE-BOP PRESERVATION SOCIETY

71 Dawn DNLS 3027 THE BE-BOP PRESERVATION SOCIETY (LP, gatefold sleeve with insert) . . . 40

GILBERT BECAUD

59 HMV POP 574 The Day The Rains Came/Les Marches De Provence . . . 7
59 HMV POP 574 The Day The Rains Came/Les Marches De Provence (78) . . . 10

SIDNEY BECHET

50 Melodisc 1103 Some Of These Days/Black & Blue (78) . . . 7
50 Melodisc 1105 I Told You Once, I Told You Twice/Georgia (78) . . . 7
54 Vogue V 2391 Royal Garden Blues/Mon Homme . . . 6
58 Vogue V 2394 Theme From The "Threepenny Opera"/Army Song . . . 5
59 Vogue V 9141 Petit Fleur/Dans La Rue D'Antibes . . . 15
59 Vogue V 9157 Le Marchand de Poissons/Si Tu Vois Ma Mere . . . 5
60 Philips JAZ 110 My Woman's Blues/What A Dream (p/s) . . . 5
55 Vogue EPV 1020 SOUVENIRS OF NEW ORLEANS (EP) . . . 8
55 Melodisc EPM 7-51 SIDNEY BECHET WITH HUMPHREY LYTTELTON'S BAND (EP) . . . 20
56 Melodisc EPM 7-62 BECHET/SPANIER BIG FOUR (EP, with Mugsy Spanier) . . . 10
56 Melodisc EPM 7-68 BECHET-SPANIER IN NEW YORK, BECHET-LYTTELTON IN LONDON (EP) . . . 10
64 Melodisc MLP 12-148 REQUIEM A BECHET (LP) . . . 20
(see also Humphrey Lyttelton, Mezz Mezzrow)

BECHET-NICHOLAS BLUE FIVE

50 Jazz Parade E1 Old Stack O' Lee Blues/Bechet's Fantasy (12" 78) . . . 7

BECHET-SPANIER BIG FOUR

50 Melodisc 8001 Four Or Five Times/China Boy (12" 78) . . . 8

BECK

94 Geffen GFS 67 Loser/Alcohol/Fume (p/s) . . . 12
94 Geffen GFSJB 67 Loser/Loser (jukebox issue, no p/s) . . . 12
94 Geffen GFSTD 67 Loser/Totally Confused/Corvette Bummer/MTV Makes Me Want To Smoke Crack (Lounge Act Version) (CD) . . . 12
94 Geffen GFS 74 Pay No Mind (Snoozer)/Special People (withdrawn) . . . 60
94 Geffen GFSC 74 Pay No Mind (Snoozer)/Special People (cassette, unreleased)
94 Geffen GFST 74 Pay No Mind (Snoozer)/Special People/Trouble All My Days/ Super Golden (Sunchild) (12", p/s, withdrawn) . . . 20
94 Geffen GFST 74 Pay No Mind (Snoozer)/Special People/Trouble All My Days/ Super Golden (Sunchild) (CD, withdrawn) . . . 10
94 Geffen GFS 19235 Beercan/Spanking Room (p/s, 1500 copies) . . . 25
96 Geffen GFS 22183 Devil's Haircut/Lloyd Price Express (p/s) . . . 7
96 Geffen GFS 22205 The New Pollution/Electric Music And The Summer People (p/s) . . . 7
97 Geffen GFS 22253 Sissyneck/Feather In Your Cap (p/s) . . . 7
97 Select SELECT 12 Clock/The Little Drum Machine Boy/Totally Confused (with/without *Select* mag) . . . 10/8
97 Geffen GFS 22293 Deadweight (Edit)/Erase The Sun (p/s) . . . 7
98 Geffen GFS 22365 Tropicalia (LP Version)/Halo Of Gold (p/s) . . . 7
99 Geffen 497182-7 Sexxlaws/Salt In The Wound (picture disc, stickered p/s) . . . 6
00 Geffen 497312-7 Mixed Bizness/(Dirty Bixin Mizness Remix) (gatefold p/s) . . . 5
97 Geffen GFSTD 22205 New Pollution/Electric Music And The Summer People (p/s) . . . 8
96 Geffen GED 24908 ODELAY (CD, with bonus track "Diskobox" & unlisted track "Clock") . . . 18

GORDON BECK (QUARTET)

68 Morgan MJ 1 GYROSCOPE (LP) . . . 400
69 M. Minor MMLP/SMLP 21 EXPERIMENTS WITH POPS (LP, as Gordon Beck Quartet) . . . 150
69 M. Minor MMLP/SMLP 22 HALF A JAZZ SIXPENCE (LP) . . . 125
69 Major Minor SMLP 88 DR. DOOLITTLE LOVES JAZZ (LP) . . . 50
72 Dire FO 341 BECK-MATTHEWSON-HUMAIR TRIO (LP) . . . 50
(see also Seven Ages Of Man)

MINT VALUE £

JEFF BECK

67	Columbia DB 8151	Hi-Ho Silver Lining/Beck's Bolero	15
67	Columbia DB 8227	Tallyman/Rock My Plimsoul	15
68	Columbia DB 8359	Love Is Blue (L'Amour Est Bleu)/I've Been Drinking	12
69	Columbia DB 8590	Plinth (Water Down The Drain)/Hangman's Knee (unissued)	
72	Epic EPC 7720	Got The Feeling/Situation	8
75	Epic EPC 3334	She's A Woman/It Doesn't Really Matter	12
80	Epic EPC 8806	The Final Peace/Space Boogie	8
80	Epic EPCA 1009	The Final Peace/Scatter Brain/Too Much To Lose/Led Boots (12", p/s)	12
82	Rak RRP 3	Hi Ho Silver Lining/Beck's Bolero/Rock My Plimsoul (picture disc)	6
68	Columbia S(C)X 6293	TRUTH (LP, 1st pressing, blue/black labels, mono/stereo)	55/40
69	Columbia S(C)X 6351	BECK-OLA (LP, 1st pressing, mono/stereo)	35/28
69	Columbia SCX 6293	TRUTH (LP, 2nd pressing, silver/black labels, mono/stereo)	15
69	Columbia SCX 6351	BECK-OLA (LP, 2nd pressing, silver/black labels, mono/stereo)	12
72	Epic EPC 64619	ROUGH AND READY (LP, yellow label)	18
72	Epic EPC 64899	JEFF BECK GROUP (LP, yellow label)	20
72	Epic EQ 30973	ROUGH AND READY (LP, quadrophonic)	22
74	CBS EQ 31331	JEFF BECK GROUP (LP, quadrophonic)	25
76	Epic EPC 32067	WIRED (LP)	12

(see also Yardbirds, Beck Bogert Appice, Donovan, Rod Stewart, Cozy Powell, Honeydrippers, Buddy Guy with Jeff Beck)

BECK, BOGERT & APPICE

73	Epic S EPC 1251	Black Cat Moan/Livin' Alone	7
73	CBS EPC 22001	BECK, BOGERT & APPICE (LP)	15
75	CBS EQ 32140/Q 65455	BECK, BOGERT & APPICE (LP, quadrophonic)	20

(see also Jeff Beck, Vanilla Fudge, Cactus)

HAROLD BECKETT

71	Philips 6308 026	FLARE UP (LP)	110
72	RCA SF 8225	WARM SMILES (LP)	65
73	RCA SF 8264	THEME FOR FEGA (LP)	25
75	Cadillac SGC 1004	JOY UNLIMITED (LP)	30
76	Ogun OG 800	MEMORIES OF BACARES (LP, as Harry Beckett's Joy Unlimited)	15
70s	Ogun OG 020	GOT IT MADE (LP, as Harry Beckett's Joy Unlimited)	12

(see also Graham Collier, Galliard, Ninesense)

STUART BECKETT

60s	Sherwood SRS 1001	Kariline/Breakthrough	30

JENNY BECKETT

65	Parlophone R 5373	My Love And I/Lock Away Your Love	7

(KEE)LYN BECKFORD

68	Island WI 3144	Combination/Hey Little Girl	30
69	Jackpot JP 707	Kiss Me Quick/MRS. MILLER: Feel It	15
69	Big Shot BI 521	Suzie Wong (as K. Beckford)/SWINGING KINGS: Deebo	25
71	G.G. GG 4514	Groove Me/Groove Version (as Keeling Beckford)	20

THEO(PHILUS) BECKFORD

61	Blue Beat BB 33	Jack And Jill Shuffle/Little Lady (as Theophilus Beckford & Clue J. & His Blues Blasters)	30
61	Blue Beat BB 50	Georgie And The Old Shoe/That's Me (as Theo Beckford & City Slickers)	25
62	Blue Beat BB 87	Walking Down King Street/The Clock (B-side actually by Sir D's Group)	25
62	Blue Beat BB 132	Bringing In The Sheep (song actually "Bringing In The Sheaves")/Run Away	25
62	Island WI 026	I Don't Want You (actually by King Edward's All Stars)/Seven Long Years	25
63	Island WI 106	Daphney/Boller Man	25
64	Blue Beat BB 250	She's Gone/Old Flame (as Cotheo Beckford, B-side act. by Frederick Hibbert)	25
64	Blue Beat BB 257	Don't Worry To Cry/Love Me Or Leave Me (as Theophilus Beckford, B-side actually by Lloyd Clarke)	25
64	Blue Beat BB 287	On Your Knees/Now You're Gone (with Yvonne Harrison)	25
65	Blue Beat BB 303	Dig The Dig (as Basil Gabbidon)/Don't Let Me Cry No More	25
65	Black Swan WI 452	Take Your Time/STRANGER COLE: Happy-Go-Lucky	25
65	Island WI 238	Trench Town People/PIONEERS: Sometime	25
65	Island WI 243	You Are The One Girl/Grudgeful People	25
65	Island WI 246	If Life Was A Thing/L. CLARKE: Parro Saw The Light (B-side actually "Pharaoh Saw The Light" by Lloyd Clarke)	25
65	Island WI 248	What A Whoe/Bajan Girl	25
68	Nu Beat NB 009	Easy Snappin'/ERIC MORRIS: My Lonely Days	15
69	Crab CRAB 25	Brother Ram Goat (as T. Beckford)/STARLIGHTS: What A Condition	15

(see also Eric Barnet[t], Maytals, Clue J & His Bluesblasters)

BOB BECKHAM

59	Brunswick 05808	Just As Much As Ever/Your Sweet Love	10
60	Brunswick 05822	Crazy Arms/Beloved	15
60	Brunswick 05835	Mais Oui/Only The Broken Hearted	5
60	Brunswick 05837	Nothing Is Forever/Two Wrongs Don't Make A Right	5
60	Brunswick 05837	Nothing Is Forever/Two Wrongs Don't Make A Right (78)	5

DAVID BEDFORD

70	Argo ZRG 638	MUSIC FOR ALBION MOONLIGHT (LP, 1 side by Elizabeth Lutyens)	25
72	Dandelion 2310 165	NURSE'S SONG WITH ELEPHANTS (LP, gatefold sleeve)	25

(see also Coxhill/Bedford Trio, Kevin Ayers & Whole World, Mike Oldfield)

BEDLAM

73	Chrysalis CFB 1	I Believe In You/Whiskey And Wine	8
73	Chrysalis CHR 1048	BEDLAM (LP)	25

(see also Cozy Powell, Ace Kefford Stand, Big Bertha)

BEDROCKS

68	Columbia DB 8516	Ob-La-Di, Ob-La-Da/Lucy	6

MINT VALUE £

EDWIN BEE
68 Decca F 12781 I've Been Loving You/Call For My Baby . . . 6

MOLLY BEE
57 London HLD 8400 Since I Met You, Baby/I'll Be Waiting For You . . . 40
57 London HLD 8400 Since I Met You, Baby/I'll Be Waiting For You (78) . . . 10
58 Capitol CL 14849 Going Steady (With A Dream)/Magic Mirror . . . 10
58 Capitol CL 14880 Don't Look Back/Please Don't Talk About Me When I'm Gone . . . 5
58 Capitol CL 14949 After You've Gone/Five Points Of A Star . . . 5
65 MGM MGM 1280 Single Girl Again/Keep It A Secret . . . 10

BEE BEE CEE
77 Rel RE 48-S You Gotta Know Girl/We Ain't Listening (p/s) . . . 70

BEEFEATERS
64 Pye International 7N 25277 Please Let Me Love You/Don't Be Long . . . 120
70 Elektra 2101 007 Please Let Me Love You/Don't Be Long (reissue) . . . 30
(see also Byrds)

BEE GEES
67 Polydor 56727 Spicks And Specks/I Am The World . . . 12
67 Polydor 56161 New York Mining Disaster 1941/I Can't See Nobody . . . 5
67 Polydor 56178 To Love Somebody/Close Another Door . . . 5
67 Polydor 56192 Massachusetts/Barker Of The U.F.O. . . . 5
67 Polydor 56220 World/Sir Geoffrey Saved The World . . . 5
68 Polydor 56229 Words/Sinking Ships . . . 5
68 Polydor 56242 Jumbo/The Singer Sang His Song . . . 5
68 Polydor 56273 I've Gotta Get A Message To You/Kitty Can . . . 5
69 Polydor 56304 Odessa Parts 1 & 2 (unissued)
69 Polydor 56304 First Of May/Lamplight . . . 5
69 Polydor 56331 Tomorrow Tomorrow/Sun In The Morning . . . 5
69 Polydor 56343 Don't Forget To Remember/The Lord . . . 5
70 Polydor 56377 I.O.I.O./Sweetheart . . . 5
70 Polydor 2001 104 Lonely Days/Man For All Seasons . . . 5
71 Polydor 2058 115 How Can You Mend A Broken Heart/Country Woman . . . 5
77 RSO 2090224 Children Of The World/Boogie Child . . . 5
67 Polydor 582/583 012 BEE GEES FIRST (LP) . . . 18
68 Polydor 582/583 020 HORIZONTAL (LP) . . . 18
68 Polydor 236 221 RARE PRECIOUS AND BEAUTIFUL (LP) . . . 18
68 Polydor 236 513 RARE PRECIOUS AND BEAUTIFUL VOL. 2 (LP) . . . 18
68 Polydor 582/583 036 IDEA (LP) . . . 18
69 Polydor 236 556 RARE PRECIOUS AND BEAUTIFUL VOL. 3 (LP) . . . 18
69 Polydor 582 049/050 ODESSA (2-LP, felt cover) . . . 30
70 Polydor 2383 010 CUCUMBER CASTLE (LP) . . . 15
70 Polydor 2310 069 TWO YEARS ON (LP) . . . 15
71 Polydor 2383 052 TRAFALGAR (LP) . . . 15
72 Polydor 2383 139 TO WHOM IT MAY CONCERN (LP) . . . 12
(see also Barry Gibb, Robin Gibb, Maurice Gibb, Humpy Bong, Fut)

BEEKEEPERS
81 Rundown ACE 40 PLATFORM FIVE EP . . . 10

MARK BEER
81 My China TAO 001 DUST ON THE ROAD (LP) . . . 15

BEES (UK)
01 We Love You ARMOUR 120 YOU GOT TO LEAVE EP (p/s, 500 only) . . . 8

BEES
67 Blue Beat BB 386 Jesse James Rides Again/The Girl In My Dreams . . . 15
68 Columbia Blue Beat DB 111 The Prisoner From Alcatraz/The Ska's The Limit . . . 10

BEES MAKE HONEY
73 EMI EMI 2078 Knee Trembler/Caldonia . . . 5
72 EMI EMC 3013 MUSIC EVERY NIGHT (LP) . . . 15

BEEZ
79 Edible SNACK 001 Easy/Vagrant (gatefold p/s) . . . 65
78 Edible SNACK 002 THE BEEZ EP: Do The Suicide (no p/s) . . . 65

B.E.F. (British Electric Foundation)
91 Ten TEN 386 Free (Edit)/Secret Life Of Arabia (stickered p/s, as B.E.F. featuring Billy MacKenzie, unissued, 200 copies only) . . . 50
80 Virgin V 2888 MUSIC FOR STOWAWAYS (cassette) . . . 12
80 Virgin V 2888 MUSIC FOR STOWAWAYS (LP, unissued, white label test pressing with press release) . . . 30
81 Virgin BEF 1 MUSIC FOR LISTENING TO (LP, export issue) . . . 12
82 Virgin VV 2219 MUSIC OF QUALITY & DISTINCTION VOL. 1 (5 x 7" box set & insert) . . . 12
(see also Heaven 17, Billy MacKenzie)

BEGGARS FARM
84 White Rabbit WR 1001 THE DEPTH OF A DREAM (LP) . . . 25

BEGGARS HILL
76 Moonshine MS 60 BEGGARS HILL (LP, private pressing) . . . 190

BEGGARS OPERA
70 Vertigo 6059 026 Sarabande/Think . . . 15
72 Vertigo 6059 060 Hobo/Pathfinder . . . 12
73 Vertigo 6059 088 Two Timing Woman/Lady Of Hell Fire . . . 8
74 Vertigo 6059 105 Classical Gas/Sweet Blossom Woman . . . 6
70 Vertigo 6360 018 ACT ONE (LP, swirl label, gatefold sleeve) . . . 30
71 Vertigo 6360 054 WATERS OF CHANGE (LP, swirl label, gatefold sleeve) . . . 30
72 Vertigo 6360 073 PATHFINDER (LP, swirl label, foldout poster cover) . . . 30
73 Vertigo 6360 090 GET YOUR DOG OFF ME! (LP, 'spaceship' label) . . . 15

MINT VALUE £

BEGINNING OF THE END

71	Atlantic 2091 097	Funky Nassau Parts 1 & 2 (initially red label)	8/6
71	Atlantic K 40304	FUNKY NASSAU (LP, gatefold sleeve)	25

BRENDAN BEHAN

60	HMV 7EG 8491	THE HOSTAGE (EP)	12
60	Argo RG 239	THE HOSTAGE (LP)	15

DOMINIC BEHAN

59	Decca F 11147	The Bells Of Hell/The Captains And The Kings	5
59	Decca F 11147	The Bells Of Hell/The Captains And The Kings (78)	10
60	Topic STOP 115	The Patriot Game/Erin Go Brath (p/s)	5
64	Piccadilly 7N 35172	Liverpool Lou/Love Is Where You Find It	5
58	Collector JEL 3	SONGS OF THE STREETS (EP)	18
60	Topic 12T 35	DOWN BY THE LIFFEYSIDE — IRISH STREET BALLADS (LP)	18
61	Topic 12T 44	EASTER WEEK AND AFTER — SONGS OF "THE TROUBLES" (LP)	18
66	Pye NPL 18134	IRELAND SINGS (LP)	15
69	Marble Arch MAL 1123	ARKLE (LP)	15

(see also Ewan MacColl)

BIX BEIDERBECKE & HIS GANG

60	Philips JAZ 116	Since My Best Gal Turned Me Down/At The Jazz Band Ball	5
55	Columbia SEG 7523	BIX BEIDERBECKE AND HIS ORCHESTRA (EP)	12
56	Columbia SEG 7577	BIX BEIDERBECKE (EP)	12
55	Columbia 33SL 1035	THE GREAT BIX (10" LP)	20

(HARRY) BELAFONTE

54	HMV 7M 202	Hold 'Em Joe/Suzanne (Every Night When The Sun Goes Down)	5
54	HMV 7M 224	I'm Just A Country Boy/Pretty As A Rainbow	5
55	Capitol CL 14312	Close Your Eyes/I Still Get A Thrill (Thinking Of You)	5
57	HMV POP 308	Banana Boat Song (Day-O)/Jamaica Farewell	5
57	HMV POP 339	Mama Looka Boo Boo/Don't Ever Love Me	5
57	HMV POP 360	Scarlet Ribbons (For Her Hair)/Hold 'Em Joe	5
57	RCA RCA 1007	Island In The Sun/Coconut Woman	5
58	RCA RCA 1033	Judy Drowned/Lucy's Door	5
58	RCA RCA 1035	Lead Man Holler/Haiti Cherie	5
59	RCA RCA 1116	Darlin' Cora/Turn Around	5
59	RCA RCA 1125	Fifteen/Round The Bay Of Mexico	5
61	RCA RCA 1247	Hole In The Bucket (with Odetta)/Chickens	5
56	Capitol EAP1 619	CLOSE YOUR EYES (EP)	8
57	HMV 7EG 8211	CALYPSO (EP)	8
57	HMV 7EG 8259	MATHILDA MATHILDA (EP)	8
57	HMV DLP 1147	THE VERSATILE MR. BELAFONTE (10" LP)	15
57	HMV CLP 1122	MARK TWAIN AND OTHER FOLK FAVOURITES (LP)	15
57	RCA RC 24005	BELAFONTE SINGS OF THE CARIBBEAN (10" LP)	12
59	RCA RD 27129	PORGY AND BESS (LP, with Lena Horne)	12
59	RCA SF 5050	BELAFONTE AT CARNEGIE HALL (LP, stereo)	12
60	RCA SF 5058	MY LORD, WHAT A MORNIN'! (LP, stereo)	12
61	RCA SF 5061	SWING DAT HAMMER (LP, stereo)	12
61	RCA SF 5088	BELAFONTE RETURNS TO CARNEGIE HALL (LP, stereo)	12

(see also Lena Horne)

BELBORN

01	World Serpent WS7 005	Seelenruhe/Phoenix (picture disc)	5

BEL CANTOS

65	R&B MRB 5003	Feel Aw Right Parts 1 & 2	25

BELFAST GYPSIES

66	Island WI 3007	Gloria's Dream/Secret Police	50
77	Sonet SNTF 738	THEM BELFAST GYPSIES (LP)	35

(see also Them, Jackie McAuley, Freaks Of Nature)

ED 'TEX' BELIN

63	Starlite STEP 39	ED 'TEX' BELIN (EP)	18
67	Starlite GRK 509	ED 'TEX' BELIN (EP, reissue)	12

ALEXANDER BELL

67	CBS 2977	Alexander Bell Believes/Hymn ... With Love	10

ARCHIE BELL & THE DRELLS

68	Atlantic 584 185	Tighten Up/Dog Eat Dog	12
68	Atlantic 584 217	I Can't Stop Dancing/You're Such A Beautiful Child	10
71	Atlantic 2091 156	Tighten Up/I Can't Stop Dancing/(There's Gonna Be A) Showdown	8
72	Atlantic K 10210	Here I Go Again/A World Without Music	6
73	Atlantic K 10263	There's Gonna Be A Showdown/Tighten Up	6
76	Portrait TA 7254	Don't Let Love Get You Down/Where Will You Go When The Party's Over/ The Soul City Walk (12")	8
68	Atlantic	TIGHTEN UP (LP)	50
72	Atlantic K 40454	HERE I GO AGAIN (LP)	20

BELINDA BELL

73	Columbia DB 8995	If Only You Believe/Stone Valley	5
73	Columbia SCXA 9255	STONE VALLEY (LP, gatefold sleeve)	16
73	One Up OU 2009	MUSIC OF W. GULGOWSKI (LP)	12

BENNY BELL & BLOCK BUSTERS

57	Parlophone R 4372	The Sack Dress/Dr. Jazz	15

CAREY BELL

60s	Delmark DS 622	CAREY BELL'S BLUES HARP (LP)	12

CHARLES BELL & CONTEMPORARY JAZZ QUARTET

63 London HA-K/SH-K 8095 ANOTHER DIMENSION (LP) . . . 15

ERIC BELL BAND

81 Hobo HOS 016 Lonely Man/Anyone Seen My Baby (p/s) . . . 30
(see also Thin Lizzy, Noel Redding Band)

FREDDIE BELL & BELLBOYS

56 Mercury MT 122 Giddy-Up-A Ding Dong/I Said It And I'm Glad (78) . . . 10
57 Mercury MT 141 Hucklebuck/Rompin' And Stompin' (78) . . . 10
57 Mercury MT 146 Teach You To Rock/Take The First Train Out Of Town (78) . . . 10
57 Mercury MT 149 Big Bad Wolf/Rockin' The Polonaise (78) . . . 10
57 Mercury MT 159 Rockin' Is My Business/You're Gonna Be Sorry (78) . . . 10
56 Mercury MEP 9508 ROCK WITH THE BELL BOYS (EP) . . . 35
57 Mercury MEP 9512 ROCK WITH THE BELL BOYS VOL. 2 (EP) . . . 60

FREDRICK BELL

68 Nu Beat NB 004 Rocksteady Cool/CARLTON ALPHONSO: I Have Changed . . . 20

GARY BELL

67 CBS 202234 Is This What I Get For Loving You?/To Keep You . . . 18
67 CBS 2646 Anyway That You Want Me/Leave It To Me . . . 10

GRAHAM BELL

66 Polydor 56067 How Can I Say I Don't Love You/If You're Gonna Go . . . 7
72 Charisma CB 201 Too Many People/Before You're A Man . . . 5
73 Charisma CB 209 You Need A 60 Minute Man/The Whole Town Wants You Hung . . . 5
75 Charisma CB 250 You Need A 60 Minute Man/That's The Way It Is . . . 5
72 Charisma CAS 1061 GRAHAM BELL (LP) . . . 15
(see also Heavy Jelly, Griffin, Every Which Way, Skip Bifferty, Bell & Arc)

MADELINE BELL

63 HMV POP 1215 I Long For Your Love/Because You Didn't Care . . . 12
64 Columbia DB 7257 You Don't Love Me No More/Don't Cross Over To My Side Of The Street . . . 12
65 Columbia DB 7512 Daytime/Don't Cry My Heart . . . 10
65 Philips BF 1448 What The World Needs Now Is Love/I Can't Wait To See My Baby's Face . . . 15
66 Philips BF 1501 Don't Come Running To Me/I Got Carried Away . . . 15
66 Philips BF 1526 One Step At A Time/You Won't See Me . . . 7
67 Philips BF 1611 Picture Me Gone/Go Ahead On . . . 30
68 Philips BF 1656 I'm Gonna Make You Love Me/I'm Gonna Leave You . . . 10
68 Philips BF 1688 Thinkin'/Don't Give Your Love Away . . . 6
68 Philips BF 1726 Hold It/What Am I Supposed To Do? . . . 7
69 Philips BF 1799 We're So Much In Love/How Much Do I Love You . . . 6
71 Philips 6006 082 If You Didn't Hear Me The First Time/You Walked Away . . . 5
67 Philips (S)BL 7818 BELLS A POPPIN' (LP) . . . 30
68 Philips SBL 7865 DOIN' THINGS (LP) . . . 30
(see also Seven Ages Of Man, Underground, Ian Green [Revelation])

SIMON BELL

78 Pye 7N 46050 Givin' It Plenty/Love Like Lightning . . . 8

WILLIAM BELL

67 Atlantic 584 076 Never Like This Before/Soldier's Goodbye . . . 8
69 Atlantic 584 259 Everyday Will Be Like A Holiday/Ain't Got No Girl . . . 7
67 Stax 601 019 Eloise (Hang On In There)/One Plus One . . . 6
68 Stax 601 038 A Tribute To A King/Every Man Oughta Have A Woman . . . 6
69 Stax STAX 110 I Forgot To Be Your Lover/Bring The Curtain Down . . . 6
69 Stax STAX 121 My Whole World Is Falling Down/All God's Children Got Soul . . . 7
69 Stax STAX 128 Happy/Johnny I Love You . . . 12
69 Atco 228 003 A TRIBUTE TO A KING (LP) . . . 35
69 Stax SXATS 1016 BOUND TO HAPPEN (LP) . . . 25
71 Stax 2363 002 BOUND TO HAPPEN (LP, reissue) . . . 12
71 Stax 2362 009 WOW . . . WILLIAM BELL (LP) . . . 18
72 Stax 2362 027 PHASES OF REALITY (LP) . . . 22
(see also Judy Clay & William Bell)

BELLA & ME

67 Columbia DB 8243 Whatever Happened To The Seven Day Week/Help Me Break This Habit . . . 12

GEORGE BELLAMY

65 Parlophone R 5282 Where I'm Bound/How Could I Ever . . . 35
72 Chapter One CH 167 Maman/Come To The Party . . . 12
(see also Tornados)

PETER BELLAMY

68 Argo MAINLY NORFOLK (LP) . . . 22
69 Xtra XTRA 1075 FAIR ENGLAND'S SHORE (LP) . . . 35
69 Topic 12T 200 THE FOX JUMPS OVER THE PARSON'S GATE (LP, blue label) . . . 18
70 Argo ZFB 11 OAK, ASH AND THORN (LP) . . . 25
72 Argo ZFB 37 WON'T YOU GO MY WAY (LP) . . . 18
72 Argo ZFB 81 MERLIN'S ISLE OF GRAMARYE (LP) . . . 18
74 Trailer LER 2089 TELL IT LIKE IT IS (LP) . . . 15
77 Free Reed FRR 014 BARRACK-ROOM BALLADS (LP) . . . 12
79 Topic 12TS 400 BOTH SIDES THEN (LP) . . . 12
83 Fellside FE 032 PETER BELLAMY WITH FRIENDS: KEEP ON KIPLING (LP) . . . 15
(see also Young Tradition)

BELL & ARC

71 Charisma CB 170 She Belongs To Me/Dawn . . . 6
71 Charisma CAS 1053 BELL & ARC (LP, gatefold sleeve) . . . 22
(see also Skip Bifferty, Arc, Every Which Way, Graham Bell)

MINT VALUE £

BELL BROTHERS

68	Action ACT 4510	Tell Him No/Throw Away The Key	15

BELLE & SEBASTIAN

97	Jeepster JPR 7001	Dog On Wheels/The State I Am In (p/s, 1,000 only)	5
97	Jeepster JPR 7003	A Century Of Fakers/Le Pastie De La Bourgeoisie (p/s)	5
96	Elektric Honey EHRLP 5	TIGERMILK (LP, 1,000 only)	70

BELLES

70	President PT 311	Don't Pretend/Words Can't Explain	15

BELLFIELD

73	Downtown DT 514	Sugar Plum/Sugar Plum Dub	6

BELL NOTES

59	Top Rank JAR 102	I've Had It/Be Mine	15
59	Top Rank JAR 102	I've Had It/Be Mine (78)	10
59	Top Rank JAR 147	Old Spanish Town/She Went That-A-Way	10
59	Top Rank JAR 147	Old Spanish Town/She Went That-A-Way (78)	10
59	Top Rank JAR 201	That's Right/Betty Dear	20

BELLS OF JOY

55	Vogue V 2357	I'm Gonna Press On/How Sweet It Is (78)	10

BELL SOUNDS

59	HMV POP 685	Marching Guitars/Chloe	5

LOUIS BELLSON (ALL STARS/QUINTET/BAND/OCTET)

56	Columbia Clef SEG 10030	BOOGIE WOOGIE PIANO AND DRUMS NO. 1 (EP)	10
56	Columbia Clef SEG 10052	BOOGIE WOOGIE PIANO AND DRUMS NO. 2 (EP)	10
53	Capitol LC 6568	JUST JAZZ (LP)	15
57	Columbia Clef C 9040	DRUMORAMA (10" LP)	20
58	Columbia Clef CX 10142	AT THE FLAMINGO (LP)	20
59	HMV CLP 1343	THE BRILLIANT BELLSON SOUND (LP)	20
61	Columbia SCX 3418	AROUND THE WORLD IN PERCUSSION (LP)	20
66	HMV CLP/CSD 3558	THUNDERBIRD (LP)	20
70	Pye NSPL 18349	LOUIE IN LONDON (LP, as Louie Bellson)	20
72	Parlophone PCS 7151	CONVERSATIONS (LP)	20

(see also Duke Ellington)

BELL-TONES

62	Columbia DB 4848	Selina/Did You Ever See A Dream Walking?	10

TONY BELLUS

59	London HL 8933	Robbin' The Cradle/Valentine Girl	45
59	London HL 8933	Robbin' The Cradle/Valentine Girl (78)	22

BELLY

92	4AD AD 2018	Gepetto/Sexy S (p/s, with 2 postcards, 2,000 only)	6
93	4AD AD 3001	Feed The Tree/Dream On Me (p/s, with 2 postcards)	6
95	4AD CADD 5004CD	KING (CD, with A5 book pack)	18

(see also Throwing Muses)

BELMONTS

61	Pye International 7N 25094	Tell Me Why/Smoke From Your Cigarette	40
62	Stateside SS 128	Come On Little Angel/How About Me?	25

(see also Dion & Belmonts)

BELOVED

86	Flim Flam HARP 2	A Hundred Words (Radio Mix)/Slow Drowning (freebie)	6
86	Flim Flam HARP 2T	A Hundred Words/Slow Drowning/In Trouble And Shame (12", p/s)	8
86	Flim Flam HARP 3	This Means War/If Only (p/s)	6
86	Flim Flam HARP 3T	This Means War/Let It Begin/Saints Preserve Us (12", p/s)	8
87	Flim Flam HARP 5T	HAPPY NOW: A Kiss Goodbye/If Pennies Came/Righteous Me (12", p/s)	10
87	Flim Flam HARP 7ET	Forever Dancing/Forever Dancing (Remix)/Surprise Me (12", p/s)	12
88	WEA YZ 311T	Loving Feeling (Feeling Lovely Mix)/Acid Love (Love & Ecstasy Mix) (12", p/s)	12
88	WEA YZ 311CD	Loving Feeling/Acid Love (Original Mix)/Loving Feeling (Feeling Lovely Mix) (3" CD with adaptor, picture case)	15
88	WEA SAM 481	Acid Love/Mixes (12", promo only)	35
89	WEA YZ 357CD	Your Love Takes Me Higher/Paradise (My Darling, My Angel)/Your Love Takes Me Higher (Rise Up Higher)/(Beautiful Mix) (3" CD with adaptor, 5" case)	15
89	WEA YZ 414T	The Sun Rising/The Sun Rising (Gentle Night)/The Sun Rising (Eurovisionary)/The Sun Rising (Deeply Satisfying) (12", p/s)	10
89	WEA YZ 414TP	The Sun Rising/The Sun Rising (Gentle Night)/The Sun Rising (Eurovisionary)/The Sun Rising (Deeply Satisfying) (12", picture disc)	15
90	WEA YZ 414TX	The Sun Rising (Remixes) (12" EP, p/s)	18
90	WEA YZ 414 TZ	The Sun Rising (Mixes) (12", p/s, unreleased)	50
89	WEA YZ 414CD	The Sun Rising/The Sun Rising (Gentle Night)/The Sun Rising (Eurovisionary)/ The Sun Rising (Deeply Satisfying) (3" CD, gatefold card sleeve)	15
90	WEA YZ 426CD	Hello/Hello Honky Tonk/Godfrey's Tonic/Hello Dolly (CD)	8
90	WEA YZ 482X	Time After Time/Time After Time — Through The Round Window (pic. disc, p/s)	7
90	WEA YZ 482CD	Time After Time (Mixes) (CD)	12
90	WEA YZ 541CD	It's Alright Now (7" Mix)/(Rattling Good Time)/(Back To Basics Instrumental) (CD, slimline jewel case)	15
93	WEA SAM 1328	Rock To The Rhythm Of Love (Mixes) (12", promo only)	20
95	WEA SAM 1464	1000 Years From Today (Mixes) (12", promo only)	30
95	WEA SAM 1621	Crystal Wave (12" 1-sided promo only)	20
96	East West EW 043CD	Deliver Me (3.56)/Deliver Me (Extended)/(Eau De Livami Vocal)/ (Salt Lake City Vocal)/(Coco Dub)/(Robodisco Dub) (CD, withdrawn)	15
96	WEA BSE1	Physical Love (Remix)/Three Steps To Heaven (Remix) (12" promo only)	30
87	Flim Flam HARPLP 2	WHERE IT'S AT (LP, with bonus 7")	15

MINT VALUE £

BELT & BRACES ROADSHOW BAND
75 Belt & Braces Roadshow BELT & BRACES ROADSHOW BAND (LP, with lyric sheet) . . . 15

BELTONES
68 Trojan TR 628 No More Heartaches/I'll Follow You . . . 10
69 Duke DU 17 Home Without You/Why Pretend . . . 6
69 High Note HS 017 Mary Mary/Going Away . . . 8
69 High Note HS 023 A Broken Heart/AFROTONES: All For One . . . 10
72 Ackee ACK 150 Wrapped Up In Love/SOUND DIMENSION: Pasero . . . 10
(see Bop & Beltones, Trevor Shield)

JOHN BELTRAN
96 Peacefrog PF 049 TEN DAYS OF BLUE (2-LP) . . . 15

JESSE BELVIN
59 RCA RCA 1119 Guess Who/Funny . . . 20
59 RCA RCA 1119 Guess Who/Funny (78) . . . 10

BEN
71 Vertigo 6360 052 BEN (LP, gatefold sleeve, swirl label) . . . 100

PAT BENATAR
79 Chrysalis CHS 2373 If You Think You Know How To Love Me/So Sincere (p/s) . . . 6
80 Chrysalis CHS 2403 We Live For Love/I Need A Lover (p/s) . . . 8
80 Chrysalis CHS 2474 Hit Me With Your Best Shot/You Better Run/Heartbreaker/ We Live For Love (p/s, some on red vinyl) . . . 8/6
81 Chrysalis CHS 2511 Treat Me Right/Hell Is For Children (p/s, clear vinyl) . . . 5
81 Sounds FREEBIE No. 1 Promises In The Dark (Edit)/MICHAEL SCHENKER GROUP: Let Sleeping Dogs Lie (flexidisc in white printed sleeve, free with *Sounds* magazine) . . . 6/5
81 Chrysalis CHS 2529 Fire And Ice/Hard To Believe (p/s, clear vinyl) . . . 5
81 Chrysalis CHSP 2529 Fire And Ice/Hard To Believe (picture disc) . . . 5
83 Chrysalis CHSP 2662 Shadows Of The Night/The Victim (shaped picture disc) . . . 12
83 Chrysalis CHS 12 2662 Shadows Of The Night/The Victim (12", p/s, blue vinyl) . . . 8
84 Chrysalis CHSP 2747 Love Is A Battlefield/Hell Is For Children (live) (picture disc) . . . 6
84 Chrysalis CHSP 2821 We Belong/Suburban King (picture disc) . . . 5
85 Chrysalis PATP 2 Shadows Of The Night/Hit Me With Your Best Shot (shaped pic disc & plinth) . . . 5
88 Chrysalis PAT 6 Don't Walk Away (gatefold p/s, red vinyl) . . . 5
81 Chrysalis CHR 1346 PRECIOUS TIME (LP, with poster) . . . 12
82 Chrysalis PCHR 1396 GET NERVOUS (LP, picture disc) . . . 15
83 Chrysalis CHRP 1451 LIVE FROM EARTH (LP, picture disc) . . . 15

STEVE BENBOW
68 L'gue Against Cruel Sports Tattered Doll (mail-order only) . . . 6
59 Collector STEVE BENBOW AND THE FOLK FOUR (EP) . . . 12
62 HMV CLP 1603 STEVE BENBOW SINGS (LP) . . . 18
63 HMV CLP 1687 I TRAVEL THE WORLD (LP) . . . 15
67 Decca LK/SKL 4881 OF SITUATIONS AND PREDICAMENTS (LP) . . . 15

RALF BENDIX & LITTLE ELIZABETH
65 Columbia DB 7774 Sag Mir Deine Sorgen/Baby Sittin' Boogie . . . 8

BENNY BENNETT
50s Seeco LDS 024 BENNY BENNETT AND HIS ORCHESTRA (LP) . . . 15

BOBBY BENNETT (U.K.)
67 CBS 202511 Just Say Goodbye/She Believes In Me . . . 7
68 Columbia DB 8435 All My Life Is You/To Give (The Reason I Live) . . . 7
69 Columbia DB 8532 Music Mother Made/You're Ready Now . . . 22

BOBBY BENNETT (U.S.)
69 London HL 10274 Big New York/Baby, Try Me . . . 10

BOYD BENNETT & HIS ROCKETS (WITH BIG MOE)
78s
55 Parlophone R 4002 Everlovin'/Boogie At Midnight (with Big Moe) . . . 30
55 Parlophone R 4063 Seventeen/Little Ole You-All (as Boyd Bennett & His Rockets) . . . 25
56 Parlophone R 4121 My Boy — Flat Top/Banjo Rock And Roll (with Big Moe) . . . 25
56 Parlophone R 4167 Blue Suede Shoes/Oo-Oo-Oo (with Big Moe) . . . 25
56 Parlophone R 4214 The Groovy Age/Hit That Jive, Jack (as Big Moe with Boyd Bennett & His Rockets) . . . 20
56 Parlophone R 4252 The Most/Rockin' Up A Storm (as Boyd Bennett & His Rockets) . . . 20
58 Parlophone R 4423 Click Clack/Move (as Boyd Bennett & His Rockers) . . . 45
59 Mercury AMT 1031 Tear It Up/Tight Tights (as Big Moe & His Orchestra) . . . 40
SINGLES
55 Parlophone MSP 6161 Everlovin'/Boogie At Midnight (with Big Moe) . . . 325
55 Parlophone MSP 6180 Seventeen/Little Ole You-All (as Boyd Bennett & His Rockets) . . . 275
56 Parlophone MSP 6203 My Boy — Flat Top/Banjo Rock And Roll (with Big Moe) . . . 325
56 Parlophone MSP 6233 Blue Suede Shoes/Oo-Oo-Oo (with Big Moe) . . . 275
56 Parlophone R 4214 The Groovy Age/Hit That Jive, Jack (as Big Moe with Boyd Bennett & His Rockets) . . . 275
56 Parlophone R 4252 The Most/Rockin' Up A Storm (as Boyd Bennett & His Rockets) . . . 275
58 Parlophone R 4423 Click Clack/Move (as Boyd Bennett & His Rockets) . . . 250
59 Mercury AMT 1031 Tear It Up/Tight Tights (as Big Moe & His Orchestra) . . . 85
(see also Moon Mullican)

BRIAN BENNETT
67 Columbia DB 8294 Canvas/Slippery Jim De Grize . . . 20
74 Fontana 6007 040 Chase Side Shoot-Up/Pegasus . . . 20
76 DJM DJS 10714 Thunderbolt/Clearing Skies (promos in p/s) . . . 12/5
77 DJM DJS 10756 Saturday Night Special/Farewell To A Friend (promos in p/s) . . . 12/5
77 DJM DJS 10791 The Girls Back Home/Jonty Jump (as the Brian Bennett Band) . . . 8
78 DJM DJS 10843 Pendulum Force/Ocean Glide . . . 5

MINT VALUE £

82 DJM DJS 10981 Top Of The World/Soul Ice . . . 8
67 Columbia S(C)X 6144 CHANGE OF DIRECTION (LP) . . . 50
69 Col. Studio Two TWO 268 THE ILLUSTRATED LONDON NOISE (LP) . . . 60
77 DJM DJF 20499 ROCK DREAMS (LP, as the Brian Bennett Band) . . . 15
78 DJM DJF 20532 VOYAGE (LP) . . . 12
(see also Shadows, Thunder Company, Wasp, Marty Wilde, Krewcats, Collage, Alan Skidmore, Big Jim Sullivan, Heat Exchange, Julian [Scott])

BRUCE BENNETT

71 Big BG 311 If You Don't Mind/Lenore (both actually by Dobby Dobson) . . . 7

CAROLE BENNETT

56 Capitol CL 14652 The Little Magician/I Was Your Only Love . . . 5
57 Capitol CL 14692 Play The Music/Miser's Gold . . . 15
57 Capitol CL 14725 Haunted Lover/Let The Chips Fall (Where They May) . . . 20

CLIFF BENNETT & REBEL ROUSERS

61 Parlophone R 4793 You've Got What I Like/I'm In Love With You . . . 40
61 Parlophone R 4836 That's What I Said/When I Get Paid . . . 35
62 Parlophone R 4895 Poor Joe/Hurtin' Inside (Twist) . . . 35
63 Parlophone R 5046 Everybody Loves A Lover/My Old Stand-By . . . 20
63 Parlophone R 5080 You Really Got A Hold On Me/Alright . . . 10
63 Parlophone DP 560 Poor Joe/Hurtin' Inside (Twist) (export issue, black label) . . . 20
64 Parlophone DP 561 When I Get Paid/That's What I Said (export issue, black label) . . . 20
64 Parlophone R 5119 Got My Mojo Working/Beautiful Dreamer . . . 10
64 Parlophone R 5173 One Way Love/Slow Down . . . 10
65 Parlophone R 5229 I'll Take You Home/Do You Love Him? . . . 10
65 Parlophone R 5259 Three Rooms Of Running Water/If Only You'd Reply . . . 10
65 Parlophone R 5317 I Have Cried My Last Tear/As Long As She Looks Like You . . . 10
66 Parlophone R 5406 You Can't Love 'Em All/Need Your Loving Tonight . . . 10
66 Parlophone R 5466 Eyes For You/Hold On I'm Coming . . . 10
66 Parlophone R 5489 Got To Get You Into My Life/Baby Each Day . . . 5
66 Parlophone R 5534 Never Knew Lovin' Could Be So Doggone Good/Don't Help Me Out . . . 5
67 Parlophone R 5565 I'm Sorry/I'll Take Good Care Of You . . . 5
67 Parlophone R 5598 I'll Be There/Use Me . . . 5
65 Parlophone GEP 8923 CLIFF BENNETT AND THE REBEL ROUSERS (EP) . . . 40
65 Parlophone GEP 8936 TRY IT BABY (EP) . . . 30
66 Parlophone GEP 8955 WE'RE GONNA MAKE IT (EP) . . . 40
64 Parlophone PMC 1242 CLIFF BENNETT AND THE REBEL ROUSERS (LP, yellow/black label) . . . 40
66 M. For Pleasure MFP 1121 DRIVIN' YOU WILD (LP) . . . 15
66 EMI Regal REG 1039 CLIFF BENNETT (LP, export issue) . . . 25
67 Parlophone PMC/PCS 7017 GOT TO GET YOU INTO OUR LIFE (LP, yellow/black label) . . . 25

CLIFF BENNETT BAND

68 Parlophone R 5666 Take Your Time/House Of A Thousand Dolls . . . 12
68 Parlophone R 5691 You're Breaking Me Up (And I'm Wasting Away)/I Hear Her Voice . . . 12
68 Parlophone R 5711 Lonely Weekends/Good Times . . . 12
68 Parlophone R 5728 One More Heartache/Nobody Runs Forever . . . 15
68 Parlophone R 5749 Back In The USSR/This Man . . . 15
68 Parlophone PMC/PCS 7054 BRANCHES OUT (LP, yellow/black label) . . . 30

CLIFF BENNETT'S REBELLION

71 CBS 7231 Amos Moses/Movin' And Travelin' On . . . 7
71 CBS 64487 CLIFF BENNETT'S REBELLION (LP) . . . 20
(see also Charles Hodges, Rebel Rousers, Toefat, Screaming Lord Sutch & Savages)

DICKIE BENNETT

55 Decca F 10595 There, But For The Grace Of God Go I/Stars Shine In Your Eyes . . . 5
56 Decca F 10697 Dungaree Doll/Can't We Be Partners (After The Dance) . . . 12
56 Decca F 10782 You Don't Know Me/Cry Upon My Shoulder . . . 5

DUSTER BENNETT

68 Blue Horizon 57-3141 It's A Man Down There/Things Are Changing . . . 18
69 Blue Horizon 57-3148 Raining In My Heart/Jumpin' For Joy . . . 15
69 Blue Horizon 57-3154 Bright Lights, Big City/Fresh Country Jam (with His House Band) . . . 20
69 Blue Horizon 57-3164 I'm Gonna Wind Up Endin' Up Or I'm Gonna End Up Windin' Up With You/ Rock Of Ages, Cleft For Me . . . 15
70 Blue Horizon 57-3173 I Chose To Sing The Blues/If You Could Hang Your Washing Like You Hang Your Lines . . . 10
70 Blue Horizon 57-3179 Act Nice And Gentle/I Want You To Love Me . . . 10
74 Rak RAK 177 Comin' Home/Pretty Little Thing . . . 15
68 Blue Horizon 7-63208 SMILING LIKE I'M HAPPY (LP, with His House Band, i.e. Fleetwood Mac) . . . 50
69 Blue Horizon 7-63221 BRIGHT LIGHTS... (LP, gatefold sleeve) . . . 50
70 Blue Horizon 7-63868 12 DB's (LP) . . . 50
(see also Fleetwood Mac)

JOE BENNETT & SPARKLETONES

57 HMV POP 399 Black Slacks/Boppin' Rock Boogie . . . 250
57 HMV POP 399 Black Slacks/Boppin' Rock Boogie (78) . . . 45
58 HMV POP 445 Rocket/Penny Loafers And Bobby Socks . . . 250
58 HMV POP 445 Rocket/Penny Loafers And Bobby Socks (78) . . . 40

JO JO BENNETT

67 Doctor Bird DB 1097 The Lecture/Cantelope Rock (with Fugitives) . . . 60
67 Doctor Bird DB 1117 Rocksteady/Real Gone Loser (with Fugitives) . . . 40
70 Explosion EX 2029 Groovy Jo Jo/Ten Steps To Soul (both actually with Mudie's All Stars) . . . 20
70 Trojan TR 7774 Leaving Rome/In The Nude (both with Mudie's All Stars) . . . 20
71 Moodisc MU 3514 Snowbird/MUDIE'S ALLSTARS: Change The Tide . . . 12
71 Moodisc HME 108 Poison Ivy/MUDIE'S ALLSTARS: Ivy Poison . . . 12
70 Trojan TBL 133 GROOVY JO JO (LP, with Mudie's Allstars) . . . 50
(see also Fugitives, I Roy)

KIM BENNETT

55 Decca F 10449 Softly Softly/ROLAND SHAW ORCHESTRA: Trumpeter's Lullaby . . . 8
55 Decca F 10460 Melody Of Love/Ding Dong . . . 8
55 Decca F 10599 The Kentuckian Song/Overnight . . . 7
56 Decca F 10706 No, Not Much/You Can't Keep Running . . . 7
(see also Roland Shaw)

LEE BENNETT & SUNLINERS

64 Decca F 12024 Poor Bachelor Boy/Fool, Fool, Fool . . . 6

RAY BENNETT

62 Decca F 11550 Go Away Little Girl/Twistin' To The Blues . . . 10
62 Decca DFE 8516 INTRODUCING RAY BENNETT (EP) . . . 40

ROY BENNETT

68 Blue Cat BS 146 I Dangerous/DEE SET: I Know A Place . . . 10

RUDI BENNETT

68 Decca F 12741 I'm So Proud/WHISTLING JACK SMITH: Havah Nagilah . . . 6
(see also Whistling Jack Smith)

TONY BENNETT

52 Columbia 38926 Our Lady Of Fatima/Just Say I Love Her (78) . . . 8
53 Columbia SCM 5048 Congratulations To Someone/Take Me . . . 15
53 Philips PB 689 Sold To The Man With The Broken Heart/One Kiss Away From Heaven (78) . . . 10
54 Columbia 39745 Here In My Heart/I'm Lost Again . . . 12
57 Philips JK 1008 Whatever Lola Wants/Heart (jukebox issue) . . . 20
53 Columbia B 2620 TONY BENNETT SPOTLITE (EP) . . . 15
54 Columbia B 2079 TONY BENNETT (EP) . . . 12
55 Philips BBE 12009 TONY BENNETT (EP) . . . 15
57 Columbia B 2582 ONE FOR MY BABY (EP) . . . 12
58 Philips BBE 12223 TONY BENNETT — PHILIPS TV SERIES (EP) . . . 12
60 Philips BBE 12338 HOMETOWN, MY HOMETOWN (EP) . . . 12
55 Philips BBR 8051 CLOUD 7 (10" LP) . . . 30
56 Philips BBR 8089 THE VOICE OF YOUR CHOICE (10" LP) . . . 30
57 Philips BBL 7138 TONY BENNETT SHOWCASE (LP) . . . 18
57 Philips BBL 7219 THE BEAT OF MY HEART (LP) . . . 15
58 Philips BBL 7219 LONG AGO AND FAR AWAY (LP) . . . 15
60 Philips BBL 7308 IN PERSON! (LP, with Count Basie Orch., with fake audience noise, mono) . . . 15
60 Philips SBBL 542 IN PERSON! (LP, with Count Basie Orch., with fake audience noise, stereo) . . . 15
60 Philips BBL 7413 TO MY WONDERFUL ONE (LP) . . . 15
60 Philips BBL 7452 ALONE TOGETHER (LP) . . . 15
61 Philips BBL 7455 SINGS A STRING OF HAROLD ARLEN (LP, also stereo SBBL 609) . . . 14/16
61 Philips BBL 7479 TONY SINGS FOR TWO (LP) . . . 15
61 Philips BBL 7495 MY HEART SINGS (LP) . . . 15
63 CBS BPG 62205 THIS IS ALL I ASK (LP) . . . 12
64 CBS BPG 62245 THE MANY MOODS OF TONY (LP) . . . 12
64 CBS BPG 62296 WHEN LIGHTS ARE LOW (LP) . . . 12
64 CBS BPG 62486 WHO CAN I TURN TO (LP) . . . 12
(see also Count Basie, John Barry)

VAL BENNETT

68 Island WI 3113 Jumping With Mr. Lee/ROY SHIRLEY: Keep Your Eyes On The Road . . . 40
68 Island WI 3146 The Russians Are Coming (Take Five)/LESTER STERLING: Sir Lee's Whip . . . 40
68 Trojan TR 611 Spanish Harlem/ROY SHIRLEY: If I Did Know . . . 20
69 Trojan TR 640 Baby Baby/Barbara . . . 15
69 Crab CRAB 6 Reggae City/CANNON KING: Mellow Trumpet
(B-side actually by Carl 'King Cannon Ball' Bryan) . . . 15
69 Camel CA 24 Midnight Spin/SOUL CATS: Money Money . . . 15
(see also Roy Shirley, Max Romeo, Derrick Morgan, Clancy Eccles, Harry J Allstars, George A Penny, Lloyd Terrell, Uniques, Versatiles)

JOHNNY BENNINGS & HIS RHYTHM & BLUES BAND

54 Esquire 10-376 Third Degree Blues/Timber (78) . . . 25

BENNY & TINA

69 Mercury MF 1133 This Love Is Real/Over My Dead Body . . . 5

BARRY BENSON

66 Parlophone R 5446 Stay A Little While/That's For Sure . . . 10
66 Parlophone R 5484 Not A One Girl Guy/Sunshine Child . . . 5
66 Parlophone R 5544 Always Waitin'/My Friend And I . . . 5
67 Parlophone R 5578 Cousin Jane/Meet Jacqueline . . . 5
67 Page One POF 034 I Can't Wait/Oh No . . . 5

BOBBY BENSON & HIS COMBO

58 Philips PB 854 Taxi Driver, I Don't Care/Gentleman Bobby . . . 10

GARY BENSON

66 Pye 7N 17032 This Man's Got No Luck/I'm So Tired . . . 5

GEORGE BENSON (QUARTET)

66 CBS (S)BPG 62817 IT'S UPTOWN (LP, as George Benson Quartet) . . . 15
67 CBS (S)BPG 62971 THE GEORGE BENSON COOKBOOK (LP) . . . 15

MARIE BENSON & THE LONDONAIRES

55 Decca F 10452 Mambo Italiano/Mobile . . . 8
55 Philips PB 528 Sooty/Mr. Dumpling (78) . . . 8

MICHAEL BENTINE

72 Polydor 2058 294 Wine Tasting Man/Olympic Showjumping . . . 5
62 Parlophone PMC 1179 IT'S A SQUARE WORLD (LP, also stereo PCS 3031) . . . 20/22
67 RCA Victor RD 7885 SQUARE BASHING (LP) . . . 15
(see also Goons)

MINT VALUE £

BRIAN BENTLEY & THE BACHELORS

60 Philips PB 1085 Wishing Well/Please Make Up Your Mind. . . . 15
60 Philips PB 1086 First Flight East/Sunday Break 5
62 Salvo SLO 1813 Caramba/Nellie Dean (99 copies only). . . . 18

JAY BENTLEY & THE JET SET

64 Vocalion VN 9230 Watusi '64/I'll Get You. . . . 10

BENTLEY BROTHERS

59 Top Rank JAR 208 Ma (She's Making Eyes At Me)/Yes, We Have No Bananas. . . . 5

BROOK BENTON

58 RCA RCA 1044 A Million Miles From Nowhere/Devoted 25
58 RCA RCA 1044 A Million Miles From Nowhere/Devoted (78) 10
58 Mercury AMT 1014 It's Just A Matter Of Time/Hurtin' Inside 5
58 Mercury AMT 1014 It's Just A Matter Of Time/Hurtin' Inside (78). . . . 10
59 Mercury AMT 1043 Endlessly/So Close 5
59 Mercury AMT 1043 Endlessly/So Close (78). . . . 10
59 Mercury AMT 1061 Thank You Pretty Baby/With All Of My Heart 10
59 Mercury AMT 1068 So Many Ways/I Want You Forever. . . . 5
60 Mercury AMT 1097 The Ties That Bind/Hither And Thither And Yon 5
60 Mercury AMT 1109 Kiddio/The Same One 10
60 Mercury AMT 1121 Fools Rush In/Somebody You'll Want Me To Want You 5
61 Mercury AMT 1134 For My Baby/Think Twice. . . . 5
61 Mercury AMT 1148 The Boll Weevil Song/Your Eyes 5
61 Mercury AMT 1157 Frankie And Johnny/It's Just A House Without You 5
61 Mercury AMT 1168 Revenge/Really Really 5
62 Mercury AMT 1172 Walk On The Wild Side/Somewhere In The Used To Be. . . . 10
62 Mercury AMT 1178 Hit Record/Thanks To The Fool 10
62 Mercury AMT 1187 Lie To Me/The Touch Of Your Hand 5
62 Mercury AMT 1194 Hotel Happiness/Still Waters Run Deep 5
62 Mercury AMT 1203 I Got What I Wanted/Dearer Than Life 5
63 Mercury AMT 1208 My True Confession/Tender Years 5
63 Mercury AMT 1212 Two Tickets To Paradise/Don't Hate Me. . . . 10
63 Mercury AMT 1217 Baby You Got It Made/Stop Foolin' (with Damita Jo). . . . 10
64 Mercury MF 806 Going Going Gone/After Midnight. . . . 5
64 Mercury MF 822 Too Late To Turn Back Now/Another Cup Of Coffee 5
64 Mercury MF 828 A House Is Not A Home/Come On Back 5
64 Mercury MF 842 Do It Right/Please, Please Make It Easy 5
68 Atlantic 584 222 Do Your Own Thing/I Just Don't Know What To Do With Myself 5
69 Atlantic 584 266 Touch 'Em With Love/She Knows What To Do For Me 5
69 Atlantic 584 267 Nothing Can Take The Place Of You/Woman Without Love. . . . 5
58 RCA RCX 169 BROOK BENTON (EP, tri centre) 30
58 Fontana TFE 17151 BROOK BENTON AT HIS BEST (EP) 18
59 Mercury ZEP 10023 THE CARESSING VOICE OF BROOK BENTON (EP) 10
60 Mercury ZEP 10046 MAKE A DATE WITH BROOK BENTON (EP) 10
60 Mercury ZEP 10076 I'M IN THE MOOD FOR LOVE. . . . 10
60 Mercury ZEP 10091 WHEN I FALL IN LOVE (EP, also stereo [SEZ 19009]) 10/15
61 Mercury ZEP 10107 WHEN YOU'RE IN LOVE (EP, also stereo [SEZ 19019]) 10/15
61 Mercury ZEP 10125 SO WARM (EP, also stereo [SEZ 19024]) 10/15
58 Mercury MMC 14015 IT'S JUST A MATTER OF TIME (LP). . . . 25
59 Mercury MMC 14022 ENDLESSLY (LP) 25
60 Mercury MMC 14042 I LOVE YOU IN SO MANY WAYS (LP). . . . 20
60 Mercury MMC 14060 SONGS I LOVE TO SING (LP, also stereo [CMS 18041]). . . . 18/22
61 Mercury MMC 14090 THE BOLL WEEVIL SONG (LP, also stereo [CMS 18060]) 18/22
61 Mercury MMC 14108 THERE GOES THAT SONG AGAIN (LP, also stereo [CMS 18068]). . . . 18/22
62 Mercury MMC 14124 GOLDEN HITS (LP). . . . 15
62 Mercury 20024 MCL BORN TO SING THE BLUES (LP). . . . 18
63 Mercury 20040 MCL IT'S JUST A MATTER OF TIME (LP). . . . 18
63 Mercury 20053 MCL THIS BITTER EARTH (LP) 18

BROOK BENTON & DINAH WASHINGTON

60 Mercury AMT 1083 Baby (You've Got What It Takes)/I Do 15
60 Mercury AMT 1099 A Rockin' Good Way/I Believe 20
69 Mercury MF 1100 A Rockin' Good Way/I Do. . . . 5
61 Mercury ZEP 10120 A ROCKING GOOD WAY (EP, also stereo SEZ 19022). . . . 40
64 Mercury 20069 MCL THE TWO OF US (LP). . . . 15

STEVE BERESFORD

75 Incus INCUS 15 TEATIME (LP) 50

BERETS

70 Avant Garde AVS 116 THE MASS FOR PEACE (LP, with insert). . . . 25

INGRID BERGMAN

56 Brunswick OE 9252 THE PIED PIPER OF HAMELIN (EP, tri-centre) 12

BERKELEY KITES

68 Polydor 56742 Hang Up City/Mary-Go-Round 8
69 Polydor 56770 Alice In Wonderland/What Goes Up Must Come Down. . . . 8

MILTON BERLE

56 Vogue Coral Q 72197 In The Middle Of The House/Buffalo 10

BERLIN RITZ

80 Big Muff BM 001 Crazy Nights/You're Where I Belong (no p/s) 50

BERMUDAS

64 London HLN 9894 Donnie/Chu Sen Ling. . . . 18

BERNADETTE

67 Rim RIM 2 Come Kiss Me Love/Let Me Do The Talking 15

MINT VALUE £

KENNY BERNARD (& WRANGLERS)

65	Pye 7N 15920	The Tracker/You Gotta Give (with Wranglers)	20
66	Pye 7N 17131	Nothing Can Change This Love/What Love Brings	30
67	Pye 7N 17233	Ain't No Soul (Left In These Old Shoes)/Hey Woman	30
67	CBS 2936	Somebody/Pity My Feet	75
68	CBS 3860	Victim Of Perfume And Lace/A Change Is Gonna Come	15

(see also Kenny & Wranglers, Wranglers, Cat's Pyjamas)

ROD BERNARD

59	London HLM 8849	This Should Go On Forever/Pardon, Mr. Gordon	30
59	London HLM 8849	This Should Go On Forever/Pardon, Mr. Gordon (78)	10
59	Mercury AMT 1070	One More Chance/Shedding Teardrops Over You	12

BERNIE & BUZZ BAND

68	Decca F 22829	The House That Jack Built/PETE KELLY'S SOULUTION: Midnight Confessions (export issue)	18
68	Deram DM 181	When Something's Wrong With My Baby/Don't Knock It	35

(see also Pete Kelly's Soulution)

ELMER BERNSTEIN

56	Brunswick 05544	Clark Street Parts 1 & 2 (gold or silver print on label)	10/6
59	Capitol CL 15101	Staccato's Theme/The Jazz At Waldo's	5
61	United Artists/HMV POP 889	The Magnificent Seven/The Lonely Rebel	5
63	MGM MGM 1238	Rat Race/Saints & Sinners	5
66	United Artists UP 1163	The Magnificent Seven/Return Of The Seven	5
60	Capitol EAP1 1287	STACCATO (EP)	8
56	Brunswick LAT 8101	THE MAN WITH THE GOLDEN ARM (LP, soundtrack)	25
57	Brunswick LAT 8195	SWEET SMELL OF SUCCESS (LP, soundtrack)	25
57	London HA-P 2076	MEN IN WAR (LP, soundtrack)	75
58	London HA-D 2074/5	THE TEN COMMANDMENTS (2-LP, soundtrack)	40
58	London HA-D 2111	DESIRE UNDER THE ELMS (LP, soundtrack)	25
58	London HA-T 2125	GOD'S LITTLE ACRE (LP, soundtrack)	30
58	Capitol LCT 6165	KINGS GO FORTH (LP, soundtrack)	15
59	Capitol LCT 6180	SOME CAME RUNNING (LP, soundtrack)	25
62	MGM MGM-C 891	WALK ON THE WILD SIDE (LP, soundtrack)	20
63	MGM MGM-C 934	TO KILL A MOCKINGBIRD (LP, soundtrack)	15
63	United Artists ULP 1041	THE GREAT ESCAPE (LP, soundtrack, mono/stereo)	20
64	MGM MGM-C 984	THE CARPETBAGGERS (LP, soundtrack)	15
64	London HA-A/SH-A 8219	THE CARPETBAGGERS (LP, soundtrack)	15
65	CBS (S)BPG 62558	THE SONS OF KATIE ELDER (LP, soundtrack, feat. Johnny Cash)	30/40
65	United Artists SULP 1106	THE HALLELUJAH TRAIL (LP, soundtrack)	15
66	United Artists (S)ULP 1140	CAST A GIANT SHADOW (LP, soundtrack, feat. Vince Hill)	18
66	United Artists ULP 1144	THE TEN COMMANDMENTS (reissue, single disc)	12
66	United Artists (S)ULP 1154	HAWAII (LP, soundtrack)	15
67	United Artists (S)ULP 1156	RETURN OF THE SEVEN (LP, soundtrack)	15
67	RCA Victor RD 7792	THE SILENCERS (LP, soundtrack, feat. Vikki Carr)	45
67	Fontana TL 5306	BABY, THE RAIN MUST FALL (LP, soundtrack)	40
68	United Artists (S)ULP 1190	THE SCALPHUNTERS (LP, soundtrack)	15
69	Paramount SPFL 254	WHERE'S JACK? (LP, soundtrack, feat. Mary Hopkin)	22
70	Capitol E-ST 263	TRUE GRIT (LP, soundtrack, feat. Glen Campbell)	18
74	Philips 9299 225	GOLD (LP, soundtrack)	15

CHUCK BERRY

78s

56	London HLU 8275	Down Bound Train/No Money Down (gold label)	50
57	London HLN 8375	You Can't Catch Me/Havana Moon (gold label)	30
57	London HLU 8428	Roll Over Beethoven/Drifting Heart	30
57	Columbia DB 3951	School Day (Ring! Ring! Goes The Bell)/Deep Feeling	30
57	London HLM 8531	Rock And Roll Music/Blue Feeling	30
58	London HLM 8585	Sweet Little Sixteen/Reelin' And Rockin'	30
58	London HLM 8629	Johnny B. Goode/Around And Around	40
58	London HL 8677	Beautiful Delilah/Vacation Time	40
58	London HL 7055	Carol/Hey Pedro (export single)	40
58	London HL 8712	Carol/Hey Pedro	40
58	London HLM 8767	Sweet Little Rock And Roller/Jo Jo Gunne	50
59	London HLM 8853	Almost Grown/Little Queenie	75
59	London HLM 8921	Back In The U.S.A./Memphis, Tennessee	75

SINGLES

56	London HLU 8275	No Money Down/Down Bound Train (gold lettering, existence unconfirmed)	600+
56	London HLU 8275	No Money Down/Down Bound Train (silver lettering on label, triangular or round centre)	350/200
57	London HLN 8375	You Can't Catch Me/Havana Moon (gold lettering on label, later silver)	325/165
57	London HLU 8428	Roll Over Beethoven/Drifting Heart	100
57	Columbia DB 3951	School Day (Ring! Ring! Goes The Bell)/Blue Feeling	100
57	London HLM 8531	Rock And Roll Music/Blue Feeling	100
58	London HLM 8585	Sweet Little Sixteen/Reelin' And Rockin'	40
58	London HLM 8629	Johnny B. Goode/Around And Around	40
58	London HL 8677	Beautiful Delilah/Vacation Time	45
58	London HL 8712	Carol/Hey Pedro	45
58	London HL 7055	Carol/Hey Pedro (export issue)	40
58	London HLM 8767	Sweet Little Rock And Roller/Jo Jo Gunne	25
59	London HLM 8853	Almost Grown/Little Queenie	30
59	London HLM 8921	Back In The U.S.A./Memphis, Tennessee	25

(The above London 45s were originally issued with triangular centres; later silver top label/round centre pressings are worth half to two-thirds these values.)

60	London HLM 9069	Let It Rock/Too Pooped To Pop	25
60	London HLM 9159	Bye Bye Johnny/Mad Lad	25
61	Pye International 7N 25100	I'm Talkin' 'Bout You/Little Star (blue label, later red/yellow)	25/10

MINT VALUE £

Year	Label / Cat. No.	Title	Value
63	Pye International 7N 25209	Go Go Go/Come On	8
63	Pye International 7N 25218	Memphis, Tennessee/Let It Rock	8
63	Pye International 7N 25228	Run Rudolph Run/Johnny B. Goode	10
64	Pye International 7N 25236	Nadine (Is It You?)/O Rangutang	8
64	Pye International 7N 25242	No Particular Place To Go/Liverpool Drive	8
64	Pye International 7N 25257	You Never Can Tell/Brenda Lee	10
64	Pye International 7N 25271	Little Marie/Go Bobby Soxer	10
65	Pye International 7N 25285	The Promised Land/The Things I Used To Do	10
65	Chess CRS 8006	I Got A Booking/Lonely School Days	10
65	Chess CRS 8012	Dear Dad/My Little Lovelight	10
65	Chess CRS 8022	It Wasn't Me/It's My Own Business	10
66	Chess CRS 8037	Ramona Say Yes/Lonely School Days	10
66	Mercury MF 958	Club Nitty Gritty/Laugh And Cry	10
67	Mercury MF 994	Back To Memphis/I Do Really Love You	10
68	Mercury MF 1057	St. Louis To Frisco/Ma Dear	10
69	Mercury MF 1102	Back To Memphis/Roll Over Beethoven	10
68	Chess CRS 8075	Johnny B. Goode/Sweet Little Sixteen	5
69	Chess CRS 8089	No Particular Place To Go/It Wasn't Me	5
72	Chess 6145 007	Rock And Roll Music/Johnny B. Goode/School Days	5
72	Chess 6145 019	My Ding-A-Ling (Live)/Let's Boogie	5
73	Chess 6145 020	Reelin' And Rockin' (Live)/I Will Not Let You Go	5
73	Chess 6145 027	South Of The Border (Live)/Bio	5
75	Chess 6145 038	Shake Rattle And Roll/I'm Just A Name	5
79	Atlantic K 11354	Oh What A Thrill/California	5

EPs

Year	Label / Cat. No.	Title	Value
56	London REU 1053	RHYTHM AND BLUES WITH CHUCK BERRY (maroon/gold label, tri-centre)	150
56	London REU 1053	RHYTHM AND BLUES WITH CHUCK BERRY (later pressing, maroon/silver label, round centre)	50
60	London REM 1188	REELIN' AND ROCKIN' (maroon or gold label, tri or round centre)	200/100
63	Pye Intl. NEP 44011	CHUCK BERRY	20
63	Pye Intl. NEP 44013	THIS IS CHUCK BERRY	20
64	Pye Intl. NEP 44018	THE BEST OF CHUCK BERRY	20
64	Pye Intl. NEP 44028	CHUCK BERRY HITS	20
64	Pye Intl. NEP 44033	BLUE MOOD	20
65	Chess CRE 6002	THE PROMISED LAND	30
65	Chess CRE 6005	COME ON	30
66	Chess CRE 6012	I GOT A BOOKING	30
66	Chess CRE 6016	YOU CAME A LONG WAY FROM ST. LOUIS	30

LPs

Year	Label / Cat. No.	Title	Value
58	London HA-M 2132	ONE DOZEN BERRYS	130
62	Pye Intl. NPL 28019	NEW JUKE BOX HITS	40
63	Pye Intl. NPL 28024	CHUCK BERRY	22
63	Pye Intl. NPL 28027	CHUCK BERRY ON STAGE	18
63	Pye Intl. NPL 28028	MORE CHUCK BERRY	18
64	Pye Intl. NPL 28031	THE LATEST AND THE GREATEST	22
64	Pye Intl. NPL 28039	YOU NEVER CAN TELL	22
65	Chess CRL 4005	CHUCK BERRY IN LONDON	20
65	Chess CRL 4506	FRESH BERRYS	20
66	Golden Guinea GGL 0352	CHUCK BERRY (reissue of NPL 28024)	18
66	Chess CRL 4548	CHUCK BERRY'S GREATEST HITS	12
66	Marble Arch MAL 611	CHUCK BERRY (2nd reissue of NPL 28024)	12
67	Mercury 20102 (S)MCL	CHUCK BERRY'S GOLDEN HITS (re-recordings, mono/stereo)	12
67	Mercury 20110 (S)MCL	CHUCK BERRY IN MEMPHIS	15
67	Mercury 20112 (S)MCL	LIVE AT THE FILLMORE AUDITORIUM — SAN FRANCISCO	15
69	Mercury 20162 (S)MCL	CONCERTO IN B. GOODE	15
72	Chess 6310 113	BACK HOME	12
72	Chess 6310 115	SAN FRANCISCO DUES	12
72	Chess 6310 122	THE LONDON CHUCK BERRY SESSIONS	12
72	Philips Int. 6619 008	ST. LOUIE TO FRISCO TO MEMPHIS (2-LP)	20
72	Chess 6641 018	GOLDEN DECADE (2-LP, gatefold sleeve)	18
73	Chess 6499 650	BIO	12
75	Chess 9109 101	CHUCK BERRY '75	12
79	Atlantic K 50648	ROCK IT	12
81	Everest CBR 1007	CHUCK BERRY LIVE	12

CHUCK BERRY/BO DIDDLEY

Year	Label / Cat. No.	Title	Value
63	Pye Intl. NEP 44009	CHUCK AND BO (EP)	20
63	Pye Intl. NEP 44012	CHUCK AND BO, VOL. 2 (EP)	20
64	Pye Intl. NEP 44017	CHUCK AND BO, VOL. 3 (EP)	22
73	Chess 6145 012	BIG DADDIES (EP)	30
64	Pye Intl. NPL 28047	TWO GREAT GUITARS (LP, mono)	40

(see also Bo Diddley)

DAVE BERRY (& CRUISERS)

Year	Label / Cat. No.	Title	Value
63	Decca F 11734	Memphis Tennessee/Tossin' & Turnin' (with Cruisers)	10
63	Decca F 11803	My Baby Left Me/Hoochie Coochie Man (B-side with Cruisers)	10
64	Decca F 11876	Baby It's You/Sweet And Lovely	10
64	Decca F 11937	The Crying Game/Don't Gimme No Lip Child	5
64	Decca F 12020	One Heart Between Two/You're Gonna Need Somebody	10
65	Decca F 12103	Little Things/I've Got A Tiger By The Tail	5
65	Decca F 12188	This Strange Effect/Now	12
65	Decca F 12258	I'm Gonna Take You There/Just Don't Know	5
66	Decca F 12337	If You Wait For Love/Hidden	5
66	Decca F 12435	Mama/Walk, Walk, Talk, Talk	5
66	Decca F 12513	Picture Me Gone/Ann	5
67	Decca F 12579	Stranger/Stick By The Book	5
67	Decca F 12651	Forever/And I Have Learned To Dream	5

MINT VALUE £

68	Decca F 12739	Just As Much As Ever/I Got A Feeling	5
68	Decca F 12771	(Do I Figure) In Your Life/Latisha	10
69	Decca F 12905	Oh What A Life (by Dave Berry & Sponge)/Huma Luma	5
70	Decca F 12999	Change Our Minds/Long Walk To D.C.	5
70	Decca F 13080	Chaplin House/Trees	5
72	CBS 7780	Movin' On (Turn Around)/Don't Bring Me Down	5
88	Flagstaff 002	Out Of Time/Serenade To Alice (p/s, 200 only)	5
64	Decca DFE 8601	DAVE BERRY (EP)	20
66	Ace Of Clubs ACL 1218	ONE DOZEN BERRIES (LP, also stereo SCL 1218)	20
65	Decca DFE 8625	CAN I GET IT FROM YOU (EP)	20
64	Decca LK 4653	DAVE BERRY (LP)	50
66	Decca LK 4823	THE SPECIAL SOUND OF DAVE BERRY (LP)	25
68	Decca LK/SKL 4932	DAVE BERRY '68 (LP)	35
87	Butt BUTT 007	HOSTAGE TO THE BEAT (LP, 1,000 only)	10

(see also Cruisers)

LEN & BARBARA BERRY

60s	Greenwich Village GVR 229	THE PORTWAY PEDDLERS (LP)	25

MIKE BERRY (& THE OUTLAWS)

61	Decca F 11314	Will You Love Me Tomorrow/My Baby Doll (with The Outlaws)	35
61	HMV POP 912	Tribute To Buddy Holly/What's The Matter (with The Outlaws)	18
62	HMV POP 979	It's Just A Matter Of Time/Little Boy Blue (backing group miscredited as Admirals, actually The Outlaws)	18
62	HMV POP 1042	Every Little Kiss/How Many Times	20
62	HMV POP 1105	Don't You Think It's Time/Loneliness (with The Outlaws) (blue or black label)	10/8
63	HMV POP 1142	My Little Baby/You'll Do It, You'll Fall In Love	20
63	HMV POP 1194	It Really Doesn't Matter/Try A Little Bit Harder	18
64	HMV POP 1257	This Little Girl/On My Mind	20
64	HMV POP 1284	Lovesick/Letter Of Love	20
64	HMV POP 1314	Who Will It Be/Talk (with Innocents)	20
64	HMV POP 1362	Two Lovers/Don't Try To Stand In My Way	10
65	HMV POP 1449	That's All I Ever Wanted From You/She Didn't Care	10
65	HMV POP 1494	It Comes And Goes/Gonna Fall In Love	10
66	HMV POP 1530	Warm Baby/Just Thought I'd 'Phone	10
67	Polydor 56182	Raining In My Heart/Eyes	10
72	York SYK 516	Going Down To Virginia/Love Her	10
72	York SYK 530	Drift Away/Keep Your Eyes On The Road	10
63	HMV 7EG 8793	IT'S TIME FOR MIKE BERRY (EP, with Outlaws)	45
63	HMV 7EG 8808	A TRIBUTE TO BUDDY HOLLY (EP)	45
72	York FYK 409	AMBUSH (LP)	20

(see also Outlaws, Le Roys, Shepperton Flames, Innocents [U.K], UK Jones)

RICHARD BERRY & PHARAOHS

64	Ember EMB EP 4527	RHYTHM AND BLUES VOL. 3 (EP)	200

BERRY STREET STATION

75	Crystal CR 7024	Chocolate Sugar/All I Want Is You	8

JON BEST

65	Decca F 12077	Young Boy Blues/Living Without Love	15

PETE BEST FOUR

64	Decca F 11929	I'm Gonna Knock On Your Door/Why Did I Fall In Love With You?	65

(see also Beatles, Lee Curtis & All Stars)

BETA BAND

97	Regal REG 16	CHAMPION VERSIONS EP: Dry The Rain/I Know/B+A/Dog's Got A Bone (12", p/s, 1,000 only)	50
98	Regal REG 18	THE PATTY PATTY SOUND EP: Inner Meet Me/The House/The Monolith/ She's The One (2 x 12", p/s, 1,000 only)	20
98	Regal REG 18	THE PATTY PATTY SOUND EP: Inner Meet Me/The House/The Monolith/ She's The One (CD, card slipcase)	20

BETTERDAYS

65	Polydor BM 56024	Don't Want That/Here 'Tis	350
91	N.T.B. 001	HOWL OF THE STREETS (EP, numbered p/s)	8
92	N.T.B. 1002	DOWN ON THE WATERFRONT (EP, numbered p/s)	8

HAROLD BETTERS

65	Sue WI 378	Do Anything You Wanna (Parts 1 & 2)	25

BEVERLEY

66	Deram DM 101	Happy New Year/Where The Good Times Are	15
67	Deram DM 137	Museum/DENNY CORDELL ENSEMBLE: A Quick One For Sanity	20

(see also John & Beverley Martyn, Levee Breakers)

BEVERLEY SISTERS

55	Decca F 10539	I Remember Mama/I've Been Thinking	10
55	Decca F 10603	Humming Bird/Have You Ever Been Lonely?	5
55	Decca F 10641	My Heart Goes A-Sailing/Teddy Bear	5
56	Decca F 10705	Willie Can/I've Started Courtin'	10
56	Decca F 10729	Rickshaw Boy/You Ought To Have A Wife	5
56	Decca F 10770	Born To Be With You/It's Easy	5
56	Decca F 10813	Come Home To My Arms/Doodle-Doo-Doo	5
57	Decca F 10832	I Dreamed/Mama From The Train (A Kiss, A Kiss)	5
57	Decca F 10853	Greensleeves/I'll See You In My Dreams	5
57	Decca F 10893	Mr. Wonderful/Blow The Wind Southerly	5
57	Decca F 10909	Bye, Bye Love/It's Illegal, It's Immoral, Or It Makes You Fat	5
57	Decca F 10943	Riding Down From Bangor/The Young Cavaliero	5
58	Decca F 10971	Long Black Nylons/Without You	20
56	Columbia SEG 7602	THREE'S COMPANY (EP)	10

MINT VALUE £

56 Decca DFE 6307 THE BEVERLEY SISTERS (EP) 10
57 Decca DFE 6401 THE BEVERLEY SISTERS NO. 2 (EP) 10
57 Decca DFE 6402 THE BEVERLEY SISTERS NO. 3 (EP) 10
58 Decca DFE 6512 THE BEVERLEY SISTERS NO. 4 (EP) 10
50s Decca DFE 6611 THE BEVS FOR CHRISTMAS (EP) 10
55 Philips BBR 8052 A DATE WITH THE BEVS (10" LP) 20
60 Columbia 33SX 1285 THE ENCHANTING BEVERLEY SISTERS (LP, also stereo [SCX 3351]) 15/20
60 Ace Of Clubs ACL 1048 THOSE BEVERLEY SISTERS (LP) 10

BEVERLEY'S ALLSTARS

65 Black Swan WI 449 Go Home/THEO BECKFORD: Ungrateful People 30
69 Trojan TR 683 Double Shot/Gimme Gimme Gal (B-side act. "Banana Water" by Mellotones) 15
70 Trojan TR 7729 Moon Dust/Fat Cat (both sides actually by Ansell Collins) 12
(see also Clarendonians, Gaylads, Ken Boothe, Glen Brown, Desmond Dekker, Bob Marley, Maytals, Melodians, Derrick Morgan, Pioneers, Rockstones, Bruce Ruffin, Delroy Wilson)

FRANK BEVERLY & BUTLERS

79 Inferno HEAT 4 If That's What You Wanted/Love (Your Pain Goes Deep) 8

BEVERLY HILLBILLIES

66 Starlite GRK 602 THE FABULOUS BEVERLY HILLBILLIES (LP) 20

BEVERLY HILLS BLUES BAND

76 Warner Bros K 16752 Just Because/If I Can Just Get Through Tonight 7
(see also Four Seasons)

BEVIS FROND

88 Freakbeat/Lyntone African Violets/THE STEPPES: History Hates No Man (flexidisc free with *Freakbeat* fanzine) 8/6
88 Bucketfull/Brains BOB 21 High In A Flat/DREAM SYNDICATE: Blind Willie McTell (free with *Bucketfull Of Brains* issue 27, 33rpm, yellow die-cut sleeve) 12/10
90 Clawfist PIS 1 Sexorcist/WALKINGSEEDS: Reflection In A Tall Mirror (p/s, mail-order only) 5
87 Woronzow WOO 3 MIASMA (LP) 12
87 Woronzow WOO 4 INNER MARSHLAND (LP) 8
87 Woronzow WOO 5 1/2 BEVIS THROUGH THE LOOKING GLASS — THE GREAT MAGNET DISASTER (2-LP, 500 only, originals all signed, with booklet; counterfeits unsigned) 50
88 Woronzow WOO 8 TRIPTYCH (LP) 12
90 Woronzow WOO 13 MAGIC EYE (LP, featuring Twink, 200 only) 12
91 Woronzow WOO 16 NEW RIVER HEAD (2-LP, 1st 500 with EP & insert) 18/12
92 Woronzow WOO 18 LONDON STONE (LP) 12
92 Woronzow WOO 26 SUPERSEEDER (2-LP) 15
93 Woronzow WOO 22 SPRAWL (2-LP, gatefold sleeve, with insert) 15
97 Woronzow WOO 406 NORTH CIRCULAR (3-LP, with insert, 750 only, signed & numbered) 25
(see also Von Trap Family, Room 13)

PAUL BEVOIR

85 Dance Network WORK 2 THE HAPPIEST DAYS OF YOUR LIFE (LP) 12
(see also Jetset)

RODNEY BEWES

69 Revolution REV 1003 Remember When/Dear Mother Love Albert 10
70 Revolution Pop REVP 1001 Dear Mother Love Albert/Meter Maid 10
(see also Highly Likely)

B-52's

79 Island WIP 6527 6060-842/Hero Worship (p/s) 5
80 Island PWIP 6551 Planet Claire/There's A Moon In The Sky (Called The Moon) (picture disc) 5
80 Island WIP 6579 Give Me Back My Man/Give Me Back My Man (Version) (p/s, mispressed, B-side plays "Strobe Light") 8
80 Island WIP 6685 Strobe Light/Dirty Back Road (in blue/black plastic bag) 8
86 Island BFTR/BFTL/BFTP 1 Rock Lobster/Planet Claire (set of 3 x 10" x 7" picture discs ['rock'/'lobster'/'planet'], each with same tracks, in printed PVC folder) 12
90 Reprise W 9917P Love Shack/Planet Claire (live)/Rock Lobster (live) (picture disc, promo only) 10
79 Island ILPS 9580 THE B-52's (LP, with bonus single "Rock Lobster"/"52 Girls" [PSR 438]) 15
80 Island ILPS 9622 WILD PLANET (LP, in plastic bag with badge) 15

MAURICIO BIANCHI

81 Sterile SR 2 SYMPATHY FOR A GENOCIDE (LP, 200 only) 70

GENE BIANCO GROUP

53 London L 1209 Limehouse Boogie/Harpin' Boogie (78) 10
60 Vogue V 9167 Alarm Clock Rock/Harp Rock Boogie 30

BIBBY

65 Blue Beat BB 289 Rub It Down/Wicked Man (actually by Harris Seaton) 20
(see also B.B. Seaton, Horace Seaton)

BIDDU

67 Regal Zonophone RZ 3002 Daughter Of Love/Look Out Here I Come 7
69 Polydor 56323 Started Me Thinking/Where In The World 6

BIFF BANG POW!

84 Creation CRE 003 Fifty Years Of Fun/Then When I Scream (foldaround sprayed p/s in poly bag) . . . 35
84 Creation CRE 007 There Must Be A Better Life/The Chocolate Elephant Man (foldaround p/s in poly bag) 35
90 Caff CAFF 13 Sleep/TIMES: Extase (p/s, with insert) 20
89 Creation CRELP 046 THE ACID HOUSE ALBUM (LP, hand-sprayed sleeve) 12
(see also Laughing Apple, Times)

BIFFY CLYRO

00s Beggars Banquet BBQ 352 27/Instruction/Breathe Her (CD) 8
00s Beggars B'quet BBQ 335CD Justboy/Being Gabriel/Unsubtle (CD) 8

MINT VALUE £

BIG AMONGST SHEEP
83 Rock Solid RSS 01 ASTROPOP (12" EP, p/s) 12
82 Rock Solid RSR 2001 TERMINAL VELOCITY (LP) 60
(see also Inner City Unit, Silverwing)

BIG BARON
60 Top Rank JAR 404 Swinging Bells (Oberon Jump)/Romance 15

BIG BEN BANJO BAND
66 Columbia DB 8069 Beatle Medley For Mums And Pops Parts 1 & 2 6
(see also Billie Anthony, Norrie Paramor & His Orchestra)

BIG BEN TRAD BAND
61 Columbia 33SX 1356 BIG BEN TRAD BAND (LP) 30

BIG BERTHA featuring ACE KEFFORD
69 Atlantic 584 298 This World's An Apple/Gravy Booby Jamm 25
(see also Cozy Powell, Ace Kefford Stand, Bedlam, Youngblood)

BIG BLACK
87 Blast First BFFP 24 He's A Whore/The Model (p/s) 5
85 Homestead HMS 007 RACER-X (12" EP, with insert) 8
87 Blast First BFFP 14T HEADACHE (12" p/s, 1,000 only, free 45, "Heartbeat"/"Things To Do Today"/"I Can't Believe") 10
87 NOT 2 (BUT 1) SOUND OF IMPACT (LP, matt sleeve, no'd up to 1,000, with 8-page booklet) 30
87 NOT 2 (BUT 1) SOUND OF IMPACT (LP, laminated sleeve, numbered from 1,001-1,500, with 8-page booklet) 20
87 NOT 2 (BUT 1) SOUND OF IMPACT (LP, unnumbered, with 8-page booklet) 10
92 Touch & Go TG 81 PIGPILE (LP, boxed set with video & T-shirt with insert) 30
(see also Rapeman)

BIG BOB
59 Top Rank JAR 185 Your Line Was Busy/What Am I 50

BIG BOPPER
58 Mercury AMT 1002 Chantilly Lace/The Purple People Eater Meets The Witchdoctor 20
58 Mercury AMT 1002 Chantilly Lace/The Purple People Eater Meets The Witchdoctor (78) 15
59 Mercury AMT 1017 Big Bopper's Wedding/Little Red Riding Hood 30
59 Mercury AMT 1017 Big Bopper's Wedding/Little Red Riding Hood (78) 15
59 Mercury AMT 1046 It's The Truth, Ruth/That's What I Am Talking About 35
59 Mercury ZEP 10004 THE BIG BOPPER (EP) 100
59 Mercury ZEP 10027 PINK PETTICOATS (EP) 150
58 Mercury MMC 14008 CHANTILLY LACE (LP) 150
74 Contour 6870 531 CHANTILLY LACE (LP) 10

BIG BORIS
72 RCA RCA 2197 Big Country/Devil's Drive 7

BIG BOY PETE
68 Camp 602 005 Cold Turkey/My Love Is Like A Spaceship 65
96 Tenth Planet TP 026 HOMAGE TO CATATONIA (LP) 18
(see also Miller, Pete Miller)

BIG BROTHER & HOLDING COMPANY
67 Fontana TF 881 Bye Bye Baby/All Is Loneliness 18
68 CBS 3683 Piece Of My Heart/Turtle Blues (some in p/s) 20/7
68 London HLT 10226 Down On Me/Call On Me 10
67 Fontana (S)TL 5457 BIG BROTHER & THE HOLDING COMPANY (LP, with Janis Joplin, mono/stereo) 45/35
68 CBS (S)63392 CHEAP THRILLS (LP, with Janis Joplin, laminated single sleeve, mono/stereo) 65/30
69 London HA-T/SH-T 8377 BIG BROTHER & THE HOLDING COMPANY (LP, reissue, mono/stereo) 22
71 CBS S 64118 BE A BROTHER (LP) 18
(see also Janis Joplin, Nick Gravenites)

BIG CARROT
73 EMI EMI 2047 Blackjack/Squint Eye Mangle 30
(see also Marc Bolan/T. Rex)

BIG COUNTRY
84 Mercury COUNT 5-5 Wonderland/Giant//Lost Patrol (Live – parts 1 & 2) (2 x 7") 10
84 Mercury MERD 185 Where The Rose Is Sown/Belief In The Small Man//Wonderland (Live)/In A Big Country (Live)/Auld Lang Syne (Live) (2 x 7") 10
(see also Skids)

BIG DAVE (Cavanaugh) & HIS ORCHESTRA
54 Capitol CL 14195 Loosely With Feeling/The Cat From Coos Bay (triangular centre) 18
55 Capitol CL 14245 Rock And Roll Party/Your Kind Of Love (triangular centre) 35

BIG FLAME
84 Laughing Gun PLAQUE 001 Sink/The Illness/Sometimes (p/s, with insert) 10

BARRY BIGGS
70 Dynamic DYN 401 Got To Be Mellow/Love Grows 12
(see also Bob & Marcia)

BIG IN JAPAN
77 Eric's ERICS 0001 Big In Japan/CHUDDIE NUDDIES: Do The Chud (p/s) 10
78 Zoo CAGE 1 FROM Y TO Z AND NEVER AGAIN (EP, foldout p/s) 15
(see also Pink Industry/Military, Holly, Holly Johnson, Yachts, Bill Drummond, Creatures, Siouxsie & Banshees, Lightning Raiders)

MINT VALUE £

BIG JOE (Joseph Spalding)
74 Dip DL 5007 Selassie Skank/Version . . . 15
74 Dip DL 5008 Weed Specialist/CHERRY & DUB MASTER: Rub A Daughter . . . 12
74 Dip DL 5027 Hog In A Me Minty/Sweet Melody . . . 18
75 Fab FAB 243 American Pum Pum/Tape White Wash . . . 5

BIG LUCKY, BIG AMOS & DONALD HINES
72 London SHU 8425 RIVER TOWN BLUES (LP) . . . 20

BIG MAYBELLE
57 London HLC 8447 I Don't Want To Cry/All Of Me . . . 50
57 London HLC 8447 I Don't Want To Cry/All Of Me (78) . . . 25
59 London HLC 8854 Baby, Won't You Please Come Home/Say It Isn't So . . . 30
59 London HLC 8854 Baby, Won't You Please Come Home/Say It Isn't So (78) . . . 18
65 London HL 9941 Careless Love/My Mother's Eyes . . . 18
67 CBS 2735 Turn The World Around The Other Way/I Can't Wait Any Longer . . . 30
67 CBS 2926 Mama (He Treats Your Daughter Mean)/Keep That Man . . . 30
68 Direction 58-3312 Quittin' Time/I Can't Wait Any Longer . . . 30
67 CBS 62999 THE PURE SOUL OF BIG MAYBELLE (LP) . . . 75

BIG MOE with BOYD BENNETT & ROCKETS
(see under Boyd Bennett)

BIG MOOSE (Walker)
60s Python PKM 01 Ramblin' Woman/Puppy Howl Blues . . . 25

BIG NOISE
90s President PCOM 1111 BIG NOISE (CD) . . . 18
(see also Gary Numan)

BIGROUP
70s Peer Intl. Library PIL 009 BIG HAMMER (LP, library disc) . . . 150

BIG SLEEP
71 Pegasus PEG 4 BLUEBELL WOOD (LP, gatefold sleeve) . . . 40
(see also Eyes Of Blue, Ancient Grease, Gentle Giant, Man, Ritchie Francis, Gary Pickford-Hopkins)

BIG STAR
78 Stax STAX 504 September Gurls/Mod Lang . . . 7
78 Aura AUS 103 Kizza Me/Dream Lover (p/s) . . . 7
78 Aura AUS 107 Jesus Christ/Big Black Car . . . 7
78 Stax SXSP 302 RADIO CITY/BIG STAR (2-LP) . . . 18
78 Aura AUL 703 THIRD ALBUM (LP) . . . 12
(see also Alex Chilton, Box Tops)

BIG THREE (U.K.)
63 Decca F 11614 Some Other Guy/Let True Love Begin . . . 18
63 Decca F 11689 By The Way/Cavern Stomp . . . 10
63 Decca F 11752 I'm With You/Peanut Butter . . . 18
64 Decca F 11927 If You Ever Change Your Mind/You've Got To Keep Her Under Hand . . . 25
73 Polydor 2058 343 Some Other Guy/Let It Rock/If You Gotta Make A Fool Of Somebody . . . 10
63 Decca DFE 8552 AT THE CAVERN (EP) . . . 25
73 Polydor 2383 199 RESURRECTION (LP) . . . 25
(see also Escorts, Paddy Klaus & Gibson, Johnny Gustafson, Faron's Flamingos, Johnny & John)

BIG THREE (U.S.)
68 Roulette RCP 5002 THE BIG THREE FEATURING MAMA CASS (LP) . . . 30
(see also Mama Cass [Elliot], Mamas & Papas)

BIG YOUTH
72 Blue Beat BB 424 Chi Chi Run/JOHN HOLT: OK Fred . . . 15
73 Downtown DT 497 Dock Of The Bay/CRYSTALITES: Bass And Drums (Version) . . . 15
73 Gayfeet CS 206 Medicine Doctor/Facts Of Life . . . 15
73 Prince Buster PB 46 Chi Chi Run/Drums And Bass (Version) . . . 12
73 Prince Buster PB 48 Leggo Beast/Leave Your Skeng . . . 12
73 Prince Buster PB 50 Cain And Abel/Cain And Abel (Version) . . . 20
73 Grape GR 3040 Foreman Versus Frazier/Foreman Versus Frazier Round Two . . . 18
73 Grape GR 3044 JA To UK/JA To UK (Version) . . . 12
73 Grape GR 3051 Opportunity Rock/Double Attack . . . 15
73 Grape GR 3061 Concrete Jungle/Screaming Tonight . . . 8
73 Green Door GD 4051 Cool Breeze/CRYSTALITES: Windstorm . . . 20
73 Summit SUM 8542 A So We Say (with Dennis Brown)/WINSTON SCOTLAND: Scarface . . . 8
74 Harry J. HJ 6682 Ride On Ride On/Wild Goose Chase (both with Dennis Brown) . . . 6
75 Attack ATT 8104 Mammy Hot And Daddy Cold/GROOVEMASTERS: Some Like It Dread . . . 10
75 Dip DL 5097 Big Youth Dread/Another Version . . . 10
75 Lucky DL 5103 Natty Warning/Version . . . 8
75 Klik KLP 9001 Dread Locks Dread . . . 15
76 Lucky LY 6001 Get Up Stand Up/Version (with Dennis Brown) . . . 6
72 Fab MS 8 CHI CHI RUN (LP) . . . 40
73 Trojan TRLS 61 SCREAMING TARGET (LP, orange & white label) . . . 30
76 Trojan TRLS 123 NATTY CULTURAL DREAD (LP) . . . 25
76 Trojan TRLS 137 HIT THE ROAD JACK (LP) . . . 20
(see also Upsetters, Keith Hudson)

BIG YOUTH & KEITH HUDSON
73 Pyramid PYR 7055 Can You Keep A Secret/HORACE ANDY & EARL FLUTE: Peter And Judas . . . 25
(see also Keith Hudson)

BIKINIS
58 Columbia DB 4149 Bikini/Boogie Rock And Roll . . . 25
58 Columbia DB 4149 Bikini/Boogie Rock And Roll (78) . . . 10

MINT VALUE £

(Mr.) ACKER BILK (& HIS PARAMOUNT JAZZ BAND)

Year	Label	Title	£
56	Tempo A 134	Dippermouth Blues/Where The River Shannon Flows	5
60	Pye 7NJ 2029	Marching Through Georgia/Delia Gone	5
60	Melodisc 1547	Goodnight Sweet Prince/East Coast Trot	5
60	Pye 7NJ 2034	Blaze Away/Higher Ground (p/s)	5
60	Pye 7NJ 2035	Under The Double Eagle/Easter Parade (p/s)	5
61	Columbia SCD 2155	Stars And Stripes Forever/Creole Jazz (p/s)	5
62	Columbia SCD 2176	Gotta See Baby Tonight/If You Were The Only Girl In The World (p/s)	5
62	Columbia SEG 8178	BAND OF THIEVES (EP)	10
58	77 LEU 12/1	ACKER'S EARLY DAYS (LP)	15
58	Pye Nixa NJT 513	ACKER BILK REQUESTS (10" LP)	20
59	Columbia 33S 1141	THE NOBLE ART OF ACKER BILK (10" LP)	12
60	Pye NJL 22	THE MR ACKER BILK OMNIBUS (LP)	25
60	Columbia 33SX 1205	SEVEN AGES OF ACKER (LP)	25
60	Columbia 33SX 1248	ACKER (LP)	25
60	Society SOC 908	MY EARLY DAYS (LP)	15
61	Columbia 33SX 1304	A GOLDEN TREASURY OF BILK (LP, also stereo [SCX 3366])	12
61	Columbia 33SX 1348	LANDSDOWNE FOLIO (LP)	25
62	Columbia 33SX 1456	BEAU JAZZ (LP)	12
63	Columbia 33SX 1525	CALL ME MISTER (LP)	25
65	Columbia 33SX 1747	ACK'S BACK (LP)	25
67	Columbia S(C)X 6241	THE VERITABLE MR BILK (LP)	25
70	Starline SRS 5026	EXPO' 70 (LP)	12

(see also Michael London)

BILL & COO

Year	Label	Title	£
75	Bradley's BRAD 7513	Smoochy Smoochy/Always I Love You	7

(see also Twinkle)

BILLIE & EDDIE

Year	Label	Title	£
59	Top Rank JAR 249	The King Is Coming Back/Come Back, Baby	25

BILLION DOLLAR BABIES

Year	Label	Title	£
77	Polydor 2391 273	BATTLE AXES (LP)	12

(see also Alice Cooper)

BILLY & ESSENTIALS

Year	Label	Title	£
63	London HLW 9657	Over The Weekend/Maybe You'll Be There	50

BILLY & LILLIE (& Billy Ford & Thunderbirds)

Year	Label	Title	£
58	London HLU 8564	La Dee Dah/BILLY FORD'S THUNDERBIRDS: The Monster	30
58	London HLU 8564	La Dee Dah/BILLY FORD'S THUNDERBIRDS: The Monster (78)	10
58	London HLU 8630	Creepin', Crawlin', Cryin'/Happiness (with Billy Ford & Thunderbirds)	40
58	London HLU 8630	Creepin', Crawlin', Cryin'/Happiness (with Billy Ford & Thunderbirds) (78)	10
58	London HLU 8689	The Greasy Spoon/Hangin' On To You (with Billy Ford & Thunderbirds)	25
58	London HLU 8689	The Greasy Spoon/Hangin' On To You (with Billy Ford & Thunderbirds) (78)	10
59	London HLU 8795	I Promise You/Lucky Ladybug	25
59	London HLU 8795	I Promise You/Lucky Ladybug (78)	20
59	Top Rank JAR 157	Bells, Bells, Bells/Honeymoonin' (as Billie & Lillie)	10
59	Top Rank JAR 157	Bells, Bells, Bells/Honeymoonin' (as Billie & Lillie) (78)	20

BIM & BAM

Year	Label	Title	£
70	Crab CRAB 48	The Pill (with Clover)/TOMMY McCOOK: Spring Fever	12
70	Crab CRAB 49	Immigrant Plight (w/ Clover)/PETER AUSTIN & HORTENSE: Bang Shangalang	12
73	Gayfeet GS 201	Fatty/Landlord	8

BIM, BAM & CLOVER

Year	Label	Title	£
70	Trojan TR 7754	Party Time Parts 1 & 2	7

UMBERTO BINDI

Year	Label	Title	£
60	Oriole CB 1577	Il Nostro Concerto/Un Giorno Un Mese Un Anno	10

BINGO

Year	Label	Title	£
73	Polydor 2066 365	We Can't Get Enough/Mumblin' Man	10

SONNY BINNS (& RUDIES)

Year	Label	Title	£
69	Downtown DT 420	The Untouchables/Lazy Boy	12
69	Downtown DT 424	Wheels/Night Train	12
70	Escort ES 818	Boss A Moon (as S. Binns)/BUNNY LEE ALLSTARS: Brotherly Love	12

(see also Rudies)

TONY BINNS

Year	Label	Title	£
71	Explosion EX 2044	Love I Madly/Musical Shower	10
71	Explosion EX 2046	Humpty Dumpty/Got To Get A Message	8

BIONIC BOOGIE

(see under Gregg Diamond)

BIOTA

Year	Label	Title	£
85	Recommended DYS 12 & 13	RACKABONES (LP, with inserts)	40

STANLEY & JEFFREY BIRD

Year	Label	Title	£
60	HMV POP 702	Johnny At The Crossheads/Betty, Betty (Go Steady With Me)	12

BIRD LEGS & PAULINE

Year	Label	Title	£
66	Sue WI 4014	Spring/In So Many Ways	30

BIRDS

Year	Label	Title	£
64	Decca F 12031	You're On My Mind/You Don't Love Me (You Don't Care)	140
65	Decca F 12140	Leaving Here/Next In Line	85
65	Decca F 12257	No Good Without You Baby/How Can It Be	105
85	Demon WEST 901	THESE BIRDS ARE DANGEROUS (LP)	20

(see also Birds Birds, Ron Wood, Faces, Creation, Ashton Gardner & Dyke)

MINT VALUE £

BIRDS & BRASS

70 Rediffusion ZS 57 SOUNDSATIONAL (LP) ... 25
74 Rediffusion 0100 171 ... ARE BACK (LP) ... 30

BIRDS BIRDS

66 Reaction 591 005 Say Those Magic Words/Daddy Daddy ... 500+
(see also Birds, Gods)

BIRDS OF A FEATHER

69 Page One POF 156 Blacksmith Blues/Sing My Song And Pray ... 10
70 Page One POF 179 All God's Children Got Soul/Get It Together ... 7
72 Jam JAM 23 You Know Me Better/Summer Has Gone ... 6
72 DJM DJS 243 Thank You/Baby Don't You Bring Me Down ... 6
70 Page One POLS 027 BIRDS OF A FEATHER (LP) ... 40
(see also Chanters, Chanter Sisters)

JANE BIRKIN & SERGE GAINSBOURG

69 Fontana TF 1042 Je T'Aime, Moi Non Plus/Jane B (initially with p/s) ... 10/6
69 Major Minor MM 645 Je T'Aime, Moi Non Plus/Jane B (reissue) ... 5
72 Philips 6009 201 La Decadanse/Les Langues De Chat ... 8
74 Antic K 11511 Je T'Aime, Moi Non Plus/Jane B (2nd reissue, 'nude' p/s) ... 7
69 Fontana STL 5493 JANE BIRKIN AND SERGE GAINSBOURG (LP) ... 40

BIRMINGHAM

71 Grosvenor GRS 1011 BIRMINGHAM (LP) ... 100
(see also Dave Peace Quartet)

BIRTH CONTROL

71 Charisma CAS 1036 BIRTH CONTROL (LP) ... 20

BIRTHDAY PARTY

80 4AD AD 12 The Friend Catcher/Waving My Arms/Cat Man (p/s) ... 8
81 4AD AD 111 Release The Bats/Blast Off (p/s) ... 8
81 4AD AD 114 Mr. Clarinet/Happy Birthday (p/s) ... 8
81 (no cat. no.) Mr. Clarinet/Missing Link (sold at gigs only) ... 50
82 Masterbag BAG 005 Dead Joe (flexidisc free with *Masterbag* magazine issue 15) ... 8/6
(see also Nick Cave & Bad Seeds, Roland S. Howard & Lydia Lunch)

DICKIE BISHOP & SIDEKICKS

57 Decca F 10869 Cumberland Gap/No Other Baby ... 18
57 Decca F 10959 The Prisoner's Song/Please Remember Me ... 10
58 Decca F 10981 Skip To My Lou/No Other Baby ... 12
58 Decca F 11028 They Can't Take That Away From Me/Jumpin' Judy ... 12
(see also Chris Barber's Skiffle Group)

TOMMY BISHOP'S RICOCHETS

65 Decca F 12238 I Should Have Known/On The Other Hand ... 15
(see also Rock 'n' Roll Revival Show)

BISHOPS

(see under Count Bishops)

BITCH

79 Hurricane FIRE 5 Big City/Wild Kids (p/s) ... 20

BITCH

81 Rutland RX 101 First Bite/Maggie (some with p/s & promo insert) ... 15/20

BITCHES SIN

81 Neat NEAT 09 Always Ready For Love/Sign Of The Times (p/s) ... 8
83 Quiet QT 001 No More Chances/Overnight/Ice Angels (12", p/s) ... 25
83 Terminal TCAS 21 OUT OF MY MIND (EP, cassette, 6-track) ... 8
82 Heavy Metal HMRLP 4 PREDATOR (LP, textured sleeve) ... 18

BITCH MAGNET

91 Caff CAFF 14 Sadie/Ducks And Drakes (p/s, with insert) ... 8

BIZ

93 Warp WARP LP 9 ELECTRO SOMA (LP, orange vinyl) ... 12

BIZET BOYS

89 Parlophone RIDE 1 Ride 'Em Cowboy/Ride 'Em Cowboy (Speechless) (p/s) ... 5
89 Parlophone 12RIDE 1 Ride 'Em Cowboy (A Classic Mix)/Ride 'Em Cowboy (Opera House Mix)/ Ride 'Em Cowboy (3 M's Much More Mix) (12", p/s) ... 10
(see also Sigue Sigue Sputnik)

BJÖRK

93 One Little Indian BJDJ 101 One Day (Endorphin Mix)/(Springs Eternal Mix) (10", die-cut sleeve, promo only, 2,000 copies) ... 20
93 One Little Indian BJDJ 102 Violently Happy (12" Mix)/(Basso Hitto Dubo) (10", die-cut sleeve, promo only, 2,000 copies) ... 20
94 One Little Indian BJDJ 103 Come To Me (Black Dog Productions)/Anchor Song (Black Dog Productions) (10", die-cut sleeve, promo only, 2,000 copies) ... 30
93 One Little Indian BJDJ 104 Human Behaviour (The Underworld Dub 1)/(The Underworld Dub 2) (10", die-cut sleeve, promo only, 1,000 copies) ... 20
93 One Little Indian 112TP 12P Human Behaviour (Speedy J. Close To Human Mix)/(Dom T. Mix)/ (Bassheads Edit) (12", promo only) ... 15
93 One Little Indian 112TP 12DJ Human Behaviour (The Underworld Mix)/(The Underworld Dub) (12", promo only) ... 15
93 One Little Indian BJDJ 123 One Day (Adrenalin — Far Removed) (12", 1-sided, promo only, 1,000 copies) .. 25
93 O. L. Indian BJDJ 124/125 BIG TIME SENSUALITY (12" EP, double pack, promo only, 500 copies) ... 20
93 O. L. Indian BJDJ 124/125g BIG TIME SENSUALITY (12" EP, double pack, promo only, 1,000 copies) ... 18
95 One L. Indian 162 TP12P ARMY OF ME (12" EP, remix double pack, single p/s, promo copies) ... 8
95 One L. Indian 162 TP12GM ARMY OF ME (Graham Massey Mix) (12", white label, no p/s, promo only) ... 8

Year	Label	Title	Value
96	O. Little Indian 193TP12DM	Enjoy/Possibly Maybe (12", 1,000 only, numbered p/s)	18
96	O. Little Indian 193TP12TD	POSSIBLY MAYBE (12" EP, 1,000 only, numbered p/s)	12
97	O. L. Indian TPLP 81	JOGA (12" triple-pack, inner sleeves, p/s)	12
97	O. L. Indian 20 TP7 BOX	JOGA (CD box set, 3 x CD singles & 1-track video, 3,000 only)	35
97	O. L. Indian 20 TP7 BOX 212	BACHELORETTE (CD box set, 3 x CD singles & 1-track video, 3,000 only)	25
93	One Little Indian TPLP 31L	DEBUT (LP, 5,000 with 16-page lyric booklet)	18/10
94	One Little Indian 152TP 7	THE BEST MIXES FROM THE ALBUM "DEBUT" FOR THOSE PEOPLE WHO DON'T BUY WHITE LABELS (mini-LP)	20
95	One L. Indian TPLP 51L	POST (LP, pink vinyl, with inner sleeve)	18
95	One L. Indian TPLP 51CDX	POST (CD, digipak w/poster & lyric book, some copies in PVC purse)	18/15

(see also Sugarcubes, Kukl)

BLACK

Year	Label	Title	Value
81	Rox ROX 17	Human Features/Electric Church (p/s)	10

BILL BLACK'S COMBO

Year	Label	Title	Value
59	Felsted AF 129	Smokie Parts 1 & 2	20
59	Felsted AF 129	Smokie Parts 1 & 2 (78)	15
60	London HLU 9090	White Silver Sands/The Wheel	12
60	London HLU 9156	Josephine/Dry Bones	10
60	London HLU 9212	Don't Be Cruel/Rollin'	10
61	London HLU 9267	Blue Tango/Willie	10
61	London HLU 9306	Hearts Of Stone/Royal Blue	10
61	London HLU 9383	Ole Buttermilk Sky/Yogi	10
61	London HLU 9436	Movin'/Honky Train	12
61	London HLU 9479	Twist-Her/My Girl Josephine	8
62	London HLU 9594	So What/Blues For The Red Boy	8
62	London HLU 9645	Joey's Song/Hot Taco	8
63	London HLU 9721	Do It — Rat Now/Little Jasper	8
63	London HLU 9788	Monkey-Shine/Long Gone	8
64	London HLU 9855	Comin' On/Soft Winds	8
64	London HLU 9903	Tequila/Raunchy	10
64	London HLU 9925	Little Queenie/Boo-Ray	25
68	London HLU 10216	Turn On Your Love Light/Ribbon Of Darkness	5
60	London REU 1277	BILL BLACK'S COMBO (EP)	30
63	London REU 1369	THE UNTOUCHABLE SOUND OF BILL BLACK (EP)	30
62	London HA-U 2310	SOLID AND RAUNCHY (LP)	40
62	London HA-U 2427	LET'S TWIST (LP, also stereo SAH-U 6222)	25/30
62	London HA-U 2433	MOVIN' (LP)	25
63	London HA-U 8080	THE UNTOUCHABLE SOUND OF BILL BLACK (LP)	25
63	London HA-U 8113	GREATEST HITS (LP)	18
64	London HA-U 8187	PLAYS CHUCK BERRY (LP)	35
68	London HA-U/SH-U 8367	BILL BLACK'S BEAT GOES ON (LP)	15
69	London HA-U/SH-U 8373	TURN ON YOUR LOVE LIGHT (LP)	15
69	London HA-U/SH-U 8389	SOULIN' THE BLUES (LP)	15

(see also Elvis Presley)

CILLA BLACK

Year	Label	Title	Value
63	Parlophone R 5065	Love Of The Loved/Shy Of Love	10
64	Parlophone R 5101	Anyone Who Had A Heart/Just For You	5
64	Parlophone R 5133	You're My World/Suffer Now I Must	6
64	Parlophone R 5162	It's For You/He Won't Ask Me	6
65	Parlophone R 5225	You've Lost That Lovin' Feelin'/Is It Love?	6
65	Parlophone R 5265	I've Been Wrong Before/I Don't Want To Know	6
66	Parlophone R 5395	Love's Just A Broken Heart/Yesterday	6
66	Parlophone R 5427	Alfie/Night Time Is Here	6
66	Parlophone R 5463	Don't Answer Me/The Right One Is Left	6
66	Parlophone R 5515	A Fool Am I (Dimmelo Parlami)/For No One	6
67	Parlophone R 5608	What Good Am I?/Over My Head	6
67	Parlophone R 5652	I Only Live To Love You/From Now On	8
68	Parlophone R 5674	Step Inside Love/I Couldn't Take My Eyes Off You	6
68	Parlophone R 5706	Where Is Tomorrow/Work Is A Four Letter Word	10
69	Parlophone R 5759	Surround Yourself With Sorrow/London Bridge	8
69	Parlophone R 5785	Conversations/Liverpool Lullaby	6
69	Parlophone R 5820	If I Thought You'd Ever Change Your Mind/It Feels So Good	6
70	Parlophone R 5879	Child Of Mine/That's Why I Love You	7
71	Parlophone R 5924	Something Tells Me (Something's Gonna Happen Tonight)/La La La Lu	5
72	Parlophone R 5938	The World I Wish For You/Down In The City	7
72	Parlophone R 5972	You, You, You/Silly Wasn't I?	6
74	EMI EMI 2107	Baby We Can't Go Wrong/Someone	5
74	EMI EMI 2169	I'll Have To Say I Love You In A Song/Never Run Out (Of You)	5
74	EMI EMI 2227	He Was A Writer/Anything That You Might Say	5
75	EMI EMI 2278	Alfie Darling/Little Bit Of Understanding	5
75	EMI EMI 2328	I'll Take A Tango/To Know Him Is To Love Him	5
64	Parlophone GEP 8901	ANYONE WHO HAD A HEART (EP)	18
64	Parlophone GEP 8916	IT'S FOR YOU (EP)	20
66	Parlophone GEP 8954	CILLA'S HITS (EP)	20
67	Parlophone GEP 8967	TIME FOR CILLA (EP)	35
65	Parlophone PMC 1243	CILLA (LP, mono, yellow/black label)	20
65	Parlophone PCS 3063	CILLA (LP, stereo, yellow/black label)	30
66	Parlophone PMC 7004	CILLA SINGS A RAINBOW (LP, mono, yellow/black label)	18
66	Parlophone PCS 7004	CILLA SINGS A RAINBOW (LP, stereo, yellow/black label)	25
66	Parlophone TA-PMC 7004	CILLA SINGS A RAINBOW (reel-to-reel tape, mono only)	12
68	Parlophone PMC 7041	SHER-OO! (LP, mono, yellow/black label)	18
68	Parlophone PCS 7041	SHER-OO! (LP, stereo, yellow/black label)	18
68	Parlophone TA-PMC 7041	SHER-OO! (reel-to-reel tape, mono only)	12
68	Parlophone PMC/PCS 7065	THE BEST OF CILLA BLACK (mono/stereo, yellow/black label)	15

MINT VALUE £

68	Parlophone TA-PCS 7065	THE BEST OF CILLA BLACK (reel-to-reel tape, mono only)	12
68	Parlophone PMC/PCS 7079	SURROUND YOURSELF WITH CILLA (LP, mono/stereo, yellow/black label)	15

(Any black and silver label reissues of the above LPs from the 70s are worth half these values.)

69	Parlophone PCS 7103	SWEET INSPIRATION (LP)	12
70	Parlophone PCS 7128	IMAGES (LP)	12
73	Parlophone PCS 7155	DAY BY DAY WITH CILLA (LP)	12

'FLIP' BLACK & BOYS UPSTAIRS

59 Capitol CL 15037 — For You My Lover/Tell Her Mister Moon — 8

FRANK BLACK

93 4AD CADD 3004 — FRANK BLACK (LP, die-cut screen-printed sleeve, with lyric inner) — 12

(see also Pixies)

JEANNE BLACK

60 Capitol CL 15131 — He'll Have To Stay/JEANNE & JANIE: Under Your Spell Again — 10
60 Capitol CL 12456 — Lisa/ JEANNE & JANIE: Journey of Love — 12

(see also Janie, Jeanne & Janie)

MATT BLACK & THE DOODLEBUGS

76 Punk BCS 0005 — Punky Xmas/Nightmare (no p/s) — 15

STANLEY BLACK & HIS PIANO ORCHESTRA

63 Decca F 11624 — Hand In Hand/Lullaby Of The Stars — 8

BLACK ABBOTTS

70 Chapter One CH 123 — She Looked Away/I Don't Mind — 7
71 Evolution E 3001 — How About Me/Everybody Needs A Little Sunshine — 7
71 Evolution E 3004 — Love Is Alive/The Painter — 15

BLACK ACE

61 XX MIN 701 — BLACK ACE (EP) — 25
62 Heritage HLP 1006 — BLACK ACE (LP) — 90

BLACK ANGELS

84 Gull GULP 1041 — KICKDOWN (LP) — 12

BLACK AXE

80 Metal MELT 1 — Highway Rider/Red Lights (some in p/s) — 15/6

BLACKBEARD

80 More Cut RDC 2002 — I WAH DUB (LP) — 20

BLACK BEATLES

70 Pama PM 804 — Reggae And Shout/LENOX BROWN: The Green Hornet — 8

BLACKBIRDS

68 Saga OPP 3 — No Destination/Space (company sleeve, possibly promo only) — 25
68 Saga FID 2113 — NO DESTINATION (LP) — 30

BLACK, BROWN & BEIGE

72 Regal Zonophone RZ 3051 — We Are The Champions/What Is A Man — 5

TONY BLACKBURN

65 Fontana TF 562 — Don't Get Off That Train/Just To Be With You Again — 12
65 Fontana TF 601 — Is There Another Way To Love You/Here Today Gone Tomorrow — 6
66 Fontana TF 729 — Green Light/Winter Is Through — 6
67 MGM MGM 1375 — So Much Love/In The Night — 6
68 MGM MGM 1394 — She's My Girl/Closer To A Dream — 5
69 MGM MGM 1467 — It's Only Love/Janie — 5
69 Polydor 56360 — Blessed Are The Lonely/Wait For Me — 5
71 RCA RCA 2067 — Is It Me Is It You/Happy — 5
71 RCA RCA 2109 — Chop Chop/If You Were A Dream — 6
68 MGM C(S) 8062 — TONY BLACKBURN SINGS (LP) — 20
70 Fontana SFL 13161 — TONY BLACKBURN MEETS MATT MONRO (LP, Blackburn and Monro have 6 tracks each) — 12

BLACKBYRDS

74 Fantasy FTC 113 — Do It Fluid/Summer Love — 8
75 Fantasy FTC 114 — Walking In Rhythm/Baby — 6
75 Fantasy FTC 117 — I Need You/All I Ask — 6
76 Fantasy FTC 122 — Rock Creek Park/Flying High — 8
76 Fantasy FTC 129 — Happy Music/Love So Fine — 6
85 Streetwave SWAVE 3 — Rock Creek Park/Walking In Rhythm (12") — 12
75 Fantasy FT 9444 — BLACKBYRDS (LP) — 20
75 Fantasy FT 522 — FLYING START (LP) — 15
76 Fantasy FTA 3003 — CITY LIFE (LP) — 15
77 Fantasy FT 534 — ACTION (LP) — 15
79 Fantasy FT 555 — NIGHT GROOVES — THE BEST OF THE BLACKBYRDS (LP) — 15

(see also Donald Byrd)

BLACK CAT BONES

70 Decca Nova SDN 15 — BARBED WIRE SANDWICH (LP) — 80

(see also Leaf Hound, Brian Short, Free, Foghat)

BLACK COUNTRY THREE

66 Transatlantic TRA 140 — BLACK COUNTRY THREE (LP) — 50

(see also Jon Raven)

BLACK CROWES

90 Def American DEFA 4 — Jealous Again/Thick'n'Thin (p/s) — 5
90 Def American DEFA 412 — Jealous Again/Thick'n'Thin/Waitin' Guilty (12", p/s) — 8
90 Def American DEFAP 412 — Jealous Again/Thick'n'Thin/Waitin' Guilty (12", picture disc) — 10
90 Def American DEFAC 4 — Jealous Again/Thick'n'Thin/Waitin' Guilty (CD) — 8
90 Def American DEFAP 612 — Hard To Handle/Jealous Again (Acoustic)/Twice As Hard (live) (12", crow-shaped picture disc with plinth) — 12

MINT VALUE £

90	Def American DEFAC 6	Hard To Handle/Jealous Again (Acoustic)/Twice As Hard (Remix) (CD)	8
91	Def American DEFAP 712	Twice As Hard/Jealous Again (live)/Could I've Been So Blind (live) (12", picture disc with insert)	8
91	Def American DEFA 812	Jealous Again/She Talks To Angels/She Talks To Angels (live) (12", p/s with patch, some sealed)	10/8
91	Def American DEFAC 812	Jealous Again/She Talks To Angels (live)/Could I've Been So Blind (live) (CD)	8
91	Def American DEFAP 10	Hard To Handle/Stare It Cold (live) (shaped picture disc)	8

BLACK DOG

91	GPR GENP(X) 2	PARALLEL EP (12", p/s)	30
92	Black Dog Prods BDP 001	VIRTUAL EP (12", p/s)	100
92	Black Dog Prods BDP 002	AGE OF SLACK (12", p/s)	100
92	Black Dog Prods BDP 003	BLACK DOG EP (12", p/s, 500 only)	80
92	GPR GENP(X) 3	VIR 2 L (12", custom sleeve)	45
92	GPR GENP(X) 9	VANTOOL EP (12", custom sleeve)	40
93	GPR GENP(X) 17	COST II (12", custom sleeve)	20
93	Rising High RSN 046	BLACK DOG PRODUCTIONS (12", 4-track, p/s)	25
91	GPR GPR 004	PARALLEL SQUELCH (LP)	40
92	GPR GPRLP 1	TEMPLE OF TRANSPARENT BALLS (2-LP, some with poster)	30/25
93	GPR GPRCD 1	TEMPLE OF TRANSPARENT BALLS (CD)	25
95	GPR GPRLP 15	PARALLEL (2-LP)	35
95	GPR GPRCD 15	PARALLEL (CD)	30
95	Warp PUPLP 1	SPANNERS (2-LP)	40
95	Warp WAP LP 8LTD	BYTES (LP, bronze vinyl)	60

(see also Alter Ego, Plaid, Repeat, Unexplored Beats, Shiva)

BLACK DYKE MILLS BAND

68	Apple APPLE 4	Thingumybob/Yellow Submarine	50

BLACK DYNAMITES

60	Top Rank JAR 319	Brush Those Tears/Lonely Cissy	25

BLACK EASTER

82	Illuminated KILL 13	READY TO ROCK (EP, p/s)	5

BLACK FLAG

81	Alt. Tentacles VIRUS 9	Six Pack/I've Heard It All Before/American Waste (p/s)	12
84	SST SST 12001	Family Man/I Won't Stick Any Of You Unless And Until I Can Stick All Of You (12", p/s)	10

BLACKFOOT

79	Atlantic K 11368	Highway Song/Road Fever	5
79	Atlantic K 11447	Train Train/Baby Blue	5
80	Atco K 11610	On The Run/Streetfighter (p/s)	7
80	Atco K 11636	Every Man Should Know (Queenie)/Highway Song	5
81	Atco K 11673	Good Morning/Payin' For It Now (p/s)	7
82	Atco K 11686T	Dry Country/Too Hard To Handle//On The Run/Train Train (double pack, gatefold sleeve)	5
82	Atco K 11760	Highway Song/Rollin' 'n' Tumblin'/Flyman (p/s, 6 different 45s, recorded live at Glasgow, Edinburgh, Newcastle, Liverpool, Manchester or Birmingham)	each 6
83	Atco B 9880P	Send Me An Angel/Driving Fool (shaped picture disc)	8

(see also Lynyrd Skynyrd)

J.D. BLACKFOOT

71	Mercury 6338 031	THE ULTIMATE PROPHECY (LP)	60

BLACKFOOT SUE

72	Jam JAM 13	Standing In The Road/Celestial Plain	5
72	Jam JAM 29	Sing Don't Speak/2 B Free	5
73	Jam JAM 44	Summer/Morning Light	5
73	Jam JAM 53	Get It All To Me/My Oh My	5
74	DJM DJS 296	Bye Bye Birmingham/Messiah	5
74	DJM DJS 326	You Need Love/Tobago Rose	5
75	DJM DJS 411	Moonshine/Corrie	5
73	Jam JAL 104	NOTHING TO HIDE (LP)	18
75	DJM DJLPS 455	GUN RUNNING (LP, withdrawn)	45

BLACKJACK

80	Polydor POSP 76	Without Your Love/Heart Of Mine (p/s)	20
79	Polydor 2391 411	BLACKJACK (LP)	20
80	Polydor	WORLDS APART (LP)	12

(see also Michael Bolotin, Michael Bolton)

BLACKJACKS

63	Pye 7N 15586	Woo Hoo/Red Dragon	18

(see also Pat Harris & Blackjacks)

BLACK KNIGHTS

65	Columbia DB 7443	I Gotta Woman/Angel Of Love	25

HONOR BLACKMAN

68	CBS 3896	Before Today/I'll Always Be Loving You (some in p/s)	55/25
64	Decca LK/SKL 4642	EVERYTHING I'VE GOT (LP, mono/stereo)	60

(see also Patrick MacNee & Honor Blackman)

RITCHIE BLACKMORE (ORCHESTRA)

65	Oriole CB 314	Getaway/Little Brown Jug	250

(see also Outlaws, Neil Christian & Crusaders, Deep Purple, [Ritchie Blackmore's] Rainbow, Rally Rounders, Green Bullfrog, Rock Aid Armenia)

BLACK NASTY

80	Grapevine GRP 140	Cut Your Motor Off/Keep On Stepping	8

MINT VALUE £

BLACK OAK ARKANSAS

75 Atlantic K 10621 Fancy Nancy/Keep On 7
71 Atlantic 2400 180 BLACK OAK ARKANSAS (LP) 12

BLACK RIDERS

85 Plastic Head GILP 555 CHOSEN FEW (LP) 15

BLACK REBEL MOTORCYCLE CLUB

01 Virgin VUS 224 Whatever Happened To My Rock 'n' Roll (Punk Song)/Red Eyes And Tears// Fail Safe/Down Here (double pack, gatefold p/s) 10
01 Virgin VUSCD 224 Whatever Happened To My Rock 'n' Roll (Punk Song)/Red Eyes And Tears/ Fail Safe/Down Here/Whatever Happened To My Rock 'n' Roll (Video) (CD, card sleeve) 8
01 Virgin VUSCDJ 224 Whatever Happened To My Rock 'n' Roll (Punk Song)/Red Eyes And Tears/ US Government/Fail Safe (promo-only, withdrawn) 15
01 Virgin VUS 234 Love Burns/At My Door (gatefold p/s) 8

BLACK ROSE

82 Teesbeat TB 5 Sucker For Your Love/No Point Runnin' (some in p/s) 125/35
83 Bullet BOLT 3 BLACK ROSE (12" EP) 8
83 Bullet BOLT 6 WE'RE GONNA ROCK YOU (12" EP) 8
84 Bullet BOL 9 Boys Will Be Boys/Liar (p/s, some with patch) 35
85 Neat NEAT 4812 Nightmare/Need A Lot Of Lovin'/Rock Me Hard (12", p/s) 8
84 Bullet BULP 3 BOYS WILL BE BOYS (LP) 12
87 Neat NEAT 1034 WALK IT HOW YOU TALK IT (LP, with lyric insert) 12

BLACK SABBATH

70 Fontana TF 1067 Evil Woman/Wicked World 90
70 Vertigo V2 Evil Woman/Wicked World (reissue, Vertigo 'swirl' sleeve) 20
70 Vertigo 6059 010 Paranoid/The Wizard (Vertigo 'swirl' sleeve) 20
72 Vertigo 6059 061 Tomorrow's Dream/Laguna Sunrise (Vertigo 'swirl' sleeve) 18
72 Phonogram DJ 005 Children Of The Grave/STATUS QUO: Roadhouse Blues (100 promo copies only) 375
73 WWA WWS 002 Sabbath Bloody Sabbath/Changes (company sleeve) 8
75 NEMS 6165 300 Am I Going Insane? (Radio)/Hole In The Sky (no p/s) 10
78 Vertigo SAB 001 Never Say Die/She's Gone (p/s) 7
78 Vertigo SAB 002 Hard Road/Symptom Of The Universe (purple or black vinyl) .... each 6
80 Vertigo SAB 412 Die Young/Heaven And Hell (extended live) (12", p/s) 8
81 Vertigo SAB 512 Mob Rules/Die Young (live) (12", p/s) 10
82 Vertigo SABP 6 Turn Up The Night/Lonely Is The Word (picture disc) 5
82 Vertigo SABP 612 Turn Up The Night/Lonely Is The Word (12", picture disc) 8
86 Vertigo SABDJ 12 In For The Kill/Turn To Stone/Heart Like A Wheel (12", promo only) 15
87 Vertigo SABAF 1 4 SONGS FROM THE ETERNAL IDOL (12", p/s, promo only) 12
89 I.R.S. EIRS CB 107 Headless Cross (Edit)/Cloak And Dagger (signed label, stickered PVC sleeve) 6
89 I.R.S. EIRSPD 115 Devil And Daughter (1-sided picture disc) 5
89 I.R.S. EIRSB 115 Devil And Daughter (box set, 1-sided disc with stencil, insert & 2 postcards) 8
92 I.R.S. EIRSDJ 180 Master Of Insanity (edit)/Time Machine/Neon Knights (live)/TV Crimes (live)/ Die (live)/Children Of The Sea (live) (CD, no p/s, promo only) 12
70 Vertigo VO 6 BLACK SABBATH (LP, 1st pressing, with black gatefold sleeve and lyric printed on cross; swirl label) 50-60
70 Vertigo VO 6 BLACK SABBATH (LP, 2nd pressing, with white gatefold sleeve and Dunbar credit for 'Warning'; swirl label, some with laminated sleeve) 40/35
70 Vertigo 6360 011 PARANOID (LP, gatefold sleeve, swirl label) 35
71 Vertigo 6360 050 MASTER OF REALITY (LP in box cover, swirl label, some with poster) 60/25
72 Vertigo 6360 071 BLACK SABBATH VOL. 4 (LP, gatefold sleeve with booklet, initially with swirl label, later with 'spaceship' label) 30/15
85 Nems BSBLP 001 THE SABBATH COLLECTION (7-LP box set) 50
88 Castle BSBCD 001 THE BLACK SABBATH CD COLLECTION (6-CD box set with badge & book, numbered, 3,000 only) 40
89 I.R.S. EIRSAPD 1002 HEADLESS CROSS (LP, picture disc, with bonus track "Cloak And Dagger") 18
90 I.R.S. EIRSACV 1038 TYR (LP, picture disc with sticker insert & 2 bonus live tracks) 18

(see also Ozzy Osborne, Dio, Elf, Cozy Powell, Quartz, Phenomena, Rock Aid Armenia)

BLACK SCIENCE ORCHESTRA

96 Junior Boys Own JBO 22 THE ALTERED STATES EP (12") 10

BLACKTHORN

77 WHM 1921 BLACKTHORN (LP) 60
78 WHM 1923 BLACKTHORN II (LP) 100

CHARLES BLACKWELL ORCHESTRA

61 HMV POP 977 Taboo/Midnight In Luxembourg 15
62 Columbia DB 4839 Supercar/Persian Theme 30
62 Columbia DB 4919 Freight Train/Death Valley 10
63 Columbia DB 4994 High Noon/For Me And My Gal 7
63 Columbia DB 7066 El Toro/Hawaiian War Chant 7
63 Columbia DB 7139 The Hokey Croakey/Lost Patrol 7
65 Columbia DB 7501 Meditation/La Bamba 7
67 United Artists UP 1187 Sailor From Gibraltar (Joe Le Rouge)/Hoi 7
60 Triumph TRY 4000 THOSE PLUCKING STRINGS (LP, unreleased, white label test pressings only) 1000

OTIS BLACKWELL

58 London HLE 8616 Make Ready For Love/When You're Around 40
58 London HLE 8616 Make Ready For Love/When You're Around (78) 45

RORY BLACKWELL & HIS BLACKJACKS

57 Parlophone R 4326 Bye Bye Love/Such A Shame 30
57 Parlophone R 4326 Bye Bye Love/Such A Shame (78) 15

MINT VALUE £

SCRAPPER BLACKWELL

67 Collector JEN 7 — SCRAPPER BLACKWELL (EP) — 10
63 '77' LA 12/4 — BLUES BEFORE SUNRISE (LP) — 40
60s Xtra XTRA 5011 — MR SCRAPPER'S BLUES (LP) — 20

BLACKWELLS (U.K.)

65 Columbia DB 7442 — Why Don't You Love Me/All I Want Is Your Love — 35

BLACKWELLS (U.S.)

60 London HLW 9135 — Unchained Melody/Mansion On The Hill — 15
61 London HLW 9334 — Love Or Money/Big Daddy And The Cat — 15

BLACK 2

70 CBS 5031 — Come To The Sabbat/Way To Power — 20
71 CBS 7596 — Wish You Would/Accident — 12
70 CBS 63948 — SACRIFICE (LP, gatefold sleeve) — 20
70 CBS 64133 — BLACK WIDOW II (LP) — 20
72 CBS 64562 — BLACK WIDOW III (LP, with inner) — 20
(see also Pesky Gee, Agony Bag)

ANDY BLADE

80 SMS SMS 001 — Break The News/Girl With The Goods (p/s) — 10
(see also Eater)

BLADES

80 Energy NRG 3 — Hot For You/The Reunion (p/s; Irish with paper labels; later UK with plastic labels, in plastic sleeve) — 20/15
81 Energy NRG 5 — Ghost Of A Chance/Real Emotion (p/s; Irish with paper labels; UK with plastic labels, in plastic sleeve) — 20/12
84 Reekus RKS 013 — The Last Man In Europe (p/s) — 12
85 Reekus RKS 15 — Those Were The Days (p/s) — 10
85 Reekus RKSY 15 — Those Were The Days (picture disc) — 12
86 Reekus RKS 017 — Downmarket/Truth Don't Hurt (as Blades with Paul Cleary) — 10
84 Reekus RKLP 1 — THE LAST MAN IN EUROPE (LP) — 20
86 Reekus RKLP 3 — RAY TOWN REVISITED (LP) — 20
(see also Partisans)

BLADES OF GRASS

67 Stateside SS 2040 — Happy/That's What A Boy Likes — 8
68 Stateside SS 2101 — Charlie And Fred/You Won't Find That Girl — 8

BLAH BLAH BLAH

79 Absurd ABSURD 1 — In The Army/Why Diddle? (p/s) — 5
80s Lyntone LYN 17627 / Good Vibes H 002 — Heavenly View/ST. VITUS DANCE: Meet Mohammed (1-sided 33rpm flexidisc with *Helden* fanzine) — 6/5
81 Some Bizzare — BLAH BLAH BLAH (LP, unreleased, stickered sleeve, white label test pressings only) — 40

HAL BLAINE (& YOUNG COUGARS)

64 RCA RCA 1379 — Gear Stripper/Challenger II (with Young Cougars) — 20
64 RCA RD/SF 7624 — DEUCES, T'S, ROADSTERS AND DRUMS (LP, mono/stereo) — 40/50

VIVIAN BLAINE

54 Parlophone MSP 6070 — Changing Partners/Lonely — 10

BLAIR

79 Miracle M4 — Night Life/Virgo Princess (12") — 10

BEVERLEY BLAIR

58 Mercury 7MT 209 — With Love We Live/Tony — 20

HENRY BLAIR

50s Capitol EAP 1-3003 — SPARKY'S MAGIC PIANO (EP) — 10

SALLY BLAIR

58 MGM MGM 1000 — Whatever Lola Wants (Lola Gets)/Daddy — 20

GARRY BLAKE

66 Columbia DB 7885 — Strawberries And Cream/Look Out Now! — 6
66 Columbia DB 7977 — Wait Until Dark/Jungle Juice — 6
66 Columbia DB 8074 — The Danny Scipio Theme/Celebration Day — 7
68 Studio Two TWO 237 — A SWINGING PARTY (LP) — 15

KARL BLAKE

80 Daark Inc. 1 — TANK DEATH (C-60 cassette) — 12
81 Daark Inc. 2 — THE NEW POLLUTION (C-60 cassette) — 12
83 Glass GLASS 013 — THE PREHENSILE TAPES (LP) — 12
92 Tak Tak Tak TAK 07 — MANDIBLES (cassette, 500 only) — 12
(see also Lemon Kittens, Shock Headed Peters, Underneath, Gland Shrouds, Homunculus, Fur Fur, Sol Invictus)

KEITH BLAKE

68 Blue Cat BS 102 — Musically/I'm Moving On — 30
(see also Overtakers, Uniques)

TIM BLAKE

78 Barclay Towers BAR 711 — Generator Laserbeam/Woodland Voice (p/s) — 8
78 Barclay Towers CLAY 7005 — BLAKE'S NEW JERUSALEM (LP) — 18
(see also Gong, Hawkwind)

WINSTON BLAKE & M-SQUAD

71 Green Door GD 4003 — Carrol Street/ANSELL COLLINS & M-SQUAD: Carol St. Version — 12

ART BLAKEY JAZZ MESSENGERS

60 Fontana TFE 17257 — BLUES MARCH (EP) — 10
61 Fontana TFE 17337 — I REMEMBER CLIFFORD (EP) — 10
61 Fontana TFE 17364 — ARE YOU REAL (EP, with Lee Morgan & Benny Golson) — 10

MINT VALUE £

61	Fontana TFL 5116	OLYMPIA CONCERT (LP)	20
62	HMV CLP 1532	ART BLAKEY JAZZ MESSENGERS (LP, also stereo CSD 1423)	15/20
62	Fontana TFL 5184	DANGEROUS FRIENDSHIPS (LP, soundtrack)	18
63	United Artists (S)ULP 1017	THREE BLIND MICE (LP, mono/stereo)	15/20
64	Riverside RLP 438	CARAVAN (LP)	15
64	HMV CLP 1760	A JAZZ MESSAGE (LP)	15
64	Riverside RLP 464	UGETSU (LP)	25
65	Limelight (S)LML 4000	'S MAKE IT (LP)	12
66	Limelight (S)LML 4012	SOUL FINGER (LP)	12
66	Limelight (S)LML 4021	BUTTERCORN LADY (LP)	12
67	Limelight (S)LML 4023	HOLD ON, I'M COMIN' (LP)	12
67	Atlantic 590 009	BLUE MONK (LP, with Thelonious Monk)	15
69	Storyville 673 013	KYOTO (LP)	12
70	Polydor 545 116	RIGHT DOWN FRONT (LP)	12
74	Prestige PR 10047	CHILD'S DANCE (LP)	12
74	Milestone ML 47008	THERMO (LP)	12

(see also Annie Ross)

ART BLAKEY/MILES DAVIS

66	Fontana FJL 135	L'ASCENSEUR POUR L'ECHAFAUD/FEMME DISPARAISSANTE (LP, soundtrack, 1 side each)	50

(see also Thelonious Monk, Miles Davis)

MEL BLANC

56	Capitol Junior CJ 104	Bugs Bunny & Aladdin's Lamp parts 1 & 2 (78, with p/s)	7
56	Capitol Junior CJ 107	Bugs Bunny & The Pirate parts 1 & 2 (78, with p/s)	7
56	Capitol Junior CJ 108	Bugs Bunny & The Grow-Small Juice parts 1 & 2 (78, with p/s)	7
56	Capitol Junior CJ 109	Woody Woodpecker Meets Davy Crockett/Davy Crockett (78)	8
56	Capitol Junior CJ 110	Pied Piper Pussy Cat (Parts 1 & 2) (78)	8
56	Capitol Junior CJ 117	Tweety Pie Pts 1 & 2 (78)	8
58	Capitol CL 14950	I Taut I Taw A Puddy Cat/K-K-K-Katy	15
60	Warner Bros WB 26	Tweety's Twistmas Twouble/I Keep Hearing Those Bells	5

BURT BLANCA

60	Zodiac ZR 004	Texas Rider/Shamash	20

BLANCMANGE

80	Blaah Music MFT-1	IRENE AND MAVIS (EP, gatefold p/s)	25
82	Lyntone LYN 1183/84	Living On The Ceiling/Sad Day (excerpt)/PASSAGE: Born Every Minute (33rpm black flexidisc free with *Melody Maker* magazine)	6/5
84	London BLAPX 8	(The) Day Before You Came/Feel Me/All Things Are Nice (Version) (12", picture disc, existence unconfirmed)	
82	London SHPD 8552	HAPPY FAMILIES (LP, picture disc)	12
84	London SHPD 8554	MANGE TOUT (LP, picture disc)	12
85	London 820 301-2	BELIEVE YOU ME (CD)	20

BILLY BLAND

60	London HL 9096	Let The Little Girl Dance/Sweet Thing	20
71	Atlantic 2091 130	Let The Little Girl Dance/Chicken Hop	10

BOBBY BLAND

61	Vogue V 9178	Cry Cry Cry/I've Been Wrong So Long	30
61	Vogue V 9182	Lead Me On/Hold Me Tenderly	30
61	Vogue V 9188	Don't Cry No More/St. James Infirmary	30
62	Vogue V 9190	You're The One (That I Need)/Turn On Your Love Light	30
62	Vogue V 9192	Blue Moon/Who Will The Next Fool Be?	30
64	Vocalion VP 9222	Ain't Nothing You Can Do/Honey Child	25
64	Vocalion VP 9229	After It's Too Late/Share Your Love With Me	20
65	Vocalion VP 9232	Yield Not To Temptation/How Does A Cheating Woman Feel?	25
65	Vocalion VP 9251	These Hands (Small But Mighty)/Today	30
66	Vocalion VP 9262	I'm Too Far Gone (To Turn Around)/ If You Could Read My Mind	25
66	Vocalion VP 9273	Good Time Charlie/Good Time Charlie (Working His Groove Bag)	20
68	Sue WI 4044	That Did It/A Touch Of The Blues	30
69	Action ACT 4524	Rockin' In The Same Old Boat/Wouldn't You Rather Have Me?	18
69	Action ACT 4538	Gotta Get To Know You/Baby I'm On My Way	25
69	Action ACT 4548	Share Your Love With Me/Honey Child	18
69	Action ACT 4553	Chains Of Love/Ask Me 'Bout Nothing But The Blues	18
74	ABC ABC 4014	Ain't No Love In The Heart Of The City/Twenty Four Blues	8
75	ABC ABC 4030	I Wouldn't Treat A Dog (The Way You Treat Me)/ I Ain't Gonna Be The First To Cry	8
77	ABC ABC 4186	The Soul Of A Man/If I Weren't A Gambler	8
63	Vocalion VEP 170153	YIELD NOT INTO TEMPTATION (EP)	60
64	Vocalion VEP 170157	BOBBY BLAND (EP)	60
60	Vogue VA 160183	TWO STEPS FROM THE BLUES (LP)	90
61	Vocalion VA 160183	TWO STEPS FROM THE BLUES (LP)	60
61	Vogue/Vocalion VAP 8027	AIN'T NOTHING YOU CAN DO (LP)	75
61	Vogue VAP 160183	TWO STEPS FROM THE BLUES (LP)	60
64	Vocalion VAP 8027	AIN'T NOTHING YOU CAN DO (LP)	60
63	Vogue/Vocalion VAP 8034	CALL ON ME/ THAT'S THE WAY LOVE IS (LP)	75
64	Vocalion VAP 8034	CALL ON ME/ THAT'S THE WAY LOVE IS (LP)	50
65	Vocalion VAP 8034	CALL ON ME/THAT'S THE WAY LOVE IS (LP)	60
60s	Vogue VAP 8034	CALL ON ME/THAT'S THE WAY LOVE IS (LP, later issue)	45
66	Vocalion VAP 8041	HERE'S THE MAN (LP)	75
68	Island ILP 974	A TOUCH OF THE BLUES (LP)	60
69	Action ACLP 6006	A PIECE OF GOLD (LP)	40
73	ABC ABCL 5044	HIS CALIFORNIA ALBUM (LP)	12
74	ABC ABCL 5053	DREAMER (LP)	12
74	Polydor 2383 257	BLUES FOR MR. CRUMP (LP, with tracks by Junior Parker & Howlin' Wolf)	20
75	ABC ABCL 5139	GET ON DOWN WITH BOBBY BLAND (LP)	12

MINT VALUE £

BOBBY BLAND & B.B. KING
74 ABC ABCD 605 TOGETHER FOR THE FIRST TIME (2-LP) 15
(see also B.B. King)

B,L&G
71 Birds Nest BN 3 Live In The Mountains/Janie Slow Down 10
(see also Trevor Burton, Denny Laine, Steve Gibbons)

MARCIE BLANE
62 London HLU 9599 Bobby's Girl/A Time To Dream 22
63 London HLU 9673 What Does A Girl Do/How Can I Tell Him 20
63 London HLU 9744 Little Miss Fool/Ragtime Sound 20
63 London HLU 9787 You Gave My Number To Billy/Told You So 20
63 London REU 1393 MARCIE BLANE (EP) 125

BLANKS
79 Void SRTS/79/CUS/560 The Northern Ripper/Understand (p/s) 60
(see also Destructors)

BLARNEY SISTERS
67 GO AJ11407 The Greatest Blessing/Golden Band 15

BLAZE
99 Slip And Slide SLIP 99 Wishing You Were Here/(mixes) (2x12") 18

BLAZER, BLAZER
78 Logo GO 362 Cecil B. Devine/Warsaw/Six O'Clock In The Morning (p/s) 10

BLAZERS
58 Fontana TFR 6010 ROCK AND ROLL (10" LP) 100

BLAZING SONS
83 Cool Ghoul COOL 002 Chant Down The National Front/N.F. Dub (no p/s) 10
(see also Phantom)

BLEACH BOYS
78 Tramp THF 002 Chloroform/You've Got Nothing (no p/s) 35
85 Zombie International ZOMBO 103010 Stocking-Clad Nazi Death Squad Bitches/Death Before Disco/ Gimme That Neutron Taste (12", p/s) 25

BLEAK HOUSE
80s Buzzard BUZZ 1 Rainbow Warrior/Isandlhwana/Inquisition (some in p/s) 100/30
82 Buzzard BUZZ 2 LIONS IN WINTER (Chase The Wind/No Reply/Down To Zero/ Flight Of The Salamander) (EP, p/s with insert) 90

BLEECHERS
69 Trojan TR 679 Ease Up/You're Gonna Feel It 12
69 Upsetter US 314 Come Into My Parlour/MELOTONES: Dry Up Your Tears 12
70 Col. Blue Beat DB 118 Send Me The Pillow (That You Dream On)/Adam And Eve 12
71 Duke DU 118 Put It Good/J.J. ALLSTARS: Good Good Version 12
(see also Busty Brown, Upsetters)

PETER BLEGVAD
80 Recommended RRA 5.75 Alcohol (p/s, 1-sided, other side etched) 5
(see also Slapp Happy)

BLENDELLS
64 Reprise RS 20291 La La La La La La/Huggies Bunnies 8
64 Reprise RS 20340 Dance With Me/Get Your Baby 8

CARLA BLEY
72 JCOA JT 4001 ESCALATOR OVER THE HILL (3-LP, with Paul Haines & Jack Bruce) 20
74 Watt WATT 1 TROPIC APPETITES (LP) 12
(see also Jazz Composers Orchestra, Michael Mantler, Jack Bruce)

PAUL BLEY TRIO
69 Fontana SFJL 929 TOUCHING (LP) 50
(see also Bley-Peacock Synthesizer Show, Annette Peacock)

ARCHIE BLEYER & HIS ORCHESTRA
54 London HL 8035 Amber/Julie's Jump 35
54 London HL 8035 Amber/Julie's Jump (78) 10
54 London HL 8111 The Naughty Lady Of Shady Lane/While The Vesper Bells Were Ringing 35
54 London HL 8111 The Naughty Lady Of Shady Lane/While The Vesper Bells Were Ringing (78) 10
55 London HLA 8176 Hernando's Hideaway/S'il Vous Plait 35
56 London HLA 8243 Nothin' To Do/JANET BLEYER: 'Cause You're My Lover 25
56 London HLA 8243 Nothin' To Do/JANET BLEYER: 'Cause You're My Lover (78) 12
56 London HLA 8263 Bridge Of Happiness/You Tell Me Your Dream, I'll Tell You Mine 25
56 London HLA 8263 Bridge Of Happiness/You Tell Me Your Dream, I'll Tell You Mine (78) 12

BLEY-PEACOCK SYNTHESIZER SHOW
72 Polydor 2425 043 REVENGE (LP) 50
(see also Annette Peacock, Paul Bley)

BLIND BLAKE
50 Tempo R 23 Hey Hey Daddy Blues/Brownskin Mama Blues (78) 15
50 Tempo R 40 Southern Rag/CC Pill Blues (78) 20
54 Jazz Collector L 97 Hot Potatoes/Southbound Rag (78) 15
58 Ristic LP 18 THE LEGENDARY BLIND BLAKE (10" LP) 60
50s Jazz Collector JLP 2001 THE LEGENDARY BLIND BLAKE (10" LP, reissue) 30
67 Riverside RLP 8804 BLUES IN CHICAGO (LP) 30
60s Whoopee 101 BLIND BLAKE 1927-30 (LP) 15
(see also Paramount Allstars)

BLIND BLAKE/CHARLIE JACKSON
50s Heritage HLP 1011 BLIND BLAKE AND CHARLIE JACKSON (LP, 99 only) 90

MINT VALUE £

BLIND BLAKE/RAMBLIN' THOMAS
59 Jazz Collector JEL 4 THE MALE BLUES VOLUME 3 (EP) 20

BLIND FAITH
69 Island (no cat. no.) Change Of Address From June 23rd 1969 (promo issue, 500 only) 200
69 Polydor 583 059 BLIND FAITH (LP, gatefold sleeve) 25
(see also Stevie Winwood, Ginger Baker, Eric Clapton)

BLIND FURY
85 Roadrunner RR 9814 OUT OF REACH (LP) 12

BLINKERS
69 Pye 7N 17752 Original Sin/Dreams Secondhand 60

BLINKY & EDWIN STARR
69 Tamla Motown TMG 720 Oh How Happy/Ooo Baby Baby (unissued, demos only) 150
70 Tamla Motown TMG 748 Oh How Happy/Ooo Baby Baby 8
70 T. Motown (S)TML 11131 JUST WE TWO (LP, as Edwin Starr & Blinky) 25
(see also Edwin Starr)

BLISS
69 Chapter One CH 107 Courtyards In Castile/Lifetime 10

MELVIN BLISS
77 Contempo CS 2013 Reward/Synthetic Substitute 20

BLITZ
81 No Future OI 1 ALL OUT ATTACK (EP, rubber-stamped labels, 500 only) 25
81 No Future OI 1 ALL OUT ATTACK (EP, reissue, white labels, later printed labels) 15/10
82 No Future OI 6 Never Surrender/Razor In The Night (p/s) 12
82 No Future OI 16 Warriors/Youth (p/s) 12
82 No Future PUNK 1 VOICE OF A GENERATION (LP, with inner sleeve) 22
(see also Rose Of Victory)

BLITZ BOYS
80 Told You So TYS 001 Eddy's New Shoes/Eddie's Friend/She Told My Friends (foldover p/s) 60

BLITZKRIEG
81 Neat NEAT 10 Buried Alive/Blitzkrieg (p/s) 110
91 Roadrunner R 09302 10 YEARS OF BLITZKRIEG (EP) 10
85 Neat NEAT 1023 A TIME OF CHANGES (LP) 40

BLITZKRIEG
82 No Future OI 8 LEST WE FORGET (EP) 18

BLITZKRIEG BOP
77 Mortonsound MTN 3172/3 Let's Go/Nine Till Five/Bugger Off (p/s, 500 only) 55
77 Lightning GTL 504 Let's Go (re-recorded)/Life Is Just A So-So/Mental Case (p/s) 15
78 Lightning GTL 543 U.F.O./Bobby Joe (p/s) 20

BLOATED TOADS
79 Shattered SHAT 4 Why/Essential In Some Form/Happy Home/Yankee TV Victim (p/s, with insert) . . . 5

BLODWYN PIG
69 Island WIP 6059 Dear Jill/Sweet Caroline 10
69 Island WIP 6069 Walk On The Water/Summer Day 10
70 Chrysalis WIP 6078 Same Old Story/Slow Down 10
89 private release A TASTE OF THINGS TO COME (cassette, 50 only, sold at gigs) 25
69 Island ILPS 9101 AHEAD RINGS OUT (LP, gatefold sleeve, pink or 'pink rim palm tree' label) . . 20/12
70 Chrysalis ILPS 9122 GETTING TO THIS (LP, gatefold sleeve) 15
(see also Mick Abrahams, Jethro Tull)

BLOND
69 Fontana TF 1040 (I Will Bring You) Flowers In The Morning/I Wake Up And Call 25
69 Fontana STL 5515 THE LILAC YEARS (LP, gatefold sleeve) 110
(see also Tages)

BLONDE ON BLONDE
69 Pye 7N 17637 All Day All Night/Country Life 50
70 Ember EMB S 279 Castles In The Sky/Circles (some in p/s) 18/8
72 Ember EMB S 316 Sad Song For An Easy Lady/Happy Families 6
69 Pye NSPL 18288 CONTRASTS (LP, gatefold sleeve) 60
70 Ember NR 5049 RE-BIRTH (LP, gatefold sleeve) 30
71 Ember NR 5058 REFLECTIONS ON A LIFE (LP, gatefold sleeve) 30
70s Ember LP 7005 BLONDE ON BLONDE (LP, unissued, test pressings only) . . . . 100+

BLONDIE
77 Private Stock PVT 90 X Offender/In The Sun (unissued, promos or stock copies, no p/s) . . . . 750+
77 Private Stock PVT 105 In The Flesh/X Offender (no p/s) 20
77 Chrysalis CHS 2180 Rip Her To Shreds/In The Flesh/X Offender (p/s) 8
77 Chrysalis CHS 2180-12 Rip Her To Shreds/In The Flesh/X Offender (12", green labels, '75p' p/s) 8
78 Chrysalis CHS 2204 Denis (Denee)/Contact In Red Square (red p/s) 5
78 Chrysalis CHS 2242 Picture This/Fade Away (And Radiate) (p/s, yellow vinyl) 5
78 Chrysalis CHE 2266 Hanging On The Telephone/Will Anything Happen (p/s, export issue) 6
78 Chrysalis CHE 2275 Heart Of Glass/Rifle Range (p/s, export issue with "pain in the ass" lyrics) 8
80 Flexi FLX 146 Speaking From The Studio (Blondie Fan Club flexidisc) 15
82 Lyntone LYN 10840/1 Yuletown Throwdown (Rapture) (with Freddie)/
BRATTLES: The Christmas Song/SNUKY TATE: Santa's Agent
(33rpm blue or orange vinyl flexi with *Flexipop* issue 15) 8/5
89 Chrysalis CHSP 12 3342 Call Me (Remix)/Backfired (Remix)/Call Me (1989) (12", picture disc) 8
98 EMI 12 ATOM 150 ATOMIC 98 (Remixes) (12", p/s, withdrawn) 15
98 EMI CD ATOM 150 ATOMIC 98 (Remixes) (CD, withdrawn) 18
76 Private Stock PVLP 1017 BLONDIE (LP) 18
82 Chrysalis PCDL 1384 THE HUNTER (LP, picture disc) 15

MINT VALUE £

89	Chrysalis CHR 1658	THE 12" MIXES (2-LP)	15
89	Chrysalis CCD 1658	THE 12" MIXES (CD)	18
95	Chrysalis CD CHR 6105	BEAUTIFUL – THE REMIX ALBUM (CD)	18
98	Chysalis 4949962	ATOMIC (CD)	18

(see also Debbie Harry, New York Blondes, Wind In The Willows, Rodney & Brunettes)

BLOOD

83	No Future OI 22	Megalomania/Calling The Shots/Parasite In Paradise (p/s)	15
83	Noise NOY 1	Stark Raving Normal/Mesrine (p/s)	10
82	Noise NOYZLP 1	FALSE GESTURES FOR A DEVIOUS PUBLIC (LP)	20
85	Conquest QUEST 3	SE PARARE NEX (LP)	15
89	Link Classics CLINK 5	FALSE GESTURES FOR A DEVIOUS PUBLIC (LP, reissue, red vinyl)	15

BLOODROCK

71	Capitol CL 15670	D.O.A./Children's Heritage	5
71	Capitol E-ST 491	BLOODROCK 2 (LP)	12
71	Capitol E-ST 765	BLOODROCK 3 (LP)	12

BLOOD, SWEAT & TEARS

68	CBS 3563	I Can't Quit Her/House In The Country	15
69	CBS 4116	You've Made Me So Very Happy/The Blues, Part 2	5
69	CBS 4220	Spinning Wheel/More And More	5
68	CBS 63296	CHILD IS THE FATHER TO THE MAN (LP)	15

(see also Al Kooper, David Clayton-Thomas)

ROGER BLOOM'S HAMMER

67	CBS 202654	Out Of The Blue/Life's A Gamble	12
67	CBS 2848	Polly Pan/Fifteen Degree Temperature Rise	6

MIKE BLOOMFIELD

69	CBS 63652	IT'S NOT KILLING ME (LP)	20

(see also Barry Goldberg Reunion, Stephen Stills, K.G.B.)

MIKE BLOOMFIELD & AL KOOPER

69	CBS 4094	The Weight/59th Street Bridge Song	10
69	CBS 66216	THE LIVE ADVENTURES OF MIKE BLOOMFIELD AND AL KOOPER (2-LP)	20

(see also Al Kooper, Paul Butterfield Blues Band, Electric Flag)

BLOSSOMS

58	Capitol CL 14833	Move On/He Promised Me	50
58	Capitol CL 14856	Little Louie/Have Faith In Me	40
58	Capitol CL 14947	No Other Love/Baby Daddy-O	40
68	MGM MGM 1435	Tweedle Dee/You Got Me Hummin'	15
71	Pama PM 814	Stand By/Soul And Inspiration	22
73	Mojo 2027 013	Touchdown/It's All Up To You	8

(see also Darlene Love, Allisons [U.S.])

BLOSSOM TOES

67	Marmalade 598 002	What On Earth/Mrs Murphy's Budgerigar/Look At Me I'm You (some in p/s)	70/25
68	Marmalade 598 009	I'll Be Your Baby Tonight/Love Is	25
68	Marmalade 598 012	Postcard/Everyone's Leaving Me Now	22
69	Marmalade 598 014	Peace Loving Man/Up Above My Hobby Horse's Head	20
69	Marmalade 598 022	New Day/Love Bomb (unissued, existence unconfirmed)	
67	Marmalade 607/608 001	WE ARE EVER SO CLEAN (LP)	80
69	Marmalade 608 010	IF ONLY FOR A MOMENT (LP)	100

(see also B.B. Blunder, Stud, Kevin Westlake)

MICHAEL BLOUNT

70	CBS 7022	Sometimes/Angelina Baby	6
72	York SYK 519	Beautiful Morning/Feathered Cloud	6
72	York SYK 28	Tackle And Sack/Pretty Face	6
72	York SKY 535	Rosie/Trombone Man	6
71	CBS 64230	PATCHWORK (LP)	18
72	York FYK 401	SOUVENIRS (LP)	15
73	York FYK 414	FANTASIES (LP)	15

BLOW MONKEYS

82	Parasol PAR 1	Live Today Love Tomorrow/In Cold Blood (no p/s)	6
87	RCA MONKX 6	(Celebrate) The Day After You (Election Mix)/It's Not Unusual (live)/ Beautiful Child/The Smile On Her Face (Sweet Murder) (10", with Curtis Mayfield, withdrawn 'Thatcher' p/s, 'General Election Party Edition')	10
88	RCA PD 42232	It Pays To Be Short (4.40)/The Love Of Which I Dare Not Speak/Hingway!/ It Pays To Belong (8.41) (CD, in numbered gold circular tin box)	8

(see also Curtis Mayfield)

BLOWZABELLA

70s	Special Delivery SPD 1028	VANILLA (LP)	25
70s	Plant Life PLR 051	IN COLOUR (LP)	25

BLUE

73	RSO 2090 109	Red Light Song/Look Around	6
73	RSO 2090 114	Little Jody/The Way Things Are	6
73	RSO 2394 105	BLUE (LP)	15

(see also Poets)

BABBITY BLUE

65	Decca F 12053	Don't Make Me/I Remembered How To Cry	10
65	Decca F 12149	Don't Hurt Me/Question	10

BOBBY BLUE

70	Duke DU 86	Going In Circles (actually by Lloyd Charmers)/Doggone Right (actually by Bobby Davis)	7

MINT VALUE £

DAVID BLUE

67	Elektra EKL 4003	DAVID BLUE (LP, red label)	30
72	Asylum SYL 9001	STORIES (LP)	15
73	Asylum SYL 9009	NICE BABY AND THE ANGEL (LP)	15
75	Asylum SYL 9025	COMIN' BACK FOR MORE (LP)	12
76	Asylum K 53056	CUPID'S ARROW (LP)	12

PAMELA BLUE

63	Decca F 11761	My Friend Bobby/Hey There Stranger	125

TIMOTHY BLUE

68	Spark SRL 1014	The Room At The Top Of The Stairs/She Won't See The Light	15

BLUE ACES

64	Pye 7N 15672	Land Of Love/Love Song Of The Waterfall	10
64	Pye 7N 15713	I Beat You To It/I Just Can't Help Loving You	10
65	Pye 7N 15821	Ain't What You Say/You Don't Care	10
65	Columbia DB 7755	Tell Me What You're Gonna Do/All I Want	100
66	Columbia DB 7954	That's All Right/Talk About My Baby	95

(see also Riot Squad)

BLUE & FERRIS

68	Blue Cat BS 147	You Stole My Money/Tell Me The Reason	40

BLUE ANGEL

80	Polydor POSP 212	I'm Gonna Be Strong/Anna Blue (no p/s)	6
81	Polydor POSP 241	I Had A Love/Can't Blame Me	6
84	Polydor POSP 212	I'm Gonna Be Strong/Anna Blue (p/s, reissue)	10
80	Polydor 2391 486	BLUE ANGEL (LP)	25

(see also Cyndi Lauper)

BLUE BEARD

71	Ember EMB S 302	Country Man/Sly Willy (some in p/s)	20/10
71	Ember LT 7004	BLUE BEARD (LP, unreleased, test pressings only)	200

BLUEBEATS

64	Ember EMB EP 4525	THE FABULOUS BLUEBEATS VOL. 1 (EP)	50
64	Ember EMB EP 4526	THE FABULOUS BLUEBEATS VOL. 2 (EP)	50

BLUEBEATERS

64	Piccadilly 7N 35181	Little David/Ain't Got A Care	7

BLUEBELLS

82	London LON(F) 14/ Lyntone LYN 12361	Forevermore/Aim In Life (p/s, with free 33rpm clear vinyl flexidisc "Everybody's Somebody's Fool")	6

(see also McClusky Brothers)

BLUE-BELLES

62	HMV POP 1029	I Sold My Heart To The Junkman/Itty Bitty Twist	40

(see also Patti LaBelle & Blue Belles)

BLUEBERRIES

65	Mercury MF 894	It's Gonna Work Out Fine/Please Don't Let Me Know	30

BLUE BLOOD

70	Sonet SNTF 615	BLUE BLOOD (LP)	20

BLUE BLUDD

87	Blud Donor no cat. No.	LIQUOR 'N' POKER (EP)	20

BLUE CHEER

68	Philips BF 1646	Summertime Blues/Out Of Focus	18
68	Philips BF 1684	Just A Little Bit/Gypsy Ball	10
68	Philips BF 1711	Feathers From Your Tree/Sun Cycle	10
69	Philips BF 1778	West Coast Child Of Sunshine/When It All Gets Old	10
71	Philips 6051 010	Pilot/Babaji	7
68	Philips (S)BL 7839	VINCEBUS ERUPTUM (LP, mono/stereo)	50/35
68	Philips SBL 7860	OUTSIDEINSIDE (LP, gatefold sleeve)	35
69	Philips SBL 7896	NEW! IMPROVED! (LP)	25
69	Philips 6336 001	BLUE CHEER (LP)	25
71	Philips 6336 004	B.C. #5 THE ORIGINAL HUMAN BEING (LP)	35

(see also Leigh Stephens, Group B)

BLUE CHIPS

65	Pye 7N 15970	I'm On The Right Side/You're Good To Me	25
66	Pye 7N 17111	Some Kind Of Lovin'/I Know A Boy	25
66	Pye 7N 17155	Tell Her/Good Lovin' Never Hurt	25

BLUE DIAMONDS

60	Decca F 21292	Ramona/All Of Me	6
60	Decca DFE 6675	I'M FOREVER BLOWING BUBBLES (EP)	15

BLUE EPITAPH

74	Holyground HG 117	ODE (LP, 99 copies only)	225
91	Holyground HG 117	ODE (LP, reissue, folded gatefold sleeve)	18

(see also Magus)

BLUE FLAMES

63	R&B JB 114	J.A. Blues/Orange Street	60
63	R&B JB 126	Stop Right Here/Rik's Tune	60

(see also Georgie Fame & Blue Flames)

BLUE GOOSE

75	Anchor ANC 1015	Loretta/Call On Me	5
75	Anchor ANCL 2005	BLUE GOOSE (LP)	12

(see also Badfinger, Curtis Knight & Zeus, Motörhead)

MINT VALUE £

BLUE JEANS

69 Columbia DB 8555 Hey Mrs. Housewife/Sandfly . . . 25
(see also Swinging Blue Jeans, Ray Ennis & Blue Jeans)

BLUE MAGIC

74 Atlantic K 10494 Sideshow/Just Don't Want To Be Lonely . . . 5
75 Atlantic K 10553 Three Ring Circus/Spell . . . 5
(see also Margie Joseph)

BLUE MAXI

70 Major Minor MM 705 Here Comes Summer/Famous Last Words . . . 6
(see also Jean-Jacques Burnel & Dave Greenfield)

BLUE MEN

60 Triumph RGXST 5000 I HEAR A NEW WORLD (PART ONE) (EP) . . . 425
60 Triumph RGXST 5001 I HEAR A NEW WORLD (PART TWO) (EP, only sleeves exist) . . . sleeve 50
60 Triumph TRX ST 9000 I HEAR A NEW WORLD (LP, unreleased, white label demos only) . . . 1,300
(see also Joe Meek, Peter Jay & Blue Men, Rodd-Ken & Cavaliers)

BLUE MOUNTAIN BOYS

63 Oriole CB 1774 Drop Me Gently/One Small Photograph Of You . . . 8

BLUE MOVIES

79 ROK ROK 9 Mary Jane/THE NOISE: Criminal (company sleeve) . . . 15

BLUE NILE

81 RSO RSO 84 I Love This Life/The Second Act (p/s) . . . 25
84 Linn LKS 1 Stay/Saddle The Horses (white p/s) . . . 8
84 Linn LKS 1-12 Stay/Saddle The Horses (12", white p/s) . . . 12
84 Linn LKS 1 Stay (Remix)/Saddle The Horses (p/s) . . . 5
84 Linn LKSD 1 Stay (Remix)/Saddle The Horses//Tinsel Town In The Rain/ Heatwave (Instrumental) (p/s, double pack) . . . 8
84 Linn LKS 1-12 Stay (Extended Remix)/Saddle The Horses (12", p/s) . . . 8
84 Linn LKS 2 Tinsel Town In The Rain/Heatwave (Instrumental) (p/s) . . . 5
84 Linn LKS 2-12 Tinsel Town In The Rain (Extended)/Regret/Heatwave (Instrumental) (12", p/s) . . . 8
89 Linn LKYCD 4 Headlights On The Parade (CD, collector's pack) . . . 8
80s Linn flexidisc (demonstration disc) . . . 20

BLUENOTES

60 Top Rank JAR 291 I Don't Know What It Is/You Can't Get Away From Love . . . 10

BLUE ORCHIDS

81 Rough Trade RT 065 Disney Boys/The Flood (p/s) . . . 5
81 Rough Trade RT 067 Work/The House That Faded Out (p/s) . . . 5
82 Rough Trade RT 117T AGENTS OF CHANGE (12" EP, in carrier bag) . . . 8
84 Rough Trade ROUGH 37 GREATEST HITS (LP) . . . 12
(see also Nosebleeds, Fall)

BLUE ÖYSTER CULT

76 CBS 4483 (Don't Fear) The Reaper/R U Ready 2 Rock . . . 5
76 CBS 4483 (Don't Fear) The Reaper/Tattoo Vampire (promo with different B-side) . . . 10
78 CBS 5689 Going Through The Motions/Searching For The Celine . . . 5
78 CBS 12-6333 (Don't Fear) The Reaper (12") . . . 8
79 CBS 7763 Mirrors/Lonely Teardrops (clear vinyl) . . . 5
81 CBS A 1453 Burnin' For You/Heavy Metal (p/s) . . . 5
81 CBS A 13 1453 Burnin' For You/Heavy Metal/The Black & Silver (12", p/s) . . . 8
83 CBS A 3937 Take Me Away/Feel The Thunder (p/s) . . . 5
83 CBS TA 3937 Take Me Away/Feel The Thunder/Burnin' For You/Doctor Music (12", p/s) . . . 8
84 CBS A 4117 Shooting Shark/Dragon Lady (p/s) . . . 5
84 CBS TA 4117 Shooting Shark/Dragon Lady (12", p/s) . . . 8
89 CBS 652 985-2 Astronomy/Magna Of Illusion/(Don't Fear) The Reaper (CD, card sleeve) . . . 8
73 CBS 64904 BLUE ÖYSTER CULT (LP) . . . 12
80 CBS 86120 CULTOSAURUS ERECTUS (LP, with poster) . . . 12

BLUE PHANTOM

72 Kaleidoscope KAL 101 DISTORTIONS (LP) . . . 55

BLUE RIDGE RANGERS

73 Fantasy FTC 105 Hearts Of Stone/Somewhere Listening For My Name . . . 6
73 Fantasy FTC 110 You Don't Own Me/Back In The Hills . . . 6
73 Fantasy FT 511 BLUE RIDGE RANGERS (LP) . . . 18
(see also John Fogerty, Creedence Clearwater Revival)

BLUE RIVERS & MAROONS

67 Columbia Blue Beat DB 103 Witchcraft Man/Searching For You Baby . . . 12
68 Spectrum SP 105 Take It Or Leave It/I've Been Pushed Around . . . 8
68 Columbia S(C)X 6192 BLUE BEAT IN MY SOUL (LP) . . . 50

BLUE RONDOS

64 Pye 7N 15734 Little Baby/Baby I Go For You . . . 50
65 Pye 7N 15833 Don't Want Your Lovin' No More/What Can I Do . . . 45

BLUES BAND

80 Blues Band BBBP 101 OFFICIAL BOOTLEG ALBUM (LP, numbered, with autographs, 3000 only) . . . 15
(see also Paul Jones, McGuinness-Flint, Manfred Mann)

BLUESBREAKERS

(see under John Mayall & Bluesbreakers)

BLUES BUSTERS

71 Jay Boy BOY 44 I Can't Stop/Inspired To Love You . . . 6

BLUES BY FIVE

64 Decca F 12029 Boom Boom/I Cried . . . 80

MINT VALUE £

BLUES COUNCIL

65 Parlophone R 5264 — Baby Don't Look Down/What Will I Do 80

BLUES 5

64 Studio 36 (no cat. no.) — Hey Baby/When You're In Love 130

BLUES IMAGE

70 Atlantic 2091 009 — Ride Captain Ride/Pay My Dues 5
71 Atlantic 2400 120 — RED, WHITE AND BLUES IMAGE (LP) 12

BLUES INCORPORATED

(see under Alexis Korner)

BLUES MAGOOS

66 Mercury MF 954 — (We Ain't Got) Nothin' Yet/Gotta Get Away 25
67 Fontana TF 848 — One By One/Love Seems Doomed 15
71 Probe PRO 522 — Can't Get Enough Of You/Sea Breeze Express 5
66 Fontana (S)TL 5402 — BLUES MAGOOS (LP, mono/stereo) 60/50
71 Probe SPB 1024 — GULF COAST BOUND (LP) 15

BLUES MASTERS

63 Island WI 078 — 5 O'Clock Whistle/African Blood (both sides actually by Baba Brooks) 35

BLUESOLOGY

65 Fontana TF 594 — Come Back Baby/Time's Getting Tougher Than Tough 300
66 Fontana TF 668 — Mister Frantic/Everyday (I Have The Blues) 350

(see also Stu Brown & Bluesology, Elton John, Long John Baldry, Elton Dean, Mark Charig)

BLUES PROJECT

67 Verve Forecast VS 1505 — I Can't Keep From Crying/The Way My Baby Walks 25
67 Verve (S)VLP 6004 — PROJECTIONS (LP) 15
72 Capitol E-ST 11017 — THE BLUES PROJECT (LP) 12

(see also Al Kooper, Tommy Flanders, Seatrain)

BLUE STARS

56 Felsted SD 80033 — Lullaby Of Birdland/Les Lavandieres Du Portugal (78) 7
58 Felsted PDL 85037 — MEET THE BLUE STARS (LP) 12

BLUE STARS

65 Decca F 12303 — Please Be A Little Kind/I Can Take It 220

BLUE STEAM

78 Rip Off RIP 5 — Lizard King/Cortina Cowboys (p/s) 10

BLUE SYSTEM

90 RCA PB 43733 — Magic Symphony/Magic Symphony (Power Edit) (p/s) 8
90 RCA PT 43734 — Magic Symphony (Power Mix)/Magic Symphony (Fun Mix)/ Magic Symphony (7" Mix) (12", p/s) 12
90 RCA PD 43734 — Magic Symphony (7" Mix)/Magic Symphony (Fun Mix)/ Magic Symphony (Power Mix) (CD) 25

BLUETONES

95 Superior Quality TONE 001 — Slight Return/The Fountainhead (blue vinyl, plain white sleeve in stickered polythene bag, 2,000 only, sold by mail-order & at gigs, some numbered) 20/15
95 Superior Quality TONE 001 — Slight Return/The Fountainhead (red vinyl, foldover p/s in poly bag, 1,000 only, export issue to Japan) 20
95 Superior Qual. BLUE 001X — Are You Blue Or Are You Blind?/String Along (p/s, numbered, 4,000 only) 5
95 Superior Q. BLUE 002CD — Bluetonic/Colorado Beetle/Glad To See Y'Back Again? (CD) 8
96 Superior Qual. BLUE 003X — Slight Return/Don't Stand Me Down (red vinyl, export issue to Japan with Japanese text on rear of p/s) 25
96 Superior Q. BLUE 005DJ — Cut Some Rug (CD, 1-track promo with 'classroom' inlay, withdrawn) 8

BLUE VELVET BAND

69 Warner Bros WS 1802 — SWEET MOMENTS WITH THE BLUE VELVET BAND (LP, gatefold sleeve) 12

BLUEWATER FOLK

70s Folk Heritage — BLUEWATER FOLK (LP) 60
70s Moonraker MOO 1 — BUGS, BLACK PUDDINGS AND CLOGS (LP, with insert) 12
70s Moonraker MOO 2 — A LANCASHIRE LIFE (LP, with insert) 12

BLUE YOGURT

70 Penny Farthing PEN 732 — Lydia/Umbrella Man 6

COLIN BLUNSTONE

71 Epic EPC 7095 — Mary, Won't You Warm My Bed/I Hope I Didn't Say Too Much Last Night 5
71 Epic EPC 7520 — Caroline Goodbye/Though You Are Far Away 5
72 Epic EPC 7765 — Say You Don't Mind/Let Me Come Closer (p/s) 7
72 Epic EPC 8434 — I Don't Believe In Miracles/I've Always Had You 5
73 Epic EPC 1197 — How Could We Dare To Be Wrong?/Time's Runnin' Out 5
73 Epic EPC 1775 — Wonderful/Beginning 6
74 Epic EPC 2413 — It's Magical/Summersong 6
76 Epic EPC 4576 — When You Close Your Eyes/Good Guys Don't Always Win 5
76 Epic EPC 4752 — Planes/Dancing In The Dark 5
76 Epic EPC 5009 — Beautiful You/It's Hard To Say Goodbye 5
77 Epic EPC 5199 — Lovin' And Free/Dancing In The Dark 5
78 Epic EPC 6320 — I'll Never Forget You/You Are The Way For Me 5
78 Epic EPC 6535 — Ain't It Funny/Who's That Knocking 5
78 Epic EPC 6793 — Photograph/Touch And Go 5
81 Panache PAN 1 — Miles Away/MITCHELL-COE MYSTERIES: Excerpts From "Exiled" (p/s) 5
71 Epic EPC 64557 — ONE YEAR (LP, textured sleeve) 15
72 Epic EPC 65278 — ENNISMORE (LP, textured sleeve) 15
74 Epic EPC 65805 — JOURNEY (LP) 12

			MINT VALUE £
76	Epic EPC 81592	PLANES (LP, with lyric insert)	12
78	Epic EPC 82835	NEVER EVEN THOUGHT (LP, with lyric insert)	15

(see also Zombies, Neil MacArthur, Mitchell-Coe Mysteries)

BLUNT INSTRUMENT

78	Diesel DCL 01	No Excuse/Interrogation (p/s)	5

BLUR

90	Food FOOD 26	She's So High (Edit)/I Know (p/s)	6
90	Food TCFOOD 26	She's So High (Edit)/I Know (cassette)	6
90	Food 12FOOD 26	She's So High (Definitive)/Sing/I Know (Extended) (12", p/s)	15
90	Food CDFOOD 26	She's So High/I Know (Extended)/Down (CD)	25
91	Food FOOD 29	There's No Other Way/Inertia (p/s)	8
91	Food TCFOOD 29	There's No Other Way/Inertia (cassette)	5
91	Food 12FOOD 29	There's No Other Way (Extended)/Inertia/Mr. Briggs/I'm All Over (12", p/s)	25
91	Food 12 FOODX 29	There's No Other Way (The Blur Remix)/Won't Do It/ Day Upon Day (live) (12", p/s lists '12 FOODDX 29')	35
91	Food CDFOOD 29	There's No Other Way/Inertia/Mr. Briggs/I'm All Over (CD)	25
91	Food FOOD 31	Bang/Luminous (p/s)	8
91	Food TCFOOD 31	Bang/Luminous (cassette)	5
91	Food 12FOOD 31	Bang (Extended)/Explain/Luminous/Uncle Love (12", p/s)	10
91	Food CDFOOD 31	Bang/Explain/Luminous/Beserk (CD)	20
91	Food 12BLUR 4	High Cool (Easy Listening Mix)/Bad Day (Leisurely Mix) (12", blue & gold company sleeve, promo, 1,000 only)	15
92	Food FOOD 37	Popscene/Mace (p/s)	6
92	Food TCFOOD 37	Popscene/Mace (cassette)	5
92	Food 12FOOD 37	Popscene/I'm Fine/Mace/Garden Central (12", p/s)	18
92	Food CDFOOD 37	Popscene/Mace/Badgeman Brown (CD)	20
92	Food BLUR 6	The Wassailing Song (1-sided gig freebie, no p/s, 500 only)	60
92	Food TCFOOD 40	For Tomorrow/Into Another/Hanging Over (cassette)	5
92	Food 12FOOD 40	For Tomorrow (Visit To Primrose Hill Extended)/Into Another/ Hanging Over/Peach (12", p/s)	18
92	Food CDFOOD 40	For Tomorrow (Visit To Primrose Hill Extended)/Peach/Bone Bag (CD, double jewel case)	20
92	Food CDSFOOD 40	For Tomorrow (Single Version)/When The Cows Come Home/ Beachcoma/For Tomorrow (Acoustic Version) (CD)	20
93	Food FOODS 45	Chemical World/Maggie May (red vinyl, paper labels, p/s)	5
93	Food 12FOOD 45	Chemical World/Es Schmecht/Young And Lovely/My Ark (12", p/s with print)	15
93	Food CDFOODS 45	Chemical World (Reworked)/Never Clever (live)/Pressure On Julian (live)/ Come Together (live) (CD, double jewel case)	15
93	Food CDFOOD 45	Chemical World/Young And Lovely/Es Schmecht/My Ark (CD)	12
93	Food FOODS 46	Sunday Sunday/Tell Me, Tell Me (B-side as "Blur featuring Seymour") (yellow vinyl, p/s)	6
93	Food 12FOODS 46	Sunday Sunday/Long Legged/Mixed Up (B-sides as "Blur featuring Seymour") (12", p/s with print)	8
93	Food CDFOOD 46	Sunday Sunday/Dizzy/Fried/Shimmer (CD, final 3 tracks as B-sides as "Blur featuring Seymour")	15
93	Food CDFOODX 46	THE SUNDAY SUNDAY POPULAR COMMUNITY SONG CD: Sunday Sunday/Daisy Bell/Let's All Go Down The Strand (CD)	15
94	Food FOODS 47	Girls And Boys/Magpie/People In Europe (p/s, numbered)	5
94	Food CDFOOD 47	Girls And Boys/People In Europe/Peter Panic (CD, slimline jewel case)	10
94	Food CDFOODS 47	Girls And Boys/Magpie/Anniversary Waltz (CD, digipak)	8
94	Food CDFOOD 50	To The End/Girls And Boys (Pet Shop Boys 7" Remix)/Girls And Boys (Pet Shop Boys 12" Remix) (CD, slimline jewel case)	12
94	Food CDFOOD 53	Parklife/Beard/To The End (French Version) (CD, slimline jewel case)	8
95	Food CDFOODDJ 59	This Is A Low (CD, promo only, plain card sleeve with set of 4 stamps)	10
95	Food 12FOODDJ 63	Country House (12", promo only, 1-sided, die-cut p/s)	10
95	Food 12FOODDJ 69	The Universal/Entertain Me (The Live It! Remix) (12", promo only, die-cut p/s)	12
96	Fan Club DEATH 1	Death Of A Party (demo) (CD, 1-track, card p/s, fan club issue, 3250 only)	25
97	Food 12BLURDJ 7	On Your Own (Crouch End Broadway Mix) (12", 1-sided, promo only)	20
97	Fan Club LOVE 001	I Love Her (CD, card p/s, fan club issue, 3,500 only)	25
97	Food FOOD 89	Beetlebum/Woodpigeon Song (limited edition red vinyl, p/s)	6
97	Food FOOD 107	M.O.R. (Road Version)/Swallows In The Heatwave (ltd. edition orange vinyl, p/s)	8
97	Food CDFOODDJ 109	Death Of A Party (7" Remix)/(Well Blurred Remix)/(Billy Whiskers Mix)/ (Album Version) (CD, promo only, card p/s)	8
99	Food CD FOOD DJ 117	Tender (LP version)/(radio edit) (CD, silver foil pack, promo only)	8
97	Food CDIN 106	BLURB (CD, interview, promo only)	20
99	Food FOOD CDJX 29	13 (CD in duffelbag with folder, photos, ski-hat and biography, promo only)	70

BLURT

80	Test Pressing TP 1	My Mother Was A Friend Of An Enemy Of The People/Get (p/s)	5
81	Armageddon AS 013	The Fish Needs A Bike/This Is My Royal Wedding Souvenir (p/s)	5

HENRY BLYTHE

56	Oriole MG 20009	AN INVESTIGATION INTO REINCARNATION (LP)	22

JIMMY BLYTHE

54	London AL 3527	SOUTH SIDE BLUE PIANO (10" LP)	25
54	London AL 3529	SOUTH SIDE CHICAGO JAZZ (10" LP)	25

ENID BLYTON

53	HMV BD 1297	Noddy & Big Ears Go Shopping/Noddy Builds His House (78, picture label)	8
53	HMV BD 1298	Noddy At The Police Court/Noddy Lets The Animals Out Of The Ark (78, picture label)	8
53	HMV BD 1299	Noddy's Adventures With His Car/Noddy Is Naughty (78, picture label)	8
57	HMV 7EG 8260	NODDY STORIES (EP)	10

MINT VALUE £

B-MOVIE

Year	Label & Cat. No.	Title	Value £
80	Dead Good DEAD 9	TAKE THREE (EP)	20
80	Dead Good BIG DEAD 12	NOWHERE GIRL (12" EP, with insert, 800 only)	20
81	Lyntone LYN 10410	Remembrance Day/SOFT CELL: Metro Mr X (red or green flexidisc with *Flexipop* magazine, issue 12)	12/6
81	Deram DM 443	Marilyn Dreams/Film Music (Part 1) (p/s)	5
81	Deram DMX 443	Marilyn Dreams/Film Music (Part 1) (12", p/s)	8
88	Wax 12 WAX 3	Nowhere Girl/Remembrance Day (12", p/s, 250 on orange vinyl, numbered)	10
88	Wax 12 WAX 3	Nowhere Girl/Remembrance Day (12", p/s, pink or black vinyl, numbered)	10/7
88	Wax 12 WAX 4	Polar Opposites/Taxi Driver (12", clear vinyl or picture disc)	each 8
88	Wax CD WAX 4	Polar Opposites/Taxi Driver (CD)	15
88	Wax WAXLP 1P	THE DEAD GOOD TAPES (LP, picture disc)	12
88	Wax WAXCD 1	THE DEAD GOOD TAPES (CD)	18
91	Dead Good GOOD 3	REMEMBRANCE DAYS (LP, with 7" "The Fool"/"Swinging Lights" [CHEAP 1])	12

BMX BANDITS

Year	Label & Cat. No.	Title	Value £
86	53rd & 3rd AGARR 3	Sad?/E102 (p/s, some with comic)	10/5
86	53rd & 3rd AGARR 312	Sad?/E102/The Cat From Outer Space (live)/Strawberry Sunday (live)/ Groovy Good Luck Friend (live) (12", p/s)	10
87	53rd & 3rd AGARR 6	What A Wonderful World/The Day Before Tomorrow (p/s)	6
87	53rd & 3rd AGARR 612	What A Wonderful World/The Day Before Tomorrow/ Johnny Alucard/Sad?/Sandy's Wallet (12", p/s)	8
92	Sunflower SUN 006	GORDON KEEN & HIS BMX BANDITS EP (p/s, red vinyl)	8

(see also Soup Dragons, Boy Hairdressers, Teenage Fanclub, Vaselines)

EDDIE BO

Year	Label & Cat. No.	Title	Value £
73	Action ACT 4609	Check Your Bucket Parts 1 & 2	50

BO & PEEP

Year	Label & Cat. No.	Title	Value £
64	Decca F 11968	Young Love/The Rise Of The Brighton Surf	40

(see also Andrew Oldham Orchestra)

BOARDS OF CANADA

Year	Label & Cat. No.	Title	Value £
94	Music 70 THS 012	HOOPER'S BAY (12" or cassette EP)	150/50
96	Skam SKA 8	High Scores/Turquoise Hexagon Sun/Nlagon/June 9th/ See Ya Later/Everything You Do Is A Balloon (12", p/s)	8
98	Skam KMAS 1	Aquarius/Chinook (p/s, with insert, 1,000 only)	50
95	Music 70 BOARD 1	2ISM (LP or cassette, 100 copies only of each)	150/80

BOARDWALKERS

Year	Label & Cat. No.	Title	Value £
60s	own label J.C. 1	A Miracle/Any Man's Girl	200

(see also Warren Davis)

BOATMEN

Year	Label & Cat. No.	Title	Value £
70s	Sweet Folk SFA 018	STRAIGHT FROM THE TUNNEL'S MOUTH (LP)	30

BOB (Relf) & EARL (Nelson)

Year	Label & Cat. No.	Title	Value £
65	Sue WI 374	Harlem Shuffle/I'll Keep Running Back	20
65	Sue WI 393	Baby I'm Satisfied/The Sissy	20
67	Sue WI 4030	Don't Ever Leave Me/Fancy Free	20
69	Island WI 6053	Harlem Shuffle/I'll Keep Running Back (reissue)	10
69	B&C CB 102	Dancin' Everywhere/Baby It's Over	10
69	Warner Bros WB 6059	Everybody Jerk/He's A Playbrother	10
70	Uni UN 519	Pickin' Up Love's Vibrations/Uh, Uh, Naw Naw Naw	5
72	Jay Boy BOY 72	I Can't Get Away/I'll Keep Running Back	5
72	Jay Boy BOY 73	My Little Girl/His & Her Shuffle (as Bob & Earl Band)	5
73	Contempo C 4	Harlem Shuffle/Harlem Shuffle (Instrumental Version)	5
67	Sue ILP 951	HARLEM SHUFFLE (LP)	125
69	Joy JOYS 199	TOGETHER (LP)	15
69	B&C BCB 1	BOB AND EARL (LP)	15
71	Jay Boy JSX 2004	HARLEM SHUFFLE (LP)	15

(see also Bob Relf, Jackie Lee, Earl Nelson, Hollywood Flames)

BOB & JERRY

Year	Label & Cat. No.	Title	Value £
58	Pye International 7N 25003	Ghost Satellite/Nothin'	18
58	Pye International N 25003	Ghost Satellite/Nothin' (78)	10
61	Philips PB 1205	Dreamy Eyes/We're The Guys	6

BOB (Andy) & MARCIA (Griffiths)

Year	Label & Cat. No.	Title	Value £
70	Bamboo BAM 40	Really Together/BOB ANDY: Desperate Lover	20
70	Harry J. HJ 6605	Young, Gifted And Black/JAY BOYS: Young, Gifted & Black (Instrumental)	6
70	Escort ES 824	Young, Gifted And Black/BARRINGTON BIGGS: My Cheri Amour	6
71	Trojan TR 7818	Pied Piper/Save Me	5
72	Trojan TR 7854	But I Do/I Don't Care	5
70	Trojan TBL 122	YOUNG, GIFTED & BLACK (LP)	25
72	Trojan TRLS 26	PIED PIPER (LP)	20

(see also Bob Andy, Marcia Griffiths)

BOB & TYRONE

Year	Label & Cat. No.	Title	Value £
69	Coxsone CS 7086	I Don't Care/LASCELLES PERKINS: Little Green Apples	30

BOB(B)ETTES

Year	Label & Cat. No.	Title	Value £
57	London HLE 8477	Mr. Lee/Look At The Stars	75
57	London HLE 8477	Mr. Lee/Look At The Stars (78)	20
58	London HLE 8597	Come-A Come-A/Speedy	80
58	London HLE 8597	Come-A Come-A/Speedy (78)	25
60	London HLE 9173	I Shot Mr. Lee/Untrue Love	45
60	London HLE 9248	Have Mercy Baby/Dance With Me Georgie	35
60	Pye International 7N 25060	I Shot Mr. Lee/Billy (as Bobettes)	40
72	Action ACT 4603	That's A Bad Thing To Know/All In Your Mind	18

BOBBIE & VERA

Year	Label & Cat. No.	Title	Value £
69	Decca F 12897	I Know That He Knows/City Of Dreams	5

MINT VALUE £

BOBBSEY TWINS
57 London HLA 8474 A Change Of Heart/Part-Time Gal . . . 40
57 London HLA 8474 A Change Of Heart/Part-Time Gal (78) . . . 15

BOBBY & DAVE
71 Ackee ACK 116 Build My World Around You/LIZZY & TONY BOP: Sammy Version . . . 15
(see also Dave Barker, Lizzy & Dennis)

BOBBY & JIM
58 Capitol CL 14877 Carry My Books/A Lover Can Tell . . . 7

BOBBY & LAURIE
66 Parlophone R 5480 Hitch Hiker/You'll Come 'Round . . . 15

BOBBY & MIDNITES
84 CBS 26046 WHERE THE BEAT MEETS THE STREET (LP). . . . 25
(see also Bob Weir, Grateful Dead)

BOBCATS
67 Pye 7N 17242 Can't See For Looking/Let Me Get By . . . 15

BOBO MR. SOUL
73 London HLU 10418 Hitch Hiking To Heartbreak/She's My Woman . . . 6

FRIDA BOCCARA
69 Philips BF 1765 Through The Eyes Of A Child/So Fair . . . 15

BOCKY & VISIONS
65 Atlantic AT 4049 I Go Crazy/Good Good Lovin' . . . 35

BODAST
81 Cherry Red BRED 12 THE BODAST TAPES FEATURING STEVE HOWE (LP) . . . 12
(see also Steve Howe, Tomorrow)

BODGER'S MATE
78 Cottage COT 521 BRIGHTER THAN USUAL (LP) . . . 25

BODIES
79 Waldo's HS 007 Art Nouveau/Machinery (poster p/s, 5 different colours) . . . 5

BODKIN
72 West CSA 104 BODKIN (LP, private pressing in posthumously-designed sleeve). . . . 300

BODY
81 Recession THE BODY ALBUM (LP, private pressing with booklet) . . . 50

BODYSNATCHERS
80 2-Tone CHS TT 9 Let's Do Rocksteady/Ruder Than You
(paper label, company PVC sleeve) . . . 6
80 2-Tone CHS TT 12 Easy Life/Too Experienced (paper label, company PVC sleeve) . . . 6

BOEING DUVEEN & BEAUTIFUL SOUP
68 Parlophone R 5696 Jabberwock/Which Dreamed It (some with p/s) . . . 175/80

BOFFALONGO
70 United Artists UP 35144 Dancing In The Moonlight/Endless Questions . . . 7
71 United Artists UAG 29130 BEYOND YOUR HEAD (LP). . . . 20

LUCILLE BOGAN
57 Jazz Collector L 90 Sweet Man, Sweet Man/Down In Boogie Alley (78). . . . 8

DIRK BOGARDE
65 Fontana TF 615 Darling/MOVIE SOUNDS: Pavanne For Diane . . . 10
60 Decca LK 4373 LYRICS FOR LOVERS (LP). . . . 15

BOGDON
81 Black Label GB 3 Oh Eddie/Reet Petite (p/s) . . . 10
81 Brilliant HIT 1 Who Do You Think You Are?/Take Me Back (p/s). . . . 10
(see also Whitesnake, Bernie Marsden)

BOGEYMEN
93 Detour DR 008 Let Me Give You My Love/You've Got No Scruples/Gimme A Little Sign
(p/s, 100 on blue vinyl). . . . 5

BOGIES
64 private press (no cat. no.) THE BOGIES ON CAMPUS (LP). . . . 200
64 private press (no cat. no.) BYE BYE BOGIES (LP). . . . 200

ERIC BOGLE
70s Autogram ALLP 211 LIVE IN PERSON (LP) . . . 20

LEE BOGLE
71 Black Swan BW 1406 Tomorrow's Dreams/SWANS: Hot Pants Reggae . . . 8

HAMILTON BOHANNON
75 Brunswick BR 16 South African Man/Have A Good Day . . . 5
78 Mercury 6167 700 Let's Start The Dance/I Wonder Why . . . 5
78 Mercury 9199 830 Let's Start The Dance/I Wonder Why (12"). . . . 10
79 London HLX10582 Let's Start The Dance Again/Version (12") . . . 10
83 Compleat CTL1 Let's Start The Dance III/Instrumental (12"). . . . 12
75 Brunswick BRLS 3013 SOUTH AFRICAN MAN (LP). . . . 12

HOUSTON BOINES
66 Blue Horizon 45 BH 1006 Superintendent Blues/Monkey Motion (99 copies only) . . . 110

BOLA 1
95 Skam SKA 5 Forcasa 3/Krak Jakomo/Metalurg 2/Ballom
(12", custom sleeve). . . . 60

MINT VALUE £

MARC BOLAN

Year	Label/Cat. No.	Title/Details	Value
65	Decca F 12288	The Wizard/Beyond The Rising Sun (some as "Marc Bölan"; demos £250)	400
66	Decca F 12413	The Third Degree/San Francisco Poet (demos £300)	420
66	Parlophone R 5539	Hippy Gumbo/Misfit (demos £300)	500
72	Track 2094 013	Jasper C. Debussy/Hippy Gumbo/The Perfumed Garden Of Gulliver Smith (p/s, withdrawn)	60
81	Rarn MBFS 001C	Sing Me A Song/Endless Sleep (Extended Version)/The Lilac Hand Of Menthol Dan (12", no p/s, clear vinyl, handwritten labels)	8
81	Rarn MBFS 001P	Sing Me A Song/Endless Sleep (Extended Version)/The Lilac Hand Of Menthol Dan (12" picture disc, misprinted with black rim; also white rim)	15/7
81	Rarn MBFS 001P	Sing Me A Song/Endless Sleep (Extended Version)/The Lilac Hand Of Menthol Dan (12", picture disc misprinted back-to-front)	20
81	Cherry Red CHERRY 29	You Scare Me To Death/The Perfumed Garden Of Gulliver Smith (initial copies with bronze label, glossy p/s & free flexidisc [Lyntone LYN 10086])	7
81	Cherry Red CHERRY 29	You Scare Me To Death/The Perfumed Garden Of Gulliver Smith (later pressing with silver label/matt p/s)	5
81	Cherry Red CHERRY P29	You Scare Me To Death/The Perfumed Garden Of Gulliver Smith (picture disc)	6
81	Cherry Red CHERRY 32	Cat Black/Jasper C. Debussy (p/s)	5
82	Cherry Red CHERRY 39	The Wizard/Beyond The Rising Sun/Rings Of Fortune (p/s)	5
72	Track 2406 101	HARD ON LOVE (LP, unreleased, white label test pressing, 2 copies only)	500+
72	Track 2406 009	HARD ON LOVE (LP, unrel, 2-sided EMIdisc acetate with "swearing intro")	2000
74	Track 2410 201	THE BEGINNING OF DOVES (LP)	20
81	Cherry Red PERED 20	YOU SCARE ME TO DEATH (LP, picture disc)	12
81	Cherry Red ERED 20	YOU SCARE ME TO DEATH (LP, gatefold sleeve; early copies with booklet stapled into sleeve; later copies with loose booklet)	each 12
89	Media Motion MEDIA 2	THE BEGINNING OF DOVES (LP, reissue, 750 only, withdrawn)	12

(see also Marc Bolan/T. Rex, Marc Bolan & Gloria Jones, Toby Tyler, John's Children, Big Carrot, Dib Cochran & The Earwigs)

MARC BOLAN & GLORIA JONES

Year	Label/Cat. No.	Title/Details	Value
77	EMI EMI 2572	To Know You Is To Love You/City Port	20

(see also Gloria Jones)

MARC BOLAN/T. REX

SINGLES

Year	Label/Cat. No.	Title/Details	Value
70	Octopus OCTO 1	Ride A White Swan/Summertime Blues/Jewel (unreleased, handwritten white label, 2 test pressings only)	2,500
70	Fly BUG 1	Ride A White Swan/Is It Love/Summertime Blues (p/s, purple labels, later with mustard labels)	15/7
71	Fly BUG 6	Hot Love/Woodland Rock/King Of The Mountain Cometh (mustard labels, later with 'fly' design)	10/5
71	Fly BUG 10	Get It On/There Was A Time/Raw Ramp (p/s, black label with silver 'fly' logo)	15
70s	Fly BUG 10	Get It On/There Was A Time/Raw Ramp (p/s, black label with white 'fly' or later silver 'fly' text)	each 5
71	Fly GRUB 1	Electric Warrior Preview Single: Jeepster/Life's A Gas (gig freebie, originally in pink envelope sleeve, later standard paper sleeve)	175/125
71	Fly BUG 16	Jeepster/Life's A Gas (white 'fly' label, or scarce issue w/out 'GRUB 1A' ref.)	5/4
72	EMI T REX 101	Telegram Sam/Cadillac/Baby Strange	5
72	Magni Fly ECHO 102	One Inch Rock/The Woodland Bop/The Throat Of Winter (unreleased, rejected 1-sided test pressing for B-side of "Debora"/"One Inch Rock", stamped white label)	125
72	Magni Fly ECHO 102	Debora/One Inch Rock/The Woodland Bop/Seal Of Seasons (p/s)	5
72	EMI MARC 2	Children Of The Revolution/Jitterbug Love/Sunken Rags	5
72	EMI MARC 3	Solid Gold Easy Action/(5th Dimension track) (mispressing)	15
72	EMI MARC 3	Solid Gold Easy Action/(Partridge Family track) (mispressing)	15
72	EMI SPRS 346	Chariot Choogle/The Slider (promo only, 'T. Rex' picture label or white label)	350/250
72	Lyntone	Christmas Time/Wanna Spend My Christmas With You/ Christmas/Everybody Knows It's Christmas (fan club flexi, some with letter in brown envelope)	40/25
73	EMI MARC 5	The Groover/Midnight	5
73	EMI MARC 6	Truck On (Tyke)/Sitting Here	5
74	EMI MARC 7	Teenage Dream/Satisfaction Pony (credited to 'Marc Bolan & T. Rex' or 'Marc Bolan')	5/4
74	EMI MARC 8	Light Of Love/Explosive Mouth	5
74	EMI MARC 9	Zip Gun Boogie/Space Boss	5
75	EMI MARC 10	New York City/Chrome Sitar	5
75	EMI MARC 11	Dreamy Lady/Do You Wanna Dance?/Dock Of The Bay (as T. Rex Disco Party)	5
75	EMI MARC 12	Christmas Bop/Telegram Sam/Metal Guru (unreleased, A- & B-side paper labels exist, 2 sets only)	labels 1,000
76	EMI MARC 13	London Boys/Solid Baby	5
76	Cube BUG 66	Hot Love/Get It On	5
76	EMI MARC 14	I Love To Boogie/Baby Boomerang	5
76	EMI MARC 15	Laser Love/Life's An Elevator	5
77	EMI MARC 16	The Soul Of My Suit/All Alone	5
77	EMI MARC 17	Dandy In The Underworld/Groove A Little/Tame My Tiger (p/s)	6
77	EMI MARC 18	Celebrate Summer/Ride My Wheels (p/s)	7
78	EMI MARC 19	Crimson Moon/Jason B. Sad (p/s)	5
77	Cube ANT 1	BOLAN'S BEST PLUS ONE (EP, p/s)	5
78	Cube ANT 2	Hot Love/Raw Ramp/Lean Woman Blues (p/s, misprinted "Raw Amp", sleeve credits 'Bolan', label credits 'T.Rex')	5
78	Cube BINT 1	Steve Dixon Interview (free with initial copies of compilation LP [HIFLD 1])	7
79	Cube ANTS 001	Life's A Gas/Find A Little Wood/Once Upon The Seas Of Abyssinia/ Blessed Wild Apple Girl (12", p/s)	12
81	Cube/Dakota	Christmas Jingle/Sailors Of The Highway (MBFS fan club flexidisc)	5

MINT VALUE £

82	Marc ABOLAN 2	THE CHILDREN OF RARN (10" EP, p/s, 33rpm, gatefold sleeve with 12-page lyric book)	25
82	Marc SBOLAN 13	Mellow Love/Foxy Box/Lunacy's Back (p/s, blue vinyl, as Marc Bolan)	5
82	Rarn MBFS RAP 2	Deep Summer/Oh Baby/One Inch Rock (unreleased version) (12", p/s, blue vinyl)	10
83	Marc SBOLAN 12EP	CHRISTMAS BOP EP (12", p/s, OMBFS only, extra tracks: acoustic versions of "King Of The Rumbling Spires" & "Savage Beethoven")	8
83	Marc SBOLAN 14PD	Think Zinc/Till Dawn/Magical Moon (picture disc)	5
84	Marc On Wax SPS 1	Mister Motion (1-sided, from "Child Of The Revolution — 14 Greats" LP, p/s)	6
84	Cube BUG 99	Sailor Of The Highway/Do You Remember (white labels, promo only)	10
84	Cube HBUG 99	RARE MAGIC (12" EP)	8
85	Cambra MAIN 1	(Whatever Happened To The) Teenage Dream (Ext.)/Solid Gold Segue (picture disc free with "Mainman" LP)	5
85	Marc PTANX 1	Megarex 1/Megarex 1 (shaped picture disc, with free plinth)	8
87	Marc MARCX 1	Children Of The Revolution (remix)/The Slider (remix)/Tear For The High Star (tribute by Dave Ash-B) (shaped picture disc)	8
94	Edsel MBPROMO 1	T. REX (CD, picture disc, 4-track sampler, tri-fold digipak, promo only)	18
97	Edsel MARC 20-50	20th Century Boy/Carsmile Smith & The Old One/ All My Love/Dandy In The Underworld (CD, gig freebie)	12

LPs

70	Fly HIFLY 2	T. REX (semi-gatefold sleeve)	15
71	Fly HIFLY 6	ELECTRIC WARRIOR (unreleased version with "Jeepster" on side 2, 1 test pressing copy only, with Marc's annotations on white sleeve)	600
71	Fly HIFLY 6	ELECTRIC WARRIOR (with poster & inner sleeve; some with stickered sleeve)	15
72	Fly HIFLY 8	BOLAN BOOGIE (1-sided test pressing with "The Visit" instead of "Jewel")	300
72	Fly HIFLY 8	BOLAN BOOGIE	12
72	EMI BLN 5001	THE SLIDER (with lyric inner sleeve)	12
73	EMI BLN 5002	TANX (with poster & inner sleeve)	15
73	EMI BLN 5003	GREAT HITS (with poster)	12
74	EMI BNLA 7751	ZINC ALLOY AND THE HIDDEN RIDERS OF TOMORROW (with 3-way numbered promo fold-out sleeve & inner, given as competition prize with letter from *Pink* or *Mirabelle* magazines, 1,000 only)	250
74	EMI BNLA 7751	ZINC ALLOY AND THE HIDDEN RIDERS OF TOMORROW (with 3-way promo fold-out sleeve & inner, without letter; numbered or un-numbered copies)	200/175
74	EMI BNLA 7751	ZINC ALLOY AND THE HIDDEN RIDERS OF TOMORROW (commercial gatefold sleeve with lyric inner sleeve)	15
75	EMI BNLA 7752	BOLAN'S ZIP GUN (diamond-cut sleeve & inner sleeve)	18
76	EMI BLNA 5004	FUTURISTIC DRAGON (with lyric inner sleeve)	12
77	EMI BLNA 5005	DANDY IN THE UNDERWORLD (with round-cut sleeve & lyric inner sleeve)	10
78	Cube HIFLD 1	MARC: THE WORDS AND MUSIC OF MARC BOLAN 1947-1977 (2-LP, gatefold sleeve, with free single [BINT 1])	20
81	Marc ABOLAN 1P	T. REX IN CONCERT (picture disc, 2 designs)	12
82	Cube/Dakota ICSX 1004	ACROSS THE AIRWAVES (picture disc)	12
82	Marc ABOLAN 3P	ELECTRIC WARRIOR (picture disc)	12
84	Marc ABOLAN 5	T. REXTASY (with 12" "Jam (live)"/ "Elemental Child (live)" [ABOLAN 5F], Official Fanclub only)	15
86	Marc On Wax WARRIOR 1/4	HISTORY OF T. REX (4-LP, numbered picture disc set, some with free fanclub T-shirt)	30/25

(see also Marc Bolan, Tyrannosaurus Rex, Dib Cochran & the Earwigs, John's Children, Big Carrot)

TOMMY BOLIN

76	Nemperor K 10730/NE 4	The Grind/Homeward Strut	10
75	Atlantic K 50208	TEASER (LP, some stickered)	18/15
76	CBS S 81612	PRIVATE EYES (LP)	12

(see also James Gang, Deep Purple)

SIMON BOLIVAR ORCHESTRA

56	London HLG 8245	Meringue Holiday/Shy	20

BOLLARDS

70s	Bumkin Records	BOLLARDS (LP)	15

MICHAEL BOLOTIN

75	RCA SF 8451	MICHAEL BOLOTIN (LP)	15

(see also Blackjack, Michael Bolton)

MICHAEL BOLTON

88	CBS 651 387-2	(Sittin' On) The Dock Of The Bay (Lightning Bolton Mix)/ (Perc-Apella Version)/Call My Name (CD, card sleeve)	8

(see also Blackjack, Michael Bolotin)

BOLT THROWER

89	Earache MOSH 13	REALM OF CHAOS (LP, picture disc)	12

BOMBADIL

72	Harvest HAR 5056	Breathless/When The City Sleeps (p/s)	10
75	Harvest HAR 5095	Breathless/When The City Sleeps (p/s, reissue)	6

(see also Barclay James Harvest)

BOMBAY DUCKS

80	Complete Control CON 1	Sympathy For The Devil/1-0-6-9 (p/s)	10
80s	United Dairies UD 05	DANCE MUSIC (LP)	18
80s	Eraserhead C-60	ANYONE CAN BE ENO (cassette)	12
80s	Eraserhead C-30	A RETROSPECTIVE LOOK AT THE BOMBAY DUCKS (cassette with mask)	12

MINT VALUE £

BON-BONS
55 London HL 8139 That's The Way Love Goes/Make My Dreams Come True . . . 65
55 London HL 8139 That's The Way Love Goes/Make My Dreams Come True (78) . . . 15
56 London HLU 8262 Circle/Frog On A Log . . . 65
56 London HLU 8262 Circle/Frog On A Log (78) . . . 18

BOBBY BOND
61 Pye International 7N 25081 You're A Livin' Doll/Sweet Love . . . 10
69 Warner Bros WB 7292 One More Mile, One More Town/If You're Leaving Me . . . 5

BRIGITTE BOND
64 Blue Beat BB 212 Oh Yeah Baby/Blue Beat Baby . . . 30

GRAHAM BOND (ORGANISATION)
64 Decca F 11909 Long Tall Shorty/Long Legged Baby (as Graham Bond Organization) . . . 50
65 Columbia DB 7471 Wade In The Water/Tammy (as Graham Bond Organisation) . . . 45
65 Columbia DB 7528 Tell Me (I'm Gonna Love Again)/Love Come Shining Through (as Graham Bond Organisation) . . . 40
65 Columbia DB 7647 Lease On Love/My Heart's In Little Pieces (as Graham Bond Organisation) . . . 35
66 Columbia DB 7838 St James Infirmary/Soul Tango (as Graham Bond Organisation) . . . 35
67 Page One POF 014 You've Gotta Have Love Babe/I Love You . . . 50
70 Warner Bros WB 8004 Walking In The Park/Springtime In The City (solo) . . . 12
71 Vertigo 6059 042 Twelve Gates To The City/Water Water (as Graham Bond with Magick) . . . 10
65 Columbia 33SX 1711 THE SOUND OF '65 (LP, 1st pressing, with '33SX' on blue/black label) . . . 170
65 Columbia 33SX 1750 THERE'S A BOND BETWEEN US (LP, 1st pressing, with '33SX' on blue/black label) . . . 150
66 Columbia SX 1711 THE SOUND OF '65 (LP, 2nd pressing, with 'SX' on blue/black label) . . . 110
66 Columbia SX 1750 THERE'S A BOND BETWEEN US (LP, 2nd pressing, with 'SX' on blue/black label) . . . 110
69 Columbia SX 1711 THE SOUND OF '65 (LP, 3rd pressing, with boxed logo on silver/black label) . . . 60
69 Columbia SX 1750 THERE'S A BOND BETWEEN US (LP, 3rd pressing, with boxed logo on blue/black label) . . . 60

(N.B., all of the above LPs have '33SX' on the sleeve, but only the 1st pressings have '33SX' on the label)

71 Warner Bros WS 3001 SOLID BOND (2-LP) . . . 40
71 Vertigo 6360 021 HOLY MAGICK (LP, gatefold sleeve, swirl label, as Graham Bond & Magick) . . . 35
71 Vertigo 6360 042 WE PUT OUR MAGICK ON YOU (LP, gatefold sleeve, swirl label, as Graham Bond With Magick) . . . 35
72 Philips 6382 010 BOND IN AMERICA (2-LP, solo [individual discs: 6499 200/1]) . . . 25
72 Philips 6382 010 THIS IS GRAHAM BOND (LP, solo) . . . 12

(see also Jack Bruce, Dick Heckstall-Smith, Ginger Baker, Duffy Power, Who, Don Rendell, Steve York's Camelo Pardalis)

GRAHAM BOND & PETE BROWN
71 Greenwich GSS 104 Lost Tribe/Macumbe/Milk Is Turning Sour In My Shoes (maxi-single) . . . 25
72 Chapter One CHSR 813 TWO HEADS ARE BETTER THAN ONE (LP) . . . 80

(see also Pete Brown)

ISABEL BOND
68 Major Minor MM 565 Cry/When A Woman Loves A Man (some in p/s) . . . 12/6
69 Major Minor MM 627 Don't Forget About Me/You'll Never Get The Chance Again . . . 20
68 Major Minor MMLP 28 THE HEART AND SOUL OF ISABEL BOND (LP) . . . 20

JACKI BOND
65 Columbia DB 7719 My Sister's Boy/Now I Know . . . 15
66 Strike JH 302 Tell Him To Go Away/Don't You Worry . . . 15
66 Strike JH 320 He Say/Why Can't I Love Him . . . 20

JANE BOND & UNDERCOVER MEN
86 Dreamworld BIG DREAM 1 POLITICALLY CORRECT (LP) . . . 12

JOHNNY BOND
50 MGM MGM 262 Music Music Music (Put Another Nickel In) (with Orchestra)/Rag Mop (78) . . . 15
60 London HLU 9189 Hot Rod Jalopy/Five-Minute Love Affair . . . 25
60 London HL 7100 Hot Rod Lincoln/Five-Minute Love Affair (export issue) . . . 20
65 London HLB 9957 Ten Little Bottles/Eleven More Months And Ten More Days (B-side with Cowboy Copas) . . . 10
62 Stateside SL 10008 THAT WILD, WICKED BUT WONDERFUL WEST (LP) . . . 20
63 London HA-B 8098 LIVE IT UP (LP, as Johnny Bond & His Friends On Stage) . . . 20
65 London HA-B 8228 THE SONGS THAT MADE HIM FAMOUS (LP) . . . 25
66 London HA-B 8272 FAMOUS HOT RODDERS I HAVE KNOWN (LP) . . . 20
67 London HA-B 8269 THE MAN WHO COMES AROUND (LP) . . . 15

JOHNNY BOND'S RED RIVER VALLEY BOYS
51 Columbia DB 2844 Love Song In 32 Bars/CHAMP BUTLER: Dear, Dear, Dear (78) . . . 10

(see also Champ Butler)

JOYCE BOND
67 Airborne NBP 0011 It's Alright/Mrs. Soul . . . 30
66 Island WI 3019 Tell Me What It's All About/Tell Me Right Now . . . 20
67 Island WIP 6010 Do The Teasy/Sugar . . . 12
67 Island WIP 6018 This Train/Not So With Me . . . 12
68 Island WIP 6051 Ob-La-Di, Ob-La-Da/Robin Hood Rides Again . . . 10
68 Pama PM 718 Back To School/They Wish . . . 12
69 Pama PM 771 Mr. Pitiful/Let's Get Married (as Joyce Bond & Little John) . . . 15
70 Upfront UPF 5 Wind Of Change/First In Line . . . 7
71 Trojan TR 7837 Help Me Make It Through The Night/Reconsider Our Love . . . 15
68 Island ILP 968 SOUL AND SKA (LP, mono only) . . . 140

MARGARET BOND
55 Decca F 10506 You'll Always Be My Lifetime Sweetheart/Where Is The One For Me . . . 8
55 Decca F 10555 My Love's A Gentle Man/Mirror, Mirror . . . 8
55 Decca F 10632 There's Always A First Time/Dancing In My Socks . . . 8
57 Parlophone R 4283 Your Love Is My Love/Goodnight My Love, Pleasant Dreams . . . 6
57 Parlophone R 4312 The Wind In The Willow/Young And In Love . . . 6

MINT VALUE £

OLIVER BOND

66	Parlophone R 5476	I Saw You All Alone/Let Me Love You	15

(see also Oliver Bone)

RONNIE BOND

69	Page One POF 123	Anything For You/Carolyn	40

(see also Troggs)

(GARY) 'U.S.' BONDS

60	Top Rank JAR 527	New Orleans/Please Forgive Me (as U.S. Bonds)	20
61	Top Rank JAR 566	Not Me/Give Me One More Chance (as U.S. Bonds)	10
61	Top Rank JAR 575	Quarter To Three/Time Ole Story (as U.S. Bonds)	10
61	Top Rank JAR 581	School Is Out/One Million Tears	10
61	Top Rank JAR 595	School Is In/Trip To The Moon	10
62	Top Rank JAR 602	Dear Lady Twist/Havin' So Much Fun	15
62	Top Rank JAR 615	Twist Twist Senora/Food Of Love	15
62	Stateside SS 111	Seven Day Weekend/Gettin' A Groove	15
62	Stateside SS 125	Copy Cat/I'll Change That Too	15
63	Stateside SS 144	Mixed Up Faculty/I Dig This Station	15
63	Stateside SS 179	Where Did That Naughty Little Girl Go?/Do The Limbo With Me	15
63	Stateside SS 219	What A Dream/I Don't Wanta Wait	15
64	Stateside SS 271	New Orleans/Quarter To Three	12
64	Stateside SS 308	My Sweet Baby Rose/Ella Is Yella	12
67	Stateside SS 2025	Send Her To Me/Workin' For My Baby	12
61	Top Rank 35/114	DANCE 'TIL QUARTER TO THREE WITH U.S. BONDS (LP)	50
62	Stateside SL 10001	TWIST UP CALYPSO (LP)	30
63	Stateside SL 10037	THE GREATEST HITS OF GARY (U.S.) BONDS (LP)	30

OLIVER BONE & SOUNDS MAXIMUM

66	Parlophone R 5527	Knock On Wood/Jugger Tea	10

(see also Oliver Bond)

BROTHER BONES & HIS SHADOWS

60	Oriole CB 1030	Sweet Georgia Brown/Margie	7

BONGO HERMAN (Davis)

70	Songbird SB 1018	True Grit/True Grit Version 2 (both credited with Les Crystalites but actually with Les & Crystalites)	25
71	Songbird SB 1060	BONGO HERMAN & LES BUNNY: Know For I/CRYSTALITES: Version (B-side actually titled 'Know Fari')	18
71	Songbird SB 1066	BONGO HERMAN & LES & BUNNY: Salaam (Peace)/CRYSTALITES: Scraper	18
72	Big BG 332	Eternal Drums/ERROL DUNKLEY: Darling Ooh Wee (both actually by Hugh Roy Junior)	15
72	Green Door GD 4049	African Breakfast/BONGO HERMAN & LES AND BUNNY: Chairman Of The Board	15
72	Songbird SB 1069	We Are Praying/CRYSTALITES: Version	10

BONGO LES & HERMAN

71	Songbird SB 1050	Home Sweet Home/Hail I	15

(see also Heptones, Scotty, Meditators)

BON JOVI

84	Vertigo VER 11	She Don't Know Me/Breakout (p/s)	22
84	Vertigo VERX 11	She Don't Know Me/Breakout (12", p/s)	30
84	Vertigo VER 14	Runaway/Breakout (live) (p/s)	22
84	Vertigo VERX 14	Runaway/Breakout (live)/Runaway (live) (12", p/s)	30
85	Vertigo VER 19	In And Out Of Love/Roulette (live) (p/s)	10
85	Vertigo VERP 19	In And Out Of Love/Roulette (live) (picture disc)	35
85	Vertigo VERX 19	In And Out Of Love/Roulette (live)/Shot Through The Heart (live) (12", p/s)	15
85	Vertigo VER 22	The Hardest Part Is The Night/Always Run To You (p/s)	12
85	Vertigo VERDP 22	The Hardest Part Is The Night/Always Run To You//Tokyo Road (live)/ Shot Through The Heart (live) (double pack, gatefold p/s)	18
85	Vertigo VERX 22	The Hardest Part Is The Night/Always Run To You/Tokyo Road (live) (12", p/s)	18
85	Vertigo VERXR 22	Red Hot And Two Parts Live: The Hardest Part Is The Night/ Tokyo Road (live)/In And Out Of Love (live) (12", p/s, red vinyl)	30
86	Vertigo VERP 26	You Give Love A Bad Name/Let It Rock (10", shaped picture disc)	30
86	Vertigo VERX 26	You Give Love A Bad Name/Let It Rock/Borderline (12", p/s with poster)	12
86	Vertigo VERXR 26	You Give Love A Bad Name/Let It Rock/ The Hardest Part Is The Night (live)/Burning For Love (live) (12", p/s, blue vinyl)	18
86	Vertigo VERPA 28	Livin' On A Prayer/Wild In The Streets (p/s, with patch)	10
86	Vertigo VERP 28	Livin' On A Prayer/Wild In The Streets (picture disc)	18
86	Vertigo VERXR 28	Livin' On A Prayer/Wild In The Streets/Edge Of A Broken Heart (12", green vinyl, p/s)	12
86	Vertigo VERXG 28	Livin' On A Prayer/Wild In The Streets/Only Lonely (live)/ Runaway (live) (12", gatefold p/s)	18
88	Mercury 080 042-2	Livin' On A Prayer/Borderline/Let It Rock/Wild In The Streets (CD Video)	20
87	Vertigo JOVS 1	Wanted Dead Or Alive/Shot Through The Heart (p/s, with metal stickers)	8
87	Vertigo JOVPB 112	Wanted Dead Or Alive/Shot Through The Heart/Social Disease (12", poster p/s)	18
87	Vertigo JOVR 112	Wanted Dead Or Alive/Shot Through The Heart/Social Disease/ Get Ready (live) (12", p/s, silver vinyl)	15
87	Vertigo JOVCD 1	Wanted Dead Or Alive (Full Version)/(Radio Edit)/(Acoustic) (CD, promo only)	30
87	Vertigo JOVR 212	Never Say Goodbye/Raise Your Hands/Wanted Dead Or Alive (Acoustic Version) (12", yellow vinyl, PVC sleeve)	12
87	Vertigo	Never Say Goodbye (CD video)	25
87	Vertigo	Wanted Dead Or Alive (CD video)	25
87	Vertigo 080 042-2	Livin' On A Prayer/Borderline/Let It Rock/Wild In The Streets (CD video)	25
88	Vertigo JOVS 3	Bad Medicine/99 In The Shade (fold-out photofile p/s)	8
88	Vertigo JOVR 312	Bad Medicine/You Give Love A Bad Name/Livin' On A Prayer (live) (12", embossed p/s)	8

MINT VALUE £

88	Vertigo JOVCD 3	Bad Medicine/Lay Your Hands On Me/99 In The Shade (CD, card sleeve)	12
88	Vertigo JOVS 4	Born To Be My Baby/Love For Sale (gold 'calendar' card envelope pack)	8
88	Vertigo JOVR 412	Born To Be My Baby/Love For Sale/Wanted Dead Or Alive (live) (12", gatefold p/s)	8
88	Vertigo JOVP 412	Born To Be My Baby/Love For Sale/Wanted Dead Or Alive (live) (12", picture disc)	12
88	Vertigo JOVCD 4	Born To Be My Baby/Love For Sale/Runaway/Livin' On A Prayer (CD)	12
89	Vertigo JOVPB 5	I'll Be There For You/Homebound Train (p/s, with poster)	5
89	Vertigo JOVCD 5	I'll Be There For You/Homebound Train/Borderline/Edge Of A Broken Heart (CD, card sleeve)	12
89	Vertigo JOVS 661	Lay Your Hands On Me/Bad Medicine (live) (red vinyl, stickered PVC sleeve)	6
89	Vertigo JOVS 662	Lay Your Hands On Me/Bad Medicine (live) (white vinyl, stickered PVC sleeve)	6
89	Vertigo JOVS 663	Lay Your Hands On Me/Bad Medicine (live) (blue vinyl, stickered PVC sleeve)	7
89	Vertigo JOVS 661-663	Lay Your Hands On Me/Bad Medicine (live) (3 x 7", red, blue or white vinyl, paper box set)	22
89	Vertigo JOVP 610	Lay Your Hands On Me/Bad Medicine (live)/Blood On Blood (10", picture disc with insert)	10
89	Vertigo JOVCD 6	Lay Your Hands On Me/You Give Love A Bad Name/Let It Rock (CD)	12
89	Vertigo JOVR 712	Living In Sin/Love Is War/The Boys Are Back In Town (12", white vinyl with stickered card insert)	12
89	Vertigo JOVCD 7	Living In Sin/Love Is War/Ride Cowboy Ride/Stick To Your Guns (CD, box set)	18
92	Vertigo JOVCD 8	Keep The Faith/I Wish Everyday Could Be Like Christmas/ Little Bit Of Soul (CD, digipak)	10
92	Vertigo JOVLH 9	Bed Of Roses/Bed Of Roses (jukebox issue, no p/s)	6
92	Vertigo JOVCD 9	Bed Of Roses/Lay Your Hands On Me (live)/Tokyo Road (live)/ I'll Be There For You (live) (CD, slimline jewel case)	10
93	Vertigo JOVMB 10	In These Arms/Bed Of Roses (Acoustic) (cassette, pull-apart outer card slipcase with tour pass)	6
93	Vertigo JOVD 11	Sleep When I'm Dead/Blaze Of Glory/You Give Love A Bad Name/ Bad Medicine (CD, digipak)	10
94	Vertigo JOVBX 13	Dry County/Stranger In This Town (live)/Blood Money (live) (gold CD, digipak)	8
94	Vertigo JOVJB 14	Always (edit)/Always (jukebox issue, no p/s)	6
94	Vertigo JOVCD 14	ALWAYS (CD EP, digipak)	12
94	Vertigo JOVJB 15	Someday I'll Be Saturday Night/Always (live) (jukebox issue, no p/s)	7
94	Vertigo JOVP 15	Someday I'll Be Saturday Night (picture disc, with insert)	5
94	Vertigo JOVDD 15	Someday I'll Be Saturday Night/Good Guys Don't Always Wear White/ Someday I'll Be Saturday Night (live) (CD, in red circular tin)	8
94	Vertigo JOVJB 16	Please Come Home For Christmas/Back Door Santa (jukebox issue, no p/s)	6
94	Vertigo JOVP 16	Please Come Home For Christmas/Back Door Santa (picture disc)	7
88	Vertigo VERHP 38	SLIPPERY WHEN WET (LP, picture disc with poster)	15
88	Vertigo VERHP 62	NEW JERSEY (LP, picture disc, stickered PVC sleeve)	15
89	Vertigo JOVI 1989	ESSENTIAL (CD, 8-track sampler, promo only)	25

JON BON JOVI

90	Vertigo JBJ 212	Miracle/Dyin' Ain't Much Of A Livin'/Interview With Jon Bon Jovi (12", p/s, with poster & numbered sticker)	15
90	Vertigo JBJP 212	Miracle/Dyin' Ain't Much Of A Livin'/Going Back (live) (12", picture disc with insert)	18

JUKE BOY BONNER

69	Blue Horizon 57-3163	Runnin' Shoes/Jackin' In My Plans	30
60s	Jan & Dil JR 451	MORE DOWN HOME BLUES (EP)	25
68	Flyright LP 3501	THE ONE MAN TRIO (LP)	30
69	Liberty LBS 83319	THINGS AIN'T RIGHT (LP)	30

GRAHAM BONNET

72	RCA RCA 2230	Rare Specimen/Whisper In The Night	8
73	RCA RCA 2380	Trying To Say Goodbye/Castles In The Air	5
74	DJM DJS 328	Back Row In The Stalls/Ghost Writer In My Eye	8
77	Ring O' 2017 105	It's All Over Now, Baby Blue/Heroes On My Picture Wall (company sleeve)	10
77	Ring O' 2017 106	Danny/Rock Island Line (company sleeve, some in promo p/s)	15/10
77	Ring O' 2017 110	Goodnight And Goodmorning/Wino Song (company sleeve)	10
78	Ring O' 2017 114/POSP 2	Warm Ride/10/12 Observation (company sleeve)	8
78	Ring O' POSP 002	Warm Ride/10/12 Observation (12", company sleeve)	15
81	Lyntone LYN 10138/9	Night Games/POLECATS: We Say Yeah/THIN LIZZY: Song For Jimmy/WAY OF THE WEST: Monkey Love (orange flexi with *Flexipop* mag, issue 10)	12/8
81	Vertigo VER 1	Night Games/Out On The Water (p/s)	5
81	Vertigo VER 2	Liar/Bad Days Are Gone (p/s)	5
81	Vertigo VER 4	That's The Way That It Is/Don't Tell Me To Go (p/s)	6
77	Ring O' 2320 103	GRAHAM BONNET (LP, with inner sleeve)	18
81	Vertigo 6302 151	LINE UP (LP, with inner sleeve)	12

(see also Marbles, Rainbow, Cozy Powell, Forcefield, Fut, Michael Schenker Group, Jon Lord)

GRAHAM BONNEY

65	Columbia DB 7773	My Little World Is All Blue/Why Can't We Be Friends	10
66	Columbia DB 7843	Super Girl/Hill Of Lovin'	12
66	Columbia DB 7934	Baby's Gone/Later Tonight	10
66	Columbia DB 8005	No One Knows/Mixed Up Baby Girl	12
67	Columbia DB 8111	Thank You Baby/Briony	5
67	Columbia DB 8142	Happy Together/That Bad Day	5
67	Columbia DB 8283	Papa Joe/My Jenny	5
68	Columbia DB 8338	By The Way I Love You/Devil's Child	5
68	Columbia DB 8382	I'll Be Your Baby Tonight/Back From Baltimore	5
68	Columbia DB 8464	Frenzy/Something I've Got To Tell You	5
69	Columbia DB 8531	Get Ready/Fly Me High Lorelei	12
69	Columbia DB 8592	Leanda Angeline/Mixing The Wine	5
70	Columbia DB 8648	Sign On The Dotted Line/Words We Said	10
70	Columbia DB 8687	When Evelyn Was Mine/Sunny Has Gone	10
66	Columbia SX 6052	SUPER GIRL (LP)	35

(see also Riot Squad)

MINT VALUE £

BONNIE & SKITTO

63	Island WI 122	Get Ready (actually by Vikings [alias Maytals])/ DON DRUMMOND: The Rocket	30

BONNIE & TREASURES

65	London HLU 9998	Home Of The Brave/Our Song	50

BONO & GAVIN FRIDAY

94	Island CID 593	In The Name Of The Father (7" Edit)/(12" Remix)/(12" Beats Mix)/ (LP Instrumental) (CD)	15

(see also U2, Virgin Prunes)

BONZO DOG (DOO-DAH) BAND

66	Parlophone R 5430	My Brother Makes The Noises For The Talkies/ I'm Gonna Bring A Watermelon To My Gal Tonight	35
66	Parlophone R 5499	Alley Oop/Button Up Your Overcoat	30
67	Liberty LBF 15040	Equestrian Statue/The Intro And The Outro	12
68	Liberty LBF 15144	Urban Spaceman/Canyons Of Your Mind (initially with spoken intro to A-side)	12/7
69	Liberty LBF 15201	Mr. Apollo/Ready Mades	8
69	Liberty LBF 15273	I Want To Be With You/We Were Wrong	10
70	Liberty LBF 15314	You Done My Brain In/Mr. Slater's Parrot	8
74	United Artists UP 35662	Mr. Slater's Parrot/Noises For The Leg	5
92	China WOK 2021	No Matter Who You Vote For The Government Always Gets In/ NEIL INNES: Them (promo only)	7
92	China WOK CD 2021	No Matter Who You Vote For The Government Always Gets In/ Urban Spaceman/The Intro/NEIL INNES: Them (CD)	12
67	Liberty LBL/LBS 83056	GORILLA (LP, some with booklet)	35/20
68	Liberty LBL/LBS 83158E	THE DOUGHNUT IN GRANNY'S GREENHOUSE (LP, gatefold sleeve, some with booklet)	35/20
69	Liberty LBS 83257	TADPOLES (LP, die-cut sleeve, some with insert)	40/25
69	Liberty LBS 83290	KEYNSHAM (LP, gatefold sleeve)	30
72	United Artists UAS 29288	LET'S MAKE UP AND BE FRIENDLY (LP)	20
74	United Artists UAD 60071/2	THE HISTORY OF THE BONZOS (2-LP, gatefold sleeve with booklet)	25

(see also Vivian Stanshall, Neil Innes, Grimms, Roger Ruskin Spear, Topo D. Bill, New Vaudeville Band)

BETTY BOO

79	Grapevine GRP 125	Say It Isn't So/Say It Isn't So (Instrumental)	8

BOOGALOOS

69	President PT 253	Rule Britannia/Love Is Blind	6

JAMES BOOKER

61	Vogue V 9177	Cool Turkey/Gonzo	20
63	Vocalion VEP 170154	GONZO (EP)	65

BOOKER T. & THE M.G.s

62	London HLK 9595	Green Onions/Behave Yourself	22
63	London HLK 9670	Jelly Bread/Aw' Mercy	15
63	London HLK 9784	Chinese Checkers/Plum Nellie	15
65	Atlantic AT 4033	Boot-Leg/Outrage	10
66	Atlantic AT 4063	Be My Lady/Red Beans And Rice	12
66	Atlantic 584 044	My Sweet Potato/Booker Loo	8
66	Atlantic 584 060	Jingle Bells/Winter Wonderland	8
67	Atlantic 584 088	Green Onions/Boot-Leg	10
67	Stax 601 009	Hip Hug Her/Summertime (initially dark blue label; later light blue)	10/7
67	Stax 601 018	Groovin'/Slim Jenkins' Place	8
67	Stax 601 026	Chinese Checkers/Plum Nellie (reissue)	8
68	Stax STAX 102	Soul Limbo/Heads Or Tails	6
69	Stax STAX 119	Time Is Tight/Hang 'Em High	6
69	Stax STAX 127	Soul Clap '69/Mrs. Robinson	6
69	Stax STAX 136	The Horse/Slum Baby	6
71	Stax 2025 026	Melting Pot/Kinda Easy Like	10
72	Stax 2025 074	Jamaica This Morning (as the MGs)/Fuquawi	6
63	London REK 1367	R&B WITH BOOKER T (EP)	35
64	Atlantic AET 6002	R&B WITH BOOKER T VOL. 2 (EP)	30
64	London HA-K 8182	GREEN ONIONS (LP)	60
65	Atlantic ATL 5027	SOUL DRESSING (LP)	40
66	Atlantic 587/588 033	GREEN ONIONS (LP, reissue)	15
67	Atlantic 587 047	SOUL DRESSING (LP, reissue)	15
67	Stax 589 002	AND NOW! (LP)	18
68	Stax 589 013	SOUL CHRISTMAS (LP)	15
68	Stax 230 002/231 002	DOIN' OUR THING (LP)	15
68	Stax (S)XATS 1001	SOUL LIMBO (LP)	15
69	Atco 228 004	GET READY (LP)	15
69	Stax (S)XATS 1005	UPTIGHT (LP, soundtrack, with Judy Clay)	18
69	Stax (S)XATS 1015	THE BOOKER T. SET (LP)	15
69	Atco 228 015	THE BEST OF BOOKER T. AND THE M.G.s (LP)	15
70	Stax SXATS 1031	McLEMORE AVENUE (LP)	15
71	Stax 2325 030	MELTING POT (LP)	12
71	Stax 2362 002	GREATEST HITS (LP)	12
75	Stax STX 1037	MEMPHIS SOUND (LP)	12

(see also Mar-Keys, Steve Cropper, Albert King, Judy Clay)

BOOMERANGS

64	Fontana TF 507	Rockin' Robin/Don't Let Her Be Your Baby	30
65	Fontana TF 555	Another Tear Falls/Fun Fun Fun	20

BOOMERANGS

66	Pye 7N 17049	Dream World/Upgraded	10

MINT VALUE £

PAT BOONE

78s

59	London HLD 8775	I'll Remember Tonight/The Mardi Gras March	5
59	London HLD 8824	There's Good Rockin' Tonight/With The Wind And The Rain In Your Hair	5
59	London HLD 8855	For A Penny/Wang Dang Taffy-Apple Tango	5
59	London HLD 8910	Rock Boll Weevil/Twixt Twelve And Twenty	5
59	London HLD 8974	A Fool's Hall Of Fame/Brightest Wishing Star	5
60	London HLD 9029	Beyond The Sunset/The Faithful Heart	5
60	London HLD 9067	(Welcome) New Lovers/Words	5
60	London HLD 9184	Delia Gone/Candy Sweet	10

SINGLES

55	London HLD 8172	Ain't That A Shame/Tennessee Saturday Night	40
55	London HLD 8197	At My Front Door/No Arms Can Ever Hold You	25
56	London HLD 8233	Gee Whittakers/Take The Time	25
56	London HLD 8253	I'll Be Home/Tutti Frutti	25
56	London HLD 8291	Long Tall Sally/Just As Long As I'm With You	45
56	London HLD 8303	I Almost Lost My Mind/I'm In Love With You	15
56	London HLD 8316	Two Hearts, Two Kisses/Rich In Love	30
56	London HLD 8346	Friendly Persuasion (Thee I Love)/Chains Of Love	22

(The above 45s were originally issued with gold lettering labels; later silver lettering copies are worth half these values.)

57	London HLD 8370	Don't Forbid Me/Anastasia	12
57	London HLD 8404	Why Baby Why/I'm Just Waiting For You	15
57	London HLD 8445	Love Letters In The Sand/Bernadine	10
57	London HLD 8479	Remember You're Mine/There's A Goldmine In The Sky	10
57	London HLD 8512	April Love/When The Swallows Come Back To Capistrano	8
57	London HLD 8520	White Christmas/Jingle Bells	8
58	London HLD 8574	A Wonderful Time Up There/It's Too Soon To Know	6
58	London HLD 8640	Sugar Moon/Cherie, I Love You	6
58	London HLD 8675	If Dreams Came True/That's How Much I Love You	6
58	London HLD 8739	Gee, But It's Lonely/For My Good Fortune	6
59	London HLD 8775	I'll Remember Tonight/The Mardi Gras March	6
59	London HLD 8824	There's Good Rockin' Tonight/With The Wind And The Rain In Your Hair	6
59	London HLD 8855	For A Penny/Wang Dang Taffy-Apple Tango	6
59	London HLD 8910	Rock Boll Weevil/Twixt Twelve And Twenty	6
59	London HLD 8974	A Fool's Hall Of Fame/Brightest Wishing Star	6

(The above 45s were originally issued with triangular centres; later round centre copies are worth two-thirds these values.)

60	London HLD 9029	Beyond The Sunset/The Faithful Heart	5
60	London HLD 9067	(Welcome) New Lovers/Words	5
60	London HLD 9138	Walking The Floor Over You/Spring Rain	5
60	London HLD 9184	Delia Gone/Candy Sweet	5
60	London HLD 9238	Dear John/Alabam	7
61	London HLD 9299	The Exodus Song/There's A Moon Out Tonight	5
61	London HLD 9350	Moody River/A Thousand Years	6
61	London HLD 9420	Big Cold Wind/That's My Desire	5
61	London HLD 9461	Johnny Will/(If I'm Dreaming) Just Let My Dream	5
62	London HLD 9504	I'll See You In My Dreams/Pictures In The Fire	5
62	London HLD 9543	Quando Quando Quando/Willing And Eager	5
62	London HLD 9573	Speedy Gonzales/The Locket	5
62	London HLD 9620	The Main Attraction/Amore Baciami	5
64	Dot DS 16658	Beach Girl/Little Honda	10
67	Dot DS 26752	As Tears Go By/Something About You	5
69	Polydor 56763	July, You're Just A Woman/Break My Mind	5

EXPORT SINGLES

56	London HL 7007	I'll Be Home/Tutti Frutti	25
56	London HL 7010	Long Tall Sally/Just As Long As I'm With You	25
56	London HL 7012	I Almost Lost My Mind/I'm In Love With You	15
56	London HL 7015	Friendly Persuasion (Thee I Love)/Chains Of Love	15
57	London HL 7019	Love Letters In The Sand/Bernadine	12
58	London HL 7033	A Wonderful Time Up There/It's Too Soon To Know	12
58	London HL 7041	Sugar Moon/Cherie, I Love You	12
58	London HL 7051	If Dreams Came True/That's How Much I Love You	12
58	London HL 7059	Gee, But It's Lonely/For My Good Fortune	12
59	London HL 7070	With The Wind And The Rain In Your Hair/There's Good Rocking Tonight	12
59	London SLD 4002	For A Penny/Wang Dang Taffy-Apple Tango (both tracks stereo)	55
61	London HLD 7112	Moody River/The Exodus Song	12
63	London HL 7118	Send Me The Pillow You Dream On/(You've Got) Personality	20
63	London HLD 7121	Mexican Joe/In The Room	25

EPs

56	London RE-D 1063	PAT BOONE SINGS THE HITS	12
57	London RE-D 1069	PAT 'ON MIKE'	10
57	London RE-D 1086	PAT BOONE SINGS THE HITS NO. 2	12
57	London RE-D 1095	A CLOSER WALK WITH THEE	8
57	London RE-D 1109	FOUR BY PAT	10
58	London RE-D 1112	PAT BOONE SINGS THE HITS NO. 3	12
58	London RE-D 1128	WHITE CHRISTMAS	8
58	London RE-D 1132	PAT PART ONE	12
58	London RE-D 1133	PAT PART TWO	12
58	London RE-D 1139	PAT'S VOICE (export issue)	10
58	London RE-D 1166	SINGS IRVING BERLIN	10
59	London RE-D 1244	JOURNEY TO THE CENTRE OF THE EARTH	12
61	London RE-D 1294	ALL HANDS ON DECK	10
62	London RE-D 1335	PAT BOONE'S LATEST AND GREATEST NO. 2	12
63	London RE-D 1384	ALWAYS YOU AND ME	12
63	London RE-D 1391	PAT SINGS MOVIE THEMES	12

LPs

57 London HA-D 2024 PAT'S BIG HITS . . . 25
57 London HA-D 2030 HOWDY! . . . 15
57 London HA-D 2049 PAT! . . . 15
58 London HA-D 2078 APRIL LOVE (soundtrack, with Shirley Jones & Lionel Newman Orchestra) . . . 15
58 London HA-D 2082 SINGS IRVING BERLIN (also stereo SAH-D 6038) . . . 15/18
58 London HA-D 2098 PAT'S BIG HITS, VOL. 2 . . . 15
58 London HA-D 2127 STARDUST (also stereo SAH-D 6001) . . . 15/18
59 London HA-D 2144 YES INDEED! (also stereo SAH-D 6010) . . . 15/18
59 London HA-D 2161 PAT SINGS (stereo edition SAH-D 6013 unissued) . . . 15
60 London HA-D 2204 TENDERLY (also stereo SAH-D 6053) . . . 15/18
60 London HA-D 2210 SIDE BY SIDE (with Shirley Boone, also stereo SAH-D 6057) . . . 15/18
60 London HA-D 2265 MOONGLOW (also stereo SAH-D 6085) . . . 15/18
61 London HA-D 2305 THIS AND THAT . . . 15
61 London HA-D 2354 THE GREAT GREAT GREAT PAT BOONE (also stereo SAH-D 6155) . . . 15/18
61 London HA-D 2382 MOODY RIVER (also stereo SAH-D 6182) . . . 15/18
62 London HA-D 2452 I'LL SEE YOU IN MY DREAMS (also stereo SAH-D 6240) . . . 15/18
62 London HA-D/SH-D 8031 PAT BOONE'S GOLDEN HITS (mono/stereo) . . . 15/18
63 London HA-D/SH-D 8053 I LOVE YOU TRULY (with Shirley Boone, mono/stereo) . . . 15/18
63 London HA-D/SH-D 8073 DAYS OF WINE AND ROSES (mono/stereo) . . . 15/18
63 London HA-D/SH-D 8109 SINGS ... GUESS WHO? (mono/stereo) . . . 30/35
64 London HA-D/SH-D 8153 THE TOUCH OF YOUR LIPS (mono/stereo) . . . 15/18
65 Dot (D)DLP 3594 BOSS BEAT . . . 15
66 Dot (D)DLP 3650 MY TENTH ANNIVERSARY WITH DOT RECORDS . . . 12
(see also Fontane Sisters)

BOO RADLEYS

90 Action TAKE 4 ICHABOD AND I (LP) . . . 12

ANTHONY BOOTH

69 Tangerine DP 0008 Till Death Do Us Part/September Days . . . 7

BARRY BOOTH

68 Pye NPL 18216 DIVERSIONS! (LP) . . . 18
(see also Monty Python)

KEN BOOTHE

66 Island WI 3020 The Train Is Coming/This Is Me . . . 40
66 Island WI 3035 I Don't Want To See You Cry/Baby I Need You (B-side actually by Wailers) . . . 90
66 Ska Beat JB 248 You're No Good/SOULETTES: Don't Care What The People Say . . . 60
67 Doctor Bird DB 1110 Say You/LYN TAITT & JETS: Smokey Places . . . 30
67 Coxsone CS 7006 Lonely Teardrops/Oowee Baby . . . 22
67 Coxsone CS 7020 Home Home Home/SOUL BROTHERS: Windell . . . 35
67 Caltone TONE 107 The One I Love/You Left The Water Running . . . 75
67 Studio One SO 2000 Feel Good/Mustang Sally . . . 35
67 Studio One SO 2012 Puppet On A String/ROLAND ALPHONSO: Look Away . . . 40
67 Studio One SO 2014 Fatty Fatty (actually Heptones)/Mother Word (actually by Delroy Wilson) . . . 30
67 Studio One SO 2026 Why Did You Leave (actually by Leroy Sibbles)/Don't Try To Reach Me (actually by Gaylads) . . . 30
68 Studio One SO 2039 When I Fall In Love/HEPTONES: Christmas Time . . . 30
68 Studio One SO 2041 The Girl I Left Behind/TERMITES: My Last Love . . . 25
68 Studio One SO 2053 Tomorrow/Movin' Away . . . 30
68 Fab FAB 63 I Remember Someone/Can't You See? . . . 85
68 Coxsone CS 7041 Everybody Knows/GAYLADS: I'm Free . . . 30
69 Coxsone CS 7094 Sherry/I've Got You . . . 22
69 Studio One SO 2073 You're On My Mind/RICHARD ACE & SOUND DIMENSIONS: Love To Cherish . . . 30
69 High Note HS 003 Lady With The Starlight/LESLIE BUTLER & COUNT OSSIE: Gay Drums . . . 45
69 Bamboo BAM 4 Pleading/SOUND DIMENSION: Call 1143 . . . 20
69 Bamboo BAM 8 Be Yourself/SOUND DIMENSION: Rathid . . . 20
70 Trojan TR 7716 Why, Baby Why/Keep My Love From Fading . . . 7
70 Trojan TR 7756 Freedom Street/BEVERLEY'S ALLSTARS: Freedom Version . . . 8
70 Trojan TR 7772 It's Gonna Take A Miracle/Now I Know . . . 8
70 Trojan TR 7780 Drums Of Freedom/BEVERLEY'S ALLSTARS: Version . . . 8
70 Gas GAS 169 Give To Me/Why . . . 8
70 Jackpot JP 748 You Left The Water Running/PHIL PRATT ALL STARS: Cut Throat . . . 18
70 Punch PH 30 Artibella/PRATT ALLSTARS: Version Of Artibella . . . 12
70 Punch PH 33 Morning/Morning (Version) . . . 8
71 Punch PH 70 Stop Your Crying/CONSCIOUS MINDS: Suffering Through The Nation . . . 6
71 Banana BA 352 Original Six (Parts 1 & 2) . . . 15
71 Summit SUM 8518 I Wish It Could Be Peaceful Again/BEVERLEY'S ALLSTARS: Peaceful Version . . . 8
71 Summit SUM 8519 Your Feeling And Mine/BEVERLEY'S ALLSTARS: Your Feeling Version . . . 8
71 Big Shot BI 590 So Nice/So Nice Version . . . 8
71 Green Door GD 4002 Medley Version/Medley Version 2 . . . 8
71 Dynamic DYN 411 Hallelujah/Trying To Reach . . . 8
72 Dynamic DYN 453 Tears From My Eyes/CONSCIOUS MINDS: Tears From My Eyes Version . . . 5
72 Pama Supreme PS 369 Look What You've Done/LLOYD CHARMERS: Look What You've Done Version . . . 8
73 Trojan TR 7893 Is It Because I'm Black/Black, Gold And Green . . . 15
73 Green Door GD 4053 Silver Words/Rasta God Version . . . 6
74 Trojan TR 7920 Everything I Own/Drum Song . . . 5
74 Trojan TR 7944 Crying Over You/Now You Can See Me Again . . . 5
75 Fab FAB 270 Thinking/Moving Away . . . 20
67 Studio One SOL 9001 MR. ROCK STEADY (LP) . . . 175
73 Trojan TRLS 58 BLACK, GOLD AND GREEN (LP) . . . 30
(see also Stranger & Ken, Keith Hudson, Gaylads, Richard Ace, Lloyd & Ken)

BOOTLES

64 Vocalion VN 9216 I'll Let You Hold My Hand/Never Till Now . . . 20

MINT VALUE £

BOOTS

68	CBS 3550	Even The Bad Times Are Good/The Animal In Me	18
68	CBS 3833	Keep Your Lovelight Burning/Give Me One More Chance	20
70	Youngblood YB 1018	You Better Run/A To D	5

DAVE BOOTS

60s	Solent SM 013	GREEN SATIN AND GOLD (LP)	110

BOOTSY'S RUBBER BAND

77	Warner Bros K 16964T	Pinocchio Theory/Psychoticbumpschool/What's A Telephone (12")	10
78	Warner Bros K 17196T	Bootzilla/Hollywood Squares (12", p/s)	10
76	Warner Bros K 56200	STRETCHIN' OUT IN BOOTSY'S RUBBER BAND (LP)	15
77	Warner Bros K 56302	AHH... THE NAME IS BOOTSY, BABY! (LP, gatefold sleeve)	15
78	Warner Bros K 56424	BOOTSY? PLAYER OF THE YEAR (LP, gatefold sleeve)	12
79	Warner Bros K 56615	THE BOOT IS MADE FOR FONK-N (LP, with inner sleeve)	12
81	Warner Bros K 56998	THE ONE GIVETH, THE COUNT TAKETH AWAY (LP)	12

(see also Parliament, Funkadelic)

RANNY BOP

70	Gas GAS 155	Pipe Dream/Suck Suck	7

BOP & BELTONES

67	Coxsone CS 7012	Treat Me Good/PETER TOUCH & WAILERS: Dancing Time (B-side actually also by Bop & Beltones)	50

(see also Beltones, Soul Vendors, Jackie Mittoo)

VICTOR BORGE

51	Columbia DC 536	Phonetic Punctuation parts 1 & 2 (78, export issue)	7
58	Phillips BBE 12154	PHONETIC PUNCTUATION (EP)	8

BILLY BORLYNN

60	Philips PB 1031	Baby Listens/Liebelei	7
60	Philips PB 1057	Every Step Of The Way/It Takes Time	7

BORN B.C.

82	Xcentric Noise FIRST 1	THE POWER & THE PRIVILEGE (EP)	8

BOSS

86	Power House (no cat. no.)	One Good Reason/Wake Up Children (p/s, with lyric sheet)	6

BOSS ATTACK

71	Fab FAB 187	Hell-El/TEARDROPS: Let Me Be Free	15

BOSS COMBO

62	Coral LVA 9205	GOLDEN ROCK AND ROLL INSTRUMENTALS (LP)	22

BOSS GUITARS

65	London HA-R/SH-R 8237	PLAY THE WINNERS (LP)	18

EARL BOSTIC (ORCHESTRA)

SINGLES

54	Parlophone MSP 6075	Off Shore/What! No Pearls	15
54	Parlophone MSP 6089	Deep Purple/Smoke Rings	15
54	Parlophone MSP 6105	Melancholy Serenade/Don't You Do It	15
54	Parlophone MSP 6110	Jungle Drums/Danube Waves	15
54	Parlophone MSP 6119	Mambolino/Blue Skies	15
54	Parlophone MSP 6131	These Foolish Things/Mambostic	15
54	Parlophone CMSP 8	Cherokee/The Song Is Ended (export issue)	20
55	Parlophone MSP 6162	Melody Of Love/Sweet Lorraine	15
56	Vogue V 2145	Flamingo/Sleep	15
56	Vogue V 2148	Moonglow/Ain't Misbehaving	15
56	Parlophone R 4208	The Bo-Do Rock (with Bill Doggett)/Mean To Me	20
56	Parlophone R 4232	For All We Know/Beyond The Blue Horizon	10
57	Parlophone R 4263	I Hear A Rhapsody/Harlem Nocturne	10
57	Parlophone R 4278	Bubbins Rock/Indiana (with Bill Doggett)	15
57	Parlophone R 4305	Avalon/Too Fine For Crying (B-side with Bill Jones)	8
57	Parlophone R 4370	Temptation/September Song	6
58	Parlophone R 4460	Over The Waves Rock/Twilight Time	10
62	Ember JBS 708	Tuxedo Junction/Air Mail Special	15
66	Island WI 271	Honeymoon Night/PATSY COLE: Disappointed Bride	15

EPs

54	Parlophone GEP 8506	FLAMINGO	15
55	Parlophone GEP 8513	LINGER AWHILE	15
55	Parlophone GEP 8520	EARL BOSTIC AND HIS ALTO SAX	15
55	Vogue EPV 1010	EARL BOSTIC	25
56	Vogue EPV 1111	VELVET SUNSET	15
56	Parlophone GEP 8539	WRAP IT UP	15
56	Parlophone GEP 8548	EARL'S IMAGINATION	10
56	Parlophone GEP 8565	ALTO SAX AND MAMBO STRINGS	10
56	Parlophone GEP 8571	MUSIC A LA BOSTIC NO. 1	10
56	Parlophone GEP 8574	MUSIC A LA BOSTIC NO. 2	10
57	Parlophone GEP 8603	MUSIC A LA BOSTIC NO. 3	10
57	Parlophone GEP 8637	BOSTIC IN HARLEM	10
58	Parlophone GEP 8701	BOSTIC BEAT	25
58	Parlophone GEP 8741	ROCKING WITH BOSTIC	25
58	Parlophone GEP 8754	ALTO MAGIC	10
50s	Parlophone CGEP 1	EARL BOSTIC (export issue)	12
50s	Parlophone CGEP 10	EARL BOSTIC (export issue)	12

10" LPs

54	Vogue LDE 100	EARL BOSTIC AND HIS ORCHESTRA	30
54	Parlophone PMD 1016	EARL BOSTIC AND HIS ALTO SAX	30
56	Parlophone PMD 1040	EARL BOSTIC AND HIS ALTO SAX NO. 2	30

MINT VALUE £

58	Parlophone PMD 1054	BOSTIC MEETS DOGGETT (with Bill Doggett)	35
58	Parlophone PMD 1068	BOSTIC ROCKS	35
59	Parlophone PMD 1071	BOSTIC SHOWCASE OF SWINGING DANCE HITS	30
59	Parlophone PMD 1074	SWEET TUNES OF THE FANTASTIC FIFTIES	30
59	Parlophone PMD 1115	SWEET TUNES OF THE ROARIN' TWENTIES	25
59	Parlophone PMD 1117	SWEET TUNES OF THE SWINGIN' THIRTIES	25
59	Parlophone PMD 1119	SWEET TUNES OF THE SENTIMENTAL FORTIES	25
60	Parlophone PMC 1125	PLAYS THE HIT TUNES OF THE BIG BROADWAY SHOWS (12" LP)	20

(see also Bill Doggett, Sonny Carter)

BOSTON

78	Epic 12 6653	Don't Look Back/The Journey (12", p/s)	8
79	Epic EPC 7888	Don't Look Back/More Than A Feeling/Smokin' (p/s)	5
76	Epic EPC 81611	BOSTON (LP)	12
76	Epic EPCH 81611	BOSTON (LP, audiophile pressing)	15
76	Epic EPC 81611	BOSTON (LP, picture disc)	15
78	Epic E 9945050	DON'T LOOK BACK (LP, picture disc)	12
86	MCA MCGP 6017	THIRD STAGE (LP, picture disc)	18
92	MCA MC 19066	THIRD STAGE (CD, in slip case)	18
94	Epic EK 64402	BOSTON (CD, in slip case)	18
94	MCA MCGP	WALK ON (LP, picture disc)	18

BOSTON CRABS

65	Columbia DB 7586	Down In Mexico/Who?	25
65	Columbia DB 7679	As Long As I Have You/Alley Oop	20
66	Columbia DB 7830	Gin House/You Didn't Have To Be So Nice	18

BOSTON DEXTERS

64	Contemporary CR 101	Matchbox/La Bamba	175
64	Contemporary CR 102	You've Been Talking About Me/Nothing's Gonna Change Me	90
64	Contemporary CR 103	What Kind Of Girl Are You/I've Got Troubles Of My Own	90
65	Columbia DB 7498	I Believe To My Soul/I've Got Something To Tell You	40
65	Columbia DB 7641	Try Hard/No More Tears	35

(see also Buzz, Tam White)

BOSTON POPS ORCHESTRA

68	RCA RCA 1683	And I Love Her/A Hard Day's Night	6

BO STREET RUNNERS

64	Decca F 11986	Bo Street Runner/Tell Me	35
65	Columbia DB 7488	Tell Me What You're Gonna Do/And I Do Just What I Want	85
65	Columbia DB 7640	Baby Never Say Goodbye/Get Out Of My Way	50
66	Columbia DB 7901	Drive My Car/So Very Woman (featuring Mike [Too Much] Patto)	75
64	Oak RGJ 131	BO STREET RUNNERS (EP, 49 copies only)	1,500+

(see also [Mike] Patto, Timebox, Chicago Line, Cheynes, Fleetwood Mac)

CONNIE BOSWELL

54	Brunswick 05319	T-E-N-N-E-S-S-E-E (Spells ...)/If I Give My Heart To You	12
55	Brunswick 05397	How Important Can It Be?/Fill My Heart With Happiness	10

ERIC BOSWELL

70	Gayfeet GS 204	Little Donkey (actually by Lou & Maxine)/ Hope And Joy (actually by Lou Sparkes)	12

(see also Lou Sparkes)

EVE BOSWELL

SINGLES

53	Parlophone MSP 6006	Sugar Bush/Moon Above Malaya (China Nights)	30
55	Parlophone MSP 6158	Ready, Willing And Able/Pam-Poo-Dey	18
55	Parlophone MSP 6160	The Heart You Break (May Be Your Own)/Tika Tika Tok	18
56	Parlophone MSP 6208	Young And Foolish/Where You Are	18
56	Parlophone MSP 6220	It's Almost Tomorrow/Cookie	18
56	Parlophone MSP 6250	Saries Marias/Come Back My Love	15
56	Parlophone R 4230	True Love/Where In The World Is Billy?	12
57	Parlophone R 4275	Rock Bobbin' Boats/Tra La La	18
57	Parlophone R 4299	Chantez, Chantez/She Said (Aunt Magnolia)	12
57	Parlophone R 4328	With All My Heart/Sugar Candy	10
57	Parlophone R 4341	The Gypsy In My Soul/Stop Whistlin' Wolf	10
57	Parlophone R 4362	Swedish Polka (Chickadee)/Tell My Love	7
58	Parlophone R 4401	(I Love You) For Sentimental Reasons/Bobby	7
58	Parlophone R 4414	I Do/Love Me Again	10
58	Parlophone R 4455	Left Right Out Of Your Heart/Voom-Ba-Voom	7
58	Parlophone R 4479	More Than Ever (Come Prima)/I Know Why	7
58	Parlophone R 4492	Christmas Lullaby/The Christmas Tree	10
59	Parlophone R 4517	If I Had A Talking Picture Of You/Piccaninny	7
59	Parlophone R 4544	Wimoweh Cha Cha/Boegoeberg Se Dam	7
59	Parlophone R 4555	Once Again/You Are Never Far Away From Me	6
60	Parlophone R 4618	Misty/Turnabout Heart	6
69	Morgan MRS 19	This Is My Love/Lonely In A Crowd	6

EPs

57	Parlophone GEP 8601	THE ENCHANTING EVE	18
58	Parlophone GEP 8690	EVE BOSWELL'S SHOWCASE	18
58	Parlophone GEP 8717	EVE BOSWELL'S SHOWCASE NO. 2	18

LPs

56	Parlophone PMD 1039	SUGAR AND SPICE (10")	40
57	Parlophone PMC 1038	SENTIMENTAL EVE	35
59	Parlophone PMC 1105	FOLLOWING THE SUN AROUND	35
76	EMI EMC 3147	SUGAR BUSH '76	12

MINT VALUE £

SIMON BOSWELL

75	Transatlantic TRA 307	MIND PARASITES (LP)	12

(see also Advertising)

BOTHY BAND

70	Polydor 2383 417	OLD HAG YOU HAVE KILLED ME (LP)	15
79	Polydor 2383 530	AFTERHOURS (LP, with lyric insert)	12

PERRY BOTKIN

60	Brunswick 05838	The Executioner Theme/Waltz Of The Hunter	5

(see also Charles Boyer)

BOULEVARD

79	Chopper CHOP 5D	MAGIC MAN (12", red vinyl, no p/s)	10
81	Boulevard VARD 1	Dawn Raid/Take It Or Leave It (p/s)	50

BOW BELLS

65	Polydor 56030	Not To Be Taken/I'll Try Not To Hold It Against You	5
66	Parlophone R 5520	Belinda/When You're In	7

(see also Nola York)

JIMMY BOWEN

57	Columbia DB 3915	I'm Stickin' With You/Ever Lovin' Fingers	80
57	Columbia DB 3915	I'm Stickin' With You/Ever Lovin' Fingers (78)	18
57	Columbia DB 3984	Warm Up To Me, Baby/I Trusted You	60
57	Columbia DB 3984	Warm Up To Me, Baby/I Trusted You (78)	15
57	Columbia DB 4027	Cross Over/It's Shameful	35
57	Columbia DB 4027	Cross Over/It's Shameful (78)	15
58	Columbia DB 4184	The Two Step/By The Light Of The Silvery Moon	22
58	Columbia DB 4184	The Two Step/By The Light Of The Silvery Moon (78)	10
65	Reprise RS 23043	The Eagle (demos & some issues list "The Golden Eagle")/Spanish Cricket	30
67	Reprise RS 20592	Raunchy (with Chorus & Orchestra)/ It's Such A Pretty World Today (wth Singers)	5
58	Columbia SEG 7757	MEET JIMMY BOWEN (EP)	120
58	Columbia SEG 7793	MEET JIMMY BOWEN NO. 2 (EP)	120

BEN BOWERS

55	Columbia SCM 5192	The Kentuckian Song/The Man From Laramie	15
56	Columbia SCM 5260	To You, My Love/I'm Still A King To You	10
57	Parlophone R 4317	Country Boy (with His Royal Jamaicans)/ Rum And Coconut Water (Rum And Coca-Cola)	8
57	Parlophone R 4317	Country Boy (with His Royal Jamaicans)/ Rum And Coconut Water (Rum And Coca-Cola) (78)	12
59	Pye N 15175	Naughty Little Flea/Donkey City (78)	8
57	Pye Jazz NJE 1001	BIG BEN BLUES (EP, with His Bluesicians)	12
58	Pye NEP 24069	KINGS OF CALYPSO VOL. 4 (EP)	8

DAVID BOWIE

SINGLES

66	Pye 7N 17020	Can't Help Thinking About Me/And I Say To Myself (with Lower Third)	140
66	Pye 7N 17079	Do Anything You Say/Good Morning Girl	175
66	Pye 7N 17157	I Dig Everything/I'm Not Losing Sleep	175
66	Deram DM 107	Rubber Band/The London Boys	140
67	Deram DM 123	The Laughing Gnome/The Gospel According To Tony Day (with inverted matrix number on label)	65
67	Deram DM 135	Love You Till Tuesday/Did You Ever Have A Dream	170
69	Philips BF 1801	Space Oddity/Wild Eyed Boy From Freecloud (unreleased p/s, only 2 or 3 copies known to exist)	3,000+
69	Philips BF 1801	Space Oddity/Wild Eyed Boy From Freecloud (mono; stereo 45s unconfirmed)	10
70	Mercury MF 1135	The Prettiest Star/Conversation Piece	130
70	Mercury 6052 026	Memory Of A Free Festival Parts 1 & 2	130
71	Mercury 6052 049	Holy Holy/Black Country Rock	150
72	RCA RCA 2160	Changes/Andy Warhol	5
72	RCA RCA 2199	Starman/Suffragette City (some in p/s)	60/5
72	RCA RCA 2263	John, I'm Only Dancing/Hang Onto Yourself (original pressing with slow 'acoustic guitar' version; later pressings have faster version with sax, £3)	5
72	Pye 7NX 8002	Do Anything You Say/I Dig Everything/I Can't Help Thinking About Me/ I'm Not Losing Sleep (p/s)	10
72	RCA RCA 2302	The Jean Genie/Ziggy Stardust	5
73	RCA RCA 2352	Drive-In Saturday/Round And Round	5
73	RCA RCA 2316	Life On Mars?/The Man Who Sold The World (some in p/s)	10/5
73	Deram DM 123	The Laughing Gnome/The Gospel According To Tony Day (reissue, matrix number correct way up on label)	5
74	RCA RCA 2424	Sorrow/Amsterdam	5
74	RCA LPBO 5009	Rebel Rebel/Queen Bitch	5
74	RCA LPBO 5021	Rock'N'Roll Suicide/Quicksand	5
74	RCA APBO 0293	Diamond Dogs/Holy Holy	5
74	RCA/Mainman/ Lyntone LYN 2929	Bowie's Greatest Hits (excerpts from Knock On Wood/ Space Oddity/The Man Who Sold The World/Life On Mars?/ Starman/Jean Genie/Sorrow/Diamond Dogs) (33rpm 1-sided flexidisc with *Record Mirror/Popswop* magazine)	18/8
74	RCA RCA 2466	Knock On Wood/Panic In Detroit	5
75	RCA RCA 2523	Young Americans/Suffragette City	5
75	Decca F 13579	The London Boys/Love You Till Tuesday	10
75	RCA RCA 2579	Fame/Right	5
75	RCA RCA 2593	Space Oddity/Changes/Velvet Goldmine (p/s)	10
76	RCA RCA 2726	Suffragette City/Stay (p/s)	15

			MINT VALUE £
77	RCA BOW-1E	From The New Album 'Low" (excerpts from Speed Of Life, Breaking Glass, What In The World, Sound And Vision, Be My Wife & A New Career In A New Town; demo only)	500
77	RCA PB 0905	Sound And Vision/A New Career In A New Town	5
77	RCA PB 1017	Be My Wife/Speed Of Life	5
77	RCA PB 1121	'Heroes'/V-2 Schneider	5
78	RCA PB 1190	Beauty And The Beast/Sense Of Doubt (some with p/s)	5/8
79	RCA BOW 2	Boys Keep Swinging/Fantastic Voyage (p/s)	5
79	RCA BOW 3	DJ/Repetition (p/s, some on green vinyl)	15/5
79	RCA BOW 4	John, I'm Only Dancing (Again)/John, I'm Only Dancing (p/s)	5
79	RCA BOW 12-4	John, I'm Only Dancing (Again) (Extended)/John, I'm Only Dancing (12", p/s)	8
80	RCA BOW 5	Alabama Song/Space Oddity (poster p/s)	5
80	RCA BOW 6	Ashes To Ashes/Move On (with 3 different p/s & 4 different sheets of 9 stamps)	5
81	RCA BOW 8	Scary Monsters/Because You're Young (p/s)	5
81	RCA BOWC 8	Scary Monsters/Because You're Young (cassette, card sleeve)	8
81	RCA BOW 9	Up The Hill Backwards/Crystal Japan (p/s)	5
81	RCA BOWC 9	Up The Hill Backwards/Crystal Japan (cassette, card sleeve)	8
82	RCA BOW 11	IN BERTHOLT BRECHT'S "BAAL" (EP, foldout p/s)	6
82	RCA BOW 100	FASHIONS (10 x 7" picture discs in plastic wallet [BOWP 101-110], each £4)	40
82	RCA BOWT 12	Peace On Earth/Little Drummer Boy/Fantastic Voyage (12", p/s, picture labels, with Bing Crosby)	8
83	EMI America 45-TCEA 152	Let's Dance/Cat People (cassette)	5
83	EMI America EAP 157	China Girl/Shake It (picture disc)	6
83	EMI America 12 EA 158	Modern Love/Modern Love (Live) (12", p/s with poster)	8
84	EMI America EA 187	Tonight/Tumble And Twirl (poster p/s)	5
85	EMI America EAP 195	Loving The Alien (Remixed Version)/Don't Look Down (Remixed Version) (shaped picture disc)	15
85	EMI America 12 EAG 195	Loving The Alien (Extended Dance Mix)/ Don't Look Down (Extended Dance Mix)/ Loving The Alien (Extended Dub Mix) (12", gatefold p/s with poster)	8
86	Virgin VSS 838	Absolute Beginners/Absolute Beginners (Dub Mix) (square picture disc)	10
86	EMI America EAP 216	Underground (Edited Version)/Underground (Instrumental) (shaped picture disc)	15
86	Virgin VSS 906	When The Wind Blows/When The Wind Blows (Instrumental) (shaped pic disc)	10
87	EMI America 12 EAX 230	Day-In Day-Out (Remix)/(Extended Dub Mix)/Julie (12", stickered black p/s)	8
87	EMI America EAP 237	Time Will Crawl (Single Version)/Girls (Single Edit) (poster p/s)	6
87	EMI America 12 EAX 237	Time Will Crawl (Dance Crew Mix)/(Dub)/Girls (Japanese Version) (12", p/s)	8
87	EMI America EAP 239	Never Let Me Down/'87 And Cry (picture disc)	5
88	Virgin CDT 20	Absolute Beginners (Full Length Version)/(Dub Mix) (3" CD, card sleeve)	10
90	EMI USA CD FAME 90	FAME 90 (Remixes) (CD)	8
93	BMG Arista 136977	Jump They Say (Radio Edit)/Pallas Athena (Don't Stop Praying Mix) (jukebox issue, no p/s)	7
93	Arista 13942-2	Jump They Say (7" Version)/Pallas Athena (Don't Stop Praying Mix) (CD, double jewel case with booklet)	8
93	BMG Arista 177057	Buddha Of Suburbia/Dead Against It (p/s)	5
93	BMG Arista 18168-2	Buddha Of Suburbia/Dead Against It (CD, holographic disc)	8
97	RCA 307031	The Heart's Filthy Lesson (Alternative Mix)/(Bowie Mix)/(Rubber Mix)/ (Simple Text Mix)/(Filthy Mix) (12", picture disc)	8
95	RCA 329407	Strangers When We Meet (Edit)/The Man Who Sold The World (live) (green vinyl, stickered card p/s)	5
95	RCA 353847	Hallo Spaceboy (Remix)/The Heart's Filthy Lesson (Radio Edit) (pink vinyl, stickered card p/s)	5
97	RCA 512347	Seven Years In Tibet (Edit)/Seven Years In Tibet (Mandarin Version) (p/s, clear vinyl)	5
97	RCA 51254-2	Seven Years In Tibet (Edit)/Seven Years In Tibet (Mandarin Version) Pallas Athena (Live) (CD, digipak)	8
97	RCA 39741-1	Telling Lies (Paradox Mix)/Telling Lies (Feelgood & Adam F Mix) (12", p/s)	8
99	Virgin VSP 1767	Survive/Seven (live) (picture disc)	10
02	Positiva (no cat. no.)	Loving The Alien/mixes (CD-R, as 'The Scumfrog Vs. Bowie')	10

LPs

67	Deram DML/SML 1007	DAVID BOWIE (mono/stereo)	200/250
69	Philips SBL 7912	DAVID BOWIE (gatefold sleeve)	250
70	Decca PA 58	THE WORLD OF DAVID BOWIE (mono)	22
72	Decca SPA 58	THE WORLD OF DAVID BOWIE (stereo, 'curly hair' cover)	12
71	Mercury 6338 041	THE MAN WHO SOLD THE WORLD (with 'dress' cover)	325
71	Mercury 6338 041	THE MAN WHO SOLD THE WORLD (cassette, with 'dress' cover)	75
71	RCA SF 8244	HUNKY DORY (orange label with lyric sheet)	12
72	RCA SF 8287	THE RISE AND FALL OF ZIGGY STARDUST AND THE SPIDERS FROM MARS (orange label with lyric inner sleeve)	12
72	RCA LSP 4813	SPACE ODDITY (reissue of SBL 7912 in different sleeve, orange label with lyric inner sleeve & poster)	15
72	RCA LSP 4816	THE MAN WHO SOLD THE WORLD (orange label with inner sleeve & poster)	15
73	RCA RS 1001	ALADDIN SANE (orange label, gatefold sleeve & lyric inner sleeve, some with fan club membership card)	16/12
74	RCA APL 1-0576	DIAMOND DOGS (orange label, gatefold sleeve)	12
74	RCA APL 2-0771	DAVID LIVE (2-LP, gatefold sleeve, orange label, photos on inners)	18
76	RCA APLI 1327	STATION TO STATION (with original colour proof sleeve)	500+
76	RCA RS 1055	CHANGESONEBOWIE (with 'sax' version of "John I'm Only Dancing")	25
78	RCA PL 02913	STAGE (2-LP, gatefold sleeve, some yellow vinyl)	20/12
77	RCA INTS 5065	LOW (red vinyl, semi-official 'factory custom pressing')	500
80	RCA BOW LP 2	SCARY MONSTERS (AND SUPER CREEPS) (purple vinyl, semi-official 'factory custom pressing')	600
80	K-Tel NE 1111	THE BEST OF BOWIE (with incorrect tracklisting)	12
81	RCA BL 43606	CHRISTIANE F. WIR KINDER VOM BAHNOF ZOO (soundtrack)	12

			MINT VALUE £
83	EMI America AMLP 3029	LET'S DANCE (picture disc)	10
84	RCA BOPIC 1	ALADDIN SANE (picture disc with numbered insert)	15
84	RCA BOPIC 2	HUNKY DORY (picture disc with numbered insert)	15
84	RCA BOPIC 3	ZIGGY STARDUST (picture disc with numbered insert)	15
84	RCA BOPIC 4	PIN-UPS (picture disc with numbered insert)	15
84	RCA BOPIC 5	DIAMOND DOGS (picture disc with numbered insert)	15
95	RCA 307021	EXCERPTS FROM OUTSIDE (with 12" booklet & lyric sheet)	15
97	RCA 44949	EARTHLING (gatefold sleeve)	15

CDs

84	Deram 800 087-2	DAVID BOWIE (withdrawn with white title)	70
84	RCA PD 89002	STAGE (2-CD, withdrawn)	50
84	RCA PD 84234	LODGER (withdrawn)	20
84	RCA PD 83856	LOW (withdrawn)	25
84	RCA PD 83857	'HEROES' (withdrawn)	25
85	RCA PD 84623	HUNKY DORY (withdrawn)	25
85	RCA PD 84654	THE MAN WHO SOLD THE WORLD (withdrawn)	30
85	RCA PD 84702	THE RISE AND FALL OF ZIGGY STARDUST AND THE SPIDERS FROM MARS (withdrawn)	25
85	RCA PD 84813	SPACE ODDITY (withdrawn)	30
85	RCA PD 84653	PIN-UPS (withdrawn)	25
85	RCA PD 83890	ALADDIN SANE (withdrawn)	25
85	RCA PD 80998	YOUNG AMERICANS (withdrawn)	25
85	RCA PD 81327	STATION TO STATION (withdrawn)	30
85	RCA PD 81732	CHANGESONEBOWIE (withdrawn)	40
85	RCA PD 83856	LOW (withdrawn)	25
85	RCA PD 83889	DIAMOND DOGS (withdrawn)	25
86	RCA PD 82743	PETER AND THE WOLF (withdrawn)	20
85	RCA PD 83647	SCARY MONSTERS (AND SUPER CREEPS) (withdrawn)	30
84	RCA PD 84202	CHANGESTWOBOWIE (withdrawn)	35
84	RCA PD 94792	GOLDEN YEARS (withdrawn)	35
84	RCA PD 84919	FAME AND FASHION (ALL TIME GREATEST HITS) (withdrawn)	55
93	EMI BOWIE 1	SELECTIONS FROM THE SINGLES COLLECTION 10-track sampler, card p/s, promo only)	20
93	Arista 17822-2	THE BUDDHA OF SUBURBIA (special edition in clear plastic case, with novel)	20
99	Virgin CDVX 2900	'hours...' (hologram sleeve)	18

PROMOS

90	BMG BOW 908	SO FAR (CD, 8-track sampler for "Sound & Vision" box set)	35
91	Rykodisc VRCD 0142	BOWIE / ENO: IT'S TIME TO LISTEN (CD, 9-track sampler from Ryko reissues; includes "Sound + Vision", "Be My Wife", "Some Are", "Heroes", "Joe The Lion", "Abdulmajid", "DJ", "Boys Keep Swinging", "Look Back In Anger")	20
93	BMG MEAT 1	Pallas Athena (12", white label, no p/s, includes two exclusive Meat Beat Manifesto remixes)	45
93	Back To Basics HOME 1	Night Flights/(B-side by Moodswings) (12")	20
95	RCA HALLO 2	Hallo Spaceboy (12" Remix) (12", 1-sided, no p/s)	20
95	BMG SOLO 1	EXCLUSIVE TOUR CD: Strangers When We Meet/MORRISSEY: The Boy Racer (Outside Tour CD)	70
96	RCA SPACE 2	Hallo Spaceboy (12" Remix) (1-sided 12", some copies listed as RCA HALLO 2, no p/s)	35
96	RCA SPACE 3	Hallo Spaceboy (Double Click Mix)/Hallo Spaceboy (Instrumental)/ Hallo Spaceboy (Lost In Space Mix) (12", no p/s)	65
99	Virgin CDVDJ 2900	'hours...' (CD, card sleeve)	20
99	EMI CDLRL 015	ALBUM SAMPLER (CD, 17-track sampler, promo only)	25
99	EMI QUEENWL 28	Under Pressure (Remixes) (with Queen) (12", white label, unreleased mix, promo only)	60

(see also Davie Jones & King Bees, Davy Jones & Lower Third, Manish Boys, Arnold Corns, Spiders From Mars, Mick Ronson, Queen, Tin Machine, Tao Jones Index, Bing Crosby)

BOWMAN-HYDE PLAYERS

61	Parlophone PMC 1155	SING ME A SOUVENIR (LP)	40

ALAN BOWN (SET)

65	Pye 7N 15934	Can't Let Her Go/I'm The One	30
66	Pye 7N 17084	Baby Don't Push Me/Everything's Gonna Be Alright	30
66	Pye 7N 17148	Headline News/Mister Pleasure	40
66	Pye 7N 17192	Emergency 999/Settle Down	60
67	Pye 7N 17256	Gonna Fix You Good (Everytime You're Bad)/I Really Really Care	30
67	Music Factory CUB 1	We Can Help You/Magic Handkerchief (as the Alan Bown!)	12
67	MGM MGM 1355	Toyland/Technicolour Dream	12
68	MGM MGM 1387	Story Book/Little Lesley	12
69	Deram DM 259	Still As Stone/Wrong Idea	10
69	Deram DM 278	Gypsy Girl/All I Can	10
70	Island WIP 6091	Pyramid/Crash Landing	7
75	CBS 3721	Rockford Files/I Don't Know	6
68	Music Factory CUB LM/LS 1	OUTWARD BOWN (LP)	50
69	Deram DML/SML 1049	THE ALAN BOWN! (LP)	30
70	Island ILPS 9131	LISTEN (LP)	18

(see also Robert Palmer, John Barry Seven, Bronco, Jonesy)

ALAN BOWN SET/JIMMY JAMES & VAGABONDS

68	Pye N(S)PL 18156	LONDON SWINGS — LIVE AT THE MARQUEE CLUB (LP, 1 side each)	40

(see also Jimmy James & Vagabonds)

ANDREW BOWN

70	Parlophone R 5856	Tarot (Theme From 'Ace Of Wands')/Lulli Rides Again	50

(see also Andy Bown)

MINT VALUE £

ANDY BOWN

73 GM GMS 1 — Sweet William/I Won't Let You Down . . . 5
74 GM GMS 19 — New York Satyricon Zany/Party Games . . . 5
75 GM GMS 9039 — Supersonic/Feeling Better . . . 5
77 EMI EMI 2571 — Love Love Love/Blood On The Keys . . . 5
77 EMI EMI 2657 — Good Enough Reason/317 Manhattan Blues . . . 5
79 EMI EMI 2906 — Another Shipwreck/Another Night With You . . . 6
79 EMI EMI 2943 — Good Advice/One More Chance . . . 5
81 EMI EMI 5245 — Say It Was Magic/One Forward Two Back Again (some in p/s) . . . 10/5
82 EMI EMI 5312 — Marianne/One Forward Two Back Again . . . 5
82 EMI EMI 5372 — Help Me/Marianne (p/s) . . . 8
72 Mercury 6310 002 — GONE TO MY HEAD (LP) . . . 12
73 GM GML 1001 — SWEET WILLIAM (LP) . . . 12
77 EMI EMC 3176 — COME BACK ROMANCE, ALL IS FORGIVEN (LP, with inner sleeve) . . . 12
79 EMI EMC 3283 — GOOD ADVICE (LP) . . . 12

(see also Andrew Bown, Herd, Judas Jump, Status Quo, Rossi & Frost, Storyteller)

BRENDAN BOWYER (& ROYALS)

65 HMV POP 1481 — The Wonder Of You/Fun Fun Fun . . . 6
66 HMV POP 1521 — The Fly/Answer Me . . . 6
67 King KG 1059 — Sitting In The Sun/Da Doo Ron Ron (as Brendan Bowyer & Royals) . . . 6
68 King KG 1078 — Woman Woman/Lady Willpower (as Brendan Bowyer & Royals) . . . 6

DAVID BOX

64 London HLU 9874 — If You Can't Say Something Nice/Sweet Sweet Day . . . 20
64 London HLU 9924 — Little Lonely Summer Girl/No One Will Ever Know . . . 20

(see also Crickets)

BOX CAR RACER

00s MCA MCS 40290 — I Feel So/Cat Like Thief (picture disc) . . . 8

(see also Blink 182)

BOXER

75 Virgin V 2049 — BELOW THE BELT (LP, with uncensored full-frontal back cover) . . . 12
76 Virgin V 2073 — BLOODLETTING (LP, withdrawn) . . . 80

(see also Patto, Timebox)

BOXEROS

61 Palette PG 9023 — El Señor Ping Pong/Y Viva El Cha Cha . . . 6

BOX TOPS

67 Stateside SS 2044 — The Letter/Happy Times . . . 12
67 Stateside SS 2070 — Neon Rainbow/She Knows How . . . 10
68 Bell BLL 1001 — Cry Like A Baby/The Door You Closed To Me . . . 7
68 Bell BLL 1017 — Choo Choo Train/Fields Of Clover . . . 7
68 Bell BLL 1035 — I Met Her In Church/People Gonna Talk . . . 7
69 Bell BLL 1045 — Sandman/Sweet Cream Ladies, Forward March . . . 7
69 Bell BLL 1063 — I Shall Be Released/I Must Be The Devil . . . 7
69 Bell BLL 1068 — Soul Deep/The Happy Song . . . 7
69 Bell BLL 1084 — Turn On A Dream/Together . . . 7
70 Bell BLL 1097 — You Keep Tightening Up On Me/Come On Honey . . . 7
73 London HLU 10402 — Sugar Creek Woman/It's All Over . . . 7
68 Stateside (S)SL 10218 — THE LETTER/NEON RAINBOW (LP) . . . 35
68 Bell MBLL/SBLL 105 — CRY LIKE A BABY (LP) . . . 22
69 Bell MBLL/SBLL 108 — NON-STOP (LP) . . . 22
69 Bell SBLL 120 — DIMENSIONS (LP) . . . 18
70 Bell MBLL/SBLL 129 — SUPER HITS (LP) . . . 15
70 Bell BELLS 149 — BOX TOPS (LP) . . . 18

(see also Big Star, Alex Chilton)

EL BOY

57 Columbia DB 3927 — Jack, Jack, Jack/Tonight My Heart She Is Crying . . . 7

DENNY BOYCE & HIS ORCHESTRA/RHYTHM

57 Oriole CB 1358 — One Man Went To Rock/Thunderstorm (78) . . . 5
58 Oriole CB 1458 — Bad Boy/When Your Hair Has Turned To Silver . . . 10
58 Oriole CB 1458 — Bad Boy/When Your Hair Has Turned To Silver (78) . . . 5

TOMMY BOYCE

65 MGM MGM 1287 — Pretty Thing/I Don't Have To Worry 'Bout You . . . 10

TOMMY BOYCE & BOBBY HART

67 A&M AMS 705 — Out And About/My Little Chickadee . . . 5
67 A&M AMS 710 — Sometimes She's A Little Girl/Love Every Day . . . 5
68 A&M AMS 714 — I Wonder What She's Doing Tonight?/Ambushers . . . 5
68 A&M AMS 722 — Goodbye Baby/Where Angels Go Trouble Follows . . . 5
68 A&M AMS 729 — Alice Long (You're Still My Favourite Girlfriend)/P.O. Box 9847 . . . 5
67 A&M AML 907 — TEST PATTERNS (LP) . . . 15

(see also Monkees, Tommy Boyce)

EDDIE BOYD

66 Blue Horizon 45 BH 1009 — It's So Miserable To Be Alone/Empty Arms . . . 150
67 Blue Horizon 57-3137 — The Big Boat/Sent For You Yesterday (with Fleetwood Mac) . . . 30
62 Esquire EP 247 — BOYD'S BLUES (EP, as Eddie Boyd Blues Combo) . . . 70
65 Fontana SFJL 905 — FIVE LONG YEARS (LP) . . . 50
67 Decca LK/SKL 4872 — EDDIE BOYD AND HIS BLUES BAND FEATURING PETER GREEN (LP) . . . 125
68 Blue Horizon 7-63202 — 7936 SOUTH RHODES (LP, with Fleetwood Mac) . . . 75
68 Storyville SLP 4054 — IN CONCERT (LP) . . . 30

(see also Fleetwood Mac)

MINT VALUE £

EDDIE BOYD/BUDDY GUY
66 Chess CRE 6009 WITH THE BLUES (EP, 2 tracks each) ... 35
(see also Buddy Guy)

FRANKLYN BOYD
57 Nestles NR 01 Bye, Bye Love (78, 1-sided card flexi) ... 7
57 Nestles NR 05 Teddy Bear (78, 1-sided card flexi) ... 7

JIMMY BOYD
53 Columbia SCM 5072 I Saw Mommy Kissing Santa Claus/Little Train A-Chuggin' In My Heart ... 40

WILLIAM BOYD
56 Capitol Junior CJ 100 Hopalong Cassidy & The Mail Train Robbery parts 1 & 2 (78, with p/s) ... 7
56 Capitol Junior CJ 103 Hopalong Cassidy & The Big Ranch Fire parts 1 & 2 (78, with p/s) ... 7

CHARLES BOYER
65 London HL 10002 Where Does Love Go/PERRY BOTKIN JR: Theme From Where Does Love Go ... 6
65 London HAT 8268 WHERE DOES LOVE GO (LP) ... 15

BOYFRIENDS
78 United Artists UP 36424 I'm In Love Today/Saturday Night (p/s) ... 10
78 United Artists UP 36442 Jenny/Don't Ask Me To Explain (p/s) ... 10
78 United Artists UP 36478 Last Bus Home/Romance (p/s) ... 10
(see also Vibrators)

BOYFRIENDS
82 Plastic PRES 001 Boyfriend/Give A Little, Take A Little (p/s) ... 40

BOY GEORGE
87 Virgin CDEP 9 To Be Reborn/Where Are You Now? (CD, gatefold card p/s) ... 12
88 Virgin BOY 105-12 Live My Life/Live My Life (Klub Mix)/Live My Life (12" Club Remix) (12", poster sleeve) ... 8
88 Virgin BOYT 106 No Clause 28 (Space Face Full Remix)/(Space Face Full Dub)/ (Full Version) (3" CD, in 5" slimline jewel case, with adaptor) ... 10
88 Virgin BOYCD 106 No Clause 28 (5" CD) ... 8
89 Virgin BOYCD 107 Don't Cry/Leave In Love/Don't Cry (Full Version)/A Boy Called Alice (3" CD) ... 10
89 Virgin BOYCD 108 Don't Take My Mind On A Trip/I Go Where I Go/Girlfriend/ What Becomes Of The Broken Hearted (3" CD, card p/s) ... 12
98 More Protein PROT 112 Sad (Mixes)/Butterfly (Mixes) ... 12
98 More Protein (no cat. no.) Open House With Boy George & Family (CD-ROM, available at selected concerts) ... 25
94 Virgin VSCDG 1490 THE DEVIL IN SISTER GEORGE EP: Miss Me Blind (Return To Gender Mix)/Generations Of Love (Ramp Club Mix)/ Am I Losing Control (Metal Bird Mix)/Love Hurts (Disco Moment Mix)/ Everything I Own (Redemption Extension Mix) (CD, digipak) ... 10
95 Spaghetti CIO CD THE CRYING GAME (CD EP) ... 8
98 Back Door BDCD 01 THE UNRECOUPABLE ONE MAN BANDIT (CD, 1st issue) ... 18
(see also Culture Club, Jesus Loves You)

BOY HAIRDRESSERS
88 53rd & 3rd AGARR T12 Golden Showers/Tidalwave/The Assumption As An Elevator (12", p/s) ... 25
(see also Teenage Fanclub, BMX Bandits, Clouds)

BOY KRAZY
91 Polydor PZCD 158 That's What Love Can Do (Extended Version)/One Thing Leads To Another/ That's What Love Can Do (7" version) (CD, p/s) ... 10
91 Polydor 828 403-2 BOY KRAZY (CD) ... 20

BILLY BOYLE
62 Decca F 11503 My Baby's Crazy 'Bout Elvis/Held For Questioning ... 25
63 Decca F 11709 I'm Coming Home/Sunday's Child ... 10
63 Columbia DB 7111 Lovers Hill/She's New To You ... 5
63 Columbia DB 7127 Hootin' In The Kitchen/Lover's Hill ... 5
64 Columbia DB 7294 Walk, Walk, Walkin'/My Baby Tonight (with Le Roys) ... 5
(see also Le Roys)

A. BOYNE
70 Punch PH 36 Oh My Darling (actually Audley Rollins)/DENNIS SMITH: Ball Of Confusion ... 10

BOYS (Jamaica)
69 Duke DU 19 Easy Sound/AFROTONES: Freedom Sound ... 12
(see also Harry J. Allstars)

BOYS (U.K.)
63 Parlophone R 5027 Polaris/Jumpin' ... 22

BOYS (U.K.)
64 Pye 7N 15726 It Ain't Fair/I Want You ... 100
(see also Sandra Barry & Boys, Action)

BOYS (U.K.)
77 NEMS NES 102 I Don't Care/Soda Pressing (p/s) ... 15
77 NEMS NES 111 First Time/Whatcha Gonna Do/Turning Grey (p/s) ... 15
78 NEMS NES 116 Brickfield Nights/Teacher's Pet (p/s) ... 10
79 Safari SAFE 21 Kamikaze/Bad Days (p/s, some with booklet) ... 7/5
80 Safari SAFE 23 Terminal Love/I Love Me (p/s) ... 5
80 Safari SAFE 27 You Better Move On/Schoolgirls (p/s) ... 5
80 Safari SAFE 31 Weekend/Cool (p/s) ... 5
80 Safari SAFE 33 Let It Rain/Lucy (p/s) ... 6
77 NEMS NES 6001 THE BOYS (LP) ... 15
78 NEMS NEL 6015 ALTERNATIVE CHARTBUSTERS (LP) ... 15
79 Safari 1-2 BOYS TO HELL WITH THE BOYS (LP, with songbook & stickered sleeve) ... 12
(see also Yobs, Rowdies, Hollywood Brats)

BOYS (U.K.)
88 private pressing — Happy Days/Standard Avenue/Learn How To Dance (p/s) 8
(see also Ocean Colour Scene)

BOYS BLUE
65 HMV POP 1427 — You Got What I Want/Take A Heart 55
(see also Jeff Elroy & Boys Blue)

BOYS OF THE LOUGH
73 Trailer LER 2086 — THE BOYS OF THE LOUGH (LP) 15
74 Trailer LER 2090 — SECOND ALBUM (LP) 15

BOYS TOWN STEEL ORCHESTRA
52 Sagomes SG 126 — Woman Police/Is It Yes? Is It No? (78) 7

BOYS WONDER
87 Sire W 8195 — Shine On Me/Stop It (p/s) 5
87 Sire W 8293 — What Now, Earthman?/Ten Million Ton Headache (p/s) 5
88 Boys Wonder BW 1 — Goodbye Jimmy Dean/Hot Rod (p/s) 5
90 Flat OUTS 001 — Eat Me, Drink Me/Harley Davidson (p/s) 5
89 Flat OUTA 002 — RADIO WONDER (LP) 12
(see also Corduroy)

BOYZONE
94 Polydor 853 246-2 — Working My Way Back To You (Radio Edit)/(12" POD Hi NRG Mix)/ Father And Son (CD, Irish-only) 18

BOZ
66 Columbia DB 7832 — You're Just The Kind Of Girl I Want/Isn't That So 10
66 Columbia DB 7889 — Meeting Time/No (Ah) Body Knows The Blues 10
66 Columbia DB 7941 — Pinocchio/Stay As You Are 8
66 Columbia DB 7972 — The Baby Song/Carry On Screaming 8
68 Columbia DB 8406 — I Shall Be Released/Down In The Flood 7
68 Columbia DB 8468 — Light My Fire/Back Against The Wall 10
(see also King Crimson)

JANET BRACE
55 Brunswick 05272 — Teach Me Tonight/My Old Familiar Heartache 10

BRACKEN
79 Look LKLP 6438 — PRINCE OF THE NORTHLANDS (LP, private pressing, with insert) 85

PROF. ALEX BRADFORD
63 London REU 1357 — TOO CLOSE TO HEAVEN (EP) 22
63 Stateside SL 10047 — ONE STEP (LP) 25
(see also Bradford Singers)

BOBBY BRADFORD
73 Emanem 302 — LOVE'S DREAM (LP) 30

BRADFORD SINGERS
62 Stateside SL 10026 — BLACK NATIVITY (LP) 30
64 Stateside SL 10083 — ANGEL ON VACATION (LP) 25
(see also Prof. Alex Bradford)

GEORGE BRADLEY & HIS BAND
65 HMV POP 1459 — Breakout/Vendetta 10

JAN BRADLEY
63 Pye International 7N 25182 — Mama Didn't Lie/Lovers Like Me 50

MARTIN BRADLEY
80 Greenwich Village GVR 205 — TIME CAN'T STAND STILL (LP) 15

OWEN BRADLEY (ORCHESTRA/QUINTET)
56 Brunswick 05528 — Theme From "The Threepenny Opera"/Lights Of Vienna (with Orchestra) 5
57 Brunswick 05700 — White Silver Sands/Midnight Blues (as Owen Bradley Quintet) 5
58 Brunswick 05736 — Big Guitar/Sentimental Dream (as Owen Bradley Quintet) 20
60 Brunswick LAT 8327 — THE BIG GUITAR (LP) 30

BRADLEY STRYDER
92 Rephlex CAT 001 — BRADLEY'S BEAT (12" EP, logo sleeve) 20
96 Rephlex CAT 020 — BRADLEY'S ROBOT (12" EP, poster p/s) 10

DON BRADSHAW-LEATHER
72 Distance DIST 101 — DISTANCE BETWEEN US (2-LP, gatefold sleeve, private pressing) 40
(supposedly by Robert John Godfrey)

BUDDY BRADSHAW
59 Capitol CL 15036 — Nothing You Can Say/Tonight I Walk Alone 15
(see also Owen Gray)

SONNY BRADSHAW (& YOUNG JAMAICA)
61 Duke DK 1003 — Yellow Birds/Festival Jump Up 12
71 Big Shot BI 576 — Wig Wam/Peace And Love (as Sonny Bradshaw & Young Jamaica) 10

TINY BRADSHAW & HIS ORCHESTRA
52 Vogue V 2146 — Breaking Up The House/Walk That Mess (78) 8
54 Parlophone CMSP 3 — South Of The Orient/Later (export issue) 30
54 Parlophone MSP 6118 — The Gypsy/Spider Web 20
55 Parlophone DP 418 — Bradshaw Boogie/Walkin' The Chalk Line (78, export issue) 15
55 Parlophone DP 427 — Choice/Light (78, export issue) 10
55 Parlophone MSP 6145 — Overflow/Don't Worry 'Bout Me 20
55 Parlophone R 3959 — Overflow/Don't Worry 'Bout Me (78) 12
54 Parlophone GEP 8507 — TRAIN KEPT A ROLLING (EP) 50
56 Parlophone GEP 8552 — POMPTON TURNPIKE (EP) 30
50s Parlophone CGEP 2 — TINY BRADSHAW (export EP) 25

MINT VALUE £

TINY BRADSHAW ORCHESTRA/WYNONIE HARRIS
70 Polydor 623 273 KINGS OF RHYTHM AND BLUES (LP, 1 side each) 25
(see also Wynonie Harris)

BOB BRADY & CONCHORDS
68 Bell BLL 1025 Everybody's Goin' To The Love-In/It's Been A Long Time Between Kisses 20
70 Bell BLL 1114 Everybody's Goin' To The Love-In/It's Been A Long Time Between Kisses (reissue) 7

PHIL BRADY & RANCHERS
65 Rex R 11011 Little Rose/Just One More Time 6
(see also Ranchers)

PHIL BRADY & THE RANCH SET
67 Go AJ 11406 Lonesome For You 20

VICTOR BRADY
70 Polydor BROWN RAIN (LP) 22

BRADY BUNCH
73 Paramount SPFL 284 MEET THE BRADY BUNCH (LP) 15

RUBY BRAFF
55 Vogue LAE 12051 HUSTLIN' AND BUSTLIN' 15
71 Polydor 2460 127 HEAR ME TALKIN'! (LP) 12

AL 'TNT' BRAGGS
66 Vocalion VP 9278 Earthquake/How Long (Do You Hold On) 20
68 Action ACT 4506 Earthquake/How Long (Do You Hold On) (reissue) 12
69 Action ACT 4526 I'm A Good Man/I Like What You Do To Me 15
65 Vocalion VEP 170163 AL 'TNT' BRAGGS (EP) 80

ERNEL BRAHAM
66 Rio R 79 Musical Fight/EDWARDS ALLSTARS: Pipeline 30
(see also Kent Walker)

BRAIN
67 Parlophone R 5595 Nightmares In Red/Kick The Donkey 70
87 Bam Caruso OPRA 63 Nightmares In Red/SRC: Black Sheep (jukebox edition, die-cut company sleeve) 10
(see also Giles Giles & Fripp, Trendsetters Ltd, League Of Gentlemen)

BRAINBOX
69 Parlophone R 5775 Woman's Gone/Down Man 12
70 Parlophone R 5842 So Helpless/To You 8
70 Parlophone PCS 7094 BRAINBOX (LP) 50
(see also Jan Akkerman, Hunters, Focus)

BRAINCHILD
70 A&M AMS 805 Cage/Autobiography 6
70 A&M AMLS 979 HEALING OF THE LUNATIC OWL (LP) 35

BRAINIAC 5
80 Roach RR 5002 Working/Feel (p/s) 10
78 Roach RREP 5001 MUSHY DOUBT (EP, 33rpm, p/s) 10

BRAINSTORM
79 Miracle M5 Lovin' Is Really My Game/Stormin' (12", no p/s) 40

WILFRED BRAMBELL
63 Parlophone R 5058 Secondhand/Ragtime Ragabone Man 15
71 CBS 7062 The Decimal Song/Time Marches On 8

WILFRED BRAMBELL & HARRY H. CORBETT
63 Pye 7N 15588 Steptoe And Son At Buckingham Palace (Parts 1 & 2, some in p/s) 10/5
63 Pye NEP 24169 THE FACTS OF LIFE (EP) 10
64 Pye NPL 18081 STEPTOE AND SON (LP) 12
65 Pye NPL 18101 STEPTOE A LA CARTE (LP) 12
65 Pye NPL 18135 LOVE AND HAROLD STEPTOE (LP) 25
66 Pye NPL 18153 GEMS FROM THE STEPTOE SCRAP HEAP (LP) 25

DELANEY BRAMLETT
64 Vocalion VP 9227 Heartbreak Hotel/You Never Looked Sweeter 15
65 Vocalion VP 9237 Liverpool Lou/You Have No Choice 10
(see also Delaney & Bonnie, King Curtis with Delaney & Friends)

BRAM STOKER
72 Windmill WMD 117 HEAVY ROCK SPECTACULAR (LP) 20

BILL BRAMWELL
58 Starlite ST45 004 My Old Man/Shoutin' In That Amen Corner 8
60 Decca F 11309 Candid Camera Theme/Frederika 8

BRAN
74 Sain 1038M AIL DDECHRA (LP) 65
76 Sain 1070M HEDFAN (LP) 65
78 Sain 1120M GWRACH Y HOS (LP, with inner sleeve) 65

BRAND
64 Piccadilly 7N 35216 I'm A Lover Not A Fighter/Hear 'Em Talking (unissued)
64 Piccadilly 7N 35216 I'm A Lover Not A Fighter/Zulu Stomp 125

BRAND NEW HEAVIES
91 Acid Jazz JAZID 39P Never Stop (12", company sleeve, withdrawn) 30
92 Acid Jazz JAZID 23 THE BRAND NEW HEAVIES (LP) 12

BILL BRANDON
73 Mercury 6052 186 I Am Free Of Your Love/(Take Another Little) Piece Of My Heart 5

JOHNNY BRANDON

56 Parlophone MSP 6238 Rock-A-Bye Baby/Lonely Lips . . . 50
56 Parlophone R 4207 Shim Sham Shuffle/I Didn't Know . . . 50
56 Decca F 10778 Glendora/Song For A Summer Night . . . 15
57 Decca F 10858 Nothing Is Too Good For You/A Sort-Of-A-Feeling . . . 15
59 Top Rank JAR 241 Santa Claus Jnr./I Heard A Bluebird Sing . . . 10
55 Pye NEP 24003 JOHNNY BRANDON HITS (EP) . . . 20

KIRK BRANDON & PACK OF LIES

87 SS SS1N2/SS2N1 KIRK BRANDON AND THE PACK OF LIES (EP) . . . 7
(see also Theatre Of Hate, Spear Of Destiny, Senate, Pack)

TONY BRANDON

68 MGM MGM 1401 Candy Kisses/Get Going Baby . . . 6

VERN BRANDON

62 Decca F 11472 Let Me Be The One/Gotta Know The Reason . . . 20

BRAND X

79 Charisma CB 340 Soho/Dance Of The Illegal Aliens (no p/s) . . . 5
79 Charisma CB 340-12 Soho/Dance Of The Illegal Aliens/Noddy Goes To Sweden/ Pool Room Blues (12", p/s) . . . 8
(see also Phil Collins)

BRANDY BOYS

65 Columbia DB 7507 Gale Winds/Don't Come Knocking At My Door . . . 12

BRANDY WINE BRIDGE

77 Cottage COT 311 THE GREY LADY (LP) . . . 25
78 Cottage COT 321 AN ENGLISH MEADOW (LP, hand-drawn sleeve with insert) . . . 25

BRANDY WINE SINGERS

68 President PT 204 Mandy/Two Little Boys . . . 6

JOHNNY BRANTLEY'S ALL STARS

58 London HLU 8606 The Place/Pot Luck . . . 25
58 London HLU 8606 The Place/Pot Luck (78) . . . 15

BRASS ALLEY

(see under Various Artists EPs)

ANDRÉ BRASSEUR

65 Pye International 7N 25332 Early Bird Satellite/Special 230 . . . 10
67 CBS 202557 The Kid/Holiday . . . 25
71 CBS 2557 The Kid/Holiday (reissue) . . . 5
66 CBS 62858 TASTY (LP) . . . 18

BRASS INCORPORATED

70 Pye International 7N 25520 At The Sign Of The Swinging Cymbal/Just Like That . . . 15

BRASS TACKS

68 Big T BIG 110 I'll Keep On Holding On/Let The Sunshine In . . . 20
68 Big T BIG 114 Maxwell Ferguson/Sunshine After The Rain . . . 35

BRATZ

80 A Famous Record AFR 1 The Bratz Are Coming/Coast To Coast/Everyone Wants To Be Elvis (p/s) . . . 6

BOB BRAUN

62 Brunswick 05875 Till Death Do Us Part/So It Goes . . . 6

RICHARD BRAUTIGAN

69 Zapple ZAPPLE 03 LISTENING TO RICHARD BRAUTIGAN (LP, unreleased, acetates exist) . . . 750+

LOS BRAVOS

66 Decca F 22419 Black Is Black/I Want A Name . . . 6
66 Decca F 22484 I Don't Care/Don't Be Left Out In The Cold . . . 6
66 Decca F 22529 Going Nowhere/Brand New Baby . . . 7
67 Decca F 22615 I'm All Ears/You'll Never Get The Chances Again . . . 7
67 Decca F 22682 Like Nobody Else/Wearing A Smile . . . 7
68 Decca F 22765 Bring A Little Lovin'/Make It Last . . . 20
69 Decca F 22853 Save Me, Save Me/Baby I Love You Because I Need You . . . 12
70 Decca F 13064 People Talking Around/Every Dog Has His Night . . . 7
66 Decca LK 4822 BLACK IS BLACK (LP) . . . 30
68 Decca LK/SKL 4905 LOS BRAVOS (LP) . . . 30
(see also Mike Kennedy)

ANTHONY BRAXTON & DEREK BAILEY

73 Emanem 601 DUO (2-LP) . . . 30
84 Incus INCUS 43 ROYAL VOLUME 1 (LP) . . . 20
(see also Derek Bailey)

PRISCILLA BRAZIER

74 Dovetail DOVE 9 PRISCILLA BRAZIER (LP) . . . 40
76 Key KL 038 SOMETHING BEAUTIFUL (LP) . . . 35

BREAD

69 Elektra EKSN 45071 London Bridge/Dismal Day . . . 6
69 Elektra EKS 74044 BREAD (LP) . . . 15
(see also David Gates, Pleasure Fair)

BREAD & BEER BAND

69 Decca F 12891 Dick Barton Theme (The Devil's Gallop)/Breakdown Blues . . . 90
72 Decca F 13354 Dick Barton Theme (The Devil's Gallop)/Breakdown Blues (reissue) . . . 40
69 Rubbish (no cat. no.) THE BREAD AND BEER BAND (LP, 1 copy known to exist) . . . 2,000+
(see also Elton John, Caleb)

MINT VALUE £

BREAD, LOVE & DREAMS

69 Decca F 12958 — Virgin Kiss/Switch Out The Sun — 18
69 Decca LK/SKL 5008 — BREAD, LOVE AND DREAMS (LP) — 85
70 Decca LK/SKL 5048 — THE STRANGE TALE OF CAPTAIN SHANNON AND THE HUNCHBACK FROM GIGHA (LP) — 85
71 Decca SKL 5081 — AMARYLLIS (LP) — 200
(see also Human Beast)

BREAKAWAYS

62 Pye 7N 15471 — He's A Rebel/Wishing Star — 15
63 Pye 7N 15585 — That Boy Of Mine/Here She Comes — 15
64 Pye 7N 15618 — That's How It Goes/He Doesn't Love Me — 15
65 Pye 7N 15973 — Danny Boy/Your Kind Of Love — 15
67 CBS 2833 — Sacred Love/Don't Be A Baby — 15
68 MCA MU 1018 — Santo Domingo/So In Love Are We — 5
(see also Vernons Girls, Burt Bacharach Orchestra, Mike Patto, Ken Cope, Sharades, De Laine Sisters)

BREAKDOWN

77 MCP 001 — MEET ME ON THE HIGHWAY (LP, private pressing with insert) — 25

BREAKTHRU'

68 Mercury MF 1066 — Ice Cream Tree/Julius Caesar — 12

BREAKWATER

86 Arista ARIST 12674 — Say You Love Me Girl/Work It Out (12", p/s) — 12

PATRICIA BREDIN

59 Top Rank JAR 257 — Till The Right Times Comes/I Live To Love You — 7

BREEDERS

02 4AD no cat. no. — HUFFER (EP, CD-R) — 12
93 4AD CADD 3014 — LAST SPLASH (LP, with free 7" "Grungé New Year") — 12
(see also Pixies)

JIMMY BREEDLOVE

57 London HLE 8490 — Over Somebody Else's Shoulder/That's My Baby — 120
57 London HLE 8490 — Over Somebody Else's Shoulder/That's My Baby (78) — 50
62 Pye International 7N 25121 — You're Following Me/Fabulous — 15
75 Pye Disco Demand DDS 110 — I Can't Help Loving You/I Saw You — 5
(see also Cues)

BUDDY BREGMAN & HIS ORCHESTRA

56 HMV 7MC 40 — Theme From "Picnic"/Riviera (export issue) — 12

JACQUES BREL

65 Fontana TL 5330 — JACQUES BREL (LP) — 18
66 Fontana TL 5391 — JACQUES BREL VOL. 2 (LP) — 18
67 Fontana TL 5429 — JACQUES BREL '67 (LP) — 18
68 Fontana SFJL 967 — A L'OLYMPIA (LP) — 20

BRELLO CABAL

67 CBS 3214 — Margarine Flavoured Pineapple Chunk/Follow That — 6
(see also Anita Harris)

BEVERLEY BREMERS

72 Wand WN 18 — Get Smart Girl/Don't Say You Don't Remember — 10
72 Wand WN 28 — We're Free/Colours Of Love — 5
72 Wand WN 34 — I'll Make You Music/I Made A Man Out Of You Jimmy — 5

BRENDA & TABULATIONS

67 London HL 10127 — Dry Your Eyes/The Wash — 25
67 London HL 10174 — When You're Gone/Hey Boy — 22
68 Direction 58-3678 — Baby You're So Right For Me/To The One I Love — 10
69 Action ACT 4541 — That's In The Past/I Can't Get Over Her — 30
70 London HL 10325 — A Child No One Wanted/'Scuse Uz Y'all — 7
71 CBS 7279 — Right On The Tip of My Tongue/Always And Forever — 7
73 Epic EPC 1361 — One Girl Too Late/The Magic Of Your Love — 6
69 Action ACLP 6003 — DRY YOUR EYES (LP) — 60

BRENDON

76 Magnet MAG 80 — Gimme Some/Changing My Life Won't Do — 6

BUDDY BRENNAN QUARTET

60 London HLU 9049 — Big River/The Chase — 10

ROSE BRENNAN

55 HMV 7M 299 — Ding Dong/Sincerely — 15
55 HMV 7M 328 — Wake The Town And Tell The People/Ten Little Kisses — 10
56 HMV 7M 360 — You Are My Love/My Dublin Bay — 10
56 HMV 7M 383 — Band Of Gold/My Believing Heart — 10
57 HMV POP 302 — Without Love (There Is Nothing)/Tra La La — 12
59 Top Rank JAR 152 — Johnny Let Me Go/My Summer Diary — 6
59 Top Rank JAR 152 — Johnny Let Me Go/My Summer Diary (78) — 10
61 Philips PB 1193 — Tall Dark Stranger/This Girl With The Wistful Eyes — 5

WALTER BRENNAN

60 London HLD 9148 — Dutchman's Gold/Back To The Farm — 10
62 Liberty LIB 55436 — Old Rivers/Epic Ride Of John H Glenn — 7
62 Liberty LIB 55477 — Houdini/The Old Kelly Place — 6
63 Liberty LIB 55508 — Mama Sang A Song/Who Will Take Gramma — 6
64 Liberty LBY 1249 — GUNFIGHT AT THE OK CORRAL (LP) — 25

BERNIE BRENT'S COMBO

60s Honey Hit TB 4501 — BERNIE BRENT'S COMBO (EP) — 8

FRANKIE BRENT

57 Pye N 15102 Rockin' Shoes/I Ain't Never Gonna Do You No Good (78) . . . 15
57 Pye N 15103 Be My Girl/Rang Dang Doo (78) . . . 15

TONY BRENT

53 Columbia SCM 5042 Have You Heard?/Strange Love . . . 10
53 Columbia SCM 5057 Which Way The Wind Blows/My One And Only Heart . . . 10
54 Columbia SCM 5135 I Understand Just How You Feel/The Magic Tango . . . 10
54 Columbia SCM 5146 Nicolette/Tell Me, Tell Me . . . 10
55 Columbia SCM 5160 It's A Woman's World/Give Me The Right To Be Wrong . . . 10
55 Columbia SCM 5170 Open Up Your Heart (with Anne Warren)/Hearts Of Stone (with Coronets) . . . 10
55 Columbia SCM 5188 Mirror, Mirror/Love And Kisses . . . 10
55 Columbia SCM 5200 With Your Love/On A Little Balcony In Spain . . . 10
56 Columbia SCM 5245 Sooner Or Later (Love Comes Along)/Pick Yourself A Star . . . 10
56 Columbia SCM 5272 My Little Angel/What A Heavenly Night For Love . . . 10
56 Columbia DB 3844 Cindy, Oh Cindy/Two Innocent Hearts . . . 10
57 Columbia DB 3884 Amore/If Wishes Were Horses . . . 10
57 Columbia DB 3918 Butterfly/How Lonely Can One Be? . . . 10
57 Columbia DB 3950 Dark Moon/The Game Of Love (A-One And A-Two) . . . 10
57 Columbia DB 3987 Deep Within Me/Why Ask For The Moon . . . 10
57 Columbia DB 4043 Love By The Jukebox Light/We Belong Together . . . 10
58 Columbia DB 4066 Don't Save Your Love (For Me)/The Clouds Will Soon Roll By . . . 5
58 Columbia DB 4128 Chanson D'Amour/Little Serenade . . . 5
58 Columbia DB 4177 Girl Of My Dreams/Don't Play That Melody . . . 5
59 Columbia DB 4238 Call Me/I Surrender, Dear . . . 5
59 Columbia DB 4304 Why Should I Be Lonely?/My Little Room . . . 5
59 Columbia DB 4357 Forever, My Darling (Pledging My Love)/Worried Mind . . . 5
60 Columbia DB 4402 Oh, So Wunderbar/Just As Much As Ever . . . 5
60 Columbia DB 4478 Your Cheatin' Heart/Come On In . . . 5
60 Columbia DB 4514 I'm Alone Because I Love You/Just A-Wearyin' For You . . . 5
61 Columbia DB 4610 Until The Real Thing Comes Along/Ten Lonely Weekends . . . 5
61 Columbia DB 4657 Is It Too Late?/You Made Me Care . . . 5
58 Columbia SEG 7824 TONY CALLS THE TUNE (EP) . . . 10
58 Columbia SEG 7869 TIME FOR TONY (EP) . . . 10
59 Columbia SEG 8019 OFF STAGE (EP) . . . 10
59 Columbia SEG 8040 OFF STAGE NO. 2 (EP) . . . 10
58 Columbia 33S 1125 OFF STAGE (10" LP) . . . 10
60 Columbia 33SX 1200 TONY TAKES FIVE (LP, also stereo SCX 3288) . . . 10
60s Columbia 33SX 5001 TONY'S BIG HITS (LP) . . . 10
(see also Coronets)

TONY BRENT & JULIE DAWN

53 Columbia SCM 5029 Ding Dong Boogie/When Are We Gonna Get Married? . . . 10
(see also Julie Dawn)

BRENT FORD & NYLONS

78 Brumbeat 19th Nervous Breakdown/Big Rock Candy Mountain (handmade foldout p/s) . . . 50

BRENTWOOD ROAD ALLSTARS

70 Bamboo BAM 23 Love At First Sight/MAYTALS: Life Could Be A Dream . . . 25
70 Bamboo BAM 25 Soul Shake/Moon Ride . . . 25

GERRY BRERETON

53 Parlophone MSP 6056 From Here To Eternity/If You've Never Been In Love . . . 10
54 Parlophone MSP 6081 The Book/Somewhere Someone (Is Saying A Prayer) . . . 8
55 Columbia SCM 5195 A Million Helping Hands/Fair Sets The Wind For Love . . . 7
(see also Eddie Calvert)

BERNARD BRESSLAW

58 HMV POP 522 Mad Passionate Love/You Need Feet . . . 5
58 HMV POP 522 Mad Passionate Love/You Need Feet (78) . . . 8
59 HMV POP 599 Charlie Brown/The Teenager's Lament . . . 5
59 HMV POP 599 Charlie Brown/The Teenager's Lament (78) . . . 10
59 HMV POP 669 Ivy Will Cling/I Found A Hole . . . 5
59 HMV POP 669 Ivy Will Cling/I Found A Hole (78) . . . 15
59 HMV 7EG 8439 I ONLY ARSKED (EP) . . . 10

PAUL BRETT('S SAGE)

70 Pye 7N 17974 Three D Mona Lisa/Mediterranean Lazy Heat Wave . . . 7
71 Dawn DNX 2508 Reason For Your Askin'/Everlasting Butterfly/Savannah Ladies/ To Everyman (Freedom) (p/s) . . . 10
71 Dawn DNS 1010 Goodbye Forever/Good Old Fashioned Funky Kind Of Music . . . 6
72 Dawn DNS 1021 Dahlia/Cottage Made For Two . . . 6
73 Bradley's BRAD 301 Mr. Custer/Good Times, Hard Times . . . 6
73 Bradley's BRAD 305 Summer Driftin'/Clocks (p/s) . . . 7
70 Pye NSPL 18347 PAUL BRETT SAGE (LP) . . . 22
71 Dawn DNLS 3021 JUBILATION FOUNDRY (LP, gatefold sleeve, as Paul Brett's Sage) . . . 18
72 Dawn DNLS 3032 SCHIZOPHRENIA (LP, foldout sleeve, as Paul Brett's Sage) . . . 25
73 Bradley's BRADL 1001 PAUL BRETT (LP, envelope sleeve with inner) . . . 18
73 Bradley's BRADL 1004 CLOCKS (LP) . . . 18
75 PF private pressing PHOENIX FUTURE (LP, 500 only) . . . 20
70s private pressing MUSIC MANIFOLD (LP, library issue) . . . 25
(see also Elmer Gantry's Velvet Opera, Fire)

STEVE BRETT & MAVERICKS

65 Columbia DB 7470 Wishing/Anything That's Part Of You . . . 85
65 Columbia DB 7581 Sad, Lonely And Blue/Candy . . . 100
65 Columbia DB 7794 Sugar Shack/Chains On My Heart . . . 140
(see also 'N Betweens, Slade)

MINT VALUE £

TONY BREVETT

71	Supreme SUP 224	Don't Get Weary/BREVETT ALLSTARS: Version	12
74	Dip DL 5028	You Don't Love Me/Version	7

(see also Melodians, Glen Adams)

TERESA BREWER

78s

50	London L 562	Copper Canyon/'Way Back Home (with Bobby Wayne)	10
50	London L 563	Ol' Man Mose/I Beeped When I Shoulda Bopped!	8
50	London L 678	Choo'n Gum/Honky Tonkin' (with Johnny Lyttel)	8
50	London L 696	The Picnic Song/Let's Have A Party (B-side with Snooky Lanson, Claire Hogan & Bobby Wayne)	12
50	London L 768	Cincinnati Dancing Pig/Punky Punkin	8
50	London L 794	Molasses Molasses/Grizzly Bear	10
50	London L 873	The Thing/I Guess I'll Have To Dream The Rest	8
51	London L 878	A Penny A Kiss — A Penny A Hug/Hello (with Snooky Lanson)	10
51	London L 967	I've Got The Craziest Feeling/If You Want Some Lovin'	10
51	London L 969	The Picnic Song/Let's Have A Party (with Snooky Lanson)	10
51	London L 970	Counterfeit Kisses/Lonesome Gal	10
51	London L 1085	I Wish I Wuz/If You Don't Marry Me	8
54	Vogue Coral Q 2001	Jilted/Le Grand Tour De L'Amour	8
54	Vogue Coral Q 2011	Skinny Minnie (Fishtail)/I Had Someone Else Before I Had You	10
54	Vogue Coral Q 2029	Au Revoir/Danger Signs	8
55	Vogue Coral Q 72066	Tweedlee Dee/Rock Love	10
57	Vogue Coral Q 72278	Lula Rock-A-Hula/Teardrops In My Heart	10
57	Vogue Coral Q 72292	You Send Me/Born To Love	8
58	Coral Q 72301	Careless Caresses/Mutual Admiration Society	8
58	Coral Q 72320	Saturday Dance/I Think The World Of You	10
58	Coral Q 72336	Pickle Up A Doodle/The Rain Falls On Ev'rybody	8
58	Coral Q 72340	The Hula Hoop Song/So Shy	8
58	Coral Q 72349	I Like Christmas/Jingle Bell Rock	12
58	Coral Q 72354	Satellite/The One Rose (That's Left In My Heart)	10
59	Coral Q 72364	Heavenly Lover/Fair Weather Sweetheart	12
59	Coral Q 72375	Bye Bye Baby Goodbye/Chain Of Friendship	12
59	Coral Q 72383	Bill Bailey, Won't You Please Come Home/Mexicali Rose	12

SINGLES

54	Vogue Coral Q 2011	Skinny Minnie (Fishtail)/I Had Someone Else Before I Had You	30
54	Vogue Coral Q 2029	Au Revoir/Danger Signs	25
55	Vogue Coral Q 72043	Let Me Go, Lover (with Lancers)/Baby, Baby, Baby	40
55	Vogue Coral Q 72065	How Important Can It Be?/What More Is There To Say?	20
55	Vogue Coral Q 72066	Tweedlee Dee/Rock Love	30
55	Vogue Coral Q 72077	Pledging My Love/I Gotta Go Get My Baby	20
55	Vogue Coral Q 72083	You're Telling Our Secret/Time	20
55	Vogue Coral Q 72098	The Banjo's Back In Town/How To Be Very, Very Popular	18
56	Vogue Coral Q 72130	A Good Man Is Hard To Find/It's Siesta Time	18
56	Vogue Coral Q 72139	Rememb'ring/My Sweetie Went Away	18
56	Vogue Coral Q 72146	A Tear Fell/Bo Weevil	18
56	Vogue Coral Q 72172	A Sweet Old-Fashioned Girl/Goodbye, John	12
56	Vogue Coral Q 72199	Keep Your Cotton Pickin' Paddies Offa My Heart/ So Doggone Lonely	10
56	Vogue Coral Q 72213	Crazy With Love/The Moon Is On Fire	12
57	Vogue Coral Q 72224	Nora Malone/When I Leave The World Behind	12
57	Vogue Coral Q 72239	I'm Drowning My Sorrows/How Lonely Can One Be	10
57	Vogue Coral Q 72251	Empty Arms/The Ricky-Tick Song	10
57	Vogue Coral Q 72278	Lula Rock-A-Hula/Teardrops In My Heart	15
57	Vogue Coral Q 72292	You Send Me/Born To Love	15
58	Coral Q 72301	Careless Caresses/Mutual Admiration Society	10
58	Coral Q 72320	Saturday Dance/I Think The World Of You	10
58	Coral Q 72336	Pickle Up A Doodle/The Rain Falls On Ev'rybody	10
58	Coral Q 72340	The Hula Hoop Song/So Shy	10
58	Coral Q 72349	I Like Christmas/Jingle Bell Rock	10
58	Coral Q 72354	Satellite/The One Rose (That's Left In My Heart)	10
59	Coral Q 72364	Heavenly Lover/Fair Weather Sweetheart	10
59	Coral Q 72375	Bye Bye Baby Goodbye/Chain Of Friendship	15
59	Coral Q 72383	Bill Bailey, Won't You Please Come Home/Mexicali Rose	6
60	Coral Q 72386	Peace Of Mind/Venetian Sunset	6
60	Coral Q 72396	How Do You Know It's Love/If There Are Stars In My Eyes	6
60	Coral Q 72405	Anymore/That Piano Man	6
60	Coral Q 72418	Have You Ever Been Lonely/When Do You Love Me	6
60	Coral Q 72447	Pretty Lookin' Boy/Your Cheatin' Heart	6

EPs

50s	London BEP 6039	TERESA BREWER WITH THE ALL STARS (export issue)	20
50s	London BEP 6041	TERESA BREWER WITH JACK PLEIS AND THE ALL STARS (export issue)	20
59	Coral FEP 2013	HULA HOOP TIME WITH TERESA BREWER	20
59	Coral FEP 2036	WHEN YOUR LOVER HAS GONE PART 1	20
59	Coral FEP 2037	WHEN YOUR LOVER HAS GONE PART 2	20
59	Coral FEP 2038	WHEN YOUR LOVER HAS GONE PART 3	20
60	Coral FEP 2047	TERESA BREWER AND THE DIXIELAND BAND PART 1	20
60	Coral FEP 2048	TERESA BREWER AND THE DIXIELAND BAND PART 2	20
60	Coral FEP 2061	HOW DO YOU KNOW IT'S LOVE	20

LPs

51	London H-APB 1006	SHOWCASE (10")	35
57	Coral LVA 9020	MUSIC! MUSIC! MUSIC!	25
58	Coral LVA 9075	FOR TEENAGERS IN LOVE	25
58	Coral LVA 9091	AT CHRISTMAS TIME	30
59	Coral LVA 9095	TIME FOR TERESA BREWER	20

59 Coral LVA 9100 WHEN YOUR LOVER HAS GONE (also stereo SVL 3003) 20/22
59 Coral LVA 9107 TERESA BREWER AND THE DIXIELAND BAND 20
60 Coral LVA 9129 RIDIN' HIGH 20
60 Coral LVA 9131 MY GOLDEN FAVOURITES. 20
60 Coral LVA 9138 NAUGHTY NAUGHTY NAUGHTY 20
61 Coral LVA 9145 SONGS EVERYBODY KNOWS 20
62 Coral LVA 9152 ALOHA FROM TERESA 20
62 Coral LVA 9204 DON'T MESS AROUND WITH TESS 20
67 Wing WL 1157 TERRIFIC TERESA BREWER! 12
(see also Snooky Lanson)

BREWER & SHIPLEY

71 Kama Sutra 2013 015 One Toke Over The Line/People Love Each Other 5
70 Kama Sutra 2361 001 TARKIO ROAD (LP) 15
71 Kama Sutra 2361 005 WEEDS (LP) 15
72 Kama Sutra 2319 021 SHAKE OFF THE DEMON (LP) 12

BREWER'S DROOP

72 RCA RCA 2216 Sweet Thing/Heart Of Stone/It Ain't The Meat — It's The Motion (p/s) 6
72 RCA SF 8301 OPENING TIME (LP) 18

BRIAR

82 Happy Face MM 142 Rainbow (To The Skies)/Crying In The Rain (p/s) 15
87 PRT BRIAR 1 Edge Of A Broken Heart/Don't Forget Me When You're On Your Own (p/s) 5
87 PRT BRIART 1 Edge Of A Broken Heart/Don't Forget Me When You're On Your Own (shaped picture disc, some with headband) 15/10
87 PRT BRIARP 1 Edge Of A Broken Heart/La Bamba/ Don't Forget Me When You're On Your Own (shaped picture disc) 8
87 UK UKPT 003 Frankie (12", p/s) 8
89 Shotgun Charlie SCR 1 Gimme All You Got/Stop Me Foolin' Around (with p/s) 8
92 Shotgun Charlie SCR 2 All She Wants/To My Door (p/s) 5
85 Heavy Metal HMRLP 41 TOO YOUNG (LP, with 7" & poster) 12
87 UK UKALP 002 CROWN OF THORNS (LP) 15

BRIDES OF FUNKENSTEIN

78 Atlantic K 50545 FUNK OR WALK (LP) 15
(see also Parliament, Funkadelic)

BOBBY BRIDGER

70 Beacon BEA 149 The World Is Turning On/Why Do I Love You 6
70 Beacon BEA 159 Sugar Shaker/You're In Love 6
(see also Errol Sobers)

DEE DEE BRIDGEWATER

80 Elektra K12 490 Lonely Disco Dancer/One In A Million Guy (12", no p/s) 12

MARC BRIERLEY

68 CBS 3857 Hold On, Hold On, The Garden Sure Looks Good Spread On The Floor/ Autograph Of Time 8
69 CBS 4191 Stay A Little Longer Merry Ann/Flaxen Hair 7
69 CBS 4632 Lady Of The Light/Sunny Weather 7
70 CBS 5266 Be My Brother/If You Took The Bandage Off 6
60s Transatlantic TRAEP 147 MARC BRIERLEY (EP) 50
67 CBS 63478 WELCOME TO THE CITADEL (LP) 80
69 CBS 63835 HELLO (LP) 30

ANNE BRIGGS

63 Topic TOP 94 THE HAZARDS OF LOVE (EP, with leaflet) 160
71 Topic 12TS 207 ANNE BRIGGS (LP) 150
71 CBS 64612 THE TIME HAS COME (LP) 115
(see also A.L. Lloyd)

BILLY BRIGGS

51 Columbia DB 2938 Chew Tobacco Rag (No. 2)/Alarm Clock Boogie (78) 15

DUGGIE BRIGGS

78 It IT 3 Punk Rockin' Granny/I'm A Flasher (p/s) 12
78 It ITEP 5 THE DUGGIE BRIGGS FLASHES ON IT AGAIN (EP) 18

LILLIAN BRIGGS

55 Philips PB 522 I Want You To Be My Baby/Give Me A Band And My Baby (78) 10
60 Coral Q 72408 Not A Soul (Blanket Roll Blues)/Smile For The People 5

BRIGHOUSE & RASTRICK BAND

51 Jamco BR 1401 West Riding/Chit Chat Polka (78) 7
51 Jamco BR 1403 Melody In F/Senator (78) 7

GREG BRIGHT

69 private pressing ROOM BY GREG (LP) 200

LEN BRIGHT COMBO

86 Empire LEN 1 Someone Must've Nailed Us Together/Mona (p/s) 6
(see also Wreckless Eric, Milkshakes)

BRIGHTER

89 Sarah SARAH 019 Around The World In 80 Days (p/s, with inserts) 8

BRIGHTON HORNS

66 Stateside SS 526 Surf Dell'amore/High Midnight 8

BRIGHTWATER

70s Myrrh MYR 1030 A BAND FOR ALL SEASONS (LP) 20

MINT VALUE £

BRILLIANT CORNERS
84 SS20 SS21 She's Got Fever/Black Water (red or pink p/s) . . . 15/30
84 SS20 SS22 Big Hip/Tangled Up In Blue (p/s) . . . 10
88 McQueen MCQLP SOMEBODY UP THERE LIKES ME (LP, with inner) . . . 15

BRIMSTONE
71 Deram DM 322 Keyhole Jake/The Monkey Song . . . 6
71 Decca DF 13222 If Ever You See Me/Work Out . . . 5

LOS BRINCOS
67 Page One POF 023 Lola/Passport (1st 5,000 in p/s) . . . 40/20
67 Page One POF 031 Nobody Wants You Now/Train . . . 15

BRINDLEY BRAE
70s Harmony DB 0002 VILLAGE MUSIC (LP, private pressing with insert) . . . 35
(see also Bev Pegg, Away From The Sand)

BRINSLEY SCHWARZ
70 United Artists UP 35118 Shining Brightly/What Do You Suggest . . . 8
71 Liberty LBY 15419 Country Girl/Funk Angel . . . 10
72 United Artists UP 35312 Country Girl/Funk Angel (reissue) . . . 7
73 United Artists UP 35588 Speedo/I Worry . . . 6
74 United Artists UP 35642 I've Cried My Last Tear/Bringdown . . . 6
74 United Artists UP 35700 (What's So Funny 'Bout) Peace, Love And Understanding/ Ever Since You're Gone . . . 7
75 United Artists UP 35768 Everybody/I Like You, I Don't Love You . . . 6
75 United Artists UP 35812 There's A Cloud In My Heart/I Got The Real Thing . . . 6
70 United Artists UAS 29111 BRINSLEY SCHWARZ (LP, gatefold sleeve) . . . 30
70 Liberty LBG 83427 DESPITE IT ALL (LP, gatefold sleeve) . . . 25
72 United Artists UAS 29217 SILVER PISTOL (LP, some with poster) . . . 20/12
72 United Artists UAS 29374 NERVOUS ON THE ROAD (LP) . . . 18
73 United Artists UAS 29489 PLEASE DON'T EVER CHANGE (LP) . . . 22
74 United Artists UAS 29641 THE NEW FAVOURITES OF BRINSLEY SCHWARZ (LP) . . . 12
(see also Kippington Lodge, Hitters, Knees, Limelight, Nick Lowe, Ernie Graham, Rumour, Chilli Willi & Red Hot Peppers, Ducks Deluxe)

BRITISH ELECTRIC FOUNDATION
(see under B.E.F.)

BRITISH SEA POWER
01 Golden Chariot BSP 01 Fear Of Drowning/A Wooden Horse (CD, 500 only) . . . 30
01 Rough Trade RTRADE S032 Remember Me/A Lovely Day Tomorrow (p/s, 500 only) . . . 10
01 Rough Trade RTRADE SCD 048 The Lonely/Spirit Of St. Louis (CD) . . . 10
02 Rough Trade RTRADES 069 Childhood Memories/Favours In The Beetroot Fields (p/s, 1000 only) . . . 8
03 Rough Trade RTRADE S092 Carrion/Apologies To Insect Life (handdrawn, textured sleeve, 1264 only) . . . 12
03 Rough Trade RTRADES 125 Remember Me/The Scottish Wildlife Experience (handdrawn sleeve) . . . 10

BRITISH LIONS
78 Vertigo 6059 192 One More Chance To Run/Booster (p/s) . . . 5
78 Vertigo 6059 201 International Heroes/Eat The Rich . . . 5
78 Vertigo 9102 019 BRITISH LIONS (LP, with inner sleeve) . . . 12
(see also Mott The Hoople, Medicine Head)

BRITISH WALKERS
65 Pye International 7N 25298 I Found You/Diddley Daddy . . . 40

BRITT
66 Piccadilly 7N 35273 You Really Have Started Something/Leave My Baby Alone . . . 18
(see also Britt Ekland)

ELTON BRITT
54 HMV HMV JO 401 That's How The Yodel Was Born/My Heart Was Made For You (78, export issue) . . . 8

MAY BRITT
59 Top Rank JAR 230 Falling In Love Again/Lola-Lola . . . 8

TINA BRITT
65 London HLC 9974 The Real Thing/Teardrops Fell . . . 35

BUDDY BRITTEN & REGENTS
62 Piccadilly 7N 35075 My Pride, My Joy/Long Gone Baby . . . 15
62 Decca F 11435 Don't Spread It Around/The Beat Of My Heart . . . 12
63 Oriole CB 1827 If You Gotta Make A Fool Of Somebody/Money . . . 18
63 Oriole CB 1839 Hey There/I'll Cry No More . . . 15
63 Oriole CB 1859 My Resistance Is Low/When I See You Smile . . . 15
63 Oriole CB 1889 Money/Sorrow Tomorrow . . . 18
64 Oriole CB 1911 I Guess I'm In The Way/Zip-A-Dee-Doo-Dah . . . 18
65 Piccadilly 7N 35241 She's About A Mover/Since You've Gone . . . 15
65 Piccadilly 7N 35257 Right Now/Jailer Bring Me Water . . . 5
(see also Regents)

BOBBIE BRITTON (& KEYNOTES)
54 Decca F 10288 Wanted/Lost (as Bobbie Britton & Keynotes) . . . 7
55 Decca F 10563 Learnin' The Blues/Strange Lady In Town (with Ted Heath Music) . . . 7
56 Decca F 10777 Autumn Concerto/The Fool Of The Year (with Ted Heath Music) . . . 7
(see also Ted Heath, Keynotes, Steve Stannard, Neville Taylor)

CHRIS BRITTON
69 Page One POLS 022 AS I AM (LP) . . . 200
(see also Troggs)

BROADCAST

Year	Label/Cat. No.	Title	Value
96	Wurlitzer Jukebox WJ 6	Accidentals/We've Got Time (p/s, some with sticker)	10/8
96	Duophonic DS 45-14	Living Room/Phantom (wraparound p/s, 1,500 only)	12
96	Duophonic DS 45-16	THE BOOK LOVERS EP (12", p/s, 2,000)	8
96	Duophonic DS 45-CD 16	THE BOOK LOVERS EP (CD, 2,500 only)	8
96	Warp	WORK AND NON-WORK (LP, promo-only, die-cut sleeve)	12

BROADSIDE

Year	Label/Cat. No.	Title	Value
71	Lincolnshire Ass. LA 4	THE GIPSY'S WEDDING DAY (10" LP)	55
73	Topic 12TS 228	THE MOON SHONE BRIGHT (As The Broadside From Grimsby) (LP, blue label)	30
75	Guildhall GHS 5	SONGS FROM THE STOCKS (LP)	80
75	Guildhall GHS 12	DRIVE THE DARK AWAY (LP)	55

DAVE BROCK

Year	Label/Cat. No.	Title	Value
83	Flicknife FLS 024	Social Alliance/Raping Robots In The Street (p/s)	5
83	Flicknife FLS 024P	Social Alliance/Raping Robots In The Street (picture disc)	8
84	Flicknife SHARP 018	EARTHED TO THE GROUND (LP)	12
88	Flicknife SHARP 042	AGENT OF CHAOS (LP)	12

(see also Dr. Technical & Machines, Hawkwind)

NORAH BROCKSTEDT

Year	Label/Cat. No.	Title	Value
60	Top Rank JAR 353	Big Boy/Tell Me No Lies	12

BROKEN BONES

Year	Label/Cat. No.	Title	Value
85	Fall Out FALL 020	Decapitated/Problem/Liquidated Brains (p/s)	5
85	Fall Out FALL 034P	Seeing Through My Eyes/The Point Of Agony/It's Like (picture disc)	5
85	Fall Out FALL 10034	Seeing Through My Eyes/The Point Of Agony/It's Like/Decapitated/Part 2/ Death Is Imminent (10", p/s)	7

BROKEN GLASS

Year	Label/Cat. No.	Title	Value
75	Capitol E-ST 11510	BROKEN GLASS (LP)	12

JOHN BROMLEY

Year	Label/Cat. No.	Title	Value
68	Polydor 56224	What A Woman Does/My My	10
68	Polydor 56287	And The Feeling Goes/Sweet Little Princess	10
69	Polydor 56305	Melody Fayre/Sugar Love	30
69	Polydor 56340	Hold Me Woman/Weather Man	10
69	Atlantic 584 289	Kick A Tin Can/Wonderland Avenue U.S.A.	10
69	Polydor 583 048	SING (LP)	25

(see also Fleur De Lys, Three People)

BRONCO

Year	Label/Cat. No.	Title	Value
70	Island ILPS 9124	COUNTRY HOME (LP, gatefold sleeve, pink or 'pink rim palm tree' label)	45/15
71	Island ILPS 9161	ACE OF SUNLIGHT (LP, gatefold sleeve, 'pink rim palm tree' label)	18
73	Polydor 2383 215	SMOKIN' MIXTURE (LP)	15

(see also Alan Bown Set)

BRONX CHEER

Year	Label/Cat. No.	Title	Value
70	Parlophone R 5865	Drive My Car/Foxtrot	8
71	Dawn DNX 2512	Barrelhouse Player/Surprising Find/Whether Or Not/Party For One (p/s)	8
72	Dawn DNS 1019	Hold On To Me/Late Date	6
72	Dawn DNLS 3004	GREATEST HITS VOLUME 3 (LP, gatefold sleeve)	15

BRONZ

Year	Label/Cat. No.	Title	Value
84	Bronze BRO 178	Send Down An Angel/Tiger (p/s)	5
84	Bronze BROX 178	Send Down An Angel/Tiger/Stranded (12", p/s)	8
80s	Lyntone LYN 14383	Taken By Storm (flexidisc)	5

MICHAEL BROOK

Year	Label/Cat. No.	Title	Value
92	4AD TAD 2011	LIVE AT THE AQUARIUM (CD, digipak)	18

PATTI BROOK (& DIAMONDS)

Year	Label/Cat. No.	Title	Value
60	Pye 7N 15300	Since You've Been Gone/That's The Way It's Gonna Be (as Patti Brook & Diamonds)	10
61	Pye 7N 15339	When The Red Red Robin/Look What You've Done To Me	5
62	Pye 7N 15422	I Love You, I Need You/Unloved, Unwanted	10

TONY BROOK & BREAKERS

Year	Label/Cat. No.	Title	Value
64	Columbia DB 7279	Meanie Genie/Ooh Poo Pah Doo (some in p/s)	140/105
65	Columbia DB 7444	Love Dances On/I Won't Hurt You	18

BROOK BROTHERS

Year	Label/Cat. No.	Title	Value
60	Top Rank JAR 349	Green Fields/How Will It End?	6
60	Top Rank JAR 409	Please Help Me, I'm Falling/When Will I Be Loved	8
60	Pye 7N 15298	Say The Word/Everything But Love	5
61	Pye 7N 15333	Warpaint/Sometimes	10
61	Pye 7N 15352	Little Bitty Heart/Tell Her	5
61	Pye 7N 15369	Ain't Gonna Wash For A Week/One Last Kiss	10
61	Pye 7N 15387	Married/I Love Girls	10
62	Pye 7N 15409	He's Old Enough To Know Better/Win Or Lose	10
62	Pye 7N 15415	Too Scared/Tell Tale	10
62	Pye 7N 15441	Just Another Fool/Double Trouble	12
62	Pye 7N 15453	Welcome Home Baby/So Long	10
62	Pye 7N 15463	I Can't Make Up My Mind/Town Girl	10
63	Pye 7N 15498	Trouble Is My Middle Name/Let The Good Times Roll	10
63	Pye 7N 15527	I'm Not Jimmy/Side By Side (with RBQ)	5
63	Pye 7N 15570	Crosswords/Whistle To The Wind	5
61	Pye NEP 24140	BROOK BROTHERS HIT PARADE (EP)	30
61	Pye NEP 24148	BROOK BROTHERS HIT PARADE VOLUME 2 (EP)	30
62	Pye NEP 24155	BROOK BROTHERS (EP)	25
61	Pye NPL 18067	BROOK BROTHERS (LP)	55

(see also Brooks)

MINT VALUE £

BROOKLYN

80	Rondelet ROUND 3	I Wanna Be A Detective (p/s)	30
81	Rondelet ROUND 6	Hollywood/Late Again (p/s)	15
80	Rondelet ABOUT 3	YOU NEVER KNOW WHAT YOU'LL FIND (LP)	30

BROOKLYN BRIDGE

68	Pye International 7N 25473	From My Window I Can See/Little Red Boat By The River	7
69	Buddah 201 029	The Worst That Could Happen/Your Kite, My Kite	8
70	Buddah 2011 010	Free As The Wind/He's Not A Happy Man	6
70	Buddah 2011 034	Down By The River/Look Again	6

(see also Johnny Maestro)

BROOKS

64	Decca F 11868	Once In A While/Poor Poor Plan	10

(see also Brook Brothers)

BABA BROOKS

63	Island WI 078	5 O'Clock Whistle/African Blood (by Blues Masters)	50
63	Island WI 096	Bank To Bank (Parts 1 & 2)	50
63	Island WI 127	Three Blind Mice/BILLY & BOBBY: We Ain't Got Nothing	40
63	R&B JB 125	Water Melon Man/STRANGER COLE: Things Come To Those Who Wait	40
64	Black Swan WI 137	Portrait Of My Love/STRANGER COLE: Goodbye Peggy	30
64	Black Swan WI 412	Jelly Beans/ERIC MORRIS: Sampson	30
64	Black Swan WI 414	Key To The City/ERIC MORRIS: Solomon Grundie	40
64	Black Swan WI 434	Spider/Melody Jamboree	30
64	Black Swan WI 438	Cork Foot/HERSANG COMBO: B.B.C. Channel 2	30
65	Black Swan WI 442	Musical Workshop/DUKE WHITE: Be Wise	30
65	Black Swan WI 444	Bus Strike/DUKE WHITE: Sow Good Seeds	30
65	Black Swan WI 451	Ethiopia/ARCHIBALD TROTT: Promised Land	30
65	Black Swan WI 466	Baby Elephant Walk/DON DRUMMOND: Don's Special	30
65	Ska Beat JB 220	One Eyed Giant (with His Band)/DYNAMITES: Walk Out On Me	30
65	Island WI 229	Guns Fever/DOTTY & BONNIE: Don't Do It	50
65	Island WI 233	Independent Ska/STRANGER & CLAUDETTE: Seven Days	30
65	Island WI 235	Duck Soup/ZODIACS: Renegade	30
65	Island WI 239	Vitamin A/ALTON ELLIS: Dance Crasher	30
65	Island WI 241	Teenage Ska/ALTON ELLIS: You Are Not To Blame	40
65	Rio R 061	Shenk I Sheck (& Band)/SHENLEY & HIACYNTH: Set Me Free	40
66	Doctor Bird DB 1042	The Clock (& Band)/LYN TAITT & COMETS & SILVERTONES: Raindrops	40
66	Doctor Bird DB 1046	Jam Session (with His Band)/CONQUERORS: What A Agony	40
67	Ska Beat JB 268	One Eyed Giant (with His Band)/DYNAMITES: Walk Out On Me (reissue)	30

(see also Blues Masters, Eric Brooks, Stranger & Patsy, Riots, Joey Smith, Saints, Richard Brothers, Derrick Morgan, Lord Tanamo, Lord Brisco, Hippy Boys, Roy Panton, Higgs & Wilson, Vinley Gayle, Joe White, Stranger & Patsy)

CHUCK BROOKS

69	Soul City SC 116	Black Sheep/I've Got To Get Myself Together	20

D. BROOKS

70	Big BG 304	Oh Me Oh My (actually "Every Time" by Hi-Tals)/ANSEL COLLINS: Staccato (actually "Every Time Version" by Rupie Edwards Allstars)	12

DALE BROOKS

65	King KG 1025	Army Green/Reminds Me Of You	10
66	Stateside SS 553	I Wanna Be Your Girl/Like Other Girls Do	30

DONNIE BROOKS

60	London HLN 9168	Mission Bell/Do It For Me	12
60	London HLN 9168	Mission Bell/Do It For Me (78)	80
60	London HLN 9253	Doll House/Round Robin	12
61	London HLN 9361	That's Why/Memphis	10
62	London HLN 9572	Oh, You Beautiful Doll/Just A Bystander	10
61	London HA-N 2391	THE HAPPIEST DONNIE BROOKS (LP)	60

ELKIE BROOKS

64	Decca F 11928	Something's Got A Hold On Me/Hello Stranger	18
64	Decca F 11983	Nothing Left To Do But Cry/Strange Though It Seems	22
65	Decca F 12061	The Way You Do The Things You Do/Blue Tonight	20
65	HMV POP 1431	He's Gotta Love Me/When You Appear	22
65	HMV POP 1480	All My Life/Can't Stop Thinking Of You	12
66	HMV POP 1512	Baby Let Me Love You/Stop The Music	12
69	NEMS 56-4136	Come September/If You Should Go	5
74	Island WIP 6187	Rescue Me/Sweet Nuthin's	5
74	Chrysalis CHS 2069	Sacrifice/ALICE COOPER: I'm Flash (p/s, unissued, promo only)	35

(see also Dada, Vinegar Joe, Steve York's Camelo Pardalis, Elki & Owen)

HADDA BROOKS

50	London L 684	I Hadn't Anyone 'Till You/Hadda's Boogie (78)	10

NORMAN BROOKS & G-BOYS

54	London L 1166	Hello Sunshine/You're My Baby	30
54	London L 1202	Somebody Wonderful/You Shouldn't Have Kissed Me The First Time	30
54	London L 1228	A Sky-Blue Shirt And A Rainbow Tie/This Waltz With You	35
54	London HL 8015	I'm Kinda Crazy/I'd Like To Be In Your Shoes, Baby	35
54	London HL 8041	I Can't Give You Anything But Love (solo)/GO-BOYS: Johnny's Tune	35
54	London HL 8041	I Can't Give You Anything But Love (solo)/GO-BOYS: Johnny's Tune (78)	8
54	London HL 8051	Candy Moon/My 3-D Sweetie	35
55	London HL 8115	Back In Circulation/Lou Lou Louisiana	35
54	London RE-P 1004	PRESENTING NORMAN BROOKS VOLUME 1 (EP)	40
55	London RE-P 1021	BABY MINE (EP)	40

PAM BROOKS

70	Big BG 307	Oh Me Oh My/ANSELL COLLINS: Staccato	18

BROOKS & JERRY

68	Direction 58-3267	I Got What It Takes Parts 1 & 2	10

BIG BILL BROONZY/CHICAGO BILL

51	Vogue V 2068	Back Water Blues/Lonesome Road Blues (78)	15
51	Vogue V 2073	In The Evenin'/Low Land Blues (78)	15
51	Vogue V 2074	John Henry/Blues In 1890 (78)	15
51	Vogue V 2075	Big Bill Blues/Hey Hey Baby (78)	15
51	Vogue V 2076	House Rent Stomp/The Moppin' Blues (78)	15
51	Vogue V 2077	Black, Brown And White/Feelin' Low Down (78)	15
52	Vogue V 2078	Make My Getaway/What I Used To Do (78)	15
52	Melodisc 1191	Keep Your Hands Off Her/Stump Blues (78, as Chicago Bill)	15
52	Melodisc 1203	Five Foot Seven/Plough Hand Blues (78, as Chicago Bill)	15
50s	private pressing	Keep Your Hand On Your Heart/T For Texas (78)	25
56	Pye Jazz NJ 2012	When Do I Get To Be Called A Man/Mindin' My Own Business (78)	15
57	Pye Jazz NJ 2016	Southbound Train/It Feels So Good (78)	15
58	Vogue V 2351	Guitar Shuffle/When Did You Leave Heaven	20
61	Storyville A 44053	Midnight Special/Black Brown And White	10
55	Vogue EPV 1024	HEY BUD BLUES (EP)	18
56	Vogue EPV 1074	SINGS THE BLUES (EP)	20
56	Vogue EPV 1107	GUITAR SHUFFLE (EP)	20
56	Pye Jazz NJE 1005	MISSISSIPPI BLUES VOLUME 1 (EP)	12
56	Pye Jazz NJE 1015	MISSISSIPPI BLUES VOLUME 2 (EP)	12
56	Melodisc EPM7 65	KEEP YOUR HANDS OFF (EP)	12
57	Pye Jazz NJE 1047	SOUTHERN SAGA (EP)	12
57	Columbia SEG 7674	BIG BILL BROONZY SINGS THE BLUES (EP)	18
57	Tempo EXA 61	BILL BAILEY WON'T YOU PLEASE COME HOME (EP)	12
58	Columbia SEG 7790	BIG BILL BROONZY SINGS THE BLUES NO. 2 (EP)	18
60	Mercury ZEP 10065	WALKIN' DOWN A LONESOME ROAD (EP)	12
60	Mercury ZEP 10093	HOLLERIN' BLUES (EP)	25
62	Storyville SEP 383	BLUES ANTHOLOGY VOLUME 3 (EP)	12
64	Mercury 10003 MCE	BLUES-GOSPEL-SPIRITUAL (EP)	15
57	Vogue LAE 12009	BIG BILL BLUES (LP)	35
57	Philips BBL 7113	BIG BILL BROONZY (LP)	40
58	Vogue LAE 12063	THE BLUES (LP)	35
58	Pye Nixa Jazz NJL 16	TRIBUTE TO BIG BILL (LP)	30
59	Tempo TAP 23	AN EVENING WITH BIG BILL BROONZY (LP)	35
61	HMV CLP 1544	LAST SESSION PART 1 (LP)	20
62	HMV CLP 1551	LAST SESSION PART 2 (LP)	20
62	HMV CLP 1562	LAST SESSION PART 3 (LP)	20
65	Storyville SLP 143	AN EVENING WITH BROONZY (LP)	15
65	Fontana 688 206ZL	TROUBLE IN MIND (LP)	22
66	Mercury 20044 MCL	REMEMBERING BROONZY — THE GREATEST MINSTREL OF THE AUTHENTIC BLUES (LP)	15
66	Storyville SLP 188	BLUES IN EUROPE (LP)	15
67	Storyville 670 154	PORTRAITS IN BLUES VOLUME 2 (LP)	20
69	CBS Realm 52648	BIG BILL'S BLUES (LP)	12
69	Xtra XTRA 1093	SINGS COUNTRY BLUES (LP)	12
78	Spotlite SPJ 900	TROUBLE IN MIND (LP, reissue)	12

(see also Chicago Bill)

BIG BILL BROONZY & PETE SEEGER

64	Xtra XTRA 1006	IN CONCERT (LP)	25
66	Verve Folkways VLP 5006	IN CONCERT (LP, reissue, also stereo SVLP 506)	12/15

(see also Pete Seeger)

BIG BILL BROONZY/SONNY BOY WILLIAMSON [I]

65	RCA Victor RD 7685	BIG BILL AND SONNY BOY (LP)	60

(see also Sonny Boy Williamson [I])

BIG BILL BROONZY, SONNY TERRY & BROWNIE McGHEE

64	Xtra XTRA 1004	BIG BILL BROONZY/SONNY TERRY/BROWNIE McGHEE (LP)	30

(see also Sonny Terry & Brownie McGhee, Washboard Sam)

BROTH

71	Mercury 6338 032	BROTH (LP)	25

BROTHER BARON

70s	Fab FAB 281	Your Love/Your Love Version	6

BROTHER BUNG

68	Avenue BEV 1054	BLUES CRUSADE (EP)	25

(see also Bob Pearce, Fresh)

BROTHER DAN ALLSTARS

68	Trojan TR 601	Donkey Returns/Tribute To Sir K.B.	15
68	Trojan TR 602	Eastern Organ/JIVERS: Our Love Will Last	15
68	Trojan TR 603	Hold Pon Them/OWEN GRAY: Answer Me	15
68	Trojan TR 607	Read Up/Gallop	12
68	Trojan TR 608	Another Saturday Night/Bee's Knees	12
68	Trojan TBL 101	LET'S CATCH THE BEAT (LP)	50
69	Trojan TRL 1	FOLLOW THAT DONKEY (LP)	30

(see also Audrey, Pooch Jackson)

BROTHER D & THE COLLECTIVE EFFORT

80	Island IPR 2005	How We Gonna Make The Black Nation Rise (12")	10

BROTHERHOOD

69	Philips BF 1766	Paper Man/Give It To Me Now	6

BROTHERHOOD OF BREATH

74	Ogun OG 100	LIVE AT WILLISAU (LP, with Chris McGregor)	18

(see also Chris McGregor's Brotherhood Of Breath, Mark Charig)

MINT VALUE £

BROTHERHOOD OF MAN

69 Deram DM 276 Love One Another/A Little Bit Of Heaven . . . 6
70 Deram DM 317 This Boy/You Can Depend On Me . . . 5
71 Deram DM 327 Reach Out Your Hand/Better Tomorrow . . . 8
71 Deram DM 335 You And I/Sing In The Sunshine . . . 5
71 Deram DM 341 California Sunday Morning/Do Your Thing . . . 5
72 Deram DM 361 Say A Prayer/Follow Me . . . 5
72 Deram DM 366 Rock Me Baby/Hang On . . . 5
73 Deram DM 385 Happy Ever After/We Can Make It . . . 5
74 Dawn DNS 1055 When Love Catches Up With You/How Can You Love (p/s) . . . 6
76 Pye 7N 45569 Save Your Kisses For Me/Let's Love Together (p/s) . . . 5
70 Deram SML 1066 UNITED WE STAND (LP) . . . 25
72 Deram SML 1089 BROTHERHOOD OF MAN (LP) . . . 15
75 Dawn DNLS 3063 GOOD THINGS HAPPENING (LP) . . . 12
(see also Sue & Sunny, Sue & Sunshine, Stockingtops)

BROTHERLY LOVE

67 CBS 2978 Ocean Of Tears/Mister Average Man . . . 6
73 CBS 1403 I Love Everything About You/Tip Of My Tongue . . . 6
(see also Car[r]ols)

BROTHERS

67 London HLU 10158 Love Story/The Girl's Alright . . . 7

BROTHERS

75 People PEO 118 In The Pocket/Everybody Loves A Winner . . . 5
75 People PLEO 25 DISCO SOUL (LP) . . . 15

BROTHERS & SISTERS (U.K.)

68 private pressing ARE WATCHING YOU (LP) . . . 130

BROTHERS & SISTERS (U.S.)

69 CBS 4583 Mighty Quinn/Chimes Of Freedom . . . 5
69 CBS 63746 DYLAN'S GOSPEL (LP) . . . 12

BROTHERS FOUR

60 Philips PB 1009 Greenfields/East Virginia . . . 7
60 Philips PB 1072 Beautiful Brown Eyes/The Green Leaves Of Summer . . . 6
64 CBS BPG 62282 SIGNS OF OUR TIMES (LP) . . . 15
66 CBS BPG 62313 GREATEST HITS (LP) . . . 12

BROTHERS GRIMM

65 Decca F 12224 Lost Love/Make It Or Break It . . . 8
66 Ember EMB 222 A Man Needs Love/Looky Looky . . . 65
(see also Barry & Tony)

BROTHERS KANE

66 Decca F 12448 Walking In The Sand/Won't You Stay Long . . . 18
(see also Sarstedt Brothers, Peter Lincoln, Peter Sarstedt, Clive Sands, Wes Sands, Eden Kane)

BROTHERS TWO

68 Action ACT 4513 Here I Am, In Love Again/I'm Tired Of You Baby . . . 20

BROTHERS WILLIAM

65 Parlophone R 5293 Linda Jane Blues/Honey Love . . . 6

AYSHEA BROUGH

71 RCA RCA 2105 Master Jack/Both Sides Now . . . 5
(see also Ayshea)

PETER BROUGH & ARCHIE ANDREWS

53 HMV BD 1306 The Little Fir Tree/I Saw Mommy Kissing Santa Claus (78, picture label) . . . 12

EDGAR BROUGHTON BAND

69 Harvest HAR 5001 Evil/Death Of An Electric Citizen . . . 10
70 Harvest HAR 5015 Out Demons Out/Momma's Reward . . . 7
70 Harvest HAR 5021 Up Yours!/Officer Dan . . . 8
70 Harvest HAR 5032 Apache Drop Out/Freedom . . . 7
71 Harvest HAR 5040 Hotel Room/Call Me A Liar . . . 8
72 Harvest HAR 5049 Gone Blue/Someone/Mr. Crosby . . . 8
69 Harvest SHVL 757 WASA WASA (LP, gatefold sleeve) . . . 30
70 Harvest SHVL 772 SING BROTHER SING (LP, gatefold sleeve, with lyric insert) . . . 30
71 Harvest SHVL 791 THE EDGAR BROUGHTON BAND (LP, gatefold sleeve) . . . 25
72 Harvest SHTC 252 IN SIDE OUT (LP, gatefold sleeve with lyric sheet) . . . 25
73 Harvest SHVL 810 OORA (LP, wraparound card sleeve in clear artwork plastic bag) . . . 20

AL BROWN (Jamaica)

71 Banana BA 360 No Soul Today/RUFFIANS: Where Did I Go Wrong (B-side actually "Bang Shang Alang" by Peter Austin & Hortense Ellis) . . . 20
71 Fab FAB 186 Ain't Got No Soul/TEARDROPS: I Got A Feeling . . . 15

AL BROWN'S TUNETOPPERS (U.S.)

60 Top Rank JAR 374 The Madison/Mo' Madison . . . 6

(CRAZY WORLD OF) ARTHUR BROWN

65 Lyntone LYN 770/1 You Don't Know (as Arthur Brown & Diamonds)/DIAMONDS: You'll Be Mine (Reading University Rag Week flexidisc) . . . 60
67 Track 604 008 Devil's Grip/Give Him A Flower . . . 12
68 Track 604 022 Fire!/Rest Cure (push-out or large centre) . . . 6/5
68 Track 604 026 Nightmare/What's Happening (some copies list "Music Man" as B-side) . . . 6
74 Gull GULS 4 Gypsies/Dance . . . 5
75 Gull GULS 13 We Gotta Get Out Of This Place/Here I Am . . . 5
77 Gull SIXPACK 4 SIX-PACK/SIX TRACK (EP, picture disc, die-cut sleeve with stand, 5,000 only) . . . 6

MINT VALUE £

68	Track 612 005/613 005	THE CRAZY WORLD OF ARTHUR BROWN (LP, mono/stereo)	40/30
74	Gull GULP 1008	DANCE (LP, with insert)	12
77	Gull GUD 2003/4	THE LOST EARS (2-LP, gatefold sleeve, as Arthur Brown's Kingdom Come)	25
78	Gull GULP 1023	CHISHOLM IN MY BOSOM (LP)	12

(see also Kingdom Come, Nick Greenwood, Atomic Rooster, Crane/Farlowe)

BEN BROWN

67	Polydor 56198	Ask The Lonely/Sidewinder	35

BOOTS BROWN & HIS BLOCKBUSTERS

58	RCA RCA 1078	Cerveza/Juicy	10
59	RCA RCA 1102	Jim Twangy/Trollin'	10
59	RCA RCA 1102	Jim Twangy/Trollin' (78)	10

(see also Shorty Rogers)

BUNNY BROWN

72	Songbird SB 1073	Fat Boy/Fat Boy — Version	15

(see also Noel Brown, Winston Scotland)

BUSTER BROWN

60	Melodisc 1559	Fannie Mae/Lost In A Dream	65
65	Sue WI 368	Fannie Mae/Lost In A Dream (reissue)	20
67	Island WI 3031	My Blue Heaven/Two Women	20
69	Blue Horizon 57-3147	Sugar Babe/I'm Going, But I'll Be Back	15
60s	XX MIN 713	B. AND BUSTER BROWN (EP, with B. Brown)	20

BUSTY BROWN

68	Doctor Bird DB 1158	Here Comes The Night/Don't Look Back	30
69	Upsetter US 304	What A Price/How Can I Forget?	12
69	Upsetter US 308	To Love Somebody/BLEECHERS: Farmer's In The Den	12
69	Punch PH 10	Broken Heart/Tribute To A King	12
70	Punch PH 38	Greatest Love/I Love You Madly	12
70	Escort ES 822	Fight For Your Right/MEDITATORS: Soul Fight (Busty Top A Pop) (B-side actually "Soul Fight" by Busty Brown)	18
70	Escort ES 845	Man Short (with Gaytones)/DAVE BARKER: She Want It	15
70	Gas GAS 154	I Love You Madly/Greatest Love	12
70	High Note HS 048	Man Short (with Gaytones)/GAYTONES: Another Version	15
71	Punch PH 72	You Inspire Me/UPSETTERS: Version	6
71	Pama Supreme PS 356	Throw Away Your Gun/TWINKLE BROTHERS: Sad Song	18

(see also Llans Thelwell, John Holt, David Isaacs)

CHARLES BROWN (BAND)

56	Vogue V 9061	I'll Always Be In Love With You/Soothe Me	600
56	Vogue V 9061	I'll Always Be In Love With You/Soothe Me (78)	150
57	Vogue V 9065	Confidential/Trouble Blues	600
57	Vogue V 9065	Confidential/Trouble Blues (78)	150
61	Parlophone R 4848	It's Christmas All Year Round/Christmas Question	45

(see also Brown Brothers)

CLARENCE 'GATEMOUTH' BROWN

65	Vocalion VE 170161	CLARENCE 'GATEMOUTH' BROWN (EP)	80
72	Python PLP 26	CLARENCE 'GATEMOUTH' BROWN VOL. 1: 1948-1953 (LP)	25
72	Python PLP 27	CLARENCE 'GATEMOUTH' BROWN VOL. 2: 1956-1965 (LP)	25

CLIFFORD BROWN (& HIS GROUP)

56	Emarcy ERE 1501	SWEET CLIFFORD (EP, as Clifford Brown & His Group)	10
58	Emarcy ERE 1565	STUDY IN BROWN VOL. 1 (EP, as Clifford Brown & His Group)	8
58	Emarcy ERE 1566	STUDY IN BROWN VOL. 2 (EP, as Clifford Brown & His Group)	8
58	Emarcy ERE 1572	CLIFFORD BROWN AND MAX ROACH (EP)	8
54	Esquire EP 3	CLIFFORD BROWN & ART FARMER WITH THE SWEDISH ALLSTARS (EP)	8
54	Esquire EP 4	AND ART FARMER WITH THE SWEDISH ALLSTARS VOL. 2 (EP)	8
55	Esquire EP 71	CLIFFORD BROWN WITH TADD DAMERON'S BAND (EP)	8
55	Vogue EPV 1027	GIGI GRYCE — CLIFFORD BROWN ORCHESTRA (EP)	8
55	Vogue EPV 1041	CONCEPTION (EP)	8
56	Vogue EPV 1119	CLIFFORD BROWN ENSEMBLE (EP)	8
54	Vogue LDE 042	CLIFFORD "BROWNIE" BROWN QUARTET (10" LP)	25
55	Vogue LDE 121	THE CLIFFORD BROWN SEXTET (10" LP)	25
58	Emarcy EJL 1278	STUDY IN BROWN (LP)	20

(see also Art Farmer, Sonny Rollins, Max Roach)

DENNIS BROWN

70	Bamboo BAM 56	Love Grows/SOUND DIMENSION: Less Problem	30
70	Banana BA 309	No Man Is An Island/SOUL SISTERS: Another Night	30
71	Banana BA 336	Never Fall In Love/Make It With You	30
71	Ocean OC 001	Little Green Apples/SOUND DIMENSION: Version	10
72	Duke DU 139	What About The Half/What About The Half Version	15
72	Explosion EX 2068	Black Magic Woman/PHILL PRATT ALL STARS: Black Magic Woman Pt 2	15
72	Pressure Beat PR 5513	Money In My Pocket/JOE GIBBS ALLSTARS: Money Love	20
72	Randy's RAN 526	Cheater/TOMMY McCOOK & IMPACT ALLSTARS: Harvest In The East	10
72	Randy's RAN 528	Meet Me On The Corner (actually unknown instrumental)/ IMPACT ALLSTARS: Version	18
72	Songbird SB 1074	Silhouettes/CRYSTALITES: Version	8
73	Ashanti ASH 402	It's Too Late/Song My Mother Used To Sing	10
73	Jackpot JP 813	He Can't Spell/CRYSTALITES: Acid Version	10
73	Smash SMA 2327	Concentration/Version	7
73	Trojan TRLS 57	SUPER REGGAE & SOUL HITS (LP)	22
75	Trojan TRLS 107	JUST DENNIS (LP)	15

(see also Big Youth & Dennis Brown, Hugh Roy, Big Youth, Sound Dimension)

DUSTY BROWN

61	Starlite ST45 058	Please Don't Go/Well You Know	35

MINT VALUE £

ED BROWN

64 London HA 8149 THE JOHN FITZGERALD KENNEDY MEMORIAL ALBUM (LP, unissued)

ERROL BROWN & CHOSEN FEW

72 Songbird SB 1082 People Make The World Go Round/People Make The World Go Round (Version) . . 8

FAITH BROWN

70 CBS 4728 Lock Me In/The Game Of Love . . . 5
71 Penny Farthing PEN 766 Any Way That You Want Me/City Wine . . . 5
72 Regal Zonophone RZ 3063 Take Me With You/If We Only Have Love . . . 5
(see also Carrolls)

FAY BROWN

55 Columbia SCM 5185 Unchained Melody/I Was Wrong . . . 15

FRIDAY BROWN(E)

66 Parlophone R 5396 Getting Nowhere/And (To Me He Meant Everything) (as Friday Browne) . . . 10
66 Fontana TF 736 32nd Love Affair/Born A Woman . . . 40
67 Fontana TF 851 Ask Any Woman/Outdoor Seminar . . . 8
69 Fontana TF 996 Stand By Your Man/I Want To Rain . . . 6
72 Philips 6006 239 Shake A Hand/Everything's Alright . . . 5
73 Philips 6006 324 Groovy Kind Of Love/Salford . . . 5
71 Philips 6308 074 FRIDAY BROWN (LP) . . . 20
(see also Marianne & Mike, High Society, Manchester Mob, Graham Gouldman)

FUNKY BROWN

72 Sioux SI 018 African (Indian Reservation)/JUMBO STERLING: Elizabethan Reggae . . . 6

GABRIEL BROWN

77 Policy Wheel PW 4592 GABRIEL BROWN AND HIS GUITAR (LP, withdrawn) . . . 15

GEORGIA BROWN

55 Decca F 10489 My Crazy L'il Mixed Up Heart/Before We Know It . . . 8
55 Decca F 10551 I Love To Dance With You/That's All I Need . . . 8
55 Decca F 10616 I Went To The Village/Wrong Again . . . 8
63 Decca SKL 4586 SINGS GERSHWIN (LP) . . . 15

GERRY BROWN'S JAZZMEN

61 Fontana TFL 5165 IT'S TRAD TIME! (LP) . . . 20

GLEN BROWN

68 Blue Cat BS 131 Way Of Life (with Joe White & Trevor)/
KARL BRYAN & LYN TAITT: I'm So Proud . . . 40
70 Summit SUM 8502 Collie And Wine/BEVERLEY'S ALLSTARS: Version . . . 10
70 Songbird SB 1021 Love I/CRYSTALITES: Heavy Load . . . 12
72 Songbird SB 1081 Smokey Eyes (with Crystalites)/Smokey Eyes (Version) . . . 20
73 Downtown DT 507 Two Wedding Skank/BARRY SIMPSON: Sugar Down Deh . . . 15

GLENMORE BROWN & HOPETON LEWIS

68 Fab FAB 42 Girl You're Cold/Soul Man . . . 20
(see also Hopeton Lewis & Glenmore Brown)

HENRY BROWN

50s Jazz Collector L 15 Henry Brown Blues/Twenty-First Street Blues (78, reissue) . . . 5
50s Jazz Collector L 31 Blues Stomp/Blind Boy Blues (78) . . . 8
50 Jazz Collector L 55 It Hurts So Good (with Ike Rodgers)/Screenin' The Blues (78) . . . 10
50s Jazz Collector L 70 Deep Morgan Blues/Eastern Chimes Blues (78) . . . 8
61 '77' LA 12-5 HENRY BROWN BLUES (LP) . . . 40

HUX BROWN & SCOTTY

71 High Note HS 056 Unbelievable Sounds/GAYTONES: Unbelievable Sounds Version . . . 25

HYLO BROWN (& TIMBERLINERS)

59 Capitol CL 15075 You Can't Relive The Past/Thunder Clouds Of Love . . . 5
60 Capitol CL 15139 I've Waited As Long As I Can/Just Any Old Love . . . 5
63 London HAB/SHB 8094 BLUEGRASS GOES TO COLLEGE (LP) . . . 15

IRVING BROWN

70 Bamboo BAM 36 Today/SOUND DIMENSION: Young Gifted And Black Version . . . 20
70 Bamboo BAM 58 I'm Still Around/Run Come . . . 20
70 Bamboo BAM 61 Let's Make It Up (actually by Larry Marshall)/BURNING SPEAR: Free . . . 25
71 Bamboo Now BN 1003 Now I'm Alone/Funky Night . . . 20
(see also Larry Marshall)

IVOR BROWN

54 London Calypso CAY 101 Chiquita Banana/Re-Incarnation (The Bed Bug) (78) . . . 7
54 London Calypso CAY 108 Wolves Of Today/Little Fly (78) . . . 7
54 London Calypso CAY 109 I'm My Own Grandpa/My Little Boy (78) . . . 7

JACKIE BROWN

72 High Note HS 057 One Night/GAYTONES: One Night Version . . . 10
72 High Note HS 060 Last Dance/GAYTONES: Last Dance Version . . . 10

JAMES BROWN (& FAMOUS FLAMES)

SINGLES

60 Parlophone R 4667 Think/You've Got The Power (with Famous Flames) . . . 40
60 Fontana H 273 This Old Heart/Wonder When You're Coming Home . . . 30
62 Parlophone R 4922 Night Train/Why Does Everything Happen To Me (with Famous Flames) . . . 40
62 Parlophone R 4952 Shout And Shimmy/Come Over Here (with Famous Flames) . . . 40
63 London HL 9730 Prisoner Of Love/Choo-Choo (Locomotion) (with Famous Flames) . . . 20
63 London HL 9775 These Foolish Things/(Can You) Feel It (Part 1) (with Famous Flames) . . . 20
64 Philips BF 1368 Out Of Sight/Maybe The Last Time (& His Orchestra) . . . 18
64 Sue WI 360 Night Train/Why Does Everything Happen To Me (with Famous Flames) . . . 18
65 London HL 9945 Have Mercy Baby/Just Won't Do Right (with Famous Flames) . . . 18
65 London HL 9990 Papa's Got A Brand New Bag Parts 1 & 2 (with Famous Flames) . . . 15

			MINT VALUE £
65	Ember EMB S 216	Tell Me What You're Gonna Do/Lost Someone (some in p/s)	35/18
65	Philips BF 1458	Try Me/Papa's Got A Brand New Bag	10
66	Philips BF 1481	New Breed Parts 1 & 2	10
66	Pye International 7N 25350	I Got You (I Feel Good)/I Can't Help It (I Just Do-Do-Do) (with Famous Flames)	10
66	Pye International 7N 25367	Ain't That A Groove Parts 1 & 2 (with Famous Flames)	10
66	Pye International 7N 25371	It's A Man's Man's Man's World/Is It Yes Or Is It No? (with Famous Flames)	10
66	Pye International 7N 25379	Money Won't Change You Parts 1 & 2 (with Famous Flames)	12
66	Pye International 7N 25394	Don't Be A Drop-Out/Tell Me That You Love Me (with Famous Flames)	10
67	Pye International 7N 25411	Bring It Up/Nobody Knows (with Famous Flames)	10
67	Pye International 7N 25418	Kansas City/Stone Fox (with Famous Flames)	8
67	Pye International 7N 25423	Let Yourself Go/Good Rockin' Tonight (with Famous Flames)	8
67	Pye International 7N 25430	Cold Sweat Parts 1 & 2 (with Famous Flames)	10
67	Pye International 7N 25441	Get It Together Parts 1 & 2 (with Famous Flames)	8
68	Polydor 56740	I Can't Stand Myself/There Was A Time	7
68	Polydor 56743	I Got The Feelin'/If I Ruled The World	7
68	Polydor 56744	Licking Stick, Licking Stick Parts 1 & 2	7
68	Polydor 56752	Say It Loud, I'm Black And I'm Proud Parts 1 & 2	8
68	Polydor 56540	That's Life/Please, Please, Please (with Famous Flames)	15
68	Polydor 56541	Say It Loud, I'm Black And I'm Proud Parts 1 & 2 (reissue)	7
69	Polydor 56776	Mother Popcorn Parts 1 & 2	7
69	Polydor 56780	The World Parts 1 & 2	7
69	Polydor 56783	Let A Man Come In And Do The Popcorn/Sometimes	7
69	Polydor 56787	There Was A Time/I Can't Stand Myself (When You Touch Me)	7
70	Polydor 56793	Ain't It Funky Now Parts 1 & 2	7
70	Polydor 2001 018	It's A New Day/Georgia On My Mind	7
70	Polydor 2001 071	Get Up, I Feel Like Being A Sex Machine Parts 1 & 2 (paper or plastic label)	7/6
70	Polydor 2001 097	Call Me Super Bad Parts 1, 2 & 3	7
71	Polydor 2001 163	Soul Power Parts 1, 2 & 3	7
71	Polydor 2001 190	I Cried/Get Up, Get Into It, Get Involved	7
71	Polydor 2001 213	Hot Pants (She Got To Use What She Got To Get What She Wants) Parts 1, 2 & 3	7
71	Polydor 2001 223	Make It Funky Parts 1 & 2	6
71	Mojo 2093 006	Hey America!/Brother Rapp (Part 1)	8
71	Polydor 2066 153	I'm A Greedy Man Parts 1 & 2	6
72	Polydor 2066 185	King Heroin/Theme From King Heroin	15
72	Polydor 2066 210	There It Is Parts 1 & 2	8
72	Polydor 2066 216	Honky Tonk Parts 1 & 2	6
72	Polydor 2066 231	Get On The Good Foot Parts 1 & 2	6
72	Polydor 2066 283	What My Baby Needs Now Is A Little More Lovin'/ This Guy's In Love With You (with Lyn Collins)	6
73	Polydor 2066 285	I've Got A Bag Of My Own/I Know It's True	6
73	Polydor 2141 008	Papa's Got A Brand New Bag/Out Of Sight/ It's A Man's Man's Man's World (p/s)	8
73	Polydor 2066 296	I Got Ants In My Pants Parts 1, 15 & 16	6
73	Polydor 2066 329	Think/Something	6
73	Polydor 2066 370	Woman Parts 1 & 2	6
74	Polydor 2066 411	Stone To The Bone/Sexy, Sexy, Sexy	6
74	Polydor 2066 485	My Thang/The Payback	6
74	Polydor 2066 513	It's Hell/Papa Don't Take No Mess	6
75	Polydor 2066 520	Funky President (People It's Bad)/Cold Blooded	7
76	Polydor 2066 642	Hot (I Need To Be Loved, Loved, Loved)/Superbad, Superslick (Part 1)	6
76	Polydor 2066 687	Get Up Offa That Thing/Release The Pressure	6
77	Polydor 2066 763	Bodyheat Parts 1, 15 & 16	6
77	Polydor 2066 834	Honky Tonk/Brother Rapp	6
78	Polydor 2066 915	Eyesight/I Never, Never, Never Will Forget	6
78	Polydor 2066 984	Nature Parts 1 & 2	6
79	Polydor POSP 24	For Goodness Sakes, Look At Those Cakes/ Get Up, I Feel Like Being A Sex Machine (red or silver label)	5
79	Polydor POSPX 24	Get Up, I Feel Like Being A Sex Machine/For Goodness Sakes, Look At Those Cakes (12")	10
79	Polydor POSPX 68	It's Too Funky In Here/Are We Really Dancing? (12")	10
79	Polydor STEP 2	Star Generation/Let The Boogie Do The Rest	5
79	Polydor STEPX 2	Star Generation/Let The Boogie Do The Rest (12")	8
80	Polydor POSP 121	Regrets/Stone Cold Drag	5
80	RCA RCAT 28	Rapp Payback (Where Iz Moses?) (Parts 1 & 2) (12")	8
81	RCA RCAT 44	Stay With Me/Smokin' And Drinkin' (12")	8
81	RCA RCAT 65	Funky Man (Parts 1 & 2)/Mashed Potatoes (12")	8
88	Urban URBX 13	She's The One/Funky President (People It's Bad)/Funky Drummer (9.13)/ Funky Drummer (Bonus Beats Reprise) (12", die-cut title sleeve)	10
88	Urban URBA 13	She's The One (Funky Drummer Remix)/Funky President (People It's Bad)/ Funky Drummer/Funky Drummer (Bonus Beats Reprise) (12")	10
88	Urban URBA17	Payback (Final Mixdown)/Give It Up Or Turn It Loose/Coldsweat (12")	20
88	Urban URBX 17 DJ	Coldcut Meets The Godfather (12" promo, same as "The Payback Mix")	10
88	Polydor 080 430-2	Give It Up Or Turn It Loose (Remix)/ The Payback Mix — Keep On Doing What You're Doing, But Make It Funky/ Cold Sweat/The Payback — Part 1 (CDV)	8

EPs

64	London RE 1410	JAMES BROWN AND THE FAMOUS FLAMES	55
64	Ember EMB EP 4549	I DO JUST WHAT I WANT	45
66	Pye Intl. NEP 44059	I GOT YOU	40
66	Pye Intl. NEP 44068	I'LL GO CRAZY	40
67	Pye Intl. NEP 44072	PRISONER OF LOVE	40
67	Pye Intl. NEP 44076	HOW LONG DARLING	40
67	Pye Intl. NEP 44088	BRING IT UP	40
70	Polydor 580 701	TURN IT LOOSE	45

MINT VALUE £

LPs

Year	Label / Cat. No.	Title	Value
64	London HA 8177	PURE DYNAMITE! (as James Brown & Famous Flames)	60
64	London HA 8184	LIVE AT THE APOLLO (as James Brown & Famous Flames)	60
64	Ember EMB 3357	TELL ME WHAT YOU'RE GONNA DO	45
64	Philips BL 7630	SHOWTIME	35
65	London HA 8203	UNBEATABLE 16 HITS	70
65	London HA 8231	PLEASE, PLEASE, PLEASE (as James Brown & Famous Flames)	80
65	Philips BL 7664	GRITS AND SOUL	40
65	London HA 8240	JAMES BROWN TOURS THE U.S.A. (with Famous Flames)	65
66	London HA 8262	PAPA'S GOT A BRAND NEW BAG (as James Brown & Famous Flames)	45
66	Philips BL 7697	JAMES BROWN PLAYS JAMES BROWN TODAY AND YESTERDAY	30
66	Pye Intl. NPL 28074	I GOT YOU (I FEEL GOOD)	50
66	Philips BL 7718	JAMES BROWN PLAYS NEW BREED	25
66	Pye Intl. NPL 28079	IT'S A MAN'S MAN'S WORLD	45
66	Pye Intl. NPL 28097	THE JAMES BROWN CHRISTMAS ALBUM	75
67	Pye Intl. NPL 28093	MIGHTY INSTRUMENTALS	35
67	Philips (S)BL 7761	HANDFUL OF SOUL	25
67	Pye Intl. NPL 28099	PAPA'S GOT A BRAND NEW BAG (reissue)	25
67	Pye Intl. NPL 28100	MR. EXCITEMENT	55
67	Polydor 582 703	THE JAMES BROWN SHOW (live)	22
67	Pye Intl. NPL 28103	SINGS RAW SOUL	20
67	Pye Intl. NPL 28104	LIVE AT THE GARDEN	40
68	Philips (S)BL 7823	JAMES BROWN PLAYS THE REAL THING	25
68	Polydor 623 017	JAMES BROWN'S GREATEST HITS	15
68	Polydor 623 032	MR. DYNAMITE	18
68	Polydor 184 100	MR. SOUL	18
68	Polydor 184 136	I CAN'T STAND MYSELF	25
69	Polydor 184 148	SOUL FIRE	20
69	Polydor 184 159	KING OF SOUL	18
60s	Polydor 2852 002	THE SOUL OF JAMES BROWN (reissue of "I Can't Stand Myself")	25
69	Mercury 20133 SMCL	JAMES BROWN SINGS OUT OF SIGHT	35
69	Polydor 583 729/30	LIVE AT THE APOLLO VOLUME TWO (2-LP)	25
69	Polydor 583 741	SAY IT LOUD — I'M BLACK AND I'M PROUD	25
69	Polydor 583 765	THE BEST OF JAMES BROWN	15
69	Polydor 583 768	IT'S A MOTHER	30
69	Polydor 643 317	THIS IS ... JAMES BROWN	18
70	Polydor 583 742	GETTIN' DOWN TO IT	25
70	Polydor 184 319	THE POPCORN	30
70	Polydor 2343 010	AIN'T IT FUNKY	35
70	Polydor 2612 005	LIVE AT THE APOLLO VOLUME TWO (2-LP, reissue)	18
70	Polydor 2334 009	PAPA'S GOT A BRAND NEW BAG	15
71	Polydor 2625 004	SEX MACHINE (2-LP)	25
71	Polydor 2310 022	SOUL ON TOP	25
71	Polydor 2310 029	IT'S A NEW DAY	25
71	Polydor 2310 089	SUPER BAD	20
71	Polydor 2343 036	SOUL BROTHER, NUMBER ONE	15
71	Polydor 2425 086	HOT PANTS	15
72	Philips 6336 201	THIS IS ... JAMES BROWN (reissue)	12
72	Polydor 2659 011	REVOLUTION OF THE MIND: RECORDED LIVE AT THE APOLLO VOL. III (2-LP)	35
72	Polydor 2391 033	THERE IT IS	30
72	Phillips 6336 201	THIS IS ... JAMES BROWN (reissue)	12
72	Contour 2870 116	PRISONER OF LOVE	15
73	Polydor 2659 018	GET ON THE GOOD FOOT (2-LP)	30
73	Polydor 2391 057	SOUL CLASSICS (also issued as record club edition [ACB 00222])	15
73	Polydor 2490 117	BLACK CAESAR (soundtrack)	50
73	Polydor 2391 084	SLAUGHTER'S BIG RIP-OFF (soundtrack)	50
74	Polydor 2391 116	SOUL CLASSICS VOLUME TWO	15
74	Polydor 2659 030	THE PAYBACK (2-LP)	40
74	Polydor 2659 036	IT'S HELL (2-LP)	40
75	Polydor 2391 164	REALITY	15
75	Polydor 2391 166	SOUL CLASSICS VOLUME THREE	15
75	Polydor 2391 175	SEX MACHINE TODAY	20
75	Polydor 2482 184	LIVE AT THE APOLLO (reissue)	12
75	Polydor 2391 197	EVERYBODY'S DOIN' THE HUSTLE AND DEAD ON THE DOUBLE BUMP	15
76	Polydor 2391 214	HOT	12
76	Polydor 2391 228	GET UP OFFA THAT THING	15
77	Polydor 2391 258	BODYHEAT	15
77	Polydor 2391 300	MUTHA'S NATURE (by James Brown & the New J.B.'s)	12
78	Polydor 2391 342	JAM 1980s	12
79	Polydor 2391 384	TAKE A LOOK AT THOSE CAKES	12
79	Polydor 2391 412	THE ORIGINAL DISCO MAN	12
80	Polydor 2391 446	PEOPLE	12
80	RCA LP 5006	SOUL SYNDROME	12
81	Polydor POLS 1029	THE THIRD COMING	12
85	Polydor 821 231-1	AIN'T THAT A GROOVE — THE J.B. STORY 1966-69	15
85	Polydor 821 232-1	DOING IT TOO DEATH — THE J.B. STORY 1970-73	15
86	Boiling Point 827 439-1	DEAD ON THE HEAVY FUNK — THE J.B. STORY 1974-76	15
86	Polydor 829 417-1	JAMES BROWN'S FUNKY PEOPLE VOL. 1 (with other artists)	15
88	Urban URBLP 14	JAMES BROWN'S FUNKY PEOPLE VOL. 2 (with other artists)	15
88	Urban URBLP 11	IN THE JUNGLE GROOVE (2-LP)	18
91	Polydor 849 108-2	STAR TIME (4-CD, with booklet)	35

(see also Lyn Collins, JBs, Maceo & All King's Men, Nat Kendrick & Swans)

JAMES BROWN (Jamaica)

Year	Label / Cat. No.	Title	Value
71	Punch PH 76	Don't Say/TRANS AM ALLSTARS: Don't Say Version	8
72	Ashanti ASH 408	Mama Don't Want To See You/Mama Don't Want To See You Version	7

MINT VALUE £

JERICHO BROWN

60 Warner Bros WB 14 Don'tcha Know (That I Love You)/Look For A Star . . . 10
64 Warner Bros WB 141 I'm Watching You/Wisdom Of A Fool . . . 5

JIM EDWARD BROWN

66 RCA RCX 7179 INTRODUCING JIM EDWARD BROWN (EP) . . . 12
(see also Browns)

JIM EDWARD (BROWN) & MAXINE BROWN

55 London HL 8123 Itsy Witsy Bitsy Me/Why Am I Falling? . . . 45
55 London HL 8123 Itsy Witsy Bitsy Me/Why Am I Falling? (78) . . . 15
55 London HLU 8166 Your Love Is Wild As The West Wind/Draggin' Mainstreet . . . 45
55 London HLU 8166 Your Love Is Wild As The West Wind/Draggin' Mainstreet (78) . . . 15
55 London HLU 8200 You Thought I Thought/Here Today And Gone Tomorrow (B-side with Bonnie) . . . 40
55 London HLU 8200 You Thought I Thought/Here Today And Gone Tomorrow (78, B-side with Bonnie) . . . 15
55 London R-EP 1024 COUNTRY SONGS (EP) . . . 25
55 London R-EU 1044 COUNTRY SONGS VOLUME 3 (EP) . . . 25

JOE BROWN (& BRUVVERS)

59 Decca F 11185 People Gotta Talk/Comes The Day (solo, triangular centre) . . . 18
60 Decca F 11207 Darktown Strutter's Ball/Swagger (solo) . . . 10
60 Decca F 11246 Jellied Eels/Dinah . . . 12
60 Pye 7N 15322 Shine/The Switch . . . 5
61 Piccadilly 7N 35000 Crazy Mixed Up Kid/Stick Around . . . 5
61 Piccadilly 7N 35005 Good Luck & Goodbye/I'm Henery The Eighth I Am . . . 5
62 Piccadilly 7N 35024 What A Crazy World We're Living In/Popcorn . . . 5
62 Decca F 11496 Comes The Day/People Gotta Talk (reissue) . . . 5
62 Piccadilly 7N 35047 A Picture Of You/A Lay-About's Lament . . . 5
62 Piccadilly 7N 35058 Your Tender Look/The Other Side Of The Town . . . 5
62 Piccadilly 7N 35082 It Only Took A Minute/All Things Bright And Beautiful . . . 5
63 Piccadilly 7N 35106 That's What Love Will Do/Hava Nagila (The Hora) . . . 5
63 Piccadilly 7N 35129 Nature's Time For Love/The Spanish Bit . . . 5
63 Piccadilly 7N 35138 Sally Ann/There's Only One Of You . . . 5
63 Piccadilly 7N 35150 Little Ukelele/Hercules Unchained . . . 5
64 Piccadilly 7N 35163 You Do Things To Me/Everybody Calls Me Joe . . . 5
64 Piccadilly 7N 35194 Don't/Just Like That . . . 5
65 Pye 7N 15784 Teardrops In The Rain/Lonely Circus . . . 5
65 Pye 7N 15888 Sicilian Tarantella/Thinkin' That I Loves You . . . 5
65 Pye 7N 15983 Charlie Girl/My Favourite Occupation . . . 5
66 Pye 7N 17074 Sea Of Heartbreak/Mrs O's Theme . . . 5
66 Pye 7N 17135 Little Ray Of Sunshine/Your Loving Touch . . . 5
66 Pye 7N 17184 A Satisfied Mind/Stay A Little While . . . 5
67 Pye 7N 17339 With A Little Help From My Friends/Show Me Around . . . 5
68 MCA MU 1003 Bottle Of Wine/Blue Tuesday . . . 5
68 MCA MU 1030 Davy The Fat Boy/Katerine . . . 5
69 MCA MU 1082 Sweet Music/Suzanne . . . 5
70 Penny Farthing PEN 718 Molly Perkins/Captain Of My Love Ship . . . 5
70 Penny Farthing PEN 747 Come Up And See Me Sometime/Give Me Muddy Water . . . 5

JOE BROWN/MARK WYNTER

63 Piccadilly NEP 24167 JUST FOR FUN (EP, soundtrack, 2 tracks each) . . . 15
64 Golden Guinea WO 1 BIG HITS OF JOE BROWN AND MARK WYNTER (EP) . . . 10
63 Golden Guinea GGL 0179 JOE BROWN/MARK WYNTER (LP, 6 tracks each) . . . 10
(see also Mark Wynter)

JOHNNY BROWN

61 Philips PB 1119 Walkin' Talkin' Kissin' Doll/Sundown . . . 10

KAY BROWN

56 Brunswick 05595 Me 'N' You 'N' The Moon/What Do You Think It Does To Me? . . . 10

KENT BROWN & RAINBOWS

68 Fab FAB 53 When You Going To Show Me How/Come Ya Come Ya . . . 10
(see also Kent & Jeannie, Sir D's Group)

LENNOX BROWN

72 Green Door GD 4023 High School Serenade/WINSTON SCOTLAND: On The Track (1st issue) . . . 7
72 Bullet BU 501 High School Serenade/WINSTON SCOTLAND: On The Track (2nd issue) . . . 7
(see also Jeff Barnes, Peter Tosh)

LES BROWN & HIS BAND OF RENOWN

54 Vogue Coral Q 2034 Ramona/Hot Point . . . 10
54 Vogue Coral Q 2042 St. Louis Blues Mambo/Moon Song . . . 10
55 Vogue Coral Q 72049 The Man That Got Away/Doodle-Doo-Doo . . . 10
55 Capitol CL 14331 Frenesi/Perfidia . . . 7
55 Capitol CL 14350 He Needs Me/Simplicity . . . 7
55 Vogue Coral Q 72107 Lullaby Of Birdland/Bernie's Tune . . . 7
56 Vogue Coral Q 72123 Hong Kong Blues (with Hoagy Carmichael & Band Of Renown)/It's All Right With Me . . . 8
56 Vogue Coral Q 72215 Flamingo/Midnight Sun . . . 7
56 Capitol CL 14512 Sincerely Yours/Take Back Your Mink . . . 5
56 Capitol CL 14611 That Certain Feeling/Hit The Road To Dreamland . . . 5
56 Capitol CL 14631 Talk About A Party/Ancient History . . . 6
57 Capitol CL 14675 Priscilla/The Best Years Of My Life . . . 8
57 Capitol CL 14706 Original Joe/If I Had The Money . . . 5
57 Vogue Coral Q 72242 Forty Cups Of Coffee/I'm Forever Blowing Bubbles . . . 12
57 Vogue Coral Q 72242 Forty Cups Of Coffee/I'm Forever Blowing Bubbles (78) . . . 12
54 Vogue Coral LVC 10002 LES DANCE (10" LP) . . . 18
55 Vogue Coral LVC 10017 INVITATION (10" LP) . . . 18
55 Vogue Coral LVC 10033 LES BROWN (10" LP) . . . 18

MINT VALUE £

MAXINE BROWN

61 London HLU 9286 All In My Mind/Harry, Let's Marry . . . 40
62 HMV POP 1102 Am I Falling In Love/Promise Me Anything . . . 70
63 Stateside SS 188 Ask Me/Yesterday's Kisses . . . 30
64 Pye International 7N 25272 Oh No Not My Baby/You Upset My Soul . . . 20
65 Pye International 7N 25299 It's Gonna Be Alright/You Do Something To Me . . . 15
65 Pye International 7N 25317 One Step At A Time/Anything For A Laugh . . . 25
67 Pye International 7N 25410 I've Got A Lot Of Love Left In Me/Hold On (I'm Comin') (B-side with Chuck Jackson) . . . 15
67 Pye International 7N 25434 Since I Found You/Gotta Find A Way . . . 12
70 Major Minor MM 709 Reason To Believe/I Can't Get Along Without You . . . 12
73 Avco 6105 022 Picked Up, Packed Up And Put Away/Bella Mia . . . 6
75 Pye Disco Demand DDS 117 One In A Million/Let Me Give You My Lovin' . . . 15
(see also Chuck Jackson & Maxine Brown)

NAPPY BROWN (& HIS BAND)

55 London HL 8145 Don't Be Angry/It's Really You . . . 500
55 London HL 8145 Don't Be Angry/It's Really You (78) . . . 30
55 London HLC 8182 Pitter Patter/There'll Come A Day . . . 400
55 London HLC 8182 Pitter Patter/There'll Come A Day (78) . . . 20
57 London HLC 8384 Little By Little/I'm Getting Lonesome (& His Band) (gold or silver lettering on label) . . . 325/175
57 London HLC 8384 Little By Little/I'm Getting Lonesome (& His Band) (78) . . . 20
58 London HLC 8760 It Don't Hurt No More/My Baby . . . 70
58 London HLC 8760 It Don't Hurt No More/My Baby (78) . . . 20

NOEL BROWN

50s Parlophone MP 134 Take Me Back To Africa/Virgin Islands (Get Happy In A Hurry) (78, export) . . . 10
68 Island WI 3149 Man's Temptation/Heartbreak Girl . . . 22
69 Songbird SB 1012 By The Time I Get To Phoenix/Heartbreak Girl . . . 10
70 Bullet BU 423 By The Time I Get To Phoenix/Heartbreak Girl (reissue) . . . 6
(see also Bunny Brown)

O'CHI BROWN

85 Magnet MAGT 288 Whenever You Need Somebody (Mixes)/I Play Games (12", p/s) . . . 10
85 Magnet MAGT 288R Whenever You Need Somebody (Pull It Off Mixes)/I Play Games (12" promo) . . . 18
86 Magnet MAGT 296 100% Pure Pain (Mixes)/I Just Want To Be Loved (12", p/s) . . . 10
86 Magnet MAGT 296R 100% Pure Pain (Mixes)/I Just want To Be Loved (12", p/s) . . . 15
86 Magnet MAGT 297 Two Hearts Beating As One (Mixes)/Another Broken Heart (12", p/s) . . . 10
86 Magnet MAGT 297R Two Hearts Beating As One (Mixes)/Another Broken Heart (12", p/s) . . . 15
87 Magnet MAGDT 9 Whenever You Need Somebody/Mixes (12", promo) . . . 18

OSCAR BROWN JNR

61 Philips PB 1097 But I Was Cool/Dat Dere . . . 5
61 Philips BBL 7478 SIN AND SOUL (LP) . . . 15
73 Atlantic K 40452 MOVIN' ON (LP) . . . 12

PAMELA BROWN

70 Joe JRS 8 People Are Running/CRITICS: School Days . . . 15

PETE BROWN('S PIBLOKTO)

69 Parlophone R 5767 The Week Looked Good On Paper/Morning Call (as Pete Brown & His Battered Ornaments, promo p/s) . . . 60
69 Parlophone R 5767 The Week Looked Good On Paper/Morning Call (as Pete Brown & His Battered Ornaments) . . . 22
69 Harvest HAR 5008 Living Life Backwards/High Flying Electric Bird (as Pete Brown & Piblokto!) . . . 15
70 Harvest HAR 5023 Can't Get Off The Planet/Broken Magic (with His Battered Ornaments) . . . 15
70 Harvest HAR 5028 Flying Hero Sandwich/My Last Band (as Pete Brown & Piblokto!) . . . 25
69 Harvest SHVL 752 A MEAL YOU CAN SHAKE HANDS WITH IN THE DARK (LP, as Pete Brown & His Battered Ornaments, mono or stereo) . . . 100
70 Harvest SHVL 768 THE ART SCHOOL DANCE GOES ON FOREVER (LP, as Pete Brown & Piblokto!) . . . 100
70 Harvest SHVL 782 THOUSANDS ON A RAFT (LP, as Pete Brown & Piblokto!) . . . 80
73 Deram SML 1103 THE NOT FORGOTTEN ASSOCIATION (LP, with Graham Bond) . . . 80
77 Harvest SHSM 2017 MY LAST BAND (LP, as Pete Brown & Piblokto) . . . 20
82 Discs Intl. INTLP 1 PARTY IN THE RAIN (LP, with Ian Lynn, private pressing) . . . 30
(see also Battered Ornaments, Graham Bond & Pete Brown, Deke Leonard)

PINEY BROWN

54 Esquire 10-330 That's Right Little Girl/EDDIE CHAMBLEE: Blues For Eddie (78) . . . 15

POLLY BROWN

73 Pye NSPL 18396 POLLY BROWN (LP) . . . 18
(see also Pickettywitch)

RANDY BROWN

80 Casablanca CANL 190 I Wanna Make Love To You/We Ought To Be Doin' It (12", p/s) . . . 12

ROY BROWN

57 London HLP 8398 I'm Sticking With You/Party Doll (gold label print, later silver) . . . 650/400
57 London HLP 8398 I'm Sticking With You/Party Doll (78) . . . 60
57 London HLP 8448 Saturday Night/Everybody . . . 750
57 London HLP 8448 Saturday Night/Everybody (78) . . . 75

RUTH BROWN (& HER RHYTHMAKERS)

55 London HL 8153 Mambo Baby/Mama (He Treats Your Daughter Mean) (with Rhythmakers) . . . 350
55 London HL 8153 Mambo Baby/Mama (He Treats Your Daughter Mean) (as Ruth Brown & Her Rhythmakers) (78) . . . 30
55 London HLE 8210 As Long As I'm Moving/R.B. Blues (with Her Rhythmakers) . . . 350
55 London HLE 8210 As Long As I'm Moving/R.B. Blues (with Her Rhythmakers) (78) . . . 30
56 London HLE 8310 I Want To Do More/Sweet Baby Of Mine . . . 200
56 London HLE 8310 I Want To Do More/Sweet Baby Of Mine (78) . . . 30

MINT VALUE £

57	London HLE 8401	Mom Oh Mom/I Want To Be Loved (But Only By You)	175
57	London HLE 8401	Mom Oh Mom/I Want To Be Loved (But Only By You) (78)	50
57	Columbia DB 3913	Lucky Lips/My Heart Is Breaking Over You	350
57	Columbia DB 3913	Lucky Lips/My Heart Is Breaking Over You (78)	30
57	London HLE 8483	When I Get You Baby/One More Time	90
57	London HLE 8483	When I Get You Baby/One More Time (78)	45
58	London HLE 8552	A New Love/Look Me Up	90
58	London HLE 8552	A New Love/Look Me Up (78)	30
58	London HLE 8645	Just Too Much/Book Of Lies	100
58	London HLE 8645	Just Too Much/Book Of Lies (78)	30
58	London HLE 8757	This Little Girl's Gone Rockin'/Why Me	60
58	London HL 7061	This Little Girl's Gone Rockin'/Why Me (export issue)	60
58	London HLE 8757	This Little Girl's Gone Rockin'/Why Me (78)	20
59	London HLE 8887	Jack O' Diamonds/I Can't Hear A Word You Say	55
59	London HLE 8887	Jack O' Diamonds/I Can't Hear A Word You Say (78)	60
59	London HLE 8946	I Don't Know/Papa Daddy	45
59	London HLE 8946	I Don't Know/Papa Daddy (78)	70
60	London HLE 9093	Don't Deceive Me/I Burned Your Letter	30
61	London HLK 9304	Sure 'Nuff/Here He Comes	35
64	Brunswick 05904	Yes Sir That's My Baby/What Happened To You	18
76	President PT 457	Sugar Babe/Stop Knocking	5
55	London REE 1038	THE QUEEN OF R&B (EP)	225
63	Philips BE 12537	GOSPEL TIME (EP)	45
60	London Jazz LTZ-K 15187	LAST DATE WITH RUTH BROWN (LP)	80
62	Philips 652 012 BL	ALONG COMES RUTH (LP)	60
63	Philips 652 020 BL	GOSPEL TIME (LP)	45
64	Atlantic ATL 5007	THE BEST OF RUTH BROWN (LP, plum label)	150
76	President PTLS 1067	SUGAR BABE (LP)	18

RUTH BROWN/JOE TURNER

56	London REE 1047	THE KING AND QUEEN OF R&B (EP, 2 tracks each)	225

SAMMI BROWN

68	Fontana TF 947	Daydream/Stop The Music	6

SANDY BROWN('S JAZZ BAND)

51	S&M SN 1002	Irish Black Bottom/Alexander (78)	8
58	Tempo A 124	African Queen/Special Delivery (as Sandy Brown's Jazz Band)	7
53	Esquire EP 28	SANDY BROWN'S JAZZ BAND (EP)	15
55	Tempo EXA 13	SANDY BROWN'S JAZZ BAND (EP)	15
55	Tempo EXA 33	SANDY BROWN'S JAZZ BAND (EP)	15
56	Tempo EXA 49	TRADITIONAL JAZZ SCENE '56 (EP)	15
57	Nixa NJE 1054	BLUE McJAZZ (EP)	12
57	NIxa NJE 1056	AFRO McJAZZ (EP)	12
53	Esquire 20-022	SANDY BROWN (10" LP, with Bobby Mickleburgh)	20
56	Tempo TAP 3	SANDY'S SIDEMEN PLAYING COMPOSITIONS BY AL FAIRWEATHER (LP)	90
57	Nixa Jazz Today NJL 9	McJAZZ (LP)	25
66	Fontana TE1 7473	SANDY BROWN ALL STARS (LP)	20
69	Fontana SFJL 921	HAIR AT ITS HAIRIEST (LP, as Sandy Brown & His Gentlemen Friends)	50
71	77 SEU 12/49	WITH THE BRIAN LEMON TRIO (LP)	15

(see also Wally Fawkes, Sandy & Teachers, Al Fairweather)

SAVOY BROWN

(see under 'S')

SHIRLEY BROWN

75	Stax STXS 2019	Woman To Woman/Yes Sir, Brother	6
75	Stax STXS 2032	I Can't Give You Up/It Ain't No Fun	5
75	Stax STX 1031	WOMAN TO WOMAN (LP)	15

(see also Oliver Sain)

STU BROWN & BLUESOLOGY

67	Polydor 56195	Since I Found You Baby/Just A Little Bit	350

(see also Bluesology, Elton John)

TEDDY BROWN

70	Trojan TR 7793	What Greater Love/Lady Love	6
71	Trojan TR 7827	Walk The World Away/Senorita Rita	6

TINY BROWN

50	Capitol CL 13306	No More Blues/Slow-Motion Baby (78)	18

VEDA BROWN

74	Stax STXS 2008	Short Stopping/I Can See Every Woman's Man But Mine	7

VERNON BROWN

71	Mojo 2093 002	I'm A Lover/Of Your Life	6

VIC BROWN COMBO

63	Rio R 7	Swanee River/Robert E. Lee	18

(se also Alan Martin)

VINCENT BROWN

70	Gas GAS 128	Look What You're Going To Do/Hold On To What You Have Got	12

WATSON T. BROWN (& EXPLOSIVE)

68	President PT 207	Some Lovin'/Home Is Where Your Heart Lies	6
68	President PT 221	Crying All Night/I Close My Eyes	6
70	Bell BLL 1109	Will You Still Love Me Tomorrow/Save The Last Dance For Me (solo)	6

(see also Explosive)

WILLIAM BROWN

71	Ackee ACK 128	I'm Alone/BELTONES: Soul People	7

BROWN BROTHERS

59 Vogue V 9131 Let The Good Times Roll/You're Right, I'm Left. 200
59 Vogue V 9131 Let The Good Times Roll/You're Right, I'm Left (78) 100
(see also Charles Brown)

DUNCAN BROWNE

68 Immediate IM 070 On The Bombsite/Alfred Bell 18
70 Bell BLL 1119 Resurrection Joe/Final Asylum 6
73 Rak RAK 162 Send Me The Bill/My Only Son 6
78 Logo GO 329 Wild Places/Camino Real. 6
68 Immediate IMSP 018 GIVE ME, TAKE YOU (LP, with insert). 225
73 RAK SRKA 6754 DUNCAN BROWNE (LP, gatefold sleeve). 18

GEORGE BROWNE

54 Parlophone CMSP 6 Calypso Mambo/The Peanut Vendor (export issue) 10
54 Parlophone CMSP 17 Somebody Bad Stole De Wedding Bell (Who's Got De Ding Dong?)/
Matilda, Matilda! (export issue) 10
57 Columbia DB 3940 Sound Barrier/Te-Le-Le 7
57 Columbia DB 3940 Sound Barrier/Te-Le-Le (78). 10
56 Melodisc MLP 509 HE LIKE IT SHE LIKE IT (10" LP). 12
(see also Humphrey Lyttelton)

IVAN BROWNE & HIS CALYPSO MUSIC

54 London Calypso CAY 109 I'm My Own Grandpa/My Little Boy (78) 8

JACKSON BROWNE

86 Elektra EKR 35P For America (Edit)/Till I Go Down (Statue Of Liberty-shaped picture disc). 5
86 Elektra EKR 42P In The Shape Of A Heart/Voice Of America (heart-shaped picture disc) 5
74 Asylum K2 43007 LATE FOR THE SKY (LP, quadrophonic) 15

SANDRA BROWNE (& BOYFRIENDS)

63 Columbia DB 4998 By Hook Or By Crook/Johnny Boy (as Sandra Browne & Boyfriends) 15
63 Columbia DB 7109 You'd Think He Didn't Know Me/Mama Never Told Me 15
65 Columbia DB 7465 Knock On Any Door/I Want Love 15

TEDDY BROWN(E)

59 Capitol CL 15059 A Corner In Paradise/The Everglades 12
61 Starlite ST45 033 Pretty Little Baby/Genevieve (as Teddy Brown) 20

THOMAS F. BROWNE

71 Vertigo 6325 250 WEDNESDAY'S CHILD (LP, gatefold sleeve, swirl label). 55
(see also Gary Wright)

TOM BROWNE

80 Arista ARIST 12357 Funkin' For Jamaica (N.Y.)/Her Silent Smile (12"). 8

DUKE BROWNER

79 Grapevine GRP 145 Crying Over You/Crying Over You (Instrumental) 10
(see also Kaddo Strings)

BROWNHILL'S STAMP DUTY

69 Columbia DB 8625 Maxwell's Silver Hammer/My Woman's Back 7

BROWNS

59 RCA RCA 1140 The Three Bells/Heaven Fell Last Night 10
59 RCA RCA 1140 The Three Bells/Heaven Fell Last Night (78) 10
59 RCA RCA 1157 Scarlet Ribbons (For Her Hair)/Blue Bells Ring 10
59 RCA RCA 1157 Scarlet Ribbons (For Her Hair)/Blue Bells Ring (78). 10
60 RCA RCA 1176 Teen-Ex/The Old Lamplighter 10
60 RCA RCA 1193 Margo (The Ninth Of May)/Lonely Little Robin 10
60 RCA RCA 1218 Send Me The Pillow You Dream On/You're So Much A Part Of Me. 7
60 RCA RCX 587/SRC 7036 IN THE COUNTRY (EP, mono/stereo) 25/35
59 RCA RD 27153/SF 5052 SWEET SOUNDS BY THE BROWNS (LP, mono/stereo) 30/45
(see also Jim Edward & Maxine Brown)

BROWN'S FERRY FOUR

54 Parlophone DP 374 I Need The Prayers/Through The Pearly Gates (with Clyde Moody, export 78) 7
54 Parlophone CMSP 11 I Need The Prayers/Through The Pearly Gates (with Clyde Moody, export issue) . 25
(see also Delmore Brothers, Grandpa Jones, Merle Travis)

BROWN SUGAR

70s Lovers Rock CJ 613 I'm In Love With A Dreadlocks/Version 15

ANNETTE (Reis) & VICTOR BROX

65 Fontana TF 536 I've Got The World In A Jug/Wake Me And Shake Me. 15
74 Sonet SNTF 663 ROLLIN' BACK (LP) 20
(see also Aynsley Dunbar Retaliation)

DAVE BRUBECK (QUARTET)

53 Vogue 45-2156 A Foggy Day/Lyons Busy 8
53 Vogue 45-2157 Mam'selle/Me And My Shadow 8
53 Vogue 45-2158 Frenesi/At A Perfume Counter. 8
53 Vogue 45-2159 Body And Soul/Let's Fall In Love 8
53 Vogue 45-2160 I'll Remember April/Singin' In The Rain. 8
53 Vogue 45-2161 Lullaby In Rhythm/You Stepped Out Of A Dream. 8
54 Vogue V 2171 At A Perfume Counter/Me And My Shadow 8
54 Vogue V 2206 Frenesi/Mam'selle 8
60 Philips JAZ 106 I'm In A Dancing Mood/Lover (p/s) 5
61 Fontana H 339 Take Five/Blue Rondo A La Turk 5
61 CBS AAG 102 The Unsquare Dance/Camptown Races 5
62 Fontana H 352 It's A Raggy Waltz/Blue Shadows In The Street 5
54 Vogue LDE 090 DAVE BRUBECK TRIO (10" LP). 20
54 Vogue LDE 095 DAVE BRUBECK QUARTET (10" LP). 20
54 Vogue LDE 104 DAVE BRUBECK QUARTET VOL. 2 (10" LP) 20

MINT VALUE £

55	Vogue LDE 114	DAVE BRUBECK QUARTET VOL. 3 (10" LP)	20
57	Fontana TFL 5017	DAVE DIGS DISNEY (LP)	15
57	Philips BBL 7147	AT NEWPORT (LP, with J.J. Johnson and Kei Winding)	12
59	Vogue LAE 12008	THE FABULOUS DAVE BRUBECK TRIO AND OCTET (LP)	15
59	Fontana TFL 5071	GONE WITH THE WIND (LP, also stereo STFL 501)	12
60	Vogue LAE 12114	DAVE BRUBECK QUARTET FEATURING PAUL DESMOND (LP)	15
66	CBS 62643	MY FAVOURITE THINGS (LP)	12
67	CBS 62921	ANYTHING GOES — THE MUSIC OF COLE PORTER (LP)	12

(see also Jimmy Rushing, Carmen McRae)

JACK BRUCE

65	Polydor BM 56036	I'm Getting Tired (Of Drinking And Gambling)/Rootin' Tootin'	50
71	Polydor 2058 153	The Consul At Sunset/Letter Of Thanks	15
74	RSO 2090 141	Keep It Down/Golden Days	5
69	Polydor 583 058	SONGS FOR A TAILOR (LP, gatefold sleeve)	25
70	Polydor 2343 033	THINGS WE LIKE (LP)	18
71	Polydor 2310 070	THINGS WE LIKE (LP, reissue)	12
71	Polydor 2310 107	HARMONY ROW (LP, gatefold sleeve)	12
74	RSO 2394 143	OUT OF THE STORM (LP, with insert)	12

(see also Alexis Korner's Blues Incorporated, Cream, Manfred Mann, Graham Bond Organisation, John Mayall, West Bruce & Laing, Lifetime, Rocket 88, Carla Bley, Duffy Power, Cozy Powell)

LENNY BRUCE

69	Transatlantic TRA 195	BERKELEY CONCERT (2-LP)	18

TOMMY BRUCE (& BRUISERS)

60	Columbia DB 4453	Ain't Misbehavin'/Got The Water Boilin' (with Bruisers)	10
60	Columbia DB 4498	Broken Doll/I'm On Fire (with Bruisers)	15
60	Columbia DB 4532	On The Sunny Side Of The Street/My Little Girl (with Bruisers)	10
61	Columbia DB 4581	You Make Love So Well/I'm Crazy 'Bout My Baby (with Bruisers)	10
61	Columbia DB 4682	Love, Honour And Oh! Baby/I'm Gonna Sit Right Down And Write	10
62	Columbia DB 4776	Babette/Honey Girl, You're Lonely	10
62	Columbia DB 4850	Horror Movies/It's You	15
62	Columbia DB 4927	Buttons And Bows/London Boys	5
63	Columbia DB 7025	Let's Do It, Let's Fall In Love/Two Feet Left	5
63	Columbia DB 7132	Lavender Blue/Sixteen Years Ago Tonight	5
64	Columbia DB 7241	Let It Be Me/No More	5
64	Columbia DB 7387	Over Suzanne/It's Drivin' Me Wild	10
65	Polydor BM 56006	Boom Boom/Can Your Monkey Do The Dog (with Bruisers)	15
66	RCA RCA 1535	Monster Gonzales/I Hate Getting Up In The Morning	18
68	CBS CBS 3405	I've Been Around Too Long/Where The Colour Of The Soil Is Different	6
68	CBS CBS 3937	Heartbreak Melody/The Reason Why	6
61	Columbia SEG 8077	KNOCKOUT (EP)	175

BRUCE & ROBIN ROCKERS

66	Marble Arch MAL 626	THE BATMAN THEME (LP)	22

CLAUDIA BRÜCKEN

90	Island 12ISX 471	Absolut[e] (Bastille Mix)/Absolut[e] (Shooting Star Mix) (12", remix, stickered title sleeve, promo only)	8
90	Island CID 471	Absolut[e] (Original)/Absolut[e] (Shooting Star)/Whisper (CD, g/fold card p/s)	10
91	Island CID 479	Kiss Like Ether (Electrical Embrace)/Kiss Like Ether (As Pure)/I, Dream (Recurring)/Kiss Like Ether (Earth Mood Magic) (CD, gatefold card p/s)	10
91	Island CID 9971	LOVE & A MILLION OTHER THINGS (CD)	20

(see also Propaganda, Act, Glenn Gregory & Claudia Brücken)

HEIDI BRÜHL

60	Philips PB 1095	Ring Of Gold/I'll Belong To You Forever (some in p/s)	12/6
63	Philips 345 579 BF	Marcel/Talk It Over With Someone	12

BRUISERS

63	Parlophone R 5042	Blue Girl/Don't Cry	20
63	Parlophone R 5092	Your Turn To Cry/Give It To Me	20

(see also [Peter] Lee Stirling & Bruisers)

BRUMBEATS

64	Decca F 11834	Cry Little Girl, Cry/I Don't Understand	22

BEAU BRUMMEL ESQUIRE

65	Columbia DB 7447	I Know Know Know/Shoppin' Around	8
65	Columbia DB 7538	The Next Kiss/Come And Get Me	8
65	Columbia DB 7675	A Better Man Than I/Teardrops	8
66	Columbia DB 7878	You Don't Know What You've Got/Take Me Like I Am	7

GEORGE BRUNIS

54	London AL 3536	NEW ORLEANS RHYTHM KINGS (LP)	20

BRUNNING (HALL) SUNFLOWER BLUES BAND

68	Saga FID 2118	BULLEN STREET BLUES (LP, as Brunning Sunflower Blues Band)	20
69	Saga EROS 8132	TRACKSIDE BLUES (LP)	50
70	Saga EROS 8150	I WISH YOU WOULD (LP, as Brunning Sunflower Blues Band)	50
71	Gemini GM 2010	THE BRUNNING/HALL SUNFLOWER BLUES BAND (LP)	60

(see also Five's Company, Fleetwood Mac, Leaf Hound)

TONY BRUNO

68	Capitol CL 15534	What's Yesterday/Small Town, Bring Down	15

BRUTE FORCE

69	Apple APPLE 8	King Of Fuh/Nobody Knows (unissued)	600+

BRUTUS

75	Purple PUR 126	Payroll/New Deal Princess	7

MINT VALUE £

CARL BRYAN

69 Trojan TR 673 — Red Ash/SILVERTONES: Bluebirds Flying Over 15
69 Duke DU 13 — Soul Pipe/Overproof 15
69 Camel CA 22 — Run For Your Life/TWO SPARKS: When We Were Young 12
69 Gas GAS 133 — Stagger Back/The Creeper 15
69 Gas GAS 134 — Walking The Dead/TREVOR & KEITH: Got What You Want 12
(see also Cannon Ball & Johnny Melody, King Cannon, Vincent Foster, Hugh Malcolm, King Cannonball, Glen Brown, Shenley Duffas, Alton Ellis, Kid Gungo, Jackie Mittoo, Johnny Moore, Joe White, Royals)

DORA BRYAN

55 HMV POP 133 — My Only Love With Men/Why Did You Call Me Lily (78) 8
63 Fontana TF 427 — All I Want For Christmas Is A Beatle/If I Were A Fairy 6

FITZVAUGHN BRYAN'S ORCHESTRA

60 Melodisc 45-1560 — Evening News/Hold Up Your Head And Smile (with Kenrick Patrick) 10

RAD BRYAN

71 Techniques TE 909 — Jumping Jack/ANSELL COLLINS: Point Blank 12
71 Bullet BU 463 — Shock Attack/Cuban Waltz 18
71 Big Shot BI 559 — Just Do The Right Things/Corporal Jones 10
71 Big Shot BI 591 — I'll Be Right There (actually by Techniques)/PLAYBOYS: Hot Pants Rock 10
71 Big Shot BI 592 — My Best Girl/My Best Girl Version 10
72 Attack ATT 8040 — Standing In The Rain (actually by Neville Grant)/Standing In The Rain Version .. 10

V. BRYAN ORCHESTRA

55 Kay CRS 028 — Tan Tan — Calypso/CYRIL DIAS: Brass Crown (Vocal: Lord Superior) (78) 10

WES BRYAN

58 London HLU 8607 — Lonesome Love/Tiny Spaceman 40
58 London HLU 8607 — Lonesome Love/Tiny Spaceman (78) 20
59 London HLU 8978 — Honey Baby/So Blue Over You 50
59 London HLU 8978 — Honey Baby/So Blue Over You (78) 20

BRYAN & BRUNELLES

65 HMV POP 1394 — Jacqueline/Louie Louie 55

ANITA BRYANT

59 London HLL 8983 — Six Boys And Seven Girls/The Blessings Of Love 12
60 London HLL 9075 — Little George (Got The Hiccoughs)/Love Look Away 12
60 London HLL 9114 — Paper Roses/Mixed Emotions 5
60 London HLL 9171 — In My Little Corner Of The World/Just In Time 5
60 London HLL 9171 — In My Little Corner Of The World/Anyone Would Love You (unissued)
60 London HLL 9219 — One Of the Lucky Ones/The Party's Over 8
60 London HLL 9247 — Wonderland By Night/Pictures 8
61 London HLL 9281 — Till There Was You/A Texan And A Girl From Mexico 8
61 London HLL 9353 — Do-Re-Mi/An Angel Cried 8
61 Philips BF 1182 — The Wedding/Seven Kinds Of Lonesome 8
66 CBS 202026 — Another Year, Another Love/My Mind's Playing Tricks On Me Again 40
62 CBS AAG 20005 — KISSES SWEETER THAN WINE (EP) 20
61 London HA-L 2381 — IN MY LITTLE CORNER OF THE WORLD (LP) 65

BOOD & FILEECE (Boudleaux & Felice) BRYANT

51 MGM MGM 452 — Overweight Blues/I Dreamed Of A Wedding (78) 8

BOUDLEAUX BRYANT

60 Polydor NH 66952 — Hot Spot/Touché (with Sparks) 10
(see also Bood & Fileece Bryant)

DON BRYANT

70 London HA-U/SH-U 8409 — PRECIOUS SOUL (LP) 22

JOHN BRYANT

65 Fontana H 625 — Tell Me What You See/Poor Unfortunate Me 12

LAURA K. BRYANT

58 London HLU 8551 — Bobby/Angel Tears 40
58 London HLU 8551 — Bobby/Angel Tears (78) 20

MARIE/MARGARET BRYANT

52 Lyragon J 701 — Tomato/Rhumboogie Anna (78) 8
52 Lyragon J 709 — Little Boy/STERLING BETTANCOURT: Blue Basin Sam (78) 8
52 Parlophone R 3592 — Ain't Misbehavin'/Beale Street Blues (78) 8
54 London Calypso CAY 105 — Don't Touch Me Nylon/Water Melon (78) 8
54 London Calypso CAY 107 — Mary's Lamb/Noisy Spring (78) 8
54 Lyragon J 724 — The Lost Watch (Tick Tick)/S. BETTANCOURT: Beater Pam (78) 10
54 Lyragon J 725 — My Handy Man/RUSSEL HENDERSON: Bacchanal (78) 10
54 Lyragon J 726 — Banana Woman/"SHAKE" KEANE: Creole Honey (78) 10
61 Kalypso XX 27 — Water Melon/Tomato 6
61 Kalypso XX 28 — Don't Touch Me Nylon/Little Boy 6
61 Kalypso XXEP 7 — CALYPSOS TOO HOT TO HANDLE (EP) 12
60s Melodisc MLP 12 132 — DON'T TOUCH ME NYLONS (LP, with or without sleeve) 25/15
60s Fab MLP 12 132 — DON'T TOUCH ME NYLONS (LP, reissue) 12

MATT BRYANT & LINDA JOYCE

60 Embassy WB 420 — Goodness Gracious Me/STEVE STANNARD & HIS GROUP: Man Of Mystery 6
(see also Maureen Evans)

RAY BRYANT TRIO/COMBO

60 Pye International 7N 25052 — Little Susie Parts 2 & 4 6
60 Philips PB 1003 — Little Susie Parts 1 & 3 6
60 Philips PB 1014 — The Madison Time Parts 1 & 2 10

RUSTY BRYANT

57 London HB-D 1066 — RUSTY BRYANT (10" LP) 100

MINT VALUE £

SANDRA BRYANT

67	Major Minor MM 523	Girl With Money/Golden Hours	7
68	Major Minor MM 553	Out To Get You/There's No Lock Upon My Door	8

GAVIN BRYARS

75	Obscure 1	THE SINKING OF THE TITANIC (LP)	12

(see also Brian Eno)

CALUM BRYCE

68	Condor PS 1001	Lovemaker/I'm Glad	200

BERYL BRYDEN('S BACK-ROOM SKIFFLE)

56	Decca F 10823	Casey Jones/Kansas City Blues	40
56	Decca F 10823	Casey Jones/Kansas City Blues (78)	25
57	Decca (no cat. no.)	Rock Me/This Train (test pressing, with Alexis Korner & Cyril Davies)	150+
56	Melodisc EPM 7-69	BERYL BRYDEN WITH FATTY GEORGE'S JAZZ BAND (EP)	10

(see also Alexis Korner, Cyril Davies)

BETSY BRYE

59	Columbia DB 4350	Sleep Walk/Daddy Daddy (Gotta Get A Phone In My Room)	25

YUL BRYNNER

67	Fontana TFL 6085	THE GYPSY AND I (LP)	12

B.T.

94	Perfecto SAM 1517	EMBRACING THE SUNSHINE (Original & Sasha Mixes) (12", double pack, promo only)	20
94	Perfecto SAM 1652	LOVING YOU MORE (12", double pack, promo only)	12
95	Perfecto SAM 1688	TRIPPING THE LIGHT FANTASTIC (12", 1-sided LP sampler, promo only)	25
95	Perfecto SAM 1690	DIVINITY (12", 1-sided LP sampler, promo only)	15
95	Perfecto SAM 1691	QUARK (12", 1-sided LP sampler, promo only)	15

B.T.B.-4

68	Liberty LBF 15067	Do It To 'Em/Sparrows And Daisies	6

B.T. EXPRESS

75	Pye International 7N 25674	Express (Parts 1 & 2)	6
75	Pye International 7N 25682	Once You Get It/This House Is Smokin'	8
75	Pye Intl. NSPL 28207	DO IT (TIL YOU'RE SATISFIED) (LP)	15
75	EMI International INA 1501	NON-STOP (LP)	15

B.T.P. FOLDERS

80	Future Earth FER 005	Radio/All Of A Sudden (p/s)	50

B12

93	Warp WAPLP 9LTD	ELECTRO — SOMA (2-LP, orange vinyl)	60
93	B12 09 CASSETTE	PRELUDE PART 1 (cassette, 400 only)	50
93	B12 09 CD	PRELUDE PT 1 (CD, 500 only)	50
93	B12 CD 1	REDCELL & STASIS (CD, 1500 only)	25
94	B12 15	B12 (12", 4-track promo only, 10 copies pressed)	80

(see also Redcell, Musicology)

BUBA & SHOP ASSISTANTS

85	Villa 21 002	Something To Do/Dreaming Backwards (p/s, with insert in poly bag)	25

(see also Shop Assistants, Pastels)

BUBBLES

63	Duke DK 1001	Bopping In The Barnyard/The Wasp	20
63	Duke DK 1001	The Wasp/Bopping In The Barnyard (matrix: DK 1001A-1, plays "Rocking Crickets" by Hot Toddy's)	20

BUCCA

82	Plant Life PLR 039	THE HOLE IN THE HARPERS HEAD (LP)	20

LINDSAY BUCKINGHAM

81	Mercury MER 85	Trouble/That's How We Do It In L.A. (p/s)	5
82	Mercury MER 96	The Visitor (Bwana)/A Satisfied Mind (p/s)	6
82	Mercury MER 102	Mary Lee Jones/September Song (p/s)	6
83	Mercury MER 150	Holiday Road/Mary Lee Jones (p/s)	8
84	Mercury MER 168	Go Insane/Play In The Rain (p/s)	5
84	Mercury MERX 168	Go Insane/Play In The Rain (12", p/s)	12
84	Mercury MER 176	Slow Dancing/D.W. Suite (p/s)	5
92	Mercury MER 371	Countdown/This Nearly Was Mine (p/s)	5
92	Mercury MERCD 371	Countdown/This Nearly Was Mine/Surrender The Rain/Trouble (CD)	8
92	Mercury MER 380	Soul Drifter/Say You'll Meet Again (p/s)	5
92	Mercury MER 380 CD	Soul Drifter/Say You'll Meet Again/This Nearly Was Mine (live)/ Street Of Dreams (live) (CD)	8

BUCKINGHAM-NICKS

74	Polydor 2066 398	Don't Let Me Down Again/Races Are Run	15
76	Polydor 2066 700	Don't Let Me Down Again/Crystal	10
73	Polydor 2391 013	BUCKINGHAM-NICKS (LP, with insert, some with stickered sleeve)	40/35
81	Polydor 2482 378	BUCKINGHAM-NICKS (LP, reissue with insert)	25

(see also Lindsay Buckingham, Stevie Nicks, Fleetwood Mac)

BUCKINGHAMS (U.K.)

65	Pye 7N 15848	I'll Never Hurt You No More/She Lied	8
65	Pye 7N 15921	To Be Or Not To Be/I Was Your First Guy	7

BUCKINGHAMS (U.S.)

67	Stateside SS 588	Kind Of A Drag/You Make Me Feel So Good	10
68	CBS 2640	Don't You Care/Why Don't You Love Me	15
68	CBS 3559	Back In Love Again/You Misunderstand Me	8

JEFF BUCKLEY

95 Columbia 662042 1 — Last Goodbye (Edit)/Lover, You Should've Come Over (Live And Acoustic In Japan)/Tongue (Live) (10", p/s, 5000 only) . . . 12
93 Big Cat ABB 61XCD — LIVE AT SIN-E EP (Mojo Pin/Eternal Life/Je N'en Connais Pas La Fin/The Way Young Lovers Do (CD) . . . 12
95 Columbia 661107 2 — THE GRACE EP (Grace (Edit)/Tongue/Kanga-Roo/Grace) (CD) . . . 8
94 Columbia 475928 — GRACE (LP) . . . 12
98 Columbia 3C 67228 — SKETCHES (FOR MY SWEETHEART, THE DRUNK) (3-LP, gatefold sleeve) . . . 20
00 Columbia 4979721 — MYSTERY WHITE BOY LIVE 95-96 (LP) . . . 12

SEAN BUCKLEY & BREADCRUMBS

65 Stateside SS 421 — It Hurts Me When I Cry/Everybody Knows . . . 80

TIM BUCKLEY

67 Elektra EKSN 45008 — Aren't You The Girl/Strange Street Affair Under Blue . . . 12
67 Elektra EKSN 45018 — Morning Glory/Knight-Errant . . . 7
68 Elektra EKSN 45023 — Once I Was/Phantasmagoria In Two . . . 7
68 Elektra EKSN 45031 — Wings/I Can't See You . . . 7
68 Elektra EKSN 45041 — Pleasant Street/Carnival Song . . . 7
70 Straight S 4799 — Happy Time/So Lonely . . . 7
66 Elektra EKL/EKS 4004 — TIM BUCKLEY (LP, orange label) . . . 60
67 Elektra EKL/EKS 318 — GOODBYE AND HELLO (LP, orange label, gatefold sleeve) . . . 40
68 Elektra EKS 74045 — HAPPY SAD (LP, orange label) . . . 30
69 Straight STS 1060 — BLUE AFTERNOON (LP) . . . 30
70 Elektra 2410 005 — LORCA (LP) . . . 30
71 Straight STS 1064 — STARSAILOR (LP) . . . 30
72 Warner Bros K 46176 — GREETINGS FROM L.A. (LP, gatefold sleeve) . . . 20
74 Discreet K 49201 — SEFRONIA (LP) . . . 20
74 Discreet K 59204 — LOOK AT THE FOOL (LP) . . . 25
91 Strange Fruit SFPS082 — THE PEEL SESSIONS: Morning Glory/Coming Home To You/ Sing A Song For You/Hallucinations/Troubadour/Once I Was (12", p/s) . . . 10

VERNON BUCKLEY

73 Grape GR 3057 — Mr Softhand/G.G. ALLSTARS: Dub . . . 6
73 Grape GR 3058 — Ital Queen/G.G. ALLSTARS: Dub . . . 6

MILT BUCKNER & HIS MUSIC

56 Capitol CL 14662 — Night Mist/Good Time Express . . . 8

TEDDY BUCKNER & HIS BAND

56 Vogue V 2369 — Oh, Didn't He Ramble/Battle Hymn Of The Republic . . . 8
56 Vogue V 2375 — When The Saints Go Marching In/West End Blues . . . 8
57 Vogue V 2414 — Sweet Georgia Brown/That's My Home . . . 8

BUCKY & STRINGS

62 Salvo SLO 1807 — Lolita's On The Loose/Lonely Island (99 copies only) . . . 30

BUD & HIS BUDDIES

58 Starlite ST45 006 — June, July And August/Sing A Little Sweeter . . . 12

BUD & TRAVIS

59 London HLU 8965 — Bonsoir Dame/Truly Do . . . 10
59 London HLU 8965 — Bonsoir Dame/Truly Do (78) . . . 15
60 London HLG 9211 — The Ballad Of The Alamo/The Green Leaves Of Summer . . . 10
61 London HA-G 2328 — BUD AND TRAVIS IN CONCERT (LP, also stereo SAH-G 6128) . . . 18/20

ROY BUDD

65 Pye 7N 15807 — Birth Of The Budd/M'Ghee M'Ghee . . . 8
66 Parlophone R 5514 — Summer Samba/Bahama Sound . . . 5
67 Pye 7N 17279 — Mr Rose/Summer Rain . . . 10
68 Pye 7N 17652 — Pavanne/Whizz Ball . . . 6
69 Pye 7N 17773 — Tijuana Piano/Lead On . . . 6
70 Pye 7N 17987 — Borsalino (Theme)/It Only Goes To Show . . . 8
70 Pye 7N 45051 — Carter (Theme)/Plaything (some in p/s) . . . 100/60
67 Pye N(S)PL 18177 — PICK YOURSELF UP — THIS IS ROY BUDD (LP) . . . 50
67 Pye N(S)PL 18195 — THE SOUND OF MUSIC (LP) . . . 20
68 Pye NPL 18212 — AT NEWPORT (LP) . . . 60
69 Pye N(S)PL 18305 — LEAD ON (LP) . . . 25
71 Pye NSPL 18348 — PLAYS SOLDIER BLUE AND OTHER THEMES (LP) . . . 50
71 Pye NSPL 18354 — BUDD 'N' BOSSA (LP) . . . 40
71 Pye NSPL 18373 — GREAT SONGS AND THEMES FROM GREAT FILMS (LP) . . . 70
72 Pye NSPL 18389 — CONCERTO FOR HARRY — SOMETHING TO HIDE (LP, soundtrack) . . . 60
72 Polydor 2383 102 — KIDNAPPED (LP, soundtrack, with Mary Hopkin) . . . 25
73 Pye NSPL 18398 — FEAR IS THE KEY (LP, soundtrack) . . . 120
76 Bradley's BRADS 8002 — DIAMONDS (LP, soundtrack) . . . 60
70s Pye NSPL 19494 — EVERYTHING'S COMING UP (LP) . . . 50
80 EMI EMC 3340 — THE SEA WOLVES (LP, soundtrack) . . . 18

BUDDY & JUNIORS

(see under Buddy Guy)

BUDDY & SKETTO

62 Dice 45/CC 7 — Little Schoolgirl/Hush Baby . . . 25

(see also Father Sketto, Ruddy & Sketto, Sketto Rich)

BUDGIE

71 MCA MK 5072 — Crash Course In Brain Surgery/Nude Disintegrating Parachutist Woman . . . 15
72 MCA MK 5085 — Whisky River/Guts . . . 10
74 MCA MCA 133 — Zoom Club (Edited Version)/Wondering What Everyone Knows . . . 8
75 MCA MCA 175 — I Ain't No Mountain/Honey . . . 8
78 A&M AMS 7342 — Smile Boy Smile/All At Sea . . . 8
80 Active BUDGE — Wildfire/Wildfire (promo only) . . . 12

MINT VALUE £

80	Active BUDGE 1	IF SWALLOWED DO NOT INDUCE VOMITING (12" EP)	12
80	Active BUDGE 2	Crime Against The World/Hellbender (p/s)	8
81	RCA BUDGE 3	Keeping A Rendezvous/Apparatus (p/s)	5
81	RCA BUDGE 3	Keeping A Rendezvous/Apparatus (picture disc)	5
81	RCA BUDGE 4	I Turned To Stone (Part 1)/I Turned To Stone (Part 2) (orange vinyl)	6
82	RCA RCA 271	Bored With Russia/Don't Cry (poster p/s)	6
82	RCA RCAP 271	Bored With Russia/Don't Cry (picture disc)	5
71	MCA MKPS 2018	BUDGIE (LP, pink/red label, initially with poster)	40/25
71	MCA MKPS 2018	BUDGIE (LP, later pressing with blue/black label)	20
73	MCA MCF 2506	BUDGIE (LP, reissue, rainbow label)	12
72	MCA MKPS 2023	SQUAWK (LP, blue/black label)	15
73	MCA MDKS 8010	NEVER TURN YOUR BACK ON A FRIEND (LP, blue/black label, g/fold sleeve)	15
74	MCA MCF 2546	IN FOR THE KILL (LP)	12
75	MCA MCF 2723	BANDOLIER (LP)	12
75	MCA MCF 2766	THE BEST OF BUDGIE (LP)	12
76	A&M AMLH 68377	IF I WAS BRITANNIA I'D WAIVE THE RULES (LP)	12
78	A&M AMLH 64675	IMPECKABLE (LP)	12
80	Active ACTLP 1	POWER SUPPLY (LP, with insert)	12
81	RCA RCALP 3046	POWER SUPPLY (LP, reissue, with different back sleeve)	12
81	RCA RCALP 6003	NIGHT FLIGHT (LP)	12
81	Cube HIFLY 36	BEST OF BUDGIE (LP)	12
82	RCA RCALP 6054	DELIVER US FROM EVIL (LP)	12

(see also Tredegar, Phenomena, George Hatcher Band)

DENNIS BUDLIMAR

67	Fontana TL 5307	THE CREEPER (LP)	18

BUENA VISTAS

66	Stateside SS 525	Hot Shot/T.N.T.	20

BUFFALO

81	Heavy Metal HEAVY 3	Battle Torn Heroes/Women Of The Night (p/s)	30
82	Heavy Metal HEAVY 15	Mean Machine/The Rumour (p/s)	25

BUFFALO SPRINGFIELD

67	Atlantic 584 077	For What It's Worth (Stop Hey What's That Sound)/ Do I Have To Come Right Out And Say It	8
67	Atlantic 584 145	Rock'n'Roll Woman/A Child's Claim To Fame	8
68	Atlantic 584 165	Expecting To Fly/Everydays	10
68	Atlantic 584 189	Uno-Mundo/Merry-Go-Round	8
69	Atco 226 006	Pretty Girl Why/Questions	8
72	Atlantic K 10237	Bluebird/Mr Soul/Rock'n'Roll Woman/Expecting To Fly (p/s)	7
67	Atlantic 587/588 070	BUFFALO SPRINGFIELD (LP, plum label, mispressing, lists "For What It's Worth" but plays "Baby Don't Scold Me"; matrix no. ends '1'; mono/stereo)	60/45
67	Atlantic 587/588 070	BUFFALO SPRINGFIELD (LP, plum label, plays "For What It's Worth", mono/stereo)	40/30
68	Atlantic 587/588 091	BUFFALO SPRINGFIELD AGAIN (LP, plum label, mono/stereo)	40/30
69	Atco 228 024	LAST TIME AROUND (LP, plum label, gatefold sleeve)	18
69	Atco 228 012	RETROSPECTIVE (LP, plum label)	12
70	Atlantic 2464 012	EXPECTING TO FLY (LP, plum label)	18
72	Atlantic K 40014	BUFFALO SPRINGFIELD AGAIN (LP, reissue, green & orange label)	18
72	Atlantic K 40077	LAST TIME AROUND (LP, reissue, green & orange label, gatefold sleeve)	12
73	Atlantic K 30028	BEGINNINGS (ATLANTIC MASTERS) (LP, green & orange label)	12

(see also Neil Young, Stephen Stills, Poco, Au-Go-Go Singers, Crosby Stills Nash & Young)

BUFFALO TOM

89	Caff CAFF 6	Enemy/Deep In The Ground (p/s)	25

BUFF MEDWAYS

00s	Transcopic TRAN 012	A Strange Kind Of Happyness/BILLY CHILDISH: Hound Dog (p/s, 500 only)	7
00s	Transcopic TRAN 015	Troubled Mind/BILLY CHILDISH: Leave My Kitten Alone (p/s, 500 only)	7

BUFFOONS

67	Columbia DB 8317	My World Fell Down/Tomorrow Is Another Day	15

BUGALOOS

71	Capitol E-SW 621	THE BUGALOOS (LP)	18

BULLAMAKANKA

83	BBC REL 454	Dr Who Is Gonna Fix It/Harlequin	6

JOHN BULL BREED

66	Polydor BM 56065	Can't Chance A Breakup/I'm A Man	300

BULLDOG BREED

69	Deram DM 270	Portcullis Gate/Halo In My Hair	40
70	Deram Nova (S)DN 5	MADE IN ENGLAND (LP)	100

(see also Flies)

BULLDOGS

64	Mercury MF 808	John, Paul, George And Ringo/What Do I See	18

BULLET

71	Purple PUR 101	Hobo/Sinister Minister	8

(see also Hard Stuff)

BULLET

75	Contour 2870 437	THE HANGED MAN (LP, TV soundtrack)	60

BULLSEYE

80	Kennet K1	No. 10,553/Why Don't You Let Me Know	8

MINT VALUE £

BULLY WEE (BAND)

Year	Label/Cat. No.	Title	Value
75	Folksound	BULLYWEE (LP)	20
76	Red Rag RRR 007	THE ENCHANTED LADY (LP)	15
70s	Red Rag RRR 017	SILVERMINES (LP, as Bullywee Band)	12
81	Jigsaw SAW 1	THE MADMAN OF GOTHAM (LP)	20

B. BUMBLE & STINGERS

Year	Label/Cat. No.	Title	Value
61	Top Rank JAR 561	Bumble Boogie/School Day Blues	12
62	Top Rank JAR 611	Nut Rocker/Nautilus	8
62	Stateside SS 113	Apple Knocker/The Moon And The Sea	10
62	Stateside SS 131	Dawn Cracker/Scales	10
63	Stateside SS 192	Baby Mash/Night Time Madness	10
67	Mercury MF 977	Silent Movies/Twelfth Street Rag	10
72	Pye International 7N 25597	Down At Mother's Place/Manhattan Spiritual	8
62	Stateside SE 1001	THE PIANO STYLINGS OF B. BUMBLE (EP)	20

(see also Kim Fowley)

BUMBLE BEE SLIM

Year	Label/Cat. No.	Title	Value
60s	Fontana 688 138ZL	BEE'S BACK IN TOWN (LP)	35

BUMBLES

Year	Label/Cat. No.	Title	Value
72	Purple PUR 107	Beep Beep/Buzz Off (some in promo-only p/s)	25/8

BUNCH

Year	Label/Cat. No.	Title	Value
67	CBS 202506	We're Not What We Appear To Be/You Never Came Home	55
67	CBS 2740	Don't Come Back To Me/You Can't Do This	25
67	CBS 3060	Looking Glass Alice/Spare A Shilling	100
68	CBS 3692	Birthday/Still	20
68	CBS 3709	Birthday/Still (reissue)	10

(see also Peter & The Wolves, Sounds Around, John Pantry)

BUNCH

Year	Label/Cat. No.	Title	Value
69	Beacon BEA 128	Red Rover, Red Rover/Happy Like This	5

BUNCH

Year	Label/Cat. No.	Title	Value
72	Island WIP 6130	When Will I Be Loved/Willie And The Hand Jive	8
72	Island ILPS 9189	ROCK ON (LP, some with 1-sided flexi: "Let There Be Drums" [WI 4002])	40/18

(see also Fairport Convention, Sandy Denny, Richard & Linda Thompson, Ashley Hutchings, Trevor Lucas)

BUNCH OF FIVES

Year	Label/Cat. No.	Title	Value
66	Parlophone R 5494	Go Home Baby/At The Station	70

(see also Viv Prince, Egg, Hullaballoos, Junior's Eyes, Outsiders [U.K.])

BUNDLE

Year	Label/Cat. No.	Title	Value
70	Polydor 2058 029	Dirty La Rue/Progressive Underground	15

ROGER BUNN

Year	Label/Cat. No.	Title	Value
70	Major Minor SMLP 70	PIECE OF MIND (LP)	55

BUNNIES

Year	Label/Cat. No.	Title	Value
66	Decca F 12350	Thumper/Ja Da	5

BINGY BUNNY & BONGO LES

Year	Label/Cat. No.	Title	Value
73	Ackee ACK 506	International Scout/International Scout Version	12

(see also Bongo Les, Mediators)

BUNNY & RUDDY

Year	Label/Cat. No.	Title	Value
68	Nu Beet NB 007	Rhythm & Soul/MONTY MORRIS: True Romance	25
68	Nu Beat NB 011	On The Town/MONTY MORRIS: Simple Simon	18

BOB BUNTING

Year	Label/Cat. No.	Title	Value
68	Transatlantic TRA 166	YOU'VE GOT TO GO DOWN THIS WAY (LP)	45

VASHTI BUNYAN

Year	Label/Cat. No.	Title	Value
70	Philips 6308 019	JUST ANOTHER DIAMOND DAY (LP)	350

(see also Vashti, Fairport Convention, Dave Swarbrick, Robin Williamson)

ERIC BURDON (BAND)

Year	Label/Cat. No.	Title	Value
75	Capitol E-ST 11359	SUN SECRETS (LP, as Eric Burdon Band)	12
75	Capitol E-ST 11426	STOP (LP, as Eric Burdon Band)	12
78	Polydor 2302 078	SURVIVOR (LP, with 8-page booklet)	12
80	Polydor 2344 147	DARKNESS — DARKNESS (LP)	12

ERIC BURDON & THE ANIMALS

Year	Label/Cat. No.	Title	Value
66	Decca F 12502	Mama Told Me Not To Come/See See Rider (unreleased)	
66	Decca F 12502	Help Me Girl/See See Rider (amended issue with new A-side)	8
67	MGM MGM 1340	When I Was Young/A Girl Named Sandoz	12
67	MGM MGM 1344	Good Times/Ain't That So	8
67	MGM MGM 1359	San Franciscan Nights/Gratefully Dead	10
68	MGM MGM 1373	Sky Pilot (Parts 1 & 2)	10
68	MGM MGM 1412	Monterey/Anything	12
69	MGM MGM 1461	Ring Of Fire/I'm An Animal	15
69	MGM MGM 1481	River Deep Mountain High/Help Me Girl	18
67	MGM C(S) 8052	WINDS OF CHANGE (LP)	25
68	MGM C(S) 8074	THE TWAIN SHALL MEET (LP)	30
68	MGM C(S) 8105	LOVE IS (LP)	30
71	MGM 2619 002	LOVE IS (2-LP; individual LP nos.: 2354 006/7)	40

(see also Animals, Stud, Zoot Money's Big Roll Band)

ERIC BURDON & WAR

Year	Label/Cat. No.	Title	Value
70	Polydor 2001 072	Spill The Wine/Magic Mountain	5
71	Liberty LBF 15434	They Can't Take Away Our Music/Home Cookin'	5
71	United Artists UP 35217	Paint It Black/Spirit	5
70	Polydor 2310 041	ERIC BURDON DECLARES WAR (LP)	20
70	Liberty LDS 8400	BLACKMAN'S BURDON (2-LP, some with banned track "P.C. 3")	30/25
76	ABC ABCL 5207	LOVE IS ALL AROUND (LP)	12

(see also War)

MINT VALUE £

ERIC BURDON & JIMMY WITHERSPOON

71	United Artists UP 35287	Soledad/Headin' For Home	7
71	United Artists UAG 29251	GUILTY! (LP, gatefold sleeve)	15

(see also Jimmy Witherspoon)

DAVE BURGESS (TRIO)

55	London HLB 8175	I Love Paris/Five Foot Two, Eyes Of Blue (Has Anybody Seen My Girl)	35
55	London HLB 8175	I Love Paris/Five Foot Two, Eyes Of Blue (Has Anybody Seen My Girl) (78)	10
58	Oriole CB 1413	I'm Available/Who's Gonna Cry?	110
58	Oriole CB 1413	I'm Available/Who's Gonna Cry? (78)	10

JOHN BURGESS

60s	Topic 12 T 199	KING OF THE HIGHLAND PIPERS (LP)	15

SONNY BURGESS

60	London HLS 9064	Sadie's Back In Town/A Kiss Goodnight	250

JIM BURGETT

61	Philips PB 1133	Let's Investigate/The Living Dead	45

CHRIS DE BURGH

75	A&M AMS 7148	Hold On/Sin City	6
75	A&M AMS 7185	Flying/Watching The World	6
76	A&M AMS 7196	Lonely Sky/The Song For You	5
76	A&M AMS 7224	Patricia The Stripper/Old Friend	5
76	A&M AMS 7267	A Spaceman Came Travelling/Just A Poor Boy (initially in p/s)	7
77	A&M AMS 7320	Broken Wings/I Will	6
78	A&M AMS 7336	Discovery/Round And Around	6
78	A&M AMS 7347	Spanish Train/Perfect Day (initially in p/s)	6
80	A&M AMS 7546	Shadows And Lights/Walls Of Silence (initially in p/s)	6
80	A&M AMS 7562	The Traveller/Eastern Wind (initially in p/s)	6
81	A&M AMS 8160	Waiting For The Hurricane/Broken Wings (p/s)	5
82	A&M AMS 8268	The Getaway/Living On The Island (p/s)	5
84	A&M AMX 202	I Love The Night/Moonlight And Vodka (12", p/s)	8
80s	A&M C DE B 1	Sailor/Lonely Sky (p/s, clear vinyl, numbered)	7

KEVIN BURKE

78	Rockburgh ROC 105	IF THE CAP FITS (LP)	25

SOLOMON BURKE

61	London HLK 9454	Just Out Of Reach/Be Bop Grandma	40
62	London HLK 9512	Cry To Me/I Almost Lost My Mind	60
62	London HLK 9560	Down In The Valley/I'm Hanging Up My Heart For You	20
63	London HLK 9715	If You Need Me/You Can Make It If You Try	20
63	London HLK 9763	Can't Nobody Love You/Stupidity	30
64	London HLK 9849	He'll Have To Go/Rockin' Soul	20
64	London HLK 9887	Goodbye Baby (Baby Goodbye)/Someone To Love Me	20
64	Atlantic AT 4004	Everybody Needs Somebody To Love/Looking For My Baby	20
64	Atlantic AT 4014	The Price/More Rockin' Soul	15
65	Atlantic AT 4022	Got To Get You Off My Mind/Peepin'	12
65	Atlantic AT 4030	Maggie's Farm/Tonight's The Night	20
65	Atlantic AT 4044	Someone Is Watching/Dance, Dance, Dance	10
65	Atlantic AT 4061	Only Love (Can Save Me Now)/Little Girl That Loves Me	12
66	Atlantic AT 4073	Baby Come On Home/No, No, No, I Can't Stop Lovin' You Now	10
66	Atlantic 584 005	I Feel A Sin Comin' On/Mountain Of Pride	8
66	Atlantic 584 026	Keep Lookin'/Suddenly	8
67	Atlantic 584 100	Keep A Light In The Window Till I Come Home/Time Is A Thief	8
67	Atlantic 584 122	Take Me (Just As I Am)/I Stayed Away Too Long	8
68	Atlantic 584 191	I Wish I Knew (How It Would Feel To Be Free)/It's Just A Matter Of Time	7
68	Atlantic 584 204	Save It/Meet Me In Church	7
68	Bell BLL 1047	Uptight Good Woman/I Can't Stop (No No No)	6
69	Bell BLL 1062	Proud Mary/What Am I Living For	6
74	Anchor ABC 4002	Midnight And You/I Have A Dream	6
63	London REK 1379	TONIGHT MY HEART SHE IS CRYING (EP)	75
65	Atlantic AET 6008	ROCK'N'SOUL (EP)	55
63	London HA-K 8018	SOLOMON BURKE'S GREATEST (LP)	85
64	Atlantic ATL 5009	ROCK'N'SOUL (LP)	65
66	Atlantic 587/588 016	THE BEST OF SOLOMON BURKE (LP)	50
66	Atlantic 590 004	KING OF ROCK'N'SOUL (LP, reissue)	22
68	Atlantic 587 105	KING SOLOMON (LP)	35
68	Atlantic 587/588 117	I WISH I KNEW (LP)	30
69	Bell MBLL/SBLL 118	PROUD MARY (LP)	20
72	MGM 2315 048	THE ELECTRONIC MAGNETISM (LP)	18

(see also Soul Clan)

SONNY BURKE (U.K.)

64	Black Swan WI 457	I Love You Still/It's Always A Pleasure	25
64	Black Swan WI 458	City In The Sky/Everyday I Love You More	22
65	Black Swan WI 469	Glad/Jeanie	20
65	Black Swan WI 470	Dance With Me/My Girl Can't Cook	25
65	Black Swan WI 471	Wicked People/Good Heaven Knows	22
66	Blue Beat BB 363	Blue Island/You Came And Left	18
67	Blue Beat BB 371	Look In Her Eyes/LLOYD CLARKE: Love Is Strange	20
68	Island ILP 972	THE SOUNDS OF SONNY BURKE (LP, mono only)	150

(see also Bob Andy, Gaylads, Ken Parker, Eddie Thornton Outfit, Glen Adams, Stranger Cole, Gaylads, Sonny & Yvonne)

DAVE BURLAND

71	Trailer LER 2029	A DALESMAN'S LITANY (LP, red label)	25
72	Trailer LER 2082	DAVE BURLAND (LP)	20
75	Rubber RUB 012	SONGS AND BUTTERED HAYCOCKS (LP)	18
79	Rubber RUB 036	YOU CAN'T FOOL THE FAT MAN (LP)	15
80	Rubber RUB 012/036	DOUBLE TAKE (2-LP, reissue)	18

MINT VALUE £

SASCHA BURLAND
61 Philips PB 1152 — Gorilla Walk/Hole In My Soul ... 6

BURMOE BROTHERS
85 Wild Blue Yonder WBY 121 — Skin/Leber Oder Lippenstift/Under The Blanket Of Love (12", p/s) ... 15

(see also Marc Almond, Nick Cave)

BURN
00s Virgin HUTCDP 146 — Facing The Music (1-sided, numbered gold-embossed p/s, 1000 only) ... 20

JEAN-JACQUES BURNEL
79 United Artists UP 36500 — Freddie Laker (Concorde And Eurobus)/Ozymandias (p/s) ... 5

80 United Artists BP 361 — Girl From The Snow Country/Ode To Joy (live)/ Do The European (live) (p/s, unissued) ... 500

88 Stranglers Information Service S.I.S. 003 — Goebbels, Mosley, God And Ingrams (fan club flexidisc, with issue 27 of *Strangled* fanzine) ... 8/5

88 Mau Mau P MAU 601 — EUROMAN COMETH (LP, picture disc reissue) ... 12

JEAN-JACQUES BURNEL & DAVE GREENFIELD
84 Epic EPCA 4076 — Rain And Dole And Tea/Consequences (p/s) ... 6

84 Epic EPC 25707 — FIRE AND WATER (LP) ... 12

(see also, Blue Maxi, Stranglers)

FRANCES BURNETT
59 Coral Q 72374 — Please Remember Me/How I Miss You So (triangular or round centre) ... 50/40

59 Coral Q 72374 — Please Remember Me/How I Miss You So (78) ... 15

REV. J.C. BURNETT/REV. GATES/REV. MOSELEY
60 Fontana TFE 17265 — TREASURES OF NORTH AMERICAN NEGRO MUSIC VOLUME 6: PREACHERS AND CONGREGATIONS (EP) ... 22

KING BURNETT
75 Dip DL 5056 — I Man Free/UPSETTERS: Version ... 18

75 Dip DL 5073 — Key Card/UPSETTERS: Domino Game ... 18

DORSEY BURNETTE
60 London HLN 9047 — Juarez Town/(There Was A) Tall Oak Tree ... 22

60 London HLN 9160 — Hey Little One/Big Rock Candy Mountain ... 30

61 London HLN 9365 — (It's No) Sin/Hard Rock Mine ... 20

65 Tamla Motown TMG 534 — Jimmy Brown/Everybody's Angel ... 65

69 Liberty LBF 15190 — The Greatest Love/Thin Little, Simple Little, Plain Little Girl ... 5

63 London RE-D 1402 — DORSEY BURNETTE SINGS (EP) ... 75

63 London HA-D 8050 — DORSEY BURNETTE (LP) ... 100

(see also Johnny & Dorsey Burnette)

JOHNNY BURNETTE (TRIO)
78s
56 Vogue Coral Q 72177 — Tear It Up/You're Undecided (as Johnny Burnette & Rock'N'Roll Trio) ... 175

57 Vogue Coral Q 72227 — Honey Hush/Lonesome Train (as Johnny Burnette Trio) ... 170

57 Vogue Coral Q 72283 — Touch Me/Eager Beaver Baby (as Johnny Burnette Trio) ... 170

60 London HLG 9172 — Dreamin'/Cincinnati Fireball ... 600

96 Cruisin' The 50s CASB 003 — The Train Kept A Rollin'/Sweet Love On My Mind (300 copies only) ... 50

SINGLES
56 Vogue Coral Q 72177 — Tear It Up/You're Undecided (as Johnny Burnette & Rock'N'Roll Trio) ... 500

57 Vogue Coral Q 72227 — Honey Hush/Lonesome Train (as Johnny Burnette Trio) ... 500

57 Vogue Coral Q 72283 — Touch Me/Eager Beaver Baby (as Johnny Burnette Trio) ... 200

60 London HLG 9172 — Dreamin'/Cincinnati Fireball ... 15

60 London HLG 9254 — You're Sixteen/I Beg Your Pardon ... 10

61 London HLG 9315 — Little Boy Sad/Pledge Of Love ... 10

61 London HLG 9388 — Girls/I've Got A Lot Of Things To Do ... 10

61 London HLG 9453 — God Country And My Baby/Honestly I Do ... 15

61 London HLG 9458 — Settin' The Woods On Fire/I'm Still Dreaming ... 18

61 London HLG 9473 — Big Big World/The Fool ... 18

62 Liberty LIB 55416 — Clown Shoes/The Way I Am ... 10

62 Liberty LIB 55489 — Damn The Defiant/Lonesome Waters ... 12

66 Liberty LIB 10235 — Dreamin'/Little Boy Sad ... 10

62 Pye International 7N 25158 — I Wanna Thank Your Folks/The Giant ... 10

63 Pye International 7N 25187 — Remember Me/Time Is Not Enough ... 10

63 Capitol CL 15322 — All Week Long/It Isn't There ... 25

64 Capitol CL 15347 — Sweet Suzie/Walking Talking Doll ... 35

EXPORT SINGLES
60 London HLG 7104 — You're Sixteen/Settin' The Woods On Fire ... 35

61 London HL 7109 — Little Boy Sad/I Go Down To The River ... 40

EPs
60 London RE-G 1263 — DREAMING ... 75

61 London RE-G 1291 — LITTLE BOY SAD ... 80

61 London RE-G 1309 — BIG BIG WORLD ... 85

61 London RE-G 1327 — GIRLS ... 85

63 Liberty LEP 2091 — HIT AFTER HIT ... 85

64 Capitol EAP 20645 — FOUR BY BURNETTE ... 175

LPs
56 Coral LVC 10041 — ROCK AND ROLL TRIO (10", as Johnny Burnette Trio) ... 750

61 London HA-G 2306 — DREAMIN' ... 60

61 London HA-G 2349 — YOU'RE SIXTEEN ... 50

61 London HA-G 2375 — JOHNNY BURNETTE SINGS (also stereo SAH-G 6175) ... 100/120

62 Liberty LBY 1006 — BURNETTE'S HITS AND OTHER FAVOURITES ... 50

64 Liberty LBY 1231 — THE JOHNNY BURNETTE STORY ... 70

			MINT VALUE £
66	Ace Of Hearts AH 120	ROCK AND ROLL TRIO (reissue, as Johnny Burnette Trio)	20
68	Sunset SLS 50007E	DREAMIN'	15
68	Coral CP 10	TEAR IT UP (as Johnny Burnette Trio)	30
71	Coral CP 61	ROCK AND ROLL TRIO (2nd reissue, as Johnny Burnette Trio)	12
74	United Artists UAS 29643	TENTH ANNIVERSARY ALBUM	12

(see also Johnny & Dorsey Burnette)

JOHNNY & DORSEY BURNETTE

63	Reprise R 20153	Hey Sue/It Don't Matter Much	45

(see also Johnny Burnette, Dorsey Burnette)

SMILEY BURNETTE

50	Capitol CL 13388	Rudolph The Red-Nosed Reindeer/Grandaddy Frog (78)	10
54	London HL 8071	Lazy Locomotive/That Long White Line	75
54	London HL 8071	Lazy Locomotive/That Long White Line (78)	30
54	London HL 8085	Chuggin' On Down "66"/Mucho Gusto	75
54	London HL 8085	Chuggin' On Down "66"/Mucho Gusto (78)	30

BURNING SPEAR

75	Fab FAB 240	Foggy Road/Version	12
75	Island ILPS 9377	MARCUS GARVEY (LP)	15

(see also Irving Brown, King Cry Cry)

BURNIN' RED IVANHOE

71	Warner Bros K 44062	BURNIN' RED IVANHOE (LP)	50
72	Dandelion 2310 145	W.W.W. (LP, gatefold sleeve)	55

JAN BURNNETTE

62	Oriole CB 1716	I Could Have Loved You So Well/The Miracle Of Life	15
62	Oriole CB 1742	All At Once/Does My Heartache Show?	10
62	Oriole CB 1761	Teddy/Trust In Me	15
63	Oriole CB 1807	The Boy I Used To Know/Unimportant Things	15
63	Oriole CB 1841	Till I Hear The Truth From You/Fall In Love	10
64	Oriole CB 1905	Let Me Make You Smile Again/No Regrets	15
64	Oriole CB 1920	Too Young/The Four Winds And The Seven Seas	15
64	Oriole CB 1949	Love, Let Me Not Hunger/The One I Love (Belongs To Somebody Else)	10

DENNIS BURNS

(see Mark Perry)

EDDIE 'GUITAR' BURNS

72	Action ACMP 100	BOTTLE UP AND GO (LP)	25
75	Big Bear BEAR 7	DETROIT BLACKBOTTOM (LP)	12

JACKIE BURNS & BELLES

63	MGM MGM 1226	He's My Guy/I Do The Best I Can	100

JIMMY BURNS

79	Grapevine GRP 118	I Really Love You/I Love You Girl	15

LISA BURNS

78	MCA MCF 2849	LISA BURNS (LP)	18

RANDY BURNS

68	Fontana STL 5520	EVENING OF THE MAGICIAN (LP)	20

RAY BURNS

53	Columbia SCM 5077	Rags To Riches/Begorrah	8
54	Columbia SCM 5153	I Can't Tell A Waltz From A Tango/Lonely Nightingale	8
55	Columbia DB 3640	That's How A Love Song Was Born/The Voice (78)	5
56	Columbia DB 3811	Condemned For Life (With A Rock And Roll Life)/The Mare Piccola	40
57	Columbia DB 3966	Wonderful! Wonderful!/Bernadine	6
58	Columbia DB 4107	Are You Sincere/The Best Dream Of All	6
55	Columbia SEG 7594	RAY BURNS (EP)	20

(see also Ruby Murray, Ronnie Harris, Diana Decker, Ray Martin)

WILFRED BURNS

53	MGM SP 1059	There Was An Old Lady/Broken Horseshoe	8

HAROLD BURRAGE

65	Sue WI 353	I'll Take One/A Long Ways Together	30
68	President PT 130	You Made Me So Happy/Take Me Now	22

KENNY BURRELL

61	Esquire 32-140	ALL NIGHT LONG (LP, as Kenny Burrell All Stars)	30
64	Verve VLP 9058	BLUE BLASH (LP, with Jimmy Smith)	30
65	Verve VLP 9099	GUITAR FORMS (LP)	30
66	Stateside SL 10163	CRASH! (LP, with Brother Jack McDuff)	20
68	Verve (S)VLP 9217	BLUES, THE COMMON GROUND (LP)	25
69	Verve SVLP 9246	NIGHT SONG (LP)	15
70	Verve SVLP 9250	ASPHALT CANYON SUITE (LP)	15

(see also Brother Jack McDuff, Jimmy Smith)

WILLIAM S. BURROUGHS

80	Industrial IR 0016	NOTHING HERE NOW BUT THE RECORDINGS (LP)	30

BUDDY BURTON

(see under Dixie Four)

HAL BURTON

58	Embassy WB 290	Rave On/Big Man (78)	12
58	Embassy WB 308	Move It/Susie Darling	25

GARY BURTON (QUARTET)

68	RCA Victor SF 7923	LOFTY FAKE ANAGRAM (LP)	20
69	RCA Victor SF 8015	GENUINE TONGUE FUNERAL (LP)	20

MINT VALUE £

71	Atlantic 2400 107	GOOD VIBES (LP)	18
72	Atlantic K 40305	ALONE AT LAST (LP)	12
72	Atlantic K 40378	PARIS ENCOUNTER (LP, with Stefan Grappelli)	12

(see also Michael Gibbs)

JAMES BURTON

71	A&M AMLS 64293	THE GUITAR SOUNDS OF JAMES BURTON (LP)	65

(see also Jim & Joe, Shindogs)

TOMMY BURTON COMBO

64	Blue Beat BB 237	Lavender Blue/I'm Walking	20

TREVOR BURTON

71	Wizard WIZ 103	Fight For My Country/Janie Slow Down	20

(see also B,L&G; Uglys, Move, Balls, Denny Laine, Danny King's Mayfair Set, Magic Christians, Idle Race)

BURUNDI STEPHENSON BLACK

71	Barclay BAR 3	Burundi Black Parts 1 & 2 (some with p/s)	8/4

BURZUM

94	Misanthropy 001	HVIS LYSET TAR OSS (LP)	18
94	Misanthropy 002	DET SOM ENGANG VAR (LP)	18

LOU BUSCH & HIS ORCHESTRA

56	Capitol CL 14504	Zambesi/Rainbow's End	15

(see also Joe 'Fingers' Carr)

ERNIE BUSH

75	Contempo CS 2020	Breakaway/(Version 2)	6

KATE BUSH

78	EMI EMI 2719	Wuthering Heights/Kite (p/s)	35
78	EMI EMI 2806	The Man With The Child In His Eyes/Moving (p/s)	18
78	EMI EMI 2887	Hammer Horror/Coffee Homeground (p/s)	8
79	EMI EMI 2911	Wow/Fullhouse (p/s)	8
79	EMI MIEP 2991	KATE BUSH ON STAGE (EP, gatefold sleeve)	12
79	EMI PSR 442/3	KATE BUSH ON STAGE (EP, double pack, gatefold sleeve, promo only)	65
80	Sound For Industry SFI 562	Selected Highlights from "Never Forever" (flexidisc, black vinyl)	12
80	Sound For Industry SFI 562	Selected Highlights from "Never Forever" (square flexidisc, black vinyl)	12
81	EMI EMI 5201	Sat In Your Lap/Lord Of The Reedy River (p/s)	5
82	EMI EMI 5350	There Goes A Tenner/Ne T'Enfuis Pas (thick card, p/s)	8
84	EMI KBS 1	THE SINGLE FILE (13 x 7" box set with lyric booklet)	130
85	EMI KB 1	Running Up That Hill/Under The Ivy (gatefold p/s)	5
85	EMI 12 KB 2	Cloudbusting (Organon Mix)/Burning Bridges/My Lagan Love (12", p/s)	8
86	EMI KBP 4	The Big Sky (Single Mix)/Not This Time (picture disc)	12
89	EMI CDEM 102	The Sensual World/(Instrumental)/Walk Straight Down The Middle (CD)	8
89	EMI EMPD 119	This Woman's Work/Be Kind To My Mistakes (picture disc, with insert, PVC sl.)	5
89	EMI 12EMP 119	This Woman's Work/Be Kind To My Mistakes/I'm Still Waiting (12", poster p/s)	8
89	EMI CDEM 119	This Woman's Work/Be Kind To My Mistakes/I'm Still Waiting (CD)	10
90	EMI CDEM 134	Love And Anger/Ken/The Confrontation/ One Last Look Around The House (CD)	10
91	Rocket TRICD 2	Rocket Man/Candle In The Wind/Rocket Man (Instrumental) (CD, digipak)	10
93	EMI GIRL 1	Rubberband Girl (CD, 1-track "lyrical teaser", promo only)	15
93	EMI EM 280	Eat The Music/Big Stripey Lie (p/s, picture labels, release cancelled, 17 copies only)	1,500
93	EMI 12EMPD 280	Eat The Music/Eat The Music (Madagascan Remix)/Big Stripey Lie (12", picture disc, unissued)	
93	EMI CDEM 280	Eat The Music/(Madagascan Remix)/Big Stripey Lie (CD, unissued)	
93	EMI MUSIC 1	Eat The Music (CD, 1-track promo for unissued single, no inlay, withdrawn)	150
93	EMI CDEM 297	Moments Of Pleasure/December Will Be Magic Again/Experiment IV (CD, box set with 4 prints)	8
94	EMI EMPD 355	And So Is Love/Rubberband Girl (USA Mix) (picture disc, PVC sleeve, with 60" x 40" poster, unnumbered or 5,000 numbered)	25/8
79	EMI EM CP 3223	THE KICK INSIDE (LP, picture disc, stickered sleeve)	50
79	EMI EM CP 3223	THE KICK INSIDE (LP, picture disc, stickered sleeve, second pressing with "manufactured in the U.K. by EMI Records Ltd" wording)	40
79	EMI EM CP 3223	THE KICK INSIDE (LP, picture disc, mispress with same picture both sides)	150
90	EMI KBBX 1	THIS WOMAN'S WORK (9-LP, box set)	100
90	EMI CKBBX 1	THIS WOMAN'S WORK (cassette, box set)	40
90	EMI CDKBBX 1	THIS WOMAN'S WORK (CD, box set)	100

(see also Peter Gabriel & Kate Bush, Lesley Duncan)

RAY BUSH & AVON CITIES' SKIFFLE

56	Tempo A 146	Hey Hey Daddy Blues/Green Corn	25
56	Tempo A 146	Hey Hey Daddy Blues/Green Corn (78)	15
56	Tempo A 149	Fisherman's Blues/This Little Light Of Mine	25
56	Tempo A 149	Fisherman's Blues/This Little Light Of Mine (78)	15
57	Tempo A 156	How Long, How Long, Blues/Julian Johnson	22
57	Tempo A 156	How Long, How Long, Blues/Julian Johnson (78)	15
57	Tempo A 157	Lonesome Day Blues/I Don't Know	20
57	Tempo A 157	Lonesome Day Blues/I Don't Know (78)	15
57	Tempo EXA 40	RAY BUSH & AVON CITIES' SKIFFLE (EP)	30
57	Tempo EXA 50	RAY BUSH & AVON CITIES' SKIFFLE NO. 2 (EP)	30

(see also Avon Cities Jazz Band)

BUSH BOYS

59	Capitol CL 15082	A Broken Vow/Never Before	7

BUSH TETRAS

81	Fetish FET 007	Things That Go Boom In The Night/Das Ah Riot (p/s)	6
82	Fetish FE 15	Can't Be Funky (unissued, stamped white label only, custom plain sleeve)	10
82	Fetish FET 16EP	RITUALS (12" EP)	15

BUSINESS

81 Secret SHH 123 Harry May/National Insurance Blacklist (p/s) ... 12
82 Secret SHH 132 SMASH THE DISCOS EP: Day-O (The Banana Boat Song)/Disco Girls/ Smash The Disco (p/s) ... 10
83 Secret SHH 150 OUT OF BUSINESS (12" EP, unissued, white label promo, 10 copies only) ... 100+
85 Wonderful World Of... 121 Get Out Of My House/All Out Tonight/Foreign Girl/Outlaw (12", p/s) ... 25
85 Diamond DIA 001 Drinking N Driving/H-Bomb (live) (p/s) ... 15
85 Diamond DIA 001T Drinking N Driving/H-Bomb (live)/Hurry Up Harry/Drinking 'N' Driving (original version) (12", p/s) ... 25
80s Link LINK 1201 DO A RUNNER (12" EP) ... 12
83 Secret SEC 11 SUBURBAN REBELS (LP) ... 20
83 Syndicate SYNLP 2 1980-81 OFFICIAL BOOTLEGS (LP) ... 30
84 Syndicate SYNLP 6 LOUD, PROUD 'N' PUNK, LIVE (LP) ... 20
85 Harry May SE 13 SATURDAY HEROES (LP) ... 20
86 Dojo DOJO LP 35 SINGALONGABUSINESS (LP) ... 15
88 Link LINK LP 035 WELCOME TO THE REAL WORLD (LP) ... 12
90 Link LRMO 1 IN AND OUT OF BUSINESS (LP, mail-order, 550 only) ... 20

(see also UK)

BUSKERS

73 Rubber RUB 007 LIFE OF A MAN (LP) ... 18
75 Hawk HALPX 142 THE BUSKERS (LP) ... 15

GEORGE HENRY BUSSEY/JIM BUNKLEY

71 Revival RVS 1003 GEORGE HENRY BUSSEY/JIM BUNKLEY (LP) ... 15

BUSTERS

63 Stateside SS 231 Bust Out/Astronauts ... 25

BUSTER('S) ALLSTARS

64 Blue Beat BB 244 Prince Royal/COSMO: One God ... 25
64 Blue Beat BB 269 The Tickler/COSMO: Rice And Badge ... 25
65 Blue Beat BB 294 Eye For Eye/South Virginia ... 25
65 Blue Beat BB 322 Happy Independence 65/STRANGER COLE: When The Party Is Over ... 25
65 Blue Beat BB 333 When The Party Is Over/Matilda (with Stranger Cole) ... 25
66 Blue Beat BB 342 Cincinnatti Kid/Sammy Dead ... 75
67 Blue Beat BB 372 Sounds And Pressure/My Darling (both actually by Hopeton Lewis) ... 40
67 Blue Beat BB 384 Take It Easy/Why Must I Cry (both actually by Hopeton Lewis) ... 30
69 Fab FAB 101 Pum Pum A Go Kill You/Oh Lady Oh ... 15
70 Fab FAB 124 The Rebel/The Preacher ... 15

(see also Prince Buster, Teddy King, Little Darling, Khandars, Higgs & Wilson, Owen Gray, Charmers, Fitzroy D Long, Maytals, Derrick Morgan, Eric Morris, Personalities, Roy & Millie, Zoot Simms, Spanish Boys, Spanish Town Skabeats)

BUSTER'S GROUP

61 Starlite ST45 052 Buster's Shack/ERIC MORRIS: Search The World ... 40

(see also Prince Buster, Rico, Owen Gray)

BUSTY & COOL

62 Blue Beat BB 144 Mr Policeman/What A World ... 25

TONY BUTALA

62 Salvo SLO 1801 Long Black Stockings/Rumors (99 copies only) ... 50

BUTCHER

82 Inept INEPT 002 On The Ground/Grow Up Don't Blow Up (p/s) ... 5

(see also Intestines)

EDDIE BUTCHER

76 Free Reed FRR 003 I ONCE WAS A DAYSMAN (LP, with insert) ... 12

SAM BUTERA (& WITNESSES)

58 HMV POP 476 Good Gracious Baby/It's Better Than Nothing At All ... 45
58 HMV POP 476 Good Gracious Baby/It's Better Than Nothing At All (78) ... 15
58 Capitol CL 14913 Bim Bam/Twinkle In Your Eye (as Sam Butera & Witnesses) ... 250
59 Capitol CL 14988 Handle With Care/French Poodle ... 20
64 Prima PR 1003 Skinnie Minnie/Little Liza Jane ... 10
56 HMV 7EG 8087 SAX SERENADE (EP) ... 40
60 London HA-D 2288 THE RAT RACE (LP, as Sam Butera & Witnesses) ... 30

(see also Louis Prima)

BILLY BUTLER (& ENCHANTERS)

69 Soul City SC 113 The Right Track/Boston Monkey ... 25
74 Epic S EPC 2508 The Right Track/Can't Live Without Her ... 6

CHAMP BUTLER

56 Vogue Coral Q 72163 The Joshua Tree/Down In Mexico ... 10

(see also Johnny Bond's Red River Valley Boys)

JERRY BUTLER

60 Top Rank JAR 389 I Found A Love/A Lonely Soldier ... 40
60 Top Rank JAR 531 He Will Break Your Heart/Thanks To You ... 50
61 Top Rank JAR 562 Find Another Girl/When Trouble Calls ... 30
61 Columbia DB 4743 Moon River/Aware Of Love ... 20
62 Stateside SS 121 Make It Easy On Yourself/It's Too Late ... 22
63 Stateside SS 158 You Can Run But You Can't Hide/I'm The One ... 22
63 Stateside SS 170 You Go Right Through Me/The Wishing Star ... 18
63 Stateside SS 195 Whatever You Want/You Won't Be Sorry ... 18
64 Stateside SS 252 Need To Belong/Give Me Your Love ... 18
64 Stateside SS 300 Giving Up On Love/I've Been Trying ... 18
65 Fontana TF 553 Good Times/I've Grown Accustomed To Her Face ... 15
65 Fontana TF 588 I Can't Stand To See You Cry/Nobody Needs Your Love ... 15

65	Mercury MF 932	Love (Oh, How Sweet It Is)/Loneliness	15
66	Sue WI 4003	I Stand Accused/I Don't Want To Hear Anymore	35
66	Sue WI 4009	Just For You/Believe In Me	30
67	Mercury MF 964	I Dig You Baby/Some Kinda Magic	12
67	Mercury MF 1005	Mr. Dream Merchant/'Cause I Love You So	10
68	Mercury MF 1035	Never Give You Up/Beside You	10
68	Mercury MF 1058	Hey Mr Western Union Man (Send A Telegram)/Just Can't Forget About You	12
69	Mercury MF 1078	Are You Happy/Strange I Still Love You	7
69	Mercury MF 1094	Only The Strong Survive/Just Because I Really Love You	10
69	Mercury MF 1122	Moody Woman/Go Away And Find Yourself	10
69	Mercury MF 1132	A Brand New Me/What's The Use Of Breaking Up	10
70	President PT 299	Make It Easy On Yourself/Moon River	7
72	Mercury 6052 036	One Night Affair/What's So Good About It (You're My Baby)	6
72	Mercury 6052 119	Moody Woman/A Brand New Me	6
72	Mercury 6052 155	I Only Have Eyes For You/Ain't Understanding Mellow	6
72	Mercury 6052 168	One Night Affair/What's So Good About It (You're My Baby) (reissue)	6
63	Stateside SL 10032	HE WILL BREAK YOUR HEART (LP)	100
63	Stateside SL 10050	FOLK SONGS (LP)	60
68	Fontana (S)TL 5246	LOVE ME (LP)	40
68	Mercury 20118 (S)MCL	MR. DREAM MERCHANT (LP)	30
69	Mercury 20144 (S)MCL	SOUL GOES ON (LP)	30
69	Mercury 20154 (S)MCL	THE ICE MAN COMETH (LP)	30
70	Joy JOYS 171	MAKE IT EASY ON YOURSELF (LP)	15
72	Mercury 6338 102	SPICE OF LIFE (LP)	18
72	Mercury 6430 401	THE VERY BEST OF JERRY BUTLER (LP)	12

(see also Betty Everett & Jerry Butler, Impressions, Gene & Jerry)

LESLIE BUTLER (& FUGITIVES)

67	Island WI 3069	Hornpipe Rock Steady/You Don't Have To Say You Love Me	40
67	Doctor Bird DB 1083	Winchester Rocksteady (with Fugitives)/ ASTON CAMPBELL & CONQUERORS: Ramona	35
68	High Note HS 008	Top Cat/WEBBER SISTERS: Stars Above	25
68	High Note HS 009	Revival/GAYLADS: Over The Rainbow's End	18

(see also Ken Boothe, Fugitives, Gaylads)

BUTTERCUPS

68	Pama PM 742	If I Love You/Loving You	12
69	Pama PM 760	Come Put My Life In Order/If I Love You	12

BILLY BUTTERFIELD & HIS ORCHESTRA

55	London HLF 8181	The Magnificent Matador/Sugar Blues Mambo	35
55	London HLF 8181	The Magnificent Matador/Sugar Blues Mambo (78)	10

(PAUL) BUTTERFIELD BLUES BAND

66	London HLZ 10100	Come On In/I Got A Mind To Give Up Living	15
67	Elektra EKSN 45007	All These Blues/Never Say No	8
67	Elektra EKSN 45020	Run Out Of Time/One More Heartache	12
68	Elektra EKSN 45047	Get Yourself Together/Mine To Love	8
69	Elektra EKSN 45069	Where Did My Baby Go/In My Own Dream	8
70	Elektra 2101 012	Love March/Love Disease	6
65	Elektra EKL/EKS 294	PAUL BUTTERFIELD BLUES BAND (LP, orange label)	40
66	Elektra EKL/EKS 315	EAST — WEST (LP, orange label)	45
67	Elek. EKL 4015/EKS 74015	THE RESURRECTION OF PIGBOY CRABSHAW (LP, orange label)	35
68	Elektra EKL 4025	IN MY OWN DREAM (LP, orange label, also stereo EKS 74025)	30
69	Elektra EKS 74053	KEEP ON MOVIN' (LP)	18
71	Elektra EKD 2001	LIVE (2-LP)	20
72	Elektra K 62011	GOLDEN BUTTER (LP, gatefold sleeve)	12

(see also John Mayall's Bluesbreakers, Mike Bloomfield)

BUTTERFLIES

68	President PT 192	Love Me Forever/He's Got Everything	10

BUTTERFLYS

64	Red Bird RB 10009	Goodnight Baby/The Swim	30

BUTTERSCOTCH

70	RCA 1983	Surprise, Surprise/In This World Of Loving You	6

BUTTERSCOTCH CABOOSE

68	Bell BLL 1023	Melinda/Let A Little Sunshine In	6

BUTTHOLE SURFERS

84	Alt. Tentacles VIRUS 22	BUTTHOLE SURFERS (mini-LP, black & white sleeve)	8
89	Blast First BFF P41	WIDOWMAKER! (10" EP, with Reading Festival insert)	8
91	Rough Trade R 2081 2601	PIOUGHD (LP, with bonus 12")	12

BUTTONDOWN BRASS

67	Fontana LPS 16255	HA HA HA (HEE-HEE-HEE) (LP)	15
76	DJM DJS 22046	FUNK IN HELL (LP)	40
77	DJM DJS 22076	COPS N'ROBBERS (LP)	15

(see also Ray Davies & Buttondown Brass)

SHEILA BUXTON

55	Columbia SCM 5193	Thank You For The Waltz/Just Between Friends	5
57	Columbia DB 3887	Perfect Love/I Love You Baby (My Baby Loves Me)	5
57	Columbia DB 4051	The In-Between Age/Charm	5
57	Columbia DB 4051	The In-Between Age/Charm (78)	8
59	Top Rank JAR 113	Soldier, Won't You Marry Me?/Li Per Li	5
59	Top Rank JAR 113	Soldier, Won't You Marry Me?/Li Per Li (78)	8

MINT VALUE £

59 Top Rank JAR 144 The Valley Of Love/The Wonder Of You . . . 5
59 Top Rank JAR 144 The Valley Of Love/The Wonder Of You (78) . . . 10
59 Top Rank JAR 240 All I Do Is Dream Of You/Shakedown. . . . 5
60 Top Rank JAR 356 Sixteen Reasons/Goodnight, God I Love You . . . 10
(see also Craig Douglas)

BUZZ

66 Columbia DB 7887 You're Holding Me Down/I've Gotta Buzz . . . 250
(see also Boston Dexters, Tam White)

BUZZ

79 Redball RR 06 Insanity/Him Not Me/Sick At Heart (p/s) . . . 50

BUZZ & BUCKY

65 Stateside SS 428 Tiger A Go Go/Bay City . . . 30
(see also Ronny & The Daytonas)

BUZZCOCKS

77 New Hormones ORG 1 SPIRAL SCRATCH (EP, plastic labels, p/s doesn't credit Howard Devoto) . . . 30
77 United Artists UP 36316 Orgasm Addict/Whatever Happened To...? (p/s). . . . 6
78 United Artists UP 36433 Love You More/Noise Annoys (p/s) . . . 5
78 United Artists UP 36455 Ever Fallen In Love (With Someone You Shouldn't've?)/Just Lust (p/s, mispressed with Gerry Rafferty track on B-side) . . . 10
78 United Artists UP 36471 Promises/Lipstick (p/s) . . . 5
78 New Hormones ORG 1 SPIRAL SCRATCH (EP, reissue, p/s credits Howard Devoto, paper label) . . . 10
78 United Artists UALP 15 Moving Away From The Pulsebeat (12", 1-sided, die-cut co. sl., promo only) . . . 20
79 United Artists UP 36499 Everybody's Happy Nowadays/Why Can't I Touch It? (p/s, available in 3 different colours) . . . each 5
79 United Artists UP 36541 Harmony In My Head/Something's Gone Wrong Again (p/s) . . . 5
80 United Artists BP 365 Why She's A Girl From The Chainstore/Are Everything (p/s) . . . 6
91 New Hormones ORG 1 SPIRAL SCRATCH (EP, 2nd reissue, promo only 7") . . . 10
91 Planet Pacific PPAC 3T Alive Tonight/Serious Crime/Last To Know/Successful Street (12", p/s) . . . 8
93 Essential ESS 2025 Innocent/Who'll Help Me To Forget (p/s) . . . 5
93 Essential ESST 2025 Innocent/Who'll Help Me To Forget/Inside (12", p/s) . . . 8
93 Essential ESST 2031 Do It/Trash Away (Live)/All Over You (Live) (12", p/s) . . . 8
95 One Stop Music ONE 7001 Noise Annoys/Isolation (live) (p/s, 1,500 only) . . . 5
78 United Artists UAG 30159 ANOTHER MUSIC IN A DIFFERENT KITCHEN (LP, black inner sleeve, initially in printed carrier bag) . . . 25/12
78 United Artists UAG 30159 ANOTHER MUSIC IN A DIFFERENT KITCHEN (LP, mispressing without "I Need") . . . 15
78 United Artists UAG 30197 LOVE BITES (LP, with embossed sleeve with insert) . . . 12
79 United Artists UAG 30260 A DIFFERENT KIND OF TENSION (LP, with inner sleeve). . . . 12
89 Absolutely Free FREELP 02 LIVE AT THE ROXY (LP). . . . 20
91 Document DLP 2 TIME'S UP (LP, mock bootleg, with bonus 33rpm interview single [FDLP 2]) . . . 20
(see also Pete Shelley, Things, Stevie's Buzz)

JAKI BYARD

68 Transatlantic PR 7463 FREEDOM TOGETHER! (LP) . . . 15

DON BYAS & HIS RHYTHM

56 Vogue V 2390 On The Way To Your Heart/The Portuguese Washerwomen . . . 8

BYE LAWS

68 Pye 7N 17481 Then You Can Tell Me Goodbye/Come On Over To My Place . . . 8
69 Pye 7N 17701 Run Baby Run/To Sir With Love . . . 8

MAX BYGRAVES

53 HMV 7M 112 Cowpuncher's Cantata/True Loves And False Lovers . . . 10
53 HMV 7M 113 Little Sir Echo/Bygraves Boogie . . . 25
53 HMV 7M 114 The Travelling Salesman/Ten Bottles Of Gin . . . 10
53 HMV 7M 134 Lovely Dollar Lolly (with Peter Brough & Archie Andrews)/ The Red Robin Cantata . . . 10
53 HMV 7M 145 Time To Dream/The Queen Of Ev'ryone's Heart . . . 10
53 HMV 7M 154 Big 'Ead/Say "Si Si" (B-side with Peter Brough & Archie Andrews). . . . 10
54 HMV 7M 180 She Was A Good Girl (As Good Girls Go)/The Jones Boy . . . 10
54 HMV 7M 194 (The Gang That Sang) Heart Of My Heart/Once She's Got You Up (B-side with Tanner Sisters). . . . 10
54 HMV 7M 220 Friends And Neighbours (with Tanner Sisters)/Chip Chopper Charlie. . . . 10
54 HMV 7M 237 Gilly Gilly Ossenfeffer Katzenelle etc./Third Little Turning On The Right. . . . 10
54 HMV 7M 238 Bank Of Sunshine/Little Johnny Rainbow . . . 10
56 HMV 7M 357 The Ballad Of Davy Crockett/A Good Idea — Son . . . 10
56 HMV 7M 368 Out Of Town/Fingers Crossed . . . 10
56 HMV 7M 388 Nothin' To Do/Lift Boy . . . 10
56 HMV 7M 400 Seventeen Tons/Try Another Cherry Tree . . . 10
59 Decca F 11119 Napoli-Napoli/Old Tymes Square. . . . 5
59 Decca F 11148 Last Night I Dreamed/Bobbikin's Lullaby . . . 5
59 Decca F 11176 Jingle Bell Rock/Who Made The Morning . . . 10
59 Decca F 11176 Jingle Bell Rock/Who Made The Morning (78). . . . 10
60 Decca F 11214 Fings Ain't Wot They Used T'Be/When The Thrill Has Gone . . . 6
60 Decca F 11214 Fings Ain't Wot They Used T'Be/When The Thrill Has Gone (78) . . . 12
60 Decca F 11251 Consider Yourself/Tra-La-La I'm In Love . . . 5
61 Decca F 11350 Bells Of Avignon/Tin Pan Alley . . . 5
55 HMV 7EG 8061 PETER BROUGH, ARCHIE ANDREWS AND MAX BYGRAVES (EP). . . . 8
56 HMV 7EG 8203 A GOOD IDEA SON (EP) . . . 5
60s Lantern MB 103 SINGS CHRISTMAS GREETINGS (EP) . . . 5
60s Lantern MB 201 IT'S YOUR BIRTHDAY (EP). . . . 5
(see also Joan Regan)

MINT VALUE £

JUNIOR BYLES

71 Bullet BU 499 Beat Down Babylon/UPSETTERS: Version . . . 18
71 Upsetter US 365 Palace Called Africa/UPSETTERS: Earthquake . . . 20
72 Upsetter US 387 Festival Da Da/UPSETTERS: Version . . . 18
72 Pama PM 857 Fever/GROOVERS: Soul Sister
(B-side actually by Heptones) . . . 18
72 Dynamic DYN 432 Pharaoh Hiding/Hail To Power . . . 7
72 Randy's RAN 523 King Of Babylon/UPSETTERS: Nebuchadnezzer . . . 18
72 Punch PH 109 Pharaoh Hiding/UPSETTERS: Hail To Power . . . 18
73 Pama PM 878 Education Rock/KEN McKAY: Nobody Knows . . . 7
74 Magnet MAG 27 Curly Locks/Now Generation . . . 8
74 Dip DL 5035 Curly Locks/Now Generation . . . 10
75 Dip DL 5074 Long Way/All The Way . . . 10
75 Ethnic ETH 26 Mumbling And Grumbling/King Size Mumble . . . 7
72 Trojan TRL 52 BEAT DOWN BABYLON (LP, beware of Canadian imports) . . . 45
(see also King Chubby, Lloyd Terrell, Dennis Alcapone, Upsetters, Bob Marley, Lee & Junior)

JAMES BYNUM

79 Grapevine GRP 117 Time Passes By/Love You . . . 8

BOBBY BYRD

71 Mojo 2001 118 I Need Help Parts 1 & 2 . . . 10
71 Mojo 2027 003 I Know You Got Soul/If You Don't Work You Can't Eat . . . 10
71 Mojo 2093 004 Hot Pants ... I'm Coming, I'm Coming, I'm Coming/Hang It Up . . . 10
72 Mojo 2093 013 Keep On Doin' What You're Doin'/Let Me Know . . . 10
72 Mojo 2093 017 If You Got A Love You'd Better Keep Hold Of It/
You've Got To Change Your Mind . . . 10
72 Mojo 2093 020 Never Get Enough/My Concerto . . . 8
73 Warner Bros K 16291 Try It Again/I'm On The Move . . . 8
73 Mojo 2093 028 Saying It And Doing It Are Two Different Things/VICKI ANDERSON: Don't
Throw Your Love In Garbage/In The Land Of Milk And Honey . . . 12
75 Seville SEV 1003 Back From The Dead/The Way To Get Down . . . 8
75 Seville SEV 1005 Headquarters/Headquarters (Instrumental Version) . . . 8
76 Contempo CS 2096 Here For The Party/Thank You For Your Love . . . 8
87 Urban URB 8 I Know You Got Soul/Hot Pants . . . 7
87 Urban URBX 8 I Know You Got Soul/Hot Pants ... I'm Coming, I'm Coming, I'm Coming/
I Know You Got Soul (Version)
(12", die-cut company sleeve) . . . 10
72 Mojo 2918 002 I NEED HELP — LIVE (LP) . . . 65
(see also JB's, James Brown, Anna King & Bobby Byrd, Vicki Anderson)

C. BYRD & SIR D.'s GROUP

60 Blue Beat BB 49 Baa Baa Black Sheep/LLOYD & CECIL: Come Over Here . . . 40

CHARLIE BYRD

62 Riverside RLP 436 BOSSA NOVA PELOS PASSAROS (LP) . . . 15
66 CBS 62610 TRAVELLIN' MAN LIVE (LP) . . . 10
66 CBS 62958 BYRDLAND (LP) . . . 10

DONALD BYRD

66 Verve VS 532 Boom Boom/See See Rider . . . 8
80 United Artists UP 622 Dominoes/Wind Parade . . . 5
(see also Blackbyrds, Art Farmer)

GARY BYRD (& THE G.B.E.)

83 Motown TMG 1312 The Crown/(Instrumental Version) (12", p/s) . . . 8

MICHAEL BYRD & COMMERCIALS

80 Another AN 002 SELL OUT BEFORE THE FALL OUT (EP, gatefold p/s, 500 copies only) . . . 6
(see also Cardiac Arrest, Selecter)

RUSSELL BYRD

64 Sue WI 305 Hitch Hike Parts 1 & 2 . . . 50

BYRDS

65 CBS 201765 Mr. Tambourine Man/I Knew I'd Want You . . . 6
65 CBS 201796 All I Really Want To Do/Feel A Whole Lot Better . . . 6
65 CBS 202008 Turn! Turn! Turn! (To Everything There Is A Season)/
She Don't Care About Time . . . 6
66 CBS 202037 Set You Free This Time/It Won't Be Wrong . . . 12
66 CBS 202067 Eight Miles High/Why . . . 10
66 CBS 202259 5D (Fifth Dimension)/Captain Soul . . . 8
66 CBS 202295 Mr Spaceman/What's Happening?!?! . . . 10
67 CBS 202559 So You Want To Be A Rock'n'Roll Star/Everybody's Been Burned . . . 10
67 CBS 2648 My Back Pages/Renaissance Fair . . . 10
67 CBS 2924 Lady Friend/Don't Make Waves . . . 15
67 CBS 3093 Goin' Back/Change Is Now . . . 12
68 CBS 3411 You Ain't Goin' Nowhere/Artificial Energy . . . 8
68 CBS 3752 I Am A Pilgrim/Pretty Boy Floyd . . . 8
69 CBS 4055 Bad Night At The Whiskey/Drug Store Truck Drivin' Man . . . 10
69 CBS 4284 Lay Lady Lay/Old Blue . . . 10
69 CBS 4572 Wasn't Born To Follow/Child Of The Universe . . . 8
70 CBS 4753 Jesus Is Just Alright/It's All Over Now Baby Blue . . . 7
71 CBS 5322 Chestnut Mare/Just A Season . . . 7
71 CBS 7253 I Trust/This Is My Destiny . . . 7
72 CBS 7712 America's Great National Pastime/Farther Along (unreleased)
73 Asylum AYM 516 Things Will Be Better/For Free (promos in p/s) . . . 12/6
73 Asylum AYM 517 Full Circle/Long Live The King . . . 6
66 CBS EP 6069 THE TIMES THEY ARE A' CHANGIN' (EP) . . . 22
66 CBS EP 6077 EIGHT MILES HIGH (EP) . . . 30
90 CBS 656544 5 FOUR DIMENSIONS EP (CD, picture disc) . . . 8

65	CBS (S)BPG 62571	MR TAMBOURINE MAN (LP, mono/stereo)	35/25
66	CBS (S)BPG 62652	TURN! TURN! TURN! (LP, mono/stereo)	40/35
66	CBS (S)BPG 62783	FIFTH DIMENSION (LP, mono/stereo)	40/35
67	CBS (S)BPG 62988	YOUNGER THAN YESTERDAY (LP, mono/stereo)	40/35
68	CBS BPG 63107	THE BYRDS' GREATEST HITS (LP, mono)	12
68	CBS (S)BPG 63169	THE NOTORIOUS BYRD BROTHERS (LP, mono/stereo)	35/30
68	CBS 63353	SWEETHEART OF THE RODEO (LP, mono/stereo)	30/25
69	CBS 63545	DR BYRDS & MR HYDE (LP, mono)	15

(Original copies of the above LPs were issued with rough-textured, plain orange labels & laminated sleeves; later copies are worth two-thirds these values.)

71	Bumble GEXP 8001	PRE-FLYTE (LP)	20
73	Asylum SYLA 8754	THE BYRDS (LP, gatefold sleeve)	12

(see also Beefeaters, Roger McGuinn, David Crosby, Gene Clark, Gram Parsons, Gene Parsons, Skip Battin, Earl Scruggs, Flying Burrito Brothers, Evergreen Blueshoes, Dillard & Clark, Kentucky Colonels)

JERRY BYRNE

76	Specialty SON 5011	Lights Out/Honey Baby	5

PACKIE BYRNE (& BONNIE SHALJEAN)

69	EFDSS LP 1009	PACKIE BYRNE (LP)	22

EDD/EDWARD BYRNES

60	Warner Bros WB 5	Kookie, Kookie (Lend Me Your Comb) (with Connie Stevens)/You're The Top	8
60	Warner Bros WB 27	Lonely Christmas/Yulesville (as Edd Byrnes)	8
60	Warner Bros WEP 6010	KOOKIE (EP, also stereo WSEP 2010)	20/15
63	Warner Bros W(S)EP 6108	KOOKIE VOLUME 2 (EP)	25

(see also Connie Stevens)

MARTIN BYRNES

70	Leader LEA 2004	BYRNES (LP)	15

PAUL BYRON

60	Decca F 11210	Pale Moon/Year Ago Tonight	10

SOL BYRON & IMPACTS

60s	Flamingo PR 5027	Pride And Joy/Thou Shall Not Steal	18

BYSTANDERS

65	Pylot WD 501	That's The End/This Time	150
66	Piccadilly 7N 35330	(You're Gonna) Hurt Yourself/Have I Offended The Girl	22
66	Piccadilly 7N 35351	My Love — Come Home/If You Walk Away	30
67	Piccadilly 7N 35363	98.6/Stubborn Kind Of Fellow	18
67	Piccadilly 7N 35382	Royal Blue Summer Sunshine Day/Make Up Your Mind	30
67	Piccadilly 7N 35399	Pattern People/Green Grass	20
68	Pye 7N 17476	When Jezamine Goes/Cave Of Clear Light	35
68	Pye 7N 17540	This World Is My World/Painting The Time	20

(see also Man)

BYZANTIUM

73	A&M AMS 7064	What A Coincidence/My Seasons Changing With The Sun	7
72	private pressing	LIVE AND STUDIO ('BLACK AND WHITE') (LP, 100 only)	150
72	A&M AMLH 68104	BYZANTIUM (LP, some with poster)	50/30
73	A&M AMLH 68163	SEASONS CHANGING (LP, poster sleeve)	45

(see also Ora)

FANTASTIC JOHNNY C

67	London HL 10169	Boogaloo Down Broadway/Look What Love Can Make You Do	10
68	London HL 10212	Hitch It To The Horse/Cool Broadway	10
69	Action ACT 4543	Is There Anything Better Than Making Love/New Love	20
75	Island USA 8	Don't Depend On Me (Parts 1 & 2)	8
69	Action ACLP 6001	BOOGALOO DOWN BROADWAY (LP)	55

ROY C

66	Island WI 273	Shotgun Wedding/I'm Going To Make It	18
66	Island WI 273	Shotgun Wedding/High School Dropout (different B-side)	12
67	Ember EMB S 230	Twistin' Pneumonia/Tear Avenue	15
66	Ember NR 5055	THE SHOTGUN WEDDING MAN (LP)	45
75	Mercury 9100 017	SEX AND SOUL (LP)	15

CABARET VOLTAIRE

79	Rough Trade RT 018	Nag Nag Nag/Is That Me (p/s)	10
79	Rough Trade RT 035	Silent Command/Chance Versus Causality (p/s)	10
80	Rough Trade RT 060	Seconds Too Late/Control Addict (p/s)	8
81	Rough Trade RT 096	Eddie's Out/Walls Of Jericho (12", p/s, with bonus 7" "Jazz The Glass"/ "Burnt To The Ground" [pink die-cut sleeve, RT 095] in plastic wallet)	8
82	Masterbag BAG 004	Gut Level (live) (flexidisc free with ***Masterbag*** magazine)	7/5
76	(no label or cat. no.)	LIMITED EDITION (private cassette)	60

(see also Richard H. Kirk, Hafler Trio, Peter Hope & Richard H. Kirk, Stephen Mallinder, UV Pop, Pressure Co., Eric Random)

MINT VALUE £

CABLES
68 Coxsone CS 7072 What Kind Of World?/My Broken Heart . . . 30
68 Studio One SO 2060 Baby Why?/Be A Man . . . 30
68 Studio One SO 2071 Love Is A Pleasure/Cheer Up . . . 30
69 Studio One SO 2085 Got To Find Someone/ALEXANDER HENRY: Please Be True . . . 30
69 Bamboo BAM 12 So Long/PRESSURE BOYS: More Love . . . 12
70 Bamboo BAM 19 How Can I Trust You?/SOUND DIMENSIONS: How Can I Trust You? (Inst.) . . . 12
70 Trojan TR 7792 Salt Of The Earth/Ring A Bell . . . 12
70 Harry J. HJ 6614 Didn't I/JAY BOYS: Tilly . . . 8
70 Harry J. HJ 6620 Feel Alright/Equal Rights . . . 7
71 Big Shot BI 598 A Sometime Girl/IN CROWD BAND: A Sometime Girl Version . . . 6
72 Jackpot JP 787 Come On/Come On Version . . . 6
73 Attack ATT 8053 Give Me A Chance/JAH FISH: King Of Zion . . . 6
(see also K. Drummond, Dingle Brothers, Alton Ellis)

CABOOSE
70 Stax STAX 151 Black Hands, White Cotton/In My Hour Of Need . . . 6

CACOPHONY
87 Roadrunner RR 349577 SPEED METAL SYMPHONY (LP) . . . 12
88 Roadrunner RR 9577 GO OFF (LP, as Marty Friedman, Jason Becker & Cacophony) . . . 12
(see also Marty Friedman, Megadeth)

CACTUS
70 Atco 2400 020 CACTUS (LP) . . . 20
71 Atco 2400 114 ONE WAY ... OR ANOTHER (LP, reissue of above LP) . . . 18
72 Atlantic K 40307 RESTRICTIONS (LP) . . . 12
72 Atlantic K 50013 'OT AND SWEATY (LP) . . . 12
(see also Vanilla Fudge, Leaf Hound, Beck Bogert Appice)

ALAN CADDY
64 HMV POP 1286 Tornado/Workout . . . 40
(see also Tornados)

CADETS (U.K.)
63 Decca F 11677 Hello Trouble/Our First Quarrel . . . 10
64 Pye 7N 15693 Chapel Of Love/I Gave My Wedding Dress Away . . . 10
65 Pye 7N 15769 Are You Teasing Me?/My Heart Skips A Beat . . . 8
65 Pye 7N 15852 Jealous Heart/Right Or Wrong . . . 12
65 Pye 7N 15947 Baby Roo/Raining In My Heart . . . 8
66 Pye 7N 17024 If I Had My Life To Live Over/Best Of All . . . 8
66 Pye 7N 17167 At The Close Of A Long Long Day/True Love . . . 8
69 Pye 7N 17762 Dying Ranger/Storeen Bawn . . . 8

CADETS (U.S.)
56 London HLU 8313 Stranded In The Jungle/I Want You (gold or silver label lettering) . . . 700/425
56 London HLU 8313 Stranded In The Jungle/I Want You (78) . . . 85

CADILLAC
86 CBS A 7180 Valentino/Valentino (p/s) . . . 8

EARL CADILLAC & HIS ORCHESTRA
59 Vogue V 9133 Zon, Zon, Zon/Il Suffit D'Une Melodie . . . 18
59 Vogue V 9133 Zon, Zon, Zon/Il Suffit D'Une Melodie (78) . . . 20
59 Vogue V 9138 The Fish Seller/Tremendo Cha Cha Cha (Plegaria) . . . 18
59 Vogue V 9138 The Fish Seller/Tremendo Cha Cha Cha (Plegaria) (78) . . . 20

CADILLACS
59 London HLJ 8786 Peek-A-Boo/Oh, Oh, Lolita . . . 50
59 London HLJ 8786 Peek-A-Boo/Oh, Oh, Lolita (78) . . . 20

SUSAN CADOGAN
74 Dip DL 5030 Hurt So Good/UPSETTERS: Loving Is Good . . . 7
75 Lucky LY 5078 Feeling Right/Congratulations . . . 7

CAEDMON
78 private pressing CAEDMON (LP, with insert, some with bonus 7": "Beyond The Second Mile"/"Give Me Jesus") . . . 500/350

CAERN
70s Gem DES 1015 A COLLECTION OF SCOTCH FOLK (LP) . . . 18

CAESAR & CLEO
65 Reprise R 20419 Love Is Strange/Let The Good Times Roll (some in p/s) . . . 25/15
65 Reprise R 30056 CAESAR AND CLEO (EP, 2 tracks each by Caesar & Cleo and Sonny & Cher) . . . 15
(see also Sonny & Cher)

CAESARS
65 Decca F 12251 On The Outside Looking In/Can You Blame Me? . . . 15
66 Decca F 12462 Five In The Morning/It's Superman . . . 12

CAESARS
00s Dolores 5468797 Fun And Games/Crackin' Up/Only You/Since You've Been Gone . . . 8

CAFE SOCIETY
75 Konk KOS 5 Whitby Two-Step/Maybe It's Me . . . 6
75 Konk KONK 102 CAFE SOCIETY (LP, with inner sleeve) . . . 15
(see also Tom Robinson Band, Claire Hamill)

BUTCH CAGE/MABEL LEE WILLIAMS
60s Storyville SLP 129 COUNTRY BLUES (LP) . . . 20

AUBREY CAGLE
62 Starlite ST45 082 Come Along Little Girl/Blue Lonely World . . . 250

JAMES CAGNEY
70 United Artists UP 36385 Yankee Doodle Dandy/Over There (B-side with Frances Langford) (p/s) 8

JEREMY CAHILL
70s Solent September Blues/Yesterday 15
(see also Shide & Acorn)

PATRICIA CAHILL
70 Deram DM 320 Little Altar Boy/Rain 7
71 Deram DM 324 Colm Ban/Eighteen 7
70 Deram Nova SDN 22 SUMMER'S DAUGHTER (LP) 30
72 Rex RPS 104 IRELAND (LP) 15

CAIN
68 Page One POF 054 Her Emotion/Take Me Back One Time 30

CAIN
80s private pressing CAIN (2-LP) 30

TUBAL CAINE
70 Attack ATT 8023 I'm A Drifter Part 1/CIMARONS: I'm A Drifter Part 2 7

AL CAIOLA (ORCHESTRA)
56 London HLC 8285 Flamenco Love/From The Heart 20
61 London HLT 9294 The Magnificent Seven/The Lonely Rebel 12
61 London HLT 9325 Bonanza/Bounty Hunter 12
61 HMV POP 884 Bonanza/Bounty Hunter (as Al Caiola Orchestra, reissue) 10
61 HMV POP 889 The Magnificent Seven/The Lonely Rebel (as Al Caiola Orchestra) 10
62 Oriole CB 1732 Mambo Jambo/Twistin' At The Woodchoppers Mill 10
66 United Artists UEP 1018 HIT T.V. THEMES (EP) 15
56 London HA-C 2017 DEEP IN A DREAM (LP) 20
57 London HA-C 2022 SERENADE IN BLUE (LP) 20
64 United Artists ULP 1090 TUFF GUITAR (LP) 20
66 United Artists (S)ULP 1115 SOUNDS FOR SPIES AND PRIVATE EYES (LP) 35

CAIRN
70s GES 1015 A COLLECTION OF SCOTCH FOLK (LP) 15

JOHN CAIRNEY
57 HMV POP 424 Two Strangers/A Certain Girl I Know (with Sammy San) 7
68 Waverley SLP 543 Please/Deep Purple 6

FORRIE CAIRNS
62 Fontana 267240 TF Salty Dog/Cockles And Mussels 7

CAIRO
80 Absurd ASK 15 Movie Stars/Cuthbert's Birthday Treat (p/s) 5

CAJUN MOON
76 Chrysalis CHR 1116 CAJUN MOON (LP) 18

CAKE
68 MCA MUPS 303 THE CAKE (LP) 15
69 MCA MUPS 390 A SLICE OF CAKE (LP) 15

J.J. CALE
66 Liberty LIB 55881 Outside Lookin' In/In Our Time 15
72 A&M AMS 7018 Cajun Moon/Starbound 6
72 A&M AMS 7022 After Midnight/Crazy Mama 6
72 A&M AMLS 68105 NATURALLY (LP, tan label) 15
72 A&M AMLS 68157 REALLY (LP, tan label) 15
79 Shelter ISA 5018 FIVE (LP, with bonus single "Katy Cool"/"Juan And Maria Juarez Blues" [JJ-1]) . 12
(see also Leathercoated Minds)

JOHN CALE
74 Island WIP 6202 The Man Who Couldn't Afford To Orgy/Sylvia Said 10
77 Illegal IL 003 ANIMAL JUSTICE (EP) 6
77 Illegal IL 003 ANIMAL JUSTICE (12" EP) 10
77 Illegal IL 006 Jack The Ripper In The Moulin Rouge/Memphis (unissued, test pressings only) 25
81 A&M AMS 8130 Dead Or Alive/Honi Soit 5
83 Ze IS 113 Close Watch/I Keep A Close Watch (p/s) 5
84 Ze IS 157 Caribbean Sunset/(same) (unissued, promo only) 8
84 Ze IS 197 Ooh La La/Magazines (p/s) 5
71 CBS 64256 VINTAGE VIOLENCE (LP, orange label) 18
71 CBS 64259 CHURCH OF ANTHRAX (LP, with Terry Riley) 18
72 Reprise K 44212 ACADEMY IN PERIL (LP) 15
73 Reprise K 44239 PARIS 1919 (LP, with lyric insert) 15
75 Island ILPS 9350 HELEN OF TROY (LP) 12
77 Island ILPS 9459 GUTS (LP) 12
(see also Velvet Underground, Nico, Terry Riley, Ayers Cale Nico & Eno, Judy Nylon)

CALEB (Quaye)
67 Philips BF 1588 Baby Your Phrasing Is Bad/Woman Of Distinction 400
(see also Mirage, Hookfoot, Bread & Beer Band, Elton John)

CALEDONIANS
69 Fab FAB 103 Funny Way Of Laughing/Don't Please 10
(see also Clarendonians, Prince Buster)

CALENDAR
75 All Platinum 6146 308 Hypertension Parts 1 & 2 6

CALIFORNIA IN-CROWD
66 Fontana TF 779 Questions And Answers/Happiness In My Heart 40

MINT VALUE £

CALIFORNIA MUSIC

74 RCA RCA 2488 Don't Worry Baby/Ten Years Harmony . . . 8
76 RCA RCA 2661 Jamaica Farewell/California Farewell . . . 8
78 RSO 014 I Can Hear Music/Love's Supposed To Be That Way (as California) . . . 5
(see also Bruce Johnston, Beach Boys)

CALIFORNIANS

67 CBS 2263 Golden Apples/Little Ship With A Red Sail . . . 55
67 Decca F 12678 Follow Me/What Love Can Do . . . 12
67 Decca F 12712 Sunday Will Never Be The Same/Can't Get You Out Of My Mind . . . 7
68 Decca F 12758 Congratulations/What Is Happy, Baby? . . . 7
68 Decca F 12802 Out In The Sun/The Sound . . . 7
69 Fontana TF 991 Mandy/The Cooks Of Cake And Kindness . . . 80
69 Fontana TF 1052 Sad Old Song/Weep No More . . . 8
69 Chapter One CH 112 You've Got Your Troubles/Early Morning Sun . . . 7
(see also Warren Zevon)

CALLAN & JOHN

69 CBS 4447 House Of Delight/Long Shadow Day . . . 22

CALL GIRLS

88 53rd & 3rd AGAR 001 Primal World/VATICAN SHOTGUN SCARE: Thick Fat Heat Source (p/s) . . . 8

(MISSISSIPPI) JOE CALLICOTT

68 Blue Horizon 7-63227 PRESENTING THE COUNTRY BLUES (LP) . . . 75
71 Revival RVS 1002 DEAL GONE DOWN (LP, as Joe Callicott) . . . 25

TERRY CALLIER

79 Elektra K 12372 Sign Of The Times/Occasional Rain . . . 8
90 Acid Jazz JAZID 27T I Don't Want To See Myself (Without You)/(If I Could Make You) Change Your Mind (12") . . . 60
78 Elektra K 52096 FIRE ON ICE (LP) . . . 20
79 Elektra K 52140 TURN YOU TO LOVE (LP) . . . 25

CALLIES

71 Rubber RUB 002 ON YOUR SIDE (LP, gatefold sleeve) . . . 18

CALLINAN-FLYNN

72 Mushroom 150 MR 18 FREEDOM'S LAMENT (LP) . . . 175

JO CALLIS

81 Pop: Aural POP 12 Woah Yeah/Sinistrale/Dodo Boys (p/s) . . . 5
(see also Rezillos, Shake, Human League)

CAB CALLOWAY

66 Stateside SS 509 History Repeats Itself/After Taxes . . . 7
58 Gala 45XP 1016 CAB CALLOWAY (EP) . . . 10
60 Fontana TFE 17216 CAB CALLOWAY (EP) . . . 22
70s Vintage Jazz VEP 22 CABULOUS CALLOWAY (EP) . . . 10
70s Vintage Jazz VEP 35 CABULOUS CALLOWAY VOL. 2 (EP) . . . 10

CALUM BRYCE

68 Conder PS 1001 Love-Maker/I'm Glad . . . 125

EDDIE CALVERT

53 Columbia SCM 5003 My Yiddishe Momme/Hora Staccato . . . 8
53 Columbia SCM 5004 Ave Maria/Just A-Wearyin' For You (as Eddie Calvert Orchestra) . . . 8
54 Columbia SCM 5129 My Son, My Son/Sherpa Song . . . 8
55 Columbia SCM 5168 Cherry Pink And Apple Blossom White/Roses Of Picardy . . . 15
56 Columbia SCM 5237 The Man With The Golden Arm/Memories Of You . . . 6
56 Columbia SCM 5277 Moonglow & Theme From "Picnic"/If I Loved You . . . 6
58 Melodisc EPM 7 MISERLOU (EP) . . . 10
55 Columbia SEG 7591 GOLDEN MELODIES OF THE GOLDEN TRUMPET (EP) . . . 10
56 Columbia SEG 7637 GOLDEN TRUMPET — GOLDEN MELODIES No. 2 (EP) . . . 10
(see also Gerry Brereton)

ROBERT CALVERT

72 United Artists UP 35543 Ejection/Catch A Falling Starfighter (p/s) . . . 15
79 Wake Up WUR 5 Cricket Star (p/s, 33rpm flexidisc, as Robert Calvert & 1st XI) . . . 10
80 Flicknife FLS 204 Lord Of The Hornets/The Greenfly & The Rose (purple print p/s) . . . 10
81 Flicknife FLS 204 Lord Of The Hornets/The Greenfly & The Rose (reissue, black print p/s) . . . 5
74 United Artists UAG 29507 CAPTAIN LOCKHEED AND THE STARFIGHTERS (LP, gatefold sleeve, with booklet and inner sleeve) . . . 25
75 United Artists UAG 29852 LUCKY LIEF AND THE LONGSHIPS (LP, gatefold sleeve) . . . 20
81 A-Side IF 0311 HYPE (SONGS OF TOM MAHLER) (LP) . . . 15
84 Flicknife SHARP 021 FREQ (LP) . . . 12
86 Demi Monde DMLP 1010 TEST TUBE CONCEIVED (LP) . . . 12
86 Harbour (no cat. no.) THE CELLAR TAPES VOLUME ONE (cassette only) . . . 15
86 Harbour (no cat. no.) THE CELLAR TAPES VOLUME TWO (cassette only) . . . 15
88 Harbour (no cat. no.) ROBERT CALVERT READS THE EARTH RITUAL (cassette, limited edition) . . . 15
88 Harbour (no cat. no.) LIVE AT THE QUEEN ELIZABETH HALL (cassette, possibly unreleased) . . . 20+
88 Beat Goes On BGOLP 2 LUCKY LIEF AND THE LONGSHIPS (LP, gatefold sleeve, reissue) . . . 12
88 Beat Goes On BGOLP 5 CAPTAIN LOCKHEED AND THE STARFIGHTERS (LP, gatefold sleeve with booklet, reissue) . . . 12
89 Clear BLACK 1 ROBERT CALVERT AT THE QUEEN ELIZABETH HALL (LP, mail order only, with badge, poster & T-shirt, gatefold sleeve) . . . 40
92 Cyborg (no cat. no.) REVENGE (cassette only) . . . 12
(see also Hawkwind, Imperial Pompadours, Catapilla, Adrian Wagner, John Stevens Away)

TABBY CALVIN & ROUNDERS

56 Capitol CL 14640 False Alarm/I Came Back To Say I'm Sorry . . . 10

CAMARATA

Year	Label	Title	Value
59	Top Rank JAR 160	Love Theme Sleeping Beauty/Medley Sleeping Beauty (as Walt Disney Studio Orchestra)	10
59	Top Rank JAR 160	Love Theme Sleeping Beauty/Medley Sleeping Beauty (78, as Walt Disney Studio Orchestra)	20
59	Top Rank JAR 162	On The Trail/Trumpeter's Prayer (as Tutti's Trumpets)	6
59	Top Rank JAR 162	On The Trail/Trumpeter's Prayer (78, as Tutti's Trumpets)	10
65	London SHU 8257	THINK YOUNG! (LP, as Camarata Orchestra)	15
70	Deram SML 1053	THE VELVET GENTLEMAN: THE MUSIC OF ERIK SATIE (LP)	40

CAMBODIANS

Year	Label	Title	Value
70	Duke DU 101	Coolie Man/J.J. ALLSTARS: Coolie Version	10

CAMEL

Year	Label	Title	Value
73	MCA MUPS 1177	Never Let Go/Curiosity	6
80	Decca FR 13871	Your Love Is Stranger Than Mine/Neon Magic (p/s)	6
84	Decca CAMEL 1	Cloak And Dagger Man/Pressure Point (p/s)	5
73	MCA MUPS 473	CAMEL (LP, black/blue label)	18
74	Deram SML 1107	MIRAGE (LP, with insert)	15
75	Decca Gama SKL-R 5207	MUSIC INSPIRED BY THE SNOW GOOSE (LP, with insert)	12
76	Decca Gama TXS-R 115	MOON MADNESS (LP, textured sleeve)	12

(see also Pete Bardens, Gong/Camel, Hatfield & The North)

CAMEL DRIVERS

Year	Label	Title	Value
68	Pye International 7N 25471	Sunday Morning 6 O'Clock/Give It A Try	8

CAMEO

Year	Label	Title	Value
78	Casablanca CAN 121	It's Serious/Inflation (12")	8
80	Casablanca CAN 199	On The One/Cameosis (12")	8
77	Casablanca CAL 2015	CARDIAC ARREST (LP)	12
78	Casablanca CAL 2026	WE ALL KNOW WHO WE ARE (LP)	12

CAMEOS

Year	Label	Title	Value
63	Columbia DB 7092	Powercut/High Low And Lonesomely	45
64	Columbia DB 7201	My Baby's Coming Home/Where E'er You Walk	40

CAMEOS

Year	Label	Title	Value
67	Toast TT 503	A Pretty Shade Of Blue/You Didn't Have To Be So Nice	8
68	Toast TT 508	On The Good Ship Lollipop/The Love Of A Boy	8

CAMERA OBSCURA

Year	Label	Title	Value
80	Small Wonder SMALL 28	Destitution/Race In Athens (p/s)	6

DION CAMERON & THREE TOPS

Year	Label	Title	Value
66	Rio R 111	Lord Have Mercy/Get Ready	15

(see also Dion & Three Tops)

G.C. CAMERON

Year	Label	Title	Value
76	Tamla Motown TMG 1033	Me And My Life/Act Like A Shotgun	7

(see also Detroit Spinners)

ISLA CAMERON

Year	Label	Title	Value
64	Transatlantic TRAEP 109	LOST LOVE (EP)	25

(see also Ewan MacColl)

JOHN CAMERON (QUARTET)

Year	Label	Title	Value
67	Columbia DB 8120	You Owe Me/Walk Small (solo)	8
69	Deram DM 256	Troublemaker/Off Centre	100
67	Columbia SCX 6116	COVER LOVER (LP)	15
69	Deram DML/SML 1044	OFF CENTRE (LP)	75

(see also Frog)

JOHNNY CAMERON

Year	Label	Title	Value
60	Top Rank JAR 396	I Double Dare You/Fantasy	10

RAY CAMERON

Year	Label	Title	Value
67	Island WIP 6003	Doin' My Time/Getaway, Getaway Car	10

CAMOUFLAGE

Year	Label	Title	Value
90	Atlantic	STRANGERS THOUGHTS (CD video)	50
90	Atlantic	THE GREAT COMMANDMENT (CD)	30

CAMPAG VELOCET

Year	Label	Title	Value
97	Fierce Panda NING 41	Drencrom [Velocet Synthemesc]/REGULAR FRIES: Dust It, Don't Bust It (p/s, 1,500 only)	10
97	Rabid Badger NANG 1	IT'S THE TEENAGE ARGOT . . . EP (12", p/s, 1,000 only)	8

ALEX CAMPBELL

Year	Label	Title	Value
65	Transatlantic TRASP 4	Been On The Road So Long/The Night Visiting Song (some in p/s)	10/6
68	Saga OPP 2	Victoria Dines Alone/Pack Up Your Sorrows	6
63	Arc ARC 36	OUT WEST WITH ALEX CAMPBELL (EP)	8
63	Society SOC 912	WAY OUT WEST (LP)	15
63	Society SOC 960	FOLK SESSION (LP)	15
64	Fidelity FID 2171	FOLK SESSION (LP, reissue)	12
64	Xtra XTRA 1064	ALEX CAMPBELL (LP, with Martin Carthy)	22
65	Polydor 623 035	IN COPENHAGEN (LP)	18
67	Saga ERO 8021	ALEX CAMPBELL AND HIS FRIENDS (LP, with Sandy Denny)	30
71	Ad-Rhythm/Tepee ARPS 1	THIS IS ALEX CAMPBELL VOL. 1 (LP)	30
71	Ad-Rhythm/Tepee ARPS 2	THIS IS ALEX CAMPBELL VOL. 2 (LP)	30
71	Boulevard 4007	16 BEST LOVED SONGS OF BONNIE SCOTLAND (LP)	15
72	Boulevard 4073	AT HIS BEST (LP)	20
76	Look LKLP 6043	NO REGRETS (LP)	12
79	Burlington BURL 002	ALEX CAMPBELL, ALAN ROBERTS AND DOUGIE MACLEAN (LP)	12
87	Sundown SDLP 2048	WITH THE GREATEST RESPECT (2-LP, reissue of "This Is..." Vols. 1 & 2)	18

(see also Sandy Denny)

MINT VALUE £

AMBROSE ADEKOYA CAMPBELL'S WEST AFRICAN RHYTHM BROTHERS

52 Melodisc SP 1 — Sing The Blues/Omo Lo' Fu Ja (78) — 7

BILL & PETE CAMPBELL

71 Duke DU 123 — Come On Home Girl/You Are Mine — 7

CAT CAMPBELL & NICKY THOMAS

72 Pressure Beat PB 5511 — Hammering/PETER TOSH: Medicine Man — 22

CHOKER CAMPBELL

65 Tamla Motown TMG 517 — Mickey's Monkey/Pride And Joy (as Choker Campbell's Big Band) — 100
65 Tamla Motown TML 11011 — HITS OF THE SIXTIES (LP, as Choker Campbell & His 16-Piece Band) — 140

CHRISTINE CAMPBELL

62 Parlophone R 4881 — Wherever I Go/Near Your Heart (red label, later black) — 5

CORNELL CAMPBELL

63 Island WI 039 — Rosabelle/Turndown Date (B-side actually "Under The Old Oak Tree") — 25
63 Island WI 083 — Each Lonely Night/ROLAND ALPHONSO: Steamline — 25
64 Port-O-Jam PJ 4008 — Jericho Road (with Dimple Hinds)/DON DRUMMOND & GROUP: Roll On Sweet Don — 60
64 Rio R 38 — Gloria/I'll Be True — 18
72 Dynamic DYN 446 — My Confession/AGGROVATORS: Version — 12
72 Green Door GD 4042 — Dearest Darling/Star Dust — 15
72 Jackpot JP 801 — Queen And The Minstrel/Put Yourself In My Place — 12
73 Jackpot JP 809 — Pity The Children/You're No Good — 15
73 Jackpot JP 814 — Harry Hippy/Just One Kiss — 6
73 Green Door GD 4057 — Give Me Love/Help Them O Lord — 12
73 Duke DU 158 — Shotgun Wedding/Girl Of My Dreams — 6
73 Duke DU 159 — The Very Best I Can/Heading For The Mountains — 6
73 Ackee ACK 513 — Give Me A Love/SHORTY PERRY: Message Of Love — 6
72 Trojan TBL 199 — CORNELL CAMPBELL (LP) — 50

(see also Eternals, Don Cornel & Eternals, Clarendonians, Charmers, Stranger & Patsy, GG Allstars)

DAVID CAMPBELL

67 Transatlantic TRA 141 — DAVID CAMPBELL (LP) — 25
72 Decca SKL 5139 — SUN WHEEL (LP) — 18

ETHNA CAMPBELL

64 Mercury MF 804 — What's Easy For Two Is Hard For One/Again — 18
64 Mercury MF 816 — Girls Like Boys/Five Minutes More — 10
60s Philips 6382138 — FOR THE GOOD TIMES (LP) — 15

GLEN CAMPBELL

61 Top Rank JAR 596 — Turn Around, Look At Me/Brenda — 18
62 Capitol CL 15268 — Too Late To Worry, Too Blue To Cry/How Do I Tell My Heart Not To Break? — 8
62 Capitol CL 15278 — Here I Am/Long Black Limousine — 8
63 Capitol CL 15295 — Prima Donna/Oh My Darling — 8
67 Speciality SPE 1002 — Satisfied Mind/Can't You See I'm Trying — 7
68 Ember EMB S 252 — I Wanna Live/Hey Little One — 5
68 Ember EMB S 255 — Dreams Of The Everyday Housewife/Combine — 5
68 Ember EMB S 258 — Straight Life/That's Not Home — 5
69 Ember EMB S 261 — Wichita Lineman/Back In The Race (p/s) — 6
69 Ember EMB S 263 — Galveston/Everytime I Itch I Wind Up Scratching You — 6
69 Capitol CL 15615 — True Grit/Hava Nagila — 6
66 London HA-F/SH-F 8291 — SWINGING 12-STRING (LP) — 18
75 Capitol E-SW 11336 — REUNION (LP & inner sleeve, with Jimmy Webb) — 15

(see also Sagittarius, Jimmy Slade)

CAMPBELL FAMILY

65 Topic 12T 120 — THE SINGING CAMPBELLS — TRADITIONS OF AN ABERDEEN FAMILY (LP, blue label) — 25

IAN CAMPBELL (FOLK) GROUP

63 Topic STOP 102 — The Sun Is Burning/The Crow On The Cradle (some in title p/s) — 15/7
64 Decca F 11802 — Marilyn Monroe/The Bells Of Rhymney — 7
65 Transatlantic TRASP 2 — Kelly From Killane/Boys Of Wexford (with Boys From Wexford) — 7
65 Transatlantic TRASP 5 — The Times They Are A-Changin'/Across The Hills (some in p/s) — 20/12
66 Transatlantic TRASP 6 — Come Kiss Me/The First Time I Ever Saw Your Face (some in p/s) — 12/7
66 Transatlantic TRASP 7 — Guantanamera/Mary Anne — 6
66 Transatlantic TRASP 10 — One Eyed Reilly/Snow Is Falling (solo) — 6
67 Big T BIG 103 — Lover Let Me In/Private Harold Harris (as Ian Campbell Four) — 6
69 Major Minor MM 639 — Break My Mind/Govan Cross Special (solo) — 6
62 Topic TOP 82 — SONGS OF PROTEST (EP) — 15
64 Decca DFE 8592 — IAN CAMPBELL FOLK GROUP (EP) — 15
65 Transatlantic TRAEP 128 — SAMPLER (EP) — 12
63 Transatlantic TRA 110 — THIS IS THE IAN CAMPBELL FOLK GROUP (LP) — 40
64 Transatlantic TRA 118 — ACROSS THE HILLS (LP) — 30
64 Contour 2870 314 — PRESENTING THE IAN CAMPBELL FOLK GROUP (LP, reissue of 1st LP) — 12
68 Transatlantic TRA 163 — THE CIRCLE GAME (LP) — 22
68 Xtra XTRA 1074 — TAM O'SHANTER (LP, as Ian Campbell & John Dunkerley) — 18
69 Transatlantic TRASAM 4 — THE IAN CAMPBELL FOLK GROUP SAMPLER (LP) — 15
69 Transatlantic TRASAM 12 — SAMPLER 2 (LP, as Ian Campbell Folk Four) — 12
69 MFP SMFP 1349 — IAN CAMPBELL & FOLK GROUP WITH DAVE SWARBRICK (LP) — 12
71 Argo ZFB 13 — THE SUN IS BURNING (LP) — 35
72 Pye PKL 5506 — SOMETHING TO SING ABOUT (LP) — 20

(see also Dave Swarbrick)

JEAN CAMPBELL

60 Embassy WB 372 — The Big Hurt/I Can't Begin To Tell You (78) — 8
60 Embassy WB 395 — Sweet Nuthin's/PAUL RICH: Standing On The Corner (78) — 8
60 Embassy WB 398 — Robot Man/BOBBY BRENT: Lucky Five (78) — 8

MINT VALUE £

60	Embassy WB 407	I'm Sorry/Everybody's Somebody's Fool (78)	10
60	Embassy WB 408	Paper Roses/Train Of Love (78)	10
60	Embassy WB 417	My Heart Has A Mind Of Its Own/I Want To Be Wanted (78)	10

JIMMY CAMPBELL

69	Fontana TF 1009	On A Monday/Dear Marge (some in p/s)	10/6
70	Fontana TF 1076	Lyanna/Frankie Joe	6
70	Fontana 6007 025	Don't Leave Me Now/So Lonely Without You	6
69	Fontana STL 5508	SON OF ANASTASIA (LP)	20
70	Vertigo 6360 010	HALF BAKED (LP, gatefold sleeve, swirl label)	20
72	Philips 6308 100	JIMMY CAMPBELL'S ALBUM (LP)	15

(see also Kirkbys, 23rd Turnoff, Rockin' Horse)

JO-ANN CAMPBELL

58	London HLU 8536	Wait A Minute/It's True	60
58	London HLU 8536	Wait A Minute/It's True (78)	20
60	HMV POP 776	Bobby, Bobby, Bobby/A Kookie Little Paradise	18
61	HMV POP 873	Motorcycle Michael/Puka Puka Pants	18
62	HMV POP 1003	You Made Me Love You/I Changed My Mind Jack	18
62	Columbia DB 4889	Sloppy Joe/I'm The Girl From Wolverton Mountain	10
62	Cameo Parkway CP 237	Mr Fix It Man/Let Me Do It My Way	15
63	Cameo Parkway CP 249	Mother Please/Waiting For Love	15

JUNIOR CAMPBELL

74	Deram SML 1106	SECOND TIME AROUND (LP)	22

(see also Marmalade, Clan, Dean Ford & Gaylords)

MURRAY CAMPBELL

58	Philips PB 880	Hey Cabby/One Day I'll Buy A Trumpet (78)	10
58	Philips PB 774	Shangri-La/Balmoral Melody (78)	8

ROY CAMPBELL (& JAZZBO JASPERS)

68	Giant GN 41	Another Saturday Night/Wonderful World (with Jazzbo Jaspers)	7
68	Jolly JY 003	Suzette/Engine Engine Number Nine	7

PATRICK CAMPBELL-LYONS

73	Sovereign SOV 115	Everybody Should Fly A Kite/I Think I Want Him Too	15
73	Sovereign SOV 119	Out On The Road/Me And My Friend	15
77	Electric WOT 12	That's What My Guru Said Last Night/The Whistling Fiddler	5
81	Public PUB 006	Naked Robots Watching Breakfast TV	5
73	Sovereign SVNA 7258	ME AND MY FRIEND (LP, gatefold sleeve)	80
81	Public PUBL 1	THE ELECTRIC PLOUGH (LP)	15

(see also Nirvana [U.K.], Pica, Hat & Tie, Aquila)

CAN

73	United Artists UP 35506	Spoon/I'm So Green	6
73	United Artists UP 35596	Moonshake/Future Days (Edit)	6
74	United Artists UP 35749	Dizzy Dizzy (Edit)/Splash (Edit)	6
76	Virgin VS 153	I Want More/... And More	5
76	Virgin VS 166	Silent Night/Cascade Waltz	5
77	Virgin VS 172	Don't Say No/Return	5
78	Lightning LIG 545	Can-Can/Can Be	5
69	United Artists UAS 29094	MONSTER MOVIE (LP, burgundy label)	35
70	United Artists UAS 29283	SOUNDTRACKS (LP)	30
71	Utd. Artists UAD 60009/10	TAGO MAGO (2-LP, flip-top sleeve)	40
72	United Artists UAS 29414	EGE BAMYASI (LP, with inner sleeve)	30
73	United Artists UAS 29505	FUTURE DAYS (LP)	15
74	United Artists UAG 29673	SOON OVER BABALUMA (LP, original silver sleeve)	25
74	United Artists USP 103	LIMITED EDITION (LP)	18
75	Virgin V 2041	LANDED (LP)	15
76	Caroline CAD 3001	UNLIMITED EDITION (2-LP, gatefold sleeve)	30
76	Sunset SLS 50400	OPENER (LP, reissue of "Monster Movie")	12
77	Virgin V 2071	FLOW MOTION (LP)	15
77	Virgin V 2079	SAW DELIGHT (LP, with insert)	15
78	United Artists UDM 105/6	CANNABALISM (2-LP, gatefold sleeve)	25
78	Laser LASL 2	CAN (LP)	12

CANAAN

73	Dovetail DOVE 3	CANAAN (LP)	35
76	Myrrh MYR 1042	OUT OF THE WILDERNESS (LP, with inner sleeve)	22

LOS CANARIOS

67	Major Minor MM 502	Three Two One Ah/What Can I Do For You	15
67	Major Minor MM 532	Get On Your Knees/Keep On The Right Side	10

CANDIDO

57	HMV DLP 1182	THE VOLCANIC (10" LP)	20
79	Salsoul SSLP 1517	DANCIN' AND PRANCIN' (LP)	12

CANDLE FACTORY

70s	CAVS	NIGHTSHIFT (LP, private pressing)	55

CONTE CANDOLI

56	London Jazz LZ-N 14010	SINCERELY, CONTE (10" LP)	15
56	London Jazz LTZ-N 15036	TOOTS SWEET (LP)	12

PETER CANDOLI & HIS ORCHESTRA

56	Capitol CL 14615	St. Louis Blues — Boogie/The Big Top (Entry Of The Gladiators)	10
60	Warner Bros WB 2	Sunset Strip Cha-Cha/DON RALKE: 77 Sunset Strip	6

CANDY

69	Grape GR 3017	Ace Of Hearts/BILLY JACK: Bet Yer Life I Do	7

PENNY CANDY

60	Top Rank JAR 328	Come On Over/They Said	10

MINT VALUE £

CANDY & KISSES

65	Cameo Parkway C 336	The 81/Two Happy People	80
85	Kent TOWN 104	Mr Creator/CHUCK JACKSON: Hand It Over (withdrawn)	20

CANDY CHOIR

66	Parlophone R 5472	Silence Is Golden/Shake Hands (And Come Out Crying)	18
67	CBS 3061	Children And Flowers/Marianne	8
68	CBS 3305	Alexander's Ragtime Band/No Grey Skies	8
70	Polydor 56369	Why Do You Cry My Love/Lucky Jim	6

(see also Summer Set, Barry Ryan)

CANDY DATES

65	Pye 7N 15944	A Day Just Like That/Well I Do	10

CANDYMEN

67	HMV POP 1612	Georgia Pines/Movies In My Mind	8

CANE

78	Lightning GIL 31	3 BY 3 EP (p/s)	15

BOB CANN

70s	Topic 12TS 275	WEST COUNTRY MELODEON (LP)	18

CANNED HEAT

68	Liberty	Rollin' And Tumblin'/Bullfrog Blues (unreleased)	
68	Liberty LBF 15090	On The Road Again/The World In A Jug	8
69	Liberty LBF 15169	Going Up The Country/One Kind Favour	8
69	Liberty LBF 15200	Time Was/Low Down	8
69	Liberty LBF 15255	Poor Moon/Sic 'Em Pigs	8
69	Liberty LBF 15302	Let's Work Together/I'm Her Man	8
70	Liberty LBF 15350	Sugar Bee/Shake It And Break It	8
70	Pye International 7N 25513	Spoonful/Big Road Blues	8
70	Liberty LBF 15395	Future Blues/Skat	6
70	Liberty LBF 15429	Christmas Blues/Do Not Enter	6
71	Liberty LBF 15439	Wooly Bully/My Time Ain't Long	6
72	United Artists UP 35348	Rockin' With The King (with Little Richard)/I Don't Care What You Tell Me	6
73	United Artists UP 35562	Keep It Clean/You Can Run But You Sure Can't Hide	6
67	Liberty LBL/LBS 83059E	CANNED HEAT (LP)	30
68	Liberty LBL/LBS 83103	BOOGIE WITH CANNED HEAT (LP)	25
69	Liberty LDS 84001E	LIVING THE BLUES (2-LP, gatefold sleeve)	35
69	Liberty LBS 83239	HALLELUJAH (LP, gatefold sleeve)	20
70	Pye Intl. NSPL 28129	VINTAGE HEAT (LP)	18
70	Liberty LBS 83303	CANNED HEAT COOKBOOK (LP)	18
70	Liberty LBS 83333	CANNED HEAT '70 CONCERT (RECORDED LIVE IN EUROPE) (LP, g/fold sleeve)	12
70	Liberty LBS 83364	FUTURE BLUES (LP, gatefold sleeve)	15
71	Liberty LPS 103/4	HOOKER'N'HEAT (2-LP, gatefold sleeve, with John Lee Hooker)	30
72	United Artists UAG 29304	HISTORICAL FIGURES AND ANCIENT HEADS (LP, gatefold sleeve)	12
73	United Artists UAS 29455	THE NEW AGE (LP)	12
74	Atlantic K 50026	ONE MORE RIVER TO CROSS (LP)	12

(see also Harvey Mandel)

CANNIBAL & HEADHUNTERS

65	Stateside SS 403	Land Of A Thousand Dances/I'll Show You How To Love Me	22
67	CBS 62942	LAND OF A 1000 DANCES (LP)	35

CANNIBALS

78	Big Cock F-UK 1	Good Guys/Nothing Takes The Place Of You (printed paper bag sleeve)	6
85	Hit Records REEBEE 2	Christmas Rock 'n' Roll/New Year's Eve Song (doublepack in stocking)	7

(see also Count Bishops, Stoned Aid)

ACE CANNON

62	London HLU 9498	Tuff/Sittin'	10
62	London HLU 9546	Blues Stay Away From Me/Blues In My Heart	8
63	London HLU 9745	Cottonfields/Mildew	8
64	London HLU 9866	Searchin'/Love Letters In The Sand	8
67	London HLU 10105	Wonderland By Night/As Time Goes By	6
70	London HA-U/SH-U 8407	ACE OF SAX (LP)	20

CONROY CANNON

69	Pama PM 769	Oh Happy Day/Can't Get Along Without You	8

FREDDY CANNON

59	Top Rank JAR 135	Tallahassee Lassie/You Know	30
59	Top Rank JAR 135	Tallahassee Lassie/You Know (78)	35
59	Top Rank JAR 207	Okefenokee/Kookie Hat	10
59	Top Rank JAR 247	Way Down Yonder In New Orleans/Fractured	10
60	Top Rank JAR 309	California, Here I Come/Indiana	10
60	Top Rank JAR 334	Chattanooga Shoeshine Boy/Boston (My Home Town)	10
60	Top Rank JAR 369	The Urge/Jump Over	10
60	Top Rank JAR 407	Happy Shades Of Blue/Guernavaca Choo Choo	10
60	Top Rank JAR 518	Humdinger/My Blue Heaven	10
61	Top Rank JAR 548	Muskrat Rumble/Two Thousand 88	10
61	Top Rank JAR 568	Buzz Buzz A Diddle It/Opportunity	25
61	Top Rank JAR 579	Transistor Sister/Walk To The Moon	10
61	Top Rank JAR 592	For Me And My Gal/Blue Plate Special	10
62	Top Rank JAR 609	Teen Queen Of The Week/Wild Guy	10
62	Stateside SS 101	Palisades Park/June July And August	7
62	Stateside SS 118	What's Gonna Happen When Summer's Done/Broadway	7
62	Stateside SS 134	If You Were A Rock & Roll Record/The Truth Ruth	15
63	Stateside SS 155	Come On And Love Me/Four Letter Man	8
63	Stateside SS 183	The Ups And Downs Of Love/It's Been Nice	8
63	Stateside SS 201	Patty Baby/Betty Jean	15

MINT VALUE £

63 Stateside SS 220 Everybody Monkey/Oh Gloria 10
64 Stateside SS 260 That's The Way Girls Are/Do What The Hippies Do 10
64 Warner Bros WB 123 Abigail Beecher/All American Girl 7
64 Stateside SS 298 Sweet Georgia Brown/What A Party 10
65 Warner Bros WB 5645 Action/Beechwood City 10
66 Warner Bros WB 5693 The Dedication Song/Come On Come On 7
69 London HLK 10252 Beautiful Downtown Burbank/If You Give Me A Title 7
60 Top Rank JKP 2058 THE EXPLOSIVE FREDDY (BOOM! BOOM!) CANNON (EP) 40
60 Top Rank JKP 2066 FOUR DIRECT HITS (EP) 40
61 Top Rank JKP 3010 ON TARGET (EP) 35
62 Stateside SE 1002 BLAST OFF WITH FREDDY CANNON (EP) 50
60 Top Rank 25/018 THE EXPLOSIVE FREDDY CANNON (LP) 35
61 Top Rank 35/106 FREDDY CANNON SINGS HAPPY SHADES OF BLUE (LP) 60
61 Top Rank 35/113 FREDDY CANNON FAVOURITES (LP) 60
63 Stateside SL 10013 BANG ON (LP) 60
64 Stateside SL 10062 STEPS OUT (LP) 70
64 Warner Bros WM/WS 8153 FREDDY CANNON (LP) 35
(see also Danny & Juniors)

JUDY CANNON

65 Pye 7N 15900 The Very First Day I Met You/Hello Heartache 45

SEAN CANNON

60s Cottage COT 411 ROVING JOURNEYMAN (LP) 15

CANNON BALL & JOHNNY MELODY

69 Big Shot BI 518 Parapinto/Cool Hand Luke 12
(see also Carl Bryan, King Cannon, Johnny Moore, Jackie Mittoo, Royals)

CANNONBALLS

61 Coral Q 72428 Cannonball Caboose/New Orleans Beat 10
61 Coral Q 72431 Lullaby Of Birdland/Calliope Boogie 10

CANNON BROTHERS

65 Brit WI 1003 Turn Your Eyes To Me/Don't Stop Now 18

CANNONS

60 Decca F 11269 I Didn't Know The Gun Was Loaded/My Guy's Come Back 10
61 Columbia DB 4724 Bush Fire/Juicy 20

CANNON'S JUG STOMPERS

66 Tax LP 2 CANNON'S JUG STOMPERS/CLIFFORD'S LOUISVILLE JUG BAND (LP, 1 side each) 22

CANNY FETTLE

75 Tradition TSR 023 VARRY CANNY (LP) 30
77 Tradition TSR 027 TRIP TO HARROGATE (LP) 18

EDDIE CANTOR

61 Capitol EAP1 20113 MA HE'S MAKING EYES AT ME (EP) 12

CAPABILITY BROWN

72 Charisma CB 193 Wake Up Little Sister/Windfall 6
73 Charisma CB 207 Midnight Cruiser/Silent Sounds 6
73 Charisma CB 217 Liar/Keep Death Off The Road 6
70s Charisma BCP 7 War (p/s) 6
72 Charisma CAS 1056 FROM SCRATCH (LP) 20
73 Charisma CAS 1068 VOICE (LP) 20
(see also Unit 4+2, Tony Rivers & Castaways)

JIM CAPALDI

74 Island WIP 6198 It's All Up To You/Whale Meat Again 6
72 Island ILPS 9187 OH HOW WE DANCED (LP, gatefold sleeve) 15
77 Island ILPS 9497 PLAY IT BY EAR (LP) 15
(see also Hellions, Traffic)

CAPE KENNEDY CONSTRUCTION CO.

69 President PT 265 The First Steps On The Moon/Armageddon 40

CAPERCAILLIE

91 Survival ZD 44342 Fear A Bhata (Oh My Boatman)/A Cur Nan Gobhar As A Chreig/Shanbally Castle/Caberfaidh/Fear A Bhata (CD remix) 8
91 Survival ZD 44594 Coisich A Ruin (Walk My Beloved) (7" Version)/ Outlaws/The Islay Ranters' Reels (A & B)/ Coisich A Ruin (Walk My Beloved) (Extended 12" Version) (CD) 8
91 Survival ZB 44897 Waiting For The Wheels To Turn/Breislach (Delerium) 5
91 Survival ZT 44898 Waiting For The Wheels To Turn/Breisleach/Dr. MacPhail's (12" p/s) 10
92 Survival 74321-11587-2 Waiting For The Wheel To Turn/Breisleach (live)/ Kenny McDonald's Jigs (live)/Waiting For The Wheel To Turn (Edit) (CD, withdrawn, no inlay) 12
92 Survival ZD 45394 A PRINCE AMONG ISLANDS (EP) 8
93 Survival (no cat. no.) Four Stone Walls/Hi Ri'm Bo/Stinging Rain (CD, digipak, promo only) 8
84 Etive/ERC 333 CASCADE (cassette) 15
84 Etive/SRT 4KL 178 CASCADE (LP) 20
87 Grampian TV GPN 1001 THE BLOOD IS STRONG (LP, with insert) 12
87 Green Linnet SIF 1077 CROSSWINDS (LP, with insert) 12
(see also Etives)

CAPES & MASKS

65 Nevis NEV R005 COMIC BOOK HEROES (LP) 25
65 Fontana TL 5339 COMIC BOOK HEROES (LP) 70

CAPES OF GOOD HOPE

66 Stateside SS 577 Winter's Children/If My Monique Could Only Dance 6

MINT VALUE £

CAPITOLS (U.K.)
66 Pye 7N 17025 — Honey And Wine/Boulavogue 12

CAPITOLS (U.S.)
66 Atlantic 584 004 — Cool Jerk/Hello Stranger 18

(see also Three Caps)

ANDY CAPP
69 Treasure Isle TI 7052 — Pop-A-Top/RICO: The Lion Speaks 12
70 Duke DU 69 — The Law Parts 1 & 2 6
70 Duke DU 71 — Poppy Show/Pop-A-Top (Part 2) 6

AL CAPPS
73 Stateside SS 2214 — Shangri-La/Magician 7

CAPREEZ
79 Grapevine GRP 113 — How To Make A Sad Man Glad/It's Good To Be Home Again 8

DANNY CAPRI
55 Capitol CL 14265 — Desirable/I Do, I Do 10
55 Capitol CL 14302 — Don't Make A Liar Out Of Me/Angelica 15

CAPRICORN
70 MCA MK 5050 — Liverpool Hello/How Did You Find Me 6

(see also Marty Wilde)

CAPRIS
61 Columbia DB 4605 — There's A Moon Out Tonight/Indian Girl 110

CAPTAIN AMERICA
92 Paperhouse PAPER 016 T — FLAME ON! (12" EP, p/s) 8

CAPTAIN & TENNILLE
78 A&M AMS 7350 — I'm On My Way/We Never Really Say Goodbye 5

CAPTAIN BEEFHEART & HIS MAGIC BAND
SINGLES
68 Pye International 7N 25443 — Yellow Brick Road/Abba Zabba 50
68 A&M AMS 726 — Moonchild/Who Do You Think You're Fooling 45
73 Reprise K 14233 — Too Much Time/My Head Is My Only House Unless It Rains 6
74 Virgin VS 110 — Upon The My-Oh-My/Magic Be 5
78 Buddah BDS 466 — Sure 'Nuff 'N Yes I Do/Electricity 7
78 MCA MCA 366 — Hard Workin' Man (Jack Nitzsche featuring Captain Beefheart)/ JACK NITZSCHE: Coke Machine 6

EPs
71 A&M AME 600 — DIDDY WAH DIDDY (promo only) 375
79 Virgin SIXPACK 1 — SIX-PACK/SIX TRACK (picture disc, die-cut p/s with stand, 5,000 only) 18
82 Virgin VS 534 12 — LIGHT REFLECTED OFF THE OCEANS OF THE MOON (12" EP, p/s) 12
84 A&M AMY 226 — THE LEGENDARY A&M SESSIONS (12" EP/mini-LP, "Diddy Wah Diddy" EP plus "Where I Am, I Always Am") 15
86 Edsel BLIMP 902 — THE LEGENDARY A&M SESSIONS (12" EP, reissue) 15

ORIGINAL LPs
68 Pye Intl. NPL 28110 — SAFE AS MILK (mono, flipback sleeve) 75
68 Liberty LBL/LBS 83172 — STRICTLY PERSONAL (gatefold sleeve, mono/stereo) 50/35
69 Straight STS 1053 — TROUT MASK REPLICA (2-LP, gatefold sleeve) 60
70 Straight STS 1063 — LICK MY DECALS OFF, BABY 50
71 Buddah 2365 002 — MIRROR MAN (gatefold die-cut sleeve) 40
72 Reprise K 44162 — THE SPOTLIGHT KID (tan 'riverboat' label, some with lyric card insert) 25/20
72 Reprise K 54007 — CLEAR SPOT (PVC sleeve with card insert) 30
74 Virgin V 2015 — UNCONDITIONALLY GUARANTEED ('two virgins' label) 20
74 Virgin V 2023 — BLUEJEANS & MOONBEAMS ('two virgins' label) 15
79 Virgin V 2149 — SHINY BEAST (BAT CHAIN PULLER) 18
80 Virgin V 2172 — DOC AT THE RADAR STATION 18
82 Virgin V 2237 — ICE CREAM FOR CROW (with inner sleeve) 18

REISSUE LPs
70 Buddah 2349 002 — DROPOUT BOOGIE (stereo reissue of "Safe As Milk") 20
73 Reprise K 44244 — LICK MY DECALS OFF, BABY 25
74 Buddah BDLP 4004 — MIRROR MAN 20
75 Reprise K 64026 — TROUT MASK REPLICA (2-LP, gatefold sleeve, tan 'riverboat' label, matt sleeve) 25
70s Reprise K 64026 — TROUT MASK REPLICA (2-LP, gatefold sleeve, 2nd re-pressing, tan 'riverboat' label, soft laminated sleeve) 20
76 Reprise K 84006 — TWO ORIGINALS OF CAPTAIN BEEFHEART (2-LP, reissue of "Lick My Decals Off, Baby" & "The Spotlight Kid") 25
77 Pye FILD 008 — THE FILE SERIES (2-LP, reissue of "Safe As Milk" & "Mirror Man", die-cut sleeve with inners) 18

(see also Mu, Frank Zappa, Jack Nitzsche)

CAPTAIN BEYOND
72 Capricorn K 47503 — CAPTAIN BEYOND (LP) 30

(see also Deep Purple)

CAPTAIN LOCKHEED & THE STARFIGHTERS
73 United Artists UP 35543 — Ejection/Catch A Falling Starfighter (p/s) 25
73 United Artists UP 35543 — Ejection/Catch A Falling Starfighter (different mix of A-side, no p/s) 10

(see also Robert Calvert)

CAPTAIN SCARLET
(see under Century 21)

MINT VALUE £

C.A. QUINTET

83	Psycho PSYCHO 12	TRIP THROUGH HELL (LP, reissue of U.S. 60s LP)	15

CARAVAN

69	Verve VS 1518	A Place Of My Own/Ride	45
70	Decca F 13063	If I Could Do It All Over Again, I'd Do It All Over You/Hello, Hello	15
71	Decca F 23125	Love To Love You (And Tonight Pigs Will Fly)/Golf Girl	15
75	Decca FR 13599	Stuck In A Hole/Lover	5
76	BTM SBT 104	All The Way (With John Wayne's Single-Handed Liberation Of Paris)/ Chiefs And Indians (p/s)	6
77	Arista ARIST 110	Better By Far/Silver Strings	5
80	Kingdom KV 8009	Heartbreaker/It's Never Too Late (p/s)	6
68	Verve (S)VLP 6011	CARAVAN (LP, 'pillar' sleeve, mono/stereo)	150
70	Decca SKL 5052	IF I COULD DO IT ALL OVER AGAIN, I'D DO IT ALL OVER YOU (LP)	30
71	Deram SDL-R 1	IN THE LAND OF GREY AND PINK (LP, gatefold sleeve)	30
72	Deram SDL 8	WATERLOO LILY (LP, gatefold sleeve)	30
72	MGM 2353 058	CARAVAN (LP, reissue)	35
73	Deram SDL-R 12	FOR GIRLS WHO GROW PLUMP IN THE NIGHT (LP, gatefold sleeve)	18
74	Deram SML 1110	CARAVAN AND THE NEW SYMPHONIA (LIVE AT DRURY LANE) (LP)	18
75	Decca SKLR 5210	CUNNING STUNTS (LP)	15

(see also Gringo, Matching Mole, Hatfield & The North, Spiro Gyra)

CARAVELLES

63	Decca F 11697	You Don't Have To Be A Baby To Cry/The Last One To Know	6
63	Decca F 11758	I Really Don't Want To Know/I Was Wrong	8
64	Decca F 11816	Have You Ever Been Lonely?/Gonna Get Along Without Ya Now	8
64	Fontana TF 466	You Are Here/How Can I Be Sure?	8
64	Fontana TF 509	I Don't Care If The Sun Don't Shine/I Like A Man	7
64	Polydor NH 59034	True Love Never Runs Smooth/Georgia Boy	7
66	Polydor 56137	Hey Mama You've Been On My Mind/New York	12
67	Polydor 56156	I Want To Love You Again/I Had To Walk Home Myself	6
68	Pye 7N 17654	The Other Side Of Love/I Hear A New Kind Of Music	7
63	Decca LK 4565	THE CARAVELLES (LP)	40

(see also Lois Lane)

GUY CARAWAN

58	Pye Nixa 7N 15132	Old Man Atom (Talking Atomic Blues)/Michael Row The Boat Ashore	7
58	Pye Nixa N 15132	Old Man Atom (Talking Atomic Blues)/Michael Row The Boat Ashore (78)	12

(see also Peggy Seeger & Guy Carawan)

CARCASS

88	Earache MOSH 06	REEK OF PUTREFACTION (LP)	20
90	Earache MOSH 18P	SYMPHONIES OF SICKNESS (LP, picture disc)	25

CARDBOARD ORCHESTRA

69	CBS 4176	Zebady Zak/Mary Tell Me Why	8
69	CBS 4633	Nothing But A Sad Sad Show/Yes I Heard A Little Bird	8

(see also Zior, Monument)

CARDIAC ARREST

79	Another Record AN 1	Running In The Street/T.V. Friends (p/s, 500 only)	10

CARDIAC ARREST

79	Tortch TOR 002	A BUS FOR A BUS ON A BUS (EP)	50

(see also Cardiacs)

CARDIACS

81	private label	TOY WORLD (cassette)	20
81	private label	THE OBVIOUS IDENTITY (cassette)	20
86	Alphabet ALPH 002	SEASIDE TREATS (12" EP, with poster & lyric insert)	25
87	Alphabet ALPH 006	THERE'S TOO MANY IRONS IN THE FIRE (12" EP, with poster)	8
88	Alphabet ALPH 008	Is This The Life/I'm Eating In Bed (p/s)	7
88	Alphabet ALPHT 008	Is This The Life/Loosefish Goosegash/I'm Eating In Bed (12", p/s)	10
88	Alphabet ALPH 009	Susannah's Still Alive/Blind In Safety And Leafy In Love (p/s)	5
91	Alphabet ALPH 015	DAY IS GONE (12" EP, with lyric sheet)	8
80s	Alphabet ALPH 000	ARCHIVE CARDIACS (cassette, fan club issue, compilation of "Toy World" & "The Obvious Identity")	10
83	Alphabet ALPH 01	THE SEASIDE (13-track cassette, colour inlay)	30
86	Alphabet ALPH 003	MR & MRS SMITH & MR DRAKE (cassette, fan club issue)	10
87	Alphabet ALPH 004	BIG SHIP (mini LP, with lyric insert)	12
87	Alphabet ALPH 005	RUDE BOOTLEG — LIVE AT READING '86 (LP, stamped sleeve with insert)	15
87	Alphabet ALPH MC005	RUDE BOOTLEG — LIVE AT READING '86 (cassette)	12
88	Torso CD 060	A LITTLE MAN AND A HOUSE AND THE WHOLE WORLD WINDOW (CD)	20

(see also Cardiac Arrest)

CARDIGANS

58	Mercury AMT 1007	Poor Boy/Each Other	10
58	Mercury AMT 1007	Poor Boy/Each Other (78)	20

CARDIGANS

95	Stockholm PO 345	Carnival/Mr. Crowley (Live) (p/s)	5
95	Stockholm PO 336	Sick & Tired/Plain Parade (p/s)	5
95	Stockholm PZCD 336	Sick & Tired/Plain Parade/Laika/Pooh Song (CD, card sleeve)	8
95	Stockholm 577 824-7	Rise & Shine/Pike Bubbles (p/s)	5
96	Trampolene 575 966-7	Been It/(Censored Radio Edit) (p/s, brown vinyl)	6
96	Stockholm 575 528 7	Lovefool/Nasty Sunny Beam (p/s, white vinyl)	5
99	Simply Vinyl SVLP 114	LIFE (LP, reissue)	15
96	Stockholm CARDBOXCD 1	FIRST BAND ON THE MOON (CD, box set with poster & T-shirt)	20
00	Simply Vinyl SVLP 175	GRAN TURISMO (LP, 180gm vinyl)	18

MINT VALUE £

PROMOS

97	Motor 571 661 1	Your New Cuckoo/(remixes) (12", title sleeve)	8
99	Stockholm CARDI 5	Erase\Rewind (Cut La Rock Vocal Mix)/(NÂid Remix) (12", die-cut title sleeve, also as white label)	10
99	Stockholm CARDI 7	Hanging Around (NÂid Remix)/My Favourite Game (Faithless Mix) (12", no p/s)	8
96	Stockholm	HIGHLIGHTS FROM THE CARDIGANS CATALOGUE (CD-R)	25
96	Stockholm MOON 1	FIRST BAND ON THE MOON ALBUM SAMPLER (CD, card sleeve)	10
98	Stockholm CARD INT 1	INTERVIEW DISC (CD, card sleeve, with outer plastic sleeve & 3 photo-cards)	18

CARDINALS

72	Nelmwood Audio	ON TOP OF THE WORLD (LP)	22

JACK CARDWELL

54	Parlophone CMSP 24	Whiskey, Women And Loaded Dice/Slap-Ka-Dab (export issue)	35
54	Parlophone DP 400	Whiskey, Women And Loaded Dice/Slap-Ka-Dab (78, export issue)	8
54	Parlophone CMSP 27	Blue Love/Diddle Diddle Dumpling (export issue)	35
54	Parlophone DP 406	Blue Love/Diddle Diddle Dumpling (78, export issue)	8
50s	Parlophone DP 424	Ko Ko Mo (I Love You So)/Are You Mine? (with Jackie Hill) (78)	15

CARE

83	Arista KBIRD 2	Flaming Sword/Misericorde (picture disc)	5

(see also Wild Swans, Lotus Eaters, Lightning Seeds)

CAREFREES

63	Oriole CB 1916	We Love You Beatles/Hot Blooded Lover	20
64	Oriole CB 1931	Aren't You Glad You're You/Paddy Wack	12

DAVE CAREY (JAZZ BAND)

53	Columbia SCM 5030	Broken Wings/Oh, Happy Day (as David Carey)	10
56	Tempo A 122	Kater Street Rag/Kansas City Kitty	8
56	Tempo A 133	I've Found A New Baby/Brown Skin Mama	8
56	Tempo A 138	Sunset Cafe Stomp/Sweet Georgia Brown	8
56	Tempo A 150	Ida, Sweet As Apple Cider/Button Up Your Overcoat	8
61	Philips PB 1158	Bingo (I'm In Love)/Paddlin' Madelin' Home (some in p/s)	10/6
56	Tempo EXA 38	DAVE CAREY JAZZ BAND (EP)	15
56	Tempo EXA 43	DAVE CAREY JAZZ BAND (EP)	15
56	Tempo EXA 51	DAVE CAREY JAZZ BAND (EP)	12
55	Tempo LAP 4	DAVE CAREY JAZZ BAND (LP)	18
57	Tempo TAP 16	JAZZ AT THE RAILWAY ARMS (LP)	25

MARIAH CAREY

90	Columbia 655 932-0	Vision Of Love/Sent From Up Above (p/s)	5
90	Columbia 655 932-2	Vision Of Love/Sent From Up Above/Medley (CD)	20
90	Columbia 656 149-7	Love Takes Time/Sent From Up Above (p/s)	6
90	Columbia 656 364-6	Love Takes Time/You Need Me/Vanishing (12", p/s)	10
90	Columbia 656 364-2	Love Takes Time/Vanishing/You Need Me (CD)	20
90	Columbia 656 364-5	Love Takes Time/Vanishing/You Need Me/Vision Of Love (CD, picture disc)	30
91	Columbia 656 583-7	Someday/Alone In Love (p/s)	5
91	Columbia 656 583-6	Someday (7" House Mix)/(12" Jackswing Mix)/(Pianoapercaloopaperlla Mix) (12", p/s)	10
91	Columbia 656 583-2	Someday (7" Jackswing Mix)/(12" Jackswing Mix)/Love/Love Takes Time (CD)	20
91	Columbia 656 583-5	Someday (7" Jackswing Mix)/Vision Of Love/Love Takes Time/Alone In Love (CD, picture disc)	30
91	Columbia 656 931-2	There's Got To Be A Way (Album Version)/(12" Remix)/(ALT Vocal Club Mix) (CD)	25
91	Columbia 656 931-5	There's Got To Be A Way/(Album Version)/(7" Remix)/Someday (7" Jackswing Mix)/Vision Of Love (CD, picture disc)	30
91	Columbia 657 403-2	Emotions/Vanishing/Vision Of Love (CD)	15
92	Columbia 657 662-7	Can't Let Go (Edit)/To Be Around You (p/s)	5
92	Columbia 657 662-6	Can't Let Go (Edit)/To Be Around You/The Wind (12", p/s)	8
92	Columbia 657 662-2	Can't Let Go (Edit)/To Be Around You/The Wind (CD, slimline jewel case)	18
92	Columbia 657 941-6	Make It Happen (Extended Version)/(Dub Version)/(C&C Classic Mix)/(LP Version) (12", p/s)	8
92	Columbia 657 941-2	Make It Happen (Radio Edit)/(Ext. Version)/(Dub)/(C&C Classic Mix)/(LP Version) (CD)	15
92	Columbia 658 137-9	I'll Be There (live)/Vision Of Love (live)/If It's Over/All In Your Mind (CD, picture disc)	18
95	Columbia XPR 2129	Joy To The World (Celebration Mix)/(Flava Mix)/(Club Mix)/(Crash Dub Crash)/(LP Version)(12", title p/s, promo only)	15
97	Columbia XPR 2378	Fly Away (Fly Away Club Mix)/(Def 'B' Fly Mix) (12", p/s, promo only)	15
97	Columbia XPR 2380	The Roof (Remix With Mobb Deep)/Underneath The Stars/Breakdown/Babydoll (12", title p/s, promo only)	18
98	Columbia XPR 2396	The Roof (Full Crewe's Club Mix)/(Full Crewe Club Mix)/(Mobb Deep Remix)/(Full Crewe Radio Mix) (12", title p/s, promo only)	15
98	Columbia XPR 2398	The Roof (Funky Club Mix)/(Radio Mix)/(After Hours Mix)/(Bass Man Mix) (12", title p/s, promo only)	15
98	Columbia XPR 2409	My All (Full Crewe Main Mix)/(Full Crewe Radio Edit)/(Full Crewe Main Mix Without Rap)/(Full Crewe Main Mix Instrumental) (12", title p/s, promo only)	12
01	Virgin VUSTDJX 211	Loverboy (10 mixes) (CD-R, paper title sleeve)	65

TONY CAREY

84	MCA MCA 873	Fine Fine Day/Say It's Over (p/s)	6
84	MCA MCFC 3212	SOME TOUGH CITY (LP, with inner sleeve)	12

(see also Rainbow, Planet P Project)

CAREY & LLOYD

72	Attack ATT 8032	Do It Again (as Carey/Lloyd)/GARY RANGLIN: Watch It	6
72	Grape GR 3025	Come Down Part 1/DYNAMITES: Come Down Part 2	6

(see also Carey Johnson, Lloyd Young, Lloyd & Carey)

MINT VALUE £

HENSON CARGILL

68 Monument MON 1015 | Skip A Rope/Very Well-Travelled Man . . . 6

PATRICK CARGILL

71 Hit HIT 16 | Father Dear Father/Theme (Instrumental) . . . 6

CARIBBEANS

69 Doctor Bird DB 1181 | Let Me Walk By/AMBLINGS: Tell Me Why . . . 18
69 Crab CR 14 | Please Please/MATADORS: The Destroyer . . . 8

CARIBBEATS

66 Ska Beat JB 246 | The Bells Of St. Mary's/WINSTON RICHARDS: Loki . . . 22
67 Double D DD 101 | Highway 300/I Think Of You (actually by Merlene McKenzie) . . . 15
67 Double D DD 103 | I'll Try/If I Did Look . . . 15
(see also Bobby Aitken, Itals)

CARIBS

60 Starlite ST45 012 | Taboo/Mathilda Cha Cha Cha! . . . 12

CARIFTA ALLSTARS

72 Green Door GD 4040 | The Harder They Come (actually by Charlie Ace)/Time Is Still Here . . . 8

CARL & COMMANDERS

61 Columbia DB 4719 | Farmer John/Cleanin' Up . . . 20

BELINDA CARLISLE

86 I.R.S. IRM 118 | Mad About You/I Never Wanted A Rich Man (p/s) . . . 6
86 I.R.S. IRMT 118 | Mad About You/(Extended Mix)/I Never Wanted A Rich Man (12", p/s) . . . 10
88 I.R.S. DIRM 118 | Mad About You/I Never Wanted A Rich Man/Mad About You (Extended Mix) (3" CD) . . . 45
87 Virgin VSCD 1036 | Heaven Is A Place On Earth/We Can Change/Heaven Is A Place On Earth (Heavenly Version)/Heaven Is A Place On Earth (Acapella Version) (CD) . . . 22
88 Virgin VSP 1046 | I Get Weak/Should I Let You In (poster p/s) . . . 8
88 Virgin VST 1046 | I Get Weak (12" Version)/I Get Weak (7" Version)/Should I Let You In? (12", p/s, with poster) . . . 12
88 Virgin VSCD 1046 | I Get Weak (7" Version)/Should I Let You In/I Get Weak (12" Version) (CD, picture disc) . . . 22
88 Virgin VSTY 1074 | Circle In The Sand/(Beach Party Mix)/(Seaside Groove Mix) (12", picture disc) . . . 15
88 Virgin VSCD 1074 | Circle In The Sand (7" Version)/(Seaside Mood Groove Mix)/(Sandblast Multi-Mix)/(Beach Party Mix) (CD) . . . 12
88 Virgin VSX 1114 | World Without You (Remix)/Nobody Owns Me (box set, 2 cards & lyric sheet) . . . 12
88 Virgin VSTP 1114 | World Without You (Extended World-wide Mix)/World Without You (7" Remix)/Nobody Owns Me (12", poster p/s) . . . 12
88 Virgin VSCD 1114 | World Without You (Extended World-wide Mix)/World Without You (7" Remix)/World Without You (Panavision Mix) (CD) . . . 12
88 Virgin VSTA 1150 | Love Never Dies... (Full Length Version)/I Feel Free (live)/Heaven Is A Place On Earth (live) (12", p/s with advent calendar) . . . 12
88 Virgin VSCD 1150 | Love Never Dies... (Full Length Version)/I Feel Free (live)/Circle In The Sand (live)/Heaven Is A Place On Earth (live) (CD, with prints) . . . 12
89 Virgin VSP 1210 | Leave A Light On/Shades Of Michaelangelo/Leave A Light On (Extended Mix) (foldout poster p/s) . . . 5
89 Virgin VSCD 1210 | Leave A Light On (7" Version)/Shades Of Michaelangelo/Leave A Light On (Extended Mix) (3" CD in card sl., also 5" CD in jewel case [662 719/211], £25) . . . 10
89 Virgin VSX 1230 | La Luna/Whatever It Takes ('Xmas' pack, gatefold p/s) . . . 7
89 Virgin VSTP 1230 | La Luna/La Luna (Extended Dance Mix)/La Luna (12" Dub Mix) (12", poster p/s) . . . 12
89 Virgin VSCD 1230DJ | La Luna/Whatever It Takes (3" CD, picture disc, promo only) . . . 60
89 Virgin VSCDT 1230 | La Luna (Single Version)/La Luna (Extended Dance Mix)/La Luna (12" Dub Mix) (5" CD, slimline jewel case) . . . 22
90 Virgin VSTP 1244 | Runaway Horses/Heaven Is A Place On Earth (live)/Circle In The Sand (Beach Party Mix) (12", foldout poster pack) . . . 12
90 Virgin VSCD 1244 | Runaway Horses/Heaven Is A Place On Earth (live)/Circle In The Sand (Beach Party Mix) (3" CD, card sleeve) . . . 8
90 Virgin VSCDT 1244 | Runaway Horses/Heaven Is A Place On Earth (Live)/Circle In The Sand (Beach Party Mix) (5" CD, slimline jewel case) . . . 18
90 Virgin VSTD 1264 | Vision Of You (7" Version)/Leave A Light On (Kamikaze Mix)/I Feel Free (12" Extended Mix) (CD) . . . 8
90 Virgin VSTA 1291 | (We Want) The Same Thing (Extended Summer Remix)/Circle In The Sand (Sand Blast Multi Mix) (12", box set with 6 stickers) . . . 8
90 Virgin VSCDP 1291 | (We Want) The Same Thing (Summer Mix)/Circle In The Sand (Sand Blast Multi Mix)/Shades Of Michaelangelo (CD, picture disc) . . . 10
90 Virgin VSCDX 1323 | Summer Rain/Summer Rain (Justin Strauss Mix)/Leave A Light On (Kamikazee Mix) (CD, digipak with prints in video-style case) . . . 15
87 Virgin VSCD 1036 | HEAVEN ON EARTH (CD, picture disc, stickered case) . . . 35
(see also Go-Go's, Smithereens)

BILL CARLISLE & CARLISLES

59 Mercury AMT 1063 | Down Boy/Union Suit . . . 40
64 Hickory 45-1254 | Shanghai Rooster/Big John Henry's Girl . . . 7

CARLISLE BROTHERS

59 Parlophone GEP 8799 | FRESH FROM THE COUNTRY (EP) . . . 30

DON CARLOS ORCHESTRA

53 HMV GV 183 | Chilli Sauce — Samba/Maria Christina — Mambo (78, export issue) . . . 10
54 HMV 7 MC 4 | Delicado/Anything Can Happen (export issue) . . . 10
56 HMV 7 MC 48 | The Bandit/Mexicana (export issue) . . . 10
60 Top Rank JAR 376 | Mustapha/Josita . . . 7
58 Pye Nixa NPT 19028 | CHA-CHA-CHA-CARLOS (10" LP) . . . 18

MINT VALUE £

DAVE CARLSEN
73 Spark SRLP 110 — A PALE HORSE (LP) . . . 35

RAY CARLSON
67 MGM MGM 1362 — Speak No Sorrow/It's Getting Me Down Girl . . . 7

(LITTLE) CARL CARLTON
68 Action ACT 4501 — Competition Ain't Nothin'/Three Way Love . . . 45
68 Action ACT 4514 — 46 Drums 1 Guitar/Why Don't They Leave Us Alone . . . 20
69 Action ACT 4537 — Look At Mary Wonder/Bad For Each Other (as Carl Carlton) . . . 18
75 ABC ABC 4040 — Smokin' Room/Signed, Sealed, Delivered, I'm Yours (as Carl Carlton) . . . 6

EDDIE CARLTON
76 Cream CRM 5001 — It Will Be Done (Parts 1 & 2) . . . 8

CARLTON & HIS SHOES
68 Coxsone CS 7065 — Love Me Forever/Happy Land . . . 35
68 Studio One SO 2062 — This Feeling/You And Me (Love Is A Treasure) . . . 22
70s Studio One PSOL 003 — LOVE ME FOREVER (LP) . . . 80
(see also Lee 'Scratch' Perry, Roy & Enid)

CARMEN
74 Regal Zonophone RZ 3086 — Flamenco Fever/Lonely House . . . 6
74 Regal Zonophone RZ 3090 — Bulerias/Stepping Stone . . . 6
73 R. Zonophone SRZA 8518 — FANDANGOS IN SPACE (LP, gatefold sleeve) . . . 25
75 R. Zonophone SLRZ 1040 — DANCING ON A COLD WIND (LP, with inner sleeve) . . . 35

HOAGY CARMICHAEL
55 Vogue Coral Q 72078 — Crazy Otto Rag/Happy Hoagy's Medley . . . 8
55 Vogue Coral Q 72095 — Lazy River/I'm Just Wild About Mary . . . 7
56 Vogue Coral Q 72123 — Hong Kong Blues/LES BROWN: It's All Right With Me . . . 7
56 Vogue Coral Q 72206 — I Walk The Line/Flight To Hong Kong . . . 7
50s HMV 7EG 8037 — STARDUST (EP) . . . 12
54 Brunswick OE 9023 — THE STARDUST ROAD (EP) . . . 10
58 Vogue VE 170113 — HOAGY CARMICHAEL (EP) . . . 12

IAN CARMICHAEL
57 HMV POP 406 — Lucky Jim (How I Envy Him)/Tomorrow, Tomorrow . . . 6

CARMITA
58 Fontana H 160 — The Crowd/Waterwagon Blues . . . 6
58 Fontana H 160 — The Crowd/Waterwagon Blues (78) . . . 12

CARNABY
65 Piccadilly 7N 35272 — Jump And Dance/My Love Will Stay . . . 100

CARNABY STREET POP ORCHESTRA & CHOIR
69 Carnaby CNLS 6003 — CARNABY STREET POP (LP) . . . 55

CARNATIONS
65 Blue Beat BB 285 — Mighty Man/What Are You Selling . . . 20

JUDY CARNE
61 Decca F 11347 — Late Last Evening (with David Kernan)/A Plea For The Throne (with Betty Marsden & Pip Hinton) ('On The Brighter Side' cast) . . . 8
69 Reprise RS 20680 — Right, Said Fred/Sock It To Me . . . 12

CARNEGY HALL
68 Polydor 56224 — The Bells Of San Francisco/Slightly Cracked . . . 12

CARNIVAL
67 Columbia DB 8255 — The Big Bright Green Pleasure Machine/Silver Dreams And Scarlet Memories . . . 7
70 Liberty LBF 15252 — Son Of A Preacher Man/Walk On By . . . 6
70 Liberty LBS 83305 — THE CARNIVAL (LP) . . . 18

CAROL & MEMORIES
66 CBS 202086 — Tears On My Pillow/Crying My Eyes Out . . . 20

BOBBI CAROL
63 Fontana 267 260TF — Will You Love Me Tomorrow/It Doesn't Matter . . . 8

CAROLE & SHERRY
62 Fontana 270 107 TF — I Ain't Ready Yet/Like I Gotta Get Away . . . 10

CAROLINA SLIM
72 Flyright LP 4702 — CAROLINA BLUES AND BOOGIE (LP) . . . 20

CAROLINES
65 Polydor BM 56027 — Love Made A Fool Of Me/Believe In Me . . . 6

CAROLLS
65 Polydor BM 56046 — Give Me Time/Darling I Want You So Much . . . 15
(see also Carols, Carrolls)

CAROLS
70 Revolution REV 013 — Everyday I Have To Cry Some/FIRE SESSION: Sleeping Reggae . . . 5
(see also Carolls, Carrolls)

THELMA CARPENTER
61 Coral Q 72422 — Yes, I'm Lonesome Tonight/Gimme A Little Kiss . . . 10
61 Coral Q 72442 — Back Street/I Ought To Know . . . 10

CARPENTERS
71 A&M AMS 832 — Love Is Surrender/For All We Know . . . 6
71 A&M AMS 851 — Rainy Days And Mondays/Saturday . . . 5
71 A&M AMS 868 — Merry Xmas Darling/Bless The Beasts And The Children . . . 6
72 A&M AMS 885 — Hurting Each Other/Maybe It's You . . . 5

MINT VALUE £

CARPENTER'S APPRENTICE
72 SRS 12107 CHANGES (LP, with insert) . . . 120

CARPET BAGGERS
67 Spin SP 2006 Flea Teacher/On Sunday . . . 10

CARPETTES
77 Small Wonder SMALL 3 RADIO WUNDERBAR (EP) . . . 12
78 Small Wonder SMALL 9 Small Wonder?/2 Ne 1 (p/s) . . . 15
79 Beggars Banquet BEG 27 I Don't Mean It/Easy Way Out (p/s) . . . 10
80 Beggars Banquet BEG 32 Johnny Won't Hurt You/Frustration Paradise/Keys To Your Heart/ Total Insecurity (double pack) . . . 10
80 Beggars Banquet BEG 47 Nothing Ever Changes/You Never Realise/ Frustration Paradise (live (p/s) . . . 10
80 Beggars Banquet BEG 49 The Last Lone Ranger/Love So Strong/Fan Club (p/s) . . . 10
79 Beggars Banquet BEGA 14 FRUSTRATION PARADISE (LP) . . . 12
80 Beggars Banquet BEGA 21 FIGHT AMONGST YOURSELVES (LP) . . . 18

CATHY CARR
56 London HLH 8274 Ivory Tower/Please, Please Believe Me . . . 40
56 Vogue Coral Q 72175 Heartbroken/I'll Cry At Your Wedding . . . 10
59 Columbia DB 4270 First Anniversary/With Love . . . 10
59 Columbia DB 4270 First Anniversary/With Love (78) . . . 10
59 Columbia DB 4317 I'm Gonna Change Him/The Little Things You Do . . . 10
60 Columbia DB 4408 Little Sister/Dark River . . . 15
63 Stateside SS 147 Sailor Boy/The Next Time The Band Plays A Waltz . . . 15

IAN CARR
(see under Nucleus)

JAMES CARR
66 Stateside SS 507 You've Got My Mind Messed Up/That's What I Want To Know . . . 60
66 Stateside SS 535 Love Attack/Coming Back To Me Baby . . . 40
66 Stateside SS 545 You're Pouring Water On A Drowning Man/Forgetting You . . . 20
67 Stateside SS 2001 The Dark End Of the Street/Loveable Girl . . . 20
67 Stateside SS 2038 Let It Happen/A Losing Game . . . 20
67 Stateside SS 2052 I'm A Fool For You/Gonna Send You Back To Georgia . . . 20
68 Bell BLL 1004 A Man Needs A Woman/Stronger Than Love . . . 12
69 B&C CB 101 Freedom Train/That's The Way Love Turned Out For Me . . . 7
72 Mojo 2092 053 Freedom Train/That's What I Want To Know . . . 10
67 Stateside SL 10205 YOU GOT MY MIND MESSED UP (LP) . . . 120
69 Bell MBLL/SBLL 113 A MAN NEEDS A WOMAN (LP) . . . 45

JOE 'FINGERS' CARR
54 Capitol CL 14169 Piccadilly Rag/Fiddle-A-Delphia . . . 5
55 Capitol CL 14359 The Barky-roll Stomp/Deep In The Heart Of Texas (with Carr-Hops) . . . 5
55 Capitol CL 14372 Give Me A Band And My Baby/Zig-A-Zig (with Joy-Riders) . . . 5
56 Capitol CL 14520 Memories Of You/Henderson Stomp (with Carr-Hops) . . . 5
56 Capitol CL 14535 Let Me Be Your Honey, Honey/Ragtime Cowboy Joe (with Carr-Hops) . . . 5
56 Capitol CL 14587 The Portuguese Washerwoman/Stumbling . . . 5
(see also Lou Busch, Vicki Young)

JOHNNY CARR (& CADILLACS)
64 Decca F 11854 Remember That Night/Respectable . . . 20
65 Fontana TF 600 Do You Love That Girl?/Give Him A Little Time . . . 18
66 Fontana TF 681 Then So Do I/I'm Just A Little Bit Shy (solo) . . . 12
67 Fontana TF 823 Things Get Better/You Got Me Baby (solo) . . . 10

LEROY CARR
58 Fontana TFE 17051 TREASURES OF NORTH AMERICAN NEGRO MUSIC VOLUME 1 (EP) . . . 25
64 RCA RCX 7168 R.C.A. VICTOR RACE SERIES VOL. 2 (EP) . . . 18
63 CBS BPG 62206 BLUES BEFORE SUNRISE (LP) . . . 45

LINDA CARR
67 Stateside SS 2058 Everytime/Trying To Be Good For You . . . 30

MIKE CARR
68 Columbia SCX 6248 UNDER PRESSURE (LP) . . . 20
73 Ad-Rhythm ARPS MIKE CARR (LP) . . . 18

ROMEY CARR
70 Columbia DB 8710 These Things Will Keep Me Loving You/Stand Up And Fight . . . 15

VALERIE CARR
58 Columbia DB 4083 You're The Greatest/Over The Rainbow . . . 6
58 Columbia DB 4131 When The Boys Talk About The Girls/Padre . . . 6
58 Columbia DB 4225 Bad Girl/Look Forward . . . 6
58 Columbia DB 4225 Bad Girl/Look Forward (78) . . . 6
59 Columbia DB 4365 The Way To My Heart/I'm Only Asking . . . 6
59 Columbia SEG 7860 VALERIE CARR (EP) . . . 12
59 Columbia 33S 1137 VALERIE CARR (10" LP) . . . 25
61 Columbia 33SX 1228 EV'RY HOUR, EV'RY DAY OF MY LIFE (LP, also stereo SCX 3307) . . . 20

VIKKI CARR
64 Liberty LBY 1208 DISCOVERY (LP) . . . 18
65 Liberty LBY 1284 ANATOMY OF LOVE (IP) . . . 18
68 Liberty LBL 83037 IT MUST BE HIM (LP) . . . 12
68 Liberty LBL 83099 VIKKI (LP) . . . 12
69 Liberty LBS 83180 FOR ONCE IN MY LIFE (LP) . . . 12

WYNONA CARR
61 Reprise R 20033 I Gotta Stand Tall/My Faith . . . 15

MINT VALUE £

DAVID CARRADINE
75 Jet JETLP 10 GRASSHOPPER (LP) . . . 12

JOE 'KING' CARRASCO & THE CROWNS
80 Stiff CROWN 1 Bueno/Tuff Enuff (vinyl 78, p/s) . . . 15

CARRICK FOLK FOUR
65 Thistle TM 90 Radio Scotland/Blue Nose . . . 6

ANDREA CARROLL
63 London HLX 9772 It Hurts To Be Sixteen/Why Am I So Shy . . . 15

BARBARA CARROLL
59 London HLR 8981 North By Northwest/Far Away . . . 15

BERNADETTE CARROLL
64 Stateside SS 311 Party Girl/I Don't Wanna Know . . . 18

BOB CARROLL
55 MGM SP 1132 I Love You So Much It Hurts/My Dearest, My Darling, My Love . . . 10
56 London HLU 8299 Red Confetti, Pink Balloons And Tambourines/Handwriting On The Wall . . . 50
56 London HLU 8299 Red Confetti, Pink Balloons And Tambourines/Handwriting On The Wall (78) . . . 8
58 London HLT 8724 Hi Yo Silver/Tonto The Brave . . . 20
58 London HLT 8724 Hi Yo Silver/Tonto The Brave (78) . . . 15
59 London HLT 8888 I Can't Get You Out Of My Heart/Since I'm Out Of Your Arms . . . 15
59 London HLT 8888 I Can't Get You Out Of My Heart/Since I'm Out Of Your Arms (78) . . . 12

CATHY CARROLL
62 Warner Bros WB 72 Poor Little Puppet/Love And Learn . . . 12

DIAHANN CARROLL
59 London HLT 8788 The Big Country/Guiding Light . . . 20
59 London HLT 8788 The Big Country/Guiding Light (78) . . . 10

DON CARROLL
57 Capitol CL 14812 At Your Front Door/The Gods Were Angry With Me . . . 10
58 Capitol CL 14823 In My Arms/The Things I Might Have Been . . . 5

GINA CARROLL
65 Decca F 12297 Bye Bye Big Boy/Down The Street . . . 20

JOHNNY CARROLL & HOT ROCKS
56 Brunswick 05580 Corrine Corrina/Wild Wild Women . . . 750
56 Brunswick 05580 Corrine Corrina/Wild Wild Women (78) . . . 100
56 Brunswick 05603 Crazy, Crazy Lovin'/Hot Rock . . . 750
56 Brunswick 05603 Crazy, Crazy Lovin'/Hot Rock (78) . . . 100
74 UK USA 1 Black Leather Rebel/Be-Bop-A-Lula (as Johnny Carroll & Blue Caps) . . . 10

PAT CARROLL
72 Pye International 7N 25592 To The Sun/Out Of My Mind . . . 7

RONNIE CARROLL
60 Philips PB 1004 Footsteps/Where My True Love Walks . . . 5
62 Philips PB 1222 Ring-A-Ding Girl/The Girls In Their Summer Dresses . . . 5
62 Philips 326 550 BF If Only Tomorrow/Think Of Her (p/s) . . . 5
(see also Millicent Martin)

TONI CARROLL
58 MGM MGM 987 Dreamsville/I've Never Felt This Way Before . . . 15
58 MGM EP 689 THIS ONE IS TONI (EP) . . . 18

CARROLLS
66 Polydor BM 56081 Surrender Your Love/The Folk I Love . . . 8
68 CBS 3414 So Gently Falls The Rain/Nice To See You Darling . . . 5
68 CBS 3710 Ever Since/Come On . . . 7
68 CBS 3875 A Lemon Balloon And A Blue Sky/Make Me Belong To You . . . 10
69 CBS 4401 We're In This Thing Together/We Know Better . . . 5
(see also Carols, Carolls, Faith Brown, Brotherly Love)

BEN CARRUTHERS & DEEP
65 Parlophone R 5295 Jack O' Diamonds/Right Behind You . . . 45

CHAD CARSON
63 HMV POP 1156 They Were Wrong/Stop Picking On Me . . . 50

DEL CARSON
59 Decca F 11135 Jean/I Told Myself A Lie . . . 6
59 Decca F 11135 Jean/I Told Myself A Lie (78) . . . 12

JOHNNY CARSON
60 Fontana H 243 Fraulein/I Wish It Were You . . . 12
60 Fontana H 259 The Train Of Love/First Proposal . . . 12
60 Fontana H 277 You Talk Too Much/Now And Always . . . 12
62 Ember EMB S 150 Teenage Bachelor/Are You Anyone's Girl? . . . 18
63 Ember EMB S 161 The Tears Came Rolling Down/One Track Mind . . . 18

KAY CARSON
56 Capitol CL 14565 Those Who Have Loved/The Fellow Over There . . . 10
56 Capitol CL 14634 There's A Shadow Between Us/This Man . . . 10
(see also Kit Carson)

KEN CARSON
55 London HLF 8213 Hawkeye/I've Been Working On The Railroad . . . 30
55 London HLF 8213 Hawkeye/I've Been Working On The Railroad (78) . . . 15
56 London HLF 8237 Let Her Go, Let Her Go/The Song Of Daniel Boone (The Daddy Of Them All) . . . 10
56 London HLF 8237 Let Her Go, Let Her Go/The Song Of Daniel Boone (The Daddy Of Them All) (78) 18

MINT VALUE £

KIT CARSON
56 Capitol CL 14524 Band Of Gold/Cast Your Bread Upon The Waters ... 12
(see also Kay Carson)

MINDY CARSON
58 Philips PB 822 The Sentimental Touch/I Was Born ... 6

MINDY CARSON & GUY MITCHELL
53 Columbia SCM 5022 That's A Why/Train Of Love ... 40
(see also Guy Mitchell)

VINCE CARSON
55 HMV 7M 313 Sweetie, Sweet, Sweet Sue/My Possession ... 8

ANITA CARTER
58 London HLA 8693 Blue Doll/Go Away Johnnie ... 25
60 London HLW 9102 Moon Girl/Mama Don't Cry At My Wedding ... 18

BENNY CARTER
54 HMV 7M 189 Blue Mountain/Sunday Afternoon ... 5
62 HMV CLP 1624/CSD1480 FURTHER DEFINITIONS (LP, mono/stereo) ... 20
66 HMV CLP/CSD 3576 FURTHER DEFINITIONS (LP, mono/stereo) ... 20
(see also Helen Humes)

BETTY CARTER
63 London HLK 9748 The Good Life/Nothing More To Look Forward To ... 12
(see also Ray Charles)

CAROLINE CARTER
65 Decca F 12239 The Ballad Of Possibilities/We Want Love ... 10

CAROLYN CARTER
65 London HL 9959 It Hurts/I'm Thru ... 35

CHRIS CARTER
81 Industrial IRC 32 THE SPACE BETWEEN (cassette) ... 12
85 C.T.I. CTILP 3 MONDO BEAT (LP) ... 12
(see also Throbbing Gristle, Chris & Cosey)

CLARENCE CARTER
68 Atlantic 584 154 Thread The Needle/Don't Make My Baby Cry ... 12
68 Atlantic 584 176 Looking For A Fox/I Can't See Myself (Crying About You) ... 12
68 Atlantic 584 187 Funky Fever/Slip Away ... 10
68 Atlantic 584 223 Too Weak To Fight/Let Me Comfort You ... 10
69 Atlantic 584 248 Snatchin' It Back/Making Love (At The Dark End Of The Street) ... 10
69 Atlantic 584 272 The Feeling Is Right/You Can't Miss When You Can't Measure ... 10
70 Atlantic 584 309 Take It Off Him And Put It On Me/The Few Troubles I've Had ... 10
70 Atlantic 2091 030 Patches/I Can't Leave Your Love Alone ... 10
71 Atlantic 2091 045 It's All In Your Mind/Willie And Laura Mae Jones ... 10
71 Atlantic 2091 093 The Court Room/Getting The Bills (But No Merchandise) ... 10
71 Atlantic 2091 139 Slipped, Tripped And Fell In Love/I Hate To Love And Run ... 10
68 Atlantic 588 152 THIS IS CLARENCE CARTER (LP) ... 25
69 Atlantic 588 172 THE DYNAMIC CLARENCE CARTER (LP) ... 25
69 Atlantic 588 191 TESTIFYIN' (LP) ... 22
70 Atlantic 2400 027 PATCHES (LP) ... 20

HAL CARTER FIVE
62 Oriole CB 1709 Come On And Twist Me/Twistin' Time Is Here ... 10

HERBIE CARTER
68 Duke DU 4 Happy Time (actually by Keble Drummond)/BOYS: Smashville ... 7

JEAN CARTER & CENTREPIECES
68 Stateside SS 2114 No Good Jim/And None ... 12

JOHN CARTER & RUSS ALQUIST
68 Spark SRL 1017 The Laughing Man/Midsummer Dreaming ... 35
(see also Carter-Lewis & Southerners, Ivy League, Flowerpot Men)

MARTIN CARTER
72 Tradition TSR 012 UPS & DOWNS (LP) ... 40

MEL CARTER
63 Pye International 7N 25212 When A Boy Falls In Love/So Wonderful ... 12
66 Liberty LIB 66113 Hold Me, Thrill Me, Kiss Me/Sweet Little Girl ... 30
65 Liberty LIB 66138 (All Of A Sudden) My Heart Sings/When I Hold The Hand Of The One I Love ... 15
66 Liberty LIB 66148 Love Is All We Need/I Wish I Didn't Love You So ... 15
66 Liberty LIB 66165 Band Of Gold/Detour ... 15
66 Liberty LIB 66183 You You You/If You Lose Her ... 12

MOTHER MAYBELLE CARTER
64 London HA-R 8214 QUEEN OF THE AUTOHARP (LP) ... 15

WILF CARTER
53 HMV JO 331 Sweet Little Lover/Huggin' Squeezin' Kissin' Teasin' (78, export issue) ... 8

SHEILA CARTER & EPISODE SIX
66 Pye 7N 17194 I Will Warm Your Heart/Incense ... 35
(see also Episode, Episode Six)

SONNY CARTER with EARL BOSTIC & HIS ORCHESTRA
55 Parlophone MSP 6167 There Is No Greater Love/Oh Baby ... 30
55 Parlophone R 4015 There Is No Greater Love/Oh Baby (78) ... 10
(see also Earl Bostic)

SYDNEY CARTER
66 Elektra EPK 801 LORD OF THE DANCE (EP) ... 18

MINT VALUE £

CARTER FAMILY

55	Brunswick OE 9168	MOUNTAIN MUSIC VOL. 2 (EP)	12
62	RCA RCX 7100	THE ORIGINAL AND GREAT CARTER FAMILY VOL. 1 (EP)	10
62	RCA RCX 7101	THE ORIGINAL AND GREAT CARTER FAMILY VOL. 2 (EP)	10
62	RCA RCX 7102	THE ORIGINAL AND GREAT CARTER FAMILY VOL. 3 (EP)	10
63	RCA RCX 7109	THE ORIGINAL AND GREAT CARTER FAMILY VOL. 4 (EP)	10
63	RCA RCX 7110	THE ORIGINAL AND GREAT CARTER FAMILY VOL. 5 (EP)	10
63	RCA RCX 7111	THE ORIGINAL AND GREAT CARTER FAMILY VOL. 6 (EP)	10
63	Ace Of Hearts AH 58	A COLLECTION OF FAVOURITES (LP)	12

CARTER-LEWIS & SOUTHERNERS

61	Piccadilly 7N 35004	So Much In Love/Back On The Scene	35
61	Ember EMB S 145	Two Timing Baby/Will It Happen To Me?	50
62	Piccadilly 7N 35085	Here's Hopin'/Poor Joe	40
62	Ember EMB S 165	Tell Me/My Broken Heart	50
63	Oriole CB 1835	Sweet And Tender Romance/Who Told You?	20
63	Oriole CB 1868	Your Momma's Out Of Town/Somebody Told My Girl	20
64	Oriole CB 1919	Skinny Minnie/Easy To Cry	35

(see also Ivy League, Flowerpot Men, White Plains, John Carter & Russ Alquist, Jimmy Page, Dawn Chorus)

MARTIN CARTHY

76	Topic STOP 7002	The Bonny Lass Of Anglesey/Palaces Of Gold	6
65	Fontana (S)TL 5269	MARTIN CARTHY (LP)	30
71	Philips 6308 049	LANDFALL (LP)	25
72	Pegasus PEG 12	SHEARWATER (LP, with insert)	20
72	Philips 6282 022	THIS IS MARTIN CARTHY (LP)	18
74	Deram SML 1111	SWEET WIVELSFIELD (LP)	15

MARTIN CARTHY & DAVE SWARBRICK

67	Fontana TE 17490	NO SONGS (EP)	35
66	Fontana STL 5362	SECOND ALBUM (LP)	25
67	Fontana STL 5434	BYKER HILL (LP)	25
68	Fontana STL 5477	BUT TWO CAME BY (LP)	25
70	Fontana STL 5529	PRINCE HEATHEN (LP)	25
71	Pegasus PEG 6	SELECTIONS (LP, gatefold sleeve)	20

(see also Dave Swarbrick, Three City Four, Steeleye Span, Leon Rosselson, Alex Campbell, Nigel Denver)

CARTOONE

69	Atlantic 584 240	Knick Knack Man/A Penny For The Sun	8
69	Atlantic 588 174	CARTOONE (LP)	25

(see also Jimmy Page)

FLIP CARTRIDGE

66	London HLU 10076	Dear Mrs Applebee/Don't Take The Lovers From The World	10

DAVE CARTWRIGHT

70	Harmony DB 0001	MIDDLE OF THE ROAD (LP, private pressing with insert)	25
72	Transatlantic TRA 255	A LITTLE BIT OF GLORY (LP)	15
73	Transatlantic TRA 267	BACK TO THE GARDEN (LP)	15
75	Transatlantic TRA 284	DON'T LET YOUR FAMILY DOWN (LP)	15

(see also Bev Pegg, Away From The Sand)

DICK CARUSO

60	MGM MGM 1077	Two Long Years/Yes Sir, That's My Baby	10
60	MGM MGM 1099	Pretty Little Dancin' Doll/We've Never Met	10

ALAN CARVELL

76	United Artists UP 36124	Georgia On My Mind/Never Give Your Love (To A New York Woman)	5

(see also Steve Allan, Carvells, Five Sapphires, Telegrams)

CARVELLS

77	Creole CR 143	The L.A. Run/Your Sweet Love	5
78	Rocket ROKN 540	Skateboard Queen/Skateboard Surfing	6
78	Rocket ROKN 544	Skateboard Riders/Skateboard King	6
78	Rocket ROLL 15	SKATEBOARD RAMPAGE (LP)	18

(see also Steve Allan, Alan Carvell, Five Sapphires, Telegrams)

CASABLANCA

74	Rocket PIGL 7	CASABLANCA (LP, die-cut sleeve with inner lyric sleeve)	18

(see also Trees)

CASANOVAS

00s	Singles Society 7STAS 3320	Nasty/Too Cool (numbered die-cut p/s, 500 only)	10

CASCADES

63	Warner Bros WB 88	Rhythm Of The Rain/Let Me Be	7
63	Warner Bros WB 98	Shy Girl/The Last Leaf	8
63	Warner Bros WB 103	I Wanna Be Your Lover/My First Day Alone	8
63	RCA Victor RCA 1358	Cinderella/A Little Like Loving	7
64	RCA Victor RCA 1378	Jeannie/For Your Sweet Love	7
65	Liberty LIB 55822	I Bet You Won't Stay/She'll Love Again	7
66	Stateside SS 515	Cheryl's Goin' Home/Truly Julie's Blues	8
69	Uni UN 508	Maybe The Rain Will Fall/Naggin' Cries	6
63	Warner Bros WEP/WSE 6106	RHYTHM OF THE RAIN (EP, mono/stereo)	40/55
63	Warner Bros WM 8127	RHYTHM OF THE RAIN (LP, mono/stereo)	40/50

AL CASEY & K.C. ETTES

63	Pye International 7N 25215	Surfin' Hootenanny/Easy Picking	18

(see also Sanford Clark, Duane Eddy)

MINT VALUE £

HOWIE CASEY & SENIORS

62	Fontana H 364	Double Twist/True Fine Mama	25
62	Fontana H 381	I Ain't Mad At You/Twist At The Top	20
63	Fontana TF 403	The Boll Weevil Song/Bony Moronie	20
62	Fontana TFL 5108	TWIST AT THE TOP (LP)	75
65	Wing WL 1022	LET'S TWIST (LP, reissue of "Twist At The Top")	25

(see also Freddie Starr)

ALVIN CASH (& REGISTERS)

65	Stateside SS 386	Twine Time/The Bump (as Alvin Cash & Crawlers)	35
66	Stateside SS 543	Philly Freeze/No Deposits, No Returns (as Alvin Cash & Registers)	22
68	President PT 115	Philly Freeze/No Deposits, No Returns (as Alvin Cash & Registers) (reissue)	8
68	President PT 119	Alvin's Boo-Ga-Loo/Let's Do Some Good Timing (as Alvin Cash & Registers)	12
68	President PT 129	Doin' The Ali Shuffle/Feel So Good	12
68	President PT 147	Charge/Diff'rent Strokes For Diff'rent Folks	15
71	President PT 351	Twine Time/Twine Awhile	10
72	President PT 383	Barracuda/Do It One More Time	10
67	President PTL 1000	THE PHILLY FREEZE (LP)	50

JOHNNY CASH (& TENNESSEE TWO)

78s

57	London HL 8358	I Walk The Line/Get Rhythm	25
57	London HLS 8427	Train Of Love/There You Go	25
57	London HLS 8461	Next In Line/Don't Make Me Go	25
57	London HLS 8514	Home Of The Blues/Give My Love To Rose	30
58	London HLS 8586	Big River (with Tennessee Two)/Ballad Of A Teenage Queen	25
58	London HLS 8656	Guess Things Happen That Way/Come In, Stranger	20
58	London HLS 8709	The Ways Of A Woman In Love/You're The Nearest Thing To Heaven	30
59	Philips PB 874	All Over Again/What Do I Care	50
59	Philips PB 897	Don't Take Your Guns To Town/I Still Miss Someone	55
59	London HLS 8789	It's Just About Time/I Just Thought You'd Like To Know	35
59	London HLS 8847	Luther Played The Boogie/Thanks A Lot	40
59	Philips PB 928	Frankie's Man, Johnny/You Dreamer You	35
59	London HLS 8928	Katy Too/I Forgot To Remember To Forget	45
59	Philips PB 953	I Got Stripes/Five Feet High And Rising	55
59	London HLS 8979	You Tell Me/Goodbye, Little Darlin', Goodbye	50
59	Philips PB 979	The Little Drummer Boy/I'll Remember You	65

SINGLES

57	London HL 8358	I Walk The Line/Get Rhythm (gold label lettering, later silver)	100/60
57	London HLS 8427	Train Of Love/There You Go	40
57	London HLS 8461	Next In Line/Don't Make Me Go	45
57	London HLS 8514	Home Of The Blues/Give My Love To Rose	40
58	London HLS 8586	Big River (with Tennessee Two)/Ballad Of A Teenage Queen	35
58	London HLS 8656	Guess Things Happen That Way/Come In, Stranger (with Tennessee Two)	15
58	London HLS 8709	The Ways Of A Woman In Love/You're The Nearest Thing To Heaven (with Tennessee Two)	18
59	Philips PB 874	All Over Again/What Do I Care	10
59	Philips PB 897	Don't Take Your Guns To Town/I Still Miss Someone	10
59	London HLS 8789	It's Just About Time/I Just Thought You'd Like To Know (with Tennessee Two)	20
59	London HLS 8847	Luther Played The Boogie/Thanks A Lot	25
59	Philips PB 928	Frankie's Man, Johnny/You Dreamer You	10
59	London HLS 8928	Katy Too/I Forgot To Remember To Forget	20
59	Philips PB 953	I Got Stripes/Five Feet High And Rising	10
59	London HLS 8979	You Tell Me/Goodbye, Little Darlin', Goodbye	15
59	Philips PB 979	The Little Drummer Boy/I'll Remember You	5
60	London HLS 9070	Straight A's In Love/I Love You Because	15
60	Philips PB 1017	Seasons Of My Heart/Smiling Bill McCall	5
60	London HLS 9182	Down The Street To 301/Story Of A Broken Heart	15
60	Philips PB 1075	Going To Memphis/Loading Coal	10
61	London HLS 9314	Oh Lonesome Me/Life Goes On	10
61	Philips PB 1148	The Rebel — Johnny Yuma/Forty Shades Of Green	5
61	Philips PB 1200	Tennessee Flat-Top Box/Tall Man	10
63	CBS AAG 159	Ring Of Fire/I'd Still Be There	5
63	CBS AAG 173	The Matador/Still In Town	5
63	CBS AAG 200	Understand Your Man/Dark As A Dungeon	5
65	CBS 201741	Orange Blossom Special/All God's Children Ain't Free	5
65	CBS 201760	It Ain't Me Babe/Time And Time Again	5
65	CBS 201809	Ring Of Fire/Streets Of Laredo	5
66	CBS 202046	The One On The Right Is On The Left/Cotton Pickin' Hands	5
66	CBS 202256	Everybody Loves A Nut/Austin Prison	5
67	CBS 202546	You Beat All I Ever Saw/Put The Sugar To Bed	5
67	CBS 3268	Rosanna's Going Wild/Long-Legged Guitar-Pickin' Man (with June Carter)	5
68	CBS 3438	Certain Kind Of Hurtin'/Another Song To Sing	5
68	CBS 3549	Folsom Prison Blues (live)/The Folk Singer	5
68	CBS 3878	Daddy Sang Bass/He Turned The Water Into Wine	5
69	CBS 4460	A Boy Named Sue (live) /San Quentin (live)	5
69	CBS 4638	Blistered/See Ruby Fall	5
76	CBS S 4287	One Piece At A Time/Go On Blues	5

EXPORT SINGLES

57	London HL 7020	Next In Line/Don't Make Me Go	35
57	London HL 7023	Home Of The Blues/Give My Love To Rose	35
58	London HL 7032	Ballad Of A Teenage Queen/Big River	25
58	London HL 7053	The Ways Of A Woman In Love/You're The Nearest Thing To Heaven	25
57	London HL 7131	Folsom Prison Blues/I Walk The Line	30

MINT VALUE £

EPs

58 London RES 1120 JOHNNY CASH (triangular or round centre) 40/20
59 London RES 1193 JOHNNY CASH SINGS HANK WILLIAMS (triangular or round centre) 40/20
59 London RES 1212 COUNTRY BOY (triangular or round centre) 35/20
59 London RES 1230 JOHNNY CASH NO. 2 (triangular or round centre). 35/20
60 Philips BBE 12377 THE TROUBADOR 20
60 Philips BBE 12318 GRANDFATHER'S CLOCK 20
60 Philips BBE 12395 SONGS OF OUR SOIL 20
61 Philips BBE 12494 STRICTLY CASH. 20
64 CBS AGG 20050 FORTY SHADES OF GREEN 15
64 CBS EP 5576 FABULOUS JOHNNY CASH. 15
64 CBS EP 5735 ORANGE BLOSSOM SPECIAL 15
64 CBS EP 5744 EVERYBODY LOVES A NUT 15
64 CBS EP 5964 RING OF FIRE. 15
65 CBS EP 6061 IT AIN'T ME BABE 15
66 CBS EP 6073 MEAN AS HELL! — BALLADS FROM THE TRUE WEST (with Statler Brothers & Carter Family) 15
65 CBS EP 6109 SONGS OF KATIE ELDER 15
65 CBS EP 6147 HAPPINESS IS YOU 15
69 CBS EP 6601 FOLSOM PRISON BLUES 12
72 CBS EP 9155 LITTLE FAUSS AND BIG HALSY 10

LPs

59 London HA-S 2157 SINGS THE SONGS THAT MADE HIM FAMOUS. 35
59 London HA-S 2179 WITH HIS HOT AND BLUE GUITAR 45
59 Philips BBL 7298 THE FABULOUS JOHNNY CASH (also stereo SBBL 554) 22/30
59 Philips BBL 7353 SONGS OF OUR SOIL 22
59 Philips BBL 7373 HYMNS BY JOHNNY CASH 30
60 Philips BBL 7358 NOW THERE WAS A SONG! (also stereo SBBL 580) 20/25
60 Philips BBL 7417 RIDE THIS TRAIN 18
61 CBS (S)BPG 62042 THE FABULOUS JOHNNY CASH (mono/stereo) 12/15
62 CBS (S)BPG 62015 HYMNS FROM THE HEART (mono/stereo) 12/15
62 CBS (S)BPG 62073 THE SOUND OF JOHNNY CASH (mono/stereo). 12/15
63 CBS BPG 62119 BLOOD SWEAT AND TEARS 15
63 CBS (S)BPG 62171 RING OF FIRE (mono/stereo) 12/15
63 CBS (S)BPG 62284 THE CHRISTMAS SPIRIT (mono/stereo). 12/15
64 CBS (S)BPG 62371 I WALK THE LINE (mono/stereo). 12/15
64 CBS (S)BPG 62463 BITTER TEARS (mono/stereo) 12/15
65 CBS (S)BPG 62501 ORANGE BLOSSOM SPECIAL (mono/stereo) 12/15
65 Fontana FJS 301 JOHNNY CASH'S COUNTRY ROUND-UP (4 tracks only) 12
65 London HA-S 8220 THE ORIGINAL SUN SOUND OF JOHNNY CASH 35
65 CBS (S)BPG 62538 BALLADS OF THE TRUE WEST VOL. 1 15
65 CBS (S)BPG 62575 RIDE THIS TRAIN 12
65 CBS (S)BPG 62591 BALLADS OF THE TRUE WEST VOL. 2 15
66 London HA-S 8253 LONESOME ME 30
66 CBS (S)BPG 62717 EVERYBODY LOVES A NUT. 12
66 CBS (S)BPG 62760 HAPPINESS IS YOU 12
67 CBS (S)BPG 62972 FROM SEA TO SHINING SEA. 12
67 CBS (S)BPG 63105 CARRYIN' ON 12
68 CBS 63308 AT FOLSOM PRISON (mono). 12
84 Charley SUN BOX-105 THE SUN YEARS (5-LP box set) 30

CASH PUSSIES

79 The Label TLR 010 99% Is Shit/Cash Flow (p/s). 6
(see also Sex Pistols)

CASINO ROYALES

67 London HLU 10122 When I Tell You That I Love You/Love In The Open Air 6

CASINOS

67 Ember EMB S 241 That's The Way/Too Good To Be True. 35
67 President PT 123 Then You Can Tell Me Goodbye/I Still Love You 10
68 President PT 140 To Be Loved/Tailor Made 6
68 President PT 156 When I Stop Dreaming/Please Love Me 6
68 President PTL 1007 THEN YOU CAN TELL ME GOODBYE (LP) 25

TONY CASO

68 London HL 10178 Shadow On The Ground/I Don't Care Who Knows It. 6

MAMA CASS

(see under Mama Cass Elliot, Mamas & Papas, Mugwumps, Big Three)

CASSETTE

79 1 track CAS 001 THE FAST FORWARD EP: What's The Point/Product/All The Rage. 10

CASSETTES

81 Zip ZIP 101 Reverberate/Don't Label Me (die-cut sleeve) 7

DAVID CASSIDY

71 Bell BELL 1189 Cherish/All I Wanna Do Is Touch You. 8
85 Arista ARISD 589 The Last Kiss/The Letter (shaped picture disc with calendar, 6500 only) 6
85 Arista ARIST 12589 The Last Kiss/The Letter (12", signed p/s) 7
85 Arista ARISD 620 Romance (Let Your Heart Go)/(Instrumental Mix) (with Samantha Fox) (picture disc) 8
(see also Partridge Family, Samantha Fox)

STEVE CASSIDY

63 Ember EMB S 177 Ecstasy/I'm A Worrying 8

TED CASSIDY

65 Capitol CL 15423 The Lurch/Wesley. 25

CAST

94 (no label) GRA 001 CAST SAMPLER (Sandstorm/Follow Me Down/Tell It Like It Is) (10", white label, white stamped sleeve, promo only, 700 copies) 25
(see also La's)

CASTANARC
74 Peninsula PENCIL 10 JOURNEY TO THE EAST (LP, private pressing) . . . 18

CASTAWAYS
65 London HL 10003 Liar Liar/Sam . . . 40

CASTE
68 President PT 211 Don't Cast Aside/One Step Closer . . . 6

JOEY CASTELL
57 Decca F 10966 I'm Left, You're Right, She's Gone/Tryin' To Get To You . . . 125
57 Decca F 10966 I'm Left, You're Right, She's Gone/Tryin' To Get To You (78) . . . 50

CASTELLS
61 London HLN 9392 Sacred/I Get Dreamy . . . 22
62 London HLN 9551 So This Is Love/On The Street Of Tears . . . 25

CASTELLS
67 Masquerade MA 500 Two Lovers/Jerusalem . . . 6

LEE CASTLE & BARONS
64 Parlophone R 5151 A Love She Can Count On/Foolin' . . . 18

ROY CASTLE
58 Pye 7N 15173 In My Heart/Mister Music Man . . . 6
58 Pye N 15173 In My Heart/Mister Music Man (78, vinyl pressing) . . . 8
59 Pye 7N 15215 The Chosen Few/Bimbo . . . 6
59 Pye N 15215 The Chosen Few/Bimbo (78, vinyl pressing) . . . 8
60 Philips PB 1087 Little White Berry/Crazy Little Thorn . . . 8
65 CBS 201736 Doctor Terror's House Of Horrors/Voodoo Girl (with Tubby Hayes) . . . 150
68 Olga OLE 12 Wonderful World/For All The World . . . 7
71 United Artists UP 35254 Maybe That's Your Problem/Thick As Thieves (with Dilys Watling) . . . 6
60s Philips EPs . . . each 10
61 Philips BBL 7457 CASTLEWISE (LP, also stereo SBBL 626) . . . 20/15

CASTLE ROCK
73 FEST 002 NOTTINGHAM CASTLE FESTIVAL FRINGE (LP, private pressing) . . . 60

CASTLE SISTERS (Jamaica)
66 Ska Beat JB 257 Stop Your Lying/Don't Be A Fool . . . 25

CASTLE SISTERS (USA)
59 Columbia DB 4335 Drifting And Dreaming/Lucky Girl . . . 6

CAST OF THOUSANDS
66 Stateside SS 546 My Jenny Wears A Mini/Girl Do What You Gonna Do . . . 15

CASTON & MAJORS
75 Tamla Motown TMG 938 Child Of Love/No One Will Know . . . 10
(see also Radiants)

JIMMY CASTOR (BUNCH)
66 Philips BF 1543 Hey Leroy, Your Mama's Callin'/Hamhock's Espanol . . . 12
67 Philips BF 1590 Magic Saxophone/Just You Girl . . . 18
71 Mercury 6052 110 Hey Leroy, Your Mama's Callin'/Hamhock's Espanol (reissue) . . . 8
73 RCA Victor APD1 0103 DIMENSION III (LP, quadrophonic) . . . 18
74 Atlantic K 50052 THE EVERYTHING MAN (LP) . . . 15
76 Atlantic K 50295 E-MAN GROOVIN' (LP) . . . 15

FRANKIE CASTRO
56 Mercury MT 114 Goodbye, So Long, I'm Gone/Too Much (78) . . . 20

CASUAL FOUR
60s Specially Made For Us 102 I Can Tell/Love Potion No. 9 . . . 50

CASUALEERS
74 Pye Disco Demand DDS 103 Dance Dance Dance/Something About This Girl . . . 5

CASUALS
65 Fontana TF 635 If You Walk Out/Please Don't Hide . . . 10
68 Decca F 12737 Adios Amor (Goodbye My Love)/Don't Dream Of Yesterday . . . 6
68 Decca F 22784 Jesamine/I've Got Something Too . . . 6
68 Decca F 22852 Toy/Touched (some in p/s) . . . 15/6
69 Decca F 22900 Fools Paradise/7 X 7 . . . 6
69 Decca F 22943 Sunflower Eyes/Never My Love . . . 6
69 Decca F 22969 Caroline/Naughty Boy . . . 8
70 Decca F 23027 My Name Is Love/I Can't Say . . . 6
71 Decca F 23112 Someday Rock 'n' Roll Lady/A Letter Every Day . . . 6
72 Parlophone R 5959 Tara Tiger Girl/Nature's Girl . . . 6
74 Dawn DNS 1069 Witch/Good Times . . . 6
69 Decca LK-R/SKL-R 5001 HOUR WORLD (LP) . . . 35

JOHNNY CASWELL
85 Kent TOWN 106 You Don't Love Me No More/STEINWAYS: You've Been Leading Me On . . . 10

CATAPILLA
71 Vertigo 6360 029 CATAPILLA (LP, gatefold sleeve, swirl label) . . . 125
72 Vertigo 6360 074L CHANGES (LP, gatefold sleeve, swirl label) . . . 200

CATATONIA
94 Crai CRAI C 039L Hooked/Fall Beside Her/Difrydreulyd (cassette) . . . 8
94 Crai CRAICD 039 Hooked/Fall Beside Her/Difrydreulyd (CD) . . . 12
94 Rough Trade 45rev33 Whale/You Can (p/s, 'Singles Club' release) . . . 20
95 Nursery NYS 12L Bleed/This Boy Can't Swim (red vinyl, numbered p/s, 1,000 only) . . . 12
95 Nursery NYSCD 12 Bleed/This Boy Can't Swim/Painful (CD) . . . 12
95 Blanco Y Negro SAM 1746 Blow The Millennium Blow/Beautiful Sailor (p/s, white vinyl Xmas 45, freebie) . . . 15

MINT VALUE £

96	Blanco Y Negro NEGAT 8X	Lost Cat/To And Fro (yellow vinyl, p/s)	6
96	Blanco Y Negro NEG 85X	Sweet Catatonia/Tourist (no'd p/s, clear vinyl, 5,000 only)	8
96	Blanco Y Negro NEG 93	You've Got A Lot To Answer For/Do You Believe In Me (red vinyl)	6
96	Blanco Y Negro NEG 97	Bleed/This Boy Can't Swim (p/s, reissue, red vinyl)	5
96	Blanco Y Negro NEG 97CD1	Bleed/This Boy Can't Swim/Painful (CD, reissue, one of a pair)	8
97	Blanco Y Negro NEG 107	I Am The Mob/Jump Or Be Sane (orange vinyl)	5
98	Blanco Y Negro NEG 109	Mulder & Scully/No Stone Unturned (blue vinyl, with poster)	5
99	Blanco Y Negro NEG 116CDDJ	Karaoke Queen (CD, card sleeve, withdrawn, promo only)	15
93	Crai C 039L	FOR TINKERBELL EP (cassette)	10
93	Crai CD 039B	FOR TINKERBELL EP (CD)	12
96	Blanco Y Negro 16305-1	WAY BEYOND BLUE (LP, deleted after one week, with free 7")	18
98	Blanco Y Negro 20834-1	INTERNATIONAL VELVET (LP, 1,000 only, with free 12")	20

CATCH (featuring Marilyn Middleton)

76	London HLZ 10543	Mr. Nice Guy/Mephisto's Nightmare	8

CATCH

77	Logo GO 103	Borderline/Black Blood (company sleeve)	30

(see also Eurythmics)

GEORGE CATES & HIS ORCHESTRA

55	Vogue Coral Q 72106	Autumn Leaves (with Steve Allen)/High And Dry	6
56	Vogue Coral Q 72162	Moonglow/Theme From "Picnic"/Rio Batucada	12

(see also Steve Allen & Orchestra)

CATFISH

70	CBS 64006	GET DOWN (LP, orange label)	20
71	Epic 64408	LIVE CATFISH (LP)	15

CATHEDRAL

95	Earache MOSH 130	THE CARNIVAL BIZARRE (2 x 10" LP, gatefold sleeve)	12

CATHERINE WHEEL

91	Wilde Club WILDE 4	SHE'S MY FRIEND (12", p/s, barcode on sleeve)	8
91	Wilde Club WILDE 5	PAINFUL THING EP (12", p/s)	8

RAY CATHODE (BBC RADIOPHONICS)

62	Parlophone R 4901	Time Beat/Waltz In Orbit	12

(see also BBC Radiophonic Workshop, George Martin)

CAT IRON

69	Xtra XTRA 1087	CAT IRON (LP)	30

CAT MOTHER & ALL NIGHT NEWSBOYS

69	Polydor 56543	Good Old Rock'N'Roll/Bad News	12
70	Polydor 2066 026	I Must Be Dreaming/Last Go Round	6
69	Polydor 184 300	THE STREET GIVETH AND THE STREET TAKETH AWAY (LP)	25
70	Polydor 2425 021	ALBION DOO-WAH (LP, gatefold sleeve)	18
72	United Artists UAG 29313	CAT MOTHER & ALL NIGHT NEWS BOYS (LP, gatefold sleeve)	18
73	United Artists UAG 29381	LAST CHANCE DANCE (LP)	12

CATS

69	Baf BAF 1	Swan Lake/Swing Low	15
69	Baf BAF 2	My Girl/The Hog	10
69	Baf BAF 3	The Hig/Blues For Justice	10
69	Baf BAF 4	William Tell/Love Walk Right In	10

CATS

67	Parlophone R 5558	What A Crazy Life/Hopeless Try	5
68	Parlophone R 5663	What Is The World Coming To/How Could I Be So Blind?	5
69	Columbia DB 8524	I Gotta Know What's Going On/Lea	5
69	Columbia DB 8571	Why/Mandy, My Dear	5
70	Columbia DB 8655	Marian/Somewhere Up There	5
71	Columbia DB 8748	I Love You, I Do/Where Have I Been Wrong	5
71	Columbia DB 8816	One Way Mind/Country Woman	5
72	Columbia DB 8850	Dance, Dance, Dance/My Friend Joe	5
72	Columbia DB 8909	Let's Dance/I've Been In Love Before	5
71	Columbia SCX 6459	TAKE ME WITH YOU (LP)	15

CATS EYES

68	Deram DM 190	Smile Girl For Me/In A Fantasy World	10
68	Deram DM 209	I Thank You Marianne/Turn Around	8
69	Deram DM 251	Where Is She Now?/Tom Drum	20
70	MCA MK 5028	Loser/Circus	5
70	MCA MK 5043	Circus/Come Away Melinda	5
70	MCA MK 5056	The Wizard/Hey (Open Your Eyes)	10

CAT'S PYJAMAS

68	Direction 58-3235	Virginia Waters/Baby I Love You	20
68	Direction 58-3482	Camera Man/House For Sale	20

(see also Kenny Bernard)

CLEM CATTINI ORK

65	Decca F 12135	No Time To Think/Impact	40

(see also Tornados, Aquarian Age, Rumplestiltskin, Spaghetti Head, Sounds Nice)

NADIA CATTOUSE

61	Parlophone R 4725	The Boy Without A Heart/Long Time, Boy	7
65	Parlophone R 5240	Port Mahon/A Little More Oil	7
66	Reality RE 503	Beautiful Barbados/Turn Around	12
60s	Church Miss. Soc. LIV/SP/81	The Larder/PAULINE FILBY: I'm Hungry	20
66	Reality RY 1001	NADIA CATTOUSE (LP)	50
70	RCA Victor SF 8070	EARTH MOTHER (LP)	45

MINT VALUE £

CAUSTIC WINDOW

92 Rephlex CAT 004 JOYREX J4 EP (12", 6-track) ... 25
92 Rephlex CAT 005 JOYREX J5 EP (12, 4-track, black or white vinyl) ... 40/30
93 Rephlex CAT 009 i JOYREX J9 EP (10", picture disc, with bonus track "HMNA", 300 only) ... 60
93 Rephlex CAT 009 ii JOYREX J9 EP (12" 4-track, initially in card mailer with bag of "space dust") ... 35/25
(see also Aphex Twin)

EDDIE CAVE & FYX

66 Pye 7N 17161 Fresh Out Of Tears/It's Almost Good ... 40

NICK CAVE (& BAD SEEDS)

84 Mute 7 MUTE 32 In The Ghetto/The Moon Is In The Gutter (p/s) ... 5
85 Mute 7 MUTE 30 Tupelo/The Six Strings That Drew Blood (p/s) ... 5
86 Lyntone LYN 18038 Scum (green vinyl flexidisc, some with poster, concert freebie) ... 12/15
88 Mute MUTE 86 Oh Deanna/The Girl At The Bottom Of My Class (no p/s, DJ-only) ... 6
92 Mute LMUTE 140 Straight To You/Jack The Ripper (Acoustic Version) (limited issue, p/s) ... 5
92 Mute MUTE 148 I Had A Dream, Joe/The Good Son (live) (numbered p/s, 2,000 only) ... 7
94 Mute MUTE 160 Do You Love Me? (Single Version)/Cassiel's Song/Sail Away (silver vinyl, p/s, 1,000 copies) ... 8
94 Mute MUTE 169 Loverman (Single Version)/(I'll Love You) Till The End Of The World (picture disc, 2,000 only) ... 8
94 Mute MUTE 172 Red Right Hand/That's What Jazz Is To Me (red vinyl, p/s, with 2 different stickers & labels, 2,000 only) ... 8
97 Mute RCD STUMM 138 MURDER BALLADS (CD, 4-track sampler, promo only) ... 10
86 Mute STUMM 34 YOUR FUNERAL ... MY TRIAL (2 x 12", with lyric inner sleeves) ... 10
88 Mute LSTUMM 52 TENDER PREY (LP, with bonus spoken word 12" "And The Ass Saw The Angel" [P STUMM 52]: "Autumn"/ "Animal Static"/"Mah Sanctum"/"Lamentation", 5,000 only) ... 15
90 Mute LSTUMM 76 THE GOOD SON (LP, with bonus 7" "Acoustic Versions From Tender Prey" [P STUMM 76]: "The Mercy Seat"/"City Of Refuge"/"Deanna") ... 12
90 Mute CDSTUMM 76 THE GOOD SON (CD, with bonus CD "Acoustic Versions From Tender Prey" [P STUMM 76]: "The Mercy Seat"/"City Of Refuge"/"Deanna") ... 18
92 Mute LSTUMM 92 HENRY'S DREAM (LP, with photographic print) ... 12
93 LCD STUMM 122 LIVE SEEDS (CD, with book in slip case) ... 15
94 Mute LSTUMM 123 LET LOVE IN (LP, with set of postcards or poster) ... 12
96 Mute CAVESPEAK 1CD MURDER BALLADS: THE INTERVIEW (CD, promo only) ... 20
97 Mute CAVESPEAK 2CD THE BOATMAN'S CALL: THE INTERVIEW (CD, promo only) ... 18
(see also Birthday Party, Annie Hogan, Burmoe Brothers)

ANDY CAVELL

62 HMV POP 1024 Hey There Cruel Heart/Lonely Soldier Boy ... 35
62 HMV POP 1080 Always On Saturday/Hey There, Senorita ... 35
63 Pye 7N 15539 Andy/There Was A Boy ... 50
64 Pye 7N 15610 Shut Up/Tell The Truth ... 40

JIMMY CAVELLO & HIS HOUSE ROCKERS

57 Vogue Coral Q 72226 Rock, Rock, Rock/The Big Beat ... 250
57 Vogue Coral Q 72226 Rock, Rock, Rock/The Big Beat (78) ... 50
57 Vogue Coral Q 72240 Foot Stompin'/Ooh-Wee ... 250
57 Vogue Coral Q 72240 Foot Stompin'/Ooh-Wee (78) ... 50
(see also Alan Freed)

CAVE OF THE LIVING STREAMS

74 UHC 1 SIXTEEN SONGS (LP, private pressing) ... 75

MONTE CAZAZZA

79 Industrial IR 0005 To Mom On Mother's Day/Candy Man (p/s, with outer polystyrene sleeve & insert, 2,500 only) ... 12
80 Industrial IR 0010 SOMETHING FOR NOBODY (EP) ... 8
81 Industrial IRC 28 LIVE AT LEEDS FAN CLUB (cassette) ... 10
(see also Psychic TV)

C.C.S. (Collective Consciousness Society)

70 Rak RAK 104 Whole Lotta Love/Boom Boom ... 6
72 Rak RAK 126 Brother/Mister What You Can't Have I Can Get ... 6
70 Rak SRAK 6751 C.C.S. (LP, gatefold sleeve) ... 20
72 Rak SRAK 503 C.C.S. (LP) ... 18
73 Rak SRAK 504 THE BEST BAND IN THE LAND (LP) ... 15
(see also Alexis Korner)

CEDARS

68 Decca F 22720 For Your Information/Hide If You Want To Hide ... 40
68 Decca F 22772 I Like The Way/I Don't Know Why ... 40
(see also Seaders)

CELIA & THE MUTATIONS

77 United Artists UP 36262 Mony Mony/Mean To Me (p/s) ... 6
77 United Artists UP 36318 You Better Believe Me/Round And Around (p/s) ... 8
(see also Stranglers, Tonight)

CELLOPHANE

(see under Selofane)

CELTIC FROST

84 Noise N 0017 MORBID TALES (mini LP, some with poster) ... 30/20

CENOTAPH CORNER

76 Cottage COT 501 UPS AND DOWNS (LP) ... 20
79 Cottage COT 031 EVERY DAY BUT WEDNESDAY (LP) ... 25

MINT VALUE £

CENTIPEDE

71	RCA Neon NE 9	SEPTOBER ENERGY (2-LP)	75
74	RCA DPS 2054	SEPTOBER ENERGY (2-LP, reissue, different cover)	20

(see also Mark Charig, Ian Carr, Elton Dean, Zoot Money, Alan Skidmore, Keith Tippett, Julie Tippetts, Mike Patto, Robert Wyatt)

CENTURION

82	Centurion 0001	Two Wheels/Bitch (private pressing)	50
82	Centurion 0001	Two Wheels/Bitch (private pressing, mislabelled 'Nikki')	30

CENTURY 21 (Gerry Anderson TV spin-offs)

65	Century 21 MA 100	JOURNEY TO THE MOON (EP)	15
65	Century 21 MA 101	INTO ACTION WITH TROY TEMPEST (EP)	15
65	Century 21 MA 102	A TRIP TO MARINEVILLE (EP)	15
65	Century 21 MA 103	INTRODUCING THUNDERBIRDS (EP)	15
65	Century 21 MA 104	MARINA SPEAKS (EP)	15
65	Century 21 MA 105	TV CENTURY 21 THEMES (EP)	15
66	Century 21 MA 106	THE DALEKS (EP)	50
66	Century 21 MA 107	F.A.B. (EP)	18
66	Century 21 MA 108	THUNDERBIRD 1 (EP)	18
66	Century 21 MA 109	THUNDERBIRD 2 (EP)	18
66	Century 21 MA 110	THE STATELY HOME ROBBERIES (EP)	25
66	Century 21 MA 111	LADY PENELOPE & OTHER TV THEMES (EP)	25
66	Century 21 MA 112	THUNDERBIRD 3 (EP)	25
66	Century 21 MA 113	THUNDERBIRD 4 (EP)	25
66	Century 21 MA 114	THE PERILS OF PENELOPE (EP)	30
66	Century 21 MA 115	TOPO GIGIO IN LONDON (EP)	45
67	Century 21 MA 116	GREAT THEMES FROM GERRY ANDERSON'S THUNDERBIRDS (EP)	30
67	Century 21 MA 117	SPACE AGE NURSERY RHYMES (EP)	35
67	Century 21 MA 118	LADY PENELOPE AND PARKER (EP)	35
67	Century 21 MA 119	BRAINS AND TIN TIN (EP)	35
67	Century 21 MA 120	INTERNATIONAL RESCUE (EP)	35
67	Century 21 MA 121	THUNDERBIRDS (EP)	35
67	Century 21 MA 122	LADY PENELOPE (EP)	35
67	Century 21 MA 123	BRAINS (EP)	35
67	Century 21 MA 124	BRINK OF DISASTER (EP)	35
67	Century 21 MA 125	ATLANTIC INFERNO (EP)	35
67	Century 21 MA 126	RICOCHET (EP)	35
67	Century 21 MA 127	TINGHA & TUCKER & THE WOMBAVILLE BAND (EP)	35
67	Century 21 MA 128	ONE MOVE & YOU'RE DEAD (EP)	35
67	Century 21 MA 129	30 MINUTES AFTER NOON (EP)	35
67	Century 21 MA 130	TINGHA & TUCKER IN NURSERY RHYME TIME (EP)	35
67	Century 21 MA 131	INTRODUCING CAPTAIN SCARLET (EP)	30
67	Century 21 MA 132	CAPTAIN SCARLET AND THE MYSTERONS (EP)	30
67	Century 21 MA 133	CAPTAIN SCARLET IS INDESTRUCTIBLE (EP)	25
67	Century 21 MA 134	CAPTAIN SCARLET OF SPECTRUM (EP)	25
67	Century 21 MA 135	CAPTAIN SCARLET VS. CAPTAIN BLACK (EP)	25
67	Century 21 MA 136	THEMES FROM GERRY ANDERSON'S CAPTAIN SCARLET (EP)	25
65	Century 21 LA 100	JOURNEY TO THE MOON (LP)	70
66	Century 21 LA 1	THE WORLD OF TOMORROW (LP)	50
66	Century 21 LA 2	LADY PENELOPE PRESENTS (LP)	50
66	Century 21 LA 3	JEFF TRACY INTRODUCES INTERNATIONAL RESCUE (LP)	50
66	Century 21 LA 4	LADY PENELOPE INVESTIGATES (LP)	50
66	Century 21 LA 5	THE TINGHA & TUCKER CLUB SONG BOOK (LP)	50
67	Century 21 LA 6	FAVOURITE TELEVISION THEMES (LP)	50
68	Marble Arch MAL 770	TV FAVOURITES VOL. 1 (LP)	20
68	Marble Arch MAL 771	TV FAVOURITES VOL. 2 (LP)	20

(see also Barry Gray, Dr. Who)

FRANK CHACKSFIELD & HIS ORCHESTRA

53	Parlophone MSP 6018	Quiet Rhythm Blues/Junior Miss	6
54	Decca F 10354	Smile (Theme From "Modern Times")/Piper In The Heather	6
56	Decca F 10689	In Old Lisbon (Lisboa Antigua)/Memories Of You	6
56	Decca F 10743	The Donkey Cart/The Banks Of The Seine	6
59	Decca F 11146	Java Boogie/A Paris Valentine	7
59	Decca F 11146	Java Boogie/A Paris Valentine (78)	6
62	Decca F 11439	The Sky At Night/Face To Face	6
58	Decca LK 4174	SOUTH SEA ISLAND MAGIC (LP)	18

CHAD (STUART) & JEREMY (CLYDE)

64	Ember EMB S 180	Yesterday's Gone/Lemon Tree (as Chad Stuart & Jeremy Clyde)	7
64	Ember EMB S 186	Early In The Morning/Like I Love You Today (as Chad Stuart & Jeremy Clyde)	7
64	United Artists UP 1062	Summer Song/No Tears For Johnnie (as Chad Stuart & Jeremy Clyde)	5
64	United Artists UP 1070	Willow Weep For Me/If She Was Mine	5
65	Ember EMB S 205	If I Loved You/No Tears For Johnnie	5
65	CBS 201769	Before And After/Evil-Hearted Me	10
65	CBS 201814	I Don't Want To Lose You/Pennies	7
66	Ember EMB S 217	What Do You Want With Me/Donna Donna	5
66	CBS 202035	Teenage Failure/Early Mornin' Rain	5
66	CBS 202279	Distant Shores/Last Night	5
66	CBS 202397	You Are She/I Won't Cry	5
64	Ember EMB EP 4543	YESTERDAY'S GONE (EP)	20
65	United Artists UEP 1008	CHAD STUART AND JEREMY CLYDE (EP)	22
65	Ember NR 5021	SING FOR YOU (LP)	25
66	Ember NR 5031	SECOND ALBUM (LP)	25
66	Ember (ST)NR 5036	THE BEST OF CHAD AND JEREMY (LP)	12
68	Regal SREG 1087	CHAD & JEREMY (LP)	18

(see also John Barry, Jeremy Clyde)

MINT VALUE £

ERNIE CHAFFIN

57 London HLS 8409 Feelin' Low/Lonesome For My Baby 150
57 London HLS 8409 Feelin' Low/Lonesome For My Baby (78) 25

CHAINO

59 London SAH-D 6078 AFRICANA (LP) 12

CHAINSAW

80 Square SQSP 2 Police And Politicians (p/s) 45
80 Pot Belly EJSP 9462 Lonely Without You/On The Highway 35
84 GMC CS 001 Long Legged Woman/Midnight Blue 30
84 Thunderbolt THBE 1006 MASSACRE (12" EP) 8

CHAIRMEN OF THE BOARD

70 Invictus INV 501 Give Me Just A Little More Time/Since The Days Of Pigtails 5
70 Invictus INV 504 You've Got Me Dangling On A String/Patches 5
71 Invictus INV 507 Everything's Tuesday/Bless You 5
71 Invictus INV 511 Pay To The Piper/When Will She Tell Me She Needs Me? 5
71 Invictus INV 516 Chairman Of The Board/Hanging On To A Memory 5
71 Invictus INV 516 Chairman Of The Board/When Will She Tell Me She Needs Me? (different B-side) 5
72 Invictus INV 519 Working On A Building Of Love/Try On My Love For Size 5
72 Invictus INV 524 Elmo James/Bittersweet 5
72 Invictus INV 527 I'm On My Way To A Better Place/So Glad You're Mine 5
73 Invictus INV 530 Finders Keepers/Finders Keepers (Instrumental) 5
70 Invictus SVT 1002 CHAIRMEN OF THE BOARD (LP) 30
71 Invictus SVT 1003 IN SESSION (LP) 30
72 Invictus SVT 1006 BITTERSWEET (LP) 20
73 Invictus SVT 1009 GREATEST HITS (LP) 15
74 Invictus 65868 SKIN I'M IN (LP) 20
(see also Showmen, General Johnson, Norman Johnson)

CHAKACHAS

61 RCA RCA 1264 Twist Twist/Baila La Bamba 6
72 Polydor 2121 093 Jungle Fever/Chaka Cha 5
72 Polydor 2489 050 JUNGLE FEVER (LP) 18
73 Young Blood SYB 3003 CHAKACHAS (LP) 15

GEORGE CHAKIRIS

59 Saga SAG 45-2905 Cool/I Got Rhythm 8
60 Triumph RGM 1010 Heart Of A Teenage Girl/I'm Always Chasing Rainbows 45

BRYAN CHALKER('S NEW FRONTIER)

70 Amity OTS 502 Ned Kelly/Four Girls From The Town Of Boston 6
72 Columbia DB 8883 Daddy Sang Bass/Lot 69 6
72 Chapter One SCH 179 Help Me Make It Through The Night/Eskimo Song 6
73 Chapter One SCH 185 Daisy A Day/Life Gets Tee-jus, Don't It 6
71 Avenue AVE 071 THE HANGING OF SAMUEL HALL (LP, as Bryan Chalker's New Frontier) 30
72 Chapter One CMS 1010 BRYAN CHALKER'S NEW FRONTIER (LP) 18
73 Chapter One CMS 1017 BRYAN CHALKER (LP) 18
74 Chapter One CMS 1020 DADDY SING ME A SONG (LP, as Brian Chalker & The Road Band) 15

CHALLENGER

81 CMC CM 0001 So Sure Of Yourself 20

CHALLENGERS (U.K.)

61 Parlophone R 4773 Cry Of The Wild Goose/Deadline 15

CHALLENGERS (U.S.)

63 Stateside SS 177 Torquay/Bulldog 15
65 Vocalion V 9253 The Man From U.N.C.L.E./The Streets Of London 20
66 Vocalion V 9270 Walk With Me/How Could I 12
63 Stateside SL 10030 SURFBEAT (LP) 60
67 Vocalion VA-N/SAV-N 8069 WIPE OUT (LP, mono/stereo) 55/75
(see also Surfaris)

RICHARD CHAMBERLAIN

62 MGM MGM-EP 776 HITS (EP) 10
62 MGM MGM-EP 778 I'LL BE AROUND (EP) 12
62 MGM MGM-EP 781 DREAM (EP) 12
63 MGM MGM-C 923 SINGS (LP) 18
64 MGM MGM-C 1009 JOY IN THE MORNING (LP) 18

CHAMBER POP ENSEMBLE

68 Decca F 12789 Walk Away Renee/59th Street Bridge Song (Feeling Groovy) 6
68 Decca LK/SKL 4933 CHAMBER POP ENSEMBLE (LP) 20

JAMES CHAMBERS

71 Summit SUM 8523 Bongo Man/KEN BOOTHE: Now I Know 10
(see also Jimmy Cliff)

CHAMBERS BROTHERS

66 Vocalion VL 9267 Love Me Like The Rain/Pretty Girls Everywhere 20
66 Vocalion VL 9276 Call Me/Seventeen 20
67 CBS 202565 All Strung Out Over You/Falling In Love 8
68 Direction 58-3215 Up Town/Love Me Like The Rain 7
68 Direction 58-3671 Time Has Come Today/Dinah 10
68 Direction 58-3760 Time Has Come Today/Dinah (reissue) 7
68 Direction 58-3865 I Can't Turn You Loose/Do Your Thing 7
69 Direction 58-4098 Are You Ready/You Got The Power To Turn Me On 6
69 Direction 58-4318 People Get Ready/No, No, No, Don't Say Goodbye 6
69 Direction 58-4367 Wake Up/Everybody Needs Someone 7
70 Direction 58-4846 Love Peace And Happiness/If You Want Me To 7

MINT VALUE £

70 Direction 58-5033 Let's Do It/To Love Somebody . . . 7
71 CBS 5389 Funky/Love, Peace And Happiness . . . 12
71 CBS 7689 By The Hair On My Chinny Chin Chin/Heaven . . . 6
66 Vocalion VA-L/SAV-L 8058 PEOPLE GET READY (LP) . . . 65
68 Liberty LBS83272 SHOUT! (LP, blue label) . . . 25
68 Direction 8-63407 THE TIME HAS COME (LP) . . . 30
69 Direction 8-63451 A NEW TIME — A NEW DAY (LP) . . . 30
70 Direction 8-66228 LOVE PEACE AND HAPPINESS (Live At Bill Graham's Fillmore West) (2-LP) . . . 30
70 Liberty LBS 83276 FEELIN' THE BLUES (LP) . . . 18
71 CBS 64156 A NEW GENERATION (LP) . . . 15

EDDIE CHAMBLEE & HIS RHYTHM & BLUES BAND

53 Esquire 10-329 All Out/TOMMY DEAN R&B BAND: Scamon Boogie (78) . . . 10
53 Esquire 10-330 Blues For Eddie/PINEY BROWN: That's Right, Little Girl (78) . . . 15
54 Esquire 10-340 Cradle Rock/Back Street (78) . . . 15

CHAMELEONS

82 Epic EPCA 2210 In Shreds/Less Than Human (p/s) . . . 15
83 Statik STAT 30 As High As You Can Go/Pleasure And Pain (p/s) . . . 6
83 Statik STAT 3012 As High As You Can Go/Pleasure And Pain/Paper Tigers (12", p/s) . . . 10
83 Statik TAK 6 A Person Isn't Safe Anywhere These Days/Thursday's Child (p/s) . . . 7
83 Statik TAK 6/12 A Person Isn't Safe Anywhere These Days/Thursday's Child/ Prisoners Of The Sun (12", p/s) . . . 10
85 Statik TAK 29 In Shreds/Nostalgia (p/s) . . . 7
85 Statik TAK 29/12 In Shreds/Less Than Human/Nostalgia (12", p/s) . . . 10
85 Statik TAK 35 Singing Rule Britannia (While The Walls Close In)/Singing Rule Britannia (Radio 1 'Saturday Live' Session Version) (p/s) . . . 6
85 Statik TAK 35/12 Singing Rule Britannia (While The Walls Close In)/Singing Rule Britannia (Radio 1 'Saturday Live' Session Version) (12", p/s) . . . 8
86 Geffen GEF 4 Tears/Paradiso (p/s) . . . 5
86 Geffen GEF 4F/SAM 287 Tears/Paradiso//Swamp Thing/Inside Out (double pack, gatefold p/s) . . . 8
86 Geffen GEF 4T Tears/Paradiso/Inside Out (12", p/s) . . . 8
86 Geffen GEF 10 Swamp Thing/John, I'm Only Dancing (p/s) . . . 5
86 Geffen GEF 10T Swamp Thing/John, I'm Only Dancing/Tears (Original Arrangement) (12", p/s) . . . 8
90 Glass Pyramid EMC 1 TONY FLETCHER WALKED ON WATER (12" EP) . . . 20
90 Glass Pyramid EMCD 1 TONY FLETCHER WALKED ON WATER (CD EP) . . . 20
85 Statik STATLP 17 SCRIPT OF THE BRIDGE (LP, picture disc) . . . 20
85 Statik STATLP 22 WHAT DOES ANYTHING MEAN? BASICALLY (LP, gatefold sleeve, with insert) . . 12

(see also Sun & Moon, Reegs)

TEDDY CHAMES

68 Blue Cat BS 141 I Want It Girl/She Is Gone (actually by Teddy Charmes) . . . 10

CHAMPIONS

63 Oriole CB 1854 Circlorama/Pinky . . . 15

CHAMPS (Jamaica)

64 Blue Beat BB 267 Walk Between Your Enemies/Do What I Say . . . 22

CHAMPS (U.S.)

58 London HLU 8580 Tequila/Train To Nowhere . . . 18
58 London HLU 8580 Tequila/Train To Nowhere (78) . . . 12
58 London HL 8655 Midnighter/El Rancho Rock . . . 18
58 London HL 8655 Midnighter/El Rancho Rock (78) . . . 15
58 London HL 8715 Chariot Rock/Subway . . . 18
58 London HL 8715 Chariot Rock/Subway (78) . . . 8
59 London HLH 8811 Beatnik/Gone Train . . . 15
59 London HLH 8811 Beatnik/Gone Train (78) . . . 20
59 London HLH 8864 Caramba/Moonlight Bay . . . 15
59 London HLH 8864 Caramba/Moonlight Bay (78) . . . 25
60 London HLH 9052 Too Much Tequila/Twenty Thousand Leagues . . . 12
61 London HLH 9430 Cantina/Panic Button . . . 12
62 London HLH 9506 Tequila Twist/Limbo Rock . . . 12
62 London HLH 9539 Experiment In Terror/La Cucaracha . . . 15
62 London HLH 9604 Limbo Dance/Latin Limbo . . . 12
59 London RE 1176 FOUR BY THE CHAMPS (EP) . . . 35
59 London RE-H 1209 ANOTHER FOUR BY THE CHAMPS (EP) . . . 35
59 London RE-H 1223 STILL MORE BY THE CHAMPS (EP) . . . 40
61 London RE-H 1250 KNOCKOUTS! (EP) . . . 60
58 London HA-H 2152 GO CHAMPS GO! (LP) . . . 60
59 London HA-H 2184 EVERYBODY'S ROCKIN' WITH THE CHAMPS (LP) . . . 60
62 London HA-H 2451 GREAT DANCE HITS (LP, early issues with flipback cover) . . . 50/35

JACQUI CHAN

60 Pye 7N 15273 But No One Knows/Gentlemen Please! . . . 7

(see also Simon Dupree & Big Sound)

ROB CHANCE & CHANCES-R

67 CBS 3130 At The End Of The Day/I've Got The Power . . . 12

(see also Chances-R)

CHANCES ARE

67 Columbia DB 8144 Fragile Child/What Went Wrong . . . 35

CHANCES-R

67 CBS 202614 Talking Out The Back Of My Head/I Aimed Too High . . . 12
67 CBS 2940 Do It Yourself/Turn A New Leaf Over . . . 12

(see also Ron Chance & Chances-R)

DANY CHANDELLE

65 Columbia DB 7540 Lying Awake/I Love You . . . 30

MINT VALUE £

BARBARA CHANDLER

63	London HLR 9823	Do You Really Love Me Too?/I Live To Love You	18
64	London HLR 9861	I'm Going Out With The Girls/Lonely New Year	18

E.J. CHANDLER

80	Destiny DS 1026	I Can't Stand To Lose You/Believe In Me	5

GENE CHANDLER

62	Columbia DB 4793	Duke Of Earl/Kissing In The Kitchen	20
63	Stateside SS 185	Rainbow/You Threw A Lucky Punch	20
64	Stateside SS 331	Just Be True/A Song Called Soul	20
64	Stateside SS 364	Bless Our Love/London Town	15
65	Stateside SS 388	What Now/If You Can't Be True (Find A Part Time Love)	18
65	Stateside SS 401	You Can't Hurt Me No More/Everybody Let's Dance	18
65	Stateside SS 425	Nothing Can Stop Me/The Big Lie	50
65	Stateside SS 458	Good Times/No One Can Love You (Like I Do)	18
66	Stateside SS 500	(I'm Just A) Fool For You/Buddy Ain't It A Shame	18
66	Chess CRS 8047	I Fooled You This Time/Such A Pretty Thing	40
67	Coral Q 72490	The Girl Don't Care/My Love	20
68	Soul City SC 102	Nothing Can Stop Me/The Big Lie (reissue)	15
69	Action ACT 4551	I Can't Save It/I Can Take Care Of Myself	35
69	President PT 234	Duke Of Earl/Stand By Me	7
70	Mercury 6052 033	Groovy Situation/Not The Marrying Kind	6
71	Mercury 6052 098	You're A Lady/Stone Cold Feeling	6
76	Brunswick BR 39	There Was A Time/ARTISTICS: I'm Gonna Miss You	6
65	Fontana TL 5247	DUKE OF EARL (LP)	80
67	Coral LVA 9236	THE GIRL DON'T CARE (LP)	55
69	MCA MUPS 367	THERE WAS A TIME (LP)	25
69	Action ACLP 6010	LIVE ON STAGE (LP)	55
71	Mercury 6338 037	SITUATION (LP)	18
74	Joy JOYS 136	A GENE CHANDLER ALBUM (LP)	15

GENE CHANDLER & BARBARA ACKLIN

69	MCA Soul Bag BAG 1	Little Green Apples/Will I Find Love	7
74	Brunswick BR 30	From The Teacher To The Preacher/Little Green Apples	10

(see also Barbara Acklin, Gene & Jerry)

JEFF CHANDLER

54	Brunswick 05264	I Should Care/More Than Anyone	10
55	Brunswick 05380	Everything Happens To Me/Always	10
55	Brunswick 05417	My Prayer/When Spring Comes	10
55	Brunswick 05441	Foxfire/Shaner Maidel	10
55	Brunswick 05465	Only The Very Young/A Little Love Can Go A Long, Long Way	10
57	London HLU 8484	Half Of My Heart/Hold Me	10
57	London HLU 8484	Half Of My Heart/Hold Me (78)	10
58	London HA-U 2100	JEFF CHANDLER SINGS TO YOU (LP)	50

KAREN CHANDLER

55	Vogue Coral Q 72091	The Price You Pay For Love/The Man In The Raincoat	10
56	Brunswick 05570	Love Is The $64,000 Question/(I'm Just A) Beginner	10
56	Brunswick 05596	Tonight You Belong To Me/Crazy Arms (with Jimmy Wakely)	10
56	Brunswick 05596	Tonight You Belong To Me/Crazy Arms (with Jimmy Wakely) (78)	10
57	Brunswick 05662	Your Wild Heart/It's An International Language	10
57	Brunswick 05662	Your Wild Heart/It's An International Language (78)	10
62	Salvo SLO 1803	My Own True Love/You Made Me Love You (99 copies only)	15

(see also Jimmy Wakely)

KENNY CHANDLER

63	Stateside SS 166	Heart/Wait For Me	15
68	Stateside SS 2110	Beyond Love/Charity	50

LEN CHANDLER

67	CBS 62931	TO BE A MAN (LP)	15

LORRAINE CHANDLER

75	Black Magic BM 105	Love You Baby/What Can I Do	5

CHANDONS

68	RCA RCA 1704	Timber/Never Been Loved Before	5

CHANGIN' TIMES

68	Bell BLL 1009	When The Good Sun Shines/Show Me The Way To Go Home	6

BRUCE CHANNEL

62	Mercury AMT 1171	Hey! Baby/Dream Girl	10
62	Mercury AMT 1177	Number One Man/If Only I Had Known	10
62	Pye International 7N 25137	Run Romance Run/Don't Leave Me	25
63	London HLU 9776	I Don't Wanna/Blue And Lonesome	15
64	London HLU 9841	Going Back To Louisiana/Forget Me Not	15
67	Stateside SS 2066	Mr. Bus Driver/It's Me	5
68	Bell BLL 1010	Keep On/Barbara Allen	5
68	Bell BLL 1030	Try Me/Water The Family Tree	5
68	Bell BLL 1038	Mr. Bus Driver/Trouble With Sam	5
68	Sonet SON 2001	Hey! Baby '68/Come On Baby	5
62	Mercury MMC 14104	HEY! BABY! (LP)	80
68	Bell MBLL/SBLL 1110	KEEP ON (LP)	25

CHANNEL 4

79	Ripping RIP 1	Vampire/Channel 4 (numbered p/s with insert)	6

CHANNEL 3

82	No Future OI 11	I've Got A Gun/Manzanar/Mannequin (p/s)	10

MINT VALUE £

CHANTAYS

63	London HLD 9696	Pipeline/Move It	15
64	King KG 1018	Beyond/I'll Be Back Someday	20
66	Dot DS 26757	Pipeline/Move It (reissue)	5
63	London RED 1397	PIPELINE (EP)	50
63	London HA-D/SH-D 8087	PIPELINE (LP, mono/stereo)	55/70
74	Contour 2870 389	PIPELINE (LP, reissue)	12

CHANTELLES

65	Parlophone R 5271	I Want That Boy/London My Home Town	18
65	Parlophone R 5303	The Secret Of My Success/Sticks And Stones	10
65	Parlophone R 5350	Gonna Get Burned/Gonna Give Him Some Love	12
66	Parlophone R 5431	I Think Of You/Please Don't Kiss Me	10
66	Polydor 56119	There's Something About You/Just Another Fool	15
67	CBS 2777	Blue Mood/The Man I Love	12

(see also Lana Sisters)

CHANTELS

58	London HLU 8561	Maybe/Come My Little Baby	550
58	London HLU 8561	Maybe/Come My Little Baby (78)	30
62	London HLL 9428	Look In My Eyes/Glad To Be Back	50
62	London HLL 9480	Well I Told You/Still	30
62	London HLL 9532	Here It Comes Again/Summertime	40
63	Capitol CL 15297	Swamp Water/Eternally	30
70	Roulette RO 514	Maybe/He's Gone	5

(see also Richard Barrett)

CHANTER

77	Expert ELP 1	SUBURBAN ETHNIA (LP, private pressing)	12

IRENE CHANTER

75	Polydor 2058 608	Make Me Happy/Funky Music	6

(see also Birds Of A Feather, Chanters, Chanter Sisters)

CHANTERS

66	CBS 202454	Every Night (I Sit And Cry)/Where	7
67	CBS 202616	You Can't Fool Me/All Day Long	15
68	CBS 3400	What's Wrong With You/Right By Your Side	6
68	CBS 3668	My Love Is For You/Mississippi Paddleboat	8

(see also Birds Of A Feather, Chanter Sisters, Irene Chanter)

CHANTER SISTERS

76	Polydor 2058 679	Halfway To Paradise/My Love	8

(see also Birds Of A Feather, Chanters, Irene Chanter)

CHANTS (U.K.)

63	Pye 7N 15557	I Don't Care/Come Go With Me	15
64	Pye 7N 15591	I Could Write A Book/A Thousand Stars	15
64	Pye 7N 15643	She's Mine/Then I'll Be Home	12
64	Pye 7N 15691	Sweet Was The Wine/One Star	10
66	Fontana TF 716	Come Back And Get This Loving Baby/Love Light	10
67	Decca F 12650	A Lover's Story/Wearing A Smile	12
67	Page One POF 016	Ain't Nobody Home/For You	10
68	RCA Victor RCA 1754	A Man Without A Face/Baby I Don't Need Your Love	50
69	RCA Victor RCA 1823	I Get The Sweetest Feeling/Candy	10
76	Chipping Norton CHIP 2	I've Been Trying/Lucky Old Me	25

(see also Real Thing)

CHANTS (U.S.)

58	Capitol CL 14876	Close Friends/Lost And Found	25

CHAOS

79	Chaotic Records VD 1	Summer Of Hate/I Want To Be Left Alone (p/s)	50

(originals have a rim around the label — counterfeits have no rim)

CHAOS & JULIA SET

93	Recoil RCL 001	VOL. 1 (12", plain sleeve)	15
93	Recoil RCL 002	VOL. 2 — FEAR OF THE FUTURE (12", plain sleeve)	15

(see also Global Communications)

CHAOS U.K.

82	Riot City RIOT 6	BURNING BRITAIN (EP)	8
82	Riot City RIOT 12	LOUD, POLITICAL AND UNCOMPROMISING (EP)	10

CHAOTIC DISCHORD

82	Riot City RIOT 10	FUCK THE WORLD (EP)	10
83	Riot City RIOT 22	NEVER TRUST A FRIEND (EP)	7
83	Beat The System	SAD SOCIETY (EP)	8
83	Riot City CITY 004	FUCK RELIGION, FUCK POLITICS, AND FUCK THE LOT OF YOU (LP)	12
84	Syndicate SYNLP 12	FUCK OFF YOU CUNT WHAT A LOAD OF BOLLOCKS (LP)	12
88	Not Very Nice GRR 3RV	VERY FUCKIN' BAD (LP)	12

HARRY CHAPIN

73	Elektra K 42155	SHORT STORIES (LP, gatefold sleeve)	18
74	Elektra 7E 1012	VERITIES & BALDERDASH (LP)	15
78	Elektra K 52089	LIVING ROOM SUITE (LP)	18

PAUL CHAPLAIN & HIS EMERALDS

60	London HLU 9205	Shortnin' Bread/Nicotine	30

MICHAEL CHAPLIN

65	Decca F 12142	I Am What I Am/Restless	6

MINT VALUE £

CHARLES CHAPLIN
57 HMV POP 370 — The Spring Song/Mandolin Serenade . . . 10

COLIN CHAPMAN
60s CCLP 1001 — FOLK SONGS VOL 1 (LP) . . . 18

GENE CHAPMAN
63 Starlite ST45 102 — Oklahoma Blues/Don't Come Crying . . . 150

GRADY CHAPMAN
60 Mercury AMT 1107 — Sweet Thing/I Know What I Want . . . 20

MICHAEL CHAPMAN
69 Harvest HAR 5002 — It Didn't Work Out/Mozart Lives Upstairs . . . 7
69 Harvest SHVL 755 — RAINMAKER (LP, gatefold sleeve) . . . 20
70 Harvest SHVL 764 — FULLY QUALIFIED SURVIVOR (LP, gatefold sleeve) . . . 20
70 Harvest SHVL 786 — WINDOW (LP, gatefold sleeve) . . . 20
71 Harvest SHVL 798 — WRECKED AGAIN (LP, gatefold sleeve) . . . 20
73 Deram SML 1105 — MILLSTONE GRIT (LP) . . . 18
74 Deram SML 1114 — DEAL GONE DOWN (LP) . . . 15
76 Decca SKL-R 5242 — SAVAGE AMUSEMENT (LP, with lyric sheet) . . . 12
70s Standard ESL 146 — GUITARS (LP, library issue) . . . 50

CHAPS
62 Parlophone R 4979 — Poppin' Medley (Parts 1 & 2) . . . 22
(see also Outlaws)

CHAPTER FIVE
66 CBS 202395 — Anything You Do Is Alright/You Can't Mean It . . . 550
67 CBS 2696 — One In A Million/Hey Hey (unissued, demos only) . . . 180

CHAPTER FOUR (U.K.)
60s GSP 11009/10 — CHAPTER FOUR (EP, no p/s) . . . 90

CHAPTER FOUR (U.K.)
80 Bridge BR 001 — HANGING AROUND STERLING (LP) . . . 35

CHAPTER FOUR (U.S.)
66 United Artists UP 1143 — In My Life/In Each Other's Arms . . . 175
(see also Jay & Americans)

CHAPTERS
65 Pye 7N 15815 — Can't Stop Thinking About Her/Dance Little Lady . . . 50

CHAPTER THREE (U.K.)
67 CBS 2971 — Cold And Lonely Hours/Wrecking Crew . . . 7

CHAQUITO & HIS ORCHESTRA
60 Fontana H 265 — Never On Sunday/Song Of Orpheus . . . 6
72 Philips 6006 225 — Hawaii 5-0/Ironside . . . 6
72 Philips 6308 087 — TV THRILLERS (LP) . . . 15
(see also Johnny Gregory)

CHARGE
70 private pressing — Zeugma/Boring Song (art sleeve) . . . 20

CHARGE
73 SRT private pressing — CHARGE (LP, 1 known copy) . . . 500+
92 Kissing Spell KSLP 9205 — CHARGE (LP, reissue, revised sleeve, 500 only) . . . 12

CHARGE
81 Test Pressing — You Deserve More Than A Maybe (p/s, 500 only) . . . 20
82 Test Pressing TP 3 — Kings Cross/Brave New World (p/s) . . . 6

MARK CHARIG
77 Ogun OG 710 — PIPEDREAM (LP) . . . 15
(see also Bluesology, B.B. Blunder, Reg King, Centipede, Keith Tippett, Julie Tippett, Brotherhood Of Breath, Elton Dean, Ninesense)

CHARIOT
84 Shades SHADE 2 — ALL ALONE AGAIN (EP) . . . 12
84 Shades SHADE 1 — THE WARRIOR (LP) . . . 20
86 Shades SHADE 4 — BURNING AMBITION (LP) . . . 15

CHARLATANS (U.K.)
89 Dead Dead Good no cat.no — OCTOBER '89 (demo cassette, sold at gigs) . . . 20
90 Dead Dead Good GOOD ONE TWELVE — Indian Rope/You Can Talk To Me/Who Wants To Know (12", 1st issue with barcode on p/s) . . . 10
90 Dead Dead Good SIT 70T — The Only One I Know/Imperial 109 (Edit)/Everything Changed (12", p/s) . . . 10
90 Dead Dead Good SIT 74T — Then/Taurus Moaner/Then (Alternate Take)/Taurus Moaner (Instrumental) (12", p/s) . . . 10
91 D. D. G. GOOD 1CD — Indian Rope/You Can Talk To Me/Who Wants To Know (CD) . . . 10
90 Situation Two SIT 70CD — The Only One I Know/Imperial 109 (Edit)/Everything Changed/ You Can Talk To Me (CD) . . . 8
90 Situation Two SIT 74T — Then/Taurus Moaner/Then (Alternate Take)/Taurus Moaner (Instrumental) (12", mispressing with vocal version of "Taurus Moaner" on both sides) . . . 8
90 Situation Two SIT 74T — Polar Bear/Taurus Moaner (12", white label test pressing, around 10 only) . . . 80
90 Situation Two SIT 74CD — Then/Taurus Moaner/Then (Alternate Take)/Taurus Moaner (Instrumental) (CD) . . . 8
91 Situation Two SIT 76CD — Over Rising/Way Up There/Opportunity Three/Happen To Die (CD) . . . 8
91 Beggars Banquet CHAR 1 — Happen To Die (1-sided, green die-cut sleeve, promo only) . . . 10
92 Situation Two SIT 88T — Weirdo/Theme From "The Wish"/Sproston Green (U.S. Version)/ Weirdo (Alternate Take) (12", with art print) . . . 8
92 Situation Two SIT 88CD — Weirdo/Theme From "The Wish"/Sproston Green (U.S. Version)/ Weirdo (Alternate Take) (CD) . . . 8
93 Beggars Banquet CHAR 7 — Subterranean (live) (CD, free with *109* fan club magazine) . . . 12/8

MINT VALUE £

94	Beggars Banquet BBQ 31CD1	I Never Want An Easy Life If Me And He Were Ever To Get There/ Only A Boho/Subterranean/Can't Get Out Of Bed (Demo Version) (CD, oblong box set with 3 postcards, numbered)	15
92	Situation Two SIT 97CD2	LIVE APRIL '92 (CD EP, shrinkwrapped with plastic g/fold box [ONE CD TWO])	8
96	Beggars Banq. BBQ 301DJ	One To Another (Radio Edit) (CD, promo)	12
01	12 KEY 1	Love Is The Key (orig. version)/Love Is The Key (So Solid Remix)/ The Bell And The Butterfly (12", no p/s, white label promo)	8
90	Situation Two SITU 30L	SOME FRIENDLY (LP, 'some friendly edition' in white PVC sleeve with inner)	12
91	Live Live Good CB 2	ISOLATION 21.2.91 (LP, official live bootleg, sold via fan club, 1,000 only)	20
92	Situation Two SITU 37	BETWEEN 10TH AND 11TH (CD, box set with cassette & video, promo only)	35
94	Beggars Banquet BBCD 147	UP TO OUR HIPS (CD, box set with cassette & video, promo only)	35

(see also Electric Crayons, Makin' Time)

CHARLATANS (U.S.)

69	Philips SBL 7903	THE CHARLATANS (LP)	70

(see also Mike Wilhelm, Tongue & Groove)

BOBBY CHARLES

56	London HLU 8247	See You Later, Alligator/On Bended Knee	2,600
56	London HLU 8247	See You Later, Alligator/On Bended Knee (78)	150
72	Bearsville K 45516	BOBBY CHARLES (LP)	15
77	Chess CXMP 2009	BOBBY CHARLES (LP)	12

DON CHARLES

62	Decca F 11424	Walk With Me My Angel/Crazy Man, Crazy	10
62	Decca F 11464	The Hermit Of Misty Mountain/Moonlight Rendezvous	15
62	Decca F 11528	It's My Way Of Loving You/Guess That's The Way It Goes	18
63	Decca F 11602	Angel Of Love/Lucky Star	20
63	Decca F 11645	Heart's Ice Cold/Daybreak	20
63	HMV POP 1271	Tower Tall/Look Before You Love	5
64	HMV POP 1307	If You Don't Know I Ain't Gonna Tell Ya/Voice On The Phone	5
64	HMV POP 1332	Big Talk From A Little Man/She's Mine	15
65	HMV POP 1382	Forgetting Me, Loving Him/A Long Time Ago	7
65	HMV POP 1420	Dream On Little Dreamer/We Only Live Once	7
65	HMV POP 1478	I Could Conquer The World/Time Will Tell	7
66	HMV POP 1542	Out Of This Cold/From The Beginning	7
67	Parlophone R 5564	So Let It Be/Bring Your Love To Me	7
67	Parlophone R 5596	Have I Told You Lately/Time Waits For Nobody	7
68	Parlophone R 5659	If I Had The Chance/(I've Got Everything) I've Got You	7
68	Parlophone R 5688	The Drifter/Great To Be Livin'	40
68	Parlophone R 5712	Your Name Is On My Heart/How Can I	6
63	Decca DFE 8530	DON CHARLES (EP)	100
67	Parlophone PMC/PCS 7021	HAVE I TOLD YOU LATELY (LP, mono/stereo)	35/45

JIMMY CHARLES

60	London HLU 9206	A Million To One/Hop Scotch Hop	25
63	Windsor WPS 120	Pitter Patter/How You Gonna Treat Me Now	7

JOHN CHARLES

60	Cetra SP 785	Sixteen Tons/Love In Portofino	5
60	Cetra SP 786	La Fine (The End)/Non Dimenticar	5

RAY CHARLES

78s

58	London HLE 8768	Rockhouse (Parts 1 & 2)	20
59	London HLE 8917	What'd I Say (Parts 1 & 2)	30
59	London HLE 9009	I'm Movin' On/I Believe To My Soul	40
60	HMV POP 792	Georgia On My Mind/Carry Me Back To Old Virginny	110

SINGLES

58	London HLE 8768	Rockhouse (Parts 1 & 2)	35
59	London HLE 8917	What'd I Say (Parts 1 & 2)	25
59	London HLE 9009	I'm Movin' On/I Believe To My Soul	18
60	London HLE 9058	Let The Good Times Roll/Don't Let The Sun Catch You Cryin'	18
60	HMV POP 774	Sticks And Stones/Worried Life Blues	15
60	London HLK 9181	Tell The Truth/You Be My Baby	15
60	HMV POP 792	Georgia On My Mind/Carry Me Back To Old Virginny	7
60	London HLK 9251	Come Rain Or Come Shine/Tell Me You'll Wait For Me	7
61	HMV POP 825	Ruby/Hard Hearted Hannah	8
61	HMV POP 838	Them That Got/I Wonder	25
61	London HLK 9364	Early In The Mornin'/A Bit Of Soul	15
61	HMV POP 862	One Mint Julep/Let's Go	15
61	HMV POP 935	Hit The Road Jack/The Danger Zone	10
61	London HLK 9435	I Wonder Who/Hard Times	12
62	HMV POP 969	Unchain My Heart/But On The Other Hand Baby	10
62	HMV POP 1017	Hide Nor Hair/At The Club	10
63	HMV POP 1133	Don't Set Me Free/The Brightest Smile In Town	10
63	HMV POP 1202	No One/Without Love (There Is Nothing)	6
63	HMV POP 1221	Busted/Making Believe	8
64	HMV POP 1251	That Lucky Old Sun/Mississippi Mud	6
64	HMV POP 1272	Baby Don't You Cry/My Heart Cries For You	6
64	HMV POP 1315	My Baby Don't Dig Me/Something's Wrong	6
64	HMV POP 1333	No One To Cry To/A Tear Fell	6
64	HMV POP 1350	Smack Dab In The Middle/I Wake Up Crying	7
65	HMV POP 1383	Makin' Whoopee/Move It On Over	6
65	HMV POP 1392	Cry/Teardrops From My Eye	6
65	HMV POP 1414	Light Out Of Darkness/Please Forgive And Forget	6
65	HMV POP 1437	I Gotta Woman/Without A Song	7
65	HMV POP 1457	Love's Gonna Live Here/I'm A Fool To Care	6
65	HMV POP 1484	The Cincinnati Kid/That's All I Am To You	6

MINT VALUE £

66	HMV POP 1502	Crying Time/When My Dreamboat Comes Home	6
66	HMV POP 1519	Together Again/You're Just About To Lose Your Clown	6
66	HMV POP 1537	Let's Go Get Stoned/The Train	7
66	HMV POP 1551	I Chose To Sing The Blues/Hopelessly	20
66	HMV POP 1566	Please Say You're Fooling/I Don't Need No Doctor	45
67	Atlantic 584 093	What'd I Say/I Got A Woman	5
67	HMV POP 1589	You Win Again/Bye Bye Love	6
67	HMV POP 1595	Somebody Oughta Write A Book About It/Here We Go Again	6
67	HMV POP 1607	In The Heat Of The Night/Something's Got To Change	7
67	Stateside SS 2071	Yesterday/Never Had Enough Of Nothing Yet	6
68	Stateside SS 2120	Eleanor Rigby/Understanding	6
71	Tangerine 6121 001	Booty Butt/Zig Zag	7
EPs			
59	London Jazz EZK 19043	THE GREAT RAY CHARLES	15
59	London Jazz EZK 19048	SOUL BROTHERS (with Milt Jackson)	15
61	London REK 1306	WHAT'D I SAY	15
61	London REK 1317	RAY CHARLES AT NEWPORT	15
62	HMV 7EG 8729	HIT THE ROAD JACK	15
62	HMV 7EG 8781	I CAN'T STOP LOVING YOU	10
63	HMV 7EG 8783	THE BALLAD STYLE OF RAY CHARLES	10
63	HMV 7EG 8801	THE SWINGING STYLE OF RAY CHARLES	10
63	HMV 7EG 8807	BABY IT'S COLD OUTSIDE (with Betty Carter)	10
63	HMV 7EG 8812	TAKE THESE CHAINS FROM MY HEART	10
63	London REB 1407	THE ORIGINAL RAY CHARLES VOLUME ONE	15
63	London REB 1408	THE ORIGINAL RAY CHARLES VOLUME TWO	15
63	London REB 1409	THE ORIGINAL RAY CHARLES VOLUME THREE	15
64	HMV 7EG 8841	BUSTED	10
64	HMV 7EG 8861	RAY CHARLES SINGS	10
64	Realm REP 4001	THE YOUNG RAY CHARLES	10
66	HMV 7EG 8932	RAY CHARLES LIVE IN CONCERT	10
66	HMV 7EG 8951	RAY CHARLES SINGS SONGS OF BUCK OWENS	10
LPs			
58	London Jazz LTZ-K 15134	THE GREAT RAY CHARLES	40
59	London Jazz LTZ-K 15146	SOUL BROTHERS (with Milt Jackson, also stereo SAH-K 6030)	25/35
59	London Jazz LTZ-K 15149	RAY CHARLES AT NEWPORT (also stereo SAH-K 6008)	25/35
59	London HA-E 2168	YES INDEED	40
59	London HA-E 2226	WHAT'D I SAY	35
60	London Jazz LTZ-K 15190	THE GENIUS OF RAY CHARLES	35
60	HMV CLP 1387/CSD 1320	THE GENIUS HITS THE ROAD (mono/stereo)	18/25
60	London HA-K 2284	RAY CHARLES IN PERSON	25
61	HMV CLP 1449/CSD 1362	DEDICATED TO YOU (mono/stereo)	15/18
61	HMV CLP 1475/CSD 1384	GENIUS + SOUL = JAZZ (mono/stereo)	15/18
62	HMV CLP 1520/CSD 1414	RAY CHARLES AND BETTY CARTER (mono/stereo)	15/18
62	London Jazz LJZ-K 15238	THE GENIUS SINGS THE BLUES	25
62	HMV CLP 1580/CSD 1451	MODERN SOUNDS IN COUNTRY & WESTERN (mono/stereo)	22/25
63	HMV CLP 1613/CSD 1477	MODERN SOUNDS IN COUNTRY & WESTERN VOL. TWO (mono/stereo)	15/18
63	London HA-K 8022	THE ORIGINAL RAY CHARLES	25
63	London HA-K 8023	THE RAY CHARLES STORY VOL. 1	15
63	London HA-K 8024	THE RAY CHARLES STORY VOL. 2	15
63	London HA-K 8035	THE GENIUS AFTER HOURS	20
63	HMV CLP 1626/CSD 1482	GREATEST HITS (mono/stereo)	15/18
63	London HA-K/SH-K 8045	SOUL MEETING (with Milt Jackson)	18
63	HMV CLP 1678	INGREDIENTS IN A RECIPE FOR SOUL	16
63	Realm RM 101	RAY CHARLES IN R&B GREATS	15
64	HMV CLP 1728/CSD 1537	SWEET AND SOUR TEARS (mono/stereo)	15/18
64	HMV CLP 1795/CSD 1566	HAVE A SMILE WITH ME (mono/stereo)	15/18
65	HMV CLP 1872/CSD 1696	LIVE IN CONCERT (mono/stereo)	15/18
65	HMV CLP 1914/CSD 1630	C&W MEETS R&B mono/stereo)	15/18
66	HMV CLP/CSD 3533	CRYIN' TIME (with Raelets)	15
66	HMV CLP/CSD 3574	RAY'S MOODS	15
67	Atlantic 587/588 056	HALLELUJAH I LOVE HER SO	12
67	HMV CLP/CSD 3630	RAY CHARLES INVITES YOU TO LISTEN	15

(see also Raelets, Milt Jackson)

SONNY CHARLES (& CHECKMATES LTD)

67	Ember EMB S 240	Mastered The Art Of Love/Please Don't Take My World Away	22
69	A&M AMS 752	Black Pearl/Lazy Susan	12

(see also Checkmates Ltd)

CHARLES, PAULETTE & GEE

71	G.G. GG 4515	Shock And Shake (Version 3)/WINSTON WRIGHT: Roll On (Version 2) (as Charlie, Paulette & Gee)	7
71	G.G. GG 4517	Rock And Shake (Version 3) (actually "Lover's Affair" by Charlie Ace & Maytones)/Roll On (Version 2) (actually "My Love And I" by Winston Wright)	6

(see also Charlie Ace)

DICK CHARLESWORTH (& HIS CITY GENTS)

61	Top Rank JAR 558	Billy Boy/Night Fall	6
61	Top Rank 35-104	MEET THE GENTS (LP)	15
62	HMV CLP 1495	YES INDEED IT'S THE GENTS (LP)	25

CHARLIE & MELODIANS

(see under Charlie Ace)

CHARLIE PARKAS

80	Paranoid Plastics PPS 1	The Ballad Of Robin Hood/Space Invaders (p/s)	8

(see also Alberto Y Lost Trios Paranoias)

MINT VALUE £

CHARLIE, PAULETTE & GEE
(see under Charles, Paulette & Gee)

CHARLOTTES
88 Molesworth HUNTS 5 — Are You Happy Now/How Can You Say (foldover p/s) ... 6
90 Subway Org. SUBWAY 27T — LOVE IN THE EMPTINESS (12" EP) ... 8

CHARMER
56 Melodisc MEL 1353 — Back To Back, Belly To Belly/Is She Is Or Is She Ain't (78) ... 15

CHARMERS (Jamaica)
61 Blue Beat BB 42 — Lonely Boy/I Am Going Back Home ... 20
62 Blue Beat BB 114 — Crying Over You/Now You Want To Cry ... 20
63 Blue Beat BB 157 — Time After Time/Done Me Wrong (with Prince Buster's Band) ... 20
63 R&B JB 118 — Angel Love/My Heart ... 20
63 R&B JB 121 — Oh Why Baby/ROLAND ALPHONSO: Perhaps ... 20
64 R&B JB 151 — What's The Use/I Am Through ... 20
64 R&B JB 156 — In My Soul/Beware ... 20
64 Blue Beat BB 204 — I'm Back/It's A Dream ... 20
64 Blue Beat BB 238 — Waiting For You/You Are My Sunshine ... 20
64 Blue Beat BB 251 — Dig Then Prince (actually Dip Them Prince)/Girl Of My Dreams (as The Charmer) 20
65 Blue Beat BB 279 — Nobody Takes My Baby Away From Me/
BUSTER ALLSTARS: Mules Mules Mules ... 20
66 Blue Beat BB 345 — Oh My Baby/STRANGER COLE: When The Party Is Over ... 20
66 Ska Beat JB 237 — Best Friend/MAYTALS: My Darling ... 20
66 Rio R 78 — You Don't Know/CORNELL CAMPBELL & ROY PANTON: Sweetest Girl ... 20
68 Coxsone CS 7043 — Things Going Wrong/KEN BOOTHE: You Keep Me Hanging On ... 30
68 Treasure Isle TI 7036 — Keep On Going (actually by Lloyd Charmers)/SILVERTONES: Don't Say No ... 22
70 Duke DU 87 — Colour Him Father/Version ... 12
70 Trojan TR 7773 — Sweeter She Is (actually by Lloyd Charmers, Dave Barker & Slim Smith)/
Fire Fire (actually by Lloyd Charmers) ... 6
70 Explosion EX 2026 — Can I Get Next To You?/Big Five ... 7
70 Explosion EX 2035 — Sweet Back/Music Talk (actually by Lloyd Charmers) ... 7
71 Explosion EX 2045 — Skinhead Train/TONY & CHARMERS: Everstrong (B-side with Tony Binns) ... 25
71 Explosion EX 2055 — Reggae In Wonderland/Wonder — Version
(both actually by Byron Lee & Dragonaires) ... 7
71 Supreme SUP 220 — Just My Imagination/Gotta Get A Message To You (actually by Dave Barker) ... 7
71 Green Door GD 4000 — Rasta Never Fails (actually by Lloyd Charmers & Ken Boothe)/
CHARMERS ALL STARS: Rasta Version ... 7
71 Green Door GD 4001 — One Big Unhappy Family/CONSCIOUS MINDS: Africa Is Paradise ... 12
71 Pama Supreme PS 340 — Red Head Duck/Jingle Jangle ... 6
(see also Spanishtown Skabeats, Lloyd & Ken, Lloydie & Lowbites, Lloyd Terrell)

CHARMERS (U.S.)
58 Vogue V 9095 — He's Gone/Oh! Yes ... 450
58 Vogue V 9095 — He's Gone/Oh! Yes (78) ... 40

LLOYD CHARMERS
67 Coxsone CS 7023 — Time Is Getting Hard/TONY GREGORY: I Sit By The Shore ... 25
69 Duke DU 15 — Cooyah/UNIQUES: Forever ... 15
69 Duke DU 16 — Follow This Sound/Why Pretend ... 12
69 Duke DU 25 — 5 To 5/SOUL STIRRERS: Come See About Me ... 12
69 Duke DU 36 — Safari (The Far East)/Last Laugh ... 12
69 Songbird SB 1001 — Ling Ting Tong/LLOYD ROBINSON: Sweet Sweet ... 10
69 Songbird SB 1007 — Duckey Luckey/In The Spirit ... 10
69 Camel CA 30 — Confidential/TOMMY COWAN: House In Session ... 8
69 Explosion EX 2001 — Death A Come/Zylon ... 8
70 Explosion EX 2032 — Vengeance/Look A-Py-Py ... 10
70 Explosion EX 2034 — Ready Talk/There Is Something About You ... 7
70 Trojan TR 7788 — Oh Me Oh My/I Did It ... 12
70 Bullet BU 435 — Dollars And Bonds/Sounds Familiar ... 7
70 Bullet BU 442 — Reggae A Bye Bye/DAVE BARKER:Doctor Jekyll ... 7
70 Escort ES 836 — Hi Shan/Soul At Large ... 12
70 Smash SMA 2302 — Big Red Bum Ball/BUNNIE LEE ALLSTARS: Big Bum Ball Version ... 7
73 Green Door GD 4064 — Save The People (as L. Charmers)/SCOTTY: Salvation Train ... 10
74 Harry J. HJ 6662 — I'm Gonna Love You Just A Little Bit More/Have I Sinned ... 6
71 Pama Supreme PS 339 — Shaft/Harry's Mood ... 8
71 Pama Supreme PS 346 — Show Business/DEBBY & LLOYD: Gloria ... 6
72 Pama Supreme PS 355 — Desiderata/Desiderata Music ... 6
70 Trojan TTL 25 — REGGAE IS TIGHT (LP) ... 30
70 Trojan TTL 30 — REGGAE CHARM (LP) ... 30
70 Pama SECO 25 — HOUSE IN SESSION (LP, with Hippy Boys) ... 70
(see also Charmers, Lloyd Tyrell/Terrell, Ken Boothe, Hippy Boys, Wayne Howard, Martia Riley, Eric Donaldson)

CHARMETTES
63 London HLR 9820 — Please Don't Kiss Me Again/What Is A Tear ... 40

CHARMS (Jamaica)
64 Island WI 154 — Carry, Go, Bring Home (actually by Justin Hinds & Dominoes)/
Hill And Gully (actually by L. Reid's Group) ... 20
66 Rio R 98 — Everybody Say Yeah/This World Is Yours ... 20

CHARMS (U.S.)
55 Parlophone MSP 6155 — Hearts Of Stone/Ko Ko Mo (I Love You So) ... 675
55 Parlophone R 3988 — Hearts Of Stone/Ko Ko Mo (I Love You So) (78) ... 40
55 Parlophone DP 412 — Hearts Of Stone/Bazoom, I Need Your Lovin' (78) (export issue) ... 40
55 Parlophone DP 423 — Two Hearts/The First Time We Met (78) (export issue) ... 100
(see also Otis Williams & Charms, Tiny Topsy, Harmonizing Four)

MINT VALUE £

CHARTBUSTERS
64 London HLU 9906 She's The One/Slippin' Thru Your Fingers . . . 18
64 London HLU 9934 Why/Stop The Music . . . 12

LINCOLN CHASE
57 London HLU 8495 Johnny Klingeringding/You're Driving Me Crazy (What Did I Do) . . . 20
57 London HLU 8495 Johnny Klingeringding/You're Driving Me Crazy (What Did I Do) (78) . . . 10
61 Philips PB 1103 Miss Orangutang/Walking Slowly . . . 25

CHASERS
65 Decca F 12302 Hey Little Girl/That's What They Call Love (some in p/s) . . . 100/50
66 Parlophone R 5451 Inspiration/She's Gone Away . . . 100
67 Philips BF 1546 The Ways Of A Man/Summer Girl . . . 15

CHATEAUX
83 Ebony EBON 13 CHAINED AND DESPERATE (LP) . . . 12
84 Ebony EBON 18 FIRE POWER (LP) . . . 12
85 Ebony EBON 31 HIGHLY STRUNG (LP) . . . 12

ROBERT CHAUVIGNY
59 Top Rank JAR 142 The Bottle Theme/French Rockin' Waltz (Eux) . . . 7
59 Top Rank JAR 142 The Bottle Theme/French Rockin' Waltz (Eux) (78) . . . 12

CHEAP BOOTS
70 Fontana 6001 020 Baby I Do Need You/Come And Stay With Me . . . 6

CHEAP TRICK
77 Epic S EPC 5701 I Want You To Want Me/Oh Boy (Instrumental Version) . . . 5
78 Epic S EPC 6199 So Good To See You/You're All Talk (withdrawn) . . . 20
79 Epic S EPC 7144 Voices/Surrender (withdrawn) . . . 5
79 Epic S EPC 7258 I Want You To Want Me (live)/I Want You To Want Me (studio) (DJ only) . . . 6
79 Epic CT-1 Dream Police/Voice/I'll Be With You Tonight (sampler, promo only) . . . 10
88 Epic 652 896-0 Don't Be Cruel (Remix)/I Know What I Want (shaped picture disc) . . . 5
88 Epic 652896 6 Don't Be Cruel (Remix)/I Know What I Want (Live)/Ain't That A Shame/ California Man (12", p/s) . . . 10
88 Epic 652 896-2 Don't Be Cruel (Remix)/I Know What I Want (live)/Ain't That A Shame (live)/ California Man (CD) . . . 8
88 Epic 653 005-3 Don't Be Cruel (Remix)/Dream Police/Way Of The World/ I Know What I Want (live) (3" CD) . . . 8
88 Epic 651 466-0 The Flame/Through The Night (shaped picture disc) . . . 5
88 Epic 651 466-2 The Flame (Album Version)/Through The Night/I Want You To Want Me/ If You Want My Love (CD, card sleeve) . . . 8
88 Epic 654 851-3 Solid Gold: The Flame/I Want You To Want Me/Surrender (3" CD, gatefold p/s) . . . 8
78 Epic EPC 86083 AT THE BUDOKAN (LP, yellow vinyl, with booklet) . . . 12
79 Epic EPC 11-83522 DREAM POLICE (LP, picture disc) . . . 12
82 Epic EPC 85740 ONE ON ONE (LP, red vinyl with insert) . . . 12
82 Epic EPC 11-85740 ONE ON ONE (LP, picture disc) . . . 15

CHEATIN' HEARTS
66 Columbia DB 8048 Zip-Tease/The Bad Kind . . . 12

CHUBBY CHECKER
59 Top Rank JAR 154 The Class/Schooldays, Oh, Schooldays . . . 45
59 Top Rank JAR 154 The Class/Schooldays, Oh, Schooldays (78) . . . 20
60 Columbia DB 4503 The Twist/Toot . . . 10
60 Columbia DB 4541 The Hucklebuck/Whole Lotta Shakin' Goin' On . . . 15
61 Columbia DB 4591 Pony Time/Oh Susannah . . . 12
61 Columbia DB 4652 Good Good Loving/Mess Around . . . 15
61 Columbia DB 4691 Let's Twist Again/Everything's Gonna Be All Right . . . 7
61 Columbia DB 4728 The Fly/That's The Way It Goes . . . 10
62 Columbia DB 4808 Slow Twistin'/The Lose Your Inhibitions Twist . . . 7
62 Columbia DB 4876 Dancin' Party/Gotta Get Myself Together . . . 7
62 Pye International 7N 25160 Dancin' Party/Gotta Get Myself Together (reissue) . . . 7
62 Cameo Parkway P 806 What Do You Say/Something To Shout About . . . 7
62 Cameo Parkway P 824 Let's Twist Again/The Twist . . . 6
62 Cameo Parkway P 849 Limbo Rock/Hitch Hiker . . . 7
63 Cameo Parkway P 862 Let's Limbo Some More/Twenty Miles . . . 7
63 Cameo Parkway P 873 Black Cloud/Birdland . . . 8
63 Cameo Parkway P 879 Twist It Up/Surf Party . . . 10
64 Cameo Parkway P 907 Hey Bobba Needle/Spread Joy . . . 12
64 Cameo Parkway P 920 Lazy Elsie Molly/Rosie . . . 8
64 Cameo Parkway P 922 She Wants T'Swim/You Better Believe It Baby . . . 8
65 Cameo Parkway P 936 Lovely, Lovely/The Weekend's Here . . . 15
65 Cameo Parkway P 949 (At The) Discotheque/Do The Freddie . . . 40
65 Cameo Parkway P 959 Everything's Wrong/Cu Ma La Be Stay . . . 25
65 Cameo Parkway P 965 Two Hearts Make One Love/You Just Don't Know (What You Do To Me) . . . 75
65 Cameo Parkway P 989 Hey You Little Boogaloo/Pussy Cat . . . 18
69 Buddah 201 045 Back In the U.S.S.R./Windy Cream . . . 5
71 London HL 10331 Let's Go Down/Goodbye Victoria . . . 5
76 London HLU 10515 (At The) Discotheque/Slow Twistin' . . . 6
78 London HLU 10557 You Just Don't Know (What You Do To Me)/ Two Hearts Make One Love (reissue) . . . 10
62 Columbia SEG 8155 KING OF THE TWIST (EP) . . . 12
63 Cameo Parkway CPE 550 DANCING PARTY (EP) . . . 15
61 Columbia 33SX 1315 TWIST WITH CHUBBY CHECKER (LP) . . . 35
61 Columbia 33SX 1341 FOR TWISTERS ONLY (LP) . . . 30
61 Columbia 33SX 1365 IT'S PONY TIME (LP) . . . 30

			MINT VALUE £
62	Columbia 33SX 1445	TWIST ALONG WITH CHUBBY CHECKER (LP)	20
62	Golden Guinea GGL 0236	TWISTIN' ROUND THE WORLD (LP)	22
63	Cameo Parkway P 7014	ALL THE HITS (LP)	22
63	Cameo Parkway P 7020	LIMBO PARTY (LP)	20
63	Cameo Parkway P 7036	CHUBBY CHECKER (LP)	25
71	London SHZ 8419	CHEQUERED (LP)	12

CHUBBY CHECKER & BOBBY RYDELL

62	Columbia DB 4802	Teach Me To Twist/Swingin' Together	15
62	Cameo Parkway C 205	Jingle Bell Rock/What Are You Doing New Year's Eve?	10
64	Cameo Parkway CPE 554	CHUBBY CHECKER AND BOBBY RYDELL IN LONDON (EP)	15
62	Columbia 33SX 1424	CHECKER AND RYDELL (LP)	20
63	Cameo Parkway C 1063	GOLDEN HITS (LP)	20

CHUBBY CHECKER & DEE DEE SHARP

62	Cameo Parkway C 1029	DOWN TO EARTH (LP)	50

(see also Dream Lovers, Bobby Rydell, Dee Dee Sharp)

CHECKERS

54	Parlophone DP 403	Over The Rainbow/CECIL YOUNG QUARTET: Oooh-Diga-Gow (78, export issue)	65

CHECKMATES

61	Piccadilly 7N 35010	Rockin' Minstrel/Pompeii	12
63	Decca F 11603	You've Gotta Have A Gimmick Today/Westpoint	22
64	Decca F 11844	Sticks And Stones/Please Listen To Me	30
65	Decca F 12114	Around/I've Got To Know Now	15
65	Parlophone R 5337	Stop That Music/I've Been In Love Before	18
66	Parlophone R 5402	(You Got) The Gamma Goochie/It Ain't Right	20
66	Parlophone R 5495	Every Day Is Just The Same/I'll Be Keeping The Score	18
61	Pye NPL 18061	THE CHECKMATES (LP)	40

(see also Original Checkmates)

CHECKMATES LTD

67	Ember EMB S 235	Do The Walk (The Temptation Walk)/Glad For You	12
69	A&M AMS 747	Love Is All I Have To Give/I Never Should Have Lied	8
69	A&M AMS 769	Proud Mary/Spanish Harlem	8
69	A&M AMLS 943	LOVE IS ALL I HAVE TO GIVE (LP)	25
70	Ember NR 5048	LIVE AT CAESAR'S PALACE (LP)	18

(see also Sonny Charles & Checkmates Ltd)

CHEEKY

80	Woodbine St. WSR 005	Don't Mess Around/Get Outa My 'Ouse (no p/s)	100

CHEERS

54	Capitol CL 14189	Bazoom (I Need Your Lovin')/Arrivederci	45
54	Capitol CL 14189	Bazoom (I Need Your Lovin')/Arrivederci (78)	10
55	Capitol CL 14248	Bernie's Tune/Whadaya Want?	25
55	Capitol CL 14248	Bernie's Tune/Whadaya Want? (78)	10
55	Capitol CL 14280	Blueberries/Can't We Be More Than Friends	30
55	Capitol CL 14280	Blueberries/Can't We Be More Than Friends (78)	10
55	Capitol CL 14337	I Must Be Dreaming/Fancy Meeting You Here	40
55	Capitol CL 14337	I Must Be Dreaming/Fancy Meeting You Here (78)	10
55	Capitol CL 14377	Black Denim Trousers And Motorcycle Boots/Some Night In Alaska	60
55	Capitol CL 14377	Black Denim Trousers And Motorcycle Boots/Some Night In Alaska (78)	10
56	Capitol CL 14561	Chicken/Don't Do Anything	25
56	Capitol CL 14561	Chicken/Don't Do Anything (78)	10
56	Capitol CL 14601	Que Pasa Muchacha/BERT CONVY: Heaven On Earth	22
56	Capitol CL 14601	Que Pasa Muchacha/BERT CONVY: Heaven On Earth (78)	10
56	Capitol EAP1 584	THE CHEERS (EP)	80

(see also Bert Convy [& Thunderbirds])

CHEETAHS

64	Philips BF 1362	Mecca/Goodnight Kiss	15
65	Philips BF 1383	Soldier Boy/Johnny	15
65	Philips BF 1412	Goodbye Baby (Baby Goodbye)/That's How It Goes	15
65	Philips BF 1453	Whole Lotta Love/Party	15
66	Philips BF 1499	The Russian Boat Song/Gamble	15

(see also Carl Wayne & Cheetahs)

CHELSEA

77	Step Forward SF 2	Right To Work/The Loner (p/s, originals in card p/s)	15/8
77	Step Forward SF 5	High Rise Living/No Admission (p/s)	10
78	Step Forward SF 8	Urban Kids/No Flowers (p/s)	8
80	Step Forward SF 14	No One's Coming Outside/What Would You Do (p/s)	5
80	Step Forward SF 15	Look At the Outside/Don't Get Me Wrong (p/s)	5
80	Step Forward SF 16	No Escape/Decide (p/s)	5
82	Step Forward SF 22	Stand Out/Last Drink (picture disc)	5
84	Chelsea CH 001	Give Me More/Sympathy For The Devil (p/s)	5
79	Step Forward SFLP 2	CHELSEA (LP, with inner sleeve)	20
81	Step Forward SFLP 5	ALTERNATIVE HITS (LP)	20
82	Step Forward SFLP 7	EVACUATE (LP)	15
84	Picasso PIK 003	LIVE AND WELL (LP)	12

CHELSEA LADS

66	CBS 202047	English Tea/Hump A Dink	5

CHEMICAL ALICE

81	Acidic GNOME 1	The Judge/Goodnight Vienna/Lands Of Home/Henry The King (12", p/s)	50

(see also Marillion)

MINT VALUE £

CHEMICAL BROTHERS

91	Eastern Bloc	Sea Of Beats/Sea Of Beats (Justin Robertson Mix) (12", p/s, as Ariel)	30
91	Deconstruction PT 44888	Rollercoaster/Mustn't Grumble/Mustn't Grumble (God's Grumble Mix) (12", as Ariel)	20
93	Dust Brothers DB's 333	Song To The Siren (12", as Dust Brothers, no p/s, 500 only)	50
93	Junior Boys Own JBO 10	Song To The Siren/Song To The Siren (Sabres Of Paradise Mixes) (12", p/s)	20
94	Boys Own COLLECT 004	14TH CENTURY SKY EP (12", no p/s, as Dust Brothers)	20
94	Junior Boys Own JBO 20	MY MERCURY MOUTH EP (12", JBO sleeve, as Dust Brothers)	20
95	Junior Boys Own CHEMS TI	Leave Home/Leave Home (Sabres Of Paradise)/Let Me In Mate (12", p/s)	25
95	Junior Boys Own CHEMS TXI	Leave Home (Underworld Mix One)/Leave Home (Underworld Mix Two) (12", p/s)	15

CHEQUERED PAST

85	Heavy Metal America HMUSA53	CHEQUERED PAST (LP, picture disc, 1,000 only)	30

(see also Steve Jones)

CLIFTON CHENIER

69	Action ACT 4550	Black Gal/Frogs Legs	15
70	Specialty SNTF 5012	BAYOU BLUES (LP)	15
70	Harvest MHSP 4002	CLIFTON CHENIER'S VERY BEST (LP)	30
79	Flyright FLY 539	ZYDECO BLUES (LP, with other artists)	15

CHER

65	Liberty LIB 66114	All I Really Want To Do/I'm Gonna Love You	5
66	Liberty LIB 66136	Where Do You Go/See See Rider	6
66	Liberty LIB 66160	Bang Bang (My Baby Shot Me Down)/Our Day Will Come	5
66	Liberty LIB 12034	I Feel Something In The Air/Come To Your Window	7
66	Liberty LIB 12038	Sunny/She's No Better Than Me	6
67	Liberty LIB 12046	Mama (When My Dollies Have Babies)/Behind The Door	6
67	Liberty LBF 15038	You Better Sit Down Kids/Elusive Butterfly	6
69	Atlantic 584 278	Walk On Gilded Splinters/Tonight I'll Be Staying Here With You	6
69	Atco 226 003	For What It's Worth/Hangin' On	6
71	MCA MU 1137	Classified 1A/Don't Put It On Me	5
72	MCA MU 1148	The Way Of Love/Fire And Rain	5
72	MCA MU 1158	Living In A House Divided/One Honest Man	5
72	MCA MU 1168	Don't Hide Your Love/First Time	5
75	Phil Spector Intl. 2010 006	A Love Like Yours (with Nilsson)/Hangin' On	12
76	Phil Spector Intl. 2010 013	A Woman's Story/Baby I Love You	10
99	Almighty	Dov'e L'Amore (Mixes) (CD-R)	75
00	Eternal SAM 00295	If I Could Turn Back Time (Mixes)/Believe (Almighty Definitive Mix)/ One By One (Junior Vasquez Club Vocal) (12" promo double pack)	25
66	Liberty LEP 4047	THE HITS OF CHER (EP)	20
65	Liberty (S)LBY 3058	ALL I REALLY WANT TO DO (LP, mono/stereo)	18/22
66	Liberty (S)LBY 3072	THE SONNY SIDE OF CHER (LP, mono/stereo)	18/22
66	Liberty (S)LBY 3081	CHER (LP, mono/stereo)	18/22
68	Liberty LBL/LBS 83051	WITH LOVE, CHER (LP)	15
68	Liberty LBL/LBS 83105E	GOLDEN GREATS (LP)	15
68	Liberty LBL 83156E	BACKSTAGE (LP)	12
69	Atco 226 026/228 026	3614 JACKSON HIGHWAY (LP, gatefold sleeve, mono/stereo)	15/12
71	MCA MUPS 438	CHER (LP)	12
72	MCA MUPS 459	FOXY LADY (LP)	12
73	MCA MUPS 484	BITTERSWEET WHITE LIGHT (LP)	12

(see also Sonny & Cher, Caesar & Cleo, Nilsson)

VIVIENNE CHERING

66	Decca F 12360	I'll Do My Crying Tomorrow/Make My Dreams Come True	10

(see also Flip & Dateliners)

CHEROKEES (U.S.)

61	Pye International 7N 25066	Cherokee/Harlem Nocturne	15

CHEROKEES (U.K.)

64	Decca F 11915	You've Done It Again Little Girl/Girl Girl Girl	12
64	Columbia DB 7341	Seven Daffodils/Are You Back In My World Now	12
65	Columbia DB 7473	Wondrous Place/Send Me All Your Love	12
65	Columbia DB 7704	I Will Never Turn My Back On You/Dig A Little Deeper	12
66	Columbia DB 7822	Land Of A 1000 Dances/Everybody's Needs	20

(see also Lee Diamond)

CHERRY

80s	Crashed Records CAR 91	He's A Bum/He Rides With Me	7

DON CHERRY

56	Brunswick 05538	Wanted Someone To Love/The Thrill Is Gone	8
57	Philips PB 755	I Keep Running Away From You/A Ferryboat Called Minerva (78)	5
57	Philips JK 1013	The Last Dance/Don't You Worry (jukebox edition)	15
58	Philips PB 816	Another Time, Another Place/The Golden Age	6
59	Philips PB 911	Hasty Heart/I Look For A Love	6
59	Philips PB 911	Hasty Heart/I Look For A Love (78)	15
66	London HLU 10045	I Love You Drops/Don't Change	6
56	Philips BBL 7128	SWINGIN' FOR TWO (LP)	12

(see also John Coltrane, Jazz Composers Orchestra)

CHERRY PEOPLE

68	MGM MGM 1438	And Suddenly/Imagination	35
69	MGM MGM 1472	Gotta Get Back/I'm The One Who Loves You	8
69	MGM MGM 1489	Light Of Love/On To Something New	8
75	Black Magic BM 112	And Suddenly/Imagination (reissue)	8

MINT VALUE £

CHERRY PIES
64 Black Swan WI 448 — Do You Keep Dreaming/Sweeter Than Cherry Pie ... 18

CHERRY SMASH
67 Track 604 017 — Sing Songs Of Love/Movie Star ... 12
68 Decca F 12838 — Goodtime Sunshine/Little Old Country Home Town ... 18
69 Decca F 12884 — Fade Away Maureen/Green Plant ... 25

FRANKIE CHERVAL
62 MGM MGM 1183 — How Come/Tag Along ... 12

PETE CHESTER
60 Pye 7N 15305 — Ten Swinging Bottles/Whole Lotta Shakin' On The Range (with Consulates) ... 35
61 Pye International 7N 25074 — Three Old Maids/Forest Fire (as Pete Chester & Group) ... 35
(see also Five Chesternuts)

VIC CHESTER
57 Decca F 10882 — Rock-A-Billy/First Date, First Kiss, First Love ... 22
57 Decca F 10882 — Rock-A-Billy/First Date, First Kiss, First Love (78) ... 10

CHESTERFIELDS
85 Subway Organisation GVP 007 — Nose Out Of Joint/SHOP ASSISTANTS: Home Again (33rpm flexidisc, with *The Underground* issue 4, *Screed* or *The Legend!* fanzine) ... 8/6
86 Subway Org. SUBWAY 5 — A GUITAR IN YOUR BATH (EP, wraparound p/s in poly bag) ... 7
87 Subway Org. SUBORG 003 — KETTLE (LP) ... 12
87 Subway Org. SUBORG 005 — WESTWARD HO (LP) ... 12

MORRIS CHESTNUT
79 Grapevine GRP 128 — Too Darn Soulful/You Don't Love Me Anymore ... 8

CHEVIOT RANTERS
73 Topic 12TS 222 — THE CHEVIOT HILLS (LP) ... 18
74 Topic 12TS 245 — CHEVIOT BARN DANCE (LP) ... 18

CHEVLONS
66 Pye 7N 17145 — Too Long Alone/It's My Problem ... 8

CHEVRONS
60 Top Rank JAR 308 — Lullaby/Day After Forever ... 12

CHEVY
80 Avatar AAA 104 — Too Much Loving/See The Light (company sleeve) ... 20
80 Avatar AAA 107 — The Taker/Life On The Run (p/s) ... 20
81 Avatar AAA 114 — Just Another Day/Rock On ... 12
80 Avatar AALP 5001 — THE TAKER (LP, gatefold sleeve with inner sleeve) ... 25

CHEYNES
63 Columbia DB 7153 — Respectable/It's Gonna Happen To You ... 75
64 Columbia DB 7368 — Going To The River/Cheyne-Re-La ... 70
65 Columbia DB 7464 — Down And Out/Stop Running Around ... 75
(see also Peter Bardens, Peter B's, Fleetwood Mac, Mark Leeman Five, Bo Street Runners)

CHEYNES
71 Bell BLL 1144 — April Fool/Gotta Get Back ... 6

CHIC
84 Atlantic AT 9604 — Chic Cheers/Savoir Faire/Dance Dance Dance (12") ... 8
86 Atlantic K 11209 — Le Freak/Savoir Faire/Chic (12") ... 8
87 Atlantic AT 9198 — Jack The Freak/Savoir Faire (12") ... 8
88 Atlantic AT 9107 — Good Times/Warm Summer Nights (12", p/s) ... 8

CHICAGO
69 CBS 4381 — Questions 67 And 68/Listen ... 6
69 CBS 4503 — I'm A Man (Parts 1 & 2) (withdrawn) ... 20
69 CBS 66221 — CHICAGO TRANSIT AUTHORITY (2-LP, orange label) ... 18
71 CBS 66405 — IV (AT CARNEGIE HALL) (4-LP, orange label) ... 25

CHICAGO BILL
(see under Big Bill Broonzy)

CHICAGO LINE
66 Philips BF 1488 — Shimmy Shimmy Ko Ko Bop/Jump Back ... 100
(see also Mike Patto, Bo Street Runners, Viv Prince)

CHICAGO LOOP
66 Stateside SS 564 — (When She Needs Good Lovin') She Comes To Me/This Must Be The Place ... 7

CHICK with TED CAMERON & D.J.'s
60 Pye 7N 15292 — Early In The Morning/Cool Water ... 40

CHICKEN SHACK
67 Blue Horizon 57-3135 — It's OK With Me Baby/When My Left Eye Jumps ... 18
68 Blue Horizon 57-3143 — Worried About My Woman/Six Nights In Seven ... 18
68 Blue Horizon 57-3146 — When The Train Comes Back/Hey Baby ... 12
69 Blue Horizon 57-3153 — I'd Rather Go Blind/Night Life ... 12
69 Blue Horizon 57-3160 — Tears In The Wind/The Things You Put Me Through ... 12
70 Blue Horizon 57-3168 — Maudie/Andalucian Blues ... 12
70 Blue Horizon 57-3176 — Sad Clown/Tired Eyes ... 12
73 Deram DM 381 — Time Goes Passing By/Poor Boy ... 8
73 Deram DM 396 — You Know You Could Be Right/The Loser ... 8
74 CBS 1832 — I'd Rather Go Blind/Sad Clown ... 6
68 Blue Horizon 7-63203 — FORTY BLUE FINGERS FRESHLY PACKED AND READY TO SERVE (LP) ... 40
69 Blue Horizon 7-63209 — O.K. KEN? (LP, gatefold sleeve) ... 35
69 Blue Horizon 7-63218 — 100 TON CHICKEN (LP) ... 35

MINT VALUE £

70 Blue Horizon 7-63861 ACCEPT CHICKEN SHACK (LP, gatefold sleeve) 35
72 Deram SDL 5 IMAGINATION LADY (LP, gatefold sleeve) 35
73 Deram SML 1100 UNLUCKY BOY (LP) 35
74 Deram SDL 8008 GOODBYE CHICKEN SHACK (LP) 30
(see also Errol Dixon, Fleetwood Mac, Christine Perfect, Carmen Macrae)

CHICKEN SHED

77 Colby AJ 370 ALICE (LP) 70

CHICKS

63 Oriole CB 1828 What Are Boys Made Of?/Over The Mountain 15

CHIEFS

58 London HLU 8624 Apache/Dee's Dream 35
58 London HLU 8624 Apache/Dee's Dream (78) 35
58 London HLU 8720 Enchiladas!/Moments To Remember 25
58 London HLU 8720 Enchiladas!/Moments To Remember (78) 25

CHIEFTAINS

64 Claddagh CC 2 THE CHIEFTAINS (LP) 12
69 Claddagh CC 7 THE CHIEFTAINS VOL. 2 (LP) 12
72 Claddagh CC 10 THE CHIEFTAINS VOL. 3 (LP) 12
73 Claddagh CC 14 THE CHIEFTAINS VOL. 4 (LP) 12

CHIFFONS

63 Stateside SS 172 He's So Fine/Oh! My Lover 10
63 Stateside SS 202 One Fine Day/Why Am I So Shy 10
63 Stateside SS 230 A Love So Fine/Only My Friend 10
64 Stateside SS 254 I Have A Boyfriend/I'm Gonna Dry Your Eyes 15
64 Stateside SS 332 Sailor Boy/When Summer's Through 15
65 Stateside SS 437 Nobody Knows What's Going On (In My Mind But Me)/
The Real Thing 25
66 Stateside SS 512 Sweet Talkin' Guy/Did You Ever Go Steady 10
66 Stateside SS 533 Out Of This World/Just A Boy 15
66 Stateside SS 559 Stop, Look And Listen/March 15
67 Stateside SS 578 My Boyfriend's Back/I Got Plenty Of Nuttin' 20
64 Stateside SE 1012 THEY'RE SO FINE (EP) 80
63 Stateside SL 10040 THE CHIFFONS (LP) 100
66 Stateside S(S)L 10190 SWEET TALKIN' GUY (LP) 80
72 London ZGP 125 SWEET TALKIN' GUY (LP, reissue) 12
75 Philips SON 005 THE CHIFFONS GREATEST HITS (LP) 12
84 Impact ACT 002 DOO LANG, DOO LANG (LP) 12
85 Impact ACT 007 FLIPS, FLOPS & RARITIES (LP) 15
(see also Four Pennies)

LORRAINE CHILD

64 Decca F 11969 You/Not This Time 15

SONNY CHILDE (& T.N.T.)

65 Decca F 12218 Giving Up On Love/Mighty Nice 15
66 Polydor 56108 Two Lovers/Ain't That Good News 15
66 Polydor 56141 Heartbreak/I Still Love You (as Sonny Childe & T.N.T.) 15
66 Polydor 582 003 TO BE CONTINUED (LP) 35

CHILD HAROLDS

68 Trident TRA 201 Diary Of My Mind/Loophole 30

BILLY CHILDISH

87 Hangman HANG 9-UP THE 1982 CASSETTES (LP, pink & black sleeve) 15
(see also Milkshakes, Thee Mighty Caesars, Buff Medways)

DR. A.A. CHILDS & CONGREGATION

50s Esquire 10-414 The Healing Prayer (Parts 1 & 2) (78) 12
60 Starlite ST45 009 The Healing Prayer (Parts 1 & 2) 6

CHI-LITES

69 Beacon BEA 119 Pretty Girl/Love Bandit 30
71 MCA MU 1138 (For God's Sake) Give More Power To The People/Trouble's A' Comin' 6
73 Brunswick BR 7 Stoned Out Of My Mind/Someone Else's Arms 8
70 MCA MUPS 397 GIVE IT AWAY (LP) 15
71 MCA MUPS 437 (FOR GOD'S SAKE) GIVE MORE POWER TO THE PEOPLE (LP) 15
72 MCA MUPS 457 A LONELY MAN (LP) 15
(see also Jackie Wilson)

CHILLIWACK

71 London HLU 10327 Everyday/Sundown 5
71 London SHU 8418 CHILLIWACK (LP) 12
(see also Collectors, Electric Prunes)

CHILLI WILLI & RED HOT PEPPERS

75 Mooncrest MOON 40 Breathe A Little/Friday Song 6
72 Revelation REV 002 KINGS OF THE ROBOT RHYTHM (LP) 20
74 Mooncrest CREST 21 BONGOS OVER BALHAM (LP) 15
(see also Brinsley Schwarz, Jo-Ann Kelly)

CHILLUM

71 Mushroom 100 MR 11 CHILLUM (LP, with photo insert) 70
(see also Secondhand)

ALEX CHILTON

80 Aura AUS 117 Hey! Little Child/No More The Moon Shines Lorena (p/s) 8
(see also Box Tops, Big Star)

MINT VALUE £

CHIMES (U.S.)
61 London HLU 9283 — Once In A While/Summer Night — 35

CHIMES featuring DENISE (U.K.)
63 Decca F 11783 — Say It Again/Can This Be Love? — 6
64 Decca F 11885 — I'll Be Waiting, I'll Be Here/Hello Heartache — 6
(see also Little Frankie)

CHIMNEYS
80 Tagmemics 45-003 — Do The Big Baby/Take Your Brain Out For A Walk (p/s, 500 only) — 15

TSAI CHIN
62 Decca LK 4501 — THE WORLD OF TSAI CHIN (LP) — 18
65 Decca LK 4717 — THE WESTERN WORLD OF TSAI CHIN (LP) — 15

CHINA DOLL
80 Wessex WEX 273 — Oysters And Wine/Past Tense (p/s) — 200

CHINA DOLLS
82 Speed FIRED 1 — One Hit Wonder/Ain't Love Ain't Bad (p/s) — 100
(see also Slade, Dummies)

CHINA STREET
78 Criminal CRM 1 — You're A Ruin/(I Wanna Be) Your M.P. (foldout lyric p/s in poly bag & badge) — 10

CHINATOWN
81 Airship AP 138 — Short And Sweet/How Many Times (p/s) — 60
81 Airship AP 343 — PLAY IT TO DEATH (LP) — 85

CHINAWITE
83 Future Earth FER 014 — Blood On The Streets/Ready To Satisfy (p/s) — 30

KES CHINS
62 Starlite ST45 089 — Annie/Moody — 8

CHIPMUNKS
(see under David Seville)

GEORGE CHISHOLM & BLUENOTES
56 Beltona BL 2671 — Honky Tonk/D.R. Rock (with Bert Weedon) — 10
56 Beltona BL 2671 — Honky Tonk/D.R. Rock (with Bert Weedon) (78) — 8
56 Decca LK 4147 — CHIS (LP) — 20
60s Philips SBBL 612 — TRAD TREAT (LP) — 18
64 Wing WL 1043 — TRAD SPECIAL (LP) — 18
60s 77 SEU 12/43 — ALONG THE CHISHOLM TRAIL (LP) — 20
60s Philips BL 7694 — MUSIC FOR ROMANTICS (LP) — 15
67 Columbia SCX 6195 — THE MAGNIFICENT SEVEN (LP) — 20
(see also Bert Weedon)

CHITINIOUS ENSEMBLE
72 Deram SML 1093 — CHITINIOUS ENSEMBLE (LP) — 100

CHOCOLATE BOYS
74 Decca F 13556 — El Bimbo/Voltaire Pier — 6

CHOCOLATE FROG
68 Atlantic 584 207 — Butchers And Bakers/I Forgive You — 22
(see also Fleur De Lys)

CHOCOLATE MILK
75 RCA RCA 2592 — Action Speaks Louder Than Words/Ain't Nothing But A Thing — 10
75 RCA RCAT 2592 — Action Speaks Louder Than Words/Ain't Nothing But A Thing (12") — 20
77 RCA PL 11830 — COMIN' (LP) — 20

CHOCOLATE WATCH BAND
67 Decca F 12649 — The Sound Of The Summer/The Only One In Sight — 25
67 Decca F 12704 — Requiem/What's It To You — 25

CHOIR
68 Major Minor MM 537 — It's Cold Outside/I'm Going Home — 45
68 Major Minor MM 557 — When You Were With Me/Changin' My Mind — 30
(see also Raspberries)

CHOPYN
75 Jet LPO 8 — GRAND SLAM (LP) — 12
(see also Ann Odell, Ray Russell)

CHORALERNA
60s Myrrh MYRRH 1047 — LET THERE BE LIGHT (LP) — 20
60s Key KL 018 — POWER (LP) — 20

CHORDETTES
78s
54 Columbia DB 3553 — Mr. Sandman/I Don't Wanna See You Cryin' (78) — 25
55 London HLA 8169 — Humming Bird/Lonely Lips (78) — 12
56 London HLA 8217 — Dudelsack Polka/I Told A Lie (78) — 12
56 London HLA 8264 — Eddie My Love/Our Melody (78) — 12
56 London HLA 8302 — Born To Be With You/Love Never Changes (78) — 8
56 London HLA 8323 — Lay Down Your Arms/Teenage Goodnight (78) — 8
57 London HLA 8473 — Echo Of Love/Just Between You And Me (78) — 12
57 London HLA 8497 — Like A Baby/Soft Sands (78) — 15
58 London HLA 8566 — Baby Of Mine/Photographs (78) — 15
58 London HLA 8584 — Lollipop/Baby, Come-A-Back-A (78) — 10
58 London HLA 8654 — Love Is A Two-Way Street/I Don't Know, I Don't Care (78) — 15
59 London HLA 8809 — We Should Be Together/No Other Arms, No Other Lips (78) — 20
59 London HLA 8926 — A Girl's Work Is Never Done/No Wheels (78) — 25

MINT VALUE £

45s

54	Columbia SCM 5158	Mr. Sandman/I Don't Wanna See You Cryin'	225
55	London HLA 8169	Humming Bird/Lonely Lips	65
56	London HLA 8217	Dudelsack Polka/I Told A Lie	50
56	London HLA 8264	Eddie My Love/Our Melody (triangular or round centre)	75/40
56	London HLA 8302	Born To Be With You/Love Never Changes	50
56	London HA 7011	Born To Be With You/Love Never Changes (export issue)	35
56	London HLA 8323	Lay Down Your Arms/Teenage Goodnight	40
57	London HLA 8473	Echo Of Love/Just Between You And Me	45
57	London HLA 8497	Like A Baby/Soft Sands	35
58	London HLA 8566	Baby Of Mine/Photographs	30
58	London HLA 8584	Lollipop/Baby, Come-A-Back-A	10
58	London HLA 8654	Love Is A Two-Way Street/I Don't Know, I Don't Care	15
59	London HLA 8809	We Should Be Together/No Other Arms, No Other Lips	12
59	London HLA 8926	A Girl's Work Is Never Done/No Wheels (B-side with Jeff Crom & Jackie Ertel)	20
61	London HLA 9400	Never On Sunday/Faraway Star	10
62	London HLA 9519	The White Rose Of Athens/Adios (Goodbye My Love)	8
60	London RE-A 1228	THE CHORDETTES (EP)	70
58	London HA-A 2088	THE CHORDETTES (LP)	125
62	London HA-A 2441	THE CHORDETTES SING (LP)	60

CHORDS (U.K.)

79	Polydor 2059 141	Now It's Gone/Don't Go Back (p/s)	6
80	Polydor POSP 101	Maybe Tomorrow/I Don't Wanna Know/Hey Girl (p/s)	6
80	Polydor POSP 146	Something's Missing/This Is What They Want (p/s)	6
80	Polydor 2059 258	The British Way Of Life/The Way It's Got To Be (p/s)	6
80	Polydor POSP 185	In My Street/I'll Keep On Holding On (p/s)	6
81	Polydor POSP 270	One More Minute/Who's Killing Who (p/s)	6
81	Polydor POSP 288	Turn Away Again/Turn Away Again (Again) (p/s)	5
80	Polydor Super POLS 1019	SO FAR AWAY (LP, some with stickered sleeve & 7" "Now It's Gone"/ "Things We Said" [KRODS 1])	30/15

(see also Rage)

CHORDS (U.S.)

54	Columbia SCM 5133	Sh-Boom (Life Could Be A Dream)/Little Maiden	2,000
54	Columbia DB 3512	Sh-Boom (Life Could Be A Dream)/Little Maiden (78)	100

CHORDS FIVE

67	Island WI 3044	I'm Only Dreaming/Universal Vagrant	90
68	Polydor 56261	Same Old Fat Man/Hold On To Everythin' You've Got	45
69	Jay Boy BOY 6	Some People/Battersea Fair	30

(see also Smoke)

CHOSEN FEW (U.K.)

65	Pye 7N 15905	It Won't Be Around You Anymore/Big City	20
65	Pye 7N 15942	So Much To Look Forward To/Today, Tonight & Tomorrow	20

(see also Alan Hull, Lindisfarne, Skip Bifferty)

CHOSEN FEW (Jamaica)

70	Songbird SB 1031	Time Is Hard/CRYSTALITES: Time Is Hard Part Two	12
70	Songbird SB 1032	Going Back Home/CRYSTALITES: Going Back Home Part Two	10
70	Songbird SB 1046	Why Can't I Touch You/INNER CIRCLE BAND: Touch You Version	12
71	Songbird SB 1061	Shaft/Shaft (Version)	10
71	Songbird SB 1067	Everybody Just A Stall/Everybody (Version)	8
72	Songbird SB 1070	Do Your Thing/Your Thing (Version)	18
72	Trojan TR 7864	Ebony Eyes/Ebony Eyes (Version)	6
72	Trojan TR 7882	Everybody Plays The Fool/You're A Big Girl Now	12
73	Trojan TR 7894	Am I Black Enough For You/Message From A Blackman	6
73	Duke DU 162	Children Of The Night/LLOYD CHARMERS: For The Good Times	7
73	Duke DU 163	Stoned In Love/MIKE CHUNG & NOW GENERATION: Stoned In Love (Version)	7
73	Duke DU 164	It's Too Late/MIKE CHUNG & NOW GENERATION: It's Too Late (Version)	7
73	Trojan TRLS 56	HIT AFTER HIT (LP)	30

CHOSEN FEW (U.S.)

74	Action ACT 4623	Funky Butter/Wondering	10
76	Polydor 2058 721	I Can Make Your Dreams Come True/Pretty Face	10
78	Polydor 2058 975	You Mean Everything To Me/It Won't Be Long	10

CHOU PAHROT

79	Klub KEP 101	Buzgo Tram Chorus/Gwizgweela Gwamhnoo/Lemons (p/s)	10
79	Klub KLP 19	LIVE (LP, private pressing)	12

CHRIS & COSEY/CREATIVE TECHNOLOGY INSTITUTE

81	Rough Trade RT 078	October (Love Song)/Little Houses (p/s)	5
81	Rough Trade RTT 078	October (Love Song)/Little Houses (12", p/s)	7
80s	Electronic Sound Maker	Sweet Surprise (magazine with free cassette)	20
84	Intl. One CTI 002	Conspiracy International/The Gift Of Tongues/The Need (p/s)	7
84	C.T.I. CTI 1	HAMMER HOUSE EP (12")	10
84	C.T.I. CTI 2	GIFT OF TONGUES (12")	10
85	Rough Trade RTT 148	Sweet Surprise 1 (1984)/2 (1985) (12", p/s, with Annie Lennox & Dave Stewart)	8
91	World Serpent WS7 004	Passion (p/s, 1-sided, other side etched)	5
80s	Sinn And Form	City Of Spirit (cassette magazine)	10
81	Rough Trade ROUGH 34	HEARTBEAT (LP, with insert)	12
81	Rough Trade COPY 008	HEARTBEAT (cassette, with 2 extra tracks "Pressure Drop" & "Tight Fit")	12
82	Rough Trade ROUGH 44	TRANCE (LP)	12

(see also Throbbing Gristle, Chris Carter, Eurythmics, Cosey Fanni Tutti)

MINT VALUE £

CHRIS & STUDENTS
61 Parlophone R 4806 Lass Of Richmond Hill/Ducks Away From My Fishin' . . . 20

PETER CHRIS & OUTCASTS
66 Columbia DB 7923 Over The Hill/The Right Girl For Me . . . 40

BOBBY CHRISTIAN & HIS ORCHESTRA
57 Oriole CB 1384 Enough Man/Crickets On Parade (possibly unissued) . . . 20+
57 Oriole CB 1384 Enough Man/Crickets On Parade (78) . . . 15

FUD CHRISTIAN ALL STARS
71 Big Shot BI 571 Never Fall In Love (actually by Winston Heywood)/
Never Fall In Love Version . . . 12

HANS CHRISTIAN
68 Parlophone R 5676 All Of The Time/Never My Love . . . 50
68 Parlophone R 5698 (The Autobiography Of) Mississippi Hobo/Sonata Of Love . . . 90
(see also Jon Anderson, Yes)

LIZ CHRISTIAN
67 CBS 202520 Suddenly You Find Love/Make It Work Out . . . 55
69 Spark SRL 1004 Call My Name/Think Of You Baby . . . 8
(see also James Royal)

MARIA CHRISTIAN
85 MCA MCA 974 Wait Until The Weekend Comes/(Instrumental) (p/s) . . . 15

NEIL CHRISTIAN (& CRUSADERS)
62 Columbia DB 4938 The Road To Love/The Big Beat Drum . . . 35
63 Columbia DB 7075 A Little Bit Of Someone Else/Get A Load Of This (with Crusaders) . . . 15
66 Strike JH 301 That's Nice/She's Got The Action . . . 10
66 Strike JH 313 Oops/She Said Yeah . . . 10
66 Strike JH 319 Two At A Time/Wanna Lover . . . 10
67 Pye 7N 17372 You're All Things Bright And Beautiful/I'm Gonna Love You Baby . . . 15
73 Youngblood YB 1044 That's Nice/She's Got The Action . . . 6
66 Columbia SEG 8492 A LITTLE BIT OF SOMETHING ELSE (EP) . . . 85
(see also Christian's Crusaders, Guy Hamilton, Jimmy Page, Ritchie Blackmore, Nicky Hopkins, Miki Dallon, Screaming Lord Sutch)

CHRISTIAN DEATH
83 No Future FL 2 ONLY THEATRE OF PAIN (LP, with insert) . . . 25
86 Jungle NOS 006 OFFICIAL ANTHOLOGY OF LIVE BOOTLEGS (LP, black & yellow sleeve) . . . 25
86 Jungle NOS 006 OFFICIAL ANTHOLOGY OF LIVE BOOTLEGS (LP, pink vinyl) . . . 12

JOHN CHRISTIAN DEE
68 Pye 7N 17566 Take Me Along/The World Can Pack Its Bags And Go Away . . . 6
69 Decca F 12901 The World Can Pack Its Bags And Go Away/Stick To Your Guns . . . 6
70 London HLH 10317 Come Forward The Man/Mr. & Mrs. Jones . . . 6

CHRISTIAN'S CRUSADERS
64 Columbia DB 7289 Honey Hush/One For The Money . . . 40
(see also Neil Christian & Crusaders)

CHRISTIE
71 CBS 9130 Everything's Gonna Be Alright/Freewheelin' Man/Magic Highway (p/s) . . . 6
70 CBS 64108 CHRISTIE (LP) . . . 15
71 CBS 64397 FOR ALL MANKIND (LP) . . . 15
(see also Acid Gallery, Epics, Outer Limits)

JOHN CHRISTIE
74 Polydor 2058 496 4th Of July (written by Paul McCartney)/Old Enough To Know Better
(some in p/s) . . . 30/15
74 Polydor 2058 528 Everybody Knows/How Does It Feel (p/s) . . . 6

LOU CHRISTIE
63 Columbia DB 4983 The Gypsy Cried/Red Sails In The Sunset . . . 18
63 Columbia DB 7031 Two Faces Have I/All That Glitters Isn't Gold . . . 15
63 Columbia DB 7096 How Many Teardrops/You And I (Have A Right To Cry) . . . 15
66 MGM MGM 1297 Lightnin' Strikes/Cryin' In The Streets . . . 10
66 MGM MGM 1308 Rhapsody In The Rain/Trapeze . . . 8
66 MGM MGM 1317 Painter/Du Ronda . . . 8
66 MGM MGM 1325 If My Car Could Only Talk/Song Of Lita . . . 15
66 Colpix PX 735 Merry Go Round/Guitars And Bongos . . . 10
67 King KG 1036 Outside The Gates Of Heaven/All That Glitters Isn't Gold . . . 8
67 CBS 2718 Shake Hands And Walk Away Cryin'/Escape . . . 12
67 CBS 2922 Gina/Back To The Days Of The Romans . . . 10
69 Buddah 201 057 I'm Gonna Make You Mine/I'm Gonna Get Married . . . 7
69 Buddah 201 073 She Sold Me Magic/Are You Gettin' Any Sunshine? . . . 7
70 Buddah 201 081 Love Is Over/Generation . . . 6
70 Buddah 2011 016 Sweet London Lady/Down When It's Up, Up When It's Down . . . 6
70 Buddah 2011 052 Indian Lady/Glory River . . . 6
71 Buddah 2011 074 Waco/Lighthouse . . . 6
71 Buddah 2011 111 I'm A Song, Sing Me/Paper Me . . . 6
71 Buddah 2011 127 Why Do Fools Fall In Love?/I'm Gonna Get Married . . . 6
72 Buddah 2011 148 Shuffle On Down To Pittsburgh/I'm Gonna Get Married . . . 8
73 CTI CTS 4002 Beyond The Blue Horizon/Hey You Cajun . . . 8
76 Elektra SEPC 4471 Riding In My Van/Summer In Malibu . . . 7
66 MGM MGM-C(S) 8008 LIGHTNIN' STRIKES (LP) . . . 35
66 Colpix PXL 551 STRIKES AGAIN (LP) . . . 30
69 Buddah 203 029 I'M GONNA MAKE YOU MINE (LP) . . . 12
71 Buddah 2318 035 PAINT AMERICA LOVE (LP) . . . 12
74 CTI CTL 24 LOU CHRISTIE (LP) . . . 15

MINT VALUE £

CHRISTIE BROTHERS STOMPERS

59 Parlophone GEP 8719 TOGETHER AGAIN (EP) . . . 18
60 Esquire EP233 RUM & COCA COLA (EP) . . . 25
60 Esquire EP243 STOMPIN' (EP) . . . 25

KEITH CHRISTIE

54 Esquire 20-047 HOMAGE TO THE DUKE (LP) . . . 20

TONY CHRISTIE (& TRACKERS)

66 CBS 202097 Life's Too Good To Waste/Just The Two Of Us . . . 10
67 MGM MGM 1365 Turn Around/When Will I Ever Love Again? . . . 10
68 MGM MGM 1386 I Don't Want To Hurt You Anymore/Say No More . . . 10
68 MGM MGM 1440 My Prayer/I Need You . . . 10
73 MCA MKS 5101 Avenues And Alleyways/I Never Was A Child . . . 7

DEREK CHRISTIEN

70 Major Minor MM 676 When A Woman Has A Baby/Please Don't Go Away . . . 6
70 Major Minor MM 713 Suddenly There's A Valley/I'll Be Coming Home . . . 100
(see also Christien Brothers)

CHRISTIEN BROTHERS

69 Major Minor MM 628 I Reached For You/Answer Me . . . 7

KEITH CHRISTMAS

69 RCA Victor SF 8059 STIMULUS (LP, with Mighty Baby) . . . 65
70 B&C CAS 1015 FABLE OF THE WINGS (LP) . . . 18
71 B&C CAS 1041 PIGMY (LP, gatefold sleeve) . . . 18
74 Manticore K 53503 BRIGHTER DAY (LP. with inner sleeve) . . . 18
76 Manticore K 53509 STORIES FROM THE HUMAN ZOO (LP, with insert) . . . 15
(see also Mighty Baby, Magic Muscle)

JUNE CHRISTY

55 Capitol CL 14355 Pete Kelly's Blues/Kicks . . . 10
55 Capitol EAP 516 SOMETHING COOL (EP) . . . 12
54 Capitol LC 6682 SOMETHING COOL (10" LP) . . . 22
56 Capitol T 725 JUNE CHRISTY (LP) . . . 18
57 Capitol T 833 JUNE — FAIR AND WARMER (LP) . . . 18
58 Capitol T 902 GONE FOR THE DAY (LP) . . . 18
58 Capitol T 1006 JUNE CHRISTY (LP) . . . 18
59 Capitol (S)T 1076 JUNE'S GOT RHYTHM (LP) . . . 18
59 Capitol (S)T 1114 THE SONG IS JUNE (LP) . . . 18
59 Capitol T 1202 JUNE CHRISTY RECALLS THOSE KENTON DAYS (LP) . . . 18
60 Capitol (S)T 1308 BALLADS FOR NIGHT PEOPLE (LP) . . . 18
61 Capitol (S)T 1398 COOL SCHOOL (LP, with Joe Castro Quartet) . . . 18
63 Capitol (S)T 1693 BEST OF (LP) . . . 15
(see also Stan Kenton)

CHROME

80 Siren/Red RS 12007 READ ONLY MEMORY (12" EP, some with poster) . . . 12/10
80 Beggars Banquet BEG 36 New Age/Information (p/s) . . . 6
81 D. F. O. T. Mountain Y3 INWORLDS (12" EP) . . . 12
82 D. F. O. T. Mountain Z17 Firebomb/Shadows Of A Thousand Years (p/s) . . . 8
80 Beggars Banquet BEGA 15 RED EXPOSURE (LP, with inner sleeve) . . . 12
80 Beggars Banquet BEGA 18 HALF MACHINE LIP MOVES (LP, some with poster insert) . . . 15/12
81 D. F. O. T. Mountain X6 BLOOD ON THE MOON (LP, with inner sleeve) . . . 12
82 D. F. O. T. Mountain X18 3RD FROM THE SUN (LP, with insert) . . . 12

CHRON GEN

81 Gargoyle GRGL 780 PUPPETS OF WAR (EP) . . . 7
81 Gargoyle/Fresh GRGL 780 PUPPETS OF WAR (EP, reissue, silver & black label) . . . 6
81 Step Forward SF 19 Reality/Subway Sadist (p/s) . . . 5
82 Secret SEC 3 LIVING NEXT DOOR TO ALICE (EP, some with *Chronic Generation Oi* magazine No. 1) . . . 8/5
82 Secret SHH 129 Jet Boy Jet Girl/Abortions/Subway Sadist (p/s) . . . 5
82 Secret SHH 139 Outlaw/Behind Closed Doors/Disco (p/s) . . . 5
83 Secret SEC 3 CHRONIC GENERATION (LP, some with free 7") . . . 15/12

CHROMING ROSE

90 EMI 5667 93774 LOUIS XIV (LP, some as picture disc) . . . 12

CHUBBY & HONEYSUCKERS

66 Rio R 75 Emergency Ward/LEN & HONEYSUCKERS: One More River . . . 12

CHUBUKOS

73 Mainstream MSS 303 Witch Doctor Bump/House Of The Rising Funk . . . 10

CHUCK & BETTY

59 Brunswick 05815 Sissy Britches/Come Back Little Girl . . . 45
59 Brunswick 05815 Sissy Britches/Come Back Little Girl (78) . . . 15

CHUCK (Josephs) & DOBBY (Dobson)

60 Blue Beat BB 19 Til The End Of Time/DUKE REID & HIS GROUP: What Makes Honey . . . 18
60 Blue Beat BB 23 Cool School/DUKE REID & HIS GROUP: Joker . . . 18
61 Starlite ST45 043 Sad Over You/Sweeter Than Honey . . . 18
61 Starlite ST45 044 Lovey Dovey/Sitting Square . . . 18
61 Blue Beat BB 39 Du Du Wap/I Love My Teacher (with Aubrey Adams & Du Droppers) . . . 18
61 Blue Beat BB 59 Oh Fanny/Running Around . . . 18
64 Blue Beat BB 246 Tell Me/I'm Going Home . . . 18

CHUCK & GARY

58 HMV POP 466 Teenie Weenie Jeanie/Can't Make Up My Mind . . . 60
58 HMV POP 466 Teenie Weenie Jeanie/Can't Make Up My Mind (78) . . . 20

MINT VALUE £

CHUCK & GIDEON
63 Parlophone R 5011 — Cherry Berry Lips/The Tender Touch 10

CHUCK & JOE WHITE
(see under Joe White)

CHUCKLES
72 Duke DU 144 — Reggae Limbo/ZAP POW: Broken Contract 8

CHUCKS
63 Decca F 11569 — Loo Be Loo/Anytime Is The Right Time 8
63 Decca F 11617 — Mulberry Bush/That's All I Need 8
63 Decca F 11777 — The Hitch Hiker/Humpity Dumpity 8
64 Decca DFE 8562 — THE CHUCKS (EP) 45

MIKIE CHUNG & NOW GENERATION
72 Green Door GD 4032 — Breezing/NOW GENERATION: Breezing — Version 8
73 Duke DU 163 — Stoned In Love/CHOSEN FEW: Stoned In Love 7
73 Duke DU 164 — It's Too Late/CHOSEN FEW: It's Too Late 7

CHURCH
82 Carrere CAR 212 — Unguarded Moment/Busdriver (p/s) 5
82 Carrere CAR 247 — Almost With You/Life Speeds Up (p/s) 5
82 Carrere CAR EP 257 — Unguarded Moment/Interlude/Golden Dawn/Sisters (10", p/s) 8
83 Carrere CHURCH R5A — Different Man/I Am A Rock (no p/s) 7
86 Bucketfull Of Brains BOB 9 — Warm Spell (hard vinyl test pressing, 20 copies only) 20
88 Arista 659 778CD — Under The Milky Way/Musk/The Warm Spell (CD, picture disc) 8
83 Carrere CHURCH 5 — SING SONGS (12" EP) 10
88 Arista 208895 — STARFISH (LP, with bonus 5-track numbered 12") 15

EUGENE CHURCH
59 London HL 8940 — Miami/I Ain't Goin' For That (triangular or round centre) 75/40
59 London HL 8940 — Miami/I Ain't Goin' For That (78) 30

CHICK CHURCHILL
73 Chrysalis CHR 1051 — YOU AND ME (LP) 18
(see also Ten Years After, Cozy Powell, Jethro Tull, Bernie Marsden)

SAVANNAH CHURCHILL
53 Brunswick 05218 — Shake A Hand/Shed A Tear (78) 25
61 London HLW 9273 — I Want To Be Loved/Time Out For Tears 12

SIR WINSTON CHURCHILL
65 HMV ALP 2081 — THE STATE FUNERAL OF WINSTON CHURCHILL (LP) 12
65 Decca LXT 6200 — THE VOICE OF WINSTON CHURCHILL (LP) 12

CICCONE YOUTH
86 Blast First BFFP 8 — INTO THE GROOVE(Y) EP: Tuff Titty Rap/Into The Groove/Burning Up (12") 10
88 Blast First BFUS 28P — WHITEY ALBUM PROMO (EP, promo only) 10
(see also Sonic Youth)

CICERO
92 Spaghetti CIOCD 1 — Heaven Must Have Sent You Back To Me/(Melt Mix)/Pukka (Elevation Mix) (CD) 12
92 Spaghetti CIOCD 3 — Love Is Everywhere/Love Is Everywhere (Extended)/Mind Gap (Extended) (CD) 8
92 Spaghetti CIOCD 4 — That Loving Feeling (7" Mix)/That Loving Feeling (Extended Mix)/ Splatt (Extended Mix) (CD) 8
92 Spaghetti CIAOCD 5 — Heaven Must Have Sent You Back To Me (Remix)/ (Extended Remix)/Jungilism (CD) 8
93 Spaghetti 513 428-1 — FUTURE BOY (LP) 12
93 Spaghetti 513 428-2 — FUTURE BOY (CD) 18
(see also Pet Shop Boys)

DIANE CILENTO
55 Polygon P 1186 — A Fool & His Heart/The Lily Watkins Tune (78) 7

CIGARETTES
78 Dead Good KEVIN 1 — THE CIGARETTES (EP, unreleased)
79 Company CIGCO 008 — They're Back Again, Here They Come/I've Forgot My Number/ All We Want Is Your Money (gatefold p/s, red or later black labels) 70/60
80 Dead Good DEAD 10 — Can't Sleep At Night/It's The Only Way To Live (Die) (p/s) 40

CIM(M)AR(R)ONS
70 Hot Rod HR 105 — Grandfather Clock/Kick Me Or I Kick You (as Cimarrons) 10
70 Reggae REG 3003 — Bad Day At Black Rock (with Cimmaron Kid)/Fragile 10
71 Big Shot BI 562 — Funky Fight/You Turned Me Down 10
71 Spinning Wheel SW 107 — Soul For Sale/Bogus-ism 7
71 Downtown DT 486 — Oh Mammy Blue/Oh Mammy Blue — Version 6
71 Downtown DT 487 — Holy Christmas/Silent Night/White Christmas 6
82 IMP IMPS 50 — With A Little Luck/Peggy Sue (p/s) 12
(see also Reaction, Winston Groovy)

CINDERELLAS
59 Brunswick 05794 — Mister Dee-Jay/Yum Yum Yum 40
59 Brunswick 05794 — Mister Dee-Jay/Yum Yum Yum (78) 10
60 Philips PB 1012 — The Trouble With Boys/Puppy Dog 20

CINDERELLAS
64 Colpix PX 11026 — Baby, Baby (I Still Love You)/Please Don't Wake Me 80
(see also Cookies)

CINDERS
63 Warner Bros WB 86 — The Cinnamon Cinder/C'mon Wobble 15
(see also Darlene Love)

CINDY & LINDY
57 HMV POP 409 — The Language Of Love/Tell Me Something Sweet . . . 10
59 Coral Q 72368 — Saturday Night In Tiajuana/The Wonder That Is You . . . 10

CINEMATICS
80s Pulsebeat CINE 001 — FAREWELL TO THE PLAYGROUND (EP, foldover p/s) . . . 25
(see also Razorcuts)

CINNAMON
69 Beacon BEA 111 — You Won't See Me Leaving/Leaves Of Love . . . 6

CINNAMON QUILL
69 Morgan MRS 17 — Girl On A Swing/Take It Or Leave It . . . 20
69 Morgan MRS 21 — Candy/Hello, It's Me . . . 30

CIRCLE
60s Circle GR 1 — IN AID OF THE MILLFIELD BUILDING FUND (EP, private pressing) . . . 150

CIRCLES
66 Island WI 279 — Take Your Time/Don't You Love Me No More . . . 65
(see also Plastic Penny, Savages, Tony Dangerfield & Thrills, Screaming Lord Sutch)

CIRCLES
72 Sioux SIOUX 017 — Mammy Blue/POOCH JACKSON & HARRY J. ALLSTARS: King Of The Road . . . 6
(see also Bob Andy)

CIRCLES
79 Graduate GRAD 4 — Opening Up/Billy (p/s) . . . 20
80 Vertigo ANGRY 1 — Angry Voices/Summer Nights (p/s) . . . 8
80 Chrysalis CHS 2418 — Opening Up/Billy (p/s, reissue) . . . 8
85 Graduate GRAD 17 — Circles/Summer Nights (p/s) . . . 18

CIRCUS
67 Parlophone R 5633 — Gone Are The Songs Of Yesterday/Sink Or Swim . . . 18
68 Parlophone R 5672 — Do You Dream/House Of Wood . . . 40
69 Transatlantic TRA 207 — CIRCUS (LP, gatefold sleeve) . . . 50
(see also Philip Goodhand-Tait)

CIRCUS MAXIMUS
67 Vanguard VSD 79260 — CIRCUS MAXIMUS (LP) . . . 30
68 Vanguard VSD 79274 — NEVERLAND REVISITED (LP) . . . 30

CIRKUS
80 Guardian GRCA 4 — Melissa/Amsterdam/Pick Up A Phone (EP) . . . 20
73 RCB 1 — CIRKUS ONE (LP, private pressing with gatefold sleeve) . . . 100
77 Shock SHOCK 1 — FUTURE SHOCK (LP) . . . 45

CIRRUS
81 Jet JET 123 — Rollin' On/Keep On Rolling (p/s, 'Yorkie™'-shaped brown vinyl) . . . 5

CITATIONS
63 Columbia DB 7068 — Moon Race/Slippin' And Slidin' . . . 30

CITY OF WESTMINSTER STRING BAND
68 Pye 7N 17620 — A Touch Of Velvet And A Sting Of Brass/Tommy Tucker . . . 8

CITY RAMBLERS SKIFFLE GROUP
57 Tempo A 158 — Ella Speed/2.19 Blues . . . 20
57 Tempo A 158 — Ella Speed/2.19 Blues (78) . . . 15
57 Tempo A 161 — Mama Don't Allow/Tom Dooley . . . 18
57 Tempo A 161 — Mama Don't Allow/Tom Dooley (78) . . . 15
57 Tempo A 165 — Delia's Gone/Boodle-Am Shake . . . 20
57 Tempo A 165 — Delia's Gone/Boodle-Am Shake (78) . . . 15
50s Topic TRC 101 — Round And Round The Picket Lines/Nine Hundred Miles (78, with Hylda Sims) . . 12
57 Storyville SEP 327 — I WANT A GIRL (EP) . . . 45
57 Storyville SEP 345 — I SHALL NOT BE MOVED (EP) . . . 45
57 Tempo EXA 59 — I WANT A GIRL (EP) . . . 40
57 Tempo EXA 71 — GOOD MORNING BLUES (EP) . . . 40
57 Tempo EXA 77 — DELIA'S GONE (EP) . . . 40
(see also Henrik Johansen)

CITY SMOKE
66 Mercury MF 971 — Sunday Morning/A Little Bit Of Love . . . 6

CITY WAITES
74 EMI EMI 2149 — The Fox/One Of My Aunts . . . 7
74 EMI EMC 3027 — A GORGEOUS GALLERY OF GALLANT INVENTIONS (LP) . . . 30
76 Decca SKL 5264 — THE CITY WAITES (LP) . . . 40
81 Hyperion A 66008 — HOW THE WORLD WAGS (LP, gatefold sleeve, some with Hyperion insert) . . . 60

C-JAM BLUES
66 Columbia DB 8064 — Candy/Stay At Home Girl . . . 22

CLAGUE
69 Dandelion S 4493 — Mandy Lee/Bottle Up And Go (with Kevin Coyne) . . . 10
(see also Coyne-Clague, Kevin Coyne, Siren)

CLAN
72 Deram DM 356 — Pretty Belinda/Ode To Karen . . . 7
(see also Junior Campbell)

CLANCY'S ALLSTARS
68 Pama PM 722 — C.N. Express Parts 1 & 2
(B-side actually "You Were Meant For Me" by Lee Perry) . . . 30
(see also Owen Gray)

MINT VALUE £

JIMMY CLANTON

58	London HLS 8699	Just A Dream/You Aim To Please (as Jimmy Clanton & His Rockets)	30
58	London HLS 8699	Just A Dream/You Aim To Please (78)	20
58	London HL 7066	A Letter To An Angel/A Part Of Me (as Jimmy Clanton & Aces) (export issue)	30
59	London HLS 8779	A Letter To An Angel/A Part Of Me (as Jimmy Clanton & Aces)	30
59	London HLS 8779	A Letter To An Angel/A Part Of Me (78)	15
59	Top Rank JAR 189	My Own True Love/Little Boy In Love	25
59	Top Rank JAR 189	My Own True Love/Little Boy In Love (78)	15
60	Top Rank JAR 269	Go, Jimmy, Go/I Trusted You	20
60	Top Rank JAR 382	Another Sleepless Night/I'm Gonna Try	15
60	Top Rank JAR 509	Come Back (To Me)/Wait	15
61	Top Rank JAR 544	What Am I Gonna Do/If I	15
62	Stateside SS 120	Venus In Blue Jeans/Highway Bound	15
63	Stateside SS 159	Darkest Street In Town/Dreams Of A Fool	12
65	Stateside SS 410	Hurting Each Other/Don't Keep Your Friends Away	20
69	London HLP 10289	Curly/I'll Never Forget Your Love	6
59	London RES 1224	JUST A DREAM (EP)	100

CLAP

79	SRTS SRTS/79/CUS	Hey Little Girl/20 Watts Of Power (p/s)	40

CLAPHAM SOUTH ESCALATORS

81	Upright UP YOUR 1	Get Me To The World On Time/Leave Me Alone/Cardboard Cut Outs (p/s)	8

(see also Meteors)

ERIC CLAPTON

66	Purdah 45-3502	Lonely Years/Bernard Jenkins (with John Mayall, 500 copies only)	300
70	Polydor 2001 096	I Am Yours (unissued)	
70	Polydor 2001 096	After Midnight/Easy Now	12
74	RSO 2090 139	Willie And The Hand Jive/I Can't Hold Out Much Longer (p/s)	6
76	RSO 2090 208	Hello Old Friend/All Our Pastimes (p/s)	12
80	RSO JON 1	Wonderful Tonight (live)/Further On Up The Road (live) (promo only)	15
80	RSO JONX 1	Wonderful Tonight (live)/Further On Up The Road (live) (12", numbered p/s)	15
81	RSO RSO 75	Another Ticket/Rita Mae (p/s)	8
83	Duck W 9651	Slow Down Linda/Crazy Mountain Hop (p/s)	6
83	Duck W 9701P	The Shape You're In/Crosscut Saw (picture disc)	8
85	Duck W 8954	She's Waiting/Jail Bait (p/s)	10
87	Duck W 8461F	Behind The Mask/Grand Illusion//Crossroads (live)/White Room (live) (double pack, gatefold p/s)	8
87	Duck W 8397F	It's In The Way That You Use It/Bad Influence//Behind The Mask/ Grand Illusion (double pack, shrinkwrapped with sticker)	10
87	Duck W 8299TP	Tearing Us Apart (with Tina Turner)/Hold On/Run (live) (12", p/s)	7
88	Polydor PZCD 8	After Midnight (Extended Version)/I Can't Stand It/Whatcha Gonna Do/ Sunshine Of Your Love (CD, card sleeve)	12
89	BBC RSL 178	Edge Of Darkness/Shoot Out (with Michael Kamen, p/s)	8
89	BBC 12 RSL 178	Edge Of Darkness/Shoot Out/Obituary/Escape From Northmoor/ Oxford Circus/Northmoor (with Michael Kamen, 12", p/s)	10
89	BBC CD RSL 178	Edge Of Darkness/Shoot Out/Obituary/Escape From Northmoor/ Oxford Circus/Northmoor (with Michael Kamen, 3" CD with adaptor, 5" case)	15
89	Duck W 2644B	Bad Love/I Shot The Sheriff (live) (box set with family tree & 2 colour prints)	6
90	Duck W 2644CD	Bad Love/Badge (live)/Let It Rain (live) (CD)	12
90	Duck W 9981B	No Alibis/Running On Faith (box set with 2 live photos & metal Strat badge)	6
90	Duck W 9981CD	No Alibis/Running On Faith/Behind The Mask (live)/Cocaine (CD)	10
90	Duck W 9970CD	Pretending/Hard Times/Knock On Wood/Behind The Sun (CD)	10
70	Polydor 2383 021	ERIC CLAPTON (LP)	12
73	RSO 2479 702	CLAPTON (LP, withdrawn)	55
74	RSO QD 4801	461 OCEAN BOULEVARD (LP, quadrophonic)	18
82	RSO RSDX 3	TIME PIECES (2-LP, unissued)	
83	WEA W 37734	MONEY AND CIGARETTES (cassette, with interview)	12
84	Aston PD 20118	TOO MUCH MONKEY BUSINESS (LP, picture disc, with Yardbirds)	15
99	Reprise SAM 00189	A SELECTION FROM THE BEST OF (CD, 9-track sampler, promo only)	20

(see also Yardbirds, John Mayall, Cream, Blind Faith, Delaney & Bonnie, Derek & The Dominos, Viv Stanshall, King Curtis, Randy Crawford)

ALAN CLARE GROUP

62	Parlophone R 4938	Screwball/Love For Sale	7
65	Pye 7N 15764	Dog's Body/Mulligatawny	7
56	Decca DFE 6368	THE IMPROVISATIONS OF... (EP)	40
56	Decca DFE 6391	ALAN CLARE TRIO WITH BOB BURNS (EP)	35
58	Decca LK 4260	JAZZ AROUND THE CLOCK (LP)	40
68	Decca SKL 4965	YOUNG GIRL (LP)	15

KENNY CLARE

67	Columbia DB 8216	If I Were A Buddy Rich Man/Hum-Drum	6

KENNY CLARE & RONNIE STEPHENSON

67	Columbia SCX 6168	DRUM SPECTACULAR (LP, with Tubby Hayes, also mono Columbia SX 6168)	30

CLARENDONIANS

65	Ska Beat JB 219	Muy Bien (My Friend)/You Are A Fool	22
66	Ska Beat JB 261	Doing The Jerk/You Won't See Me	22
66	Island WI 284	Try Me One More Time/Can't Keep A Good Man Down	22
66	Island WI 3005	I'll Never Change/Rules Of Life	22
67	Island WI 3032	Shoo-Be-Doo-Be (I Love You)/Sweet Heart Of Beauty	22
67	Island WI 3041	You Can't Be Happy/Goodbye Forever	22
67	Studio One SO 2004	The Table's Going To Turn/I Can't Go On	30
67	Studio One SO 2007	He Who Laughs Last/GAYLADS: Just A Kiss From You	30
67	Studio One SO 2017	Love Me With All Your Heart/Love Don't Mean Much To Me	30
67	Rio R 112	Rudie Bam Bam/Be Bop Boy	18

MINT VALUE £

67 Rio R 115 Musical Train/Lowdown Girl . . . 18
68 Caltone TONE 114 Baby Baby/Bye Bye Bye . . . 15
69 Duke DU 97 Come Along/Try To Be Happy . . . 10
69 Gas GAS 131 When I Am Gone/She Brings Me Joy . . . 7
70 Trojan TR 7714 Lick It Back/BEVERLEY'S ALLSTARS: Busy Bee . . . 8
70 Trojan TR 7719 Baby Don't Do It/BEVERLEY'S ALLSTARS: Touch Down . . . 8
71 Green Door GD 4009 Seven In One (Medley) (both sides) . . . 6
72 Attack ATT 8039 Bound In Chains/STUD ALLSTARS: Version . . . 6
72 Pama PM 847 This Is My Story/VAL BENNETT: Caledonia . . . 6
73 Pama PM 856 Good Hearted Woman/CORNELL CAMPBELL: What Happens . . . 6
73 Techniques TE 925 Just One Look/Sinner Man . . . 6
73 Dragon DRA 1006 Walking Up A One Way Street/DYNAMITES: Instrumental . . . 7

(see also Lee & Clarendonians, Desmond Baker & Clarendonians, Four Aces, Prince Buster, Dennis Walks)

ALICE CLARK

69 Action ACT 4520 You Got A Deal/Say You'll Never . . . 20

CHRIS CLARK

67 Tamla Motown TMG 591 Love's Gone Bad/Put Yourself In My Place . . . 35
67 Tamla Motown TMG 624 From Head To Toe/The Beginning Of The End . . . 30
68 Tamla Motown TMG 638 I Want To Go Back There Again/I Love You . . . 25
68 T. Motown (S)TML 11069 SOUL SOUNDS (LP) . . . 110

CLAUDINE CLARK

62 Pye International 7N 25157 Party Lights/Disappointed . . . 15
63 Pye International 7N 25186 Walk Me Home From The Party/Who Will You Hurt? . . . 15
67 Sue WI 4039 The Strength To Be Strong/Moon Madness . . . 25

DAVE CLARK FIVE

62 Ember EMB S 156 Chaquita/In Your Heart (grey/pink or red/yellow labels) . . . 55/45
62 Piccadilly 7N 35088 First Love/I Walk The Line . . . 45
62 Piccadilly 7N 35500 That's What I Said/I Knew It All The Time . . . 45
63 Columbia DB 7011 The Mulberry Bush/Chaquita . . . 30
63 Columbia DB 7112 Do You Love Me/Doo-Dah . . . 8
63 Columbia DB 7154 Glad All Over/I Know You . . . 6
64 Columbia DB 7210 Bits And Pieces/All Of The Time . . . 6
64 Columbia DB 7291 Can't You See That She's Mine/Because . . . 6
64 Columbia DB 7335 Thinking Of You Baby/Whenever You're Around . . . 6
64 Columbia DB 7377 Any Way You Want It/Crying Over You . . . 7
65 Columbia DB 7453 Everybody Knows/Say You Want Me . . . 8
65 Columbia DB 7503 Reelin' And Rockin'/Little Bitty Pretty One . . . 7
65 Columbia DB 7580 Come Home/Mighty Good Loving (some in p/s) . . . 18/7
65 Columbia DB 7625 Catch Us If You Can/Move On . . . 7
65 Columbia DB 7744 Over And Over/I'll Be Yours . . . 7
66 Columbia DB 7863 Try Too Hard/All Night Long . . . 10
66 Columbia DB 7909 Look Before You Leap/Please Tell Me Why . . . 10
66 Columbia DB 8028 Nineteen Days/I Need Love . . . 7
67 Columbia DB 8152 You Got What It Takes/Sitting Here Baby . . . 7
67 Columbia DB 8194 Tabatha Twitchit/Man In A Pin-Striped Suit (some in export p/s) . . . 18/6
67 Columbia DB 8286 Everybody Knows/Concentration Baby . . . 6
68 Columbia DB 8342 No One Can Break A Heart Like You/You Don't Want My Lovin' . . . 6
68 Columbia DB 8465 The Red Balloon/Maze Of Love . . . 6
68 Columbia DB 8505 Live In The Sky/Children . . . 6
69 Columbia DB 8545 The Mulberry Tree/Small Talk . . . 7
69 Columbia DB 8591 Get It On Now/Maze Of Life (unreleased, acetates exist)
69 Columbia DB 8624 Put A Little Love In Your Heart/34-06 . . . 6
69 Columbia DB 8638 Good Old Rock'N'Roll Medley (Parts 1 & 2) (some in p/s) . . . 10/6
70 Columbia DB 8660 Everybody Get Together/Darling I Love You . . . 6
70 Columbia DB 8681 Julia/Five By Five . . . 10
70 Columbia DB 8689 Here Comes Summer/Break Down And Cry . . . 6
70 Columbia DB 8724 Play More Good Old Rock'N'Roll Medley (Parts 1 & 2) (some in p/s) . . . 10/6
71 Columbia DB 8749 Southern Man/If You Wanna See Me Cry . . . 7
71 Columbia DB 8791 Won't You Be My Lady/Into Your Life . . . 7
72 Columbia DB 8963 All Time Greats Medley (Glad All Over/Do You Love Me/Bits & Pieces/ Glad All Over)/Wild Weekend (p/s) . . . 15
75 EMI EMI 2307 Here Comes Summer/Break Down & Cry (reissue) . . . 5
77 Polydor 2058 953 Everybody Knows/Always Me (some in p/s) . . . 12/6
64 Columbia SEG 8289 THE DAVE CLARK FIVE (EP) . . . 20
65 Columbia SEG 8381 THE HITS OF THE DAVE CLARK FIVE (EP) . . . 30
65 Columbia SEG 8447 WILD WEEKEND (EP) . . . 35
64 Columbia 33SX 1598 SESSION WITH THE DAVE CLARK FIVE (LP, blue/black label) . . . 30
64 Ember FA 2003 DAVE CLARK FIVE AND THE WASHINGTON D.C.'s (LP) . . . 40
65 EMI Regal REG 2017 IN SESSION (LP, export issue) . . . 45
65 Columbia SX 1756 CATCH US IF YOU CAN (LP, soundtrack, blue/black label) . . . 45
67 Columbia SX 6105 THE DAVE CLARK FIVE'S GREATEST HITS (LP, blue/black label) . . . 25
68 Columbia SX 6207 EVERYBODY KNOWS (LP, blue/black label) . . . 35
68 M. For Pleasure MFP 1260 A SESSION WITH THE DAVE CLARK FIVE (LP, reissue, different sleeve) . . . 12
69 Columbia SX 6309 5 BY 5 1964-69: 14 TITLES BY THE DAVE CLARK FIVE (LP, blue/black label) . . . 35
70 Columbia SCX 6437 IF SOMEBODY LOVES YOU (LP) . . . 30

(see also Dave Clark & Friends, Smith D'Abo, Mike Smith, Washington D.C.s)

DAVE CLARK & FRIENDS

71 Columbia DB 8834 Draggin' The Line/One Eyed, Blues Suited, Gun Totin' Man . . . 7
72 Columbia DB 8862 Think Of Me/Right Or Wrong . . . 10
72 Columbia DB 8907 Rub It In/I'm Sorry Baby . . . 6
73 EMI EMI 2013 Sweet City Woman/Love Comes But Once . . . 6
73 EMI EMI 2082 Sha-Na-Na/I Don't Know . . . 6
72 Columbia SCX 6494 DAVE CLARK AND FRIENDS (LP) . . . 22

(see also Dave Clark Five)

DEE CLARK

Year	Label/Cat. No.	Title	£
59	London HL 8802	Nobody But You/When I Call On You	30
59	London HL 8802	Nobody But You/When I Call On You (78)	15
59	London HL 8915	Just Keep It Up (And See What Happens)/ Whispering Grass(Don't Tell The Trees)	35
59	London HL 8915	Just Keep It Up (And See What Happens)/Whispering Grass (Don't Tell The Trees) (78)	15
59	Top Rank JAR 196	Hey, Little Girl/If It Wasn't For Love	30
59	Top Rank JAR 196	Hey, Little Girl/If It Wasn't For Love (78)	15
60	Top Rank JAR 284	How About That/Blues Get Off My Shoulder	18
60	Top Rank JAR 373	At My Front Door/Cling-A-Ling	22
60	Top Rank JAR 501	Gloria/You're Looking Good	15
61	Top Rank JAR 551	Your Friends/Because I Love You	12
61	Top Rank JAR 570	Raindrops/I Want To Love You	15
62	Columbia DB 4768	Don't Walk Away From Me/You're Telling Our Secrets	40
63	Stateside SS 180	I'm A Soldier Boy/Shook Up Over You	20
64	Stateside SS 355	Heartbreak/Warm Summer Breeze	15
65	Stateside SS 400	T.C.B./It's Impossible	15
70	Liberty LBF 15334	Where Did All The Good Times Go?/24 Hours Of Loneliness	10
60	Top Rank BUY 044	HOW ABOUT THAT! (LP)	30
70	Joy JOYS 130	YOU'RE LOOKING GOOD (LP)	15

DOTTY CLARK

Year	Label/Cat. No.	Title	£
61	London HLX 9418	It's Been A Long, Long Time/That's A Step In The Right Direction	10

GENE CLARK

Year	Label/Cat. No.	Title	£
67	CBS 202523	Echoes/I Found You	20
74	Asylum AYM 536	No Other/The True One	6
74	Asylum AYM 540	Life's Greatest Fool/From A Silver Phial	6
88	Bucketfull of Brains BOB 18	Gypsy Rider/SEERS: Flyaway (flexidisc with Bucketfull Of Brains magazine, issue 24)	7/5
92	Demon GENE 1	GENE CLARK AND CARLA OLSON SING 3 SONGS BY THE BYRDS (CD, picture disc, no inlay, promo only)	12
67	CBS 62934	GENE CLARK WITH THE GOSDIN BROTHERS (LP)	35
72	A&M AMLS 64297	WHITE LIGHT (LP)	22
74	Asylum SYL 9020	NO OTHER (LP)	18
77	RSO 2394 175	TWO SIDES TO EVERY STORY (LP)	12
84	Making Waves SPIN 122	FIREBYRD (LP)	12

(see also Byrds, Dillard & Clark)

GUY CLARK

Year	Label/Cat. No.	Title	£
75	RCA Victor APL1-130	OLD NO. 1 (LP)	15
76	RCA Victor RS 1097	TEXAS COOKIN' (LP)	15

JAMES CLARK(E) + SOUNDS

Year	Label/Cat. No.	Title	£
68	Fontana TF 918	"A Man Of Our Times" T.V. Series Theme/Spring Bossa	6
68	Fontana SFJL 966	A MAN OF OUR TIMES (LP)	25

JIMMY 'SOUL' CLARK

Year	Label/Cat. No.	Title	£
76	Black Magic BM 115	Sweet Darlin'/Sweet Darlin' (Instrumental)	6

MICHAEL CLARK

Year	Label/Cat. No.	Title	£
66	Liberty LIB 5893	None Of These Girls/Work Out	20

NOBBY CLARK

Year	Label/Cat. No.	Title	£
76	Epic S EPC 4381	Steady Love/Give Me The Heart	10

PAUL CLARK & FRIENDS

Year	Label/Cat. No.	Title	£
77	Myrrh MYR 1054	GOOD TO BE HOME (LP, with inner sleeve)	18
78	Myrrh MYR 1059	HAND TO THE PLOUGH (LP)	18

PETULA CLARK

78s

Year	Label/Cat. No.	Title	£
59	Pye Nixa N 15208	Where Do I Go From Here?/Mama's Talking Soft	10
59	Pye Nixa N 15220	Adonis/If I Had My Way	10
59	Pye Nixa N 15230	Dear Daddy/Through The Livelong Day	12
59	Pye N 15244	I Love A Violin/Guitare Et Tambourin	18

SINGLES

Year	Label/Cat. No.	Title	£
57	Pye Nixa 7N 15096	With All My Heart/Gonna Find Me A Bluebird	22
57	Pye Nixa 7N 15112	Alone/Long Before I Knew You	8
58	Pye Nixa 7N 15126	Baby Lover/The Little Blue Man	8
58	Pye Nixa 7N 15135	Love Me Again/In A Little Moment	10
58	Pye Nixa 7N 15152	St. Tropez (Sur La Plage)/Devotion	12
58	Pye Nixa 7N 15168	I Wish I Knew/Fibbin'	10
59	Pye Nixa 7N 15182	Ever Been In Love/Lucky Day	10
59	Pye Nixa 7N 15191	Watch Your Heart/Suddenly	10
59	Pye Nixa 7N 15208	Where Do I Go From Here?/Mama's Talking Soft	12
59	Pye Nixa 7N 15220	Adonis/If I Had My Way	12
59	Pye Nixa 7N 15230	Dear Daddy/Through The Livelong Day	15
59	Pye 7N 15244	I Love A Violin/Guitare Et Tambourin	15
60	Pye 7N 15281	Cinderella Jones/All Over Now	6
61	Pye 7N 15324	Sailor/My Heart	5
61	Pye 7N 15337	Something Missing/Isn't This A Lovely Day?	8
61	Pye 7N 15355	Welcome Home/Les Gens Diront	8
61	Pye 7N 15361	Romeo/You're Getting To Be A Habit With Me	5
61	Pye 7N 15389	My Friend The Sea/With All My Love	5
62	Pye 7N 15407	I'm Counting On You/Some Other World	6
62	Pye 7N 15437	Whistlin' For The Moon/Tender Love	6
62	Pye 7N 15448	Ya Ya Twist/Si C'est Oui, C'est Oui	5

62 Pye 7N 15456 Jumble Sale/Too Late. . . . 5
62 Pye 7N 15478 The Road/No Love, No Nothin' 6
63 Pye 7N 15495 I Will Follow Him/Darling Cheri 6
63 Pye 7N 15517 Valentino/Imagination 6
63 Pye 7N 15522 Chariot/Casanova. . . . 5
63 Pye 7N 15551 Let Me Tell You/Be Good To Me 6
63 Pye 7N 15573 Baby It's Me/This Is Goodbye 6
64 Pye 7N 15606 Thank You/Crying Through A Sleepless Night 8
64 Pye 7N 15639 In Love/Forgetting You (J'ai Tout Oublié) 6
64 Pye 7N 15668 True Love Never Runs Smooth/Saturday Sunshine 6
65 Pye 7N 15722 Downtown/You'd Better Love Me. . . . 5
65 Pye 7N 15772 I Know A Place/Jack And John 5
65 Pye 7N 15864 You'd Better Come Home/My Heart. . . . 5
65 Pye 7N 15945 Round Every Corner/Two Rivers. . . . 5
65 Pye 7N 15991 You're The One/Gotta Tell The World (some in export p/s). . . . 15/5
66 Pye 7N 17038 My Love/Where I'm Going 5
66 Pye 7N 17071 A Sign Of The Times/Time For Love 6
66 Pye 7N 17133 I Wouldn't Live Without Your Love/Your Way Of Life. . . . 5
66 Pye 7N 17187 Who Am I/Love Is A Long Journey 6
66 Pye 7N 17218 Colour My World/I'm Begging You. . . . 6
67 Pye 7N 17258 This Is My Song/The Show Is Ours. . . . 5
67 Pye 7N 17325 Don't Sleep In The Subway/Here Comes The Morning 5
67 Pye 7N 17377 The Cat In The Window/Fancy Dancin' Man 6
67 Pye 7N 17416 The Other Man's Grass/At The Crossroads. . . . 5
68 Pye 7N 17466 Kiss Me Goodbye/I've Got Love Going For Me. . . . 5
68 Pye 7N 17580 Don't Give Up/Everytime I See A Rainbow 5
68 Pye 7N 17646 I Want To Sing With Your Band/Look To The Sky. . . . 5
69 Pye 7N 17733 Happy Heart/Love Is The Only Thing. . . . 5
69 Pye 7N 17779 Look At Mine/You And I. . . . 5
69 Pye 7N 17840 No One Better Than You/Things Bright And Beautiful 5
70 Pye 7N 17973 Melody Man/Big Love Sale 5
71 Pye 7N 45026 The Song Of My Life/For Love. . . . 5
71 Pye 7N 45091 The World Song/I Know What Love Is About 5
71 Pye 7N 45112 I Don't Know How To Love Him/Song Went Wrong. . . . 5
72 Polydor 2058 295 Wedding Song (There Is Love)/Song Without End 6
73 Polydor 2058 413 Lead Me On/Taking It On (both with Sacha Distel) 12
74 Polydor 2058 519 Let's Sing A Love Song/I'm The Woman You Need 8
75 Polydor 2058 560 I Am Your Song/Super Loving Lady. . . . 12
75 Pye 7N 45473 Wind Of Change (edit)/Memories Are Made Of This. . . . 6
75 Pye 7N 45506 What I Did For Love/I Believe In Love 6
76 Pye 7N 45650 Downtown (Disco Version)/Two Rivers 8
78 Lyntone Put A Little Sunbeam In Your Life (flexidisc for Sunbeam cars). . . . 6

EPs

56 Pye Nixa NEP 24006 CHILDREN'S CHOICE 20
56 Pye Nixa NEP 24016 PETULA CLARK HIT PARADE. . . . 25
57 Pye Nixa NEP 24056 PETULA CLARK HIT PARADE NO. 2 15
57 Pye Nixa NEP 24060 YOU ARE MY LUCKY STAR PART 1 22
57 Pye Nixa NEP 24061 YOU ARE MY LUCKY STAR PART 2 22
57 Pye Nixa NEP 24062 YOU ARE MY LUCKY STAR PART 3 22
58 Pye Nixa NEP 24080 PETULA CLARK HIT PARADE NO. 3 18
58 Pye Nixa NEP 24089 PETULA CLARK SINGS IN FRENCH 15
58 Pye Nixa NEP 24094 A CHRISTMAS CAROL (also stereo NSEP 85001) 15/30
59 Pye NEP 24121 ENCORE. . . . 15
61 Pye NEP 24137 PETULA CLARK HIT PARADE 4 18
61 Pye NEP 24150 PETULA CLARK HIT PARADE 5 18
61 Pye NEP 24163 PETULA CLARK'S HITS. . . . 10
62 Pye NEP 24157 PET-OOH-LA-LA. . . . 15
63 Pye NEP 24182 EN FRANÇAIS 12
64 Pye NEP 24189 ENCORE EN FRANÇAIS. . . . 12
64 Pye NEP 24194 PETULA SINGS 'HELLO DOLLY!' IN FRENCH 10
65 Pye NEP 24206 DOWNTOWN. . . . 10
65 Pye-Vogue VRE 5004 LES DISQUES D'OR DE LA CHANSON 18
65 Pye-Vogue VRE 5007 PETULA CLARK CHANTE EN ITALIEN 22
65 Pye NEP 24233 YOU'RE THE ONE (existence unconfirmed) . . . . 30+
66 Pye NEP 24237 CALL ME 15
66 Pye NEP 24246 MY LOVE 12
66 Pye NEP 24259 JUST SAY GOODBYE. . . . 15
66 Pye NEP 24266 I COULDN'T LIVE WITHOUT YOUR LOVE 15
67 Pye NEP 24279 THIS IS MY SONG 12
66 Pye-Vogue VRE 5019 L'AGENT SECRET 18
66 Pye-Vogue VRE 5023 HELLO MISTER BROWN 18
67 Pye-Vogue VRE 5025 C'EST MA CHANSON. . . . 18
67 Pye NEP 24280 THE MANY FACES OF PETULA CLARK 15
67 Pye NEP 24286 Here, There And Everywhere 15
68 Pye-Vogue VRE 5026 L'Amour Viendra. . . . 15
68 Pye-Vogue VRE 5028 Dis-Moi Au Revoir 15
68 Pye NEP 24301 Don't Give Up. . . . 15

LPs

56 Pye Nixa NPT 19002 PETULA CLARK SINGS (10"). . . . 80
56 Pye Nixa NPT 19014 A DATE WITH PET (10") 60
57 Pye Nixa NPL 18007 YOU ARE MY LUCKY STAR. . . . 50
59 Pye Nixa NPL 18039 PETULA CLARK IN HOLLYWOOD 45
62 Pye NPL 18070 IN OTHER WORDS — PETULA CLARK 35
63 Pye NPL 18098 PETULA 20
64 Pye-Vogue VRL 3001 LES JAMES DEAN 30

MINT VALUE £

65 Pye NPL 18114 DOWNTOWN 12
65 Pye NPL 18123 SINGS THE INTERNATIONAL HITS 12
65 Pye-Vogue VRL 3010 PETULA '65 (in French) 25
66 Pye-Vogue VRL 3016 HELLO PARIS VOL. 1 25
66 Pye-Vogue VRL 3019 HELLO PARIS VOL. 2 25
66 Pye-Vogue VRL 3022 PETULA '66 18
67 Pye N(S)PL 18171 COLOUR MY WORLD (original track listing, with "England Swings" & "Reach Out I'll Be There") 15
67 Pye N(S)PL 18171 COLOUR MY WORLD (revised track listing, with "This Is My Song" & "The Show Is Over") 12
67 Pye-Vogue VRL 3030 C'EST MA CHANSON 15
68 Warner Bros WF(S) 2550 FINIAN'S RAINBOW (soundtrack) 25
68 Pye-Vogue VRLS 3035 PETULA CLARK A PARIS 20

ROY CLARK

59 HMV POP 581 Please Mr. Mayor/Puddin' 100
59 HMV POP 581 Please Mr. Mayor/Puddin' (78) 40
63 Capitol CL 15288 In The Mood/Texas Twist 15
63 Capitol CL 15317 Tips Of My Fingers/Spooky Movies 10
69 Dot DOT 126 Yesterday When I Was Wrong/Just Another Man 6
69 Dot DOT 131 September Song/For All The Life Of Me 6
62 Capitol (S)T 1780 THE LIGHTNING FINGERS OF ROY CLARK (LP) 30

SANFORD CLARK

56 London HLD 8320 The Fool/Lonesome For A Letter (with Al Casey) (gold label print, later silver) 200/85
56 London HL 7014 The Fool/Lonesome For A Letter (with Al Casey) (export issue) 50
56 London HLD 8320 The Fool/Lonesome For A Letter (78) 18
59 London HLW 8959 Run, Boy Run/New Kind Of Fool (triangular or round centre) 35/20
59 London HLW 8959 Run, Boy Run/New Kind Of Fool (78) 65
60 London HLW 9026 Son-Of-A-Gun/I Can't Help It (If I'm Still In Love With You) 20
60 London HLW 9095 Go On Home/Pledging My Love 20
68 Ember EMB S 250 Shades/Once Upon A Time 8
57 London RED 1105 PRESENTING SANFORD CLARK (EP) 75
60 London REW 1256 LOWDOWN BLUES (EP) 75
72 Ember CW 131 THEY CALL ME COUNTRY (LP) 15
(see also Al Casey)

TERRY CLARK

60s Myrrh MYR 1071 WELCOME (LP) 15

ALLAN CLARKE

72 RCA RCA 2244 You're Losing Me/A Coward By Name 10
73 EMI EMI 2024 Who/I Look In Your Eyes 6
74 EMI EMI 2133 Sideshow/Don't Let Me Down Again 6
75 EMI EMI 2352 Born To Run/Why Don't You Call 6
76 EMI EMI 2491 Living In Love/People Of That Kind 6
78 Polydor 2058 979 I Don't Know When I'm Beat/The Passenger 8
78 Polydor 2059 025 I'm Betting My Life On You/I Wasn't Born Yesterday 5
82 Forever FORE 3 Someone Else Will/Castles In The Wind 10
72 RCA SF 8283 MY REAL NAME IS 'AROLD (LP) 15
73 EMI EMA 752 HEADROOM (LP) 15
74 EMI EMC 3041 ALLAN CLARKE (LP) 15
76 EMI EMC 3130 I'VE GOT TIME (LP) 15
(see also Hollies)

ANNETTE CLARKE

73 Techniques TE 925 Just One Look/Sinner Man 6

DAVE CLARKE

94 Bush 1012 Red 1 (of 3) (Protective Custody)/Zeno Xero (12", p/s, red vinyl) 12
94 Bush 1015 Red 2 (of 3) (Wisdom To The Wise)/Gonk (12", p/s, red vinyl) 10

JOHN COOPER CLARKE

79 Epic S EPC 12 7009 ¡Gimmix!/I Married A Monster From Outer Space (Third Version) (p/s, triangular disc, orange vinyl) 5
79 Epic S EPC 7982 Splat/Twat/Sleepwalk (double-grooved A-side, p/s, with Epic inner sleeve) 5
78 Rabid TOSH 103 INNOCENTS (EP, orange p/s, green labels) 5
78 Rabid TOSH 103 INNOCENTS (EP, 2nd pressing, blue foldout p/s, blue labels) 5
78 CBS 83132 DISGUISE IN LOVE (LP) 18
80 Epic EPC 84083 SNAP, CRACKLE [&] BOP (LP, with 48-page book in sleeve pocket) 15

JOHNNY CLARKE

74 Explosion EX 2089 None Shall Escape The Judgement/Every Rasta Is A Star 6
74 Pyramid PYR 7013 My Desire/Lemon Tree 6
75 Attack ATLP 1015 ENTER INTO HIS GATES WITH PRAISE (LP) 12
75 Vulcan VULP 001 PUT IT ON (LP) 12

KENNY CLARKE (with Francy Boland Big Band)

57 Columbia SEG 7830 KENNY CLARKE QT. (EP) 25
63 London HA-K 8085 JAZZ IS UNIVERSAL (LP, with Francy Boland Big Band) 10

LINDA CLARKE

67 Decca F 12709 Your Hurtin' Kinda Love/Send Me The Pillow You Dream On 6
68 Decca F 12787 Society's Child/Rain In My Heart 15

LLOYD CLARKE

62 Blue Beat BB 99 Good Morning/Now I Know A Reason (with Smithie's Sextet) 20
62 Blue Beat BB 104 Fool's Day/You're A Cheat (with Reco's All Stars) 20
62 Island WI 007 Love You The Most/LLOYD ROBINSON: You Said You Loved Me 22
62 Island WI 045 Japanese Girl/He's Coming 22
63 Rio R 16 Love Me/Half As Much 15

			MINT VALUE £
64	Rio R 23	Stop Your Talking/A Penny	15
64	Rio R 24	Fellow Jamaican/PATRICK & GEORGE: My Love	15
68	Island WI 3116	Summertime/VAL BENNETT: Soul Survivor	20
68	Blue Cat BS 136	Young Love/UNTOUCHABLES: Wall Flower	18
70	Escort ERT 849	Chicken Thief/STRANGER COLE: Tomorrow	7
71	Black Swan BW 1405	Love You The Most/LOW BITES:Version	18

(see also Derrick & Lloyd, Theo Beckford, Soulettes, Delroy Wilson, Laurel Aitken, Sonny Burke, Uniques)

TONY CLARKE

64	Pye International 7N 25251	Ain't Love Good, Ain't Love Proud/Coming Back Strong	18
65	Chess CRS 8011	The Entertainer/This Heart Of Mine	20
69	Chess CRS 8091	The Entertainer/Ain't Love Good, Ain't Love Proud	15
74	Chess 6145 030	Landslide/The Entertainer	5

CLARK-HUTCHINSON

70	Decca Nova (S)DN-R 2	A = MH²(LP)	35
70	Deram SML 1076	RETRIBUTION (LP)	35
71	Deram SML 1090	GESTALT (LP)	35

(see also Sam Gopal, Vamp, Upp)

CLARK SISTERS

59	London HLD 8791	Chicago/Opus 1	10
59	London HLD 8791	Chicago/Opus 1 (78)	12
58	London RE-D 1198	SING, SING, SING (EP)	15
58	London HA-D 2128	SING, SING, SING (LP)	22
59	London HA-D 2177	THE CLARK SISTERS SWING AGAIN (LP, also stereo SAH-D 6025)	20/25

CLASH

77	CBS S CBS 5058	White Riot/1977 (p/s, 'The Clash' or 'The CLASH' on label)	10
77	CBS CL 1	CAPITAL RADIO (EP, *NME* freebie, p/s)	40
77	CBS S CBS 5293	Remote Control/London's Burning (live) (p/s)	10
77	CBS S CBS 5664	Complete Control/The City Of The Dead (p/s)	8
78	CBS S CBS 6383	(White Man) In Hammersmith Palais/The Prisoner (initially green, then pink, blue or yellow die-cut sleeve)	7
79	CBS S CBS 7324	THE COST OF LIVING (EP, gatefold p/s & inner sleeve)	10
79	CBS S CBS 8087	London Calling/Armagideon Time (p/s, green or red shaded sleeve, white or yellow/orange label)	6
(All the early Clash singles were re-pressed in 1979 with picture sleeves.)			
81	CBS A12 1133	The Magnificent Seven/The Magnificent Dance (12", p/s with sticker sheet)	8
81	CBS S 2309	Know Your Rights/First Night Back In London (p/s, with free sticker)	8
82	CBS A 2479	Rock The Casbah/Long Time Jerk (p/s, with free stickers)	8
82	CBS A 11 2479	Rock The Casbah/Long Time Jerk (picture disc)	10
82	CBS A 2646	Should I Stay Or Should I Go/Straight To Hell (p/s, with free sticker)	8
82	CBS A 11 2646	Should I Stay Or Should I Go/Straight To Hell (picture disc)	7
82	CBS A 12 2646	Should I Stay Or Should I Go/Straight To Hell (12", p/s with stencil)	8
88	CBS CLASHB 2	London Calling/Brand New Cadillac/Rudie Don't Fail (box set)	7
91	Columbia 656 667-5	Should I Stay Or Should I Go/London Calling/ Train In Vain/I Fought The Law (CD in tin)	10
91	Columbia 656 814-5	Rock The Casbah/Tommy Gun/(White Man) In Hammersmith Palais/ Straight To Hell (CD in tin)	10
91	Columbia 656 946-5	London Calling/Clampdown/The Call Up/London's Burning (CD in tin)	8
78	CBS 82431	GIVE 'EM ENOUGH ROPE (LP, promo-only package with poster in folder)	75

(see also 101'ers, Big Audio Dynamite, Janie Jones & Lash, Tymon Dogg, Ellen Foley, Futura 2000)

CLASSICS (Jamaica)

69	Doctor Bird DB 1190	Worried Over Me/LAUREL AITKEN: Rice And Peas	18
70	New Beat NB 061	Same Old Feeling/So Much Love	10
70	New Beat NB 071	History Of Africa/Honeybee	7
70	Pama PM 830	Sex Education/POWER: Soul Flash	7
71	Punch PH 79	Cheerio Baby/Civilization	7

CLASSICS (U.S.)

61	Mercury AMT 1152	Life Is But A Dream/That's The Way	100
63	Stateside SS 215	Till Then/Enie Minie Mo	30
66	Capitol CL 15470	Pollyanna/Cry Baby	20

CLASSICS IV

68	Liberty LBF 15051	Spooky/Poor People	8
69	Liberty LBF 15177	Stormy/Twenty Four Hours Of Loneliness	10
69	Liberty LBF 15196	Traces/Mary, Mary Row Your Boat	6
69	Liberty LBF 15231	Everyday With You Girl/Sentimental Lady	6

(see also Dennis Yost & Classics IV)

CLASSMATES

63	Decca F 11736	Let's Get Together Tonight/It's No Game	7
63	Decca F 11779	Go Tell It On The Mountain/Give Me A Girl	7
64	Decca F 11806	In Morocco/I Feel	7
64	Decca F 12047	Go Away/Pay Day	12

CLAUDETTE (& CORPORATION)

69	Jackpot JP 712	Let's Fall In Love/PROPHETS: Purple Moon	10
70	Grape GR 3020	Skinheads A Bash Them (with Corporation)/ CORPORATION: Walkin' Thru Jerusalem	100

(see also Corporation)

CASSIUS CLAY

64	CBS AAG 190	Stand By Me/I Am The Greatest	25
66	CBS 202190	Stand By Me/I Am The Greatest (reissue)	10
63	CBS BPG 62274	I AM THE GREATEST! (LP)	45

JUDY CLAY

67	Stax 601 022	You Can't Run Away From Your Heart/It Takes A Lotta Good Love	10

(see also Billy Vera & Judy Clay, Booker T. & M.G.'s)

MINT VALUE £

JUDY CLAY & WILLIAM BELL

68 Stax STAX 101 Private Number/Love, Aye 'Tis. 10
69 Stax STAX 115 My Baby Specialises/Left Over Love. 7
(see also William Bell, Billy Vera & Judy Clay)

OTIS CLAY

67 President PT 121 It's Easier Said Than Done/Flame In Your Heart 6
68 President PT 132 I'm Satisfied/I Testify 6
68 President PT 148 That's How It Is/Show Place. 12
68 President PT 176 A Lasting Love/Got To Find A Way 6
69 Atlantic 584 282 Baby Jane/You Hurt Me For The Last Time 65
72 London HLU 10397 Trying To Live My Life Without You/Let Me Be The One 6
74 London HLU 10467 You Did Something To Me/It Was Jealousy 6
73 London SH-U 8446 TRYING TO LIVE MY LIFE WITHOUT YOU (LP) 22

TOM CLAY

72 Tamla Motown TMG 801 What The World Needs Now/The Victors 5

CLAY FAV

79 own label CONSIGNMENT STOCK (EP, no p/s) 40

ALASDAIR CLAYRE

67 Elektra EUK 255 ALASDAIR CLAYRE (LP) 55
76 Acorn CF 252 ADAM AND THE BEASTS (LP). 25

ADAM CLAYTON & LARRY MULLEN

96 Mother MUM 75 Theme From Mission: Impossible/Theme From Mission: Impossible (Junior's Hard Mix Edit) (jukebox issue, no p/s, promo only). 8
96 Mother 12MUMDJ 75-1 THEME FROM MISSION: IMPOSSIBLE — REMIXES BY JUNIOR VASQUEZ (12", brown die-cut sleeve with title sticker, promo only). 15
96 Mother 12MUMDJ 75-2 THEME FROM MISSION: IMPOSSIBLE — REMIXES BY GOLDIE & ROB PLAYFORD (12", grey die-cut sleeve with title sticker, promo only) 15
96 Mother MUMCD 75DJ Theme From Mission: Impossible/(Junior's Hard Mix Edit)/ (Junior's Hard Mix)/Mission Accomplished — Cut The Red Not The Blue/ (Dave Clarke's Remix)/(Guru Mix) (CD, digipak, promo only). 20
(see also U2)

BUCK CLAYTON

57 Pye/Vanguard PPT 12006 BUCK MEETS RUBY (10" LP, with Ruby Braff). 12
60 Philips BBL 7317 SONGS FOR SWINGERS (LP) 12
66 77 LEU 12/11 LE VRAI BUCK CLAYTON VOLUME 1 (LP, with Humphrey Lyttelton's Band). 12
66 77 LEU 12/18 LE VRAI BUCK CLAYTON VOLUME 2 (LP, with Humphrey Lyttlelon's Band). 12
68 CBS Realm RM 52078 A BUCK CLAYTON JAM SESSION (LP). 12
(see also Humphrey Lyttelton, Jimmy Rushing)

DOCTOR CLAYTON

65 RCA Victor RCX 7177 RCA RACE SERIES VOLUME 6 (EP) 20
70 RCA Intl. INTS 1176 PEARL HARBOUR BLUES (LP). 20

MERRY CLAYTON

70 A&M AMS 802 Gimme Shelter/Good Girls. 6
73 Ode ODS 66301 Acid Queen/Underture (p/s). 15
70 A&M AMLS 995 GIMME SHELTER (LP) 15
72 A&M AMLS 67012 MERRY CLAYTON (LP). 15
(see also Raelets)

PAUL CLAYTON

61 London HLU 9285 Wings Of A Dove/So Long (It's Been Good To Know You) 15
61 London REU 1276 PAUL CLAYTON (EP) 120

STEVE CLAYTON

56 Vogue Coral Q 72200 Two Different Worlds/It Happened Again. 8
57 Vogue Coral Q 72253 The Boy With The Golden Kazoo/I Wanna Put My Arms Around You. 8
60 London HLU 9033 Let's Tell Them Now/They Say In Time. 8

VIKKI CLAYTON

88 Dambuster DAM 021 LOST LADY FOUND (LP) 20
(see also Fairport Convention)

CLAYTON SQUARES

65 Decca F 12250 Come And Get It/And Tears Fell 40
66 Decca F 12456 There She Is/Imagination. 150
(see also Liverpool Scene, Andy Roberts, Mike Hart)

DAVID CLAYTON-THOMAS

72 CBS 64755 DAVID CLAYTON-THOMAS (LP, plain orange label) 15
72 CBS 65237 TEQUILA SUNRISE (LP, plain orange label) 15
73 RCA SF 8381 DAVID CLAYTON-THOMAS (LP, gatefold sleeve). 15
(see also Blood Sweat & Tears)

CLEAR BLUE SKY

70 Vertigo 6360 013 CLEAR BLUE SKY (LP, gatefold sleeve, swirl label). 90
90 Saturn SRLP 101 DESTINY (LP). 12

CLEAR LIGHT

67 Elektra EKSN 45019 Black Roses/She's Ready To Be Free 12
68 Elektra EKSN 45027 Night Sounds Loud/How Many Days Have Passed. 8
67 Elektra EKL 4011 CLEAR LIGHT (LP, orange label, also stereo EKS 74011) 40

CLEARLIGHT

75 Virgin V 2029 SYMPHONY (LP, stickered sleeve). 15
75 Virgin V 2039 FOREVER BLOWING BUBBLES (LP) 15
(see also Gong, Steve Hillage)

CLEAR SPOT
98 Duophonic Super 45s — Psycho's Blues/Moonman Bop (33rpm, 300 copies on blue vinyl, 1700 on black, p/s) . . . 8/6
(see also Stereolab)

CLEARWAYS
64 Columbia DB 7333 — I'll Be Here/I've Just Got A Letter . . . 7

JOHN CLEESE (& 1948 CHOIR)
67 Pye 7N 17336 — The Ferret Song — From 'At Last The 1948 Show'/The Rhubarb Tart Song . . . 10
67 Parlophone PMC 7024 — I'M SORRY I'LL READ THAT AGAIN (LP) . . . 20
(see also Monty Python)

CLEFS
62 Salvo SLO 1810 — Don't Cry/The Dream Train Special (99 copies only) . . . 20

CLEFTONES
56 Columbia DB 3801 — You Baby, You/Little Girl Of Mine . . . 550
56 Columbia DB 3801 — You Baby, You/Little Girl Of Mine (78) . . . 50
61 Columbia DB 4678 — Heart And Soul/How Do You Feel . . . 165
61 Columbia DB 4720 — (I Love You) For Sentimental Reasons/Deed I Do . . . 110
63 Columbia DB 4988 — Lover Come Back To Me/There She Goes . . . 60

PAT CLEMENCE
64 HMV POP 1360 — While I Live/Since I Don't Have You . . . 6

JACK CLEMENT
58 London HLS 8691 — Ten Years/Your Lover Boy . . . 85
58 London HLS 8691 — Ten Years/Your Lover Boy (78) . . . 50

SOUL JOE CLEMENTS
69 Plexium PXM 10 — Smoke And Ashes/Ever, Ever . . . 120

CLEO
64 Decca F 11817 — To Know Him Is To Love Him/ANDREW OLDHAM ORCHESTRA: There Are But Five Rolling Stones . . . 35
(see also Andrew Oldham Orchestra, This 'N' That)

CLERKS
80 Rok ROK VIII/VII — No Good For Me/HAZARD: Gotta Change My Life (company sleeve) . . . 6
84 Puddisc SRT8 KS 1538 — Dancing With My Girl/On The Telephone/All I Want Is You (p/s) . . . 5

CLEVELANDS
64 Philips BF 1315 — Big Town/Lonely, Weary And Blue . . . 7
64 Philips BF 1342 — Little Girl In Calico/Everything Is Fine . . . 7

CLIENTELLE
79 Quest BRS 003 — Can't Forget (p/s) . . . 125
81 Banana BANANA 505 — DESTINATION UNKNOWN (LP) . . . 120

JIMMY CLIFF
62 Blue Beat BB 78 — I'm Sorry (with Cavaliers Combo)/BLUE BEATS: Roarin' (with Red Price) . . . 25
62 Island WI 012 — Hurricane Hatty/Dearest Beverley . . . 25
62 Island WI 016 — Miss Jamaica/Gold Digger . . . 22
62 Island WI 025 — Since Lately/I'm Free . . . 25
63 Island WI 062 — My Lucky Day/One-Eyed Jacks . . . 22
63 Island WI 070 — King Of Kings/SIR PERCY: Oh Yeah . . . 22
63 Island WI 112 — Miss Universe/The Prodigal . . . 22
63 Black Swan WI 403 — The Man/You Are Never Too Old . . . 25
64 Stateside SS 342 — One Eyed Jacks/King Of Kings . . . 18
66 Fontana TF 641 — Call On Me/Pride And Passion . . . 15
67 Island WIP 6004 — Aim And Ambition/Give And Take . . . 10
67 Island WIP 6011 — I Got A Feeling/Hard Road To Travel . . . 10
67 Island WIP 6024 — That's The Way Life Goes/Thank You . . . 10
68 Island WIP 6039 — Waterfall/Reward . . . 18
69 Trojan TR 690 — Wonderful World, Beautiful People/Hard Road To Travel (some in p/s) . . . 8/7
70 Trojan TR 7722 — Vietnam/She Does It Right . . . 7
70 Trojan TR 7745 — Suffering/Come Into My Life . . . 7
70 Trojan TR 7745 — Those Good Good Old Days/Pack Up Hang Ups . . . 7
70 Trojan TR 7767 — You Can Get It If You Really Want/Be Aware . . . 7
70 Island WIP 6087 — Wild World/Be Aware . . . 6
70 Island WIP 6097 — Synthetic World/I Go To Pieces . . . 6
71 Island WIP 6103 — Goodbye Yesterday/Breakdown . . . 6
71 Island WIP 6100 — Sitting In Limbo/The Bigger They Come . . . 6
72 Island WIP 6132 — Trapped/Struggling Man . . . 6
68 Island ILP 962 — HARD ROAD TO TRAVEL (LP) . . . 60
69 Trojan TRLS 16 — JIMMY CLIFF (LP) . . . 20
71 Island ILPS 9159 — ANOTHER CYCLE (LP) . . . 15
(see also Jackie Edwards & Jimmy Cliff, James Chambers)

CLIFF & HANK
(see under Cliff Richard)

BUZZ CLIFFORD
61 Fontana H 297 — Baby Sittin' Boogie/Driftwood (blue or black label) . . . 10/8
61 Fontana H 312 — Three Little Fishes/Simply Because . . . 7
62 Columbia DB 4903 — More Dead Than Alive/Nobody Loves Me Like You . . . 10
61 Fontana TFL 5147 — BABY SITTIN' WITH BUZZ CLIFFORD (LP, also stereo [STFL 567]) . . . 80/110

JOHN & JULIA CLIFFORD
77 Topic 12TS 311 — THE HUMOURS OF LISHEEN (LP) . . . 22

MINT VALUE £

LINDA CLIFFORD

74	Paramount PARA 3051	After Loving You/Check Out Your Heart	6
78	Curtom K 17163	If My Friends Could See Me Now/Runaway Love	6
78	Curtom K 17163T	If My Friends Could See Me Now/Runaway Love (12")	8
79	RSO RSO 37	Don't Give It Up/Don't Let Me Have Another Bad Dream (12")	8

CLIFFTERS

62	Philips PB 1242	Django/Amapola (Pretty Little Poppy)	12

BILL CLIFTON

60	Melodisc 1554	You Don't Think About Me/Mail Carrier's Warning	8
63	Decca F 11793	Beatle Crazy/Little Girl Dressed In Blue	10
58	Mercury MEP 9546	BILL CLIFTON AND THE DIXIE MOUNTAIN BOYS (EP)	18
62	London HA-B 8004	CARTER FAMILY MEMORIAL ALBUM (LP)	18
62	London HA-B 8020	THE BLUEGRASS SOUND OF BILL CLIFTON (LP)	18
63	London HA-B 8070	SOLDIER SING ME A SONG (LP)	18
64	London HA-B 8193	CODE OF THE MOUNTAINS (LP)	18
67	London HA-U 8325	MOUNTAIN RAMBLINGS (LP)	18

BILL CLIFTON & JIM EANES

60s	Melodisc EPM 7102	BLUE RIVER HOEDOWN (EP)	18

CLIMAX (CHICAGO) BLUES BAND

69	Parlophone R 5809	Like Uncle Charlie/Loving Machine	20
70	Harvest HAR 5029	Reap What I've Sowed/Spoonful	7
71	Harvest HAR 5041	Towards The Sun/Everyday (as Climax Chicago)	7
72	Harvest HAR 5065	Mole On The Dole/Like Uncle Charlie (as Climax Chicago)	6
73	Harvest HAR 5067	Shake Your Love/You Make Me Sick	6
69	Parlophone PMC/PCS 7069	CLIMAX CHICAGO BLUES BAND (LP, yellow/black label)	50
70	Parlophone PCS 7084	PLAYS ON (LP)	40
70	Harvest SHSP 4009	A LOT OF BOTTLE (LP)	25
71	Harvest SHSP 4015	TIGHTLY KNIT (LP)	18
72	Harvest SHSP 4024	RICH MAN (LP)	18

PATSY CLINE

57	Brunswick 05660	A Poor Man's Roses (Or A Rich Man's Gold)/Walkin' After Midnight	90
57	Brunswick 05660	A Poor Man's Roses (Or A Rich Man's Gold)/Walkin' After Midnight (78)	35
61	Brunswick 05855	I Fall To Pieces/Lovin' In Vain	15
61	Brunswick 05861	Crazy/Who Can I Count On	25
62	Brunswick 05866	She's Got You/Strange	10
62	Brunswick 05869	When I Get Through With You/Imagine That	10
62	Brunswick 05874	So Wrong/You're Stronger Than Me	10
62	Brunswick 05878	Heartaches/Why Can't He Be You	8
63	Brunswick 05883	Leavin' On Your Mind/Tra Le La Le La Triangle	12
63	Brunswick 05888	Sweet Dreams/Back In My Baby's Arms	15
63	Decca 31262	Blue Moon Of Kentucky/Faded Love (export)	50
62	Brunswick OE 9490	SWEET DREAMS (EP)	35
62	Brunswick LAT 8394	SHOWCASE (LP)	35
62	Brunswick LAT/STA 8510	SENTIMENTALLY YOURS (LP, mono/stereo)	25/35
63	Brunswick LAT 8549	A TRIBUTE TO PATSY CLINE (LP)	35
64	Brunswick LAT/STA 8589	A PORTRAIT OF PATSY CLINE (LP, mono/stereo)	30/35
65	Ember CW 16	IN MEMORIAM (LP)	15
65	Fontana FJL 302	TODAY TOMORROW AND FOREVER (LP)	20
66	Fontana FJL 309	I CAN'T FORGET YOU (LP)	20
68	Ember CW 134	WALKING AFTER MIDNIGHT (LP)	12
68	MCA MUP 316	THE SOUND OF PATSY CLINE (LP)	15
68	MCA MUP(S) 326	HEARTACHES (LP)	15
69	MCA MUP(S) 350	ALWAYS (LP)	12
70	MCA MUPS 378	THAT'S HOW A HEARTACHE BEGINS (LP)	12

CLINIC

97	Aladdin's Cave Of Golf GOLF001	IPC Subeditors Dictate Our Youth/Porno/D.I.Y. (p/s, 500 copies only)	20
98	Aladdin's C.O.G. GOLF002	Monkey On Your Back/D.T. (p/s, 500 copies only)	6
98	Aladdin's C.O.G. GOLF003	Cement Mixer/Kimberley (p/s, 1,000 copies only)	5

BUDDY CLINTON

60	Top Rank JAR 287	Across The Street From Your House/How My Prayers Have Changed	15

GEORGE CLINTON

79	ABC ABC 4053	Please Don't Run From Me/Life And Breath	6

(do not see also Parliament, Funkadelic)

LARRY CLINTON

79	Grapevine GRP 120	She's Wanted In Three States/If I Knew	8

CLINTONES

73	Ackee ACK 515	Equal Rights/Version	6

CLIQUE (U.K.)

65	Pye 7N 15786	She Ain't No Good/Time Time Time	90
65	Pye 7N 15853	We Didn't Kiss, Didn't Love, But Now We Do/You've Been Unfair	140
60s	private pressing	THE CLIQUE (EP, no p/s)	550+

(see also Hammersmith Gorillas)

CLIQUE

93	Detour DR 006	THE EARLY DAYS EP (EP, purple, orange or blue p/s, 130 on green vinyl; rest on black, white or yellow vinyl	6/5
94	Detour DR 014	Reggie/She Doesn't Need You Anymore (p/s, red vinyl)	5
94	Detour DR 014	Reggie/She Doesn't Need You Anymore (pic disc, 200 only)	7

CLIQUE (U.S.)

69	London HLU 10286	Sugar On Sunday/Superman	30

JIMMY CLITHEROE
65 Parlophone R 5387 They All Blame Jim/Jim Plays Hookies . . . 7

CLIVE & GLORIA
63 R&B JB 113 Change Of Plan/Little Gloria . . . 15
64 R&B JB 173 Money Money Money/Have I Told You Lately . . . 15
64 King KG 1004 Do The Ska/You Made Me Cry . . . 20

CLIVE & NAOMI
65 Ska Beat JB 181 You Are Mine/Open The Door . . . 25
(see also Desmond Dekker)

CLOCK DVA
81 Fetish FET 008 Four Hours (Re-mixed)/Sensorium (p/s) . . . 8
85 Fetish FET 008 FOUR HOURS EP (12", p/s) . . . 8
80 private cassette DEEP FLOOR (cassette) . . . 12
80 private cassette FRAGMENT DVATION (cassette) . . . 12
81 Fetish FR 2002 THIRST (LP, with insert) . . . 12
81 Industrial IRC 31 WHITE SOULS IN BLACK SUITS (cassette, with booklet) . . . 15

CLOCKHOUSE
83 Picturesque PIC 1 Vanishing Point/Everyman (p/s) . . . 7

CLOCKWORK CRIMINALS
82 Ace ACE 38 YOUNG AND BOLD (EP) . . . 12

CLOCKWORK ORANGES
66 Ember EMB S 227 Ready Steady/After Tonight . . . 20

CLOCKWORK SOLDIERS
84 Rot ASS 5 Wet Dreams/Suicide/In The Name Of Science (p/s) . . . 5

BETTY CLOONEY
55 HMV 7M 311 I Love You A Mountain/Can't Do Without You . . . 15
(see also Rosemary Clooney)

ROSEMARY CLOONEY
51 Columbia DB 2892 Alice In Wonderland Medley (Parts 1 & 2) (78) . . . 10
53 Columbia SCM 5019 Half As Much/Botch-A-Me (Ba-Ba-Baciami Piccina) . . . 22
53 Columbia SCM 5027 If I Had A Penny/You're After My Own Heart . . . 18
53 Columbia SCM 5028 On The First Warm Day/If Teardrops Were Pennies . . . 18
53 Columbia SCM 5040 (Remember Me) I'm The One Who Loves You/Lover's Gold . . . 18
53 Columbia SCM 5049 Blues In The Night/Who Kissed Me Last Night? . . . 15
54 Columbia SCM 5093 I Still Feel The Same About You (with Betty Clooney)/ Why Fight The Feeling . . . 15
56 Philips JB 100 The Teddy Bear's Picnic/Kitty Kat's Party (78, picture label) . . . 12
57 Philips PB 744 You Can't Lose The Blues With Colours/That's How It Is (78) . . . 8
57 Philips JK 1010 Mangos/All The Pretty Little Horses (jukebox issue) . . . 18
58 Philips PB 792 I Can't Stop Crying/Love And Affection (78) . . . 10
58 Philips PB 800 I Could Have Danced All Night/I've Grown Accustomed To Your Face . . . 6
58 Philips PB 800 I Could Have Danced All Night/I've Grown Accustomed To Your Face (78) . . . 8
58 MGM MGM 990 The Loudenboomer Bird/It's A Boy . . . 6
58 MGM MGM 990 The Loudenboomer Bird/It's A Boy (78) . . . 8
59 Philips PB 900 Tonight/Come Rain Or Come Shine . . . 6
59 Philips PB 900 Tonight/Come Rain Or Come Shine (78) . . . 15
59 Coral Q 72357 Diga Me (Deega May-Tell Me)/A Touch Of The Blues . . . 7
59 Coral Q 72357 Diga Me (Deega May-Tell Me)/A Touch Of The Blues (78) . . . 10
59 MGM MGM 1010 Love Eyes/Flattery (B-side with Jose Ferrer) . . . 6
60 Coral Q 72388 Love, Love Away/I Wish I Were In Love Again . . . 6
60 MGM MGM 1062 For You/I Wonder . . . 6
60 RCA RCA 1203 Many A Wonderful Moment/Vaya, Vaya . . . 6
54 Columbia SEG 7552 ROSEMARY CLOONEY AND HARRY JAMES (EP) . . . 12
55 Philips BBE 12004 ROSEMARY CLOONEY (EP) . . . 15
56 Philips BBE 12051 SINGS SONGS FOR THE YOUNG AT HEART (EP) . . . 15
60 Coral FEP 2045 SWING AROUND ROSIE VOL. 1 (EP) . . . 15
60 Coral FEP 2046 SWING AROUND ROSIE VOL. 2 (EP) . . . 15
54 Philips BBR 8022 WHITE CHRISTMAS (10" LP) . . . 30
55 Philips BBR 8047 ROSEMARY CLOONEY (10" LP) . . . 30
56 Philips BBR 8073 AT THE LONDON PALLADIUM (10" LP) . . . 30
56 Philips BBL 7090 HEY BABY (LP, with Duke Ellington) . . . 20
57 Philips BBL 7156 RING AROUND ROSIE (LP, with Hi-Lo's) . . . 20
57 Philips BBL 7191 CHILDREN'S FAVOURITES (LP) . . . 20
59 Philips BBL 7301 SHOWCASE OF HITS (LP) . . . 20
59 Coral LVA 9112 SWING AROUND ROSIE (LP) . . . 20
61 RCA RD 27189 CLAP HANDS, HERE COMES ROSIE! (LP, also stereo SF 5075) . . . 15
61 MGM C 838 SWINGS SOFTLY (LP) . . . 15

ROSEMARY CLOONEY & MARLENE DIETRICH
53 Columbia SCM 5010 Too Old To Cut The Mustard/Good For Nothin' . . . 20
(see also Marlene Dietrich, Betty Clooney, Bob Hope & Rosemary Clooney, Guy Mitchell)

CLOSE LOBSTERS
89 Caff CAFF 4 Just Too Bloody Stupid/All The Little Boys And Girls (p/s) . . . 8

CLOUD
75 Kingsway DOVE 16 FREE TO FLY (LP) . . . 20
77 Kingsway DOVE 44 WATERED GARDEN (LP, gatefold sleeve) . . . 30
70s private pressing THE RESTING PLACE (LP) . . . 25
85 Songs Of Fellow. SFR103 THE PROMISE (LP) . . . 15

MINT VALUE £

CLAUDE CLOUD

55 MGM MGM 820 — Cloudburst/One Bone (78, as Claude Cloud & Thunderclaps) . . . 22
57 MGM MGM 946 — The Beat/Around The Horn (as Claude Cloud & His Orchestra) . . . 15
55 MGM MGM-EP 517 — LET'S GO CATSTATIC NO. 1 (EP, as Claude Cloud & Thunderclaps) . . . 40
56 MGM MGM-D 142 — ROCK 'N' ROLL (10" LP) . . . 100
(see also Sonny Thompson, Sam 'The Man' Taylor)

CLOUD NINE

90s Acid Jazz JAZID 87P — I Feel It (12", p/s, promo-only, withdrawn) . . . 30
90s Acid Jazz JAZID 78 — MILLENNIUM (LP, withdrawn) . . . 50

CLOUDS

69 Island WIP 6055 — Heritage/Make No Bones About It . . . 15
69 Island WIP 6067 — Scrapbook/Carpenter . . . 15
69 Island ILPS 9100 — THE CLOUDS SCRAPBOOK (LP, pink label or 'pink rim palm tree') . . . 35/15
71 Chrysalis ILPS 9151 — WATERCOLOUR DAYS (LP, gatefold sleeve, 'pink rim palm tree' label) . . . 20

CLOUDS

86 Sha La La Ba Ba Ba 001 — Throwaway/CLOUDS: Jenny Nowhere (p/s, flexi free with various fanzines) . . . 8/6
88 Subway Org. SUBWAY 12 — Tranquil/Get Out Of My Dream (p/s) . . . 5
88 Subway Org. SUBWAY 12T — Tranquil/Get Out Of My Dream/Village Green (12", p/s) . . . 8
(see also Boy Hairdressers, Teenage Fanclub)

CLOUT

90 Mooncrest JWL 1000 — We'll Bring The House Down/Jim Jam (p/s) . . . 7
(see also Slade)

CLOVEN HOOF

82 Elemental EM 001 — OPENING RITUAL (12" EP) . . . 80
84 Neat NEAT 1013 — CLOVEN HOOF (LP) . . . 15
86 Trojan CH 002 — FIGHTING BACK (LP, some with poster) . . . 15

CLOVER

70 Liberty LBF 15341 — Wade In The Water/Stealin' . . . 10
77 Vertigo LYN 4277 — There Is No Substitute For Real Magic (flexidisc, promo only) . . . 7
69 Liberty LBS 83340 — CLOVER (LP) . . . 25
71 Liberty LBS 83487 — FORTY-NINER (LP) . . . 22
77 Vertigo 6360 145 — UNAVAILABLE (LP) . . . 12
77 Vertigo 6360 155 — LOVE ON THE WIRE (LP) . . . 12
(see also Huey Lewis & News)

CLOVERLEAFS

56 MGM MGM 933 — Step Right Up And Say Howdy/With Plenty Of Money And You (Gold Digger's Lullaby) . . . 8
(see also Art Mooney)

CLOVERS

56 London HLE 8229 — Nip Sip/If I Could Be Loved By You (gold or silver label lettering) . . . 900/450
56 London HLE 8229 — Nip Sip/If I Could Be Loved By You (78) . . . 40
56 London HLE 8314 — Love, Love, Love/Hey, Doll Baby . . . 600
56 London HLE 8314 — Love, Love, Love/Hey, Doll Baby (78) . . . 40
56 London HLE 8334 — From The Bottom Of My Heart/Your Tender Lips . . . 650
56 London HLE 8334 — From The Bottom Of My Heart/Your Tender Lips (78) . . . 40
58 London HL 7048 — Wishing For Your Love/All About You (export issue) . . . 240
58 London HL 7048 — Wishing For Your Love/All About You (78, export issue) . . . 40
58 HMV POP 542 — In The Good Old Summertime/Idaho . . . 35
58 HMV POP 542 — In The Good Old Summertime/Idaho (78) . . . 20
59 London HLT 8949 — Love Potion No. 9/Stay Awhile (triangular or round centre) . . . 55/30
59 London HLT 8949 — Love Potion No. 9/Stay Awhile (78) . . . 30
60 London HLT 9122 — Lovey/One Mint Julep . . . 45
60 London HLT 9154 — Easy Lovin'/I'm Confessin' (That I Love You) . . . 35
61 HMV POP 883 — Honey Dripper/Have Gun . . . 25
68 Atlantic 584 160 — Your Cash Ain't Nothin' But Trash/I've Got My Eyes On You . . . 15
69 Atlantic 587 162 — LOVE BUG (LP) . . . 60

CLUB QUINTET

60 Top Rank JAR 362 — Caravelle (Secret Serenade)/Bluer Than Blue . . . 6

CLUES

81 Clues CLU 001 — NO VACANCIES (EP) . . . 10

CLUTHA (FOLK GROUP)

71 Argo ZFB 18 — SCOTIA! (LP, as Clutha Folk Group) . . . 15
74 Topic 12TS 242 — SCOTS BALLADS, SONGS AND DANCE TUNES (LP, as Clutha) . . . 12

JEREMY CLYDE

65 CBS 201823 — I Love My Love/Anytime . . . 6
(see also Chad & Jeremy)

CLYDE VALLEY STOMPERS

56 Beltona BL 2648 — Uist Tramping Song/Keep Right On To The End Of The Road (78) . . . 8
56 Beltona BL 2649 — I Love A Lassie/Old Rustic Bridge By The Mill (78) . . . 8
56 Beltona BL 2650 — Old Time Religion/Pearly Gates (78) . . . 8
57 Decca FJ 10897 — Bill Bailey Won't You Please Come Home (with Mary McGowan)/Milenberg Joys . . . 10
57 Decca FJ 10897 — Bill Bailey Won't You Please Come Home (with Mary McGowan)/Milenberg Joys (78) . . . 8
62 Parlophone R 4928 — Peter And The Wolf/Loch Lomond . . . 7
60 Pye NJL 23 — HAVE TARTAN — WILL TRAD (LP) . . . 35
(see also Ian Menzies)

C.M.J.

68	Impression IMP 102	I Can't Do It All By Myself/Nothing At All	45
71	Mother MOT 3	La La La/Step Around It	12
65	Impression EPIM 501	THE C.M.J. TRIO (EP)	80
69	Impression IMPL 1001	C.M.J. LIVE AT THE BANKHOUSE (LP, private pressing)	110

C.M.U. (Contemporary Music Unit)

72	Transatlantic BIG 508	Heart Of The Sun/Doctor Am I Normal?	10
71	Transatlantic TRA 237	OPEN SPACES (LP, gatefold sleeve)	50
72	Transatlantic TRA 259	SPACE CABARET (LP)	35

COACHMEN

59	Vogue V 9154	Those Brown Eyes/Bald Mountain	5
59	Vogue V 9154	Those Brown Eyes/Bald Mountain (78)	7
61	Vogue VAE 170149	HERE COME THE COACHMEN (EP)	8
60	Vogue VA 16062	HERE COME THE COACHMEN (LP)	12

COACHMEN

66	Columbia DB 8057	Gabrielle/Seasons In The Sun	8

COAL PORTERS

92	Bucketfull/Brains BOB 32	Watching Bluegrass Burn/R.E.M.: Academy Fight Song (live) (p/s, vinyl or flexi, free with *Bucketfull Of Brains* magazine, 39/40)	12/5

(see also Long Ryders, Spinning Whighats)

COASTERS

57	London HLE 8450	Searchin'/Young Blood	75
57	London HL 7021	Searchin'/Young Blood (export issue)	30
57	London HLE 8450	Searchin'/Young Blood (78)	15
58	London HLE 8665	Yakety Yak/Zing! Went The Strings Of My Heart	20
58	London HLE 8665	Yakety Yak/Zing! Went The Strings Of My Heart (78)	15
58	London HLE 8729	The Shadow Knows/Sorry But I'm Gonna Have To Pass	60
58	London HLE 8729	The Shadow Knows/Sorry But I'm Gonna Have To Pass (78)	20
59	London HLE 8819	Charlie Brown/Three Cool Cats	15
59	London HL 7073	Charlie Brown/Three Cool Cats (export issue)	15
59	London HLE 8819	Charlie Brown/Three Cool Cats (78)	15
59	London HLE 8882	Along Came Jones/That Is Rock And Roll (silver top label)	20
59	London HLE 8882	Along Came Jones/That Is Rock And Roll (78)	15
59	London HLE 8938	Poison Ivy/I'm A Hog For You	18

(The above 45s were originally issued with triangular centres, later round centre copies are worth half to two-thirds these values.)

59	London HLE 8938	Poison Ivy/I'm A Hog For You (78)	20
60	London HLE 9020	What About Us/Run Red Run	20
60	London HLE 9020	What About Us/Run Red Run (78)	20
60	London HLK 9111	Besame Mucho (Parts 1 & 2)	25
60	London HLK 9111	Besame Mucho (Parts 1 & 2) (78)	25
60	London HLK 9151	Wake Me, Shake Me/Stewball	20
60	London HLK 9208	Shoppin' For Clothes/The Snake And The Bookworm	25
61	London HLK 9293	Wait A Minute/Thumbin' A Ride	15
61	London HLK 9349	Little Egypt/Keep On Rolling	15
61	London HLK 9413	Girls! Girls! Girls! (Parts 1 & 2)	15
62	London HLK 9493	(Ain't That) Just Like Me/Bad Blood	15
64	London HLK 9863	T'Ain't Nothin' To Me/Speedo's Back In Town	15
66	Atlantic 584 033	She's A Yum Yum/Saturday Night Fish Fry	10
67	Atlantic 584 087	Searchin'/Yakety Yak	10
67	CBS 2749	Soul Pad/Down Home Girl	15
68	Direction 58-3701	She Can/Everybody's Woman	15
71	Parlophone R 5931	Love Potion No. 9/D.W. Washburn	5
72	Stateside SS 2201	Cool Jerk/Talkin' 'Bout A Woman (withdrawn)	18
59	London REE 1203	THE COASTERS (EP)	60
60	London HA-E 2237	GREATEST HITS (LP)	100
63	London HA-K 8033	COASTIN' ALONG WITH THE COASTERS (LP)	90
66	Atlantic 588 134	COASTIN' ALONG WITH THE COASTERS (LP, reissue)	25
67	Atlantic 590 015	ALL TIME GREATEST HITS (LP)	20
71	Joy JOYS 189	HUNGRY (LP)	20
74	London SHZ 8460	ON BROADWAY (LP)	18

COAST ROAD DRIVE

74	Deram SML 1113	DELICIOUS AND REFRESHING (LP)	35

C.O.B. (Clive's Original Band)

72	Polydor 2058 260	Blue Morning/Bones	30
71	CBS 69010	SPIRIT OF LOVE (LP, gatefold sleeve)	70
72	Polydor Folk Mill 2383 161	MOYSHE McSTIFF & THE TARTAN LANCERS OF THE SACRED HEART (LP, gatefold sleeve)	250

(see also Famous Jug Band, Incredible String Band)

COBBLERS LAST

79	Banshee BAN 1012	BOOT IN THE DOOR (LP, with insert)	110

COBBS

69	Amalgamated AMG 845	Hot Buttered Corn/COUNT MACHUKI: It Is I	15
69	Amalgamated AMG 849	Space Daughter/LLOYD & DEVON: Reggae Baby	15

JUNIE COBB'S HOMETOWN BAND

59	Collector JDL 38	Chicago Buzz/East Coast Trot	10

MINT VALUE £

BILLY COBHAM

73	Atlantic K 40406	SPECTRUM (LP, gatefold sleeve)	15
74	Atlantic K 50098	TOTAL ECLIPSE (LP)	15
74	Atlantic K 50037	CROSSWINDS (LP)	15
75	Atlantic K 50147	SHABAZZ (LP)	15
75	Atlantic K 50185	A FUNKY SIDE OF THINGS (LP)	15

COBRA

78	Rip Off RIP 3	Graveyard Boogie/Looking For A Lady (p/s)	30

(see also Speed)

COCHISE

70	United Artists UP 35134	Watch This Space/59th St. Bridge Song	6
70	Liberty LBS 15425	Love's Made A Fool Of You/Words Of A Dying Man	6
71	Liberty LBF 15460	Why I Sing The Blues/Jed Colider	6
70	United Artists UAS 29117	COCHISE (LP, gatefold sleeve)	20
70	Liberty LBS 83428	SWALLOW TALES (LP)	15
72	United Artists UAS 29286	SO FAR (LP)	15

(see also B.J. Cole, Mick Grabham)

DIB COCHRAN & EARWIGS

70	Bell BLL 1121	Oh Baby/Universal Love	700

(see also Marc Bolan, Tyrannosaurus Rex, Tony Visconti, Rick Wakeman)

EDDIE COCHRAN

78s

57	London HLU 8386	20 Flight Rock/Dark Lonely Street	80
57	London HLU 8433	Sittin' In The Balcony/Completely Sweet	110
58	London HLU 8702	Summertime Blues/Love Again	100
59	London HLU 8792	C'mon Everybody/Don't Ever Let Me Go	120
59	London HLU 8880	Teenage Heaven/I Remember	225
59	London HLU 8944	Somethin' Else/Boll Weevil Song	275
60	London HLW 9022	Hallelujah, I Love Her So/Little Angel	350
60	London HLG 9115	Three Steps To Heaven/Cut Across Shorty	550
95	Cruisin' The 50s CASS 001	Three Steps To Heaven/Cut Across Shorty (reissue, 300 only)	40
96	Cruisin' The 50s CASB 004	Week-End/Cherished Memories (reissue, 400 only)	30

SINGLES

57	London HLU 8386	20 Flight Rock/Dark Lonely Street (triangular centre; also silver-top label with triangular centre; later round centre)	200/50
57	London HLU 8433	Sittin' In The Balcony/Completely Sweet	400
58	London HLU 8702	Summertime Blues/Love Again	30
59	London HLU 8792	C'mon Everybody/Don't Ever Let Me Go	30
59	London HLU 8880	Teenage Heaven/I Remember	40
59	London HL 7082	Teenage Heaven/Boll Weevil Song (export issue)	80
59	London HLU 8944	Somethin' Else/Boll Weevil Song	50
60	London HLW 9022	Hallelujah, I Love Her So/Little Angel (triangular centre, later round)	50/20

(The above singles were originally issued with triangular centres, later round centre copies are worth half these values unless stated.)

60	London HLG 9115	Three Steps To Heaven/Cut Across Shorty	20
60	London HLG 9196	Sweetie Pie/Lonely	40
61	London HLG 9362	Weekend/Cherished Memories	25
61	London HLG 9460	Jeannie, Jeannie, Jeannie/Pocketful Of Hearts	40
61	London HLG 9464	Pretty Girl/Teresa	40
61	London HLG 9467	Undying Love/Stockin's 'n' Shoes	50
62	Liberty LIB 10049	Never/Think Of Me	15
63	Liberty LIB 10088	My Way/Rock And Roll Blues	15
63	Liberty LIB 10108	Drive-In Show/I Almost Lost My Mind	20
64	Liberty LIB 10151	Skinny Jim/Nervous Breakdown	60
66	Liberty LIB 10233	C'mon Everybody/Summertime Blues	12
66	Liberty LIB 10249	Three Stars/Somethin' Else	60
67	Liberty LIB 10276	Three Steps To Heaven/Eddie's Blues	50
68	Liberty LBF 15071	Summertime Blues/Let's Get Together	15
68	Liberty LBF 15109	Somethin' Else/Milk Cow Blues	10
70	Liberty LBF 15366	C'mon Everybody/Mean When I'm Mad	10
72	United Artists UP 35361	Somethin' Else/Three Steps To Heaven	5
72	United Artists UP 35408	Summertime Blues/Cotton Picker	5
79	Rockstar RSR-SP 3001	What'd I Say/Milk Cow Blues (p/s)	5
79	Rockstar RSR-SP 3002	Skinny Jim/Half Loved (p/s)	5
80	United Artists FREE 16	"20TH ANNIVERSARY ALBUM" SAMPLER (no p/s)	8

EPs

59	London REU 1214	C'MON EVERYBODY (orange sleeve, triangular or round centre)	110/70
59	London REU 1214	C'MON EVERYBODY (yellow sleeve, silver-top label, round centre)	125
60	London REU 1239	SOMETHIN' ELSE (triangular or round centre)	125/90
60	London REG 1262	EDDIE'S HITS	90
61	London REG 1301	CHERISHED MEMORIES OF EDDIE COCHRAN	90
62	Liberty LEP 2052	NEVER TO BE FORGOTTEN	50
63	Liberty LEP 2090	CHERISHED MEMORIES (VOL.1)	50
63	Liberty LEP 2111	C'MON EVERYBODY (reissue)	45
63	Liberty LEP 2122	SOMETHIN' ELSE (reissue)	45
63	Liberty LEP 2123	CHERISHED MEMORIES OF EDDIE COCHRAN (reissue)	45
63	Liberty LEP 2124	EDDIE'S HITS (reissue)	45
64	Liberty LEP 2165	C'MON AGAIN	65
64	Liberty LEP 2180	STOCKIN'S 'N' SHOES	55

LPs

58	London HA-U 2093	SINGIN' TO MY BABY (initially with laminated rear sleeve)	250/165
60	London HA-G 2267	THE EDDIE COCHRAN MEMORIAL ALBUM	100
62	Liberty LBY 1109	CHERISHED MEMORIES	50

MINT VALUE £

63	Liberty LBY 1127	THE EDDIE COCHRAN MEMORIAL ALBUM (reissue)	40
63	Liberty LBY 1158	SINGIN' TO MY BABY (reissue)	50
64	Liberty LBY 1205	MY WAY	60
68	Liberty LBL/LBS 83009	THE EDDIE COCHRAN MEMORIAL ALBUM (2nd reissue)	15
68	Liberty LBL/LBS 83072E	CHERISHED MEMORIES (reissue)	18
68	Liberty LBL 83104	MY WAY (reissue in different sleeve)	18
68	Liberty LBL/LBS 83152	SINGIN' TO MY BABY (2nd reissue in different sleeve)	15
70	Liberty LBS 83337	THE VERY BEST OF EDDIE COCHRAN	12
71	United Artists UAS 29163	THE LEGENDARY EDDIE COCHRAN	12
72	United Artists UAD 60017/18	THE LEGENDARY MASTER SERIES (2-LP, with booklet)	25
72	United Artists UAS 29380	ON THE AIR	15
79	United Artists UAK 30244	THE SINGLES ALBUM (with bonus 7": "Pretty Girl"/"Think Of Me" & poster)	15
79	Charly CR 30168	A LEGEND IN OUR TIME	12
80	United Artists UP ECSP 20	20TH ANNIVERSARY ALBUM (4-LP, box set)	50
88	Liberty ECB 1	THE EDDIE COCHRAN BOX SET (6-LP box set with booklet)	45

HANK COCHRAN

68	Monument LMO 5020	HEART OF HANK (LP)	15

JACKIE LEE COCHRAN

57	Brunswick 05669	Ruby Pearl (with Jimmy Pruett)/Mama Don't You Think I Know	2,000
57	Brunswick 05669	Ruby Pearl (with Jimmy Pruett)/Mama Don't You Think I Know (78)	150

BRUCE COCKBURN

71	True North WTN 003	HIGH WINDS WHITE SKY (LP)	15
71	True North TNX 7	SUNWHEEL DANCE (LP)	15

JOE COCKER

64	Decca F 11974	I'll Cry Instead/Precious Words	75
68	Regal Zonophone RZ 3006	Marjorine/New Age Of The Lily	10
68	Regal Zonophone RZ 3013	With A Little Help From My Friends/Something's Coming On	8
69	Regal Zonophone RZ 3024	Delta Lady/She's So Good To Me	8
70	Regal Zonophone RZ 3027	The Letter/Space Captain	8
70	Fly BUG 3	Cry Me A River/Give Peace A Chance (p/s)	8
71	Fly BUG 9	High Time We Went/Black-Eyed Blues	6
72	Magni Fly ECHO 103	With A Little Help From My Friends/Delta Lady/The Letter (p/s)	8
72	Cube BUG 25	Woman To Woman/Midnight Rider (with Chris Stanton Band)	6
83	Island WIP 6818	Ruby Lee/Talking Back To The Night (export issue)	8
60s	Oak	JOE COCKER (EP, existence unconfirmed)	500+
67	Action ACT 002 EP	RAG GOES MAD AT THE MOJO (33rpm EP, 2 tracks by Joe Cocker's Blues Band, in conjunction with Sheffield University rag magazine *Twikker*)	90
69	Regal Zono. SLRZ 1006	WITH A LITTLE HELP FROM MY FRIENDS (LP)	40
69	Regal Zono. SLRZ 1011	JOE COCKER! (LP)	35
71	Fly HIFLY 3	COCKER HAPPY (LP)	12
74	Fly HIFLY 18	I CAN STAND A LITTLE RAIN (LP)	12

(see also Grease Band, Made In Sheffield)

COCKNEY REBEL

(see under Steve Harley/Cockney Rebel)

COCKNEY REJECTS

79	Small Wonder SW 19	Flares'N'Slippers/Police Star/I Wanna Be A Star (p/s)	8
79	EMI EMI 5008	I'm Not A Fool/East End (p/s)	5
80	EMI EMI 5035	Bad Man!/The New Song (p/s)	5
80	Zonophone Z 2	The Greatest Cockney Rip-Off/Hate Of The City (p/s, yellow vinyl)	5
80	Zonophone Z 4	I'm Forever Blowing Bubbles/West Side Boys (p/s)	8
80	Zonophone Z 6	We Can Do Anything/15 Nights (p/s)	6
80	Zonophone Z 10	We Are The Firm/War On The Terraces (p/s)	8
81	Zonophone Z 20	Easy Life/Motorhead/Hang 'Em High (p/s)	5
80	Zonophone ZONO 101	GREATEST HITS VOLUME 1 (LP)	18
80	Zonophone ZONO 102	GREATEST HITS VOLUME 2 (LP, with inner sleeve & poster)	15
81	Zonophone ZEM 101	GREATEST HITS VOLUME 3 (LIVE AND LOUD) (LP)	15

COCKNEYS

64	Philips BF 1303	After Tomorrow/I'll Cry Each Night	18
64	Philips BF 1338	After Tomorrow/I'll Cry Each Night (reissue)	15
64	Philips BF 1360	I Know You're Gonna Be Mine/Oh No You Won't	18

COCK SPARRER

77	Decca FR 13710	Runnin' Riot/Sister Suzie (no p/s; demos in p/s £100)	20
77	Decca FR 13732	We Love You/Chip On My Shoulder (no p/s)	15
77	Decca LFR 13732	We Love You/Chip On My Shoulder (12" p/s, with photo insert, 7,500 only)	18
82	Carrere CAR 255	England Belongs To Me/Argy Bargy (p/s)	40
83	Razor RAZ 9	SHOCK TROOPS (LP)	50
84	Syndicate SYNLP 7	RUNNIN' RIOT IN 84	40
86	Razor RAZ 26	TRUE GRIT (LP)	25

(see also Little Roosters, Guttersnipes)

COCKTAIL CABINET

67	Page One POF 046	Puppet On A String/Breathalyser	30

COCTEAU TWINS

83	4AD AD 303	Peppermint Pig/Laugh Lines (p/s)	12
84	4AD AD 314	Sugar Hiccup (1-sided, promo only)	15
88	4AD CAD 807	BLUE BELL KNOLL (LP, tri-foldout sleeve)	12

(see also This Mortal Coil, Felt)

C.O.D.s

66	Stateside SS 489	Michael (The Lover)/Cry No More	25

MINT VALUE £

JAMIE COE

Year	Label/Cat. No.	Title	Value
59	Parlophone R 4600	Summertime Symphony/There's Gonna Be A Day	165
60	Parlophone R 4621	School Day Blues/I'll Go On Loving You	90
61	HMV POP 991	How Low Is Low/Little Dear Little Darling	20
63	London HLX 9713	The Fool/I've Got That Feeling Again	20

PETER & CHRIS COE

Year	Label/Cat. No.	Title	Value
72	Trailer LER 2077	OPEN THE DOOR AND LET US IN (LP)	25
76	Trailer LER 2098	OUT OF SEASON, OUT OF RHYME (LP)	20
79	Highway SHY 7007	GAME OF ALL FOURS (LP)	15

(see also Bandoggs)

TONY COE (QUINTET)

Year	Label/Cat. No.	Title	Value
61	Philips B 10784L	SWINGIN' TILL THE GIRLS COME HOME (LP)	75
67	Columbia SCX 6170	TONY'S BASEMENT (LP)	100

TONY COE & BRIAN LEMON TRIO

Year	Label/Cat. No.	Title	Value
68	'77' SEU 12/41	TONY COE AND BRIAN LEMON TRIO (LP)	60

(see also Robert Farnon & Tony Coe)

JACK & CHARLIE COEN

Year	Label/Cat. No.	Title	Value
77	Topic 12TS 337	THE BRANCH LINE (LP)	22

COFFEE BAR SKIFFLERS

Year	Label/Cat. No.	Title	Value
58	Embassy WEP 1008	SKIFFLE SESSION (EP)	12

(see also Chas McDevitt Skiffle Group)

DENNIS COFFEY

Year	Label/Cat. No.	Title	Value
72	A&M AMS 7010	Getting It On/Ride Sally Ride	6
70	A&M AMLS 68035	EVOLUTION (LP)	18
71	A&M AMLS 68072	GOIN' FOR MYSELF (LP)	18
74	Sussex LPSX 9	INSTANT COFFEY (LP)	15

ALMA COGAN

78s

Year	Label/Cat. No.	Title	Value
52	HMV B 10280	Would You/To Be Worthy Of You	12
52	HMV B 10307	To Be Loved By You/The Homing Waltz (with Larry Day)	10
52	HMV B 10319	Pretty Bride (Sew, Sew, Sew, Sew)/Waltz Of Paree (Sous Le Ciel De Paris)	10
52	HMV B 10338	Blue Tango/Half As Much	5
52	HMV B 10344	I Went To Your Wedding/You Belong To Me	7
52	HMV B 10370	Take Me In Your Arms And Hold Me/Wyoming Lullaby	7
53	HMV B 10449	Till I Waltz Again With You/Happy Valley Sweetheart	7
53	HMV B 10460	If I Had A Penny/Hold Me, Thrill Me, Kiss Me	5
53	HMV B 10464	On The First Warm Day (with Les Howerd)/LES HOWERD: The Windsor Waltz	5
53	HMV B 10505	Till They've All Gone Home/Hug Me A Hug (with Les Howerd)	5
53	HMV B 10530	If I Had A Golden Umbrella/Mystery Street	5
53	HMV B 10590	My Love, My Love/Wasted Tears	7
54	HMV B 10615	Ricochet (Rick-O-Shay)/The Moon Is Blue	5
54	HMV B 10743	Skinnie Minnie (Fishtail)/What Am I Going To Do, Ma (The Doo-Ma Song)	7
54	HMV B 10761	This Ole House/Skokiaan	7
54	HMV B 10802	(Don't Let The) Kiddygeddin/Mrs. Santa Claus	7
55	HMV B 10832	Mambo Italiano/The Naughty Lady Of Shady Lane	5
55	HMV B 10848	Tweedlee-Dee/More Than Ever Now	7
56	HMV POP 223	Why Do Fools Fall In Love?/(The Same Thing Happen With) The Birds And The Bees?	7
57	HMV POP 317	Whatever Lola Wants (Lola Gets)/Lucky Lips	7
57	HMV POP 367	Fabulous/Summer Love	7
58	HMV POP 450	Sugartime/Gettin' Ready For Freddy	7
58	HMV POP 482	Stairway Of Love/Comes Love	7
58	HMV POP 500	Sorry, Sorry, Sorry/Fly Away Lovers	7
58	HMV POP 531	There's Never Been A Night/If This Isn't Love	7
59	HMV POP 573	Last Night On The Back Porch/Mama Says	9
59	HMV POP 670	We Got Love/I Don't Mind Being All Alone	20

SINGLES

Year	Label/Cat. No.	Title	Value
53	HMV 7M 166	Over And Over Again/Isn't Life Wonderful (with Les Howerd)	35
53	HMV 7M 106	I Went To Your Wedding/You Belong To Me	40
53	HMV 7M 107	To Be Loved By You/The Homing Waltz (B-side with Larry Day)	40
54	HMV 7M 173	Ricochet (Rick-O-Shay)/The Moon Is Blue	40
54	HMV 7M 188	Bell Bottom Blues/Love Me Again	60
54	HMV 7M 196	Make Love To Me/Said The Little Moment	35
54	HMV 7M 219	The Little Shoemaker/Chiqui-Chaqui (Chick-ee Chock-ee)	40
54	HMV 7M 228	Little Things Mean A Lot/Canoodlin' Rag	45
54	HMV 7M 239	Skinnie Minnie (Fishtail)/What Am I Going To Do, Ma (The Doo-Ma Song)	75
54	HMV 7M 269	This Ole House/Skokiaan	45
54	HMV 7M 271	I Can't Tell A Waltz From A Tango/Christmas Cards	35
55	HMV 7M 286	Paper Kisses/Softly, Softly	35
55	HMV 7M 293	Chee-Chee-Oo-Chee (Sang The Little Bird)/Tika Tika Tok	35
55	HMV 7M 301	Tweedlee-Dee/More Than Ever Now	35
55	HMV 7M 316	Got'n Idea/Give A Fool A Chance	35
55	HMV 7M 337	Never Do A Tango With An Eskimo/Twenty Tiny Fingers	40
56	HMV 7M 367	Love And Marriage/Sycamore Tree	35
56	HMV 7M 415	Why Do Fools Fall In Love?/ (The Same Thing Happen With) The Birds And The Bees?	50
56	HMV POP 239	Mama Teach Me To Dance/I'm In Love Again	30
56	HMV POP 261	In The Middle Of The House/Two Innocent Hearts	40
57	HMV POP 284	You, Me And Us/Three Brothers	30
57	HMV POP 317	Whatever Lola Wants (Lola Gets)/Lucky Lips	40
57	HMV POP 336	Chantez, Chantez/Funny, Funny, Funny	25
57	HMV POP 367	Fabulous/Summer Love	30

			MINT VALUE £
57	HMV POP 392	That's Happiness/What You've Done To Me	20
57	HMV POP 415	Party Time/Please Mister Brown (Mister Jones, Mister Smith)	20
58	HMV POP 433	The Story Of My Life/Love Is	15
58	HMV POP 450	Sugartime/Gettin' Ready For Freddy	15
58	HMV POP 482	Stairway Of Love/Comes Love	15
58	HMV POP 500	Sorry, Sorry, Sorry/Fly Away Lovers	10
58	HMV POP 531	There's Never Been A Night/If This Isn't Love	12
59	HMV POP 573	Last Night On The Back Porch/Mama Says	12
59	HMV POP 608	Pink Shoelaces/The Universe	12
59	HMV POP 670	We Got Love/I Don't Mind Being All Alone	8
60	HMV POP 728	O Dio Mio/Dream Talk	8
60	HMV POP 760	The Train Of Love/The 'I Love You' Bit	12
60	HMV POP 815	Must Be Santa/Just Couldn't Resist Her With Her Pocket Transistor	10
61	Columbia DB 4607	Cowboy Jimmy Joe/Don't Read This Letter	8
61	Columbia DB 4679	With You In Mind/Ja-Da	8
61	Columbia DB 4749	All Alone/Keep Me In Your Heart	8
62	Columbia DB 4794	She's Got You/In The Shade Of The Old Apple Tree	8
62	Columbia DB 4912	Goodbye Joe/I Can't Give You Anything But Love	8
63	Columbia DB 4965	Tell Him/Fly Me To The Moon (Bossa Nova)	8
63	Columbia DB 7059	Hold Out Your Hand You Naughty Boy/Just Once More	8
64	Columbia DB 7233	The Tennessee Waltz/I Love You Too Much	15
64	Columbia DB 7390	It's You/I Knew Right Away	10
65	Columbia DB 7619	Love Is A Word/Now That I've Found You (unissued)	
65	Columbia DB 7652	Snakes And Snails (And Puppy Dog Tails)/How Many Days, How Many Nights	12
65	Columbia DB 7757	Let Her Go/Yesterday (unissued)	
65	Columbia DB 7786	Eight Days A Week/Help!	10
66	Columbia DB 8088	Now That I've Found You/More	15
80	HMV POP 2015	Dreamboat/Twenty Tiny Fingers	6
EPs			
55	HMV 7EG 8122	THE GIRL WITH A LAUGH IN HER VOICE	25
55	HMV 7EG 8151	THE GIRL WITH A LAUGH IN HER VOICE NO. 2	30
56	HMV 7EG 8169	THE GIRL WITH A LAUGH IN HER VOICE NO. 3	30
57	HMV 7EG 8437	SHE LOVES TO SING	40
LPs			
58	HMV CLP 1152	I LOVE TO SING	65
61	HMV CLP 1459	OLIVER! (with others, also stereo CSD 1370)	40/55
61	Columbia 33SX 1345	ALMA SINGS WITH YOU IN MIND (also stereo SCX 3391)	60/100
62	Columbia 33SX 1469	HOW ABOUT LOVE! (also stereo SCX 3459)	60/100
67	Columbia SX 6130	ALMA	50

(see also Ronnie Hilton, Angela & Fans, Billy Cotton)

ALMA COGAN & RONNIE HILTON

57	HMV 7EG 8352	THE HITS FROM 'MY FAIR LADY' (EP, 1 side each)	12

(see also Ronnie Hilton)

ALMA COGAN & FRANKIE VAUGHAN

54	HMV 7M 226	Do, Do, Do, Do, Do, Do, Do It Again/Jilted	35
54	HMV B 10712	Do, Do, Do, Do, Do, Do, Do It Again/Jilted (78)	10

(see also Frankie Vaughan)

DON COGAN

58	MGM MGM 984	The Fountain Of Love/I'm Takin' Over	25
58	MGM MGM 984	The Fountain Of Love/I'm Takin' Over (78)	8

SHAYE COGAN

58	Columbia DB 4055	Billy Be Sure/Doodle Doodle Doo	15
60	MGM MGM 1063	Mean To Me/They Said It Couldn't Be Done	100

(see also Buddy Morrow)

ALAN COHEN BAND

72	Argo ZDA 159	BLACK, BROWN AND BEIGE (LP)	65

LEONARD COHEN

68	CBS 3337	Suzanne/So Long, Marianne	7
69	CBS 4245	Bird On The Wire/Seems So Long Ago, Nancy	8
71	CBS 7292	Joan Of Arc/Diamonds In The Mine	7
74	CBS 2494	Bird On The Wire (live)/Tonight Will Be Fine (live)	7
74	CBS 2699	Lover Lover Lover/Who By Fire	6
76	CBS 4306	Suzanne/Take This Longing	6
77	CBS 5882	Memories/Don't Go Home With Your Hard-On	6
78	CBS 6095	True Love Leaves No Traces/I Left A Woman Waiting	6
72	CBS EP 9162	McCABE AND MRS MILLER (EP, p/s)	10
68	CBS (S)BPG 63241	SONGS OF LEONARD COHEN (LP, orange label, some with stickered sleeve; mono/stereo)	20/15
68	CBS 63241	SONGS OF LEONARD COHEN (LP, orange label, re-pressing w/out prefix)	15/12

COIL

79	North'ton Wood H. HAV 1	Motor Industry/Alcoholic Stork (p/s)	15

COIL

85	F & F/K.422 FFK 512	Panic/Tainted Love/Aqua Regis (12", red or black vinyl, 'hair'-textured p/s)	35/20
86	Force & Form/K.422 ROTA 121	The Anal Staircase/Blood From The Air/Ravenous (12", p/s, some on clear vinyl)	35/20
87	Solar Lodge 001	HELLRAISER (10" EP, coloured vinyl [clear or pink, 500 each], or black)	35/20
90	Shock SX 002	Wrong Eye/Scope (pink p/s, signed & lettered A-Z, 26 only)	75
90	Shock SX 002	Wrong Eye/Scope (974 w/ no'd white p/s; or 1,000 w/ unno'd yellow p/s)	25
90	Shock SX 002	Wrong Eye/Scope (green p/s, 300 only, some with gold/black sticker)	40
92	Clawfist 22	Airborne Bells/Is Suicide A Solution (p/s, 1,250 only)	40
94	Loci S1	Themes From Blue (p/s, 23 on yellow vinyl, 1,000 on blue vinyl)	150/80
94	Eskaton 001	Nasa Arab/First Dark Ride (12", stickered plain black sleeve, 2,500 only)	30

MINT VALUE £

95 Eskaton 003 — PHILM (10" EP, with poster, 2,000 only, 50 on clear vinyl in handmade p/s) . . . 80/30
86 Threshold ROTA 1 — HORSE ROTORVATOR (LP, with A5 card insert & stickers) . . . 40
87 Threshold House LOCI 1 — GOLD IS THE METAL (LP, red vinyl; with bonus 7": "The Wheel"/"The Wheal", unfinished proof sleeve without writing, 25 only) . . . 175
87 Threshold House LOCI 1 — GOLD IS THE METAL (LP, red [150 only] or clear vinyl [500 only], with inner sleeve; with bonus 7": "The Wheel"/"The Wheal") . . . 60/35
87 Threshold House LOCI 1 — GOLD IS THE METAL (LP, box set with 7", "The Wheel"/"The Wheal", poster & booklet in black linen folder, embossed sleeve, autographed, 55 only) . . . 500
87 Threshold House LOCI CD1 — GOLD IS THE METAL (CD, 1,000 only) . . . 20
90 Normal NORMAL 77 — GOLD IS THE METAL (LP, black vinyl re-pressing with 7": "The Wheel"/"Keel Hauler") . . . 35
93 Loci CD 4b — STOLEN AND CONTAMINATED SONGS (CD, 1st edit with different artwork) . . . 400
90s Loci CD 6 — ANGELIC CONVERSATION (CD, gold disc, 1,000 only) . . . 18
95 Eskaton 007 — WORSHIP THE GLITCH (2 x 10" LP, as Coil Vs. Elph, with insert, 2,000 only, 50 with white optical plastic cover) . . . 70/30
95 Eskaton 006 — WORSHIP THE GLITCH (CD, as Coil Vs. Elph, 500 only in black optical plastic) . . . 30

(see also Psychic TV, Throbbing Gristle, Current 93, Thighpaulsandra)

COINS

69 Toast TT 513 — Love Power/You Can't Get Away From It . . . 6
69 Toast TT 515 — Don't You Know It's Just A Game, Love? (actually by Miss White & Mr. Green)/Crying Over You . . . 6

ALVADEAN COKER

55 London HLU 8191 — Do Dee Oodle De Do I'm In Love/We're Gonna Bop . . . 375
55 London HLU 8191 — Do Dee Oodle De Do I'm In Love/We're Gonna Bop (78) . . . 40

SANDY COKER & HIS BAND

54 London HL 8109 — Meadowlark Melody/Toss Over . . . 80
54 London HL 8109 — Meadowlark Melody/Toss Over (78) . . . 18

RIC COLBECK QUARTET

70 Fontana 6383 001 — THE SUN IS COMING UP (LP) . . . 30

COLD BLOOD

70 Atlantic 584 319 — You Got Me Hummin'/If You Will . . . 6
70 Atlantic 588 218 — COLD BLOOD (LP, plum/red label) . . . 20
71 Atlantic 2400 102 — SISYPHUS (LP, gatefold sleeve, plum/red label) . . . 20
74 Warner Bros K 56047 — LYDIA (LP) . . . 15

BEN COLDER

64 MGM MGM-EP 791 — MAKE THE WORLD GO BY (EP) . . . 18

(see also Sheb Wooley)

COLDPLAY

98 private pressing HGCD 633 — SAFETY EP: Bigger, Stronger/No More Keeping My Feet On The Ground/Such A Rush (CD, 500 only) . . . 500
99 Fierce Panda NING 68 — Brothers And Sisters (wraparound p/s, 1000 only) . . . 60
99 EMI EMI CDR 6528 — THE BLUE ROOM EP (Bigger, Stronger/Don't Panic/See You Soon/High Speed/Such A Rush) (CD, digipak) . . . 50
00 Parlophone R 6536 — Shiver/For You/Careful Where You Stand (p/s) . . . 15
00 Parlophone R 6549 — Trouble/Brothers And Sisters (p/s, numbered, stickered poly outer) . . . 20
01 EMI EMI 879080 2 — Don't Panic/You Only Live Twice/Bigger, Stronger (CD, digipak) . . . 8
01 fan club no cat. no — MINCE SPIES (CD EP, 1000 only, given away with *Coldplayground* fanzine) . . . 100
02 Parlophone 5515497 — The Scientist/1:36/I Ran Away (p/s) . . . 6
03 Parlophone R 6594 — Clocks/Crest Of Waves (p/s) . . . 6
03 Parlophone 12 R 6594 — REMIXES (12", die-cut sleeve, 1000 only) . . . 45
00 Parlophone 5277831 — PARACHUTES (LP) . . . 15
02 EMI EMI 5405041 — A RUSH OF BLOOD TO THE HEAD (LP, gatefold sleeve, with inner) . . . 12

B.J. COLE

73 United Artists UAS 29418 — NEW HOVERING DOG (LP) . . . 15

(see also Cochise)

BOBBY COLE

68 CBS 3626 — Mister Bo Jangles/Bus 22 To Jerusalem . . . 6

CINDY COLE

65 Columbia DB 7519 — A Love Like Yours/He's Sure The Boy I Love . . . 18
66 Columbia DB 7973 — Just Being Your Baby (Turns Me On)/Lonely City Blue Boy . . . 30

(see also Jeannie & Big Guys)

CLAY COLE

62 London HLP 9499 — Twist Around The Clock/Don't Twist . . . 10

COZY COLE

58 London HL 8750 — Topsy (Parts 1 & 2) . . . 10
58 London HL 7065 — Topsy (Parts 1 & 2) (export issue) . . . 10
58 London HL 8750 — Topsy (Parts 1 & 2) (78) . . . 10
59 Mercury AMT 1015 — St. Louis Blues/Father Co-operates . . . 10
59 Mercury AMT 1015 — St. Louis Blues/Father Co-operates (78) . . . 10
59 London HL 8843 — Turvy (Parts 1 & 2) . . . 12
59 London HL 8843 — Turvy (Parts 1 & 2) (78) . . . 15
62 Coral Q 72457 — Big Noise From Winnetka (Parts 1 & 2) . . . 10
57 MGM MGM-EP 622 — COZY COLE ALL STARS (EP) . . . 15

DON COLE & ALLEYNE

65 Fontana TF 522 — Gotta Find My Baby/Something's Gotta Hold Of Me . . . 8

JERRY COLE

65 Capitol CL 15397 — Every Window In The City/Come On Over To My Place . . . 20

KEITH COLE

71 Big BG 315 — Musical Attack/RUPIE EDWARDS ALLSTARS: Shack Attack . . . 7
71 Big BG 316 — Music Alone Version 3/RUPIE EDWARDS ALLSTARS: Behold Another Version . . . 7

KING COLE TRIO/QUINTET
(see under Nat 'King' Cole)

LLOYD COLE & COMMOTIONS
84 Welcome To L. Vegas LC 1 Are You Ready To Be Heartbroken?/Down At The Mission (p/s, withdrawn) 30

NAT COLE
70 Jackpot JP 717 Pack Of Cards/RITA & NAT COLE: Spread Joy 7
70 Jackpot JP 718 Love Making/SONNY BINNS & RITA: My Love 7
70 Jackpot JP 722 Sugar Sugar/SONNY BINNS & RITA: Sign Off 7
70 Explosion EX 2022 In The Summertime/Apollo Moon Walk 7
70 Creole CR 1002 Me And My Life/Instrumental 6
(see also Rita Alston)

(NAT) 'KING' COLE
78s
50 Melodisc 8011 Heads/It Had To Be You (as King Cole Quintet) 12
50 Melodisc 8012 Pro-Sky/I Can't Give You Anything But Love (as King Cole Quintet) 12
54 Vogue V 2214 Nat's Kicks (Parts 1 & 2) (as Nat 'King' Cole Quintet) 10
54 Capitol CL 14172 I Am In Love/There Goes My Heart 7
55 Capitol CL 14215 Long Long Ago/Open Up The Doghouse (with Dean Martin) 15
58 Capitol CL 14820 Angel Smile/Back In My Arms 7
58 Capitol CL 14853 With You On My Mind/The Song Of Raintree County 7
58 Capitol CL 14898 Come Closer To Me/Nothing In The World 7
58 Capitol CL 14937 Non Dimenticar (Don't Forget)/Bend A Little My Way 7
59 Capitol CL 14987 Madrid/Give Me Your Love 7
59 Capitol CL 15017 You Made Me Love You/I Must Be Dreaming 12
59 Capitol CL 15056 Midnight Flyer/Sweet Bird Of Truth 10
59 Capitol CL 15087 Buon Natale/The Happiest Little Christmas Tree 20

SINGLES
54 Capitol CL 14149 Smile (Theme From 'Modern Times')/Make Her Mine 22
54 Capitol CL 14155 Unbelievable/Hajji Baba (Persian Lament) 18
54 Capitol CL 14172 I Am In Love/There Goes My Heart 18
54 Capitol CL 14203 If I Give My Heart To You/Hold My Hand 18
54 Capitol CL 14207 Papa Loves Mambo/Teach Me Tonight 20
55 Capitol CL 14215 Long Long Ago/Open Up The Doghouse (with Dean Martin) 20
55 Capitol CL 14235 A Blossom Fell/Alone Too Long 20
55 Capitol CL 14251 The Sand And The Sea/Darling, Je Vous Aime Beaucoup 18
55 Capitol CL 14295 If I May (with Four Knights)/I Envy 18
55 Capitol CL 14317 Annabelle/I'd Rather Have The Blues ('Kiss Me Deadly' Theme) 18
55 Capitol CL 14327 My One Sin/Don't Hurt The Girl 20
55 Capitol CL 14364 Love Is A Many-Splendored Thing/Autumn Leaves 18
55 Capitol CL 14378 Someone You Love/Forgive My Heart 18
(The above 45s were originally issued with triangular centres. Later round centre copies are worth around half these values.)
56 Capitol CL 14513 Dreams Can Tell A Lie/Ask Me 15
56 Capitol CL 14529 Nothing Ever Changes (My Love For You)/I'm Gonna Laugh You Out Of My Life . . 8
56 Capitol CL 14573 Too Young To Go Steady/Never Let Me Go 10
56 Capitol CL 14621 Love Me As Though There Were No Tomorrow/That's All There Is To That (as Nat 'King' Cole & Four Knights) 10
56 Capitol CL 14632 My Dream Sonata/I Just Found Out About Love 6
56 Capitol CL 14661 To The Ends Of The Earth/Toyland 6
57 Capitol CL 14678 Night Lights/Dame Crazy 6
57 Capitol CL 14688 You Are My First Love/Ballerina 6
57 Capitol CL 14709 When I Fall In Love/Calypso Blues 8
57 Capitol CL 14733 When Rock And Roll Came To Trinidad/It's All In The Game 10
57 Capitol CL 14765 My Personal Possession (as Nat 'King' Cole & Four Knights)/Send For Me 8
57 Capitol CL 14787 Stardust/Love Letters 7
58 Capitol CL 14820 Angel Smile/Back In My Arms 6
65 Capitol CL 15411 The Ballad Of Cat Ballou/They Can't Make Her Cry (with Stubby Kaye) 6

EPs
55 Capitol EAP 1-514 TENTH ANNIVERSARY ALBUM PART 1 12
55 Capitol EAP 2-514 TENTH ANNIVERSARY ALBUM PART 2 12
55 Capitol EAP 3-514 TENTH ANNIVERSARY ALBUM PART 3 12
55 Capitol EAP 4-514 TENTH ANNIVERSARY ALBUM PART 4 12
55 Capitol EAP 1-633 MOODS IN SONG 12
56 Capitol EAP 1010 LOVE IS A MANY-SPLENDORED THING 12
56 Capitol EAP 1036 THE CHRISTMAS SONG 12
56 Capitol EAP 1040 STRIP FOR ACTION 12
57 Capitol EAP 1-801 NIGHT LIGHTS 10
57 Capitol EAP 1-813 AROUND THE WORLD (with Nelson Riddle) 10
58 Capitol EAP 1-824 LOVE IS THE THING PART 1 10
58 Capitol EAP 2-824 LOVE IS THE THING PART 2 10
58 Capitol EAP 3-824 LOVE IS THE THING PART 3 10
58 Capitol EAP 1-960 LOOKING BACK 10
58 Capitol EAP 1-993 ST. LOUIS BLUES PART 1 12
58 Capitol EAP 2-993 ST. LOUIS BLUES PART 2 12
58 Capitol EAP 3-993 ST. LOUIS BLUES PART 3 12
58 Capitol EAP 1-782 AFTER MIDNIGHT PART 1 10
58 Capitol EAP 2-782 AFTER MIDNIGHT PART 2 10
58 Capitol EAP 3-782 AFTER MIDNIGHT PART 3 10
58 Capitol EAP 4-782 AFTER MIDNIGHT PART 4 10

LPs
53 Capitol LC 6569 CAPITOL PRESENTS NAT KING COLE (10") 30
53 Capitol LC 6587 CAPITOL PRESENTS NAT KING COLE AND HIS TRIO VOLUME 1 (10") 25
53 Capitol LC 6593 CAPITOL PRESENTS NAT KING COLE AT THE PIANO (10") 25
53 Capitol LC 6594 CAPITOL PRESENTS NAT KING COLE AND HIS TRIO VOLUME 2 (10") 25
53 Capitol LC 6627 NAT KING COLE SINGS FOR TWO IN LOVE (10") 25

			MINT VALUE £
54	Capitol LCT 6003	NAT KING COLE TENTH ANNIVERSARY ALBUM	22
56	Capitol LC 6818	BALLADS OF THE DAY (10")	20
56	Capitol LC 6830	THE PIANO STYLE OF NAT KING COLE (10")	20
56	Brunswick LAT 8123	IN THE BEGINNING (as King Cole Trio)	22
57	Capitol (S)LCT 6129	LOVE IS THE THING	15
57	Capitol LCT 6133	AFTER MIDNIGHT (as Nat King Cole & His Trio)	15
57	Capitol LCT 6142	THIS IS NAT KING COLE	15
58	Capitol (S)LCT 6149	JUST ONE OF THOSE THINGS	15
58	Capitol (S)LCT 6156	ST LOUIS BLUES — SONGS OF W.C. HANDY	18
59	Capitol (S)LCT 6173	THE VERY THOUGHT OF YOU (mono/stereo)	12/15
59	Capitol (S)LCT 6176	WELCOME TO THE CLUB (mono/stereo)	12/15
59	Capitol (S)LCT 6182	TO WHOM IT MAY CONCERN (mono/stereo)	12/15
60	Capitol (S)W 1220	A MIS AMIGOS (mono/stereo)	12/15
60	Capitol (S)W 1444	THE MAGIC OF CHRISTMAS (mono/stereo)	12/15
61	Capitol (S)W 1392	WILD IS LOVE (mono/stereo)	12/15
61	Capitol (S)W 1331	TELL ME ALL ABOUT YOURSELF (mono/stereo)	12/15
61	Capitol (S)W 1574	THE TOUCH OF YOUR LIPS (mono/stereo)	12/15
65	Capitol (S)W340	CAT BALLOU AND OTHER MOTION PICTURE SONGS	15

(see also Dean Martin, Four Knights)

(NAT) 'KING' COLE and GLORIA WOOD

53	Capitol CL 13919	Red Canary/Hello Sunshine (78)	7

PATSY COLE

66	Island WI 271	Disappointed Bride/EARL BOSTIC: Honeymoon Night	18

ROCKY COLE

61	Oriole CB 1635	Heaven And Earth/Huey's Song	6

STRANGER COLE

63	R&B JB 133	Out Of Many/Nothing Tried	22
63	Island WI 110	Stranger At The Door/Conqueror	22
63	Island WI 114	Last Love/STRANGER & KEN: Hush Baby	25
63	Island WI 126	We Are Rolling/Millie Maw	22
64	Island WI 137	Goodbye Peggy (actually plays "Goodbye Peggy Darling" by Roy Panton)/ BABA BROOKS: Portrait Of My Love	22
64	R&B JB 129	Morning Star/Beat Up Your Gum	18
64	Island WI 133	Til My Dying Days/STRANGER & PATSY: I Need You	22
64	Black Swan WI 413	Uno Dos Tres (act. with Ken Boothe)/Look (B-side actually by unknown artist)	22
64	Black Swan WI 415	Summer Day/Loving You Always (both actually by Dottie & Bonnie)	22
64	Black Swan WI 435	Little Boy Blue/ERIC MORRIS: Words Of Wisdom	22
65	Ska Beat JB 192	Pussy Cat/MAYTALS: Sweet Sweet Jenny	20
65	Island WI 169	Koo Koo Doo (with Owen & Leon)/GLORIA & DREAMLETTS: Stay Where You Are	22
65	Island WI 177	Run Joe (with Baba Brooks)/Make Believe	22
65	Blue Beat BB 322	When The Party Is Over/BUSTER'S ALLSTARS: Happy Independence '65	20
65	Blue Beat BB 333	Matilda (actually with Prince Buster)/BUSTER'S ALL STARS: When The Party Is Over	22
66	Doctor Bird DB 1025	We Shall Overcome/Do You Really Love Me (as Stranger Cole & Seraphines)	25
66	Doctor Bird DB 1040	Drop The Ratchet/Oh Yee Mahee (as Stranger Cole & Conquerors)	25
67	Doctor Bird DB 1066	You Took My Love (actually by Patsy Todd)/FUGITIVES: Living Soul	25
68	Island WI 3154	Jeboza Macoo/Now I Know (B-side actually with Gladdy Anderson)	55
68	Amalgamated AMG 801	Just Like A River (as Stranger Cole & Gladdy)/LEADERS: Hope Someday	18
69	Amalgamated AMG 838	What Mama Na Want She Get/We Two	18
69	Duke DU 27	Glad You're Living/Help Wanted	10
69	Unity UN 501	Last Flight To Reggae City (w/ Tommy McCook)/JUNIOR SMITH: Watch Dem Go	8
69	Unity UN 514	When I Get My Freedom/Life Can Be Beautiful	7
69	Escort ES 810	Pretty Cottage/To Me	10
69	Escort ES 819	Leana Leana/Na Na Na	7
69	Escort ES 826	Loneliness/Remember	7
70	Escort ES 830	Little Things/Till The Well Runs Dry	6
70	Escort ES 831	Everything With You/Picture On The Wall	6
70	Escort ES 832	Pussy/Let Me In	6
70	Pama PM 790	Come Dance With Me/Dance With Me	7
71	Camel CA 72	Crying Every Night/DENNIS ALCAPONE & DELROY WILSON: It Must Come	10
71	Escort ERT 849	Tomorrow/SONNY BURKE: Chicken Thief	7
72	Tropical AL 0011	Mail Man (with Charlie Ace)/Mail Man (Version)	7
72	Jackpot JP 791	My Confession/LASCELS & HORTENSE: The Might Organ	6
72	Pama PM 848	The House Where Bombo Lives/Our High School Dance	6

(see also Stranger, Stranger & Gladys, Stranger & Patsy, Stranger & Ken, Rob Walker, Charmers, Lloyd Clarke, Don Drummond, Tommy McCook, Ernest Wilson, Delroy Wilson, Lester Sterling, Baba Brooks, Roland Alphonso)

BOBBY COLEMAN

66	Pye International 7N 25365	(Baby) You Don't Have To Tell Me/Pleasure Girl	70

FITZROY COLEMAN

61	Starlite ST45 064	Lucilla/Caribbean Sunset	12

LONNIE COLEMAN & JESSE ROBERTSON

56	London HLU 8335	Dolores Diane/Oh Honey, Why Don'tcha	75
56	London HLU 8335	Dolores Diane/Oh Honey, Why Don'tcha (78)	15

ORNETTE COLEMAN

60	Contemporary LAC 12228	TOMORROW IS THE QUESTION (LP)	20
61	London Jazz LTZ-K 15199	CHANGE OF THE CENTURY (LP, also stereo SAH-K 5099)	18
61	London Jazz LTZ-K 15228	THIS IS OUR MUSIC (LP, also stereo SAH-K 6181)	18
62	London Jazz LTZ-K 15241	THE ORNETTE COLEMAN QUARTET (LP, also stereo SAH-K 6235)	18
67	CBS 66023	CHAPPAQUA SUITE (2-LP)	18
68	Polydor 623 246/7	AN EVENING WITH ORNETTE COLEMAN (2-LP)	15

MINT VALUE £

ROGER COLEMAN

60 Top Rank JAR 311 Nobody's Fool/Endlessly . . . 10

COLETTE & BANDITS

65 Stateside SS 416 A Ladies Man/Lost Love . . . 10

COLLAGE

73 Studio Two TWO 410 MISTY (LP) . . . 35
(see also Brian Bennett)

COLLECTIVE HORIZONTAL

79 Dolmen DO 1 COLLECTIVE HORIZONTAL EP (gatefold p/s, stickered white labels) . . . 5

COLLECTORS (Canada)

70 London HLU 10304 I Must Have Been Blind/The Beginning . . . 6
69 Warner Bros WS 1774 GRASS AND WILD STRAWBERRIES (LP) . . . 25
(see also Chilliwack, Electric Prunes)

COLLECTORS (U.K.)

80 Central Collection COL 1 Different World/Talking Hands (p/s) . . . 6

COLLEGE BOYS (Jamaica)

64 Blue Beat BB 202 Love Is A Treasure/Someone Will Be There . . . 22

COLLEGE BOYS (U.K.)

64 Columbia DB 7306 I Just Don't Understand/I'm Gonna Cry . . . 20
67 Pye 7N 17294 Good Times/San Antonio Rose . . . 8

GRAHAM COLLIER SEXTET/SEPTET

67 Deram DML/SML 1005 DEEP DARK BLUE CENTRE (LP) . . . 70
69 Fontana SFJL 922 DOWN ANOTHER ROAD (LP) . . . 50
70 Fontana 6309 006 SONGS FOR MY FATHER (LP, as Graham Collier Music featuring Harry Beckett) . . . 65
71 Philips 6308 051 MOSAICS (LP, live, as Graham Collier Music featuring Harry Beckett) . . . 60
72 Saydisc SDL 244 PORTRAITS (LP) . . . 30
(see also Harry Beckett)

MITTY COLLIER

64 Pye International 7N 25275 I Had A Talk With My Man/Free Girl . . . 25

ALBERT COLLINS

69 Liberty LBS 83238 LOVE CAN BE FOUND ANYWHERE (LP) . . . 35
73 Tumbleweed TW 3501 THERE'S GOTTA BE A CHANGE (LP) . . . 25

ANSEL(L) COLLINS

69 Trojan TR 699 Night Of Love/DERRICK MORGAN: Copy Cat . . . 10
69 Trojan TR 7712 Cotton Dandy/CARL DAWKINS: Don't Get Weary . . . 7
70 Trojan TR 7729 Moon Dust/Fat Cat . . . 15
70 Trojan TR 7730 Monkey (Version I)/(Version II) (plays "High Voltage"/"High Voltage Version"; B-side actually by Beverley All Stars) . . . 15
70 J-Dan JDN 4401 Cock Robin/KING DENNIS: Seven Zero . . . 8
70 Techniques TE 907 Top Secret/Crazy Rhythm (both actually by Winston Wright) . . . 15
71 Techniques TE 913 Nuclear Weapon/TECHNIQUES ALL STARS: La, La, La . . . 15
(see also Dave & Ansell Collins, Conquerors, Lloyd Young, Prince Buster, Les Foster, Ethiopians, Eternals, Pam Brooks, Dennis Alcapone, Rad Bryan)

BOOTSY COLLINS

(see under Bootsy's Rubber Band)

DAVE & ANSELL COLLINS

(see under 'D')

DONIE COLLINS SHOWBAND

68 Pye 7N 17682 Get Down With It/I Can't Help Myself (Sugar Pie Honey Bunch) . . . 10

DOROTHY COLLINS

51 MGM MGM 354 Me And My Imagination/I'm Playing With Fire (78) . . . 8
52 Brunswick 05010 So Madly In Love (with Gordon Jenkins Orchestra)/GORDON JENKINS, ORCHESTRA & CHORUS: Just Say The Word (78) . . . 8
53 Brunswick 05042 Jump Back Honey/I Will Still Love You (with Snooky Lanson) (78) . . . 10
53 Brunswick 05051 If'n/Puppy Love (with Raymond Scott Orchestra) (78) . . . 8
55 Vogue Coral Q 72111 My Boy — Flat Top/In Love . . . 40
55 Vogue Coral Q 72111 My Boy — Flat Top/In Love (78) . . . 12
56 Vogue Coral Q 72116 Moments To Remember/Love And Marriage . . . 12
56 Vogue Coral Q 72116 Moments To Remember/Love And Marriage (78) . . . 8
56 Vogue Coral Q 72137 Seven Days/Manuello . . . 25
56 Vogue Coral Q 72137 Seven Days/Manuello (78) . . . 10
56 Vogue Coral Q 72173 Treasure Of Love/He's Got Me, Hook, Line And Sinker . . . 20
56 Vogue Coral Q 72173 Treasure Of Love/He's Got Me, Hook, Line And Sinker (78) . . . 12
56 Vogue Coral Q 72193 Love Me As Though There Were No Tomorrow/Rock And Roll Train . . . 40
56 Vogue Coral Q 72193 Love Me As Though There Were No Tomorrow/Rock And Roll Train (78) . . . 15
56 Vogue Coral Q 72198 The Italian Theme/Cool It, Baby . . . 35
56 Vogue Coral Q 72198 The Italian Theme/Cool It, Baby (78) . . . 15
56 Vogue Coral Q 72208 The Twelve Gifts Of Christmas/Mr. Santa . . . 15
57 Vogue Coral Q 72232 Baby Can Rock/Would You Ever . . . 25
57 Vogue Coral Q 72232 Baby Can Rock/Would You Ever (78) . . . 15
57 Vogue Coral Q 72252 Mr. Wonderful/I Miss You Already . . . 10
57 Vogue Coral Q 72262 Four Walls/Big Dreams . . . 8
57 Vogue Coral Q 72262 Four Walls/Big Dreams (78) . . . 8
57 Vogue Coral Q 72287 Soft Sands/Sing It, Children, Sing It . . . 8
59 Top Rank JAR 259 Baciare, Baciare/Everything I Have Is Yours . . . 7
60 Top Rank JAR 401 Banjo Boy/Tintarella Di Luna . . . 7
60 Top Rank JAR 523 Unlock Those Chains/I'll Be Yours, You'll be Mine . . . 7
55 London REP 1025 DOROTHY COLLINS SINGS (EP) . . . 30
57 Coral LVA 9058 AT HOME WITH DOROTHY AND RAYMOND (LP) . . . 30

MINT VALUE £

EDWYN COLLINS

87	Creation CRE 047T	Don't Shilly Shally/If Ever You're Ready (7" & 12", white label test pressing only)	40/35
87	Elevation ACIDB 6	My Beloved Girl/50 Shades Of Blue (Acoustic Version)/Clouds (Fogging Up My Mind)/What's The Big Idea? (box set with 3 postcards)	6

(see also Orange Juice, Paul Quinn & Edwyn Collins)

GLENDA COLLINS

60	Decca F 11280	Take A Chance/Crazy Guy	15
61	Decca F 11321	Oh How I Miss You Tonight/Age For Love	18
61	Decca F 11417	Head Over Heels In Love/Find Another Fool	15
63	HMV POP 1163	I Lost My Heart In The Fairground/I Feel So Good	85
63	HMV POP 1233	If You Gotta Pick A Baby/In The First Place	50
64	HMV POP 1283	Baby It Hurts/Nice Wasn't It	70
64	HMV POP 1323	Lollipop/Everybody's Got To Fall In Love	60
65	HMV POP 1439	Johnny Loves Me/Paradise for Two	60
65	HMV POP 1475	Thou Shall Not Steal/Been Invited To A Party	50
66	Pye 7N 17044	Something I've Got To Tell You/My Heart Didn't Lie	75
66	Pye 7N 17150	It's Hard To Believe It/Don't Let It Rain On Sunday	90
90	Document CSAP LP 108	BEEN INVITED TO A PARTY (LP)	20
90	Document CSAP CD 108	BEEN INVITED TO A PARTY (LP)	20

JUDY COLLINS

66	London HLZ 10029	I'll Keep It With Mine/Thirsty Boots	10
67	Elektra EKSN 45011	In My Life/Hard Lovin' Loser	8
69	Elektra EKSN 45053	Some Day Soon/My Father	8
69	Elektra EKSN 45073	Chelsea Morning/Pretty Polly	7
69	Elektra EKSN 45077	Turn, Turn, Turn/Mr. Tambourine Man	7
65	Elektra EKL 209	MAID OF CONSTANT SORROW (LP)	35
65	Elektra EKS 7300	FIFTH ALBUM (LP, orange label)	18
68	Elektra EKL 4012	WILD FLOWERS (LP, orange label, also stereo EKS 74012)	18
69	Elektra EKL 4033	WHO KNOWS WHERE THE TIME GOES (LP, gatefold sleeve, orange label; also stereo EKS 74033)	18

KEANYA COLLINS

78	Grapevine GRP 108	Barnabus Collins — Love Bandit/I Call You Daddy	8

LYN COLLINS

64	Sabre SA 0002	What Am I Gonna Do Without You?/When A Girl Meets A Bad, Bad Boy	18
74	Polydor 2066 490	Rock Me Again And Again And Again/Wide Awake In A Dream	25
74	Mojo 2093 029	Think (About It)/Me And My Baby Got Our Own Thing Going	10
88	Urban URBX 15	Rock Me Again And Again And Again (12")	10
72	Polydor 2918 006	THINK (ABOUT IT) (LP)	40
88	Urban URBLP 7	LYN COLLINS (THE FEMALE PREACHER) (LP)	15

(see also James Brown)

PETER COLLINS

70	Decca F 13048	Get In A Boat/Girl By The Sea	7
70	Decca Nova SDN 21	PETER COLLINS (LP)	25

PHIL COLLINS

81	Virgin VSK 102	In The Air Tonight/The Roof Is Leaking (12-page cartoon booklet p/s)	8
87	Bold Reprieve BRM 007P	Deep Green (1-sided, promo only)	25
90	Virgin VSCDX 1305	Do You Remember? (live)/Doesn't Anybody Stay Together Anymore (live)/The Roof Is Leaking (live) (CD, picture disc, 'carousel' pack)	15

(see also Genesis, Flaming Youth, Brand X, Peter Banks)

PHIL COLLINS & MARILYN MARTIN

85	Virgin VSS 818	Separate Lives/Only You Know And I Know (white vinyl & poster in wallet)	5
85	Virgin VSSD 818	Separate Lives/Only You Know And I Know (2 interlocking picture discs)	5

(see also Brand X, Peter Banks, Genesis, Flaming Youth, Marilyn Martin)

RODGER COLLINS

67	Vocalion VF 9285	She's Looking Good/I'm Serving Time	12

SHIRLEY COLLINS

60	Collector JEI 1508	SINGS IRISH (EP)	60
60	Collector JEB 3	THE FOGGY DEW (EP)	60
60	Collector JEB 5	ENGLISH SONGS (EP)	60
64	Collector JEB 9	ENGLISH SONGS VOL. 2 (EP, with Robin Hall)	60
63	Topic TOP 95	HEROES IN LOVE (EP)	60
59	Folkways FG 3564	FALSE TRUE LOVERS (LP)	110
60	Argo RG 150	SWEET ENGLAND (LP)	120
64	Decca LK 4652	FOLK ROOTS, NEW ROUTES (LP, with Davy Graham, some may have insert)	125
67	Topic 12T 170	THE SWEET PRIMEROSES (LP, originally with blue label)	40/25
68	Polydor 583 025	THE POWER OF THE TRUE LOVE KNOT (LP, with Incredible String Band)	65
71	Pegasus PEG 7	NO ROSES (LP, gatefold sleeve, with Albion Country Band)	35
74	Topic 12T 238	ADIEU TO OLD ENGLAND (LP, originally with blue label)	35/22
75	Deram SML 1117	A FAVOURITE GARLAND (LP)	35
76	Harvest SHSM 2008	AMARANTH (LP)	22
78	Topic 12T 380	FOR AS MANY AS WILL (LP)	18
83	Hannibal HNBL 1327	THE POWER OF THE TRUE LOVE KNOT (LP, reissue)	12

SHIRLEY & DOLLY COLLINS

69	Harvest SHVL 754	ANTHEMS IN EDEN (LP, gatefold sleeve)	50
70	Harvest SHVL 771	LOVE, DEATH AND THE LADY (LP, gatefold sleeve)	70
76	Harvest SHSM 2008	ANTHEMS IN EDEN (LP, gatefold sleeve, reissue)	18

(see also Davy Graham, Albion Country Band, Conundrum)

SIR COLLINS

(see under 'S')

TOMMY COLLINS

58 Capitol CL 14838 Think It Over Boys/All Of The Monkeys Ain't In The Zoo 10
58 Capitol CL 14838 Think It Over Boys/All Of The Monkeys Ain't In The Zoo (78).......... 8
58 Capitol CL 14894 Let Down/It Tickles.......... 8
59 Capitol CL 15076 Little June/A Hundred Years From Now.......... 10
60 Capitol CL 15118 Wreck Of The Old '97/You Belong In My Arms 7
57 Capitol T 776 WORDS AND MUSIC COUNTRY STYLE (LP).......... 25
59 Capitol T 1196 THIS IS TOMMY COLLINS (LP).......... 25

COLLINS BAND & BOB STACKIE

68 Collins Downbeat CRC 0017 Bob Stackie In Soho/LORD CHARLES & HIS BAND: Jamaican Bits And Pieces.......... 45
(see also Sir Collins)

JOE COLMAN

90 Blast First FU10 INFERNAL MACHINE (LP, picture disc, 1,000 only).......... 18

COLONEL

75 Ring O' 2017 104 Cokey Cokey/Away In A Manger (company sleeve) 10

COLONEL

80 Virgin VS 380 Too Many Cooks (In The Kitchen)/I Need Protection (p/s) 6
(see also XTC, Mr. Partridge)

JERRY COLONNA

54 Brunswick 05243 Ebb Tide/The Velvet Glove 15
54 Brunswick 05342 It Might As Well Be Spring/Ja-Da.......... 12
55 Parlophone MSP 6165 Let Me Go, Lover/I Want To Love You, Cara Mia 10
55 London HL 8143 Chicago Style/Baffi 40
55 London HL 8143 Chicago Style/Baffi (78) 10
56 HMV 7M 369 The Shifting, Whispering Sands/Waltz Me Around 10
59 London HA-U 2190 LET'S ALL SING (LP).......... 30
65 Ace Of Hearts AH 102 JERRY COLONNA AND GROUCHO MARX (LP) 15

COLORADOS

64 Oriole CB 1972 Lips Are Redder On You/Who You Gonna Hurt?.......... 30

COLORS OUT OF TIME

81 Monsters In Orbit TVEYE 1 Rock Section/Mambo Girls/Dancing With You (hand-made p/s).......... 6
82 Monsters In Orbit TVEYE 5 She Spins/The Ocean (p/s) 5

COLOR TAPES

79 Wavelength HURT 4 Cold Anger/Leaves Of China (p/s).......... 6

COLOSSEUM

69 Fontana TF 1029 Walking In The Park/Those About To Die.......... 10
69 Fontana STL 5510 THOSE WHO ARE ABOUT TO DIE SALUTE YOU (LP, gatefold sleeve).......... 30
69 Vertigo VO 1 VALENTYNE SUITE (LP, gatefold sleeve, swirl label & inner bag) 35
70 Vertigo 6360 017 DAUGHTER OF TIME (LP, gatefold sleeve, some with large swirl label & bag). 40/35
(see also Dick Heckstall-Smith, Chris Farlowe, Greenslade, John Mayall, Howard Riley Trio, Tempest, Mogul Thrash)

COLOURBOX

82 4AD AD 215 Breakdown/Tarantula (p/s).......... 7
82 4AD BAD 215 Breakdown/Tarantula (12", p/s) 10
83 4AD AD 314 Breakdown (Second Version)/Tarantula (Second Version) (different p/s) 6
83 4AD BAD 314 Breakdown (Second Version)/Tarantula (Second Version) (12", different p/s).......... 8
86 4AD 605 The Official Colourbox World Cup Theme/Philip Glass (p/s) 5
85 4AD CAD 508 COLOURBOX (LP, stickered sleeve, 10,000 only, with bonus LP MAD 509).......... 20
(see also M/A/R/R/S)

COLOURED RAISINS

70 Trojan TR 7700 One Way Love/No More Heartaches 7
(see also Raisins)

COLOURFIELD

84 Chrysalis COLF D2 Thinking Of You/Wild Flames//Little Things/Thinking Of You (double pack).......... 6
85 Chrysalis COLF D4 Castles In The Air/Your Love Was Smashing//I Can't Get Enough Of You Baby/Castles In The Air (Instrumental Mix) (double pack, gatefold p/s) 6
87 Chrysalis CCD 1546 DECEPTION (CD) 25
89 Chrysalis CHR 1480 VIRGINS AND PHILISTINES (CD).......... 60
(see also Specials)

COLOURFUL SEASONS

68 MGM MGM 1433 Out Of The Blue/It's Gonna Break My Heart 6

COLO(U)RS OF LOVE

68 Page One POF 060 I'm A Train/Up On A Cotton Cloud.......... 8
68 Page One POF 086 Just Another Fly/Twenty Ten 8
69 Page One POF 124 Mother Of Convention/Music Mother Made.......... 8

CHRISTOPHER COLT

68 Decca F 12726 Virgin Sunrise/Girl In The Mirror 30

TONY COLTON('S BIG BOSS BAND)

64 Decca F 11879 Lose My Mind/So Used To Loving You (solo) 25
65 Pye 7N 15886 I Stand Accused/Further On Down The Track (with Big Boss Band) 110
66 Pye 7N 17046 You're Wrong There Baby/Have You Lost Your Mind 25
66 Pye 7N 17117 I've Laid Some Down In My Time/Run Pony Rider 40
68 Columbia DB 8385 In The World Of Marnie Dreaming/Who Is She? (solo) 15
(see also Poet & One Man Band, Head Hands & Feet, Real McCoy, Peter B's)

JOHN COLTRANE

60 Esquire EP 229 SOUL OF 'TRANE (EP).......... 10
61 Esquire EP 239 BASS BLUES (EP) 10
64 Fontana 469 203TE WHILE MY LADY SLEEPS (EP) 10

MINT VALUE £

58	Esquire 32-079	THE FIRST TRANE (LP)	18
58	Esquire 32-089	SOUL TRANE (LP)	18
59	Esquire 32-091	TRANEING IN (LP)	18
60	London Jazz LTZ-K 15197	GIANT STEPS (LP)	18
61	Esquire 32-129	LUSH LIFE (LP)	18
61	London Jazz LTZ-K 15219	COLTRANE JAZZ (LP, also stereo SAH-K 6162)	18
62	London Jazz LTZ-K 15232	BAGS AND TRANE (LP, also stereo SAH-K 6192)	18
62	Columbia 33SX 1399	THE BIRDLAND STORY VOL. 1: ECHOES OF AN ERA (LP)	15
62	London Jazz LTZ-K 15239	OLE COLTRANE (LP, also stereo SAH-K 6223)	18
62	HMV CLP 1548	AFRICA/BRASS (LP, also stereo CSD 1431)	15
62	Storyville SLP 28	JOHN COLTRANE & DAVE CHAMBERS (LP)	15
62	HMV CLP 1590	LIVE AT THE VILLAGE VANGUARD (LP, also stereo CSD 1456)	15
63	United Artists (S)ULP 1018	COLTRANE TIME (LP)	15
63	London HA-K/SH-K 8017	COLTRANE PLAYS THE BLUES (LP, as John Coltrane Group)	18
63	Esquire 32-179	STANDARD COLTRANE (LP)	18
63	HMV CLP 1629	COLTRANE (LP, also stereo CSD 1483)	15
63	HMV CLP 1647	BALLADS (LP, also stereo CSD 1496)	15
63	HMV CLP 1657	DUKE ELLINGTON & JOHN COLTRANE (LP, also stereo CSD 1502)	15
64	HMV CLP 1695	IMPRESSIONS (LP, also stereo CSD 1509)	15
64	HMV CLP 1700	JOHN COLTRANE WITH JOHNNY HARTMAN (LP)	15
64	Realm RM 157	ON WEST 42ND STREET (LP)	12
64	Realm RM 181	TRANE RIDE (LP)	12
64	HMV CLP 1741	LIVE AT BIRDLAND (LP, also stereo CSD 1544)	15
65	HMV CLP 1799	CRESCENT (LP, also stereo CSD 1567)	15
65	Stateside SL 10124	BLACK PEARLS (LP)	15
65	HMV CLP 1869	A LOVE SUPREME (LP, also stereo CSD 1605)	15
65	Atlantic ATL/SAL 5022	MY FAVOURITE THINGS (LP)	15
65	Realm RM 52226	TANGANYIKA STRUT (LP)	12
65	HMV CLP 1897	COLTRANE PLAYS (LP, also stereo CSD 1619)	15
66	Stateside SL 10162	BAHIA (LP)	15
66	HMV CLP/CSD 3543	ASCENSION (LP, as John Coltrane Orchestra)	15
66	HMV CLP/CSD 3551	NEW THING AT NEWPORT (LP, with Archie Shepp)	15
66	Atlantic 587/588 004	THE AVANT-GARDE (LP, with Don Cherry)	15
66	HMV CLP/CSD 3575	MEDITATIONS (LP)	15
67	Atlantic 587/588 039	COLTRANE'S SOUND (LP)	15
67	HMV CLP/CSD 3599	COLTRANE LIVE AT THE VILLAGE VANGUARD AGAIN! (LP)	15
67	HMV CLP/CSD 3617	OM (LP, withdrawn)	25
67	HMV CLP/CSD 3617	KULU SE MAMA (LP)	15
68	Transatlantic PR 7280	DAKAR (LP)	15
68	Transatlantic PR 7378	LAST TRANE (LP)	15
68	Impulse MIPL/SIPL 502	EXPRESSION (LP)	15
69	Atlantic 588 139	THREE LITTLE WORDS (LP)	15
69	Impulse MIPL/SIPL 515	COSMIC MUSIC (LP, by Alice & John Coltrane)	15
70	Impulse SIPL 522	SELFLESSNESS (LP)	15
71	Probe SPB 1025	AFRO BLUE (LP)	12
72	Prestige PR 24003	JOHN COLTRANE (2-LP)	15
73	CBS PR 24014	MORE LASTING THAN BRONZE (2-LP)	15
74	Atlantic K 60052	THE ART OF JOHN COLTRANE: THE ATLANTIC YEARS (2-LP)	15
74	CBS PR 24037	BLACK PEARLS (2-LP)	15

(see also Miles Davis, Thelonious Monk, Cannonball Adderley, Don Cherry, Archie Shepp)

COLTS

65	Pye 7N 15955	San Miguel/Where Has Our Love Gone?	7

COLUMBIA BOYS

68	Pye 7N 17513	Baby Come Back/Born To Lose	8
69	Pye 7N 17763	That's My Pa/She Thinks I Still Care	7

COLUMBUS

70	Deram DM 294	Ev'rybody Loves The U.S. Marshall/Tired	10

KEN COLYER('S JAZZMEN)

55	Decca F 10504	Early Hours/Cataract Rag	15
55	Decca F 10519	If I Ever Cease To Love/The Entertainer	15
55	Decca F 10565	It Looks Like A Big Time Tonight/Red Wing	15
56	Tempo A 117	Just A Closer Walk With Thee/Sheik Of Araby	15
56	Tempo A 120	If I Ever Cease To Love You/Isle Of Capri	15
56	Tempo A 126	My Bucket's Got A Hole In It/Wabash Blues	15
56	Tempo A 136	Maryland, My Maryland/The World Is Waiting For The Sunrise	15
56	Decca FJ 10755	All The Girls Go Crazy About The Way I Walk/Dippermouth Blues	15
61	Columbia DB 4676	The Happy Wanderer/Maryland, My Maryland	8
55	Decca DFE 6268	AND BACK TO NEW ORLEANS VOL. 1 (EP)	20
55	Decca DFE 6299	AND BACK TO NEW ORLEANS VOL. 2 (EP)	15
55	Vogue EPV 1202	KEN COLYER IN NEW ORLEANS (EP)	12
55	Tempo EXA 26	KEN COLYER JAZZMEN (EP)	12
56	Melodisc EPM7 59	KEN COLYER JAZZMEN AND THE CRANE RIVER JAZZ BAND (EP)	20
56	Vogue EPV 1102	KEN COLYER IN NEW ORLEANS (EP)	15
56	Tempo EXA 31	KEN COLYER JAZZMEN (EP)	12
57	Tempo EXA 53	KEN COLYER IN NEW ORLEANS (EP)	12
58	Decca DFE 6435	KEN COLYER AND HIS OMEGA BRASS (EP)	10
58	Decca DFE 6466	THEY ALL PLAYED RAGTIME (EP)	20
59	Esquire EP 233	RUM AND COCA COLA (EP, with Christie Brothers Stompers)	12
60	Storyville SEP 301	KEN COLYER JAZZMEN (EP)	22
60	Storyville SEP 305	KEN COLYER'S JAZZMEN (EP)	15
60	Storyville SEP 309	KEN COLYER'S JAZZMEN (EP)	12
60	Decca DFE 6645	WALKING THE BLUES (EP, also stereo STO 143)	20/25
60	Columbia SEG 8038	THIS IS JAZZ (EP)	15
61	Storyville SEP 392	TRAD JAZZ SCENE IN EUROPE VOL. 2 (EP)	15

MINT VALUE £

61 Storyville SEP 412 WILDCAT BLUES (EP) . . . 12
61 Columbia SEG 8104 THIS IS JAZZ VOL. 1 NO. 2 (EP) . . . 18
61 Esquire EP 243 STOMPING (EP) . . . 12
62 Columbia SEG 8145 THIS IS JAZZ VOL. 2 (EP) . . . 12
62 Columbia SEG 8180 TOO BUSY (EP) . . . 20
60s Melodisc EPM7 105 KEN COLYER (EP) . . . 20
66 K.C. KCS 11EP GREEN CORN (EP) . . . 12
54 Decca LF 1152 NEW ORLEANS TO LONDON (10" LP) . . . 60
54 Decca LF 1196 BACK TO THE DELTA (10" LP, as Ken Colyer's Jazzmen & Skiffle Group) . . . 45
55 Vogue LDE 161 KEN COLYER IN NEW ORLEANS (10" LP) . . . 30
56 Tempo LAP 11 KEN COLYER'S JAZZMEN (10" LP) . . . 35
57 Decca LK 4178 CLUB SESSION (LP) . . . 18
58 Decca LF 1301 IN GLORY LAND (10" LP, as Ken Colyer & His Omega Brass Band) . . . 25
59 Decca LF 1319 COLYER IN HAMBURG (10" LP) . . . 25
59 Decca LK 4294 PLAYS STANDARDS (LP) . . . 18
60 Columbia 33SX 1220 THIS IS JAZZ (LP) . . . 30
61 Columbia 33SX 1297 THIS IS JAZZ VOL. 2 (LP, also stereo SCX 3360) . . . 25
61 Columbia 33SX 1363 THIS IS THE BLUES VOL. 1 (LP) . . . 60
63 Society SOC 914 COLYER'S PLEASURE (LP) . . . 25
64 77 LEU 12/7 KEN COLYER AND THE ORIGINAL CRANE RIVER BAND (LP) . . . 30
64 77 LEU 12/10 THE REAL KEN COLYER (LP) . . . 25
65 K.C. KCS 1001 WANDERING (LP) . . . 50

KEN COLYER'S SKIFFLE GROUP

55 Decca F 10631 Down By The Riverside/Take This Hammer . . . 22
55 Decca F 10631 Down By The Riverside/Take This Hammer (78) . . . 6
56 Decca FJ 10711 Streamline Train/Go Down Old Hannah . . . 22
56 Decca FJ 10711 Streamline Train/Go Down Old Hannah (78) . . . 6
56 Decca FJ 10751 Down Bound Train/Mule Skinner . . . 18
56 Decca FJ 10772 Old Riley/Stack O'Lee Blues . . . 15
57 Decca FJ 10889 The Grey Goose/I Can't Sleep . . . 15
57 Decca FJ 10926 Sporting Life/House Rent Stomp . . . 12
57 Decca FJ 10926 Sporting Life/House Rent Stomp (78) . . . 6
57 Decca FJ 10972 Ella Speed/Go Down Sunshine . . . 15
57 Decca FJ 10972 Ella Speed/Go Down Sunshine (78) . . . 8
55 Decca DFE 6286 KEN COLYER'S SKIFFLE GROUP (EP, various coloured sleeves) . . . 22
58 Decca DFE 6444 KEN COLYER'S SKIFFLE GROUP NO. 2 (EP) . . . 20
60 Decca DFE 6563 KEN COLYER'S SKIFFLE GROUP IN HAMBURG (EP) . . . 25

(see also Crane Skiffle Group)

COMBAT 84

82 Victory VIC 1 ORDERS OF THE DAY (EP, wraparound p/s) . . . 20
83 Victory VIC 2 Rapist/The Right To Choose/Barry Prudom (p/s) . . . 20

COMBINATIONS

72 Punch PH 99 1 2 3 A B C/Zee . . . 6

COME

79 Come Org. WDC 88001 Come Sunday/Shaved Slits . . . 15
79 Come Org. WDC 88203 PRESENT RAMPTON (LP) . . . 40
81 Come Org. WDC 881012 I'M JACK (LP, orange vinyl with insert) . . . 30

(see also Whitehouse, New Order)

RORY COMMADORE

(see under Tindersticks)

COMMANCHES

64 Pye 7N 15609 Tomorrow/Missed Your Loving . . . 12

(see also Bobby Allen)

COMMANDERS

55 Brunswick 05366 The Elephants' Tango/Commanders Overture . . . 7
55 Brunswick 05433 The Cat From Coos Bay/Camptown Boogie . . . 8
55 Brunswick 05467 The Monster/Cornball No. 1 . . . 8

(see also Louis Armstrong)

COMMENDABLES

80s Lip CC 1 London E1/Decaying House . . . 10

COMMERCIALS

81 Fast Product COM 1 Sixteen Again And Again/The Heroine Dies/Simon (p/s) . . . 8

COMMITTED

79 Ace ACE 006 Crash Victim/British Crimes/Fast Lane/Advertising . . . 150

COMMITTEE

68 Liberty LBF 15154 Hard Way/Hey You . . . 15

COMMITTEE

69 Pye 7N 17826 Sleep Tight Honey/Memories Of Melinda . . . 6

COMMODORES

55 London HLD 8209 Riding On A Train/Uranium . . . 950
55 London HLD 8209 Riding On A Train/Uranium (78) . . . 60
56 London HLD 8251 Speedo/Whole Lotta Shakin' Goin' On . . . 950
56 London HLD 8251 Speedo/Whole Lotta Shakin' Goin' On (78) . . . 60

COMMODORES

69 Atlantic 584 273 Keep On Dancing/Rise Up . . . 7

(see also Lionel Richie)

COMMON ROUND

70s Galliard GAL 4015 FOUR PENCE A DAY (LP) . . . 15

MINT VALUE £

PERRY COMO

78s

56 HMV POP 191 Juke Box Baby/The Things I Didn't Do . . . 6
59 RCA RCA 1126 I Know/You Are In Love . . . 10
59 RCA RCA 1156 A Still Small Voice/No Well On Earth . . . 6
60 RCA RCA 1170 Delaware/I Know What God Is . . . 20

SINGLES

53 HMV 7M 102 The Ruby And The Pearl/My Love And Devotion . . . 15
53 HMV 7M 110 Some Enchanted Evening/Bali Ha'i . . . 18
53 HMV 7M 118 Don't Let The Stars Get In Your Eyes/To Know You (Is To Love You) (B-side with Fontane Sisters) . . . 50
53 HMV 7M 124 Wild Horses/Please Believe Me . . . 18
53 HMV 7M 138 My Lady Loves To Dance/A Bushel And A Peck (B-side with Betty Hutton) . . . 18
53 HMV 7M 149 My One And Only Heart/Say You're Mine Again . . . 18
53 HMV 7M 155 Hello, Young Lovers/We Kiss In A Shadow . . . 15
53 HMV 7M 163 Pa-Paya Mama/Why Did You Leave Me? . . . 15
54 HMV 7M 175 You Alone/Surprising . . . 15
54 HMV 7M 200 Idle Gossip/Look Out The Window . . . 30
54 HMV 7M 215 Wanted/Give Me Your Hand . . . 18
54 HMV 7M 241 Hit And Run Affair/If You Were Only Mine . . . 15
54 HMV 7M 263 There Never Was A Night So Beautiful/Papa Loves Mambo . . . 18
54 HMV 7M 278 Frosty The Snowman/The Twelve Days Of Christmas . . . 15
55 HMV 7M 296 Ko Ko Mo (I Love You So)/You'll Always Be My Lifetime Love . . . 15
55 HMV 7M 305 Door Of Dreams/Nobody . . . 12
55 HMV 7M 326 There's No Place Like Home For The Holidays/Tina Marie . . . 15
56 HMV 7M 366 Fooled/The Rose Tattoo . . . 12
56 HMV 7M 404 Hot Diggity (Dog Ziggity Boom)/My Funny Valentine . . . 18
56 HMV 7MC 39 Hot Diggity (Dog Ziggity Boom)/Juke Box Baby (export issue) . . . 60
56 HMV POP 240 Glendora/More . . . 15
56 HMV 7MC 49 Glendora/More (export issue) . . . 18
56 HMV POP 271 Moonlight Love/Chincherinchee . . . 12
57 HMV POP 304 Somebody Up There Likes Me/Dream Along With Me (I'm On My Way To A Star) . . . 10
57 HMV 7MC 51 Somebody Up There Likes Me/Dream Along With Me (I'm On My Way To A Star) (export issue) . . . 12
57 HMV POP 328 Round And Round/My House Is Your House . . . 12
57 RCA RCA 1001 The Girl With The Golden Braids/My Little Baby . . . 8
57 HMV POP 369 Silk Stockings/Childhood Is A Meadow . . . 10
57 HMV POP 394 As Time Goes By/All At Once You Love Her . . . 10
57 RCA RCA 1016 Marching Along To The Blues/Dancin' . . . 6
57 RCA RCA 1027 Just Born (To Be Your Baby)/Ivy Rose . . . 6
58 RCA RCA 1036 Magic Moments/Catch A Falling Star . . . 6
58 RCA RCA 1055 Kewpie Doll/Dance Only With Me . . . 12
58 RCA RCA 1062 I May Never Pass This Way Again/Prayer For Peace . . . 5

EPs

54 HMV 7EG 8013 PERRY COMO . . . 8
56 HMV 7EG 8171 SO SMOOTH . . . 8
56 HMV 7EG 8192 COMO SWINGS . . . 10
57 HMV 7EG 8244 WITH A SONG IN MY HEART . . . 10

LPs

54 HMV DLP 1026 PERRY COMO SINGS (10") . . . 30
57 RCA RD 27035 WE GET LETTERS . . . 15
57 RCA RD 27070 WE GET LETTERS VOL. 2 . . . 18
57 RCA RD 27078/SF 5011 DEAR PERRY (mono/stereo) . . . 15/20
57 RCA RD 27082 SINGS MERRY CHRISTMAS MUSIC . . . 15
58 RCA RD 27100 COMO'S GOLDEN RECORDS . . . 15
58 RCA RD 27106/SF 5021 WHEN YOU COME TO THE END OF THE DAY (mono/stereo) . . . 15/20
58 RCA RD 27139/SF 5045 SINGS THE SONGS OF CHRISTMAS (mono/stereo) . . . 15/20
59 RCA RD 27154/SF 5053 COMO SWINGS (mono/stereo) . . . 15/20
60 RCA RD 27206/SF 5089 FOR THE YOUNG AT HEART (mono/stereo) . . . 15/20
61 RCA RD 27232 SING TO ME, MR. C . . . 15
63 RCA Victor RD 7582 THE SONGS I LOVE . . . 15
66 RCA Victor RD 7802 LIGHTLY LATIN . . . 15
66 RCA Victor RD 7836 IN ITALY . . . 15

(see also Fontane Sisters, Betty Hutton)

LES COMPAGNONS DE LA CHANSON

53 Columbia SCM 5005 The Three Bells (The Jimmy Brown Song)/Ave Maria . . . 20
53 Columbia SCM 5056 The Galley Slave/Dreams Never Grow Old . . . 15

COMPANY

80 Incus INCUS 36 FABLES (LP) . . . 50
80 Incus INCUS 38 FICTIONS (LP) . . . 50
82 Incus INCUS 46 EPIPHANY (LP) . . . 50
82 Incus INCUS 47 EPIPHANIES (LP) . . . 50
83 Incus INCUS 51 TRIOS (LP) . . . 50

COMPANY

79 United Artists BP 326 We Wish You Well/Right Time For Love . . . 30

(see also Whitesnake)

COMPLEX

70 CLPM 001 COMPLEX (LP, private pressing, 99 copies only) . . . 1,500
71 Deroy THE WAY WE FEEL (LP, private pressing, 99 copies only) . . . 800

(see also Monsoon, Misfits)

COMPROMISE

66 CBS 202050 You Will Think Of Me/Love Minus Zero . . . 7

COMSAT ANGELS
79 Junta JUNTA 1 Red Planet/I Get Excited/Specimen No. 2 (p/s, later reissued on red vinyl) 6/8

BOBBY COMSTOCK (& COUNTS)
59 Top Rank JAR 223 The Tennessee Waltz/Sweet Talk 10
60 London HLE 9080 Jambalaya/Let's Talk It Over (as Bobby Comstock & Counts) 20
63 Stateside SS 163 Let's Stomp/I Want To Do It 15
63 Stateside SS 221 Susie Baby/Take A Walk 12
65 United Artists UP 1086 I'm A Man/I'll Make You Glad 20

COMUS
71 Dawn DNX 2506 Diana/In The Lost Queen's Eyes/Winter Is A Coloured Bird (p/s) 25
71 Dawn DNLS 3019 FIRST UTTERANCE (LP, gatefold sleeve with lyric sheet) 105
74 Virgin V 2018 TO KEEP FROM CRYING (LP) 20
(see also Gong, Henry Cow, Esperanto Rock Orchestra)

CON-CHORDS
65 Polydor BM 56059 You Can't Take It Away/Let Me Walk With You 20

CONCORDE
70 Attack ATT 8020 Let Me Out/I Belong To You 12

CONCORDS
66 Emblem JDR 303 SOUL PURPOSE (LP) 25

CONCORDS
69 Blue Cat BS 170 Buttoo/I Need Your Loving 15

CONDEMNED 84
86 RFB SIN 2 Oi Ain't Dead!/Under Her Thumb/Follow The Leader/The Nutter (12", p/s, blue vinyl) 25
87 RFB SIN 3 IN SEARCH OF THE NEW BREED (12" EP) 25
88 Oi! OIR 003 BATTLE SCARRED (LP) 22

EDDIE CONDON
60 Philips JAZ 115 Heebies Jeebies/What-cha-call-'em Blues (as Eddie Condon & All-Stars) 6
62 Stateside SL 10005 JAM SESSIONS AT COMMODORE (LP, as Eddie Condon & Group) 15
62 Stateside SL 10010 CONDON A LA CARTE (LP) 15

JEFF CONDON
63 MGM MGM 1221 (Walkin' In) Freddy's Footsteps/Never You Mind 7

HOWIE G. CONDOR
65 Fontana TF 613 Big Noise From Winnetka/The Fix 10

CONEY ISLAND KIDS
55 London HLJ 8207 Baby, Baby You/Moonlight Beach 50
55 London HLJ 8207 Baby, Baby You/Moonlight Beach (78) 15

CONFLICT
82 Crass 221984/1 THE HOUSE THAT MAN BUILT (EP, foldout poster p/s) 6
82 Xntrix XN 2001 LIVE AT THE CENTRE IBERICO (EP, with insert) 6
83 Corp. Christi CHRIST IT'S 4 A Nation Of Animal Lovers/Liberate (poster p/s) 6
85 Mortarhate MORT 15 The Battle Continues (both sides) (p/s, different colours, with insert) 5
88 FUND 1 FROM PROTEST TO RESISTANCE (LP, mail order, w/l, stickered plain sleeve) . . . 12

ARTHUR CONLEY
67 Atlantic 584 083 Sweet Soul Music/Let's Go Steady 10
67 Atlantic 584 121 Shake, Rattle And Roll/You Don't Have To See Me 10
67 Atlantic 584 143 Whole Lotta Woman/Love Comes And Goes 10
68 Atlantic 584 175 Funky Street/Put Our Love Together 10
68 Atlantic 584 197 People Sure Act Funny/Burning Fire 10
68 Atlantic 584 224 Aunt Dora's Love Soul Shack/Is That You Love 10
69 Atco 226 004 Star Revue/Love Sure Is A Powerful Thing 7
70 Atco 226 011 They Call The Wind Maria/Hurt 6
70 Atlantic 2091 025 All Day Singing/God Bless 6
71 Atlantic 2091 106 Sweet Soul Music/Shake, Rattle And Roll 6
71 Atlantic 2091 120 I'm Living Good/I'm So Glad You're Here 6
72 Capricorn K 17506 Rita/More Sweet Soul Music 6
67 Atlantic 587 069 SWEET SOUL MUSIC (LP) 30
68 Atlantic 587 084 SHAKE, RATTLE AND ROLL (LP) 25
68 Atlantic 587/588 128 SOUL DIRECTION (LP) 25
69 Atco 228 019 MORE SWEET SOUL (LP) 18
(see also Soul Clan)

BRIAN CONNELL & ROUND SOUND
66 Mercury MF 956 Just My Kind Of Loving/Something You've Got 10
66 Mercury MF 991 The Same Thing's Happened To Me/Mister Porter 10
68 Philips BF 1661 What Good Am I/Just Another Wedding Day 10
68 Philips BF 1718 I Know/Mister Travel Company 10

RAY CONNIFF & ROCKIN' RHYTHM BOYS
55 Vogue Coral QW 5001 Piggy Bank Boogie/Short Stuff 20
55 Vogue Coral QW 5001 Piggy Bank Boogie/Short Stuff (78) 10
68 CBS (S)BPG 63276 HOW TO SAVE A MARRIAGE AND RUIN YOUR LIFE (LP, soundtrack) 20

BILLY CONNOLLY
85 Audiotrax ATX 10 Freedom (with Chris Tummings & Singing Rebels Band)/ JIMMY HELMS: Celebration (some in p/s) 20/8
72 Transatlantic TRA 258 LIVE! (LP) 12
76 Transatlantic GAR 1 THE CONNOLLY GOLDEN GIFT BOX (2-LP box set: "Live!" & "Solo Concert") . . 15
(see also Humblebums; George Harrison, Ringo Starr & Eric Clapton appear on "Freedom")

MINT VALUE £

BRIAN CONNOLLY

82 Carrere CAR 231 Hypnotised/Fade Away (p/s) 18
(see also Sweet)

CHRIS CONNOR

59 London HLE 8869 Hallelujah I Love Him So/I Won't Cry Anymore 12
59 London HLE 8869 Hallelujah I Love Him So/I Won't Cry Anymore (78) 20
60 London HLK 9124 I Only Want Some/That's My Desire 10
56 London EZ-N 19010 CHRIS CONNOR SINGS LULLABYS OF BIRDLAND (EP, with Ellis Larkin Trio) . . . 15
57 London RE-N 1093 LONDON'S GIRL FRIENDS — NO. 2 (EP) 18
56 London HA-K 2030 PRESENTING CHRIS CONNOR (LP, also stereo SAH-K 6032) 25
56 London LZ-N 14007 SINGS LULLABYS FOR LOVERS (10" LP) 20
57 London HB-N 1074 CHRIS (10" LP) 30
57 London HA-K 2066 HE LOVES ME, HE LOVES ME NOT (LP) 22
60 London LZ-N 14036 THIS IS CHRIS (10" LP) 25
60 London LTZ-K 15142 A JAZZ DATE WITH (LP) 25
60 London LTZ-K 15151 CHRIS CRAFT (LP) 15
60 London Jazz LTZ-K 15183 THE BALLAD OF THE SAD CAFÉ (LP) 20
60 London Jazz LTZ-K 15185 WITCHCRAFT (LP) 20
60 London Jazz LTZ-K 15195 CHRIS IN PERSON (LP, also stereo SAH-K 6088) 20
61 London SAH-K 6190 DOUPLE EXPOSURE (LP, with Maynard Ferguson) 15

EDRIC CONNOR

57 Oriole CB 1362 Manchester United Calypso/Yorumba Highlife (78) 75

KENNETH CONNOR

59 Top Rank JAR 138 Rail Road Rock/Ramona 10
59 Top Rank JAR 138 Rail Road Rock/Ramona (78) 12

CAROL CONNORS

62 London HLN 9619 Big Big Love/Two Rivers 18
(see also Teddy Bears)

CONNY

61 Columbia DB 4714 No One Can Tell Me I'm Too Young/Lovable 20
62 Columbia DB 4845 Gino/Midi-Midinette 20

CONQUERORS

67 Doctor Bird DB 1119 Won't You Come Home Now?/Oh That Day 25
67 Treasure Isle TI 7035 Lonely Street/I Fell In Love 20
69 Amalgamated AMG 832 Secret Weapon (actually by Ansell Collins)/Jumpy Jumpy Girl 18
69 High Note HS 016 If You Can't Beat Them/Anywhere You Want To Go 12
69 High Note HS 025 National Dish/Mr D.J. 12
(see also Stranger Cole & Conquerors, Baba Brooks)

JESS CONRAD

60 Decca F 11236 Cherry Pie/There's Gonna Be A Day 8
60 Decca F 11259 Unless You Meant It/Out Of Luck 10
61 Decca F 11315 Mystery Girl/The Big White House 8
61 Decca F 11348 This Pullover/Why Am I Living? 10
61 Decca F 11375 Oh You Beautiful Doll/I See You 7
61 Decca F 11394 Walkaway/Every Breath I Take 7
61 Decca F 11412 Twist My Wrist/Hey Little Girl (some in p/s) 15/7
62 Decca F 11511 Pretty Jenny/You Can Do It If You Try 7
63 Decca F 11620 It's About Time/As You Like It 7
63 Columbia DB 4969 Take Your Time/I Know You 7
64 Columbia DB 7223 Pussycat/Tempted 7
65 Columbia DB 7561 Things I'd Like To Say/Don't Turn Around 7
65 Pye 7N 15849 Hurt Me/It Can Happen To You 35
69 President PT 269 Other Side Of Life/See The Tinker Ride 6
70 President PT 292 Crystal Ball Dream/Pussycat 6
71 President PT 357 Here She Comes Again/My Idea 6
60 Decca DFE 6666 JESS CONRAD (EP) 25
62 Decca DFE 6702 TWIST MY WRIST (EP) 25
63 Decca DFE 8524 THE HUMAN JUNGLE (EP) 25
61 Decca LK 4390 JESS FOR YOU (LP) 50
(see also Guvners)

TONY CONRAD & FAUST

72 Caroline C 1501 OUTSIDE THE DREAM SYNDICATE (LP) 18
(see also Faust)

CONSCIOUS MINDS

71 Big BG 318 Jamaican Boy/Brainwash 10
71 Ackee ACK 141 Paul, Marcus And Norman/Version 7
71 Punch PH 97 Paul, Marcus And Norman/Version (reissue) 6
71 Escort ERT 857 Peace Treaty/Brainwash 7
(see also Ken Boothe, Jamaicans, B.B. Seaton, Charmers)

CONSORTIUM

68 Pye 7N 17635 All The Love In The World/Spending My Life Saying Goodbye 8
69 Pye 7N 17725 When The Day Breaks/Day The Train Never Came 15
69 Pye 7N 17797 Beggar Man/Cynthia Serenity 7
69 Pye 7N 17841 I Don't Want Her Anymore/The House Upon The Hill 7
70 Trend TNT 52 Melanie Cries Alone/Copper Coloured Years 7

CONSUMATES

68 Coxsone CS 7054 What Is It/ROLAND ALPHONSO: Musical Happiness 25

CONTACT

79 Object Music OM 11 FUTURE/PAST (EP) 5
(see also Passage)

CONTINENTALS
62 Island WI 010 — Going Crazy/Give Me All Your Love 22

CONTINUUM
70 RCA Victor SF 8157 — CONTINUUM (LP) 20
71 RCA Victor SF 8196 — AUTUMN GRASS (LP, gatefold sleeve) 25

CONTOURS
62 Oriole CB 1763 — Do You Love Me/Move Mister Man 20
63 Oriole CB 1799 — Shake Sherry/You Better Get In Line 45
63 Oriole CB 1831 — Don't Let Him Be Your Baby/It Must Be Love 55
64 Stateside SS 299 — Can You Do It/I'll Stand By You 40
65 Stateside SS 381 — Can You Jerk Like Me/That Day She Needed Me 35
65 Tamla Motown TMG 531 — First I Look At The Purse/Searching For A Girl 45
66 Tamla Motown TMG 564 — Determination/Just A Little Misunderstanding 50
67 Tamla Motown TMG 605 — It's So Hard Being A Loser/Your Love Grows More Precious Every Day 25
70 Tamla Motown TMG 723 — Just A Little Misunderstanding/First I Look At The Purse 8
65 Tamla Motown TME 2002 — THE CONTOURS (EP) 100
63 Oriole PS 40043 — DO YOU LOVE ME (LP) 250

CONTRABAND
74 Transatlantic BIG 518 — Lady For Today/On The Road 6
74 Transatlantic TRA 278 — CONTRABAND (LP, with lyric insert) 25
(see also Mae McKenna)

CONTRAST
69 Orange OAS 202 — Hey That's No Way To Say Goodbye/We Can Make It If We Try 8

CONTRASTS featuring BOB MORRISON
64 Parlophone R 5095 — I Can't Get You Out Of My Mind/Click When You're In Love 6
64 Parlophone R 5190 — Call Me/Come On Let's Go 7
68 Monument MON 1018 — What A Day/Lonely Child 10
(see also Bill Forbes)

CONTROLLED BLEEDING
86 Sterile SR 11 — HEADCRACK (LP) 20

CONUNDRUM & RICHARD HARVEY
78 Streetsong No. 1 — Black Birds Of Brittany/SHIRLEY COLLINS & ANNIE POWER: The Mariners Farewell (poster p/s) 18
(see also Bert Jansch, Shirley Collins)

CONVAIRS
66 HMV POP 1549 — Tomorrow Is A Long Time/Midnight Mary 12

BERT CONVY & THUNDERBIRDS
55 London HLB 8190 — C'mon Back/Hoo Bop De Bow 165
55 London HLB 8190 — C'mon Back/Hoo Bop De Bow (78) 40
56 Capitol CL 14601 — Heaven On Earth/CHEERS: Que Pasa Muchacha 25
56 Capitol CL 14601 — Heaven On Earth/CHEERS: Que Pasa Muchacha (78) 18
(see also Cheers, Thunderbirds)

CONNIE CONWAY
60 London HA-W 2214 — CONNIE CONWAY (LP) 22

MIKE CONWAY
68 Plexium PXM 1 — Reign Of King Sadness/I'm Gonna Get Me A Woman 7

RUSS CONWAY
60 Columbia DB 4418 — Royal Event/Rule Britannia! (78) 8
(see also John Barry, Billy Cotton, Ronnie Harris, Olivers)

STEVE CONWAY
55 Columbia SEG 7573 — MEMORIES OF STEVE CONWAY (EP, company sleeve) 10
56 Columbia SEG 7649 — MORE MEMORIES OF STEVE CONWAY (EP) 12

JIMMY CONWELL
72 Jay Boy BOY 64 — Cigarette Ashes/Second Hand Happiness 6

COO-COO RACHAS
59 Capitol CL 15024 — Chili Beans/Track Down 15

RY COODER
71 Reprise RS 23497 — How Can A Poor Man Stand Such Times And Live/Goin' To Brownsville 7
82 Warners K 17952F/SAM 149 — Gypsy Woman/Alimony//Teardrops Will Fall/It's All Over Now (double pack) 5
71 Reprise RSLP 6402 — RY COODER (LP) 22
72 Reprise K 44142 — INTO THE PURPLE VALLEY (LP, with lyric sheet) 18
(see also Don Everly)

ENGLAND COOK
72 Explosion EX 2063 — Samba Girl/NOW GENERATION: Samba (Version) 6

LITTLE JOE COOK (U.K.)
65 Sue WI 385 — Stormy Monday Blues (Parts 1 & 2) 40
(see also Chris Farlowe, Beazers)

LITTLE JOE COOK (U.S.)
68 Sonet SON 2002 — Don't You Have Feelings?/Hold On To Your Money 10
74 Sonet SON 2041 — Hold On To Your Money/Don't You Have Feelings? (reissue, sides reversed) 5

PETER COOK
65 Pye 7N 15847 — Georgia/There And Bach Again 40
(see also Peter London)

MINT VALUE £

PETER COOK

65	Decca F 12182	The Ballad Of Spotty Muldoon/Lovely Lady Of The Roses	18
61	Parlophone PMC 1145	BEYOND THE FRINGE (LP, with other artists)	20
63	Parlophone PMC 1190	BRIDGE ON THE RIVER WYE (LP, with other artists; also stereo PCS 3036)	20/25
63	Parlophone PMC 1198	PETER COOK PRESENTS THE ESTABLISHMENT (LP, with other artists)	20
65	Decca LK 4722	PETER COOK PRESENTS MISTY MR. WISTY (LP)	25
65	Transatlantic TRA 131	PRIVATE EYE'S BLUE RECORD (LP, with other artists)	25

PETER COOK & DUDLEY MOORE

62	Parlophone R 4969	Excerpts From "Beyond The Fringe": Sitting On The Bench/The End Of The World (with Alan Bennett & Jonathan Miller)	15
65	Decca F 12158	Goodbyeee (& Dudley Moore Trio)/DUDLEY MOORE TRIO: Not Only But Also	10
66	Decca F 12380	Isn't She A Sweetie/Bo Dudley	12
67	Decca F 12551	The L.S. Bumble Bee/The Bee Side	30
67	Decca F 12710	Bedazzled/Love Me	30
65	Parlophone GEP 8940	PETER COOK AND DUDLEY MOORE (EP)	12
65	Decca DFE 8644	BY APPOINTMENT (EP)	12
65	Decca LK 4703	NOT ONLY PETER COOK BUT ALSO DUDLEY MOORE (LP)	22
66	Decca LK 4785	ONCE MOORE WITH COOK (LP)	22
68	Decca LK/SKL 4923	BEDAZZLED (LP, soundtrack)	150
68	Decca LK 4981	GOODBYE AGAIN (LP, excerpts from TV series)	20
71	Decca LK 5080	NOT ONLY BUT ALSO (LP)	20

(see also Dudley Moore Trio)

PAUL COOKE

71	Ackee ACK 129	That Girl Was Mine/No Harm	6

ROGER (JAMES) COOKE

68	NEMS 56 3719	If I Didn't Have You/I Know It's You	7
69	Columbia DB 8510	Not That It Matters Anymore/Paper Chase	6
69	Columbia DB 8556	Stop/Someday	6
69	Columbia DB 8596	Smiling Through My Tears/Ain't That A Wonderful Thing (with Eve Graham)	6
71	Columbia DB 8761	If You Would Stay/Mama Packed A Picnic Tea	6
71	Columbia DB 8806	People I Gotta Dream/Today I Killed A Man I Didn't Know	6
70	Columbia SCX 6388	STUDY (LP)	20
72	Regal Zono. SRZA 8508	MEANWHILE ... BACK AT THE WORLD (LP, gatefold sleeve)	20
73	Regal Zono. SLRZ 1035	MINSTREL IN FLIGHT (LP)	20

(see also David & Jonathan)

SAM COOKE

57	London HLU 8506	You Send Me/Summertime	40
57	London HLU 8506	You Send Me/Summertime (78)	15
58	London HLU 8615	That's All I Need To Know/I Don't Want To Cry	60
58	London HLU 8615	That's All I Need To Know/I Don't Want To Cry (78)	15
58	HMV POP 568	Love You Most Of All/Win Your Love For Me	45
58	HMV POP 568	Love You Most Of All/Win Your Love For Me (78)	15
59	HMV POP 610	Everybody Likes To Cha Cha Cha/The Little Things You Do	45
59	HMV POP 610	Everybody Likes To Cha Cha Cha/The Little Things You Do (78)	15
59	HMV POP 642	Only Sixteen/Let's Go Steady Again	15
59	HMV POP 642	Only Sixteen/Let's Go Steady Again (78)	15
59	HMV POP 675	There, I've Said It Again/One Hour Ahead Of The Posse	40
60	London HLU 9046	Happy In Love/I Need You Now	55
60	RCA RCA 1184	Teenage Sonata/If You Were The Only Girl	20
60	HMV POP 754	Wonderful World/Along The Navajo Trail	30
60	RCA RCA 1202	Chain Gang/I Fall In Love Everyday	15
61	RCA RCA 1221	Sad Mood/Love Me	15
61	RCA RCA 1230	That's It, I Quit, I'm Movin' On/What Do You Say	15
61	RCA RCA 1242	Cupid/Farewell, My Darling	12
61	RCA RCA 1260	Feel It/It's Alright	12
62	RCA RCA 1277	Twisting The Night Away/One More Time	10
62	RCA RCA 1296	Bring It On Home To Me/Having A Party	8
62	RCA RCA 1310	Nothing Can Change This Love/Somebody Have Mercy	8
63	RCA RCA 1327	Send Me Some Loving/Baby Baby Baby	12
63	RCA RCA 1341	Another Saturday Night/Love Will Find A Way	8
63	RCA RCA 1361	Frankie And Johnny/Cool Train	10
63	RCA RCA 1367	Little Red Rooster/Shake Rattle And Roll	15
64	RCA RCA 1386	Good News/Basin Street Blues	10
64	RCA RCA 1405	Good Times/Tennessee Waltz	12
64	RCA RCA 1420	Cousin Of Mine/That's Where It's At	15
65	RCA RCA 1436	Shake/A Change Is Gonna Come	15
65	RCA RCA 1452	It's Got The Whole World Shakin'/Ease My Troublin' Mind	12
65	RCA RCA 1476	Sugar Dumpling/Bridge Of Tears	15
68	RCA RCA 1701	Another Saturday Night/DUANE EDDY: Dance With The Guitar Man (w/drawn)	15+
69	RCA RCA 1817	Cupid/Farewell, My Darling (reissue)	6
63	RCA RCX 7117	HEART AND SOUL (EP)	35
64	RCA RCX 7128	SWING SWEETLY (EP)	50
58	HMV CLP 1261	SAM COOKE (LP, with Bumps Blackwell Orchestra)	130
59	HMV CLP 1273	ENCORE (LP)	100
61	RCA RD 27190	COOKE'S TOUR (LP, also stereo SF 5076)	45/60
61	RCA RD 27215	HITS OF THE FIFTIES (LP, also stereo SF 5098)	45/60
61	RCA RD 27222	SWING LOW (LP)	50
62	RCA RD 27245	MY KIND OF BLUES (LP, also stereo SF 5120)	50/65
62	RCA RD 27263	TWISTIN' THE NIGHT AWAY (LP, also stereo SF 5133)	50/65
63	RCA RD/SF 7539	MR. SOUL (LP, mono/stereo)	50/60
63	RCA RD/SF 7583	NIGHT BEAT (LP)	50/75
64	RCA RD/SF 7635	AIN'T THAT GOOD NEWS (LP, mono/stereo)	40/55
65	RCA RD/SF 7674	AT THE COPA (LP, mono/stereo)	40/55
65	RCA RD/SF 7730	SHAKE (LP, mono/stereo)	45/60

65 London HA-U 8232 THE SOUL STIRRERS FEATURING SAM COOKE (LP) . . . 100
66 RCA RD/SF 7764 TRY A LITTLE LOVE (LP) . . . 45
66 Immediate IMLP 002 THE WONDERFUL WORLD OF SAM COOKE (LP) . . . 60
69 RCA Intl. INTS 1005 THE ONE AND ONLY SAM COOKE (LP) . . . 12
70 RCA Intl. INTS 1080 THE LATE AND GREAT SAM COOKE (LP) . . . 12
74 BBC SAM COOKE AND OTHERS (LP, for radio use) . . . 90

COOKIES

62 London HLU 9634 Chains/Stranger In My Arms . . . 20
63 London HLU 9704 Don't Say Nothin' Bad About My Baby/Softly In The Night . . . 20
63 Colpix PX 11012 Will Power/I Want A Boy For My Birthday . . . 20
64 Colpix PX 11020 Girls Grow Up Faster Than Boys/Only To Other People . . . 25
(see also Earl-Jean, Cinderellas, Dorothy Jones)

COOL

69 DeWolfe DW/LP 3136 POP SOUNDS (LP, music library only) . . . 35
(see also Elastic Band)

JOE COOL & KILLERS

77 Ariola ARO 165 I Just Don't Care/My Way . . . 6
(see also Killers)

OLIVER COOL

60 Columbia DB 4552 Oliver Cool/I Like Girls . . . 7
61 Columbia DB 4616 Give Me The Summertime/I Said Yeah . . . 7

COOL BREEZE

71 Patheway PAT 103 People Ask What Love Is/There'll Be No More Sad Tomorrows . . . 20
72 Decca F 13324 Summertime Sunshine/Sing Out Your Love . . . 6
75 Bus Stop BUS 1023 Do It Some More/Citizen Jones . . . 6

COOL CATS

68 Jolly JY 007 What Kind Of Man/HELMSLEY MORRIS: Little Things . . . 35
69 Jolly JY 009 Hold Your Love/ALVA LEWIS: Hang My Head And Cry . . . 18

COOLERS

73 Bread BR 1112 The Youth Of Today/TYRONE TAYLOR: Close Observation . . . 6

EDDIE COOLEY & DIMPLES

57 Columbia DB 3873 Priscilla/Got A Little Woman . . . 250
57 Columbia DB 3873 Priscilla/Got A Little Woman (78) . . . 30

SPADE COOLEY & HIS FIDDLIN' FRIENDS

51 Brunswick 04812 Horse Hair Boogie/Down Yonder (78) . . . 6

RITA COOLIDGE

83 A&M AM 007 All Time High/All Time High (Extended Instrumental) (p/s) . . . 6
83 Scanlite BOND 1 All Time High/All Time High (Extended Instrumental) (p/s) . . . 12

COOL MEN

58 Parlophone GEP 8739 COOL FOR CATS NO. 1 (EP) . . . 25
58 Parlophone GEP 8752 COOL FOR CATS NO. 2 (EP) . . . 25

COOL STICKY

68 Amalgamated AMG 825 Train To Soulsville/ERIC MONTY MORRIS: Cinderella (actually by Errol Dunkley) . . . 20

CHRIS COOMBES

65 Holyground HG 110 WHERE IT'S AT (EP, 99 only) . . . 35

ALICE COOPER

71 Straight W 7209 Eighteen/Body . . . 75
71 Warner Bros K 16127 Under My Wheels/Desperado . . . 8
72 Warner Bros K 16188 School's Out/Gutter Cat (p/s) . . . 10
72 Warner Bros K 16214 Elected/Luney Tune (p/s) . . . 12
72 Warner Bros K 16248 Hello Hurray/Generation Landslide . . . 7
73 Warner Bros/ Lyntone LYN 2585/6 Slick Black Limousine/Extracts From: Unfinished Sweet/Elected/No More Mr Nice Guy/Billion Dollar Babies/I Love The Dead (33rpm flexi free with *NME*) . . . 12/6
73 Warner Bros K 16262 No More Mr. Nice Guy/Raped And Freezin' . . . 6
74 Warner Bros K 16345 Teenage Lament '74/Hard Hearted Alice . . . 6
74 Warner Bros K 16127 Under My Wheels/Desperado (reissue) . . . 6
74 Warner Bros K 16409 School's Out/No More Mr. Nice Guy/Elected/Billion Dollar Babies (maxi-45) . . . 7
74 Chrysalis CHS 2069 I'm Flash/ELKIE BROOKS: Sacrifice (p/s, promo only) . . . 35
75 Anchor ANC 1012 Department Of Youth/Cold Ethyl (p/s) . . . 6
75 Anchor ANC 1018 Only Women Bleed/Devil's Food . . . 5
75 Anchor ANC 1025 Welcome To My Nightmare/Black Widow . . . 5
75 Anchor ANE 7001 Welcome To My Nightmare/Department Of Youth/Black Widow/ Only Women Bleed (EP, p/s) . . . 6
75 Anchor ANE 12001 Welcome To My Nightmare/Department Of Youth/Black Widow/ Only Women Bleed (12" EP, p/s) . . . 10
76 Warner Bros K 16792 I Never Cry/Got To Hell (p/s) . . . 10
77 Warner Bros K 16935 (No More) Love At Your Convenience/It's Hot Tonight (p/s, gothic type on label) . . . 6
80 Warner Bros K 17598 Clones (We're All)/Model Citizen (p/s) . . . 7
82 Warner Bros K 17940 For Britain Only/Under My Wheels (live) (p/s) . . . 8
82 Warner Bros K 17940M For Britain Only/Under My Wheels (live) (picture disc, unreleased)
82 Warner Bros K 17940T For Britain Only/Under My Wheels (live)/Who Do You Think We Are? (live)/ Model Citizen (live) (12", p/s) . . . 12
83 Warner Bros ALICE 1T I Love America/Fresh Blood/Pass The Gun Around (12", p/s) . . . 12
86 MCA MCA 1090 He's Back (The Man Behind The Mask)/Billion Dollar Babies (poster p/s) . . . 6
89 Epic ALICE 3 Bed Of Nails/I'm Your Gun (p/s, with poster) . . . 8
89 Epic ALICEP 3 Bed Of Nails/I'm Your Gun/Go To Hell (live) (12", picture disc) . . . 8

MINT VALUE £

89	Epic ALICEC 3	Bed Of Nails/I'm Your Gun/Go To Hell (live)/Only Women Bleed (live) (CD, card sleeve)	10
89	Epic 655 061-2	Poison/Trash/Ballad Of Dwight Fry (live)/I Got A Line On You (CD, 'bottle' pack)	12
89	Epic ALICEP 4	House Of Fire/This Maniac's In Love With You (shaped picture disc)	6
89	Epic ALICEQ 4	House Of Fire/Poison (live)/Spark In The Dark (live)/Under My Wheels (live) (12", with tour poster)	8
89	Epic ALICEC 4	House Of Fire/This Maniac's In Love With You/Billion Dollar Babies (live)/ Under My Wheels (live) (CD, card sleeve)	8
91	Epic 657 438-9	Love's A Loaded Gun/Fire/Eighteen (live) (CD, gun-shaped p/s)	12
69	Straight STS 1051	PRETTIES FOR YOU (LP, purple label, gatefold sleeve)	60
69	Straight STS 1061	EASY ACTION (LP, purple label, gatefold sleeve)	55
71	Straight STS 1065	LOVE IT TO DEATH (LP, purple label, gatefold sleeve)	50
71	Warner Bros K 56005	KILLER (LP, green label, gatefold sleeve with perforated foldout calendar)	20
72	Warner Bros K 56007	SCHOOL'S OUT (LP, green label, 'desktop' gatefold sleeve, with 'paper panties' inner)	45
73	Warner Bros K 56013	BILLION DOLLAR BABIES (LP, green label, gatefold embossed sleeve with attached perforated cards, with $ billion note & inner sleeve)	22
73	Warner Bros K 46177	LOVE IT TO DEATH (LP, reissue, green label, gatefold sleeve)	18
73	Warner Bros K 66021	SCHOOL DAYS (2-LP, gatefold sleeve, reissue of STS 1051 & 1061)	18
74	Warner Bros K 56018	MUSCLE OF LOVE (LP, 'cardboard box' sleeve, with insert & inner sleeve)	15

(see also Billion Dollar Babies)

GARNELL COOPER & KINFOLKS

63	London HL 9757	Green Monkey/Long Distance	18

HENRY COOPER

76	DJM DJS 10734	Knock Me Down With A Feather/Knocked Out For Your Love (p/s)	10/6

LES COOPER & SOUL ROCKERS

62	Stateside SS 142	Wiggle Wobble/Dig Yourself	12

MARTY COOPER CLAN

63	RCA Victor RD 7596	NEW SOUNDS — OLD GOODIES (LP)	15

MIKE COOPER

70	Dawn DNX 2501	Your Lovely Ways (Parts 1 & 2)/Watching You Fall (Parts 1 & 2) (p/s)	7
71	Dawn DNX 2511	Too Late Now/The Ballad Of Fulton Allen/Good Times (p/s)	7
72	Dawn DNS 1022	Time In Hand/Schwabisch Hall	6
60s	Saydisc SD 137	UP THE COUNTRY BLUES (EP)	70
68	Matchbox SDM 159	THE INVERTED WORLD (LP, with Ian A. Anderson)	85
69	Pye NSPL 18281	OH REALLY!? (LP)	25
70	Dawn DNLS 3005	DO I KNOW YOU? (LP)	15
70	Dawn DNLS 3011	TROUT STEEL (LP, some with poster insert)	20/15
71	Dawn DNLS 3026	PLACES I KNOW (LP, with insert)	15
72	Dawn DNLS 3031	THE MACHINE GUN COMPANY (LP)	15
74	Fresh Air 6370 500	LIFE AND DEATH IN PARADISE (LP)	12

(see also Ian A. Anderson, Heron)

TOMMY COOPER

61	Palette PG 9019	Don't Jump Off The Roof Dad/How Come There's No Dog Day?	25
67	Pye 7N 17259	Happy Tommy/Tom Tom The Piper's Son	7

COOPER TEMPLE CLAUSE

03	BMG MORNING 32	Promises Promises/Our Eyes Are Bright (p/s)	5
00s	private pressing	The Crayon Demos/Who Needs Enemies?/Let's Kill Music/Devil Walks In The Sand Demos (CD-R, in hand-crayoned sleeve)	100
00s	Morning MORNING 11	Let's Kill Music/Girl Ink Age (p/s)	7
00s	Morning MORNING 27	A.I.M. (1-track promo-only CD, avaiable on mail order from *NME*)	15
01	Morning MORNING 2	THE HARDWARE EP (Way Out West/Sister Soul//The Devil Walks In The Sand/ Solitude) (2 x 7", 1 black and 1 white vinyl, poly sleeves in box, 500 only)	40
01	Morning MORNING 6	THE WARFARE EP (Panzer Attack/ I'll Still Write/I'll Still Write [Acoustic]/Mansell) (2 x 7", 1 black and white 1 vinyl in box, 1000 only)	15
01	Morning MORNING 5	THE WARFARE EP (Panzer Attack/ I'll Still Write/Mansell) (CD, digipak)	12
02	Morning MORNING 20	SEE THIS THROUGH AND LEAVE (6 x 7", limited, numbered box set)	20

COWBOY COPAS

51	Vogue V 9001	The Feudin' Boogie (with Grandpa Jones)/Strange Little Girl (78)	12
53	Parlophone R 3708	It's No Sin To Love You/I've Grown So Used To You (78)	10
53	Parlophone R 3756	Doll Of Clay/If Wishes Were Horses (78)	10
54	Parlophone CMSP 10	I Can't Go On/A Wreath On The Door Of My Heart (export issue)	35
54	Parlophone DP 373	I Can't Go On/A Wreath On The Door Of My Heart (78, export issue)	10
54	Parlophone MSP 6079	Tennessee Senorita/If You Will Let Me Be Your Love	30
54	Parlophone R 3812	Tennessee Senorita/If You Will Let Me Be Your Love (78)	12
54	Parlophone DP 384	Look What I Got/Will You Forget (78, export issue)	10
54	Parlophone DP 390	The Man Upstairs/He Stands By The Window (78, export issue)	10
54	Parlophone MSP 6109	A Heartbreak Ago/The Blue Waltz	30
54	Parlophone R 3880	A Heartbreak Ago/The Blue Waltz (78)	10
55	Parlophone MSP 6164	I'll Waltz With You In My Dreams/Return To Sender	30
55	Parlophone R 4005	I'll Waltz With You In My Dreams/Return To Sender (78)	12
60	Melodisc M 1566	Alabam/I Can	18
55	Parlophone GEP 8527	FAVOURITE COWBOY SONGS (EP)	18
56	Parlophone GEP 8575	WESTERN STYLE (EP)	18
50s	Parlophone CGEP 3	COWBOY COPAS (EP, export issue)	18
62	Top Rank JKP 3014	COUNTRY MUSIC (EP)	18
63	Stateside SE 1003	COUNTRY HITS (EP)	15
64	London R-ED 1418	THE UNFORGETTABLE COWBOY COPAS VOLUME 1 (EP)	15
64	London R-ED 1419	THE UNFORGETTABLE COWBOY COPAS VOLUME 2 (EP)	15
64	London R-ED 1420	THE UNFORGETTABLE COWBOY COPAS VOLUME 3 (EP)	15
61	Melodisc MLP 12-119	COWBOY COPAS (LP)	35

MINT VALUE £

63 Stateside SL 10035 SONGS THAT MADE HIM FAMOUS (LP) 15
63 London HA-B 8088 COUNTRY ENTERTAINER NO. 1 (LP) 25
64 London HA-B 8180 STARS OF THE GRAND OLE OPRY — COWBOY COPAS (LP) 20
64 Ember CW 105 OPRY STAR SPOTLIGHT ON COWBOY COPAS (LP) 12
(see also Johnny Bond)

JULIAN COPE

84 Mercury MADOX 004 Head Hang Low/Elegant Chaos/Strasbourg/Lunatic And Fire Pistol (excerpts), (tracks by Spirit) (flexidisc sampler, printed plain sleeve) 5
85 Mercury MER 1822 Sunspots/I Went On A Chourney//Mik Mak Mok/Land Of Fear (double pack) 6
86 Island ISBN 290 World Shut Your Mouth/World Shut Your Mouth (Trouble Funk Remix)// Umpteenth Unnatural Blues/Levitation (double pack box set with biography, photos & stickers) 8
87 Antar 4503 Interview/Christmas Mourning/Transmitting (fan club box set, with card, biography, membership card, letter, photos & stickers) 7
91 Island JC 1 Safesurfer/If You Love Me At All (33rpm, sold at gigs, stickered white sleeve) . . . 12
94 K.A.K. (no cat. no.) Paranormal In The West Country (Original Version)/(String Quartet Version)/ (Acoustic Version)/(Krankenhausmusik Version) (mail-order only via offer with "Queen Elizabeth" LP) 12
87 Island ILPS 9861 SAINT JULIAN (LP, with free 12" interview LP [JCCLP 1]) 12
(see also Teardrop Explodes, Rabbi Joseph Gordan)

KEN COPE & BREAKAWAYS

63 Pye 7N 15524 Hands Off, Stop Muckin' About/Why Am I So Shy 6
(see also Breakaways)

SUZY COPE

61 HMV POP 941 Teenage Fool/Juvenile Delinquent 25
62 HMV POP 1047 Not Never Not Now/Kisses And Tears 25
63 HMV POP 1167 Biggity Big/Doing What You Know Is Wrong 25
65 CBS 201792 You Can't Say I Never Told You/And Now I Don't Want You. 25

AL(L)AN COPELAND

57 Vogue Coral Q 72237 Feeling Happy/You Don't Know 15
57 Vogue Coral Q 72277 How Will I Know?/Will You Still Be Mine 8
59 Pye International 7N 25007 Flip Flop/Lots More Love (as Allan Copeland) 18
59 Pye International N 25007 Flip Flop/Lots More Love (78, as Allan Copeland) 25

KEN COPELAND

57 London HLP 8423 Pledge Of Love/MINTS: Night Air. 300
57 London HLP 8423 Pledge Of Love/MINTS: Night Air (78) 40

COPPER FAMILY

71 Leader LED 2067 A SONG FOR EVERY SEASON (LP, sampler, tracks from 4-LP set). 40

COPPERFIELD

69 Instant IN 004 Any Old Time/I'm No Good For Her 12
69 Parlophone R 5818 I'll Hold Out My Hand/Far Away Love 6
(see also Quartz)

COPS 'N ROBBERS

64 Decca F 12019 St. James Infirmary/There's Gotta Be A Reason. 55
65 Pye 7N 15870 I Could Have Danced All Night/Just Keep Right On 30
65 Pye 7N 15928 It's All Over Now Baby Blue/I've Found Out 30
(see also Fairies)

COPY CATS

69 Bullet BU 419 Copy Cat (with Derrick Morgan)/BUNNY LEE ALL STARRS: Hot Lead 7

CORAL

02 Deltasonic XPCD 2729 Machines Have No Emotions/Skeleton Key (Video)/The Coral (On The Road Movie) (CD-Rom) 20
02 Deltasonic DLT 005 Goodbye/Travelling Circus (numbered p/s). 5
03 Deltasonic DLT 010 Don't Think You're The First/See Through Bergerac (numbered p/s) 6
01 Deltasonic DLT 1 SHADOWS FALL EP (Shadows Fall/The Ballad Of Simon Diamond/A Sparrow's Song) (CD, 1000 only) 80
01 Deltasonic DLTCD 3 THE OLDEST PATH EP (The Oldest Path/God Knows/Short Balled/Flys (CD, 1000 only, picture disc) 40
02 Deltasonic 6725222 SKELETON KEY EP (Dressed Like A Cow/Darkness/Sheriff John Brown/ Skeleton Key [video]) (CD, with sticker) 15
02 Deltasonic DLTLP 006 THE CORAL (LP, with inner) 12

CORBAN

78 Acorn AC 002 A BREAK IN THE CLOUDS (LP, with insert) 18

HARRY H. CORBETT

62 Pye 7N 15468 Junk Shop/The Isle Of Clerkenwell 10
63 Pye 7N 15552 Like The Big Guys Do/The Green Eye 10
63 Pye 7N 15584 The Table And The Chair/Things We Never Had 10
67 Decca F 12714 Flower Power Fred/(I'm) Saving All My Love (with Unidentified Flower Objects) . 15
71 Columbia DB 8840 Harry You Love Her/It's The End Of A Beautiful Night 7
(see also Wilfred Brambell, Wilfred Brambell & Harry H. Corbett, Faraway Folk)

MIKE CORBETT & JAY HIRSH

71 Atlantic 2400 141 MIKE CORBETT & JAY HIRSH (LP, gatefold sleeve) 20
(see also Mr. Flood's Party)

RONNIE CORBETT

68 Columbia DB 8512 Big Man/Fancy You Fancying Me. 7
70 Philips 6006 070 It's All Going Up, Up, Up/Put On A Happy Face 6

CORBY & CHAMPAGNE

66 Pye 7N 17203 Time Marches On/I'll Be Back 6

MINT VALUE £

JASON CORD

69	Chapter One CH 102	I've Got My Eyes On You/I Can't Take No More Of Your Lies	6
69	Chapter One CH 110	Why Shouldn't I/Spring Never Came Twice	6

FRANK CORDELL & HIS ORCHESTRA

56	HMV 7M 397	Port-Au-Prince/"Double Cross" TV Theme	8
56	HMV 7M 419	Sadie's Shawl/Flamenco Love	15
61	HMV POP 824	The Black Bear/Darling Charlie	10
61	HMV POP 852	Theme From 'The Rebel'/Ou La La	7
63	HMV CSD 1475	HERE THIS! (LP)	15

PHIL CORDELL

69	Warner Bros WB 8001	Pumping The Water/Red Lady	7

(see also Thursday's Children)

CORDES

65	Cavern Sound IMSTL 1	Give Her Time/She's Leaving	60

LOUISE CORDET

62	Decca F 11476	I'm Just A Baby/In A Matter Of Moments	8
62	Decca F 11524	Sweet Enough/Someone Else's Fool	6
63	Decca F 11673	Around And Around/Which Way The Wind Blows	10
64	Decca F 11824	Don't Let The Sun Catch You Crying/Loving Baby	10
64	Decca F 11875	Don't Make Me Over/Two Lovers	15
62	Decca DFE 8515	THE SWEET BEAT OF LOUISE CORDET (EP)	60

CORDUROY

93	Acid Jazz JAZID 68T	Something In My Eye/Ponytail/Electric Soup (12")	15
90s	Acid Jazz JAZID 119T	Summer In My Eye (12", company sleeve, withdrawn)	35

(see also Boys Wonder)

CORDUROYS

66	Planet PLF 122	Tick Tock/Too Much Of A Woman	40

CHICK COREA (& RETURN TO FOREVER)

72	ECM ECM 1018/9	PARIS CONCERT FEBRUARY 1971 (2-LP, as Corea & Braxton & Holland)	15
74	Atlantic K 60081	INNER SPACE (2-LP)	18
74	People PLEO 9	SUNDANCE (LP)	18

(see also Return To Forever)

PADDY COREA

72	Explosion EX 2066	Soul And Inspiration/STAGS: You Must Be Trying My Faith	6

CORKSCREW

79	Highway SHY 7005	FOR OPENERS (LP)	25

CORNBREAD & JERRY

61	London HLG 9352	L'il Ole Me/Loco Moto	12

DON CORNEL & ETERNALS

70	Moodisc MU 3506	Christmas Joy/WINSTON & RUPERT: Musically Beat	7

CORNELIUS BROTHERS & SISTER ROSE

71	United Artists UP 35218	Treat Her Like A Lady/Over At My Place	6
72	United Artists UP 35378	Too Late To Turn Back Now/Lift Your Love Higher	15
73	United Artists UP 35502	I'm Never Gonna Be Alone Anymore/Let's Stay Together	8

DON CORNELL

51	HMV JO 212	I Need You So/It Couldn't Happen To A Sweeter Girl (78)	8
54	Vogue Coral Q 2013	Hold My Hand/I'm Blessed	45
54	Vogue Coral Q 2037	S'Posin'/I Was Lucky	20
55	Vogue Coral Q 72058	No Man Is An Island/All At Once	18
55	Vogue Coral Q 72070	Give Me Your Love/When You Are In Love	18
55	Vogue Coral Q 72071	Athena/Size 12	18
55	Vogue Coral Q 72073	Stranger In Paradise/The Devil's In Your Eyes	40
55	Vogue Coral Q 72080	Unchained Melody/Most Of All	20
55	Vogue Coral Q 72080	Unchained Melody/Most Of All (78)	6
55	Vogue Coral Q 72104	Love Is A Many Splendored Thing/The Bible Tells Me So	22
56	Vogue Coral Q 72132	There Once Was A Beautiful/Make A Wish	18
56	Vogue Coral Q 72144	Teenage Meeting (Gonna Rock It Right)/I Still Have A Prayer	35
56	Vogue Coral Q 72144	Teenage Meeting (Gonna Rock It Right)/I Still Have A Prayer (78)	10
56	Vogue Coral Q 72152	Rock Island Line/Na-Ne Na-Na	22
56	Vogue Coral Q 72152	Rock Island Line/Na-Ne Na-Na (78)	10
56	Vogue Coral Q 72164	But Love Me (Love But Me)/Fort Knox	18
56	Vogue Coral Q 72203	All Of You/Heaven Only Knows	15
57	Vogue Coral Q 72218	See-Saw/From The Bottom Of My Heart	20
57	Vogue Coral Q 72234	Let's Be Friends/Afternoon In Madrid	15
57	Vogue Coral Q 72257	Sittin' In The Balcony/Let's Get Lost	30
57	Vogue Coral Q 72257	Sittin' In The Balcony/Let's Get Lost (78)	12
57	Vogue Coral Q 72276	Mama Guitar/A Face In The Crowd	30
57	Vogue Coral Q 72276	Mama Guitar/A Face In The Crowd (78)	15
57	Vogue Coral Q 72291	There's Only You/Non Dimenticar	12
58	Coral Q 72308	Before It's Time To Say Goodnight/Mailman, Bring Me No More Blues	20
58	Coral Q 72308	Before It's Time To Say Goodnight/Mailman, Bring Me No More Blues (78)	15
58	Coral Q 72313	I've Got Bells On My Heart/Keep God In The Home	12
58	Coral Q 72313	I've Got Bells On My Heart/Keep God In The Home (78)	15
59	Pye International 7N 25041	Sempre Amore/Forever Couldn't Be Long Enough	12
59	Pye International N 25041	Sempre Amore/Forever Couldn't Be Long Enough (78)	12
59	London HLD 8937	This Earth Of Mine/The Gang That Sang "Heart Of My Heart"	12
59	London HLD 8937	This Earth Of Mine/The Gang That Sang "Heart Of My Heart" (78)	20
54	Vogue Coral LVC 10004	DON CORNELL FOR YOU (10" LP)	35
56	Coral LVA 9037	LET'S GET LOST (LP)	40

MINT VALUE £

JERRY CORNELL

55 London HL 8157 — Please Don't Talk About Me When I'm Gone/St. Louis Blues . . . 55

LYN CORNELL

60 Decca F 11227 — Like Love/Demon Lover . . . 20
60 Decca F 11260 — Teaser/What A Feeling . . . 12
60 Decca F 11277 — Never On Sunday/Swain Kelly . . . 6
60 Decca F 11301 — The Angel And The Stranger/Xmas Stocking . . . 6
61 Decca F 11326 — The Sweet Life (La Dolce Vita)/When Is Someday . . . 7
61 Decca F 11374 — Surely In Love/Adios My Love . . . 7
62 Decca F 11430 — African Waltz/Moanin' . . . 8
62 Decca F 11469 — I Sold My Heart To The Junkman/Step Up And Rescue Me . . . 15
63 Decca F 11775 — Sally Go Round The Roses/You Can Kiss Me If You Like . . . 10

CORNFLAKES

62 Fontana 267 227TF — Oh, Listen To The Band/Moonstruck . . . 8

ARNOLD CORNS

71 B&C CB 149 — Moonage Daydream/Hang Onto Yourself (as 'The Arnold Corns') . . . 60
72 B&C CB 189 — Hang Onto Yourself/Man In The Middle . . . 40
74 Mooncrest MOON 25 — Hang Onto Yourself/Man In The Middle (reissue) . . . 15
(see also David Bowie)

CORONADOS

64 London HL 9895 — Love Me With All Your Heart/Querida . . . 10
67 Stateside SS 2043 — Johnny B. Goode/Shook Me Down . . . 8

CORONETS

54 Columbia SCM 5117 — Do, Do, Do, Do, Do, Do, Do It Again/I Ain't Gonna Do It No More . . . 12
56 Columbia SCM 5235 — Lizzie Borden/My Believing Heart . . . 8
56 Columbia SCM 5261 — There's No Song Like An Old Song/The Magic Touch . . . 12
56 Columbia DB 3827 — Someone To Love/The Rocking Horse Cowboy . . . 8
56 Columbia SEG 7603 — RHYTHM AND BLUES (EP, as Coronets with Eric Jupp Orchestra) . . . 15
56 Columbia SEG 7621 — THE PERFECT COMBINATION (EP, as Coronets with Eric Jupp Orchestra) . . . 10
56 Columbia SEG 7714 — SONG SHOW (EP) . . . 10
(see also Chris Sandford & Coronets, Tony Brent, Ronnie Harris, Benny Hill, Eric Jupp, Lee Lawrence)

CORONETS

68 Stresa BEV SP 1104/1105 — I Wonder Why/You're Leaving Tomorrow . . . 45

CORPORATION (Jamaica)

70 Grape GR 3022 — Sweet Musille/Walking Thru' Jerusalem . . . 10
(see also Claudette & Corporation, Billy Jack)

CORPORATION (U.S.)

69 Capitol E-T/E-ST 175 — THE CORPORATION (LP) . . . 25

CORRIE FOLK TRIO/CORRIES

63 Waverley SLP 530 — Love Is Teasing/O, Waly Waly (p/s) . . . 8
63 Waverley ELP 129 — CORRIE FOLK TRIO (EP) . . . 20
63 Waverley ELP 131 — YON FOLK SONGS IS FOR THE BURDS (EP) . . . 20
63 Waverley ELP 132 — MORE FOLK SONGS FOR THE BURDS (EP) . . . 15
65 Waverley ZLP 2042 — CORRIE FOLK TRIO WITH PADDIE BELL (LP, also stereo SZLP 2043) . . . 20
65 Waverley ZLP 2050 — THE PROMISE OF THE DAY (LP) . . . 20

CORRS

95 Atlantic A 5727CD — Runaway/Leave Me Alone (CD) . . . 8
96 Atlantic A 5662 CD — Love To Love You (radio edit)/Rainy Day/Carraroe Jig (CD, includes 6 cards) . . . 10
97 Atlantic A 5661 CD — Love To Love You (radio edit)/Rainy Day/Carraroe Jig/Runaway (LP version) (CD) . . . 8
97 Atlantic AT 0018 CDX — I Never Loved You Anyway (Radio Edit)/What I Know/ I Never Loved You Anyway (Acoustic) (CD, includes 3 cards) . . . 8
99 Atlantic PC1/C01 — Lifting Me (Mixes)/Interactive CD-Rom Interview . . . 15
98 Atlantic 80917 2 — TALK ON CORNERS (CD, with 4 prints & cassette) . . . 15

Promos

97 East West 19417 — 6 SONGS FROM THE ALBUM "TALK ON CORNERS" (CD, unmixed versions) . . . 20
98 Atlantic SAM 3233 — DREAMS (remixes) (12", p/s) . . . 20

CORSAIRS (Jamaica)

70 Unity UN 558 — Goodnight My Love/Lover Girl . . . 7

CORSAIRS (U.K.)

67 CBS 202624 — Pay You Back With Interest/I'm Gonna Shut You Down . . . 15

CORSAIRS (U.S.)

62 Pye International 7N 25142 — I'll Take You Home/Sitting On Your Doorstep (with Jay 'Bird' Uzzel) . . . 8

BOB CORT (SKIFFLE GROUP)

57 Decca FJ 10831 — It Takes A Worried Man To Sing A Worried Blues/Don't You Rock Me Daddy-O . . . 20
57 Decca FJ 10831 — It Takes A Worried Man To Sing A Worried Blues/ Don't You Rock Me Daddy-O (78) . . . 7
57 Decca F 10892 — Six-Five Special/Roll Jen Jenkins . . . 20
57 Decca F 10892 — Six-Five Special/Roll Jen Jenkins (78) . . . 6
57 Decca F 10899 — Maggie May/Jessamine (with Liz Winters) . . . 8
57 Decca F 10905 — Schoolday (Ring! Ring! Goes The Bell)/Ain't It A Shame (To Sing Skiffle On Sunday) . . . 20
57 Decca F 10951 — 'Bob Cort Skiffle Party' Medley (Parts 1 & 2) . . . 12
58 Decca F 10989 — The Ark (Noah Found Grace In The Eyes Of God)/Yes! Suh! . . . 15
59 Decca F 11109 — Foggy Foggy Dew/On Top Of Old Smokey (solo) . . . 7
59 Decca F 11109 — Foggy Foggy Dew/On Top Of Old Smokey (solo) (78) . . . 8
59 Decca F 11145 — Waterloo/Battle Of New Orleans (solo) . . . 12
59 Decca F 11145 — Waterloo/Battle Of New Orleans (solo) (78) . . . 6
59 Decca F 11160 — Kissin' Time/I'm Gonna Get Married (solo) . . . 10

MINT VALUE £

59 Decca F 11160	Kissin' Time/I'm Gonna Get Married (solo) (78)	6
William Timpson Ltd no cat. no.	The Shop In The Cellar (1-sided 78, 200 only)	15
60 Decca F 11197	El Paso/A Handful Of Gold (solo)	6
60 Decca F 11256	Mule Skinner Blues/The Ballad Of Walter Williams (solo)	15
60 Decca F 11256	Mule Skinner Blues/The Ballad Of Walter Williams (solo) (78)	9
60 Decca F 11285	The Ballad Of The Alamo/Five Brothers (solo)	7
59 Decca DFE 6630	BARRACK ROOM BALLADS (EP)	12
61 Decca DFE 6686	BOB CORT'S GENTLEFOLK (EP, as Bob Cort's Gentlefolk)	10
57 Decca LK 4222	AIN'T IT A SHAME (LP)	30
59 Decca LK 4301	ESKIMO NELL (LP)	25

(see also Liz Winters & Bob Cort)

DAVE 'BABY' CORTEZ

59 London HLU 8852	The Happy Organ/Love Me As I Love You	15
59 London HLU 8852	The Happy Organ/Love Me As I Love You (78)	7
59 London HLU 8919	The Whistling Organ/I'm Happy	8
59 London HLU 8919	The Whistling Organ/I'm Happy (78)	5
60 Columbia DB 4404	Piano Shuffle/Dave's Special	8
60 London HLU 9126	Deep In The Heart Of Texas/You're Just Right	15
62 Pye International 7N 25159	Rinky Dink/Getting Right	15
66 Roulette RK 7001	Countdown/Summertime	6
60 London RE-U 1233	DAVE 'BABY' CORTEZ (EP)	40
64 London HA-U 8142	THE GOLDEN HITS OF DAVE 'BABY' CORTEZ (LP)	35

CORTINAS

68 Polydor 56255	Phoebe's Flower Shop/Too Much In Love	18

(see also Octopus)

CORTINAS

77 Step Forward SF 1	Fascist Dictator/Television Families (p/s, first 1,000 in card sleeve)	20/12
78 Step Forward SF 6	Defiant Pose/Independence (p/s)	12
78 Step Forward SF 6	Defiant Pose/Independence (12", pink die-cut sleeve)	12
78 CBS CBS 6759	Heartache/Ask Mr. Waverley (p/s)	8
78 CBS CBS 82831	TRUE ROMANCES (LP, with photo insert)	20

LEE CORVETTE

62 Decca	The Heart You Break (May Be Your Own)/Tender Love	10

CORVETTES

82 Bitchin BIT 100	Surf, Don't Walk/She'll Be Blonde (p/s)	6
84 Bitchin BIT 101	Girls Cars Girls Sun Girls Surf Girls Fun Girls/The Beach Is Not Enough (p/s)	6

LARRY CORYELL

69 Vanguard SVRL 19051	LADY CORYELL (LP)	18
69 Vanguard SVRL 19059	CORYELL (LP)	18
71 Vanguard 6359 005	SPACES (LP)	18

(see also Jazz Composers Orchestra)

BILL COSBY

67 Warner Bros WB 7072	Little Ole Man (Uptight! Everything's Alright)/Don'cha Know (some in p/s)	10/6
65 Warner Bros W(S) 1567	I STARTED OUT AS A CHILD (LP)	15
66 Warner W(S) 1634	WONDERFULNESS (LP)	15
68 Warner W(S) 1770	IT'S TRUE, IT'S TRUE (LP)	15

COSMIC BABY/VANGELIS

94 East West SAM 1484	A TRIBUTE TO BLADERUNNER (12", double pack, promo only)	40

(see also Vangelis)

COSMIC EYE

72 Regal Zono. SLRZ 1030	DREAM SEQUENCE (LP)	120

COSMO

63 Blue Beat BB 175	Gypsy Woman/Do Unto Others	18
64 Blue Beat BB 244	One God/BUSTER'S ALL STARS: Prince Royal (actually "Reincarnation")	22
64 Blue Beat BB 269	Rice And Badgee/BUSTER'S ALL STARS: The Tickler	22

(see also Cosmo & Dennis, Denzil Dennis)

FRANK COSMO

63 Island WI 058	Revenge/Laughin' At You (B-side actually with Bobby Aitken)	25
63 Island WI 073	Dear Dreams/Go Go Go	18
63 Island WI 100	Merry Christmas/Greetings From Beverley's	20
63 R&B JB 119	I Love You/DON DRUMMOND: Close Of Play	22
64 Island WI 135	Better Get Right/Ameletia	25
64 Black Swan WI 446	Alone/Beautiful Book	22

(see also Two Kings)

COSMO & DENNIS (alias Denzil)

62 Blue Beat BB 145	Bed Of Roses/Tonight And Evermore (as Cosmo & Denzil)	22
65 Blue Beat BB 296	Sweet Rosemarie/Lollipop I'm In Love	20
65 Blue Beat BB 312	Come On Come On/I Don't Want You	18

(see also Cosmo)

COSMOTHEKA

70s Shy SHY 7001	WINES & SPIRITS (LP)	25

DON COSTA, HIS ORCHESTRA & CHORUS

55 London HLF 8186	Love Is A Many Splendoured Thing/Safe In The Harbour	40
59 London HLT 8992	I Walk The Line/Cat Walk	12
59 London HLT 8992	I Walk The Line/Cat Walk (78)	25
60 London HLT 9137	Theme From "The Unforgiven"/Streets Of Paris	10

MINT VALUE £

60 London HLT 7103 — Theme From "The Unforgiven"/FERRANTE & TEICHER: Theme From "The Apartment" (export issue) . . . 12
60 London HLT 9195 — Never On Sunday/The Sound Of Love . . . 8
61 London HLT 9320 — The Misfits/Chi Chi . . . 10

SAM COSTA

61 Palette PG 9026 — I'm Changing My Hat To A Bowler/Oh Dear . . . 6

JACK COSTANZO

61 London HLG 9401 — Theme From Route 66/Naked City Theme . . . 8

JACK COSTANZO & TUBBY HAYES

62 Fontana TFL 5190/ STFL 598 — COSTANZO PLUS TUBBS — EQUATION IN RHYTHM (LP, mono/stereo) . . . 60/30

(see also Tubby Hayes)

CELIA COSTELLO

75 Leader LEE 4054 — CELIA COSTELLO (LP, with insert) . . . 20

DANNY COSTELLO

57 Oriole CB 1393 — Like A Brook Gets Lost In A River/That's Where I Shine . . . 7

DAY COSTELLO

71 Spark SRL 1042 — The Long And Winding Road/Free (Unlimited Horizons) . . . 10

(see also Ross McManus)

ELVIS COSTELLO (& ATTRACTIONS)

77 Stiff BUY 14 — Alison/Welcome To The Working Week (p/s, A-side mispress on white vinyl) . . . 300
77 Stiff BUY 15 — Red Shoes/Mystery Dance (p/s, mispress, plays "Dream Tobacco" by Max Wall) . 20

(The above singles were later re-pressed with 'Made In England' on label; these are worth £3 each.)

78 Radar ADA 24 — Radio Radio/Tiny Steps (12", promo-only, 500 pressed) . . . 15
78 Radar RG 1 — Talking In The Dark/Wednesday Week (p/s, gig freebie) . . . 6
80 F-Beat XX 5P — New Amsterdam/Just A Memory/Dr Luther's Assistant/Ghost Train (picture disc) . . . 6
80 2-Tone CHS TT 7 — I Can't Stand Up For Falling Down/Girls Talk (unreleased, later a gig freebie, more common issue has XX1 in run-off groove, 13,000 pressed) . . . 20/12
80 Stiff GRAB 3 — STIFF SINGLES FOUR PACK (BUY 11, 14, 15 & 20 in clear plastic wallet) . . . 12
81 F-Beat XX 17 — A Good Year For The Roses/Your Angel Steps Out Of Heaven (withdrawn p/s) . . 10
93 Demon ECPROMO 1 — TWO AND A HALF YEARS IN 31 MINUTES (CD, fold-out digipak, promo only) . . . 10
94 Demon ECPROMO 2 — HIGHLIGHTS FROM ALMOST BLUE AND IMPERIAL BEDROOM (CD, fold-out digipak, promo only) . . . 10
95 Demon ECPROMO 3 — SELECTIONS FROM THE KING OF AMERICA (CD, fold-out digipak, promo only) . . . 10
78 Radar RAD 3 — THIS YEAR'S MODEL (LP, with free 7" "Stranger In The House"/"Neat Neat Neat" (live) [die-cut company sleeve, SAM 83], 50,000 pressed; 1st 5,000 shrinkwrapped & stickered) . . . 12
79 Radar RAD 15 — ARMED FORCES (LP, foldout stickered sleeve with free EP "Live At Hollywood High" [p/s, SAM 90] & postcards) . . . 12
79 Radar RAD 15 — ARMED FORCES (LP, mispress, plays "[What's So Funny 'Bout] Peace, Love & Understanding" instead of "Two Little Hitlers"; sticker on insert) . . . 15
86 IMP FIEND CD 21 — ARMED FORCES (CD, with 'Peace, Love & Understanding") . . . 18
94 Warner Bros PRO-CD 6955 — BRUTAL YOUTH WORDS AND MUSIC PROGRAMME (CD, promo only) . . . 18

(see also Nick Lowe, George Jones, Coward Brothers)

BILLY COTTON (& HIS ORCHESTRA/BAND)

54 Decca F 10299 — Friends And Neighbours/The Kid's Last Fight . . . 22
54 Decca F 10377 — This Ole House/Somebody Goofed . . . 12
55 Decca F 10630 — The Dam Busters March/Bring Your Smile Along . . . 8
65 Walt Disney/S. County DIS 2 — Never Smile At A Crocodile/Second Star To The Right . . . 7
67 Philips BF 1551 — Thunderbirds Theme/Zero X (as Billy Cotton Band) . . . 15
53 Decca LF 1124 — SOLDIERS OF THE QUEEN (10" LP) . . . 20
54 Decca LF 1185 — WAKEY, WAKEY! (10" LP) . . . 20
61 Columbia 33SX 1383 — WAKEY, WAKEY! (LP, Billy Cotton Bandshow with Alma Cogan & Russ Conway) . . . 25

(see also Alma Cogan, Russ Conway)

JAMES COTTON (BLUES BAND)

78 Buddah BDS 471 — Rock'n'Roll Music/Help Me . . . 6
68 Vanguard SVRL 19035 — CUT YOU LOOSE! (LP, as James Cotton Blues Band) . . . 25

JIMMY COTTON

62 Columbia SEG 8141 — CHRIS BARBER PRESENTS JIMMY COTTON (EP) . . . 25
62 Columbia SEG 8189 — CHRIS BARBER PRESENTS JIMMY COTTON NO. 2 (EP) . . . 25

(see also James Cotton Blues Band, Alexis Korner)

MIKE COTTON (SOUND)

62 Columbia DB 4910 — The Tinker/Zulu Warrior (as the Mike Cotton Jazz Band . . . 10
63 Columbia DB 7029 — Swing That Hammer/Heartaches (as Mike Cotton Jazzmen) . . . 10
63 Columbia DB 7134 — Midnite Flyer/One Mint Julep (as Mike Cotton Band) . . . 10
64 Columbia DB 7267 — I Don't Wanna Know/This Little Pig . . . 40
64 Columbia DB 7382 — Round And Round/Beau Dudley . . . 50
65 Columbia DB 7623 — Make Up Your Mind/I've Got My Eye On You . . . 35
66 Polydor BM 56096 — Harlem Shuffle/Like That . . . 18
62 Columbia SEG 8144 — COTTON PICKING (EP) . . . 35
63 Columbia SEG 8190 — THE WILD AND THE WILLING (EP) . . . 35
64 Columbia 33SX 1647 — MIKE COTTON SOUND (LP) . . . 450+

(see also Lucas & Mike Cotton Sound, Satisfaction)

JOHN(NY) COUGAR

78 Riva RIVA 14 — I Need A Lover/Born Reckless (as Johnny Cougar, p/s) . . . 7
78 Riva RIVA 16 — Factory/Alley Of The Angels (as Johnny Cougar, p/s) . . . 10

(see also John Cougar Mellencamp)

MINT VALUE £

COUGARS

63 Parlophone R 4989 Saturday Night At The Duckpond/See You In Dreamland . . . 15
63 Parlophone R 5038 Red Square/Fly-By-Nite . . . 15
64 Parlophone R 5115 Caviare And Chips/While The City Sleeps . . . 25
63 Parlophone GEP 8886 SATURDAY NIGHT WITH THE COUGARS (EP) . . . 50

ROGER COULAM QUARTET

67 CBS 52399 ORGAN IN ORBIT (LP) . . . 20
70 Fontana 16009 BLOW HOT, BLOW COLD (LP) . . . 20

DENIS COULDRY (& SMILE)

68 Decca F 12734 James In The Basement (solo)/DENIS COULDRY & NEXT COLLECTION: I Am Nearly There . . . 12
68 Decca F 12786 Penny For The Wind/Tea And Toast, Mr. Watson? (as Denis Couldry & Smile) . . . 15
(see also Felius Andromeda)

DENNIS COULSON

73 Elektra K 42148 DENNIS COULSON (LP, gatefold sleeve) . . . 15

COULSON, DEAN, McGUINNESS, FLINT

72 DJM DJLPS 424 LO AND BEHOLD (LP, gatefold sleeve) . . . 18
(see also Manfred Mann, McGuinness Flint, Dennis Coulson, Lyle McGuinness Band)

PHIL COULTER ORCHESTRA

68 Pye 7N 17511 Congratulations/Gold Rush . . . 22

COUNCIL COLLECTIVE

84 Polydor MINEX 1 Soul Deep (Club Mix)/Soul Deep (12", stickered black die-cut sleeve) . . . 8
(see also Style Council, Jimmy Ruffin)

COUNT

74 Purple PUR 122 Gazaroody/The So, So Long . . . 10

(COUNT) BISHOPS

75 Chiswick SW 1 SPEEDBALL (EP, 1st 1,000 in glossy p/s, promos £10) . . . 8
78 Chiswick NS 35 Mr Jones/Human Bean/Route 66/Too Much Too Soon (unissued, test pressings only, as Bishops) . . . 18
77 Chiswick WIK 1 THE COUNT BISHOPS (LP) . . . 12
78 Chiswick CH 7 LIVE AT THE ROUNDHOUSE (10" mini-LP) . . . 12
(see also Cannibals)

COUNT BUSTY & RUDIES

68 Melody MRC 003 You Like It/The Reggay . . . 10

COUNT DOWNE & ZEROS

64 Ember EMB S 189 Hello My Angel/Don't Shed A Tear . . . 45
(see also Peter & Headlines)

COUNTDOWNS

63 United Artists UP 1024 Mouse On The Moon/The Big Safari . . . 10
(see also John Barry)

COUNT FIVE

66 Pye International 7N 25393 Psychotic Reaction/They're Gonna Get You . . . 40

COUNT OSSIE & HIS MYSTIC REVELATION

71 Ashanti ASH 404 Rasta Reggae/Samia . . . 15
71 Moodisc MU 3515 Whispering Drums/SLIM SMITH & UNIQUES: Give Me Some More Loving . . . 15
71 Moodisc HM 105 Whispering Drums/SLIM SMITH & UNIQUES: Give Me Some More Loving . . . 15
74 Ashanti NTI 1301 GROUNATION (3-LP, with Mystic Revelation Of Rastafari) . . . 35
(see also Jackie Estick, Gaylads, Soul Defenders)

COUNT PRINCE

(see under Count Prince Miller)

COUNTRY BOY

64 Blue Beat BB 236 I'm A Lonely Boy (actually by Shenley Duffas)/EDWARD'S ALL STARS: He's Gone Ska . . . 20

COUNTRY CATS

56 Parlophone DP 521 Mountain Mambo/Hot Strings (78, export issue) . . . 12

COUNTRY FOLK

70s Thule SLP 101 THE COUNTRY FOLK (LP, private pressing) . . . 70

COUNTRY FUNK

70 Polydor 248 2018 COUNTRY FUNK (LP) . . . 22

COUNTRY GAZETTE

72 United Artists UAG 29404 TRAITOR IN OUR MIDST (LP) . . . 15
73 United Artists UAS 29491 DON'T GIVE UP YOUR DAY JOB (LP) . . . 15
(see also Flying Burrito Brothers)

COUNTRY GENTLEMEN

63 Decca F 11766 Greensleeves/Baby Jean . . . 40
(see also High Society, Peter Cowap)

COUNTRY HAMS

74 EMI EMI 2220 Walking In The Park With Eloise/Bridge On The River Suite (p/s, red & brown label) . . . 55
82 EMI EMI 2220 Walking In The Park With Eloise/Bridge On The River Suite (p/s, reissue, beige label) . . . 15
(see also Paul McCartney/Wings, Chet Atkins, Floyd Cramer)

COUNTRY JOE & THE FISH

67 Fontana TF 882 Not So Sweet Martha Lorraine/Love . . . 15
69 Vanguard VA 3 Here I Go Again/It's So Nice To Have Love . . . 7
70 Vanguard 6076 250 I-Feel-Like-I'm-Fixin'-To-Die Rag/Maria . . . 10

MINT VALUE £

67 Fontana TFL 6081 ELECTRIC MUSIC FOR THE MIND AND BODY (LP) 40
68 Fontana TFL 6086 I-FEEL-LIKE-I'M-FIXIN'-TO-DIE (LP)........ 35
68 Vanguard SVRL 19006 TOGETHER (LP)........ 20
69 Vanguard SVRL 19026 ELECTRIC MUSIC FOR THE MIND AND BODY (LP, reissue)........ 15
69 Vanguard SVRL 19029 I-FEEL-LIKE-I'M-FIXIN'-TO-DIE (LP, reissue) 15
69 Vanguard SVRL 19048 HERE WE ARE AGAIN (LP) 20
70 Vanguard SVRL 19058 THE BEST OF COUNTRY JOE AND THE FISH (LP)........ 15
70 Vanguard 6359 002 C.J. FISH (LP)........ 18
73 Vanguard VSD 27/28 THE LIFE AND TIMES OF (2-LP, gatefold sleeve, quadrophonic/stereo) 20/15
80 Piccadilly PIC 3009 THE EARLY YEARS (LP, private pressing, withdrawn) .... 50+
(see also Country Joe McDonald)

COUNTRY JUG
72 Decca F 13270 I'm Sorry/Do You Wanna?/Flying 22
(see also Ray Dorset)

COUNTRYMEN
62 Piccadilly 7N 35029 I Know Where I'm Going/Swamp Legend 6
62 Piccadilly 7N 34012 I KNOW WHERE I'M GOING (EP)........ 12
62 Piccadilly NPL 38003 A FLYING VISIT BY THE COUNTRYMEN (LP) 15

COUNTRYMEN
69 Jayboy BOY 3 After All/White Rose Of Athens........ 6

COUNTS
72 Janus 6146 013 (Why Not) Start All Over Again/Thinking Single........ 6

COUNT VICTORS
62 Coral Q 72456 Peepin' 'N' Hidin'/Don't Laugh At Me ('Cos I'm A Fool) 22
63 Coral Q 72462 Road Runner/Lorie........ 18

WAYNE/JAYNE COUNTY (& ELECTRIC CHAIRS)
77 Illegal IL 002 Stuck On You/Paranoia Paradise/The Last Time (p/s)........ 8
77 Sweet F.A. WC 1 Fuck Off/On The Crest (p/s)........ 12
78 Safari SAFE 1 Eddie And Sheena/Rock And Roll Cleopatra (p/s, some with cartoon insert).... 10
78 Safari SAFE 6 I Had Too Much To Dream Last Night/Fuck Off (unissued)
78 Safari WC 2 BLATANTLY OFFENZIVE (EP, gold vinyl) 8
78 Safari SAFE 9 Trying To Get On The Radio/Evil Minded Momma (p/s)........ 5
79 Illegal IL 005 Thunder When She Walks/What You Got (p/s)........ 5
78 Safari SAFELS 13 Berlin (Long Version)/Waiting For The Marines/Midnight Pal (12", p/s, pink vinyl) . 8
83 Safari WCP 3 Fuck Off/Toilet Love (picture disc) 7
78 Safari GOOD 1 STORM THE GATES OF HEAVEN (LP, multicoloured or grey marbled vinyl)..... 12
(see also Mystere Five's)

DIANA COUPLAND
59 HMV POP 690 Love Him/I Am Loved........ 6

COURIERS
66 Ember EMB S 218 Take Away/Done Me Wrong (some with p/s)........ 120/30
(see also William E. Kimber)

COURIERS
69 Ash ALP 201 PACK UP YOUR SORROWS (LP) 30

TOM COURTENAY
63 Decca F 11729 Mrs. Brown You've Got A Lovely Daughter/Knocking On The Door........ 8

COURT MARTIAL
82 Riot City RIOT 5 GOTTA GET OUT (EP) 5
82 Riot City RIOT 11 NO SOLUTION (EP) 5

BILL COURTNEY
59 RCA RCA 1142 Judy Is/Without Her Love 8
59 RCA RCA 1142 Judy Is/Without Her Love (78)........ 10
60 Columbia DB 4512 Petticoats Fly/Blanket On The Beach 7

COURTYARD MUSIC GROUP
74 Deroy JUST OUR WAY OF SAYING HELLO (LP, private pressing) 200

COUSIN EMMY & HER KINFOLK
56 Brunswick OE 9258 KENTUCKY MOUNTAIN BALLADS VOL. 1 (EP)........ 18
56 Brunswick OE 9259 KENTUCKY MOUNTAIN BALLADS VOL. 2 (EP)........ 18

COUSINS (Belgium)
61 Palette PG 9011 Kili Watch/Feugo 12
61 Palette PG 9017 Bouddha/Kana Kapila 12
62 Palette PG 9035 Anda/Danseuse 12

COUSINS (U.K.)
64 Decca F 11924 Yes Sir That's My Baby/Two Lovely Black Eyes 8

DAVE COUSINS
72 A&M AMS 7032 Going Home/Ways And Means 6
72 A&M AMLS 68118 TWO WEEKS LAST SUMMER (LP)........ 20
79 Old School SLURP 1 OLD SCHOOL SONGS (LP, private pressing with Brian Willoughby)........ 25
80 Passport PVC 8901 OLD SCHOOL SONGS (LP, reissue with different sleeve) 15
(see also The Strawbs)

DON COVAY (& GOODTIMERS)
61 Pye International 7N 25075 Pony Time/Love Boat 25
61 Philips PB 1140 Shake Wid The Shake/Every Which Way 35
62 Cameo Parkway C 239 The Popeye Waddle/One Little Boy Had Money 30
64 Atlantic AT 4006 Mercy, Mercy/Can't Stay Away 12
65 Atlantic AT 4016 Take This Hurt Off Me/Please Don't Let Me Know........ 12
65 Atlantic AT 4056 See Saw/I Never Get Enough Of Your Love........ 12

			MINT VALUE £
66	Atlantic AT 4078	Sookie Sookie/Watching The Late Late Show	12
66	Atlantic 584 025	You Put Something In Me/Iron Out The Rough Spots	8
66	Atlantic 584 059	See Saw/Somebody's Got To Love You	8
67	Atlantic 584 082	Shingaling '67/I Was There	10
67	Atlantic 584 094	Sookie Sookie/Mercy Mercy	8
67	Atlantic 584 114	40 Days — 40 Nights/The Usual Place	12
70	Atlantic 2091 018	Everything I Do Goin' Be Funky/Key To The Highway	10
65	Atlantic ATL 5025	MERCY! (LP, plum label)	100
67	Atlantic 587 062	SEE-SAW (LP)	35
69	Atlantic K 50225	HOUSE OF BLUE LIGHT (LP)	25
73	Mercury 6338 211	SUPERDUDE (LP)	15
75	Mercury 9100 010	HOT BLOOD (LP)	15

(see also Soul Clan)

DAVID COVERDALE

77	Purple PUR 133	Hole In The Sky/Blindman	12
78	Purple PUR 136	Breakdown/Only My Soul	12
90	Epic 656 292 7	Last Note Of Freedom/HANS ZIMMER: Car Building (poster p/s)	10
90	Epic 656 292 6	Last Note Of Freedom/HANS ZIMMER: Car Building (12", p/s)	8
93	EMI EMPD 279	Take A Look At Yourself (with Jimmy Page)/ Waiting On You (picture disc in numbered p/s)	6
93	EMI CDEMS 270	TAKE ME FOR A LITTLE WHILE (CD EP, in box with colour prints)	8
77	Purple TPS 3509	DAVID COVERDALE'S WHITESNAKE (LP)	12
77	Purple TPS 3509TC	DAVID COVERDALE'S WHITESNAKE (LP, white label promo, plain sleeve, with insert)	25
78	Purple TPS 3513	NORTHWINDS (LP, with inner sleeve)	12

(see also Whitesnake, Deep Purple, Wizard's Convention, Roger Glover, Jimmy Page)

JULIAN COVEY & MACHINE

67	Island WIP 6009	A Little Bit Hurt/Sweet Bacon	45
67	Island WIP 6442	A Little Bit Hurt/Sweet Bacon (reissue)	10

JULIE COVINGTON

70	Columbia DB 8649	The Magic Wasn't There/The Way Things Ought To Be	15
70	Columbia DB 8705	Tonight Your Love Is Over/If I Had My Time Again	15
72	RCA RCA 2181	Day By Day/With Me It Goes Deeper	6
71	Columbia SCX 6466	THE BEAUTIFUL CHANGES (LP)	110

(see also Rock Follies)

PETER COWAP

70	Pye 7N 17976	Crickets/Wicked Melinda	6
71	Pye 7N 45042	The Man With The Golden Gun/Tampa, Florida	6
71	Pye 7N 45071	Safari/Oh Soloman	6

(see also 10cc, Country Gentlemen)

NOEL COWARD

54	Philips BB 2001	Mad Dogs & Englishmen/A Room With A View (78)	7
54	Philips BB 2002	Poor Little Rich Girl/Uncle Harry (78)	7

COWBOY

71	Atlantic 2466 022	REACH FOR THE SKY (LP)	15
72	Atlantic K 40312	5'LL GETCHA TEN (LP, with insert)	15

COWBOY CHURCH SUNDAY SCHOOL

55	Brunswick 05371	Open Up Your Heart/The Lord Is Counting On You	10
55	Brunswick 05455	Go On By/The Little Black Sheep	8
56	Brunswick 05533	These Bad Bad Kids/A Handful Of Shame	8
56	Brunswick 05598	It Is No Secret/Don't Send Those Kids To Sunday School	8

COWBOYS INTERNATIONAL

79	Virgin VS 253	Aftermath/Pt. 2 (orange vinyl, p/s)	10

(see also Public Image Ltd.)

COWSILLS

67	MGM MGM 1353	The Rain, The Park And Other Things/River Blue	18
68	MGM MGM 1383	We Can Fly/A Time For Remembrance	10
68	MGM MGM 1400	In Need Of A Friend/Mr. Flynn	10
68	MGM MGM 1424	Indian Lake/Newspaper Blanket	10
68	MGM MGM 1441	Poor Baby/Meet Me At The Wishing Well	8
69	MGM MGM 1469	Hair/What Is Happy	8
69	MGM MGM 1484	The Prophecy Of Daniel And John The Divine/Gotta Get Away From It All	8
69	MGM MGM 1490	Love American Style/Silver Threads And Golden Needles	8
71	London HLU 10329	On My Side/There Is A Child	8
67	MGM C/CS 8059	THE COWSILLS (LP)	30
68	MGM CS 8077	WE CAN FLY (LP)	25
68	MGM CS 8095	CAPTAIN SAD AND HIS SHIP OF FOOLS (LP)	25
68	Fontana SFL 13055	THE COWSILLS AND THE LINCOLN PARK ZOO (LP)	25
71	London SH-U 8421	ON MY SIDE (LP)	15

BILLY COX

71	Pye Intl. NSPL 25158	NITRO FUNCTION (LP)	40

(see also Jimi Hendrix)

HARRY COX

65	EFDSS LP 1004	ENGLISH FOLK SINGER (LP)	22

IDA COX

52	Jazz Collector L 22	Graveyard Dream Blues/Weary Way Blues (78)	10
52	Jazz Collector L76	Mama Do Shee Blues/Worried Mama Blues (78)	10
59	Fontana TFE 17136	IDA COX (EP)	25
54	London AL 3517	SINGS THE BLUES (10" LP)	60
60s	Riverside RLP 374	BLUES FOR RAMPART STREET (LP)	40

MINT VALUE £

74	Fountain FB 301	IDA COX VOLUME 1 (LP)	15
75	Fountain FB 304	VOLUME 2: 1923-1924 (LP)	15
75	Gannet GEN 5371-5376	PARAMOUNT RECORDINGS (6-LP box set)	40

(see also Ma Rainey)

IDA COX/ETHEL WATERS

50s	Poydras 104	IDA COX AND ETHEL WATERS (EP)	35

MICHAEL COX

59	Decca F 11166	Boy Meets Girl/Teenage Love	25
59	Decca F 11166	Boy Meets Girl/Teenage Love (78)	18
59	Decca F 11182	Too Hot To Handle/Serious	25
59	Decca F 11182	Too Hot To Handle/Serious (78)	18
60	Triumph RGM 1011	Angela Jones/Don't Want To Know (company sleeve)	18
60	Ember EMB S 103	Angela Jones/Don't Want To Know (export issue)	10
60	HMV POP 789	Along Came Caroline/Lonely Road	25
61	HMV POP 830	Teenage Love/Linda	20
61	HMV POP 905	Sweet Little Sixteen/Cover Girl	25
62	HMV POP 972	Young Only Once/Honey Cause I Love You	30
62	HMV POP 1065	Stand Up/In April	30
63	HMV POP 1137	Don't You Break My Heart/Hark Is That A Cannon I Hear	30
63	HMV POP 1220	Gee What A Party/See That Again	30
64	HMV POP 1293	Rave On/Just Say Hello	35
65	HMV POP 1417	Gypsy/It Ain't Right	25
66	Parlophone R 5436	I Hate Getting Up In The Morning/Love 'Em And Leave 'Em	6
67	Parlophone R 5580	I'll Always Love You/You Never Can Tell (Till You Try)	7

SONNY COX

70	Pama PM 815	Choking Kind/Chocolate Candy	8

WALLY COX

61	Vogue V 9175	I Can't Help It/The Heebie Jeebees	30
74	Pye Disco Demand DDS 105	This Man/I've Had Enough	8

LOL COXHILL

78	Chiltern Sound CS 100	MURDER IN THE AIR (12" EP)	35
71	Dandelion DSD 8008	EAR OF THE BEHOLDER (2-LP, gatefold sleeve, also with cat. no. 69001)	60
72	Mushroom 150 MR 23	TOVERBAL SWEET (LP)	60
73	Caroline C 1503	COXHILL MILLER (LP, with Stephen Miller)	25
74	Caroline C 1507	THE STORY SO FAR ... OH REALLY? (LP, with Stephen Miller)	30
75	Caroline C 1514	LOL COXHILL & WELFARE STATE (LP)	18
75	Caroline C 1515	FLEAS IN THE CUSTARD (LP)	30
76	Ogun OG 510	DIVERSE (LP)	15
78	Ogun OG 525	THE JOY OF PARANOIA (LP)	15
78	Ictus 0008	MOOT (LP)	30
80	Pipe PIPE 1	SLOW MUSIC (LP)	25

(see also Stephen Miller & Lol Coxhill, Kevin Ayers, Steve York's Camelo Pardalis)

COXHILL BEDFORD DUO

71	Polydor 2001 253	Pretty Little Girl (Parts 1 & 2)	6
72	Dandelion 2058 214	Mood/WILL DANDY & DANDYLETTES: Sonny Boy/Oh Mein Papa	6

(see also David Bedford, Lol Coxhill)

JIM COYLE & MAL SHARPE

63	Warner Bros WM 8130	THE ABSURD IMPOSTERS (LP)	15

KEVIN COYNE

72	Dandelion 2001 357	Cheat Me/Flowering Cherry	7
80	Virgin VGD 3504	SANITY STOMP (EP, double pack)	8
72	Dandelion 2310 228	CASE HISTORY (LP)	50
73	Virgin VD 2501	MARJORY RAZORBLADE (2-LP)	22

(see also Clague, Coyne-Clague, Siren, Gordon Smith)

COYNE-CLAGUE

69	Dandelion S 4494	The Stride/I Wonder Where	8

(see Clague, Kevin Coyne)

CRABBY APPLETON

70	Elektra 2101 006	Go Back/Try	6
71	Elektra EK 45716	Grabon/Can't Live My Life	6
70	Elektra EKS 74067	CRABBY APPLETON (LP)	20
71	Elektra EKS 74106	ROTTEN TO THE CORE (LP)	20

CRACK

80	JSO EAT 4	Making The Effort/Easy Street	8

CRACK

82	RCA RCA 214	Don't You Ever Let Me Down/I Can't Take It (die-cut 'Battle of the Bands' sleeve)	25
82	RCA RCA 255	Going Out/The Troops Have Landed (p/s)	15
83	RCA CRACK 1	All Or Nothing/I Caught You Out (p/s)	20

CRACKED MIRROR

83	CMLP 001	CRACKED MIRROR (LP, private pressing, 200 only)	80

CRACKERS

69	Fontana TF 995	Honey Do/It Happens All The Time	12

(see also Merseys)

CRACK THE SKY

76	Lifesong ELS 45016	We Want Mine/Invaders From Mars	8
76	Lifesong LSLP 6005	ANIMAL NOTES (LP, with inner sleeve)	15

MINT VALUE £

SARAH CRACKNELL

87 3 Bears TED 001 Love Is All You Need/Coastal Town (p/s) . . . 20
97 Gut CDGUT 7 Goldie (Radio Edit)/(Original Version)/Empire State High/ Aussie Soap Girl (CD, slimline jewel case, withdrawn). . . 20
(see also St. Etienne, 50 Year Void, Lovecut D.B.)

(BILLY) 'CRASH' CRADDOCK

59 Philips PB 966 Boom Boom Baby/Don't Destroy Me (as 'Crash' Craddock). . . 30
59 Philips PB 966 Boom Boom Baby/Don't Destroy Me (78) . . . 15
60 Philips PB 1006 Since She Turned Seventeen/I Want That (as 'Crash' Craddock) . . . 25
60 Philips PB 1092 Good Time Billy (Is A Happiness Fool)/Heavenly Love. . . 18
61 Mercury AMT 1146 How Lonely He Must Be/Truly True . . . 12

CRADLE OF FILTH

94 Cacophonous NIHIL1 THE PRINCIPLE OF EVIL MADE FLESH (LP) . . . 18
98 Music For Nations MFN 242 CRUELTY AND THE BEAST (LP) . . . 12

CRAIG

65 King KG 1022 Ain't That A Shame/International Blues. . . 18

CRAIG

66 Fontana TF 665 A Little Bit Of Soap/Ready Steady Let's Go . . . 55
66 Fontana TF 715 I Must Be Mad/Suspense . . . 340
(see also Galliard)

PAUL CRAIG

66 CBS 202406 Midnight Girl/Autumn. . . 10

DON CRAINE'S NEW DOWNLINERS SECT

67 Pye 7N 17261 I Can't Get Away From You/Roses . . . 210
(see also Downliners Sect)

FLOYD CRAMER

54 London HL 8012 Fancy Pants/Five Foot Two Eyes Of Blue . . . 55
54 London HL 8012 Fancy Pants/Five Foot Two Eyes Of Blue (78). . . 8
54 London HL 8062 Jolly Cholly/Oh! Suzanna. . . 65
54 London HL 8062 Jolly Cholly/Oh! Suzanna (78) . . . 8
55 London HLU 8195 Rag-A-Tag/Aunt Dinah's Quiltin' Party. . . 40
55 London HLU 8195 Rag-A-Tag/Aunt Dinah's Quiltin' Party (78) . . . 10
58 RCA RCA 1050 Flip Flop And Bop/Sophisticated Swing . . . 25
58 RCA RCA 1050 Flip Flop And Bop/Sophisticated Swing (78) . . . 12
60 RCA RCA 1211 Last Date/Sweetie Baby . . . 7
61 RCA RCA 1231 On The Rebound/Mood Indigo. . . 6
61 RCA RCA 1241 San Antonio Rose/I Can Just Imagine. . . 5
61 RCA RCA 1259 Hang On/Your Last Goodbye. . . 6
62 RCA RCA 1275 Chattanooga Choo Choo/Let's Go. . . 6
62 RCA RCA 1284 Lovesick Blues/First Hurt . . . 6
62 RCA RCA 1301 Hot Pepper/For Those That Cry . . . 6
62 RCA RCA 1311 Swing Low/Losers Weepers. . . 5
55 London REP 1023 PIANO HAYRIDE (EP, with Louisiana Hayride Band) . . . 50
63 RCA RCX 7120 THAT HANDSOME PIANO (EP) . . . 18
61 RCA RD 27221/SF 5103 ON THE REBOUND (LP, mono/stereo) . . . 15/18
62 RCA RD 27250/SF 5124 AMERICA'S BIGGEST SELLING PIANIST (LP, mono/stereo). . . 15/18
62 RCA RD 27260/SF 5130 GETS ORGAN-IZED (LP) . . . 15
62 RCA RD/SF 7518 I REMEMBER HANK WILLIAMS (LP) . . . 15
63 RCA RD/SF 7540 SWING ALONG WITH FLOYD CRAMER (LP). . . 15
63 RCA RD/SF 7575 COMING ON (LP) . . . 15
64 RCA RD/SF 7622 COUNTRY PIANO — CITY STRINGS (LP) . . . 12
64 RCA RD/SF 7646 AT THE CONSOLE (LP) . . . 12
65 RCA RD 7665 THE BEST OF FLOYD CRAMER (LP). . . 12
65 RCA RD/SF 7748 CLASS OF '65 (LP). . . 12
(see also Country Hams)

FLOYD CRAMER/HOUSTON ROBERTS

65 Fontana FJL 308 FLOYD CRAMER/HOUSTON ROBERTS (LP, one side each). . . 12

CRAMP

78 Rip Off RIP 7 She Doesn't Love Me/Suzy Lie Down (p/s) . . . 10

CRAMPS

79 Illegal ILS 12013 GRAVEST HITS (12" EP, blue or black vinyl) . . . 30/8
80 Illegal ILS 0017 Fever/Garbage Man (withdrawn 1st 'full band' p/s; re-pressed in different p/s with 4 separate shots) . . . 20/10
80 Illegal ILS 021 Drug Train/Love Me/I Can't Hardly Stand It (p/s). . . 10
81 IRS PFS 1003 Goo Goo Muck/She Said (p/s, yellow vinyl) . . . 10
81 IRS PFSX 1008 The Crusher/Save It/New Kind Of Kick (12", p/s) . . . 12
85 Big Beat NS 110 Can Your Pussy Do The Dog?/Blue Moon Baby (p/s, orange see-through vinyl) . . . 5
86 Big Beat NS 115 What's Inside A Girl/Give Me A Woman (p/s, purple vinyl) . . . 5
86 Big Beat NS 115 What's Inside A Girl/Get Off The Road/Give Me A Woman (12", p/s, white vinyl). . 10
89 Enigma ENVPD 17 Bikini Girls With Machine Guns/Jackyard Backoff (picture disc). . . 8
89 Enigma ENV 19 All Women Are Bad/King Of The Drapes/Teenage Rage/High School Hellcats (12", pic disc) . . . 10
80 Illegal ILP 005 SONGS THE LORD TAUGHT US (LP, white label with "Drug Train" in place of "T.V. Set") . . . 100
80 Illegal ILP 005 SONGS THE LORD TAUGHT US (LP, with "T.V. Set"). . . 15
81 IRS SP 70016 PSYCHEDELIC JUNGLE (LP). . . 15
83 Illegal ILP 012 OFF THE BONE (LP, white label, with different mix of "Drug Train", around 50 copies pressed, unreleased) . . . 100+
83 Illegal ILP 012 OFF THE BONE (LP, with 3-D sleeve & glasses). . . 15
83 Illegal ILP 012 OFF THE BONE (LP, picture disc with extra track) . . . 15

MINT VALUE £

84	Big Beat NED 6	SMELL OF FEMALE (LP, red see-through vinyl)	15
84	Big Beat BEDP 6	SMELL OF FEMALE (LP, picture disc)	15
86	Big Beat WIKA 46	A DATE WITH ELVIS (LP, with poster)	12
86	Big Beat WIKA 46	A DATE WITH ELVIS (LP, blue vinyl)	20
91	Big Beat WIKPD 101	LOOK MOM NO HEAD (LP, picture disc)	15
91	Windsong WINDSONG 4	LUX (3 x 12" box set, with poster, T-shirt & book, numbered, withdrawn)	50

CRANBERRIES

91	Xeric XER 014	Uncertain/Nothing Left At All (p/s)	15
91	Xeric XER 014T	Uncertain/Nothing Left At All/Pathetic Senses/Them (12", p/s)	20
91	Xeric XER 014CD	Uncertain/Nothing Left At All/Pathetic Senses/Them (CD)	30
92	Island IS 548	What You Are/Dreams (p/s)	15
92	Island 12IS 548	What You Are/Liar/Dreams (12", p/s, with postcard)	20

TONY CRANE

65	Polydor BM 56008	Ideal Love/Little You	8
66	CBS 202022	Even The Bravest/I Still Remember	10
67	Pye 7N 17337	Anonymous Mr Brown/In This World	12
68	Pye 7N 17517	Scratchin' Ma Head/Patterns In The Sky	15

(see also Bob Miller, Merseys/Merseybeats)

CRANE/FARLOWE

73	Dawn DNS 1034	Can't Find A Reason/Moods	7

(see also Atomic Rooster, Crazy World Of Arthur Brown, Chris Farlowe, Katmandu)

CRANE RIVER JAZZ BAND

50	Modern Messages MM 335/6	Crane River Woman/Low Down Blues (78)	7
51	Delta D 6	If I Ever Cease To Love/Gipsy Lament (78)	8
51	Esquire 12-013	Eh, La Bas!/CHRIS BARBER'S JAZZ BAND: Oh, Didn't He Ramble (78)	10
51	Melodisc 1027	Eh, La-Bas!/Just A Closer Walk With Thee (78)	8
53	Parlophone MSP 6008	Lily Of The Valley/Till We Meet Again	15
57	77 LP/4	ORIGINAL CRANE RIVER JAZZ BAND (LP)	60
57	77 LP/5	ORIGINAL CRANE RIVER JAZZ BAND (LP)	45
57	77 LP/17	ORIGINAL CRANE RIVER JAZZ BAND (LP)	45
57	77 LP/18	ORIGINAL CRANE RIVER JAZZ BAND (LP)	50

(see also Ken Colyer)

CRANES SKIFFLE GROUP

57	Embassy WB 238	Freight Train/Cumberland Gap (78)	8

(see also Ken Colyer, Chas McDevitt)

CRASH

82	Crash EJSP 9819	FIGHT FOR YOUR LIFE (EP, no p/s)	8

CRASHERS

69	Amalgamated AMG 834	Hurry Come Up/Off Track	12

CRASS

78	Small Wonder WEENY 2	THE FEEDING OF THE 5000 (12" EP, with 4-page insert & poster)	15
78	Crass 621984	THE FEEDING OF THE 5000 (12" EP, reissue with "Reality Asylum")	8
79	Crass 521984/1	Reality Asylum/Shaved Women (brown cardboard gatefold p/s; later in white newspaper foldout sleeve)	10/5
80	Crass/Xntrix 421984/1	Bloody Revolutions/POISON GIRLS: Persons Unknown (foldout p/s)	8
80	Crass 421984/5	Nagasaki Nightmare/Big A Little A (foldout p/s, some with patch)	6/5
81	Crass 421984/6	Rival Tribal Rebel Revel/Bully Boys Out Fighting (flexdisc with *Toxic Graffiti* fanzine)	10/5
81	Crass 421984/6	Rival Tribal Rebel Revel/Bully Boys Out Fighting (hard vinyl promo, p/s)	25
81	Crass COLD TURKEY 1	Merry Crassmass/Merry Crassmass — Have Fun (p/s)	5
82	Crass 221984/6	How Does It Feel (To Be The Mother Of 1000 Dead?)/The Immortal Death/ Don't Tell Me You Care (foldout p/s)	8
83	Crass 121984/3	Sheep Farming In The Falklands/Gotcha! (live) (foldout p/s with lyric insert)	6
83	(no label)	Gotcha! (clear flexidisc)	10
83	Crass 121984/4	Who Dunnit? (Parts 1 & 2) (p/s, brown vinyl)	5
82	Crass BOLLOX 2U2	CHRIST THE ALBUM (2-LP, box set with booklet)	20

(see also Joy De Vivre, Eve Libertine, Poison Girls)

CRAVATS

78	The Cravats CH 004	Gordon/Situations (p/s)	12
79	Small Wonder SMALL 15	The End/Burning Bridges/I Hate The Universe (p/s)	8
80	Small Wonder SMALL 24	Precinct/Who's In Here With Me? (p/s, some with free flexidisc ["Fireman"/ A FLUX IN 3D: Divide])	8/6
80	Small Wonder SMALL 25	You're Driving Me Mad/I Am The Dregs (p/s)	10
81	Small Wonder SMALL 26	Off The Beach/And The Sun Shone On (p/s)	8
82	Crass 221984/2	RUB ME OUT (EP, 21" x 14" poster p/s)	8
85	Reflex 12 RE 10	THE LAND OF THE GIANTS (12" EP)	10
80	Small Wonder CRAVAT 1	THE CRAVATS IN TOYTOWN (LP, with inner sleeve)	15

CAROLYN CRAWFORD

65	Stateside SS 384	When Someone's Good To You/My Heart	115

HANK CRAWFORD

63	London HAK 8103	SOUL OF THE BALLAD (LP)	30

JAMES 'SUGARBOY' CRAWFORD

73	Chess 6145 024	Jock-o-mo (Iko Iko)/BOBBY CHARLES: See You Later, Alligator	6

JIMMY CRAWFORD

60	Columbia DB 4525	Long Stringy Baby/Unkind	50
61	Columbia DB 4633	Love Or Money/Does My Heartache Show	15
61	Columbia DB 4717	I Love How You Love Me/Our Last Embrace	7
62	Columbia DB 4841	I Shoulda Listened To Mama/A Boy Without A Girl	12
62	Columbia DB 4895	Thank You/There'll Be No Goodbyes	12
63	Columbia DB 4957	Another Of Your Toys/Young And Afraid	8
63	Columbia DB 7175	Don't Worry About Bobby/Take This Rose	12

MINT VALUE £

JOHNNY CRAWFORD

62	Pye International 7N 25145	Cindy's Birthday/Patti Ann	10
62	London HL 9605	Your Nose Is Gonna Grow/Something Special	10
62	London HL 9638	Rumors/No One Really Loves A Clown	10
63	London HL 9669	Proud/Lonesome Town	10
64	London HL 9836	Judy Loves Me/Living In The Past	10
62	London RE 1343	JOHNNY CRAWFORD (EP)	30
64	London RE 1416	WHEN I FALL IN LOVE (EP)	30
63	London HA 8060	RUMORS (LP)	50
64	London HA 8197	JOHNNY CRAWFORD — HIS GREATEST HITS (LP)	50

MICHAEL CRAWFORD

65	United Artists UP 1095	The Knack/Oh That Girl	10

ROSETTA CRAWFORD

51	Vocalion V 1002	Stop It Joe/My Man Jumped Salty On Me (78)	12

CRAWFORD BROTHERS

57	Vogue V 9077	Midnight Mover Groover/Midnight Happenings	250
57	Vogue V 9077	Midnight Mover Groover/Midnight Happenings (78)	75
59	Vogue V 9140	It Feels Good/I Ain't Guilty (triangular or round centre)	275/200
59	Vogue V 9140	It Feels Good/I Ain't Guilty (78)	100

CRAWLING CHAOS

80	Factory FAC 17	Sex Machine/Berlin (p/s)	15

CRAYS

65	Polydor BM 56033	Nancy's Minuet/Don't Pity Me	6

PEE WEE CRAYTON

78	Vanguard VSD 6566	THINGS I USED TO DO (LP)	15

CRAZE

79	Cobra COB 3	Motions/Spartans (p/s)	5
80	Harvest HAR 5200	Motions/Spartans (reissue in different p/s)	5
80	Harvest HAR 5205	Lucy/Stop Living In The Past (p/s)	6

(see also Skunks, Hard Corps)

CRAZY CAVAN AND THE RHYTHM ROCKERS

73	Crazy Rhythm CR 01	Teddy Boy Boogie/Bop Little Baby	8
74	Crazy Rhythm CR 02	Teddy Boy Rock'N'Roll/Rockabilly Star/Wildest Cat In Town/ Little Teddy Girl	10

CRAZY ELEPHANT

69	Major Minor MM 609	Gimme Gimme Good Lovin'/Dark Part Of My Mind	5
69	Major Minor MM 623	Sunshine Red Wine/Pam	5
70	Major Minor MM 672	There's A Better Day Coming/Space Buggy	5
69	Major Minor SMLP 62	CRAZY ELEPHANT (LP)	20

CRAZY FEELINGS

67	Polydor NH 56723	Please Lie/Time Is Running Out	6

CRAZY HORSE

72	Reprise RSLP 6438	CRAZY HORSE (LP)	18
72	Reprise K 44171	LOOSE (LP, gatefold sleeve)	15

(see also Neil Young, Nils Lofgren, Jack Nitzsche)

CRAZY ROCKERS

64	King KG 1001	Third Man Theme/Mama Papa	7

PAPA JOHN CREACH

71	Grunt FTR 1003	PAPA JOHN CREACH (LP)	15
73	Grunt FTR 1009	FILTHY (LP)	15

(see also Jefferson Airplane)

CREAM

66	Reaction 591 007	Wrapping Paper/Cat's Squirrel	15
66	Reaction 591 011	I Feel Free/N.S.U.	12
67	Reaction 591 015	Strange Brew/Tales Of Brave Ulysses	12
68	Polydor 56258	Anyone For Tennis (The Savage Seven Theme)/Pressed Rat And Warthog	10
68	Polydor 56286	Sunshine Of Your Love/SWLABR	7
68	Polydor 56300	White Room/Those Were The Days	7
69	Polydor 56315	Strange Brew/Wrapping Paper (unissued)	
69	Polydor 56315	Badge/What A Bringdown	7
71	Polydor 2058 120	I Feel Free/Wrapping Paper	6
72	Polydor 2058 285	Badge/What A Bringdown (reissue)	6
66	Reaction 593/594 001	FRESH CREAM (LP, mono/stereo)	55/35
67	Reaction 593/594 003	DISRAELI GEARS (LP, sleeve laminated on front & back, mono/stereo)	45/35
68	Reaction 593/594 003	DISRAELI GEARS (LP, sleeve laminated on front only, mono/stereo)	40/30
68	Polydor 582/583 031/2	WHEELS OF FIRE (2-LP, gatefold sleeve, mono/stereo; set no. 2612 001)	50/40
68	Polydor 582/583 033	WHEELS OF FIRE — IN THE STUDIO (LP, mono/stereo)	30/20
68	Polydor 582/583 040	WHEELS OF FIRE — LIVE AT THE FILLMORE (LP, mono/stereo)	30/20
69	Polydor 583 053	GOODBYE (LP, gatefold sleeve)	20
69	Polydor 583 060	THE BEST OF CREAM (LP)	12
70	Polydor 2383 016	LIVE CREAM (LP)	12
71	Polydor 2855 002	CREAM ON TOP (LP, mail-order compilation)	60
72	Polydor 2383 119	LIVE CREAM VOL. 2 (LP)	12
75	Polydor 2384 067	CREAM (LP, reissue of "Fresh Cream" with 2 extra tracks)	12
75	RSO 2394 179	GOODBYE (LP, gatefold sleeve, reissue)	12
80	RSO 2658 142	CREAM (7-LP set including "Fresh Cream", "Disraeli Gears", "Wheels Of Fire", "Goodbye", "Live Cream" & "Live Cream Vol. 2")	40
92	UFO CR 1	CREAM IN GEAR (96-page book packaged with "Disraeli Gears" CD)	20

(see also Eric Clapton, Jack Bruce, Ginger Baker, Blind Faith)

MINT VALUE £

CREAMERS

89 Fierce FRIGHT 045 Sunday Head/Think I'm Gonna Be Sick (p/s) . . . 10

JOAN CREARY

71 Fab FAB 181 Your Best Friend/Version . . . 7

CREATION (U.K.)

66 Planet PLF 116 Making Time/Try And Stop Me (some in company sleeves) . . . 40/30
66 Planet PLF 119 Painter Man/Biff Bang Pow (some in company sleeves) . . . 40/30
67 Polydor 56177 If I Stay Too Long/Nightmares . . . 40
67 Polydor 56207 Life Is Just Beginning/Through My Eyes . . . 70
68 Polydor 56230 How Does It Feel To Feel/Tom Tom . . . 55
68 Polydor 56246 Midway Down/The Girls Are Naked . . . 50
73 Charisma CB 213 Making Time/Painter Man . . . 8
77 Raw RAW 4 Making Time/Painter Man (reissue, p/s) . . . 10
84 Edsel E 5006 Making Time/Uncle Bert (p/s) . . . 10
73 Charisma Perspective CS 8 THE CREATION '66-67 (LP) . . . 40
82 Edsel ED 106 HOW DOES IT FEEL TO FEEL (LP, with foldout insert) . . . 15
(see also Mark Four, Birds, Ashton Gardner & Dyke, Kennedy Express, Eddy Phillips, Smiley, Spectrum)

CREATION (U.S.)

72 Stateside SS 2205 I Got The Fever/Soul Control . . . 10
(see also Prophets)

CREATIONS

67 Rio R 133 Meet Me At Eight/Searching . . . 15
68 Amalgamated AMG 818 Holding Out/Get On Up . . . 15
69 Punch PH 2 Mix Up Girl/Qua Kue Shut . . . 10
(see also Little Roys)

CREATOR & NORMA

63 Island WI 105 We Will Be Lovers/Come On Pretty Baby . . . 18

CREATURES

66 CBS 202048 Turn Out The Light/It Must Be Love . . . 8
66 CBS 202350 String Along/Night Is Warm . . . 8
67 CBS 2666 Looking At Tomorrow/Someone Needs You . . . 8

CREATURES

81 Polydor POSPG 354 WILD THINGS (double pack EP, gatefold p/s; picture labels) . . . 5
83 Wonderland SHE 1 Miss The Girl/Hot Springs In The Snow (p/s) . . . 5
98 Sioux 1V Sad Cunt/Sad Cunt (Chix'n'Dix mix) (p/s) . . . 5
98 Sioux 2 ERASER CUT (10" EP, p/s) . . . 7
(see also Siouxsie & Banshees)

CREEDENCE CLEARWATER REVIVAL

69 Liberty LBF 15223 Proud Mary/I Put A Spell On You (withdrawn) . . . 20
69 Liberty LBF 15223 Proud Mary/Born On The Bayou . . . 6
69 Liberty LBF 15230 Bad Moon Rising/Lodi . . . 6
69 Liberty LBF 15250 Green River/Commotion . . . 6
70 Liberty LBF 15283 Down On The Corner/Fortunate Son . . . 6
70 Liberty LBF 15310 Travellin' Band/Who'll Stop The Rain . . . 6
70 Liberty LBF 15354 Up Around The Bend/Run Through The Jungle (initially in p/s) . . . 10/5
70 Liberty LBF 15384 Long As I Can See The Light/Lookin' Out My Back Door (initially in p/s) . . . 10/5
71 Liberty LBF 15440 Have You Ever Seen The Rain/Hey Tonight . . . 5
71 United Artists UP 35210 Hey Tonight/Have You Ever Seen The Rain (reissue) . . . 6
71 United Artists UP 35261 Sweet Hitch-Hiker/Door To Door . . . 6
72 Fantasy F 676 Someday Never Comes/Tearin' Up The Country . . . 5
72 Fantasy FTC 101 Born On The Bayou/I Put A Spell On You . . . 5
73 Fantasy FTC 104 It Came Out Of The Sky/Side O' The Road . . . 5
69 Liberty LBS 83259 CREEDENCE CLEARWATER REVIVAL (LP) . . . 20
69 Liberty LBS 83261 BAYOU COUNTRY (LP) . . . 20
69 Liberty LBS 83273 GREEN RIVER (LP) . . . 20
70 Liberty LBS 83338 WILLY AND THE POORBOYS (LP) . . . 20
70 Liberty LBS 83388 COSMO'S FACTORY (LP) . . . 20
71 Liberty LBG 83400 PENDULUM (LP, gatefold sleeve) . . . 15
(see also Golliwogs, John Fogerty, Tom Fogerty, Blue Ridge Rangers)

CREEPERS

66 Blue Beat BB 366 Beat Of My Soul/LLOYD ADAMS: I Wish Your Picture Was You . . . 18

CREME CARAMEL

69 Pye International 7N 25495 My Idea/Excursion . . . 6

CRESCENDOS

58 London HLU 8563 Oh Julie/My Little Girl . . . 60
58 London HLU 8563 Oh Julie/My Little Girl (78) . . . 20

CRESCENTS

58 Columbia DB 4093 Wrong/Baby, Baby, Baby . . . 110
58 Columbia DB 4093 Wrong/Baby, Baby, Baby (78) . . . 20

CRESCENTS

64 London HLN 9851 Pink Dominos/Breakout . . . 20

CRESSIDA

70 Vertigo VO 7 CRESSIDA (LP, gatefold sleeve, swirl label) . . . 100
71 Vertigo 6360 025 ASYLUM (LP, gatefold sleeve, swirl label) . . . 120

CRESTAS

65 Fontana TF 551 To Be Loved/When I Fall In Love . . . 25

MINT VALUE £

CRESTERS

64	HMV POP 1249	I Just Don't Understand/I Want You	15
64	HMV POP 1296	Put Your Arms Around Me/Do It With Me	15

(see also Mike Sagar & Cresters, Richard Harding)

CRESTS

59	London HL 8794	Sixteen Candles/Beside You	80
59	London HL 8794	Sixteen Candles/Beside You (78)	40
59	Top Rank JAR 150	Flower Of Love/Molly Mae	20
59	Top Rank JAR 150	Flower Of Love/Molly Mae (78)	25
59	Top Rank JAR 168	Six Nights A Week/I Do	25
59	Top Rank JAR 168	Six Nights A Week/I Do (78)	35
59	London HL 8954	The Angels Listened In/I Thank The Moon	50
59	London HL 8954	The Angels Listened In/I Thank The Moon (78)	40
60	Top Rank JAR 302	A Year Ago Tonight/Paper Crown	30
60	Top Rank JAR 372	Step By Step/Gee (But I'd Give The World)	30
60	HMV POP 768	Always You/Trouble In Paradise	35
60	HMV POP 808	Isn't It Amazing/Molly Mae	30
61	HMV POP 848	Model Girl/We've Got To Tell Them	22
62	HMV POP 976	Little Miracles/Baby I Gotta Know	25
63	London HLU 9671	Guilty/Number One With Me	25

(see also Johnny Maestro)

CREW

69	Plexium PXM 12	Marty/Danger Signs	7
70	Decca F 13000	Cecilia/1970	7

CREW-CUTS

53	Mercury MB 3135	Crazy 'Bout You Baby/Angela Mia (78)	10
54	Mercury MB 3140	Sh-Boom/I Spoke Too Soon (78)	10
54	Mercury MB 3159	Oop-Shoop/Do Me Good, Baby (78)	12
54	Mercury MB 3177	Twinkle Toes/Dance Mr. Snowman Dance (78)	8
54	Mercury MB 3185	Barking Dog/All I Wanna Do (78)	12
55	Mercury MB 3202	Earth Angel/Ko Ko Mo (78)	8
55	Mercury MB 3222	Unchained Melody/Two Hearts, Two Kisses (78)	10
55	Mercury MB 3228	Don't Be Angry/Chop Chop Boom (78)	14
56	Mercury MT 100	Angels In The Sky/Seven Days (78)	10
56	Mercury 7MT 2	Angels In The Sky/Seven Days (export issue)	25
56	Mercury MT 108	A Story Untold/Honey Hair, Sugar Lips, Eyes Of Blue (78)	12
56	Mercury MT 127	Rebel In Town/Bei Mir Bist Du Shoen (78)	14
57	Mercury MT 140	Young Love/Little By Little (78)	15
57	Mercury MT 161	Susie-Q/Such A Shame (78)	20
57	Mercury MT 178	I Sit In My Window/Hey, You Face (78)	15
58	RCA RCA 1075	Hey, Stella!/Forever, My Darling	30
58	RCA RCA 1075	Hey, Stella!/Forever, My Darling (78)	30
56	Mercury MEP 9002	PRESENTING THE CREW-CUTS (EP)	60
56	Mercury MPT 7501	THE CREW-CUTS ON PARADE (10" LP)	100

BOB CREWE (GENERATION)

60	London HLI 9077	Water Boy/Voglio Cantare (solo)	6
64	Stateside SS 356	Maggie Maggie May/We Almost Made It	6
67	Stateside SS 582	Music To Watch Girls By/Girls On The Rocks	12
67	Stateside SS 2032	You Only Live Twice/A Lover's Concerto	10
67	Philips BL 7788	PLAY THE FOUR SEASONS HITS (LP, as Bob Crewe Orch.)	18
67	Stateside SL 10210	MUSIC TO WATCH GIRLS BY (LP)	30
68	Stateside S(S)L 10260	BARBARELLA (LP, soundtrack)	80

BERNARD CRIBBINS

60	Parlophone R 4712	Folk Song/My Kind Of Someone (B-side with Joyce Blair)	7
62	Parlophone R 4869	The Hole In The Ground/Winkle Picker Shoes	6
62	Parlophone R 4923	Right Said Fred/Quietly Bonkers	6
62	Parlophone R 4961	Gossip Calypso/One Man Band	6
67	Parlophone R 5603	When I'm Sixty-Four/Oh My Word	10
62	Parlophone GEP 8859	THE HOLE IN THE GROUND (EP)	18
62	Parlophone PMC 1186	A COMBINATION OF CRIBBINS (LP, also stereo [PCS 3035])	each 25

CRICKETS featuring Buddy Holly

78s

57	Vogue Coral Q 72279	That'll Be The Day/I'm Lookin' For Someone To Love	15
57	Coral Q 72298	Oh Boy!/Not Fade Away	15
58	Coral Q 72279	That'll Be The Day/I'm Lookin' For Someone To Love	15
58	Coral Q 72307	Maybe Baby/Tell Me How	15
58	Coral Q 72329	Think It Over/Fool's Paradise	15
58	Coral Q 72343	It's So Easy/Lonesome Tears	15

SINGLES

57	Vogue Coral Q 72279	That'll Be The Day/I'm Lookin' For Someone To Love	22
57	Coral Q 72298	Oh Boy!/Not Fade Away	20
58	Coral Q 72279	That'll Be The Day/I'm Lookin' For Someone To Love (2nd issue)	20
58	Coral Q 72307	Maybe Baby/Tell Me How	20
58	Coral Q 72329	Think It Over/Fool's Paradise	20
58	Coral Q 72343	It's So Easy/Lonesome Tears	20

(All the above 45s were originally issued with triangular centres; later round centre copies are worth around half these values.)

68	Decca AD 1012	Oh, Boy/That'll Be The Day (export issue)	75
68	MCA MU 1017	Oh, Boy/That'll Be The Day (as Crickets featuring Buddy Holly)	8

EPs

58	Coral FEP 2003	THE SOUND OF THE CRICKETS (triangular or round centre)	45/30
59	Coral FEP 2014	IT'S SO EASY (triangular or round centre)	45/30

MINT VALUE £

60	Coral FEP 2060	FOUR MORE BY THE CRICKETS	40
60	Coral FEP 2062	THAT'LL BE THE DAY	40

LP

58	Vogue Coral LVA 9081	THE CHIRPING CRICKETS (Vogue-Coral labels & Coral sleeve)	110
58	Coral LVA 9081	THE CHIRPING CRICKETS (re-pressing with Coral labels & sleeve)	65

(see also Buddy Holly)

CRICKETS

78s

59	Coral Q 72365	Love's Made A Fool Of You/Someone, Someone	75
59	Coral Q 72382	When You Ask About Love/Deborah	100
60	Coral Q 72395	More Than I Can Say/Baby My Heart (existence unconfirmed)	

SINGLES

59	Coral Q 72365	Love's Made A Fool Of You/Someone, Someone	15
59	Coral Q 72382	When You Ask About Love/Deborah	15
60	Coral Q 72395	More Than I Can Say/Baby My Heart	15
61	Coral Q 72417	Peggy Sue Got Married/Don'tcha Know	15
61	Coral Q 72440	I Fought The Law/A Sweet Love	15
61	London HLG 9486	He's Old Enough To Know Better/I'm Feeling Better	15
62	Liberty LIB 55441	Don't Ever Change/I Am Not A Bad Guy	8
62	Liberty LIB 55495	Little Hollywood Girl/Parisian Girl	15
63	Liberty LIB 10067	My Little Girl/Teardrops Fall Like Rain	8
63	Liberty LIB 10092	Don't Try To Change Me/Lost And Alone	15
63	Liberty LIB 10113	Right Or Wrong/You Can't Be In Between	8
64	Liberty LIB 10145	Lonely Avenue/Playboy	8
64	Liberty LIB 55696	(They Call Her) La Bamba/All Over You	8
64	Liberty LIB 10174	I Think I've Caught The Blues/We Gotta Get Together	8
66	Liberty LIB 55603	April Avenue/Don't Say You Love Me	12
68	Liberty LBF 15089	My Little Girl/Lonely Avenue	8
72	United Artists UP 35457	Don't Ever Change/Playboy	8
73	Philips 6006 269	My Rockin' Days/Lovesick Blues	10
73	Philips 6006 294	Hayride/Wasn't It Nice In New York City (some in p/s)	25/15
74	Mercury 6008 006	Ooh Las Vegas/Rhyme And Time	6
79	Rollercoaster RRC 2001	Cruise In It/Rock Around With Ollie Vee (1st 2,000 with 'single photo' p/s)	8/5
87	Rollercoaster RRC 2007	Forever In Mind/The Weekend/Your M-M-Memory/Three-Piece (tri-centre in overprinted p/s)	8
88	MPL/CBS TSH 1	T-Shirt/Hollywould (p/s)	10
88	MPL/CBS TSHT 1	T-Shirt/Hollywould (12", p/s)	15
88	MPL/CBS CDTSHT 1	T-Shirt/Hollywould (CD)	25

EPs

60	Coral FEP 2053	THE CRICKETS (initially triangular centre, later round centre)	75/40
61	Coral FEP 2064	THE CRICKETS DON'T EVER CHANGE	40
63	Liberty (S)LEP 2094	STRAIGHT NO STRINGS (mono/stereo)	35/60
64	Liberty LEP 2173	COME ON	40
77	Rollercoaster RRCEP 0001	MILLION DOLLAR MOVIE (shared with Sonny Curtis; test pressings only)	12

LPs

61	Coral LVA 9142	IN STYLE WITH THE CRICKETS	60
62	Liberty (S)LBY 1120	SOMETHING OLD, SOMETHING NEW, SOMETHING BLUE, SOMETHING ELSE! (mono/stereo)	40/50
65	Liberty LBY 1258	THE CRICKETS — A COLLECTION	40
71	CBS 64301	ROCKIN' FIFTIES, ROCK 'N' ROLL	20
73	Philips 6308 149	BUBBLEGUM, POP, BALLADS & BOOGIES	25
74	Mercury 6310 007	A LONG WAY FROM LUBBOCK	25
75	MCA MCFM 2710	BACK IN STYLE	15

(see also Buddy Holly, Jerry Allison & Crickets, Ivan, Sonny Curtis, Earl Sinks, Sinx Mitchell, David Box)

CRICKETS & BOBBY VEE

63	Liberty LEP 2084	JUST FOR FUN (EP)	25
63	Liberty (S)LEP 2116	BOBBY VEE MEETS THE CRICKETS (EP, mono/stereo)	35/50
63	Liberty LEP 2149	BOBBY VEE MEETS THE CRICKETS VOL. 2 (EP)	35
62	Liberty (S)LBY 1086	BOBBY VEE MEETS THE CRICKETS (LP, mono/stereo)	25/40

(see also Bobby Vee)

CRIME

80	Punk Products PP 1	Johnny Come Home/Generation Gap (p/s)	100

CRIMINAL CLASS

82	Inferno HELL 7	Fighting The System/Soldier (p/s)	8

CRISIS

79	Peckham Action NOTH 1	No Town Hall (Southwark)/Holocaust/P.C. One Nine Eight Four (p/s)	15
79	Ardkor CRI 002	UK '79/White Youth (p/s)	10
80	Ardkor CRI 003	HYMNS OF FAITH (12" EP)	20
81	Ardkor CRI 004	Alienation/Brückwood/Hospital (p/s, with insert)	10
82	Crisis NOTH 1/CRI 002	HOLOCAUST UK (12" EP)	15

(see also Death In June, Current 93, Theatre Of Hate)

CRISIS

70s	private pressing	ANOTHER FINE MESS (LP)	35

CRISPY AMBULANCE

79	Aural Assault AAR 001	From The Cradle To The Grave/4 Minutes From The Frontline (glossy or matt p/s)	15/8
81	Factory FAC 32	Unsightly And Serene: Not What I Expected/Deaf (10", p/s)	8
83	CBST 7	THE BLUE AND YELLOW OF THE YACHT CLUB (cassette)	8
83	CBST 8	OPEN GATES OF FIRE (cassette)	8
89	Temps Moderne LTMV:X	FIN (LP)	12

(see also Ram Ram Kino)

MINT VALUE £

GARY CRISS

62	Stateside SS 104	Our Favourite Melodies/Welcome Home To My Heart	12
62	Stateside SS 123	My Little Heavenly Angel/The Girl That I Told You About	10
63	Stateside SS 164	Long Lonely Nights/I Still Miss You So	10
63	Stateside SS 265	Sweet, Warm And Soft/Little Joe	10
65	Stateside SS 427	Hands Off Buddy/If This Is Goodbye	12

PETER CRISS

79	Casablanca CAN 139	You Matter To Me/Hooked On Rock And Roll (p/s, green vinyl with mask)	30
79	Casablanca CAN 139	You Matter To Me/Hooked On Rock And Roll (p/s, black vinyl)	15
80	Mercury 6302 065	OUT OF CONTROL (LP)	15

(see also Kiss)

LINDA CRISTAL

59	Coral Q 72350	Strictly For Pleasure (A Perfect Romance)/It's Better In Spanish	7
59	Coral Q 72350	Strictly For Pleasure (A Perfect Romance)/It's Better In Spanish (78)	8

CRISTINA

80	Island/Ze WIP 6560	Is That All There Is?/Jungle Love (withdrawn)	6
80	Island/Ze 12WIP 6560	Is That All There Is?/Jungle Love (12", withdrawn)	10

BOBBY CRISTO & REBELS

64	Decca F 11913	The Other Side Of The Track/I've Got You Out Of My Mind	40

MARY CRISTY

76	Polydor 2056 513	Thank You For Rushing Into My Life/We Can't Hide This Time	10

CRITICS & NYAH SHUFFLE

70	Joe JRS 1	Behold/SEXY FRANKIE: Tea, Patty, Sex And Ganja	8

CRITICS GROUP

66	Argo ZDA 46	A MERRY PROGRESS TO LONDON (LP, with insert)	18
68	Argo ZDA 82	THE FEMALE FROLIC (LP, with insert)	18
68	Argo DA 86	WATERLOO PETERLOO (LP, with insert)	15

CRITTERS

66	London HLR 10047	Younger Girl/Gone For Awhile	15
66	London HLR 10071	Mr. Dieingly Sad/It Just Won't Be That Way	15
66	London HLR 10101	Bad Misunderstanding/Forever Or No More	15
67	London HLR 10119	Marryin' Kind Of Love/New York Bound	10
67	London HLR 10149	Don't Let The Rain Fall Down On Me/Walk Like A Man Again	12
67	London HA-R 8302	THE CRITTERS (LP)	40

JIM CROCE

72	Vertigo 6073 251	Operator/Rapid Roy	6
72	Vertigo 6360 700	YOU DON'T MESS AROUND WITH JIM (LP, gatefold sleeve, swirl label)	20
72	Vertigo 6360 702	I GOT A NAME (LP)	18
70s	Life Song 35000	TIME IN A BOTTLE (LP)	15
70s	Life Song INT 14052	GREATEST CHARACTER (LP)	12
70s	Life Song 135004	LIFE & TIMES (LP)	18

CROCHETED DOUGHNUT RING

67	Polydor 56204	Two Little Ladies (Azalea And Rhododendron)/Nice	40
67	Deram DM 169	Havana Anna/Happy Castle	40
68	Deram DM 180	Maxine's Parlour/Get Out Your Rock And Roll Shoes	25

(see also Force Five, Doughnut Ring, Fingers, Daddy Lindberg)

CROCODILE RIDE

80s	Thunderball Surfacer 002	Ex-Hipster/Satellite/14 ICED BEARS: Falling Backwards/World I Love (Speed Mix) (1,000 only, numbered & stickered mailer)	8

CROFTERS

69	Say Disc SD 113	PILL FERRY (EP)	10
69	Beltona SBE 103	CROFTERS (LP)	15

TONY CROMBIE

54	Decca F 10424	Stop It All/All Of Me (& His Orchestra)	6
55	Decca F 10454	Perdido/Love You Madly (& His Orchestra)	6
55	Decca F 10547	Early One Morning/Flying Home (& His Orchestra)	6
55	Decca F 10592	Flying Hickory/String Of Pearls (& His Orchestra)	6
55	Decca F 10637	I Want You To Be My Baby (with Annie Ross)/Three Little Words	6
55	Decca F 10637	I Want You To Be My Baby (with Annie Ross)/Three Little Words (78)	6
56	Columbia DB 3822	Teach You To Rock/Short'nin' Bread Rock (as Tony Crombie & Rockets)	40
56	Columbia DB 3822	Teach You To Rock/Short'nin' Bread Rock (78)	10
56	Columbia DB 3859	Sham Rock/Let's You And I Rock (as Tony Crombie & Rockets)	35
56	Columbia DB 3859	Sham Rock/Let's You And I Rock (78)	12
57	Columbia DB 3880	Rock, Rock, Rock/The Big Beat (as Tony Crombie & Rockets) (78)	14
57	Columbia DB 3881	Lonesome Train (On A Lonesome Track)/We're Gonna Rock Tonight (78, as Tony Crombie & Rockets)	20
57	Columbia DB 3921	London Rock/Brighton Rock (as Tony Crombie & Rockets)	35
57	Columbia DB 3921	London Rock/Brighton Rock (78)	20
57	Columbia DB 4000	Sweet Beat/Sweet Georgia Brown (as Tony Crombie & His Sweet Beat)	10
57	Columbia DB 4000	Sweet Beat/Sweet Georgia Brown (78)	10
58	Columbia DB 4076	Dumplin's/Tw'on Special	10
58	Columbia DB 4076	Dumplin's/Tw'on Special (78)	10
58	Columbia DB 4145	Unguaua/Piakukaungchung (as Tony Crombie Men)	7
58	Columbia DB 4145	Unguaua/Piakukaungchung (as Tony Crombie Men) (78)	8
58	Columbia DB 4189	Rock-Cha-Cha/The Gigglin' Gurgleburp (as Tony Crombie Men)	6
58	Columbia DB 4189	Rock-Cha-Cha/The Gigglin' Gurgleburp (as Tony Crombie Men) (78)	10
59	Columbia DB 4253	Champagne Cha Cha/Shepherd's Cha Cha (as Tony Crombie Men)	5
59	Columbia DB 4253	Champagne Cha Cha/Shepherd's Cha Cha(as Tony Crombie Men) (78)	10
59	Top Rank JAR 182	"Man From Interpol" Theme/Interpol Cha Cha Cha & Chase (as Tony Crombie Orchestra)	5

MINT VALUE £

59	Top Rank JAR 182	"Man From Interpol" Theme/Interpol Cha Cha Cha & Chase (78, as Tony Crombie Orchestra)	20
62	Ember JBS 706	Gutbucket/Just Like Old Times	6
56	Decca DFE 6247	PRESENTING TONY CROMBIE NO. 1 (EP)	12
56	Decca DFE 6281	PRESENTING TONY CROMBIE NO. 2 (EP)	12
57	Columbia SEG 7676	ROCK ROCK ROCK (EP)	80
57	Columbia SEG 7686	LET'S YOU AND I ROCK (EP)	80
61	Decca DFE 6670	FOUR FAVOURITE FILM THEMES (EP)	8
59	Columbia SEG 7882	SWINGIN' DANCE BEAT NO. 1 (EP)	10
59	Columbia SEG 7896	SWINGIN' DANCE BEAT NO. 2 (EP)	10
59	Columbia SEG 7918	ATMOSPHERE (EP, as Tony Crombie & His Men)	10
56	Columbia 33S 1117	TONY CROMBIE & HIS SWEETBEAT (10" LP)	40
57	Columbia 33S 1108	ROCKIN' WITH TONY CROMBIE & ROCKETS (10" LP)	100
58	Columbia SCX 3262	ATMOSPHERE (LP)	40
59	Top Rank 35/043	MAN FROM INTERPOL (LP, TV series music, by Tony Crombie & Band)	25
60	Top Rank BUY 027	DRUMS! DRUMS! DRUMS! (LP, as Tony Crombie & His Band)	30
61	Tempo TAP 30	JAZZ INC. (LP)	100
61	Decca SKL 4114	SWEET WIDE AND BLUE (LP)	30
61	Decca LK 4385	TWELVE FAVOURITE FILM THEMES (LP, also stereo SKL 4127)	40
61	Ember EMB 3336	WHOLE LOTTA TONY (LP)	60

(see also Annie Ross, Ray Ellington, London Jazz Quartet)

BILL CROMPTON

58	Fontana H 152	A Hoot An' A Holler/The Popocatepetl Beetle	12
58	Fontana H 152	A Hoot An' A Holler/The Popocatepetl Beetle (78)	10
59	Fontana H 178	Out Of Sight, Out Of Mind/My Lover	10
59	Fontana H 178	Out Of Sight, Out Of Mind/My Lover (78)	10

CROMWELL

75	Cromwell WELL 006	First Day	20
75	Cromwell WELL 005	AT THE GALLOP (LP, private pressing)	140

(see also Establishment)

LINK CROMWELL (Lenny Kaye)

66	London HLB 10040	Crazy Like A Fox/Shock Me	20

(see also Patti Smith Group)

ANDREW CRONSHAW

77	Trailer LREP 1	CLOUD VALLEY (EP)	10
74	Xtra XTRA 1139	A IS FOR ANDREW, Z IS FOR ZITHER (LP)	15

CROOKED OAK

76	Folkland FL 0102	FROM LITTLE ACORNS GROW (LP, 500 only)	70
79	Eron ERON 019	THE FOOT O'WOR STAIRS (LP)	25

CROOKS

79	Blue Print BLU 2002	Modern Boys/The Beat Goes On (die-cut p/s)	6
80	Blue Print BLU 2006	All The Time In The World/Bangin' My Head (p/s)	8
80	Blue Print BLUP 5002	JUST RELEASED (LP)	12

DAVID CROOKS

70	Jackpot JP 759	I Won't Hold It Against You (actually by Dave Barker)/ BOBBY JAMES: King Of Hearts	7

(see also Dave Barker)

STEVE CROPPER

70	Stax STAX 147	Funky Broadway/Crop Dustin'	10
69	Stax SXATS 1008	WITH A LITTLE HELP FROM MY FRIENDS (LP)	22

STEVE CROPPER & ALBERT KING

69	Stax SXATS 1020	JAMMED TOGETHER (LP, with Pops Staples)	18

(see also Booker T. & M.G.'s, Albert King)

BING CROSBY

78s

59	Brunswick 05790	Rain/Church Bells	10
59	Philips PB 921	Say One For Me/I Couldn't Care Less	10

SINGLES

54	Brunswick 03384	White Christmas/Let's Start The New Year Right	10
54	Brunswick 03929	Silent Night, Holy Night/Adeste Fideles	7
54	Brunswick 05224	What A Little Moonlight Can Do/Down By The Riverside (with Gary Crosby)	8
54	Brunswick 05244	Changing Partners/Y'All Come	15
54	Brunswick 05269	Secret Love/My Love, My Love	12
54	Brunswick 05277	Young At Heart/I Get So Lonely	8
54	Brunswick 05304	If There's Anybody Here (From Out Of Town)/Back In The Old Routine (with Donald O'Connor)	7
54	Brunswick 05315	Cornbelt Symphony/The Call Of The South (with Gary Crosby)	7
54	Brunswick 05339	Count Your Blessings Instead Of Sheep/What Can You Do With A General	12
54	Brunswick 05354	White Christmas/Snow (with Danny Kaye, Peggy Lee & Trudy Stevens)	8
55	Brunswick 05377	The Song From "Desiree" (We Meet Again)/I Love Paris	6
55	Brunswick 05385	Tobermory Bay/The River (Sciummo)	6
55	Brunswick 05403	Dissertation On The State Of Bliss (with Patty Andrews)/It's Mine, It's Yours	6
55	Brunswick 05404	The Search Is Through/The Land Around Us	6
55	Brunswick 05410	Stranger In Paradise/Who Gave You The Roses	6
55	Brunswick 05419	Ohio/A Quiet Girl	6
55	Brunswick 05430	Jim, Johnny And Jonas/Nobody	6
55	Brunswick 05451	All She'd Say Was "Umh"/She Is The Sunshine Of Virginia	6
55	Brunswick 05486	Angel Bells/There's Music In You	6
55	Brunswick 05501	Let's Harmonize/Sleigh Bell Serenade	6
56	Brunswick 05511	Farewell/Early American	6
56	Brunswick 05543	In A Little Spanish Town/Ol' Man River	6

			MINT VALUE £
56	Brunswick 05558	No Other Love/Sleepy Time Gal	6
56	Brunswick 05585	Honeysuckle Rose/Swanee	6
56	Brunswick 05620	Christmas Is A-Comin'/Is Christmas Only A Tree	6
56	Capitol CL 14643	Now You Has Jazz (with Louis Armstrong)/LOUIS ARMSTRONG: High Society Calypso	10
56	Capitol CL 14645	True Love (with Grace Kelly)/Well, Did You Evah? (with Frank Sinatra)	6
57	Brunswick 05674	Around The World/VICTOR YOUNG ORCHESTRA: Around The World	6
57	Capitol CL 14761	Man On Fire/Seven Nights A Week	6
57	London HLR 8504	Never Be Afraid/I Love You Whoever You Are	7
57	London HLR 8513	How Lovely Is Christmas/My Own Individual Star	7
57	Brunswick 05726	Chicago/Alabamy Bound	6
58	Philips PB 817	Straight Down The Middle/Tomorrow's My Lucky Day	15
58	Brunswick 05760	Love In A Home/In The Good Old Summer Time	6
58	Brunswick 05764	It's Beginning To Look Like Christmas/I Heard The Bells	6
58	Brunswick 05770	Gigi/The Next Time It Happens	6
59	Brunswick 05790	Rain/Church Bells	6
59	Philips PB 921	Say One For Me/I Couldn't Care Less	6
59	Gala GSP 801	My Own Individual Star/Never Be Afraid	6
60	Brunswick 05840	Happy Birthday & Auld Lang Syne/Home Sweet Home	6
60	MGM MGM 1098	The Second Time Around/Incurably Romantic	6
62	Decca F 21452	Let's Not Be Sensible (with Joan Collins)/Team Work (with Bob Hope)	8
65	Brunswick 05928	Where The Blue Of The Night/Goodnight Sweetheart	6
68	MCA MU 1010	Around The World/VICTOR YOUNG ORCHESTRA: Around The World	6
EPs			
54	Brunswick OE 9003	BING SINGS HITS	8
55	Brunswick OE 9027	GARY CROSBY AND FRIEND (with Gary Crosby)	8
56	Brunswick OE 9292	SONGS I WISH I HAD SUNG VOL. 2	8
58	Philips BBE 12142	BING	8
58	Brunswick OE 9353	TO BALI AND MOROCCO (with Bob Hope)	8
58	Brunswick OE 9359	BING AND THE DIXIELAND BANDS (1 track with Conee Boswell)	8
59	Columbia SEG 7522	TRY A LITTLE TENDERNESS	8
59	Fontana TFE 17178	PLEASE	8
59	Fontana TFE 17179	REMEMBER	8
59	RCA SRC 7013	GOING PLACES (stereo, with Rosemary Clooney)	8
61	MGM MGM-ES 3515	BING AND SATCHMO (stereo, with Louis Armstrong)	8
LPs			
51	Brunswick LA 8513	SINGS COLE PORTER SONGS (10")	15
51	Brunswick LA 8514	STARDUST (10")	15
51	Brunswick LA 8529	EL BINGO — A SELECTION OF LATIN AMERICAN FAVOURITES (10")	15
52	Brunswick LA 8505	SINGS JEROME KERN SONGS (10")	15
54	Columbia 33S 1036	CROSBY CLASSICS (10")	15
56	Brunswick LAT 8106	SHILLELAGHS AND SHAMROCKS	12
52	Brunswick LA 8558	BING AND CONNIE (10", with Connie Boswell)	12
53	Brunswick LA 8571	STEPHEN FOSTER SONGS (10")	12
53	Brunswick LA 8579	BING CROSBY AND THE DIXIELAND BANDS (10")	12
53	Brunswick LA 8584	THE QUIET MAN (10")	12
53	Brunswick LA 8585	AULD LANG SYNE (10")	12
53	Brunswick LA 8592	HOLIDAY INN (10", with Fred Astaire)	12
53	Brunswick LA 8595	BLUE OF THE NIGHT (10")	12
53	Brunswick LA 8600	BING CROSBY SINGS VICTOR HERBERT SONGS (10")	12
53	Brunswick LA 8602	BLUE SKIES (10", with Fred Astaire)	12
53	Brunswick LA 8606	WHEN IRISH EYES ARE SMILING (10")	12
53	Brunswick LA 8620	DOWN MEMORY LANE (10")	12
53	Brunswick LA 8624	DOWN MEMORY LANE VOL. 2 (10")	12
54	Brunswick LA 8645	LE BING — SINGS HITS OF PARIS (10")	12
54	Brunswick LA 8656	'WAY BACK HOME (10")	12
54	Brunswick LA 8666	GEORGE GERSHWIN SONGS (10")	12
54	Brunswick LA 8673	SOME FINE OLD CHESTNUTS (10")	12
54	Brunswick LA 8674	BING SINGS THE HITS (10")	12
54	Brunswick LA 8675	SONG HITS FROM BROADWAY SHOWS (10")	12
54	Brunswick LA 8684	YOURS IS MY HEART ALONE (10")	12
54	Brunswick LA 8686	MERRY CHRISTMAS (10")	12
54	Brunswick LA 8687	CROSBY COLLECTOR'S CLASSICS VOL. 1 (10")	12
54	Brunswick LAT 8051-8055	BING — A MUSICAL AUTOBIOGRAPHY (5-LP box set)	30
55	Brunswick LA 8714	COUNTRY GIRL/LITLE BOY LOST (10")	12
55	Brunswick LA 8723	CROSBY COLLECTOR'S CLASSICS VOL. 2 (10")	12
55	Brunswick LA 8724	COUNTRY STYLE (10")	12
55	Brunswick LA 8726	CROSBY COLLECTOR'S CLASSICS VOL. 3 (10")	12
55	Brunswick LA 8727	CROSBY COLLECTOR'S CLASSICS VOL. 4 (10")	12
55	Brunswick LA 8730	FAVOURITE HAWAIIAN SONGS (10")	12
55	Brunswick	FAVOURITE HAWAIIAN SONGS VOL. 2 (10")	12
55	Brunswick LA 8741	BING THE EARLY THIRTIES VOL. 2 (10")	12
56	Brunswick LAT 8138	SONGS I WISH I'D SUNG	12
56	Brunswick LAT 8152	HOME ON THE RANGE	12
56	HMV CLP 1088	BING SINGS WHILST BREGMAN SWINGS	12
57	Brunswick LAT 8154	HIGH TOR (with Julie Andrews)	12
57	Brunswick LAT 8216	A CHRISTMAS SINGS WITH BING	12
57	Brunswick LAT 8217	NEW TRICKS	12
58	Brunswick LAT 8228	BING AND THE DIXIELAND BANDS	12
58	Brunswick LAT 8253	TWILIGHT ON THE TRAIL	12
58	Fontana TFR 6000	DER BINGLE (10")	15
59	Brunswick LAT 8278	WHEN IRISH EYES ARE SMILING	12
59	Brunswick LAT 8281	BING CROSBY SINGS	12

MINT VALUE £

59	Philips BBL 7335	SAY ONE FOR ME (soundtrack, with Debbie Reynolds)	12
57	RCA RD 27032	BING WITH A BEAT (with Bob Scobey's Frisco Jazz Band)	12
61	MGM C 844	BING AND SATCHMO (with Louis Armstrong)	12
62	Brunswick BING 1-15	BING'S HOLLYWOOD (15 LPs)	each 12
65	Reprise R 6106	RETURN TO PARADISE ISLAND	12

(see also Gary Crosby, Louis Armstrong, Bob Hope, Fred Astaire, Peggy Lee)

BOB CROSBY & HIS BOBCATS

59	London HLD 8828	Petite Fleur/Such A Long Night	8
59	London HLD 8828	Petite Fleur/Such A Long Night (78)	20
60	London HLD 9228	The Dark At The Top Of The Stairs/Night Theme	7
60	London HA-D 2293	BOB CROSBY'S GREAT HITS (LP, also stereo SAH-D 6105)	15/18

(see also Modernaires)

DAVID CROSBY

93	Atlantic A 7360	Hero/Coverage/Fare Thee Well (CD)	8
71	Atlantic 2401 005	IF I COULD ONLY REMEMBER MY NAME (LP, gatefold sleeve, red/plum label)	18

(see also Byrds, Crosby [Stills] Nash [& Young])

GARY CROSBY

54	Brunswick 05340	Mambo In The Moonlight/Got My Eyes On You	10
55	Brunswick 05365	Palsy Walsy/Loop-De-Loop Mambo (with Cheer Leaders)	10
55	Brunswick 05378	Ready, Willing And Able/There's A Small Hotel	15
55	Brunswick 05400	Ko Ko Mo (I Love You So)/Struttin' With Some Barbecue (w/ Louis Armstrong)	10
55	Brunswick 05400	Ko Ko Mo (I Love You So)/Struttin' With Some Barbecue (78, with Louis Armstrong)	10
55	Brunswick 05446	Ayuh Ayuh/Mississippi Pecan Pie	12
55	Brunswick 05496	Truly/Give Me A Band And My Baby (B-side with Paris Sisters)	10
56	Brunswick 05546	Yaller Yaller Gold/Get A Load O' Me	10
56	Brunswick 05574	Easy Street/Lazybones (with Louis Armstrong)	7
56	Brunswick 05574	Easy Street/Lazybones (78, with Louis Armstrong)	8
56	Brunswick 05633	Yaller Yaller Gold/Noah Found Grace In The Eyes Of God (with Dreamers)	6
58	HMV POP 550	Judy, Judy/Cheatin' On Me	40
58	HMV POP 550	Judy, Judy/Cheatin' On Me (78)	15
59	HMV POP 648	The Happy Bachelor/This Little Girl Of Mine	6
57	Vogue VA 160118	GARY CROSBY (LP)	20

(see also Bing Crosby, Louis Armstrong)

CROSBY & NASH

72	Atlantic K 10192	Southbound Train/Whole Cloth	7
72	Atlantic K 50011	GRAHAM NASH & DAVID CROSBY (LP, foldout sleeve)	20

CROSBY, STILLS & NASH

69	Atlantic 584 283	Marrakesh Express/Helplessly Hoping	10
69	Atlantic 584 304	Suite: Judy Blue Eyes/Long Time Gone	8
69	Atlantic 588 189	CROSBY, STILLS & NASH (LP, gatefold sleeve, with lyric sheet)	22

CROSBY, STILLS, NASH & YOUNG

70	Atlantic 2091 002	Teach Your Children/Country Girl	7
70	Atlantic 2091 010	Woodstock/Helpless	8
70	Atlantic 2091 023	Ohio/Find The Cost Of Freedom	7
70	Atlantic 2091 039	Our House/Deja Vu	10
88	Atlantic A 9003TX	American Dream/Compass/Soldiers Of Peace/Ohio (12", p/s)	8
70	Atlantic 2401 001	DÉJA VU (LP, gatefold sleeve, pasted-on photo on front, plum/red label)	25
71	Atlantic 2657 007	FOUR WAY STREET (2-LP, gatefold sleeve with lyric sheet)	25

(see also David Crosby, Stephen Stills [Manassas], Graham Nash, Neil Young)

CROSS

87	Virgin VS 1007	Cowboys And Indians (4.20)/Love Lies Bleeding (She's A Wicked Wily Waitress) (p/s)	10
87	Virgin VSTC 1007	Cowboys And Indians (Full Length Version)/Love Lies Bleeding (She's A Wicked Wily Waitress) (cassette)	15
87	Virgin VST 1007	Cowboys And Indians (Full Length Version 5.53)/Love Lies Bleeding (She's A Wicked Wily Waitress) (12", p/s)	20
87	Virgin CDEP 10	Cowboys And Indians (4.20)/Cowboys And Indians (Full Length Version 6.12)/ Love Lies Bleeding (She's A Wicked Wily Waitress) (CD, promo only)	100
88	Virgin VS 1026	Shove It! (7" Version)/Rough Justice (p/s)	10
88	Virgin VST 1026	Shove It! (Extended Mix)/Shove It! (Metropolix)/Rough Justice (12", p/s)	22
88	Virgin CDEP 20	Shove It! (7" Version)/Rough Justice/Cowboys And Indians (4.20)/ Shove It! (Extended Mix) (CD)	30
88	Virgin VS 1062	Heaven For Everyone/Love On A Tightrope (Like An Animal) (p/s)	12
88	Virgin VST 1062	Heaven For Everyone/Love On A Tightrope (Like An Animal)/Contact (12", p/s)	20
88	Virgin VS 1100	Manipulator/Stand Up For Love (p/s)	15
88	Virgin VST 1100	Manipulator (Extended)/Stand Up For Love/Manipulator (7" Version) (12", p/s)	30
88	Virgin VVCS 7	Love On The Tightrope (Like An Animal)/(tracks by Phil Collins, China Crisis & Donny Osmond) (3" CD sampler, gatefold sleeve)	10
90	Parlophone R 6251	Power To Love (3.28)/Passion For Trash (p/s)	10
90	Parlophone 12R 6251	Power To Love (Extended Version)/Passion For Trash/ Power To Love (7" Version) (12", p/s)	18
90	Parlophone CDR 6251	Power To Love (Extended Version)/Passion For Trash/ Power To Love (7" Version) (CD)	30
87	Virgin V 2477	SHOVE IT! (LP, 8 tracks, with inner sleeve)	12
90	Parlophone PCS 7342	MAD, BAD AND DANGEROUS TO KNOW (LP)	20
90	Parlophone CDPCS 7342	MAD, BAD AND DANGEROUS TO KNOW (CD)	75
90	(no label)	OFFICIAL BOOTLEG (fan club-only cassette, featuring Brian May)	20
91	(no label)	LIVE IN GERMANY (fan club-only cassette)	15

(see also Roger Taylor, Queen)

MINT VALUE £

JIMMIE CROSS

66	Red Bird RB 10042	Super Duper Man/Hey Little Girl	22
78	Wanted Cult 101	I Want My Baby Back/Play The Other Side (p/s)	8

(Keith) CROSS & (Peter) ROSS

71	Decca F 13224	Can You Believe It?/Blind Willie Johnson	7
72	Decca F 13316	Peace In The End/Prophets Guiders	7
72	Decca SKL 5129	BORED CIVILIANS (LP)	50

(see also T2)

CROSSBEATS

67	Pilgrim PSR 7003	Step Aside/Forgive Me (p/s or art sleeve)	8
60s	Pilgrim PSR 7004	Busy Man/Change (p/s)	6
60s	Pilgrim KLP 12	CRAZY MIXED UP GENERATION (LP)	20

ANDRAE CROUCH (& DISCIPLES)

70s	Light LS 7014	JUST ANDRAE (LP)	15
70s	Light LS 7018	DISCIPLES LIVE AT CARNEGIE HALL (LP)	15
70s	Light LS 7019	KEEP ON SWINGIN' (LP)	15
70s	Light LS 7025	TAKE ME BACK (LP)	15
70s	Myrrh MYR 1188	NO TIME TO LOSE (LP)	15

CROW

70	Stateside SS 2159	Evil Woman, Don't Play Your Games With Me/Gonna Leave A Mark	6
70	Stateside SS 2171	Slow Down/Cottage Cheese	6
70	Stateside SS 2180	Don't Try To Lay No Boogie Woogie On The King Of Rock And Roll/Satisfied	6
75	Right On R101	Your Autumn Of Tomorrow/Uncle Funk	5
70	Stateside SSL 10301	CROW MUSIC (LP)	12
70	Stateside SSL 10310	CROW BY CROW (LP)	12

SHERYL CROW

93	A&M 580 380-7	Run, Baby, Run/All By Myself (p/s)	7
93	A&M 580 380-4	Run, Baby, Run/All By Myself (cassette)	5
93	A&M 580 381-2	Run, Baby, Run/All By Myself/The Na-Na Song/Reach Around Jerk (CD)	15
94	A&M 580 462-7	What Can I Do For You (Radio Edit)/Volvo Cowgirl 99 (p/s)	6
94	A&M 580 462-4	What Can I Do For You (Radio Edit)/Volvo Cowgirl 99 (cassette)	5
94	A&M 580 462-7	What Can I Do For You (Radio Edit)/What Can I Do For You (LP Version)/ Volvo Cowgirl 99/I Shall Believe (CD)	10
94	A&M 580 568-7	Run, Baby, Run/Leaving Las Vegas (Acoustic Version) (p/s)	6
94	A&M 580 569-2	Run, Baby, Run/Leaving Las Vegas (Acoustic Version)/ All By Myself/Reach Around Jerk (CD)	10
94	A&M 581 147-2	Run, Baby, Run/Can't Cry Anymore/Reach Around Jerk/I Shall Believe (CD, 'The Nashville Sessions', box set with poster & no'd 'obi')	15
94	A&M 580 644-7	Leaving Las Vegas/Leaving Las Vegas (Live In Nashville) (p/s, with postcard)	5
94	A&M 580 645-2	Leaving Las Vegas/I Shall Believe (Live In Nashville)/What Can I Do For You (Live At Borderline) (CD, stickered digipak with space for 2nd CD)	10
96	A&M 581 902-7	If It Makes You Happy (Edit)/All I Wanna Do (jukebox issue, no p/s)	7
96	A&M SCJB 2	Strong Enough/All I Wanna Do (Remix) (jukebox issue, no p/s)	7
96	A&M 580 918-7	Strong Enough/No One Said It Would Be Easy (p/s)	5
95	A&M 540 368-2/ 540 126-2-18	TUESDAY NIGHT MUSIC CLUB (CD, 2nd issue, with patchwork/montage cover and bonus 6-track CD "Sheryl Crow Live" [540 367-2])	25

CROWBAR

84	Skinhead SKIN 1	Hippie Punks/White Riot (p/s)	35

CROWD

79	SRT SRTS/79/CUS 377	Ronnie (Is A Headbanger)/A Little Of What I Fancy/Let's Fly Together (p/s)	6

CROWDED HOUSE

87	Capitol CDCL 416	World Where You Live (Extended Version)/Something So Strong/ Don't Dream It's Over/That's What I Call Love (CD, card sleeve)	15
88	Capitol CDCL 498	Better Be Home Soon/Kill Eye/Don't Dream It's Over (live)/ Better Be Home Soon (CD)	18
88	Capitol CDCL 509	Sister Madly/Mansion In The Slums/Something So Strong (live) (CD)	18
92	Capitol CDCL 655	Four Seasons In One Day (LP)/Dr. Livingstone/Recurring Dream/ Anyone Can Tell (CD, in collector's box)	10
91	Capitol CDP 793 559-2	WOODFACE (CD, foldout pack)	18
92	Capitol CH 1/2	LIVE AT THE TOWN AND COUNTRY CLUB, LONDON, NOVEMBER 9 1991 (2-CD, in PVC gatefold wallet & inserts, promo only)	70
92	Capitol CH 1/2	LIVE AT THE TOWN AND COUNTRY CLUB, LONDON, NOVEMBER 9 1991 (2-CD, in 5" x 5" black box with sampler cassette, promo only)	80
96	EMI FINNTERVIEW 2	THE FINAL INTERVIEW...? (CD, promo only)	18

(see also Split Enz, Tim Finn)

CROWDY CRAWN

(see under Brenda Wootton)

CROWFOOT

70	Paramount PARA 3008	California Rock 'N' Roll/Maybe I Can Learn To Live	5
70	Paramount SPFL 265	CROWFOOT (LP)	12

CROWNS

68	Pama PM 725	I Know, It's Alright/I Surrender	10
68	Pama PM 736	Jerking The Dog/Keep Me Going	12
68	Pama PM 745	She Ain't Gonna Do Right/I Need Your Loving	10
68	Pama PM 759	Since You Been Gone/Call Me	10
68	Pama PMLP 6	MADE OF GOLD (LP)	40

CROWS

54	Columbia SCM 5119	Gee/I Love You So	3,000
54	Columbia DB 3478	Gee/I Love You So (78)	250

MINT VALUE £

TREVOR CROZIER'S BROKEN CONSORT
72 Argo AFB 60 PARCEL OF OLD CRAMS (LP) 15

CRUCIFIXION
80 Miramar MIR 4 The Fox/Death Sentence (no p/s) 80
82 Neat NEAT 19 Take It Or Leave It/On The Run (p/s) 5
84 Neat NEAT 37 Green Eyes/Moon Rising/Jailbait (p/s) 5
84 Neat NEAT 3712 Green Eyes/Jailbait/Moon Rising (12", p/s, some on purple or green vinyl) 18/8

ARTHUR 'BIG BOY' CRUDUP
64 RCA RCA 1401 My Baby Left Me/I Don't Know It 35
64 RCA RCX 7161 RHYTHM AND BLUES VOL. 4 (EP) 25
69 Blue Horizon 7-63855 MEAN OLE FRISCO (LP) 100
70 Delmark DS 614 LOOK ON YONDERS WALL (LP) 25
71 Delmark DS 621 CRUDUP'S MOOD (LP) 25
72 RCA RD 8224 THE FATHER OF ROCK 'N' ROLL (LP) 25
74 United Artists UAS 29092 ROEBUCK MAN (LP) 20

CRUISERS
65 Decca F 12098 It Ain't Me Babe/Baby What You Want Me To Do 25
(see also Dave Berry, Godley & Creme)

SIMON CRUM
58 Capitol CL 14965 Country Music Is Here To Stay/Stand Up, Sit Down, Shut Your Mouth 25
59 Capitol CL 15077 I Fell Out Of Love With Love/Morgan Poisoned The Water Hole 12
61 Capitol CL 15183 Enormity In Motion/Cuzz Yore So Sweet 15
(see also Ferlin Husky)

RAY CRUMLEY
77 Magnet MAG 103 It's Uncanny/All The Way In Love With You 25

CRUSADERS
71 Rare Earth SRE 3001 OLD SOCKS NEW SHOES (LP) 15
72 Blue Thumb ILPS 9218 CRUSADERS (2-LP) 15
73 Mowest MWS 7004 HOLLYWOOD (LP) 20
75 ABC ABCD 607 SOUTHERN COMFORT (2-LP) 15
(see also Jazz Crusaders)

CRUX/CRASH
82 No Future OI 18 KEEP ON RUNNING (12" EP) 15

CRY
87 Crazy Flowerpot CFP 001 Party After Dark (some with p/s) 80/15
87 Crazy Flowerpot CFP 002 Give Her An Ice Cream (no p/s) 20

CRYAN' SHAMES
(see under Shames)

CRYER
80 Happy Face MM 124 The Single/Hesitate (p/s, with 2 inserts) 65

BARRY CRYER
58 Fontana H 139 The Purple People Eater/Hey! Eula 15
58 Fontana H 139 The Purple People Eater/Hey! Eula (78) 10
58 Fontana H 151 Nothin' Shakin'/Seven Daughters 18
58 Fontana H 151 Nothin' Shakin'/Seven Daughters (78) 12
59 Fontana H 177 Angelina/Kissin' 15
59 Fontana H 177 Angelina/Kissin' (78) 15

CRYIN' SHAMES
66 Decca F 12340 Please Stay/What's News Pussycat 22
66 Decca F 12425 Nobody Waved Goodbye/You 35
(see also Paul & Ritchie & Cryin' Shames, Gary Walker & Rain)

CRYING SHAMES
80 Logo GO 385 That's Rock'n'Roll/Too Late (p/s) 12

CRYSTALITES
69 Big Shot BI 510 Biafra/Drop Pan 7
69 Nu Beat NB 036 Splash Down/Finders Keepers 12
69 Songbird SB 1015 Musical Madness Parts 1 & 2 10
69 Songbird SB 1016 The Bad Parts 1 & 2 10
69 Explosion EX 2002 Doctor Who (Parts 1 & 2) 10
69 Explosion EX 2003 Barefoot Brigade/Slippery 10
69 Explosion EX 2005 Bombshell/Bag-A-Wire (B-side actually by Bobby Ellis & Crystalites) 15
69 Explosion EX 2006 A Fistful Of Dollars/The Emperor (B-side actually by Bobby Ellis & Crystalites) 15
70 Explosion EX 2010 The Bad/The Bad Version 15
70 Bullet BU 424 A Fistful Of Dollars/BOBBY ELLIS: Crystal 15
70 Songbird SB 1017 The Undertaker/Stop That Man (B-side actually "Easy Ride" by Ike Bennett & Crystalites) 15
70 Songbird SB 1020 Lady Madonna/Ghost Rider 8
70 Songbird SB 1024 Isies/Isies (Version 2) 8
70 Songbird SB 1025 Stranger In Town/Stranger In Town (Version 2) 8
70 Songbird SB 1030 Sic Him Rover/Drop Pon 8
70 Songbird SB 1034 Overtaker (Version I)/Overtaker (Version II) 10
70 Songbird SB 1035 Undertaker's Burial/Ghost Rider 6
71 Songbird SB 1057 Earthly Sounds/Version 6
73 Grape GR 3050 Blacula/Version 8
(see also Chosen Few, Scotty, Ramon & Crystalites, Kingstonians, Bongo Herman, Denzil Laing, Derrick Harriot, Ethiopians, Dennis Brown, Glen Brown, Big Youth)

MINT VALUE £

CRYSTALS

62	Parlophone R 4867	There's No Other Like My Baby/Oh Yeah Maybe Baby	150
62	London HLU 9611	He's A Rebel/I Love You Eddie	18
63	London HLU 9661	He's Sure The Boy I Love/Walking Along (La-La-La)	15
63	London HLU 9732	Da Doo Ron Ron/Git It	10
63	London HLU 9773	Then He Kissed Me/Brother Julius	10
64	London HLU 9837	Little Boy/Uptown (withdrawn)	75
64	London HLU 9852	I Wonder/Little Boy	40
64	London HLU 9909	All Grown Up/PHIL SPECTOR GROUP: Irving (Jaggered Sixteenths)	15
65	United Artists UP 1110	My Place/You Can't Tie A Girl Down	40
69	London HLU 10239	Da Doo Ron Ron/He's A Rebel	5
74	Warners/Spector K 19010	Da Doo Ron Ron/Then Kissed Me (blue vinyl)	5
76	Phil Spector Intl. 2010 020	All Grown Up/The Twist	6
63	London RE-U 1381	DA DOO RON RON (EP)	100
63	London HA-U 8120	HE'S A REBEL (LP)	150

(see also Darlene Love, Bob B. Soxx & Blue Jeans, Phil Spector)

C.S.A.

96	Squariel Records SQ003	Don't/'Till I Waltz Again With You (p/s)	6

JOE CUBA SEXTET

66	Pye International 7N 25401	Bang! Bang!/Push, Push, Push	20

CUBAN HEELS

78	Housewives' Choice JY 1/2	Downtown/Do The Smoke Walk (p/s)	30

CUBY & BLIZZARDS

68	Philips BF 1638	Distant Smile/Don't Know Which Way To Go	15
68	Philips BF 1719	Windows Of My Eyes/Checkin' Up On My Baby	10
69	Philips BF 1827	Apple Knocker's Flophouse/Go Down Sunshine	15
69	Philips (S)BL 7874	DESOLATION (LP)	50
69	Philips SBL 7918	APPLE KNOCKERS FLOPHOUSE (LP)	40

'CUDDLY' DUDLEY (Heslop)

59	HMV POP 586	Lots More Love/Later	18
59	HMV POP 586	Lots More Love/Later (78)	18
60	HMV POP 725	Too Pooped To Pop/Miss In-Between	22
61	Ember EMB S 136	Sitting On A Train/One Thing I Like	12
62	Piccadilly 7N 35090	Monkey Party/The Ferryboat Ride (as Cudley Dudley)	12
64	Oriole International ICB 9	Blarney Blues/Peace On Earth	12
64	Oriole International ICB 10	Way Of Life/When Will You Say You'll Be Mine	12

CUDDLY TOYS

81	Parole PURLE 9	Astral Joe/Slowdown (p/s)	12
81	Fresh FRESH 10	Mothman/Jo In The Girls (p/s, with 5 stickers)	12
81	Fresh FRESH 20	Astral Joe/Slowdown (p/s, reissue)	12
81	Fresh FRESH 25	Someone's Crying/Bring On The Ravers (p/s)	8

(see also Raped)

CUES

56	Capitol CL 14501	Burn That Candle/O My Darlin'	260
56	Capitol CL 14501	Burn That Candle/O My Darlin' (78)	30
56	Capitol CL 14651	Crackerjack/The Girl I Love (featuring Jimmy Breedlove)	230
56	Capitol CL 14651	Crackerjack/The Girl I Love (78)	30
57	Capitol CL 14682	Prince Or Pauper/Why	200
57	Capitol CL 14682	Prince Or Pauper/Why (78)	25

(see also Jimmy Breedlove)

CUFF-LINKS

70	MCA MU 1128	Robin's World/Lay A Little Love On Me	6
70	MCA MUP(S) 398	TRACY (LP)	18

XAVIER CUGAT

54	Columbia SCMC 2	Spanish Dance/The Bells Of San Raquel (export issue)	6
54	Columbia SCMC 4	Yo Ta Namora/Anna Boroco Tinde (export issue)	6
54	HMV 7MC 35	Mi Espanan/Society Conga (export issue)	6
63	Mercury AMT 1202	Watermelon Man/Swinging Shepherd Blues	10
65	Brunswick STA 8647	DANCE PARTY (LP)	12

CULPEPPER'S ORCHARD

72	Polydor 2480 123	SECOND SIGHT (LP)	100

JAMIE CULLUM TRIO

99	own label	HEARD IT ALL BEFORE (CD, private pressing, 700 only)	150

CULT

80s	Beggars Banquet 235H	Sun King/Edie (Ciao Baby)/She Sells Sanctuary (12", holographic plastic sl.)	12
84	B. Banquet BEGA 57P	DREAMTIME (LP, picture disc)	12
84	B. Banquet BEGA 57	DREAMTIME (white label test pressing, with unique version of "Go West")	30
80s	Beggars Banquet	ELECTRIC (LP, gold vinyl)	15
91	Beggars Banquet CBOX 1	SINGLES COLLECTION (10-CD box set, picture discs with booklet)	30

(see also Death Cult, Lonesome No More, Theatre Of Hate, Studio Sweethearts)

CULT FIGURES

79	Rather GEAR 4/RT 020	Zip Nolan (Highway Patrolman)/P.W.T. (Playing With Toys)/ Zip Dub (gatefold p/s)	8

(see also Swell Maps)

CULT HERO

79	Fiction FICS 006	I'm A Cult Hero/I Dig You (p/s, 2,000 only)	50

(see also Cure)

MINT VALUE £

CULT MANIAX

82 Elephant Rock — Blitz/Lucy Looe (p/s) . . . 6
82 Next Wave NXT 2/BAK 1 — Frenzie/The Russians Are Coming/Black Horse/Death March (p/s) . . . 6

CULTURE CLUB

82 Virgin VSY 518 — Do You Really Want To Hurt Me/Do You Really Want To Hurt Me (Dub Version) (picture disc) . . . 5
82 Virgin (no cat. no.) — I'll Tumble 4 Ya/BLUE RONDO: Change (blue 1-sided flexi with *Noise* mag) . . . 6
82 Virgin VSY 558 — Time (Clock Of The Heart)/White Boys Can't Control It (picture disc) . . . 5
83 Virgin VSY 571 — Church Of The Poison Mind/Man Shake (picture disc) . . . 5
83 Virgin VSY 612 — Karma Chameleon/That's The Way (picture disc) . . . 5
84 Virgin VSY 657 — It's A Miracle/Love Twist (picture disc) . . . 5
84 Virgin VS 694 — The War Song/La Cancion De Guerra (red vinyl) . . . 5
84 Virgin VSY 694 — The War Song/La Cancion De Guerra (picture disc, withdrawn) . . . 65
86 Virgin VSX 845 — Move Away/Sexuality (5", picture disc, 33rpm, with booklet & gatefold p/s) . . . 5
86 Virgin VSY 861 — God Thank You Woman/From Luxury To Heartache (picture disc) . . . 18
82 Virgin VP 2232 — KISSING TO BE CLEVER (LP, picture disc, with insert) . . . 12
83 Virgin VP 2285 — COLOUR BY NUMBERS (LP, picture disc) . . . 12
84 Virgin VP 2330 — WAKING UP WITH THE HOUSE ON FIRE (LP, picture disc, with insert) . . . 12

(see also Boy George, Jesus Loves You, The Edge)

CULVER STREET PLAYGROUND

68 President PT 145 — Alley Pond Park/A Decent Sort Of Guy . . . 12

CUMBERLAND THREE

60 Columbia DB 4460 — Johnny Reb/Come Along Julie . . . 6
64 Parlophone R 5113 — The Cumberland Crew/Chilly Winds . . . 6
61 Columbia 33SX 1302 — FOLK SCENE, U.S.A. (LP, also stereo SCX 3364) . . . 15
61 Columbia 33SX 1318 — CIVIL WAR ALMANAC — YANKEES (LP) . . . 15
61 Columbia 33SX 1325 — CIVIL WAR ALMANAC — REBELS (LP) . . . 15
64 Parlophone PMC 1233 — INTRODUCING (LP) . . . 12

(see also John Stewart)

BARBARA CUMMINGS

67 London HLU 10110 — She's The Woman/There's Something Funny Going On . . . 8

DAVID CUNNINGHAM

80 Piano PIANO 001 — GREY SCALE (LP) . . . 12

H. CUNNINGHAM

71 Tropical AL 004 — Ethiopian Son/TROPICAL ALLSTARS: Version 2 . . . 5

RUPERT CUNNINGHAM

70 Duke DU 98 — Funky/Sugar Cane . . . 5

CUPIDS

58 Vogue V 9102 — Now You Tell Me/Lillie Mae . . . 850
58 Vogue V 9102 — Now You Tell Me/Lillie Mae (78) . . . 150

CUPID'S INSPIRATION

68 NEMS 56-3500 — Yesterday Has Gone/Dream . . . 8
68 NEMS 56-3702 — My World/Everything Is Meant To Be . . . 8
69 Bell BLL 1069 — The Sad Thing/Look At Me . . . 8
70 CBS 4722 — Without Your Love/Different Guy . . . 7
70 CBS 4994 — Are You Growing Tired Of My Love/Sunshine . . . 7
69 NEMS 6-63553 — YESTERDAY HAS GONE (LP, as Cupid's Inspiration Featuring T. Rice-Milton) . . . 30

(see also Gordon Haskell, Paper Blitz Tissue)

CUPOL

80 4AD BAD 9 — Like This For Ages/Kluba Cupol (12", p/s, 45/33rpm) . . . 12

(see also Wire)

CUPPA T

67 Deram DM 144 — Miss Pinkerton/Brand New World . . . 12
68 Deram DM 185 — Streatham Hippodrome/One Man Band . . . 12

(see also Overlanders)

CUPS

68 Polydor 56777 — Good As Gold/Life And Times . . . 12

(see also Gallagher & Lyle)

MIKE CURB CONGREGATION

70 Polydor 2058 075 — Burning Bridges/Sweet Gingerbread Man . . . 8

CURE

SINGLES

78 Small Wonder SMALL 11 — Killing An Arab/10.15 Saturday Night (p/s, 15,000 only, beware of counterfeits) . . 28
79 Fiction FICS 001 — Killing An Arab/10.15 Saturday Night (p/s, reissue) . . . 17
79 Fiction FICS 002 — Boys Don't Cry/Plastic Passion ('soldier' p/s) . . . 17
79 Fiction FICS 005 — Jumping Someone Else's Train/I'm Cold (p/s) . . . 22
80 Fiction FICS 010 — A Forest/Another Journey By Train (p/s or 'radiophonic' die-cut sleeve) . . . 14/10
80 Fiction FICSX 010 — A Forest (Extended Version)/Another Journey By Train (12", p/s) . . . 28
81 Fiction FICS 012 — Primary/Descent (p/s) . . . 12
81 Fiction FICSX 012 — Primary (Extended)/Descent (12", p/s) . . . 22
81 Fiction FICS 014 — Charlotte Sometimes/Splintered In Her Head (p/s) . . . 10
81 Fiction FICSX 014 — Charlotte Sometimes/Splintered In Her Head/Faith (live) (12", p/s) . . . 17
82 Fiction FICS 015 — The Hanging Garden/Killing An Arab (live) (p/s) . . . 10
82 Fiction FICG 015 — The Hanging Garden/100 Years//A Forest/Killing An Arab (double pack, gatefold p/s, 5,000 only) . . . 14
82 Lyntone LYN 12011 — Lament (1-sided flexidisc, red or green vinyl) . . . 32/10
82 Lyntone LYN 12011 — Lament (1-sided flexidisc, red or green vinyl, with *Flexipop* issue 22) . . . 38/14
82 Fiction FICSX 017 — Let's Go To Bed (Extended)/Just One Kiss (Extended) (12", p/s) . . . 10
83 Fiction FICS 018 — The Walk/The Dream (paper labels, poster p/s) . . . 14

			MINT VALUE £
83	Fiction FICS 018	The Walk/The Dream (plastic labels, standard p/s)	6
83	Fiction FICSP 018	The Walk/The Dream (picture disc)	32
83	Fiction FICSX 018	Upstairs Room/The Dream/The Walk/Lament//Let's Go To Bed (Extended)/ Just One Kiss (Extended) (12" double pack, shrinkwrapped with sticker)	22
83	Fiction FICSP 019	The Lovecats/Speak My Language (picture disc, PVC sleeve)	28
84	Fiction FIXSP 020	The Caterpillar/Happy The Man (picture disc, printed PVC sleeve)	28
85	Fiction FICSX 22	In Between Days/The Exploding Boy/A Few Hours After This (12", p/s)	10
85	Fiction 080182-2	In Between Days/The Exploding Boy/A Few Hours After This/ Six Different Ways (live)/Push (live) (CD Video)	38
85	Fiction FICSG 23	Close To Me (Remix)/A Man Inside My Mouth (poster p/s; some copies with blue & white 'Head On The Door' sticker)	10/8
85	Fiction FICST 23	HALF AN OCTOPUS: Close To Me (Remix)/A Man Inside My Mouth/New Day/ Stop Dead (10" EP, p/s)	14
85	Fiction 080180-2	Close To Me (12" Remix)/A Man Inside My Mouth/Stop Dead/ New Day (CD Video)	38
86	Fiction FICSX 24	Boys Don't Cry (New Voice Club Mix)/Pill Box Tales/Do The Hansa (12", p/s)	10
87	Fiction FICSG 25	Why Can't I Be You?/A Japanese Dream//Six Different Ways (live)/ Push (live) (numbered double pack, gatefold p/s)	12
87	Fiction FICS 26	Catch/Breathe (p/s, in carrier bag)	7
87	Fiction FICSP 26	Catch/Breathe (clear vinyl, printed PVC sleeve)	12
87	Fiction FICSE 26	Catch/Breath/Kyoto Song (live)/A Night Like This (live) (12")	10
87	Fiction 080186-2	Catch/Breathe/A Chain Of Flowers/Icing Sugar (Remix) (CD Video)	38
87	Fiction FICS 27	Just Like Heaven/Snow In Summer (p/s, numbered, white vinyl)	10
87	Fiction FICS 27	Just Like Heaven/Snow In Summer (p/s, mispress, A-side plays both sides)	18
87	Fiction FICSP 27	Just Like Heaven/Snow In Summer (picture disc in custom PVC sleeve)	18
87	Fiction FICSX 27	Just Like Heaven/Snow In Summer/Sugar Girl (12", p/s)	8
87	Fiction FIXCD 27	Just Like Heaven (Remix)/Snow In Summer/Sugar Girl (CD, card sleeve)	22
88	Fiction FIXCD 28	Hot Hot Hot!!! (Extended Remix)/Hot Hot Hot!!! (Remix)/Hey You!!! (Extended Remix) (CD, card sleeve with insert for *10 Imaginary Years* book)	22
89	Fiction FICSG 29	Lullaby (Remix)/Babble (gatefold p/s, numbered with sticker)	7
89	Fiction FICSP 29	Lullaby (Remix)/Babble (clear vinyl, numbered printed 'spider web' PVC sleeve)	14
89	Fiction FICVX 29	Lullaby (Remix)/Babble/Out Of Mind (12", pink vinyl, numbered with stickers)	18
89	Fiction FICCD 29	Lullaby (Remix)/Babble/Out Of Mind/Lullaby (Extended Remix) (3" CD, gatefold p/s)	18
89	Fiction FICSG 30	Lovesong/2 Late ('The Love Box' set with linen print)	12
89	Fiction FICCD 30	Lovesong (7" Mix)/2 Late/Fear Of Ghosts/Lovesong (Extended Mix) (CD)	12
90	Fiction FICPA 34	Pictures Of You (Remix)/Last Dance (live) (p/s, green vinyl, no'd sticker)	7
90	Fiction FICPA 34	Pictures Of You (Remix)/Last Dance (live) (p/s, green vinyl, mispress, plays "Last Dance" both sides)	22
90	Fiction FICPB 34	Pictures Of You (Remix)/Prayers For Rain (p/s, purple vinyl, numbered sticker)	10
90	Fiction FIXPA 34	Pictures Of You (Extended Remix)/Last Dance (live)/Fascination Street (live) (12", p/s, green vinyl, numbered sticker)	10
90	Fiction FIXPB 34	Pictures Of You (Strange Mix)/Prayers For Rain (live)/Disintegration (live) (12", p/s, purple vinyl, numbered sticker)	14
90	Fiction FICCDA 34	Pictures Of You (Remix)/Last Dance (live)/Fascination Street (live) (CD)	10
90	Fiction FICCDB 34	Pictures Of You (Strange Mix)/Prayers For Rain (live)/Disintegration (live) (CD)	12
90	Fiction FICSX 35	Never Enough (Big Mix)/Harold & Joe/Let's Go To Bed (Milk Mix) (12", p/s)	8
90	Fiction FICDP 35	Never Enough (Big Mix)/Harold & Joe/Let's Go To Bed (Milk Mix) (CD, with window sticker, numbered slimline jewel case)	12
90	Fiction 080184-2	Why Can't I Be You? (12" Remix)/A Japanese Dream (5.40 Remix)/Hey You!!! (CD Video)	38
91	Fiction FICDR 36	Close To Me (Closer Mix)/Just Like Heaven (Dizzy Mix)/Why Can't I Be You (12" remix) (CD, with poster, shrinkwrapped with card insert & numbered sticker)	12
92	Fiction FICCD 39	High/This Twilight Garden/Play/High (Higher Mix) (CD, box set)	10
92	Fiction FICPA 42	Friday I'm In Love/Halo/Scared Of You/Friday I'm In Love (Strangelove Mix) (12", p/s, numerous different coloured or marbled vinyls)	10
96	Fiction FICDD 53	Gone! (Radio Mix)/(Critter Mix)/(Ultraliving Mix)/ (Spacer Mix) (CD, 3-CD inlay)	12

PROMOS

79	Fiction	Boys Don't Cry	40
79	Fiction CUR 1	Grinding Halt/Meat Hook (12", stickered sleeve)	55
81	Fiction FICS 12	Primary (1-sided, no p/s)	22
82	Lyntone LYN 12011	Lament (hard vinyl test pressing, no p/s)	100
82	Fiction CURE 1	One Hundred Years/The Hanging Garden (12", p/s, promo/gig freebie)	55
88	Fiction FICSDJ 28	Hot Hot Hot!!! (Remix)/Hey You!!! (Remix) (die-cut title p/s)	12
84	Fiction KAREN 1	THE TOP (12", 1-sided, 3-track sampler)	50
94	Fiction FICCS 50	LOST WISHES (cassette, 4-track, mail order only)	50
96	Fiction FICSTX 53	Gone! (Ultraliving Mix) (12", same track both sides, with 'DJ' insert)	12
97	Fiction FICSX 54	Wrong Number (Single Mix)/(ISDN Mix)/(Digital Exchange Mix)/ (Dub Analogue Exchange Mix)/(Crossed Line Mix)/(Engaged Mix)/ (P2P Mix) (12", double pack, p/s, promo only)	22
89	Fiction DISIN 1	DISINTEGRATION (CD, 4-track sampler)	18
89	Fiction CIFCD 3	STRANGER THAN FICTION (CD, 6-track sampler, 1000 only)	110
90	Fiction CUREPROCD 1	MIXED UP (CD, 4-track sampler)	12
90	Fiction CUREPROCD 3	THE CURE — AN INTERVIEW (CD)	20
92	Fiction CURE 1	CLASSIC CURE: Love Cats/Close To Me (Closer Mix)/Lovesong/ Charlotte Sometimes/Lullaby/Why Can't I Be You/A Forest (CD, sampler, inlay)	20
93	Fiction SHOWPRO 1	SHOWPRO: Just Like Heaven/Doing The Unstuck (CD, 2-track sampler)	18
93	Fiction PARISPRO 01	PARISPRO: Catch/Play For Today (CD, 2-track sampler)	22
97	Fixtion FIXCD.COM 1	FIVE SWING LIVE (CD, 5-track sampler, available via the internet, 5,000 only)	28

LPs

79	Fiction FIX 1	THREE IMAGINARY BOYS (with inner sleeve, postcard & badge)	32
80	Fiction FIXC 6	FAITH/CARNAGE VISORS (original double-play cassette, b&w cover, paper labels)	12

MINT VALUE £

84	Fiction FIXS 9	THE TOP (with badge & poster, green inner sleeve)	18
84	Fiction FIXS 9	THE TOP (with promo plastic snake & top)	32
86	Fiction 815 011-2	BOYS DON'T CRY (CD, original non-picture disc, with "Object" & "World War" & without "So What")	28
87	Fiction FIXH 13/FIXHA 13	KISS ME, KISS ME, KISS ME (with bonus orange vinyl 6-track 12" [FIXHA 13], in custom PVC sleeve)	45
89	Fiction FIXHP 14	DISINTEGRATION (picture disc, printed PVC sleeve)	22
90	Fiction FIXCD 17	ENTREAT (CD, exclusive to HMV, card p/s, yellow photo)	22
92	Fiction 513 600-0	LIMITED EDITION CD BOX (15 x CD hinged box set, 2,500 only)	190

(see also Cult Hero, Siouxsie & Banshees, Glove, Fools Dance, Tim Pope, Lockjaw, Obtainers)

MARTIN CURE & PEEPS

67	Philips BF 1605	It's All Over Now/I Can Make The Rain Fall Up	40

(see also Peeps, Rainbows)

JOHNNY CURIOUS & STRANGERS

78	Illegal IL 009	In Tune/Road To Cheltenham/Pissheadsville/Jennifer (p/s)	10
79	Bugle BLAST 2	Someone Else's Home/Backwards In The Night (p/s)	12

CURIOSITY SHOPPE

68	Deram DM 220	Baby I Need You/So Sad	70

CURRANT KRAZE

70	Deram DM 292	Lady Pearl/Breaking The Heart Of A Good Man	5

CURRENT 93

83	L.A.Y.L.A.H. L.A.Y. 1	Lashtal/Salt/Caresse (12", white p/s [reissued in 1988 with dark p/s and "1988" on label])	22/18
85	L.A.Y.L.A.H. L.A.Y. 14	NIGHTMARE CULTURE (12" EP, with Sickness Of Snakes [i.e. Coil feat. Boyd Rice]; matt black & red sleeve)	22
87	L.A.Y.L.A.H. L.A.Y. 18	HAPPY BIRTHDAY PIGFACE CHRISTUS (12" EP)	22
87	Maldoror MAL 108	Crowleymass/Christmassacre/Crowleymass (Mix Mix Mix) (12", p/s)	28
88	Yangki 002	FAITH'S FAVOURITES EP (Ballad Of The Pale Girl/NURSE WITH WOUND: Swamp Rat) (12", laminated p/s)	28
88	Maldoror MAL 088	The Red Face Of God/The Breath And The Pain Of God (12", p/s, with insert, 666 only)	40
89	Yangki 003	DEATH OF THE CORN (12" EP, with Sol Invictus; 'art' sleeve)	18
90	Harbinger 001	No Hiding From The Blackbird/NURSE WITH WOUND: Burial Of The Stoned Sardine (p/s, remixed reissue of giveaway 7")	12
90	Shock SX 003	She Is Dead And All Fall Down/God Has Three Faces And Wood Has No Name (folded sleeve in bag, 1,000 only, 26 signed/lettered)	45/22
90	Cerne 004	This Ain't The Summer Of Love/SOL INVICTUS: Abbatoirs Of Love (live in Japan, gig freebie, 93 only with insert & gig ticket, 200 without insert)	60/25
92	Durtro DURTRO 004	LOONEY RUNES (12", live EP, 2,000 only, with poster)	22
94	Ptolemaic Terrascope POT6	Broken Birds Fly/RANDY CALIFORNIA: The American Society/The Whale Song (free with *Ptolemaic Terrascope* mag)	10/8
94	Durtro DURTRO 022	THE FIRE OF THE MIND (CD EP, free with book 'Simply Being')	55
95	Durtro DURTRO 025	Tamlin/How The Great Satanic Glory Faded (12", numbered with insert, 2,000 only)	28
95	Durtro DURTRO 025	Tamlin/How The Great Satanic Glory Faded (CD, numbered, 3,000 only)	18
95	Durtro DURTRO 028	Where The Long Shadows Fall (12", 1-sided clear vinyl with insert, 2,000 only)	18
96	Durtro DURTRO 033	The Seven Seals/(various artists) (CD, mail order)	18
84	L.A.Y.L.A.H. LAY 008	DOGS BLOOD RISING (LP; CDs £18)	25
86	Maldoror UDO 22M	IN MENSTRUAL NIGHT (LP, 25 with handmade inserts & cover)	115/22
86	United Dairies UD 022	IN MENSTRUAL NIGHT (LP, picture disc)	28
87	L.A.Y.L.A.H. LAY 20	SWASTIKAS FOR NODDY (LP, with insert)	25
88	Maldoror MAL 666	CHRIST AND THE PALE QUEENS MIGHTY IN SORROW (3-sided LP, with inserts, 93 copies only)	110
88	Maldoror MAL 777	IMPERIUM (LP, black label, with insert, later copies have white label)	28/18
89	Maldoror MAL 093	DAWN (LP)	60
89	Durtro DURTRO 001	LIVE AT BAR MALDOROR (LP, white label, 1,000 only)	55
80s	Maldoror MAL 123	NATURE UNVEILED (LP, some with insert & free 7": "No Hiding From The Blackbird/NURSE WITH WOUND: Burial Of The Sardine")	30/20
90	United Dairies UD 029	EARTH COVERS EARTH (mini-LP)	35
90	Cerne 00123	THE CERNE BOX SET (3-LP set, includes "Horse"; other LPs by Sol Invictus & Nurse With Wound, 2,000 only)	70
90	United Dairies UD 033CD	CROOKED CROSSES FOR THE NODDING DOG (CD)	18
90	NER BADVC 693	1888 (LP, split with Death In June, 500 each on clear & red vinyl; also on black vinyl)	35/25
92	Durtro DURTRO 006	ISLAND (LP, with insert, 2,000 only)	22
92	Durtro DURTRO 011	THUNDER PERFECT MIND (2-LP, with insert)	22
94	Durtro DURTRO 018	OF RUINE, OR SOME BLAZING STARRE (LP, blue vinyl w/insert, 2,000 only)	18
94	Durtrohoho 019	LUCIFER OVER LONDON (LP, red vinyl with insert, 2,000 only)	20
96	Durtro DURTRO 026	ALL THE PRETTY LITTLE HORSES (LP, clear vinyl with insert, 2,000 only)	12
96	United Dairies UDOR 4	WHEN THE MAY RAIN COMES \ (CD, mail order, free with 'Ultrasonic Seraphim' [2-CD by SAND])	15
01	United Durtro UDOR 8	BRIGHT YELLOW MOON (CD, with Nurse With Wound, first 1,000 with bonus CD)	28

(see also Nurse With Wound, 23 Skidoo, Psychic TV, Crisis, Death In June, Sol Invictus, Steven Stapleton & David Tibet, Tibet & Stapleton)

CLIFFORD CURRY

69	Action ACT 4549	She Shot A Hole In My Soul/We're Gonna Hate Ourselves In The Morning	18
69	Pama PM 793	You Turn Out The Light/Good Humour Man	10
69	Pama PM 797	I Can't Get A Hold Of Myself/Ain't No Danger	25

TIM CURRY

74	UK UK 67	Sweet Transvestite/Time Warp	7

MINT VALUE £

CURTAINS
95 Detour DR 025 — In My Street/Family Affair (p/s, blue vinyl, 100 only) 7

DAN CURTIN
94 Peacefrog PF 018X — PARALLEL EP (12", sampler, plain sleeve) 15
94 Peacefrog PF 018 — THE SILICON DAWN (2-LP) 18
94 Peacefrog PF 018CD — THE SILICON DAWN CD (CD) 15
95 Peacefrog PF 023 — PURVEYORS OF FINE FUNK — HEIGHTS TRAX VOL 1 EP (12", plain sleeve) 15
95 Peacefrog PF 024 — DREAMS NOT OF TODAY EP (12", plain sleeve) 10
95 Peacefrog PF 032 — PURVEYORS OF FINE FUNK — HEIGHTS TRAX VOL 2 EP (12", plain sleeve) 10
95 Peacefrog PF 038 — WEB OF LIFE (2-LP) 18
96 Peacefrog PF 058 — PURVEYORS OF FINE FUNK VOL 3 EP (12", plain sleeve) 10
97 Peacefrog PF 064 — PURVEYORS OF FINE FUNK VOL 4 EP (12", plain sleeve) 8

ALLEN CURTIS
64 Hickory 45-1226 — Fireball Mail/The Hole He Said He'd Dig For Me 8

CHRIS CURTIS
66 Pye 7N 17132 — Aggravation/Have I Done Something Wrong 40
(see also Searchers)

DENNY CURTIS
68 Plexium PXM 2 — Crying Over You/You Don't Love Me No More 6
69 Plexium PXM 6 — Message/You Gotta Be Mine 6

JOHNNY CURTIS
66 Parlophone R 5529 — Our Love's Disintegrating/(I'd Be) A Legend In My Time 40
67 Parlophone R 5582 — Jack And The Beanstalk/Go On Back 20
68 Major Minor MM 564 — Pickin' Up Pebbles/Gentle On My Mind 7

KING CURTIS
(see under 'K')

LEE CURTIS (& ALL STARS)
63 Decca F 11622 — Little Girl/Just One More Dance (solo) 15
63 Decca F 11690 — Let's Stomp/Poor Unlucky Me 20
64 Decca F 11830 — What About Me/I've Got My Eyes On You 15
64 Philips BF 1385 — Ecstasy/A Shot Of Rhythm And Blues 15
(see also Pete Best Four)

MAC CURTIS
57 Parlophone R 4279 — The Low Road/You Ain't Treatin' Me Right 1,600
57 Parlophone R 4279 — The Low Road/You Ain't Treatin' Me Right (78) 220
74 Polydor 2310 293 — ROCKABILLY KINGS (LP, with Charlie Feathers) 25

SONNY CURTIS
60 Coral Q 72400 — The Red Headed Stranger/Talk About My Baby 35
64 Colpix PX 11024 — A Beatle I Want To Be/So Used To Loving You 18
64 Liberty LIB 55710 — Bo Diddley Bach/I Pledged My Love To You 20
85 Songworks S1 — I Think I'm In Love/A Whole Lot Less To Me Than Meets The Eye 5
85 Songworks S2 — Heart Of Gold/Why Did You Say 'I Do' To Me 5
(see also Crickets)

DAVE CURTISS & TREMORS
63 Philips BF 1257 — You Don't Love Me/Sweet Girl Of Mine 8
63 Philips BF 1285 — What Kind Of Girl Are You?/Dreamer's Funfair 8
64 Philips BF 1330 — Summertime Blues/I'm A Hog For You Baby 8

ROCKY CURTISS & HARMONY FLAMES
59 Fontana TFE 17172 — U.S.A. HIT PARADE (EP) 50

CURTISS MALLDOON
71 Regal Zonophone 3038 — You Make Me Happy (And You Make Me Sad)/Amber Man 5
72 Purple PUR 106 — One Way Ticket/Next Time 7

BOBBY CURTOLA (& MARTELLS)
61 Columbia DB 4672 — Don't You Sweetheart Me/My Heart's Tongue-Tied (solo) 18
62 London HL 9577 — Fortune Teller/Johnny Take Your Time (solo) 18
62 London HL 9639 — Aladdin/I Don't Want To Go On Without You (solo) 18
63 Decca F 11670 — Gypsy Heart/I'm Sorry 15
63 Decca F 11725 — Three Rows Over/Indian Giver 15

CURVE
91 Anxious ANXP 27 — Blindfold/Ten Little Girls (picture disc) 6
93 Anxious — FALLING FREE — APHEX TWIN REMIX (12", 1-sided promo only, 500 only) 60
93 Anxious ANXCDS 42 — BLACKERTHREETRACKERTWO EP (CD, with Future Sound Of London mix) 8

CURVED AIR
71 Warner Bros WB 8023 — It Happened Today/What Happens When You Blow Yourself Up 8
72 Warner Bros K 16164 — Sarah's Concern/Phantasmagoria 6
84 Pearl Key PK 07350 — Renegade/We're Only Human (p/s) 10
70 Warner Bros K 56004 — AIR CONDITIONING (LP, picture disc, 10,000 only) 40/20
70 Warner Bros WSX 3012 — AIR CONDITIONING (LP, green label) 18
70 Warner Bros K 56004 — AIR CONDITIONING (LP, green label) 12
71 Warner Bros K 46090 — SECOND ALBUM (LP, die-cut 'leaves' fold-out sleeve, green label) 15
72 Warner Bros K 46158 — PHANTASMAGORIA (LP, green label, with inner lyric card) 18
73 Warner Bros K 46224 — AIR CUT (LP, green label, gatefold sleeve) 18
(see also Kirby, Sonja Kristina, [Darryl Way's] Wolf, Trace, Legs, Stretch)

ADGE CUTLER & WURZELS
67 Columbia SX 6126 — ADGE CUTLER AND THE WURZELS (LP) 12
67 Columbia SX 6165 — ADGE CUTLER'S FAMILY ALBUM (LP) 12
68 Columbia S(C)X 6263 — CUTLER OF THE WEST (LP) 12
69 Columbia S(C)X 6367 — CARRY ON CUTLER (LP) 12

MINT VALUE £

IVOR CUTLER TRIO

67	Parlophone R 5624	I Had A Little Boat/A Great Grey Grasshopper	7
59	Fontana TFE 17144	OF Y'HUP (EP)	25
61	Decca DFE 6677	GET AWAY FROM THE WALL (EP)	25
61	Decca LK 4405	WHO TORE YOUR TROUSERS? (LP)	60
67	Parlophone PCS 7040	LUDO (LP)	50

T. TOMMY CUTRER (& GINNY WRIGHT)

54	London HL 8093	Mexico Gal/Wonderful World (B-side with Ginny Wright)	60
54	London HL 8093	Mexico Gal/Wonderful World (78, B-side with Ginny Wright)	20

(see also Ginny Wright)

CUTTERS

59	Decca F 11110	I've Had It/Rockaroo	18
59	Decca F 11110	I've Had It/Rockaroo (78)	18

(see also Neville Taylor & Cutters)

CYANIDE

78	Pye 7N 46048	I'm A Boy/Do It (p/s)	35
78	Pye 7N 46094	Mac The Flash/Hate The State (demo copies in p/s)	60/15
79	Pinnacle PIN 23	Fireball/Your Old Man (p/s)	45
78	Pye NSPL 18554	CYANIDE (LP)	40

CYAN THREE

66	Decca F 12371	Since I Lost My Baby/Face Of A Loser	20

CYBERMEN

78	Rockaway AERE 101	THE CYBERMEN (EP, available in 2 different sleeves)	40
79	Rockaway LUV 002	You're To Blame/It's You I Want (with inserts)	10

CYCLONES

64	Oriole CB 1898	Nobody/Little Egypt	40

CYCLONES

71	Banana BA 338	My Sweet Lord/DENNIS BROWN: Silky (B-side actually by Monty Alexander & Cyclones)	12

CYLOB

95	Rephlex CAT 015	INDUSTRIAL FOLKSONGS (12", initially in polystyrene sleeve)	12

CYMANDE

73	Alaska ALA 4	The Message/Zion I	10
73	Alaska ALA 10	Bras/Ras Tafarian Folk Song	10
74	Contempo CS 2019	Brothers On The Slide/Pon De Dungle	10
73	Alaska ALKA 100	CYMANDE (LP)	20
74	Contempo CLP 508	PROMISED HEIGHT (LP)	25

JOHNNY CYMBAL

60	MGM MGM 1106	It'll Be Me/Always, Always	25
63	London HLR 9682	Mr Bass Man/Sacred Lovers Vow	12
63	London HLR 9731	Teenage Heaven/Cinderella Baby	20
63	London HLR 9762	Dum Dum Dee Dum/Surfing At Tijuana	18
64	London HLR 9911	Mitsou/Robinson Crusoe On Mars	18
65	United Artists UP 1093	Go V.W. Go/Sorrow And Pain	25
63	London RER 1375	MISTER BASS MAN (EP)	45
64	London RER 1406	CYMBAL SMASHES (EP)	45

(see also Derek)

CYMBALINE

65	Pye 7N 15916	Please Little Girl/Coming Home Baby	30
65	Mercury MF 918	Top Girl/Can You Hear Me?	25
66	Mercury MF 961	I Don't Want It/Where Did Love Go Wrong	8
66	Mercury MF 975	Peanuts And Chewy Macs/Found My Girl	8
67	Philips BF 1624	Matrimonial Fears/You Will Never Love Me	30
68	Philips BF 1681	Down By The Seaside/Fire	15
69	Philips BF 1749	Turn Around/Come Back Baby	8

CYMERONS

64	Decca F 11976	I'll Be There/Making Love To Another	15
66	Polydor 56098	Everyday (Will Change)/I Can See You	7

CYNIC

83	Cynic CYN 1	Suicide/No Time At All (no p/s)	130

CYNTHIA & ARCHIE

64	R&B JB 168	Every Beat/DELROY WILSON: Sammy Dead	25

CYRKLE

66	CBS 202064	Red Rubber Ball/How Can I Leave Her	7
66	CBS 202246	Turn Down Day/Big Little Woman	7
67	CBS 202516	Bony Maronie/Please Don't Ever Leave Me	7
67	CBS 202577	I Wish You Could Be There/The Visit (She Was Here)	7
67	CBS 2790	We Had A Good Thing Goin'/Two Rooms	7
67	CBS 2917	Penny Arcade/Words	7
67	CBS 62977	NEON (LP)	30

CZAR

70	Philips 6006 071	Oh Lord I'm Getting Heavy/Why Don't We Be A Rock'n'Roll Band	30
70	Fontana 6309 009	CZAR (LP)	130

(see also Hungry Wolf)

HOLGER CZUKAY

(see under Jah Wobble, Can)

MINT VALUE £

KIM D
65 Pye 7N 15953 — The Real Thing/Come On Baby 15
(see also Kim Davis)

ROB D
95 Mo' Wax MW 037 — Clubbed To Death/(Mixes) (12", p/s) 25

TONY D & SHAKEOUTS
64 Piccadilly 7N 35168 — Is It True/Never Let Her Go 25

DA BAND
78 Rip Off RIP 2 — I Like It/Pirate's Lullaby (p/s) 20

DA BIZ
80 Small Operations SO 002 — On The Beach/This Is No Audition (p/s) 10
80 Sire SIR 4045 — On The Beach/This Is No Audition (p/s, reissue) 6

MIKE D'ABO
69 Immediate IM 075 — See The Little People — Gulliver's Travels/Anthology Of Gulliver's Travels Part 2 (withdrawn) 20
70 Uni UNS 525 — Let It Roar/California Line 7
70 Bell BLL 1134 — Miss Me In The Morning/Arabella, Cinderella 6
72 A&M AMS 7016 — Belinda/Little Miss Understood 6
74 A&M AMS 7121 — Fuel To Burn/Hold On Darlin' 6
70 Uni UNLS 114 — D'ABO (LP, gatefold sleeve) 18
72 A&M AMLH 68097 — DOWN AT RACHEL'S PLACE (LP, with inner sleeve) 12
74 A&M AMLH 63634 — BROKEN RAINBOWS (LP) 12
(see also Manfred Mann, Band Of Angels, Gulliver's Travels, Smith & D'Abo)

RITA DACOSTA
75 Contempo CS 2060 — Don't Bring Me Down/No! No! No! 20

DADA
71 Atco 2400 030 — DADA (LP) 22
(see also Robert Palmer, Elkie Brooks, Paul Korda, Vinegar Joe)

DADDY LONGLEGS
70 Warner Bros WB 8012 — High Again/To The Rescue (Wet Putso) 5
70 Warner Bros WS 3004 — DADDY LONGLEGS (LP) 20
71 Vertigo 6360 038 — OAKDOWN FARM (LP, gatefold sleeve, swirl label) 35
72 Polydor 2371 261 — THREE MUSICIANS (LP) 15
73 Polydor 2371 323 — SHIFTING SANDS (LP) 15
(see also Daylight)

DADDY-O'S
58 Oriole CB 1454 — Got A Match?/Have A Cigar 18
58 Oriole CB 1454 — Got A Match?/Have A Cigar (78) 8

DADDY'S ACT
67 Columbia DB 8242 — Eight Days A Week/Gonna Get You 18

D.A.F. (Deutsche Amerikanische Freundschaft)
81 Virgin VS 418 — Der Mussolini/Der Räuber Und Der Prinz (co. sleeve, possibly promo only) 5
81 Virgin VS 418-12 — Der Mussolini/Der Räuber Und Der Prinz (12", p/s, original issue) 8

CALVIN DAFOS
66 Blue Beat BB 347 — Brown Sugar/I'm Gone 20
69 Doctor Bird DB 1174 — Lash Them/CDs: Medicine Master 18

DAFT PUNK
94 Soma 014 — ALIVE/THE NEW WAVE (12" EP, company sleeve) 20
95 Soma 025 — DA FUNK (12" EP, company sleeve) 15

DAGABAND
80 Rutland RX 100 — Test Flight/Images (p/s) 5
83 MHM A-M 094 — Second Time Around/Reds Under The Beds/I Can See For Miles (p/s) 25

DAGGERMEN
86 Empire UPW 258J — INTRODUCING THE DAGGERMEN (EP, die-cut company sleeve) 10
86 Own Up DAG 001 — DAGGERS IN MY MIND (LP) 12
(see also James Taylor Quartet)

ETIENNE DAHO
89 Virgin VS 1180 — Stay With Me/Bleu Comme Toi (p/s) 5

DAILY FLASH
84 Psycho PSYCHO 32 — I FLASH DAILY (LP) 15

TONY DAINES
63 Fontana TF 433 — Chapel In The Moonlight/Echo Of Footsteps 8
64 Fontana TF 472 — Too Late/I Told You So 7

MINT VALUE £

DAISY CHAINSAW

90s Deva 82TP7	Pink Flower/Room Eleven (p/s)	8
90s Deva 82TP12	Pink Flower/All The Kids Agree/Room Eleven (12", p/s)	8
90s Deva/One Little Indian 92TP12	Hope Your Dreams Come True/Propeller Punch/Queue For Transatlantic Alien (12", p/s)	8
90s One Little Indian 100TP7	Love Me Forever/Diamond Of The Desert (white vinyl, p/s)	7

DAISY PLANET

60s Oak (no cat. no.)	DAISY PLANET (EP, no p/s)	60

DAKOTA JIM

66 Blue Beat BB 358	Only Soul Can Tell (actually by Slim Smith)/DAKOTA'S ALLSTARS: Call Me Master (actually by Prince Buster All Stars)	35

(see also Slim Smith)

DAKOTA OAK

01 Twisted Nerve TN 021	How Danny's Friends Became A Force For Good/How Danny's Sorrowing Friends Defied Conventions/Helpless (wraparound p/s in outer)	5

DAKOTAS

63 Parlophone R 5044	The Cruel Sea/The Millionaire	10
63 Parlophone R 5064	Magic Carpet/Humdinger	12
64 Parlophone R 5203	Oyeh/My Girl Josephine	25
67 Page One POF 018	I'm 'N 'Ardworkin' Barrow Boy/Seven Pounds Of Potatoes	25
68 Philips BF 1645	I Can't Break The News To Myself/The Spider And The Fly	70
63 Parlophone GEP 8888	MEET THE DAKOTAS (EP)	45

(see also Billy J. Kramer & Dakotas)

MICHAEL D'ALBUQUERQUE

74 RCA SF 8383	WE MAY BE CATTLE BUT WE ALL HAVE NAMES (LP, with lyric sheet)	15
76 Warner Bros K 56276	STALKING THE SLEEPER (LP)	12

(see also E.L.O., Michael Albuquerque)

DALE & GRACE

63 London HL 9807	I'm Leaving It Up To You/That's What I Like About You	15
64 London HL 9857	Stop And Think It Over/Bad Luck	15
69 London HL 10249	I'm Leaving It Up To You/Love Is Strange	8
64 London RE 1428	DALE AND GRACE NO. 1 (EP)	40
64 London RE 1429	DALE AND GRACE NO. 2 (EP)	40
64 London RE 1430	DALE AND GRACE NO. 3 (EP)	40

ALAN DALE

55 Vogue Coral Q 72072	Cherry Pink And Apple Blossom White/I'm Sincere	10
55 Vogue Coral Q 72089	Sweet And Gentle/You Still Mean The Same To Me	10
55 Vogue Coral Q 72105	Rockin' The Cha-Cha/Wham! (There I Go In Love Again)	18
55 Vogue Coral Q 72105	Rockin' The Cha-Cha/Wham! (There I Go In Love Again) (78)	8
56 Vogue Coral Q 72121	Robin Hood/Lisbon Antigua	10
56 Vogue Coral Q 72121	Robin Hood/Lisbon Antigua (78)	10
56 Vogue Coral Q 72156	Dance On/Mr. Moon	10
56 Vogue Coral Q 72156	Dance On/Mr. Moon (78)	7
56 Vogue Coral Q 72166	The Birds And The Bees/I Promise	10
56 Vogue Coral Q 72191	Be My Guest/Pardners (with Buddy Hackett)	10
56 Vogue Coral Q 72194	The Test Of Time/I Cry More	10
56 Vogue Coral Q 72194	The Test Of Time/I Cry More (78)	10
57 Vogue Coral Q 72225	Don't Knock The Rock/Your Love Is My Love	30
57 Vogue Coral Q 72225	Don't Knock The Rock/Your Love Is My Love (78)	10
57 Vogue Coral Q 72231	The Girl Can't Help It/Lonesome Road	30
57 Vogue Coral Q 72231	The Girl Can't Help It/Lonesome Road (78)	12
58 MGM MGM 986	Volare/Weeping Willow In The Wind	6

(see also Johnny Desmond)

DICK DALE & HIS DELTONES

63 Capitol CL 15296	Peppermint Man/Surf Beat	20
63 Capitol CL 15320	The Scavenger/Wild Ideas	20
88 Pulch Wave PSC 666	Pick And Play/The Wedge (p/s)	6
63 Capitol T 1886	SURFERS' CHOICE (LP)	65
63 Capitol T/ST 1930	KING OF THE SURF GUITAR (LP, mono/stereo)	60/80

GLEN DALE

66 Decca F 12475	Good Day Sunshine/Make Me Belong To You	8
68 Page One POF 059	I've Got You On My Mind/Now I See You	6
68 Page One POF 105	I've Got Something Too/Something's Gotten Hold Of My Heart	6

(see also Fortunes)

JIM DALE

57 Parlophone R 4329	Piccadilly Line/I Didn't Mean It	10
57 Parlophone R 4343	Be My Girl/You Shouldn't Do That	10
57 Parlophone R 4356	All Shook Up/Wandering Eyes (with Vipers & King Brothers)	15
57 Parlophone R 4376	Just Born (To Be Your Baby)/Crazy Dream	8
58 Parlophone R 4402	Sugartime/Don't Let Go	10
58 Parlophone R 4402	Sugartime/Don't Let Go (78)	6
58 Parlophone R 4424	Tread Softly Stranger/Jane Belinda	8
59 Parlophone R 4522	Gotta Find A Girl/The Legend Of Nellie D.	7
59 Parlophone R 4522	Gotta Find A Girl/The Legend Of Nellie D. (78)	7
60 Academy AD 001	Somewhere There's A Someone/If You Come Back	6
62 Piccadilly 7N 35039	One Boy, One Girl/My Resistance is Low	5
63 Piccadilly 7N 35100	Start All Over Again/It's For Them	5
69 Pye 7N 17839	Twinky/Plenty More Days	8
73 United Artists UA 35483	Milligan's Blues/It's Gonna Be A Good War	6
57 Parlophone GEP 8656	JIM DALE (EP)	40
58 Parlophone PMD 1055	JIM (10" LP)	80

MINT VALUE £

PAUL DALE BAND

82 KA KA 6/PAUL 1 Alright On The Night/Hold On (p/s, some on clear vinyl) ... 12/6
(see also Marseille)

SYD DALE ORCHESTRA

65 Decca F 22300 C'mon In/Disc A Go Go ... 8

DALEKS

(see under Century 21)

DALE SISTERS

60 HMV POP 781 The Kiss/Billy Boy, Billy Boy ... 12
61 Ember EMB S 140 My Sunday Baby/All My Life ... 15
62 Ember EMB S 151 Secrets/Road To Love ... 10

DÄLEX

81 Dodgy DODGY 1 Juvenile/Action Man Touched (p/s) ... 6

BASIL DALEY

68 Studio One SO 2054 Hold Me Baby/HEPTONES: I Got A Feeling ... 18

JIMMY DALEY & DING-A-LINGS

57 Brunswick 05648 Rock, Pretty Baby/Can I Steal A Little Love ... 100
57 Brunswick 05648 Rock, Pretty Baby/Can I Steal A Little Love (78) ... 30

SALVADOR DALI

62 Decca SET 230 DALI IN VENICE (LP, gatefold sleeve with booklet) ... 75

DALLAS BOYS

67 Major Minor MM 534 He Won't Love You (Like I Do)/What Do You Know About Losin' ... 6
(see also Five Dallas Boys)

DALLIONS

62 Oriole CB 1794 Teardrops In The Rain/Loop De Loop ... 8

MIKI DALLON

65 RCA RCA 1438 Do You Call That Love?/Apple Pie ... 20
65 RCA RCA 1478 I Care About You/I'll Give You Love ... 60
66 Strike JH 306 Cheat And Lie/(I'm Gonna Find A) Cave ... 30
66 Strike JH 318 What Will Your Mama Say Now?/Two At A Time ... 8
(see also Neil Christian & Crusaders)

DAVID & MARIANNE DALMOUR

60s Columbia 33SX 1715 INTRODUCING (LP) ... 30

DALTONS

67 Fab FAB 30 Never Kiss You Again/RIGHTEOUS FLAMES: When A Girl Loves A Boy ... 12
(see also Prince Buster)

ROGER DALTREY

73 Track 2094 014 Thinking/There Is Love ... 5
75 A&M AMS 7206 Orpheus Song/Love's Dream ... 5
75 Lyntone LYN 3176/7 Wagner's Dream/Love's Theme/RICK WAKEMAN: Count Your Blessings (flexidisc with *19* magazine) ... 10/6
77 Polydor 2058 896 One Of The Boys/You Better Put Something Inside Me ... 6
77 Polydor 2058 948 Say It Ain't So Joe/Satin And Lace (withdrawn, existence unconfirmed)
77 Polydor 2121 319 Written On The Wind/Dear John ... 6
78 Polydor 2058 986 Say It Ain't So Joe/The Prisoner ... 6
86 10 TEND 81 Under A Raging Moon/Move Better In The Night//Behind Blue Eyes/5:15 (double pack, gatefold p/s) ... 8
86 10 TENG 8110 Under A Raging Moon (6.43)/Move Better In The Night/Under A Raging Moon/5:15 (10" double pack, gatefold p/s) ... 10
86 10 TENG 8112 Under A Raging Moon (6.43)/Move Better In The Night/Under A Raging Moon (4.30) (12", gatefold p/s) ... 8
86 10 TEND 103 The Pride You Hide/Don't Talk To Strangers//Pictures Of Lily (live)/Break Out (double pack) ... 8
80 Polydor POLD 5034 McVICAR (LP, soundtrack, some on clear vinyl) ... 20/15
(see also Who, High Numbers, McEnroe & Cash)

TONI DALY

66 Columbia DB 8043 Like The Big Man Said/You Can't Get No Water ... 8
(see also Antoinette)

DALYS

65 Fontana TF 546 Me Japanese Boy/Never Kind Of Love ... 6
65 Fontana TF 637 She's My Girl/When Love Has Gone ... 6
66 Strike JH 317 Don't Go Breaking My Heart/Little Stranger ... 7
67 Fontana TF 809 Sweet Maria/Leaving Time ... 6
67 Fontana TF 841 A Fistful Of Dollars/Man With No Name ... 7
68 Fontana TF 907 Let Me Go Lover/A Place In The Sun ... 6
69 Fontana TF 988 Early Morning Rain/Chanson D'Amour ... 6

DAMASCUS

80s private pressing OPEN YOUR EYES (12" EP, later with different back sleeve, some with insert) ... 100/75
(see also Thin End Of The Wedge)

DAMITA JO

54 HMV 7MC 2 I'd Do It Again/Do I, Do I, Do I (B-side with Steve Gibson) (export issue) ... 20
54 HMV JO 390 I'd Do It Again/Do I, Do I, Do I (B-side with Steve Gibson) (78, export issue) ... 10
60 Mercury AMT 1085 Widow Walk/Dearest Darling ... 6
60 Mercury AMT 1116 I'll Save The Last Dance For You/Forgive ... 6
60 Mercury AMT 1133 Keep Your Hands Off Him/Hush, Somebody's Calling My Name ... 6
61 Mercury AMT 1141 Do What You Want/Sweet Georgia Brown ... 5
61 Mercury AMT 1155 I'll Be There/Love Laid Its Hands On Me ... 5

MINT VALUE £

61	Mercury ZEP 10118	I'LL SAVE THE LAST DANCE FOR YOU (EP)	18
61	Mercury MMC 14089	I'LL SAVE THE LAST DANCE FOR YOU (LP, also stereo [CMS 18059])	25
62	Mercury MMC 14105	LIVE AT THE DIPLOMAT (LP)	25
66	Columbia S(C)X 6094	MIDNIGHT SESSION (LP)	15

DAMNED

76	Stiff BUY 6	New Rose/Help! (first pressing with push-out centre & 'Delga' credit on p/s)	15
76	Stiff BUY 6	New Rose/Help! (p/s, later issues)	5
77	Stiff BUY 10	Neat Neat Neat/Stab Yor Back/Singalongascabies (glossy p/s, first pressing with push-out centre & gothic lettering; later centres solid)	15/6
77	Stiff DAMNED 1	Stretcher Case Baby/Sick Of Being Sick (p/s, *NME* competition & gig freebie)	40
77	Stiff BUY 18	Problem Child/You Take My Money (p/s, originally with press-out centre)	7/5
77	Stiff BUY 24	Don't Cry Wolf/One Way Love (20,000 on pink vinyl, no p/s; later black vinyl)	7/5
77	Stiff BUY 24	Don't Cry Wolf/One Way Love (Dave Vanian-designed p/s, existence unconfirmed)	
78	Dodgy Demo Co. SGS 105	Love Song/Burglar (mail order issue/gig freebie, plain sleeve, stickered labels)	18
79	Chiswick CHIS 112	Love Song/Noise Noise Noise/Suicide (red vinyl, 4 different sleeves)	each 6
79	Chiswick CHIS 112	Love Song/Noise Noise Noise/Suicide (4 different sleeves)	each 5
79	Chiswick CHIS 116	Smash It Up/Burglar (p/s)	5
79	Chiswick CHIS 120	I Just Can't Be Happy Today/Ballroom Blitz/The Turkey Song (p/s)	5
80	Chiswick CHIS 130	White Rabbit/Rabid (Over You)/Seagulls (unissued in U.K., Europe-only, 2 x 1-sided white-label test pressings exist, hand-written labels)	400+
80	Chiswick CHIS 135	The History Of The World Part 1/I Believe The Impossible/Sugar And Spite (p/s)	5
80	Chiswick CHIS 12 135	The History Of The World Part 1/I Believe The Impossible/ Sugar And Spite (12", p/s)	8
80	Chiswick CHIS 139	There Ain't No Sanity Clause/Hit Or Miss/Looking At You (live) (p/s)	5
81	NEMS TRY 1	FRIDAY THE 13TH (EP, p/s)	5
81	NEMS TRY 1	FRIDAY THE 13TH (12" EP)	8
81	Stiff GRAB 2	FOUR PACK (4 x 7" [BUY 6, 10, 18 & 24], in a plastic wallet)	25
82	Big Beat NS 75	Love Song/Noise Noise Noise/Suicide (3 different sleeves, blue vinyl)	5
82	Big Beat NS 76	Smash It Up/Burglar (p/s, red vinyl)	6
82	Big Beat NS 77	Wait For The Blackout/CAPTAIN SENSIBLE & SOFTIES: Jet Boy, Jet Girl (p/s, red/black 'Damned' labels)	5
82	Big Beat NSP 77	Wait For The Blackout/CAPTAIN SENSIBLE & SOFTIES: Jet Boy, Jet Girl (picture disc)	5
82	Big Beat NS 80	Lively Arts/Teenage Dream (p/s, green vinyl)	6
82	Bronze BRO 149	Lovely Money/Lovely Money (Disco Mix)/I Think I'm Wonderful (p/s)	6
82	Bronze BROP 149	Lovely Money/Lovely Money (Disco Mix)/I Think I'm Wonderful (picture disc)	7
82	Bronze BRO 156	Dozen Girls/Take That/Mine's A Large One, Landlord/Torture Me (p/s)	6
82	Big Beat NS 80	Lively Arts/Teenage Dream (p/s, some on green vinyl)	8/5
82	Bronze BRO 159	Generals/Disguise/Citadel Zombies (p/s)	10
83	Big Beat NS 85	White Rabbit/Rabid (Over You)/Seagulls (p/s)	5
84	Plus One DAMNED 1P	Thanks For The Night/Nasty (picture disc)	5
84	Plus One DAMNED 1	Thanks For The Night/Nasty (p/s, 1,000 each on red, white & blue vinyl)	each 6
84	Plus One DAMNED 1T	Thanks For The Night/Nasty/Do The Blitz (12", no'd p/s, multicoloured vinyl)	10
84	Plus One DAMNED 1T	Thanks For The Night/Nasty ('woman'-shaped pic disc with plinth, 1,000 only)	15
85	MCA GRIM 1	Grimly Fiendish/Edward The Bear (autographed gatefold p/s, 1,000 only)	8
85	MCA GRIMP 1	Grimly Fiendish/Edward The Bear (picture disc)	5
85	MCA GRIMT 1	Grimly Fiendish (Spic'n'Span Mix)/Edward The Bear (12", autographed p/s)	10
85	MCA GRIM 2/GRIMY 2	Edition Premier: The Shadow Of Love/Nightshift/Let There Be Rats/ Wiped Out (double pack)	5
85	MCA GRIM 3	Is It A Dream (Wild West End Mix)/Street Of Dreams (live) (p/s, with 5 badges)	5
86	MCA GRIMT 4	Eloise/Temptation/Beat Girl (12", p/s, 2,000 on blue vinyl)	8
86	Stiff BUY 6/BUYDJ 6A	New Rose/Help!//I'm So Bored (1-sided) (double pack, stickered PVC sleeve with insert, 1st disc on white vinyl, 2nd disc actually plays "I Fall" [live])	8
86	Stiff BUY 6	New Rose/Help! (reissue, red vinyl, PVC sleeve, with card insert)	6
91	Deltic DELT 7T	Fun Factory/CAPTAIN SENSIBLE: Freedom/Pasties/A Riot On Eastbourne Pier (12" p/s, blue vinyl, mail-order only, 2000 only)	8
77	Stiff SEEZ 1	DAMNED DAMNED DAMNED (LP)	12
77	Stiff SEEZ 1	DAMNED DAMNED DAMNED (LP, 2,000 with Eddie & Hot Rods photograph on rear sleeve; some shrinkwrapped with title sticker)	130/50
79	Chiswick CWK 3011	MACHINE GUN ETIQUETTE (LP, with inner sleeve)	12
81	Ace DAM 1	THE BEST OF THE DAMNED (LP, red or blue vinyl)	12
82	Ace DAM 2	MACHINE GUN ETIQUETTE (LP, reissue, blue or white/clear vinyl with inner)	12
82	Ace DAM 3	THE BLACK ALBUM (LP, single reissue, 12,000 with lyrics & poster)	12
82	Big Beat NED 1	LIVE SHEPPERTON 1980 (LP, with 'Collectors Catalogue', 5,000 only)	12
83	Stiff MAIL 2	DAMNED DAMNED DAMNED/MUSIC FOR PLEASURE (2-LP, reissue, gatefold sleeve, mail-order, 5000 only)	20
83	Damned DAMU 2	LIVE IN NEWCASTLE (LP, 5,000 by mail-order only)	15
83	Damned PDAMU 2	LIVE IN NEWCASTLE (LP, picture disc, 5,000 only)	15
85	MCA MCFW 3275	PHANTASMAGORIA (LP, white vinyl, with inner)	12
86	Stiff GET 4	THE CAPTAIN'S BIRTHDAY PARTY — LIVE AT THE ROUNDHOUSE (mini-LP, 45rpm, blue vinyl, stickered plain white sleeve)	12
86	Stiff MAIL 2	DAMNED, DAMNED, DAMNED/MUSIC FOR PLEASURE (2-LP, reissue, yellow vinyl, 4000 by mail-order only)	18
86	Dojo DOJOPD 46	STRAWBERRIES (LP, reissue picture disc)	12
87	Demon PFIEND 91	DAMNED DAMNED DAMNED (LP, reissue picture disc)	12
87	Demon FIEND 108	MUSIC FOR PLEASURE (LP, reissue, orange vinyl)	12
89	Essential ESCLP 008	FINAL DAMNATION (LP, green vinyl, with poster)	12
92	Reviever RRLP 159	LIVE AT THE LYCEUM (LP, clear vinyl)	12

(see also Captain Sensible, Rat Scabies, Rat & Whale, Edge, Magic Michael, Maxim's Thrash, Naz Nomad & Nightmares, Auntiepus, Disco Brothers, Phantom Chords, Tank, Eddie & Hot Rods, U.F.O., Tanz Der Youth)

KENNY DAMON

65	Mercury MF 907	While I Live/Fountain In Capri	10
66	Mercury MF 936	World Of No Return/You Are Everything That's Beautiful	6
68	Mercury MF 1014	Turn Her Away/Till Then My Love	6

(see also Kenny Roberts)

MINT VALUE £

RUSS DAMON

64 Stateside SS 258 Hip Huggers/Heaven Sent 12

STUART DAMON

70 Reflection REF L7 STUART 'CHAMPION' DAMON (LP) 25

DAMON & NAOMI

97 Earworm WORM 3 The Navigator/Awake In A Muddle (p/s) 5

(see also Galaxie 500)

VIC DAMONE

57 MGM MGM 949 And This Is My Beloved (with Howard Keel)/Night Of My Nights 6
57 MGM MGM 950 Stranger In Paradise (with Ann Blyth)/ANN BLYTH:Baubles, Bangles And Pearls . 6
58 Philips PB 866 Ooooh, My Love/Forever New (78) 7
59 Philips PB 889 Separate Tables/Gigi (78) 7
54 Mercury EP1 3121 WALKING MY BABY BACK HOME (EP) 12
57 Philips BBE 12099 VIC DAMONE (EP) 8
58 Philips BBE 12197 DAMONE FAVOURITES (EP) 8
58 Philips BBE 12222 VIC DAMONE (EP) 8
58 Mercury MEP 9534 THE VOICE OF VIC DAMONE (EP) 8
59 Mercury ZEP 10022 YOURS FOR A SONG (EP) 8
59 Philips BBE 12245 DO I LOVE YOU (EP) 8
61 Philips BBE 12502 ON THE SWINGERS SIDE (EP) 8
62 Capitol EAP1 1646 LINGER AWHILE (EP) 8
57 Mercury MPT 7514 ALL-TIME SONG HITS (10" LP) 25
57 Philips BBL 7144 THAT TOWERING FEELING! (LP) 15
58 Philips BBL 7259 CLOSER THAN A KISS (LP) 15
60 Philips BBL 7347 THIS GAME OF LOVE (LP) 12
62 Capitol (S)T 1646 LINGER AWHILE (LP) 12
62 Capitol (S)T 1691 STRANGE ENCHANTMENT (LP) 12
62 Capitol (S)T 1748 THE LIVELY ONES (LP) 12
63 Capitol (S)T 1811 MY BABY LOVES TO SWING (LP) 12
63 Capitol (S)T 1944 THE LIVELIEST (LP) 12
64 Capitol (S)T 2133 ON THE STREET WHERE YOU LIVE (LP) 12

(see also Howard Keel, Easy Riders)

VIC DANA

62 Liberty LIB 51 I Will/Proud 15
62 Liberty LIB 58 (A Girl Need) To Love And Be Loved/Time Can Change 5
62 Liberty LIB 64 Very Good Year For Girls/Looking For Me 5
63 Liberty LIB 10190 Red Roses For A Blue Lady/My World 5
63 Liberty LIB 73 Danger/Heart, Hand And Teardrop 5
64 Liberty LIB 92 Warm And Tender/Shangri-La 5
65 Liberty LIB 309 Moonlight And Roses/What'll I Do 5
65 Liberty LIB 313 Crystal Chandelier/What Now My Love (Et Maintenant) 6
66 Liberty LIB 319 I Love You Drops/Sunny Skies 6
66 Liberty LIB 322 Million And One/My Baby Wouldn't Leave Me 6

DANCE CHAPTER

80 4AD AD 18 Anonymity/New Dance (p/s, some with card insert) 8/6
81 4AD BAD 115 CHAPTER II (12" EP, most with mismatched A&B-side labels) 10
85 Pleasantly Surprised PS 10 WHEN THE SPIRIT MOVES THEM (cassette, in bag with inserts) 15

DANCER, PRANCER & NERVOUS

59 Capitol CL 15097 The Happy Reindeer/Dancer's Waltz (some with p/s) 12/6

(see also Singing Reindeer)

DANCING DID

79 Fruit & Veg F&V 1 Dancing Did/Lorry Pirates (p/s) 8
80 Fruit & Veg F&V 2 The Haunted Tearooms/Squashed Things On The Road (p/s) 5
82 Stiff BUY 136 The Lost Platoon/The Human Chicken (withdrawn 'cavalry' p/s) 8

DANDO SHAFT

70 Youngblood YB 1012 Cold Wind/Cat Song 10
72 RCA RCA 2246 Sun Clog Dance/This Gift 10
70 Youngblood SSYB 6 AN EVENING WITH DANDO SHAFT (LP) 60
71 RCA Neon NE 5 DANDO SHAFT (LP, gatefold sleeve) 65
72 RCA Victor SF 8256 LANTALOON (LP, initially with poster) 80/45
77 Rubber RUB 034 KINGDOM (LP) 30

(see also Hedgehog Pie)

DANDY (& SUPERBOYS)

64 Dice CC 21 Rudie Don't Go/It's Just Got To Be 12
65 Dice CC 24 You Got To Pray/I Got To Have You (as Dandy & Barbara) 12
65 Blue Beat BB 308 To Love You/I'm Looking For Love 15
65 Blue Beat BB 319 Hey Boy Hey Girl/So Long Baby (as Dandy & Del) 15
65 Blue Beat BB 327 My Baby/I'm Gonna Stop Loving You 15
65 Blue Beat BB 336 I Found Love/You've Got Something Nice 15
66 Dice CC 29 The Operation/A Little More Ska 15
66 Ska Beat JB 247 The Fight/Do You Know 18
67 Ska Beat JB 269 One Scotch One Bourbon One Beer/Maximum Pressure 18
67 Ska Beat JB 273 Rudie A Message To You/Til Death Do Us Part 18
67 Ska Beat JB 279 You're No Hustler/No No 18
67 Giant GN 3 My Time Now/East Of Suez (with Superboys) 15
67 Giant GN 5 Puppet On A String/Have Your Fun (with Superboys) 10
67 Giant GN 7 We Are Still Rude/Let's Do Rocksteady (with Superboys) 10
67 Giant GN 10 Somewhere My Love/My Kind Of Love (with Superboys) 10
67 Giant GN 15 There Is A Mountain/This Music Got Soul (with Superboys) 8
68 Giant GN 20 Charlie Brown/Groovin' At The Cue (as Dandy & Charlie Griffiths) 10
68 Giant GN 27 Sweet Ride/Up The Hill (with Superboys) 10
68 Giant GN 30 Tears On My Pillow/Mad Them (with Superboys) 10

68 Giant GN 36 I'm Back With A Bang Bang/Jungle Walk (with Superboys) . . . 10
68 Trojan TR 618 The Toast/Kicks Out . . . 10
68 Trojan TR 629 Sentence (as Dandy & Lee)/LEE PERRY: You Crummy . . . 10
69 Columbia Blue Beat DB 112 Play It Cool/Rude With Me . . . 10
68 Downtown DT 401 Move Your Mule/Reggae Me This . . . 7
69 Downtown DT 402 Come Back Girl/Shake Me Wake Me . . . 7
69 Downtown DT 404 Tell Me Darling/Cool Hand Luke . . . 7
69 Downtown DT 406 Doctor Sure Shot/Put On Your Dancing Shoes . . . 7
69 Downtown DT 410 Reggae In Your Jeggae/DREAMERS: Reggae Shuffle . . . 7
69 Downtown DT 411 You Don't Care/Tryer (both sides with Audrey) . . . 7
69 Downtown DT 415 Rocksteady Gone/Walking Down . . . 7
69 Downtown DT 416 I'm Your Puppet/Water Boy . . . 7
69 Downtown DT 421 Games People Play/AUDREY: One Fine Day . . . 7
69 Downtown DT 429 People Get Ready/RUDIES: Near East . . . 7
69 Downtown DT 434 Be Natural, Be Proud/Who Do You Want To Run To . . . 7
69 Downtown DT 437 Come On Home/Love Is All You Need . . . 7
69 Downtown DT 442 Everybody Loves A Winner/Try Me One More Time . . . 7
69 Downtown DT 445 Let's Come Together (with Israelites)/JAKE WADE: Music Fever . . . 7
69 Downtown DT 453 Won't You Come Home/Baby Make It Soon . . . 7
70 Downtown DT 456 Raining In My Heart/First Note . . . 7
70 Downtown DT 458 Build Your Love (On Solid Foundation)/Let's Talk It Over . . . 7
70 Downtown DT 462 Morning Side Of The Mountain (as Dandy & Audrey)/AUDREY: Show Me Baby . . . 7
70 Downtown DT 468 How Glad I Am/I'm So Glad (as Dandy & Audrey) . . . 7
70 Trojan TR 7800 Take A Letter Maria/You're Coming Back . . . 6
71 Downtown DT 483 Could It Be True/Your Eyes Are Dreaming (as Dandy & Jackie) . . . 6
71 Downtown DT 484 Daddy's Home/Everyman . . . 6
71 Trojan TR 7816 Same Old Fashioned Way/Out Of Many, One People . . . 6
72 Trojan TR 7857 What Do You Want To Make Those Eyes At Me For/Talking About Sally . . . 6
67 Giant GNL 1000 ROCKSTEADY WITH DANDY (LP) . . . 75
68 Trojan TRL 2 DANDY RETURNS (LP) . . . 30
69 Trojan TRL 17 I NEED YOU (LP, with Audrey) . . . 25
70 Trojan TTL 26 YOUR MUSICAL DOCTOR (LP) . . . 18
70 Trojan TBL 118 MORNINGSIDE OF THE MOUNTAIN (LP, with Audrey) . . . 22

(see also Bobby Thompson, Sugar & Dandy, Rub A Dubs, Don Martin, Boy Friday, Audrey, Little Sal with Dandy & Superboys)

CHRIS DANE
55 London HLA 8165 Cynthia's In Love/My Ideal . . . 45
55 London HLA 8165 Cynthia's In Love/My Ideal (78) . . . 10

JERRY DANE
60 Decca F 11234 You're My Only Girl/Nothing But The Truth . . . 7
60 Decca F 11284 Let's/Awhile In Love . . . 8
63 Windsor WPS 127 Everybody Go Wild/Watcha Want (p/s) . . . 15/8

PATRICK DANE
65 Columbia DB 7466 In My Baby's Eyes/The Only One (with Quiet Five) . . . 6
65 Columbia DB 7749 Go Out And Get Somebody/Go On Your Way (with Club '69) . . . 6
68 MGM MGM 1403 When You Lose The One You Love/Home (as Patrick Dane & Mark 7) . . . 6

(see also Quiet Five)

SHELLEY DANE
60 Pye International 7N 25064 Hannah Lee/This Is The Time In My Life . . . 6

CAL DANGER
62 Fontana 267 225 TF Restless/Teenage Girlie Blues . . . 75

A.P. DANGERFIELD
68 Fontana TF 935 Conversations (In A Station Light Refreshment Bar)/Further Conversations . . . 25

KEITH DANGERFIELD
68 Plexium P 1237 No Life Child/She's A Witch . . . 200

TONY DANGERFIELD & THRILLS
64 Pye 7N 15695 I've Seen Such Things/She's Too Way Out . . . 30

(see also Savages, Circles)

DANI
74 Pye International 7N 25667 La Vie A 25 Ans/Pour Que Ça Dure (p/s) . . . 6
74 Pye International 7N 25667 That Old Familiar Feeling/Pour Que Ça Dure . . . 12

DANIEL IN THE LION'S DEN
70 Trojan TR 7797 Dancing In The Sun/LION'S DEN: Chick A Bow . . . 6

DANIELLE
66 Philips BF 1532 I'm Gonna Marry The Boy/Magic Carpet Of Love . . . 8
67 Philips BF 1574 Oh Mama/Come A Little Closer . . . 7

BILLY DANIELS
51 London L 1003 That Old Black Magic/Love Is A Lovely Thing (78) . . . 7
56 Vogue V 2386 I Live For You/Medley: Easy To Love, etc. . . . 7
56 Oriole CB 1087 I Get A Kick Out Of You/Too Marvelous For Words . . . 7
56 Oriole CB 1095 That Old Black Magic/I Concentrate On You . . . 7
60 Vogue V 9172 That Old Black Magic/My Yiddishe Mamma . . . 15
56 Mercury MEP 9001 BILLY DANIELS (EP) . . . 15
58 HMV 7EG 8485 BEST OF BILLY DANIELS (EP) . . . 10
60 Mercury ZEP 10066 THAT OLD BLACK MAGIC (EP) . . . 12
53 Oriole/Mercury MG 10003 TORCH HOUR (10" LP, Oriole label with stickered U.S. Mercury sleeve) . . . 30
54 Mercury MG 25103 TORCH HOUR (10" LP, reissue) . . . 20
54 Mercury MG 25163 SONGS AT MIDNIGHT (10" LP) . . . 25
56 Mercury MPT 7006 TORCH HOUR (10" LP, 2nd reissue) . . . 15
56 Mercury MPT 7505 SONGS AT MIDNIGHT (10" LP, reissue) . . . 18
56 Vogue LAE 12021 AT THE CRESCENDO (LP) . . . 15
58 HMV DLP 1174 YOU GO TO MY HEAD (10" LP) . . . 15
58 HMV CLP 1200 THE MASCULINE TOUCH (LP) . . . 15

MINT VALUE £

JOE DANIELS' JAZZ GROUP

54	Parlophone MSP 6111	I Wish I Could Shimmy Like My Sister Kate/Susie	7
54	Parlophone MSP 6129	Little Brown Jug/Mountain Wine	7
54	Parlophone MSP 6143	Crazy Rhythm/The Champagne Touch	7
56	Parlophone R 4236	"Dixieland Party (No. 2)" Medley (both sides)	6
57	Parlophone R 4273	When The Saints Go Marching In/Spanish Shawl (solo)	6
57	Parlophone R 4324	Avalon/New Orleans Parade	6
57	Parlophone R 4330	Oi! Oi! Oi!/Bottle Beatin' Blues	6
57	Parlophone R 4378	"Juke Box Jazz" Medley (both sides)	6

JULIUS DANIELS

65	RCA RCX 7175	R.C.A. VICTOR RACE SERIES VOL. 4 (EP)	20

MAXINE DANIELS

57	Oriole CB 1366	Coffee-Bar Calypso/Cha-Cha Calypso	10
58	Oriole CB 1402	I Never Realised/Moonlight Serenade	10
58	Oriole CB 1440	You Brought A New Kind Of Love To Me/Somebody Else Is Taking My Place	10
58	Oriole CB 1449	When It's Springtime In The Rockies/My Summer Heart	10
58	Oriole CB 1462	Passionate Summer/Lola's Heart	10

MIKE DANIELS & HIS BAND

57	Columbia 33SX 1256	MIKE ON MIKE (LP)	45

REV R.A. DANIELS

51	Capitol CL 13530	He's The Lily Of The Valley/I Shall Wear A Crown (78)	30

ROLY "YO YO" DANIELS

60s	Stardisc SD 101	Yo Yo Boy/The Teacher (p/s)	15
61	Parlophone R 4759	Late Last Evening/Bella Bella Marie	7
62	Decca F 11501	Yo Yo Boy/The Teacher (reissue)	8

SAM DANIELS

63	Sway SW 003	Tell Me Baby/ERNIE FAULKENER: Beautiful Girl (both with Planets)	12

JOHNNY DANKWORTH ORCHESTRA

53	Parlophone MSP 6026	Honeysuckle Rose (with Cleo Laine)/Swingin'	10
53	Parlophone MSP 6032	Moon Flowers/Two Ticks	10
53	Parlophone MSP 6037	I Get A Kick Out Of You (with Frank Holder)/Easy Living (with Cleo Laine)	10
54	Parlophone MSP 6067	S' Wonderful/Younger Every Day	10
54	Parlophone MSP 6077	The Slider/It's The Talk Of The Town	10
54	Parlophone MSP 6083	The Jerky Thing/My Buddy	10
54	Parlophone MSP 6092	Runnin' Wild/Oo-Be-Doop	10
54	Parlophone MSP 6113	Perdido/Four Of A Kind	10
54	Parlophone MSP 6139	Bugle Call Rag/You Go To My Head	10
55	Capitol CL 14285	Singin' In The Rain/Non-Stop London	10
56	Parlophone MSP 6255	Experiments With Mice/Applecake	12
57	Parlophone R 4274	All Clare/Melbourne Marathon	8
57	Parlophone R 4294	Duke's Joke/Coquette	8
57	Parlophone R 4321	Big Jazz Story/Firth Of Fourths	8
58	Parlophone R 4456	The Colonel's Tune/Jim And Andy's	8
59	Top Rank JAR 209	We Are The Lambeth Boys/Duet For 16	10
59	Top Rank JAR 209	We Are The Lambeth Boys/Duet For 16 (78)	8
61	Columbia DB 4590	African Waltz/Moanin'	5
61	Columbia DB 4695	The Avengers/Chano	20
61	Columbia DB 4751	String Of Camels/Winter Wail	5
62	Columbia DB 4852	Cannonball/S.O. Blues	6
62	Columbia DB 4943	Opato/Abandonado	5
63	Fontana TF 422	The Avengers/Off The Cuff	18
64	Fontana TF 512	Beefeaters/Down A Tone	40
65	Fontana TF 643	Sands Of The Kalahari/Night Thoughts	6
66	Fontana TF 675	Return From The Ashes/Piano Theme	5
66	Fontana TF 700	Modesty Blaise Theme/The Frost Report	7
67	Fontana TF 805	(Ain't That) Just Like A Woman/Accident	6
73	Philips 6006 337	Tomorrows World/Bitter Lemons	6
78	BBC RESL 63	Telford's Change/Serenade For Sylvia (p/s)	8
61	Columbia SEG 8137	AFRICAN WALTZ (EP)	15
58	Parlophone GEP 8653	DANKWORTH WORKSHOP NO. 1 (EP)	25
58	Parlophone GEP 8697	DANKWORTH WORKSHOP NO. 2 — EXPERIMENTS WITH DANKWORTH (EP)	12
60	Columbia SEG 8037	THE CRIMINAL (EP, soundtrack; also stereo ESG 7825)	20/35
56	Parlophone PMD 1042	JOURNEY INTO JAZZ (10" LP)	20
58	Parlophone PMC 1076	THE VINTAGE YEARS (LP)	20
59	Parlophone PMC 1043	FIVE STEPS TO DANKWORTH (LP)	20
60	Top Rank 25/019	LONDON TO NEWPORT (LP)	50
61	Columbia 33SX 1280	JAZZ ROUTES (LP, also stereo SCX 3347)	35
63	Columbia 33SX 1572	CURTAIN UP (LP)	15
64	Fontana TL/STL 5203	WHAT THE DICKENS! (LP)	30
64	Encore ENC 165	FROM 7 ON (LP)	20
65	Fontana TL/STL 5229	THE ZODIAC VARIATIONS (LP, mono/stereo)	15/30
67	Stateside S(S)L 10213	FATHOM (LP, soundtrack)	45
68	Fontana TL 5445	THE $1,000,000 COLLECTION (LP)	20
72	Philips 6308 122	FULL CIRCLE (LP)	25
73	Philips 6308 169	LIFELINE (LP)	25
80s	Sepia RRT 1007	FAIR OAK FUSIONS (LP)	15
80s	Sepia RSR 1008	PRELUDE TO A KISS (LP)	20

(see also Cleo Laine, Philip Green, Tony Mansell, Kenny Wheeler & Johnny Dankworth, Frank Holder, Pinewood Studio Orchestra)

JOHNNY DANKWORTH SEVEN

50	Jazz Parade B 8	Lightly Politely/Marmaduke (78)	7
51	Vogue B 9	Strike Up The Band/Little Benny (78)	7

MINT VALUE £

DANLEERS

58	Mercury AMT 1003	One Summer Night/Wheelin' And A-Dealin'	200
58	Mercury AMT 1003	One Summer Night/Wheelin' And A-Dealin' (78)	50

DANNY & THE JUNIORS

58	HMV POP 436	At The Hop/Sometimes (When I'm All Alone)	15
58	HMV POP 436	At The Hop/Sometimes (When I'm All Alone) (78)	10
58	HMV POP 467	Rock And Roll Is Here To Stay/School Boy Romance	35
58	HMV POP 467	Rock And Roll Is Here To Stay/School Boy Romance (78)	20
58	HMV POP 504	Dottie/In The Meantime	25
58	HMV POP 504	Dottie/In The Meantime (78)	25
60	Top Rank JAR 510	Twistin' U.S.A./Thousand Miles Away	15
61	Top Rank JAR 552	Pony Express/Daydreamer	15
61	Top Rank JAR 587	Back To The Hop/The Charleston Fish	15
62	Top Rank JAR 604	Twistin' All Night Long/Twistin' England (with Freddy Cannon)	15
63	London HL 9666	Oo-La-La-Limbo/Now And Then	12
68	Stateside SS 2117	At The Hop/LLOYD PRICE: (You've Got) Personality	5

C. DANOVAN

73	Randy's RAN 529	Sweet Caroline/IMPACT ALL STARS: Caroline (Version)	5

DANSE SOCIETY

81	Society SOC 3-81	The Clock/Continent (brown, black & white foldout p/s)	15
81	Society SOC 3-81	The Clock/Continent (re-pressing, black & white foldout p/s)	5
81	Pax PAX 2	There Is No Shame In Death/Dolphins/These Frayed Edges (12", p/s, blue or black vinyl)	20/6
82	Pax SOC 5	Woman's Own/We're So Happy (p/s)	8
82	Pax PAX 5	Woman's Own/Continent/We're So Happy/Belief (12", with spined p/s)	10

DANSETTE DAMAGE

78	Shoestring LACE 001	New Musical Express/The Only Sound (p/s)	120
79	Pinnacle PIN 30	2001$\frac{3}{4}$ Approximately/Must Be Love (p/s)	8
94	Shoestring BLOO 2LP	SOLD AS SEEN (LP, gatefold sleeve)	15

DANTALIAN'S CHARIOT

67	Columbia DB 8260	The Madman Running Through The Fields/The Sun Came Bursting Through My Cloud	125
95	Tenth Planet TP 015	CHARIOT RISING (LP, numbered, 1,000 only)	25

(see also Zoot Money's Big Roll Band)

DANTE

61	Brunswick 05857	Bye Bye Baby/That's Why	10

DANTE & EVERGREENS

60	Top Rank JAR 402	Alley-Oop/The Right Time	30

RONNIE DANTE

64	Stateside SS 351	Don't Stand Up In A Canoe/If You Love Me Laurie	6

TROY DANTE (& INFERNOS)

63	Decca F 11639	The Face/Give Me Some More	8
63	Decca F 11746	It's Alright/Tell Me (as Troy Dante & Infernos)	8
64	Fontana TF 445	Tell Me When/It Had To Be (as Troy Dante & Infernos)	8
64	Fontana TF 477	This Little Girl/Loving Eyes (as Troy Dante & Infernos)	18
64	Fontana TF 498	Baby/Tell Me Now	8
65	Fontana TF 541	I Wish I Knew/Sad Tears	8
66	Polydor NH 56110	I'll Never Know/Security	7
68	Columbia DB 8381	My Friend The Scarecrow/Emma May Kingston	7

JOE DARENSBOURG & HIS DIXIE FLYERS

58	Vogue V 2409	Yellow Dog Blues/Careless Love	6
58	Vogue LAE 12149	JOE DARENSBOURG & HIS DIXIE FLYERS (LP)	15

DARIEN SPIRIT

73	Charisma CAS 1065	ELEGY TO MARILYN (LP)	20

BOBBY DARIN

78s

56	Brunswick 05561	Rock Island Line/Timber (as Bobby Darin & Jaybirds)	50
58	London HLE 8666	Splish Splash/Judy Don't Be Moody	30
58	London HLE 8679	Early In The Morning/Now We're One	45
58	London HLE 8737	Queen Of The Hop/Lost Love	45
59	London HLE 8793	Mighty Mighty Man/You're Mine (as Bobby Darin with Rinky Dinks)	50
59	London HLE 8815	Plain Jane/While I'm Gone	50
59	London HLE 8867	Dream Lover/Bullmoose	35
59	London HLK 8939	Mack The Knife/Was There A Call For Me	25
60	London HLK 9034	La Mer (Beyond The Sea)/That's The Way Love Is	50
60	London HLK 9086	Clementine/Down With Love	60
60	London HLK 9142	Bill Bailey Won't You Please Come Home/Tall Story	75

SINGLES

56	Brunswick 05561	Rock Island Line/Timber (as Bobby Darin & Jaybirds)	170
58	London HLE 8666	Splish Splash/Judy Don't Be Moody	30
58	London HLE 8679	Early In The Morning/Now We're One (as Rinky-Dinks featuring Bobby Darin)	45
58	London HLE 8737	Queen Of The Hop/Lost Love	25
58	London HL 7060	Queen Of The Hop/Lost Love (export issue)	25
59	London HLE 8793	Mighty Mighty Man/You're Mine (as Bobby Darin with Rinky Dinks)	35
59	London HLE 8815	Plain Jane/While I'm Gone	30
59	London HL 7078	Plain Jane/Dream Lover (export issue)	30
59	London HLE 8867	Dream Lover/Bullmoose	8
59	London HLK 8939	Mack The Knife/Was There A Call For Me	8
60	London HLK 9034	La Mer (Beyond The Sea)/That's The Way Love Is	7

(The above 45s were originally issued with triangular centres, later round centre pressings are worth around two-thirds these values.)

			MINT VALUE £
60	London HLK 9086	Clementine/Down With Love	6
60	London HLK 9142	Bill Bailey Won't You Please Come Home/Tall Story	6
60	Brunswick 05831	Hear Them Bells/The Greatest Builder	15
60	London HLK 9197	Beachcomber/Autumn Blues (credited to 'Bobby Darin At The Piano')	10
60	Lonson HLK 9215	Somebody To Love/I'll Be There	6
61	London HLK 9303	Lazy River/Oo-Ee-Train	6
61	London HLK 9375	Nature Boy/Look For My True Love	6
61	London HLK 9407	Theme From "Come September"/Walk Bach To Me (with Orchestra)	10
61	London HLK 9429	You Must Have Been A Beautiful Baby/Sorrow Tomorrow	6
61	London HLK 9474	Multiplication (From "Come September")/Irresistible You	6
62	London HLK 9540	What'd I Say/Ain't That Love	6
62	London HLK 9575	Things/Jailer Bring Me Water	6
62	Capitol CL 15272	If A Man Answers/A True, True Love	7
62	London HLK 9624	Baby Face/You Know How	6
63	London HLK 9663	I've Found A New Baby/Keep A-Walkin'	8
63	Capitol CL 15286	You're The Reason I'm Living/Now You're Gone	7
63	Capitol CL 15306	Eighteen Yellow Roses/Not For Me	8
63	Capitol CL 15328	Be Mad Little Girl/Since You've Been Gone	10
64	Capitol CL 15338	I Wonder Who's Kissing Her Now/As Long As I'm Singing	7
64	Atlantic AT 4002	Milord/Golden Earrings	7
64	Capitol CL 15360	The Things In This House/Wait By The Water	7
65	Capitol CL 15401	When I Get Home/Lonely Road	7
65	Capitol CL 15414	Gyp The Cat/That Funny Feeling	7
65	Atlantic AT 4046	We Didn't Ask To Be Brought Here/Funny What Love Can Do	10
66	Atlantic 584 014	Mame/Walking In The Shadow Of Love	7
66	Atlantic 584 051	If I Were A Carpenter/Rainin'	6
67	Atlantic 584 063	The Girl That Stood Beside Me/Reason To Believe	7
67	Atlantic 584 079	Lovin' You/Amy	7
67	Atlantic 584 105	The Lady Came From Baltimore/I Am	7
67	Atlantic 584 147	At The Crossroads/She Knows	6
68	Bell BLL 1040	Change/Long Line Rider	6
69	Bell BLL 1090	Sugar-Man/Jive	6
70	Major Minor MM 697	Maybe We Can Get It Together/RX-Pyro (Prescription: Fire) (as Bob Darin)	6
74	Mowest MW 3014	Blue Monday/Moritat: Mack The Knife	6
EPs			
59	London REE 1173	BOBBY DARIN	70
59	London REE 1225	BOBBY DARIN NO. 2	50
60	London REK 1243	THAT'S ALL	25
61	London REK 1286	FOR TEENAGERS ONLY	40
61	London REK 1290	UP A LAZY RIVER	22
61	London REK 1310	TWO OF A KIND (with Johnny Mercer)	35
61	London REK 1321	THE 25TH DAY OF DECEMBER	50
61	London REK 1334	LOVE SWINGS	25
62	London REK 1338	TWIST WITH BOBBY DARIN	22
62	London REK 1342	THINGS!	22
65	Atlantic AET 6013	MILORD	22
LPs			
58	London HA-E 2140	BOBBY DARIN	60
59	London HA-E 2172	THAT'S ALL	30
59	London HA-K 2235	THIS IS DARIN (also stereo SAH-K 6067)	25/35
60	London HA-K 2291	DARIN AT THE COPA (also stereo SAH-K 6103)	25/35
60	London HA-K 2311	FOR TEENAGERS ONLY	45
61	London HA-K 2363	TWO OF A KIND (with Johnny Mercer; also stereo SAH-K 6164)	30/40
61	London HA-K 2372	THE BOBBY DARIN STORY	30
61	London HA-K 2394	LOVE SWINGS (also stereo SAH-K 6194)	25/35
62	London HA-K 2456	DARIN SINGS RAY CHARLES (also stereo SAH-K 6243)	30/40
62	Capitol T 1791	OH! LOOK AT ME NOW	25
62	London HA-K 8030	THINGS AND OTHER THINGS	35
63	London HA-K/SH-K 8102	IT'S YOU OR NO-ONE (mono/stereo)	35/45
63	Capitol T 1826	EARTHY	20
63	Capitol T 1866	YOU'RE THE REASON I'M LIVING	25
63	Capitol (S)T 1942	EIGHTEEN YELLOW ROSES & 11 OTHER HITS (mono/stereo)	30/40
64	Capitol (S)T 2007	GOLDEN FOLK HITS (mono/stereo)	30/40
65	Capitol T 2194	FROM HELLO DOLLY TO GOODBYE CHARLIE	20
65	Atlantic ATL 5014	BOBBY DARIN WINNERS	30
65	Capitol T 2322	I WANNA BE AROUND	30
66	Capitol T 2571	THE BEST OF BOBBY DARIN	20
66	Atlantic 587/588 014	SINGS THE SHADOW OF YOUR SMILE	22
66	Atlantic 587/588 020	IN A BROADWAY BAG (MAME)	18
66	Atlantic 587/588 051	IF I WERE A CARPENTER	18
67	Atlantic 587 065	THE BOBBY DARIN STORY	18
67	Atlantic 587 073	SOMETHING SPECIAL	40
67	Atlantic 587 076	INSIDE OUT	18
67	Atlantic 587 089	SINGS DR. DOOLITTLE	15
69	Bell MBLL/SBLL 112	BORN WALDEN ROBERT CASSOTTO	15
69	Bell SBLL 128	COMMITMENT	20

(see also Rinky Dinks)

DARK

72	SIS 0102	DARK ROUND THE EDGES (LP, private pressing, 12 copies with colour gatefold sleeve & booklet)	1,800
72	SIS 0102	DARK ROUND THE EDGES (LP, private pressing, 8 copies with black & white gatefold sleeve)	1,300
72	SIS 0102	DARK ROUND THE EDGES (LP, private pressing, 40 copies with single black & white sleeve)	1,000
90	Swank	DARK ROUND THE EDGES (LP, reissue, U.K. pressing marketed in U.S.)	30

MINT VALUE £

91 Swank/Darkside 001 DARK ROUND THE EDGES (LP, as above, with different insert, 225 only) 25
92 Kissing Spell KSCD 9204 DARK ROUND THE EDGES (CD, with 8-page booklet, 1,500 only). 20
95 Acme AC 8009LP ARTEFACTS FROM THE BLACK MUSEUM (LP, 500 only, with insert) 15

DARKER SHADE OF BLACK

71 Jackpot JP 758 War/JEFF BARNES: People's Version 7

DARKNESS

02 Must Destroy DUSTY 001CD I Believe In A Thing Called Love/Love On The Rocks With No Ice/Love Is Only A Feeling (CD) 100
03 Must Destroy DESTROYER 6 Get Your Hands Off My Woman (Clean Version)/(Dirty Version)/Best Of Me (p/s, 2000 only). 50
03 Must Destroy DUSTY 006 CD Get Your Hands Off My Woman (Clean Version)/(Dirty Version)/Best Of Me (CD) . 40
03 Must Destroy DESTROYER 10 Growing On Me/How Dare You Call This Love (p/s) 15
03 Must Destroy DUSTY 010 CD Growing On Me/How Dare You Call This Love/Bareback (CD) 8
03 Must Destroy DARK 01 I Believe In A Thing Called Love/Makin' Out (picture disc, sticker-sealed PVC sleeve, with inlay). 10
03 Must Destroy DARK 02 Christmas Time (Don't Let The Bells End)/I Love You 5 Times (die-cut picture disc, with insert). 12
03 Must Destroy 50466 74521 PERMISSION TO LAND (LP). 12

DARKSIDE

90 Situation 2 SIT 66T HIGH RISE LOVE EP (12") 8
90 Situation 2 SIT 72T Waiting For The Angels (12"). 8
91 Situation 2 DARK 3 ALWAYS A PLEASURE EP (12") 8
90 Situation 2 SITU 29P ALL THAT NOISE (LP, picture disc, die-cut sleeve). 18
91 Acid Ray DARK 2 PSYCHEDELIZE SUBURBIA (LP, mail-order only, with poster). 12
93 Situation 2 SITU 34P MELOMANIA (LP, picture disc, die-cut sleeve) 12

(see also Spacemen 3)

DARK STAR

81 Avatar AAA 105 Lady Of Mars/Rock 'N' Romancin' (company sleeve) 12
81 Steel Strike no cat. no. Lady Of Mars/Rock 'N' Romancin' (12", 250 pressed). 90
81 Avatar AALP 5003 DARK STAR (LP, some with patch). 22/18
87 FM WKFMLP 97 REAL TO REEL (LP) 15

DARKTHRONE

91 Peaceville VILE 22 SOULSIDE JOURNEY (LP, picture disc) 25
92 Peaceville VILE 28 A BLAZE IN THE NORTHERN SKY (LP). 40
93 Peaceville VILE 35 UNDER A FUNERAL MOON (LP) 40
94 Peaceville VILE 43 TRANSILVANIAN HUNGER (LP). 40

DARLETTES

70 President PT 317 Lost/Sweet Kind Of Loneliness 15

DARLING BUDS

87 Darling Buds DAR 1 If I Said/Just To Be Seen (p/s, some with insert, 2,000 only) 15/8
88 Bonk On 001 Spin/BUBBLEGUM SPLASH track (flexidisc free with *So Naive* fanzine) 8/6
89 Flexi FLX 448 Valentine (live)/That's The Reason (live) (fan club flexidisc) 5
90 Native NTV 54 Shame On You/Valentine//It's All Up To You/Spin//Think Of Me/ That's The Reason (triple-pack in envelope sleeve) 8

BILL DARNEL

55 London HLU 8204 My Little Mother/Bring Me A Bluebird (with Frank Weir & His Orchestra) 45
55 London HLU 8204 My Little Mother/Bring Me A Bluebird (with Frank Weir & His Orchestra) (78) 6
56 London HLU 8234 The Last Frontier/Rock-A-Boogie Baby. 50
56 London HLU 8234 The Last Frontier/Rock-A-Boogie Baby (78) 8
56 London HLU 8267 Guilty Lips/Ain't Misbehavin'. 40
56 London HLU 8292 Tell Me More/Satin Doll 40
56 London HLU 8292 Tell Me More/Satin Doll (78). 8

(see also Frank Weir & His Orchestra)

GLENN DARRELL

54 London HL 8023 Write And Tell Me Why/Don't Let Me Down (78) 8

GUY DARRELL (& MIDNIGHTERS)

63 Oriole CB 1932 Go Home Girl/You Won't Come Home (as Guy Darrell & Midnighters) 12
64 Oriole CB 1964 Sorry/Sweet Dreams (as Guy Darrell & Midnighters) 12
65 CBS 201806 Stupidity/One Of These Days. 10
66 CBS 202033 Somewhere They Can't Find Me/It Takes A Lot To Laugh 10
66 CBS 202082 I've Been Hurt/Blessed 20
66 CBS 202296 Big Louie/My Way Of Thinking. 7
67 CBS 202510 Hard Lovin'/I've Never Had A Love Like That 7
67 CBS 202642 Crystal Ball/Didn't I 7
67 Piccadilly 7N 35406 Evil Woman/What You Do About That 20
67 Pye 7N 17435 Cupid/What's Happened To Our Love 7
68 Pye 7N 17586 Skyline Pigeon/Everything 7
69 Page One POF 120 Turn To Me/What's Her Name. 5
69 Page One POF 141 Birds Of A Feather/Keep The Rain From My Door 5
69 Page One POF 155 How Are You/Turtle Turquoise And The Hare (as Guy Darrell Syndicate). 5
72 CBS 53364 GUY DARRELL (LP) 25

JAMES DARREN

59 Pye International 7N 25019 Gidget/There's No Such Thing (as Jimmy Darren) 15
59 Pye International N 25019 Gidget/There's No Such Thing (as Jimmy Darren) (78). 10
59 Pye International 7N 25034 Angel Face/I Don't Wanna Lose You (as Jimmy Darren). 12
59 Pye International N 25034 Angel Face/I Don't Wanna Lose You (as Jimmy Darren) (78) 15
60 Pye International 7N 25059 Because They're Young/Let There Be Love 7
61 Pye International 7N 25116 Goodbye Cruel World/Valerie. 7

MINT VALUE £

62	Pye International 7N 25125	Her Royal Majesty/If I Could Only Tell You	7
62	Pye International 7N 25138	Conscience/Dream Big	7
62	Pye International 7N 25155	Mary's Little Lamb/The Life Of The Party	7
62	Pye International 7N 25168	Too Young To Go Steady/Hail To The Conquering Hero	7
63	Pye International 7N 25170	Pin A Medal On Joey/I'll Be Loving You	7
63	Colpix PX 708	Backstage/Gegetta	6
65	Warner Bros WB 5648	Because You're Mine/Millions Of Roses	7
66	Warner Bros WB 5689	Tom Hawk/I Want To Be Lonely	7
67	Warner Bros WB 5874	All/Misty Morning Eyes	7
59	Pye Intl. NEP 44004	P.S. I LOVE YOU (EP)	20
62	Pye Intl. NEP 44008	JAMES DARREN HIT PARADE (EP)	20
63	Pye Intl. NPL 28021	LOVE AMONG THE YOUNG (LP)	35

JEANNIE DARREN & SECOND CITY SOUND

69	Major Minor MM 611	River Deep, Mountain High/Julie	5

MAXINE DARREN

65	Pye 7N 15796	How Can I Hide It From My Heart/Don't You Know	10

CHRIS DARROW

73	United Artists UAG 29453	CHRIS DARROW (LP)	12
74	United Artists UAG 29634	UNDER MY OWN DISGUISE (LP)	12

(see also Kaleidoscope)

DARTELLS

63	London HLD 9719	Dartell Stomp/Hot Pastrami	22

BARRY DARVELL

60	London HL 9191	Geronimo Stomp/How Will It End?	80

DARWIN'S THEORY

67	Major Minor MM 503	Daytime/Hosanna	50

NITAE DASGUPTA

72	Mushroom 100 MR 22	SONGS OF INDIA (LP)	40

DAS SCHNITZ

79	Ellie Jay EJSP 9249	4 AM (EP, custom sleeve)	100

DATE WITH SOUL

67	Stateside SS 2062	Yes Sir, That's My Baby/PRISCILLA: He Noticed Me	85

(see also Jack Nitzsche, Brian Wilson, Sonny & Cher, Darlene Love/Blossoms, Jackie De Shannon, the Paris Sisters)

DATSUNS

02	Cargo 7SN 013	In Love/Little Bruise (p/s, 3000 only)	10

DAUGHTERS OF ALBION

69	Fontana STL 5486	DAUGHTERS OF ALBION (LP)	18

CLAUDE DAUPHIN

59	Top Rank JAR 195	From The French/JOE PARADISE TRIO: From The French	8

DAVE & ANSELL COLLINS

72	Techniques TE 915	Karate/Doing Your Own Thing	7
72	Rhino RNO 106	Keep On Trying/Give Me Some Light	6
73	Rhino RNO 111	Hot Line/Sunshine Rock (label credits 'Dave Collins')	6
71	Trojan TBL 162	DOUBLE BARREL (LP)	15

(see also Ansel Collins, Les Foster & Ansell Collins, Dave Barker)

DAVE DAVANI & D MEN

63	Columbia DB 7125	Don't Fool Around/She's The Best For Me	15
64	Decca F 11896	Midnight Special/Sho' Know A Lot About Love	20

DAVE DAVANI (FOUR)

65	Parlophone R 5329	Top Of The Pops/Workin' Out	18
66	Parlophone R 5490	Tossin' And Turnin'/Jupe	40
66	Parlophone R 5525	One Track Mind/On The Cooler Side	30
72	Philips 6006 195	King Kong Blues/Come Back Baby (solo)	8
65	Parlophone PMC 1258	FUSED (LP)	70

DAVE & DIAMONDS

65	Columbia DB 7692	I Walk The Lonely Night/You Do Love (some in p/s)	35/15

(see also Dave Russell)

DAVE & DON

67	Polydor 56212	What A Feeling/That's My Way	6

BOB DAVENPORT (& RAKES)

60	Collector JEB 4	GEORDIE SONGS (EP)	15
62	Topic TOP 83	WOR GEORDIE (EP, with Rakes)	15
66	Columbia SX 1786	BOB DAVENPORT AND THE RAKES (LP, with Rakes)	20

ALAN DAVEY

87	Hawkfan HWFB 3/4	THE ELF EP (double pack, 2 x 7" with insert in wraparound p/s in poly bag)	12

(see also Hawkwind)

(Shaun) DAVEY & (James) MORRIS

73	York FYK 417	DAVEY AND MORRIS (LP, with insert)	110

(see also Strawbs)

DAVID

69	Philips BF 1776	Please Mister Postman/Light Of Your Mind	50
70	Fontana TF 1081	I'm Going Back/Selppin	7

ALAN DAVID

64	Decca F 11956	I Want So Much To Know You/I Can't Go Wrong	7
65	Decca F 12130	Crazy 'Bout My Baby/A Thousand Years Too Late	7
67	Polydor BM 56201	Flower Power/Completely Free	6
65	Decca LK 4674	ALAN DAVID (LP)	25

DAVID & EMBERS

63	Decca F 11717	What Is This/Teddy Bear Special	7

(see also Embers)

DAVID & GIANTS

68	Capitol CL 15915	Ten Miles High/Super Love	6

DAVID & JONATHAN

67	Columbia S(C)X 6031	DAVID AND JONATHAN (LP)	25

(see also Roger Cook, Edison Lighthouse, White Plains)

DAVID & ROZAA

70	Philips 6006 040	Time Of Our Life/We Can Reach An Understanding	18
71	Philips 6006 094	The Spark That Lights The Flame/Two Can Share	18

(see also David Essex)

DIANNE DAVIDSON

72	Janus 6146 019	Sympathy/All I Wanted	6
72	Janus 6146 021	Ain't Gonna Be Treated This Way/All I Wanted (All The Time)	5
72	Janus 6310 209	BACKWOODS WOMAN (LP)	15

FRANKIE DAVIDSON & HI MARKS

61	Starlite ST45 5037	You're Driving Me Crazy/I Care For You (B-side with Unicords)	20
61	London HL 9309	Detour/Just For Today	10
68	Decca F 22780	Hector The Trash Collector/Somebody Come And Take My Wife	6

TOMMY DAVIDSON

56	London HLU 8219	Half Past Kissing Time/I Don't Know Yet But I'm Learning	100
56	London HLU 8219	Half Past Kissing Time/I Don't Know Yet But I'm Learning (78)	20

HUTCH DAVIE

58	London HLE 8667	At The Woodchopper's Ball/Honky Tonk Train Blues (& His Honky Tonkers)	10
58	London HLE 8667	At The Woodchopper's Ball/Honky Tonk Train Blues (78)	5
60	London HLE 9076	Sweet Georgia Brown/Heartaches	5
62	Pye International 7N 25149	But I Do/Time Was (& Orchestra)	5
60	London HA-E 2216	MUCH HUTCH (LP)	20

ALUN DAVIES

65	Parlophone R 5384	Girls Were Made To Love And Kiss/Rose Marie	6
68	Mercury MF 1043	One Day Soon/Pretend You Don't See Her	6
72	CBS 65108	DAYDO (LP)	15

(see also Cat Stevens)

BOB DAVIES

63	London HLU 9767	Rock'N'Roll Show/With You Tonight	30

CYRIL DAVIES (R&B ALLSTARS)

63	Pye International 7N 25194	Country Line Special/Chicago Calling	30
63	Pye International 7N 25221	Preachin' The Blues/Sweet Mary	40
69	Pye 7N 17663	Country Line Special/Sweet Mary	15
64	Pye Intl. NEP 44025	THE SOUND OF CYRIL DAVIES (EP)	75
57	'77' LP 2	THE LEGENDARY CYRIL DAVIES (10" LP, 99 only, with Alexis Korner)	900+
70	Folklore F-LEAT 9	THE LEGENDARY CYRIL DAVIES (LP, reissue)	150

(see also Alexis Korner, Beryl Bryden)

DAVE DAVIES

67	Pye 7N 17356	Death Of A Clown/Love Me Till The Sun Shines	7
67	Pye 7N 17429	Susannah's Still Alive/Funny Face	10
68	Pye 7N 17514	Lincoln County/There's No Life Without Love	20
69	Pye 7N 17678	Hold My Hand/Creeping Jean	20
68	Pye NEP 24289	DAVE DAVIES HITS (EP)	300

(see also Kinks)

IRVING DAVIES & METHOD MEN

62	Decca F 11456	The Method/ABC The Method	6

JACKIE DAVIES & HIS QUARTET

57	Pye Nixa N 15115	Land Of Make Believe/Over The Rainbow (78)	80

(see also Chico Arnez)

MARION DAVIES

69	Columbia DB 8589	Walk Out Of My Mind/This Is My Lonely Life	7

(see also Ladybirds)

MIAR DAVIES

64	Decca F 11805	Ten Good Reasons/I Won't Remember You	10
64	Decca F 11894	I Hear You Knocking/Navy Blue	10

NICOLA DAVIES

68	SNB 55-3627	Infatuation/My Boy	6

RAY DAVIES & BUTTONDOWN BRASS

73	Pye NSPL 41021	I BELIEVE IN MUSIC (LP)	15
75	Philips 6382 111	FLASHPOINT (LP)	15

(see also Buttondown Brass; the above is not Ray Davies of the Kinks)

RAY DAVIES

86	Virgin VS 865-12	Quiet Life/Voices In The Dark/GIL EVANS: Va Va Voom (12", p/s)	8

(see also Kinks)

MINT VALUE £

RON DAVIES
70 A&M AMLS 933 — SILENT SONG THROUGH THE LAND (LP) . . . 12

RUPERT DAVIES
63 Parlophone R 5067 — October Dreams/Smoking My Pipe (La Pipa) . . . 7

BARRINGTON DAVIS
72 Montague MONS 2 — TRACKS OF MIND (LP, with lyric insert) . . . 50

BETTE DAVIS & DEBBIE BURTON
63 London HLU 9711 — Whatever Happened To Baby Jane?/I've Written A Letter To Daddy . . . 12
76 EMI EMA 778 — MISS BETTE DAVIS (LP) . . . 20

BETTY DAVIS
75 Island USA 2011 — Shut Off The Light/He Was A Big Freak . . . 6
75 Island ILPS 9329 — NASTY GIRL (LP) . . . 22

BILLIE DAVIS
63 Decca F 11572 — Tell Him/I'm Thankful . . . 6
63 Decca F 11658 — He's The One/V.I.P. . . . 10
63 Columbia DB 7115 — Bedtime Stories/You And I . . . 15
64 Columbia DB 7195 — That Boy John/Say Nothin' Don't Tell . . . 12
64 Columbia DB 7246 — School Is Over/Give Me Love . . . 12
64 Columbia DB 7346 — Whatcha Gonna Do/Everybody Knows (as Billie Davis & Le Roys) . . . 12
65 Piccadilly 7N 35227 — Last One To Be Loved/You Don't Know . . . 7
65 Piccadilly 7N 35266 — No Other Baby/Hands Off . . . 10
66 Piccadilly 7N 35308 — Heart And Soul/Don't Take All Night . . . 10
66 Piccadilly 7N 35350 — Just Walk In My Shoes/Ev'ry Day . . . 20
67 Decca F 12620 — Wasn't It You?/Until It's Time For You To Go . . . 7
67 Decca F 12696 — Angel Of The Morning/Darling Be Home Soon . . . 6
68 Decca F 12823 — I Want You To Be My Baby/Suffer . . . 6
69 Decca F 12870 — I'll Come Home/Make The Feeling Go Away . . . 6
69 Decca F 12923 — I Can Remember/Nobody's Home To Go Home To . . . 18
69 Decca F 12977 — Nights In White Satin/It's Over . . . 15
70 Decca F 13049 — Venid Con Migo/Love (Spanish export issue) . . . 7
70 Decca F 13085 — There Must Be A Reason/Love . . . 6
72 Regal Zonophone RZ 3050 — I Tried/Touch My Love . . . 6
78 Magnet MAG 124 — Run Joey Run/East Come Easy Go . . . 6
70 Decca LK/SKL 5029 — BILLIE DAVIS (LP, mono/stereo) . . . 80/70
(see also Keith & Billie, Le Roys, Mike Sarne)

BLIND GARY DAVIS/REVEREND GARY DAVIS
63 '77' LA 12-14 — PURE RELIGION AND BAD COMPANY (LP) . . . 45
60s Fontana 688 303 ZL — HARLEM STREET SINGER (LP) . . . 30
64 Xtra XTRA 1009 — REV. GARY DAVIS/SHORT STUFF MACON (LP, 1 side each) . . . 20
66 Xtra XTRA 5014 — SAY NO TO THE DEVIL (LP) . . . 30
67 Xtra XTRA 5042 — A LITTLE MORE FAITH (LP) . . . 30
69 Fontana SFJL 914 — BRING YOUR MONEY HONEY (LP) . . . 22
71 Transatlantic TRA 244 — RAGTIME GUITAR (LP) . . . 15
72 Transatlantic TRA 249 — CHILDREN OF ZION (LP) . . . 15
74 Kicking Mule SNKD 1 — LO I BE WITH YOU ALWAYS (2-LP) . . . 18

BLIND JOHNNY DAVIS
52 MGM MGM 463 — Your Love Belongs To Me/Magic Carpet (78) . . . 15

BOBBY DAVIS (Jamaica)
71 Banana BA 344 — Return Your Love/RILEY'S ALLSTARS: Version . . . 8
(see also Barbara Dunkley)

BOBBY DAVIS (U.S.)
61 Starlite ST45 056 — I Was Wrong/Hype You Into Selling Your Head . . . 40

BONNIE DAVIS
55 Brunswick 05507 — Pepper-Hot Baby/For Always, Darling . . . 50
55 Brunswick 05507 — Pepper-Hot Baby/For Always, Darling (78) . . . 12

CLIFFORD DAVIS
69 Reprise RS 27003 — Before The Beginning/Man Of The World . . . 10
70 Reprise RS 27008 — Come On Down And Follow Me/Homework . . . 7
71 Reprise K 14282 — Before The Beginning/Man Of The World (reissue) . . . 7

DANNY DAVIS (U.K.)
60 Parlophone R 4657 — Love Me/You're My Only Girl . . . 20
60 Parlophone R 4796 — Talking In My Sleep/Lullaby Of Love . . . 15
61 Pye 7N 15391 — Tell All The World/Rumours . . . 10
62 Pye 7N 15427 — Rome Wasn't Built In A Day/Tell Me . . . 8
62 Pye 7N 15470 — Patches/September In The Rain . . . 8
(see also Marauders)

DANNY DAVIS ORCHESTRA (U.S.)
58 London HL 8766 — Trumpet Cha-Cha-Cha/Lonesome Trumpet . . . 8
65 MGM MGM 1277 — Main Theme From "The Saint"/Little Bandits Of Juarez . . . 10
64 London HAR 8204 — THEY'RE PLAYING OUR SONG (LP, with Ruby & Romantics) . . . 40
(see also Ruby & Romantics, Byron Lee)

EDDIE ('LOCKJAW') DAVIS
56 Parlophone GEP 8587 — EDDIE 'LOCKJAW' DAVIS TRIO (EP) . . . 8
57 Parlophone GEP 8678 — LOCKJAW (EP) . . . 8
58 Parlophone GEP 8685 — EDDIE 'LOCKJAW' DAVIS TRIO (EP) . . . 8
59 Esquire EP 217 — EDDIE 'LOCKJAW' DAVIS (EP) . . . 10
61 Esquire EP 237 — EDDIE 'LOCKJAW' DAVIS QUARTET (EP) . . . 10
60 Esquire 32-104 — THE EDDIE 'LOCKJAW' DAVIS COOK BOOK (LP) . . . 20
60 Esquire 32-117 — VERY SAXY (LP, with Coleman Hawkins, Arnett Cobb & Bobby Tate) . . . 20

MINT VALUE £

61	Esquire 32-128	JAWS IN ORBIT (LP)	20
64	Stateside SL 10102	THE FIRST SET — LIVE AT MINTONS (LP, with Johnny Griffin)	18

(see also Coleman Hawkins, Johnny Griffin)

EDWARD H. DAVIS

74	Sain SAIN 1016M	HEN FFORDD GYMREIG O FYW (LP)	20
76	Sain SAIN 1053M	SNEB YN BECSO DAM (LP)	15

JESSE (ED) DAVIS

71	Atlantic 2091 076	Every Night Is Saturday Night/Washita Love Child (as Jesse Davis)	6
71	Atco 2400 106	JESSE 'ED' DAVIS (LP)	15
72	Atlantic K 40329	ULULU (LP)	15

KIM DAVIS

66	Decca F 12387	Don't Take Your Lovin' Away/Feelin' Blue	20
67	CBS 202568	Tell It Like It Is/Losing Kind	12
68	CBS 3260	Until It's Time For You To Go/I Hold No Grudge	7
69	CBS 4210	Are You Ready For Love/Taste Of Excitement	7

(see also Kim D, Kim & Kinetics)

LARRY DAVIS/FENTON ROBINSON

72	Python PLP 24	LARRY DAVIS AND FENTON ROBINSON (LP, 99 copies only)	70

MAXWELL DAVIS

66	Ember FA 2040	BATMAN THEME AND OTHER BAT SONGS (LP)	35

MAXWELL STREET JIMMY DAVIS

66	Bounty BY 6009	MAXWELL STREET JIMMY DAVIS (LP)	30

MELVIN DAVIS

69	Action ACT 4531	Save It/This Love Was Meant To Be	30

MILES DAVIS

LPs

55	Esquire 20-041	MILES DAVIS QUINTET (10")	30
53	Esquire 20-017	MILES DAVIS PLAYS (10")	30
53	Esquire 20-021	MILES DAVIS ALL STARS (10")	30
54	Esquire 20-052	MILES DAVIS ALL STARS (A HIFI MODERN JAZZ JAM SESSION) (10")	30
54	Vogue LDE 064	MILES DAVIS AND HIS ORCHESTRA (10")	30
54	Esquire 20-056	MILES DAVIS ALL STARS (A SECOND HIFI MODERN JAZZ JAM SESSION) (10")	30
54	Capitol LC 6683	CLASSICS IN JAZZ (10")	30
55	Esquire 20-062	MILES DAVIS ALL STARS SEXTET (10")	30
55	Esquire 20-072	MILES DAVIS QUINTET (10")	30
56	Philips BBL 7140	'ROUND ABOUT MIDNIGHT	18
57	Fontana TFL 5007	MILES AHEAD	20
58	Fontana TFL 5035	MILESTONES	20
58	Esquire 32-068	RELAXIN' WITH THE MILES DAVIS QUARTET	25
59	Fontana TFL 5056	PORGY AND BESS (also stereo [STFL 507])	20/25
59	Esquire 32-012	THE MUSINGS OF MILES	25
60	Fontana TFL 5081	JAZZ TRACK — "L'ANSCENSEUR POUR L'ECHAFAUD"	20
60	Fontana TFL 5089	THE "MOST" OF MILES	15
60	Fontana STFL 513	KIND OF BLUE (also mono [TFL 5072])	20/15
60	Esquire 32-098	WALKIN'	18
60	Esquire 32-100	MILES DAVIS AND THE MODERN JAZZ GIANTS VOL. 2	18
60	Esquire 32-108	WORKIN' WITH THE MILES DAVIS QUINTET	18
61	Font. TFL 5100/STFL 531	SKETCHES OF SPAIN	18
61	Esquire 32-118	EARLY MILES	20
61	Esquire 32-138	STEAMIN' WITH THE MILES DAVIS QUINTET	18
61	Fontana TFL 5163	FRIDAY NIGHT AT THE BLACKHAWK, SAN FRANCISCO (VOL. 1) (with Cannonball Adderley & John Coltrane; also stereo STFL 580)	18
61	Fontana TFL 5164	SATURDAY NIGHT AT THE BLACKHAWK, SAN FRANCISCO (VOL. 2) (with Cannonball Adderley & John Coltrane; also stereo STFL 581)	18
62	Fontana TFL 5172	SOMEDAY MY PRINCE WILL COME (also stereo STFL 587)	18
62	CBS (S)BPG 62081	AT THE CARNEGIE HALL, MAY 19TH 1961	15
64	CBS (S)BPG 62170	SEVEN STEPS TO HEAVEN	15
64	CBS (S)BPG 62327	SKETCHES OF SPAIN (reissue)	12
64	CBS (S)BPG 62213	QUIET NIGHTS	15
64	CBS (S)BPG 62306	FRIDAY NIGHT AT THE BLACKHAWK (reissue)	12
64	CBS (S)BPG 62307	SATURDAY NIGHT AT THE BLACKHAWK (reissue)	12
64	Vocalion LAEF 584	BLUE MOODS	15
64	CBS (S)BPG 62389	MILES AND MONK AT NEWPORT with Thelonious Monk)	15
64	CBS (S)BPG 62390	DAVIS IN EUROPE	15
65	Stateside SL 10111	MILES DAVIS AND JOHN COLTRANE PLAY RICHARD ROGERS (with John Coltrane)	12
65	Pacific Jazz 688 204 ZL	DAVIS AND COLTRANE PLAY RICHARD RODGERS (with John Coltrane)	15
70	CBS 66236	BITCHES BREW (2-LP)	18
71	CBS 66257	MILES DAVIS AT FILLMORE (2-LP)	18
72	CBS 64575	LIVE-EVIL (2-LP)	18
72	Prestige PR 24001	MILES DAVIS (2-LP)	18
72	Prestige PR 24012	TALLEST TREES (2-LP)	18
73	CBS CQ 30997/Q 66236	BITCHES BREW (2-LP, quadrophonic)	20
73	CBS GQ 30954/Q 67219	LIVE-EVIL (2-LP, quadrophonic)	20
74	Prestige PR 24034	WORKIN' & STEAMIN' (2-LP)	18

MILES DAVIS/ART BLAKEY

66	Fontana FJL 135	L'ASCENSEUR POUR L'ECHAFAUD/LA FEMME DISPARAISSANTE (LP, soundtrack, 1 side each)	45

(see also Art Blakey, Thelonious Monk, Dizzy Gillespie, Milt Jackson, Cannonball Adderley, Charlie Parker)

MINT VALUE £

MILES DAVIS & JOHN COLTRANE

(see under Miles Davis, John Coltrane)

SAMMY DAVIS (Jnr.)

Year	Label/Cat. No.	Title	£
54	Brunswick 05326	Because Of You (Parts 1 & 2)	10
55	Brunswick 05383	The Birth Of The Blues/Love (Your Magic Spell Is Everywhere)	12
55	Brunswick 05389	Six Bridges To Cross/Glad To Be Unhappy	10
55	Brunswick 05409	And This Is My Beloved/The Red Grapes	7
55	Brunswick 05428	Love Me Or Leave Me/Something's Gotta Give	15
55	Brunswick 05450	That Old Black Magic/Give A Fool A Chance	12
55	Brunswick 05469	Hey There/My Funny Valentine	12
55	Brunswick 05478	Backtrack/It's Bigger Than You And Me	6
56	Brunswick 05518	In A Persian Market/The Man With The Golden Arm	8
56	Capitol CL 14562	Azure/Dedicated To You	6
56	Brunswick 05583	Adelaide/I'll Know	6
56	Brunswick 05594	Earthbound/Five	6
56	Brunswick 05611	Frankie And Johnny/Circus	6
56	Brunswick 05617	You're Sensational/Don't Let Her Go	6
56	Brunswick 05629	All Of You/Just One Of Those Things	12
57	Brunswick 05637	The Golden Key/All About Love	6
57	Brunswick 05647	Dangerous/The World Is Mine Tonight	6
57	Brunswick 05668	Too Close For Comfort/Jacques D'Iraque	6
57	Brunswick 05694	Goodbye, So Long, I'm Gone/French Fried Potatoes And Ketchup	6
57	Brunswick 05717	Mad Ball/The Nearness Of You	6
57	Brunswick 05724	Long Before I Knew You/Never Like This	6
58	Brunswick 05732	I'm Comin' Home/Hallelujah, I Love Her	6
59	Brunswick 05778	That's Anna/I Never Got Out Of Paris (78)	7
60	Brunswick 05830	Happy To Make Your Acquaintance/Baby, It's Cold Outside (with Carmen McRae)	6
64	Reprise R 20227	The Shelter Of Your Arms/Falling In Love With You	6
64	Reprise R 20289	Not For Me/Bang Bang	8
69	MCA MK 5016	Rhythm Of Life/Pompeii Club/Rich Man's Frug	15
76	20th Century BTC 2292	Baretta's Theme/I Heard A Song	6
50	Brunswick OE 9445	BOY MEETS GIRL (EP, with Carmen McRae)	8
56	Capitol EAP1 555	SAMMY DAVIS JNR. (EP)	8
56	Brunswick LAT 8088	JUST FOR LOVERS (LP)	15
56	Brunswick LAT 8153	STARRING SAMMY DAVIS (LP)	15
57	Brunswick LAT 8157	HE'S LOOKING AT YOU (LP)	12
57	Brunswick LAT 8215	SAMMY SWINGS (LP)	12
58	Brunswick LAT 8248	IT'S ALL OVER BUT THE SWINGIN' (LP)	12
59	Brunswick LAT 8296	SAMMY AT THE TOWN HALL, NEW YORK (LP, also stereo STA 3012)	12/15
59	Brunswick LAT 8308	PORGY AND BESS (LP, with Carmen McRae, also stereo STA 3017)	12/15
60	Brunswick LAT 8330	SAMMY AWARDS (LP)	12
60	Brunswick LAT 8352	I GOTTA RIGHT TO SWING (LP)	12
64	Reprise R 6126/R(9) 6126	CALIFORNIA SUITE (LP)	12
66	Reprise RLP/RSLP 6214	SOUNDS OF '66 (LP)	12
70	Tamla Motown STML 11160	SOMETHING FOR EVERYONE (LP)	22

(see also Dean Martin)

SILKIE DAVIS

Year	Label/Cat. No.	Title	£
70	Torpedo TOR 2	Conversations/TWINKLE: Peace & Tranquility	5
70	Torpedo TOR 12	When I Was A Little Girl/I'm So Lonely	5

SKEETER DAVIS

Year	Label/Cat. No.	Title	£
60	RCA Victor RCA 1201	No Never/(I Can't Help You) I'm Falling Too	8
61	RCA Victor RCA 1222	My Last Date With You/Someone I'd Like To Forget	6
63	RCA Victor RCA 1328	The End Of The World/Somebody Loves You	8
63	RCA Victor RCA 1345	I'm Saving My Love/Somebody Else On Your Mind	6
63	RCA Victor RCA 1363	I Can't Stay Mad At You/It Was Only My Heart	10
64	RCA Victor RCA 1384	He Says The Same Things To Me/How Much	6
64	RCA Victor RCA 1398	Now You're Gone/Gonna Get Along Without You Now	6
65	RCA Victor RCA 1474	Sun Glasses/He Loved Me Too Little	6
64	RCA Victor RCX 7153	SILVER THREADS AND GOLDEN NEEDLES (EP)	22
63	RCA Victor RD/SF 7563	THE END OF THE WORLD (LP, mono/stereo)	25/30
63	RCA Victor RD/SF 7604	CLOUDY, WITH OCCASIONAL TEARS (LP, mono/stereo)	20/25
64	RCA Victor RD 7676	LET ME GET CLOSE TO YOU (LP)	20
69	RCA Victor SF 8068	MARY FRANCES (LP)	20

SKEETER DAVIS & BOBBY BARE

Year	Label/Cat. No.	Title	£
65	RCA RD 7711	TUNES FOR TWO (LP)	20

(see also Bobby Bare)

SMILEY DAVIS

Year	Label/Cat. No.	Title	£
53	London L 1189	Big Mamou/Play Girl (78, actually by Smiley Lewis)	130

SPENCER DAVIS (GROUP)

Year	Label/Cat. No.	Title	£
64	Fontana TF 471	Dimples/Sittin' And Thinkin'	30
64	Fontana TF 499	I Can't Stand It/Midnight Train	25
65	Fontana TF 530	Every Little Bit Hurts/It Hurts Me So	15
65	Fontana TF 571	Strong Love/This Hammer	15
65	Fontana TF 632	Keep On Running/High Time Baby	7
66	Fontana TF 679	Somebody Help Me/Stevie's Blues	7
66	Fontana TF 739	When I Come Home/Trampoline	7
66	Fontana TF 762	Gimme Some Loving/Blues In F	7
67	Fontana TF 785	I'm A Man/I Can't Get Enough Of It	12
67	Fontana TF 854	Time Seller/Don't Want You No More	10
67	United Artists UP 1203	Mr. Second Class/Sanity Inspector	6
68	United Artists UP 2213	After Tea/Moonshine	6
68	United Artists UP 2226	Short Change/Picture Of Heaven	8
73	Vertigo 6059 087	Livin' In A Back Street/Sure Need A Helping Hand	6

65	Fontana TE 17444	YOU PUT THE HURT ON ME (EP)	25
65	Fontana TE 17450	EVERY LITTLE BIT HURTS (EP)	30
66	Fontana TE 17463	SITTIN' AND THINKIN' (EP)	35
65	Fontana TL 5242	THEIR FIRST LP (LP)	45
66	Fontana TL 5295	THE SECOND ALBUM (LP)	45
66	Fontana TL 5359	AUTUMN '66 (LP)	45
67	Fontana TL 5443	THE BEST OF THE SPENCER DAVIS GROUP (LP, unissued)	
67	United Artists (S)ULP 1186	HERE WE GO ROUND THE MULBERRY BUSH (LP, soundtrack, with Traffic, mono/stereo)	35/30
68	United Artists (S)ULP 1192	WITH THEIR NEW FACE ON (LP, mono/stereo)	30/25
68	Wing WL 1165	EVERY LITTLE BIT HURTS (LP, reissue of "Their First LP")	15
68	Island ILP 970/ILPS 9070	THE BEST OF THE SPENCER DAVIS GROUP FEATURING STEVIE WINWOOD (LP, plain pink label, flipback sleeve; sleeve lists "Please Do Something" but plays "Together Till The End Of Time"; mono/stereo)	20/15
69	CBS 63842	LETTERS FROM EDITH (LP, unissued, 50 white label test pressings only)	200+
71	United Artists UAS 29177	IT'S BEEN SO LONG (LP, solo with Peter Jameson, 'envelope' cover)	12
72	United Artists UAS 29361	MOUSETRAP (LP, solo)	12
73	Vertigo 6360 088	GLUGGO (LP, gatefold sleeve)	12
74	Vertigo 6360 105	LIVIN' IN A BACK STREET (LP)	12
88	Island ILPS/CID 9919	STEVIE WINWOOD: THE SPENCER DAVIS GROUP YEARS (LP & CD, unissued)	

(see also Stevie Winwood, Traffic, Anglos, Blind Faith, Ray Fenwick, Pete York, Hardin & York, Murgatroyd Band, Mirage, Portobello Explosion, Shotgun Express)

STEVE DAVIS

68	Fontana TF 922	Takes Time To Know Her/She Said Yeah	50

TYRONE DAVIS

68	Stateside SS 2092	What If A Man/Bet You Win	18
69	Atlantic 584 253	Can I Change My Mind/A Woman Needs To Be Loved	12
69	Atlantic 584 265	Is It Something You've Got?/Undying Love	12
69	Atlantic 584 288	All The Waiting Is Not In Vain/Need Your Lovin' Everyday	12
70	Atlantic 2091 003	Turn Back The Hands Of Time/I Keep Coming Back	15
71	Atlantic 2091 078	Could I Forget You/Just My Way Of Loving You	10
71	Atlantic 2091 131	One Way Ticket/We Got A Love	10
72	Atlantic K 10207	Can I Change My Mind/Turn Back The Hands Of Time/One Way Ticket	8
73	Brunswick BR 4	Without You In My Life/How Could I Forget You	10
73	Brunswick BR 6	There It Is/You Wouldn't Believe	10
74	Brunswick BR 10	I Wish It Was Me/You Don't Have To Beg To Stay	10
76	Brunswick BR 31	Turning Point/Don't Let It Be Too Late	10
77	Brunswick BR 40	Ever Lovin' Girl/Forever	10
70	Atlantic 588 209	CAN I CHANGE MY MIND (LP)	30
71	Atlantic 2465 021	TURN BACK THE HANDS OF TIME (LP)	25
73	Brunswick BRLS 3002	I HAD IT ALL THE TIME (LP)	25
73	Brunswick BRLS 3005	GREATEST HITS (LP)	18

WALTER DAVIS

64	RCA RCX 7169	R.C.A. VICTOR RACE SERIES VOL. 3 (EP)	20
70	RCA Intl. INTS 1085	THINK YOU NEED A SHOT (LP)	20

WARREN DAVIS MONDAY BAND

67	Columbia DB 8190	Wait For Me/I Don't Wanna Hurt You	18
67	Columbia DB 8270	Love Is A Hurtin' Thing/Without Fear	15

(see also Boardwalkers)

DAVIS SISTERS

53	HMV B 10582	Rock-A-Bye Boogie/I Forgot More Than You'll Ever Know (78)	15

BRIAN DAVISON

70	Charisma CAS 1021	BRIAN DAVISON'S EVERY WHICH WAY (LP, pink label)	12

(see also Habits, Nice, Every Which Way)

WILD BILL DAVISON

55	Melodisc MLP 501	WILD BILL DAVISON (LP)	15

TIM DAWE

69	Straight ST(S) 1058	PENROD (LP)	25

CARL DAWKINS

67	Rio R 136	All Of A Sudden/Running Shoes	15
67	Rio R 137	Baby I Love You/Hard Time	15
68	Blue Cat BS 114	I Love The Way You Are/DERMOTT LYNCH: I Can't Stand It	15
68	Duke DU 3	I'll Make It Up/J.J. ALL STARS: One Dollar Of Music	10
69	Nu Beat NB 030	Rodney's History/DYNAMITES: Tribute To Drumbage	10
70	Duke DU 93	Get Together/FAMILY MAN: Instalment Plan	10
70	Duke DU 95	This Land/J.J. ALL STARS: Land Version	10
70	Trojan TR 7765	Satisfaction/Things A Get Bad To Worse	7
71	Big Shot BI 570	Perseverence/J.J. ALL STARS: Perseverence (Version)	15
71	Explosion EX 2051	I Feel Good/J.J. ALL STARS: I Feel Good Version Two	6
71	Explosion EX 2059	Make It Great/STONE: What A Day	6
71	New Beat NB 086	Walk A Little Prouder/YOUTH PROFESSIONALS: Walk (Version)	6
72	Duke DU 133	My Whole World/Men A Broken Heart	6

(see also Rass Dawkins, Untouchables, Winston Wright, Ansell Collins, Roland Alphonso, West Indians)

HORRELL DAWKINS

66	Ska Beat JB 240	Cling To Me/Butterfly	22

JIMMY DAWKINS

73	Mojo 2027 011	The Things I Used To Do/Put It On The Hawg	8
71	Delmark DS 623	FAST FINGERS (LP)	20
78	Sonet SNTF 758	TRANSATLANTIC 770 (LP)	15

MINT VALUE £

RASS DAWKINS (& WAILERS)
71 Upsetter US 368 Picture On The Wall/UPSETTERS: Picture Version 22
(see also Bob Marley/Wailers, Carl Dawkins)

JULIE DAWN
53 Columbia SCM 5035 Wild Horses/A Whistling Kettle And A Dancing Cat 10
(see also Tony Brent & Julie Dawn, Cyril Stapleton)

DAWN & DEEJAYS
65 RCA RCA 1470 These Are The Things About You/I Will Think Of You 10

DAWNBREAKERS
65 Decca F 12110 Let's Live/Lovin' For You 10

DAWN CHORUS
69 MCA MK 5004 A Night To Be Remembered/Crying All Night 8
(see also Carter-Lewis)

DAWN CHORUS
85 Dawn DAWN 1 Teenage Kicks/Dream Lover (p/s) 12

DAWN TRADER
80 AFE 1980 NO ONE GONNA BETTER ME (EP, private pressing) 60

DAWNWATCHER
80 Dawnwatcher DWS 001 Spellbound 150
82 Dawnwatcher DWS 002 Backlash (p/s) 30

DAWNWIND
76 Amron ARN 5003 LOOKING BACK ON THE FUTURE (LP, private pressing) 100

DONNA DAWSON
73 Trojan TR 7892 You Can't Buy Me Love/First Cut Is The Deepest 6

LES DAWSON SYNDICATE
(see under Johnny Stevens and Les Dawson Syndicate)

LESLEY DAWSON
66 Mercury MF 924 Pastel Shades Of Love/The Time Has Come 6
67 Mercury MF 946 Just Say Goodbye/Just A Passing Phase 8
67 Mercury MF 965 Run For Shelter/I'll Climb On A Rainbow 15

DANIELLE DAX
83 Initial IRC 009 POP-EYES (LP, with 'Meat Harvest' cover & lyric sheet) 20
(see also Lemon Kittens)

DAY
94 Detour DR 019 Another Country/Gospel (p/s, 100 on green vinyl) 7

BING DAY
59 Mercury AMT 1047 I Can't Help It/Mama's Place 110

BOBBY DAY (& SATELLITES)
57 HMV POP 425 Little Bitty Pretty One/When The Swallows Come Back To Capistrano (as Bobby Day & Satellites) 165
57 HMV POP 425 Little Bitty Pretty One/When The Swallows Come Back To Capistrano (78) 25
58 London HL 8726 Rockin' Robin/Over And Over 22
58 London HL 8726 Rockin' Robin/Over And Over (78) 20
59 London HL 8800 The Bluebird, The Buzzard And The Oriole/Alone Too Long 50
59 London HL 8800 The Bluebird, The Buzzard And The Oriole/Alone Too Long (78) 35
59 London HL 8964 Love Is A One Time Affair/Ain't Gonna Cry No More 22
59 London HL 8964 Love Is A One Time Affair/Ain't Gonna Cry No More (78) 30
60 London HLY 9044 My Blue Heaven/I Don't Want To 22
61 Top Rank JAR 538 Over And Over/Gee Whiz 15
65 Sue WI 388 Rockin' Robin/Over And Over (reissue) 25

DORIS DAY

78s
59 Philips PB 923 Be Prepared/It Happened To Jane 8
59 Philips PB 949 The Tunnel Of Love/Run Away, Skidaddle, Skidoo 10
59 Philips PB 958 Possess Me/Roly Poly 10

SINGLES
53 Columbia SCM 5038 April In Paris/Your Mother And Mine (with Four Lads) 25
53 Columbia SCM 5039 That's What Makes Paris Paree/I Know A Place 25
53 Columbia SCM 5044 A Bushel And A Peck/If I Were A Bell 25
53 Columbia SCM 5045 The Second Star To The Right (with Four Lads)/ I'm Gonna Ring The Bell Tonight 25
53 Columbia SCM 5059 The Cherries/Papa, Won't You Dance With Me? 25
53 Columbia SCM 5062 Mister Tap-Toe/Why Should We Both Be Lonely? 25
53 Columbia SCM 5067 We Kiss In A Shadow/Something Wonderful 25
53 Columbia SCM 5075 That's The Way He Does It/Cuddle Up A Little Closer 25
54 Columbia SCM 5087 A Load Of Hay/It Had To Be You 25
55 Columbia SCM 5171 Just One Of Those Things/Sometimes I'm Happy 20
57 Philips JK 1020 Twelve O'Clock Tonight/Today Will Be Yesterday Tomorrow! (jukebox issue) 25
57 Philips JK 1031 The Party's Over/Rickety-Rackety Rendezvous (jukebox issue) 20
58 Philips PB 799 A Very Precious Love/Teacher's Pet 6
58 Philips PB 843 Everybody Loves A Lover/Instant Love 6
58 Philips PB 863 Love In A Home/Blues In The Night 6
59 Philips PB 910 Love Me In The Daytime/He's So Married 6
59 Philips PB 923 Be Prepared/It Happened To Jane 6
59 Philips PB 949 The Tunnel Of Love/Run Away, Skidaddle, Skidoo 6
59 Philips PB 958 Possess Me/Roly Poly 6
64 CBS AAG 183 Move Over Darling/Twinkle Lullaby 8
64 CBS AAG 219 Oowee Baby/The Rainbow's End 15

MINT VALUE £

64 CBS AAG 231 — Send Me No Flowers/Love Him . . . 6
65 CBS 201808 — Catch The Bouquet/Summer Has Gone . . . 6
65 CBS 201898 — Do Not Disturb/Au Revoir Is Goodbye With A Smile . . . 6
66 CBS 202229 — Glass Bottomed Boat/Soft As The Starlight . . . 6

EPs

54 Columbia SEG 7507 — CANADIAN CAPERS (company sleeve) . . . 12
54 Columbia SEG 7515 — WE KISS IN A SHADOW (company sleeve) . . . 12
54 Columbia SEG 7531 — NOBODY'S SWEETHEART (company sleeve) . . . 12
54 Columbia SEG 7546 — SOMETIMES I'M HAPPY (company sleeve) . . . 12
55 Columbia SEG 7572 — VOCAL GEMS FROM THE FILM "YOUNG MAN OF MUSIC" . . . 12
55 Philips BBE 12007 — DORIS DAY . . . 15
55 Philips BBE 12011 — I'LL NEVER STOP LOVING YOU . . . 15
56 Philips BBE 12089 — DORIS DAY NO. 2 . . . 15
57 Philips BBE 12151 — DAY DREAMS . . . 15
58 Philips BBE 12167 — DORIS . . . 15
58 Philips BBE 12187 — THE SONG IS YOU . . . 15
58 Philips BBE 12213 — DREAM A LITTLE DREAM OF ME . . . 15
59 Philips BBE 12298 — LET'S FLY AWAY (also stereo SBBE 9006) . . . 15/18
59 Philips BBE 12339 — PILLOW TALK . . . 12
60 Philips BBE 12388 — YOU CAN'T HAVE EVERYTHING (also stereo SBBE 9021) . . . 15/18
61 Philips SBBE 9034 — SHOW TIME NO. 1 (stereo) . . . 15
62 CBS AGG 20009 — I HAVE DREAMED . . . 12
62 CBS AGG 20018 — DUET (with André Previn Trio) . . . 10
63 CBS AGG 20029 — DUET NO. 2 (with André Previn Trio) . . . 10
64 CBS AGG 20048 — MOVE OVER DARLING . . . 10

LPs

54 Columbia 33S 1038 — LULLABY OF BROADWAY (10", 2 different sleeve designs) . . . each 30
54 Philips BBR 8026 — THE VOICE OF YOUR CHOICE (10") . . . 20
55 Philips BBR 8040 — YOUNG AT HEART (10", with Frank Sinatra) . . . 25
55 Philips BBL 7047 — LOVE ME OR LEAVE ME . . . 30
56 Philips BBR 8094 — DORIS DAY FAVOURITES (10") . . . 20
56 Philips BBR 8104 — CALAMITY JANE (10", with Howard Keel) . . . 20
57 Philips BBL 7120 — DAY DREAMS . . . 25
57 Philips BBL 7137 — DORIS AND FRANK (6 tracks each by Doris Day & Frank Sinatra) . . . 25
57 Philips BBL 7142 — DAY BY DAY . . . 30
58 Philips BBL 7175 — DAY IN HOLLYWOOD . . . 22
58 Philips BBL 7197 — THE PYJAMA GAME (with other artists, 5 tracks by Doris Day) . . . 15
58 Philips BBL 7211 — DAY BY NIGHT . . . 30
58 Philips BBL 7247 — HOORAY FOR HOLLYWOOD VOL. 1 . . . 25
58 Philips BBL 7248 — HOORAY FOR HOLLYWOOD VOL. 2 . . . 20
59 Philips BBL 7296 — CUTTIN' CAPERS (also stereo SBBL 540) . . . 18/22
59 Philips BBL 7297 — SHOWCASE OF HITS . . . 15
59 Philips SBBL 519 — HOORAY FOR HOLLYWOOD (stereo reissue) . . . 22
59 Philips SBBL 548 — DAY BY NIGHT (stereo reissue) . . . 22
60 Philips BBL 7377 — WHAT EVERY GIRL SHOULD KNOW (also stereo SBBL 563) . . . 15/18
60 Philips SBBL 537 — IN THE STILL OF THE NIGHT . . . 20
60 Philips BBL 7392 — SHOW TIME (also stereo SBBL 577) . . . 15/18
61 Philips BBL 7471 — BRIGHT AND SHINY (also stereo SBBL 619) . . . 25/30
61 Philips BBL 7496 — I HAVE DREAMED (also stereo SBBL 643) . . . 25/30
62 CBS (S)BPG 62053 — BRIGHT AND SHINY (reissue, mono/stereo) . . . 12/15
62 CBS (S)BPG 62057 — I HAVE DREAMED (reissue, mono/stereo) . . . 12/15
62 CBS (S)BPG 62010 — DUET (with André Previn Trio, mono/stereo) . . . 14/16
63 CBS (S)BPG 62101 — YOU'LL NEVER WALK ALONE (mono/stereo) . . . 25/30
63 CBS (S)BPG 62129 — ANNIE GET YOUR GUN (with Robert Goulet, mono/stereo) . . . 14/16
64 CBS (S)BPG 62226 — LOVE HIM (mono/stereo) . . . 25/30
65 CBS (S)BPG 62461 — WITH A SMILE AND A SONG . . . 25
65 CBS (S)BPG 62502 — LATIN FOR LOVERS . . . 18
66 CBS (S)BPG 62562 — SENTIMENTAL JOURNEY . . . 15
66 CBS BPG 62785 — SINGS HER GREAT MOVIE HITS . . . 15
66 CBS (S)BPG 62712 — THE DORIS DAY CHRISTMAS ALBUM . . . 15

(see also Four Lads, Frank Sinatra, Frankie Laine, Howard Keel)

DORIS DAY & JOHNNIE RAY

53 Columbia SCM 5033 — Ma Says, Pa Says/A Full Time Job . . . 30

(see also Johnnie Ray)

JACKIE DAY

67 Sue WI 4040 — Before It's Too Late/Without A Love . . . 175

JILL DAY

55 Parlophone MSP 6169 — Sincerely/Chee-Chee-Oo Chee (Sang The Little Bird) . . . 18
55 Parlophone MSP 6177 — Promises/Whistlin' Willie . . . 15
56 HMV 7M 362 — I Hear You Knocking/Far Away From Everybody . . . 20
56 HMV 7M 391 — A Tear Fell/Holiday Affair . . . 15
56 HMV POP 254 — Happiness Street (Corner Sunshine Square)/Somewhere In The Great Beyond . . 10
57 HMV POP 288 — I Dreamed/Give Her My Love When You See Her . . . 10
57 HMV POP 320 — Mangos/Cinco Robles (Five Oaks) . . . 10

KENNY DAY

60 Top Rank JAR 339 — Teenage Sonata/My Love Doesn't Love Me At All (some with p/s) . . . 10/6
61 Top Rank JAR 400 — Why Don't We Do This More Often/The Sheik Of Morocco (some with p/s) . . . 10/6

MURIEL DAY

69 CBS 4115 — The Wages Of Love/Thinking Of You . . . 12
69 Page One POF 151 — Optimistic Fool/Nine Times Out Of Ten . . . 25

TANYA DAY & NU-NOTES

64 Polydor NH 52331 — His Lips Get In The Way/I Get So Lonely . . . 6

MINT VALUE £

TERRY DAY

62	CBS AAG 104	That's All I Want/I Waited Too Long	18

(see also Rip-Chords, Rogues)

DAY BROTHERS

60	Oriole CB 1575	Angel/Just One More Kiss	18

JOHNNY DAYE

69	Stax STAX 111	Stay Baby Stay/I Love Love	6

DAYLIGHT

71	RCA RCA 2106	Lady Of St. Clare/Wednesday People	10
71	RCA SF 8194	DAYLIGHT (LP)	45

(see also Daddy Longlegs)

DAYLIGHTERS

64	Sue WI 343	Oh Mom! (Teach Me How To Uncle Willie)/Hard-Headed Girl	35

DAY OF THE PHOENIX

70	Greenwich GLSPR 1002	WIDE OPEN N-WAY (LP)	30
72	Chapter One CNSR 812	THE NEIGHBOUR'S SON (LP)	40

DAYTRIPPERS

71	Trojan TR 7839	The Birds And The Bees/My Family	5

DAYTON

83	Capitol 12 CL 318	The Sound Of Music/Eyes On You/Love You Anyway (12", p/s)	8
83	Capitol EST 712 2971	FEEL THE MUSIC (LP)	20

DAZZLE

75	DJM DJS 384	Jim'll Fix It/Leave It Up To Jim	6

DBX

93	Peacefrog PF 015	ALIEN EP (12", plain sleeve)	20
94	Peacefrog PF 022	Losing Control/Beat Phreak/Live Wire/Spock's Brain (12", plain sleeve)	30
95	Peacefrog PR 025	LOSING CONTROL REMIXES (12", plain sleeve)	25

D.C. 10's

80	Certain Euphoria ACE 451	Bermuda/I Can See Through Walls	10

BOBBY DEACON

60	Pye 7N 15270	Fool Was I/Where's My Love	18
60	Pye 7N 15299	I Love You So/Your Kisses Are Fine	15

GEORGE DEACON & MARION ROSS

73	Xtra XTRA 1130	SWEET WILLIAM'S GHOST (LP, with lyric insert)	150

DEACON BLUE

88	CBS CD DEAC 5	When Will You (Make My Telephone Ring) (Remix)/That Brilliant Feeling No. 2/ Punch And Judy Man/Disney World (CD, card sleeve)	10
88	CBS CP DEAC 5	When Will You (Make My Telephone Ring)/That Brilliant Feeling No. 2/ Punch And Judy Man/Disney World (CD, picture disc)	8
88	CBS 450 549-0	RAINTOWN (LP, with bonus LP "Riches" [XPR 1361] & sticker)	15
88	CBS XPR 1361	RICHES (LP, white embossed sleeve, available separately via fan club)	12

(see also Ricky Ross)

DEADBEATS

80	Red Rhino RED 3	Choose You/Julie's New Boyfriend (p/s)	8

DEAD BOYS

77	Sire SRE 1004	Sonic Reducer/Down In Flames (no p/s)	25
77	Sire 6078 609	Sonic Reducer/Little Girl/Down In Flames (12", p/s)	15
78	Sire SRE 1029	Tell Me/Not Anymore/Ain't Nothin' To Do (p/s)	25
77	Sire 9103 329	YOUNG, LOUD & SNOTTY (LP)	25
78	Sire SRK 6054	WE HAVE COME FOR YOUR CHILDREN (LP)	15
87	Line LILP 400200	NIGHT OF THE LIVING DEAD BOYS (LP)	15

(see also Stiv Bators, Lords Of The New Church, Wanderers)

DEAD ELVIS

95	Concrete HARD 612	Opium Shuffle (Skank Mix)/(Dead Elvis Mix) (12", p/s)	15

(see also Death In Vegas)

DEAD KENNEDYS

80	Fast Products FAST 12	California Uber Alles/Man With The Dogs (p/s, moulded or paper labels)	5
81	Statik STAT EP 2	IN GOD WE TRUST (12" EP, with insert)	8
81	Cherry Red CHERRY 13	Holiday In Cambodia/Police Truck ('digger' p/s)	5
81	Cherry Red CHERRY 13	Holiday In Cambodia/Police Truck ('burning man' p/s, with lyric sheet)	6
81	Cherry CHERRY 16	Kill The Poor/In-Sight (p/s, with badge)	5
81	Cherry CHERRY 24	Too Drunk To Fuck/The Prey (p/s, with lyric sheet)	5
82	Statik STAT 24	Nazi Punks Fuck Off/Moral Majority (p/s)	5
81	Cherry Red B RED 10	FRESH FRUIT FOR ROTTING VEGETABLES (LP, with insert & 'Heads' pic on rear)	18
87	Alternative Tent. VIRUS 57	GIVE ME CONVENIENCE... (LP, with "Buzzbomb From Pasadena" flexidisc)	15

(see also East Bay Ray, Lard)

DEADLY TOYS

79	Bonhard/Hunt DT 1	Nice Weather/Roll On Doomsday/I'm Logical/Deadly Mess Around (EP, some in hand made gatefold sleeve)	25

DEAD MAN'S SHADOW

80	Hog HOG 1	Neighbours/Poxy Politics/War Ploys/Morons (p/s)	5
81	Subversive ANARCHO 1	HEATHROW TOUCHDOWN (EP, 1 side by Action Pact)	6
82	Rondelet ROUND 16	BOMB SCARE (EP)	6
84	Criminal Damage CRILP 110	TO MOHAMMED ... A MOUNTAIN (LP)	12

MINT VALUE £

DEAD OR ALIVE

80 Inevitable INEV 005 I'm Falling/Flowers (foldout p/s) . . . 12
81 Inevitable INEV 008 Number Eleven/Name Game (live) (p/s) . . . 8
82 Black Eyes BE 1 It's Been Hours Now/Whirlpool/Nowhere To Nowhere/ It's Been Hours Now (Alternative Mix) (12", p/s) . . . 15
82 Black Eyes BE 2 The Stranger/Some Of That (p/s) . . . 8
83 Epic A 3399 Misty Circles/Misty Circles (Instrumental) (p/s) . . . 6
83 Epic TA 3399 Misty Circles (Dance Mix)/Misty Circles (Dub Mix)/Selfish Side (12", p/s) . . . 10
83 Epic A 3676 What I Want/The Stranger (Remix) (white 'floppy hat' p/s, withdrawn) . . . 25
83 Epic A 3676 What I Want/The Stranger (black p/s) . . . 6
83 Epic TA 3676 What I Want (Dance Mix)/The Stranger (12", p/s, some with poster) . . . 15/8
84 Epic A 4069 I'd Do Anything/Anything (Dub) (p/s) . . . 5
84 Epic QA 4069 I'd Do Anything/Anything (Dub)/Give It To Me (10", p/s) . . . 10
84 Epic TA 4069 I'd Do Anything/Misty Circles/What I Want/Give It To Me (12", p/s) . . . 10
84 Epic WA 4271 That's The Way (I Like It)/Keep That Body Strong (That's The Way) (picture disc) . . 6
84 Epic TA 4271 That's The Way (I Like It) (Extended Version)/Keep That Body Strong (That's The Way) (12", p/s) . . . 8
84 Epic A 4510 What I Want (Remix)/The Stranger (poster p/s) . . . 10
84 Epic TA 4510 What I Want (Dance Mix)/The Stranger (12", p/s, some with poster) . . . 10/8
84 Epic XPR 1257 MIGHTY MIX: Wish You Were Here/What I Want/Do It/Misty Circles/ Absolutely Nothing/Sit On It/You Make Me Wanna/That's The Way (I Like It) (12", white label, promo only) . . . 12
84 Epic You Spin Me Round (Big Ben Mix) (1-sided, stickered p/s, promo only) . . . 15
84 Epic TX 4861/TA 4510 You Spin Me Round (Like A Record) (Murder Mix)/Misty Circles (Extended Mix)// What I Want (Dance Mix)/The Stranger (12", p/s, double pack, shrinkwrapped) . . . 15
85 Epic A 6086 Lover Come Back To Me/Far Too Hard (blue p/s, withdrawn) . . . 60
85 Epic WA 6086 Lover Come Back To Me/Far Too Hard (fan-shaped picture disc with plinth) . . . 10
85 Epic QTA 6086 Lover Come Back To Me (Extended Remix)/Far Too Hard (12", poster p/s) . . . 15
87 Epic XPR 1328 CLEAN AND DIRTY: Something In My House (Mortevicar Mix)/ Something In My House (Naughty XXX Mix) (12", white label, plain white sleeve) . . . 50
88 Epic BURNSQ 4 Turn Around And Count 2 Ten (I Had A Disco Dream Mix)/Something In My House (Instru-Mental)/Then There Was You/Come Inside (12", p/s) . . . 18
88 Epic BURNSC 4 Turn Around And Count 2 Ten/Something In My House (Instru-Mental)/ Turn Around And Count 2 Ten (I Love BPM Mix)/ (Instru-Mental) (CD, picture disc) . . . 18
89 Epic BURNSC 5 Come Home With Me Baby (Remix)/Come Home With Me Baby (12" Version)/ (Deadhouse Dub 12") (CD) . . . 10

(see also Nightmares In Wax, Sisters Of Mercy, Pauline Murray & Invisible Girls, International Chrysis, Mission)

DEAD SEA FRUIT

67 Camp 602 001 Kensington High Street/Put Another Record On . . . 12
68 Camp 602 004 Love At The Hippiedrome/My Naughty Bluebell . . . 12
67 Camp 603 001 DEAD SEA FRUIT (LP) . . . 90

DEAD WRETCHED

82 Inferno HELL 2 NO HOPE FOR ANYONE (EP) . . . 40
82 Inferno HELL 5 Convicted/Infiltrator (p/s) . . . 10

BILL DEAL & RHONDELLS

69 MGM MGM 1466 May I/Day By Day My Love Grows Stronger . . . 5
69 MGM MGM 1479 I've Been Hurt/I've Got My Needs . . . 8
69 MGM MGM 1488 What Kind Of Fool Do You Think I Am/Are You Ready For This . . . 5

DEALER

83 Windrush WR 1030 Better Things To Do/Suspected Foul Play (p/s) . . . 120
86 Ebony EBON 42 FIRST STRIKE (LP) . . . 12

ALAN DEAN

55 MGM SP 1116 The Song From "Desiree"/Tonight, My Love . . . 6
55 MGM SP 1139 Remember Me, Wherever You Go/Love Is All That Matters . . . 6
56 MGM SP 1173 Without You/Take A Bow . . . 6
57 Columbia DB 3932 Rock 'n' Roll Tarantella/Life Is But A Dream . . . 20
57 Columbia DB 3932 Rock 'n' Roll Tarantella/Life Is But A Dream (78) . . . 8

ALAN DEAN & HIS PROBLEMS

64 Decca F 11947 The Time It Takes/Dizzy Heights . . . 18
65 Pye 7N 15749 Thunder And Rain/As Time Goes By . . . 60

LITTLE BILLY DEAN

67 Strike JH 325 That's Always Like You/Tic Toc . . . 25

BOBBY DEAN

65 Parlophone R 5254 More And More/Saint James' Infirmiary . . . 8

DEREK DEAN & FRESHMEN

66 Pye 7N 17037 So This Is Love/King Cole Yenka . . . 8

(see also Derek & Freshmen)

ELTON DEAN

71 CBS 64539 ELTON DEAN (LP) . . . 45
77 Ogun OG 610 THE CHEQUE IS IN THE MAIL (LP, with Joe Gallivan & Kenny Wheeler) . . . 15

(see also Bluesology, Soft Machine, Centipede, Ninesense, Julie Tippetts, Hugh Hopper, Mike Hugg, Reg King, Keith Tippett)

EMIL DEAN

68 Island WIP 6033 This Is Our Anniversary/Lonely Boy . . . 6

(see also Nirvana [UK])

MINT VALUE £

HAZELL DEAN

Year	Label/Cat. No.	Title	£
75	Decca F 13613	Our Day Will Come/Instrumental	12
76	Decca F 13668	Got You Where I Want You/You Were There	12
77	Decca F 13683	Look What I've Found At The End Of A Rainbow/Where Are We Going	12
77	Decca F 13736	No One's Ever Gonna Love You (The Way That I Love You)/ Just One More Time	12
77	Decca F 13751	Who Was That Lady (I Saw You With)/One Bad Mistake	12
83	Proto ENATX 109	Searchin' (Megamix)/Searchin' (Nightclubbing Mix) (12")	18
83	Proto ENATX 109	Searchin' (Megamix)/Searchin' (Nightclubbing Mix) (12", blue vinyl)	25
84	Proto ENAT 109	Searchin' (Original Version)/Searchin' (US Megamix) (12", red vinyl, p/s)	12
84	Proto ENAT 114	Evergreen/Jealous Love (12", p/s)	10
84	Proto ENAT 114	Evergreen/Jealous Love (12" green vinyl, p/s)	12
84	Proto ENAT 119	Whatever I Do (Wherever I Go)/(Dub Mix)/Young Boy In The City (12", p/s & poster)	10
85	Proto ENAP 123	No Fool (For Love)/(Instrumental) (heart-shaped picture disc)	6
85	Parlophone 12RA 6107	They Say It's Gonna Rain (Zulu Mix)/I Can't Get You Out Of My Mind (12", p/s)	10
85	Parlophone 12R 6107	They Say It's Gonna Rain (Indian Summer Mix)/I Can't Get You Out Of My Mind (12", p/s & poster)	10
86	EMI 12EMI 5560	E.S.P. (Extra Sensual Persuasion)/(Extended Dance Mix)/Image In The Mirror (Extended Mix) (12", p/s)	8
86	EMI 12EMI 5584	Stand Up (Extended Version)/Love Ends Love Parts (12", p/s)	8
86	EMI 12EMID 5584	Stand Up (Extended Version)/Love Ends Love Parts//Whatever I Do (Wherever I Go) (Extended Ver.)/Searchin' (Extended Ver.) (12" doublepack, g/fold p/s)	10
86	EMI 12EMIX 5584	Searchin'/Whatever I Do/Stand Up (High As A Kite Mix)/(Ext. Ver.) (12")	12
88	EMI 12EMIX 45	Who's Leaving Who (Mixes)/Whatever I Do (Extended Version) (12", p/s)	10
88	EMI 12EMIX 62	Maybe (We Should Call It A Day) (Extra Beat Boys Remix)/No Fool (For Love) (The Murray Mix) (12", p/s)	10
88	EMI CDEM 62	Maybe (We Should Call It A Day)/Who's Leaving Who (Bob's Tambourine Mix)/ Maybe (We Should Call It A Day) (CD)	15
88	EMI 12 EMX 71	Turn It Into Love (7" Version)/You're Too Good To Be True/Megamix (12", p/s)	10
88	EMI CDEM 71	Turn It Into Love (7" Version)/Turn It Into Love (Extended Version)/ You're Too Good To Be True (CD)	15
89	Lisson DOLEQ 12R	Love Pains (mixes)/More Than Words Can Say (12", p/s)	10
91	Lisson DOLEQ 19R	Better Off Without You/Better Off Without You (Lickin' Mix)/Are You Man Enough (12", p/s)	10
91	Lisson DOLED 19R	Better Off Without You/Better Off Without You (Lickin' Mix)/Are You Man Enough (12", p/s)	12
92	EMI 12JUN 10	Searchin' (Ian Levine Ext'd Version)/Whatever I Do (Wherever I Go) (Extended Version)/Back In My Arms (Ext'd Ver.)/No Fool For Love (Ext'd Ver.) (12")	12
81	Carlin Music Corp. CMC 100488	THE SOUND OF BACHARACH & DAVID (LP, promo only)	50
	EMI CDP 790304-2	ALWAYS (CD)	18

JIMMY DEAN

Year	Label/Cat. No.	Title	£
59	Philips PB 940	Weekend Blues/Sing Along	8
59	Philips PB 940	Weekend Blues/Sing Along (78)	8
60	Philips PB 984	There's Still Time, Brother/Thanks For The Dream	6
61	Philips PB 1187	Big Bad John/I Won't Go Hunting With You Jake	5
61	Philips PB 1210	To A Sleeping Beauty/The Cajun Queen	5
62	Philips PB 1223	Smoke Smoke (Smoke) That Cigarette/Dear Ivan	7
62	CBS AAG 107	Steel Men/Little Bitty Big John	5
62	CBS AAG 122	Little Black Book/Please Pass The Biscuits	6
61	Philips BBE 12501	JIMMY DEAN (EP)	20
66	CBS EP 6075	THE BEST OF JIMMY DEAN (EP)	20
63	CBS	PORTRAIT OF JIMMY DEAN (LP)	15
65	Fontana FJL 303	GOLDEN FAVOURITES (LP)	12

NORA DEAN

Year	Label/Cat. No.	Title	£
69	Upsetter US 322	The Same Thing You Gave To Daddy/UPSETTER PILGRIMS: A Testimony	12
70	Trojan TR 7735	Barbwire/BARONS: Calypso Mama	7
71	Randy's RAN 508	Want Man/RANDY'S ALL STARS: Man	5
71	High Note HS 050	I Must Get A Man/The Valet	5
71	Bullet BU 472	Peace Begins Within/SLICKERS: Go Back Home	8
71	Gas GAS 165	Greedy Boy/KEITH: Please Stay (B-side actually by Slim Smith)	7
72	Big Shot BI 611	Night Food Reggae/PROPHETS: Jaco	6
73	Bread BR 1117	Mama/Man A Walk And Talk	6

(see also Hugh Roy)

PAUL DEAN (& SOUL SAVAGES)

Year	Label/Cat. No.	Title	£
64	Polydor NH 59102	She Can Build A Mountain/A Day Gone By (probably unreleased)	
65	Decca F 12136	You Don't Own Me/Hole In The Head (as Paul Dean & Thoughts)	18
66	Reaction 591 002	She Can Build A Mountain/A Day Gone By (as Paul Dean & Soul Savages)	15

(see also Oscar, Thoughts)

PAULA DEAN & NYAH SHUFFLE

Year	Label/Cat. No.	Title	£
70	Joe's JRS 2	Since I Met You Baby/Jug Head	8

ROGER DEAN'S LYSIS

Year	Label/Cat. No.	Title	£
77	Mosaic GCM 762	LYSIS LIVE (LP)	12
77	Mosaic GCM 774	CYCLE (LP)	12

TERRI DEAN

Year	Label/Cat. No.	Title	£
59	Top Rank JAR 141	I'm Confessin' (That I Love You)/I Blew Out The Flame	10
59	Top Rank JAR 141	I'm Confessin' (That I Love You)/I Blew Out The Flame (78)	8
59	Top Rank JAR 179	Adonis/You Treat Me Like A Boy	10
59	Top Rank JAR 179	Adonis/You Treat Me Like A Boy (78)	8

MINT VALUE £

DEAN & JEAN

64	Stateside SS 249	Tra La La La Suzy/I Love The Summertime	20
64	Stateside SS 283	Hey Jean Hey Dean/Please Don't Tell Me How	18
64	Stateside SS 313	Thread Your Needle/I Wanna Be Loved	20

(see also Brenda Lee Jones)

DEAN & MARK

64	Hickory 45-1227	With Tears In My Eyes/Kissin' Games	12
64	Hickory 45-1249	When I Stop Dreaming/There Oughta Be A Law	12
65	Hickory 45-1294	Just A Step Away/Fallen Star	12

(see also Newbeats, Larry Henley)

JASON DEANE

66	King KG 1049	Make Believe/Don't Ever Want To See You No More	25
67	King KG 1060	Down In The Street/Ain't Got No Love	35

(see also Jason Dene)

PETER DE ANGELIS ORCHESTRA & CHORUS

58	London HL 8743	The Happy Mandolin/Holiday In Naples	6
58	London HL 8743	The Happy Mandolin/Holiday In Naples (78)	7

DEANO

65	Columbia DB 7728	Just A Child In This World/Little Miss With-It	10
66	Columbia DB 7898	Starlight, Starbright/I'm So Happy	10
66	Columbia DB 7965	Please Don't Talk To The Lifeguard/When You Wish Upon A Star	12
67	Columbia DB 8233	What's The Matter With The Matador?/Baby, Let Me Be Your Baby	10
65	Columbia SEG 8470	DEANO (EP)	35

BLOSSOM DEARIE

66	Fontana TF 719	I'm Hip/Wallflower Lonely, Cornflower Blue	6
67	Fontana TF 788	Sweet Georgie Fame/One Note Samba	8
67	Fontana TF 886	Once I Loved/Sunny	6
67	Fontana TF 934	The Music Played/Discover Who I Am	6
68	Fontana TF 986	Hey John/59th Street Bridge Song	6
67	Fontana TL 5399	SWEET BLOSSOM DEARIE (LP)	30
67	Fontana TL 5352	BLOSSOM TIME AT RONNIE'S (LP)	50
67	Fontana STL 5454	SOON IT'S GONNA RAIN (LP)	30
70	Fontana 6309 015	THAT'S THE WAY I WANT IT TO BE (LP)	35

DEARLY BELOVED

66	CBS 202398	Peep Peep Pop Pop/It Is Better	10

DEAR MR. TIME

70	Square SQ 3	Prayer For Her/Light Up A Light	12
71	Square SQA 101	GRANDFATHER (LP)	80

DEATH ADDICT

83	Stench STN 1	Killing Time/Dead And Buried (p/s)	12

DEATH CULT

83	Situation 2 SIT 29	God's Zoo/God's Zoo (These Times) (p/s)	5
83	Situation 2 SIT 29 T	God's Zoo/God's Zoo (These Times) (12", p/s)	8

(see also Cult)

DEATH IN JUNE

84	New European SA 29634	Heaven Street/We Drive East/In The Night Time (12", 2,000 with brown/gold embossed/textured sleeve, later 2,000 with blue/white sleeve)	50/40
84	New European SA 30634	State Laughter/Holy Water (p/s)	40
84	New European BADVC 6	She Said Destroy/The Calling (p/s)	25
84	New European 12BADVC 6	The Calling/She Said Destroy/Doubt To Nothing (12", p/s with insert)	40
85	New European BADVC 69	Born Again/The Calling (Mk II)/Carousel (Bolt Mix) (12", p/s)	25
85	New European BADVC 73	...And Murder Love/A.M.L. (Instrumental) (p/s)	25
85	New European 12BADVC73	Come Before Christ And Murder Love/Torture By Roses (12", p/s)	30
87	New European BADVC 10	To Drown A Rose/Zimmerit/Europa/The Gates Of Heaven (10", p/s)	20
88	Cenaz CENAZ 09	Born Again/The Calling (Mk II)/Carousel (Remix) (12" picture disc, 1st pressing with silver print & rim, 970 only; 2nd pressing bronze)	25/20
94	Twilight Command NERO I	SUNDOGS (Rose Clouds Of Holocaust/13 Years Of Carrion) (p/s with sticker)	7
92	New European BADVC 8	CATHEDRAL OF TEARS (12" EP, picture disc with sticker)	20
93	New European BADVC 63	PARADISE RISING (12" EP)	18
96	Twil. Command NERO XIII	Kapo!/Occidental Martyr (p/s)	18
85	New European BADVC 3	THE GUILTY HAVE NO PRIDE (LP)	25
80s	Leprosy UBADVC 4	BURIAL (LP, 'quilted' sleeve, brown, pink, white & other coloured vinyl)	30
90s	Leprosy UBADVC 4	BURIAL (LP, textured sleeve, various coloured vinyls)	30
92	Leprosy UBADVC 4	BURIAL (LP, standard sleeve, green vinyl)	30
85	New European BADVC 13	NADA (LP, blue or brown sleeve; also picture disc)	40/25/15
86	New European BADVC 726	LESSON ONE: MISANTHROPY (LP, embossed sleeve with insert)	20
87	New European BADVC 11	BROWN BOOK (LP, textured sleeve with inner & insert; export copies had extra inserts & postcards)	35/25
88	New European BADVC 9	THE WORLD THAT SUMMER (2-LP, gatefold textured sleeve)	30
88	New European BADVC 88	WALL OF SACRIFICE (LP, red sleeve or green/yellow sleeve)	60/40
89	New European BADVC 93	93 DEAD SUN WHEELS (mini-LP, with Current 93)	20
92	Leprosy LEPER 2	NIGHT AND FOG (LP, red vinyl, 1,000 only)	30
93	New European BADVC 36	BUT WHAT ENDS WHEN THE SYMBOLS SHATTER (LP, with inner & insert, 500 on purple vinyl, 3,000 on black vinyl)	35/20
93	New Euro'n BADVCCD 36	BUT WHAT ENDS WHEN THE SYMBOLS SHATTER (CD, gold disc digipak, 5,000 only)	20
93	New Euro'n BADVCCD 96	SOMETHING IS COMING (2-CD, digipak, 5,000 only)	25
94	New European BADVC 38	ROSE CLOUDS OF HOLOCAUST (LP, with insert & inner)	12
94	New Euro'n BADVCCD 38	ROSE CLOUDS OF HOLOCAUST (CD, digipak, 5,000 only)	20
95	New European BADVC 39	BLACK WHOLE OF LOVE (box set with 12", 10", 7" & CDs with inserts)	30
96	New European BADVC 96	SOMETHING IS COMING (2-LP, textured sleeve with insert)	15

(see also Crisis, Current 93, Boyd Rice & Friends, Sol Invictus)

MINT VALUE £

DEATH IN VEGAS

99 Concrete YAWNING 1 Blood Yawning (12", 1-sided promo-only, etched, p/s) . . . 8
00 Concrete HARD 4510 One More Time (featuring Bobby Gillespie) (1-sided 10", red vinyl, p/s) . . . 7
01 Concrete SCORPIO 1 Scorpio (12", no p/s, 1-sided DJ white label, 1,000 copies only) . . . 20
02 Concrete HARD 5112 Leather Girls (Original Mix)/Natja (LAMF Mix)/Natja (Zoo Station) (12", double pack, p/s) . . . 10

(see also Dead Elvis)

DEATH SENTENCE

82 Beat The System DEATH 1 DEATH & PURE DESTRUCTION (EP) . . . 6

DEBONAIRES (U.K.)

66 Pye 7N 17151 A Love Of Our Own/The Night Meets The Dawn . . . 7
66 Pye 7N 17204 Crying Behind Your Smile/Forever More . . . 7

DEBONAIRES (U.S.)

70 Track 604 035 I'm In Love Again/Headache In My Heart . . . 22

DEBONAIRS

63 Parlophone R 5054 That's Right/When True Love Comes Your Way . . . 7

DEBS

65 Mercury MF 888 Sloopy's Gonna Hang On/Under A Street Light . . . 18

DEB-TONES

59 RCA RCA 1137 Knock, Knock — Who's There?/I'm In Love Again . . . 25
59 RCA RCA 1137 Knock, Knock — Who's There?/I'm In Love Again (78) . . . 20

DEBUTANTES

80 Rok ROK XVII/XVIII Man In The Street/INNOCENT BYSTANDERS: Where Is Johnny (company sleeve) . . . 6

DECAMERON

73 Vertigo 6360 097 SAY HELLO TO THE BAND (LP) . . . 12

VINNI DE CAMPO

50 London L 960 Bring Back The Thrill/Faithful (78) . . . 7

YVONNE DE CARLO

55 Capitol CL 14380 Take It Or Leave It/Three Little Stars . . . 8

PAULO DE CARVALHO

74 Pye International 7N 25647 (And Then) After Love/E Depois Do Adeus (p/s) . . . 10

DE CASTRO SISTERS

54 London HL 8104 Teach Me Tonight/It's Love . . . 50
55 London HL 8137 Boom Boom Boomerang/Let Your Love Walk In . . . 50
55 London HL 8137 Boom Boom Boomerang/Let Your Love Walk In (78) . . . 8
55 London HL 8158 I'm Bewildered/To Say You're Mine . . . 50
55 London HL 8158 I'm Bewildered/To Say You're Mine (78) . . . 8
55 London HLU 8189 If I Ever Fall In Love/Cuckoo In The Clock . . . 40
55 London HLU 8189 If I Ever Fall In Love/Cuckoo In The Clock (78) . . . 6
55 London HLU 8212 Christmas Is A-Comin'/Snowbound For Christmas . . . 40
56 London HLU 8228 Give Me Time/Too Late Now . . . 40
56 London HLU 8228 Give Me Time/Too Late Now (78) . . . 10
56 London HLU 8296 No One To Blame But You/Cowboys Don't Cry . . . 40
56 London HLU 8296 No One To Blame But You/Cowboys Don't Cry (78) . . . 10
58 HMV POP 527 Who Are They To Say?/When You Look At Me . . . 12
58 HMV POP 527 Who Are They To Say?/When You Look At Me (78) . . . 15
59 HMV POP 583 Teach Me Tonight Cha Cha/The Things I Tell My Pillow . . . 10
59 HMV POP 583 Teach Me Tonight Cha Cha/The Things I Tell My Pillow (78) . . . 18
61 Capitol CL 15199 Red Sails In The Sunset/Bells . . . 8

DECISIONS

68 MCA MU 1027 In The Shade Of Your Love/Constable Jones . . . 5

DIANA DECKER

54 Columbia SCM 5083 Oh, My Papa/Crystal Ball . . . 18
54 Columbia SCM 5096 The Happy Wanderer/Till We Two Are One . . . 15
54 Columbia SCM 5120 Jilted/The Man With The Banjo . . . 15
54 Columbia SCM 5123 Kitty In The Basket/Never Never Land . . . 12
54 Columbia SCM 5130 Mama Mia/Percy The Penguin . . . 15
54 Columbia SCM 5145 Sisters/Abracadabra . . . 15
55 Columbia SCM 5166 Open The Window Of Your Heart/The Violin Song . . . 12
55 Columbia SCM 5173 Apples, Peaches And Cherries/Paper Valentine . . . 40
56 Columbia SCM 5246 Rock-A-Boogie Baby/Willie Can . . . 35

(see also Ray Burns, Ruby Murray)

DECORATORS

81 New Hormones ORG 5 Twilight View/Reflections (p/s) . . . 5

DE COURCY'S

65 Egmont EGM 9220 SALUTE TO THE SHADOWS (LP) . . . 15

DE DANAAN

82 Cara CARA 1 Hey Jude/St. Jude's Hornpipe/Trip To Taum Reel/Teetotaller . . . 5
75 Polydor 2904 005 DE DANAAN (LP) . . . 15
77 Decca SKL-R 5287 DE DANAAN — SELECTED JIGS AND REELS (LP) . . . 20
80 Decca SKL 5318 BANKS OF THE NILE (LP) . . . 12

DEDICATED MEN'S JUG BAND

65 Piccadilly 7N 35245 Boodle-Am-Shake/Come On Boys . . . 6
66 Piccadilly 7N 35283 Don't Come Knocking/Out Time Blues . . . 6

DEDRINGER

80	DinDisc DIN 10	Sunday Drivers/We Don't Mind (p/s)	5
80	DinDisc DIN 11	Innocent 'Till Proven Guilty/Maxine//Took A Long Time/ We Don't Mind (double pack)	10
81	DinDisc DIN 12	Direct Line/She's Not Ready (p/s)	5
82	Neat NEAT 18	Hot Lady/Hot Licks And Rock'N'Roll (p/s)	5
81	DinDisc DID 7	DIRECT LINE (LP)	15
83	Neat NEAT 1009	SECOND RISING (LP, with inner sleeve)	12

DAVE DEE

70	Fontana TF 1074	My Woman's Man/Gotta Make You Part Of Me	6
70	Fontana 6007 021	Annabella/Kelly	6
70	Philips 6006 061	Everything About Her/If I Believed In Tomorrow	6
71	Philips 6006 100	Wedding Bells/Sweden	6
71	Philips 6006 154	Hold On/Mary Morning, Mary Evening	6
71	Philips 6006 180	Swingy/Don't You Ever Change Your Mind	6

(see also Dave Dee, Dozy, Beaky, Mick & Tich)

DAVE DEE, DOZY, BEAKY, MICK & TICH

65	Fontana TF 531	No Time/Is It Love	25
65	Fontana TF 586	All I Want/It Seems A Pity	22
65	Fontana TF 630	You Make It Move/I Can't Stop	8
66	Fontana TF 671	Hold Tight!/You Know What I Want	5
66	Fontana TF 711	Hideaway/Here's A Heart	5
66	Fontana TF 746	Bend It/She's So Good	5
66	Fontana TF 775	Save Me/Shame	5
67	Fontana TF 798	Touch Me Touch Me/Marina	5
67	Fontana TF 830	Okay!/He's A Raver	5
67	Fontana TF 873	Zabadak!/The Sun Goes Down	5
68	Fontana TF 903	The Legend Of Xanadu/Please	12
74	Antic K 11510	She's My Lady/Babeigh	6
67	Fontana TE 17488	LOOS OF ENGLAND (EP)	12
66	Fontana TL 5350	DAVE DEE, DOZY, BEAKY, MICK & TICH (LP)	20
66	Fontana (S)TL 5388	IF MUSIC BE THE FOOD OF LOVE PREPARE FOR INDIGESTION (LP)	20
67	Fontana (S)TL 5441	GOLDEN HITS OF DAVE DEE, DOZY, BEAKY, MICK & TICH (LP)	15
68	Fontana (S)TL 5471	IF NO-ONE SANG (LP)	20
69	Fontana SFL 13002	DDDBM&T (LP)	20
70	Fontana SFL 13173	TOGETHER (LP)	15

(see also Dozy Beaky Mick & Tich [D,B,M & T], Dave Dee)

JEANNIE DEE

69	Beacon BEA 115	Come Into My Arms/Sun Shine On Me	7
69	Beacon BEA 142	Don't Go Home My Little Darling/Come See About Me	12

JOEY DEE & STARLI(GH)TERS

61	Columbia DB 4758	Peppermint Twist (Parts 1 & 2)	10
62	Columbia DB 4803	Hey, Let's Twist/Roly Poly	10
62	Columbia DB 4842	Shout (Parts 1 & 2)	10
62	Columbia DB 4862	Ya Ya/Fanny Mae	10
62	Columbia DB 4905	What Kind Of Love Is This?/Wing Ding	10
63	Columbia DB 4955	I Lost My Baby/Keep Your Mind On What You're Doin'	7
63	Columbia DB 7005	Baby You're Driving Me Crazy/Help Me Pick Up The Pieces	7
63	Columbia DB 7055	Hot Pastrami With Mashed Potatoes (Parts 1 & 2)	10
63	Columbia DB 7102	Dance, Dance, Dance/Let's Have A Party (features Ronettes uncredited)	10
63	Columbia DB 7277	Down By The Riverside/Getting Nearer (features Ronettes uncredited)	10
61	Columbia 33SX 1406	DOIN' THE TWIST LIVE AT THE PEPPERMINT LOUNGE (LP)	25
62	Columbia 33SX 1461	BACK AT THE PEPPERMINT LOUNGE (LP)	25
62	Columbia 33SX 1502	ALL THE WORLD IS TWISTIN' (LP)	25
63	Columbia 33SX 1532	JOEY DEE (LP)	25
63	Columbia 33SX 1607	DANCE DANCE DANCE (LP, with Starlighters, also with Ronettes uncredited)	30

(see also Young Rascals)

JOHNNIE DEE

65	Columbia DB 7612	Frankie's Angel/Everything's Upside Down	7

JOHNNY DEE

57	Oriole CB 1367	Sittin' In The Balcony/A-Plus Love	140
57	Oriole CB 1367	Sittin' In The Balcony/A-Plus Love (78)	35

(see also John D. Loudermilk)

KIKI DEE

63	Fontana TF 394	Early Night/Lucky High Heels	15
63	Fontana TF 414	I Was Only Kidding/Don't Put Your Heart In His Hand	10
64	Fontana TF 443	Miracles/That's Right, Walk On By	18
64	Fontana TF 490	(You Don't Know) How Glad I Am/Baby I Don't Care	12
65	Fontana TF 596	Runnin' Out Of Fools/There He Goes	10
66	Fontana TF 669	Why Don't I Run Away From You?/Small Town	15
67	Fontana TF 792	I'm Going Out (The Same Way I Came In)/We've Got Everything Going For Us	10
67	Fontana TF 833	I/Stop And Think	8
67	Fontana TF 870	Excuse Me/Patterns	8
68	Fontana TF 926	Can't Take My Eyes Off You/Hungry Heart	8
68	Fontana TF 983	Now The Flowers Cry/On A Magic Carpet Ride	65
70	Tamla Motown TMG 739	The Day Will Come Between Sunday And Monday/ My Whole World Ended (The Moment You Left Me)	15
73	Rocket PIG 2	Lonnie And Josie/The Last Good Man In My Life	7
65	Fontana TE 17443	KIKI DEE (EP)	35
66	Fontana TE 17470	KIKI DEE IN CLOVER (EP)	30
68	Fontana (S)TL 5455	I'M KIKI DEE (LP)	40
70	Tamla Motown STML 11158	GREAT EXPECTATIONS (LP)	55

(see also Elton John)

MINT VALUE £

LENNY DEE

55	Brunswick 05440	Plantation Boogie/Birth Of The Blues	7

RICKY DEE & EMBERS

62	Stateside SS 136	Workout/JOHN MOBLEY: Tunnel Of Love	15

SANDRA DEE

61	Brunswick 05858	Tammy Tell Me True/Let's Fall In Love	10

SIMON DEE

69	Chapter One CH 105	Julie/Whatever Happened To Us?	6

TAMMI DEE

71	Downtown DT 479	Val/MUSIC DOCTORS: Bank Raid	8

TOMMY DEE

59	Melodisc 1516	Three Stars/TEEN JONES (TONES): I'll Never Change (tri or round centre)	75/50
59	Melodisc 1516	Three Stars/TEEN JONES (TONES): I'll Never Change (78)	25

DEE & DYNAMITES

60	Philips PB 1081	Blaze Away/South Bound Gasser	12

MAURICE DEEBANK

84	Cherry Red MRED 61	INNER THOUGHT ZONE (LP)	12

(see also Felt)

DEEJAYS

65	Polydor BM 56034	Dimples/Coming On Strong	50
65	Polydor BM 56501	Blackeyed Woman/I Just Can't Go To Sleep	110

ANTHONY DEELEY

68	Pama PM 728	Anytime Man/Don't Change Your Mind About Me	7

ANGELA DEEN

64	Fontana TF 491	There's So Much About My Baby That I Love/Gotta Hand It To The Boy	10

CAROL DEENE

61	HMV POP 922	Sad Movies/Don't Forget	10
62	HMV POP 973	Norman/On The Outside Looking In	6
62	HMV POP 1027	Johnny Get Angry/Somebody's Smiling	6
62	HMV POP 1058	Some People/Kissin'	6
62	HMV POP 1086	James/It Happened Last Night	7
63	HMV POP 1123	Let Me Do It My Way/Growin' Up	10
63	HMV POP 1200	Oh Oh Oh Willie/I Want To Stay Here	7
64	HMV POP 1275	Who's Been Sleeping In My Bed?/Love Is Wonderful	10
64	HMV POP 1337	Very First Kiss/Hard To Say Goodnight	10
65	HMV POP 1405	Most People Do/I Can't Forget Someone Like You	7
65	Columbia DB 7743	He Just Don't Know/Up In The Penthouse	10
66	Columbia DB 7890	Dancing In Your Eyes/Please Don't Be Unfaithful Again	7
67	Columbia DB 8107	Love Not Have I/Time	7
68	CBS 3206	When He Wants A Woman/I'm Not Crying	6
69	Conquest CXT 102	One More Chance/Invisible Tears	6
70	World Records ST 1031	A LOVE AFFAIR (LP)	15

DEEP END

78	private pressing	BEGGED AND BORROWED (LP, listed as CPLP 016)	15

DEEP FEELING

70	Page One POF 165	Do You Love Me/Move On	5
70	Page One POF 177	Skyline Pigeon/We've Thrown It All Away	6
71	DJM DJLPS 419	DEEP FEELING (LP)	50

DEEP FREEZE

70s	Guardian GRL 43	Keeping You In Furs/Don't Look Back	5

DEEP FREEZE MICE

80s	Cordelia ERICAT 002	THESE FLOORS ARE SMOOTH (EP)	10
80s	Cordelia ERICAT 004	HANG ON CONSTANCE LET ME HEAR THE NEWS (EP)	8
80s	Cordelia ERICAT 013	RAIN IS WHEN THE EARTH IS TELEVISION (EP)	7
80s	Cordelia ERICAT 016	NEURON MUSIC (12" EP)	8
79	Mole Embalming MOLE 1	MY GERANIUMS ARE BULLETPROOF (LP, 1st 200 with paste-on sleeve, 8-page booklet & various A4 inserts)	60/30
81	Mole Embalming MOLE 2	TEENAGE HEAD IN MY REFRIGERATOR (LP)	30
81	Mole Embalming MOLE C2	HEGEL'S BRAIN (cassette)	12
81	Inedible MOLE 3	GATES OF LUNCH (LP)	15
83	Mole Embalming MOLE 4	SAW A RANCH BURNING LAST NIGHT (LP)	15

DEEP PURPLE

68	Parlophone R 5708	Hush/One More Rainy Day (some in promo-only p/s)	350/35
68	Parlophone R 5745	Kentucky Woman/Wring That Neck (withdrawn)	50+
69	Parlophone R 5763	Emmaretta/Wring That Neck	35
69	Harvest HAR 5006	Hallelujah (I Am The Preacher)/April Part 1 (some in promo-only p/s)	250/20
70	Harvest PSR 325	Concerto, 1st Movement (edit)/Concerto, 2nd Movement (edit) (promo, possibly some commercial)	30
70	Harvest HAR 5020	Black Night/Speed King	6
71	Harvest HAR 5033	Strange Kind Of Woman/I'm Alone	6
71	Harvest HAR 5045	Fireball/Demon's Eye	6
72	Purple PUR 102	Never Before/When A Blind Man Cries	6
74	Purple PUR 117	Might Just Take Your Life/Coronarias Redig	7
76	Purple PUR 130	You Keep On Moving/Love Child	7
77	Purple PUR 132	Smoke On The Water/Woman From Tokyo/Child In Time (10,000 with p/s)	7
85	Polydor POSPP 719	Perfect Strangers (edit)/Son Of Alerik (edit) (picture disc)	7
87	Polydor POSPP 843	Call Of The Wild/Strange Ways (12", picture disc)	10
88	Polydor POC 4	Hush ('88 Re-recording)/Dead Or Alive (Live) (blue vinyl, p/s)	5

88 Polydor RX 4 | Hush ('88 Re-recording)/Dead Or Alive (Live)/Bad Attitude (12", gatefold p/s) 8
88 Polydor PZCD 4 | Hush ('88 Re-recording)Dead Or Alive/Bad Attitude (CD) 12
88 Polydor 080 088-2 | Bad Attitude/Black And White/Unwritten Law/Strangeways (CD Video). 25
90 RCA PT 49224 | Love Conquers All (Edit)/Truth Hurts (die-cut picture disc, with insert) 7
95 EMI 7243 8 82214 67 | Black Night (Remix)/Black Night (Original Mix)/Speed King (12", purple vinyl, numbered limited edition) 8
77 Purple PUR 135 | NEW LIVE AND RARE VOL. 1 (EP, 15,000 on purple vinyl). 8
78 Purple PUR 137 | NEW LIVE AND RARE VOL. 2 (EP) 8
80 Harvest SHEP 101 | NEW LIVE AND RARE VOL. 3 (EP) 8
68 Parlophone PMC/PCS 7055 | SHADES OF DEEP PURPLE (LP, yellow/black label, mono/stereo). 90/60
69 Parlophone PCS 7055 | SHADES OF DEEP PURPLE (LP, stereo repressing, white/black label) 20
69 Harvest SHVL 751 | THE BOOK OF TALIESYN (LP). 50
69 Harvest SHVL 759 | DEEP PURPLE (LP, laminated gatefold sleeve). 50
70 Harvest SHVL 767 | CONCERTO FOR GROUP AND ORCHESTRA (LP, laminated gatefold sleeve) . . . 25
70 Harvest SHVL 777 | IN ROCK (LP, laminated gatefold sleeve) 25
71 Harvest SHVL 793 | FIREBALL (LP, textured gatefold sleeve, with insert) 15
72 Purple TPSA 7504 | MACHINE HEAD (LP, laminated gatefold sleeve, with lyric insert). 12
73 Purple TPSA 7508 | WHO DO WE THINK WE ARE (LP, laminated gatefold sleeve, with insert). 12
74 Purple Q4TPS 7504 | MACHINE HEAD (LP, laminated gatefold sleeve, quadrophonic) 35
74 Purple TPS 3505 | BURN (LP) 12
74 Purple TPS 3508 | STORMBRINGER (LP) 12
75 Purple TPSA 7515 | COME TASTE THE BAND (LP, gatefold sleeve with inner) 12
78 Harvest SHSM 2026 | THE SINGLES A's AND B's (LP, purple vinyl) 20
79 Purple TPS 3514 | THE MARK 2 PURPLE SINGLES (LP, purple vinyl) 15
80 Harvest SHSM 2016 | SHADES OF DEEP PURPLE (LP, 'dismembered doll-limb' sleeve, withdrawn) . . . 75
84 Polydor POLHP 16 | PERFECT STRANGERS (LP, picture disc, with extra track & die-cut sleeve) 12
84 Polydor DEEP 1A | DEEP PURPLE INTERVIEW (LP, 1-sided, promo-only, stickered white sleeve) . . . 15
85 EMI EJ 26 0343 0 | IN ROCK (LP, picture disc with poster) 15
85 EMI EJ 34 0344 0 | FIREBALL (LP, picture disc with poster). 15
85 EMI EG 26 0345 0 | MACHINE HEAD (LP, picture disc with poster) 15
85 EMI PUR 1/E 2606131 | DEEP PURPLE — ANTHOLOGY (2-LP, blue vinyl) 30
86 Polydor DEEP 2A | HOUSE OF BLUE LIGHT (interview LP, promo-only, plays same both sides, stickered black sleeve) 15
87 Polydor 831 318-2 | HOUSE OF BLUE LIGHT (CD) 20
88 Connoisseur VSOP 125 | SCANDINAVIAN NIGHTS (2-LP, gatefold sleeve, with booklet). 18
91 EMI 96129 | ANTHOLOGY (3-LP) 20
93 BMG 74321 15420-1 | THE BATTLE RAGES ON (LP, with inner sleeve). 15
95 EMI 7243 8 34019 18 | DEEP PURPLE IN ROCK (2-LP, purple vinyl, gatefold sleeve with inners). 15
97 EMI DEEPP 3 | MACHINE HEAD (2-LP, 'EMI 100' remixed anniversary edition, purple vinyl, gatefold sleeve, with insert) 18
97 EMI LPCENT 25 | SHADES OF DEEP PURPLE (LP, 'EMI 100', 180gm vinyl edition, yellow/black label) 15
97 EMI DEEPP 2 | FIREBALL (2-LP, gatefold sleeve with inners & limited edition print) 15
98 EMI PP 074 | VERY BEST OF (2-LP, purple vinyl). 18
98 EMI 7243 8 57864 19 | MADE IN JAPAN (2-LP, numbered, purple vinyl, gatefold sleeve with inners) 15
99 Harvest 7243 4 99469 10 | BOOK OF TALIESYN (LP, 180gm vinyl, gatefold sleeve in stickered PVC outer). . 15

(see also Ritchie Blackmore, Rainbow, Gillan, [David Coverdale's] Whitesnake, Tommy Bolin, [Sheila Carter &] Episode Six, Jon Lord, Roger Glover, Green Bullfrog, Wizard's Convention, Elf, Maze, M.I. Five, Warhorse, Captain Beyond, John Lawton, Hell Preachers Inc., Glen Hughes, Trapeze, Leading Figures, Paice Ashton & Lord, Silverhead, Pete York Percussion Band)

DEEP RIVER BOYS

54 HMV 7M 174 | Sweet Mama Tree Top Tall/A Kiss And Cuddle Polka 22
54 HMV 7M 280 | Shake, Rattle And Roll/St. Louis Blues 40
56 HMV 7M 361 | Rock-A-Beatin' Boogie/Just A Little Bit More! 40
56 HMV POP 263 | That's Right/Honey Honey 20
57 HMV POP 395 | Whole Lotta Shakin' Goin' On/There's A Goldmine In The Sky 30
57 HMV POP 395 | Whole Lotta Shakin' Goin' On/There's A Goldmine In The Sky (78). 6
58 HMV POP 449 | Not Too Old To Rock And Roll/Slow Train To Nowhere 22
58 HMV POP 449 | Not Too Old To Rock And Roll/Slow Train To Nowhere (78) 8
58 HMV POP 537 | Itchy Twitchy Feeling/I Shall Not Be Moved. 20
58 HMV POP 537 | Itchy Twitchy Feeling/I Shall Not Be Moved (78) 8
59 Top Rank JAR 172 | Nola/Kissin' 6
59 Top Rank JAR 172 | Nola/Kissin' (78) 8
59 Top Rank JAR 174 | I Don't Know Why (I Just Do)/Timbers Gotta Roll (with Harry Douglass) 6
60 Top Rank JAR 352 | Go Galloway, Go/Dum Dum De Dum (with Harry Douglass). 5
62 HMV POP 1081 | Settle Down/Ashes Of Roses. 8
55 Nixa 45EP 113 | GO ON BOARD LITTLE CHILDREN (EP) 8
55 Nixa 45EP 114 | SWING LOW SWEET CHARIOT (EP) 8
55 Nixa 45EP 130 | WALK TOGETHER CHILDREN (EP) 8
55 Nixa 45EP 131 | EZEKIEL SAW THE WHEEL (EP) 8
55 HMV 7EG 8133 | DEEP RIVER BOYS (EP) 8
57 HMV 7EG 8321 | ROMANCE A LA MODE (EP) 8
57 HMV 7EG 8445 | NEGRO SPIRITUALS (EP) 8
54 Nixa XLTY 135 | SPIRITUALS SUNG BY THE DEEP RIVER BOYS (10" LP). 25
54 Nixa XLTY 138 | SPIRITUALS SUNG BY THE DEEP RIVER BOYS (10" LP). 25
60 Top Rank 35/108 | THE BLUE DEEPS (LP) 25

(see also Fats Waller, Harry Douglass & Deep River Boys)

DEEP SET

68 Pye 7N 17594 | That's The Way Life Goes/Hello Amy. 7
69 Major Minor MM 607 | I Started A Joke/Spicks And Specks. 10

DEEP SIX

66 Liberty LIB 55882 | Counting/When Morning Breaks 6

DEEP SWITCH

86 SWITCH 1 | NINE INCHES OF GOD (LP, private pressing) 20

MINT VALUE £

DEEP TIMBRE
72 Westwood WR 5006 DEEP TIMBRE (LP) . . . 40

SAM DEES
69 Major Minor MM 655 If It's All Wrong (It's All Right)/Don't Keep Me Hangin' On . . . 18
75 Atlantic K 10676 Fragile, Handle With Care/Save The Love At Any Cost . . . 22
89 RCA PB 43129 After All/Always Something (p/s) . . . 10
75 Atlantic K 50142 THE SHOW MUST GO ON (LP) . . . 30

SAM DEES & BETTYE SWANN
76 Atlantic K 10719 Storybook Children/Just As Sure . . . 10
(see also Bettye Swann)

DEE SET
68 Blue Cat BS 146 I Know A Place/ROY BENNETT: I Dangerous . . . 15

DEFENDANTS
80s Edible EAT 001 Headmaster/Such A Spiv (stickered insert cover & stickered labels) . . . 12

DEFENDERS
68 Doctor Bird DB 1104 Set Them Free/Don't Blame The Children (actually by Lee Perry & Sensations) . . 25
(see also Lee Perry)

DEF LEPPARD
79 Bludgeon Riffola SRT/CUS/232 THE DEF LEPPARD EP: Ride Into The Sun/Getcha Rocks Off/The Overture (red label, p/s with lyric insert, 150 only) . . . 300
79 Bludgeon Riffola SRT/CUS/232 THE DEF LEPPARD EP: Ride Into The Sun/Getcha Rocks Off/The Overture (red label, with/without p/s, 850 only) . . . 250/60
79 Bludgeon Riffola MSB 001 Ride Into The Sun/Getcha Rocks Off/The Overture (reissue, yellow label, 15,000 pressed, no p/s) . . . 18
79 Phonogram 6059 240 Getcha Rocks Off/Ride Into The Sun/The Overture (2nd reissue, no p/s) . . . 10
79 Phonogram 6059 240 Getcha Rocks Off/Ride Into The Sun/The Overture (mispressing, both sides play "The Overture") . . . 40
79 Phonogram 6059 247 Wasted/Hello America (p/s) . . . 12
80 Phonogram LEPP 1 Hello America/Good Morning Freedom (p/s) . . . 12
81 Phonogram LEPP 2 Let It Go/Switch 625 (p/s, 10,000 shrinkwrapped with patch) . . . 15/12
82 Phonogram LEPP 3 Bringin' On The Heartbreak/Me And My Wine (p/s) . . . 35
82 Phonogram LEPP 312 Bringin' On The Heartbreak/Me And My Wine/You Got Me Runnin' (12", p/s) . . . 20
83 Phonogram VER 5 Photograph/Bringin' On The Heartbreak (p/s) . . . 10
83 Phonogram VERP 5 Photograph/Bringin' On The Heartbreak (camera-shaped fold-out/pop-up sleeve, 500 only) . . . 25
83 Phonogram VERX 5 Photograph/Bringin' On The Heartbreak/Mirror, Mirror (12", p/s) . . . 20
83 Phonogram VER 6 Rock Of Ages/Action! Not Words (p/s) . . . 7
83 Phonogram VERP 6 Rock Of Ages/Action! Not Words (guitar-shaped picture disc) . . . 35
83 Phonogram VERQ 6 Rock Of Ages/Action! Not Words (foldout 'rock box' cube sleeve, 500 only) . . . 40
83 Phonogram VERX 6 Rock Of Ages/Action! Not Words (12", p/s) . . . 18
83 Phonogram VERDJ 8 Too Late/Foolin' (p/s, DJ-only promo with rear band photo in football kit) . . . 150
83 Phonogram VER 8 Too Late For Love/Foolin' (p/s) . . . 12
83 Phonogram VERX 8 Too Late For Love/Foolin'/High And Dry (12", p/s) . . . 20
84 Phonogram VER 9 Photograph/Bringin' On The Heartbreak (reissue, 'wallet' p/s) . . . 10
84 Phonogram VERG 9 Photograph/Bringin' On The Heartbreak (g/fold printed 'wallet' p/s, 500 only) . . . 40
84 Phonogram VERX 9 Photograph/Bringin' On The Heartbreak/Mirror, Mirror (12", p/s) . . . 20
87 Phonogram LEPX 1 Animal/Animal (Extended Mix)/Tear It Down (12", p/s, black vinyl) . . . 8
87 Phonogram LEPC 1 Animal/Animal (Extended Mix)/Tear It Down (12", p/s, red vinyl) . . . 20
87 Phonogram LEPCD 1 Animal/Women/Animal (Extended Mix)/Tear It Down (CD, no'd, 1,000 only) . . . 30
87 Phonogram LEPS 2 Pour Some Sugar On Me/I Wanna Be Your Hero (tri-shaped picture disc in silver 12" foldout p/s with tour dates) . . . 15
87 Phonogram LEPMC 2 Pour Some Sugar On Me/I Wanna Be Your Hero (cassette) . . . 7
87 Phonogram LEPX 2 Pour Some Sugar On Me (Extended Version)/Pour Some Sugar On Me/I Wanna Be Your Hero (12", p/s) . . . 8
87 Phonogram LEPPX 2 Pour Some Sugar On Me (Extended Version)/Pour Some Sugar On Me (Extended)/I Wanna Be Your Hero (12", picture disc, unissued)
87 Phonogram LEPMC 333 Hysteria/Ride Into The Sun (1987 Version) (cassette) . . . 8
87 Phonogram LEPS 3 Hysteria/Ride Into The Sun (1987 Version) (p/s, shrinkwrapped with patch) . . . 10
87 Phonogram LEPX 3 Hysteria/Ride Into The Sun (1987 Version)/Love And Affection (live) (12", p/s) . . . 8
87 Phonogram LEPX 313 Hysteria/Ride Into The Sun (1987 Version)/Love And Affection (live) (12", envelope box sleeve with poster & international discography, 5,000 only) . . 15
87 Phonogram LEPCD 3 Hysteria/Ride Into The Sun (1987 Version)/Love And Affection (live)/I Wanna Be Your Hero (CD, 5,000 only with titles in red, numbered) . . . 15
88 Phonogram LEPP 4 Armageddon It! (The Atomic Mix)/Ring Of Fire (poster p/s) . . . 7
88 Phonogram LEPX 4 Armageddon It!/Armageddon It! (The Atomic Mix)/Ring Of Fire (12", p/s) . . . 8
88 Phonogram LEPXB 4 Armageddon It!/Armageddon It! (The Atomic Mix)/Ring Of Fire (12", numbered box set with poster, enamel badge & 5 postcards, 5,000 only) . . 18
88 Phonogram LEPCD 4 Armageddon It! (The Atomic Mix)/Ring Of Fire/Animal/Pour Some Sugar On Me (CD, picture disc) . . . 15
88 Phonogram LEPG 5 Love Bites/Billy's Got A Gun (live) (no'd gatefold p/s with 8-page lyric book) . . . 8
88 Phonogram LEPX 5 Love Bites/Billy's Got A Gun (live)/Excitable (Orgasmic Mix) (12", p/s) . . . 8
88 Phonogram LEPXB 5 Love Bites/Billy's Got A Gun (live)/Excitable (Orgasmic Mix) (12", box set with 4 cardboard inserts, 5,000 only) . . . 18
88 Phonogram LEPCD 5 Love Bites/Rocket (The Lunar Mix)/Billy's Got A Gun (live) (CD, card sleeve) . . . 15
89 Phonogram LEPC 6 Rocket/Release Me (foldout 'Brit' pack, envelope sleeve with 3 inserts) . . . 8
89 Phonogram LEPXP 6 Rocket (The Lunar Mix)/(Radio Edit)/Release Me (12", picture disc, some numbered) . . . 15/10
89 Phonogram LEPX 6 Rocket (The Lunar Mix)/Release Me/Rock Of Ages (live) (12", p/s) . . . 8
89 Phonogram LEPXC 6 Rocket (The Lunar Mix)/Release Me/Rock Of Ages (live) (12", calendar pack) . . . 20
89 Phonogram LEPCD 6 Rocket (The Lunar Mix)/Rock Of Ages (live)/Release Me (CD) . . . 15
92 Phonogram DEFXP 7 Let's Get Rocked/Only After Dark/Too Late For Love (live) (12", picture disc, with insert) . . . 10

92 Phonogram DEFCD 7 — Let's Get Rocked/Only After Dark/Women (live) (CD, picture disc, in box with space for 4 CDs) . . . 20
88 Bludgeon Riffola 080 458-2 — Love Bites/Rocket (Lunar Mix)/Billy's Got A Gun (live)/ Love Bites (Video) (CD Video) . . . 30
89 Bludgeon Riffola 080 034-2 — Rock Of Ages/Stagefright/Billy's Got A Gun/Too Late For Love/ Rock Of Ages (Video) (CD Video) . . . 30
89 Bludgeon Riffola 080 626-2 — Animal (Extended Version)/Animal/Tear It Down/Animal (Video) (CD Video) . . . 30
90 Bludgeon Riffola 080 990-2 — Rocket (Radio Edit)/Release Me/Rock Of Ages/Rocket (Video) (CD Video) . . . 30
87 Phonogram HYSPD 1 — HYSTERIA (LP, picture disc) . . . 15
89 Phonogram 836 606-2 — THE FOUR ALBUMS (4-CD box set, with booklet) . . . 50
92 Phonogram 510 978-1 — ADRENALIZE (LP, picture disc, 5,000 only, numbered, die-cut sleeve) . . . 15
94 Phonogram (no cat. no.) — ADRENALIZE — MAHOGANY BOX SET (CD, picture disc, with interview picture CD, 3 booklets, signed/no'd certificate, signed photo & plectrum, 1,000 only) . . 200
95 Mercury DLINT 3 — 1980-1995 VAULT — AN INTERVIEW WITH JOE ELLIOT & RICK SAVAGE (CD, promo only) . . . 30

(see also Lucy, Gogmagog)

ZION DE GALLIER

68 Parlophone R 5686 — Me/Winter Will Be Cold . . . 15
68 Parlophone R 5710 — Dream Dream Dream/Geraldine . . . 18

(see also Mark Wirtz)

GLORIA DE HAVEN

55 Brunswick 05369 — So This Is Paris/The Two Of Us . . . 10
55 Brunswick 05457 — Red Hot Pepper Pot/Won't You Save Me? . . . 15
59 Oriole CB 1524 — Dearly Beloved/Life . . . 8

DE-HEMS

72 President PT 388 — Don't Cross That Line/Lover Let Me Go . . . 8

DE JOHN SISTERS

57 Mercury MT 174 — What Am I/Where Would I Be . . . 10
60 London HLT 9127 — Yes Indeed/Be Anything (But Be Mine) . . . 10

DEK & JERRY

66 Philips BF 1494 — What's The Matter With Me?/Don't Waste Your Time . . . 8

DESMOND DEKKER (& ACES)

63 Island WI 054 — Honour Your Mother And Father (as Desmond Decker & Beverley's Allstars)/ Madgie ('63) (with Beverley's Allstars) . . . 15
63 Island WI 111 — Parents/Labour For Learning (solo) . . . 25
64 Island WI 158 — Jeserine/King Of Ska (as Desmond Dekkar & His Cherry Pies) . . . 25
64 Black Swan WI 455 — Dracula (as Desmond Dekkar)/DON DRUMMOND: Spitfire . . . 30
65 Island WI 181 — Get Up Adine (as Desmond Dekkar, actually with Four Aces)/Be Mine Forever (as Patsy & Desmond; song is act. "Down Down Down" by Clive & Naomi) . . . 30
65 Island WI 202 — This Woman (as Desmond Dekker & Four Aces)/ LEE PERRY & UPSETTERS: Si Senora (B-side actually by Ossie & Upsetters) . . 18
67 Pyramid PYR 6003 — Wise Man/ROLAND ALPHONSO: Middle East . . . 12
67 Pyramid PYR 6004 — 007 (Shanty Town)/ROLAND ALPHONSO: El Torro . . . 7
67 Pyramid PYR 6006 — It's A Shame/ROLAND ALPHONSO: On The Move . . . 12
67 Pyramid PYR 6008 — Rudy Got Soul/ROLAND ALPHONSO: The Cat . . . 20
67 Pyramid PYR 6011 — Rude Boy Train/ROLAND ALPHONSO: Nothing For Nothing . . . 20
67 Pyramid PYR 6012 — Mother's Young Girl/SOUL BROTHERS: Confucious . . . 40
67 Pyramid PYR 6017 — Unity/Sweet Music . . . 12
67 Pyramid PYR 6020 — Sabotage/Pretty Africa . . . 12
67 Pyramid PYR 6020 — Sabotage/It Pays . . . 12
67 Pyramid PYR 6026 — It Pays/Young Generation . . . 12
68 Pyramid PYR 6031 — Beautiful And Dangerous/I've Got The Blues . . . 12
68 Pyramid PYR 6035 — Bongo Gal/Shing A Ling . . . 12
68 Pyramid PYR 6037 — To Sir, With Love/Fu Manchu . . . 30
68 Pyramid PYR 6044 — Mother Pepper/Don't Blame Me . . . 12
68 Pyramid PYR 6047 — Hey Grandma/Young Generation . . . 12
68 Pyramid PYR 6051 — Music Like Dirt (Intensified)/Coconut Water . . . 12
68 Pyramid PYR 6054 — It Mek/Writing On The Wall . . . 10
68 Pyramid PYR 6058 — Israelites/BEVERLEY'S ALLSTARS: The Man . . . 6
68 Pyramid PYR 6059 — Christmas Day/I've Got The Blues . . . 10
69 Pyramid PYR 6068 — It Mek/Problems . . . 6
69 J.J. PYR 6058 — Israelites/BEVERLEY'S ALLSTARS: The Man (reissue, mis-labelled copy) . . . 6
70 Trojan TR 7777 — You Can Get It If You Really Want/Perseverance . . . 6
70 Trojan TR 7802 — The Song We Used To Sing/Get Up Little Suzie . . . 6
71 Trojan TR 7847 — Lightning Stick/Troubles And Miseries . . . 6
72 Trojan TR 7876 — It Gotta Be So/The First Time For A Long Time . . . 6
73 Rhino RNO 115 — Sing A Little Song/I'm A Busted Lad . . . 6
67 Doctor Bird DLM 5007 — 007 SHANTY TOWN (LP) . . . 130
69 Doctor Bird DLM 5013 — THE ISRAELITES (LP, solo) . . . 130
69 Trojan TTL 4 — THIS IS DESMOND DEKKAR (LP, label credits Dekker) . . . 25
70 Trojan TBL 146 — YOU CAN GET IT IF YOU REALLY WANT (LP) . . . 20
73 Trojan TRLD 401 — DOUBLE DEKKER (2-LP) . . . 20

(all the above LPs have orange labels)
(see also Al Barry, Skatalites, Maytals)

GEORGE DEKKER

71 Trojan TR 7879 — Time Hard/SYDNEY, GEORGE & JACKIE: Fall In Love . . . 6

DEL AMITRI

82 Lyntone LYN 1548 — What She Calls It (flexi, free with *Stand & Deliver* mag) . . . 20
83 No Strings NOSP 1 — Sense Sickness/The Difference Is (p/s) . . . 90
85 Chrysalis CHS 2859 — Sticks And Stones Girl/This King Is Poor (p/s) . . . 5
85 Chrysalis CHS 12 2859 — Sticks And Stones Girl/This King Is Poor/The Difference Is (12", p/s) . . . 8
85 Chrysalis CHS 2925 — Hammering Heart/Lines Running North (p/s) . . . 5

MINT VALUE £

85 Chrysalis CHS 12 2925 Hammering Heart/Lines Running North/Brown Eyed Girl (12", p/s) 15
89 A&M AM 527 Stone Cold Sober/The Return Of Maggie Brown/Talk It To Death (p/s) 10
89 A&M CDEE 527 Stone Cold Sober/The Return Of Maggie Brown/Talk It To Death (3" CD) 8
89 A&M AMY 515 Kiss This Thing Goodbye/No Holding On/Slowly, It's Coming Back (12", p/s) 8
89 A&M CDEE 515 Kiss This Thing Goodbye/No Holding On/Slowly, It's Coming Back (3" CD, card sleeve) 18
80s Fan Club Charlie's Bar (flexi, 1-track) 10
90 A&M AMX 589 Spit In The Rain/Scared To Love/The Return Of Maggie Brown/Talk It To Death (10", in box with lyric insert) 12
92 A&M AMY 884 Be My Downfall/Whiskey Remorse/Lighten Up The Load/The Heart Is A Bad Design (10", with poster) 7
97 A&M 582 365-2 Medicine/Driving With The Brakes On (Live)/Move Away Jimmy Blue (live)/The Ones That You Love... (live) (CD, slimline jewel case, withdrawn) 10
97 A&M 582 367-2 Medicine/Roll To Me (Live At Leeds)/Here & Now (Live At Leeds)/Hatful Of Rain (Live At Leeds) (CD, slimline jewel case, withdrawn) 10
97 A&M 582 369-2 Medicine/Some Other Sucker's Parade (Live At Leeds)/Always The Last To Know (Live At Leeds)/Stone Cold Sober (Live At Leeds) (CD, slimline jewel case, withdrawn) 10
97 A&M 582 4332 Some Other Sucker's Parade/Driving With The Brakes On (Live At Leeds)/Move Away Jimmy Blue (Live At Leeds)/The Ones That You Love Lead You Nowhere (Live At Leeds) (CD, with postcards) 10
97 A&M 582 4352 Some Other Sucker's Parade (Version)/Roll To Me (Live At Leeds)/Here & Now (Live At Leeds)/Hatful Of Rain (Live At Leeds) (CD) 8

DELACARDOS

61 HMV POP 890 Hold Back The Tears/Mister Dillon 90

DE LAINE SISTERS

62 Piccadilly 7N 35070 It Might As Well Rain Until September/Puppet On A String 10
(see also Ladybirds, Breakaways)

ERIC DELANEY BAND

60 Parlophone R 4646 Bass Drum Boogie/Let's Get Organised 6
62 Parlophone R 4925 Manhattan Spiritual/Down Home 7
50s Pye HI-FI DELANEY (10" LP) 25

ERIC DELANEY'S BIG BEAT SIX

65 Pye 7N 15782 The Big Beat/Big Noise From Winnetka 6

DELANEY & BONNIE (& FRIENDS)

69 Elektra EKSN 45066 Get Ourselves Together/Soldiers Of The Cross (withdrawn) 20+
69 Apple SAPCOR 7 THE ORIGINAL DELANEY & BONNIE (LP, unreleased, no sleeve) 800
69 Elektra EKS 74039 THE ORIGINAL DELANEY & BONNIE — ACCEPT NO SUBSTITUTE (LP, commercial release of above LP) 15
69 Stax SXATS 1029 HOME (LP) 15
70 Atlantic 2400 013 ON TOUR WITH ERIC CLAPTON (LP) 15
71 Atco 2400 029 TO BONNIE FROM DELANEY (LP) 12
71 London ZGL 113 GENESIS (LP) 12
71 Atlantic 2400 119 MOTEL SHOT (LP) 12
72 CBS 64959 TOGETHER (LP) 12
74 Stax 2362 001 HOME (LP, reissue) 12
(see also Eric Clapton, Delaney Bramlett, King Curtis with Delaney & Friends, Shindogs)

DEL-CAPRIS

79 Grapevine GRP 112 Hey Little Way Out Girl (actually by Construction)/EULA COOPER: Beggars Can't Be Choosey (p/s) 8

DELFONICS

68 Bell BLL 1005 La La Means I Love You/Can't Get Over Losing You 10
68 Bell SBLL 106 LA-LA MEANS I LOVE YOU (LP) 20
69 Bell SBLL 121 THE SOUND OF SEXY SOUL (LP) 20
71 Bell SBLL 137 THE DELFONICS (LP) 12
74 Bell BELLS 245 ALIVE AND KICKING (LP) 12

TERESA DEL FUEGO

81 Satril HH 155 Don't Hang Up/Wonder Wonder (no p/s) 8
(see also Swing Out Sister)

DELGADOS

95 Chemikal Underground CHEM 001 Monica Webster/Brand New Car (p/s) 6
95 Radar SCAN 07 THE LAZARWALKER EP (p/s) 10
96 Chemikal Underground CHEM 004 Cinecentre/Thirteen Gliding Prices/Mule Emulator (p/s) 5
96 Boa HISS 4 Liquidation Girl/VAN IMPE: Piranha (hand-painted brown paper bag p/s, 500 only) 15

DELICATES

59 London HLT 8953 Ronnie Is My Lover/Black And White Thunderbird 120
59 London HLT 8953 Ronnie Is My Lover/Black And White Thunderbird (78) 40
60 London HLT 9176 Too Young To Date/The Kiss 80

DELICATESSAN

67 Vocalion VN 9286 The Red Baron's Revenge/The Dog Fight (Der Hundkampf) 10

DELITES

80 Grapevine GRP 127 Lover/Tell Me Why 8

JOHNNY DE LITTLE

61 Columbia DB 4578 Not Guilty/They 8
62 Columbia DB 4907 Lover/You Made Me Love You 8
63 Columbia DB 7023 Days Of Wine And Roses/Ride On 8
63 Columbia DB 7044 The Wind And The Rain/Unchained Melody 12
65 CBS 201790 The Knack/What To Do With Laurie 8
(see also John Barry)

DELIVERANCE

87 Metalworks VOV 664 DEVIL'S MEAT (LP) 15
89 Metalworks VOV 673 EVIL FRIENDSHIP (LP, lyric inner) 15
90 Metalworks VOV 679 THE BOOK OF LIES (LP) 15

DENNIS D'ELL

67 CBS 202605 It Breaks My Heart In Two/Better Use Your Head (withdrawn; demos £140) 220
67 Decca F 12647 A Woman Called Sorrow/The Night Has A Thousand Eyes (as Denny D'Ell) 8
76 Polydor 2058 715 Home Is Home/Morning Without You (as Denis D'Ell) 7
(see also Honeycombs)

JIMMY DELL

58 RCA RCA 1066 Teeny Weeny/BARRY DE VORZON: Barbara Jean 65
58 RCA RCA 1066 Teeny Weeny/BARRY DE VORZON: Barbara Jean (78) 35

PETE DELLO & FRIENDS

71 Nepentha 6437 001 INTO YOUR EARS (LP, gatefold sleeve) 140
(see also Honeybus, Lace, Red Herring, Leah, John Killigrew, Magic Valley, Grant Tracy & Sunsets, Sunsets)

DELLS

63 Pye International 7N 25178 The (Bossa Nova) Bird/Eternally 20
67 Chess CRS 8066 O-O I Love You/There Is 12
68 Chess CRS 8071 Wear It On Our Face/Please Don't Change Me Now 15
68 Chess CRS 8079 Stay In My Corner/Love Is So Simple 12
68 President PT 223 It's Not Unusual/Stay In My Corner 6
68 Chess CRS 8084 Always Together/I Want My Momma 6
69 Chess CRS 8099 I Can Sing A Rainbow/Love Is Blue-Hallelujah Baby 6
69 Chess CRS 8102 Oh What A Night/Believe Me 8
69 President PT 270 Oh What A Night/Moving On 7
69 Chess CRS 8105 On The Dock Of The Bay/When I'm In Your Arms 7
72 Chess 6145 008 It's All Up To You/Oh, My Dear 6
73 Chess 6145 022 Give Your Baby A Standing Ovation/Run For Cover 8
68 Chess CRLS 4554 GREATEST HITS (LP) 22
69 Chess CRLS 4555 LOVE IS BLUE/OH, WHAT A NIGHT (LP) 30
71 Joy JOYS 186 OH WHAT A NIGHT (LP) 15

DELKOM

91 Wau! Mr Modo MWS 034R Superjack — Orbital Infusion 2000/Neutron 9000 Mix (12", 500 only) 15

ELAINE DELMAR

59 Fontana H 227 I Loves You Porgy/Porgy (78) 7
70 CBS 5329 Hurt So Bad/The Train 5

DELMORE BROTHERS

58 Parlophone GEP 8728 COUNTRY AND WESTERN (EP) 40
(see also Brown's Ferry Four, Grandpa Jones, Merle Travis)

DELMONTES

80s Rational RATE 3 Don't Cry Your Tears/So It's Not To Be (yellow or blue p/s) 8

AL DE LORY

65 London HLU 9999 Yesterday/Traffic Jam 20
70 Capitol CL 15644 Song From M*A*S*H/Feeling Of Love 5

DELROY & SPORTY

71 Banana BA 322 Lovers Version/DUDLEY SIBLEY: Having A Party 12

DELROY & TENNORS

71 Camel CA 62 Donkey Shank/MURPHY'S ALL STARS: Donkey Track 10

DELTA CATS

69 Bamboo BAM 3 I Can't Re-Live (song actually "I Can't Believe")/I've Been Hurt 15
(see also Thrillers)

DELTA 5

79 Rough Trade RT 31 Mind Your Own Business/Now That You've Gone (p/s) 7
80 Rough Trade RT 41 Anticipation/You (p/s) 7
81 Rough Trade RT 61 Try/Colour (p/s) 7

DELTA KINGS

61 London RE-R 1318 AT SUNDOWN (EP) 10
61 London Jazz LTZ-R 15204 AT SUNDOWN (LP, also stereo SAH-R 6118) 15/18

DELTA RHYTHM BOYS

51 London L 1145 Blow Out The Candle/All The Things You Are (78) 12
54 Brunswick 05353 Mood Indigo/Have A Hope, Have A Wish, Have A Prayer 10
52 Esquire 15-001 DELTA RHYTHM BOYS WITH THE METRONOME ALLSTARS (10" LP) 25

DELTAS

64 Blue Beat BB 265 Georgia/The Party 22
65 Blue Beat BB 275 The Visitor/SKATALITES: Hanging The Beam 25

DELTA SKIFFLE GROUP

57 Esquire 10-504 Skip To My Lou/John Brown's Body (78) 8
57 Esquire 10-507 K.C. Moan/Pick A Bale Of Cotton (78) 8
58 Esquire 10-517 Ain't You Glad?/Open Up Them Pearly Gates (78) 10
58 Esquire EP 162 DELTA SKIFFLE GROUP (EP) 55

DELTONES (Jamaica)

71 Green Door GD 4010 Chopsticks/DES BRYAN: Belmont Street 10
72 Trojan TRM 9001 Chopsticks/I Got It/Put It On 6

DELTONES (U.K.)

70 Columbia DB 8719 Gimme Some Lovin'/Have A Little Talk With Myself 18

MINT VALUE £

DEL-TONES (U.S.)
59 Top Rank JAR 171 Moonlight Party/Rockin' Blues ... 75
59 Top Rank JAR 171 Moonlight Party/Rockin' Blues (78) ... 30
(see also Beau-Marks)

MILTON DE LUGG ORCHESTRA
65 Columbia DB 7474 The Addams Family Theme/The Alfred Hitchcock Theme ... 15
66 Columbia DB 7762 The Munsters Theme/The Addams Family Theme ... 15
(see also Beau-Marks)

DELUSION
80s Wizzo WIZZO 2 Pessimists Paradise/Desert Island (gatefold p/s) ... 8

DEL(L)-VIKINGS
57 London HLD 8405 Come Go With Me/How Can I Find A True Love (gold or silver label lettering) 150/65
57 London HLD 8405 Come Go With Me/How Can I Find A True Love (78) ... 15
57 London HLD 8464 Whispering Bells/Little Billy Boy ... 65
57 London HLD 8464 Whispering Bells/Little Billy Boy (78) ... 12
57 Mercury MT 169 Cool Shake/Jitterbug Mary (78) ... 30
58 Mercury 7MT 199 The Voodoo Man/Can't Wait ... 65
58 Mercury MT 199 The Voodoo Man/Can't Wait (78) ... 30
59 Mercury AMT 1027 Flat Tyre/How Could You ... 55
59 Mercury AMT 1027 Flat Tyre/How Could You (78) ... 45
62 HMV POP 1072 Confession Of Love/Kilimanjaro ... 30
63 HMV POP 1145 An Angel Up In Heaven/The Fishing Chant ... 30
71 Contour 2870 388 COME GO WITH ME (LP) ... 15
(see also Chuck Jackson)

LEO DE LYON
54 MGM SP 1087 The Band Played On/Say It Isn't So ... 7
60 Oriole CB 1561 Rich In Love/The Blue Train ... 7
60 Oriole MG 20053 LEO DE LYON (LP) ... 18

RALPH DE MARCO
59 London HLL 9010 Old Shep/More Than Riches ... 10
59 London HLL 9010 Old Shep/More Than Riches (78) ... 25

DEMENSIONS
60 Top Rank JAR 505 Over The Rainbow/Nursery Rhyme Rock ... 75
61 Coral Q 72437 Count Your Blessings Instead Of Sheep/Again ... 18

(ROD) DEMICK & (HERBIE) ARMSTRONG
70 Decca F 13056 We're On The Right Track/Dreaming (as Demick-Armstrong) ... 6
71 Mam MAM 10 If I Ever Get To You/Girl ... 5
71 Mam MAM-AS 1001 LITTLE WILLY RAMBLE (LP) ... 12
72 A&M AMLH 68908 LOOKIN' THROUGH (LP) ... 12
(see also Wheels, James Brothers, Fox)

DEMOB
81 Round Ear ROUND 1 Anti Police/Teenage Adolescence (foldout p/s, later standard p/s) ... 12/10
81 Round Ear EAR 3 No Room For You/Think Straight/New Breed (p/s) ... 10

DEMON
81 Clay CLAY 4 Liar/Wild Woman (p/s, red vinyl) ... 8
82 Carrere CAR 226 One Helluva Night/Into The Nightmare (picture disc) ... 6
83 Clay CLAY 25 The Plague/The Only Sane Man (p/s) ... 6
84 Clay CLAY 41 Wonderland/Blackheath (p/s) ... 6
84 Clay 12CLAY 41 Wonderland/Blackheath/Nowhere To Run (12", p/s) ... 8
88 Clay CLAY 48D Tonight (The Hero Is Back)/Hurricane//Night Of The Demon/
Don't Break The Circle (double pack) ... 5
83 Clay CLAYLP 6 THE PLAGUE (LP, gatefold sleeve, with insert) ... 15
83 Clay CLAYLP 6P THE PLAGUE (LP, picture disc) ... 20
90 Sonic SONICLP 1 NIGHT OF THE DEMON (LP) ... 12
90 Flametrader LP 1 ONE HELLUVA NIGHT (2-LP) ... 18

DEMON FUZZ
70 Dawn DNX 2504 I Put A Spell On You/Message To Mankind/Fuzz Oriental Blues (some in p/s) ... 8/5
70 Dawn DNLS 3013 AFREAKA! (LP) ... 30

DEMON PACT
81 Slime PACT 1 Eaten Alive/Raiders (p/s) ... 50
81 Slime PACT 2 Escape/Demon Pact (unreleased, labels only)

DEMON PREACHER
78 Illegal SRTS/CUS/78110 Royal Northern (N7)/Laughing At Me/
Steal Your Love/Dead End Kidz (numbered p/s) ... 25
78 Small Wonder SMALL TEN Little Miss Perfect/Perfect Dub (p/s) ... 10
(see also Demons, Alien Sex Fiend, Fenzyx)

DEMONS (Jamaica)
69 Big Shot BI 523 You Belong To My Heart/Bless You ... 10

DEMONS (U.K.)
80 Crypt Music DEM 1 Action By Example/I Wish I Was A Dog (p/s) ... 12
(see also Alien Sex Fiend, Demon Preacher)

DEMONSTRATORS
64 Warner Bros WB 132 Sweet Violets/Ultra Violet ... 15

JASON DENE
66 Parlophone R 5485 Opportunity/It's Me ... 7
(see also Jason Deane)

TERRY DENE

57	Decca F 10895	A White Sport Coat/The Man In The Phone Booth	40
57	Decca F 10895	A White Sport Coat/The Man In The Phone Booth (78)	6
57	Decca F 10914	Start Movin'/Green Corn	25
57	Decca F 10938	Come And Get It/Teenage Dream	25
57	Decca F 10964	Lucky Lucky Bobby/Baby, She's Gone	25
57	Decca F 10964	Lucky Lucky Bobby/Baby, She's Gone (78)	8
58	Decca F 10977	The Golden Age/C'Min And Be Loved	20
58	Decca F 10977	The Golden Age/C'Min And Be Loved (78)	6
58	Decca F 11016	Stairway Of Love/Lover, Lover!	12
58	Decca F 11016	Stairway Of Love/Lover, Lover! (78)	6
58	Decca F 11037	Seven Steps To Love/Can I Walk You Home	18
58	Decca F 11037	Seven Steps To Love/Can I Walk You Home (78)	6
58	Decca F 11076	Who Baby Who/Pretty Little Pearly	20
58	Decca F 11076	Who Baby Who/Pretty Little Pearly (78)	8
59	Decca F 11100	I've Got A Good Thing Going/Bimbombey	15
59	Decca F 11100	I've Got A Good Thing Going/Bimbombey (78)	8
59	Decca F 11136	There's No Fool Like A Young Fool/I've Come Of Age	15
59	Decca F 11136	There's No Fool Like A Young Fool/I've Come Of Age (78)	10
59	Decca F 11154	Thank You Pretty Baby/A Boy Without A Girl	20
59	Decca F 11154	Thank You Pretty Baby/A Boy Without A Girl (78)	12
60	Oriole CB 1562	Geraldine/Love Me Or Leave Me	25
61	Oriole CB 1594	Like A Baby/Next Stop Paradise	22
63	Aral PS 107	The Feminine Look/Fever (all in p/s)	20
82	Logo GO 412	Paralysed/Lorna/The Girl In The Long Black Dress	5
57	Decca DFE 6427	TERRY DENE (EP, issued without p/s)	50
58	Decca DFE 6459	THE GOLDEN DISC (EP)	45
58	Decca DFE 6507	TERRY DENE NO. 1 (EP)	45
66	Herald ELR 107	TERRY DENE NOW (EP)	20
72	Pilgrim JLPS 175	IF THAT ISN'T LOVE (LP)	12
73	Pilgrim JLPS 188	CALL TO THE WIND (LP)	12
74	Decca SPA 368	I THOUGHT TERRY DENE WAS DEAD (LP)	15

DENE BOYS

57	HMV POP 374	Bye Bye Love/Love Is The Thing	20
58	HMV POP 455	Skylark/I Walk Down The Street	10
58	HMV POP 455	Skylark/I Walk Down The Street (78)	8

DENE FOUR

59	HMV POP 666	Hush-a-bye/Something New	22

(see also Dene Boys)

DENIGH

80	Ace ACE 16	No Way/Running (no p/s)	80

DENIMS

65	CBS 201807	I'm Your Man/Ya Ya	70

CLAUDE DENJEAN

71	Decca PFS 4212	MOOG! (LP)	12

ROGER DENISON

66	Parlophone R 5545	I'm On An Island/I'm Running Out Of Time	12
67	Parlophone R 5566	She Wanders Through My Mind/This Just Doesn't Seem To Be My Day	8

WADE DENNING & PORT WASHINGTONS

67	MGM MGM 1339	Tarzan's March/Batman	15

D.D. (Denzil) DENNIS

70	Crab CRAB 60	Having A Party/Man With Ambition	7
70	Pama Supreme PS 301	My Way/Happy Days	7
71	Punch PH 93	Christmas Message/Cool It Girl	7
71	Pama Supreme PS 330	I'm A Believer/I'll Make The Way Easy	7
74	Pama Supreme PS 391	Women And Money/UPSETTERS: Ten Cent Skank	8

(see also Denzil Dennis)

DENZIL DENNIS

63	Blue Beat BB 181	Seven Nights In Rome/Love Is For Fools	18
68	Trojan TR 614	Donkey Train/Down By The Riverside	12
68	Trojan TR 615	Me Nah Worry/Hush Don't You Cry	12
68	Jolly JY 011	Oh Carol/Where Has My Little Girl Gone	12
70	Pama Supreme PS 304	Painful Situation/Nothing Has Changed	7
71	Pama Supreme PS 350	South Of The Border/GRAHAM: Long Island	12
72	Pama Supreme PS 375	Mama We're All Crazy Now/ROY SHIRLEY: A Lady's A Man's Best Friend	7
72	Duke DU 142	I Forgot To Be Your Lover/I've Got To Settle Down	7
73	Grape GR 3059	People Got To Be Friends/Ups And Downs (actually by Pat Rhoden)	7

(see also D.D. Dennis, Cosmo & Dennis, Denzil & Pat, Denzil & Jennifer, Les & Silkie)

JACKIE DENNIS

58	Decca F 10992	La Dee Dah/You're The Greatest	12
58	Decca F 11011	Miss Valerie/My Dream	18
58	Decca F 11011	Miss Valerie/My Dream (78)	6
58	Decca F 11033	The Purple People Eater/You-Oo	18
58	Decca F 11033	The Purple People Eater/You-Oo (78)	6
58	Decca F 11060	More Than Ever (Come Prima)/Linton Addie	12
58	Decca F 11060	More Than Ever (Come Prima)/Linton Addie (78)	6
58	Decca F 11090	Gingerbread/Lucky Ladybug	12
58	Decca F 11090	Gingerbread/Lucky Ladybug (78)	6
59	Top Rank JAR 129	Summer Snow/Night Bird	10
59	Top Rank JAR 129	Summer Snow/Night Bird (78)	6
58	Decca DFE 6513	JACKIE DENNIS NO. 1 (EP)	45

MINT VALUE £

DENNIS & LIZZY

70	Camel CA 56	Everybody Bawlin'/Mr Brown	10
73	Pyramid PYR 7002	Ba-Ba-Ri-Ba-Shank/TOMMY McCOOK ALL STARS: Buck And The Preacher	10

(see also Dennis Alcapone, Lizzy & Dennis)

DENNISONS

63	Decca F 11691	(Come On) Be My Girl/Little Latin Lupe Lu	20
64	Decca F 11880	Walkin' The Dog/You Don't Know What Love Is	25
64	Decca F 11990	Nobody Like My Babe/Lucy (You Sure Did It This Time)	20

DENNY & WILSON

72	Hillcrest HCT 6	Hey Hey Girl/CARLTON ALPHONSO: Girl I Love You	6

MARTIN DENNY (& HIS ORCHESTRA)

59	London HLU 8860	Quiet Village/Llama Serenade	7
59	London SLW 4004	Quiet Village/Llama Serenade (stereo export issue)	35
59	London HLU 8860	Quiet Village/Llama Serenade (78)	6
59	London HLU 8976	The Enchanted Sea/Martinique	6
59	London HLU 8976	The Enchanted Sea/Martinique (78)	8
62	Liberty LIB 55470	A Taste Of Honey/The Brighter Side	6
60	London REU 1241	THE EXOTIC SOUNDS OF MARTIN DENNY (EP)	20
58	London HB-U 1079	EXOTICA (10" LP, mono only)	40
58	London SAH-U 6004	FORBIDDEN ISLAND (LP, stereo only)	35
59	London HA-U 2196	AFRO-DESIA (LP, also stereo SAH-U 6048)	20/30
60	London HA-U 2208	QUIET VILLAGE (LP, also stereo SAH-U 6055)	25/30
60	London SAH-W 6062	EXOTICA (12" LP, stereo reissue with extra tracks "Busy Port" & "Waipio")	25
60	London HA-G 2253	EXOTICA — VOL. 2 (LP, also stereo SAH-G 6076)	25/30
60	London HA-W 2239	EXOTICA — VOL. 3 (LP, also stereo SAH-W 6069)	25/30
60	London HA-G 2281	THE ENCHANTED SEA (LP, also stereo SAH-G 6098)	25/30
61	London HA-G 2317	THE SILVER SCREEN (LP, also stereo SAH-G 6122)	15/18
61	London HA-G 2387	EXOTIC PERCUSSION (LP, also stereo SAH-G 6187)	15/18
62	London HA-G 2417	ROMANTICA (LP, also stereo SAH-G 6215)	15/18
64	Liberty LBY 1241	HAWAII TATTOO (LP)	18
65	Liberty (S)LBY 1221	LATIN VILLAGE (LP)	12
65	Liberty (S)LBY 1267	SPANISH VILLAGE (LP)	12
66	Liberty (S)LBY 1276	20 GOLDEN HAWAIIAN HITS (LP)	12
66	Liberty (S)LBY 1301	MARTIN DENNY PLAYS (LP)	12
66	Liberty (S)LBY 1354	HAWAII TOUCH (LP)	15
68	Sunset SLS 50002	SAYONARA (LP)	12

SANDY DENNY

72	Island WIP 6141	Here In Silence/Man Of Iron (theme from *Pass Of Arms* film, some in p/s)	25/40
72	Island WIP 6142	Listen Listen/Tomorrow Is A Long Time	6
73	Island WIP 6176	Whispering Grass/Friends (some in p/s)	6/10
74	Island WIP 6195	Like An Old Fashioned Waltz (unissued)	
76	Mooncrest MOON 54	Make Me A Pallet On Your Floor/This Train	6
77	Island WIP 6391	Candle In The Wind/Still Waters Run Deep (unissued, promo only)	30
67	Saga EROS 8041	SANDY AND JOHNNY (LP, with Johnny Silvo)	30
70	Saga EROS 8153	SANDY DENNY (LP)	35
71	Island ILPS 9165	THE NORTH STAR GRASSMAN AND THE RAVENS (LP, gatefold sleeve, 'pink rim palm tree' label)	22
72	Island ILPS 9207	SANDY (LP, gatefold sleeve, originally with 'pink rim palm tree' label)	12/20
73	Island ILPS 9258	LIKE AN OLD FASHIONED WALTZ (LP, gatefold sleeve, 'pink rim palm tree' label)	20
73	Hallmark SHM 813	ALL OUR OWN WORK (LP, with Strawbs)	15
77	Island ILPS 9433	RENDEZVOUS (LP, with insert)	12
78	Mooncrest CREST 28	THE ORIGINAL SANDY DENNY (LP)	20
85	Island SDSP 100	WHO KNOWS WHERE THE TIME GOES? (4-LP box set)	30
97	Strange Fruit SFRSCD 006	THE BBC SESSIONS 1971-73 (CD, limited edition)	25

(see also Fairport Convention, Bunch, Strawbs, Fotheringay, Alex Campbell, Trevor Lucas, Richard Thompson)

SUSAN DENNY

65	Melodisc MEL 1596	Don't Touch Me/Johnny	15

DENTISTS

85	Spruck SP 003	Strawberries Are Growing In My Garden (And It's Wintertime)/ Burning The Thoughts From My Skin/Doreen (p/s)	10
85	Spruck SP 004	YOU AND YOUR BLOODY ORANGES (12" EP, p/s)	10
86	Tambourine SP 006	DOWN AND OUT IN PARIS AND CHATHAM (12" EP, brown/white or group p/s)	8
87	Tambourine URINE 3	Writhing On The Shagpile/Just Like Oliver Reed/A Strange Way To Go About Things/Calm You Down/The Turquoise Castle (12", p/s)	8
85	Spruck SPR 001	SOME PEOPLE ARE ON THE PITCH THEY THINK IT'S ALL OVER IT IS NOW (LP)	15

MICKEY DENTON

61	London HLX 9398	The Steady Kind/Now You Can't Give Them Away	12

KARL DENVER

61	Decca F 11360	Marcheta/Joe Sweeney	5
61	Decca F 11395	Mexicali Rose/Bonny Scotland	5
62	Decca F 11420	Wimoweh/Gypsy Davy	6
62	Decca F 11431	Never Goodbye/Highland Fling	5
62	Decca F 11470	A Little Love, A Little Kiss/Lonely Sailor	5
62	Decca F 11505	Blue Weekend/My Mother's Eyes	6
62	Decca F 11553	Dry Tears/Pastures Of Plenty	6
63	Decca F 11608	Can You Forgive Me/Love From A Heart Of Gold	6
63	Decca F 11674	Indian Love Call/My Melancholy Baby	6
63	Decca F 11720	Still/My Canary Has Circles Under His Eyes	5
64	Decca F 11828	My World Of Blue/The Green Grass Grows All Round	6

MINT VALUE £

64	Decca F 11905	Love Me With All Your Heart/Am I That Easy To Forget?	6
64	Decca F 12025	Sally/Swanee River	6
65	Mercury MF 878	Cry A Little Sometimes/Today Will Be Yesterday Tomorrow	8
65	Mercury MF 904	Marta/I'll Never Forget To Remember	8
65	Mercury MF 926	The Tips Of My Fingers/I'm Alone Because I Love You	8
68	Page One POF 063	You've Still Got A Place In My Heart/I Still Miss Someone (as Karl Denver Trio)	10
62	Decca DFE 8501	BY A SLEEPY LAGOON (EP)	15
62	Decca DFE 8504	KARL DENVER HITS (EP)	10
61	Ace Of Clubs ACL 1098	WIMOWEH (LP)	20
62	Ace Of Clubs ACL 1131	KARL DENVER (LP)	20
63	Decca LK 4540	LIVE AT THE YEW TREE (LP)	30
64	Decca LK 4596	WITH LOVE (LP)	30

NIGEL DENVER

66	Decca LK 4728	MOVIN' ON (LP, featuring Martin Carthy)	50
67	Major Minor MMLP 1	SCOTTISH REPUBLICAN SONGS (LP)	25
68	Decca SKL 4943	FOLK OLD AND NEW (LP)	25

DENZIL & JENNIFER

70	Escort ES 824	Young, Gifted And Black/OWEN GRAY: I Am Satisfied	7

DENZIL (Dennis) & PAT (Rhoden)

69	Downtown DT 403	Dream/Sincerely	7

DEODATO

74	CTI CTL 21	IN CONCERT (LP, with Airto)	12

(see also Airto)

SIDNEY DE PARIS' BLUE NOTE JAZZ MEN

50	Jazz Parade E2	Ballin' The Jack/Who's Sorry Now (12" 78)	7

WILBUR DE PARIS' NEW ORLEANS BAND

59	London HLE 8816	Petite Fleur/Over And Over Again	7

DEPECHE MODE

81	Lyntone LYN 10209	Sometimes I Wish I Was Dead/FAD GADGET: King Of The Flies (red flexidisc free with *Flexipop* magazine, issue 11)	25/15
81	Lyntone LYN 10209	Sometimes I Wish I Was Dead/FAD GADGET: King Of The Flies (test pressing)	250
81	Mute MUTE 013	Dreaming Of Me/Ice Machine (p/s)	5
83	Mute L12BONG 2	Get The Balance Right/My Secret Garden (live)/See You (live)/ Satellite (live) (12", numbered p/s)	10
83	Mute L12BONG 3	Everything Counts/Boys Say Go (live)/New Life (live)/Nothing To Fear (live)/ The Meaning Of Love (live) (12", numbered p/s)	10
83	Mute L12BONG 4	Love In Itself (2)/Just Can't Get Enough (live)/Photograph Of You (live)/ Shout (live)/Photographic (live) (12", numbered p/s)	10
84	Mute L12BONG 5	People Are People (On-U-Sound Remix)/In Your Memory/ People Are People (12", numbered in die-cut p/s)	10
84	Mute L12BONG 6	Master And Servant (On-U-Sound Science Fiction Dancehall Classic)/ Are People People?/(Set Me Free) Remotivate Me (12", numbered p/s)	10
85	Mute L12 BONG 8	Edit The Shake/Master And Servant (live)/Flexible (Pre-Deportation Mix)/ Something To Do (Metal Mix) (12", p/s)	10
85	Mute 7BONG 9	It's Called A Heart/Fly On The Windscreen (p/s, sealed with poster)	5
85	Mute D12BONG 9	It's Called A Heart (Mixes)/Fly On The Windscreen (Mixes) (12", p/s, dbl-pack)	10
86	Mute CBONG 11	A Question Of Lust (Flood Mix)/If You Want (live)/Shame (live)/ Blasphemous Rumours (live) (cassette in 7" pack with book & badge)	8
86	Mute L12BONG 12	A Question Of Time (Mixes)/Black Celebration (Black Tulip Mix)/More Than A Party (Live Remix) (12", p/s)	8
87	Mute L12 BONG 13	Strangelove (Blind Mix)/PIMPF/Strangelove (Pain Mix)/Agent Orange (12", p/s)	8
87	Mute CDBONG 13	Strangelove (Maxi-Mix)/Strangelove (Midi-Mix)/Strangelove (LP Mix)/ PIMPF/Agent Orange (CD, card p/s)	8
87	Mute CBONG 14	Never Let Me Down Again (Split Mix)/(Aggro Mix)/Pleasure Little Treasure (Glitter Mix) (cassette with 'overlay')	5
87	Mute L12BONG 14	Never Let Me Down Again (Tsangarides Mix)/Pleasure Little Treasure (Join Mix)/To Have And To Hold (Spanish Taster) (12", p/s)	8
87	Mute CDBONG 14	Never Let Me Down Again (Split Mix)/Pleasure Little Treasure (Join Mix)/ To Have And To Hold (Spanish Taster)/Never Let Me Down Again (Aggro Mix) (CD in pouch)	12
88	Mute L12BONG 15	Behind The Wheel (Beatmasters Remix)/Route 66 (Casuality Mix) (12", p/s)	8
89	Mute 10BONG 16	Everything Counts (Absolute Mix)/(1983 12" Mix)/Nothing (US 7" Mix) (10", envelope p/s, with 2 postcards & window sticker)	12
89	Mute L12BONG 16	Everything Counts (Tim Simenon & M. Saunders Remix)/Nothing (Justin Strauss Remix)/Strangelove (Tim Simenon & M. Saunders Remix) (12", p/s)	8
89	Mute LCDBONG 16	Everything Counts (Tim Simenon & M. Saunders Remix)/Nothing (Justin Strauss Remix)/Strangelove (Tim Simenon & M. Saunders Remix) (3" CD, 'filofax page' p/s)	15
89	Mute GBONG 17	Personal Jesus/(Acoustic)/Dangerous (Hazchemix) (gatefold p/s with photos)	5
89	Mute L12BONG 17	Personal Jesus (Mixes)/Dangerous (Hazchemix) (12", p/s)	8
89	Mute LCDBONG 17	Personal Jesus (Pump Mix)/Personal Jesus (Telephone Stomp Mix)/ Dangerous (Hazchemix) (3" CD)	15
90	Mute XL12BONG 18	Enjoy The Silence (The Quad: Final Mix) (12", 1-side etched, p/s)	10
90	Mute LCDBONG 18	Enjoy The Silence (Bassline): Bassline/Harmonium/Ricki Tick Tick Mix/ Memphisto (CD)	10
90	Mute XLCDBONG 18	Enjoy The Silence (The Quad: Final Mix) (3" CD, 1-track)	25
90	Mute L12BONG 19	Policy Of Truth (Trancentral Mix)/Policy Of Truth (Pavlov's Dub)/ Kaleid (remix) (12", gatefold p/s)	8
90	Mute L12BONG 20	World In My Eyes (Dub In My Eyes)/(Mode To Joy)/Happiest Girl (The Pulsating Orbital Mix) (12", p/s with inner, in sealed blue PVC pack)	10

MINT VALUE £

90	Mute LCDBONG 20	World In My Eyes (Dub In My Eyes)/World In My Eyes (Mode To Joy)/ Happiest Girl (The Pulsating Orbital Vocal Mix)/Sea Of Sin (Sensoria)/ World In My Eyes (Mayhem Mode)/Happiest Girl (Jack Mix) (CD)	25
91	Mute DMBX 1	1 (6-CD single box set, with booklet)	25
91	Mute DMBX 2	2 (6-CD single box set, with booklet)	25
91	Mute DMBX 3	3 (6-CD single box set, with booklet)	25
94	Mute XLCDBONG 24	In Your Room (Mixes)/Higher Love (Adrenaline Mix) (CD)	10
02	Mute MUTE 12BONG 33	Goodnight Lovers (ISAN Falling Leaf Mix)/When The Body Speaks (Acoustic Version)/The Dead Of Night (Electronicat Remix) (12", red vinyl, p/s)	25
87	Mute STUMM 47	MUSIC FOR THE MASSES (LP, clear vinyl)	20
87	Mute STUMM 47	MUSIC FOR THE MASSES (LP, with bonus 12" "Strangelove (Maximix)"/ "Never Let Me Down Again (Split Mix)" [HMV 1])	30
88	Mute CDSTUMM 5	SPEAK AND SPELL (CD)	18
89	Mute CD TUMM 100	101 (2-CD, tri-fold card sleeve, with booklet in slip case)	20
89	Mute (no cat. no.)	B-SIDES (4-LP set, plain white box, unreleased, test pressings only)	1,000
93	Mute LCDSTUMM 106	SONGS OF FAITH AND DEVOTION LIVE (CD, in slipcase with photo-book)	20
98	Mute MUTEL 5	SINGLES 86-98 (3-LP box set, numbered, with booklet)	25
PROMOS			
86	Mute BONG 12	A Question Of Time (Edit)/Black Celebration (Live) (white label)	70
87	Mute BONG 13R	Strangelove (Radio Edit)/Strangelove (p/s)	80
87	Mute DANCE BONG 13	Strangelove (Blind Mix)/(Fresh Ground Mix) (12", promo-only remix)	50
87	Mute BONG 14R	Never Let Me Down Again/Pleasure Little Treasure	70
87	Mute P12BONG 14	Never Let Me Down Again (Split Mix)/Pleasure Little Treasure (Glitter Mix)/ Never Let Me Down Again (Aggro Mix) (12")	10
87	Mute DJBONG 15	Behind The Wheel (DJ Remix)/Behind The Wheel (LP Mix)	90
89	Mute BONG 17	Personal Jesus/Dangerous (censored black rear p/s)	40
89	Mute PP12BONG 16	Strangelove (Hijack Mix)/Nothing (12")	18
89	Mute BONG 16R	Everything Counts (Live – Radio Edit)/Nothing (Live Mix) (stickered p/s)	20
90	Mute BONG 18	Enjoy The Silence/Memphisto ('A' label)	25
90	Mute RCDBONG 18	Enjoy The Silence (7")/Memphisto (7") (CD)	25
90	Mute CDBONG 19R	Policy Of Truth (7" Version)/Kaleid (Remix) (CD)	25
90	Mute PSTUMM 64	VIOLATOR (12" EP, 4-track sampler)	15
90	Mute 12BONG 20	World In My Eyes (Oil Tank Mix)/Happiest Girl (Kiss-A-Mix)/Sea Of Sin (Sensoria) (12", white label, numbered, stickered sleeve)	25
93	Mute PL12BONG 23	Rush (Spiritual Guidance Mix)/Rush (Amylnitrate Mix)/Rush (Wild Planet Vocal Mix) (12")	50
97	Mute BONG 26	It's No Good (Club 69 Future Mix)/It's No Good (Club 69 Future Dub)/ It's No Good (Club 69 Funk Dub) (12")	60
97	Mute PL12BONG 26	It's No Good (Club 69 mixes) (12")	70
97	Mute XLCDBONG 26	It's No Good (Live) (CD)	70
97	Mute P12BONG 28	Useless (CJ Bolland Funky Sub Mix)/Useless (the Kruder & Dorfmeister Session™) (12", die-cut p/s)	18
98	Mute P12BONG 29	Only When I Lose Myself (Dan The Automator Mix)/Only When I Lose Myself (Subsonic Legacy Mix)/Painkiller (Kill The Pain — DJ Shadow Vs Depeche Mode)/Headstar (12", die-cut p/s)	10
01	Mute P12BONG 30	Dream On (Bushwacka Tough Guy mixes) (12", p/s)	18
01	Mute P12BONG 30	Dream On (Dave Clarke Club Mix)/Dream On (Bushwacka Blunt Mixes) (12", p/s)	18
01	Mute P12BONG 30	Dream On (Octagon Man mixes)/(Dave Clarke Acoustic Mix)/Dream On (Kid 606 Mix) (12", p/s)	18
01	Mute PL12BONG 31	I Feel Loved (Danny Tenaglia mixes) (12", p/s)	20
01	Mute PL12BONG 32	Freelove (Deep Dish Freedom Mix)/Freelove (Josh Wink Vocal Interpretation)/Freelove (Deep Dish Freedom Dub)/Freelove (Powder Productions Remix) (12", doublepack, p/s)	25
87	Mute (no cat. no.)	THE B-SIDES (4-LP test pressings in title box)	800+
87	Mute (no cat. no.)	THE B-SIDES (4-cassette set)	250+
90	Mute (no cat. no.)	VIOLATOR (LP, CD & cassette in 12" x 12" picture box with insert)	140
93	Mute VERBONG 1	SONGS OF FAITH & DEVOTION (interview CD)	70
93	Mute (no cat. no.)	SONGS OF FAITH & DEVOTION (4-CD box set)	300
94	Mute DEPRO 1	DEPRO 1 (13-track compilation CD)	90
97	Mute BXSTUMM 148	ULTRA (box set, with CD, T-shirt, stickers & EPK video, soap box pack)	150
98	Mute (no cat. no.)	THE SINGLES 86>98 (15" x 6" box set, with 3 CDs, video tape & cards)	120
01	Mute IPKSTUMM 190	EXCITER (interview CD with bonus multimedia disc)	70
01	Mute BCDSTUMM 190	EXCITER (interview CD with bonus multimedia disc, in long box)	110

DEPRAVED

86	Children Of Rev. GURT 6	COME ON DOWN (LP, with lyric inner)	12

DEPRESSIONS

77	Barn 2014 112	Living On Dreams/Family Planning (p/s)	20
78	Barn 2014 119	Messing With Your Heart/Street Kid (p/s)	18
78	Barn 2014 122	Get Out Of This Town/Basement Daze (p/s)	10
78	Barn 2314 105	THE DEPRESSIONS (LP)	15

DEPUTIES

66	Strike JH 305	Given Half A Chance/Where Do People Go	10

DEPUTY DAWG

96	Peacefrog P F053	GUN SLINGER EP (12", plain sleeve)	10

(see also Luke Slater)

DEREK

68	London HLZ 10230	Cinnamon/This Is My Story	10

(see also Johnny Cymbal)

MINT VALUE £

DEREK & THE DOMINOES
70 Polydor 2058 057 Tell The Truth/Roll It Over (withdrawn) . . . . . . 80+
71 Polydor 2058 130 Layla/Bell Bottom Blues (original, red paper label) 5
74 RSO 2090 104 Why Does Love Got To Be Sad?/Presence Of The Lord 5
82 RSO RSO 87 Layla/ERIC CLAPTON: Wonderful Tonight (p/s). 5
82 RSO RSOX 87 Layla/ERIC CLAPTON: Wonderful Tonight (live) (12", p/s) 8
71 Polydor 2625 005 LAYLA AND OTHER ASSORTED LOVE SONGS (2-LP). 20
(see also Eric Clapton, Bobby Whitlock)

DEREK & FRESHMEN
65 Oriole CB 305 Gone Away/I Stand Alone 15
(see also Derek Dean & Freshmen)

FRANK DE ROSA & HIS ORCHESTRA
58 London HLD 8576 Big Guitar/Irish Rock 30
58 London HLD 8576 Big Guitar/Irish Rock (78) 6

DERRICK (Morgan) & JENNIFER
70 Crab CRAB 47 Need To Belong/Let's Have Some Fun 8
70 Crab CRAB 54 Rocking Good Way/Wipe These Tears 8
(see also Derrick Morgan)

DERRICK (Morgan) & LLOYDS (Clarke)
62 Blue Beat BB 135 Love And Leave Me (actually by Lloyd Clarke)/Merry Twist (actually "Whistle Stop Tour" by Roy Richards) 22
(see also Derrick Morgan, Lloyd Clarke)

DERRICK (Morgan) & NAOMI (Campbell)
65 Island WI 193 Two Of A Kind/I Want A Lover (credited to Derrick Morgan) 25
65 Ska Beat JB 185 Heart Of Stone/DERRICK MORGAN: Let Me Go 22
65 Ska Beat JB 188 I Wish I Were An Apple/DERRICK MORGAN: Around The Corner 25
(see also Derrick Morgan, Naomi, Don Drummond)

DERRICK (Morgan) & PATSY (Todd)
61 Blue Beat BB 57 Feel So Fine/ROLAND ALPHONSO & GROUP: Mean To Me. 22
61 Blue Beat BB 65 Baby Please Don't Leave Me/Let The Good Times Roll 18
62 Blue Beat BB 97 Love Not To Brag/DRUMBAGO'S ALL STARS: Duck Soup 25
62 Blue Beat BB 100 In My Heart (actually by Derrick Morgan)/BELL'S GROUP: Kingston 13 22
62 Blue Beat BB 106 Oh Shirley/BASIL GABIDON'S GROUP: Sam The Fisherman (B-side actually by Roland Alphonso). 20
62 Blue Beat BB 121 Crying In The Chapel/Come Back My Love 25
62 Blue Beat BB 123 Oh My Love/Let's Go To The Party. 22
62 Island WI 018 Housewife's Choice/Gypsy Woman 15
63 Blue Beat BB 152 Little Brown Jug/Mow Sen Wa (with Lloyd Clarke) 25
63 Blue Beat BB 160 Trying To Make You Mine (actually "Baby Please Don't Leave Me" by Derrick Morgan)/Hold Me 25
63 Island WI 055 Sea Wave/Look Before You Leap 20
64 Blue Beat BB 207 Lover Boy/The Moon 20
64 Blue Beat BB 224 Steal Away/Money 20
64 Blue Beat BB 247 Troubles/Right (B-side actually "Baby Face"). 22
65 Blue Beat BB 291 You I Love/Let Me Hold Your hand (song actually "Steal Away") 22
65 Blue Beat BB 318 Eternity/Want My Baby. 22
65 Island WI 224 The National Dance/DESMOND DEKKER & FOUR ACES: Mount Zion 25
66 Island WI 288 I Found A Queen/It's True My Darling 20
68 Nu Beat NB 008 Hey Boy, Hey Girl/Music Is The Food Of Life. 15
(see also Derrick Morgan, Patsy Todd)

DERRICK (Morgan) & PAULETT
69 Nu Beat NB 027 I'll Do It/Give You My Love 15
(see also Derrick Morgan, Paulette)

DERRICK (Morgan) & PAULINE (Morgan)
68 Pyramid PYR 6027 You Never Miss Your Water/DERRICK MORGAN: Got You On My Mind 15
68 Pyramid/J.J. PYR 6063 Don't Say/DERRICK MORGAN: Johnny Pram Pram 15
(see also Derrick Morgan, Patsy Todd, Basil Gabbidon)

DERRICK & SOUNDS
68 Pye 7N 17601 Power Of Love/I'll Take You Home 5
69 Pye 7N 17709 My Sly Sadie/I Can't Lose That Girl 5
69 Pye 7N 17801 Morning Papers And Margarine/Winter Of Your Love 5

DERRINGERS
61 Capitol CL 15189 (If You Cry) True Love, True Love/Sheree. 18

GLEN DERRY ORCHESTRA
61 Oriole CB 1609 Blue Sax/Beatnik 8

HENRI DES
70 United Artists UP 35109 Return/Retour. 18

DES (Bryan) ALLSTARS
70 Grape GR 3014 Night Food Reggae/Walk With Des 7
70 Grape GR 3015 If I Had A Hammer/Hammer Reggae 7
70 Grape GR 3016 Henry The Great/Black Scorcher 8

SUGAR PIE DE SANTO
64 Pye International 7N 25249 Soulful Dress/Use What You Got 22
64 Pye International 7N 25267 I Don't Wanna Fuss/I Love You So Much. 22
66 Chess CRS 8034 There's Gonna Be Trouble/In The Basement (B-side with Etta James) 22
69 Chess CRS 8093 Soulful Dress/There's Gonna Be Trouble 12
(see also Etta James & Sugar Pie De Santo)

MINT VALUE £

MICHAEL DES BARRES

74 Purple PUR 123 — Leon/New Moon Tonight . . . 8

(see also Silverhead, Detective, Phoenix)

DESCENDANTS

67 CBS 202545 — Garden Of Eden/Lela . . . 60

DESECRATION

88 TPC — WHO'S IN CONTROL (EP, pink, green or black vinyl, with flexi) . . . 8

DESECTORS

70 GAS GAS 137 — King Kong/Please Stay . . . 6

DESERT WOLVES

87 Ugly Man UGLY 6T — Love Shattered Lives/Stopped In My Tracks/Desolation/ Sunday Morning (12", p/s) . . . 10
88 Ugly Man UGLY 9 — Speak To Me Rochelle/Besotted (p/s) . . . 6
88 Ugly Man UGLY 9T — Speak To Me Rochelle/Mexico/Besotted/La Petite Rochelle (12", p/s) . . . 12

JACKIE DE SHANNON

62 Liberty LIB 55497 — You Won't Forget Me/I Don't Think So Much . . . 20
63 Liberty LIB 55563 — Needles And Pins/Did He Call Today Mama? . . . 20
64 Liberty LIB 55645 — When You Walk In The Room/Till You Say You'll Be Mine . . . 15
64 Liberty LIB 10165 — Dancing Silhouettes/Hold Your Head High . . . 10
64 Liberty LIB 10175 — Don't Turn Your Back On Me/Be Good Baby . . . 12
65 Liberty LIB 10192 — She Don't Understand Him Like I Do/The Prince . . . 10
65 Liberty LIB 10202 — What The World Needs Now Is Love/It's Love Baby . . . 7
65 Liberty LIB 12019 — A Lifetime Of Loneliness/I Remember The Boy . . . 10
66 Liberty LIB 66171 — Come And Get Me/Splendour In The Grass . . . 7
66 Liberty LIB 66202 — I Can Make It With You/To Be Myself . . . 7
66 Liberty LIB 66224 — Come On Down/Find Me Love . . . 18
68 Liberty LBF 15133 — The Weight/Effervescent Blue . . . 7
69 Liberty LBF 15238 — Put A Little Love In Your Heart/Always Together . . . 7
70 Liberty LBF 15281 — Love Will Find A Way/I Let Go Completely . . . 7
70 Liberty LBF 15324 — What The World Needs Now/Keep Me In Mind . . . 7
72 Atlantic K 10184 — Vanilla Olay/I Wanna Roo You . . . 6
72 Atlantic K 10241 — Only Love Can Break Your Heart/Would You Like To Learn To Dance . . . 6
65 Liberty LEP 2233 — JACKIE (EP) . . . 35
64 Liberty LBY 1182 — THIS IS JACKIE DE SHANNON (LP) . . . 18
65 Liberty LBY 1245 — DON'T TURN YOUR BACK ON ME (LP) . . . 20
65 Liberty LBY 3063 — THIS IS JACKIE DE SHANNON (LP) . . . 20
66 Liberty (S)BLY 3085 — ARE YOU READY FOR THIS? (LP) . . . 20
68 Liberty LBS 83117E — GREAT PERFORMANCES (LP) . . . 20
69 Liberty LBS 83148E — ME ABOUT YOU (LP) . . . 20
70 Liberty LBS 83304 — PUT A LITTLE LOVE IN YOUR HEART (LP) . . . 20
72 Atlantic K 40396 — JACKIE (LP) . . . 15

(see also Date With Soul)

DESIGN

70 CBS 5112 — Willow Stream/Coloured Mile . . . 7
71 Epic EPC 7119 — Jet Song/Minstrel's Theme . . . 10
72 Regal Zonophone RZ 3044 — Colour All The World/Lazy Song . . . 7
72 Regal Zonophone RZ 3060 — Mayday/Yellow Bird . . . 7
73 Regal Zonophone RZ 3082 — One Sunny Day/End Of The Party . . . 7
71 Epic EPC 64322 — DESIGN (LP) . . . 15
71 Epic EPC64653 — TOMORROW IS SO FAR AWAY (LP, with insert) . . . 30
73 Regal Zono. SLRZ 1037 — DAY OF THE FOX (LP) . . . 25

DESIRELESS

88 CBS CD DESI 2 — Voyage Voyage (Britmix)/Voyage Voyage (Euro Remix)/ Destin Fragile (Instrumental) (CD) . . . 8
88 CBS CD DESI 3 — John (Extended Remix)/Voyage Voyage (Remix)/Qui Peut Savoir (CD) . . . 10
88 CBS 565 902-9 — FRANCOIS (CD) . . . 22

JOHNNY DESMOND

53 MGM SP 1042 — A Bushel And A Peck/ART LUND: If I Were A Bell . . . 10
54 Vogue Coral Q 2019 — The High And The Mighty/Got No Time . . . 10
55 Vogue Coral Q 72055 — Don't/There's No Happiness For Me (with Alan Dale & Buddy Greco) . . . 10
55 Vogue Coral Q 72076 — Play Me Hearts And Flowers/I'm So Ashamed . . . 10
55 Vogue Coral Q 72090 — Togetherness/A Straw Hat And A Cane . . . 10
55 Vogue Coral Q 72099 — Yellow Rose Of Texas/You're In Love With Someone . . . 10
55 Vogue Coral Q 72110 — Land Of The Pharaohs/This Too Shall Pass . . . 8
56 Vogue Coral Q 72115 — Sixteen Tons/Ballo Italiano . . . 8
56 Vogue Coral Q 72153 — Without You/I'll Cry Tomorrow . . . 8
56 Vogue Coral Q 72170 — A Little Love Can Go A Long Way/Please Don't Forget Me . . . 8
56 Vogue Coral Q 72190 — "The Proud Ones" Theme/I Only Know I Love You . . . 8
56 Vogue Coral Q 72207 — A Girl Named Mary/"Run For The Sun" Theme . . . 8
57 Vogue Coral Q 72235 — Where The River Meets The Sea/18th Century Music Box (B-side with Jimmy Saunders) . . . 10
57 Vogue Coral Q 72246 — That's Where I Shine/I Just Want You To Want Me . . . 8
57 Vogue Coral Q 72261 — A White Sports Coat (And A Pink Carnation)/Just Lookin' . . . 10
57 Vogue Coral Q 72261 — A White Sports Coat (And A Pink Carnation)/Just Lookin' (78) . . . 8
57 Vogue Coral Q 72269 — Shenandoah Rose/Consideration . . . 8
58 MGM MGM 994 — Hot Cha Cha/I'll Close My Eyes . . . 5
59 Philips PB 890 — Willingly/Apple (When Ya Gonna Fall From The Tree?) . . . 5
60 Coral Q 72398 — The Most Happy Fella/LANCERS: Joey, Joey, Joey . . . 5
60 Philips PB 1044 — Hawk/Playing The Field . . . 25
62 Top Rank JAR 612 — Twistin' Rose Of Texas/ Hello Honey . . . 10
56 Vogue Coral LVA 9035 — SOUVENIR D'ITALIE (LP) . . . 25

MINT VALUE £

LORRAE DESMOND (& REBELS)

54	Decca F 10375	Hold My Hand/On The Waterfront	12
54	Decca F 10398	Far Away (My Love Is Far Away)/No One But You	12
54	Decca F 10404	I Can't Tell A Waltz From A Tango/For Better, For Worse (with Johnston Brothers)	12
55	Decca F 10461	A Boy On Saturday Night/Why — Oh Why?	12
55	Decca F 10510	Don't/Where Will The Baby's Dimple Be?	12
55	Decca F 10533	Stowaway/Heartbroken (B-side with Johnston Brothers)	10
55	Decca F 10612	You Should Know/Wake The Town And Tell The People	10
56	Parlophone R 4239	Written On The Wind/A House With Love In It	8
57	Parlophone R 4287	You Won't Be Around/Play The Music (as Lorrae Desmond & Rebels)	8
57	Parlophone R 4320	Kansas City Special/Preacher, Preacher (as Lorrae Desmond & Rebels)	8
57	Parlophone R 4361	Ding-Dong Rock-a-billy Weddin'/Cabin Boy (as Lorrae Desmond & Rebels)	25
57	Parlophone R 4361	Ding-Dong Rock-a-billy Weddin'/Cabin Boy (78)	6
58	Parlophone R 4400	Two Ships/Little David	7
58	Parlophone R 4430	Down By The River/The Secret Of Happiness	7
58	Parlophone R 4463	Soda Pop Hop/Blue, Blue Day	15
58	Parlophone R 4463	Soda Pop Hop/Blue, Blue Day (78)	12
59	Parlophone R 4534	Tall Paul/Wait For It	12
59	Parlophone R 4534	Tall Paul/Wait For It (78)	12
60	Parlophone R 4670	Tell Me Again/Get Your Daddie's Car Tonight	8

MIKE DESMOND

57	Columbia DB 3954	Young And In Love/Two Loves (as Michael Desmond)	7
57	Columbia DB 4018	Chances Are/If You're Not Completely Satisfied (as Michael Desmond)	7
59	Top Rank JAR 225	If I Were The Sky/Tua	6
60	Top Rank JAR 298	The Happy Muleteer/Oh, So Wunderbar	6

PAUL DESMOND

60	RCA 1373	Take Ten/Embarcadero	7
61	Warner Bros WS 8020	PAUL DESMOND & FRIENDS (LP, stereo)	12

(see also Gerry Mulligan, Dave Brubeck)

DESOLATION ANGELS

84	AM AM 266	Valhalla/Boadicea (p/s)	40
85	Thameside TRR 111	DESOLATION ANGELS (LP)	50

DESPERATE BICYCLES

77	Refill RR 1	Smokescreen/Handlebars (p/s, same tracks both sides)	12
77	Refill RR 2	The Medium Was Tedium/Don't Back The Front (p/s, same tracks both sides)	12
78	Refill RR 3	NEW CROSS NEW CROSS (EP)	7
78	Refill RR 4	Occupied Territory/Skill (p/s)	7
78	Refill RR 7	Grief Is Very Private/Obstructive/Conundrum (some copies may be in p/s)	8
80	Refill RR 6	REMORSE CODE (LP)	15

DESSIE & JOHN

69	Downtown DT 440	Boss Sound/Everything Is Alright	10

DESTROY ALL MONSTERS

79	Cherry Red CHERRY 3	Bored/You're Gonna Die (p/s, red vinyl)	5
79	Cherry Red CHERRY 7	Meet The Creeper/November 22nd 1963 (p/s)	5
79	Cherry Red CHERRY 9	Nobody Knows/What Do I Get? (p/s)	5

(see also MC5)

DESTROYER

81	Clean Kill SJP 829	Evil Place/Stand And Deliver (no p/s)	50

DESTROYERS

70	Amalgamated AMG 856	Niney Special/Danger Zone	12
70	Pressure Beat PR 5505	Pressure Tonic/Machuki's Cooking (B-side actually with Count Machuki)	12

(see also Soul Brothers, Nicky Thomas)

DESTRUCTORS (V)

82	Carnage BOOK 2	Meaningless Names/AK 47/Police State/Dachau/Death Squad (p/s)	5
82	Carnage Benelux KILL 2	Religion/Soldier Boy/Agent Orange/Corpse Gas (p/s)	5
80s		EXORCISE THE DEMONS OF YOUTH (EP, with insert)	8

(see also Blanks)

DETAILS

80	Energy NRG 2	Keep On Running/Run'ins (p/s)	5
80	Energy NRG 002	Keep On Running/Run'ins (12", stickered plain sleeve, promo only)	8

DETECTIVE

78	Swansong SS 8504	IT TAKES ONE TO KNOW ONE (LP, with inner sleeve)	12

(see also Michael Des Barres)

DETERGENTS

65	Columbia DB 7513	Leader Of The Laundromat/Ulcers	18
65	Columbia DB 7591	I Don't Know/The Blue Kangaroo	10

DETONATORS

78	Local LR 1	Need Love Tonight/Great Big Ghetto/Shoob Shooby Do/ Give Me A Helping Hand (p/s)	6

DETOURS

68	CBS 3213	Run To Me Baby/Hangin' On	30
68	CBS 3401	Whole Lotta Lovin'/Pieces Of You	55

(see also Gene Latter)

DETROIT with MITCH RYDER

72	Paramount PARA 3022	It Ain't Easy/Long Neck Goose	5
72	Paramount SPFL 277	DETROIT (LP)	20

(see also Mitch Ryder)

MINT VALUE £

DETROIT EMERALDS

71 Pye International 7N 25544 Do Me Right/Just Now And Then . . . 8
71 Janus 6146 004 Wear This Ring/I Bet You Get The One . . . 5
72 Janus 6146 007 You Want It, You Got It/Till You Decide To Come Home . . . 5
72 Janus 6146 015 Do Me Right/Baby Let Me Take You In My Arms . . . 8
72 Janus 6146 020 Feel The Need In Me/And I Love Her . . . 8
71 Janus 6310 204 DO ME RIGHT (LP) . . . 20
72 Janus 6310 207 YOU WANT IT, YOU GOT IT (LP) . . . 20
73 Janus 6309 101 ABE, JAMES AND IVORY (LP) . . . 12

DETROITS

70 Fontana 6438 006 'TIS US OURSELVES (LP) . . . 12

DETROIT SPINNERS

65 Tamla Motown TMG 514 Sweet Thing/How Can I? (demos credited to either 'Spinners' or 'Detroit Spinners') . . . 150/65
65 Tamla Motown TMG 514 Sweet Thing/How Can I? (stock copies credited to 'Spinners') . . . 200
65 Tamla Motown TMG 523 I'll Always Love You/Tomorrow May Never Come (as 'Spinners' or 'Detroit Spinners') . . . 60/50
67 Tamla Motown TMG 627 For All We Know/I'll Always Love You (1st pressing with tall, narrow print) . . . 20/18
70 Tamla Motown TMG 755 It's A Shame/Together We Can Make Such Sweet Music (unissued)
70 Tamla Motown TMG 755 It's A Shame/Sweet Thing (as Motown Spinners) . . . 12
71 Tamla Motown TMG 766 Together We Can Make Such Sweet Music/Truly Yours (as Motown Spinners) . . . 6
80 Atlantic K 11558 Split Decision/Now That You're Mine Again . . . 8
80 Atlantic K 11558 Split Decision/Now That You're Mine Again (12") . . . 25
68 T. Motown (S)TML 11060 THE DETROIT SPINNERS (LP) . . . 55
71 T. Motown STML 11182 SECOND TIME AROUND (LP, as Motown Spinners) . . . 15
(see also Spinners, G.C. Cameron)

DEUCE COUP

67 Mercury MF 1013 A Clown In One Town/Angela (some in p/s) . . . 12/6

DEUCE OF HEARTS

66 CBS 202345 Closer Together/The Times They Are A Changin' . . . 7

JIMMY DEUCHAR

58 Tempo A 167 Bewitched/My Funny Valentine (as Jimmy Deuchar & His Pals) . . . 6
58 Tempo A 167 Bewitched/My Funny Valentine (78, as Jimmy Deuchar & His Pals) . . . 8
55 Tempo EXA 18 JIMMY DEUCHAR ENSEMBLE (EP) . . . 40
56 Esquire EP 93 JIMMY DEUCHAR QUARTET (EP) . . . 40
56 Esquire EP 103 JIMMY DEUCHAR QUARTET (EP) . . . 40
58 Tempo EXA 79 OPUS DE FUNK (EP, as Jimmy Deuchar Sextet) . . . 40
58 Tempo EXA 81 SWINGIN' IN STUDIO TWO (EP) . . . 40
59 Tempo EXA 88 WAIL (EP, with Victor Feldman Quintet) . . . 40
54 Esquire 20-059 DIG DEUCHAR, DON'T DANCE (LP) . . . 80
55 Tempo LAP 2 JIMMY DEUCHAR ENSEMBLE (10" LP) . . . 250
56 Tempo TAP 4 TOP TRUMPETS (LP) . . . 250
56 Vogue LDE SHOWCASE (LP) . . . 60
58 Tempo TAP 20 PAL JIMMY (LP) . . . 300
(see also Victor Feldman)

BIG PETE DEUCHAR/DEUKER

63 Fontana 267 278 TF Google Eye/There's A Hand Leading Me (as Big Pete Deuchar) . . . 10
65 Columbia DB 7763 Goin' In Training/I Saw Your Face In The Moon . . . 8

DEVIANTS

68 Stable STA 5601 You Got To Hold On/Let's Loot The Supermarket . . . 30
67 Underground Imp. IMP 1 PTOOFF! (LP, foldout sleeve, private pressing via *IT* magazine) . . . 150
68 Stable SLP 007 DISPOSABLE (LP, gatefold sleeve) . . . 85
69 Transatlantic TRA 204 THE DEVIANTS THREE (LP, some with booklet) . . . 80/60
69 Decca LK-R/SKL-R 4993 PTOOFF! (LP, reissue) . . . 50
84 Psycho PSYCHO 25 HUMAN GARBAGE (LIVE AT DINGWALLS '84) (LP) . . . 15
(see also Mick Farren, Pink Fairies, Larry Wallis)

DEVIL'S HOLE GANG

70s Slow Burning Fuse SSSS 1 Free The People/Isn't It/Something To Look Forward To (p/s, with insert) . . . 12

JOHNNY DEVLIN (& DETOURS)

64 Pye 7N 15598 Sometimes/If You Want Someone (as Johnny Devlin & Detours) . . . 10
66 CBS 202085 Hung On You/Prove It . . . 10
66 CBS 202339 My Strength; Heart Of Soul/I Can't Get You Off My Mind . . . 10
67 CBS 202452 Tender Lovin' Care/Five O'Clock World . . . 10
67 CBS 2751 Hurtin'/You Gotta Tell Me . . . 8

DEVO

78 Stiff DEV 1 Jocko Homo/Mongoloid (foldout p/s) . . . 5
78 Stiff DEV 2/BOY 1 (I Can't Get No) Satisfaction/Sloppy (I Saw My Baby Getting) (p/s) . . . 5
78 Stiff BOY 1 (I Can't Get No) Satisfaction/Sloppy (I Saw My Baby Getting) (12", stickered p/s) . 8
78 Stiff ODD 1 BE STIFF (12" EP, white label) . . . 8
79 Elevator NICE 1 Mechanical Man/Blockhead/Blackout/Auto-Modern (official bootleg, no'd p/s) . . . 6
78 Virgin V 2106 Q: ARE WE NOT MEN? (LP, various colour vinyls) . . . 12
78 Virgin VP 2106 Q: ARE WE NOT MEN? (LP, picture disc, with 'Flimsy Wrap' 33rpm 1-sided flexidisc [VDJ 27/Lyntone LYN 6260]) . . . 12

DEVON (Russell) & TARTANS

68 Nu Beat NB 021 Let's Have Some Fun/Making Love . . . 10
(see also Tartans)

DEVON (Russell) & SEDRIC (Myton)

69 Blue Cat BS 158 What A Sin Thing/Short Up Dress . . . 18

DEVONNES

75 UK USA 5 I'm Gonna Pick Up My Toys/Limits . . . 8

MINT VALUE £

BARRY DE VORZON

58 RCA RCA 1066 Barbara Jean/JIMMY DELL: Teeny Weeny . . . 60
58 RCA RCA 1066 Barbara Jean/JIMMY DELL: Teeny Weeny (78) . . . 35
60 Philips PB 993 Betty Betty (Go Steady With Me)/Across The Street . . . 22
(see also Barry & Tamerlanes, Jimmy Dell)

DEVOTED

68 Page One POF 076 I Love George Best/United (initially in p/s) . . . 15/7

DEVOTIONS

64 Columbia DB 7256 Rip Van Winkle/I Love You For Sentimental Reasons . . . 75

JANINE DE WAYLENE & HER MARTENOT

60 Top Rank JAR 363 Faces In The Dark/Martenot Theme/Farewell Christina . . . 7

DEWDROPS

67 Blue Beat BB 381 Somebody's Knocking/By And By . . . 18

BRIAN DEWHURST

75 Folk Heritage FHR 075 THE HUNTER & THE HUNTED (LP) . . . 20

KEITH DEWHURST & ALBION BAND

80 Charisma CDS 4020 LARK RISE TO CANDLEFORD (A COUNTRY TAPESTRY) (LP, soundtrack) . . . 12
(see also Albion Band)

FAY DEWITT

54 London HL 8021 Misirlou/Snap Snap Snap Your Fingers (78) . . . 6

DANNY DEXTER

63 London HLU 9690 Sweet Mama/Go On . . . 20

EDDIE DEXTER & HIS BAND

55 Capitol CL 14371 Moonlight/The Verse Of Stardust . . . 8

RAY DEXTER & LAYABOUTS

62 Decca F 11538 The Coalman's Lament/Lonely Weekend . . . 30

DEXYS MIDNIGHT RUNNERS

85 Mercury DEXYS 13 An Extract From 'This Is What She's Like'/'This Is What She's Like' Finale (p/s) . . . 6
85 Mercury DEXYSD 13 An Extract From 'This Is What She's Like'/'This Is What She's Like' Finale// Marguerita Time/Reminisce Part One (double pack, gatefold p/s) . . . 10
89 Mercury 080 628-2 Come On Eileen/The Celtic Soul Brothers/Jackie Wilson Said (I'm In Heaven When You Smile)/Liars A To E (CD Video) . . . 8
85 Mercury DEXYS 1310 This Is What She's Like/Marguerita Time (10", p/s) . . . 10
(see also Killjoys, Kevin Rowland)

TRACEY DEY

64 Stateside SS 287 Go Away/Gonna Get Along Without You Now . . . 15

BARRY D'FANO

62 Palette PG 9038 Message Of Love/The Kiss That Broke My Heart . . . 10

DHARMA B featuring ACE OF CLUBS

90s Acid Jazz JAZID 35T Everything Is Going To The Beat (12", company sleeve) . . . 20

DHARMA BLUES BAND

69 Major Minor SMPC 5017 DHARMA BLUES (LP) . . . 55

DIALS (Jamaica)

69 Duke DU 48 Bye Bye Love/It's Love . . . 7
69 Duke DU 49 Love Is A Treasure/DIAMONDS: I Want To Be . . . 7

DIALS (U.K.)

79 Wessex WEX 266 Maxine/Hey Denise (p/s) . . . 7

BRIAN DIAMOND & THE CUTTERS

63 Decca F 11724 Jealousy Will Get You Nowhere/Brady Brady . . . 18
64 Fontana TF 452 Shake, Shout And Go/Whatcha Gonna Do Now Pretty Baby . . . 18
65 Pye 7N 15779 Big Bad Wolf/See If I Care . . . 15
65 Pye 7N 15952 Bone Idol/Sands Of Time . . . 15

(GREGG DIAMOND'S) BIONIC BOOGIE

79 Polydor PB 50 Chains/Hot Butterfly . . . 5
79 Polydor POSPX 50 Chains/Hot Butterfly (12") . . . 10
88 Urban URBX 16 Hot Butterfly/Mess Up The Boogie/When The Shit Hits The Fan (12", p/s) . . . 8
79 Polydor 2391 322 BIONIC BOOGIE (LP) . . . 12

JERRY DIAMOND

57 London HLE 8496 Sunburned Lips/Don't Trust Love . . . 40
57 London HLE 8496 Sunburned Lips/Don't Trust Love (78) . . . 12

LEE DIAMOND (& CHEROKEES)

61 Fontana H 310 I'll Step Down/Josephine (as Lee Diamond & Cherokees) . . . 18
61 Fontana H 345 Stop Your Crying/You'll Want Me . . . 18
(see also Cherokees)

NEIL DIAMOND

66 London HLZ 10049 Solitary Man/Do It . . . 12
66 London HLZ 10072 Cherry, Cherry/I'll Come Running . . . 12
66 London HLZ 10092 I Got The Feelin' (Oh No No)/The Boat That I Row . . . 10
67 London HLZ 10111 You Got To Me/Someday Baby . . . 10
67 London HLZ 10126 Girl, You'll Be A Woman Soon/You'll Forget . . . 10
67 London HLZ 10151 Thank The Lord For The Night Time/The Long Way Home . . . 10
67 London HLZ 10161 Kentucky Woman/The Time Is Now . . . 8
68 London HLZ 10177 New Orleans/Hanky Panky . . . 8
68 London HLZ 10187 Red Red Wine/Red Rubber Ball . . . 8
68 Uni UN 503 Brooklyn Roads/Holiday Inn Blues . . . 5

68	MCA MU 1033	Two-Bit Manchild/Broad Old Woman	5
69	MCA MU 1070	Brother Love's Travelling Salvation Show/A Modern Day Version Of Love	5
69	MCA MU 1087	Sweet Caroline (Good Times Never Seemed So Good)/Dig In	5
71	President PT 335	Kentucky Woman/Cherry, Cherry/I Thank The Lord For The Night Time (p/s)	7
71	Uni UN 536	Stones/Crunchy Granola Suite	5
87	CBS 651 201-7	I Dreamed A Dream/Sweet Caroline (box set with calendar)	6
66	London HA-Z 8307	THE FEEL OF NEIL DIAMOND (LP)	50
74	CBS Q 69067	SERENADE (LP, quadrophonic)	15
76	CBS Q 86004	BEAUTIFUL NOISE (LP, quadrophonic)	15
81	World Records ALBUM 91	THE BEST OF NEIL DIAMOND (4-LP box set, mail-order only)	25
96	Sony Publishing XPCD 708	THE NEIL DIAMOND SONG BOOK (CD, promo only)	25

DIAMOND BOYS

62	Parlophone GIB 102	Fool In Love/New Orleans (export issue)	30
63	RCA RCA 1351	Hey Little Girl/What'd I Say	15

(see also Albert Ammons)

DIAMOND HEAD

80	Happy Face MMDH 120	Shoot Out The Lights/Helpless (p/s)	15
80	Media SCREEN 1	Sweet And Innocent/Streets Of Gold (p/s)	15
81	DHM DHM 004	Waited Too Long/Play It Loud (p/s)	7
81	DHM DHM 005	DIAMOND LIGHTS EP (Diamond Lights/ We Won't Be Back/I Don't Got/It's Electric) (12", p/s)	30
82	MCA DHM 101	FOUR CUTS (EP, p/s)	7
82	MCA DHMT 101	FOUR CUTS (12" EP, with insert)	12
82	MCA DHM 102/MSAM 23	In The Heat Of The Night/Play It Loud (live)//Sweet And Innocent (live)/ (Interview With Tommy Vance) (double pack, gatefold p/s)	8
82	MCA DHMT 102	In The Heat Of The Night (Full Length Version)/Play It Loud (live) (12", p/s)	10
83	MCA DHM 103	Makin' Music/(Andy Peebles Interview) (p/s)	8
83	MCA DHMT 103	Makin' Music/(Andy Peebles Interview) (12", p/s)	15
83	MCA DHM 104	Out Of Phase/The Kingmaker (p/s)	5
83	MCA DHMP 104	Out Of Phase/The Kingmaker (picture disc)	6
83	MCA DHMT 104	Out Of Phase/The Kingmaker/Sucking My Love (live) (12", p/s)	30
92	Bronze	Wild In The Streets (12", p/s, 1 side etched)	8
80	DHM MMDHLP 105	LIGHTNING TO THE NATIONS (LP, plain or printed white labels, plain white sleeve, sold at gigs, a few signed in blue ink & available via *Sounds*)	60/50
81	MCA DH 1001	LIVING ON BORROWED TIME (LP, gatefold sleeve with inner sleeve, some with poster & fan club insert)	22/15
83	MCA DH 1002	CANTERBURY (LP)	12
86	Metal Masters METALP 110	BEHOLD THE BEGINNING (LP, remixed reissue of 1st LP)	15
87	FM WKFMLP 92	AM I EVIL (LP, with inner sleeve)	20

DIAMONDS (Jamaica)

72	Songbird SB 1079	Mash Up/DYNAMITES: Mash Up (Version)	6

(see also Dymonds, Sir Collins Band)

DIAMONDS (U.K.)

63	Philips BF 1264	The Lost City/Chasey Chasey	15

DIAMONDS (U.S.)

55	Vogue Coral Q 72109	Black Denim Trousers And Motorcycle Boots/Nip Sip	50
55	Vogue Coral Q 72109	Black Denim Trousers And Motorcycle Boots/Nip Sip (78)	25
55	Mercury MT 121	Love, Love, Love/Ev'ry Night About This Time (78)	22
57	Mercury MT 148	Little Darlin'/Faithful And True (78)	10
57	Mercury MT 167	Don't Say Goodbye/Words Of Love (78)	15
57	Mercury MT 179	Oh, How I Wish/Zip Zip (78)	15
58	Mercury 7MT 187	Silhouettes/Honey Bird	40
58	Mercury MT 187	Silhouettes/Honey Bird (78)	15
58	Mercury 7MT 195	The Stroll/Land Of Beauty	35
58	Mercury MT 195	The Stroll/Land Of Beauty (78)	15
58	Mercury 7MT 207	Don't Let Me Down/High Sign	35
58	Mercury MT 207	Don't Let Me Down/High Sign (78)	18
58	Mercury 7MT 208	Straight Skirts/Patsy	50
58	Mercury MT 208	Straight Skirts/Patsy (78)	20
58	Mercury 7MT 233	Where Mary Go?/Kathy-O	8
58	Mercury MT 233	Where Mary Go?/Kathy-O (78)	15
58	Mercury AMT 1004	Eternal Lovers/Walking Along	12
58	Mercury AMT 1004	Eternal Lovers/Walking Along (78)	15
59	Mercury AMT 1024	She Say (Oom Dooby Doom)/From The Bottom Of My Heart	12
59	Mercury AMT 1024	She Say (Oom Dooby Doom)/From The Bottom Of My Heart (78)	30
60	Mercury AMT 1086	Tell The Truth/Real True Love	25
61	Mercury AMT 1156	One Summer Night/It's A Doggone Shame	15
57	Mercury MEP 9515	PRESENTING THE DIAMONDS (EP)	35
57	Mercury MEP 9523	THE DIAMONDS VOL. 1 (EP)	45
58	Mercury MEP 9527	THE DIAMONDS VOL. 2 (EP)	45
58	Mercury MEP 9530	THE DIAMONDS VOL. 3 (EP)	45
59	Mercury ZEP 10003	DIG THE DIAMONDS (EP)	45
59	Mercury ZEP 10020	THE DIAMONDS MEET PETE RUGOLO (EP)	22
59	Mercury ZEP 10026	DIAMONDS ARE TRUMPS (EP)	45
60	Mercury ZEP 10053	STAR STUDDED DIAMONDS (EP)	45
61	Mercury ZEP 10097	PETE RUGOLO LEADS THE DIAMONDS (EP, also stereo SEZ 10912)	25/35
57	Mercury MPT 7526	THE DIAMONDS (10" LP)	150
60	Mercury MMC 14039	SONGS FROM THE OLD WEST (LP)	22

(see also Pete Rugolo)

DIAMOND TWINS

66	HMV POP 1508	Crying The Night Away/Start The World Spinning Again	6

(see also Sonia Kent)

MINT VALUE £

DIANE & JAVELINS

66 Columbia DB 7819 — Heart And Soul/Who's The Girl 50

(PAUL) DI'ANNO

84 FM VHF 1 — Heart User/Road Rat (p/s) 8
84 FM WKFM LP1 — DI'ANNO (LP, blue vinyl) 15
84 FM WKFM PD1 — DI'ANNO (LP, picture disc) 18
(see also Gogmagog, Iron Maiden)

DIATONES

61 Starlite ST45 057 — Ruby Has Gone/Oh Baby Come Dance With Me 100

CYRIL DIAZ & HIS ORCHESTRA

55 Kay CRS 003 — Lazy Man Paul (with Lord Christo)/JOHNNY GOMEZ & ORCHESTRA: Johnny Nightmare (78) 7
57 Kay CRS 028 — Brass Crown (with Lord Superior)/V. BRYAN ORCHESTRA: Tan-Tan (78) 7
57 Kay CRS 033 — Merengue Maraval/CYRIL DIAZ COMBO: Merengue Balisier (78) 7

MANU DIBANGO

73 London HL 10423 — Soul Makossa/Lily 8
73 London SH 8451 — O BOSO (LP) 20
75 Creole CRLP 503 — MAKOSSA MUSIC (LP) 15
78 Decca SKL-R 5296 — AFROVISION (LP) 12
79 Decca SKL-R 5303 — MANU '76 (LP) 12

LLOYD DICE

70 Joe JRS 5 — Trial Of Pama Dice/JOE: Jughead Returns 12
(see also Trevor Lloyd)

DICE THE BOSS

69 Duke/Joe DU 51 — Gun The Man Down/JOE MANSANO: The Thief 10
69 Duke/Joe DU 52 — But Officer/JOE'S ALL STARS: Reggae On The Shore 10
70 Duke/Joe DU 57 — Your Boss D.J./TITO SIMON: Read The News 10
70 Joe's JRS 17 — The Informer/Cool It 8
70 Explosion EX 2017 — Funky Monkey/JOE'S ALL STARS: Funky Monkey Version 8
70 Explosion EX 2020 — Funky Duck/Dunkier Than Duck 8
(see also Pama Dice, Joe The Boss)

PAMA DICE

69 Jackpot JP 715 — Honky Tonk Popcorn/Bongo Man 12
69 Jackpot JP 716 — Sin, Sun And Sex/Reggae Popcorn 5
(see also Dice The Boss, Joe The Boss)

DICK & DEE DEE

61 London HLG 9408 — The Mountain's High/I Want Someone 12
62 London HLG 9483 — Goodbye To Love/Swing Low 12
62 Liberty LIB 55412 — Tell Me/Will You Always Love Me 8
63 Warner Bros WB 96 — Young And In Love/Say To Me 8
63 Warner Bros WB 111 — Where Did The Good Times Go/Guess Our Love Must Show 8
63 Warner Bros WB 119 — Turn Around/Don't Leave Me 8
64 Warner Bros WB 126 — All My Trails/Don't Twice, It's All Right 10
64 Warner Bros WB 138 — Remember When/You Were Mine 10
64 Warner Bros WB 145 — Thou Shalt Not Steal/Just 'Round The River Bend 8
65 Warner Bros WB 156 — Be My Baby/Room 404 10
65 Warner Bros WB 5671 — Use What You've Got/P.S. 1402 8
63 Warner Bros WM/WS 8132 — YOUNG AND IN LOVE (LP, mono/stereo) 40/50
63 Warner Bros WM/WS 8150 — TURN AROUND (LP, mono/stereo) 35/45

DOLES DICKEN'S BAND

58 London HLD 8639 — Piakukaungchung (Pie-ah-coo-ka-ung-chung)/Our Melody 10

DICKENS

80 Hawkmoon ROCK 101 — STANDING OUT (LP, private pressing) 12
(see also Ice)

CHARLES DICKENS

65 Pye 7N 15887 — That's The Way Love Goes/In The City 10
65 Pye 7N 15938 — I Stand Alone/Hey Little Girl 10
66 Immediate IM 025 — So Much In Love/Our Soul Brothers 20
(see also Habits)

LITTLE JIMMY DICKENS

54 Columbia DC 670 — Then I Had To Turn Around/Hot Diggity Dog (78, export issue) 12
65 CBS 201969 — May The Bird Of Paradise Fly Up Your Nose/My Eyes Are Jealous 6

DICKIES

78 A&M AMS 7368 — Paranoid/I'm OK, You're OK (p/s, clear, black or milky vinyl) 5/6/7
78 A&M AMS 7373 — Eve Of Destruction/Doggie Do (p/s, pink or black vinyl) 5
78 A&M AMS 7391 — Give It Back/You Drive Me Ape (p/s, white or black vinyl) 5
78 A&M AMS 7403 — Silent Night/The Sounds Of Silence (p/s, white or black vinyl) 6/5
79 A&M AMS 7431 — Banana Splits/Hideous/Got It At The Store (p/s, opaque or translucent yellow vinyl; also black vinyl) 5/7/6
79 A&M AMS 7469 — Nights In White Satin/Waterslide (p/s, white vinyl) 5
79 A&M AMS 7491 — Manny, Moe And Jack/She Loves Me Not (p/s, black vinyl only) 10
80 A&M AMS 7504 — Fan Mail/Tricia Toyota (I'm Stuck In A Pagoda) (opaque or translucent red vinyl, poster p/s) 8
80 A&M AMS 7544 — Gigantor/Bowling With Bedrock Barney (yellow vinyl, p/s with full colour or b&w reverse) 10
90 Overground OVER 12 — Just Say Yes/Ayatollah You So (p/s with lyric sheet, mauve, blue or white vinyl, 2,000 of each colour) 6
90 Overground OVER 12 — Just Say Yes/Ayatollah You So (black vinyl test pressing, 50 only) 15

MINT VALUE £

90	Overground OVER 017	Roadkill (flexidisc available on 'Just Say Yes' European Tour, no p/s, 5000 only)	5
95	Plastic Head HOLE 008	Make It So/Oh Baby (p/s, black vinyl, 1,000 only)	6
79	A&M AMLE 64742	THE INCREDIBLE SHRINKING DICKIES (LP, black or yellow vinyl)	each 14
79	A&M AMLE 64742	THE INCREDIBLE SHRINKING DICKIES (LP, blue or orange vinyl, with black or red-and-black on sleeve)	18/22
79	A&M AMLH 68510	DAWN OF THE DICKIES (LP, blue or black vinyl)	20/14

(see also Chuck Wagon)

BRUCE DICKINSON

90	EMI EM 138	Tattooed Millionaire/Ballad Of Mutt (paper label, glossy p/s)	6
90	EMI EMPD 138	Tattooed Millionaire/Ballad Of Mutt (shaped picture disc)	12
90	EMI EMCD 138	Tattooed Millionaire/Ballad Of Mutt/Wind Of Change (CD)	10
90	EMI EMPD 142	All The Young Dudes/Darkness Be My Friend (shaped picture disc with plinth)	12
90	EMI EMCD 142	All The Young Dudes/Darkness Be My Friend/Sin City (CD picture disc)	12
90	EMI EMPD 151	Dive! Dive! Dive!/Riding With The Angels (live)/Sin City (live)/ Black Night (live) (12", picture disc)	12
90	EMI EMCD 151	Dive! Dive! Dive!/Riding With The Angels (live)/Sin City (live)/ Black Night (live) (CD)	10
94	EMI EM 341	Shoot All The Clowns/Over And Out (p/s, clear vinyl with insert)	5

(see also Iron Maiden, Samson, Xero, Rock Aid Armenia)

VIC DICKINSON & JOE THOMAS GROUPS

57	Pye/Vanguard PPT 12005	VIC DICKINSON SEPTET (10" LP)	12
60	London Jazz LTZ-K 15182	MAINSTREAM (LP, also stereo SAH-K 6066)	12
66	Fontana FJL 404	SHOWCASE (solo LP)	12
66	Fontana FJL 406	SHOWCASE VOLUME 2 (solo LP)	12

BARBARA DICKSON

74	RSO 2090 144	Here Comes The Sun/The Long And Winding Road	5
69	Trailer LER 3002	THE FATE O'CHARLIE (LP)	45
70	Decca SKL 5041	THRO' RECENT YEARS (LP, with Archie Fisher)	35
71	Decca SKL 5058	DO RIGHT WOMAN (LP)	45
72	Decca SKL 5116	FROM THE BEGGAR'S MANTLE FRINGED WITH GOLD (LP)	40
74	RSO 2394 141	JOHN, PAUL, GEORGE, RINGO AND BERT (LP, with London cast)	30

DICTATORS with TONY & HOWARD

63	Oriole CB 1934	So Long Little Girl/Say Little Girl	15

(see also Tony & Howard)

DICTATORS

77	Asylum K 13091	Search And Destroy/Sleepin' With The TV On (no p/s)	8
77	Asylum K 53061	MANIFEST DESTINY (LP)	12

BO DIDDLEY

59	London HLM 8913	The Great Grandfather/Crackin' Up	75
59	London HLM 8913	The Great Grandfather/Crackin' Up (78)	35
59	London HLM 8975	Say Man/The Clock Strikes Twelve	75
59	London HLM 8975	Say Man/The Clock Strikes Twelve (78)	40
60	London HLM 9035	Say Man, Back Again/She's Alright	75
60	London HLM 9112	Road Runner/My Story	55
62	Pye Intl. 7N 25165	You Can't Judge A Book By The Cover/I Can Tell	18
63	Pye Intl. 7N 25193	Who Do You Love?/The Twister	15
63	Pye Intl. 7N 25210	Bo Diddley/Detour	15
63	Pye Intl. 7N 25216	You Can't Judge A Book By The Cover/I Can Tell (reissue)	12
63	Pye Intl. 7N 25217	Pretty Thing/Road Runner	15
63	Pye Intl. 7N 25227	Bo Diddley Is A Lover/Doin' The Jaguar	12
64	Pye Intl. 7N 25235	Memphis/Monkey Diddle	12
64	Pye Intl. 7N 25243	Mona/Gimme Gimme	15
64	Pye Intl. 7N 25258	Mama Keep Your Big Mouth Shut/Jo-Ann	12
65	Chess CRS 8000	Hey Good Lookin'/You Ain't Bad (As You Claim To Be)	12
65	Chess CRS 8014	Somebody Beat Me/Mush Mouth Millie	12
65	Chess CRS 8021	Let The Kids Dance/Let Me Pass	12
66	Chess CRS 8026	500% More Man/Stop My Monkey	12
66	Chess CRS 8036	We're Gonna Get Married/Easy	12
67	Chess CRS 8053	Ooh Baby/Back To School	10
67	Chess CRS 8057	Wrecking My Love Life/Boo-Ga-Loo Before You Go	15
68	Chess CRS 8078	Another Sugar Daddy/I'm High Again	10
69	Chess CRS 8088	Bo Diddley 1969/Soul Train	10
72	Chess 6145 002	I Said Shut Up Woman/I Love You More Than You'll Ever Know	6
56	London RE-U 1054	RHYTHM AND BLUES WITH BO DIDDLEY (EP, gold label lettering)	225
63	Pye Intl. NEP 44014	HEY! BO DIDDLEY (EP)	22
64	Pye Intl. NEP 44019	THE STORY OF BO DIDDLEY (EP)	22
64	Pye Intl. NEP 44031	BO DIDDLEY IS A LUMBERJACK (EP)	25
64	Pye Intl. NEP 44036	DIDDLING (EP)	25
65	Chess CRE 6008	I'M A MAN (EP)	30
66	Chess CRE 6023	ROOSTER STEW (EP)	30
59	London HA-M 2230	GO BO DIDDLEY (LP)	300
62	Pye Jazz NJL 33	BO DIDDLEY IS A GUNSLINGER (LP)	40
63	Pye Intl. NPL 28025	HEY! BO DIDDLEY (LP)	25
63	Pye Intl. NPL 28026	BO DIDDLEY (LP)	25
63	Pye Intl. NPL 28029	BO DIDDLEY RIDES AGAIN (LP)	25
63	Pye Intl. NPL 28032	BO DIDDLEY'S BEACH PARTY (LP)	22
64	Pye Intl. NPL 28034	BO DIDDLEY IN THE SPOTLIGHT (LP)	35
64	Pye Intl. NPL 28049	16 ALL-TIME HITS (LP)	25
64	Chess CRL 4002	HEY GOOD LOOKIN' (LP)	35
65	Chess CRL 4507	LET ME PASS (LP)	35
67	Chess CRL 4525	THE ORIGINATOR (LP)	35

MINT VALUE £

68	Chess CRL 4529	SUPER BLUES (LP, with Muddy Waters & Little Walter)	40
68	Chess CRL 4537	THE SUPER SUPER BLUES BAND (LP, with Muddy Waters & Howlin' Wolf)	50
73	Chess 6499 476	THE LONDON SESSIONS (LP)	18

(see also Chuck Berry & Bo Diddley)

DIDDY MEN

65	Columbia DB 7782	The Song Of The Diddy Men/Hello Doddy	8

DIDJITS

95	Touch & Go RCRPA 11	Pigs (1-sided white label)	5

DIE ELECTRIC EELS

78	Rough Trade RT 008	Agitated/Cyclotron (p/s)	15

DIESEL M

94	Choci's Chewns CCB 001	M FOR MULTIPLE (12", blue vinyl, 666 only)	40
95	Choci's Chewns DDL 001	M FOR MANGOES (12", red vinyl, 666 only)	40

(see also µ-Ziq)

MARLENE DIETRICH

52	Columbia SCM 5010	Too Old To Cut The Mustard/Good For Nothing (with Rosemary Clooney)	25
53	Philips PB 164	Dot's Nice — Donna Fights/It's The Same (with Rosemary Clooney) (78)	6
54	Philips PB 314	Besides/Land, Sea And Air (with Rosemary Clooney) (78)	6
55	Philips PB 472	I Am A Camera Theme/Peter (78)	6
57	London HLD 8492	Near You/Another Spring, Another Love	15
57	London HLD 8492	Near You/Another Spring, Another Love (78)	6
63	HMV POP 1196	Lili Marlene/Sag Mir Wo Die Blumen Sind?	6
65	HMV POP 1379	Where Have All The Flowers Gone?/Blowin' In The Wind	6
65	Pye 7N 15770	Go Away From My Window/Shir Hatan	6
57	HMV 7EG 8257	MARLENE DIETRICH IN 'THE BLUE ANGEL' (EP)	25
58	London RED 1146	MARLENE DIETRICH (EP)	20
64	HMV 7EG 8844	RETURNS TO GERMANY (EP)	12
53	Brunswick LA 8591	SOUVENIR ALBUM (10" LP)	25
54	Philips BBR 8006	AT THE CAFÉ DE PARIS (10" LP, introduced by Noel Coward)	25
59	Philips BBL 7322	LILI MARLENE (LP)	15
60	Philips BBL 7386	DIETRICH IN RIO (LP, also stereo SBBL 571)	15/18
63	HMV CLP 1659	RETURNS TO GERMANY (LP)	15
60s	Philips	other LPs	15

(see also Rosemary Clooney)

DIF JUZ

81	4AD BAD 109	HU/RE/MI/CS (12" EP)	15
81	4AD BAD 116	VIBRATING AIR: Heset/Diselt/Gunet/Soarn (12" EP)	12
83	Red Flame RFM 24	WHO SAYS SO (LP)	15
85	Pleasantly Surprised PS 9	TIME CLOCK TURNS BACK (cassette, with inserts)	40

RICHARD DIGANCE

70s	Coast COASTAL 4	SONG FROM A BOOK (LP)	12

DIGA RHYTHM BAND

76	United Artists UAG 29975	DIGA RHYTHM BAND (LP)	22

(see also Grateful Dead, Mickey Hart, Jerry Garcia)

STEVE DIGGLE

80	Faulty Products FEP 7000	Fifty Years Of Comparative Wealth/Shut Out The Light/ Here Comes The Fire Brigade (unreleased)	

(see also Buzzcocks, Flag Of Convenience)

MOSES & JOSHUA (DILLARD)

67	Stateside SS 2059	My Elusive Dreams/What's Better Than Love (as Moses & Joshua Dillard)	18
68	Bell BELL 1018	Get Out Of My Heart/They Don't Want Us Together (as Moses & Joshua)	10
72	Mojo 2092 054	My Elusive Dreams/Get Out Of My Heart	8

DILLARD & CLARK

69	A&M AMS 764	Radio Song/Why Not Your Baby	6
69	A&M AMLS 939	THE FANTASTIC EXPEDITION OF DILLARD & CLARK (LP)	15
69	A&M AMLS 966	THROUGH THE MORNING, THROUGH THE NIGHT (LP)	15

(see also Gene Clark, Byrds, Dillards)

DILLARDS

65	Capitol CL 15420	Nobody Knows/Ebo Walker	7
69	Elektra EKSN 45048	Reason To Believe/Nobody Knows	7
69	Elektra EKSN 45062	She Sang Hymns Out Of Tune/Single Saddle	6
69	Elektra EKSN 45081	Rainmaker/West Montana Hanna	6
68	Elektra EKS 74035	WHEATSHEAF SUITE (LP)	15
69	Polydor 236 559	BACK PORCH BLUE GRASS (LP)	15
70	Elektra EKS 74054	COPPERFIELDS (LP)	15
72	United Artists UAG 29366	ROOTS AND BRANCHES (LP)	12
73	United Artists UAS 29516	TRIBUTE TO THE AMERICAN DUCK (LP)	12

(see also Dillard & Clark)

DILLINGER

73	Duke DU 149	Headquarters (as Dellenger)/CHENLEY DUFFAS: Black Girl In My Bed	12
73	Downtown DT 512	Tighten Up Skank/Middle East Rock	8
79	Island ISL 976	Cokane In My Brain/Power	10

(see also David Isaacs)

TODD DILLINGHAM

95	Woronzow WOO 25	SGT. KIPPER (2-LP)	18

MINT VALUE £

PHYLLIS DILLON

66	Doctor Bird DB 1061	Don't Stay Away (as Phillis Dillon)/TOMMY McCOOK & SUPERSONICS: What Now	40
67	Trojan TR 006	This Is A Lovely Way/Thing Of The Past (as Phyllis Dellon)	22
67	Treasure Isle TI 7003	This Is A Lovely Way/Thing Of The Past	20
67	Treasure Isle TI 7015	Perfidia/It's Rocking Time	20
68	Treasure Isle TI 7041	I Wear This Ring/Don't Touch Me Tomato	18
69	Trojan TR 651	Love Is All I Had/Boys And Girls Reggae (as Phillis Dylon)	10
69	Trojan TR 671	The Right Track/TOMMY McCOOK & SUPERSONICS: Moonshot	10
69	Trojan TR 686	Lipstick On Your Collar (as Phillis Dillon)/TOMMY McCOOK & SUPERSONICS: Tribute To Rameses	8
70	Duke Reid DR 2508	This Is Me/Skabuvie (act. "If Your Name Is Andy"/"Ska Vovi" by Dorothy Reid)	8
70	Duke DU 76	Walk Through This World/The Rooster	8
71	Treasure Isle TI 7058	One Life To Live, One Love To Give/TOMMY McCOOK: My Best Dress	12
71	Treasure Isle TI 7070	Midnight Confession/TOMMY McCOOK & SOUL SYNDICATE: Version	12
72	Sioux SI 009	In The Ghetto/NYAH EARTH: Knight Of The Long Knives	12
72	Trojan TRL 41	ONE LIFE TO GIVE (LP)	35

DIMENSIONALS

53	London L 1217	Sleepy Time Gal/DON BAKER/DIMENSIONALS: Drinkin' Pop-Sodee Odee (78)	30

DIMENSIONS

65	Parlophone R 5294	Tears On My Pillow/You Don't Have To Whisper	35

DIMPLES

66	Decca F 12537	The Love Of A Lifetime/My Heart Is Tied To You	35

(see also Gospel Garden, Amazing Blondel)

DIMPLES & EDDIE with RICO's COMBO

62	Planetone RC 3	Fleet Street/Good Bye World	18

D INFLUENCE

90s	Acid Jazz JAZID 30T	I'm The One (12", p/s)	15

DINGER

85	Face Value FVRA 221	Air Of Mystery/I Love To Love (no p/s)	35

(see also Erasure)

DINGLE BROTHERS

71	Dynamic DYN 418	You Don't Know/CABLES: Rich Man, Poor Man	6

BOB DINI

53	London L 1213	Too Long/Remember Me (78)	8
54	London HL 8019	Good-bye My Love/Sometime (78)	10

MARK DINNING

60	MGM MGM 1053	Teen Angel/Bye Now Baby	15
60	MGM MGM 1069	You Win Again/A Star Is Born (A Love Is Dead)	10
60	MGM MGM 1101	The Lovin' Touch/Come Back To Me (My Love)	10
61	MGM MGM 1125	Top Forty, News, Weather And Sport/Suddenly	12
62	MGM MGM 1148	In A Matter Of Moments/What Will My Mary Say	10
62	MGM MGM 1155	All Of This For Sally/The Pickup	10
65	Hickory 45-1293	Dial AI 1-4883/I'm Glad We Fell In Love	8

DINNING SISTERS

55	Polygon P 1161	Goofus/Mama (He Treats Your Daughter Mean) (78)	12
55	London HLF 8179	Drifting And Dreaming/Truly	55
55	London HLF 8179	Drifting And Dreaming/Truly (78)	20
56	London HLF 8218	Hold Me Tight/Uncle Joe	55
56	London HLF 8218	Hold Me Tight/Uncle Joe (78)	15

(see also 'Tennessee' Ernie Ford)

KENNY DINO

61	HMV POP 960	Your Ma Said You Cried In Your Sleep Last Night/Dream A Girl	12

DINO, DESI & BILLY

65	Reprise R 20367	I'm A Fool/So Many Ways	8
66	Reprise R 23047	Not The Loving Kind/Chimes Of Freedom	8

DINOSAUR JR

88	Blast First BFFP 30	Freak Scene/Keep The Glove (p/s)	8
88	Blast First BFFP 30	Freak Scene (censored)/Keep The Glove (plain white labels, no p/s, promo only)	15
89	The Catalogue CAT 069/2	Just Like Heaven/LUNACHICKS: Get Off The Road (33rpm square flexidisc free with *The Catalogue* magazine)	10/6
89	Blast First BFFP 47	Just Like Heaven/Throw Down	7
89	Blast First BFFP 47T	Just Like Heaven/Throw Down/Chunks (A Last Rites Tune) (12", p/s)	10
89	Blast First BFFP 47CD	Just Like Heaven/Throw Down/Chunks (A Last Rites Tune)/Freak Scene (Uncensored Version)/Keep The Glove (CD, picture disc)	12
97	Trade 2 TRDSC 009	I'm Insane (2000 copies pressed)	8
97	WEA (no cat. no.)	TAKE A RUN AT THE SUN (CD-R, 3-track sampler, unique sleeve)	10

DIO

75	Purple PUR 128	Sitting In A Dream (as Ronnie Dio featuring Roger Glover & Guests)/ JOHN LAWTON: Little Chalk Blue	10
83	Vertigo DIOP 2	Rainbow In The Dark/Stand Up And Shout (live) (picture disc)	7
84	Vertigo DIOP 4	Mystery/Eat Your Heart Out (live) (picture disc)	6
85	Vertigo DIOD 5	Rock'n'Roll Children/Sacred Heart (gatefold p/s)	5
85	Vertigo DIOW 512	Rock'n'Roll Children/We Rock (live)/The Last In Line (live) (12", white vinyl, stickered PVC sleeve)	8
85	Vertigo DIOFP 6	Hungry For Heaven/King Of Rock And Roll (p/s, with poster & sticker)	5
85	Vertigo DIOP 6	Hungry For Heaven/King Of Rock And Roll (dragon-shaped picture disc)	8
85	Vertigo DIOW 612	Hungry For Heaven/The Message (12", white vinyl)	8

Year	Label / Cat. No.	Title	Value £
86	Vertigo DIOEP 7	THE DIO EP (double pack)	5
86	Vertigo DIOP 710	THE DIO EP (10", shaped picture disc)	8
86	Vertigo DIO 712	THE DIO EP (12", p/s with family tree)	8
87	Vertigo DIOP 912	Hey Angel/Why Are They Watching Me?/Rock'n'Roll Children/Mystery (12", picture disc with insert)	8
86	Vertigo VERB 40	INTERMISSION (mini-LP with postcards & discography, stickered sleeve)	12

(see also Elf, Rainbow, Roger Glover, Black Sabbath, John Lawton)

DION (& BELMONTS)

78s

Year	Label / Cat. No.	Title	Value £
58	London HL 8646	I Wonder Why/Teen Angel (as Dion & Belmonts)	80
58	London HL 8718	I Can't Go On (Rosalie)/No One Knows (as Dion & Belmonts)	55
59	London HL 8799	Don't Pity Me/Just You (as Dion & Belmonts)	55
59	London HLU 8874	A Teenager In Love/I've Cried Before (as Dion & Belmonts)	65
59	Pye International 7N 25038	A Lover's Prayer/Every Little Thing I Do (as Dion & Belmonts)	85
60	London HLU 9030	Where Or When/That's My Desire (as Dion & Belmonts)	120

SINGLES

Year	Label / Cat. No.	Title	Value £
58	London HL 8646	I Wonder Why/Teen Angel (as Dion & Belmonts)	60
58	London HL 8718	I Can't Go On (Rosalie)/No One Knows (as Dion & Belmonts)	55
59	London HL 8799	Don't Pity Me/Just You (as Dion & Belmonts)	50
59	London HL 8874	A Teenager In Love/I've Cried Before (mispressing as Dion & Delmonts)	45
59	London HLU 8874	A Teenager In Love/I've Cried Before (as Dion & Belmonts)	40

(The above 45s were originally issued with triangular centres, round-centre re-pressings are worth two-thirds these values.)

Year	Label / Cat. No.	Title	Value £
59	Pye International 7N 25038	A Lover's Prayer/Every Little Thing I Do (as Dion & Belmonts)	50
60	London HLU 9030	Where Or When/That's My Desire (as Dion & Belmonts)	25
60	Top Rank JAR 368	When You Wish Upon A Star/My Private Joy (as Dion & Belmonts)	20
60	Top Rank JAR 503	In The Still Of The Night/Swinging On A Star (as Dion & Belmonts)	20
60	Top Rank JAR 521	Lonely Teenager/Little Miss Blue	20
61	Top Rank JAR 545	Havin' Fun/North-East End Of The Corner	15
61	Top Rank JAR 586	Runaround Sue/Runaway Girl	12
62	HMV POP 971	The Wanderer/The Majestic	12
62	HMV POP 1020	Lovers Who Wander/(I Was) Born To Cry	10
62	Stateside SS 115	Little Diane/Lost For Sure	10
62	Stateside SS 139	Love Came To Me/Little Girl	8
63	CBS AAG 133	Ruby Baby/He'll Only Hurt You	10
63	Stateside SS 161	Sandy/Faith	20
63	CBS AAG 145	This Little Girl/The Loneliest Man In The World	8
63	Stateside SS 209	Come Go With Me/King Without A Queen	15
63	CBS AAG 161	Be Careful Of Stones That You Throw/I Can't Believe (That You Don't Love Me Anymore)	10
63	CBS AAG 169	Donna, The Prima Donna/You're Mine	8
63	CBS AAG 177	Drip Drop/No One's Waiting For Me	10
64	CBS AAG 188	I'm Your Hoochie Coochie Man/The Road I'm On (Gloria)	12
64	CBS AAG 224	Johnnie B. Goode/Chicago Blues	15
65	CBS 201728	Sweet, Sweet Baby/Unloved, Unwanted Me (as Dion Di Mucci)	12
65	CBS 201780	Spoonful/Kickin' Child	12
66	HMV POP 1565	My Girl The Month Of May/Berimbau (as Dion & Belmonts)	15
67	HMV POP 1586	Movin' Man/For Bobbie (as Dion & Belmonts)	12
68	London HLP 10229	Abraham, Martin And John/Daddy Rollin'	8
69	London HLP 10277	Both Sides Now/You Better Watch Yourself (Sonny Boy)	7
70	Warner Bros WB 7356	If We Only Have Love/Natural Man	7
70	Warner Bros WB 7401	Your Own Back Yard/Sit Down, Old Friend	7
71	Warner Bros WB 6120	Close To It All/Windows	7
71	Warner Bros K 16100	Peaceful Place/Sunniland	7
72	Warner Bros K 16132	Sanctuary/Brand New Morning	7
75	Phil Spector Intl. 2010 012	Born To Be With You/Good Lovin' Man	5

EPs

Year	Label / Cat. No.	Title	Value £
62	HMV 7EG 8749	SWINGALONG WITH DION	100
63	Stateside SE 1006	DION'S HITS	60

LPs

Year	Label / Cat. No.	Title	Value £
59	London HA-U 2194	PRESENTING DION AND THE BELMONTS (as Dion & Belmonts)	325
60	Top Rank 25-027	THE TOPPERMOST — VOL. 1 (as Dion & Belmonts, with others)	75
61	HMV CLP 1539	RUNAROUND SUE	100
63	Stateside SL 10034	LOVERS WHO WANDER	80
63	CBS (S) BPG 62137	RUBY BABY (mono/stereo)	22/25
64	CBS (S) BPG 62203	DONNA THE PRIMA DONNA (mono/stereo)	22/25
67	HMV CLP 3618	TOGETHER AGAIN (as Dion & Belmonts, also stereo CSD 3618)	40
70	London HA-P/SH-P 8390	DION	18
70	Warner Brothers WS 1826	SIT DOWN OLD FRIEND	18
71	Warner Brothers WS 1872	YOU'RE NOT ALONE	18
72	Warner Brothers K 46122	SANCTUARY	18
72	Warner Brothers K 46199	SUITE FOR LATE SUMMER	18
73	Warner Brothers K 46208	REUNION — LIVE AT MADISON SQUARE GARDEN, 1972 (with Belmonts)	15
75	Phil Spector Intl. 2307 002	BORN TO BE WITH YOU	12

(see also Belmonts)

DION (Cameron) & THREE TOPS

Year	Label / Cat. No.	Title	Value £
67	Doctor Bird DB 1101	Miserable Friday/This World Has A Feeling	25
72	Big BG 331	Three Tops Time/UNDERGROUND PEOPLE: Tops (Version)	8

(see also Three Tops)

CELINE DION

Year	Label / Cat. No.	Title	Value £
91	Epic 656 326-7	Where Does My Heart Beat Now?/I Feel Too Much (p/s)	6
91	Epic 656 326-6	Where Does My Heart Beat Now?/I'm Loving Every Moment With You/ I Feel Too Much (12", p/s)	8
91	Epic 656 326-2/5	Where Does My Heart Beat Now?/I'm Loving Every Moment With You/ I Feel Too Much (CD, card sleeve or jewel case)	each 15

MINT VALUE £

91	Epic 657 333-7	The Last To Know/Unison (p/s)	5
91	Epic 657 333-0	The Last To Know/Unison (poster p/s)	10
91	Epic 657 333-2	The Last To Know/Unison/If We Could Start Over (CD)	12
92	Epic 657 660-7	Beauty And The Beast (duet with Peabo Bryson)/ The Beast Lets Belle Go (Instrumental) (p/s)	5
92	Epic 657 660-2	Beauty And The Beast (duet with Peabo Bryson)/ The Beast Lets Belle Go (Instrumental) (CD)	8
92	Epic 657 660-5	Beauty And The Beast (duet with Peabo Bryson)/The Beast Lets Belle Go (Instrumental) (CD, textured blue digipak)	15
92	Epic 658 192-7	If You Asked Me To/Love You Blind (p/s)	5
92	Epic 658 192-2	If You Asked Me To/Where Does My Heart Beat Now/Love You Blind (CD)	10
92	Epic 658 778-2	Love Can Move Mountains (Remix)/Love Can Move Mountains (Club Mix)/ Cry Just A Little/Beauty And The Beast (duet with Peabo Bryson) (CD)	15
91	Epic 467 203-1	UNISON (LP)	15
92	Epic 471 508-1	CELINE DION (LP, some with bonus track "Where Does My Heart Beat Now")	15
92	Epic 471 508-2	CELINE DION (CD)	18

DIPLOMATS

67	Caltone TONE 108	Meet Me At The Corner/Do It To Me Baby (by Lloyd & Groovers)	25
68	Caltone TONE 109	Going Alone/My Heart My Soul (by Lloyd & Groovers)	25
68	Caltone TONE 112	Strong Man/Listen To The Music (by Lloyd & Groovers)	25

DIPLOMATS

68	Direction 58-3899	I Can Give You Love/I'm So Glad I Found You	10

(see also Sam, Erv & Tom)

DIPLOMATS

82	Exchange EX 1	Memories Of You/I'll Keep Holding On (p/s)	7

(see also Scene)

DIRECT HITS

82	Whaam! WHAAM 007	Modesty Blaise/Sunny Honey Girl (p/s)	15
85	Direct POP 001	Christopher Cooper/She Really Didn't Care (p/s)	7
84	Whaam! BIG 7	BLOW UP (LP)	30

(see also Exits)

DIRECTION

93	Detour DR 003	Yesterday/The Kids Wanna New Direction (p/s, 1,000 only)	10

DIRECTIONS

79	Tortch TOR 004	Three Bands Tonite/On The Train (p/s, some with badge)	80/75

(see also Big Sound Authority)

DIRE STRAITS

82	Vertigo DSTR 101	Private Investigations/Badges Posters Stickers T-Shirts (10", p/s)	7
84	Vertigo DSTR 610	Love Over Gold (live)/Solid Rock (live) (10", p/s)	7
85	Vertigo DSTR 910	So Far Away/Walk Of Life (10", p/s)	7
85	Vertigo DSTR 1010	Money For Nothing/Love Over Gold (live) (10", p/s)	7
85	Vertigo DSPIC 10	Money For Nothing/Love Over Gold (live) (shaped picture disc with plinth)	8
85	Vertigo DSPIC 11	Brothers In Arms/Going Home — Theme From 'Local Hero' (Live Version) (oblong picture disc in stickered PVC sleeve)	12
85	Vertigo DSTR 1110	Brothers In Arms/Going Home — Theme From *Local Hero* (Live Version) (10", p/s)	7
85	Vertigo 884 285-2	Brothers In Arms (short)/Going Home (live)/Brothers In Arms (long)/ Why Worry (CD, promo only)	50
88	Vertigo DSCD 15	Sultans Of Swing/Portobello Belle (live)/Romeo And Juliet/ Money For Nothing (CD, card sleeve)	10
88	Vertigo 080 130-2	Money For Nothing (Full Length Version)/One World/So Far Away (CD Video)	20
88	Vertigo 080 134-2	Walk Of Life/Why Worry (LP Version)/Ride Across The River (CD Video)	20
89	Vertigo 080 128-2	Sultans Of Swing/Wild West End/Down The Waterline (CD Video)	20
89	Vertigo 080 132-2	Brothers In Arms (Full Length Version)/Your Latest Trick/ Ride Across The River (CD Video)	20
89	Vertigo 080 136-2	Twisting By The Pool/Two Young Lovers/If I Had You/ Twisting By The Pool (live) (CD Video)	20
82	Vertigo HS 6359 034	MAKING MOVIES (LP, half-speed master recording)	15
82	Vertigo HS 9102 021	DIRE STRAITS (LP, half-speed master recording)	15

(see also Mark Knopfler, David Knopfler)

DIRK & STIG

78	Ring O' 2017 109/DIB 1	Ging Gang Goolie/Mr. Sheene (unissued)	
79	EMI EMI 2852	Ging Gang Goolie/Mr. Sheene (p/s, black or khaki vinyl)	18/10

(see also Rutles, Neil Innes)

DIRTY BLUES BAND

68	Stateside S(S)L 10234	DIRTY BLUES BAND (LP)	30
69	Stateside S(S)L 10268	STONE DIRT (LP)	22

(see also Baconfat)

DIRTY DOG

78	Lightning GIL 511	Let Go Of My Hand/Shouldn't Do It/Gonna Quit/Guitar In My Hand (p/s)	15

DIRTY HARRY

73	Unity UN 573	Big Haire/YOUNG DOUG: Skank In Skank	5

DIRTY STRANGERS

89	Thrill TH 3	Bathing Belles/Oh Yeah/Hands Up (p/s, featuring Keith Richards)	8

(see also Rolling Stones)

DIRTY TRICKS

75	Polydor 2383351	DIRTY TRICKS (LP)	20

DISCHARGE

80 Clay CLAY 1 Realities Of War/They Declare It/But After The Gig/Society's Victim (p/s) 7
80 Clay CLAY 3 Fight Back/War's No Fairy Tale/Always Restrictions/You Take Part In Creating This System/Religion Instigates (p/s) 6
80 Clay CLAY 5 Decontrol/It's No TV Sketch/Tomorrow Belongs To Us (p/s) 6
81 Clay CLAY 6 Never Again/Death Dealers/Two Monstrous Nuclear Stock-Piles (p/s) 6
81 Clay PLATE 2 WHY (12" EP) 10
82 Clay CLAY 14 State Violence, State Control/Doomsday (p/s) 12
83 Clay CLAY 29 Price Of Silence/Born To Die In The Gutter (p/s) 7
82 Clay CLAYLP 3 HEAR NOTHING, SEE NOTHING, SAY NOTHING (LP) 18
84 Clay CLAYLP 12 NEVER AGAIN (LP, red vinyl) 18

DISCO BROTHERS

76 United Artists THE DISCO BROTHERS/THE TARTAN HORDE (EP, p/s) 6
(see also Nick Lowe, Tartan Horde, Roogalator, Damned, Brinsley Schwartz)

DISCO STUDENTS

79 Yeah Yeah Yeah UHHUH 1 South Africa House/Kafkaesque (no p/s) 15
80 Yeah Yeah Yeah UHHUH 2 A Boy With A Penchant For Open-Necked Shirts/Pink Triangles/Credit (no p/s) . . 15

DISCO 2000

87 KLF Comms. D 2001 I Gotta CD (7" Edit) (unissued, white labels only) 20
87 KLF Comms. D 2000 I Gotta CD/I Love Disco 2000 (12", p/s) 15
(see also J.A.M.s, KLF, Timelords, Bill Drummond, Space)

DISCO ZOMBIES

79 South Circular SGS 106 Drums Over London/Heartbeats Love (black, white & pink or black, white & green handmade wraparound p/s) 30
79 Uptown/Wizzo WIZZO 1 THE INVISIBLE (EP) 15
81 Dining Out TUX 2 Here Come The Buts/Mary Millington (p/s) 15
(see also Steppes, Fifty Fantastics)

DISCS

65 Columbia DB 7477 Not Meant To Be/Come Back To Me 7

BABA DISE

69 Gas GAS 118 Wanted/SENSATIONS: I'll Always Love You 10

DISORDER

80 Durham B. Centre BOOK 1 Reality Crisis/1984 (oversized p/s) 15

DISORDER

80 Ace ACE 12 Air Raid/Law And Disorder (1st 100 in custom 'war book' p/s) 80/50
81 Disorder ORDER 1 Complete Disorder/Insane Youth/Today's World/Violent Crime (p/s) 6
81 Disorder ORDER 2 Distortion To Deafness/More Than Fights/Daily Life/You've Got To Be Someone (p/s) 5
82 Disorder 12ORDER 3 PERDITION (12" EP) 8
83 Disorder ORDER 4 MENTAL DISORDER (EP) 6
84 Disorder 12 ORDER 5 THE SINGLES COLLECTION (12" EP) 10

TOM DISSIVELT

65 Philips BL 7681 FANTASY IN ORBIT (LP) 40

DISTANT COUSINS

66 CBS 202352 She Ain't Loving You/Here Today, Gone Tomorrow 18
67 CBS 2800 Mister Sebastian/Empty House 7

DISTRACTIONS

79 Factory FAC 12 Time Goes By So Slow/Pillow Fight (p/s) 15
79 TJM TJM 2 YOU'RE NOT GOING OUT DRESSED LIKE THAT (12" EP) 12

DISTRIBUTORS

80 Tap TAP 1 TV Me/Wireless (various foldover p/s) 6
81 Red Rhino RED 9 Hold/Get Rid Of These Things/Wages For Lovers (12", p/s) 8

DIVINE

84 Proto ENAT 118 You Think You're A Man/You Think You're A Man (Remix)/Give It Up (12", p/s) . . . 15

DIVINE COMEDY

91 Setanta SET 008 Timewatch/Jerusalem/The Rise And Fall (12", p/s) 25
92 Setanta SET 011 Europop: New Wave/Intifada/Monitor/Timewatch/Jerusalem/The Rise And Fall (12", p/s) 22
92 Setanta SET 011CD Europop: New Wave/Intifada/Monitor/Timewatch/Jerusalem/The Rise And Fall (CD) 45
93 Setanta CAO 008 Lucy/The Pop Singer's Fear Of The Pollen Count/I Was Born Yesterday (mail order, p/s) 18
93 Setanta CAO 009 Your Daddy's Car (Demo)/THE GLEE CLUB: Free To Believe (33 rpm clear vinyl flexi) 18
93 Setanta DC 001 Indulgence No. 1: Hate My Way/Untitled Melody/Europe By Train (picture disc) . . 25
94 Setanta DC 002 Indulgence No. 2: A Drinking Song/When The Lights Go Out All Over Europe/Tonight We Fly (handfinished wraparound p/s, stamped labels) 25
98 TC 12TC BJD 001 I've Been To A Marvellous Party (Mixes) (12", p/s, double pack promo) 22
90 Setanta SETLPM 002 FANFARE FOR THE COMIC MUSE (LP, with inner sleeve) 55
90 Setanta SETCD 002 FANFARE FOR THE COMIC MUSE (CD) 75
93 Setanta SETLP 011 LIBERATION (LP) 15
93 Setanta SETCD 011 LIBERATION (CD) 20
94 Setanta SETCD 013 PROMENADE (CD, with bonus 4-track live CD) 45
97 Setanta SETCDL 036 A SHORT ALBUM ABOUT LOVE (numbered boxed digipak, with 3 postcards) . . . 22
98 Setanta SET CDL 057 FIN DE SIÈCLE (CD, gatefold digipak with lyric booklet) 20
99 Setanta SETCDL 100 A SECRET HISTORY (2-CD, with hardback book) 25

MINT VALUE £

DIXIE BELLES

63	London HLU 9797	Down At Papa Joe's/Rock, Rock, Rock	15
64	London HLU 9842	Southtown, U.S.A./Why Don't You Set Me Free?	10
64	London REU 1434	THE DIXIE BELLES (EP)	25
64	London HA-U/SH-U 8152	DOWN AT PAPA JOE'S (LP, with Cornbread & Jerry)	30

DIXIE CUPS

64	Pye International 7N 25245	Chapel Of Love/Ain't That Nice	10
64	Red Bird RB 10006	People Say/Girls Can Tell (some copies on Pye label)	10/8
64	Red Bird RB 10012	You Should Have Seen The Way He Looked At Me/No True Love	10
64	Red Bird RB 10017	Little Bell/Another Boy Like Mine	10
65	Red Bird RB 10024	Iko Iko/Gee Baby Gee	10
65	Red Bird RB 10032	Gee The Moon Is Shining Bright/I'm Gonna Get You Yet	20
65	HMV POP 1453	Two Way Poc A Way/That's Where It's At	15
66	HMV POP 1524	What Kind Of Fool/Danny Boy	15
66	HMV POP 1557	Love Ain't So Bad (After All)/Daddy Said No	10
71	Buddah 2011 079	Chapel Of Love/People Say	5
65	Red Bird RB 20100	CHAPEL OF LOVE (LP)	70
66	HMV CLP 1916	RIDING HIGH (LP)	45

DIXIE DRIFTER

65	Columbia DB 7710	Soul Heaven/Three Chairs Theme	12

DIXIE FOUR

60s	Rarities RA 3	THE DIXIE FOUR (EP)	25

DIXIE HUMMINGBIRDS

64	Vogue V 2422	Have A Talk With Jesus/In The Morning	18
64	Vogue LAE-P 588	PRAYER FOR PEACE (LP)	45

DIXIELANDERS

63	Vocalion V 9209	Cyclone/Mardyke	35

DIXIELAND JUG BLOWERS

54	HMV 7M 223	Memphis Shake/Boodle-Am-Shake	15
54	HMV 7M 233	Hen Party Blues/Carpet Alley Breakdown	15

(see also Johnny Dodds)

ERROL DIXON

60	Blue Beat BB 27	Midnight Track/Anytime Anywhere	20
61	Blue Beat BB 46	Mama Shut Your Door/Too Much Whisky	20
62	Blue Beat BB 86	Bad Bad Woman/Early This Morning	15
62	Island WI 017	Morning Train/Lonely Heart	25
63	Island WI 069	I Love You/Tell Me More	25
63	Carnival CV 7001	Oo Wee Baby/Twisting And Shaking	10
63	Carnival CV 7004	Mean And Evil Woman/Tutti Frutti	10
64	Oriole CB 1945	Rocks In My Pillow/Give Me More Time (as Errol Dixon & Bluebeaters)	40
66	Blue Beat BB 337	Gloria/Heavy Shuffle	18
66	Blue Beat BB 344	You're No Good/Midnight Bus	18
66	Rainbow RAI 104	I Need Someone To Love/I Want (as Errol Dixon & Goodtime Band)	18
66	Fab EP 1	I Need Someone To Love/I Want (reissue)	12
67	Ska Beat JB 271	Midnight Party/It Makes No Difference	20
67	Direct DS 5002	I Don't Want/The Hoop	10
67	Decca F 12613	Six Questions/Not Again	15
67	Decca F 12717	True Love Never Runs Smooth/What Ya Gonna Do (B-side with Judy Kay)	15
68	Decca F 12826	Back To The Chicken Shack (as Big City Blues Of Errol Dixon)/ I Done Found Out	18
69	Doctor Bird DB 1197	Why Hurt Yourself/She Started To Scream	18
70	Gas GAS 148	Something On Your Mind/I Need Love	8
65	Decca DFE 8626	SINGS FATS (EP, with Honeydrippers)	60
68	Decca LK/SKL 4962	BLUES IN THE POT (LP, with Chicken Shack)	80
70	Transatlantic TRA 225	THAT'S HOW YOU GOT KILLED BEFORE (LP)	30

(see also Chicken Shack)

HUGH DIXON

64	London HA-U 8188	FRANTIC GUITARS (LP)	15

JEFF DIXON

67	Coxsone CS 7015	The Rock/HAMBOYS: Harder On The Rock	25
68	Studio One SO 2051	Tickle Me/ENFORCERS: Forgive Me	22

TEX DIXON

70	Ackee ACK 111	Funky Trombone/Crying Horn	7
70	Ackee ACK 112	My Ring/Here I Am	7

WILLIE DIXON & ALLSTARS

56	London HLU 8297	Walking The Blues/Crazy For My Baby	2,000
56	London HLU 8297	Walking The Blues/Crazy For My Baby (78)	220
64	Pye International 7N 25270	Crazy For My Baby/Walkin' The Blues (reissue)	30
74	London HA-O 8465	CATALYST (LP, unreleased)	

DIXXY SISTERS

54	Columbia SCM 5105	Spin The Bottle Polka/The Game Of Broken Hearts	15

DJ KRUSH

95	Mo' Wax MW 033	A Whim/89.9 Megamix (12", stickered p/s)	15
95	Mo' Wax MWCD 033	A Whim/89.9 Megamix (CD, in slipcase, with inner)	8
95	Mo' Wax MW 042	Meiso/(mixes) (12", p/s)	8
96	Mo' Wax MW 060	Only The Strong Survive/(mixes) (12", p/s)	10
93	Mo' Wax MWLP 001	JAZZ HIP JAP (LP)	30
94	Mo' Wax MWLP 025	STRICTLY TURNTABLIZED (2-LP)	15
95	Mo' Wax MWLP 039	MEISO (2-LP, die-cut sleeve)	20

(see also DJ Shadow)

MINT VALUE £

DJ SHADOW

93	Mo' Wax MW 014	In/ Flux/Hindsight (12", plain sleeve, with obi sticker, with the Groove Robbers)	50
93	Mo' Wax MW 014	In/ Flux/Hindsight (12", reissue, title sleeve, with the Groove Robbers)	15
93	Mo' Wax MW 014	In/ Flux/Hindsight (12" picture disc, plastic sleeve, with the Groove Robbers)	50
93	Mo' Wax MWCD 014	In/ Flux/Hindsight (CD, with the Groove Robbers)	10
94	Mo' Wax MW 024	Lost And Found/DJ KRUSH: Kemuri (12", p/s)	15
94	Mo' Wax MWCD 024	Lost And Found/DJ KRUSH: Kemuri (CD)	10
94	Mo' Wax MW 027	What Does Your Soul Look Like (parts 1, 3 & 4) (p/s)	15
96	Mo' Wax MW 057	Midnight In A Perfect World (remixes)/Mutual Slump (12", p/s)	12
96	Mo' Wax MWCD 057	Midnight In A Perfect World (remixes)/Mutual Slump (CD, card sleeve with inner)	15
96	Mo' Wax MW 058	Stem/Red Bus Needs To Leave (p/s)	10
97	Mo' Wax MW 063s	High Noon/Organ Donor (Extended Overhaul) (p/s)	10
97	Mo' Wax MW 063	High Noon/Devil's Advocate/Organ Donor (Extended Overhaul) (p/s)	10
97	Mo' Wax MWCD 063	High Noon/Devil's Advocate/Organ Donor (Extended Overhaul) (CD)	10
98	Mo' Wax MW 059	ENDTRODUCING (LP)	20

(see also Q-Bert, U.N.K.L.E.)

D'JURANN JURANN

74	Dawn DNS 1068	Streakin'/Oh! Janine	10

(see also Paul King, King Earl Boogie Band, Mungo Jerry)

JED(RZEZ) DMOCHOWSKI

83	Whaam! WHAAM 009	Sha-La-La-La (Dance With Me)/Ruined City (with or without 'Jed' on p/s)	8/10
82	Whaam! WHAAM 84	STALLIONS OF MY HEART (LP)	12

(see also V.I.P.'s)

DNA

90	Raw Bass 12 RBASS 006	LA SERENISSIMA (12" EP)	10

DNV

79	New Pleasures Z2	Mafia/Death In Venice/Goodbye 70s (foldout p/s)	20

(see also Another Pretty Face, Funhouse, Waterboys, TV21)

D.O.A.

93	Alt. Tentacles VIRUS 120	It's Not Unusual/Dead Men Tell No Tales (yellow vinyl)	5
81	Alt. Tentacles VIRUS 7	POSITIVELY D.O.A. (EP)	7
83	Alt. Tentacles VIRUS 31	BLOODIED BUT UNBOWED — THE DAMAGE TO DATE 1978-84 (12" EP)	8
84	Alt. Tentacles VIRUS 24	WAR ON 45 (12" EP)	8
85	Alt. Tentacles VIRUS 42	DON'T TURN YOUR BACK (ON DESPERATE TIMES) (LP)	12
85	Alt. Tentacles VIRUS 44	LET'S WRECK THE PARTY (LP, with insert & small 'spy' logo)	12

CARL DOBKINS JNR.

59	Brunswick 05804	My Heart Is An Open Book/My Pledge To You	12
59	Brunswick 05804	My Heart Is An Open Book/My Pledge To You (78)	15
59	Brunswick 05811	If You Don't Want My Lovin'/Love Is Everything	25
59	Brunswick 05811	If You Don't Want My Lovin'/Love Is Everything (78)	15
60	Brunswick 05817	Lucky Devil/(There's A Little Song A-Singing) In My Heart	12
60	Brunswick 05832	Exclusively Yours/One Little Girl	10
60	Brunswick LAT 8329	CARL DOBKINS JNR. (LP)	80

BOBBY DOBSON

69	Punch PH 4	Strange/Your New Love	8

(see also Dobby Dobson)

BONNIE DOBSON

69	RCA RCA 1901	I'm Your Woman/I Got Stung	6
70	RCA SF 8079	BONNIE DOBSON (LP)	15
72	Argo ZFB 79	BONNIE DOBSON (LP)	45
76	Polydor 2383 400	MORNING DEW (LP)	15

DOBBY DOBSON (& DELTAS)

65	King KG 1008	Cry A Little Cry/Diamonds And Pearls (as Dobby Dobson & Deltas)	12
67	Trojan TR 011	Loving Pauper/TOMMY McCOOK & SUPERSONICS: Sir Don	18
68	Studio One SO 2068	Walking In The Footsteps/SOUL VENDORS: Studio Rock	30
68	Coxsone CS 7058	Seems To Me I'm Losing You/GAYLADS: Red Rose	25
69	Blue Cat BS 171	Strange/Your New Love	18
69	Punch PH 12	The Masquerade Is Over/Love For Ambition	6
70	Success RE 906	Crazy/RUPIE EDWARDS ALL STARS: Your New Love	6
70	Big BG 303	That Wonderful Sound/I Wasn't Born Yesterday	6
70	Big BG 310	Halfway To Paradise/Utopia	5
71	Dynamic DYN 426	Carry That Weight/More Weight	5
69	Pama SECO 33	STRANGE (LP)	50
70	Trojan TBL 145	THAT WONDERFUL SOUND (LP)	30

(see also Bobby Dobson, Chuck & Dobby, Bruce Bennett, Ernest Wilson & Freddy)

LYN DOBSON

74	Fresh Air 6370 501	JAM SANDWICH (LP)	15

(see also Manfred Mann, Soft Machine, Miller Anderson)

ROY DOCKER

68	Domain D3	Mellow Moonlight/MUSIC THROUGH SIX: Riff Raff	10
69	Pama PM 750	When/Go	6
69	Pama PM 756	I'm An Outcast/Everyday Will Be A Holiday	8

DOCTOR & THE MEDICS

82	Whaam! WHAAM 6	The Druids Are Here/The Goats Are Trying To Kill Me (p/s)	5

DOCTOR BROWN

95	Magic Gnome	ANOTHER REALM (LP, 500 only)	15

MINT VALUE £

DR. CALCULUS

86 10 DIX 45 DESIGNER BEATNIK (LP) 10
86 10 DIXCD 45 DESIGNER BEATNIK (CD) 25
(see also Stephen 'Tin Tin' Duffy)

DOCTOR DARK

76 Target TGT 102 Red Hot Passion/Instrumental (no p/s) 7
(see also Snivelling Shits)

DOCTOR FATHER

70 Pye 7N 17977 Umbopo/Roll On. 7
(see also 10cc, Godley & Creme, Hotlegs)

DR. FEELGOOD & THE INTERNS (U.S.)

62 Columbia DB 4838 Dr. Feelgood/Mister Moonlight. 25
64 Columbia DB 7228 The Doctor's Doogie/Blang Dong 25
66 CBS 202099 Don't Tell Me No Dirty/Where Did You Go 20
68 Capitol CL 15569 Sugar Bee/You're So Used To It. 20
64 Columbia SEG 8310 DR. FEELGOOD AND THE INTERNS (EP) 70
(see also Piano Red)

DR. FEELGOOD (U.K.)

74 United Artists UP 35760 Roxette/(Get Your Kicks On) Route 66 (no p/s). 5
75 United Artists UP 35815 She Does It Right/I Don't Mind (no p/s). 5
75 United Artists UP 35857 Back In The Night/I'm A Man 5
77 United Artists UP 36304 She's A Windup/Hi-Rise (p/s). 5
77 United Artists 12UP 36304 She's A Windup/Hi-Rise/Homework (12", die-cut sleeve) 8
77 United Artists UP 36332 Baby Jane/Looking Back. 7
77 United Artists 12UP 36332 Baby Jane/Looking Back/You Upset Me Baby (live) (12", p/s) 8
79 United Artists UP 36468 Milk And Alcohol/Every Kind Of Vice (p/s, brown or white vinyl). 5
79 United Artists X/Y/ZUP 36506 As Long As The Price Is Right/Down At The (Other) Doctors (p/s, either black, blue, brown or violet vinyl, 3 different p/s designs) . . . . . . each 5
86 Stiff BUY 253 Don't Wait Up/Something Good (shrink-wrapped with bonus 45: "Back In The Night"/"Milk And Alcohol" [FBUY 56]) (p/s) 6
75 United Artists UAS 29727 DOWN BY THE JETTY (LP, mono only) 12
75 United Artists UAS 29880 MALPRACTICE (LP) 12
76 United Artists UAS 29990 STUPIDITY (LP initially with stickered covers & bonus 7": "Riot In Cell Block No. 9"/"Johnny B. Goode" [FEEL 1]) 12
79 United Artists UAK 30239 AS IT HAPPENS (LP, with inner sleeve & bonus 7" "Encore EP": "Riot In Cell Block No. 9"/"The Blues Had A Baby And They Named It Rock'N'Roll"/ "Lights Out"/"Great Balls Of Fire" [p/s, FEEL 2], with inner sleeve) 12
(see also Wilko Johnson, Lew Lewis, Oil City Sheiks)

DR. HOOK

73 CBS 1037 The Cover Of "Radio Times" (1-sided, promo only, by Dr. Hook & Friends). 75
78 Capitol CL 15992 The Radio/Only Sixteen/I'm A Lamb (p/s) 8
78 Capitol PSLP 314 FOR YOU FROM DR. HOOK (EP, promo only) 10
71 CBS 64754 DR. HOOK AND THE MEDICINE SHOW (LP, plain orange label). 15
71 CBS 65132 SLOPPY SECONDS (LP, plain orange label) 15
71 CBS 65560 BELLY UP (LP, plain orange label). 12

DR. JOHN (The Night Tripper)

70 Atco 2091 019 Wash Mama Wash/Mama Roux 6
72 Atlantic K 10158 Iko Iko/Huey Smith Medley 6
72 Atlantic K 10214 Wang Dang Doodle/Big Chief 5
73 Atlantic K 10291 Right Place, Wrong Time/I Been Hoodooed. 10
73 Atlantic K 10329 Such A Night/Life. 8
68 Atlantic 587/588 147 GRIS GRIS (LP, plum label, mono/stereo) 30
69 Atco 228 018 BABYLON (LP, plum label). 18
70 Atco 2400 015 REMEDIES (LP, plum label) 18
71 Atlantic 2400 161 THE SUN, MOON AND HERBS (LP, plum label, gatefold sleeve with insert) 25
72 Atlantic K 40384 GUMBO (LP, green & orange label, gatefold sleeve). 15
72 Atlantic K 40168 GRIS GRIS (LP, reissue, green & orange label). 15
72 Atlantic K 40250 THE SUN, MOON AND HERBS (LP, reissue, green & orange label, gatefold sleeve with insert) 15
73 Atco K 50017 IN THE RIGHT PLACE (LP, U.K. disc in U.S. stickered 3-way gatefold sleeve). 20
73 CBS 65659 TRIUMVIRATE (LP, with John Hammond & Mike Bloomfield). 15
74 Atlantic K 50035 DESITIVELY BONNAROO (LP). 15
75 United Artists UAG 29902 HOLLYWOOD BE THY NAME (LP, with inner sleeve) 15
75 DJM DJSLM 2019 CUT ME WHILE I'M HOT (ANYTIME, ANYPLACE) (LP) 12

DR. K'S BLUES BAND

68 Spark SRLP 101 DR. K'S BLUES BAND (LP) 60

DR. MARIGOLD'S PRESCRIPTION

68 Pye 7N 17493 My Old Man's A Groovy Old Man/People Get Ready 7
69 Pye 7N 17832 You've Got To Build Your Love/My Picture Of Love 7
70 Bell BLL 1096 Breaking The Heart Of A Good Man/Night Hurries On By 7
70 Bell BLL 1126 Sing Along, Sing Along, Sing Along/Father Jim 7
71 Bell BLL 1149 Muddy Water/Come With Me 7
69 Marble Arch MALS 1222 PICTURES OF LIFE (LP) 12
73 Pye/Santa Ponsa PNL 501 HELLO GIRL (LP, as Dr. Marigold's). 12

DR. OCTAGON

96 Mo' Wax MWLP 046 OCTAGONECOLOGYST (3-LP) 25

DOCTOR ROCKIT

96 Clear CLR 411 READY TO ROCKIT EP (2 x 10", p/s) 15

DR. STRANGELY STRANGE

69 Island ILPS 9106 KIP OF THE SERENES (LP, pink label, later 'palm-tree' with remix) 90/100
70 Vertigo 6360 009 HEAVY PETTING (LP, gatefold sleeve, swirl label; beware of counterfeits) 90
(see also Sweeney's Men, Gary Moore)

DR. TECHNICAL & MACHINES

83 Hawkfan HWFB 1 Zones/Processed (1-sided with insert, mail-order issue, no p/s) 12
(see also Dave Brock, Hawkwind)

DR. WEST'S MEDICINE SHOW & JUNK BAND

67 CBS 202492 The Eggplant That Ate Chicago/You Can't Fight City Hall Blues 8
67 CBS 202658 Gondoliers, Shakespeares, Overseers/Daddy I Know. 8
68 Page One POF 061 Bullets La Verne/Jigsaw. 35
70 Page One POF 176 Gondoliers, Shakespeares, Overseers/Daddy I Know (reissue) 6
69 Page One POLS 017 THE EGGPLANT THAT ATE CHICAGO (LP). 40
(see also Norman Greenbaum)

DR. WHO

76 Argo ZSW 564 DR. WHO AND THE PESCATONS (LP, spoken word,
read by Tom Baker & Elizabeth Sladen) 15
79 BBC REC 364 GENESIS OF THE DALEKS (LP, spoken word) 15
81 RNIB TALKING BOOK (reel-to-reel tape, read by Gabriel Wolf) 20
82 BBC 2LP-22001 DOCTOR WHO COLLECTOR'S EDITION (2-LP, includes
"Genesis Of The Daleks" [BBC 22364], "Sound Effects" [BBC 22316],
& bonus 7" "Doctor Who"/"The Astronauts" [RESL 451], with poster) 30
(see also BBC Radiophonic Workshop, Century 21, Jon Pertwee)

DR. Z

70 Fontana 6007 023 Lady Ladybird/People In The Street. 40
71 Vertigo 6360 048 THREE PARTS TO MY SOUL (LP, gatefold sleeve, swirl label) 200

PAT DODD

59 Pye International 7N 25030 Stag Party/Odds'n'Dodds 7
59 Pye International N 25030 Stag Party/Odds'n'Dodds (78) 12

DODD'S ALLSTARS

69 Coxsone CS 7096 Mother Aitken (actually by Lord Power)/What A Love (actually by Denzil Laing) . 25

JOHNNY DODDS

51 HMV B 10082 Bucktown Stomp/Weary City Stomp (78) 8
52 HMV B 10223 Blue Washboard Stomp/Bull Fiddle Blues (78) 25
52 Vocalion V 1003 After You've Gone/Come On And Stomp Stomp Stomp (78) 10
52 Vocalion V 1008 Weary Blues/New Orleans Stomp (78). 10
52 Vocalion V 1022 When Erastus Plays His Old Kazoo/Joe Turner Blues (78). 10
53 Vocalion V 1025 San/New St. Louis Blues (78, mispressing) 30
53 Vocalion V 1025 Oh! Lizzie (A Lover's Lament)/Clarinet Wobble (78) 10
53 London AL 3505 JOHNNY DODDS VOLUME 1 (10" LP) 15
54 London AL 3513 JOHNNY DODDS VOLUME 2 (10" LP) 15
55 Vogue Coral LRA 10025 JOHNNY DODDS VOL. 1 (10" LP) 25
55 HMV DLP 1073 JOHNNY DODDS WASHBOARD STOMP (10" LP) 20
56 Philips BBL 7136 JOHNNY DODDS AND KID ORY (LP). 12
56 London AL 3555 JOHNNY DODDS VOLUME 3 (10" LP) 18
57 London AL 3560 JOHNNY DODDS VOLUME 4 (10" LP) 18
(see also Dixieland Jugblowers)

MALCOLM DODDS

59 Brunswick 05774 This Is Real (This Is Love)/I'll Always Be With You 5
59 Brunswick 05796 Tremble/Deep Inside 5

NELLA DODDS

65 Pye 7N 25281 Come See About Me/You Don't Love Me Anymore. 35
65 Pye 7N 25291 Finders Keepers, Losers Weepers/A Girl's Life. 25

DODGERS

60 Downbeat CHA 2 Let's Make A Whole Lot Of Love/You Make Me Happy 25

DODO RESURRECTION

72 Elegiac SNT 7926 NOSTRADAMUS (LP, private pressing, with fold-out 'treatise' insert). 2,500
(see also Underwater Hairdressers)

DODO'S

67 Polydor BM 56153 I Made Up My Mind/Can't Make It Out 35

ERNIE K-DOE

(see under 'K')

DOGFEET

71 Reflection HRS 7 Sad Story/On The Road 35
71 Reflection HRS 12 Since I Went Away/Evil Woman 35
70 Reflection REFL 8 DOGFEET (LP) 350
94 Kissing Spell CA 36001 DOGFEET (LP, reissue) 15

TYMON DOGG

81 Ghost Dance GHO 1 Lose This Skin (featuring the Clash)/Indestructable (p/s). 6
(see also Timon, Clash)

DOGGEREL BANK

73 Charisma CB 220 Tiny Seed Of Love/Down On The Farm 5
73 Charisma CAS 1079 SILVER FACES (LP) 12
75 Charisma CAS 1102 MISTER SKILLCORN DANCES (LP). 18

BILL DOGGETT

55 Parlophone DP 411 Gumbo/Tara's Theme (78, export issue) 20
55 Parlophone DP 432 Christmas Song/Winter Wonderland (78, export issue) 20
56 Parlophone CMSP 39 Honky Tonk (Parts 1 & 2) (gold label lettering, export issue) 18

Year	Label / Cat. No.	Title	MINT VALUE £
56	Parlophone R 4231	Honky Tonk (Parts 1 & 2) (gold label lettering, later silver)	30/18
56	Parlophone R 4231	Honky Tonk (Parts 1 & 2) (78)	6
57	Parlophone R 4265	Slow Walk/Peacock Alley	15
57	Parlophone R 4265	Slow Walk/Peacock Alley (78)	8
57	Parlophone R 4306	Ram-Bunk-Shush/Blue Largo	15
57	Parlophone R 4306	Ram-Bunk-Shush/Blue Largo (78)	8
57	Parlophone R 4379	Hot Ginger/Soft	18
57	Parlophone R 4379	Hot Ginger/Soft (78)	10
58	Parlophone R 4413	Leaps And Bounds (Parts 1 & 2)	10
58	Parlophone R 4413	Leaps And Bounds (Parts 1 & 2) (78)	12
60	Parlophone R 4629	Smokie/Evening Dreams	10
61	Warner Bros WB 32	The Hully Gully Twist/Jackrabbit	10
61	Warner Bros WB 46	You Can't Sit Down (Parts 1 & 2)	15
57	Parlophone GEP 8644	HONKY TONK (EP)	30
57	Parlophone GEP 8674	PLAYS DUKE ELLINGTON (EP)	12
58	Parlophone GEP 8711	BILL DOGGETT (EP)	12
58	Parlophone GEP 8727	RAINBOW RIOT (EP)	12
59	Parlophone GEP 8771	A JOLLY CHRISTMAS (EP)	12
58	Parlophone PMD 1067	DAME DREAMING (10" LP)	35
59	Parlophone PMD 1073	DANCE AWHILE WITH DOGGETT (10" LP)	35
60	Parlophone PMC 1118	DOGGETT'S BIG CITY DANCE PARTY (LP)	20
60	Parlophone PMC 1124	ON TOUR (LP)	18
61	Warner Bros WM 402	3046 PEOPLE DANCED 'TIL 4 A.M. (LP, live, as Bill Doggett & His Combo)	15
62	Parlophone PMC 1165	BACK WITH MORE BILL DOGGETT (LP)	20
62	Warner Bros WM 4056	THE BAND WITH THE BEAT (LP, with His Combo, also stereo WS 8056)	12/15
65	HMV CLP 1884	WOW (LP)	15

(see also Ella Fitzgerald, Earl Bostic)

DOGROSE

Year	Label / Cat. No.	Title	MINT VALUE £
73	Satril SAT 6	All For The Love Of City Lights/Each Other	6
72	Satril SATL 4002	ALL FOR THE LOVE OF DOGROSE (LP)	22

DOGS D'AMOUR

Year	Label / Cat. No.	Title	MINT VALUE £
88	China WOL 7	THE (UN)AUTHORISED BOOTLEG (LP)	30

THE DOG THAT BIT PEOPLE

Year	Label / Cat. No.	Title	MINT VALUE £
71	Parlophone R 5880	Lovely Lady/Merry-Go-Round	25
71	Parlophone PCS 7125	THE DOG THAT BIT PEOPLE (LP)	240

(see also Norman Haines, Locomotive)

DOGWATCH

Year	Label / Cat. No.	Title	MINT VALUE £
79	Bridgehouse BHLP 002	PENFRIEND (LP, with insert)	20

NED DOHENY

Year	Label / Cat. No.	Title	MINT VALUE £
81	CBS 9481	To Prove My Love/On The Swing Shift (p/s)	8
81	CBS 13-9481	To Prove My Love/On The Swing Shift (12", p/s)	10

DOKKEN

Year	Label / Cat. No.	Title	MINT VALUE £
82	Carrere CAR 229	We're Illegal/Paris Is Burning (p/s)	5
82	Carrere CAL 136	BREAKIN' THE CHAINS (LP)	12

JOE DOLAN

Year	Label / Cat. No.	Title	MINT VALUE £
67	Piccadilly 7N 35368	House With The Whitewashed Gable/Work Day Blues	6
67	Pye 7N 17354	Tar And Cement/Time Of My Life	7

RAMBLIN' JIMMY DOLAN

Year	Label / Cat. No.	Title	MINT VALUE £
51	Capitol CL 13600	Wine, Women, And Pink Elephants /GENE O'QUIN: Boogie Woogie Fever (78)	10
53	Capitol CL 13982	The Wheel That Does The Squeakin'/Playin' Dominoes And Shootin' Dice (78)	10

DOLE

Year	Label / Cat. No.	Title	MINT VALUE £
78	Ultimate ULT 402	New Wave Love/Hungry Men No Longer Steal Sheep But Are There Hanging Judges? (die-cut p/s)	20

MICKY DOLENZ

Year	Label / Cat. No.	Title	MINT VALUE £
67	London HLH 10117	Don't Do It/FINDERS KEEPERS: (We Wear) Lavender Blue	15
67	London HLH 10152	Huff Puff/OBVIOUS: Fate	15
73	MGM 2006 265	Daybreak/Love War	10
74	MGM 2006 392	Ooh She's Young/Love War	10
79	Chrysalis CHS 2297	Love Light/Alicia (p/s)	6
83	A&M BUGSY 1	Tomorrow/BUGSY MALONE GANG: Fat Sam's Grand Slam (with poster)	10

(see also Monkees)

ANDY DOLL

Year	Label / Cat. No.	Title	MINT VALUE £
62	Starlite ST45 068	Wild Desire/Wyat	12
63	Starlite STLP II	ON STAGE (LP, by Andy Doll Band & Guests)	15

LINDA DOLL & SUNDOWNERS

Year	Label / Cat. No.	Title	MINT VALUE £
64	Piccadilly 7N 35166	Bonie Maronie/He Don't Want Your Love Anymore	12

DOLLIES

Year	Label / Cat. No.	Title	MINT VALUE £
65	CBS 201788	You Touch Me Baby/I Can't Go On	10

DOLPHIN

Year	Label / Cat. No.	Title	MINT VALUE £
76	Private Stock PVT 52	Then I Kissed Her/The Glyderes	5
76	Private Stock PVT 67	Goin' Back/Think Ahead	7
77	Private Stock PVT 91	Only Seventeen/Take Care Of The Ocean	5
77	Private Stock PVT 122	Imagination Dancing/The Actress	5
80	Gale 5	Hey Joe/Dubby Dubby	5
77	Private Stock PVLP 1055	GOODBYE (LP)	12
80	Gale GALELP 02	MOLECULES (LP)	12

ERIC DOLPHIN QUINTET

Year	Label / Cat. No.	Title	MINT VALUE £
61	Esquire 32-123	THE ERIC DOLPHIN QUINTET (LP)	25

DOLPHINS

65 Stateside SS 375 Hey Da Da Dow/I Don't Want To Go On Without You . . . 12

ERIC DOLPHY

69 Transatlantic PR 7311 OUTWARD BOUND (LP) . . . 12

ERIC DOLPHY & BOOKER LITTLE

66 Stateside SL 10160 ERIC DOLPHY AND BOOKER LITTLE MEMORIAL ALBUM (LP) . . . 15

BILLY DOLTON

61 Parlophone R 4733 Winkie Doll/Girls . . . 15

DOME

81 Dome DOME 3 Jasz (1-sided flexidisc) . . . 6
80 4AD CAD 16 3R4 (mini-LP) . . . 12
80 Dome DOME 1 DOME ONE (LP) . . . 15
80 Dome DOME 2 DOME 2 (LP) . . . 12
81 Dome DOME 3 DOME 3 (LP) . . . 12
(see also Wire, Gilbert & Lewis)

ANNA DOMINO

86 Factory FAC 158 Summer (p/s) . . . 12

FATS DOMINO

78s

54 London HL 8007 Rose Mary/You Said You Love Me . . . 65
54 London HL 8063 Little School Girl/You Done Me Wrong . . . 55
54 London HL 8096 Don't Leave Me This Way/Something's Wrong . . . 50
55 London HL 8124 Love Me/Don't You Hear Me Calling You . . . 40
55 London HL 8133 Thinking Of You/I Know . . . 25
55 London HLU 8173 Ain't That A Shame/La La . . . 12
56 London HLU 8256 Bo Weevil/Don't Blame It On Me . . . 18
56 London HLU 8280 I'm In Love Again/My Blue Heaven . . . 10
56 London HLU 8309 When My Dream Boat Comes Home/So Long . . . 12
56 London HLU 8330 Blueberry Hill/I Can't Go On (Rosalie) . . . 10
57 London HLU 8356 Honey Chile/Don't You Know . . . 12
57 London HLP 8377 Blue Monday/What's The Reason I'm Not Pleasing You . . . 12
57 London HLP 8407 I'm Walkin'/I'm In The Mood For Love . . . 12
57 London HLP 8449 The Valley Of Tears/It's You I Love . . . 12
57 London HLP 8471 What Will I Tell My Heart/When I See You . . . 12
57 London HLP 8519 Wait And See/I Still Love You . . . 12
58 London HLP 8575 The Big Beat (from the film)/I Want You To Know . . . 12
58 London HLP 8628 Sick And Tired/No, No . . . 12
58 London HLP 8663 Little Mary/The Prisoner's Song . . . 15
58 London HLP 8727 Young School Girl/It Must Be Love . . . 20
58 London HLP 8759 Whole Lotta Loving/Coquette . . . 20
59 London HLP 8822 When The Saints Go Marching In/Telling Lies . . . 30
59 London HLP 8865 Margie/I'm Ready . . . 35
59 London HLP 8942 I Want To Walk You Home/I'm Gonna Be A Wheel Some Day . . . 45
59 London HLP 9005 Be My Guest/I've Been Around . . . 55
60 London HLP 9073 Country Boy/If You Need Me . . . 65
60 London HLP 9163 Walking To New Orleans/Don't Come Knockin' . . . 110

SINGLES

55 London HL 8124 Love Me/Don't You Hear Me Calling You . . . 175
55 London HL 8133 Thinking Of You/I Know . . . 150
55 London HLU 8173 Ain't That A Shame/La La . . . 70
56 London HLU 8256 Bo Weevil/Don't Blame It On Me . . . 100
56 London HLU 8280 I'm In Love Again/My Blue Heaven . . . 90
56 London HLU 8309 When My Dream Boat Comes Home/So Long . . . 70
56 London HLU 8330 Blueberry Hill/I Can't Go On (Rosalie) . . . 70
57 London HLU 8356 Honey Chile/Don't You Know . . . 70
57 London HLP 8377 Blue Monday/What's The Reason I'm Not Pleasing You . . . 60
(The above 45s were originally issued with triangular centres & gold lettering labels; later silver-label re-pressings are worth around half these values.)
57 London HLP 8407 I'm Walkin'/I'm In The Mood For Love . . . 25
57 London HLP 8449 The Valley Of Tears/It's You I Love . . . 25
57 London HLP 8471 What Will I Tell My Heart/When I See You . . . 25
57 London HLP 8519 Wait And See/I Still Love You . . . 22
58 London HLP 8575 The Big Beat (From The Film)/I Want You To Know . . . 20
58 London HLP 8628 Sick And Tired/No, No . . . 20
58 London HLP 8663 Little Mary/The Prisoner's Song . . . 22
58 London HLP 8727 Young School Girl/It Must Be Love . . . 25
58 London HLP 8759 Whole Lotta Loving/Coquette . . . 22
59 London HLP 8822 When The Saints Go Marching In/Telling Lies . . . 18
(HLP 8407 through to 8822 45s were issued with triangular centres & silver lettering on all-black labels; later copies are worth around half these values.)
59 London HLP 8865 Margie/I'm Ready (triangular centre & silver-top label, later round centre) . . . 15/8
59 London HLP 8942 I Want To Walk You Home/I'm Gonna Be A Wheel Some Day (tri or round) . . . 18/10
59 London HLP 9005 Be My Guest/I've Been Around (triangular or round centre) . . . 40/12
(All subsequent London 45s were issued with round centres & silver-top labels.)
60 London HLP 9073 Country Boy/If You Need Me . . . 12
60 London HLP 9133 Tell Me That You Love Me/Before I Grow Too Old . . . 15
60 London HLP 9163 Walking To New Orleans/Don't Come Knockin' . . . 12
60 London HLP 9198 Three Nights A Week/Put Your Arms Around Me, Honey . . . 12
60 London HLP 9244 My Girl Josephine/Natural Born Lover . . . 10
61 London HLP 9301 What A Price/Ain't That Just Like A Woman . . . 15
61 London HLP 9327 Fell In Love On Monday/Shu-Rah . . . 15
61 London HLP 9374 It Keeps Rainin'/I Just Cry . . . 30
61 London HLP 9415 Let The Four Winds Blow/Good Hearted Man . . . 12

MINT VALUE £

61	London HLP 9456	What A Party/Rockin' Bicycle	12
62	London HLP 9520	Jambalaya/You Win Again	10
62	London HLP 9557	My Real Name/My Heart Is Bleeding	15
62	London HLP 9590	Dance With Mr. Domino/Nothing New (Same Old Thing)	15
62	London HLP 9616	Did You Ever See A Dream Walking/Stop The Clock	15
63	London HLP 9738	You Always Hurt The One You Love/Trouble Blues	12
63	HMV POP 1164	There Goes My Heart Again/Can't Go On Without You	12
63	HMV POP 1197	When I'm Walkin'/I've Got A Right To Cry	10
63	HMV POP 1219	Red Sails In The Sunset/Song For Rosemary	7
63	HMV POP 1265	Just A Lonely Man/Who Cares	10
64	HMV POP 1281	I Don't Want To Set The World On Fire/Lazy Lady	7
64	HMV POP 1303	If You Don't Know What Love Is/Something You Got Baby	22
64	HMV POP 1324	Mary Oh Mary/Packin' Up	7
64	HMV POP 1370	Kansas City/Heartbreak Hill	8
65	Mercury MF 869	(I Left My Heart) In San Francisco/I Done Got Over It	12
65	Mercury MF 873	What's That You Got?/It's Never Too Late	10
65	HMV POP 1421	Why Don't You Do Right?/Wigs	8
67	HMV POP 1582	I'm Livin' Right/I Don't Want To Set The World On Fire	8
67	Liberty LBF 12055	It Keeps Rainin'/Blue Monday	7
68	Liberty LBF 15098	Walking To New Orleans/Blueberry Hill	5
68	Reprise RS 20696	Honest Mamas Love Their Papas Better/One For The Highway (withdrawn)	12
68	Reprise RS 20763	Lady Madonna/One For The Highway	18
69	Reprise RS 20810	Everybody's Got Something To Hide Except Me And My Monkey/ So Swell When You're Well	8
69	Liberty LBF 15274	I'm Ready/The Fat Man	10
69	Mercury MF 1104	What's That You Got?/Jambalaya (On The Bayou)	8
78	Sonet SON 2168	Sleeping On The Job/After Hours	5

EXPORT SINGLES

57	London HL 7028	Wait And See/I Still Love You	35
58	London HL 7040	Sick And Tired/No, No	35
58	London HL 7054	The Big Beat (from the film)/Little Mary	35

EPs

55	London RE-P 1022	BLUES FOR LOVE (1st pressing with gold lettering label, later silver)	80/40
56	London RE-U 1062	BLUES FOR LOVE VOL. 2 (1st pressing with gold label, later silver)	70/40
57	London RE-U 1073	FATS (export issue, plain sleeve)	130
57	London RE-P 1079	HERE COMES FATS VOL. 1	45
58	London RE-P 1080	HERE COMES FATS VOL. 2	45
58	London RE-P 1115	CARRY ON ROCKIN' PART 1	60
58	London RE-P 1116	CARRY ON ROCKIN' PART 2	60
58	London RE-P 1117	BLUES FOR LOVE VOL. 3	40
58	London RE-P 1121	BLUES FOR LOVE VOL. 4	40
58	London RE-P 1138	HERE COMES FATS VOL. 3	40
59	London RE-P 1206	THE ROCKIN' MR. D VOL. 1	40
59	London RE-P 1207	THE ROCKIN' MR. D VOL. 2	40

(The above EPs were originally issued with triangular centres; round-centre re-pressings are worth two-thirds these values.)

60	London RE-P 1261	BE MY GUEST	35
60	London RE-P 1265	THE ROCKIN' MR. D VOL. 3	35
62	London RE-P 1340	WHAT A PARTY	35
64	HMV 7EG 8862	RED SAILS IN THE SUNSET	30
65	Liberty LEP 4026	MY BLUE HEAVEN	30
66	Liberty LEP 4045	ROLLIN'	30

LPs

56	London HA-U 2028	FATS' ROCK AND ROLLIN'	100
56	London HA-P 2041	CARRY ON ROCKIN'	100
57	London HA-P 2052	HERE STANDS FATS DOMINO	100
56	London HA-P 2073	THIS IS FATS DOMINO	70
58	London HA-P 2087	THIS IS FATS	70
58	London HA-P 2135	THE FABULOUS "MR. D"	60
59	London HA-P 2223	LET'S PLAY FATS DOMINO	60
60	London HA-P 2312	A LOT OF DOMINOES!	50
61	London HA-P 2364	I MISS YOU SO	50
61	London HA-P 2420	LET THE FOUR WINDS BLOW	50
61	London HA-P 2426	WHAT A PARTY	50
62	London HA-P 2447	TWISTIN' THE STOMP	50
63	London HA-P 8039	JUST DOMINO	50
63	London HA-P 8084	WALKING TO NEW ORLEANS	50
63	HMV CLP 1690	HERE COMES FATS DOMINO (also stereo CSD 1520)	30/40
63	HMV CLP 1740	FATS ON FIRE (also stereo CSD 1543)	30/40
65	Liberty LBY 3033	MILLION SELLERS BY FATS VOL. 1	18
65	Liberty LBY 3046	MILLION SELLERS BY FATS VOL. 2	18
65	HMV CLP 1821	GETAWAY WITH FATS DOMINO (also stereo CSD 1580)	22/30
65	Mercury (S)MCL 20070	DOMINO '65 (mono/stereo)	15
68	Stateside (S)SL 10240	FANTASTIC FATS	12

DOMINOES (Jamaica)

68	Melody MRC 002	A Tribute (actually by Ann Reid)/Hooray (actually by Uniques)	10

DOMINOES (U.K.)

58	Reading Rag LYN 545	Bye Bye Johnny/Yakety Yak	15

DOMINOES (U.S.)

51	Vogue V 9012	Sixty Minute Man/I Can't Escape From You (78)	40
52	Vogue V 2135	Have Mercy, Baby/That's What You're Doing To Me (78)	40
67	Vogue V 212	Sixty Minute Man/I Can't Escape From You	25
56	Vogue EPV 1113	RHYTHM AND BLUES (EP, 2 tracks by Swallows)	325

(see also Billy Ward & Dominoes, Clyde McPhatter, Jackie Wilson)

SAM DONAHUE & HIS ORCHESTRA
55 Capitol CL 14349 Saxaboogie/September In The Rain. . . . 18

TROY DONAHUE
63 Warner Bros WB 111 Live Young/Somebody Loves Me. . . . 10

MIKE DONALD
71 Folk Heritage FHR 021 YORKSHIRE SONGS OF THE BROAD ACRES (LP). . . . 25

ERIC DONALDSON
71 Dynamic DYN 420 Cherry Oh Baby/LLOYD CHARMERS: Sir Charmers Special . . . 8
71 Dynamic DYN 423 Love Of The Common People/DRAGONAIRES: The Dragon's Net . . . 10
71 Dynamic DYN 425 Just Can't (Happen This Way)/Just Can't (Happen This Way) Version . . . 6
72 Dynamic DYN 431 I'm Indebted/I'm Indebted (Version). . . . 6
72 Dynamic DYN 439 Miserable Woman/The Lion Sleeps . . . 6
72 Dynamic DYN 445 Blue Boot/Blue Boot (Version). . . . 6
72 Dynamic DYN 452 Little Did You Know/Little Did You Know (Version) . . . 5
73 Dragon DRA 1017 What A Festival/I ROY & ERIC: Festival Version . . . 5
73 Dragon DRA 1018 The Way You Do The Things You Do/Version . . . 5
73 Dragon DRA 1020 Watch What You're Doing To Me/You Must Believe Me . . . 5
73 Dragon DRA 1027 A Weh We A Go Go/SOUL DEFENDERS: Version . . . 5
72 Trojan TRL 42 ERIC DONALDSON (LP). . . . 15
(see also Prunes, Satchmo)

DON & DEWEY
64 London HL 9897 Get Your Hat/Annie Lee . . . 30
66 Cameo Parkway CP 750 Soul Motion/Stretchin' Out. . . . 30
67 Sue WI 4032 Soul Motion/Stretchin' Out (reissue) . . . 25
71 Specialty SNTF 5006 DON AND DEWEY (LP) . . . 15
(see also Don 'Sugarcane' Harris, Dewey Terry)

DON & GOODTIMES
67 Columbia DB 8199 I Could Be So Good To You/And It's So Good. . . . 7
67 Columbia DB 8266 Happy And Me/If You Love Her, Cherish Her And Such . . . 7

DON & JUAN
62 London HLX 9529 What's Your Name?/Chicken Necks. . . . 40

DON & PETE
66 Columbia DB 7881 And I'm Crying Again/Time Will Tell . . . 5

DONAYS
62 Oriole CBA 1770 Devil In His Heart/Bad Boy. . . . 125

DON, DICK & JIMMY
54 Columbia SCM 5110 Brand Me With Your Kisses/Angela Mia. . . . 20
55 London HL 8117 You Can't Have Your Cake And Eat It Too/That's What I Like . . . 40
55 London HL 8117 You Can't Have Your Cake And Eat It Too/That's What I Like (78) . . . 8
55 London HL 8144 Make Yourself Comfortable/(Whatever Happened To The) Piano Players (That Played Like This). . . . 25
55 London HL 8144 Make Yourself Comfortable/(Whatever Happened To The) Piano Players (That Played Like This) (78) . . . 8
56 HMV POP 280 That's The Way I Feel/Two Voices In The Night . . . 10
55 London RE-U 1043 DON, DICK AND JIMMY (EP) . . . 40

DOROTHY DONEGAN
56 MGM MGM-EP 532 DOROTHY DONEGAN TRIO (EP) . . . 8

LONNIE DONEGAN
78s
56 Decca FJ 10695 Diggin' My Potatoes/Bury My Body (Lonnie Donegan Skiffle Group) . . . 6
56 Oriole CB 1329 The Passing Stranger/TOMMY REILLY: The Intimate Stranger. . . . 12
56 Columbia DB 3850 On A Christmas Day/Take My Hand, Precious Lord . . . 8
58 Pye Nixa N 15165 Lonnie's Skiffle Party Parts 1 & 2 . . . 8
58 Pye Nixa N 15172 Tom Dooley/Rock O' My Soul . . . 6
59 Pye Nixa N 15181 Does Your Chewing Gum Lose Its Flavour/Aunt Rhody . . . 7
59 Pye Nixa N 15198 Fort Worth Jail/Whoa Buck . . . 10
59 Pye Nixa N 15206 Battle Of New Orleans/Darling Corey . . . 8
59 Pye N 15219 Kevin Barry/My Laggan Love (Irish-only issue) . . . 15
59 Pye N 15223 Sal's Got A Sugar Lip/Chesapeake Bay . . . 15
59 Pye N 15237 San Miguel/Talking Guitar Blues . . . 15
60 Pye N 15256 My Old Man's A Dustman/The Golden Vanity . . . 20
60 Pye N 15267 I Wanna Go Home (The Wreck Of The John B)/ Jimmy Brown The Newsboy. . . . 25
60 Pye N 15275 Lorelei/In All My Wildest Dreams. . . . 35

SINGLES
55 Decca F 10647 Rock Island Line/John Henry (as Lonnie Donegan Skiffle Group) (tri-centre) . . . 25
56 Decca FJ 10695 Diggin' My Potatoes/Bury My Body (as Lonnie Donegan Skiffle Group) (tri-centre) . . . 25
56 Columbia DB 3850 On A Christmas Day/Take My Hand, Precious Lord (as Lonnie Donegan with Chris Barber's Jazz Band) . . . 40
57 Pye Nixa 7N 15116 Jack O' Diamonds/Ham 'N' Eggs . . . 8
58 Pye Nixa 7N 15129 The Grand Coolie Dam/Nobody Loves Like An Irishman . . . 10
58 Pye Jazz 7NJ 2006 Midnight Special/When The Sun Goes Down . . . 25
58 Pye Nixa 7N 15148 Sally, Don't You Grieve/Betty, Betty, Betty . . . 6
58 Pye Nixa 7N 15158 Lonesome Traveller/Times Are Getting Hard Boys . . . 6
58 Pye Nixa 7N 15165 Lonnie's Skiffle Party (Parts 1 & 2) . . . 6
58 Pye Nixa 7N 15172 Tom Dooley/Rock O' My Soul . . . 6
59 Pye Nixa 7N 15198 Fort Worth Jail/Whoa Buck . . . 6
59 Pye 7N 15219 Kevin Barry/My Laggan Love (Irish-only issue) . . . 25
59 Pye 7N 15223 Sal's Got A Sugar Lip/Chesapeake Bay . . . 6

MINT VALUE £

59 Pye 7N 15237 San Miguel/Talking Guitar Blues . . . 6
60 Pye 7N 15275 Lorelei/In All My Wildest Dreams. . . . 6
60 Pye 7N 15312 Lively/Black Cat (Cross My Path Today) . . . 6
60 Pye 7N 15315 Virgin Mary/Beyond The Sunset . . . 6
61 Pye 7N 15330 (Bury Me) Beneath The Willow/Leave My Woman Alone. . . . 6
61 Pye 7N 15371 Michael Row The Boat/Lumbered . . . 6
61 Pye 7N 15410 The Comancheros/Ramblin' Round. . . . 6
62 Pye 7N 3109 The Comancheros/So Long (Medley)
(export issue, 'sombrero' or 'chair' p/s) . . . 18/15
62 Pye 7N 15424 The Party's Over/Over The Rainbow . . . 6
62 Pye 7N 15446 I'll Never Fall In Love Again/Keep On The Sunny Side . . . 6
62 Pye 7N 15455 Pick A Bale Of Cotton/Steal Away (some in p/s) . . . 15/6
62 Pye 7N 15493 The Market Song/Tit-bits
(with Max Miller & Lonnie Donegan Group) . . . 6
63 Pye 7N 15514 Losing By A Hair/Trumpet Sounds . . . 5
63 Pye 7N 15530 It Was A Very Good Year/Rise Up. . . . 6
63 Pye 7N 15564 Lemon Tree/I've Gotta Girl So Far . . . 6
63 Pye 7N 15579 500 Miles Away From Home/This Train . . . 6
64 Pye 7N 15669 Beans In My Ears/It's A Long Road To Travel . . . 6
64 Pye 7N 15679 Fisherman's Luck/There's A Big Wheel. . . . 6
65 Pye 7N 15803 Get Out Of My Life/Won't You Tell Me . . . 6
65 Pye 7N 15893 Louisiana Man/Bound For Zion . . . 6
66 Pye 7N 15993 World Cup Willie/Where In This World Are We Going (some in p/s). . . . 50/20
66 Pye 7N 17109 I Wanna Go Home/Black Cat (Cross My Path Today) . . . 6
67 Pye 7N 17232 Aunt Maggie's Remedy/(Ah) My Sweet Marie . . . 6
68 Columbia DB 8371 Toys/Relax Your Mind. . . . 7
69 Decca F 12984 My Lovely Juanita/Who Knows Where The Time Goes . . . 7

EPs

56 Decca DFE 6345 THE LONNIE DONEGAN SKIFFLE GROUP (tri-centre, later round). . . . 25/12
56 Jazz Today JTE 107 BACKSTAIRS SESSION . . . 30
56 Pye Nixa Jazz NJE 1014 BACKSTAIRS SESSION (reissue) . . . 15
56 Pye Nixa Jazz NJE 1017 SKIFFLE SESSION. . . . 12
57 Pye Nixa NEP 24031 HIT PARADE. . . . 12
57 Pye Nixa NEP 24040 HIT PARADE VOL. 2 . . . 12
58 Pye Nixa NEP 24067 HIT PARADE VOL. 3 . . . 12
58 Pye Nixa NEP 24075 DONEGAN ON STAGE . . . 15
58 Pye Nixa NEP 24081 HIT PARADE VOL. 4 . . . 15
59 Pye Nixa NEP 24104 HIT PARADE VOL. 5 . . . 15
59 Pye Nixa NEP 24107 RELAX WITH LONNIE. . . . 18
59 Pye Nixa NEP 24114 HIT PARADE VOL. 6 . . . 15
60 Pye Nixa NEP 24127 YANKEE DOODLE DONEGAN . . . 15
61 Pye Nixa NEP 24134 HIT PARADE VOL. 7 . . . 18
61 Pye Nixa NEP 24149 HIT PARADE VOL. 8 . . . 18

LPs

56 Pye Nixa NPT 19012 LONNIE DONEGAN SHOWCASE (10") . . . 25
57 Pye Nixa NPT 19027 LONNIE (10", also stereo NSPT 84000) . . . 22/50
58 Pye NPL 18034 TOPS WITH LONNIE. . . . 20
59 Pye NPL 18043 LONNIE RIDES AGAIN . . . 20
61 Pye NPL 18063 MORE TOPS WITH LONNIE . . . 20
62 Pye NPL 18073 SING HALLELUJAH . . . 30
62 Golden Guinea GGL 0135 GOLDEN AGE OF DONEGAN . . . 12
63 Golden Guinea GGL 0170 GOLDEN AGE OF DONEGAN VOL. 2. . . . 12
65 Pye NPL 18126 THE LONNIE DONEGAN FOLK ALBUM. . . . 30
70 Decca SKL 5068 LONNIEPOPS — LONNIE DONEGAN TODAY . . . 15
78 Chrysalis CHR 1158 PUTTIN' ON THE STYLE. . . . 12

(see also Monty Sunshine, Chris Barber, Max Miller)

DONKEYS

80 Rhesus GO APE 102 What I Want/Four Letters (yellow or orange label, p/s). . . . 20
80 Rhesus GO APE 3 No Way/You Jane (p/s) . . . 20
80 Rhesus GO APE 105 Don't Go/Living Legends (p/s). . . . 20
80 Back Door DOOR 006 No Way/You Jane (reissue, p/s) . . . 7
80 Deram DM-R 431 What I Want/Four Letters (reissue, p/s). . . . 8
81 MCA MCA 682 Don't Go/Living Legends (reissue, p/s). . . . 5
81 MCA MCA 721 Let's Float/Watched By Everyone (p/s) . . . 7
81 MCA MCA 737 Listen To Your Radio/Watched By Everyone (as Donkees) (p/s). . . . 7

JIMMY DONLEY

57 Brunswick 05715 South Of The Border/The Trail Of The Lonesome Pine . . . 20
59 Brunswick 05807 The Shape You Left Me In/What Must I Do . . . 120
59 Brunswick 05807 The Shape You Left Me In/What Must I Do (78) . . . 25

DONNA & FREEDOM SINGERS

70 Bamboo BAM 53 Oh Me Oh My (actually by Jerry Jones)/JACKIE MITTOO: Gold Mine . . . 15

DONNAS

03 East West AT 0148 Take It Off/Hyperactive/Rock 'n' Roll Machine (p/s,
some on picture disc with die-cut sleeve) . . . 15/5
03 East West AT 0156 Who Invited You/Mama's Boy (p/s) . . . 5

RAL DONNER

61 Parlophone R 4820 You Don't Know What You've Got/So Close To Heaven . . . 15
61 Parlophone R 4859 Please Don't Go/I Didn't Figure On Him . . . 18
62 Parlophone R 4889 I Don't Need You/She's Everything (I Wanted You To Be) . . . 20
62 Stateside SS 109 Bells Of Love/Loveless Life. . . . 18
63 Reprise R 20141 I Got Burned/A Tear In My Eye. . . . 35

DONNIE & DREAMERS

61 Top Rank JAR 571 Count Every Star/Dorothy . . . 40

MINT VALUE £

DONOVAN

65	Pye 7N 15801	Catch The Wind/Why Do You Treat Me Like You Do	6
65	Pye 7N 15866	Colours/To Sing For You	6
65	Pye 7N 15984	Turquoise/Hey Gyp (Dig The Slowness)	7
66	Pye 7N 17067	Josie/Little Tin Soldier	6
66	Pye 7N 17088	Remember The Alamo/The Ballad Of A Crystal Man	15
66	Pye 7N 17241	Sunshine Superman/The Trip	7
67	Pye 7N 17267	Mellow Yellow/Preachin' Love	6
67	Pye 7N 17403	There Is A Mountain/Sand And Foam	6
68	Pye 7N 17457	Jennifer Juniper/Poor Cow	6
68	Pye 7N 17537	Hurdy Gurdy Man/Teen Angel	6
68	Pye 7N 17660	To Susan On The West Coast Waiting/Atlantis (unreleased)	
68	Pye 7N 17660	Atlantis/I Love My Shirt	6
69	Pye 7N 17778	Goo Goo Barabajagal (Love Is Hot)/Bed With Me (with Jeff Beck Group)	12
69	Pye 7N 17778	Barabajagal/Trudi (shortened A-side title & retitled B-side)	8
70	Dawn DNS 1006	Ricki Ticki Tavi/Roots Of Oak (as Donovan with Open Road)	6
70	Dawn DNS 1006	Riki Tiki Tavi (shortened spelling of A-side)/Roots Of Oak (with Open Road)	5
70	Dawn DNS 1007	Celia Of The Seals (with Danny Thompson)/Mr. Wind	6
72	private pressing	The Music Makers (one-sided, paper sleeve, 50 only)	50
73	Epic EPC 1471	I Like You/Earth Sign Man	5
73	Epic EPC 1644	Maria Magenta/Intergalactic Laxative (p/s)	8
73	Epic EPC 1960	Sailing Homeward/Lazy Daze (p/s)	6
74	Epic EPC 1960	Sailing Homeward/Yellow Star (p/s, reissue with different B-side; some copies list both Donovan & Andrew Oldham as producers)	each 6
75	Epic EPC 2661	Rock'n'Roll With Me/Divine Daze Of Deathless Delight (some in p/s)	30/6
75	Epic EPC 3037	Rock And Roll Souijer/Love Of My Life	5
77	Rak RAK 265	The Light/The International Man (some in p/s)	8/5
92	Silhouette MDCDKR 3	Newest Bath Guide/Moira MacCavendish/Brother Sun, Sister Moon (CD)	18
65	Pye NEP 24219	THE UNIVERSAL SOLDIER (EP, some incorrectly list 'Summer 1955' instead of 'Summer 1965' as date on rear sleeve)	each 12
65	Pye NEP 24229	COLOURS (EP)	22
66	Pye NEP 24239	DONOVAN VOL. 1 (EP)	22
68	Pye NEP 24287	CATCH THE WIND (EP)	22
68	Pye NEP 24299	HURDY GURDY DONOVAN (EP)	22
65	Pye NPL 18117	WHAT'S BIN DID AND WHAT'S BIN HID (LP, some with misprinted Side 2 label)	30
65	Pye NPL 18128	FAIRYTALE (LP, some copies with blank rear sleeve)	25
66	World Records ST 951	DONOVAN (LP)	15
67	Pye NPL 18181	SUNSHINE SUPERMAN (LP)	30
68	Pye N(S)PL 20000	A GIFT FROM A FLOWER TO A GARDEN (2-LP, black or navy blue box set, separate halves or with taped hinge; with 12 inserts in folder, mono/stereo)	55/45
68	Pye N(S)PL 18237	DONOVAN IN CONCERT (LP, mono/stereo)	20/18
69	Pye N(S)PL 18283	DONOVAN'S GREATEST HITS (LP, gatefold sleeve with booklet, mono/stereo)	15/12
70	Dawn DNLS 3009	OPEN ROAD (LP, gatefold sleeve)	20
71	Dawn DNLD 4001	H.M.S. DONOVAN (2-LP, gatefold sleeve, some with foldout poster)	55/22
73	Pye 11PP 102	FOUR SHADES ("H.M.S. Donovan"/"Greatest Hits"/"Open Road") (4-LP box set)	50
73	Epic EPC 65490	COSMIC WHEELS (LP, gatefold sleeve with inner sleeve & poster)	12
90	Permanent PERMLP 2	DONOVAN RISING (LP, 500 only)	20
97	American Recordings 74321 39743 2	SUTRAS (CD)	18

(see also Jeff Beck, Open Road)

JASON DONOVAN

88	PWL PWLT 17R	Nothing Can Divide Us (mixes) (12", p/s)	12
88	PWL PWLCD 17	Nothing Can Divide Us (7" Version)/(Dub Mix)/(Instrumental) (CD)	15
89	PWL PWLT 32R	Too Many Broken Hearts (mixes)/Wrap My Arms Around You (12", p/s)	12
89	PWL PWCD 32	Too Many Broken Hearts/(Instrumental)/Wrap My Arms Around You (CD)	15
89	PWL PWCD 39	Sealed With A Kiss/Just Call Me Up/Too Many Broken Hearts (Techno Remix) (CD)	8
89	PWL PWCD 43	Every Day (I Love You More) (7" Version)/(Extended)/ I Guess She Never Loved Me (CD)	10
90	PWL PWLT 58R	Another Night (mixes) (12", picture disc)	12
93	Polydor PZCD 295	Angel (Forever In Your Debt)/Shout About/Symptoms Of A Real Love (7" Mix)/ Symptoms Of A Real Love (12" Mix) (CD, withdrawn)	10

(see also Kylie Minogue)

DONTELLS

65	Fontana TF 566	In Your Heart/Nothing But Nothing	55
74	President PT 373	In Your Heart/Nothing But Nothing (reissue)	12

DICKY DOO & DON'TS

58	London HLU 8589	Click Click/Did You Cry	25
58	London HLU 8589	Click Click/Did You Cry (78)	15
58	London HLU 8754	Leave Me Alone/Wild, Wild Party (with Orchestra)	35
58	London HLU 8754	Leave Me Alone/Wild, Wild Party (with Orchestra) (78)	30
60	Top Rank JAR 318	Wabash Cannonball/WEST TEXAS MARCHING BAND: The Drums Of Richard A Doo	25

DOOF

80	Doof	EXIST (10" mini-LP, with booklet)	8

(see also Exhibit A)

DOOLEY SISTERS

55	London HL 8128	Ko Ko Mo (I Love You So)/Heart Throb	60
55	London HL 8128	Ko Ko Mo (I Love You So)/Heart Throb (78)	8

MINT VALUE £

JOHN DOONAN

72	Leader LEA 2043	FLUTE FOR THE FEIS (LP)	15
72	Leader LEA 2043	FLUTE FOR THE FEIS (LP, reissue)	15

DOOR & THE WINDOW

79	NB Records NB 3	He Feels Like A Doris/I Like Sound/Innocent/Dig/Production Line (white label with stickers & insert p/s in poly bag)	5
80	NB Records NB 5	DETAILED TWANG (LP, blank labels)	12
80	NB Records NB 9	MUSIC AND MOVEMENT (live cassette)	12

(see also Alternative TV)

DOORS

SINGLES

67	Elektra EKSN 45009	Break On Through (To The Other Side)/End Of The Night	40
67	Elektra EKSN 45012	Alabama Song (Whisky Bar)/Take It As It Comes	20
67	Elektra EKSN 45014	Light My Fire/The Crystal Ship	18
67	Elektra EKSN 45017	People Are Strange/Unhappy Girl	18
67	Elektra EKSN 45022	Love Me Two Times/Moonlight Drive	12
68	Elektra EKSN 45030	We Could Be So Good Together/The Unknown Soldier	12
68	Elektra EKSN 45037	Hello, I Love You/Love Street	8
69	Elektra EKSN 45050	Touch Me/Wild Child	10
69	Elektra EKSN 45059	Wishful Sinful/Who Scared You?	10
69	Elektra EKSN 45065	Tell All The People/Easy Ride	10
70	Elektra 2101 004	You Make Me Real/The Spy	7
70	Elektra 2101 008	Roadhouse Blues/Blue Sunday	7
71	Elektra EK 45726	Love Her Madly/(You Need Meat) Don't Go No Further	6
71	Elektra K 12021	Riders On The Storm/The Changeling	6
72	Elektra K 12036	Tightrope Ride/Variety Is The Spice Of Life	5
72	Elektra K 12048	Ships — Sails/In The Eye Of The Sun	5
72	Elektra K 12059	Get Up And Dance/Tree Trunks	5
79	Elektra K 12215/SAM 94	Love Me Two Times/Hello, I Love You// Ghost Song/Roadhouse Blues (double pack)	8
83	Elektra E 9974T	Gloria/Love Me Two Times (12", p/s with poster)	10
89	Elektra 969 344-2	Riders On The Storm/The End (3" CD, card sleeve)	8
91	Elektra EKR 125TW	Light My Fire/People Are Strange/Soul Kitchen (12", p/s, with poster)	8
92	Final Vinyl FV 1/2	INTERVIEW TAPES (2 x 7" box set, with 7 inserts, numbered, 500 only)	10

ORIGINAL LPs

67	Elektra EKL 4007	THE DOORS (orange label, also stereo EKS 74007)	60/30
68	Elektra EKL 4014	STRANGE DAYS (textured orange label, inner sleeve, also stereo EKS 74014)	60/30
68	Elektra EKL 4024	WAITING FOR THE SUN (orange label, gatefold sleeve with insert, also stereo EKS 74024)	60/30
69	Elektra EKS 75005	THE SOFT PARADE (orange label, gatefold sleeve, with lyric sheet)	25
70	Elektra EKS 75007	MORRISON HOTEL (orange label, gatefold sleeve)	20
70	Elektra 2665 002	ABSOLUTELY LIVE (2-LP, orange label, gatefold sleeve)	20
71	Elektra EKS 74079	13 ('butterfly' label, compilation)	15
71	Elektra K 42090	L.A. WOMAN ('butterfly' label, round-cornered, die-cut PVC 'window' sleeve & yellow inner sleeve)	15
71	Elektra K 42104	OTHER VOICES ('butterfly' label, gatefold sleeve)	15
72	Elektra K 62009	WEIRD SCENES INSIDE THE GOLDMINE (2-LP, 'butterfly' label, gatefold sleeve)	20
72	Elektra K 62116	FULL CIRCLE ('butterfly' label, gatefold sleeve)	15

REISSUE LPs

70	Elektra EKS 74024	WAITING FOR THE SUN ('butterfly' label, gatefold sleeve)	15
71	Elektra K 42012	THE DOORS ('butterfly' label)	15
71	Elektra K 42016	STRANGE DAYS ('butterfly' label)	15
71	Elektra K 42079	THE SOFT PARADE ('butterfy' label, gatefold sleeve, with lyric sheet)	15
72	Elektra K 42080	MORRISON HOTEL ('butterlfly' label, gatefold sleeve)	15
72	Elektra K 75011	L.A. WOMAN ('butterfly' label, standard sleeve)	12
74	Elektra K 42090	L.A. WOMAN ('butterfly' label, standard sleeve)	12
78	Elektra K 52111	AN AMERICAN PRAYER ('butterfly' label, gatefold sleeve, with 8-page booklet)	25

CDs

85	Elektra 960 345-2	THE BEST OF THE DOORS (2-CD)	20
87	Elektra K 262005	ABSOLUTELY LIVE (2-CD, withdrawn)	25
87	Elektra 960 269-2	ALIVE, SHE CRIED	18
87	Elektra 960 741-2	LIVE AT THE HOLLYWOOD BOWL	18
88	HMV C 8816	L.A. WOMAN (HMV box set, 2,500 only, numbered with booklet)	18
91	Elektra 7559 61082-2	IN CONCERT (2-CD)	20
98	Elektra 7559 62295-2	THE DOORS BOX SET VOL. I (2-CD, with booklet)	25
98	Elektra 7559 62296-2	THE DOORS BOX SET VOL. II (2-CD, with booklet)	25

(see also Ray Manzarek)

DOORS OF PERCEPTION

91	Lizard Nation LN 002	ACID DREAMS (12" EP, includes Jim Morrison sample, withdrawn)	8
91	Lizard Nation LN 001	SO JOIN MR. DREAMS (LP, with inner sleeve, some with booklet, 850 only)	15/12
92	Lizard Nation LN 005	LORDS SO STRANGE R. (LP, test pressings only)	12

MIKE DORANE & CIMARONS

71	Ackee ACK 144	Penguin Funk/Ad-Lib	7

DOREEN (Campbell) & ALL STARS

67	Rainbow RAI 114	Rude Girls/Please Stay	12

DOREEN (Shaffer) & JACKIE (Opel)

65	Ska Beat JB 208	Welcome Home/You And I	22

(see also Jackie & Doreen)

KENNY DOREHAM & SONNY ROLLINS

58	London LTZU 15133	JAZZ CONTRASTS (LP)	20

DORIAN

70 Ember EMB S 285 Psychedelic Lipstick/Help For My Waiting 6

DORIS

81 ABCD ABCD 1 Sitting Here Waiting (no p/s) 5
82 ABCD ABCD 3 GYPSY LADY (LP, actually credited to A Band Called Doris) 250

DORIS

98 EMI/Mr. Bongo MRBLP 010 DID YOU GIVE THE WORLD SOME LOVE TODAY, BABY? (LP, reissue of Swedish 60s LP) 12

HAROLD DORMAN

60 Top Rank JAR 357 Mountain Of Love/To Be With You 25
61 London HLS 9386 There They Go/I'll Stick By You 30

STACY DORNING

74 Scratchy CHR 1070 STACY DORNING (LP, with Duncan Browne) 12

DOROTHY

80 Industrial IR 0014 I Confess/Softness (p/s) 8

RALPH DORPER

83 Operation Twilight OPT 18 THE ERASERHEAD EP (12") 12
(see also Propaganda)

CHRIS DORS

61 Fontana H 329 That's When Your Heartaches Begin/They Called It Love 12

DIANA DORS

53 HMV B 10613 I Feel So Mmm.../A Kiss And A Cuddle (78) 20
60 Pye 7N 15242 April Heart/Point Of No Return 10
60 Pye N 15242 April Heart/Point Of No Return (78) 25
64 Fontana TF 506 So Little Time/It's Too Late 15
66 Polydor BM 56111 Security/Gary 10
77 EMI EMI 2705 Passing By/It's A Small World 8
82 Nomis NOM 1 Where Did They Go/It's You Again (with Gary Dors) 8
60 Pye NPL 18044 SWINGIN' DORS (LP, foldout sleeve, red vinyl) 75

RAY DORSET (WITH MUNGO JERRY)

72 Dawn DNS 1018 Cold Blue Excursion/I Need It (solo) 10
77 Polydor 2230 103 MUNGO BOX (EP, as Ray Dorset & Mungo Jerry, p/s) 8
79 Polydor 2059 127 Dancin' In The Street/Rockin' On The Road (as Ray Dorset & Mungo Jerry, p/s) . . . 8
79 Satellite RAY 001 Forgotten Land/New Way Of Life (solo, unreleased; 100 promos only) 10
81 Stagecoach TRI 101 Knocking On Heaven's Door/Hazel Eyes (as Ray Dorset with Mungo Jerry) 8
72 Dawn DNLS 3033 COLD BLUE EXCURSION (LP, solo; gatefold sleeve with lyric inner) 15
(see also Mungo Jerry, Good Earth, County Jug, Macon Jug, Katmandu, Insiders, Panache, Made In England)

DORSETS

65 Sue WI 391 Pork Chops/Cool It 35

GERRY DORSEY

59 Decca F 11108 Mister Music Man/Crazy Bells 15
59 Decca F 11108 Mister Music Man/Crazy Bells (78) 15
59 Parlophone R 4595 I'll Never Fall In Love Again/Every Day Is A Wonderful Day 10
61 Parlophone R 4739 Big Wheel/The Sentimental Joker 10
64 Pye 7N 15622 Baby I Do/Take Your Time 10
65 Hickory 45-1337 Baby Turn Around/Things I Wanna Do 15

JACK DORSEY ORCHESTRA

65 Polydor 56020 Dance Of The Daleks/Likely Lads 18
68 Pye 7N 17501 Soul Coaxing/Elizabeth's Waltz 8

JIMMY DORSEY ORCHESTRA

57 HMV POP 324 So Rare/Sophisticated Swing 10
57 HMV POP 383 Jay-Dee's Boogie Woogie/June Night 20
54 Columbia 33S 1026 DIXIE BY DORSEY (10" LP) 12

LEE DORSEY

62 Top Rank JAR 606 Do-Re-Mi/People Gonna Talk 20
65 Sue WI 367 Do-Re-Mi/Ya Ya 22
65 Stateside SS 441 Ride Your Pony/The Kitty Cat Song 10
65 Stateside SS 465 Work Work Work/Can You Hear Me 10
66 Sue WI 399 Messed Around/When I Meet My Baby 22
66 Stateside SS 485 Get Out Of My Life, Woman/So Long 10
66 Stateside SS 506 Confusion/Neighbour's Daughter 8
66 Stateside SS 528 Working In A Coalmine/Mexico 5
66 Stateside SS 552 Holy Cow/Operation Heartache 5
67 Stateside SS 593 Rain Rain Go Away/Gotta Find A Job 6
67 Stateside SS 2017 My Old Car/Why Wait Until Tomorrow 6
67 Stateside SS 2055 Go-Go Girl/I Can Hear You Callin' 6
68 President PT 226 Ya Ya/Give Me You 6
68 Bell BLL 1006 Can You Hear Me/Cynthia 6
69 Bell BLL 1051 I'm Gonna Sit Right Down And Write Myself A Letter/Little Baby 6
69 Bell BLL 1060 Ride Your Pony/Get Out Of My Life, Woman 6
69 Bell BLL 1074 Everything I Do Gonh Be Funky/There Should Be A Book 12
71 Mojo 2066 063 Occapella/Yes We Can Part 1 5
72 Mojo 2093 009 Freedom For The Stallion/If She Won't (Find Someone Who Will) 5
66 Stateside SE 1038 RIDE YOUR PONY (EP) 25
66 Stateside SE 1043 YOU'RE BREAKING ME UP (EP) 30
65 Sue ILP 924 THE BEST OF LEE DORSEY (LP) 70
66 Stateside S(S)L 10177 LEE DORSEY — RIDE YOUR PONY (LP) 25
66 Stateside S(S)L 10192 THE NEW LEE DORSEY (LP) 25
71 Polydor 2489 006 YES WE CAN (LP) 15

MINT VALUE £

LEE DORSEY & BETTY HARRIS

69	Buffalo BFS 1002	Love Lots Of Lovin'/Take Care Of Your Love	15

(see also Betty Harris)

TOMMY DORSEY ORCHESTRA

58	RCA RD 27069	FRANKIE AND TOMMY (LP, with Frank Sinatra)	20

(see also Frank Sinatra, Jo Stafford)

D.O.S.E.

95	Colosseum TOGA 001TJX	Plug Myself In (with Mark E. Smith) (p/s, numbered, 1-sided, 500 only)	5

(see also Fall)

JOHNNY DOT & DASHERS

62	Salvo SLO 1805	I Love An Angel/Just For You (99 copies only)	25

DOTTY & BONNIE

64	Rio R 43	I'm So Glad/DOUGLAS BROTHERS: Got You On My Mind	15
64	Island WI 143	Your Kisses/Why Worry	18
64	Island WI 148	Dearest/Tears Are Falling	18
65	Ska Beat JB 183	Foul Play/ROLAND ALPHONSO & GROUP: Yard Broom	30
67	Ska Beat JB 274	I'll Know/Love Is Great	22

(see also Bonnie Frankson, Eric Morris, Don Drummond, Skatalites, Baba Brooks)

DOUBLE FEATURE

67	Deram DM 115	Baby Get Your Head Screwed On/Come On Baby	50
67	Deram DM 165	Handbags And Gladrags/Just Another Lonely Night	18

DOUBLES with GAY BLADES

59	HMV POP 613	Hey Girl!/Little Joe	110

SUZANNE DOUCET

68	Liberty LBF 15150	Swan Song/Cry My Heart	12

DOUGHNUT RING

68	Deram DM 215	Dance Around Julie/The Bandit	35

(see also Crocheted Doughnut Ring)

JOHNNY DOUGHTY

77	Topic 12TS 324	ROUND RYE BAY FOR MORE (LP, with insert)	15

CARL DOUGLAS (& BIG STAMPEDE)

66	Go AJ 11401	Crazy Feeling/PETER PERRY SOUL BAND: Keep It To Myself	18
67	Go AJ 11408	Let The Birds Sing/Something For Nothing	40
67	United Artists UP 1206	Nobody Cries/Serving A Sentence Of Life (solo)	90
68	United Artists UP 2227	Sell My Soul To The Devil/Good Hard Worker	15
71	CBS 7101	Do You Need My Love/Lean On Me	7
72	Blue Mountain BM 1007	Somebody Stop This Madness/Ain't No Use (as Karl Douglas)	6

CHIC DOUGLAS

58	Fontana H 121	I'm Not Afraid Anymore/Jo-Ann	10

CRAIG DOUGLAS

58	Decca F 11055	Nothin' Shakin'/Sitting In A Tree House	20
58	Decca F 11055	Nothin' Shakin'/Sitting In A Tree House (78)	8
58	Decca F 11075	Go Chase A Moonbeam/Are You Really Mine	18
58	Decca F 11075	Go Chase A Moonbeam/Are You Really Mine (78)	6
59	Top Rank JAR 110	Come Softly To Me/Golden Girl	7
59	Top Rank JAR 110	Come Softly To Me/Golden Girl (78)	10
59	Top Rank JAR 133	Teenager In Love/The 39 Steps	7
59	Top Rank JAR 133	Teenager In Love/The 39 Steps (78)	12
59	Top Rank JAR 159	Only Sixteen/My First Love Affair	6
59	Top Rank JAR 159	Only Sixteen/My First Love Affair (78)	15
59	Top Rank JAR 204	The Riddle Of Love/Wish It Were Me	6
59	Top Rank TR 5004	Battle Of New Orleans/Dream Lover/SHEILA BUXTON: Personality/ Where Were You On Our Wedding Day/BERT WEEDON: I Need Your Love Tonight ('King-Size' 7", special sleeve)	15
60	Top Rank JAR 268	Pretty Blue Eyes/Sandy	6
60	Top Rank JAR 340	Heart Of A Teenage Girl/New Boy	6
60	Top Rank JAR 406	Oh, What A Day/Why, Why, Why	6
60	Top Rank JAR 515	Where's The Girl (I Never Met)/My Hour Of Love	6
61	Top Rank JAR 543	The Girl Next Door/Hey Mister Conscience	6
61	Top Rank JAR 555	A Hundred Pounds Of Clay/Hello Spring	12
61	Top Rank JAR 556	A Hundred Pounds Of Clay (censored version)/Hello Spring (some in p/s)	20/7
61	Top Rank JAR 569	Time/After All	6
61	Top Rank JAR 589	No Greater Love/We'll Have A Lot To Tell	6
62	Top Rank JAR 603	A Change Of Heart/Another You	7
62	Top Rank JAR 610	When My Little Girl Is Smiling/Ring A Ding	7
62	Columbia DB 4854	Our Favourite Melodies/Rainbows	7
62	Decca F 11523	Oh Lonesome Me/Please Don't Take My Heart	6
63	Decca F 11575	Town Crier/I'd Be Smiling Now	6
63	Decca F 11665	Danke Shoen/Teenage Mona Lisa	6
63	Decca F 11722	I'm So Glad I Found Her/Love Her While She's Young	6
63	Decca F 11763	Counting Up The Kisses/From Russia With Love	6
64	Fontana TF 458	Silly Boy/Love Leave Me Alone	10
64	Fontana TF 475	Come Closer/She's Smiling At Me (as Craig Douglas & Tridents)	15
65	Fontana TF 525	Across The Street/Party Girl	10
65	Fontana TF 580	Around The Corner/Find The Girl	10
66	Fontana TF 690	I'm On The Outside Looking In/Knock On Any Door	8
69	Pye 7N 17746	How Do You Feel About That/Then	7
69	Pye 7N 17863	Raindrops Keep Falling On My Head/Don't Mind If I Cry	8
71	Crystal CR 7011	All Kinds Of People/Evenin' Rain	6
76	Cube BUG 72	Who's Sorry Now/Both Sides Now	5

MINT VALUE £

77	Cube BUG 76	Turn Away/Baby Blue	5
59	Top Rank JKR 8033	CRAIG SINGS FOR 'ROXY' (EP)	25
60	Decca DFE 6633	CRAIG (EP)	30
62	Decca DFE 8509	CUDDLE UP WITH CRAIG (EP)	18
63	Columbia SEG 8219	CRAIG MOVIE SONGS (EP)	35
60	Top Rank BUY 049	CRAIG DOUGLAS (LP)	60
61	Top Rank 35-103	BANDWAGON BALL (LP)	45
62	Columbia 33SX 1468	OUR FAVOURITE MELODIES (LP)	80
81	Jackson JKS 5	OH LONESOME ME (LP)	12

(see also Bert Weedon)

DONNA DOUGLAS

58	Fontana H 158	The Shepherd/I'm Dancing With Tears In My Eyes	10
59	Fontana H 223	Six Boys And Seven Girls/Into Each Life Some Rain Must Fall	8
59	Fontana H 223	Six Boys And Seven Girls/Into Each Life Some Rain Must Fall (78)	6
61	Piccadilly 7N 35014	Tammy Tell Me True/Memory Lane	8
62	Piccadilly 7N 35031	The Message In A Bottle/If This Is Love	10
62	Piccadilly 7N 35042	Matelot/All The Other Girls	8
63	Piccadilly 7N 35111	It's A Pity To Say Goodnight/Do I Know	8
63	Piccadilly 7N 35135	He's So Near/Turn Around	8
64	Pye 7N 15654	Blue Star/Java Jones	8

JACK DOUGLAS

68	Columbia DB 8393	Swannee River/Call Alf	8

JOHNNY DOUGLAS (& HIS ORCHESTRA/COMBO)

54	Decca F 10276	Ballet Of The Bells/Solfeggio (as Johnny Douglas & His Orchestra)	6
63	Speyside SK 1501	Ski Jump/Clementine (as Johnny Douglas Combo)	6
65	RCA 1444	Crack In The World/Time	12

KIRK DOUGLAS & MELLOMEN

55	Brunswick 05408	A Whale Of A Tale/And The Moon Grew Brighter And Brighter	15

LEW DOUGLAS & HIS ORCHESTRA

54	MGM SP 1093	Caesar's Boogie/Turn Around Boy	15

MARK DOUGLAS

62	Ember EMB S 166	It Matters Not/Upside Down	75

NORMA DOUGLAS

57	London HLZ 8475	Be It Resolved/Joe He Gone	25
57	London HLZ 8475	Be It Resolved/Joe He Gone (78)	6

ROB & DEAN DOUGLAS

67	Deram DM 132	I Can Make It With You/Phone Me	40

DOUGLAS BROTHERS

66	Rio R 57	Valley Of Tears/CHARMERS: Where Do I Turn	15
66	Rio R 63	Down And Out/RONALD WILSON: Lonely Man	15

(see also Dotty & Bonnie)

HARRY DOUGLASS & DEEP RIVER BOYS

60	Top Rank JAR 352	Dum Dum De Dum/Go Galloway, Go	7

(see also Deep River Boys)

RONNIE DOVE

64	Stateside SS 314	Sweeter Than Sugar/I Believed In You	7
64	Stateside SS 346	Say You/Let Me Stay Today	7
64	Stateside SS 366	Right Or Wrong/Baby, Put Your Arms Around Me	7
65	Stateside SS 392	Hello Pretty Girl/Keep It A Secret	7
65	Stateside SS 412	One Kiss For Old Times' Sake/Bluebird	8
65	Stateside SS 436	A Little Bit Of Heaven/If I Live To Be A Hundred	8
65	Stateside SS 462	I'll Make All Your Dreams Come True/I Had To Lose You	7
65	Stateside SS 480	Kiss Away/Where In The World	7
66	Stateside SS 492	When Liking Turns To Loving/I'm Learning How To Smile Again	7
66	Stateside SS 510	Let's Start All Over Again/That Empty Feeling	7
66	Stateside SS 524	Happy Summer Days/Long After	7
66	Stateside SS 542	I Really Don't Want To Know/Years Of Tears	7
66	Stateside SS 571	Cry/Autumn Rhapsody	7
70	Stateside SS 2003	One More Mountain To Climb/All	7
70	Stateside SS 2018	My Babe/Put My Mind At Ease	7
70	Stateside SS 2047	I Want To Love You For What You Are/I Thank You For Your Love	7
70	Stateside SS 2086	Dancin' Out Of My Heart/Back From Baltimore	7
68	Stateside SS 2119	Mountain Of Love/Never Gonna Cry (The Way I'll Cry Tonight)	8
65	Stateside SL 10149	RONNIE DOVE (LP)	35

DOVELLS

61	Columbia DB 4718	The Bristol Stomp/Out In The Cold Again	20
62	Columbia DB 4810	Do The New Continental/Mopitty Mope Stomp	20
62	Columbia DB 4877	Bristol Twistin' Annie/The Actor	20
62	Cameo Parkway P 845	Hully Gully Baby/Your Last Chance	10
63	Cameo Parkway P 861	You Can't Run Away From Yourself/Save Me Baby	10
63	Cameo Parkway P 867	You Can't Sit Down/Stompin' Everywhere	15
63	Cameo Parkway P 882	Betty In Bermudas/Dance The Froog	12
63	Cameo Parkway P 901	Be My Girl/Dragster On The Prowl	18
79	London HAU 8515	CAMEO PARKWAY SESSIONS (LP)	12

(see also Len Barry)

DOVES

98	Manchester MANC 9	Seven Day Smile (with Jane Weaver)/ANDY VOTEL & JANE WEAVER: Gutter Girl (p/s)	10
98	Manchester MANCCD 9	Seven Day Smile (with Jane Weaver)/ANDY VOTEL & JANE WEAVER: Gutter Girl/ JANE WEAVER: You're Not The Only Person That I Used To Know (CD)	12

MINT VALUE £

99	Casino CHIP 003	Here It Comes/Meet Me At The Pier/(Acoustic Version) (10", p/s)	30
02	Heavenly HVN 111-10	There Goes The Fear/Hit The Ground Running (10", p/s)	8
02	Heavenly HVN 126-10	Caught By The River/The Sulphur Man (Rebelski Remix)/Where We're Calling From (Hebden Bridge Remix) (numbered p/s, 3,000 only)	6
98	Casino CHIP 001	CEDAR EP: Cedar Room/Rise/Zither (10", wraparound p/s)	70
99	Casino CHIP 002	SEA EP (10", p/s)	15
99	Casino CHIP 002CD	SEA EP (CD, gatefold card sleeve)	40

(see also Badly Drawn Boy, Sub Sub, Jane Weaver v Doves)

BRENT DOWE

71	Summit SUM 8521	Knock Three Times/GAYLADS: This Time I Won't Hurt You	6
71	Summit SUM 8525	Put Your Hand In The Hand/Miracle (B-side actually "It Took A Miracle Version" by Beverley's All Stars)	6
71	Summit SUM 8530	Freedom Train/BEVERLEY'S ALL STARS: Freedom Train (Version)	6
73	Green Door GD 4061	Reggae Makossa/No Nola (B-side actually by Melodians)	6

(see also Melodians)

JOE DOWELL

61	Mercury AMT 1161	The Bridge Of Love/Just My Love	7
62	Mercury AMT 1180	Little Red Rented Rowboat/The One I Left For You	7
60s	Wing	WOODEN HEART (LP)	20

DOWLANDS

62	Oriole CB 1748	Little Sue/Julie (as Dowlands & Soundtracks)	45
62	Oriole CB 1781	Big Big Fella/Don't Ever Change	130
63	Oriole CB 1815	Break Ups/A Love Like Ours	45
63	Oriole CB 1892	Lonely Johnny (song actually titled "Lucky Johnny")/ Do You Have To Have Me Blue?	750
64	Oriole CB 1897	All My Loving/Hey Sally (as Dowlands & Soundtracks)	15
64	Oriole CB 1926	I Walk The Line/Happy Endings	40
64	Oriole CB 1947	Wishing And Hoping/You Will Regret It	80
65	Columbia DB 7547	Don't Make Me Over/Someone Must Be Feeling Sad	40

DOWNBEATS

61	Starlite ST45 051	Thinkin' Of You/Midnight Love	25

BRUCE DOWNER

71	Summit SUM 8524	Free The People (actually by Bruce Ruffin)/BEVERLEY'S ALL STARS: Free The People (Version)	6

BOB DOWNES

70	Vertigo 6059 011	No Time Like The Present/Keep Off The Grass	7
70	Philips SBL 7922	BOB DOWNES' OPEN MUSIC (LP)	110
70	Vertigo 6360 005	ELECTRIC CITY (LP, gatefold sleeve, swirl label)	40
73	Ophenian BDOM 001	DIVERSIONS (LP)	15
74	Ophenian BDOM 002	EPISODES AT 4AM (LP, with insert)	15
75	Ophenian BDOM 003	HELLS ANGELS (LP)	15

DEIRDRE DOWNES & BROADSIDERS

69	Pye 7N 17781	Lady Mary/Did He Mention My Name	7

DOWN HOME

70s	Lismor Folk LIFL 7011	FIDDLE MUSIC VOLUME ONE (LP)	15

BIG AL DOWNING

64	Sue WI 341	Yes I'm Loving You/Please Come Home	35

DOWNLINERS SECT

64	Columbia DB 7300	Baby What's Wrong/Be A Sect Maniac	25
64	Columbia DB 7347	Little Egypt/Sect Appeal	25
64	Columbia DB 7415	Find Out What's Happening/Insecticide	25
65	Columbia DB 7509	Wreck Of The Old '97/Leader Of The Sect	25
65	Columbia DB 7597	I Got Mine/Waiting In Heaven Somewhere	25
65	Columbia DB 7712	Bad Storm Coming/Lonely And Blue	25
66	Columbia DB 7817	All Night Worker/He Was A Square	25
66	Columbia DB 7939	Glendora/I'll Find Out	55
66	Columbia DB 8008	The Cost Of Living/Everything I've Got To Give	30
64	Contrast Sound RBCSP 1	NITE IN GREAT NEWPORT STREET (EP)	300
65	Columbia SEG 8438	THE SECT SING SICK SONGS (EP)	125
78	Charly CEP 119	DOWNLINERS SECT (EP, reissue of "The Sect Sing Sick Songs")	10
64	Columbia 33SX 1658	THE SECT (LP)	100
65	Columbia 33SX 1745	THE COUNTRY SECT (LP)	90
66	Columbia S(C)X 6028	THE ROCK SECT'S IN (LP, mono/stereo)	90/110

(see also Don Crane's Downliners Sect)

DOWN TO EARTH

71	Downtown DT 485	Under The Boardwalk/Under The Boardwalk (Version) (B-side actually "Double Barrel Version")	7

DOWNTOWN ALL STARS

69	Downtown DT 426	Everybody Feel Good/RUDIES: Downtown Jump	7

DOYAL & GROVES (MELODY BOYS)

60	Top Rank JKP 2057	COUNTRY AND WESTERN EXPRESS VOL. 3 (EP)	8

GENE DOZIER & UNITED FRONT

74	Mercury 6167 007	Give The Women What They Want/The Best Girl I Ever Had	20

LAMONT DOZIER

74	Probe PRO 618	Trying To Hold On To My Woman/We Don't Want Nobody To Come	8
74	Anchor ABC 4003	Fish Ain't Bitin'/Breaking Out All Over	5
75	Anchor ABC 4056	All Cried Out/Rose	5
77	Warner Bros K 16942	Going Back To My Roots/Going Back To My Roots (Version)	5
81	CBS A 1235	To Cool Me Out/Starting Over	5

MINT VALUE £

74	ABC ABCL 5042	OUT HERE ON MY OWN (LP)	18
75	ABC ABCL 5096	BLACK BACH (LP)	18
77	Warner Bros K 56396	PEDDLIN' MUSIC ON THE SIDE (LP)	15

(see also Holland & Dozier)

DOZY, BEAKY, MICK & TICH (D.B.M.&T.)

69	Fontana TF 1061	Tonight Today/Bad News	6
70	Fontana 6007 022	Mr. President/Frisco Annie (as D.B.M.&T)	5
70	Philips 6006 066	Festival/Leader Of A Rock'N'Roll Band	5
71	Philips 6006 114	I Want To Be There/For The Use Of Your Son (as D.B.M.&T)	5
72	Philips 6006 198	They Won't Sing My Song/Soukie	5
70	Philips 6308 029	FRESH EAR (LP, gatefold sleeve, credited to D.B.M.&T)	20

(see also Dave Dee Dozy Beaky Mick & Tich)

DRAGON

76	Acorn CF 268	DRAGON (LP, gatefold sleeve)	30

DRAGONFLY

74	Retreat RTS 257	Gondola/Almost Abandoned (demo)	15
75	Retreat RTS 261	Driving Around The World/Since I Left My Home	8
74	Retreat RTL 6002	ALMOST ABANDONED (LP)	15

DRAGONFLY

80s	Dragonfly DF 001	SILENT NIGHTS EP (p/s, private pressing)	300

DRAGONSFIRE

82	Belltree BTR 001	RISING PHOENIX (LP, with insert)	25

(see also Spinning Wheel)

DRAG SET

66	Go AJ 11405	Get Out Of My Way/Day And Night	200

(see also Open Mind)

DRAGSTER

81	Heavy Metal HEAVY 4	Ambition/Won't Bring You Back (p/s)	30

CHARLIE DRAKE

58	Parlophone R 4461	Splish Splash/Hello, My Darlings	12
58	Parlophone R 4478	Volare/Itchy Twitchy Feeling	16
58	Parlophone R 4496	Tom Thumb's Tune/Goggle Eye Ghee	7
58	Parlophone R 4496	Tom Thumb's Tune/Goggle Eye Ghee (78)	8
59	Parlophone R 4552	Sea Cruise/Starkle, Starkle Little Twink	12
59	Parlophone R 4552	Sea Cruise/Starkle, Starkle Little Twink (78)	10
60	Parlophone R 4675	Naughty/Old Mr. Shadow	7
60	Parlophone R 4701	Mr. Custer/Glow Worm	7
61	Parlophone R 4824	My Boomerang Won't Come Back/She's My Girl	6
62	Parlophone R 4875	Tanglefoot/Drake's Progress	6
62	Parlophone R 4918	I Bent My Assigai/Sweet Freddy Green	6
63	Parlophone R 5057	I've Lost The End Of My Yodel/I Can Can't I	6
64	Parlophone R 5143	I'm Too Heavy For The Light Brigade/The Reluctant Tight-Rope Walker	6
64	Parlophone R 5209	Charles Drake 007/Bumpanology (Bump Head Blues)	6
71	Columbia DB 8829	Puckwudgie/Toffee And Tears	6
75	Charisma CB 270	You Never Know/I'm Big Enough For Me (produced by Peter Gabriel)	8
76	Sol Doon SDRO 24S	Super Punk/Someone	5
58	Parlophone GEP 8720	HELLO MY DARLINGS (EP)	20
60	Parlophone GEP 8812	NAUGHTY CHARLIE DRAKE (EP)	15
64	Parlophone GEP 8903	HITS FROM THE MAN IN THE MOON (EP)	15
69	Music F. Pleasure MFP 1310	HELLO MY DARLINGS (LP)	12

NICK DRAKE

79	Island RSS 7	Introduction/Hazy Jane II/Time Has Told Me/Fruit Tree/Rider On The Wheel ("Fruit Tree" sampler, 1-sided promo only)	250
69	Island ILPS 9105	FIVE LEAVES LEFT (LP, 1st pressing, pink label, black 'circle' logo, g/fold sleeve)	500+
69	Island ILPS 9105	FIVE LEAVES LEFT (LP, gatefold sleeve, 2nd pressing, 'pink rim label, 'palm tree' logo)	200+
70	Island ILPS 9134	BRYTER LAYTER (LP, 'pink rim label, 'palm tree' logo)	250+
72	Island ILPS 9184	PINK MOON (LP, 'pink rim label, 'palm tree' logo, gatefold sleeve)	250+
79	Island NDSP 100	FRUIT TREE (3-LP, box set with booklet)	60
85	Island ILPS 9826	HEAVEN IN A WILD FLOWER (THE BEST OF NICK DRAKE) (LP)	22
86	Hannibal HNBX 5302	FRUIT TREE (4-LP, expanded reissue with booklet)	75
87	Hannibal HNBL 1318	TIME OF NO REPLY (LP)	18
89	Island ILPS 9105	FIVE LEAVES LEFT (LP, reissue, 'blue with white palm tree' label)	18
89	Island ILPS 9134	BRYTER LAYTER (LP, reissue, 'blue with white palm tree' label)	18
89	Island ILPS 9184	PINK MOON (LP, reissue, 'blue with white palm tree' label)	18
91	Hannibal HNCD 5402	FRUIT TREE (4-CD, with booklet in 12" x 12" box)	70

PETE DRAKE

63	Philips BF 1332	Forever/Sleep Walk	10

DRAMATICS

72	Stax 2025 053	Whatcha See Is Whatcha Get/Thankful For Your Love	8
72	Stax 2025 101	In The Rain/Get Up And Get Down	6
73	Stax 2025 117	Toast To A Fool/Your Love Was Strange	12
73	Stax 2025 181	Hey You, Get Off My Mountain/Devil Is Dope	6
76	ABC ABC 4101	You're Fooling You/I'll Make It So Good	6
72	Stax 2362 025	WHATCHA SEE IS WHATCHA GET (LP)	20
74	Stax STX 1021	A DRAMATIC EXPERIENCE (LP)	20
75	ABC ABCL 5121	DRAMATIC JACKPOT (LP, gatefold sleeve)	12
75	ABC ABCL 5150	DRAMA V (LP, gatefold sleeve)	12

MINT VALUE £

DRAMATIS

82 Rocket XPRES 79-12 The Shame (Dance Party Mix 1)/Only Find Rewind (12", p/s, with poster). 8
(see also Gary Numan, Paul Gardiner)

BARRY DRANSFIELD

72 Polydor Folk Mill 2383 160 BARRY DRANSFIELD (LP). 240
(see also Robin & Barry Dransfield, Dransfields)

ROBIN DRANSFIELD

80 Topic 12TS 414 TIDEWAVE (LP) 18
(see also Robin & Barry Dransfield, Dransfields)

ROBIN & BARRY DRANSFIELD

70 Trailer LER 2011 THE ROUT OF THE BLUES (LP) 30
71 Trailer LER 2026 LORD OF ALL I BEHOLD (LP). 30
(see also Robin Dransfield, Barry Dransfield, Dransfields)

DRANSFIELDS

76 Transatlantic TRA 322 THE FIDDLER'S DREAM (LP) 22
77 Free Reed 018 POPULAR TO CONTRARY BELIEF (LP) 15
78 Transatlantic TRA 386 BOWIN' AND SCRAPIN' (LP) 15
(see also Robin & Barry Dransfield, Robin Dransfield, Barry Dransfield)

RUSTY DRAPER

56 Mercury MT 113 Rock And Roll Ruby/House Of Cards (78). 12
56 Mercury MT 128 In The Middle Of The House/Pink Cadillac (78) 10
57 Mercury MT 137 Giant (from the film)/Tiger Lilly (with Jack Halloran Singers) (78) 7
57 Mercury MT 147 Let's Go Calypso/Should I Never Love Again (78) 7
58 Mercury MT 194 Buzz Buzz Buzz/I Get The Blues When It Rains (78). 12
58 Mercury 7MT 211 Gamblin' Gal/That's My Doll. 15
58 Mercury MT 211 Gamblin' Gal/That's My Doll (78) 8
58 Mercury 7MT 229 Chicken-Pickin' Hawk/June, July And August. 15
58 Mercury MT 229 Chicken-Pickin' Hawk/June, July And August (78) 7
59 Mercury AMT 1019 Shoppin' Around/With This Ring 30
59 Mercury AMT 1019 Shoppin' Around/With This Ring (78) 12
59 Mercury AMT 1034 The Sun Will Always Shine/Hey Li Lee Li Lee Li. 7
60 Mercury AMT 1101 Mule Skinner Blues/Please Help Me, I'm Falling. 8
60 Mercury AMT 1110 Luck Of The Irish/It's A Little More Like Heaven. 6
61 Mercury AMT 1127 Jealous Heart/Ten Thousand Years Ago 10
63 London HLU 9786 Night Life/That's Why I Love You Like I Do 12
65 London HLU 9989 Folsom Prison Blues/You Can't Be True, Dear 12
56 Mercury MEP 9506 PRESENTING RUSTY DRAPER (EP). 30
59 Mercury ZEP 10016 RUSTY DRAPER (EP). 22
60 Mercury ZEP 10059 RUSTY IN GAMBLING MOOD (EP) 25
60 Mercury ZEP 10095 MULE SKINNER BLUES (EP). 25
64 London RE-U 1431 RUSTY DRAPER NO. 1 (EP). 22
64 London RE-U 1432 RUSTY DRAPER NO. 2 (EP). 22
60 Mercury MMC 14040 HITS THAT SOLD A MILLION (LP) 30

DREAD AT THE CONTROLS

77 Hawkeye HALP 001 DUB (LP). 12

DREAMERS

68 Columbia DB 8340 The Maybe Song/The Long Road 10
(see also Freddie & Dreamers)

DREAMERS

69 Downtown DT 407 Sweet Chariot/Let's Go Downtown 7
69 Downtown DT 408 I Second That Emotion/Dear Love. 7

DREAMLETS

65 Ska Beat JB 182 Really Now/SKATALITES: Street Corner 30

DREAMLOVERS

61 Columbia DB 4711 When We Get Married/Just Because 175
(see also Chubby Checker)

DREAM MERCHANTS

67 Decca F 12617 Rattler/I'll Be With You In Apple Blossom Time. 8

DREAM POLICE

70 Decca F 12998 I'll Be Home (In A Day Or So)/Living Is Easy 10
70 Decca F 13078 Our Song/Much Too Much 6
70 Decca F 13105 I've Got No Choice/What's The Cure For Happiness? 6

DREAMS

68 United Artists UP 2249 I Will See You There/A Boy Needs A Girl. 7
69 CBS 4247 Baby I'm Your Man/Softly, Softly 7
69 Dolphin 4432 Casatschok/Don't You Ask Me. 7
70 CBS 64203 DREAMS (LP). 20
72 CBS 64597 IMAGINE MY SURPRISE (LP). 20

DREAM SYNDICATE

88 Bucketfull Of Brains BOB 21 Blind Willie McTell/THE BEVIS FROND: High In A Flat (free with *Bucketfull Of Brains* issue 27, 33rpm, yellow die-cut sleeve) 10/6

DREAM THEATER

93 East West Another Day/Status Seeker (live) (cassette) 12
94 East West A 5835 Lie/Space-Dye Vest/To Live Forever/Another Day (live) (p/s) 8
94 East West A 5835 T Lie/Take The Time (Demo)/Space-Dye Vest (12", p/s) 20
94 East West A 5835 CD Lie/Space-Dye Vest/To Live Forever/Another Day (live) (CD) 8
89 MCA MCF 3445 WHEN DREAM AND DAY UNITE (LP) 12
92 Atco 7567 92148 1 IMAGES AND WORDS (LP) 15

MINT VALUE £

DREAMTIMERS
61 London HLU 9368 — The Dancin' Lady/An Invitation . . . 25

DREAM WEAVERS
56 Brunswick 05515 — It's Almost Tomorrow/You've Got Me Wondering (gold label lettering, later silver) . . . 40/25
56 Brunswick 05568 — A Little Love Can Go A Long, Long Way/Into The Night (featuring Wade Buff) . . . 22
56 Brunswick 05607 — You're Mine/Is There Somebody Else? (featuring Wade Buff) . . . 15

DREGS
79 Disturbing DRO 1 — THE DREGS EP (p/s, numbered, stamped sleeve, 500 only) . . . 50

LEN DRESSLAR
56 Mercury 7MT 3 — Chain Gang/These Hands (export issue) . . . 15

JOHN DREVAR('S EXPRESSION)
67 MGM MGM 1367 — The Closer She Gets/When I Come Home . . . 70
68 Polydor BM 56290 — What Greater Love/I've Decided (solo) . . . 8

ALAN DREW
63 Columbia DB 7090 — Here Comes The Rain/Always The Lonely One . . . 6

PATTI DREW
68 Capitol CL 15557 — Workin' On A Groovy Thing/Without A Doubt . . . 10
68 Capitol CL 15575 — Hard To Handle/Just Can't Forget About You . . . 7

DREXCIYA
93 Rephlex CAT 017 — 3 — MOLECULAR ENHANCEMENT (12", 4-track) . . . 15
95 Warp WAP 57 — THE JOURNEY HOME (12", company sleeve) . . . 20

DRIFTERS (U.K.)
59 Columbia DB 4263 — Feelin' Fine/Don't Be A Fool (With Love) . . . 50
59 Columbia DB 4263 — Feelin' Fine/Don't Be A Fool (With Love) (78) . . . 50
59 Columbia DB 4325 — Driftin'/Jet Black . . . 45
(see also Shadows, Cliff Richard, Jet Harris, Tony Meehan)

DRIFTERS (U.S.)
78s
56 London HLE 8344 — Soldier Of Fortune/I Gotta Get Myself A Woman . . . 90
58 London HLE 8686 — Moonlight Bay/Drip-Drop . . . 60
59 London HLE 8892 — There Goes My Baby/Oh, My Love . . . 90
59 London HLE 8988 — Dance With Me/True Love, True Love . . . 100
60 London HLE 9081 — This Magic Moment/Baltimore . . . 120

SINGLES
56 London HLE 8344 — Soldier Of Fortune/I Gotta Get Myself A Woman . . . 1,500
58 London HLE 8686 — Moonlight Bay/Drip-Drop . . . 150
59 London HLE 8892 — There Goes My Baby/Oh, My Love . . . 30
59 London HLE 8988 — Dance With Me/True Love, True Love . . . 20
60 London HLE 9081 — This Magic Moment/Baltimore . . . 15
60 London HLK 9145 — Lonely Winds/Hey Senorita . . . 15
60 London HLK 9201 — Save The Last Dance For Me/Nobody But Me . . . 10
61 London HLK 7114 — Save The Last Dance For Me/This Magic Moment (export issue) . . . 22
61 London HLK 7115 — I Count The Tears/Dance With Me (export issue) . . . 22
61 London HLK 9287 — I Count The Tears/Sadie My Lady . . . 10
61 London HLK 9326 — Some Kind Of Wonderful/Honey Bee . . . 15
61 London HLK 9382 — Please Stay/No Sweet Lovin' . . . 15
61 London HLK 9427 — Sweets For My Sweet/Loneliness Or Happiness . . . 12
62 London HLK 9500 — Room Full Of Tears/Somebody New Dancin' With You . . . 12
62 London HLK 9522 — When My Little Girl Is Smiling/Mexican Divorce . . . 10
62 London HLK 9554 — Stranger On The Shore/What To Do . . . 10
62 London HLK 9626 — Up On The Roof/Another Night With The Boys . . . 8
63 London HLK 9699 — On Broadway/Let The Music Play . . . 20
63 London HLK 9750 — Rat Race/If You Don't Come Back . . . 20
63 London HLK 9785 — I'll Take You Home/I Feel Good All Over . . . 10
64 London HLK 9848 — Vaya Con Dios/In The Land Of Make Believe . . . 10
64 London HLK 9886 — One Way Love/Didn't It . . . 10
64 Atlantic AT 4001 — Under The Boardwalk/I Don't Want To Go On Without You . . . 10
64 Atlantic AT 4008 — I've Got Sand In My Shoes/He's Just A Playboy . . . 12
64 Atlantic AT 4012 — Saturday Night At The Movies/Spanish Lace . . . 8
65 Atlantic AT 4019 — At The Club/Answer The Phone . . . 12
65 Atlantic AT 4023 — Come On Over To My Place/Chains Of Love . . . 12
65 Atlantic AT 4034 — Follow Me/The Outside World . . . 18
65 Atlantic AT 4040 — I'll Take You Where The Music's Playing/Far From The Maddening Crowd . . . 10
66 Atlantic AT 4062 — We Gotta Sing/Nylon Stockings . . . 18
66 Atlantic AT 4084 — Memories Are Made Of This/My Island In The Sun . . . 10
66 Atlantic 584 020 — Up In The Streets Of Harlem/You Can't Love 'Em All . . . 25
67 Atlantic 584 065 — Baby What I Mean/Aretha . . . 12
68 Atlantic 584 152 — I'll Take You Where The Music's Playing/On Broadway . . . 7
68 Atlantic 584 195 — Still Burning In My Heart/I Need You Now . . . 7
69 Atlantic 584 246 — Saturday Night At The Movies/Under The Boardwalk . . . 6
71 Atlantic 2091 064 — A Rose By Any Other Name/Be My Lady . . . 6
76 Atlantic K 10700 — You Gotta Pay Your Dues/Black Silk . . . 6
79 Epic EPC 7806 — Pour Your Little Heart Out Parts 1 & 2 . . . 12

EPs
61 London RE-K 1282 — THE DRIFTERS' GREATEST HITS . . . 45
63 London RE-K 1355 — THE DRIFTERS . . . 45
63 London RE-K 1385 — DRIFTIN' . . . 45
64 Atlantic AET 6003 — DRIFTIN' VOL. 2 . . . 35
65 Atlantic AET 6012 — TONIGHT . . . 35

MINT VALUE £

LPs

Year	Label/Cat. No.	Title	Mint Value £
60	London HA-K 2318	THE DRIFTERS' GREATEST HITS	65
62	London HA-K 2450	SAVE THE LAST DANCE FOR ME	75
65	Atlantic ATL 5015	OUR BIGGEST HITS	40
65	Atlantic ATL/STL 5023	THE GOOD LIFE WITH THE DRIFTERS (mono/stereo)	40/55
66	Atlantic ATL/STL 5039	I'LL TAKE YOU WHERE THE MUSIC'S PLAYING (mono/stereo)	40/55
67	Atlantic 587 038	BIGGEST HITS	18
67	Atlantic 587 061	I'LL TAKE YOU WHERE THE MUSIC'S PLAYING (reissue)	18
67	Atlantic 590 010	SOUVENIRS	25
67	Atlantic 587 063	SAVE THE LAST DANCE FOR ME (reissue)	25
68	Atlantic 587/588 103	THE DRIFTERS' GOLDEN HITS	15
68	Atlantic 587 123	ROCKIN' AND DRIFTIN'	35
68	Atlantic 587 144	GOOD GRAVY (as Clyde McPhatter & Drifters)	40
69	Atlantic 587/588 160	UP ON THE ROOF	20

(see also Clyde McPhatter, Ben E. King, Bobby Hendricks)

DRIFTING SLIM

Year	Label/Cat. No.	Title	Mint Value £
66	Blue Horizon 45-1005	Good Morning Baby/My Sweet Woman (99 copies only)	80

DRIFTWOOD

Year	Label/Cat. No.	Title	Mint Value £
70	Decca F 13084	Shylock Bay/The Wind Cries Above You	6
71	Decca F 13139	Say The Right Things/Still I'll Stay With You	6
70	Decca SKL 5069	DRIFTWOOD (LP)	40

(see also Neil Harrison)

JIMMY DRIFTWOOD

Year	Label/Cat. No.	Title	Mint Value £
60	RCA RCX 191	COUNTRY GUITAR VOL. 13 (EP)	8
60	RCA RCX 193	TALL TALES IN SONG VOL. 1 (EP)	10
60	RCA RCX 195	TALL TALES IN SONG VOL. 2 (EP)	10
60	RCA RCX 198	TALL TALES IN SONG VOL. 3 (EP)	10
61	RCA RD 27226	SONGS OF BILLY YANK AND JOHNNY REB (LP)	12

JULIE DRISCOLL

Year	Label/Cat. No.	Title	Mint Value £
63	Columbia DB 7118	Take Me By The Hand/Stay Away From Me	40
65	Parlophone R 5296	Don't Do It No More/I Know You	35
66	Parlophone R 5444	I Didn't Want To Have To Do It/Don't Do It No More	20
67	Parlophone R 5588	I Know You Love Me Not/If You Should Ever Leave Me	20
67	Marmalade 598 005	Save Me	15
71	Polydor 2480 074	JULIE DRISCOLL — 1969 (LP)	40
72	Polydor 2383 077	JULIE DRISCOLL — 1969 (LP, reissue)	15

JULIE DRISCOLL, BRIAN AUGER & TRINITY

Year	Label/Cat. No.	Title	Mint Value £
68	Marmalade 598 006	This Wheel's On Fire/A Kind Of Love In	10
68	Marmalade 598 011	Road To Cairo/Shadows Of You	10
69	Marmalade 598 018	Take Me To The Water/Indian Rope Man	20
67	Marmalade 607/608 002	OPEN (LP, mono/stereo)	90/80
68	M. For Pleasure MFP 1265	JOOLS/BRIAN (LP, tracks shared by Julie Driscoll & Brian Auger)	30
69	Marmalade 608 005/6	STREET NOISE (2-LP)	200
69	Marmalade 608 014	STREET NOISE PART 1 (LP)	60
69	Marmalade 608 015	STREET NOISE PART 2 (LP)	60

(see also Brian Auger & Trinity, Working Week, Julie Tippetts, B.B. Blunder)

DRISCOLLS

Year	Label/Cat. No.	Title	Mint Value £
80s	Woosh	Father's Name Is Dad/STRAWBERRY STORY: Tell Me Now (p/s)	7

DRIVE

Year	Label/Cat. No.	Title	Mint Value £
78	NRG NE 467	Jerkin'/Push'N'Shove (no p/s)	90

DRIVE

Year	Label/Cat. No.	Title	Mint Value £
90	First Strike FST 007	No Girls/Peephole (hand-made numbered gatefold p/s with insert)	8
92	First Strike FST 020L	This Ain't No Picnic/My World (p/s, white vinyl in bag, numbered, 120 only)	5

DRIVE

Year	Label/Cat. No.	Title	Mint Value £
93	Ninja Tune DRIVE 1	Curfew (Beatmasters 12" Mix)/(Rebel Funk Mix)/(Beatmasters Instrumental) (12", p/s)	8
93	Ninja Tune DRIVE CD 1	Curfew (Rebel Radio Mix)/(Beatmasters 12" Mix)/(Rebel Funk Mix) (Beatmasters Instrumental) (CD)	10

(see also All Saints)

DRIVERS

Year	Label/Cat. No.	Title	Mint Value £
83	Greyhound GRK 701	Talk All Night/Sister (p/s)	6
84	Nouveau NMS 5	Things/Stolen Treasure (p/s)	6
83	Greyhound GRK 3301	SHORT CUTS (LP)	12

(see also Nick Van Eede)

DRIZABONE

Year	Label/Cat. No.	Title	Mint Value £
91	4th & Broadway BRW 223	Real Love/Instrumental Version	50

D-ROK

Year	Label/Cat. No.	Title	Mint Value £
91	Warhammer DROK 08722	Get Out Of My Way (D-Mix)/Renegade/Get Out Of My Way (Airnix) (12", p/s)	10
91	Warhammer DROK 08724	Get Out Of My Way (D-Mix)/Renegade/Get Out Of My Way (Airnix) (CD)	10
91	Warhammer DROK 08710	OBLIVION (LP)	12

(see also Brian May)

FRANK D'RONE

Year	Label/Cat. No.	Title	Mint Value £
60	Mercury AMT 1123	Strawberry Blonde (The Band Rocked On)/Time Hurries By	10
59	Mercury ZEP 10033	FRANK D'RONE SINGS (EP)	15
59	Mercury ZEP 10083	BLUE SERENADE (EP)	10
59	Mercury ZEP 10116	THE BAND ROCKED ON (EP)	30
60	Mercury MMC 14053	AFTER THE BALL (LP)	30

DRONES
77 Valer VRS 1 — Bone Idle/I Just Wanna Be Myself (gatefold p/s, made in France or England) . . 12/6
77 Fifth Avenue CAS 107 — Bone Idle/I Just Wanna Be Myself (cassette, flip-open 'cigarette box' sleeve). . . . 30
77 Valer VRSP 1 — Be My Baby/Lift Off The Bans (12", white label, unreleased) 50
77 Valer — Be My Baby (Take Two)/The Clique (white label, unrel., many autographed). 20
77 Ohms GOOD MIX 1 — TEMPTATIONS OF A WHITE COLLAR WORKER (EP, different coloured sleeves, some with writing on inner sleeve) 15
80 Fabulous JC 4 — Can't See/Fooled Today (p/s). 7
77 Valer VRLP 1 — FURTHER TEMPTATIONS (LP). 30

DROWNING CRAZE
81 Situation 2 SIT 3 — Storage Case (p/s) 10
81 Situation 2 SIT 13 — Trance/I Love The Fjords (p/s) 10
82 Situation 2 SIT 16 — Heat (p/s) 10

DRUG ADDIX
78 Chiswick SW 39 — MAKE A RECORD (EP) 10
(see also Kirsty MacColl)

DRUG SQUAD
80 Bathroom Floor BFR 001 — Operation Julie/Switchcleaner (p/s). 6

DRUGSTORE
93 Honey — Alive (yellow vinyl flexidisc) 6
93 Honey HON 1 — Alive/Gravity (p/s, 500 only). 6

DRUID
75 EMI EMC 3081 — TOWARDS THE SUN (LP, with inner sleeve) 12
76 EMI EMC 3128 — FLUID DRUID (LP, with inner sleeve). 12

DRUID CHASE
67 CBS 3053 — Take Me In Your Garden/I Wanna Get My Hands On You. 22

DRUIDS
63 Parlophone R 5097 — Long Tall Texan/Love So Blue 120
64 Parlophone R 5134 — It's Just A Little Bit Too Late/See What You've Done. 120

DRUIDS
71 Argo ZFB 22 — BURNT OFFERING (LP). 90
73 Argo ZFB 39 — PASTIME WITH GOOD COMPANY (LP) 90
(see also Giles Farnaby's Dream Band)

DRUMBAGO
63 Island WI 085 — I Am Drunk (actually by Raymond Harper & Drumbago's Group)/Sea Breeze (actually by Sammy & Drumbago's Group). 25
68 Blue Cat BS 145 — Reggae Jeggae (with Blenders)/TYRONE TAYLOR: Delilah 18
69 Trojan TR 638 — Dulcemania (with Dynamites)/CLANCY ECCLES: China Man 10
(see also Derrick Patsy, Dennis Walks)

BILL DRUMMOND
87 Creation CRE 039T — King Of Joy/The Manager (12", p/s). 20
(see also Big In Japan, Lori & Chameleons, J.A.M.s, KLF, Disco 2000, Timelords)

DON DRUMMOND
62 Island WI 021 — Schooling The Duke/Bitter Rose (as Don Drummond Orchestra; B-side is actually by Shenley Duffus). 30
63 Black Swan WI 406 — Scrap Iron/DRAGONAIRE: Prevention. 25
63 Blue Beat BB 179 — Reload/Far East 20
63 Island WI 094 — Scandal/My Ideal (B-side actually by W. Sparks). 25
63 R&B JB 103 — Royal Flush/MAYTALS: Matthew Mark. 30
63 R&B JB 105 — The Shock/TONETTES: Tell Me You're Mine 22
64 Ska Beat JB 178 — Silver Dollar/TOMMY McCOOK: My Business. 30
64 Island WI 149 — Eastern Standard Time/DOTTY & BONNIE: Sun Rises 22
64 Island WI 153 — Musical Storeroom/STRANGER COLE: He Who Feels 22
64 Island WI 162 — Garden Of Love/STRANGER COLE: Cherry May 35
65 Island WI 192 — Stampede (with Drumbago)/JUSTIN HINDS & DOMINOES: Come Bail Me 22
65 Island WI 204 — Coolie Baby/LORD ANTICS: You May Stray. 22
65 Island WI 208 — Man In The Street/RITA & BENNY: You Are My Only Love 30
65 Island WI 242 — University Goes Ska/DERRICK & NAOMI: Pain In My Heart. 35
69 Studio One SO 2078 — Heavenless/GLEN BROWN & DAVE BARKER: Lady Lovelight. 40
69 Trojan TR 678 — Memory Of Don/JOHN HOLT: Darling I Love You 15
69 Studio One SO 9008 — THE BEST OF DON DRUMMOND (LP). 110
69 Trojan TTL 23 — MEMORIAL ALBUM (LP) 35
(see also Joe White, Rhythm Aces, Roy & Millie, Movers, Desmond Dekker, Shenley Duffas, Hi-Tones, Duke Reid, Soul Brothers, Baba Brooks, Bonnie & Skitto, Eric Morris, Pioneers, Stranger & Patsy, Techniques, Winston Wright)

DON DRUMMOND JUNIOR
67 Caltone TONE 104 — Sir Pratt Special/HEMSLEY MORRIS: Love Is Strange 30
68 Caltone TONE 124 — Dirty Dozen/PHIL PRATT: Reach Out. 40
70 Jackpot JP 710 — Memory Of Don Drummond/TOBIES: Resting. 12
(see also Vincent Gordon)

K. DRUMMOND
73 Jackpot JP 810 — Your Pretty Face/Your Pretty Face (Version). 5
(see also Cables)

PETE DRUMMOND & THE VHF BAND
72 Warner Bros K 16232 — Rocking At The BBC/Goodbye (vinyl 78). 20

ROY DRUSKY
59 Brunswick 05785 — Wait 'N' See/Just About That Time. 10
61 Brunswick 05856 — Three Hearts In A Tangle/I'd Rather Loan You Out 7

MINT VALUE £

DRY ICE

69	B&C CB 115	Running To The Convent/Nowhere To Go	15

(see also Pluto)

DRY RIB

79	Clockwork COR 001	THE DRY SEASON (EP, 33rpm, photocopied foldover p/s, screen-printed labels)	30

(see also Television Personalities, Times, L'Orange Mechanik)

AMANCIO D'SILVA

69	Columbia S(C)X 6322	INTEGRATION (LP)	55
71	Columbia SCX 6465	REFLECTIONS (LP)	55

(see also Cosmic Eye)

D-TRAIN

82	Prelude EPCA 12-2016	You're The One For Me/You're The One For Me (Version) (12", p/s)	8

DUALS

61	London HL 9450	Stick Shift/Cruising	40

DUBLINERS

60s	Transatlantic TRAEP 136	MAINLY BLARNEY (EP)	8
66	Transatlantic TRA 139	FINNEGAN WAKES (LP)	20
68	Major Minor GOL 200	THE DUBLINERS (LP)	12
67	Major Minor SMLP 3	A DROP OF THE HARD STUFF (LP)	12
68	Major Minor SMLP 34	AT IT AGAIN (LP)	12
69	Columbia SCX 6380	AT HOME WITH THE DUBLINERS (LP)	15
70	Columbia SCX 6423	REVOLUTION (LP)	12
73	Polydor 2383 235	PLAIN AND SIMPLE (LP, gatefold sleeve)	12
74	Polydor 2383 266	THE DUBLINERS LIVE (LP)	12

DUBS

57	London HLU 8526	Could This Be Magic/Such Lovin'	225
57	London HLU 8526	Could This Be Magic/Such Lovin' (78)	40
58	London HL 8684	Gonna Make A Change/Beside My Love	375
58	London HL 8684	Gonna Make A Change/Beside My Love (78)	60

DIANE DUCANE

79	Contact WN 2	Better Late Than Never/One Day	12

JOHN DU CANN

77	Arista ARIST 128	Throw Him In Jail/Street Stutter	5
77	Arista ARIST 145	Where's The Show/Hang Around	5
79	Vertigo 6059 241	Don't Be A Dummy/If I'm Makin' (p/s)	5
77	Arista SPARTY 1027	THE WORLD'S NOT BIG ENOUGH (LP, unreleased)	

(see also Attack, Andromeda, Five Day Week Straw People, Atomic Rooster, Hard Stuff, Status Quo)

DUCHESS

53	London L 1172	Ragging The Scale/Kitten On The Keys (78)	6

DUCKS DELUXE

73	RCA RCA 2438	Coast To Coast/Bring Back That Packard Car	6
74	RCA LPBO 5019	Fireball/Saratoga Suzie	5
74	RCA RCA 2477	Love's Melody/Two Time Twister	5
75	RCA RCA 2531	I Fought The Law/Cherry Pie	5
74	RCA LPL1 5008	DUCKS DELUXE (LP)	12
74	RCA SF 8402	TAXI TO THE TERMINAL ZONE (LP)	12
82	Blue Moon BMLP 001	LAST NIGHT OF A PUB ROCK BAND (2-LP)	15

(see also Motors, Tyla Gang, Brinsley Schwarz)

DUDLEY

60	Vogue V 9171	Lone Prairie Rock/El Pizza	20

DAVE DUDLEY

63	United Artists UP 1029	Six Days On The Road/I Feel A Cry Coming On	12
67	Mercury MF 1003	Trucker's Prayer/Don't Come Cryin' To Me	7
68	Mercury MF 1037	There Ain't No Easy Run/Why Can't I Be With You? (It's A Shame)	6

ROBERTA DUDLEY

50	Tempo R 22	Krooked Blues/When You're Alone (78)	15
51	Poydras 3	Krooked Blues/When You're Alone (shellac 45)	8

(see also Kid Ory)

DU-ETTES

72	President PT 382	Every Beat Of My Heart/Sugar Daddy	10
72	President PT 398	Please Forgive Me/Lonely Days	10

SHENLEY DUFFAS

62	Island WI 036	Give To Get/What You Gonna Do (as S. Duffas; B-side actually with Millie Small)	15
63	Island WI 063	Fret Man Fret/Doreen	15
63	Island WI 093	What A Disaster/I Am Rich	15
63	Island WI 115	Know The Lord/TOMMY McCOOK: Ska Ba	30
63	Island WI 125	Easy Squeal/Things Ain't Going Right	15
63	R&B JB 134	No More Wedding Bells/Let Them Fret	15
64	R&B JB 146	Big Mouth/FRANKIE ANDERSON: Peanut Vendor	18
64	R&B JB 152	Christopher Columbus/CARL BRYAN ORCHESTRA: Barber Chair	18
64	R&B JB 154	Mother-In-Law/DON DRUMMOND & GROUP: Festival	18
64	Black Swan WI 440	Digging A Ditch/He's Coming Down	18
64	Black Swan WI 443	Gather Them In/Crucifixion	20
64	Rio R 41	I Will Be Glad/Heariso (as Shandly Duffus)	18
65	Island WI 182	La La La/UPCOMING WILLOWS: Jonestown Special	30
65	Island WI 184	You Are Mine/UPCOMING WILLOWS: Red China	30
65	Island WI 186	Rukumbine/One Morning	15

MINT VALUE £

72	Upsetter US 380	Bet You Don't Know/UPSETTERS: Ring Of Fire	18
72	Dynamic DYN 451	Peace (with Soul Avengers)/UPSETTERS: Peace — Version	7
72	Grape GR 3031	Sincerely/Sincerely — Version (with Upsetters)	8

(see also Chenley Duffus, Billy Dyce)

CHENLEY DUFFUS

72	Pama PM 859	At The End/Good Night My Love	8

(see also Shenley Duffas)

DUFFY

73	Chapter One SCHR 184	The Joker/Running Away	18
70	Chapter One CHSR 814	SCRUFFY DUFFY (LP)	100

STEPHEN 'TIN TIN' DUFFY

85	10	She Loves Me/She Loves It (p/s, withdrawn)	60
85	10	Baby Impossible (p/s, withdrawn)	60
86	10 TENP 91	I Love You (Aversion)/I Love You/Love Is Driving Me Insane (gatefold p/s with poster, withdrawn)	6
86	10 TIN 91-12	I Love You/Love Is Driving Me Insane/I Love You (The Inversion)/ Wednesday Jones/Icing On The Kake/Kiss Me (12", p/s)	8
86	10 TIND 5-10	I Love You (Inversion)/Wednesday Jones (Dixie)//Icing On The Cake/ Kiss Me (10", double pack, gatefold p/s)	7
86	10 DIXCD 29	BECAUSE WE LOVE YOU (CD)	30

(see also Hawks, Dr. Calculus, Lilac Time)

DUFFY'S DESTRUCTION

92	Lost IT 6	Please Sir, I've Got Mange/Your Mind Is InThis Jar (p/s)	7

DUFFY'S NUCLEUS

67	Decca F 22547	Hound Dog/Mary Open The Door	45

(see also Duffy Power, Pentangle, John McLaughlin)

DON DUGGAN

68	Pye 7N 17633	Let Her Dance/Westmeath Bachelor (with Savoys)	8

BILLY DUKE

62	Ember EMB S 153	Walking Cane/Amen	7
62	Ember EMB S 160	Ain't She Pretty/Timbuctu	7
64	London HLU 9907	While The Bloom Is On The Rose/I'm The Lonesomest Guy In Town	10
65	London HLU 9960	Sugar'N'Spice/Prisoner Of Love	10

DENVER DUKE & JEFFREY NULL BLUEGRASS BOYS

63	Starlite STEP 33	DENVER DUKE & JEFFREY NULL BLUEGRASS BOYS (EP)	15

DON DUKE

60	Embassy WB 402	Please Don't Tease/Made You (78)	8
60	Embassy WB 405	When Will I Be Loved/Look For A Star (78)	8
60	Embassy WB 414	Only The Lonely/Chain Gang (78)	10
60	Embassy WB 416	So Sad (To See Good Love Go Bad)/Please Help Me I'm Falling (78)	8
60	Embassy WB 418	Dreamin'/Let's Think About Living (78)	10

(see also Dick Jordan, Bud Ashton)

DORIS DUKE

71	Mojo 2092 005	To The Other Woman/I Don't Care Anymore	8
71	Mojo 2092 017	If She's Your Wife Who Am I?/It Sure Was Fun	8
73	Mainstream MSS 302	Business Deal/Nobody But You	8
76	Contempo CX15	Woman Of The Ghetto/TAMIKO JONES: Let It Flow	12
71	Mojo 2916 001	I'M A LOSER (LP)	35
71	Mojo 2916 006	A LEGEND IN HER OWN TIME (LP)	35
75	Contempo CRM 111	A LEGEND IN HER OWN TIME (LP, reissue)	15
75	Contempo CLP 519	WOMAN (LP)	18

GEORGE DUKE

71	Sunset SLS 50232	LIVE IN LOS ANGELES (LP)	12
74	BASF BAP 5064	THE AURA WILL PREVAIL (LP)	12
75	BASF BAP 5071	I LOVE THE BLUES, SHE HEARD MY CRY (LP)	12
80	Epic EPC 84311	A BRAZILIAN LOVE AFFAIR (LP)	12

PATTY DUKE

65	United Artists UP 1103	Don't Just Stand There/Everything But Love	12
65	United Artists UP 1116	Say Something Funny/Funny Little Butterflies	7
65	United Artists (S)ULP 1123	DON'T JUST STAND THERE (LP, mono/stereo)	40

DUKE ALL STARS

68	Blue Cat BS 111	Letter To Mummy And Daddy (Parts 1 & 2)	20

DUKE & DUCHESS

55	London HLU 8206	Borrowed Sunshine/Get Ready For Love (with Sir Hubert Pimm)	40
55	London HLU 8206	Borrowed Sunshine/Get Ready For Love (with Sir Hubert Pimm) (78)	7

(see also Sir Hubert Pimm)

DUKE'S NOBLEMEN

68	Philips BF 1691	City Of Windows/Thank You For Your Loving	5

AGGIE DUKES

57	Vogue V 9090	John John/Well Of Loneliness	450
57	Vogue V 9090	John John/Well Of Loneliness (78)	90

DUKES OF DIXIELAND

62	CBS BPG 62014	BREAKIN' IT UP ON BROADWAY (LP)	15

MINT VALUE £

DUKES OF STRATOSPHEAR

85 Virgin VS 763 — The Mole From The Ministry/My Love Explodes (no p/s) 5
87 Virgin VSY 982 — You're A Good Man Albert Brown/Vanishing Girl (p/s, 5,000 on multi-coloured vinyl) 5
85 Virgin WOW 1 — 25 O'CLOCK (LP) 12
87 Virgin VP 2440 — PSONIC PSUNSPOT (LP, gatefold sleeve, 5,000 on multi-coloured vinyl) 25
(see also XTC, Mr. Partridge)

DULCIMER

71 Nepentha 6437 003 — AND I TURNED AS I HAD TURNED AS A BOY (LP, gatefold sleeve) 50
80 Happy Face MMLP 1021 — A LAND FIT FOR HEROES (LP, private pressing) 18

LIZA DULITTLE

68 Pye 7N 17590 — I've Got To Get A Grip Of Myself/Did You Hear A Heart Break Last Night? 8
(see also Margo & Marvettes)

DUM

74 RAK RAK 179 — In The Mood/Watching The Clock 6
(see also Mud)

DUMAINES

55 HMV 7EG 8119 — JAZZOLA EIGHT (EP) 8

DUMB ANGELS

88 Fierce FRIGHT 033 — Love And Mercy/Love And Mercy (p/s, numbered) 35
(see also Pooh Sticks)

DUMBELLES

80 Polydor POSP 209/EGO 3 — Giddy Up/A Christmas Dream (no p/s) 10
(see also Roxy Music)

JOHN DUMMER (BLUES BAND)

68 Mercury MF 1040 — Travelling Man/40 Days (as John Dummer Blues Band) 20
69 Mercury MF 1119 — Try Me One More Time/Riding At Midnight (as John Dummer Blues Band) 15
70 Fontana 6007 027 — Happy/Nightingale (unissued in U.K.; France-only)
70 Philips 6006 111 — Nine By Nine/Going In The Out (credited to either Famous Music Band or John Dummer Band) 12
71 Philips 6006 176 — Medicine Weasel/The Endgame (with Nick Pickett) 7
73 Vertigo 6059 074 — Ooblee-Doobee Jubilee/The Monkey Speaks His Mind (as John Dummer Oobleedooblee Band) 6
69 Mercury SMCL 20136 — CABAL (LP) 90
69 Mercury SMCL 20167 — JOHN DUMMER BAND (LP) 135
70 Philips 6309 008 — FAMOUS MUSIC BAND (LP) 55
72 Philips 6382 039 — THIS IS THE JOHN DUMMER BLUES BAND (LP) 40
73 Philips 6382 040 — VOLUME II — TRY ME ONE MORE TIME (LP) 40
72 Vertigo 6360 055 — BLUE (LP, gatefold sleeve, swirl label) 90
73 Vertigo 6360 083 — OOBLEEDOOBLEE JUBILEE (LP, as John Dummer Oobleedooblee Band, swirl label) 40
(see also Nick Pickett, Dave Kelly, Famous Music Band, Tony McPhee)

DUMMIES

79 Cheapskate FWL 001 — When The Lights Are Out/She's The Only Woman (no p/s) 8
80 Pye 7P 163 — When The Lights Are Out/She's The Only Woman (no p/s, reissue) 8
80 Cheapskate CHEAP 003 — Didn't You Used To Use To Be You?/Miles Out To Sea (p/s) 10
81 Cheapskate CHEAP 014 — Maybe Tonite/When I'm Dancin' I Ain't Fightin' (p/s) 12
(see also China Dolls, Slade)

DUMPY'S RUSTY NUTS

81 Cool King CNK 006 — Just For Kicks/Ride With Me (p/s, reissued as Dumpy's Rusty Bolts) 8/5
82 Cool King CK 008 — Boxhill Or Bust/It's Got To Be Blues (p/s, initially with free patch) 6/5
90 A Side DRN 21 — Run Run Run/Rock City (withdrawn, promos more common) 5
84 Landslide LDLP 101 — SOMEWHERE IN ENGLAND (LP) 12

DUNAMIS

79 Daybreak DB 2602 — I CAN FLY (LP, some signed) 20/15

AYNSLEY DUNBAR (RETALIATION)

67 Blue Horizon 3109 — Warning/Cobwebs (some in p/s) 60/25
68 Liberty LBF 15132 — Watch 'N' Chain/Roamin' And Ramblin' 15
68 Liberty LBL/LBS 83154 — AYNSLEY DUNBAR RETALIATION (LP, mono/stereo) 50
68 Liberty LBL/LBS 83177 — DR. DUNBAR'S PRESCRIPTION (LP, mono/stereo) 50
69 Liberty LBS 83223 — RETALIATION (LP) 50
70 Liberty LBS 83316 — REMAINS TO BE HEARD (LP, textured sleeve) 60
71 Warner Bros WS 3010 — BLUE WHALE (LP) 22
71 Warner Bros K 46062 — BLUE WHALE (LP, reissue) 12
(see also John Mayall & Bluesbreakers, Heavy Jelly, Annette & Victor Brox, Exchekers)

SCOTT DUNBAR

71 Ahura Mazda AMS SDS 1 — FROM LAKE MARY (LP) 30

JOHNNY DUNCAN (& BLUE GRASS BOYS)

57 Columbia DB 3925 — Kaw-Liga/Ella Speed (gold label lettering, later silver) 25/15
57 Columbia DB 3925 — Kaw-Liga/Ella Speed (78) 12
57 Columbia DB 3959 — Last Train To San Fernando/Rock-A-Billy Baby (gold label lettering, later silver) 25/12
57 Columbia DB 3996 — Blue, Blue Heartache/Jig Along Home 12
57 Columbia DB 4029 — Footprints In The Snow/Get Along Home, Cindy 10
58 Columbia DB 4074 — Goodnight Irene/If You Love Me Baby 20
58 Columbia DB 4074 — Goodnight Irene/If You Love Me Baby (78) 6
58 Columbia DB 4118 — Itching For My Baby/I Heard The Bluebirds Sing 18
58 Columbia DB 4118 — Itching For My Baby/I Heard The Bluebirds Sing (78) 10
58 Columbia DB 4167 — All Of The Monkeys Ain't In The Zoo/More And More 12
58 Columbia DB 4167 — All Of The Monkeys Ain't In The Zoo/More And More (78) 8

MINT VALUE £

58 Columbia DB 4179 My Lucky Love/Geisha Girl ... 10
58 Columbia DB 4179 My Lucky Love/Geisha Girl (78) ... 10
59 Columbia DB 4282 Rosalie/This Train ... 12
59 Columbia DB 4282 Rosalie/This Train (78) ... 12
59 Columbia DB 4311 Kansas City/That's All Right Darlin' ... 15
59 Columbia DB 4311 Kansas City/That's All Right Darlin' (78) ... 15
60 Columbia DB 4415 Any Time/Yellow, Yellow Moon (solo) ... 7
61 Pye 7N 15358 Tobacco Road/Sleepy-Eyed John (solo) ... 10
61 Pye 7N 15380 The Legend Of Gunga Din/Hannah (solo) ... 10
62 Pye 7N 15420 A Long Time Gone/Waitin' For The Sandman (solo) ... 10
63 Columbia DB 7164 The Ballad Of Jed Clampett/Will You Be Mine?
(as Johnny Duncan & Kingpins) ... 10
64 Columbia DB 7334 Dang Me/Which Way Did He Go? (solo) ... 6
66 Columbia DB 7833 My Little Baby/I Thank My Lucky Stars (solo) ... 5
57 Columbia SEG 7708 JOHNNY DUNCAN AND HIS BLUE GRASS BOYS (EP) ... 25
57 Columbia SEG 7773 JOHNNY DUNCAN AND HIS BLUE GRASS BOYS NO. 2 (EP) ... 25
58 Columbia SEG 7753 FOOTPRINTS IN THE SNOW (EP) ... 25
58 Columbia SEG 7850 TENNESSEE SING SONG (EP) ... 25
57 Columbia 33S 1122 TENNESSEE SONG BAG (10" LP) ... 50
58 Columbia 33S 1129 JOHNNY DUNCAN SALUTES HANK WILLIAMS (10" LP) ... 45
61 Columbia 33SX 1328 BEYOND THE SUNSET (LP) ... 30
68 M. For Pleasure MFP 1032 BEYOND THE SUNSET (LP, reissue) ... 12
(see also Chris Barber's Skiffle Group)

LESLEY DUNCAN (& JOKERS)

63 Parlophone R 5034 I Want A Steady Guy/Movin' Away (as Lesley Duncan & Jokers) ... 10
64 Parlophone R 5106 Tell Me/You Kissed Me Boy ... 10
64 Mercury MF 830 When My Baby Cries/Did It Hurt? ... 10
65 Mercury MF 847 Just For The Boy/See That Guy ... 10
65 Mercury MF 876 Run To Love/Only The Lonely And Me ... 10
65 Mercury MF 939 Hey Boy/I Go To Sleep ... 10
69 CBS 4585 Sing Children Sing/Exactly Who You Are ... 5
79 CBS 8061 Sing Children Sing/Rainbow Games (p/s, with Kate Bush) ... 10
82 Korova KOW 22 Masters Of War/Another Light Goes Out (p/s) ... 5
71 CBS 64202 SING CHILDREN SING (LP) ... 15
72 CBS 64807 EARTH MOTHER (LP) ... 15
74 GM GML 1007 EVERYTHING CHANGES (LP) ... 15
(see also Mitchell/Coe Mysteries)

TOMMY DUNCAN

66 Sue WI 4002 Dance, Dance, Dance/Let's Try It Over Again ... 35

TOMMY DUNCAN & HIS WESTERN ALL STARS

50 Capitol CL 13261 Gamblin' Polka Dot Blues/Chattanooga Shoe Shine Boy (78) ... 12

BARBARA DUNKLEY

71 Banana BA 342 We'll Cry Together/BOBBY DAVIS: Got To Get Away ... 6

DELROY DUNKLEY

70 Hot Rod HR 109 I Wish You Well/TONY & DELROY: Impossible Love ... 7

ERROL(L) DUNKLEY

67 Rio R 109 Love Me Forever/VIETNAM ALLSTARS: The Toughest ... 45
67 Rio R 131 You're Gonna Need Me/Seek And You'll Find ... 30
68 Island WI 3150 Once More/I'm Not Your Man ... 20
68 Amalgamated AMG 800 Please Stop Your Lying/Feel So Fine
(B-side actually by Tommy McCook & Band) ... 30
68 Amalgamated AMG 805 I'm Going Home/I'm Not Your Man ... 30
68 Amalgamated AMG 807 The Scorcher/Do It Right Tonight ... 30
68 Amalgamated AMG 820 Love Brother/I Spy ... 12
69 Fab FAB 117 I'll Take You In My Arms/KING CANNON: Daphney Reggae ... 8
70 Unity UN 554 My Special Prayer/Never Hurt The One You Love ... 7
70 Banana BA 302 Satisfaction/CECIL LOCKE: Sing Out Loud ... 15
71 Big BG 324 Deep Meditation/RUPIE EDWARDS ALL STARS: Meditation Version ... 18
71 Big BG 327 Three In One/RUPIE EDWARDS ALL STARS: One In Three ... 6
71 Nu Beat NB 091 Three In One/RUPIE EDWARDS ALL STARS: One In Three ... 6
71 Explosion EX 2053 O Lord/KEITH with IMPACT ALL STARS: Raindrops
(B-side actually "My Baby" by Lloyd Charmers) ... 6
72 Camel CA 87 Black Cinderella/PHIL PRATT ALLSTARS: Our Anniversary
(B-side actually Tropic Shadows) ... 12
73 Grape GR 3039 Why Did You Do It/One Love ... 8
73 Count Shelley CS 3039 Girl You Cried/Where Must I Go ... 5
70s Attack AT 1003 YOU NEVER KNOW (LP) ... 30
73 Attack ATLP 1003 DARLING OOH (LP) ... 20
(see also Errol & His Group, Gaynor & Erroll], Mister Versatile, Don Lee, Ken Parker, Bongo Herman)

BLIND WILLIE DUNN'S GIN BOTTLE FOUR with KING OLIVER

54 Columbia SCM 5100 Jet Black Blues/Blue Blood Blues ... 25
54 Columbia DB 3440 Jet Black Blues/Blue Blood Blues (78) ... 18
(see also Eddie Lang & Lonnie Johnson)

GEORGE DUNN

73 Leader LEE 4042 GEORGE DUNN (LP, with insert) ... 18

CATHAL DUNNE

79 Epic SEPC 7190 Happy Man/Sweet Woman Of Mine (p/s) ... 5

TONY DUNNING (& TREMELOS)

60 Palette PG 9006 Seventeen Tomorrow/Be My Girl ... 10
61 Palette PG 9018 Pretend/Don't Bother To Call ... 10
61 Palette PG 9027 Under Moscow Skies/Sixteen Candles ... 10

MINT VALUE £

CHAMPION JACK DUPREE

Year	Label / Cat. No.	Title	Value
51	Jazz Parade B 16	Fisherman's Blues/County Jail Special (78)	30
62	Storyville A 45051	Whiskey Head Woman/Shirley May	20
67	Decca F 12611	Barrelhouse Woman/Under Your Hood	22
67	Blue Horizon 45-1007	Get Your Head Happy/Easy Is The Way (with T.S. McPhee)	130
68	Blue Horizon 57-3140	I Haven't Done No-One No Harm/How Am I Doing It (with Stan Webb)	22
69	Blue Horizon 57-3152	Ba'la Fouche/Kansas City	22
69	Blue Horizon 57-3158	I Want To Be A Hippy/Goin' Back To Louisiana	22
61	Storyville SEP 381	BLUES ANTHOLOGY VOL. 1 (EP)	30
64	RCA RCX 7137	RHYTHM AND BLUES VOL. 1 (EP)	30
64	Decca DFE 8586	LONDON SPECIAL (EP, with Keith Smith Climax Band)	60
65	Ember EMB 4564	JACK DUPREE (EP)	25
60s	XX MIN 716	CHAMPION JACK DUPREE (EP)	20
59	London Jazz LTZ-K 15171	BLUES FROM THE GUTTER (LP)	85
61	London Jazz LTZ-K 15217	CHAMPION JACK'S NATURAL AND SOULFUL BLUES (LP, also stereo SAH-K 6151)	80/110
65	Storyville SLP 145	TROUBLE TROUBLE (LP)	35
65	Xtra XTRA 1028	CABBAGE GREENS (LP)	25
65	Storyville SLP 161	PORTRAITS IN BLUES (LP)	35
66	Decca LK/SKL 4747	FROM NEW ORLEANS TO CHICAGO (LP)	90
67	Storyville 670 194	CHAMPION JACK DUPREE (LP)	40
67	Decca SKL 4871	CHAMPION JACK DUPREE AND HIS BIG BLUES BAND (LP)	90
68	Blue Horizon 7-63206	WHEN YOU FEEL THE FEELING YOU WAS FEELING (LP)	80
69	Blue Horizon 7-63214	SCOOBYDOOBYDOO (LP)	80
70	Sonet SNTF 614	THE INCREDIBLE CHAMPION JACK DUPREE (LP)	18
72	Sonet SNTF 626	LEGACY OF THE BLUES (LP)	18
75	Atlantic K 40526	BLUES FROM THE GUTTER (LP)	12

(see also T.S. McPhee)

CHAMPION JACK DUPREE/JIMMY RUSHING

Year	Label / Cat. No.	Title	Value
64	Ember CJS 800	TWO SHADES OF BLUE (LP)	40

(see also Jimmy Rushing)

CHAMPION JACK DUPREE & KING CURTIS

Year	Label / Cat. No.	Title	Value
73	Atlantic K 40434	BLUES FROM MONTREUX (LP)	12

(see also King Curtis)

SIMON DUPREE & BIG SOUND

Year	Label / Cat. No.	Title	Value
66	Parlophone R 5542	I See The Light/It Is Finished	10
67	Parlophone R 5574	Reservations/You Need A Man	10
67	Parlophone R 5594	Day Time, Night Time/I've Seen It All Before	10
67	Parlophone R 5646	Kites/Like The Sun Like The Fire (with Jacqui Chan)	8
68	Parlophone R 5670	For Whom The Bell Tolls/Sleep	6
68	Parlophone R 5697	Part Of My Past/This Story Never Ends	8
68	Parlophone R 5727	Thinking About My Life/Velvet And Lace	8
69	Parlophone R 5757	Broken Hearted Pirates/She Gave Me The Sun	10
69	Parlophone R 5816	The Eagle Flies Tonight/Give It All Back	10
67	Parlophone PMC/PCS 7029	WITHOUT RESERVATIONS (LP, yellow & black label)	55
69	Parlophone PCS 7029	WITHOUT RESERVATIONS (LP, re-pressing, silver & black label)	22

(see also Moles, Gentle Giant, Jacqui Chan)

DUPREES

Year	Label / Cat. No.	Title	Value
62	HMV POP 1073	You Belong To Me/Take Me As I Am	35
62	Stateside SS 143	My Own True Love/Ginny	18
63	London HLU 9678	I'd Rather Be Here In Your Arms/I Wish I Could Believe You	22
63	London HLU 9709	Gone With The Wind/Let's Make Love Again	20
63	London HLU 9774	Why Don't You Believe Me?/My Dearest One	20
63	London HLU 9813	Have You Heard?/Love Eyes	20
64	London HLU 9843	It's No Sin/The Sand And The Sea	20
65	CBS 201803	Around The Corner/They Said It Couldn't Be Done	15
66	CBS 202028	She Waits For Him/Norma Jean	12
68	MGM MGM 460	My Special Angel/Ring Of Love	10
70	Polydor 2058 077	Check Yourself/The Sky's The Limit	15

DURAN DURAN

Year	Label / Cat. No.	Title	Value
81	EMI EMI 5137	Planet Earth/Late Bar (glossy p/s)	6
81	EMI 12EMI 5137	Planet Earth (Night Version)/Planet Earth/Late Bar (12", p/s)	8
81	EMI EMI 5168	Careless Memories/Khanada (p/s)	6
81	EMI 12EMI 5168	Careless Memories/Fame/Khanada (12", p/s)	8
81	EMI 12EMI 5206	Girls On Film (Night Version)/Girls On Film/Faster Than Light (12", p/s)	8
81	EMI EMI 5254	My Own Way/Like An Angel (p/s)	5
81	EMI 12EMI 5254	My Own Way (Night Version)/Like An Angel/My Own Way (Short Version)(12", p/s)	8
82	EMI 12EMI 5327	Save A Prayer/Hold Back The Rain (12" remix) (12", p/s)	8
82	EMI 12EMI 5346	Rio (Part 1)/Rio (Part 2)/My Own Way (12", p/s)	8
83	Flexi (no cat. no.)	The Smash Hits Interview (flexidisc free with *Smash Hits*)	8/5
84	EMI DURANP 2	The Reflex/Make Me Smile (poster p/s)	6
84	EMI 12 DURANP 2	The Reflex (Dance Mix)/Make Me Smile/The Reflex (12", picture disc)	10
84	EMI DURAN (A-E) 3	The Wild Boys/Cracks In The Pavement (Live) (5 different p/s)	5
85	Parlophone DURANG 007	A View To A Kill/A View To A Kill (That Fatal Kiss) (white vinyl, gatefold p/s)	6
86	Parlophone TCDDNX 45	Notorious (Latin Rascals Mix)/Winter Marches On/Notorious (cassette)	5
86	Parlophone 12 DDNX 45	Notorious (Latin Rascals Mix)/Winter Marches On/Notorious (12", p/s)	10
87	Parlophone TRADEX 1	Skin Trade/We Need You (poster p/s)	8
87	Parlophone TC TRADE 1	Skin Trade (Stretch Mix)/We Need You/Skin Trade (cassette in 'video' case)	10
87	Parlophone TOUR 1	Meet El Presidente/Vertigo (Do The Demolition) (non-gatefold p/s)	8
87	Parlophone CDTOUR 1	The Presidential Suite: Meet El Presidente (extended)/Meet El Presidente (Meet El Beat)/Meet El Presidente/Vertigo (Do The Demolition) (CD, gatefold card sleeve)	10

MINT VALUE £

88 Parlophone 12 YOUR 1 — I Don't Want Your Love (Big Mix)/(7" Mix)/(Album Version) (12", p/s) ... 8
88 Parlophone 12 YOUR S1 — I Don't Want Your Love (Big Mix)/I Don't Want Your Love (Album Version) (12", p/s, 1 side etched) ... 8
88 Parlophone CD YOUR 1 — I Don't Want Your Love (7" Mix)/I Don't Want Your Love (Album Version)/ I Don't Want Your Love (Big Mix) (CD, stickered case) ... 10
88 Parlophone 12DDX 11 — All She Wants Is (US Master Mix)/All She Wants Is (45 Mix)/I Believe — All I Need To Know (Medley) (12", p/s) ... 8
88 Parlophone 12DDDJ 11 — All She Wants Is (Euro Dub Mix)/All She Wants Is (45 Mix)/All She Wants Is (US Master Mix)/All She Wants Is (House Dub) (12", p/s, promo only) ... 15
88 Parlophone CDDD 11 — All She Wants Is (45 Mix)/Skin Trade (Parisian Mix)/I Believe — All I Need To Know (Medley) (3" CD) ... 15
89 Parlophone DDA/B/C 12 — Do You Believe In Shame?/The Krush Brothers LSD Edit//Do You Believe In Shame?/God (London)/This Is How A Road Gets Made/Palomino// Do You Believe In Shame?/Drug — It's Just A State Of Mind (triple-pack, foldout p/s & 3 cards) ... 18
89 Parlophone 10DD 12 — Do You Believe In Shame?/The Krush Brothers LSD Edit/Notorious (live) (10", numbered or unnumbered p/s) ... 10/8
89 Parlophone CDDD 12 — Do You Believe In Shame?/The Krush Brothers LSD Edit/Notorious (live)/ God (London)/This Is How A Road Gets Made (3" CD) ... 20
89 Parlophone CDDD 13 — Burning The Ground/Decadance/Decadance (Extended Mix) (CD, 2,000 only) ... 35
90 Parlophone 12DD 14 — Violence Of Summer (The Rock Mix)/Violence Of Summer (The Dub)/ (The Story Mix) (12", p/s) ... 8
90 Parlophone CDDD 14 — Violence Of Summer (LP Version)/Violence Of Summer (The Power Cut Down Mix)/Violence Of Summer (The Story Mix) (CD, slimline case) ... 8
90 Parlophone 12DDG 15 — Serious/Yo Bad Azizi/Water Babies (12", gatefold p/s) ... 8
90 Parlophone 12DDS 15 — Serious/Yo Bad Azizi/Water Babies (12", p/s, etched disc with poster) ... 8
90 Parlophone CDDD 15 — Serious/Yo Bad Azizi/Water Babies (CD) ... 12
93 Parlophone CDDDS 16 — Ordinary World (Single Version)/Save A Prayer/Skin Trade/ My Antarctica (CD, fold-out pack, withdrawn) ... 25
93 Parlophone CDDPD 16 — Ordinary World (Single Version)/The Reflex/Hungry Like The Wolf/ Girls On Film (CD, picture disc) ... 8
93 Parlophone CDDDS 17 — Come Undone (Edit)/Ordinary World (Acoustic Version)/Come Undone (FGI Phumpin' 12")/Come Undone (La Fin De Siecle) (CD, digipak) ... 10
93 Parlophone CDDD 17 — Come Undone/Rio/Is There Something I Should Know/A View To A Kill (CD) ... 10
95 Parlophone 12DD DJ 007 — White Lines (70's Club Mix)/(Oakland Funk Mix)/(Album Version) (12", pearl vinyl, promo only) ... 20
94 Parlophone CDDDB 35 — DURAN DURAN (2-CD, fold-out digipak with 2 booklets) ... 25

PROMOS

81 EMI 12EMI 5137 — Planet Earth (1-sided 12") ... 25
87 Parlophone CLUBTOUR 1 — THE PRESIDENTIAL SUITE EP (12") ... 18
88 Parlophone 12YOURDJ 1 — I Don't Want Your Love (Big Mix)/ (Dub Mix) (12") ... 20
88 Parlophone 12DDDJ 11 — All She Wants Is (Euro Dub Mix)/(Mixes) (12") ... 20
93 Parlophone 12DDDJ 17 — Come Undone (FGI Phumpin' 12" Mix)/(Mixes) (12") ... 25
93 Parlophone CDDDDJ 17 — Come Undone (Edit)/(Mixes)/Ordinary World (Acoustic Versions) (CD) ... 20
95 Parlophone CDINTPR 01 — Perfect Day (CD export promo, pink title sleeve) ... 15
97 Parlophone BARBDJ 97 — Electric Barbarella (Radio Edit)/(Album Version) (CD, card sleeve) ... 20
97 Virgin VSTDJ 1639 — Out Of My Mind/(Mixes) (12", stickered title sleeve) ... 15
98 Parlophone 12GOF 1 — Girls On Film (Tall Paul Mix)/(Instrumental) (12") ... 18
98 EMI GREATEST 001 — GREATEST (CD, card sleeve) ... 20

(see also Arcadia, Power Station)

JIMMY DURANTE

55 Brunswick 05395 — Pupalina (My Little Doll)/Little People ... 10
55 Brunswick 05445 — It's Bigger Than Both Of Us (with Patty Andrews)/ When The Circus Leaves Town ... 10
55 Brunswick 05495 — Swingin' With Rhythm And Blues (with Peter Lawford)/ I Love You, I Do (with Eddie Jackson) ... 10
60 Brunswick 05829 — Shine On Harvest Moon/The Best Things In Life Are Free ... 7
63 Warner Bros WB 112 — September Song/Young At Heart ... 7
64 Warner Bros WB 149 — Old Man Time/I Came Here To Swim ... 6
54 MGM EPC 2 — JIMMY DURANTE (EP, export issue) ... 18
57 MGM MGM-EP 508 — JIMMY DURANTE (EP) ... 15
57 MGM MGM-EP 597 — SCHNOZZLES (EP) ... 15
52 MGM MGM-D 102 — IN PERSON (10" LP) ... 30
53 Brunswick LA 8582 — JIMMY DURANTE SINGS (10" LP) ... 30
57 Brunswick LAT 8216 — CLUB DURANTE (LP) ... 20

(see also Ethel Merman, Groucho Marx)

ALLISON DURBIN

69 Decca LK-R/SKL-R 4996 — I HAVE LOVED ME A MAN (LP) ... 40

JUDITH DURHAM

67 Columbia DB 8207 — The Olive Tree/The Non Performing Lion Quickstep ... 6
67 Columbia DB 8290 — Again And Again/Memories ... 10
70 A&M AMS 777 — The Light Is Dark Enough/Wanderlove ... 6
69 Columbia S(C)X 6374 — FOR CHRISTMAS WITH LOVE (LP) ... 15
70 A&M AMLS 967 — GIFT OF SONG (LP) ... 15
71 A&M AMLS 2011 — CLIMB EV'RY MOUNTAIN (LP) ... 12

(see also Seekers, Keith Potger)

KENNY DURHAM

58 London LTZU 15133 — JAZZ CONTRASTS (LP, with Sonny Rollins) ... 20

TERRY DURHAM

69 Deram DML/SML 1042 — CRYSTAL TELEPHONE (LP, with insert) ... 22

(see also Storyteller)

MINT VALUE £

DURUTTI COLUMN

82 Factory FAC 64 — I Get Along Without You Very Well/Prayer (p/s) 7
80 Factory FACT 14 — THE RETURN OF THE DURUTTI COLUMN (LP, with sandpaper sleeve, some with Martin Hannett's "Testcard" flexidisc [FACT 14C]) 50/35
83 Factory FACT 74 — ANOTHER SETTING (LP, with perfumed cut-out insert) 12
83 VU VINI 1 — LIVE AT THE VENUE LONDON (LP) 18
88 Factory FACT 244 — VINI REILLY (LP, with free p/s 7" "I Know Very Well How I Got My Note Wrong" [FAC 244++] by Vincent Gerard & Steven Patrick) 20
88 Factory FACD 244 — VINI REILLY (CD, with 3" CD "I Know Very Well How I Got My Note Wrong" [FAC CD 244++] by Vincent Gerard & Steven Patrick) 30

(see also Nosebleeds, Gammer & His Familiars, Morrissey)

IAN DURY (& THE BLOCKHEADS)

78 Stiff BUY 2712 — What A Waste/Wake Up (12", plain white sleeve) 20
78 Stiff BUY 38 — Hit Me With Your Rhythm Stick/There Ain't Half Been Some Clever Bastards (red vinyl, p/s, one copy known) 400
78 Stiff FREEBIE 1 — Sex And Drugs And Rock And Roll/England's Glory/Two Steep Hills (p/s, free at *NME* party/competition) 8
77 Stiff SEEZ 4 — NEW BOOTS AND PANTIES!! (LP, with bonus track 'Sex And Drugs And Rock And Roll') 20
77 Stiff SEEZ 4 — NEW BOOTS AND PANTIES!! (LP, limited edition gold vinyl) 25

(see also Kilburn & The High Roads, Greatest Show On Earth, Loving Awareness)

ANDREW DURYER

75 Real RR 2003 — BALLADS OF A WANDERER (LP) 25

JEAN DUSHON

65 Chess CRL 4000 — MAKE WAY FOR JEAN DUSHON (LP) 40

DUSK

71 Bell BLL 1167 — I Hear Those Church Bells Ringing/I Cannot See To See You 8

PAT DUSKY AND MARINES

67 Stardust STP 1 — I Fall To Pieces/This Can Be The Night 6

LA DÜSSELDORF

78 Radar ADA 5 — La Düsseldorf/Silver Cloud (unissued, white label promo only) 25
81 Albion ION 1025 — Tintarella Di (some might have p/s) 10

DUST BROTHERS

93 Dust Brothers DB's 333 — Song To The Siren (12", no p/s, 500 only) 50
93 Junior Boys Own JBO 10 — Song To The Siren/Song To The Siren (Sabres Of Paradise Mixes) (12", p/s) 20
94 Boys Own COLLECT 004 — 14TH CENTURY SKY EP (12", no p/s) 20
94 Junior Boys Own JBO 20 — MY MERCURY MOUTH EP (12", JBO sleeve) 20

(see also Chemical Brothers)

SLIM DUSTY

58 Columbia DB 4212 — A Pub With No Beer/Once When I Was Mustering (with His Country Rockers) 8
59 Columbia DB 4294 — The Answer To A Pub With No Beer/Winter Winds (with His Bushlanders) 6
60 Columbia SEG 8009 — SLIM DUSTY AND HIS COUNTRY ROCKERS (EP) 25
63 Decca LK 4551 — SLIM DUSTY SINGSONG (LP) 20

DUTCH SWING COLLEGE BAND

51 Saturn EGX 106 — Alexander's Ragtime Band/Birthday Blues (78 picture disc) 75

JACQUES DUTRONC

66 Vogue VRS 7015 — Et Moi, Et Moi, Et Moi/Mini-Mini-Mini 12
66 Vogue VRS 7021 — Les Cactus/L'Espace D'Une Felle 7
66 Vogue VRS 7024 — J'Aime Les Filles/L'Idole 6
67 Vogue VRS 7027 — Le Plus Difficile/Les Rois De La Reforme 6
67 Vogue VRL 3029 — JACQUES DUTRONC (LP) 25

JOSE DUVAL

57 London HLR 8458 — Message Of Love/That's What You Mean To Me 25

MARK DWAYNE

62 Oriole CB 1712 — Remember Me Huh/Poorest Boy In Town 12
62 Oriole CB 1744 — Today's Teardrops/Little Bitty Heart 12

DYAKS

78 Bonaparte BONE 2 — Gutter Kids/It's A Game (p/s) 5

BILLY DYCE

72 G.G. GG 4532 — Be My Guest/HUGH ROY: Way Down South 7
72 G.G. GG 4534 — Take Warning/TYPHOON ALL STARS: Warning (Version) 8
72 G.G. GG 4537 — Time Is Still Here/G.G. ALL STARS: Time — Version 7
72 Pama PM 835 — Be My Guest/HUGH ROY: Way Down South 7
73 Pama PM 874 — Woman Smarter/SHENLEY DUFFAS: Standing On The Hill 6
73 Bread BR 1115 — You Need Love (with Millions)/G.G. ALL STARS: Love — Dub 6

DYKE & BLAZERS

67 Pye International 7N 25413 — Funky Broadway (Parts 1 & 2) 18

BOB DYLAN

SINGLES

65	CBS 201751	The Times They Are A-Changin'/Honey, Just Allow Me One More Chance	7
65	CBS 201753	Subterranean Homesick Blues/She Belongs To Me	7
65	CBS 201781	Maggie's Farm/On The Road Again	7
65	CBS 201811	Like A Rolling Stone/Gates Of Eden	7
65	CBS 201811	Like A Rolling Stone (Parts 1 & 2) (demo only)	110
65	CBS 201824	Positively 4th Street/From A Buick 6	7
66	CBS 201900	Can You Please Crawl Out Your Window/Highway 61 Revisited	12
66	CBS 202053	One Of Us Must Know (Sooner Or Later)/Queen Jane Approximately	20
66	CBS 202307	Rainy Day Women Nos. 12 & 35/Pledging My Time	8
66	CBS 202258	I Want You/Just Like Tom Thumb's Blues (live)	12

(Some of the above singles were reissued with four-figure catalogue numbers, e.g. CBS 1811, which are worth around £6 each.)

66	CBS 2700	Leopard-Skin Pill-Box Hat/Most Likely You Go Your Way And I'll Go Mine (p/s)	55
66	CBS 2700	Leopard-Skin Pill-Box Hat/Most Likely You Go Your Way And I'll Go Mine	10
67	CBS 2476	Mixed Up Confusion/Corrine Corrina (unissued in U.K.)	
69	CBS 4219	I Threw It All Away/The Drifter's Escape	5
70	CBS 5122	Wigwam/Copper Kettle (The Pale Moonlight)	6
71	CBS 7329	Watching The River Flow/Spanish Is The Loving Tongue	6
71	CBS 7688	George Jackson (Acoustic)/George Jackson (Big Band Version)	8
73	CBS 1158	Just Like A Woman/I Want You (p/s, 'Hall Of Fame Hits' series)	6
74	CBS 2006	A Fool Such As I/Lily Of The West	6
74	Island WIP 6168	On A Night Like This/Forever Young	6
75	CBS 3160	Tangled Up In Blue/If You See Her, Say Hello	6
75	CBS 3665	Million Dollar Bash/Tears Of Rage	6
76	CBS 3878	Hurricane (Part 1)/(Full Version) (some list 'Pt 1'/'Pt 2'; with/without p/s)	8/5
76	CBS 3945	Lay Lady Lay/I Threw It All Away (p/s)	5
76	CBS 4113	Mozambique/Oh Sister	5
76	CBS 4859	Stuck Inside Of Mobile With The Memphis Blues Again/Rita May (p/s; demos have "Rita May" as A-side, p/s)	12/8
78	CBS 12-6499	Baby Stop Crying/New Pony (12", p/s)	8
78	CBS 12-6718	Is Your Love In Vain?/We Better Talk This Over (12", p/s)	8
78	CBS 6935	Changing Of The Guard/Sènor	5
81	CBS A 1406	Heart Of Mine/Let It Be Me	5
83	CBS A 3916	Union Sundown/Angels Flying Too Close To The Ground (p/s)	5
84	CBS A 4055	Jokerman/Licence To Kill (p/s, embossed or standard label)	5
84	CBS A 4055	Jokerman (Special Faded Radio Version)/Licence To Kill (p/s, promo only)	12
85	CBS GA 5020	Highway 61 Revisited (live)/It Ain't Me Babe (live) (gatefold p/s)	8
85	CBA TA 6469	When The Night Comes Falling Down (Full Length Version)/Dark Eyes (12", p/s)	8
86	MCA 23633	Band Of The Hand/M. RUBINI: Theme From Joe's Death (12", p/s)	8
87	CBS 651 148-6	The Usual/Got My Mind Made Up/They Killed Him (12", p/s; mispressing, 3rd track plays either "Drifting Too Far From Shore" or "Precious Memories")	8
89	CBS 655 358-2	Everything Is Broken/Where Teardrops Fall/Dead Man Dead Man/ Ugliest Girl In The World (CD, card sleeve)	8
89	CBS 655 358-3	Everything Is Broken/Where Teardrops Fall/Dead Man Dead Man/ Ugliest Girl In The World (3" CD, gatefold sleeve)	8
90	CBS 655 643-2	Political World/Ring Them Bells/Silvio/All Along The Watchtower (live) (CD)	8
90	CBS 655 643-5	Political World/Caribbean Wind/You're A Big Girl Now/It's All Over Now, Baby Blue (live 17/5/66) (CD, picture disc, no front inlay)	8

EPs

65	CBS EP 6051	DYLAN	40
66	CBS EP 6070	ONE TOO MANY MORNINGS	45
66	CBS EP 6078	MR TAMBOURINE MAN	45

ORIGINAL LPs

62	CBS (S)BPG 62022	BOB DYLAN (mono/stereo)	25
63	CBS (S)BPG 62193	THE FREEWHEELIN' BOB DYLAN (mono/stereo)	30
63	CBS (S)BPG 62251	THE TIMES THEY ARE A-CHANGIN' (mono/stereo)	30
64	CBS (S)BPG 62429	ANOTHER SIDE OF BOB DYLAN (mono/stereo)	30
65	CBS (S)BPG 62515	BRINGING IT ALL BACK HOME (mono/stereo)	30
65	CBS (S)BPG 62572	HIGHWAY 61 REVISITED (mono/stereo)	30
66	CBS (S)BPG 66012	BLONDE ON BLONDE (2-LP, 8 or 9 photos on inside gatefold sleeve, mono/stereo)	60/40
67	CBS BPG 62847	BOB DYLAN'S GREATEST HITS (mono)	15
68	CBS (S)BGP 63252	JOHN WESLEY HARDING (mono/stereo)	22/18

*(The above LPs were originally issued with rough textured labels & flipback sleeves, **without** 'CBS Records' credit on rear sleeve & with inner sleeves advertising other CBS LPs.)*

69	CBS (M/S) 63601	NASHVILLE SKYLINE (mono/stereo)	22/15
74	Island ILPS 9261	PLANET WAVES ('pink rim palm tree' label, with inner sleeve)	12
75	CBS 69097	BLOOD ON THE TRACKS (orange label, red inner with painting or liner notes on rear sleeve)	each 12/15

REISSUE LPs

69	CBS 66012	BLONDE ON BLONDE (2-LP, with 8 or 9 photos on inside gatefold sleeve)	20
70s	CBS 66012	BLONDE ON BLONDE (2-LP, with 12 or 15 photos on inside gatefold sleeve)	15

(The above stereo reissues have smooth orange labels, with 'CBS Records' credit on rear sleeve & with ad. inner sleeves.)

70s	CBS Q 63601	NASHVILLE SKYLINE (quadrophonic)	15
76	CBS Q 86003	DESIRE (quadrophonic)	15

PROMOS

88	CBS SAMPCD 1224	FOREVER YOUNG (CD, 18 tracks)	40
90	CBS XPCD 116	FOREVER YOUNG (CD, 13 tracks)	40

(see also Dick Farina, Band, George Harrison, Traveling Wilburys, Doug Sahm, Earl Scruggs)

MINT VALUE £

DYMONDS
71 Big BG 326 Girl You Are Too Young/RUPIE EDWARDS ALL STARS: Version. 6

DYNAMIC CORVETTES
75 Contempo CS 2059 Funky Music Is The Thing (Parts 1 & 2). 7

DYNAMIC GANG (Bob Andy & Marcia Griffiths)
71 Moodisc MU 3511 I'll Never Believe In You/LLOYD WILLIS: Black Attack 6

DYNAMICS (Jamaica)
68 Blue Cat BS 104 My Friends/NEVILLE IRONS: Soul Glide 20
69 Punch PH 1 The Burner/Juckie Juckie (B-side actually by Tommy McCook & Carl Bryan). . . . 10

DYNAMICS (U.S.)
63 London HLX 9809 Misery/I'm The Man 45
64 King KG 1007 So In Love With Me/Say You Will 18
69 Atlantic 584 270 Ice Cream Song/The Love That I Need 10

DYNAMITES
69 Duke DU 30 John Public/CLANCY ECCLES: Fire Corner (B-side actually by King Stitt) 8
69 Duke DU 31 I Don't Care (actually by Dingle Brothers)/CLANCY ECCLES: Shoo-Be-Do 8
69 Clandisc CLA 200 Mr. Midnight (Skokiaan)/KING STITT: Who Yeah 8
70 Clandisc CLA 212 Black Beret/BARRY & AFFECTIONS: Love Me Tender 10
70 Clandisc CLA 219 Sha La La La/Pop It Up 10
71 Clandisc CLA 237 Hello Mother/FABULOUS FLAMES: Hi-De-Ho 7
69 Trojan/Clandisc TTL 21 FIRE CORNER (LP, with King Stitt) 25

(see also Clancy Eccles & Dynamites, Baba Brooks, Dennis Alcapone, Diamonds, Joe Higgs, Silvertones, Carl Dawkins, Chris Leon, Hopeton Lewis, Melodians, Cynthia Richards, Soul Twins, Stranger & Gladys, Carey & Lloyd)

DYNATONES
59 Top Rank JAR 149 Steel Guitar Rag/The Girl I'm Searching For. 25
59 Top Rank JAR 149 Steel Guitar Rag/The Girl I'm Searching For (78) 20

DYNATONES
66 Pye International 7N 25389 The Fife Piper/And I Always Will 45

ALAN DYSON
68 Pye NPL 18218 THE STILL SMALL VOICE OF ALAN DYSON (LP). 12

RONNIE DYSON
74 CBS 2430 We Can Make It Last Forever/Just A Little Love From Me 8

VINCE EAGER (& THE VAGABONDS)
58 Decca F 11023 Tread Softly Stranger & Yea Yea (as Vince Eager & The Vagabonds; unissued, 2 x 1-sided demos only). . . . . each 25
58 Parlophone R 4482 Five Days, Five Days/No More 30
58 Parlophone R 4482 Five Days, Five Days/No More (78) 15
59 Parlophone R 4531 When's Your Birthday, Baby?/The Railroad Song 20
59 Parlophone R 4531 When's Your Birthday, Baby?/The Railroad Song (78) 30
59 Parlophone R 4550 This Should Go On Forever/No Other Arms, No Other Lips. 20
59 Top Rank JAR 191 Makin' Love/Primrose Lane 7
59 Top Rank JAR 191 Makin' Love/Primrose Lane (78) 70
60 Top Rank JAR 275 Why/El Paso 6
60 Top Rank JAR 307 No Love Have I/Lonely Blue Boy. 8
61 Top Rank JAR 539 (I Wanna) Love My Life Away/I Know What I Want 6
61 Top Rank JAR 593 The World's Loneliest Man/Created In A Dream 6
63 Piccadilly 7N 35110 Any Time Is The Right Time/Heavenly 6
63 Piccadilly 7N 35157 I Shall Not Be Moved/It's Only Make Believe. 5
58 Decca DFE 6504 VINCE EAGER AND THE VAGABONDS NO. 1 (EP) 110
71 Avenue AVE 093 VINCE EAGER PAYS TRIBUTE TO ELVIS PRESLEY (LP) 15

EAGLE
70 Pye International 7N 25530 Kickin' It Back To You/Come In, It's All For Free 7
69 Pye Intl. NSPL 28138 COME UNDER NANCY'S TENT (LP) 30

EAGLES (Jamaica)
69 Songbird SB 1006 Rudam Bam/Prodigal Boy (B-side actually "Any Little Bit" by Crystals). 8
72 Duke Reid DR 2522 Your Enemies Can't Hurt You/Version 7
73 Techniques TE 927 Rub It Down/TOMMY McCOOK ALL STARS: Rub It Down — Version 6

(see also Jamaican Eagles, Roy Richards)

EAGLES (U.K.)
62 Pye 7N 15451 Bristol Express/Johnny's Tune 10
62 Pye 7N 15473 Exodus: The Main Theme/March Of The Eagles 10
62 Pye 7N 15503 The Desperados/Special Agent 10
63 Pye 7N 15550 Come On Baby (To The Floral Dance)/Theme From Station Six Sahara 10
63 Pye 7N 15571 Eagles Nest/Poinciana (unreleased)
64 Pye 7N 15613 Andorra/Moonstruck 10
64 Pye 7N 15650 Write Me A Letter/Wishin' And Hopin'. 18
62 Pye NEP 24166 NEW SOUND T.V. THEMES (EP) 18
63 Pye NPL 18084 SMASH HITS (LP). 50

(see also Valerie Mountain)

EAGLES (U.S.)

72	Asylum AYM 505	Take It Easy/Get You In The Mood (promo only p/s)	8
88	Elektra EKR 10CD	Hotel California/Pretty Maids All In A Row/Hotel California (live) (3" CD)	8
89	Asylum 969 341-2	Take It Easy/One Of These Nights/Desperado/Lyin' Eyes (edit) (3" CD, card sleeve)	8
75	Asylum K 53003	DESPERADO (LP, audiophile pressing, mail-order via *Hi-Fi Today* mag)	25

SNOOKS EAGLIN

60s	Storyville A 45056	Country Boy/Alberta	12
60s	Storyville SEP 386	BLUES ANTHOLOGY VOL. 6 (EP)	20
61	Heritage HLP 1002	SNOOKS EAGLIN (LP, 99 only)	80
63	Storyville SLP 119	NEW ORLEANS STREET SINGER (LP)	20
64	Storyville SLP 140	VOL. 2 — BLUES FROM NEW ORLEANS (LP)	20
70s	Storyville 670 146	PORTRAITS IN BLUES VOLUME 1 (LP)	20

JIM EANES

59	Melodisc 1530	Christmas Doll/It Won't Seem Like Christmas	15

EARCANDY

93	Poor Person Prod. PPPR 1	SPACE IS JUST A PLACE (LP, handmade sleeve, 500 only)	15
94	Poor Person Prod. PPPR 2	TIME IS JUST A STATE OF MIND (LP, handmade sleeve)	15
95	Poor Person Prod. PPPR 5	SOUND IS JUST THE WAY YOU EAR IT (LP, handmade sleeve with insert, numbered, 600 only)	15
95	Poor Person Prod. PPPR 8	TASTING 1,2,3, TASTING (LP, handmade sleeve & insert, numbered, 500 only)	15

ROBERT EARL

58	Philips PB 805	I May Never Pass This Way Again/Someone	6
58	Philips PB 867	More Than Ever (Come Prima)/No One But You (In My Heart)	6
59	Philips PB 891	The Wonderful Secret Of Love/The Boulevard Of Broken Dreams	6
59	Philips PB 960	The Test Of Time/The Key (78)	6
58	Philips BBE 12032	ROBERT EARL (EP)	15
59	Philips BBE 12240	THE WONDERFUL SECRET OF LOVE (EP)	15
60	Philips BBL 7394	SHOWCASE (LP)	20

EARL & DEAN

66	Strike JH 323	Slowly Goin' Out Of My Head/Little Buddy	7

CHARLES EARLAND

76	Mercury 6167 360	Intergalactic Love Song/From My Heart To Yours	5
76	Mercury 6167 414	We All Live In The Jungle/Intergalactic Love Song	5
78	Mercury 6167 703	Let The Music Play/Broken Heart	5
78	Mercury 9199 831	Let The Music Play/Broken Heart (12")	10
70s	Prestige PR 10041	INTENSITY (LP)	12
76	Mercury SRM 11049	ODYSSEY (LP)	12

KENNETH EARLE

60	Decca F 11205	The New Frankie And Johnny/40-30-40	10
60	Decca F 11224	Standing On The Corner/Put Your Arms Around Me, Honey	5

EARL-JEAN

64	Colpix PX 729	I'm Into Somethin' Good/We Love And Learn	18
64	Colpix PX 748	Randy/They're Jealous Of Me	25

(see also Cookies)

EARLS

63	Stateside SS 153	Remember Then/Let's Waddle	40
63	London HL 9702	Never/I Keep-A Tellin' You	50
71	Atlantic 2091 129	Remember Then/I Believe	7

EARLS OF SUAVE

92	Camden Town GNAR 002	A Cheat/Who Will The Next Fool Be (p/s)	5
94	Vinyl Japan PAD 16	In My Dreams/Somebody Buy Me A Drink (p/s)	5

EARTH

69	CBS 4671	Resurrection City/Comical Man	35
69	Decca F 22908	Stranger Of Fortune/Everybody Sing The Song	15

EARTH & FIRE

70	Polydor 56790	Seasons/Paradise	20
71	Nepentha 6129 001	Invitation/Wild And Exciting	18
72	Polydor 2001 356	Memories/From The End To The Beginning	6
73	Polydor 2001 435	Maybe Tomorrow/Theme From Atlantis	6
74	Polydor 2121 235	Love Of Life/Tuffy The Cat	6
71	Nepentha 6437 004	EARTH AND FIRE (LP, gatefold sleeve)	200
73	Polydor 2310 262	ATLANTIS (LP)	18
75	Polydor 2925 033	TO THE WORLD A FUTURE (LP)	15

EARTH BAND

(see under Manfred Mann's Earth Band)

EARTH BOYS

59	Capitol CL 14979	Barbara Ann/Space Girl	18

EARTHLINGS

65	Parlophone R 5242	Landing Of The Daleks/March Of The Robots	40

EARTH OPERA

68	Elektra EKSN 45035	Close Your Eyes And Shut The Door/Dreamless	8
69	Elektra EKSN 45049	American Eagle Tragedy/When You Were Full Of Wonder	7
69	Elektra EKSN 45061	Alfie Finney/Home To You	7
68	Elektra EKS 74016	EARTH OPERA (LP, gatefold sleeve)	40
69	Elektra EKS 74038	GREAT AMERICAN EAGLE TRAGEDY (LP)	22

(see also Rowan Brothers)

MINT VALUE £

EARTHQUAKE

74	Cloud One HIT 4	Friday On My Mind/Madness	5
75	United Artists UP 35787	Tall Order For A Short Guy/Mr Security	5
75	United Artists UAS 29853	LIVE (LP)	12

EARTHQUAKERS

67	Stateside SS 2050	Whistling In The Sunshine/Dreaming In The Moonlight	8

EARTHQUAKES

69	Duke DU 54	Pair Of Wings/I Can't Stop Loving You	10
69	Duke DU 56	Earthquake/Simmering	10

(see also Sir Collins & Earthquakes)

EARTH, WIND & FIRE

71	Warner Bros WB 6125	Help Somebody/Love Is Life	6
73	CBS 1792	Evil/Clover	5
74	CBS 2033	Keep Your Head To The Sky/Build Your Nest	5
74	CBS 2284	Mighty Mighty/Drum Song	5
74	CBS 2782	Kalimba Story/The Nine Chee Bit	5
71	Warner Bros WS 1905	EARTH, WIND & FIRE (LP, with insert)	35
73	CBS 65208	LAST DAYS AND TIME (LP)	15
73	CBS Q 65604	HEAD TO THE SKY (LP, quadrophonic)	15
73	CBS 65604	HEAD TO THE SKY (LP)	12
74	CBS 65844	OPEN OUR EYES (LP, with inner sleeve)	12
75	CBS 80575	THAT'S THE WAY OF THE WORLD (LP, gatefold sleeve with inner)	12

TIM EASLEY

68	Bell BLL 1036	Susie Q (Parts 1 & 2)	8

EAST BAY RAY

84	Alt. Tentacles VIRUS 34	Trouble In Town/Poisonheart (p/s)	5

(see also Dead Kennedys)

EASTER & TOTEM

84	Smoking Beagle/Lyntone LYN 11873/4	HIP REPLACEMENT (LP)	12

EAST MAIN ST. EXPLOSION

69	Fontana TF 1039	Hop, Skip And Jump/Little Jackie Horner	6

EAST OF EDEN

68	Atlantic 584 198	King Of Siam/Ballad Of Harvey Kaye	25
69	Deram DM 242	Northern Hemisphere/Communion	18
70	Deram DM 297	Jig-A-Jig/Marcus Junior	5
71	Deram DM 338	Ramadhan/In The Snow For A Blow/Better Git It In Your Soul/ Have To Whack It Up A Bit	15
72	Harvest HAR 5055	Boogie Woogie 'Flu/Last Dance Of The Clown (p/s)	12
73	United Artists UP 35567	Sin City Girls/All Our Yesterdays	8
69	Deram DML/SML 1038	MERCATOR PROJECTED (LP, mono/stereo)	40/35
70	Deram SML 1050	SNAFU (LP)	30
71	Decca SPA 157	WORLD OF EAST OF EDEN (LP)	12
71	Harvest SHVL 792	EAST OF EDEN (LP)	28
71	Harvest SHVL 796	NEW LEAF (LP)	25

BUGSY EASTWOOD

68	President PT 209	Blackbird Charlie/My Sun	6

(see also Exception)

CLINT EASTWOOD

62	Cameo Parkway C 240	Rowdy/Cowboy Wedding Song (some in p/s)	25/15

EASYBEATS

66	United Artists UP 1144	Come And See Her/Make You Feel Alright (Women)	20
66	United Artists UP 1157	Friday On My Mind/Made My Bed, Gonna Lie In It	8
66	United Artists UP 1175	Who'll Be The One?/Saturday Night	12
67	United Artists UP 1183	Heaven And Hell/Pretty Girl	12
67	United Artists UP 1201	The Music Goes Round My Head/Come In, You'll Get Pneumonia	12
68	United Artists UP 2209	Hello, How Are You?/Falling Off The Edge Of The World	10
68	United Artists UP 2219	The Land Of Make-Believe/We All Live Happily	10
68	United Artists UP 2243	Good Times/Lay Me Down And Die	10
69	Polydor 56335	St. Louis/Can't Find Love	8
70	Polydor 2001 028	(Who Are My) Friends?/Rock'n'Roll Boogie	10
67	United Artists (S)ULP 1167	GOOD FRIDAY (LP)	100
68	United Artists (S)ULP 1193	VIGIL (LP)	60
70	Polydor Special 2482 010	FRIENDS (LP)	60
70s	Hallmark HM 609	EASYBEATS (LP, reissue of "Good Friday")	12

(see also Paintbox, Haffy's Whisky Sour, Harry Vanda, Grapefruit)

EASY RIDERS

58	Philips PB 823	Salute To Windjammer/Kari Waits For Me	5
58	Philips PB 823	Salute To Windjammer/Kari Waits For Me (78)	10
60	London HLR 9204	Young In Love/Saturday's Child	8
60	London HA-R 2323	REMEMBER THE ALAMO (LP, also stereo SAH-R 6126)	16/18

(see also Terry Gilkyson & Easy Riders, Vic Damone, Frankie Laine)

EASY STREET

76	Polydor 2058807	Feels Like Heaven/Shadows On The Wall (no p/s)	10
70s	Muscle Music AP 591	Person To Person/Easy Come Easy Go	30
77	Polydor 2383 444	UNDER THE GLASS (LP)	15

EASYWORLD

90s	Fierce Panda NING 103	Hundredweight/U Make Me Want To Drink Bleach (orange vinyl, 500 only)	15
90s	Zomba 9253377	Try Not To Think/Everyone Knows (die-cut, numbered p/s, 500 only)	8

EATER

77	The Label TLR 001	Outside View/You (p/s)	10
77	The Label TLR 003	Thinkin' Of The USA/Space Dreamin'/Michael's Monetary System (p/s)	10
77	The Label TLR 004	Lock It Up/Jeepster (p/s)	10
77	The Label TLR 004/12	Lock It Up/Jeepster (12", p/s)	8
78	The Label TLR 007	GET YOUR YO-YO'S OUT (EP, white vinyl; blue, green or red p/s)	8
78	The Label TLR 007	GET YOUR YO-YO'S OUT (12" EP, white vinyl; (blue, green or red p/s)	10
78	The Label TLR 009	What She Wants She Needs/Reaching For The Sky (p/s)	6
78	The Label TLRLP 001	THE ALBUM (LP, with inner sleeve)	30
85	De Lorean EAT 1	THE HISTORY OF EATER (LP, 1,000 each on red, white & blue vinyl, with bonus 7" [EAT FREEBIE 1])	12
85	De Lorean EAT 1	THE HISTORY OF EATER (LP, green vinyl)	12

(see also Andy Blade)

EATHOPIANS

69	Nu Beat NB 038	Buss Your Mouth (actually "Contention" by Ethiopians)/REGGAE BOYS: Rough Way Ahead (B-side actually by Keith Blake & Hi-Tals)	12

(see also Ethiopians)

KOOKIE EATON

68	Condor PS 1002	Cream Machine/Joke B-Side	5

EAZIE RYDER

78	Graduate GRAD 1	Motorbikin'/City Lights (p/s)	20

EBONIES

68	Philips BF 1648	Never Gonna Break Your Heart Again/Shoeshine Boy	10

EBONYS

71	CBS 7384	You're The Reason Why/Sexy Ways	8

EBONY SISTERS

69	Bullet BU 401	Let Me Tell You Boy/RHYTHM RULERS: Mannix (B-side actually by Rhythm Rulers)	8
70	Bullet BU 420	Each Time/BUNNY LEE ALLSTARS: Boss Walk	10

(see also Sister)

KATJA EBSTEIN

70	Liberty LBF 15317	No More Love For Me/Without Love	15

ECCENTRICS

65	Pye 7N 15850	What You Got/Fe Fi Fo Fum	40

CLANCY ECCLES (& DYNAMITES)

61	Blue Beat BB 34	River Jordan/I Live And I Love (with Hersan & His City Slickers)	22
61	Blue Beat BB 67	Freedom/More Proof	25
63	Island WI 044	Judgement/Baby Please (B-side actually with Paulette)	22
63	Island WI 098	Glory Hallelujah/Hot Rod (B-side actually by Roland Alphonso)	22
65	Ska Beat JB 194	Sammy No Dead/Roam Jerusalem	20
65	Ska Beat JB 198	Miss Ida/KING ROCKY: What Is Katty	20
67	Doctor Bird DB 1156	Feel The Rhythm/Easy Snapping (B-side actually by Theo Beckford)	20
67	Pama PM 701	What Will Your Mama Say/Darling Don't Do That	15
68	Pama PM 712	The Fight/Great	22
68	Nu Beat NB 006	Festival '68/I Really Love You	15
69	Trojan TR 639	Sweet Africa/Let Us Be Lovers	12
69	Trojan TR 647	Bangarang Crash/DYNAMITES: Rahthid	12
69	Trojan TR 648	Constantinople/Deacon Sun	12
69	Trojan TR 649	Demonstration/VAL BENNETT: My Girl	12
69	Trojan TR 658	Fattie Fattie/SILVERSTARS: Last Call	12
69	Duke DU 9	Auntie Lulu/SLICKERS: Bag A Boo	8
69	Duke DU 31	Shoo-Be-Do/DYNAMITES: I Don't Care (B-side actually by Dingle Brothers)	8
69	Clandisc CLA 201	The World Needs Loving/DYNAMITES: Dollar Train (B-side actually by Clancy Eccles)	10
69	Clandisc CLA 206	Dance Beat/KING STITT: The Ugly One	10
70	Clandisc CLA 209	Open Up/HIGGS & WILSON: Agane (B-side actually "Again")	10
70	Clandisc CLA 211	Promises/Real Sweet (both sides with Dynamites)	10
70	Clandisc CLA 212	Black Beret (with Dynamites)/BARRY & AFFECTIONS: Love Me Tender	10
70	Clandisc CLA 213	Phantom/Skank Me (both sides with Dynamites) (B-side actually by Barry & Affections)	10
70	Clandisc CLA 214	Africa/Africa Part Two (both sides with Dynamites)	10
70	Clandisc CLA 221	Unite Tonight/Uncle Joe	8
70	Clandisc CLA 227	Credit Squeeze/DYNAMITES: Credit Squeeze	8
71	Clandisc CLA 231	Sweet Jamaica/DYNAMITES: Going Up West	8
71	Clandisc CLA 232	Rod Of Correction/Rod Of Correction Version	8
71	Clandisc CLA 235	John Crow Skank/KING STITT: Merry Rhythm	8
71	Clandisc CLA 236	Power For The People/DYNAMITES: Power For The People — Version	8
71	Pama Supreme PS 332	What Will Your Mama Say/TIGER: United We Stand	6
72	Clandisc CLA 239	Hallelujah, Free At Last/DYNAMITES: Sha-La-La	8
69	Trojan TTL 72	FREEDOM (LP)	35
70	Clandisc TBL 124	HERBSMAN REGGAE (LP)	30

(see also Dynamites, Drumbago, Marlene Webber, Westmorelites)

JIMMY ECHO

65	Columbia DB 7629	After Tonight/Practise What You Preach	6

ECHO & THE BUNNYMEN

79	Zoo CAGE 004	The Pictures On My Wall/Read It In Books (p/s, original issue with yellow or grey labels, with "The Revenge Of Voodoo Billy" scratched in B-side run-off)	6
80	Korova KOW 1	Rescue/Simple Stuff (2 different p/s designs)	each 6
80	Korova KOW 1T	Rescue/Simple Stuff/Pride (12", p/s)	8
80	Korova KOW 11	The Puppet/Do It Clean (p/s, limited issue)	7

			MINT VALUE £
81	Korova KOW 15T	A Promise/Broke My Neck (Long Version) (12", p/s)	8
83	Korova KOW 26	The Cutter/Way Out And Up We Go/Zimbo (12", with bonus Peel Session cassette [KOW 26C])	10
83	Korova KOW 26T	The Cutter/Way Out And Up We Go/Zimbo (live) (12", with poster)	8
84	Korova KOW 35F/ SAM 202	Seven Seas/All You Need Is Love//The Killing Moon/Stars Are Stars/ Villiers Terrace (numbered double pack, gatefold p/s)	6
88	Korova KOW 43P	Bring On The Dancing Horses/Over Your Shoulder ('cow'-shaped picture disc in stickered PVC sleeve)	8
88	Korowa KOW 43F/SAM 269	Bring On The Dancing Horses/Over Your Shoulder/Villiers Terrace/Monkeys (double pack)	6
87	WEA YZ 134	The Game/Lost And Found (unreleased alternate p/s without title, promo only)	7
87	WEA YZ 144B	Lips Like Sugar/Rollercoaster (box set with 3 postcards)	6
91	Imaginary FREE 001	Foggy Notion/MOCK TURTLES: Pale Blue Eyes (no p/s, promo only)	5
81	Korova KODE 1	CROCODILES (LP, with bonus 7", "Do It Clean"/"Read It In Books" [SAM 128] & inner sleeve)	12
83	Korova KODE 6	PORCUPINE (LP, with bonus Peel Session cassette [KOW 26C])	15
85	Korova KODE 13	SONGS TO LEARN AND SING (LP, with lyric booklet & 7": "The Pictures On My Wall"/"Read It In Books" [p/s, yellow/blue labels, CAGE 004], no "Voodoo Billy" run-off groove message; some signed)	25/12
85	Korova KODE 13P	SONGS TO LEARN AND SING (LP, picture disc)	12

(see also Ian McCulloch, Will Sergeant)

ECHO BASE

84	DEP International DEP 14	Out Of My Reach/Splash Down (p/s)	15
85	DEP International DEP 19	Puppet At The Go Go/Genius + Soul = Jazz (p/s)	15
85	DEP International LPDEP 9	BUY ME (LP)	18

(see also Ocean Colour Scene)

ECHOES (U.K.)

62	Fontana 267254 TF	Cloak And Dagger/Sounds Like Winter	8
62	Fontana TF 392	The Happy Whistler/Sticks And Stones	7
63	Fontana TF 415	The Jog/Marching Thru'	8
64	Fontana TF 439	My Little Girl/More	8
64	Philips BF 1370	Don't You Believe Them/I'll Get Over You	7
66	Philips BF 1480	Got To Run/Thanks A Lot	7
68	Philips BF 1687	Searchin' For You Baby/Listen To Me Baby	18

ECHOES (U.S.)

60	Top Rank JAR 399	Born To Be With You/My Guiding Light	20
61	Top Rank JAR 553	Baby Blue/Boomerang	22

ECHOES & CELESTIALS (Jamaica)

61	Hornet H 1004	Are You Mine/I'll Love You Forever	18
62	Blue Beat BB 89	Are You Mine/I'll Love You Forever (reissue)	20

BILLY ECKSTINE

53	MGM SP 1011	Kiss Of Fire/I Apologise	15
53	MGM SP 1020	Come To The Mardi Gras/Be Fair	7
53	MGM SP 1040	Coquette/A Fool In Love	6
53	MGM SP 1055	I've Never Been In Love Before/I'll Know	6
53	MGM SP 1060	St. Louis Blues (Parts 1 & 2) (as Billy Eckstine & Metronome All Stars)	6
54	MGM SP 1082	Tenderly/Fortune Telling Cards	8
54	MGM SP 1084	Rendezvous/Don't Get Around Much Anymore	6
54	MGM SP 1095	Seabreeze/Sophisticated Lady	6
54	MGM SP 1101	No One But You/I Let A Song Go Out Of My Heart	15
54	MGM SP 1107	Beloved/Olay Olay (The Bullfighter's Song)	6
55	MGM SP 1117	Mood Indigo/Do Nothin' Till You Hear From Me	6
55	MGM SP 1124	What More Is There To Say?/Prelude To A Kiss	6
55	MGM SP 1136	Love Me Or Leave Me/The Life Of The Party	8
55	MGM SP 1140	More Than You Know/La De Do De Do (Honey Bug Song)	6
56	MGM SP 1153	Farewell To Romance/Lost In Loveliness	6
56	MGM SP 1167	Good-bye/You've Got Me Crying Again	6
56	MGM SP 1170	The Show Must Go On/You'll Get Yours	6
56	MGM MGM 925	Solitude/I Got It Bad (And That Ain't Good)	6
57	MGM MGM 948	A Man Doesn't Know/My Fickle Heart	6
57	HMV POP 341	Pretty, Pretty/Blue Illusion	6
57	MGM MGM 970	Bring Back The Thrill/Over The Rainbow	6
58	Mercury 7MT 191	Boulevard Of Broken Dreams/If I Can Help Somebody	6
58	Mercury 7MT 224	Vertigo/In The Rain	6
58	Mercury MT 224	Vertigo/In The Rain (78, vinyl pressing)	8
58	Mercury AMT 1008	Prisoner Of Love/Funny	5
58	Mercury AMT 1008	Prisoner Of Love/Funny (78)	10
59	Mercury AMT 1018	Gigi/Trust In Me	6
59	Mercury AMT 1018	Gigi/Trust In Me (78)	10
59	Columbia DB 4334	I Want A Little Girl/Lonesome Lover Blues (with Count Basie Orchestra)	5
59	Columbia DB 4334	I Want A Little Girl/Lonesome Lover Blues (78, with Count Basie Orchestra)	10
60	Columbia DB 4407	Anything You Wanna Do (I Wanna Do With You)/Like Wow	5
62	Ember JBS 703	Good Jelly Blues/If That's The Way You Feel	5
65	Tamla Motown TMG 533	Had You Been Around/Down To Earth	80
69	Mercury MF 1103	I Apologise/My Foolish Heart (p/s)	5
69	Mercury MF 1106	Gigi/Coquette (p/s)	5
54	MGM EPC 6	BILLY ECKSTINE (EP, export issue)	12
55	MGM MGM-EP 511	BILLY ECKSTINE (EP)	12
55	MGM MGM-EP 523	THE CASHMERE VOICE (EP)	12
57	MGM MGM-EP 598	FOUR GREAT STANDARDS (EP)	12
57	Parlophone GEP 8672	A DATE WITH RHYTHM (EP, with His All Star Band)	12
57	Mercury ZEP 10005	THE BEST OF MISTER B. NO. 1 (EP)	12
57	Mercury ZEP 10110	BOULEVARD OF BROKEN DREAMS (EP)	12
60	Emarcy JAZZYEP 9509	THE BEST OF MISTER B. NO. 2 (EP)	12

MINT VALUE £

61 Columbia SEG 8042 BASIE-ECKSTINE INCORPORATED (EP; also stereo ESG 7827). 12/15
54 MGM MGM-D 126 TENDERLY (10" LP) 20
56 MGM MGM-D 138 THAT OLD FEELING (10" LP). . . . 20
58 MGM MGM-D 151 A WEAVER OF DREAMS (10" LP) 20
59 Mercury MMB 12002 BILLY ECKSTINE'S IMAGINATION (LP) 15
60 Mercury MMC 14043 BILLY'S BEST (LP) 15
60 Columbia 33SX 1249 ONCE MORE WITH FEELING (LP, also stereo SCX 3322) 15
61 Columbia 33SX 1327 NO COVER, NO MINIMUM (LP, also stereo SCX 3381) 15
62 Ember EMB 3338 MR. B (LP) 12
62 Mercury MMC 14100 AT BASIN STREET EAST (LP, also stereo CMS 18066) 12/15
64 Mercury 20012 MCL NOW SINGING 12 GREAT MOVIES (LP). . . . 15
66 T. Motown (S)TML 11025 THE PRIME OF MY LIFE (LP, mono/stereo) 55/65
67 T. Motown (S)TML 11046 MY WAY (LP, mono/stereo) 45/55
68 Fontana SFL 13039 AT BASIN STREET EAST (LP, reissue) 12
69 T. Motown (S)TML 11101 GENTLE ON MY MIND (LP) 40
71 Stax 2362 013 STORMY (LP) 12
72 Stax 2325 084 SENIOR SOUL (LP) 12

(see also Sarah Vaughan & Billy Eckstine)

ECLECTION

68 Elektra EKSN 45033 Nevertheless/Mark Time 12
68 Elektra EKSN 45040 Another Time, Another Place/Betty Brown 12
68 Elektra EKSN 45042 Please/Saint George And The Dragon 12
68 Elektra EKSN 45046 Please (Mark II)/In The Early Days 10
76 Elektra K 12196 Nevertheless/Please 5
68 Elektra EKL 4023 ECLECTION (LP, gatefold sleeve, also stereo EKS 74023) 100

(see also Fotheringay, Dorris Henderson, Trevor Lucas, Mogul Thrash)

ECSTASY CLUB

88 Hardware HWR 001 JESUS LOVES THE ACID (EP) 15

ECSTASY, PASSION & PAIN

74 Pye International 7N 25641 Don't Burn Your Bridges Behind You/I Wouldn't Give You Up 6
74 Pye International 7N 25660 Good Things Don't Last Forever/Born To Lose You 6
74 Pye International 7N 25669 Ask Me/I'll Take The Blame 10
74 Pye Intl. NSPL 28204 ECSTASY, PASSION & PAIN (LP) 20

ECTOMORPH

90s Woronzow WOO 15 THE FURIOUS SLEEPER (LP, with poster & inserts, 500 only) 20

JASON EDDIE & THE CENTREMEN

65 Parlophone R 5388 Whatcha Gonna Do Baby/Come On Baby (as Jason Eddie & the Centremen) . . 150
66 Parlophone R 5473 Singing The Blues/True To You (as Jason Eddie & the Centremen) 175
69 Tangerine DP 0010 Heart And Soul/Playing The Clown (solo) 50

EDDIE & THE CRAZY JETS

64 King KG 1000 Come On Let's Slop/Down By The Riverside 7

EDDIE & THE HOT RODS

76 Island WIP 6270DJ Writing On The Wall/Cruisin' (In The Lincoln) (promos in generic title p/s) 15
76 Island WIP 6270 Writing On The Wall/Cruisin' (In The Lincoln) (some in black & white p/s) 15/5
76 Island WIP 6306 Wooly Bully/Horseplay (Weary Of The Schmaltz) (p/s) 8
76 Island IEP 2 LIVE AT THE MARQUEE (EP, p/s) 6
76 Island WIP 6354 Teenage Depression/Shake 6
77 Island WIP 6388 I Might Be Lying/Ignore Them 6
77 Island WIP 6401 Do Anything You Wanna Do/Schoolgirl Love (p/s) 6
77 Island 12WIP 6401 Do Anything You Wanna Do/Schoolgirl Love (12", white stickered sleeve) 8
77 Island IEP 5 AT THE SPEED OF SOUND (EP, p/s) 5
77 Island IEP 5 AT THE SPEED OF SOUND (12", plain sleeve) 8
77 Island WIP 6411 Quit This Town/Distortion May Be Expected (p/s) 5
77 Island WIP 6438 Life On The Line/Do Anything You Wanna Do (live) (p/s) 5
77 Island 12WIP 6438 Life On The Line/Do Anything You Wanna Do (live)/(I Don't Know)
What's Really Going On (live)/Why Can't It Be (live) (12", p/s) 8
76 Island ILPS 9457 TEENAGE DEPRESSION (LP, with poster) 15
94 Windsong WINCD 062 BBC RADIO ONE LIVE IN CONCERT (CD, withdrawn) 20

(see also Rods, Rob Tyner & Hot Rods, Lew Lewis)

EDDIE & JERRY

72 Hillcrest HCT 4 Hail Rasta Man Hail/UPSETTERS: Scorcher 5

EDDIE'S CROWD

66 CBS 202078 Baby Don't Look Down/Take It Easy Baby 70

DUANE EDDY (& THE REBELS)

78s

58 London HL 8669 Rebel-Rouser/Stalkin' 20
58 London HL 8723 Ramrod/The Walker (as Duane Eddy & Rebels, actually by Al Casey) 30
58 London HL 8764 Cannonball/Mason-Dixon Lion (as Duane Eddy & Rebels) 30
59 London HLW 8821 The Lonely One/Detour 50
59 London HLW 8879 Peter Gunn/Yep! 40
59 London HLW 8929 Forty Miles Of Bad Road/The Quiet Three 50
59 London HLW 9007 Some Kind-A Earthquake/First Love, First Tears 60
60 London HLW 9050 Bonnie Came Back/Movin 'N' Groovin' 80
60 London HLW 9104 Shazam!/The Secret Seven 120
60 London HLW 9162 Because They're Young/Rebel Walk 100

SINGLES

58 London HL 8669 Rebel-Rouser/Stalkin' (initially with triangular centre, later round centre) 15/7
58 London HL 8723 Ramrod/The Walker (as Duane Eddy & Rebels, actually by Al Casey
tri-centre or round centre) 12/7
58 London HL 8764 Cannonball/Mason-Dixon Lion (as Duane Eddy & Rebels, tri or round centre) . 12/7
59 London HLW 8821 The Lonely One/Detour (triangular centre or round centre) 12/7

(see also Patrick Campbell-Lyons)

			MINT VALUE £
59	London HLW 8879	Peter Gunn/Yep! (triangular or round centre)	10
59	London HLW 8929	Forty Miles Of Bad Road/The Quiet Three (triangular or round centre)	10/6
59	London HLW 9007	Some Kind-A Earthquake/First Love, First Tears	7
60	London HLW 9050	Bonnie Came Back/Movin 'N' Groovin'	7
60	London HLW 9104	Shazam!/The Secret Seven	7
60	London HLW 9162	Because They're Young/Rebel Walk	7
60	London HLW 9225	Kommotion/Theme For Moon Children	7
61	London HLW 9257	Pepe/Lost Friend	6
61	London HLW 9324	Theme From Dixie/The Battle	7
61	London HLW 9370	Ring Of Fire/Gidget Goes Hawaiian	7
61	London HLW 9406	Drivin' Home/My Blue Heaven	7
61	London HLW 9477	The Avenger/Londonderry Air	8
61	Parlophone R 4826	Caravan (Parts 1 & 2) (actually by Al Casey)	10
62	RCA RCA 1288	Deep In The Heart Of Texas/Saints And Sinners	7
62	RCA RCA 1300	The Ballad Of Paladin/Wild Westerner	6
62	RCA RCA 1316	(Dance With The) Guitar Man/Stretchin' Out (with Rebelettes)	6
63	RCA RCA 1329	Boss Guitar/Desert Rat (with Rebelettes)	7
63	RCA RCA 1344	Lonely Boy, Lonely Guitar/Joshin'	7
63	RCA RCA 1357	You're Baby's Gone Surfin'/Shuckin'	8
63	RCA RCA 1369	My Baby Plays The Same Old Song On His Guitar All Night Long/ Guitar'd And Feather'd	8
64	RCA RCA 1389	The Son Of Rebel Rouser/The Story Of Three Loves	8
64	RCA RCA 1425	Guitar Star/The Iguana	8
65	Colpix PX 779	Trash/South Phoenix	12
65	Colpix PX 788	The House Of The Rising Sun/Don't Think Twice, It's All Right	12
66	Reprise RS 20504	Daydream/This Guitar Was Made For Twangin'	15
67	Reprise RS 20557	Monsoon/Roarin'	15
68	Reprise RS 20690	Niki Hoeky/Velvet Nights (Theme From "Elvira Madigan")	15
68	RCA RCA 1701	Dance With The Guitar Man/SAM COOKE: Another Saturday Night (withdrawn)	15
68	London HLW 10191	Peter Gunn/Rebel-Rouser	5
69	CBS 3962	Break My Mind/Loving Bird	8
75	Target 101	Love Confusion/Love Is A Warm Emotion	10
87	Capitol CL 463	Rockestra Theme/Blue City (p/s)	5
87	Capitol 12 CL 463	Rockestra Theme/Rockestra Theme (Version)/Blue City (12", p/s)	8
EXPORT SINGLES			
58	London HL 7057	Ramrod/The Walker (as Duane Eddy & Rebels)	18
59	London HL 7072	The Lonely One/Detour	18
59	London HL 7076	Yep!/Three-30-Blues	30
59	London SLW 4001	Peter Gunn/Yep! (stereo)	90
59	London HL 7080	Forty Miles Of Bad Road/The Quiet Three	18
60	London HL 7090	Bonnie Come Back/Lost Island	30
60	London HL 7096	Because They're Young/Rebel Walk	15
EPs			
58	London RE 1175	REBEL ROUSER (as Douane Eddy)	20
59	London RE-W 1216	THE LONELY ONE	18
59	London RE-W 1217	YEP!	18
60	London RE-W 1252	BECAUSE THEY'RE YOUNG	15
60	London RE-W 1257	TWANGY	15
61	London RE-W 1287	PEPE	15
61	London RE-W 1303	DUANE EDDY PLAYS MOVIE THEMES	15
61	London RE-W 1341	TWANGY NO. 2	20
63	RCA RCX 7115	A COUNTRY TWANG	25
63	RCA RCX 7129	MR. TWANG	35
64	RCA RCX 7146	TWANGIN' UP A SMALL STORM	40
65	Colpix PXE 304	COTTONMOUTH	50
LPs			
58	London HA-W 2160	HAVE 'TWANGY' GUITAR, WILL TRAVEL	30
59	London HA-W 2191	ESPECIALLY FOR YOU (also stereo SAH-W 6045 with different version of "Tuxedo Junction")	22/30
60	London HA-W 2236	THE "TWANG'S" THE "THANG!" (also stereo SAH-W 6068)	18/30
60	London HA-W 2285	SONGS OF OUR HERITAGE (gatefold sleeve, also stereo SAH-W 6119)	22/30
61	London HA-W 2325	A MILLION DOLLARS' WORTH OF TWANG	25
61	London HA-W 2373	GIRLS, GIRLS, GIRLS (also stereo SAH-W 6173)	22/30
62	London HA-W 2435	A MILLION DOLLARS' WORTH OF TWANG VOL. 2	30
62	RCA RD 27264/SF 5134	TWISTIN' AND TWANGIN' (mono/stereo)	22/25
62	RCA RD/SF 7510	TWANGY GUITAR — SILKY STRINGS (mono/stereo)	15/22
63	RCA RD/SF 7545	DANCE WITH THE GUITAR MAN (mono/stereo)	18/22
63	RCA RD/SF 7560	TWANG A COUNTRY SONG (mono/stereo)	18/22
63	RCA RD/SF 7568	TWANGIN' UP A STORM (mono/stereo)	18/22
64	RCA RD/SF 7621	LONELY GUITAR (mono/stereo)	22/25
64	RCA RD/SF 7656	WATER SKIING (mono/stereo)	25/30
65	RCA RD/SF 7689	TWANGIN' THE GOLDEN HITS (mono/stereo)	18/20
65	RCA RD/SF 7754	TWANGSVILLE (mono/stereo)	22/30
65	Colpix PXL 490	DUANE A-GO-GO-GO	20
66	Colpix PXL 494	DUANE EDDY DOES BOB DYLAN	20
67	Reprise R(S)LP 6218	THE BIGGEST TWANG OF THEM ALL (mono/stereo)	15/18
67	Reprise RLP 6240	THE ROARIN' TWANGIES (mono only)	30
67	G. Guinea GG(S)L 10337	DUANE DOES BOB DYLAN (reissue, mono/stereo)	15/22
70	Valiant VS 108	THE BIGGEST TWANG OF THEM ALL	12
70	London ZGW 105	MOVIN' 'N' GROOVIN'	12
75	GTO GTLP 002	GUITAR MAN	12
84	Magnum Force MFM 023	REBEL ROUSIN' (Duane Eddy Convention anniversary issue, with overprinted labels, 200 only)	12

(see also Lee Hazlewood)

PEARL EDDY
54 HMV 7M 262 Devil Lips/That's What A Heart Is For ... 15

EDDY & TEDDY
61 London HLU 9367 Bye Bye Butterfly/Star Crossed Lovers ... 15

EDDYSONS
68 Olga OLE 010 Ups And Downs/Sweet Memories ... 7

DAVID EDE BAND
60 Pye 7N 15280 Easy Go/The Blue Bird (as David Ede & Rabin Rock) ... 10
61 Pye 7N 15329 Obsession/Bootnik ... 10
61 Pye 7N 15370 Last Night/Ding Dong John (as David Ede & Go Man Go Men) ... 30
61 Pye 7N 15394 Twelfth Street Rag/No Hats On Ilkley ... 10
62 Pye 7N 15417 Twistin' Those Meeces To Pieces/Twistin' The Trad ... 10
(see also Oscar Rabin)

TONI EDEN
60 Columbia DB 4409 Teen Street/No One Understands (My Johnny) ... 25
60 Columbia DB 4458 Grown Up Dreams/Whad'ya Gonna Do ... 18
60 Columbia DB 4527 Will I Ever/The Waitin' Game ... 15
61 Decca F 11342 Send Me/Interesting Facts ... 10

EDEN'S CHILDREN
68 Stateside (S)SL 10235 EDEN'S CHILDREN (LP) ... 45

EDEN STREET SKIFFLE GROUP
57 Headquarter & General Stores (no cat. no.) SKIFFLE ALBUM NO. 1 (10 x 7" 78rpm clear flexidiscs in p/s) ... 90

EDGE
78 Albion ION 4 Macho Man/I'm Cold (p/s) ... 5
79 Hurricane FIRE 3 Downhill/American Excess (p/s, white vinyl) ... 6
79 Chiltern Sound CSLP UNEASY PEACE (LP) ... 15
80 Hurricane FLAK 102 SQUARE 1 (LP) ... 15
(see also Damned, Culture Club)

THE EDGE with SINÉAD O'CONNOR
86 Virgin VS 897 Heroine (Theme From "Captive")/Heroine (Mix II) (p/s) ... 5
86 Virgin VS 897-12 Heroine (Theme From "Captive")/Heroine (Mix II) (12", p/s) ... 8
86 Virgin V 2401 CAPTIVE (LP, soundtrack) ... 12
(see also U2, Jah Wobble)

EDISON LIGHTHOUSE
71 Bell BLL 1153 What's Happening/Take A Little Time ... 6
72 Bell BLL 1206 Find Mr. Zebedee?/Reconsider, My Belinda ... 6
(see also Flowerpot Men, White Plains, David & Jonathan, First Class)

HARRY 'SWEETS' EDISON SEXTET
60 HMV POP 720 Hollering At The Watkins/K.M. Blues ... 6
56 Vogue LDE 118 HARRY EDISON QUARTET (LP) ... 15

LADA EDMUND JR
75 MCA MU 172 The Larue/Soul Au Go-Go ... 8

DAVE EDMUNDS (& ROCKPILE)
71 Regal Zonophone RZ 3032 I'm-A Comin' Home/Country Roll ... 15
71 Regal Zonophone RZ 3037 Blue Monday/I'll Get Along ... 15
72 Regal Zonophone RZ 3059 Down, Down, Down/It Ain't Easy ... 15
73 Rockfield ROC 1 Baby I Love You/Maybe ... 6
73 Rockfield ROC 2 Born To Be With You/Pick Axe Rag (with Mickie Gee) ... 7
74 Rockfield ROC 4 Need A Shot Of Rhythm And Blues/Let It Be Me ... 7
75 Rockfield ROC 6 I Ain't Never/Some Other Guy ... 7
76 Swan Song SSK 19408 Here Comes The Weekend/As Lovers Do ... 5
76 Swan Song SSK 19409 Where Or When/New York's A Lonely Town ... 5
77 Swan Song SSK 19410 Ju Ju Man/What Did I Do Last Night? ... 5
77 Swan Song SSK 19411 I Knew The Bride/Back To Schooldays ... 5
78 Swan Song SSK 19413 Deborah/What Looks Best On You ... 5
79 Swan Song SSK 19418 Girls Talk/Bad Is Bad (p/s, clear vinyl) ... 5
90 Capitol 10CL 568 King Of Love/Stay With Me Tonight (45rpm)/King Of Love (78 rpm) (10", p/s) ... 20
90 Capitol 12CL 568 King Of Love/Stay With Me Tonight/Every Time I See Her (12", p/s) ... 8
71 Regal Zono. SRZA 8503 ROCKPILE COLLECTION (LP, unreleased)
72 Regal Zono. SLRZ 1026 ROCKPILE (LP) ... 30
75 Rockfield RRL 101 SUBTLE AS A FLYING MALLET (LP) ... 15
82 Arista SPART 1184 DE 7TH (LP, with bonus EP "Live At The Venue" [JUKE 1]) ... 12
(see also Image, Human Beans, Love Sculpture, Rockpile, Andy Fairweather-Low)

EDOUARD
66 CBS 202200 My Name Is Edouard/N'aie Pas Peur Antoinette (p/s) ... 10

EDSELS
61 Pye International 7N 25086 Rama Lama Ding Dong/Bells ... 130

IAN EDWARD & ZODIACS
(see under Ian & Zodiacs)

(KING) EDWARDS GROUP
63 Island WI 040 Dear Hearts/Oh Mary (B-side actually by Ransford Barnett) ... 20
63 Island WI 047 Russian Roulette (actually by King Edwards All Stars)/You're Mine (actually by Douglas Brothers) ... 25
63 Island WI 082 He Gave You To Me/Kings Priests And Prophets (both actually by The Schoolboys) ... 18
63 Island WI 087 Hey Girl/Skies Are Grey (both actually by Ransford Barnett) ... 15

MINT VALUE £

ADINA EDWARDS

72 Dynamic DYN 454 Talk About Love/Don't Forget To Remember . . . 6
60s Tabernacle TLP 1005 JESUS IS MINE (LP) . . . 20
(see also Coxsone Dodd)

BOBBY EDWARDS

61 Top Rank JAR 584 You're The Reason/I'm A Fool Loving You . . . 15

BRENT EDWARDS

63 Pye International 7N 25197 Pride/Over The Weekend . . . 12

CHUCK EDWARDS

68 Soul City SC 104 Downtown Soulville/I Need You . . . 15

GARY EDWARDS (COMBO)

62 Oriole CB 1700 Twist Or Bust/The Franz Liszt Twist (as Gary Edwards Combo) . . . 12
62 Oriole CB 1717 The Method/Twistful Thinkin' . . . 8
62 Oriole CB 1733 Africa/One Fifteen A.M. . . . 12
62 Oriole CB 1759 Hopscotch/Theme For A Broken Dream . . . 20

(WILFRED) JACKIE EDWARDS

60 Starlite ST45 016 We're Gonna Love/Your Eyes Are Dreaming (as Wilfred Edwards & Caribs) . . . 12
60 Starlite ST45 026 I Know/Tell Me Darling (as Wilfred Edwards) . . . 12
61 Starlite ST45 046 Whenever There's Moonlight/Heaven Just Knows (as Wilfred Edwards) . . . 12
61 Starlite ST45 062 More Than Words Can Say/I Love You No More (as Wilfred Edwards) . . . 12
62 Starlite ST45 076 Little Bitty Girl/Never Go Away (as Wilfred Edwards) . . . 12
62 Island WI 008 All My Days/Hear Me Cry (as Wilfred Jackie Edwards) . . . 12
62 Island WI 019 One More Week/Tears Like Rain (as Wilfred Edwards) . . . 12
62 Decca F 11547 Lonely Game/Suddenly . . . 8
63 Black Swan WI 404 Why Make Believe/Do You Want Me (as Wilfred Jackie Edwards & Velvetts) . . . 15
64 Black Swan WI 416 The Things You Do/Little Smile (as Wilfred Jackie Edwards) . . . 15
64 Fontana TF 465 Sea Cruise/Little Princess . . . 15
64 Sue WI 329 Stagger Lee/Pretty Girl . . . 22
65 Aladdin WI 601 He'll Have To Go/Gotta Learn To Love Again . . . 12
65 Aladdin WI 605 Hush/I Am In Love With You No More . . . 12
65 Aladdin WI 611 The Same One/I Don't Know . . . 12
65 Island WI 255 White Christmas/My Love And I . . . 10
66 Island WI 270 Sometimes/Come On Home . . . 15
66 Island WI 274 L-O-V-E/What's Your Name . . . 10
66 Island WI 287 Think Twice/Oh Mary . . . 10
66 Island WI 3006 I Feel So Bad/I Don't Want To Be Made A Fool Of . . . 100
66 Island WI 3018 Royal Telephone/It's No Secret . . . 8
67 Island WI 3030 Only A Fool Breaks His Own Heart/The End . . . 8
67 Island WIP 6008 Come Back Girl/Tell Him You Lied . . . 5
68 Island WIP 6026 Julie On My Mind/If This Is Heaven . . . 5
68 Island WI 3157 You're My Girl/Heaven Only Knows . . . 10
69 Direction 58-4096 Why Must I Be Alone/I'm Gonna Make You Cry . . . 5
69 Direction 58-4402 Too Experienced/Someone To Love . . . 5
69 Direction 58-4630 Oh Manio/Here We Go Again . . . 5
70 CBS 5147 Tell Me Why Say Goodbye/Walter Walter . . . 5
71 Horse HOSS 1 I Must Go Back/Baby I Want To Be Near You (some in p/s) . . . 8/5
66 St. Mary's IEP 701 SACRED HYMNS VOL. 1 (EP, some in p/s) . . . 35/18
66 St. Mary's IEP 702 SACRED HYMNS VOL. 2 (EP, with St. Mary's label, some in p/s) . . . 35/18
66 St. Mary's IEP 702 SACRED HYMNS VOL. 2 (EP, with red-and-white Island label; some in p/s) . . . 35/18
66 Island IEP 708 HUSH! (EP) . . . 30
64 Island ILP 906 THE MOST OF WILFRED JACKIE EDWARDS (LP) . . . 40
64 Island ILP 912 STAND UP FOR JESUS (LP) . . . 40
66 Island ILP 931 COME ON HOME (LP) . . . 40
66 Island ILP 936 THE BEST OF JACKIE EDWARDS (LP) . . . 40
66 Island ILP 940 BY DEMAND (LP) . . . 40
67 Island ILP(S) 960 PREMATURE GOLDEN SANDS (LP) . . . 40
69 Island IWP 4 PUT YOUR TEARS AWAY (LP) . . . 40
69 Direction 8-63977 LET IT BE ME (LP) . . . 18
70 Trojan TTL 40 THE MOST OF WILFRED JACKIE EDWARDS (LP, as Wilfred Jackie Edwards) . . . 15
70 Trojan TTL 45 COME ON HOME (LP) . . . 15
70 Trojan TTL 46 BY DEMAND (LP) . . . 15
70 Trojan TTL 57 PREMATURE GOLDEN SANDS (LP, reissue) . . . 15
(see also Wilfred & Millicent, Wilfred & Millie, Jackie & Millie)

JACKIE EDWARDS & JIMMY CLIFF

68 Island WIP 6036 Set Me Free/Here I Come . . . 6
68 Island WIP 6042 You're My Girl/Heaven Only Knows . . . 6
(see also Jackie & Millie, Millie, Jimmy Cliff, Wilfred & Millie)

JIMMY EDWARDS (U.K.)

60 Fontana H 260 I've Never Seen A Straight Banana/Rhymes . . . 10
60 Fontana TFE 17296 JIMMY EDWARDS SINGS "PA GLUM" (EP) . . . 25
60 Fontana TFL 5103 TAKE IT FROM HERE (LP, with Dick Bentley & June Whitfield) . . . 35
(see also Joy Nichols)

JIMMY EDWARDS (U.S.)

58 Mercury 7MT 193 Love Bug Crawl/Honey Lovin' . . . 550
58 Mercury MT 193 Love Bug Crawl/Honey Lovin' (78) . . . 125

JIMMY EDWARDS (& PROFILE)

79 Warner Bros K 17415 Nora's Diary/Call Me A Fraud (features Sham 69) (p/s) . . . 20
79 Warner Bros K 17464 Twentieth Century Time/Seven Hail Marys (features Pretenders) (p/s) . . . 6
80 Polydor 2059 240 Toys/Hard Heart (p/s) . . . 5
80 Polydor 2059 256 Cabaret/Drag It Back (p/s, solo) . . . 5
81 Polydor POSP 240 In The City/Five Minute Girl (p/s, solo) . . . 5
(see also Time U.K., Pretenders, Sham 69)

MINT VALUE £

JONATHAN & DARLENE EDWARDS

58	Philips PB 789	It's Magic (as Jonathan Edwards)/It Might As Well Be Spring (78)	6
57	Philips BBE 12155	THE PIANO ARTISTRY OF JONATHAN EDWARDS (EP)	8
58	Philips BBE 12179	THE PIANO ARTISTRY OF JONATHAN EDWARDS NO. 2 (EP)	8
60	Philips BBL 7412	JONATHAN & DARLENE EDWARDS IN PARIS (LP, also stereo SBBL 590)	10/12

(see also Gordon MacRae, Jo Stafford)

MILL EDWARDS

73	Action ACT 4617	I Found Myself/Don't Forget About Me	7

PAUL EDWARDS

76	Cottage COT 301	LONGSTONE FARM (LP)	15

R. EDWARDS & SOCIAL EAGLES

73	Dip DL 5014	One Sunday Morning/Version Sunday Morning (with Allstars)	6
73	Dip DL 5014	One Sunday Morning/AFRICAN BROTHERS: Mysterious Nature (2nd issue, different B-side)	10

RUPIE EDWARDS (ALL STARS)

62	Blue Beat BB 90	Guilty Convict/Just Because (as Rupert Edwards & Smithie's Sextet)	22
68	Doctor Bird DB 1163	I Can't Forget/I'm Writing Again	22
69	Crab CRAB 35	Long Lost Love/Uncertain Love	10
70	Crab CRAB 41	Sharp Pan Ya Machete/Redemption	10
70	Explosion EX 2030	Full Moon/Baby	6
70	Explosion EX 2031	Love At First Sight/I Need Your Care	6
71	Bullet BU 494	I'm Gonna Live Some Life/RUPIE EDWARDS ALLSTARS: Rock 'In'	6
71	Nu Beat NB 082	Black Man/Tell The People	8
71	Nu Beat NB 091	One In Three/ERROLL DUNKLEY: Three In One	6
71	Big BG 320	Soulful Stew/Soulful Stew — Version Two (as Rupie Edwards Allstars)	8
71	Big BG 324	Deep Meditation (version)/ERROLL DUNKLEY: Deep Meditation	18
71	Big BG 327	One In Three/ERROLL DUNKLEY: Three In One	6
72	Big BG 333	Press Along/Press Along — Version (as Rupie Edwards Allstars)	6
72	Big BG 335	Jimmy As Job Card (actually titled "Jimmy Has A Job Card")/ Riot (as Rupie Edwards Allstars)	10
72	Big BG 337	Christmas Parade (actually by Rupie Edwards Allstars)/ UNDERGROUND PEOPLE: Santa	5

(see also R. Edwards & Social Eagles, Gaylads, Heptones, Ethiopians, Dymonds, Dobby Dobson, Keith Cole, Country Boy, Keith Cole, Laurel Aitken, Dennis Alcapone, Gregory Isaacs, Itals, Hugh Roy, Kingstonians, Little George, Mediators, Max Romeo, I Roy, B.B. Seaton, Soul Kings, Joe White)

SAMUEL EDWARDS

69	Blue Cat BS 159	Want It Want It/SPARKERS: Israel	18

TOM EDWARDS

57	Vogue Coral Q 72236	What Is A Teen Age Girl?/What Is A Teen Age Boy?	8

TOMMY EDWARDS

52	MGM MGM 466	It's All In The Game/My Concerto (78)	8
52	MGM MGM 540	Easy To Say/Greatest Sinner Of Them All (78)	8
52	MGM MGM 567	Piano Bass And Drums/Sinner Or Saint (78)	8
53	MGM MGM 598	(Now And Then, There's) A Fool Such As I/Take These Chains From My Heart (78)	10
53	MGM SP 1030	(Now And Then, There's) A Fool Such As I/Take These Chains From My Heart	12
56	MGM SP 1168	Baby, Let Me Take You Dreaming/MARION SISTERS: Life Could Not Be Better	18
56	MGM MGM 894	Baby, Let Me Take You Dreaming/MARION SISTERS: Life Could Not Better Be (78)	8
58	MGM MGM 989	It's All In The Game/Please Love Me Forever	6
58	MGM MGM 995	Mr. Music Man/Love Is All We Need	6
58	MGM MGM 995	Mr. Music Man/Love Is All We Need (78)	8
59	MGM MGM 1006	Please, Mr. Sun/The Morning Side Of The Mountain	6
59	MGM MGM 1006	Please, Mr. Sun/The Morning Side Of The Mountain (78)	12
59	MGM MGM 1020	My Melancholy Baby/It's Only The Good Times	6
59	MGM MGM 1020	My Melancholy Baby/It's Only The Good Times (78)	18
59	MGM MGM 1032	I've Been There/I Looked At Heaven	6
59	MGM MGM 1045	(New In) The Ways Of Love/Honestly And Truly	6
60	MGM MGM 1065	Don't Fence Me In/I'm Building Castles Again	6
60	MGM MGM 1080	I Really Don't Want To Know/Unloved	6
60	MGM MGM 1097	Blue Heartaches/It's Not The End Of Everything	6
60	MGM MGM 1113	As You Desire Me/Suzie Wong	6
61	MGM MGM 1130	The Golden Chain/That's The Way With Love	6
62	MGM MGM 1156	The Tables Are Turning/I'll Cry You Out Of My Heart	6
59	MGM MGM-EP 707	I'VE BEEN THERE (EP)	35
60	MGM MGM-EP 712	THE WAYS OF LOVE (EP)	35
59	MGM MGM-C 774	IT'S ALL IN THE GAME (LP)	55
59	MGM MGM-C 791	FOR YOUNG LOVERS (LP)	40
60	MGM MGM-C 824	YOU STARTED ME DREAMING (LP)	40

TYRONE EDWARDS

74	Invictus S INV 2542	Can't Get Enough Of You/You Took Me From A World Outside	7

VINCE EDWARDS (U.K.)

67	United Artists UP 1179	I Can't Turn Back Time/The Lively One	8
68	United Artists UP 2230	County Durham Dream/It's The Same Old Song	6
68	United Artists UP 2236	Aquarius/Hair	5

VINCE EDWARDS (U.S.)

58	Capitol CL 14825	Widget/Lollipop	6
64	Colpix PX 771	No Not Much/See That Girl (p/s)	10
62	Brunswick OE 9498	VINCE EDWARDS SINGS (EP)	10
62	Brunswick LAT 8515	VINCE EDWARDS SINGS (LP)	12
60s	United Artists	BEN CASEY (LP)	12

MINT VALUE £

WILFRED EDWARDS
(see under Jackie Edwards)

EDWARDS HAND
71 RCA SF 8154 — STRANDED (LP) . . . 22
73 Regal Zono. SRZA 8513 — RAINSHINE (LP, unissued, demos only) . . . 100+
(see also Picadilly Line)

EDWICK RUMBOLD
66 CBS 202393 — Specially When/Come Back . . . 60
67 Parlophone R 5622 — Shades Of Grey/Boggle Woggle . . . 70

E.F. BAND
80 Rok ROK XI/XII — Another Day Gone/SYNCHROMESH: October Friday (die-cut co. sleeve) . . . 30
80 Aerco/EF Band EF 1 — Night Angel/Another Day Gone (some with p/s) . . . 30/15
80 Redball RR 026 — Self Made Suicide/Sister Syne (some with wraparound p/s) . . . 30/7
80 Redball RR 036 — The Devil's Eye/Comprende (some with wraparound p/s) . . . 25/7
83 Bullet CULP 2 — DEEP CUT (LP) . . . 15

WALTER EGAN
77 United Artists UP 36245 — Only The Lucky/I'd Rather Have Fun . . . 5

WILLIE EGANS
60s XX MIN 714 — WILLIE EGANS (EP) . . . 20
70s Flyright LP 6000 — ROCKS, BOOGIES AND ROLLS (LP) . . . 15

JULIE EGE
71 CBS 5431 — Love/In One Of Your Weaker Moments . . . 10

JOSEPH EGER
70 Charisma CAS 1008 — CLASSICAL HEADS (LP) . . . 15

EGG
69 Deram DM 269 — Seven Is A Jolly Good Time/You Are All Princes . . . 20
70 Deram Nova (S)DN 14 — EGG (LP) . . . 30
71 Deram SML 1074 — THE POLITE FORCE (LP) . . . 35
74 Caroline C 1510 — THE CIVIL SURFACE (LP) . . . 25
(see also Hatfield & The North, Arzachel, Bunch Of Fives, Khan)

EGGY
69 Spark SRL 1024 — Hookey/You're Still Mine . . . 20

EGYPT
88 HTD 7HTD 1 — Crazy Horses /Got No Fear (p/s) . . . 10
88 HTD HTD LP 1 — EGYPT (LP, with inner) . . . 15

EIFFEL TOWER
69 Chappell LPC 1032 — THE EIFFEL TOWER (LP, library edition) . . . 50

8-EYED SPY
82 Fetish FE 19 — Diddy Wah Diddy/Dead You Me B Side (p/s) . . . 12
81 Fetish FR 2003 — 8-EYED SPY (LP) . . . 20
(see also Lydia Lunch)

EIGHTH DAY
71 Invictus INV 514 — She's Not Just Another Woman/I Can't Fool Myself . . . 7
72 Invictus INV 521 — Eeny Meeny Miny Mo/Rocks In My Head . . . 7

801
76 Island ILPS 9444 — 801 LIVE (LP) . . . 12
(see also Phil Manzanera, Roxy Music, Brian Eno)

EIGHTH WONDER
85 CBS QTX 6594 — Stay With Me/Loser In Love/Open Your Mind (12", poster p/s) . . . 8
87 CBS PHONE P1 — When The Phone Stops Ringing (Single Version)/Let Me In (picture disc) . . . 5
88 CBS SCARE Y1 — I'm Not Scared/I'm Not Scared (Disco Mix)/J'ai Pas Peur (10", p/s, with PSB) . . . 18
88 CBS SCAREC 1 — I'm Not Scared (Disco Mix)/I'm Not Scared/J'ai Pas Peur (CD, with PSB) . . . 25
(see also Pet Shop Boys, Rock Aid Armenia)

EIGHTIES LADIES
86 Music Of Life MOLIF 6 — Turned On To You/Turned On To You (Alternative Mix) (12", p/s) . . . 15
(see also Roy Ayers)

808 STATE
88 Creed STATE 003 — Let Yourself Go (303 Mix)/Let Yourself Go (D50 Mix)/Deepville (12", plain stickered sleeve) . . . 10
89 ZTT ZANG 1TX — Pacific — 909 (Mellow Birds Mega Edit)/Bonus Bird Beats/Cobra Bora (12", plain stickered sleeve) . . . 10
89 ZTT ZANG 1CD — Pacific 202/Pacific State Origin/Pacific 303/Cobra Bora Shortcut (3" CD) . . . 12
89 ZTT ZANG 2CD — THE EXTENDED PLEASURES OF DANCE EP (CD, withdrawn) . . . 30
91 ZTT ZANG 14CD — IN YER FACE EP (CD) . . . 8
91 ZTT ZANG 19CD — Ooops!/Ski Family/808091 (live) (CD, featuring Björk) . . . 8
93 ZTT SAM 933 — 10 X 10 (Vox Mix)/10 X 10 (Beats Version) (12", promo only) . . . 8
88 Creed STATE 002 — NEWBUILD (LP) . . . 20
(see also Hit Squad)

EINSTÜRZENDE NEUBAUTEN
85 Some Bizzare BART 12 — Yü-Gung/Seelebrennt/Sand (12", p/s) . . . 10
85 Some Bizzare BART 451 — Das Schaben/Das Schaben (LP freebie, no p/s) . . . 8

EIRE APPARENT
67 Track 604 019 — Follow Me/Here I Go Again . . . 20
69 Buddah 201 039 — Rock'N'Roll Band/Yes I Need Someone . . . 30
72 Buddah 2011 117 — Rock'N'Roll Band/Yes I Need Someone (reissue) . . . 10
69 Buddah 203 021 — SUN RISE (LP, featuring Jimi Hendrix) . . . 60
(see also Ernie Graham, Henry McCulloch)

MINT VALUE £

EJECTED

82	Riot City RIOT 14	HAVE YOU GOT 10p? (EP)	10
82	Riot City RIOT 19	NOISE FOR THE BOYS (EP)	10
83	Riot City RIOT 28	PRESS THE BUTTON (EP)	8
82	Riot City CITY 003	A TOUCH OF CLASS (LP)	25
83	Riot City CITY 007	THE SPIRIT OF REBELLION (LP)	25

BRITT EKLAND

79	Jet JET 161	Do It To Me (Once More With Feeling)/Private Party (gatefold p/s)	5
79	Jet JETP 161	Do It To Me (Once More With Feeling)/Private Party (picture disc)	10
79	Jet JET 12161	Do It To Me (Once More With Feeling)/Private Party (12", foldout p/s)	8

(see also Britt)

EKSEN TRICK BRICK BAND

78	Aerco AERL 17	SKY STORY (LP, with insert)	30

EKSEPTION

70	Philips 318 992 BF	Air/Dharma For One	5
72	Philips 6012 219	Ava Maria/Dharma For One	5
69	Philips 6314 001	BEGGAR JULIAN'S TIME TRIP (LP)	15
70	Philips 6314 005	EKSEPTION (LP)	18
71	Philips 6423 005	EKSEPTION III (LP)	15
72	Philips 6423 019	00.04 (LP)	15
72	Philips 6423 042	V (LP)	15
74	Philips 6423 079	CLASSICS IN POP (LP)	12
75	Philips 6423 082	MIND MIRROR (LP)	12
75	Philips 6314 044	EKSEPTIONAL CLASSICS (LP)	12

MARGARET ELAINA

73	Bullet BU 522	Ben/RICHIE & NOW GENERATION: Laughing Stock Version	5

ELAINE

63	Columbia DB 7091	I Never Wonder Where My Baby Goes/Look But Don't Touch	10

ELASTICA

93	Deceptive BLUFF 003	Stutter/Pussycat (numbered die-cut sleeve, 1,500 only)	22
94	Deceptive BLUFF 004	Line Up/Vaseline (numbered die-cut sleeve, 1,500 only)	8
94	Deceptive BLUFF 010	Connection/See That Animal (numbered die-cut sleeve, 3,000 only)	7
95	Deceptive BLUFF 011	Waking Up/Gloria (numbered die-cut sleeve, 5,000 only)	7
95	Deceptive BLUFF 011	Waking Up/Gloria (12", p/s)	8
95	Deceptive BLUFF 014LP	ELASTICA (LP, with flexidisc & booklet, no'd & stickered sleeve, 5,000 only)	15

(see also Suede)

ELASTIC BAND

68	Decca F 12763	Think Of You Baby/It's Been A Long Time Baby	25
68	Decca F 12815	Do Unto Others (From "Mr. Rose" T.V. Series)/8½ Hours Of Paradise	25
69	Decca Nova (S)DN 6	EXPANSIONS ON LIFE (LP, mono/stereo)	50/40

(see also Mayfield's Mule, Sweet, Andy Scott, Love Affair, Northwind)

ELASTICK BAND

67	Stateside SS 2056	Spazz/Papier Mache (unissued, demos only)	300
68	Decca F 12815	Do Unto Others/8 Half Hours Of Paradse	35

ELASTIC OZ BAND

(see under Bill Elliott)

DONNIE ELBERT

58	Parlophone R 4403	Let's Do The Stroll/Wild Child	125
58	Parlophone R 4403	Let's Do The Stroll/Wild Child (78)	75
65	Sue WI 377	A Little Piece Of Leather/Do Wat'cha Wanna	25
65	Sue WI 396	You Can Push It (Or Pull It)/Lily Lou	22
67	CBS 2807	Get Ready/Along Came Pride	8
68	Polydor BM 56234	In Between The Heartaches/Too Far Gone	18
68	Polydor BM 56265	This Old Heart Of Mine (Is Weak For You)/Run Little Girl	10
68	New Wave NW 001	Baby Please Come Home/Without You	7
69	Deram DM 235	Without You/Baby Please Come Home (reissue)	6
69	R&B UP 2000	Without You/(different B-side) (white label test pressing only)	8
72	Epic EPC 7943	Get Ready/Alone Came Pride	6
72	Mojo 2092 040	This Old Heart Of Mine (Is Weak For You)/Good To Me	6
72	Jay Boy BOY 70	Half As Old/Baby Let Me Love You Tonite	6
97	Joe Boy JBV 1	So Soon/Can't Get Over Losing You (p/s with numbered certificate, 300 only)	18
69	Polydor 236 560	TRIBUTE TO A KING (LP)	22
73	Ember EMB 3421	THE ROOTS OF DONNIE ELBERT (LP)	18

ELBOW

02	V2 VVR 5016160	Powder/(Nady Votel Mix)/About Time (Acoustic Version) (10", p/s)	8
00	UglyMan UGLY 25	THE ANY DAY NOW EP: Any Day Now (Radio Edit)/Wurzel/George Lassoes The Moon/Don't Mix Your Drinks (CD)	8

ELCORT

66	Parlophone R 5447	Tammy/Searchin'	12

ERIC ELDER

70	Philips 6006 081	San Tokay/Sunflower	5

ELDORADOS (Jamaica)

70	Bullet BU 428	Savage Colt/The Clea Hog	8

ELDORADOS (Rhodesia)

63	Decca DFE 8543	THE ELDORADOS (EP)	110

ELDORADOS (U.S.)

72	Mojo 2092 050	Loose Booty (Parts 1 & 2)	8

MINT VALUE £

ROY ELDRIDGE & CLAUDE BOLLING

56 Vogue V 2373 — Wild Man Blues/Fireworks . . . 12

ROY ELDRIDGE QUINTET

58 Columbia/Clef SEB 10085 — DIXIELAND BLUES (EP) . . . 8
60 HMV 7EG 8682 — SWINGING ON THE TOWN (EP) . . . 8
55 Columbia/Clef 33C 9005 — ROY ELDRIDGE QUINTET (LP) . . . 15

ELECAMPANE

75 Dame Jane ODJ 1 — WHEN GOD'S ON THE WATER (LP, private pressing with insert) . . . 120
78 Dame Jane ODJ 2 — FURTHER ADVENTURES OF MR PUNCH (LP, private pressing with booklet) . . . 50

ELECTRIC BANANA

67 De Wolfe DW/LP 3040 — ELECTRIC BANANA (LP, 10", original issue, tricolour label) . . . 80
67 De Wolfe DWLP 3040 — ELECTRIC BANANA (LP, second issue, with other artists) . . . 30
68 De Wolfe DWLP 3069 — MORE ELECTRIC BANANA (LP) . . . 65
69 De Wolfe DWLP 3123 — EVEN MORE ELECTRIC BANANA (LP) . . . 45
73 De Wolfe DWLP 3284 — HOT LICKS (LP) . . . 40
76 De Wolfe DWLP 3381 — THE RETURN OF THE ELECTRIC BANANA (LP) . . . 25
79 Butt NOTT 001 — THE SEVENTIES (LP) . . . 18
80 Butt NOTT 003 — THE SIXTIES (LP) . . . 18
97 Tenth Planet TP 031 — THE ELECTRIC BANANA BLOWS YOUR MIND (LP, numbered, 1,000 only) . . . 15

(see also Pretty Things, Zac Zolar & Electric Banana)

ELECTRIC CHAIRS

(see under Wayne/Jayne County)

ELECTRIC CRAYONS

89 Emergency MIV 3 — Hip Shake Junkie/Happy To Be Hated (p/s) . . . 15

(see also Charlatans)

ELECTRIC EELS (U.S.)

(see under Die Electric Eels)

ELECTRIC FLAG

68 CBS 3584 — Groovin' Is Easy/Over-Lovin' You . . . 7
69 CBS 4066 — Sunny/Soul Searchin' . . . 7
68 CBS 62394 — A LONG TIME COMIN' (LP) . . . 18
69 CBS 63462 — THE ELECTRIC FLAG — AN AMERICAN MUSIC BAND (LP) . . . 20
71 CBS 64337 — THE BEST OF ELECTRIC FLAG (LP) . . . 12
75 Atlantic K 50090 — THE BAND KEPT PLAYING (LP) . . . 12

(see also Mike Bloomfield, Buddy Miles, Barry Goldberg)

ELECTRIC GUITARS

81 Fried Egg EGG 12 — Health/The Continental Shelf (p/s, with insert) . . . 5

ELECTRICIANS

67 Columbia DB 8228 — Champion House Theme/DON HARPER & ELECTRICIANS: Shin Bone . . . 7

(see also Don Harper)

ELECTRIC INDIAN

69 United Artists UP 35039 — Keem-O-Sabe/Broad Street . . . 8

(see also Len Barry)

ELECTRIC JOHNNY

61 London HLU 9384 — Black-Eyes Rock/Johnny On His Strings . . . 40

ELECTRIC LIGHT ORCHESTRA (E.L.O.)

SINGLES

72 Harvest HAR 5053 — 10538 Overture/1st Movement (Jumping Biz) . . . 6
72 Harvest HAR 5063 — Roll Over Beethoven/Manhattan Rumble (49th Street Massacre) (with withdrawn B-side) . . . 12
72 Harvest HAR 5063 — Roll Over Beethoven/Queen Of The Hours . . . 5
73 Harvest HAR 5077 — Showdown/In Old England Town (Boogie 2) (Instrumental) . . . 8
74 Warner Brothers K 16349 — Ma-Ma-Ma Belle/Oh No Not Susan . . . 5
75 Warner Bros K 16510 — Can't Get It Out Of My Head/Illusions In G Major . . . 6
75 Jet JET 764 — Evil Woman/10538 Overture (live) . . . 5
76 Jet JET 769 — Night Rider/Daybreaker (live) . . . 6
76 Jet JET 779 — Strange Magic/Showdown (live) . . . 5
76 Jet UP 36184 — Livin' Thing/Fire On High (blue vinyl) . . . 8
77 Jet UP 36209 — Rockaria!/Poker (p/s) . . . 5
77 Jet UP 36254 — Telephone Line/Poor Boy (The Greenwood)/King Of The Universe . . . 5
77 Harvest HAR 5121 — Showdown/Roll Over Beethoven (p/s) . . . 5
77 Harvest HAR 12-5121 — Showdown/Roll Over Beethoven (12", p/s) . . . 10
77 Harvest PSLP 213 — Showdown/Roll Over Beethoven (12", promo-only art sleeve) . . . 12
77 Jet UP 36313 — Turn To Stone/Mr. Kingdom (p/s) . . . 5
77 Jet UP 36342 — Mr. Blue Sky/One Summer Dream (p/s, some on blue vinyl) . . . 6/5
78 Jet SJET 100 — Rockaria!/Poker (reissue) . . . 5
78 Jet SJET 101 — Telephone Line/Call Boy (reissue) . . . 5
78 Jet SJET 103 — Turn To Stone/Mr. Kingdom (reissue) . . . 5
78 Jet SJET 104 — Mr. Blue Sky/One Summer Dream (reissue) . . . 5
78 Jet SJET 109 — Wild West Hero/Eldorado (p/s) . . . 5
78 Jet SJET 12-109 — Wild West Hero/Eldorado (12", yellow vinyl, die-cut company sleeve, 'Jet' or picture labels) . . . 12/10
78 Jet SJET 121 — Sweet Talkin' Woman/Bluebird Is Dead (mauve or black vinyl, p/s) . . . 6/5
78 Jet SJET 12-121 — Sweet Talkin' Woman/Bluebird Is Dead (12", mauve vinyl, p/s) . . . 12
78 Jet ELO 1 — THE ELO EP (p/s) . . . 6
79 Jet SJET 144 — Shine A Little Love/Jungle (white or black vinyl, p/s) . . . 7/5
79 Jet SJET 12-144 — Shine A Little Love/Jungle (12", black vinyl, company sleeve) . . . 20
79 Harvest HAR 5179 — Roll Over Beethoven/Showdown (p/s) . . . 5
79 Harvest 12HAR 5179 — Roll Over Beethoven/Showdown (12", p/s) . . . 8
79 Jet SJET 150 — The Diary Of Horace Wimp/Down Home Town (p/s) . . . 6

MINT VALUE £

79	Jet JET 153	Don't Bring Me Down/Dreaming Of 4000 (p/s)	5
79	Jet SJET 153	Don't Bring Me Down/Dreaming Of 4000 (with different prefix, no p/s)	5
79	Jet JET 166	Confusion/Last Train To London (p/s, some with sticker)	7/5
80	Jet SJET 179	I'm Alive/Drum Drums (p/s)	5
80	Jet JET 185	Xanadu/Fool Country (gatefold p/s, red or Jet label, with Olivia Newton-John)	8
80	Jet JET 10-185	Xanadu/Fool Country (10", pink vinyl, die-cut p/s, with Olivia Newton-John)	15
80	Jet JET 195	All Over The World/Midnight Blue (p/s)	5
80	Jet JET 10-195	All Over The World/Midnight Blue (10", blue vinyl, die-cut p/s)	15
80	Jet JET 7004	Don't Walk Away/Across The Border (p/s)	6
81	Jet ELO 2	Mr Blue Sky/Across The Border/Telephone Line/Don't Bring Me Down (withdrawn, some in p/s)	35/30
81	Jet JET 7011	Hold On Tight/When Time Stood Still (p/s)	7
81	Jet JET 7015	Twilight/Julie Don't Live Here Any more (p/s)	5
81	Jet JET 7018	Ticket To The Moon/Here Is The News (p/s)	7
81	Jet JET 12-7018	Ticket To The Moon/Here Is The News (12", picture disc)	15
82	Jet JET 7021	The Way Life's Meant To Be/Wishing (p/s, B-side without black text)	5
83	Jet JET A3500	Rock'n'Roll Is King/After All (p/s, silver or Jet labels)	6/5
83	Jet JET TA 3500	Rock'n'Roll Is King/After All/Time After Time (12", p/s)	8
83	Jet A 3720	Secret Messages/Buildings Have Eyes (p/s, silver or Jet labels)	6/5
83	Jet JET 7038	Secret Messages/Buildings Have Eyes (p/s, U.K. export to Holland)	5
83	Jet PA 3720	Secret Messages/Buildings Have Eyes (picture disc, stickered PVC sleeve)	10
83	Jet A 3869	Four Little Diamonds/Letter From Spain (p/s)	5
83	Jet TA 3869	Four Little Diamonds/Letter From Spain/The Bouncer (12", p/s)	12
84	EMI/Gold G 45 22	10538 Overture/Roll Over Beethoven (p/s)	5
86	Epic EPC A 6844	Calling America/Caught In The Trap (p/s)	5
86	Epic QTA 6844	Calling America/Caught In The Trap/Destination Unknown (12", p/s)	10
86	Epic EPC A 7090	So Serious/Matter Of Fact (p/s)	5
86	Epic QTA 7090	So Serious/Matter Of Fact/Matter Of Fact (Alternate Lyrics) (12", p/s)	10
86	Epic EPCA 7317	Getting To The Point/Secret Lives (p/s)	6
86	Epic QTA 7317	Getting To The Point/Secret Lives/E.L.O. Megamix (12", p/s)	12

LPs

71	Harvest SHVL 797	ELECTRIC LIGHT ORCHESTRA (gatefold sleeve, with inner sleeve & lyric insert)	12
73	Harvest Q4SHVL 797	ELECTRIC LIGHT ORCHESTRA (quadrophonic, promo only)	75
73	Harvest SHVL 806	ELECTRIC LIGHT ORCHESTRA II (gatefold sleeve)	12
73	Warner Bros K 56021	ON THE THIRD DAY (cut-out gatefold sleeve)	12
76	Jet JETLP 19	OLE ELO (withdrawn)	15
77	Jet UAG 30091	ON THE THIRD DAY (new mix, new sleeve & inner sleeve)	15
78	Jet JETBX 1	THREE LIGHT YEARS (3-LP, boxed set of "On The Third Day", "Eldorado" & "Face The Music", with booklet & inserts)	18
78	Jet JETLP 200	A NEW WORLD RECORD (red vinyl, with inner sleeve)	12
78	Jet JETLP 201	FACE THE MUSIC (green vinyl, with inner sleeve)	12
78	Jet JETLP 202	ON THE THIRD DAY (clear vinyl, with inner sleeve)	12
78	Jet JETLP 203	ELDORADO (yellow vinyl, with inner sleeve)	12
78	Jet JETDP 400	OUT OF THE BLUE (2-LP, clear or dark blue vinyl, with inner sleeves, with cut-out spaceship, poster & insert)	15
82	Jet JETBX 2	FOUR LIGHT YEARS (4-LP, box set of "A New World Record", "Out Of The Blue" [2-LP] & "Discovery", with booklet & insert)	20
85	Epic EP 32700	THE NIGHT THE LIGHT WENT ON (IN LONG BEACH)	15

(see also Idle Race, Jeff Lynne, Move, Roy Wood, Michael D'Albuquerque, Wilson Gale & Co., Tandy-Morgan)

ELECTRIC PRUNES

66	Reprise RS 20532	I Had Too Much To Dream (Last Night)/Luvin'	25
67	Reprise RS 20564	Get Me To The World On Time/Are You Lovin' Me More (But Enjoying It Less)	25
67	Reprise RS 20607	The Great Banana Hoax/Wind-Up Toys	18
67	Reprise RS 23212	A Long Day's Flight/The King Is In His Counting House	15
68	Reprise RS 20652	Everybody Knows You're Not In Love/You Never Had It Better	30
73	Elektra K 12102	I Had Too Much To Dream (Last Night)/KNICKERBOCKERS: Lies	7
79	Radar ADA 16	I Had Too Much To Dream (Last Night)/Luvin' (p/s)	8
67	Reprise R(S)LP 6248	THE ELECTRIC PRUNES (LP, mono/stereo)	65
68	Reprise R(S)LP 6275	MASS IN F MINOR (LP, mono/stereo)	45
68	Reprise RSLP 6316	RELEASE OF AN OATH (LP)	45
73	Reprise K 34003	MASS IN F MINOR (LP, reissue)	12
97	Heartbeat HB 67	STOCKHOLM '67 (LP, gatefold sleeve with booklet)	20

ELECTRIC SOFT PARADE

03	BMG 8287658787	Things I've Done Before (white vinyl, numbered, stickered sleeve)	5

ELECTRIC TOILET

83	Psycho PSYCHO 8	IN THE HANDS OF KARMA (LP, reissue of U.S. LP)	15

ELECTRIX

79	ELX 001	HOLLAND (EP)	6

ELECTRONIC

89	Factory FAC 257	Getting Away With It (white label test pressing)	15
89	Factory FAC 257	Getting Away With It (Full Length Version)/Getting Away With It (Inst.) (12", p/s)	10
89	Factory FACD 257	Getting Away With It (Full Length Version)/Getting Away With It (Instrumental) Getting Away With It (Extended Version) (CD)	10
91	Factory FACD 287	Get The Message (7" Mix)/The Message (12" Mix)/Free Will (CD)	10
93	Parlophone 10RD 6311	Disappointed (7" Mix)/Disappointed (12" Remix) (10", promo only)	12
93	Parlophone CDR 6311	Disappointed (7" Mix)/Disappointed (12" Remix)/Disappointed (Original Mix)/Idiot Country Two (CD, card p/s)	8
96	Parlophone no cat. no.	Forbidden City (1-track promo CD, special sleeve)	10

(see also New Order, Smiths, Pet Shop Boys)

ELECTROSCOPE

97	Wurlitzer Jukebox WJ 19	THE VANISHING PULSAR PLANET EP (p/s)	5
97	Wurlitzer Jukebox WJ 23	SOMMERSO EP (p/s)	5

MINT VALUE £

ELECTROTUNES

80	Cobra COS 5	If This Ain't Love/Bodywork (p/s)	5

ELEGANTS

58	HMV POP 520	Little Star/Getting Dizzy	25
58	HMV POP 520	Little Star/Getting Dizzy (78)	25
58	HMV POP 551	Please Believe Me/Goodnight	60
58	HMV POP 551	Please Believe Me/Goodnight (78)	40

ELEKTRIC MUSIC

93	East West YZ 755	TV/Television (p/s)	8
93	East West YZ 755T	TV/Television (12", p/s)	10
93	East West YZ 755CD	TV/Television (CD)	8
93	East West SAM 1252	Lifestyle (Edit-Style Mix)/(Club-Style Mix)/(Phoneme-Style Mix) (10", promo)	50

(see also Kraftwerk)

ELENA

65	Columbia DB 7598	Evening Time/Road Of Love	12

ELEPHANT BAND

72	Mojo 2092 036	Stone Penguin/Groovin' At The Apollo	25

ELEPHANT'S MEMORY

69	Buddah 201055	Crossroads Of The Stepping Stones/Yoghurt Song	6
69	Buddah 201067	Old Man Willow/Jungle Gym At The Zoo	6
70	CBS 5207	Mongoose/I Couldn't Dream	6
72	Apple APPLE 45	Power Boogie/Liberation Special (double-A-side)	10
69	Buddah 203 022	ELEPHANT'S MEMORY (LP)	18
72	Apple SAPCOR 22	ELEPHANT'S MEMORY (LP, gatefold sleeve with inner sleeve)	25

(see also John Lennon, Yoko Ono)

ELERI, JANET & DIANE

70s	Fanfare FR 2196	THE ANSWER (LP)	100

11.59

74	Dovetail DOVE 4	THIS IS OUR SACRIFICE OF PRAISE (LP, with insert)	80

ELEVENTH HOUR

75	20th Century BTC 2215	Hollywood Hot/Hollywood Hotter	5

ELF

74	Purple PUR 118	L.A. 59/Ain't It All Amusing	10
74	Purple TPS 3506	CAROLINA COUNTRY BALL (LP)	22

(see also Roger Glover, Dio, Rainbow, Deep Purple, Black Sabbath)

ELFLAND ENSEMBLE

77	Chrysalis CHS 2151	Too Much Magic (feat. Derek Brimstone)/Lizarel (featuring Mary Hopkin) (p/s)	6
77	Chrysalis CHS 2193	Beyond The Fields We Know/Alveric's Journey	5

(see also Mary Hopkin)

ELGINS

66	Tamla Motown TMG 551	Put Yourself In My Place/Darling Baby	55
66	Tamla Motown TMG 583	Heaven Must Have Sent You/Stay In My Lonely Arms	25
67	Tamla Motown TMG 615	It's Been A Long Long Time/I Understand My Man	25
68	Tamla Motown TMG 642	Put Yourself In My Place/Darling Baby (reissue)	18
71	Tamla Motown TMG 771	Heaven Must Have Sent You/Stay In My Lonely Arms (reissue)	6
71	Tamla Motown TMG 787	Put Yourself In My Place/It's Gonna Be Hard Times	6
68	T. Motown (S)TML 11081	DARLING BABY (LP)	90

ELIAS & HIS ZIG-ZAG JIVE FLUTES

58	Columbia DB 4109	Tom Hark/Ry-Ry	10
58	Columbia DB 4146	Zeph Boogie/Vucka' Magcwabeni (Back From The Dead)	10
58	Columbia DB 4146	Zeph Boogie/Vucka' Magcwabeni (Back From The Dead) (78)	8

ELIAS HULK

70	Youngblood SSYB 8	UNCHAINED (LP)	250

ELIGIBLES

59	Capitol CL 15067	Faker, Faker/24 Hours (Till My Date With You)	8
59	Capitol CL 15098	The Little Engine/My First Christmas With You	8
60	Capitol CL 15203	Young Is My Lover/East Of West Berlin	7
60	Capitol (S)T 1310	ALONG THE TRAIL (LP)	18
61	Capitol (S)T 1411	LOVE IS A GAMBLE (LP)	18

ELIJAH

71	Ackee ACK 121	Selassie High/Mount Zion	6

ELIMINATORS

66	Pye NPL 18160	GUITARS AND PERCUSSION (LP)	30

ELIXIR

85	Elixir ELIXIR 1	Treachery (Ride Like The Wind)/Winds Of Time (folded p/s with insert)	80
86	Elixir ELIXIR 2	THE SON OF ODIN (LP, private pressing with insert)	50
90	Sonic SONICLP 9	LETHAL POTION (LP)	12

ELIZABETH

73	Paramount PARA 3032	Stop Killing Me With Kindness/Oh Bird	6
68	Vanguard SVRL 19010	ELIZABETH (LP)	35

ELKI & OWEN & RIM RAM BAND

69	Revolution REV 004	Groovie Kinda Love	8

(see also Elkie Brooks, Owen Gray)

JIMMY ELLEDGE

62	RCA RCA 1274	Swanee River Rocket/Funny How Time Slips Away	12
65	Hickory 45-1363	Pink Dally Rue/Legend In My Time	7
64	RCA RCX 7132	FUNNY HOW TIME SLIPS AWAY (EP)	45

ELLI

67	Parlophone R 5575	Never Mind/I'll Be Looking Out For You	6

YVONNE ELLIMAN

71	MCA MK 5063	I Don't Know How To Love Him/Jesus Christ Superstar Overture	7
73	Purple PUR 114	I Can't Explain/Hawaii	20
73	Purple TPS 3504	FOOD OF LOVE (LP)	30

DUKE ELLINGTON & HIS (FAMOUS) ORCHESTRA

78s

51	Columbia DC 573	Fancy Dan/The Hawk Talks (export issue)	7
52	Vogue V 2080	Caravan/Indian Summer	8
52	Vogue V 2087	She/The Happening	8
59	Philips PB 946	Anatomy Of A Murder/Flirtibird	15

SINGLES

53	HMV 7M 156	Otto Make That Riff Staccato/Time's A-Wastin'	7
54	HMV 7MC 1	Flamingo/Jump For Joy (export issue)	6
54	HMV 7MC 9	In A Sentimental Mood/I Let A Song Go Out Of My Heart (export issue)	6
54	HMV 7M 170	The Flaming Sword/BARNEY BIGARD ORCHESTRA: A Lull At Dawn	7
54	Capitol CL 14186	Smile/If I Give My Heart To You	7
55	Capitol CL 14229	Twelfth Street Rag (Mambo)/Chile Bowl	7
55	Capitol CL 14260	Tyrolean Tango/All Day Long	6
55	Columbia SCM 5182	Brown Betty/Ting-A-Ling	7
59	Philips PB 946	Anatomy Of A Murder/Flirtibird	5
59	Philips PB 243	Skin Deep (Parts 1 & 2) (with Louis Bellson)	12
60	Philips JAZ 101	Malletoba Skank/All Of Me (p/s)	5
60	Philips JAZ 117	Duke's Place/Jones (p/s)	5

EPs

54	Columbia SEG 7538	DUKE ELLINGTON	8
54	Columbia SEG 7579	DUKE ELLINGTON	8
54	Columbia SEG 7563	DUKE ELLINGTON	8
54	Capitol EAP1 477	THE DUKE PLAYS ELLINGTON	8
54	Capitol EAP2 477	THE DUKE PLAYS ELLINGTON PT. 2	8
54	HMV 7EG 8033	DUKE ELLINGTON AND HIS ORCHESTRA	8
55	HMV 7EG 8158	DUKE ELLINGTON AND AL HIBBLER	8
55	Capitol EAP1 521	ELLINGTON '55	8
55	Capitol EAP2 521	ELLINGTON '55	8
55	Capitol EAP3 521	ELLINGTON '55	8
55	Vogue EPV 1051	DUKE ELLINGTON — BILLY STRAYHORN	8
55	Vogue EPV 1060	DUKE ELLINGTON AND THE CORONETS	8
55	Philips BBE 12002	DUKE ELLINGTON — BETTY ROCHE	8
56	Capitol EAP2 637	DANCE TO THE DUKE NO. 2	8
56	Capitol EAP3 637	DANCE TO THE DUKE NO. 3	8
56	HMV 7EG 8189	DUKE ELLINGTON AND JIMMY BLANTON	8
57	HMV 7EG 8209	DUKE ELLINGTON PRESENTS IVIE ANDERSON	8
57	Capitol EAP 1004	DANCE TO THE DUKE	8
57	Decca DFE 6376	THE DUKE IN LONDON	8
58	RCA RCX 1006	DUKE ELLINGTON	8
59	RCA RCX 1022	CARAVAN	8
59	Fontana TFE 17117	HARLEM TWIST (with Lonnie Johnson Harlem Footwarmers & Chicago Footwarmers)	8
61	Capitol EAP1 20114	ULTRA DELUXE	8

LPs

53	HMV DLP 1007	ELLINGTON'S GREATEST (10")	18
53	Columbia 33SX 1022	MASTERPIECES	15
53	Vogue LDE 035	DUKE ELLINGTON AND THE CORONETS (10")	18
53	Capitol LC 6616	PREMIERED BY ELLINGTON (10")	18
54	Capitol LC 6670	THE DUKE PLAYS ELLINGTON (10")	18
54	HMV DLP 1025	GREAT ELLINGTON SOLOISTS (10")	15
54	HMV DLP 1034	ELLINGTON HIGHLIGHTS, 1940 (10")	18
54	Columbia 33S 1044	JAZZ COCKTAIL (10")	15
54	Capitol LCT 6008	ELLINGTON '55	15
54	Philips BBL 7003	ELLINGTON UPTOWN	15
55	HMV DLP 1070	PERFUME SUITE/BLACK BROWN AND BEIGE (10")	18
55	HMV DLP 1094	SATURDAY NIGHT FUNCTION (10")	15
55	Vogue Coral LRA 10027	DUKE ELLINGTON AND HIS ORCHESTRA VOL. 1 (10")	18
55	Vogue Coral LRA 10028	DUKE ELLINGTON AND HIS ORCHESTRA VOL. 2 (10")	18
55	Philips BBR 8044	MOOD ELLINGTON (10")	18
56	London AL 3551	THE DUKE — 1926 (10")	18
56	London Jazz LTZ-N 15029	HISTORICALLY SPEAKING — THE DUKE	15
56	Capitol T 679	ELLINGTON SHOWCASE	15
57	Philips BBL 7133	AT NEWPORT	15
57	Philips BBL 7152	AT NEWPORT WITH BUCK CLAYTON	12
57	London LTZ N 15078	PRESENTS	12
58	HMV DLP 1172	A BLUES SERENADE (10")	18
59	RCA RD 27134	IN A MELLOW TONE	12
59	HMV CLP 1316	BACK TO BACK (with Johnny Hodges)	12
60	Philips SBBL 514	ANATOMY OF A MURDER (soundtrack)	15
60	Philips SBBL 543	AT THE BALL MASQUE	12
60	Philips BBL 7355	FESTIVAL SESSION (also stereo SBBL 556)	12
60	Philips BBL 7381	BLUES IN ORBIT (also stereo SBBL 567)	12
61	Philips BBL 7418	THE NUTCRACKER SUITE (also stereo SBBL 594)	12
61	Philips BBL 7443	ELLINGTON UPTOWN	12
61	HMV CLP 1374	SIDE BY SIDE (with Johnny Hodges)	12
61	Parlophone PMC 1116	HISTORICALLY SPEAKING	12
61	Parlophone PMC 1136	DUKE ELLINGTON PRESENTS...	12

MINT VALUE £

MARC ELLINGTON

68	Philips BF 1665	I Shall Be Released/Mrs. Whittle	7
69	Philips BF 1742	Did You Give The World Some Love Today Baby/Bless The Executioner	6
69	Philips BF 1779	Four In The Morning/Peggy Day	6
71	Charisma CB 161	Alligator Man/Song For A Friend	6
69	Philips (S)BL 7883	MARC ELLINGTON (LP)	20
71	Charisma CAS 1033	RAINS, REINS OF CHANGES (LP, with lyric insert)	22
72	Philips 6308 120	A QUESTION OF ROADS (LP)	18
72	Xtra XTRA 1154	MARC TIME (LP, with Fairport Convention)	25
73	Philips 6308 143	RESTORATION (LP)	15

(see also Fairport Convention, Matthews Southern Comfort)

RAY ELLINGTON QUARTET

53	Columbia SCM 5050	The Little Red Monkey/Kaw-Liga	15
54	Columbia SCM 5088	All's Going Well (My Lady Montmorency) (with Marion Ryan)/Ol' Man River	15
54	Columbia SCM 5104	Rub-A-Dub-Dub/The Owl Song	15
54	Columbia SCM 5147	A.B.C. Boogie/Christmas Cards	25
55	Columbia SCM 5177	Ko Ko Mo (I Love You So)/Woodpecker	25
55	Columbia SCM 5187	Play It Boy, Play/The Irish Were Egyptians Long Ago	15
55	Columbia SCM 5199	Cloudburst/Pet	12
56	Columbia SCM 5250	Hold Him Tight/Who's Got The Money?	12
56	Columbia SCM 5274	Keep The Coffee Hot/Lucky 13	12
56	Columbia DB 3821	Stranded In The Jungle/Left Hand Boogie	25
56	Columbia DB 3821	Stranded In The Jungle/Left Hand Boogie (78)	8
56	Columbia DB 3838	Giddy-Up-A Ding Dong/The Green Door	25
56	Columbia DB 3838	Giddy-Up-A Ding Dong/The Green Door (78)	8
57	Columbia DB 3905	Marianne/That Rock 'N' Rollin' Man	25
57	Columbia DB 3905	Marianne/That Rock 'N' Rollin' Man (78)	8
57	Columbia DB 4013	Don't Burn Me Up/Swaller-Tail Coat	10
57	Columbia DB 4013	Don't Burn Me Up/Swaller-Tail Coat (78)	8
58	Columbia DB 4057	Living Doll/Long Black Nylons (solo)	25
58	Columbia DB 4057	Living Doll/Long Black Nylons (solo) (78)	12
58	Pye Nixa 7N 15159	The Sultan Of Bezaaz/You Gotta Love Somebody	8
58	Pye Nixa N 15159	The Sultan Of Bezaaz/You Gotta Love Somebody (78)	8
59	Pye Nixa 7N 15189	Chip Off The Old Block/Charlie Brown	15
59	Pye Nixa N 15189	Chip Off The Old Block/Charlie Brown (78)	12
59	Oriole CB 1512	Carina/I Was A Little Too Lonely	7
59	Oriole CB 1512	Carina/I Was A Little Too Lonely (78)	10
60	Ember EMB S 102	The Madison/Jump Over (with Tony Crombie Orchestra) (p/s with insert)	20
60	Ember EMB S 114	Très Jolie/Dracula's Three Daughters	8
63	Ember EMB S 172	Too Old To Cut The Mustard/She Lied	7
64	Ember EMB S 188	Rhythm Of The World/If You Can't Say Something Nice	7

(see also Tony Crombie, Marion Ryan)

ELLINGTONS

79	Grapevine GRP 114	(I'm Not) Destined To Become A Loser/MILLIONAIRES: You've Got To Love Your Baby	10

DEREK & DOROTHY ELLIOT

72	Trailer LER 2023	DEREK & DOROTHY ELLIOT (LP)	15
76	Tradition TSR 025	YORKSHIRE RELISH (LP)	15

MAMA CASS (ELLIOT)

68	RCA Victor RCA 1726	Dream A Little Dream Of Me/Midnight Voyage (as Mama Cass)	8
68	Stateside SS 8002	California Earthquake/Talkin' To Your Toothbrush	6
69	Stateside SS 8014	I Can Dream Can't I?/Move A Little Closer Baby	6
69	Stateside SS 8021	It's Getting Better/Who's To Blame? (as Mama Cass)	6
69	Stateside SS 8031	Make Your Own Kind Of Music/Lady Love	6
70	Stateside SS 8039	New World Coming/Blow Me A Kiss	6
70	Stateside SS 8057	A Song That Never Comes/I Can Dream, Can't I?	6
71	Probe PRO 512	Good Times Are Comin'/Welcome To The World	6
71	Probe PRO 519	Easy Come, Easy Go/Ain't Nobody Else Like You	6
68	Stateside S(S)L 5004	DREAM A LITTLE DREAM (LP)	22
69	Stateside S(S)L 5014	BUBBLEGUM, LEMONADE AND SOMETHING FOR MAMA (LP)	18

(see also Mamas & Papas, Big Three, Dave Mason & Cass Elliot, Mugwumps)

BERN ELLIOTT (& FENMEN)

63	Decca F 11770	Money/Nobody But Me	10
64	Decca F 11852	New Orleans/Everybody Needs A Little Love	10
64	Decca F 11970	Good Times/What Do You Want With My Baby (as Bern Elliott & Klan)	10
65	Decca F 12051	Guess Who/Make It Easy On Yourself (solo)	12
65	Decca F 12171	Lipstick Traces/Voodoo Woman (solo)	10
64	Decca DFE 8561	BERN ELLIOTT AND THE FENMEN (EP)	30

(see also Fenmen)

BILL ELLIOTT & ELASTIC OZ BAND

71	Apple APPLE 36	God Save Us/Do The Oz (initially with p/s)	40/18

(see also Splinter, John Lennon/Yoko Ono)

JACK ELLIOTT

69	Leader LEA 4001	JACK ELLIOTT OF BIRTLEY (LP, with booklet)	20

(see also Elliotts Of Birtley)

MARI ELLIOTT

76	GTO GT 58	Silly Billy/Half Past One	15

(see also Poly Styrene, X Ray Spex)

MIKE ELLIOTT

72	Ackee ACK 151	Milk And Honey/Burst A Shirt	7

PETER ELLIOTT

57	Parlophone R 4355	To The Aisle/All At Once (You Love Her)	8
58	Parlophone R 4457	Devotion/No Fool Like An Old Fool	6
59	Parlophone R 4514	Call Me/Flamingo	5
59	Parlophone R 4529	The Young Have No Time/Over And Over	5
59	Parlophone R 4529	The Young Have No Time/Over And Over (78)	8
61	Top Rank JAR 390	Waiting For Robert E. Lee/Toot Toot Tootsie	6
66	Strike JH 311	Thinking/Song Is Love	5
60s	Honey Hit TB 123	The Devil's Workshop/Three Little Peggies (p/s)	7

(RAMBLIN') JACK ELLIOTT

54	Topic TRC 98	Talking Miner Blues/Pretty Boy Floyd (78)	25
65	Fontana TF 575	More Pretty Girls/Roll On Buddy (as Ramblin' Jack Elliott)	7
65	Columbia DB 7593	Rusty Jigs And Sandy Sam/Rocky Mountain Belle (as Ramblin' Jack Elliott)	7
60	Columbia SEG 8046	KID STUFF (EP)	35
63	Collector JEA 5	RAMBLING JACK ELLIOTT (EP)	25
64	Collector JEA 6	BLUES AND COUNTRY (EP)	25
55	Topic T 5	WOODY GUTHRIE'S BLUES (8" mini-LP)	40
57	Topic 10T 15	JACK TAKES THE FLOOR (10" LP)	40
59	Columbia 33SX 1166	RAMBLIN' JACK ELLIOT IN LONDON (LP)	50
59	Encore ENC 194	IN LONDON (LP)	25
60	Columbia 33SX 1291	RAMBLIN' JACK ELLIOTT SINGS WOODY GUTHRIE & JIMMIE RODGERS (LP)	55
65	Fontana TFL 6044	JACK ELLIOTT (LP)	25
65	Stateside SL 10143	JACK ELLIOTT COUNTRY STYLE (LP)	25
66	Stateside SL 10167	SINGS THE SONGS OF WOODY GUTHRIE (LP)	22
70	Reprise RSLP 6387	BILL DURHAM SACKS AND RAILROAD SACKS (LP)	18

SHAWN ELLIOTT

62	Stateside SS 124	Goodbye My Lover/Ain't That A Shame	8
63	Stateside SS 174	Sincerely And Tenderly/Why Don't You Love Me Anymore	8
64	Rio R 51	Shame And Scandal In The Family/My Girl	12
64	Columbia DB 7418	My Girl/Shame And Scandal In The Family (reissue)	10

ELLIOTTS OF BIRTLEY

69	Xtra XTRA 1091	A MUSICAL PORTRAIT OF A DURHAM MINING FAMILY (LP)	15

(see also Jack Elliott)

ELLIOTT'S SUNSHINE

68	Philips BF 1649	Is It Too Late/'Cause I'm Lonely	7

ELLIS

(see under Steve Ellis)

ALTON ELLIS (& FLAMES)

65	Island WI 239	Dance Crasher (with Flames)/BABA BROOKS: Vitamin A	30
65	Island WI 241	You Are Not To Blame/BABA BROOKS: Teenage Ska	25
66	Doctor Bird DB 1044	Blessings Of Love/Nothing Sweeter (as Alton & Flames)	25
66	Doctor Bird DB 1049	The Preacher (as Alton & Flames)/LYNN TAITT & COMETS: Tender Loving Care	22
66	Doctor Bird DB 1055	Shake It (with Flames)/SILVERTONES: Whoo Baby	25
66	Doctor Bird DB 1059	Girl I've Got A Date (with Flames)/LYN TAITT & TOMMY McCOOK: The Yellow Basket	25
67	Island WI 3046	Cry Tough (with Flames)/TOMMY McCOOK & SUPERSONICS: Mr Solo	30
67	Treasure Isle TI 7004	Rocksteady (with Flames)/TOMMY McCOOK & SUPERSONICS: Wall Street Shuffle	22
67	Treasure Isle TI 7010	Duke Of Earl/All My Tears (with Flames)	25
67	Treasure Isle TI 7016	Ain't That Loving You/TOMMY McCOOK/SUPERSONICS: Tommy's Rocksteady	22
67	Treasure Isle TI 7030	Oowee Baby/How Can I (with Flames)	18
67	Treasure Isle TI 7044	Willow Tree/I Can't Stop Now	22
67	Trojan TR 004	Ain't That Loving You (with Flames)/TOMMY McCOOK & SUPERSONICS: Comet Rocksteady	22
67	Trojan TR 009	Wise Birds Follow Spring/TOMMY McCOOK & SUPERSONICS: Soul Rock	22
67	Studio One SO 2028	I Am Just A Guy/SOUL VENDORS: Just A Little Bit Of Soul	22
67	Studio One SO 2033	Only Sixteen/Baby (both actually by Heptones)	25
68	Studio One SO 2037	Live And Learn/HEPTONES: Cry Baby Cry	22
68	Trojan TR 630	I Can't Stand It/Trying To Reach My Goal	15
68	Trojan TR 642	Breaking Up/Party Time	15
68	Nu Beat NB 010	I Can't Stand It/Tonight	12
68	Nu Beat NB 013	Bye Bye Love/MONTY MORRIS: My Lonely Days	12
68	Nu Beat NB 014	La La Means I Love You/Give Me Your Love	15
68	Pama PM 707	The Message/Some Talk	10
68	Pama PM 717	My Time Is The Right Time/JOHNNY MOORE: Tribute To Sir Alex	10
68	Coxsone CS 7071	A Fool/SOUL VENDORS: West Of The Sun	30
69	Studio One SO 2084	Change Of Plans/CABLES: He'll Break Your Heart (B-side act. by Mad Lads)	20
69	Gas GAS 105	Diana/Some Talk	8
69	Bamboo BAM 2	Better Example/DUKE MORGAN: Lick Olt Back	10
69	Duke DU 14	Diana/Personality	10
70	Duke DU 72	Remember That Sunday/TOMMY McCOOK & SUPERSONICS: Last Lick	7
70	Gas GAS 151	Suzie/Life Is Down In Denver (some copies credit Alton Ellis & Flames)	6
70	Gas GAS 161	Deliver Us/NEVILLE HINDS: Originator	6
70	Duke Reid DR 2501	What Does It Take To Win Your Love/TOMMY McCOOK: Reggae Meringue	12
70	Duke Reid DR 2512	You Made Me So Very Happy/TOMMY McCOOK & SUPERSONICS: Continental	10
70	Bamboo BAM 29	Tumbling Tears/SOUND DIMENSION: Today Version	10
70	Techniques TE 903	It's Your Thing/TECHNIQUES ALL STARS: Get Left	8
70	Techniques TE 905	I'll Be Waiting/TECHNIQUES ALL STARS: I'll Be Waiting Version	8
71	Banana BA 318	Sunday Coming/CARL BRYAN: Sunday Version	10
71	Banana BA 330	Bam Bye/Keep On Yearning	10
71	Banana BA 347	Hey World/Harder And Harder	10
71	Gas GAS 164	Back To Africa/NEVILLE HINDS: Originator	6
71	Fab FAB 165	Good Good Loving/Since I Fell For You	22

MINT VALUE £

71 Bullet BU 466 Black Man's Pride/LEROY PALMER: Groove With It . . . 15
71 Bullet BU 485 Don't Care/True Born African . . . 6
71 Smash SMA 2319 A Little Loving/DELROY WILSON & ALTON ELLIS: Loving Version . . . 7
71 Smash SMA 2320 I'll Be There/ITALS: Rude Boy Train . . . 7
71 Big Shot BI 589 Be True/Be True — Version . . . 5
72 Big Shot BI 602 I'm Trying/Luna's Mood . . . 5
72 Spur SP 3 All That We Need Is Love/KEITH HUDSON: Better Love . . . 30
72 Grape GR 3029 Big Bad Boy/HUDSON'S ALLSTARS: Big Bad Version . . . 7
72 Ackee ACK 145 Oppression/Oppression Version (both with Zoot Simms) . . . 22
72 Ackee ACK 148 Let's Stay Together/Version . . . 15
72 Ackee ACK 502 Too Late To Turn Back Now/IMPACT ALLSTARS: Version . . . 12
72 Jackpot JP 796 Play It Cool/AGGROVATORS: King Of The Zozas . . . 6
72 Camel CA 94 Wonderful World/FAB DIMENSION: Wonderful Version . . . 6
72 Pama PM 840 Girl I've Got A Date/Eat Bread . . . 5
72 Pama Supreme PS 347 Moon River/I Can't Find Out . . . 5
72 Pama Supreme PS 361 Working On A Groovy Thing/HARLESDEN SKANKERS: Version . . . 6
73 Ackee ACK 511 Alton's Official Daughter/Aquarius Dub (both with Herman) . . . 15
73 Harry J. HJ 6653 Deliver Us To Africa/Nyah Medley . . . 5
73 Pyramid PYR 7003 Truly/LLOYD COXSONE SIX: Cruising . . . 5
67 Coxsone CSL 8008 SINGS ROCK AND SOUL (LP) . . . 110
71 Bamboo BDLPS 214 SUNDAY COMING (LP) . . . 65
73 Count Shelly SSLO 02 ALTON ELLIS'S GREATEST HITS (LP) . . . 40
(see also Alton & Eddy, Hortense Ellis, Hortense & Alton, Flames [Jamaica], Righteous Flames, Tony Gordon)

BOBBY ELLIS

68 Island WI 3136 Dollar A Head (with Crystalites)/RUDY MILLS: I'm Trapped . . . 25
74 Dragon DRA 1033 Up Park Camp/Verse 4 . . . 6
(see also Jerry Lewis, Derrick Harriot, Rudy Mills, Crystalites, Keith & Tex, Eric Morris, Roy Richards, Soul Vendors)

DON ELLIS (ORCHESTRA)

69 CBS 4518 Eli's Comin'/House In The Country . . . 5
67 Fontana (S)TL 5426 'LIVE' AT MONTEREY (LP) . . . 12
68 Liberty LBL/LBS 83060 THE DON ELLIS ORCHESTRA LIVE (LP) . . . 12
68 CBS 63230 ELECTRIC BATH (LP) . . . 40
68 CBS 63356 SHOCK TREATMENT (LP) . . . 12
69 CBS 63503 AUTUMN (LP) . . . 12
69 CBS 63680 THE NEW DON ELLIS BAND GOES UNDERGROUND (LP) . . . 12
71 CBS 66261 DON ELLIS AT FILLMORE (2-LP) . . . 18
72 CBS GQ 30927 TEARS OF JOY (LP, quadrophonic) . . . 12

HERB ELLIS-JIMMY GIUFFRE ALL STARS

60 HMV POP 721 Goose Grease/My Old Flame . . . 5

HORTENSE ELLIS

63 R&B JB 101 I'll Come Softly/I'm In Love (with Alton Ellis) . . . 20
65 Blue Beat BB 295 I've Been A Fool/Hold Me Tenderly . . . 25
67 Fab FAB 20 Somebody Help Me (with Buster's All Stars)/
PRINCE BUSTER & ALL STARS: Rock & Shake . . . 15
70 Bullet BU 427 Last Date/PAT SATCHMO: Cherry Pink . . . 7
70 Gas GAS 160 To The Other Man/MUSIC BLENDERS: Raindrops . . . 7
70 Techniques TE 908 To The Other Man/TECHNIQUES ALL STARS: To The Other Man Version . . . 7
72 Green Door GD 4035 Bringing In The Sheaves (with Stranger Cole)/Version . . . 6
(see also Hortense & Alton, Hortense & Delroy, Hortense & Jackie, Alton Ellis, Duke Reid, Three Tops, Jackie Opal)

JO-JO ELLIS

72 Fury FY 302 The Fly/Perdona Mia . . . 30

LARRY ELLIS

58 Felsted AF 110 Buzz Goes The Bee/Nothing You Can Do . . . 18
58 Felsted AF 110 Buzz Goes The Bee/Nothing You Can Do (78) . . . 25

MATTHEW ELLIS

71 Regal Zonophone RZ 3033 Avalon/You Are . . . 6
71 Regal Zonophone RZ 3039 Birthday Song/Salvation . . . 6
72 Regal Zonophone RZ 3045 Palace Of Plenty/Two By Two . . . 6
71 Regal Zono. SRZA 8501 MATTHEW ELLIS (LP) . . . 18
72 Regal Zono. SRZA 8505 AM I...? (LP) . . . 30
(see also Procol Harum, Chris Spedding)

SHIRLEY ELLIS

63 London HLR 9824 The Nitty Gritty/Give Me A List . . . 10
65 London HLR 9946 The Name Game/Whisper To Me Wind . . . 8
65 London HLR 9961 The Clapping Song/This Is Beautiful . . . 7
65 London HLR 9973 The Puzzle Song/I See It, I Like It, I Want It . . . 8
66 London HLR 10021 Ever See A Diver Kiss His Wife While The Bubbles Bounce About Above
The Water?/Stardust . . . 7
67 CBS 202606 Soul Time/Waitin' . . . 25
67 CBS 2817 Sugar Let's Shing-A-Ling/How Lonely Is Lonely . . . 12
71 CBS 7463 Soul Time/Waitin' (reissue) . . . 5
77 CBS 4901 Soul Time/Waitin' (2nd reissue, coloured vinyl) . . . 5
67 CBS (S)BPG 63044 SOUL TIME WITH SHIRLEY ELLIS (LP) . . . 50

(STEVE) ELLIS

70 CBS 4992 Loot/More More More . . . 6
70 CBS 5199 Evie/Fat Crow . . . 5
71 CBS 7037 Take Your Love/Jingle Jangle Jasmine . . . 5
71 CBS 7411 Hold On/Goody Goody Dancing Shoes . . . 5
72 Epic EPC 8318 Good To Be Alive/Morning Paper (as Ellis) . . . 5
73 Epic SEPC 1627 Open Road/Leaving In The Morning (as Ellis) . . . 5
73 Epic EPC 1803 Loud And Lazy Love Song/Goodbye Boredom (as Ellis) . . . 5
74 Epic SEPC 1052 El Doomo/Your Game (as Ellis) . . . 6

MINT VALUE £

88 Ocean OCN 2 Hot Lips/Little One (withdrawn) . . . 6
72 Epic EPC 64878 RIDING ON THE CREST OF A SLUMP (LP, as Ellis) . . . 18
73 Epic EPC 65650 WHY NOT? (LP, as Ellis) . . . 15
(see also Love Affair, Widowmaker, Zoot Money, Peter Bardens)

ANDY ELLISON

68 Track 604 018 It's Been A Long Time/JOHN'S CHILDREN: Arthur Green . . . 70
68 CBS 3357 Fool From Upper Eden/Another Lucky Lie . . . 50
68 S.N.B. 55-3308 You Can't Do That/Casbah . . . 70
68 S.N.B. 55-3308 You Can't Do That/Cornflake Zoo (second issue, different B-side) . . . 80
(see also John's Children, Jet, Radio Stars)

LORRAINE ELLISON

66 Warner Bros WB 5850 Stay With Me/I Got My Baby Back (re-pressed in 1969) . . . 10
68 Warner Bros WB 2094 Try (Just A Little Bit Harder)/In My Tomorrow . . . 6
70 Warner Bros WB 7394 You've Really Got A Hold On Me/You Don't Know Anything About Love . . . 6
71 Mercury 6052 073 Call Me Anytime You Need Some Lovin'/Please Don't Teach Me To Love You . . . 15
70 Warner Bros WS 1821 STAY WITH ME (LP) . . . 30

ELMERHASSEL

95 Stagedive DIVE 03 Pride In Ipswich (p/s) . . . 5
90s Dirter 7DPR 10 Almost At One (p/s) . . . 6

ELMER HOCKETT'S HURDY GURDY

68 Parlophone R 5716 Fantastic Fair/MOOD MOSAIC: The Yellow Spotted Capricorn . . . 10
(see also Mood Mosaic, Mark Wirtz)

ELOY

83 Heavy Metal HMINT 1 Fools/Heartbeat (p/s) . . . 5
83 Heavy Metal HMPD 1 Fools/Heartbeat (picture disc) . . . 8
83 Heavy Metal HMPD 1 Fools/Heartbeat (clear vinyl) . . . 8
82 Heavy Metal HMILP 1 PLANETS (LP, clear vinyl with inner sleeve) . . . 12
82 Heavy Metal HMIPD 1 PLANETS (LP, picture disc) . . . 18
82 Heavy Metal HMILP 3 TIME TO TURN (LP, clear vinyl with inner sleeve) . . . 12
82 Heavy Metal HMIPD 3 TIME TO TURN (LP, picture disc) . . . 18
83 Heavy Metal HMIPD 12 PERFORMANCE (LP, picture disc) . . . 12
84 Heavy Metal HMIPD 21 METROMANIA (LP, picture disc) . . . 18
84 Heavy Metal HMICD 21 METROMANIA (CD) . . . 20
85 IMS MILCH 014 CODENAME WILDGEESE (LP, soundtrack) . . . 12
89 FM Revolver REV PD120 RA (LP, picture disc) . . . 15

EL PAS(S)O

71 Big Shot BI 572 Out De Light, Baby/Mosquito I (both actually by Dennis Alcapone) . . . 12
71 Punch PH 61 Mosquito One/Out De Light (reissue) . . . 10
(see also Dennis Alcapone)

JEFF ELROY & BOYS BLUE

66 Philips BF 1533 Honey Machine/Three Woman . . . 20
(see also Boys Blue)

ELTI-FITS

70s Worthing Street WSEF 1 GOING STRAIGHT (EP, various foldover picture sleeves) . . . 6

ELVES

70 MCA MU 1114 Amber Velvet/West Virginia . . . 7

CAROL ELVIN

63 Columbia DB 7095 'Cos I Know/C'mon Over . . . 10
65 Parlophone R 5228 Don't Leave Me/'Cos I Love You . . . 10

LEE & JAY ELVIN

59 Fontana H 191 So The Story Goes/When You See Her . . . 22
59 Fontana H 191 So The Story Goes/When You See Her (78) . . . 18
(see also Jerry Lordan)

EMANON

77 Clubland SJP 777 Raging Pain/Rip A Bough (stamped sleeve) . . . 30

BOBBIE EMBER

65 Polydor BM 56062 Why Can't You Bring Me Home/When Love Isn't There . . . 7

EMBERS

63 Decca F 11625 Chelsea Boots/Samantha . . . 20
(see also David & Embers, Three's A Crowd)

EMBRACE

96 Fierce Panda NING 29 All You Good Good People/My Weakness Is None Of Your Business (p/s, 1,300 only, some numbered) . . . 50/45
97 Hut HUTT 84 FIREWORKS EP (12", p/s) . . . 8
97 Hut CDHUT 46 THE GOOD WILL OUT (CD, digipak with blue cloth cover) . . . 25
98 Hut HUTDX 103/109 THE ABBEY ROAD SESSIONS (2-CD, gatefold card sleeve, with inners) . . . 35
98 BBC BOX SET EMBRACE EPS (6 x 12"s in black box, numbered, 100 only) . . . 200
00 Hut CDPHUT 60 DRAWN FROM MEMORY (CD in embossed tin, with sticker) . . . 30

EMBRYO

80 Rampant RAM 001 I'm Different/You Know He Did (p/s) . . . 8
(see also Jump Squad)

EMCEE 5

62 Columbia SEG 8153 LET'S TAKE FIVE (EP) . . . 45

EMERALDS (U.K.)

65 Decca F 12096 Don't Listen To Your Friends/Say You're Mine . . . 7
65 Decca F 12304 King Lonely The Blue/Someone Else's Fool . . . 55

MINT VALUE £

EMERALDS (U.S.)

64	London HL 9839	Donkey Kick Back/Sittin' Bull	10

EMERGENCY

83	Riot City RIOT 21	POINTS OF VIEW (EP)	5

KEITH EMERSON

76	Manticore K 13513	Honky Tonk Train Blues/Barrel House Shake Down (p/s)	6
80	Atlantic K 11612	Taxi Ride (Rome)/Mater Tenebrarum (p/s)	6
81	MCA MCA 697	I'm A Man/Nighthawks Main Title Theme (p/s)	7
80	Atlantic K 50753	INFERNO (LP, soundtrack)	12
81	MCA MCF 3107	NIGHTHAWKS (LP, soundtrack)	12

(see also Emerson Lake & Palmer, Nice, V.I.P.'s, Rock Aid Armenia)

EMERSON, LAKE & PALMER

73	Lyntone/Manticore LYN 2762	Brain Salad Surgery/(excerpts from "Brain Salad Surgery" LP) (flexidisc in gatefold p/s free with *NME*)	15/7
74	Manticore K 13503	Jerusalem/When The Apple Blossoms Bloom In The Windmills Of Your Mind, I'll Be Your Valentine (some with p/s)	10/6
77	Atlantic K 10946	Fanfare For The Common Man/Brain Salad Surgery (p/s)	6
77	Atlantic K 10946T	Fanfare For The Common Man (Album Version)/Brain Salad Surgery (12", p/s)	15
70	Island ILPS 9123	EMERSON, LAKE AND PALMER (LP, pink label, later 'pink rim palm tree')	20/15
71	Island ILSP 9155	TARKUS (LP, gatefold sleeve)	12
71	Island HELP 1	PICTURES AT AN EXHIBITION (LP, gatefold sleeve)	12
72	Island ILPS 9186	TRILOGY (LP, gatefold sleeve)	12
73	Manticore K 53501	BRAIN SALAD SURGERY (LP, gatefold sleeve with poster)	15

(see also Emerson Lake & Powell, Nice, Keith Emerson, Greg Lake, Shame, Asia, King Crimson, Stray Dog)

EMERSON, LAKE & POWELL

86	Polydor POSP 804	Touch And Go/Learning To Fly (p/s)	5
86	Polydor POSPX 804	Touch And Go/Learning To Fly/The Locomotion (12", p/s)	10

(see also Emerson Lake & Palmer, Cozy Powell)

DICK EMERY

62	Philips 326559 BF	A Cockney Christmas/(All I Want For Christmas Is) My Two Front Teeth	6
63	Philips BF 1272	I (Who Have Nothing)/Walk With Me, My Angel	6
69	Pye 7N 17644	If You Love Her/Day After Day	6
70	Pye 7N 17888	With Ageing/Wonderful World Of Love	5
72	Pye 7N 45202	You Are Awful/Dance Dance	6
73	Pye 7N 45288	You're Just As Lovely Today/Our Young Idea	5
69	Pye NSPL 18277	DICK EMERY SINGS (LP)	12

EMILY

87	Sha La La 007	The Old Stone Bridge/REMEMBER FUN: Hey Hey Hate (flexidisc, p/s)	7
87	Big Fun BIG FUN 001	The Old Stone Bridge/What The Fool Said (flexidisc)	7
88	Esurient PACE 5	Stumble/Boxing Day Blues/Rachel (p/s, with insert)	5

EMJAYS

59	Top Rank JAR 145	All My Love All My Life/Cross My Heart	60
59	Top Rank JAR 145	All My Love All My Life/Cross My Heart (78)	60

EMMET SPICELAND

68	Page One POF 089	Lowlands Low/Bunclody	7
69	Page One POF 143	So Long Marianne/In Search Of Franklin	7
68	Page One POLS 011	THE FIRST (LP)	70
77	Hawk HALP 166	THE EMMET SPICELAND ALBUM (LP, reissue of above LP)	35

EMMETT

65	Columbia DB 7582	Baby Ain't No Lie/Hard Travelling	7
65	Columbia DB 7695	Nancy/Kilkenny Mountains	6

FRED EMNEY

58	Decca DFE 6554	FRED EMNEY (EP)	15

EMOTIONS

69	Downtown DT 446	Give Me Love/HORACE FAITH: Daddy's Home	10

EMOTIONS (Jamaica)

66	Ska Beat JB 263	Rude Boy Confession/Heartbreaking Gypsy	30
67	Caltone TONE 100	A Rainbow/TONY & DOREEN: Just You And I	20
68	Caltone TONE 118	Soulful Music/No Use To Cry	20
68	Caltone TONE 129	Careless Hands/TOMMY McCOOK & SUPERSONICS: Caltone Special	20
69	High Note HS 018	The Storm/Easy Squeeze	10
69	High Note HS 026	Rum Bay/PATSY: Find Someone	8
70	Supreme SUP 209	Halleluiah/MATADOR ALLSTARS: Boat Of Joy	6

(see also Romeo & Emotions, Horace Faith)

EMOTIONS (U.K.)

65	Polydor BM 56025	Lonely Man/Line Shooter	6

EMOTIONS (U.S.)

62	London HLR 9640	Echo/Come Dance Baby	40
63	London HLR 9701	L-O-V-E/A Million Reasons	50
63	Stateside SS 237	A Story Untold/One Life One Love One You	30

EMOTIONS (U.S.)

69	Stax STAX 123	So I Can Love You/Got To Be The Man	7
69	Stax STAX 134	I Like It/Best Part Of A Love Affair	15
69	Deep Soul DS 9104	Somebody New/Brushfire	30
75	Stax STXS 2020	Baby I'm Through/I Wanna Come Back	6
70	Stax SXATS 1030	SO I CAN LOVE YOU (LP)	30
77	CBS 81639	FLOWERS (LP)	12
77	CBS 82065	REJOICE (LP)	12

EMPEROR
77 Private Stock — EMPEROR (LP) — 12

EMPEROR (Norway)
93 Candlelight 002 — EMPEROR (LP) — 15
95 Candlelight 008 — IN THE NIGHTSIDE ECLIPSE (LP) — 12
98 Candlelight 023 — ANTHEMS TO THE WELKIN AT DUSK (LP, gatefold sleeve) — 12
99 Candlelight 035 — EQUILIBRIUM IX (LP, gatefold sleeve) — 12

EMPERORS
66 Stateside SS 565 — Karate/I've Got To Have Her — 15
69 Pama PM 786 — Karate/I've Got To Have Her (reissue) — 7

EMPEROR'S NEW CLOTHES
90s Acid Jazz JAZID 128T — Dark Light (12", company sleeve) — 20

EMPIRE
81 Dinosaur DE 004 — Hot Seat/All These Things (p/s) — 12
80 White Line DE 001 — EXPENSIVE SOUND (LP) — 12
(see also Generation X)

ENCHANTED FOREST
68 Stateside SS 2080 — You're Never Gonna Get My Lovin'/Suzanne — 12

ENCHANTERS
67 Warner Bros WB 2054 — We Got Love/I've Lost All Communications — 12

THE END
65 Philips BF 1444 — I Can't Get Any Joy/Hey Little Girl — 20
68 Decca F 22750 — Shades Of Orange/Loving, Sacred Loving — 40
69 Decca LK-R/SKL-R 5015 — INTROSPECTION (LP) — 110
96 Tenth Planet TP 025 — IN THE BEGINNING ... THE END (LP, gatefold sleeve, numbered, 1,000 only) — 15
97 Tenth Planet TP 033 — RETROSPECTION (LP, numbered, 1,000 only) — 15
(see also Tucky Buzzard, Bill Wyman, Innocents, Bobby Angelo, Tuxedo)

ENDEVERS
68 Decca F 12817 — Remember When We Were Young/Taking Care Of Myself — 30
68 Decca F 12859 — She's My Girl/She's That Kind Of Girl — 30
69 Decca F 12939 — Sunny And Me/I Really Hope You Do — 10

SERGIO ENDRIGO
68 Pye International 7N 25502 — Marianne/Il Dolce Paese — 10

MELVIN ENDSLEY
57 RCA RCA 1004 — I Like Your Kind Of Love/Is It True? — 45
57 RCA RCA 1004 — I Like Your Kind Of Love/Is It True? (78) — 15
58 RCA RCA 1051 — I Got A Feelin'/There's Bound To Be — 40
58 RCA RCA 1051 — I Got A Feelin'/There's Bound To Be (78) — 20

ENEMY
81 Tin Tin NM 1 — 50,000 Dead/Society's Fool/Neutral Ground (p/s) — 8
82 Fallout FALL 001 — Fallen Hero/Tomorrow's Warning/Prisoner Of War (p/s, with inner) — 7
82 Fallout FALL 004 — Punks Alive/Piccadilly Sidetracks/Twist And Turn (p/s, orange vinyl) — 7
83 Fallout FALL 014 — Last Rites/Why Not (p/s) — 5
84 Rot ASS 9 — Last But Not Least/Images (live) (p/s) — 6

ENERGY
83 Aros AROS 11233 — Nowhere To Hide/Fight For Your Freedom (no p/s) — 75
81 GRN 1 — CONQUER THE WORLD: Conquer The World/Make It/Law Breaker (EP, no p/s) — 100
80s BIPS BECK 927 — ENERGISED (EP) — 80

ENERGY IQ
80 Optimistic OPT 008 — THROUGH THE PLUGHOLE (EP) — 6

SCOTT ENGEL
58 Vogue V 9125 — Blue Bell/Paper Doll — 450
58 Vogue V 9125 — Blue Bell/Paper Doll (78) — 150
59 Vogue V 9145 — The Livin' End/Good For Nothin' (with Count Dracula & Boys) — 550
59 Vogue V 9145 — The Livin' End/Good For Nothin' (with Count Dracula & Boys) (78) — 200
59 Vogue V 9150 — Charlie Bop/All I Do Is Dream Of You — 400
59 Vogue V 9150 — Charlie Bop/All I Do Is Dream Of You (78) — 160
66 Liberty LEP 2261 — SCOTT ENGEL (EP) — 50
(see also Scott Walker, Walker Brothers)

SCOTT ENGEL & JOHN STEWART
66 Capitol CL 15440 — I Only Came To Dance With You/Greens — 30
(see also Scott Walker, Walker Brothers)

ENGINE
87 Beak BEAK 1 — Getting Away From It All (p/s) — 5
88 BH SIXFIFTY 1 — WELL OILED (LP) — 12

ENGLAND
76 Deroy DER 1356 — ENGLAND (LP, private pressing) — 400

ENGLAND
77 Arista ARIST 88 — Pariffinalea/Nanagram — 6
77 Arista ARTY 153 — GARDEN SHED (LP) — 40

ENGLAND'S GLORY
73 Venus VEN 105 — ENGLAND'S GLORY (LP, private pressing, pink label, 25 copies only; beware of white label counterfeits) — 250
87 Five Hours Back TOCK 4 — ENGLAND'S GLORY (LP, stickered sleeve) — 12
(see also Only Ones)

MINT VALUE £

ENGLAND SISTERS

60 HMV POP 710 Heartbeat/Little Child . . . 50

ENGLISH

81 Albion ION 1008 Hooray For The English/When You Fly (p/s) . . . 10

BARBARA JEAN ENGLISH

74 Contempo CS 2031 Breaking Up A Happy Home/Guess Who . . . 6
75 Contempo CS 2062 I'm Living In A Lie/Key In The Mailbox . . . 6

ERROL(L) ENGLISH

70 Big Shot BI 547 I Don't Want To Love You/Love Is Pure . . . 6
70 Big Shot BI 548 Once In My Life/Rabbit In A Cottage . . . 6
70 Torpedo TOR 8 Open The Door To Your Heart/That Will Do . . . 6
70 Torpedo TOR 9 Where You Lead Me/Hitchin' A Ride . . . 6
70 Torpedo TOR 16 Sad Girl/Welcome Me Back Home . . . 6
70 Torpedo TOR 22 Sha La La La Lee/BOVVER BOYS: A.G.G.R.O. . . . 12
71 Duke DU 99 Sometimes (with Champions)/Sugar Cane . . . 6
(see also Junior English, Errol & Champions)

JUNIOR ENGLISH

69 Camel CA 35 Nobody Knows (with Tony Sexton)/Somewhere . . . 6
71 Pama PM 828 Jesamine/SYDNEY ALL STARS: The Flash . . . 6
72 Pama PM 841 Miss Playgirl/Once In My Life . . . 5
72 Pama PM 866 I Don't Want To Die/Land Of Sea And Sand . . . 5
72 Pama PM 869 Daniel/Perfidia . . . 5
72 Banana BA 368 Anniversary/Girls Like You . . . 6
73 Pama Supreme PS 381 Garden Party/Version . . . 5
(see also Errol English)

ENGLISH ROSE

70 Polydor 2058 040 Yesterday's Hero/To Jackie . . . 6
(see also Neat Change, Love Affair)

ENGLISH SUBTITLES

79 Small Wonder SMALL 22 Time Tunnel/Sweat/Reconstruction (p/s) . . . 5
82 Glass 007/10 SEC 21 Tannoy/Cars On Fire (folded p/s in bag with insert) . . . 6
82 Glass GLASS LP 013 ORIGINAL DIALOGUE (LP, with inner sleeve) . . . 12

ENID

SINGLES

76 Buk BUK 3002 The Lovers/In The Region Of The Summer Stars . . . 15
77 EMI International INT 534 Jubilee/Omega (p/s) . . . 5
77 EMI International INT 540 Golden Earrings/Omega (p/s) . . . 12
79 Pye 7P 106 Dambusters March — Land Of Hope And Glory/The Skye Boat Song (p/s, blue vinyl) . . . 10
80 Pye 7P 187 Fool/Tito (p/s) . . . 10
80 EMI EMI 5109 Golden Earrings/665 The Great Bean (p/s) . . . 10
81 Bronze BRO 127 When You Wish Upon A Star/Jessica (p/s) . . . 10
81 Bronze BRO 134 Heigh Ho/Twinkle Twinkle Little Star (p/s) . . . 8
82 Rak RAK 349 And Then There Were None/Letter From America (p/s) . . . 6
84 EMI 12EMI 5505 And Then There Were None/Letter From America/Raindown (12", p/s) . . . 10
86 Sedition EDIT 3314 Itchycoo Park/Sheets Of Blue (p/s) . . . 5
86 Sedition EDITL 3314 Itchycoo Park/Sheets Of Blue (12", p/s) . . . 10
90 Enid ENID 7999 Salome/Salomee (p/s) . . . 5
90 Enid ENID 6999 Salome/Salomee (12", p/s) . . . 8

LPs

76 Buk BULP 2014 IN THE REGION OF THE SUMMER STARS (1st issue, white label, with insert, without mention of "Enid" on front cover; distributed by Decca) . . . 20
77 Buk BULP 2014 IN THE REGION OF THE SUMMER STARS (2nd issue, black label, with "Enid" on front cover) . . . 15
77 Honeybee INS 3005 IN THE REGION OF THE SUMMER STARS (3rd issue, brown label, some with poster) . . . 15/12
77 Honeybee INS 3012 AERIE FAIRIE NONSENSE . . . 15
79 Pye NSPH 18593 TOUCH ME (with insert) . . . 12
79 Pye NH 116 SIX PIECES (with insert, 2,000 only) . . . 15
84 The Enid ENID 1 LIVE AT HAMMERSMITH VOL. I (5,500 only) . . . 15
84 The Enid ENID 2 LIVE AT HAMMERSMITH VOL. II (2,000 only) . . . 15
84 The Enid ENID 3 SOMETHING WICKED THIS WAY COMES . . . 12
84 The Enid ENID 4 SIX PIECES ('enhanced' version, 3,500 only) . . . 15
84 The Enid ENID 5 TOUCH ME ('enhanced' version, 4,000 only) . . . 15
84 The Enid ENID 6 AERIE FAERIE NONSENSE (remixed/re-recorded version) . . . 12
84 The Enid ENID 7 IN THE REGION OF THE SUMMER STARS (remastered & re-recorded version) . . . 15
84 The Enid ENID 8 THE SPELL (2-LP, 45rpm, gatefold sleeve) . . . 15
84 The Stand LE 1 "THE LIVERPOOL ALBUM" (untitled mini-album, sold at gigs, 800 only) . . . 30
84 The Stand THE STAND 1 THE STAND (fan club issue, 5,000 only, some autographed) . . . 40+/30
85 The Stand THE STAND 2 THE STAND 1985-1986 (fan club issue, 2,000 only, some autographed) . . . 25+/20
85 The Enid ENID 9 FAND (with re-recorded version of "Fand" track, 3,000 only) . . . 15
86 The Enid ENID 10 SALOME . . . 12
87 Dojo DOJOLP 24 LOVERS AND FOOLS (2-LP) . . . 15
94 The Enid AHOE 1 AN ALTERNATIVE HISTORY VOL 1 (LP, green vinyl, numbered, with insert, 1,000 only) . . . 15
94 The Enid AHOE 2 AN ALTERNATIVE HISTORY VOL 2 (LP, pink vinyl, numbered, with insert, 1,000 only) . . . 15

(Cassette copies of the above Enid-label albums with Lodge Recording Studios inlays are worth £15 each; copies with typewritten & colour-cover inlays are worth £10 each.)

CASSETTES

77 Honeybee TC-INS 3012 AERIE FAIRIE NONSENSE (1,000 only) ... 12
79 Pye ZCNH 116 SIX PIECES (500 only) ... 12
87 Dojo DOJOC 24 LOVERS AND FOOLS ... 20
86 The Enid (no cat. no.) INNER PIECES ... 12
86 The Enid (no cat. no.) INNER VISIONS ... 12
86 The Enid (no cat. no.) AT HAMMERSMITH 17TH OCTOBER 1986 (official bootleg, typed inlay) ... 12
87 The Enid (no cat. no.) AT HAMMERSMITH 30TH OCTOBER 1987 (official bootleg, typed inlay) ... 12
80s The Enid (no cat. no.) INTRODUCING THE ENID (5-track sampler, typed inlay) ... 8
(see also Robert John Godfrey, Godfrey & Stewart, William Arkle, Glen Baker, Kim Wilde)

ETHEL ENNIS

64 RCA SF 7654 ONCE AGAIN (LP) ... 15

RAY ENNIS & BLUE JEANS

68 Columbia DB 8431 What Have They Done To Hazel?/Now That You've Got Me (You Don't Seem To Want Me) ... 25
(see also Swinging Blue Jeans, Blue Jeans)

SEAMUS ENNIS

68 Ember FA 2054 THE BONNY BUNCH OF ROSES (LP, reissue) ... 12
70 Leader LEA 2003 SEAMUS ENNIS (LP) ... 12
74 Topic 12TS 250 THE WANDERING MINSTREL (LP) ... 12
76 Free Reed FROO 1/2 FORTY YEARS OF IRISH PIPING (2-LP with insert) ... 18

BRIAN ENO

74 Island WIP 6178 Seven Deadly Finns/Later On ... 8
75 Island WIP 6233 The Lion Sleeps Tonight (Wimoweh)/I'll Come Running ... 8
78 Polydor 2001 762 The King's Lead Hat/R.A.F. (B-side with Snatch) ... 5
89 Virgin CDT 41 Another Green World/Dover Beach/Deep Blue Day (3" CD, g/fold card sleeve) ... 8
74 Island ILPS 9268 HERE COME THE WARM JETS (LP) ... 12
74 Island ILPS 9309 TAKING TIGER MOUNTAIN (BY STRATEGY) (LP) ... 12
75 Island ILPS 9351 ANOTHER GREEN WORLD (LP) ... 12
75 Island HELP 22 EVENING STAR (LP, as Fripp & Eno) ... 12
75 Obscure OBS 3 DISCREET MUSIC (LP) ... 12
76 Editions EG EGM 1 MUSIC FOR FILMS (LP, private pressing) ... 100
77 Polydor 2302 071 BEFORE AND AFTER SCIENCE (LP, with 4 Peter Schmidt prints) ... 15
83 EG EGBS 002 WORKING BACKWARDS 1983-1973 (9-LP box set with "Music For Films, Vol. 2" LP & "Rarities" 12") ... 40
(see also Eno Moebius Roebius, Ayers Cale Nico & Eno, Roxy Music, Passengers, Robert Fripp, Lady June, David Toop, Gavin Bryars, Toto)

BRIAN ENO & DAVID BYRNE

81 EG EGO 1 The Jezebel Spirit/Regiment (p/s) ... 10
(see also David Byrne, Talking Heads)

ENO, MOEBIUS, ROEBIUS

76 Sky SKY 120 AFTER THE HEAT (LP) ... 12
(see also Brian Eno)

ENORMOUS ROOM

86 Sharp CAL 5 100 Different Words/Sylvia's Children/Melanie And Martin/ You Wrote A Book (12", p/s) ... 8
86 Medium Cool MC 001 I Don't Need You/Melanie And Martin (flexidisc, p/s) ... 6

ENOS & SHEILA

68 Blue Cat BS 138 Tonight You're Mine/UNTOUCHABLES: Your Love ... 22
(see also Enos McLeod)

ENOUGH'S ENOUGH

68 Tattoo TT 101 Please Remember/Look Around You Baby ... 280

ENSLAVED

90s Candlelight 001MLP HORDANES LAND (EP) ... 80

ENTICERS

72 Atlantic 2091 136 Calling For Your Love/Storyteller ... 25

ENTOMBED

89 Earache MOSH 21P LEFT HAND PATH (LP, picture disc) ... 12

JOHN ENTWISTLE('S OX)

71 Track 2094 008 I Believe In Everything/My Size ... 10
75 Decca FR 13567 Mad Dog/Cell No.7 (as John Entwistle's Ox) ... 8
81 WEA K 79249P Too Late The Hero/I'm Coming Back (picture disc, some autographed) ... 8/5
71 Track 2406 005 SMASH YOUR HEAD AGAINST THE WALL (LP) ... 25
72 Track 2406 104 WHISTLE RYMES (LP) ... 25
75 Decca TXS 114 MAD DOG (LP, as John Entwistle's Ox) ... 22
(see also Who, Rigor Mortis)

ENYA

87 BBC RESL 201 I Want Tomorrow/The Celts Theme (p/s) ... 7
87 BBC CDRSL 201 I Want Tomorrow/The Celts Theme/To Go Beyond I/To Go Beyond II (CD) ... 25
88 WEA YZ 312 CD Orinoco Flow/Smaotin.../Out Of The Blue (3" CD) ... 18
88 WEA YZ 356 CD Evening Falls/Oiche Chiun (Silent Night)/Morning Glory (3" CD) ... 15
89 WEA YZ 368 CD Storms In Africa (Part II)/Storms In Africa (Part I) (3" CD, card sleeve) ... 15
89 WEA YZ 368 CDX Storms In Africa (Part II)/The Celts/Aldebaran/Storms In Africa (Part I) (5" CD, picture disc) ... 20
91 WEA YZ 580 CD Exile/On Your Shore/Watermark/River (CD, slimline jewel case) ... 10
91 WEA YZ 604 CDX Caribbean Blue/Orinoco Flow/As Baile/Oriel Window (CD, digipak) ... 8
91 WEA YZ 635 T How Can I Keep From Singing/O'che Chi'n (Silent Night) (12", metallic p/s) ... 8

MINT VALUE £

92	WEA YZ 640 CDX	Book Of Days/Watermark/On Your Shore/Exile (CD, box set with 4 prints)	12
92	WEA YZ 705 CDX	The Celts/O'che Chi'n (Silent Night)/Storms In Africa (Pt. II)/ Eclipse (CD,with 4 prints)	8
95	WEA WEA023 CDX	ANYWHERE IS (CD EP, limited edition)	10
87	BBC REB 605	ENYA (LP)	15
87	BBC BBCCD 605	ENYA (CD)	35
93	WEA WX 274	WATERMARK (LP)	12
93	WEA 2292-43875-8	WATERMARK (mini-disc)	18
90s	WEA WX 431903175572	SHEPHERDS' MOONS (LP)	15

EPICS (U.K.)

65	Pye 7N 15829	There's Just No Pleasing You/My Little Girl	7
66	Pye 7N 17053	Just How Wrong Can You Be/Blue Turns To Grey	8
68	CBS 3564	Travelling Circus/Henry Long	8

(see also Acid Gallery, Christie, T. Rex)

EPICS (Jamaica)

70	Bamboo BAM 37	Your Love/Driving Me Crazy	6

EPILEPTICS

80	Stortbeat/Mirror BEAT 8	1970'S EP (black & white p/s, stencilled white labels)	12
81	Spiderleg SDL 1	1970'S EP (re-recorded, printed labels, folded different printed b&w p/s)	8
81	Spiderleg SDL 2	LAST BUS TO DEBDEN (EP, hand-written labels & photocopied p/s)	10
81	Spiderleg SDL 2	LAST BUS TO DEBDEN (EP, with printed labels in printed card gatefold p/s)	7

(see also Licks, Flux Of Pink Indians)

EPISODE

68	MGM MGM 1409	Little One/Wide Smiles	30

(see also Episode Six)

EPISODE SIX

66	Pye 7N 17018	Put Yourself In My Place/That's All I Want	18
66	Pye 7N 17110	I Hear Trumpets Blow/True Love Is Funny That Way	18
66	Pye 7N 17147	Here, There And Everywhere/Mighty Morris Ten	18
67	Pye 7N 17244	Love, Hate, Revenge/Baby Baby Baby	18
67	Pye 7N 17330	Morning Dew/Sunshine Girl	18
67	Pye 7N 17376	I Can See Through You/When I Fall In Love	18
68	Chapter One CH 103	Lucky Sunday/Mr. Universe	18
69	Chapter One CH 104	Mozart Versus The Rest/Jak D'Or	15
87	PRT PYL 6026	PUT YOURSELF IN MY PLACE (LP)	12

(see also Episode, Sheila Carter & Episode Six, Neo Maya, Roger Glover, Jon Lord, Gillan, Deep Purple, Quatermass)

MINNIE EPPERSON

68	Action ACT 4503	Grab Your Clothes (And Get On Out)/No Love At All	35

PRESTON EPPS

59	Top Rank JAR 140	Bongo Rock/Bongo Party	18
59	Top Rank JAR 140	Bongo Rock/Bongo Party (78)	8
59	Top Rank JAR 180	Bongos In Pastel/Doin' The Cha Cha Cha	7
59	Top Rank JAR 180	Bongos In Pastel/Doin' The Cha Cha Cha (78)	10
60	Top Rank JAR 345	Bongo Boogie/Flamenco Boogie	12
60	Top Rank JAR 413	Bongo Bongo Bongo/Hully Gully Bongo	10
60	Top Rank JAR 522	Bongola/Blue Bongo	7
70	President PT 294	Bongo Rock/SANDY NELSON: Teen Beat	6
60	Top Rank JKP 2060	RUSHING FOR PERCUSSION (EP, with Sandy Nelson)	20

(see also Sandy Nelson)

EQUALS

67	President PT 117	I Won't Be There/Fire	8
67	President PT 135	Baby, Come Back/Hold Me Closer	5
67	President PT 158	Give Love A Try/Another Sad And Lonely Night	7
68	President PT 180	I Get So Excited/Skies Above	5
68	President PT 200	Laurel And Hardy/The Guy Who Made Her A Star	5
68	President PT 222	Softly Softly/Lonely Rita	5
69	President PT 240	Michael And The Slipper Tree/Honey Gum	6
69	President PT 260	Viva Bobby Joe/I Can't Let You Go	6
69	President PT 275	Rub A Dub Dub/After The Lights Go Down Low	6
70	President PT 303	I Can See But You Don't Know/Gigolo Sam	60
70	President PT 325	Black Skin Blue Eyed Boys/Happy Birthday Girl	6
70	President PT 345	Help Me Simone/Love Potion	6
73	President PT 414	Diversion/Here Today Gone Tomorrow	6
75	President PT 436	Georgetown Girl/We've Got It All Worked Out	6
76	Mercury 6007 104	Kaiwana Sunshine Girl/Soul Mother	6
76	Mercury 6007 106	Funky Like A Train/If You Didn't Miss Me	15
76	Mercury 6007 107	Funky Like A Train/If You Didn't Miss Me (12")	20
77	Mercury 6007 139	Irma La Douce/Ar'e Harry	6
77	President PT 464	Beautiful Clown/Daily Love	6
78	Ice GUY 5	Red Dog/Something Beautiful	6
88	Club JAB 58	Funky Like A Train/Born Ya!/Funky Like A Train (extended) (reissue)	7
88	Club JABX 58	Funky Like A Train/Born Ya!/Funky Like A Train (extended) (12", reissue)	12
68	President PTE 1	BABY COME BACK (EP)	20
68	President PTE 2	THE EQUALS (EP)	20
67	President PTL 1006	UNEQUALLED EQUALS (LP)	22
68	President PTL 1015	EQUALS EXPLOSION (LP)	20
68	President PTL(S) 1020	SENSATIONAL EQUALS (LP)	20
68	President PTL(S) 1025	SUPREME (LP)	18
69	President PTLS 1030	THE EQUALS STRIKE AGAIN (LP)	18

MINT VALUE £

69 President PTLS 1050 BEST OF THE EQUALS (LP) 18
70 President PTLS 1038 AT THE TOP (LP). 18
76 Mercury 9109 601 BORN YA! (LP) 25
78 Ice ICEL 1002 MYSTIC SISTER (LP) 25
(see also Little Grants & Eddie, Pyramids, Hickory, Little Brother Grant, Zappata Schmitt, Seven Letters/Syramip, Thirty-Second Turn-Off)

EQUATIONS
69 Fontana TF 1035 Waiting On The Shores Of Nowhere/You Stood Beside Me 6

EQUINOX
73 Boulevard BLVD 4118 HARD ROCK (LP). 18

EQUIPE 84
67 Major Minor MM 517 Auschwitz/Twenty Ninth Of September. 20

ERASURE
SINGLES
85 Mute L12MUTE 40 Who Needs Love (Like That) (Mexican Mix)/Push Me Shove Me (Tacos Mix) (12", p/s) 30
85 Mute L12MUTE 42 Heavenly Action (Yellow Brick Mix)/Don't Say No (Ruby Red Mix) (12", p/s, L12 cat. no. must be listed on sleeve & label). 60
85 Mute DMUTE 42 Heavenly Action/Don't Say No (Ruby Red Mix)//Who Needs Love (Like That) (Mexican Mix)/Push Me Shove Me (Tacos Mix) (12", shrinkwrapped double pack). 30
86 Mute 12MUTE 45 Oh L'Amour/March On Down The Line/Gimme! Gimme! (12", 'Thomas The Tank Engine' p/s, withdrawn) 15
86 Mute L12MUTE 45 Oh L'Amour (Funky Sisters Mix)/March On Down The Line/ Gimme! Gimme! Gimme! (Remix) (12", p/s) 12
86 Mute DMUTE 51 Sometimes/Sexuality//Who Needs Love (Like That)/Push Me Shove Me (double pack, with insert, shrinkwrapped with sticker) 8
86 Mute DMUTE 51 Sometimes/Sexuality//Oh L'Amour/March On Down The Line (double pack, with insert, shrinkwrapped with sticker) 8
87 Mute CDMUTE 56 It Doesn't Have To Be/Sometimes/Oh L'Amour/Heavenly Action/Who Needs Love (Like That)/Gimme! Gimme! Gimme!/In The Hall Of The Mountain King (CD, 7"-sized 'tray' p/s). 10
88 Mute LCDMUTE 93 Crackers International II: Stop! (Mark Saunders Remix)/Knocking On Your Door (Mark Saunders Remix)/God Rest Ye Merry Gentlemen (3" CD, Xmas pack with card & gift label, 6" x 3" sleeve) 20
90 Mute XL12MUTE 99 Supernature (Mark Saunders Remix)/You Surround Me (Gareth Jones Remix)/ Supernature (Daniel Miller & Phil Legg Remix) (12", envelope p/s). 10
90 Mute XL12MUTE 109 Blue Savannah (Der Deutsche Mix II)/Blue Savannah (Der Deutsche Mix I) (12", 1-sided, numbered envelope p/s) 10
94 Mute MUTE 166 I Love Saturday/Dodo/Because You're So Sweet (unreleased, p/s only) 50

LPs
99 Mute EBX 1 ERASURE 1 (5-CD box set) 30
99 Mute EBX 2 ERASURE 2 (5-CD box set) 30

PROMOS
86 Mute P12MUTE 45 Oh L'Amour/March On Down The Line/Gimme! Gimme! Gimme! (12", plain white sleeve, dark blue vinyl). 20
90 Mute ERAS 1 Push Me Shove Me (Moonbeam Mix)/(Catatonic Mix)/Senseless (Avalon Mix) (12", p/s) 20
90 Mute ERAS 2 ERAS 2: Who Needs Love Like That (Winnie Cooper Mix)/ Ship Of Fools (Orbital South Seas Isles Of Holy Beats Mix) (12", die-cut title sleeve) 18
90 Mute ERAS 3 Sometimes (Danny Rampling Mix) (12", die-cut title sleeve) 20
91 Mute P12MUTE 125 Chorus (Youth's Agreessive Dance Mix)/(Pure Dance Mix)/Snappy (Martyn Phillips Mix)/Snappy (Justin Robertson Mix) (12", green label, no p/s) 12
90s Mute P12MUTE 195 Don't Say Your Love Is Killing Me (Tall Paul Mix)/(John Pleased Wimmin Flashback Vox) Oh L'Amour (Tin Tin Out Remix)/(Matt Darey Mix) (12", white label test pressing with press release & release sheet, 10 copies only). 70
92 Mute ERAS 4 ABBA-ESQUE EP: Voulez Vous (Brain Stem Death Dest Mix)/Lay All Your Love On Me (No Panties Mix)/Take A Chance On Me (Take A Trance On Me)/ SOS (Perimeter Mix) (12") 25
94 Mute PL12 MUTE 166 Ghost (12", 1-sided). 15
97 Mute P12 MUTE 208 Rain (Blue Amazon Twisted Circles Mix)/In My Arms (Dekkard Dub)/ Sometimes (John "00" Flemings Full Vocal Club Mix)/Sometimes (John "00" Flemings Give It Some Welly Dub Mix) (12", p/s) 10
97 Mute PL12 MUTE 208 Rain (John Of The Pleased Wimmin Vocal Mix)/(John Of The Pleased Wimmin Dub)/Sometimes (John "00" Flemings Full Vocal Club Mix)/ In My Arms (BBE Mix) (12", p/s) 10
92 Mute ERAS 5 POP (CD, 19-track compilation, without "Take A Chance On Me" & "Who Needs Love Like That [Hamburg Mix]", numbered, promo only) 40
92 Mute ERAS INT 1 POP (CD, interview disc) 50
96 Mute ERAS SAY 1 I SAY I SAY I SAY I SAY (CD, interview disc). 50
96 Mute ERAS SAY 2 ERASURE (CD, interview disc) 50
96 Mute ERAS SAY 3 COWBOY (CD, interview disc). 50
(see also Depeche Mode, Dinger)

ERAZERHEAD
81 Test Pressing TP 4 Ape Man/Wipeout/Rock And Roll Zombie (p/s). 5
82 Flicknife FLS 208 Shell Shock/She Can Dance (p/s) 5
82 Flicknife FLS 210 Teenager In Love/All For Me (p/s) 5

EREHWON
81 Harvest HAR 5213 Tiny Goddess/The Hero (p/s). 5
(see also Patrick Campbell-Lyons)

MINT VALUE £

ERIC (Sykes) & HATTIE (Jacques)
63 Decca LK 4507 ERIC, HATTIE AND THINGS (LP) 25
(see also Eric Sykes & Hattie Jacques)

ERIC HYSTERIC & ESOTERICS
80 Wasted Vinyl WASTE 1 Tropical Vision/Dance And Sing (p/s) 5

ROKY ERICKSON (& THE ALIENS)
77 Virgin VS 180 Bermuda/The Interpreter (p/s) 10
80 CBS 8888 Creature With The Atom Brain/The Wind And More (with The Aliens) 8
80 CBS 9055 Mine Mine Mind/Bloody Hammer (Acoustic Version) (p/s, with The Aliens) 8
87 B'full Of Brains BOB 13 Don't Shake Me Lucifer (live) (flexidisc free with ***Bucketfull Of Brains*** mag) 6/5
87 Five Hours Back TOCK 7P CASTING THE RUNES (LP, picture disc) 25
(see also 13th Floor Elevators)

ERIK
93 PWL PWCD 252 Looks Like I'm In Love Again (mixes) (CD) 8
93 PWL PWLT 270 The Devil & The Deep Blue Sea (mixes) (12", p/s, withdrawn) 10
93 PWL PWCD 270 The Devil & The Deep Blue Sea (mixes) (CD, withdrawn) 15

ERROL (English) & CHAMPIONS
70 Jackpot JP 732 Lonely Boy/Da Boo 7
70 Jackpot JP 738 Lonely Boy/TONY & CHAMPIONS: All Of My Life 7
(see also Errol English)

ERROL (Dunkley) & HIS GROUP
65 Blue Beat BB 284 Gypsy/Miss May (actually by Errol Dunkley & Roy Shirley) 22
(see also Errol Dunkley)

ERROL (Dunkley) & U ROY
72 Punch PH 105 Darling Ooh Wee/GOD SONS: Merry Up Version 10

ERSATZ
81 Raw RAW 35 Motorbody Love/One Good Reason/Gimme A Chance (poster p/s) 6
80s Leisure Sounds SRS 32 Smile In Shadow/House Of Cards (p/s) 6

BLUEGRASS ERWIN
59 Top Rank JAR 252 I Won't Cry Alone/I Can't Love You 7

ESCALATORS
83 Big Beat NS 86 Something's Missing/The Edge (p/s) 8
83 Big Beat NS 87 The Munsters Theme/Monday (p/s) 6

ESCORTS (Jamaica)
70 Big Shot BI 535 I'm So Afraid/Mother Nature 7
74 Fab FAB 245 Sixpense/Loving Feeling 7
(see also Sensations)

ESCORTS (U.K.)
64 Fontana TF 453 Dizzy Miss Lizzy/All I Want Is You 22
64 Fontana TF 474 The One To Cry/Tell Me Baby 22
64 Fontana TF 516 I Don't Want To Go On Without You/Don't Forget To Write 20
65 Fontana TF 570 C'Mon Home Baby/You'll Get No Lovin' That Way 22
66 Fontana TF 651 Let It Be Me/Mad Mad World 22
66 Columbia DB 8061 From Head To Toe/Night Time 35
(see also Big Three, Paddy Klaus & Gibson, Swinging Blue Jeans, Terry Sylvester)

ESCORTS (U.S.)
63 Coral Q 72458 Submarine Race Watching/Somewhere 18

ESCORTS (U.S.)
75 Contempo CLP 521 ALL WE NEED IS ANOTHER CHANCE (LP) 15

ESCORTS & KAY JUSTICE
54 Columbia SCM 5132 If You Took Your Love From Me/Yes, Indeed 12

ESCOURTS
76 Alaska ALA 1014 Disrespect Can Wreck/Bam A Lam A Boogie 8

ESG
81 Factory FAC 34 You're No Good/UFO (p/s) 35

ESPERANTO ROCK ORCHESTRA
73 A&M AMLH 68175 ESPERANTO ROCK ORCHESTRA (LP) 12
(see also Keith Christmas, Comus)

ESPRIT DE CORPS
73 Jam JAM 24 If (Would It Turn Out Wrong)/Picture On The Wall 15
73 Jam JAM 32 Lonely/Do You Remember Me 10
(see also David Ballantyne, Just Plain Smith, Just Plain Jones)

ESPRIT DE CORPS
80s Come 0001 Anxiety/The Tea Cup Song (hand-made silk-screened sleeve) 10

ESQUERITA
58 Capitol CL 14938 Rockin' The Joint/Esquerita And The Voola 110
72 Specialty SPE 6603 WILDCAT SHAKEOUT (LP) 40

ESQUIRES
67 Stateside SS 2048 Get On Up/Listen To Me 12
68 Stateside SS 2077 And Get Away/Everybody's Laughing 10
73 Action ACT 4618 My Sweet Baby/Henry Ralph 8
68 London HA-Q/SH-Q 8356 GET ON UP AND GET AWAY (LP) 20

ESQUIVEL
63 Reprise R 6046 MORE OF OTHER WORLDS, OTHER SOUNDS (LP) 15

MINT VALUE £

ESSENTIAL LOGIC

78	Cells SELL ONE	Aerosol Burns/World Friction (p/s)	8
79	Rough Trade RT29	Popcorn Boy/Flora Force (p/s)	12
80	Rough Trade RT50	Eugene (p/s)	10
81	Rough Trade RT74	Fanfare In The Garden/The Captain (p/s)	7

(see also X-Ray Spex)

ESSEX

63	Columbia DB 7077	Easier Said Than Done/Are You Going My Way	18
63	Columbia DB 7122	A Walkin' Miracle/What I Don't Know Won't Hurt Me (with Anita Humes)	15
63	Columbia DB 7178	She's Got Everything/Out Of Sight, Out Of Mind	12
63	Columbia 33SX 1593	EASIER SAID THAN DONE (LP)	60
64	Columbia 33SX 1613	A WALKIN' MIRACLE (LP)	60

DAVID ESSEX

65	Fontana TF 559	And The Tears Came Tumbling Down/You Can't Stop Me Loving You	45
65	Fontana TF 620	Can't Nobody Love You/Baby I Don't Mind	45
66	Fontana TF 680	This Little Girl Of Mine/Brokenhearted	45
66	Fontana TF 733	Thigh High/De Boom Lay Boom	40
68	Uni UN 502	Love Story/Higher Than High	20
68	Pye 7N 17621	Just For Tonight/Goodbye	20
69	Decca F 12935	That Takes Me Back/Lost Without Linda	35
69	Decca F 12967	The Day The Earth Stood Still/Is It So Strange?	35
73	CBS 1693	Rock On/On And On (p/s)	5
73	CBS 1902	Lamplight/We All Insane (p/s)	5
74	CBS 2176	America/Dance Little Girl (p/s)	6
74	CBS 2492	Gonna Make You A Star/Window (p/s)	5
74	CBS 2828	Stardust/Miss Sweetness (p/s)	5
75	CBS 3425	Rollin' Stone/Coconut Ice (p/s)	5
75	CBS 3572	Hold Me Close/Good Old Rock & Roll (p/s)	5
75	CBS 3676	If I Could/Funfair (p/s)	5
75	Sound For Industry SFI 200	Hello It's Me (fan club flexidisc)	15
76	CBS 4050	City Lights/St. Amie (p/s)	6
76	CBS 4486	Coming Home/Good Lovin' (p/s, some copies b/w "Won't Get Burned Again")	6
78	CBS 6063	Stay With Me Baby/Lend Me Your Comb (p/s)	5
78	CBS 6705	Brave New World/Street Fight (p/s)	5
79	Mercury 6007 202	Imperial Wizard/Midnight Train (p/s, blue vinyl)	5
79	Mercury 6007 220	20 Flights Up/Are You Still My True Love (p/s)	5
79	Vertigo 6059 233	M.O.D./M.O.D. (2) (as M.O.D., songwriting credited to D. Cook, p/s, some allegedly mispressed on 2-Tone label)	75+/7
80	United Artists UP 605	World/I Who Am I (p/s)	6
80	Mercury BIKE 1	Silver Dream Machine (Part 1)/(Part 2) (p/s)	5
80	Mercury HOT 1	Hot Love/Rock And Roll Me (p/s)	5
80	Mercury BIKE 2	The Race/Suzuki Warlord (p/s)	5
80	Mercury MER 47	On My Bike/Swim Against The Flow (p/s)	6
80	Mercury MER 55	Heart On My Sleeve/I Don't Want To Go To The Disco (p/s)	5
81	Mercury MER 72	Be-Bop-A-Lula/Secret Lover (p/s)	5
81	Mercury MER 77	Sunshine Girl/Don't Leave Me This Way (p/s)	5
81	Mercury MER 82	The Magician/Life Support System (p/s)	5
82	Mercury MER 100	Sweethearts/Hold On Me (p/s)	5
82	Mercury MER 118	No Substitutes/She's My World (p/s)	5
83	Mercury ESSEP 1	The Smile/Slave (picture disc)	7
83	Mercury ESSEX 12	The Smile/Slave (12", p/s)	8
83	Mercury ESSEX 22	You're In My Heart/Come On Little Darlin'//A Winter's Tale/Verity (double pack gatefold p/s, some with inner picture sleeve)	8/6
87	Arista RISCD 11	Myfanwy (Long Version)/Myfanwy/Myfanwy (Love Theme) (CD, card sleeve)	10
89	CBS 654 948-0	Rock On (Shep Pettibone Remix)/The Zone (poster p/s)	5
89	CBS 654 948-2	Rock On (Shep Pettibone Remix)/Rock On (Dub Mix)/Rock On (7" Version)/ The Zone (CD, card sleeve)	8
89	Lamplight CDLAMP 6	The Sun Ain't Gonna (Anymore) (Extended)/(7" Version)/ Heart Beats Like A Drum/Heaven Knows (CD)	8
79	Mercury 9109 616	IMPERIAL WIZARD (LP, blue vinyl)	12

(see also David & Rozaa, Us)

ESSJAY

71	DJM DJS 254	Twins Of Evil/Fastback	8

NEVILLE ESSON

61	Blue Beat BB 37	Lover's Jive/Wicked And Dreadful (with Clue J. & His Blues Busters)	20

ESTABLISHMENT

81	Foetain	BAD CATHOLICS (LP)	30

(see also Cromwell)

GLORIA ESTEFAN

89	Epic 653195 0	Can't Stay Away From You/Let It Loose (reissue, poster p/s)	7
89	Epic 653195 7	Can't Stay Away From You/Let It Loose (shaped picture disc)	10
89	Epic 653195 2	Can't Stay Away From You/Let It Loose/Primitive (CD, card sleeve)	8
89	Epic 655054 9	Don't Wanna Lose You/Words Get In The Way (live) (poster p/s)	7
89	Epic 655054 1	THE BALLADS TWELVE INCH: Don't Wanna Lose You/Anything For You/ Can't Stay Away From You/Words Get In The Way (12" p/s)	8
89	Epic 655054 3	Don't Wanna Lose You/Si Voy A Perderte/Words Get In The Way (live) (3" CD)	8
89	Epic 655287 8	Oye Mi Canto (Hear My Voice) (English Version) (Def 12" Mix (8.18)/ Oye Mi Canto (Hear My Voice) (English Version) (Def Dub Mix) (5.12)/ Oye Mi Canto (Hear My Voice) (English Version) (House Mix) (4.33) (12", p/s)	8
89	Epic 655287 5	Oye Mi Canto (Spanish Version) (Edit)/Anything For You (Spanish Version)/ Words Get In The Way (Spanish Version)/Si Voy A Perderte (Don't Wanna Lose You) (Spanish Version) (CD, picture disc)	20
89	Epic 655450 0	Get On Your Feet/1-2-3 (live) ('Tour Souvenir' issue with 4 postcards)	7

MINT VALUE £

Year	Label/Cat. No.	Title	Value
89	Epic 655450 5	Get On Your Feet (Pop Vocal)/Get On Your Feet (Special Mix)/1-2-3 (live) (12", calendar gatefold p/s)	8
89	Epic 655450 8	Get On Your Feet (House Vocal) (6.50)/Get On Your Feet (House Techno Dub) (5.30)/Get On Your Feet (Deep Bass Vocal) (5.29) (12", p/s)	12
89	Epic 655450 2	Get On Your Feet (7" Version)/Get On Your Feet (Pop Vocal)/ 1-2-3 (live)/Don't Wanna Lose You (Portuguese) (CD, card sleeve)	8
90	Epic 655728 7	Here We Are/Don't Let The Sun Go Down On Me (envelope pack, with print)	8
90	Epic 655982 0	Cuts Both Ways/You Made A Fool Of Me (poster p/s)	6
91	Epic 656574 0	Coming Out Of The Dark/Desde La Oscuridad (Spanish Version) (frame pack with 2 prints)	5
91	Epic 656773 0	Seal Our Fate/Seal Our Fate (Remix Edit) (foldout tour souvenir pack with 2 prints, postcards & poster)	5
91	Epic 656968 0	Remember Me With Love/Your Love Is Bad For Me (pull-out portrait pack with 4 photos & lyrics)	5

(see also Gloria Estefan & Miami Sound Machine)

GLORIA ESTEFAN & MIAMI SOUND MACHINE

Year	Label/Cat. No.	Title	Value
84	Epic A 4800	Prisoner Of Love/Toda Tuya (Toda Dia Eva Dia De Indio) (p/s)	5
84	Epic TX 4800	Prisoner Of Love/Toda Tuya (Toda Dia Eva Dia De Indio)/ Prisoner Of Love (instrumental) (12", p/s)	8
85	Epic A 6537	Bad Boy (Club Mix)/Movies (p/s)	5
85	Epic QTA 6537	Bad Boy (Club Mix)/Bad Boy (Rubber-Club-Dub-Mix)/Movies (12", p/s)	8
85	Epic TA 6361	Conga! (Dance Mix)/Conga! (Instrumental)/Mucho Money (12", p/s)	8
86	Epic A 6956	Falling In Love (Uh-Oh)/Surrender Paradise (p/s)	5
86	Epic 650251 7	Falling In Love (Uh-Oh) (Remix)/Surrender Paradise (p/s)	5
86	Epic TA 6956	Falling In Love (Uh-Oh)/Conga! (The Stronga-Conga Remix)/ Surrender Paradise (p/s)	8
87	Epic 650805 7	Rhythm Is Gonna Get You/Give It Up ('red dress' p/s)	5
87	Epic 650805 8	Rhythm Is Gonna Get You/Rhythm Is Gonna Get You (Dub Mix)/Give It Up (12", 'red dress' p/s)	8
87	Epic 651125 7	Betcha Say That/Love Toy (p/s)	5
87	Epic 651125 8	Betcha Say That/Betcha Say That (Dub)/Love Toy (12", p/s)	8
87	Epic 651125 9	Betcha Say That/Love Toy/The Megamix (Rhythm Is Gonna Get You/ Conga/Dr. Beat/Betcha Say That/Bad Boy) (12", p/s)	10
88	Epic 650805 7	Rhythm Is Gonna Get You/Give It Up (reissue, 'Stakeout' p/s)	8
88	Epic 650805 8	Rhythm Is Gonna Get You/Rhythm Is Gonna Get You (Dub Mix)/ Give It Up (12", reissue, white 'Stakeout' p/s)	8
88	Epic 650805 9	Rhythm Is Gonna Get You (7.09)/Rhythm Is Gonna Get You (live)/ Give It Up (12", reissue, black 'Stakeout' p/s)	15
88	Epic 651444 0	Can't Stay Away From You/Let It Loose (poster p/s)	20
88	Epic 651444 7	Can't Stay Away From You/Let It Loose ('dreamy' p/s)	5
88	Epic 651444 8	Can't Stay Away From You/Let It Loose/Primitive Love (12", 'dreamy' p/s)	8
88	Epic 651444 9	Can't Stay Away From You/Let It Loose/Bad Boy (Remix) (12", 'dreamy' p/s)	10
88	Epic 651444 2	Can't Stay Away From You/Rhythm Is Gonna Get You/Surrender (Remix) (3" CD with adaptor in 5" p/s)	10
88	Epic 651444 2	Can't Stay Away From You/Rhythm Is Gonna Get You/Surrender (Remix) (5" CD)	8
88	Epic 651673 9	Anything For You (English)/Words Get In The Way/The Megamix (Rhythm Is Gonna Get You/Conga/Dr. Beat/Betcha Say That/Bad Boy) (12", p/s)	8
88	Epic 651673 2	Anything For You (English Version)/Anything For You (Spanish Version)/ The Megamix: Rhythm Is Gonna Get You/Conga!/Dr. Beat/Betcha Say That/ Bad Boy (CD, card sleeve)	8
88	Epic 652958 0	1-2-3/Surrender (poster p/s)	8
88	Epic 652958 1	1-2-3 (The Dancing By Numbers Mix)/Anything For You (English/Spanish Version)/Surrender (Remixed By Humberto Gatica) (12", p/s)	8
88	Epic 652958 2	1-2-3 (Extended Version)/1-2-3 (Dub Mix)/Surrender/ Primitive Love (CD, card sleeve)	8
88	Epic 654534 7	Rhythm Is Gonna Get You/Give It Up (reissue, badge shrinkwrapped to p/s)	10
88	Epic 654514 0	Rhythm Is Gonna Get You/Give It Up (calendar gatefold p/s)	8
88	Epic 654514 9	Rhythm Is Gonna Get You/Give It Up (poster p/s)	8
88	Epic 654514 8	Rhythm Is Gonna Get You/Rhythm Is Gonna Get You (live)/Give It Up (12", p/s)	8
88	Epic 654514 2	Rhythm Is Gonna Get You (Special Version)/Conga! (Dance Mix)/Give It Up (CD, card sleeve)	8

(see also Gloria Estefan, Miami Sound Machine)

'SLEEPY' JOHN ESTES

Year	Label/Cat. No.	Title	Value
66	Delmark DJB 3	SLEEPY JOHN'S GOT THE BLUES (EP)	30
63	Esquire 32-195	THE LEGEND OF SLEEPY JOHN ESTES (LP)	50
63	'77' LA 12-27	TENNESSEE JUG BUSTERS — BROKE AND HUNGRY (LP)	35
65	Storyville SLP 172	PORTRAITS IN BLUES VOLUME 10 (LP)	30
72	Delmark DS 619	ELECTRIC SLEEP (LP)	18

JOHN ESTES/FURRY LEWIS/WILL SHADE

Year	Label/Cat. No.	Title	Value
71	Revival RVS 1008	OLD ORIGINAL TENNESSEE BLUES (LP)	20

JACKIE ESTICK

Year	Label/Cat. No.	Title	Value
61	Blue Beat BB 64	Boss Girl/COUNT OSSIE & GROUP: Cassavubu	25
63	Island WI 042	Since You've Been Gone/Daisy I Love You	30
66	Ska Beat JB 256	The Ska/Daisy I Love You	25

DEON ESTUS

Year	Label/Cat. No.	Title	Value
89	Mika MIKAG 2	Heaven Help Me/It's A Party/Love Can't Wait (poster p/s)	5
89	Mika MIKCD 2	Heaven Help Me/It's A Party/Love Can't Wait/Me Or The Rumours (Instrumental) (CD, card p/s)	12

(see also George Michael)

ETCETERAS

Year	Label/Cat. No.	Title	Value
64	Oriole CB 1950	Where Is My Love/Bengawan Solo	15
64	Oriole CB 1973	Little Lady/Now I Know	20

ETERNALS (Jamaica)

69	Coxsone CS 7091	Queen Of The Minstrels/Stars	25
70	Moodisc MU 3506	Christmas Joy/WINSTON & RUPERT: Musically Beat	7
71	Moodisc MU 3507	Push Me In The Corner/MUDIE'S ALL STARS: Mudie's Madness (B-side actually by Ansell Collins)	12
71	Moodisc MU 3508	Keep On Dancing/HAZEL WRIGHT: My Jealous Eyes	10

(see also Don Cornel & Eternals)

ETERNALS (U.S.)

59	London HL 8995	Rockin' In The Jungle/Rock 'N' Roll Cha-Cha (triangular or round centre)	140/90
59	London HL 8995	Rockin' In The Jungle/Rock 'N' Roll Cha-Cha (78)	50

ETERNAL TRIANGLE

69	Decca F 12954	Turn To Me/Windows	5
69	Decca F 12979	I Guess The Lord Must Be In New York City/Perfumed Candle	5

ETERNITY'S CHILDREN

68	Capitol CL 15558	Mrs Bluebird/Little Boy	18

ETHEL THE FROG

80	Best SRTSFMR 014	Eleanor Rigby/Fight Back	110
80	EMI EMI 5041	Eleanor Rigby/Fight Back (reissue)	10
80	EMI EMC 3329	ETHEL THE FROG (LP, with Terry Hopkinson & Doug Sheppard)	15

ETHIOPIANS

66	Ska Beat JB 260	Live Good (credited to the Etheopians)/SOUL BROTHERS: Soho	35
66	Island WI 3015	I Am Free/SOUL BROTHERS: Shanty Town	25
67	Rio R 110	Owe Me No Pay Me/SHARKS: I Wouldn't Baby	18
67	Rio R 114	I'm Gonna Take Over Now/JACKIE MITTOO: Home Made	25
67	Rio R 123	What To Do/JACKIE MITTOO: Got My Bugaloo	35
67	Rio R 126	Dun Dead A'Ready/BOB ANDY: Stay In My Lonely Arms	25
67	Rio R 130	Train To Skaville/You Are The Girl (B-side actually by Gladiators)	22
67	Doctor Bird DB 1092	I Need You/Do It Sweet	22
67	Doctor Bird DB 1096	The Whip/Cool It, Amigo	22
67	Doctor Bird DB 1103	Stay Loose, Mama/The World Goes Ska	22
68	Doctor Bird DB 1141	Come On Now/Sh'Boom	22
68	Doctor Bird DB 1147	Engine 54/Give Me Your Love	50
68	Doctor Bird DB 1148	Train To Glory/You Got The Dough	22
68	Doctor Bird DB 1169	Everything Crash/I'm Not Losing You	20
68	Crab CRAB 2	Fire A Muss Tail/Blacker Black (B-side actually by Count Ossie)	12
68	Crab CRAB 5	Reggie Hit The Town/Ding Dong Bell	12
69	Crab CRAB 7	I Am A King/What A Big Surprise	12
69	Doctor Bird DB 1172	Not Me/Cut Down	15
69	Doctor Bird DB 1185	Hong Kong Flu/Clap Your Hands	25
69	Doctor Bird DB 1186	What A Fire/You	18
69	Doctor Bird DB 1199	Everyday Talking/Sharing You	18
69	Trojan TR 666	Woman Capture Man/One	7
69	Trojan TR 697	Well Red/J.J. ALLSTARS: R.F.K.	7
69	Nu Beat NB 031	My Testimony/J.J. ALL STARS: One Dollar Of Soul	10
69	Duke DU 35	My Girl/ANSELL COLLINS: Bigger Boss	8
70	Duke DU 61	Mek You Go On So/WINSTON WRIGHT & J.J. ALL STARS: Neck Tie	8
70	Duke Reid DR 2507	Mother's Tender Care/TOMMY McCOOK: Soldier Man	5
70	Bamboo BAM 26	Walkie Talkie/SOUND DIMENSION: Moan And Groan	10
70	Bamboo BAM 38	You'll Want To Come Back/JACKIE MITTOO: Baby Why (Instrumental) (B-side actually by Sound Dimension)	10
70	J.J. JJ 3302	Wreck It Up/Don't Go	8
70	J.J. JJ 3303	Hong Kong Flu/Everything Crash	6
70	Gas GAS 142	Satan Girl/MATADORS: The Pum	6
70	High Note HS 042	Praise For I (actually "Praise Fari")/GAYTONES: Charrie Part II	8
70	Songbird SB 1040	No Baptism/CRYSTALITES: No Baptism (Version Two)	7
70	Songbird SB 1047	Good Ambition/CRYSTALITES: Ambition Version	6
71	Randy's RAN 509	Mi Want Girl/RANDY'S ALL STARS: Girl — Version	7
71	Randy's RAN 510	True Man, Free Man/RANDY'S ALL STARS: Truthful — Version	7
71	Randy's RAN 512	Mr. Tom/Sad News	7
71	Fab FAB 180	Monkey Money/Version	8
71	Treasure Isle TI 7067	Pirate/TOMMY McCOOK & SOUL SYNDICATE: Depth Charge	8
71	Songbird SB 1059	What A Pain/CRYSTALITES: Pain Version	6
71	Songbird SB 1062	Lot's Wife/DERRICK HARRIOTT: Slave	6
71	Songbird SB 1064	Best Of Five (Parts 1 & 2)	6
71	Big Shot BI 569	He's Not A Rebel/J.J. ALL STARS: He's Not A Rebel — Version	15
71	Big Shot BI 574	The Selah/Don't Let Me Go	6
71	Duke DU 102	Drop Him/J.J. ALL STARS: Drop Him Version	6
71	Duke DU 108	Rim Bim Bam/RANDY'S ALL STARS: Rim Bim Bam Version	7
71	Explosion EX 2050	Starvation/TROJAN ALL STARS: Starvation Version	6
71	G.G. GG 4519	Love Bug/Sound Of Our Forefathers	7
71	Supreme SUP 221	Love Bug/Sound Of Our Forefathers	6
71	Supreme SUP 226	Starvation/MAXIE & GLEN: Jordan River	6
71	Big BG 330	Solid As A Rock/RUPIE EDWARDS ALL STARS: Solid As A Rock Version	6
71	Punch PH 96	Solid As A Rock/RUPIE EDWARDS ALL STARS: Solid As A Rock Version	5
72	G.G. GG 4533	Israel Want To be Free/TYPHOON ALL STARS: Israel (Version)	6
72	Prince Buster PB 38	You Are For Me/Playboy	8
72	Techniques TE 919	Promises/TIVOLIS: Promises — Version	6
73	Harry J. HJ 6646	The Word Is Love/The Word Is Love — Version	5
74	Harry J. HJ 6663	Buy You A Ring/Pray Muma	5
75	Dragon DRA 1032	Knowledge Is Power/Power Version	5
68	Doctor Bird DLM 5011	THE ETHIOPIANS GO ROCK STEADY/ENGINE 54 (LP)	200
69	Trojan TTL 10	REGGAE POWER (LP)	30
70	Trojan TBL 112	WOMAN CAPTURE MAN (LP)	50

(see Eathopians, Soul Brothers, Soul Vendors, Hamliins)

MINT VALUE £

ETIVES

81 Ayrespin AYRC 106 A BREATH OF FRESH AIR (cassette) . . . 20
84 Ayrespin AYRC 015 AN GAOL A THUG MI OG (MY LOVE OF EARLY DAYS) (LP) . . . 20
84 Ayrespin AYRC 015 AN GAOL A THUG MI OG (MY LOVE OF EARLY DAYS) (cassette) . . . 12
(see also Capercaillie)

ETTA (James) & HARVEY (Fuqua)

60 London HLM 9180 If I Can't Have You/My Heart Cries . . . 60
(see also Etta James, Moonglows, Harvey & Moonglows)

JACK EUBANK'S ORCHESTRA

61 London HLU 9312 What'd I Say/Chiricahua . . . 10
62 London HLU 9501 Searchin'/Take A Message To Mary . . . 10

EUGENE & BURST

71 Supreme SUP 225 Let It Fall/DENZIL & BURST: Can't Change . . . 5

EUGENIUS

93 Creation CAUG 005 Caesar's Vein (p/s) . . . 7
93 Creation CAUG 008CD EASTER BUNNY EP (CD) . . . 8
(see also Teenage Fanclub)

EUROPEANS

79 Heartbeat PULSE 2 Europeans/Voices (p/s) . . . 5

EUROPEANS

82 A&M AMS 8245 Animal Song/Someone's Changing (p/s) . . . 5
83 A&M AM 113 Aeious/Voice On The Telephone (p/s) . . . 5
83 A&M AM 138 Recognition/New Industry (p/s) . . . 7
83 A&M AM 158 American People/Going To Work (p/s) . . . 5
83 A&M AMX 158 American People/Going To Work/Someone's Changing/New Industy (12", p/s) . . . 8
84 A&M AM 184 Typical/Falling (p/s) . . . 5
84 A&M AM 201 Listen/Climb The Wall (p/s) . . . 5
84 A&M AMX 201 Listen/Climb The Wall (12", p/s) . . . 8
83 A&M AMLX 68558 VOCABULARY (LP) . . . 12
84 A&M SCOT 1 LIVE (LP) . . . 12
84 A&M AMA 5034 RECURRING DREAMS (LP) . . . 12
(see also Marillion)

EURYTHMICS

81 RCA RCA 68 Never Gonna Cry Again/Le Sinistre (p/s) . . . 8
81 RCA RCAT 68 Never Gonna Cry Again (Extended)/Le Sinistre (Extended) (12", p/s) . . . 25
81 RCA RCA 115 Belinda/Heartbeat, Heartbeat (p/s) . . . 15
82 RCA RCA 199 This Is The House/Home Is Where The Heart Is (p/s) . . . 15
82 RCA RCAT 199 This Is The House/Your Time Will Come (live)/Never Gonna Cry Again/ 4/4 In Leather (live)/Take Me To Your Heart (live) (12", p/s) . . . 35
82 RCA RCA 230 The Walk/Step On The Beast/The Walk (Part 2) (p/s) . . . 12
82 RCA RCAT 230 The Walk/Invisible Hands/Dr Trash/The Walk (Part 2) (12", printed die-cut sl.) . . . 35
82 RCA DA 1 Love Is A Stranger/Monkey, Monkey (with reverse print on rear of p/s) . . . 5
82 RCA DAP 1 Love Is A Stranger/Monkey, Monkey (picture disc) . . . 5
82 RCA DAT 1 Love Is A Stranger/Let's Just Close Our Eyes/Monkey, Monkey (12", blue p/s) . . . 8
83 RCA DAP 2 Sweet Dreams (Are Made Of This)/I Could Give You (A Mirror) (picture disc) . . . 6
83 RCA DAT 2 Sweet Dreams (Are Made Of This)/I Could Give You (A Mirror)/ Baby's Gone Blue (12", p/s) . . . 8
83 RCA DAP 3 Who's That Girl?/You Take Some Lentils ... And You Take Some Rice (picture disc) . . . 7
83 RCA DAT 3 Who's That Girl?/You Take Some Lentils ... And You Take Some Rice/ ABC (Freeform) (12", p/s) . . . 8
83 RCA DA 4/EUC 001 Right By Your Side/Right By Your Side (Party Mix) (stickered p/s) . . . 5
83 RCA EUC 001 INTRO SPEECH: "Intro Speech"/"Step On The Beast"/ "Invisible Hands"/"Angel (Dub)"/"Satellite Of Love") . . . 30
83 RCA DAP 4 Right By Your Side/Right By Your Side (Party Mix) (picture disc) . . . 6
83 RCA DAT 4 Right By Your Side/Right By Your Side (Special Mix)/ Pluse Something Else (12", p/s) . . . 8
84 RCA DAP 5 Here Comes The Rain Again/Paint A Rumour (picture disc) . . . 5
84 RCA DAT 5 Here Comes The Rain Again/This City Never Sleeps (live)/ Paint A Rumour (Long Version) (12", p/s) . . . 8
84 Virgin VSY 728-12 Sexcrime (1984) (Extended Mix)/Sexcrime (1984) (Single Version)/ I Did It Just The Same (12" picture disc) . . . 10
85 Virgin VSY 734 Julia/Ministry Of Love (picture disc in pop-up p/s) . . . 8
85 Virgin VSY 734-12 Julia (Extended Version)/Ministry Of Love (12", picture disc, unissued)
85 RCA PB 40375 It's Alright (Baby's Coming Back)/Conditioned Soul ('video still' p/s) . . . 5
85 RCA PB 40375/PB 40101 It's Alright (Baby's Coming Back)/Conditioned Soul//Would I Lie To You?/ Here Comes That Sinking Feeling (double pack, with free coloured vinyl 7") . . . 12
85 RCA PB 40376/PB 40102 It's Alright (Baby's Coming Back)/Conditioned Soul/Tous Les Garçons Et Les Filles//Would I Lie To You? (E.T. Mix)/Would I Lie To You? (Extended Remix)/ Here Comes That Sinking Feeling (12", double pack, gatefold PVC sleeve; 2nd on coloured vinyl) . . . 10
85 RCA BYTI 100 I Love You Like A Ball And Chain (mono)/I Love You Like A Ball And Chain (stereo) (promo only) . . . 8
86 RCA DA 8 Thorn In My Side/In This Town (p/s, with shrinkwrapped enamel badge) . . . 6
86 RCA DA 9P The Miracle Of Love/When Tomorrow Comes (live) (shaped picture disc) . . . 8
87 RCA DA 11P Beethoven (I Love To Listen To)/Heaven (poster p/s) . . . 5
87 RCA DA 11CD Beethoven (I Love To Listen To)/Heaven/Beethoven (I Love To Listen To) (Dance Mix) (CD, card sleeve) . . . 8
87 RCA DAT 14P Shame (Dance Mix)/I've Got A Lover (Back In Japan)/Shame (12", p/s & print) . . . 8
87 RCA DA 14CD Shame (Dance Mix)/I've Got A Lover (Back In Japan)/There Must Be An Angel (Playing With My Heart) (live) (CD) . . . 8
88 RCA DA 15X I Need A Man/I Need You/There Must Be An Angel (Playing With My Heart) (live)/

MINT VALUE £

		Missionary Man (live) (10", p/s)	8
88	RCA DA 15CD	I Need A Man/Missionary Man (Live Version)/I Need You/I Need A Man (Macho Mix) (CD, picture disc in numbered metal tin)	8
88	RCA DA 16CD	You Have Placed A Chill In My Heart (Remix)/Do You Want To Break Up? (Dance Mix)/Here Comes The Rain Again (Live Version)/You Have Placed A Chill In My Heart (Acoustic Version) (CD, numbered black metal tin)	8
88	Virgin CDT 22	Sexcrime (1984) (Extended 12" Remix)/Julia (Extended 12" Remix)/I Did It Just The Same (3" CD, gatefold card sleeve)	10
88	Virgin CDF 22	Sexcrime (1984) (Extended 12" Remix)/Julia (Extended 12" Remix)/I Did It Just The Same (5" CD)	8
89	RCA DACD 17	Revival (E.T. Mix)/Precious/Revival (Extended Dance Mix) (CD)	8
89	RCA DACD 20	Don't Ask Me Why/Rich Girl/When The Day Goes Down (Acoustic Version)/ Don't Ask Me Why (Acoustic Version) (CD, numbered 7" box with poster)	8
90	RCA DACD 24	The King And Queen Of America/There Must Be An Angel (Playing WIth My Heart) (live)/I Love You Like A Ball And Chain (live)/See No Evil (CD, in numbered wood box)	12
83	Lyntone LYN 13916	A CHRISTMAS MESSAGE (fan club flexidisc, no p/s)	8
84	Lyntone LYN 15292	A YULETIDE MESSAGE TO ALL OUR PALS (fan club flexidisc, no p/s)	8
87	Lyntone (no cat. no.)	DAVE AND ANNIE'S CHRISTMAS MESSAGE '87 (fan club flexidisc, no p/s)	6
89	Flexi FLX 880	DAVE AND ANNIE'S CHRISTMAS MESSAGE '89 (fan club flexidisc, foldout p/s)	6
90	Flexi FLX 1000	DAVE AND ANNIE'S CHRISTMAS MESSAGE '90 (fan club flexidisc, foldout p/s)	6
00	BMG BMGSM 2	PEACE IS JUST A WORD (CD EP, with *The Sunday Times Magazine*)	12
83	RCA RCALP 6063	SWEET DREAMS (LP, picture disc)	12
83	RCA PL 70109	TOUCH (LP, picture disc)	12
00	Parlophone (no cat. no.)	PEACE (CD, promo, with book)	60

(see also David A. Stewart, ACatch, Chris & Cosey, Longdancer, Stewart & Harrison)

JOHN EVAN BAND

90	A New Day NRS/CD 1	THE JOHN EVAN BAND LIVE '66 (CD, 500 only)	50

(see also Jethro Tull)

BARBARA EVANS

59	RCA RCA 1122	Souvenirs/Pray For Me, Mother (78)	15
59	RCA RCA 1122	Souvenirs/Pray For Me, Mother (triangular centre)	25
61	Mercury AMT 1151	Charlie Wasn't There/Nothing You Can Do	6

CHRISTINE EVANS

65	Philips BF 1406	Growing Pains/Someone In Love	6
66	Philips BF 1496	Somewhere There's Love/Right Or Wrong	10
67	Melodisc MEL 1620	I'm Gonna Tell Tony/Someone In Love	10

DAVE EVANS

71	Village Thing VTS 6	THE WORDS IN BETWEEN (LP)	12
72	Village Thing VTS 14	ELEPHANTASIA (LP)	12
74	Kicking Mule SNKF 107	SAD PIG DANCE (LP, with booklet)	12

GIL EVANS ORCHESTRA

60	Vogue EPV 1266	GREAT JAZZ STANDARDS (EP)	10
60	Vogue LAE 12234	GREAT JAZZ STANDARDS (LP)	15
75	RCA LSA 3192	PLAYS THE MUSIC OF JIMI HENDRIX (LP)	15

JOHN EVANS

62	Palette PG 9040	Melodie Pour Madame/Cry Me A River	10

LARRY EVANS

56	London HLU 8269	Crazy 'Bout My Baby/Henpecked	650
56	London HLU 8269	Crazy 'Bout My Baby/Henpecked (78)	125

MAUREEN EVANS

78s

59	Embassy WB 348	Lipstick On Your Collar/What A Diff'rence A Day Made	10
59	Embassy WB 356	Broken-Hearted Melody/Plenty Good Lovin'	10
59	Embassy WB 371	Among My Souvenirs/Happy Anniversary	12
59	Oriole CB 1517	Don't Want The Moonlight/The Years Between	10
60	Oriole CB 1533	The Big Hurt/I Can't Begin To Tell You	15
60	Oriole CB 1540	Love, Kisses And Heartaches/We Just Couldn't Say Goodbye	15
60	Oriole CB 1550	Paper Roses/Please Understand	20

SINGLES

58	Embassy WB 300	Carolina Moon/Stupid Cupid	10
58	Embassy WB 303	Fever/Born Too Late	10
58	Embassy WB 309	The Hula Hoop Song/Hoopa Hoola	6
58	Embassy WB 313	I'll Get By/Someday (You'll Want Me To Want You)	6
58	Embassy WB 316	You Always Hurt The One You Love/The Day The Rains Came	6
58	Embassy WB 319	To Know Him Is To Love Him/Kiss Me, Honey Honey, Kiss Me	10
59	Embassy WB 344	Goodbye Jimmy, Goodbye/May You Always	6
59	Embassy WB 348	Lipstick On Your Collar/What A Diff'rence A Day Made	10
59	Embassy WB 356	Broken-Hearted Melody/Plenty Good Lovin'	6
59	Embassy WB 371	Among My Souvenirs/Happy Anniversary	6
59	Oriole CB 1517	Don't Want The Moonlight/The Years Between	7
60	Oriole CB 1533	The Big Hurt/I Can't Begin To Tell You	8
60	Oriole CB 1540	Love, Kisses And Heartaches/We Just Couldn't Say Goodbye	7
60	Oriole CB 1550	Paper Roses/Please Understand	10
61	Oriole CB 1563	Mama Wouldn't Like It/My Little Corner Of The World	7
61	Oriole CB 1578	As Long As He Needs Me/Where Is Love?	7
61	Oriole CB 1581	Till/Why Don't You Believe Me	7
61	Oriole CB 1613	My Foolish Heart/Oh Gypsy Oh Gypsy	7
62	Oriole CB 1743	Never In A Million Years/We Had Words	7
62	Oriole CB 1760	Like I Do/Starlight Starbright	6
63	Oriole CB 1804	Pick The Petals/Melancholy Me	10
63	Oriole CB 1806	Tomorrow Is Another Day/Acapulco Mexico	7

MINT VALUE £

63	Oriole CB 1851	What A Difference A Day Made/Oh What A Guy	7
63	Oriole CB 1875	Like You Used To Do/As You Love Her	6
64	Oriole CB 1906	I Love How You Love Me/John John	8
64	Oriole CB 1939	He Knows I Love Him Too Much/Don't Believe Him	7
64	Oriole CB 1969	Get Away/I've Often Wondered	7
65	CBS 201733	All The Angels Sing/Speak Sugar Speak	7
65	CBS 201752	Never Let Him Go/Poco Sole	8
67	CBS 202621	Somewhere There's Love/It Takes A Little Time	8
68	CBS 3222	I Almost Called Your Name/Searching For Home	8
63	Oriole EP 7076	MELANCHOLY ME (EP)	40
63	Oriole PS 40046	LIKE I DO (LP)	40

(see also Matt Bryant & Linda Joyce)

PAUL EVANS (& CURLS)

59	London HLL 8968	Seven Little Girls Sitting In The Back Seat/Worshipping An Idol (with Curls)	12
59	London HLL 8968	Seven Little Girls Sitting In The Back Seat/Worshipping An Idol (78)	40
60	London HLL 9045	Midnite Special/Since I Met You, Baby	25
60	London HLL 9129	Happy-Go-Lucky Me/Fish In The Ocean	10
60	London HLL 9183	Brigade Of Broken Hearts/Twins	10
60	London HLL 9239	Hushabye Little Guitar/Blind Boy	15
62	London HLR 9636	The Bell That Couldn't Jingle/Gilding The Lily	7
63	London HLR 9770	Even Tan/Ten Thousand Years	12
63	London RE-R 1349	PAUL EVANS (EP)	110
60	London HA-L 2248	PAUL EVANS SINGS THE FABULOUS TEENS (LP)	140

RUSSELL EVANS & NITEHAWKS

66	Atlantic 584 010	Send Me Some Cornbread/The Bold	10

EVEN DOZEN JUG BAND

66	Bounty BY 6023	THE EVEN DOZEN JUG BAND (LP)	25

(see also Lovin' Spoonful, John Sebastian)

BETTY EVERETT

64	Stateside SS 259	You're No Good/Chained To Your Love	20
64	Stateside SS 280	It's In His Kiss (The Shoop Shoop Song)/Hands Off	15
64	Stateside SS 321	I Can't Hear You/Can I Get To Know You	20
64	Fontana TF 520	Getting Mighty Crowded/Chained To A Memory	15
64	King KG 1002	Happy I Long To Be/Your Loving Arms	12
65	Sue WI 352	I've Got A Claim On You/Your Love Is Important To Me	35
68	President PT 215	It's In His Kiss (The Shoop Shoop Song)/Getting Mighty Crowded	7
69	President PT 251	You're No Good/Hands Off	7
69	MCA Soul Bag BAG 3	I Can't Say No To You/Better Tomorrow Than Today	8
69	MCA MU 1055	There'll Come A Time/Take Me	7
70	Uni UN 517	Sugar/Hold On	7
71	Liberty LBF 15428	I Got To Tell Somebody/Why Are You Leaving Me	7
72	President PT 372	Trouble Over The Weekend/The Shoe Doesn't Fit	7
65	Fontana TL 5236	IT'S IN HIS KISS (LP)	60
68	Joy JOYS 106	IT'S IN HIS KISS (LP, reissue)	15
69	Uni UNLS 109	THERE'LL COME A TIME (LP)	30

BETTY EVERETT & JERRY BUTLER

64	Stateside SS 339	Let It Be Me/Ain't That Lovin' You Baby	15
65	Fontana TF 528	Smile/Love Is Strange	10
68	President PT 214	Let It Be Me/Smile	6
69	President PT 252	Our Day Will Come/Just Be True	6
65	Fontana TL 5237	DELICIOUS TOGETHER (LP)	50
68	Joy JOYS 123	DELICIOUS TOGETHER (LP, reissue)	18

(see also Jerry Butler)

KENNY EVERETT

68	MGM MGM 1421	It's Been So Long/Without Her	7
69	Deram DM 245	Nice Time/And Now For A Little Train Number	7

(see also Kenny & Cash)

VINCE EVERETT

65	Fontana TF 606	Bless You/'Til I Lost You	12
67	Fontana TF 818	Endlessly/Who's That Girl?	12
68	Fontana TF 915	Every Now And Then/Barbarella	15

EVERGREEN BLUES

67	Mercury MF 1012	Midnight Confessions/(Yes) That's My Baby	6
68	Mercury MF 1025	Laura (Keep Hangin' On)/Yesterday's Coming	6
68	Mercury 20122 SMCL	7 DO ELEVEN (LP)	18

EVERGREEN BLUESHOES

69	London HA-U/SH-U 8399	THE BALLAD OF THE EVERGREEN BLUESHOES (LP)	22

(see also Skip Battin, Byrds)

EVERLY BROTHERS

78s

57	London HLA 8440	Bye Bye, Love/I Wonder If I Care As Much	10
57	London HLA 8498	Wake Up Little Susie/Maybe Tomorrow	10
58	London HLA 8554	Should We Tell Him/This Little Girl Of Mine	15
58	London HLA 8618	All I Have To Do Is Dream/Claudette	10
58	London HLA 8685	Bird Dog/Devoted To You	12
58	London HLA 8781	Problems/Love Of My Life	25
59	London HLA 8863	Poor Jenny/Take A Message To Mary	35
59	London HLA 8934	('Til) I Kissed You/Oh, What A Feeling	65
60	London HLA 9039	Let It Be Me/Since You Broke My Heart	150
60	Warner Bros WB 1	Cathy's Clown/Always It's You	220
60	London HLA 9157	When Will I Be Loved/Be-Bop-A-Lula	120
60	Warner Bros WB 19	Lucille/So Sad (To Watch Good Love Go Bad)	300

MINT VALUE £

SINGLES

57	London HLA 8440	Bye Bye, Love/I Wonder If I Care As Much	25/10
57	London HLA 8498	Wake Up Little Susie/Maybe Tomorrow	18/10
58	London HLA 8554	Should We Tell Him/This Little Girl Of Mine	30/12
58	London HLA 8618	All I Have To Do Is Dream/Claudette	10/8
58	London HLA 8685	Bird Dog/Devoted To You	10/8
58	London HLA 8781	Problems/Love Of My Life	10/8
59	London HLA 8863	Poor Jenny/Take A Message To Mary	12/8
59	London HLA 8934	('Til) I Kissed You/Oh, What A Feeling	12/8
60	London HLA 9039	Let It Be Me/Since You Broke My Heart	18/10

(Where two prices are listed above, the first refers to original triangular centres, the second to later round centres.)

60	Warner Bros WB 1	Cathy's Clown/Always It's You	7
60	London HLA 9157	When Will I Be Loved/Be-Bop-A-Lula	10
60	Warner Bros WB 19	Lucille/So Sad (To Watch Good Love Go Bad)	6
60	London HLA 9250	Like Strangers/Leave My Woman Alone	10
61	Warner Bros WB 33	Walk Right Back/Ebony Eyes	6
61	Warner Bros WB 42	Temptation/Stick With Me Baby	6
61	Warner Bros WB 50	Muskrat/Don't Blame Me	6
62	Warner Bros WB 56	Crying In The Rain/I'm Not Angry	6
62	Warner Bros WB 67	How Can I Meet Her?/That's Old Fashioned	7
62	Warner Bros WB 79	No One Can Make My Sunshine Smile/Don't Ask Me To Be Friends	7
63	Warner Bros WB 94	So It Will Always Be/Nancy's Minuet	7
63	Warner Bros WB 99	It's Been Nice/I'm Afraid	7
63	Warner Bros WB 109	The Girl Sang The Blues/Love Her	7
64	Warner Bros WB 129	Ain't That Lovin' You Baby/Hello Amy	8
64	Warner Bros WB 135	The Ferris Wheel/Don't Forget To Cry	6
64	Warner Bros WB 143	You're The One I Love/Ring Around My Rosie (withdrawn)	18
64	Warner Bros WB 146	Gone, Gone, Gone/Torture	12
65	Warner Bros WB 154	You're My Girl/Don't Let The Whole World Know	7
65	Warner Bros WB 158	That'll Be The Day/Give Me A Sweetheart	12
65	Warner Bros WB 161	The Price Of Love/It Only Costs A Dime	6
65	Warner Bros WB 5628	The Price Of Love/It Only Costs A Dime (reissue)	7
65	Warner Bros WB 5639	I'll Never Get Over You/Follow Me	7
65	Warner Bros WB 5649	Love Is Strange/Man With Money	6
66	Warner Bros WB 5682	It's All Over/I Used To Love You (unissued)	
66	Warner Bros WB 5743	(You Got) The Power Of Love/Leave My Girl Alone	12
66	Warner Bros WB 5754	I've Been Wrong Before/Hard Hard Year	18
67	Warner Bros WB 7520	Bowling Green/I Don't Want To Love You	18
67	Warner Bros WB 7062	Mary Jane/Talking To The Flowers	18
67	Warner Bros WB 7088	Love Of The Common People/A Voice Within	18
68	Warner Bros WB 7192	It's My Time/Empty Boxes	15
68	Warner Bros WB 7226	Milk Train/Lord Of The Manor	18
69	Warner Bros WB 6056	Cathy's Clown/Walk Right Back	7
70	Warner Bros WB 6074	Good Golly, Miss Molly/Oh, Boy!	18
70	Warner Bros WB 7425	Yves/Human Race	18
72	RCA Victor RCA 2232	Ridin' High/Stories We Could Tell	15
73	RCA Victor RCA 2286	Not Fade AwayLay It Down	8
77	Warner Bros K 17004	Silent Treatment/Dancing On My Feet	5
80	Old Gold SET 1	THE EVERLY BROTHERS SINGLES SET (15 x p/s 7", box set with book)	30

EPs

58	London RE-A 1113	THE EVERLY BROTHERS	35
58	London RE-A 1148	THE EVERLY BROTHERS — NO. 2	35
58	London RE-A 1149	THE EVERLY BROTHERS — NO. 3	40
59	London RE-A 1174	THE EVERLY BROTHERS — NO. 4	40
59	London RE-A 1195	SONGS OUR DADDY TAUGHT US PART 1	45
59	London RE-A 1196	SONGS OUR DADDY TAUGHT US PART 2	45
59	London RE-A 1197	SONGS OUR DADDY TAUGHT US PART 3	45
60	London RE-A 1229	THE EVERLY BROTHERS — NO. 5	40

(Prices for the above EPs refer to original triangular centre labels, round-centre editions are worth two-thirds these values.)

61	Warners W(S)EP 6034	ESPECIALLY FOR YOU (mono/stereo)	35/70
61	London RE-A 1311	THE EVERLY BROTHERS — NO. 6	45
62	Warners W(S)EP 6049	FOREVERLY YOURS (mono/stereo)	35/75
62	Warners W(S)EP 6056	IT'S EVERLY TIME (mono/stereo)	35/75
63	Warners W(S)EP 6107	A DATE WITH THE EVERLY BROTHERS VOL. 1 (mono/stereo)	40/85
63	Warners W(S)EP 6109	A DATE WITH THE EVERLY BROTHERS VOL. 2 (mono/stereo)	40/85
63	Warners W(S)EP 6111	INSTANT PARTY VOL. 1 (mono/stereo)	40/85
63	Warners W(S)EP 6113	INSTANT PARTY VOL. 2 (mono/stereo)	40/85
63	Warners W(S)EP 6115	BOTH SIDES OF AN EVENING — FOR DANCING VOL. 1 (mono/stereo)	45/90
64	Warners W(S)EP 6117	BOTH SIDES OF AN EVENING — FOR DREAMING VOL. 2 (mono/stereo)	45/90
64	Warners WEP 6128	THE EVERLY BROTHERS SING GREAT COUNTRY HITS VOL. 1	45
64	Warners WEP 6131	THE EVERLY BROTHERS SING GREAT COUNTRY HITS VOL. 2	45
64	Warners WEP 6132	THE EVERLY BROTHERS SING GREAT COUNTRY HITS VOL. 3	45
65	Warner Bros WEP 6138	BOTH SIDES OF AN EVENING — FOR FUN VOL. 3	45
65	Warner Bros WEP 604	THE PRICE OF LOVE	30
65	Warner Bros WEP 608	ROCK'N'SOUL VOL. 1	30
65	Warner Bros WEP 609	ROCK'N'SOUL VOL. 2	30
66	Warner Bros WEP 610	LOVE IS STRANGE	45
66	Warner Bros WEP 612	PEOPLE GET READY	45
66	Warner Bros WEP 618	WHAT AM I LIVING FOR?	50
67	Warner Bros WEP 622	LEAVE MY GIRL ALONE	50
67	Warner Bros WEP 623	SOMEBODY HELP ME	45
72	Warner Bros K 16209	CRYING IN THE RAIN	10
74	Warner Bros K 16407	WAKE UP LITTLE SUSIE	10

EVERLY BROTHERS

MINT VALUE £

LPs

58	London HA-A 2081	THE EVERLY BROTHERS	75
58	London HA-A 2150	SONGS OUR DADDY TAUGHT US	75
60	Warner Bros WM 4012	IT'S EVERLY TIME (also stereo WS 8012)	30/45
60	London HA-A 2266	THE FABULOUS STYLE OF THE EVERLY BROTHERS	40
60	Warner Bros WM 4028	A DATE WITH THE EVERLY BROTHERS (also stereo WS 8028)	35/50
61	Warner Bros WM 4052	BOTH SIDES OF AN EVENING (also stereo WS 8052)	30/45
62	Warner Bros WM 4061	INSTANT PARTY (also stereo WS 8061)	30/45
62	Warner Bros WM/WS 8108	THE GOLDEN HITS OF THE EVERLY BROTHERS (mono/stereo)	18/20
62	Warner Bros WM/WS 8116	CHRISTMAS WITH THE EVERLY BROTHERS AND THE BOYS TOWN CHOIR (mono/stereo)	40/50
63	Warner Bros WM/WS 8138	SING GREAT COUNTRY HITS (mono/stereo)	30/40
64	Warner Bros WM/WS 8163	THE VERY BEST OF THE EVERLY BROTHERS (mono/stereo)	12/15
65	Warner Bros WM/WS 8169	GONE GONE GONE (mono/stereo)	30/40
65	Warner Bros WM/WS 8171	ROCK 'N' SOUL (mono/stereo)	30/40
65	Warner Bros W(S) 1471	THE GOLDEN HITS OF THE EVERLY BROTHERS (reissue, mono/stereo)	12/15
65	Warner Bros W(S) 1554	THE VERY BEST OF THE EVERLY BROTHERS (reissue, mono/stereo)	12/15
65	Warner Bros W(S) 1578	ROCK 'N' SOUL (reissue)	20/25
65	Warner Bros W(S) 1605	BEAT 'N' SOUL	30
65	Warner Bros W(S) 1620	IN OUR IMAGE (mono/stereo)	30/40
67	Warner Bros W(S) 1646	TWO YANKS IN ENGLAND (mono/stereo)	30/40
67	Warner Bros W(S) 1676	THE HIT SOUND OF THE EVERLY BROTHERS (mono/stereo)	30/40
67	Warner Bros W(S) 1708	THE EVERLY BROTHERS SING (mono/stereo)	30/40
68	Warner Bros W(S) 1752	ROOTS	22
70	Warner Bros WS 1858	THE EVERLY BROTHERS SHOW (2-LP)	20
70	Valiant VS 109	GONE GONE GONE (reissue)	12
71	Warner Bros K 46128	ROOTS (reissue)	12
72	RCA Victor SF 8270	STORIES WE COULD TELL	12
73	RCA Victor SF 8332	PASS THE CHICKEN AND LISTEN	12
77	Warner Bros K 56415	THE NEW ALBUM	12
80	Marks & Spencer IMP 111	THE VERY BEST OF THE EVERLY BROTHERS	40
90	Knight EVYLP 47004	PERFECT HARMONY (multi-LP box set)	20

(see also Don Everly, Phil Everly)

DON EVERLY

74	Ode ODS 66046	Warmin' Up The Band/Evelyn Swing	6
76	DJM DJS 10692	Yesterday Just Passed Away Again/Never Like This	6
77	DJM DJS 10760	So Sad/Love At Last Sight (p/s)	6
77	DJM DJS 10842	Brother Juke Box/Oh What A Feeling	5
71	A&M AMLS 2007	DON EVERLY (LP, with Ry Cooder)	22
74	Ode ODE 77023	SUNSET TOWERS (LP, with Heads, Hands & Feet)	22

PHIL EVERLY

73	RCA RCA 2409	The Air That I Breathe/God Bless Older Ladies	6
74	Pye 7N 45398	Invisible Man/It's True	6
74	Pye 7N 45415	Sweet Music/Goodbye Line	5
75	Pye 7N 45544	Better Than Now/You And I Are A Song	5
80	Epic EPC 9575	Dare To Dream Again/Lonely Days, Lonely Nights	5
83	Capitol CL 2276	She Means Nothing To Me (with Cliff Richard)/A Man And A Woman (p/s)	5
73	RCA SF 8370	STAR SPANGLED SPRINGER (LP)	22
74	Pye NSPL 18448	THERE'S NOTHING TOO GOOD FOR MY BABY (LP)	22
75	Pye NSPL 18473	MYSTIC LINE (LP)	18

(see also Cliff Richard)

EVERREADY'S

80	Taaga TAG 3	Don't Do It Again/Martian Girl (gatefold p/s)	15

LENNY EVERSONG

57	Vogue Coral Q 72255	Jezebel/Jealousy	10

EVERYBODY'S CHILDREN

70	Fontana TF 1070	Time Is Now/Abide With Me	5

EVERY MOTHER'S SON

67	MGM MGM 1341	Come And Take A Ride In My Boat/I Believe In You	15
67	MGM MGM 1350	Put Your Mind At Ease/Proper Four Leaf Clover	12
67	MGM MGM 1372	Pony With The Golden Mane/Dolls In The Clock	8
67	MGM C(S) 8044	EVERY MOTHER'S SON (LP)	30
68	MGM C(S) 8061	EVERY MOTHER'S SON'S BACK (LP)	30

EVERYONE

71	Charisma CB 146	Trouble At The Mill/Radio Lady	5
71	Charisma CAS 1028	EVERYONE (LP)	12

(see also Andy Roberts)

EVERYONE ELSE

79	Woodbine St WSR 001	Schooldays/Brainwashed/Out Of My Mind/Don't Call Us (p/s)	125

EVERYONE INVOLVED

72	Arcturus ARC 3	The Circus Keeps On Turning/Motor Car Madness	30
72	Arcturus ARC 4	EITHER OR (LP, private pressing, embossed plain white sleeve with inserts)	200

EVERYTHING BUT THE GIRL

82	Cherry Red CHERRY 37	Night And Day/Feeling Dizzy/On My Mind (yellow p/s)	5
83	Cherry Red 12CHERRY 37	Night And Day/Feeling Dizzy/On My Mind (12", p/s)	8
89	Cherry Red CDCHERRY 37	Night And Day/Feeling Dizzy/On My Mind (CD)	8
84	Blanco Y Negro NEG 1	Each And Every One/Laugh You Out The House/Never Could Have Been Worse (12", p/s)	8
84	Blanco Y Negro NEG 6T	Native Land/Riverbed Dry/Easy As Sin/Gun Cupboard Love/ Don't You Go (12", stickered p/s)	8
86	Blanco Y Negro NEG 23F	Don't Leave Me Behind/Alfie//Come On Home (Acoustic)/ Always On My Mind (live) (double pack, gatefold p/s)	5

MINT VALUE £

88 Blanco Y Negro NEG 30CD These Early Days/Those Early Days (Demo)/Dyed In The Grain/ Another Day Another Dollar (3" CD) ... 10
88 Blanco Y Negro NEG 33CD I Always Was Your Girl/Hang Out The Flags/Home From Home/ Almost Blue (3" CD) ... 10
88 Blanco Y Negro NEG 34CD I Don't Want To Talk About It/Oxford Street/I Don't Want To Talk About It (Instrumental)/Come On Home (3" CD) ... 8
88 Blanco Y Negro NEG 37CD Love Is Here Where I Live/Living On Honeycomb/How About Me?/ Each And Every One (3" CD) ... 8
88 Blanco Y Negro NEG 39CD These Early Days (Dave Bascombe Remix)/Dyed In The Grain/ No Place Like Home/Another Day, Another Dollar (3" CD) ... 8
90 Blanco Y Negro NEG 40CD Driving (Radio Edit)/Me And Bobby D/Downtown Train/Driving (Full Version) (CD) 8
90 Blanco Y Negro NEG 44CD Take Me/Take Me (Hamblin Remix)/Driving (Acoustic Version)/Take Me (Love Mix)(CD) 8
91 Blanco Y Negro NEG 51CD Old Friends/Apron Strings (live)/Politics Aside (Instrumental)/ Back To The Old House (live) (CD) ... 8
91 Blanco Y Negro NEG 53CD Twin Cities (Wildwood Mix)/Meet Me In The Morning (live)/ Twin Cities (The Green Plains A Cappella Mix)/Mine (CD) ... 8
96 Blanco Y Negro SAM 1936 Driving (Masters At Work Extended 12") (Masters At Work Dub)/ (Acapella) (T's Master Mix)(T's Frozen Sun Mix)/(Underdog Vocal Mix)/ (Underdog Instrumental Mix) (12", double pack, stickered title p/s) ... 8
97 Virgin VSTXDJ 1589 Wrong (Mood II Swing Dub)/(Deep Dish Remix) (12", stickered sleeve) ... 8
97 Virgin VSTDJ 1589 Wrong (Todd Terry Remix)/(Everything But The Drums)/(Deep Dish Remix)/ (Tee's Beats)/(EBTG Original Mix)/(Deep Dish Dub) (12", double pack, stickered sleeve) ... 10

(see also Ben Watt, Marine Girls, Tracey Thorn)

EVERYTHING IS EVERYTHING

69 Vanguard VA 1 Witchi Tai To/Oooh Baby ... 10
68 Vanguard SVRL 19036 EVERYTHING IS EVERYTHING (LP) ... 18

EVERY WHICH WAY

70 Charisma BD 1 Go Placidly ... 6

(see also Brian Davison, Griffin, Heavy Jelly, Skip Bifferty, Graham Bell, Bell & Arc)

EWAN (McDermott) & DENVER

67 Giant GN 17 I Want You So Bad/ERIC McDERMOTT: I'm Gonna Love You ... 8

EWAN (McDermott) & JERRY (McCarthy)

67 Blue Beat BB 385 Oh Babe/Dance With Me (with Carib Beats) ... 15
67 Giant GN 5 The Right Track/We Got To Be One ... 10
67 Giant GN 10 Rock Steady Train/My Baby Is Gone ... 10
67 Giant GN 14 Tennessee Waltz/You've Got Something ... 10

DON EWELL

57 Tempo TAP 7 PIANO SOLOS OF KING OLIVER CREOLE JAZZ BAND TUNES (LP) ... 15

(see also Mama Yancey/Don Ewell)

EX

86 Ron Johnson ZRON 11 '1936' THE SPANISH REVOLUTION (double pack with book) ... 7

EX/ALERTA

84 CNT CNT 017 THE RED DANCE PACKAGE (12", split EP) ... 8

EXCALIBUR

88 Clay PLATE 1 HOT FOR LOVE (Hot For Love/Early In The Morning/Come On And Rock/ Death's Door (12" EP) ... 8
90 Active 12ATV 101 Carole Ann (12", p/s) ... 8
85 Conquest QUEST 5 THE BITTER END (mini-LP) ... 18

EXCEL

79 ARSS XL1 If It Rains/Rolling Home/She's One Of The Boys/Rock Show (EP, p/s) ... 20
80 Polydor POSP 110 What Went Wrong?/Junita (p/s) ... 8

EXCELS

67 Atlantic 584 133 California On My Mind/The Arrival Of Mary ... 15

EXCELSIOR SPRING

69 Instant IN 002 Happy Miranda/It ... 18

EXCEPTION(S)

67 CBS 202632 The Eagle Flies On Friday/Girl Trouble ... 40
67 CBS 2830 Gaberdine Saturday Night Street Walker/Sunday Night At The Prince Rupert ... 20
68 President PT 181 Rub It Down/It's Snowing In The Desert ... 6
68 President PT 205 Helicopter/Back Room ... 6
68 President PT 218 Tailor Made Babe/Turn Over The Soil ... 6
69 President PT 236 Jack Rabbit/Keep The Motor Running ... 6
69 President PT 271 Pendulum/Don't Torture Your Mind ... 6
69 President PTLS 1026 THE EXCEPTIONAL EXCEPTION (LP) ... 25

(see also Bugsy Eastwood, Fotheringay, Fairport Convention)

EXCEPTIONS

65 Decca F 12100 What More Do You Want?/Soldier Boy ... 18

(see also Orchids)

EXCHECKERS

64 Decca F 11871 All The World Is Mine/It's All Over ... 18

(see also Aynsley Dunbar Retaliation)

EXCITERS

63 United Artists UP 1011 Tell Him/Hard Way To Go ... 15
63 United Artists UP 1017 He's Got The Power/Drama Of Love ... 18
63 United Artists UP 1026 Get Him/It's So Exciting ... 15
64 United Artists UP 1041 Do-Wah-Diddy/If Love Came Your Way ... 18
65 Columbia DB 7479 I Want You To Be My Boy/Tonight, Tonight ... 15

MINT VALUE £

65	Columbia DB 7544	Just Not Ready/Are You Satisfied	15
65	Columbia DB 7606	Run Mascara/My Father	15
66	London HLZ 10018	A Little Bit Of Soap/I'm Gonna Get Him Someday	12
66	London HLZ 10038	You Better Come Home/Weddings Make Me Cry	20
69	United Artists UP 2274	Do Wah Diddy Diddy/Hard Way To Go	10
71	Jay Boy BOY 38	Soul Motion/You Know It Ain't Right	10
65	United Artists UEP 1005	DO WAH DIDDY DIDDY (EP)	90
64	United Artists ULP 1032	THE EXCITERS (LP)	100

EXCURSION

69	Gemini GMX 5029	NIGHT TRAIN (LP)	18

EXECUTIVE(S)

64	Columbia DB 7323	March Of The Mods/Why, Why, Why	7
64	Columbia DB 7393	Strictly For The Beat/No Room For Squares	6
65	Columbia DB 7573	It's Been So Long/You're For Me (as Executives)	6
65	Columbia DB 7770	Return Of The Mods/How Sad	8
66	Columbia DB 7919	Lock Your Door/In My Arms (as Executives)	6

EXECUTIVE(S)

67	CBS 202652	Smokey Atmosphere/Sensation	10
67	CBS 3067	Ginza Strip/I'll Always Love You	10
68	CBS 3431	Tracy Took A Trip/Gardena Dreamer (as Executive, some with promo only p/s)	35/20
69	CBS 4013	I Ain't Got Nobody/To Kingdom Come (as Executive)	10

EXECUTIVES

80	Attrix RB 05	Shy Little Girl/Never Go Home/JOHNNIE & LUBES: I Got Rabies/ Terror In The Parking Lot (p/s)	7

EXECUTIVE SUITE

75	Cloud One HIT 1	When The Fuel Runs Out/(instrumental)	7
77	Polydor 2001 597	When The Fuel Runs Out/(instrumental) (reissue)	5

EXHIBIT A

80	Irrelevant Wombat DAMP 1	NO ELEPHANTS THIS SIDE OF THE WATFORD GAP (EP, with insert)	15
80	Irrelevant Wombat DAMP 2	DISTANCE (EP)	15

(see also Doof)

EXILE

77	Boring BO 1	DON'T TAX ME (EP, p/s)	35
78	Charly CYS 1033	The Real People/Tomorrow Today/Disaster Movie (p/s)	10

EXILES

66	Topic 12T 143	FREEDOM, COME ALL YE (LP)	15
67	Topic 12T 164	THE HALE AND THE HANGED (LP)	15

EXITS

78	Way Out WOO 1	YODELLING (EP, numbered, gatefold p/s, hand-stamped labels)	60

EXITS

78	Red Lightning GIL 519	The Fashion Plague/Cheam (p/s, labels on wrong sides)	80

(see also Direct Hits)

EXIT STANCE

80s	Fight Back FIGHT 4	Crimes Against Humanity (p/s)	5

EXODUS (Jamaica)

71	Duke DU 103	Pharaoh's Walk/Little Caesar	6
72	Sioux SI 001	Pharaoh's Walk No. 9/SAMMY JONES: Worried Over You	5
72	Sioux SI 010	Julia Sees Me/LLOYD THE MATADOR: The Train (Engine 54)	8

EXORDIUM

70s	Face To Face FTF 1001	TROUBLE WITH ADAM (LP, private pressing)	20

EXOTICS

64	Decca F 11850	Cross My Heart/Ooh La La	8

EXOTICS

68	Columbia DB 8418	Don't Lead Me On/You Can Try	7

EXPELAIRES

79	Zoo CAGE 007	To See You/Frequency (p/s)	5

(see also Mission)

EXPELLED

82	Riot City RIOT 8	Dreaming/No Life, No Future/What Justice (p/s)	6
82	Riot City RIOT 17	Government Policy/Make It Alone (p/s)	6
84	Riot City 12RIOT 33	THE SINGLES (12" EP)	8

EXPERIMENTS WITH ICE

81	United Dairies EX 001	EXPERIMENTS WITH ICE (LP)	20

EXPLICIT CORPSE

81	Gistol	That Day Before.../I Gotta Gistol (stickered white labels, plastic gatefold p/s)	5

EXPLOITED

81	Exploited EXP 001	Army Life/Fuck The Mods/Crashed Out (p/s)	6
81	Exploited EXP 002	Exploited Barmy Army/I Believe In Anarchy/What You Gonna Do? (p/s)	6
81	Exploited EXP 003	EXTRACTS FROM EDINBURGH NITE CLUB (EP)	6
81	Secret SHH 110	Dogs Of War/Blown To Bits (live) (p/s)	5
81	Secret SHH 112	Army Life/Fuck The Mods/Crashed Out (p/s, reissue)	5
81	Secret SHH 120	Dead Cities/Hitler's In The Charts Again/Class War (p/s)	5
83	Blurg/Pax PAX 15	Rival Leaders/Army Style/Singalongabushell (p/s)	6
81	Exploited EXP 1001	PUNK'S NOT DEAD (LP)	12
81	Exploited EXP 1002	ON STAGE (LP)	12

MINT VALUE £

EXPLORER

84	Rock Shop RSR 006	EXPLODING (LP)	40

EXPLOSIVE

68	President PT 221	Crying All Night/I Close My Eyes	6
69	President PT 244	Cities Make The Country Colder/Step Out Of Line	20
69	President PT 262	Who Planted Thorns In Miss Alice's Garden?/I Get My Kicks From Living	6
70	President PT 286	I'm Gonna Use What I Got To Get What I Need/Am I A Fool? (with Del Taylor)	6
70	President PT 302	This Ain't The Road To Freedom/Today Is Today	6
71	Plexium PXM 20	Hey Presto, Magic Man/Get It Together	6
71	Plexium PXM 24	Love Doesn't Come Easy/See You In The Morning	6

(see also Watson T. Browne & Explosive)

EXPORT

79	Atlantic K 11344	Julie Bitch/Nice To Know You	15
80	His Master's Vice VICE 2	You've Got To Rock/Wheeler Dealer (title sleeve)	18
80	His Master's Vice VICE 1	EXPORT (LP)	18

EXPOZER

80	Hit Hard HARD 1	Rock Japan/Exposed At Last (p/s)	12
80	Hit Hard	EXPOSED AT LAST (LP)	12

EXTERNAL MENACE

82	Beat The System MENACE 1	YOUTH OF TODAY (EP)	7
83	Beat The System MENACE 2	NO VIEWS (EP)	7

EXTREEM

66	Strike JH 326	On The Beach/Don't You Ignore Me	12

EXTREME NOISE TERROR/CHAOS U.K.

86	Manic Ears ACHE 01	EAR SLAUGHTER — RADIOACTIVE (LP)	12

EXUMA

71	Mercury 6052 080	Damn Fool/You Don't Know What's Going On	6
72	Mercury 6052 112	We Got To Go/Zandoo	6
70	Mercury 6338 018	EXUMA (LP)	15

EYE FULL TOWER

67	Polydor BM 56734	How About Me?/Carol Cartoon	7

EYELESS IN GAZA

80	Ambivalent Scale ASR 2	Kodak Ghosts Run Amok/China Blue Vision/The Feeling's Mutual (wraparound p/s)	25
81	Cherry Red CHERRY 20	Invisibility/Three Kittens/Plague Of Years (p/s, with insert)	7
81	Cherry Red CHERRY 31	Others/Jane Dancing/Ever Present/Avenue With Trees (p/s)	5
82	Cherry Red CHERRY 47	Veil Like Calm/Taking Steps (p/s)	8
83	Cherry Red CHERRY 63	Sun Bursts In (p/s)	7
81	Cherry Red BRED 18	CAUGHT IN THE FLUX (LP, with bonus 12" EP [12 BRED 18], with inner)	12
82	Cherry Red BRED 36	DRUMMING THE BEATING HEART (LP)	12
86	Cherry Red BRED 69	BACK FROM THE RAINS (LP, with inner)	12

(see also Martyn Bates)

EYES

65	Mercury MF 881	When The Night Falls/I'm Rowed Out	200
66	Mercury MF 897	The Immediate Pleasure/My Degeneration	140
66	Mercury MF 910	Man With Money/You're Too Much	160
65	Mercury MF 934	Good Day Sunshine/Please Don't Cry	100
66	Mercury 10035 MCE	THE ARRIVAL OF THE EYES (EP)	400+
84	Bam Caruso KIRI 028	BLINK (LP, 2 different sleeves)	each 18
87	Bam Caruso MARI 038	SCENE BUT NOT HEARD (mini-LP)	15

(see also Pupils)

EYES OF BLUE

66	Deram DM 106	Heart Trouble/Up And Down	20
67	Deram DM 114	Supermarket Full Of Cans/Don't Ask Me To Mend Your Broken Heart	20
68	Mercury MF 1049	Largo/Yesterday	10
69	Mercury SMCL 20134	THE CROSSROADS OF TIME (LP)	35
69	Mercury SMCL 20164	IN FIELDS OF ARDATH (LP)	35

(see also Ancient Grease, Big Sleep, Man, Ritchie Francis, Gary Pickford-Hopkins)

EYNESBURY GIANT

78	Ultimate URL 602	FROM THE CASK (LP, with insert)	20

E-ZEE POSSEE

89	More Protein PROCD 1	Everything Starts With An 'E' (Edit)/(Sir Frederick Leighton Remix) (CD)	15

WILL EZELL

50s	Signature 910	Heifer Dust/Barrelhouse Woman (78)	7
50s	Signature 911	Old Mill Blues/Mixed Up Rag (78)	7
50	Tempo R 31	Old Mill Blues/Mixed Up Rag (78)	7
54	London AL 3539	GIN MILL JAZZ (10" LP)	25
73	Gannet 12-002	CHICAGO PIANO (LP)	12

(see also Paramount Allstars)

EZY MEAT

84	Electric Storm ES 0001	NOT FOR WIMPS (LP, with insert, Irish only)	50
86	Electric Storm ES 0002	ROCK YOUR BRAINS OUT (LP, with insert, Irish only)	40

EZY RIDER

82	English Steel	POWER (LP)	150

SHELLEY FABARES

62	Pye International 7N 25132	Johnny Angel/Where's It Gonna Get Me? (blue label, later yellow label)	15/10
62	Pye International 7N 25133	She Can't Find Her Keys/Very Unlikely (with Paul Peterson)	12
62	Pye International 7N 25151	Johnny Loves Me/I'm Growing Up	12
62	Pye International 7N 25166	The Things We Did Last Summer/Breaking Up Is Hard To Do	12
63	Pye International 7N 25184	Telephone (Won't You Ring)/Big Star	12
65	Fontana TF 592	My Prayer/Pretty Please	12

(see also Paul Peterson & Shelley Fabares)

FABIAN

59	HMV POP 587	I'm A Man/Hypnotized	35
59	HMV POP 587	I'm A Man/Hypnotized (78)	50
59	HMV POP 612	Turn Me Loose/Stop Thief!	30
59	HMV POP 643	Tiger/Mighty Cold (To A Warm, Warm Heart)	25
59	HMV POP 659	Got The Feeling/Come On And Get Me	18
60	HMV POP 695	Hound Dog Man/This Friendly World	18
60	HMV POP 724	String Along/About This Thing Called Love	10
60	HMV POP 778	I'm Gonna Sit Right Down And Write Myself A Letter/ Strollin' In The Springtime	10
60	HMV POP 800	Tomorrow/King Of Love	10
60	HMV POP 810	Kissin' And Twistin'/Long Before	10
61	HMV POP 829	You Know You Belong To Somebody Else/Hold On	10
61	HMV POP 869	Grapevine/David And Goliath	10
61	HMV POP 934	You're Only Young Once/The Love That I'm Giving To You	10
59	HMV CLP 1301	HOLD THAT TIGER (LP)	75
60	HMV CLP 1345	THE FABULOUS FABIAN (LP)	60
61	HMV CLP 1433	YOUNG AND WONDERFUL (LP, also stereo CSD 1352)	45/65

FABIONS

69	Bullet BU 410	V. Rocket/Smile (B-side actually "My Baby" by Tennors)	12

FABLE

70	Penny Farthing PEN 725	Minstrel Song/She Said Yes	5
71	Penny Farthing PEN 751	With A Boy Like You/She Said Yes	5
74	Magnet MAG 5002	FABLE (LP)	12

FABULOUS COUNTS

71	Mojo 2092 021	Get Down People/Lunar Funk	10

FABULOUS DIALS

63	Pye International 7N 25200	Bossa Nova Stomp/Forget Me Not	25

FABULOUS FLAMES

70	Clandisc CLA 224	Holly Holy/LORD CREATOR: Kingston Town	10
71	Trojan TR 7822	Growing Up/Lovitis	5

(see also Dynamites)

FABULOUS IMPACT

90	Kent 6T 6	Baby Baby, I Want You/HAMPTONS: No No No No No No Not My Girl (100 Club 6Ts allnighter anniversary disc)	15

FABULOUS SHADES

71	Tropical AL 005	Lonely Man/Version 2	6

FABULOUS SWINGTONES

58	HMV POP 471	Geraldine/You Know Baby	350
58	HMV POP 471	Geraldine/You Know Baby (78)	50

FABULOUS TALBOT BROTHERS

50s	Melodisc M 1507	Bloodshot Eyes/She's Got Freckles	15
50s	Melodisc M 1507	Bloodshot Eyes/She's Got Freckles (78)	10

FACES

70	Warner Bros WB 8005	Flying/Three-Button Hand-Me-Down	7
70	Warner Bros WB 8014	Wicked Messenger/Nobody Knows (unissued)	
70	Warner Bros WB 8018	Had Me A Real Good Time/Rear Wheel Skid	8
73	Warner Bros K 16247	Cindy Incidentally/Skewiff (Mend The Fuse) (with lyric insert, no p/s)	6
73	Warner Bros K 16281	Borstal Boys (withdrawn, any pressed?)	10+
73	NME SF1 139	Dishevelment Blues/Ooh La La Preview (flexidisc free with *NME*)	12/6
74	Warner Bros K 16494	You Can Make Me Dance, Sing Or Anything/As Long As You Tell Him (credited to Rod Stewart and the Faces, p/s)	7
77	Riva RIVA 8	THE FACES (EP, p/s)	5
70	Warner Bros WS 3000	FIRST STEP (LP, orange label, gatefold sleeve)	22
71	Warner Bros WS 3011	LONG PLAYER (LP, blue & silver label, stitched die-cut '78rpm' style sleeve)	15
71	Warner Bros K 46053	FIRST STEP (LP, reissue, green label, gatefold sleeve)	18
71	Warner Bros K 56006	A NOD IS AS GOOD AS A WINK ... TO A BLIND HORSE (LP, green label, some with poster)	20/12
72	Warner Bros K 46064	LONG PLAYER (LP, reissue, blue & silver label, stitched die-cut '78rpm'-style sleeve)	15
73	Warner Bros K 56011	OOH-LA-LA (LP, green label, 'Faces' sleeve with lyric poster)	15
73	Warner Bros K 56172	SNAKES AND LADDERS: BEST OF (LP)	12

74 Warner Bros K 46053 FIRST STEP (LP, 2nd reissue, 'Burbank' label, gatefold sleeve) . . . 12
74 Warner Bros K 56006 A NOD IS AS GOOD AS A WINK ... TO A BLIND HORSE (LP, reissue, 'Burbank' label) . . . 12
74 Warner Bros K 56011 OOH-LA-LA (LP, 'Burbank' label, 'Faces' sleeve, some with lyric poster) . . . 15/12
75 Warner Bros K 66027 TWO ORIGINALS OF . . . (2-LP, reissue of "First Steps" & "Long Player", gatefold sleeve) . . . 18
(see also Small Faces, Rod Stewart, Ronnie Lane & Slim Chance, Ron Wood, Jeff Beck Group, Kenney Jones)

FACTORY
68 MGM MGM 1444 Path Through The Forest/Gone . . . 700
69 CBS 4540 Try A Little Sunshine/Red Chalk Hill . . . 280
(see also Peter & Wolves, Norman Conquest, John Pantry)

FACTORY
70 Oak RGJ 718 Time Machine/Castle On The Hill (99 copies only) . . . 240
(see also Velvet Hush)

FACTORY
82 Future Earth FER 011 You Are The Music/History Of The World (silver die-cut sleeve) . . . 20

FACTOTUMS
65 Immediate IM 009 In My Lonely Room/Run In The Green And Tangerine Flaked Forest . . . 30
65 Immediate IM 022 You're So Good To Me/Can't Go Home Anymore My Love . . . 30
66 Piccadilly 7N 35333 Here Today/In My Room . . . 18
66 Piccadilly 7N 35355 I Can't Give You Anything But Love/Absolutely Sweet Marie . . . 18
67 Pye 7N 17402 Cloudy/Easy Said, Easy Done . . . 15
69 CBS 4140 Mr And Mrs Regards/Driftwood . . . 12

FADELA
88 Factory FAC 197 N'sel Fik/Ateni Bniti (12") . . . 10

FADERS
79 Rip Off RIP 8 Cheatin'/Library Book (in bag p/s) . . . 50

FAD GADGET
81 Lyntone LYN 10209 King Of The Flies/DEPECHE MODE: Sometimes I Wish I Was Dead (red vinyl flexidisc free with *Flexipop* magazine, issue 11) . . . 25/10

FADING COLOURS
66 Ember EMB S 229 (Just Like) Romeo And Juliet/Billy Christian . . . 20
67 Ember EMB S 237 Be With Me/You're No Use . . . 7
(see also Orange Seaweed)

FAERIE SYMPHONY
77 Decca F 13735 Dance Of The Theena Shee (Daoine Sidhe)/The Unseelie Court . . . 5
(see also Tom Newman)

BRIAN FAHEY (& HIS ORCHESTRA)
59 Parlophone R 4655 Street Of A Thousand Bongos/Waltz For Beatniks . . . 7
60 Parlophone R 4686 At The Sign Of The Swingin' Cymbal/The Clanger . . . 18
62 Parlophone R 4909 At The Sign Of The Swingin' Cymbal/The Clanger (reissue, as Brian Faye & His Orchestra) . . . 12
65 Parlophone R 5262 Gidian's Way/Love Theme From "In Harm's Way" . . . 12
65 United Artists UP 1115 Twang/You Can't Catch Me . . . 7
67 Parlophone R 5615 The Plank/Stay On the Island . . . 8
68 Columbia DB 8447 Late Night Extra/Oh The Pity Of It All . . . 10
69 Major Minor MM 656 Open House/Countdown . . . 18
67 Studio Two TWO 175 TIME FOR TV (LP) . . . 25

JOHN FAHEY
67 Transatlantic TRA 173 THE TRANSFIGURATION OF BLIND JOE DEATH (LP, some with booklet) . . . 20/15
68 Vanguard SVRL 19033 YELLOW PRINCESS (LP) . . . 15
68 Vanguard SVRL 19055 REQUIA (LP) . . . 15
69 Takoma SNTF 607 BLIND JOE DEATH (LP) . . . 12
69 Takoma SNTF 608 DEATH CHANTS, WALTZES & MILITARY BREAKDOWNS) (LP) . . . 12
72 Reprise K 44213 OF RIVERS AND RELIGION (LP) . . . 12
73 Reprise K 44246 AFTER THE BALL (LP) . . . 12
74 Takoma SNTF 675 JOHN FAHEY, PETER LANG AND LEO KOTTKE (LP) . . . 12
(see also Leo Kottke)

JAD FAIR
80 Armageddon AEP 003 THE ZOMBIES OF MORA-TAU (EP, die-cut p/s with insert) . . . 15
(see also Half Japanese)

JAD FAIR & PASTELS
91 Paperhouse PAPER 013T THIS COULD BE THE NIGHT EP (12", p/s) . . . 15
92 Paperhouse PAPER 018CD HE CHOSE HIS COLOURS WELL (CD EP) . . . 10
(see also Pastels)

WERLY FAIRBURN & DELTA BOYS
56 London HLC 8349 I'm A Fool About Your Love/All The Time . . . 1,000
56 London HLC 8349 I'm A Fool About Your Love/All The Time (78) . . . 150

JOHNNY FAIRE
58 London HLU 8569 Bertha Lou/Till The Law Says Stop . . . 550
58 London HLU 8569 Bertha Lou/Till The Law Says Stop (78) . . . 100

FAIRFIELD PARLOUR
70 Vertigo 6059 003 Bordeaux Rosé/Chalk On The Wall . . . 20
70 Vertigo 6059 008 Just Another Day/Caraminda/I Am All The Animals/Song For You . . . 20
76 Prism PRI 1 Bordeaux Rosé/Baby Stay For Tonight . . . 8
90s Bucketfull Of Brains Nursey Nursey (free with ***Bucketfull Of Brains***, issue 29) . . . 5
70 Vertigo 6360 001 FROM HOME TO HOME (LP, gatefold sleeve, swirl label) . . . 80
90s U.F.O. no cat. number FROM HOME TO HOME (LP, reissue) . . . 15
(see also Kaleidoscope [U.K.], I Luv Wight)

MINT VALUE £

FAIRIES

64	Decca F 11943	Don't Think Twice, It's Alright/Anytime At All	100
65	HMV POP 1404	Get Yourself Home/I'll Dance	240
65	HMV POP 1445	Don't Mind/Baby Don't	100

(see also Twink, Cops 'N Robbers)

FAIRPORT CONVENTION

SINGLES

67	Track 604 020	If I Had A Ribbon Bow/If (Stomp)	45
68	Island WIP 6047	Meet On The Ledge/Throwaway Street Puzzle (pink label)	12
69	Island WIP 6064	Si Tu Dois Partir/Genesis Hall	6
70	Island WIP 6089	Now Be Thankful/Sir B. McKenzie's Daughter's Lament	10
70	Polydor 2058 014	If (Stomp)/Chelsea Morning	12
71	Island WIP 6128	John Lee/The Time Is Near (some in p/s)	12/6
73	Island WIP 6155	Rosie/Knights Of The Road	5
75	Island WIP 6241	White Dress/Tears (some in p/s)	12/6
78	Hawk HASP 423	Jam's O'Donnell's Jig/The Last Waltz (Irish-only)	20
79	Simons PMW 1	Rubber Band/The Bonny Black Hare	12
86	Sunrise Bong 1	Quazi B Goode/MIKE SILVER: Where Would You Rather Be Tonight	10
87	Island IF 324	Meet On The Ledge (Re-recorded)/Sigh Bheg Sigh Mhor (live)	5
87	Island 12IF 324	Meet On The Ledge (Re-recorded)/John Barleycorn (live)/ Sigh Bheg Sigh Mhor (live) (12", p/s, some with poster)	10/8

POLYDOR LP

68	Polydor 582/583 035	FAIRPORT CONVENTION (mono/stereo)	90/70

ISLAND LPs

69	Island ILPS 9092	WHAT WE DID ON OUR HOLIDAYS (1st pressing, pink label with black 'circle' logo; 2nd pressing, pink label with black 'block' logo)	50/40
69	Island ILPS 9092	WHAT WE DID ON OUR HOLIDAYS (3rd pressing, pink label with 'i' logo)	20
69	Island ILPS 9092	WHAT WE DID ON OUR HOLIDAYS (4th pressing, pink rim label with 'palm tree' logo)	15
69	Island ILPS 9102	UNHALFBRICKING (1st pressing, pink label with black 'circle' logo)	40
69	Island ILPS 9102	UNHALFBRICKING (2nd pressing, pink label with black 'block' logo)	25
69	Island ILPS 9102	UNHALFBRICKING (3rd pressing, pink label with 'i' logo)	22
70	Island ILPS 9102	UNHALFBRICKING (4th pressing, pink rim label with 'palm tree' logo)	15
69	Island ILPS 9115	LIEGE AND LIEF (gatefold sleeve, 1st pressing, pink label with 'i' logo)	20
70	Island ILPS 9115	LIEGE AND LIEF (gatefold sleeve, 2nd pressing, pink rim label with 'palm tree' logo)	15
70	Island ILPS 9130	FULL HOUSE (white label test pressing, with "Poor Will & The Jolly Hangman")	225+
70	Island ILPS 9130	FULL HOUSE (1st pressing, gatefold sleeve lists "Poor Will & The Jolly Hangman")	20
70	Island ILPS 9130	FULL HOUSE (2nd pressing, gatefold sleeve without reference to "Poor Will & The Jolly Hangman")	18
70	Island ILPS 9130	FULL HOUSE (gatefold sleeve, 3rd pressing, pink rim label with 'palm tree' logo)	15
71	Island ILPS 9162	ANGEL DELIGHT (gatefold sleeve with 'stuck-on' photos, pink rim label)	15
71	Island ILPS 9176	BABBACOMBE LEE (gatefold sleeve, with innersleeve and booklet, some with sticker)	30/15
72	Island ICD 4	THE HISTORY OF FAIRPORT CONVENTION (2-LP, with 12-page booklet & blue ribbons; later with book & green, red or light blue ribbons)	20/18
73	Island ILPS 9208	ROSIE	12
73	Island ILPS 9246	FAIRPORT NINE (gatefold sleeve)	12
74	Island ILPS 9285	LIVE CONVENTION (with insert)	12
75	Island ILPS 9313	RISING FOR THE MOON (with insert, 'palm tree' label)	12
75	Island ISS 2	FAIRPORT TOUR SAMPLER (free in *NME* competition, 500 only)	120
76	Island ILPS 9389	GOTTLE O' GEER	15
76	Island HELP 28	LIVE AT THE L.A. TROUBADOR 1974	25

OTHER LPs

77	Vertigo 9102 015	BONNY BUNCH OF ROSES (gatefold sleeve)	18
78	Vertigo 9102 022	TIPPLER'S TALES (with lyric insert)	15
79	Woodworm BEAR 22	FAREWELL FAREWELL (gatefold sleeve)	25
79	Simons GAMA 1	FAREWELL FAREWELL (reissue, gatefold sleeve)	20
82	Woodworm WR 001	MOAT ON THE LEDGE — LIVE 1981	12
82	Woodworm (no cat. no.)	AIRING CUPBOARD TAPES (cassette)	12
83	Woodworm WRC 1	AT 2 (AIRING CUPBOARD TAPES 2) (cassette)	20
84	Woodworm (no cat. no.)	THE BOOT (2-cassette in video box, 1,000 only)	25
87	Woodworm (no cat. no.)	THE OTHER BOOT (2-cassette in video box, 1,000 only)	25
88	Woodworm (no cat. no.)	THE THIRD LEG (2-cassette in video box, 1,000 only)	25
88	Woodworm WR 011	BONNY BUNCH OF ROSES (reissue)	12
89	BGO BGOCD 72	TIPPLER'S TALES (CD)	20
92	Vertigo 512882	BONNY BUNCH OF ROSES / TIPPLERS TALES (CD)	30

(see also Richard Thompson, Ian Matthews, Dave Swarbrick, Sandy Denny, Ashley Hutchings, Trevor Lucas, Albion Band, Bunch, Fotheringay, Vashti Bunyan, Trader Horne, Thieves, Pyramid, Allan Taylor, Krysia, Marc Ellington, Brian Maxine, Steeleye Span, Vikki Clayton)

FAIR WARNING

87	Areba ERA 2	ROCKING AT THE SPEED OF LIGHT EP (12", p/s)	30

FAIRWAYS (featuring Gary Street)

69	Mercury MF 1116	Yoko Ono/I Don't Care	10

FAIR WEATHER

70	RCA RCA 1977	Natural Sinner/Haven't I Tried?	6
70	RCA RCA 2040	Road To Freedom/Tutti Frutti	8
71	RCA Neon NE 1000	Lay It On Me/Looking For The Red Label Pt 2	12
71	RCA Neon NE 1	BEGINNING FROM AN END (LP)	45

(see also Andy Fairweather-Low, Amen Corner, Wynder K. Frog)

MINT VALUE £

AL FAIRWEATHER

57 Columbia SEG 7653 AL FAIRWEATHER'S JAZZ BAND (EP) . . . 8
58 Tempo EXA 63 AL FAIRWEATHER'S JAZZMEN (EP, with Henrick Johansen) . . . 10
62 Columbia SEG 8157 STUDY IN BROWN (EP, with Sandy Brown) . . . 15
62 Columbia SEG 8181 GROOVER WAILIN' (EP, with Sandy Brown) . . . 12
58 Nixa NJT 511 FAIRWEATHER FRIENDS (LP) . . . 30
60 Columbia 33SX 1159 AL AND SANDY (LP) . . . 20
60 Columbia 33SX 1221 AL'S PALS (LP) . . . 30
61 Columbia 33SX 1306 DOCTOR McJAZZ (LP, also stereo SCX 3367, with Sandy Brown) . . . 40/50
63 Columbia 33SX 1509 THE INCREDIBLE McJAZZ (LP, with Sandy Brown's All Stars) . . . 40
(see also Sandy Brown, Henrik Johansen, Albert Nicholas)

ANDY FAIRWEATHER-LOW

76 A&M AMLH 64602 BE BOP'N'HOLLA (LP, blue vinyl) . . . 12
(see also Amen Corner, Fair Weather, Gary Pickford-Hopkins & Friends, Dave Edmunds & Rockpile)

FAIRY'S MOKE

75 Deroy 1175 FAIRY'S MOKE (LP, private pressing, actually various artists LP) . . . 150
(see also Baby Sunshine)

FAIRYTALE

67 Decca F 12644 Guess I Was Dreaming/Run And Hide . . . 100
67 Decca F 12665 Lovely People/Listen To Mary Cry . . . 80

ADAM FAITH (& ROULETTES)

78s

58 HMV POP 438 (Got A) Heartsick Feeling/Brother Heartache And Sister Tears . . . 65
58 HMV POP 557 High School Confidential/Country Music Holiday . . . 75
59 Top Rank JAR 126 Ah, Poor Little Baby!/Runk Bunk . . . 75
59 Parlophone R 4591 What Do You Want?/From Now Until Forever . . . 40
60 Parlophone R 4623 Poor Me/The Reason . . . 40

SINGLES

58 HMV POP 438 (Got A) Heartsick Feeling/Brother Heartache And Sister Tears . . . 110
58 HMV POP 557 High School Confidential/Country Music Holiday . . . 100
59 Top Rank JAR 126 Ah, Poor Little Baby!/Runk Bunk (blue or orange label) . . . 25/50
59 Parlophone R 4591 What Do You Want?/From Now Until Forever . . . 5
60 Parlophone R 4665 Made You/When Johnny Comes Marching Home . . . 5
62 Parlophone R 4864 Lonesome/Watch Your Step . . . 6
62 Parlophone R 4964 Baby Take A Bow/Knocking On Wood . . . 6
63 Parlophone R 4990 What Now/What Have I Got . . . 6
63 Parlophone R 5039 Walkin' Tall/Just Mention My Name . . . 6
63 Parlophone R 5091 We Are In Love/Made For Me (with Roulettes) . . . 6
64 Parlophone R 5109 If He Tells You/Talk To Me . . . 6
64 Parlophone R 5138 I Love Being In Love With You/It's Alright (with Roulettes) . . . 6
64 Parlophone R 5174 I Just Don't Know/Only One Such As You . . . 6
64 Parlophone R 5201 A Message To Martha (Kentucky Bluebird)/It Sounds Good To Me . . . 6
65 Parlophone R 5235 Stop Feeling Sorry For Yourself/I've Gotta See My Baby . . . 6
65 Parlophone R 5260 Hand Me Down Things/Talk About Love . . . 6
65 Parlophone R 5289 Someone's Taken Maria Away/I Can't Think Of Anyone Else (with Roulettes) . . . 6
65 Parlophone R 5349 I Don't Need That Kind Of Lovin'/I'm Used To Losing You . . . 6
66 Parlophone R 5398 Idle Gossip/If You Ever Need Me . . . 8
66 Parlophone R 5412 To Make A Big Man Cry/Here's Another Day . . . 10
66 Parlophone R 5516 Cheryl's Goin' Home/Funny Kind Of Love . . . 10
67 Parlophone R 5556 What More Can Anyone Do/You've Got A Way With Me . . . 15
67 Parlophone R 5635 Cowman Milk Your Cow/Daddy, What'll Happen To Me . . . 25
67 Parlophone R 5649 To Hell With Love/Close The Door . . . 12
68 Parlophone R 5673 You Make My Life Worth While/Hey Little Lovin' Girl . . . 15

EPs

60 Parlophone GEP 8811 ADAM'S HIT PARADE . . . 12
60 Parlophone GEP 8824 ADAM NO. 1 (also stereo SGE 2014) . . . 12/20
60 Parlophone GEP 8826 ADAM NO. 2 (also stereo SGE 2015) . . . 12/20
60 Parlophone GEP 8831 ADAM NO. 3 (also stereo SGE 2018) . . . 12/20
61 Parlophone GEP 8841 ADAM'S HIT PARADE VOL. 2 . . . 12
62 Parlophone GEP 8851 ADAM FAITH NO. 1 . . . 15
62 Parlophone GEP 8852 ADAM FAITH NO. 2 . . . 15
62 Parlophone GEP 8854 ADAM FAITH NO. 3 (with John Barry) . . . 15
62 Columbia SEG 8138 BEAT GIRL (2 Faith tracks, with John Barry Orchestra) . . . 35
62 Parlophone GEP 8862 ADAM'S HIT PARADE VOL. 3 . . . 15
63 Parlophone GEP 8877 ADAM'S LATEST HITS . . . 15
64 Parlophone GEP 8893 TOP OF THE POPS (with Roulettes) . . . 18
64 Parlophone GEP 8904 FOR YOU — ADAM . . . 15
65 Parlophone GEP 8929 A MESSAGE TO MARTHA — FROM ADAM . . . 18
65 Parlophone GEP 8939 SONGS AND THINGS . . . 20

LPs

60 Columbia 33SX 1225 BEAT GIRL (soundtrack, with John Barry Orchestra) . . . 50
60 Parlophone PMC 1128 ADAM (also stereo PCS 3010) . . . 20/30
61 Parlophone PMC 1162 ADAM FAITH (also stereo PCS 3025) . . . 20/30
62 Parlophone PMC 1192 FROM ADAM WITH LOVE (also stereo PCS 3038) . . . 15/20
63 Parlophone PMC 1213 FOR YOU — ADAM (also stereo) . . . 20/30
64 Parlophone PMC 1228 ON THE MOVE (with Roulettes) . . . 40
65 Parlophone PMC 1249 FAITH ALIVE! (with Roulettes) . . . 80
60 EMI Regal (S)REG 1033 ADAM (mono/stereo export issue in different sleeve) . . . 18/22
(see also Roulettes, John Barry)

AUSTIN FAITH

71 Dynamic DYN 407 634 5789/DYNAMIC BOYS: Warm And Tender Love . . . 7
(see also Austin Faithful)

MINT VALUE £

GEORGE FAITH

77 Black Swan ILPS 9504 — TO BE A LOVER (LP) . . . 20

HORACE FAITH

69 B&C CB 104 — Spinning Wheel/Like I Used To Do . . . 7
69 Downtown DT 446 — Daddy's Home/EMOTIONS: Give Me A Love . . . 7
70 Trojan TR 7766 — Susie Is Sorrow/DERRICK PEPPER: Don't Go . . . 6
70 Trojan TR 7790 — Black Pearl/Help Me Help Myself . . . 6
70 A&M AMS 817 — Shame And Scandal In The Family/REGGAE STRINGS: Reggae Strings . . . 6

PERCY FAITH ORCHESTRA

60 Philips PB 989 — Theme From 'A Summer Place'/Go-Go-Po-Go . . . 6
64 CBS AAG 226 — The Virginian/Judy . . . 7
59 Philips BBE 12397 — FAMOUS FILM THEMES (EP) . . . 8
66 CBS 62663 — THEMES FOR THE IN CROWD (LP) . . . 15
66 CBS SS 62779 — BIG BAM BOOM!!! (LP) . . . 12

AUSTIN FAITHFUL

68 Blue Cat BS 140 — Uncle Joe/Can't Understand . . . 15
68 Pyramid PYR 6016 — I'm In A Rocking Mood/ROLAND ALPHONSO: Stream Of Life . . . 15
69 Pyramid PYR 6028 — Eternal Love/ROLAND ALPHONSO: Goodnight My Love . . . 12
69 Pyramid PYR 6042 — Ain't That Peculiar?/Miss Anti-Social . . . 10
(see also Austin Faith)

MARIANNE FAITHFULL

64 Decca F 11923 — As Tears Go By/Greensleeves . . . 6
64 Decca F 12007 — Blowin' In The Wind/The House Of The Rising Sun . . . 7
65 Decca F 12075 — Come And Stay With Me/What Have I Done Wrong? . . . 7
65 Decca F 12162 — This Little Bird/Morning Sun . . . 6
65 Decca F 12193 — Summer Nights/The Sha La La Song . . . 7
65 Decca F 12268 — Yesterday/Oh Look Around You . . . 7
66 Decca F 12408 — Tomorrow's Calling/That's Right Baby . . . 7
66 Decca F 12443 — Counting/I'd Like To Dial Your Number . . . 10
66 Decca F 22524 — Is This What I Get For Loving You?/Tomorrow's Calling . . . 10
69 Decca F 12889 — Something Better/Sister Morphine (withdrawn) . . . 50
75 NEMS NES 004 — Dreamin' My Dreams/Lady Madalene . . . 6
76 NEMS NES 013 — All I Wanna Do In Life/Wrong Road Again . . . 6
77 NEMS NES 014 — Wrong Road Again/The Way You Want Me To Be . . . 6
78 NEMS NES 117 — The Way You Want Me To Be/That Was The Day (Nashville) . . . 6
79 Island WIP 6491 — The Ballad Of Lucy Jordan/Brain Drain . . . 6
80 Island 12WIP 6542 — Broken English/Why D'Ya Do It? (12", p/s) . . . 10
80 Decca F 13890 — As Tears Go By/Come And Stay With Me/This Little Bird/Summer Nights (p/s) . . . 6
65 Decca DFE 8624 — GO AWAY FROM MY WORLD (EP) . . . 35
65 Decca LK 4688 — COME MY WAY (LP) . . . 50
65 Decca LK 4689 — MARIANNE FAITHFULL (LP) . . . 50
66 Decca LK 4778 — NORTH COUNTRY MAID (LP) . . . 50
67 Decca LK/SKL 4854 — LOVEINAMIST (LP) . . . 75
69 Decca (S)PA 17 — THE WORLD OF MARIANNE FAITHFULL (LP, mono/stereo) . . . 15/12
76 NEMS NEL 6007 — DREAMIN' MY DREAMS (LP) . . . 15

FAITH, HOPE & CHARITY

70 Crewe CRW 3 — So Much Love/Life Won't Be The Same Without You . . . 6
70 Crewe CRW 3 — So Much Love/Let's Try It Over . . . 5

FAITH NO MORE

88 Slash LASH 17 — We Care A Lot/Spirit (p/s) . . . 6
88 Slash LASHX 17 — We Care A Lot/Spirit/Chinese Arithmetic (Radio Mix) (12", p/s) . . . 8
88 Slash LASH 18 — Annie's Song (Remix)/Greed (p/s) . . . 10
88 Slash LASHP 18 — Annie's Song (Remix)/Greed (picture disc) . . . 10
88 Slash LASHX 18 — Anne's Song (Remix)/Greed (12", p/s) . . . 12
89 Kerrang! FIEND 3 — Sweet Emotion/(Balaam & The Angel track) (flexidisc with *Kerrang!* mag) . . . 10/6
90 Slash LASPD 21 — Epic/War Pigs (live) (shaped picture disc) . . . 8
90 Slash LASCD 21 — Epic/War Pigs (live)/Surprise You're Dead (live)/Chinese Arithmetic (live) (CD, card sleeve) . . . 10
90 Slash LASCD 24 — From Out Of Nowhere/Woodpecker From Mars (live)/The Real Thing (live)/ Epic (live) (CD, card sleeve) . . . 8
90 Slash LASPD 26 — Epic/Falling To Pieces (live) (shaped picture disc, 12" insert in PVC sleeve) . . . 6
90 Slash LASPD 26 — Epic/Falling To Pieces (live)/Epic (live)/As The Worm Turns (live) (CD) . . . 8
90 London/Slash 850 228 — KING FOR A DAY, FOOL FOR A LIFETIME (7 x 7" box set) . . . 30
89 Slash 828 217-1 — THE REAL THING (LP, picture disc) . . . 18

FAKES

79 Deep Cuts DEEP TWO — Production/Look-Out (p/s) . . . 5

TAV FALCO'S PANTHER BURNS

(see under Panther Burns)

EDDIE FALCON

60 Columbia DB 4420 — The Young Have No Time To Lose/My Thanks To You . . . 7
61 Columbia DB 4646 — Linda Rose/If Ever I Should Fall In Love . . . 7

FALCONS (U.K.)

64 Philips BF 1297 — Stampede/Kazutzka . . . 15

FALCONS (U.S.)

59 London HLT 8876 — You're So Fine/Goddess Of Angels . . . 120
59 London HLT 8876 — You're So Fine/Goddess Of Angels (78) . . . 70
62 London HLK 9565 — I Found A Love/Swim (some labels credit B-side as "Swin") . . . 60
(see also Wilson Pickett, Eddie Floyd)

MINT VALUE £

THE FALL

Year	Label	Title	£
78	Step Forward SF 7	BINGO-MASTERS' BREAKOUT! (EP)	10
78	Step Forward SF 9	It's The New Thing/Various Times (p/s)	8
79	Step Forward SF 11	Rowche Rumble/In My Area (p/s)	6
80	Step Forward SF 13	Fiery Jack/Second Dark Age/Psykick Dancehall 2 (black-and-white or yellow p/s)	10/8
80	Rough Trade RT 048	How I Wrote Elastic Man/City Hobgoblins (p/s)	6
80	Rough Trade RT 056	Totally Wired/Putta Block (p/s)	8
81	Rough Trade RT 071	SLATES (10" EP, 33rpm)	10
81	Kamera ERA 001	Lie Dream Of A Casino Soul/Fantastic Life (p/s)	5
82	Kamera ERA 004	Look, Know/I'm Into C.B. (p/s)	6
82	Rough Trade RT 133	The Man Whose Head Expanded/Ludd Gang (p/s)	6
82	Kamera ERA 014	Marquis Cha Cha/Papal Visit (p/s, B-side plays "Room To Live", withdrawn)	30
83	Rough Trade RT 143	Kicker Conspiracy/Wings//Container Drivers/New Puritan (g/fold double pack)	10
84	Beggars Banquet BEG 116	C.R.E.E.P./Pat-Trip Dispenser (p/s)	10
84	Beggars Banquet BEG 116T	C.R.E.E.P./(Extended Version)/Pat-Trip Dispenser (12", p/s, green vinyl)	12
84	B. Banquet BEG 116TP	C.R.E.E.P./(Extended Version)/Pat-Trip Dispenser (12", p/s, with art print)	8
84	Beggars Banquet BEG 120E	CALL FOR ESCAPE ROUTE (7"/12" double pack EP)	8
85	Beggars Banquet BEG 150	Cruiser's Creek (p/s)	6
85	Beggars Banquet BEG 150T	Cruiser's Creek (12", p/s)	10
87	Beggars Banquet BEG 187H	There's A Ghost In My House/Haf Found Bormann (hologram p/s)	5
87	Beggars Banquet BEG 200P	Hit The North (Parts 1 & 2) (picture disc, printed PVC sleeve)	5
87	Beggars Banquet BEG 200T	Hit The North (Parts 1 & 2) (12", gatefold sleeve)	8
87	Beggars Banquet BEG 206B	Victoria/Tuff Life Boogie (box set with inserts & badge)	5
88	Beggars Banquet FALL 2B	Jerusalem (Remix)/Acid Priest 2088 (Remix)//Big New Prinz (Remix)/ Wrong Place Right Time No. 2 (Remix) (double pack box set, with postcard)	5
88	Beggars Banquet FALL 2CD	Jerusalem (Remix)/Acid Priest 2088 (Remix)//Big New Prinz (Remix)/ Wrong Place, Right Time No. 2 (Remix) (3" CD, double pack, gatefold wallet, 4,000 only)	10
90	Cog Sinister SINCD 4	Telephone Thing/British People In Hot Weather/Telephone Dub (CD)	8
90	Cog Sinister SINR 5	Popcorn Double Feature/Zandra (p/s)	6
90	Cog Sinister SINCD 5	Popcorn Double Feature/Arms Control Poseur/Butterflies/Brains (CD)	8
90	Cog Sinister SINDJ 6	White Lightning (stickered sleeve)	5
94	Permanent 10SPERM 14	15 Ways (10", p/s)	10
79	Step Forward SFLP 1	LIVE AT THE WITCH TRIALS (LP)	12
79	Step Forward SFLP 4	DRAGNET (LP, with insert)	15
80	Rough Trade ROUGH 10	TOTALE'S TURNS (IT'S NOW OR NEVER) (LP)	12
80	Rough Trade ROUGH 18	GROTESQUE (AFTER THE GRAMME) (LP)	14
81	Step Forward SFLP 6	THE EARLY YEARS 1977-79 (LP)	15
82	Chaos LIVE 006	LIVE AT ACKLAM HALL (cassette)	12
82	Kamera KAM 005	HEX ENDUCTION HOUR (LP)	12
83	Rough Trade 062	PERVERTED BY LANGUAGE (LP)	14

(see also D.O.S.E.)

FALLEN ANGELS (U.K.)

Year	Label	Title	£
84	Fallout FALL 12 027	INNER PLANET LOVE (mini-LP)	10

(see also Knox, Hanoi Rocks, Troops Of Tomorrow)

FALLEN ANGELS (U.S.)

Year	Label	Title	£
67	London HL 10166	I Don't Want To Fall/Most Children Do	6
68	London HA-Z/SH-Z 8359	THE FALLEN ANGELS (LP)	25

JOHNNY FALLIN

Year	Label	Title	£
59	Capitol CL 15043	Party Kiss/The Creation Of Love	40
59	Capitol CL 15091	Wild Streak/If I Could Write A Love Song	45

FALLING LEAVES

Year	Label	Title	£
65	Parlophone R 5233	She Loves To Be Loved/Not Guilty	60
66	Decca F 12420	Beggar's Parade/Tomorrow Night	30

FALLOUT

Year	Label	Title	£
83	Mouth Too Small To F. F2	SALAMI TACTICS (EP)	5
84	I FLP 2	BUTCHERY (10" EP, with lyric inner)	8

FALLOUT CLUB

Year	Label	Title	£
79	Secret SHH104	The Falling Years/The Beat Boys (p/s)	14
81	Happy Birthday UR3	Dream Soldiers/Pedestrial Walk Way (p/s)	14

FALSE IDOLS

Year	Label	Title	£
78	Old Knew Wave BOG 005	Broken Judy/Marbled Hands/H-Brain (tri-fold p/s)	5
78	Old Knew Wave BOG 007	Ego Wino/Good Night (p/s, pink vinyl)	5

AGNETHA FALTSKOG

Year	Label	Title	£
82	Epic EPC A 2824	Never Again/Just For The Fun (p/s, with Tomas Ledin)	12
83	Epic EPC A 3436	The Heat Is On/Man (p/s)	8
83	Epic EPC WA 3436	The Heat Is On/Man (picture disc)	30
83	Epic EPC A 3622	Wrap Your Arms Around Me/Take Good Care Of The Children (p/s)	8
83	Epic EPC TA 3622	Wrap Your Arms Around Me/The Heat Is On/ Take Good Care Of The Children (Extended) (12", p/s)	15
83	Epic EPC A 3812	Can't Shake Loose/To Love (p/s)	8
83	Epic EPC A 3812	Can't Shake Loose/To Love (poster p/s)	15
83	Epic EPC WA 3812	Can't Shake Loose/To Love (picture disc)	25
85	Epic EPC A 6133	I Won't Let You Go/You're There (p/s)	8
85	Epic EPC TA 6133	I Won't Let You Go (Extended)/You're There (12", p/s)	15
86	Sonet SON 2317	The Way You Are/Fly Like The Eagle (p/s, with Ola Hanansson)	10
88	WEA YZ 170	The Last Time/Are You Gonna Throw It All Away (p/s)	8
88	WEA YZ 170T	The Last Time (Extended Remix)/The Last Time/ Are You Gonna Throw It All Away (12", p/s)	15
88	WEA YZ 177	I Wasn't The One (Who Said Goodbye)/If You Need Somebody Tonight (p/s, with Peter Cetera)	8

MINT VALUE £

88	WEA YZ 177T	I Wasn't The One (Who Said Goodbye) (Extended Version)/(Yo No Fui [Quien Dijo Adios])/If You Need Somebody Tonight (12", p/s, with Peter Cetera)	15
88	WEA YZ 300	Let It Shine/Maybe It Was Magic (p/s)	8
88	WEA YZ 300T	Let It Shine (Extended)/('Bright' Mix)/Maybe It Was Magic (12", p/s)	15
98	Polydor POLPROCD 2	The Queen Of Hearts (Nar Du Tar Mej I Din Fam) (CD, promo only)	40
74	Embassy EMB 31094	AGNETHA (LP)	80

(see also Abba)

GEORGIE FAME (& THE BLUE FLAMES)

SINGLES

64	Columbia DB 7193	Do The Dog/Shop Around	20
64	Columbia DB 7255	Green Onions/Do-Re-Mi	12
64	Columbia DB 7328	Bend A Little/I'm In Love With You (solo)	20
64	Columbia DB 7428	Yeh Yeh/Preach And Teach (some copies list "Yeah, Yeah" on label)	each 6
64	Columbia DB 7428	Yeh Yeh/Preach And Teach (99 promo copies only with p/s)	65+
65	Columbia DB 7494	In The Meantime/Telegram	12
65	Columbia DB 7633	Like We Used To Be/It Ain't Right	10
65	Columbia DB 7727	Something/Outrage	8
66	Columbia DB 7946	Getaway/El Bandido	8

(All the above singles credited to Georgie Fame & Blue Flames unless stated; the singles listed below were solo.)

66	Columbia DB 8015	Sunny/Don't Make Promises	7
66	Columbia DB 8096	Sitting In The Park/Many Happy Returns	7
67	CBS 202587	Because I Love You/Bidin' My Time (p/s)	8
67	CBS 2945	Try My World/No Thanks (p/s)	8
67	CBS 3124	The Ballad Of Bonnie And Clyde/Beware Of The Dog (p/s)	8
69	CBS 4295	Peaceful/Hideaway (with John Barry)	7
69	CBS 4659	Seventh Son/Fully Booked	6
70	CBS 5035	Entertaining Mr. Sloane/Somebody Stole My Thunder	50
70	CBS 5131	Fire And Rain/Someday Man	6
86	Ensign ENYX 605	Samba (mixes)/Willow King (12", p/s)	8
86	Ensign ENYR 605	Samba (mixes)/New York Afternoon (12", p/s, with Mondo Kane)	10

EPs

64	Columbia SEG 8334	RHYTHM AND BLUEBEAT	55
64	Columbia SEG 8382	RHYTHM AND BLUES AT THE FLAMINGO	30
64	Columbia SEG 8393	FAME AT LAST	25
65	Columbia SEG 8406	FATS FOR FAME	30
65	Columbia SEG 8454	MOVE IT ON OVER	30
66	Columbia SEG 8518	GETAWAY	25
67	CBS EP 6363	KNOCK ON WOOD	25

LPs

64	Columbia 33SX 1599	RHYTHM AND BLUES AT THE FLAMINGO	90
64	Columbia 33SX 1638	FAME AT LAST	30
66	Columbia SX 6043	SWEET THINGS	35
66	Columbia SX 6076	SOUND VENTURE	35
67	Columbia SX 6120	HALL OF FAME	22
67	CBS (S)BPG 63018	TWO FACES OF FAME	22
68	CBS (S) 63293	THE THIRD FACE OF FAME (mono/stereo)	18/15
69	CBS (S) 63650	GEORGIE DOES HIS OWN THING WITH STRINGS (mono/stereo)	18/15
69	CBS S 63786	SEVENTH SON	20
71	CBS S 64350	GOING HOME	18
72	Reprise K 44183	ALL ME OWN WORK	20
74	Island ILPS 9293	GEORGIE FAME	25

(see also Blue Flames, Jimmy Nicol, Perry Ford & Sapphires)

FAMILY

67	Liberty LBF 15031	Scene Thru The Eye Of A Lens/Gypsy Woman (mispress, B-side plays "Let Me Be Good To You" by Otis Redding)	80
67	Liberty LBF 15031	Scene Thru The Eye Of A Lens/Gypsy Woman	175
68	Reprise RS 23270	Me My Friend/Hey Mr. Policeman	15
68	Reprise RS 23315	Second Generation Woman/Home Town	15
69	Reprise RS 27001	No Mule's Fool/Good Friend Of Mine (initially in p/s)	15/5
70	Reprise RS 27005	Today/Song For Lots (initially in p/s)	15/5
70	Reprise RS 27009	The Weaver's Answer/Strange Band/Hung Up Down (initially in p/s)	8/5
71	Reprise K 14090	In My Own Time/Seasons (initially in p/s)	8/5
71	Reprise SAM 1	Larf And Sing/Children (promo only)	15
72	Reprise K 14196	Burlesque/The Rockin' R's	7
72	Reprise K 14218	My Friend The Sun/Glove	7
73	Raft RA 18501	Boom Bang/Stop This Car	7
73	Raft RA 18503	Sweet Desiree/Drink To You	7
68	Reprise R(S)LP 6312	MUSIC IN A DOLL'S HOUSE (LP, with insert, mono/stereo)	80/40
69	Reprise RLP 6340	FAMILY ENTERTAINMENT (LP, mono, some with poster)	50/25
69	Reprise RSLP 6340	FAMILY ENTERTAINMENT (LP, stereo, some with poster)	25/18
70	Reprise RSLP 9001	A SONG FOR ME (LP, with lyric sheet, later copies without boat label £15)	25

(The above LPs were originally issued with 'steamboat' label designs, later pressings with same cat. no. are worth £2 less.)

70	Reprise RSX 9005	ANYWAY (LP, custom polythene sleeve)	15
71	Reprise RMP 9007	OLD SONGS NEW SONGS (LP)	15
71	Reprise K 54003	FEARLESS (LP)	12
72	Reprise K 54006	BANDSTAND (LP, 'window' sleeve)	15
73	Raft RA 58501	IT'S ONLY A MOVIE (LP)	12

(see also Farinas, Stud, Mogul Thrash, Hellions, Ashton Gardner & Dyke, Revolution, Streetwalkers)

FAMILY CAT

89	Bad Girl BGRIFC 01	Tom Verlaine (Demo Version) (gig freebie flexidisc, hand-sprayed p/s & insert)	5
91	Bad Girl BGRLT 009T	Color Me Grey/I Must Have Been Blind/Great Ugly Place (12", p/s)	8

(see also P.J. Harvey)

MINT VALUE £

FAMILY CIRCLE
69 Attack AT 8001 Phoenix Reggae/BIG L: Music Box . . . 8

FAMILY DOGG
67 MGM MGM 1360 Family Dogg/The Storm . . . 10
68 Fontana TF 921 I Wear A Silly Grin/Couldn't Help It . . . 10
68 Fontana TF 968 Brown-Eyed Girl/Let It Rain . . . 7
69 Bell BLL 1055 A Way Of Life/Throw It Away . . . 6
69 Bell BLL 1077 Arizona/The House In The Heather . . . 6
70 Bell BLL 1100 When Tomorrow Comes Today/This Unhappy Heart Of Mine . . . 6
71 Bell BLL 1139 Coat Of Many Colours/Jesus Loves You . . . 6
69 Bell SBLL 122 A WAY OF LIFE (LP, with members of Led Zeppelin) . . . 25
72 Polydor 2318 061 THE VIEW FROM ROWLAND'S HEAD (LP) . . . 15
(see also Steve Rowland, Albert Hammond, Christine Holmes)

FAMILY FODDER
79 Parole/Fresh PURL 4 Playing Golf/My Baby Takes Valium (p/s) . . . 5

FAMILY MAN (Aston Barrett)
70 Escort ERT 834 Midnight Sunshine/GREGORY & STICKY: You Are My Sunshine . . . 6
72 Downtown DT 491 Herb Tree/STUDIO SOUND: Holy Poly (reissue) . . . 6
(see also Hippy Boys, Upsetters, Bob Marley & Wailers, Carl Dawkins)

FAMILY PLANN
75 President PT 441 Sexy Summer/Can You Get Into The Music . . . 5

FAMOUS ECCLES & MISS FREDA THING
56 Parlophone R 4251 My September Love/JIM MORIARTY: You Gotta Go Oww! . . . 15
(see also Spike Milligan, Goons)

FAMOUS JUG BAND
69 Liberty LBF 15224 The Only Friend I Own/A Leaf Must Fall . . . 8
69 Liberty LBS 83263 SUNSHINE POSSIBILITIES (LP) . . . 40
70 Liberty LBS 83355 CHAMELEON (LP) . . . 30
(see also Incredible String Band, C.O.B.)

FAMOUS MUSIC BAND
69 Philips 6006 111 Nine By Nine/Going In The Out (with John Dummer) . . . 8
(see also John Dummer)

FANATICS
89 Chapter 22 12 CHAP 38 SUBURBAN LOVE SONGS (12" EP) . . . 25
(see also Ocean Colour Scene)

FAN-CLUB
78 M&S SJP 791B Avenue/Night Caller (p/s, photocopied insert) . . . 15
(see also Transvision Vamp)

FANCY
73 Atlantic K 10383 Wild Thing/Fancy (some with p/s) . . . 8/5
76 Arista ARIST 32 Music Maker/Bluebird . . . 8
74 Antic K 51502 WILD THING (LP) . . . 12
75 Arista ARTY 102 SOMETHING TO REMEMBER (LP) . . . 12
(see also Ray Fenwick, Judas Priest)

FANDANGO
(see Nic Simper's Fandango, under 'S')

FANNY
70 Reprise RSLP 6416 FANNY (LP) . . . 12
72 Reprise K 44144 CHARITY BALL (LP) . . . 12

FANS
79 Fried Egg EGG 3 Giving Me That Look in Your Eyes/Stay The Night/He'll Have To Go (p/s) . . . 45
79 Albion ION 0004 True (dayglo inner, inc bonus 7" & lyric sheet) . . . 20
80 Albion FAN 01 Cars And Explosions/Dangerous Goodbyes (p/s) . . . 20
81 Fried Egg EGG 10 You Don't Live Here Anymore/Following You (p/s) . . . 30

FANTASIA
67 Stateside SS 2031 Gotta Get Away/She Needs My Love . . . 7

FANTASTIC BAGGYS
76 United Artists UP 36142 Summer Means Fun/JAN & DEAN: Surf City/Sidewalk Surfin' . . . 10
(see also Jan & Dean, Bruce Johnston)

FANTASTIC FOUR
68 Tamla Motown TMG 678 I Love You Madly/I Love You Madly (Instrumental) . . . 18
69 T. Motown (S)TML 11105 THE FANTASTIC FOUR (LP) . . . 40

FANTASTIC JOHNNY C
(see under 'C')

FANTASTICS
68 MGM MGM 1434 Baby Make Your Own Sweet Music/Who Could Be Lovin' You . . . 20
68 MGM MGM 1434DJ Baby Make Your Own Sweet Music/ Who Could Be Lovin' You (DJ promo) . . . 30
69 Deram DM 264 Face To Face With Heartache/This Must Be My Rainy Day . . . 6
70 Deram DM 283 Waiting Round For Heartaches/Ask The Lonely . . . 6
71 Deram DM 334 For Old Times Sake/Exodus Main Theme . . . 6
71 Mojo 2027 004 Baby Make Your Own Sweet Music/Who Could Be Lovin' You? (reissue) . . . 6
(see also Velours)

FANTASY
73 Polydor 2058 405 Politely Insane/I Was Once Aware . . . 35
73 Polydor 2383 246 PAINT A PICTURE (LP, gatefold sleeve) . . . 200+

MINT VALUE £

BARRY FANTONI

66 Fontana TF 707 Little Man In A Little Box/Fat Man . . . 25
67 Columbia DB 8238 Nothing Today/The Spanish Lady Tango . . . 7

FAPARDOKLY

83 Psycho PSYCHO 5 FAPARDOKLY (LP, 300 only) . . . 15
(see also Mu)

FARAWAY FOLK

70s Tabitha TAB 3 Shadow Of A Pie/Folsom Prison Blues/Rent A Man/Soulful Shade Of Blue . . . 14
70s RA EP 7001 INTRODUCING THE FARAWAY FOLK (EP) . . . 40
70s RA LP 6006ST LIVE AT THE BOLTON (LP) . . . 55
72 RA LP 6012ST TIME AND TIDE (LP) . . . 80
73 RA LP 6019 ON THE RADIO (LP) . . . 25
74 RA LP 6022 ONLY AUTHORISED EMPLOYEES TO BREAK BOTTLES
(LP, with Harry H. Corbett) . . . 35
75 RA LP 6029 SEASONAL MAN (LP, gatefold sleeve with insert) . . . 150
80s RA BATTLE OF THE DRAGONS (cassette) . . . 15
(see also Harry H. Corbett)

FAR CRY

69 Vanguard SVRL 19041 THE FAR CRY (LP) . . . 25

DON FARDON

67 Pye International 7N 25437 (The Lament Of The Cherokee) Indian Reservation/Dreamin' Room . . . 8
68 Pye International 7N 25475 (The Lament Of The Cherokee) Indian Reservation/Dreamin' Room (reissue) . . . 6
69 Pye International 7N 25483 We Can Make It Together/Coming On Strong . . . 6
69 Pye International 7N 25486 Good Lovin'/Ruby's Pictures On My Wall . . . 6
69 Young Blood YB 1007 It's Been Nice Loving You/Let The Love Live . . . 7
70 Young Blood YB 1010 Belfast Boy/Echoes Of The Cheers . . . 30
71 Young Blood YB 1013 Delta Queen/Hometown Baby . . . 5
71 Young Blood YB 1021 Girl/Sandiago . . . 5
71 Young Blood YB 1027 Follow Your Drum/Get Away John . . . 5
70 Young Blood SYB 4 I'VE PAID MY DUES! (LP) . . . 18
70 Young Blood SSYB 13 RELEASED (LP) . . . 18
(see also Sorrows)

FAR EAST FAMILY BAND

75 Vertigo 6370 850 NIPPONJIN (LP) . . . 20

DICK FARINA & ERIC VON SCHMIDT

63 Folklore F-LEUT/7 DICK FARINA & ERIC VON SCHMIDT (LP, featuring 'Blind Boy Grunt') . . . 75
(see also Bob Dylan, Richard & Mimi Farina)

RICHARD & MIMI FARINA

65 Fontana STFL 6060 CELEBRATIONS FOR A GREY DAY (LP) . . . 18
65 Fontana STFL 6075 REFLECTIONS IN A CRYSTAL WIND (LP) . . . 18
73 Vanguard VSD 21/22 THE BEST OF RICHARD & MIMI FARINA (2-LP) . . . 18
(see also Dick Farina & Eric Von Schmidt)

FARINAS

64 Victor Buckland Sound Studio Bye Bye Johnny/All You Gotta Do/Twist And Shout
(as James King & Farinas) . . . 500
64 Fontana TF 493 You'd Better Stop/I Like It Like That . . . 65
(see also Family)

CHRIS FARLOWE (& THUNDERBIRDS)

62 Decca F 11536 Air Travel/Why Did You Break My Heart? . . . 50
63 Columbia DB 7120 I Remember/Push Push (as Chris Farlowe & Thunderbirds) . . . 30
64 Columbia DB 7237 Girl Trouble/Itty Bitty Pieces (as Chris Farlowe & Thunderbirds) . . . 30
64 Columbia DB 7311 Just A Dream/What You Gonna Do?
(as Chris Farlow & Thunderbirds) . . . 22
64 Columbia DB 7379 Hey, Hey, Hey, Hey/Hound Dog (as Chris Farlow & Thunderbirds) . . . 20
65 Columbia DB 7614 Buzz With The Fuzz/You're The One (withdrawn,
as Chris Farlow & Thunderbirds, demos more common £105) . . . 200
65 Immediate IM 016 The Fool/Treat Her Good . . . 15
66 Immediate IM 023 Don't Just Look At Me/Think . . . 18
66 Immediate IM 035 Out Of Time/Baby Make It Soon . . . 10
66 Columbia DB 7983 Just A Dream/Hey, Hey, Hey, Hey . . . 15
66 Immediate IM 038 Ride On Baby/Headlines . . . 10
67 Immediate IM 041 My Way Of Giving/You're So Good To Me . . . 15
67 Immediate IM 049 Yesterday's Papers/Life Is But Nothing . . . 8
67 Immediate IM 056 Moanin'/What Have I Been Doin'? . . . 8
67 Immediate IM 065 Handbags And Gladrags/Everyone Makes A Mistake . . . 10
68 Immediate IM 066 The Last Goodbye/Paperman Fly In The Sky (B-side with Thunderbirds) . . . 12
68 Immediate IM 071 Paint It Black/I Just Need Your Lovin' . . . 12
69 Immediate IM 074 Dawn/April Was The Month . . . 12
70 Polydor 2066 017 Black Sheep/Fifty Years . . . 6
70 Polydor 2066 046 Put Out The Light/Questions (as Chris Farlowe & Hill) . . . 5
75 Polydor 2066 650 We Can Work It Out/Only Women Bleed . . . 5
75 Virgin SV 102 Out Of Time/Handbags And Gladrags//Yesterday's Papers/
Ride On Baby (double pack) . . . 5
78 Beeb BEEB 022 Gangsters (as Chris Farlowe & Dave Greenslade)/
DAVE GREENSLADE'S GANGSTERS: Sarah Gant Theme . . . 6
65 Decca DFE 8665 CHRIS FARLOWE (EP) . . . 90
65 Immediate IMEP 001 FARLOWE IN THE MIDNIGHT HOUR (EP) . . . 50
66 Immediate IMEP 004 CHRIS FARLOWE HITS (EP) . . . 40
66 Island IEP 709 STORMY MONDAY (EP) . . . 135
66 Columbia SX 6034 CHRIS FARLOWE AND THE THUNDERBIRDS (LP) . . . 150
66 Immediate IMLP 005 14 THINGS TO THINK ABOUT (LP) . . . 60
66 Immediate IMLP 006 THE ART OF CHRIS FARLOWE (LP) . . . 60

67	EMI Regal REG 2025	CHRIS FARLOWE (LP, export issue)	35
68	Immediate IMLP/IMCP 010	THE BEST OF CHRIS FARLOWE VOLUME ONE (LP)	25
69	Immediate IMLP 021	THE LAST GOODBYE (LP)	70
70	Polydor 2425 029	FROM HERE TO MAMA ROSA (LP, as Chris Farlowe & Hill)	20
75	Polydor 2469 259	THE CHRIS FARLOWE BAND LIVE (LP)	15

(see also Thunderbirds, Beazers, Little Joe Cook, Crane/Farlowe, Atomic Rooster, Colosseum, Dave Greenslade, Spectrum)

ART FARMER

56	Vogue EPV 1045	ART FARMER (EP, as Art Farmer New Jazz All Stars)	8
54	Esquire 20-033	ART FARMER SEXTET — WORK OF ART (10" LP)	15
55	Esquire 32-037	MUSIC FOR THAT WILD PARTY (LP)	12
56	Esquire 32-072	TWO TRUMPETS (LP, with Donald Byrd)	12
59	London SAH-T 6028	MODERN ART (LP)	12
60	London Jazz LTZ-T 15184	BRASS SHOUT (LP)	12
60	London Jazz LTZ-T 15198	THE AZTEC SUITE (LP)	12
61	Esquire 32-120	EARTHY (LP)	12
64	London HA-K/SH-K 8135	INTERACTION (LP, as Art Farmer Quartet featuring Jim Hall)	12

(see also Clifford Brown, Benny Golson, Donald Byrd)

JULES FARMER

59	London HLP 8967	Love Me Now/Part Of Me (Is Still With You)	15
59	London HLP 8967	Love Me Now/Part Of Me (Is Still With You) (78)	30

MYLENE FARMER

89	Polydor 080 360-2	Ainsi Soit Je... (Maxi Remix)/Ainsi Soit Je... (Lamentations)/ Ainsi Soit Je... (Classic Bonus Beats) (CD Video, export only)	45

FARMLIFE

82	Dining Out TUX 19	Susie's Party/Simple Men	6
83	Whaam! WHAAM 13	Big Country 1 & 2 (unreleased; Echantillan test pressings only)	40

GILES FARNABY'S DREAM BAND

73	Argo AFW 112	Newcastle Brown/29th Of May	12
73	Argo ZDA 158	GILES FARNABY'S DREAM BAND (LP)	60

(see also Druids)

ROBERT FARNON ORCHESTRA

63	Philips BF 326563	Theme From The Dick Powell Show/Nervous	5
72	MCA MCA 117	Colditz March/That Italian Summer	5
58	Decca DFE 6470	JOURNEY INTO MELODY (EP)	8
55	Decca LK 4119	CANADIAN IMPRESSIONS (LP)	20
56	Vogue Coral LVA 9003	GENTLEMEN MARRY BRUNETTES (LP, soundtrack)	35
60	Delyse ECB 3157/DS 6057	CAPTAIN HORATIO HORNBLOWER (LP, soundtrack, mono/stereo)	60/75
64	Philips SBL 7634	CAPTAIN FROM CASTILE (LP, soundtrack)	12
68	Philips SBL 7867	SHALAKO (LP, soundtrack)	15

(see also Jack Saunders)

ROBERT FARNON & TONY COE

70	Chapter One CHS 804	POP MAKES PROGRESS (LP)	25

(see also Tony Coe)

FARON'S FLAMINGOS

63	Oriole CB 1834	Do You Love Me?/See If She Cares	20
63	Oriole CB 1867	Shake Sherry/Give Me Time	22

(see also Big Three, Mojos)

WAYNE FARO'S SCHMALTZ BAND

69	Deram DM 222	There's Still Time/Give It Time	12

GARY FARR (& THE T-BONES)

65	Columbia DB 7608	Give All She's Got/Don't Stop And Stare (as Gary Farr & T-Bones)	50
68	Marmalade 598 007	Everyday/Green (with Kevin Westlake)	10
69	Marmalade 598 017	Hey Daddy/The Vicar And The Pope	15
71	CBS 5430	Revolution Of The Seasons/Old Man Boulder	8
65	Columbia SEG 8414	DEM BONES, DEM BONES, DEM T-BONES (EP)	150
69	Marmalade 608 013	TAKE SOMETHING WITH YOU (LP)	80
71	CBS 64138	STRANGE FRUIT (LP, with Richard Thompson & Mighty Baby)	40

(see also T-Bones, Richard Thompson, Mighty Baby, Meic Stevens, Kevin Westlake & Gary Farr)

MARY ANN FARRAR & SATIN SOUL

76	Brunswick BR 38	Stoned Out Of My Mind/Living In The Footsteps Of Another Girl	5

BILLY FARRELL

58	Philips PB 828	Yeah Yeah/Someday (You'll Want Me To Want You)	20

DO & DENA FARRELL

57	HMV POP 427	Young Magic/New Love Tonight	15
57	HMV POP 427	Young Magic/New Love Tonight (78)	10

MICK FARREN

78	Logo GO 321	Half Price Drinks/I Don't Want To Go This Way	6
79	Logo GO 345	Broken Statue/It's All In The Picture	5
78	Stiff LAST 4	ALL SCREWED UP (EP, as Mick Farren & Deviants)	8
70	Transatlantic TRA 212	MONA (THE CARNIVOROUS CIRCUS) (LP)	55
78	Logo LOGO 2010	VAMPIRES STOLE MY LUNCH MONEY (LP, with lyric insert)	35
84	Psycho PSYCHO 20	MONA (THE CARNIVOROUS CIRCUS) (LP, reissue)	25

(see also Deviants, Twink)

MIA FARROW

68	Dot DOT 116	Lullaby From Rosemary's Baby (Parts 1 & 2)	8

MINT VALUE £

FASCINATIONS			
67	Stateside SS 594	Girls Are Out To Get You/You'll Be Sorry	75
68	Sue WI 4049	Girls Are Out To Get You/You'll Be Sorry (reissue)	35
71	Mojo 2092 004	Girls Are Out To Get You/You'll Be Sorry (2nd reissue)	12
71	Mojo 2092 018	I'm So Lucky He Loves Me/Say It Isn't So	7
FASCINATORS			
58	Capitol CL 14942	Chapel Bells/I Wonder Who	350
59	Capitol CL 15062	Oh, Rose Marie/Fried Chicken And Macaroni	150
FASHIONS			
68	Stateside SS 2115	I.O.U. (A Lifetime Of Love)/When Love Slips Away	15
69	Evolution E 2444	I.O.U. (A Lifetime Of Love)/He Gives Me Love	8
FAST BREEDERS & RADIO ACTORS			
78	Nuke NUKE 235	Nuclear Waste/Digital Love (some in p/s, with insert)	15/10
(see also Radio Actors)			
FAST CARS			
79	Streets Ahead SA 3	The Kids Just Wanna Dance/You're So Funny (p/s)	250
FAST EDDIE			
82	Well Suspect BLAM 001	My Babe/Help Me/Sweet Sensations (p/s)	8
FAST SET			
80	Axis AXIS 1	Junction One/Children Of The Revolution (p/s)	15
FAT			
71	RCA LSA 3009	FAT (LP)	18
FATAL CHARM			
79	Company CR 005	Paris/Glitterbit/Out Of My Head	8
FATAL MICROBES			
79	Small Wonder SMALL 20	Violence Grows/Beautiful Pictures/Cry Baby (p/s)	5
(see also Pete Fender)			
FATAL MICROBES/POISON GIRLS			
79	Small Wonder WEENY 3	FATAL MICROBES MEET THE POISON GIRLS (12" EP, with insert)	8
(see also Poison Girls)			
FATBACK BAND			
75	Polydor 2066 494	Keep On Steppin'/Breakin' Up Is Hard To Do	5
75	Polydor 2066 524	Wicky Wacky/Can't Fight The Flame	5
75	Polydor 2066 590	Yum, Yum (Gimme Some)/Trompin'	5
75	Polydor 2066 637	(Are You Ready) Do The Bus Stop/Got To Learn How To Dance	5
76	Polydor 2066 682	Par-r-rty Time/Put Your Love In My Tender Care	5
75	Polydor 2391 143	KEEP ON STEPPIN' (LP)	15
75	Polydor 2391 184	YUM, YUM (LP)	15
FAT CITY			
69	Probe SPB 1008	REINCARNATION (LP)	15
FATHER'S ANGELS			
68	MGM MGM 1459	Don't Knock It/Bok To Bach	150
75	Black Magic BM 103	Bok To Bach/Disco Trucking	6
FAT MATTRESS			
69	Polydor 56352	Naturally/Iridescent Butterfly	8
69	Polydor 56367	Magic Forest/Bright New Way	12
70	Polydor 2058 053	Highway/Black Sheep Of The Family	12
69	Polydor 582/583 056	FAT MATTRESS (LP, open-out sleeve)	25
70	Polydor 2383 025	FAT MATTRESS II (LP)	20
(see also Noel Redding Band, Jimi Hendrix Experience, Flowerpot Men)			
FATS & CHESSMEN			
62	Pye International 7N 25122	Big Ben Twist/Old Macdonald Had A Twist	7
ERIC FATTER			
69	Camel CA 20	Since You've Been Gone (actually Eric Fratter)/WINSTON HINES: Cool Down (B-side actually by Winston Hinds)	8
(see also Eric Fratter, Afrotones)			
FAT TRUCKERS			
01	Cercle CERCLE 002	Teenage Daughter/Multiplex (black die-cut sleeve, 500 only)	6
01	Roadtrain (no cat. no.)	Superbike/Favver's Plimsolls (die-cut p/s, 1000 only)	6
FAT TULIPS			
88	Sweet William BILLY 001	You Opened My Eyes/ROSEHIPS: Ask Johnny Dee (33rpm flexi, p/s w/insert)	10
ERNIE FAULKNER			
63	Sway SW 003	Beautiful Girl/SAM DANIELS: Tell Me Baby (both with The Planets)	12
FAUST			
72	Faust/Polydor 2001-299	It's A Bit Of A Pain / So Far	8
79	Recommended RR 2.5	It's A Bit Of A Pain / So Far (p/s, reissue)	5
96	Die Stadt 011	Right Between Yr Eyes (p/s, Uberschall Festival single,with Stereolab and Foetus)	20
90	Chemical Imbalance CI 08	Live In Hamburg (issued free with Chemical Imbalance magazine)	25
97	CRDC 11	Mikrowaves, Magic Brew And R Be Yr Ey (10", p/s)	8
79	Recommended RR 1.5	EXTRACTS FROM FAUST PARTY 3: Extract 1 / Extract 4 (EP)	12
80	Recommended RR 6.5	EXTRACTS FROM FAUST PARTY 3: Extract 2 / Extract 6 (EP)	12
71	Polydor 2310 142	FAUST (LP, initially on clear vinyl, with clear sleeve & clear insert)	50/25
72	Polydor 2310 196	SO FAR (LP, with 9 prints in wallet)	50
73	Virgin VC 501	THE FAUST TAPES (LP)	15
73	Virgin V 2004	FAUST IV (LP)	15

MINT VALUE £

79	Recommended R.R. 2	SO FAR (LP, reissue, with 10 insert prints, numbered, 600 only)	20
80	Recommended RR 6	THE FAUST TAPES (LP, plastic bag cover)	20
90	Table Of The Elements 26	CONCERTS 1: LIVE IN HAMBURG (CD)	30
93	Virgin V 2004	FAUST IV (LP, reissue)	12
94	Table Of The Elements 27	CONCERTS 2: LIVE IN LONDON (CD)	30

(see also Tony Conrad & Faust)

FAVOURITES

80	4 Play FOUR 002	S.O.S./Favourite Shoes (p/s)	10
80	4 Play FOUR 003	Angelica/Cold (p/s)	8

FAVOURITE SONS

65	Mercury MF 911	That Driving Beat/Walkin' Walkin' Walkin'	140

WALLY FAWKES (& HIS TROGLODYTES)

57	Decca FJ 10855	Petite Fleur/Baby Brown (with Sandy Brown Quintet)	12
57	Decca FJ 10936	Sent For You Yesterday And Here You Came Today/Why Can't You Behave	8
58	Decca F 11002	The Pilot Fish And The Whale/Pale Blues	8
56	Decca DFE 6192	TAKIN' IT EASY — VOL 1 (EP, with Bruce Turner)	15
56	Decca DFE 6193	TAKIN' IT EASY — VOL 2 (EP, with Bruce Turner)	15
57	Decca DEF 6407	AND HIS TROGLODYTES (EP)	15
60	Decca DFE 6600	FLOOK DIGS JAZZ (EP)	20
61	Decca STO 136	A NIGHT AT THE SIX BELLS (EP)	25
56	Decca LF 1214	TAKIN' IT EASY (LP, with Bruce Turner)	20
58	Decca LF 312	FAWKES ON HOLIDAY (LP)	20

(see also Sandy Brown)

CHARLIE FAWN

80	Warner Bros K 17566	Always Something There To Remind Me/Poet For A Generation	8

BILL FAY

67	Deram DM 143	Some Good Advice/Screams In The Ears	50
70	Deram Nova SDN 12	BILL FAY (LP)	40
71	Deram SML 1079	TIME OF THE LAST PERSECUTION (LP)	110

BRIAN FAYE & ORCHESTRA

(see under Brian Fahey)

FRANCIS FAYE

61	Vogue V 9186	I Wish I Could Shimmy Like My Sister Kate/Night And Day	18
61	HMV POP 898	Frenesi/Miserlou	7
65	Stateside SL 10129	YOU GOTTA GO! GO! GO! (LP)	18

LITTLE RITA FAYE

53	MGM MGM 671	Rock City Boogie/Wait A Little Longer (78)	10
53	MGM MGM 697	I Fell Out Of The Christmas Tree/I'm A Problem Child (78)	7

F.B.I. (FOLK BLUES INC.)

66	Eyemark EMS 1006	Don't Hide/When The Ship Comes In	22
73	A&M AMS 7050	I Wonder What She's Doing Tonight/Boogaloo Boo-Boo	10
76	Good Earth GD 6	F.B.I./The Time Is Right To Leave The City	10
77	Good Earth GDS 802	F.B.I. (LP)	85

FEARN'S BRASS FOUNDRY

68	Decca F 12721	Don't Change It/John White	20
68	Decca F 12835	Now I Taste The Tears/Love, Sink And Drown	10

FEAR OF FALLING

83	Excellent XL 7	Like A Lion/You My Prodigal Son (p/s)	30

CHARLIE FEATHERS/MAC CURTIS

74	Polydor 2310 293	ROCKABILLY KINGS (LP, withdrawn)	25

(see also Mac Curtis)

FEATURES

70s	Progress PR 01	Drab City/Job Satisfaction	60

FEATURES

80	ASM HIT 06	She Makes Me Blue/Don't Let Them Know	20
81	AFM PET 01	Monday-Friday/Cue The Next Army	20

FEDERALMEN

70	London HLU 10303	Soul Serenade/Scorcher	7

FEDERALS (U.K.)

63	Parlophone R 4988	Brazil/In A Persian Market	15
63	Parlophone R 5013	Boot Hill/Keep On Dancing With Me	15
64	Parlophone R 5100	The Climb/Dance With A Dolly	15
64	Parlophone R 5139	Marlena/Please Believe Me	15
64	Parlophone R 5193	Twilight Time/Lost And Alone	15
65	Parlophone R 5320	Bucket Full Of Love/Leah	18

(see also Winston's Fumbs, Yes)

FEDERALS (Jamaica)

67	Island WI 3126	Penny For Your Song/I've Passed This Way Before	22
68	Island WI 3152	Shocking Love/By The River	22
69	High Note HS 024	Wailing Festival/Me And My Baby (B-side actually "By The River")	12
70	Camel CA 40	In This World/You Better Call On Me (B-side actually "Shocking Love")	8

FEEDER

96	Echo ECS 13	TWO COLOURS: Pictures Of Rain/Chicken On A Bone (p/s, clear vinyl)	35
96	Echo ECS 13	TWO COLOURS: Pictures Of Rain/Chicken On A Bone (CD, 1,000 only)	35
96	Echo ECS 27	Stereo World/My Perfect Day (p/s)	45
97	Echo ECS 32	Tangerine/Rhubarb (die-cut p/s)	12

MINT VALUE £

97	Echo ECS 36	Cement/Pictures Of Pain (red vinyl, p/s)	12
97	Echo ECS 42	Crash/Here In The Bubble (clear vinyl, numbered p/s)	8
97	Echo ECS 44	High/Wishing For The Sun (sky blue vinyl, p/s)	7
98	Echo ECS 052	Suffocate/Eclipse (purple vinyl, p/s)	8
99	Echo ECS 75	Day In Day Out/Dance To Disco/Honeyfuzz (white vinyl, p/s)	10
01	Echo ECS 116	Turn/Come Back Around (purple vinyl, p/s)	8
97	Echo ECSCD 36	CEMENT EP (CD, digipak)	15
96	Echo ECHLP 9	SWIM (LP)	20

FEELIES

79	Stiff (no cat. no.)	Facé La/The Boy With Perpetual Nervousness/ Everybody's Got Something To Hide (Except Me And My Monkey) (flexidisc, promo only, free with *Be Stiff* fanzine issue 6, 5,000 only)	6/4
79	Rough Trade RT 24	Facé La/Raised Eyebrows (p/s)	7
80	Stiff BUY 65	Everybody's Got Something To Hide/Original Love (p/s)	7

FELDER'S ORIOLES

65	Piccadilly 7N 35247	Down Home Girl/Misty	30
65	Piccadilly 7N 35269	Sweet Tasting Wine/Turn On Your Lovelight	18
66	Piccadilly 7N 35311	I Know You Don't Love Me No More/Only Three Can Pay	18
66	Piccadilly 7N 35332	Back Street/Something You Got	18

(see also V.I.P.s, Mike Patto)

MARTY FELDMAN

68	Pye 7N 17643	Funny He Never Married/Travel Agency (with Tim Brooke-Taylor)	6
68	Decca F 12857	A Joyous Time Of Year/B Side	6
68	Pye NPL 18258	MARTY (LP)	25
69	Decca LK/SKL 4983	I FEEL A SONG GOING OFF (LP)	22

VICTOR FELDMAN BIG BAND/QUARTET

55	Tempo A 127	Elegy/Maenya (78)	7
56	Tempo A 142	Big Top/Cabaletto	5
57	Tempo A 154	Jackpot/You Are My Heart's Desire	5
55	Tempo EXA 29	BIG BAND (EP)	50
57	Tempo EXA 57	VICTOR FELDMAN IN LONDON — THE QUARTET VOLUME 1 (EP)	60
57	Tempo EXA 67	VICTOR FELDMAN IN LONDON VOLUME 2 (EP)	60
58	Tempo EXA 85	MUTUAL ADMIRATION (EP, with Dizzy Reece)	50
50s	Esquire EP 43	MODERN JAZZ QUARTET (EP)	40
50s	Esquire EP 54	MODERN JAZZ QUARTET (EP)	20
50s	Esquire EP 64	MODERN JAZZ QUINTET/SEXTET (EP)	25
50s	Esquire EP 84	MODERN JAZZ QUARTET/SEXTET (EP)	20
50s	Esquire EP 104	MODERN JAZZ QUARTET (EP)	40
50s	Esquire EP 114	VIC FELDMAN ENCORE (EP)	15
50s	Esquire 20 - 046	MULTIPLE TALENTS (LP)	30
55	Esquire 20 - 064	EXPERIMENT IN TIME (LP)	40
55	Tempo LAP 5	VICTOR FELDMAN'S SEXTET (10" LP)	150
56	Tempo LAP 6	VICTOR FELDMAN MODERN JAZZ QUARTET (10" LP)	120
57	Tempo TAP 8	VICTOR FELDMAN IN LONDON VOL. 1 (LP)	120
57	Tempo TAP 12	VICTOR FELDMAN IN LONDON VOL. 2 (LP)	100
58	Tempo TAP 19	TRANSATLANTIC ALLIANCE (LP)	200
59	Contemporary LAC 12172	THE ARRIVAL OF VICTOR FELDMAN (LP)	15

(see also Dizzy Reece)

VICTOR FELDMAN, TERRY GIBBS & LARRY BUNKER

60	Top Rank 30/007	VIBES TO THE POWER OF THREE (LP)	18

JOSE FELICIANO

68	RCA RCA 1715	Light My Fire/California Dreamin'	8
68	RCA RCA 1769	Hi Heel Sneakers/Hitchcock Railway	5
69	RCA RCA 1871	And The Sun Will Shine/Rain	5

FELIUS ANDROMEDA

67	Decca F 12694	Meditations/Cheadle Heath Delusions	45

(see also Denis Couldry)

JULIE FELIX

65	Decca DFE 8613	SINGS BOB DYLAN & WOODY GUTHRIE (EP)	15
64	Decca LK 4626	JULIE FELIX (LP)	20
65	Decca LK 4683	SINGS DYLAN AND GUTHRIE (LP)	18
65	Decca LK 4724	SECOND ALBUM (LP)	15
66	Decca LK 4820	THIRD ALBUM (LP)	15
66	Fontana TL 5386	CHANGES (LP)	15
60s	Fontana SFL 13117	GOING TO THE ZOO (LP)	12

MIKE FELIX

66	Pye 7N 17058	You Belong To Me/Booga Dee	22
67	Decca F 12701	Blueberry Hill/I Don't Think You Want Me Anymore	8

FELIX & HIS GUITAR

59	London HLU 8875	Chili Beans/Puerto Rican Riot	12
59	London HLU 8875	Chili Beans/Puerto Rican Riot (78)	15

FELT

79	Shanghai S79/CUS 321	Index/Break It (p/s, early copies have notes on rear sleeve)	60/50
81	Cherry Red CHERRY 26	Something Sends Me To Sleep/Red Indians/Something Sends Me To Sleep (Version)/Red Indians (p/s)	15
82	Cherry Red CHERRY 45	My Face Is On Fire/Trails Of Colour Dissolve (p/s)	12
83	Cherry Red CHERRY 59	Penelope Tree/A Preacher In New England (p/s)	10
83	Cherry Red 12CHERRY 59	Penelope Tree/A Preacher In New England/ Now Summer's Spread Its Wings Again (12", p/s)	12
84	Cherry Red CHERRY 78	Mexican Bandits/The World Is As Soft As Lace (p/s)	8
84	Cherry Red CHERRY 81	Sunlight Bathed The Golden Glow/Fortune (p/s)	15

84 Cherry Red 12CHERRY 81 Sunlight Bathed The Golden Glow/Fortune/Sunlight Strings (12", p/s) 15
85 Cherry Red 12CHERRY 89 Primitive Painters/Cathedral (12", p/s, with Liz Frazer). 10
86 Creation CRE 027 Ballad Of The Band/I Didn't Mean To Hurt You (p/s) 8
86 Creation CRE 032 Rain Of Crystal Spires/I Will Die With My Head In Flames (p/s) 8
88 Cherry Red CDCHERRY 89 Primitive Painters/Cathedral (reissue, picture CD) 10
88 Creation CRE 060 Space Blues/Tuesday's Secret (ltd. ed. die-cut company sleeve). 6
89 él GPO F44 Get Out Of My Mirror (flexidisc) 7
89 él GPO 44 Get Out Of My Mirror (hard vinyl test pressing, 200 only) 20

(see also Versatile Newts, Maurice Deebank, Cocteau Twins)

FEMININE TOUCH featuring DUKE DURRELL

76 Paladin PAL 11 You Make Me Come Alive/You Make Me Come Alive (Instrumental) 5

JAYMES FENDA & VULCANS

64 Parlophone R 5210 Mistletoe Love/The Only Girl 15

JAN FENDER

71 Prince Buster PB 5 Sea Of Love/PRINCE BUSTER: Heaven Help Us All 12
71 Fab FAB 164 Sweet P/CLIFF & ORGANIZERS: Mr Brown. 10
71 Fab FAB 166 Holly Holy Version/Old Kentrone Version (as Jal Fender). 10

PETE FENDER

81 Xntrix 2002 FOUR FORMULAS (EP, some in 8" silk-screened book p/s) 30/8

(see also Fatal Microbes, Omega Tribe)

FENDER BENDERS

79 Sticky SL 001 Big Green Thing/Hillman Hunter Paranoia (textured p/s, various colours) 6

FENDERMEN

60 Top Rank JAR 395 Mule Skinner Blues/Torture 10
60 Top Rank JAR 513 Don't You Just Know It/Beach Party 10

FENMEN

64 Decca F 11955 Rag Doll/Be My Girl 18
65 Decca F 12269 I've Got Everthing You Need Babe/Every Little Day Now 12
66 CBS 202075 California Dreamin'/Is This Your Way?. 12
66 CBS 202236 Rejected/Girl Don't Bring Me Down. 25

(see also Bern Elliott & Fenmen, Pretty Things, Zac Zolar & Electric Banana)

PETER FENTON

66 Fontana TF 748 Marble Breaks, Iron Bends/Small Town 15

SHANE FENTON (& FENTONES)

61 Parlophone R 4827 I'm A Moody Guy/Five Foot Two, Eyes Of Blue. 8
62 Parlophone R 4866 Walk Away/Fallen Leaves On The Ground. 10
62 Parlophone R 4883 It's All Over Now/Why Little Girl 10
62 Parlophone R 4921 Cindy's Birthday/It's Gonna Take Magic 8
62 Parlophone R 4951 Too Young For Sad Memories/You're Telling Me 8
63 Parlophone R 4982 I Ain't Got Nobody/Hey Miss Ruby 8
63 Parlophone R 5020 A Fool's Paradise/You Need Love (solo) 8
63 Parlophone R 5047 Don't Do That/I'll Know (solo) 8
64 Parlophone R 5131 Hey, Lulu/I Do, Do You? 8
72 Fury FY 305 Eastern Seaboard/Blind Fool. 25
74 Contour 2870 409 GOOD ROCKIN' TONIGHT (LP) 15

(see also Fentones)

FENTONES

62 Parlophone R 4899 The Mexican/Lover's Guitar 15
62 Parlophone R 4937 The Breeze And I/Just For Jerry 12

(see also Shane Fenton)

FENWAYS

65 Liberty LIB 66082 Walk/Whip And Jerk. 10

RAY FENWICK

78 Mercury 6007 176 Queen Of The Night/I Wanna Boogie 6
71 Decca SKL 5090 KEEP AMERICA BEAUTIFUL, GET A HAIRCUT (LP). 50

(see also Spencer Davis Group, After Tea, Fancy, Ian Gillan Band, Wizard's Convention, Murgatroyd Band, Marlon, Forcefield, Syndicats, South Coast Ska Kings, Rupert's People)

FERDIA

78 Polydor 2904 012 A SIGH FOR OLD TIMES (LP) 15

FERDINAND & DILL

70 Pama PM 805 Take Back Your Nicklet/Blueberry Hill 6

DOTTIE FERGUSON

57 Mercury MT 182 Happy Happy Birthday Baby/Darling, It's Wonderful (78) 10

H-BOMB FERGUSON

54 Esquire 10-372 Feel Like I Do/My Love (78) 35

HELENA FERGUSON

67 London HLZ 10164 Where Is The Party?/My Terms 30

JESSIE LEE FERGUSON & OUTER LIMITS

69 Pye International 7N 25492 New Shoes/Puttin' It On, Puttin' It Off 8

JOHNNY FERGUSON

60 MGM MGM 1059 Angela Jones/Blue Serge And White Lace 12
61 MGM MGM 1119 No One Can Love You/The Valley Of Love. 8

MINT VALUE £

MAYNARD FERGUSON ORCHESTRA

58 Emarcy EJL 1270 JAM SESSION (LP). . . . 22
58 Emarcy EJL 1275 AROUND THE HORN (LP) 22
58 Emarcy EJL 1287 DIMENSIONS (LP) 22
59 Columbia 33SX 1146 MESSAGE FROM NEWPORT (LP) 18
60 Mercury MMC 14050 THE BOY WITH LOTS OF BRASS (LP, also stereo CMS 18034) 15
60 Columbia 33SX 1210 MESSAGE FROM BIRDLAND (LP, also stereo SCX 3245). . . . 15
60 Columbia 33SX 1270 JAZZ FOR DANCING (LP, also stereo SCX 3338) 15
61 Columbia 33SX 1301 NEWPORT SUITE (LP, also stereo SCX 3368). . . . 15
62 Columbia 33SX 1439 MAYNARD 62 (LP) 18
66 Fontana TL 5274 BLUES REAR (LP) 25
66 Fontana TL 5293 COLOR HIM WILD (LP). . . . 25
67 Fontana TL 5310 SEXTET (LP). . . . 30
68 Atlantic 2464008 FREAKY (LP) 25
69 CBS 63514 BALLAD STLYE OF MAYNARD FERGUSON (LP) 150
70 CBS 64101 WORLD OF (M.F. HORN) (LP). . . . 25
71 CBS 64432 ALIVE AND WELL IN LONDON (LP). . . . 25
72 CBS 65027 M.F. HORN 2 (LP) 25
73 CBS 65589 M.F. HORN 3 (LP) 25
73 CBS 65952 M.F. HORN 4 (LIVE AT JIMMYS) (LP). . . . 35

ALEX FERGUSSON

80 Red RS 003 Stay With Me Tonight/Brushing Your Hair (p/s) 5
94 own label ALEX FERGUSSON (LP, white label, plain cover with postcard, 500 only) 12
(see also ATV)

FERKO STRING BAND

55 London HL 8140 Alabama Jubilee/Sing A Little Melody. . . . 30
55 London HLF 8183 Ma (She's Making Eyes At Me)/You Are My Sunshine 30
55 London HLF 8215 Happy Days Are Here Again/Deep In The Heart Of Texas. . . . 25
55 London HLF 8215 Happy Days Are Here Again/Deep In The Heart Of Texas (78) 7
58 London HL 7052 Happy Days Are Here Again/Alabama Jubilee (export issue). . . . 18
56 London RE-F 1041 PHILADELPHIA MUMMERS PARADE VOL. 1 (EP). . . . 15
56 London RE-F 1052 PHILADELPHIA MUMMERS PARADE VOL. 2 (EP). . . . 15
57 London HB-C 1064 THE FERKO STRING BAND VOL. 1 (10" LP) 20

FERMENA

71 Pama PM 839 Come What May/Version (B-side with Ranny). . . . 5
73 Pama PM 879 Wonderful Dreams/Version 5

PHIL FERNANDO

58 Pye Nixa 7N 15142 Blonde Bombshell/Make Ready for Love 10
58 Pye Nixa N 15142 Blonde Bombshell/Make Ready for Love (78). . . . 8
62 Palette PG 9029 Do The High Life/High Life Girl 8

ANDY FERNBACH

69 Liberty LBL/LBS 83233 IF YOU MISS YOUR CONNEXION (LP) 100
(see also Groundhogs)

MAJA FERNICK

72 Philips 6006 196 Give Me Your Love Again/Flowers In The City. . . . 8

FERRANTE & TEICHER

60 London HLT 9164 Theme From "The Apartment"/Lonely Room 5
60 London HLT 7103 Theme From "The Apartment"/DON COSTA & HIS ORCHESTRA: Theme From "The Unforgiven" (export issue) 7
61 London HLT 9298 Theme From "Exodus"/Twilight. . . . 5
61 London HLT 7105 Theme From "Exodus"/Twilight (export issue). . . . 10
65 United Artists UP 1097 The Knack/Country Boy. . . . 7
61 HMV/Utd. Artists 7EG 8700 EXODUS (EP) 10

DIANE FERRAZ & NICKY SCOTT

66 Columbia DB 7824 Me And You/Don't Pretend. . . . 8
66 Columbia DB 7897 You've Got To Learn/Like You As You Are 8
66 Columbia DB 7963 Sh-Boom, Sh-Boom/Allah Mobish. . . . 8
(see also Nicky Scott)

JOE FERRER & HIS DEVILS BOYS

61 Oriole CB 1629 Rockin' Crickets/Blue Guitar 18

EUGENE FERRIS

66 Planet PLF 112 There Was A Smile In Your Eyes/Soft Moonlight. . . . 35

GEORGE FERRIS

71 Ackee ACK 117 With Every Dream/Diana 6

FERRIS WHEEL

67 Pye 7N 17387 I Can't Break The Habit/Number One Guy. . . . 10
68 Pye 7N 17538 Let It Be Me/You Look At Me 8
68 Pye 7N 17631 The Na Na Song/Three Cool Cats 8
69 Polydor 56366 Can't Stop Now/I Know You Well 6
67 Pye NPL 18203 CAN'T BREAK THE HABIT (LP). . . . 25
70 Polydor 583 066 FERRIS WHEEL (LP) 15
(see also Linda Lewis, West Five)

BRYAN FERRY

73 Island WIP 6170 A Hard Rain's Gonna Fall/2 HB 5
74 Island WIP 6196 The 'In' Crowd/Chance Meeting (initially in p/s). . . . 8/5
74 Island WIP 6205 Smoke Gets In Your Eyes/Another Time, Another Place. . . . 5
75 Island WIP 6234 You Go To My Head/Re-Make, Re-Model (no p/s) 5
75 Island WIP 6234 You Go To My Head/Re-Make, Re-Model (DJ copies in generic promo p/s). . . . 20
76 Island IEP 1 EXTENDED PLAY (EP, p/s). . . . 6

78 Polydor PPSP 10 Hold On I'm Coming/Take Me To The River (12", unissued, promo only, numbered stamped p/s). . . . 20
85 E.G. FERPX 2 Don't Stop The Dance (Special 12" Remix)/Slave To Love (Special 12" Remix)/Nocturne (12", picture disc, printed PVC sleeve). . . . 10
88 Virgin CDT 10/EGOCD 41 Let's Stick Together/Shame Shame Shame/Chance Meeting/ Sea Breezes (3" CD, card sleeve) 10
88 Virgin CDEP 8 The Right Stuff (4.25)/(6.40)/(Dub Mix) (CD, gatefold sleeve) 10
88 Virgin CDEP 19 Kiss And Tell/Kiss And Tell (Dub Mix)/Zamba/Kiss And Tell (Dance Mix) (CD) 8
88 Virgin VSCD 1066 Limbo (Latin Mix)/Bête Noire (Instrumental)/Limbo (Brooklyn Dub Mix) (CD in 6" x 5" cardboard box) 10
88 E.G. EGOCD 44 Let's Stick Together (Westside '88 Mix)/Trash/Sign Of The Times/Casanova (CD). 10
89 E.G. EGOCD 46 The Price Of Love (The R&B '89 Remix)/Don't Stop The Dance (Special 12" Remix)/Slave To Love (12" Remix)/Loner (3" CD, card sleeve) 10
89 E.G. EGOCD 48 He'll Have To Go/Take Me To The River/Broken Wings/Carrickfergus (3" CD, card sleeve) 10
73 Island (no cat. no.) THESE FOOLISH THINGS (2 x 7", white label test pressings) 250
73 Island ILPS 9239 THESE FOOLISH THINGS (LP, unissued gatefold sleeve). . . . 500
76 Island ILPS 9367 LET'S STICK TOGETHER (LP, original issue) 12
78 Polydor POLD 5003 THE BRIDE STRIPPED BARE (LP, original with A//3 P matrix, includes 'Broken Wings', white label test pressings only, some in different proof gatefold sleeve). . . . 200/400

(see also Roxy Music)

CATHERINE FERRY

76 Barclay BAR 42 One, Two, Three/1, 2, 3 12

FESTIVAL

78 Nevis NEV 107 Something In Your Smile/Let's Make Love 45

FEVER TREE

68 MCA MU 1043 San Francisco Girls/Come With Me. . . . 10
68 Uni UNLS 102 FEVER TREE (LP). . . . 25
68 MCA MUPS 347 ANOTHER TIME, ANOTHER PLACE (LP). . . . 30

FICKLE FINGER

69 Page One POF 150 Fickle Lizzie-Anne/Cellophane Mary Jane. . . . 12
(see also Matchmakers, Mark Wirtz)

FICKLE PICKLE

70 Fontana TF 1069 Millionaire/Sam And Sadie. . . . 8
70 Philips 6006 038 Maybe I'm Amazed/Sitting On A Goldmine 6

FI-DELS

72 Jay Boy BOY 69 Try A Little Harder/You Never Do Right. . . . 8
70s DJM DJS 689 Try A Little Harder/KEYMAN STRINGS: Instrumental Version 8

KEITH FIELD

68 Polydor 56278 The Day That War Broke Out/Stop Thief 15

ALAN FIELDING

58 Fontana H 124 Just Remember/Don't Say Goodbye 6
60 Decca F 11261 I'll Never Understand/I Love Suzie Brown. . . . 6
61 Decca F 11487 Scatter Brain/I've Got To Learn To Forget 6
62 Decca F 11404 How Many Nights, How Many Days/Building Castles In The Air. . . . 7
62 Decca F 11518 Too Late To Worry Too Blue To Cry/You Reap Just What You Sow 7

FENELLA FIELDING

66 Columbia DB 8056 Big Bad Mouse/Later 10

JERRY FIELDING & HIS ORCHESTRA

54 London HL 8017 When I Grow Too Old To Dream/Button Up Your Overcoat 50
55 London HL 7001 Faintly Reminiscent/Blues Serenade (export issue). . . . 20
55 London HL 7002 Pea-nut Vendor/Can't Help Lovin' Dat Man (export issue) 20
55 London HL 7003 Tea For Two/Here In My Arms (export issue) 20
55 London HL 7004 I'm In Love/Blue Prelude (export issue) 20
55 Brunswick 05399 The Gypsy In My Soul/The Glory Of Love. . . . 10
55 London RE-P 1026 DANCE DATE VOL. 1 (EP) 18
54 London H-APB 1022 FAINTLY REMINISCENT (10" LP). . . . 20
54 London H-APB 1027 PLAYS A DANCE CONCERT (10" LP) 20

FIELD MICE

88 Sarah SARAH 012 Emma's House/When You Sleep/Fabulous Friend/The Last Letter (p/s). . . . 12
89 Caff CAFF 2 I Can See Myself Alone Forever/Everything About You (foldaround p/s in poly bag with insert) 25
88 Sarah SARAH 18 Sensitive/When Morning Comes To Town/Penguins (foldout p/s, with poster) 10
91 Sarah SARAH 44 September's Not So Far Away/Hello And Goodbye (p/s, with insert). . . . 10

FIELDS

69 Uni UNLS 104 FIELDS (LP) 35

FIELDS

71 CBS 7555 Friends Of Mine/Three Minstrels 6
71 CBS 69009 FIELDS (LP, with/without poster) 45/30
(see also Rare Bird)

BILLY FIELDS

55 MGM SP 1126 Sincerely/Thrilled 6
59 Mercury AMT 1067 The Greatest Love In The World/No Other Love 6

MINT VALUE £

ERNIE FIELDS & HIS ORCHESTRA

59	London HL 8985	In The Mood/Christopher Columbus (some with tri-centre)	12/7
59	London HL 8985	In The Mood/Christopher Columbus (78)	25
60	London HL 9100	Chattanooga Choo Choo/Workin' Out	10
60	London HL 9227	Raunchy/My Prayer	8
60	London RE 1260	SAXY (EP)	50
60	London HA 2263	IN THE MOOD (LP)	50

GRACIE FIELDS

55	Decca F 10614	Twenty/Summertime In Venice	6
56	Decca F 10824	A Letter To A Soldier/The Sweetest Prayer In All The World	6
57	Columbia DB 3953	Around The World/Far Away	6
52	Decca LF 1080	NOW IS THE HOUR (10" LP, original pressing)	18
53	Decca LF 1140	GRACIE FIELDS (10" LP)	20
57	Conquest CL 1001	OUR GRACIE (LP)	15

IRVING FIELDS TRIO & ORCHESTRA

54	Parlophone CMSP 9	Mr. Piano Player/Cuban Carnival (export issue)	10
58	Oriole CB 1436	Ragtime Rock/Syncopated Sadie	6
58	Oriole CB 1436	Ragtime Rock/Syncopated Sadie (78)	8

KANSAS FIELDS & MILTON SEALEY

56	Ducretet DEP 95017	KANSAS FIELDS & MILTON SEALEY (EP)	12

FIELDS OF THE NEPHILIM

84	Tower N1	BURNING THE FIELDS (12" EP, red/black p/s)	25
85	Tower N1/Jung. JUNG 28T	BURNING THE FIELDS (12" EP, green p/s with insert & band photo label)	8
85	Tower N1/Jung. JUNG 28T	BURNING THE FIELDS (12" EP, green & other coloured vinyl export issue)	8
86	Situation 2 SIT 42	Power/Secrets (7", white label promos only, stickered plain sleeve)	15
87	Situation 2 SIT 46	Preacher Man/Laura II (p/s, some with Beggars Banquet sticker)	35/25
87	Situation 2 SIT 48	Blue Water/In Every Dream Home A Heartache (p/s)	10
87	Situation 2 SIT 48T	Blue Water (Electrostatic)/In Every Dream Home A Heartache (live)/ Blue Water (Hot Wire) (12", p/s, some with poster)	15/8
87	House Of Dolls HOD 15	Dawnrazor (on free EP with *House Of Dolls* magazine, issue 15)	8/6
89	Situation 2 SIT 57	Psychonaut/Celebrate (Second Seal) (blue/green p/s)	6
90	Beggars Banquet BEG 250	Sumerland/Phobia (live) (no p/s)	5
88	Situation 2 SITU 22	THE NEPHILIM (LP, gatefold sleeve, with inner)	12
88	Situation 2 SITU 22L	THE NEPHILIM (LP, 2 x 45rpm 12", gatefold sleeve, numbered)	20

FIESTAS

59	London HL 8870	So Fine/Last Night I Dreamed	40
59	London HL 8870	So Fine/Last Night I Dreamed (78)	45
71	Atlantic 2091 121	So Fine/Broken Heart	6

FIFTEENTH

86	Tanz TANZ 3	ANDELAIN (12" EP)	10

FIFTH AVENUE

65	Immediate IM 002	The Bells Of Rhymney/Just Like Anyone Would Do	30

(see also Denny Gerrard, Warm Sounds)

FIFTH AVENUE BAND

69	Reprise RSPL 6369	FIFTH AVENUE BAND (LP)	20

FIFTH COLUMN

66	Columbia DB 8068	Benjamin Day/There's Nobody There	20

(see also Gerry Rafferty)

5TH DIMENSION

67	Liberty LIB 12051	Go Where You Wanna Go/Too Poor To Die	18
67	Liberty LIB 12056	Another Day, Another Heartache/Rosecrans Blvd.	8
67	Liberty LBF 15014	Up Up And Away/Pattern People	10
68	Liberty LBF 15052	Carpet Man/Magic Garden	10
68	Liberty LBF 15072	Stoned Soul Picnic/Sailboat Song	7
68	Liberty LBF 15081	Ticket To Ride/Orange Air	6
68	Liberty LBF 15143	Sweet Blindness/Good News	5
69	Liberty LBF 15180	California Soul/I'll Never Be The Same Again	5
69	Liberty LBF 15193	Aquarius — Let The Sun Shine In/Don'tcha Hear Me Callin' To Ya	6
69	Liberty LBF 15288	Wedding Bell Blues/Let It Be Me	6
70	Liberty LBF 15356	I'll Be Lovin' You Forever/Train Keep On Movin'	15
70	Bell BLL 1137	One Less Bell To Answer/Feelin' Alright	6
76	ABC ABC 4118	Love Hangover/Will You Be There	10
67	Liberty LBL/LBS 83038	UP UP AND AWAY (LP)	18
68	Liberty LBL/LBS 83098E	MAGIC GARDEN (LP)	18
68	Liberty LBL/LBS 83155E	STONED SOUL PICNIC (LP)	20
69	Liberty LBS 83205	AGE OF AQUARIUS (LP)	18
70	Liberty LBS 83228	THE FANTASTIC 5TH DIMENSION (LP)	15

FIFTH ESTATE

67	Stateside SS 2034	Ding Dong The Witch Is Dead/Rub A Dub	10
67	Stateside SS 2068	Heigh Ho/It's Waiting There For You	8
68	Stateside SS 2105	Do Drop In/That's Love	7
69	Stateside SS 2125	Coney Island Sally/Tomorrow Is My Turn	7

FIFTY FANTASTICS

79	South Circular SGS 108	God's Got Religion/STEPPES: The Beat Drill (white label)	10
80	Dining Out TUX 5	God's Got Religion/The Beat Drill (reissue, foldout p/s, handdone labels)	8

(see also Steppes, Disco Zombies)

FIFTY FOOT HOSE

69	Mercury SLML 4030	CAULDRON (LP)	100

MINT VALUE £

50 YEAR VOID
92 BLADE 1 — Blade's Love Machine (1-sided 12", white label promo, 100 only) ... 30+
(see also St. Etienne, Sarah Cracknell)

FIGGY DUFF
80 Dingles DIN 326 — FIGGY DUFF (LP) ... 25
85 Celtic CM 023 — AFTER THE TEMPEST (LP, with insert) ... 20

FILBERT'S FOIBLES
94 Easycore SILK 4 — Fondle My Fondant Fancies/Petit Fours Whores (p/s) ... 5

PAULINE FILBY
60s Church Miss. Soc. LIV/SP/81 — I'm Hungry/NADIA CATTOUSE: The Larder ... 20
68 Herald ELR 1081 — MY WORLD BY PAULINE FILBY (EP) ... 30
69 Herald LLR 567 — SHOW ME A RAINBOW (LP) ... 75
(see also Narnia, Accolade, Gordon Giltrap)

FILE UNDER POP
79 Rough Trade RT 011 — Heathrow/Corrugate/Heathrow SLB (p/s) ... 6
(see also AK Process)

FILTHY FELCHER
02 Glem GLEM-O 3 — Sordid Suckle/MacDonald's Milkshake (p/s) ... 6

FILTHY PHIL & FAST EDDIE
89 Receiver RRLP 124 — NAUGHTY OLD SANTA'S CHRISTMAS CLASSICS (LP) ... 15
(see also Motörhead)

FILTHY RICH
87 JM TR 102 — She's 17 (p/s) ... 25
(see also Trident)

FINAL CONFLICT
89 Futuresound VFS 001 — My England/Across The Room (stickered white sleeve) ... 20
86 Futuresound FS 001 — CHANNEL 8 (cassette) ... 8
86 Futuresound FS 001 — EP (EP) ... 10
86 Futuresound FS 002 — THE TIME HAS ARRIVED (EP, with 22-page booklet) ... 10

FINAL PROGRAM
81 Program FINAL 001 — PROTECT AND SURVIVE (EP) ... 6

FINAL TOUCH
70s Myrrh MYR 1188 — LOVE SONG (LP) ... 15

FINCH
78 Rockburgh ROC 103 — GALLEONS OF PASSION (LP) ... 15

FINDERS KEEPERS (U.K.)
66 CBS 202249 — Light/Power Of Love (withdrawn, promos may exist) ... 60+
66 CBS 202249 — Light/Come On Now ... 15
67 Fontana TF 892 — On The Beach/Friday Kind Of Monday ... 25
68 Fontana TF 938 — Sadie (The Cleaning Lady)/Without Her ... 15
(see also Trapeze, Glenn Hughes, News)

FINDERS KEEPERS (U.S.)
67 London HLH 10117 — Lavender Blue/MICKEY DOLENZ: Don't Do It ... 15

FINGERS
66 Columbia DB 8026 — I'll Take You Where The Music's Playing/My Way Of Thinking ... 10
67 Columbia DB 8112 — All Kinds Of People/Circus With A Female Clown ... 30
(see also Crocheted Doughnut Ring, Legend)

LEE FINN & RHYTHM MEN
63 Starlite ST45 103 — High Class Feelin'/Pour Me A Glass Of Wine ... 175

MICKEY FINN & BLUE MEN
(see under 'M')

SIMON FINN
70 Mushroom 100 MR 2 — PASS THE DISTANCE (LP, with lyric insert) ... 90

TIM FINN
83 Epic A 3932 — Fraction Too Much Friction/Below The Belt (p/s) ... 5
86 Virgin VS 849-12 — No Thunder No Fire No Rain (Extended Version)/ No Thunder No Fire No Rain/Searching The Streets (12", p/s) ... 8
86 Virgin VS 866-12 — Carve You In Marble/Hole In My Heart (12", p/s) ... 8
89 Capitol CDCL 542 — How'm I Gonna Sleep?/Cruel Black Crow (live)/ Six Months In A Leaky Boat (live) (CD) ... 8
94 Capitol — LIVE AT THE BORDERLINE (CD, promo only) ... 25
(see also Split Enz, Crowded House)

LARRY FINNEGAN
62 HMV POP 1022 — Dear One/Candy Lips ... 18
62 London HLU 9613 — Pretty Suzy Sunshine/It's Walkin' Talkin' Time ... 20
65 Ember EMB S 207 — The Other Ringo (A Tribute To Ringo Starr)/ When My Love Passes By (p/s) ... 20/10

MIKE FINNIGAN
78 CBS 6656 — Just One Minute More/Blood Is Thicker Than Water ... 8

FINN MACCUILL
77 private pressing — SINK YE SWIM YE (LP) ... 80

MINT VALUE £

FIRE

68	Decca F 12753	Father's Name Is Dad/Treacle Toffee World	200
68	Decca F 12856	Round The Gum Tree/Toothie Ruthie	30
70	Pye NSPL 18343	THE MAGIC SHOEMAKER (LP)	275
97	Tenth Planet TP 029	UNDERGROUND AND OVERHEAD: THE ALTERNATE FIRE (LP, gatefold sleeve, numbered, 1,000 only)	18

(see also Strawbs, Paul Brett's Sage)

FIREBALLS

59	Top Rank JAR 218	Torquay/Cry Baby	18
60	Top Rank JAR 276	Bulldog/Nearly Sunrise	18
60	Top Rank JAR 354	Foot-Patter/Kissin'	15
60	Top Rank JAR 507	Vaquero (Cowboy)/Chief Whoopin'-Koff	15
61	Pye International 7N 25092	Quite A Party/Gunshot	12
62	Stateside SS 106	Rik-A-Tik/Yacky Doo	10
63	Stateside SS 151	Carioca/Find Me A Golden Street	10
65	Stateside SS 417	Baby What's Wrong/Yummie Yama Papa	10
67	Stateside SS 2095	Bottle Of Wine/Ain't That Rain	8
68	Stateside SS 2106	Goin' Away/Groovy Motions	8
69	Stateside SS 2134	Come On, React!/Woman Help Me	8
69	London HLZ 10260	Long Green/Light In The Window	7
61	Top Rank 35/105	VAQUERO (LP)	75
68	Stateside S(S)L 10237	BOTTLE OF WINE (LP)	30
69	London HA/SH 8396	COME ON, REACT! (LP)	20

(see also Jimmy Gilmer, Buddy Holly)

FIREBALL XL5

(see under Century 21)

FIREBRAND

85	What WR 71	Never Felt This Way Before/I'm Leaving (p/s)	75

FIRECLOWN

83	Fireclown FC 1001	INVASION EP (Magic/Poor Man/Invasion) (10", no p/s)	12

FIRE ENGINES

80	Codex Comms. CDX 01	Get Up And Use Me/Everything's Roses (p/s)	15
81	Pop:Aural POP 010	Candy Skin/Meat Whiplash (foldout p/s in poly bag)	8
81	Pop:Aural POP 013	Big Gold Dream/Sympathetic Anaesthetic (p/s)	6
81	Pop:Aural POP 01312	Big Gold Dream/Sympathetic Anaesthetic/New Thing In Cartons (12", non-gatefold p/s; gatefold p/s £5)	7
81	Accessory ACC 001	LUBRICATE YOUR LIVING ROOM (LP, in plastic bag)	12

FIRE EXIT

79	Time Bomb Explosion 1	Timewall/Talkin' About Myself (p/s, stamped labels)	10

FIREFLIES

59	Top Rank JAR 198	You Were Mine/Stella Got A Fella	18
59	Top Rank JAR 198	You Were Mine/Stella Got A Fella (78)	30
60	London HLU 9057	I Can't Say Goodbye/What Did I Do Wrong	55

FIREHOUSE FIVE PLUS TWO

56	Good Time Jazz GV 2192	Runnin' Wild/Lonesome Railroad Blues	5
50s	Good Time Jazz GV 2396	Mississippi Rag/Five Foot Two, Eyes Of Blue (78)	7
50s	Good Time Jazz LDG 036	GOES SOUTH VOL. 1 (10" LP)	12
50s	Good Time Jazz LDG 079	GOES SOUTH VOL. 2 (10" LP)	12
50s	Good Time Jazz LDG 094	GOES SOUTH VOL. 3 (10" LP)	12
50s	Good Time Jazz LDG 169	GOES SOUTH VOL. 4 (10" LP)	12
50s	Good Time Jazz LDG 183	FIREHOUSE FIVE (10" LP)	12
50s	Good Time Jazz LAG 12079	THE FIREHOUSE FIVE PLUS TWO (LP)	12
50s	Good Time Jazz LAG 12089	THE FIREHOUSE FIVE PLUS TWO VOL. 2 (LP)	12

FIRE ISLAND

92	Boys Own BOIX 11	In Your Bones/Fire Island (12", 4-track)	20

FIREMAN

99	Hydra HYPRO 12 008	Fluid (12", p/s, promo only)	50
99	Hydra HYPRO CD 008	Fluid (CD, promo only)	60
93	Parlophone FIRE 1	STRAWBERRIES OCEANS SHIPS FOREST (2-LP, clear vinyl, numbered white sleeve, with inners, promo only)	50
93	Parlophone PCSD 145	STRAWBERRIES OCEANS SHIPS FOREST (2-LP, clear vinyl, red sleeve, with inners)	35
93	Parlophone PCSD 145	STRAWBERRIES OCEANS SHIPS FOREST (CD)	25
98	Hydra 4970551	RUSHES (LP)	30

(see also Paul McCartney)

FIRE SESSION

70	Revolution REV 10	Souvenir/Bad Girl	6
70	Revolution REV 13	Sleeping Reggae/CAROLS: Everyday I Have To Cry Some	6
70	Revolution REV 14	Death Of The Ugly One/Big Feet	6

FIRESIGN THEATRE

68	CBS 65129	WAITING FOR THE ELECTRICIAN OR SOMEONE LIKE HIM (LP)	15
68	CBS 65130	HOW TO BE IN TWO PLACES AT ONCE WHEN YOU'RE NOT ANYWHERE AT ALL? (LP)	15
72	CBS CQ 30737	FIRESIGN THEATRE (LP, quadrophonic)	15

FIRESTONES

62	Decca F 11436	Party Twist (Medley) (Parts 1 & 2)	6

FIRING SQUAD

64	Parlophone R 5152	A Little Bit More/Bull Moose	30

MINT VALUE £

FIRKIN THE FOX
84 Woodworm WR 005 BEHIND BARS (LP) . . . 25

FIRM
85 Atlantic A 9586P Radioactive/Together (shaped picture disc) . . . 10
85 Atlantic AT 9586 Radioactive/Together/City Sirens/Live In Peace (12", p/s) . . . 8
86 Atlantic A 9458 All The King's Horses/Fortune Hunter (p/s) . . . 5
85 Atlantic 781 239-2 THE FIRM (CD) . . . 18
86 Atlantic 781 628-2 THE FIRM MEAN BUSINESS (CD) . . . 18
(see also Jimmy Page, Rock Aid Armenia)

FIRST AID
77 Decca TXS 117 NOSTRADAMUS (LP) . . . 22

FIRST CHOICE
73 Pye International 7N 25613 This Is The House Where Love Died/One Step Away (unissued, demos may exist) . . . 70
74 Bell BLL 1376 The Player (Parts 1 & 2) . . . 6
73 Bell BELLS 229 ARMED AND EXTREMELY DANGEROUS (LP) . . . 18

FIRST CLASS
74 UK UKAL 1008 THE FIRST CLASS (LP) . . . 15
76 UK UKAL 1022 S.S.T. (LP) . . . 15
(see also White Plains, Edison Lighthouse, Brotherhood Of Man, Carter-Lewis & Southerners, Ivy League)

FIRST EDITION
68 Reprise RS 20655 Just Dropped In (To See What Condition My Condition Was In)/ Shadow In The Corner Of Your Mind . . . 8
68 Reprise RS 20693 Charlie The Fer'de Lance/Look Around I'll Be There . . . 5
69 Reprise RS 20799 But You Know I Love You/Homemade Lies . . . 5
68 Reprise RSLP 6276 THE FIRST EDITION (LP) . . . 12
(see also Kenny Rogers)

FIRST GEAR
64 Pye 7N 15703 A Certain Girl/Leave My Kitten Alone . . . 175
65 Pye 7N 15763 The 'In' Crowd/Gotta Make Their Future Bright . . . 40

FIRST IMPRESSION
67 Saga SOC 1045 BEAT CLUB (LP) . . . 15

FIRST IMPRESSION/GOOD EARTH
68 Saga FID 2117 SWINGING LONDON (LP) . . . 15
(see also Good Earth, Mungo Jerry)

FIRST IMPRESSIONS
65 Pye 7N 15797 I'm Coming Home/Looking For Her . . . 15
(see also Legends)

FIRST OFFENCE
88 Metal Other OTH 11 FIRST OFFENCE (LP, some with insert) . . . 30/25

FIRST STEPS
80 English Rose ER I The Beat Is Back/She Ain't In Love/Let's Go Cuboids (p/s, with insert) . . . 70
81 English Rose ER III Anywhere Else But Here/Airplay/I Got The News (p/s) . . . 60

CLARE FISCHER
62 Fontana 688124 ZL FIRST TIME OUT (LP) . . . 25

WILD MAN FISCHER
69 Reprise RSLP 6332 AN EVENING WITH WILD MAN FISCHER (gatefold sleeve) . . . 35
(see also Frank Zappa)

FISCHERMAN'S FRIEND
91 EG OP 51 MONEY (12", with "Orb Clubmix", 500 only) . . . 15

FISH
89 EMI 12EMPD 109 State Of Mind/The Voyeur (I Like To Watch)/State Of Mind (Presidential Mix) (12", picture disc) . . . 8
89 EMI CDEM 109 State Of Mind (Album Version)/The Voyeur (I Like To Watch)/ State Of Mind (Presidential Mix) (CD) . . . 8
90 EMI EMPD 135 A Gentleman's Excuse Me/Whiplash (shaped picture disc) . . . 5
90 EMI 12EMPD 135 A Gentleman's Excuse Me/Whiplash/A Gentleman's Excuse Me (Demo Version) (12", picture disc) . . . 8
91 Polydor FISHS 1 Internal Exile/Carnival Man (12" picture disc, numbered die cut sleeve) . . . 8
91 Polydor FISHS 2 Credo/Credo (7" Mix)/Poet's Moon (12", box set with poster & numbered seal) . . . 8
91 Polydor FISHCD 2 Credo/Credo (7" Mix)/Poet's Moon (CD, picture disc, signed numbered digipak) . 15
90 EMI EMDPD 1015 VIGIL IN A WILDERNESS OF MIRRORS (LP, picture disc) . . . 12
(see also Marillion)

ARCHIE FISHER
68 Xtra XTRA 1070 ARCHIE FISHER (LP) . . . 22
70 Decca SKL 5057 ORFEO (LP) . . . 30
82 Celtic Music CM 007 ARCHIE FISHER (LP, reissue) . . . 15
(see also Barbara Dickson)

CHIP FISHER
59 Parlophone R 4604 Poor Me/No One . . . 18
59 RCA RCX 143 AT THE SUGAR BOWL (EP) . . . 75

EDDIE FISHER
53 HMV 7M 101 I'm Yours/That's The Chance You Take . . . 20
53 HMV 7M 115 Everything I Have Is Yours/You'll Never Know . . . 25
53 HMV 7M 116 Trust In Me/Forgive Me . . . 15
53 HMV 7M 117 Outside Of Heaven/Lady Of Spain . . . 30

			MINT VALUE £
53	HMV 7M 125	Even Now/If It Were Up To Me	15
53	HMV 7M 126	Downhearted/Am I Wasting My Time On You	22
53	HMV 7M 133	I'm Walking Behind You (with Sally Sweetland)/Hold Me	30
53	HMV 7M 146	Just Another Polka/When I Was Young (Yes, Very Young)	15
53	HMV 7M 159	Wish You Were Here/A Fool Was I	25
53	HMV 7M 168	Many Times/With These Hands	12
54	HMV 7M 172	Oh My Papa/(I Never Missed You) Until You Said "Goodbye"	18
54	HMV 7M 185	How Deep Is The Ocean?/That Old Feeling	15
54	HMV 7M 201	April Showers/Just To Be With You	15
54	HMV 7M 212	I'm In The Mood For Love/A Girl, A Girl	15
54	HMV 7M 235	May I Sing To You?/My Friend	15
54	HMV 7M 242	How Do You Speak To An Angel?/My Arms, My Heart, My Love	15
54	HMV 7M 251	I Need You Now/Heaven Was Never Like This	15
54	HMV 7M 257	They Say It's Wonderful/Green Years	15
54	HMV 7M 266	Count Your Blessings Instead Of Sheep/White Christmas	15
55	HMV 7M 294	(I'm Always Hearing) Wedding Bells/A Man Chases A Girl	15
56	HMV 7M 353	Magic Fingers/My One And Only Love	12
56	HMV 7M 374	Dungaree Doll/If It Hadn't Been For You	20
56	HMV 7M 402	Without You/No Other One	12
56	HMV 7M 421	Sweet Heartaches/What Is This Thing Called Love?	12
56	HMV POP 273	Cindy, Oh Cindy/Fanny	18
57	HMV POP 296	Some Day Soon/All About Love	6
57	HMV POP 342	Tonight My Heart She Is Crying/Blues For Me	6
57	RCA RCA 1009	A Second Chance/Slow Burning Love	6
58	RCA RCA 1030	Sayonara/That's The Way It Goes	6
58	RCA RCA 1061	Kari Waits For Me/I Don't Hurt Anymore	6
58	RCA RCA 1061	Kari Waits For Me/I Don't Hurt Anymore (78)	8
59	RCA RCA 1147	The Last Mile Home/I'd Sail A Thousand Seas	5
61	London HL 9469	Tonight/Breezin' Along With The Breeze	6
54	HMV 7EG 8026	NIGHT AND DAY (EP)	12
54	HMV 7EG 8046	APRIL SHOWERS (EP)	12
55	HMV 7EG 8146	HOW DEEP IS THE OCEAN (EP)	12
55	HMV 7EG 8156	EDDIE FISHER SINGS NO. 3 — TAKE MY LOVE (EP)	12
56	HMV 7EG 8207	BUNDLE OF JOY (EP, with Debbie Reynolds)	10
54	HMV DLP 1040	TIME FOR ROMANCE (10" LP)	25
55	HMV DLP 1074	MY SERENADE IS YOU (10" LP)	25
56	HMV CLP 1095	SINGS ACADEMY AWARD WINNING SONGS (LP)	15
59	RCA Camden CDN 123	HEART! (LP)	12

FAYE FISHER

65	Columbia DB 7575	Our Love/I Just Don't Know What To Say	7
65	Columbia DB 7732	Oh Heartache You're Bothering Me/It's You	7

MATTHEW FISHER

73	RCA APL1 0195	JOURNEY'S END (LP)	15

(see also Procol Harum, Green Bullfrog)

RAY FISHER

72	Trailer LER 2038	THE BONNY BIRDY (LP, red label, later yellow)	20/15

SONNY FISHER

77	Ace NST 59	Rockin' Daddy/I Can't Lose (78)	30

TONI FISHER

60	Top Rank JAR 261	The Big Hurt/Memphis Belle	7
60	Top Rank JAR 341	How Deep Is The Ocean/Blue, Blue, Blue	8
62	London HLX 9564	West Of The Wall/What Did I Do	10

FISHER BROTHERS

64	London HLN 9928	Big Round Wheel/By The Time You Read This Letter	10

FISHER FAMILY

60s	Topic TOP 67	FAR OVER THE FORTH (EP)	8
66	Topic 12T 137	THE FISHER FAMILY (LP)	15

FISHERFOLK

70s	Celebration CR 1007	WORSHIP WITH THE FISHERFOLK (LP)	18
70s	Celebration CR 1025	THE SUN'S GONNA SHINE (LP)	15
70s	Celebration CR 1028	JOY IN THE MORNING (LP)	18
70s	Celebration CR 1030	WILLING TO ROW (LP)	18

FIST

80	Neat NEAT 04	Name Rank And Serial Number/You'll Never Get Me In One Of Those (p/s, some with poster insert)	10/8
80	MCA MCA 615	Name Rank And Serial Number/You'll Never Get Me (In One Of Those) (p/s, reissue, some with poster insert)	30/20
80	MCA MCA 640	Forever Amber/Brain Damage (p/s)	12
81	MCA MCA 663	Collision Course/Law Of The Jungle (some in p/s)	100/30
82	Neat NEAT 021	The Wanderer/Too Hot (p/s)	10
80	MCA MCF 3082	TURN THE HELL ON (LP)	15
85	Neat NEAT 1003	BACK WITH A VENGEANCE (LP, some on yellow vinyl)	30/15

JOHN FITCH & ASSOCIATES

71	Beacon BEA 117	Romantic Altitude/Stoned Out Of It	15

FITS

82	Rondelet ROUND 13	Think For Yourself: Burial/Straps (p/s)	10
83	Corpus Christi ITS 9	Tears Of A Nation/Bravado/Breaking Point (p/s)	6
84	Trapper FIT 1	Action/Achilles Heel (p/s)	7

85 Trapper FIT 2 — Fact Or Fiction/Give Away (p/s) 5
81 Beat The System FIT 1 — YOU SAID WE'D NEVER MAKE IT (EP, wraparound p/s) 8
82 Rondelet ROUND 30 — THE LAST LAUGH (EP) 10
82 Rondelet ABOUT 6 — NOTHING AND NOWHERE (LP) 12
85 Trapper FIT 3 — FACT OR FICTION (mini-LP) 10

FITZ & COOLERS

68 Nu Beat NB 003 — Cover Me/Darling 12

ELLA FITZGERALD

78

59 Brunswick 05783 — My Happiness/A Satisfied Mind 8

SINGLES

54 Brunswick 05324 — Who's Afraid (Not I, Not I, Not I)/I Wished On The Moon (with Gordon Jenkins) . . 10
55 Brunswick 05392 — Lullaby Of Birdland/Later 10
55 Brunswick 05427 — Moanin' Low/Take A Chance On Love 10
55 Brunswick 05468 — Lover, Come Back To Me/Old Devil Moon 10
55 Brunswick 05473 — Pete Kelly's Blues/Hard Hearted Hannah 10
55 Brunswick 05477 — Soldier Boy/Air Mail Special (with Bill Doggett) 10
56 Brunswick 05514 — My One And Only Love/(Love Is) The Tender Trap 10
56 Brunswick 05539 — Ella's Contribution To The Blues/Early Autumn 10
56 Brunswick 05584 — You'll Never Know/But Not Like Mine 10
56 HMV POP 266 — The Silent Treatment/The Sun Forgot To Shine This Morning 10
57 HMV POP 290 — A Beautiful Friendship/Too Young For The Blues 8
57 HMV POP 316 — Hotta Chocolatta/Stay There 7
57 HMV POP 348 — Johnny One Note/To Keep My Love Alive 7
57 HMV POP 373 — Ev'ry Time We Say Goodbye/Manhattan 7
57 HMV POP 380 — Goody Goody/A Tisket, A Tasket 7
58 HMV POP 486 — The Swingin' Shepherd Blues/Midnight Sun 7
58 HMV POP 499 — Beale Street Blues/St. Louis Blues 6
58 HMV POP 518 — Your Red Wagon/Trav'lin Light 6
59 Brunswick 05783 — My Happiness/A Satisfied Mind 6
59 HMV POP 657 — But Not For Me/You Make Me Feel So Young 7
59 HMV POP 686 — The Christmas Song/You Make Me Feel So Young 7
60 HMV POP 701 — Like Young/Beat Me Daddy Eight To The Bar 7
60 HMV POP 719 — It's All Right With Me/Don'cha Go Way Mad (with Oscar Peterson) 6
60 HMV POP 736 — Mack The Knife/Lorelei 7
60 HMV POP 782 — How High The Moon (Parts 1 & 2) 10
60 HMV POP 809 — Good Morning Blues/Jingle Blues 6
60 HMV POP 817 — We Three Kings Of Orient Are/White Christmas 7
61 HMV POP 849 — The Lady Is A Tramp/Misty 6
64 Verve VS 502 — Desafinado/Stardust 6
65 Verve VS 519 — Can't Buy Me Love/Sweetest Sound 8
65 Verve VS 524 — Why Was I Born/All The Things You Are 5
66 Stateside SS 569 — These Boots Were Made for Walkin'/Stardust 7
69 Reprise RS 20850 — Get Ready/Open Your Window 10
69 Polydor 56767 — Hey Jude/Sunshine Of Your Love 5
71 Reprise RS 23507 — I Heard It Through The Grapevine/Days Of Wine & Roses 5

LPs

53 Brunswick LA 8581 — SOUVENIR ALBUM (10") 25
54 Brunswick LA 8648 — ELLA SINGS GERSHWIN (10") 25
55 Brunswick LAT 8056 — ELLA — SONGS IN A MELLOW MOOD 18
56 Brunswick LAT 8091 — SWEET AND HOT 18
56 Brunswick LAT 8115 — LULLABIES OF BIRDLAND 18
56 HMV CLP 1083 — THE COLE PORTER SONGBOOK VOLUME 1 18
56 HMV CLP 1084 — THE COLE PORTER SONGBOOK VOLUME 2 18
57 Brunswick LAT 8223 — ELLA AND HER FELLAS 18
57 HMV CLP 1116 — THE RODGERS AND HART SONGBOOK VOLUME 1 18
57 HMV CLP 1117 — THE RODGERS AND HART SONGBOOK VOLUME 2 18
58 HMV CLP 1166 — LIKE SOMEONE IN LOVE 15
58 HMV CLP 1183 — THE IRVING BERLIN SONGBOOK VOLUME ONE 12
58 HMV CLP 1184 — THE IRVING BERLIN SONGBOOK VOLUME TWO 12
58 HMV CLP 1213/1214 — THE DUKE ELLINGTON SONGBOOK NUMBER ONE (2-LP) 18
58 HMV CLP 1227/1228 — THE DUKE ELLINGTON SONGBOOK NUMBER TWO (2-LP) 18
59 HMV CLP 1267 — ELLA SWINGS LIGHTLY 12
59 HMV CLP 1338 — SINGS GERSHWIN VOL. 1 (also stereo CSD 1292) 12/15
59 HMV CLP 1339 — SINGS GERSHWIN VOL. 2 12
60 HMV CLP 1347 — SINGS GERSHWIN VOL. 3 (also stereo CSD 1299) 12/15
60 HMV CLP 1348 — SINGS GERSHWIN VOL. 4 (also stereo CSD 1300) 12/15
60 HMV CLP 1353 — SINGS GERSHWIN VOL. 5 (also stereo CSD 1304) 12/15
60 HMV CSD 1287 — SWEET SONGS FOR SWINGERS 12
60 HMV CLP 1391 — ELLA IN BERLIN — MACK THE KNIFE 12
60 HMV CLP 1396 — SONGS FROM THE FILM "LET NO MAN WRITE MY EPITAPH" 12
60 HMV CLP 1397 — ELLA WISHES YOU A SWINGING CHRISTMAS 12
61 HMV CLP 1383 — HELLO LOVE! (also stereo CSD 1315) 12/15
63 Verve VLP 9020 — RHYTHM IS MY BUSINESS 12
65 Verve VLP 9083 — ELLA AT JUAN-LES-PINS 12

(see also Oscar Peterson, Count Basie, Ink Spots)

ELLA FITZGERALD & LOUIS ARMSTRONG

53 Brunswick 05112 — Who Walks In When I Walk Out/Would You Like To Take A Walk (78) 8
56 HMV CLP 1098 — ELLA AND LOUIS (LP) 12
57 HMV CLP 1146 — ELLA AND LOUIS AGAIN NO. 1 (LP) 12
57 HMV CLP 1147 — ELLA AND LOUIS AGAIN NO. 2 (LP) 12
59 HMV CLP 1245 — PORGY AND BESS (LP) 12
59 HMV CLP 1246 — PORGY AND BESS (LP) 12

(see also Louis Armstrong)

MINT VALUE £

ELLA FITZGERALD/BILLIE HOLIDAY
58 Columbia Clef 33CX 10100 AT NEWPORT (LP) 20

G.F. FITZGERALD
70 Uni UNLS 115 MOUSEPROOF (LP, with insert). 60
(see also Sam Gopal)

PATRICK FITZGERALD
77 Small Wonder SMALL 4 SAFETY PIN STUCK IN MY HEART (EP, with lyrics). 5
78 Small Wonder SMALL 6 Buy Me, Sell Me/The Little Dippers/Trendy/The Backstreet Boys (p/s) 5
78 Small Wonder WEENY ONE THE PARANOID WARD/THE BEDROOM TAPES (EP, mono/stereo, 33rpm) 7
78 Small Wonder WEENY ONE THE PARANOID WARD/THE BEDROOM TAPES (12" EP) 10
79 Polydor 2383 533 GRUBBY STORIES (LP). 12

MAGGIE FITZGIBBON
59 Pye International N 25047 Kookaburra/The Right Kind Of Man (78) 12

FITZROY (Sterling) & HARRY
70 Bullet BU 439 Freedom Street/Freedom Street Version 7
70 Escort ERT 827 Pop A Top Train/Doing The Moonwalk 10

FIVE AMERICANS
66 Pye International 7N 25354 I See The Light/The Outcasts. 20
66 Pye International 7N 25373 Evol — Not Love/Don't Blame Me 35
67 Stateside SS 2012 Western Union/Now That It's All Over 10
67 Stateside SS 2036 Sound Of Love/Sympathy 8
68 Stateside SS 2097 7.30 Guided Tour/See-Saw Man 8

5 A.M. EVENT
66 Pye 7N 17154 Hungry/I Wash My Hands (In Muddy Water) 200

FIVE & A PENNY
68 Polydor 56282 You Don't Know Where Your Interest Lies/Mary Go Round 25

FIVE BLIND BOYS
64 Vocalion EPVP 1276 NEGRO SPIRITUALS (EP, 2 tracks by Spirits Of Memphis) 25
64 Vocalion EPVP 1282 FIVE BLIND BOYS (EP) 25

FIVE BLOBS
58 Philips PB 881 The Blob/Saturday Night In Tijuana. 20
58 Philips PB 881 The Blob/Saturday Night In Tijuana (78) 15

FIVE BY FIVE
68 Pye International 7N 25477 Fire/Hang Up 35

FIVE CARD STUD
67 Philips BF 1567 Beg Me/Once 15

FIVE CHESTERNUTS
58 Columbia DB 4165 Jean Dorothy/Teenage Love 200
58 Columbia DB 4165 Jean Dorothy/Teenage Love (78). 110
(see also Shadows, Pete Chester)

FIVE COUNTS
62 Oriole CB 1769 Watermelon Walk/Spanish Nights 20

FIVE CRESTAS
66 Excel ES SP 288/289 How Sweet It Is (To Be Loved By You)/You Used To Love Me (private pressing). . 65

FIVE DALLAS BOYS
57 Columbia DB 4005 Shangri-La/By The Fireside 8
57 Columbia DB 4041 I Never Had The Blues/All The Way 8
58 Columbia DB 4102 26 Miles (Santa Catalina)/Sail Along, Silv'ry Moon 8
58 Columbia DB 4154 Big Man/Lonesome Traveller 8
58 Columbia DB 4231 Fatty Patty/Do You Wanna Jump Children?. 10
58 Columbia DB 4231 Fatty Patty/Do You Wanna Jump Children? (78) 8
59 Columbia DB 4244 Gigi/The Mocking Bird 5
59 Columbia DB 4244 Gigi/The Mocking Bird (78) 8
59 Columbia DB 4313 Morning Papers/I'm Aware. 5
60 Columbia DB 4445 Boston Tea Party/Ramona 5
61 Columbia DB 4599 One Finger, One Thumb/Nice To Know You Care 5
60 Columbia SEG 8035 THE FIVE DALLAS BOYS (EP). 18
(see also Dallas Boys)

FIVE DAY RAIN
70 private pressing FIVE DAY RAIN (LP, no sleeve, 15 copies only). . . . . 500+
93 private pressing FIVE DAY RAIN (LP, re-pressing in signed, numbered sleeve,
signed note in run-out groove & letter of authenticity, 25 only). 80
94 Background HBG 123 FIVE DAY RAIN (LP, reissue) 12
(see also Scots Of St. James, Hopscotch, One Way Ticket, Glencoe)

FIVE DAY WEEK STRAW PEOPLE
68 Saga FID 2123 FIVE DAY WEEK STRAW PEOPLE (LP). 80
(see also Attack, Andromeda, John Du Cann)

FIVE DE MARCO SISTERS
53 MGM SP 1043 Bouillabasse/I'm Never Satisfied. 15
54 Brunswick 05349 Love Me/Just A Girl That Men Forget 18
55 Brunswick 05425 Dreamboat/Two Hearts, Two Kisses (Make One Love) 18
55 Brunswick 05474 The Hot Barcarolle/Sailor Boys Have Talk To Me In English. 15
56 Brunswick 05526 Romance Me/This Love Of Mine 15

FIVE DU-TONES
63 Stateside SS 206 Shake A Tail Feather/Divorce Court. 18
68 President PT 134 Shake A Tail Feather/Divorce Court (reissue) 8

MINT VALUE £

FIVE EMPREES

65 Stateside SS 470 Little Miss Sad/Hey Lover 15

FIVE FLEETS

58 Felsted AF 103 Oh What A Feeling/I Been Cryin' 300
58 Felsted AF 103 Oh What A Feeling/I Been Cryin' (78) 90

FIVE GO DOWN TO THE SEA

83 Kabuki KAFIVE 5 KNOT A FISH (EP) 6
84 Abstract 12 ABS 027 THE GLEE CLUB (12" EP) 8
85 Creation CRE 021T Singing In Braille/Aunt Nelly/Silk Brain Worm/Women (12", p/s) 8

FIVE HAND REEL

76 Rubber RUB 019 FIVE HAND REEL (LP, with lyric insert). 12

FIVE KEYS

54 Capitol CL 14184 Ling, Ting, Tong/I'm Alone (78). 45
55 Capitol CL 14313 The Verdict/Make Me Um Pow Pow (triangular centre) 500
55 Capitol CL 14313 The Verdict/Make Me Um Pow Pow (78). 50
55 Capitol CL 14325 (Close Your Eyes) Take A Deep Breath/Doggone It, You Did It (tri centre) 450
55 Capitol CL 14325 (Close Your Eyes) Take A Deep Breath/Doggone It, You Did It (78). 40
56 Capitol CL 14545 Gee Whittakers!/'Cause You're My Lover 300
56 Capitol CL 14545 Gee Whittakers!/'Cause You're My Lover (78) 30
56 Capitol CL 14582 She's The Most/I Dreamt I Dwelt In Heaven 275
56 Capitol CL 14582 She's The Most/I Dreamt I Dwelt In Heaven (78) 30
56 Capitol CL 14639 That's Right/Out Of Sight, Out Of Mind 175
56 Capitol CL 14639 That's Right/Out Of Sight, Out Of Mind (78) 20
57 Capitol CL 14686 The Wisdom Of A Fool/Now Don't That Prove I Love You? 175
57 Capitol CL 14686 The Wisdom Of A Fool/Now Don't That Prove I Love You? (78) 25
57 Capitol CL 14736 Four Walls/Let There Be You 100
57 Capitol CL 14736 Four Walls/Let There Be You (78). 25
57 Capitol CL 14756 The Blues Don't Care/This I Promise You 125
57 Capitol CL 14756 The Blues Don't Care/This I Promise You (78) 35
58 Capitol CL 14829 From Me To You/Whippety Whirl 150
58 Capitol CL 14829 From Me To You/Whippety Whirl (78). 45
58 Capitol CL 14967 One Great Love/Really-O Truly-O. 150
57 Capitol T 828 THE FIVE KEYS ON STAGE! (LP). 150

FIVE MILES OUT

73 Action ACT 4614 Super Sweet Girl Of Mine/Set Your Mind Free. 7

FIVE OF DIAMONDS

65 Oak RGJ 150 FD FIVE OF DIAMONDS (EP). 375

FIVE OR SIX

81 Cherry Red CHERRY 19 Another Reason/The Trial (p/s) 5
81 Cherry Red 12CHERRY 23 POLAR EXPOSURE (12" EP). 8
82 Cherry Red 12CHERRY 43 FOUR FROM FIVE OR SIX (12" EP). 8
82 Cherry Red FRIZBEE 2 A THRIVING AND HAPPY LAND (LP). 12

FIVEPENNY PIECE

69 Columbia DB 8558 Hang The Flag Out Mrs Jones/Little Boy Little Girl 5
72 Columbia SCX 6488 FIVEPENNY PIECE (LP) 12
73 Columbia SCX 6536 MAKIN' TRACKS (LP) 15
70s EMI EMC 3077 WISH YOU WERE HERE (LP) 12
70s EMI EMC 3234 BOTH SIDES OF (LP) 12
70s One Up OU 2050 ON STAGE (LP). 12

FIVE ROYALES

60 Ember EMB S 124 Dedicated To The One I Love/Miracle Of Love. 100

FIVE SAPPHIRES

78 Rocket ROKN 539 Love Music/Where Did All The Good Times Go 6
79 Warner Bros K 17307 Duke Of Earl/Oh My Darlin' 5
79 Warner Bros K 17360 Once In A While/Falling In Love. 5

(see also Steve Allan, Alan Carvell, Carvells, Telegrams)

FIVE SATINS

57 London HL 8501 To The Aisle/Wish I Had My Baby 950
57 London HL 8501 To The Aisle/Wish I Had My Baby (78). 140
59 Top Rank JAR 199 Wonderful Girl/Weeping Willow 40
59 Top Rank JAR 239 Shadows/Toni My Love 40
60 MGM MGM 1087 Your Memory/I Didn't Know 65

FIVE'S COMPANY

66 Pye 7N 17118 Sunday For Seven Days/The Big Kill. 10
66 Pye 7N 17162 Some Girls/Big Deal. 6
66 Pye 7N 17199 Session Man/Dejection 18
69 Saga FID 2151 THE BALLAD OF FRED THE PIXIE (LP). 18

(see also Brunning Hall Sunflower Blues Band)

FIVE SMITH BROTHERS

54 Decca F 10403 A.B.C. Boogie/Veni-Vidi-Vici (with Dennis Wilson Quartet) 18
55 Decca F 10507 Paper Valentine/You're As Sweet Today (As Yesterday) 15
55 Decca F 10527 Don't Worry/I'm In Favour Of Friendship. 15
56 Decca F 10698 You Took My Heart (My Only Heart)/The Grass Is Green 10

(see also Smith Brothers)

MINT VALUE £

FIVE STAIRSTEPS (& CUBIE)
68 Pye International 7N 25448 A Million To One/Something's Missing (with Cubie) . . . 12
69 Buddah 201 026 Stay Close To Me/I Made A Mistake (with Cubie) . . . 12
69 Buddah 201 070 We Must Be In Love/Little Young Lovers (with Cubie) . . . 12
70 Buddah 201 083 Dear Prudence/O-o-h Child . . . 12
70 Buddah 2011 036 O-o-h Child/Who Do You Belong To? . . . 12
70 Buddah 2011 053 Because I Love You/America — Standing . . . 8
(see also Stairsteps)

FIVE STEPS BEYOND
67 CBS 202490 Not So Young Today/Meanwhile Back In My Heart . . . 12
95 Tenth Planet TP 019 FAINT HEARTS AND FAIR MAIDS (LP, 600 only) . . . 12
96 Tenth Planet TP 021 SMILE (LP, with A4 booklet, 600 only) . . . 12

FIVE THIRTY/5:30
85 Other 12 OTH 2 Catcher In The Rye/Weight Of The World/Mood Suite/ Suburban Town (12", p/s, as Five Thirty) . . . 15
85 East West WX 530 BED (LP, as 5:30) . . . 12

FIVE TOWNS
67 Direction 58-3115 It Isn't What You've Got/Advice . . . 8

FIXER
78 Rainbow RSL 116 Bright And Rosy (no p/s) . . . 75

FIZZBOMBS
87 Narodnik NRK 003 Sign On The Line/The Lines That (p/s) . . . 8
87 Wild Rumpus SHEP 001 You Worry Me/JESSE GARON & DESPERADOS: Hank Williams Is Dead (p/s, flexidisc) . . . 6
88 Calculus KIT 002 THE SURFIN' WINTER EP (p/s) . . . 5
88 Calculus KIT 002T THE SURFIN' WINTER EP (12", p/s) . . . 8

ROBERTA FLACK
69 Atlantic 584 294 Compared To What/Hey, That's No Way To Say Goodbye . . . 6
73 Atlantic K 10282 Killing Me Softly With His Song/Just Like A Woman . . . 5
69 Atlantic 588 204 FIRST TAKE (LP, with Donny Hathaway) . . . 15
71 Atlantic K 40040 FIRST TAKE (LP, reissue) . . . 12
71 Atlantic K 40097 CHAPTER TWO (LP) . . . 12
72 Atlantic K 40297 QUIET FIRE (LP) . . . 12
73 Atlantic K 50021 KILLING ME SOFTLY (LP) . . . 12
75 Atlantic K 50049 FEEL LIKE MAKIN' LOVE (LP) . . . 12
(see also Donny Hathaway)

FLACK OFF
80 Sofa FLACK OFF EP: COCKTAILS AT SIX . . . 20

FLAG OF CONVENIENCE
82 Sire SIR 4057 Life On The Telephone/The Other Man's Sin (no p/s) . . . 5
(see also Steve Diggle, Buzzcocks)

FLAIRS
57 Oriole CB 1392 Swing Pretty Mama/I'd Climb The Hills And Mountains . . . 550
57 Oriole CB 1392 Swing Pretty Mama/I'd Climb The Hills And Mountains (78) . . . 100

LES FLAMBEAUX
65 HMV POP 1456 Cachita/Greensleeves . . . 5
71 Mushroom 100 MR 13 LES FLAMBEAUX (LP, 2 different sleeve designs) . . . 18

FLAME
70 Stateside SS 2183 See The Light/Get Your Mind Made Up . . . 12
71 Stateside SSL 10312 THE FLAME (LP) . . . 30
(see also Flames [South Africa], Beach Boys)

FLAME
77 RCA PC 12160 QUEEN OF THE NEIGHBOURHOOD (LP) . . . 12
(see also Aerosmith)

FLAME 'N' KING & BOLD ONES
79 Grapevine GRP 123 Ho Happy Day/Ain't Nobody Jivin' . . . 10

FLAMES
64 Island WI 130 He's The Greatest/Someone Going To Bawl (both actually by the Maytals) . . . 30
64 Island WI 136 Little Flea/Good Idea (both actually by the Maytals) . . . 30
64 Island WI 138 When I Get Home/Neither Silver Nor Gold (both actually by the Maytals) . . . 30
64 Island WI 139 Broadway Jungle/Beat Lied (both actually by the Maytals) . . . 30
(see also Maytals, Vikings)

FLAMES
64 Blue Beat BB 205 Helena Darling/My Darling (both actually by Plamers) . . . 18

FLAMES
68 Nu Beat NB 020 Mini Really Fit Dem/Soul Train (both actually by Alton Ellis & Flames) . . . 10
73 Ackee ACK 528 Feeling Good/Zig Zag . . . 6
(see also Alton Ellis & Flames, Righteous Flames, Larry Marshall)

FLAMES (South Africa)
68 Flame FAN 101/1 Streamliner/Follow The Sun (p/s) . . . 22
68 Page One FOR(S) 009 BURNING SOUL (LP) . . . 40
(see also Flame, Beach Boys)

FLAMING EMERALDS
78 Grapevine GRP 104 Have Some Everybody/Have Some Everybody (Instrumental) . . . 10

MINT VALUE £

JOHNNY FLAMINGO

57 Vogue V 9089 My Teen-Age Girl/When I Lost You. . . . 100
57 Vogue V 9089 My Teen-Age Girl/When I Lost You (78) 35
58 Vogue V 9100 So Long/Make Me A Present Of You 75
58 Vogue V 9100 So Long/Make Me A Present Of You (78). . . . 45

FLAMINGOS

57 London HLN 8373 Would I Be Crying?/Just For A Kick 600
57 London HLN 8373 Would I Be Crying?/Just For A Kick (78). . . . 140
57 Brunswick 05696 The Ladder Of Love/Let's Make Up 550
57 Brunswick 05696 The Ladder Of Love/Let's Make Up (78) 125
59 Top Rank JAR 213 Love Walked In/Yours. . . . 40
60 Top Rank JAR 263 I Only Have Eyes For You/I Was Such A Fool 100
60 Top Rank JAR 367 Nobody Loves Me Like You/You, Me And The Sea 40
60 Top Rank JAR 519 Mio Amore/At Night 35
66 Philips BF 1483 Boogaloo Party/Nearness Of You 18
69 Philips BF 1786 Boogaloo Party/Nearness Of You (reissue, some in p/s) 15/7
69 Philips SBL 7906 HITS NOW AND THEN (LP). . . . 30

FLAMIN' GROOVIES

71 Kama Sutra 2013 031 Teenage Head/Evil-Hearted Ada 10
72 Kama Sutra 2013 042 Gonna Rock Tonite/Keep A-Knockin'/SHA NA NA:
Rock'n'Roll Is Here To Stay/At The Hop/Duke Of Earl. . . . 6
72 United Artists UP 35392 Slow Death/Talahassie Lassie (some in promo only p/s) 25/7
72 United Artists UP 35464 Married Woman/Get A Shot Of Rhythm And Blues. . . . 8
76 Sire 6198 086 Don't You Lie To Me/She Said Yeah/Shake Some Action (p/s) 5
76 Sire 6078 602 Shake Some Action/Teenage Confidential
(p/s, 2 different versions of A-side). . . . 8
76 Kama Sutra KSS 707 Teenage Head/Headin' For The Texas Border 6
78 Sire 6078 619 Feel A Whole Lot Better/Paint It Black/Shake Some Action (p/s). . . . 7
78 Sire 6078 619 Feel A Whole Lot Better/Paint It Black/Shake Some Action (12", p/s) 8
78 Sire SIR 4002 Move It/When I Heard Your Name 6
79 Sire SIR 4018 Absolutely Sweet Marie/Werewolves Of London/Next One Crying (p/s) 6
76 United Artists REM 406 SLOW DEATH (EP). . . . 8
71 Kama Sutra 2683 003 FLAMIN' GROOVIES (2-LP) 15
77 Sire 9103 251 SHAKE SOME ACTION (LP). . . . 12
78 Sire 9103 333 THE FLAMIN' GROOVIES NOW! (LP) 12
(see also Mike Wilhelm)

FLAMING YOUTH

69 Fontana TF 1057 Guide Me Orion/From Now On (Immortal Invisible) 22
70 Fontana 6001 002 Every Man, Woman And Child/Drifting 18
70 Fontana 6001 003 From Now On/Space Child. . . . 18
69 Fontana STL 5533 ARK II (LP, with plastic window sleeve) 40
(see also Genesis, Phil Collins, Jackson Heights)

FLAMMA-SHERMAN

68 SNB 55-3488 No Need To Explain/Bassa Love 8
68 SNB 55-3769 Love Is In The Air/Super Day 7
69 SNB 55-4142 Move Me/Where Is He. . . . 20

BUD FLANAGAN

59 Columbia DB 4265 Strollin'/Home Is Where Your Heart Is 6
59 Columbia DB 4265 Strollin'/Home Is Where Your Heart Is (78) 7
69 Pye 7N 17854 Who Do You Think You're Kidding, Mr Hitler (Dad's Army Theme)/
BERNARD BEDFORD & CHORUS: It Ain't Gonna Rain No Mo! 10
75 Pye 7N 45530 Who Do You Think You're Kidding, Mr Hitler (Dad's Army Theme)/
BERNARD BEDFORD & CHORUS: It Ain't Gonna Rain No Mo! (reissue) 5
59 Columbia SEG 7876 BUD (EP) 10

FLANAGAN & ALLEN

53 Columbia SEG 7709 TOGETHER AGAIN (EP). . . . 10
53 Columbia 33S 1010 FLANAGAN AND ALLEN (10" LP) 15
53 Decca LF 1125 FAVOURITES (10" LP) 15

FLANAGAN BROTHERS

58 Vogue Coral Q 72342 Salton City/Early One Evening 20
58 Vogue Coral Q 72342 Salton City/Early One Evening (78). . . . 12

MICHAEL FLANDERS (& DONALD SWANN)

57 Parlophone R 4354 A Gnu/Misalliance 5
59 Parlophone R 4528 The Little Drummer Boy/DONALD SWANN: The Youth Of The Heart 5
57 Parlophone PMC 1033 AT THE DROP OF A HAT (LP, also stereo PCS 3001) 12
61 Parlophone PMC 1164 BESTIARY OF FLANDERS AND SWANN (LP). . . . 12
64 Parlophone PMC 1216 AT THE DROP OF ANOTHER HAT (LP, also stereo [PCS 3052]) . . . . each 12

TOMMY FLANDERS

69 Verve SVLP 6020 MOONSTONE (LP) 18
(see also Blues Project)

FLARES

61 London HLU 9441 Foot Stompin'/Hotcha Cha-Cha Brown 25
63 London HA-U 8034 FOOT STOMPIN' HITS (LP). . . . 75

FLASH

72 Sovereign SOV 105 Small Beginnings/Morning Haze 7
73 Sovereign SOV 116 Watch Your Step/Lifetime. . . . 7
72 Sovereign SVNA 7251 FLASH (LP). . . . 15
72 Sovereign SVNA 7255 FLASH IN THE CAN (LP, some in unissued 'band in studio' proof sleeve) 25/15
73 Sovereign SVNA 7260 OUT OF OUR HANDS (LP). . . . 15
(see also Peter Banks, Yes)

MINT VALUE £

FLASH & BOARD OF DIRECTORS

68 Bell BLL 1007 — Busy Signal/Love Ain't Easy . . . 6

FLASHPOINT

87 private pressing FP 01 — NO POINT OF REFERENCE (LP) . . . 40

FLAT EARTH SOCIETY

83 Psycho PSYCHO 17 — WALEECO (LP) . . . 15

FLATMATES

86 Subway Organisation SUBWAY 6 — I Could Be In Heaven/Tell Me Why/So In Love With You (foldaround p/s with insert in poly bag) . . . 6
88 Subway Org. SUBWAY 17T — Shimmer/On My Mind/If Not For You/Bad (12", p/s, with 'flat sharing guide') . . . 8

(Lester) FLATT & (Earl) SCRUGGS

65 CBS 201793 — Ballad Of Jed Clampett/Gonna Give Myself A Ball . . . 7
67 CBS 3038 — Foggy Mountain Breakdown/California Uptight Band . . . 5
67 Mercury MF 1007 — Foggy Mountain Breakdown/My Cabin In Caroline . . . 5
61 Mercury ZEP 10106 — C & W TRAIL BLAZERS NO. 4 (EP) . . . 15
64 Mercury 10010 MCE — COUNTRY AND WESTERN ACES (EP) . . . 15
62 Philips BBL 7516 — SONGS OF THE FAMOUS CARTER FAMILY (LP) . . . 12
63 CBS BPG 62095 — FOLK SONGS OF OUR LAND (LP) . . . 12
63 CBS BPG 62259 — AT CARNEGIE HALL (LP) . . . 12

LINDA FLAVELL

66 Decca F 12312 — And The Trouble With Me Is You/Over And Over . . . 10

FLAVOUR

68 Direction 58-3597 — Sally Had A Party/Shop Around . . . 10

LOS FLECHAZOS

94 Detour Records DRO 13 — Try It/You Drove Me Crazy (p/s, 100 red vinyl) . . . 7

GREGORY FLECKNER QUINTET

96 Clear CLR 418 — Oi, That's My Bird (12", with Plaid & Dr Rockit mixes, p/s) . . . 12

(FABULOUS) FLEE-REKKERS/FLEE-RAKKERS

60 Triumph RGM 1008 — Green Jeans/You Are My Sunshine (as Fabulous Flee-Rakkers) . . . 35
60 Top Rank JAR 431 — Green Jeans/You Are My Sunshine (reissue, as Fabulous Flea-Rakkers) . . . 60
60 Pye 7N 15288 — Sunday Date/Shiftless Sam . . . 15
60 Pye 7N 15326 — Blue Tango/Bitter Rice . . . 15
61 Piccadilly 7N 35006 — Lone Rider/Miller Like Wow . . . 18
62 Piccadilly 7N 35048 — Stage To Cimarron/Twistin' The Chestnuts . . . 18
62 Piccadilly 7N 35081 — Sunburst/Black Buffalo . . . 20
63 Piccadilly 7N 35109 — Fireball/Fandango . . . 20
61 Pye NEP 24141 — THE FABULOUS FLEE-REKKERS (EP) . . . 70

(see also Ricky Wayne & Fabulous Flee-Rakkers)

(PETER GREEN'S) FLEETWOOD MAC

SINGLES

67 Blue Horizon 57-3051 — I Believe My Time Ain't Long/Rambling Pony (as Peter Green's Fleetwood Mac, initially with p/s) . . . 80/18
68 Blue Horizon 57-3138 — Black Magic Woman/The Sun Is Shining . . . 10
68 Blue Horizon 57-3139 — Need Your Love So Bad/Stop Messin' Around . . . 10
68 Blue Horizon 57-3145 — Albatross/Jigsaw Puzzle Blues . . . 6
69 Immediate IM 080 — Man Of The World/EARL VINCE & VALIANTS: Somebody's Gonna Get Their Head Kicked In Tonight . . . 10
69 Blue Horizon 57-3157 — Need Your Love So Bad/Black Magic Woman (unissued)
69 Blue Horizon 57-3157 — Black Magic Woman/No Place To Go (unissued)
69 Blue Horizon 57-3157 — Need Your Love So Bad/No Place To Go . . . 6
69 CBS 3051 — I Believe My Time Ain't Long/Rambling Pony (reissue) . . . 6
69 Reprise RS 27000 — Oh Well (Parts 1 & 2) . . . 6
70 Reprise RS 27007 — The Green Manalishi (With The Two-Prong Crown)/World In Harmony (initially with p/s) . . . 30/8
71 Reprise RS 27010 — Dragonfly/The Purple Dancer . . . 5
71 CBS/Blue Horizon 3145 — Albatross/Jigsaw Puzzle Blues (reissue) . . . 5
72 Reprise K 14194 — Spare Me A Little Of Your Love/Sunny Side Of Heaven . . . 5
73 Reprise K 14280 — Did You Ever Love Me?/The Derelict . . . 5
73 CBS 1722 — Black Magic Woman/Stop Messin' Around . . . 5
73 CBS 8306 — Albatross/Need Your Love So Bad (p/s, 'Hall Of Fame Hits' reissue) . . . 5
74 Reprise K 14315 — For Your Love/Hypnotised . . . 5
75 Reprise K 14388 — Heroes Are Hard To Find/Born Enchanter . . . 5
75 DJM DJS 10620 — Man Of The World/DANNY KIRWAN: Second Chapter . . . 5
75 Reprise K 14403 — Warm Ways/Blue Letter (initially with p/s) . . . 12/5
76 Reprise K 14413 — Over My Head (Edit)/I'm So Afraid . . . 5
76 Reprise K 14430 — Rhiannon/Sugar Daddy (initially with p/s) . . . 12/5
76 Reprise K 14447 — Say You Love Me/Monday Morning . . . 5
77 Warner Bros K 16872 — Go Your Own Way/Silver Springs (p/s) . . . 10
77 Warner Bros K 16930 — Don't Stop/Gold Dust Women . . . 5
77 Warner Bros K 16969 — Dreams/Songbird . . . 5
77 Warner Bros K 17013 — You Make Loving Fun/Never Going Back Again . . . 5
79 Warner Bros K 17468 — Tusk/Never Make Me Cry ('dog' or 'plain' p/s) . . . each 5
79 Warner Bros K 17533 — Sara/That's Enough For Me (p/s) . . . 6
80 Warner Bros K 17577 — Not That Funny/Save Me A Place (p/s) . . . 5
80 Warner Bros K 17614 — Think About Me/Honey Hi (p/s) . . . 5
81 Warner Bros K 17746 — The Farmer's Daughter/Dreams (live) (p/s) . . . 7
82 Warner Bros K 17965 — Hold Me/Eyes Of The World (p/s) . . . 5
82 Warner Bros K 17997 — Gypsy (Edit)/Cool Water (p/s) . . . 5
82 Warner Bros FLEET 1P — Oh Diane/Rhiannon/The Chain (picture disc) . . . 10
83 Warner Bros W 9848 — Can't Go Back/That's Alright (p/s) . . . 5
83 Warner Bros W 9848T — Can't Go Back/Rhiannon/Tusk/Over And Over (12", p/s) . . . 10

87	Warner Bros W 8398	Big Love/You And I Part 1//The Chain/Go Your Own Way (gatefold double pack)	12
87	Warner Bros W 8398TP	Big Love (Extended)/You And I Part 1 (12", picture disc)	15
87	Warner Bros W 8317TP	Seven Wonders (Extended Remix)/Book Of Miracles (Instrumental)/ Seven Wonders (Dub) (12", picture disc)	10
87	Warner Bros W 8291	Little Lies/Ricky (picture disc)	5
87	Warner Bros W 8291TP	Little Lies (Extended)/Little Lies (Dub)/Ricky (12", picture disc)	10
88	Warner Bros W 8143CD	Everywhere/When I See You Again/Rhiannon/Say You Love Me (3" CD with adaptor, 5" case)	8
88	Warner Bros W 8114B	Family Man/Down Endless Street (box set, with 2 colour prints)	8
88	Warner Bros W 8114T	Family Man (Extended Vocal Mix)/Family Party Bonus Beats/ You And I Part II (12", p/s)	8
88	Warner Bros W 7860CD	Isn't It Midnight?/Mystified/Say You Love Me/Gypsy (3" CD w/ adaptor, 5" case)	8
88	Warner Bros W 7644CD	As Long As You Follow/Oh Well (live)/Gold Dust Woman (3" CD with adaptor, 5" case)	8
89	Warner Bros W 7528CD	Hold Me/No Questions Asked/I Loved Another Woman (live) (3" CD, gatefold p/s)	8
89	CBS 6546137	Albatross/Man Of The World (p/s)	10
89	CBS 654 613-6	Albatross/Man Of The World/Black Magic Woman/Love That Burns (12", p/s)	8
89	CBS 654 613-2	Albatross/Black Magic Woman/Love That Burns (CD, card sleeve)	20
89	CBS 655 171-3	Solid Gold: Albatross/Black Magic Woman/Need Your Love So Bad/ I'd Rather Go Blind (3" CD, gatefold card sleeve, as Fleetwood Mac & Christine Perfect)	8
90	Warner Bros W 9866CDX	Save Me/Another Woman (live)/Everywhere (live) (CD, foldout sleeve)	8
90	Warner Bros W 9739CDX	In The Back Of My Mind (edit)/Lizard People/Little Lies (live)/The Chain (live) (CD, foldout sleeve)	8

LPs

68	Blue Horizon 7-63200	PETER GREEN'S FLEETWOOD MAC (mono/stereo)	50/40
68	Blue Horizon 7-63205	MR. WONDERFUL (gatefold sleeve)	35
69	Blue Horizon 7-63215	THE PIOUS BIRD OF GOOD OMEN	30
69	Reprise RSLP 9000	THEN PLAY ON (gatefold sleeve)	15
70	Reprise RSLP 9004	KILN HOUSE (gatefold sleeve, some with insert)	15/12
71	CBS Blue Horizon 63875	THE ORIGINAL FLEETWOOD MAC	15
71	CBS 69011	GREATEST HITS (plain orange label)	12
72	Reprise K 44181	BARE TREES	25
77	Reprise K 54043	FLEETWOOD MAC (white vinyl with lyric sheet)	18
77	Warner Bros K 56344	RUMOURS (white vinyl with lyric sheet)	18
90	Warner Bros 7599-26206-2	BEHIND THE MASK (picture disc, box set, with print & graphics software)	20

(see also Mick Fleetwood's Zoo, Peter Green, Stevie Nicks, Buckingham-Nicks, Jeremy Spencer, Christine Perfect, Danny Kirwan, John Mayall, Otis Spann, Eddie Boyd, Duster Bennett, Chicken Shack, Shotgun Express, Bo Street Runners, Cheynes, Tramp, Brunning Hall Sunflower Blues Band)

FLEETWOODS

59	London HLU 8841	Come Softly To Me/I Care So Much	15
59	London HLU 8841	Come Softly To Me/I Care So Much (78)	22
59	London HLU 4003	Come Softly To Me/I Care So Much (stereo export issue)	60
59	London HLU 8895	Graduation's Here/Oh Lord Let It Be Me	18
59	London HLU 8895	Graduation's Here/Oh Lord Let It Be Me (78)	40
59	Top Rank JAR 202	Mr. Blue/You Mean Everything To Me	12
59	Top Rank JAR 202	Mr. Blue/You Mean Everything To Me (78)	55
60	Top Rank JAR 294	Outside My Window/Magic Star (some in p/s)	20/10
60	Top Rank JAR 383	Runaround/Truly Do	10
61	London HLG 9341	Tragedy/Little Miss Sad One	15
61	London HLG 9426	He's The Great Imposter/Poor Little Girl	12
62	Liberty LIB 62	They Tell Me It's Summer/Lovers By Night Strangers By Day	12
63	Liberty LIB 75	Goodnight My Love Pleasant Dreams/Jimmy Beware	12
64	Liberty LIB 93	Ruby Red Baby Blue/Lonesome Town	15
65	Liberty LIB 10191	Almost There/Before And After (Losing You)	15
60	Top Rank BUY 028	MR BLUE (LP, with 3 tracks by other artists)	30
61	London HA-G 2388	SOFTLY (LP, also stereo SAH-G 6188)	65/85
61	London HA-G 2419	DEEP IN A DREAM (LP)	75

MICK FLEETWOOD'S ZOO

81	RCA RCA 118	You Weren't In Love/O-Niamali (p/s)	5
83	RCA RCA 360	I Want You Back/Put Me Right (p/s)	8

(see also Fleetwood Mac)

HELEN FLEMING

66	Blue Beat BB 341	Eve's Ten Commandments/Don't Take Your Love Away	12

JOY FLEMING

75	Antic K 11518	A Bridge Of Love/Divorcee	5
76	Private Stock PVT 54	Are You Ready For Love/Alabama Standby	10

WADE FLEMONS

59	Top Rank JAR 206	Slow Motion/Walkin' By The River	15
60	Top Rank JAR 327	What's Happening?/Goodnight, It's Time To Go	15
60	Top Rank JAR 371	Easy Lovin'/Whoops Now	15

FLESHEATERS

81	Initial IRC 007	A MINUTE TO PRAY, A SECOND TO DIE (LP)	18

FLESH VOLCANO

87	Some Bizzare SLUT 1	Slut/The Universal Cesspool/Bruisin' Chain (12", p/s)	10

(see also Marc Almond, Foetus)

DARROW FLETCHER

66	London HLU 10024	The Pain Gets A Little Deeper/My Judgement Day	75

MINT VALUE £

DON FLETCHER

66	Vocalion VP 9271	Two Wrongs Don't Make A Right/I'm So Glad	20

GUY FLETCHER

69	Pye 7N 17765	Magic Woman/All Fall Down	6

SAM FLETCHER

59	MGM MGM 1024	Time Has A Way/No Such Luck	7
60	RCA RCA 1255	Tall Hope/You're So Far Away From Home	7

FLEUR-DE-LYS

65	Immediate IM 020	Moondreams/Wait For Me	200
66	Immediate IM 032	Circles/So Come On	500
66	Polydor 56124	Mud In Your Eye/I've Been Trying	420
67	Polydor 56200	I Can See A Light/Prodigal Son	60
68	Polydor 56251	The Gong With The Luminous Nose/Hammer Head	100
68	Atlantic 584 193	Stop Crossing The Bridge/Brick By Brick (Stone By Stone)	40
69	Atlantic 584 243	You're Just A Liar/One Girl City	70

(see also John Bromley, Terry Durham, Tony & Tandy, Sharon Tandy, Rupert's People, Shyster, Quotations, Bryn Haworth, Chocolate Frog, Gordon Haskell, Waygood Ellis)

VIC FLICK SOUND

70	Chapter One CH 136	Hang On/Wonderful World	8
71	Chapter One CH 155	Quest For Love/Clarice	6

FLIES

66	Decca F 12533	I'm Not Your Stepping Stone/Talk To Me	165
67	Decca F 12594	House Of Love/It Had To Be You	60
68	RCA RCA 1757	The Magic Train/Gently As You Feel	35

(see also Bulldog Breed, T2)

SHELBY FLINT

61	Warner Bros WB 30	Angel On My Shoulder/Somebody	10
66	London HLT 10068	Cast Your Fate To The Wind/The Lilly	20

FLINTLOCKS

66	Decca F 12412	What Goes On?/I Walked Right Into A Heaven	7

FLINTSTONES

64	HMV POP 1266	Safari/Work Out	20

BUNNY FLIP

72	Pressure Beat PB 5510	Shanky Dog (actually "Skanky Dog" by Winston Scotland)/ JOE GIBBS & NOW GENERATION: Boney Dog	8

(see also Winston Scotland)

FLIP & DATELINERS

64	HMV POP 1359	My Johnny Doesn't Come Around Anymore/Please Listen To Me	60

(see also Vivienne Chering)

FLIPPER

81	Alt. Tentacles VIRUS 8	Ha Ha Ha/Love Canal (p/s, with insert)	8

FLIPS

62	London HLU 9490	Rockin' Twist/Oh, You Beautiful Doll — Twist	18

FLIRTATIONS

68	Deram DM 195	Someone Out There/How Can You Tell Me?	7
68	Deram DM 195DJ	Someone Out There/How Can You Tell Me?	15
68	Deram DM 216	Nothing But A Heartache/Christmas Time Is Here Again	25
69	Deram DM 252	What's Good About Goodbye My Love?/Once I Had A Love	6
70	Deram DM 281	Keep On Searchin'/Moma I'm Coming Home	6
70	Deram DM 295	Can't Stop Loving You/Everybody Needs Somebody	6
71	Deram DM 329	Give Me Love/This Must Be The End Of The Line	6
72	Deram DM 351	Need Your Lovin'/I Wanna Be There	7
71	Polydor 2058 167	Little Darlin'/Take Me In Your Arms And Love Me	18
72	Polydor 2058 249	Love A Little Longer/Hold On To Me Babe	6
74	Polydor 2058 295	Dirty Work/No Such Thing As A Miracle	6
73	Mojo 2092 058	Why Didn't I Think Of That?/Oh Mia Bamba	6
78	Casino Classics CC 1	Little Darling (I Need You)/LENNY GAMBLE: I'll Do Anything For You	5
98	London Traffic TRAF 1	Nothing But A Heartache (1-sided, reissue promo, 500 only)	8
69	Deram DML/SML 1046	SOUNDS LIKE THE FLIRTATIONS (LP)	40

(see also Pearly Gates, Gypsies)

FLO & EDDIE

73	Reprise K 14261	Afterglow/Carlos And De Bull	6
72	Reprise K 44201	THE PHLORESCENT LEECH AND EDDIE (LP)	15
73	Reprise K 44234	FLO AND EDDIE (LP)	15

(see also Turtles, Frank Zappa/Mothers Of Invention)

FLOATING BRIDGE

69	Liberty LBS 83271	FLOATING BRIDGE (LP)	40

FLOCK

70	CBS 4932	Tired Of Waiting For You/Store Bought — Store Thought	5
69	CBS 63733	THE FLOCK (LP, orange label)	15
70	CBS 64055	DINOSAUR SWAMPS (LP, orange label, gatefold sleeve)	12

FLOCK OF SEAGULLS

(see under A Flock Of Seagulls)

DICK FLOOD

59	Felsted AF 125	The Three Bells/Far Away	7
59	Felsted AF 125	The Three Bells/Far Away (78)	15

FLORIBUNDA ROSE

67 Piccadilly 7N 35408 — One Way Street/Linda Loves Linda ... 20
(see also Scrugg, John T. Kongos)

FLOWCHART

90s Enraptured RAPT 4505 — Rainbow Hello/ALPHASTONE: Astro (p/s) ... 8
90s Enraptured RAPT 4527 — NO. 7 IN THE STRESS FREE SERIES: Gip Part One/Gip Part 2 (in box) ... 10

FLOWERED UP

90 Heavenly 10 HVN 3 — It's On — Feel The Pain (10", p/s, 1 side etched) ... 8
90 Heavenly HVN 3 — It's On/Sonia (p/s) ... 5
90 Heavenly HVN 003CD — It's On/Sonia/Egg Rush (CD) ... 8
91 FFRR FUPCD 2 — It's On/Egg Rush/Take It (live) (CD) ... 8
91 Heavenly FUPXR 1 — Take It/I'll Be Your Dog/Take It (live)/Phobia (12", p/s, with print) ... 8
90 The Catalogue CAT 084 — It's On (The Posh Facker Mix)/SAINT ETIENNE: Only Love Can Break Your Heart (remixed by Flowered Up) (square flexidisc with *The Catalogue* mag) ... 7/5
92 Heavenly HVN 16 — Weekender (12.53) (12", 1-sided, p/s) ... 10
92 Heavenly HVN 16X — Weatherall's Weekender (Andy Weatherall Remix) (12", p/s) ... 20
92 Heavenly HVN 16CD — Weekender (12.53) (CD, 1-track) ... 10

FLOWERPOT MEN

67 Deram DM 142 — Let's Go To San Francisco (Parts 1 & 2) ... 7
68 Page One POF 065 — Mighty Quinn/Voices From The Sky ... 10
67 Deram DM 160 — A Walk In The Sky/Am I Losing You? ... 10
68 Deram DM 183 — A Man Without A Woman/You Can Never Be Wrong ... 10
69 Deram DM 248 — In A Moment Of Madness/Young Birds Fly ... 10
(see also Ivy League, Friends, Carter-Lewis & Southerners, Edison Lighthouse, Fat Mattress, Gordon Haskell, Kestrels, One & One)

LLOYD FLOWERS & RECO'S RHYTHM GROUP

62 Blue Beat BB 88 — I'm Going Home/Lover's Town ... 20

PHIL FLOWER(S)

69 A&M AMS 766 — Like A Rolling Stone/Keep On Sockin' It Children ... 12
70 A&M AMS 784 — Every Day I Have To Cry/If It Feels Good Do It (miscredited as Phil Flower) ... 22

(Lloyd) FLOWERS & ALVIN (Ranglin)

72 Explosion EX 2067 — Howdy And Tenky/SHORTY PERRY: Sprinkle Some Water ... 5
72 Grape GR 3028 — In De Pum Pum/MAYTONES: If Loving You Was Wrong ... 6
72 Bullet BU 512 — Howdy And Tenky/SHORTY PERRY: Sprinkle Some Water ... 5
73 Duke DU 150 — Rastaman Going Back Home/LITTLE YOUTH: Barble Dove Skank ... 5

FLOWER SERMON

92 Rough Trade 45REV 13 — Sugar Lullaby (p/s with insert) ... 8

FLOWER SHOPPE

72 Polydor 2066 096 — You've Come A Long Way/Kill The Monster ... 8

FLOWER TRAVELLING BAND

71 Atlantic 2091 128 — Satori (Enlightment) (Parts 1 & 2) ... 20

BOBBY FLOYD

72 Pama PM 860 — Sound Doctor/YOUNG DILLINGER: Doctor Skank ... 18

EDDIE FLOYD

66 Atlantic 584 041 — Knock On Wood/Got To Make A Comeback ... 8
67 Stax 601 001 — Raise Your Hand/I've Just Been Feeling Bad (dark or light blue label) ... 8/5
67 London HL 10129 — Set My Soul On Fire/Will I Be The One? ... 10
67 Speciality SPE 1001 — Never Get Enough Of Your Love/Bye Bye Baby ... 10
67 Stax 601 016 — Things Get Better/Good Love, Bad Love ... 10
67 Stax 601 024 — On A Saturday Night/Under My Nose ... 10
68 Stax 601 035 — Big Bird/Holding On With Both Hands ... 10
68 Stax STAX 104 — I've Never Found A Girl (To Love Me Like You Do)/I'm Just The Kind Of Fool ... 10
69 Stax STAX 108 — Bring It On Home To Me/Sweet Things You Do ... 8
69 Stax STAX 116 — I've Got To Have Your Love/Girl I Love You ... 5
69 Stax STAX 125 — Don't Tell Your Mama/Consider Me ... 5
70 Stax STAX 153 — My Girl/Laurie ... 5
72 Polydor 2025 098 — Yum Yum Yum/I Want Some/Tears Of Joy ... 5
74 Stax STXS 2005 — Soul Street/The Highway Man ... 5
81 I-Spy SEE 9 — The Beat Song/London ('I-Spy' sleeve) ... 5
67 Stax 589 006 — KNOCK ON WOOD (LP) ... 35
68 Stax (S)XATS 1003 — I'VE NEVER FOUND A GIRL (LP) ... 30
69 Atco 228 014 — KNOCK ON WOOD (LP, reissue) ... 18
69 Stax SXATS 1023 — YOU'VE GOT TO HAVE EDDIE (LP) ... 20
71 Stax 2363 010 — YOU'VE GOT TO HAVE EDDIE (LP, reissue) ... 15
74 Stax STX 1002 — SOUL STREET (LP) ... 12
(see also Falcons, Primettes/Eddie Floyd)

FLUFF

72 Decca F 13305 — The Sun Ain't Gonna Shine (Anymore)/Let's Get Back Together ... 7

FLUX (OF PINK INDIANS)

81 Crass 321984/2 — NEU SMELL (EP, foldout poster sleeve) ... 8
85 Spiderleg SDL 16 — TAKING A LIBERTY (EP, as Flux, with booklet sleeve) ... 6
83 Spiderleg SDL 8 — STRIVE TO SURVIVE CAUSING THE LEAST SUFFERING POSSIBLE (LP, with booklet) ... 15
84 Spiderleg SDL 13 — THE FUCKING CUNTS TREAT US LIKE PRICKS (2-LP) ... 18
(see also Epileptics, Licks)

FLYING BURRITO BROTHERS

69 A&M AMS 756 — The Train Song/Hot Burrito No. 1 ... 8
70 A&M AMS 794 — Older Guys/Down In The Churchyard ... 5
70 A&M AMS 816 — Tried So Hard/Lazy Days ... 6

MINT VALUE £

Year	Label / Cat. No.	Title	Value
72	A&M AMS 871	White Line Fever/Colorado	5
69	A&M AML(S) 931	THE GILDED PALACE OF SIN (LP)	15
70	A&M AMLS 983	BURRITO DELUXE (LP)	15
71	A&M AMLS 64295	THE FLYING BURRITO BROTHERS (LP)	12
72	A&M AMLS 64343	LAST OF THE RED-HOT BURRITOS (LP)	12
73	Bumble GEXD 301	LIVE IN AMSTERDAM (2-LP)	15

(see also Byrds, Gram Parsons, Gene Parsons, Stephen Stills & Manassas, Rick Roberts, Country Gazette, Skip Battin)

FLYING CIRCUS

Year	Label / Cat. No.	Title	Value
71	Harvest SHSP 4010	PREPARED IN PEACE (LP)	15

FLYING MACHINE

Year	Label / Cat. No.	Title	Value
69	Pye 7N 17722	Smile A Little Smile For Me/Maybe We've Been Loving Too Long	7
69	Pye 7N 17722	Baby Make It Soon/Smile A Little Smile For Me	6
69	Pye 7N 17811	Send My Baby Home Again/Look At Me, Look At Me	6
70	Pye 7N 17914	Hanging On The Edge Of Sadness/Flying Machine	7
70	Pye 7N 45001	The Devil Has Possession Of Your Mind/Hey Little Girl	5
70	Pye 7N 45093	Yes I Understand/Pages Of Your Life	5
70	Pye NSPL 18328	DOWN TO EARTH WITH THE FLYING MACHINE (LP)	22

(see also Pinkertons, Pinkerton's Assorted Colours, Tony Newman)

FLYING SAUCER ATTACK

Year	Label / Cat. No.	Title	Value
92	Heartbeat FSA 6	Soaring High/Standing Stone (p/s, 500 only, 1st few with autographed postcards; later with various different designs)	25/20
93	Heartbeat FSA 61	Wish/Oceans (p/s, 700 only)	15
94	Domino RUG 23	Land Beyond The Sun/Everywhere Was Everything (p/s, hand-painted rear sleeve, 500 only)	8
95	Planet PUNK 008	Beach Red Lullaby/Second Hour (p/s, 1,300 only)	6
96	Enraptured RAPT 4505	At Night/JESSAMINE: From Hereto And Now Otherwise (500 on clear vinyl, 2500 black)	12/8
98	Earworm WORMSC 1	Land Beyond The Sun (2 -Track Version)/Instrumental For Silence (green vinyl, 500 only)	6
94	Heartbeat FSA 62	FLYING SAUCER ATTACK (LP, 1,000 only)	20

FLYING SAUCERS

Year	Label / Cat. No.	Title	Value
76	Nevis NEV LP 114	PLANET OF THE DRAPES (LP)	12

FLYING SQUAD

Year	Label / Cat. No.	Title	Value
78	CBS	FLYING SQUAD (LP)	12

ERROL FLYNN

Year	Label / Cat. No.	Title	Value
55	Philips PB 380	Lily Of Laguna/We'll Gather Lilacs (B-side with Patrice Wymore) (78)	12

STEVE FLYNN

Year	Label / Cat. No.	Title	Value
67	Parlophone R 5625	Mr Rainbow/Let's Live For Tomorrow	25
68	Parlophone R 5689	Your Life And My Life/Come Tomorrow	8

(see also Mark Wirtz)

FLY ON THE WALL

Year	Label / Cat. No.	Title	Value
79	Next Wave NEXT 1	DEVON DUMB (EP, numbered)	20

FLYS

Year	Label / Cat. No.	Title	Value
78	EMI EMI 2747	Love And A Molotov Cocktail/Can I Crash Here?/Civilisation (p/s)	10
78	EMI EMI 2795	Fun City/E.C. 4 (p/s)	10
78	EMI EMIY 2867	Waikiki Beach Refugees/We Don't Mind The Rave (p/s, yellow vinyl)	10
79	EMI EMI 2907	Beverley/Don't Moonlight On Me (p/s)	6
79	EMI EMI 2936	Name Dropping/Fly V Fly (p/s, some on green vinyl)	15
79	EMI EMI 2979	Living In The Sticks/We Are The Lucky Ones (p/s)	8
79	Parlophone R 6030	16 Down/Night Creatures/Lois Lane/Today Belongs To Me (p/s)	5
77	Zama ZA 10 EP	BUNCH OF FIVE (33rpm EP, die-cut p/s)	125
80	Parlophone R 6063	FOUR FROM THE SQUARE (EP, p/s, demos £20)	7

FLYTE REACTION

Year	Label / Cat. No.	Title	Value
91	Woronzow W0014	SONGS IN A CIRCLE (LP)	15
92	Splendid SPLEN 001	STRAWBERRY LIP SALVATION (LP)	12
93	Splendid SPLEN 002	SPECTRAL FOOTWEAR (LP)	12
95	Splendid SPLEN 003	CREATE A SMILE (LP)	12

FOCAL POINT

Year	Label / Cat. No.	Title	Value
68	Deram DM 186	Love You Forever/Sycamore Sid	35

FOCUS

Year	Label / Cat. No.	Title	Value
71	Polydor 2001 134	House Of The King/Black Beauty	7
71	Blue Horizon 2094 006	Hocus Pocus/Janis	15
72	Blue Horizon 2096 008	Tommy/Focus II	15
76	Polydor 2001 640	House Of The King/O Avendrood	5
71	Polydor 2344 003	IN AND OUT OF FOCUS (LP, gatefold sleeve)	12
72	Blue Horizon 2096 002	MOVING WAVES (LP, with poster)	18
72	Polydor 2659 016	FOCUS III (2-LP, gatefold sleeve)	15
73	Polydor 2443 118	LIVE AT THE RAINBOW (LP, gatefold sleeve)	12

(see also Jan Akkerman, Brainbox, Robin Lent)

FOCUS THREE

Year	Label / Cat. No.	Title	Value
67	Columbia DB 8279	10,000 Years Behind My Mind/The Sunkeeper	50

FOETUS & CHROME CRANKS

Year	Label / Cat. No.	Title	Value
94	PCP 011-2	Vice Squad Dick/Little Johnny Jewel (p/s)	20

FOETUS ART TERRORISM

Year	Label / Cat. No.	Title	Value
84	Self Imm. WOMB FAT 11.12	Calamity Crush/Catastrophe Crunch (12")	20

FOETUS CORRUPTUS

Year	Label / Cat. No.	Title	Value
91	Rifle RIFLE 1	RIFE (2-LP, stickered black sleeve)	20

FOETUS INC.

90	Big Cat ABB 16T	Butterfly Potion/Free James Brown (12")	20
90	Self Imm. WOMB 6	SINK (LP)	25

FOETUS INTERRUPTUS

88	Self Imm. WOMB FIP 5	THAW (LP)	20

FOETUS ÜBER FRISCO

82	Self Immolation WOMB 125/SUSC 12	Custom Built For Capitalism/1.0.4.5./Birthday (12", p/s)	20
85	Self Imm. WOMB UNC 7.12	Finely Honed Machine/Sick Minutes (12")	20

FOETUS UNDER GLASS

85	Self Imm. WOMB S201	Spite Your Face/OKFM (p/s)	20

(see also You've Got Foetus On Your Breath, Philip & His Foetus Vibrations, Scraping Foetus Off The Wheel, Flesh Volcano)

FOGCUTTERS

64	Liberty LIB 55793	Cry Cry Cry/You Say	15

JOHN FOGERTY

74	Fantasy FTC 111	Comin' Down The Road/Ricochet	5
75	Fantasy FTC 119	Rockin' All Over The World/The Wall	5
75	Fantasy FTC 120	Almost Saturday Night/Sea Cruise	5
76	Fantasy FTC 133	You Got The Magic/Evil Thing	5
75	Fantasy FT 526	JOHN FOGERTY (LP)	15

(see also Creedence Clearwater Revival, Blue Ridge Rangers)

TOM FOGERTY

71	United Artists UP 35264	Goodbye Media Man (Parts 1 & 2)	5
72	Fantasy F 680	Cast The First Stone/Lady Of Fatima	5
73	Fantasy FTC 109	Joyful Resurrection/Heartbeat	5
72	Fantasy FAN 9407	TOM FOGERTY (LP)	15

(see also Creedence Clearwater Revival, Ruby)

FOGGY

72	York SYK 534	How Come The Sun/Take Your Time	7
73	York SYK 542	Kitty Starr/She's Far Away (p/s)	8
72	York FYK 411	SIMPLE GIFTS (LP, with insert, featuring Strawbs)	60
75	Canon CNN 5759	PATCHWORK (LP)	45

(see also Strawbs, Foggy Dew-O)

FOGGY DEW-O

68	Decca F 12776	Reflections/Grandfather's Clock	8
71	York SYK 503	Me And Bobby McGee/Feelin' Groovy	6
68	Decca LK/SKL 4940	THE FOGGY DEW-O (LP)	15
70	Decca LK/SKL 5035	BORN TO TAKE THE HIGHWAY (LP)	12
71	Decca Eclipse ECS 2118	THE FOGGY DEW-O (LP, reissue)	12

(see also Strawbs, Foggy)

FOGHAT

72	Bearsville K 15501	What A Shame/Hole To Hide In	5
74	Bearsville K 15511	Long Way To Go/Ride Ride Ride	5
74	Bearsville K 15517	Step Outside (Edit)/Mabellene	5
76	Bearsville K 15522	Slow Ride (Edit)/Save Your Loving (For Me)	5
77	Bearsville K 15537	I Just Want To Make Love To You (Live Edit)/Fool For The City (Live Edit)	5
79	Bearsville WIP 6582	Third Time Lucky/Somebody's Been Sleeping In My Bed	5
72	Bearsville K 45503	FOGHAT (LP)	15
73	Bearsville K 45514	FOGHAT — ROCK'N'ROLL (LP)	12

(see also Black Cat Bones, Savoy Brown, Warren Philips & The Rockets)

FOIL

97	13th Hour HOUR 011	Don't Come Around/Brand New Brain/Molina (p/s, blue vinyl, 1000 only)	7
97	13th Hour HOUR 013	Reviver Gene/Sedate Me (green vinyl, 500 only)	7
97	Mute 13THLP 05	SPREAD IT ALL AROUND (LP, clear vinyl, with inner sleeve)	12

ELLEN FOLEY (& CLASH)

81	Epic EPC A 9522	The Shuttered Palace/Beautiful Waste Of Time (p/s)	6
81	Epic EPC A 1160	Torchlight/Game Of A Man (p/s)	5
81	Epic SEPC 84809	SPIRIT OF ST. LOUIS (LP, with inner sleeve)	12

(see also Clash)

RED FOLEY

53	Brunswick 05076	Hot Toddy/ROBERTA LEE & HARDROCK GUNTER: Sixty Minute Man (78)	7
54	Brunswick 05307	Pin Ball Boogie/Jilted (78)	15
54	Brunswick 05321	Skinnie Minnie (Fishtail)/Thank You For Calling	15
55	Brunswick 05508	Croce Di Oro (Cross Of Gold) (with Betty Foley)/The Night Watch	20
55	Brunswick 05363	Hearts Of Stone/RED FOLEY & BETTY FOLEY: Never	20
60	Brunswick LAT 8343	SING ALONG WITH RED FOLEY (LP, also stereo STA 3034)	20/25

(see also Roberta Lee)

RED FOLEY & ERNEST TUBB

55	Brunswick OE 9148	COUNTRY DOUBLE DATE (EP, with Minnie Pearl)	20
57	Brunswick LAT 8206	RED AND ERNIE (LP)	25

(see also Ernest Tubb)

SIMON FOLEY

77	Look LKLP 6324	TO STRIVE WITH PRINCES (LP, with booklet)	20

FOLKAL POINT

72	Midas MR 003	FOLKAL POINT (LP)	425

FOLK DEVILS

84	Ganges RAY 1	Hank Turns Blue/Chewin' The Fat (some with p/s)	15/8

MINT VALUE £

CALVIN FOLKES

63	Rio R 5	Someone/Kentucky Home	15
63	Rio R 8	You'll Never Know/Is It Time?	15
64	Port-O-Jam PJ 4117	My Bonnie/What A Day	12
64	Port-O-Jam PJ 4118	Hello Everybody/IRVING SIX: King's Boogie	12

FOLK(S) BROTHERS

61	Blue Beat BB 30	Carolina/I Met A Man (original, blue label, as Folks Brothers)	12
60s	Fab BB 30	Carolina (as Folks Brothers)/ERIC 'HUMPTY DUMPTY' MORRIS: Humpty Dumpty	6
70s	Blue Beat BB 30	Carolina/I Met A Man (reissue, white label, as Folk Brothers)	6

FOLKLANDERS

60s	Urban PB 001	TWO LITTLE FISHES (EP)	10

FOLKLORE

75	Homespun HPL 104	FIRST OF FOLKLORE (LP, Ireland-only)	40

FOLK SONG CLUB

65	white label (no cat. no.)	IMPERIAL COLLEGE (LP, private pressing)	150

FOLKWAYS

72	Folk Heritage	NO OTHER NAME (LP)	12

EDDIE FONTAINE

55	HMV 7M 304	Rock Love/All My Love Belongs To You (with Neal Hefti & Excels)	375
55	HMV B 10852	Rock Love/All My Love Belongs To You (with Neal Hefti & Excels) (78)	75
56	Brunswick 05624	Cool It, Baby/Into Each Life Some Rain Must Fall	200
56	Brunswick 05624	Cool It, Baby/Into Each Life Some Rain Must Fall (78)	50
58	London HLM 8711	Nothin' Shakin' (But The Leaves On The Trees)/Don't Ya Know	30
58	London HLM 8711	Nothin' Shakin' (But The Leaves On The Trees)/Don't Ya Know (78)	45

ARLENE FONTANA

59	Pye International 7N 25010	I'm In Love/Easy	12
59	Pye International N 25010	I'm In Love/Easy (78)	8

WAYNE FONTANA & THE MINDBENDERS

63	Fontana TF 404	Hello! Josephine/Road Runner	25
63	Fontana TF 418	For You, For You/Love Potion No.9	12
64	Fontana TF 436	Little Darlin'/Come Dance With Me	15
64	Fontana TF 451	Stop Look And Listen/Duke Of Earl	10
64	Fontana TF 497	Um, Um, Um, Um, Um, Um/First Taste Of Love	6
65	Fontana TF 535	The Game Of Love/Since You've Been Gone	6
65	Fontana TF 579	It's Just A Little Bit Too Late/Long Time Comin'	10
65	Fontana TF 611	She Needs Love/Like I Did	8
69	Fontana H 1022	Um, Um, Um, Um, Um, Um/The Game Of Love (p/s)	8
64	Fontana TE 17421	ROAD RUNNER (EP)	50
64	Fontana TE 17435	UM, UM, UM, UM, UM, UM (EP)	22
65	Fontana TE 17449	THE GAME OF LOVE (EP)	22
65	Fontana TE 17453	WALKING ON AIR (EP)	55
64	Fontana TL 5230	WAYNE FONTANA AND THE MINDBENDERS (LP)	60
65	Fontana TL 5257	ERIC, RICK, WAYNE, BOB — IT'S WAYNE FONTANA AND THE MINDBENDERS (LP)	50
67	Wing WL 1166	WAYNE FONTANA AND THE MINDBENDERS (LP, reissue)	15
69	Fontana SFL 13106	WAYNE FONTANA AND THE MINDBENDERS (LP, 2nd reissue)	12

(see also Wayne Fontana, Mindbenders)

WAYNE FONTANA

65	Fontana TF 642	It Was Easier To Hurt Her/You Made Me What I Am Today	7
66	Fontana TF 684	Come On Home/My Eyes Break Out In Tears	7
66	Fontana TF 737	Goodbye Bluebird/The Sun's So Hot Today	7
66	Fontana TF 770	Pamela Pamela/Something Keeps Calling Me Back	7
67	Fontana TF 827	24 Sycamore/From A Boy To A Man	7
67	Fontana TF 866	The Impossible Years/In My World	7
67	Fontana TF 889	Gina/We All Love The Human Race	7
68	Fontana TF 911	Storybook Children/I Need To Love You	7
68	Fontana TF 933	The Words Of Bartholomew/Mind Excursion	7
68	Fontana TF 976	Never An Everyday Thing/Waiting For A Break In The Clouds	8
69	Fontana TF 1008	Dayton Ohio 1903/Say Goodbye To Yesterday	8
69	Fontana TF 1054	Charlie Cass/Linda (withdrawn issue)	20+
69	Fontana TF 1054	We're Building A Love/Charlie Cass	10
69	Fontana H 1027	Come On Home/Pamela Pamela (p/s)	10
70	Philips 6006 035	Give Me Just A Little More Time/I'm In Love (withdrawn)	25+
73	Warner Bros K 16269	Together/One Man Woman	6
66	Fontana (S)TL 5351	WAYNE ONE (LP)	25
69	Fontana SFL 13144	WAYNE ONE (LP, reissue)	12

(see also Mindbenders)

FONTANE SISTERS

78s

51	HMV B 10021	Tennessee Waltz/As We Are Today	10
54	HMV B 10765	Please Play Our Song/Mexican Joe	10
54	London HL 8099	Happy Days And Lonely Nights/If I Didn't Have You	15
55	London HL 8113	Hearts Of Stone/Bless Your Heart	15
55	London HL 8126	Rock Love/You're Mine	15
55	London HLD 8177	Seventeen/If I Could Be With You	12
55	London HLD 8211	Rolling Stone/Daddy-O	12
56	London HLD 8225	Adorable/Playmates	15
56	London HLD 8265	Eddie My Love/Yum Yum	12
56	London HLD 8289	I'm In Love Again/You Always Hurt The One You Love	15
56	London HLD 8318	Voices (with narration by Pat Boone)/Willow Weep For Me	10

MINT VALUE £

56	London HLD 8343	Silver Bells/Nuttin' For Christmas	15
57	London HLD 8378	The Banana Boat Song/Lonesome Lover Blues	10
57	London HLD 8415	Please Don't Leave Me/Still	15
57	London HLD 8488	Fool Around/Which Way To Your Heart?	15
58	London HLD 8621	Chanson D'Amour (Song Of Love)/Cocoanut Grove	12
59	London HLD 8861	Billy Boy/Encore D'Amour	20

SINGLES

54	London HL 8099	Happy Days And Lonely Nights/If I Didn't Have You	90
55	London HL 8113	Hearts Of Stone/Bless Your Heart	100
55	London HL 8126	Rock Love/You're Mine	90
55	London HLD 8177	Seventeen/If I Could Be With You	90
55	London HLD 8211	Rolling Stone/Daddy-O	75
56	London HLD 8225	Adorable/Playmates	55
56	London HLD 8265	Eddie My Love/Yum Yum	55
56	London HL 7009	Eddie My Love/Yum Yum (export issue)	40
56	London HLD 8289	I'm In Love Again/You Always Hurt The One You Love (gold lettering label, later silver)	45/25
56	London HLD 8318	Voices (with narration by Pat Boone)/Willow Weep For Me (gold lettering label, later silver)	40/20
56	London HLD 8343	Silver Bells/Nuttin' For Christmas	25
57	London HLD 8378	The Banana Boat Song/Lonesome Lover Blues (gold or silver lettering)	30/20
57	London HLD 8415	Please Don't Leave Me/Still	25
57	London HLD 8488	Fool Around/Which Way To Your Heart?	25
58	London HLD 8621	Chanson D'Amour (Song Of Love)/Cocoanut Grove	15
59	London HLD 8861	Billy Boy/Encore D'Amour	15
60	London HLD 9037	Listen To Your Heart/Please Be Kind	10
60	London HLD 9078	Theme From "A Summer Place"/Darling, It's Wonderful	10

EPs

55	London RE-D 1029	FONTANE SISTERS NO. 1	70
55	London RE-D 1037	FONTANE SISTERS NO. 2	60

LP

57	London HA-D 2053	THE FONTANES SING	130

(see also Pat Boone, Perry Como)

SAM FONTEYN

66	Parlophone R 5519	Lost In Space/BERNARD SHARPE: Jorrocks	10

BILLY FONTEYNE

63	Oriole CB 1917	Little Child/Look Before You Leap	12

FOO FIGHTERS

95	Roswell CL 753	This Is A Call/Winnebago	12
95	Roswell 12CL 753	This Is A Call/Winnebago/Podunk (12", luminous vinyl)	25
95	Roswell CDCL 753	This Is A Call/Winnebago/Podunk (CD)	8
95	Roswell CL 757	I'll Stick Around/How I Miss You (red vinyl)	15
95	Roswell 12CL 757	I'll Stick Around/How I Miss You (12" p/s)	18
95	Roswell CL 762	For All The Cows/Watershed (blue vinyl)	8
95	Roswell CDCL 762	For All The Cows/(live version)/Watershed (live) (CD)	8
95	Roswell CL 768	Big Me/Floaty/Gas Chamber (white vinyl)	6
97	Roswell CL 788	Monkey Wrench/Up In Arms (red vinyl)	7
97	Roswell CL 792	Everlong/Drive Me Wild (blue vinyl)	5
97	Roswell CL 796	My Hero/Dear Lover (red vinyl, stickered poly sleeve, with insert)	12
03	BMG 82876-52256-7	Low/Never Talking To You Again (Live Version) (numbered p/s, 3,000 only)	5
99	BMG 749582	GENERATOR (CD EP)	8
95	Roswell EST 2266	FOO FIGHTERS (LP)	25

FOOL

69	Mercury MF 1111	We Are One/Shining Light	10
69	Mercury SMCL 20138	THE FOOL (LP)	25

FOOLS DANCE

87	L. T. T. Slaughter LTS 22	They'll Never Know/Empty Hours (p/s)	10
87	L. T. T. Slaughter LTS 22T	They'll Never Know/The Collector/Empty Hours/The Ring (12", p/s)	15
85	Top Hole Turn TURN 19	FOOLS DANCE (mini-LP)	20
86	Top Hat TH 22	FOOLS DANCE (mini-LP, reissue)	15
86	L. T. T. Slaughter LTS 18	FOOLS DANCE (mini-LP, 2nd reissue)	12

(see also Cure, Stranglers)

CHUCK FOOTE

62	London HLU 9495	You're Running Out Of Kisses/Come On Back	15

FOOT IN COLD WATER

73	Island WIP 6162	(Isn't Love Unkind) In My Life/Deep Freeze	6
74	Elektra K 52011	OR ALL AROUND US (LP)	18

FORBES

77	Power Exchange PX 253	The Beatles/Sweet Kiss Of Fire	7

BILL FORBES

58	Columbia DB 4232	My Cherie/God's Little Acre	10
59	Columbia DB 4269	Once More/Believe In Me	15
59	Columbia DB 4386	Too Young/It's Not The End Of The World	15
61	Columbia DB 4566	You're Sixteen, You're Beautiful/Backward Child	12
61	Columbia DB 4619	That's It, I Quit, I'm Moving On/Big City Boy	12
61	Columbia DB 4747	Goodbye Cruel World/Next Time	12
62	Columbia DB 4855	Laughter Or Tears/Like A Good Girl Should	8
62	Columbia DB 4945	Poker Face/Marianne	8

(see also Contrasts)

MINT VALUE £

FORCEFIELD

87 President PT 551 Smoke On The Water/Shine It On Me (p/s) 5
88 President PT 578 Heartache/I Lose Again (Instrumental Version) (p/s) 5
(see also Cozy Powell, Graham Bonnet, Ray Fenwick, Whitesnake)

FORCE FIVE

64 United Artists UP 1051 Don't Make My Baby Blue/Shaking Postman 15
65 United Artists UP 1089 Yeah, I'm Waiting/I Don't Want To See You Again 30
65 United Artists UP 1102 Baby Don't Care/Come Down To Earth 30
65 United Artists UP 1118 I Want You Babe/Gee Too Tiger 35
66 United Artists UP 1141 Don't Know Which Way To Turn/Baby Let Your Hair Down 40
(see also Crocheted Doughnut Ring)

FORCE WEST

65 Decca F 12223 I Can't Give What I Haven't Got/Why Won't She Stay 12
66 Columbia DB 7908 Gotta Find Another Baby/Talkin' About Our Love 15
66 Columbia DB 7963 When The Sun Comes Out (Weatherman)/Gotta Tell Somebody 12
67 Columbia DB 8174 All The Children Sleep/Desolation 15
68 CBS 3632 I'll Walk In The Rain/What's It To Be? 8
68 CBS 3798 I'll Be Moving On/Like The Tide, Like The Ocean 8
69 CBS 4385 Sherry/Mister Blue 8

CLINTON FORD

78s

58 Oriole CB 1425 Sweet Sixteen/Eleven More Months And Ten More Days 7
58 Oriole CB 1427 Jesus Remember Me/In The Sweet Bye & Bye (with Hallelujah Skiffle Group) 12
59 Oriole CB 1483 I Cried A Tear/(You Were Only) Teasin' 7
59 Oriole CB 1500 Old Shep/Nellie Dean Rock 12
59 Oriole CB 1516 Lovesick Blues/Give A Little, Take A Little 12
59 Oriole CB 1518 Silver Threads Among The Gold/Red Indian Christmas Carol 9

SINGLES

58 Oriole CB 1425 Sweet Sixteen/Eleven More Months And Ten More Days 6
59 Oriole CB 1483 I Cried A Tear/(You Were Only) Teasin' 6
59 Oriole CB 1500 Old Shep/Nellie Dean Rock 6
59 Oriole CB 1516 Lovesick Blues/Give A Little, Take A Little 5
59 Oriole CB 1518 Silver Threads Among The Gold/Red Indian Christmas Carol 5
61 Oriole CB 1551 Mustapha/Two Brothers 5
61 Oriole CB 1612 Oh By Jingo/Get Out And Get Under 5
61 Oriole CB 1623 Too Many Beautiful Girls/Everybody's Doing It 5
62 Oriole CB 1706 Fanlight Fanny/Dreamy City Lullaby 6
62 Oriole CB 1747 Under The Bamboo Tree/Who's Next In Line 5
62 Oriole CB 1768 Opening Night In Loveland/Madam Moscovitch 5
63 Oriole CB 1798 Popsy Wopsy/You Can Tell Her Anything 5
63 Oriole CB 1884 Rainbow/On Mother Kelly's Doorstep 5
64 Columbia DB 7220 Southtown U.S.A./Honey Baby 5
64 Columbia DB 7413 Oh, Johnny! Oh, Johnny! Oh!/Since I Found You 5
66 Piccadilly 7N 35343 Dandy/Why Don't Women Like Me 5
67 Piccadilly 7N 35361 Run To The Door/Best Job Yet 5
67 Piccadilly 7N 35378 This Song Is Just For You/Take Care On The Road 5
67 Piccadilly 7N 35404 Dance With A Dolly (With A Hole In Her Stocking)/Streets Of Laredo 5
67 Pye 7N 17428 Last One To Say Goodnight/Greatest Clown 5
68 Pye 7N 17521 Cathy I Love You/American Girl 5
68 Pye 7N 17572 Give A Little Take A Little/West Wind Blow Me Home 5
68 Pye 7N 17628 Sounds Of Goodbye/Try A Little Tenderness 5
69 Pye 7N 17718 Moonlight Brings Memories/Now That You've Gone 5
69 Pye 7N 17766 Cielito Lindo/Lonelyville 5
69 Pye 7N 17838 Angel In My Pocket/Lorena 5
70 Pye 7N 45079 Turn The Good Times On/The Pockets Of One Little Boy 5

EP

67 Piccadilly NEP 34057 DANDY 12

LPs

62 Oriole PS 40021 CLINTON FORD (with George Chisholm Allstars) 12
63 Columbia 33SX 1560 THE MELODY MAN (also stereo SCX 3496) 12/15
64 Realm RM 147 BY JINGO 12
65 Columbia 33SX 1689 LISTEN WITH US (also stereo SCX 3529) 15/20
67 Pye NPL 18210 CLINTON THE CLOWN 15
67 Piccadilly N(S)PL 38028 DANDY 15
67 Piccadilly N(S)PL 38034 BIG WILLY BROKE JAIL TONIGHT 15
(see also Hallelujah Skiffle Group)

DEAN FORD (& GAYLORDS)

64 Columbia DB 7264 Twenty Miles/What's The Matter With Me? 22
64 Columbia DB 7402 Mr Heartbreak's Here Instead/I Won't 22
65 Columbia DB 7610 The Name Game/That Lonely Feeling 22
75 EMI EMC 3079 DEAN FORD (LP) 15
(see also Gaylords, Marmalade, Junior Campbell)

DEE DEE FORD

60 London HLU 9245 Good-Morning Blues/I Just Can't Believe 60
(see also Don Gardner & Dee Dee Ford)

EDDIE/EDDY FORD

72 Pressure Beat PB 5512 You Wrong Fe Trouble Joshua/KENNETH POWER: Joshua Row Us Home 6
73 Duke Reid DR 2523 Guess I This Riddle/Riddle Version (as Eddie Ford) 5

EMILE FORD (& THE CHECKMATES)

59 Pye 7N 15225 What Do You Want To Make Those Eyes At Me For?/Don't Tell Me Your Troubles .. 6
59 Pye N 15225 What Do You Want To Make Those Eyes At Me For?/
Don't Tell Me Your Troubles (78) 18

MINT VALUE £

60	Pye 7N 15245	On A Slow Boat To China/That Lucky Old Sun	6
60	Pye N 15245	On A Slow Boat To China/That Lucky Old Sun (78)	15
60	Pye 7N 15268	You'll Never Know What You're Missin' 'Til You Try/Still	8
60	Pye 7N 15279	Red Sails In The Sunset/Afraid	6
60	Pye 7N 15282	Them There Eyes (solo)/Question	5
60	Pye 7N 15314	Counting Teardrops/White Christmas	6
61	Pye 7N 15331	A Kiss To Build A Dream On/What Am I Gonna Do	6
61	Piccadilly 7N 35003	Half Of My Heart/Gypsy Love (solo)	8
61	Piccadilly 7N 35007	Hush, Somebody's Calling My Name/After You've Gone	8
61	Piccadilly 7N 35019	The Alphabet Song/Keep A-Lovin' Me (solo)	8
62	Piccadilly 7N 35033	I Wonder Who's Kissing Her Now/Doin' The Twist (solo)	8
62	Piccadilly 7N 35078	Your Nose Is Gonna Grow/Rains Come	8
63	Piccadilly 7N 35116	Doin' What You Do To Me/Hold Me Thrill Me Kiss Me	8
69	Decca F 12959	Set Me Free/Don't Remind Me (export issue)	18
59	Pye NEP 24119	EMILE (EP)	15
60	Pye NEP 24124	EMILE FORD HIT PARADE (EP)	15
60	Pye NEP 24133	EMILE FORD HIT PARADE VOL. 2 (EP)	20
60	Pye NPL 18049	NEW TRACKS WITH EMILE (LP)	30
61	Piccadilly NPL 38001	EMILE (LP)	35

FRANKIE FORD

59	London HL 8850	Sea Cruise/Roberta (with Huey 'Piano' Smith & Clowns) (black triangular centre, later silver-top triangular centre)	60/40
59	London HL 8850	Sea Cruise/Roberta (with Huey 'Piano' Smith & Clowns) (78)	90
59	Top Rank JAR 186	Alimony/Can't Tell My Heart (What To Do) (with Huey 'Piano' Smith & Clowns)	12
59	Top Rank JAR 186	Alimony/Can't Tell My Heart (What To Do) (78)	70
60	Top Rank JAR 282	Cheatin' Woman/HUEY 'PIANO' SMITH & CLOWNS: Don't You Just Know Kokomo	20
60	Top Rank JAR 299	Time After Time/I Want To Be Your Man	10
60	London HLP 9222	You Talk Too Much/If You've Got Troubles	22
65	Sue WI 366	Sea Cruise/Roberta (with Huey 'Piano' Smith & Clowns) (reissue)	20
65	Sue WI 369	What's Going On?/Watchdog	35
78	Chiswick NS 38	Sea Cruise/Alimony (p/s)	5

(see also Huey 'Piano' Smith)

JASON FORD & THE BULLDOGS

62	Piccadilly 7N 35193	Nobody Knows/Am I The One	10

JON FORD

68	Philips BF 1690	Two's Company, Three's A Crowd/Place In Your Heart	7
69	Philips BF 1791	I Know It's Love/Look Before You Leap	6
69	Philips BF 1817	Ice Cream Man/This Was The Time	6
70	Philips BF 1833	Yesterday When I Was Young/Running Around	6
70	Philips 6006 030	You've Got Me Where You Want Me/You're All Alone Tonight	55

LITA FORD & OZZY OSBOURNE

89	Dreamland A 49396	Close My Eyes Forever (Remix)/Under The Gun (p/s)	5
89	Dreamland PA 49396	Close My Eyes Forever (Remix)/Under The Gun/Blueberry (12", picture disc)	8
89	Dreamland PA 49396	Close My Eyes Forever (Remix)/Under The Gun/Blueberry (3" CD, g/fold p/s)	10

(see also Ozzy Osbourne, Runaways)

MIKE FORD & THE CONSULS

63	Piccadilly 7N 35127	Jumping Jeremiah/The Greenman	15

PERRY FORD (& SAPPHIRES)

59	Parlophone R 4573	Bye, Bye Baby, Goodbye/She Came As A Stranger	7
60	Parlophone R 4633	Crazy Over You/Garden Of Happiness	7
60	Parlophone R 4683	Don't Weep (Little Lady)/Little Grown-Up	8
62	Decca F 11497	Baby, Baby (Don't You Worry)/Prince Of Fools (with Sapphires & Blue Flames)	10

(see also Ivy League, Georgie Fame)

RICKY FORD (& TENNESSEANS)

63	Parlophone R 5018	Sweet And Tender Romance/Cheat Cheat	10
64	Parlophone R 5230	You Are My Love/Long Way From Home (with Tennesseans)	7

'TENNESSEE' ERNIE FORD

SINGLES

54	Capitol CL 14005	Give Me Your Word/River Of No Return	15
54	Capitol CL 14006	Catfish Boogie/Kiss Me Big	25
55	Capitol CL 14261	His Hands/I Am A Pilgrim	8
55	Capitol CL 14273	Losing You/There Is Beauty In Everything	8
56	Capitol CL 14500	Sixteen Tons/You Don't Have To Be A Baby To Cry	15
56	Capitol CL 14506	The Ballad Of Davy Crockett/Farewell	15
56	Capitol CL 14557	That's All/Bright Lights And Blonde-Haired Women	8
56	Capitol CL 14616	Who Will Shoe Your Pretty Little Foot?/Gaily The Troubadour	5
56	Capitol CL 14657	First Born/Have You Seen Her?	5
57	Capitol CL 14691	The Watermelon Song/One Suit	5
57	Capitol CL 14734	The Lonely Man/False Hearted Girl	5
57	Capitol CL 14759	In The Middle Of An Island/Ivy League	5
58	Capitol CL 14846	Down Deep/Bless Your Pea Pickin' Heart	5
58	Capitol CL 14896	Love Makes The World Go 'Round/Sunday Barbecue	5
59	Capitol CL 14972	Glad Rags/Sleepin' At The Foot Of The Bed	5
59	Capitol CL 15010	Blackeyed Susie/Code Of The Mountains	5
61	Capitol CL 15210	Little Red Rockin' Hood/I Gotta Have My Baby Back	8

EPs

56	Capitol EAP 1014	SIXTEEN TONS	15
57	Capitol EAP 1-639	'TENNESSEE' ERNIE FORD	12
60	Capitol EAP1 1227	GATHER ROUND	12
61	Capitol EAP1 20067	ANTICIPATION BLUES	20

MINT VALUE £

LPs

52 Capitol LC 6573 CAPITOL PRESENTS (10") ... 30
56 Capitol LC 6825 THIS LUSTY LAND (10") ... 15
58 Capitol T 888 OL' ROCKIN' ERN ... 30
60 Capitol T 1380 SIXTEEN TONS ... 25
(see also Dinning Sisters)

'TENNESSEE' ERNIE FORD & BETTY HUTTON
54 Capitol CL 14133 This Must Be The Place/The Honeymoon's Over (green label) ... 15

FORD THEATRE
69 Stateside SSL 10288 TIME CHANGES (LP) ... 15

EDDIE 'BUSTER' FOREHAND
69 Action ACT 4519 Young Boy Blues/You Were Meant For Me ... 15

FOREIGNER
77 Atlantic K 10986 Cold As Ice/I Need You (ice-coloured clear vinyl, printed PVC sleeve) ... 5
78 Atlantic K 11167 Hot Blooded/Tramontaine (red vinyl, printed PVC sleeve) ... 5
79 Atlantic K 11236 Blue Morning, Blue Day/I Have Waited So Long (picture disc) ... 5
85 Atlantic A 9596 I Want To Know What Love Is/Street Thunder ('F'-shaped picture disc) ... 6
(see also J&B, State Of Mickey & Tommy, Spooky Tooth)

FORERUNNERS
64 Solar SRP 100 Bony Maronie/Pride ... 50

FORERUNNERS
60s Key KL 008 THE FORERUNNERS (LP) ... 20
60s Key KL 004 RUNNING BACK (LP) ... 20

JOHN FOREMAN
70s Reality RY 1004 THE 'OUSES IN BETWEEN (LP) ... 12

FOREST
69 Harvest HAR 5007 Searching For Shadows/Mirror Of Life ... 18
69 Harvest SHVL 760 FOREST (LP) ... 90
70 Harvest SHVL 784 FULL CIRCLE (LP) ... 65
88 Zap! ZAP 3 FULL CIRCLE (LP, reissue) ... 12

FOR(R)ESTERS
65 Polydor 56038 Broken Hearted Clown/Lonely Boy ... 8
65 Polydor 56057 How Can I Tell Her/So Shy ... 8
66 Polydor 56104 Early Morning Hours/World Is Mine ... 8
66 Columbia DB 8040 Sometimes When You're Lonely/Today Or Tomorrow (as Forresters) ... 7
66 Columbia DB 8086 Mr. Smith/Ship On The Sea (as Foresters) ... 6
67 Columbia DB 8176 Comin' Home In The Evening/Sunshine's On Its Way (as Foresters) ... 6

FOREVER AMBER
69 Advance (no cat. no.) THE LOVE CYCLE (LP, private pressing, 99 copies only) ... 1,000+

FOREVER MORE
70 RCA RCA 2024 Put Your Money On A Pony/Yours ... 6
70 RCA SF 8016 YOURS FOREVER MORE (LP) ... 20
71 RCA LSA 3015 WORDS ON BLACK PLASTIC (LP) ... 18
(see also Scots Of St. James, Hopscotch)

FORGEMASTERS
89 WARP WAP 1 TRACK WITH NO NAME (12", p/s) ... 10

FORK IN THE ROAD
70 Ember EMB S 311 I Can't Turn Around/Skeleton In My Closet ... 160

FORMAT
69 CBS 4600 Maxwell's Silver Hammer/Music Man ... 7
(see also Fourmost)

FORMATIONS
68 MGM MGM 1399 At The Top Of The Stairs/Magic Melody ... 85
71 Mojo 2027 001 At The Top Of The Stairs/Magic Melody (reissue) ... 8

GEORGE FORMBY
55 Decca DFE 6144 GEORGE FORMBY AND HIS UKULELE GUITAR (EP) ... 12
56 Decca DFE 6328 GEORGE FORMBY AND HIS UKULELE GUITAR, NO. 2 (EP) ... 12
56 Decca DFE 6355 GEORGE FORMBY AND HIS UKULELE GUITAR, NO. 3 (EP) ... 12
61 Ace Of Clubs ACL 1062 GEORGE FORMBY SOUVENIR (LP) ... 12
63 Ace Of Clubs ACL 1145 TURNED OUT NICE AGAIN (LP) ... 12

FORMERLY FAT HARRY
71 Harvest SHSP 4016 FORMERLY FAT HARRY (LP) ... 20

FORMINX
65 Vocalion V 9235 Jenka Beat/Geronimo Jenka ... 35
(see also Aphrodite's Child, Vangelis)

FORMULA
65 HMV POP 1438 Close To Me/If Ever ... 8

FORMULA 1
65 Warner Bros WB 155 I Just Can't Go To Sleep/Sure Know A Lot About Love ... 25

ANDY FORRAY
68 Parlophone R 5715 Sarah Jane/Don't Care Anymore ... 7
68 Parlophone R 5729 The Proud One/Messin' Round With Me ... 7
68 Decca F 12733 Epitaph To You/Dream With Me ... 50
69 Fontana TF 999 Let The Sunshine In/Baby Is Coming ... 6

HELEN FORREST
56 Capitol CL 14594 Taking A Chance On Love/I Love You Much Too Much ... 7

JANE FORREST
56 Columbia SCM 5213 Sincerely Yours/A Girl Can't Say 10

JIMMY FORREST
54 Vogue V 2282 Flight 3D/Sophisticated Lady (78) 10

SHARON FORRESTER
73 Ashanti ASH 403 Silly Wasn't I?/NOW-GEN: Silly Wasn't I? — Version. 6

THOMAS FORSTNER
89 Ariola 112 298 Song Of Love/Nur Ein Lied (p/s, withdrawn). 5
89 Ariola 662 298 Song Of Love (12" Version)/Nur Ein Lied/Song Of Love (7") (CD, withdrawn). 8

BRUCE FORSYTH
62 Piccadilly 7N 35086 The Oh-Be-Joyfuls/I Like People 5
64 Piccadilly 7N 35189 The Mysterious People/You've Just Found Out 5
65 Pye 7N 15879 Hush Hush Sweet Charlotte/Don't Say Goodbye 5
68 Mercury MF 1047 Star/Do, Do, Do. 5
68 Pye 7N 17460 I'm Backing Britain/There's Not Enough Love In The World (p/s). 6
69 Decca F 12940 When You Gotta Go/By The Fireside 5
60 Parlophone GEP 8807 I'M IN CHARGE (EP). 18
60 Parlophone PMC 1132 MR ENTERTAINMENT (LP, also stereo PCS 3031) 15/18

FORTES MENTUM
68 Parlophone R 5684 Saga Of A Wrinkled Man/Mr. Partridge Passed Away Today 25
68 Parlophone R 5726 I Can't Go On Loving You/Humdiggle We Love You 12
69 Parlophone R 5768 Gotta Go/Marrakesh. 12
(see also Angel Pavement, Pussy)

LANCE FORTUNE
60 Pye 7N 15240 Be Mine/Action (with Johnny Prendy, alias John Barry) 8
60 Pye 7N 15240 Be Mine/Action (78, with Johnny Prendy, alias John Barry). 25
60 Pye 7N 15260 All On My Own/This Love I Have For You 10
60 Pye 7N 15297 I Wonder/Will You Still Be My Girl? 10
61 Pye 7N 15347 Who's Gonna Tell Me?/Love Is The Sweetest Thing 10

RITA FORTUNE
74 CBS 2603 Sisters And Brothers/(Part 2). 6

FORTUNES
63 Decca F 11718 Summertime Summertime/I Love Her Still (as Fortunes & Cliftones) (some in p/s) 40/18
64 Decca F 11809 Caroline/If You Don't Want Me Now 25
64 Decca F 11912 Come On Girl/I Like The Look Of You 12
64 Decca F 11985 Look Homeward Angel/I'll Have My Tears To Remind Me 12
65 Decca F 12173 You've Got Your Troubles/I've Got To Go. 6
65 Decca F 12243 Here It Comes Again/Things I Should Have Known 6
66 Decca F 12321 This Golden Ring/Someone To Care 7
66 Decca F 12429 You Gave Me Somebody To Love/Silent Street 8
66 Decca F 12485 Is It Really Worth Your While?/Am I Losing My Touch. 8
67 Decca F 12612 Our Love Has Gone/Truly Yours. 8
67 United Artists UP 1188 The Idol/His Smile Was A Lie. 6
68 United Artists UP 2218 Loving Cup/Hour At The Movies 6
68 United Artists UP 2239 Seasons In The Sun/Louise 6
69 Decca F 12874 Here It Comes Again/Our Love Has Gone. 5
69 United Artists UP 35054 Lifetime Of Love/Sad Sad Sad (withdrawn, existence unconfirmed)
69 United Artists UP 35054 Books And Films/Sad Sad Sad 7
71 Capitol CL 15671 Here Comes That Rainy Day Feeling Again/Bad Side Of Town. 7
65 Decca LK/SKL 4736 THE FORTUNES (LP, mono/stereo). 35/60
72 Capitol ST 21891 THE FORTUNES (LP) 15
(see also Glen Dale)

45's
79 Chopper CHEAP 5 Couldn't Believe A Word/Lonesome Lane (no p/s) 7
79 Stiff BUY 52 Couldn't Believe A Word/Lonesome Lane (no p/s, reissue) 5

48 CHAIRS
79 Absurd ABSURD 3 Snap It Around/Psycle Sluts (p/s) 5

49 AMERICANS
80 No Bad NB 4 THE HIT ALBUM (14-track EP). 6
80 Choo Choo Train CHUG 2 TOO YOUNG TO BE IDEAL (12" EP). 10
80 Choo Choo Train CHUG 1 EL PLURIBUS UNUM (LP) 12

FORUM
67 London HLM 10120 The River Is Wide/I Fall In Love (All Over Again) 8
70 B&C CB 119 The River Is Wide/I Fall In Love (All Over Again) (reissue). 5

SHIRLEY FORWOOD
57 London HLD 8402 Two Hearts (With An Arrow Between)/Juke Box Lovers. 35
57 London HLD 8402 Two Hearts (With An Arrow Between)/Juke Box Lovers (78) 7

BOBBY FOSTER
70 Bread BR 1101 Tell Me Why You Say Goodbye/YOUTH: I'll Make Him Believe In You 6

JACKIE FOSTER
63 Planetone RC 13 Oh Leona/I Fell In Love 15

JOHN FOSTER
66 Island ILP 939 JOHN FOSTER SINGS (LP) 35

LARRY FOSTER & SOUL EXPLOSION
70 Fab FAB 130 Boom Biddy Boom/Next To Me (actually by Sugar Simone). 7
(see also Sugar Simone)

MINT VALUE £

LES FOSTER

70	Torpedo TOR 7	Run Like A Thief/Nobody's Fool	6

LES FOSTER & ANSELL COLLINS

73	Camel CA 102	The Man In Your Life/Version	5

(see also Dave & Ansell Collins, Sugar Simone, Lance Hannibal)

LESLIE FOSTER

69	Jolly JY 022	Muriel/Nowhere To Hide	6

VINCENT FOSTER

69	Escort ES 803	Shine Eye Gal/Who Nest (B-side actually "Who Next" by Carl Bryan)	6

FOTHERINGAY

70	Island WIP 6085	Peace In The End/Winter Winds	15
70	Island ILPS 9125	FOTHERINGAY (LP, pink label/'i' logo, gatefold sleeve)	50
70	Island ILPS 9125	FOTHERINGAY (LP, later issue, pink rim label/'palm tree' logo, gatefold sleeve)	20

(see also Sandy Denny, Trevor Lucas, Eclection, Exception[s], Fairport Convention, Mick Greenwood)

MR FOUNDATION

(see under 'M')

FOUNDATIONS

67	Pye 7N 17366	Baby, Now That I've Found You/Come On Back To Me	7
68	Pye 7N 17417	Back On My Feet Again/I Can Take Or Leave Your Loving	6
68	Pye 7N 17503	Any Old Time (You're Lonely And Sad)/We Are Happy People	6
68	Pye 7N 17636	Build Me Up Buttercup/New Direction	6
69	Pye 7N 17702	In The Bad Bad Old Days/Give Me Love	6
69	Pye 7N 17809	Born To Live, Born To Die/Why Did You Cry	6
69	Pye 7N 17849	Baby I Couldn't See/Penny, Sir	6
70	Pye 7N 17904	Take A Girl Like You/I'm Gonna Be A Rich Man	6
70	Pye 7N 17956	I'm Gonna Be A Rich Man/Who Am I?	6
71	MCA MCA 5075	Stoney Ground/I'll Give You Love	8
70s	Summit SU 100	Where Were You When I Needed Your Love/Love Me Nice 'n Easy	6
78	Psycho P 2603	Closer To Loving You/Change My Life	150+
68	Pye NEP 24297	IT'S ALL RIGHT (EP)	25
67	Pye NPL 18206	FROM THE FOUNDATIONS (LP)	20
68	Pye NPL 18227	ROCKING THE FOUNDATIONS (LP)	20
69	Pye N(S)PL 18290	DIGGING THE FOUNDATIONS (LP)	20

(see also Pluto)

JAMES FOUNTAIN

76	Cream CRM 5002	Seven Day Lover/Malnutrition	10

PETE FOUNTAIN

60	Coral Q 72389	Do You Know What It Means To Miss New Orleans?/A Closer Walk	5
60	Coral Q 72404	Columbus Stockade Blues/Sentimental Journey	5
60	Coral Q 72404	Columbus Stockade Blues/Sentimental Journey (78)	12
59	Tempo EXA 93	DIXIELAND ALL STARS (EP)	8
71	Xtra XTRA 1120	NEW ORLEANS ALL STARS (LP)	12

(see also Brenda Lee)

THE 4

64	Decca F 11999	It's Alright/There's Nothing Like It	15

FOUR ACES (Jamaica)

65	Island WI 178	Hoochy-Koochy-Kai-Po/River Bank Coberly Again	20
65	Island WI 178	Hoochy-Koochy-Kai-Po/SKATALITES: Sucu Sucu (different B-side)	22
65	Island WI 179	Sweet Chariot/Peace And Love	20
65	Island WI 180	Little Girl/CLARENDONIANS: Day Will Come	20

(see also Desmond Dekker)

FOUR ACES (U.K.)

60s	Anton/E.R.S. EAG 178/179	Why Do You/Fortune Teller (private pressing)	250+

FOUR ACES (U.S.)

54	Brunswick 05256	The Gang That Sang "Heart Of My Heart"/Heaven Can Wait	10
54	Brunswick 05308	Three Coins In The Fountain/Wedding Bells (Are Breaking Up This Gang Of Mine)	25
54	Brunswick 05322	It Shall Come To Pass/Dream	8
54	Brunswick 05348	It's A Woman's World/The Cuckoo Bird In The Pickle Tree	12
54	Brunswick 05355	Mister Sandman/(I'll Be With You) In Apple Blossom Time	25
55	Brunswick 05379	Melody Of Love/There Is A Tavern In The Town	12
55	Brunswick 05401	There Goes My Heart/Take Me In Your Arms	8
55	Brunswick 05418	Stranger In Paradise/You'll Always Be The One	20
55	Brunswick 05429	Sluefoot/I'm In The Mood For Love	8
55	Brunswick 05480	Love Is A Many Splendored Thing/Shine On Harvest Moon	22
55	Brunswick 05504	Jingle Bells/The Christmas Song (Merry Christmas To You)	7
56	Brunswick 05562	To Love Again/Charlie Was A Boxer	6
56	Brunswick 05566	The Gal With The Yaller Shoes/Of This I'm Sure	6
56	Brunswick 05573	If You Can Dream/It's The Talk Of The Town	6
56	Brunswick 05589	A Woman In Love/I Only Know I Love You	8
56	Brunswick 05601	Dreamer/Let's Fall In Love	5
56	Brunswick 05613	You Can't Run Away From It/Written On The Wind	5
56	Brunswick 05623	Friendly Persuasion (Thee I Love)/Someone To Love	7
57	Brunswick 05651	Heart/What A Difference A Day Made	6
57	Brunswick 05663	Bahama Mama/You're Mine	6
57	Brunswick 05695	Three Sheets To The Wind/Yes, Sir, That's My Baby	5
57	Brunswick 05712	Half Of My Heart/When My Sugar Walks Down The Street	5
58	Brunswick 05743	Rock And Roll Rhapsody/I Wish I May, I Wish I Might	7
58	Brunswick 05743	Rock And Roll Rhapsody/I Wish I May, I Wish I Might (78)	8
58	Brunswick 05758	Hangin' Up A Horseshoe/Two Arms, Two Lips, One Heart!	7

MINT VALUE £

58	Brunswick 05758	Hangin' Up A Horseshoe/Two Arms, Two Lips, One Heart! (78)	8
58	Brunswick 05767	The World Outside/The Christmas Tree	7
58	Brunswick 05767	The World Outside/The Christmas Tree (78)	12
59	Brunswick 05773	The World Outside/The Inn Of The Sixth Happiness	8
59	Brunswick 05773	The World Outside/The Inn Of The Sixth Happiness (78)	8
59	Brunswick 05812	Waltzin' Matilda/Roses Of Rio	8
59	Brunswick 05812	Waltzin' Matilda/Roses Of Rio (78)	10
50s	Decca A 73010	I'm Yours/I Understand (export issue)	15
54	Brunswick OE 9090	PRESENTING THE FOUR ACES (EP)	12
55	Brunswick OE 9157	MOOD FOR LOVE VOL. 1 (EP)	12
55	Brunswick OE 9192	MOOD FOR LOVE VOL. 2 (EP)	12
57	Brunswick OE 9324	ACES SING FILM TITLES (EP)	10
59	Brunswick OE 9458	THE FOUR ACES (EP)	12
53	Brunswick LA 8614	JUST SQUEEZE ME (10" LP)	30
57	Brunswick LAT 8221	SHUFFLIN' ALONG (LP)	20
58	Brunswick LAT 8249	HITS FROM HOLLYWOOD (LP)	20
59	Brunswick STA 3014	THE SWINGIN' ACES (LP, stereo)	20

(see also Al Alberts)

FOUR COINS

58	Fontana H 101	My One Sin/A Broken Promise (78)	10
58	Fontana H 168	The World Outside/Be Still My Heart	8

4 DEGREES

65	Oak RGJ 187	4 DEGREES (LP, 1-sided, no sleeve)	425

FOUR DOLLS

57	Capitol CL 14778	Three On A Date/Proud Of You	15
57	Capitol CL 14778	Three On A Date/Proud Of You (78)	7
58	Capitol CL 14845	Whoop-A-Lala/I'm Following You	12
58	Capitol CL 14845	Whoop-A-Lala/I'm Following You (78)	8

FOUR ESCORTS

54	HMV 7M 277	Loop De Loop Mambo/Love Me	12

FOUR ESQUIRES

55	London HL 8152	The Sphinx Won't Tell/Three Things (A Man Must Do)	55
55	London HL 8152	The Sphinx Won't Tell/Three Things (A Man Must Do) (78)	10
56	London HLA 8224	Adorable/Thunderbolt	50
56	London HLA 8224	Adorable/Thunderbolt (78)	10
57	London HL 8376	Look Homeward Angel/Santo Domingo (unreleased)	
57	London HL 8376	Look Homeward Angel/Santo Domingo (78) (unreleased)	
58	London HLO 8533	Love Me Forever/I Ain't Been Right Since You Left	18
58	London HLO 8579	Always And Forever/I Walk Down The Street	15
58	London HLO 8579	Always And Forever/I Walk Down The Street (78)	7
58	London HL 8746	Hideaway/Repeat After Me	12
58	London HL 8746	Hideaway/Repeat After Me (78)	15
59	Pye Intl. 7N 25012	Non E Cosi/Land Of You And Me	6
59	Pye Intl. 7N 25027	Act Your Age/So Ends The Night	6
59	Pye Intl. N 25027	Act Your Age/So Ends The Night (78)	12
60	Pye Intl. 7N 25049	Wouldn't It Be Wonderful/Wonderful One	6

FOUR EVERS

66	CBS 202549	A Lovely Way To Say Goodnight/The Girl I Wanna Bring Home	25

FOUR FRESHMEN

54	Capitol CL 14196	Love Turns Winter To Spring/Mood Indigo	7
55	Capitol CL 14338	Day By Day/How Can I Tell Her	7
56	Capitol CL 14580	Love Is Just Around The Corner/Angel Eyes (as Four Freshmen & Five Trombones)	5
56	Capitol CL 14610	Graduation Day/Lonely Night In Paris	7
56	Capitol CL 14633	You're So Far Above Me/He Who Loves And Runs Away	5
54	Capitol LC 6685	VOICES IN MODERN (10" LP)	15

FOUR FULLER BROTHERS

69	MCA MU 1068	Bitter Honey/Groupie	7

FOUR GEES

67	President PT 160	Ethiopia/Rough Rider	6

FOUR GIBSON GIRLS

58	Oriole CB 1447	No School Tomorrow/June, July And August	18
58	Oriole CB 1453	Safety Sue/VARIOUS ARTISTS: Safety Sue	15
58	Oriole CB 1453	Safety Sue/VARIOUS ARTISTS: Safety Sue (78)	8

FOUR GRADS

57	Conquest CE 1007	THE FOUR GRADS PART 1 (EP)	10
57	Conquest CE 1017	THE FOUR GRADS PART 2 (EP)	10

FOUR GUYS

55	Vogue Coral Q 72054	Half Hearted Kisses/Mine	15

(see also Modernaires)

FOUR INSTANTS

66	Society	DISCOTHEQUE (LP)	15

FOUR JACKS

58	Decca F 10984	Hey! Baby/The Prayer Of Love	15
58	Decca F 10984	Hey! Baby/The Prayer Of Love (78)	8
58	Decca DFE 6460	HEY! BABY (EP)	40

FOUR JACKS & A JILL

68	RCA Victor RCA 1669	Master Jack/I Looked Back	6

MINT VALUE £

FOUR JONES BOYS

55	Decca F 10568	A Real Romance/When I Let You Go	7
55	Decca F 10671	Moments To Remember/Sing-ing-ing-ing	7
56	Decca F 10717	Tutti Frutti/Are You Satisfied?	20
56	Decca F 10717	Tutti Frutti/Are You Satisfied? (78)	7
56	Decca F 10789	Happiness Street (Corner Of Sunshine Square)/Someone To Love	8
56	Decca F 10829	Priscilla/It Isn't Right	10

(see also Jones Boys, Annette Klooger)

FOUR JUST MEN

64	Parlophone R 5186	That's My Baby/Things Will Never Be The Same	80

(see also Just Four Men, Wimple Winch)

FOUR KENTS

68	RCA RCA 1705	The Moving Finger Writes/Searchin'	8

FOUR KESTRELS

61	Decca F 11333	Sound Off/Can't Say I Do	6

FOUR KINSMEN

67	Decca F 22671	It Looks Like The Daybreak/Forget About Him	8

(see also Kinsmen)

FOUR KNIGHTS

54	Capitol CL 14076	I Get So Lonely/Till Then	25
54	Capitol CL 14154	Easy Street/In The Chapel In The Moonlight	20
54	Capitol CL 14204	I Don't Wanna See You Cryin'/Saw Your Eyes	18
55	Capitol CL 14244	Honey Bunch/Write Me, Baby	35
55	Capitol CL 14290	Inside Out/Foolishly Yours	15
56	Capitol CL 14516	Guilty/You	12
59	Coral Q 72355	Foolish Tears/O' Falling Star	15
59	Coral Q 72355	Foolish Tears/O' Falling Star (78)	10
55	Capitol EAP1 506	THE FOUR KNIGHTS (EP)	60
53	Capitol LC 6604	SPOTLIGHT SONGS (10" LP)	50

(see also Nat 'King' Cole)

FOUR LADS

57	Philips JK 1021	Golly/I Just Don't Know (jukebox issue)	12
57	Philips PB 769	The Eyes Of God/His Invisible Hand (78)	7
58	Philips PB 839	Enchanted Island/Guess What The Neighbours'll Say	5
58	Philips PB 839	Enchanted Island/Guess What The Neighbours'll Say (78)	10
59	Philips PB 894	The Girl On Page 44/The Mocking Bird	5
60	Philips PB 1000	Standing On The Corner/Sunday	6
60	Philips PB 1020	You're Nobody 'Til Somebody Loves You/Goona Goona	5
55	Philips BBE 12044	MOMENTS TO REMEMBER (EP)	10
61	London RE-R 1289	FOUR LADS FOUR HITS (EP)	12
62	London HA-R 2413	DIXIELAND DOIN'S (LP, also stereo SAH-R 6213)	12/15

(see also Johnnie Ray, Frankie Laine, Doris Day)

FOUR LEAVED CLOVER

65	Oak RGJ 207	Alright Girl/Why	380

FOUR MACS

64	Parlophone R 5204	Come Back Silly Girl/Darlin'	6

(see also Sands Of Time)

FOUR MATADORS

66	Columbia DB 7806	A Man's Gotta Stand Tall/Fast Cars And Money	70

FOURMOST

63	Parlophone R 5056	Hello Little Girl/Just In Case	6
63	Parlophone R 5078	I'm In Love/Respectable	7
64	Parlophone R 5128	A Little Loving/Waiting For You	7
64	Parlophone R 5157	How Can I Tell Her/You Got That Way	8
64	Parlophone R 5194	Baby I Need Your Loving/That's Only What They Say	8
65	Parlophone R 5304	Everything In The Garden/He Could Never	7
65	Parlophone R 5379	Girls Girls Girls/Why Do Fools Fall In Love?	8
66	Parlophone R 5491	Here, There And Everywhere/You've Changed	12
66	Parlophone R 5528	Auntie Maggie's Remedy/Turn The Lights Down	15
68	CBS 3814	Apples, Peaches, Pumpkin Pie/He Could Never	15
69	CBS 4041	Rosetta/Just Like Before	25
69	CBS 4461	Easy Squeezy/Do I Love You?	20
72	Phoenix SNIX 126	Goodnight Sweet Dreams/Memphis	5
64	Parlophone GEP 8892	THE SOUND OF THE FOURMOST (EP)	65
64	Parlophone GEP 8917	THE FOURMOST (EP)	80
65	Parlophone PMC 1259	FIRST AND FOURMOST (LP)	90
75	Fourmost SOF 001	THE FOURMOST (LP, private pressing, signed sleeve)	12

(see also Format)

FOURMYULA

69	Columbia DB 8549	Honey Chile/Come With Me	7

FOUR PALMS

58	Vogue V 9116	Jeanie, Joanie, Shirley, Toni/Consideration	600
58	Vogue V 9116	Jeanie, Joanie, Shirley, Toni/Consideration (78)	150

FOUR PENNIES (U.K.)

63	Philips BF 1296	Do You Want Me To/Miss Bad Daddy	7
64	Philips BF 1322	Tell Me Girl/Juliet	5
64	Philips BF 1322	Juliet/Tell Me Girl (A- & B-sides supposedly flipped after original release)	10
64	Philips BF 1349	I Found Out The Hard Way/Don't Tell Me You Love Me	6
64	Philips BF 1366	Black Girl/You Went Away	7
65	Philips BF 1398	The Way Of Love/A Place Where No-One Goes	7

MINT VALUE £

65	Philips BF 1435	Until It's Time For You To Go/Till Another Day	8
66	Philips BF 1469	Trouble Is My Middle Name/Way Out Love	7
66	Philips BF 1491	Keep The Freeway Open/Square Peg	8
66	Philips BF 1519	No Sad Songs For Me/Cats	10
64	Philips BBE 12561	THE FOUR PENNIES (EP)	20
64	Philips BBE 12562	SPIN WITH THE PENNIES (EP)	22
64	Philips BBE 12570	THE SWINGING SIDE OF THE FOUR PENNIES (EP)	22
64	Philips BBE 12571	THE SMOOTH SIDE OF THE FOUR PENNIES (EP)	18
64	Philips BL 7642	TWO SIDES OF THE FOUR PENNIES (LP)	60
66	Philips BL 7734	MIXED BAG (LP)	130
67	Wing WL 1146	JULIET (LP)	25

(see also Lionel Morton, Fritz Mike & Mo)

FOUR PENNIES (U.S.)

63	Stateside SS 198	My Block/Dry Your Eyes	30
63	Stateside SS 244	When The Boy's Happy (The Girl's Happy Too)/Hockaday Part 1	25
79	Ensign ENY 23	When The Boy's Happy/CARLO: Little Orphan Girl	5

(see also Chiffons)

FOUR + ONE

65	Parlophone R 5221	Time Is On My Side/Don't Lie To Me	85

(see also In Crowd, Tomorrow, Keith West)

FOUR PREPS

57	Capitol CL 14727	Falling Star/Where Wuz You	6
57	Capitol CL 14747	I Cried A Million Tears/Moonstruck In Madrid	6
57	Capitol CL 14768	Again 'n' Again 'n' Again/Promise Me Baby	6
57	Capitol CL 14783	Band Of Angels/How About That?	6
58	Capitol CL 14815	26 Miles (Santa Catalina)/Fools Will Be Fools	8
58	Capitol CL 14873	Big Man/Stop, Baby	7
58	Capitol CL 14914	Lazy Summer Night/Summertime Lies	7
59	Capitol CL 14992	The Riddle Of Love/She Was Five And He Was Ten	7
59	Capitol CL 15032	Cinderella/Gidget	8
59	Capitol CL 15044	The Big Surprise/Try My Arms	7
59	Capitol CL 15065	I Ain't Never/Memories, Memories	7
60	Capitol CL 15110	Listen Honey (I'll Be Home)/Down By The Station	7
60	Capitol CL 15128	Got A Girl/(Wait Till You) Hear It From Me	7
61	Capitol CL 15182	Calcutta/Gone Are The Days	7
61	Capitol CL 15217	More Money For You And Me (Medley)/Swing Down Chariot	8
57	Capitol EAP1 862	DREAMY EYES (EP)	15
58	Capitol EAP1 1015	TWENTY SIX MILES (EP)	18
59	Capitol EAP1 1064	BIG MAN (EP)	18
59	Capitol EAP1 1139	LAZY SUMMER NIGHT (EP)	15
61	Capitol EAP4 1647	CAMPUS ENCORES (EP)	12
59	Capitol T 1216	DANCING AND DREAMING (LP)	15
61	Capitol T 1291	DOWN BY THE STATION (LP)	15
61	Capitol T 1566	ON THE CAMPUS (LP)	18
61	Capitol (S)T 1647	CAMPUS ENCORE (LP)	15
62	Capitol (S)T 1814	CAMPUS CONFIDENTIAL (LP)	15
63	Capitol (S)T 1976	SONGS FOR A CAMPUS PARTY (LP)	15
64	Capitol (S)T 2169	HOW TO SUCCEED IN LOVE (LP)	15

4 SAXOPHONES IN 12 TONES

56	Vogue V 2355	Fantastic/Frankly Speaking	7

FOUR SEASONS

SINGLES

62	Stateside SS 122	Sherry/I've Cried Before	8
63	Stateside SS 145	Big Girls Don't Cry/Connie-O	8
63	Stateside SS 169	Walk Like A Man/Lucky Ladybug	8
63	Stateside SS 194	Ain't That A Shame/Soon (I'll Be Home Again)	8
63	Stateside SS 216	Candy Girl/Marlena	12
63	Stateside SS 241	Santa Claus Is Coming To Town/Christmas Tears	15
64	Stateside SS 262	Peanuts/Silhouettes	12
64	Philips BF 1317	Dawn (Go Away)/No Surfin' Today	7
64	Philips BF 1334	Ronnie/Born To Wander	7
64	Stateside SS 315	Alone/Long Lonely Nights	7
64	Philips BF 1347	Rag Doll/Silence Is Golden	6
64	Stateside SS 343	Since I Don't Have You/Sincerely	10
65	Philips BF 1364	Save It For Me/Funny Face	7
65	Philips BF 1372	Big Man In Town/Little Angel	7
65	Philips BF 1395	Bye Bye Baby (Baby Goodbye)/Searching Wind	7
65	Philips BF 1411	Toy Soldier/Betrayed	7
65	Philips BF 1420	Girl Come Running/Cry Myself To Sleep	7
65	Philips BF 1439	Let's Hang On!/On Broadway Tonight	6
66	Philips BF 1474	Working My Way Back To You/Too Many Memories	6
66	Philips BF 1493	Opus 17 (Don't Worry 'Bout Me)/Beggar's Parade	7
66	Philips BF 1511	I've Got You Under My Skin/Huggin' My Pillow	8
67	Philips BF 1538	Tell It To The Rain/Show Girl	7
67	Philips BF 1556	Beggin'/Dody	7
67	Philips BF 1584	C'mon Marianne/Let's Ride Again	7
67	Philips BF 1600	Around And Around/WONDER WHO: Lonesome Road	8
67	Philips BF 1621	Watch The Flowers Grow/Raven	8
68	Philips BF 1651	Will You Love Me Tomorrow?/Silhouettes	7
68	Philips BF 1685	Saturday's Father/Goodbye Girl	7
69	Philips BF 1743	Electric Stories/Pity	12
69	Philips BF 1763	Rag Doll/Working My Way Back To You (p/s)	7
71	Philips 6051 018	Rag Doll/Let's Hang On/I've Got You Under My Skin (maxi-single)	5
71	Warner Bros K 16107	Whatever You Say/Sleeping Man (withdrawn, 300 only)	20

MINT VALUE £

EPs

64	Stateside SE 1011	THE FOUR SEASONS SING	40
68	Philips MCP 1000	HITS OF THE FOUR SEASONS (cassette, in plastic tray, card p/s)	10

LPs

63	Stateside SL 10033	SHERRY AND 11 OTHERS	35
63	Stateside SL 10042	AIN'T THAT A SHAME	40
63	Stateside SL 10051	THE FOUR SEASONS' GREETINGS	35
64	Philips BL 7611	BORN TO WANDER	20
64	Philips BL 7621	DAWN (GO AWAY) AND 11 OTHER GREAT SONGS	20
64	Philips BL 7643	RAG DOLL	18
65	Philips BL 7663	ENTERTAIN YOU	20
65	Philips (S)BL 7687	SING BIG HITS BY BURT BACHARACH ... HAL DAVID ... BOB DYLAN	18
65	Philips BL 7699	WORKING MY WAY BACK TO YOU	18
66	Philips (S)BL 7719	GOLD VAULT OF HITS	15
67	Philips (S)BL 7751	SECOND VAULT OF GOLDEN HITS	15
67	Philips (S)BL 7752	LOOKIN' BACK	15
67	Philips (S)BL 7753	CHRISTMAS ALBUM	25
69	Philips (S)BL 7880	THE GENUINE IMITATION LIFE GAZETTE	18
76	Private Stock DAPS 1001	THE FOUR SEASONS STORY	12

(see also Beverly Hills Blues Band, Frankie Valli, Wonder Who)

FOUR SENSATIONS

52	London L 1137	Heaven Knows Why/Believing In You (78)	25
52	Melodisc P 216	Raindrops/When Honeymoon Lane Becomes Memory Lane (78)	8

FOUR SIGHTS

64	Columbia DB 7227	But I Can Tell/And I Cry	12

4-SKINS

81	Clockwork Fun CF 101	One Law For Them/Brave New World (p/s)	18
81	Secret SHH 125	Yesterday's Heroes/Justice/Get Out Of My Life (p/s)	15
82	Secret SHH 141	Lowlife/Bread Or Blood (p/s)	35
82	Secret SEC 4	THE GOOD, THE BAD AND THE 4-SKINS (LP, with photo inner)	15
83	Syndicate SYN 1	A FISTFUL OF ... 4-SKINS (LP)	15
84	Syndicate SYN LP 5	FROM CHAOS TO 1984 (LP)	20

(see also Plastic Gangsters)

FOUR SPICES

57	MGM MGM 944	Armen's Theme (Yesterday And You)/Fire Engine Boogie	125
57	MGM MGM 944	Armen's Theme (Yesterday And You)/Fire Engine Boogie (78)	15

FOUR SQUARES

64	Hollick & Taylor HT 1009	FOUR SQUARES (EP)	65

(see also Pink People)

FOURTEEN (14)

68	Olga OLE 002	Through My Door/Meet Mr. Edgar	12
68	Olga OLE 006	Umbrella/Drizzle (Rain)	12
68	Olga S 051	Easy To Fool/Frosty Stars On A Window Pane	10

14 ICED BEARS

86	Frank COPPOLA 101	Inside/Blue Suit/Cut (hand-printed paper bag sleeve)	25
87	Frank CAPRA 202	Like A Dolphin/Balloon Song/Train Song/Lie To Choose (12", p/s)	10
87	Penetration	Balloon Song (flexidisc)	8
87	Penetration 001	Lie To Choose/SPLENDOUR IN THE GRASS: Twist Me (flexidisc)	6
88	Sarah SARAH 005	Come Get Me/Unhappy Days/Sure To See (poster p/s)	15
89	Thunderball 7TBL 2	Mother Sleep (7", unreleased, Mayking test pressings only)	25
90s	Thunderball Surfacer 002	Falling Backwards/World I Love/CROCODILE RIDE: Ex-Hipster/Satellite (Speed Mix) (numbered & stickered mailer, 1,000 only)	8

FOUR TONES

58	Decca F 11074	Voom Ba Voom/Rickshaw Boy	15
58	Decca F 11074	Voom Ba Voom/Rickshaw Boy (78)	8

FOUR TOPHATTERS

55	London HLA 8163	Leave-a My Gal Alone/Go Baby Go	300
55	London HLA 8163	Leave-a My Gal Alone/Go Baby Go (78)	35
55	London HLA 8198	Forty Five Men In A Telephone Booth/Wild Rosie	300
55	London HLA 8198	Forty Five Men In A Telephone Booth/Wild Rosie (78)	20

FOUR TOPS

SINGLES

64	Stateside SS 336	Baby I Need Your Lovin'/Call On Me	45
65	Stateside SS 371	Without The One You Love (Life's Not Worthwhile)/Love Has Gone	40
65	Tamla Motown TMG 507	Ask The Lonely/Where Did You Go?	45
65	Tamla Motown TMG 515	I Can't Help Myself/Sad Souvenirs	15
65	Tamla Motown TMG 528	It's The Same Old Song/Your Love Is Amazing	20
65	Tamla Motown TMG 542	Something About You/Darling I Hum Our Song	20
66	Tamla Motown TMG 553	Shake Me, Wake Me (When It's Over)/Just As Long As You Need Me	28
66	Tamla Motown TMG 568	Loving You Is Sweeter Than Ever/I Like Everything About You	15
66	Tamla Motown TMG 579	Reach Out, I'll Be There/Until You Love Someone (small print, later large)	12/7
67	Tamla Motown TMG 589	Standing In The Shadows Of Love/Since You've Been Gone (small print, later large)	15/8
67	Tamla Motown TMG 601	Bernadette/I Got A Feeling	8
67	Tamla Motown TMG 612	Seven Rooms Of Gloom/I'll Turn To Stone	12
67	Tamla Motown TMG 623	You Keep Running Away/If You Don't Want My Love	10
67	Tamla Motown TMG 634	Walk Away Renee/Mame	8
68	Tamla Motown TMG 647	If I Were A Carpenter/Your Love Is Wonderful	7
68	Tamla Motown TMG 665	Yesterday's Dreams/For Once In My Life	7
68	Tamla Motown TMG 675	I'm In A Different World/Remember When	7
69	Tamla Motown TMG 698	What Is A Man?/Don't Bring Back Memories	8

MINT VALUE £

69 Tamla Motown TMG 710 Do What You Gotta Do/Can't Seem To Get You Out Of My Mind . . . 12
70 Tamla Motown TMG 736 It's All In The Game/Love (Is The Answer) . . . 6
70 Tamla Motown TMG 752 Still Water (Love)/Still Water (Peace) . . . 6
71 Tamla Motown TMG 770 Just Seven Numbers (Can Straighten Out My Life)/I Wish I Were Your Mirror . . . 6
71 Tamla Motown TMG 785 Simple Game/You Stole My Love . . . 5
72 Tamla Motown TMG 803 Bernadette/I Got A Feeling/It's The Same Old Song . . . 5
72 Tamla Motown TMG 829 I'll Turn To Stone/Love Feels Like Fire . . . 5
72 Probe PRO 575 Keeper Of The Castle/Jubilee With Soul . . . 5
73 Probe PRO 596 Are You Man Enough/Peace Of Mind . . . 6
74 Probe PRO 612 I Just Can't Get You Out Of My Mind/Am I My Brother's Keeper . . . 10
75 ABC ABC 4057 Seven Lonely Nights/I Can't Hold On Much Longer . . . 5

EPs

66 Tamla Motown TME 2012 THE FOUR TOPS . . . 25
67 Tamla Motown TME 2018 FOUR TOP HITS . . . 22

LPs

65 Tamla Motown TML 11010 THE FOUR TOPS . . . 60
66 T. Motown (S)TML 11021 SECOND ALBUM (mono/stereo) . . . 40/50
66 T. Motown (S)TML 11037 FOUR TOPS ON TOP (mono/stereo) . . . 30/40
67 T. Motown (S)TML 11041 FOUR TOPS LIVE! (mono/stereo) . . . 30/40
67 T. Motown (S)TML 11056 REACH OUT . . . 25
68 T. Motown (S)TML 11061 FOUR TOPS GREATEST HITS . . . 18
69 T. Motown (S)TML 11087 YESTERDAY'S DREAMS . . . 22
69 T. Motown (S)TML 11113 FOUR TOPS NOW . . . 22
70 T. Motown (S)TML 11138 SOUL SPIN (mono/stereo) . . . 22/18
70 Tamla Motown STML 11149 STILL WATERS RUN DEEP . . . 15
71 Tamla Motown STML 11173 CHANGING TIMES . . . 15
71 Tamla Motown STML 11195 GREATEST HITS VOL. 2 . . . 15
72 Tamla Motown STML 11206 NATURE PLANNED IT . . . 12
73 Probe SPB 1064 KEEPER OF THE CASTLE . . . 15
73 Probe SPB 1077 SHAFT IN AFRICA (soundtrack, with Johnny Pate) . . . 25
73 Probe SPBA 6277 MAIN STREET PEOPLE . . . 12
74 Probe SPBA 6283 MEETING OF THE MINDS . . . 12
74 ABC ABCL 5035 SHAFT IN AFRICA (soundtrack, reissue) . . . 15
74 ABC ABCL 5062 LIVE AND IN CONCERT . . . 12
75 ABC ABCL 5132 NIGHT LIGHTS HARMONY . . . 12

(see also Supremes & Four Tops)

FOUR TUNES

54 London L 1231 I Gambled With Love/Marie (78) . . . 70
54 London HL 8050 Do, Do, Do, Do, Do Do It Again/My Wild Irish Rose (78) . . . 18
55 London HL 8151 I Sold My Heart To A Junkman/The Greatest Feeling In The World . . . 125
55 London HL 8151 I Sold My Heart To A Junkman/The Greatest Feeling In The World (78) . . . 30
55 London HLJ 8164 Tired Of Waitin'/L'Amour, Toujours L'Amour (Love Everlasting) . . . 60
55 London HLJ 8164 Tired Of Waitin'/L'Amour, Toujours L'Amour (Love Everlasting) (78) . . . 25

FOUR VOICES

56 Philips PB 591 Geronimo/Lovely One (78) . . . 8
58 Philips PB 864 Tell Me You're Mine/Tight Spot . . . 6
58 Philips PB 864 Tell Me You're Mine/Tight Spot (78) . . . 12

FOUR WINDS

58 London HLU 8556 Short Shorts/Five Minutes More . . . 45
58 London HLU 8556 Short Shorts/Five Minutes More (78) . . . 20

KIM FOWLEY

66 Parlophone R 5521 Lights/Something New And Different . . . 18
66 CBS 202243 They're Coming To Take Me Away Ha-Haaa!!/You Get More For Your Money On The Flip Side Of This Record Talking Blues . . . 10
66 CBS 202338 Lights (The Blind Can See)/Something New And Different (reissue) . . . 12
66 Island WI 278 The Trip/Beautiful People . . . 15
72 Action ACT 4606 Born To Make You Cry/Thunder Road . . . 7
73 Capitol CL 15743 International Heroes/E.S.P. Reader . . . 5
78 Mercury 6005 009 Control/Rubber Rainbow . . . 5
79 Illegal ILS 012 Rubber Rainbow/In My Garage (p/s) . . . 5
80 Island WIP 6555 1989: Waiting For The Next Ten Years/1987: Lost Like A Lizard In Snow . . . 5
73 Capitol E-ST 11159 INTERNATIONAL HEROES (LP) . . . 12

(see also Freaks Of Nature, Hollywood Argyles, Napoleon XIV, B. Bumble & Stingers)

HARRY FOWLER & MARIO FABRIZI

61 HMV POP 891 Buddies/HARRY FOWLER: Follow Flogger . . . 8

FOX

68 CBS 3381 Mister Carpenter/Seek And You Find . . . 60

(see also Top Topham, Dave Mason)

FOX

70 Fontana 6007 016 Second Hand Love/Butterfly . . . 20
70 Fontana 6309 007 FOR FOX SAKE (LP) . . . 65

FOX

75 GTO GTLP 006 TAILS OF ILLUSION (LP) . . . 12
77 GTO GTLP 020 BLUE HOTEL (LP) . . . 12

(see also Wooden Horse, Demick & Armstrong)

FOX

81 BBC RESL 115 Electro People/If You Don't Want My Peaches . . . 8

DON FOX

57 Decca F 10927 Be My Girl/You'll Never Go To Heaven . . . 10
57 Decca F 10955 The Majesty Of Love/Party Time . . . 10
58 Decca F 10983 Pretend You Don't See Her/Wasteland . . . 10

MINT VALUE £

58	Decca F 11057	She Was Only Seventeen/When You're A Long, Long Way Away	10
60	Triumph RGM 1022	T'ain't What You Do/Out There	40
61	Oriole CB 1643	Don't Fool With Love/If You Go	8
60s	Honey Hit TB 125	Three Swinging Clicks/I Found The Girl I Love In My Home Town (some in p/s)	15/7

SAMANTHA FOX

84	Lamborghini LMG 10	Aim To Win/17 And Holding (p/s)	5
84	Lamborghini LMG 10	Aim To Win/17 And Holding (12", p/s)	8
84	Lamborghini LMG 10	Aim To Win/17 And Holding (12", picture disc)	12
86	Jive FOXYP 5	Nothing's Gonna Stop Me Now/Dream City (picture disc)	5
87	Jive FOXYR 5	Nothing's Gonna Stop Me Now (Extended Mix)/Dream City/Want You To Want Me (12", p/s)	10
87	Jive FOXYS 5	Nothing's Gonna Stop Me Now (Extended Mix)/Dream City/Want You To Want Me (12" picture disc)	10
87	Jive FOXTB 5	Nothing's Gonna Stop Me Now (Extended Mix)/Dream City/Want You To Want Me (12", box set)	10
87	Jive FOXY CD 8	True Devotion/Even In The Darkest Hours/Fox Hunt Mix featuring "I Surrender (To The Spirit Of The Night)"/Touch Me (I Want Your Body)/ Nothing's Gonna Stop Me Now (CD)	10
88	Jive FOXY CD 9	Naughty Girls (Need Love Too) (Special Extended Version)/ (Instrumental Edit)/Dream City (CD, picture disc)	10
89	Jive FOXY CD 11	I Only Wanna Be With You/Nothing's Gonna Stop Me Now/I Only Wanna Be With You (Extended Version)/Confession (CD, in circular tin)	10
89	Jive FOXY CD 12	I Wanna Have Some Fun (7" Version)/Lovin' Don't Grow On Trees/I Wanna Have Some Fun (Have Some Fun Mix)/Out Of Our Hands (CD, in tin)	10
88	Jive HIPR 39	TOUCH ME (LP, picture disc)	12

(see also David Cassidy)

ROY FOXLEY & HIS LEVEE RAMBLERS

50	Tailgate 4 & 5	South/Weary Blues (78)	7

BRUCE FOXTON

86	Harvest HAR 5239	Play This Game To Win/Welcome To The Hero (p/s)	5

(see also Jam)

FOXX

71	MCA MUPS 419	REVOLT OF EMILY YOUNG (LP)	15

INEZ FOXX

63	Sue WI 301	Mockingbird/He's The One You Love (actually by Inez & Charlie Foxx)	20
64	Sue WI 304	Jaybirds/Broken-Hearted Fool (actually by Inez & Charlie Foxx)	25
64	Sue WI 314	Ask Me/Hi Diddle Diddle (actually by Inez & Charlie Foxx)	25
64	Sue WI 323	Hurt By Love/Confusion (actually by Inez & Charlie Foxx)	25
71	Pye International 7N 25546	You Shouldn't Have Set My Soul On Fire/Live For Today	7
73	Stax 2025 151	You Hurt Me For The Last Time/Watch The Dog (That Brings The Bone)	7

INEZ & CHARLIE FOXX

64	Sue WI 307	Competition/Here We Go Round The Mulberry Bush (as Charlie & Inez Foxx)	22
64	Sue WI 356	La De Da I Love You/Yankee Doodle Dandy	25
65	London HLC 9971	My Momma Told Me/I Feel Alright	10
65	London HLC 10009	Hummingbird/If I Need Anyone (Let It Be You)	10
66	Stateside SS 556	Come By Here/No Stranger To Love	22
67	Stateside SS 586	Tightrope/My Special Prayer	25
67	Direction 58-2712	I Ain't Goin' For That/Undecided	8
67	Direction 58-3192	(1, 2, 3, 4, 5, 6, 7) Count The Days/A Stranger I Don't Know	8
68	Direction 58-3816	Come On In/Baby Drop Your Dime	8
69	Direction 58-4042	Baby Give It To Me/You Fixed My Heartache	8
69	London HLC 10250	Mockingbird/Hummingbird (unissued)	
69	United Artists UP 2269	Mockingbird/Hurt By Love	8
69	United Artists UP 35013	La De Da I Love You/Don't Do It No More	7
71	Pye International 7N 25561	Tightrope/Baby Take It All	6
64	Sue ILP 911	MOCKINGBIRD (LP)	80
65	London HA-C 8241	INEZ AND CHARLIE FOXX (LP, plum label, later black)	70/40
68	Direction 8-63085	COME BY HERE (LP)	30
68	Direction 8-63281	GREATEST HITS (LP)	22
69	United Artists UA(S) 29025	MOCKINGBIRD (LP)	15
71	Pye PKL 4406	GREATEST HITS (LP)	12

JOHN FOXX

80	Island Music/Smash Hits	My Face (yellow vinyl 1-sided flexidisc free with *Smash Hits* magazine)	10/5
80	Virgin VS 338	No-One Driving/Glimmer//This City/Mr. No (double pack, gatefold p/s)	6
80	Virgin VS 338	No-One Driving (2.53 DJ Version)/Glimmer//This City/Mr. No (double pack, stickered gatefold p/s, matrix no. VS 338 A5DJ)	15
80	Virgin VS 360	Burning Car/20th Century (picture disc)	5
82	Virgin VSY 513	Endlessly/Young Man (picture disc)	5
83	Virgin VSD 543	Endlessly/Ghosts On Water//Dance With Me/A Kind Of Wave (double pack)	5
84	Virgin VSD 615	Your Dress/Woman On A Stairway//Lifting Sky/Annexe (double pack)	5
84	Virgin VSP 645	Like A Miracle/Wings And A Wind (shaped picture disc)	8
85	Virgin VS 771	The Stars On Fire/What Kind Of Girl (p/s, with bonus single)	5
87	Virgin CDV 2355	IN MYSTERIOUS WAYS (CD)	20

(see also Ultravox)

FRABJOY & RUNCIBLE SPOON

69	Marmalade 598 019	I'm Beside Myself/Animal Song	25

(see also Godley & Creme, Doctor Father, Hotlegs, Mockingbirds, 10cc)

FRAME

66	RCA RCA 1556	My Feet Don't Fit In His Shoes/She	15
67	RCA RCA 1571	Doctor Doctor/I Can't Go On	60
70	Pye 7N 45213	Rockin' Machine/One More Time	7

FRAMES

Year	Label/Cat.	Title	£
79	Brain Booster BBC 2	False Accusations/69 (no p/s)	6

PETER FRAMPTON

Year	Label/Cat.	Title	£
72	A&M AMS 7025	It's A Plain Shame/Oh For Another Day	5
75	A&M AMS 7174	Show Me The Way/Crying Clown	5
81	A&M AMS 8154	Breaking All The Rules/Night Town (p/s)	7
85	Virgin VSS 827	Lying/You Know So Well (shaped disc)	7
72	A&M AMLS 68099	WIND OF CHANGE (LP)	15
74	A&M AMLH 6369	SOMETHING'S HAPPENING (LP)	12
75	A&M AMLH 64512	FRAMPTON (LP)	12

(see also Preachers, Herd, Humble Pie, Frampton's Camel, Moon's Train)

FRAMPTON'S CAMEL

Year	Label/Cat.	Title	£
73	A&M AMS 7069	All Night Long/Don't Fade Away	5
73	A&M AMLH 68150	FRAMPTON'S CAMEL (LP, with poster)	15

(see also Peter Frampton, Parrish & Gurvitz)

PETER FRANC

Year	Label/Cat.	Title	£
73	Dawn DNS 1033	I'll Move Along/Song For Every Season	6
73	Dawn DNS 1039	Ballad Of the Superstar/Strange Kind Of Woman	6
74	Dawn DNS 1088	Flag Of Convenience/At Home With You	6
73	Dawn DNLS 3043	PROFILE (LP)	18
73	Dawn DNLS 3051	EN ROUTE (LP)	15

FRANCIS

Year	Label/Cat.	Title	£
67	Blue Beat BB 379	Warn The People (actually by Willie Francis)/SWINGERS: Simpleton (actually by Peter Tosh & Crackers)	50
72	Fab FAB 182	Rocking Machine/SOUL CLANS: Flying Rhythm	10
73	Fab FAB 251	Locks/Version	10

B. FRANCIS

Year	Label/Cat.	Title	£
65	Ska Beat JB 193	Judy Crowned/Who Crunch	18

BOBBY FRANCIS

Year	Label/Cat.	Title	£
67	Doctor Bird DB 1153	Chain Gang/Venus	18

(see also Winston Francis)

CLAIRE FRANCIS

Year	Label/Cat.	Title	£
66	Polydor 56079	I've Got My Own Thing Going/Here I Go Again	7
67	Polydor 56142	But I Don't Care/If You Don't Know	7

CONNIE FRANCIS

78s

Year	Label/Cat.	Title	£
56	MGM MGM 902	My First Real Love (with Jaybirds)/Believe In Me (Crede Mi)	60
56	MGM MGM 932	My Sailor Boy/Everyone Needs Someone	15
57	MGM MGM 945	Little Blue Wren/I Never Had A Sweetheart	35
57	MGM MGM 962	Eighteen/Faded Orchid	35
58	MGM MGM 998	You Always Hurt The One You Love/In The Valley Of Love	8
59	MGM MGM 1001	My Happiness/Happy Days And Lonely Nights	15
59	MGM MGM 1012	If I Didn't Care/Toward The End Of The Day	30
59	MGM MGM 1018	Lipstick On Your Collar/Frankie	30
59	MGM MGM 1036	Plenty Good Lovin'/You're Gonna Miss Me	30
59	MGM MGM 1046	Among My Souvenirs/Do You Love Me Like You Kiss Me?	40

SINGLES

Year	Label/Cat.	Title	£
56	MGM SP 1169	My First Real Love (with Jaybirds)/Believe In Me (Crede Mi)	200
56	MGM MGM 932	My Sailor Boy/Everyone Needs Someone	85
57	MGM MGM 945	Little Blue Wren/I Never Had A Sweetheart	60
57	MGM MGM 962	Eighteen/Faded Orchid	65
58	MGM MGM 975	Who's Sorry Now?/You Were Only Fooling (While I Was Falling In Love)	6
58	MGM MGM 982	I'm Sorry I Made You Cry/Lock Up Your Heart	6
58	MGM MGM 985	Carolina Moon/Stupid Cupid	10
58	MGM MGM 993	I'll Get By/Fallin'	7
58	MGM MGM 998	You Always Hurt The One You Love/In The Valley Of Love	7
59	MGM MGM 1001	My Happiness/Happy Days And Lonely Nights	7
59	MGM MGM 1012	If I Didn't Care/Toward The End Of The Day	10
59	MGM MGM 1018	Lipstick On Your Collar/Frankie	7
59	MGM MGM 1036	Plenty Good Lovin'/You're Gonna Miss Me	7
59	MGM MGM 1046	Among My Souvenirs/Do You Love Me Like You Kiss Me?	7
60	MGM MGM 1060	Valentino/It Would Be Worth It	7
60	MGM MGM 1070	Mama/Teddy (withdrawn; demos more common, £40)	60
60	MGM MGM 1076	Mama/Robot Man	6
60	MGM MGM 1086	Everybody's Somebody's Fool/Jealous Of You	6
60	MGM MGM 1100	My Heart Has A Mind Of Its Own/Malaguena	6
60	MGM MGM 1111	Many Tears Ago/Senza Mama (With No-One)	7
61	MGM MGM 1121	Where The Boys Are/Baby Roo	7
61	MGM MGM 1136	Breakin' In A Brand New Broken Heart/Someone Else's Boy	6
61	MGM MGM 1138	Together/Too Many Rules	6
61	MGM MGM 1145	Baby's First Christmas/I'm Falling In Love With You Tonight	7
62	MGM MGM 1151	Don't Cry On My Shoulder/Mr. Twister	8
62	MGM MGM 1157	Don't Break The Heart That Loves You/Ain't That Better Baby?	7
62	MGM MGM 1165	Vacation/It's Gonna Take Me Some Time	10
62	MGM MGM 1171	Playin' Games/I Was Such A Fool	8
62	MGM MGM 1185	I'm Gonna Be Warm This Winter/Pretty Little Baby	7
62	MGM MGM 1193	Follow The Boys/Tonight's My Night	7
63	MGM MGM 1202	If My Pillow Could Talk/Lollipop Lips	7
63	MGM MGM 1207	Drownin' My Sorrows/Look At Him	7
63	MGM MGM 1212	Your Other Love/Whatever Happened To Rosemary	7
63	MGM MGM 1220	The Summer Of His Years/My Buddy	7
63	MGM MGM 1224	Blue Winter/Souvenirs	7

MINT VALUE £

63	MGM MGM 1236	Be Anything (But Be Mine)/Tommy	7
64	MGM MGM 1253	Don't Ever Leave Me/Waiting For You	7
65	MGM MGM 1265	Forget Domani/I Don't Want To Be No Better Off	12
65	MGM MGM 1271	My Child/No One Ever Sends Me Roses	7
65	MGM MGM 1282	Roundabout/Love Is Me, Love Is You	10
66	MGM MGM 1293	Jealous Heart/Can I Rely On You?	8
66	MGM MGM 1295	The Phoenix Love Theme — Senza Fine/Bossa Nova Hand Dance	8
66	MGM MGM 1305	Love Is Me, Love Is You/I'd Let You Break My Heart All Over Again	8
66	MGM MGM 1320	Somewhere My Love (Lara's Theme)/Letter From A Soldier (Dear Mama)	8
66	MGM MGM 1327	Spanish Nights And You/Games That Lovers Play	8
67	MGM MGM 1334	Another Page/Souvenir D'Italie	8
67	MGM MGM 1336	Time Alone Will Tell/Born Free	8
67	MGM MGM 1347	My Heart Cries For You/If My Friends Could See Me Now (Medley)	8
68	MGM MGM 1381	My World Is Slipping Away/Till We're Together	8
68	MGM MGM 1407	Why Say Goodbye?/Addio Mi Amore	8
68	MGM MGM 1446	Somebody Else Is Taking My Place/Brother Can You Spare A Dime?	8
69	MGM MGM 1471	The Wedding Cake/Overhill Underground	12
69	MGM MGM 1483	Who's Sorry Now?/Vacation	7
69	MGM MGM 1493	Mr. Love/Zingara	10
71	MGM 2006 052	Lipstick On Your Collar/Who's Sorry Now?/Robot Man	8
73	MGM 2006 221	Lipstick On Your Collar/Frankie	5
73	GSF GSZ 10	The Answer/Paint The Rain	6
75	MGM 1110 004	Who's Sorry Now?/Mama	5
75	MGM 1110 005	Stupid Cupid/Carolina Moon	5
78	Polydor 2066 881	Burning Bridges/Let's Go Where The Good Times Go	6
78	United Artists UP 36430	Where The Boys Are/A-Ba-Ni-Bi	6
78	United Artists UP 26463	My Mother's Eyes/Lovin' Man	6
79	Polydor POSP 75	Three Good Reasons/What's Wrong With My World?	5

EPs

56	MGM MGM-EP 658	A GIRL IN LOVE	30
58	MGM MGM-EP 677	HEARTACHES	20
58	MGM MGM-EP 686	CONNIE FRANCIS	30
59	MGM MGM-EP 697	IF I DIDN'T CARE	25
60	MGM MGM-EP 711	YOU'RE MY EVERYTHING	35
60	MGM MGM-EP 717	ROCK AND ROLL MILLION SELLERS NO. 1	35
60	MGM MGM-EP 720	ROCK AND ROLL MILLION SELLERS NO. 2	30
60	MGM MGM-EP 731	ROCK AND ROLL MILLION SELLERS NO. 3	25
60	MGM MGM-EP 742	FIRST LADY OF RECORD (laminated or matt rear sleeve)	18
61	MGM MGM-EP 756	WHERE THE BOYS ARE	25
61	MGM MGM-EP 759	CONNIE FRANCIS FAVOURITES	30
61	MGM MGM-EP 760	SINGS ITALIAN FAVOURITES	30
63	MGM MGM-EP 769	CONNIE'S AMERICAN HITS	30
63	MGM MGM-EP 773	HEY RING-A-DING	35
63	MGM MGM-EP 775	WHAT KIND OF FOOL AM I?	30
63	MGM MGM-EP 780	MALA FEMMENA	30
63	MGM MGM-EP 783	FROM ITALY ... WITH LOVE	35
65	MGM MGM-EP 789	SINGS FOR MAMA	35
66	MGM MGM-EP 792	JEALOUS HEART	35

LPs

58	MGM MGM-D 153	WHO'S SORRY NOW? (10")	75
59	MGM MGM-C 782	MY THANKS TO YOU	35
59	MGM MGM-C 786	THE EXCITING CONNIE FRANCIS	25
59	MGM MGM-C 797	CHRISTMAS WITH CONNIE	40
60	MGM MGM-C 804	ROCK AND ROLL MILLION SELLERS NO. 1	45
60	MGM MGM-C 812	COUNTRY AND WESTERN GOLDEN HITS	35
60	MGM MGM-C 819	FUN SONGS FOR CHILDREN	60
60	MGM MGM-C 821	SINGS ITALIAN FAVOURITES (also stereo CS 6002)	20/25
60	MGM MGM-C 831	CONNIE'S GREATEST HITS	15
60	MGM MGM-C 836	SPANISH AND LATIN AMERICAN FAVOURITES (also stereo CS 6012)	18/22
61	MGM MGM-C 845	SINGS JEWISH FAVOURITES (also stereo CS 6021)	18/22
61	MGM MGM-C 854	MORE ITALIAN FAVOURITES (also stereo CS 6029)	18/22
61	MGM MGM-C 861	AT THE COPA (also stereo CS 6035)	18/22
61	MGM MGM-C 870	SONGS TO A SWINGIN' BAND (also stereo CS 6044)	18/22
61	MGM MGM-C 875	SINGS 'NEVER ON SUNDAY' AND OTHER TITLE SONGS FROM MOTION PICTURES (also stereo CS 6047)	18/22
61	MGM MGM-C 879	DO THE TWIST	50
62	MGM MGM-C 883	SINGS FOLK SONG FAVOURITES (also stereo CS 6054)	18/22
62	MGM MGM-C 898	SINGS IRISH FAVOURITES (also stereo CS 6056)	25/30
62	MGM MGM-C 916	COUNTRY MUSIC CONNIE STYLE (also stereo CS 6062)	20/25
63	MGM MGM-C 930	MODERN ITALIAN HITS (also stereo CS 6067)	18/22
63	MGM MGM-C 931	FOLLOW THE BOYS (also stereo CS 6068)	18/22
63	MGM MGM-C 940	SINGS AWARD-WINNING MOTION PICTURE HITS (also stereo CS 6070)	18/22
64	MGM MGM-C 958	GREATEST AMERICAN WALTZES (also stereo CS 6075)	18/22
64	MGM MGM-C 970	16 OF CONNIE'S BIGGEST HITS	15
65	MGM MGM-C 983	LOOKING FOR LOVE (also stereo CS 6079)	20
65	MGM MGM-C 998	A NEW KIND OF CONNIE... (also stereo CS 6080)	18
65	MGM MGM-C 1003	SINGS GREAT COUNTRY FAVOURITES (with Hank Williams Jnr, also stereo CS 6081)	20/22
65	MGM MGM-C 1006	SINGS 'FOR MAMA' (also stereo CS 6082)	20/22
65	MGM MGM-C 1012	SINGS THE ALL-TIME INTERNATIONAL HITS (also stereo CS 6083)	18/22
66	MGM MGM-C(S) 8006	WHEN THE BOYS MEET THE GIRLS (soundtrack, mono/stereo)	18/22
66	MGM MGM-C(S) 8009	JEALOUS HEART	20
66	MGM MGM-C(S) 8027	MOVIE GREATS OF THE SIXTIES	20
66	MGM MGM-C(S) 8036	LIVE AT THE SAHARA IN LAS VEGAS	20
66	World Record Club TP 618	MY THANKS TO YOU	12
67	MGM MGM-C 8041	THE BEST OF CONNIE FRANCIS	15

68 MGM MGM-C(S) 8050 LOVE ITALIAN STYLE (mono/stereo) . . . 18/22
68 MGM MGM-C(S) 8054 MY HEART CRIES FOR YOU (mono/stereo) . . . 18/22
68 MGM MGM-C(S) 8086 CONNIE AND CLYDE . . . 20
69 MGM MGM-C(S) 8110 HAWAII CONNIE . . . 40
70 MGM MGM-CS 8117 SINGS THE SONGS OF LES REED . . . 20
73 MGM 2353 072 GREAT SONGS OF THE SIXTIES . . . 12
74 MGM ACB 00143 SINGS GREAT COUNTRY HITS (Audio Club Of Great Britain issue) . . . 12
75 MGM ACB 00167 SINGS GREAT COUNTRY HITS VOL. 2 (Audio Club Of G.B. issue) . . . 15
76 MGM ACB 00195 THE SPECIAL MAGIC OF CONNIE FRANCIS (Audio Club Of G.B. issue) . . . 12
78 United Artists ULP 30182 WHO'S HAPPY NOW? (withdrawn sleeve with different lettering) . . . 150
78 United Artists ULP 30182 WHO'S HAPPY NOW? . . . 12
81 R/Digest GBCF-A-106 THE BEST OF CONNIE FRANCIS (4-LP) . . . 20

CONNIE FRANCIS & MARVIN RAINWATER

58 MGM MGM 969 The Majesty Of Love/You My Darling You . . . 45
58 MGM MGM 969 The Majesty Of Love/You My Darling You (78) . . . 30
(see also Marvin Rainwater)

(KING) JOE FRANCIS

65 Blue Beat BB 323 Wicked Woman/King Joe's Ska (as King Joe Francis) . . . 15
66 Ska Beat JB 262 Scarborough Ska/I Got A Scar (as Joe Francis & Ricky Logan & Snowballs) . . . 18
66 Rio R 90 Have My Body (song actually "Have Mercy Baby")/Everybody's Got To Know (as King Joe Francis & Hijackers) . . . 15
67 Rainbow RAI 114 My Granny/Pull It Out (as J. Francis & Rico's Boys) . . . 12

JOHNNIE FRANCIS

55 Decca F 10440 Funny Thing/Give Me The Right . . . 7

LEE FRANCIS

65 Decca F 12148 Ciao/If He Wants Me . . . 7
(see also Vernons Girls)

NAT FRANCIS

66 Blue Beat BB 346 Mama Kiss Him Goodnight/Tra La La (with Prince Buster Junior & Sunsets) . . . 20
66 Blue Beat BB 361 Just To Keep You (credited to B. Junior)/You Only Want My Money . . . 15
67 Blue Beat BB 376 Seven Nights Of Love/Feeling Blue . . . 18

RITCHIE FRANCIS

72 Pegasus PEG 11 SONGBIRD (LP) . . . 25
(see also Eyes Of Blue, Big Sleep)

STEVE FRANCIS

64 King KG 1012 Watch Your Step/Lovey Dovey . . . 6

WILBERT FRANCIS & VIBRATORS

66 Ska Beat JB 267 Memories Of You/CHUCK JACQUES: Now That You're Gone . . . 20
(see also Little Willie, Vibrators [Jamaica])

WILLIE FRANCIS

69 Bullet BU 415 Motherless Children/I Am Not Afraid . . . 8
71 Escort ERT 848 Burn Them/Poor Boy . . . 7
71 Pama PM 829 Oh What A Mini/Version . . . 6
(see also Martin Riley)

WINSTON FRANCIS

69 Coxsone CS 7089 Reggae And Cry/FREEDOM SINGERS: Easy Come Easy Go (B-side actually by Righteous Flames) . . . 25
69 Studio One SO 2086 The Games People Play/ALBERT GRIFFITHS: The Kicks . . . 22
69 Punch PH 5 Too Experienced/JACKIE MINTO: Mule Jerk (B-side actually by Jackie Mittoo) . . 12
69 Bamboo BAM 10 The Same Old Song/SOUND DIMENSION: Rattle On . . . 18
70 Bamboo BAM 46 Turn Back The Hands Of Time/Soul Bowl . . . 18
70 Bamboo BAM 48 California Dreaming/JACKIE MITTOO & SOUND DIMENSION: Soul Stew . . . 10
72 Camel CA 99 Ten Times Sweeter Than You/Fat Boy . . . 6
73 Fab FAB 271 Mr Fix It/Version . . . 7
74 Ashanti ASH 415 California Dreaming/SOUND DIMENSION: Soul Food (reissue) . . . 8
70 Bamboo BDLP 207 MR FIX IT (LP) . . . 60
71 Bamboo BDLPS 216 CALIFORNIA DREAMING (LP) . . . 50
(see also Bobby Francis, Jerry & Freedom Singers, Zimm & Dee Dee)

JACQUELINE FRANCOIS

59 Philips BBL 7273 THE SWEET LANGUAGE OF LOVE (LP) . . . 15

JACKSON C. FRANK

65 Columbia DB 7795 Blues Run The Game/Can't Get Away From My Love . . . 50
65 Columbia 33SX 1788 JACKSON C. FRANK (LP) . . . 200
78 B&C BCLP 4 AGAIN (LP, reissue of above LP) . . . 35

FRANK & BARBARIANS

62 Oriole CB 1758 The Bouncer/Concerto In The Stars . . . 10
(see Frank Barber)

FRANKIE & CLASSICALS

67 Philips BF 1586 I Only Have Eyes For You/What Shall I Do? . . . 150
74 Pye Intl. DDS 101 What Shall I Do?/Goodbye Love, Hello Sadness . . . 10

FRANKIE & JOHNNY

66 Decca F 22376 Never Gonna Leave You/I'll Hold You . . . 105
66 Parlophone R 5518 Climb Ev'ry Mountain/I Wanna Make You Understand . . . 12
78 Inferno HEAT 8 I'll Hold You/Never Gonna Leave You (reissue) . . . 7
(see also Maggie Bell)

FRANKIE & LARRY

60 Capitol CL 15153 Not Yet/A Fool For You . . . 15

MINT VALUE £

FRANKIE & TIMEBREAKERS

68 Philips BF 1696 — I'll Be Home/Is There Anybody ... 7

FRANKIE GOES TO HOLLYWOOD

SINGLES

Year	Label/Cat. No.	Title	Value
83	ZTT P ZTAS 1	Relax (Move)/One September Monday (picture disc)	6
83	ZTT 12 ZTAS 1	Relax (Original Mix)/Ferry Across The Mersey/Relax Bonus (Again) (12", ZTT sleeve or standard p/s)	18
83	ZTT 12 ZTAS 1	Relax (Original Mix)/Ferry Across The Mersey/Relax Bonus (Again) (12", ZTT sleeve or standard p/s, some copies play at 33rpm but list 45rpm)	15
83	ZTT 12 ZTAS 1 (matrix no.: 1A 2U)	Relax (Sex Mix [alias 8.20 "New York Mix"])/Ferry Across The Mersey Relax Bonus (Again) (12", p/s, 45rpm)	12
83	ZTT 12 ZTAS 1 (matrix no.: 1A 5U)	Relax (Sex Mix)/Ferry Across The Mersey/Relax Bonus (Again) (12", p/s, 45rpm, different 'U.S. chequered' p/s)	8
83	ZTT 12P ZTAS 1	Relax (Sex Mix)/Ferry Across The Mersey/Relax Bonus (Again) (12", picture disc)	8
83	ZTT CTIS 102	Relax: The Party Trick (Acting Dumb)/The Special Act (Adapted From The Sex Mix)/The U.S. Mix (Come Dancing)/The Single (The Act)/Later On (From One September Monday)/Gerry Marsden's Ferry Across The Mersey (And Here I'll Stay) (cassette)	8
84	ZTT P ZTAS 3	Two Tribes (We Don't Want To Die)/One February Friday (picture disc)	6
84	ZTT CTIS 103	TWO TRIBES (KEEP THE PEACE) (cassette)	5
84	ZTT P ZTAS 5	The Power Of Love/The World Is My Oyster (picture disc)	5
84	ZTT 12X ZTAS 5	The Power Of Love/The World Is My Oyster/Welcome To The Pleasuredome (Pleasurefix)/The Only Star In Heaven (Starfix) (12", g/fold p/s with 5 photos)	8
84	ZTT CTIS 105	The Power Of Love (Extended Version)/Trapped And Scrapped/Holier Than Thou (cassette, picture 'envelope' box)	8
85	ZTT ZTAS 7	Welcome To The Pleasure Dome (Altered Reel) (actually plays "Video Mix 5.05")/Happy Hi Get It On (p/s, blue label)	10
85	ZTT P ZTAS 7	Welcome To The Pleasure Dome (Alternative Reel ["Fruitiness Mix"])/ Happy Hi/Get It On (apple-shaped picture disc)	7
85	ZTT CTIS 107	Welcome To The Pleasure Dome (Soundtrack From Bernard Rose Video)/ Happy Hi (All In The Mind)/Get It On/How To Remake The World (cassette)	5
86	ZTT ZTAX 22	Rage Hard (Stamped)/(Don't Lose What's Left) Of Your Little Mind (p/s)	5
86	ZTT ZTD 22	Rage Hard/(Don't Lose What's Left) Of Your Little Mind ('pop-up fists' p/s)	5
86	ZTT 12 ZTAQ 22	Rage Hard/Suffragette City/(Don't Lose What's Left) Of Your Little Mind (extended) (12", stickered p/s with poster)	8
86	ZTT 12 ZTAX B 22	Rage Hard (++ Mix)/Roadhouse Blues/(Don't Lose What's Left) Of Your Little Mind (extended) (12", in 'action series 22' box)	8
86	ZTT ZCID 22	Rage Hard +/Rage Hard ++/Rage Hard*/(Don't Lose What's Left) Of Your Little Mind/Suffragette City/Roadhouse Blues (CD, card sleeve)	10
86	ZTT ZCID 25	WARRIORS OF THE WASTELAND (Compacted) (CD EP, card sleeve)	8
87	ZTT ZTE 26	Watching The Wildlife (Die Letzen Tag Der Menscheit Mix)/ Watching The Wildlife/The Waves (12", p/s)	8
87	ZTT CTIS 26	Watching The Wildlife (Cassetted) (EP, cassette, includes "Condom Mix" & "Orchestral Wildlife")	5
00	ZTT ZTT 154TX3	Two Tribes (Almighty Remix) (12", 1-sided, white label)	10

PROMOS

Year	Label/Cat. No.	Title	Value
83	ZTT ZTAS 1DJ	Relax — The Last Seven Inches/One September Monday (white label, stamped label, no p/s)	8
84	ZTT XZTAS 3DJ	Two Tribes (Carnage)/Relax (U.S. Mix) (12", ZTT sleeve)	12
84	ZTT XZIP 1	Two Tribes (Hibakusha)/War (Hide Yourself)/Two Tribes/ One February Friday (12", ZTT sleeve)	18
84	ZTT ZTAS 5 DJ-A	The Power Of Love (5.28)/The World Is My Oyster (12")	18
86	ZTT 12 ZTAK 25	Warriors (The Attack Mix) (12", white label, featuring Gary Moore)	18
93	ZTT SAM 1231	Relax (Ollie J. Remix) (6.38)/(Trip-Ship Edit) (6.12)/(Ollie J.'s Seven Inches)/ (Jam & Spoon Hi-N-R-G Mix) (7.55)/(C Jam & Spoon Trip-O-Matic Fairy Tale Space Mix) (7.52)/(MCMXCIII) (3.45) (12", double pack, gatefold sleeve)	15
93	ZTT SAM 1275	Welcome To The Pleasuredome (Brothers In Rhythm Rollercoaster Mix) (15.15)/ (Pleasurefix — Original 12" Mix) (9.55)/(Elevatorman's Top Floor Club Mix) (6.02)/(Elevatorman's Deep Down Bass-Ment Dub) (6.00) (12", double pack, gatefold sleeve, promo sleeve)	10
94	ZTT SAM 1331	Two Tribes (The Intermission Mixes): (Legend Mix)/(Legend Instrumental)/ (Workout Mix)/(Workout Instrumental) (12", stickered title sleeve)	10
94	ZTT (no cat. no)	Two Tribes (808 State Remix) (10", 1-sided red vinyl)	15
00	ZTT ZTT 166TP	Welcome To The Pleasuredome (mixes) (12", double pack, p/s)	20

(see also Holly, Holly Johnson, Spitfire Boys)

ARETHA FRANKLIN

SINGLES

Year	Label/Cat. No.	Title	Value
61	Fontana H 271	Love Is The Only Thing/Today I Sing The Blues (with Ray Bryant Combo)	15
61	Fontana H 343	Rock-A-Bye Your Baby With A Dixie Melody/Operation Heartbreak	10
65	CBS 201732	Can't You Just See Me/You Little Miss Raggedy Anne	18
67	CBS 202468	Cry Like A Baby/Swanee	7
67	CBS 3059	Take A Look/Lee Cross	7
67	Atlantic 584 084	I Never Loved A Man (The Way I Love You)/Do Right Woman – Do Right Man	6
67	Atlantic 584 115	Respect/Save Me	6
67	Atlantic 584 127	Baby I Love You/Going Down Slow	7
67	Atlantic 584 141	(You Make Me Feel Like A) Natural Woman/Never Let Me Go	6
67	Atlantic 584 157	(I Can't Get No) Satisfaction/Night Life (withdrawn B-side)	6
67	Atlantic 584 157	Chain Of Fools/(I Can't Get No) Satisfaction	6
68	Atlantic 584 172	Since You've Been Gone/Ain't No Way	10
68	Atlantic 584 186	Think/You Send Me	7
68	Atlantic 584 206	I Say A Little Prayer/See-Saw	6
69	Atlantic 584 239	Don't Let Me Lose This Dream/The House That Jack Built	6
69	Atlantic 584 252	The Weight/The Tracks Of My Tears	5

MINT VALUE £

69 Atlantic 584 285 | Share Your Love With Me/Pledging My Love/The Clock . . . 5
69 Atlantic 584 306 | Eleanor Rigby/It Ain't Fair . . . 6
70 Atlantic 584 322 | Call Me/Son Of A Preacher Man . . . 8
70 Atlantic 2091 027 | Don't Play That Song/The Thrill Is Gone . . . 5
70 Atlantic 2091 042 | Border Song (Holy Moses)/You And Me (unissued)
70 Atlantic 2091 044 | Oh No, Not My Baby/You And Me . . . 5
71 Atlantic 2091 063 | You're All I Need To Get By/The Border Song . . . 5
71 Atlantic 2091 111 | I Say A Little Prayer/(I Can't Get No) Satisfaction . . . 5
71 Atlantic 2091 127 | A Brand New Me/Spirit In The Dark . . . 5
71 Atlantic 2091 168 | Rock Steady/Oh Me, Oh My . . . 12
72 Atlantic K 10154 | Daydreaming / I've Been Loving You Too Long . . . 7
72 Atlantic K 10224 | Rock Steady/All The King's Horses . . . 7
86 Arista ARIDP 624 | Freeway Of Love/Until You Say You Love Me//Jump To It/ Zoomin' To The Freeway (double pack) . . . 5
86 Arista ARIST 22624 | Freeway Of Love (Pink Cadillac Mix)/Until You Say You Love Me (p/s, pink vinyl) . . 8
86 Arista ARIST 22657 | Another Night / Kind Of Man//Another Night (Nightlife Mix) (double pack) . . . 6
86 Arista ARIST 22678 | Jumpin' Jack Flash/Who's Zoomin' Who//Sweet Bitter Love/Integrity (double pack) . . . 20+
89 Arista 112 377 | Through The Storm (with Elton John)/Come To Me (picture disc) . . . 5
89 Arista 612 185 | Through The Storm (with Elton John)/Come To Me/Oh Happy Day (live) (with Mavis Staples) (12", p/s) . . . 8
89 Arista 162 185 | Through The Storm (with Elton John)/Come To Me/Oh Happy Day (live) (with Mavis Staples) (3" CD, card sleeve) . . . 8
89 Arista 612 545 | It Isn't, It Wasn't, It Ain't Never Gonna Be (Extended) (with Whitney Houston)/ (Hip-Hop Remix)/Think 89 (12", p/s) . . . 8
89 Arista 612 683 | It Isn't, It Wasn't, It Ain't Never Gonna Be (with Whitney Houston)/ (After Hours Club Mix)/(New Jack Swing Dub Mix (12", no p/s) . . . 8
89 Arista 662 545 | It Isn't, It Wasn't, It Ain't Never Gonna Be (Single Remix) (with Whitney Houston)/ (Extended Remix)/(Hip-Hop Remix)/Think 89 (12", p/s) . . . 8

EP

62 Fontana TE 467217 | TODAY I SING THE BLUES . . . 30

LPs

61 Fontana TFL 5173 | ARETHA . . . 40
65 CBS (S)BPG 62566 | YEAH!!! — IN PERSON . . . 20
67 CBS (S)BPG 62744 | SOUL SISTER . . . 20
67 Atlantic 587/588 066 | I NEVER LOVED A MAN . . . 20
67 CBS (S)BPG 62969 | TAKE IT LIKE YOU GIVE IT . . . 20
67 CBS 63160 | LEE CROSS . . . 20
67 Atlantic 587/588 085 | ARETHA ARRIVES . . . 15
67 CBS 64536 | GREATEST HITS . . . 18
68 Atlantic 587/588 099 | LADY SOUL . . . 18
68 CBS 63269 | TAKE A LOOK AT ARETHA FRANKLIN . . . 15
68 Atlantic 587/588 114 | ARETHA NOW . . . 15
68 CBS 63064 | GREATEST HITS VOL. 2 . . . 15
68 Atlantic 587/588 149 | ARETHA IN PARIS — LIVE AT THE OLYMPIA . . . 22
69 Atlantic 588 169 | SOUL '69 . . . 15
69 Atlantic 588 182 | ARETHA'S GOLD . . . 15
69 Chess (S)CRL 54550 | SONGS OF FAITH . . . 15
70 Atlantic 2400 004 | THIS GIRL'S IN LOVE WITH YOU . . . 15
70 Atlantic 2464 007 | I SAY A LITTLE PRAYER . . . 15
70 Atlantic 2400 021 | DON'T PLAY THAT SONG . . . 18
71 Atlantic 2400 136 | LIVE AT THE FILLMORE WEST (gatefold sleeve) . . . 15
71 Atlantic 2400 188 | GREATEST HITS . . . 12
72 Atlantic K 40095 | SPIRIT IN THE DARK . . . 15
72 Atlantic K 40323 | YOUNG, GIFTED AND BLACK . . . 12
72 Atlantic K 60023 | AMAZING GRACE (2-LP) . . . 15
73 Atlantic K 40504 | HEY NOW HEY (THE OTHER SIDE OF THE SKY) . . . 12
74 Atlantic K 50031 | LET ME IN YOUR LIFE . . . 12
75 Atlantic K 50093 | WITH EVERYTHING I FEEL IN ME . . . 12
75 Atlantic K 50159 | YOU . . . 12
76 Atlantic K 56248 | SPARKLE (soundtrack, with Curtis Mayfield) . . . 12

ARETHA FRANKLIN & WHITNEY HOUSTON

89 Arista 612 545 | It Isn't, It Wasn't, It Ain't Never Gonna Be (Extended) (with Whitney Houston)/(Hip-Hop Remix)/Think 89 (12") . . . 8
89 Arista 612 683 | It Isn't, It Wasn't, It Ain't Never Gonna Be (with Whitney Houston)/(After Hours Club Mix)/(New Jack Swing Dub Mix) (12") . . . 8
89 Arista 662 545 | It Isn't, It Wasn't, It Ain't Never Gonna Be (Single Remix) (with Whitney Houston)/(Extended Remix)/(Hip-Hop Remix)/Think 89 (CD) . . . 8

(see also Whitney Houston)

CAROLYN FRANKLIN

69 RCA Victor RCA 1851 | Boxer/I Don't Want To Lose You . . . 7
70 RCA Victor RCA 2009 | All I Want To Be Is Your Woman/You Really Didn't Mean It . . . 5
69 RCA RD/SF 8035 | BABY DYNAMITE! (LP) . . . 15
70s Joy JOYS 180 | THE FIRST TIME I CRIED (LP) . . . 12

ERMA FRANKLIN

67 London HLZ 10170 | Piece Of My Heart/Big Boss Man . . . 18
68 London HLZ 10201 | Open Up Your Soul/I Just Ain't Ready For Love . . . 10
68 London HLZ 10220 | The Right To Cry/Don't Catch The Dog's Bone . . . 10
69 Soul City SC 118 | Don't Wait Too Long/Time After Time . . . 15
69 MCA MU 1073 | Gotta Find Me A Lover (24 Hours A Day)/Change My Thoughts From You . . . 7
71 Jay Boy BOY 36 | I Just Ain't Ready For Love/The Right To Cry . . . 6
71 Jay Boy BOY 41 | Piece Of My Heart/Big Boss Man (reissue) . . . 6
70 MCA MUP MUPS 394 | SOUL SISTER (LP) . . . 35

MINT VALUE £

MARIE FRANKLIN
68 MGM MGM 1455 You Ain't Changed/Don'tcha Bet No Money . . . 8

GORDON FRANKS
62 Parlophone R 4910 Rag Trade Rag/Sid's Tune . . . 6
62 Parlophone R 4929 Outbreak Of Murder/Johnny's Tune . . . 8
63 Decca F 11587 Sam Benedict Theme/Sweet And Sour . . . 6

JOHNNY FRANKS
55 Melodisc P 230 Tweedle Dee/Shake, Rattle And Roll (78) . . . 25
56 Melodisc 1355 Rock Candy Baby/Sing-ing-ing (78) . . . 10
58 Melodisc 1459 Good Old Country Music/Cheatin' On Me . . . 8
58 Melodisc 1459 Good Old Country Music/Cheatin' On Me (78) . . . 25

BONNIE (BLUE) FRANKSON
68 Jolly JY 014 Loving You/Shoo Be Do (both with Joe Nolan Band) . . . 10
69 Jolly JY 021 London City/Dearest (both with Joe Nolan & Dynamic Heatwave) . . . 10
69 Columbia Blue Beat DB 114 Dearest/London City . . . 12
73 Ackee ACK 512 Getting Things Together/Version . . . 6
(see also Dotty & Bonnie)

FRANTIC ELEVATORS
79 TJM TJM 5 Voice In The Dark/Passion/Every Day I Die (p/s) . . . 40
80 TJM TJM 6 Hunchback Of Notre Dame/See Nothing And Everything/Don't Judge Me (unreleased; demos only) . . . 150+
80 Eric's ERIC'S 6 You Know What You Told Me/Production Prevention (p/s) . . . 50
81 Crackin' Up CRAK 1 Searching For The Only One/Hunchback Of Notre Dame (p/s) . . . 20
82 No Waiting WAIT 1 Holding Back The Years/Pistols In My Brain (p/s) . . . 20
87 TJM TJM 101 THE EARLY YEARS (mini-LP) . . . 20
88 Receiver KNOB 2 THE EARLY YEARS (mini-LP, reissue with new sleeve & interview disc, as Mick Hucknall & Frantic Elevators) . . . 18
(see also Simply Red)

FRANTIC SPIDERS
93 Hometown FRANTIC 001 YOU'RE DEAD EP (p/s, with inserts) . . . 7

ANDY FRASER BAND
75 CBS 80731 THE ANDY FRASER BAND (LP) . . . 12
75 CBS 81027 IN YOUR EYES (LP) . . . 12
(see also Free, Sharks)

JIMMY FRASER
97 Sony NSTA1 Of Hopes And Dreams And Tombstones/PATTI AUSTIN: Are You Ready For Love (promo, 500 only) . . . 8

JOHN FRASER
58 Pye N 15098 Bye Bye Love/Why Don't They Understand? (78) . . . 8
58 Pye 7N 15118 Trolley Stop/Don't Take Your Love From Me . . . 5
58 Pye N 15118 Trolley Stop/Don't Take Your Love From Me (78) . . . 8
59 Pye 7N 15212 Bye Bye, Baby, Goodbye/Golden Cage . . . 20
59 Pye N 15212 Bye Bye, Baby, Goodbye/Golden Cage (78) . . . 20
58 Pye NEP 24068 PRESENTING JOHN FRASER (EP) . . . 20

NORTON FRASER
57 Columbia DC 709 Rock Around The Clock/Bongalulu (78) (export issue) . . . 12

FRATERNITY BROTHERS
59 HMV POP 582 Passion Flower/A Nobody Like Me (B-side with Gil Fields) . . . 8
59 HMV POP 582 Passion Flower/A Nobody Like Me (78, B-side with Gil Fields) . . . 10

FRATERNITY OF MAN
70 Stateside SS 2166 Don't Bogart Me/Wispy Paisley Skies . . . 6

ERIC FRATTER
69 Trojan TR 655 Since You've Been Gone/AFROTONES: Things I Love . . . 8
(see also Eric Fatter)

FRAYS
65 Decca F 12153 Keep Me Covered/Walk On . . . 140
65 Decca F 12229 My Girl Sloopy/For Your Precious Love . . . 50
(see also Mike Patto)

NORMA FRAZER
65 Ska Beat JB 223 Heartaches/Everybody Loves A Lover . . . 20
67 Coxsone CS 7017 The First Cut Is The Deepest/BUMPS OAKLEY: Rag Doll . . . 18
67 Studio One SO 2024 Come By Here/WAILERS: I Stand Predominate . . . 70
68 Coxsone CS 7060 Respect/Time . . . 25
(see also Sound Dimension, Righteous Homes, Viceroys, Tommy McCook)

DALLAS FRAZIER
66 Capitol CL 15445 Elvira/That Ain't No Stuff . . . 10
66 Capitol CL 15457 Just A Little Bit Of You/Walkin' Wonder . . . 8
59 Capitol EAP 1035 DALLAS FRAZIER (EP) . . . 20

FRAZIER CHORUS
87 4AD BAD 708 Sloppy Heart/Typical (12", p/s) . . . 8
87 Virgin VSCD 1192 Sloppy Heart/Anarchy In The UK/String/Typical (3" CD in heart-shaped box) . . . 15
91 Virgin CDV 2654 RAY (CD, with bonus remix CD) . . . 30

FREAKS OF NATURE
66 Island WI 3017 People! Let's Freak Out/The Shadow Chasers . . . 60
(see also Kim Fowley, Belfast Gypsies, Jackie McAuley)

MINT VALUE £

STAN FREBERG

54 Capitol CL 14187 Sh-Boom (Life Could Be A Dream) (with The Toads)/C'est Ci Bon. 35
55 Capitol CL 14316 The Lone Psychiatrist/The Honey-Earthers (with Daws Butler) 22
56 Capitol CL 14509 The Yellow Rose Of Texas/Rock Around Stephen Foster 20
56 Capitol CL 14571 The Great Pretender/The Quest For Bridey Hammerschlaugen (B-side with June Foray) 20
56 Capitol CL 14608 Heartbreak Hotel/Rock Island Line 30
57 Capitol CL 14712 Banana Boat (Day-O)/Tele-vee-shun 18
58 Capitol CL 14966 Green Chritma (with Daws Butler)/The Meaning Of Christmas (with Jud Conlon Chorale). 15
60 Capitol CL 15122 The Old Payola Roll Blues (with Jesse White)/ Sh-Boom (Life Could Be A Dream) 15
55 Capitol EAP1 496 ANY REQUESTS (EP). 12
56 Capitol EAP1 628 THE REAL SAINT GEORGE (EP). 15
61 Capitol EAP1 1101 OMAHA (EP). 12
61 Capitol EAP1 20050 THE GREAT PRETENDER (EP) 15
61 Capitol EAP1 20115 FREBERG AGAIN (EP, with Daws Butler) 12
57 Capitol T 777 A CHILD'S GARDEN OF FREBERG (LP) 30
58 Capitol LCT 6170 THE BEST OF THE STAN FREBERG SHOWS (LP) 15
58 Capitol LCT 6171 THE BEST OF THE STAN FREBERG SHOWS VOL. 2 (LP). 18
61 Capitol W 1573 PRESENTS THE UNITED STATES OF AMERICA (LP) 18
64 Capitol T 2020 THE BEST OF STAN FREBERG (LP) 15

JOHN FRED & HIS PLAYBOY BAND

67 Pye International 7N 25442 Judy In Disguise (With Glasses)/When The Lights Go Out 5
68 Pye International 7N 25453 Hey Hey Bunny/No Letter Today 7
68 Pye International 7N 25462 We Played Games/Lonely Are The Lonely. 6
68 Pye International 7N 25470 Little Dum Dum/Tissue Paper 6
68 CBS 3475 Shirley/High Heel Sneakers 10
69 MCA MU 1088 Silly Sarah Carter/Back In The USSR 5
67 Pye Intl. NPL 28111 AGNES ENGLISH (LP) 22

FRED BANANA COMBO

78 Warm AWMR 2004 No Destination Blues/Jerk Off All Nite Long (p/s) 5

FREDDIE & THE DREAMERS

63 Columbia DB 7032 If You Gotta Make A Fool Of Somebody/Feel So Blue 7
64 Columbia DB 7214 Over You/Come Back When You're Ready 5
64 Columbia DB 7286 I Love You Baby/Don't Make Me Cry 5
64 Columbia DB 7322 Just For You/Don't Do That To Me 5
65 Columbia DB 7526 A Little You/Things I'd Like To Say. 5
65 Columbia DB 7720 Thou Shalt Not Steal/I Don't Know 6
65 Columbia DC 763 A Windmill In Old Amsterdam/A Love Like You (export issue). 15
66 Columbia DB 7857 If You've Gotta Minute Baby/When I'm Home With You. 7
66 Columbia DB 7929 Playboy/Some Day. 7
66 Columbia DB 8033 Turn Around/Funny Over You 7
67 Columbia DB 8137 Hello, Hello/All I Ever Want Is You 7
67 Columbia DB 8200 Brown And Porter's (Meat Exporters) Lorry/Little Brown Eyes 12
68 Columbia DB 8496 Little Big Time/FREDDIE GARRITY: You Belong To Me. 12
68 Columbia DB 8517 It's Great/Gaberdine Mac 12
69 Columbia DB 8606 Get Around Downtown Girl/What To Do 12
71 Philips 6006 098 Susan's Tuba/You Hurt Me Girl 7
78 Polydor 2059 041 Here We Go/I Saw Ya 7
63 Columbia SEG 8275 IF YOU GOTTA MAKE A FOOL OF SOMEBODY (EP). 18
63 Columbia SEG 8287 SONGS FROM THE FILM "WHAT A CRAZY WORLD" (EP) 20
64 Columbia SEG 8302 YOU WERE MADE FOR ME (EP) 18
64 Columbia SEG 8323 OVER YOU (EP). 18
64 Columbia SEG 8349 FREDDIE SINGS JUST FOR YOU (EP) 18
65 Columbia SEG 8403 READY, FREDDIE, GO! (EP) 22
65 Columbia SEG 8457 FREDDIE AND THE DREAMERS (EP) 22
63 Columbia 33SX 1577 FREDDIE AND THE DREAMERS (LP) 30
64 Columbia 33SX 1663 YOU WERE MAD FOR ME (LP). 30
65 Columbia SX 1785 SING ALONG PARTY (LP) 25
66 Columbia S(C)X 6069 IN DISNEYLAND (LP, mono/stereo). 30/35
67 Columbia SX 6177 KING FREDDIE AND THE DREAMING KNIGHTS (LP) 35
67 M. For Pleasure MFP 1168 HITS WITH FREDDIE AND THE DREAMERS (LP, repackage of 33SX 1663) 12
60s World Record Club ST 928 SING ALONG PARTY (LP, reissue). 15
71 World Record Club ST 1050 IN DISNEYLAND (LP, reissue) 12

(see also Freddie Garrity, Dreamers)

FREDDIE & THE DREAMERS/PETER & GORDON

64 Columbia SEG 8337 JUST FOR YOU (EP, 2 tracks each) 20

(see also Peter & Gordon)

DOTTY FREDERICK

59 Top Rank JAR 106 Ricky/Just Wait. 40
59 Top Rank JAR 106 Ricky/Just Wait (78) 15

TOMMY FREDERICK & HI-NOTES

58 London HLU 8555 Prince Of Players/I'm Not Pretending 60
58 London HLU 8555 Prince Of Players/I'm Not Pretending (78). 20

BILL FREDERICKS

78 Polydor 2059 035 Almost/Wind Of Change 7

DOLORES FREDERICKS

56 Brunswick 05540 Cha Cha Joe/Whole Lotta Shakin' Goin' On 30

MARC FREDERICKS

56 London HLD 8281 Mystic Midnight/Symphony To Anne. 35

MINT VALUE £

FRED LOCKS

78 Tribesman TM 20 Love & Only Love/Stricker Ishion 12
78 Revelations FRW 375 Love & Harmony/Joy & Harmony (featuring Brigadier Jerry) (p/s). 10
78 Lloyd Coxsone LC 001 Voice Of The Poor/LEVI ROOTS: Poor Man's Story. 10

FREE (Holland)

69 Philips BF 1738 Soul Party/Down To The Bone 6
69 Philips BF 1754 Keep In Touch/Taking It Away 22

FREE (U.K.)

69 Island WIP 6054 Broad Daylight/The Worm 50
69 Island WIP 6062 I'll Be Creepin'/Sugar For Mr Morrison 50
70 Island WIP 6082 All Right Now/Mouthful Of Grass (pink label). 8
70 Island WIP 6093 The Stealer/Lying In The Sunshine 8
71 Island WIP 6100 My Brother Jake/Only My Soul 6
72 Island WIP 6129 Little Bit Of Love/Sail On. 6
72 Island WIP 6146 Wishing Well/Let Me Show You 6
73 Island WIP 6160 Travellin' In Style/Easy On My Soul. 6
76 Island WIP 6351 The Hunter/Worry. 6
85 Island 12 IS 221 Wishing Well/Woman (live)/Walk In My Shadow (live) (12", p/s) 10
78 Island IEP 6 THE FREE EP (p/s). 6
82 Island PIEP 6 THE FREE EP (12", picture disc) 10
69 Island ILPS 9089 TONS OF SOBS (LP, gatefold sleeve, 1st pressing, pink label/ black & orange 'circle' logo) 75
69 Island ILPS 9089 TONS OF SOBS (LP, gatefold sleeve, 2nd pressing, pink label/black 'block' logo) 30
70 Island ILPS 9089 TONS OF SOBS (LP, gatefold sleeve, 3rd pressing, pink label/'i' logo) 20
71 Island ILPS 9089 TONS OF SOBS (LP, gatefold sleeve, 4th pressing, pink rim label/ 'palm tree' logo) 15
69 Island ILPS 9104 FREE (LP, gatefold sleeve, 1st pressing, pink label/'i' logo). 40
70 Island ILPS 9104 FREE (LP, gatefold sleeve, 2nd pressing, pink rim label/'palm tree' logo). 15
70 Island ILPS 9120 FIRE AND WATER (LP, 1st pressing, pink label/'i' logo) 35
70 Island ILPS 9120 FIRE AND WATER (LP, 2nd pressing, pink rim label/'palm tree' logo) 15
70 Island ILPS 9138 HIGHWAY (LP) 12
71 Island ILPS 9160 LIVE (LP, in envelope sleeve with inner) 15
72 Island ILPS 9192 FREE AT LAST (LP) 12
73 Island ILPS 9217 HEARTBREAKER (LP, with inner sleeve) 12
74 Island ISLD 4 THE FREE STORY (2-LP, with 4-page booklet, numbered) 20
(see also Paul Kossoff, Rabbit, Kossoff Kirke Tetsu & Rabbit, Sharks, Andy Fraser Band, Black Cat Bones, Rock Aid Armenia)

FREE AGENTS

80 Groovy STP 1 FREE AGENTS (LP, 1000 only, hand-made sleeve) 20
(see also Pete Shelley, Eric Random)

ALAN FREED & HIS ROCK'N'ROLL BAND

57 Vogue Coral Q 72219 Teen Rock/Right Now, Right Now (with Alan Freed's Rock'n'Rollers) 125
57 Vogue Coral Q 72219 Teen Rock/Right Now, Right Now (78). 25
57 Vogue Coral Q 72230 Rock'n'Roll Boogie/Teener's Canteen (with Alan Freed's Rock'n'Rollers). 125
57 Vogue Coral Q 72230 Rock'n'Roll Boogie/Teener's Canteen (78) 25
56 Vogue Coral LVA 9033 ROCK'N'ROLL DANCE PARTY VOL. 1 (LP, featuring Modernaires) 75
57 Vogue Coral LVA 9066 ROCK'N'ROLL DANCE PARTY VOL. 2 (LP, with Jimmy Cavello) 100
(see also Jimmy Cavello)

FREE DESIGN

69 Project 3 HEAVEN/EARTH (LP) 25

FREEDOM

68 Mercury MF 1033 Where Will You Be Tonight/Trying To Get A Glimpse Of You (some in p/s) 35/15
69 Plexium PXM 3 Escape While You Can/Kandy Kay. 15
70 Probe PRO 504 Frustrated Woman/Man Made Laws. 5
71 Vertigo 6059 051 Thanks/Miss Little Louise 10
70 Probe SPBA 6252 FREEDOM (LP). 20
71 Vertigo 6360 050 THROUGH THE YEARS (LP, gatefold sleeve, swirl label) 40
72 Vertigo 6360 072 FREEDOM IS MORE THAN A WORD (LP, gatefold sleeve, swirl label) 80
(see also Procol Harum, Snafu)

FREEDOM GROUP

72 Randy's RAN 525 Sing A Song Of Freedom (actually by Max Romeo)/IMPACT ALLSTARS: Song Of Freedom (Version). 7

FREEDOM SINGERS (Jamaica)

67 Studio One SO 2010 Have Faith/Work Crazy. 22
70 Bamboo BAM 21 Give Peace A Chance/SOUND DIMENSION: In Cold Blood 15
(see also Winston Francis)

FREEDOM SINGERS (U.K.)

70 New Beat NB 059 Election (with Live Stocks)/FLECE & LIVE SHOCKS: Tomorrow's World. 8
71 New Beat NB 074 Your Testimony/Train Coming 5

FREE FERRY

69 CBS 4456 Mary, What Have You Become?/Friend 8
70 CBS 4647 Haverjack Drive/Flying. 5

FREEFORM

95 Skam SKA 3 Fane/Recut/Rail/Siamese Telebox/The Brink/Many/Freeform Dub (12") 30

ALAN FREEMAN AND THE TALMY STONE BAND

62 Decca F 11543 Madison Time/Madison Time 5

ART FREEMAN

66 Atlantic 584 053 Slippin' Around/Can't Get You Out Of My Mind. 135

MINT VALUE £

BOBBY FREEMAN

58 London HLJ 8644 Do You Want To Dance?/Big Fat Woman . . . 35
58 London HLJ 8644 Do You Want To Dance?/Big Fat Woman (78) . . . 25
58 London HLJ 8721 Betty Lou Got A New Pair Of Shoes/Starlight . . . 50
58 London HLJ 8721 Betty Lou Got A New Pair Of Shoes/Starlight (78) . . . 30
59 London HLJ 8782 Shame On You Miss Johnson/Need Your Love . . . 50
59 London HLJ 8782 Shame On You Miss Johnson/Need Your Love (78) . . . 30
59 London HLJ 8898 Mary Ann Thomas/Love Me . . . 45
59 London HLJ 8898 Mary Ann Thomas/Love Me (78) . . . 35
60 London HLJ 9031 Sinbad/Ebb Tide (The Sea) . . . 15
60 Parlophone R 4684 (I Do The) Shimmy Shimmy/You Don't Understand Me . . . 18
64 Pye International 7N 25260 C'mon And Swim (Parts 1 & 2) . . . 20
64 Pye International 7N 25280 S-W-I-M/That Little Old Heartbreaker Me . . . 25
66 Pye International 7N 25347 The Duck/Cross My Heart . . . 25
66 Pye International 7N 25347 The Duck/The Devil (2nd issue with different B-side) . . . 15

BUD FREEMAN

58 Fontana TFE 17082 CHICAGO STYLE (EP, as Bud Freeman & Orchestra) . . . 8
59 Parlophone GEP 8783 THE JAZZ SCENE (EP, as Bud Freeman & Trio) . . . 8
59 Top Rank JKR 8021 JAZZ FOR SALE VOL. 1 (EP, as Bud Freeman & Quartet) . . . 8
54 Columbia 33S 1016 COMES JAZZ (10" LP) . . . 12
55 Capitol LC 6706 CLASSICS IN JAZZ (10" LP) . . . 12
66 Fontana TL 5370 BUD FREEMAN ESQ. (LP) . . . 25
68 Fontana TL 5414 FREEMAN & CO (LP) . . . 25
73 Philips 6308 254 SONG OF THE TENOR (LP) . . . 20

CAROL FREEMAN

67 CBS 202579 The Rolling Sea/Leaving You Now . . . 12

ERNIE FREEMAN

57 London HLP 8523 Raunchy/Puddin' . . . 18
57 London HLP 8523 Raunchy/Puddin' (78) . . . 8
57 London HL 7029 Dumplin's/Beautiful Weekend (export issue) . . . 18
58 London HLP 8558 Dumplin's/Beautiful Weekend . . . 18
58 London HLP 8558 Dumplin's/Beautiful Weekend (78) . . . 12
58 London HLP 8660 Indian Love Call/Summer Serenade . . . 12
58 London HLP 8660 Indian Love Call/Summer Serenade (78) . . . 12
60 London HLP 9041 Big River/Night Sounds . . . 8
65 London HLP 9944 Raunchy '65/Jivin' Around . . . 8
56 London RE-U 1059 ERNIE FREEMAN AND HIS RHYTHM GUITAR (EP) . . . 55
59 London RE-P 1210 ERNIE FREEMAN VOL. 2 (EP) . . . 40
(see also Sir Chauncey)

EVELYN FREEMAN EXCITING VOICES

69 London HLU 10287 I Heard The Voice/I Dreamed Last Night . . . 5

GEORGE FREEMAN

71 Jay Boy BOY 54 I'm Like A Fish/Why Are You Doing This To Me . . . 25

MARGARET FREEMAN

61 Starlite ST45 040 Forbidden Fruit/Mister Ting A Ling . . . 12

PAUL FREEMAN

71 Punch PH 82 Don't Give Up/UPSETTERS: Give Up (Version) . . . 10

RUSS FREEMAN & CHET BAKER QUARTET

60 Vogue EPV 1255 RUSS FREEMAN & CHET BAKER QUARTET (EP) . . . 10
(see also Chet Baker)

FREE MOVEMENT

72 CBS 7768 The Harder I Try/Comin' Home . . . 25

FREE 'N EASY

68 Oak RGJ 628 FREE 'N EASY (LP, private pressing [Warren Coley W.C.P. 001]) . . . 110

FREE SOULS

64 Blue Beat BB 264 I Want To Be Free/Angel . . . 20

FREESTYLE ORCHESTRA

89 SBK 12SBKDJ 7011 Keep On Pumping It Up (12", promo only) . . . 15

FREEWHEELERS

65 HMV POP 1406 Why Do You Treat Me Like A Fool?/Ad Lib Blues . . . 8

FREEZE

79 A1.A.1.1.A.1 IN COLOUR (EP, p/s) . . . 10
80 A1 A.1.1.S.1 Celebration/Cross-Over . . . 8

ACE FREHLEY

78 Casablanca CAN 135 New York Groove/Snow Blind (p/s, blue vinyl with mask) . . . 35
78 Casablanca CAN 135 New York Groove/Snow Blind (no p/s, black vinyl) . . . 20
87 Atlantic A 9255T Into The Night/Fractured Too/Breakout (12", p/s) . . . 10
(see also Kiss)

DON FRENCH

59 London HLW 8884 Lonely Saturday Night/Goldilocks . . . 140
59 London HLW 8884 Lonely Saturday Night/Goldilocks (78) . . . 50
59 London HLW 8989 Little Blonde Girl/I Look Into My Heart . . . 165
59 London HLW 8989 Little Blonde Girl/I Look Into My Heart (78) . . . 65

RAY FRENCH

66 Pye 7N 17215 Since I Lost My Baby/Gun Me Down . . . 12

MINT VALUE £

FRENCH IMPRESSIONISTS

82	Operation Twilight OPT 20	Santa Baby/Jingle Bell Rock (p/s)	15
82	Operation T'light 12OPT 20	Santa Baby/Jingle Bell Rock (12", p/s)	10

(see also Aztec Camera)

FRENCH REVOLUTION

69	Decca F 22898	Nine Till Five/Why?	90

FRENZ

70	Sugar SU 101	Mee Lei Moi/I Hear Music	5

FRENZY

81	Frenzy FRENZY 1	This Is The Last Time/Gypsy Dancer (no p/s)	100
81	Frenzy FRENZY 3	Without You/Thanks For Nothing (no p/s)	150
84	Nervous NEP 002	Robot Riot/All Alone (p/s)	20
84	Nervous 12 NEP 002	Robot Riot/All Alone/Cry Or Die/Torment (12", p/s, 1st 500 on blue vinyl)	20/10
86	ABC EYE T7	I See Red/Whose Life/Don't Give Up (12", p/s)	10
85	Nervous NERD 016	HALL OF MIRRORS (LP, orange or black vinyl)	15

FRESH

70	RCA RCA 2003	Stoned In Saigon/Just A Note	6
70	RCA SF 8122	FRESH OUT OF BORSTAL (LP)	15
71	RCA LSA 3027	FRESH TODAY (LP)	12

(see also Paul Korda, Brother Bung, Fruit Machine)

FRESH

92	Magnet MAG 1008CD	Did I Say "Ti Amo" (mixes) (CD)	12

FRESH AIR

69	Pye 7N 17736	Running Wild/Stop, Look, Listen	100
72	Philips 6006 187	It Takes Too Long/Here Comes Summer	6
72	Columbia DB 8872	Bye Bye Jane/It's All Over	6

FRESHIES

78	Razz RAZZXEP 1	BAISER (EP, with Chris Sievey solo tracks, 33rpm, no'd, handwritten labels)	35
79	Razz RAZZXEP 2	STRAIGHT IN AT NO. 2 (EP, handwritten labels with inserts, 1,000 only, numbered, green or orange p/s)	15
79	Razz RAZZ 3	THE MEN FROM BANANA ISLAND WHOSE STUPID IDEAS NEVER CAUGHT ON IN THE WESTERN WORLD AS WE KNOW IT (EP, black & white photocopied p/s or numbered blue p/s)	each 10
79	Razz RAZZ 5	We're Like You/CHRIS SIEVEY: Hey (p/s)	8
80	Absurd A9	Octopus/Sheet Music	8
80	Razz RAZZ 6	Yellow Spot/If It's News (p/s)	8
80	Razz RAZZ 7	No Money/Oh Girl (p/s)	8
80	Razz RAZZ 8	RED INDIAN MUSIC (EP, with Chris Sievey)	88
80	Razz RAZZ 11	I'm In Love With The Girl On The Virgin Manchester Megastore Checkout Desk/Singalong Version (p/s, some with free lyric book)	12/8
80	Razz RAZZ 12	I'm In Love With The Girl On The Manchester Checkout Desk (Radio Version)/ Singalong Version ('bleeped') (white label radio issue, 200 only)	10
80	Razz RAZZ 13	One To One/House Beautiful (unreleased)	
81	MCA MCA 693	Wrap Up The Rockets And It's Gonna Get Better/Tell Her I'm Ill (12")	8
81	MCA MCAS 693	Wrap Up The Rockets And It's Gonna Get Better/Tell Her I'm Ill (cassette)	8
81	CV CVS 1	If You Really Love Me... Buy Me A Shirt/I Am A Walrus (p/s)	10
81	HANNA 1	Virgin Megastore/Wrap Up The Rockets/Buy Me A Shirt/Tell Her I'm Ill/ Frank Talks To Chris (Conversation) (12", white label, stickered sleeve)	8
78	Razz RAZZC 1	ALL SLEEP'S SECRETS (12-track cassette)	12
79	Razz RAZZCS-2	MANCHESTER PLAYS (cassette, radio sessions & interview, 1,000 only)	12
79	Razz RAZZCS-3	SING THE GIRLS FROM BANANA ISLAND... (16-track cassette, 1,000 only)	12
80	Razz CS-4	ROUGH AND READY (12-track cassette, 1,000 only)	12
81	Razz CS-5	LONDON PLAYS (cassette, live & radio sessions, 1,000 only)	12
85	ETS 1	JOHNNY RADAR STORY (20-track cassette, some with bonus Frank Sidebottom 8-track: "Firm Favourites")	15/12
85	ETS 1	JOHNNY RADAR STORY (LP, vinyl test pressing of cassette)	40
85	ETS 3	EARLY RAZZ (cassette)	12
85	ETS 4	STUDIO OUT-TAKES (cassette)	12

(see also Chris Sievey, Going Red?)

FRESH MAGGOTS

71	RCA RCA 2150	Car Song/What Would You Do	20
71	RCA SF 8205	FRESH MAGGOTS (LP)	200

FRESH MEAT

73	Deram DMR 384	Never Mind The Money/Candy Eyes	6

FRESHMEN

67	Pye 7N 17432	Papa Oom Mow Mow/Let's Dance	8
68	Pye 7N 17592	Go Granny Go/Look At The Sunshine	12
69	Pye 7N 17689	Just To See You Smile/Indian Lake	8
69	Pye 7N 17757	She Sang Hymns Out Of Tune/Mr. Beverly's Heavy Days	8
70	CBS 4842	Halfway To Where/Time Hasn't Changed Her	6
70	CBS 5168	Banquet For The World/Time Hasn't Changed Her	6
71	CBS 7241	One Bad Thing/Everywhere There Is Love	6
72	CBS 7694	Swanee River/Take The Time It Takes	6
68	Pye N(S)PL 18263	MOVIN' ON (LP)	50
70	CBS 64099	PEACE ON EARTH (LP)	30

FRESH WINDOWS

67	Fontana TF 839	Fashion Conscious/Summer Sun Shines	80

FRIDA

82 Epic EPC A 2603 — I Know There's Something Going On/Threnody (p/s) . . . 8
82 Epic EPC A 2863 — To Turn To Stone/I Got Something (p/s) . . . 12
83 Epic EPC A 3435 — Here We'll Stay/Strangers (p/s) . . . 8
83 Epic EPC A 3983 — Time/I Am A Seeker (p/s, with B.A. Robertson) . . . 8
84 Epic EPC A 4717 — Shine/That's Tough (p/s) . . . 8
84 Epic EPC TA 4717 — Shine (6.27 Version)/That's Tough (12", p/s) . . . 15
84 Epic EPC A 4886 — Heart Of The Country/Slowly (p/s) . . . 12
84 Epic EPC TA 4886 — Heart Of The Country/Slowly/I Know There's Something Going On (Extended) (12", p/s) . . . 20

(see also Abba)

BOY FRIDAY (& GROOVERS)

70 Downtown DT 470 — Version Girl/Grumble Man . . . 12
71 Downtown DT 471 — Music So Good/Right Track (both with Groovers) . . . 8
71 Downtown DT 472 — Sounds I Remember/JOAN LONG: Reconsider Our Love . . . 6
71 Downtown DT 473 — Take A Message Ruby/Second Note . . . 8
71 Downtown DT 476 — There'll Always Be Sunshine/Sunshine Track . . . 7
71 Downtown DT 477 — Hot Pants Girl/Raunchy . . . 6
71 Downtown DT 481 — El Raunchy/Conversation (as Boy Friday & Collins) . . . 6
71 J-Dan JDN 4416 — I Don't Want No War/Third Note Swing . . . 7
71 J-Dan JDN 4418 — Situation Version/OUR BAND: Keep Tracking . . . 7

(see also Dandy & Superboys)

CAROL FRIDAY

65 Parlophone R 5297 — Gone Tomorrow/Show Me The Way . . . 8
65 Parlophone R 5369 — Everybody I Know/Wasted Days . . . 20
67 Parlophone R 5567 — Big Sister/I Look Around Me . . . 10

FRIDAY KNIGHTS

60 Oriole CB 1579 — Poor Man's Roses/Don't Open That Door . . . 7

FRIDGE

98 Earworm WORM 37 — Deadly Cube/PORTAL: Hydro-Electric (tracing paper p/s) . . . 8

FRIDGES

80 Ink-Ink II 01 — Lynn Freeze/Shower Of B's/That's Why I Took Up The Harmonica/ No Room! (p/s, with insert) . . . 5

KINKY FRIEDMAN

74 Vanguard VSD 79333 — SOLD AMERICAN (LP) . . . 12
75 ABC ABCL 5134 — KINKY FRIEDMAN (LP) . . . 12
76 Epic EPC 81640 — LASSO FROM EL PASO (LP) . . . 12

MARTY FRIEDMAN

86 Shrapnel RR 95291 — DRAGON'S KISS (LP) . . . 12

(see also Megadeth, Cacophony)

PERRY FRIEDMAN

60 Topic TOP 56 — VIVE LA CANADIENNE (EP) . . . 8

BRIAN JOSEPH FRIEL

74 Dawn DNLS 3054 — BRIAN JOSEPH FRIEL (LP) . . . 12
75 Dawn DNLS 3064 — ARRIVERDERCI ARDROSSAN (LP) . . . 12

TERRY FRIEND & FRIENDS

77 Tramp (no cat. no.) — COME THE DAY (LP, private pressing, 100 only) . . . 40

(see also Stonefield Tramp)

FRIEND & LOVER

68 Verve VS 1515 — Reach Out Of The Darkness/Time Is On Your Side . . . 10

FRIENDLY HOPEFULS

81 Abstract ABS 004 — Tribute To The Punks Of '76/Tribute To The Punks Of '76 (Disco Dub Mix) (p/s, coloured vinyl) . . . 5

FRIENDLY PERSUASION

74 Rare Earth RES 120 — Remember (Sha La La)/I'll Always Do The Best I Can . . . 5

FRIENDS

68 Deram DM 198 — Piccolo Man/Mythological Sunday . . . 25

(see also Flowerpot Men, Ivy League)

FRIENDS

70 United Artists UP 35146 — Futz/Costa Del Sol . . . 5

FRIENDS

74 Merlin HF 4 — FRIENDS (LP, white label test pressing, 1 copy only!) . . . 1,500+

(see also Ithaca, Alice Through The Looking Glass, Agincourt, Tomorrow Come Someday, BBC Radiophonic Workshop)

FRIENDS

83 Rock Shop RSR 002 — Night Walker/Wasted Time (no p/s) . . . 25

FRIENDS AGAIN

83 Moonboot MOON 1 — Honey At The Core/Lucky Star (p/s) . . . 6
84 Mercury FAEP 1 — THE FRIENDS AGAIN EP: Lullaby No. 2 Love On Board/Wand You Wave/ Thank You For Being An Angel//Sunkissed (New Version)/ State Of Art (Remix) (double pack, stickered gatefold p/s) . . . 6

FRIENDSHIP

70 B&C CB 133 — The World Is Going To Be A Better Place/Million Hearts . . . 5

FRIENDS OF DISTINCTION

69 RCA 1838 — Grazing In The Grass/I Really Hope You Do . . . 6
70 RCA 1952 — Love Or Let Me Be Lonely/This Generation . . . 6
71 RCA LSP 4408 — WHATEVER (LP) . . . 15

MINT VALUE £

FRIENDS O' MINE

72	Westwood WRS 021	FRIENDS O' MINE (LP, 250 copies only)	110

(see also Mark Kjeldsen)

FRIJID PINK

70	Deram DM-R 288	The House Of The Rising Sun/Drivin' Blues	7
70	Deram DM 309	Sing A Song Of Freedom/End Of The Line	7
70	Deram DM 321	Heartbreak Hotel/Bye Bye Blues	8
71	Deram DM 332	Music For The People/Sloony	8
71	Deram DM 336	We're Gonna Be There (When Johnny Comes Marching Home)/Shortly Kline	7
71	Deram DM 347	Lost Son/I Love Her	7
70	Deram SML 1062	FRIJID PINK (LP)	40
70	Deram SML 1077	DEFROSTED (LP)	40

(Robert) FRIPP & (Brian) ENO

73	Island HELP 16	NO PUSSYFOOTIN' (LP)	12
75	Island HELP 22	EVENING STAR (LP)	12

(see also Giles Giles & Fripp, King Crimson, Brian Eno, Roxy Music, David Sylvian & Robert Fripp)

JACKIE FRISCO

63	Decca F 11566	You Can't Catch Me/Sugar Baby	12
63	Decca F 11692	When You Ask About Love/He's So Near	8

VONNIE FRITCHIE

55	London HLU 8178	Sugar Booger Avenue/There I Stood (To Throw Old Shoes And Rice)	60

FRED FRITH

74	Caroline C 1508	GUITAR SOLOS (LP)	12
76	Caroline C 1518	GUITAR SOLOS 2 (LP)	12

(see also Henry Cow)

FRITZ, MIKE & MO

65	Philips BF 1427	Somebody Stole The Sun/Let Me Hear Your Voice	10
65	Philips BF 1441	What Colour Is A Man?/So Now You're Gone	8

(see also Four Pennies)

LEFTY FRIZZELL

51	Columbia MC 3412	Shine Shave Shower/Look What Thoughts Will Do (78, export issue)	20
51	Columbia MC 3420	How Long Will It Take (To Stop Loving You)/Give Me More, More, More (78, export issue)	8
51	Columbia MC 3422	Travellin' Blues/I Want To Be With You Always (78, export issue)	20
51	Columbia MC 34328	Don't Stay Away (Till Love Grows Cold)/You're Here, So Everything's All Right (78, export issue)	8
52	Columbia FB 3632	Always Late (With Your Kisses)/Mom & Dad's Waltz (78)	20
63	CBS BPG 62188	THE ONE AND ONLY LEFTY FRIZZELL (LP)	15
66	CBS BPG 62595	THE SAD SIDE OF LOVE (LP)	15

EDGAR FROESE

74	Virgin V 2016	AQUA (LP)	12

(see also Tangerine Dream)

FROG

73	Jam JAM 39	Witch Hunt (Theme From Psychomania)/Living Dead (die-cut company sleeve)	100

(see also John Cameron)

WYNDER K. FROG

(see under 'W')

RAYMOND FROGGATT

68	Polydor 56249	Callow-La-Vita/Lost Autumn	6
68	Polydor 56274	Just A Little Bit Of Love/ABC Gold Fish	6
68	Polydor 56284	The Red Balloon/Lost Autumn	6
68	Polydor 56294	Rosalind/Roly	6
69	Polydor 56314	Ring Ting A Ling/Anything You Want To	6
69	Polydor 56334	Movin' Down South/It's Only Me	6
69	Polydor 56358	Lazy Jack/Hasn't The Lord Blessed Us?	6
70	Polydor 2058 028	Matter Of Pride/Fisher Boy	5
71	Bell BLL 1156	Singer/Church Fête (as Froggatt)	5
72	Bell BLL 1209	Rachel/Kentucky Sue	5
72	Bell BLL 1261	Running Water/Rock'n'Roll Song	5
74	Reprise K 14328	Roadshow/Salt	5
75	Jet JET 749	Try To Get You Into My Life/This Could Last All Night	5
69	Polydor 583 044	THE VOICE AND WRITING OF RAYMOND FROGGATT (LP)	25
72	Bell BELLS 207	BLEACH (LP)	25
74	Reprise K 44257	ROGUES AND THIEVES (LP)	15

(see also Monopoly)

FROGMEN

61	Oriole CB 1617	Underwater/Mad Rush (withdrawn)	50+

FROGMORTON

76	Philips 6006 506	White Swans/Uncivilised Man	5
76	Philips 6308 261	AT LAST (LP)	20

JANE FROMAN

55	Capitol CL 14208	The Song From "Desiree" (We Meet Again)/Mine	6
55	Capitol CL 14209	The Finger Of Suspicion Points At You/My Shining Hour	12
55	Capitol CL 14254	I Wonder/I'll Never Be The Same	12
56	Capitol CL 14658	You'll Never Walk Alone/One Little Candle	5
56	Capitol EAP1 600	JANE FROMAN (EP)	8
56	Capitol EAP1 889	SONGS AT SUNSET (EP)	8
56	Capitol EAP2 889	SONGS AT SUNSET (EP)	8
56	Capitol EAP3 889	SONGS AT SUNSET (EP)	8

MINT VALUE £

52 Capitol LC 6554 WITH A SONG IN MY HEART (10" LP) . . . 18
53 Capitol LC 6605 YOURS ALONE (10" LP) . . . 18

FRONT
77 The Label TLR 005 System/Queen's Mafia (p/s) . . . 8

DOM FRONTIERE & HIS ORCHESTRA
57 London HLU 8385 Jet Rink Ballad/Uno Mas . . . 40
57 London HLU 8385 Jet Rink Ballad/Uno Mas (78) . . . 8

FRONT LINE
65 Atlantic AT 4057 I Don't Care/Got Love . . . 35

FROST
69 Vanguard SVRL 19056 ROCK AND ROLL MUSIC (LP) . . . 22
69 Vanguard SVRL 19052 FROST MUSIC (LP) . . . 22

DAVID FROST (& others)
66 Parlophone R 5441 Zookeeper/Deck Of Cards . . . 6
66 Parlophone PMC 7005 THE FROST REPORT ON BRITAIN (LP) . . . 18
67 Pye NPL 18199 THE FROST REPORT ON EVERYTHING (LP) . . . 15

MAX FROST & TROOPERS
68 Capitol CL 15565 Shape Of Things To Come/Free Lovin' . . . 25

FROST LANE
71 Cutty Wren MM 1 FROST LANE (LP, actually various artists LP) . . . 40

FRUGAL SOUND
66 Pye 7N 17062 Norwegian Wood/Cruel To Be Kind . . . 10
66 Pye 7N 17129 Just Outside The Door/I'm On Your Side . . . 6
67 RCA Victor RCA 1556 Backstreet Girl/Reason To Believe . . . 6
67 RCA Victor RCA 1595 Abilene/Love Is A New Face . . . 5
68 RCA Victor RCA 1659 All Strung Out/Miss Mary . . . 5

FRUIT EATING BEARS
78 DJM DJS 857 Door In My Face/Going Through The Motions (company sleeve) . . . 75
78 Raw RAW 9 Chevy Heavy (p/s) . . . 25

FRUIT GUMS
70 Fab FAB 138 Sweet Pork/Crying All Night . . . 6

FRUIT MACHINE
69 Spark SRL 1003 Follow Me/Cuddly Toy . . . 40
69 Spark SRL 1027 I'm Alone Today/Sunshine Of Your Love (some in title p/s) . . . 140/80
(see also Rare Bird)

FRUMPY
71 Philips 6003 133 Life Without Pain/Morning . . . 5
71 Philips 6305 067 ALL WILL BE CHANGED (LP) . . . 15
72 Philips 6305 098 FRUMP 2 (LP, black & blue vinyl) . . . 20
(see also Atlantis)

FRUUPP
74 Dawn DNS 1087 Prince Of Heaven/Jaunting Car . . . 10
73 Dawn DNLS 3053 FUTURE LEGENDS (LP) . . . 25
74 Dawn DNLS 3058 SEVEN SECRETS (LP, with lyric insert) . . . 25
74 Dawn DNLH 2 THE PRINCE OF HEAVEN'S EYES (LP, some with book) . . . 35/25
75 Dawn DNLS 3070 MODERN MASQUERADES (LP, with lyric insert) . . . 25

FUCHSIA
71 Pegasus PEG 8 FUCHSIA (LP) . . . 180

FUD (Christian) & DEL
73 Duke DU 165 Beef Sticker/PRINCE HERON: Ten Commandments . . . 6
73 Songbird SB 1086 Dr. Fud/FUD CHRISTIAN ALLSTARS: La-Fud-Del Skank . . . 6

FUD CHRISTIAN ALLSTARS
71 Big Shot BI 571 Never Fall In Love (actually by Winston Heywood)/
Never Fall In Love Version . . . 7
(see also Linkers, Ansel Linkers)

FUGI
71 Blue Horizon 2096 005 Red Moon (Parts 1 & 2) . . . 22

FUGITIVE
81 private pressing FMR 050 Need My Freedom . . . 20

FUGITIVES (Jamaica)
67 Doctor Bird DB 1082 Musical Pressure/LESLIE BUTLER & FUGITIVES: Winchester Rocksteady . . . 22
(see also Jo Jo Bennett & Fugitives, Two Kings, Jo Jo Bennett, Stranger Cole)

FUGITIVES (U.S.)
61 Vogue V 9176 Freeway/Fugitive . . . 35

FUGS
68 Big T BIG 115 Crystal Liaison/When The Mode Of The Music Changes . . . 8
68 Transatlantic TRA 180 TENDERNESS JUNCTION (LP, some with poster) . . . 30/18
68 Transatlantic TRA 181 IT CRAWLED INTO MY HAND, HONEST (LP) . . . 18
69 Fontana (S)TL 5501 VIRGIN FUGS (LP) . . . 22
69 Fontana (S)TL 5513 THE FUGS ... FIRST ALBUM (LP) . . . 22
69 Fontana (S)TL 5524 FUGS II (LP) . . . 22
69 Reprise RSLP 6359 THE BELLE OF AVENUE A (LP) . . . 15
75 ESP-Disk ESP 2018 ROUNDERS SCORE (LP) . . . 12

HIROSHI FUKUMURA
80 Champagne HUNT UP THE WIND (LP) . . . 12

MINT VALUE £

FULHAM FURIES
78 GM GMS 9050 These Boots Are Made For Walking/Under Pressure (no p/s) 35
(see also Lurkers)

BLIND BOY FULLER
57 Philips BBL 7512 BLIND BOY FULLER 1935-40 (LP) 45
68 Matchbox SDR 143 BLIND BOY FULLER ON DOWN VOLUME 1 (LP) 20
69 Matchbox SDR 168 BLIND BOY FULLER ON DOWN VOLUME 2 (LP) 20
60s Flyright LP 105 CAROLINA BLUES (LP) 12

GIL FULLER & DIZZY GILLESPIE
66 Fontana 688 147 ZL MAN FROM MONTEREY (LP) 12
(see also Dizzy Gillespie)

BOBBY FULLER FOUR
66 London HLU 10030 I Fought The Law/Little Annie Lou 25
66 London HLU 10041 Love's Made A Fool Of You/Don't You Ever Let Me Know 20
73 President PT 394 Another Sad And Lonely Night/Only When I Dream 10
67 President PTL 1003 MEMORIAL ALBUM (LP) 40
(see also Randy Fuller)

JERRY FULLER
59 London HLH 8982 The Tennessee Waltz/Charlene 12
59 London HLH 8982 The Tennessee Waltz/Charlene (78) 25
61 London HLN 9439 Guilty Of Loving You/First Love Never Dies 10
62 Salvo SLO 1802 Lipstick And Rouge/Mother Goose At The Bandstand (99 copies only) 150

JESSE FULLER
65 Good Time Jazz GV 2426 San Francisco Bay Blues/New Midnight Special 7
67 Good Time Jazz GV 2427 Runnin' Wild/The Monkey And The Engineer 7
67 Fontana TF 821 Going Back To My Old Used To Be/Bye And Bye 15
58 Good Time Jazz LAG 12159 JESSE FULLER (LP) 18
60 Good Time Jazz LAG 12279 LONE CAT (LP) 18
60 Topic 10T 59 WORKING ON THE RAILROAD (10" LP) 25
63 Good Time Jazz LAG 574 SAN FRANCISCO BAY BLUES (LP) 15
65 Stateside SL 10154 JESSE FULLER'S FAVOURITES (LP) 15
66 Fontana TL 5313 SESSION WITH JESSE FULLER (LP) 18
66 Topic 12T 134 MOVE ON DOWN THE LINE (LP) 25
66 Stateside SL 10166 SAN FRANCISCAN BAY BLUES (LP, reissue) 12
60s Vocalion VRLP 574 SAN FRANCISCO BAY BLUES (LP) 18
60s Evolution Z 1004 LIVE IN LONDON (LP) 15

JOHNNY FULLER
73 Speciality SON 5017 Haunted House/Swinging At The Creek 6

RANDY FULLER
67 President PT 111 It's Love, Come What May/The Things You Do 12
(see also Bobby Fuller Four)

WALTER 'GIL' FULLER
51 Vogue V 2037 The Scene Changes/Mean To Me (78) 8

FULL MOON
89 private pressing LUNAR 13 FULL MOON (LP, private pressing) 12
90 private pressing LUNAR 14 A LIVE ENCOUNTER (LP, private pressing) 15

FULL TIME MEN
86 Shigaku SHIG 1T I Got Wheels/One More Time/Way Down South (12", p/s) 8
(see also R.E.M.)

LOWELL FULSON/FULSOM
53 London L 1199 I Love My Baby/The Blues Came Rollin' In (78) 55
65 Sue WI 375 Too Many Drivers/Key To Your Heart 25
66 Sue WI 4023 Talking Woman/Blues Around Midnight 40
66 Outasite 45-502 Stop And Think/Baby (with Leon Blue) 70
66 Polydor 56515 Black Nights/Little Angel 18
67 Fontana TF 795 Tramp/Pico 25
76 Jet JET 770 Do You Love Me?/Monday Morning 6
69 Fontana SFJL 920 SAN FRANCISCO BLUES (LP) 40
69 Polydor 2384 038 IN A HEAVY BAG (LP, as Lowell Fulsom) 22

FUMBLE
72 Sovereign SOV 110 Hullo Mary Lou/Hanging On 5
73 Sovereign SOV 118 Million Seller/Get Up 5
73 Sovereign SOV 121 Alexandra Park/Mama I Can't Tell You 5
72 Sovereign SVNA 7254 FUMBLE (LP, gatefold sleeve) 18
74 RCA SF 8403 POETRY IN LOTION (LP) 12

FUNBOY FIVE
80s Cool Cat Daddy-O PHUN 1 Life After Death/Compulsive Eater (foldover p/s) 6

FUNERAL FOR A FRIEND
02 Mighty Atom MTY 338 Between Order And Model/Juno/Red Is The New Black (CD) 35
03 Infectious EW 269 Juneau/Getaway Plan (white vinyl, p/s) 10
03 Infectious EW 269CD 1 Juneau/Getaway Plan (CD, card sleeve) 8
03 Warner EW 274 She Drove Me To Daytime TV/Bullet Theory (blue vinyl, p/s) 8
00s Infectious INFEC 126S Four Ways — This Year's Most Open Heartbreak/She Drove Me To Daytime Television//Kiss And Make Up (All Bets Are Off)/Escape Artists Never Die (2 x 7", red vinyl, gatefold p/s) 10
00s Infectious INFEC 12CDS Four Ways — This Year's Most Open Heartbreak/She Drove Me To Daytime Television/Kiss And Make Up (All Bets Are Off)/Escape Artists Never Die (CD, 2000 only) 10

FUN FOUR
80 NMC NMC 010 Singing In The Showers/By Products/Elevator Crush (p/s) . . . 25
(see also Orange Juice)

FUNGUS
73 Fungus FUN 1 Premonitions Parts 1 & 2 (private pressing) . . . 200+
(see also Secondhand, Seventh Wave)

FUNHOUSE
82 Ensign ENY 222 Out Of Control/This Could Be Hell (p/s) . . . 6
82 Ensign ENYT 222 Out Of Control (Full Version)/This Could Be Hell (12", p/s) . . . 10
(see also Another Pretty Face, DNV, Waterboys)

FARLEY 'JACKMASTER' FUNK
86 London LONX 105 Love Can't Turn Around (12", featuring Darryl Pandy) . . . 10

FUNKADELIC
70 Pye International 7N 25519 I Got A Thing, You Got A Thing, Everybody's Got A Thing/Fish, Chips & Sweat . . 10
71 Pye International 7N 25548 You & Your Folks, Me & Mine/Funky Dollar Bill . . . 10
71 Janus 6146 001 Can You Get To That/Back In Our Minds . . . 7
78 Warner Bros K 17246 One Nation Under A Groove (Parts 1 & 2) . . . 5
78 Warner Bros K 17246T One Nation Under A Groove (Parts 1 & 2) (12") . . . 10
79 Warner Bros K 17321 Cholly (Funk Getting Ready To Roll)/Into You . . . 5
79 Warner Bros K 17494 (Not Just) Knee Deep (Parts 1 & 2) . . . 8
81 Warner Bros K 17786 The Electric Spanking Of War Babies/(Instrumental Mix) (p/s) . . . 5
81 Warner Bros K 17786T The Electric Spanking Of War Babies/(Instrumental Mix) (12") . . . 8
70 Pye Intl. NSPL 28137 FUNKADELIC (LP) . . . 40
71 Pye Intl. NSPL 28144 FREE YOUR MIND AND YOUR ASS WILL FOLLOW (LP) . . . 40
71 Janus 6310 201 MAGGOT BRAIN (LP) . . . 40
75 20th Century W 215 LET'S TAKE IT TO THE STAGE (LP) . . . 12
78 Warner Bros K 56299 HARDCORE JOLLIES (LP) . . . 15
78 Warner Bros K 56539 ONE NATION UNDER A GROOVE
(LP, some with free 12" "One Nation Under A Groove") . . . 15/12
79 Warner Bros K 56712 UNCLE JAM WANTS YOU (LP, gatefold sleeve) . . . 15
81 Warner Bros K 56299 THE ELECTRIC SPANKING OF WAR BABIES (LP) . . . 12
(see also Parliament, Parlet, Brides Of Funkenstein, Bootsy's Rubber Band, Dolby's Cube, P-Funk Allstars)

FUNKEES
76 Black Magic BM 114 Abraka/Ole . . . 6
75 Contempo CS 2058 Tu Lay/Cool It Down . . . 6

FUNKMASTERS
84 Master Funk MF4 It's Over/(Versions) (12") . . . 8

FUNKY BOTTOM CONGREGATION
69 Beacon BEA 122 Hare-Krishna/Things About Yourself . . . 6

FUNKY JUNCTION
73 Stereo Gold Award MER 373 PLAY TRIBUTE TO DEEP PURPLE (LP) . . . 15

FINBAR & EDDIE FUREY
72 Dawn DNS 1025 Her Father Didn't Like Me Anyway/Reynardine . . . 5
68 Transatlantic TRA 168 FINBAR AND EDDIE FUREY (LP) . . . 20
69 Xtra XTRA 1077 TRADITIONAL IRISH PIPE MUSIC (LP) . . . 20
69 Transatlantic TRA 191 THE LONESOME BOATMAN (LP) . . . 18
72 Dawn DNLS 3037 THE DAWNING OF THE DAY (LP, with lyric insert) . . . 20

FINBAR FUREY & BOB STEWART
76 Crescent ARS 110 TOMORROW WE PART (LP) . . . 12

FUR FUR
80s Daark Inc. D.I. 7 FUR FUR (cassette) . . . 12
(see also Karl Blake, Danielle Dax, Lemon Kittens, Gland Shrouds)

FURRY DICE
80 White Line WHLS 001 Rudi Don't Take Your Love To Town/K.G.B. (p/s) . . . 6

TOMMY FURTADO
57 London HLA 8418 Sun Tan Sam/Isabella . . . 30
57 London HLA 8418 Sun Tan Sam/Isabella (78) . . . 8

BILLY FURY
78s
59 Decca F 11102 Maybe Tomorrow/Gonna Type A Letter . . . 100
59 Decca F 11128 Margo/Don't Knock Upon My Door . . . 150
59 Decca F 11158 Angel Face/Time Has Come . . . 200
59 Decca F 11189 My Christmas Prayer/Last Kiss . . . 300
SINGLES
59 Decca F 11102 Maybe Tomorrow/Gonna Type A Letter (triangular centre, later round) . . . 25
59 Decca F 11128 Margo/Don't Knock Upon My Door (triangular centre, later round) . . . 25/30
59 Decca F 11158 Angel Face/Time Has Come (triangular centre, later round) . . . 30/20
59 Decca F 11189 My Christmas Prayer/Last Kiss (triangular centre, later round) . . . 65/35
60 Decca F 11200 Colette/Baby How I Cried (triangular centre, later round) . . . 40/15
60 Decca F 11237 That's Love/You Don't Know (as Billy Fury & Four Jays) . . . 20
60 Decca F 11267 Wondrous Place/Alright, Goodbye . . . 25
60 Decca F 11311 A Thousand Stars/Push Push . . . 12
61 Decca F 11334 Don't Worry/Talkin' In My Sleep (with Four Kestrels) . . . 15
61 Decca F 11349 Halfway To Paradise/Cross My Heart . . . 10
61 Decca F 11384 Jealousy/Open Your Arms . . . 10
61 Decca F 11409 I'd Never Find Another You/Sleepless Nights . . . 10
62 Decca F 11437 Letter Full Of Tears/Magic Eyes . . . 10
62 Decca F 11458 Last Night Was Made For Love/King For Tonight . . . 10
62 Decca F 11485 Once Upon A Dream/If I Lose You . . . 10

			MINT VALUE £
62	Decca F 11508	Because Of Love/Running Around	10
63	Decca F 11582	Like I've Never Been Gone/What Do You Think You're Doing Of?	10
63	Decca F 11655	When Will You Say I Love You?/All I Wanna Do Is Cry	10
63	Decca F 11701	In Summer/I'll Never Fall In Love Again	10
63	Decca F 11744	Somebody Else's Girl/Go Ahead And Ask Her	10
63	Decca F 11792	Do You Really Love Me Too?/What Am I Gonna Do?	10
64	Decca F 11888	I Will/Nothin' Shakin' (But The Leaves On The Trees) (some B-sides list "Nothin' Shakin' ")	each 15
64	Decca F 11939	It's Only Make Believe/Baby What Do You Want Me To Do?	15
64	Decca F 40719	Hippy Hippy Shake/Glad All Over (export-only, some with p/s)	80/50
65	Decca F 12048	I'm Lost Without You/You Better Believe It, Baby	10
65	Decca F 12178	In Thoughts Of You/Away From You	10
65	Decca F 12230	Run To My Lovin' Arms/Where Do You Run?	10
66	Decca F 12325	I'll Never Quite Get Over You/I Belong To The Wind	10
66	Decca F 12409	Don't Let A Little Pride Stand In Your Way/Didn't See The Real Thing Come Along	12
66	Decca F 12459	Give Me Your Word/She's So Far Out She's In	15
67	Parlophone R 5560	Hurtin' Is Loving/Things Are Changing	18
67	Parlophone R 5605	Loving You/I'll Go Along With It Now	12
67	Parlophone R 5634	Suzanne In The Mirror/It Just Don't Matter Now	15
67	Parlophone R 5658	Beyond The Shadow Of A Doubt/Baby Do You Love Me?	12
68	Parlophone R 5681	Silly Boy Blue/One Minute Woman	30
68	Parlophone R 5723	Phone Box/Any Morning Now	18
68	Parlophone R 5747	Lady/Certain Things	18
69	Parlophone R 5788	I Call For My Rose/Bye Bye	18
69	Parlophone R 5819	All The Way To The U.S.A./Do My Best For You	25
70	Parlophone R 5845	Why Are You Leaving?/Old Sweet Roll (Hi-De-Ho)	35
70	Parlophone R 5874	Paradise Alley/Well ... All Right	40
72	Fury FY 301	Will The Real Man Please Stand Up/At This Stage	25
74	Warner Bros WB 16402	I'll Be Your Sweetheart/Fascinating Candle Flame	30
76	NEMS NES 018	Halfway To Paradise/Turn My Back On You	12
81	Polydor POSP 355	Be Mine Tonight/No Trespassers (p/s)	10
82	Polydor POSP 488	Love Or Money/Love Sweet Love (p/s)	8
82	Polydor POSP 528	Devil Or Angel/Don't Tell Me Lies ('guitar' or 'microphone' p/s)	8/15
83	Polydor POSP 558	Forget Him/Your Words (p/s)	10
83	Polydor POSP 558	Let Me Go Lover/Your Words (same p/s as above but diff. A-side, 500 only)	35
83	Lyntone LYN 13078/BF 1	Devil Or Angel/Lost Without You (flexi free within memorial concert booklet)	20/6
83	private pressing	BILLY FURY IN INTERVIEW WITH STUART COLEMAN (10", 500 white label copies only, 1st 200 numbered)	40/35

EPs

59	Decca DFE 6597	MAYBE TOMORROW (triangular centre, orange/red p/s)	90
59	Decca DFE 6597	MAYBE TOMORROW (round centre, orange/red or yellow p/s)	75/60
61	Decca DFE 6694	BILLY FURY	60
62	Decca DFE 6699	BILLY FURY NO. 2	60
62	Decca DFE 6708	PLAY IT COOL	35
62	Decca DFE 6708	PLAY IT COOL (export issue, blue/green 'crouching' cover)	100+
62	Decca DFE 8505	BILLY FURY HITS	30
63	Decca DFE 8525	BILLY FURY AND THE TORNADOS	40
63	Decca DFE 8558	AM I BLUE	45
65	Decca DFE 8641	BILLY FURY AND THE GAMBLERS	125
73	Ronco MR EP 001	LONG LIVE ROCK (with others, no p/s)	30
83	Decca DFE 8686	MY CHRISTMAS PRAYER	15

LPs

60	Decca LF 1329	THE SOUND OF FURY (10")	200+
60	Ace Of Clubs ACL 1047	BILLY FURY	35
61	Ace Of Clubs ACL 1083	HALFWAY TO PARADISE	35
63	Decca LK 4533	BILLY	40
63	Decca LK 4548/SKL 4548	WE WANT BILLY! (with Tornados, mono/stereo)	40/55
65	Decca LK 4677	I'VE GOTTA HORSE (soundtrack)	70
67	Ace Of Clubs ACL 1229	THE BEST OF BILLY FURY	25
71	Decca SPA 188	THE WORLD OF BILLY FURY (mono/stereo)	each 15
72	Decca SPA 575	THE WORLD OF BILLY FURY VOLUME 2	20
76	Decca DPA 3033/4	THE BILLY FURY STORY (2-LP)	15
81	Decca LFT 1329	THE SOUND OF FURY (10", reissue)	20
83	Red Bus BUSLP 1003	THE MISSING YEARS	15

(see also Tornados, Gamblers)

FURYS

63	Stateside SS 182	Never More/Zing! Went The Strings Of My Heart	12
72	Jay Boy BOY 61	What Is Soul?/I Lost My Baby	6
72	Jay Boy BOY 68	I'm Satisfied With You/Just A Little Mixed Up	7

FURY'S TORNADOES

74	Warner Bros K 16442	Telstar '74/I Would Give You Anything	10

(see also Billy Fury)

F.U.S.E.

93	Warp WAP38	TRAIN TRACS (12", some white vinyl, p/s)	15/10
93	Warp LP12LTD	DIMENSION INTRUSION (2-LP, white vinyl)	30

FUSION

79	Plastic Fantastic PFUL 1104	COLD OUTSIDE EP (12")	8
80	Telephone TEL 101	TILL I HEAR FROM YOU (LP, blue vinyl)	20

(see also Nik Kershaw)

FUSION ORCHESTRA

73	EMI EMI 2056	When My Mama's Not At Home/Nuthouse Rock	6
73	EMI EMA 758	A SKELETON IN ARMOUR (LP, gatefold sleeve)	35

FUT

70 Beacon BEA 160 — Have You Heard The Word/Futting Around ... 30
(see also Graham Bonnet, Bee Gees, Marbles, Maurice Gibb, Steve & Stevie; this record has NO Beatles involvement)

FUTUREHEADS

03 Fantastic Plastic FP 7035 — 1-2-3-NUL! EP: Carnival Kids/Ticket/Cabaret/A Picture Of Dorian Gray (p/s, with sticker and badge) ... 10
00s Project Cosmonaut PCOS 001 — Nul Book Standard — Park Inn/Robot/My Rules/Stupid And Shallow (p/s) ... 20
00s Fantastic Plastic FP 7036 — First Day/Balsch/Piece Of Crap (red or clear vinyl, p/s, 500 only) ... 7

FUTURE KINGS OF SPAIN

00s Red Flag RF 01CDS — A Place For Everything And Everything In Its Place/Your Starlight/Love Of The Common Man (CD, card sleeve) ... 10

FUTURE PAST

91 B12 03 — Our Paths Meet/Harmony Park/Your Hand In My Mind/Dance Intellect/ TV People (12", black vinyl) ... 40

FUTURES

75 Buddah BDS 430 — You Better Be Certain/No One Could Compare ... 6
75 Buddah BDLP 4031 — CASTLES IN THE SKY (LP) ... 12

FUTURE SOUND OF LONDON

SINGLES

91 Jumpin' & Pumpin' TOT 17 — Papua New Guinea/Papua New Guinea (Andrew Weatherall Mix) (p/s) ... 8
94 Virgin PROMO 500 — Slider/Snake Hips/You're Creeping Me Out/Herd Killing/Live In New York (double pack, promo only, 500 copies) ... 30

12" SINGLES

91 Jumpin' & Pumpin' 12TOT 11 — PULSE: Bring On The Pulse/In The Mind Of A Child/ Hardhead/Pulse State ... 12
91 Jumpin' & Pumpin' 12TOT 16 — PULSE 3: Tingler/Owl/Bite The Bullet/Calcium ... 12
91 Jumpin' & Pumpin' 12TOT 17 — Papua New Guinea (Dali Mix)/(Dumb Child Of Q Mix)/ (Qube Mix) (p/s) ... 12
92 Jumpin' & Pumpin' 12TOT 17R — Papua New Guinea (Andrew Weatherall Mix)/(Dub Mix)/(Journey To Pyramid)/ (Monsoon Mix)/(Graham Massey Mix)/(Dumb Child Of Q Mix) (p/s) ... 12
94 Virgin VST 1540P — Far Out Son Of Lung And The Ramblings Of A Madman/ Snake Hips/Smokin' Japanese Babe/Amoeba (white vinyl, promo only) ... 30
95 Virgin SEMTEX DJ 1 — Semtex (Part 1)/Semtex (Part 2)/We Have Explosive/Semtex (stamped sleeve, promo only, 500 copies) ... 15
97 Virgin VSTDJ 1616 — We Have Explosive Mantronix Plastik Formula (Mix 1)/(Mix 2) (stickered sleeve, promo only) ... 8
97 Virgin VSTXDJ 1616 — We Have Explosive (Original Mix)/(Leon Mar Mix)/ (Oil Funk Mix)/(Part 4)/(Part 5) (stickered black sleeve, promo only) ... 8

12" EPs

91 Jumpin' & Pumpin' 12TOT 15 — PRINCIPALS OF MOTION EP ... 12
91 Jumpin' & Pumpin' 12TOT 18 — SMART SYSTEMS EP ... 12
92 Jumpin' & Pumpin' 12TOT 25 — PULSE 4 (I'm Not Gonna Let You Do It/The Creator/Shrink/ 18 Space Virus) ... 12
92 Union City UCRT 11 — METROPOLIS EP ... 12
93 Virgin VST 1478 — CASCADE EP ... 12

CD SINGLES

92 Jumpin' & Pumpin' CDSTOT 17 — Papua New Guinea/(Andrew Weatherall Mix)/(Dub Mix)/ (Journey To Pyramid)/(Graham Mix)/ (Dumb Child Of Of Q)/(Hamish McDonald Mix) ... 12
93 Virgin VSCDT 1478 — Cascade (Part 1)/(Part 2)/(Part 3)/(Part 4)/(Part 5)/Short Form ... 8
96 Virgin VCD 1605 — MY KINGDOM (5 mixes & radio edits, card slipcase, promo only) ... 10
96 Virgin VSCDDJ 1805 — My Kingdom (Media Mix)/(Part 4) (card sleeve, promo only) ... 10

ALBUMS

92 Jumpin'/Pumpin' LPTOT 2 — ACCELERATOR (2-LP) ... 15
94 Virgin V 2755 — ISDN (LP, embossed, fold-out black sleeve with insert) ... 30
94 Virgin CDV 2755 — ISDN (CD, embossed black wallet) ... 25
97 Virgin ISDNSHOW 1 — ISDN SHOW (CD, promo only, no inlay) ... 25
(see also Amorphous Androgynous, Art Science Technology, Humanoid, Humanoid featuring Sharon Benson, Intelligent Communications, Mental Cube, Metropolis, Pulse Systems, Semi Real, Smart Systems, Yage, Stakker)

FUZZ

71 Mojo 2092 003 — I Love You For All Seasons (Parts 1 & 2) ... 7
71 Mojo 2092 008 — Like An Open Door/Leave It All Behind ... 7
71 Mojo 2916 010 — FUZZ (LP) ... 30

FUZZ FACE

68 Page One POF 065 — Mighty Quinn/Voices From The Sky ... 6

FUZZTONES

85 ABC S 006 — She's Wicked/Epitaph For A Head (p/s) ... 6

FUZZY DUCK

71 MAM MAM 37 — Double Time Woman/Just Look Around You ... 15
71 MAM MAM 51 — Big Brass Band/One More Hour ... 15
71 MAM AS 1005 — FUZZY DUCK (LP, with poster) ... 125
90 Reflection MM 05 — FUZZY DUCK (LP, reissue with booklet & single "Double Time Woman"/ "One More Hour" [MMS 01]) ... 15
(see also Andromeda, Greatest Show On Earth)

MINT VALUE £

FX

79	own label	THE SOUTH'S GONNA RISE AGAIN (EP)	100+

FYNN McCOOL

70	RCA RCA 1956	U.S. Thumbstyle/Diamond Lil	8
70	RCA SF 8112	FYNN McCOOL (LP, gatefold sleeve)	50

(see also Shakespears, Grapefruit, Sleepy)

TOMMY G & CHARMS

67	London HLB 10107	I Know What I Want/I Want You So Bad	40

WINSTON G (& WICKED)

65	Parlophone R 5266	Please Don't Say/Like A Baby	35
66	Parlophone R 5330	Until You Were Gone/That Way Too (as Winston G. & Wicked)	15
66	Decca F 12444	Cloud Nine/I'll Make You Cry Tomorrow	18
67	Decca F 12559	Mother Ferguson's Love Dust/Judge And Jury	22
67	Decca F 12623	Riding With The Milkman/Bye Bye Baby	22

B(ASIL) GABBIDON

61	Blue Beat BB 069-A	Warpaint Baby (miscredited to B. Cabbidon & Buster's Group)/ I Was Wrong (miscredited to Chuck & Dobbie with Buster's Group)	18
62	Blue Beat BB 111-A	Ivoree/Lover Man	15
62	Blue Beat BB 124	Independence Blues/For My Love (as B. Gabbidon)	15
62	Blue Beat BB 129-A	Our Melody/Going Back To Ja (with Randy's All Stars)	15
62	Island WI 033	I Found My Baby (actually by Roy Braham)/No Fault Of Mine	22
63	Island WI 076	I Bet You Don't Know/3 x 7	22
63	Island WI 089	St. Louis Woman/Get On The Ball	20
63	Blue Beat BB 155-A	Eana Mena/Since You Are Gone (with Prince Buster All Stars)	15
63	Blue Beat BB 161	I'll Find Love (with Prince Buster All Stars)/ MELLOW LARKS: What You Gonna Do?	15
65	Blue Beat BB 288	Tick Tock (actually by Theo Beckford)/The Streets Of Glory (actually by Theo Beckford & Yvonne Harrison)	15

(see also Derrick Patsy & Basil, Mellow Larks, Derrick Morgan)

PETER GABRIEL

77	Charisma CB 301	Solsbury Hill/Moribund The Burgermeister (p/s)	10
77	Charisma CB 302	Modern Love/Slowburn (no p/s, 'nude' picture label, withdrawn)	40
78	Charisma CB 311	D.I.Y./Perspective (p/s, purple label, Irish-only sleeve)	10
78	Charisma CB 311	D.I.Y./Perspective (p/s, silver label, possibly Irish-only sleeve)	10
78	Charisma CB 319	D.I.Y. (Remix)/Mother Of Violence/Teddy Bear (no p/s, withdrawn)	25
78	Sound For Industry SFI 381	Solsbury Hill (live) (1-sided flexidisc, concert freebie)	8
80	Charisma CB 354	Games Without Frontiers/The Start/I Don't Remember (p/s)	5
80	Charisma CB 370	Biko/Shosholoza/Jetzt Kommt Die Flut (p/s, 33rpm)	5
80	Charisma CB 360	No Self Control/Lead A Normal Life (p/s)	8
82	Charisma SHOCK 1	Shock The Monkey/Soft Dog (Instrumental) (p/s)	8
82	Charisma SHOCK 1	Shock The Monkey/Shock The Monkey (Instrumental) (same p/s as above)	30
82	Charisma SHOCK 122	Shock The Monkey/Soft Dog (Instrumental) (picture disc)	10
82	Charisma SHOCK 12	Shock The Monkey/Soft Dog (Instrumental) (12", p/s)	8
82	Charisma SHOCK 350	Shock The Monkey/Shock The Monkey (Instrumental) (12", same p/s as above [SHOCK 12])	20
82	Charisma CB 405	I Have The Touch/Across The River (p/s)	15
83	Charisma GAB 12	I Don't Remember (live)/Solsbury Hill (live)/Kiss Of Life (live) (12", shrinkwrapped stickered double pack, with 12" white label [GAB 122], "Games Without Frontiers"/"Schnappschuss (Ein Familienfoto)", no p/s)	12
86	Charisma/Virgin PGT 112	Sledgehammer (Dance Mix)/Don't Break This Rhythm/Sledgehammer (Album Version)/Biko (Original 12" Mix) (cassette, silver card box)	10
87	Charisma/Virgin GAIL 312	Big Time (Extended Version)/Curtains/No Self Control (live)/ Across The River/Big Time (7" Version) (CD, gatefold card p/s)	8
88	Charisma/Virgin CDT 4	Sledgehammer/Don't Break This Rhythm/ I Have The Touch ('85 Remix) (3" CD, card p/s)	8
88	Charisma/Virgin CDT 33	Solsbury Hill/Moribund The Burgermeister/Solsbury Hill (live) (3" CD, card p/s)	8
92	Virgin PGS 7	Digging In The Dirt/Bashi-Bazouk (black label, jukebox issue)	7
92	Virgin PGSDG 712	Digging In The Dirt/Digging In The Dirt (Instrumental)/Quiet Steam/ Bashi-Bazouk (12", p/s, withdrawn)	15
92	Virgin PGSDG 7	Digging In The Dirt/Digging In The Dirt (Instrumental)/Quiet Steam/ Bashi-Bazouk (CD, picture disc in box with lyric sheet)	10
92	Virgin PGSDX 8	Steam/Games Without Frontiers (Massive DB Mix)/Steam (Oh, Oh, Let Off Steam Mix)/Games Without Frontiers (live) (CD in fold-out house-shaped box)	12
92	Virgin PGS 9	Blood Of Eden/Mercy Street (p/s)	5
92	Virgin PGSDX 9	Blood Of Eden/Mercy Street/Sledgehammer (CD, foldout sleeve with booklet)	12
92	Virgin PGSDX 10	Kiss That Frog (Edit)/Across The River/Kiss That Frog (Mindbender Mix Edit)/ Shakin' The Tree (Bottrill Remix) (CD, digipak with postcards)	8
80	Reformation RSR 113	CHROMEDOME (LP)	25
86	Virgin PGCDP 5	SO (CD, picture disc)	18

(see also Genesis, Youssou 'Ndour & Peter Gabriel, Colin Scot, Charlie Drake)

PETER GABRIEL & KATE BUSH

86 Charisma/Virgin PGSP 2 Don't Give Up/In Your Eyes (Special Mix) (poster p/s in stickered PVC sleeve) . . . 15
86 Charisma/Virgin PGS 212 Don't Give Up/In Your Eyes (Special Mix)/This Is The Picture (Excellent Birds) (12", p/s) . . . 8
(see also Kate Bush)

RUSS GABRIEL

95 Input Neuron INMD(X)1 FUTURE FUNK VOL. 1 (12", double pack, p/s) . . . 15

GABRIEL & ANGELS

63 Stateside SS 150 That's Life That's Tough/Don't Wanna Twist No More . . . 15

GABRIELLI BRASS

65 Polydor 56031 Angel Cake/Cat Walk . . . 5
65 Polydor 56047 Ride Your Pony/Anyone Who Had A Heart . . . 6
68 Polydor 56252 'Canterbury Tales' Theme/Working My Way Back To You . . . 6

GABY & CABLES

72 Duke DU 129 Only Love Can Make You Smile/Only Love Version . . . 7
(see also Gaby & Wilton)

GABY & WILTON

72 Camel CA 92 Only Love/CHARLEY ACE: The Ten Commandments Of Joshua . . . 8
(see also Gaby & Cables)

GADGETS

83 Glass GLASS 026 We Had No Way Of Knowing/Acid Bath (unissued)
83 Glass GLASS 12026 We Had No Way Of Knowing/Acid Bath (12", unissued)
79 Final Solution FSLP 001 GADGETREE (LP, with insert, blue or beige picture on sleeve) . . . 20
80 Final Solution FSLP 002 LOVE, CURIOSITY, FRECKLES & DOUBT (LP) . . . 20
83 Glass GLALP 006 THE BLUE ALBUM (LP, with inner sleeve) . . . 12
83 Glass GLAMC 006 THE BLUE ALBUM (cassette) . . . 12
(see also The The, Matt Johnson, Colin Lloyd Tucker, Plain Characters)

MEL GADSON

60 London HLX 9105 Comin' Down With Love/I'm Gettin' Sentimental Over You . . . 20

GAGALACTYCA

90 Holyground HG 1135/ Magic Mixture MM 3 GAGALACTYCA (LP, with booklet, actually by Lightyears Away & Thundermother, 425 only) . . . 18
(see also Bill Nelson, David John & Mood)

MAJOR YURI GAGARIN

61 Britone MK 100 CONQUEST OF SPACE (EP) . . . 25

GAGS

79 Look LKLP 6312 DEATH IN BUZZARD'S GULCH (LP) . . . 30

BASIL GAIL

70 Bullet BU 454 I Wish/Black Is Black . . . 6

SLIM GAILLARD (QUARTET/TRIO)

50 Parlophone R 3291 Jam Man/JOHNNY OTIS: Harlem Nocturne (78) . . . 40
51 Vogue V 2029 Voot Boogie/Queen's Boogie (78) . . . 10
51 Vogue V 2044 Central Avenue Breakdown/Sighing Boogie (78) . . . 10
56 Parlophone GEP 8595 SLIM GAILLARD NO. 1 (EP) . . . 22
56 Columbia Clef SEB 10046 MUSICAL AGGREGATIONS (EP) . . . 25
60 London RED 1251 SLIM GAILLARD RIDES AGAIN (EP) . . . 30
(see also Meade 'Lux' Lewis & Slim Gaillard)

DONNA GAINES

71 MCA MK 5060 Sally Go Round The Roses/So Said The Man . . . 6
(see also Donna Summer)

GAINORS

58 London HLU 8734 The Secret/Gonna Rock Tonite . . . 120
58 London HLU 8734 The Secret/Gonna Rock Tonite (78) . . . 35

GALACTIC FEDERATION

66 Polydor BM 56093 The March Of The Sky People/Moon Shot . . . 35

GALACTIC SYMPOSIUM

80 Vague VOG 2 Money/In The Navy (gatefold p/s) . . . 6

GALADRIEL

82 Pennine PPS 191 AIRBORNE (LP, with insert) . . . 12

GALAHAD

87 private pressing G 1001 Dreaming From The Inside/The Opiate (p/s, 500 only) . . . 15

DIAMANDA GALAS

82 Y Y 18 LITANIES DU SATAN (LP) . . . 12
86 Mute STUMM 33 SAINT OF THE PIT (12" EP, p/s with inner) . . . 8

GALAXIE 500

89 Chemical Imbalance C 1005 Oblivious/tracks by other artists (free with issue 8 of *Chemical Imbalance* magazine) . . . 8
89 Catalogue CAT 075 Victory Garden/STRAIGHTJACKET FITS: Hail (1-sided flexi free with *The Catalogue* magazine) . . . 5
90 Caff CAFF 9 Rain/Don't Let Your Youth Go To Waste (p/s, with insert in bag) . . . 25
89 Schemer 8905 CD TODAY (CD, with 2 extra tracks) . . . 15
89 Rough Trade ROUGH 146 ON FIRE (LP) . . . 12
90 Rough Trade ROUGH 156 THIS IS OUR MUSIC (LP, with sticker and 3 postcards) . . . 12

MINT VALUE £

90	Rough Trade ROUGHCD 156	THIS IS OUR MUSIC (CD, trifold case)	15
91	Rough Trade ROUGH 146L	ON FIRE (LP, reissue with shrinkwrapped CD single)	15
96	Rykodisc RCD 10355	GALAXIE 500 (4-CD box set with booklet)	25

(see also Damon & Naomi)

GALAXIES

60	Capitol CL 15158	The Big Triangle/Until The Next Time	15

DAVID GALBRAITH

57	Columbia DB 3947	Heartbreak Is New To Me/Miracle In Milan	7
58	Columbia DB 4226	Do I Love You/Tonight	6
58	Columbia DB 4226	Do I Love You/Tonight (78)	8

EDDIE GALE

69	Blue Note BST 84294	GHETTO MUSIC (LP)	12

SANDRA GALE

63	Ember EMB S 162	Hello Heartbreak/If She's Right For You	6

SUNNY GALE

53	HMV 7M 147	Teardrops On My Pillow/Send My Baby Back To Me	15
54	HMV 7M 243	Goodnight, Well It's Time To Go/Close To Me	15
55	HMV 7M 344	C'est La Vie/Looking Glass	15
57	Brunswick 05659	Two Hearts (With An Arrow Between)/Maybe You'll Be There	8
57	Brunswick 05661	Come Go With Me/Please Go	10
58	Brunswick 05753	A Certain Smile/Just Friends	10
58	Brunswick 05753	A Certain Smile/Just Friends (78)	8
61	London HLU 9322	Please Love Me Forever/Sunny	10

GALE BROTHERS

66	Parlophone R 5535	Every Day Of My Life/All Strung Out	6

GALENS

63	London HLH 9804	Baby I Do Love You/Love Bells	25

FRANCE GALL

65	Philips BF 1408	Poupée De Cire, Poupeé De Son/Le Coeur Qui Jazze	10
88	WEA YZ 316 CD	Ella Elle L'a (CD, slimline jewel case)	15

RORY GALLAGHER

79	Chrysalis CHS 2364	Philby/Hellcat/Country Mile (p/s, coloured vinyl)	5
80	Chrysalis CHS 2453	Wayward Child/Keychain (p/s, coloured vinyl)	5
71	Polydor 2383 044	RORY GALLAGHER (LP)	25
71	Polydor 2383 076	DEUCE (LP)	20
72	Polydor 2383 112	LIVE! IN EUROPE (LP, gatefold sleeve)	20
73	Polydor 2383 189	BLUEPRINT (LP)	20
73	Polydor 2383 230	TATTOO (LP)	15
74	Polydor 2659 031	IRISH TOUR '74 (2-LP)	15
87	Capo/Demon XFIEND 98	DEFENDER (LP, with bonus 7", "Seems To Me"/"No Peace For The Wicked")	12

(see also Taste, Killing Floor, Joe O'Donnell)

GALLAGHER-LYLE

67	Polydor BM 56170	Trees/In The Crowd	10
72	Capitol ST 21906	GALLAGHER AND LYLE (LP)	18

(see also James Galt, McGuinness Flint, Cups)

GALLAHADS

55	Capitol CL 14282	Ooh-Ah/Careless	15
55	Capitol CL 14282	Ooh-Ah/Careless (78)	8

GALLANTS

64	Capitol CL 15366	Happy Beat/Rhino	6
65	Capitol CL 15408	"Man From U.N.C.L.E." Theme/Vagabond	15

GALLERY

69	Midas	THE WIND THAT SHAKES THE BARLEY (LP)	300

GALLIANO

88	Acid Jazz JAZID 1	Frederick Lies Still/I Love You Baby (1st pressing, with large centre hole)	15

GALLIARD

70	Deram DM 306	I Wrapped Her In Ribbons/The Hermit And The Knight	8
70	Deram Nova (S)DN 4	STRANGE PLEASURE (LP)	150
70	Deram SML 1075	NEW DAWN (LP)	150

(see also Craig)

GALLIARDS

60	Topic STOP 101	Black And White/Bahnuah	6

BOB GALLION

59	MGM MGM 1028	Out Of A Honky Tonk/You Take The Table And I'll Take The Chairs	12
60	MGM MGM 1057	Froggy Went A Courtin'/Hey! Joe	12
65	Hickory 45-1300	I Don't Have The Right (To Disagree)/Thank The Devil For Hideaways	7

GALLON DRUNK

93	Clawfist XPIG 21	Known, Not Wanted/TINDERSTICKS: We Have All The Time In The World ('singles club' release, p/s, 1,400 only)	15

GALLOW GLASS CEILI BAND

60s	Top Rank RX 30314	COME TO THE CEILI (LP)	20

FRANK GALLUP

58	HMV POP 509	Got A Match?/I Beg Your Pardon	7
58	HMV POP 509	Got A Match?/I Beg Your Pardon (78)	7

JAMES GALT
65 Pye 7N 15936 Comes The Dawn/My Own Way . . . 12
65 Pye 7N 17021 With My Baby/A Most Unusual Feeling . . . 35
(see also Gallagher-Lyle)

GAMBLERS
63 Decca F 11780 You've Really Got A Hold On Me/Can I See You Tonight? . . . 10
64 Decca F 11872 Nobody But Me/It's So Nice . . . 15
65 Decca F 12060 Now I'm All Alone/Find Out What's Happening . . . 20
66 Decca F 12399 Doctor Goldfoot (And His Bikini Machine)/It Seems So Long . . . 18
67 Parlophone R 5557 Cry Me A River/Who Will Buy . . . 20
(see also Billy Fury)

GAME
65 Pye 7N 15889 But I Do/Gotta Keep On Moving Baby . . . 70
66 Decca F 12469 Gonna Get Me Someone/Gotta Wait . . . 150
67 Parlophone R 5553 The Addicted Man/Help Me Mummy's Gone (withdrawn) . . . 1000
67 Parlophone R 5569 It's Shocking What They Call Me/Help Me Mummy's Gone . . . 300

DOUGLAS GAMLEY
60 Delyse/Envoy VOY 9142 PIANO PLAYTIME (LP) . . . 12

GAMMER & HIS FAMILIARS
84 Gammer GAMMER 5 Will The New Baby/All Above (12", p/s) . . . 8
(see also Durutti Column)

GANDALF THE GREY
80s Heyoka THE GREY WIZARD AM I (LP, reissue of U.S. LP) . . . 25

RON WARREN GANDERTON
(see under Sound Ceremony)

LITTLE JIMMY GANDY
69 Roulette RO 510 Cool Thirteen/I'm Not Like The Others . . . 8

GANGBUSTERS
63 Fontana TF 419 The Memory Of Your Face/When We Met . . . 8

GANG OF ANGELS
94 Shotgun CDBOR 012 Hello Goodbye/Jim Jam (CD) . . . 8
(see also Slade)

GANG OF FOUR
80 Fast Product FAST 5 DAMAGED GOODS (EP, original with b&w labels, some with sticker) . . . 8/5

GANGSTERS
79 Stortbeat A45/B45 Harlow Town/Record Company (p/s) . . . 10
79 Stortbeat BEAT 3 Best Friend/Best Friend Dub (p/s) . . . 8
79 Stortbeat BEAT 2 GANGSTERS (LP) . . . 20

GANGSTERS
80 Big Bear BB 25 Rudi The Red Nose Reindeer/White Christmas . . . 5
80 Big Bear BB 28 Wooly Bully/We Are The Gangsters . . . 5
80 Big Bear 12BB 28 Wooly Bully/We Are The Gangsters (12") . . . 8

GANIM'S ASIA MINORS
58 London HLE 8637 Daddy Lolo/Halvah . . . 12

CECIL GANT
74 Flyright LP 4710 ROCK LITTLE BABY (LP) . . . 15
75 Flyright LP 4714 CECIL'S BOOGIE (LP) . . . 12
79 Magpie 1816 KILLER DILLER BOOGIE (LP) . . . 12

CLENTT GANT
60 Starlite ST45 023 I'm Just A Lucky So-And-So/I Need You So . . . 10

DON GANT
65 Hickory 45-1297 Early In The Morning/Don't Ya Even Cry . . . 10

ELMER GANTRY'S (VELVET) OPERA
67 Direction 58-3083 Flames/Salisbury Plain . . . 15
68 Direction 58-3481 Mary Jane/Dreamy . . . 10
69 Direction 58-3924 Volcano/A Quick 'B' . . . 10
68 Direction 8-63300 ELMER GANTRY'S VELVET OPERA (LP) . . . 50
(see also Velvet Opera, Stretch, Strawbs, Hudson-Ford, Paul Brett's Sage)

GANTS
65 Liberty LIB 55829 Road Runner/My Baby Don't Care . . . 35
67 Liberty LIB 55940 I Wonder/Greener Days . . . 15

GARBAGE
SINGLES
95 Discordant CORD 001 Vow/Torn Apart (embossed metal 'G' logo sleeve, with insert, 3,000 pressed [934 issued], stickered, some sealed) . . . 55/65
95 Discordant CORD 001 Vow/Torn Apart (plain black embossed 'G' logo sleeve, with insert in poly bag, 500 only, some sealed) . . . 20/25
95 Mushroom SX 1138 Subhuman/1 Crush (embossed rubber 'G' logo sleeve, with SX 1138 insert, some in white 'G' logo carrier bag, 3,000 only; some with incorrect insert [S 1138]) . . . 27/32
95 Mushroom S 1138 Subhuman/1 Crush (embossed card 'G' logo sleeve, with insert, 2,000 pressed [1,000 issued]) . . . 20
95 Mushroom D 1138 Subhuman/1 Crush/Vow (CD, embossed inlay, stickered case, 3,000 only) . . . 20
95 Mushroom SX 1199 Only Happy When It Rains/Girl Can't Come/Sleep (double-grooved B-side, stickered 'hologram prismaboard' 'G' logo sleeve, with inner sleeve & insert; some in blue 'G' logo carrier bag, 5,000 only) . . . 12

MINT VALUE £

95 Mushroom SX 1199 — Only Happy When It Rains/Girl Can't Come/Sleep (as above, shrinkwrapped) — 12
95 Mushroom SX 1237 — Queer/Queer (Adrian Sherwood Remix) (p/s, in stickered 'crystal' outer 'G' logo sleeve, 5,000 only, some with 12" pink 'Garbage' carrier bag) — 10
96 Mushroom SX 1271 — Stupid Girl/Dog New Tricks (The Pal Mix) (jukebox issue, white label, no p/s) — 7
96 Mushroom SX 1271/1237 — Stupid Girl/Queer (jukebox issue, white label, stamped 'Garbage' logo, no p/s) — 10
96 Mushroom SX 1271 — Stupid Girl/Dog New Tricks (The Pal Mix) (stickered red 'Tak-Tile' cloth 'G' logo sleeve, some with stickered shrinkwrap, 10,000 only) — 7/10
96 Mushroom SX 1271 — Stupid Girl/Dog New Tricks (The Pal Mix) (stickered blue 'Tak-Tile' cloth 'G' logo sleeve, some with stickered shrinkwrap, 10,000 only) — 10/12
96 Mushroom SX 1494 — Milk (The Wicked Mix)/(The Tricky Remix) (embossed/hologram 'G' logo sleeve, with inner sleeve & poster, sealed) — 6
96 Mushroom DJMILK 1 — RABBIT IN THE MOON MILK (Udder Edit)/(Got It Mix)/(Butchered Vegas Mix)/ (12", die-cut white embossed 'G' logo sleeve, day-glo yellow inner sleeve, 500 only) — 18
96 Mushroom DJMILK 2 — GOLDIE MILK ('Completely Trashed' Mix)/('VIP Refuge Trash Your Shit') (12", die-cut white embossed 'G' logo sleeve, day-glo orange inner sleeve, 500 only) — 18
96 Mushroom DJMILK 3 — MASSIVE ATTACK MILK ('D' Mix)/('Trance' Mix) (12", die-cut white embossed 'G' logo sleeve, day-glo pink inner sleeve, 500 only) — 18

LPs

95 Mushroom L 31450 — GARBAGE (as 2 x 45rpm 12", with inner sleeves) — 15
95 Mushroom LX 31450 — GARBAGE (as 6 x 7" singles in box set with 3 inserts [now import only], most sealed) — 15/18

PROMOS

95 Mushroom (no cat. no.) — Subhuman/1 Crush/Vow (cassette, black embossed inlay) — 35
95 Mushroom (no cat. no.) — Vow/Queer/Only Happy When It Rains/Fix Me Now/As Heaven Is Fine (cassette, black embossed inlay) — 35
95 Mushroom TRASH 02 — Vow/Subhuman/1 Crush (CD, embossed rubber sleeve with insert, promo only) — 65
96 Mushroom TRASH 09/010 — Stupid Girl (Red Snapper Mix)/(Dreadzone Mix) (12", hand-stamped label, plain black die-cut sleeve, 1,000 only) — 18
96 Mushroom TRASH 011 — Stupid Girl Remixes (Todd Terry)/(Danny Saber) (CD, no inlay, 500 only; 125 distributed) — 25
96 Mushroom MILK CDP — Milk (Wicked Mix)/(The Siren Mix)/(Album Version) (CD, hologram inlay) — 20
96 Mushroom CDP (no cat no.) — Milk (Garbage Wicked Mix)/(Goldie Completely Trashed Mix)/ (Massive Attack Massive Mix)/(The Tricky Mix)/ (Rabbit In The Moon Utter Mix) (CD, hologram inlay) — 20
98 Mushroom TRASH 17 — Push It (1-track CD, shaped card sleeve, in resealable foil bag) — 12
98 Mushroom TRASH 16 — THIS IS A PROMOTIONAL ITEM: Stupid Girl/Only Happy When It Rains/ Queer/Milk (CD, card sleeve in resealable foil bag) — 20
98 Mushroom TRASH 19 — VERSION 2.0 (CD/CD-ROM, stickered, embossed shaped card sleeve with insert, promo only) — 22
01 Mushroom TRASH 33 — PREVIOUS GARBAGE (CD sampler, card title sleeve) — 22

(see also Goodbye Mr. MacKenzine)

GARBO

82 Rarn RARN 201 — Dancing Strange/Why Don't You Call Me?/Everyday Hallucinations (p/s) — 200

GARBO'S CELLULOID HEROES

78 Big Bear BB 13 — Only Death Is Fatal/Won't You Come to my Funeral (p/s) — 10

VIN GARBUTT

72 Trailer LER 2078 — THE VALLEY OF TREES (LP, red label) — 15
75 Trailer LER 2081 — THE YOUNG TIN WHISTLE PEST (LP, red label) — 12

DIGNO GARCIA Y SUS CARIOS

61 Palette PG 9024 — Brigitte Bardot/Morena — 8
66 Pye 7N 17172 — Guantanamera/The Bird — 5

JERRY GARCIA

71 Douglas DGL 69013 — HOOTEROLL? (LP, with Howard Wales) — 15
72 Warner Bros K 46139 — GARCIA (LP) — 12
74 Round RX 59301 — GARCIA (LP) — 12
76 United Artists UAG 29921 — REFLECTIONS (LP) — 12

(see also Grateful Dead, Diga Rhythm Band, Old & In The Way)

RUSS GARCIA ORCHESTRA

58 London — FANTASTICA! (10" LP) — 30

GARDEN ODYSSEY (ENTERPRISE)

69 Deram DM 267 — Sad And Lonely/Sky Pilot (8/M/1) (as Garden Odyssey Enterprise) — 20
72 RCA RCA 2159 — Joker/Have You Ever Been To Georgia (as Garden Odyssey) — 6

(see also Graham Gouldman)

PAUL GARDINER

81 Beggars Banquet BEG 61 — Stormtrooper In Drag/Night Talk (p/s) — 5
81 Beggars Banquet BEG 61T — Stormtrooper In Drag/Night Talk (12", unreleased, white label promos only) — 350+
84 Numa NU 1 — Venus In Furs/No Sense (p/s) — 5
84 Numa NUM 1 — Venus In Furs (Extended Mix)/No Sense/Venus In Furs (7" Mix) (12", p/s) — 10

(see also Dramatis, Tubeway Army, Gary Numan)

AVA GARDNER

53 MGM SP 1005 — Can't Help Lovin' Dat Man/Bill — 10

BORIS GARD(I)NER (& LOVE PEOPLE)

69 High Note HS 010 — Lucky Is The Boy/Bobby Sox To Stockings — 25
69 Doctor Bird DB 1205 — Elizabethan Reggae/Hooked On A Feeling — 18
69 Duke DU 21 — Never My Love/The Bold One — 12
70 Treasure Isle TI 7056 — Hooked On A Feeling/MESSAGE: Turn Around Twice — 15
70 Big Shot BI 537 — Sweet Soul Special/Memories Of Love (with Love People) — 7
70 Big Shot BI 538 — Darkness/Watch This Music (B-side actually "Keep Out") (with Love People) — 7

MINT VALUE £

70	Big Shot BI 539	Hot Shot/Watch This Music (with Love People)	7
70	Dynamic DYN 404	Commanding Wife/Band Of Gold (as Boris Gardner & Happening)	6
70	Trojan TR 7753	Dynamic Pressure/Reggae Me Dis, Reggae Me Dat	6
70	Trojan TBL 121	REGGAE HAPPENING (LP)	30

DAVE GARDNER

58	Brunswick 05740	Hop Along Rock/All By Myself (B-side with Anita Kerr Singers)	30
58	Brunswick 05740	Hop Along Rock/All By Myself (B-side with Anita Kerr Singers) (78)	8

DON GARDNER & DEE DEE FORD

62	Stateside SS 114	I Need Your Loving/Tell Me	15
62	Stateside SS 130	Don't You Worry/I'm Coming Home To Stay	18
68	Soul City SC 101	Don't You Worry/I'm Coming Home To Stay (reissue)	15

(see also Baby Washington & Don Gardner, Dee Dee Ford)

JOANNE GARDNER

70s	Polydor	JOANNE GARDNER (LP)	15

JOHNNY GARFIELD

65	Pye 7N 15758	Stranger In Paradise/Anyone Can Lose A Heart	45

(Art) GARFUNKEL

74	CBS CQ 31474/Q 69021	ANGEL CLARE (LP, quadrophonic)	12

(see also Simon & Garfunkel, Tom & Jerry)

FRANK GARI

60	London HLU 9277	I Ain't Got A Girl/Utopia	10

JUDY GARLAND

53	MGM SP 1001	A Couple Of Swells/Medley: I Love A Piano/Snooky Ookums/When The Midnight Choo Choo Leaves (with Fred Astaire)	8
56	MGM SP 1157	Look For The Silver Lining/Who?	8
57	Capitol CL 14789	Rock-a-bye Your Baby With A Dixie Melody/After You've Gone	6
57	Capitol CL 14790	I Feel A Song Coming On/Just Imagine	6
57	Capitol CL 14791	By Myself/It's Lovely To Be Back In London	6
55	Philips BBE 12012	BORN IN A TRUNK — SELECTIONS FROM A STAR IS BORN (EP)	10
56	MGM MGM-EP 568	IF YOU FEEL LIKE SINGING (EP)	10
56	MGM MGM-EP 641	EASTER PARADE — EXCERPTS (EP, with Fred Astaire & Peter Lawford)	10
56	MGM MGM-EP 672	WORDS AND MUSIC — SOUNDTRACK EXCERPTS (EP, 1 track with June Allyson & Mickey Rooney)	10
59	Capitol EAP1 1036	JUDY IN LOVE (EP)	8
59	Capitol EAP2 1036	JUDY IN LOVE (EP)	8
59	Capitol EAP3 1036	JUDY IN LOVE (EP)	8
59	Capitol EAP7 1569	JUDY AT CARNEGIE HALL (EP)	8
59	Capitol EAP8 1569	JUDY AT CARNEGIE HALL (EP)	8
60	Capitol EAP1 20051	A GARLAND FOR JUDY (EP)	8
55	Brunswick LA 8725	JUDY AT THE PALACE (10" LP)	25
55	MGM MGM-D 134	BORN TO SING (10" LP)	25
55	Philips BBL 7007	A STAR IS BORN (LP, soundtrack)	15
56	Capitol LCT 6103	MISS SHOW BUSINESS (LP)	15
57	Capitol LCT 6121	JUDY (LP)	15
57	Capitol LCT 6136	ALONE (LP)	15
59	Capitol (S)T 1036	JUDY IN LOVE (LP, mono/stereo)	12/15
59	Capitol (S)T 1118	AT THE GROVE (LP, mono/stereo)	12/15
59	Capitol (S)T 1188	THE LETTER (LP, mono/stereo)	12/15
61	Capitol (S)T 1467	JUDY! THAT'S ENTERTAINMENT (LP, mono/stereo)	12/15
63	Capitol T 1999	THE HITS OF JUDY GARLAND (LP)	12
63	Ace Of Hearts AH 11	GREATEST PERFORMANCES (LP)	12

(see also Fred Astaire)

ERROL GARNER

60	Philips JAZ 103	Cheek To Cheek/The Way You Look Tonight (p/s)	6
60	Philips JAZ 105	Lullaby Of Birdland/Easy To Love (p/s)	6
56	London RE-U 1066	THE PIANO WIZARDRY OF ERROL GARNER (EP)	12
60s	Realm REP 4006	UNDECIDED (EP)	8
53	Vogue LDE 034	ERROL GARNER TRIO VOLUME ONE (10" LP)	15
54	Felsted EDL 87002	MARGIE (10" LP)	15
54	Philips BBR 8002	PLAYS FOR DANCING (10" LP)	15
55	Philips BBR 8045	SOLO FLIGHT (10" LP)	15
55	Philips BBL 7034	GONE GARNER GONEST (LP)	12
55	Columbia 33S 1050	PIANO MOODS (10" LP)	15
55	Columbia 33S 1059	PIANO GEMS (10" LP)	15
55	Oriole MG 26042	GONE WITH GARNER (10" LP)	15
55	Felsted EDL 87015	PASSPORT TO FAME (10" LP)	15

REGGIE GARNER

76	Capitol CL 15874	Hot Line/Blessed Be The Name Of My Baby	7

BLIND LEROY GARNET

52	Jazz Collector L 74	Chain 'Em Down/Louisiana Glide (78)	12

COL GARNET

66	Page One POF 002	With A Girl Like You/Monday Monday	12

ALF GARNETT (& FAMILY)

67	CBS 202607	All/Among My Souvenirs	6
68	Pye NPL 18192	SEX AND OTHER THOUGHTS (LP)	18

GALE GARNETT

64	RCA RCA 1418	We'll Sing In The Sunshine/Prism Song	10
65	RCA RCA 1451	I'll Cry Alone/Where Do You Go To Go Away?	60
65	RCA RD 7726	MY KIND OF FOLK SONGS (LP)	30
66	RCA RD 7750	LOVIN' PLACE	20

MINT VALUE £

LAURENT GARNIER

93 Warp WAP 36 — A BOUT DE SOUFFLE (12", company sleeve) 8

JESSE GARON & DESPERADOS

(see under 'J')

LIEF GARRETT

79 Scotti Brothers K 11449 — Same Goes For You/Give In (p/s) 8

VERNON GARRETT

67 Stateside SS 2006 — If I Could Turn Back The Hands Of Time/You And Me Together 22
67 Stateside SS 2026 — Shine It On/Things Are Lookin' Better 15
68 Action ACT 4508 — Shine It On/Things Are Lookin' Better (reissue) 12

DAVID GARRICK

65 Piccadilly 7N 35231 — Go/When The World Was Our Own 7
65 Piccadilly 7N 35263 — One Little Smile/We Must Be In Love 7
66 Piccadilly 7N 35317 — Lady Jane/Let's Go Somewhere 8
66 Piccadilly 7N 35335 — Dear Mrs Applebee/You're What I'm Living For 8
67 Piccadilly 7N 35371 — I've Found A Love/(You Can't Hide) A Broken Heart 6
67 Piccadilly 7N 35377 — A Certain Misunderstanding/I'm Looking Straight At You 6
67 Piccadilly 7N 35402 — Don't Go Out In The Rain (You're Gonna Melt, Sugar)/ Theme For A Wishing Heart 6
67 Pye 7N 17409 — Ave Maria/Please Stay 6
67 Pye 7N 17409 — Ave Maria/You Don't Know (different B-side) 6
68 Pye 7N 17509 — Rainbow/I'll Be Home 7
68 Pye 7N 17610 — A Little Bit Of This (And A Little Bit Of That)/Flutterby Butterfly 6
69 Pye 7N 17685 — Maypole Mews/Like To Get To Know You Better 6
69 Pye 7N 17820 — Poor Little Me/Molly With The Hair Like Silver 6
69 Columbia DB 8680 — Bake Me A Woman/House In The Heather 6
71 Columbia DB 8784 — Mary In The Morning/Beautiful People 6
67 Piccadilly NEP 34056 — DAVID (EP) 50
66 Piccadilly N(S)PL 38024 — A BOY CALLED DAVID (LP, mono/stereo) 25/30
67 Piccadilly N(S)PL 38035 — DON'T GO OUT INTO THE RAIN, SUGAR (LP) 22
68 Pye N(S)PL 18223 — BLOW UP — LIVE! (LP, unreleased)
68 Marble Arch MAL 822 — A BOY CALLED DAVID (LP, reissue) 12

MICHAEL GARRICK

65 Argo EAF/ZFA 92 — ANTHEM — MICHAEL GARRICK QUINTET (EP, mono/stereo) 50
66 Argo EAF 115 — BEFORE NIGHT/DAY (EP) 50
63 Airborne — CASE OF JAZZ (LP) 65
64 Airborne — MOONSCAPE (LP) 300
64 Argo ZDA 26/27 — POETRY AND JAZZ IN CONCERT (2-LP, with Norma Winstone) 60
65 Argo (Z)DA 33 — OCTOBER WOMAN (LP, as Michael Garrick Quintet, with Joe Harriott) 50
65 Argo (Z)DA 36 — PROMISES (LP, as Michael Garrick Sextet, with Ian Carr) 60
68 Argo (Z)DA 88 — BLACK MARIGOLDS (LP, as Michael Garrick Septet) 50
68 Airborne NBP 0021 — JAZZ PRAISES AT ST. PAULS (LP) 40
69 Argo ZPR 264/5 — POETRY AND JAZZ IN CONCERT 250 (2-LP, as Michael Garrick Quintet) 50
70 Argo ZDA 135 — HEART IS A LOTUS (LP, as Michael Garrick Sextet with Norma Winstone) 50
72 Argo ZDA 153 — COLD MOUNTAIN (LP, as Michael Garrick Trio) 50
72 Argo ZDA 154 — HOME STRETCH BLUES (LP, as Michael Garrick Band with Norma Winstone) 50
73 Impulse AS 49 — ILLUMINATION (LP, as Michael Garrick Sextet) 25
74 Argo ZDA 163 — TROPPO (LP) 45

(see also Ian Carr, Norma Winstone, Joe Harriott, Garrick's Fairground)

GARRICK'S FAIRGROUND

71 Argo AFW 105 — Epiphany/Blessed Are The Peacemakers 10
72 Argo ZAGF 1 — MR. SMITH'S APOCALYPSE (LP) 70

(see also Michael Garrick)

FREDDIE GARRITY

68 Columbia DB 8348 — Little Red Donkey/So Many Different Ways 8
74 Bus Stop BUS 1017 — Hello Kids/It's Good For You 8
74 Bus Stop BUS 1022 — The Chicken Song/Pooh Pooh Pooh 8
70 Starline SRS 5019 — OLIVER IN THE OVERWORLD (LP, soundtrack) 20
71 CBS 70096 — OLIVER IN THE UNDERWORLD (LP, reissue soundtrack) 12

(see also Freddie & Dreamers)

ROBIN GARSIDE & PAUL GOUGH

77 Northern Sound NSR 01 — SEA SONGS (LP) 15

ROBIN GARTON & HIS BAND

58 Martello MC 100 — Topsy/Jump For Me 5

REX GARVIN & MIGHTY CRAVERS

66 Atlantic 584 028 — Sock It To 'Em J.B. (Parts 1 & 2) 12
67 Atlantic 584 097 — I Gotta Go Now (Up On The Floor)/Believe It Or Not 15

JOHN GARY

59 Top Rank JAR 177 — Let Them Talk/Tell My Love 8
59 Top Rank JAR 177 — Let Them Talk/Tell My Love (78) 12
60 Top Rank JAR 392 — Little Things Mean A Lot/Ever Since I Met Lucy 8

GARY & ARIELS

64 Fontana TF 476 — Say You Love Me/Town Girl 12

(see also Garry Mills)

GARY & STU

72 Carnaby 6151 003 — Sweet White Dove/Good Lady Fair 10
72 Carnaby 6302 012 — HARLAN FARE (LP) 35

(see also Koobas, March Hare)

GAS

80	Polydor POSP 192	It Shows In Your Face/Tomorrow (p/s)	35
81	Polydor POSP 296	Treatment/That's It (12", p/s)	30
81	Polydor POSP 344	The Finger/Knock It Down (p/s)	25
81	Polydor POLE 1052	EMOTIONAL WARFARE (LP)	20

GASKIN

81	Rondelet ROUND 7	I'm No Fool/Sweet Dream Maker (p/s)	25
82	Rondelet ROUND 21	Mony Mony/Queen Of Hams (p/s)	18
81	Rondelet ABOUT 4	END OF THE WORLD (LP, gatefold sleeve)	25
82	Rondelet ABOUT 8	NO WAY OUT (LP, with inner)	20

GASLIGHT

70	SDE 32732	GASLIGHT (2-LP, private pressing, gatefold sleeve with inserts, 2nd disc by Gaslight Choir)	75

GASOLINE BAND

72	Cube HIFLY 9	GASOLINE BAND (LP)	12

GASS

65	Parlophone R 5344	One Of These Days/I Don't Know Why	15
66	Parlophone R 5456	The New Breed/In The City	35
67	CBS 202647	Dream Baby (How Long Must I Dream?)/Jitterbug Sid	20
71	Polydor 2058 147	Something's Got To Change Your Ways/Mr Banana	6
70	Polydor 2383 022	JUJU (LP, featuring Peter Green)	45
71	Polydor 2383 035	CATCH MY SOUL — THE ROCK-OTHELLO (LP, cast recording featuring Gass)	20

GASS COMPANY

68	President PT 170	Everybody Needs Love/Nightmare	30

(see also Wake)

GAS WORKS

73	Regal Zonophone RZ 3075	Standing Stiff/Keep On Rolling	6
73	Regal Zonophone RZ 3080	God's Great Spaceship/Cider With Rosie	6
73	Regal Zono. SRLZ 1036	GAS WORKS (LP)	18

DAVID GATES

60	Top Rank JAR 504	The Happiest Man Alive/The Road That Leads To Love	40
73	Elektra K 42150	DAVID GATES — FIRST (LP)	15

(see also Bread)

PEARLY GATES

74	Polydor 2058 443	Johnny And The Juke-Box/They Were Good Times	6
78	Bronze BRO 61	Burnin' Love (Parts 1 & 2)	5

(see also Flirtations, Gypsies)

RAY GATES

66	Decca F 12502	It's Such A Shame/Have You Ever Had The Blues	40

REV. J.M. GATES

50s	Square M3	Need Of Prayer/Death's Black Train Is Coming (78)	10

GATES OF EDEN

66	Pye 7N 17195	Too Much On My Mind/I'm Warning You	18
67	Pye 7N 17252	In Your Love/Snoopy Versus The Red Baron	12
67	Pye 7N 17278	1 To 7/Hey Now	20

GATEWAY SINGERS

57	Brunswick LAT 8176	PUTTIN' ON THE STYLE (LP)	18

GATHERERS

73	Duke DU 153	Words Of My Mouth/UPSETTERS: Version	35

LUCHO GATICA

54	Parlophone CMSP 16	Besame Mucho/Las Muchachas De La Plaza De Espana (export issue)	8

GATOR CREEK

71	Mercury 6052 058	Danny's Song/Take A Look	6
71	Mercury 6338 035	GATOR CREEK (LP)	15

DICK GAUGHAN

72	Trailer LER 2072	NO MORE FOREVER (LP, red label)	12

GEORGES GAVARENTZ

69	Philips SBL 7898	THEY CAME TO ROB LAS VEGAS (LP, soundtrack)	80

JIMMY GAVIN

57	London HLU 8478	I Sit In My Window/Lonely Chair	80
57	London HLU 8478	I Sit In My Window/Lonely Chair (78)	20

JOHNNY GAVOTTE

60	Parlophone R 4631	It's Not Too Late/Can't Forget	10

BETSY GAY

50	Capitol CL 13300	Country Washburne — Chug-A-Lug/Whoa Sailor (78)	8
50	Capitol CL 13315	Honky Tonkin'/DEUCE SPRIGGENS: Red Hot Mama (78)	8
51	Capitol CL 13425	Cigars, Cigarettes, Souvenirs/That Ain't In My Catalogue (78)	8

ELAINE GAY

54	Parlophone MSP 6140	Love/Instantly	10
55	Parlophone R 3997	Rock Love/Ebony Eyes (78)	10

MAC GAYDEN

73	EMI EMA 760	McGAVOCK GAYDEN (LP)	20

(see also Area Code 615)

BILLY GAYE & GAYTONES

73	Waverley SLP 501	Oh Honey Love Me/I'll Never Say Never Again	5

MINT VALUE £

MARVIN GAYE

Year	Label / Cat. No.	Title	Mint Value £
63	Oriole CBA 1803	Stubborn Kind Of Fellow/It Hurt Me Too	100
63	Oriole CBA 1846	Pride And Joy/One Of These Days	70
63	Stateside SS 243	Can I Get A Witness?/I'm Crazy 'Bout My Baby	50
64	Stateside SS 284	You're A Wonderful One/When I'm Alone I Cry	40
64	Stateside SS 326	Try It Baby/If My Heart Could Sing	40
64	Stateside SS 360	How Sweet It Is (To Be Loved By You)/Forever	40
65	Tamla Motown TMG 510	I'll Be Doggone/You've Been A Long Time Coming	45
65	Tamla Motown TMG 524	Pretty Little Baby/Now That You've Won Me	35
65	Tamla Motown TMG 539	Ain't That Peculiar?/She's Got To Be Real	25
66	Tamla Motown TMG 552	One More Heartache/When I Had Your Love	25
66	Tamla Motown TMG 563	Take This Heart Of Mine/Need Your Lovin' (Want You Back)	25
66	Tamla Motown TMG 574	Little Darlin' (I Need You)/Hey Diddle Diddle	25
67	Tamla Motown TMG 618	Your Unchanging Love/I'll Take Care Of You	22
68	Tamla Motown TMG 640	You/Change What You Can	18
68	Tamla Motown TMG 676	Chained/At Last (I Found A Love)	18
69	Tamla Motown TMG 686	I Heard It Through The Grapevine/Need Somebody	7
69	Tamla Motown TMG 705	Too Busy Thinking 'Bout My Baby/Wherever I Lay My Hat	7
69	Tamla Motown TMG 718	That's The Way Love Is/Gonna Keep On Tryin' Till I Win Your Love	7
70	Tamla Motown TMG 734	Abraham, Martin And John/How Can I Forget?	8
71	Tamla Motown TMG 775	What's Going On?/God Is Love	6
71	Tamla Motown TMG 796	Save The Children/Little Darling (I Need You)	7
72	Tamla Motown TMG 802	Mercy Mercy Me/Bad Tomorrows	6
72	Tamla Motown TMG 817	Inner City Blues/Wholly Holy	10
73	Tamla Motown TMG 846	Trouble Man/Don't Mess With Mister 'T'	12
74	Tamla Motown TMG 882	Come Get To This/Distant Lover	12
85	CBS DA 4894	Sanctified Lady/Sanctified Lady (Instrumental)//Sexual Healing/ Rockin' After Midnight (double pack)	5
86	Motown ZB 40758	The World Is Rated X/Lonely Lover	5
66	Tamla Motown TME 2016	MARVIN GAYE (EP)	65
67	Tamla Motown TME 2019	ORIGINALS FROM MARVIN GAYE (EP)	55
64	Stateside SL 10100	MARVIN GAYE (LP)	175
65	Tamla Motown TML 11004	HOW SWEET IT IS TO BE LOVED BY YOU (LP)	100
65	Tamla Motown TML 11015	HELLO BROADWAY (LP)	100
66	T. Motown (S)TML 11022	A TRIBUTE TO THE GREAT NAT KING COLE (LP, mono/stereo)	70/90
66	T. Motown (S)TML 11033	MOODS OF MARVIN GAYE (LP, mono/stereo)	50/70
68	T. Motown (S)TML 11065	MARVIN GAYE'S GREATEST HITS (LP)	20
69	T. Motown (S)TML 11091	IN THE GROOVE (LP)	40
69	T. Motown (S)TML 11119	M.P.G. (LP)	22
69	T. Motown (S)TML 11123	MARVIN GAYE AND HIS GIRLS (LP, with T. Terrell, M. Wells & K. Weston)	25
70	T. Motown (S)TML 11136	THAT'S THE WAY LOVE IS (LP)	20
71	Tamla Motown STML 11190	WHAT'S GOING ON? (LP, initially with lyric sheet)	18/12
72	Tamla Motown STML 11201	THE HITS OF MARVIN GAYE (LP)	12
73	Tamla Motown STML 11225	TROUBLE MAN (LP, soundtrack)	18
78	Tamla Motown TMSP 6008	HERE, MY DEAR (2-LP)	20
76	Tamla Motown STML 12025	I WANT YOU (LP)	12

MARVIN GAYE & TAMMI TERRELL

Year	Label / Cat. No.	Title	Mint Value £
67	Tamla Motown TMG 611	Ain't No Mountain High Enough/Give A Little Love	18
67	Tamla Motown TMG 625	Your Precious Love/Hold Me Oh My Darling	15
67	Tamla Motown TMG 635	If I Could Build My Whole World Around You/If This World Were Mine	12
68	Tamla Motown TMG 655	Ain't Nothin' Like The Real Thing/Little Ole Boy, Little Ole Girl	8
68	Tamla Motown TMG 668	You're All I Need To Get By/Two Can Have A Party	7
69	Tamla Motown TMG 681	You Ain't Livin' Till You're Lovin'/Oh How I'd Miss You	8
69	Tamla Motown TMG 697	Good Lovin' Ain't Easy To Come By/Satisfied Feelin'	7
69	Tamla Motown TMG 715	The Onion Song/I Can't Believe You Love Me (demos in p/s £40)	5
68	T. Motown (S)TML 11062	UNITED (LP)	40
68	T. Motown (S)TML 11084	YOU'RE ALL I NEED (LP)	35
70	T. Motown (S)TML 11132	EASY (LP)	22
70	T. Motown (S)TML 11153	GREATEST HITS (LP)	15

MARVIN GAYE & MARY WELLS

Year	Label / Cat. No.	Title	Mint Value £
64	Stateside SS 316	Once Upon A Time/What's The Matter With You, Baby?	25
64	Stateside SL 10097	TOGETHER (LP)	120

MARVIN GAYE & KIM WESTON

Year	Label / Cat. No.	Title	Mint Value £
64	Stateside SS 363	What Good Am I Without You?/I Want You Around	25
67	Tamla Motown TMG 590	It Takes Two/It's Got To Be A Miracle (This Thing Called Love) (1st pressing with narrow print; later issues with wider print)	15/10
67	T. Motown (S)TML 11049	TAKE TWO (LP, mono/stereo)	45/50

(see also Diana Ross, Tammi Terrell, Mary Wells, Kim Weston)

GAYLADS

Year	Label / Cat. No.	Title	Mint Value £
64	R&B JB 159	There'll Come A Day/BILLY COOKE: Iron Bar	22
64	R&B JB 165	What Is Wrong With Me?/Whap Whap	22
66	Island WI 281	Goodbye Daddy/Your Eyes	25
66	Island WI 291	You Never Leave Him/Message To My Girl	25
66	Island WI 3002	Stop Making Love/They Call Her Dawn	20
66	Doctor Bird DB 1014	Lady With The Red Dress/Dinner For Two	30
66	Doctor Bird DB 1031	You Should Never Do That/WINSTON STEWART: I Don't Know Why I Love You	25
66	Rymska RA 104	You Should Never Do That/TECHNIQUES: So Many Times	25
67	Island WI 3022	Don't Say No/SONNY BURKE: You Rule My Heart	22
67	Island WI 3025	You No Good Girl/Yes Girl	22
67	Studio One SO 2002	Tears From My Eyes/Never Let Your Country Down	30
67	Studio One SO 2013	I Am Going To Cool It (actually by Little Roy)/ MELODIANS: Let's Join Together	30
67	Studio One SO 2017	Love Me With All Your Heart/I Don't Care	30

MINT VALUE £

67 Rio R 125 — Put On Your Style/SOUL BROTHERS: Soul Serenade. . . . 22
68 Blue Cat BS 110 — Go Away/SOUL VENDORS: Julie On My Mind. . . . 20
68 Doctor Bird DB 1124 — It's Hard To Confess/I Need Your Loving 25
68 Doctor Bird DB 1145 — She Want It/Joy In The Morning 22
68 Fab FAB 62 — Looking For A Girl/Aren't You The Guy 30
68 Hi Note HS 001 — A B C Rocksteady/LESLIE BUTLER & COUNT OSSIE: Soul Drums. . . . 20
69 Trojan TR 688 — You Had Your Chance/Wha' She Do Now. . . . 12
69 Upsetter US 323 — The Same Things/I Wear My Slanders 12
70 Trojan TR 7703 — There's A Fire/Last Time 6
70 Trojan TR 7738 — That's What Love Will Do/This Time I Won't Hurt You 8
70 Trojan TR 7743 — Young, Gifted And Black/BEVERLEY'S ALLSTARS: Moon Glow 8
70 Trojan TR 7763 — Tell The Children The Truth/Something Is Wrong Somewhere 6
70 Trojan TR 7771 — Soul Sister/BEVERLEY'S ALLSTARS: Soul Version 6
70 Trojan TR 7782 — It's All In The Game/BEVERLEY'S ALLSTARS: Version II 6
70 Trojan TR 7799 — Fire And Rain/Cold And Lonely Night. . . . 5
71 Ackee AC 141 — Accept My Apologies (actually by B.B. Seaton & Ken Boothe)/ My Version (actually by Conscious Minds) 6
71 Big BG 319 — Can't Hide The Feeling/RUPIE EDWARDS ALLSTARS: Version 6
71 Camel CA 79 — Seven In One Medley (Parts 1 & 2) 6
71 Summit SUM 8514 — My Jamaican Girl/BEVERLEY'S ALLSTARS: Version 5
71 Bullet BU 462 — My Love/Stranger Love 5
74 Dip DL 5009 — You Made A Mistake/Shower Of Blessings 5
67 Coxsone CSL 8005 — ROCKSTEADY (LP) 100
67 Coxsone CSL 8006 — SUNSHINE IS GOLDEN (LP) 70

(see also Gaylords, Rockstones, Delano Stewart, Ken Boothe, B.B. Seaton, Brent Dowe, Dobby Dobson, Jackie Mittoo, Heptones, Clarendonians, Soul Vendors)

JEANNE GAYLE

52 Capitol CL 13814 — Takes Two To Tango/It Wasn't God Who Made Honky Tonk Angels (78, with Cliffie Stone's Music) 8
52 Capitol CL 13847 — Bim Bam Baby/Butterflies (78, with Cliffie Stone's Music). . . . 8

VINLEY GAYLE

64 Black Swan WI 453 — Go-Go/BABA BROOKS: Take Five 22

GAYLET(T)S

68 Island WI 3129 — Silent River Runs Deep/You're My Kind Of Man 22
68 Island WI 3141 — I Like Your World/Lonely Feeling 22
68 Big Shot BI 502 — If You Can't Be Good/Something About My Man. . . . 12
69 Big Shot BI 516 — Son-Of-A-Preacher-Man/That's How Strong My Love Is 12
70 London HLJ 10302 — Son-Of-A-Preacher-Man/I Like Your World. . . . 7

(see also Bob Andy)

GAYLORDS (U.S.)

55 Mercury MB 3226 — Mambo Rock/Plantation Boogie (78). . . . 8
58 Mercury AMT 1006 — Flamingo L'Amore/I'm Longin' For Love 5
58 Mercury AMT 1006 — Flamingo L'Amore/I'm Longin' For Love (78) 8
59 Mercury AMT 1023 — Again/How About Me 5
59 Mercury AMT 1023 — Again/How About Me (78) 12
59 Mercury AMT 1049 — Sweet Than You/Homin' Pigeon 5
60 Mercury MMC 14032 — THAT'S AMORE (LP) 12

GAYLORDS (Jamaica)

66 Island WI 269 — Chipmunk Ska/What Is Wrong? (both actually by Gaylads) 22

(see also Gaylads)

GAYLORDS (U.K.)

66 Columbia DB 7805 — He's A Good Face But He's Down And Out/You Know It Too 18

(see also Dean Ford & Gaylords, Marmalade)

WILTON 'BOGEY' GAYNAIR QUARTET

61 Tempo EXA 103 — BLUE BOGEY VOLUME ONE (EP) 25
59 Tempo TAP 25 — BLUE BOGEY (LP) 150

GAYNOR (Junior English) & ERROL (Dunkley)

65 Blue Beat BB 286 — My Queen/ROLAND ALPHONSO: Roland Plays Prince (B-side actually "Hanging The Beam" by Skatalites) 30

(see also Errol Dunkley)

GLORIA GAYNOR

78 Polydor 2066922 — For The First Time In My Life/This Love Affair 40
87 Fanfare CDFAN 11 — Be Soft With Me Tonight (mixes) (CD) 12

MEL GAYNOR

55 Decca F 10497 — Just A Man/How Important Can It Be? 8
55 Decca F 10542 — With You Beside Me/Oh, My Love 8
55 Decca F 10618 — Bella Notte/Sweet Kentucky Rose 8

(see also Oscar Rabin)

MITZI GAYNOR

59 Top Rank JAR 258 — Happy Anniversary/Play For Keeps. . . . 5
60 Top Rank JAR 289 — I Don't Regret A Thing/The Touch Of Time 5
58 HMV 7EG 8460 — MITZI (EP). . . . 12

ROSEMARY GAYNOR

55 Columbia SCM 5196 — Ain't That A Shame/A Happy Song 12

PAUL GAYTEN

57 London HL 8503 — Yo, Yo, Walk/TUNE WEAVERS: Happy Happy Birthday Baby. . . . 180
57 London HL 8503 — Yo, Yo, Walk/TUNE WEAVERS: Happy Happy Birthday Baby (78) 40
59 London HLM 8998 — The Hunch/Hot Cross Buns 100
59 London HLM 8998 — The Hunch/Hot Cross Buns (78) 30

MINT VALUE £

GAYTONES (Jamaica)

70 High Note HS 037 — Target (actually "Musical Fight" by Crashers)/PATSY: Find Someone (song actually "True Love") — 15
70 High Note HS 048 — Ten To One/Another Version — 8
71 High Note HS 055 — Heart Of The Knights/One Toke Over The Line (B-side actually by Stranger & Gladdy) — 12
71 Green Door GD 4016 — Jamaican Hilite (Parts 1 & 2) — 6
73 Smash SMA 2330 — Blackman Kingdom Come/Swing And Dine (B-side actually by Melodians) — 7

(see also Righteous Flames, Max Romeo, Ethiopians, Jackie Brown, Jean & Gaytones, Huxbrown & Scotty, Charlie Ace, Delano Stewart, Teddy & Conquerors)

GAYTONES (U.S.)

73 Action ACT 4610 — Soul Makossa/Soul Makossa (Version) — 15

GBH

82 Clay CLAY 8 — No Survivors/Self Destruct/Big Women (p/s) — 6
82 Clay CLAY 11 — Sick Boy/Slit Your Own Throat/Am I Dead Yet? (p/s) — 6
82 Clay CLAY 16 — Give Me Fire/Mantrap (p/s) — 6
82 Clay CLAY 16P — Give Me Fire/Mantrap (picture disc) — 8
83 Clay CLAY 22 — Catch 23/Hellhole (p/s) — 6
84 Clay CLAY 36 — Do What You Do/Four Men (p/s) — 6
82 Clay CLAYLP 4 — CITY BABY ATTACKED BY RATS (LP) — 15

G-CLEFS

56 Columbia DB 3851 — Ka-Ding Dong/Darla, My Darlin' — 725
56 Columbia DB 3851 — Ka-Ding Dong/Darla, My Darlin' (78) — 35
61 London HLU 9433 — I Understand/Little Girl I Love You — 5
62 London HLU 9530 — A Girl Has To Know/(There Never Was A Dog Like) Dad — 15
62 London HLU 9563 — Make Up Your Mind/Call Me Away — 15

GEDDES AXE

80 ACS ACS 1 — Return Of The Gods/Wildfire/Aftermath (p/s, with insert) — 20
81 Steel City AXE 1 — Sharpen Your Wits/Rock 'N' Roll (p/s) — 50
82 Bullet BOLT 4 — Escape From New York/Day The Wells Ran Dry/Six Six Six (12", p/s) — 8

ROY GEE

70 J-Dan JDN 4412 — Consider Me/You Walked Away — 8
70 J-Dan JDN 4413 — Try To Understand/I'd Rather Go Blind — 7

RON GEESIN

65 RRG 319/320 — RON GEESIN (EP, handmade p/s, 100 only) — 65
67 Transatlantic (S)TRA 161 — A RAISE OF EYEBROWS (LP) — 40
72 KPM KPM 1102 — ELECTROSOUND (LP, library issue, 1,000 only) — 20
73 Ron Geesin RON 28 — AS HE STANDS (LP) — 15
75 KPM KPM 1154 — ELECTROSOUND VOL. 2 (LP, library issue, 1,000 only) — 20
75 Ron Geesin RON 31 — PATRUNS (LP) — 15
77 Ron Geesin RON 323 — RIGHT THROUGH (LP) — 15
77 KPM KPM 1201 — ATMOSPHERES (LP, library issue, 1,000 only) — 20

(see also Bridget St. John, Pink Floyd, Original Downtown Syncopators, Amory Kane)

RON GEESIN & ROGER WATERS

70 Harvest SHSP 4008 — MUSIC FROM THE BODY (LP, soundtrack; initially green labels with Waters/Geesin photos; later with black labels) — 20/12

(see also Roger Waters, Pink Floyd)

J. GEILS BAND

72 Atco 2400 196 — THE MORNING AFTER (LP) — 12

HERB GELLER QUARTET

56 London RE-U 1067 — SENSATIONAL SAX OF HERB GELLER (EP) — 12

GEMAGE

80 private pressing BGA 1 — Story So Far/Bring Me Death (no p/s) — 50

GEMINI (Portugal)

78 Philips 6031 070 — Dal-Li-Dou (Falling In Love)/Dal-Li-Dou — 12

GEMINI (U.K.)

65 Columbia DB 7638 — Space Walk/Goodbye Joe (demos may credit the 'Original Tornados') — 40

(see also Tornados)

GEMINI (U.K.)

81 Airship AP 345 — COUNTER BALANCE (LP) — 150

GENE

94 Costermonger COST 1 — For The Dead/Child's Body (p/s, 1,994 numbered copies only) — 25
94 Costermonger COST 2 — Be My Light, Be My Guide/This Is Not My Crime (numbered p/s) — 12
94 Costermonger COST 2CD — Be My Light, Be My Guide/This Is Not My Crime/I Can't Help Myself (CD) — 10

GENE & DEBBE

67 London HLE 10165 — Go With Me/Torch I Carry — 7
68 London HLE 10179 — Playboy/I'll Come Running — 10
68 London HLE 10203 — Lovin' Season/Love Will Give Us Wings — 7

GENE & EUNICE

56 Vogue V 9062 — I Gotta Go Home/Have You Changed Your Mind? — 175
56 Vogue V 9062 — I Gotta Go Home/Have You Changed Your Mind? (78) — 65
57 Vogue V 9066 — Move It Over, Baby/This Is My Story — 150
57 Vogue V 9066 — Move It Over, Baby/This Is My Story (78) — 65
57 Vogue V 9071 — Let's Get Together/I'm So In Love With You — 150
57 Vogue V 9071 — Let's Get Together/I'm So In Love With You (78) — 65
57 Vogue V 9083 — Doodle Doodle Doo/Don't Treat Me This Way — 150
57 Vogue V 9083 — Doodle Doodle Doo/Don't Treat Me This Way (78) — 70
58 Vogue V 9106 — I Mean Love/The Angels Gave You To Me — 150

MINT VALUE £

58 Vogue V 9106 — I Mean Love/The Angels Gave You To Me (78) 70
58 Vogue V 9126 — Strange World/The Vow 50
58 Vogue V 9126 — Strange World/The Vow (78) 70
(The above 45s were originally issued with triangular centres; later issues with round centres are worth about half the values listed.)
59 Vogue V 9136 — Bom Bom Lulu/Hi Diddle Diddle 100
59 Vogue V 9136 — Bom Bom Lulu/Hi Diddle Diddle (78) 100
59 London HL 8956 — Poco-Loco/Go-On Kokomo 45
59 London HL 8956 — Poco-Loco/Go-On Kokomo (78) 125

GENE & GENTS

68 Pye 7N 17532 — C'mon Everybody/Hound Dog 7

GENE & JERRY

71 Mercury 6052 050 — You Just Can't Win/Sho' Is Groovin' 7
71 Mercury 6052 087 — Everybody Is Waiting/Ten And Two 7
71 Mercury 6338 051 — ONE AND ONE (LP) 18
(see also Gene Chandler, Jerry Butler)

GENE LOVES JEZEBEL

82 Situation 2 SIT 18T — Shavin' My Neck/Sun & Insanity/Machismo/Glad To Be Alive (12", p/s) 12
82 Situation 2 SIT 20 — Screaming (For Emaline) (p/s) 12
82 Situation 2 SIT 24 — Bruises/Punch Drunk (p/s) 8

GENERAL JOHNSON

(see under 'J')

GENERAL STRIKE

79 Canal CANAL 01 — Part 1: My Body/Part 2: (Parts Of) My Body (p/s) 5
84 Touch — GENERAL STRIKE (cassette in PVC wallet with inserts) 6

GENERAL WOLF

86 SRT SRT 6KS 1085 — I Believe In Love/Take A Dream (p/s) 8

GENERATION GAP

69 Pye 7N 17845 — She's Coming Home/Reach The Top 6
70 Pye 7N 17979 — Any Old Time You're Lonely And Sad/Rainbows 'N' Sorrows 6

GEN(ERATION) X

77 Generation X GX 101 — Your Generation/Listen! (white label test pressing, official bootleg sold at gigs, no p/s) 30
77 Chrysalis CHS 2165 — Your Generation/Day By Day (p/s, original copies with 'A' on label have band credits on front) 6/5
77 Chrysalis CHS 2165 — Your Generation/Day By Day (sleeve only, unissued, featuring 'pre-peroxide' Billy Idol; 1 copy known to exist) 200
77 Chrysalis CHS 2189 — Wild Youth/Wild Dub (Version) (p/s) 8
77 Chrysalis CHS 2189 — Wild Youth/Wild Dub (Version) (p/s, mispressing, plays "No No No", B-side matrix: CHS 2189 B/1) 25
78 Chrysalis CHS 2207 — Ready Steady Go/No No No (p/s) 5
79 Chrysalis CHS(A) 2261 — King Rocker/Gimme Some Truth (pink vinyl, Tony James p/s) 8
79 Chrysalis CHS(B) 2261 — King Rocker/Gimme Some Truth (red vinyl, Billy Idol p/s) 6
79 Chrysalis CHS(C) 2261 — King Rocker/Gimme Some Truth (yellow vinyl, Mark Laff p/s) 10
79 Chrysalis CHS(D) 2261 — King Rocker/Gimme Some Truth (orange vinyl, Bob Andrews p/s) 8
79 Chrysalis CHS 2261 — King Rocker/Gimme Some Truth (black vinyl, Bob Andrews p/s) 6
79 Chrysalis CHS 2310 — Valley Of The Dolls/Shakin' All Over (p/s, marbled brown vinyl) 8
79 Chrysalis CHS 2330 — Friday's Angels/Trying For Kicks/This Heat (p/s, red or black vinyl) 8/25
81 Chrysalis CHS 2488 — Dancing With Myself/Untouchables/King Rocker/Rock On (as Gen X, p/s, some on clear vinyl) 18/8
78 Chrysalis CHR 1169 — GENERATION X (LP, with 'T-shirt offer' wraparound) 35
85 Chrysalis CCD 1169 — GENERATION X (CD) 25
85 Chrysalis CCD 1193 — VALLEY OF THE DOLLS (CD) 25
(see also Billy Idol, Sigue Sigue Sputnik, Empire, Westworld)

GENERATOR (featuring Gary Numan)

94 JVO JVOT 001 — Are 'Friends' Electric? (Eccentric Mix)/Bring Back The Love/Going Home (12", p/s) 8
94 JVO JVO 001 — Are 'Friends' Electric? (Radio Mix)/Are 'Friends' Electric? (Eccentric Mix)/Bring Back The Love/Going Home (CD) 8
(see also Gary Numan)

GENESIS

SINGLES

68 Decca F 12735 — The Silent Sun/That's Me (promos £200) 275
68 Decca F 12775 — A Winter's Tale/One Eyed Hound (promos £250) 300
69 Decca F 12949 — Where The Sour Turns To Sweet/In Hiding (promos £250) 300
70 Charisma GS 1/2 — Looking For Someone/Visions Of Angels (promo only) 500
71 Charisma CB 152 — The Knife (Parts 1 & 2) (some in p/s) 325/60
72 Charisma CB 181 — Happy The Man/Seven Stones (some belated copies in p/s; beware counterfeits) 325/60
73 Charisma (no cat. no.) — Twilight Alehouse (1-sided flexidisc free with *Zig Zag* & later via fan club, [black vinyl, white label test pressings exist — £70] with/without magazine) 35/20
74 Charisma CB 224 — I Know What I Like (In Your Wardrobe)/Twilight Alehouse 5
74 Charisma CB 238 — Counting Out Time/Riding The Scree 8
75 Charisma CB 251 — The Carpet Crawlers/Evil Jam ("The Waiting Room" live) 20
76 Charisma CB 277 — A Trick Of The Tail/Ripples (purple or silver label) 8/5
77 Charisma CB 300 — Your Own Special Way/It's Yourself 6
78 Charisma CB 309 — Follow You, Follow Me/Ballad Of Big (p/s) 5
78 Charisma CB 315 — Many Too Many/The Day The Light Went Out/Vancouver (p/s) 8
80 Charisma CB 369 — Misunderstanding/Evidence Of Autumn (p/s) 8
81 Charisma CB 39 — Keep It Dark/Naminanu (p/s) 5

MINT VALUE £

81 Charisma CB 391-12 Keep It Dark/Naminanu/Abacab (Long Version) (12", p/s) . . . 8
82 Charisma CB 393 Man On The Corner/Submarine (blue label, some with p/s). . . 70/5
82 Charisma GEN 1 3 X 3 (Paperlate/You Might Recall/Me And Virgil) (EP, picture disc). . . 7
82 Lyntone LYN 11806 The Lady Lies (live) (green flexidisc free with *Flexipop* mag, issue 21) . . . 12/7
83 Lyntone LYN 13143 Firth Of Fifth (live edit) (flexidisc, some with numbered gatefold p/s) . . . 20/5
83 Charisma/Virgin TATA Y-1 That's All/Taking It All Too Hard (shaped picture disc). . . 20
84 Charisma/Virgin ALS 1 Illegal Alien/Turn It On Again (live) (shaped picture disc) . . . 20
84 Charisma/Virgin CB 300 Your Own Special Way/It's Yourself (blue label reissue, no p/s) . . . 6
84 Charisma/Virgin CB 356 Turn It On Again/Behind The Lines Part 2 (blue label reissue, no p/s). . . 6
84 Charisma/Virgin CB 369 Misunderstanding/Evidence Of Autumn (blue label reissue, no p/s). . . 6
86 Charisma/Virgin GENSY 1 Invisible Touch/The Last Domino (clear vinyl, foldout p/s). . . 6
86 Charisma/Virgin GENSY 2-12 In Too Deep (Unedited)/Do The Neurotic (Unedited) (12" picture disc in stickered sleeve) . . . 10
86 Virgin SNEG 3-12 Land Of Confusion/Land Of Confusion (Extended)/Feeding The Fire/ Do The Neurotic (CD, gatefold p/s) . . . 10
87 Virgin GENSG 412 Tonight, Tonight, Tonight (Edit)/In The Glow Of The Night/ Paperlate/Tonight, Tonight, Tonight (12" Remix) (12", gatefold p/s) . . . 8
87 Virgin CDEP 1 Tonight, Tonight, Tonight (Edit)/In The Glow Of The Night/ Invisible Touch (12" Remix)/Tonight, Tonight, Tonight (CD, gatefold p/s) . . . 40
87 Virgin DRAW 412 Tonight, Tonight, Tonight (Edit)/In The Glow Of The Night/Paperlate/ Tonight, Tonight, Tonight (12" Remix) (CD, gatefold p/s) . . . 10
87 Virgin GENS 512 Throwing It All Away (live)/I'd Rather Be You/Invisible Touch (live) (12", p/s) . . . 8
88 Virgin CDT 5 Mama (Long Version)/It's Gonna Get Better (Long Version) (3" CD, card p/s) . . . 8
88 Charisma/Virgin CDT 40 SPOT THE PIGEON EP (Match Of The Day/Pigeons/Inside And Out) (3" CD, card sleeve) . . . 10
88 Charisma/Virgin CDF 40 SPOT THE PIGEON EP (Match Of The Day/Pigeons/Inside And Out) (5" export CD, card sleeve) . . . 8
89 Virgin VVD 359 Domino: (Part 1) In The Glow Of The Night/(Part 2) The Last Domino (3" CD free with "Invisible Touch Tour" video). . . 20
91 Virgin GENDG7 I Can't Dance/On The Shoreline/That's All (live)/In Too Deep (live) (CD, with limited edition history & discography booklet). . . 8
92 Virgin GENDG 8 Hold On My Heart/Way Of The World/Your Own Special Way (live) (CD, digipak with 4 postcards). . . 10
92 Virgin GENDX 9 Jesus He Knows Me (Single Mix)/Hearts On Fire/Land Of Confusion (Rehearsal Version) (CD, 'Invisible Series' box set w/ space for other CDs). . . 10
92 Virgin GENS 10 Invisible Touch (live)/Abacab (live) (no'd gatefold p/s) . . . 8
92 Virgin GENDX 10 Invisible Touch (live)/Abacab (live)/The Brazilian (live) (CD, numbered box with booklet) . . . 10
98 Virgin GENCDJ 6 CALLING ALL STATIONS (CD, 7-track sampler, promo only) . . . 8
99 Virgin SAMPGEN 8 TURN IT ON AGAIN (CD, 3-track sampler, promo only) . . . 20

LPs

69 Decca LK 4990 FROM GENESIS TO REVELATION (mono, with lyric sheet, unboxed logo) . . . 480
69 Decca SKL 4990 FROM GENESIS TO REVELATION (stereo, with lyric sheet, unboxed logo). . . 150
70 Decca SKL 4990 FROM GENESIS TO REVELATION (stereo, with lyric sheet, boxed logo). . . 30
70 Charisma CAS 1020 TRESPASS (original pink scroll label & gatefold sleeve with lyric sheet) . . . 20
71 Charisma CAS 1052 NURSERY CRYME (original pink scroll label, gatefold sleeve). . . 20
72 Charisma CAS 1052 NURSERY CRYME (2nd pressing, 'tour' label, gatefold sleeve) . . . 65
74 Decca SKL 4990 IN THE BEGINNING (reissue of 1st LP, 'snake' sleeve with lyric insert). . . 15
75 Charisma CGS 102 GENESIS COLLECTION VOLUME ONE (2-LP, boxed set of "Trespass" & "Nursery Cryme" in original sleeves, with poster) . . . 80
75 Charisma CGS 103 GENESIS COLLECTION VOLUME TWO (2-LP, boxed set of "Foxtrot" & "Selling England By The Pound", with poster) . . . 80

(see also Flaming Youth, Phil Collins, Mike Rutherford, Peter Gabriel, Steve Hackett, Anthony Phillips, Brand X, Quiet World)

GENEVEVE

66 CBS 202061 Once/Just A Whisper (some in p/s) . . . 18/8
66 CBS 202096 Nothing In The World/Summer Days . . . 7
67 CBS 202524 That Can't Be Bad/I Love Him, I Need Him . . . 7

GENGHIS KHAN (Germany)

79 Ariola ARO 163 Genghis Khan/Desert Land (unissued; promos may exist)
79 CBS 12-7317 Genghis Khan/Desert Land (12", clear vinyl with p/s insert) . . . 8

GENGHIS KHAN (U.K.)

83 Genghis Khan GK 1 DOUBLE DEALIN' (If Heaven Is Hell/Highway Passion//Midnight Rendezvous Mean Streak) (EP, double pack). . . 80
83 Wabbit WAB 61/63 Love You/Lady Lady//Mongol Nation/Gone For A Drive (double pack). . . 40

GENOCIDE

79 Safari SAP 2 IMAGES OF DELUSION (EP) . . . 8

GENTILES (U.K.)

68 Pye 7N 17530 Goodbye Baby/Marlena . . . 8

GENTILES (Jamaica)

70 High Note HS 046 Your Destiny/Lock Love Away (actually by Melodians) . . . 12

(see also Melodians)

JOHNNY GENTLE

59 Philips PB 908 Wendy/Boys And Girls (Were Meant For Each Other) . . . 12
59 Philips PB 908 Wendy/Boys And Girls (Were Meant For Each Other) (78). . . 8
59 Philips PB 945 Milk From The Coconut/I Like The Way . . . 10
59 Philips PB 945 Milk From The Coconut/I Like The Way (78) . . . 15
60 Philips PB 988 Darlin' Won't You Wait/This Friendly World . . . 8
60 Philips PB 1069 After My Laughter Came Tears/Sonja . . . 8
61 Philips PB 1142 Pick A Star/Darlin' . . . 8
59 Philips BBE 12345 THE GENTLE TOUCH (EP). . . 70

(see also Darren Young)

MINT VALUE £

TIM GENTLE & HIS GENTLEMEN
65 Oriole CB 1988 — Without You/Someone's In The Kitchen With Dinah 15

GENTLE GIANT
73 WWA WWP 1001 — In A Glass House/An Inmate's Lullaby 12
74 WWA WWS 017 — The Power And The Glory/Playing The Game 12
77 Chrysalis CHS 2160 — I'm Turning Around/Just The Same (live) 6
77 Chrysalis CHS 2181 — Two Weeks In Spain/Free Hand 5
78 Chrysalis CHS 2245 — Thank You/Spooky Boogie 5
79 Chrysalis CHS 2270 — Words From The Wise/No Stranger 5
70 Vertigo 6360 020 — GENTLE GIANT (LP, gatefold sleeve, swirl label, later 'spaceship' label) 35/12
71 Vertigo 6360 041 — ACQUIRING THE TASTE (LP, gatefold sleeve, swirl or 'spaceship' label) 30/12
72 Vertigo 6360 070 — THREE FRIENDS (LP, gatefold sleeve, swirl label, later 'spaceship' label) 30/12
72 Vertigo 6360 080 — OCTOPUS (LP, gatefold sleeve, swirl label) 25
73 WWA WWA 002 — IN A GLASS HOUSE (LP, silk-screen cover, with photo insert & lyric inner) 20
74 WWA WWA 010 — THE POWER AND THE GLORY (LP, with insert) 18
75 Chrysalis CHR 1093 — FREE HAND (LP, green label, with insert) 12
75 Vertigo 6641 334 — GIANT STEPS — THE FIRST FIVE YEARS (2-LP) 15
76 Chrysalis CHR 1115 — INTERVIEW (LP, green label, with lyric inner sleeve) 12
77 Chrysalis CTY 1133 — LIVE (PLAYING THE FOOL) (2-LP, with 12-page booklet) 15
77 Chrysalis CHR 1152 — THE MISSING PIECE (LP, with inner sleeve) 20
78 Chrysalis CHR 1186 — GIANT FOR A DAY (LP, with mask insert & lyric inner sleeve) 12
80 Chrysalis CHR 1285 — CIVILIAN (LP, with lyric inner sleeve) 12

(see also Simon Dupree & Big Sound)

GENTLE INFLUENCE
69 Pye 7N 17666 — Never Trust In Tomorrow/Easy To Love 10
69 Pye 7N 17743 — Always Be A Part Of My Living/Captain Reale 10

GENTLE PEOPLE
67 Columbia DB 8276 — It's Too Late/Sea Of Heartbreak 12

GENTLE PEOPLE
95 Rephlex CAT 040R — JOURNEY (12", Aphex Twin Remix) 8

GENTLE TOUCH
65 London HLR 10175 — Among The First To Know/Merry Go Round 6

BILL GENTLES
69 Gas GAS 104 — Long Life/SCHOOLBOYS: O Tell Me 8
70 Pama PM 801 — What A Woman/Sleepy Cat 6
70 Punch PH 54 — Fight The Good Fight/Fight Beat 6
71 Escort ERT 853 — Bachelor Boy/SCORPIONS: Colour Rites 6
72 Bullet BU 506 — Pure In Heart/Clean Hands 5

(see also Bill Jentles, Bill Jenties)

ART GENTRY
72 Mojo 2092 048 — Breakthrough/Wonderful Dream 7

BOBBIE GENTRY
67 Capitol CL 15511 — Ode To Billie Joe/Mississippi Delta 6
67 Capitol (S)T 2830 — ODE TO BILLIE JOE (LP) 15
68 Capitol (S)T 2842 — THE DELTA SWEETE (LP) 12
69 Capitol E-(S)T 155 — TOUCH 'EM WITH LOVE (LP) 12

BO GENTRY & RITCHIE CORDELL
69 CBS 4299 — Stone Go-Getter/Hung Up 5

GENTRYS
65 MGM MGM 1284 — Keep On Dancing/Make Up Your Mind 12
66 MGM MGM 1296 — Brown Paper Sack/Spread It On Thick 25
66 MGM MGM 1312 — Everyday I Have To Cry/Don't Let It Be 12
68 Bell BLL 1012 — I Can't Go Back To Denver/You Better Come Home 7

GENTS
81 Posh POSH 001 — The Faker/The Pink Panther 20
82 Kosmic KOS 6886 — Schooldays/True Stories (some with p/s) 8/5
83 Posh POSH 007 — Revenge/Girl (p/s) 5
85 Posh no cat. no. — Lambs To The Slaughter/Friday On My Mind 5
80s Posh MEGA 1 — Revenge/Over Me/The Gent (p/s) 5
77 GG no cat. no. — HOW IT ALL BEGAN (LP) 12

GEOFFREY
78 Music Bank BECK 694 — ABH (Who Wants To Listen To Punk Rock?)/Colt 45 Rock (p/s) 15

GEORDIE
72 Regal Zonophone RZ 3067 — Don't Do That/Francis Was A Rocker 12
73 EMI EMI 2008 — All Because Of You/Ain't It Just Like A Woman 6
73 EMI EMI 2031 — Can You Do It/Red Eyed Lady 5
73 EMI EMI 2048 — Electric Lady/Geordie Stomp 5
73 EMI EMI 2100 — Black Cat Woman/Geordie's Lost His Liggy 5
82 EMI EMI 2031 — Nutbush City Limits/No Sweat (p/s) 20
73 EMI EMC 3001 — HOPE YOU LIKE IT (LP) 12
74 EMI EMA 764 — DON'T BE FOOLED BY THE NAME (LP) 15
76 EMI EMC 3134 — SAVE THE WORLD (LP) 18
83 Neat NEAT 1008 — NO SWEAT (LP) 15

(see also Influence, AC/DC)

BARBARA GEORGE
62 London HL 9513 — I Know/Love 20
64 Sue WI 316 — Send For Me/Bless You 35

EARL GEORGE
73 Count Shelly CS 025 — Gonna Give Her All The Love/PRINCE JAZZBO: Wise Shepherd 5

MINT VALUE £

LLOYD GEORGE

62	London HLP 9562	Lucy Lee/Sing Real Loud	75

GEORGETTES

58	London HL 8548	Love Like A Fool/Oh Tonight	50
58	London HL 8548	Love Like A Fool/Oh Tonight (78)	35
60	Pye International 7N 25058	Down By The River/A Pair Of Eyes	12

GEORGIA SLIM/WALTER ROLAND

59	Jazz Collector JEL 2	THE MALE BLUES VOL. 1 (EP)	20

GEORGIA TOM

60s	Riverside RLP 8803	GEORGIA TOM AND FRIENDS (LP)	22

(see also Paramount Allstars)

GEORGIE'S VARSITY 5

61	Vogue Pop V 9189	When My Sugar Walks Down The Street/Five Foot Two, Eyes Of Blue	8

GERALDINE FIBBERS

94	Hut HUT 49	Marmalade/Get Thee Gone (p/s)	5

GERBILS

98	Earworm WORM 14	Lucky Girl/Big White Limo (p/s, 1,000 only)	5

WESLEY GERMS

72	Upsetter US 390	Whiplash/UPSETTERS: Whiplash Version	10

GERONIMO BLACK

72	Uni UNLS 126	GERONIMO BLACK (LP)	22
74	MCA MCF 2683	GERONIMO BLACK (LP, reissue)	12

(see also Frank Zappa/Mothers Of Invention)

DENNY GERRARD

70	Deram Nova SDN 10	SINISTER MORNING (LP, with High Tide)	50

(see also Warm Sounds, High Tide, Open Road, Fifth Avenue, High Tide)

GERRY & THE HOLOGRAMS

79	Absurd ABSURD 4	Gerry And The Holograms/Increased Resistance (p/s)	5
79	Absurd ABSURD 5	The Emperor's New Music (unplayable record, glued into p/s)	8

GERRY & THE PACEMAKERS

63	Columbia DB 4987	How Do You Do It?/Away From You	5
63	Columbia DB 7041	I Like It/It's Happened To Me	5
63	Columbia DB 7126	You'll Never Walk Alone/It's All Right	5
64	Columbia DB 7189	I'm The One/You've Got What I Like	5
64	Columbia DB 7268	Don't Let The Sun Catch You Crying/Show Me That You Care	5
64	Columbia DB 7353	It's Gonna Be Alright/It's Just Because	7
64	Columbia DB 7437	Ferry Cross The Mersey/You You You	5
65	Columbia DB 7504	I'll Be There/Baby, You're So Good To Me	5
65	Columbia DB 7738	Walk Hand In Hand/Dreams	8
66	Columbia DB 7835	La La La/Without You	8
66	Columbia DB 8044	Girl On A Swing/A Fool To Myself	10
74	DJM DJS 298	Remember (The Days Of Rock And Roll)/There's Still Time	7
78	EMI EMI 2814	Ferry Cross The Mersey/Don't Let The Sun Catch You Crying (promo p/s)	5
63	Columbia SEG 8257	HOW DO YOU DO IT? (EP)	22
64	Columbia SEG 8295	YOU'LL NEVER WALK ALONE (EP, initially in misprinted sleeve listing "It's All Right" instead of "Jambalaya" on front)	25/22
64	Columbia SEG 8311	I'M THE ONE (EP)	22
64	Columbia SEG 8346	DON'T LET THE SUN CATCH YOU CRYING (EP)	25
64	Columbia SEG 8367	IT'S GONNA BE ALRIGHT (EP)	25
65	Columbia SEG 8388	GERRY IN CALIFORNIA (EP)	40
65	Columbia SEG 8397	HITS FROM 'FERRY CROSS THE MERSEY' (EP)	35
65	Columbia SEG 8426	RIP IT UP (EP)	45
63	Columbia 33SX 1546	HOW DO YOU LIKE IT? (LP, also stereo SCX 3492)	30/45
65	Columbia 33SX 1693	FERRY CROSS THE MERSEY (LP, soundtrack, with Cilla Black & Fourmost, also stereo SCX 3544)	30/40
67	M. For Pleasure MFP 1153	YOU'LL NEVER WALK ALONE (LP, reissue of "How Do You Like It", different sleeve)	12
65	EMI Regal REG 2018	YOU'LL NEVER WALK ALONE (LP, export issue)	35

(see also Gerry Marsden)

GESCOM

94	Skam SKA 2	Dan One/Five/Cicada/Sciew Spo (12", card folder p/s)	40
95	Skam SKA 3	Snackwitch/Mag (12", printed card folder p/s)	40
95	Clear CLR 408	THE SOUNDS OF MACHINES OUR PARENTS USED (12", p/s)	50
96	Skam SKA 7	KEY NELL 1/2/3/4 (12", bubblewrap sleeve)	15

(see also Autechre)

GESTURES

65	Stateside SS 379	Run Run Run/It Seems To Me	20

STAN GETZ (QUARTET/QUINTET)

78s

50	Melodisc MEL 1109	Five Brothers/Four & One More (78, as Stan Getz Tenor Sax Stars)	7
55	Columbia LB 10002	The Way You Look Tonight/Stars Fell On Alabama (78)	7

SINGLES

60	HMV POP 735	With The Wind And The Rain In Your Hair/I Hadn't Anyone Till You	5
62	Verve POP 1061	Jazz Theme From Dr. Kildare/Desafinado (with Charlie Byrd)	5
63	Verve VS 506	Carnival/Blanco Samba	6

EPs

50s	Esquire EP 16	STAN GETZ QUARTET	8
50s	Esquire EP 48	STAN GETZ QUARTET	8

MINT VALUE £

50s Esquire EP 133 STAN GETZ IN RETROSPECT (as Stan Getz Quartet) 8
50s Esquire EP 134 THE BROTHERS (as Stan Getz & His Four Brothers) 8
50s Esquire EP 173 STAN GETZ QUARTET 8
50s Esquire EP 194 DON'T GET SCARED 8
54 Vogue EPV 1016 STAN GETZ QUARTET 10
55 Columbia SEB 10001 THE ARTISTRY OF STAN GETZ NO. 1 8
55 Columbia SEB 10021 THE ARTISTRY OF STAN GETZ NO. 2 8
56 Vogue EPV 1084 THE BROTHERS — STAN GETZ VOL. 1 8
56 Columbia SEB 10034 'TIS AUTUMN (as Stan Getz Quintet) 8
57 Columbia SEB 10063 THE ARTISTRY OF STAN GETZ NO. 3 8
57 Columbia SEB 10076 MINOR BLUES 8
57 Columbia SEB 10089 COOL SOUNDS 8
58 Columbia SEB 10117 MORE COOL SOUNDS (as Stan Getz Group) 8
59 HMV 7EG 8556 STAN GETZ/OSCAR PETERSON TRIO 8
59 HMV 7EG 8596 STAN GETZ/DIZZY GILLESPIE SEXTET 8
60 HMV 7EG 8641 STAN GETZ/OSCAR PETERSON TRIO NO. 2 8
61 HMV 7EG 8689 COOL VELVET (also stereo GES 5828) 8/10
63 Verve VEP 5009 DESAFINADO (with Charlie Byrd) 8
64 Verve VEP 5014 THE GIRL FROM IPANEMA (with Joao Gilberto) 8

LPs

53 Esquire 20-007 STAN GETZ PLAYS (10" 25
54 Vogue LDE 089 AT STORYVILLE (10" 25
55 Vogue LDE 147 STAN GETZ QUARTET (10") 25
55 Columbia Clef 33CX 10000 AT THE SHRINE NO. 1 (as Stan Getz Quintet) 15
55 Columbia Clef 33CX 10001 AT THE SHRINE NO. 2 (as Stan Getz Quintet) 15
62 HMV CLP 1577 FOCUS (also stereo CSD 1448) 12/15
62 World Record Club T 341 THE STEAMER 12
63 World Record Club T 467 THE SOFT SWING 12
63 Verve (S)VLP 9013 JAZZ SAMBA (with Charlie Byrd, mono/stereo) 12/15
63 Verve VLP 9024 BIG BAND BOSSA NOVA 12
63 Verve (S)VLP 9038 JAZZ SAMBA ENCORE! (with Luiz Bonfa, mono/stereo) 12/15
64 Verve VLP 9065 GETZ—GILBERTO 12
64 Verve VLP 9069 REFLECTIONS 12
64 Verve VLP 9081 GETZ AU GO GO 12
65 M. For Pleasure MFP 1023 INTERPRETATIONS 12
65 Verve VLP 9132 GETZ—GILBERTO NO. 2 12
66 Verve VLP 9139 CRAZY RHYTHM 12
64 Columbia 33SX 1686 THE MODERN WORLD OF GETZ 12
65 Columbia 33SX 1707 THE GETZ AGE 12
65 MGM MGM-C(S) 8001 MICKEY ONE (soundtrack, mono/stereo, with booklet) 20/25
66 Stateside SL 10161 GREATEST HITS 12
67 Verve 2317 062 THE SPECIAL MAGIC OF STAN GETZ AND BURT BACHARACH 12

(see also Dizzy Gillespie, Gil Fuller & Dizzy Gillespie, Astrud Gilberto, Joao Gilberto, Johnny Smith)

G-FORCE

80 Jet JET 183 Hot Gossip/Because Of Your Love (p/s) 20
80 Jet JET 194 You/Trust You Lovin' (no p/s) 12
80 Jet JET 7005 White Knuckles/Rockin' And Rollin'/I Look At You (p/s) 15
80 Jet JETLP 229 G-FORCE (LP, with inner sleeve and patch) 20
80 Jet JETPD 229 G-FORCE (LP, picture disc) 18

(see also Gary Moore, Johnny Gustafson)

G.G. ALLSTARS

70 Explosion EX 2012 Champion/MAYTONES: Funny Man 8
70 Explosion EX 2014 Barabus/This Kind Of Life 8
70 Explosion EX 2023 Man From Carolina/Gold On Your Dress (B-side actually by Slickers) 8
70 Explosion EX 2024 African Melody/Serious Love (B-side actually by Maytones) 6
70 Explosion EX 2025 Ganja Plane/Deep River 7
70 Gas GAS 153 So Alive/Mercy Mr D.J. 7
70 Escort ERT 835 African Melody/Man From Carolina 6
70 G.G. GG 4501 Music Keep On Playing (actually by Cornell Campbell)/
Music Keep On Playing Version 7
71 G.G. GG 4508 Cleanliness Version 2/MAYTONES: Cleanliness 7
71 G.G. GG 4510 Rocking On The G.G. Beat (actually by Maytones)/WINSTON WRIGHT:
Rocking On The G.G. Beat Version II 8
71 G.G. GG 4511 Lonely Nights (actually by Eric Donaldson & West Indians)/
MAYTONES: Let The Version Play 6
71 G.G. GG 4513 All One Nation (actually by Maytones)/VAL BENNETT: Judgement Warrant 8
71 G.G. GG 4526 Rod Of Righteousness (actually "Stretch Forth His Hand" by Jah Huntly)/
DENNIS ALCAPONE: King Of Kings (B-side actually "King Of Glory") 6
72 G.G. GG 4530 Donkey Face Version/MAYTONES: Donkey Face 6
72 Pama PM 846 I'm Feeling Lonely Version/MAYTONES: I'm Feeling Lonely 6
73 Bullet BU 528 People Get Funny Version/MAYTONES: People Get Funny 5
70 Trojan TBL 129 MAN FROM CAROLINA (LP) 25

(see also Paulette & Gee, Billy Dyce, Maytones, Charlie Ace, Monty Morris, Starlights, Lloyd & Carey, Gladdy & Stranger, Heptones, Shorty Perry, Barbara Jones)

G.G.F.H.

94 Peaceville CC8 Welcome To The Process (green vinyl) 15

G.G. RHYTHM SECTION

69 Blue Cat BS 165 T.N.T./MAYTONES: Botheration 15

AMOS GHERKIN QUARTET

70 Parlophone R 5872 Blakey And Me/Theme From An Unmade Silent Movie 5

MINT VALUE £

GHETTO CHILDREN
73 CBS 1450 I Just Gotta Find Somebody To Love Me/Rat-a-tat-tat ... 5

WESS & DORI GHEZZI
75 Bradleys BRAD 7515 Fallin'/Era ... 8

GHOST
69 Gemini GMS 007 When You're Dead/Indian Maid ... 25
70 Gemini GMS 014 I've Got To Get To Know You/For One Second ... 22
88 Bam Caruso OPRA 088 Time Is My Enemy/POETS: I Love Her Still (company sleeve, promo only) ... 6
70 Gemini GME 1004 WHEN YOU'RE DEAD — ONE SECOND (LP, some with extra track, "I've Got To Get To Know Her") ... 160/130
87 Bam Caruso KIRI 077 FOR ONE SECOND (LP, reissue of "When You're Dead" with extra track) ... 12
(see also Velvett Fogg, Shirley Kent, Virginia Tree)

GHOST DANCE
86 Karbon KAR 604 The Grip Of Love/Where Spirits Fly (p/s) ... 5
(see also Skeletal Family, All About Eve, Sisters Of Mercy)

BILL GIANT
61 MGM MGM 1135 Better Let Her Go/When I Grow Too Old To Dream ... 12

GIANT CRAB
68 Uni UN 509 Hot Line Conversation/E.S.P. ... 6

GIANTS
60s Polydor LPHM 46426 IN GERMANY (LP, also stereo SLPHM 237626) ... 25/30

GIANT SAND
87 B'full Of Brains BOB 14 Wishing Well/PAUL ROLAND: Madhouse (Demo) (hard vinyl test pressing) ... 6

GIANT SUNFLOWER
67 CBS 2805 February Sunshine/Big Apple ... 15
67 CBS 3033 Mark Twain/What's So Good About Goodbye? ... 10

BARRY GIBB
70 Polydor 2058 030 I'll Kiss Your Memory/This Time ... 8
84 Polydor POSPP 695 Shine Shine/She Says ('mirror' picture disc) ... 5
(see also Bee Gees)

MAURICE GIBB
70 Polydor 2058 013 Railroad/I've Come Back ... 8
(see also Bee Gees, Fut)

ROBIN GIBB
69 Polydor 56337 Saved By The Bell/Alexandria Good Time (withdrawn) ... 20
69 Polydor 56337 Saved By The Bell/Mother And Jack ... 7
69 Polydor 56368 One Million Years/Weekend ... 8
70 Polydor 56371 August October/Give Me A Smile ... 7
84 Polydor POSPG 668 Another Long Night In New York/I Believe In Miracles (with free single) ... 5
69 Polydor 583 085 ROBIN'S REIGN (LP) ... 30
(see also Bee Gees)

DOUG GIBBONS
65 Decca F 12122 I've Got Tears To Remind Me/I Found Out ... 6

STEVE GIBBONS (BAND)
71 Wizard WIZ 102 Alright Now/Lay Some Lovin' Down ... 10
82 RCA RCA 174 Loving Me, Loving You/That Makes It Tough/No Money Down (picture disc) ... 5
71 Wizard SWZA 5501 SHORT STORIES (LP) ... 45
(see also Uglys, Magic Christians, B,L&G)

CALY GIBBS
71 Amalgamated AMG 870 Seeing Is Believing/JOE GIBBS ALLSTARS: Ghost Capturer ... 18
(see also Carlton Gibbs)

CARLTON GIBBS
70 Amalgamated AMG 872 Ghost Walk/Joy Stick ... 18

GEORGIA GIBBS
55 Mercury MB 3196 Tweedle Dee/You're Wrong, All Wrong (78) ... 7
55 Mercury MB 3223 Dance With Me Henry/Ballin' The Jack (78) ... 8
55 Vogue Coral Q 72088 Ballin' The Jack/I Still Feel The Same About You ... 15
56 Mercury MT 110 Kiss Me Another/Rock Right (78) ... 7
56 Vogue Coral Q 72182 If I Were A Bell/I'll Know ... 10
57 RCA RCA 1011 Sugar Candy/I'm Walking The Floor Over You ... 10
57 RCA RCA 1011 Sugar Candy/I'm Walking The Floor Over You (78) ... 7
58 RCA RCA 1029 Great Balls Of Fire/I Miss You ... 25
58 RCA RCA 1029 Great Balls Of Fire/I Miss You (78) ... 15
58 Mercury 7MT 210 Arriverderci Roma/24 Hours A Day ... 15
58 Columbia DB 4201 The Hula Hoop Song/Keep In Touch ... 10
59 Columbia DB 4259 The Hucklebuck/Better Loved You'll Never Be ... 10
60 London HLP 9098 The Stroll That Stole My Heart/Seven Lonely Days ... 10
65 Stateside SS 423 Let Me Cry On Your Shoulder/Venice Blues ... 5
55 Mercury EP-1-3265 THE MAN THAT GOT AWAY (EP) ... 15
56 Mercury MEP 9505 SWEET GEORGIA GIBBS (EP) ... 15
57 Mercury MEP 9516 SWEET GEORGIA GIBBS VOL. 2 (EP) ... 15
56 Mercury MPT 7500 SINGS THE OLDIES (10" LP) ... 40
57 Mercury MPT 7511 HER NIBS MISS GIBBS (10" LP) ... 40
57 Mercury MPL 6508 SWINGING WITH HER NIBS (LP) ... 22

JOE GIBBS (& DESTROYERS)
70 Amalgamated AMG 855 Nevada Joe (act. by Johnny Lover)/Straight To The Head (act. by Destroyers) ... 18
70 Amalgamated AMG 858 Franco Nero (actually by Count Machuki & Destroyers)/ Version Two (actually by Destroyers) ... 18

MINT VALUE £

70	Amalgamated AMG 859	Rock The Clock/Version Two	15
70	Amalgamated AMG 860	Let It Be/Turn Back The Hands Of Time (both actually by Nicky Thomas)	12
70	Amalgamated AMG 865	Hijacked/Life Is Down In Denver	18
70	Amalgamated AMG 867	Movements/Caesar	15
70	Amalgamated AMG 868	Gift Of God (actually by Lizzy)/The Rapper	10
70	Pressure Beat PR 5504	News Flash/Version Two	10
73	Jackpot JP 811	Ration/Version (as Joe Gibbs All Stars)	8

(see also Lizzy, Reggae Boys, Bunny Flip, Destroyers, Dennis Brown, Caly Gibbs, Nicky Thomas)

MICHAEL GIBBS

70	Deram DML/SML 1063	MICHAEL GIBBS (LP)	55
71	Deram SML 1087	TANGLEWOOD '63 (LP)	55
72	Polydor 2683 011	JUST AHEAD (2-LP)	55
74	Polydor 2383 252	IN THE PUBLIC INTEREST (LP, with Gary Burton)	45
70s	Bronze ILPS 9353	ONLY CHROME ... WATERFALL (LP)	25

(see also Neil Ardley, Gary Burton)

TERRY GIBBS BIG BAND

59	Mercury CMS 18016	LAUNCHING A NEW BAND (LP)	15
61	HMV/Verve CLP 1560	THE EXCITING TERRY GIBBS BIG BAND (LP, also stereo CSD 1439)	12/15

DON GIBSON

56	MGM SP 1177	Sweet Dreams/The Road Of Life Alone	150
56	MGM MGM 909	Sweet Dreams/The Road Of Life Alone (78)	15
58	RCA RCA 1056	Oh Lonesome Me/I Can't Stop Lovin' You	15
58	RCA RCA 1056	Oh Lonesome Me/I Can't Stop Lovin' You (78)	10
58	RCA RCA 1073	Blue Blue Day/Too Soon	15
58	RCA RCA 1073	Blue Blue Day/Too Soon (78)	10
58	RCA RCA 1098	Give Myself A Party/Look Who's Blue	20
58	RCA RCA 1098	Give Myself A Party/Look Who's Blue (78)	10
59	RCA RCA 1110	A Stranger To Me/Who Cares?	15
59	RCA RCA 1110	A Stranger To Me/Who Cares? (78)	14
59	RCA RCA 1150	Don't Tell Me Your Troubles/Heartbreak Avenue	15
59	RCA RCA 1150	Don't Tell Me Your Troubles/Heartbreak Avenue (78)	18
59	RCA RCA 1158	Big Hearted Me/I'm Movin' On	12
59	RCA RCA 1158	Big Hearted Me/I'm Movin' On (78)	20

(The above RCA 45s were originally issued with triangular centres; later round-centre copies are worth half these values.)

60	RCA RCA 1183	Just One Time/I May Never Get To Heaven	12
60	RCA RCA 1200	Far Far Away/A Legend In My Time	12
60	RCA RCA 1217	Sweet Dreams/The Same Street	7
61	RCA RCA 1243	Sea Of Heartbreak/I Think It's Best (To Forget Me)	8
62	RCA RCA 1272	Lonesome Number One/The Same Old Trouble	7
62	RCA RCA 1297	I Can Mend Your Broken Heart/I Let Her Get Lonely	7
63	RCA RCA 1335	Head Over Heels In Love With You/It Was Worth It	8
65	RCA RCA 1456	Again/You're Going Away	8
66	RCA RCA 1524	(Yes) I'm Hurting/My Whole World Is Hurt	8
67	RCA RCA 1626	All My Love/No Doubt About It (as Don Gibson & Jordanaires)	8
68	RCA RCA 1680	Ashes Of Love/Good Morning Dear	8
60	RCA RCX 1050	BLUE AND LONESOME (EP)	18
62	RCA RCX 213	LOOK WHO'S BLUE (EP)	18
62	RCA RCX 214	THAT GIBSON BOY (EP)	18
63	RCA RCX 7122	MAY YOU NEVER BE ALONE (EP)	18
60	RCA RD 27158	THE GIBSON BOY (LP)	60
62	RCA Victor RD/SF 7506	SOME FAVOURITES OF MINE (LP)	25
63	RCA Victor RD/SF 7576	I WROTE A SONG (LP)	25
64	RCA Victor RD 7641	GOD WALKS THESE HILLS (LP)	25

GINNY GIBSON

55	MGM SP 1121	Like Ma-a-d/Once There Was A Little Girl	12
58	MGM MGM 953	Whatever Lola Wants (Lola Gets)/If Anything Should Happen	15

JODY GIBSON & MULESKINNERS

59	Parlophone R 4579	Kissin' Time/Man On My Trail	15
60	Parlophone R 4645	If You Don't Know/So You Think You've Got Troubles	15

LORNE GIBSON TRIO

62	Decca F 11519	Little Black Book/What Kind Of Love Is This?	5
63	Decca F 11684	Some Do, Some Don't (Some Will, Some Won't)/Heaven's Above	5
64	Decca F 11814	Hang Up The Phone/I Think It's Best To Forget Me	5
64	Decca F 12005	The Girl I Loved/Don't Go Near The Indians	5
65	Decca F 12102	Red Roses For A Blue Lady/Talking To Your Picture	5
65	Decca F 12290	I'll Give You Me/As Lovers Do	5
66	Decca F 12357	A Little Lovin' Light/When Baby Says Goodbye	5
66	Decca F 12450	Jingle Jangle/Roses From A Stranger (solo)	5
69	RCA RCA 1917	Eva Magdalena/A Thing Called Love	5

STEVE GIBSON & RED CAPS

57	HMV POP 417	Silhouettes/Flamingo	175
57	HMV POP 417	Silhouettes/Flamingo (78)	25

WAYNE GIBSON (& DYNAMIC SOUNDS)

63	Decca F 11713	Linda Lu/Beachcomber	18
64	Decca F 11800	Come On Let's Go/Pop The Whip	18
64	Pye 7N 15680	Kelly/See You Later Alligator	15
65	Pye 7N 15798	Portland Town/Please Baby Please	10
65	Parlophone R 5357	Ding Dong The Witch Is Dead/In The Night	10
65	Columbia DB 7683	One Little Smile/Baby, Baby, Baby Pity Me	30
66	Columbia DB 7911	Under My Thumb/It Always Happens (Icey) (solo)	35
66	Columbia DB 7998	For No One/He's Got The Whole World In his Hands (solo)	10
75	Pye 7N 45455	Yesterday's Papers/Don't Waste Time Following Me (solo)	5

MINT VALUE £

GIBSONS

65 CBS 202015 Any Time That You're Lonely/Born To Be Free . . . 7
66 CBS 202063 Come Summertime/Summer Affair . . . 7
66 Deram DM 103 Two Kinds Of Lovers/Hey Girl . . . 6
67 Deram DM 119 The Magic Book/You Know I Need Your Lovin' . . . 7
67 Major Minor MM 524 Night And Day/City Life . . . 10
67 Major Minor MM 538 Lazy Summer Day/She's Not Like Any Girl . . . 10
67 Major Minor MM 547 Only When You're Lonely/Ode To A Dolls House . . . 7

GIDIAN (& UNIVERSALS)

66 Columbia DB 7826 Try Me Out/There Isn't Anything . . . 20
66 Columbia DB 7916 Fight For Your Love/See If She Cares . . . 8
66 Columbia DB 8041 Feeling/Don't Be Sentimental (as Gidian & Universals) . . . 10
70 UPC UPC 107 That's Love/We Are The Happiest . . . 6
(see also Universals, Chris Lamb & Universals)

GIFT

81 Venus ORBIT 1 Crashing Down/It'll End In Tears (p/s) . . . 20

GIFTED CHILDREN

81 Whaam! WHAAM 001 Painting By Numbers/Lichtenstein Girl (p/s) . . . 30
(see also Television Personalities)

GIGGETTY

78 Pye 7N 46136 Black Country Christmas/Motorway Mess . . . 12
75 GE 100 DAWN TO DUSK IN THE BLACK COUNTRY (LP, with insert) . . . 50
77 Bridge GE 101 TAMBOURINE (LP) . . . 40
80 Bridge GE 103 BLACK COUNTRY TIME (LP, also listed as Revolver REV LP1) . . . 40

GILBERTO GIL

71 Famous SFM 1001 GILBERTO GIL (LP) . . . 18

GILBERT

67 CBS 3089 Disappear/You . . . 18
68 CBS 3399 What Can I Do?/You . . . 18
69 Major Minor MM 613 Mister Moody's Garden/I Wish I Could Cry . . . 20
(see also Gilbert O'Sullivan)

HERSCHEL BURKE GILBERT

63 London HLD 9655 Dick Powell Theme/Nervous Teaser Theme . . . 7

GEORGE GILBERT

74 Mime LPMS 7041 MEDWAY FLOWS SOFTLY (LP, with insert) . . . 15

GILBERT & LEWIS

81 4AD AD 106 Ends With The Sea/Hung Up To Dry Whilst Building An Arch (p/s) . . . 6
82 Cherry Red BRED 27 MZUI (LP, PVC cover, insert sleeve) . . . 12
(see also Wire, Dome, Cupol)

ASTRUD GILBERTO

64 Verve VS 520 Girl From Ipanema (with Stan Getz)/STAN GETZ & JOAO GILBERTO: Blowin' In The Wind . . . 7
66 Verve VEP 5019 AND ROSES AND ROSES (EP, with Antonio Carlos Jobim) . . . 12
66 Verve (S)VLP 9163 A CERTAIN SMILE AND A CERTAIN KIND OF SADNESS (LP) . . . 15
69 Verve (S)VLP 9242 I HAVEN'T GOT ANYTHING BETTER TO DO (LP) . . . 15
72 C.T.I. CTL 1 GILBERTO WITH TURRENTINE (LP, with Stanley Turrentine) . . . 12
(see also Stan Getz, Stanley Turrentine)

JOAO GILBERTO

61 Parlophone PMC 1248 BOSSA-FINADO (LP) . . . 15
(see also Stan Getz)

GILDED CAGE

69 Tepee TPR 1003 Long Long Road (For The Broken Heart)/Baby Grumpling . . . 35
(see also She Trinity)

COSMO GILE

60 Top Rank JAR 410 Bambina D'Amsterdam/Tintarella Di Luna . . . 8

GILES, GILES & FRIPP

68 Deram DM 188 One In A Million/Newly-Weds . . . 60
68 Deram DM 210 Thursday Morning/Elephant Song . . . 50
68 Deram DML/SML 1022 THE CHEERFUL INSANITY OF GILES, GILES AND FRIPP (LP, mono/stereo) . . . 80/70
70 Deram SPA 423 THE CHEERFUL INSANITY OF GILES, GILES AND FRIPP (LP, stereo reissue) . . . 25
(see also Brain, Trendsetters Ltd, League Of Gentlemen, King Crimson, Fripp & Eno, McDonald & Giles)

TOM GILFELLON

72 Trailer LER 2079 LOVING MAD TOM (LP, red label) . . . 15
76 Topic 12TS 282 IN THE MIDDLE OF THE TUNE (LP, blue label) . . . 15

GILGAMESH

75 Caroline CA 2007 GILGAMESH (LP) . . . 20
(see also Hugh Hopper)

TERRY GILKYSON & EASY RIDERS

58 Philips JK 1007 Marianne/Goodbye Chaquita (jukebox issue) . . . 15
60 Fontana TFE 17326 STROLLING BLUES (EP) . . . 15
60 Fontana TFE 17327 LONESOME RIDER (EP) . . . 15
61 London RER 1333 ROLLIN' (EP) . . . 18
53 Brunswick LA 8618 GOLDEN MINUTES OF FOLK MUSIC (10" LP) . . . 25
61 London HA-R 2301 ROLLIN' (LP, also stereo SAH-R 6111) . . . 15/18
61 London HA-R 2323 REMEMBER THE ALAMO (LP, as Easyriders Including Terry Gilkyson) . . . 15
(see also Easy Riders)

MINT VALUE £

(IAN) GILLAN (BAND)

78	Island R 553-B	Twin Exhausted (live)/Smoke On The Water (live)/ILLUSION: Madonna Blue/Revolutionary (12", promo only, as Ian Gillan Band)	20
78	Island WIP 6423	Mad Elaine/Mercury High (as Ian Gillan Band, company sleeve)	8
79	Acrobat BAT 2	Vengeance/Smoke On The Water (p/s)	6
79	Acrobat BAT 1212	She Tears Me Down/Puget Sound/Vengeance/Mr. Universe (12", stickered card sleeve, promo only)	15
80	Virgin VS 355	Sleeping On The Job/Higher And Higher (p/s, with free patch)	5
80	Virgin VS 362	No Easy Way/Handles On Her Hips/Might As Well Go Home (p/s)	5
80	Virgin VS 377	Trouble/Your Sister's On My List (poster p/s)	5
80	Virgin VS 377	Trouble/Your Sister's On My List//Mr Universe (live)/Vengeance (live)/ Smoke On The Water (live) (double pack, gatefold p/s)	6
81	Virgin VSK 103	Mutually Assured Destruction/The Maelstrom (gatefold p/s, with booklet)	5
81	Sounds FREEBIE No. 2	I'll Rip Out Your Spine (extract)/PROFESSIONALS: Little Boys In Blue (extract) (33rpm 1-sided flexi, printed die-cut sleeve, free with *Sounds* paper)	8/5
81	Lyntone LYN 10599	Higher And Higher/Spanish Guitar (1-sided blue flexi with *Flexipop* magazine 13)	10/6
81	Lyntone LYN 10599	Higher And Higher/Spanish Guitar (same tracks both sides, hard vinyl test pressing, handwritten white labels)	35
82	Virgin VSY 465	Restless/On The Rocks (live) (picture disc)	5
82	Virgin VSY 519	Living For The City/Purple Sky (picture disc, mispressed, B-side plays "Breaking Chains", some with explanatory sticker)	5
82	Virgin VSY 519	Living For The City/Purple Sky (picture disc)	7
82	Virgin VS 537	Long Gone/Figi (foldout p/s)	5
82	Kerrang!	Purple Sky/GARY MOORE: Wishing Well/TELEPHONE: Squeeze (flexidisc free with *Kerrang!* magazine)	12/5
88	Virgin VS 1088	South Africa/John (p/s, as Ian Gillan)	5
88	Virgin TVS 1088	South Africa (extended mix)/South Africa/John (12", p/s, as Ian Gillan)	10
90	Teldec YZ 513	No Good Luck/Love Gun (p/s, as Ian Gillan)	5
90	Teldec YZ 513 (TW)	No Good Luck/Love Gun/Rock'N'Roll Girls (12", "In Rock" or portrait p/s) .. each	8
90	Teldec SAM 678	Talking To You/Moonshine (12", clear vinyl promo, in PVC wallet with insert & postcard)	8
91	East West SAM 906	Toolbox/Hang Me Out To Dry/Dirty Dog/Pictures Of Hell (12" promo, black sl.)	8
76	Polydor/Oyster 2490 136	CHILD IN TIME (LP, gatefold sleeve, as Ian Gillan Band)	15
77	Island ILPS 9511DJ	IAN GILLAN BAND SAMPLER (LP, 1-sided promo for "Scarabus", company sleeve)	25
78	Island ILPS 9545	LIVE AT THE BUDO-KAN (LP, unissued)	
80	Virgin V 2171	GLORY ROAD (LP, with bonus LP "For Gillan Fans Only" [VDJ 32], stickered, embossed sleeve & inner sleeves)	12
82	Virgin VP 2238	MAGIC (LP, picture disc in die-cut sleeve with insert)	12

(see also Episode Six, Deep Purple, Ray Fenwick, Split Knee Loons, John McCoy, Johnny Gustafson, Bernie Tormé, Thunderstick, Jerusalem, Quatermass, Strapps, Colin Towns, White Spirit, Zzebra, Rock Aid Armenia)

DANA GILLESPIE

65	Pye 7N 15872	Donna Donna/It's No Use Saying If	12
65	Pye 7N 15962	Thank You Boy/You're A Heartbreak Man	8
67	Pye 7N 17280	Pay You Back With Interest/Adam Can You Beat That	8
68	Decca F 12847	You Just Gotta Know My Mind/He Loves Me, He Loves Me Not	10
74	RCA RCA 0211	Weren't Born A Man/All Gone	8
74	RCA RCA 2466	Andy Warhol/Dizzy Heights	10
75	RCA RCA 2489	Really Love That Man/Hold Me Gently	5
69	Decca SKL 5012	BOX OF SURPRISES (LP)	50
73	RCA APL1 0354	WEREN'T BORN A MAN (LP)	20
74	RCA APL1 0682	AIN'T GONNA PLAY NO SECOND FIDDLE (LP)	15

DIZZY GILLESPIE (QUINTET)

56	Vogue V 2116	The Champ (Parts 1 & 2)	5
59	HMV 7EG 8574	Constantinople/Willow Weep For Me	7
60	HMV POP 705	Doddlin'/Dizzy's Blues	5
55	Vogue EPV 1022	DIZZY GILLESPIE (EP)	8
55	Vogue EPV 1049	DIZZY GILLESPIE WITH STRINGS (EP)	8
56	Vogue EPV 1078	DIZZY GILLESPIE (EP)	8
56	Vogue EPV 1094	THE CHAMP — DIZZY GILLESPIE (EP)	8
56	Vogue EPV 1157	DIZZY GILLESPIE AND HIS ORCHESTRA (EP)	8
56	Vogue EPV 1158	DIZZY GILLESPIE AND HIS ORCHESTRA (EP)	8
57	Columbia Clef SEB 10075	PILE DRIVER (EP)	8
57	Columbia Clef SEB 10096	BIRKS WORKS (EP)	8
60	HMV 7EG 8577	MELLOW SOUNDS (EP, as Dizzy Gillespie Quintet)	8
61	HMV 7EG 8646	MORE MELLOW SOUNDS (EP, as Dizzy Gillespie Quintet)	8
63	Philips 430 793BE	NEW SOUND IN JAZZ (EP)	8
64	Philips BE 12552	BE BOP (EP)	8
65	Philips BE 12583	FILM THEMES (EP)	8
66	Verve VRE 5022	ALWAYS (EP)	8
60	Esquire EP 193	DIZZY WITH STRINGS (EP, with Operatic Strings)	8
52	Esquire 20-003	OPERATIC STRINGS (10" LP)	20
53	Vogue LDE 017	DIZZY GILLESPIE PLAYS (10" LP)	20
53	Vogue LDE 033	DIZZY GILLESPIE PLAYS — JOHNNY RICHARDS CONDUCTS (10" LP)	20
54	Vogue LDE 039	PARIS CONCERT (10" LP)	20
54	Vogue LDE 076	DIZZY GILLESPIE AND ORCHESTRA (10" LP)	20
54	HMV DLP 1047	DIZZY GILLESPIE AND HIS ORCHESTRA (10" LP)	20
54	Felsted EDL 87006	DIZZY GILLESPIE'S OPERATIC STRINGS — JEALOUSY (10" LP)	20
55	Vogue LDE 135	DIZZY GILLESPIE AND HIS ORCHESTRA (10" LP)	20
55	Columbia Clef 33CX 10002	DIZZY GILLESPIE AND HIS ORCHESTRA (LP)	15
58	Columbia Clef 33CX 10144	DIZZY IN GREECE (LP)	20
59	HMV CLP 1318	HAVE TRUMPET, WILL TRAVEL (LP)	15
60	HMV CLP 1381	THE GREATEST TRUMPET OF THEM ALL (LP)	12

			MINT VALUE £
61	HMV CLP 1431	PORTRAIT OF DUKE ELLINGTON (LP)	12
62	HMV CLP 1484	GILLESPIANA (LP, also stereo CSD 1392)	12/15
62	Verve VLP/SVLP 9016	CARNEGIE HALL CONCERT (LP)	12
63	Realm RM 114	THE DIZZY GILLESPIE STORY VOL. 1 (LP)	12
63	Realm RM 118	THE DIZZY GILLESPIE STORY VOL. 2 (LP)	12
65	M. For Pleasure MFP 1041	THE CHAMP (LP)	12
67	Fontana TL 5343	OPERATIC STRINGS (LP, reissue)	12
71	Pye PKL 4403	SOULED OUT (LP)	12
73	Mainstream MSL 1010	DIZZY GILLESPIE & MITCHELL RUFF DUO (LP)	12
70s	Pablo 231 0794	FREE RIDE (LP)	12

(see also Miles Davis, Lalo Schifrin)

DIZZY GILLESPIE & STAN GETZ

60	HMV 7EG 8596	DIZZY GILLESPIE/STAN GETZ SEXTET (EP)	8
55	Columbia Clef 33C 9009	DIZZY GILLESPIE — STAN GETZ SEXTET (LP)	12
55	Columbia 33C 9027	MORE OF (10" LP)	15

(see also Stan Getz)

DIZZY GILLESPIE & CHARLIE PARKER

57	Columbia Clef SEB 10087	ONE MORE TIME: WITH BIRD AND DIZ (EP)	8
61	Vogue LAE 12252	DIZ 'N BIRD IN CONCERT (LP)	15

(see also Charlie Parker)

DIZZY GILLESPIE & HIS ORCHESTRA

54	Felsted 82001	Blue & Sentimental/Moon Nocturne (78)	8

DIZZY GILLESPIE & ORCHESTRA/DON BYAS QUARTET

57	MGM MGM-EP 579	DIZZ AND DON (EP, 2 tracks each)	8

DIZZY GILLESPIE/KAI WINDING'S BIRDLANDERS

58	MGM MGM-EP 681	TWO BY TWO (EP, 2 tracks each)	8

HUGH GILLESPIE

78	Topic 12TS 364	CLASSIC RECORDINGS OF IRISH TRADITIONAL FIDDLE MUSIC (LP)	12

JAZZ GILLUM

66	RCA Victor RD 7816	JAZZ GILLUM 1938-1947 (LP)	22
70	RCA Intl. INTS 1177	YOU GOT TO REAP WHAT YOU SOW (LP)	15
71	Xtra XTRA 1111	BLUES BY JAZZ GILLUM, WITH ARBEE STIDHAM AND MEMPHIS SLIM (LP)	15

JIMMY GILMER & FIREBALLS

62	London HLD 9632	I'm Gonna Go Walkin'/Born To Be With You (as Chimmy Gilmer)	15
63	London HLD 9789	Sugar Shack/My Heart Is Free	10
64	London HLD 9827	Daisy Petal Pickin'/When My Tears Have Dried	10
64	London HLD 9872	Ain't Gonna Tell Nobody/Young Am I	12
64	London HLD 9898	Look At Me/I'll Send For You	15
65	Dot DS 16666	Thunder 'N' Lightnin'/Cry Baby (unissued)	
65	Stateside SS 418	Thunder 'N' Lightnin'/What Do You Do	15
65	Stateside SS 472	She Belongs To Me/Rambler's Blues	10
68	London HL 10232	Three Squares/Baby	6
64	London HA-D/SH-D 8150	SUGAR SHACK (LP)	50
65	Dot DLP 3577	BUDDY'S BUDDY — BUDDY HOLLY SONGS BY JIMMY GILMER (LP)	50

(see also Fireballs, Jim & Monica)

DAVE GILMOUR

78	Harvest HAR 5167	There's No Way Out Of Here/Deafinitely (no p/s)	7
84	Harvest HAR 5226	Blue Light (LP Version)/Cruise (blue or red titles on p/s)	each 5
84	Harvest 12HAR 5226	Blue Light (LP Version)/Cruise (12", p/s)	10
84	Harvest HAR 5229	Love On The Air/Let's Get Metaphysical (p/s)	5
84	Harvest HARP 5229	Love On The Air/Let's Get Metaphysical (shaped picture disc)	12
84	Harvest 12HAR 5229	Love On The Air/Let's Get Metaphysical (12", p/s)	8

(see also Pink Floyd, Joker's Wild, Rock Aid Armenia)

PETER GILMORE

60	HMV POP 740	Follow That Girl/Come Away	8

JAMES GILREATH

63	Pye International 7N 25190	Little Band Of Gold/I'll Walk With You	12
63	Pye International 7N 25213	Lollipops, Lace And Lipstick/Mean Ole River	12

GORDON GILTRAP (BAND)

73	Philips 6006 344	No Way Of Knowing/I See A Road	15
79	Cube BUG 89	The Waltons Theme/Birds Of A Feather (p/s)	5
79	Electric LWOP 29	Fear Of The Dark/Catwalk Blues/Inner Dream (12", picture disc)	8
68	Transatlantic TRA 175	GORDON GILTRAP (LP)	30
69	Transatlantic TRA 202	PORTRAIT (LP)	25
71	MCA MKPS 2020	A TESTAMENT OF TIME (LP)	20
73	Philips 6308 175	GILTRAP (LP, with lyric insert)	20
76	Electric TRIX 2	VISIONARY (LP, with insert)	12
77	Electric TRIX 4	PERILOUS JOURNEY (LP, with insert)	12
78	Electric TRIX 7	FEAR OF THE DARK (LP, gatefold sleeve)	15
81	Themes International	THEMES (LP, by Gordon Giltrap Band, library issue)	18
82	KPM KPM 1292	SOUNDWAVES (LP, by Gordon Giltrap Band, library issue)	18
82	KPM KPM 1330	IN AT THE DEEP END (LP, by Gordon Giltrap Band, library issue)	18

(see also Accolade, Pauline Filby, Catherine Andrews)

GINGER ALE

70	Famous FAM 102	In The Sand/Get Off My Life Woman	5

GINGER JUG BAND

70s	GJB 001	GINGER JUG BAND (LP, private pressing)	22

GINGER SNAPS

65	RCA RCA 1483	The Sh Down Down Song/I've Got Faith In Him	15

MINT VALUE £

HERMIONE GINGOLD & GILBERT HARDING
53 Philips PB 104 — Oh, Grandma/Takes Two To Tango (78) . . . 8

GINGRINI
73 Harry J. HJ 6647 — Zion 'lah/Zion 'lah (Version) . . . 6

GINHOUSE
71 Charisma CAS 1031 — GINHOUSE (LP) . . . 55

GINKS
65 Summit ATL 4176 — A TRIBUTE TO THE BEATLES (LP) . . . 15

GINO & GINA
58 Mercury 7MT 230 — Pretty Baby/Love's A Carousel . . . 45
58 Mercury MT 230 — Pretty Baby/Love's A Carousel (78) . . . 18

ALLEN GINSBERG
60s Cape Goliard — Wales: A Visitation (single issued with book of same title) . . . 25
65 Better Books (no cat. no.) — ALLEN GINSBERG READING AT BETTER BOOKS (LP) . . . 80
65 Love Books Ltd. LB 0001 — ALLEN GINSBERG, LAURENCE FERLINGHETTI, GREGORY CORSO & ANDREI VOZNESENSKY READING AT THE ARCHITECTURAL ASSOCIATION (LP) . . . 80
68 Transatlantic TRA 192 — GINSBERG'S THING (LP) . . . 25
(see also Ginsbergs)

GINSBERGS
67 Saga Psyche PSY 3002 — THE GINSBERGS AT THE ICA (LP) . . . 15
(see also Allen Ginsberg)

GIORGIO
66 Page One POF 003 — Full Stop/Believe Me . . . 6
67 Page One POF 028 — How Much Longer Must I Wait/Bla Bla Diddly . . . 6
69 MCA MCA 1094 — Happy Birthday/Looky Looky . . . 5
(see also Giorgio Moroder, Giorgio & Marco's Men)

GIORGIO & MARCO'S MEN
66 Polydor 56101 — Girl Without A Heart/Run Run . . . 7
68 Electratone EP 1003 — Baby I Need You/Maureen . . . 65

GIPSY LOVE
72 BASF BAP 5026 — GIPSY LOVE (LP) . . . 22

CHUCK GIRARD
60s Myrrh MYR 1025 — CHUCK GIRARD (LP) . . . 15
60s Myrrh MYR 1065 — WRITTEN ON THE WIND (LP) . . . 15

MARTINE GIRAULD
92 Opaz OP 001SRH — REVIVAL (12" EP, p/s) . . . 8

GIRL
79 Jet JET 159 — My Number/My Number (Version) (clear vinyl, PVC sleeve, some with 2 stickers) 6/5
79 Jet JET 159 — My Number/My Number (Version) (black vinyl, promo only) . . . 5
80 Jet JET 169 — Do You Love Me?/Strawberries (p/s) . . . 7
80 Jet JET 176 — Hollywood Tease (Remix)/You Really Got Me/My Number (some in poster p/s) . . 7/5
80 Jet JET 191 — Love Is A Game/Little Miss Ann (white vinyl, patch & sticker in PVC sleeve) . . . 8
80 Jet JET 10 191 — Love Is A Game/Little Miss Ann (10", white vinyl with sticker in PVC sleeve) . . . 8
82 Jet JET 7019 — Old Dogs/Passing Clouds (p/s) . . . 5
80 Jet JETLP 224 — SHEER GREED (LP, stickered sleeve with inner) . . . 15
82 Jet JETLP 238 — WASTED YOUTH (LP, with inner sleeve) . . . 12
(see also Def Leppard, Bernie Tormé)

GIRLFRIENDS
63 Colpix PX 712 — Jimmy Boy/For My Sake . . . 50

GIRLIE
69 Treasure Isle TI 7053 — Boss Cocky/LOVE SHOCKS: Musical True . . . 15
69 Bullet BU 400 — Madame Straggae/LAUREL AITKEN: Stupid Married Man . . . 8
69 Duke DU 42 — African Meeting (as Girlie & Junior)/JOSH: Higher And Higher . . . 7
70 Joe JRS 7 — Small Change/Mind Your Business (as Girlie & Joe [Mansano]) . . . 8
70 Ackee ACK 124 — Decimilization/Decimilization Version (as Girlie & Paul) . . . 6
(see also Laurel Aitken & Girlie)

GIRLS AT OUR BEST
80 Records RR 001 — Getting Nowhere Fast/Warm Girls (p/s) . . . 10
81 Rough Trade RT 055 — Politics/It's Fashion (p/s) . . . 5
81 Happy Birthday UR 4 — Go For Gold/I'm Beautiful Now (p/s) . . . 8
81 Happy Birthday UR 6 — Fast Boyfriends/This Train (p/s) . . . 8
81 Happy Birthday RULP 1 — PLEASURE (LP, with lyric insert, 1st 10,000 with free 'pleasure bag' with 2 postcards, sticker & stencil) . . . 12/10

GIRLSCHOOL
79 City NIK 6 — Take It All Away/It Could Be Better (p/s, red vinyl, pink p/s, b&w front photo) . . . 7
79 City NIK 6 — Take It All Away/It Could Be Better (p/s, black vinyl, orange p/s) . . . 5
79 Mulligan LUNS 723 — Take It All Away/It Could Be Better (Irish version, no p/s, red vinyl) . . . 10
81 Bronze BROX 118 — Hit And Run/Tonight/Tush (10" EP) . . . 8
81 Bronze BROX 126 — C'mon Let's Go/Tonight/Demolition Boys (10" EP) . . . 8
82 Bronze BRO 144 — THE WILDLIFE EP: Don't Call It Love/Wildlife/Don't Stop (red vinyl, p/s) . . . 5
81 Bronze BRON 534 — HIT AND RUN (LP, red vinyl) . . . 15
85 Mercury 824611 M1 — RUNNING WILD (LP) . . . 12
(see also Motörhead, Killjoys)

GIRL TALK
84 Innervision IVST 4 — Can The Rhythm (mixes) (12", p/s) . . . 12

MINT VALUE £

GIST
81 Rough Trade RT 58 This Is Love/Yanks (p/s) . . . 8
81 Rough Trade RT 85 Love At First Sight/Light Aircraft (p/s) . . . 7
83 Rough Trade RT 125 Fool For A Valentine/Fool For A Version (p/s) . . . 7

GITTE
64 Columbia DB 7440 The Heart That You Break (May Be Your Own)/Seems Just Like Old Times . . . 10

JIMMY GIUFFRE
55 Capitol LC 6699 JIMMY GIUFFRE (10" LP) . . . 15
57 London Jazz LTZK 15059 THE JIMMY GIUFFRE CLARINET (LP) . . . 12
58 London Jazz LTZK 15130 JIMMY GIUFFRE (LP) . . . 12
58 London Jazz LTZK 15137 TRAV'LIN' LIGHT (LP) . . . 12
(see also Shelly Manne)

GLADDY (Anderson) & FOLLOWERS
69 Blue Cat BS 172 Judas/The World Come To An End . . . 18
(see also Stranger & Glady)

GLADDY (Anderson) & STRANGER (Cole)
73 Pama PM 872 Dedicated To Illiteracy/G.G. ALLSTARS: Dub . . . 8
(see also Gladstone Anderson, Stranger Cole, Stranger & Glady)

GLADIATORS
63 HMV POP 1134 Tovaritch/Bleak House . . . 20
(see also Nero & Gladiators)

GLADIATORS
68 Direction 58-3854 Girl Don't Make Me Wait/Can't Get Away From Heartbreak . . . 8
69 Direction 58-4308 Waiting On The Shores Of Nowhere/I'll Always Love You . . . 8
69 Direction 58-4507 As Long As I Live/Everything . . . 6
69 Direction 58-4660 Twelfth Of Never/Lovin' My Baby Back Home . . . 6

GLADIATORS (Jamaica)
69 Doctor Bird DB 1114 The Train Is Coming/So Fine . . . 25
69 Studio One SO 2072 Hello Carol/RICHARD ACE: More Reggae . . . 30
69 Bamboo BAM 7 Anywhere/SOUND DIMENSION: Baby Face . . . 12
70 Duke DU 58 My Girl (actually by Glen Adams)/You Were To Be . . . 10
72 Ackee ACK 149 Sonia/SOUND DIMENSION: Solas . . . 12

GLADIATORS
72 Pye 7N 45155 Tiptoe Through The Tulips/When We All Go In The Ring (p/s) . . . 5

GLADIATORS (Jamaica)
70s Rock Steady Rev. REVR 12 Unusual Reggae/Andue . . . 5

GLADIOLAS
57 London HLO 8435 Little Darlin'/Sweetheart, Please Don't Go . . . 260
57 London HLO 8435 Little Darlin'/Sweetheart, Please Don't Go (78) . . . 60
(see also Maurice Williams & Zodiacs)

GLAND SHROUDS
80s Daark Inc. D.I. 3 STAFF IN CONFIDENCE/TOYSHOP UNIVERSAL (cassette) . . . 12
(see also Karl Blake, Lemon Kittens, Fur Fur)

GLASER BROTHERS
69 MGM MGM-CS 8115 NOW COUNTRY (LP) . . . 12

GLASGOW
84 Neat NEAT 40 Stranded/Heat Of The Night (p/s) . . . 15
84 Clydebank CLY 001 GLASGOW'S MILES BETTER (12" EP) . . . 12

GLASS
82 Glass GLASS1 New Colours/Sweet Entropy (p/s) . . . 22

PHILIP GLASS
70s Chatham Square LP 1001/2 MUSIC WITH CHANGING PARTS (2-LP) . . . 25
70s Chatham Square LP 1003 MUSIC IN FIFTHS/MUSIC IN A SIMILAR MOTION (LP) . . . 15
70s Folkways FTS 33902 TWO PAGES (LP) . . . 12
76 Cardine LA 2010 MUSIC IN 12 (PARTS 1 & 2) (LP) . . . 12
78 Shandar SHAN 83515 SOLO MUSIC (LP) . . . 12
(see also Ray Manzarek)

GLASS HARP
72 MCA MUPS 431 GLASS HARP (LP) . . . 15
72 MCA MUPS 449 SYNERGY (LP) . . . 15
73 MCA MUPS 470 IT MAKES ME GLAD (LP) . . . 12

GLASS HOUSE
70 Invictus INV 506 Stealing Moments From Another Woman's Life/If It Ain't Love, It Don't Matter . . . 7
71 Invictus INV 510 I Can't Be You/He's In My Life . . . 7

GLASS MENAGERIE
68 Pye 7N 17518 She's A Rainbow/But That's When I Start To Love Her . . . 12
68 Pye 7N 17568 You Didn't Have To Be So Nice/Let's All Run To The Sun . . . 8
68 Pye 7N 17615 Frederick Jordan/I Said Goodbye To Me . . . 175
69 Polydor 56318 Have You Forgotten Who You Are/Do You Ever Think? . . . 6
69 Polydor 56341 Do My Thing Myself/Watching The World Pass By . . . 6
(see also Paladin, Toe-Fat)

GLASS OPENING
68 Plexium P 1236 Silver Bells And Cockle Shells/Does It Really Matter . . . 420

TOM GLAZER & DO-RE-MI CHILDREN'S CHORUS
63 London HLR 9742 On Top Of Spaghetti/Battle Hymn Of The Children . . . 8
63 London HLR 9817 It's A Mad, Mad, Mad, Mad World/Dance With The Dolly . . . 10

JACKIE GLEASON (& ORCHESTRA)
55 Capitol CL 14289 Rain/I'll Never Be The Same (with Orchestra) . . . 6
55 Capitol CL 14363 Autumn Leaves/Oo! What You Do To Me (with Orchestra) . . . 6
60 Brunswick 04775 What Is A Boy?/What Is A Girl? . . . 7
69 MCA MU 1108 What Is A Boy?/What Is A Girl? (reissue) . . . 5
56 Capitol EAP 1-871 TO A SLEEPING BEAUTY (EP) . . . 10

CAPTAIN GLEASON'S GARDEN BAND
55 Capitol CL 14323 In The Good Old Summertime/The Band Played On . . . 6
(see also Jackie Gleason)

GLEN (Brown) & LLOYD (Robinson)
66 Ska Beat JB 250 Live And Let Others Die/Too Late . . . 30
67 Doctor Bird DB 1099 Feel Good Now/What You've Got (credited as Lloyd Glen) . . . 30

GLENCOE
72 Epic EPC 8383 Look Me In The Eye/Telephonia . . . 6
72 Epic EPC 65207 GLENCOE (LP) . . . 15
73 Epic EPC 65717 SPIRIT OF GLENCOE (LP) . . . 15
(see also Hopscotch, Five Day Rain, Greatest Show On Earth, Loving Awareness)

DARRELL GLENN
54 HMV 7MC 23 In The Chapel In The Moonlight/Once And Only Once (export issue) . . . 18

GLIDE
95 Ochre OCH 003 EXCERPTS FROM A SPACE AGE FREAK OUT (Part 1) (orange vinyl, p/s) . . . 5
(see also Echo & Bunnymen)

GLITTERHOUSE
68 Stateside SS 2129 Barbarella/BOB CREWE: An Angel Is Love . . . 12
68 Stateside SS 2129 Barbarella/Love Drags Me Down (different B-side) . . . 15

GLOBAL COMMUNICATIONS
93 Evolution EVO 04 KEONGAKU EP (12", 4-track, plain sleeve) . . . 15
94 Dedicated DEDLP 014L 76: 14 (2-LP, gatefold sleeve with bonus 12") . . . 25
94 Dedicated DEDLP 014 76: 14 (2-LP, gatefold sleeve) . . . 18
94 Dedicated DEDCD 014L 76: 14 (CD, gatefold, wraparound sleeve) . . . 20
94 Dedicated DEDCD 014 76: 14 (CD) . . . 18
96 Dedicated DED 21LP REMOTION — THE GLOBAL COMMUNICATIONS REMIX ALBUM (LP) . . . 25
(see also Mystic Institue, Link, Reload, Reload & E621, Chaos & Julia Set, Jedi Knights)

GLOBAL VILLAGE TRUCKING COMPANY
76 Caroline C 1516 GLOBAL VILLAGE TRUCKING COMPANY (LP, with insert) . . . 15

GLOBE SHOW
69 Page One POF 128 Yes Or No/Gettin' On Back . . . 7
(see also Chris Shakespeare Globe Show)

GLOBE TROTTERS
54 Parlophone CMSP 18 At Sundown/My Gal Sal (export issue) . . . 15
50s Parlophone DP 347 Darktown Strutters' Ball/Satan Takes A Holiday (78, export issue) . . . 7
54 Parlophone GEP 8528 SATURDAY NIGHT HOP (EP) . . . 20

GLOBETROTTERS
70 RCA RCA 2017 Gravy/Cheer Me Up . . . 6
71 RCA SF 8158 THE GLOBETROTTERS (LP) . . . 15

GLOOMYS
68 Columbia DB 8391 Daybreak/Queen And King . . . 12
71 DJM DJS 240 I'm A Bum/Let Me Dream . . . 6

GLORIA MUNDI
78 RCA PB 5068 Fight Back/Do It (p/s) . . . 5
78 RCA PL2 5157 I INDIVIDUAL (LP, with inner sleeve) . . . 12
79 RCA PL2 5244 THE WORD IS OUT (LP, with lyric inner) . . . 12

GLORIES
67 CBS 2786 I Stand Accused (Of Loving You)/Wish They Could Write A Song . . . 15
67 Direction 58-3084 Give Me My Freedom/Security . . . 10
68 Direction 58-3300 Sing Me A Love Song/Oh Baby That's Love . . . 6
68 Direction 58-3646 My Sweet Sweet Baby/Stand By (I'm Comin' Home) . . . 6

GLOVE
83 Wonderland SHE 3 Like An Animal/Mouth To Mouth (p/s, some sleeves with centre holes) . . . 7
83 Wonderland SHEX 3 Like An Animal (Club, What Club? Mix)/Like Animal/Mouth To Mouth (12", p/s, some sleeves with centre hole) . . . 10
83 Wonderland SHE 5 Punish Me With Kisses/The Tightrope (p/s) . . . 12
83 Wonderland SHELP 2 BLUE SUNSHINE (LP, with inner sleeve) . . . 12
83 Wonderland SHELP 2 BLUE SUNSHINE (LP, mispressing with double-printed sleeve) . . . 20
(see also Cure, Siouxsie & Banshees, Creatures)

ROGER GLOVER (& GUESTS)
74 Purple PUR 125 Love Is All/Old Blind Mole/Magician Moth . . . 10
84 Safari SAF EP 1 Love Is All/Old Blind Mole/Magician Moth (p/s, reissue) . . . 5
84 Polydor POSP 678 The Mask/So Remote (p/s, solo) . . . 6
74 Purple TPSA 7514 THE BUTTERFLY BALL (AND THE GRASSHOPPER'S FEAST) (LP, g/fold sleeve) 18
78 Polydor 2391 306 ELEMENTS (LP, solo) . . . 12
84 Polydor POLD 5139 THE MASK (LP, solo, with insert) . . . 12
(see also [Sheila Carter &] Episode [Six], Deep Purple, Elf, Eddie Hardin, Whitesnake, Rainbow, Glenn Hughes, John Lawton, Wizard's Convention, Marlon, Green Bullfrog, David Coverdale, Dio)

JEREMY GLUCK
86 Flicknife SHARP 037 I KNEW BUFFALO BILL (LP) . . . 15
(see also Barracudas)

MINT VALUE £

GMT
91 Mausoleum BONE 12-83102 One By One (12", p/s) ... 10

GNAC
98 Earworm WORM 29 The Moustache/Armchair Thriller (p/s, black vinyl) ... 6

GNANK
99 Gnank GNANK 01 Gnank Gnank/Oi, Gnank (p/s) ... 8

GNASHER
74 Purple PUR 119 Medina Road/Easy Meat ... 8

GNIDROLOG
72 RCA SF 8261 IN SPITE OF HARRY'S TOE-NAIL (LP) ... 45
72 RCA SF 8322 LADY LAKE (LP, some with insert) ... 100/45

GNOMES OF ZURICH
66 Planet PLF 121 Please Mr Sun/I'm Coming Down With The Blues (with custom 'Planet' sleeve) ... 40/35
67 CBS 202556 Hang On Baby/Blues For My Baby ... 30
67 CBS 2694 High Hopes/Pretender ... 30
67 RCA Victor RCA 1606 Second Fiddle/Publicity Girl ... 22

G-NOTES
58 Oriole CB 1456 Ronnie/I Would ... 20
58 Oriole CB 1456 Ronnie/I Would (78) ... 12

GOAT
82 Real Kavoom ARK 1 REAL KAVOOM (12" EP) ... 8

GOBBLEDEGOOKS
64 Decca F 12023 Now And Again/Where Have You Been ... 15

GOBBLINZ
79 Pinnacle P 8454 London/Women In Love (p/s) ... 80
80s Bacon SLICE 01 Love Me Too/All Of This And More (no p/s) ... 80

GO-BETWEENS
80 Postcard 80-4 I Need Two Heads/Stop Before You Say It (brown label & brown co. sleeve) ... 15
80 Postcard 80-4 I Need Two Heads/Stop Before You Say It (yellow label & cream co. sleeve) ... 18
80 Postcard 81-9 Your Turn My Turn (company sleeve) ... 8
82 Rough Trade RT 108 Hammer The Hammer/By Chance (p/s) ... 5
83 Rough Trade RT 124 Cattle And Cane/Heaven Says (p/s) ... 5
83 Rough Trade RT 114 Man O'Sand To Girl O'See/This Girl Black Girl (p/s) ... 5
87 Beggars Banquet BEG 183D Right Here/When People Are Dead/A Little Romance//Don't Call Me Gone/ A Little Romance (live) (double pack) ... 5
88 B. Banquet BEG 218B Streets Of Your Town/Wait Until June (box set) ... 8

GOBLIN
79 EMI EMC 3222 SUSPIRIA (LP, soundtrack) ... 40

VIC GODARD (& SUBWAY SECT)
80 Oddball/MCA 585 Split Up The Money/Out Of Touch (p/s, with Subway Sect) ... 7
81 Rough Trade RT 068 Stop That Girl/Instrumentally Scared/Vertical Integration (p/s, w/Subway Sect) ... 7
81 Club Left CLUB 1 Stamp Of A Vamp/Hey Now (I'm In Love) (p/s, with Subway Sect) ... 7
85 El Benelux EL 4 Holiday Hymn/Nice On The Ice (p/s) ... 7
85 El Benelux EL 4T Holiday Hymn/Nice On The Ice/Stop That Girl/Ice On The Volcano/ T.R.O.U.B.L.E. (12", p/s) ... 10
93 Postcard DUBH 937 Won't Turn Back/Won't Turn Back (Version) (p/s, 1,000 only) ... 7
80 Oddball/MCA MCF 3070 WHAT'S THE MATTER BOY? (LP, with Subway Sect) ... 18
82 London SH 8549 SONGS FOR SALE (LP, with Subway Sect) ... 18
85 Rough Trade ROUGH 56 A RETROSPECTIVE (LP, with Subway Sect) ... 18
85 MCA/El 01 HOLIDAY HYMN (LP, 10 test pressings only; abandoned issue of "T.R.O.U.B.L.E.") ... 30+
86 Rough Trade ROUGH 86 T.R.O.U.B.L.E. (LP) ... 12
93 Postcard DUBH 936 END OF THE SURREY PEOPLE (LP) ... 12
(see also Subway Sect)

KEITH & DONNA GODCHAUX
75 Round RX 104 KEITH & DONNA GODCHAUX (LP) ... 18
(see also Grateful Dead)

GEOFF GODDARD
61 HMV POP 938 Girl Bride/For Eternity ... 55
62 HMV POP 1068 My Little Girl's Come Home/Try Once More ... 60
63 HMV POP 1160 Saturday Dance/Come Back To Me ... 45
63 HMV POP 1213 Sky Men/Walk With Me My Angel ... 140

HUGH GODFREY
67 Coxsone CS 7001 A Dey Pon Dem/SOUL BROTHERS: Take Ten ... 22
67 Studio One SO 2008 My Time/MARCIA GRIFFITHS: Hound Dog ... 35
67 Studio One SO 2015 Go Tell Him/MARCIA GRIFFITHS: After Laughter ... 25
(see also Soul Brothers)

RAY GODFREY
78 Grapevine GRP 111 Come And Get These Memories/I'm The Other Half Of You ... 8

ROBERT JOHN GODFREY
74 Charisma CAS 1084 FALL OF HYPERION (LP) ... 30
80s Nuage (no cat. no.) REVERBERATIONS (cassette) ... 12
(see also Enid, Godfrey & Stewart, Don Bradshaw)

GODFREY & STEWART

86 The Enid ENID 11 THE SEED AND THE SOWER (LP) . . . 15
86 The Enid ENID 11 THE SEED AND THE SOWER (cassette) . . . 12
80s The Stand HEARTLP JOINED BY THE HEART (LP, fan club issue, 2,000 only) . . . 20
86 The Enid (no cat. no.) JOINED BY THE HEART (cassette) . . . 12
80s The Stand HEARTC JOINED BY THE HEART (cassette, fan club issue) . . . 12
(see also Robert John Godfrey, Enid)

GODIEGO

78 Satril SATL 4009 THE WATER MARGIN (LP, TV soundtrack) . . . 12

GODLEY & CREME

68 Blinkers 1215 Goodnight Blinkers/Hello Blinkers (die-cut sleeve) . . . 30
79 Mercury SAMP 017 5 O'Clock/The Flood//Lost Weekend/Honolulu (double pack sampler, promo) . . . 10
81 Polydor POSP 322 Under Your Thumb (Short Version)/Power Behind The Throne (2,000 only with p/s) . . . 5
85 Polydor POSP 372 Cry/Love Bombs (picture disc) . . . 5
85 Polydor 080 101 2 Cry/Love Bombs/Cry (CD Video) . . . 12
81 Polydor POLD 543 ISMISM (LP, white sleeve with die-cut holes) . . . 12
(see also Mockingbirds, Hotlegs, 10cc, Dave Berry, Frabjoy & Runcible Spoon, Cruisers, Whirlwinds, Doctor Father)

GODS

67 Polydor 56168 Come On Down To My Boat Baby/Garage Man . . . 140
68 Columbia DB 8486 Baby's Rich/Somewhere In The Street . . . 30
69 Columbia DB 8544 Hey! Bulldog/Real Love Guaranteed . . . 35
69 Columbia DB 8572 Maria/Long Time, Sad Time, Bad Time . . . 35
68 Columbia S(C)X 6286 GENESIS (LP) . . . 150
70 Columbia SCX 6372 TO SAMUEL A SON (LP) . . . 130
76 Harvest SHSM 2011 GODS (LP) . . . 25
(see also Uriah Heep, Shame, Toe-Fat, Birds Birds)

GOD'S GIFT

79 Newmarket no cat. no. THESE DAYS (EP) . . . 10
81 New Hormones ORG 14 Soldiers/Anthony Perkins/No God/The Hunger Of Millions (12", p/s) . . . 8
83 Pleasantly Surprised PS 7 FOLIE A QUATRE (cassette, in bag with inserts) . . . 12

GOD SONS

72 Green Door GD 4024 Merry Up/Merry Up — Version . . . 10
(see also Errol & U Roy, Carl Masters)

GOD SPEED! YOU BLACK EMPEROR

99 Constellation CST 006 SLOW RIOT FOR NEW ZERO KANADA (12" EP) . . . 15
99 Kranky KRANK 034 SLOW RIOT FOR NEW ZERO KANADA (CD EP) . . . 8

GODZ

67 Fontana STL 5500 CONTACT WITH THE GODZ (LP) . . . 25
69 Fontana STL 5512 GODZ II (LP) . . . 25

GOGMAGOG

85 F. For Thought YUMT 109 I Will Be There/Living In A Timewarp/It's Illegal, It's Immoral, It's Unhealthy But It's Fun (12", p/s & insert) . . . 30
(see also Iron Maiden, Di'Anno, Def Leppard, Whitesnake, Gillan, White Spirit)

GO-GO's (U.K.)

64 Oriole CB 1982 I'm Gonna Spend My Christmas With A Dalek/Big Boss Man (some in p/s) . . . 45/30

GO-GO's (U.S.)

80 Stiff BUY 78 We Got The Beat/How Much More (p/s) . . . 5
81 I.R.S. PFP 1007 Our Lips Are Sealed/Surfing And Spying (p/s, pink vinyl) . . . 10
81 I.R.S. GONP 101 Automatic/Tonite (picture disc) . . . 7
90 A&M AMP 712 Cool Jerk/We Got The Beat (picture disc) . . . 5
90 A&M AMCD 712 Cool Jerk/We Got The Beat (CD) . . . 8
(see also Belinda Carlisle, Jane Wiedlin)

GOING RED?

81 Razz CLEAN 1 Some Boys/Tune Kevin's Strings (p/s) . . . 8
81 MCA MCA 673 Some Boys/Tune Kevin's Strings (reissue, p/s) . . . 5
(see also Freshies, Chris Sievey, Jilted John)

HERBIE GOINS & NIGHT-TIMERS

66 Parlophone R 5478 No. 1 In Your Heart/Cruisin' . . . 100
66 Parlophone R 5533 The Incredible Miss Brown/Comin' Home To You . . . 45
67 Parlophone PMC 7026 NUMBER ONE IN YOUR HEART (LP) . . . 150
(see also Night-Timers, Alexis Korner's Blues Incorporated)

HARRY GOLD with NORRIE PARAMOR ORCHESTRA

54 Columbia SCM 5144 Be Good To Me/Frou Frou . . . 10
(see also Norrie Paramor)

MARTY GOLD

70 Avco Embassy 6466 001 MOOG PLAYS THE BEATLES (LP) . . . 12

BARRY GOLDBERG (REUNION)

68 Pye International 7N 25465 Another Day/Capricorn Blues (as Barry Goldberg Reunion) . . . 7
68 Pye Intl. NSPL 28116 BARRY GOLDBERG REUNION (LP) . . . 20
69 Buddah 203 020 TWO JEWS BLUES (LP, with Mike Bloomfield) . . . 15
71 Buddah 2318 038 BLASTS FROM MY PAST (LP) . . . 12
(see also Electric Flag, Mike Bloomfield)

GOLDEBRIARS

64 Columbia DB 7384 Sea Of Tears/I've Got To Love Somebody . . . 10

MINT VALUE £

GOLDEN APPLES OF THE SUN

65 Decca F 12194 | Monkey Time/Chocolate Rolls, Tea And Monopoly (unissued, test pressings only) . . . 80+
65 Immediate IM 010 | Monkey Time/Chocolate Rolls, Tea And Monopoly . . . 40

GOLDEN CRUSADERS

64 Columbia DB 7232 | I'm In Love With You/Always On My Mind . . . 15
64 Columbia DB 7357 | Hey Good Lookin'/Come On, Come On . . . 15
65 Columbia DB 7485 | I Don't Care/That Broken Heart Is Mine . . . 15

GOLDEN DAWN

88 Sarah SARAH 009 | My Secret World/Spring-Heeled Jack/The Railway Track (p/s, with poster) . . . 12
89 Sarah SARAH 017 | George Hamilton's Dead (p/s, with poster) . . . 12

GOLDEN EARRING(S)

68 Capitol CL 15552 | I've Just Lost Somebody/The Truth About Arthur (as Golden Earrings) . . . 10
68 Capitol CL 15567 | Dong Dong Di Ki Di Gi Dong/Wake Up — Breakfast (as Golden Earrings) . . . 10
69 Major Minor MM 601 | Just A Little Peace In My Heart/Remember My Friend (as Golden Earrings) . . . 8
69 Major Minor MM 633 | It's Alright But It Could Be Better/Where Will I Be (as Golden Earrings) . . . 8
70 Major Minor MM 679 | Another Forty-Five Miles/I Can't Get Hold Of Her . . . 8
70 Polydor BM 56514 | That Day/Words I Need . . . 15
70 Polydor 2001 073 | Back Home/This Is The Time Of Year . . . 8
72 Polydor 2001 346 | Buddy Joe/Avalanche . . . 5
73 Track 2094 116 | Radar Love/Just Like Vince Taylor . . . 5
74 Track 2094 121 | Instant Poetry/From Heaven, From Hell . . . 5
74 Track 2094 126 | Candy's Going Bad/She Flies On Strange Wings . . . 5
75 Track 2094 130 | Ce Soir/Lucky Number . . . 5
76 Polydor 2001 626 | Sleepwalking/Babylon (no p/s) . . . 5
77 Polydor 2121 312 | Bombay/Faded Jeans (no p/s) . . . 5
77 Polydor 2121 335 | Radar Love (live)/Just Like Vince (live) (12", p/s) . . . 8
83 Mercury MER 122 | Twilight Zone/King Dark (p/s) . . . 5
83 Mercury MERX 122 | Twilight Zone/King Dark (12", blue or yellow p/s) . . . 8
84 Carrere CAR 321 | When The Lady Smiles/Orwell's Year (p/s) . . . 5
84 Carrere CART 321 | When The Lady Smiles/Orwell's Year (12", p/s) . . . 8
69 Major Minor SMLP 65 | EIGHT MILES HIGH (LP) . . . 35
71 Polydor 2310 135 | SEVEN TEARS (LP) . . . 20
72 Polydor 2310 210 | TOGETHER (LP) . . . 18
73 Track 2406 109 | HEARING EARRING (LP, braille sleeve) . . . 15
73 Track 2406 112 | MOONTAN (LP, gatefold sleeve with insert) . . . 15
75 Track 2406 117 | SWITCH (LP) . . . 15
76 Polydor 2430 330 | TO THE HILT (LP, gatefold sleeve with insert) . . . 15
77 Polydor 2344 059 | CONTRABAND (LP, with insert) . . . 15

GOLDEN FLEECE

67 Decca F 12669 | Athens 6 a.m./Girl From Syracuse . . . 6

GOLDEN GATE QUARTET

53 Columbia SCM 5054 | Moses Smote The Waters/Bones, Bones, Bones . . . 5
56 Columbia SEG 7700 | SINGS GREAT SPIRITUALS (EP) . . . 8
58 Fontana TFR 6009 | THAT GOLDEN CHARIOT (10" LP) . . . 20
59 Columbia 33SX 1172 | SHOUT FOR JOY! (LP) . . . 15
50s Columbia 33CSX 9 | NEGRO SPIRITUALS (LP) . . . 15
61 Columbia 33SX 1370 | GET ON BOARD (LP) . . . 15

GOLDEN GATE STRINGS

65 Columbia DB 7634 | Mr. Tambourine Man/With God On Our Side . . . 12

GOLDEN HORDE

80s Hot Wire HWS 855 | Young And Happy/Little UFO/Fiona (p/s) . . . 5
85 Hot Wire WAY OUT 1 | DIG THAT CRAZY GRAVE (EP) . . . 5
85 Hot Wire/I.D. NOSE 7 | THE CHOCOLATE BISCUIT CONSPIRACY (LP) . . . 12

GOLDFRAPP

00 Mute 12MUTE 247 | Lovely Head/(Stare Mesto Mix)/(Miss World Mix) (12", p/s) . . . 20
00 Mute 12MUTE 253 | Utopia/(New Ears Mix)/(Sunroof Mix) (12", p/s) . . . 12
01 Mute 12MUTE 259 | Human/(Calexico Instrumental)/(Massey's Neanderthal Mix) (12", p/s) . . . 12
00 Mute STUMM 188 | FELT MOUNTAIN (LP, with inner) . . . 12

GOLDIE (& GINGERBREADS)

65 Decca F 12070 | Can't You Hear My Heartbeat/Little Boy . . . 15
65 Decca F 12126 | That's Why I Love You/Skip . . . 15
65 Decca F 12199 | Sailor Boy/Please Please . . . 15
66 Immediate IM 026 | Goin' Back/Headlines (solo) . . . 15
66 Fontana TF 693 | I Do/Think About The Good Times (solo) . . . 15
69 Decca F 12931 | Can't You Hear My Heartbeat/That's Why I Love You . . . 6

(see also Ten Wheel Drive)

JOHN GOLDING

74 Cottage 101S | DISCARDED VERSE (LP, 2,000 only) . . . 12

VIVIEN GOLDMAN

81 Window WIN 1 | Launderette/Private Armies (gatefold p/s, with PiL) . . . 7
81 Window 12WIN 1 | Launderette/Private Armies (12", p/s, with PiL) . . . 8

(see also Public Image Ltd)

BOBBY GOLDSBORO

63 Stateside SS 193 | The Runaround/The Letter . . . 15
63 United Artists UP 1046 | See The Funny Little Clown/Hello Loser . . . 8
64 United Artists UP 1054 | Whenever He Holds You/If She Was Mine . . . 8
65 United Artists UP 1079 | Little Things/I Just Can't Go On Pretending . . . 15
65 United Artists UP 1091 | Voodoo Woman/It Breaks My Heart . . . 7

MINT VALUE £

65 United Artists UP 1104 If You Wait For Love/If You've Got A Heart. . . . 7
66 United Artists UP 1120 Broomstick Cowboy/Ain't Got Time For Happy 7
66 United Artists UP 1128 It's Too Late/I'm Goin' Home 12
66 United Artists UP 1135 I Know You Better Than That/When Your Love Has Gone 7
66 United Artists UP 1146 Take Your Love/Longer Than Forever 12
67 United Artists UP 1156 It Hurts Me/Pity The Fool 7
67 United Artists UP 1166 No Fun At The Fair/Hold On. . . . 7
67 United Artists UP 1177 Too Many People/Goodbye To All You Women 25
68 United Artists UP 2223 Autumn Of My Life/She Chased Me. . . . 7
69 United Artists UP 2264 Love Arrester/Dissatisfied Man 7
69 United Artists UP 35034 Muddy Mississippi Line/Richer Man Than I. . . . 6
69 United Artists UP 35053 Letter To Emily/Tomorrow Is Forgotten 6
65 United Artists UEP 1006 LITTLE THINGS (EP). . . . 40
66 United Artists UEP 1016 THE TALENTED BOBBY GOLDSBORO (EP) 40
65 United Artists ULP 1118 I CAN'T STOP LOVING YOU (LP) 30
66 United Artists (S)ULP 1135 IT'S TOO LATE (LP) 35
67 United Artists (S)ULP 1163 SOLID GOLDSBORO — GREATEST HITS (LP) 22
68 United Artists (S)ULP 1195 HONEY (LP, black label). . . . 22
68 United Artists (S)ULP 1206 WORD PICTURES (LP). . . . 18
69 United Artists UAS 29008 TODAY (LP). . . . 15

GOLDSMITH

83 Bedlam BLM 001 Life Is Killing Me/Music Man (p/s) 50

JERRY GOLDSMITH

(see under Soundtrack LPs)

GOLGOTHA

84 Golgotha GOTH 002 DANGEROUS GAMES (Dangerous Games/Old England's Green/Air/
The Great Divide (EP, no p/s). . . . 100
90 Communique CMGLP 003 UNMAKER OF WORLDS (EP, p/s) 15

GOLIARD

76 Broadside BRO 127 FORTUNE MY FOE (LP, with booklet) 15

GOLIATH

70 CBS 5312 Port And Lemon Lady/I Heard About A Friend 7
70 CBS 64229 GOLIATH (LP). . . . 50

GOLLIWOGS

66 Vocalion VF 9266 Brown-Eyed Girl/You Better Be Careful. . . . 40
67 Vocalion VF 9283 Fragile Child/Fight Fire 40
72 Fantasy FAN 5996 GOLLIWOGS (LP, pressed in U.S. for U.K. distribution) 15
(see also Creedence Clearwater Revival)

BENNY GOLSON

81 CBS A 1223 The New Killer Joe/Walkin' And Stalkin' 5
81 CBS 12A 1223 The New Killer Joe/Walkin' And Stalkin' (12"). . . . 8
59 Esquire 32-125 GONE WITH GOLSON (LP). . . . 15
60 Esquire 32-105 GROOVIN' WITH GOLSON (LP) 15

BENNY GOLSON & ART FARMER

62 Pye International 7N 25120 Blues March/Serenata 5
65 Stateside SL 10150 STOCKHOLM SOJOURN (LP) 12
(see also Art Farmer)

GONADS

82 Secret SHH 131 PURE PUNK FOR NOW PEOPLE (EP). . . . 8
82 Secret SHH 134 PEACE ARTISTS (EP) 6
83 Razor RZS 103 DELILAH (THE PUNK EPIC) (EP). . . . 5

GONDOLIERS

58 Starlite ST45 001 Fly, Seagull, Fly/God's Green Acres 12

NAT GONELLA & HIS GEORGIA JAZZ BAND

60 Columbia DB 4465 Show Me The Way To Go Home/My Gal Sal. . . . 8
58 Columbia 33S 1146 SALUTE TO SATCHMO (10" LP) 50
61 Columbia 33SX 1380 THE NAT GONELLA STORY (LP). . . . 50

RON GONELLA

60s Lismor LILP 5017 FIDDLER'S FANCY (LP) 12

GONG

71 Philips 6332 033 CONTINENTAL CIRCUS (LP, soundtrack) 30
73 Virgin V 2002 RADIO GNOME INVISIBLE PART 1 — THE FLYING TEAPOT
(LP, originally with black & white label design) 15/12
73 Virgin V 2007 RADIO GNOME INVISIBLE PART 2 — ANGEL'S EGG
(LP, gatefold sleeve, initially with b&w label; some with book) 30/12
74 Virgin VC 502 CAMEMBERT ELECTRIQUE (LP). . . . 12
74 Virgin V 2019 YOU (LP, with lyric insert) 12
76 Virgin V 2046 SHAMAL (LP) 12
77 Virgin V 2074 GAZEUSE! (LP, with poster). . . . 15
77 Virgin VGD 3501 LIVE ETC. (2-LP, with cut-out cover & inner sleeves) 18
78 Virgin V 2099 EXPRESSO II (LP, with inner). . . . 12
(see also Mother Gong, Gilli Smyth & Mother Gong, Daevid Allen, Steve Hillage, Clearlight, Radio Actors, Sphynx, Tim Blake, Comus)

GONG/CAMEL/HENRY COW/GLOBAL TRUCKING COMPANY

73 Greasy Truckers GT 4997 GREASY TRUCKERS (2-LP, 1 side each; with insert) 20
(see also Camel, Henry Cow, Global Trucking Company)

GONKS

64 Decca F 11984 The Gonk Song/That's All Right, Mamma 30
(see also Twinkle)

MINT VALUE £

RON GONNELLA

70s LISMOR LILP 5017 — FIDDLERS FANCY (LP) ... 12

PAUL GONSALVES

64 Vocalion LAE 587 — BOOM JACKIE BOOM CHICK (LP) ... 150
70 Deram SML 1064 — HUMMINGBIRD (LP) ... 40
73 Black Lion 2460 191 — JUST A-SITTIN' AND A-ROCKIN' (LP, with Ray Nance) ... 12
(see also Tubby Hayes & Paul Gonsalves)

GONZALEZ

74 EMI EMI 2706 — I Haven't Stopped Dancing Yet/Carnival (12") ... 8
74 EMI EMC 3046 — GONZALEZ (LP) ... 25
75 EMI EMC 3100 — OUR ONLY WEAPON IS OUR MUSIC (LP) ... 15

BELLE GONZALEZ

72 Columbia DB 8852 — Bottles/I Hate Sunday ... 7
65 Jupiter JEPOC 37 — POETS SET IN JAZZ (EP, as Belle Gonzalez & Sextet) ... 15
66 Jupiter JEPOC 39 — CONTEMPORARY POETS SET IN JAZZ (EP) ... 15
72 Columbia SCX 6484 — BELLE (LP) ... 50
(see also Mark Wirtz)

DOUGLAS GOOD & GINNY PLENTY

68 Stateside SS 2104 — Sunny And Me/Living In A World Of Make Believe ... 6

JACK GOOD'S FAT NOISE

60 Decca F 11233 — The Fat Washerwoman/The Fat Noise ... 10

GOODBYE MR MACKENZIE

84 Scruples YTS 1 — Death Of A Salesman/LINDY BERGMAN: Locked Inside Your Prison (no p/s, 500 only) ... 25
86 Precious Org. JEWEL 2 — The Rattler/Candlestick Park (p/s) ... 6
86 Precious Org. JEWEL 2T — The Rattler/Candlestick Park/The End (12", p/s) ... 10
86 Clandestine MACK 1 — Face To Face/Secrets/Good Deeds (12", p/s, 1,000 only) ... 10
88 Capitol CLCD 501 — Goodbye Mr MacKenzie (extended)/Green Turn Red/Knockin' On Joe (CD) ... 10
88 Capitol CLCD 513 — Open Your Arms (extended)/Secrets/Amsterdam/Pleasure Search CD) ... 10
89 Capitol CDCL 522 — The Rattler/Here Comes Deacon Brodie/Calton Hall/Drunken Sailor (CD) ... 10
89 Capitol CLCD 538 — Goodwill City (5.03)/I'm Sick Of You/What's Got Into You/Insidious Thing (CD) ... 10
90 Parlophone PCS 7345 — HAMMER AND TONGS (LP, unreleased, white label test pressings only) ... 40
(see also Garbage)

GOOD EARTH

68 Saga FID 2112 — IT'S HARD ROCK AND ALL THAT (LP) ... 22
70 Saga FID 8157 — IN THE SUMMERTIME (LP, with tracks by Macon Jug) ... 15
72 Boulevard 4078 — RAY DORSET'S BEST (LP, 4 tracks by Good Earth & 6 tracks by Macon Jug) ... 12
(see also First Impression/Good Earth, Mungo Jerry, Ray Dorset)

GOODEES

69 Stax STAX 113 — Condition Red/Didn't Know Love Was So Good ... 12

GOOD GUYS

70 Duke DU 82 — Death Rides/Destruction ... 7
70 Duke DU 83 — Wreck It Up/Dynamic Groove ... 7
70 Duke DU 84 — Happiness/Latissimo ... 8
(see also Byron Lee & Dragonaires)

PHILIP GOODHAND-TAIT (& STORMSVILLE SHAKERS)

66 Parlophone R 5448 — I'm Gonna Put Some Hurt On You/It's A Lie (with Stormsville Shakers) ... 15
66 Parlophone R 5498 — No Problem/What More Do You Want (with Stormsville Shakers) ... 20
66 Parlophone R 5547 — You Can't Take Love/J.C. Greaseburger (solo) ... 15
69 Decca F 12868 — Love Has Got Hold Of Me/Too Pleased To Help ... 8
70 DJM DJS 230 — Jeannie/Run See The Sun ... 5
71 DJM DJS 236 — Oh Rosanna/I Didn't Know Myself ... 5
71 DJM DJLPS 411 — REHEARSAL (LP) ... 12
71 DJM DJLPS 416 — I THINK I'LL WRITE A SONG (LP) ... 12
72 DJM DJLPS 425 — SONGFALL (LP, gatefold sleeve) ... 12
73 DJM DJLPS 432 — PHILIP GOODHAND-TAIT (LP) ... 12
75 DJM DJLPS 453 — JINGLE JANGLE MAN (LP) ... 12
(see also Circus, Larry Williams, Love Affair)

CUBA GOODING

83 London LONX 41 — Happiness Is Just Around The Bend/(Version) (12") ... 8

JOHNNY GOODISON

70 Deram DM 319 — A Little Understanding/One Mistake ... 7
(see also Quotations, Johnny B. Great)

GOODLETTSVILLE FIVE

64 London HLW 9854 — Eef/Baly's Gone Eefing ... 8

JOHN GOODLUCK

74 Tradition TSR 015 — SUFFOLK MIRACLE (LP, with insert) ... 30

BENNY GOODMAN

53 Columbia SCM 5053 — Temptation Rag/Bugle Call Rag ... 6
55 Capitol CL 14258 — Jumpin' At The Woodside/Let's Dance ... 6
56 Columbia SCM 5239 — King Porter Stomp/Memories Of You ... 6
56 HMV 7M 380 — Don't Be That Way/Down South Camp Meeting ... 6
56 Capitol CL 14531 — Goody Goody/Sometimes I'm Happy ... 5
56 Capitol CL 14570 — Don't Be That Way/And The Angels Sing ... 5
60 Philips JAZ 107 — Liza/Slipped Disc (p/s) ... 5
58 Philips BBE 12172 — PEGGY WITH BENNY (EP, with Peggy Lee) ... 8
52 Capitol LC 6526 — SESSION FOR SIX (10" LP, as The Benny Goodman Sextet) ... 12
52 Capitol LC 6557 — EASY DOES IT (10" LP) ... 15

MINT VALUE £

52 Capitol LC 6565 AFTER HOURS (10" LP) . . . 15
53 Capitol LC 6601 THE BENNY GOODMAN BAND (10" LP) . . . 15
53 Capitol LC 6620 THE GOODMAN TOUCH (10" LP) . . . 15
54 Columbia 33S 1048 SESSION FOR SEXTET (10" LP) . . . 15
54 Capitol LC 6680 CLASSICS IN JAZZ (10" LP) . . . 15
54 Philips BBL 7000 CARNEGIE HALL JAZZ CONCERT (LP, auto-coupling) . . . 12
54 Philips BBL 7001 CARNEGIE HALL JAZZ CONCERT (LP, auto-coupling) . . . 12
55 Philips BBR 8064 LET'S HEAR THE MELODY (10" LP) . . . 15
55 Philips BBL 7009 1937-1938 JAZZ CONCERT NO. 2 (LP, auto-coupling) . . . 12
55 Philips BBL 7010 1937-1938 JAZZ CONCERT NO. 2 (LP, auto-coupling) . . . 12
55 Philips BBL 7043 PRESENTS EDDIE SAUTER ARRANGEMENTS (LP) . . . 12
56 Philips BBL 7073 MAKES HISTORY (LP) . . . 12
56 Brunswick LAT 8102 THE BENNY GOODMAN STORY VOLUME ONE (LP) . . . 12
56 Brunswick LAT 8103 THE BENNY GOODMAN STORY VOLUME TWO (LP) . . . 12
58 Fontana TFR 6006 BENNY GOODMAN SEXTET (10" LP) . . . 18

DAVE GOODMAN & FRIENDS

78 The Label TLR 008 Justifiable Homicide/Take Down Your Fences (p/s, 1st 15,000 on red vinyl) . . . 7
(N.B. rumoured copies with 'Steve Jones & Paul Cook' credit on the sleeve DO NOT exist)
(see also Sex Pistols)

GOOD MISSIONARIES

80 Kif KIF'S 1 Good Missionary (Parts 1 & 2) (p/s) . . . 5
80 Unnormality NORM 001 VIBING UP THE SENILE WORLD (The Good Missionary Part 1 [live]/
The Good Missionary Part/Kif Kif's Free Freak Out [live]) (EP, 1,000 only) . . . 5
81 Unnormality NORM 002 DERANGED IN HASTINGS (Keep Going Backwards/Attitudes)
(EP, with printed insert, PVC sleeve) . . . 5
79 Deptford Fun City DLP 04 FIRE FROM HEAVEN (LP) . . . 12
80 Conventional (no cat. no.) SPONTANEOUS EMISSIONS (studio/live cassette) . . . 12
(see also Mark Perry, Alternative TV)

GOOD RATS

69 London HLR 10237 The Hobo/The Truth Is Gone . . . 6

GOOD SHIP LOLLIPOP

69 Ember EMB S 276 Maxwell's Silver Hammer/How Does It Feel (some in p/s) . . . 12/6

GOOD TIME LOSERS

67 Fontana TF 791 Trafalgar Square/Where Did My Heart Go . . . 6

GOODTIMERS

62 Fontana H 360 It's Twistin' Time/Twisting Train . . . 10

GOOD VIBRATIONS

70 Ember EMB S 270 Call Me Lightning/Nantucket Ferry . . . 6

ROD GOODWAY

90 Woronzow WOO 12 ETHEREAL COUNTERBALANCE (LP) . . . 18

RON GOODWIN CONCERT ORCHESTRA

53 Parlophone MSP 6035 Limelight/The Song From Moulin Rouge . . . 15
53 Parlophone MSP 6055 Tropical Mirage/The Man Between . . . 15
54 Parlophone MSP 6103 The Sons Of The High Seas/Guadalcanal March . . . 15
54 Parlophone MSP 6115 Cara Mia/Three Coins In The Fountain . . . 15
54 Parlophone MSP 6136 Midnight Blue/On The Waterfront . . . 15
56 Parlophone 45 R-4235 War And Peace/The Christmas Tree . . . 12
57 Parlophone R 4297 Skiffling Strings (Swinging Sweetheart)/I'll Find You . . . 12
58 Parlophone R 4608 Lolita/All Strung Up . . . 10
61 Parlophone R 4821 Murder She Says/Double Scotch . . . 8
64 Parlophone R 5146 633 Squadron/Love Theme From 633 Squadron . . . 6
65 Parlophone R 5181 Girl With A Dream/Of Human Bondage . . . 5
65 Parlophone R 5394 The Early Bird/The Alphabet Murders . . . 6
66 Parlophone R 5501 The Trap/Operation Crossbow . . . 7
67 Parlophone R 5618 The Magnificent Two/Venus Waltz . . . 5
72 Columbia DB 8938 Pathfinders March/Aces High . . . 6
55 Parlophone GEP 8555 RON GOODWIN AND HIS CONCERT ORCHESTRA (EP) . . . 10
58 Parlophone GEP 8662 RON GOODWIN SPECIALS (EP) . . . 8
58 Parlophone GEP 8699 RON GOODWIN SPECIALS NO. 2 (EP) . . . 8
60 Parlophone SGE 2010 THE SMOOTH SOUND (EP, stereo) . . . 8
54 Parlophone PMD 1014 FILM FAVOURITES (10" LP) . . . 15
56 Parlophone PMD 1038 MUSIC TO SET YOU DREAMING (10" LP) . . . 15
58 Parlophone PCS 3002 MUSIC FOR AN ARABIAN NIGHT (LP) . . . 15
58 Parlophone PCS 3006 OUT OF THIS WORLD! (LP) . . . 25
64 United Artists ULP 1071 633 SQUADRON (LP, soundtrack) . . . 15
65 Stateside SL 10136 THOSE MAGNIFICENT MEN IN THEIR FLYING MACHINES (LP, soundtrack) . . . 30
66 Polydor 582 004 THE TRAP (LP, soundtrack) . . . 50
68 Stateside (S)SL 10259 DECLINE AND FALL ... OF A BIRDWATCHER (LP, soundtrack) . . . 110
69 Paramount SPFL 255 MONTE CARLO OR BUST! (LP, soundtrack) . . . 45
69 MGM MGM-C(S) 8102 WHERE EAGLES DARE (LP, soundtrack) . . . 12
69 United Artists UAS 29019 BATTLE OF BRITAIN (LP, soundtrack) . . . 15
72 Studio 2 TWO 373 PLAY BURT BACHARACH (LP) . . . 12
73 Studio Two TWOX 1007 SPELLBOUND (LP) . . . 12
76 EMI EMC 3148 ESCAPE FROM THE DARK (LP, soundtrack) . . . 30
78 Studio Two TWOSP 108 THE FIRST 25 YEARS (2-LP) . . . 18
(see also 20th Century Fox Orchestra, Parlophone Pops Orchestra)

GOOFERS

55 Vogue Coral Q 72051 Hearts Of Stone/You're The One . . . 60
55 Vogue Coral Q 72051 Hearts Of Stone/You're The One (78) . . . 15
55 Vogue Coral Q 72074 Flip, Flop And Fly/My Babe . . . 60
55 Vogue Coral Q 72074 Flip, Flop And Fly/My Babe (78) . . . 15

			MINT VALUE £
55	Vogue Coral Q 72094	Goofy Drybones/Nare	35
55	Vogue Coral Q 72094	Goofy Drybones/Nare (78)	12
56	Vogue Coral Q 72124	Sick! Sick! Sick!/Twenty One	30
56	Vogue Coral Q 72124	Sick! Sick! Sick!/Twenty One (78)	25
56	Vogue Coral Q 72171	Tear Drop Motel/Tennessee Rock And Roll	40
56	Vogue Coral Q 72171	Tear Drop Motel/Tennessee Rock And Roll (78)	25
57	Vogue Coral Q 72267	Wow!/Push, Push, Push Cart	30
57	Vogue Coral Q 72267	Wow!/Push, Push, Push Cart (78)	25
57	Vogue Coral Q 72289	The Dipsy Doodle/Take This Heart	30
57	Vogue Coral Q 72289	The Dipsy Doodle/Take This Heart (78)	15

GOONS

56	Decca F 10756	I'm Walking Backwards For Christmas/Bluebottle Blues	15
56	Decca F 10780	The Ying Tong Song/Bloodnok's Rock 'N' Roll Call	15
57	Decca F 10885	Eeh! Ah! Oh! Ooh!/I Love You	12
57	Decca F 10945	A Russian Love Song/Whistle Your Cares Away	10
57	Decca F 10945	A Russian Love Song/Whistle Your Cares Away (78)	6
79	Lyntone	SCHOOL LEAVERS GOING TO COLLEGE (EP, flexidisc for Barclays Bank)	8
56	Decca DFE 6396	THE GOONS (EP)	18
64	Decca LF 1332	UNCHAINED MELODIES (10" LP)	25
59	Parlophone PMC 1108	BEST OF THE GOON SHOWS (LP)	15
60	Parlophone PMC 1129	BEST OF THE GOON SHOWS (NO. 2) (LP)	15
75	EMI EMC 3082	VERY BEST OF (LP)	12

(see also Peter Sellers, Spike Milligan, Harry Secombe, Michael Bentine, Famous Eccles, Eric Sykes)

SAM GOPAL

69	Stable STA 5602	Horse/Back Door Man (unissued, existence unconfirmed)	
69	Stable SLE 8001	Escalator/Angry Faces/Cold Embrace/The Sky is Burning (LP sampler)	50
69	Stable SLE 8001	ESCALATOR (LP, gatefold sleeve)	110

(see also Hawkwind, Motörhead, Vamp, Isaac Guillory, Clark-Hutchinson, G. F. Fitzgerald)

RABBI JOSEPH GORDAN

(see under 'R')

PETE(R) GORDENO

61	Fontana H 319	Be My Girl/Haven't Got Time (as Pete Gordeno)	12
62	Parlophone R 4862	I Got Eyes/You're Following Me	10
62	Parlophone R 4931	Down By The Riverside/The Boys Kept Hanging Around	8
65	Decca F 12088	Have You Looked Into Your Heart/Don't Come To Me	8
69	Decca F 12947	Everybody Knows/Man And Wife Time	8
68	MCA MU 1009	Shout It From The Hilltop/Born To Be Wanted	5
69	MCA MU 1058	My Girl Maria/I Appreciate	5
70	Decca PA 78	THE WORLD OF PETER GORDENO (LP)	15

GORDON

(see under Gordon Waller)

ANITA GORDON

55	Brunswick 05456	Lonesome Like Nobody Knows/His Hands	10

BARRY GORDON

56	MGM MGM 928	I Can't Whistle/The Milkman's Polka	10
56	MGM MGM 935	Rock Around Mother Goose/Nuttin' For Christmas	20

CURTIS GORDON

57	Mercury MT 163	Sixteen/Cry, Cry (78)	15

DEXTER GORDON

65	Realm RM 191	DEXTER RIDES AGAIN (LP)	12
60s	Fontana Jazz FJL 907	MASTER SWINGERS (LP, with Wardell Gray)	15
71	Black Lion 2460 108	MONTMARTRE COLLECTION VOL. 1 (LP)	12

(see also Wardell Gray)

JOE GORDON (FOLK FOUR)

59	HMV POP 600	Gotta Travel On/Ho Ro My Nutbrown Maid	6
59	HMV POP 600	Gotta Travel On/Ho Ro My Nutbrown Maid (78)	6
59	HMV POP 634	Dream Lover/Dance To Your Daddy	15
59	HMV POP 634	Dream Lover/Dance To Your Daddy (78)	10
60	HMV POP 737	Football Crazy/By The Bright Shining Light Of The Moon	5
59	HMV 7EG 8454	JOE GORDON FOLK HOUR (EP)	15

LONNIE GORDON

90	Supreme SUPETX 159	Happenin' All Over Again (mixes) (12")	10
90	Supreme CDSUPE 167	BEYOND YOUR WILDEST DREAMS (mixes) (CD EP)	15
90	Supreme SUPETX 181	If I Have To Stand Alone (Imsomniac Mix)/If I Have To Stand Alone (Tuesday Mix) (12")	10
90	Supreme CDSUPE 181	IF I HAVE TO STAND ALONE (mixes) (CD EP)	15
91	Supreme CDSU 6	IF I HAVE TO STAND ALONE (CD, withdrawn)	50

NOELE GORDON

74	UK UK 76	To My Daughter/WERNER TAUTZ ORCHESTRA: Dream Concerto	5
81	EMI 5218	After All These Years/Goodbye (p/s)	8

PHIL GORDON

55	Brunswick 05481	Get A Load Of That Crazy Walk/Strip Polka	8
56	Brunswick 05545	Down The Road Apiece/I'm Gonna Move To The Outskirts Of Town	30

ROBERT GORDON WITH LINK WRAY

77	Private Stock PVTS 127	Endless Sleep & The Fool/The Fool (B-side plays at 78rpm)	15

(see also Link Wray)

RONNIE GORDON

63	R&B JB 127	Shake Some Time/Comin' Home	22

MINT VALUE £

ROSCO(E) GORDON

60	Top Rank JAR 332	Just A Little Bit/Goin' Home (as Rosco Gordon)	30
63	Stateside SS 204	Just A Little Bit/What I Wouldn't Do	25
65	Vocalion V-P 9245	Keep On Doggin'/Bad Dream	25
65	Island WI 256	Surely I Love You/What You Do To Me	25
66	Island WI 272	No More Doggin'/Goin' Home	30

TONY GORDON

73	Grape GR 3056	Be True (actually by Alton Ellis)/Navajo Trail	6

(see also Alton Ellis)

VINCENT GORDON

69	Coxsone CS 7085	Soul Trombone/LARRY & ALVIN: Your Cheating Heart	25
69	Duke DU 37	Everybody Bawlin'/SILVERTONES: Come Look Here	12
69	Crab CRAB 16	Walking By/VICEROYS: Promises Promises	10
74	Big Shot BI 630	Come Go With Me/SKIN, FLESH & BONES: Dub Ali Dub	6
75	DIP DLP 5001	MUSICAL BONES (LP, plain sleeve, white label)	35

(see also Don Drummond Junior)

CHARLIE GORE

54	Parlophone CMSP 19	I'll Find Somebody/Heaven Sent You To Me (export issue)	22
54	Parlophone DP 379	I'll Find Somebody/Heaven Sent You To Me (78)	8
54	Parlophone CMSP 26	Two Of A Kind/It's A Long Walk Back To Town (export issue)	22
54	Parlophone DP 397	Two Of A Kind/It's A Long Walk Back To Town (78)	8
54	Parlophone CMSP 30	I Didn't Know/Oh! Mis'rable Love (export issue)	22

(see also Hawkshaw Hawkins, Ruby Wright)

LESLEY GORE

63	Mercury AMT 1205	It's My Party/Danny	8
63	Mercury AMT 1210	Judy's Turn To Cry/Just Let Me Cry	8
63	Mercury AMT 1213	She's A Fool/The Old Crowd	8
64	Mercury MF 803	You Don't Own Me/Run Bobby Run	10
64	Mercury MF 810	That's The Way Boys Are/That's The Way The Ball Bounces	10
64	Mercury MF 821	I Don't Wanna Be A Loser/It's Gotta Be You	10
64	Mercury MF 829	Maybe I Know/Wonder Boy	10
64	Mercury MF 837	Sometimes I Wish I Were A Boy/Hey Now	10
65	Mercury MF 846	The Look Of Love/Little Girl Go Home	10
65	Mercury MF 862	Sunshine Lollipops And Rainbows/You've Come Back	10
65	Mercury MF 872	My Town, My Guy And Me/Girl In Love	10
65	Mercury MF 889	I Won't Love You Anymore (Sorry)/No Matter What You Do	10
66	Mercury MF 902	Young Love/I Just Don't Know If I Can	10
66	Mercury MF 963	California Nights/I'm Going Out (The Same Way I Came In)	10
66	Mercury MF 984	I'm Fallin' Down/Summer And Sandy	10
68	Mercury MF 1017	Magic Colours/It's A Happening World	10
75	A&M AMS 7184	Immortality/Give It To Me, Sweet Thing	5
64	Mercury 10017 MCE	LESLEY GORE (EP)	40
63	Mercury MMC 14127	I'LL CRY IF I WANT TO (LP)	40
63	Mercury 20001 MCL	SINGS OF MIXED-UP HEARTS (LP)	30
64	Mercury 20020 MCL	BOYS BOYS BOYS (LP)	30
64	Mercury 20033 MCL	GIRL TALK (LP)	30
65	Mercury 20071 MCL	MY TOWN, MY GUY & ME (LP)	25
65	Mercury 20076 MCL	ALL ABOUT LOVE (LP)	30
67	Wing WL 1183	GIRL TALK (LP, reissue)	15

GORGONI, MARTIN & TAYLOR

72	Buddah 2011-137	Toly Toly Guyluesha/I Can Make You Cry	7
72	Buddah 2318 067	GORGONI, MARTIN AND TAYLOR (LP)	15

GORKY'S ZYGOTIC MYNCI

93	Ankst ANKST/GZM 040	PATIO (10" EP)	15
94	Ankst ANKST 048	Merched Yn Neud Gwallt Eu Gilydd/Bocs Angelica/ When You Laugh At Your Own Garden In A Blazer (p/s)	6
95	Ankst ANKST 053	Pentref Wrth Y Môr/The Game Of Eyes/Cwpwrdd Sadwrn (p/s)	6
95	Ankst ANKST 058	Gewn Ni Gorffen/12 Impressionistic Soundscapes (clear vinyl, die-cut p/s, mail order only, 1,000 copies)	10
96	Ankst ANKST 068	AMBER GAMBLER EP (10", p/s)	8
98	Mercury ANKST GZM 5	Let's Get Together (In Our Minds)/Billy And The Sugarloaf Mountain/Hwiangerdd Mar (numbered p/s)	7

JOHN GORMAN

73	Island WIP 6151	WPC Hodges/I Remember	5
77	DJM DJF 20491	GO MAN GORMAN (LP)	12

(see also Scaffold, Grimms)

EYDIE GORMÉ

54	Vogue Coral Q 2014	Frenesi/Climb Up The Wall	15
54	Vogue Coral Q 2027	Tea For Two/Sure	12
55	Vogue Coral Q 72067	Give A Fool A Chance/A Girl Can't Say (unissued)	
55	Vogue Coral Q 72092	Give A Fool A Chance/A Girl Can't Say	12
55	Vogue Coral Q 72103	Soldier Boy/What Is The Secret Of Your Success?	12
56	London HL 8227	Sincerely Yours/Come Home	25
57	HMV POP 400	Kiss In Your Eyes/Your Kisses Kill Me	7
58	HMV POP 432	Love Me Forever/Until They Sail	10
58	HMV POP 493	You Need Hands/The Gentleman Is A Dope	6
58	HMV POP 513	Gotta Have Rain/To You, From Me	6
58	HMV POP 529	Dormi, Dormi, Dormi/Be Careful, It's My Heart	6
59	HMV POP 577	Separate Tables/The Voice Of My Heart	6
59	HMV POP 616	I'm Yours/Don't Take Your Love From Me	6
60	HMV POP 767	The Dance Is Over/Too Young To Know	20
62	CBS AAG 105	Yes, My Darling Daughter/Sonny Boy	6

MINT VALUE £

63 CBS AAG 131 Blame It On The Bossa Nova/Guess I Should Have Loved Him More 6
63 CBS AAG 149 Don't Try To Fight It Baby/Theme From Light Fantastic 10
63 CBS AAG 170 Everybody Go Home/The Message 7
64 CBS AAG 215 I Want You To Meet My Baby/Can't Get Over (The Bossa Nova) 6
67 CBS 202470 Everybody Go Home/The Message (reissue) 5
59 HMV 7EG 8547 LOVE IS A SEASON (EP, also stereo [GES 5789]) 10/15
59 HMV 7EG 8562 I'LL REMEMBER APRIL (EP, also stereo [GES 5795]) 10/15
59 HMV 7EG 8409 EXCITING EYDIE (EP) 10
59 HMV 7EG 8474 FINE AND DANDY (EP) 8
59 HMV 7EG 8515 WHEN YOUR LOVER HAS GONE (EP) 8
64 CBS AGG 20047 THE SWEETEST SOUNDS (EP) 8
58 Coral LVA 9086 EYDIE GORME'S DELIGHT (LP) 15
58 HMV CLP 1156 EYDIE GORME (LP) 15
58 HMV CLP 1170 EYDIE SWINGS THE BLUES (LP) 15
58 HMV CLP 1201 VAMPS THE ROARING 20's (LP) 15
59 HMV CLP 1250 EYDIE IN LOVE (LP) 15
59 HMV CLP 1257 GORME SINGS SHOWSTOPPERS (LP) 12
59 HMV CLP 1290 LOVE IS A SEASON (LP) 15
60 HMV CLP 1323 ON STAGE (LP) 12
60 HMV CLP 1392/CSD 1322 EYDIE IN DIXIE-LAND (LP, mono/stereo) 12/15

(see also Steve Lawrence)

FRANK GORSHIN

66 Pye International 7N 25402 The Riddler/Never Let Her Go (some in p/s) 65/25

GOSPEL CLASSICS

68 Chess CRS 8080 More Love, That's What We Need/You Need Faith 70

GOSPELFOLK

69 Emblem 7DR 324 PRODIGAL (LP) 280

GOSPEL GARDEN

68 Camp 602 006 Finders Keepers/Just A Tear 12

(see also Dimples, Amazing Blondel)

GOSPEL OAK

70 Uni UNS 527 Recollections Of Jessica/Brown Haired Girl 6
70 Uni UNLS 113 GOSPEL OAK (LP) 20

GOSPEL PEARLS

63 Liberty LBY 1191 THE GOSPEL PEARLS (LP) 25

GOTHIC HORIZON

70 Argo AFW 102 The Jason Lodge Poetry Book/Wilhelmina Before Sunrise 18
71 Argo AFW 104 Marjorie/Song 15
72 Argo AFW 107 If You Can Smile/Thoughts 12
72 Argo AFW 108 Girl With Guitar/Can't Bear To Think About You 12
71 Argo ZFB 26 THE JASON LODGE POETRY BOOK (LP) 70
72 Argo ZDA 150 TOMORROW IS ANOTHER DAY (LP) 100

KEVIN GOULD

70s Myrrh MYR 1028 TRUE STORIES BY (LP) 18

SANDRA GOULD

63 Philips BF 1290 Hello Melvin (This Is Mama)/My Son The Surfer 5

TERRY GOULD

69 Sing SING 1001 SEVERAL KINDS OF LOVING (LP) 12

DALE GOULDER & LIZ DYER

70 Argo ZFB 10 JANUARY MAN (LP) 30
71 Argo ZFB 30 RAVEN & CROW (LP) 30

GRAHAM GOULDMAN

66 Decca F 12334 Stop! Stop! Stop! (Or Honey I'll Be Gone...)/Better To Have Loved And Lost 80
68 RCA Victor RCA 1667 Upstairs, Downstairs/Chestnut 20
69 Spark SRL 1026 Windmills Of Your Mind/Harvey's Theme (as Graham Gouldman Orchestra) 12
72 CBS 7739 Nowhere To Go/Growing Older 7

(see also 10cc, Whirlwinds, Mockingbirds, High Society, Frabjoy & Runcible Spoon, Manchester Mob, Garden Odyssey Enterprise, Friday Browne, Doctor Father)

GOVE

69 London HLE 10295 Sunday Morning Early/Death Letter Blues 12

GOVERNMENT ISSUE

83 Dischord 10¾ BOYCOTT STABB (LP, 500 only on pink vinyl) 12
85 Fountain Of Youth No. 17 THE FUN JUST NEVER ENDS (LP) 12

JOHN GRAAS SEPTET

54 London RE-P 1003 FRENCH HORN VOL. 1 (EP) 15

GRAB GRAB THE HADDOCK

84 Cherry Red 12CHERRY 83 THREE SONGS BY GRAB GRAB THE HADDOCK (12" EP) 8

(see also Marine Girls, Tracey Thorne)

MICK GRABHAM

72 United Artists UP 35391 On Fire For You Baby/Sweet Blossom Woman 5
72 United Artists UAS 29341 MICK THE LAD (LP) 12

(see also Plastic Penny, Cochise, Procol Harum)

GRACE

80 MCA MCA 628 Fire Of London/Beatnik (p/s) 5
81 MCA MCA 667 Billy Boy/Ad Mad (p/s) 15

CHARLIE GRACIE

57	Parlophone R 4290	Butterfly/Ninety-Nine Ways (initially gold lettering on label, later silver)	75/40
57	Parlophone R 4313	Fabulous/Just Lookin' (initially gold lettering on label, later silver)	80/40
57	London HL 8467	Wandering Eyes/I Love You So Much It Hurts (tri-centre)	25
57	London HLU 8521	Cool Baby/You Got A Heart Like A Rock (tri-centre)	30
57	London HLU 8521	Cool Baby/You Got A Heart Like A Rock (78)	10
58	London HLU 8596	Crazy Girl/Dressin' Up (tri-centre)	35
58	London HLU 8596	Crazy Girl/Dressin' Up (78)	12
59	Coral Q 72362	Doodlebug/Hurry Up, Buttercup (tri-centre)	30
59	Coral Q 72362	Doodlebug/Hurry Up, Buttercup (78)	22
59	Coral Q 72373	Angel Of Love/I'm A Fool, That's Why (tri-centre, later round centre)	20/15
59	Coral Q 72373	Angel Of Love/I'm A Fool, That's Why (78)	25
59	Coral Q 72381	Oh-Well-A/Because I Love You So	25
59	Coral Q 72381	Oh-Well-A/Because I Love You So (78)	40
60	Columbia DB 4477	The Race/I Looked For You	22
62	London HLU 9603	Pretty Baby/Night And Day, U.S.A.	22
65	Stateside SS 402	He'll Never Love You Like I Do/Keep My Love Next To Your Heart	60
57	Parlophone GEP 8630	THE FABULOUS CHARLIE GRACIE (EP)	60
78	London HA-U 8513	CAMEO PARKWAY SESSIONS (LP)	15

GRACIOUS!

68	Polydor 56333	Beautiful/What A Lovely Rain	22
70	Vertigo 6059 009	Once On A Windy Day/Fugue In D Minor	12
70	Vertigo 6360 002	GRACIOUS! (LP, gatefold sleeve, swirl label)	60
72	Philips Intl. 6382 004	THIS IS ... GRACIOUS!! (LP, gatefold sleeve)	70

GRADUATE

80	Precision PAR 100	Elvis Should Play Ska/Julie Julie (p/s)	12
80	Precision PAR 104	Ever Met A Day/Shut Up (p/s)	6
80	Precision PAR 111	Ambition/Bad Dreams (p/s)	6
81	Precision PAR 117	Shut Up/Ever Met A Day (reissue, no p/s)	5
80s	Blue Hat 5 BHR	Mad One/Somebody Put Out The Fire	12
80	Precision PART 001	ACTING MY AGE (LP)	15

(see also Tears For Fears)

GRADUATES

79	Graduate GRAD 1	If You Want It/Hey Young Girl (p/s)	6

BILLY GRAHAM & ESCALATORS

67	Atlantic 584 073	Ooh Poo Pah Doo/East 24th Avenue	10

BOBBY/BOBBIE GRAHAM

65	Fontana TF 521	Skin Deep/Zoom Widge And Wag (as Bobbie Graham)	15
66	Fontana TF 667	Teensville/Grotty Drums (as Bobby Graham)	15

(see also Outlaws, Jimmy Page)

CHICK GRAHAM & COASTERS

64	Decca F 11859	Education/I Know	12
64	Decca F 11932	A Little You/Dance Baby Dance	12

DAV(E)Y GRAHAM

68	Decca F 12841	Both Sides Now/Tristano	5
62	Golden Guinea GGL 0224	THE GUITAR PLAYER (LP)	30
64	Decca LK 4649	FOLK, BLUES AND BEYOND (LP)	60
64	Decca LK 4652	FOLK ROOTS, NEW ROUTES (LP, with Shirley Collins)	100
66	Decca LK 4780	MIDNIGHT MAN (LP)	60
68	Decca LK/SKL 4969	LARGE AS LIFE AND TWICE AS NATURAL (LP)	70
69	Decca LK/SKL 5011	HAT (LP)	65
70	Decca SKL 5056	HOLLY KALEIDOSCOPE (LP, as Davy Graham & Holly)	55
70	President PTLS 1039	GODINGTON BOUNDARY (LP, with Holly)	30
76	Eron ERON 007	ALL THAT MOODY (LP, private pressing)	125
81	Righteous GDC 001	FOLK ROOTS, NEW ROUTES (LP, with Shirley Collins, reissue)	15
97	Rollercoaster ROLL 2022	AFTER HOURS (10" LP)	12
99	Rollercoaster ROLL 2023	ALL THAT MOODY (10" LP, reissue)	12

DAVY GRAHAM & ALEXIS KORNER

62	Topic TOP 70	3/4 A.D. (EP, first pressing in mauve sleeve with cream label; later pressings with lilac or bronze sleeve and blue label)	225/125/100

(see also Alexis Korner)

DAVY GRAHAM/THAMESIDERS

63	Decca DFE 8538	FROM A LONDON HOOTENANNY (EP, 2 tracks each)	15

ERNIE GRAHAM

78	Stiff OFF 2	Romeo And The Lonely Girl/Only Time Will Tell (p/s)	5
71	Liberty LBS 83485	ERNIE GRAHAM (LP)	40

(see also Clancy, Eire Apparent, Brinsley Schwarz, Help Yourself, Nick Lowe)

KENNY GRAHAM'S AFRO-CUBISTS

60	Starlite ST45 013	Bongo Chant/Beguine	6
57	Pye Jazz NJE 1053	PRESENTING KENNY GRAHAM PART 1 (EP)	15
57	Esquire EP 34	CARIBBEAN SUITE (EP)	12
57	Esquire EP 68	KENNY GRAHAM'S AFRO CUBISTS (EP)	10
57	Esquire EP 83	KENNY GRAHAM'S AFRO CUBISTS (EP)	20
56	MGM MGM-C 764	MOONDOG AND SUNCAT SUITES (LP, as Kenny Graham & His Satellites)	60
57	Nixa NJL 12	PRESENTING KENNY GRAHAM (LP)	60
57	Esquire 20-012	KENNY GRAHAM AFRO CUBISTS (LP)	20
57	Esquire 20-023	CARIBBEAN SUITE (LP)	20

(see also Yolanda)

LEN GRAHAM

77	Topic 12TS 334	WIND AND WATER (LP)	12

MINT VALUE £

LEO GRAHAM

73	Upsetter US 399	News Flash/UPSETTERS: Flashing Echo	15
73	Summit SUM 8539	Three Blind Mice/UPSETTERS: Mice Skank	12

LOU GRAHAM

58	Coral Q 72322	Wee Willie Brown/You Were Mean Baby	500
58	Coral Q 72322	Wee Willie Brown/You Were Mean Baby (78)	125

LYNDA GRAHAM

62	Philips 326 552BF	As Long As The River Flows/When I'm Sixteen	8
63	Philips BF 1249	Without Your Love/Wait And See	10
64	Philips BF 1308	You'd Better Believe It/That's The Last Thing I'd Do	12

GRAHAM CENTRAL STATION

74	Warner Bros K 46206	GRAHAM CENTRAL STATION (LP)	15

(see also Sly & Family Stone)

RON GRAINER ORCHESTRA

60	Warner Bros WB 24	The Maigret Theme/Along The Boulevards (as Ron Grainer & His Music)	6
62	Fontana 267219 TF	A Kind Of Loving/Mild And Bitter Blues	8
62	Fontana 267232 TF	Johnny's Tune/Yeoman's Parade	8
62	Pye 7N 15411	Happy Joe/Old Ned	6
63	Decca F 11597	That Was The Week That Was/Petit Louis	7
63	Decca F 11640	Station Six Sahara/Indian Blues	6
64	HMV POP 1366	Not So Much A Programme, More A Way Of Life/Ascot Gavotte	10
67	Pye 7N 17383	A Man In A Suitcase/Andorra (pink label, later blue)	18
67	RCA Victor RCA 1635	The Prisoner/Happening Sunday	75
68	RCA Victor RCA 1698	Love Theme/Detective	6
69	RCA Victor RCA 1898	The Paul Temple Theme/The Jazz Age	18
72	Pye 7N 45141	Steptoe & Son/Counting The Coaster	5
79	RK 1021	Tales Of The Unexpected/Malice Aforethought (p/s)	12
87	Six Of One LYN 18284	The Age Of Elegance/Arrival: The Awakening (Six Of One fan club flexidisc)	8
60	Warner Bros WEP 6012	THEME MUSIC FROM "INSPECTOR MAIGRET" (EP)	12
79	Six Of One 6 OF 1	THE PRISONER ARRIVAL (EP, fan club issue)	30
69	RCA Intl. INTS 1020	THEMES LIKE... (LP)	12
78	RK LB 003	TALES OF THE UNEXPECTED (LP)	12

GLENDA GRAINGER

60s	Audio Fidelity AFSP 007	Mr. Kiss Kiss Bang Bang/Who	10

BILLY GRAMMER

58	London HLU 8752	Gotta Travel On/Chasing A Dream	15
58	London HLU 8752	Gotta Travel On/Chasing A Dream (78)	12
59	Felsted AF 121	Bonaparte's Retreat/The Kissing Tree	12
59	Felsted AF 121	Bonaparte's Retreat/The Kissing Tree (78)	15
59	Felsted AF 128	Willy, Quit Your Playing/It Takes You	10
59	Felsted AF 128	Willy, Quit Your Playing/It Takes You (78)	15
61	Brunswick 05851	Rainbow Round My Shoulder/Columbus Stockade Blues	8
59	Felsted GEP 1005	BILLY GRAMMER HITS (EP)	75

GERRY GRANAHAN

58	London HL 8668	No Chemise, Please/Girl Of My Dreams	30
58	London HL 8668	No Chemise, Please/Girl Of My Dreams (78)	18
60	Top Rank JAR 262	It Hurts/RICHIE ROBIN: Strange Dream	15

ROCCO GRANATA

59	Oriole CB 1525	Marina/Manuela	6
59	Oriole CB 1525	Marina/Manuela (78)	15
61	Oriole CB 1564	Julia/Rocco Cha Cha	5

GRAND FUNK RAILROAD

70	Capitol CL 15632	Heartbreaker/Please Don't Worry	6
70	Capitol CL 15661	Closer To Home/Aimless Lady	6
71	Capitol CL 15668	Inside Looking Out/Paranoid (33rpm)	5
71	Capitol CL 15689	I Can Feel Him In The Morning/Are You Ready/Mean Mistreater (33rpm maxi-single)	5
71	Capitol CL 15705	People, Let's Stop The War/Save The Land	5
72	Capitol CL 15738	Rock And Roll Soul/Flight Of Phoenix	5
69	Capitol E-ST 307	ON TIME (LP)	35
70	Capitol E-ST 406	GRAND FUNK (LP)	30
70	Capitol E-ST 471	CLOSER THAN HOME (LP)	30
71	Capitol E-SW 764	SURVIVAL (LP)	12
72	Capitol E-AS 853	E PLURIBUS FUNK (LP, circular 'silver coin' sleeve)	12
73	Capitol E-AST 11099	PHOENIX (LP, gatefold sleeve)	12
73	Capitol E-AST 11027	WE'RE AN AMERICAN BAND (LP)	12
75	Capitol E-ST 11356	ALL THE GIRLS IN THE WORLD BEWARE (LP)	12
76	Capitol E-ST 11482	BORN TO DIE (LP)	12
76	EMI EMC 1503	GOOD SINGING, GOOD PLAYING (LP)	12

GRANDISONS

63	RCA RCA 1339	All Right/True Romance	10

GRAND PRIX

80	RCA RCA 7	Thinking Of You/Feels Good (p/s)	20
83	Chrysalis PRIX 2	Shout/Keep On Believing (p/s, some with patch)	10/5
83	Chrysalis PRIXP 2	Shout/Keep On Believing (picture disc)	6
83	Chrysalis PRIXX 2	Shout (12", p/s)	15
80	RCA PL 25321	GRAND PRIX — THE FIRST ALBUM (LP)	12
82	RCA RCALP 6027	THERE FOR NONE TO SEE (LP, with lyric insert)	15

(see also McAuley Schenker Group, Praying Mantis, Stratus, Uriah Heep)

MINT VALUE £

GERRI GRANGER

63	London HLX 9759	Just Tell Him Jane Said Hello/What's Wrong With Me	12

ROY GRANGER ORCHESTRA

60	Top Rank JAR 320	Manhattan Lullaby/Lazy Baby	7

GRANNIE

71	SRT SRT 71138	GRANNIE (LP, private pressing of 99 copies only, homemade sleeve)	850

GRANNY'S INTENTIONS

67	Deram DM 158	The Story Of David/Sandy's On The Phone Again	15
68	Deram DM 184	Julie Don't Love Me Anymore/One Time Lovers	15
68	Deram DM 214	Never An Everyday Thing/Hilda The Bilda	15
70	Deram DM 293	Take Me Back/Maybe	18
70	Deram SML 1060	HONEST INJUN (LP)	55

(see also Gary Moore)

AMY GRANT

70s	Myrrh MYR 1124	AGE TO AGE (LP)	18

EARL GRANT

58	Brunswick 05762	The End/Hunky Dunky Doo	7
59	Brunswick 05779	Evening Rain/Kathy-O	5
59	Brunswick 05779	Evening Rain/Kathy-O (78)	7
59	Brunswick 05792	Last Night (I Went Out Of My Mind)/Imitation Of Life	5
59	Brunswick 05792	Last Night (I Went Out Of My Mind)/Imitation Of Life (78)	8
60	Brunswick 05824	House Of Bamboo/Two Loves Have I	12
60	Brunswick 05824	House Of Bamboo/Two Loves Have I (78)	15
60	Brunswick 05841	Not One Minute More/Building Castles	5
62	Brunswick 05865	Tender Is The Night/Honey	5
62	Brunswick 05870	Swingin' Gently/Evening Rain	5
62	Brunswick 05877	Sweet Sixteen Bars/Learnin' The Blues	5
65	Brunswick 05945	Stand By Me/After Hours	5
60	Brunswick OE 9460	EARL GRANT (EP)	8
63	Brunswick OE 9493	SWINGING GENTLY (EP)	8
59	Brunswick LAT 8297	THE END (LP)	12
60	Brunswick LAT 8332	NOTHIN' BUT THE BLUES (LP)	12
60	Brunswick LAT 8351	THE MAGIC OF EARL GRANT (LP)	12
61	Brunswick LAT 8389	EBB TIDE (LP, also stereo STA 3051)	12/15
62	Brunswick LAT 8502	EARL AFTER DARK (LP)	12

ERKEY GRANT & EARWIGS

63	Pye 7N 15521	I'm A Hog For You/I Can't Get Enough Of You	35

GOGI GRANT

55	London HLB 8192	Suddenly There's A Valley/Love Is	40
56	London HLB 8257	Who Are We/We Believe In Love	35
56	London HLB 8282	Wayward Wind/No More Than Forever	30
57	London HLB 8364	You're In Love/When The Tide Is High	25
58	London HLB 8550	The Golden Ladder/All Of Me	22
58	RCA RCA 1038	It's A Wonderful Thing To Be Loved/What A Beautiful Combination	6
58	RCA RCA 1047	Bonjour Tristesse/Johnny's Dream	6
59	RCA RCA 1101	Say A Prayer For Me Tonight/TONY MARTIN: She Is Not Thinking Of Me	5
59	RCA RCA 1105	Kiss Me Honey Honey Kiss Me/Two Dreams	7
59	RCA RCA 1105	Kiss Me Honey Honey Kiss Me/Two Dreams (78)	7
60	London HLG 9185	Goin' Home/I'm Going To Live The Life	8
56	London REB 1057	GOGI GRANT (EP, export issue)	18
57	London HA-B 2032	SUDDENLY THERE'S GOGI GRANT (LP)	50
58	RCA RD 27054	BOTH ENDS OF THE CANDLE (LP, soundtrack)	15
59	RCA RD 27097	GIGI (LP, with Tony Martin)	15
60	London HA-G 2242	IF YOU WANT TO GET TO HEAVEN — SHOUT! (LP, also stereo SAH-G 6072)	25/30

(see also Tony Martin)

JANIE GRANT

61	Pye International 7N 25093	Triangle/She's Going Steady With You	15
62	Pye International 7N 25148	That Greasy Kid Stuff/Trying To Forget You	15

JULIE GRANT

62	Pye 7N 15430	Somebody Tell Him/Ev'ry Letter You Write	10
62	Pye 7N 15447	So Many Ways/Unimportant Things	10
62	Pye 7N 15461	When You're Smiling/Lonely Sixteen	10
62	Pye 7N 15483	Up On The Roof/When You Ask About Love	10
63	Pye 7N 15508	Count On Me/Then, Only Then	8
63	Pye 7N 15526	That's How Heartaches Are Made/Cruel World	10
63	Pye 7N 15545	Don't Ever Let Me Down/Somebody Cares	10
63	Pye 7N 15590	Hello Love/It's Alright	8
64	Pye 7N 15684	Come To Me/Can't Get You Out Of My Mind	8
64	Pye 7N 15615	Every Day I Have To Cry/Watch What You Do With My Baby	10
64	Pye 7N 15652	You Are Nobody 'Til Somebody Loves You/I Only Care About You	10
65	Pye 7N 15756	Baby Baby (I Still Love You)/My World Is Empty Without You	10
65	Pye 7N 15812	Giving Up/Cause I Believe In You	10
65	Pye 7N 15884	Lonely Without You/As Long As I Know He's Mine	10
65	Pye 7N 15937	Stop/When The Lovin' Ends	10
62	Pye NEP 24171	THIS IS JULIE GRANT (EP)	40

LEE GRANT (& CAPITOLS)

66	Parlophone R 5531	Breaking Point/Don't Cry Baby (with Capitols)	20
70	Decca F 13029	A Little Love And Understanding/I Got To Get You Out Of My Mind (solo)	7

MINT VALUE £

LITTLE BROTHER (GRANT)

70 Torpedo TOR 27 Baby Don't Let Me Down/Brother Strong Man (as Little Brother) . . . 7
70 Torpedo TOR 28 Let's Do It Together/Hey Man, Why (as Little Brother Grant & Zapatta Schmidt) . . . 7
(see also Equals)

NEVILLE GRANT

73 Downtown DT 509 Sick And Tired/PRINCE DJANGO: Hot Tip . . . 20

NORMAN GRANT ORCHESTRA

61 Starlite ST45 060 Jive Medley/Speak Low . . . 7

TOP GRANT

62 Island WI 034 Searching/David & Goliath . . . 18
62 Island WI 052 Suzie/Jenny . . . 18
63 Island WI 072 Riverbank Coberley (as Top-Grant)/Nancy . . . 18
63 Island WI 074 Money Money Money/Have Mercy On Me . . . 18
63 Island WI 077 War In Africa/The Birds . . . 18
(see also Rhythm Aces)

GRANTCHESTER MEADOW

71 Amber ABR 004 Candlelight/Winter Blues . . . 15

GRAPE

92 Pencil Toast PENT 001 Baby In A Plastic Bag/Listen To Your Heart (p/s) . . . 25
(see also P.J. Harvey)

GRAPEFRUIT

68 RCA Victor RCA 1656 Dear Delilah/The Dead Boot . . . 6
68 RCA Victor RCA 1677 Elevator/Yes . . . 10
68 RCA Victor RCA 1716 C'mon Marianne/Ain't It Good . . . 6
68 Stateside-Dunhill SS 8005 Someday Soon/Theme For Twiggy . . . 7
69 Stateside-Dunhill SS 8011 Round Going Round/This Little Man . . . 7
69 RCA Victor RCA 1855 Deep Water/Come Down To The Station . . . 6
70 RCA Victor RCA 1907 Lady Godiva/Thunder And Lightning . . . 6
71 Deram DM 343 Universal Party/Sha Sha . . . 6
69 Stateside-Dunhill S(S)L 5008 AROUND GRAPEFRUIT (LP) . . . 40
69 RCA Victor SF 8030 DEEP WATER (LP) . . . 22
(see also Tony Rivers & Castaways, Easybeats, Fynn McCool, Sleepy)

GRAPEVINE

68 Liberty LBF 15063 Things Ain't What They Used To Be Anymore/Ace In The Hole . . . 6

GRASSROOTS

66 RCA Victor RCA 1532 Where Were You When I Needed You/These Are Bad Times . . . 10
67 Pye International 7N 25422 Let's Live For Today/Depressed Feeling . . . 12
67 Pye International 7N 25431 Things I Should Have Said/Tip Of My Tongue . . . 7
68 RCA Victor RCA 1682 Melody For You/Hey Friend . . . 6
68 RCA Victor RCA 1737 Midnight Confessions/Who Will You Be Tomorrow . . . 8
69 Stateside-Dunhill SS 8006 Bella Linda/Hot Bright Lights . . . 6
69 Stateside-Dunhill SS 8012 All Good Things Come To An End/Melody For You . . . 6
69 Stateside-Dunhill SS 8018 The River Is Wide/(You Gotta) Live For Love . . . 6
69 Stateside-Dunhill SS 8023 Who Will You Be Tomorrow/Midnight Confessions . . . 6
69 Stateside-Dunhill SS 8029 I'd Wait A Million Years/Fly Me To Havana . . . 10
69 Stateside-Dunhill SS 8033 Heaven Knows/Don't Remind Me . . . 6
70 Stateside-Dunhill SS 8037 Back To Dreamin' Again/Truck Drivin' Man . . . 6
70 Stateside-Dunhill SS 8048 Walking Through The Country/Melinda Love . . . 6
70 Probe PRO 503 Come On And Say It/Something's Comin' Over Me . . . 5
71 Probe PRO 515 Temptation Eyes/Keepin' Me Down . . . 5
69 Stateside S(S)L 5005 GOLDEN GRASS (LP) . . . 20
70 Stateside SSL 5012 LEAVING IT ALL BEHIND (LP) . . . 20
72 Probe SPB 1058 MOVE ALONG (LP) . . . 12
(see also P.F. Sloan)

GRASS-SHOW

96 Food FOOD 94 Freak Show/Sympathetic Television (picture disc, poster sleeve) . . . 5

GRATEFUL DEAD

67 Warner Bros WB 7186 Born Cross-Eyed/Dark Star . . . 50
70 Warner Bros WB 7410 Uncle John's Band/New Speedway Boogie . . . 12
71 Warner Bros. Truckin'/Johnny B. Goode (unissued)
72 Warner Bros K 16167 One More Saturday Night (as Grateful Dead with Bobby Ace)/Bertha . . . 7
73 Atlantic K 19301 Let Me Sing Your Blues Away/Here Comes Sunshine . . . 7
74 United Artists UP 36030 U.S. Blues/Loose Lucy . . . 6
77 Warner Bros SAM 79 Dark Star/Born Cross-Eyed (mail-order issue with *Dark Star* magazine) . . . 15
79 Arista ARIST 236 Good Lovin'/Stagger Lee . . . 6
87 Arista RIS 35 Touch Of Grey/My Brother Esau (grey vinyl, p/s) . . . 6
67 Warner Bros W(S) 1689 THE GRATEFUL DEAD (LP, mono/stereo) . . . 80/40
68 Warner Bros WS 1749 ANTHEM OF THE SUN (LP) . . . 40
69 Warner Bros WS 1790 AOXOMOXOA (LP) . . . 35
70 Warner Bros WS 1830 LIVE/DEAD (2-LP) . . . 30
70 Warner Bros WS 1869 WORKINGMAN'S DEAD (LP, matt sleeve) . . . 15
71 Warner Bros WS 1893 AMERICAN BEAUTY (LP) . . . 15
71 Warner Bros K 66009 GRATEFUL DEAD LIVE (SKULL AND ROSES) (2-LP) . . . 20
72 Polydor 2310 171 HISTORIC DEAD (LP) . . . 22
72 Polydor 2310 172 VINTAGE DEAD (LP) . . . 22
72 Warner Bros K 66019 EUROPE '72 (3-LP, triple fold-out sleeve) . . . 22
73 Warner Bros K 46246 HISTORY OF GRATEFUL DEAD (BEAR'S CHOICE) (LP) . . . 12
73 Warner Bros K 49301 WAKE OF THE FLOOD (LP) . . . 12
74 Warner Bros K 56024 SKELETONS FROM THE CLOSET: THE BEST OF GRATEFUL DEAD (LP) . . . 12
74 Warner Bros K 59302 FROM THE MARS HOTEL (LP) . . . 12

75 United Artists UAS 29895 BLUES FOR ALLAH (LP, with insert) . . . 12
76 United Artists UAD 60131/2 STEAL YOUR FACE (2-LP, gatefold sleeve, with sampler LP "For Dead Heads Only" [FREE 2] in inner sleeve) . . . 30
(see also Jerry Garcia, Mickey Hart, Kingfish, Robert Hunter, Bob Weir, Keith & Donna Godchaux, Silver [U.S.], Diga Rhythm Band)

NICK GRAVENITES
69 CBS 63818 MY LABORS (LP) . . . 22
(see also Big Brother & Holding Company)

BILLY GRAVES
59 Felsted AF 119 The Shag (Is Totally Cool)/Uncertain (export issue) . . . 18
59 Felsted AF 119 The Shag (Is Totally Cool)/Uncertain (78, export issue) . . . 20

CARL GRAVES
75 A&M AM 7151 Baby Hang Up The Phone/Walk Softly . . . 8
75 A&M AM 7180 The Next Best Thing/Something Teling Me . . . 6
76 A&M AM 7235 My Whole World Ended/Baby Don't Knock . . . 5

GRAVY TRAIN
73 Dawn DNS 1036 Strength Of A Dream/Tolpuddle Episode . . . 6
74 Dawn DNS 1058 Starbright Starlight/Good Time Thing . . . 6
75 Dawn DNS 1115 Climb Aboard The Gravy Train/Sanctuary . . . 6
70 Vertigo 6360 023 GRAVY TRAIN (LP, gatefold sleeve, swirl label) . . . 50
71 Vertigo 6360 051 BALLAD OF A PEACEFUL MAN (LP, gatefold sleeve, swirl label) . . . 120
73 Dawn DNLS 3046 SECOND BIRTH (LP) . . . 40
74 Dawn DNLH 1 STAIRCASE TO THE DAY (LP) . . . 40

BARRY GRAY (ORCHESTRA)
62 Lyntone LYN 249/250 Sabotage/Supercar Song/Supercar Twist (flexi, p/s may exist) . . . 35+/18
64 Melodisc MEL 1591 Fireball/Zero G (by Barry Gray & His Spacemakers; some in p/s) . . . 50/15
65 Pye 7N 17016 Thunderbirds/Parker — Well Done (some in p/s) . . . 35/18
67 Pye 7N 17391 Captain Scarlet/The Mysterons Theme (some in p/s) . . . 30/18
68 Pye 7N 17625 Joe 90 — Title Theme/Joe 90 — Hijacked (some in p/s) . . . 50/25
62 Golden Guinea GGL 0106 SUPERCAR — FLIGHT OF FANCY (LP, with Edwin Astley) . . . 50
67 United Artists (S)ULP 1159 THUNDERBIRDS ARE GO! (LP, soundtrack, mono/stereo) . . . 110/130
(see also Century 21, Mary Jane with Barry Gray, Richard Harvey)

CLAUDE GRAY
64 Mercury 10012 MCE COUNTRY AND WESTERN ACES (EP) . . . 20

DAVID GRAY
92 Hut HUT 23 Birds Without Wings/L's Song/The Light (12", p/s) . . . 12
92 Hut HUTCD 23 Birds Without Wings/L's Song/The Light (CD) . . . 10
93 Hut HUT 27 Shine/Brick Walls/The Rice (12", p/s) . . . 12
93 Hut HUTCD 27 Shine/Brick Walls/The Rice (CD) . . . 10
93 Hut HUT 32 Wisdom/Lovers/4AM (12", p/s) . . . 12
93 Hut HUTCD 32 Wisdom/Lovers/4AM (CD) . . . 10
99 IHT IHTCDS 001 This Year's Love/Nightblindness/Over My Head (CD) . . . 10
99 IHT IHTCDS 002 Babylon/Lead Me Upstairs (Live)/New Horizons (Live) (CD) . . . 10
99 IHT IHTCDS 003 Please Forgive Me (Radio Edit)/(Paul Hartnoll Remix) (CD) . . . 10
01 Hut CDHUTP 17 What Are You?/Falling Free/Coming Down/FLESH: Made Up My Mind (promo CD) . . . 12

DOBIE GRAY
65 London HL 9953 The "In" Crowd/Be A Man . . . 15
65 Pye International 7N 25307 See You At The Go Go/Walk With Love . . . 18
69 London HL 10268 The "In" Crowd/Be A Man (reissue) . . . 7
73 MCA MU 1184 Drift Away/City Stars . . . 8
73 MCA MU 1221 Now That I'm Without You/Loving Arms . . . 6
75 Black Magic BM 107 Out On The Floor/Be A Man . . . 10

DOLORES GRAY
53 Brunswick 05111 Big Mamou/Say You're Mine (78) . . . 8
55 Brunswick 05382 Heat Wave/After You Get What You Want, You Don't Want It . . . 12
55 Brunswick 05407 Rock Love/One . . . 25
55 Brunswick 05407 Rock Love/One (78) . . . 10
57 Capitol CL 14732 There'll Be Some Changes Made/Fool's Errand . . . 10
57 Capitol CL 14770 I'm Innocent/My Mama Likes You . . . 8
63 Philips 326 582BF Mornin' Train/Our Day Will Come . . . 7

DORIAN GRAY
67 Parlophone R 5612 Behind The Tear/Walking Down A Back Street . . . 6
68 Parlophone R 5667 I've Got You On My Mind/Move On . . . 8
68 Parlophone R 5705 Love Is All That It Should Be/Let Me Go Home . . . 6
68 Parlophone R 5732 Jingle Down A Hill/Get Goin' Baby . . . 6

HERBIE GRAY
68 Giant GN 38 We're Staying Here/Life Ska . . . 15
(see also Gene Rondo, Owen & Dandy)

JERRY GRAY & HIS ORCHESTRA
54 Brunswick 05351 The Ooh And Ah Mambo/Kettle Drum Hop . . . 8

JOHNNIE 'THE GASH' GRAY
58 Fontana H 123 Big Guitar/Tequila . . . 20
58 Fontana H 134 Apache/Zach's Tune . . . 18
58 Fontana H 134 Apache/Zach's Tune (78) . . . 10
60 Melodisc 45-1500 Any Old Iron Cha Cha/Cocktails For Two Cha Cha (with His Chunks Of Mettle) . . . 5

LORRAINE GRAY
64 Fontana TF 435 Are You Getting Tired Of Your Little Toy?/ The Boy That I Want Doesn't Want Me . . . 10
64 Fontana TF 484 The Little Girl That Cries/Talk To Him . . . 8

MINT VALUE £

OWEN GRAY

Year	Label / Cat. No.	Title	MINT VALUE £
60	Starlite ST45 015	Far Love/Please Let Me Go	30
60	Starlite ST45 019	Jenny Lee/The Plea	30
60	Blue Beat BB 8	Cutest Little Woman/Running Around (with Ken Richards Band)	20
61	Blue Beat BB 43	Sinners Weep/Get Drunk (with Hersan & His City Slickers)	15
61	Starlite ST45 032	Mash It (Parts 1 & 2)	20
62	Starlite ST45 078	I Feel Good/Someone To Help Me	18
62	Starlite ST45 088	Let Me Go Free/In My Dreams	18
62	Blue Beat BB 75	Rockin' In My Feet/Nobody Else (with Jets)	18
62	Blue Beat BB 91	Millie Girl (with Buster's Group)/DERRICK MORGAN: Headache	20
62	Blue Beat BB 103	Lonely Days/No Good Woman (with Sonny Bradshaw Quartet)	15
62	Blue Beat BB 108	Keep It In Mind/Do You Want To Jump (with Les Dawson Combo)	15
62	Blue Beat BB 113	Best Twist/Grandma-Grandpa (B-side with Hersan & His City Slickers)	18
62	Blue Beat BB 127	Pretty Girl/Twist So Fine	18
62	Blue Beat BB 136	They Got To Move/I Love Her	15
62	Blue Beat BB 139	Tree In The Meadow/Lizebella (with Buster's Group)	15
62	Island WI 002	Patricia/Twist Baby	25
62	Island WI 020	Audrey/Dolly Baby (with Ernest Rauglin [sic] Orchestra)	25
62	Island WI 030	Midnight Trail/Time Will Tell	15
62	Island WI 048	I'm Still Waiting/Last Night	15
62	Chek TD 101	Come On Baby/My One Desire	12
62	Dice CC 3	On The Beach/Young Lover	12
63	Blue Beat BB 147	Big Mabel/Don't Come Knocking (with Edwards' Groupe)	15
63	Blue Beat BB 188	Call Me My Pet/Give Me Your Love	15
63	Blue Beat BB 201	Snow Falling/Oowee Baby (as Owen Gray & His Big Brother)	12
64	Blue Beat BB 217	Draw Me Nearer/Daddy's Girl	12
65	Blue Beat BB 290	Daddy's Gone/BUSTER'S ALLSTARS: Johnny Dark	15
65	Aladdin WI 603	Gonna Work Out Fine/Dolly Baby	18
65	Aladdin WI 607	Can I Get A Witness/Linda Lu	18
65	Island WI 252	Shook Shimmy And Shake/I'm Going Back	18
65	Island WI 258	You Don't Know Like I Do/Take Me Serious (with Sound System)	15
66	Island WI 267	Paradise/Bye Bye Love	12
66	Blue Beat BB 365	I'm Gonna Say So Long/The Days I'm Living	12
67	Island WIP 6000	Help Me/Incense	18
67	Collins Downbeat CR 003	Collins Greetings/Rock It Down (with Sir Collins & Band)	40
67	Collins Downbeat CR 004	I'm So Lonely (with Sir Collins & Band)/EL RECO, SIR COLLINS & J. SATCH: Shock Steady	40
68	Collins Downbeat CR 007	Am Satisfy (with Sir Collins & Band)/BOB STACKIE & SIR COLLINS & BAND: Sweet Music	50
68	Collins Downbeat CR 010	I'm Gonna Take You Back (with Bob Stackie)/GLEN ADAMS: King Sized	40
68	Coxsone CS 7047	Give Me A Little Sign/Ain't Nobody Home	25
68	Coxsone CS 7053	Give It To Me/Isn't It So	25
68	Blue Cat BS 123	These Foolish Things/This I Promise	12
69	Blue Cat BS 156	I Can't Stop Loving You/Tell Me Darling	12
68	Trojan TR 632	Lovey Dovey/Grooving	12
69	Fab FAB 90	Three Coins In The Fountain/Tennessee Waltz	10
69	Fab FAB 96	Ay Ay Ay/Let It Be Me (with Rudies)	8
69	Fab FAB 120	Understand My Love/Apollo 12	8
69	Fab FAB 126	Swing Low/Release Me	8
69	Trojan TR 650	I Can't Stop Loving You/Tell Me Darling	8
69	Trojan TR 670	Too Experienced/I Really Loved You Baby	8
69	Duke DU 12	Reggae Dance/I Know	8
69	Duke DU 33	Seven Lonely Days/He Don't Love You Like I Do	6
69	Downtown DT 423	Groovin'/HERBIE GRAY & RUDIES: These Memories	12
69	Downtown DT 428	Lovey Dovey (with Dandy)/HERBIE GRAY & RUDIES: Kitty Wait	12
69	Camel CA 25	Girl What You Doing To Me/Woman A Grumble	8
69	Camel CA 34	Don't Take Your Love Away/Two Lovers	8
69	Camel CA 37	Every Beat Of My Heart/Don't Cry	8
70	Camel CA 50	Don't Sign The Paper/Packing Up Loneliness	8
70	Camel CA 51	Bring Back Your Love/Got To Come Back	8
70	Upfront UPF 3	Dream Lover/Mudda-Granma-Reggae (with Maximum Breed)	7
70	Bamboo BAM 47	I Can Feel It/I Don't Want (To Lose Your Love)	10
70	Crab CRAB 52	Just A Little Loving/DERRICK MORGAN: Take A Letter Maria	6
70	Pama PM 810	Sugar Dumpling/I Don't Know Why	6
70	Pama Supreme PS 299	I Am In Love Again/RANDY WILLIAMS: Version	6
70	Pama Supreme PS 302	Candida/When Will I Find My Way	6
70	Pama Supreme PS 310	You Gonna Miss Me/I Hear You Knocking	6
70	Supreme SUP 206	Surfin'/All The Love	6
70	Ackee ACK 102	No More/Don't Leave Me (both as Owen Gray & Omen)	6
71	Ackee ACK 123	Whispering Bells/CLANCY'S ALLSTARS: Whiplash (B-side actually "Jacket" by Dave Barker)	10
71	Camel CA 60	Groove Me/No Other One	7
71	Camel CA 73	Nothing Can Separate Us/Girl I Want You To Understand	6
71	Punch PH 87	Sincerely/Hold On I'm Coming	6
71	Pama Supreme PS 325	Summer Sand/Something To Remind Me	6
71	Pama Supreme PS 332	Greatest Hits (Parts 1 & 2)	6
72	Pama Supreme PS 351	Time/GRAHAM: Harlesden High Street	8
72	Pama Supreme PS 358	Hail The Man/I'll Follow You	5
72	Pama Supreme PS 360	Amazing Grace (with Graham Hawk)/SKETTO RICH: Don't Stay Out Late	5
70s	Rock Steady Rev. REV 004	Groovy Kind Of Love (with Elki & Rim Ram Band)/RIM RAM BAND: The Whistler	5
61	Starlite STLP 5	OWEN GRAY SINGS (LP)	225
63	Melodisc MLP 12-153	CUPID (LP)	65
69	Trojan TTL 24	REGGAE WITH SOUL (LP)	25
77	Trojan TRLS 139	FIRE AND BULLETS (LP)	20
78	Trojan TRLS 150	DREAMS OF OWEN GRAY (LP)	18

(see also Laurel & Owen, Gray Brothers, Elki & Owen, Owen & Milie, Owen & Dandy, Dennis Lowe, Survivors, Denzil & Jennifer, Brother Dan, Glen Adam)

MINT VALUE £

SHANE GRAY
68 Page One POF 102 — Sing Out Loud/Come Back To My Heart Again . . . 6

WARDELL GRAY
54 Brunswick LA 8646 — THE CHASE (LP, with Dexter Gordon) . . . 15
65 Stateside SL 10144 — WARDELL GRAY MEMORIAL ALBUM (VOL. 1) (LP) . . . 12
65 Stateside SL 10145 — WARDELL GRAY MEMORIAL ALBUM (VOL. 2) (LP) . . . 12

GRAY BROTHERS
68 Blue Cat BS 124 — Always/Big Man . . . 18
(see also Owen Gray)

KATHRYN GRAYSON
53 MGM SP 1002 — (All Of A Sudden) My Heart Sings/Jealousy . . . 10
53 MGM SP 1014 — Smoke Gets In Your Eyes/The Touch Of Your Hand (B-side with Howard Keel) . . . 10
54 MGM SP 1078 — I Hate Men/ANN MILLER & TOMMY RALL: Always True To You In My Way . . . 10
56 MGM EP 636 — WANTING YOU (EP) . . . 10

KATHRYN GRAYSON & HOWARD KEEL
53 MGM SP 1003 — Why Do I Love You/Make Believe . . . 10
54 MGM SP 1076 — So In Love/ANN MILLER: Too Darn Hot . . . 10
54 MGM SP 1077 — We Open In Venice (with Ann Miller & Tommy Rall)/Wunderbar/ HOWARD KEEL: Were Thine That Special Face . . . 10
54 MGM SP 1079 — So Kiss Me Kate/KEENAN WYNN & JAMES WHITMORE: Brush Up Your Shakespeare/ANN MILLER, TOMMY RALL, BOBBY VAN & BOB FOSSE: From This Moment On . . . 10
(see also Howard Keel, Ann Miller)

LARRY GRAYSON
72 York SYK 529 — Shut That Door/Slack Alice . . . 6
72 York MYK 602 — WHAT A GAY DAY (LP) . . . 18

MILTON GRAYSON
60 London HLU 9068 — Forget You/The Puppet . . . 8

RUDY GRAYZELL
54 London HL 8094 — Looking At The Moon And Wishing On A Star/ The Heart That Once Was Mine . . . 300
54 London HL 8094 — Looking At The Moon And Wishing On A Star/ The Heart That Once Was Mine (78) . . . 80

GRAZINA
62 HMV POP 1094 — Lover Please Believe Me/So What . . . 15
63 HMV POP 1149 — Don't Be Shy/Another Like You . . . 15
63 HMV POP 1212 — Be My Baby/I Ain't Gonna Knock On Your Door . . . 15
64 Giv-A-Disc LYN 568 — Stay Awhile/Let Me Go Lover . . . 12
(see also Lady Murray, Mr & Mrs Murray, Le Roys, Cliff Richard)

GREASE BAND
72 Harvest HAR 5052 — Laughed At The Judge/All I Want To Do/Jesse James . . . 6
75 Goodear EAR 602 — New Morning/Pontardawe Hop . . . 5
71 Harvest SHVL 790 — THE GREASE BAND (LP) . . . 20
75 Goodear EAR 2902 — AMAZING GREASE (LP) . . . 12
(see also Joe Cocker, Wynder K. Frog, Made In Sheffield, Henry McCullough)

JOHNNY B. GREAT (& GOODMEN)
63 Decca F 11740 — School Is In/She's A Much Better Lover Than You (with Goodmen) . . . 8
64 Decca F 11804 — Acapulco 1922/You'll Never Leave Him (solo) . . . 8
(see also Quotations, Johnny Goodison)

GREAT ACES
72 Fab FAB 191 — Gold And Silver/Liberty Rock . . . 7
72 Fab FAB 200 — Liberty Rock/Rock My Soul . . . 7
72 Fab FAB 201 — I Didn't Mean It/Boots And Shoes . . . 6
72 Fab FAB 202 — Baby Girl/Version . . . 6
73 Fab FAB 203 — Banana/My Sweet Lord . . . 6

GREAT AWAKENING
69 London HLU 10284 — Amazing Grace/Silver Waterfall . . . 6

GREATEST LITTLE SOUL BAND IN THE LAND
69 MCA Soul Bag BAG 4 — Tenement Halls/Flat, Black And Together . . . 6
69 MCA Soul Bag BAG 6 — Something For My People/Win Lose Or Draw . . . 6
(see also J.J. Jackson)

GREATEST SHOW ON EARTH
70 Harvest HAR 5012 — Real Cool World/Again And Again . . . 18
70 Harvest HAR 5026 — Tell The Story/Mountain Song . . . 6
77 Harvest HAR 5129 — Magic Touch Woman/Again And Again . . . 8
70 Harvest SHVL 769 — HORIZONS (LP) . . . 45
70 Harvest SHVL 783 — THE GOING'S EASY (LP) . . . 45
75 Harvest SHSM 2004 — THE GREATEST SHOW ON EARTH (LP) . . . 12
(see also Living Daylights, Ian Dury & Blockheads, Fuzzy Duck, Glencoe, Naturals)

GREAT METROPOLITAN STEAM BAND
69 MCA MNP/S 403 — THE GREAT METROPLITAN STEAM BAND (LP) . . . 30

GREAT SATURDAY NIGHT SWINDLE
77 CBS 82044 — GREAT SATURDAY NIGHT SWINDLE (LP, Irish-only issue) . . . 15
(see also Rosemary Taylor)

GREAT SOCIETY
68 CBS 63476 — CONSPICUOUS ONLY IN ITS ABSENCE (LP) . . . 25
(see also Jefferson Airplane)

MINT VALUE £

GREAT UNCLE FRED
67 Strike JH 324 — I'm In Love With An Ex-Beauty Queen/Singalong Version . . . 6

R.B. GREAVES
69 Atco 226 007 — Take A Letter Maria/Big Bad City. . . . 7
70 Atco 2091 013 — Fire And Rain/Ballad Of Leroy. . . . 7
71 Atlantic 2091 170 — Paperback Writer/Over You Now . . . 6
75 20th Century BTC 2191 — Come On And Get Yourself Some/BMF (Beautiful) . . . 6
70 Atco 228 034 — R.B. GREAVES (LP) . . . 18

JOE GRECH
71 Electro ES 152 — Marija L-Maltija/In-Nassab (export issue) . . . 6

BUDDY GRECO
56 Vogue Coral Q 72192 — They Didn't Believe Me/Here I Am In Love Again . . . 6
57 Vogue Coral Q 72268 — Paris Loves Lovers/Ain't No In Between. . . . 6
57 London HLR 8452 — With All My Heart/Game Of Love (with B-G Skiffle Band) . . . 15
57 London HLR 8452 — With All My Heart/Game Of Love (with B-G Skiffle Band) (78) . . . 10
58 London HLR 8613 — I've Grown Accustomed To Her Face/On The Street Where You Live (as Buddy Greco & His Quartet) . . . 6
58 London HLR 8613 — I've Grown Accustomed To Her Face/On The Street Where You Live (78, as Buddy Greco & His Quartet) . . . 12
60 Fontana H 255 — The Lady Is A Tramp/Like Young . . . 7
62 Columbia DB 4924 — Mr. Lonely/Sentimental Fool . . . 5
65 Columbia DB 7790 — Mr. Kiss Kiss Bang Bang/Passing Pastels . . . 5
60 Fontana TFE 17322 — BUDDY GRECO PLAYS AND SINGS THE LADY IS A TRAMP (EP) . . . 8
56 Vogue Coral LVA 9021 — AT MISTER KELLY'S (LP). . . . 18
60 Fontana TFL 5098 — MY BUDDY (LP) . . . 15
61 Fontana TFL 5125 — SONGS FOR SWINGING LOSERS (LP, also stereo STFL 552). . . . 15/18
62 Columbia 33SX 1441 — I LIKE IT SWINGING (LP, also stereo SCX 3445) . . . 12/15
63 Columbia 33SX 1463 — LET'S LOVE (LP, also stereo SCX 3457). . . . 12/15
63 Columbia 33SX 1478 — BUDDY AND SOUL (LP, also stereo SCX 3464) . . . 12/15
63 Columbia 33SX 1519 — BUDDY'S BACK IN TOWN (LP, also stereo SCX 3482) . . . 12/15
63 Columbia 33SX 1544 — SOFT AND GENTLE (LP, also stereo SCX 3491) . . . 12/15
64 Columbia 33SX 1590 — ONE MORE TIME (LP) . . . 12
64 Columbia 33SX 1620 — SINGS FOR INTIMATE MOMENTS (LP) . . . 12
64 Columbia 33SX 1667 — ON STAGE (LP). . . . 12
65 Columbia 33SX 1701 — MODERN SOUNDS OF HANK WILLIAMS (LP). . . . 12
65 Columbia 33SX 1766 — I LOVE A PIANO (LP) . . . 12

(see also Johnny Desmond)

JULIETTE GRECO
54 Philips BBR 8023 — JULIETTE GRECO SINGS (10" LP) . . . 22

GREEDIES
80 Vertigo GREED 1 — A Merry Jingle/A Merry Jangle (p/s) . . . 10

(see also Professionals, Thin Lizzy, Sex Pistols)

AL GREEN(E)
68 Stateside SS 2079 — Back Up Train/Don't Leave Me (as Al Greene & Soul Mates) . . . 25
69 Action ACT 4540 — Don't Hurt Me No More/Get Yourself Together (by Al Greene) . . . 10
70 London HLU 10300 — You Say It/Gotta Find A New World . . . 6
71 London HLU 10324 — I Can't Get Next To You/Ride Sally Ride. . . . 6
71 Bell BLL 1188 — Back Up Train/Don't Leave Me (as Al Green & Soul Mates, reissue) . . . 8
71 London HLU 10337 — Tired Of Being Alone / Right Now, Right Now. . . . 6
71 London HLU 10348 — Let's Stay Together/Tomorrow's Dream. . . . 6
72 London HLU 10369 — Look What You've Done For Me/I've Never Found A Girl . . . 6
72 London HLU 10382 — I'm Still In Love With You/Old Time Relovin' . . . 6
72 London HLU 10393 — You Ought To Be With Me/What Is This Feeling . . . 6
73 London HLU 10406 — Call Me/What A Wonderful Thing Love Is . . . 6
73 London HLU 10419 — Love And Happiness/So You're Leaving . . . 6
73 London HLU 10426 — Here I Am/I'm Glad You're Mine . . . 6
74 London HLU 10443 — Living For You/It Ain't No Fun To Me . . . 6
74 London HLU 10452 — Let's Get Married/So Good To Be Here . . . 6
74 London HLU 10470 — Sha La La (Make Me Happy)/School Days. . . . 6
75 London HLU 10482 — L.O.V.E./I Wish You Were Here With Me . . . 6
75 London HLU 10493 — Oh Me Oh My/Strong As Death . . . 6
75 London HLU 10511 — Full Of Fire/Could I Be The One. . . . 6
76 London HLU 10527 — Let It Shine/There's No Way. . . . 6
76 London HLU 10542 — Keep Me Crying/There Is Love . . . 6
79 Cream HCS 101 — Belle/To Sir With Love . . . 6
85 Hi HIUK 45 7003 — Never Met Anybody Like You/Higher Plane . . . 6
86 A&M AM 302 — True Love/You Brought The Sunshine. . . . 6
88 A&M AM 484 — Put A Little Love In Your Heart (with Annie Lennox)/Spheres Of Celestial Influence. . . . 6
88 A&M CDEE 484 — Put A Little Love In Your Heart (7" Version)/(Vocal Mix)/(Full Version) (with Annie Lennox)/Spheres Of Celestial Influence/A Great Big Piece Of Love (3" CD in 5" card sleeve) . . . 8
89 A&M/Breakout USA 654 — As Long As We're Together/Blessed . . . 6
69 Action ACLP 6008 — BACK UP TRAIN (LP) . . . 50
71 London SHU 8424 — AL GREEN GETS NEXT TO YOU (LP). . . . 15
72 London SHU 8430 — LET'S STAY TOGETHER (LP) . . . 15
72 London SHU 8443 — I'M STILL IN LOVE WITH YOU (LP). . . . 15
73 London SHU 8457 — CALL ME (LP). . . . 15
74 London SHU 8464 — LIVIN' FOR YOU (LP). . . . 15
74 London SHU 8479 — EXPLORES YOUR MIND (LP) . . . 15

BARRY GREEN
63 Ember JBS 713 — Together/Collective Marriage. . . . 6

BRIAN GREEN
68 Fontana SFJL 912 BRIAN GREEN DISPLAY (LP) ... 35

GARLAND GREEN
69 MCA Soul Bag BAG 9 Jealous Kinda Fella/I Can't Believe You Quit Me ... 10
75 Polydor 2066 557 Bumpin' And Stompin'/Nothing Can Take You From Me ... 6

GRANT GREEN
62 Blue Note (B)BLP 84071 GREEN STREET (LP) ... 15
63 Blue Note (B)BLP 4111 THE LATIN BIT (LP) ... 15
65 Blue Note (B)BLP 4139 AM I BLUE (LP) ... 25
66 Blue Note (B)BLP 4202 I WANT TO HOLD YOUR HAND (LP) ... 15
68 Blue Note BLP 4253 STREET OF DREAMS (LP, also stereo BST 84253) ... 12
69 Blue Note BST 84310 GOING WEST (LP) ... 15

GRIZ GREEN
58 Mercury AMT 1012 Be Happy/Morocco (78) ... 6

HUGHIE GREEN
66 Columbia DB 8085 Cuddle Up Baby/Clap Your Hands (B-side with Monica Rose) ... 8
77 Philips GB 1 Stand Up And Be Counted/Land Of Hope And Glory ... 5

IAN GREEN (REVELATION)
67 Polydor 56194 Last Pink Rose/Green Blues (solo) ... 10
69 CBS 3997 When You Love A Man/Santa Maria ... 6
69 CBS 4623 Revelation/Groover's Grave ... 6
70 CBS 63840 REVELATION (LP) ... 22
(see also Madeline Bell, Rosetta Hightower)

JESSE GREEN
77 EMI EMI 2615 Come With Me/Pt 2 ... 10

JIMMY GREEN
73 Duke DU 155 Suspicion/LLOYD'S ALL STARS: Suspicion — Version ... 7
73 Green Door GD 4062 I'll Be Standing By/LLOYD'S ALL STARS: I'll Be Standing By "Version" ... 6
(see also Jimmy London)

KATHE GREEN
69 Deram DM 279 If I Thought You'd Ever Change Your Mind/Primrose Hill ... 7
69 Deram SML 1039 RUN THE LENGTH OF YOUR WILDNESS (LP) ... 30

PETER GREEN
71 Reprise RS 27012 Heavy Heart/No Way Out ... 12
72 Reprise K 14141 Beast Of Burden/Uganda Woman (with Nigel Watson) ... 12
78 PVK PV 16 Apostle/Tribal Dance ... 8
79 PVK PV 24 In The Skies/Proud Pinto (p/s) ... 6
80 PVK PV 36 Walking In The Road/Woman Don't ... 6
80 PVK PV 41 Loser Two Times/Momma Doncha Cry ... 6
81 PVK PV 103 Give Me Back My Freedom/Lost My Love ... 6
81 PVK PV 112 Promised Land/Bizzy Lizzy ... 6
70 Reprise RSLP 9006 THE END OF THE GAME (LP, with Nigel Watson) ... 40
72 Reprise K 44106 THE END OF THE GAME (LP, with Nigel Watson, reissue) ... 12
79 PVK PVLS 101 IN THE SKIES (LP, green vinyl) ... 15
(see also Fleetwood Mac, Peter B's, Shotgun Express, John Mayall & Bluesbreakers, Gass, Peter Bardens, Katmandu)

SALLY GREEN
62 Philips PB 1243 It Hurts Too Much To Laugh/When's He Gonna Kiss Me ... 15

TOM GREEN
74 Action ACT 4621 Rock Springs Railroad Station/Endless Confusion ... 18

PHILIP GREEN & PINEWOOD STUDIO ORCHESTRA
59 Top Rank JAR 112 Sapphire (with Johnny Dankworth)/Tiger Bay ... 6
60 Top Rank JAR 355 "League Of Gentlemen" March/"Golden Fleece" Theme ... 10

GREEN ANGELS
65 Parlophone R 5390 Rockin' Red Wing/Let It Happen ... 15
66 Parlophone R 5512 An Exile's Dream/Hanningan's Hooley ... 5

NORMAN GREENBAUM
70 Reprise RS 20846 Jubilee/Skyline ... 6
70 Reprise RS 20885 Spirit In The Sky/Milk Cow (cream or mustard label) ... each 5
70 Reprise RS 20919 Canned Ham/Junior Cadillac ... 6
71 Reprise RS 21008 California Earthquake/Rhode Island Red ... 6
70 Reprise RSLP 6365 SPIRIT IN THE SKY (LP) ... 15
70 Page One POLS 017 WITH DR. WEST'S MEDICINE SHOW & JUNK BAND (LP) ... 12
(see also Dr. West's Medicine Show & Junk Band)

GREEN BEAN
69 Regal Zonophone RZ 3017 The Garden's Lovely/Sittin' In The Sunshine ... 8

GREENBEATS
64 Pye 7N 15718 If This World Were Mine/You Must Be The One ... 8
65 Pye 7N 15843 So Sad/I'm On Fire ... 7
67 Spin SP 2007 Pretty Woman/Thing ... 8

GREEN BULLFROG
72 MCA MKPS 2021 GREEN BULLFROG (LP) ... 50
(see also Deep Purple, Ritchie Blackmore, Roger Glover, Tony Ashton, Matthew Fisher)

MINT VALUE £

GREEN DAY

94	Reprise W 0257	Basket Case/Tired Of Waiting For You (p/s)	8
94	Reprise W 0257 CD	Basket Case/Longview (live)/Burnout (live)/ 2000 Light Years Away (live) (CD)	8
94	Reprise W 0257 CD2	Basket Case/On The Wagon/Tired Of Waiting For You/ 409 In Your Coffee Maker (CD)	8
95	Reprise W 0320 LC/X	Geek Stink Breath/I Want To Be On TV (p/s, red vinyl)	6

GREEN MAN

75	private pressing	WHAT AILS THEE? (LP)	200+

CLAUDE 'FATS' GREENE & ORCHESTRA

66	Island WI 290	Fats Shake 'Em Up Parts 1 & 2 (actually with Al Thomas)	15

JACK GREENE

68	Decca AD 1005	What Locks The Door/My Elusive Dreams (export issue)	8

JEANIE GREENE

69	Atlantic 584 226	Sure As Sin/I've Been A Long Time Loving You	7

KELLIE GREENE

64	Stateside SS 303	Madrigal/Foggy Day	7

LAURA GREENE

79	Grapevine GRP 135	Can't Help Loving Dat Man/It's A Good Day For A Parade	10

(see also Diane Renay)

LORNE GREENE

64	RCA RCA 1428	Ringo/Bonanza	8
63	RCA RD 7566	YOUNG... AT HEART (LP)	22
65	RCA RD 7709	THE MAN (LP)	22

LEE GREENLEE

59	Top Rank JAR 226	Cherry, I'm In Love With You/Starlight	7

GREEN RIVER

90	Tupelo TUP CD17	DRY AS A BONE EP (CD)	30

GREEN RIVER BOYS

63	Capitol ST 1810	BIG BLUEGRASS SPECIAL (LP)	20

(DAVE) GREENSLADE

73	Warner Bros K 16264	Temple Song/An English Western	5
75	Warner Bros K 16584	Catalan/Animal Farm	5
76	Warner Bros K 16828	Gangsters/Rubber Face, Lonely Eyes (as Dave Greenslade's Gangsters)	5
80	EMI EMI 5034	The Pentateuch Overture/Mischief And War (p/s, as Dave Greenslade)	5
73	Warner Bros K 46207	GREENSLADE (LP)	15
73	Warner Bros K 46259	BEDSIDE MANNERS ARE EXTRA (LP)	15
73	Warner Bros K 56055	SPYGLASS GUEST (LP, gatefold sleeve)	15
75	Warner Bros K 56126	TIME AND TIDE (LP, gatefold sleeve)	15
76	Warner Bros K 56306	CACTUS CHOIR (LP, as Dave Greenslade)	12
80	EMI EMSP 332	THE PENTATEUCH OF THE COSMOGONY (2-LP, with 47-page book, as Dave Greenslade)	35

(see also Wes Minster Five, Alan Price Set, Geno Washington & Ram Jam Band, Chris Farlowe, Colosseum, Samurai, Web)

ARTHUR GREENSLADE (& GEE MEN)

61	Decca F 11363	Rockin' Susannah/Eclipse (with Gee Men)	7
66	Columbia DB 7865	Watermelon Man/Serenade To A Broken Jaw	6
55	Brunswick OE 9171	CASK OF THE AMONTILLADO (EP)	12

GREEN TELESCOPE

86	Imaginary MIRAGE 001	Two By Two/Make Me Stay/Thinkin' About Today (p/s, various designs)	6
86	Wump BIF 4811	Face In The Crowd/Thoughts Of A Madman (p/s)	5

ELLIE GREENWICH

67	United Artists UP 1180	I Want You To Be My Baby/Goodnight, Goodnight	15
68	United Artists UP 2214	Sunshine After The Rain/A Long Time Comin'	12
70	Bell BLL 1105	I Don't Wanna Be Left Outside/Ain't That Peculiar	8
73	MGM 2315 243	LET IT BE WRITTEN, LET IT BE SUNG (LP)	22

(see also Popsicles, Raindrops [U.S.])

MICHAEL GREENWOOD

64	Oriole CB 1943	Buy Your Kid A Guitar/The Bellringer's Nightmare	5

MICK GREENWOOD

71	MCA MDKS 8003	THE LIVING GAME (LP, gatefold sleeve)	12
72	MCA MKPS 2026	TO FRIENDS (LP)	12

(see also Fotheringay)

NICHOLAS GREENWOOD

72	Kingdom KVLP 9002	COLD CUTS (LP)	400

(see also Crazy World Of Arthur Brown, Khan, Bryn Howarth)

STOCKER GREENWOOD & FRIENDS

79	Changes	BILLY + NINE (LP)	25

BIG JOHN GREER

51	HMV JO 360	Woman Is A Five Letter Word/Got You On My Mind (78, export issue)	30

GINNY GREER

57	Brunswick 05673	Five Oranges, Four Apples/Kiss Me Hello (But Never Goodbye)	6

GREG

(see under Greg Bright)

BOBBY GREGG & FRIENDS

62	Columbia DB 4825	The Jam (Parts 1 & 2)	12

BRIAN GREGORY

65 HMV POP 1412 Give Me Your Word/The Ballad Of Dick Turpin . . . 6

GLENN GREGORY & CLAUDIA BRÜCKEN

85 ZTT P ZTAS 15 When Your Heart Runs Out Of Time/(Drumless) (book-shaped picture disc) . . . 5
(see also Heaven 17, Propaganda, Act)

IA(I)N GREGORY

60 Pye 7N 15295 Time Will Tell/The Night You Told A Lie (as Ian Gregory) . . . 30
61 Pye 7N 15397 Can't You Hear The Beat Of A Broken Heart/Because . . . 25
62 Pye 7N 15435 Mr. Lovebug/Pocketful Of Dreams . . . 35
63 Columbia DB 7085 How Many Times/Yellow Teddy Bear . . . 12

JOHNNY GREGORY & HIS ORCHESTRA

60 Fontana H 251 Honky Tonk Train Blues/"Sons And Lovers" Theme (with Cascading Strings) . . . 6
60 Fontana H 286 Bonanza/Maverick . . . 10
61 Fontana H 288 Wagon Train/Bronco . . . 10
61 Fontana H 337 Sucu Sucu/Echo For Two . . . 5
61 Fontana H 341 Route 66/M Squad . . . 8
61 Fontana TFE 17325 MAVERICK! (EP) . . . 15
61 Fontana TFE 17331 BONANZA (EP) . . . 15
62 Fontana TFE 17389 THE T.V. THRILLERS (EP) . . . 15
61 Fontana TFL 5110 T.V. WESTERN THEMES (LP, also stereo STFL 538) . . . 15/20
62 Fontana TFL 5170/STFL 585 CHANNEL THRILL: THE T.V. THRILLER THEMES (LP, mono/stereo) . . . 12/15
72 Philips 6308 111 SPIES AND DOLLS (LP) . . . 25
74 United Artists UAG 29546 A MAN FOR ALL SEASONS (LP) . . . 15
76 Philips 6308 255 THE DETECTIVES (LP) . . . 12
(see also Chaquito)

TONY GREGORY

66 Doctor Bird DB 1007 Baby Come On Home/Marie Elena . . . 15
66 Doctor Bird DB 1016 Give Me One More Chance/I've Lost My Love . . . 15
67 Island WI 3029 Get Out Of My Life/SOUL BROTHERS: Sugar Cane . . . 18
67 Coxsone CS 7013 Only A Fool (Breaks His Own Heart)/Pure Soul . . . 15
71 Horse HOSS 3 Bouncing All Over The World/Tell Me . . . 6
67 Coxsone CSL 8011 TONY GREGORY SINGS (LP) . . . 55
(see also Lloyd Charmers)

GREHAN SISTERS

66 Rex EPR 5005 THE GREHAN SISTERS (EP) . . . 10
67 Transatlantic TRA 160 ON GALTYMORE MOUNTAINS (LP) . . . 15

STAN GREIG'S JAZZ BAND

59 Tempo EXA 90 STAN GREIG'S JAZZ BAND (EP) . . . 25
72 Redeffusion ZS 116 BOOGIE WOOGIE (LP) . . . 15
80s Calligraph CLGLP 004 BLUES EVERY TIME (LP) . . . 20

GREMLINS

66 Mercury MF 981 The Coming Generation/That's What I Want . . . 22
67 Mercury MF 1004 You Gotta Believe It/I Can't Say . . . 22

JOYCE GRENFELL

58 HMV 7EG 8787 AT HOME (EP) . . . 10
59 HMV 7EG 8936 OLD TYME DANCING (EP) . . . 10
54 Philips BBL 7004 REQUESTS THE PLEASURE (LP) . . . 20
62 HMV CLP 1155 JOYCE GRENFELL IN A MISCELLANY (LP) . . . 15
64 HMV CLP 1810 ENCORES (LP) . . . 12
76 One Up OU 2149 COLLECTION (LP) . . . 12
78 EMI DUO 128 THE NEW COLLECTION (2-LP) . . . 15

JOYCE GRENFELL & STANLEY HOLLOWAY

59 Caedmon TC 1104 BAB BALLADS & CAUTIONARY TALES (LP) . . . 20
(see also Stanley Holloway)

JOEL GREY

54 MGM SPC 1 Last Night In The Back Porch/Two-Faced (export issue) . . . 15
57 Capitol CL 14779 Everytime I Ask My Heart/Moonlight Swim . . . 7
58 Capitol CL 14832 Be My Next/Shoppin' Around . . . 15

RONNIE GREY & JETS

55 Capitol CL 14329 Run, Manny, Run/Sweet Baby . . . 30

GREYHOUND

71 Trojan TR 7820 Black And White/Sand In Your Shoes . . . 6
71 Trojan TR 7834 Follow The Leader/Funky Jamaica . . . 6
71 Trojan TR 7848 Moon River/I've Been Trying/Pressure Is Coming On . . . 6
72 Trojan TRLS 27 BLACK AND WHITE (LP) . . . 18
(see also Tillermen)

GRID

90 East West YZ 475 Floatation (Subsonic Grid Mix)/Floatation (Sonic Swing Mix) (p/s) . . . 5
90 East West YZ 475T Floatation (Subsonic Grid Mix)/Floatation (Sonic Swing Mix) (12", p/s) . . . 8
90 East West YZ 475CD Floatation (7" Version)/(Subsonic Grid Mix)/(Sonic Swing Mix) (CD) . . . 8
90 East West YZ 498 A Beat Called Love/A Beat Called Dub (p/s) . . . 5
90 East West YZ 498T A Beat Called Love (3.40)/A Beat Called Club/A Beat Called Dub (12", p/s) . . . 8
90 East West YZ 498CD A Beat Called Love (3.40)/A Beat Called Club/A Beat Called Dub (CD) . . . 8
91 Virgin VST 1369 Boom! (Freestyle Mix)/Boom! (707 Mix) (12", p/s) . . . 10
93 Virgin VSCDT 1427 Heartbeat (Radio Edit)/Heartbeat (Back To The Future Mix)/
Heartbeat (Purple Heart Mix)/Heartbeat (456 Mix) (CD) . . . 8
93 Virgin VSCDX 1427 Heartbeat (Brian Eno Remixes) (CD) . . . 12

MINT VALUE £

94 Deconstruction CORBY 3 Texas Cowboys (Hardkiss 'Beans Is Ready, Boys' Mix) (12", promo only). 12
89 Grid GRID 001 INTERGALACTICA (12", white label, private pressing). 15
89 Grid GRID 002 ON THE GRID (12", white label private pressing) 15
93 Virgin VSTX 1442 CRYSTAL CLEAR (Orb Mixes) (12", 4-track, clear vinyl). 10
(see also Timothy Leary Meets The Grid)

GRIDS

80 Kings Head NEW ANTHEMS (EP) 20

ROOSEVELT GRIER

68 Action ACT 4515 People Make The World/Hard To Forget. 18
69 Pama PM 774 Who's Got The Ball. 15
69 Pama PM 784 C'mon Cupid/High Society Woman 15

GRIFFIN

69 Bell BLL 1075 I Am The Noise In Your Head/Don't You Know. 30
72 MGM 2006 088 What Happens In The Darkness/Calling You 10
(see also Heavy Jelly, Skip Bifferty, Every Which Way, Bell & Arc, Happy Magazine, Ginger Baker's Airforce)

SYLVIA GRIFFIN

88 Rocket BLAST 7 Love's A State Of Mind/Forgive The Girl (p/s, features George Harrison) 15
88 Rocket BLAST 712 Love's A State Of Mind/Forgive The Girl/Lonely Heart (12", p/s, features George Harrison) 25
88 Rocket BLACD 7 Love's A State Of Mind/Forgive The Girl/Lonely Heart (CD, card sleeve, features George Harrison). 50

JOHNNY GRIFFIN BIG SOUL BAND

61 Riverside REP 3203 THE BIG SOUL BAND (EP, with Clark Terry & Bobby Timmons) 10
61 Riverside RLP 12-3331 THE BIG SOUL BAND (LP, also stereo [RLP 9331]. 25
(see also Eddie 'Lockjaw' Davis)

MERV GRIFFIN

61 London HLL 9339 The Charanga/Along Came Joe. 10

VINCENT GRIFFIN

77 Topic 12TS 338 TRADITIONAL FIDDLE MUSIC FROM COUNTY CLARE (LP) 12

VIRGIL GRIFFIN

71 Jay Boy BOY 43 La Da Da Da Da/Climbing 7

GRIFFIN BROTHERS' ORCHESTRA

52 Vogue V 2139 Weepin' And Cryin' (with Tommy Brown)/The Teaser Boogie (78) 15

ANDY GRIFFITH

55 Capitol CL 14263 Ko Ko Mo (I Love You So)/Make Yourself Comfortable 25
56 Capitol CL 14619 No Time For Sergeants/Make Yourself Comfortable 12
57 Capitol CL 14766 Mama Guitar/A Face In The Crowd 25
57 Capitol CL 14766 Mama Guitar/A Face In The Crowd (78). 15
58 Capitol CL 14936 Midnight Special/She's Bad, Bad Business (with Dixie Seven) 15
59 Capitol CL 15003 Hamlet (Parts 1 & 2). 5
56 Capitol EAP1 630 ANDY GRIFFITH (EP) 15
60 Capitol ST 1105 SHOUTS THE BLUES AND OLD TIMEY SONGS (LP, mono/stereo) 12/15

MARCIA GRIFFITHS

66 Island WI 285 Funny/KING SPARROW: Beggars Have No Choice (B-side actually by Leonard Dillon & Wailers; some copies credit Marcia Griffiths on both sides) . . . 40
67 Studio One SO 2008 Hound Dog (actually by Norma Fraser)/HUGH GODFREY: My Time 35
67 Studio One SO 2015 After Laughter/HUGH GODFREY: Go Tell Him 25
68 Coxsone CS 7035 Mojo Girl (actually Nora Dean)/HAMLINS: Tell Me That You Love Me. 25
68 Coxsone CS 7055 Feel Like Jumping/HORACE TAYLOR: Thundering Vibrations 30
68 Coxsone CS 7062 Hold Me Tight/BASIES: Home Sweet Home (B-side actually by Basses). 40
68 Studio One SO 2047 Words (as Marcia Griffiths & Jeff Dixon)/SHARKS: How Could I Live 25
68 Studio One SO 2059 Truly/SIMMS & ROBINSON: Drought. 22
69 Gas GAS 111 Tell Me Now/STAN HOPE: The Weight 12
69 High Note HS 029 Talk (Parts 1 & 2) (correct title is actually "Toil") 12
69 Escort ES 808 Don't Let Me Down/REGGAEITES: Romper Room (B-side actually by Peter Tosh) 10
69 Trojan TR 693 Put A Little Love In Your Heart/J BOYS: Jay Fever. 8
70 Harry J. HJ 6613 Put A Little Love In Your Heart/JAY BOYS: Bah Oop Ah. 7
70 Harry J. HJ 6623 Band Of Gold/JAY BOYS: Cowboy (Version II) 7
70 Bamboo BAM 59 Shimmering Star/SOUND DIMENSION: Mun-Dun-Gu (B-side actually Im & David) 15
(see also Bob & Marcia, Peter Touch/Tosh, Roy Richards, Soul Vendor, Bob Andy, Della Humphrey, Mr. Foundation, Bob Marley)

VICTOR GRIFFITHS

70 Punch PH 29 I Am Proud Of You/KING VICTOR ALL STARS: Version 7

FERRE GRIGNARD

68 Atlantic 584 158 Yellow You Yellow Me/La Si Do. 6
70 Major Minor SMLP 72 CAPTAIN DISASTER (LP). 15

CAROL GRIMES (& DELIVERY)

70 B&C CB 129 Harry Lucky/Homemade Ruin (with Delivery) 6
74 Virgin VS 109 You're The Only One/Southern Boogie 5
74 Good Ear EAR 105 Give It Everything You've Got/Let's Do It Again (with London Boogie Band) 5
75 Good Ear EAR 605 I Betcha Didn't Know That/Dynamite. 5
76 Decca FR 13674 I Betcha Didn't Know That/Dynamite (reissue) 5
77 B&C BCP 2 I Don't Wanna Discuss It/I'm Walking (with Delivery) 5
82 Polydor POSP 417 Ain't That Peculiar/Fashion Passion (p/s) 5
70 Charisma CAS 1023 FOOLS MEETING (LP, with Delivery). 70
74 Caroline CA 2001 WARM BLOOD (LP) 18
76 Decca SKL-R 5258 CAROL GRIMES (LP) 15
(see also Uncle Dog, Babylon)

JOHNNY GRIMES

54 Parlophone DP 388 — Who Would You Cry To/These Three Little Words (with Wanda Wayne) (78, export issue) . . . 7

TINY GRIMES & HIS R&B QUINTET

54 Esquire 10-349 — Annie Laurie/Hot In Harlem (78) . . . 7

GRIMMS

75 DJM DJS 393 — Backbreaker/The Masked Poet . . . 5
76 DJM DJS 679 — The Womble Bashers Of Walthamstow/ The Worst Is Yet To Come/Wiggle Waggle . . . 5
73 Island HELP 11 — GRIMMS (LP) . . . 12
73 Island ILPS 9248 — ROCKIN' DUCK (LP, gatefold sleeve) . . . 12
(see also Neil Innes, Liverpool Scene, Scaffold, Mike McGear, McGough & McGear, John Gorman, Zoot Money, Patto, Viv Stanshall, Andy Roberts, Bashers)

GRIM REAPER

83 Ebony EBON 16 — SEE YOU IN HELL (LP) . . . 20
85 Ebony EBON 32 — FEAR NO EVIL (LP) . . . 20
87 RCA PL 86250 — ROCK YOU TO HELL (LP) . . . 12

GRIN

71 CBS 5239 — We All Sung Together/See What A Love Can Do . . . 5
71 CBS 7405 — Everybody's Missin' The Sun/18 Faced Lover . . . 5
72 CBS 7757 — White Lies/Just To Have You . . . 5
73 Epic EPC 1463 — Ain't Love Nice/Love Or Else . . . 5
71 Epic EPC 64272 — GRIN (LP) . . . 18
72 Epic EPC 64652 — 1 + 1 (LP) . . . 18
73 Epic EPC 65166 — ALL OUT (LP) . . . 18
(see also Nils Lofgren)

GRINDERSWITCH

76 Capricorn 2089 030 — Picking The Blues/The Best I Can . . . 5

JANNY GRINE

70s Sparrow BIRD 104 — FREE INDEED (LP) . . . 15

GRINGO

71 MCA MKS 5067 — I'm Another Man/Soft Mud . . . 6
71 MCA MKPS 2107 — GRINGO (LP) . . . 20
(see also Caravan)

JOE GRINNE

69 Coxsone CS 7098 — Mr Editor/How I Feel (both sides actually by Melodians) . . . 22

GRISBY DYKE

69 Deram DM 232 — The Adventures Of Miss Rosemary La Page/Mary Anne She . . . 6

GRIZZARDS

98 Baban GRIZ 5 — Grizzling/The Green Griz (p/s) . . . 8

DEWEY GROOM

62 Starlite ST45 085 — Butane Blues/That's All I Want Out Of Life . . . 30
63 Starlite ST45 095 — You're Tearing My Heart Out Of Me/Walking Papers . . . 20
63 Starlite ST45 105 — Heartaches For Sale/Sometimes If I'm Lucky . . . 18

GROOP

68 CBS 3204 — Woman You're Breaking Me/Mad Over You . . . 30
68 CBS 3351 — Lovin' Tree/Night Life . . . 12
69 Bell BLL 1070 — A Famous Myth/Tears And Joys . . . 8
69 Bell BLL 1080 — The Jet Song (When The Weekend's Over)/Nobody At All . . . 10

GROOVE

69 Parlophone R 5783 — The Wind/Play The Song . . . 20

GROOVE

80 Trendy WHIP 1 — Heart Complaint/I Wanna Be Your Pygmy . . . 15

GROOVE FARM

87 Raving Pop Blast RPBGF 1 — SORE HEADS AND HAPPY HEARTS (EP, with insert & handwritten labels) . . . 10
87 Raving Pop Blast RPBGF 2 — ONLY THE MOST IGNORANT GUTLESS SHEEP-BRAINED POLTROON CAN DENY THEM NOW (EP) . . . 8
87 Raving Pop Blast RAVE 20 — BAGISM (EP, hand-painted gatefold no'd p/s with insert, home-made labels) . . . 5
87 Subway Org. SUBWAY 15T — GOING BANANAS WITH THE GROOVE FARM (12" EP) . . . 8
88 Subway Organisation SUBWAY 19T — The Big Plastic Explosion! (It's Alright, It's Alright) (Dance Mix)/Nancy Sinatra/ Baby Blue Marine/Riot On Sunset Strip/Red Dress (p/s) . . . 7
88 Subway Organisation SUBWAY 22N — Driving In Your New Car (Mini Mix)/Expanding Reindeer/ I Can't Dance With You/Epistle To Duppy (10", p/s) . . . 7
88 Subway Organisation SUBWAY 22N — Driving In Your New Car (Mini Mix)/Expanding Reindeer/I Can't Dance With You/Epistle To Duppy (12", white label promos only, with press release) . . . 20
88 Kvatch 001/LYN 18632 — Baby Blue Marine/SEA URCHINS: Clingfilm (flexi, 1,000 only, 500 with p/s) . . . 15/8
90 Woosh WOOSH 6 — Heaven Is Blue/ESMERELDA'S KITE: Vampire Girl (1-sided red flexidisc free with *Woosh* fanzine) . . . 6/5

GROOVERS

71 Camel CA 83 — Put Me Down Easy/I Want To Go Back Home . . . 6
71 Escort ERT 863 — Bend Down Low/The Burning Feeling . . . 6
(see also Lloyd & Groovers, Alva Lewis, Junior Byles, Dennis Walks)

GROOVE TUNNEL

95 Detour DR 023 — Rainy Day/How Do You Feel (p/s, white vinyl) . . . 5

MINT VALUE £

WINSTON GROOV(E)Y

69	Grape GR 3005	Leaving Me Standing/Little Girl	10
69	Grape GR 3008	Merry X-mas/I Am Lonely	8
69	Nu Beat NB 041	Island In The Sun/Work It Up	10
69	Nu Beat NB 042	Josephine/Champagne And Wine	8
70	New Beat NB 053	Standing At The Corner/You Send Me	5
70	New Beat NB 055	Yellow Bird/For Your Love	5
70	New Beat NB 058	Here Is My Heart/Birds And Flowers	5
70	New Beat NB 066	Groovin'/Sugar Mama	5
70	New Beat NB 073	Tennessee Waltz/Old Man Trouble	5
70	Attack ATT 8019	You Can't Turn Your Back On Me/PAMA DICE: The Worm	8
70	Jackpot JP 708	Funky Chicken/CIMARRONS: Part 2 (B-side actually unknown instrumental)	8
70	Jackpot JP 709	Funny/CIMARRONS: Funny Version Two	7
70	Torpedo TOR 11	Please Don't Make Me Cry/Motion On The Ocean	5
70	Crab CRAB 63	I Like The Way/Tell Me Why	5
71	Crab CRAB 64	I've Got The Find A Way To Win Mary Back/Wanna Be There	5
71	Bullet BU 471	I Wanna Be Loved/Get Back Together	5
71	Pama PM 827	Don't Break My Heart/How Long Will This Go On	5
71	Pama Supreme PS 323	Free The People/Not Now	5
72	Pama Supreme PS 349	What You Gonna Do/Why Did You Leave	5
72	Pama Supreme PS 364	Sylvia's Mother/Here Is My Heart	5
73	Explosion EX 2086	Nose For Trouble/RHYTHM RULERS: Version	5
74	Explosion EX 2088	Please Don't Make Me Cry/So Easy	5
69	Pama PMP 2011	FREE THE PEOPLE (LP)	30

(see also King Horror, Upsetters)

WALTER GROSS

54	MGM SP 1070	Blue Moon/Tenderly	7
54	MGM SP 1071	You Won't Forget Me (with India Adams)/Follow Me	7

G.G. GROSSETT

69	Crab CRAB 10	Run Girl Run/DENNIS WALKS: The Drifter	10
69	Crab CRAB 33	Greater Sounds/Live The Life I Love	7

STEFAN GROSSMAN

70	Big T BIG 133	Pretty Little Tune/Little Sally Walker	6
71	Big T BIG 140	'Joe Hill' — Themes	6
68	Fontana (S)TL 5463	AUNT MOLLY'S MURRAY FARM (LP)	22
69	Fontana STL 5485	THE GRAMERCY PARK SHEIK (LP)	22
70	Transatlantic TRA 217	YAZOO BASIN BOOGIE (LP)	15
71	Transatlantic TRA 246	THOSE PLEASANT DAYS (LP, with lyric insert)	12
72	Transatlantic TRA 257	HOT DOGS (LP)	12
73	Transatlantic TRA 274	GUITAR INSTRUMENTALS (LP)	12
75	Transatlantic TRA 293	BOOTLENECK SERENADE (LP)	12

(see also John Renbourn)

LUTHER GROSVENOR

71	Island WIP 6109	Here Comes The Queen/Heavy Day	6
72	Island WIP 6124	All The People/Waiting	6
71	Island ILPS 9168	UNDER OPEN SKIES (LP)	22

(see also Hellions, Revolution, Art, Spooky Tooth, Mott The Hoople, Widowmaker)

CARL GROSZMANN

70	Decca F 13065	Thunderbird/Missouri Woman	6
75	Ring O' 2017 103	I've Had It/C'mon And Roll	15
77	Ring O' 2017 107	Face Of A Permanent Stranger/Your Own Affair (promo p/s or company sleeve)	15/10
75	Ring O' 2320 102	CARL GROSZMANN (LP, unreleased)	

GROUND ATTACK

81	Ground Attack GAR 001	THE RED LION EP (Red Lion/Every Mother's Son) (gatefold p/s, later no p/s)	80/5

GROUNDHOGS

68	Liberty LBF 15174	You Don't Love Me/Still A Fool	25
69	Liberty LBF 15263	B.D.D./TONY McPHEE: Gasoline	15
70	Liberty LBF 15346	Eccentric Man/Status People	15
73	W. Wide Artists WWS 006	Sad Go Round/Over Blue	6
74	W. Wide Artists WWS 012	Plea Sing, Plea Sing/TONY McPHEE: Dog Me Bitch	6
76	United Artists UP 36095	Live A Little Lady/Boogie Withus	6
76	United Artists UP 36177	Pastoral Future/Live Right (as Tony McPhee & Groundhogs)	6
68	Liberty LBL/LBS 83199E	SCRATCHING THE SURFACE (LP, mono/stereo)	75/50
69	Liberty LBS 83253	BLUES OBITUARY (LP)	45
70	Liberty LBS 83295	THANK CHRIST FOR THE BOMB (LP, gatefold sleeve)	22
71	Liberty LBS 83401	SPLIT (LP, gatefold sleeve)	18
72	United Artists UAG 29347	WHO WILL SAVE THE WORLD... (LP, gatefold sleeve)	15
72	United Artists UAG 29419	HOGWASH (LP, gatefold sleeve)	15
74	United Artists UDF 31	GROUNDHOGS' BEST 1969-1972 (2-LP)	22
74	W. Wide Artists WWA 004	SOLID (LP, with lyric insert)	12
76	United Artists UAG 29917	CROSSCUT SAW (LP)	15
76	United Artists UAG 29994	BLACK DIAMOND (LP)	15
84	Psycho PSYCHO 24	HOGGIN' THE STAGE (2-LP, with EP, stickered sleeve)	25

(see also John Lee's Groundhogs, Tony McPhee, Herbal Mixture, Home, Andy Fernbach, John Lee Hooker)

GROUP

72	Charisma CB 197	Bovver Boys/Piraeus Football Club/An Open Letter To George Best	10

(see also Neil Innes)

GROUP B

67	Vocalion VF 9284	I Know Your Name Girl/I Never Really Know	22

(see also Blue Cheer)

GROUP 1850
69 Philips SBL 7884 — AGEMO'S TRIP TO MOTHER EARTH (LP) 140

GROUP IMAGE
69 Stable SLE 8005 — A MOUTH IN THE CLOUDS (LP) 30

GROUP ONE
58 HMV POP 463 — She's Neat/Made For Each Other 25
58 HMV POP 463 — She's Neat/Made For Each Other (78) 8
58 HMV POP 492 — Chanson D'Amour/Londonderry Air 10
58 HMV POP 492 — Chanson D'Amour/Londonderry Air (78) 7

GROUP SIX
59 Oriole CB 1488 — Rock-A-Boogie/Rockin' The Blues 25
59 Oriole CB 1488 — Rock-A-Boogie/Rockin' The Blues (78) 18

GROUP THERAPY
69 Philips BF 1744 — River Deep Mountain High/Remember What You Said 6
69 Philips BF 1792 — Can't Stop Lovin' You Baby/I Must Go 6
69 Philips SBL 7883 — YOU'RE IN NEED OF GROUP THERAPY (LP) 18

GROUP TWO
68 Columbia DB 8374 — It's Raining Outside/Western Man, Eastern Lady 5

GROUP X
63 Fontana 267 274 TF — There Are 8 Million Cossack Melodies — And This Is One Of Them/ Teneriffe (some in p/s) 20/12
63 Fontana TF 417 — Roti Calliope/Cross Beat 18

GROUT
78 Urinating Vicar SIDEWAYS GRA — DO IT YOURSELF (EP) .... 200+

GROW UP
80 Object Music OBJ 005 — THE BEST THING (LP) 12
81 Rough Trade GROW 1 — WITHOUT WINDS (LP) 12

GRUMBLE
73 RCA Victor RCA 2384 — Da Doo Ron Ron/Pig Bin An' Gone 5
(see also 10cc)

GRUNT FUTTOCK
72 Regal Zonophone RZ 3042 — Rock 'N' Roll Christian/Free Sole 30
(see also Move, Roy Wood)

GRUVY BEATS
70 Nu Beat NB 048 — Share Your Popcorn/LAUREL AITKEN: Mr. Popcorn 12
70 Nu Beat NB 049 — Blue Mink/LAUREL AITKEN: I've Got Your Love 8

GRYPHON
77 Harvest HAR 5125 — Spring Song/Fall Of The Leaf 6
73 Transatlantic TRA 262 — GRYPHON (LP, gatefold sleeve) 15
74 Transatlantic TRA 282 — MIDNIGHT MUSHRUMPS (LP) 15
74 Transatlantic TRA 287 — RED QUEEN TO GRYPHON THREE (LP) 15
75 Transatlantic TRA 302 — RAINDANCE (LP) 12
77 Harvest SHSP 4063 — TREASON (LP, with insert) 12
(see also Richard Harvey)

G.T.O.'s
67 Polydor 56721 — She Rides With Me/Rudy Vadoo 35
(see also Joey & Continentals)

G.T.O.'s (Girls Together Outrageously)
70 Straight STS 1059 — PERMANENT DAMAGE (LP) 90
(see also Jeff Beck, Frank Zappa)

G.T.R.
86 Arista GTR 1 — When The Heart Rules The Mind/Reach Out (poster sleeve) 6
86 Arista GTRSD 1 — When The Heart Rules The Mind/Reach Out (picture disc) 8
(see also Steve Hackett)

GUANA BATZ
84 Big Beat SW 89 — You're So Fine/Rockin' In My Coffin/Jungle Rumble/Guana Rock (p/s) 6
84 Big Beat NS 96 — The Cave/Werewolf Blues (p/s) 5
85 I.D. NOSE 4 — HELD DOWN ... AT LAST (LP) 12

GUARDIANS OF THE RAINBOW
68 President PT 186 — What Do You Do When You've Lost Your Love/Cry Alone 6

JOSE GUARDIOLA & ROSE MARY
63 HMV POP 1147 — Algo Prodigioso/Di Papa 20

GUESS WHO
65 Pye International 7N 25305 — Shakin' All Over/Till We Kissed 20
66 King KG 1044 — His Girl/It's My Pride 30
67 Fontana TF 831 — This Time Long Ago/There's No Getting Away From You 15
67 Fontana TF 861 — Miss Felicity Grey/Flying On The Ground Is Wrong 10
69 RCA RCA 1832 — These Eyes/Lightfoot 5
69 RCA RCA 1870 — Laughing/Undun 5
70 RCA RCA 1925 — No Time/Proper Stranger 5
70 RCA RCA 1943 — American Woman/No Sugar Tonight 5
70 RCA RCA 1994 — Hand Me Down World/Runnin' Down The Street 5
70 RCA RCA 2026 — Share The Land/Bus Rider 5
70 RCA SF 8037 — WHEATFIELD SOUL (LP) 15
70 RCA SF 8107 — AMERICAN WOMAN (LP) 15
71 RCA SF 8153 — SHARE THE LAND (LP) 15

MINT VALUE £

71	RCA SF 8216	SO LONG BANNATYNE (LP)	12
72	RCA SF 8269	ROCKIN' (LP)	12
73	RCA SF 8329	LIVE AT THE PARAMOUNT, SEATTLE (LP)	12
73	RCA SF 8349	ARTIFICIAL PARADISE (LP)	12

EARL GUEST

62	Columbia DB 4707	Honky Tonk Train Blues/Winkle Picker Stomp	10
62	Columbia DB 4926	The Girl From The Fair Isle/Twistin' John	7
64	Columbia DB 7212	Begin The Beguine/Foxy	10

LENNIS GUESS

75	Route RT 11	Just Ask Me/Workin' For My Baby	6

REG GUEST SYNDICATE

65	Mercury MF 927	Underworld/Guys, Guns, Dolls And Danger	70
66	Mercury 20089MCL	UNDERWORLD (LP)	50

GUGGENHEIM

72	Indigo GOLP 7001	GUGGENHEIM (LP, private pressing)	75

ISAAC GUILLORY

74	Atlantic K 40521	ISAAC GUILLORY (LP)	15

(see also Shames, Sam Gopal)

GUILLOTEENS

65	Pye International 7N 25324	I Don't Believe/Hey You	50

BONNIE GUITAR

58	London HLD 8591	A Very Precious Love/Johnny Vagabond	25
58	London HLD 8591	A Very Precious Love/Johnny Vagabond (78)	8
59	Top Rank JAR 260	Candy Red Apple/Come To Me, I Love You	8
58	London HA-D 2122	MOONLIGHT AND SHADOWS (LP)	35

GUITAR CRUSHER with JIMMY SPURRILL

69	Blue Horizon 57-3149	Since My Baby Hit The Numbers/Hambone Blues	35

(see also Wild Jimmy Spurrill)

GUITAR RED

63	Pye International 7N 25219	Just You And I/Old Fashioned Love	20

GUITAR SHORTY

72	Flyright LP 500	CAROLINA SLIDE GUITAR (LP)	15

GULLIVER

70	Elektra 2101 011	Every Day's A Lovely Day/Angelina	6
70	Elektra 2101 017	Angelina/Christine	5
70	Elektra 2410 006	GULLIVER (LP)	18

(see also Daryl Hall & John Oates)

GULLIVER'S PEOPLE

66	Parlophone R 5435	Splendour In The Grass/Took This Land	7
66	Parlophone R 5464	Fi Fo Fum/Over The Hills	6
68	Parlophone R 5709	On A Day Like This/My Life	6
69	Columbia DB 8588	Somehow, Somewhere/I Found Love	6

GULLIVER'S TRAVELS

69	Instant INLP 003	GULLIVER'S TRAVELS (LP, withdrawn)	50+

(see also Mike D'Abo, Andrew Oldham)

GUN

68	CBS 3764	Race With The Devil/Sunshine	10
68	CBS 3764	Race With The Devil/3-4 In The Middle (different B-side)	10
69	CBS 4052	Drives You Mad/Rupert's Travels	6
69	CBS 4443	Hobo/Don't Look Back	6
69	CBS 4443	Hobo/Long Hair Wild Man (different B-side)	8
70	CBS 4952	Runnin' Wild/Drown Yourself In The River	6
69	CBS 63552	GUN (LP)	25
69	CBS 63683	GUNSIGHT (LP)	30

(see also Rupert's People, Three Man Army, Knack)

GUN CLUB

82	Beggars Banquet BEG 80	Ghost On The Highway/Sex Beat (p/s)	6
82	Animal/Chry. CHCAT 2635	The Fire Of Love/Walking With The Beast (p/s)	6
83	Animal/Chrysalis GUN 1	Death Party/House On Highland Avenue/The Lie (p/s)	8
83	Animal/Chrysalis GUN 12	Death Party/House On Highland Avenue/The Lie/Light Of The World/ Come Back Jim (12", p/s)	10
88	Red Rhino RED 89	The Breaking Hands/Crabdance (p/s)	8
88	Red Rhino RED 89 12	The Breaking Hands/Crabdance/Nobody's City (12", p/s)	10
90	Fire BLAZE 47T	The Great Divide/Crabdance/St. John's Divine Part 2 (p/s)	10

(see also Kid Congo Powers)

JON GUNN

67	Deram DM 133	I Just Made Up My Mind/Now It's My Turn	12
67	Deram DM 166	If You Wish It/I Don't Want To Get Hung Up On You Babe	7

JO JO GUNNE

(see under 'J')

JIM GUNNER

60	Decca F 11276	Hoolee Jump/Footloose (as Jim Gunner & Echoes)	15
61	Fontana H 313	Desperado/Baghdad (as Jim Gunner & His Sidekicks)	15

TONY GUNNER

62	London HLU 9492	Rough Road/You Gotta Get Home	20

MINT VALUE £

GUNS FOR HIRE

80 Korova KOW 6 — My Girlfriend's Boyfriend/I'm Famous Now (p/s) 10
(see also Main T. Possee)

GUNS N' ROSES

87 Geffen GEF 22 — It's So Easy/Mr Brownstone (p/s) 12
87 Geffen GEF 22T — It's So Easy/Mr Brownstone/Shadow Of Your Love/Move To The City (12", p/s) 15
87 Geffen GEF 22TP — It's So Easy/Mr Brownstone/Shadow Of Your Love/ Move To The City (12", picture disc with stickered PVC sleeve) 50
87 Geffen GEF 30 — Welcome To The Jungle/Whole Lotta Rosie (live) (red p/s) 10
87 Geffen GEF 30T — Welcome To The Jungle/Whole Lotta Rosie (live)/It's So Easy (live)/ Knockin' On Heaven's Door (live) (12", red p/s) 25
87 Geffen GEF 30TW — Welcome To The Jungle/Whole Lotta Rosie (live)/It's So Easy (live)/ Knockin' On Heaven's Door (live) (12", poster p/s) 12
87 Geffen GEF 30P — Welcome To The Jungle/Whole Lotta Rosie (live)/It's So Easy (live)/ Knockin' On Heaven's Door (live) (12", picture disc) 40
88 Geffen GEF 43 — Sweet Child O' Mine/Out Ta Get Me (p/s, with wraparound sticker) 5
88 Geffen GEF 43TE — Sweet Child O' Mine/Out Ta Get Me/Rocket Queen (10", revolving p/s) 20
88 Geffen GEF 43TV — Sweet Child O' Mine/Out Ta Get Me/Rocket Queen (12", metallic p/s) 12
88 Geffen GEF 47 — Welcome To The Jungle/Nightrain (p/s) 5
88 Geffen GEF 47TW — Welcome To The Jungle/Nightrain/You're Crazy (Acoustic Version) (12", poster p/s) 8
88 Geffen GEF 47TV — Welcome To The Jungle/Nightrain/You're Crazy (Acoustic Version) (12", p/s, with patch) 12
88 Geffen GEF 47TP — Welcome To The Jungle/Nightrain/You're Crazy (Acoustic Version) (12", picture disc) 12
88 Geffen GEF 47CD — Welcome To The Jungle/Nightrain/You're Crazy (Acoustic Version) (3" CD with adaptor, 5" case) 15
89 Geffen GEF 50P — Paradise City/I Used To Love Her (gun-shaped clear or white picture disc) 12/15
89 Geffen GEF 50X — Paradise City/I Used To Love Her (p/s, slotted in holster p/s) 8
89 Geffen GEF 50T — Paradise City/I Used To Love Her/Anything Goes (12", p/s) 8
89 Geffen GEF 50CD — Paradise City/I Used To Love Her/Anything Goes/Sweet Child O' Mine (3" CD) 10
89 Geffen GEF 55W — Sweet Child O' Mine (Remix)/Out Ta Get Me (stickered p/s, sealed w/ tattoo) 7
89 Geffen GEF 55P — Sweet Child O' Mine/Out Ta Get Me/Rocket Queen (shaped pic disc & sticker) 15
89 Geffen GEF 55P — Sweet Child O' Mine/Out Ta Get Me/Rocket Queen (12" uncut shaped pic disc) 100
89 Geffen GEF 55T — Sweet Child O' Mine (Remix)/Move To The City/Whole Lotta Rosie (live)/ It's So Easy (live) (12", p/s) 12
89 Geffen GEF 55CD — Sweet Child O' Mine (Remix)/Move To The City/Whole Lotta Rosie (live)/ It's So Easy (live) (3" CD) 12
89 Geffen GEF 56T — Patience/Rocket Queen/W. Axl Rose Interview (12", p/s) 10
89 Geffen GEF 56CD — Patience/Rocket Queen/W. Axl Rose Interview (3" CD, gatefold card sleeve) 12
89 Geffen GEF 60X — Nightrain/Reckless Life (live) (p/s, with patch) 8
89 Geffen GEF 60P — Nightrain/Reckless Life (live) (case-shaped picture disc, stickered PVC sleeve) 15
89 Geffen GEF 60CD — Nightrain/Knockin' On Heaven's Door (live)/Reckless Life (live) (3" CD, gatefold card sleeve) 12
91 Geffen GFSTP 6 — You Could Be Mine/Civil War (12", clear vinyl with insert in PVC sleeve) 10
91 Geffen GFSTD 6 — You Could Be Mine/Civil War (CD, card p/s) 8
91 Geffen GFST 9 — Don't Cry/Don't Cry (Alternate Lyrics)/Don't Cry (Demo) (12", hologram p/s) 8
91 Geffen GFSTD 9 — Don't Cry/Don't Cry (Alternate Lyrics)/(Demo) (CD, card gatefold p/s w/ sticker) 8
91 Geffen GFSX 17 — Live And Let Die (LP Version)/Live And Let Die (live) (12", yellow/orange vinyl, die-cut p/s) 8
91 Geffen GFSTD 17 — Live And Let Die (LP Version)/Live And Let Die (live)/ Shadow Of Your Love (live) (CD, stencil p/s) 10
92 Geffen GFST 18 — November Rain/Sweet Child O' Mine (live)/Patience (live) (12", p/s, 1 side etched) 10
92 Geffen GFSTD 18 — November Rain/Sweet Child O' Mine (live)/Patience (live) (CD) 10
87 Geffen 9240 148 — APPETITE FOR DESTRUCTION (LP, withdrawn 'robot' sleeve) 12

ARTHUR GUNTER

72 Blue Horizon 2431 012 — BLUES AFTER HOURS (LP) 60
70s Contempo COLP 119 — BLACK AND BLUES (LP) 15

HARDROCK GUNTER

55 Brunswick OE 9167 — MOUNTAIN MUSIC (EP) 30
(see also Red Foley, Roberta Lee)

GURU GURU

73 Atlantic K 50022 — DON'T CALL US WE'LL CALL YOU (LP) 12
74 Atlantic K 50044 — DANCE OF THE FLAMES (LP) 12

GURU GURU/ULI TREPTE

80s United Dairies UDT 07 — LIVE 72 & 73 (cassette, 1 side each) 18

GURUS

66 United Artists UP 1160 — Blue Snow Night/Come Girl 22

JOHNNY GUSTAFSON

65 Polydor 56022 — Just To Be With You/Sweet Day 15
65 Polydor 56043 — Take Me For A Little While/Make Me Your Number One 18
(see also Big Three, Merseybeats, Quotations, Hard Stuff, Johnny & John, Ian Gillan Band, G-Force)

CARL GUSTAV & 84's

81 Convulsive CN 001 — I Want To Kill Russians/Through Birds, Through Fire, But Not Through Glass (p/s) 10

ARLO GUTHRIE

67 Reprise RS 20644 — Motorcycle Song/Now And Then 8
70 Reprise RS 20877 — Alice's Rock'N'Roll Restaurant/Coming In To Los Angeles 5
70 Reprise RS 20951 — Valley To Pray/Gabriel's Mother's Hiway Ballad No. 16 Blues (demo-only) 7
71 Reprise RS 20994 — The Ballad Of Tricky Fred/Shackles And Chains 5
67 Reprise RLP 6267 — ALICE'S RESTAURANT (LP) 20

MINT VALUE £

68	Reprise RSLP 6269	ARLO (LP)	18
69	Reprise RSLP 6346	RUNNING DOWN THE ROAD (LP)	15
70	Reprise RSLP 6411	WASHINGTON COUNTY (LP)	15

GWEN GUTHRIE

86	4th + Broadway BRW 1252	Seventh Heaven/It Should Have Been You/Getting Hot (12", p/s)	12

SHEILA GUTHRIE

63	Fontana TF 399	Mirror Mirror/It Doesn't Mean A Thing	8

WOODY GUTHRIE

51	Melodisc 1141	Ramblin' Blues/Talkin' Columbia Blues (78)	8
55	Melodisc EPM7 84	HARD AIN'T IT HARD (EP)	18
55	Melodisc EPM7 85	WORRIED MAN BLUES (EP)	18
55	Melodisc EPM7 91	HEY LOLLY LOLLY (EP)	18
55	Melodisc MLP 12-106	MORE SONGS BY GUTHRIE (LP)	50
58	Topic 12T 31	BOUND FOR GLORY (LP)	40
64	RCA RD 7642	DUST BOWL BALLADS (LP)	35
65	Xtra XTRA 1012	WOODY GUTHRIE (LP)	20
66	Xtra XTRA 1064	WOODY GUTHRIE (LP)	20
66	Xtra XTRA 1065	POOR BOY (LP)	20
66	Xtra XTRA 1067	SONGS TO GROW ON VOL. 1 (LP)	20
68	Ember CW 129	WOODY GUTHRIE (LP)	20
69	Ember CW 135	CISCO HOUSTON AND WOODY GUTHRIE (LP)	20
69	Ember CW 136	BLIND SONNY TERRY & WOODY GUTHRIE (LP)	20

GUTTERSNIPES

88	Razor GUTT 1	Addicted To Love/Love's Young Dream (p/s)	8
88	Razor RAZ 42	THE POOR DRESS UP (LP)	12

(see also Cocksparrer)

GUV'NERS

63	Piccadilly 7N 35117	Let's Make A Habit Of This/The Kissing Had To Stop	12

(see also Jess Conrad, Dickie Pride, Nelson Keene)

BARRY GUY

76	Incus INCUS 22	STATEMENTS V-XI FOR DOUBLE BASS AND VIOLONE (LP)	50

(see also Derek Bailey Barry Guy & Paul Rutherford)

BUDDY GUY

65	Chess CRS 8004	Let Me Love You Baby/Ten Years Ago	18
68	Fontana TF 951	Mary Had A Little Lamb/Sweet Little Angel	15
72	Atlantic K 10195	Honey Dripper/Man Of Many Words	6
91	Silvertone ORE 30	Mustang Sally/Trouble Don't Last (p/s)	5
65	Chess CRE 6004	CRAZY MUSIC (EP)	40
68	Vanguard SVRL 19001	COMING AT YOU (LP)	35
68	Vanguard SVRL 19002	MAN AND HIS BLUES (LP)	35
68	Vanguard SVRL 19004	BLUES TODAY (LP)	25
69	Vanguard SVRL 19008	THIS IS BUDDY GUY! (LP)	25
69	Vanguard SVRL 79290	HOT AND COOL (LP)	20
69	Chess CRL(S) 4546	I LEFT MY BLUES IN SAN FRANCISCO (LP)	35
69	Python KM 2	FIRST TIME I MET THE BLUES (LP)	40
70	Harvest SHSP 4006	BUDDY AND THE JUNIORS (LP, with Junior Mance & Junior Wells)	25
70	Red Lightnin' RL 001	IN THE BEGINNING (LP)	15
72	Atlantic K 40240	PLAY THE BLUES (LP, with Junior Wells)	18
73	Vanguard VSD 79323	HOLD THAT PLANE (LP)	18

(see also Junior Wells, Eddie Boyd/Buddy Guy)

BUDDY GUY with JEFF BECK

91	Silvertone ORE 30	Mustang Sally/Trouble Don't Last (p/s)	5

(see also Jeff Beck)

DERYCK GUYLER

71	Columbia DB 8764	(You Can't Kill An Old) Desert Rat/Ruby	10

GUYS

69	Tepee TPR SP 1001	You Go Your Way/Little Girl	10

(see also Beat Six)

GEORGE GUZMAN

69	London HA/SH 8384	INTRODUCING GEORGE GUZMAN (LP)	12

GYGAFO

89	Holyground HG 1155	LEGEND OF THE KINGFISHER (LP, 160 copies only, posthumously designed semi-gatefold sleeve with insert)	40

GYNAECOLOGISTS

81	Teesbeat TB 2	The Red Pullover/The Offence (p/s)	5

GYPP

70s	Shy Talk	GYPP (EP)	7

GYPSIES

67	CBS 201785	Jerk It/Diamonds, Rubies, Gold And Fame	30

(see also Flirtations, Pearly Gates)

GYPSY

71	United Artists UAG 29155	GYPSY (LP)	15
72	United Artists UAS 29420	BRENDA AND THE RATTLESNAKE (LP)	15

(see also Legay)

JENNY HAAN
78 EMI EMI 2949 We Drove Them All Mad/Forgotten Dreams (p/s) . . . 5
(see also Babe Ruth)

HABIBIYYA
72 Island HELP 7 IF MAN BUT KNEW (LP, with inner sleeve) . . . 35
(see also Mighty Baby)

HABITS
66 Decca F 12348 Elbow Baby/Need You . . . 25
(see also Charles Dickens, Nice, Brian Davison)

HACKENSACK
72 Island WIP 6149 Moving On/River Boat . . . 12
71 Polydor 2383 263 UP THE HARD WAY (LP, with inner sleeve) . . . 70
74 Zel UZ 003 HERE COMES THE JUDGE (LP, private pressing, as Hack & Sack) . . . 200
(see also Megaton, Tiger [U.K.], Nicky Moore Band)

BOBBY HACKETT & BILLY BUTTERFIELD
68 Verve (S)VLP 9212 BOBBY, BILLY AND BRAZIL (LP) . . . 12

STEVE HACKETT
78 Charisma CB 312 How Can I?/Kim (with Ritchie Havens) . . . 10
78 Charisma CB 318 Narnia (Remix)/Please Don't Touch . . . 8
79 Charisma CB 334 Every Day/Lost Time In Cordoba . . . 5
79 Charisma CB 341 Clocks — The Angel Of Mons/Acoustic Set . . . 5
79 Charisma CB 341-12 Clocks — The Angel Of Mons /Acoustic Set/Tigermoth (12", p/s) . . . 10
80 Charisma CB 357 The Show/Hercules Unchained (p/s) . . . 5
80 Charisma CB 368 Sentimental Institution/The Toast (p/s) . . . 5
83 Charisma CELL 12 Cell 151/Air Conditioned Nightmare/Time Lapse At Milton Keynes (12", p/s; with bonus white label 12" "Clocks — The Angel Of Mons"/ "Acoustic Set"/"Tigermoth" [CELL 13], 2,000 only) . . . 10
75 Charisma CAS 111 VOYAGE OF THE ACOLYTE . . . 12
01 Camino CAMCD 23 LIVE ARCHIVE (4-CD box set) . . . 30
01 Camino CAMCD 23 LIVE ARCHIVE (5-CD box set, limited edition with extra CD) . . . 30
(see also Peter Banks, Genesis, GTR, Quiet World)

MANOS HADJIDAKIS
62 Columbia SX 6253 LILACS OUT OF THE DEAD LAND (LP) . . . 15

HAFFY'S WHISKY SOUR
71 Deram DM 345 Shot In The Head/Bye Bye Bluebird . . . 7
(see also Easybeats, Paintbox)

HAFLER TRIO
84 Doublevision DVR 4 BANG! — AN OPEN LETTER (LP, with insert) . . . 12
86 Charrm 3 THREE WAYS OF SAYING TWO — THE NETHERLANDS LECTURES (LP, stickered sleeve with booklet) . . . 15
86 Touch T 05 THE SEA ORG (10", 'audio/visual' package with booklet) . . . 12
(see also Cabaret Voltaire)

SAMMY HAGAR
77 Capitol E-ST 11599 SAMMY HAGAR (LP, red vinyl) . . . 12
79 Capitol E-ST 11983 STREET MACHINE (LP, with free single) . . . 12
(see also Van Halen, Madonna, Montrose)

EARLE HAGEN
64 Colpix PX 740 Nancy's Theme/New Interns Watusi . . . 7

JOAN HAGER
57 Brunswick 05650 Happy Is A Girl Named Me/Run Darlin', Don't Walk . . . 12

MERLE HAGGARD & STRANGERS
68 Capitol CL 15540 The Legend Of Bonnie And Clyde/I Started Loving You Again . . . 5
66 Capitol T/ST 2453 JUST BETWEEN THE TWO OF US (LP, with Bonnie Owens) . . . 15
67 Capitol T/ST 2702 I'M A LONESOME FUGITIVE (LP) . . . 15
68 Capitol T/ST 2912 THE LEGEND OF BONNIE & CLYDE (LP) . . . 15
69 Capitol T/ST 2972 MAMA TRIED (LP) . . . 15
69 Capitol ST 21377 SAME TRAIN, A DIFFERENT TIME (LP) . . . 15
70 Capitol ST 21531 A PORTRAIT OF MERLE HAGGARD (LP) . . . 12
70 Capitol E-ST 451 THE FIGHTIN' SIDE OF ME (LP) . . . 15
71 Capitol E-ST 735 HAG (LP) . . . 12
72 Capitol E-ST 835 SOMEDAY WE'LL LOOK BACK (LP) . . . 12
72 Capitol E-ST 882 LET ME TELL YOU ABOUT A SONG (LP) . . . 12
73 Capitol E-ST 11200 I LOVE DIXIE BLUES (LP) . . . 12
76 Capitol E-ST 11544 MY LOVE AFFAIR WITH TRAINS (LP) . . . 12
77 MCA MCF 2818 MY FAREWELL TO ELVIS (LP) . . . 12
87 Premier PMP 1003 TO ALL THE GIRLS I'VE LOVED BEFORE (LP, withdrawn) . . . 20

MEL HAGUE
60s LK/LP 6558 MERRY-GO-ROUND (LP, some signed) . . . 18/12

MINT VALUE £

JOYCE HAHN

57 London HLA 8453 Gonna Find Me A Bluebird/I Saw You, I Saw You . . . 25
57 London HLA 8453 Gonna Find Me A Bluebird/I Saw You, I Saw You (78) . . . 8

PAUL HAIG

81 Rational no cat. no. DRAMA (cassette) . . . 15
82 Operation Twilight OPT 03 Running Away/Time (p/s) . . . 5
84 Island ISX 198 The Only Truth (U.S. Remix)/Instrumental/Ghost Rider (12", p/s) . . . 8
80s Masterbag no cat. no. Blue (square flexidisc free with *Masterbag* magazine) . . . 6/5
84 Island ILPS 9742 RHYTHM OF LIFE (LP) . . . 12
85 Operation Afterglow OPA 3 THE WARP OF PURE FUN (LP, inner sleeve) . . . 12
(see also Josef K, Rhythm Of Life, Juggernauts)

NORMAN HAINES (BAND)

70 Parlophone R 5871 Daffodil/Autumn Mobile (as Norman Haynes Band) . . . 25
71 Parlophone SPSR 338 Den Of Iniquity/Everything You See (Mr. Armageddon) (promo only) . . . 40
72 Parlophone R 5960 Give It To You Girl/Elaine (as Norman Haines) . . . 25
71 Parlophone PCS 7130 DEN OF INIQUITY (LP) . . . 350
(see also Avalanche, Brumbeats, The Dog That Bit People, Locomotive)

HAIR

69 Pye NSPL 18314 RAVE UP (LIVE FROM THE SHAFTESBURY THEATRE) (LP) . . . 65
(see also Alex Harvey, Hairband)

HAIR

71 Columbia SCX 6452 HAIRPIECE (LP) . . . 120

HAIRBAND

69 Bell BLL 1076 Big Louis/Travelling Song . . . 18
69 Bell SBLL 69 BAND ON THE WAGON (LP) . . . 55
(see also Alex Harvey, Hair)

HAIRCUT 100

83 Arista CLIP 5 Whistle Down The Wind (withdrawn) . . . 10+
83 Polydor HCP2 So Tired (silver vinyl, no p/s) . . . 8
82 Arista HCC 101 BLUE HAT FOR A BLUE DAY (LP, withdrawn, test pressings only) . . . 40+

HAIRPOWER

70 CBS 4961 Royal International Love-in/Be There, Be Hair . . . 5

DENNIS HALE

55 Parlophone MSP 6153 The Butterscotch Mop/S'posin' . . . 10
(see also Jack Parnell)

BILL HALEY (& HIS COMETS)

78s

53 London L 1190 Crazy Man, Crazy/Whatcha Gonna Do (as Bill Haley with Haley's Comets) (gold label lettering) . . . 25
53 London L 1216 Pat-A-Cake/Fractured (as Bill Haley with Haley's Comets, gold label) . . . 30
54 London HL 1190 Crazy Man, Crazy/Whatcha Gonna Do (as Bill Haley with Haley's Comets) (reissue, silver label lettering) . . . 25
54 London HL 1216 Pat-A-Cake/Fractured (reissue, silver label lettering, as Bill Haley with Haley's Comets) . . . 30
54 Brunswick 05338 Shake, Rattle And Roll/A.B.C. Boogie (gold or silver lettering) . . . 10/7
55 London HL 8142 Green Tree Boogie/Sundown Boogie . . . 15
55 London HLF 8161 Farewell, So Long, Goodbye/I'll Be True . . . 15
55 London HLF 8194 Ten Little Indians/Rocking Chair On The Moon . . . 15
56 Melodisc 1376 I'm Gonna Dry Ev'ry Tear With A Kiss/Why Do I Cry Over You . . . 65
57 London HLF 8371 Rock The Joint/Yes Indeed! . . . 15
57 Brunswick 05658 Forty Cups Of Coffee/Choo Choo Ch'Boogie . . . 10
57 Brunswick 05688 (You Hit The Wrong Note) Billy Goat/Rockin' Rollin' Rover . . . 12
57 Brunswick 05719 Miss You/The Dipsy Doodle . . . 20
58 Brunswick 05735 Mary, Mary Lou/It's A Sin . . . 20
58 Brunswick 05742 Skinny Minnie/How Many . . . 20
58 Brunswick 05752 Lean Jean/Don't Nobody Move . . . 25
58 Brunswick 05766 Whoa Mabel!/Chiquita Linda . . . 30
59 Brunswick 05788 I Got A Woman/Charmaine . . . 35
59 Brunswick 05805 Shaky/Caldonia . . . 40
59 Brunswick 05810 Joey's Song/Ooh! Look-A There, Ain't She Pretty . . . 40

SINGLES

54 Brunswick 05317 (We're Gonna) Rock Around The Clock/Thirteen Women . . . 60/25
54 Brunswick 05338 Shake, Rattle And Roll/A.B.C. Boogie . . . 45/22
55 Brunswick 05373 Happy Baby/Dim, Dim The Lights (I Want Some Atmosphere) . . . 45/22
55 Brunswick 05405 Birth Of The Boogie/Mambo Rock . . . 45/22
55 London HL 8142 Green Tree Boogie/Sundown Boogie . . . 160/60
55 Brunswick 05453 Two Hound Dogs/Razzle Dazzle . . . 45/22
55 London HLF 8161 Farewell, So Long, Goodbye/I'll Be True . . . 125/65
55 London HLF 8194 Ten Little Indians/Rocking Chair On The Moon . . . 140/70
55 Brunswick 05509 Rock-A-Beatin' Boogie/Burn That Candle . . . 45/22
56 Brunswick 05530 See You Later, Alligator/The Paper Boy (On Main Street, USA) . . . 40/20
(When two prices are given for the above 45s, the first refers to original gold-lettering labels & the second to later copies with silver-lettering on label.)
56 Brunswick 05565 The Saints Rock 'N' Roll/R-O-C-K . . . 20
56 Brunswick 05582 Rockin' Through The Rye/Hot Dog Buddy Buddy . . . 20
56 Brunswick 05615 Rip It Up/Teenager's Mother . . . 20
56 Brunswick 05616 Rudy's Rock/Blue Comet Blues . . . 20
57 Brunswick 05640 Don't Knock The Rock/Calling All Comets . . . 20

MINT VALUE £

57 Brunswick 05641 Hook, Line And Sinker/Goofin' Around . . . 20
57 London HLF 8371 Rock The Joint/Yes Indeed! (gold or silver label). . . . 140/70
57 Brunswick 05658 Forty Cups Of Coffee/Choo Choo Ch'Boogie . . . 20
57 Brunswick 05688 (You Hit The Wrong Note) Billy Goat/Rockin' Rollin' Rover. . . . 22
57 Brunswick 05719 Miss You/The Dipsy Doodle . . . 20
58 Brunswick 05735 Mary, Mary Lou/It's A Sin . . . 18
58 Brunswick 05742 Skinny Minnie/How Many. . . . 20
58 Brunswick 05752 Lean Jean/Don't Nobody Move . . . 18
58 Brunswick 05766 Whoa Mabel!/Chiquita Linda . . . 20
59 Brunswick 05788 I Got A Woman/Charmaine. . . . 18
59 Brunswick 05805 Shaky/Caldonia . . . 20
59 Brunswick 05810 Joey's Song/Ooh! Look-A There, Ain't She Pretty . . . 20

(The above 45s were originally issued with triangular centres; later round centres are worth half the value for earlier 45s to two-thirds for later 45s.)

60 Brunswick 05818 Puerto Rican Peddler/Skokiaan. . . . 12
60 Warner Bros WB 6 Candy Kisses/Tamiami. . . . 10
61 London HLU 9471 Spanish Twist/My Kind Of Woman. . . . 15
63 Stateside SS 196 Tenor Man/Up Goes My Love. . . . 8
64 Warner Bros WB 133 Rock Around The Clock/Love Letters In The Sand . . . 12
64 Brunswick 05910 Happy Baby/Birth Of The Boogie. . . . 15
64 Brunswick 05917 The Green Door/Yeah! She's Evil. . . . 15
68 MCA MU 1013 (We're Gonna) Rock Around The Clock/Shake, Rattle And Roll. . . . 6
68 Pye International 7N 25455 Crazy Man, Crazy/Dance With A Dolly (With A Hole In Her Stocking) . . . 18
73 Sonet SON 2016 Me And Bobby McGee/I Wouldn't Have Missed It For The World . . . 5
74 Sonet SON 2043 Crazy Man, Crazy/Lawdy Miss Clawdy . . . 5
74 MCA MCA 128 Rock Around The Clock/Rip It Up/Shake, Rattle And Roll . . . 5
74 MCA MCA 142 See You Later Alligator/Rudy's Rock. . . . 5
76 MCA MCA 263 Shake, Rattle And Roll/Razzle Dazzle/Rock-A-Beatin' Boogie . . . 5
80 Rollercoaster RRC 2004 Rock The Joint/Fractured (reissue) . . . 5
80 Sonet SON 2202 God Bless Rock And Roll/So Right Tonight . . . 5
81 Thumbs Up TU 103 Rocket 88/Tearstains On My Pillow. . . . 5

EXPORT SINGLES

54 Decca BM 05317 (We're Gonna) Rock Around The Clock/Thirteen Women . . . 80
55 Decca BM 05405 Birth Of The Boogie/Mambo Rock. . . . 65
55 Decca BM 05509 Rock-A-Beatin' Boogie/Burn That Candle . . . 65
56 Decca BM 05530 See You Later Alligator/The Paper Boy (On Main Street, USA). . . . 65
56 Decca BM 31163 The Saints Rock 'N' Roll/R-O-C-K . . . 50
56 Decca BM 31164 Rockin' Through The Rye/Hot Dog Buddy Buddy . . . 50
56 Decca BM 31171 Rip It Up/Teenager's Mother . . . 50
57 Decca BM 31174 Don't Knock The Rock/Choo Choo Ch'Boogie . . . 50
68 Decca AD 1010 (We're Gonna) Rock Around The Clock/Shake, Rattle And Roll. . . . 25

EPs

55 Brunswick OE 9129 DIM, DIM THE LIGHTS (gold lettering label, 'stage' p/s, various colours). . . . 40
55 Brunswick OE 9129 DIM, DIM THE LIGHTS (silver lettering label, 'stage' or 'cameo' p/s) . . . each 35
55 London REF 1031 ROCK AND ROLL. . . . 60
56 London REF 1049 LIVE IT UP PART 1 . . . 50
56 London REF 1050 LIVE IT UP PART 2 . . . 50
56 Brunswick OE 9214 ROCK AND ROLL WITH BILL HALEY . . . 25
56 Brunswick OE 9250 ROCK AROUND THE CLOCK. . . . 20
56 Brunswick OE 9250 ROCK AROUND THE CLOCK (round centre, different sleeve, same design as "Bill Haley" [OE 9459]). . . . 40
56 London REF 1058 LIVE IT UP PART 3 . . . 50
56 Brunswick OE 9278 ROCK'N'ROLL STAGE SHOW PART 1 . . . 35
56 Brunswick OE 9279 ROCK'N'ROLL STAGE SHOW PART 2 . . . 35
56 Brunswick OE 9280 ROCK'N'ROLL STAGE SHOW PART 3 . . . 35
58 Brunswick OE 9349 ROCKIN' THE OLDIES PART 1 . . . 50
58 Brunswick OE 9350 ROCKIN' THE OLDIES PART 2 . . . 50
58 Brunswick OE 9351 ROCKIN' THE OLDIES PART 3 . . . 50
59 Brunswick OE 9446 ROCKIN' AROUND THE WORLD . . . 60
59 Brunswick OE 9459 BILL HALEY . . . 50

(The above EPs were originally issued with triangular centres, later round-centre copies are worth two-thirds these values.)

60 Warners WEP 6001 BILL HALEY AND HIS COMETS. . . . 40
61 Warners WEP 6025 BILL HALEY'S JUKE BOX (also stereo WSEP 2025) . . . 40/60
64 Warners WEP 6133 BILL HALEY VOLUME 1 . . . 40
64 Warners WEP 6136 BILL HALEY VOLUME 2 . . . 40

LPs

55 London H-APB 1042 LIVE IT UP (10", gold or silver lettering on label). . . . 110/65
56 Brunswick LAT 8117 ROCK AROUND THE CLOCK. . . . 35
56 Brunswick LAT 8139 ROCK AND ROLL STAGE SHOW. . . . 35
57 London HA-F 2037 ROCK THE JOINT. . . . 90
57 Brunswick LAT 8219 ROCKIN' THE OLDIES . . . 65
57 Brunswick LAT 8268 ROCKIN' THE JOINT. . . . 65
59 Brunswick LAT 8295 BILL HALEY'S CHICKS (also stereo STA 3011) . . . 65/85
60 Brunswick LAT 8326 STRICTLY INSTRUMENTAL . . . 60
61 Ace Of Hearts AH 13 ROCK AROUND THE CLOCK (2 slightly different sleeves) . . . 18/15
62 Columbia 33SX 1460 TWISTIN' KNIGHTS AT THE ROUNDTABLE (LIVE!). . . . 35
62 Ace Of Hearts AH 35 ROCKIN' THE OLDIES . . . 15
64 Ace Of Hearts AH 66 BILL HALEY'S CHICKS . . . 15
64 Golden Guinea GGL 0282 ROCK THE JOINT. . . . 15
65 Xtra XTRA 1027 BILL HALEY & THE COMETS. . . . 30
65 Warner Bros W 1391 BILL HALEY'S JUKE BOX . . . 50
67 Marble Arch MAL 817 ROCK THE JOINT. . . . 12
67 Ember EMB 3386 REAL LIVE ROCK'N'ROLL. . . . 15
68 MCA MUP 318 RIP IT UP! . . . 15

MINT VALUE £

68	Ember EMB 3396	KING OF ROCK (reissued 1973)	15/12
69	Ember EMB 3401	MISTER ROCK 'N' ROLL	12
70	Valiant VS 103	BILL HALEY & THE COMETS	15
71	Coral CP 55	ROCK AROUND THE CLOCK	12
71	Sonet SNTF 623	ROCK AROUND THE COUNTRY	12
73	Sonet SNTF 645	JUST ROCK AND ROLL MUSIC	12
79	Rollercoaster ROLL 2002	ROCK THE JOINT! (10")	12

(see also Kingsmen, Jodimars, Nick Nantos & His Fireballs)

HALF JAPANESE

81	Armageddon AS 009	Spy/I Know How It Feels ... Bad/My Knowledge Was Wrong (p/s)	5
92	Paperhouse PAPER 017	Eye Of The Hurricane/Said And Done/U.S. Teens Are Spoiled Bums/ Daytona Beach	5
81	Armageddon ABOX 1	1/2 GENTLEMEN NOT BEASTS (3-LP box set with poster, booklet & lyric insert)	25
81	Armageddon ARM 7	LOUD (LP)	12

(see also Jad Fair)

HAL HOPPERS

54	London HL 8107	More Love/Do Nothin' Blues	45
54	London HL 8107	More Love/Do Nothin' Blues (78)	8
55	London HL 8129	Mother Of Pearl/Baby I've Had It	45
55	London HL 8129	Mother Of Pearl/Baby I've Had It (78)	8

ADELAIDE HALL

60	Oriole CB 1556	Common Sense/Blue Bird On My Shoulder	10

BOB HALL & ALEXIS KORNER

78	Logo GO 331	Pinetop's Boogie Woogie/All I Got Is You	12

(see also Brunning Hall Sunflower Blues Band, Alexis Korner)

CAROLINE HALL

70	Major Minor MM 689	Dream Boy/Julie	6
71	Decca F 13146	Hold My Hand/Put A Light In The Window	6

(DARYL) HALL & (JOHN) OATES

85	RCA PB 49967	Out Of Touch/Dance On Your Knees (square picture disc)	5
88	Arista 661 730	Downtown Life/Downtown Remix/Dubtown Life/ Keep On Pushin' Love (CD, withdrawn)	8
89	RCA PD 49465	Maneater/Delayed Reaction/I Can't Go For That (No Can Do)/ Unguarded Minute (3" CD, gatefold card sleeve)	8

(see also Gulliver)

DEREK HALL & MIKE COOPER

60s	Kennet KRS 766	OUT OF THE SHADES (EP)	35

DICKSON HALL (& COUNTRY ALL-STARS)

57	MGM MGM-EP 626	OUTLAWS OF THE OLD WEST (EP)	20
58	London RE-R 1158	FABULOUS COUNTRY HITS NO. 1 (EP)	20
58	London RE-R 1159	FABULOUS COUNTRY HITS NO. 2 (EP)	20
58	London RE-R 1160	FABULOUS COUNTRY HITS NO. 3 (EP)	20
60	Fontana Z 4011	ALL-TIME COUNTRY AND WESTERN HITS (LP)	15

DOLORES HALL

72	Jay Boy BOY 77	Good Lovin' Man/W-O-M-E-N	8

(see also Jackie Lee & Dolores Hall)

DORA HALL

64	King KG 1003	Hello Faithless/You've Got Me Cryin' Again	5

GERRI HALL

66	Sue WI 4026	Who Can I Run To/I Lost A Key (unissued)	

JIMMY GRAY HALL

74	Epic EPC 2312	Be That Way/Possessed By The Moon	15

JUANITA HALL

62	Storyville SEP 382	STORYVILLE BLUES ANTHOLOGY VOL. 2 (EP)	15
64	Society SOC 971	JUANITA HALL SINGS THE BLUES (LP)	15

LANI HALL

83	A&M AM 159	Never Say Never Again/Un Chanson D'Amour (p/s)	8
74	A&M AMLS 64359	SUNDOWN LADY (LP)	15

LARRY HALL

60	Parlophone R 4625	Sandy/Lovin' Tree	12
62	Salvo SLO 1811	Ladder Of Love/The One You Left Behind (99 copies only)	25

RENE HALL'S ORCHESTRA

58	London HLU 8581	Twitchy/Flippin'	60
58	London HLU 8581	Twitchy/Flippin' (78)	7

ROBIN HALL (& JIMMY MacGREGOR)

60	Collector JDS 3	Football Crazy/Rosin The Beau	7
60	Decca F 11266	Football Crazy/Rosin The Beau (reissue, p/s)	10
60	Collector JES 5	WEE MAGIC STANE (LP)	8
60	Collector JES 6	THE BONNIE LASS O'FYVIE (EP, solo)	8
60	Collector JES 7	MACPHERSON'S RANT (EP, solo)	8
61	Collector JES 9	GLASGOW STREET SONGS VOL. 3 (EP)	8
64	Collector JES 12	ROBIN HALL (EP, solo)	8
64	Collector JES 13	ROBIN HALL SINGS AGAIN (EP, solo)	8
61	Ace Of Clubs ACL 1065	SCOTTISH CHOICE (LP, with Jimmie MacGregor)	15

(see also Galliards)

MINT VALUE £

RONNIE HALL
61 Piccadilly 7N 35001 The Code Of Love/Who Cares . . . 6
62 Piccadilly 7N 35040 My Very First Love/The Day After Forever . . . 6
65 Fontana TF 569 I'll Stand Aside/I'm Getting Nowhere . . . 15

ROY HALL
56 Brunswick 05531 See You Later, Alligator/Don't Stop Now (gold label lettering) . . . 500
56 Brunswick 05531 See You Later, Alligator/Don't Stop Now (78) . . . 115
56 Brunswick 05555 Blue Suede Shoes/Luscious . . . 500
56 Brunswick 05555 Blue Suede Shoes/Luscious (78) . . . 125
56 Brunswick 05627 Diggin' The Boogie/Three Alley Cats . . . 550
56 Brunswick 05627 Diggin' The Boogie/Three Alley Cats (78) . . . 100

TONY HALL
77 Free Reed FRR 012 FIELDVOLE MUSIC (LP, with insert) . . . 20

CHANCE HALLADAY
62 Vogue V 9203 John Henry/Thirteen Women . . . 25

HALLELUJAH SKIFFLE GROUP
58 Oriole CB 1429 I Saw The Light/A Closer Walk With Thee (with Clinton Ford) . . . 20
58 Oriole CB 1429 I Saw The Light/A Closer Walk With Thee (78, with Clinton Ford) . . . 12
(see also Clinton Ford)

HALLIARD
67 Saga SOC 1058 IT'S THE IRISH IN ME (LP) . . . 35
68 Broadside BRO 106 THE HALLIARD AND JON RAVEN (LP) . . . 50
(see also Jon Raven, Nic Jones)

GERI HALLIWELL
99 EMI 12 EMDJX 542 Look At Me (Terminalhead Remix)/(Terminalhead dub) (12", die cut sleeve, promo only) . . . 12
99 EMI CDEMDJX 542 Look At Me (CD, sealed card p/s, promo only) . . . 12
99 EMI CD IN 122 Interview (CD, tri-fold digipak, promo only) . . . 20
00 EMI no cat. no. Lift Me Up (4 mixes) (CD-R, paper title sleeve) . . . 25
99 EMI DJ 521 0092 SCHIZOPHRENIC (CD, album sampler in sealed foil wallet, numbered sticker, promo only) . . . 20
(see also Spice Girls)

DICK HALLMAN
56 Brunswick 05608 Two Different Worlds/Love Me As Though There Were No Tomorrow . . . 7
60 Vogue V 9162 Born To Be Loved/Just Squeeze Me But Don't Teeze Me . . . 10

JOHNNY HALLYDAY
62 Philips BF 1238 Shake The Hand Of A Fool/Hold Back The Sun . . . 12
63 Philips 373 012BF Hey Little Girl/Caravan Of Lonely Men . . . 12
65 Philips BF 1449 Pour Moi Tu Es La Seule/They Call Him A Man . . . 15
62 Philips 432 813BE ROCKING (EP) . . . 150
66 Vogue VRE 5013 JOHNNY HALLYDAY (EP) . . . 160
61 Philips BBL 7556 SINGS AMERICA'S ROCKIN' HITS (LP) . . . 110

HALOS
61 London HLU 9424 Nag/Copycat . . . 40

CHRIS HAMALTON
53 London L 1177 Farmer's Boy Boogie/Celebration Rag (78) . . . 10
53 London L 1200 Dizzy Fingers/Saturday Rag (78) . . . 10

STUART HAMBLEN
54 HMV 7MC 20 This Ole House/When My Lord Picks Up The 'Phone (export issue) . . . 25
54 HMV JO 413 This Ole House/When My Lord Picks Up The 'Phone (78) . . . 8
55 HMV JO 434 Ole Pappy Time/The Toy Violin (78, export issue) . . . 7
55 HMV 7MC 30 Go On By/Just A Man (export issue) . . . 20
56 HMV 7M 394 Hell Train/A Few Things To Remember . . . 18

BILLY HAMBRIC
79 Grapevine GRP 139 She Said Goodbye/I Found True Love . . . 8

HAMEFARERS
60s Polydor 2384 074 A BREATH O' SHETLAND (LP) . . . 12

CLAIRE HAMILL
72 Island WIP 6122 When I Was A Child/Alice In The Streets Of Darlington . . . 6
72 Island WIP 6133 Baseball Blues/Smile Your Blues Away . . . 6
74 Konk KOS 1 Geronimo's Cadillac/Luck Of The Draw . . . 5
81 WEA K 18440 First Night In New York/Ultraviolet Light (B-side with Gary Numan) (p/s) . . . 7
72 Island ILPS 9182 ONE HOUSE LEFT STANDING (LP) . . . 15
73 Island ILPS 9225 OCTOBER (LP) . . . 15
74 Konk KONK 101 STAGE DOOR JOHNNIES (LP) . . . 12
75 Konk KONK 104 ABRACADABRA (LP, featuring Cafe Society, with insert) . . . 12
(see also Cafe Society, Gary Numan)

BILLY HAMILTON & STRANDSMEN
67 Philips BF 1622 Try To Remember/Don't You Believe It . . . 7

CHICO HAMILTON QUINTET
57 Vogue V 2407 The Sage/The Morning After . . . 6
65 HMV POP 1451 Carol's Walk/Chic Chic Chico . . . 8
58 Vogue LAE 12045 CHICO HAMILTON QUINTET IN HIFI (LP) . . . 20
68 Solid State USS 7010 THE GAMUT (LP) . . . 12

DAVID HAMILTON
70s Spectre SP 501 A Special Goodnight To You/Just For The Weekend . . . 8

EDWARD HAMILTON & ARABIANS
80 Grapevine GRP 134 Baby Don't You Weep/I'm Gonna Love You . . . 8

MINT VALUE £

GARY HAMILTON

Year	Label/Cat. No.	Title	Value
67	Decca F 12697	Let The Music Play/Don't Ask	6
69	CBS 4674	Easy Rider/Hare Krishna	6

(see also Hamilton & [Hamilton] Movement)

GAVIN HAMILTON

Year	Label/Cat. No.	Title	Value
67	King KG 1067	It Won't Be The Same/Turn The Key Softly	140

GEORGE HAMILTON IV

Year	Label/Cat. No.	Title	Value
57	London HL 8361	A Rose And A Candy Bar/If You Don't Know (gold or silver label print)	150/80
57	London HL 8361	A Rose And A Candy Bar/If You Don't Know (78)	25
57	HMV POP 429	Why Don't They Understand/Even Tho'	12
57	HMV POP 429	Why Don't They Understand/Even Tho' (78)	10
58	HMV POP 474	Now And For Always/One Heart	10
58	HMV POP 474	Now And For Always/One Heart (78)	8
58	HMV POP 505	I Know Where I'm Goin'/Who's Taking You To The Prom?	10
58	HMV POP 505	I Know Where I'm Goin'/Who's Taking You To The Prom? (78)	7
58	HMV POP 534	Your Cheatin' Heart/When Will I Know?	10
58	HMV POP 534	Your Cheatin' Heart/When Will I Know? (78)	8
60	HMV POP 813	Before This Day Ends/Loneliness Is All Around Us	6
63	RCA RCA 1353	Abilene/Oh So Many Years	6
72	Uni UNS 480	Evel Knievel/Boy From The Country	5
58	HMV CLP 1202	ON CAMPUS (LP)	22
59	HMV CLP 1263	SING ME A SAD SONG — A TRIBUTE TO HANK WILLIAMS (LP)	22

GUY HAMILTON

Year	Label/Cat. No.	Title	Value
65	HMV POP 1418	A Lifetime Of Loneliness/Give The Game Away	12

(see also Neil Christian)

M. HAMILTON

Year	Label/Cat. No.	Title	Value
67	Ska Beat JB 265	Something Gotta Ring/DENNIS LYNWARD & HIS GROUP: Jazz Session	15

MILTON HAMILTON

Year	Label/Cat. No.	Title	Value
73	Explosion EX 2069	Long Long Road/Version	5

ROY HAMILTON

Year	Label/Cat. No.	Title	Value
58	Fontana H 113	Don't Let Go/The Right To Love	25
58	Fontana H 113	Don't Let Go/The Right To Love (78)	7
58	Fontana H 143	Crazy Feelin'/In A Dream	15
58	Fontana H 143	Crazy Feelin'/In A Dream (78)	10
59	Fontana H 180	Pledging My Love/My One And Only Love	15
59	Fontana H 180	Pledging My Love/My One And Only Love (78)	12
59	Fontana H 193	I Need Your Loving/Somewhere Along The Way	12
59	Fontana H 193	I Need Your Loving/Somewhere Along The Way (78)	20
61	Fontana H 298	You Can Have Her/Abide With Me	15
61	Fontana H 320	You're Gonna Need Magic/To The One I Love	15
63	MGM MGM 1210	Theme From "The VIPs"/The Sinner	12
64	MGM MGM 1251	There She Is/The Panic Is On	140
65	MGM MGM 1268	A Thousand Tears Ago/Sweet Violet	15
66	RCA RCA 1500	And I Love Her/Tore Up Over You	10
69	Deep Soul DS 9106	Dark End Of The Street/100 Years Ago	30
59	Fontana TFE 17160	WHY FIGHT THE FEELING (EP)	20
60	Fontana TFE 17163	THE MOOD MOVES (EP)	20
61	Fontana TFE 17170	COME OUT SWINGING (EP)	20
63	Columbia 33SX 1473	GREATEST HITS (LP)	40
64	MGM MGM-C 960	WARM SOUL (LP)	40

RUSS HAMILTON

Year	Label/Cat. No.	Title	Value
57	Oriole CB 1359	We Will Make Love/Rainbow	7
57	Oriole CB 1388	Wedding Ring/I Still Belong To You	7
57	Oriole CB 1406	I Don't Know Why/My Mother's Eyes	6
58	Oriole CB 1404	Little One/I Had A Dream	6
58	Oriole CB 1451	Drifting And Dreaming/Tip-toe Through The Tulips	6
58	Oriole CB 1459	I Wonder Who's Kissing Her Now/September In The Rain	6
58	Oriole CB 1465	Things I Didn't Say/Strange Are The Ways Of Love	6
59	Oriole CB 1492	The Reprieve Of Tom Dooley/Dreaming Of You	6
59	Oriole CB 1492	The Reprieve Of Tom Dooley/Dreaming Of You (78)	7
59	Oriole CB 1506	My Unbreakable Heart/I Found You	7
59	Oriole CB 1506	My Unbreakable Heart/I Found You (78)	15
59	Oriole CB 1508	Smile, Smile, Smile (And Sing, Sing, Sing)/Shadow	7
59	Oriole CB 1508	Smile, Smile, Smile (And Sing, Sing, Sing)/Shadow (78)	10
60	Oriole CB 1527	Things No Money Can Buy/Mama	7
60	Oriole CB 1527	Things No Money Can Buy/Mama (78)	15
60	Oriole CB 1531	It's A Sin To Tell A Lie/Folks Get Married In The Spring	7
60	Oriole CB 1531	It's A Sin To Tell A Lie/Folks Get Married In The Spring (78)	10
60	MGM MGM 1096	Gonna Find Me A Bluebird/Choir Girl	6
64	Ember EMBS 184	Valley Of Love/Loneliest Boy In Town	6
64	Ember EMBS 193	We Will Make Love/No One Can Love Like You	6
58	Oriole EP 7005	RUSS HAMILTON (EP)	30
58	Oriole MG 20031	WE WILL MAKE LOVE (LP)	55

SCOTT HAMILTON

Year	Label/Cat. No.	Title	Value
66	Parlophone R 5492	Good Day Sunshine/For No One	6

HAMILTON & MOVEMENT

Year	Label/Cat. No.	Title	Value
65	Polydor BM 56026	Really Saying Something/I Won't See You Tonight	70
67	CBS 202573	I'm Not The Marrying Kind/My Love Belongs To You	35

(see also Gary Hamilton, Paul Stewart Movement)

HAMLINS

Year	Label/Cat. No.	Title	Value
67	Coxsone CS 7021	Trying To Keep A Good Man Down/BOB MARLEY: Oh My Darling	60
67	Coxsone CS 7022	Soul And Inspiration/ETHIOPIANS: Let's Get Together	25
68	Coxsone CS 7048	Sentimental Reasons/SOUL VENDORS: Last Waltz	30
68	Blue Cat BS 115	Sugar And Spice/SOUL VENDORS: Mercy Mercy Mercy	15

(see also Minstrels)

MARVIN HAMLISCH

Year	Label/Cat. No.	Title	Value
77	United Artists UP 36301	Bond 77/Ride To Atlantis	5

JACK HAMMER

Year	Label/Cat. No.	Title	Value
61	Oriole CB 1634	Young Only Once/Juliette	15
62	Oriole CB 1645	Kissin' Twist/Melancholy Boy	10
62	Oriole CB 1728	Crazy Twist/Twist Talk	12
62	Oriole CB 1753	Don't Let Baby Know/Number 2539	15
66	Polydor 56091	Thanks/Love Ladder	15
69	United Artists UP 35029	What Greater Love/The Mason Dixon Line	40
71	Youngblood YB 1023	Colour Combination/Swim	50
63	Oriole PS 40020	HAMMER + BEAT = TWIST (LP)	75+
66	Polydor	BRAVE NEW WORLD (LP)	30

HAMMERHEAD

Year	Label/Cat. No.	Title	Value
81	Linden Sounds LS 009	Time Will Tell/Lonely Man (p/s)	100

HAMMERS

Year	Label/Cat. No.	Title	Value
69	President PT 247	Baby And Me/Little Butterfly	6
69	President PT 276	Sugar Baby/Power Of Love	6

HAMMERS (Jamaica)

Year	Label/Cat. No.	Title	Value
70	Gas GAS 162	Hotter Than Scorcher/Someday Could See You	10

(see also Joan Ross)

HAMMERSMITH GORILLAS

Year	Label/Cat. No.	Title	Value
74	Penny Farthing PEN 849	You Really Got Me/Leavin' 'Ome	18
77	Raw RAW 2	You Really Got Me/Leavin' 'Ome (reissue, company sleeve)	8

(see also Clique)

PETER HAMMILL

Year	Label/Cat. No.	Title	Value
75	Charisma CB 245	Birthday Special/Shingle Song	8
78	Charisma CB 339	The Polaroid (credited to Ricky Nadir)/The Old School Tie	10
78	Charisma PH 001	Crying Wolf/This Side Of The Looking Glass (promo only)	30
81	Virgin VS 424	My Experience/Glue (p/s)	5
82	Naive NAV 3	Paradox Drive/Now More Than Ever (p/s)	6
83	Naive NAV 8	Film Noir/Seven Wonders	6
84	Charisma CB 414	Just Good Friends/Just Good Friends (Instrumental) (p/s)	5
86	Foundry FOUND 3	Painting By Numbers/You Hit Me Where I Live (p/s)	5
86	Foundry FOUND 312	Painting By Numbers (Extended)/You Hit Me Where I Live/Shell (12", p/s)	8
71	Charisma CAS 1037	FOOL'S MATE (LP, gatefold sleeve)	18
73	Charisma CAS 1067	CHAMELEON IN THE SHADOW OF THE NIGHT (LP, gatefold sleeve)	18
74	Charisma CAS 1083	THE SILENT CORNER AND THE EMPTY STAGE (LP, gatefold sl., with inner)	18
74	Charisma CAS 1089	IN CAMERA (LP, with inner sleeve)	15
75	Charisma CAS 1099	NADIR'S BIG CHANCE (LP, with inner sleeve)	15
77	Charisma CAS 1125	OVER (LP, some with inner lyric sleeve)	18/12
78	Charisma CAS 1137	THE FUTURE NOW (LP, with insert)	15
79	Charisma CAS 1146	pH 7 (LP, with inner sleeve)	15

(see also Van Der Graaf Generator, Le Orme, Rikki Nadir, Colin Scot)

ALBERT HAMMOND

Year	Label/Cat. No.	Title	Value
73	MUM MUMS 65320	IT NEVER RAINS IN SOUTHERN CALIFORNIA (LP)	12
73	MUM MUMS 65554	FREE ELECTRIC BAND (LP)	12
74	MUM MUMS 80026	ALBERT HAMMOND (LP)	12

(see also Family Dogg)

CLAY HAMMOND

Year	Label/Cat. No.	Title	Value
72	Jay Boy BOY 78	Dance Little Girl/Twin Brother	5

JOHN HAMMOND

Year	Label/Cat. No.	Title	Value
65	Fontana TF 560	Baby Won't You Tell Me/I Live The Life I Love	15
68	Atlantic 584 190	Brown Eyed Handsome Man/Crosscut Saw	10
64	Fontana TFL 6046	BIG CITY BLUES (LP)	40
65	Fontana TFL 6059	SO MANY ROADS (LP)	35
71	CBS 64365	SOURCE POINT (LP)	22
72	CBS 65051	I'M SATISFIED (LP)	22
72	Vanguard VSD 11/12	THE BEST OF JOHN HAMMOND — SOUTHERN FRIED (2-LP)	20

STEVE HAMMOND

Year	Label/Cat. No.	Title	Value
67	Pye 7N 17275	I Think We're Alone Now/Just Call My Name	5

CURLEY HAMNER & COOPER BROTHERS

Year	Label/Cat. No.	Title	Value
59	Felsted SD 80061	Twistin' And Turnin'/King And Queen	10

SUSAN HAMPSHIRE

Year	Label/Cat. No.	Title	Value
65	Decca F 12185	When Love Is True/When The World Was Our Own	10

LIONEL HAMPTON (& HIS HAMP-TONES)

Year	Label/Cat. No.	Title	Value
52	MGM MGM 468	Samson's Boogie/Helpless (78, & His Hamp-Tones, B-side with Sonny Parker)	8
57	Vogue V 2405	Flying Home/Perdido (with Just Jazz All Stars)	18
57	Vogue V 2406	Hamp's Boogie Woogie/The Blues (with Just Jazz All Stars)	20
56	MGM MGM-EP 552	LIONEL HAMPTON & HIS ORCHESTRA (EP)	12
54	Vogue EPV 1015	LIONEL HAMPTON TRIO (EP)	10
54	Brunswick OE 9007	JUST JAZZ (EP)	10
55	Brunswick OE 9108	JUST JAZZ CONCERT (EP)	10
55	Philips BBE 12017	LIONEL HAMPTON & HIS ORCHESTRA (EP)	8

MINT VALUE £

57 Vogue EPV 1161 GENE NORMAN PRESENTS JUST JAZZ — LIONEL HAMPTON AT THE PASADENA AUDITORIUM (EP) . . . 12
57 Vogue EPV 1189 LIONEL HAMPTON JAM SESSION (EP) . . . 8
57 Vogue EPV 1190 LIONEL HAMPTON AT THE PASADENA AUDITORIUM (EP) . . . 8
56 Columbia Clef SEB 10025 LIONEL HAMPTON BIG BAND (EP) . . . 8
56 Columbia Clef SEB 10028 LIONEL HAMPTON QUARTET/QUINTET (EP) . . . 8
56 Columbia Clef SEB 10045 LIONEL HAMPTON BIG BAND (EP) . . . 8
56 Columbia Clef SEB 10065 LIONEL HAMPTON QUARTET (EP) . . . 8
57 Columbia Clef SEB 10086 LIONEL HAMPTON QUARTET (EP) . . . 8
57 Columbia Clef SEB 10092 LIONEL HAMPTON BIG BAND NO. 3 (EP) . . . 8
57 Felsted ESD 3026 LIONEL HAMPTON QUINTET (EP) . . . 8
58 RCA RCX 1004 LIONEL HAMPTON (EP) . . . 8
58 Columbia Clef SEB 10108 HAMPS BOOGIE WOOGIE (EP) . . . 12
62 Oriole EP 7046 LIONEL HAMPTON ORCHESTRA (EP) . . . 12
51 Brunswick LA 8527 HAMP'S BOOGIE WOOGIE (10" LP) . . . 30
52 Brunswick LA 8551 MOONGLOW (10" LP) . . . 30
53 Vogue LDE 043 LIONEL HAMPTON'S "JAZZ TIME PARIS" VOLUME 1 (10" LP) . . . 20
54 Vogue LDE 051 NEW SOUNDS FROM EUROPE VOLUME 2 — FRANCE (10" LP) . . . 20
54 Vogue LDE 063 LIONEL HAMPTON VOLUME 3 (10" LP) . . . 20
54 Felsted EDL 87007 THE HAMP IN PARIS IN PARIS VOLUME 1 (10" LP) . . . 20
54 Felsted EDL 87008 THE HAMP IN PARIS IN PARIS VOLUME 2 (10" LP) . . . 20
55 Felsted PDL 85002 LIONEL HAMPTON AND HIS NEW FRENCH SOUND VOLUME 1 (10" LP) . . . 20
55 HMV CLP 1023 HOT MALLETS (LP) . . . 15
55 Columbia Clef 33C 9011 LIONEL HAMPTON QUARTET (10" LP) . . . 15
55 Philips BBL 7015 APOLLO HALL CONCERT 1954 (LP) . . . 15
56 Philips BBL 7119 HAMPTON AND THE OLD WORLD (LP) . . . 12
56 Oriole MG 20012 HAMP 1956 (LP) . . . 12
56 Brunswick LAT 8086 ALL AMERICAN AWARD CONCERT (LP) . . . 12
57 RCA RD 27006 JAZZ FLAMENCO (LP) . . . 12
61 Fontana Fortune Z 4053 THE ONE AND ONLY LIONEL HAMPTON (LP) . . . 12
66 World Record Club T 578 THE HIGH AND THE MIGHTY (LP) . . . 12
(see also Sonny Parker)

PAUL HAMPTON

58 Philips PB 787 Play It Cool/Classy Babe (78) . . . 20

SLIDE HAMPTON & HIS BAND

62 London HA-K/SH-K 8008 JAZZ WITH A TWIST (LP) . . . 15

HAMPTONS

(see under Fabulous Impact)

HERBIE HANCOCK

63 Blue Note 45-1887 Blind Man, Blind Man (Parts 1 & 2) . . . 18
70 Warner Bros WB 7358 Fat Mama/Wiggle-Waggle . . . 8
74 CBS 2329 Chameleon/Vein Melter . . . 5
75 CBS 3059 Palm Grease/Butterfly . . . 5
64 Blue Note (B)BLP 4109 TAKIN' OFF (LP) . . . 25
64 Blue Note (B)BLP 4126 MY POINT OF VIEW (LP) . . . 25
64 Blue Note (B)BLP 4147 INVENTIONS AND DIMENSIONS (LP) . . . 22
65 Blue Note (B)BLP 4175 EMPYREAN ISLES (LP) . . . 22
66 Blue Note BLP 4195 MAIDEN VOYAGE (LP, also stereo BST 84195) . . . 20
60s Blue Note BST 84279 SPEAK LIKE A CHILD (LP) . . . 15
60s Blue Note BST 84321 THE PRISONER (LP) . . . 15
60s Blue Note BST 89907 THE BEST OF HERBIE HANCOCK (LP) . . . 15
71 Warner Bros WS 1834 FAT ALBERT ROTUNDA (LP) . . . 25
71 Warner Bros K 46077 MWANDISHI (LP) . . . 15
72 Warner Bros K 46164 CROSSINGS (LP) . . . 15
74 Warner Bros K 46039 FAT ALBERT ROTUNDA (LP, reissue) . . . 18
74 CBS 80193 THRUST (LP) . . . 15
74 CBS 80546 DEATH WISH (LP, soundtrack) . . . 25
74 CBS 65582 SEXTANT (LP) . . . 15
74 CBS 65928 HEADHUNTERS (LP) . . . 18
75 CBS 69185 MAN CHILD (LP) . . . 15
(see also Headhunters)

SHEILA HANCOCK

63 Decca F 11618 My Last Cigarette/Landlord And Tenant . . . 7
62 Transatlantic TRA 106 PUTTING OUT THE DUSTBIN (LP) . . . 20

SHEILA HANCOCK & MALCOLM TAYLOR

66 Eyemark EMS 1007 I'm Reformed/I Got You (die cut sleeve) . . . 7

TONY HANCOCK

63 Pye 7N 15575 Wing Commander Hancock — Test Pilot/The Threatening Letters (with Kenneth Williams) . . . 15
61 Pye NEP 24146 LITTLE PIECES OF HANCOCK (EP) . . . 8
62 Pye NEP 24161 LITTLE PIECES OF HANCOCK VOL. 2 (EP) . . . 10
62 Pye NEP 24170 HANCOCK'S HALF HOUR (EP) . . . 10
63 Pye NEP 24175 THE BLOOD DONOR (EP) . . . 8
60 Pye NPL 18045 THIS IS HANCOCK (LP) . . . 15
60 Pye NPL 18054 PIECES OF HANCOCK (LP) . . . 15
61 Pye NPL 18068 THE BLOOD DONOR AND THE RADIO HAM (LP) . . . 12
63 Piccadilly FTF 38500 FACE TO FACE (LP, interview disc) . . . 75
65 Decca LK 4740 IT'S HANCOCK (LP) . . . 15
(see also Sidney James, Kenneth Williams)

OWEN HAND

61 Transatlantic TRA 127 SOMETHING NEW (LP) . . . 100
66 Transatlantic TRA I LOVED A LASS (LP) . . . 55

JOHNNY HANDLE

61	Topic TOP 78	STOTTIN' DOON THE WAAL (EP)	10

(see also Louise Killen & Johnny Handle)

HANDSOME BEASTS

81	Heavy Metal HEAVY 1	All Riot Now/Mark Of The Beast (p/s)	25
81	Heavy Metal HEAVY 2	Breaker/One In A Crowd/Crazy (wraparound p/s)	8
82	Heavy Metal HEAVY 11	Sweeties/You're One Your Own (p/s, with card sheet)	8
82	Heavy Metal HMRLP 2	BEASTIALITY (LP)	20
90	FM Revolver HMRLP 132	THE BEAST WITHIN (LP)	12

JOHN HANDY

76	Impulse IMP 7001	Hard Work/Young Enough To Dream	6
80	MCA MCA 626	Hard Work/Young Enough To Dream (reissue)	5

WAYNE HANDY

58	London HL 8547	Say Yeah/Could It Be (B-side with King Sisters)	500
58	London HL 8547	Say Yeah/Could It Be (B-side with King Sisters) (78)	100

PAUL HANFORD

60	Parlophone R 4680	Itsy Bitsy Teenie Weenie Little Polka Dot Bikini/Why Have You Changed Your Mind	7
60	Parlophone R 4694	If You Ain't Got Love/Ev'ry Little Girl	10
61	Parlophone R 4745	Everything/Cigarettes And Coffee Blues	8
61	Parlophone R 4813	Memphis Address/Flutter Flutter	10
62	Oriole CB 1779	Don't Be/Habit Of Loving You	10
63	Oriole CB 1830	Just When I Need You Most/Judy	10
63	Oriole CB 1866	The Minute You're Gone/High School Dance	10

HANGMAN'S BEAUTIFUL DAUGHTERS

87	Dreamworld DREAM 11	Love Is Blue/Popular Trend (p/s)	7
87	Dreamworld DREAM 11T	Love Is Blue/Popular Trend/Jonathan/Don't Ask My Name (12", p/s)	8
87	Yo Jo Jo 1	Darkside/Pushing Me Too Far (flexidisc, p/s)	8
88	Dreamworld BIG 5	TRASH MANTRA (mini-LP)	12

HANK & MELLOWMEN

60s	Lyntone LYN 153/154	Santa Anno/Mosology/(other artists) (Bangor University Rag flexidisc)	7
60s	Lyntone LYN 201	So In Love With You/Michael (Bangor University Rag flexidisc)	7

(see also Roger Whittaker)

MICHAEL HANLY & MICHAEL O'DONNEL

74	Polydor 2908 013	CELTIC FOLKWEAVE (LP, Ireland-only)	40

BOBBY HANNA

67	Decca F 12604	Thanks To You/Here I Stand	6
67	Decca F 12695	Blame It On Me/Goin' Where The Lovin' Is	8
68	Decca F 12738	Too Much Love/What Do I Want For Tomorrow	6
68	Decca F 12783	Written On The Wind/Everybody Needs Love	8
68	Decca F 12833	To Wait For Love (Is To Waste Your Life Away)/Is It Wrong	6
69	Decca F 22917	Winter Love (E' L'Amore)/Time	5
70	Decca PA 109	THE WORLD OF BOBBY HANNA (LP)	12

GEORGE HANNA & SARAH ANNE O'NEILL

78	Topic 12TS 372	ON THE SHORES OF LOUGH NEAGH (LP)	12

JOSH HANNA

65	Parlophone R 5385	When I Love You/Love Me, Love Me	6
66	Decca F 12532	Shut Your Mouth/Sweet To My Soul	15

HANNA BARBERA (cartoon soundtrack EPs)

66	Hanna Barbera HBE 1	FLINTSTONES — HANSEL AND GRETEL (EP)	15
66	Hanna Barbera HBE 2	UNCLE REMUS — BRER RABBIT AND THE TAR BABY (EP)	15
66	Hanna Barbera HBE 3	FLINTSTONES — GOLDILOCKS, BEAROSAURUS (EP)	15
66	Hanna Barbera HBE 4	SNAGGLEPUSS TALES — WIZARD OF OZ (EP)	15
66	Hanna Barbera HBE 5	YOGI BEAR AND BOO BOO TELL JACK AND THE BEANSTALK (EP)	15
66	Hanna Barbera HBE 6	FRED FLINTSTONE & BARNEY RUBBLE — SONG FROM MARY POPPINS (EP)	15
67	Hanna Barbera HBE 7	TOP CAT — ROBIN HOOD (EP)	15
67	Hanna Barbera HBE 8	YOGI BEAR AND BOO BOO — LITTLE RED RIDING HOOD (EP)	15
67	Hanna Barbera HBE 9	FLINTSTONES — THREE LITTLE PIGS (EP)	15
67	Hanna Barbera HBE 10	AUGIE DOGGY AND DOGGY DADDY — SONGS FROM PINOCCHIO (EP)	15
67	Hanna Barbera HBE 11	PEBBLES AND BAMM BAMM — WE WISH YOU A MERRY CHRISTMAS (EP)	15
68	Hanna Barbera HBE 12	MERRY CHRISTMAS — ORGAN AND CHIMES (EP)	12
68	Hanna Barbera HBE 13	MAGILLA GORILLA AND OGEE — ALICE IN WONDERLAND (EP)	15
68	Hanna Barbera HBE 14	PEBBLES AND BAMM BAMM — SONGS FROM THE GOOD SHIP LOLLIPOP (EP)	15

HANNIBAL

74	B&C HB 1	Winds Of Change/Winter	6
70	B&C CAS 1022	HANNIBAL (LP)	45

LANCE HANNIBAL

69	Blue Cat BS 148	Read The News/RECO & RHYTHM ACES: Return Of The Bullet	12

(see also Sugar Simone, Les Foster)

HANOI ROCKS

83	Lick LIX 1	Malibu Beach/Rebel On The Run (p/s)	5
83	Lick LIXPD 1	Malibu Beach/Rebel On The Run (picture disc)	10
84	CBS A 4513	Up Around The Bend/Until I Get You (p/s, with free transfer)	8
84	CBS DA 4513	Up Around The Bend/Until I Get You//Under My Wheels/I Feel Alright/ Train Kept A Rollin' (double pack)	10
84	CBS TA 4513	Up Around The Bend/Back To The Mystery City/Until I Get You/ Mental 84 Beat (12", p/s, with free transfer)	8
84	CBS TA 4732	Underwater World/Shakes/Magic Carpet Ride (12", p/s)	8

MINT VALUE £

84	CBS WA 4732	Underwater World/Shakes/Magic Carpet Ride (12", picture disc)	10
84	CBS WA 4685	Don't You Ever Leave Me/Oil And Gasoline/Malibu Beach (Calypso) (12", 3-D picture disc)	10
82	Lick LICLPPD4	SELF DISTRUCTION BLUES (LP, picture disc)	12
83	Lick LICLP 1	BACK TO THE MYSTERY CITY (LP, white vinyl)	12

(see also Fallen Angels, Dark, Idle Flowers, Urban Dogs, Suicide Twins)

HANSON & KARLSSON

67	Polydor 184 196	SWEDISH UNDERGROUND (LP)	15
69	Polydor 462 60	MONUMENT (LP)	15
69	Polydor 583 564	MAN AT THE MOON (LP)	18

(see also Bo Hansson)

BO HANSSON

72	Charisma CAS 1059	LORD OF THE RINGS (LP)	12

HAPPENINGS

66	Fontana TF 735	See You In September/He Thinks He's A Hero	10
66	Fontana TF 766	Go Away Little Girl/Tea Time	10
67	Pye International 7N 25501	My Mammy/I Believe In Nothing	7
67	Stateside SS 587	Goodnight My Love/Lillies By Monet	8
67	Stateside SS 2013	I Got Rhythm/You're In A Bad Way	8
67	BT Puppy BTS 45532	Why Do Fools Fall In Love/When The Summer Is Through	8
67	BT Puppy BTS 45530	My Mammy/I Believe In Nothing	6
68	BT Puppy BTS 45538	Music Music Music/When I Lock My Door	7
68	BT Puppy BTS 45540	Randy/Love Song Of Mummy And Dad	8
68	BT Puppy BTS 45543	Breaking Up Is Hard To Do/Anyway	7
68	BT Puppy BTS 45545	Crazy Rhythm/Love Song Of Mummy And Dad	6
69	BT Puppy BTS 45546	Where Do I Go, Go-Be-In (Hare Krishna)/New Day Comin'	6
83	Surf King SK 1	HARMONY BEACH (EP, private pressing)	10
67	Fontana TL 5383	BYE BYE, SO LONG, FAREWELL ... SEE YOU IN SEPTEMBER (LP)	30
67	BT Puppy BTLP 1003	PSYCLE (LP)	25
68	BT Puppy BTLPS 1004	GOLDEN HITS (LP)	18

HAPPY CONFUSION

69	Penny Farthing PEN 706	Yes Sir/Hereditary Impediment	5

HAPPY FAMILY

82	4AD AD 204	Puritans/Innermost Thoughts/The Mistake (p/s)	20
82	4AD CAD 214	THE MAN ON YOUR STREET (LP)	12

(see also Josef K, Momus)

HAPPY MAGAZINE

68	Polydor 56233	Satisfied Street/Do Right Woman Do Right Man	8
69	Polydor 56307	Who Belongs To You (Ooby Dooby Doo)/Beautiful Land	6

(see also Griffin)

HAPPY MONDAYS

86	Factory FAC 142	Freaky Dancing (Live)/The Egg (p/s)	12
87	Factory FAC 176	Tart Tart/Little Matchstick Owen's Rap (12", p/s)	10
89	Factory FAC 232	Wrote For Luck (Vince Clark Remixes) (12", p/s)	8
87	Factory FACT 170	SQUIRREL & G-MAN TWENTY FOUR HOUR PARTY PEOPLE PLASTIC FACE CARNT SMILE (WHITE OUT) (LP, with "Desmond", 5,000 in plastic sleeve)	25/15

HAPPY WANDERERS STREET BAND

57	Esquire 10-510	The Happy Wanderer/Don't Fence Me In (78)	7

HAPSHASH & THE COLOURED COAT

69	Liberty LBF 15188	Colinda/The Wall	20
67	Minit MLS 40001E	FEATURING THE HUMAN HOST AND THE HEAVY METAL KIDS (LP, with Art, initially red vinyl with insert; later copies on black vinyl)	70/40
69	Liberty LBL/LBS 83212R	THE WESTERN FLYER (LP, with Mike Batt)	30

(see also Tony McPhee, Warm Sounds, Marc Bolan/T. Rex, Art, Mike Batt)

HARBOUR LITES

65	HMV POP 1426	Come Back Silly Girl/Revenge	8
65	HMV POP 1465	I Would Give All/They Call The Wind Maria	12
66	Fontana TF 682	Run For Your Life/Lonely Journey	12

HARD CORPS

84	Hard Corps HC 01	Dirty/To Breathe (12", hand-written white labels, numbered)	25
84	Survival SUR 026	Dirty/Respirer (To Breathe) (white or printed labels, stickered plain black sleeve)	10
84	Survival SUR 12 026	Dirty/Respirer (To Breathe) (12", with sticker in plain black sleeve)	12
85	Immaculate 12 IMMAC 2	Je Suis Passée (Extended French Version)/(Extended Club Dub Mix) (12", p/s)	12
85	Polydor HARDX 1	Je Suis Passée (Extended)/(Instrumental Mix)/(Dub Mix) (12", p/s)	8
85	Polydor HARDA 1	Je Suis Passée (Hard Mix)/(French Mix)/(Dub Mix) (12", gatefold PVC sleeve, various colours, with poster)	25
85	Polydor HARD 2	To Breathe/Metal And Flesh (unreleased)	30
85	Polydor HARDX 2	To Breathe/Metal And Flesh/To Breathe (Instrumental) (12", unreleased)	40
87	Rhythm King TYPE 3T	Lucky Charm/Porte-Bonheur/Lucky Charm (The Music) (12", p/s)	8
90	Concrete P. CPPRODLP 011	METAL AND FLESH (LP, clear vinyl)	15
90	Concrete P. CPPRODCD 011	METAL AND FLESH (CD)	25

(see also Craze, Skunks, T.U.F.F.)

HARDFLOOR

92	Harthouse HARTUK 1	HARDTRANCE ACPERIENCE EP (12", 4-track)	12

EDDIE HARDIN

72	Decca F 13307	Why Does Everybody Put Me Down/Spend Your Money Honey	5
72	Decca TXS 106	HOME IS WHERE YOU FIND IT (LP)	12

(see also Hardin-York, Spencer Davis Group, Roger Glover)

MINT VALUE £

TIM HARDIN

66 Verve VS 1504 Hang On To A Dream/A Reason To Believe . . . 12
67 Verve VS 1511 The Lady Came From Baltimore/Black Sheep Boy . . . 7
68 Verve VS 1516 Don't Make Promises/Smugglin' Man . . . 7
69 CBS 4441 A Simple Song Of Freedom/Question Of Birth . . . 6
71 Verve 2009 006 If I Were A Carpenter/Hang On To A Dream . . . 6
73 CBS 1016 Do The Do/Sweet Lady . . . 6
66 Verve (S)VLP 5018 TIM HARDIN 1 (LP) . . . 30
67 Verve (S)VLP 6002 TIM HARDIN 2 (LP) . . . 30
67 Atlantic 587/588 082 THIS IS TIM HARDIN (LP, plum label) . . . 30
68 Verve (S)VLP 6010 LIVE IN CONCERT (LP) . . . 22
69 Verve (S)VLP 6016 TIM HARDIN 4 (LP) . . . 22
69 Verve (S)VLP 6019 THE BEST OF (LP) . . . 20
69 CBS (S/M) 63571 SUITE FOR SUSAN MOORE AND DAMIAN (LP, gatefold sleeve, mono/stereo) . . . 18
70 CBS 64335 BIRD ON A WIRE (LP) . . . 15
72 CBS 65209 PAINTED HEAD (LP) . . . 15
74 GM GML 1004 NINE (LP) . . . 12
74 Verve 2683 048 TIM HARDIN 1/2 (2-LP, gatefold reissue) . . . 20

(Eddie) HARDIN & (Pete) YORK

69 Bell BLL 1064 Tomorrow Today/Candlelight (as Hardin-York) . . . 7
69 Bell SBLL 125 TOMORROW TODAY (LP) . . . 22
70 Bell SBLL 136 HARDIN & YORK (THE WORLD'S SMALLEST BIG BAND) (LP) . . . 22
71 Bell SBLL 141 FOR THE WORLD (LP) . . . 22
71 Decca SKL 5095 FOR THE WORLD (LP, reissue) . . . 12
(see also Eddie Hardin, Pete York, Spencer Davis Group)

RICHARD HARDING

61 HMV POP 887 Jezebel/Temptation . . . 25
(see also Cresters, Mike Sagar & Cresters)

ROSEMARY HARDMAN (& BOB AXFORD)

69 Folk Heritage no cat. no. QUEEN OF HEARTS (LP) . . . 120
71 Trailer LER 2075 FIREBIRD (LP) . . . 25
71 Trailer LER 3018 SECOND SEASON CAME (LP, by Rosemary Hardman & Bob Axford) . . . 25
75 Alida Star Cottage JERSEY BURGER (LP) . . . 120
78 Plant Life PLR 014 EAGLE OVER BLUE MOUNTAIN (LP, with insert) . . . 20
80 Plant Life PLR 023 ROSIE HARDMAN (LP) . . . 12
83 Plant Life PLR 053 THE WEAKNESS OF EVE (LP, with lyric insert) . . . 15

HARD MEAT

69 Island WIP 6066 Rain/Burning Up Years . . . 12
70 Warner Bros WB 8010 Ballad Of Marmalade Emma And Teddy Grimes/Yesterday, Today, Tomorrow . . . 6
70 Warner Bros WS 1852 HARD MEAT (LP, with photo insert) . . . 20
70 Warner Bros WS 1879 THROUGH A WINDOW (LP) . . . 30

HARD ROAD

79 Goodstuff LP 1002 NO PROBLEM (LP, private pressing) . . . 20

HARDSHIP POST

95 Sub Pop SP 295 Watching You/Your Sunshine (red vinyl) . . . 5

HARD STUFF

72 Purple PUR 103 Jay Time/The Orchestrator . . . 7
73 Purple PUR 116 Inside Your Life/(It's) How You Do It! . . . 7
72 Purple TPSA 7505 BULLETPROOF (LP, gatefold sleeve) . . . 25
73 Purple TPSA 7507 BOLEX DEMENTIA (LP) . . . 25
(see also Andromeda, Atomic Rooster, John Du Cann, Five Day Week Straw People, Johnny Gustafson, Bullet, Quatermass)

HARD TRAVELLIN'

71 Flams Ltd PR 1065 HARD TRAVELLIN' (LP, private pressing) . . . 100+

HARDWARE

79 Narc NARC 001 Speed Unit/Wall To Wall/Walking/Fire (folded p/s) . . . 6
79 Narc NARC 002 Rubberface/Face The Flag/The Seven Minutes (p/s) . . . 5

HARDWARE

85 Reset 7REST 7 Dance/Hey (p/s) . . . 10
85 Reset 12REST 7 Dance/Hey (12", p/s) . . . 20

HARDY

71 Ackee ACK 131 Glorious Morning/Hearing's Not Seeing . . . 6

DAVE HARDY

76 Red Rag RRR 008 LEAVING THE DALES (LP) . . . 12

FRANCOISE HARDY

64 Pye 7N 15612 Catch A Falling Star/Only Friends . . . 10
64 Pye 7N 15653 Tous Les Garcons Et Les Filles/L'Amour S'en Va . . . 6
64 Pye 7N 15696 Pourtant Tu M'Aimes/Jaloux . . . 8
64 Pye 7N 15740 Et Meme/Le Temps De L'Amour . . . 8
65 Pye 7N 15802 All Over The World/Another Place . . . 6
66 Vogue VRS 7001 Just Call And I'll Be There/You Just Have To Say The Word . . . 7
66 Vogue VRS 7004 So Many Friends/However Much . . . 10
66 Vogue VRS 7010 This Little Heart/The Rose . . . 6
66 Vogue VRS 7011 La Maison Ou J'ai Grandi/Je Ne Suis La Pour Personne . . . 6
66 Vogue VRS 7014 Autumn Rendezvous/It's My Heart . . . 6
66 Vogue VRS 7020 Si C'est Ca/Je Serai La Pour Toi . . . 7
66 Vogue VRS 7025 Voila/Qui Peut Dire . . . 7
67 Vogue VRS 7026 On Se Quitte Toujours/Les Petits Garcons . . . 10
68 United Artists UP 1208 Now You Want To Be Loved/Tell Him You're Mine . . . 8
68 United Artists UP 2253 Will You Love Me Tomorrow/Loving You . . . 8

MINT VALUE £

69 United Artists UP 35011 Comment Te Dire Adieu/La Mer, Les Etoiles Et Le Vent 10
70 United Artists UP 35070 All Because Of You/Time Passing By 10
70 United Artists UP 35105 Soon Is Slipping Away/The Bells Of Avignon 10
64 Pye NEP 24188 C'EST FAB (EP) 12
64 Pye NEP 24192 FRANCOISE SINGS IN ENGLISH (EP) 12
64 Pye NEP 24193 C'EST FRANCOISE (EP) 12
60s Vogue VRE 5000 FRANCOISE (EP) 15
60s Vogue VRE 5001 FRANCOISE HARDY (EP) 15
60s Vogue VRE 5003 DIS LUI NON (EP) 15
60s Vogue VRE 5008 LE TEMPS DES SOUVENIRS (EP) 15
60s Vogue VRE 5012 CHANTE EN ALLEMAND (EP) 18
60s Vogue VRE 5015 L'AMITIE (EP) 18
60s Vogue VRE 5017 MON AMIE LA ROSE (EP) 18
60s Vogue VRE 5018 AUTUMN RENDEZVOUS (EP) 18
64 Pye NPL 18094 FRANCOISE HARDY (LP) 18
64 Pye NPL 18099 IN VOGUE (LP) 18
65 Vogue VRL 3000 FRANCOISE HARDY (LP) 25
66 Vogue VRL 3021 FRANCOISE HARDY (LP) 25
66 Vogue VRL 3023 LE MEILLEUR DE FRANCOISE HARDY (LP) 15
66 Vogue VRL 3025 SINGS IN ENGLISH (LP) 15
67 Vogue VRL 3028 FRANCOISE (LP) 15
67 Vogue VRL 3031 VOILA! FRANCOISE HARDY (LP) 20
68 United Artists SULP 1191 IL N'Y A PAS D'AMOUR HEUREUX (LP) 25
68 United Artists ULP 1207 EN ANGLAIS (LP) 35
70 United Artists UAS 29046 ONE-NINE-SEVEN-ZERO (LP) 30

LAVELL HARDY

68 Direction 58-3261 Don't Lose Your Groove/Women Of The World 10

COLIN HARE

70 Penny Farthing PEN 736 Grannie, Grannie/For Where Have You Been 7
71 Penny Farthing PEN 750 Underground Girl/Fighting For Peace 7
72 Warner Bros K 16203 Didn't I Tell You/Seek Not In The Wide World 7
71 Penny Farthing PELS 516 MARCH HARE (LP) 55
(see also Honeybus)

WINSTON HAREWOOD

71 Camel CA 64 I Will Never Fall In Love Again (actually by Winston Heywood)/
LA-FUD-DIL ALL-STARS: La-Fud-Dil (actually "La-Fud-Del") 8
(see also Winston Heywood)

RON HARGRAVE

58 MGM MGM 956 Latch On/Only A Daydream 3,250
58 MGM MGM 956 Latch On/Only A Daydream (78) 375

HARLAN COUNTY

70 Nashville 6076 002 Dr. Handy's Dandy Candy/Big Heat 5
70 Nashville 6336 002 HARLAN COUNTY (LP) 12
(see also Peter Skellern)

HARLEM HAMFATS

51 Vocalion V 1005 Weed Smoker's Dream (Why Don't You Do It Now)/
ROSETTA HOWARD: Let Your Linen Hang Low (78) 20
63 Ace Of Hearts AH 27 HARLEM HAMFATS (LP) 18

HARLEM JONNS RESHUFFLE

(see under 'J')

HARLESDEN MONKS

72 Pama Supreme PS 352 Time/Harlesden High Street 6

STEVE HARLEY (& COCKNEY REBEL)

73 EMI EMI 2051 Sebastian/Rock And Roll Parade 5
74 EMI EMI 2191 Psychomodo/Such A Dream (unreleased)
74 EMI EMI 2191 Mr Soft/Such A Dream (with 'Orchestrated by Alan Powell' credit) 5
(The above singles are credited to Cockney Rebel.)
74 EMI EMI 2233 Big Big Deal/Bed In The Corner 12
76 EMI EMI 2539 (I Believe) Love's A Prima Donna/Sidetrack One 5
77 EMI EMI 2673 The Best Years Of Our Lives (live)/Tumbling Down (live) (p/s) 6
(The above singles are credited to Steve Harley & Cockney Rebel; all subsequent singles are solo.)
77 EMI EMI 2922 Someone's Coming/Riding The Waves (For Virginia Woolf) 5
82 Chrysalis CHS 2594 I Can't Even Touch You/I Can Be Anyone (p/s) 5
89 Vital Vinyl VIT 3 When I'm With You/Theme From Babbacombe Lee (p/s) 5
93 Food For Thought The Lighthouse/Star For A Week (CD, promo only, no cat. no.) 8
(see also Anderson Harley & Batt)

LEE HARMER'S POPCORN

68 Page One POF 053 Love Is Coming/Hello Sunshine 10

HARMONIANS

70 Ackee ACK 107 Music Street/Group Of Girls 8
(see also Tony & Hippy Boys, Winston Shan)

HARMONICA FATS

63 Stateside SS 184 Tore Up/I Get So Tired 40
68 Action ACT 4507 Tore Up/I Get So Tired (reissue) 15

HARMONISERS

69 Duke DU 32 Mother Hen/WINSTON SINCLAIR: Chastise Them 10

HARMONIZING FOUR

66 Rymska RA 102 Who Knows/Heart Of Stone (actually by Charms) 18
(see also Charms)

HARMONY GRASS

68 RCA RCA 1772 Move In A Little Bit Closer Baby/Happiness Is Toy Shaped . . . 7
69 RCA RCA 1828 First Time Loving/What A Groovy Day . . . 6
69 RCA RCA 1885 I Remember/Summer Dreaming . . . 6
70 RCA RCA 1932 Mrs. Richie/Teach Me How (withdrawn) . . . 10+
70 RCA RCA 1932 Cecilia/Mrs. Richie . . . 6
70 RCA RCA 2011 Stand On Your Own Two Feet/Sing In The Sunshine . . . 6
70 RCA SF 8034 THIS IS US (LP) . . . 25
(see also Tony Rivers & Castaways)

HARMONY TRIO

69 Emblem 7DR 323 LET'S FACE IT (LP) . . . 12

JOE HARNELL

62 London HLR 9637 Harlem Nocturne/Fly Me To The Moon — Bossa Nova . . . 6
78 MCA MCA 397 The Incredible Hulk Theme/Love Theme . . . 6
62 London RER 1344 DANCE THE BOSSA NOVA (EP) . . . 12

BILLY HARNER

71 Kama Sutra 2013 029 What About The Music/Please Spare Me This Time . . . 10
71 Kama Sutra 2013 029 What About The Music/Please Spare Me This Time/What About The Music (Instrumental) (a few demos mispressed with extra track) . . . 200
72 Blue Horizon 2431 013 TRIGGER FINGER (LP) . . . 15

BUD HARPER

65 Vocalion VP 9252 Mr. Soul/Let Me Love You . . . 60

CHARLIE HARPER

80 Gem GEMS 35 Barmy London Army/Talk Is Cheap (p/s, green or yellow vinyl) . . . each 5
81 Ramkup CAC 005 Freaked/Jo (p/s) . . . 5
(see also U.K. Subs, Long Tall Shorty, Urban Dogs)

DON HARPER SEXTET

58 Pye Jazz 7NJ 2024 Hi-Diddle-Fiddle/It's The Bluest Kind Of Blues . . . 5

DON HARPER ORCHESTRA

68 Columbia DB 8519 "World Of Sport" March/England 88 . . . 6
71 Columbia DB 8843 "World Of Sport" March/England 88 (reissue) . . . 5
73 Columbia DB 9023 World Of Sport/"Dr. Who" Theme (as Don Harper's Homo Electronicus) . . . 25
(see also Electricians)

JANICE HARPER

57 HMV POP 376 Bon Voyage/Tell Me That You Love Me Tonight . . . 8
58 Capitol CL 14899 Devotion/In Time . . . 10
59 Capitol CL 14977 I Was Hoping You'd Ask Me/I'm Making Love To You . . . 7
59 Capitol CL 15026 Let Me Call You Sweetheart/Just Whistle . . . 7
59 Capitol CL 15026 Let Me Call You Sweetheart/Just Whistle (78) . . . 7
60 Capitol CL 15159 Only Once/Love Me Now, Love Me Never . . . 7
59 Capitol T 1195 WITH FEELING (LP) . . . 25

JESSIE HARPER

92 Kissing Spell KSLP 9203 GUITAR ABSOLUTION IN THE SHADE OF A MIDNIGHT SUN (LP, reissue of acetate-only album) . . . 20
(see also Human Instinct)

JOE 'HARMONICA' HARPER

58 MGM MGM 983 Lazy Train/Her Lips Were Like Velvet . . . 8
58 MGM MGM 983 Lazy Train/Her Lips Were Like Velvet (78) . . . 8

MIKE HARPER

70 Concord CON 026 You've Got Too Much Going For You/This Time . . . 15
76 RCA RCA 2719 Rip Off/I'm Crying . . . 5

ROY HARPER

SINGLES

66 Strike JH 304 Take Me Into Your Eyes/Pretty Baby (some in wraparound p/s) . . . 45/25
67 CBS 203001 Midspring Dithering/Zengem . . . 22
68 CBS 3371 Life Goes By/Nobody's Got Any Money In The Summer . . . 20
72 Harvest HAR 5059 Bank Of The Dead (Valerie's Song)/Little Lady (some in p/s) . . . 10/6
74 Harvest HAR 5080 (Don't You Think We're) Forever/Male Chauvinist Pig Blues . . . 5
74 Harvest HAR 5089 Home (live)/Home (studio) . . . 5
75 Harvest HAR 5096 When An Old Cricketer Leaves The Crease/Hallucinating Light (Acoustic Version) (p/s) . . . 5
75 Harvest HAR 5102 Grown-Ups Are Just Silly Children/Referendum (Legend) . . . 5
75 EMI PSR 407 Referendum/Another Day (live)/Tom Tiddler's Ground (live) (promo only) . . . 8
77 Harvest HAR 5120 One Of Those Days In England/Watford Gap (p/s) . . . 5
77 Harvest HAR 5140 Sail Away/Cherishing The Lonesome (as Roy Harper's Black Sheep) . . . 7
78 Harvest HAR 5160 When An Old Cricketer Leaves The Crease/Home (studio) (p/s) . . . 5
80 Harvest HAR 5203 Playing Games/First Thing In The Morning (p/s) . . . 6
80 Harvest HAR 5207 Short And Sweet/Water Sports (live)/Unknown Soldier (live) (p/s) . . . 6
82 Public PUBS 1001 No One Gets Out Here Alive/Casualty (live) (p/s) . . . 5
83 Public PUBS 1002 I Still Care/Goodbye Ladybird (p/s) . . . 6
85 B. Banquet BEG 131 Elizabeth (Short Version)/Advertisement (Short Version) (p/s) . . . 6
85 B. Banquet BEG 131T Elizabeth/Advertisement/I Hate The White Man (live) (12", p/s) . . . 8
88 Regal Zonophone HR 1 Laughing Inside/Laughing Inside (p/s, promo only; as Harry Rope) . . . 7
88 EMI EM 46 Laughing Inside/Laughing Inside (Acoustic Version) (p/s) . . . 5

ORIGINAL LPs

66 Strike JHL 105 SOPHISTICATED BEGGAR . . . 275
67 CBS (S)BPG 63184 COME OUT FIGHTING GHENGIS SMITH (mono/stereo) . . . 35/25
69 Liberty LBL/LBS 83231 FOLKJOKEOPUS (mono/stereo) . . . 40/35
69 Harvest SHVL 766 FLAT, BAROQUE AND BERSERK (gatefold sleeve; some with "H. Ash" label credit) . . . 22

MINT VALUE £

71	Harvest SHVL 789	STORMCOCK (gatefold sleeve with lyric inner)	22
73	Harvest SHVL 808	LIFEMASK (foldout 'door' sleeve, with insert)	22
74	Harvest SHSP 4027	VALENTINE (initially with lyric booklet)	30/20
74	Harvest SHDW 405	FLASHES FROM THE ARCHIVES OF OBLIVION (2-LP, gatefold sleeve)	22
75	Harvest SHSP 4046	HQ (with lyric inner sleeve)	20
77	Harvest SHSP 4060	BULLINAMINGVASE (with inner sleeve & "Watford Gap"; some with 7", "Referendum"/"Another Day" (live)/"Tom Tiddler's Ground" [PSR 407])	15/20
77	Harvest SHSP 4060	BULLINAMINGVASE (2nd pressing with "Breakfast With You")	18
77	Harvest SHSP 4077	COMMERCIAL BREAK (unreleased; test pressing with proof sleeve)	200+
78	Harvest SHSM 2025	HARPER 1970-1975	12
78	Harvest	HARPER 1970-1975 (6-LP box set)	125
80	Harvest SHVL 820	THE UNKNOWN SOLDIER (with inner sleeve)	12
82	Public PUBLP 5001	WORK OF HEART (with inner sleeve)	12
82	Public TC PUBLP 5001	WORK OF HEART (cassette on 'real time' high quality tape, different sleeve, 250 only)	12
84	Hard Up PUB 5002	BORN IN CAPTIVITY (880 only)	35
92	Hard Up HU 2	BORN IN CAPTIVITY II (LIVE) (cassette)	15

REISSUE ALBUMS

70	Young Blood SSYB 7	RETURN OF THE SOPHISTICATED BEGGAR (LP, with "Hup Hup Spiral" closed run-out groove, different sleeve)	20
73	Birth RAB 3	RETURN OF THE SOPHISTICATED BEGGAR (LP, 2nd reissue, with "Hup Hup Spiral" closed run-out groove, different sleeve)	15
75	Sunset SLS 50373	FOLKJOKEOPUS (LP)	12
77	Big Ben BBX 502	THE SOPHISTICATED BEGGAR (LP, different rear sleeve)	12
77	Embassy EMB 31544	THE EARLY YEARS (LP, reissue of "Come Out Fighting Ghengis Smith", different sleeve)	12
85	Awareness AWL 1001	BORN IN CAPTIVITY (LP, different rear sleeve)	12
86	Awareness AWL 1002	WORK OF HEART (LP, different sleeve with inner; 1st 1,000 with 2 x 7": "No One Gets Out Here Alive"/"Casualty (live)" [PUBS 1001] & "Still Care"/ "Goodbye Ladybird" [PUBS 1002]; later copies with just PUBS 1001)	15/12
86	Awareness AWL 1002	WORK OF HEART (cassette, different sleeve, 250 only on 'real time' quality tape)	12
93	Hard Up HUCD 003	FLAT, BAROQUE & BERSERK (CD, in box with 40-page booket & poster, signed)	20

(see also Rory Phare, Per Yarroh)

TIM HARPER

95	Peacefrog PF 047	I Feel A Groove (12", plain sleeve)	10

HARPER'S BIZARRE

67	Warner Bros WB 5890	59th Street Bridge Song (Feelin' Groovy)/Lost My Love Today	6
67	Warner Bros WB 7528	Come To The Sunshine/The Debutante's Ball	6
67	Warner Bros WB 7063	Anything Goes/Malibu U	6
67	Warner Bros WB 7090	Chattanooga Choo Choo/Hey You In The Crowd	6
68	Warner Bros WB 7172	Cotton Candy Sandman (Sandman's Coming)/Virginia City	6
68	Warner Bros WB 7223	Battle Of New Orleans/Green Apple Tree	6
69	Warner Bros WB 7238	I Love You, Alice B. Toklas!/Look To The Rainbow	6
70	Warner Bros WB 7388	Anything Goes/Virginia City	6
67	Warner Bros W 1693	FEELIN' GROOVY (LP)	25
67	Warner Bros W 1716	ANYTHING GOES (LP)	20
68	Warner Bros W(S) 1739	THE SECRET LIFE OF HARPER'S BIZARRE (LP)	20

SLIM HARPO

61	Pye International 7N 25098	Rainin' In My Heart/Don't Start Cryin' Now	20
63	Pye International 7N 25220	Don't Start Cryin' Now/Rainin' In My Heart	20
66	Stateside SS 491	Baby Scratch My Back/I'm Gonna Miss You (Like The Devil)	25
66	Stateside SS 527	Shake Your Hips/Midnight Blues	25
66	Stateside SS 557	I'm A King Bee/I Got Love If You Want It	25
67	Stateside SS 581	I'm Your Breadmaker Baby/Loving You (The Way I Do)	25
67	President PT 164	I'm Gonna Keep What I've Got/I've Got To Be With You Tonight	10
68	Liberty LBF 15176	Something Inside Me/PAPPA LIGHTFOOT: Wine Whisky And Women	20
68	President PT 187	Tip On In (Parts 1 & 2)	12
70	Blue Horizon 57-3175	Folsom Prison Blues/Mutual Friend	30
65	Stateside SL 10135	A LONG DRINK OF THE BLUES (LP, with Lightnin' Slim)	65
68	President PTL 1017	TIP ON IN (LP)	30
70	Blue Horizon 7-63854	HE KNEW THE BLUES (LP)	90
72	Blue Horizon 2431 013	TRIGGER FINGER (LP)	110
76	Flyright LP 520	BLUES HANGOVER (LP)	18
78	Sonet SNTF 769	HE KNEW THE BLUES (LP)	15
80	Flyright FLY 558	GOT LOVE IF YOU WANT IT (LP)	12

(see also Lightnin' Slim)

GEORGE HARRASSMENT & HOMOSEXUALS

80s	Black Noise 12 NO 6	MASAI SLEEP WALKING (LP)	12

(see also Homosexuals)

HARRIER

84	Black Horse HARR 1T	OUT ON THE STREET EP (Out On The Street/Nickels And Dimes/Shine On) (12", p/s)	12

DERRICK HARRIOT(T) (& CRYSTALITES)

62	Blue Beat BB 131	I Care/Have Faith In Me (as Derrick Harriott & Vagabonds)	18
63	Blue Beat BB 178	Be True/I Won't Cry	18
64	Island WI 157	What Can I Do (The Wedding)/Leona	18
65	Island WI 170	I Am Only Human (as Derak Harriott)/ROY PANTON: Good Man	22
65	Island WI 237	My Three Loves/The Jerk	20
65	Island WI 245	Together/Mama Didn't Lie	18
65	Ska Beat JB 199	Monkey Ska/Derrick!	22
66	Doctor Bird DB 1002	Jon Tom/AUDREY WILLIAMS: Solas Market	18
67	Island WI 3063	The Loser/Bless You	35
67	Island WI 3064	Happy Times/You My Everything	25

Year	Label / Cat. No.	Title	MINT VALUE £
67	Island WI 3077	Walk The Streets/BOBBY ELLIS: Step Softly (B-side with Desmond Miles Seven)	45
67	Island WI 3089	Solomon/BOBBY ELLIS: The Emperor (B-side with Desmond Miles Seven)	22
68	Island WI 3135	Do I Worry?/BOBBY ELLIS & CRYSTALITES: Shuntin'	22
68	Island WI 3147	Born To Love You/IKE & CRYSTALITES: Alfred Hitchcock	22
68	Island WI 3153	Tang Tang Festival Song/CRYSTALITES: James Ray	22
69	Big Shot BI 505	Standing In/Bumble Bee	15
69	Big Shot BI 511	Another Lonely Night/Been So Long	15
70	Songbird SB 1013	Riding For A Fall/I'm Not Begging	12
70	Songbird SB 1014	Sitting On Top/You Were Meant For Me	12
70	Songbird SB 1022	Go Bye Bye/Laugh It Off	12
70	Songbird SB 1028	Message From A Black Man/(Version II)	10
70	Songbird SB 1029	Psychedelic Train (w/ Chosen Few)/Psychedelic Train (Pt. 2) (with Crystalites)	10
70	Songbird SB 1033	No Man Is An Island/CRYSTALITES: No Man Is An Island Part 2	12
70	Songbird SB 1042	Groovy Situation/CRYSTALITES: The Crystal Groove	10
70	Songbird SB 1043	Psychedelic Train Chapter Three/CRYSTALITES: Groovy Situation Version II	18
71	Songbird SB 1052	Candy/CRYSTALITES: Candy Version	18
71	Songbird SB 1055	Lollipop Girl/CRYSTALITES: Lollipop Version	15
71	Songbird SB 1063	Medley In 5 (Parts 1 & 2)	7
72	Songbird SB 1065	Have You Seen Her/CRYSTALITES: Have You Seen Her — Version	7
72	Songbird SB 1068	Over The River/River (Version)	7
72	Songbird SB 1071	Since I Lost My Baby/Baby (Version)	7
72	Songbird SB 1078	Being In Love/Love (Version)	6
72	Songbird SB 1084	Don't Rock The Boat/Rock (Version)	7
73	Explosion EX 2071	Let Me Down Easy/Let Me Down Easy — Version	7
74	Harry J. HJ 6675	Some Guys Have All The Luck/Some Guys Have All The Luck — Version	6
65	Island ILP 928	THE BEST OF DERRICK HARRIOTT (LP)	150
67	Island ILP 955	DERRICK HARRIOTT'S ROCKSTEADY PARTY (LP, actually v/a LP)	200
68	Island ILP 983	THE BEST OF VOLUME TWO (LP, as Derrick Harriott & Crystalites)	150
69	Pama SECO 13	SINGS JAMAICA REGGAE (LP)	90
70	Trojan TTL 43	THE BEST OF DERRICK HARRIOTT (LP)	40
70	Trojan TTL 54	ROCKSTEADY PARTY (LP)	50
70	Trojan TBL 114	THE UNDERTAKER (LP, as Derrick Harriott & Crystalites)	35
70	Trojan TBL 141	PSYCHEDELIC TRAIN (LP, as Derrick Harriott & Crystalites)	35

JOE HARRIOTT

Year	Label / Cat. No.	Title	Value
56	Jazz Today JTE 106	WITH STRINGS (EP)	18
56	Pye Jazz NJE 1003	NO STRINGS (EP)	50
50s	Melodisc EPM7 117	COOL JAZZ WITH JOE (EP)	20
57	Columbia SEG 7665	JOE HARRIOTT QUARTET (EP)	100
59	Columbia SEG 7939	BLUE HARRIOTT (EP)	30
61	Columbia SEG 8070	A GUY CALLED JOE (EP)	25
60	Jazzland JLP 49	FREE FORM (LP)	50
62	Columbia 33SX 1477	ABSTRACT (LP)	125
63	Columbia 33SX 1627	MOVEMENT (LP)	250
64	Columbia 33SX 1692	HIGH SPIRITS (LP)	120
66	Columbia S(C)X 6025	DOUBLE QUINTET (LP, with John Mayer)	25
67	Melodisc SLP 12150	SWINGS HIGH (LP)	100
67	Columbia S(C) 6122	INDO-JAZZ FUSIONS (LP, with John Mayer)	30
68	Columbia S(C)X 6215	INDO-JAZZ FUSIONS II (LP, with John Mayer)	40
68	Columbia S(C)X 6249	PERSONAL PORTRAIT (LP)	40
69	Columbia SCX 6354	HUM-DONO (LP)	240
73	One Up OU 2011	MEMORIAL 1973 (LP)	40

(see also Tony Kinsey Trio & Joe Harriott, John Mayer, Michael Garrick)

JOE HARRIOTT/DON RENDELL QUARTET

Year	Label / Cat. No.	Title	Value
57	MGM MGM-EP 615	JAZZ BRITANNIA (EP, 2 tracks each)	25

(see also Don Rendell)

ANITA HARRIS

Year	Label / Cat. No.	Title	Value
61	Parlophone R 4830	I Haven't Got You/Mr One And Only	7
64	Vocalion V 9223	Lies/Don't Think About Love	6
65	Decca F 12082	Willingly/At Last Love	8
65	Pye 7N 15868	Trains And Boats And Planes/Upside Down	8
65	Pye 7N 15894	I Don't Know Anymore/When I Look At You	6
65	Pye 7N 15971	London Life/I Run To Hide	6
66	Pye 7N 17069	Something Must Be Done/Funny Kind Of Feeling	12
66	CBS 2724	Just Loving You/Butterfly With Coloured Wings	6
67	CBS 2991	The Playground/B.A.D. For Me	20
68	CBS 3211	Anniversary Waltz/Old Queenie Cole	6
68	CBS 3468	Tuppeny Bus Ride/Artie	6
68	CBS 3637	Dream A Little Dream Of Me/The Flying Machine	5
68	CBS 3765	Le Blon/Dusty Road	6
67	Pye NEP 24288	ANITA HARRIS (EP)	20
67	CBS EP 6359	NURSERY RHYMES FOR OUR TIMES (EP)	12
68	CBS EP 6401	DREAM A LITTLE DREAM OF ME (EP)	12
67	Marble Arch MAL 761	ANITA HARRIS (LP)	15
69	CBS 63927	CUDDLY TOY (LP)	12

(see also Brello Cabal)

ARTIE HARRIS & HIS BOYS

Year	Label / Cat. No.	Title	Value
63	Oriole CB 1816	Go Go Gaudeamus/Mexicana	8

BETTY HARRIS

Year	Label / Cat. No.	Title	Value
63	London HL 9796	Cry To Me/I'll Be A Liar	18
65	Stateside SS 475	What A Sad Feeling/I'm Evil Tonight	25
67	Stateside SS 2045	Nearer To You/12 Red Roses	20
69	Action ACT 4535	Ride Your Pony/Trouble With My Lover	15
69	Action ACLP 6007	SOUL PERFECTION (LP)	80

(see also Betty Harris & Lee Dorsey)

MINT VALUE £

BRENDA JO HARRIS

69 Roulette RO 503 I Can Remember/Play With Fire . . . 7

DON 'SUGARCANE' HARRIS

70 BASF MPS 68027 KEEP ON DRIVING (LP) . . . 12
70 BASF MPS 68028 FIDDLER ON THE ROCK (LP) . . . 12
72 BASF MPS 68029 GOT THE BLUES (LP) . . . 12
73 BASF MPS 68030 CUPFUL OF DREAMS (LP) . . . 12
(see also Don & Dewey)

EDDIE HARRIS

69 Atlantic 584 218 Listen Here/Theme — In Search Of A Movie . . . 6
69 Atlantic 584 232 It's Crazy/Live Right Now (unissued)
74 Atlantic K 10513 Is It In?/Funkarama . . . 6
75 Atlantic K 10561 I Need Some Money/Don't Want Nobody . . . 5
76 Atlantic K 10741 Get On Up And Dance/Why Must We Part . . . 5
62 Stateside SL 10009 BREAKFAST AT TIFFANY'S (LP) . . . 18
63 Stateside SL 10018 MIGHTY LIKE A ROSE (LP) . . . 18
63 Stateside SL 10049 GOES TO THE MOVIES (LP) . . . 18
65 Atlantic SAL 5045 THE IN SOUND (LP) . . . 20
69 Atlantic 588 177 SILVER CYCLES (LP) . . . 15
71 Atlantic 2466 013 FREE SPEECH (LP) . . . 12
73 Atlantic K 40123 PLUG ME IN (LP) . . . 12
73 Atlantic K 40482 SINGS THE BLUES (LP) . . . 12
73 Atlantic K 40220 THE ELECTRIFYING EDDIE HARRIS (LP) . . . 12
74 Atlantic K 50084 IS IT IN? (LP) . . . 12
75 Atlantic K 50127 I NEED SOME MONEY (LP) . . . 12

JET HARRIS

62 Decca F 11466 Besame Mucho/Chills And Fever . . . 7
62 Decca F 11488 Main Title Theme (from The Man With The Golden Arm)/Some People . . . 7
64 Decca F 11841 Big Bad Bass/Rifka . . . 7
67 Fontana TF 849 My Lady/You Don't Live Twice . . . 8
75 SRT SRT 75355 Theme For A Fallen Idol/This Sportin' Life (initial pressing) . . . 7
75 SRT SRT 75355 Theme/This Sportin' Life (later pressing with shortened A-side title) . . . 6
78 SRT SRT 77389 Guitar Man/Theme . . . 6
62 Decca DFE 8502 JET HARRIS (EP) . . . 35
78 Ellie Jay EJSP 8622 INSIDE JET HARRIS — THE LAST CONCERT (LP, 2,500 only) . . . 22
70s Q LPMM 1038 ANNIVERSARY ALBUM (LP) . . . 20
(see also Shadows, Jet Harris & Tony Meehan, Keith Meehan, Peter Rawes)

JET HARRIS & TONY MEEHAN

63 Decca F 11563 Diamonds/Footstomp . . . 7
63 Decca F 11644 Scarlett O'Hara/(Doing The) Hully Gully . . . 7
63 Decca F 11710 Applejack/The Tall Texan . . . 8
80 Decca F 13892 Diamonds/Scarlett O'Hara/Applejack/Man With The Golden Arm (p/s) . . . 5
63 Decca DFE 7099 DIAMONDS (EP, export issue, existence confirmed) . . . 100+
63 Decca DFE 8528 JET AND TONY (EP) . . . 30
76 Decca REM 1 REMEMBERING (LP) . . . 12
(see also Shadows, Jet Harris, Tony Meehan, Vipers Skiffle Group)

JOHNNY HARRIS

65 Mercury MF 942 Mynahg Hop/Here Comes The Boot . . . 5
69 Warner Bros WB 8000 Footprints On The Moon/Lulu's Theme . . . 7
70 Warner Bros WB 8016 Fragment Of Fear/Stepping Stones . . . 10
70 Warner Bros WS 3002 MOVEMENTS (LP) . . . 25
72 Warner Bros K 46054 MOVEMENTS (LP, reissue) . . . 20
73 Warner Bros K 46187 ALL TO BRING YOU MORNING (LP) . . . 12

JUNE HARRIS

65 CBS 201774 Over And Over Again/Stand Back . . . 12

MAX HARRIS

60 Fontana H 282 Gurney Slade/Hat And Cane . . . 8
69 Pye 7N 17730 Baby Love Theme/Robert's Theme . . . 10

PAT HARRIS & BLACKJACKS

63 Pye 7N 15567 The Hippy Hippy Shake/You Gotta See Your Mama Ev'ry Night . . . 18
(see also Blackjacks)

PAUL HARRIS

70 Intl. Broadcasters Society HISTORY OF OFFSHORE RADIO (LP, radio-only) . . . 12

PHIL HARRIS

54 HMV 7M 199 I Know An Old Lady/Take Your Girlie To The Movies . . . 12
54 HMV 7M 231 I Guess I'll Have To Change My Plan/The Persian Kitten . . . 12
55 HMV 7M 289 I Wouldn't Touch You With A Ten-Foot Pole/There's A Lot More . . . 12
70 Buena Vista DF 478 Thomas O'Malley Cat/SCATMAN CROTHERS: Everybody Wants To Be A Cat . . . 6
59 RCA Camden CDN 124 THAT'S WHAT I LIKE ABOUT THE SOUTH (LP) . . . 12

RICHARD HARRIS

68 RCA RCA 1699 MacArthur Park/Paper Chase . . . 5
68 Stateside SS 8001 The Yard Went On Forever/Lucky Me . . . 5
70 Stateside SS 8054 Ballad Of 'A Man Called Horse'/The Morning Of The Mourning Of Another Kennedy . . . 5
68 RCA Victor RD/SF 7947 A TRAMP SHINING (LP) . . . 15
68 Stateside (S)SL 5001 THE YARD WENT ON FOREVER (LP) . . . 15
70 Stateside SSL 5019 A TRAMP SHINING (LP, reissue) . . . 12

MINT VALUE £

ROLF HARRIS

60	Columbia DB 4483	Tie Me Kangaroo Down, Sport/Nick Teen And Al K. Hall	6
60	Columbia DB 4556	Tame Eagle/Uncomfortable Yogi	6
62	Columbia DB 4888	Sun Arise/Someone's Pinched Me Winkles	5
63	Columbia DB 4979	Johnny Day/In The Wet	5
64	Columbia DB 7349	Ringo For President/Head Hunter	7
65	Columbia DB 7669	War Canoe/Linda	5
66	Columbia DB 8014	Hev Yew Gotta Loight Boy/Animals Pop Party	5
68	Columbia DB 8475	Have A Beer/The Bloke Who Invented Beer	5
69	Columbia DB 8553	Bluer Than Blue/The Monster	6
66	Columbia SEG 8531	ROLF HARRIS FAVOURITES (EP)	10
63	Columbia S(C)X 1507	SUN ARISE (LP, mono/stereo)	16/20

RONNIE HARRIS (& CORONETS)

54	Columbia SCM 5138	Hold My Hand/No One Can Change Destiny	10
54	Columbia SCM 5139	I Love Paris/I Still Believe	10
55	Columbia SCM 5159	Don't Go To Strangers/Surprisingly (as Ronnie Harris & Coronets)	10
55	Columbia SCM 5176	Stranger In Paradise/I Wonder	10
56	Columbia SCM 5242	I've Changed My Mind A Thousand Times/Come To Me (with Coronets)	10
56	Columbia DB 3836	That's Right/A House With Love In It	12
57	Columbia DB 3877	Armen's Theme (Yesterday And You)/Dancing Chandelier	5
57	Columbia DB 3934	Dear To Me/It's Not For Me To Say (B-side with Russ Conway)	5

(see also Coronets, Ruby Murray, Ray Burns, Russ Conway)

ROY HARRIS

72	Topic 12TS 217	THE BITTER AND THE SWEET (LP, blue label)	15
75	Topic 12TS 256	CHAMPIONS OF FOLLY (LP)	20

SHAKEY JAKE HARRIS

69	Liberty LBS 83217	FURTHER ON UP THE ROAD (LP)	35
73	Polydor 2391 015	THE DEVIL'S HARMONICA (LP)	25

SUE HARRIS

78	Free Reed FRR 020	HAMMERS AND TONGUES (LP)	12

THURSTON HARRIS (& SHARPS)

57	Vogue V 9092	Little Bitty Pretty One/I Hope You Won't Hold It Against Me (with Sharps)	160
57	Vogue V 9092	Little Bitty Pretty One/I Hope You Won't Hold It Against Me (with Sharps) (78)	60
58	Vogue V 9098	Do What You Did/I'm Asking Forgiveness (as Thurston Harris & Sharps)	275
58	Vogue V 9098	Do What You Did/I'm Asking Forgiveness (78)	70
58	Vogue V 9108	Be Baba Leba/I'm Out To Getcha	300
58	Vogue V 9108	Be Baba Leba/I'm Out To Getcha (78)	65
58	Vogue V 9122	Smokey Joe's/Only One Love Is Blessed	170
58	Vogue V 9122	Smokey Joe's/Only One Love Is Blessed (78)	65
58	Vogue V 9127	Tears From My Heart/Over Somebody Else's Shoulder	130
58	Vogue V 9127	Tears From My Heart/Over Somebody Else's Shoulder (78)	100
59	Vogue V 9139	Purple Stew (as Thurston Harris & Masters)/I Hear A Rhapsody	140
59	Vogue V 9139	Purple Stew (as Thurston Harris & Masters)/I Hear A Rhapsody (78)	100
59	Vogue V 9144	You Don't Know How Much I Love You/In The Bottom Of My Heart	130
59	Vogue V 9144	You Don't Know How Much I Love You/In The Bottom Of My Heart (78)	100
59	Vogue V 9146	Hey Little Girl/My Love Will Last	160
59	Vogue V 9146	Hey Little Girl/My Love Will Last (78)	100
59	Vogue V 9149	Runk Bunk/Bless Your Heart	210
59	Vogue V 9149	Runk Bunk/Bless Your Heart (78)	110
59	Vogue V 9151	Slip-Slop/Paradise Hill	200
59	Vogue V 9151	Slip-Slop/Paradise Hill (78)	120
66	Sue WI 4016	Little Bitty Pretty One/I Hope You Won't Hold It Against Me (reissue)	30

(see also Sharps)

WEE WILLIE HARRIS

57	Decca F 10970	Rockin' At The Two 'I's/Back To School Again	35
57	Decca F 10970	Rockin' At The Two 'I's/Back To School Again (78)	25
58	Decca F 10980	Love Bug Crawl/Rosie Lee	40
58	Decca F 10980	Love Bug Crawl/Rosie Lee (78)	25
58	Decca F 11044	Got A Match/No Chemise, Please!	40
58	Decca F 11044	Got A Match/No Chemise, Please! (78)	25
60	Decca F 11217	Wild One/Little Bitty Girl	18
63	HMV POP 1198	You Must Be Joking/Better To Have Loved	10
66	Parlophone R 5504	Someone's In The Kitchen With Diana/Walk With Peter And Paul (some A-sides list 'Dina')	10
66	Polydor 56140	Listen To The River Roll Along/Try Moving Baby (writing in black or white)	10
74	Decca F 13516	Together/Rock'n'Roll Jamboree	5
58	Decca DFE 6465	ROCKING WITH WEE WILLIE (EP)	160

WYNONIE 'MR BLUES' HARRIS

51	Vogue V 2006	All She Wants To Do Is Rock/Drinkin' Wine Spo-Dee-O-Dee (78)	25
52	Vogue V 2111	Luscious Woman/Lovin' Machine (78)	35
52	Vogue V 2127	Bloodshot Eyes/Lollipop Mama (78)	20
52	Vogue V 2128	Just Like Two Drops Of Water/Good Mornin' Judge (78)	35
52	Vogue V 2133	Night Train/Do It Again Please (78)	30
52	Vogue V 2134	Rock, Mr. Blues/Put It Back (78)	30
52	Vogue V 2144	Teardrops From My Eyes/Keep On Churnin' (Till The Butter Comes) (78)	35
52	Vogue V 2166	I Like My Baby's Pudding/Adam Come And Get Your Rib (78)	30
56	Vogue V 2127	Bloodshot Eyes/Lollipop Mama (triangular centre)	125
56	Vogue V 2127	Bloodshot Eyes/Lollipop Mama (round centre)	75
56	Vogue EPV 1103	WYNONIE 'MISTER BLUES' HARRIS (EP)	175
61	Blue Beat BBEP 301	BATTLE OF THE BLUES (EP)	90

WYNONIE HARRIS/EDDIE 'CLEANHEAD' VINSON

72	Polydor 2343 048	JUMP BLUES (LP)	20

(see also Tiny Bradshaw/Wynonie Harris, Eddie 'Cleanhead' Vinson)

MINT VALUE £

HARRIS SISTERS

55 Capitol CL 14232 — Kissin' Bug/We've Been Walkin' All Night . . . 20
55 Capitol CL 14232 — Kissin' Bug/We've Been Walkin' All Night (78) . . . 12

DANNY HARRISON

62 Starlite ST45 77 — No One To Love Me/All The World is Lonely . . . 7
62 Starlite ST45 91 — Broken Love Affair/Have I Wasted My Life . . . 7
63 Starlite ST45 108 — Have You Ever Been Lonely/Mary Ann I'm Lonesome . . . 7
65 Coral Q 72479 — Speak Of The Devil/I'm A Rollin' Stone . . . 15
62 Starlite STEP 23 — INTRODUCING DANNY HARRISON (EP) . . . 22

EARL HARRISON

67 London HL 10121 — Humphrey Stomp/Can You Forgive Me . . . 45

GEORGE HARRISON

SINGLES

71 Apple R 5884 — My Sweet Lord/What Is Life (colour 'head' p/s) . . . 12
71 Apple R 5912 — Bangla-Desh/Deep Blue (some with p/s [beware of new-looking counterfeits!]) 75/5
74 Apple R 6002 — Ding Dong, Ding Dong/I Don't Care Anymore (no p/s) . . . 5
75 Apple R 6001 — Dark Horse/I Don't Care Anymore (unissued)
75 Apple R 6001 — Dark Horse/Hari's On Tour (Express) . . . 12
75 Apple R 6007 — You/World Of Stone (p/s) . . . 8
76 Apple R 6012 — This Guitar (Can't Keep From Crying)/Maya Love (no p/s) . . . 20
76 Apple R 5884 — My Sweet Lord/What Is Life (reissue, black & white 'gnome' p/s) . . . 15
76 Dark Horse K 16856 — This Song/Learning How To Love You (issued with U.S. p/s) . . . 10
77 Dark Horse K 16896 — True Love/Pure Smokey (no p/s) . . . 5
77 Dark Horse K 16967 — It's What You Value/Woman Don't You Cry For Me (no p/s) . . . 5
79 Dark Horse K 17327 — Blow Away/Soft Touch (p/s) . . . 5
79 Dark Horse K 17284 — Love Comes To Everyone/Soft Hearted Hana . . . 8
79 Dark Horse K 17423 — Faster/Your Love Is Forever (with charity stickered plain white die-cut sleeve) . . 15
79 Dark Horse K 17423 — Faster/Your Love Is Forever (picture disc, stickered PVC sleeve with insert) . . . 35
81 Dark Horse K 17807M — All Those Years Ago/Writings On The Wall (cassette) . . . 10
81 Dark Horse K 17837DJ — Teardrops (Edited Version)/Save The World (DJ promo only, no p/s) . . . 25
81 Dark Horse K 17837 — Teardrops/Save The World (p/s) . . . 10
82 Dark Horse 929 864-7 — Wake Up My Love/Greece (p/s) . . . 8
86 Ganga Publishing B.V. — Shanghai Surprise (with Vicki Brown) (unreleased, 1-sided promo only; no catalogue number, matrix: SHANGHAI 1) . . . 350
87 Dark Horse W 8178 — Got My Mind Set On You/Lay His Head (p/s, green label) . . . 8
87 Dark Horse W 8178B — Got My Mind Set On You/Lay His Head (box set with 2 postcards) . . . 20
87 Dark Horse W 8178T — Got My Mind Set On You (Extended Version)/Got My Mind Set On You (Single Version)/Lay His Head (12", p/s with poster) . . . 20
87 Dark Horse W 8178TP — Got My Mind Set On You (Extended Version)/Got My Mind Set On You (Single Version)/Lay His Head (12", picture disc) . . . 20
88 Dark Horse W 8131B — When We Was Fab/Zig Zag (box set with fold-out poster & cut-out) . . . 10
88 Dark Horse W 8131T — When We Was Fab (Unextended Version)/Zig Zag/That's The Way It Goes/ When We Was Fab (Reverse End) (12", p/s) . . . 12
88 Dark Horse W 8131TP — When We Was Fab (Unextended Version)/Zig Zag/That's The Way It Goes (Remix)/When We Was Fab (Reverse End) (12", picture disc) . . . 20
88 Dark Horse W 8131CD — When We Was Fab (Unextended Version)/Zig Zag/That's The Way It Goes (Remix)/When We Was Fab (Reverse End) (3" CD with 5" adaptor, 5" case) . . . 12
88 Dark Horse W 7913 — This Is Love/Breath Away From Heaven (p/s) . . . 8
88 Dark Horse W 7913T — This Is Love/Breath Away From Heaven/All Those Years Ago (12", p/s) . . . 15
88 Dark Horse W 7913CD — This Is Love/Breath Away From Heaven/All Those Years Ago/Hong Kong Blues (3" CD with adaptor, 5" case) . . . 12
89 Dark Horse W 2696 — Cheer Down/That's What It Takes (p/s) . . . 8
89 Dark Horse W 2696T — Cheer Down/That's What It Takes/Crackerbox Palace (12", p/s) . . . 15
89 Dark Horse W 2696CD — Cheer Down/That's What It Takes/Crackerbox Palace (3" CD, gatefold card sleeve) . . . 20
88 Genesis SGH 777 — SONGS BY GEORGE HARRISON (Limited Edition) (EP, 33rpm, issued with limited edition book Songs By George Harrison) . . . 650
88 Genesis SGHCD 777 — SONGS BY GEORGE HARRISON (CD EP, issued with limited edition book) . . . 625
92 Genesis SGH 778 — SONGS BY GEORGE HARRISON VOL. 2 (EP, with limited edition book *Songs By George Harrison Vol. 2*) . . . 375
92 Genesis SGHCD 778 — SONGS BY GEORGE HARRISON VOL. 2 (CD EP, with limited edition book) . . . 350

LPs

68 Apple (S)APCOR 1 — WONDERWALL MUSIC (soundtrack; with insert, black inner sleeve, mono/stereo) . . . 125/60
69 Zapple ZAPPLE 02 — ELECTRONIC SOUND (with inner sleeve) . . . 90
71 Apple STCH 639 — ALL THINGS MUST PASS (3-LP box set with poster & lyric inner sleeves; initial batch in U.K. box, later in U.S. box) . . . 35/25
72 Apple STCX 3385 — THE CONCERT FOR BANGLA DESH (3-LP box set, with booklet, featuring Bob Dylan) . . . 25
73 Apple PAS 10006 — LIVING IN THE MATERIAL WORLD (gatefold sleeve with inner) . . . 18
92 Apple SAPCOR 1 — WONDERWALL MUSIC (reissue, gatefold sleeve with inner sleeve) . . . 20
96 Zapple ZAPPLE 02 — ELECTRONIC SOUND (reissue, with inner sleeve . . . 20
01 Parlophone 5304741 — ALL THINGS MUST PASS (3-LP, reissue) . . . 20

CDs

87 Dark Horse 9256432 — CLOUD NINE . . . 20
87 Parlophone CDS 7466888 — ALL THINGS MUST PASS (2-CD, some without Apple logo) . . . 30/18
89 Dark Horse K 9257262 — THE BEST OF DARK HORSE 1976-1989 . . . 30
92 Dark Horse 7599269642 — LIVE IN JAPAN (2-CD) . . . 30

(see also Beatles, Traveling Wilburys, Billy Connolly & Chris Tummings, Sylvia Griffin)

KATHLEEN HARRISON

66 Columbia DB 7871 — Mrs. Thursday/Call Round Any Old Time . . . 7

MIKE HARRISON

71 Island ILPS 9170 — MIKE HARRISON (LP) . . . 15
72 Island ILPS 9209 — SMOKESTACK LIGHTNING (LP) . . . 15

(see also Spirit)

MINT VALUE £

NEIL HARRISON
74 Deram SML 1115 ALL DRESSED UP AND NOWHERE TO GO (LP) 15
(see also Driftwood)

NOEL HARRISON
65 Decca F 12001 Trees/To Ramona 7
66 Decca F 12314 A Young Girl Of Sixteen/Tomorrow Is My Turn 6
66 Decca F 12345 It's All Over Now Baby Blue/Much As I Love You 6
67 Reprise RS 20615 Suzanne/Life Is A Dream 7
68 Reprise RS 20758 Windmills Of Your Mind/Leitch On The Beach 8
69 Decca F 12918 Love Minus Zero/Just Can't Wait 6
57 HMV 7EG 8383 NOEL HARRISON (EP) 18
65 Decca DFE 8616 NOEL HARRISON (EP) 12
65 Decca DFE 8639 TO RAMONA (EP) 15
60 Philips BBL 7399 AT THE BLUE ANGEL (LP) 22
69 Reprise RSLP 6321 THE GREAT ELECTRIC EXPERIMENT IS OVER (LP) 18

REGGIE HARRISON
63 Cameo Parkway P 863 A Lonely Piano/HIPPIES: Memory Lane 20

WILBERT HARRISON
59 Top Rank JAR 132 Kansas City/Listen My Darling 20
59 Top Rank JAR 132 Kansas City/Listen My Darling (78) 25
62 Island WI 031 I'm Broke/Off To School 18
65 Sue WI 363 Let's Stick Together/Kansas City Twist 22
70 London HL 10307 Let's Work Together/Stagger Lee 12
73 Action ACT 4613 Get It While You Can/Amen 8
70 London HA/SH 8415 LET'S WORK TOGETHER (LP) 45

WILBERT HARRISON/BABY WASHINGTON
71 Joy JOYS 191 BATTLE OF THE GIANTS (LP, 1 side each) 18
(see also Baby Washington)

YVONNE HARRISON
67 Caltone TONE 102 The Chase/Take My Hand 15

DEBBIE/DEBORAH HARRY
89 Chrysalis CHSCD 3369 I Want That Man (12 Inch Remix)/(7" Version)/(Instrumental)/Bike Boy (CD) 8
89 Chrysalis CHSCD 3452 Brite Side/In Love With Love/Bugeye (CD) 8
89 Chrysalis CHSCCD 3452 Brite Side (Remix)/French Kissin' In The USA/In Love With Love/Bugeye (CD) 8
93 Chrysalis TC-CHS 4900 I Can See Clearly/Standing In My Way (B-side with Joey Ramone) (cassette) 7
99 Chrysalis CDMAN 2000 I Want That Man (radio edit)/(Almighty Definitive Mix)/D-Bop Vocal Mix (CD, card p/s, promo only) 15
(see also Wind In The Willows, Blondie, New York Blondes)

HARRY & RADCLIFFE
69 Camel CA 26 History/Just Be Alone 8
69 Punch PH 8 History/Just Be Alone 6

HARRY J. ALL STARS
69 Harry J. TR 675 Liquidator/GLEN & DAVE: La La Always Stay (green or white label) 10/8
70 Harry J. HJ 6601 The Big Three/Lavender (B-side actually "Lavender Blue" by Lloyd Robinson) 10
70 Harry J. HJ 6608 Reach For The Sky/Interrogator 10
70 Harry J. HJ 6621 Return Of The Liquidator (actually "Tons Of Gold" by Val Bennett)/All Day 15
72 Harry J. HJ 6641 Down Side Up/Down Side Up — Version 10
73 Explosion EX 2073 Chirpy Chirpy Cheep Cheep/Chirpy Chirpy (Instrumental) 10
73 Blue Mountain BM 1028 U.F.O./Reggae With The Birds 8
70 Trojan TBL 104 THE LIQUIDATOR (LP) 25
(see also Jay Boys, Bob Andy, John Holt, Lizzy)

HARSH REALITY
68 Philips PB 1710 Tobacco Ash Sunday/How Do You Feel 12
69 Philips PB 1769 Heaven And Hell/Praying For Reprieve 18
69 Philips (S)BL 7891 HEAVEN AND HELL (LP, gatefold sleeve) 95

CAJUN HART
69 Warner Bros WB 7258 Got To Find A Way/Lover's Prayer 150

DERRY HART & HARTBEATS
59 Decca F 11138 Come On Baby/Nowhere In This World 20
59 Decca F 11138 Come On Baby/Nowhere In This World (78) 15

MICKEY HART
73 Warner Bros. K 46182 ROLLING THUNDER (LP) 22
(see also Grateful Dead, Diga Rhythm Band)

MIKE HART
70 Dandelion S 4781 Yawney Morning Song/Almost Liverpool 8 7
74 Deram DM 409 Son Son/Bad News Man 6
70 Dandelion 63756 MIKE HART BLEEDS (LP) 25
72 Dandelion 2310 211 BASHER, CHALKY, PONGO AND ME (LP, as Mike Hart & Comrades) 35
(see also Clayton Squares, Liverpool Scene)

TIM HART
79 Chrysalis CHR 2335 Overseas/Hillman Avenger (p/s) 7
79 Chrysalis CHR 1218 TIM HART (LP) 12
(see also Steeleye Span)

TIM HART & MADDY PRIOR
68 Tepee TPRM 104 FOLK SONGS OF OLDE ENGLAND VOL. 1 (LP, gatefold sleeve) 65
69 Tepee TPRM 105 FOLK SONGS OF OLDE ENGLAND VOL. 2 (LP, gatefold sleeve) 65
69 Ad-Rhythm ARPS 3 FOLK SONGS OF OLDE ENGLAND VOL. 1 (LP, reissue) 30

MINT VALUE £

69	Ad-Rhythm ARPS 4	FOLK SONGS OF OLD ENGLAND VOL. 2 (LP, reissue)	30
71	Charisma CAS 1035	SUMMER SOLSTICE (LP, gatefold sleeve)	20
76	Mooncrest CREST 12	SUMMER SOLSTICE (LP, reissue, gatefold or single sleeve)	16/12

(see also Steeleye Span, Maddy Prior, Silly Sisters)

FRANK HARTE

67	Topic 12T 172	DUBLIN STREET SONGS (LP)	18
73	Topic 12T 218	THROUGH DUBLIN CITY (LP)	12

KEEF HARTLEY (BAND)

69	Deram DM 250	Leave It 'Till The Morning/Just To Cry	12
69	Deram DM 273	Waiting Around/Not Foolish, Not Wise	12
70	Deram DM 316	Roundabout (Parts 1 & 2)	10
73	Deram DM 380	Dance To The Music/You And Me	8
69	Deram DML/SML 1037	HALFBREED (LP, gatefold sleeve, 1st pressing has 'mono/stereo' holes on rear sleeve)	30
69	Deram DML/SML 1054	THE BATTLE OF N.W.6 (LP, gatefold sleeve, 1st pressing has 'mono/stereo' holes on rear sleeve)	25
70	Deram SML 1071	THE TIME IS NEAR (LP, with booklet, some in laminated sleeve)	35/25
71	Deram SDL 2	OVERDOG (LP, gatefold sleeve)	25
71	Deram SDL 4	LITTLE BIG BAND (LP, gatefold sleeve)	25
72	Deram SDL 9	SEVENTY SECOND BRAVE (LP, gatefold sleeve)	25
73	Deram SDL 13	LANCASHIRE HUSTLER (LP, gatefold sleeve)	25
74	Deram DPA 3011/2	THE BEST OF (2-LP, gatefold sleeve)	20
70s	Deram SDN 30251/2	THE BATTLE OF N.W.6/THE TIME IS NEAR (2-LP, gatefold sleeve)	20

(see also Rory Storm & Hurricanes, Artwoods, John Mayall's Bluesbreakers, Miller Anderson, Dog Soldier, Henry Lowther, Wynder K. Frog)

HARVESTERS

78	SRT/CUS/135	TWELVE YEARS ON (LP)	12
80	private pressing	A COLLECTOR'S ITEM (LP)	12

HARVEY (Fuqua) & MOONGLOWS

58	London HLM 8730	Ten Commandments Of Love/Mean Old Blues	275
58	London HLM 8730	Ten Commandments Of Love/Mean Old Blues (78)	80

(see also Moonglows, Etta & Harvey)

HARVEY BOYS

57	London HLA 8397	Nothing Is Too Good For You/Marina Girl	50
57	London HLA 8397	Nothing Is Too Good For You/Marina Girl (78)	15

(SENSATIONAL) ALEX HARVEY (BAND)

64	Polydor NH 52264	I Just Wanna Make Love To You/Let The Good Times Roll	30
64	Polydor NH 52907	Got My Mojo Working/I Ain't Worried Baby (as Alex Harvey & His Soul Band)	55
65	Polydor BM 56017	Ain't That Just Too Bad/My Kind Of Love (as Alex Harvey & His Soul Band)	45
65	Fontana TF 610	Agent 00 Soul/Go Away Baby	30
66	Fontana TF 764	Work Song/I Can Do Without Your Love	25
67	Decca F 12640	The Sunday Song/Horizon's	35
67	Decca F 12660	Maybe Some Day/Curtains For My Baby	40
69	Fontana TF 1063	Midnight Moses/Roman Wall Blues	25
72	Vertigo 6059 070	There's No Lights On The Christmas Tree Mother, (They're Burning Big Louie Tonight)/Harp	5
73	Vertigo 6059 075	Jungle Jenny/Buff's Bar Blues (as The Sensational Alex Harvey Band)	5
74	Vertigo 6059 098	The Faith Healer (Edit)/St. Anthony (as The Sensational Alex Harvey Band)	5
75	Vertigo ALEX 001	Delilah (live)/Soul In Chains (live) (p/s, as The Sensational Alex Harvey Band)	6
75	Vertigo ALEX 002	Gamblin' Bar Room Blues/Shake That Thing (p/s, as The Sensational Alex Harvey Band)	6
77	Mountain TOP 32	Mrs Blackhouse/Engine Room Boogie (p/s, as The Sensational Alex Harvey Band)	6
79	RCA PB 5199	Shakin' All Over/Wake Up Davis (p/s, as Alex Harvey - The New Band)	5
64	Polydor LPHM 46424	ALEX HARVEY AND HIS SOUL BAND (LP)	120
64	Polydor LPHM 46441	THE BLUES (LP)	150
69	Fontana (S)TL 5534	ROMAN WALL BLUES (LP)	160
73	Vertigo 6360 081	FRAMED (LP, as The Sensational Alex Harvey Band, gatefold sleeve, swirl label, later spaceship label)	130/30
73	Vertigo 6360 103	NEXT (LP, as The Sensational Alex Harvey Band, spaceship label)	12
77	K-Tel NE 984	ALEX HARVEY PRESENTS THE LOCH NESS MONSTER (LP, withdrawn, gatefold stickered sleeve, with 16-page 'descriptive diary')	40
79	RCA PL 25257	THE MAFIA STOLE MY GUITAR (LP, as Alex Harvey - The New Band)	12
83	Power Supply AMP 2	THE SOLDIER ON THE WALL (LP)	15
84	Samurai SAH 117PD	S.A.H.B. LIVE (LP, reissue, picture disc)	12

(see also Tear Gas, Hairband, Rock Workshop, Nazareth, Michael Schenker Group, Tandoori Cassette)

FREDERIC HARVEY

60s	HMV 7EG 8847	SINGS WEST COUNTRY SONGS (EP)	10

JANCIS HARVEY

73	Pilgrim King KLPS 47	DISTANCE OF DOORS (LP)	70
74	Westwood WRS 038	JANCIS HARVEY (LP)	90
75	Westwood WRS 054	TIME WAS NOW (LP)	90
76	Westwood WRS 107	A PORTRAIT OF JANCIS HARVEY (LP)	70
79	Westwood WRS 144	FROM THE DARKNESS CAME LIGHT (LP)	60

JANE HARVEY

60	Pye International 7N 25046	I'm Gonna Go Fishin'/Hundred Dreams From Now	6

LANCE HARVEY & KINGPINS

64	Pye 7N 15647	He's Telling You Lies/How Do You Fix A Broken Heart	7
64	Lyntone LYN 509	SINCE YOU WALKED OUT ON ME (Keele Rag flexidisc EP, with The Escorts)	15

MINT VALUE £

PETER HARVEY

62	Columbia DB 4873	Rainin' In My Heart/Please Don't Tell Joe	8
63	Columbia DB 7030	Wishing You The Best Of Luck My Friend/Lovin' Can Be Lonesome	6
64	Columbia DB 7192	Heart Of Ice/Trace Of A Heartache	6
64	Columbia DB 7331	Big Man In A Big House/Date With A Heartache	6

P.J. HARVEY

91	Too Pure PURE 5	Dress/Water (demo)/Dry (demo) (12")	25
92	Too Pure PURECD 5	Dress/Water (demo)/Dry (demo) (CD)	25
92	Too Pure PURES 8	Sheela-Na-Gig/Joe (p/s, 400 only)	50
92	Too Pure PURE 8	Sheela-Na-Gig/Hair (demo)/Joe (demo) (12", p/s)	22
92	Too Pure PURECD 8	Sheela-Na-Gig/Hair (demo)/Joe (demo) (CD)	25
93	Island 12IS 538	50 Ft Queenie/Mansize (demo)/Hook (demo)/Reeling (12", p/s)	15
93	Island 12IS 569	Mansize/Wang Dang Doodle/Daddy (12", p/s)	10
93	Island CID 569	Mansize/Wang Dang Doodle/Daddy (CD)	10
95	Island IS 607	Down By the Water/Lying In The Sun/Somebody's Down Somebody's Name (p/s)	7
95	Island CID 607	Down By The Water/Living In The Sun/Somebody's Down Somebody's Name (CD)	10
95	Island 12IS 614	C'Mon Billy/Darling Be There/Maniac (12", p/s)	10
95	Island IS 610	Send His Love To Me/Long Time Coming (Evening Session) (7" picture disc in 12" poster p/s)	12
95	Island CID 610	Send His Love To Me/Long Time Coming (Evening Session)/Harder (CD, with postcards in envelope pack)	10
98	Island IS 718	A Perfect Day Elise/Sweeter Than Anything/Instrumental #3 (p/s)	8
99	Island IS 730	The Wind/Nina In Ecstasy 2/Rebecca (p/s)	8
00	Island IS 769	Good Fortune/66 Promises (p/s)	8
92	Too Pure PURE(D) 10	DRY (LP, 1st 5,000 with bonus LP, "Demonstrations", inner sleeve and no'd sticker)	80/20
92	Too Pure PUREDCD 10	DRY (CD, 1st 5,000 with additional "Demonstrations" LP tracks)	80
95	Island 524-178 2	THE B-SIDES CD (picture disc CD, 2,000 only, digipak)	25
95	Island CIDZ 8035	TO BRING YOU MY LOVE & THE B-SIDES CD (2-CD)	35
99	Island DESIRE CD1	IS THIS DESIRE? (CD, interview disc, slimline case, promo only)	25

(see also Automatic Dlamini, Family Cat, Grape, John Parish & Polly Jean Harvey)

RICHARD HARVEY

83	Anderburr HX 1010	Theme From Terrahawks (3.00)/Variations On The Theme (3.17) (p/s)	5
83	Anderburr HX 21010	Theme From Terrahawks (4.50)/Variations On The Theme (7.25) (12", p/s with poster)	8
75	Transatlantic TRA 292	DIVISIONS ON A GROUND (LP)	25
79	ICL 001	A NEW WAY OF SEEING (LP, private pressing)	15

(see also Gryphon, Barry Gray)

TINA HARVEY

73	UK UK 24	Nowhere To Run/Tina's Second Song	50

HARVEY'S PEOPLE

69	Galliard GAL 4001	LOVING AND LIVING (LP)	15

CHRISTINE HARWOOD

70	Birth RAB 1	NICE TO MEET MISS CHRISTINE (LP)	45

GORDON HASKELL

69	CBS 4509	Boat Trip/Time Only Knows	12
70	CBS 4795	Oo-La-Di-Doo-Da-Day/Born To Be Together	12
69	CBS 63741	SAILIN' MY BOAT (LP)	90
72	Atlantic K 40311	IT IS AND IT ISN'T (LP, with lyric insert)	15
73	RCA	SERVE AT ROOM TEMPERATURE (LP, unissued)	200

(see also Fleur-De-Lys, Cupid's Inspiration, Flowerpot Men, King Crimson)

JACK HASKELL (& HONEY-DREAMERS)

57	London HL 8426	Around The World/Away Out West	25
58	Oriole CB 1442	The Night Of The Senior Prom/Hungry For Love (with Honey-Dreamers)	7

MICHAEL HASLAM

65	Parlophone R 5267	There Goes The Forgotten Man/My Heart Won't Say Goodbye	6

JOE HASSELVANDER

85	Pentagram DEVIL 3	LADY KILLER (LP)	15

HASSLES

67	United Artists UP 1199	You Got Me Hummin'/I'm Thinkin'	18

(see also Billy Joel)

HASTINGS OF MALAWI

81	Papal 003	VIBRANT STAPLER OBSCURES CHARACTERISTIC GROWTH (LP, red vinyl)	12

(see also Nurse With Wound)

HAT & TIE

66	President PT 105	Chance For Romance/California Jazz Club U.S.A.	15
67	President PT 122	Bread To Spend/Finding It Rough (demos credit A-side as "Bread")	100

(see also Patrick Campbell-Lyons, Nirvana [U.K.])

TONY HATCH ORCHESTRA

59	Top Rank JAR 107	Chick/Side Saddle	5
59	Top Rank JAR 107	Chick/Side Saddle (78)	7
59	Top Rank JAR 165	Rhoom Ba-Cha/Stetson	5
59	Top Rank JAR 165	Rhoom Ba-Cha/Stetson (78)	9
61	Pye International 7N 25085	Rocking Waltz/Devil's Herd	6
61	Pye International 7N 25068	Tim Frazer's Theme/Girls Of Copenhagen	6
61	Pye 7N 15408	The Ghost Squad/What's That All About	5
62	Pye 7N 15434	Ben Casey Theme/Perry Mason Theme	6
62	Pye 7N 15460	Out Of This World Theme/Cyril's Tune (some in p/s)	10/5
62	Pye 7N 15494	Theme From The Dick Powell Show/Sharon	5

MINT VALUE £

65 Pye 7N 15754 Crossroads Theme/The Marie Celeste (some in p/s) 12/7
65 Pye 7N15972 Man Alive/Crosstown Commuter 8
66 Pye 7N 17169 Crossroads Theme/Round Every Corner (some in p/s) 12/7
67 Pye 7N 17263 Comedy Tonight/You're Lovely 10
69 Pye 7N 17814 Theme From Who-Dun-It/The Champions 35
69 Pye 7N 17864 The Doctors — Theme/Love Song 6
73 Pye 7N 45210 Memories Of Summer/Best In Football 10
74 Pye 7N 45326 The World At War/Sportsnight 5
78 EMI EMI 2780 Sweeney 2/Regan's Key 20
83 Tube TUBE 003 Airline/The Hifi 6
65 Pye NPL/NSPL 18124 THE TONY HATCH SOUND (LP) 18
67 Pye NSPL 18164 A LATIN HAPPENING (LP) 12
67 Pye NSPL 18176 BEAUTIFUL IN THE RAIN (LP) 15
67 Marble Arch MALS 767 DOWNTOWN (LP) 12
68 Pye NSPL 18217 THE COOL LATIN SOUND (LP) 12
74 Pye NSPL 41029 HIT THE ROAD TO THEMELAND (LP) 15

TONY HATCH & CHERRY CHILDREN

70 Pye 7N 17912 Yoko/Bahama Sound 5

GEORGE HATCHER BAND

77 United Artists UP 36233 Black Moon Rising/Find A New Lover (p/s) 7
76 United Artists UAG 29997 DRY RUN (LP, gatefold sleeve) 12
77 United Artists EXP 100 HAVE BAND WILL TRAVEL (10" EP) 10
77 United Artists UAS 30090 TALKIN' TURKEY (LP) 12
(see also Budgie)

HATE

70 Famous SFMA 5752 HATE KILLS (LP) 40

BOBBY HATFIELD

68 Verve VS 570 Hang-Ups/Soul Cafe 8
68 Verve VS 576 Only You/The Wonder Of You 8
72 Warner Bros K 16163 Oo-Wee-Baby, I Love You/Rock'n'Roll Woman 12
(see also Righteous Brothers, Ringo Starr)

HATFIELD & THE NORTH

74 Virgin VS 116 Let's Eat (Real Soon)/Fitter Stoke Has A Bath 8
74 Virgin V 2008 HATFIELD AND THE NORTH (LP, gatefold sleeve) 25
75 Virgin V 2030 THE ROTTER'S CLUB (LP) 20
79 Virgin VR 5 AFTERS (LP, withdrawn) 40
(see also Matching Mole, Egg, Khan, Camel, National Health, Caravan)

DONNY HATHAWAY

70 Atco 226 010 The Ghetto (Parts 1 & 2) 5
72 Atlantic K 10193 The Ghetto (Parts 1 & 2)/Little Ghetto Boy 5
73 Atlantic K 10354 Love Love Love/Someday We'll Be Free 5
71 Atco 2465 019 EVERYTHING IS EVERYTHING (LP) 15
71 Atlantic 2400 143 DONNY HATHAWAY (LP) 15
72 Atco K 40063 EVERYTHING IS EVERYTHING (LP, reissue) 12
72 Atlantic K 40241 DONNY HATHAWAY (LP, reissue) 12
72 Atlantic K 40369 LIVE (LP) 15
73 Atlantic K 40487 EXTENSION OF A MAN (LP) 15
(see also Roberta Flack)

FAY HAUSER

75 Philips 6006 489 You Bring The Sun In The Morning/(Pt. 2) 5

HATS

70s Deadly Boring HAT 001 No Time Is A Good Time/Living On The Roof (p/s, with lyric insert) 5

ALAN HAVEN

64 United Artists UP 1057 Theme From "A Jolly Bad Fellow"/Jee B'ees (with John Barry) 12
65 Fontana TF 542 Image/Romance On The North Sea 8
65 Fontana TF 590 The Knack/Satin Doll (with John Barry) 12
66 Fontana TF 658 Flamingo/Shangri-La 6
67 Fontana TF 835 Image/Romance Of The North Sea (reissue) 8

RICHIE HAVENS

69 Big T BIG 119 Oxford Town/My Own Way 5
69 Verve VS 1512 Three Day Eternity/No Opportunity Necessary No Experience Needed 5
69 Verve VS 1519 Lady Madonna/Indian Rope Man 6
70 Verve VS 1521 Rocky Raccoon/Stop Pulling And Pushing Me 5
70 Verve VS 1523 There's A Hole In The Future/Minstrel From Gault 5
70 Verve VS 1524 Handsome Johnny/Sandie 5
72 Verve 2121 117 Freedom/Handsome Journey 5
68 Verve (S)VLP 6005 SOMETHIN' ELSE AGAIN (LP) 15
68 Verve (S)VLP 6008 MIXED BAG (LP) 15
69 Verve (S)VLP 6014 1983 (LP) 15
69 Verve (S)VLP 6021 STONEHENGE (LP) 15
69 Transatlantic TRA 187 ELECTRIC HAVENS (LP) 12
69 Transatlantic TRA 199 THE RICHIE HAVENS RECORD (LP) 12
71 Verve 2310 080 ALARM CLOCK (LP) 12
71 Verve 2304 050 STATE OF MIND (LP) 12
72 Polydor 2480 049 GREAT BLIND DEGREE (LP) 12

HAVENSTREET

76 Rissole (no cat. no.) THE END OF THE LINE (LP, private pressing with booklet) 75

PAT HAWES with DAVE CAREY'S RHYTHM

56 Tempo A 141 Snowy Morning Blues/Sheik Of Araby 6
56 Tempo LAP 9 PAT HAWES (10" LP) 18

GRAHAM HAWK & OWEN GRAY

72 Pama Supreme PS 360 — Amazing Grace/SKETTO RICH: Don't Stay Out Late . . . 6

HAWK & CO.

81 Epic EPC A 1735 — Nite Life/Nite Life (Version) . . . 5
82 Epic EPC A 2223 — Livin' For The Good Times/Sweet Talker . . . 5
(see also Shadows)

TOMMY HAWKE

60 Top Rank JAR 348 — Good Gravy (I'm In Love Again)/Umpteen Years (And A Million Tears) . . . 18

CHIP HAWKES

77 RCA PL 25044 — NASHVILLE ALBUM (LP) . . . 12
(see Tremeloes)

HAWKEYES

57 Capitol CL 14764 — Someone Someday/Who Is He? . . . 20

BUDDY BOY HAWKINS/WILLIAM MOORE

50s Heritage RE 102 — BUDDY BOY HAWKINS/WILLIAM MOORE (EP) . . . 50
(see also Blind Lemon Jefferson)

CAROL HAWKINS

73 Polydor 2058 387 — Listen/All For One . . . 8

COLEMAN HAWKINS

55 Brunswick 05459 — Lucky Duck/Bye 'N' Bye . . . 10
55 Brunswick OE 9166 — THE HAWK TALKS (EP) . . . 12
55 Mercury EP1 6029 — COLEMAN HAWKINS GROUP (EP) . . . 10
55 HMV 7EG 8057 — COLEMAN HAWKINS AND HIS ORCHESTRA (EP) . . . 8
55 Vogue EPV 1021 — COLEMAN HAWKINS (EP) . . . 10
56 Vogue EPV 1147 — COLEMAN HAWKINS AND HIS ORCHESTRA (EP) . . . 10
57 HMV 7EG 8230 — THE BEAN STALKS AGAIN (EP) . . . 8
58 HMV 7EG 8393 — HAWKINS ALLSTARS (EP) . . . 8
58 London Jazz EZ-C 19020 — THE HAWK RETURNS PART 1 (EP) . . . 10
58 Columbia Clef SEB 10106 — AT THE OPERA HOUSE (EP) . . . 8
59 Esquire EP 192 — BEAN AND THE BOYS (EP) . . . 10
50s London EZC 19020 — THE HAWK RETURNS PT 1 (EP) . . . 8
60 HMV 7EG 8625 — COLEMAN HAWKINS AND HIS CONFRERES (EP) . . . 8
61 Esquire EP 235 — COLEMAN HAWKINS SEXTET (EP) . . . 10
53 Capitol LC 6580 — CLASSICS IN JAZZ (10" LP) . . . 20
53 Capitol LC 6650 — CAPITOL PRESENTS COLEMAN HAWKINS AND SONNY GREER (10" LP) . . . 25
54 HMV DLP 1055 — TEN COLEMAN HAWKINS' SPECIALS (10" LP) . . . 20
59 HMC CLP 1293 — GENIUS OF COLEMAN HAWKINS (LP) . . . 18
59 Felsted FJA 7005 — THE HIGH AND MIGHTY HAWK (LP, also stereo SJA 2005) . . . 18
61 Esquire 32-095 — SOUL (LP) . . . 18
61 Esquire 32-102 — HAWK EYES (LP) . . . 18
61 Moodsville MV 7 — COLEMAN HAWKINS (LP) . . . 18
62 Swingsville SVLP 2001 — COLEMAN HAWKINS WITH THE RED GARLAND TRIO (LP) . . . 15
62 Swingsville SVLP 2005 — THE COLEMAN HAWKINS ALL STARS (LP) . . . 15
62 Swingsville SVLP 2013 — STASCH (LP) . . . 15
63 HMV CLP 1630 — DESAFINADO (LP, also stereo CSD 1484) . . . 15
64 Verve VLP 9044 — ALIVE! AT THE VILLAGE GATE (LP) . . . 15
64 HMV CLP 1689 — TODAY AND NOW (LP) . . . 15
64 CBS BPG 62157 — BACK IN BEAN'S BAG (LP, with Clark Terry) . . . 15
64 Fontana FJL 102 — SWING' (LP) . . . 15
65 Fontana TL 5273 — MEDITATION (LP) . . . 15
66 Fontana SJL 131 — CATTIN' (LP) . . . 15
71 Xtra XTRA 1119 — COLEMAN HAWKINS (LP) . . . 12
72 Black Lion 2460 159 — THE HAWK IN GERMANY (LP) . . . 12
(see also Hines & Eldridge, Milt Jackson & Coleman Hawkins, Eddie 'Lockjaw' Davis, Sir Charles Thompson)

COLEMAN HAWKINS & LESTER YOUNG

65 Stateside SL 10117 — CLASSIC TENORS (LP) . . . 12

DALE HAWKINS

57 London HL 8482 — Susie-Q/Don't Treat Me That Way . . . 525
57 London HL 8482 — Susie-Q/Don't Treat Me That Way (78) . . . 125
58 London HLM 8728 — La-Do-Dada/Cross Ties . . . 50
58 London HLM 8728 — La-Do-Dada/Cross Ties (78) . . . 60
59 London HLM 8842 — Yea-Yea/Lonely Nights . . . 50
59 London HLM 8842 — Yea-Yea/Lonely Nights (78) . . . 80
59 London HLM 9016 — Liza Jane/Back To School Blues . . . 50
59 London HLM 9016 — Liza Jane/Back To School Blues (78) . . . 110
60 London HLM 9060 — Hot Dog/Our Turn . . . 50
69 Bell SBLL 127 — L.A., MEMPHIS AND TYLER, TEXAS (LP) . . . 12
73 Checker 6467 301 — OH! SUSIE Q (LP) . . . 12

ERSKINE HAWKINS QUINTET

60 Brunswick LAT 8374 — THE HAWK BLOWS AT MIDNIGHT (LP, also stereo STA 3042) . . . 12/15

HAWKSHAW HAWKINS

51 Vogue V 9003 — Doghouse Boogie/Yesterday's Kisses (78) . . . 15
51 Vogue V 9027 — Slow Coach/Two Roads (78) . . . 12
54 Parlophone CMSP 1 — Betty Lorraine/CHARLIE GORE & LOUIS INNIS: Mexican Joe (export issue) . . . 25
50s Parlophone DP 336 — I Hope You're Crying Too/I'm A Lone Wolf (export 78) . . . 12
63 London HL 9737 — Lonesome 7-7203/Everything Has Changed . . . 8
58 Parlophone GEP 8742 — COUNTRY AND WESTERN (EP) . . . 40
58 Vogue VE 170117 — HAWKSHAW HAWKINS — COUNTRY AND WESTERN (EP) . . . 40
64 London HA 8181 — THE ALL NEW HAWKSHAW HAWKINS (LP) . . . 18
(see also Charlie Gore, Louis Innis)

MINT VALUE £

JUNE HAWKINS

55 Brunswick 05370 — Beat Out Dat Rhythm On A Drum/MURIEL SMITH & CARMEN JONES CHORUS: Dat's Love ... 8

RONNIE HAWKINS (& HAWKS)

59 Columbia DB 4319 — Forty Days (To Come Back Home)/One Of These Days ... 55
59 Columbia DB 4345 — Mary Lou/Need Your Lovin' (Oh So Bad) ... 35
60 Columbia DB 4412 — Southern Love (Whatcha-Gonna' Do)/Love Me Like You Can ... 25
60 Columbia DB 4442 — Clara/Lonely Hours ... 40
63 Columbia DB 7036 — Bo Diddley/Who Do You Love? ... 35
70 Roulette RO 512 — Who Do You Love?/Bo Diddley ... 5
70 Atlantic 584 320 — Down In The Alley/Matchbox ... 5
70 Atlantic 2091 007 — Bitter Green/Forty Days ... 5
72 Monument MNT 8292 — Cora Mae/Ain't That A Shame ... 5
60 Columbia SEG 7983 — ROCKIN' WITH RONNIE (EP, also stereo ESG 7792) ... 125/200
60 Columbia SEG 7988 — ROCKIN' WITH RONNIE (EP, also stereo ESG 7795) ... 125/200
60 Columbia 33SX 1238 — MR. DYNAMO (LP, also stereo SCX 3315) ... 140/190
60 Columbia 33SX 1295 — THE FOLK BALLADS OF RONNIE HAWKINS (LP, also stereo SCX 3358) ... 85/100
70 Roulette RCP 1003 — ARKANSAS ROCK PILE (LP, with The Band) ... 20
70 Atlantic 2400 009 — RONNIE HAWKINS (LP) ... 15
72 Monument MNT 65122 — ROCK AND ROLL RESURRECTION (LP) ... 12
(see also Band, Levon & Hawks)

SCREAMIN' JAY HAWKINS

58 Fontana H 107 — I Put A Spell On You/Little Demon (78) ... 100
65 Columbia DB 7460 — The Whammy/Strange ... 25
65 Sue WI 379 — I Hear Voices/Just Don't Care ... 40
66 Sue WI 4008 — I Put A Spell On You/Little Demon (unissued)
69 Direction 58-4097 — I Put A Spell On You/Little Demon ... 22
80 Polydor POSP 183 — I Put A Spell On You/Armpit 6 (with Keith Richards) ... 10
66 Planet PLL 1001 — THE NIGHT AND DAY OF SCREAMIN' JAY HAWKINS (LP) ... 100
69 Direction (S) 8-63481 — I PUT A SPELL ON YOU (LP, mono or stereo) ... 40
69 Mercury SMCL 20178 — WHAT THAT IS (LP) ... 22
(see also Keith Richards)

WENDELL HAWKINS TRIO

61 Parlophone PMC 1157 — MR. HAWKINS AT THE PIANO (LP) ... 12

HAWKLORDS

78 Charisma HL 1 — PSI Power/Death Trap (no p/s, promo only) ... 12
78 Charisma CB 323 — PSI Power/Death Trap (no p/s) ... 8
79 Charisma CB 332 — 25 Years/(Only) The Dead Dreams Of A Cold War Kid (no p/s) ... 6
79 Charisma CB 332 12 — 25 Years/(Only) The Dead Dreams Of A Cold War Kid/PXR 5 (12", grey vinyl; also mispressed on black vinyl) ... 10/12
82 Flicknife FLS 209 — Who's Gonna Win The War?/Time Of (p/s) ... 6
78 Charisma CDS 4014 — 25 YEARS ON (LP, with inner sleeve, some sold with separate tour book) ... 12/15
(see also Hawkwind)

HAWKS

69 Stateside SS 2147 — The Grissle/SHEEP: Hide And Seek ... 12

HAWKS

81 Five Believers FB 001 — Words Of Hope/Sense Of Ending (p/s) ... 15
(see also Lilac Time, Stephen 'Tin Tin' Duffy)

ALAN HAWKSHAW

70 Tangerine DP 0005 — Puppet On A String/Everybody Knows ... 5
79 BBC RESL 64 — Grange Hill/Stoned ... 20
72 Philips 6414 310 — ORGAN SOUNDS SUPER STEREO — ALAN HAWKSHAW PLAYS THE PHILICORDA (LP) ... 12
72 Studio Two TWO 391 — 27 TOP TV THEMES AND COMMERCIALS (LP) ... 30
72 KPM 1080 — FLUTE FOR MODERNS (with Alan Parker) (LP) ... 35
74 Polydor 2460 218 — NON-STOP HAMMOND HITS (LP) ... 12
(see also Shadows)

HAWKSWORTH-VERRELL JAZZ GROUP

56 Decca FJ 10726 — Ring Dem Bells/Always ... 6

JOHNNY HAWKSWORTH (ORCHESTRA)

65 Pye 7N 15969 — Lunar Walk/It's Murder (as Johnny Hawksworth Orchestra) ... 15
66 Columbia DB 8059 — Goal/"Goal — World Cup 1966" Theme (as Sounds Of Johnny Hawksworth) ... 6
67 Columbia DB 8129 — Wack Wack/On The Tiles ... 6
(see also Johnny's Jazz)

HAWKWIND

SINGLES

70 Liberty LBF 15382 — Hurry On Sundown/Mirror Of Illusion ... 90
72 United Artists UP 35381 — Silver Machine/Seven By Seven ('machine' art p/s) ... 12
73 United Artists (WD 3637) — Sonic Attack (1-sided promo in cloth sleeve) ... 185
73 United Artists UP 35566 — Urban Guerilla/Brainbox Pollution ... 12
73 United Artists USEP 1 — HURRY ON HAWKWIND (EP) ... 35
74 United Artists UP 35715 — The Psychedelic Warlords (Disappear In Smoke)/It's So Easy ... 8
75 United Artists UP 35808 — Kings Of Speed/Motorhead (some in p/s) ... 40/6
76 Charisma CB 289 — Kerb Crawler/Honky Dorky ... 7
77 Charisma CB 299 — Back On The Streets/The Dream Of Isis (p/s) ... 6
77 Charisma CB 305 — Quark, Strangeness & Charm/Forge Of Vulcan ... 7
78 United Artists UP 35381 — Silver Machine/Seven By Seven (reissue, black-on-white p/s) ... 5
78 United Artists 12UP 35381 — Silver Machine/Seven By Seven (12", silver p/s) ... 10
80 Bronze BRO 98 — Shot Down In The Night/Urban Guerilla (p/s) ... 5
80 Bronze BRO 98 — Shot Down In The Night/Urban Guerilla (1-sided gold vinyl flexidisc) ... 30
80 Bronze BRO 109 — Who's Gonna Win The War?/Nuclear Toy (p/s, cream or green labels) ... 12/5

			MINT VALUE £
81	RCA RCA 137	Angels Of Death/Trans-Dimensional Man (p/s)	5
82	RCA Active RCA 267	Silver Machine/Silver Machine (Full Version)/Psychedelic Warlords (p/s)	5
82	RCA Active RCAP 267	Silver Machine/(Full Version)/Psychedelic Warlords (picture disc)	10
82	Flicknife FLS 005	Motorhead/Valium Ten (p/s)	5
82	Flicknife FLST 005	Motorhead/Valium Ten (extended) (12", p/s)	8
83	United Artists UP 35381	Silver Machine/Seven By Seven (reissue, white-on-black p/s)	5
83	Liberty UPP 35381	Silver Machine/Seven By Seven (picture disc)	12
83	Liberty UPP 35381	Silver Machine/Seven By Seven (mispressed picture disc, plays Beatles' "Ask Me Why")	18
83	Flicknife FLS 214	Hawkwind And Co: Your Last Chance (p/s, sampler with Robert Calvert & Michael Moorcock)	6
83	Flicknife FLS 025	Motorway City/Master Of The Universe (p/s)	5
84	Flicknife FLEP 104	THE EARTH RITUAL PREVIEW (12" EP)	8
85	Flicknife FLS 032	Needle Gun/Arioch (p/s)	5
85	Flicknife FLST 032	Needle Gun (extended)/Arioch (p/s)	8
86	Flicknife FLS 033	Zarozinia/Assault And Battery (live) (p/s)	5
86	Samurai HW 001	Silver Machine/Magnu (motorcycle-shaped picture disc)	15
86	Flicknife FLS 034-A	Motorhead/Hurry On Sundown (p/s with insert)	5
90	Receiver REPLAY 3014	THE EARLY YEARS LIVE (12", p/s, blue vinyl)	12
93	4 Real 4R 1	SPIRIT OF THE AGE (SOLSTICE REMIXES) (12" EP)	15
93	4 Real 4R 2	DECIDE YOUR FUTURE (12" EP)	10
94	Emerg. Broadcast EBS 110	QUARK, STRANGENESS & CHARM (12" EP, clear vinyl, 200 only)	15

ALBUMS

70	Liberty LBS 83348	HAWKWIND (LP, gatefold sleeve; blue or black labels)	55
71	United Artists UAG 29202	IN SEARCH OF SPACE (LP in foldout sleeve, some with 'log book')	25/12
72	United Artists UAG 29364	DOREMI-FASOL-LATIDO (LP, with inner sleeve, some with poster)	20/12
73	Utd. Artists UAD 60037/8	SPACE RITUAL ALIVE (2-LP, foldout sleeve with inners)	30
74	United Artists UAG 29672	HALL OF THE MOUNTAIN GRILL (LP, with inner sleeve)	15
75	United Artists UAG 29766	WARRIOR ON THE EDGE OF TIME (LP, foldout pop-up sleeve with inner)	20
76	United Artists UAK 29919	ROADHAWKS (LP, gatefold sleeve with poster & sticker)	18/12
76	Mushroom	THE XENON CODEX (LP, with inner, gatefold sleeve)	15
79	Charisma CDS 4016	P.X.R.5 (LP, with family tree poster)	20
80	Charisma BG 2	REPEAT PERFORMANCE (LP)	12
80	Bronze BRON 530	LEVITATION (LP, blue vinyl)	18
81	RCA Active RCALP 6004	SONIC ATTACK (LP, with insert)	18
82	RCA Active RCALP 9004	CHURCH OF HAWKWIND (LP, with lyric booklet)	25
82	RCA Active RCALP 6055	CHOOSE YOUR MASQUES (LP)	18
84	Flicknife PSHARP 014	ZONES (LP, picture disc reissue)	15
84	Flicknife ZSHARP 019	INDEPENDENT DAYS (10" mini-LP)	8
84	Liberty SLP 1972921	HAWKWIND (LP, reissue, picture disc, die-cut)	15
84	Flicknife SHARP 022	STONEHENGE: THIS IS HAWKWIND DO NOT PANIC (LP, with 12", gatefold sleeve or single sleeve with poster)	each 18
85	Flicknife SHARP 033	CHRONICLE OF THE BLACK SWORD (LP, with inner sleeve)	12
85	Flicknife SHARP 033CD	CHRONICLE OF THE BLACK SWORD (CD, with 3 extra tracks)	18
86	Hawkfan HWFB 2	HAWKFAN 12 (LP, with poster, sticker insert & carrier bag, 600 only)	75
86	RCA NL 71150	ANGELS OF DEATH (LP)	22
86	Samurai SMR 046	APPROVED HISTORY OF HAWKWIND 1967-1982 (3-LP, pic discs & booklet)	40
87	Flicknife HWBOX 01	OFFICIAL PICTURE LOG BOOK (4-LP box set, [3 picture discs & interview disc] with badge & insert)	40
94	Emerg. Broadcast EBS 111	THE BUSINESS TRIP (2-LP, clear vinyl, 1,500 only)	18
95	Emerg. B/cast EBSLP 118	ALIEN 4 (2-LP, gatefold sleeve)	18
95	Dojo DOJO CD 244	ELECTRIC TEPEE (CD, picture disc, unreleased)	20

(see also Hawklords, Robert Calvert, Michael Moorcock, Inner City Unit, Sphynx, Dave Brock, Steve Swindells, Tim Blake, Huw Lloyd Langton Group, Alan Davey, Motörhead, Sonic Assassins, Dr. Technical & Machines, Sam Gopal, Magic Muscle, Opal Butterfly, Nik Turner, Widowmaker, Adrian Shaw)

DEANE HAWLEY

61	Liberty LIB 55359	Pocketful Of Rainbows/That Dream Could Never Be	10

GOLDIE HAWN

72	Reprise K 14211	Carey/I'll Be Your Baby Tonight	6

BRYN HAWORTH

74	Island ILPS 9287	LET THE DAYS GO BY (LP, with inner sleeve)	15

(see also Fleur De Lys, Nicholas Greenwood)

HAYDOCK'S ROCKHOUSE

66	Columbia DB 8050	Cupid/She Thinks	40
67	Columbia DB 8135	Lovin' You/Mix A Fix	40

(see also Hollies)

BILL HAYES

53	MGM SP 1036	The Donkey Song/My Ever-Lovin'	25
55	London HL 8149	The Berry Tree/Blue Black Hair	45
55	London HL 8149	The Berry Tree/Blue Black Hair (78)	8
56	London HLA 8220	Ballad Of Davy Crockett/Farewell	50
56	London HLA 8239	Kwela Kwela/The White Buffalo	40
56	London HLA 8239	Kwela Kwela/The White Buffalo (78)	7
56	London HLA 8300	Das Ist Musik/I Know An Old Lady	35
56	London HLA 8300	Das Ist Musik/I Know An Old Lady (78)	7
56	London HLA 8325	The Legend Of Wyatt Earp/That Do Make It Nice	40
56	London HLA 8325	The Legend Of Wyatt Earp/That Do Make It Nice (78)	10
57	London HL 8430	Wringle Wrangle/Westward Ho The Wagons	25
57	London HL 8430	Wringle Wrangle/Westward Ho The Wagons (78)	8
59	London HLR 8833	Wimoweh/Goin' Down The Road Feelin' Bad (with Buckle Busters)	15
59	London HLR 8833	Wimoweh/Goin' Down The Road Feelin' Bad (78, with Buckle Busters)	12
56	London RE-A 1051	GREAT PIONEERS OF THE WEST (EP)	40

MINT VALUE £

GEMMA HAYES

00s Source SOURCDSP 028 — 4:35 AM — Gotta Low/Making Waves/Evening Sun/Piano Song (CD, card sleeve) 10
00s Source SOUR 051 — Let A Good Thing Go/Pieces Of Glass (p/s) . . . 5

ISAAC HAYES

69 Stax STAX 133 — Walk On By/By The Time I Get To Phoenix . . . 5
70 Stax STAX 154 — I Stand Accused/I Just Don't Know What To Do With Myself . . . 5
71 Stax 2025 020 — You've Lost That Lovin' Feelin'/Our Day Will Come . . . 5
71 Stax 2025 029 — Never Can Say Goodbye/I Can't Help It (If I'm Still In Love With You) . . . 5
72 Stax 2025 069 — Theme From "Shaft"/Cafe Regio's . . . 5
72 Stax 2025 089 — Let's Stay Together/Ain't That Loving You (For More Reasons Than One) (with David Porter) . . . 5
72 Stax 2025 146 — Theme From *The Men*/Type Thang . . . 5
74 Stax STXS 2004 — Title Theme From *Tough Guys*/Hung Up On My Baby . . . 6
75 ABC ABC 4076 — Chocolate Chip/Chocolate Chip (Instrumental) . . . 5
76 ABC ABC 4100 — Disco Connection/St. Thomas Square . . . 5
76 ABC ABC 4111 — Rock Me Easy Baby (Parts 1 & 2) . . . 5
76 ABC ABC 4136 — Juicy Fruit (Disco Freak) (Parts 1 & 2) . . . 5
77 ABC ABE 12007 — Disco Connection/Chocolate Chip (12") . . . 8
79 Polydor POSPX 23 — Zeke The Freak/If We Ever Needed Peace (12") . . . 8
80 Polydor 2001 965 — I Ain't Ever/Love Has Been Good For Us . . . 5
86 CBS 650236-7 — Hey Girl/Ike's Rap VIII . . . 5
69 Stax SXATS 1028 — HOT BUTTERED SOUL (LP) . . . 20
70 Stax SXATS 1032 — THE ISAAC HAYES MOVEMENT (LP) . . . 18
70 Stax 2465 016 — BLUE HAYES (LP) . . . 18
71 Stax 2325 026 — TO BE CONTINUED (LP) . . . 18
71 Stax 2325 014 — THE ISAAC HAYES MOVEMENT (LP, reissue) . . . 12
71 Stax 2325 011 — HOT BUTTERED SOUL (LP, reissue) . . . 12
71 Stax 2659 007 — SHAFT — ORIGINAL SOUNDTRACK (2-LP, soundtrack, gatefold sleeve) . . . 22
72 MGM 2315 115 — SHAFT'S BIG SCORE! (LP, soundtrack) . . . 20
72 Atlantic K 40327 — IN THE BEGINNING (LP) . . . 12
72 Stax 2628 004 — BLACK MOSES (2-LP) . . . 18
74 Stax 2325 111 — JOY (LP) . . . 12
74 Stax STXD 4001/2 — TRUCK TURNER (2-LP, soundtrack) . . . 18
74 Stax STXH 5001 — TOUGH GUYS (LP, soundtrack) . . . 12
75 Stax STX 1043 — USE ME (LP) . . . 12
75 Stax STX 1036 — THE BEST OF ISAAC HAYES (LP) . . . 12
75 ABC ABCL 5129 — CHOCOLATE CHIP (LP, gatefold sleeve) . . . 12
75 ABC ABCL 5155 — GROOVE-A-THON (LP, gatefold sleeve) . . . 12

LINDA HAYES

55 Parlophone MSP 6174 — Please Have Mercy (with Platters)/Oochi Pachi (with Tony Williams) . . . 330
55 Parlophone R 4038 — Please Have Mercy (with Platters)/Oochi Pachi (with Tony Williams) (78) . . . 75
(see also Platters)

PETER LIND HAYES

60 Brunswick 05821 — Life Gets Tee-jus Don't It/Sing Me A Happy Song . . . 10
(see also Peter & Mary)

TUBBY HAYES

56 Tempo A 148 — Ode To Ernie/No, I Woodyn't . . . 10
62 Fontana H 397 — Sally/I Believe In You (as Tubby Hayes Quintet) . . . 30
55 Tempo EXA 14 — THE LITTLE GIANT (EP) . . . 40
55 Tempo EXA 17 — TUBBY HAYES AND HIS ORCHESTRA (EP) . . . 25
55 Tempo EXA 27 — THE SWINGING GIANT NO. 1 (EP, as Tubby Hayes Quartet) . . . 40
56 Tempo EXA 28 — THE SWINGING GIANT NO. 2 (EP, as Tubby Hayes Quartet) . . . 40
56 Tempo EXA 36 — MODERN JAZZ SCENE (EP, as Tubby Hayes & His Orchestra) . . . 40
57 Tempo EXA 55 — AFTER LIGHTS OUT (EP, as Tubby Hayes Quintet) . . . 50
57 Tempo EXA 75 — TUBBY HAYES AND THE JAZZ COURIERS (EP) . . . 60
58 Tempo EXA 82 — THE EIGHTH WONDER (EP, solo) . . . 60
57 Tempo TAP 6 — AFTER LIGHTS OUT (LP, as Tubby Hayes Quintet) . . . 300
57 Tempo TAP 15 — JAZZ COURIERS (LP) . . . 300
60 Tempo TAP 29 — TUBBY'S GROOVE (LP, as Tubby Hayes Quartet) . . . 400
61 Fontana TFL 5142 — TUBBS (LP, also stereo STFL 562) . . . 100
61 Ember EMB 3337 — AN EVENING WITH MR. PERCUSSION (LP, with Tony Kinsey) . . . 50
61 Fontana TFL 5183 — TUBBS IN NEW YORK (LP, also stereo STFL 595) . . . 100
63 Fontana 680 998 TL — DOWN IN THE VILLAGE (LP, also stereo 886 163TY) . . . 200
64 Fontana (S)TL 5195 — RETURN VISIT! (LP) . . . 100
64 Fontana TL 5200 — LATE SPOT AT SCOTT'S (LP) . . . 250
66 Fontana (S)TL 5221 — TUBBY TOURS (LP, with Orchestra) . . . 30
66 Fontana (S)TL 5410 — 100% PROOF (LP) . . . 75
67 Wing WL 1162 — TUBBS IN NEW YORK (LP, reissue) . . . 15
69 Fontana SFJL 911 — MEXICAN GREEN (LP) . . . 125
71 Fontana 6309 002 — THE TUBBY HAYES ORCHESTRA (LP) . . . 20
72 Philips 6382 041 — THIS IS JAZZ — 100% PROOF (LP) . . . 15
(see also Jack Constanzo & Tubby Hayes, Jazz Couriers, London Jazz Quartet, Dave Lee, Ronnie Scott, Roy Castle)

TUBBY HAYES & CLEO LAINE

61 Fontana TFL 5151 — PALLADIUM JAZZ DATE (LP, also stereo STFL 570) . . . 75
65 Wing WL 1088 — PALLADIUM JAZZ DATE (LP, reissue) . . . 25
(see also Cleo Laine)

TUBBY HAYES & PAUL GONSALVES ALLSTARS

67 Columbia SX 6003 — JUST FRIENDS (LP) . . . 100
60s World Record Club T 631 — CHANGE OF SETTING (LP) . . . 100
(see also Paul Gonsalves)

LOU HAYLES

77 Myrrh MYR 1055 — DON'T HIDE AWAY (LP) . . . 150

MINT VALUE £

DICK HAYMES

56	Capitol CL 14618	You'll Never Know/Love Walked In	6
56	Capitol CL 14659	Two Different Worlds/Love Is A Great Big Nothin'	6
57	Capitol CL 14674	Never Leave Me/New York's My Home	6
57	Capitol CL 14720	C'est La Vie/Now At Last	6
51	Brunswick LA 8516	IRVING BERLIN SONGS (10" LP)	15
51	Brunswick LA 8530	SOUVENIR ALBUM (10" LP)	15
56	Capitol LC 6823	RAIN OR SHINE (10" LP)	15

ARTHUR HAYNES

61	HMV POP 987	Not To Worry/Looking Around	8

GOLDIA HAYNES

51	Capitol CL 13486	That Great Judgement Day/Travelling (78)	10
52	Capitol CL 13550	Truth In The Gospel/Oh Lord How Long (78)	18

ROY HAYNES, PHINEAS NEWBORN, PAUL CHAMBERS TRIO

61	Esquire 32-103	WE THREE (LP)	12

STEVE HAYNES BAND

78	Black Bear BLA 2005	Back In My Arms Again/Walk On By (p/s)	20
78	Black Bear BLA 2008	Save Me Save Me/Strong Good Lovin' (p/s)	15

HAYSTACK

69	United Artists UP 35024	Letter To Josephine/Love You're Making A Fool Of Me	6
69	United Artists UP 35035	Tahiti Farewell/Pantomime People	6

JUSTIN HAYWARD

65	Pye 7N 17041	London Is Behind Me/Day Must Come	120
66	Parlophone R 5496	I Can't Face The World Without You/I'll Be Here Tomorrow	140
80	CBS 11-7731	The Eve Of The War/Horsell (12" picture disc)	8

(see also Wilde Three, Moody Blues)

RICK HAYWARD

71	Blue Horizon 2431 006	RICK HAYWARD (LP)	65

(see also Accent, Christine Perfect)

SUSAN HAYWARD

56	MGM MGM-EP 555	I'LL CRY TOMORROW — SOUNDTRACK SELECTION (EP)	15

JOE HAYWOOD

65	Island WI 218	Warm And Tender Love/I Would If I Could	15

LEON HAYWOOD

66	Vocalion VL 9280	Ain't No Use/Hey, Hey, Hey	18
67	Vocalion VL 9288	Ever Since You Were Sweet Sixteen/Skate Awhile	18
69	MCA Soul Bag BAG 5	Mellow Moonlight/Tennessee Waltz	8
70	Capitol CL 15634	I Wanna Thank You/I Was Sent To Love You	12
73	Pye International 7N 25611	La La Song/There Ain't Enough Hate Around To Make Me Turn Around	5
75	20th Century BTC 2191	Come On And Get Yourself Some/BMF (Beautiful)	5
75	20th Century BTC 2228	I Wanta Do Something Freaky To You/I Know What Love Is	6
78	Fantasy FTC 151	Baby Reconsider/Would I	10
67	Vocalion VAL 8064	SOUL CARGO (LP)	70
69	MCA MUPS 369	IT'S GOT TO BE MELLOW (LP)	20
73	Pye Intl. NSPL 28177	BACK TO STAY (LP)	15
75	20th Century BT 476	COME AND GET YOURSELF SOME (LP)	15

OFRA HAZA

87	Globe Style NST 122	Im Nin' Alu (Played In Full Mix)/Im Nin' Alu (12", extended mix)	10

HAZE

85	Gabadon GABS 003	THE EMBER (12" EP)	8
86	Gabadon GABS 5	Tunnel Vision/Shadows (p/s)	5
85	Gabadon GABC 2	CELLAR REPLAY (cassette)	10
84	Gabadon GABL 001	C'EST LA VIE (LP)	25

HAZEL

93	Sub Pop SP74 241	Jilted (blue vinyl)	5

HAZEL & JOLLY BOYS

67	Doctor Bird DB 1063	Stop Them/Deep Down	22

RONNIE HAZELHURST

78	Polydor 2384 107	SIXTEEN SMALL SCREEN GREATS (LP)	12

LEE HAZLEWOOD

60	London HLW 9223	Words Mean Nothing/The Girl On Death Row (with Duane Eddy)	35
66	MGM MGM 1310	Sand/My Autumn's Done Come	8
67	MGM MGM 1348	My Baby Cried All Night Long/These Boots Are Made For Walkin'	10
67	Reprise RS 20613	Ode To Billie Joe/Charlie Bill Nelson	7
68	Reprise RS 20667	Rainbow Woman/I Am, You Are	8
72	RCA RCA 2185	Big Red Balloon/Down From Dover	6
73	Stateside SS 2225	Poet/Come Spend The Morning	6
66	MGM MGM-CS 8014	THE VERY SPECIAL WORLD OF LEE HAZLEWOOD (LP)	30
68	Reprise RSLP 6297	LOVE AND OTHER CRIMES (LP)	25
69	London HA-N/SH-N 8398	TROUBLE IS A LONESOME TOWN (LP)	30
72	Reprise K 44161	REQUIEM FOR AN ALMOST LADY (LP)	20
74	Stateside SSL 10315	POET, FOOL OR BUM (LP)	25

(see also Nancy Sinatra & Lee Hazlewood, Duane Eddy)

MINT VALUE £

TONY HAZZARD

66	Columbia DB 7927	You'll Never Put Shackles On Me/Calling You Home	6
68	CBS 3452	Sound Of The Candyman's Trumpet/Everything's Gone Wrong	5
69	CBS 63608	DEMONSTRATION (LP)	15
71	Bronze ILPS 9174	LOUDWATER HOUSE (LP)	12
73	Bronze ILPS 9222	WAS THAT ALRIGHT THEN? (LP)	12

HEAD

79	Ellie Jay MB1	Nothing To Do In A Town Like Leatherhead/University '79	60+

MURRAY HEAD

65	Columbia DB 7635	Alberta/He Was A Friend Of Mine	8
65	Columbia DB 7771	The Bells Of Rhymney/Don't Sing No Sad Songs For Me	10
67	Columbia DB 8102	Someday Soon/You Bore Me	8
67	Immediate IM 053	She Was Perfection/Secondhand Monday	55
69	MCA MK 5019	Superstar/John 1941 (p/s, with Trinidad Singers)	7
71	MCA MKS 5019	Superstar/John 1941 (p/s, reissue)	6
73	CBS 65503	NIGEL LIVED (LP)	20
75	Island ILPS 9347	SAY IT AIN'T SO (LP, gatefold sleeve)	12

ROY HEAD (& TRAITS)

65	Pye International 7N 25340	Just A Little Bit/Treat Me Right	15
65	Vocalion VP 9248	Treat Her Right/So Long, My Love	18
66	Vocalion VP 9254	Apple Of My Eye/I Pass The Day	15
66	Vocalion VP 9269	My Babe/Pain	15
66	Vocalion VP 9274	Wigglin' And Gigglin'/Driving Wheel	18
66	London HLZ 10097	To Make A Big Man Cry/Don't Cry No More	10
70	Stateside SS 8050	Mama Mama/I'm Not A Fool Anymore	7
75	London HLD 10487	The Most Wanted Woman In Town/Gingers Breadman	8
66	Pye Intl. NEP 44053	JUST A LITTLE BIT OF ROY HEAD (EP)	35
70	Stateside SSL 5033	SAME PEOPLE (LP)	25

(see also Traits)

HEADACHE

77	Lout 001	Can't Stand Still/No Reason For Your Call (p/s)	25

HEADBANGERS

81	Magnet MAG 206	Status Rock/Headbang Boogie (p/s)	5

(see also Biddu, Leaf Hound, Weapon)

THEE HEADCOATS

90	Sub Pop SP71	Time Will Tell/Davey Crockett (Gabba Hey) (p/s)	6
92	Sub Pop SP151	Ballad Of Hollis Brown/Grizzly Bear (p/s, blue vinyl)	8

(see also Milkshakes)

HEADHUNTERS

76	Arista ARTY 116	SURVIVAL OF THE FITTEST (LP)	25
77	Arista SPART 1048	STRAIGHT FROM THE GATE (LP)	15

(see also Herbie Hancock)

HEADLESS CHICKENS

89	Hometown Atrocities 1	THE HOMETOWN ATROCITIES EP (wraparound p/s, 'kylie' or 'glossy')	200/120

(see also Radiohead)

HEADLINERS

59	Parlophone R 4593	The Bubble Car Song/Andy's Theme	8

HEADLINERS

65	Decca F 12209	That's The Way I Must Go/Four Seasons	8

HEAD MACHINE

70	Major Minor SMLP 79	ORGASM (LP)	150

(see also Uriah Heep)

HEAD OF DAVID

89	Blast First WANT 001	WHITE ELEPHANT (LP, mail-order only)	12

HEADS, HANDS & FEET

71	Island ILPS 9149	HEAD, HANDS AND FEET (LP)	20
72	Island ILPS 9185	TRACKS (LP)	20

(see also Don Everly, Tony Colton, Poet & One Man Band)

HEALEY SISTERS

64	HMV POP 1313	Give Me Back My Heart/After The Party	10

JOE HEANEY

60	Collector JEI 5	MORRISSEY AND THE RUSSIAN SOLDIER (EP)	8
63	Topic 12T 91	IRISH TRADITIONAL SONGS IN GAELIC AND ENGLISH (LP)	12

HEART

77	Arista ARISTA 140	Heartless/Here Song (withdrawn)	8
86	Capitol CLP 406	Nothin' At All (Extended Remix)/The Wolf (heart-shaped picture disc)	6
87	Capitol CLP 457	Who Will You Run To?/Nobody Home (picture disc)	10
87	Capitol CDCL 473	There's The Girl (12" Remix)/Bad Animals/There's The Girl (7" Remix) (CD)	8
88	Capitol CDCL 477	These Dreams (7" Version)/Heart Of Darkness/If Looks Could Kill (live)/ There's The Girl (Rock-A-Pella Version) (CD)	8
88	Capitol CDCL 482	Never (Extended Remix)/These Dreams (7" Version)/Heart Of Darkness/ If Looks Could Kill (live) (CD)	8
88	Capitol CDCL 487	What About Love? (Extended Version)/Shell Shock/Crazy On You/ Dreamboat Annie (CD)	8
88	Capitol CDCL 507	Nothin' At All (Ext. Remix)/I've Got The Music In Me/I Want You So Bad (CD)	8
77	Arista SPART 1024	MAGAZINE (LP, withdrawn)	15
77	Arista SPART 1024	MAGAZINE (LP, picture disc)	15
90	Capitol HGIFT 1	HEART BOX SET (3-LP: "Heart", "Bad Animals" & "Brigade" + 24pp booklet)	18

MINT VALUE £

HEART BEATS

80	Red Shadow REDS 2	Talk To Me/Don't Want Romance (p/s)	5
81	Nothing Shaking SHAD 1	Go/One Of The People (p/s, blue vinyl)	15

HEARTBREAKERS

77	Track 2094 135	Chinese Rocks/Born To Lose (p/s)	8
77	Track 2094 135T	Chinese Rocks/Born To Lose (12", p/s)	12
77	Track 2094 137	One Track Mind/Can't Keep My Eyes On You (live)/Do You Love Me (p/s)	10
77	Track 2094 142	It's Not Enough/Let Go (p/s, withdrawn)	60
79	Beggars Banquet BEG 21	Get Off The Phone (live)/I Wanna Be Loved (live) (p/s)	5
88	Jungle JUNG 38 T	SHE WANTS TO MAMBO (12" EP)	8
77	Track 2409 218	L.A.M.F. (LP)	20
81	Jungle FREUD 1	D.T.K. — LIVE AT THE SPEAKEASY (LP, white or pink vinyl)	18
84	Jungle FREUDP 4	L.A.M.F. REVISITED (LP, picture disc)	18
88	Jungle FREUDP 1	D.T.K. — LIVE AT THE SPEAKEASY (LP, reissue, picture disc)	18

(see also New York Dolls, Johnny Thunders)

HEARTS (U.K.)

64	Parlophone R 5147	Young Woman/Black Eyes	25

HEARTS (U.S.)

64	Stateside SS 268	Dear Abby/Dear Abby (Instrumental)	15

HEARTS & FLOWERS

67	Capitol CL 15492	Rock'N'Roll Gypsies/Road To Nowhere	12
68	Capitol CL 15549	She Sang Hymns Out Of Tune/Tin Angel	10

HEARTS OF SOUL

70	Columbia DB 8670	Waterman/Fat Jack	18

HEATERS

70	Upsetter US 329	Melting Pot/UPSETTERS: Kinky Mood	12

HEAT EXCHANGE

79	EMI EMI 2988	Shake Down/You're Gonna Love This (p/s)	5
79	EMI 12EMI 2988	Shake Down/You're Gonna Love This (12", p/s)	8
79	EMI EMC 3306	ONE STEP AHEAD (LP)	12

(see also Brian Bennett)

TED HEATH ORCHESTRA

78

50s	Confectioners' Benevolent Fund	Candy Queen Waltz (with Dennis Lotis)/The Girl On The Candy Box (with Dickie Valentine) (promo)	10

SINGLES

54	Decca F 10200	Seven Eleven/Lullaby Of Birdland	12
54	Decca F 10222	Creep/Slim Jim — Creep	15
54	Decca F 10246	Skin Deep/Walking Shoes	25
54	Decca F 10272	Viva Verrell/Holiday For Strings	10
54	Decca F 10273	Lush Slide/Fascinating Rhythm	10
55	Decca F 10425	Dig Deep/Asia Minor	10
55	Decca F 10447	Peg O' My Heart (Mambo)/In The Mood (For Mambo)	10
55	Decca F 10477	Haitian Ritual/Late Night Final	10
55	Decca F 10540	Bell Bell Boogie/Amethyst	10
55	Decca F 10590	Barber Shop Jump/Look For The Silver Lining	8
55	Decca F 10624	Malaguena/Cloudburst	8
56	Decca F 10683	The Man With The Golden Arm/Paris By Night	7
56	Decca F 10746	The Faithful Hussar/Siboney	8
58	Decca F 11000	Swingin' Shepherd Blues/Raunchy	7
58	Decca F 11003	Tequila/Little Serenade	7
58	Decca F 11025	Tom Hark/Cha Cha Baby	6
59	Decca F 11111	Peter Gunn/Sermonette (78)	12
59	Decca F 11155	Jazzboat/Mah Jong (78)	12
59	Decca F 11179	Swinging Ghosts/Indian Love Call (78)	12
63	Decca F 11727	Wigwam/Mairi's Wedding	5
65	Decca F 12133	Sidewinder/Hit And Miss	6

EPs

55	Decca DFE 6025	TED HEATH AND HIS MUSIC	12
55	Decca DFE 6027	TED HEATH AND HIS MUSIC NO. 2	12
55	Decca DFE 6120	LONDON PALLADIUM HIGHLIGHTS	8
55	Decca DFE 6159	FATS WALLER ALBUM NO. 2	12
55	Decca DFE 6160	SELECTIONS FROM FATS WALLER ALBUM NO. 2	8
55	Decca DFE 6189	HUNDREDTH LONDON PALLADIUM SUNDAY CONCERT VOL. 1	8
55	Decca DFE 6190	HUNDREDTH LONDON PALLADIUM SUNDAY CONCERT VOL. 2	8
55	Decca DFE 6191	HUNDREDTH LONDON PALLADIUM SUNDAY CONCERT VOL. 3	8
56	Decca DFE 6290	GERSHWIN FOR MODERNS NO. 1	8
56	Decca DFE 6300	AUSTRALIAN SUITE	12
56	Decca DFE 6304	KERN FOR MODERNS NO. 1	8
56	Decca DFE 6305	KERN FOR MODERNS NO. 2	8
56	Decca DFE 6306	KERN FOR MODERNS NO. 3	8
56	Decca DFE 6317	LONDON PALLADIUM HIGHLIGHTS	8
56	Decca DFE 6323	FOUR CLASSICS	8
56	Decca DFE 6346	LONDON PALLADIUM HIGHLIGHTS NO. 3	8
56	Decca DFE 6354	GERSHWIN FOR MODERNS NO. 2	8
56	Decca DFE 6373	LONDON PALLADIUM HIGHLIGHTS NO. 4	8
57	Decca DFE 6403	TED HEATH AND HIS MUSIC NO. 3	8
57	Decca DFE 6432	TED HEATH AND HIS MUSIC NO. 4	8
57	Decca DFE 6451	TED HEATH RECALLS THE FABULOUS DORSEYS NO. 1	8
58	Decca DFE 6487	TED HEATH AND HIS MUSIC NO. 5	8
58	Decca DFE 6500	OUR KIND OF JAZZ	8
58	Decca DFE 6509	HITS I MISSED NO. 1 (also stereo STO 103)	8/10

MINT VALUE £

58	Decca DFE 6510	TED HEATH PLAYS AL JOLSON CLASSICS NO. 1	8
58	Decca DFE 6511	OLD ENGLISH NO. 1	8
59	Decca STO 109	TED HEATH SWING SESSION (stereo)	12
59	Decca STO 113	TED HEATH SWINGS IN HI STEREO (stereo)	10
59	Decca DFE 6579	FOUR HITS FROM THE ALL TIME TOP TWELVE (also stereo STO 122)	8/12
60	Decca DFE 6625	BEAULIEU FESTIVAL SUITE (also stereo STO 135)	8/12
60	Decca DFE 6642	MY VERY GOOD FRIENDS THE BANDLEADERS	8
61	Decca STO 155	GREAT FILM HITS (stereo)	10
63	Decca STO 8532	MOMENTS AT MONTREUX (stereo)	10

LPs

51	Decca LF 1037	TEMPO FOR DANCERS (10")	22
52	Decca LF 1060	LISTEN TO MY MUSIC (10")	20
52	Decca LF 1064	SELECTION (10")	20
53	Decca LK 4062	AT THE LONDON PALLADIUM	15
53	Decca LK 4064	STRIKE UP THE BAND	15
54	Decca LK 4074	TED HEATH'S FATS WALLER ALBUM	15
54	Decca LK 4075	TED HEATH'S 100TH LONDON PALLADIUM SUNDAY CONCERT	15
54	Decca LK 4098	GERSHWIN FOR MODERNS	12
56	Decca LK 4121	KERN FOR MODERNS	12
56	Decca LK 4134	AT THE LONDON PALLADIUM VOLUME 4	12
56	Decca LK 4148	RODGERS FOR MODERNS	12
57	Decca LK 4165	AT CARNEGIE HALL	12
57	Decca LK 4167	FIRST AMERICAN TOUR	12
58	Decca LK 4275	HITS I MISSED (also stereo SKL 4003)	12/20
58	Decca LK 4280	OLDE ENGLYSHE	12
58	Decca SKL 4023	SWINGS IN HI-STEREO (stereo only)	25
59	Decca SKL 4030	SWING SESSION (stereo only)	20
59	Decca SKL 4046	SHALL WE DANCE	15
59	Decca SKL 4079	BEAULIEU JAZZ FESTIVAL (stereo only)	45
59	Decca LK 4208	ALL TIME TOP TWELVE — THE BILLBOARD (also stereo SKL 4054)	12/20
59	Decca LK 4307	PLAYS THE GREAT FILM HITS (also stereo SKL 4055)	12/20
60	Decca LK 4324	PLAYS THE BLUES (also stereo SKL 4074)	12/20
60	Decca LK 4328	THE BIG BAND DIXIE SOUND (also stereo SKL 4076)	12/20
60	Decca LK 4331	IN CONCERT (also stereo SKL 4079)	12/20
60	Decca LK 4344	MY VERY GOOD FRIENDS THE BAND LEADERS (also stereo SKL 4090)	12/20
61	Decca LK 4374	THE INSTRUMENTS OF THE DANCE ORCHESTRA (also stereo SKL 4117)	12/20
61	Decca LK 4389	GOES LATIN (also stereo SKL 4389)	12/20

(Early copies of the above stereo LPs have a "ffss" circle logo at the top of the label & blue back sleeves.)

62	Decca PFM 24004	BIG BAND PERCUSSION (also stereo PFS 34004)	12/20

(see also Joan Regan, Bobbie Britton, Johnston Brothers, Annette Klooger)

HEATHCLIFFE

68	Tangerine DP 0001	Holly Bush And Mistletoe/My World	6

HEATHER

65	King KG 1027	I'll Come Softly/No One In The Whole Wide World	7

HEAVENLY

89	Sarah SARAH 30	I Fell In Love Last Night/Over And Over (p/s)	8

HEAVEN 17

81	Wool City Rocker LYN 9296	Something's Wrong (flexidisc free with fanzine)	8/5
82	Virgin VS 483	Height Of The Fighting (He-La-Hu)/Honeymoon In New York (unissued, no p/s)	15
83	Virgin VSP 570	Temptation/We Live So Fast (picture disc)	5
83	Virgin VSP 607	Come Live With Me/Let's All Make A Bomb (picture disc)	5
83	Virgin VSP 628	Crushed By The Wheels Of Industry/(Version) (picture disc)	5
88	Virgin VSCD 1113	The Ballad Of Go Go Brown (Extended Version)/I Set You Free/ The Ballad Of Go Go Brown (7" Version)/Slow All Over (CD)	8
88	Virgin VSCD 1134	Train Of Love In Motion (7" Version)/Work/Train Of Love In Motion (The Mainline Mix)/Giving Up (3" CD, card sleeve)	8
88	Virgin CDT 19	Temptation/Who'll Stop The Rain?/We Live So Fast (3" CD, card sleeve)	8
88	Virgin CDT 21	(We Don't Need This) Fascist Groove Thang (3" CD, gatefold card sleeve)	8
84	Virgin/fan club	HOW MEN ARE (cassette, studio demo via fan club)	12
86	Virgin TCV 2383	ENDLESS (cassette, double-play in presentation box with booklet)	12

(see also B.E.F., Human League, Glenn Gregory & Claudia Brucken)

HEAVY COCHRAN

78	Psycho P 2611	I've Got Big Balls/Well, Fairly Big	5
79	Psycho P 2619	I've Got A Little Prick/It's 12 Inches Long, But I Don't Use It As A Rule	6

(see also Lieutenant Pigeon)

HEAVY DUTY BREAKS

85	Illuminated ILL 5512	Heavy Duty Breaks (Radio Version)/Bonus Beats (12", p/s)	8
85	Illuminated JAMS 49	HEAVY DUTY BREAKS (LP, remixes of other artists)	12

(see also Killing Joke)

HEAVY JELLY

69	Island WIP 6049	I Keep Singing The Same Old Song/Blue	8

(see also Skip Bifferty, Griffin, Graham Bell, Arc)

HEAVY JELLY

69	Head HDS 4001	Time Out Chewn In/The Long Wait	20
70	Island HELP	HEAVY JELLY (LP, promo only)	100
84	Psycho PSYCHO 30	TAKE ME DOWN TO THE WATER (LP, reissue of "Heavy Jelly")	12

(see also Jackie Lomax, Aynsley Dunbar Retaliation)

HEAVY METAL KIDS

74	Atlantic K 50047	HEAVY METAL KIDS (LP, with poster)	12
77	Rak SRAK 523	KITSCH (LP)	12

(see also Gary Holton, Kids)

MINT VALUE £

HEAVY PETTIN'

82 Neat NEAT 17 Roll The Dice/Love Times Love (p/s) . . . 10
83 Polydor HEPP 3 Love Times Love/Shout It Out (shaped picture disc) . . . 8
85 Polydor HEP 4 Sole Survivor/Crazy (p/s) . . . 5

HEAVYWEIGHTS

69 Spark SRL 1033 Utterly Funky/Shambala . . . 15

BOBBY HEBB

66 Philips BF 1503 Sunny/Bread . . . 6
66 Philips BF 1522 A Satisfied Mind/Love Love Love . . . 10
67 Philips BF 1541 Love Me/Baby I'm Crazy . . . 6
67 Philips BF 1570 I Love Everything About You/Some Kinda Magic . . . 6
67 Philips BF 1610 Everything Is Coming Up Roses/Bound By Love . . . 5
68 Philips BF 1702 You Want To Change Me/Dreamy . . . 25
72 Philips 6051 023 Love Love Love/Sunny . . . 7
72 Philips 6051 025 Some Kind Of Magic/Good Lovin' . . . 5
66 Philips BL 7740 SUNNY (LP) . . . 25

HEBREW CHILDREN & INNER CIRCLE

73 Ackee ACK 508 Dog And Bone/Version . . . 5

DICK HECKSTALL-SMITH (QUINTET)

57 Pye Jazz NJE 1037 VERY SPECIAL OLD JAZZ (EP, as Dick Heckstall-Smith Quintet) . . . 25
72 Bronze ILPS 9196 DUST IN THE AIR SUSPENDED MARKS THE PLACE ... WHERE A STORY ENDED (LP, gatefold sleeve with lyric inner sleeve) . . . 18

(see also Graham Bond Organisation, John Mayall & Bluesbreakers, Alexis Korner, Colosseum, Rocket 88)

JESSE HECTOR

99 No Hit NO HIT EP 1961 Fast Train To Memphis/My Bucket's Got A Hole In It/All By Myself/ Nightmares (p/s) . . . 6

HEDGEHOG PIE

76 Rubber ADUB 8 Well I Know/Go With The Flow . . . 6
76 Rubber TUB 12 THE LAMBTON WORM (EP, foldout sleeve) . . . 8
72 Rubber RUB 002 HIS ROUND (LP, with Tony Capstick) . . . 15
75 Rubber RUB 009 HEDGEHOG PIE (LP) . . . 25
75 Rubber RUB 014 GREEN LADY (LP) . . . 20
78 Rubber RUB 024 JUST ACT NORMAL (LP, with lyric insert) . . . 20

(see also Dando Shaft)

HEDGEHOPPERS ANONYMOUS

65 Decca F 12241 It's Good News Week/Afraid Of Love . . . 6
65 Decca F 12298 Don't Push Me/Please Don't Hurt Your Heart For Me . . . 7
66 Decca F 12400 Baby (You're My Everything)/Remember . . . 12
66 Decca F 12479 Daytime/That's The Time . . . 8
66 Decca F 12530 Stop Press/Little Memories . . . 10

(see also Alan Avon & Toy Shop, Jonathan King, Mick Tinsley)

HEFNER

97 Inertia INERT 0004 Car Chase/Remix (12", p/s) . . . 10
98 Sticky STICKY 23 A Hymn For The Alcohol/My Art College Days Are Over (p/s, 500 only) . . . 8
98 Too Pure PURE 64 THE HEFNER SOUL: Flowers/A Hymn For The Coffee/Broodmare/The Girl From The Coast/More Christian Girls (10" EP) . . . 10
02 Too Pure PURE 125X THE HEFNER BRAIN: When The Angels Play Their Drum Machines/Dark Hearted Discos/The Baggage Reclaim Song/Can't Help Losing You/All I'll Ever Need (10", p/s) . . . 8

NEAL HEFTI & ORCHESTRA

66 RCA Victor RCA 1521 The Batman Theme/Batman Chase . . . 25
89 RCA PB 49571PD The Batman Theme (1966 Version)/Batman Chase (picture disc) . . . 6
54 Vogue/Coral LVC 10005 SWINGIN' ON A CORAL REEF (10" LP) . . . 15
65 Warner Bros W 1599 HARLOW (LP, soundtrack) . . . 30
65 United Artists (S)ULP 1098 HOW TO MURDER YOUR WIFE (LP, soundtrack) . . . 35
66 RCA Victor RD 7795 BOEING BOEING (LP, soundtrack) . . . 30
66 United Artists (S)ULP 1141 DUEL AT DIABLO (LP, soundtrack) . . . 20
67 London HA-D 8337 BAREFOOT IN THE PARK (LP, soundtrack) . . . 30
68 Dot (S)LPD 514 THE ODD COUPLE (LP, soundtrack) . . . 30

LUCILLE HEGAMIN

73 VJM VLP 50 BLUE FLAME (LP) . . . 12

DONALD HEIGHT

66 London HLZ 10062 Talk Of The Grapevine/There'll Be No Tomorrow . . . 45
67 London HLZ 10116 Three Hundred & Sixty Five Days/I'm Willing To Wait . . . 35
71 Avco Embassy 6105 005 Dancin' To The Music Of Love/Rags To Riches To Rags . . . 10
71 Jay Boy BOY 32 Talk Of The Grapevine/There'll Be No Tomorrow (reissue) . . . 6
72 Jay Boy BOY 51 Three Hundred & Sixty Five Days/I'm Willing To Wait (reissue) . . . 5
72 Jay Boy BOY 60 We Gotta Make Up/I Can't Get Enough . . . 5

RONNIE HEIGHT

59 Decca F 11126 Come Softly To Me/So Young, So Wise . . . 18
59 Decca F 11126 Come Softly To Me/So Young, So Wise (78) . . . 30
60 London HLN 9144 The One Finger Symphony/Mem'ries & Habits . . . 7

HEINZ (& WILD BOYS)

63 Decca F 11652 Dreams Do Come True/Been Invited To A Party . . . 20
63 Decca F 11693 Just Like Eddie/Don't You Knock At My Door . . . 7
63 Decca F 11768 Country Boy/Long Tall Jack . . . 8
64 Decca F 11831 You Were There/No Matter What They Say . . . 15
64 Decca F 11920 Please Little Girl/For Loving Me This Way . . . 20
64 Columbia DB 7374 Questions I Can't Answer/The Beating Of My Heart . . . 20
65 Columbia DB 7482 Diggin' My Potatoes/She Ain't Comin' Back (with Wild Boys) . . . 35

MINT VALUE £

65	Columbia DB 7559	Don't Think Twice, It's All Right/Big Fat Spider	22
65	Columbia DB 7656	End Of The World/You Make Me Feel So Good	35
65	Columbia DB 7779	Heart Full Of Sorrow/Don't Worry Baby	35
66	Columbia DB 7942	Movin' In/I'm Not A Bad Guy	40
63	Decca DFE 8545	HEINZ (EP)	55
63	Decca DFE 8559	LIVE IT UP (EP)	40
64	Decca LK 4599	TRIBUTE TO EDDIE (LP)	80

(see also Tornados, Saints)

HELDEN

83	Zica ZICA 01	Holding On/Once Upon A Time In The ... (p/s)	10
83	Zica 12 ZICA 01	Holding On/Once Upon A Time In The ... (12", p/s)	25
83	In The City ITC 1	Holding On/HOI POLLOI: When It's History (free with *In The City* magazine)	6/8

(see also Ultravox)

HELEN & JOSEPH

72	Rediffusion RS 001	L'Imhabba/Gonna Be A Fun Day (p/s, export issue)	6

HELEN LOVE

93	Dam. Goods DAMGOOD 18	Formula One Racing Girls/Riding High (pink vinyl, p/s)	6
93	Dam. Goods DAMGOOD 27	Joey Ramoney/I Was Your Greatest Fan (green vinyl, p/s)	6
94	Dam. Goods DAMGOOD 38	Punk Boy/Punk Boy 2 (blue vinyl, p/s)	6
94	Dam. Goods DAMGOOD 42	SUMMER POP PUNK POP EP (10", pink vinyl, p/s, 500 only)	12
95	Dam. Goods DAMPUD 33	Christmas Single/(Wat Tyler track) (olive vinyl, p/s)	12
95	Dam. Goods DAMGOOD 61	Bubblegum/Let's Go (pink vinyl, p/s)	6
95	Dam. Goods DAMGOOD 80	Ahead Of The Race/Diet Cola Race (white vinyl, p/s)	5
95	Dam. Goods DAMGOOD 89	Beat Him Up/Superboy/Supergirl (blue vinyl, p/s)	5
95	Wurlitzer Jukebox WJ 4	Il Fait Beau/BELMONDO: Metroliner (flexidisc)	5
96	Dam. Goods DAMGOOD 95	We Love You/The Girl About Town/We Love You/Punk Boy (orange vinyl, p/s)	5

RICHARD HELL (& VOIDOIDS)

76	Stiff BUY 7	(I Could Live With You In) Another World/(I Belong To The) Blank Generation/ You Gotta Lose (some with p/s, numbered, 5,000 only; later re-pressed for "The Stiff Box Set" & numbered '001')	10/6
77	Sire 6078 608	Blank Generation/Love Comes In Spurts (no p/s)	8
77	Sire 6078 608	Blank Generation/Liars Beware/Who Says? (12", p/s)	10
79	Radar ADA 30	The Kid With The Replaceable Head/I'm Your Man (p/s)	7
94	Overground OVER 36	Another World/Blank Generation/Love Comes In Spurts (p/s, reissue, 2,000 only)	5
96	Codex CODE 3X	GO NOW (10", p/s, 1,000 only, etched yellow vinyl)	8
96	Codex CODE 3	GO NOW (CD, 1,000 only)	8
92	Overground OVER 24	3 NEW SONGS (EP, 134 yellow vinyl copies)	6
77	Sire 9103 327	BLANK GENERATION (LP, some with inner sleeve)	15/12
83	I.D. NOSE 2	DESTINY STREET (LP)	12

(see also Neon Boys)

HELLANBACH

84	Neat NEAT 1006	NOW HEAR THIS (LP, with inner sleeve)	12
84	Neat NEAT 1019	THE BIG ... H (LP, with insert)	12

HELLHAMMER

84	Noise N 008	APOCALYPTIC RAIDS (12" EP, 45/33rpm)	15

DAVE HELLING

65	Stateside SS 409	It Ain't Me Babe/If You're Gonna Leave Me	10
66	Planet PLF 101	Christine/The Bells (with 'Planet' company sleeve)	30/25

HELLIONS

65	Piccadilly 7N 35213	Daydreaming Of You/Shades Of Blue	22
65	Piccadilly 7N 35232	Tomorrow Never Comes/Dream Child	20
65	Piccadilly 7N 35265	A Little Lovin'/Think It Over	20

(see also Revolution, Traffic, Roaring Sixties, Jim Capaldi, Dave Mason, Luther Grosvenor, Family, Spooky Tooth)

HELL IS FOR HEROES

00s	Universal HERO 001CD	Sick/Happy (CD, card sleeve)	20
00s	Chrysalis CHS 5143	I Can Climb Mountains/Get Low (blue vinyl, p/s)	7
00s	EMI 5515397	Night Vision/Can't You Hear It (clear vinyl, p/s)	6

HELLO

72	Bell BELL 1238	You Move Me/Ask Your Mama	15
72	Bell BELL 1265	C'mon/Wench	5
73	Bell BELL 1333	Another School Day/C'mon Get Together (p/s)	6

HELL PREACHERS INC.

69	Marble Arch MALS 1169	SUPREME PSYCHEDELIC UNDERGROUND (LP)	25

BOBBY HELMS

57	Brunswick 05711	Fraulein/(Got A) Heartsick Feeling	12
57	Brunswick 05721	My Special Angel/Standing At The End of My World	15
58	Brunswick 05730	No Other Baby/The Magic Song	18
58	Brunswick 05730	No Other Baby/The Magic Song (78)	8
58	Brunswick 05741	Love My Lady/Just A Little Lonesome	18
58	Brunswick 05748	Jacqueline/Living In The Shadow Of The Past	15
58	Brunswick 05754	Schoolboy Crush/Borrowed Dreams	18
58	Brunswick 05765	Jingle Bell Rock/Captain Santa Claus	25
58	Brunswick 05765	Jingle Bell Rock/Captain Santa Claus (78)	22
59	Brunswick 05786	Miss Memory/New River Train	12
59	Brunswick 05786	Miss Memory/New River Train (78)	15
59	Brunswick 05801	Soon It Can Be Told/I Guess I'll Miss The Prom	12
59	Brunswick 05801	Soon It Can Be Told/I Guess I'll Miss The Prom (78)	18
59	Brunswick 05813	My Lucky Day/Hurry Baby	12
59	Brunswick 05813	My Lucky Day/Hurry Baby (78)	20

MINT VALUE £

61	Brunswick 05852	Sad Eyed Baby/You're The One	8
60	Brunswick OE 9461	BOBBY HELMS (EP)	65
57	Brunswick LAT 8250	SINGS TO MY SPECIAL ANGEL (LP)	100

JIMMY HELMS

63	Pye 7N 45440	Ragtime Girl/Romeo & Juliet	7
69	London HL 10255	If You Let Me/I Don't Care Who Knows It	6
73	Capitol CL 15762	My Little Devil/Magnificent Sanctuary Band	12

HELP

71	MCA MWPS 4039	SECOND COMING (LP)	60

HELPLESS HUW

78	US US 001	Still Love You (In My Heart)	5
80	US US 002	Sid Vicious Was Innocent/Going Through The Motions/ Baby We're Not In Love/When You're Weary (p/s in bag)	7

HELP YOURSELF

71	Liberty LBF 15459	Running Down Deep/Paper Leaves	8
72	United Artists UP 35355	Heaven Row/Brown Lady	8
72	United Artists UP 35466	Mommy Won't Be Home For Christmas/Johnny B. Goode	6
71	Liberty LBS 83484	HELP YOURSELF (LP)	20
72	United Artists UAS 29287	STRANGE AFFAIR (LP, with inner sleeve)	20
72	United Artists UAS 29413	BEWARE OF THE SHADOW (LP)	18
73	United Artists UDG 4001 [UAS 29487/FREE 1]	THE RETURN OF KEN WHALEY/HAPPY DAYS (2-LP, box set with individual sleeves)	30
73	United Artists UAS 29487	THE RETURN OF KEN WHALEY (LP)	15

(see also Man, Deke Leonard, Shades Of Morley Brown, Tyla Gang)

HEMLOCK

73	Deram DM 379	Mr Horizontal/Beggar Man	12
73	Deram SML 1102	HEMLOCK (LP)	55

(see also Miller Anderson, Keef Hartley Band, Dog Soldier)

BERTHA HENDERSON/ROSA HENDERSON

60	Jazz Collector JEL 14	THE FEMALE BLUES VOL. 2 (EP)	18

BILL HENDERSON

60	Top Rank JAR 412	Sweet Pumpkin/Joey, Joey, Joey	15
63	Stateside SL 10019	BILL HENDERSON (LP)	22

DICKIE HENDERSON & JUNE LAVERICK

60	Oriole CB 1536	Simpatica/It's So Nice To Sleep With No-One (78)	8

(see also June Laverick)

DORRIS HENDERSON

65	Columbia DB 7567	The Hangman/Leaves That Are Green	15
67	Fontana TF 811	Message To Pretty/Watch The Stars	10
65	Columbia SX 6001	THERE YOU GO (LP, with John Renbourn)	300+
67	Fontana (S)TL 5385	WATCH THE STARS (LP, with John Renbourn)	250

(see also Eclection, John Renbourn)

EDMONIA HENDERSON

51	Tempo R 43	Mama Don't Want A Sweet Man Any More/Hateful Blues (78)	10

FINIS HENDERSON

83	Motown TMGT 1304	Skip To My Lou/I'd Rather Be Gone/Vina Del Mar (12")	10

FLETCHER HENDERSON

50s	Jazz Collector JE 111	FLETCHER HENDERSON JAZZ GROUP (EP)	8
50s	Jazz Collector JE 115	BIG BAND STORY VOL. 1 (EP)	8
55	London AL 3547	BIRTH OF BIG BAND JAZZ (10" LP)	15
55	HMV DLP 1066	AT CONNIE'S INN (10" LP)	15
50s	Audubon AAF-AAK	FLETCHER HENDERSON (6 x 10" LP set)	60

(see also Clara Smith & Fletcher Henderson)

JOE HENDERSON

62	London HLU 9553	Snap Your Fingers/If You See Me Cry	8
63	London REU 1376	JOE HENDERSON (EP)	25

JOE 'MR. PIANO' HENDERSON

58	Pye Nixa 7N 15147	Trudie/Love Is The Sweetest Thing	6
60	Pye 7N 15257	Ooh! La! La!/Mind	7

LORNA HENDERSON

60	Oriole CB 1549	Lollipops To Lipstick/Steady Eddie	25
60	Oriole CB 1549	Lollipops To Lipstick/Steady Eddie (78)	15
60	Oriole CB 1590	A Thousand Stars/Murray, What's Your Hurry?	10

RUSS HENDERSON & HIS CALYPSO BAND

57	HMV POP 333	Waiting For The Coconuts To Fall/Nobody's Business (78)	8

(see also Marie Bryant)

SKITCH HENDERSON

59	Brunswick OE 9434	LONDON AT MIDNIGHT (EP)	10

WILLIE HENDERSON (& SOUL EXPLOSIONS)

70	MCA MU 1127	Funky Chicken/Oo Wee Baby, I Love You (with Soul Explosions)	7
73	Contempo C 18	The Dance Master (Parts 1 & 2)	6
74	Contempo CS 9005	The Dance Master (Parts 1 & 2) (reissue)	5
74	Pye International 7N 25668	Gangster Boogie Bump/Let's Merengue	5

MINT VALUE £

BOBBY HENDRICKS

Year	Label/Cat. No.	Title	£
58	London HL 8714	Itchy Twitchy Feeling/A Thousand Dreams	60
58	London HL 8714	Itchy Twitchy Feeling/A Thousand Dreams (78)	30
59	Top Rank JAR 193	Little John Green/Sincerely, Your Lover	20
61	Mercury AMT 1163	I'm Coming Home/Every Other Night	10
64	Sue WI 315	Itchy Twitchy Feeling/Thousand Dreams (reissue, as Bobby Henricks)	22

(see also Drifters)

HUGH HENDRICKS & UPSETTERS

Year	Label/Cat. No.	Title	£
70	Spinning Wheel SW 103	Land Of Kinks/O'NEIL HALL: This Man	10

JON HENDRICKS

Year	Label/Cat. No.	Title	£
56	Brunswick 05521	Four Brothers/Cloudburst (with Dave Lambert Singers)	8
68	Verve VS 572	No More/Rainbow's End	5
71	Philips 6006 088	I Got Soul/Slow Train	5
61	Vogue EPV 1268	A GOOD GIT-TOGETHER (EP)	12
60	Vogue LAE 12231	A GOOD GIT-TOGETHER (LP)	18
70	Valiant VS 140	BOSSA MAN (LP)	12
72	Philips 6438 019	LIVE (LP)	12

(see also Dave Lambert)

JIMI HENDRIX (EXPERIENCE)

SINGLES

Year	Label/Cat. No.	Title	£
66	Polydor 56139	Hey Joe/Stone Free	8
67	Track 604 001	Purple Haze/51st Anniversary (white or black label)	15/8
67	Track 604 004	The Wind Cries Mary/Highway Chile	8
67	Track 604 007	The Burning Of The Midnight Lamp/The Stars That Play With Laughing Sam's Dice	7
67	Decca F 22652	How Would You Feel/You Don't Want Me (with Curtis Knight, test pressing, unreleased)	500
67	Track 604 009	How Would You Feel/You Don't Want Me (with Curtis Knight)	10
67	London HL 10160	Hush Now/Flashing (with Curtis Knight; some in export p/s)	30/8
68	Track 604 025	All Along The Watchtower/Long Hot Summer Night	7
69	Track 604 029	Crosstown Traffic/Gypsy Eyes	10
69	Track 604 033	Let Me Light Your Fire/The Burning Of The Midnight Lamp	10
70	London HLZ 10321	Ballad Of Jimi/Gloomy Monday (with Curtis Knight)	7
70	London HL 7126	Ballad Of Jimi/Gloomy Monday (with Curtis Knight, export issue)	30
70	Track 2095 001	Voodoo Chile/Hey Joe/All Along The Watchtower (p/s; later copies have white border on sleeve; also sold without p/s)	12/8/6
71	RCA RCA 2033	No Such Animal (Parts 1 & 2) (initially in p/s, with Curtis Knight uncredited)	18/6
71	Track 2094 007	Angel/Night Bird Flying	7
71	Track 2094 010	Gypsy Eyes/Remember/Purple Haze/Stone Free (initially in p/s)	20/8
72	Polydor 2001 277	Johnny B. Goode/Little Wing	6
73	Reprise K 14286	Hear My Train A-Comin/Rock Me Baby	6
73	Polydor/Sound For Industry SFI 1572	Red House/Spanish Castle Magic (1-sided flexidisc with *Rolling Stone*)	15/5
80	Polydor 2608 001	6 SINGLES PACK (6 plain sleeve singles [2141 275-280], open-out card p/s)	20
82	CBS CBS A 2749	Fire/Are You Experienced? (p/s)	5
89	Castle Comms. HENPD 01	Hey Joe/Purple Haze/Radio One Theme (12", picture disc)	8
89	Polydor PO 33	Purple Haze/51st Anniversary (p/s, reissue)	5
89	Polydor PZCD 33	Purple Haze/51st Anniversary/All Along The Watchtower/Hey Joe (CD, card p/s)	8
90	Polydor PO 71	Crosstown Traffic/Voodoo Chile (p/s)	5
90	Polydor PO 100	All Along The Watchtower/Voodoo Chile/Hey Joe (p/s)	5
92	BMG 791 168	JIMI PLAYS BERKELEY (CD EP, available with "Jimi Plays Berkeley" video)	8

TRACK LPs

Year	Label/Cat. No.	Title	£
67	Track 612 001	ARE YOU EXPERIENCED (mono, some in laminated sleeve)	150/50
67	Track 613 001	ARE YOU EXPERIENCED (stereo, rumoured to exist)	
67	Track 612 003	AXIS: BOLD AS LOVE (laminated gatefold sleeve, some with gatefold insert, mono)	140/60
67	Track 613 003	AXIS: BOLD AS LOVE (laminated gatefold sleeve, some with gatefold insert, stereo)	95/50
68	Track 612 004/613 004	SMASH HITS (mono/stereo)	40/22
68	Track 612 008/009	ELECTRIC LADYLAND (2-LP, plain white non-gatefold sleeve, labels marked "Test Pressing", mono)	1,000+
68	Track 613 008/009	ELECTRIC LADYLAND (2-LP, lam'd g/f sl., 1st press. light blue tr'klisting, st.)	80/70
68	Track 613 010	ELECTRIC LADYLAND PART 1 (stereo only)	25
68	Track 613 017	ELECTRIC LADYLAND PART 2 (stereo only)	25
70	Track Super 2406 002	BAND OF GYPSYS (original 'puppet' sleeve)	85
70	Track Super 2406 002	BAND OF GYPSYS (repressing, gatefold 'Isle Of Wight' sleeve)	20
70	Track Super 2406 002	BAND OF GYPSYS (2nd repressing, single sleeve)	15
70	Track 2407 010	BACKTRACK 10: ARE YOU EXPERIENCED? (budget reissue, mono)	15
70	Track 2407 011	BACKTRACK 11: AXIS: BOLD AS LOVE (budget reissue, mono)	15
71	Track 2856 002	ELECTRIC JIMI HENDRIX (mail-order only Record Club release)	650
71	Track 2408 101	THE CRY OF LOVE (gatefold sleeve)	15
71	Track 2408 101	THE CRY OF LOVE (red vinyl, factory custom pressing, 3 copies only)	1,500+
88	Track/HMV C 881-16	ARE YOU EXPERIENCED (LP, box set, ltd. ed. of 2,500, no'd, with certificate)	30

POLYDOR LPs

Year	Label/Cat. No.	Title	£
71	Polydor 2302 016	ISLE OF WIGHT	12
71	Polydor 2302 018	HENDRIX IN THE WEST (gatefold sleeve)	15
72	Polydor 2302 020	WAR HEROES	15
72	Polydor 2302 023	THE CRY OF LOVE (gatefold sleeve, reissue)	12
73	Polydor 2302 268	SMASH HITS (stereo reissue)	12
73	Polydor 2480 005	BAND OF GYPSYS (reissue, different gatefold sleeve)	12
73	Polydor 2657 012	ELECTRIC LADYLAND (2-LP, laminated gatefold sleeve, reissue)	25
73	Polydor 2310 271	ELECTRIC LADYLAND PART 1 (reissue)	12
73	Polydor 2310 272	ELECTRIC LADYLAND PART 2 (reissue)	12
74	Polydor 2310 301	LOOSE ENDS	12

MINT VALUE £

75 Polydor 2310 398 — CRASH LANDING 12
75 Polydor 2310 415 — MIDNIGHT LIGHTNING 12
78 Polydor 2612 034 — THE ESSENTIAL JIMI HENDRIX (2-LP, with bonus 1-sided 33rpm 7" "Gloria" [JIMI 1] in special bag) 18
78 St. Michael 2102/0102 — JIMI HENDRIX (cat. no. also listed as Polydor 2891 139) 60
78 St. Michael/Poly. 2891 139 — JIMI HENDRIX (cassette) 25
80 Polydor 2625 040 — JIMI HENDRIX (13-LP box set [11 x LP + 1 x 2-LP]) 75
80 Polydor POLS 1023 — NINE TO THE UNIVERSE 12
84 Polydor SPDLP 3 — ELECTRIC LADYLAND (2-LP, non-laminate gatefold sleeve, 2nd reissue) 18
87 Polydor 833 004-1 — LIVE AT WINTERLAND (2-LP, with poster) 18
88 Polydor/HMV C88 LP 1-16 — ARE YOU EXPERIENCED? (box set sold via HMV stores, 1,500 only) 12
90 Polydor 847 2311 — CORNERSTONES: JIMI HENDRIX 1967-1970 12

OTHER LPs

68 London HA/SH 8349 — GET THAT FEELING (with Curtis Knight) 25
68 London HA/SH 8369 — STRANGE THINGS (with Curtis Knight) 25
71 Ember NR 5057 — EXPERIENCE — THE ORIGINAL SOUNDTRACK (gatefold sleeve) 12
71 Reprise K 40430 — LIVE AT THE MONTEREY INTERNATIONAL POP FESTIVAL (shared with Otis Redding) 30
71 Reprise K 44159 — RAINBOW BRIDGE (matt gatefold sleeve, 'steamboat' label, soundtrack) 12
72 Ember NR 5061 — MORE EXPERIENCE (soundtrack) 12
73 Reprise K 64017 — SOUNDTRACK RECORDINGS FROM THE FILM *JIMI HENDRIX* (2-LP) 18
73 Ember NR 5068 — IN THE BEGINNING (textured gatefold sleeve) 12
74 Ember EMB 3428 — LOOKING BACK WITH JIMI HENDRIX 12
75 DJM DJLMD 8011 — FOR REAL (2-LP, gatefold sleeve) 18
89 Castle Comms. HBLP 100 — LIVE AND UNRELEASED — THE RADIO SHOW (5-LP) 30

CDs

84 Track 821 993 2 — BAND OF GYPSYS 18
88 Polydor/HMV C88 LP 1-11 — ARE YOU EXPERIENCED? (box set via HMV stores, 1,500 only) 18
89 Castle Comms. HBCD 100 — LIVE AND UNRELEASED — THE RADIO SHOW (3-CD, box set) 30
89 Polydor 831 312-2 — HENDRIX IN THE WEST 18
89 Polydor 837 574-2 — LOOSE ENDS 18

(see also Eire Apparent, Jayne Mansfield, McGough & McGear, Noel Redding Band, Fat Mattress, Curtis Knight, Billy Cox, Buddy Miles, Riot Squad)

MARGIE HENDRIX

66 Mercury MF 976 — I Call You Lover But You Ain't Nothin' But A Tramp/The Question 15
67 Mercury MF 1001 — Restless/On The Right Track 20

LARRY HENLEY

64 Hickory 45-1272 — My Reasons For Living/Stickin' Up For My Baby 12
(see also Newbeats, Dean & Mark)

CHRISTIE HENNESSY

73 Westwood — CHRISTIE HENNESSY (LP) 40

HENNESSYS

69 Cambrian CLP 593 — THE ROADS AND THE MILES (LP) 60
60s Music Factory MF 106 — CARDIFF AFTER DARK (LP) 60

ADRIAN HENRI

60s Charivari — ADRIAN HENRI (LP) 12
60s Argo PLP 1194 — ADRIAN HENRI AND HUGO WILLIAMS (LP) 12
(see also Liverpool Scene, McGough & McGear)

ANN HENRY

60 Top Rank JAR 292 — Like Young/Sugar Blues 8

BOB HENRY

65 Philips BF 1450 — I Need Someone/Built Like A Man 18
(see also Robert Henry)

CLARENCE ('FROGMAN') HENRY

57 London HLN 8389 — Ain't Got No Home/Troubles Troubles (as Clarence Henry) (gold or silver lettering) 275/140
57 London HLN 8389 — Ain't Got No Home/Troubles Troubles (as Clarence Henry) (78) 55
61 Pye International 7N 25078 — (I Don't Know Why) But I Do/Just My Baby And Me 7
61 Pye International 7N 25089 — You Always Hurt The One You Love/Little Suzy 7
61 Pye International 7N 25108 — Lonely Street/Why Can't You 8
61 Pye International 7N 25115 — On Bended Knees/Standing In The Need Of Love 8
62 Pye International 7N 25123 — A Little Too Much/I Wish I Could Say The Same 10
62 Pye International 7N 25141 — Dream Myself A Sweetheart/Lost Without You 10
62 Pye International 7N 25169 — The Jealous Kind/Come On And Dance 10
64 London HLU 9936 — Little Green Frog/Have You Ever Been Lonely? 10
66 London HLU 10025 — Ain't Got No Home/Baby, Ain't That Love? 10
61 Pye Intl. NEP 44007 — CLARENCE 'FROGMAN' HENRY HIT PARADE (EP) 60
61 Pye Intl. NPL 28017 — YOU ALWAYS HURT THE ONE YOU LOVE (LP) 75

RICHARD HENRY

68 Regal Zonophone RZ 3014 — Oh Girl/Lay Your Head Upon My Shoulder 6

ROBERT HENRY

66 Philips BF 1476 — Walk Away Like A Winner/That's All I Want 40
(see also Bob Henry)

HENRY COW

73 Virgin V 2005 — THE LEGEND (LP) 20
74 Virgin V 2011 — UNREST (LP) 18
75 Virgin V 2027 — IN PRAISE OF LEARNING (LP) 18
76 Caroline CAD 3002 — CONCERTS (LP) 18
79 Broadcast BC 1 — WESTERN CULTURE (LP) 15
(see also Slapp Happy, Art Bears, Fred Frith, Gong/Henry Cow/Global Trucking Company)

MINT VALUE £

HENRY & LIZA

73 Dragon DRA 1004 — Hole Under Cratches/TIVOLIS: Hole Under Cratches (Instrumental) (actually "Hole Under Crutches") . . . 6

(see also Max Romeo)

HENRY III

67 Island WI 3078 — Thank You Girl/Take Me Back . . . 22
67 Island WI 3081 — I'll Reach The End/Won't Go Away (B-side actually "Lee's Special" by Don Tony Lee) . . . 22
67 RCA RCA 1568 — So Much Love/Sitting In The Park . . . 18
70 Dynamic DYN 402 — Out Of Time/VICEROYS: Love For Everyone (both with Hubcap & Wheels) . . . 8

(see also Uniques)

JUDY HENSKE

66 Reprise RS 20485 — Road To Nowhere/Sing A Rainbow . . . 15
65 Reprise RS 6203 — DEATH DEFYING (LP) . . . 18

JUDY HENSKE & JERRY YESTER

69 Straight STS 1052 — FAREWELL ALDEBARAN (LP) . . . 25

ROBERT HENRY HENSLEY

68 Polydor 56295 — You're Gonna See Me Cry/Montage . . . 8

NICKY HENSON

63 Parlophone R 4976 — Till I See You Cry/What Does It Mean? . . . 15

DAVID HENTSCHEL

75 Ring O' 2017 101 — Oh My My/Devil Woman . . . 8
75 Ring O' 2320 101 — ST*RTLING MUSIC (LP) . . . 12

NAT HEPBURN

60s Jump Up JU 516 — River/Political Girl . . . 6

HEP STARS

66 Decca F 22446 — Sunny Girl/No Response . . . 40
67 Olga OLE 001 — Wedding/Consolation . . . 20
68 Olga OLE 013 — Let It Be Me/Groovy Summertime (withdrawn, supposedly reissued 1969) . . . 45
68 Olga OLE 014 — Malaika/It's Nice To Be Back (some in export p/s) . . . 55/25

(see also Abba)

HEPTONES

66 Rio R 104 — Gunmen Coming To Town/TOMMY McCOOK & SUPERSONICS: Riverton City . . . 45
67 Ska Beat JB 266 — We've Got Love/I Am Lonely . . . 70
67 Caltone TONE 105 — Schoolgirls/Ain't That Bad? . . . 22
67 Studio One SO 2005 — A Change Is Gonna Come/Nobody Knows . . . 25
67 Studio One SO 2014 — Fat Girl/DELROY WILSON: Mother Word . . . 20
67 Studio One SO 2021 — If I Knew/Festival Day . . . 40
67 Studio One SO 2026 — Why Did You Leave?/GAYLADS: Don't Try To Reach Me . . . 22
67 Studio One SO 2027 — Why Must I?/SLIM SMITH: Try Again . . . 22
67 Studio One SO 2031 — Take Me (actually by The Soul Vendors)/DELROY WILSON: I'm Not A King . . . 22
67 Studio One SO 2033 — Only Sixteen/Baby . . . 20
68 Studio One SO 2040 — Tripe Girl/DELROY WILSON: Mr. D.J. . . . 22
68 Studio One SO 2049 — Cry, Baby, Cry/Mama . . . 22
68 Studio One SO 2052 — Dock Of The Bay/KING ROCKY (ELLIS): The Ruler . . . 22
68 Studio One SO 2055 — Party Time/Oil In Your Lamp . . . 22
68 Coxsone CS 7052 — Love Won't Come Easy/Gee Wee . . . 22
68 Coxsone CS 7068 — Equal Rights/Ting-A-Ling . . . 22
68 Coxsone CS 7082 — Soul Power/Love Me Always . . . 22
69 Coxsone CS 7092 — Sweet Talking/Ob-La-Di . . . 22
69 Studio One SO 2083 — I Shall Be Released/Love Me Always . . . 22
69 Bamboo BAM 11 — I Shall Be Released/Love Me Always (Power) (reissue) . . . 12
70 Bamboo BAM 28 — Young, Gifted and Black/SOUND DIMENSION: Joyland . . . 12
70 Bamboo BAM 39 — Young Generation/You Turned Away . . . 30
70 Bamboo BAM 43 — Message From A Blackman/SOUND DIMENSION: Jamaica Underground . . . 12
70 Upsetter US 339 — Hurry Up/Thanks We Get . . . 12
70 Banana BA 311 — Be A Man/U ROY: Shock Attack . . . 12
71 Banana BA 325 — Suspicious Minds/Haven't You Any Fight Left? . . . 10
71 Banana BA 349 — Freedom Line/SOUND DIMENSION: Version . . . 8
72 Green Door GD 4020 — Hypocrite/JOHNNY LOVER: Straight To The Head . . . 12
72 Prince Buster PB 37 — Our Day Will Come/PRINCE BUSTER: Protection . . . 12
72 Ashanti ASH 411 — I'm In The Mood For Love/TOMMY McCOOK & NOW GENERATION: Eight Years After . . . 8
72 Duke DU 143 — Save The Last Dance For Me/Be The One . . . 6
72 Pama PM 843 — You've Lost That Lovin' Feelin'/RUPIE EDWARDS ALLSTARS: Feeling Version . . . 6
72 Pama Supreme PS 367 — Save The Last Dance For Me/Save The Last Dance Version . . . 6
72 Ackee ACK 407 — I Miss You (Parts 1 & 2) . . . 12
73 Ackee ACK 414 — Let Me Hold Your Hand/Version . . . 5
73 Jaguar JAG 103 — Drifting Away/BONGO LES: Zion Drum . . . 8
73 Grape GR 3053 — Old Time/G.G. ALLSTARS: Dub . . . 5
73 Smash SMA 2328 — Soul Sister/IMPACT ALLSTARS: Soul Sister (Version) . . . 7
74 Pama Supreme PS 390 — Thanks We Get/Oppression (both actually by Delroy Butler) . . . 7
75 Faith FA 012 — Party Time/Version . . . 5
67 Studio One SOL 9002 — THE HEPTONES (LP) . . . 120
68 Studio One SOL 9010 — ON TOP (LP) . . . 120
72 Trojan TBL 183 — THE HEPTONES AND THEIR FRIENDS MEET THE NOW GENERATION (LP) . . . 40
75 Island ILPS 9297 — BOOK OF RULES (LP) . . . 18
76 Island ILPS 9456 — PARTY TIME (LP) . . . 15

(see also Barry Llewellyn, Soul Vendors, Ronald & Lloyd, Ed Nangle, Love Generation, Alton Ellis, Basil Daley, Ken Boothe, Jackie Mittoo)

HERB & KAY

54 Parlophone MSP 6127 This Ole House/Angels In The Sky 25
54 Parlophone CMSP 23 This Ole House/Angels In The Sky (export issue).......... 25
55 Parlophone CMSP 31 Coffee Blues/Juke Box Jig (export issue).......... 25

HERBAL MIXTURE

66 Columbia DB 8021 A Love That's Died/Tailor Made 175
66 Columbia DB 8083 Machines/Please Leave My Mind.......... 175
(see also Tony McPhee, Groundhogs)

HERBIE & ROYALISTS

68 Saga FID 2121 SOUL OF THE MATTER (LP) 25

HERBIE'S PEOPLE

65 CBS 202005 Sweet And Tender Romance/You Thrill Me To Pieces 20
66 CBS 202058 One Little Smile/You Never Know 10
67 CBS 202584 Residential Area/Humming Bird 12

HERD

65 Parlophone R 5284 Goodbye Baby, Goodbye/Here Comes The Fool.......... 35
65 Parlophone R 5353 She Was Really Saying Something/It's Been A Long Time Baby 45
66 Parlophone R 5413 So Much In Love/This Boy's Always Been True 45
67 Fontana TF 819 I Can Fly/Diary Of A Narcissist 12
67 Fontana TF 856 From The Underworld/Sweet William.......... 7
67 Fontana TF 887 Paradise Lost/Come On — Believe Me (some in p/s).......... 18/7
68 Fontana TF 925 I Don't Want Our Loving To Die/Our Fairy Tale 7
68 Fontana TF 975 Sunshine Cottage/Miss Jones.......... 8
69 Fontana TF 1011 The Game/Beauty Queen.......... 8
71 B&C CB 154 You've Got Me Hangin' From Your Lovin' Tree/I Don't Wanna Go To Sleep Again .. 6
72 Bumble GEX 1 From The Underworld/Paradise Lost/On My Way Home (maxi-single).......... 5
73 Bumble GE 120 I Don't Want Our Loving To Die/The Game 5
68 Fontana (S)TL 5458 PARADISE LOST (LP).......... 35
72 Bumble GEMP 5001 NOSTALGIA (LP) 22
(see also Peter Frampton, Humble Pie, Judas Jump, Andy Bown, Preachers)

HERE & NOW

78 Charly CYS 1055 End Of The Beginning/Choke A Koala (p/s) 5
79 Charly CEP 122 A Dog In Hell/Floating Anarchy Radio (p/s) 5
80 Charly NOW 1 Give And Take 5
78 Deptford Fun City DLP 02 WHAT YOU SEE ... IS WHAT YOU ARE (LP, 1 side by Alternative TV).......... 12
(see also Daevid Allen)

HERESY

86 Earache Thanks (flexidisc, mail-order, 2,000 only [400 each on different coloured vinyl]) .. 5
89 In Your Face FACE 4 WHOSE GENERATION? EP (gatefold p/s).......... 5

HERESY/CONCRETE SOX

87 Manic Ears MOSH 2 HERESY/CONCRETE SOX (LP, 1 side each) 12

HERETIC

84 Thunderbolt THBE 1004 BURNT AT THE STAKE EP (Water Of Vice/Keep On Telling Those Lies/
Fever Of Love/Watch Me Grow (12", p/s).......... 30

HERITAGE

81 Rondelet ROUND 8 Strange Place To Be/Misunderstood (p/s) 20
82 Rondelet ABOUT 12 REMORSE CODE (LP, with lyric insert).......... 35

HERMAN (Chin-Loy)

71 Big Shot BI 573 El Fishy/HERMAN'S ALLSTARS: Nightmare
(B-side actually "In The Spirit" by Lloyd Charmers) 8
71 Big Shot BI 577 Tar Baby (actually "Crazy Baby" by U. Roy Jr.)/TOMMY McCOOK: Archie.......... 7
71 Big Shot BI 578 New Love/AUGUSTUS PABLO: The Mood 18
71 Big Shot BI 579 East Of The River Nile Version/AUGUSTO PABLO: East Of The River Nile 25
71 Duke DU 107 To The Fields/HERMAN'S VERSION MEN: Fields Version.......... 10
71 Ackee ACK 133 Dunce Cap/AQUARIANS: Version Cap.......... 6
71 Ackee ACK 140 Youth Man/AQUARIANS: Version.......... 15
71 Explosion EX 2049 Love Brother/Uganda.......... 6
71 Escort ERT 854 Love Brother/Love Brother Version (B-side actually by Tommy McCook) 6
71 Punch PH 55 Hold The Ghost/AQUARIUS SOUL BAND: Duppy Dance 6
71 Punch PH 58 Listen To The Beat/AQUARIANS: Sounds Only.......... 6
(see also Jimbilin)

PRIEST HERMAN

64 Blue Beat BB 266 We Are Praying/BUSTER'S ALLSTARS: Dallas, Texas 20

WOODY HERMAN

78s

52 London L 1156 Celestial Blues/Early Autumn 8
52 London L 1160 Blues In Advance/Terrista 8
53 London L 1222 Men From Mars/Beau Jazz.......... 8
54 London HL 8013 Wooftie/Moten Stomp (as Woody Herman & New Third Herd) 10
54 London HL 8031 Fancy Woman/Eight Babies To Mind (as Woody Herman's Woodchoppers).......... 12
55 London HL 8122 Sorry 'bout The Whole Darned Thing/Love's A Dog (with New Third Herd) 12

SINGLES

54 London HL 8013 Wooftie/Moten Stomp (as Woody Herman & New Third Herd) 30
54 London HL 8031 Fancy Woman/Eight Babies To Mind (as Woody Herman's Woodchoppers).......... 30
54 Capitol CL 14183 Muskrat Ramble/Woodchopper's Mambo (Woody Herman & His Orchestra) 15
55 London HL 8122 Sorry 'Bout The Whole Darned Thing/Love's A Dog (with New Third Herd) 30
55 Capitol CL 14231 Mexican Hat Trick/Sleepy Serenade (as Woody Herman & His Orchestra).......... 8
55 Capitol CL 14278 My Sin Is You/Have it Your Way (with Allen Sisters) 10
55 Capitol CL 14299 Kiss The Baby/Long, Long Night (as Woody Herman & New Third Herd).......... 10
55 Capitol CL 14333 The Girl Upstairs/You're Here, My Love (as Woody Herman & His Orchestra).......... 8

MINT VALUE £

Year	Label	Title	Value
55	Capitol CL 14366	Love Is A Many Splendoured Thing/House Of Bamboo (as Woody Herman & His Orchestra & Singers)	7
56	Capitol CL 14522	Skinned/Skinned Again (as Woody Herman & His Orchestra)	5
56	Capitol CL 14578	To Love Again/For All We Know (as Woody Herman & His Orchestra)	5
57	HMV POP 371	Comes Love/Makin' Whoopee	5
60	Top Rank TR 5012	Blowin' Up A Storm/It's Coolin' Time (as Woody Herman Orchestra)	6
60	Philips JAZ 113	The Third Herd/Keen And Peachy	5
62	Ember JBS 702	Woodchoppers' Ball/Body And Soul	8
69	Chess CRS 8095	Hush/Light My Fire	8

EPs

Year	Label	Title	Value
54	London RE-P 1001	HERD FROM MARS VOL. 1 (as Woody Herman & New Third Herd)	15
55	London RE-P 1002	HERD FROM MARS VOL. 2 (as Woody Herman & New Third Herd)	15
55	Columbia SEG 7532	WOODY HERMAN AND HIS ORCHESTRA	8
55	Philips BBE 12026	WOODY HERMAN AND HIS ORCHESTRA	8
55	Capitol EAP1 556	SPECIALS	8
55	Capitol EAP1 560	THE WOODY HERMAN BAND	8
55	Capitol EAP2 560	THE WOODY HERMAN BAND	8
55	Capitol EAP3 560	THE WOODY HERMAN BAND	8
56	Capitol EAP2 658	THE WOODY HERMAN ORCHESTRA	8
56	Capitol EAP3 658	THE WOODY HERMAN ORCHESTRA	8
57	Capitol EAP 1009	ROAD BAND	8
57	Capitol EAP 1015	WOODY HERMAN'S HERD	8
57	Capitol EAP 1026	MUSIC TO DANCE TO	8

LPs

Year	Label	Title	Value
52	Capitol LC 6560	CLASSICS IN JAZZ (10")	15
52	MGM MGM-D 108	AT CARNEGIE HALL VOLUME 1 (10")	15
53	MGM MGM-D 110	AT CARNEGIE HALL VOLUME 2 (10")	15
53	London H-APB 1014	STOMPING AT THE SAVOY (10", as Woody Herman & New Third Herd)	15
54	London H-APB 1018	MEN FROM MARS (10", as Woody Herman & New Third Herd)	15
55	Columbia 33S 1060	HERE'S HERMAN (10")	12
55	Columbia 33S 1068	SEQUENCE IN JAZZ (10")	12
56	Brunswick LAT 8092	WOODCHOPPERS' BALL	12
56	Philips BBL 7123	THREE HERDS	12
57	HMV CLP 1130	SONGS FOR HIP LOVERS	15
58	Fontana TFR 6015	SUMMER SEQUENCE (10")	12
59	Top Rank 35/038	THE HERD RIDES AGAIN	12
60	Top Rank BUY 009	MOODY WOODY (as Woody Herman Orchestra featuring Charlie Byrd)	12
61	London Jazz LTZ-K 15200	AT THE MONTEREY JAZZ FESTIVAL (also stereo SAH-K 6100)	12

(see also David Rose Orchestra)

HERMAN'S HERMITS

Year	Label	Title	Value
64	Columbia DB 7338	I'm Into Something Good/Your Hand In Mine	6
64	Columbia DB 7408	Show Me Girl/I Know Why	6
65	Columbia DB 7475	Silhouettes/Can't You Hear My Heartbeat?	6
65	Columbia DB 7546	Wonderful World/Dream On	6
65	Columbia DB 7670	Just A Little Bit Better/Take Love, Give Love	6
65	Columbia DB 7791	A Must To Avoid/The Man With The Cigar	6
66	Columbia DB 7861	You Won't Be Leaving/Listen People	6
66	Columbia DB 7947	This Door Swings Both Ways/For Love	7
66	Columbia DB 8012	No Milk Today/My Reservation's Been Confirmed	7
66	Columbia DB 8076	East-West/What Is Wrong, What Is Right?	6
67	Columbia DB 8123	There's A Kind Of Hush (All Over The World)/Gaslite Street	6
67	Columbia DB 8235	Museum/Moonshine Man	6
68	Columbia DB 8327	I Can Take Or Leave Your Loving/Marcel's	6
68	Columbia DB 8404	Sleepy Joe/Just One Girl	6
68	Columbia DB 8446	Sunshine Girl/Nobody Needs To Know	6
68	Columbia DB 8504	Something's Happening/The Most Beautiful Thing In My Life	6
69	Columbia DB 8563	My Sentimental Friend/My Lady	6
68	EMI SLES 15	No Milk Today/There's A Kind Of Hush (promo only, white label)	20
68	EMI SLES 16	London Look (promo only, white label)	20
69	Columbia DB 8626	Here Comes The Star/It's Alright Now	6
70	Columbia DB 8656	Years May Come, Years May Go/Smile Please	6
71	RCA RCA 2135	She's A Lady/Gold Mandala	5
72	RCA RCA 2265	The Man/Effen Curly	5
74	Buddah BDS 700	Train/Ride On The Water (withdrawn)	30+
65	Columbia SEG 8380	HERMANIA (EP)	22
65	Columbia SEG 8440	MRS BROWN YOU'VE GOT A LOVELY DAUGHTER (EP)	20
65	Columbia SEG 8442	HERMAN'S HERMITS HITS (EP)	20
66	Columbia SEG 8477	A MUST TO AVOID (EP)	20
66	Columbia SEG 8503	MUSIC FROM THE SOUNDTRACK "HOLD ON" (EP)	22
67	Columbia SEG 8520	DANDY (EP)	22
65	Columbia 33SX 1727	HERMAN'S HERMITS (LP)	25
65	Columbia S(C)X 6303	MRS BROWN YOU'VE GOT A LOVELY DAUGHTER (LP, soundtrack, mono or stereo, some with manuscript)	25/30
66	Columbia SX 6084	BOTH SIDES OF HERMAN'S HERMITS (LP)	25
67	Columbia S(C)X 6174	THERE'S A KIND OF HUSH ALL OVER THE WORLD (LP)	25
60s	Regal SREG 1117	HERMAN'S HERMITS (LP, export issue)	30
60s	Columbia SCXC 27	THE BEST OF HERMAN'S HERMITS (LP, export issue)	30
60s	Columbia SCXC 32	THE BEST OF HERMAN'S HERMITS VOL. 2 (LP, export issue)	30
60s	Columbia SCXC 34	THERE'S A KIND OF HUSH ALL OVER THE WORLD (LP, export issue)	30
60s	Columbia SCXC 35	BLAZE (LP, export issue)	30

(see also Peter Noone)

CORRINE HERMES

Year	Label	Title	Value
83	Polydor POSPE 597	Words Of Love/Si La Vie Est Cadeau (p/s)	6

HEROES
75 United Artists UP 36016 — Grown Up/Losing You — 6
(see also Motors)

TED HEROLD
60 Polydor NH 66817 — I Don't Know Why/Moonlight — 30

HERON
70 Dawn DNS 1015 — Take Me Back Home/Minstrel And A King — 8
71 Dawn DNX 2509 — Bye And Bye/Through Time/Only A Hobo/I'm Ready To Leave (p/s) — 10
71 Dawn DNLS 3010 — HERON (LP, with insert) — 35
72 Dawn DNLS 3025 — TWICE AS NICE AT HALF THE PRICE (2-LP, some with postcard) — 35/45
(see also Mike Cooper)

MIKE HERON('S REPUTATION)
71 Island WIP 6101 — Call Me Diamond/Lady Wonder — 5
75 Neighbourhood NBH 3109 — Evie/Down On My Knees After Memphis (as Mike Heron's Reputation) — 5
78 Zoom ZUM 5 — Sold On Your Love/Portland Rose (p/s) — 5
71 Island ILPS 9146 — SMILING MEN WITH BAD REPUTATIONS (LP, gatefold sleeve) — 12
75 Neighborhood 80637 — MIKE HERON'S REPUTATION (LP) — 12
(see also Incredible String Band)

BERNARD HERRMAN
69 Phase 4 Stereo PFS 4173 — THE GREAT MOVIE THRILLERS (LP) — 20
75 Phase 4 Stereo PFS 4309 — THE FANTASY FILM WORLD OF BERNARD HERRMANN (LP) — 15
76 Phase 4 Stereo PFS 4337 — THE MYSTERIOUS FILM WORLD OF BERNARD HERRMANN (LP) — 15

KRISTIN HERSH
93 4AD KH 2 — Velvet Days (Demo)/Houdini Blues (demo) (promo only, no p/s) — 7
94 4AD CADD 4002CD — HIPS & MAKERS (CD, digipak with postcards) — 20
(see also Throwing Muses)

PAT HERVEY & TIARAS & ART SNIDER
67 President PT 110 — Can't Get You Out Of My Mind/Givin' In — 7

HERZFELD
93 Duophonic DS45 07 — Two Mothers/Who The Scroungers Are (p/s, mail order only) — 6

HESITATIONS
69 London HLR 10180 — Born Free/Push A Little Bit Harder — 20
68 London HLR 10198 — The Impossible Dream (The Quest)/Nobody Knows You When You're Down And Out — 8
68 London HA-R/SH-R 8360 — THE NEW BORN FREE (LP) — 18

CAROLYN HESTER
65 Dot DS 16750 — Ain't That Rain?/Ten Thousand Candles — 5
65 Dot DS 16751 — Playboys And Playgirls/High Flyin' Bird — 5
65 Dot DS 26750 — Come On Back/Three Young Men — 5
65 Dot DS 26751 — What Does It Get You?/Now He's Gone — 10
66 CBS 202409 — A Reason To Believe/Early Morning Rain — 5
65 Dot DLP 3604 — THAT'S MY SONG (LP) — 15
66 Dot DLP 3638 — AT TOWN HALL (LP) — 15
66 CBS (S)BPG 62033 — CAROLYN HESTER (LP) — 18
67 Realm RM 2338 — THIS LIFE I'M LIVING (LP) — 12
69 Pye Intl. NSPL 28121 — THE CAROLYN HESTER COALITION (LP) — 12

HEWETT SISTERS
59 HMV POP 567 — Baby-O/Jerri-Lee (I Love Him So) — 25
59 HMV POP 567 — Baby-O/Jerri-Lee (I Love Him So) (78) — 8

BEN HEWITT
59 Mercury AMT 1041 — You Break Me Up/I Ain't Givin' Up Nothin' — 50
59 Mercury AMT 1055 — For Quite A While/Patricia June — 30
59 Mercury AMT 1084 — I Want A New Girl Now/My Search — 50
60 Mercury ZEP 10035 — BREAK IT UP WITH BEN HEWITT (EP) — 220

GARTH HEWITT
70s Myrrh MYR 1051 — LOVE SONGS FOR THE EARTH (LP) — 18
70s Myrrh MYR 1078 — I'M GRATEFUL (LP) — 18

PETE HEWSON
83 Reset RES 2 — Take My Hand/Her (p/s) — 50
83 Reset REST 2 — Take My Hand/Her (12", p/s) — 80

ANNE HEYWOOD
59 Top Rank JAR 130 — I'd Rather Have Roses (Than Riches)/Love Is — 6
59 Top Rank JAR 130 — I'd Rather Have Roses (Than Riches)/Love Is (78) — 5

EDDIE HEYWOOD
58 Mercury 7MT 131 — Heywood's Bounce/Soft Summer Breeze — 8
64 Stateside SS 264 — Theme From The Film "The Prize"/Li'l Darlin' — 6
(see also Hugo Winterhalter)

WINSTON HEYWOOD (& HOMBRES)
71 Dynamic DYN 424 — Bam-Sa-Bo/Version — 10
72 Dynamic DYN 441 — Stop The War/Version — 6
72 Dynamic DYN 457 — Seek And You'll Find/Version — 6
73 Attack ATT 8046 — Da Doo Ron Ron/Version — 6
(see also Winston Harewood, Fud Christian All Stars)

LENNIE HIBBERT & COUNT OSSIE BAND
69 Doctor Bird DB 1113 — Pure Sole/PATSY: A Man Is Two Faced — 20
(see also Sound Dimension)

MINT VALUE £

AL HIBBLER

55	Brunswick 05420	Unchained Melody/Daybreak (gold or silver label)	35/22
55	Brunswick 05454	They Say You're Laughing At Me/I Can't Put My Arms Around A Memory	15
55	London HL 8184	Now I Lay Me Down To Dream/Danny Boy	45
55	London HL 8184	Now I Lay Me Down To Dream/Danny Boy (78)	7
55	Brunswick 05492	He/Breeze (Blow My Baby Back To Me)	10
56	Brunswick 05523	The Eleventh Hour Melody/Let's Try Again	10
56	Brunswick 05552	After The Lights Go Down Low/Stella By Starlight	10
56	Brunswick 05590	Never Turn Back/Away All Boats	6
56	Brunswick 05619	Nightfall/I'm Free	6
57	Brunswick 05653	The Town Crier/Trees	6
57	Brunswick 05703	Around The Corner From The Blues/I Complain	7
57	Columbia LB 10066	Goin' To Chicago Blues/Sent For You Yesterday And Here You Come Today (78, with Count Basie Big Band)	10
58	Brunswick 05739	When Will I Forget You?/My Heart Tells Me	6
58	Brunswick 05749	Honeysuckle Rose/Ain't Nothing Wrong With That Baby	6
58	Brunswick 05768	Love Land/Love Me Long, Hold Me Close, Kiss Me Warm And Tender	6
59	London HL 7086	Danny Boy/Now I Lay Me Down To Dream (export issue)	7
55	HMV 7EG 8158	DUKE ELLINGTON AND AL HIBBLER (EP)	8
57	HMV 7EG 8326	AL HIBBLER SINGS LOVE SONGS (EP)	8
57	Brunswick OE 9331	HERE'S HIBBLER PT. 1 (EP)	12
57	Brunswick OE 9332	HERE'S HIBBLER PT. 2 (EP)	12
57	Brunswick OE 9333	HERE'S HIBBLER PT. 3 (EP)	12
56	Brunswick LAT 8140	STARRING AL HIBBLER (LP)	25

EDDIE HICKEY

59	Decca F 11153	Lady May/Cap And Gown	10
60	Decca F 11204	Who Could Be Bluer?/Plain Jane	10
60	Decca F 11241	Another Sleepless Night/Barbara	10

ERSEL HICKEY

59	Fontana H 198	You Threw A Dart/Don't Be Afraid Of Love	65
59	Fontana H 198	You Threw A Dart/Don't Be Afraid Of Love (78)	20

DWAYNE HICKMAN

60	Capitol CL 15164	I'm A Lover, Not A Fighter/I Pass Your House	10

HICKORY

69	CBS 3963	Green Light/Key	22

(see also Equals)

COLIN HICKS (& CABIN BOYS)

57	Pye 7N 15114	Wild Eyes And Tender Lips/Empty Arms Blues (with Cabin Boys)	25
57	Pye 7N 15114	Wild Eyes And Tender Lips/Empty Arms Blues (78, with Cabin Boys)	15
57	Pye 7N 15125	La Dee Dah/Wasteland	15
57	Pye 7N 15125	La Dee Dah/Wasteland (78)	15
58	Pye 7N 15163	Little Boy Blue/Jambalaya	18
58	Pye 7N 15163	Little Boy Blue/Jambalaya (78)	25

DAN HICKS & HIS HOT LICKS

72	Blue Thumb ILPS 9204	STRIKING IT RICH (LP)	12

JIMMY HICKS

72	London HLU 10396	I'm Mr. Big Stuff/Tell Her That I Love You	12

HIDDEN STRENGTH

76	United Artists UAS 29949	HIDDEN STRENGTH (LP)	15

HIDEAWAYS

69	Action ACT 4544	Hide Out/Jolly Joe	15
71	Jay Boy BOY 29	Hide Out/Jolly Joe (reissue)	5

HI-FI

84	Butt MGLS 003	Louie Louie/Summertime	8

(see also Ian Matthews)

HI-FI FOUR

56	Parlophone MSP 6210	Band Of Gold/Davy, You Upset My Life	165
56	Parlophone R 4130	Band Of Gold/Davy, You Upset My Life (78)	15

HI FI'S

63	Piccadilly 7N 35130	Take Me Or Leave Me/I'm Struck	8
64	Pye 7N 15635	Will Yer Won't Yer/She's The One	8
64	Pye 7N 15710	I Keep Forgettin'/Why Can't I Stop Loving You?	35
65	Pye 7N 15788	Baby's In Black/Kiss And Run	15
66	Alp 595 010	It's Gonna Be Morning/I Wanna Hear You Say Yeah	50

HI-FI SEVEN

57	Nestles NR 17	Jazz In Piccadilly (There's A Tavern In The Town) (1-sided card flexi, 78rpm)	7
57	Nestles NR 19	Jazz In Piccadilly (Landlord Fill The Flowing Bowl) (1-sided card flexi, 78rpm)	7

ALEX 'HURRICANE' HIGGINS

82	Solid STOP 003	One-Four-Seven/Life's In The Pocket (p/s)	10

LIZZIE HIGGINS

75	Topic 12TS 260	UP AND AWA WI THE LAVEROCK (LP, gatefold sleeve)	12

JOE HIGGS

67	Coxsone CS 7004	Neighbour Neighbour/MELODIANS: I Should Have Made It Up	25
67	Island WI 3026	I Am The Song/Worry No More	30
68	Island WI 3131	You Hurt My Soul/LYNN TAITT: Why Am I Treated So Bad?	25
70	Clandisc CLA 208	Mademoiselle/DYNAMITES: Lion	12
71	Big BG 312	Burning Fire/RUPIE EDWARDS ALL STARS: Version	8
71	New Beat NB 087	Mother Radio/DAWN SHARON: Little Deeds	6

MINT VALUE £

71 Supreme SUP 215 Burning Fire/RUPIE EDWARDS ALL STARS: Push And Pull . . . 6
72 Sioux SI 005 The World Is Spinning Around/THE REACTION: Hallelujah . . . 5
72 Sioux SI 014 The Wave Of War/JUMBO STERLING: Shaft . . . 5
72 Sioux SI 021 Lay A Foundation/JACKIE ROWLAND: Lay A Foundation (Version) . . . 5
75 Grounation GROL 508 LIFE OF CONTRADICTION (LP) . . . 15
(see also Higgs & Wilson, Bob Marley/Wailers, Soul Vendors)

(Joe) HIGGS & (Roy) WILSON

60 Blue Beat (B)B 3 Manny Oh/When You Tell Me Baby (white label/blue writing [B3] or blue label/silver writing [BB 3]) (with Ken Richards & His Comets) . . . each 20
61 Starlite ST45 035 Pretty Baby/I Long For The Day . . . 25
61 Starlite ST45 036 Lover's Song/It Is A Day . . . 25
61 Starlite ST45 042 Come On Home/The Robe . . . 22
61 Starlite ST45 053 Sha Ba Ba/Change Of Mind . . . 22
62 Blue Beat BB 95 How Can I Be Sure/Mighty Man . . . 18
63 R&B JB 109 Let Me Know/Bye And Bye . . . 15
63 Blue Beat BB 190 If You Want Pardon/BABA BROOKS BAND: Musical Communion . . . 20
63 Island WI 081 Last Saturday Morning/Praise The Lord . . . 20
64 Rio R 29 Love Is Not For Me/Gone Is Yesterday . . . 15
65 Blue Beat BB 277 Pain In My Heart/BUSTER ALL STARS: Going West . . . 25
70 Clandisc CLA 218 Don't Mind Me/GLEN AND ROY: Angel . . . 8
(see also Clancy Eccles)

HIGH

69 CBS 4164 Long Live The High/Beggar Man Dan . . . 12

HIGH & MIGHTY

66 HMV POP 1548 Tryin' To Stop Cryin'/Escape From Cuba . . . 20

HIGH BROOM

70 Island WI 6088 Dancing In The Moonlight/Percy's On The Run . . . 15
73 Columbia DB 8969 Dancing In The Moonlight/Percy's On The Run (reissue) . . . 7
(see also Leviathan, Mike Stuart Span, Jason Crest, Holy Mackerel)

HIGH KEYS

63 London HLK 9768 Que Sera Sera/Daddy, Ooh Long Legs . . . 20

HIGH LLAMAS

98 Alpaca Park/V2 no cat. no. Blinger Suc/Sparkle Up, Sparkle Down (tour single, clear sleeve) . . . 6

HIGH LEVEL RANTERS

68 Topic 12TS 186 NORTHUMBERLAND FOR EVER (LP, blue label, 2 different sleeves) . . . 15
70 Trailer LER 2020 KEEP YOUR FEET STILL GEORDIE HINNIE (LP, red label) . . . 15
71 Trailer LER 2030 HIGH LEVEL (LP, red label) . . . 15
72 Trailer LER 2037 A MILE TO RIDE (LP) . . . 12
75 Topic 2-12TS 271/2 THE BONNY PIT LADDIE (2-LP, blue label) . . . 18
77 Broadside BRO 128 ENGLISH SPORTING BALLADS (LP, 1-side Martin Wyndham-Read, 2,000 only) . . 20
79 Topic 12TS 388 FOUR IN A BAR (LP) . . . 12

HIGHLY LIKELY

74 BBC RESL 10 Whatever Happened To You?/God Bless Everyone . . . 30
(see also Mike Hugg, Rodney Bewes)

HIGH NUMBERS

64 Fontana TF 480 Zoot Suit/I'm The Face . . . 350
80 Back Door DOOR 4 I'm The Face/Zoot Suit (reissue, die cut sleeve) . . . 20
(see also Who)

HIGH SOCIETY

66 Fontana TF 771 People Passing By/Star Of Eastern Street . . . 22
(see also Friday Browne, Graham Gouldman, Country Gentlemen, Manchester Mob)

HIGH TIDE

69 Liberty LBS 83264 SEA SHANTIES (LP, gatefold sleeve) . . . 65
70 Liberty LBS 83294 HIGH TIDE (LP) . . . 60
84 Psycho PSYCHO 26 SEA SHANTIES (LP, reissue) . . . 12
84 Psycho PSYCHO 27 HIGH TIDE (LP, reissue) . . . 12
(see also Misunderstood, Denny Gerrard, Magic Muscle, Third Ear Band)

HIGH TIDE

81 Sunday Morning (no cat. no.) Baby Dancing/Letter From A Coward (mail-order only) . . . 8

DEAN HIGHTOWER

60 HMV CLP 1360 TWANGY — WITH A BEAT (LP) . . . 50

DONNA HIGHTOWER

59 Capitol CL 15048 Lover, Come Back To Me/Because Of You . . . 7
59 Capitol CL 15049 Ain't That Love/Forgive Them . . . 7
60 Capitol ST 1273 GEE BABY (LP) . . . 25
68 Ember 2051 TAKE ONE (LP) . . . 12

ROSETTA HIGHTOWER

68 Toast TT 506 Pretty Red Balloons/How Can You Mistreat (The One You Love)? . . . 10
68 Toast TT 509 I Can't Give Back The Love I Feel For You/Big Bird . . . 30
69 CBS 4584 One Heart For Sale/What Do I Do? . . . 10
70 CBS 4758 April Fools/I'll Hold Out My Hand . . . 5
70 CBS 4988 Persuader/Come Together . . . 5
71 CBS 7068 Go Pray For Tomorrow/Give Me Just A Little More Line . . . 6
73 Philips 6006 291 The Walls Fell Down/Captain's Army . . . 6
71 CBS 64201 HIGHTOWER (LP) . . . 15
71 Rediffusion ZS 88 ROSETTA HIGHTOWER (LP) . . . 12
(see also Orlons, Ian Green [Revelation])

MINT VALUE £

HIGH TREASON

80 Burlington BURLS 001 — Saturday Night Special (no p/s) — 30

HIGHWAY

74 EMI EMC 3019 — HIGHWAY (LP) — 12
75 EMI EMA 770 — SMOKING AT THE EDGE (LP) — 12

HIGHWAYMEN

61 HMV POP 948 — The Gypsy Rover/Cotton Fields — 6
62 United Artists UP 1001 — Birdman (with narration from Burt Lancaster)/Cindy Oh Cindy — 8

HIGH WINDOWS

68 CBS 3208 — Maybe Someday/Your Eyes — 6

HILARY HILARY

80 Modern STP 2 — How Come You're So Dumb/Rich Kid Blues (p/s) — 110
(see also Roger Taylor, Queen)

RAY HILDEBRAND

70s Myrrh MST 6508 — SPECIAL KIND OF MAN (LP) — 18

DIANE HILDEBRANDE

69 Elektra EKSN 45055 — Jan's Blues/Early Morning Blues And Greens — 10

HI LITES

65 London HL 9967 — Hey Baby/Groovey — 12

HI-LITERS

58 Mercury AMT 1011 — Dance Me To Death/Cha Cha Rock — 125
58 Mercury AMT 1011 — Dance Me To Death/Cha Cha Rock (78) — 80

ALEX HILL

53 Vocalion V 1027 — Stompin' 'Em Down/Track Head Blues (78) — 15
(see also Paramount Allstars)

BENNY HILL

55 Decca F 10442 — I Can't Tell A Waltz From A Tango/Teach Me Tonight — 20
55 Decca F 10442 — I Can't Tell A Waltz From A Tango/Teach Me Tonight (78) — 8
56 Columbia SCM 5238 — Memories Are Made Of This/Who Done It? (as Benny Hill & Coronets) — 18
56 Columbia DB 3731 — Memories Are Made Of This/Who Done It? (78, as Benny Hill & Coronets) — 10
61 Pye 7N 15327 — Gather In The Mushrooms/Pepys' Diary — 7
61 Pye 7N 15359 — Transistor Radio/Gypsy Rock — 7
62 Pye 7N 15520 — Harvest Of Love/Fame — 6
65 Pye 7N 15974 — What A World/I'll Never Know — 6
66 Pye 7N 17026 — My Garden Of Love/The Andalucian Gypsies — 6
92 EMI ERNPD 1 — Ernie/Ting A Ling A Loo (shaped picture disc) — 6
61 Pye NEP 24144 — BENNY HILL PARADE VOL. 1 (EP) — 12
63 Pye NEP 24174 — THE HARVEST OF LOVE (EP) — 12
66 Pye NPL 18133 — SINGS? (LP) — 15
(see also Coronets)

BUNKER HILL & RAYMEN

62 Stateside SS 135 — Hide & Go Seek Parts 1 & 2 — 18

CHIPPIE HILL/HOCIEL THOMAS

72 Collectors Edition 1001 — CHIPPIE HILL AND HOCIEL THOMAS (LP) — 12

DAVID HILL

57 Vogue V 9076 — All Shook Up/Melody For Lovers (with Ray Ellis Orchestra) — 200
57 Vogue V 9076 — All Shook Up/Melody For Lovers (78, with Ray Ellis Orchestra) — 70
58 RCA RCA 1041 — That's Love/Keep Me In Mind (with Joe Relsman's Orchestra & Chorus) — 175
58 RCA RCA 1041 — That's Love/Keep Me In Mind (78, with Joe Relsman's Orchestra & Chorus) — 75

JESSIE HILL

60 London HLU 9117 — Ooh Poo Pah Doo Parts 1 & 2 — 25

MIKE HILL GROUP

65 Polydor BM 56016 — Silver Star/Best Of Both Worlds — 5

VINCE HILL

62 Piccadilly 7N 35043 — The Rivers Run Dry/Not Any More — 7
62 Piccadilly 7N 35068 — There You Go/Just As Long As (You Belong To Me) — 7
63 Piccadilly 7N 35108 — A Day At The Seaside/Tricks Of The Trade — 7
63 Piccadilly 7N 35118 — As It Was Written/Is There Anyone At Home — 7
63 Piccadilly 7N 35148 — Blue Velvet/Like Anything — 7
64 Piccadilly 7N 35161 — If You Knew/Fools & Lovers — 7
64 Piccadilly 7N 35192 — It's Only Make Believe/Let The Wind Blow — 7
66 Columbia SEG 8509 — FOUR SIDES OF VINCE HILL (EP) — 15
66 Columbia S(C)X 6018 — HAVE YOU MET? (LP) — 12
66 Columbia S(C)X 6046 — HEARTACHES (LP) — 12
67 Columbia S(C)X 6096 — AT THE CLUB (LP) — 12
67 Columbia S(C)X 6141 — EDELWEISS (LP) — 12
68 Columbia S(C)X 6185 — ALWAYS YOU AND ME (LP) — 12
69 Columbia S(C)X 6304 — YOU FORGOT TO REMEMBER (LP) — 12
(see also [Jackie &] Raindrops, Elmer Bernstein)

Z.Z. HILL

65 R&B MRB 5005 — Someone To Love Me/Have Mercy Someone — 30
69 Action ACT 4532 — Make Me Yours/What Am I Living For? — 22
71 Mojo 2092 019 — Faithful And True/I Think I'd Do It — 8
75 United Artists UP 35727 — I Keep On Loving You/Whoever's Thrilling You — 8
77 CBS 5553 — Love Is So Good When You're Stealin' It/Need You By My Side — 8
66 Sue IEP 711 — GIMME GIMME (EP, 2 tracks each by Z.Z. Hill & Intentions; some in p/s) — 275/100

MINT VALUE £

69	Action ACLP 6004	WHOLE LOT OF SOUL (LP)	70
72	Mojo 2916 013	THE BRAND NEW Z.Z. HILL (LP)	40
75	Contempo CLP 515	THE BRAND NEW Z.Z. HILL (LP, reissue)	18

(see also Intentions)

STEVE HILLAGE

76	Virgin VS 161	It's All Too Much/Shimmer	10
77	Virgin VS 171	Hurdy Gurdy Man/Om Nama Shivaya	5
77	Virgin VS 197	Not Fade Away/Saucer Surfing	5
77	Virgin VDJ 23	Leylines To Glassdome/GLEN PHILLIPS: Lies (p/s, gig freebie)	6
78	Virgin VS 212	Getting Better/Palm Trees (Love Guitar) (some in p/s)	8/5
78	Virgin VDJ 25	Getting Better/Palm Trees (Love Guitar) (12", p/s)	12
79	Virgin VS 313	Don't Dither, Do It/Getting In Tune (p/s)	6
82	Virgin VS 551	Alone (p/s)	6
82	Virgin VS 574	Kamikaze Eyes (p/s)	10
79	Virgin SIXPACK 2	SIX PACK/SIX TRACK (EP, picture disc, 5,000 only, die-cut p/s with stand)	8
77	Virgin V 2777	MOTIVATION RADIO (LP, with inner)	15
78	Virgin V 2098	GREEN (LP, green vinyl, with insert)	12
79	Virgin VR 1	RAINBOW DOME MUSICK (LP, clear vinyl)	12
79	Virgin VGD 3502	LIVE HERALD (2-LP)	15
83	Virgin V 2244	FOR TO NEXT (LP, with bonus instrumental LP "And Not Or")	12

(see also Gong, Khan, Arzachel, Clearlight, Radio Actors, System 7)

HILLER BROTHERS

60s	Honey Hit TB 124	Little Darlin'/Changin' My Mind (some with p/s)	10/6

JANE HILLERY

66	Columbia DB 7918	You've Got That Hold On Me/Take Me Away	20

(see also Magistrates)

MABLE HILLERY

69	Xtra XTRA 1063	IT'S SO HARD TO BE A NIGGER (LP)	30

GILLIAN HILLS

65	Vogue VRS 7005	Tomorrow Is Another Day/Look At Them	10

HILLTOPPERS

78s

52	Vogue V 9045	Trying/You Made Up My Mind (featuring Jimmy Sacca)	12
53	London L 1204	P.S. I Love You/I'd Rather Die Young	20
54	London HL 8003	Love Walked In/To Be Alone	25
54	London HL 8026	From The Vine Came The Grape/Time Will Tell	20
54	London HL 8070	Poor Butterfly/Wrapped Up In A Dream	20
54	London HL 8081	Will You Remember?/The Old Cabaret	20
54	London HL 8092	If I Didn't Care/Bettina	20
55	London HL 8116	Time Waits For No One/You Try Somebody Else	20
55	London HLD 8168	The Kentuckian Song/I Must Be Dreaming	10
55	London HLD 8208	Searching/All I Need Is You	12
56	London HLD 8255	My Treasure/Last Word In Love	12
56	London HLD 8278	Do The Bop/When You're Alone	30
56	London HLD 8298	Tryin'/D-A-R-L-I-N'	10
56	London HLD 8333	So Tired/Faded Rose	8
57	London HLD 8441	I'm Serious/I Love My Girl	12
57	London HLD 8455	A Fallen Star/Footsteps	12
57	London HLD 8528	The Joker/Chicken, Chicken	15
58	London HLD 8603	You Sure Look Good To Me/Starry Eyes	20

45s

54	London HL 8026	From The Vine Came The Grape/Time Will Tell	90
54	London HL 8070	Poor Butterfly/Wrapped Up In A Dream	90
54	London HL 8081	Will You Remember?/The Old Cabaret	80
54	London HL 8092	If I Didn't Care/Bettina	80
55	London HL 8116	Time Waits For No One/You Try Somebody Else	80
55	London HLD 8168	The Kentuckian Song/I Must Be Dreaming	60
55	London HLD 8208	Searching/All I Need Is You	65
56	London HLD 8221	Only You (And You Alone)/(It Will Have To Do) Until The Real Thing Comes Along (gold or silver label lettering)	30/20
56	London HLD 8255	My Treasure/Last Word In Love	50
56	London HLD 8278	Do The Bop/When You're Alone	120
56	London HLD 8298	Tryin'/D-A-R-L-I-N'	35
56	London HLD 8333	So Tired/Faded Rose	35
57	London HLD 8381	Marianne/You're Wasting Your Time	25
57	London HLD 8441	I'm Serious/I Love My Girl	25
57	London HLD 8455	A Fallen Star/Footsteps	25
57	London HLD 8528	The Joker/Chicken, Chicken	35
58	London HLD 8603	You Sure Look Good To Me/Starry Eyes	22
60	London HLD 9038	Alone/The Prisoner's Song	15

EPs

55	London RE-P 1012	PRESENTING THE HILLTOPPERS	45
55	London RE-D 1030	THE HILLTOPPERS VOL. 2	45
57	London RE-D 1099	THE HILLTOPPERS VOL. 3	40

LPs

57	London HA-D 2029	THE TOWERING HILLTOPPERS	50
57	London HA-D 2071	TOPS IN POPS	45

(see also Sacca, Billy Vaughn)

MINT VALUE £

HI-LO'S

Year	Label/Cat. No.	Title	Value
62	Reprise RS 20095	A Taste Of Honey/My Baby Just Cares For Me	6
57	London RE-U 1077	UNDER GLASS (EP)	15
58	London RE-R 1110	THE HI-LO'S (EP)	15
57	Philips BBE 12127	HERE ARE THE HI-LO'S (EP)	12
59	Philips BBE 12289	AND ALL THAT JAZZ (EP)	12
60	Philips BBE 12425	HERE ARE THE HI-LO'S (EP, also stereo SBBE 9035)	10/12
57	London HA-U 2026	UNDER GLASS (LP)	18
58	Philips BBL 7154	SUDDENLY IT'S THE HI-LO'S (LP)	15
59	Philips BBL 7288	AND ALL THAT JAZZ (LP)	15
60	Philips BBL 7411	ALL OVER THE PLACE (LP, also stereo SBBL 589)	12/15
60s	Omega XSD 11	IN STEREO (LP)	15
63	Reprise R 6034	HAPPEN TO FOLK SONGS (LP)	12

RONNIE HILTON

Year	Label/Cat. No.	Title	Value
55	HMV 7M 285	Prize Of Gold/A Blossom Fell	25
55	HMV 7M 303	Just Say You Love Her/My Loving Hands	10
56	HMV 7M 336	Bella Notte/He	12
56	HMV 7M 358	Young And Foolish/Moments To Remember	15
56	HMV 7M 382	The Last Frontier/Here Comes My Love	8
56	HMV 7M 390	No Other Love/It's All Been Done Before (B-side with Alma Cogan)	20
56	HMV 7M 413	Who Are We/Give Me My Ranch	12
56	HMV POP 248	A Woman In Love/I Just Found Out About Love	12
56	HMV POP 274	Two Different Worlds/Constant And True	12
57	HMV POP 291	The Wisdom Of A Fool/Amore	12
57	HMV POP 307	For Your Love/Once	10
57	HMV POP 318	Heart/Penny Serenade	8
57	HMV POP 338	Around The World/I'd Give You The World	8
57	HMV POP 364	The Miracle Of Love/Wonderful! Wonderful!	8
57	HMV POP 393	Marching Along To The Blues/She	8
57	HMV POP 422	That's Why I Was Born/The Moonraker's Song	7
58	HMV POP 437	I'll Buy You A Star/You Should Belong To Me	6
58	HMV POP 446	Magic Moments/One Blade Of Grass (In A Meadow)	6
58	HMV POP 468	I May Never Pass This Way Again/Love Walked In	6
58	HMV POP 479	On The Street Where You Live/I've Grown Accustomed To Her Face	6
58	HMV POP 497	Her Hair Was Yellow/Let Me Stay With You	6
58	HMV POP 556	The Day The Rains Came/Do I Love You (Because You're Beautiful)	6
58	HMV POP 559	The World Outside/As I Love You	5
59	HMV POP 560	Gigi (Gaston's Soliloquy)/Keep Your Kisses	5
59	HMV POP 638	The Wonder Of You/A Hundred Miles From Everywhere	5
64	HMV POP 1291	Don't Let The Rain Come Down/Send For Me	5
65	HMV POP 1378	A Windmill In Old Amsterdam/Dear Heart	5
67	HMV POP 1600	If I Were A Rich Man/Laughing Gnome	6
68	Columbia DB 8506	Glory Glory Leeds United/We Shall Not Be Moved (with Leeds United AFC)	5
55	HMV 7EG 8121	THE STAR OF SONG (EP)	12
56	HMV 7EG 8149	HEY THERE (EP)	12
57	HMV 7EG 8198	FOR THOSE IN LOVE (EP)	12
57	HMV 7EG 8202	FOR THOSE IN LOVE NO. 2 (EP)	12
58	HMV 7EG 8352	THE HITS FROM 'MY FAIR LADY' (EP, 1 side by Alma Cogan)	12
55	HMV DLP 1109	BY THE FIRESIDE (10" LP)	30
59	HMV CLP 1295	I'M BEGINNING TO SEE THE LIGHT (LP)	30

(see also Alma Cogan)

HILTONAIRES

Year	Label/Cat. No.	Title	Value
67	Coxsone CSL 8004	THE BEST OF THE HILTONAIRES (LP)	140

HIM & THE OTHERS

Year	Label/Cat. No.	Title	Value
66	Parlophone R 5510	I Mean It/She's Got Eyes That Tell Lies	800

JUSTIN HINDS/HINES (& DOMINOES)

Year	Label/Cat. No.	Title	Value
64	Ska Beat JB 176	King Samuel/River Jordan	25
65	Ska Beat JB 187	Mother Banner/DON DRUMMOND & HIS GROUP: Apanga	35
65	Island WI 171	Botheration/Satan (as Justin Hines & Dominoes)	25
65	Island WI 174	Jump Out Of The Frying Pan/Holy Dove (as Justin Hines & Dominoes)	25
65	Island WI 194	Rub Up, Push Up/The Ark	22
65	Island WI 232	Turn Them Back/TOMMY McCOOK: Rocket Ship	25
65	Island WI 236	Peace And Love/Skalarama (B-side actually by Lyn Taitt & Comets)	30
66	Doctor Bird DB 1048	The Higher The Monkey Climbs/Fight For Your Right	22
67	Island WI 3048	On A Saturday Night/Save A Bread	22
67	Treasure Isle TI 7002	Here I Stand/No Good Rudie	18
67	Treasure Isle TI 7005	Carry Go Bring Come/Fight Too Much	18
67	Treasure Isle TI 7014	On A Saturday Night/Save A Bread	18
67	Treasure Isle TI 7017	Once A Man/TOMMY McCOOK & SUPERSONICS: Persian Cat	18
68	Treasure Isle TI 7063	Botheration/VINCENT HINDS: Mouth Trombone	15
68	Treasure Isle TI 7068	Mighty Redeemer (Parts 1 & 2)	15
69	Trojan TR 652	You Should've Known Better/TOMMY McCOOK & SUPERSONICS: Third Figure	10
70	Duke Reid DR 2511	Say Me Say/I Want It	8
70	Duke DU 67	Drink Milk/Everywhere I Go (as Justin Hines & Dominoes)	8
75	Pama PM 4001	Sinners Where You Going To Hide?/If It's Love You Need	6

(see also Lyn Taitt, Skatalites, Don Drummond)

NEVILLE HINDS

Year	Label/Cat. No.	Title	Value
70	Duke Reid DR 2503	Sunday Gravy (as Neville Hines)/JOHN HOLT: Write Her A Letter	15
70	Camel CA 44	London Bridge/SCORCHERS: Things And Time (B-side act. by Wailing Souls)	10
70	Gas GAS 126	I Who Have Nothing/You Send Me	6
71	Explosion EX 2043	Delivered/Specially For You (B-side actually by Blake Boy)	6
72	Upsetter US 384	Blackman's Time/UPSETTERS: Version	8
73	Harry J HJ 6657	Musical Splendour/JOHN CROW GENERATION: Musical Drum & Bass	5

(see also Neville Irons & Byron Lee & The Dragonaires, Lloyd Robinson, Marvels, Alton Ellis)

RUPERT HINE

72 Purple PUR 105 — Hamburgers/A Varlet Lad T'was Samuel Green (Historical Moments – Part 17) . . . 6
76 Electric WOT 8 — Snakes Don't Dance Fast/Hopi Smile . . . 5
71 Purple TPSA 7502 — PICK UP A BONE (LP, with David MacIver) . . . 35
73 Purple TPSA 7509 — UNFINISHED PICTURE (LP) . . . 18
(see also Jon Pertwee)

EARL 'FATHA' HINES

51 Vogue V 304 — Daniel/Get On Board, Little Children (78, as Prof. J. Earl Hines & His Goodwill Singers) . . . 7
55 HMV 7EG 8114 — EARL HINES AND HIS ORCHESTRA (EP, 1 track with Billy Eckstine) . . . 8
57 MGM MGM-EP 573 — MIDNIGHT IN NEW ORLEANS (EP, as Earl Hines All Stars) . . . 8
56 Vogue EPV 1144 — QUINTET (EP) . . . 10
54 Mercury MG 25018 — EARL HINES AND HIS ALL STARS (10" LP) . . . 15
55 Vogue Coral LRA 10031 — FATS WALLER SONGS (10" LP) . . . 15
55 Columbia 33S 1063 — PIANO MOODS (10" LP) . . . 15
56 HMV DLP 1132 — GRAND TERRACE SWING (10" LP) . . . 12
60 MGM MGM-C 833 — EARL'S PEARLS (LP, as Earl 'Fatha' Hines Quartet) . . . 15
65 World Record Club T 539 — HINES '65 (LP) . . . 12
65 Stateside SL 10116 — SPONTANEOUS EXPLORATIONS (LP) . . . 12
67 Fontana SFJL 902 — BLUES IN THIRDS (LP) . . . 12
67 Fontana TL 5378 — JAZZ MEANS HINES! (LP) . . . 12
(see also Louis Armstrong)

FRAZER HINES

68 Major Minor MM 579 — Who's Dr. Who?/Punch And Judy Man . . . 40

JUSTIN HINES

(see under Justin Hinds)

SONNY HINES

65 King KG 1009 — Anytime, Any Day, Anywhere/Nothing Like Your Love . . . 15

HINES & ELDRIDGE

69 Mercury SMWL 21041 — HINES AND ELDRIDGE WITH COLEMAN HAWKINS VOLUME 2 (LP) . . . 12
(see also Coleman Hawkins, Earl Hines, Roy Eldridge)

HINES, HINES & DAD

68 CBS 3667 — Something Extra/Hambone . . . 5

HINGE

68 RCA RCA 1721 — Village Postman/You'd Better Go Home . . . 20

JOE HINTON

64 Vocalion VP 9224 — Funny How Time Slips Away/You Gotta Have Love . . . 15
66 Vocalion VP 9258 — Just A Kid Named Joe/Pledging My Love . . . 15
66 Vocalion VA-P 8043 — FUNNY HOW TIME SLIPS AWAY (LP) . . . 90

HI-NUMBERS

65 Decca F 12233 — Heart Of Stone/Dancing In The Street . . . 40

HIPPIES

63 Cameo Parkway P 863 — Memory Lane/REGGIE HARRISON: A Lonely Piano . . . 20

HIPPY BOYS

69 Trojan TR 668 — Love/The Whole Family . . . 12
69 Trojan TR 669 — Michael Row The Boat Ashore/Who Is Coming To Dinner . . . 12
69 Bullet BU 412 — Hog In A Me Minte/Lorna Run . . . 7
69 Bullet BU 413 — What's Your Excuse?/Tell Me Tell . . . 10
69 Camel CA 29 — Cat Nip/Cooyah (both as Hippie Boys) . . . 10
69 High Note HS 021 — Doctor No Go/Sailing (B-side actually "Faberge" by Baba Brooks & Band) . . . 10
69 High Note HS 030 — Chicken Lickin'/BABA BROOKS: Old Man Flint . . . 10
69 High Note HS 035 — Reggae Pressure/SOUL RHYTHMS: It Hurts (B-side actually Soul Rhythms) . . . 10
69 Unity UN 528 — Dreams To Remember/Peace Maker . . . 7
70 High Note HS 038 — Piccadilly Hop/Nigeria . . . 10
70 Duke DU 92 — Cloud Burst/LLOYD CHARMERS: Message From A Black Man . . . 7
71 Big Shot 580 — Voodoo/LITTLE ROY: Hard Fighter . . . 6
69 Big Shot BSLP 5005 — REGGAE WITH THE HIPPY BOYS (LP, actually on High Note label) . . . 60
(see also Upsetters, Family Man, Danny Williams, Tony, Hippy Boys, Cynthia Richards, Pioneers)

HIPSTER IMAGE

65 Decca F 12137 — Can't Let Her Go/Make Her Mine (demos £250) . . . 350

HIRSCHE NICHT AUFS SOFA

86 United Dairies UD 018 — MELCHIOR (LP, with insert) . . . 30

AL HIRT

60 HMV POP 749 — Tin Roof Blues/The Original Dixieland One Step (as Al Hirt's Jazz Band) . . . 5
63 RCA RCA 1380 — Java/I Can't Get Started . . . 5
67 RCA RCA 1590 — Theme From "The Monkees"/Tarzan March . . . 6
68 RCA RCA 1662 — Keep The Ball Rolling/Manhattan Safari . . . 5
68 RCA RCA 1685 — The Glory Of Love/Calypsoul . . . 5
68 RCA RD 7961 — UNFORGETTABLE (LP) . . . 12
(see also Ann-Margret)

HIS NAME IS ALIVE

90 4AD HNIA 1 — How Ghosts Affect Relationships/If July (promo only, no p/s) . . . 6
93 4AD HNIA 2 — Extracts From "Mouth To Mouth": In Every Ford/Lip/Drink, Dress And Ink/ Can't Go Wrong Without You/The Dirt Eaters (CD, promo only) . . . 12

HI-SPOTS

58 Melodisc 1457 — Lend Me Your Comb/I Don't Hurt Anymore . . . 22
58 Melodisc 1473 — Secretly/I Got . . . 22
58 Melodisc 1473 — Secretly/I Got (78) . . . 12

MINT VALUE £

HISS

00s	Polydor 065778-7	Triumph/Street Research (red vinyl, p/s, 750 only)	10
00s	Polydor 065778-2	Triumph/Street Research/Back On The Radio (CD)	10

ALFRED HITCHCOCK

58	London HA-P 2130	MUSIC TO BE MURDERED BY (LP, music by Jeff Alexander Orchestra, also stereo SH-P 6012)	40/50

(see Jeff Alexander)

ROBYN HITCHCOCK (& THE EGYPTIANS)

81	Armageddon AS 008	The Man Who Invented Himself/Dancing On God's Thumb (p/s, some with flexidisc "It's A Mystic Trip"/"Grooving On An Inner Plane" [4 SPURT 1])	6/8
82	Albion ION 103	America/It Was The Night/How Do You Work This Thing? (p/s)	8
82	Albion FREEBIE 1	52 Stations/COSMOPOLITANS: How To Keep Your Husband Happy/ MOTOR BOYS MOTOR: Little Boy And Fat Man/dB's: Amplifier (flexidisc free with "Groovy Decay" LP [ALB 110] or at gigs)	6
82	Midnight Music DING 2	Eaten By Her Own Dinner/Listening To The Higsons/Dr. Sticky (p/s)	7
82	Midnight Music DONG 2	Eaten By Her Own Dinner/Grooving On An Inner Plane/Messages Of The Dark The Abandoned Brain/Happy The Golden Prince (12", p/s)	10
84	Midnight Music DONG 8	The Bells Of Rhymney/Falling Leaves/Winter Love/ The Bones In The Ground (12", p/s)	8
85	Midnight Music DONG 12	Heaven/Dwarfbeat/Some Body (12", p/s)	8
85	Midnight Music DONG 17	Brenda's Iron Sledge (live)/Only The Stones Remain/ The Pit Of Souls (Part I-IV) (12", p/s)	8
83	Albion 12 ION 1036	Nightride To Trinidad (Long Version)/Kingdom Of Love/Midnight Fish (12", p/s)	10
86	Glass Fish OOZE 1	If You Were A Priest/The Crawling (p/s)	5
84	Bucketfull/Brains BOB 8	Happy The Golden Prince (flexidisc free with *Bucketfull Of Brains* mag)	8/6
84	Bucketfull/Brains BOB 8	Happy The Golden Prince (hard vinyl white label test pressing, 20 only)	30
81	Armageddon ARM 4	BLACK SNAKE DIAMOND RôLE (LP)	12

(see also Soft Boys, Knox)

HI-TENSION

77	Island IPR 2007	Hi-Tension/Girl I Bet Cha (12")	8
79	Island WIP 6493	There's A Reason/If It Moves You	5
79	Island 12 WIP 6493	There's A Reason/If It Moves You (12")	10
78	Island ILPS 9564	HI-TENSION (LP, with poster)	15

HI-TONES

62	Island WI 029	Going Steady/Darlin' Elaine	22
63	Island WI 086	Ten Virgins (actually by Angelic Brothers)/Too Young To Love (actually by Larry Marshall)	22
63	R&B JB 123	You Hold The Key/DON DRUMMOND: Rock Away	35

HIT PACK

65	Tamla Motown TMG 513	Never Say No To Your Baby/Let's Dance	110

HIT PARADE

84	JSH JSH 1	Forever/Stop (die-cut p/s)	8
84	JSH JSH 2	My Favourite Girl/It Rained On Monday Morning (die-cut p/s)	7
85	JSH JSH 3	The Sun Shines In Gerrards Cross/You Hurt Me Too (die-cut p/s)	6
85	JSH JSH 4	You Don't Love Me Then/Huevo's Mexicana (die-cut p/s with card)	6
86	JSH JSH 5	See You In Havana/Wipe Away The Tears (die-cut p/s)	5
87	JSH JSH 6	I Get So Sentimental/Sue (die-cut p/s)	5

HIT SQUAD

88	Eastern Bloc EASTERN 01	Wax On The Melt/SPM MC Tunes/Shure.4 (12", white label promo only, plain stickered sleeve)	30

(see also 808 State)

HITTERS

73	United Artists UP 35530	Hypocrite/The Version	22

(see also Brinsley Schwarz)

HOAX

80	Hologram HOAX 1	ONLY THE BLIND CAN SEE IN THE DARK (EP)	25
81	Hologram HOAX 3	SO WHAT (12" EP, p/s, blue vinyl)	15
82	Hologram HOAX 4	Quiet In The Sixpenny 5 (p/s)	10

HOBBIES OF TODAY

78	Waxworks H.O.T. WAX 01	Metal Boys/Tight Rope Walker (p/s)	5

HOBBIT

71	Deroy	FIRST AND LAST (LP, private pressing)	60

HOBBITS

68	Decca AD 1004	Daffodil Days (The Affection Song)/Sunny Day Girl (export issue)	18
68	MCA MU 1002	Daffodil Days (The Affection Song)/Sunny Day Girl	8
67	MCA MUP 301	DOWN TO MIDDLE EARTH (LP)	25

HOBBS

78	Big SOLD 4	Bop Around The Shop/(You've Got Me In A) Whirl Girl (gatefold p/s & insert)	6

HOBBY HORSE

72	Bell BELL 1248	Summertime, Summertime/Sweet And Low	10

(see also Mary Hopkin)

HOBBY SHOP

68	Columbia DB 8395	Why Must It Be This Way?/Talk To Me	8

LES HOBEAUX

57	HMV POP 377	Oh, Mary Don't You Weep/Toll The Bell Easy	20
57	HMV POP 377	Oh, Mary Don't You Weep/Toll The Bell Easy (78)	10
57	HMV POP 403	Mama Don't Allow/Hey, Hey, Daddy Blues	20
57	HMV POP 403	Mama Don't Allow/Hey, Hey, Daddy Blues (78)	10

58 HMV POP 444 Dynamo/Two Ships . . . 20
58 HMV POP 444 Dynamo/Two Ships (78) . . . 10
57 HMV 7EG 8297 SOHO SKIFFLE (EP) . . . 55

HOBOKEN
73 Oak HOBOKEN (LP, 6 copies only) . . . 300+

EDMUND HOCKRIDGE
53 Parlophone MSP 6027 Luck Be A Lady/I'll Know . . . 8
53 Parlophone MSP 6028 I've Never Been In Love Before/My Time Of Day . . . 8

CHRIS HODGE
72 Apple APPLE 43 We're On Our Way/Supersoul (initially in p/s) . . . 30/10
74 RCA LPBO 5007 Beautiful Love/Sweet Lady From The Sky . . . 6
74 DJM DJS 10337 I Love You/Old James Dean . . . 5

MARVA HODGE
70 Polydor 56792 The Ghetto/Sometimes . . . 8

CHARLES HODGES
69 Major Minor MM 654 Try A Little Love/Someone To Love . . . 20
(see also Outlaws, Cliff Bennett's Rebellion)

EDDIE HODGES
61 London HLA 9369 I'm Gonna Knock On Your Door/Ain't Gonna Wash For A Week . . . 12
62 London HLA 9505 Bandit Of My Dreams/Mugmates . . . 15
62 London HLA 9576 (Girls, Girls, Girls) Made To Love/I Make Believe It's You . . . 10
63 MGM MGM 1232 Just A Kid In Love/Avalanche . . . 8
65 Stateside SS 442 New Orleans/Hard Times For Young Lovers . . . 8
65 Stateside SS 469 Love Minus Zero — No Limit/The Water Is Over My Head . . . 12
62 London REA 1353 EDDIE HODGES (EP) . . . 75
(see also Hayley Mills & Eddie Hodges)

JOHNNY HODGES & HIS ORCHESTRA
54 Felsted 82004 Frisky/Far Away Blues (78) . . . 7
52 Vogue LD 011 JOHNNY HODGES (10" LP) . . . 25
56 Columbia/Clef C 9051 IN A TENDER MOOD (10"LP) . . . 15
57 Columbia CX 10098 ELLINGTON ALL STARS (LP) . . . 12
59 Columbia CX 10136 THE BIG SOUND (LP) . . . 12
61 HMV CLP 1430 BLUES-A-PLENTY (LP) . . . 12

HOFFNER BROTHERS
72 Bullet BU 513 The King Man Is Back/SHALIMAR ALL STARS: Version . . . 5
72 Green Door GD 4039 The King Man Is Back/SHALIMAR ALL STARS: Version (reissue) . . . 5
73 Ackee ACK 521 Open Up The Gates/Version . . . 5
73 Grape GR 3042 Let Me Dream (Parts 1 & 2) . . . 5

ANNIE HOGAN
85 Doublevision DVR 9 PLAYS KICKABYE (12" EP) . . . 15
(see also Marc Almond, Nick Cave, Soft Cell)

CLAIRE HOGAN
59 Top Rank JAR 161 Sing A Smiling Song/I Wonder . . . 6
59 Top Rank JAR 161 Sing A Smiling Song/I Wonder (78) . . . 8
(see also Teresa Brewer)

SILAS HOGAN
71 Blue Horizon 2431 008 TROUBLE AT HOME (LP) . . . 75
70s Flyright FLY 595 I'M A FREE-HEARTED MAN (LP) . . . 15

HOGARTH
68 Liberty LBF 15156 Suzie's Getting Married/I've Been Dreaming . . . 15

SMOKEY HOGG
64 Realm RM 197 I'M SO LONELY (LP) . . . 30
72 Ember EMB 3405 SINGS THE BLUES (LP) . . . 25
70s Specialty SNTF 5018 U BETTER WATCH THAT JIVE (LP) . . . 15
(see also John Lee Hooker/Lightnin' Hopkins/Smokey Hogg)

HOGS
69 Jay Boy BOY 5 It's All Coming To Me Now/Motor Cycle Rider . . . 6

SUZI JANE HOKUM
66 MGM MGM 1323 Need All The Help I Can Get/Home . . . 18

HOKUM CLONES
03 Rough Trade FOR US FU 25 Breakin' From A Jailhouse Blues/You Ain't Foolin' Me (p/s, 1000 only) . . . 5

HOKUS POKE
72 Vertigo 6360 064 EARTH HARMONY (LP) . . . 50

RON HOLDEN
60 London HLU 9116 My Babe/Love You So . . . 70

FRANK HOLDER
57 Decca F 10880 The Caterpillar Bush/Red Beans And Rice . . . 6
57 Decca F 10908 Battle Of The Century/Chinese Cricket Match . . . 6
57 Decca F 10919 Champion Calypso/Sweetie Charlie . . . 6
58 Parlophone R 4459 Bechuanaland/Nor The Moon By Midnight . . . 8
(see also Johnny Dankworth)

RAM JOHN HOLDER
67 Columbia DB 8157 I Need Somebody/She's Alright . . . 10
67 Columbia DB 8262 My Friend Jones/It Won't Be Long Before I Love You . . . 18
68 Beacon BEA 108 I Just Came To Get My Baby/Yes I Do . . . 8
69 Upfront UPF 2 Goodwill To All Mankind/BLACK VELVET: Goodwill Sermon . . . 7

MINT VALUE £

70 United Artists UP 35117 — Where Do The Dreams Go?/Miracle Happens Every Day 6
63 Melodisc MLP 12-133 — RAM BLUES GOSPEL AND SOUL (LP) 50
69 Beacon BEAS 2 — BLACK LONDON BLUES (LP) 50
70 Beacon BEAS 17 — BOOTLEG BLUES (LP) 45
(see also Ram Jam Band, Ram Holder Brothers, Geno Washington)

RAM HOLDER BROTHERS

66 Parlophone R 5471 — Just Across The River/Ram Blues 20
(see also Ram Jam Band, Ram John Holder)

HOLE

91 City Slang EFA 04070-45/ SLANG 013 — Teenage Whore/Drown Soda (p/s, lilac, clear or green vinyl, 500 of each) .... each 12
91 City Slang EFA 04070 — Teenage Whore/Drown Soda (12") 8
91 City Slang EFA 04070 CD — Teenage Whore/Drown Soda (CD) 8
93 City Slang EFA 04916-45 — Beautiful Son/Old Age/20 Years In The Dakota (purple vinyl) 8
93 City Slang EFA 04916-02 — Beautiful Son/Old Age/20 Years In The Dakota (12", green vinyl) 12
94 City Slang EFA 04936-7 — Miss World/Rock Star (Alternate Mix) (pink vinyl) 8
96 Mirromax 573 164-7 — Gold Dust Woman/N.Y. LOOSE: Spit (gatefold p/s, 2 x 1-sided 7"s, with etched B-sides, 5,000 numbered) 8
91 City Slang SLANG 012 — PRETTY ON THE INSIDE (LP, blue vinyl) 20
94 City Slang EFA 04935-1 — LIVE THROUGH THIS (LP, 3000 on white vinyl) 25/12

BILLIE HOLIDAY

56 Vogue V 2408 — Detour Ahead/Blue, Turning Grey Over You (78) 8
56 Vogue V 2408 — Detour Ahead/Blue, Turning Grey Over You 20
59 MGM MGM 1033 — Don't Worry About Me/Just One More Chance 10
55 Brunswick OE 9172 — LADY DAY VOL. 1 (EP) 12
55 Columbia Clef SEB 10009 — BILLIE HOLIDAY SINGS (EP) 10
55 Vogue EPV 1128 — BILLIE HOLIDAY (EP) 15
56 Brunswick OE 9199 — LADY DAY VOL. 2 (EP) 10
56 Brunswick OE 9251 — LADY DAY VOL. 3 (EP) 10
56 Columbia Clef SEB 10035 — AN EVENING WITH BILLIE HOLIDAY (EP) 12
56 Columbia Clef SEB 10048 — BILLIE HOLIDAY SINGS (EP) 12
59 Fontana TFE 17010 — LADY DAY (EP) 10
59 HMV 7EG 8627 — SAY IT ISN'T SO (EP) 10
60 MGM MGM-EP 715 — BILLIE HOLIDAY (EP) 10
50s Melodisc EPM7 125 — EMBRACEABLE YOU (EP) 15
60 Fontana TFE 17026 — BLUE (EP) 10
60 Fontana TFE 17214 — FABULOUS (EP) 8
60 Philips BBE 12359 — JAZZ GALLERY (EP) 12
54 Columbia 33S 1034 — BILLIE HOLIDAY (10" LP) 50
54 Brunswick LA 8676 — LOVER MAN (10" LP) 50
55 Philips BBR 8032 — FAVOURITES (10" LP) 40
56 Columbia Clef 33C 9023 — AT JAZZ AT THE PHILHARMONIC (10" LP) 20
56 Columbia Clef 33CX 10019 — MUSIC FOR TORCHING (LP) 20
57 Columbia Clef 33CX 10064 — VELVET MOOD (LP) 20
57 Columbia Clef 33CX 10076 — SOLITUDE (LP) 20
57 Columbia Clef 33CX 10092 — LADY SINGS THE BLUES (LP) 20
59 Columbia Clef 33CX 10145 — SONGS FOR DISTINGUÉ LOVERS (LP) 20
59 MGM MGM-C 792 — BILLIE HOLIDAY (LP) 20
59 Fontana TFL 5032 — LADY IN SATIN (LP) 20
60 Fontana TFL 5106 — A BILLIE HOLIDAY MEMORIAL (LP) 20
61 HMV CLP 1414 — THE UNFORGETTABLE LADY DAY (LP) 20
62 Stateside SL 10007 — BILLIE HOLIDAY (LP) 20
64 Ace Of Hearts AH 64 — THE LADY SINGS VOL. 3 (LP) 12
65 Fontana TL 5262 — ONCE UPON A TIME (LP, with Teddy Wilson) 15
66 Fontana TL 5287 — BILLIE HOLIDAY (LP) 15
66 Island ILP 929 — LAST LIVE RECORDING (LP) 60

CHICO HOLIDAY

59 RCA RCA 1117 — Young Ideas/Cuckoo Girl 30
59 RCA RCA 1117 — Young Ideas/Cuckoo Girl (78) 10
61 Coral Q 72443 — God, Country And My Baby/Fools 18
59 RCA RCX 171 — CHICO HOLIDAY (EP) 65

JIMMY HOLIDAY

63 Vocalion POP V 9206 — How Can I Forget/Janet 30
64 London HLY 9868 — I Lied/Alison 22
66 Liberty LIB 12040 — Baby I Love You/You Won't Get Away 18
67 Liberty LIB 12048 — Give Me Your Love/The Turning Point 18
67 Liberty LIB 12053 — Everybody Needs Help/I'm Gonna Move To The City 12
68 Minit MLF 11008 — Give Me Your Love/The Beauty Of A Girl In Love 8
69 Minit MLL/MLS 40010 — SPREAD YOUR LOVE (LP) 45

JIMMY HOLIDAY & CLYDIE KING

67 Liberty LIB 12058 — Ready, Willing And Able/We Got A Good Thing Goin' 25
72 United Artists UP 35371 — Ready, Willing And Able/JIMMY HOLIDAY: Give Me Your Love 7
(see also Clydie King)

JOHNNY HOLIDAY

59 London RE 1226 — SENTIMENTAL HOLIDAY (EP) 10
59 London RE 1227 — HOLIDAY FOR ROMANCE (EP) 10

HOLIDAYMAKERS

89 Woosh WOOSH 4 — Cincinnati/Seventh Valley Girl (p/s) 10
89 Maker 00IT — Gay Cowboy (12", p/s) 8

HOLIDAYS

66 Polydor 56720 — I'll Love You Forever/Makin' Up Time 125
(see also Edwin Starr)

HOLLAND

84 Ebony EBON 17	EARLY WARNING (LP)	12

BRIAN HOLLAND

74 Invictus INV 2553	I'm So Glad/I'm So Glad (Version)	8

EDDIE HOLLAND

62 Fontana H 387	Jamie/Take A Chance On Me	300
63 Oriole CBA 1808	If It's Love (It's All Right)/It's Not Too Late	450

LYNN HOLLAND

64 Ember EMB S 198	And The Angels Sing/I Can't Read Your Writing (For My Tears) (some in p/s)	12/6
65 Polydor BM 56035	Oh Darling How I Miss You/Before	6
67 Polydor 56166	One Man In My Life/Wand'rin Boy (unissued)	
67 Polydor 56187	Come And Love/May God Help You And Protect You (unissued)	
67 Polydor 236217	OH DARLING HOW I MISS YOU (LP)	25

(see also Holly)

TONY HOLLAND

63 HMV POP 1135	Sidewalk/Time Goes By	45

(Brian) HOLLAND & (Lamont) DOZIER

72 Invictus INV 525	Why Can't We Be Lovers/Don't Leave Me	5
73 Invictus INV 528	Don't Leave Me Starvin' For Your Love (Parts 1 & 2)	6

(see also Lamont Dozier, Brian Holland)

MICHAEL HOLLIDAY

78s

59 Columbia DB 4336	For You, For You/Life Is A Circus	10
59 Columbia DB 4378	Starry-Eyed/The Steady Game	20

SINGLES

56 Columbia SCM 5221	Sixteen Tons/The Rose Tattoo	22
56 Columbia SCM 5252	Nothin' To Do/Perfume, Candy And Flowers	20
56 Columbia SCM 5273	Hot Diggity (Dog Ziggity)/The Gal With The Yaller Shoes	20
56 Columbia DB 3813	The Runaway Train/Ten Thousand Miles	20
57 Columbia DB 3871	Yaller Yaller Gold/I Saw Esau	15
57 Columbia DB 3919	Love Is Strange/My House Is Your House	15
57 Columbia DB 3948	Four Walls/Wringle Wrangle	15
57 Columbia DB 3973	All Of You/It's The Good Things We Remember	15
57 Columbia DB 3992	Old Cape Cod/Love You Darlin'	12
58 Columbia DB 4058	The Story Of My Life/Keep Your Heart	7
58 Columbia DB 4087	In Love/Rooney	6
58 Columbia DB 4121	Stairway Of Love/May I?	6
58 Columbia DB 4155	I'll Always Be In Love With You/I'll Be Lovin' You, Too	6
58 Columbia DB 4188	She Was Only Seventeen/The Gay Vagabond	6
58 Columbia DB 4216	My Heart Is An Open Book/Careless Hands	6
59 Columbia DB 4255	Palace Of Love/The Girls Of County Armagh	6
59 Columbia DB 4307	Moments Of Love/Dearest	6
59 Columbia DB 4336	For You, For You/Life Is A Circus	6
59 Columbia DB 4378	Starry-Eyed/The Steady Game	6
60 Columbia DB 4437	Skylark/Dream Talk	6
60 Columbia DB 4475	Little Boy Lost/The One-Finger Symphony	6
60 Columbia DB 4548	Stay In Love/Catch Me A Kiss	6
61 Columbia DB 4604	I'm The One Who Loves You/Miracle Of Monday Morning	6
61 Columbia DB 4663	I Wonder Who's Kissing Her Now/Dream Boy, Dream	6
62 Columbia DB 4819	I Don't Want You To See Me Cry/Wishin' On A Rainbow	6
62 Columbia DB 4890	Have I Told You Lately That I Love You/It Only Takes A Minute	6
63 Columbia DB 4976	Laugh And The World Laughs With You/Iron Fence	6
63 Columbia DB 7080	Between Hello And Goodbye/Just To Be With You Again	6
63 Columbia DB 7171	Drums/Can I Forget You	6
64 Columbia DB 7327	My Last Date (With You)/Always Is A Long Long Time	6

EPs

56 Columbia SEG 7638	MY GUITAR AND ME	12
57 Columbia SEG 7683	MUSIC WITH MIKE	12
58 Columbia SEG 7752	RELAX WITH MIKE	12
58 Columbia SEG 7761	ALL TIME FAVOURITES	12
58 Columbia SEG 7818	MELODY MIKE	12
59 Columbia SEG 7836	SENTIMENTAL JOURNEY (with Edna Savage)	15
59 Columbia SEG 7892	MIKE AND THE OTHER FELLA	12
59 Columbia SEG 7972	MIKE NO. 1 (also stereo ESG 7784)	12/15
60 Columbia SEG 7986	FOUR FEATHER FALLS (also stereo ESG 7793)	25/35
60 Columbia SEG 7996	MIKE NO. 2 (also stereo ESG 7803)	12/15
61 Columbia SEG 8074	MIKE NO. 3 (also stereo ESG 7842)	12/15
61 Columbia SEG 8101	MIKE SINGS RAGTIME (also stereo ESG 7856)	12/15
61 Columbia SEG 8115	MIKE IN A SENTIMENTAL MOOD (also stereo ESG 7864)	12/15
62 Columbia SEG 8161	HAPPY HOLLIDAY	12
62 Columbia SEG 8186	MORE HAPPY HOLLIDAY	12
61 Columbia SEG 8242	MIKE SINGS COUNTRY AND WESTERN STYLE	20
64 Columbia SEG 8373	MEMORIES OF MIKE	20

LPs

58 Columbia 33S 1114	HI! (10")	25
59 Columbia 33SX 1170	MIKE	20
60 Columbia 33SX 1262	HOLLIDAY MIXTURE (also stereo SCX 3331)	15/20
61 Columbia 33SX 1354	HAPPY HOLLIDAY	18
62 Columbia 33SX 1426	TO BING FROM MIKE (also stereo SCX 3441)	15/20
64 Columbia 33SX 1586	THE BEST OF MICHAEL HOLLIDAY	15
60s World Record Club T 792	TO BING FROM MIKE	12

(see also Edna Savage)

MINT VALUE £

SU(SAN) HOLLIDAY

64	Columbia DB 7363	Dark Despair/The Other Side (demos list A-side as "[Street Of] Dark Despair")	15
64	Columbia DB 7403	Any Day Now/Don't Come Knocking At My Door	15
65	Columbia DB 7616	Sometimes/Long Haired Boy	15
65	Columbia DB 7709	Nevertheless (I'm In Love With You)/Moonglow	15
66	Columbia SX 6067	I WANNA SAY HELLO (LP, as Su Holliday)	110

(see also Susan Singer)

TIM HOLLIER

70	Fontana TF 1080	In This Room/Love Song	6
71	Philips 6006 130	Circle Is Small/In A Corner Of My Life/Time Stood Still	6
68	United Artists (S)ULP 1211	MESSAGE TO A HARLEQUIN (LP)	22
71	Philips 6308 044	SKY SAIL (LP)	18

HOLLIES

SINGLES

63	Parlophone R 5030	(Ain't That) Just Like Me/Hey, What's Wrong With Me	20
63	Parlophone R 5052	Searchin'/Whole World Over	12
63	Parlophone R 5077	Stay/Now's The Time	10
64	Parlophone R 5104	Just One Look/Keep Off That Friend Of Mine	7
64	Parlophone R 5137	Here I Go Again/Baby That's All	7
64	Parlophone R 5178	We're Through/Come On Back	6
65	Parlophone R 5232	Yes I Will/Nobody	6
65	Parlophone R 5287	I'm Alive/You Know He Did	6
65	Parlophone R 5322	Look Through Any Window/So Lonely	7
65	Parlophone R 5392	If I Needed Someone/I've Got A Way Of My Own	8
66	Parlophone R 5409	I Can't Let Go/Running Through The Night	6
66	Parlophone R 5469	Bus Stop/Don't Run And Hide	6
66	United Artists UP 1152	After The Fox (with Peter Sellers)/BURT BACHARACH: The Fox-Trot	35
66	Parlophone R 5508	Stop! Stop! Stop!/It's You	6
67	Parlophone R 5562	On A Carousel/All The World Is Love	6
67	Parlophone R 5602	Carrie Anne/Signs That Will Never Change	6
67	Parlophone R 5637	King Midas In Reverse/Everything Is Sunshine	10
68	Parlophone R 5680	Jennifer Eccles/Open Up Your Eyes	6
68	Parlophone R 5733	Listen To Me/Do The Best You Can	7
69	Parlophone R 5765	Sorry Suzanne/Not That Way At All	7
69	Parlophone R 5806	He Ain't Heavy, He's My Brother/'Cos You Like To Love Me	7
70	Parlophone R 5837	I Can't Tell The Bottom From The Top/Mad Professor Blyth	5
70	Parlophone R 5862	Gasoline Alley Bred/Dandelion Wine	5
71	Parlophone R 5905	Hey Willy/Row The Boat Together	7
72	Polydor 2058 199	The Baby/Oh Granny	7
72	Parlophone R 5939	Long Cool Woman (In A Black Dress)/Cable Car	6
72	Polydor 2058 289	Magic Woman Touch/Indian Girl	6
73	Polydor 2058 403	The Day That Curly Billy Shot Down Crazy Sam McGee/Born A Man	6
74	Polydor 2058 435	The Air That I Breathe/No More Riders	5
74	Polydor 2058 476	Son Of A Rotten Gambler/Layin' To The Music	6
74	Polydor 2058 533	I'm Down/Hello Lady Goodbye	6
75	Polydor 2058 595	Sandy (Fourth Of July, Asbury Park)/Second-Hand Hangups	6
75	EMI EMI 2353	Long Cool Woman In A Black Dress/Carrie Anne	6
76	Polydor 2058 694	Boulder To Birmingham/Crocodile Woman (She Bites)	6
76	Polydor 2058 719	Star/Love Is The Thing	6
76	Polydor 2058 779	Daddy Don't Mind/C'mon	6
76	Polydor 2058 799	Wiggle That Wotsit/Corrine	6
76	Polydor 2058 880	Hello To Romance/48 Hour Parole	6
77	Polydor 2058 906	Amnesty/Crossfire	6
78	EMI EMI 2813	Look Through Any Window/I'm Alive/Just One Look (p/s)	6
79	Polydor POSP 35	Something To Live For/Song Of The Sun	6
79	Polydor POSPX 35	Something To Live For/Song Of The Sun/The Air That I Breathe (12", p/s)	12
80	Polydor 2059 246	Soldier's Song/Draggin' My Heels	10
80	Polydor POSP 175	Heartbeat/Take Your Time	8
81	EMI EMI 5229	Holliedaze (A Medley)/Holliepops (Medley)	5
81	Polydor POSP 379	Take My Love And Run/Driver	5
82	Parlophome PMS 1001	He Ain't Heavy, He's My Brother/'Cos You Like To Love Me (p/s)	5
83	WEA U 9888	Stop! In The Name Of Love/Musical Pictures (p/s)	5
84	EMI G45 11	Just One Look/Here I Go Again (p/s)	5
84	Columbia DB 9110	Too Many Hearts Get Broken/You're All Woman (p/s)	5
84	Columbia 12DB 9110	Too Many Hearts Get Broken/You're All Woman/Laughter Turns To Tears (12", p/s)	8
87	Columbia DB 9146	This Is It/You Gave Me Strength (p/s)	5
87	Columbia 12DB 9146	This Is It/You Gave Me Strength/You're All Woman (12", p/s)	8
87	Columbia DB 9151	Reunion Of The Heart/Too Many Hearts Get Broken (p/s)	5
87	Columbia 12DB 9151	Reunion Of The Heart/Too Many Hearts Get Broken/Hollidaze (12", p/s)	8
88	EMI CDEM 74	He Ain't Heavy, He's My Brother/Carrie/The Air That I Breathe/Yes I Will (CD)	8
88	EMI CDEM 80	The Air That I Breathe/We're Through/King Midas In Reverse/He Ain't Heavy, He's My Brother (CD)	8
90	SRT 90LS 2407	Purple Rain/Naomi/Two Shadows (12", p/s, available only at gigs)	8
90	SRT 90C 2407	Purple Rain/Naomi/Two Shadows (cassette, available only at gigs)	6

EPs

64	Parlophone GEP 8909	THE HOLLIES	40
64	Parlophone GEP 8911	JUST ONE LOOK	45
64	Parlophone GEP 8915	HERE I GO AGAIN	45
64	Parlophone GEP 8927	WE'RE THROUGH	45
65	Parlophone GEP 8934	IN THE HOLLIES STYLE	50
65	Parlophone GEP 8942	I'M ALIVE	45
66	Parlophone GEP 8951	I CAN'T LET GO	55

MINT VALUE £

LPs

Year	Label	Title	Value
64	Parlophone PMC 1220	STAY WITH THE HOLLIES (also stereo PCS 3054)	45/60
65	Parlophone PMC 1235	IN THE HOLLIES STYLE	45
65	Parlophone PMC 1261	THE HOLLIES	30
66	Parlophone PMC/PCS 7008	WOULD YOU BELIEVE? (mono/stereo)	25/40
66	Parlophone PMC/PCS 7011	FOR CERTAIN BECAUSE (gatefold sleeve, mono/stereo)	25/40
67	Parlophone PMC/PCS 7022	EVOLUTION (mono/stereo)	40/55
67	Parlophone PMC/PCS 7039	BUTTERFLY (mono/stereo)	35/45
67	Parlophone TA-PMC 7039	BUTTERFLY (reel-to-reel tape, mono)	12
67	EMI Regal SREG 2024	THE HOLLIES (export compilation)	35
67	World Records ST 979	THE VINTAGE HOLLIES (stereo reissue of "In The Hollies Style")	35
68	World Records ST 1035	STAY WITH THE HOLLIES (record club reissue)	30
68	Parlophone PMC/PCS 7057	THE HOLLIES' GREATEST	15
68	Parlophone TA-PMC 7057	THE HOLLIES' GREATEST (reel-to-reel tape, mono)	12
69	Parlophone PMC/PCS 7078	THE HOLLIES SING DYLAN (mono/stereo)	30/22
69	Regal Starline SRS 5008	REFLECTION (stereo reissue of "The Hollies")	12
69	Parlophone PCS 7092	HOLLIES SING HOLLIES (gatefold sleeve)	20

(The above Parlophone LPs were originally issued with yellow/black labels; 1970s pressings with silver & black labels are worth £10 each.)

Year	Label	Title	Value
70	Parlophone PCS 7116	CONFESSIONS OF THE MIND (with colour insert)	20
71	Parlophone PAS 10005	DISTANT LIGHT (gatefold sleeve)	20
71	Regal Starline SRS 5013	STOP! STOP! STOP! (reissue of "For Certain Because")	12
71	MFP MFP 5252	THE HOLLIES (budget reissue of "Evolution")	12
72	Parlophone PCS 7148	THE HOLLIES' GREATEST HITS VOL. 2	12
72	Polydor 2383 144	ROMANY (gatefold sleeve)	20
74	Polydor 2383 262	HOLLIES (with lyric insert)	15
75	Polydor 2442 128	ANOTHER NIGHT (gatefold sleeve)	15
76	Polydor 2442 141	WRITE ON (with lyric inner)	15
76	Polydor 2383 421	RUSSIAN ROULETTE (with lyric inner)	15
78	Polydor 2383 474	A CRAZY STEAL (with lyric inner)	12
78	Parlophone PMC 7174	THE BEST OF THE HOLLIES' EPs	12
78	Parlophone PMC 7176	THE OTHER SIDE OF THE HOLLIES	18
79	Polydor 2442 160	FIVE THREE ONE — DOUBLE SEVEN O FOUR (with lyric insert)	12
79	St. Michael 2102/0101	UP FRONT (sold through Marks & Spencer in conjunction with Polydor)	45
79	St. Michael 2102/0101	UP FRONT (cassette, via Marks & Spencer/Polydor)	20
80	Polydor POLTV 12	BUDDY HOLLY (with lyric insert)	15
83	WEA 2501391	WHAT GOES AROUND	12
94	Fast Forward FFCD 822	LEGENDARY TOP TENS 1963 — 1988 (CD, sold via Avon Cosmetics)	25

(see also Allan Clarke, Graham Nash, Terry Sylvester, Haydock's Rockhouse, Peter Sellers & Sophia Loren)

BRENDA HOLLOWAY

Year	Label	Title	Value
64	Stateside SS 307	Every Little Bit Hurts/Land Of A Thousand Boys	45
65	Tamla Motown TMG 508	When I'm Gone/I've Been Good To You	90
65	Tamla Motown TMG 519	Operator/I'll Be Available	65
66	Tamla Motown TMG 556	Together Till The End Of Time/Sad Song	75
66	Tamla Motown TMG 581	Hurt A Little Everyday/Where Were You (demos credit Brenda Holiday)	35
67	Tamla Motown TMG 608	Just Look What You've Done/Starting The Hurt All Over Again	22
67	Tamla Motown TMG 622	You've Made Me So Very Happy/I've Got To Find It	22
69	Tamla Motown TMG 700	Just Look What You've Done/You've Made Me So Very Happy	15
68	T. Motown (S)TML 11083	THE ARTISTRY OF BRENDA HOLLOWAY (LP)	130

LOLEATTA HOLLOWAY

Year	Label	Title	Value
71	United Artists UP 35273	Bring It On Up/Rainbow '71'	8

PATRICE HOLLOWAY

Year	Label	Title	Value
66	Capitol CL 15484	Love And Desire/Ecstasy	70

STANLEY HOLLOWAY

Year	Label	Title	Value
59	Decca F 11140	Dark Girl Dressed In Blue/Growing Old	5
60	Columbia DB 4517	Petticoat Lane/Sing A Song Of London	5
60	Pye 7N 15302	Lily Of Laguna/A Bachelor Gay	5
61	Columbia DB 4653	Brahan Boots/Tommy The Whistler	5
59	Philips BBE 12326	MY WORD YOU DO LOOK QUEER (EP)	8
59	Pye NEP 24097	NO TREES IN THE STREET (EP)	8
60	Columbia SEG 8034	ADVENTURES WITH ALBERT (EP)	8
62	Columbia SEG 8118	BRAHN BOOTS AND OTHER FAVOURITES (EP)	8
56	Columbia 33S 1093	FAMOUS ADVENTURES WITH OLD SAM & THE RAMSBOTTOMS (10" LP)	15
58	Philips BBL 7237	'ERE'S 'OLLOWAY (LP)	12
60	Pye NPL 18056	JOIN IN THE CHORUS (LP)	12

(see also Joyce Grenfell & Stanley Holloway)

HOLLOW GROUND

Year	Label	Title	Value
80	Guardian GR/HG C57	FLYING HIGH EP (Flying High/Warlord/Rock On/Don't Chase The Dragon) (some in p/s)	150/30

HOLLOW MEN

Year	Label	Title	Value
85	Evensong EVE 107	Late Flowering Lust/Ocean Lies/Raindrop Children (p/s)	8
87	Evensong EVE 212	Gold And Ivory/Filth City Fever/Pandemonium Carousel/ Autumn Avenue (12", p/s, with postcard)	8
87	Evensong EVE 212	Gold And Ivory/Filth City Fever/Pandemonium Carousel/Autumn Avenue (12", white label test pressing in unreleased proof sleeve)	50
88	Gigantic GI 101	White Train/The Man Who Would Be King (die-cut p/s, promo only)	8
89	Blind Eye BE 007	The Drowning Man/Whisper To Me/Ivory Blues (12", p/s, with promo booklet, some signed)	8/10
86	Dead Man's Curve DMC 15	TALES OF THE RIVERBANK (LP)	12
88	Dead Man's Curve DMC 25	THE MAN WHO WOULD BE KING (LP)	12
88	D.M.C. VIVID ONE	THE MAN WHO WOULD BE KING (CD)	18

MINT VALUE £

HOLLY

65 Fontana TF 980 — On With The Game/Paradise Lost 8
(see also Lynn Holland)

HOLLY

79 Eric's ERIC'S 003 — Yankee Rose/Treasure Island/Desperate Dan (p/s) 25
79 Eric's ERIC'S 007 — Hobo Joe/Stars Of The Bars (p/s) 20
(see also Holly Johnson, Frankie Goes To Hollywood, Big In Japan)

BUDDY HOLLY

78s

56 Brunswick 05581 — Blue Days — Black Nights/Love Me 220
57 Vogue Coral Q 72293 — Peggy Sue/Everyday 100
58 Coral Q 72293 — Peggy Sue/Everyday 12
58 Coral Q 72288 — Listen To Me/I'm Gonna Love You Too 30
58 Coral Q 72325 — Rave On/Take Your Time 30
58 Coral Q 72333 — Early In The Morning/Now We're One 40
58 Coral Q 72346 — Heartbeat/Well ... All Right 45
59 Coral Q 72360 — It Doesn't Matter Anymore/Raining In My Heart 45
59 Brunswick 05800 — Rock Around With Ollie Vee/Midnight Shift 220
59 Coral Q 72376 — Peggy Sue Got Married/Crying, Waiting, Hoping 220
60 Coral Q 72392 — Heartbeat/Everyday 450

SINGLES

56 Brunswick 05581 — Blue Days — Black Nights/Love Me 800
57 Vogue Coral Q 72293 — Peggy Sue/Everyday 70
58 Coral Q 72293 — Peggy Sue/Everyday 15
58 Coral Q 72288 — Listen To Me/I'm Gonna Love You Too 25
58 Coral Q 72325 — Rave On/Take Your Time 25
58 Coral Q 72333 — Early In The Morning/Now We're One 25
58 Coral Q 72346 — Heartbeat/Well ... All Right 25
59 Coral Q 72360 — It Doesn't Matter Anymore/Raining In My Heart 15
59 Brunswick 05800 — Rock Around With Ollie Vee/Midnight Shift 40
59 Coral Q 72376 — Peggy Sue Got Married/Crying, Waiting, Hoping 20
(The above 45s were originally issued with triangular centres; reissues with round centres are worth two-thirds these values)
60 Coral Q 72392 — Heartbeat/Everyday 18
60 Coral Q 72397 — True Love Ways/Moondreams 15
60 Coral Q 72411 — Learning The Game/That Makes It Tough 12
61 Coral Q 72419 — What To Do/That's What They Say 15
61 Coral Q 72432 — Baby I Don't Care/Valley Of Tears 10
61 Coral Q 72445 — Look At Me/Mailman, Bring Me No More Blues 15
62 Coral Q 72449 — Listen To Me/Words Of Love 15
62 Coral Q 72455 — Reminiscing/Wait Till The Sun Shines, Nellie 7
63 Coral Q 72459 — Brown-Eyed Handsome Man/Slippin' And Slidin' 10
63 Coral Q 72463 — Bo Diddley/It's Not My Fault 10
63 Coral Q 72466 — Wishing/Because I Love You 10
63 Coral Q 72469 — What To Do/Umm Oh Yeah 18
64 Coral Q 72472 — You've Got Love/An Empty Cup (as Buddy Holly & The Crickets) 22
64 Coral Q 72475 — Love's Made A Fool Of You/You're The One 15
66 Coral Q 72483 — Maybe Baby/That's My Desire 40
68 Decca AD 1009 — Rave On/Peggy Sue (p/s, export reissue) 75
68 MCA MU 1012 — Peggy Sue/Rave On (reissue) 6
69 MCA MU 1059 — Love Is Strange/You're The One 10
69 MCA MU 1081 — It Doesn't Matter Anymore/Maybe Baby (reissue) 7
70 MCA MU 1116 — Rave On/Umm Oh Yeah (Dearest) 6
73 MCA MMU 1198 — That'll Be The Day/Well All Right/Every Day 6
74 MCA MCA 119 — It Doesn't Matter Anymore/True Love Ways/Brown Eyed Handsome Man 6
75 MCA MCA 207 — Oh Boy!/Every Day (as Buddy Holly & Crickets) 6
76 MCA MCA 252 — True Love Ways/It Doesn't Matter Anymore/Raining In My Heart/Moondreams (p/s) 6
76 MCA MCA 253 — Peggy Sue/Rave On/Rock Around With Ollie Vee/Midnight Shift (p/s) 6
76 MCA MCA 254 — Maybe Baby/Think It Over/That'll Be The Day/It's So Easy (p/s, as Buddy Holly & Crickets) 6
78 MCA MCA 344 — Wishing/Love's Made A Fool Of You (p/s) 6
83 MCA HR 001 — That'll Be The Day/True Love Ways (as Buddy Holly & Crickets) (with/without *The History Of Rock* issue 1; 'Made In France' or 'Made In Gt. Britain' on label) 7/5
84 MCA BHB 1 — THAT'LL BE THE DAY (10 x 7" box set, comprising BH1-10 in p/s) 45
89 MCA MCAV 1368 — Oh Boy!/Well ... All Right/Mailman Bring Me No More Blues/Everyday (10", p/s) . . 8

EPs

58 Coral FEP 2002 — LISTEN TO ME (brown cover, sleeve shows Holly *without* glasses; disc credits title as "Buddy Holly") . . . . . 400+
58 Coral FEP 2002 — LISTEN TO ME (re-pressing, various shades of green/brown p/s, shows Holly *with* glasses; disc credits title as "Buddy Holly") 40
58 Coral FEP 2005 — RAVE ON (various shades of green/brown p/s) 50
59 Coral FEP 2014 — IT'S SO EASY 50
59 Coral FEP 2015 — HEARTBEAT 50
59 Coral FEP 2032 — BUDDY HOLLY 50
59 Brunswick OE 9456 — BUDDY HOLLY NO. 1 70
59 Brunswick OE 9457 — BUDDY HOLLY NO. 2 70
(The above EPs were originally issued with triangular centres; later pressings with round-centres are worth between half and two-thirds these values.)
60 Coral FEP 2044 — THE LATE GREAT BUDDY HOLLY (tri centre) . . . . . 50+
60 Coral FEP 2044 — THE LATE GREAT BUDDY HOLLY (round centre) 30
64 Coral FEP 2065 — BUDDY — BY REQUEST 55
64 Coral FEP 2066 — THAT TEX-MEX SOUND 70
64 Coral FEP 2067 — WISHING 60
64 Coral FEP 2068 — SHOWCASE VOLUME 1 70

64	Coral FEP 2069	SHOWCASE VOLUME 2	70
65	Coral FEP 2070	BUDDY HOLLY SINGS	75

LPs

58	Vogue Coral LVA 9085	BUDDY HOLLY (Vogue-Coral labels & Coral sleeve)	125
58	Coral LVA 9085	BUDDY HOLLY	55
59	Coral LVA 9105	THE BUDDY HOLLY STORY('High Fidelity Coral' logo on sleeve)	30
60s	Coral LVA 9105	THE BUDDY HOLLY STORY (reissue, different 'roll-neck sweater' sleeve with small 'Coral' logo)	45
60	Coral LVA 9127	THE BUDDY HOLLY STORY VOL. II	25
61	Ace Of Hearts AH 3	THAT'LL BE THE DAY	15
63	Coral LVA 9212	REMINISCING	30
64	Coral LVA 9222	SHOWCASE	30
65	Coral LVA 9227	HOLLY IN THE HILLS (with Bob Montgomery, withdrawn mispressing, sleeve & label list "Wishing", plays "Reminiscing"; matrix no's end w/ 1B both sides)	50
65	Coral LVA 9227	HOLLY IN THE HILLS (corrected edition, with Bob Montgomery, plays "Wishing", matrix numbers end with 1B on one side & 2B on other)	70
67	Ace Of Hearts AH 148	BUDDY HOLLY'S GREATEST HITS	12
68	MCA MUP(S) 312	LISTEN TO ME (mono/stereo, reissue of "Buddy Holly" [LVA 9085])	25/18
68	MCA MUP(S) 313	RAVE ON (mono/stereo, reissue of "The Buddy Holly Story")	25/18
68	MCA MUP(S) 314	BROWN-EYED HANDSOME MAN (mono/stereo,reissue of "Reminiscing")	25/18
68	MCA MUP(S) 315	HE'S THE ONE (mono/stereo, reissue of "Showcase")	25/18
68	MCA MUP(S) 319	TRUE LOVE WAYS (mono/stereo, reissue of "The Buddy Holly Story, Volume II")	25/18
68	MCA MUP 320	WISHING (mono only, reissue of "Holly In The Hills")	30
69	MCA MUPS 371	GIANT	25

(The above MCA albums were originally issued with yellow labels; later variations exist with various twin-toned designs.)

70	Coral CP/CPS 47	BUDDY HOLLY'S GREATEST HITS VOL. 2 (reissue, mono/stereo)	12/8
75	World Records SM 301/5	THE BUDDY HOLLY STORY (5-LP box set)	30
79	MCA Coral CDMSP 807	THE COMPLETE BUDDY HOLLY (6-LP box set with sepia-tinted book)	35
80	Marks & Spencer IMP 114	HEARTBEAT	60
83	MCA MCM 1002	FOR THE FIRST TIME ANYWHERE	12
86	Rollercoaster ROLL 2013	SOMETHING SPECIAL FROM BUDDY HOLLY	20

(see also Crickets, Fireballs)

STEVIE HOLLY

66	Planet PLF 107	A Strange World/Little Man (initially with "Planet" company sleeve)	30/25

HOLLY GOLIGHTLY

94	Vinyl Japan PAD 13	JIGGY JIGGY (EP)	5
95	Vinyl Japan PAD 26	MARY ANN (EP)	5
96	Damaged Goods DAMGOOD 110	Come The Day/In You (picture disc)	6

HOLLY & JOEY

82	Virgin VS 478	I Got You Babe/HOLLY & THE ITALIANS: One More Dance (p/s)	12

(see also Ramones, Deborah Harry)

HOLLY & THE ITALIANS

81	Virgin VS 411	I Wanna Go Home/Fanzine (p/s)	15
81	Virgin VS 429	Just For Tonight/Baby Gets It All (p/s)	7
81	Virgin V 2186	THE RIGHT TO BE ITALIAN (LP, with lyric insert)	15

KENNY HOLLYWOOD

62	Decca F 11546	Magic Star/The Wonderful Story Of Love	30

HOLLYWOOD ARGYLES

60	London HLU 9146	Alley Oop/Sho' Knew A Lot About Love	10
60	London HLU 9146	Alley Oop/Sho' Knew A Lot About Love (78)	40
60	Top Rank JAR 530	Gun Totin' Critter Called Jack/GARY PAXTON: Bug-Eye	20

(see also Kim Fowley, Skip & Flip, Gary Paxton)

HOLLYWOOD FLAMES

57	London HL 7030	Buzz Buzz Buzz/Crazy (export issue)	40
58	London HL 8545	Buzz Buzz Buzz/Crazy	70
58	London HL 8545	Buzz Buzz Buzz/Crazy (78)	25
59	London HLW 8955	Much Too Much/In The Dark	70
59	London HLW 8955	Much Too Much/In The Dark (78)	25
60	London HLE 9071	If I Thought You Needed Me/Every Day Every Way	40

HOLLYWOOD FREEWAY

72	Threshold TH 10	I've Been Moved/Cool Calamares (unissued)	
72	Deram DM 359	I've Been Moved/Cool Calamares	6
73	Pye 7N 45273	You're The Song (That I Can't Stop Singing)/This Feeling Called Love	8

(see also Tony Rivers)

HOLLYWOOD HURRICANES

64	Prima PR 1009	Beavershot/Have Love Will Travel	6

HOLLYWOOD VINES

61	Capitol CL 15191	When Johnny Comes Slidin' Home/Cruisin'	15

MIKE HOLM

70	Major Minor MM 659	Mendocino/Cutey Girl	5

BILL HOLMAN OCTET

54	Capitol KC 65000	Cousin Jack/Plain Folks	7

EDDIE HOLMAN

65	Cameo Parkway P 960	This Can't Be True/A Free Country	50
69	Action ACT 4547	I Love You/I Surrender	55
70	Stateside SS 2160	(Hey There) Lonely Girl/It's All In The Game	12

MINT VALUE £

70	Stateside SS 2170	Since I Don't Have You/Don't Stop Now	12
72	GSF GSZ 1	My Mind Keeps Telling Me/Stranded In A Dream	6
77	Salsoul SZ 2026	This Will Be A Night To Remember/Time Will Tell	6

DAVID HOLMES

97	Go Beat GOB 6	Don't Die Just Yet (Mogwai Mix)/Holiday Girl (Arab Strap Mix) (p/s, 500 only)	18

(see also Mogwai)

CHRISTINE HOLMES

64	Mercury MF 813	This Is My Prayer/My Dream	10
64	Mercury MF 819	Play Me A Sad Song (Mr DJ)/Doesn't He Know	10
64	Mercury MF 831	Goodbye Boys Goodbye/Is It Love	10
65	Mercury MF 851	Many Things From Your Window/You'd Better Believe It	7
65	Mercury MF 887	Goin' Where The Lovin' Is/Where There's Smoke	7

(see also Family Dogg)

IVAN HOLMES

67	Columbia DB 8119	The Light, The Love And The Life/Cocaine	7

JAKE HOLMES

69	Polydor 56547	How Are You (Parts 1 & 2)	5
70	Ember EMB S 269	Saturday Night/Diner Song	5
70	Polydor 2066 040	So Close/Django And Friend	5
70	Polydor 583 579	JAKE HOLMES (LP)	25
70	Polydor 2425 036	SO CLOSE SO VERY FAR TO GO (LP)	25
72	CBS 64905	HOW MUCH TIME (LP)	20

JOE HOLMES & LEN GRAHAM

79	Topic 12TS 401	AFTER DAWNING (LP)	12

LEROY HOLMES & ORCHESTRA

68	United Artists UP 2222	The Good, The Bad And The Ugly/Live For Life	5

SALTY HOLMES

50	London L 663	I Found My Mama/Don't Shed Your Tears After I'm Gone (78)	7

RICHARD 'GROOVES' HOLMES

67	Transatlantic PR 7435	SOUL MESSAGE (LP)	12
68	Transatlantic PR 7493	RICHARD 'GROOVES' HOLMES (LP)	18

HOLOCAUST

80	Phoenix PSP 1	Heavy Metal Mania/Only As Young As You Feel (p/s)	20
80	Phoenix 12 PSP 1	Heavy Metal Mania/Love's Power/Only As Young As You Feel (12", p/s)	30
80	Phoenix 12 PSP 2	Smokin' Valves/Friend Or Foe (p/s)	10
80	Phoenix 12 PSP 2	Smokin' Valves/Friend Or Foe/Out My Book (12", p/s)	30
81	Phoenix PSP 3P	HOLOCAUST LIVE (EP)	25
82	Phoenix 12 PSP 4	Comin' Through/Don't Wanna Be A Loser/Good Thing Going (12", p/s)	30
81	Phoenix PSLP 1	THE NIGHTCOMERS (LP)	40
83	Phoenix PSPLP 4	LIVE (HOT CURRY AND WINE) (LP)	25
84	Phoenix PSPLP 5	NO MAN'S LAND (LP)	20

HOLOGRAM

82	Phoenix PSPLP 2	STEAL THE STARS (LP)	12

HOLOSADE

88	Powerstation AMP 16	HELL HOUSE (LP)	12

JOHN HOLT

63	Island WI 041	I Cried A Tear/I'll Stay	25
68	Trojan TR 643	Tonight/Oh How It Hurts (B-side actually by Paragons)	22
69	Trojan TR 661	Ali Baba/I'm Your Man	12
69	Trojan TR 674	What You Gonna Do Now/Have You Ever Been To Heaven	10
69	Trojan TR 694	Have Sympathy/HARRY J ALLSTARS: Spyrone	12
69	Trojan TR 7702	Wooden Heart/All My Life	10
70	Duke Reid DR 2506	Come Out Of My Bed/WINSTON WRIGHT: Hide And Seek	12
70	Duke DU 73	Stealing, Stealing/WINSTON WRIGHT: Stealing, Stealing (Volume 2)	8
70	Duke DU 77	The Working Kind/Open Jaw	8
70	Jackpot JP 735	A Little Tear/JEFF BARNS: Get In The Groove	7
70	Bamboo BAM 44	A Love I Can Feel/JOHNNY LAST: Long Liver Man (B-side act. by Hugh Black)	10
70	Bamboo BAM 55	A Stranger In Love/WAILERS: Jailhouse (Good Rudy)	70
70	Bamboo BAM 62	Holly Holy/Do You Love Me?	8
70	Banana BA 314	Why Can't I Touch You/SOUND DIMENSION: Touching Version	8
70	Smash SMA 2303	My Heart Is Gone/PHIL PRATT ALL STARS: Version	6
70	Smash SMA 2305	I Had A Talk With My Woman/MAXINE: Life Is Not The Same Anymore	6
70	Supreme SUP 212	Share My Rest/AL BROWN: Allways	12
70	Unity UN 548	Sometimes/BUNNY LEE ALL STARS: Lash-La-Rue	12
70	Unity UN 549	Sea Cruise/LEE'S ALL STARS: Niney's Hop	8
70	Unity UN 552	Walking Along/LEE'S ALL STARS: Warefare	10
70	Unity UN 556	Give Her All The Love/BUSTY BROWN: Nobody But You	6
71	Banana BA 340	O.K. Fred/Fancy Make-Up	10
71	Banana BA 345	Build Our Dreams/LEROY SIBBLES: Love In Our Nation	10
71	Treasure Isle TI 7061	Let's Build Our Dreams/TOMMY McCOOK & SUPERSONICS: Testify Version	18
71	Treasure Isle TI 7065	Sister Big Stuff/TOMMY McCOOK & SUPERSONICS: Black River	20
71	Treasure Isle TI 7066	Paragons Medley/TOMMY McCOOK & SUPERSONICS: Medley Version	18
71	Ashanti ASH 401	Again/MUDIES ALL STARS: Ten Steps To Soul Version	7
71	Camel CA 78	Linger A While/Version	7
71	Escort ERT 847	Knock On Your Door/URIEL ALDRIDGE: Set Me Free	6
71	Jackpot JP 772	Stick By Me/It's A Pleasure	6
71	Jackpot JP 774	It's A Jam In The Streets/A Man Needs A Woman	6
71	Jackpot JP 784	Anymore/Lost Love	6
71	Moodisc MU 3513	It May Sound Silly/MUDIE ALL STARS: Instrumental	6
71	Moodisc HM 105	It May Sound Silly/MUDIE ALL STARS: Instrumental (reissue)	6

71 Punch PH 60 — Strange Things/WINSTON WRIGHT: Want Money (B-side act. G.G. All Stars) 10
71 Smash SMA 2324 — Mother And Father Love/AGGROVATORS: Mother Love Version 6
72 Blue Beat BB 424 — O.K. Fred/BIG YOUTH: Chi Chi Run 7
72 Prince Buster PB 40 — Close To Me/Version 7
72 Prince Buster PB 41 — Get Ready/Version 7
72 Prince Buster PB 42 — Rain From The Skies/Version 7
72 Prince Buster PB 43 — The First Time/Version 7
72 Prince Buster PB 49 — For Your Love/Version 7
72 G.G. GG 4529 — Keep It Up/A Love Like Yours 6
72 Fab FAB 188 — A Little Happiness/DELROY WILSON: Diamond Rings 10
72 Jackpot JP 790 — Don't You Know/Riding For A Fall 6
72 Jackpot JP 807 — Looking Back/I'll Be There 6
72 Pama PM 845 — I'll Always Love You/SLIM SMITH: 3 x 7 Rock And Roll 6
72 Pama PM 852 — Pledging My Love/I Will Know What To Do 6
73 Fab FAB 224 — Let's Go Dancing/Version 7
73 Fab FAB 244 — Let's Go Dancing/Version (reissue) 7
73 Attack ATT 8045 — Time And The River/Version 5
73 Smash SMA 2329 — Don't Break Your Promise/I've Been Admiring You 8
73 Ackee ACK 513 — Ecstacy/Version 6
70 Bamboo BDLP 210 — A LOVE I CAN FEEL (LP) 45
70s Melodisc MLP 12170 — GREATEST HITS (LP) 40
70s Melodisc MLP 12180 — OK FRED (LP) 45
70s Melodisc MLP 12191 — JOHN HOLT & FRIENDS (LP) 45
71 Trojan TRL(S) 37 — STILL IN CHAINS (LP) 18
72 Trojan TRL(S) 43 — HOLT (LP) 18
72 Trojan TBL 184 — PLEDGING MY LOVE (LP) 18
73 Trojan TRLS 55 — THE FURTHER YOU LOOK (LP) 18
74 Attack ATLP 1010 — A LOVE I CAN FEEL (LP) 18
74 Trojan TRLS 75 — A THOUSAND VOLTS OF HOLT (LP) 18
74 Trojan TRLS 85 — DUSTY ROADS (LP) 18
75 Cactus CTLP 109 — TIME IS THE MASTER (LP) 15

(see also Jay & Joya, Little John, Neville Hinds, Jeff Barnes, Danny Simpson, Hugh Roy, U Roy Junior, Don Drummond, Interns)

GARY HOLTON

84 Magnet GARY 2 — Catch A Falling Star/Angel (star-shaped picture disc) 8

(see also Heavy Metal Kids, Kids, Slade)

ROOSEVELT HOLTS

68 Blue Horizon 7-63201 — PRESENTING THE COUNTRY BLUES (LP) 80

HOLY MACKEREL

72 CBS 8447 — Rock-A-Bye/New Black Shoes 6
72 CBS 65297 — HOLY MACKEREL (LP) 25
93 Tenth Planet TP 005 — CLOSER TO HEAVEN (LP, numbered, 500 only) 15

(see also Jason Crest, High Broom)

HOLY MODAL ROUNDERS

68 Elektra EKL 4026 — THE MORAY EELS EAT THE HOLY MODALS (LP, mono) 25
68 Elektra EKS 74026 — THE MORAY EELS EAT THE HOLY MODALS (LP, stereo) 30
70 Transatlantic TRA 7451 — HOLY MODAL ROUNDERS (LP) 25
70 Transatlantic TRA — HOLY MODAL ROUNDERS 2 (LP) 25

HOMBRES

67 Verve VS 1510 — Let It Out (Let It All Hang Out)/Go Girl Go 15

HOME

69 Bell SBLL 119 — JOLLIVER ARKANSAW (LP) 65

HOME

72 CBS 7809 — Fancy Lady, Hollywood Child/Shady Lady 6
71 CBS 64365 — PAUSE FOR A HOARSE HORSE (LP) 40
72 CBS 64752 — HOME (LP) 15
73 CBS 65550 — THE ALCHEMIST (LP) 20
70s CBS — (LP, unreleased, test pressings only) .... 150+

(see also Groundhogs, AC/DC, WIshbone Ash, Blue Rondos)

HOMER & JETHRO

54 HMV B 10581 — How Much Is That Hound Dog/Rudolph The Flat-Nosed Reindeer (78) 10
54 HMV 7M 211 — Swappin' Partners/Crazy Mix-Up Song 15
54 Parlophone CMSP 2 — Don't Let Your Sweet Love Die/When It's Long Handle Time In Tennessee (export issue) 15
59 RCA RCA 1148 — Waterloo/The Battle Of Kookamonga 6
59 RCA RCA 1148 — Waterloo/The Battle Of Kookamonga (78) 20
59 Parlophone GEP 8791 — WANTED FOR MURDER OF THE STANDARDS (EP) 18

HOMESICK JAMES

64 Sue WI 319 — Crossroads/My Baby's Sweet 30
65 Sue WI 330 — Set A Date/Can't Afford To Do It 35

HOMESICK JAMES/SNOOKY PRYOR

74 Caroline C 1502 — HOMESICK JAMES AND SNOOKY PRYOR (LP) 22

HOMOSEXUALS

78 L'Orelei PF 151 — Hearts In Exile/South South Africans (p/s, with insert) 8
79 Black Noise F12 No. 2 — Divorce Proceedings/Mecho Madness (12", plain sleeve with sticker) 10
81 Black Noise BN 1 — BIGGER THAN THE NUMBER YET MISSING THE DOT (EP, clear vinyl, fold-around hand-painted sleeve) 8
84 Recommended RR 18 — THE HOMOSEXUALS RECORD (LP, with inserts) 12

(see also George Harrassment & Homosexuals, Ice La Bas, Amos & Sara, Nancy Sesay & Melodaires, L-Voag, Sir Alick & Phraser)

MINT VALUE £

HOMUNCULUS
80s Detrimental History DHSS 4 MORGUE DREAMS (cassette) 12
(see also Karl Blake)

MINAKO HONDA
87 Columbia DB 9153 Golden Days (English Version)/Crazy Nights (English Version) (p/s, features Brian May) 35

HONDELLS
64 Mercury MF 834 Little Honda/Hot Rod High 20
65 Mercury MF 925 Younger Girl/All American Girl 18
66 Mercury MF 967 Cheryl's Goin' Home/Show Me Girl 18

HONEST MEN
69 Tamla Motown TMG 706 Cherie/Baby 18

HONEYBOY
71 Trojan TR 7835 Jamaica/ITALS: Sea Wave 7
72 Banana BA 375 Homeward Bound/Peace In The Land 7

HONEYBUS
67 Deram DM 131 Delighted To See You/The Breaking Up Scene 12
67 Deram DM 152 Do I Figure In Your Life?/Throw My Love Away 12
68 Deram DM 182 I Can't Let Maggie Go/Tender Are The Ashes 7
68 Deram DM 207 Girl Of Independent Means/How Long 12
69 Deram DM 254 She Sold Blackpool Rock/Would You Believe 10
70 Deram DM 289 Story/The Right To Choose 7
72 Bell BLL 1205 She Is The Female To My Soul/For Where Have You Been 6
73 Warner Bros K 16250 For You/Little Lovely One 8
76 Decca F 13631 I Can't Let Maggie Go/Julie In My Heart 5
70 Deram DML/SML 1056 STORY (LP) 75
73 Warner Bros K 46248 RECITAL (LP, withdrawn) .... 150+
(see also Pete Dello, Colin Hare, Lace, Magic Valley, Red Herring)

HONEYCOMBS
64 Pye 7N 15664 Have I The Right/Please Don't Pretend Again 6
64 Pye 7N 15705 Is It Because/I'll Cry Tomorrow 7
64 Pye 7N 15736 Eyes/If You've Got To Pick A Baby 12
65 Pye 7N 15781 Don't Love You No More/I'll See You Tomorrow (withdrawn, promo only) 110
65 Pye 7N 15827 Something Better Beginning/I'll See You Tomorrow 12
65 Pye 7N 15890 That's The Way/Can't Get Through To You 6
65 Pye 7N 15979 This Year, Next Year/Not Sleeping Too Well Lately 10
66 Pye 7N 17089 Who Is Sylvia?/How Will I Know 15
66 Pye 7N 17138 It's So Hard/I Fell In Love 15
66 Pye 7N 17173 That Loving Feeling/Should A Man Cry 18
69 Pye 7N 17741 Have I The Right/Please Don't Pretend Again (stereo reissue) 6
65 Pye NEP 24230 THAT'S THE WAY (EP) 45
64 Pye NPL 18097 THE HONEYCOMBS (LP) 50
65 Pye NPL 18132 ALL SYSTEMS GO! (LP) 80
66 Golden Guinea GGL 0350 THE HONEYCOMBS (LP, reissue in different sleeve) 20
(see also Lemmings, Dennis D'Ell, Martin Murray)

HONEYCONE
70 Hot Wax HWX 103 While You're Out Looking For Sugar/The Feeling's Gone 6
71 Hot Wax HWX 105 Girls It Ain't Easy/Take Me With You 6
71 Hot Wax HWX 107 Want Ads/We Belong Together 10
72 Hot Wax HWX 111 One Monkey Don't Stop No Show/Stick Up 6
72 Hot Wax HWX 112 The Day I Found Myself/When Will It End 6
72 Hot Wax HWX 116 Sittin' On A Time Bomb/It's Better To Have Loved And Lost 6
71 Hot Wax SHW 5002 HONEYCONE (LP) 15
71 Hot Wax SHW 5004 SWEET REPLIES (LP) 15
72 Hot Wax SHW 5005 SOULFUL TAPESTRY (LP) 15
73 Hot Wax SHW 5010 LOVE, PEACE AND SOUL (LP) 18

HONEYDEW
70 Argo AFW 101 Part Of This Game/To Make You Mine 5
70 Argo HONEYDEW (LP) 70

HONEYDRIPPERS
84 Es Paranza 790 220-1 THE HONEYDRIPPERS VOL. ONE (10" LP) 8
(see also Robert Plant)

HONEYEND
72 Spark SRL 1072 Heartbreaker/Beautiful Downtown 60

HONEYS
63 Capitol CL 15299 Surfin' Down The Swanee River/Shoot The Curl 60
(see also American Spring, Beach Boys)

HONEYTONES
58 London HLX 8671 Don't Look Now, But.../I Know, I Know 65
58 London HLX 8671 Don't Look Now, But.../I Know, I Know (78) 30

HONEYTREE
70s Myrrh MYR 1039 EVERGREEN (LP) 18

HONG GANG
72 Sioux SI 004 Reggae Mento/MONTEGO MELON: Swan Lake 5
73 Sioux SI 025 Smoking Wild/ROOSEVELT SINGERS: Heavy Reggae 5
(see also Bob Andy)

ROBBIN HOOD
56 MGM SP 1178 The Rock-A-Bye Blues/Beautiful, Beautiful Love 15

MINT VALUE £

HOOD

Year	Label	Title	Value
92	Fluff HONEY 4	Sirens/Fault/Your Sixth Sense (p/s, 500 only)	20
93	Fluff HONEY 6	I Didn't Think You Were Going To Hit Me In The Face/In The Trap Of Doing/ Choosing A Grimace (wraparound p/s, 500 only)	18
94	Hedonist Prods. 002 F	57 White Bread: My Last August/Experimental Film-Making (flexidisc, p/s, 1000 only)	6
95	Orgasm ORGASM 08	A Harbour Of Thoughts/Disappointed/Uneven Conversation Should Point To Cause/Forced By The Reasoning Hand/John Clyde-Evans/Silo Crash (p/s)	8
95	555 Recordings 555 01	LEE FAUST'S MILLION PIECE ORCHESTRA: Biochemistry Revision Can Wait/ England's Fine Fields/Rocck? I Can't Even Spell The Word/ Stricken Office Worker (EP, 1000 copies only)	10
96	Earworm WORM 1	SECRETS NOW KNOWN TO OTHERS: Forhead/Crow Blown West/Beware! Falling Ox/I'm Turning Into A Cart/Further Woodland/20X/Visions Of Old Machinery/ Sometimes Doomed/You Should Never Feel Alone In This World/Crushed By Life (EP, p/s, 1000 only)	10
96	Love Train PUBE 11	I've Forgotten How To Live/The Weather Side Of The Stone Mill Tower/ Dimensions TBA	10
98	Rocket Racer ROCKET 04	The Year Of Occasional Lull/Fog Projections (1000 only, numbered, 980 with black artwork, 20 with red)	5/10
98	Happy Go Lucky HGL 12	Filmed Initiative/As Evening Changed The Day (different photo on each p/s)	15
98	555 Recordings 555 13	(The) Weight/Fallen Farmer/We Are Not Promote/Impossible Calm/Feel The Rush (Coming In From The Avant Garde)/I Know What To Squander/Mast-On-Hill/ Collapsing Climate Soul (p/s)	6
94	Fluff ARC 01	CABLED LINEAR TRACTION (LP, 200 only)	25
96	Slumberland SLR 59LP	SILENT '88 (LP, with free 7")	12
97	Happy Go Lucky HAPPY 10LP	STRUCTURED DISASTERS (LP, with free 7")	12
98	Domino WIGLP 42	RUSTIC HOUSES, FORLORN VALLEYS (LP)	12
99	Slumberland SLR 46LP	CABLED LINEAR TRACTION (LP, reissue, 1100 only)	12

HOODOO RHYTHM DEVILS

Year	Label	Title	Value
78	Fantasy FTC 147	Gotta Lot Of Love In My Soul/MDR Of Love	20

HOOK

Year	Label	Title	Value
68	Uni UN 507	In The Beginning/Show You The Way	8

EARL HOOKER

Year	Label	Title	Value
69	Blue Horizon 57-3166	Boogie Don't Blot/Funky Blues	30
70	Blue Horizon 7-63850	SWEET BLACK ANGEL (LP)	90
70	Stateside SSL 10298	DON'T HAVE TO WORRY (LP)	45

(see also John Lee Hooker)

JOHN LEE HOOKER

78s

Year	Label	Title	Value
52	Vogue V 2102	Hoogie Boogie/Whistlin' And Moanin' Blues	65
54	London HL 8037	Need Somebody/Too Much Boogie	75

45s

Year	Label	Title	Value
63	Stateside SS 203	Boom Boom/Frisco Blues	20
64	Stateside SS 297	Dimples/I'm Leaving	15
64	Stateside SS 341	I Love You Honey/Send Me Your Pillow	15
64	Pye International 7N 25255	High Priced Woman/Sugar Mama	15
64	Polydor NH 52930	Shake It Baby/Let's Make It Baby	18
65	Sue WI 361	I'm In The Mood/Boogie Chillun	35
66	Chess CRS 8039	Let's Go Out Tonight/In The Mood	18
66	Planet PLF 114	Mai Lee/Don't Be Messing With My Bread (with Groundhogs)	45
70	President PT 295	Dimples/Boom Boom	5
89	Silvertone ORECD 10	The Healer (Single Version)/Rockin' Chair/No Substitute/The Healer (Album Version) (3" CD, with Carlos Santana, card sleeve)	8

EPs

Year	Label	Title	Value
60	Riverside REP 3202	WEDNESDAY EVENING	25
60	Riverside REP 3207	DEMOCRAT MAN	25
64	Stateside SE 1019	THE BLUES OF JOHN HOOKER	30
64	Stateside SE 1023	I'M JOHN LEE HOOKER	30
64	Ember EP 4561	THINKING BLUES	40
65	Pye Intl. NEP 44034	LOVE BLUES	35
65	Chess CRE 6000	DOWN AT THE LANDING	35
65	Atlantic AET 6010	JOHN LEE HOOKER	35
66	Chess CRE 6007	WALKING THE BOOGIE	35
66	Chess CRE 6014	THE JOURNEY	35
66	Chess CRE 6021	REAL FOLK BLUES VOL. 3	35
73	Impulse 9103	SERVES YOU RIGHT TO SUFFER	15

LPs

Year	Label	Title	Value
62	Riverside RLP 12-838	THE FOLK BLUES OF JOHN LEE HOOKER	40
62	Stateside SL 10014	THE FOLK LORE OF JOHN LEE HOOKER	45
63	London HA-K 8097	DON'T TURN ME FROM YOUR DOOR	60
64	Stateside SL 10053	THE BIG SOUL OF JOHN LEE HOOKER	45
64	Stateside SL 10074	I WANT TO SHOUT THE BLUES	35
64	Pye Intl. NPL 28042	HOUSE OF THE BLUES	45
64	Fontana 688 700 ZL	THE FOLK-BLUES OF HOOKER	40
65	Fontana FJL 119	BLUE!	40
65	Ember EMB 3356	SINGS THE BLUES	30
65	Riverside RLP 008	BURNING HELL	30
65	Chess CRL 4500	JOHN LEE HOOKER PLAYS AND SINGS THE BLUES	35
66	HMV CLP 5032/CSD 3542	IT SERVES YOU RIGHT TO SUFFER (mono/stereo)	45/50
66	Ember (ST)EMB 3371	DRIFTIN' THROUGH THE BLUES	30
67	Chess CRL 4527	THE REAL FOLK BLUES	30
67	HMV CLP/CSD 3612	LIVE AT THE CAFE A GO GO	30
67	Atlantic Special 590 003	DRIFTIN' BLUES	18

MINT VALUE £

Year	Label/Cat. No.	Title	Value
68	Joy JOY(S) 101	I'M JOHN LEE HOOKER	15
68	Joy JOY(S) 124	BURNIN'	15
68	Stateside (S)SL 10246	URBAN BLUES	30
69	Joy JOYS 129	TRAVELIN'	12
69	Joy JOYS 133	THE FOLKLORE OF JOHN LEE HOOKER	15
69	Stateside (S)SL 10280	SIMPLY THE TRUTH	25
69	Joy JOYS 142	CONCERT AT NEWPORT	15
69	Joy JOYS 147	THE BIG SOUL OF JOHN LEE HOOKER	15
69	Storyville 673 005	YOU'RE LEAVIN' ME BABY	15
69	Joy JOYS 152	IN PERSON	15
60s	Advent LP 2801	JOHN LEE HOOKER AND HIS GUITAR	40
70	Storyville 673 020	TUPELO BLUES	15
70	Joy JOYS 156	THE BEST OF JOHN LEE HOOKER	15
70	Stax SXATS 1025	THAT'S WHERE IT'S AT	15
71	Probe SPB 1016	IF YOU MISS 'IM . . . I GOT 'IM (with Earl Hooker)	18
71	Probe SPB 1034	ENDLESS BOOGIE	12
71	Stax 2362 017	THAT'S WHERE IT'S AT!	15
71	Xtra XTRA 1114	JOHN LEE HOOKER	15
71	United Artists UAS 29235	COAST TO COAST BLUES BAND	20
72	Specialty SNTF 5005	ALONE	12
72	Probe SPB 1057	NEVER GET OUT OF THESE BLUES ALIVE	12
73	Green Bottle GN 4002	JOHNNY LEE	15
73	Checker 6467 305	MAD MAN BLUES	12
73	Polydor 2310 256	SLIM'S STOMP	12
75	ABC ABCL 5059	FREE BEER AND CHICKEN	12
75	New World NW 6003	JOHN LEE HOOKER (reissue of above with 1 extra track)	12
75	Atlantic K 40405	DETROIT SPECIAL	12
77	DJM DJD 28026	DIMPLES (2-LP)	18

(see also Canned Heat, Carlos Santana & Buddy Miles, John Lee's Groundhogs)

JOHN LEE HOOKER/LIGHTNIN' HOPKINS/SMOKEY HOGG

Year	Label/Cat. No.	Title	Value
73	Specialty SNTF 5013	HOOKER HOPKINS HOGG (LP)	15

(see also Lightnin' Hopkins, Smokey Hogg)

STEVE HOOKER & HEAT

Year	Label/Cat. No.	Title	Value
77	Takeaway TAKE 1/ EJR 577	If You Don't Do The Business/Rock & Roll Doctor/I'm Hooked/ Marionette (stamped white sleeve with insert)	8

HOOKFOOT

Year	Label/Cat. No.	Title	Value
69	Page One POF 144	Way Of The Musician/Hookfoot	6
71	DJM DJLPS 413	HOOKFOOT (LP)	15
72	DJM DJLPS 422	GOOD TIMES A' COMIN' (LP)	12
73	DJM DJLPS 428	COMMUNICATIONS (LP)	12

(see also Loot, Caleb, Soul Agents)

MARSHALL HOOKS & CO.

Year	Label/Cat. No.	Title	Value
71	Blue Horizon 2096 002	I Want The Same Thing Tomorrow/Hookin' It	18
71	Blue Horizon 2431 003	MARSHALL HOOKS & CO. (LP)	65

HOOTEN(ANNY) SINGERS

Year	Label/Cat. No.	Title	Value
64	United Artists UP 1082	Gabrielle/Darling (most copies list artist as Hooten Singers)	35

(see also Abba, Hep Stars, Northern Lights)

BOB HOPE

Year	Label/Cat. No.	Title	Value
52	Capitol CL 13787	A 4-Legged Friend/There's A Cloud In My Valley Of Sunshine (78, with Jimmy Wakely)	10
58	London HLU 8593	Paris Holiday/Nothing In Common (with Bing Crosby)	18
58	London HLU 8593	Paris Holiday/Nothing In Common (78, with Bing Crosby)	8
59	RCA RCA 1139	Ain't A-Hankerin'/Protection (with Rosemary Clooney)	6
59	RCA RCA 1139	Ain't A Hankerin'/Protection (78, with Rosemary Clooney)	8
63	United Artists UP 1023	Call Me Bwana/The Flipside	6
58	HMV DLP 1088	EDDIE FOY AND THE SEVEN LITTLE FOYS (10" LP, soundtrack, with James Cagney)	30
63	Brunswick LAT 8539	IN RUSSIA AND ONE OTHER PLACE (LP)	18

(see also Bing Crosby, Rosemary Clooney)

LYN(N) HOPE

Year	Label/Cat. No.	Title	Value
57	Vogue V 9081	Blue Moon/Blues For Anna Bacca	45
57	Vogue V 9081	Blue Moon/Blues For Anna Bacca (78)	20
57	Vogue V 9082	Eleven Till Two/Blues For Mary	45
57	Vogue V 9082	Eleven Till Two/Blues For Mary (78)	20
58	Vogue V 9115	Temptation/The Scrunch	30
58	Vogue V 9115	Temptation/The Scrunch (78)	30
60	Blue Beat BB 21	Shockin'/Blue And Sentimental	20
57	Vogue VE 170103	LYNN HOPE AND HIS TENOR SAX (EP)	85
60	Vogue VE 170146	LYNN HOPE AND HIS TENOR SAX (EP)	100

PETER HOPE & RICHARD H. KIRK

Year	Label/Cat. No.	Title	Value
85	Doublevision DVR 15	Leather Hands (Master Mix)/(Radio Mix)/(Crash Mix) (12", p/s)	8

(see also Cabaret Voltaire, Richard H. Kirk)

HOPE OF THE STATES

Year	Label/Cat. No.	Title	Value
00s	Seeker SEEK 001	Black Dollar Bills/Everything For Everyone (Demo)/Sts'Ikel (Demo) (CD, numbered & signed, 1000 only)	10
00s	Sony 6742577	Enemies/Friends (numbered p/s)	10
00s	Sony 6742575	Enemies/Friends (CD)	8

HOPETOWN (Lewis) & GLENMORE (Brown)

Year	Label/Cat. No.	Title	Value
68	Fab FAB 43	Skinny Leg Girl/Live Like A King	22

MINT VALUE £

MARY HOPKIN

68	Apple APPLE 2	Those Were The Days/Turn Turn Turn (later copies credit Mary Hopkins)	each 5
68	Apple APPLE 2	Those Were The Days/Turn Turn Turn (blank Apple label on A-side)	10
69	Apple APPLE 7	Lontana Dagli Occhi/Game (Europe-only, unreleased in U.K.)	
69	Apple APPLE 9	Prince En Avignon/The Game (France-only, unreleased in U.K.)	
69	Apple APPLE 10	Goodbye/Sparrow	6
69	Apple APPLE 16	Que Sera Sera/Fields Of St. Etienne (unreleased)	
69	Cambrian CSP 703	Aderyn Llwyd/Y Blodyn Gwyn (p/s)	18
70	Cambrian CSP 712	Pleserau Serch/Tyrd Yn Ôl (p/s)	18
70	Apple APPLE 22	Temma Harbour/Lontano Dagli Occhi (black or green lettering on p/s)	each 5
70	Apple APPLE 26	Knock, Knock Who's There?/I'm Going To Fall In Love Again (p/s)	5
70	Apple APPLE 27	Que Sera Sera/Fields Of St. Etienne (unreleased in U.K., acetates only)	
70	Apple APPLE 30	Think About Your Children/Heritage (p/s)	6
71	Apple APPLE 34	Let My Name Be Sorrow/Kew Gardens (p/s)	18
71	Apple APPLE 39	Water, Paper And Clay/Jefferson (p/s)	22
72	Regal Zonophone RZ 3070	Mary Had A Baby/Cherry Tree Carol	5
76	Good Earth GD 2	If You Love Me (I Won't Care): (some copies list "If You Love Me")/Tell Me Now	5
77	Good Earth GD 11	Wrap Me In Your Arms/Just A Dreamer (p/s)	10
68	Cambrian CEP 414	LLAIS SWYNOL MARY HOPKIN (EP)	15
69	Cambrian CEP 420	MARY AC EDWARD (EP, with Edward Morris Jones)	15
69	Apple (S)APCOR 5	POST CARD (LP, with black inner sleeve, mono/stereo)	20/15
71	Apple SAPCOR 21	EARTH SONG — OCEAN SONG (LP, gatefold sleeve, 'Apple' inner sleeve)	25
72	Apple SAPCOR 23	THOSE WERE THE DAYS (LP, with 'Apple' inner sleeve)	70
77	Decca SPA 546	THE WELSH WORLD OF MARY HOPKIN (LP)	25
91	Apple SAPCOR 5	POST CARD (LP, reissue, gatefold sleeve with bonus 12" [SAPCOR 52])	20
92	Apple SAPCOR 21	EARTH SONG/OCEAN SONG (LP, reissue, gatefold sleeve with inner)	20

(see also Hobby Horse, Sundance, Oasis, Elfland Ensemble, Bob Johnson & Pete Knight, Roy Budd, Elmer Bernstein)

ANTHONY HOPKINS

86	Juice AA5	Distant Star/Ordinary Man (p/s)	8

JOEL & LIGHTNIN' HOPKINS

60	Heritage H 1000	BLUES FROM EAST TEXAS (LP, 99 copies only)	120

(see also Lightnin' Hopkins)

LIGHTNIN' HOPKINS

61	Bluesville BVLP 1019	LIGHTNIN' HOPKINS (LP)	65
62	'77' LA 12/1	SAM LIGHTNIN' HOPKINS — THE ROOSTER CROWED IN ENGLAND (LP)	65
63	Stateside SL 10031	LIGHTNIN' STRIKES (LP)	45
63	Realm RM 128	LIGHTNIN' HOPKINS SINGS THE BLUES (LP)	40
63	Realm RM 171	DIRTY HOUSE BLUES (LP)	40
64	Stateside SL 10076	BLUES HOOT (LP, some tracks by Sonny Terry & Brownie McGhee)	45
65	Stateside SL 10110	HOOTIN' THE BLUES (LP)	40
65	Stateside SL 10155	DOWN HOME BLUES (LP)	40
65	Fontana AH 183	THE BLUES (LP)	30
65	Fontana 688 301 ZL	LAST NIGHT BLUES (LP)	35
65	Fontana 688 801 ZL	BURNIN' IN L.A. (LP)	35
66	Fontana 688 803 ZL	BLUE BIRD BLUES (LP)	35
66	Fontana 688 807 ZL	BLUES PARTY (LP)	35
66	Ember EMB 3389	A TIME FOR BLUES (LP)	30
66	Ember EMB 3416	LIVE AT THE BIRD LOUNGE (LP)	30
67	Ember EMB 3423	I'VE BEEN BUKED AND SCORNED (LP)	30
66	Verve (S)VLP 5003	ROOTS OF HOPKINS (LP)	30
66	Verve (S)VLP 5014	LIGHTNIN' STRIKES (LP, reissue)	22
66	Saga ERO 8001	LIGHTNIN' HOPKINS (LP)	15
67	Xtra XTRA 5036	BLUES IN MY BOTTLE (LP)	22
68	Xtra XTRA 5044	GOT TO MOVE YOUR BABY (LP, reissue of Fontana 688 301 ZL)	18
68	Minit MLL/MLS 40006	EARTH BLUES (LP)	25
69	Liberty LBL 83254	KING OF DOWLING STREET (LP)	25
69	Joy JOY(S) 115	LIGHTNIN' STRIKES (LP, 2nd reissue)	15
69	Polydor 545 019	THAT'S MY STORY (LP)	18
70	Ace Of Hearts (Z)AHT 183	THE BLUES (LP)	15
70	Poppy PYS 11000	LIGHTNIN'! VOLUME 1 (LP)	18
70	Poppy PYS 11002	LIGHTNIN'! VOLUME 2 (LP)	18
71	Liberty LBS 83293	THE CALIFORNIA MUDSLIDE (AND EARTHQUAKE) (LP)	22
71	Mayfair AMLB 4000 1/2	LIGHTNIN' STRIKES (2-LP)	18
71	Blue Horizon 2431 005	LET'S WORK AWHILE (LP)	100
71	Xtra XTRA 1127	THE ROOTS OF LIGHTNIN' HOPKINS (LP)	20
71	Boulevard BLVD 4001	LIGHTNIN' HOPKINS (LP)	15
72	Carnival 2941 005	LONESOME LIGHTNIN' (LP)	15
73	Mainstream MSL 1001	DIRTY BLUES (LP)	15
74	Sonet SNTF 672	LEGACY OF THE BLUES VOLUME 12 (LP)	15
75	Mainstream MSL 1031	LOW DOWN DIRTY BLUES (LP)	15

(see also Sonny Terry & Brownie McGhee, Joel & Lightnin' Hopkins, Lightnin' Hopkins & John Lee Hooker, Big Joe Williams)

LIGHTNIN' HOPKINS & JOHN LEE HOOKER

69	Storyville 616 001	THERE'S GOOD ROCKIN' TONIGHT! (LP)	45
72	Storyville SLP 174	LIGHTNIN' HOPKINS AND JOHN LEE HOOKER (LP)	40

(see also John Lee Hooker/Lightnin' Hopkins/Smokey Hogg)

LINDA HOPKINS

61	Coral Q 72423	I Diddle Dum Dum/All In My Mind	22
62	Coral Q 72448	Mama's Doin' The Twist/My Mother's Eyes	18

LINDA HOPKINS & JACKIE WILSON

63	Coral Q 72464	Shake A Hand/Say I Do	12
65	Coral Q 72480	Yes Indeed/When The Saints Go Marching In	15

(see also Jackie Wilson)

MINT VALUE £

NICKY HOPKINS
66 CBS 202055 Mr Big/Jenni ... 18
67 Polydor 56175 Mister Pleasant/Nothing As Yet ... 18
68 MGM MGM 1419 Top Pops No. 1 (Medley)/(Part 2) ... 6
68 Fontana TF 906 High On A Hill/Trumpet Serenade (actually by Nigel Hopkins) ... 6
73 CBS CBS 1328 Speed On/Sundown In Mexico ... 5
66 CBS (S)BPG 62679 THE REVOLUTIONARY PIANO OF NICKY HOPKINS (LP) ... 35
73 CBS 65416 THE TIN MAN WAS A DREAMER (LP) ... 18
(see also Aquarian Age, Neil Christian & Crusaders, Cyril Davies R&B All-Stars, Poet & One Man Band, Quicksilver Messenger Service, Sweet Thursday)

WASH HOPKINS SINGERS
69 Action ACT 4546 He's Got Blessing/Rock In A Weary Land ... 8

HUGH HOPPER
73 CBS 65466 1984 (LP) ... 25
76 Compendium FIDARDO 4 CRUEL BUT FAIR (LP) ... 15
77 Compendium FIDARDO 7 HOPPERTUNITY BOX (LP) ... 15
78 Ogun OG 527 ROGUE ELEMENT (LP, as Hopper, Dean, Gowen, Sheen — 'Soft Heap') ... 12
(see also Caravan, Elton Dean, Gilgamesh, Isotope, Matching Mole, Ninesense, Soft Machine)

HOPSCOTCH
69 United Artists UP 2231 Look At The Lights Go Up/Same Old Fat Man ... 55
69 United Artists UP 35022 Long Black Veil/Easy To Find ... 7
(see also Scots Of St. James, Five Day Rain, Forever More, Glencoe)

HORACE & IMPERIALS
68 Nu Beat NB 012 Young Love/Days Like These ... 15

HORDEN RAIKES
72 Folk Heritage FHR 026 HORDEN RAIKES (LP) ... 20
73 Folk Heritage FHR 042 KING COTTON (LP) ... 15

HORIZON
81 SRT SRTS 81432 Stage Struck/Remember The Bad Boys ... 10

HORIZON
83 Orbit TRIP 4 Sunshine Reggae/Nightlife ... 6
(see also Mungo Jerry)

PAUL HORN
68 Liberty LBL 83084E COSMIC CONSCIOUSNESS (LP) ... 20

RODERICK HORN & DOROTHY VERNON
66 Unit Nineteen UN 19 1004 SONGS FROM THE SHEFFIELD PLAYHOUSE (EP) ... 10

JIMMY BO HORNE
80 T.K. STKR 13 7586 Is It In/Spank (12") ... 10

LENA HORNE
55 HMV 7M 309 Love Me Or Leave Me/I Love To Love ... 10
55 HMV 7M 319 It's All Right With Me/It's Love ... 10
56 HMV 7M 423 If You Can Dream/What's Right For You (Is Right For Me) ... 8
56 MGM MGM 917 Can't Help Lovin' Dat Man/The Man I Love ... 7
59 RCA RCA 1120 A New Fangled Tango/Honeysuckle Rose ... 5
59 RCA RCA 1120 A New Fangled Tango/Honeysuckle Rose (78) ... 10
65 United Artists UP 1101 The Sand And The Sea/It Had Better Be Tonight ... 5
71 Buddah 2011 078 Maybe I'm Amazed/Feels So Good ... 12
57 RCA RD 27021/SF 5007 AT THE WALDORF ASTORIA (LP, mono/stereo) ... 12/15
58 RCA RD 27063 STORMY WEATHER (LP) ... 15
59 RCA RD 27098/SF 5019 GIVE THE LADY WHAT SHE WANTS (LP, mono/stereo) ... 12/15
59 RCA RD 27141 A FRIEND OF YOURS (LP) ... 12
61 RCA RD 27255 LENA AT THE SANDS (LP, also stereo SF 5217) ... 12
63 RCA RD/SF 7530 LENA LOVELY AND ALIVE (LP) ... 12
64 Stateside S(S)L 10081 HERE'S LENA (LP) ... 12
(see also Harry Belafonte)

HANK HORNSBY
57 MGM MGM 955 Pots And Pans/Cotton ... 6
58 MGM MGM 972 The Legend Of The Birds And Bees/Girls Girls Girls ... 6
58 MGM MGM 972 The Legend Of The Birds And Bees/Girls Girls Girls (78) ... 7

HORNSEY AT WAR
70s War WAR 001 DEAD BEAT REVIVAL (EP, numbered p/s) ... 8

HORRORCOMIC
77 Lightning/B&C BVZ 0007 I'm All Hung Up On Pierrepoint/The Exorcist/Sex In The Afternoon (p/s) ... 45
78 Lightning GIL 512 I Don't Mind/England 77 (p/s) ... 80
79 B&C BCS 18 Jesus Crisis/Cut Your Throat (p/s) ... 200

HORSE
70 RCA Victor SF 8109 HORSE (LP) ... 100
(see also Saturnalia)

HORSLIPS
73 Oats OAT 1 High Reel/Furniture ... 5
79 DJM DJT 15001 Loneliness/Homesick (leaf-shaped green vinyl) ... 5
73 Oats MOO 3 HAPPY TO MEET ... SORRY TO PART (LP, booklet octagonal sleeve) ... 20
74 Oats MOO 5 THE TAIN (LP) ... 15
76 Oats MOO 9 DRIVE THE COLD WINTER AWAY (LP) ... 12

HORTENSE (Ellis) & ALTON (Ellis)
65 Island WI 230 Don't Gamble With Love/Something You Got (B-side actually by Alton Ellis & Flames) ... 22
(see also Hortense Ellis, Alton Ellis, Mr. Foundation)

MINT VALUE £

HORTENSE (Ellis) & DELROY (Wilson)

66 Rio R 119 We're Gonna Make It/SOUL BROTHERS: Ska Shuffle 25
(see also Hortense Ellis, Delroy Wilson)

HORTENSE (Ellis) & JACKIE (Opel)

64 R&B JB 138 Stand By Me/JACKIE OPEL: Solid Rock 25
(see also Hortense Ellis, Jackie Opel)

JOHNNY HORTON

59 Philips PB 932 The Battle Of New Orleans/All For The Love Of A Girl 7
59 Philips PB 932 The Battle Of New Orleans/All For The Love Of A Girl (78) 25
59 Philips PB 951 Sal's Got A Sugar Lip/Johnny Reb 10
59 Philips PB 951 Sal's Got A Sugar Lip/Johnny Reb (78) 45
59 Philips PB 976 Take Me Like I Am/I'm Ready If You're Willing 7
59 Philips PB 976 Take Me Like I Am/I'm Ready If You're Willing (78) 45
60 Philips PB 995 Sink The Bismarck!/The Same Old Tale The Crow Told Me 10
60 Philips PB 1062 North To Alaska/The Mansion You Stole 7
61 Philips PB 1130 When It's Springtime In Alaska/Mr. Moonlight 8
61 Philips PB 1132 Sleepy Eyed John/They'll Never Take Her Love From Me 10
61 Philips PB 1170 Miss Marcy/Ole Slew Foot 10
62 Philips PB 1226 Words/Honky Tonk Man 10
63 CBS AAG 132 All Grown Up/I'm A One Woman Man 10
60 Mercury ZEP 10074 THE FANTASTIC JOHNNY HORTON (EP) 55
64 Mercury 10008 MCE COUNTRY AND WESTERN ACES (EP) 40
60 Philips BBL 7464 THE SPECTACULAR JOHNNY HORTON (LP) 35
61 Philips BBL 7536 HONKY TONK MAN (LP) 35
63 London HA-U 8096 DONE ROVIN' (LP) 40
65 Fontana FJL 306 VOICE OF JOHNNY HORTON (LP) 18
60s Hallmark SHM 634 THE UNFORGETTABLE JOHNNY HORTON (LP) 12

ROBERT HORTON

60 Pye 7N 15285 (Roll Along) Wagon Train/Sail Ho! 5
60 Pye NEP 24118 SUNDAY NIGHT AT THE LONDON PALLADIUM (EP) 5

WALTER 'SHAKEY' HORTON

70 London HAK/SHK 8405 SOUTHERN COMFORT (LP, as Shakey Horton) 90
74 Xtra XTRA 1135 WALTER 'SHAKEY' HORTON WITH HOT COTTAGE (LP) 18
74 Sonet SNTF 677 BIG WALTER HORTON (LP, with Carey Bell) 15

LA/THE HOST

84 Orbitone THE HOST EP (cassette) 5
85 Quiet QU 1 The Big Sleep/Just Breaking Away (p/s) 8

HOT BUTTER

73 Pye NSPL 28169 POPCORN (LP) 12
73 Pye NSPL 28181 MORE HOT BUTTER (LP) 15

HOT CLUB

82 RAK 346 The Dirt That She Walks On Is Sacred Ground To Me/Heat (p/s) 12
82 RAK 346 The Dirt That She Walks On Is Sacred Ground To Me/Heat (12", p/s) 10
(see also Rich Kids, Spectres)

HOT CHOCOLATE (BAND)

69 Apple APPLE 18 Give Peace A Chance/Living Without Tomorrow (as Hot Chocolate Band) 45
70 Rak RAK 103 Love Is Life/Pretty Girls (with promo p/s) 8
(see also Errol Brown & Chosen Few, Tony Wilson)

HOT HOT HEAT

00s Sub Pop BUN 0457 Bandages/Apt. 101 (p/s) 6
00s Sub Pop SP 594 KNOCK KNOCK KNOCK EP: Le Le Low/5 Times Out Of 100/Have A Good Sleep/ Touch You/More For Show (12", pink vinyl, p/s) 10
00s Sub Pop SPCD 594 KNOCK KNOCK KNOCK EP (CD) 10

HOTLEGS

70 Fontana 6007 019 Neanderthal Man/You Didn't Like It Because You Didn't Think Of It 5
71 Philips 6006 140 Lady Sadie/The Loser 8
71 Philips 6308 047 THINKS: SCHOOL STINKS (LP) 20
71 Philips 6308 080 SONG (LP) 22
(see also 10cc, Mindbenders, Godley & Creme, Tristar Airbus)

HOT POTATO

73 PMTB 1 HOT POTATO (LP, private pressing) 25

HOT ROD

69 Joe's DU 41 The Judge/RON: Soul Of Soul Of Joel 10

HOT ROD ALLSTARS

69 Duke DU 59 Lick A Pop/Treasure 20
70 Duke DU 65 Paint Your Wagon/Organ Man 15
70 Duke DU 66 Return Of The Bad Man/Caysoe Reggae 20
70 Trojan TR 7732 Strong Man/Sentimental 12
70 Trojan TR 7733 Virgin Soldier/Brixton Reggae Festival 15
70 Torpedo TOR 1 Pussy Got Nine Life/BOSS SOUNDS: Lick It Back 25
70 Torpedo TOR 5 Skinheads Don't Fear/Ten Commandments From The Devil 40
70 Torpedo TOR 10 Moonhop In London/Skinhead Moondust 40
70 Torpedo TOR 14 Control Your Doggy/Follow The Stars 12
70 Hot Rod HR 104 Skinhead Speaks His Mind/CARL LEVEY: Carnaby Street 40
70 Hot Rod HR 107 Strictly Invitation/PATSY & PEGGY: Dog Your Woman 10
70 Hot Rod HR 108 Beautiful World/Shocks Of A Drugs Man 15
(see also Setters, Betty Sinclair)

HOTRODS

65 Columbia DB 7693 I Don't Love You No More/Ain't Coming Back No More 55

MINT VALUE £

HOT SPRINGS

66 Columbia DB 7821 — It's All Right/All I Know About Love 18

HOT-TODDYS

59 Pye International 7N 25020 — Shakin' And Stompin'/Rockin' Crickets 30
59 Pye International N 25020 — Shakin' And Stompin'/Rockin' Crickets (78) 30
(see also Rockin' Rebels)

HOT TUNA

72 Grunt 65-0502 — Keep On Truckin'/Water Song 5
76 Grunt RCG 1002 — It's So Easy/I Can't Be Satisfied 5
70 RCA SF 8125 — HOT TUNA (LP) 15
71 RCA LSP 4550 — ELECTRIC LIVE (FIRST PULL UP, THEN PULL DOWN) (LP) 15
72 Grunt FTR 1004 — BURGERS (LP, with purple inner sleeve) 12
(see also Jefferson Airplane)

HOT VULTURES

77 Red Rag RRR 015 — THE EAST STREET SHAKES (LP) 18
70s Plant Life PLR 018 — UP THE LINE (LP) 15

HOT WATER

78 Duff — Different Morning/Premium Bondage 8
79 Duff DWR 101 — Get Lost!/Bird's Eye View (p/s) 7

HOUGHTON WEAVERS

60s Folk Heritage FHR 106 — SIT THI DOWN (LP) 15
60s EMI HW 1002 — ALIVE & KICKING (LP) 15

HOUNDHEAD HENRY/FRANKIE JAXON

60 Jazz Collector JEL 10 — THE MALE BLUES VOLUME 6 (EP) 18

HOUR GLASS

68 Liberty LBL/LBS 83219E — THE HOUR GLASS (LP) 25
74 United Artists USD 303/4 — THE HOUR GLASS (2-LP) 18
(see also Allman Brothers)

SON HOUSE

(see under 'S')

HOUSEHOLD

67 United Artists UP 1190 — I Guess I'll Learn How To Fly/Nothing You Can Do But Cry 10
68 United Artists UP 2210 — Twenty First Summer/Winter's Coming On 10

HOUSEMARTINS

85 Go! Discs GOD 7 — Flag Day/Stand At Ease (p/s) 5
85 Go! Discs GOD 7/GOD 9 — Flag Day/Stand At Ease//Sheep/Drop Down Dead (shrinkwrapped double pack) .. 6
85 Go! Discs GODX 7 — Flag Day/Stand At Ease/Coal Train To Hatfield Main (12", p/s) 8
86 Go! Discs GODP 9 — Sheep/I'll Be Your Shelter/Drop Down Dead (picture disc) 5
86 Go! Discs GODP 11 — Happy Hour/The Mighty Ship (shaped picture disc) 5
86 Go! Discs GODP 13 — Think For A Minute/Who Needs The Limelight (shaped picture disc) 5
86 Go! Discs GODP 16 — Caravan Of Love/When I First Met Jesus (rectangular picture disc) 5
86 Go! Discs GODB 16 — THE HOUSEMARTINS' CHRISTMAS BOX SET (4 singles in foldout sleeve, some signed) 25/12
88 Go! Discs GODCD 22 — There Is Always Something There To Remind Me/Get Up Off Our Knees/ Get Up Off Our Knees (live)/Johannesburg (CD) 8
84 private pressing — THEMES FROM THE WELL-DRESSED MAN (cassette) 20
84 private pressing — THE HOUSEMARTINS FROM OUTER SPACE (cassette) 20
(see also Beautiful South)

HOUSEMASTER BALDWIN

88 Koolkat KOOLT 21 — DELTA HOUSE (12", p/s) 10
88 Koolkat KOOLT 22 — DON'T LEAD ME (12", p/s) 10

HOUSE OF LORDS

69 B&C CB 112 — In The Land Of Dreams/Ain't Gonna Wait Forever 15

HOUSE OF LOVE

87 Creation CRE 043T — Shine On/Love/Flow (12", p/s, 4,000 only) 10
87 Creation CRE 044T — Real Animal/Plastic/Nothing To Me (12", p/s, 4,000 only) 25
88 Creation CRE 053 — Christine/Loneliness Is A Gun (die-cut '99p' sleeve) 7
88 Creation CRE 057 — Destroy The Heart/Blind/Mr Jo (p/s) 8
88 Creation CRE 057T — Destroy The Heart/Blind/Mr Jo (12", p/s) 10
92 Fontana HOL 710 — YOU DON'T UNDERSTAND EP (10", limited edition, numbered sleeve) 8

BOBBI HOUSTON

74 Action ACT 4622 — I Want To Make It With You (Parts 1 & 2) 12

CISCO HOUSTON

60 Top Rank 30/028 — THE CISCO SPECIAL (LP) 50
68 Fontana FJL 412 — I AIN'T GOT NO HOME (LP) 15
69 Ember CW 135 — CISCO HOUSTON AND WOODY GUTHRIE (LP) 15

CISSY HOUSTON

70 Major Minor MM 700 — He/I Believe/I'll Be There 6
70 Major Minor MM 716 — The Long And Winding Road/Be My Baby 6
70 Pye International 7N 25537 — I Just Don't Know What To Do With Myself/This Empty Place 18
71 Pye International 7N 25545 — The Long And Winding Road/Be My Baby (reissue) 5
71 Janus 6146 003 — Darling Take Me Back/Hang On To A Dream 6
72 Janus 6146 027 — Midnight Train To Georgia/I'm So Glad I Can Love Again 6
70 Major Minor SMLP 80 — PRESENTING CISSY HOUSTON (LP) 30
71 Pye Intl. NSPL 28146 — THE LONG AND WINDING ROAD (LP) 15
78 Private Stock PVLP 1044 — THINK IT OVER (LP) 15
(see also Sweet Inspirations)

DAVID HOUSTON

55 London HL 8147 Blue Prelude/I'm Sorry I Made You Cry . . . 45
55 London HL 8147 Blue Prelude/I'm Sorry I Made You Cry (78) . . . 18
63 Columbia DB 7159 Mountain Of Love/Poor Little Angeline . . . 6
66 Columbia DB 7997 Almost Persuaded/We Got Love . . . 6

DAVID HOUSTON & TAMMY WYNETTE

67 Columbia DB 8246 My Elusive Dreams/Marriage On The Rocks . . . 8

SAM HOUSTON

65 Island WI 172 My Mother's Eyes/Danny Boy . . . 12

THELMA HOUSTON

69 Stateside SS 8026 Jumpin' Jack Flash/Sunshower . . . 10
70 Stateside SS 8036 Save The Country/I Just Can't Stay Away . . . 7
70 Stateside SS 8044 I Just Wanna Be Me/Crying In The Sunshine . . . 7
72 Tamla Motown TMG 799 I Want To Go Back There Again/Pick Of The Week . . . 5
72 Mowest MW 3001 No One's Gonna Be A Fool Forever/What If . . . 5
73 Mowest MW 3004 Black California/I'm Letting Go (withdrawn) . . . 10
69 Stateside (S)SL 5010 SUNSHOWER (LP) . . . 20
73 ABC ABCL 5061 SUNSHOWER (LP, reissue) . . . 12
73 Mowest MWS 7003 THELMA HOUSTON (LP) . . . 12

WHITNEY HOUSTON

85 Arista ARIST 12614 Someone For Me/The Greatest Love Of All (12", p/s) . . . 8
85 Arista ARIST 12625 You Give Good Love (Extended)/How Will I Know/You Give Good Love (Remix)/Someone For Me (12", p/s) . . . 8
85 Arista ARIST 640 All At Once (promo only for 'Wogan' TV show, plain sleeve, printed white label) . 10
87 Arista RISCD 1 I Wanna Dance With Somebody (Who Loves Me) (12" Remix)/Moment Of Truth/ I Wanna Dance With Somebody (Who Loves Me) (Dub Mix) (CD, card sleeve) 8
87 Arista RISCD 31 Didn't We Almost Have It All/I Wanna Dance With Somebody (Who Loves Me) (Acappella Mix)/WHITNEY HOUSTON & JERMAINE JACKSON: Shock Me (CD, card sleeve with stickered p/s) . . . 8
87 Arista RISCD 43 So Emotional (Extended Remix)/Didn't We Almost Have It All (live)/ For The Love Of You (CD, card sleeve) . . . 8
88 Arista 111 516P Love Will Save The Day/Hold Me (picture disc) . . . 5
88 Arista 111 516W Love Will Save The Day/Hold Me (tour packs, Wembley or Birmingham p/s) . each 5
88 Arista 661 516 Love Will Save The Day (Extended Club Mix)/Love Will Save The Day (Single Version)/WHITNEY HOUSTON & TEDDY PENDERGRASS: Hold Me (CD, picture disc with gatefold card sleeve) . . . 10
88 Arista 661 613 One Moment In Time/(KASHIF: Olympic Joy)/Rise To The Occasion/ One Moment In Time (Instrumental) (CD) . . . 8
86 Arista WHIT 1 WHITNEY HOUSTON (LP, box set with 10 postcards, songbook & calendar) 12
(see also J.A.M.s, Aretha Franklin & Whitney Houston)

LARRY HOVIS

58 Capitol CL 14843 Do I Love You/We Could Have Lots Of Fun . . . 7
59 Capitol CL 15083 My Heart Belongs To Only You/I Want To Fall In Love . . . 7

BRIAN HOWARD & SILHOUETTES

62 Columbia DB 4914 Somebody Help Me/Young And Evil . . . 20
63 Columbia DB 7067 The Worryin' Kind/Come To Me . . . 20
64 Fontana TF 464 Back In The U.S.A./Hooked . . . 18

JAN HOWARD

60 London HL 7088 The One You Slip Around With/I Wish I Could Fall In Love Again (export issue). . 25

JOHNNY HOWARD BAND

60 Decca F 11298 Up The Wall/Orbit . . . 6
62 Decca F 11423 Mind Reader/Spanish Gipsy Dance . . . 6
64 Decca F 11925 Rinky Dink/Java . . . 10
65 Decca F 12065 El Pussy Cat/A Tune Called Harry . . . 6
67 Deram DML/SML 1001 THE VELVET TOUCH OF JOHNNY HOWARD (LP) . . . 12

LES HOWARD

53 HMV 7M 127 Love Evermore/I Lived When I Met You . . . 10
53 HMV 7M 171 Rags To Riches/From Here To Eternity . . . 10
57 Conquest CP 103 Priscilla/Singin' The Blues (78) . . . 7

ROLAND S. HOWARD & LYDIA LUNCH

86 4AD BAD 210 Some Velvet Morning/I Fell In Love With A Ghost (12", p/s, with postcard). 12
(see also Lydia Lunch, Birthday Party)

ROSETTA HOWARD

51 Vocalion V 1005 Let Your Linen Hang Low/HARLEM HAMFATS: Weed Smoker's Dream (78) 20

JACK HOWARTH

71 Fontana 6438 040 'Ow Do (LP) . . . 12

WAYNE HOWARD

70 Explosion EX 2042 All Kinds Of Everything/Cool And Easy (B-side actually by Lloyd Charmers) 7

CATHERINE HOWE

71 Reflection HRS 11 Nothing More Than Strangers/It Comes With The Breezes . . . 18
71 Reflection REFL 11 WHAT A BEAUTIFUL PLACE (LP) . . . 200+
75 RCA Victor SF 8407 HARRY (LP) . . . 15
70s RCA Victor ARL 5013 DRAGONFLY DAYS (LP) . . . 12

STEVE HOWE

75 Atlantic K 50151 BEGINNINGS (LP, gatefold sleeve, some with embossed 'Yes' logo) 12/15
79 Atlantic K 50621 THE STEVE HOWE ALBUM (LP, gatefold sleeve) . . . 12
(see also In Crowd, Syndicats, Tomorrow, Bodast, Yes, Asia)

MINT VALUE £

EDDIE HOWELL
76 Warner Bros K 16701 Man From Manhattan/Waiting In The Wings (features members of Queen) 12
77 Warner Bros K 16866 Sweet On You/Miss Amerika (features Gary Moore) 6
(see also Queen, Gary Moore, Brian May, Freddie Mercury)

PETER HOWELL
(see under Friends, Ithaca, Alice Through The Looking Glass, Agincourt, Tomorrow Come Someday, BBC Radiophonic Workshop)

FRANKIE HOWERD
54 Decca F 10420 (Don't Let The) Kiddy Geddin/Abracadabra 15
58 Columbia DB 4230 It's All Right With Me/Song And Dance Man 10
64 Decca F 12028 Last Word On The Election/Last Word On The Election (part 2) 6
70 Pye 7N 45061 Up Je T'Aime/All Through The Night 6
71 Columbia DB 8757 Up Pompeii/Salute!. 6
63 Decca LK 4556 AT THE ESTABLISHMENT (LP) 22
60s Pye NPL SOMETHING FUNNY HAPPENED ON THE WAY TO THE FORUM (LP) 22
72 Carnival 2928 201 TELLS THE STORY OF PETER AND THE WOLF (LP) 15

CHRIS HOWLAND
58 Columbia DB 4114 Mama (Ma, He's Making Eyes At Me)/Fraulein 8
59 Columbia DB 4194 Susie Darlin'/The Rain Falls On Ev'rybody 10

HOWLIN' WOLF
61 Pye International 7N 25101 Little Baby/Down In The Bottom 25
63 Pye International 7N 25192 Just Like I Treat You/I Ain't Superstitious 25
64 Pye International 7N 25244 Smokestack Lightnin'/Going Down Slow ('Slow' or 'South' on B-side label) . . 25/18
64 Pye International 7N 25269 Little Girl/Tail Dragger 22
64 Pye International 7N 25283 Love Me Darling/My Country Sugar Mama 22
65 Chess CRS 8010 Killing Floor/Louise 15
65 Chess CRS 8016 Ooh Baby/Tell Me What I've Done 15
69 Chess CRS 8097 Evil/Tail Dragger 12
56 London REU 1072 RHYTHM AND BLUES WITH HOWLIN' WOLF (EP) 200
63 Pye Intl. NEP 44015 SMOKESTACK LIGHTNIN' (EP) 30
64 Pye Intl. NEP 44032 TELL ME (EP) 30
66 Chess CRE 6017 REAL FOLK BLUES (EP) 30
64 Chess CRL 4006 MOANIN' IN THE MOONLIGHT (LP) 60
65 Chess CRL 4508 POOR BOY (LP) 45
66 Ember EMB 3370 BIG CITY BLUES (LP) 35
67 Marble Arch MAL 665 MOANIN' IN THE MOONLIGHT (LP, reissue) 12
69 Chess CRLS 4543 THE HOWLIN' WOLF ALBUM (LP) 20
71 Syndicate Chapter SC 003 GOING BACK HOME (LP) 18
71 Chess 6310 108 MESSAGE TO THE YOUNG (LP) 18
71 Rolling Stones COC 49101 THE LONDON SESSIONS (LP) 18
71 Python PLP 13 HOWLIN' WOLF (LP) 50
(see also Hubert Sumlin)

HOWLIN' WOLF, MUDDY WATERS & BO DIDDLEY
68 Chess CRL 4537 THE SUPER SUPER BLUES BAND (LP) 50
(see also Muddy Waters, Bo Diddley)

HOWLIN' WOLF/JUNIOR PARKER/BOBBY BLAND
74 Polydor 2383 257 BLUES FOR MR. CRUMP (LP) 30

LINDA HOYLE
70 Vertigo 6059 018 Eli's Coming/United States Of Mind (as Linda Hoyle & Affinity) 20
71 Vertigo 6360 060 PIECES OF ME (LP, gatefold sleeve, swirl label) 120
(see also Affinity, Nucleus)

H.P. LOVECRAFT
67 Philips BF 1620 Wayfarin' Stranger/The Time Machine 7
68 Philips BF 1639 The White Ship (Parts 1 & 2) (unissued)
68 Philips BF 1639 The White Ship/I've Been Wrong Before 7
67 Philips (S)BL 7830 H.P. LOVECRAFT (LP) 45
68 Philips SBL 7872 H.P. LOVECRAFT II (LP, most with watermark at start of each side) 30/15
72 Philips 6336 210 THIS IS H.P. LOVECRAFT (LP) 15
72 Philips 6336 213 H.P. LOVECRAFT VOL. 2 (LP) 15

H2O
81 Spock PARA 2 Hollywood Dream/Children (with lyric insert) 6

FREDDIE HUBBARD
72 CTI CTL 5 STRAIGHT LIFE (LP) 12
73 CTI CTL 11 SKY DIVE (LP) 12
75 CTI CTI 6056 POLAR AC (LP) 12
75 Atlantic K 60053 THE ART OF FREDDIE HUBBARD: THE ATLANTIC YEARS (2-LP) 18
75 Blue Note BST 84056 GOIN' UP (LP) 12
75 Blue Note BST 84085 READY FOR FREDDIE (LP) 12
75 Blue Note BST 84115 HUB TONES (LP) 12
75 Blue Note BST 84172 BREAKING POINT (LP) 12
75 Blue Note BST 84196 BLUE SPIRITS (LP) 12
75 Blue Note BST 84207 THE NIGHT OF THE COOKERS VOL. 1 (LP) 12
75 Blue Note BST 84208 THE NIGHT OF THE COOKERS VOL. 2 (LP) 12
75 CBS 80478 HIGH ENERGY (LP) 15

HUBCAP & WHEELS
70 Dynamic DYN 403 One Pound Weight/VICEROYS: Come Dance 6
(see also Byron Lee & Dragonaires)

WENDY HUBER
65 Philips BF 1446 Come Away Melinda/I Belong To The Wind 8

MINT VALUE £

RITA & TONY HUDD

85	Burlington BURL 022	THE WOODEN LEG ALBUM (LP)	12

ROY HUDD

66	Polydor 56136	Ramsey's Men/The Day We Won The Cup (some in p/s)	50/15
67	Pye 7N 17434	Artificial Jumping Spider Seller/Sir Rhubarb Tansy	5
77	BBC RESL 47	Standing Outside The Palace/I'm Gonna Let Them Get Me Down	5

JACK HUDSON

72	Folk Heritage FHR 041	SUMMER DAYS AND YOU (LP)	20

JOHNNY HUDSON & TEENBEATS

63	Decca F 11679	Charms/Makin' Up Is So Much Fun	10

KEITH HUDSON (& CHUCKLES)

69	Big Shot BI 528	Tambourine Man/Old Fashioned Way (both actually by Ken Boothe)	18
70	Smash SMA 2311	Don't Get Me Confused/D. SMITH: Ball of Confusion (B-side actually by Dennis Alcapone)	12
71	Smash SMA 2526	Light Of Day/I Thought You Knew	12
72	Spur SP 1	Darkest Night On A Wet Looking Road/Version	40
72	Duke DU 145	Satan Side (with Chuckles)/DON T. JUNIOR: Evil Spirit	30
72	Downtown DT 492	True True To My Heart/BIG YOUTH: Ace 90 Skank	10
73	Summit SUM 8541	Melody Maker/Uncover Me	12
75	Faith FA 025	Blackbelt Jones/Version	8
75	ATRA ATLP 1002	PICK A DUB (LP)	50
77	BRD 001	BRAND (LP)	35

(see also Big Youth, Alton Ellis, Hugh Roy, Delroy Wilson)

KEITH HUDSON & I ROY

73	Randy's RAN 534	Silver Platter/Jean You Change Everything	18

(see also I Roy)

ROCK HUDSON

59	Brunswick 05816	Pillow Talk/Roly Poly	10
70	Warner Bros WB 8006	Gone With The Cowboys/Meantime	7

HUDSON-FORD

74	A&M AMS 7096	Burn Baby Burn/Angels (p/s)	5
77	Arnakata ARN 5001	REPERTOIRE (LP, for publishers' use)	20

(see also Strawbs, Monks, Elmer Gantry's Velvet Opera)

HUDSON PEOPLE

78	Hithouse HIT 1	Trip To Your Mind (Parts 1 & 2) (12")	20
79	Ensign ENY 2712	Trip To Your Mind (Parts 1 & 2) (12", reissue)	8

HUES CORPORATION

74	RCA RCA 2444	Freedom Of The Stallion/Get Off My Cloud	5
74	RCA APL1 0323	FREEDOM OF THE STALLION (LP)	12
74	RCA APL1 0775	ROCKIN' SOUL (LP)	12

HUEYS

69	London HLU 10264	Coo-Coo Over You/You Ain't No Hippie	12

HUG

75	Polydor 2383 330	NEON DREAM (LP)	12

MIKE HUGG

72	Polydor 2058 265	Blue Suede Shoes Again/Fool No More	5
73	Polydor 2058 359	Stress And Strain/Tonight	5
72	Polydor/Sound For Industry SFI 122	Bonnie Charlie/SLADE: The Whole World's Going Crazee (33rpm flexidisc free with *Music Scene* magazine)	12/8
72	Polydor 2383 140	SOMEWHERE (LP, gatefold sleeve)	12
73	Polydor 2383 213	STRESS AND STRAIN (LP)	12

(see also Manfred Mann, Hug, Highly Likely, Elton Dean)

HUGGY BEAR

93	PUSS 002	February 14th/Into The Mission (1-sided gig freebie, w/l, plain black sleeve)	5

CAROL HUGHES

58	Columbia DB 4094	Lend Me Your Comb/First Date	15

DANNY HUGHES

69	Pye 7N 17750	Hi Ho Silver Lining/I Washed My Hands In Muddy Water	15

(see also Orange Machine)

DAVID HUGHES

59	Top Rank JAR 205	Teach Me (How To Love Him)/You Would Have Done The Same	7
60	Top Rank JAR 316	Looking High, High, High/Mi Amor	8

FRED HUGHES

65	Fontana TF 583	Oo Wee Baby I Love You/Love Me Baby	18
76	Brunswick BR 37	Baby Boy/JOHNNY JONES & KING CASUALS: Purple Haze	8
76	DJM DJS 10717	Oo Wee Baby I Love You/My Cries Oh	5

'FRIDAY' HUGHES

51	MGM MGM 422	Lazy Morning/The Devil Ain't Lazy (78)	8

GLENN HUGHES

79	Safari SAFE 14	I Found A Woman/L.A. Cut Off (p/s)	5
77	Safari LONG 2	PLAY ME OUT (LP)	12

(see also Deep Purple, News, Finders Keepers, Trapeze, Roger Glover, Hughes-Thrall)

JIMMY HUGHES

63	London HL 9680	I'm Qualified/My Loving Time	25
64	Pye International 7N 25254	Steal Away/Lollipops, Lace And Lipstick	15
66	Sue WI 4006	Goodbye My Love/It Was Nice	30

MINT VALUE £

66	Atlantic 584 017	Neighbour, Neighbour/It's A Good Thing	12
67	Atlantic 584 135	Hi-Heel Sneakers/Time Will Bring You Back	12
69	Stax STAX 117	Sweet Things You Do/Let 'Em Down Baby	7
69	Stax STAX 126	I'm Not Ashamed To Beg Or Plead/Chains Of Love	12
67	Atlantic 587 068	WHY NOT TONIGHT? (LP)	60
69	Stax SXATS 1010	SOMETHING SPECIAL (LP)	30

RHETTA HUGHES

70s	Polydor 184 223	RELIGHT MY FIRE (LP)	15

HUGHES-THRALL

82	Epic EPC 25052	HUGHES-THRALL (LP)	15

(see also Glenn Hughes)

HUGO & LUIGI

57	Columbia DB 3978	Rockabilly Party/Shenandoah Rose	18
58	Columbia DB 4156	Twilight In Tennessee/Cha-Hua-Hua	8
59	RCA RCA 1127	La Plume De Ma Tante/Honolulu Lu	6
59	RCA RCA 1127	La Plume De Ma Tante/Honolulu Lu (78)	10
60	RCA RCA 1169	Just Come Home/Lonesome Stranger (78)	15

ALAN HULL

70	Big T BIG 129	We Can Swing Together/Obadiah's Grave	10
73	Charisma CB 208	Numbers (Travelling Band)/Drinking Song/One Off Pat (p/s)	6
73	Charisma CB 211	Justanothersadsong/Waiting	5
75	Warner Brothers K 16561	Dan The Plan/One More Bottle Of Wine	5
75	Warner Brothers K 16599	One More Bottle Of Wine/Squire	5
75	Warner Brothers K 16643	Crazy Woman/Golden Oldies	5
79	Rocket XPRES 12	I Wish You Well/Love Is The Answer (p/s)	5
79	Rocket XPRES 19	A Walk In The Sea/Corporation Rock	5
83	Black Crow CROS 2	Malvinas Melody/Ode To A Taxman (p/s)	5
73	Charisma CAS 1069	PIPEDREAM (LP, gatefold sleeve with booklet)	15
75	Warner Brothers K 56121	SQUIRE (LP)	12
79	Rocket TRAIN 6	PHANTOMS (LP, with inner sleeve)	12
83	Black Crow CRO 206	ON THE OTHER SIDE (LP)	12

(see also Lindisfarne, Chosen Few, Radiator)

HULLABALLOOS

64	Columbia DB 7392	I'm Gonna Love You Too/Why Do Fools Fall In Love	12
65	Columbia DB 7558	I'll Show You How To Love/Did You Ever	12
65	Columbia DB 7626	Don't Stop/I Won't Turn Away Now	12

(see also Bunch Of Fives)

GEORGE HULTGREEN

70	Warner Bros WB 8017	Say Hello/Before You Say Goodbye	6

(see Eclection, Sailor)

HUMAN BEANS

67	Columbia DB 8230	Morning Dew (Take Me For A Walk)/It's A Wonder	60

(see also Love Sculpture, Dave Edmunds)

HUMAN BEAST

70	Decca LK/SKL 5053	VOLUME ONE (LP)	180

(see also Bread Love & Dreams)

HUMAN BEINZ

67	Capitol CL 15529	Nobody But Me/Sueno	40
68	Capitol CL 15542	Turn On Your Lovelight/It's Fun To Be Clean	25

HUMAN INSTINCT

65	Mercury MF 951	Can't Stop Around/I Want To Be Loved By You My Friend	40
66	Mercury MF 972	The Rich Man/Illusions	45
67	Mercury MF 990	Go-Go/I Can't Live Without You	35
68	Deram DM 167	A Day In My Mind's Mind/Death Of The Seaside	45
68	Deram DM 177	Renaissance Fair/Pink Dawn	45

(see also Jessie Harper)

HUMAN LEAGUE

78	Fast Product FAST 4	Being Boiled/Circus Of Death (p/s, original issue with b&w picture labels)	8
79	Fast Product FAST 10	THE DIGNITY OF LABOUR (12" EP, with spoken-word flexidisc [F10x/VF 1])	10
79	Virgin VS 294	Empire State Human/Introducing (p/s)	6
80	Virgin SV 105	HOLIDAY '80 (EP, single or double pack, red & green labels, 10,000 only)	10
80	Virgin VS 351	Empire State Human/Introducing//Only After Dark/Toyota City (Long Version) (double pack, p/s, shrinkwrapped)	20
80	Virgin VS 351	Only After Dark/Toyota City (Long Version) (p/s)	8
80	Virgin VS 351	Empire State Human/Introducing (p/s, reissue)	5
80	Virgin VS 351-12	Empire State Human/Introducing (12", p/s)	12
81	Virgin VS 395	Boys And Girls/Tom Baker (gatefold or non-gatefold p/s)	each 5
81	Virgin SV 105	HOLIDAY '80 (reissue 3-track EP, blue/pink labels)	5
81	Virgin SV 105-12	HOLIDAY '80 (12", 5-track EP, withdrawn)	30+
82	Virgin VSY 522	Mirror Man/(You Remind Me Of) Gold (picture disc)	5
84	Virgin VSY 723	Louise/The Sign (Remix) (picture disc)	5
88	Virgin CDT 6	Hard Times/Love Action (I Believe In Love)/Hard Times Instrumental/ Love Action Instrumental (3" CD, card sleeve)	10
88	Virgin VSCD 1025	Love Is All That Matters (Edit)/I Love You Too Much (Dub Version)/ Love Is All That Matters (Extended Version) (CD, gatefold card sleeve)	10
88	Virgin CDT 24	(Keep Feeling) Fascination (Extended 12" version)/(Keep Feeling) Fascination (Improvisation 12" Dub Version)/Total Panic (3" CD, card sleeve)	10
90	Virgin VSCDT 1262	Heart Like A Wheel/Heart Like A Wheel (Extended Mix)/Rebound/ Heart Like A Wheel (Remix) (CD)	8

90	Virgin VSCDX 1262	Heart Like A Wheel/Heart Like A Wheel (Extended Mix)/Rebound/ A Doorway (Dub Mix) (CD, numbered)	8
90	Virgin VSCDT 1303	Soundtrack To A Generation (Edit)/(Orbit Mix)/(Instrumental)/ (Pan Belgian Mix) (CD)	8
90	Virgin VSCDX 1303	Soundtrack To A Generation (Pan Belgian Dub)/(808 Mix Instrumental)/ (Dave Dodd's Mix)/(Acappella) (CD)	12
03	Virgin 12HL 001	The Sound Of The Crowd (Trisco's PopClash Mix)/Love Action (Salmon & Jenkins Mix)/Open Your Heart (Laid Remix) (12", stickered title sleeve)	12
03	Virgin 12HL 002	The Sound Of The Crowd (Freaksblamredo)/Love Action (Brooks Red Line Vocal Mix)/(Keep Feeling) Fascination (Groove Collision TMC Mix) (12", stickered title Sleeve)	12
03	Virgin 12HL 003	Don't You Want Me (Majik Johnson Original Booty Mix)/Love Action (Salmon & Jenkins Dub)/The Sound Of The Crowd (Freaksoldskooljam) (12", stickered title Sleeve)	12
03	Virgin 10HL 004	Open Your Heart (The Strand Remix)/The Sound Of The Crowd (Extended Family Vocal Mix) (10", stickered title sleeve)	12
81	Virgin VP 2192	DARE! (LP, picture disc, die-cut sleeve with insert, black or white vinyl border)	10/12
88	Virgin CDHLP 1	GREATEST HITS (CD, picture disc)	18

(see also Heaven 17, Men, Philip Oakey & Giorgio Moroder, Respect, Jo Callis)

HUMANOID

88	Westside WSR 7	Stakker Humanoid (Part 1)/Stakker Humanoid (Part 2) (p/s)	8
88	Westside WSR 12	Stakker Humanoid/Radio Edit/Omen Mix (12", p/s)	12
88	Westside WSRT 12	HUMANOID EP (12", no p/s)	12
88	Westside WSRCD 12	HUMANOID EP (3" CD)	10
89	Westside WSR 14	Slam/Bass Invaders/Slam Edit/Slam Hip House Version (12", p/s)	12
89	Westside HUMT 2	The Deep (Into The Abyss Mix)/The Deep (Extended LP Version)/ Cry Baby/The Deep (W5 Mix) (12", p/s)	12
92	Jumpin' & Pumpin' 12TOT 27	Stakker Humanoid (12" Orginal)/(Smart Systems Remix)/(Cobain Mix '94)/ (Snowman Mix)/(The Omen Mix)/(303 Tribe)/(Outer Limits) (12", brown or black vinyl, p/s)	15/12
92	Jumpin' & Pumpin' CDSTOT 27	Stakker Humanoid (Original Mix)/(Smart Systems Remix)/(Cobain Mix '94)/ (The Omen Mix)/(303 Mix)/(Outer Limits)/(12" Original) (CD)	12
88	Westside Human 1989	GLOBAL (LP)	15
88	Westside HUMANCD 1989	GLOBAL (CD)	18

(see also Future Sound Of London, Art Science Technology)

HUMANOID featuring SHARON BENSON

89	Westside HUMT 1	TonIGHT (12", 3 mixes, p/s)	8

(see also Future Sound Of London)

HUMBLEBUMS

69	Big T BIG 122	Saturday Roundabout Sunday/Bed Of Mossy Green	6
69	Big T BIG 127	Coconut Tree/Her Father Didn't Like Me Anyway	6
70	Big T BIG 130	Shoeshine Boy/My Apartment	6
69	Transatlantic TRA 186	THE FIRST COLLECTION OF MERRY MELODIES (LP)	15
69	Transatlantic TRA 201	THE NEW HUMBLEBUMS (LP)	15
70	Transatlantic TRA 218	OPEN UP THE DOOR (LP)	15
74	Transatlantic TRA 288	THE COMPLETE HUMBLEBUMS (3-LP, box set of above albums)	20

(see also Gerry Rafferty, Billy Connolly)

HUMBLE PIE

69	Immediate IM 082	Natural Born Bugie/Wrist Job (later in p/s)	12/7
70	A&M AMS 807	Big Black Dog/Strange Days	7
72	A&M AMS 7003	Hot'n'Nasty/You're So Good For Me	6
73	A&M AMS 7052	Black Coffee/Say No More	6
73	A&M AMS 7070	Get Down To It/Honky Tonk Woman	6
73	A&M AMS 7090	Oh La De Da/Outcrowd	6
75	A&M AMS 7185	Rock'n'Roll Music/Scored Out	6
80	Jet JET 180	Fool For A Pretty Face/You Soppy Pratt (p/s)	6
69	Immediate IMSP 025	AS SAFE AS YESTERDAY IS (LP)	20
69	Immediate IMSP 027	TOWN AND COUNTRY (LP)	20
70	A&M AMLS 986	HUMBLE PIE (LP)	15
71	A&M AMLS 2013	ROCK ON (LP)	15
72	A&M AMLH 63506	PERFORMANCE — ROCKIN' THE FILLMORE (2-LP)	18
72	A&M AMLS 64342	SMOKIN' (LP)	15
73	A&M AMLD 6004	EAT IT (2-LP)	18
74	A&M AMLH 63611	THUNDERBOX (LP)	12
75	A&M AMLS 68282	STREET RATS (LP)	12

(see also Steve Marriott, Small Faces, Peter Frampton, Herd, Natural Gas)

HUMBUG

70	CBS 4811	Groovin' With Mr Bloe/Marianna	6
70	CBS 5208	I Got A Feeling (Vocal)/I Got A Feeling (Instrumental)	5

HELEN HUMES

53	Brunswick 05078	They Raided The Joint/Loud Talking Woman (78)	8
53	Brunswick 05193	I Cried For You/Mean Way Of Loving (78)	12
56	Vogue V 2048	Million Dollar Secret/If I Could Be With You One Hour Of The Day	12
56	Vogue V 2048	Million Dollar Secret/If I Could Be With You One Hour Of The Day (78)	10
59	Contemporary CV 2415	When The Saints Come Marching In/Bill Bailey, Won't You Please Come Home (with Benny Carter's All-Stars)	7
59	Contemporary CV 2415	When The Saints Come Marching In/Bill Bailey, Won't You Please Come Home (78, with Benny Carter's All-Stars)	12
61	Contemporary LAC 12245	HELEN HUMES AND THE BENNY CARTER ALL STARS (LP)	15

(see also Benny Carter, Jimmy Witherspoon/Helen Humes)

MINT VALUE £

DELLA HUMPHREY

69	Action ACT 4525	Don't Make The Good Girls Go Bad/Your Love Is All I Need	15
72	Fab FAB 183	Dreamland (actually by Marcia Griffiths)/Version	10

HUMPY BONG

70	Parlophone R 5859	Don't You Be Too Long/We're Alright 'Till Then	35

(see also Bee Gees, Morgan)

HUNDRED REASONS

02	Sony 6724407	If I Could/No. 5 (green vinyl, numbered, stickered PVC sleeve)	7
02	Columbia 6726647	Silver/Rush In (clear vinyl, numbered, stickered PVC sleeve)	7
00s	Columbia 6731457	Falter/Safe Distance (orange vinyl, numbered, stickered PVC sleeve)	7
00	Fierce Panda NING 99	EP ONE: Cerebra/Clear (Flawed) (clear vinyl, no p/s, 1000 only)	25
00	Fierce Panda NING 99	EP ONE: Cerebra/Clear (Flawed) (CD)	8
01	Sony 6713927	EP TWO: Remmus/Soapbox Rally (yellow vinyl, numbered, stickered PVC sl.)	10
01	Columbia 671392	EP TWO: Remmus/Soapbox Rally/Shine/Remmus (video) (CD)	12
01	Sony 6720787	EP THREE: I'll Find You/Sunny (red vinyl, numbered, stickered PVC sleeve)	10
01	Sony 6720782	EP THREE: Sunny/Slow Motion (CD, with video track)	8

HUNGER

84	Psycho PSYCHO 14	STRICTLY FROM HUNGER (LP, reissue of U.S. LP)	15

HUNGRY WOLF

70	Philips 6308 009	HUNGRY WOLF (LP)	75

(see also Czar, Alan Parker, Ugly Custard)

GERALDINE HUNT

69	Roulette RO 515	Never Never Leave Me/Push Sweep	12
75	EMI EMI 2275	You/It's All For You	6

MARSHA HUNT

69	Track 604 030	Walk On Gilded Splinters/Hot Rod Poppa	8
69	Track 604 034	Desdemona/Hippy Gumbo	18
70	Track 604 037	Keep The Customer Satisfied/Lonesome Holy Roller	7
73	Vertigo 6059 080	Beast Day/Somebody To Love (as Marsha Hunt's 22)	6
71	Track 2410 101	WOMAN CHILD (LP)	35

MICHAEL HUNT & JOE LEATHERLAND

67	Decca LK 4902	WATER OF TYNE (LP)	12

PEE WEE HUNT & HIS ORCHESTRA

55	Capitol CL 14225	It's Never Too Late To Fall In Love/A Room In Bloomsbury	15
55	Capitol CL 14286	Save Your Love For Me/My Extraordinary Gal	15
56	Capitol CL 14515	Petunia's Patch/Vanessa	6
56	Capitol CL 14538	Lullaby Of Birdland/It's All Been Done Before	6
56	Capitol CL 14583	Swedish Rhapsody/The Object Of My Affection	6
56	Capitol CL 14630	I'll See You In Cuba/Canoodlin' Rag	6
58	Capitol CL 14884	Miss Otis Regrets/I Love Paris	6

TOMMY HUNT

62	Top Rank JAR 605	The Door Is Open/I'm Wondering	18
68	Direction 58-3216	I Need A Woman Of My Own/Searchin' For My Baby Looking Everywhere	10
72	Polydor 2058 236	Mind, Body & Soul/One More Mountain To Climb	6
74	Pye 7N 45325	Sleep Tight Honey/Time Alone Will Tell	6
75	Spark SRL 1132	Crackin' Up/Get Out	6
85	Kent TOWN 103	The Work Song/IVORYS: Please Stay	8

(see also Ivorys)

WILLIE AMOS HUNT

67	Camp 602 003	Would You Believe/My Baby Wants To Dance	45

HUNT & TURNER

72	Village Thing VTS 11	MAGIC LANDSCAPE (LP)	22

CAROL HUNTER

73	Purple PUR 115	Look Out Cleveland/5/4 March	7
73	Purple TPS 3503	THE NEXT VOICE YOU HEAR (LP)	12

DANE HUNTER

65	Oriole CB 1985	Evergreen Tree/Too Late	6

DANNY HUNTER (& GIANTS)

60	HMV POP 722	Make It Up/Little Girl (as Danny Hunter & Giants)	20
60	HMV POP 775	Who's Gonna Walk Ya Home?/Lonely And Blue	20
61	Fontana H 300	Lost Weekend/Age For Love	15

DAVE HUNTER

68	RCA RCA 1766	She's A Heartbreaker/Love Me A Lifetime	8
69	RCA RCA 1841	Don't Throw Your Love To The Wind/Hitchcock Railway	6

GREG HUNTER

66	Parlophone R 5483	Five O'Clock World/Away From Happiness	8

IAN HUNTER

75	CBS 3486	Who Do You Love/Boy	5
76	CBS 4268	All American Alien Boy (Version)/Rape	6
76	CBS 4479	You Nearly Did Me In/A Letter From Britannia To The Union Jack	15
77	CBS 5229	Justice Of The Peace/The Ballad Of Little Star (as Ian Hunter's Overnight Angels)	8
77	CBS 5497	England Rocks/Wild 'N' Free (as Ian Hunter's Overnight Angels)	5
79	Chrysalis CHS 2324	When The Daylight Comes/Life After Death (p/s, white vinyl with mask)	5
79	Chrysalis CHS 2346	Ships/Wild East (p/s)	5
79	Chrysalis CHS 2390	Cleveland Rocks/Bastard (p/s)	5
80	Chrysalis CHS 2434	We Gotta Get Out/Medley: Once Bitten Twice Shy/Bastard/Cleveland Rocks/Sons And Daughters/One Of The Boys (live double pack, gatefold p/s)	5

MINT VALUE £

81	Chrysalis CHS 2542	Lisa Likes Rock 'n' Roll/Noises (p/s, clear vinyl)	5
83	CBS A 3541	All Of The Good Ones Are Taken/Death 'N' Glory Boys (p/s)	5
83	CBS TA 3541	All Of The Good Ones Are Taken/Death 'N' Glory Boys/Traitor (12", p/s)	8
83	CBS A 3855	Somethin's Goin' On/All Of The Good Ones Are Taken (Slow Version) (p/s)	5
83	CBS A 3855	Somethin's Goin' On (Radio Edit)/All Of The Good Ones Are Taken (Slow Version) (promo only, no p/s)	5
90	Mercury HRCD 1	American Music/Women's Intuition/Cool/Big Time (CD, with Mick Ronson, promo only)	8
77	CBS	YOU'RE NEVER ALONE WITH A SCHIZOPHRENIC (LP, unissued; later issued on Chrysalis CHR 1214)	12

(see also Mott The Hoople, At Last The 1958 Rock & Roll Show, Apex Rhythm & Blues All Stars, Mick Ronson, Roger Taylor)

IVORY JOE HUNTER

50	MGM MGM 271	I Almost Lost My Mind/S.P. Blues (78, with Orchestra)	30
56	London HLE 8261	A Tear Fell/I Need You By My Side	360
56	London HLE 8261	A Tear Fell/I Need You By My Side (78)	30
57	Columbia DB 3872	Since I Met You, Baby/You Can't Stop This Rockin' And Rollin'	250
57	Columbia DB 3872	Since I Met You, Baby/You Can't Stop This Rockin' And Rollin' (78)	25
57	London HLE 8486	Love's A Hurting Game/Empty Arms	180
57	London HLE 8486	Love's A Hurting Game/Empty Arms (78)	30
61	Capitol CL 15220	I'm Hooked/Because I Love You	30
61	Capitol CL 15226	You Better Believe It, Baby/May The Man Win	30

ROBERT HUNTER

74	Round RX 101	TALES OF THE GREAT RUM RUNNERS (LP)	12
75	Round RX 105	TIGER ROSE (LP)	12
80	Dark Star DSLP 8001	JACK O'ROSES (LP)	15

(see also Grateful Dead)

SUSAN HUNTER

55	Brunswick 05458	Not Yet/Was That The Right Thing To Do?	8

TAB HUNTER

57	London HLD 8380	Young Love/Red Sails In The Sunset (gold or silver label)	30/18
57	London HLD 8410	Ninety-Nine Ways/I Don't Get Around Much Anymore	18
58	London HLD 8535	Don't Let It Get Around/I'm Alone Because I Love You	18
60	Warner Bros WB 8	(What Can I Give) My Only Love/(I'll Be With You) In Apple Blossom Time	6
60	Warner Bros WB 20	Waitin' For The Fall/Our Love	6
61	London HLD 9381	The Wild Side Of Life/My Devotion	10
62	London HLD 9559	Born To Lose/I Can't Stop Lovin' You	8
58	London RE-D 1134	TAB HUNTER (EP)	40
61	Warner Bros WEP 6023	TAB HUNTER (EP, also stereo WSEP 2023)	25/40
60	Warner Bros WM 4008	TAB HUNTER (LP, also stereo WS 8008)	35/65
61	London HA-D 2401	YOUNG LOVE (LP, also stereo SAH-G 6201)	50/65

HUNTER MUSKETT

73	Bradleys BRAD 303	John Blair/Silver Coin (p/s)	6
70	Decca Nova SDN 20	EVERY TIME YOU MOVE (LP)	160
73	Bradleys BRADL 1003	HUNTER MUSKETT (LP)	25

HUNTERS (U.K.)

60	Fontana H 276	Teen Scene/Santa Monica Flyer	25
61	Fontana H 303	Golden Ear-rings/Tally Ho	12
61	Fontana H 323	The Storm/How's M'Chicks?	12
64	Fontana TF 514	Teen Scene/Someone Else's Baby	15
61	Fontana TFL 5140	TEEN SCENE: THE HUNTERS PLAY THE BIG HITS (LP, stereo STFL 561)	45/60
62	Fontana TFL 5175	HITS FROM THE HUNTERS (LP, also stereo STFL 572)	45/60

(see also Dave Sampson & Hunters, Maisie McDaniel)

HUNTERS (Holland)

66	RCA RCA 1541	Russian Spy And I/Spring	18

(see also Jan Akkerman, Brainbox)

HURDY GURDY

72	CBS 64781	HURDY GURDY (LP)	150

RED VINCENT HURLEY

76	Pye 7N 45583	When/Just A Little Love (p/s)	7

HURRICANES

71	Upsetter US 363	Got To Be Mine/UPSETTERS: Version	12

(see also Dave Barker)

HURRICANE STRINGS

63	Columbia DB 7027	Venus/In The Carrick	8

MIKE HURST (& METHOD)

63	Philips BF 1295	The Banjo Song/Any Chance For Me	6
64	Philips BF 1319	Carol Anne/Anytime That You Want Me	6
64	Philips BF 1353	Half Heaven Half Heartache/Look In Your Eyes	6
65	Philips BF 1389	Last Time You'll Walk Out On Me/Something Told Me	6
65	Philips BF 1424	Show Me Around/I'm Running Away	6

(see also Springfields, Remo Four, Ashton Gardner & Dyke, Sundance)

MISSISSIPPI JOHN HURT

65	Vanguard SVRL 19005	THE IMMORTAL MISSISSIPPI JOHN HURT (LP)	20
66	Vanguard SVRL 19032	MISSISSIPPI JOHN HURT (LP)	20
67	Fontana TFL 6079	MISSISSIPPI JOHN HURT (LP)	20
71	Spokane SPL 1001	THE ORIGINAL 1928 RECORDINGS (LP)	50
71	Vanguard VSD 19/20	THE BEST OF MISSISSIPPI JOHN HURT (2-LP)	18
73	Vanguard VSD 79327	LAST SESSIONS (LP)	15

MINT VALUE £

HUSH

68	Fontana TF 944	Elephant Rider/Grey	400

HüSKER Dü

84	SST SST 025	Eight Miles High/Masochism World (live) (p/s)	8
85	SST 051	Makes No Sense At All/Love Is All Around (p/s)	5
86	Warner Bros W 8746	Don't Want To Know If You're Lonely/All Work And No Play (p/s)	5
86	Warner Bros W 8746T	Don't Want To Know If You're Lonely/All Work And No Play/ Helter Skelter (live) (12", p/s)	10
86	Warner Bros W 8612	Sorry Somehow/All This I've Done For You (p/s)	5
86	Warner Bros W 8612	Sorry Somehow/All This I've Done For You//Celebrated Summer (Acoustic)/ Flexible Flyer (double pack, gatefold sleeve)	8
86	Warner Bros W 8612T	Sorry Somehow/All This I've Done For You/Celebrated Summer (Acoustic)/ Flexible Flyer/Fattie (12", p/s)	8
87	Warner Bros W 8456	Could You Be The One/Everytime (p/s)	5
87	Warner Bros W 8456T	Could You Be The One/Everytime/Charity, Chastity, Prudence, Hope (12", p/s)	10
87	Warner Bros W 8276	Ice Cold Ice/Gotta Lotta (p/s)	5
87	Warner Bros W 8276T	Ice Cold Ice/Gotta Lotta/Medley (12", p/s)	10

FERLIN HUSKY (& HIS HUSH PUPPIES)

57	Capitol CL 14702	Gone/Missing Persons (as Ferlin Husky & His Hush Puppies)	15
57	Capitol CL 14702	Gone/Missing Persons (as Ferlin Husky & His Hush Puppies) (78)	10
57	Capitol CL 14753	A Fallen Star/Prize Possession	20
57	Capitol CL 14753	A Fallen Star/Prize Possession (78)	15
57	Capitol CL 14785	This Moment Of Love/Make Me Live Again	8
57	Capitol CL 14785	This Moment Of Love/Make Me Live Again (78)	15
58	Capitol CL 14824	Wang Dang Doo/What'cha Doin' After School	20
58	Capitol CL 14824	Wang Dang Doo/What'cha Doin' After School (78)	18
58	Capitol CL 14883	Slow Down Brother/The Drunken Driver (& His Hush Puppies)	25
58	Capitol CL 14916	I Feel That Old Heartache Again/I Saw God	8
58	Capitol CL 14922	The Kingdom Of Love/Terrific Together	7
58	Capitol CL 14954	I Will/All Of The Time	5
59	Capitol CL 14995	My Reason For Living/Wrong	5
59	Capitol CL 15027	Draggin' The River/Sea Sand	5
59	Capitol CL 15094	Black Sheep/I'll Always Return	5
60	Capitol CL 15160	The Wings Of A Dove/Next To Jimmy	5
57	Capitol EAP1 718	SONGS OF THE HOME AND HEART (EP)	12
57	Capitol EAP1 837	FERLIN HUSKY HITS (EP)	15
57	Capitol EAP1 921	COUNTRY MUSIC HOLIDAY (EP)	15
59	Parlophone GEP 8795	COUNTRY ROUND UP (EP)	30
60	Capitol EAP1 1280	FERLIN'S FAVOURITES (EP)	15
60	Capitol EAP2 1280	FERLIN'S FAVOURITES (EP)	15
60	Capitol EAP3 1280	FERLIN'S FAVOURITES (EP)	15
58	Capitol T 880	BOULEVARD OF BROKEN DREAMS (LP)	22
59	Capitol T 976	SITTIN' ON A RAINBOW (LP)	22
65	Fontana FJL 304	OLE OPRY FAVOURITES (LP)	12

(see also Simon Crum)

JACQUES HUSTIN

74	EMI EMI 2143	Fleur De Liberté/Freedom For The Man	15

HUSTLER

74	A&M AMLS 68276	HIGH STREET (LP)	12
75	A&M AMLH 33001	PLAY LOUD (LP)	12

HUSTLERS

63	Philips BF 1275	Gimme What I Want/Not Much	7
64	Mercury MF 807	Be True To You/You Can't Sit Down	7
64	Mercury MF 817	Sick Of Giving/Easy To Find	20

WILLIE HUTCH

73	Tamla Motown TMG 862	Brother's Gonna Work It Out/I Choose You	6
73	Tamla Motown STMA 8003	THE MACK (LP, soundtrack)	15
73	Tamla Motown STML 11247	FULLY EXPOSED (LP)	12
74	Tamla Motown STML 11269	FOXY BROWN (LP, soundtrack)	15
74	Tamla Motown STML 11280	THE MARK OF THE BEAST (LP)	12
75	Tamla Motown STML 12015	ODE TO MY LADY (LP)	20
76	Tamla Motown STML 12023	CONCERT IN BLUES (LP)	12

ASHLEY HUTCHINGS

72	Island HELP 5	MORRIS ON (LP, actually by various folk artists)	12
76	Island HELP 24	RATTLEBONE AND PLOUGHBACK (LP)	20
76	Harvest SHSM 2012	SON OF MORRIS ON (LP, actually by various folk artists)	12
77	Harvest SHSP 4073	KICKIN' UP THE SAWDUST (LP)	20

(see also Fairport Convention, Steeleye Span, Bunch)

HUTCH HUTCHINS

77	Goodwood GM 12324	FEELS LIKE RAIN (LP)	35

SAM HUTCHINS

69	Bell BLL 1044	Dang Me/I'm Tired Of Pretending	8

LEROY HUTSON

75	Warner Bros K 16536	All Because Of You Parts 1 & 2	6
74	Buddah BDLP 4013	THE MAN (LP)	15
75	Warner Bros K 56139	HUTSON (LP)	35

J.B. HUTTO & HIS HAWKS

73	Delmark DS 617	HAWK SQUAT (LP)	12

MINT VALUE £

BETTY HUTTON

53	HMV 7M 103	Somebody Loves Me/Jealous (B-side with Pat Morgan)	15
56	Capitol CL 14568	Sleepy Head/Hit The Road To Dreamland	10
54	Capitol LC 6639	CAPITOL PRESENTS BETTY HUTTON (10" LP)	30

(see also Hutton Sisters, Perry Como, 'Tennessee' Ernie Ford)

DANNY HUTTON

66	MGM MGM 1314	Funny How Love Can Be/Dreamin' Isn't Good For You	8
65	Pye International 7N 25325	Roses And Rainbows/Monster Shindig	7

(see also Three Dog Night)

HUTTON SISTERS (Betty & Marion)

55	Capitol CL 14250	Ko Ko Mo (I Love You So)/Heart Throb	25

(see also Betty Hutton)

CHARLIE HYATT

65	Island IEP 707	RASS! (EP, as Bam & Charlie Hyatt)	25
66	Island ILP 932	KISS ME NECK (LP)	45

HYDRA

74	Capricorn 2089 008	Glitter Queen/It's So Hard	5
74	Capricorn 2429 120	HYDRA (LP)	12

HYGRADES

65	Columbia DB 7734	She Cared/We're Through	10

BRIAN HYLAND

78

60	London HLR 9161	Itsy Bitsy Teeny Weeny Yellow Polka Dot Bikini/Don't Dilly Dally, Sally	220

45s

60	London HLR 9113	Rosemary/Library Love Affair	28
60	London HLR 9161	Itsy Bitsy Teeny Weeny Yellow Polka Dot Bikini/Don't Dilly Dally, Sally	10
60	London HLR 9203	Four Little Heels/That's How Much	8
61	London HLR 9262	Lop Sided, Over Loaded/I Gotta Go ('Cause I Love You)	8
61	HMV POP 915	Let Me Belong To You/Let It Die	10
61	HMV POP 955	The Night I Cried/I'll Never Stop Wanting You	10
62	HMV POP 1013	Ginny Come Lately/I Should Be Gettin' Better	7
62	HMV POP 1051	Sealed With A Kiss/Summer Job	7
62	HMV POP 1079	Warmed Over Kisses/Walk A Lonely Mile	7
63	HMV POP 1113	I May Not Live To See Tomorrow/It Ain't That Way At All	7
63	HMV POP 1143	If Mary's There/Remember Me	7
63	HMV POP 1169	Somewhere In The Night/I Wish Today Was Yesterday	7
63	HMV POP 1188	I'm Afraid To Go Home/Save Your Heart For Me	7
63	HMV POP 1237	Let Us Make Our Own Mistakes/Nothing Matters But You	7
64	Philips BF 1326	Here's To Our Love/Two Kinds Of Girls	7
65	Philips BF 1429	Stay Away From Her/I Can't Keep A Secret	7
65	Philips BF 1486	3,000 Miles/Sometimes They Do	7
66	Philips BF 1508	The Joker Went Wild/I Can Hear The Rain	15
66	Philips BF 1528	Run, Run, Look And See/Why Did You Do It	7
67	Philips BF 1555	Hung Up In Your Eyes/Why Mine	7
67	Philips BF 1569	Holiday For Clowns/Yesterday I Had A Girl	7
67	Philips BF 1601	Get The Message/Kinda Groovy	8
69	Dot DOT 119	Tragedy/You Better Stop — And Think It Over	7
69	Dot DOT 124	A Million To One/It Could All Begin Again (In You)	7
69	Dot DOT 128	Stay And Love Me All Summer/Rainy April Morning	7
70	Uni UN 530	Gypsy Woman/You And Me (No. 2)	7
71	Uni UN 533	No Place To Run/So Long, Marianne	6
72	Uni UN 540	I Love Every Little Thing About You/With My Eyes Wide Open	6
72	Uni UN 545	Only Wanna Make You Happy/When' You're Lovin' Me	6

EP

62	HMV 7EG 8780	SEALED WITH A KISS	50

LPs

61	London HA-R 2289	THE BASHFUL BLONDE	150
62	HMV CLP 1553	LET ME BELONG TO YOU	100
63	HMV CLP 1759	COUNTRY MEETS FOLK	65
66	Philips BL 7762	THE JOKER WENT WILD	30
68	Fontana SFL 13008	HERE'S TO OUR LOVE	22
72	Uni UNLS 118	BRIAN HYLAND	15

C. HYMAN

65	Ska Beat JB 200	The Ska Rhythm/The Ska Is Moving On	20

DICK HYMAN TRIO

56	MGM SP 1164	Theme From "The Threepenny Opera"/Baubles, Bangles And Beads	8
58	MGM MGM-EP 646	DICK HYMAN SWINGS (EP)	8
69	Command SCMD 508	MOOG — THE ELECTRIC ECLECTICS OF DICK HYMAN (LP)	15
70	Command SCMD 946	THE AGE OF ELECTRONICUS (LP)	25

PHYLLIS HYMAN

79	Arista ARIST 323	You Know How To Love Me/Give A Little More (12", p/s)	10

MINT VALUE £

I AM KLOOT
00s Uglyman AMOUR 4CD Twist/86 TVs (CD) . . . 10

JANIS IAN
67 Verve Folkways VS 1503 Society's Child (Baby I've Been Thinking)/Letter To Jon . . . 20
67 Verve Folkways VS 1506 Society's Child (Baby I've Been Thinking)/Letter To Jon (reissue) . . . 7
68 Verve Folkways VS 1513 Sunflakes Fall, Snowrays Call/Insanity Comes Quietly To The Structured Mind . . . 8
67 Verve F'ways (S)VLP 6001 JANIS IAN (LP) . . . 25
67 Verve Forecast (S)VLP 6003 FOR ALL THE SEASONS OF YOUR MIND (LP) . . . 18
68 Verve Forecast (S)VLP 6009 THE SECRET LIFE OF J. EDDY FINK (LP) . . . 15
70 Verve Folkways SVLP 6023 WHO REALLY CARES? (LP) . . . 15
71 Capitol E-ST 683 PRESENT COMPANY (LP) . . . 15

IAN (Meeson) & BELINDA (Gillet)
89 Odeon ODO 112 Who Wants To Live Forever?/Who Wants To Live Forever? (Instrumental) (p/s, feat. Brian May) . . . 7
89 Odeon 12ODO 112 Who Wants To Live Forever?/Who Wants To Live Forever? (Instrumental)/ Who Wants To Live Forever? (Original Demo) (12", p/s, feat. Brian May) . . . 10
(see also Brian May)

IAN & SYLVIA
63 Fontana TF 426 Four Strong Winds/Long Lonesome Road . . . 7
65 Fontana TFL 6053 EARLY MORNING RAIN (LP) . . . 18
68 Vanguard SVRL 19004 THE BEST OF IAN & SYLVIA (LP) . . . 12

IAN (EDWARD) & ZODIACS
63 Oriole CB 1849 Beechwood 4-5789/You Can Think Again . . . 50
65 Fontana TF 548 Just The Little Things/This Won't Happen To Me (as Ian Edward with Zodiacs) . . . 35
66 Fontana TF 708 No Money, No Honey/Where Were You? . . . 30
66 Fontana TF 753 Wade In The Water/Come On Along, Girl . . . 65
65 Wing WL 1074 GEAR AGAIN — 12 HITS (LP) . . . 55
(see also Koppykats, Wellington Wade)

ICARUS
69 Spark SRL 1012 The Devil Rides Out/You're In Life . . . 50
72 Pye NSPL 28161 THE MARVEL WORLD OF ICARUS (LP) . . . 90

ICE
67 Decca F 12680 Anniversary (Of Love)/So Many Times . . . 60
68 Decca F 12749 Ice Man/Whisper Her Name (Maria Laine) . . . 70
(see also Affinity)

ICE
79 Storm SR 3307 SAGA OF THE ICE KING (LP, private pressing with booklet) . . . 160
(see also Dickens)

ICED EARTH
02 Century Media DARK GENESIS (5-CD box set, initial issues with mispressed labels) . . . 40

ICE LA BAS
80s Storm SR 12 NO 4 ICE LA BAS (12" EP, with booklet) . . . 10

ICICLE WORKS
82 Troll Kitchen WORKS 1 Nirvana/Love Hunt/Scirocco (p/s) . . . 10
83 Situation 2 SIT 22 Birds Fly (Whisper To A Scream)/Reverie Girl (p/s) . . . 5
83 B. Banquet BEG 99P Love Is A Wonderful Colour/Waterline (picture disc) . . . 5
83 Beggars Banquet BEG 99/ ICE 1 Love Is A Wonderful Colour/Waterline//In The Dance The Shamen Led/ The Devil On Horseback (double pack, gatefold p/s) . . . 5
85 B. Banquet BEG 142D/ICE 2 Seven Horses/Slingshot//Beggar's Legacy/Goin' Back (double pack) . . . 5
88 B. Banquet BEG 215CD Little Girl Lost/Evangeline/Understanding Jane/Tin Can (CD, picture disc) . . . 8
81 private pressing ASCENDING (EP, cassette) . . . 20
(see also Ian McNabb, Melting Bear)

IDEALS
61 Pye International 7N 25103 Knee Socks/Mary's Lamb . . . 45

IDES OF MARCH
66 London HLU 10058 You Wouldn't Listen/I'll Keep Searching (as I'des Of March) . . . 10
68 London HLU 10183 Hole In My Soul/Girls Don't Grow On Trees . . . 10
70 Warner Bros WB 7378 Vehicle/Lead Me Home, Gently . . . 6
70 Warner Bros WB 7403 Superman/Home . . . 6
70 Warner Bros WS 1863 THE IDES OF MARCH (LP) . . . 20
(see also Survivors)

IDIOTS
80s Blue Angle BLI 2 Operation Julie/(Why Does Politics Turn Men Into) Toads (p/s) . . . 5
(see also Tone Deaf & Idiots)

IDLE FLOWERS
84 Miles Ahead AHEAD 1 All I Want Is You/Fizz Music (p/s) . . . 8
(see also Hanoi Rocks)

IDLE RACE

67 Liberty LBF 15026 The Imposters Of Life's Magazine/Sitting In My Tree . . . 35
68 Liberty LBF 15054 The Skeleton And The Roundabout/Knocking Nails Into My House . . . 15
68 Liberty LBF 15101 The End Of The Road/The Morning Sunshine. . . . 15
68 Liberty LBF 15129 I Like My Toys/The Birthday (unissued)
69 Liberty LBF 15218 Days Of Broken Arrows/Warm Red Carpet (B-side act. "Worn Red Carpet") . . . 18
69 Liberty LBF 15242 Come With Me/Reminds Me Of You . . . 15
71 Regal Zonophone RZ 3036 Dancing Flower/Bitter Green . . . 12
76 United Artists UP 36060 The Skeleton And The Roundabout/Morning Sunshine . . . 5
68 Liberty LBL/LBS 83132 THE BIRTHDAY PARTY (LP, mono/stereo) . . . 65/45
69 Liberty LBS 83221 THE IDLE RACE (LP) . . . 90
71 Regal Zono. SLRZ 1017 TIME IS (LP) . . . 120
73 Sunset SLS 50354 ON WITH THE SHOW (LP) . . . 12
76 Sunset SLS 50381 THE BIRTHDAY PARTY (LP, reissue) . . . 15

(see also Mike Sheridan & Nightriders, Nightriders, Mike Sheridan's Lot, Lemon Tree, Jeff Lynne, Move, E.L.O., Trevor Burton, Steve Gibbons Band, Wizzard)

IDLEWILD

97 Human Condition HC 0017 Queen Of The Troubled Teens/Faster/Self Healer (p/s, 1,000 only) . . . 50
97 Fierce Panda NING 42 Chandelier/I Want To Be A Writer (p/s). . . . 30
97 Deceptive BLUFF 057 Satan Polaroid/House Alone (die-cut p/s, numbered, 1,500 only) . . . 45
98 Deceptive BLUFF 058CD CAPTAIN EP (Self Healer/Annihilate Now!/Last Night I Missed All The Fireworks/ Satan Polaroid/You Just Have To Be Who You Are) (CD) . . . 15
98 Food FOOD 111 A Film For The Future/Mince Showercap Part 1 (wraparound p/s, stickered poly outer sleeve). . . . 12
98 Food FOOD 113 Everyone Says You're So Fragile/Mince Showercap Part 2 (wraparound p/s, stickered poly outer sleeve). . . . 12
98 Food FOOD 114 I'm A Message/Mince Showercap Part 3 (p/s). . . . 12
98 Food FOOD CD114 I'm A Message/Mince Showercap Part 3/This Is Worse (CD, digipak) . . . 12
98 Food CDFOODS 114 I'M A MESSAGE EP: (I'm A Message/ Satan Polaroid/You've Lost Your Way (CD, digipak). . . . 12
00 Food FOOD 134 Roseability/Rusty (wraparound p/s, stickered poly outer) . . . 8
03 Parlophone R 6598 A Modern Way Of Letting Go/(Live Version) (numbered, foldout p/s). . . . 5
98 Food FOODLP 28 HOPE IS IMPORTANT (LP). . . . 12
00 Food FOODLP 32 100 BROKEN WINDOWS (LP, with print) . . . 12
02 Parlophone 5402431 THE REMOTE PART (LP) . . . 12

BILLY IDOL

82 Chrysalis CHS 2543 Mony Mony/Baby Talk (p/s) . . . 6
82 Chrysalis CHS 12 2543 Mony Mony/Baby Talk/Untouchables/Dancing With Myself (12", p/s). . . . 8
82 Chrysalis CHSP 2625 Hot In The City/Dead On Arrival (picture disc) . . . 6
82 Chrysalis IDOL 1 Dancing With Myself/White Wedding (p/s, clear vinyl) . . . 6
83 Chrysalis IDOL 1 White Wedding/Hot In The City (reissue, p/s, clear vinyl) . . . 6
84 Chrysalis IDOL 2 Rebel Yell/Crank Call//White Wedding/Hot In The City (double pack, gatefold p/s) . . . 5
84 Chrysalis IDOLP 2 Rebel Yell/Crank Call (square picture disc). . . . 10
84 Chrysalis IDOLD 3/ CHS 2656 Eyes Without A Face/The Dead Next Door//Dancing With Myself/ Rebel Yell (double pack). . . . 6
84 Chrysalis IDOLP 3/ CHS 2656 Eyes Without A Face/The Dead Next Door//Dancing With Myself/ Rebel Yell (12" picture disc). . . . 10
84 Chrysalis IDOL 4 Flesh For Fantasy/Blue Highway (gatefold p/s) . . . 6
84 Chrysalis IDOLX 4 Flesh For Fantasy (Extended)/Blue Highway/Flesh For Fantasy (12", p/s, with poster) . . . 8
84 Chrysalis IDOLP 4 Flesh For Fantasy (Extended)/Blue Highway/Flesh For Fantasy (12" picture disc)10
85 Chrysalis IDOL 5 White Wedding/Flesh For Fantasy (second reissue, p/s, white vinyl) . . . 5
85 Chrysalis IDOL 5 White Wedding (Shotgun Mix Parts 1& 2)/Mega-Idol-Mix (p/s, some clear vinyl in PVC sleeve). . . . 8/10
85 Chrysalis IDOLX 5 White Wedding (Shotgun Mix Parts 1& 2)/Mega-Idol-Mix (12", p/s, white vinyl). . . 12
85 Chrysalis IDOLP 5 White Wedding (Shotgun Mix Parts 1& 2)/Mega-Idol-Mix (12" picture disc) . . . 10
85 Chrysalis IDOLP 6 Rebel Yell/(Do Not) Stand In The Shadows (Live)/Blue Highway (Live) (12" picture disc). . . . 10
86 Chrysalis IDOLD 8 To Be A Lover/All Summer Single/White Wedding/Mega-Idol-Mix (double pack, gatefold p/s) . . . 6
86 Chrysalis IDOLX 8 To Be A Lover (Mercy Mix)/To Be A Lover/All Summer Single (12", p/s) . . . 8
86 Chrysalis IDOLX 8 To Be A Lover (Mercy Mix)/To Be A Lover/All Summer Single (12" picture disc). . . . 8
87 Chrysalis IDOLP 9 Don't Need A Gun/Fatal Charm (12" picture disc) . . . 8
88 Chrysalis IDOLCD 12 Hot In The City (Exterminator Mix)/Catch My Fall (Remix Fix)/ Soul Standing By/Mony Mony (live) (CD) . . . 10
88 Chrysalis IDOLB 13 Catch My Fall/All Summer Single (7" box set with badge and card) . . . 5
88 Chrysalis BILYV 1 IDOL SONGS — 11 OF THE BEST (50,000 with bonus LP). . . . 12

(see also Generation X)

IDOLS

65 Mercury MF 840 Don't Walk Away/You Don't Care . . . 15

(see also Mike Sax & Idols)

IDOLS

79 Ork NYC 2 You/Girl That I Love (p/s) . . . 8

(see also New York Dolls)

IF

70 Island WIP 6083 Raise The Level Of Your Conscious Mind/I'm Reaching Out On All Sides. . . . 8
71 United Artists UP 35263 Far Beyond/Forgotten Roads. . . . 6
72 United Artists UP 35356 You In Your Small Corner/Waterfall . . . 6
70 Island ILPS 9129 IF (LP, 1st pressing, pink label/'i' logo) . . . 35
71 Island ILPS 9129 IF (LP, 2nd pressing, pink rim label/'palm tree' logo) . . . 12
71 Island ILPS 9137 IF2 (LP, pink label, pink rim label/'palm tree' logo) . . . 20

MINT VALUE £

71	United Artists UAG 29158	IF3 (LP)	15
72	United Artists UAG 29315	IF IV (LP, gatefold sleeve with inner)	15
74	Gull GULP 1004	NOT JUST A BUNCH OF PRETTY FACES (LP)	12
75	Carley Records CR 300010	TEA BREAK OVER -- BACK ON YOUR 'EADS (LP)	15

(see also Ferris Wheel)

IF

92	MCA MCST 1627	Saturday's Angels (Justin Robertson Mixes) (12")	8

KRIS IFE

67	MGM MGM 1369	Hush/The Spectator	15
68	MGM MGM 1390	This Woman's Love/I Gotta Feeling	7
68	Music Factory CUB 3	Give And Take/Sands Of Time	8
68	Parlophone R 5741	Imagination/I'm Coming 'Round	15
69	Parlophone R 5770	Haven't We Had A Good Time?/Will I Ever Fall In Love Again?	7

(see also Quiet Five, Judd)

FRANK IFIELD

60	Columbia DB 4399	Lucky Devil/Nobody Else But You	5
60	Columbia DB 4464	Happy-Go-Lucky Me/Unchained Melody	5
60	Columbia DB 4496	Gotta Get A Date/No Love Tonight	5
61	Columbia DB 4568	That's The Way It Goes/Phoebe Snow	5
61	Columbia DB 4658	Tobacco Road/Life's A Holiday	5
67	Columbia DB 8164	You Came Along (From Out Of Nowhere)/And I Always Will Do	5
70	Decca F 13015	Three Good Reasons/I Wrapped Her In Ribbons	5
70	Decca F 13074	Easy Come, Easy Go/Tennessee Bird Walk	5
63	Columbia SEG 8262	JUST ONE MORE CHANCE (EP, also stereo [ESG 7897])	10/15
63	Columbia SEG 8288	PLEASE (EP)	10
64	Columbia SEG 8300	DON'T BLAME ME (EP)	10
64	Columbia SEG 8322	BORN FREE (EP)	10
64	Columbia SEG 8343	BLUE SKIES (EP)	10
64	Columbia SEG 8359	I SHOULD CARE (EP)	10
64	Columbia SEG 8377	FRANK IFIELD SINGS (EP)	10
64	Columbia SEG 8385	FUNNY HOW TIME SLIPS AWAY (EP)	10
65	Columbia SEG 8448	LOVE WALKED IN (EP)	10
65	Columbia SEG 8456	HONG KONG BLUES (EP)	10
66	Columbia SEG 8495	GIVE HIM MY REGARDS (EP)	12
62	Columbia SCX 3460	I'LL REMEMBER YOU (LP, stereo)	12
65	Columbia 33SX 1723	PORTRAIT IN SONG (LP, also stereo SCX 3551)	15
65	Columbia 33SX 1751	UP JUMPED A SWAGMAN (LP)	12/15
66	Columbia S(C)X 6009	BABES IN THE WOOD (LP, cast recording, mono/stereo)	15
73	Spark SRLP 111	SOMEONE TO GIVE MY LOVE TO (LP)	15/18
78	FIR FIR 3781	BARBARY COAST (LP)	15
80	FIR FIR 3782	SWEET VIBRATIONS (LP)	12
80s	FIR FIR 3783	IF LOVE MUST GO (LP)	12
80s	FIR FIR 3784	AT THE SANDCASTLE (LP)	12

'IGGINBOTTOM

69	Deram DML/SML 1051	'IGGINBOTTOM'S WRENCH (LP)	115

(see also Soft Machine)

IGGY & STOOGES

(see under Stooges, Iggy Pop)

JULIO IGLESIAS

70	Decca F 23005	Gwendolyne/Bla, Bla, Bla	8

IGNERANTS

79	Rundown ACE 008	Radio Interference/Wrong Place, Wrong Time (p/s)	30

IGNORANTS

93	Spaghetti CIOCD 8	Phat Girls (Seven Stone Diet)/Fat Girls (Clubland Frenzy)/ Fat Girls (Bedtime Binge)/Rewind (CD)	8

I.G.s

75	RCA RCA 2560	Show And Tell/I Can't Get You Out Of My Mind	20

IGUANA

72	Polydor 2383 108	IGUANA (LP)	20

IGUANAS

65	RCA RCA 1484	This Is What I Was Made For/Don't Come Runnin' To Me	30

IJAHMAN

76	Lucky LY 6016	Jah Heavy Load/Heavy Dub	10

I-JOG & TRACKSUITS

78	Tyger TYG 1	Red Box/Worrying Man (p/s)	6

IKE (B) & CRYSTALITES

68	Island WI 3134	Illya Kuryakin/Anne Marie (B-side miscredited to Bobby Ellis & Crystalites)	22
68	Island WI 3151	Try A Little Merriness/Patricia (as Ike B & Crystalites)	20

IKETTES

62	London HLU 9508	I'm Blue/Find My Baby	22
65	Stateside SS 407	Peaches'N'Cream/The Biggest Players	18
65	Stateside SS 434	(He's Gonna Be) Fine Fine Fine/How Come	18
65	Sue WI 389	Prisoner In Love/Those Words	35
66	Polydor 56506	I'm So Thankful/Don't Feel Sorry For Me	15
66	Polydor 56516	(Never More) Lonely For You/Sally Go Round The Roses	15
66	London HLU 10081	What'cha Gonna Do?/Down, Down	18
67	Polydor 56533	I'm So Thankful/Don't Feel Sorry For Me (reissue)	6
73	Mojo 2092 063	Peaches'N'Cream/Sally Go Round The Roses	8
65	Stateside SE 1033	FINE FINE FINE (EP)	100

(see also Ike & Tina Turner, P.P. Arnold)

ILANIT
77 Pye International 7N 25739 I'm No One (If You Leave Me)/I Can't Say I Love You (p/s) . . . 10

I LIFE
64 R&B JB 140 Kiss You Gave Me/No More . . . 15

ILLUSION
69 Dot DOT 122 Did You See Her Eyes?/Falling In Love . . . 8
70 Dot DOT 133 Together/Don't Push It . . . 5
70 Dot DOT 137 Let's Make Each Other Happy/Beside You (unissued)
70 Paramount PARA 3007 Let's Make Each Other Happy/Beside You . . . 5
69 Dot (S)LPD 531 ILLUSION (LP) . . . 22
70 Dot SLPD 537 TOGETHER (AS A WAY OF LIFE) (LP) . . . 20
70 Paramount SPFL 264 IF IT'S SO (LP, originally planned for Dot SLPD 539) . . . 18

ILLUSIVE DREAM
69 RCA Victor RCA 1791 Electric Garden/Back Again . . . 25
(see also Christine Perfect)

SOLOMON ILORY
63 Blue Note 45-1899 Yabe E (Farewell) (Parts 1 & 2) . . . 12

I LUV WIGHT
70 Philips 6006 043 Let The World Wash In/Mediaeval Masquerade (some in p/s) . . . 90/35
(see also Kaleidoscope, Fairfield Parlour)

IM (Cedric Brooks) & DAVID
70 Bamboo BAM 57 Candid Eye/SOUND DIMENSION: Federated Backdrop . . . 25

IMAGE
65 Parlophone R 5281 Come To The Party/Never Let Me Go . . . 35
65 Parlophone R 5352 Home Is Anywhere/I Hear Your Voice Again . . . 35
66 Parlophone R 5442 I Can't Stop Myself/Let's Make The Scene . . . 35
(see also Dave Edmunds)

IMAGES
65 Polydor 56011 I Only Have Myself To Blame/Head Over Heels . . . 30

NATALIE IMBRUGLIA
98 RCA 74321 52799-2 Torn/Contradictions/Diving In The Deep End (CD, withdrawn) . . . 12

HAMISH IMLACH
67 Xtra XTRA 1059 BEFORE AND AFTER (LP) . . . 12
68 Xtra XTRA 1069 THE TWO SIDES OF HAMISH IMLACH (LP) . . . 12
72 Xtra XTRA 1128 FINE OLD ENGLISH TORY TIMES (LP) . . . 12

IMMORTALS
69 Amalgamated AMG 851 Bongo Jah/ANSELL COLLINS: My Last Waltz . . . 10

IMMORTALS
86 MCA MCA 1057 No Turning Back/No Turning Back (The Chocks-Away Mix) (p/s) . . . 30
86 MCA MCAT 1057 No Turning Back (Joy Stick Mix)/No Turning Back/No Turning Back (The Chocks-Away Mix) (12", p/s) . . . 35
(see also Queen)

IMPAC
66 CBS 202402 Too Far Out/Rat Tat Ta Tat . . . 80

IMPACT ALL STARS
71 Bullet BU 483 Dandy Shandy Version 4/Go Back Version 3 . . . 6
71 Randy's RAN 519 Go Back Version 4/Version 3 . . . 7
71 Supreme SUP 223 Go Back/Version . . . 6
(see also Randy's All Stars, Alton Ellis, Gregory Issacs, Errol Dunkley, C. Danovan, Heptones, Dennis Brown, Horace Andy)

IMPALAS
59 MGM MGM 1015 Sorry (I Ran All The Way Home)/Fool, Fool, Fool . . . 30
59 MGM MGM 1015 Sorry (I Ran All The Way Home)/Fool, Fool, Fool (78) . . . 50
59 MGM MGM 1031 Oh, What A Fool/Sandy Went Away . . . 30
60 MGM MGM 1068 Peggy Darling/'Bye Everybody . . . 30
59 MGM MGM-EP 696 SORRY (I RAN ALL THE WAY HOME) (EP) . . . 450

IMPERIAL POMPADOURS
80 Pompadour POMP 001 ERSATZ (LP, actually Inner City Unit with Robert Calvert & Barney Bubbles) . . . 35
(see also Inner City Unit, Robert Calvert)

IMPERIALS
68 Nu Beat NB 012 Young Love/Days Like These . . . 8

IMPERIALS (Jamaica)
69 Bullet BU 417 Black Is Soul/Always With You . . . 7

IMPERIALS
72 Key KL 012 TIME TO GET IT TOGETHER (LP) . . . 18
74 Key KL 025 FOLLOW THE MAN WITH THE MUSIC (LP) . . . 15

IMPERSONATORS
69 Big Shot BI 524 Make It Easy On Yourself/I've Tried Before . . . 8
(see also Moffat Allstars)

IMPOSSIBLE DREAMERS
80 Merciful Release MR 1 Books Books Books/Not A Love Song/Waiting For The Girl/What Can You Do When You See Someone As Beautiful As You? . . . 8
82 One Hundred Things MR 5 Life On Earth/Spin (12", die-cut sleeve) . . . 8
80s One Hundred Things READY FOR RHYTHM SECTION (LP) . . . 12

IMPOSSIBLE YEARS
85 Dreamworld DREAM 1 SCENES WE'D LIKE TO SEE (12" EP) . . . 12

MINT VALUE £

IMPOSTERS

69 Mercury MF 1080 — Apache '69/Q Three 20

IMPRESSIONS

58 London HL 8697 — For Your Precious Love/Sweet Was The Wine (as Jerry Butler & Impressions) 150
58 London HL 8697 — For Your Precious Love/Sweet Was The Wine (78, as Jerry Butler & Impressions) 70
61 HMV POP 961 — Gypsy Woman/As Long As You Love Me 50
63 HMV POP 1129 — I'm The One Who Loves You/I Need Your Love 20
63 HMV POP 1226 — It's Alright/You'll Want Me Back 18
64 HMV POP 1262 — Talkin' About My Baby/Never Too Much Love 20
64 HMV POP 1295 — I'm So Proud/I Made A Mistake 15
64 HMV POP 1317 — Keep On Pushing/I Love You (Yeah) 15
64 HMV POP 1343 — You Must Believe Me/See The Real Me 15
65 HMV POP 1408 — People Get Ready/I've Been Trying 15
65 HMV POP 1429 — Woman's Got Soul/Get Up And Move 15
65 HMV POP 1446 — A Meeting Over Yonder/I Found That I've Lost 15
65 HMV POP 1472 — I Need You/Never Could You Be 15
65 HMV POP 1492 — Amen/Long Long Winter 12
66 HMV POP 1498 — You've Been Cheatin'/Just One Kiss From You 18
66 HMV POP 1516 — Since I Lost The One I Love/Falling In Love With You 12
66 HMV POP 1526 — Too Slow/No One Else 12
66 HMV POP 1545 — Can't Satisfy/This Must End 20
67 HMV POP 1581 — You Always Hurt Me/Little Girl 18
68 Stateside SS 2083 — We're A Winner/You've Got Me Runnin' 12
68 Buddah 201 021 — Fool For You/I'm Loving Nothing 8
69 Stateside SS 2139 — Can't Satisfy/You've Been Cheatin' 10
69 Buddah 201 062 — Choice Of Colors/Mighty Mighty Spade And Whitey 5
70 Buddah 2011 030 — Check Out Your Mind/Can't You See? 5
70 Buddah 2011 045 — (Baby) Turn On To Me/Soulful Love 5
71 Buddah 2011 068 — Ain't Got Time/I'm So Proud 5
71 Buddah 2011 087 — Love Me/Do You Want Me To Win 5
71 Buddah 2011 099 — Inner City Blues/Amen/Keep On Pushin' 5
72 Buddah 2011 124 — Our Love Goes On And On/This Love's For Real 5
73 Probe PRO 584 — People Get Ready/We Be Rolling On 5
65 HMV 7EG 8896 — IT'S ALL RIGHT (EP) 50
66 HMV 7EG 8954 — SOULFULLY (EP) 50
64 HMV CLP 1743 — THE NEVER ENDING IMPRESSIONS (LP) 65
65 HMV CLP 1935 — BIG SIXTEEN (LP, also stereo CSD 1642) 35/45
66 HMV CLP/CSD 3548 — RIDIN' HIGH (LP) 45
67 HMV CLP/CSD 3631 — THE FABULOUS IMPRESSIONS (LP) 45
68 Stateside (S)SL 10239 — WE'RE A WINNER (LP) 30
68 Joy JOYS 104 — FOR YOUR PRECIOUS LOVE (LP, with Jerry Butler) 15
69 Buddah 203 012 — THIS IS MY COUNTRY (LP) 18
69 Stateside (S)SL 10279 — BIG SIXTEEN (VOL. 2) (LP) 20
70 Buddah 2359 003 — THE YOUNG MOD'S FORGOTTEN STORY (LP) 22
70 Buddah 2359 009 — AMEN (LP) 15
71 Buddah 2318 017 — CHECK OUT YOUR MIND (LP) 15
72 Buddah 2318 059 — TIMES HAVE CHANGED (LP) 15
75 ABC ABCL 5104 — BIG SIXTEEN (LP, reissue) 15

(see also Curtis Mayfield, Jerry Butler)

IMPS

58 Parlophone R 4398 — Dim Dumb Blonde/Let Me Lie 20
58 Parlophone R 4398 — Dim Dumb Blonde/Let Me Lie (78) 15

INADEQUATES

59 Capitol CL 15051 — Pretty Face/Audie 25

IN-BE-TWEENS

(see under 'N Betweens)

IN CAMERA

82 4AD BAD 205 — FIN (12" EP) 10

INCAS

65 Lyntone LYN 765/6 — KEELE RAG RECORD (EP, flexidisc, with 3 other bands) 40
66 Parlophone R 5551 — One Night Stand/I'll Keep Holding On 18

INCOGNITO

81 Ensign ENYT 211 — Incognito (remix)/Shine On (live) (12") 10

INCREDIBLE BONGO BAND

73 MGM 2006 161 — Bongo Rock/Bongolia 12
72 MGM 2315 255 — BONGO ROCK (LP) 30
76 DJM DJS 20452 — BONGO ROCK (LP, reissue) 20

INCREDIBLE HOG

73 Dart ART 2026 — Lame/Tadpole 12
73 Dart 65372 — VOLUME 1 (LP) 100

INCREDIBLE KIDDA BAND

78 Psycho P 2608 — Everybody Knows/No Nerve (a few in p/s) 50/30
79 Carrere CAR 119 — Fighting My Way Back/Saturday Night Fever 150

INCREDIBLES

67 Stateside SS 2053 — There's Nothing Else To Say/Heart And Soul 150
74 Contempo CS 9008 — There's Nothing Else To Say/Another Dirty Deal 10
74 Contempo CLP 512 — HEART AND SOUL (LP) 15

INCREDIBLE STRING BAND

SINGLES

67 Elektra EKSN 45013 Way Back In The 1960s/Chinese White (white-label promo) . . . 50+
68 Elektra EKSN 45028 Painting Box/No Sleep Blues . . . 12
69 Elektra EKSN 45074 Big Ted/All Writ Down . . . 10
70 Elektra 2101 003 This Moment/Black Jack Davy . . . 6
72 Island WIP 6145 Black Jack David/Moon Hang Low . . . 5
73 Island WIP 6158 At The Lighthouse Dance/Jigs . . . 5

ORIGINAL LPs

66 Elektra EUK 254 THE INCREDIBLE STRING BAND (1st pressing, white label, green logo, black lettering) . . . 100
67 Elektra EUK 257/EUKS 7257 THE 5000 SPIRITS OR THE LAYERS OF THE ONION (mono/stereo, red label) . 35/30
68 Elektra EUK 258/EUKS 7258 THE HANGMAN'S BEAUTIFUL DAUGHTER (red label, with lyric insert) . . . 30
68 Elektra EKL 4036/7 WEE TAM/THE BIG HUGE (2-LP, red label, gatefold sleeve, with insert; also stereo EKS 74036/7) . . . 50
69 Elektra EKS 74057 CHANGING HORSES (red label, gatefold sleeve) . . . 22
70 Elektra 2469 002 I LOOKED UP (red label) . . . 22
70 Elektra 2665 001 U (2-LP, red label , gatefold sleeve, some with foldover lyric insert) . . . 25/30
70 Island ILPS 9140 BE GLAD FOR THE SONG HAS NO ENDING (pink rim label/'palm tree' logo) . . . 15
71 Island ILPS 9172 LIQUID ACROBAT AS REGARDS THE AIR (gatefold sleeve, with inner, pink rim label/'palm tree' logo) . . . 15
72 Island ILPS 9211 EARTHSPAN (with lyric inner sleeve, pink rim label/'palm tree' logo) . . . 15
73 Island ILPS 9229 NO RUINOUS FEUD (with inner sleeve, pink rim label/'palm tree' logo) . . . 12
74 Island ILPS 9270 HARD ROPE AND SILKEN TWINE (with inner sleeve, pink rim label/'palm tree' logo) . . . 12
76 Island ISLD 9 SEASONS THEY CHANGE (2-LP, gatefold sleeve) . . . 20

REISSUE LPs

66 Elektra EUK 254 THE INCREDIBLE STRING BAND (2nd pressing, red label) . . . 50
68 Elektra EKL 254 THE INCREDIBLE STRING BAND (3rd pressing, red label) . . . 20
68 Elektra EKS 7257 THE 5000 SPIRITS OR THE LAYERS OF THE ONION (red label) . . . 20
68 Elektra EKL 4036 WEE TAM (red label, also stereo EKS 74036) . . . 15
68 Elektra EKL 4037 THE BIG HUGE (red label, also stereo EKS 74037) . . . 15
71 Elektra EKS 7257 THE 5000 SPIRITS OR THE LAYERS OF THE ONION ('butterfly' label) . . . 12
71 Elektra EKS 7258 THE HANGMAN'S BEAUTIFUL DAUGHTER . . . 12
70 Elektra EKS 74061 I LOOKED UP (existence confirmed, 'butterfly' label) . . . 12
71 Elektra EKS 74065 RELICS OF THE INCREDIBLE STRING BAND ('butterfly' label) . . . 12
71 Elektra K 42002 THE HANGMAN'S BEAUTIFUL DAUGHTER ('butterfly' label, with insert) . . . 12
71 Elektra K 42037 CHANGING HORSES ('butterfly' label, gatefold sleeve) . . . 12
72 Elektra K 42021 WEE TAM ('butterfly' label) . . . 12
72 Elektra K 42022 THE BIG HUGE ('butterfly' label) . . . 12
72 Elektra K 62002 U (2-LP, 'butterfly' label, gatefold sleeve, with foldover lyric insert) . . . 18

(see also Robin Williamson, Mike Heron, Famous Jug Band, C.O.B., Shirley Collins)

IN CROWD (Jamaica)

71 Spinning Wheel SW 105 Bush Jacket/Soul Face . . . 12

IN CROWD (U.K.)

65 Parlophone R 5276 That's How Strong My Love Is/Things She Says . . . 70
65 Parlophone R 5328 Stop! Wait A Minute/You're On Your Own . . . 55
65 Parlophone R 5364 Why Must They Criticize?/I Don't Mind . . . 45

(see also Tomorrow, Keith West, Steve Howe, Four + One)

INCROWD

69 Deram DM 272 Where In The World/I Can Make Love To You . . . 15

INCUBUS

84 Guardian GRC 2165 TO THE DEVIL A DAUGHTER (LP) . . . 18

INDECENT EXPOSURE

84 Index IS A1 Riots (Single Version)/A Matter Of Time (no p/s) . . . 7

INDEPENDENTS

72 Wand WN 29 Just As Long As You Need Me (Parts 1 & 2) . . . 5
73 Pye 7N 25623 Baby I've Been Missing You/Couldn't Hear Nobody Say . . . 5
74 Pye 7N 252634 It's All Over/Sarah Lee . . . 5

INDIAN SUMMER

71 RCA Neon NE 3 INDIAN SUMMER (LP) . . . 35

(see also Ross)

LOS INDIOS TABAJARAS

63 RCA RCA 1365 Maria Elena/Jungle Dream . . . 5
64 RCA RCX 7135 A LA ORILLA DEL LAGO (EP) . . . 8
64 RCA no cat. no. LOS INDIOS TABAJARAS (LP) . . . 12

INDO JAZZMEN

68 Saga FID 2145 RAGAS AND REFLECTIONS (LP) . . . 15

INERTIA

80s Inertial ERT 1 The Screen/4 Submarine (p/s) . . . 5

INFANTES JUBILATE

68 Music Factory CUB 5 Exploding Galaxy/Take It Now . . . 55

INFA RIOT

81 Secret SHH 117 Kids Of The 80s/Still Out Of Order (p/s) . . . 6
82 Secret SHH 133 The Winner/School's Out (p/s) . . . 6
82 Secret SEC 7 STILL OUT OF ORDER (LP) . . . 15

(see also Infas)

MINT VALUE £

INFAS

84 Panache PAN 101 — Sound And Fury/Triffic Spiff Ya O.K. (p/s) 8
84 Panache PANLP 501 — SOUND AND FURY (LP) 12
(see also Infa Riot)

INFINITY PROJECT

89 Fabulous FABU 004 — HYPERACTIVE (12" EP, sponged cover) 10
90 Fabulous FABU 005 — UPHOLD THE LAW (12" EP) 10
90 Fabulous FABU 016 — TRIBADELIC MELTDOWN (12" EP) 8

IN FLAMES

72 Pama PM 842 — Rocket Man/I'm All Broke Up 6

INFLUENCE

69 Orange OAS 201 — I Want To Live/Driving Me Wild 15
(see also John Miles, Geordie, Smokestack Crumble)

INFORMATION

69 Beacon BEA 121 — Orphan/Oh Strange Man 10
70 Evolution E 2461S — Face To The Sun/Lovely To See You 15

NICK INGHAM

75 Studio Two TWOX 1045 — TERMINATOR (LP) 15

RED INGLE

50 Capitol CL 13356 — Turn Your Head Little Darlin'/You Can't Be As Fit As A Fiddle (78) 8
59 Capitol EAP 20052 — CIGAREETS, WHUSKY AND WILD WILD WOMEN (EP) 20

JORGEN INGMANN

61 Fontana H 311 — Cherokee/Anna 7
61 Fontana H 333 — Milord/Oceans Of Love 7
61 Fontana H 353 — Violetta/Pinetop's Boogie Woogie 7
62 Fontana 267 237 TF — Africa/Johnny's Tune 7
63 Columbia DB 7013 — I Loved You (Dansevise)/Little Boy (as Grethe & Jorgen Ingmann) 6
64 Columbia SEG 8340 — DRINA (EP) 20

LUTHER INGRAM

70 Stax STAX 142 — My Honey And Me/Puttin' Game Down 8
70 Stax STAX 148 — Home Don't Seem Like A Home/Ain't That Lovin' You? 8

INITIALS

64 London HLR 9860 — School Day/Song Is Number One 18

IN-KEEPERS

68 Morgan MR 109P — IN-KEEPERS (LP) 25

INK SPOTS

54 Parlophone DP 368 — Ebb Tide/Changing Partners (78, export issue) 25
54 Parlophone MSP 6063 — Here In My Lonely Room/Flowers, Mister Florist, Please 25
54 Parlophone MSP 6074 — Ebb Tide/If You Should Say Goodbye 25
54 Parlophone MSP 6126 — Planting Rice/Yesterdays 22
55 Parlophone MSP 6152 — Melody Of Love/Am I Too Late? 22
55 Parlophone R 3977 — Melody Of Love/Am I Too Late? (78) 8
56 Parlophone DP 514 — Don't Laugh At Me/Keep It Movin' (78, export issue) 8
50s Parlophone DP 428 — Someone's Rocking My Dreamboat/When You Come To The End Of The Day (78, export issue) 8
55 Brunswick OE 9158 — SWING HIGH SWING LOW VOL. 1 (EP) 10
56 Brunswick OE 9426 — THEY SOLD A MILLION NO. 10 (EP) 12
56 Brunswick OE 9427 — THEY SOLD A MILLION NO. 11 (EP) 15
57 HMV 7EG 8410 — CHARLIE FUQUA'S INK SPOTS (EP) 10
57 Parlophone GEP 8673 — YESTERDAYS (EP) 10
50s Britone LP 1003 — THE INK SPOTS (10" LP) 30
53 Brunswick LA 8590 — SOUVENIR ALBUM VOLUME ONE (10" LP) 25
55 Brunswick LA 8710 — STREET OF DREAMS (10" LP) 25
(see also Ella Fitzgerald)

AUTREY INMAN

63 Decca DFE 8571 — AMERICAN COUNTRY JUBILEE NO. 1 (EP) 15

INMATES

79 Soho SH 7 — Dirty Water/Danger Zone (gatefold p/s) 8
79 Radar ADA 47 — The Walk/Talkin' Woman (p/s) 5
81 Radar ADA 63 — (I Thought I Heard A) Heartbeat/Tallahassie Lassie (p/s) 5

INNER CITY

92 Ten TENX 408 — Praise (F.S.O.L. Conceptual)/(Intergalactic Dub)/(Mayday Mix) (12", p/s) 12
93 Virgin OVD 438 — TESTAMENT 93 (EP, remixes, printed card envelope sleeve) 10
93 Virgin CDOVD 438 — TESTAMENT 93 (CD EP) 10

INNER CITY EXPRESS

78 Ebony EYE 5 — Fat On Funk/Sho' Dig Dancin' (12") 8
78 Ebony EYE 15 — Spring Rain/Reggae Strings 6

INNER CITY UNIT

79 Riddle RID 001/ICU 45 — Solitary Ashtray/So Try As Id (Dub Version) (plain sleeve with colour insert) 8
79 Riddle RID 003 — Paradise Beach/Amyl Nitrate (company die-cut sleeve) 8
81 Avatar AAA 113 — Beer, Baccy, Bingo And Benidorm/In The Mood (Nude) (red vinyl, no p/s) 6
82 Avatar AAA 119 — Bones Of Elvis/Sid's Song (no p/s) 5
85 Jettisoundz JZ 5 — BLOOD AND BONE (12" EP, p/s) 8
79 Riddle RID 002 — PASS OUT (THE 360° PSYCHO DELERIA SOUND) (LP) 15
81 Avatar AALP 5004 — THE MAXIMUM EFFECT (LP, with insert) 12
(see also Hawkwind, Sphynx, Radio Actors, Imperial Pompadours, Catherine Andrews, Big Amongst Sheep, Nik Turner)

MINT VALUE £

INNER MINDS

70 New Beat NB 067 Witchcraft Man/Night In Cairo . . . 6
70 New Beat NB 069 Pum Pum Girl/Freedom . . . 6
71 Bullet BU 465 Arawak Version/Cuffy Cuffy . . . 6

NEIL INNES

72 United Artists UP 35358 Slush/Rawlinson's End (unissued)
73 United Artists UP 35495 How Sweet To Be An Idiot/The Age Of Desperation . . . 7
73 United Artists UP 35639 Momma B/Immortal Invisible . . . 7
74 United Artists UP 35676 Re-cycled Vinyl Blues/Fluff On The Needle . . . 7
74 United Artists UP 35745 Lie Down And Be Counted/Bandwagon . . . 7
75 United Artists UP 35772 What Noise Annoys An Oyster/Oo-Chuck-A-Mao-Mao . . . 7
77 Arista ARISTA 106 Lady Mine/Crystal Balls . . . 6
77 Arista ARISTA 123 Silver Jubilee (A Tribute)/Drama On A Saturday Night . . . 6
78 Warner Bros K 17182 Protest Song/The Hard-To-Get . . . 6
80 Polydor POSP 107 Amoeba Boogie/Theme . . . 5
80 Polydor 2059 247 Kenny And Liza/Human Race . . . 5
82 MMC MMC 100 Them/Rock Of Ages . . . 6
82 MMC MMC 103 Mr. Eurovision/Ungawa . . . 6
84 PRT 7P 298 Humanoid Boogie/Libido (p/s) . . . 6
84 PRT 12P 298 Humanoid Boogie/Libido (12", p/s) . . . 8
73 United Artists UAG 29492 HOW SWEET TO BE AN IDIOT (LP) . . . 22
82 MMC MMC 001 OFF THE RECORD (2-LP) . . . 20

(see also Grimms, Bonzo Dog [Doo Dah] Band, Rutles, World, Dirk & Stig, Group)

INN KEEPERS

71 Banana BA 328 Duppy Serenade/Sunshine Version (actually by Dennis Alcapone) . . . 15

(see also WInston Matthews)

INNOCENCE

66 Kama Sutra KAS 203 There's Got To Be A Word!/I Don't Wanna Be Around You . . . 8
66 Kama Sutra KAS 206 Mairzy Doats And Dozy Doats/Lifetime Of Lovin' You . . . 8

INNOCENT BYSTANDERS

80 Rok ROK XVII/XVIII Where Is Johnny?/DEBUTANTES: The Man In The Street (company sleeve) . . . 6

INNOCENTS (U.K.)

63 Columbia DB 7098 Stepping Stones/Grazina . . . 12
63 Columbia DB 7173 A Fine, Fine Bird/Spanish Holiday . . . 15
64 Columbia DB 7314 Stick With Me Baby/Not More Than Everything . . . 10

(see also Mike Berry, Innocents & Leroys)

INNOCENTS (U.K.)

80 Kingdom KV 8010 One Way Love/Every Wednesday Night At Eight (p/s) . . . 10

(see also Woodentops, Advertising, Secret Affair)

INNOCENTS (U.S.)

60 Top Rank JAR 508 Honest I Do/My Baby Hully Gullys . . . 35
61 Top Rank JAR 541 Gee Whiz/Please Mr Sun . . . 35

(see also Kathy Young)

INNOCENTS & LEROYS

64 Regal Zonophone RZ 502 HOT SIX: Don't Throw Your Love Away; My Girl Lollipop; I Love You Because; Not Fade Away (maxi-single, plain sleeve) . . . 12

(see also Innocents [U.K.], Le-Roys)

INQUISITIVE PEOPLE

67 Decca F 12699 Big White Chief/Rhapsody Of Spring . . . 6

INSANE

82 Insane INSANE 1 Why Die?/War And Violence (p/s) . . . 15
82 Riot City RIOT 3 Politics/Dead And Gone/Last Day (p/s) . . . 10
82 No Future OI 10 El Salvador/Nuclear War/Chinese Rock (p/s) . . . 10

INSECT TRUST

69 Capitol E-(S)T 109 THE INSECT TRUST (LP) . . . 65

INSIDERS

80 Satellite SATS 1002 Rollin' & Strollin'/She Had To Go (features Ray Dorset) . . . 10

(see also Ray Dorset)

INSPIRAL CARPETS

80s own label SONGS OF SHALLOW INTENSITY (p/s, demo cassette) . . . 12
80s own label WAITING FOR OURS (p/s, demo cassette) . . . 12
80s own label COW (p/s, demo cassette) . . . 8
87 Debris DEB 06 Garage Full Of Flowers/METRO INFINITY: Stupid Friends (flexidisc, some with ***Debris*** fanzine) . . . 7/5
88 Playtime AMUSE 2 Keep The Circle Around/Theme From Cow (p/s) . . . 15
88 Playtime AMUSE 2T PLANE CRASH (12" EP, later 'reissued' as white label without p/s) . . . 15/7
88 Playtime AMUSE 4 Butterfly/You Can't Take The Truth (unreleased, white label promos only) . . . 8
88 Playtime AMUSE 4T TRAIN SURFING (12" EP, unreleased, white label test pressings only) . . . 15
89 Cow MOO 1 PLANE CRASH (12" EP, unreleased reissue)
89 Cow MOO 2 TRAIN SURFING (12" EP, some with rear sticker & scratched-out matrix) . . . 8
89 Cow DUNG 4 Keep The Circle Around/Seeds Of Doubt/Joe/Causeway/Butterfly/26/ Garage Full Of Flowers/96 Tears (demo cassette) . . . 8

INSPIRATIONS (Jamaica)

69 Camel CA 11 Down In The Park/Love Oh Love . . . 10
69 Camel CA 21 Wonder Of Love/Cinderella . . . 8
70 Amalgamated AMG 857 Take Back Your Duck/Nothing For Nothing . . . 12
70 Amalgamated AMG 861 La La/Reggae Fever . . . 12
70 Amalgamated AMG 862 The Train Is Coming/Man Oh Man . . . 8
70 Trojan TTL 27 REGGAE FEVER (LP) . . . 35

(see also Untouchables, Niney)

MINT VALUE £

INSPIRATIONS (U.S.)

67	Polydor 56730	Touch Me, Kiss Me, Hold Me/What Am I Gonna Do With You?	120

INSTANT AGONY

82	H. Man H. Biscuit DUNK 1	THINK OF ENGLAND (EP)	5
82	H. Man H. Biscuit DUNK 2	FASHION PARADE (EP)	5
83	Flicknife FLS 022	No Sign Of Life/Taste Of Power (p/s)	5
83	Flicknife FLS 028	Nicely Does It/We Don't Need You (p/s)	5

INSTANT SUNSHINE

68	Page One POF 085	Here We Go Again/Methylated	10
68	Page One POL 007	LIVE AT TIDDY DOLS (LP)	25

INSTITUTE OF FORMAL RESEARCH

97	Bubblehead BH 005	VOLUME ONE: FILE UNDER SUBCONSCIOUS (CD, features Zoot Horn Rollo)	20

(see also Mick Taylor, Chris Spedding)

INSYNC VS MYSTERON

95	Peacefrog PF 033	AUDIBLE ILLUSION EP (12", plain sleeve)	10

INTELLIGENT COMMUNICATIONS

91	Jumpin' & Pumpin' 12TOT 15	PRINCIPLES OF MOTION EP (12", p/s)	10

(see also Future Sound Of London)

INTENSIVE CARE

84	Punishment Block CELL 1	COWARDS EP (p/s)	8
87	Back To Back BTB 001	REBBELS, ROCKETS AND RUBBERMEN (12", p/s)	12

INTENTIONS (U.K.)

72	Pye 7N 45123	There's Nobody I'd Sooner Love/Hurry On Home	5

INTENTIONS (U.S.)/Z.Z. HILL

66	Sue IEP 711	GIMME GIMME (EP, 2 tracks each by Intentions & Z.Z. Hill; 2 tracks mistakenly credited to Jackie Day on sleeve; some in p/s)	275/100

INTERNATIONAL CHRYSIS

94	PWL PWLT 303	Rebel Rebel (The Hole Mix)/Rebel Rebel (Extended Mix) (12", promo only)	15

(see also Dead Or Alive)

INTERNATIONAL PENPALS

80s	Radical Wallpaper RADWAL 001	Day They Ate Ronald Reagan (p/s)	12

INTERNS (Jamaica)

70	Jackpot JP 729	See You At Sunrise/LITTLE WONDER: Out Of Reach (B-side actually "Just Out Of Reach" by John Holt)	8

(see also Viceroys, Bob Marley & Wailers)

INTERNS (U.K.)

64	Philips BF 1320	Don't You Dare/Here There Everywhere	15
64	Philips BF 1345	Cry To Me/There's Love For You	15
66	Parlophone R 5479	Is It Really What You Want?/Just Like Me	30
67	Parlophone R 5586	Ray Of Sunshine/Please Say Something Nice	8

(see also Shadows)

INTERPOL

02	Matador OLE 546-7	PDA/Specialist (p/s)	8
02	Matador OLE 546-2	PDA/NYC/Specialist (CD, digipak, with slipcase)	8
02	fukd i.d #3 CHEM047CD	PDA: Precipitate/Roland/5 (CD, stickered card sleeve, 1,000 only)	30
02	Matador OLE 570-7	Obstacle 1/Obstacle 2 (Peel Session Version) (p/s)	10
02	Matador OLE 570-2	Obstacle 1/PDA (Morning Becomes Electric Session)/Hands Away (Peel Session) (CD)	8
00s	Matador OLE 5827	Say Hello To The Angels/NYC (p/s)	7
00s	Matador OLE 582-2	Say Hello To The Angels/NYC/NYC (Demo Version) (CD)	8
00s	Matador OLE 594-2	Obstacle 1 (Arthur Baker's Return To New York Mix [Edit])/(Return To New York Mix)/(Radio Edit) (CD)	8
00s	Matador OLE 5947	Obstacle 1 (Arthur Baker's Return To New York Mix [Edit])/(Black Session) (p/s)	6
00s	Matador OLE 5949	Obstacle 1 (Video)/Specialist (Black Session)/Leif Erikson (Black Session) (DVD)	8

IN THE NURSERY

84	Paragon VIRTUE 5	Witness To A Scream/1984 (p/s)	20
85	New European BADVC 55	Sonority — A Strength (12" EP)	12
85	Sweatbox SOX 008	Temper/Breach Birth/Joaquin/Arm Me Audacity (12", p/s)	8
87	Sweatbox SOX 019	Trinity: Elegy/Trinity: Elegy (Reprise)/Blind Me (12", p/s with inner sleeve)	8
83	Paragon VIRTUE 2	WHEN CHERISHED DREAMS COME TRUE (mini-LP, silk-screened g/fold p/s)	30

INTRA VEIN

79	Bum FP 001	Speed Of The City/Sick (printed PVC sleeve or stamped plain sleeve)	40/30

(see also Veins)

INTRIGUES

69	London HL 10293	In A Moment/Scotchman Rock	10
72	Janus 6146 008	To Make A World/Mojo Hanna	6

INTRUDERS

59	Top Rank JAR 158	Frankfurters And Sauerkraut/Creepin'	10
59	Top Rank JAR 158	Frankfurters And Sauerkraut/Creepin' (78)	10

INTRUDERS

66	London HL 10069	Up And Down The Ladder/United	35
69	Action ACT 4523	Slow Drag/So Glad I'm Yours	12
69	Ember EMB S 254	Cowboys To Girls/Turn Back The Hands Of Time	12
72	Ember EMB S 325	Cowboys To Girls/GOOD VIBRATIONS: Shake A Hand	7
85	Streetwave MKL 6	WHO DO YOU LOVE? (LP)	12

MINT VALUE £

INVADERS (Jamaica)

67	Columbia Bluebeat DB 105	Limbo Girl/Soul Of The Jungle	12
68	Columbia Bluebeat DB 109	Stop Teasing/Invaders At The Carnival	12
68	Studio One SO 2044	Soulful Music/SOUL VENDORS: Happy Organ	30
71	G.G. GG 4527	Got To Go Home/PAULETTE & GEE: How Long Will You Stay?	7

INVADERS (U.K.)

70s	Jovian ZIT 2	Launderama/Plastic Nose	5

INVICTAS

64	United Artists UP 1013	Green Bow Tie/Touch Of Orchid	10

INVITATIONS (Jamaica)

71	Crab CRAB 66	Birmingham Cat/Now You're On Your Own	8

INVITATIONS (U.S.)

65	Stateside SS 453	Hallelujah/Written On The Wall	50
65	Stateside SS 478	What's Wrong With My Baby?/Why Did My Baby Turn Bad?	70
70	Jay Boy BOY 24	How'd We Ever Get This Way?/Picking Up	5
72	Mojo 2092 055	What's Wrong With My Baby?/Why Did My Baby Turn Bad? (reissue)	5
74	Polydor 2066 366	Let's Love And Find Together/Love Has To Grow	10

INXS

81	RCA RCA 89	Just Keep Walking/Scratch (some in p/s)	40/10
83	Mercury INXS 1	Don't Change/You Never Used To Cry (p/s)	12
83	Mercury INXS 121	Don't Change/You Never Used To Cry/Golden Playpen (12", p/s)	16
83	Mercury INXS 2	The One Thing/The Sax Thing (p/s)	8
83	Mercury INXS 212	The One Thing (6.10)/Black And White (12", p/s)	12
83	Mercury INXS 222	The One Thing/Black And White/Here Comes II (12", p/s)	10
84	Mercury INXS 3	Original Sin/Jan's Song (live)/To Look At You (live) (p/s)	8
84	Mercury INXS 312	Original Sin/Original Sin (Extended Version)/Jan's Song (live)/ To Look At You (live) (12", p/s)	12
84	Philips PH 2	I Send A Message/Mechanical (p/s, some in envelope pack with postcard & biography)	20/5
84	Philips PH 212	I Send A Message (Long Distance)/Mechanical/I Send A Message (Local Call) (12", p/s)	15
86	Mercury INXSD 4	This Time/Original Sin (Extended Version)//Burn For You (Extended Mix)/ Dancing On The Jetty (double pack)	6
86	Mercury INXSC 5	What You Need/Sweet As Sin (p/s, sealed with bonus promo sampler cassette)	10
86	Mercury INXSD 512	What You Need (Remix)/Sweet As Sin/What You Need (live)//The One Thing (live)/Don't Change/Johnsons Aeroplane (12", double pack)	12
86	Mercury INXSD 6	Listen Like Thieves/Begotten//One X One/XS Verbiage (double pack)	5
86	Mercury INXSP 6	Listen Like Thieves/Begotten (flag-shaped picture disc)	10
86	Mercury INXS 612	Listen Like Thieves (Extended Remix)/Listen Like Thieves (Instrumental Remix)/Listen Like Thieves (live)/Begotten (12", p/s with poster)	8
86	Mercury INXSD 7	Kiss The Dirt/6 Knots/The One Thing (live)//This Time/ Original Sin (Long Version) (double pack)	5
87	Mercury INXCD 8	Need You Tonight/Mediate/I'm Coming (Home) (CD, card sleeve)	8
87	Mercury INXSR 9	New Sensation/Do Wot You Do (picture disc)	5
87	Mercury INXSP 912	New Sensation/Do Wot You Do/Love Is (What I Say)/Same Direction (12", poster p/s)	8
87	Mercury INXCD 9	New Sensation/Do Wot You Do/Love Is (What I Say)/ Same Direction (CD, card sleeve)	8
88	Mercury INXS 1010	Devil Inside/On The Rocks/Dancing On The Jetty/Shine Like It Does (live) (10", p/s)	7
88	Mercury INXCD 10	Devil Inside (Re-mix Version)/Devil Inside (7" Version)/On The Rocks/ What You Need (CD, card sleeve)	8
88	Mercury INXS 1100	Never Tear Us Apart/Guns In The Sky (Kick Ass Remix) (picture disc)	5
88	Mercury INXS 1110	Never Tear Us Apart/Need You Tonight/Listen Like Thieves (Extended Vocal Remix)/Guns In The Sky (Kick Ass Mix) (10", white vinyl, stickered PVC sleeve)	7
88	Mercury INXCD 11	Never Tear Us Apart/Guns In The Sky (Kick Ass Remix)/This Time (CD)	8
88	Mercury 080 396-2	Never Tear Us Apart/Guns In The Sky (Kick Ass Remix)/ Different World (7" Mix) (CD Video)	8
88	Mercury INXSG 12	Need You Tonight/Move On ('magic pack' p/s with 2 photocards)	5
88	Mercury 080 394-2	Need You Tonight/Tiny Daggers/Mediate/I'm Coming (Home)/ Need You Tonight (CD Video)	8
89	Mercury INXS 1322	Mystify/Biting Bullets/Shine Like It Does (live)/Never Tear Us Apart (live) (12", 'Global Tour' 'Special Sticker Pack', with poster & postcard)	8
89	Mercury 080 876-2	Mystify/Need You Tonight (Ben Liebrand Mix)/Shine Like It Does (live)/ Never Tear Us Apart (live)/Mystify (CD Video)	10
92	Mercury INSXP 20	Baby Don't Cry/Questions (Instrumental)/Ptar Speaks/Baby Don't Cry (Vocal & Ochestral Mix) (12", picture disc)	8
97	Mercury INXSJ 3012	Searchin' (Linslee Campbell R'n'B Mix)/(Linslee Campbell Mellow Mix) (12", printed labels, die-cut 'INXS' logo p/s, promo only)	8
97	Mercury INXSJ 3012	Searchin' (Linslee Campbell R'n'B Mix)/(Linslee Campbell Mellow Mix) (12", stamped white labels, plain titles die-cut sleeve, promo only)	8
97	Mercury INXSJJ 3012	Searchin' (Lead Station Main Mix)/(Lead Station Funk Work Mix)/ (Lead Station Wiggly Worm Mix)/(Lead Station Hydroponic Mix) (12", black title p/s, promo only)	8
97	Mercury INXCD 30	Searchin'/(Lead Station Radio Mix)/(Alex Reece Mix) (CD, part 1, withdrawn)	12
97	Mercury INXDD 30	Searchin' (CD, part 2, withdrawn)	12
97	Mercury INXSD 30	Searchin' (CD, part 3, withdrawn)	12

IONA

78	Silver Scales	CUCKOO (LP)	35
70s	Celtic Music CM 001	IONA (LP)	35

I.O.W. CHEROKEES

66	69 69EP 001	I.O.W. CHEROKEES (EP, private pressing)	10

MINT VALUE £

DON IPPOLITO ORCHESTRA

Year	Label	Title	Value
55	Parlophone MSP 6187	Camptown Racer Mambo/Can't Do It Mambo	7

IPSISSIMUS

Year	Label	Title	Value
69	Parlophone R 5774	Hold On/Lazy Woman	45

IQ

Year	Label	Title	Value
82	Red Stripe LYN 12028/9	Beef In A Box/RE-FLEX: Praying To The Beat/ASTRAKHAN: And She Smiled/ JENNY JAY: Jane (flexidisc, sampler for "Melody Maker Playback Vol. 1" LP)	8
84	Jim White/IQ PROMO 101	Awake And Nervous/Through The Corridors (12", no p/s, 500 only)	30
84	Sahara IQ 1002	Barbell Is In/Just Changing Hands (p/s)	8
84	Sahara IQ 12 1002	Barbell Is In (Lizard Mix)/Dans Le Parc Du Chateau Noir (12", p/s)	12
84	IQFREEB 1	Hollow Afternoon (1-sided, Marquee gig freebie)	35
85	Sahara IQ 1003	Corners (Remix)/Thousand Days (p/s)	8
85	Sahara IQ 12 1003	Corners/Thousand Days/The Wake (12", p/s)	12
86	STAL Other Boxer 1	Nomzamo (Demo) (1-sided fan club single)	18
86	Sahara IQSD 1	It All Stops Here/Intelligence Quotient (shaped picture disc)	18
87	RLOG Another Boxer 1	Fascination/The Bold Grenadier Pt. 1 (fan club single)	18
87	Squawk VERX 34	Promises (Extended Remix)/Promises (7" Version)/Human Nature (Edit) (12", p/s)	10
88	RLOG One More Boxer 1	A Different Magic Roundabout (Honest!)/The Big Balls Of Bert Christ (fan club single)	12
89	Squawk VERCD 42	Sold On You/Through My Fingers/Promises (As Years Go By)/ Colourflow (CD, card sleeve)	15
92	MIMP 00000001	BLUBA NEENY NOO: Last Human Gateway (Acoustic Middle Section)/ A Bit Of Love Lost (CD, fan club single, 361 copies only)	18
82	private pressing	SEVEN STORIES INTO EIGHT (cassette, different coloured sleeves, 40 numbered copies only)	10-12
83	MRC MAJ 1001	TALES FROM THE LUSH ATTIC (LP, 1,000 copies in pale or dark blue numbered sleeve)	18
84	COSL MAJ 1001	TALES FROM THE LUST ATTIC (LP, reissue in brown sleeve)	12
85	Sahara SAH 136	THE WAKE (LP)	12
85	STAL BOXER 1	NINE IN A POND IS HERE (2-LP, 1,000 copies only)	22
86	Samurai SAMR 045	LIVING PROOF (LP)	12
86	Samurai SAMRCD 045	LIVING PROOF (CD)	25
87	Squawk VERH 43	NOMZAMO (LP)	12
89	Squawk 836 429-1	ARE YOU SITTING COMFORTABLY? (LP)	12

(see also Niadem's Ghost)

IQ ZERO

Year	Label	Title	Value
79	Object Music OM 9	(Everybody Kills) Insects/Electromotion/Quirky Pop Music (p/s)	20
79	Logo GO 374	She's So Rare/Crazy Dolls (p/s)	15

IRELAND'S FREEMEN

Year	Label	Title	Value
75	Polydor 2908 017	SEAN SOUTH (LP)	15

IRISH MIST

Year	Label	Title	Value
75	SRT/Custom 012	ROSIN THE BOW (LP)	15

IRISH ROVERS

Year	Label	Title	Value
67	Brunswick STA 8679	FIRST OF THE IRISH ROVERS (LP)	12
68	MCA MUPS 310	THE UNICORN (LP)	12
69	MCA MUPS 353	LIVERPOOL LOU (LP)	12
69	MCA MUPS 389	TALES TO WARM YOUR MIND (LP)	12
70	MCA MUPS 406	LIFE OF THE ROVER (LP)	12

IRISH TRADITION

Year	Label	Title	Value
79	Green Linnet SIF 1016	THE CORNER HOUSE (LP)	15

IRON BUTTERFLY

Year	Label	Title	Value
68	Atlantic 584 188	Possession/Unconscious Power	6
69	Atlantic 584 254	Soul Experience/In The Crowds	6
70	Atlantic 2091 024	In-A-Gadda-Da-Vida/Termination	5
68	Atlantic 587/588 116	IN-A-GADDA-DA-VIDA (LP)	22
69	Atco 2465 015	HEAVY (LP)	15
69	Atco 228 011	BALL (LP, gatefold sleeve)	15
70	Atlantic 2400 014	LIVE (LP)	15
71	Atlantic 2401 003	METAMORPHOSIS (LP)	12

(see also Ramatam)

IRON MAIDEN

Year	Label	Title	Value
70	Gemini GMS 006	Falling/Ned Kelly	12

IRON MAIDEN

Year	Label	Title	Value
80	EMI EMI 5032	Running Free/Burning Ambition (p/s)	25
80	EMI EMI 5065	Sanctuary/Drifter (live)/I've Got The Fire (live) (uncensored p/s)	35
80	EMI EMI 5065	Sanctuary/Drifter (live)/I've Got The Fire (live) (censored p/s)	15
80	EMI EMI 5105	Women In Uniform/Invasion (p/s)	15
80	EMI 12EMI 5105	Women In Uniform/Phantom Of The Opera (live)/Invasion (12", p/s)	15
81	EMI EMI 5145	Twilight Zone/Wrathchild (p/s)	12
81	EMI EMI 5145	Twilight Zone/Wrathchild (p/s, red or clear vinyl)	25/30
81	EMI EMI 5145	Twilight Zone/Wrathchild (p/s, brown vinyl mispressing)	600
81	EMI TCEMI 5145	Twilight Zone/Wrathchild (cassette)	8
81	EMI EMI 5184	Purgatory/Genghis Khan (p/s)	30
82	EMI EMI 5263	Run To The Hills/Total Eclipse (p/s)	6
82	EMI EMIP 5263	Run To The Hills/Total Eclipse (picture disc)	15
82	EMI EMI 5287	The Number Of The Beast/Remember Tomorrow (live) (p/s)	5
82	EMI EMI 5287	The Number Of The Beast/Remember Tomorrow (live) (p/s, red vinyl)	12
83	EMI EMI 5378	Flight Of Icarus/I've Got The Fire (p/s)	5
83	EMI 12EMIP 5378	Flight Of Icarus/I've Got The Fire (12", picture disc)	20
83	EMI EMI 5397	The Trooper/Cross-Eyed Mary (p/s)	5

MINT VALUE £

83 EMI EMIP 5397 The Trooper/Cross-Eyed Mary (soldier-shaped picture disc) — 25
84 EMI EMI 5489 2 Minutes To Midnight/Rainbow's Gold (p/s) — 5
84 EMI 12EMI 5489 2 Minutes To Midnight/Rainbow's Gold/Mission From 'Arry (12", picture disc) — 20
84 EMI EMI 5502 Aces High/King Of Twilight (p/s) — 5
84 EMI 12EMIP 5502 Aces High/King Of Twilight/The Number Of The Beast (live) (12", picture disc) — 18
85 EMI EMI 5532 Running Free (live)/Sanctuary (live) (poster p/s) — 7
85 EMI 12EMIP 5532 Running Free (live)/Sanctuary (live)/Murders In The Rue Morgue (live) (12", picture disc) — 18
85 EMI EMI 5542 Run To The Hills (live)/Phantom Of The Opera (live) (with Xmas card) — 8
85 EMI 12EMIP 5542 Run To The Hills (live)/Phantom Of The Opera (live)/ Losfer Words (The Big 'Orra) (live) (12", picture disc) — 15
86 EMI EMIP 5583 Wasted Years/Reach Out (computer-shaped picture disc) — 15
86 EMI EMI 5589 Stranger In A Strange Land/That Girl (foldout poster p/s) — 6
86 EMI 12EMIP 5589 Stranger In A Strange Land/That Girl/Juanita (12", picture disc) — 18
88 EMI EMS 49 Can I Play With Madness/Black Bart Blues (p/s, with sticker & transfer) — 5
88 EMI EMP 49 Can I Play With Madness/Black Bart Blues (shaped picture disc) — 15
88 EMI CDEM 49 Can I Play With Madness/Black Bart Blues/Massacre (CD) — 10
88 EMI EMP 64 The Evil That Men Do/Prowler '88 (gatefold p/s) — 5
88 EMI EMP 64 The Evil That Men Do/Prowler '88 (shaped picture disc) — 10
88 EMI 12EMS 64 The Evil That Men Do/Prowler '88/Charlotte The Harlot '88 (12", poster p/s) — 8
88 EMI CDEM 64 The Evil That Men Do/Prowler '88/Charlotte The Harlot '88 (CD, picture disc) — 10
88 EMI EMS 79 The Clairvoyant (live)/The Prisoner (live) (clear vinyl, poster p/s) — 6
88 EMI EMP 79 The Clairvoyant (live)/The Prisoner (live) (shaped picture disc) — 10
88 EMI CDEM 79 The Clairvoyant (live)/The Prisoner (live)/Heaven Can Wait (live) (CD, picture disc) — 8
89 EMI EM 117 Infinite Dreams (live)/Killers (live) (with free patch) — 5
89 EMI EMPD 117 Infinite Dreams (live)/Killers (live) (shaped picture disc with insert) — 7
89 EMI 12EM 117 Infinite Dreams (live)/Killers (live)/Still Life (live) (12", poster p/s) — 8
89 EMI 12EM 117 Infinite Dreams (live)/Killers (live)/Still Life (live) (CD) — 8
90 EMI 12EMP 158 Holy Smoke/All In Your Mind/Kill Me Ce Soir (12" picture disc with insert) — 8
90 EMI 12EMP 158 Holy Smoke/All In Your Mind/Kill Me Ce Soir (12", gold vinyl test pressing, promo only) — 200+
90 EMI EM 171 Bring Your Daughter ... To The Slaughter/I'm A Mover (etched, p/s) — 6
90 EMI EMPD 171 Bring Your Daughter ... To The Slaughter/I'm A Mover (picture disc 'brain' pack) — 6
90 EMI 12EMP 171 Bring Your Daughter ... To The Slaughter/I'm A Mover (12", calendar pack) — 10
90 EMI 12EMPD 171 Bring Your Daughter ... To The Slaughter/I'm A Mover/ Communication Breakdown (12", picture disc, die-cut sleeve) — 12
92 EMI 12EMP 229 Be Quick ...Or Be Dead/Nodding Donkey Blues/Space Station No.5 (12" picture disc, with insert) — 10
92 EMI EMPD 240 From Here To Eternity/I Can't See My Feeling (shaped picture disc with insert) — 8
92 EMI EMP 263 Fear Of The Dark (live)/Tailgunner (live) (poster p/s) — 5
92 EMI EMPD 263 Fear Of The Dark (live)/Hooks In You (live) (shaped picture disc, with insert) — 8
92 EMI EMPD 263 Fear Of The Dark (live)/Hooks In You (live) (shaped picture disc, with mispressed B-side "Tailgunner" [live]) — 12
95 EMI 12EM 398 Man On The Edge/I Live My Way (12", picture disc, with poster) — 8
00 EMI no cat. no. Tommy Vance Previews: The Wicker Man/Ghost Of The Navigator/ Brave New World/Dream Of Mirrors/The Nomad (CD-R, with Thomas The Vance intros) — 100
79 Rock Hard ROK 1 THE SOUNDHOUSE TAPES (EP, p/s; counterfeits have slightly glossier sleeves) — 100
81 EMI 12EMI 5219 MAIDEN JAPAN EP (12" EP, p/s) — 15
93 EMI 12EMP 288 HALLOWED BE THY NAME EP (12", picture disc) — 8

ALBUMS

80 EMI EMC 3330 IRON MAIDEN (LP, some with poster) — 25/12
82 EMI EMCP 3400 THE NUMBER OF THE BEAST (LP, picture disc, with inner) — 50
84 EMI POWERP 1 POWERSLAVE (LP, picture disc) — 40
88 EMI EMDP 1006 SEVENTH SON OF A SEVENTH SON (LP, picture disc, with banner) — 50
90 EMI EMPD 1017 NO PRAYER FOR THE DYING (LP, picture disc, die cut sleeve) — 18
90 EMI (no cat. no.) NO PRAYER FOR THE DYING (CD, with interview cassette, photos & bio, promo only) — 75
90 EMI (no cat. no.) THE FIRST TEN YEARS — UP THE IRONS (10 x 12" double packs, box set available by mail order with tokens from records) — 65
90 EMI (no cat. no.) THE FIRST TEN YEARS — UP THE IRONS (10 x CD, box set available by mail order with tokens from records) — 65
93 EMI DON 1 LIVE AT DONINGTON (3-LP) — 20
96 EMI IPEMD 1097 BEST OF THE BEAST (4-LP box set, with inners, book and bonus tracks) — 65
96 EMI BEST 001 BEST OF THE BEAST (CD, Steve Harris interview disc, commercial CD, video, in 40cm x 30cm, flip-up 3D presentation box with 60-page book, 2 photographs, biography, promo only) — 125
98 EMI LPCENT 35 IRON MAIDEN (LP, reissue, 180gm vinyl) — 18
99 EMI EDHUNTER 666 ED HUNTER DEMO (CD-Rom, card p/s) — 25
02 EMI 538 6431 ROCK IN RIO (3-LP, picture discs, trifold sleeve) — 20
02 EMI 544 2772 EDDIE'S ARCHIVE (6-CD, tin box with insert, shot glass, pewter ring and parchment) — 80

(see also Bruce Dickinson, A.S.A.P., Di'Anno, Gogmagog, Samson, Urchin, Xero, Lionheart, Pat Travers, Stratus, Nicko McBrain, Money, White Spirit)

NEVILLE IRONS

68 Blue Cat BS 104 Soul Glide/DYNAMICS: My Friends — 30

(see also Neville Hinds)

IRON VIRGIN

74 Deram DM 416 Rebels Rule/Ain't No Clown — 10

I ROY

(see under 'R')

MINT VALUE £

ANDY IRVINE

80 Tara 3002 RAINY SUNDAYS, WINDY DREAMS (LP) 15

ANDY IRVINE & PAUL BRADY

76 Mulligan LUN 008 ANDY IRVINE & PAUL BRADY (LP) 20

WELDON IRVINE

75 Strata East SES 19749 IN HARMONY (LP) 12

LONNIE IRVING

60 Melodisc MEL 1546 Pinball Machine/I Got Blues On My Mind 35

(BIG) DEE IRWIN

64 Stateside SS 261 Donkey Walk/Someday You'll Understand Why 15
64 Colpix PX 11040 Heigh-ho/It's My Birthday 7
64 Colpix PX 11050 Personality/It's Only A Paper Moon 7
65 Stateside SS 450 You Satisfy My Needs/I Wanna Stay Right Here With You 80
68 Minit MLF 11013 I Can't Stand The Pain/My Hope To Die Girl (as Dee Irwin) 6

BIG DEE IRWIN & LITTLE EVA

63 Colpix PX 11010 Swinging On A Star/Another Night With The Boys (Little Eva uncredited) 6
64 Colpix PX 11021 I Wish You A Merry Christmas/Christmas Song 7
63 Colpix PXE 301 SWINGING ON A STAR (EP) 22
65 Golden Guinea GSGL 10497 SWINGING ON A STAR (LP) 18
(see also Little Eva, Suzi & Big Dee Irwin)

DAVID ISAACS

66 Island WI 261 I'd Rather Be Lonely/See That Man 22
68 Trojan TR 616 Place In The Sun/UPSETTER ALL STARS: Handy-Cap 22
69 Upsetter US 302 Good Father/SLIM SMITH: What A Situation 12
69 Upsetter US 305 I've Got Memories/I'm Leaving 12
69 Upsetter US 311 He'll Have To Go/Since You're Gone 12
69 Upsetter US 319 Who To Tell/BUSTY BROWN: I Can't See Myself Cry 12
69 Punch PH 6 I Can't Take It Anymore/LLOYD DOUGLAS: Anyway 10
71 Punch PH 84 You'll Be Sorry/Knock Three Times 10
71 Bullet BU 459 Just Enough/ROY PATIN: Standing (B-side actually by Roy Panton) 8
71 Tropical AL 006 Love Has Join Us/MAX ROMEO: Cross Over The Bridge (correct title for A-side is 'Love Has Joined Us') 7
73 Upsetter US 400 Stranger On The Shore/DILLINGER: John Devour 22
73 Bread BR 1118 Just Enough/We Are Neighbours 7
(see also Upsetters)

GREGORY ISAACS

70 Escort ERT 833 While There Is Life/HARRY YOUNG: Come On Over 10
70 Success RE 914 Too Late/KINGSTONIANS: You Can't Wine 8
71 Big Shot BI 584 Lonely Man/RUPIE EDWARDS ALL STARS: Lonely Man Version 8
73 Ackee ACK 522 I'm Coming Home/Version 5
73 Green Door GD 4054 Lonely Soldier/IMPACT ALL STARS: Version 8
74 Pyramid PYR 7012 Innocent People Cry/Version 8
74 Attack ATT 8081 Don't Go/Dubwise 5
75 Camel CA 2008 Lonely Days/Version 5
75 Bullet BU 555 Lonely Days/Version 5
75 Trojan TRLS 102 IN PERSON (LP) 20
(Joel Marvin, I Roy)

IKE ISAACS

74 Decca Eclipse ECS 2163 FOURTEEN GREAT T.V. THEMES (LP) 12

ISCA FAYRE

76 Candle CAN 761 THEN AROUND ME YOUNG AND OLD (LP) 15

JON ISHERWOOD

70 Decca LK/SKL 5051 A LAUGHING CRY (LP) 15

ISHMAEL & ANDY

73 Myrrh MYR 1005 READY SALTED (LP) 18

ISLAND BOYS

58 London RE-R 1122 GO CALYPSO NO. 1 (EP) 8
58 London RE-R 1123 GO CALYPSO NO. 2 (EP) 8
58 London RE-R 1124 GO CALYPSO NO. 3 (EP) 8

ISLANDERS

59 Top Rank JAR 215 The Enchanted Sea/Pollyanna 10
60 Top Rank JAR 305 Blue Train/Tornado 10

ISLANDERS

65 Fontana TF 577 It Ain't Me Babe/Four Strong Winds 10
65 Fontana TF 605 Walkin' Away/Roberta Let Your Hair Hang Down 7

JIMMY ISLE

59 London HLS 8832 Diamond Ring/I've Been Waiting 75
59 London HLS 8832 Diamond Ring/I've Been Waiting (78) 30
60 Top Rank JAR 274 Billy Boy/Oh Judy 15

ISLEY BROTHERS

59 RCA RCA 1149 Shout (Parts 1 & 2) 25
59 RCA RCA 1149 Shout (Parts 1 & 2) (78) 240
60 RCA RCA 1172 Respectable/I'm Gonna Knock On Your Door 20
60 RCA RCA 1190 How Deep Is The Ocean/He's Got The Whole World In His Hands 20
60 RCA RCA 1213 Tell Me Who/Say You Love Me Too 20
62 Stateside SS 112 Twist And Shout/Spanish Twist 18
62 Stateside SS 132 Twistin' With Linda/You Better Come Home 15
63 Stateside SS 218 Nobody But Me/I'm Laughing To Keep From Crying 18

63 United Artists UP 1034 Tango/She's Gone . . . 15
64 United Artists UP 1050 Shake It With Me Baby/Stagger Lee. . . . 18
64 Atlantic AT 4010 The Last Girl/Looking For A Love . . . 20
66 Tamla Motown TMG 555 This Old Heart Of Mine (Is Weak For You)/There's No Love Left
(1st press has narrow print on label; re-pressed 1968 with wider print). 20/10
66 Tamla Motown TMG 566 Take Some Time Out For Love/Who Could Ever Doubt My Love . . . 25
66 Tamla Motown TMG 572 I Guess I'll Always Love You/I Hear A Symphony
(1st pressing with narrow print) . . . 25/10
67 Tamla Motown TMG 606 Got To Have You Back/Just Ain't Enough Love. . . . 20
68 Tamla Motown TMG 652 Take Me In Your Arms (Rock Me A Little While)/Why When Love Is Gone . . . 18
69 Tamla Motown TMG 683 I Guess I'll Always Love You/It's Out Of The Question . . . 6
69 Tamla Motown TMG 693 Behind A Painted Smile/One Too Many Heartaches . . . 6
69 Major Minor MM 621 It's Your Thing/Don't Give It Away . . . 8
69 Tamla Motown TMG 708 Put Yourself In My Place/Little Miss Sweetness . . . 8
69 Major Minor MM 631 I Turned You On/I Know Who You Been Socking It To . . . 6
69 Tamla Motown TMG 719 Take Some Time Out For Love/Who Could Ever Doubt My Love (reissue) . . . 6
70 Stateside SS 2162 Was It Good To You?/I Got To Get Myself Together. . . . 5
71 Stateside SS 2188 Warpath/I Got To Find Me One. . . . 7
71 Stateside SS 2193 Love The One You're With/He's Got Your Love . . . 5
73 Tamla Motown TMG 877 Tell Me It's Just A Rumour, Baby/Save Me From This Misery. . . . 5
73 Epic EPC 1980 The Highways Of My Life/Don't Let Me Be Lonely Tonight. . . . 5
74 Epic EPC 2803 Need A Little Taste Of Love/If You Were There . . . 5
76 DJM DJS 640 Twist And Shout/Time After Time (reissue). . . . 5
79 RCA PC 9411 Shout/Respectable/Tell Me Who (12", p/s). . . . 8
64 RCA RCX 7149 THE ISLEY BROTHERS (EP) . . . 70
60 RCA RD 27165/SF 7055 SHOUT (LP, mono/stereo) . . . 65/90
64 United Artists ULP 1064 THE FAMOUS ISLEY BROTHERS — TWISTING AND SHOUTING (LP). . . . 80
66 Tamla Motown TML 11034 THIS OLD HEART OF MINE (IS WEAK FOR YOU) (LP, mono/stereo). . . . 35/40
68 T. Motown (S)TML 11066 SOUL ON THE ROCKS (LP) . . . 45
69 Major Minor SMLP 59 IT'S OUR THING (LP) . . . 25
69 T. Motown (S)TML 11112 BEHIND A PAINTED SMILE (LP, mono/stereo) . . . 30/25
70 Stateside SSL 10300 THE BROTHERS: ISLEY (LP). . . . 22
70 RCA Intl. INTS 1098 SHOUT (LP) . . . 12
73 Epic EPC 65740 3 + 3 (LP, gatefold sleeve) . . . 12
74 Epic EPC 80317 LIVE IT UP (LP). . . . 12
75 Epic EPC 69139 THE HEAT IS ON (LP). . . . 12
76 Epic EPC 81268 HARVEST FOR THE WORLD (LP) . . . 12

ISOLATION

73 Riverside HASLP 2083 ISOLATION (LP, private pressing with insert) . . . 400

ISOTOPE

74 Gull GULP 1002 ISOTOPE (LP). . . . 12
74 Gull GULP 1006 ILLUSION (LP) . . . 12
75 Gull GULP 1017 DEEP END (LP) . . . 12

ISRAELITES

69 Downtown DT 413 Moma Moma/Melody For Two . . . 7
69 Downtown DT 433 Seven Books/Chaka Beat . . . 7
70 J-Dan JDN 4410 Can't Help From Crying/Can't Get Used To Losing You . . . 7
(see also Music Doctors)

ITALS (Jamaica)

67 Giant GN 8 New Loving (with Soul Brothers)/I Told You Little Girl . . . 20
67 Giant GN 12 Don't Throw It Away/Make Up Your Mind (both with Carib-Beats) . . . 20
71 Big BG 325 Ba-Da-Doo-Ba-Dey/RUPIE EDWARDS ALL STARS: Version . . . 12
(see also Alton Ellis, Honeyboy)

ITALS (U.K.)

71 Black Swan BW 1404 Dawn Patrol/Whiskey Bonga (DJ and Rhythm). . . . 12
71 Black Swan BW 1407 Judgement Rock (actually by Charlie Ace)/Night West. . . . 10

ITHACA

73 Merlin HF 6 A GAME FOR ALL WHO KNOW (LP, with insert). . . . 700+
93 Background A GAME FOR ALL WHO KNOW (LP, reissue) . . . 15
(see also Friends, Alice Through The Looking Glass, Agincourt, Tomorrow Come Someday, BBC Radiophonic Workshop)

IT'S A BEAUTIFUL DAY

69 CBS 4457 White Bird/Wasted Union Blues . . . 8
70 CBS 4933 Soapstone Mountain/Do You Remember The Sun. . . . 5
73 CBS 1625 Ain't That Lovin' You Baby/Time . . . 5
69 CBS 63722 IT'S A BEAUTIFUL DAY (LP, gatefold sleeve) . . . 20
70 CBS 64065 MARRYING MAIDEN (LP). . . . 15
72 CBS 64314 CHOICE QUALITY STUFF — ANYTIME (LP) . . . 15

IT'S IMMATERIAL

84 Eternal JF 4 A Gigantic Raft In The Philipines/The Mermaid (p/s) . . . 10

IVAN

58 Coral Q 72341 Real Wild Child/Oh, You Beautiful Doll . . . 325
58 Coral Q 72341 Real Wild Child/Oh, You Beautiful Doll (78) . . . 150
(see also Jerry Allison, Crickets)

IVAN D. JUNIORS

63 Oriole CB 1874 Catch You If I Can/On My Mind . . . 15

IVANS MEADS

65 Parlophone R 5342 A Little Sympathy/The Sins Of A Family . . . 60
66 Parlophone R 5503 We'll Talk About It Tomorrow/The Bottle . . . 30

MINT VALUE £

BURL IVES

54	Columbia SCMC 5	I've Got No Use For Women/River Of Smoke (export issue)	20
56	Brunswick 05510	Ballad Of Davy Crockett/Goober Peas	10
56	Brunswick 05551	Dying Stockman/Click Go The Shears	12
56	Brunswick 05604	The Bus Stop Song/That's My Heartstrings	10
56	Decca BM 31183	Marianne/Pretty Girl (with Trinidadies) (export issue)	15
62	Brunswick 05863	A Little Bitty Tear/Shanghied	6
63	Brunswick 05868	Funny Way Of Laughin'/Mother Wouldn't Do That	7
63	HMV POP 1178	Ugly Bug Ball/On The Front Porch	6
53	Brunswick LA 8552	BALLADS AND FOLK SONGS VOL. 2 (10" LP)	15
53	Brunswick LA 8583	BALLADS AND FOLK SONGS VOL. 1 (10" LP)	15
54	Brunswick LA 8633	FOLK SONGS — DRAMATIC AND HUMOROUS (10" LP)	20
54	Brunswick LA 8641	WOMEN (10" LP)	10
55	Brunswick LAT 8048	CORONATION CONCERT (LP)	15
56	Brunswick LA 8739	AUSTRALIAN FOLK SONGS (10" LP)	20
56	Brunswick LAT 8142	DOWN TO THE SEA IN SHIPS (LP)	15
60	Brunswick LAT 8344	SONGS OF IRELAND (LP)	12
61	Brunswick LAT 8381	THE VERSATILE BURL IVES (LP)	12
62	Brunswick LAT 8395	SONGS OF THE WEST (LP)	12
62	Brunswick LAT 8404	FUNNY WAY OF LAUGHIN' (LP, also stereo STA 3063)	12/15
63	Brunswick LAT 8517	SUNSHINE IN MY SOUL (LP)	15
63	Brunswick LAT/STA 8554	SINGIN' EASY (LP, mono/stereo)	12/15
64	Brunswick LAT 8591	PEARLY SHELLS (LP)	12
66	Brunswick LAT 8665	SOMETHING SPECIAL (LP)	12
60s	American Heritage AH 14	IN THE QUIET OF THE NIGHT (LP)	15
60s	Herald LLR 528	SINGS WITH CHILDREN (LP)	15
60s	MCA Coral CDL 8008	JUNIOR CHOICE (LP)	12
60s	CBS BPG 62588	THE WAYFARING STRANGER (LP)	12
60s	CBS 31717	THE TIMES THEY ARE A-CHANGING (LP)	15
60s	Polydor 3187094	LIVE IN EUROPE (LP)	15
60s	WRC T 302	SING FAITH & JOY (LP)	12
60s	Word TWE 6001	BRIGHT & BEAUTIFUL (LP)	12
60s	Coral CP 31	CORONATION CONCERT (LP)	20
60s	Brunswick LAT 8577	TRUE LOVE (LP)	15
60s	Brunswick LAT 8142	SINGS DOWN TO THE SEA IN SHIPS (LP)	20

IVEYS

68	Apple APPLE 5	Maybe Tomorrow/And Her Daddy's A Millionaire	45
69	Apple APPLE 14	Dear Angie/No Escaping Your Love (unreleased; Europe & Japan only)	
68	Apple SAPCOR 8	MAYBE TOMORROW (LP, unissued; Europe & Japan only)	
92	Apple SAPCOR 8	MAYBE TOMORROW (LP, reissue, gatefold sleeve & bonus 12" [SAPCOR 82])	25
92	Apple SAPCOR 8	MAYBE TOMORROW (CD)	30

(see also Badfinger, Pleasure Garden)

IVOR & SHEILA

81	Eron 027	CHANGING TIMES (LP, with insert)	30

IVORIES

85	Kent TOWN 103	Please Stay/TOMMY HUNT: The Work Song	8

(see also Tommy Hunt)

JACKIE IVORY

66	Atlantic AT 4075	Hi-Heel Sneakers/Do It To Death	20
65	Atlantic ATL 5046	SOUL DISCOVERY (LP, reissued in 1966)	60/18

IVY LEAGUE

64	Piccadilly 7N 35200	What More Do You Want?/Wait A Minute	12
65	Piccadilly 7N 35222	Funny How Love Can Be/Lonely Room	6
65	Piccadilly 7N 35228	That's Why I'm Crying/A Girl Like You	6
65	Piccadilly 7N 35251	Tossing And Turning/Graduation Day	6
65	Piccadilly 7N 35267	Our Love Is Slipping Away/I Could Make You Fall In Love	5
66	Piccadilly 7N 35294	Running Round In Circles/Rain Rain Go Away	6
66	Piccadilly 7N 35326	Willow Tree/One Day	10
66	Piccadilly 7N 35348	My World Fell Down/When You're Young	15
67	Piccadilly 7N 35365	Four And Twenty Hours/Arrivederci Baby	6
67	Piccadilly 7N 35397	Suddenly Things/Tomorrow Is Another Day	7
67	Pye 7N 17386	Thank You For Loving Me/In The Not Too Distant Future	10
65	Piccadilly NEP 34038	FUNNY HOW LOVE CAN BE (EP)	25
65	Piccadilly NEP 34042	TOSSING AND TURNING (EP)	22
65	Piccadilly NEP 34046	THE HOLLY AND THE IVY LEAGUE (EP)	30
66	Piccadilly NEP 34048	OUR LOVE IS SLIPPING AWAY (EP)	40
65	Piccadilly NPL 38015	THIS IS THE IVY LEAGUE (LP)	40

(see also Carter-Lewis, White Plains, Edison Lighthouse, Flowerpot Men, Kestrels, One & One, Johnny Shadow, Perry Ford, First Class, Friends, Warm Sensations)

IVY THREE

60	London HLW 9178	Yogi/Was Judy There	18

IZZY POUND

69	Plexium PXM 9	Pumpkin Miny/Na Na Na Na	50

CLUE J. & HIS BLUES BLASTERS

60 Blue Beat BB 15 — Easy Snappin'/Goin' Home (with vocal by Theophilus Beckford) . . . 35
61 Blue Beat BB 37 — Lovers' Jive/Wicked And Dreadful (actually with Neville Esson) . . . 35
61 Blue Beat BB 60 — Little Willie/Pine Juice . . . 30

DAVID J. (& J. WALKERS)

81 4AD AD 112 — Nothing/Armour (as David Jay & René Halkett) (p/s, with lyric sheet) . . . 6
(see also Bauhaus)

HARRY J. ALL STARS

(see under 'H')

TONY J.

75 Stonehouse 001 — Telephone Line/Telephone Version . . . 5

BILLY JACK (& CIMARONS)

70 Grape GR 3018 — Let's Work Together/CORPORATION: Jam Monkey . . . 7
70 Big Shot BI 558 — Once A Man/Soul Mood (as Billy Jack & Cimarons) . . . 7
70 Big Shot BI 559 — Bet Your Life I Do/CANDY & CIMARONS: Ace Of Hearts . . . 7
(see also Candy)

BOBBY JACK

59 Top Rank JAR 190 — Tempting Me/Early Mornin' . . . 8

JACK (Bernard) & BEANSTALKS

69 Supreme SUP 203 — Work It Up/Chatty Chatty . . . 12
(see also Kingstonians)

JACKAL

86 Crim. Damage CRI 12-134 — Underneath The Arches/Thunder Machine (12", p/s) . . . 15
(see also Renegade Soundwave)

JACKIE & BRIDIE

68 Major Minor MM 562 — Come Me Little Son/We Only Needed Time . . . 6
64 Fontana TL 5212 — HOLD BACK THE DAWN (LP) . . . 25
70 Concord CONS 1002 — FOLK WORLD OF JACKIE AND BRIDIE (LP) . . . 15
71 Galliard GAL 4009 — THE PERFECT ROUND (LP) . . . 15
70s Nevis NEV LP 102 — HELLO FRIEND (LP, as Jacqui & Bridie) . . . 12
(see also Jacqueline & Bridie)

JACKIE & DOREEN

64 Ska Beat JB 168 — Every Beat Of My Heart . . . 20
65 Ska Beat JB 209 — The New Vow/Adorable You . . . 20
(see also Doreen Shaffer, Jackie Opel)

JACKIE (Edwards) & MILLIE (Small)

65 Island WI 253 — This Is My Story/SOUND SYSTEM: Never Again . . . 25
66 Island WI 265 — My Desire/MILLIE: That's How Strong My Love Is . . . 25
67 Island WIP 6012 — In A Dream/Ooh Ooh . . . 20
67 Island ILP 941 — PLEDGING MY LOVE (LP, as Jackie Edwards & Millie Small) . . . 100
68 Island ILP 963 — THE BEST OF JACKIE AND MILLIE VOLUME TWO (LP) . . . 90
70 Trojan TTL 52 — THE BEST OF JACKIE AND MILLIE VOLUME TWO (LP, reissue) . . . 18
70 Trojan TBL 155 — JACKIE & MILLIE (LP) . . . 18
(see also Wilfred & Millicent, Jackie Edwards, Millie)

JACKIE & RAINDROPS

(see under Jackie Lee & Raindrops)

JACKIE & ROY

58 Vogue V 9101 — You Smell So Good/Let's Take A Walk Around The Block . . . 50
58 Vogue V 9101 — You Smell So Good/Let's Take A Walk Around The Block (78) . . . 25
59 Vogue VE 1-70131 — JACKIE AND ROY (EP) . . . 30
58 Vogue VA 1-60111 — JACKIE AND ROY (LP) . . . 40

ALEXANDER JACKSON & TURNKEYS

65 Sue WI 386 — The Whip/Tell It Like It Is (actually "Flea Pot"/"Sweetie Lester" by Lala Wilson) . . 50

BO WEAVIL JACKSON

59 Jazz Collector JDL 127 — Some Scream High Yellow/Why Do You Moan? . . . 6

BULLMOOSE JACKSON & HIS ORCHESTRA

53 Vogue V 2129 — Nosey Joe/I Know Who Threw The Whisky In The Well (78) . . . 25

CHAD JACKSON

90 Big Wave BWRT — Hear The Drummer Get Wicked (12") . . . 8

CHRIS JACKSON

69 Soul City SC 112 — I'll Never Forget You/Forever I'll Stay With You . . . 25
70 Soul City SC 120 — Since There's No Doubt/We Will Be Together (unissued)

MINT VALUE £

CHUCK JACKSON

61	Top Rank JAR 564	I Don't Want To Cry/Just Once	40
62	Top Rank JAR 607	The Breaking Point/My Willow Tree	35
62	Stateside SS 102	Any Day Now/ED BRUCE: The Prophet	22
62	Stateside SS 127	I Keep Forgettin'/Who's Gonna Pick Up The Pieces	22
63	Stateside SS 171	Tell Him I'm Not Home/Getting Ready For The Heartbreak	25
64	Pye International 7N 25247	Beg Me/For All Time	20
64	Pye International 7N 25276	Any Day Now/The Prophet (reissue)	20
65	Pye International 7N 25287	Since I Don't Have You/Hand It Over	60
65	Pye International 7N 25301	I Need You/Chuck's Soul Brothers Twist	18
65	Pye International 7N 25321	If I Didn't Love You/Just A Little Bit Of Your Soul	18
66	Pye International 7N 25384	Chains Of Love/I Keep Forgettin'	50
67	Pye International 7N 25439	Shame On Me/Candy	30
68	Tamla Motown TMG 651	Girls, Girls, Girls/(You Can't Let The Boy Overpower) The Man In You	15
70	Tamla Motown TMG 729	Honey Come Back/What Am I Gonna Do Without You	10
73	Probe PRO 595	I Only Get The Feeling/Slowly But Surely	20
74	Probe PRO 617	I Can't Break Away/Just A Little Tear	6
75	All Platinum 6146 310	I've Got The Need/Beautiful Woman	6
75	Disco Demand DDS 116	These Chains Of Love/Any Day Now	10
85	Kent TOWN 104	Hand It Over/CANDY & KISSES: Mr Creator (withdrawn)	10
80s	Inferno SIN 1	Chains Of Love/Good Things Come To Those Who Wait/Hand It Over/ Any Day Now	20
66	Pye Intl. NPL 28082	TRIBUTE TO RHYTHM AND BLUES (LP)	50
68	T. Motown (S)TML 11071	CHUCK JACKSON ARRIVES! (LP)	70
69	T. Motown (S)TML 11117	GOIN' BACK TO CHUCK JACKSON (LP)	45
72	Probe SPB 1084	THROUGH ALL TIMES (LP)	25
74	Anchor ABCL 5040	THROUGH ALL TIMES (LP, reissue)	12

(see also Del[l]-Vikings)

CHUCK JACKSON & MAXINE BROWN

65	Pye International 7N 25308	Something You Got/Baby Take Me	25
65	Pye Intl. NPL 28091	SAYING SOMETHING (LP)	50

(see also Maxine Brown, Tammi Terrell)

DEON JACKSON

66	Atlantic AT 4070	Love Makes The World Go Round/You Said You Loved Me	30
66	Atlantic 584 012	Love Takes A Long Time Growing/Hush Little Baby	20
68	Atlantic 584 159	Ooh Baby/All On A Sunny Day	25
76	Contempo CS 9031	Love Makes The World Go Round/I Can't Go On	12

EARL JACKSON

76	ABC ABC 4110	Soul Self Satisfaction/Looking Thru' The Eyes Of Love	5

GEORGE JACKSON

69	Capitol CL 15605	Find 'Em, Fool 'Em And Forget 'Em/My Desires Are Getting The Best Of Me	18
72	London HLU 10373	Aretha, Sing One For Me/I'm Gonna Wait	6
73	London HLU 10413	Let 'Em Know You Care/Patricia	7

GORDON JACKSON

69	Marmalade 598 010	Me And My Zoo/A Day At The Cottage	10
69	Marmalade 598 021	Song For Freedom/Sing To Me Woman	10
69	Marmalade 608 012	THINKING BACK (LP)	80

(see also Traffic)

HAROLD JACKSON & TORNADOES

58	Vogue V 9105	Move It On Down The Line Parts 1 & 2	120
58	Vogue V 9105	Move It On Down The Line Parts 1 & 2 (78)	60

JACKIE JACKSON

74	T. Motown STML 11249	JACKIE JACKSON (LP)	15

(see also Jacksons, Jackson 5)

JANET JACKSON

SINGLES

83	A&M AMS 8303	Come Give Your Love To Me/The Magic Is Working (p/s)	8
83	A&M AMSX 8303	Come Give Your Love To Me/The Magic Is Working (12", p/s)	12
83	A&M AM 112	Don't Mess Up This Good Thing/Young Love (p/s)	8
83	A&M AMX 112	Don't Mess Up This Good Thing/Young Love/Forever Yours (12", p/s)	12
86	A&M AMS 337	When I Think Of You/Come Give Your Love To Me/ What Have You Done For Me Lately/Young Love (clear vinyl/picture disc double pack in PVC foldout cover)	12
86	A&M AMS 359	Control/Pretty Boy (p/s, with free cassette ["Nasty (Cool Summer Mix)"])	10
87	Breakout USAD 601	Let's Wait A While/Nasty (Cool Summer Mix Pt. 1)//Nasty (Original Mix)/ Control/Let's Wait A While (Remix)/Nasty (Cool Summer Mix Part 1 Fade) (picture disc/clear vinyl double pack in PVC foldout sleeve)	10
87	Breakout USAS 613	Funny How Time Flies (When You're Having Fun)/When I Think Of You (poster p/s)	5
89	Breakout USACD 663	Miss You Much (Mamma Mix 3.55)/Miss You Much (Mamma Mix 7.22)/ You Need Me (CD)	10
89	Breakout USACD 673	Rhythm Nation (7" Edit)/(12" House Nation Mix)/(12" United Dub) (CD)	10
90	Breakout USAB 681	Come Back To Me (7" I'm Beggin' You Mix)/Alright (7" R&B mix) (box set with metal badge & foldout poster)	6
90	Breakout USACD 681	Come Back To Me (7" I'm Beggin' You Mix)/Alright (7" R + B Mix)/ Alright (7" House Mix With Rap) (CD)	10
90	Breakout USAP 684	Escapade (We've Got It Made 7")/Escapade (Housecapade 7") (picture disc with photo & discography)	5
90	Breakout USAS 693	Alright (House Mix)/Vuelve A Mi (Come Back To Me) (shaped picture disc with plinth in printed PVC sleeve)	8

PROMOS

95 AMPM AMPMDJ 25 — Runaway (Factory Mix)/When I Think Of You (Heller & Farley Project Mix)/ Runaway (Factory Dub)/When I Think Of You (Junior Trackhead Joint)/ Runaway (Tribal Dub) (12", company sleeve) . . . 10
96 AMPM 581 697-1 — The Best Things In Life Are Free (The S-Man Salsoul Vibe)/(K-Klass 12")/ (K-Klass 7")/(Roger's Nasty Dub)/(Roger's Ill Dub)/(Roger's Deep Dub)/ (Bonus Beats) (12", with Luther Vandross, double pack, co. sleeve) . . . 10
97 Virgin VSTXDJ 1666 — Got 'Til It's Gone (Def Club Mix)/(Armand Van Helden Speedy Garagez Mix) (Def The Bass Mix)/(Def Instrumental)/(Armand Van Helden Bonus Beats) (12", double pack, title stickered sleeve) . . . 15
97 Virgin VSTDJ 1670 — Together Again: Tony Humphries Remixes/(Tony Humphries Club Mix)/ (Tony Humphries 12" Edit Mix)/(Tony Humphries FBI Dub)/ (Tony Humphries White And Black Dub) (12", title stickered sleeve) . . . 8
97 Virgin VSTDJ 1683 — I Get Lonely (Janet Vs Jason — The Club Remix)/(Janet Vs Jason — The Remix Sessions — Part 2)/(Jason's Special Sauce Dub)/ (LP Version) (12", title stickered sleeve) . . . 8

JANET JACKSON & CLIFF RICHARD

84 A&M AM 210 — Two To The Power Of Love/JANET JACKSON: Rock'n'Roll (p/s) . . . 25
84 A&M AMX 210 — Two To The Power Of Love/JANET JACKSON: Rock'n'Roll/Don't Mess Up This Good Thing (12", p/s) . . . 25

(see also Cliff Richard)

JERMAINE JACKSON

84 Epic JMJDJ 1 — Tell Me I'm Not Dreamin' (Too Good To Be True) (with Michael Jackson)/ Come To Me/Oh Mother (promo only) . . . 30
85 Arista ARIST 609 — Do What You Do/Tell Me I'm Not Dreamin' (Too Good To Be True) (last track with Michael Jackson) (p/s) . . . 5
85 Arista ARIST 12609 — Do What You Do/Tell Me I'm Not Dreamin' (Too Good To Be True) (last track with Michael Jackson) (12", p/s) . . . 8

(see also Jacksons, Jackson 5, Michael Jackson)

JERRY JACKSON

63 London HLR 9689 — Gypsy Eyes/Turn Back . . . 30
66 Cameo Parkway P 100 — It's Rough Out There/I'm Gonna Paint A Picture . . . 175

JIM JACKSON

66 RCA RCX 7182 — R.C.A. VICTOR RACE SERIES VOL. 7 (EP) . . . 18

JIMMY JACKSON('S ROCK 'N' ROLL SKIFFLE)

57 Columbia DB 3898 — California Zephyr/I Shall Not Be Moved . . . 22
57 Columbia DB 3937 — Sittin' In The Balcony/Good Morning Blues . . . 35
57 Columbia DB 3937 — Sittin' In The Balcony/Good Morning Blues (78) . . . 8
57 Columbia DB 3957 — River Line/Lonely Road . . . 18
57 Columbia DB 3988 — White Silver Sands/Build Your Love (On A Strong Foundation) (solo) . . . 10
58 Columbia DB 4085 — Love-A Love-A Love A/Photographs (solo) . . . 10
58 Columbia DB 4085 — Love-A Love-A Love A/Photographs (solo) (78) . . . 8
58 Columbia DB 4153 — Swing Down, Sweet Chariot/This Little Light Of Mine (solo) . . . 8
58 Columbia DB 4153 — Swing Down, Sweet Chariot/This Little Light Of Mine (78, solo) . . . 12
58 Columbia SEG 7750 — ROCK 'N' SKIFFLE (EP) . . . 75
58 Columbia SEG 7768 — COUNTRY AND BLUES (EP) . . . 80

J.J. JACKSON (& Greatest Little Soul Band In The Land)

67 Polydor 56718 — But It's Alright/Do The Boogaloo . . . 15
67 Strike JH 329 — Come See Me/Try Me . . . 15
67 Warner Bros WB 2082 — Sho Nuff (Got A Good Thing Going)/Here We Go Again . . . 10
68 Warner Bros WB 2090 — Down, But Not Out/Why Does It Take So Long? . . . 10
68 Warner Bros WB 6029 — Courage Ain't Strength/You Do It 'Cause You Wanna . . . 10
69 Warner Bros WB 7276 — Ain't Too Proud To Beg/But It's Alright . . . 10
71 Mojo 2092 014 — But It's Alright/Do The Boogaloo . . . 10
67 Strike JLH 104 — J.J. JACKSON WITH THE GREATEST LITTLE SOUL BAND (LP) . . . 35
69 MCA SKA 100 — GREATEST LITTLE SOUL BAND (LP) . . . 25
70 RCA Victor SF 8093 — J.J. JACKSON'S DILEMMA (LP) . . . 22

(see also Greatest Little Soul Band)

J.J. JACKSON/LINDA JONES

77 Loma/Warners K 56271 — THIS IS LOMA — VOL. 7 (LP, 1 side each) . . . 15

LEVI JACKSON

71 Columbia DB 8807 — This Beautiful Day/Don't You Be A Sinner . . . 50

(see also Solomon King)

LLOYD JACKSON

71 Pama Supreme PS 308 — Cracklin' Rosie/Little Deeds Of Kindness (B-side with Scorpions) . . . 6

MAHALIA JACKSON

51 Vogue V 301 — Since The Fire Started Burning In My Soul/In My Home Over There (78) . . . 8
51 Vogue V 302 — The Last Mile Of The Way/I'm Glad Salvation Is Free (78) . . . 7
52 Vogue V 305 — I Do, Don't You/Silent Night, Holy Night (78) . . . 8
52 Vogue V 306 — I Gave Up/Silent Night, Holy Night (78) . . . 7
55 Philips BB 2005 — A Rusty Old Halo/The Treasures Of Love (78, export issue) . . . 10
58 Philips PB 869 — For My Good Fortune/Have You Any Rivers . . . 5
58 Philips PB 869 — For My Good Fortune/Have You Any Rivers? (78) . . . 15
59 Philips PB 933 — Trouble Of The World/Tell The World About This . . . 5
60 Philips PB 1040 — Onward Christian Soldiers/The Lord's Prayer . . . 5
60 Vogue V 2418 — The Lord's Prayer/Bless This House . . . 5
60 Top Rank JKP 2038 — IN THE UPPER ROOM VOLUME 1 (EP) . . . 8
60 Top Rank JKP 2048 — IN THE UPPER ROOM VOLUME 2 (EP) . . . 8
52 Vogue LDE 005 — MAHALIA JACKSON (10" LP) . . . 35
59 Philips BBL 7289 — NEWPORT 1958 (LP, also stereo SBBL 547) . . . 12/15
60 Top Rank 30/006 — JUST AS I AM (LP) . . . 15

			MINT VALUE £
60	Philips BBL 7362	GREAT GETTIN' UP MORNING (LP)	12
60	Philips BBL 7391	THE POWER AND THE GLORY (LP, also stereo SBBL 576)	12/15
60	Philips BBL 7435	COME ON CHILDREN LET'S SING (LP)	15
61	Philips BBL 7456	I BELIEVE (LP, also stereo SBBL 610)	12/15

MICHAEL JACKSON

SINGLES

72	Tamla Motown TMG 797	Got To Be There/Maria (You Were The Only One)	5
72	Tamla Motown TMG 816	Rockin' Robin/Love Is Here And Now You're Gone	8
72	Tamla Motown TMG 826	Ain't No Sunshine/I Wanna Be Where You Are	5
72	Tamla Motown TMG 834	Ben/You Can Cry On My Shoulder	8
73	Tamla Motown TMG 863	Morning Glow/My Girl	5
74	Tamla Motown TMG 900	Music And Me/Johnny Raven	5
75	Tamla Motown TMG 946	One Day In Your Life/With A Child's Heart	5
75	Tamla Motown TMG 1006	Just A Little Bit Of You/Dear Michael	5
79	Epic S EPC 7135	You Can't Win (Part 1)/You Can't Win (Part 2) (picture disc)	12
79	Epic 12EPC 7135	You Can't Win (Part 1)/You Can't Win (Part 2) (12")	10
79	Epic 12EPC 7763	Don't Stop 'Til You Get Enough/I Can't Help It (12")	8
79	Epic 12EPC 8206	Rock With You/Get On The Floor/You Can't Win (Extended) (12")	8
81	Motown TMG 977	We're Almost There/We've Got A Good Thing Going (p/s)	5
81	Motown TMGT 977	We're Almost There (Album Version)/We've Got A Good Thing Going (12")	8
82	Epic EPCA 11-2729	The Girl Is Mine (with Paul McCartney)/ Can't Get Outta The Rain (picture disc)	15
83	Epic EPC 2906	GREATEST ORIGINAL HITS: Don't Stop 'Til You Get Enough/ She's Out Of My Life/Off The Wall/Rock With You (EP)	15
83	Epic EPCA 40-2906	GREATEST ORIGINAL HITS: Don't Stop 'Til You Get Enough/ She's Out Of My Life/Off The Wall/Rock With You (EP, cassette)	8
83	Motown TMG 986	Happy (Love Theme From 'Lady Sings The Blues')/We're Almost There (poster or standard p/s)	8/4
83	Motown EPCA 112729	Happy (Love Theme From 'Lady Sings The Blues')/We're Almost There (picture disc)	10
83	Motown CTME 2035	MOTOWN FLIP HITS — MICHAEL JACKSON: One Day In Your Life/ Got To Be There/Ben/Ain't No Sunshine (EP, cassette)	10
83	Motown M6077C	Got To Be There/Ben (cassette)	6
83	Epic EPCA 3643	Thriller/JACKSONS: Things I Do For You (live) (poster p/s)	8
83	Epic TA 3643	Thriller (Album Version)/Thriller (Remix Short Version)/JACKSONS: Things I Do For You (live) (12", 'calendar' p/s)	50
83	Epic MJ 1 (1-9)	MICHAEL JACKSON'S 9 SINGLES PACK (9 x 7", p/s, each on red vinyl, in PVC foldout wallet)	35
84	Motown TMGT 1342	Farewell My Summer Love (Extended)/Call On Me (12", die-cut sleeve)	8
84	Motown TMGT 1355	Girl You're So Together (Album Version)/Touch The One You Love/Ben/ Ain't No Sunshine (12")	8
84	Epic A 3910	P.Y.T. (Pretty Young Thing)/Working Day And Night (p/s, 2nd issue)	7
84	Epic EPC 450 127-4	THE 12" MIXES: Billie Jean/Beat It/Wanna Be Startin' Somethin'/Thriller/ P.Y.T. (Pretty Young Thing) (cassette)	8
84	Arista JMJDJ 1	Tell Me I'm Not Dreamin' (Too Good To Be True)/JERMAINE JACKSON: Come To Me/Oh Mother (promo only)	25
87	Epic 650 202-0	I Just Can't Stop Loving You (with Siedah Garratt)/Baby Be Mine (poster p/s)	10
87	Epic 650 202-6	I Just Can't Stop Loving You (with Siedah Garratt)/Baby Be Mine (12", p/s with poster)	15
87	Epic 651 100-4	Bad (Dance Extended Mix)/Bad (Dub Version)/Bad (A Capella) (cassette)	7
87	Epic 651 155-6	Bad (Dance Extended Mix With False Fade)/Bad (7" Single Mix)/Bad (Dance Radio Edit)Bad (Dub)/Bad (A Cappella) (12", p/s, red vinyl)	18
87	Epic 651 275-7	The Way You Make Me Feel/The Way You Make Me Feel (Instrumental) (p/s, with competition leaflet, stickered sleeve)	5
87	Epic 651 275-3	The Way You Make Me Feel (7" Mix)/(A Cappella)/(Dance Radio Edit)/ (Dub)/(Get Into The Groove — Put Either Side On The Turntable, Lower The Arm And See Which Your Needle Pix) (12, p/s, double-groove)	20
87	Epic 651 275-9	The Way You Make Me Feel (Dance Extended Mix)/The Way You Make Me Feel (Dub Version)/The Way You Make Me Feel (A Cappella) (CD, card p/s)	22
88	Epic 651 388-9	Man In The Mirror (Single Mix)/Man In The Mirror (Instrumental) (square-shaped picture disc)	15
88	Epic 651 388-2	Man In The Mirror (4.55)/Man In The Mirror (Album Mix)/ Man In The Mirror (Instrumental) (CD, card sleeve)	20
88	Epic 651 388-2	Man In The Mirror/Man In The Mirror (Album Mix)/Man In The Mirror (Instrumental) (3" CD with adaptor, card sleeve)	25
88	Epic 651 546-7	Dirty Diana/Dirty Diana (p/s, with 13" cardboard figure)	12
88	Epic 652 864-6	Dirty Diana/Dirty Diana (Instrumental)/Bad (Extended Dance Mix With False Fade) (12", with tour poster p/s)	15
88	Epic 651 546-9	Dirty Diana (4.42)/Dirty Diana (Instrumental)/Bad (Dance Extended Mix Includes "False Fade") (CD, card p/s)	22
88	Epic 651 546-2	Dirty Diana (4.42)/Dirty Diana (Instrumental)/Dirty Diana (Album Version) (3" CD with adaptor, card p/s)	22
88	Epic MJ 5	THE MICHAEL JACKSON BAD SOUVENIR SINGLES PACK (5 x 7" square picture discs in foldout PVC wallet, with lyric book)	40
88	Epic 652 844-9	Another Part Of Me/(Instrumental) (p/s, with Bad tour backstage pass)	12
88	Epic 652 844-0	Another Part Of Me/Another Part Of Me (Instrumental) (poster p/s)	10
88	Epic 652 844-2	Another Part Of Me (Extended Dance Mix)/(Radio Edit)/(Drum Mix)/ (A Capella) (CD, card p/s)	22
88	Epic 652 844-3	Another Part Of Me (Extended Dance Mix)/(Radio Edit)/(Dub Mix)/ (Instrumental) (3" CD with adaptor, card p/s)	22
88	Epic 653 004-2	Another Part Of Me (Extended Dance Mix)/Another Part Of Me (Radio Edit) Another Part Of Me (Drum Mix)/Another Part Of Me (A Cappella) (CD, pic disc)	30
88	Epic 653 026-0	Smooth Criminal/Smooth Criminal (Instrumental) (pack with 4 postcards)	15
88	Epic 653 170-6	Smooth Criminal (Extended Dance Mix)/ Smooth Criminal Extended (Dance Mix Dub Mix)/Smooth Criminal (A Cappella) (12" w/'Moonwalker' advent calendar)	20

MINT VALUE £

88 Epic 653 026-2 Smooth Criminal (Extended Dance Mix)/Smooth Criminal ("Annie" Mix)/ Smooth Criminal (A Cappella) (CD, card p/s) . . . 22
89 Epic 654 672-0 Leave Me Alone/Human Nature (pop-up p/s) . . . 25
89 Epic 654 672-4 Leave Me Alone/Don't Stop 'Til You Get Enough/Human Nature (cassette, 'Moonwalker' fold-out card slip case) . . . 8
89 Epic 654 672-2 Leave Me Alone (4.40)/Don't Stop 'Til You Get Enough (3.55)/Human Nature (4.05)/Wanna Be Startin' Something (Extended 6.30) (CD, card sleeve) . . . 20
89 Epic 654 672-3 Leave Me Alone (4.40)/Don't Stop 'Til You Get Enough (6.04)/ Human Nature (4.05) (3" CD, gatefold card sleeve) . . . 22
89 Tamla Motown MOTD7 0005 VINTAGE GOLD (3" CD EP, gatefold card sleeve, with Jackson 5) . . . 10
89 Epic 654 947-9 Liberian Girl (Edit)/Girlfriend (star mobile foldout card pack) . . . 15
89 Epic 654 947-4 Liberian Girl (Edit)/Girlfriend (cassette) . . . 6
89 Epic 654 947-2 Liberian Girl (Edit 3.39)/Girlfriend/The Lady In My Life/Get On The Floor (CD, card p/s) . . . 22
89 Epic 654 947-3 Liberian Girl (Edit 3.39)/Get On The Floor/Girlfriend (3" CD, g/fold card p/s) . . . 22
92 Epic MJ 4 (658 281-1/4) TOUR SOUVENIR PACK (CD, 4-picture disc, box set with booklet) . . . 40
92 Epic 658 360-7 Jam (7" Edit)/Beat It (Moby's Sub Mix) ('picture frame' pack with 2 prints) . . . 7
95 Epic 662 022 Scream (Single Edit)/Childhood (p/s, with 2 page lyric insert) . . . 10
95 Epic 662 127 Scream (Def Radio Mix)/Scream (Single Edit) (limited edition poster sleeve) . . . 7
96 Epic 662 950 They Don't Care About Us (Single Edit 4:43)/They Don't Care About Us (Love To Infinity's Walk In The Park Radio Mix) (jukebox issue, white labels, no p/s) . . . 15
96 Epic 662 950 They Don't Care About Us (LP Edit 4:10)/They Don't Care About Us (Love To Infinity's Walk In The Park Radio Mix) (jukebox issue, white labels, no p/s) . . . 15
97 Epic 663 787 Stranger In Moscow/Stranger In Moscow (Version) (jukebox issue, white labels, no p/s) . . . 10
97 Epic 664 462 Blood On The Dancefloor/Mix (jukebox issue, white labels, no p/s) . . . 10
97 Epic 664 796 History/Ghosts (jukebox issue, white labels, no p/s) . . . 20
97 Epic no cat. no. Smile (CD, withdrawn) . . . 500

PROMOS

92 Epic XPR 1733 Remember The Time: (12" Main Mix)/(New Jack Mix)/(New Jack Main Mix)/ (Silky Soul 12" Mix)/(Silky Soul Dub)/(E-Smoov's Late Nite Mix) (12", company sleeve) . . . 8
92 Epic XPR 1814 Jam: (More Than Enuff Mix)/(Roger's Club Mix)/(E-Smoov Jazzy Jam)/ (Atlanta Techno Mix)/(Roger's Underground Mix)/(Silky 12")/ (More Than Enuff Dub)/(Maurice's Jammin' Dub Mix)/(Roger's Club Dub)/ (Atlanta Techno Dub)/(Roger's Slam Jam Mix)/(Silky Dub)/(A Cappella Mix) (12", double pack, black & orange stickered white sleeve) . . . 25
92 Epic XPR 1797 Who Is It (Patience Mix)/(Patience Beats)/(Most Patient Mix)/(HIS Mix)/ (The P-Man Dub) (12", company sleeve) . . . 10
95 Epic XPR 2265 The Classic Remix Series: Wanna Be Startin' Something (Brothers In Rhythm Mix)/(Tommy D's Main Mix) (12", plain sleeve, sealed with title sticker) . . . 15
95 Epic XPR 2266 DMC Megamix (15.40)/(11.18) (12", custom sleeve) . . . 15
95 Epic XPR 2229 The Classic Remix Series: Rock With You (Frankie's Favorite Club Mix)/ (The Masters At Work Remix) (12", plain sleeve, sealed with title sticker) . . . 12
95 Epic XPCD 7222 The Classic Remix Series: Rock With You (Frankie's Favorite Club Mix Radio Edit)/(Frankie's Favorite Club Mix) (CD) . . . 20
95 Epic XPR 2184 Scream: (Classic Club Mix)/(DM R&B Extended Mix)/(Def Radio Mix)/ (Naughty Main Mix)/(Naughty Main Mix No Rap)/(Dave 'Jam' Hall's Extended Urban Remix)/(Pressurized Dub Part 1)/(Pressurized Dub Part 2)/ (Album Version)/(Single Edit No. 2)/(Naughty Pretty-Pella)/ (Naughty A Cappella) (12", double pack, red title sleeve) . . . 20
96 Epic XPR 2207 Mj Club Megamix (MJ Mega Remix)/(MJ Urban Megamix) (12", blue & purple title sleeve) . . . 15
96 Epic XPR 3020 They Don't Care About Us (The Love To Infinity Mixes): Classic Paradise Mix/ Anthem Of Love/Classic Dub/Anthem Of love Dub/Hacienda Mix (12", p/s) . . . 10
96 Epic XPR 3030 They Don't Care About Us (The R&B Mixes): Track Masters Remix/ Dallas Austin Main Mix/Charles' Full Dirty Mix/LP Edit/Love To Infinity's Walk In The Park/Track Masters' Instrumental (12", p/s) . . . 10
96 Epic XPR 3033 The Classic Remix Series: Don't Stop Til You Get Enough (Roger's Underground Solution Mix)/Beat It (Moby's Sub Mix) (12", plain sleeve sealed with title sticker) . . . 8
96 Epic SAMPCD 3598 This Time Around (DM Radio Mix)/(Dallas Radio Remix)/(Maurice's Club Around Radio Mix)/(Maurice's Hip Hop Around Mix)/ (David Mitson Clean Edit) (CD) . . . 60
97 Epic XPCD 2176 HIStory (Mix 1)/Ghosts/(HIStory (Mix 2) HIStory (Mix 3)/HIStory (Mix 4) (CD) . . . 15
97 Epic XPR 3125 Blood On The Dancefloor (TM's Switchblade Mix)/(TM's O-Postive Dub) (12", blue title p/s) . . . 8
97 Epic XPR 3136 Blood On The Dancefloor (Refugee Camp Mix)/(7" Version) (12", green title p/s) . . 8
97 Epic XPR 3149 HIStory (Marks! Philly Vocal)/(Marks! Future Dub) (12", yellow title sleeve) . . . 8
97 Epic XPR 3159 HIStory (Tony Moran's HIStory Lesson)/(Tony Moran's HIStorical Dub)
97 Epic XPR 3168 Is It Scary (Eddie's Love Mix)/(Eddie's Rub-A-Dub Mix)/(Eddie's Love Mix)/ (Radio Edit) (12", white embossed title p/s) . . . 30
97 Epic XPR 3169 HIStory (Ummah Urban Mix)/(Ummah Radio Mix)/(Tony Moran's 7" HIStory Lesson Edit)/(Ummah DJ Mix) (12", green title sleeve) . . . 8
97 Epic XPR 3196 Is It Scary (Deep Dish Dark & Scary Remix)/(Deep Dish Double-O-Jazz Dub)/ (Deep Dish Dark & Scary Remix)/(Radio Edit) (12", black embossed title p/s) . . . 35

ALBUMS

72 Tamla Motown STML 11205 GOT TO BE THERE (LP) . . . 12
73 Tamla Motown STML 11220 BEN (LP) . . . 12
73 Tamla Motown STML 11235 MUSIC AND ME (LP) . . . 12
75 Tamla Motown STMA 8022 FOREVER, MICHAEL (LP, gatefold sleeve) . . . 12
79 Epic EPC 83458/83468 OFF THE WALL (LP, gatefold sleeve, with 7" picture disc "You Can't Win (Parts 1)/(Part 2)" [S EPC 7135], some with information sheet) . . . 25
79 Epic SXPR 1207 EPIC HITS FROM THE JACKSONS & MICHAEL JACKSON (LP, promo only, stickered sleeve) . . . 18

MINT VALUE £

81	Motown PR 84	JACKSON 5: HISTORY OF MOTOWN (4-LP box set, with 1 Michael Jackson LP)	25
82	Epic EPC 11-85930	THRILLER (LP, picture disc in PVC sleeve)	25
82	Motown/Pickwick TMS 3511	AIN'T NO SUNSHINE (LP)	12
83	MCA MCA 70000	E.T. — THE EXTRA TERRESTRIAL (LP, box set with booklet & poster, narration & "Someone In The Dark", with music by John Williams)	70
82	MCA MCFP 3160	E.T. (THE EXTRA TERRESTRIAL) (LP, picture disc)	15
83	MCA CAC 70000	E.T. — THE EXTRA TERRESTRIAL (cassette, box set with booklet & poster)	30
87	Epic 450 290-0	BAD (LP, picture disc)	20
87	Epic 450 290-8	BAD GIFT PACK (cassette pack, with note pad, highlighter pen & calender)	25
87	Epic 450 290-9	BAD (CD, picture disc, some sealed in long PVC blister pack)	45/25
92	Epic 465 802-9	DANGEROUS (CD, gold disc, 10"x10" pop-up 'Collectors Edition First Printing')	30

(see also Jackson 5, Diana Ross & Michael Jackson, Paul McCartney, Jacksons, Jermaine Jackson)

MILLIE JACKSON

72	Mojo 2093 011	A Child Of God/You're The Joy Of My Life	15
72	Mojo 2093 015	Ask Me What You Want/I Just Can't Stand It	8
72	Mojo 2093 022	My Man, A Sweet Man/I Gotta Get Away (From My Own Self)	7
73	Polydor 2066 317	Breakaway/Strange Things	5
75	Polydor 2066 536	If Loving You Is Wrong/The Rap	5
75	Polydor 2006 612	Loving Arms/Left Over	5
76	Spring 2066 713	A House For Sale/There You Are	8
72	Mojo 2918 005	MILLIE JACKSON (LP)	40

(see also Elton John)

MILT JACKSON

57	Esquire EP 74	MILT JACKSON MODERN JAZZ QUARTET (EP)	8
58	London EZ-C 19004	THE MILT JACKSON SEPTET (EP)	12
62	London RE-K 1315	THE BALLAD ARTISTRY OF MILT JACKSON (EP)	8
53	Vogue LDE 044	MILT JACKSON AND HIS NEW GROUP (10" LP)	15
55	Esquire 20-042	MILT JACKSON QUINTET (10" LP)	15
55	London Jazz LZ-C 14006	MILT JACKSON QUARTET (10" LP)	15
57	London Jazz LTZ-K 15064	BALLADS AND BLUES (LP)	12
57	London Jazz LTZ-K 15074	THE JAZZ SKYLINE (LP)	12
57	London Jazz LTZ-K 15091	JACKSONSVILLE (LP)	12
57	Vogue LAE 12046	WIZARD OF THE VIBES (LP)	12
59	London Jazz LTZ-K 15141	PLENTY, PLENTY SOUL (LP)	12
59	London Jazz LTZ-T 15172	BAGS' OPUS (LP, also stereo SAH-T 6049)	12
60	London Jazz LTZ-T 15177	BAGS AND FLUTES (LP)	12
60	London Jazz LTZ-K 15196	BEAN BAGS (LP, also stereo SAH-K 6095; with Coleman Hawkins)	12
61	London Jazz LTZ-K 15220	THE ARTISTRY OF MILT JACKSON (LP, also stereo SAH-K 6163)	12
61	London Jazz LTZ-K 15232	BAGS AND TRANE (LP, with John Coltrane; also stereo SAH-K 6192)	12
61	Philips BBL 7459	MILT JACKSON (LP)	12
62	Esquire 32-134	MILT JACKSON MODERN JAZZ QUARTET/QUINTET (LP)	12
62	Riverside RLP (9)407	BAGS MEETS WES (LP, with Wes Montgomery)	12
63	Realm RM 119	THE MILT JACKSON QUARTET (LP)	12
63	HMV CLP 1589	STATEMENTS (LP, also stereo CSD 1455)	12
63	Realm RM 156	ROLL 'EM BAGS (LP)	12
64	Atlantic ATL/SAL 5012	VIBRATIONS (LP)	12
65	Mercury LML/SML 4008	IN A NEW SETTING (LP)	12
65	Mercury LML/SML 4016	AT THE MUSEUM OF MODERN ART (LP)	12
66	Mercury LML/SML 4028	BORN FREE (LP)	12
73	CTI CTL 8	CHERRY (LP, with Stanley Turrentine)	12

(see also Ray Charles, Modern Jazz Quartet, Stanley Turrentine, Miles Davis/Art Blakey, Coleman Hawkins)

PAPA CHARLIE JACKSON

50	Tempo R 30	Long Gone Lost John/I'm Looking For A Woman Who Knows How To Treat Me Right (78)	15
60	Heritage R 100	PAPA CHARLIE JACKSON (EP) 99 only	70
60	Heritage HLP 1011	PAPA CHARLIE JACKSON (LP) 99 only	100

(see also Paramount Allstars, Blind Blake)

POOCH JACKSON

72	Sioux SI 013	You Just Gotta Get Ready/BROTHER DAN: Django's Valley	5
72	Sioux SI 016	Once Bitten (with Harry J. Allstars)/KING REGGAE: Slave Driver	5

(see also Circles)

PRESTON JACKSON & HIS UPTOWN BAND

50	Tempo R 25	Trombone Man/Yearning For Mandalay (78)	8
50	Tempo R 26	It's Tight, Jim/Harmony Blues (78)	8

PYTHON LEE JACKSON

(see under 'P')

RAY JACKSON

76	EMI EMI 2514	Take Some Time/Working On	5
80	Mercury MER 3	In The Night/Waiting For The Time (p/s)	5
80	Mercury MER 8	Little Town Flirt/Make It Last (p/s)	5
80	Mercury 9109 831	IN THE NIGHT (LP, with inner sleeve)	12

(see also Lindisfarne)

ROOT & JENNY JACKSON

69	Beacon BEA 110	Please Come Home/Lean On Me	15
69	Beacon BEA 136	Let's Go Somewhere/If I Didn't Love You	10

SHAWNE JACKSON

74	Pye 7N 25636	Just As Bad As You/He May Be Your Man	5

SHIRLEY JACKSON

63	Decca F 11612	You Gotta Love And Be Loved/Don't Play Me A Love Song	7
63	Decca F 11788	Broken Home/No Greater Love Than Mine	12

MINT VALUE £

SHOVELVILLE K. JACKSON

60s Melodisc MEL 1683 Be Careful Of Stones That You Throw/Kentucky Blues ... 12

SIMONE JACKSON

62 Piccadilly 7N 35087 Pop Pop Popeye/He Ain't Got No Time For Love ... 12
63 Piccadilly 7N 35124 Ain't Gonna Kiss Ya/Slow Motion ... 12
63 Piccadilly 7N 35149 Tell Me What To Do/Done What You Know Is Wrong ... 12

STONEWALL JACKSON

59 Philips PB 941 Waterloo/Smoke Along The Track ... 12
59 Philips PB 941 Waterloo/Smoke Along The Track (78) ... 10
60 Philips PB 1073 I'm Gonna Find You/A Little Guy Called Joe ... 6
65 CBS BPG 62587 GREATEST HITS (LP) ... 10

TONY JACKSON (& VIBRATIONS)

64 Pye 7N 15685 Bye Bye Baby/Watch Your Step ... 25
64 Pye 7N 15745 This Little Girl Of Mine/You Beat Me To The Punch ... 40
65 Pye 7N 15766 Love Potion No. 9/Fortune Teller ... 50
65 Pye 7N 15876 Stage Door/That's What I Want (as Tony Jackson Group) ... 35
66 CBS 202039 You're My Number One/Let Me Know (as Tony Jackson Group) ... 40
66 CBS 202069 Never Leave Your Baby's Side/I'm The One She Really Thinks A Lot Of (solo) ... 40
66 CBS 202297 Follow Me/Walk That Walk (solo) ... 60
66 CBS 202408 Anything Else You Want/Come On And Stop (solo) ... 40
91 Strange Things STZ 5005 JUST LIKE ME (LP) ... 15
(see also Searchers)

WALTER JACKSON

65 Columbia DB 7620 Welcome Home/Blowin' In The Wind ... 18
66 Columbia DB 7949 Tear For Tear/It's An Uphill Climb To The Bottom ... 30
66 Columbia DB 8054 A Corner In The Sun/Not You ... 18
67 Columbia DB 8154 Speak Her Name/They Don't Give Medals (To Yesterday's Heroes) ... 18
70 Atlantic 584 311 Any Way That You Want Me/Life Has Its Ups And Downs ... 8
73 Brunswick BR 5 Easy Evil/I Never Had It So Good ... 6

WANDA JACKSON

59 Capitol CL 15033 You're The One For Me/A Date With Jerry ... 20
59 Capitol CL 15090 Reaching/I'd Rather Have You ... 20
60 Capitol CL 15147 Let's Have A Party/Cool Love ... 25
61 Capitol CL 15176 Mean Mean Man/Honey Bop ... 25
61 Capitol CL 15223 Right Or Wrong/Funnel Of Love ... 15
62 Capitol CL 15234 In The Middle Of A Heartache/I'd Be Ashamed ... 12
62 Capitol CL 15249 If I Cried Every Time You Hurt Me/Let My Love Walk In ... 12
58 Capitol EAP1 1041 WANDA JACKSON (EP) ... 75
62 Capitol EAP1 20353 A LITTLE BITTY TEAR (EP) ... 50
58 Capitol T 1041 WANDA JACKSON (LP) ... 140
60 Capitol T 1384 ROCKIN' WITH WANDA (LP) ... 100
61 Capitol (S)T 1511 THERE'S A PARTY GOIN' ON (LP, mono/stereo) ... 75/100
61 Capitol (S)T 1596 RIGHT OR WRONG (LP, mono/stereo) ... 50/65
62 Capitol T 1776 WONDERFUL WANDA (LP) ... 35
64 Capitol (S)T 2030 TWO SIDES OF WANDA (LP, mono/stereo) ... 50/65
64 Capitol (S)T 2306 BLUES IN MY HEART (LP) ... 15
66 Capitol (S)T 2438 SINGS COUNTRY SONGS (LP, black label) ... 12
67 Capitol (S)T 2606 SALUTES THE COUNTRY MUSIC HALL OF FAME (LP, black label) ... 12
67 Capitol (S)T 2812 YOU'LL ALWAYS HAVE MY LOVE (LP) ... 12
69 Capitol (S)T 2976 CREAM OF THE CROP (LP, with Party Timers) ... 12
73 Word WST 9514 COUNTRY GOSPEL (LP) ... 12
70s Myrrh MUR 1021 NOW I HAVE EVERYTHING (LP) ... 25

JACKSON & SMITH

65 Polydor 56051 Ain't That Loving You Baby/Every Day I Have The Blues ... 8
66 Polydor 56086 Party '66/And That's It ... 6

JACKSON BROTHERS

59 London HLX 8845 Tell Him No/Love Me ... 25
59 London HLX 8845 Tell Him No/Love Me (78) ... 20

JACKSON 5

SINGLES

70 Tamla Motown TMG 724 I Want You Back/Who's Loving You ... 6
70 Tamla Motown TMG 738 ABC/The Young Folks (some in promo only p/s) ... 60/6
70 Tamla Motown TMG 746 The Love You Save/I Found That Girl ... 6
70 Tamla Motown TMG 758 I'll Be There/One More Chance ... 6
71 Tamla Motown SFI 66 Chartbusters Volume 5: Going Back To Indiana (flexidisc) ... 8
71 Tamla Motown TMG 769 Mama's Pearl/Darling Dear (some in promo only p/s) ... 60/6
71 Tamla Motown TMG 778 Never Can Say Goodbye/She's Good ... 5
72 Tamla Motown TMG 809 Sugar Daddy/I'm So Happy ... 5
72 Tamla Motown TMG 825 Little Bitty Pretty One/Maybe Tomorrow ... 5
72 Tamla Motown TMG 833 Lookin' Through The Windows/Love Song (some in promo only p/s) ... 15/5
72 Tamla Motown TMG 837 THE CHRISTMAS EP: Santa Claus Is Coming To Town/
Someday At Christmas/Christmas Won't Be The Same This Year ... 12
73 Tamla Motown TMG 842 Doctor My Eyes/My Little Baby ... 10
73 Tamla Motown TMG 856 Hallelujah Day/To Know ... 5
73 Tamla Motown TMG 865 Skywriter/Ain't Nothin' Like The Real Thing (some in promo only p/s) ... 15/5
73 Tamla Motown TMG 878 Get It Together/Touch ... 5
74 Tamla Motown TMG 895 The Boogie Man/Don't Let Your Baby Catch You ... 5
74 Tamla Motown TMG 904 Dancing Machine/It's Too Late To Change The Time ... 5
74 Tamla Motown TMG 927 The Life Of The Party/Whatever You Got I Want ... 5
74 Lyntone LYN 2639 Talk And Sing Personally To Valentine Readers
(33rpm flexidisc free with 'Valentine' magazine) ... 15/10

MINT VALUE £

75 Rice Krispies (no cat. nos.) — Sugar Daddy/Goin' Back To Indiana/Who's Loving You/Mama's Pearl/ ABC/The Love You Save (6 different Rice Krispies cut-out card discs) .... each 30
75 Tamla Motown TMG 942 — I Am Love (Part 1)/I Am Love (Part 2) 5
75 Tamla Motown TMG 1001 — Forever Came Today/I Can't Quit Your Love 5
77 Motown TMG 1081 — JUKEBOX GEMS: Skywriter/I Want You Back/The Love You Save (EP) 8
80 Motown SPTMG 2 — THE MOTOWN 20TH ANNIVERSARY SINGLES BOX (15 x 7") 30
83 Motown CTME 2034 — MOTOWN FLIP HITS — JACKSON 5: I Want You Back/ I'll Be There/Lookin' Through The Windows/ABC (EP, cassette) 10
86 Motown 8000 — You Can Cry On My Shoulder/Instrumental (CD) 10
87 Motown ZB 41655 — THE CHRISTMAS EP: Santa Claus Is Coming To Town/ Someday At Christmas/Christmas Won't Be The Same This Year (EP, reissue) 5
89 Tamla Motown ZD 41949 — VINTAGE GOLD (3" CD, gatefold card sleeve, as Michael Jackson & Jackson 5) 10

LPs

70 T. Motown (S)TML 11142 — DIANA ROSS PRESENTS THE JACKSON 5 (flipback sleeve, mono/st.) 25/20
70 T. Motown (S)TML 11156 — ABC (flipback sleeve, mono/stereo) 50/40
70 T. Motown STML 11168 — THE JACKSON 5 CHRISTMAS ALBUM (flipback sleeve) 20
71 T. Motown STML 11174 — THIRD ALBUM (original with flipback sleeve) 18
71 T. Motown STML 11188 — MAYBE TOMORROW 15
72 T. Motown STML 11214 — LOOKIN' THROUGH THE WINDOWS 20
73 T. Motown STML 11231 — SKYWRITER 12
73 T. Motown STML 11243 — GET IT TOGETHER (with photo insert) 18
74 T. Motown STML 11275 — DANCING MACHINE 18
75 T. Motown STML 11290 — MOVING VIOLATIONS 18
76 Motown STML 12046 — JOYFUL JUKEBOX MUSIC 12
77 T. Motown TMSP 6004 — THE JACKSON 5 ANTHOLOGY (2-LP, original issue) 18
77 Motown STMX 6006 — MOTOWN SPECIAL — THE JACKSON 5 15
79 MFP MFP 50418 — ZIP-A-DEE-DOO-DAH 15
81 Motown PR 84 — JACKSON 5: HISTORY OF MOTOWN (4-LP box set, with 1 Michael Jackson LP) 30
82 Motown/Pickwick TMS 3505 — THE JACKSON 5 20

(see also Michael Jackson, Jermaine Jackson, Jacksons)

JACKSON HEIGHTS

70 Charisma JH 1 — Doubting Thomas/Insomnia 6
72 Vertigo 6059 068 — Maureen/Long Time Dying 6
70 Charisma CAS 1018 — KINGS PROGRESS (LP, pink label) 30
72 Vertigo 6360 067 — 5TH AVENUE BUS (LP, gatefold sleeve, swirl label) 45
72 Vertigo 6360 077 — RAGAMUFFIN'S FOOL (LP, swirl label, some with poster) 65/35
73 Vertigo 6360 092 — BUMP AND GRIND (LP, 'spaceship label') 15

(see also Nice)

JACKSONS

77 Epic S EPC 5063 — Enjoy Yourself (Extended Version 5.48)/Style Of Life (12", p/s) 15
78 Epic S EPC 12-6683 — Blame It On The Boogie (LP version)/Do What You Wanna (12") 10
78 Epic S EPC 12-6983 — Destiny (Full Length Album Version)/Blame It On The Boogie (Special 7-Minute Extended Disco Remix)/That's What You Get (For Being Polite) (12", p/s) 10
79 Epic EPC 12-7181 — Shake Your Body (Down To The Ground) (Special Disco Remix 8.40)/ All Night Dancin' (6.09) (12", p/s) 10
79 Epic EPC 13-7876 — Blame It On The Boogie (Album Version)/That's What You Get (For Being Polite)/Blame It On The Boogie (instrumental) (12") 10
79 Epic E 12-6983 — Blame It On The Boogie (Album Version)/That's What You Get (For Being Polite) (7 Minute Remix)/Blame It On The Boogie (12") 10
80 Epic EPC 12-9391 — Heartbreak Hotel (Album Version)/Different Kind Of Lady (12") 15
81 Epic EPC A 40-2627 — GREATEST ORIGINAL HITS: Can You Feel It/Shake Your Body (Down To The Ground)/Show You The Way To Go/Blame It On The Boogie (EP, cassette) 6
81 Epic EPC A 1294 — Walk Right Now/Your Ways (picture disc) 10
79 Epic S XPR 1207 — EPIC HITS FROM THE JACKSONS & MICHAEL JACKSON (LP, promo only) 20
84 Epic EPC 86303 — VICTORY (LP, picture disc) 35
85 Epic SAI 7561 — A TASTE OF VICTORY (LP, picture disc, promo only via Kelloggs offer) 50

(see also Jackson 5, Michael Jackson, Jermaine Jackson)

CHUBBY JACKSON'S BIG BAND

60 Top Rank TR 5015 — A Ballad For Jai/Hail, Hail, The Herd's All Here 6

JACKSON SISTERS

73 Mums MUM 18257 — I Believe In Miracles/Day In The Blue 75
87 Urban URB 4 — I Believe In Miracles/Boy You're Dynamite 10
87 Urban URBX 4 — I Believe In Miracles/Boy You're Dynamite (12", p/s) 20

JACK THE LAD

73 Charisma CB 206 — One More Dance/Draught Genius (Polka) (p/s) 6
73 Charisma CB 218 — Why Can't I Be Satisfied/Make Me Happy 5
75 Charisma CB 242 — Home Sweet Home/Big Ocean Liner 5
75 Charisma CB 253 — Gentleman Soldier/Oakey Strike Evictions 5
75 Charisma CB 264 — My Friend The Drink/Rocking Chair 5
74 Charisma CAS 1085 — IT'S JACK THE LAD (LP) 15
74 Charisma CAS 1094 — OLD STRAIGHT TRACK (LP, with lyric sheet) 15
75 Charisma CAS 1110 — ROUGH DIAMONDS (LP) 15
76 United Artists UAS 29999 — JACKPOT (LP) 12

(see also Lindisfarne)

JACKY

68 Philips BF 1647 — White Horses/Too Many Chiefs (Not Enough Indians) 8
68 Philips BF 1689 — We're Off And Running/Well That's Loving You 6
69 Page One POF 122 — Love Is Now/Never Will I Be 7
68 Philips SBL 7851 — WHITE HORSES (LP) 25

(see also Jackie & Raindrops, Raindrops, Jackie Lee, Emma Rede, Vince Hill)

MINT VALUE £

DICK JACOBS (& HIS ORCHESTRA)

56	Vogue Coral Q 72147	Saxophone/Never Come Sunday	6
56	Vogue Coral Q 72154	"The Man With The Golden Arm" Theme/Butternut	8
56	Vogue Coral Q 72204	Petticoats Of Portugal/East Of Eden	6
57	Vogue Coral Q 72245	The Big Beat/The Tower Trot	12
57	Vogue Coral Q 72260	Rock-a-billy Gal/The Golden Strings	12
57	Vogue Coral Q 72260	Rock-a-billy Gal/The Golden Strings (78)	10
57	Vogue Coral Q 72280	Fascination/Summertime In Venice	6
57	Vogue Coral LVA 9076	THE SKIFFLE SOUND (LP, as Dick Jacobs & His Skiffle Group)	45
59	Coral SVL 3008	BROADWAY SONG BOOK (LP)	15
59	Coral LVA 9102	THEMES FROM HORROR MOVIES (LP)	25

HANK JACOBS

64	Sue WI 313	So Far Away/Monkey, Hips And Rice	35

JIMMY JACOBS & NITESPOTS

60s	Gargoyle ADV 305011	SWINGIN' SOHO — JIMMY SINGS, THE NITESPOTS SWING (LP)	15

JACQUELINE & BRIDIE

64	Fontana TL 5212	HOLD BACK THE DAWN (LP)	20

(see also Jackie & Bridie)

CHUCK JACQUES & LYNN TAITT & COMETS

67	Ska Beat JB 264	Dial 609/VIBRATORS & TOMMY McCOOK & COMETS: Wait For Me	20

(see also Wilbert Francis & Vibrators)

HATTIE JACQUES

71	Avenue NUE 143	THE BUNGLES OF BOJUN (EP)	10

(see also Eric Sykes)

ILLINOIS JACQUET & HIS ORCHESTRA

56	Vogue V 2387	Blow Illinois Blow/Destination Moon	6
53	Vogue LDE 026	ILLINOIS JACQUET (10" LP)	15
56	Columbia Clef 33C 9018	ILLINOIS JACQUET (10" LP)	15
57	Columbia Clef 33CX 10085	GROOVIN' WITH JACQUET (LP)	12
50s	Melodisc MLP 12-301	JAZZ AT THE PHILHARMONIC (LP)	12

JADE

70	DJM DJS 227	Alan's Song/Amongst Anemones	8
70	DJM DJLPS 407	FLY ON STRANGE WINGS (LP)	150

JADE WARRIOR

72	Vertigo 6059 069	The Demon Trucker/Snake	15
78	Island JAD 1	Way Of The Sun/Sun Ra	5
71	Vertigo 6360 033	JADE WARRIOR (LP, gatefold sleeve, swirl label)	55
71	Vertigo 6360 062	RELEASED (LP, gatefold sleeve, swirl label)	65
72	Vertigo 6360 079	LAST AUTUMN'S DREAM (LP, gatefold sleeve, swirl label)	55
74	Island ILPS 9290	FLOATING WORLD (LP)	18
75	Island ILPS 9318	WAVES (LP)	15
76	Island ILPS 9393	KITES (LP)	15
78	Island ILPS 9552	WAY OF THE SUN (LP)	15
79	Butt BUTT 001	REFLECTIONS (LP)	12

(see also July, Joe O'Donnell)

JADIS

84	private pressing	BABOON ENQUIRIES (cassette)	12
87	private pressing DEM 1	G13/Out Of Reach (cassette)	8
88	private pressing DEM 2	Don't Keep Me Waiting/In The Dark (cassette)	8
89	private pressing	Lost For Words/This Changing Face (cassette)	8
90	Back Beat 004-12	THE JADIS ALBUM (LP, numbered)	15

MAX JAFFA (& HIS ORCHESTRA)

56	Columbia SCM 5226	China Boogie/Slap Happy	8

CHRIS JAGGER

73	GM GMS 3	Something New/Joy Of The Ride	6
73	GM GML 1003	CHRIS JAGGER — YOU KNOW THE NAME BUT NOT THE FACE (LP)	15

MICK JAGGER

70	Decca F 13067	Memo From Turner/Natural Magic (some in export p/s)	40/12
84	CBS TA 4431	State Of Shock/Your Ways (picture disc)	6
87	CBS 651028-0	Let's Work/Catch As Catch Can (poster p/s)	8
87	CBS THROW P1	Throwaway/Peace For The Wicked (picture disc)	10
87	CBS THROW C1	Throwaway (Remix)/(Vocal Dub)/Peace For The Wicked (CD, card sleeve)	15
70	United Artists UAS 29108	NED KELLY (LP, soundtrack)	35
70	Warner Bros WS 2554	PERFORMANCE (LP, soundtrack)	30
85	CBS 86310	SHE'S THE BOSS (CD)	15
87	CBS 460 123-2	PRIMITIVE COOL (CD)	15
01	Virgin no cat. no.	GODDESS IN THE DOORWAY (interview CD, promo only)	30

(see also Rolling Stones, Jacksons, Jack Nitzsche)

JAGO

72	Duke DU 134	Rebel Train/Babylon Version	8

JAGS

61	Decca F 11397	The Hunch/Cry Wolf	10

JAGS

79	Island WIP 6501	Back Of My Hand/Double Vision (p/s)	6
79	Island 12SWIP 6501	Back Of My Hand/Double Vision/Single Vision/What Can I Do? (12", p/s)	8
80	Island WIP 6531	Woman's World/Dumb Blonde (p/s)	8
80	Island WIP 6587	Party Games/She's So Considerate (p/s)	10

MINT VALUE £

80	Island WIP 6666	I Never Was A Beach Boy/Tune Into Heaven (p/s)	15
80	Island WIP 6683	The Sound Of G-O-O-D-B-Y-E/The Hurt (no p/s)	10
79	Island ILPS 9603	EVENING STANDARDS (LP)	20
81	Island ILPS 9655	NO TIE LIKE A PRESENT (LP)	20

JAGUAR

81	Heavy Metal HEAVY 10	Back Street Woman/Chasing The Dragon (p/s)	40
82	Neat NEAT 16	Axe Crazy/War Machine (p/s)	22
83	Neat NEAT 1007	POWER GAMES (LP, some on purple vinyl)	30/18
84	Roadrunner RR 9851	THIS TIME (LP)	15

JAGUARS

63	Impression IMP 101	Opus To Spring/The Beat (1,000 only)	35
65	Contest RGJ 152	We'll Live On Happily/Now You Wonder Why	300

(see also Dave Mason)

JAH FISH

72	Grape GR 3034	Vampire Rock/MOD STARS: El-Sisco Rock	8

JAH LION

76	Island ILPS 9386	COLUMBIA COLLY (LP)	25

(see also Jah Lloyd)

JAH LLOYD

73	Jaguar JAG 102	Channel One (with Douglas Boothe)/SOUL SYNDICATES:Channel Two	5
73	Jaguar JAG 104	Psalm Two/SOUL SYNDICATES: Channel Two	5
70s	His Majesty MH 1004	REGGAE STICK (LP)	20
70s	His Majesty MH 1003	DREAD LION DUB (LP)	25

(see also Jah Lion)

JAH SCOUSE

85	Better Things BETS 1	Merge/Vegan Mix (foldout p/s)	5

JAH WOBBLE

78	Virgin VS 239	STEEL LEG MEETS THE ELECTRIC DREAD (EP p/s)	7
78	Virgin VS 239-12	STEEL LEG MEETS THE ELECTRIC DREAD (12 EP, p/s)	10
78	Virgin VOLE 9	Dreadlock Don't Deal In Wedlock/Pthilius Pubis (p/s)	5
78	Virgin 12VOLE 9	Dreadlock Don't Deal In Wedlock/Pthilius Pubis (12", p/s)	8
80	Virgin VS 337	Betrayal/MR. X: Battle Of Britain (p/s)	5
80	Virgin VS 337-12	Betrayal/MR. X: Battle Of Britain (12", p/s)	8
80	Virgin VS 361-12	V.I.E.P. (12" EP)	8
81	Island WIP 6701	HOW MUCH ARE THEY? (12" EP)	8
82	Jah Wobble JAH 1	Fading/Nocturnal (p/s, as Jah Wobble With Animal)	5
82	Jah Wobble JAH 2	Long Long Way/Nocturnal (12", p/s)	8
92	East West OVAL 103 T	VISIONS OF YOU (12" EP, some with p/s)	8
94	Island CID 587	AMOR (EP, 2-CD in foldout digipak)	12
80	Virgin V 2158	THE LEGEND LIVES ON (mini-LP)	12
95	Island CID 8044	HEAVEN AND EARTH (CD)	18

(see also Bartok)

JAH WOBBLE, THE EDGE & HOLGER CZUKAY

83	Island WOB 1	Snake Charmer/Hold On To Your Dreams (p/s)	5

(see also Don Letts & Jah Wobble, Dan MacArthur, Public Image Ltd, The Edge, Orb, Can)

JAH WOOSH

75	Lucky DL 5094	Rocking Blues/Version	5
75	Lucky DL 5096	Don't Do That/That Dub	5

JAKE & FAMILY JEWELS

70	Polydor 2425 027	JAKE AND THE FAMILY JEWELS (LP)	15

JAKLIN

69	Stable SLE 8003	JAKLIN (LP)	250

JAM

SINGLES

77	Polydor 2058 866	In The City/Takin' My Love (p/s, reissues exist with red label)	10
77	Polydor 2058 903	All Around The World/Carnaby Street (p/s)	8
77	Polydor 2058 945	The Modern World/Sweet Soul Music (live)/Back In My Arms Again (live)/ Bricks And Mortar (Part) [live] (p/s)	8
78	Polydor 2058 995	News Of The World/Aunties And Uncles (Impulsive Youths)/Innocent Man (p/s)	5
78	Polydor 2059 054	David Watts/'A' Bomb In Wardour Street (plastic moulded label, p/s)	5
78	Polydor 2059 054	David Watts/'A' Bomb In Wardour Street (white paper label, no p/s)	5
78	Polydor POSP 8	Down In The Tube Station At Midnight/So Sad About Us/The Night (p/s)	5
79	Polydor POSP 34	Strange Town/The Butterfly Collector (p/s)	7
79	Polydor POSP 69	When You're Young/Smithers-Jones (p/s)	6

(The above singles were reissued twice in their picture sleeves; early originals have curved edges on sleeve openings whereas the reissues are straight. Lettering on the reissue labels tends to be fatter; reissues are worth £3-£4.)

80	Polydor 2059 266	Start!/Liza Radley (p/s)	5
81	Polydor POSP 257	Funeral Pyre/Disguises (p/s)	5
82	Polydor POSP 400	Precious (1-sided promo, company sleeve)	40
82	Polydor POSPJ 540/JAM 1	Beat Surrender/Shopping//Move On Up/Stoned Out Of My Mind/ War (double pack, gatefold p/s)	6
82	Polydor PODJ 540	Beat Surrender (DJ Version)/Shopping (promo, company sleeve)	10
83	Polydor 2059 482	That's Entertainment/Down In The Tube Station At Midnight (live) (U.K. reissue of European import, embossed p/s)	5
80	Lyntone LYN 9048/ Flexipop 002	Pop Art Poem/Boy About Town (version) (blue, yellow or green 1-sided flexi with *Flexipop* mag issue 2; add £2 with magazine & £5 with mailer p/s)	7/5/10
80	Lyntone LYN 9048	Pop Art Poem/Boy About Town (version) (same tracks both sides, hard vinyl white label, 300 only, with mail-order mailer p/s)	50/40
81	Lyntone no cat. no.	When You're Young (live) (1-sided fan club flexidisc, 33rpm)	25

82	Fan Club no cat. no.	Tales From The Riverbank (version) (33rpm 1-sided fan club flexidisc)	25
82	Polydor PAOLO 100	Move On Up (live) (flexidisc free with *Melody Maker* paper)	7/5
92	Polydor POCS 199	The Dreams Of Children/Away From The Numbers (live) (withdrawn cassette)	6
97	Polydor 2058 266	In The City (1-sided "20th anniversary party invite" promo, die-cut co. sleeve)	40
97	Polydor JAM 1	DIRECTION, REACTION, CREATION (CD, sampler, gatefold card p/s)	12

FRENCH PRESSINGS

79	Polydor POSP 83	The Eton Rifles/See Saw (no p/s)	7
80	Polydor 2059 266	Start!/Liza Radley (p/s)	7
81	Polydor POSP 257	Funeral Pyre/Disguises (no p/s)	7

MISPRESSINGS

78	Polydor 2058 995	News Of The World/Aunties And Uncles/Innocent Man (p/s, plays B-side on both sides)	40
78	Polydor POSP 6	Sandy/Can't Let You Go (by John Travolta, B-side mispressed with "So Sad About Us")	30
78	Polydor 2059 054	David Watts/'A' Bomb In Wardour Street (plastic moulded label; songwriting credit for "David Watts" mis-credited to "Ray Davis", p/s)	20
78	Polydor POSP 8	Down In The Tube Station At Midnight/So Sad About Us/The Night (p/s; with erroneous B-side reference to "All Mod Cons" LP)	15
78	Polydor POSP 8	Down In The Tube Station At Midnight/So Sad About Us/The Night (A-side plays John Travolta's "Sandy")	12
79	Polydor POSP 69	When You're Young/Smithers-Jones (p/s, with B-side on both sides)	40
80	Polydor 2059 266	Start!/Liza Radley (p/s, 1 side plays Village People's "Can't Stop The Music")	15
82	Polydor POSP 400	Town Called Malice/Precious (p/s, silver moulded label, both sides play "Precious")	30

ALBUMS

77	Polydor 2383 477	IN THE CITY (LP, with inner sleeve)	15
78	Polydor POLD 5008	ALL MOD CONS (LP, with inner sleeve)	20
79	Polydor POLD 5028	SETTING SONS (LP, embossed sleeve with tracklisting sticker on back & inner sleeve)	15
83	Polydor SNAP 1	SNAP! (2-LP, with bonus 4-track EP 'Live At Wembley' [SNAPL 45])	20
84	Polydor 821 712-2	COMPACT SNAP! (CD)	18
91	Receiver	LIVE AT THE ROXY (LP, unissued, 25 test pressings only)	150+
02	Simply Vinyl SVLP	ALL MOD CONS (LP, 180 gm vinyl, limited edition)	20

(see also Style Council, Paul Weller, Bruce Foxton, Time U.K., Sharp)

JAM ON THE MUTHA

90	Wau!/Polydor MAGXR 3	Hotel California (Orb In Cali Mix 1)/(Like Joe Never Left Mix)/(Orbitally Ambient Mix) (12", p/s)	10

JAM TODAY

80s	Stroppy Cow SCJT 1	Stereotyping/Song About Myself (p/s, with insert)	60

JAMAICA FATS

66	Blue Beat BB 368	Jacqueline/Please Come Home (actually by Al T. Joe & Celestials)	25

(see also Al T. Joe)

JAMAICAN ACTIONS

68	Coxsone CS 7070	Catch The Quinella/JACKIE MITTOO: Songbird	30

JAMAICAN CALYPSONIANS

54	Times Record UD 1005	Not Me/Rum & Coconut Water (78)	7
50s	Kalypso RL 102	Hol'im Joe/Bargie (78)	8

JAMAICAN EAGLES

73	Harry J HJ 6661	Country Living/Country Living (Version)	5

(see also Eagles)

JAMAICAN FOUNDATIONS

68	Coxsone CS 7036	Take It Cool/VICEROYS: Try Hard To Leave	25

JAMAICANS

66	Doctor Bird DB 1109	Cool Night/Ma And Pa	45
67	Trojan TR 007	Dedicated To You/The Things I Said To You	25
67	Treasure Isle TI 7007	Things You Say You Love/I've Got A Pain	25
67	Treasure Isle TI 7012	Baba Boom (Festival Song 1967) (actually by Baba Boom)/TOMMY McCOOK & SUPERSONICS: Real Cool	25
67	Treasure Isle TI 7037	Peace And Love/Woman Gone Home	25
69	Escort ES 806	Early In The Morning/Mr. Lonely	15
70	Harry J. HJ 6604	Fire Parts 1 & 2	12
71	Dynamc DYN 410	Love Uprising/My Love For You	10
71	Dynamic DYN 417	Mary/CONSCIOUS MINDS: Soldier Boy	10
71	New Beat NB 084	Mary/CONSCIOUS MINDS: Soldier Boy	10
72	Dynamic DYN 430	I Believe In Music/Music (Version)	10
72	Dynamic DYN 442	Are You Sure/Are You Sure (Version)	10
72	Dynamic DYN 456	Sunshine Love/Sunshine Version	10
74	Dragon DRA 1029	My Heart Just Keeps On Breaking/My Heart Just Keeps On Breaking (Instrumental)	10

(see also Norris Weir & Jamaicans, Tommy Cowan)

JAMAICAN SHADOWS

67	Coxsone CS 7005	Have Mercy/Blending Love	30
69	Upsetter US 320	Dirty Dozen (actually by Upsetters)/Crying Too Long	25

JAMAICA'S OWN VAGABONDS

64	Decca DFE 8588	BEHOLD (EP)	45
64	Decca LK 4617	SKA TIME (LP)	60

(see also Vagabonds, Jimmy James & Vagabonds)

MINT VALUE £

AHMED JAMAL

59 London Jazz LTZ-M 15162 BUT NOT FOR ME (LP) . . . 20
59 London Jazz LTZ-M 15170 AHMED JAMAL (LP) . . . 20
62 Pye Jazz NJL 38 ALHAMBRA (LP) . . . 15
63 Pye Jazz NJL 50 MACANUDO (LP) . . . 15
64 Chess CRL 4001 NAKED CITY THEME (LP) . . . 15
67 Chess CRL 4509 ROAR OF THE GREASE PAINT (LP) . . . 15
68 Chess CRL 4530 STANDARD-EYES (LP) . . . 15
68 Chess CRL 4532 CRY YOUNG (LP) . . . 15

JAMES

86 Sire JIM 3 Chain Mail/Hup Springs (p/s) . . . 10
86 Sire JIM 4 So Many Ways/Withdrawn (p/s) . . . 10
86 Sire JIM 4T So Many Ways/Just Hipper/Withdrawn (12", p/s) . . . 18
88 Blanco Y Negro NEG 26 Yaho/Mosquito (p/s) . . . 7
88 Blanco Y Negro NEG 26T Yaho/Mosquito/Left Out Of Her Will/New Nature (12", p/s) . . . 15
88 Blanco Y Negro NEG 31 What For/Island Swing (p/s) . . . 7
88 Blanco Y Negro NEG 31T What For (Climax Mix)/Island Swing/Not There (12", p/s) . . . 15
88 Blanco Y Negro NEG 31C What For (Climax Mix)/Island Swing/Not There (cassette, in video-style box) . . . 10
89 Rough Trade RT 225 Sit Down/Sky Is Falling (p/s) . . . 8
89 Rough Trade RTT 225 Sit Down/Goin' Away/Sky Is Falling (12", p/s, 1st 500 with postcard) . . . 12/8
89 Rough Trade RTT 225 CD Sit Down/Goin' Away/Sky Is Falling (3" CD, card sleeve) . . . 25
89 Rough Trade RT 245 Come Home/Promised Land (p/s) . . . 7
89 Rough Trade RTT 245 Come Home (Long Version)/Come Home (7" Version)/Promised Land/ Slow Right Down (Demo Version) (12", p/s) . . . 10
89 Rough Trade RTT 245 CD Come Home (Long Version)/Come Home (7" Version)/Promised Land/ Slow Right Down (Demo Version) (5" CD, card sleeve) . . . 12
90 Fontana JIMM 512 How Was It For You?/How Was It For You? (Different Mix)/Lazy/ Undertaker (12", p/s, with stencil) . . . 12
90s Lyntone Weather Change (Demo Version) (flexidisc, with tour programme) . . . 12/6
84 Factory FAC 78 JIMONE EP: What's The World/Fire So Close/Folklore (p/s) . . . 12
85 Factory FAC 138 VILLAGE FIRE: What's The World/Fire So Close/Folklore/Hymn From A Village/ If Things Were Perfect (12" EP) . . . 12
85 Factory FAC 119 JAMES II: Hymn From A Village/If Things Were Perfect (p/s) . . . 12
86 Sire JIM 3T SIT DOWN EP: Chain Mail/Uprising/Hup Springs (12", p/s) . . . 18
91 Fontana JIM 812 SIT DOWN (12" EP, recorded live at G-Mex) . . . 12
92 Fontana JIM 12 SEVEN (EP) . . . 7
89 Rough Trade ONEMAN 1LP ONE MAN CLAPPING (LP, with inner sleeve) . . . 15

B.B. JAMES

70 Upsetter US 328 Consider Me/Consider Me Version . . . 12

BOB JAMES

75 CTI CTI 6043 BOB JAMES ONE (LP) . . . 15
75 CTI CTI 6057 BOB JAMES TWO (LP) . . . 15

BOBBY JAMES & DAVE (Barker)

71 Smash SMA 2314 You Said It/AGGRO BAND: Hot Sauce . . . 15

BRIAN JAMES

68 Olga OLE 005 Come Back Silly Girl/It Just Happened That Way . . . 8

CALVIN JAMES

65 Columbia DB 7516 Some Things You Never Get Used To/Remember . . . 25
(pseudonym for George Underwood; see also Davie Jones & King Bees)

COL JAMES

62 Oriole CB 1736 Doesn't Anybody Make Short Movies/Oooh Looka There Ain't She Pretty . . . 12

DANNY JAMES

72 Southern Sound BT 100 Your Gravy Train/Devil Made Me Say That . . . 5

DICK JAMES

53 Parlophone MSP 6039 Mother Nature And Father Time/Don't You Care . . . 5
53 Parlophone MSP 6047 The Joker/Guessing . . . 12
55 Parlophone MSP 6170 Unchained Melody/Come Back (Come Back To Me) . . . 5
55 Parlophone MSP 6190 He/So Must I Love You . . . 5
56 Parlophone MSP 6199 Robin Hood/The Ballad Of Davy Crockett . . . 35
56 Parlophone MSP 6230 "Summer Sing-Song" Medley . . . 5
56 Parlophone R 4220 I Only Know I Love You/Mirabelle . . . 5
56 Parlophone R 4241 "Sing Song Time (No. 3)" Medley . . . 5
57 Parlophone R 4255 The Garden Of Eden/I Accuse . . . 5
57 Parlophone R 4314 Westward Ho The Wagons!/The Gay Cavalier . . . 5
57 Parlophone R 4375 "Skiffling Sing Song" Medley . . . 5
58 Parlophone R 4498 Daddy's Little Girl/When You're Young . . . 5
58 Parlophone R 4498 Daddy's Little Girl/When You're Young (78) . . . 8
59 Parlophone R 4606 There But For Your Love Go I/Minus One Heart . . . 5
64 Parlophone R 5212 "Sing A Song Of Beatles With Dick James" Medley (Parts 1 & 2) . . . 8

ELMORE JAMES

64 Sue WI 335 Dust My Blues/Happy Home (as Elmore James & Broom Dusters) . . . 45
65 Sue WI 383 It Hurts Me Too/Bleeding Heart . . . 35
65 Sue WI 392 Knocking At Your Door/Calling The Blues (B-side actually by Junior Wells & Earl Hooker) . . . 120
66 Sue WI 4007 I Need You/Mean Mistreating Mama . . . 30
65 Sue ILP 918 THE BEST OF ELMORE JAMES (LP) . . . 60
65 Sue ILP 927 THE ELMORE JAMES MEMORIAL ALBUM (LP) . . . 60
68 Bell MBLL/SBLL 104 SOMETHING INSIDE OF ME (LP) . . . 45
68 Ember EMB 3397 THE LATE FANTASTICALLY GREAT ELMORE JAMES (LP) . . . 25
70 United Artists UAS 29109 THE LEGEND OF ELMORE JAMES (LP) . . . 22
70 Blue Horizon 7-66230 TO KNOW A MAN (2-LP) . . . 85

MINT VALUE £

70	Blue Horizon 7-63204	TOUGH (LP, with 4 tracks by John Brim)	65
73	Polydor 2383 200	COTTON PATCH HOTFOOTS (LP, shared with Walter Horton)	15
75	DJM DJLMD 8008	ALL THEM BLUES (2-LP)	18
83	Ace CH 68	KING OF THE SLIDE GUITAR (LP, yellow vinyl)	12

ETTA JAMES

60	London HLM 9139	All I Could Do Was Cry/Tough Mary	40
60	London HLM 9234	My Dearest Darling/Girl Of My Dreams	30
61	Pye International 7N 25079	At Last/I Just Want To Make Love To You	25
61	Pye International 7N 25080	Trust In Me/Anything To Say You're Mine	18
61	Pye International 7N 25113	Dream/Fool That I Am	18
62	Pye International 7N 25131	Something's Got A Hold On Me/Waiting For Charlie To Come Home	18
62	Pye International 7N 25162	Stop The Wedding/Street Of Tears	20
63	Pye International 7N 25205	Pushover/I Can't Hold It In Any More	18
65	Sue WI 359	Roll With Me Henry/Good Rockin' Daddy	45
67	Chess CRS 8052	I Prefer You/I'm So Glad (I Found Love In You)	18
67	Chess CRS 8063	Tell Mama/I'd Rather Go Blind	18
67	Chess CRS 8069	Security/I'm Gonna Take What He's Got	15
68	Chess CRS 8076	I Got You Babe/I Worship The Ground You Walk On	12
68	Chess CRS 8082	You Got It/Fire	12
72	Chess 6145 016	Tell Mama/I'd Rather Go Blind/I Found A Love	10
74	Santa Ponsa PNS 14	Just Ask Me/99 Ways	6
74	Chess 6145 033	Out On The Streets Again/Come A Little Closer	6
78	Warner Brothers K 17173	Piece Of My Heart/Lovesick Blues	5
65	Chess CRL 4502	ETTA JAMES ROCKS THE HOUSE (LP)	70
67	Chess CRL 4524	AT LAST (LP)	55
68	Ember EMB 3390	THE SOUL OF ETTA JAMES (LP)	40
68	Chess CRL 4536	TELL MAMA (LP)	45
72	Chess 6310 126	GOLDEN DECADE (LP)	15
73	Chess 6671 003	PEACHES (2-LP)	25
78	Warner Brothers K 56492	DEEP IN THE NIGHT (LP)	12
81	Ace 10CH 33	GOOD ROCKIN' MAMA (10" LP)	12

(see also Etta & Harvey)

ETTA JAMES & SUGAR PIE DeSANTO

65	Chess CRS 8025	Do I Make Myself Clear/Somewhere Down The Line	22

(see also Sugar Pie DeSanto)

HARRY JAMES & HIS ORCHESTRA

65	Dot DS 16729	Love Theme From In Harm's Way/Green Onions	5
54	Philips BBR 8010	SOFT LIGHTS, SWEET TRUMPET (10" LP)	12
54	Columbia 33S 1014	ALLTIME FAVOURITES (10" LP)	12
54	Columbia 33S 1031	RHYTHM SESSION WITH HARRY JAMES (10" LP)	12
55	Columbia 33S 1052	TRUMPET TIME (10" LP)	12
56	Capitol LC 6800	IN HI-FI (10" LP)	12
62	MGM C 932	THE SOLID GOLD TRUMPET (LP)	12
64	MGM C 1005	DOWNBEAT (LP)	12

(see also Rosemary Clooney)

JASON JAMES

67	CBS 2705	Miss Pilkington's Maid/Count Me Out	20

JERRY JAMES & BANDITS

64	Solar SRP 101	Sweet Little Sixteen/Three Steps To Heaven	15

JESSE JAMES

54	Vocalion V 1037	Southern Casey Jones/Lonesome Day Blues (78)	15
71	Mojo 2092 016	Don't Nobody Want To Get Married/(Pt. 2)	7

JIMMY JAMES (& THE VAGABONDS)

62	Dice CC 4	Bewildered And Blue/I Don't Want To Cry (solo)	20
63	R&B JB 112	Jump Children/Tell Me (solo)	25
64	Black Swan WI 437	Thinking Of You/Shirley (solo)	30
65	Columbia DB 7653	Shoo Be Doo You're Mine/We'll Never Stop Loving You	18
66	Ska Beat JB 242	Your Love/Someday (solo)	18
66	Piccadilly 7N 35298	I Feel Alright/I Wanna Be Your Everything	12
66	Piccadilly 7N 35320	Hi Diddley Dee Dum Dum (It's A Good Good Feelin')/Come To Me Softly	12
66	Piccadilly 7N 35331	This Heart Of Mine/I Don't Wanna Cry	15
66	Piccadilly 7N 35349	Ain't Love Good, Ain't Love Proud/Don't Know What I'm Gonna Do	15
67	Piccadilly 7N 35360	I Can't Get Back Home To My Baby/Hungry For Love (solo)	12
67	Piccadilly 7N 35374	No Good To Cry/You Showed Me The Way	12
68	Pye 7N 17579	Red Red Wine/Who Could Be Loving You	8
69	Pye 7N 17719	Close The Door/Why (solo)	6
71	Trojan TR 7806	Help Yourself/Why	18
72	Bamboo BAM 67	Riverboat Jenny/If I Wasn't Black	10
72	Stateside SS 2209	A Man Like Me/Survival	7
75	Pye 7N 45524	Whatever Happened To The Love We Knew/Let's Have Fun	5
75	Pye 7N 45472	Hey Girl/I Am Somebody	30
66	Piccadilly NEP 34053	JIMMY JAMES AND THE VAGABONDS (EP)	50
66	Piccadilly NPL 38027	THE NEW RELIGION (LP)	45
68	Pye N(S)PL 18231	OPEN UP YOUR SOUL (LP)	35
68	Marble Arch MAL 823	THIS IS JIMMY JAMES (LP)	12
70	Marble Arch MAL 1244	THE NEW RELIGION (LP, reissue)	12
75	Pye NSPL 18457	YOU DON'T STAND A CHANCE IF YOU CAN'T DANCE (LP)	18

JIMMY JAMES & THE VAGABONDS/ALAN BOWN SET

67	Pye N(S)PL 18156	LONDON SWINGS — LIVE AT THE MARQUEE CLUB (LP, 1 side each)	45

(see also Vagabonds, Jamaica's Own Vagabonds, Alan Bown Set)

MINT VALUE £

JOHN JAMES

70	Transatlantic TRA 219	MORNING BRINGS THE LIGHT (LP)	15
71	Transatlantic TRA 242	JOHN JAMES (LP)	15
72	Transatlantic TRA 250	SKY IN MY PIE (LP)	15
75	Transatlantic TRA 305	HEAD IN THE CLOUDS (LP)	15
76	Kicking Mule SNKF 128	DESCRIPTIVE GUITAR INSTRUMENTALS (LP)	12
78	Kicking Mule SNKF 136	LIVE IN CONCERT (LP)	12
84	Stoptime STOP 101	ACOUSTICA ECLECTICA (LP, some signed)	20/15

JONI JAMES

53	MGM SP 1013	Why Don't You Believe Me?/Wishing Ring	25
53	MGM SP 1025	Have You Heard/Purple Shades	15
53	MGM SP 1026	Your Cheatin' Heart/I'll Be Waiting For You	18
53	MGM SP 1041	Almost Always/Is It Any Wonder?	18
53	MGM SP 1064	I'll Never Stand In Your Way/Why Can't I	18
54	MGM SP 1081	I Need You Now/You're Nearer	12
54	MGM SP 1089	I'll Be Seeing You/Am I In Love	15
54	MGM SP 1094	You're My Everything/Maybe Next Time	12
54	MGM SP 1100	In A Garden Of Roses/Every Day	12
54	MGM SP 1105	Pa Pa Pa/Mama, Don't Cry At My Wedding	12
55	MGM SP 1125	This Is My Confession/How Important Can It Be?	12
55	MGM SP 1135	When You Wish Upon A Star/Is This The End Of The Line?	12
56	MGM SP 1149	You Are My Love/My Believing Heart	12
57	MGM MGM 918	Give Us This Day/How Lucky You Are	10
57	MGM MGM 954	Only Trust Your Heart/I Need You So	8
58	MGM MGM 973	My Funny Valentine/My Darling, My Darling	7
58	MGM MGM 978	Never 'Till Now/Love Works Miracles	7
58	MGM MGM 991	There Goes My Heart/Funny	12
58	MGM MGM 991	There Goes My Heart/Funny (78)	12
59	MGM MGM 1002	There Must Be A Way/I'm Sorry For You, My Friend	8
59	MGM MGM 1002	There Must Be A Way/I'm Sorry For You, My Friend (78)	15
59	MGM MGM 1022	Perhaps/I Still Get A Thrill (Thinking Of You)	6
59	MGM MGM 1034	I Still Get Jealous/Prayer Of Love	6
59	MGM MGM 1041	Are You Sorry?/What I Don't Know Won't Hurt Me	6
59	MGM MGM 1050	Little Things Mean A Lot/I Laughed At Love	7
60	MGM MGM 1064	You Belong To Me/I Need You Now	6
60	MGM MGM 1089	We Know/They Really Don't Know You	6
60	MGM MGM 1105	Be My Love/Tall As A Tree	6
54	MGM MGM-EP 504	JONI JAMES (EP)	18
55	MGM MGM-EP 518	SINGS TO YOU (EP)	18
56	MGM MGM-EP 530	LITTLE GIRL BLUE (EP)	18
56	MGM MGM-EP 558	LOVE LETTERS (EP)	15
60	MGM MGM-EP 728	THE SONGS OF HANK WILLIAMS (EP, also stereo MGM-ES 3501)	15/18
54	MGM MGM-D 127	LET THERE BE LOVE (10" LP)	45
59	MGM MGM-C 777	ONE HUNDRED SONGS AND JONI (LP)	30
59	MGM MGM-C 785	JONI SINGS SONGS OF HANK WILLIAMS (LP)	25
60	MGM MGM-C 809	TI VOGLIO BENE (I LOVE YOU SO) (LP)	25
60	MGM MGM-C 823/CS 6005	SINGS IRISH FAVOURITES (LP, mono/stereo)	20/25
60	MGM MGM-C 825	SWINGS SWEET (LP)	22
61	MGM MGM-C 839/CS 6015	100 STRINGS AND JONI IN HOLLYWOOD (LP, mono/stereo)	20/25
63	MGM MGM-C 933	AFTER HOURS (LP)	22

MARK JAMES

67	Liberty LIB 55953	Bimbo Knows/I Can't Let You Go	7

NICKY JAMES (MOVEMENT)

65	Columbia DB 7747	Stagger Lee/I'm Hurtin' Inside (as Nicky James Movement)	30
67	Philips BF 1566	I Need To Be Needed/So Glad We Made It	7
68	Philips BF 1635	Would You Believe/Silver Butterfly	15
68	Philips BF 1694	Lookin' Through Windows/Nobody But Me	7
69	Philips BF 1755	Time/Little Bit Of Paper	8
69	Philips BF 1804	Reaching For The Sun/No Life At All	7
72	Threshold TH 12	Why/Foreign Shore	6
73	Threshold TH 16	Black Dream/She Came To Me	6
73	Threshold TH 17	I Guess I've Always Loved You/My Style	8
71	Philips 6308 069	NICKY JAMES (LP)	20
73	Threshold THS 10	EVERY HOME SHOULD HAVE ONE (LP)	15
76	Threshold THS 19	THUNDERTHROAT (LP)	12

(see also Move)

PHILIP JAMES & BLUES BUSTERS

65	Island WI 219	Wide Awake In A Dream/MAYTALS: Tell Me The Reason	60

(see also Blues Busters)

RICKY JAMES

57	HMV POP 306	Knee Deep in The Blues/Bluer Than Blue	35
57	HMV POP 306	Knee Deep in The Blues/Bluer Than Blue (78)	7
57	HMV POP 334	Party Doll/Ninety-Nine Ways	40
57	HMV POP 334	Party Doll/Ninety-Nine Ways (78)	7

ROGER JAMES FOUR

65	Columbia DB 7556	Letter From Kathy/Leave Me Alone	7
66	Columbia DB 7813	Better Than Here/You're Gonna Come Home Cryin' (withdrawn)	50
66	Columbia DB 7829	Better Than Here/You're Gonna Come Home Cryin'	30

RUBY JAMES

69	Fontana TF 1051	Gettin' Mighty Crowded/Don't Play That Song	12

SALLY JAMES

74	Philips 6006 418	Isn't It Good/Wake Me When It's Over (p/s)	7

SIDNEY JAMES (& DEAN ROGERS/LIZ FRASER)

61 Decca F 11328 The Ooter Song/Double Bunk (with Liz Fraser) . . . 15
61 HMV POP 886 Kids/One Last Kiss (with Dean Rogers) . . . 10
73 Pye 7N 4528 Our House/She's Gone (solo) (p/s) . . . 15
(see also Tony Hancock)

SKIP JAMES

65 Vanguard VSD 79219 SKIP JAMES TODAY (LP) . . . 25
67 Private PR3 1964-67 (LP, 99 copies only) . . . 45
68 Vanguard VSD 79273 DEVIL GOT MY WOMAN (LP) . . . 25
70 Spokane SPL 1003 THE ORIGINAL 1930/31 RECORDINGS (LP) . . . 45
78 Vanguard VDP 20001 I'M SO GLAD (LP) . . . 18
70s Storyville 670 185 THE GREATEST OF THE DELTA BLUES SINGERS (LP) . . . 18

SONNY JAMES

56 Capitol CL 14635 The Cat Came Back/Hello Old Broken Heart . . . 25
56 Capitol CL 14664 Twenty Feet Of Muddy Water/For Rent (One Empty Heart) . . . 18
57 Capitol CL 14683 Young Love/You're The Reason I'm In Love . . . 18
57 Capitol CL 14708 First Date, First Kiss, First Love/Speak To Me . . . 15
57 Capitol CL 14742 Dear Love/Lovesick Blues . . . 10
57 Capitol CL 14788 Love Conquered (Love Came, Love Saw)/A Mighty Lovable Man . . . 18
57 Capitol CL 14814 Uh-Huh-Mm/Why Can't They Remember? . . . 30
57 Capitol CL 14814 Uh-Huh-Mm/Why Can't They Remember? (78) . . . 15
58 Capitol CL 14848 Kathaleen/Walk To The Dance . . . 15
58 Capitol CL 14879 Are You Mine/Let's Play Love . . . 6
58 Capitol CL 14915 You Got That Touch/I Can See It In Your Eyes . . . 6
58 Capitol CL 14952 I Can't Stay Away From You/Let Me Be The One To Love You . . . 5
59 Capitol CL 14991 Yo-Yo/Dream Big . . . 12
59 Capitol CL 14991 Yo-Yo/Dream Big (78) . . . 25
59 Capitol CL 15022 Talk Of The School/The Table . . . 5
59 Capitol CL 15046 Pure Love/This Love Of Mine . . . 5
59 Capitol CL 15079 Red Mud/Who's Next In Line . . . 5
60 London HL 9132 Jenny Lou/Passin' Through . . . 10
65 Capitol CL 15377 You're The Only World I Know/Tying The Pieces Together . . . 5
57 Capitol EAP1 827 YOUNG LOVE (EP) . . . 35
64 Capitol EAP1 20654 YOU'RE THE ONLY WORLD I KNOW (EP) . . . 22
57 Capitol T 779 SOUTHERN GENTLEMAN (LP) . . . 30
57 Capitol T 867 SONNY (LP) . . . 30
58 Capitol T 988 HONEY (LP) . . . 25
63 London HA-D 8049 YOUNG LOVE (LP) . . . 70

STU(ART) JAMES (& MOJOS)

65 Decca F 12231 Wait A Minute/Wonder If She Knows (as Stu James & Mojos) . . . 20
74 Bradleys BRAD 7406 I Only Wish I Had The Time/Back To Basingstoke (Part 1) . . . 7
76 Bradleys BRAD 7614 I'm In The Mood For Love/Firefly (as Stuart James) . . . 7
(see also Mojos)

SULLIVAN JAMES BAND

66 Parlophone R 5465 Goodbye Mr. Heartache/We're Gonna Make It . . . 7

TOMMY JAMES & SHONDELLS

66 Roulette RK 7000 Hanky Panky/SHONDELLS: Thunderbolt . . . 15
66 Pye International 7N 25398 It's Only Love/Ya! Ya! . . . 10
67 Major Minor MM 511 I Think We're Alone Now/Gone Gone Gone . . . 8
67 Major Minor MM 548 Out Of The Blue/Love's Closing In On Me . . . 6
68 Major Minor MM 558 Wish It Were You/Get Out Now . . . 8
68 Major Minor MM 567 Mony Mony/One, Two, Three And I Fell . . . 7
68 Roulette RO 500 Do Something To Me/Somebody Cares . . . 5
69 Roulette RO 502 Crimson And Clover/Some Kind Of Love . . . 6
69 Roulette RO 506 Sweet Cherry Wine/Breakaway . . . 5
69 Roulette RO 507 Crystal Blue Persuasion/I'm Alive . . . 12
69 Roulette RO 511 Ball Of Fire/Makin' Good Time . . . 5
70 Roulette RO 513 She/Loved One . . . 5
70 Roulette RO 516 Come To Me/Talkin' And Signifyin' . . . 5
70 Roulette RO 518 Ball And Chain/Candy Makers (solo) . . . 5
68 Major Minor MMLP/SMLP 27 SOMETHING SPECIAL (LP) . . . 18
68 Roulette RRLP/SRLP 1 MONY MONY (LP) . . . 18
68 Roulette RRLP/SRLP 2 CRIMSON AND CLOVER (LP) . . . 18
69 Roulette RRLP/SRLP 3 CELLOPHANE SYMPHONY (LP) . . . 18
72 Roulette 2432 002 THE BEST OF TOMMY JAMES & THE SHONDELLS (LP) . . . 15
72 Roulette 2432 005 MY HEAD, MY BED AND MY RED GUITAR (LP, solo) . . . 12

TONY JAMES

68 Jolly JY 002 Treat Me Right/Me Donkey's Dead . . . 12

WINSTON JAMES

70 Hot Rod HR 106 Prison Sentence/JANET FERRON: Darling I Need You . . . 12

JAMES BOYS

68 Direction 58-3721 The Mule (Instrumental)/The Horse (Vocal) . . . 10

JAMES BROTHERS

68 Page One POF 077 I Forgot To Give You Love/The Truth About It . . . 8
68 Page One POF 088 Does It Have To Be Me/You Don't Really Love Me . . . 8
(see also Wheels)

JAMES GANG

70 Stateside SS 2158 Funk No. 48/Collage . . . 8
70 Stateside SS 2173 Stop/Take A Look Around (withdrawn) . . . 15
70 Probe PRO 502 Funk 49/Thanks . . . 6
71 Probe PRO 533 Walk Away/Yadig? . . . 5

			MINT VALUE £
70	Stateside SSL 10295	YER' ALBUM (LP)	25
70	Probe SPB 6253	RIDES AGAIN (LP)	20
71	Probe SPB 1038	THIRDS (LP)	20
71	Probe SPB 1045	LIVE IN CONCERT (LP)	15
72	Probe SPB 1056	STRAIGHT SHOOTER (LP)	15
73	Probe SPB 1065	PASSIN' THRU (LP)	15

(see also Joe Walsh, Tommy Bolin)

BOBBY JAMESON

64	Decca F 12032	All I Want Is My Baby/Each And Every Day	30
64	London HL 9921	I Wanna Love You/I'm So Lonely	25
65	Brit WI 1001	Rum-Pum/Please Mr. Mailman	18

STEPHEN JAMESON

70	Pye 7N 45189	Margie Make It March/Happiness Road	5
73	Dawn DNS 1035	Don't Say/Back Together Once Again	5
73	Dawn DNLS 3044	STEPHEN JAMESON (LP)	15

JAMESON RAID

80	Blackbird BRAID 001	The Hypnotist/The Raid/Gettin' Hotter/Straight From The Butchers (p/s)	40
81	GBH GBH 1	Seven Days Of Splendour/It's A Crime/Catcher In The Rye (p/s, with lyric sheet, white sleeve, later black sleeve)	25/20

JAMIES

58	Fontana H 153	Summertime Summertime/Searching For You	45
58	Fontana H 153	Summertime Summertime/Searching For You (78)	20
62	Columbia DB 4885	Summertime Summertime/Searching For You (reissue)	20

JAMIROQUAI

93	Acid Jazz JAZID 46	When You Gonna Learn/Too Young To Die (p/s)	25
93	Acid Jazz JAZID 46T	When You Gonna Learn/Didgin' Out/Too Young To Die (12", p/s)	15

JAMME

70	Stateside-Dunhill SSL 5024	JAMME (LP)	15

JOE JAMMER

73	Regal Zono. SRZA 8514	BAD NEWS (LP)	25

(see also Mitchell/Coe Mysteries)

J.A.M.s

(see under Justified Ancients Of Mu Mu)

JAN & ARNIE

58	London HL 8653	Jennie Lee/Gotta Getta Date	50
58	London HL 8653	Jennie Lee/Gotta Getta Date (78)	35

(see also Jan & Dean)

JAN & DEAN

59	London HLN 8936	Baby Talk/Jeanette, Get Your Hair Done	30
59	London HLN 8936	Baby Talk/Jeanette, Get Your Hair Done (78)	100
59	London HLU 8990	There's A Girl/My Heart Sings	25
59	London HLU 8990	There's A Girl/My Heart Sings (78)	120
60	London HLU 9063	Clementine/You're On My Mind	20
61	London HLH 9395	Heart And Soul/Midsummer Night's Dream	18
62	Liberty LIB 55397	A Sunday Kind Of Love/Poor Little Puppet	12
63	Liberty LIB 55531	Linda/When I Learn How To Cry	12
63	Liberty LIB 55580	Surf City/She's My Summer Girl	8
63	Liberty LIB 55613	Honolulu Lulu/Someday You'll Go Walkin' By	10
64	Liberty LIB 55641	Drag City/Schlock Rod Pt 1	12
64	Liberty LIB 55672	Dead Man's Curve/The New Girl In School	10
64	Liberty LIB 55704	The Little Old Lady From Pasadena/My Mighty GTO	10
64	Liberty LIB 55724	Ride The Wild Surf/The Anaheim, Azusa And Cucamonga Sewing Circle, Book Review And Timing Association	10
65	Liberty LIB 55727	Sidewalk Surfin'/When It's Over	10
65	Liberty LIB 55766	(Here They Come) From All Over The World/Freeway Flyer	10
65	Liberty LIB 55792	You Really Know How To Hurt A Guy/It's As Easy As 1, 2, 3	10
65	Liberty LIB 55833	I Found A Girl/It's A Shame To Say Goodbye	10
66	Liberty LIB 10225	Norwegian Wood/A Beginning From An End	20
66	Liberty LIB 55860	Batman/Bucket 'T'	15
66	Liberty LIB 10244	Popsicle/The Joker Is Wild	10
66	Liberty LIB 55923	The New Girl In School/School Day (Ring Ring Goes The Bell)	8
66	Liberty LIB 10252	Tennessee/Horace The Swinging School Bus Driver	12
67	CBS 202630	Yellow Balloon/A Taste Of Rain	18
65	Liberty LEP 2213	SURF 'N' DRAG HITS (EP)	35
66	Liberty LEP 2258	THE TITANIC TWOSOME (EP)	50
76	United Artists REM 402	REMEMBER JAN & DEAN (EP)	15
63	Liberty LBY 1163	SURF CITY AND OTHER SWINGING CITIES (LP)	35
64	Liberty LBY 1220	DEAD MAN'S CURVE/NEW GIRL IN SCHOOL (LP)	40
64	Liberty LBY 1229	RIDE THE WILD SURF (LP)	35
65	Liberty LBY 1279	GOLDEN HITS (LP)	20
65	Liberty LBY 1304	FOLK 'N' ROLL (LP)	30
66	Liberty LBY 1309	JAN AND DEAN MEET BATMAN (LP)	25
66	Liberty LBY 1339	FILET OF SOUL (A LIVE ONE) (LP)	25

(see also Legendary Masked Surfers, Fantastic Baggys, Jan & Arnie)

JAN & KELLY

62	Philips 326 567 BF	Ooh! 'E Didn't/Prepare To Meet Your Fate Mate	7
62	Philips BF 1253	I Could Have Died/Make Me A Doormat	7
63	Philips BF 1265	Ooh! I Can't/Write Me A Letter	7
64	Philips BF 1323	And Then He Kicked Me/My Country And Western Lover	10
64	Philips BF 1377	There Was A Girl/There Was A Boy/And Then There Was Nothing	7
63	Philips BE 12536	TIME FOR A LAUGH (EP)	25

MINT VALUE £

JAN & KJELD

59 Pye International 7N 25013 Buona Sera/Tiger Rag . . . 6
59 Pye International N 25013 Buona Sera/Tiger Rag (78) . . . 10
60 Ember EMB S 101 Banjo Boy/Don't Raise A Storm (some in p/s) . . . 22/10
60 Qualiton PSP 7127 Sweet Sue/Oh! Mein Papa (as Jan & Keld) . . . 6
60 Ember EMB S 109 Down By The Riverside/I Shall Not Be Moved . . . 6
60 Ember EMB 3312 THE KIDS FROM COPENHAGEN (LP, label states "The Boys From Copenhagen") . . . 22

BRUCE JANAWAY

78 Deep Range SRT/CUS/216 PURITANICAL ODES (LP, with insert) . . . 35

JAN DUKES DE GREY

70 Decca Nova (S)DN 8 SORCERERS (LP) . . . 50
71 Transatlantic TRA 234 MICE AND RATS IN THE LOFT (LP) . . . 80

JANE'S ADDICTION

88 WEA W 7520 Mountain Song/Jane Says (p/s) . . . 6
88 WEA W 7520T Mountain Song/Jane Says/Had A Dad (live) (12", p/s) . . . 8
91 WEA W 0031TP Classic Girl/No One's Leaving (live)/Ain't No Right (live) (12", picture disc, die-cut sleeve) . . . 8

PETER JANES

67 CBS 203004 Emperors And Armies/Go Home Ulla (some in p/s) . . . 10/6
68 CBS 3299 Do You Believe/For The Sake Of Time . . . 10

JANIE

61 Capitol CL 15180 You Better Not Do That/Only Girls Can Tell . . . 12
(see also Jeanne Black)

JANINE

81 Stiletto JAN 001 Crazy On You/Candy (p/s) . . . 170

JOHNNY JANIS

58 London HLU 8650 The Better To Love You/Can This Be Love . . . 15
58 London HLU 8650 The Better To Love You/Can This Be Love (78) . . . 10
60 Philips PB 1090 Gina/If The Good Lord's Willin' . . . 6
58 HMV 7EG 8365 JOHNNY JANIS (EP) . . . 25
66 London HA-U 8270 ONCE IN A BLUE MOON (LP) . . . 25

BERT JANSCH

67 Big T BIG 102 Life Depends On Love/A Little Sweet Sunshine . . . 12
73 Reprise K 14234 Oh My Father/The First Time Ever I Saw Your Face . . . 7
74 Charisma CB 240 In The Bleak Midwinter/One For Jo . . . 6
75 Charisma CB 267 Dance Lady Dance/Build Another Band . . . 5
79 Kicking Mule SCK 44 Time And Time/Una Linea Di Dolcezza (as Bert Jansch Conundrum) . . . 5
82 Logo GO 409 Heartbreak Hotel/Up To The Stars (p/s) . . . 5
66 Transatlantic EP 145 NEEDLE OF DEATH (EP) . . . 30
65 Transatlantic TRA 125 BERT JANSCH (LP) . . . 25
65 Transatlantic TRA 132 IT DON'T BOTHER ME (LP) . . . 25
66 Transatlantic TRA 143 JACK ORION (LP) . . . 40
67 Transatlantic TRA 157 NICOLA (LP) . . . 25
69 Transatlantic TRA 179 BIRTHDAY BLUES (LP) . . . 25
69 Vanguard VSD 79292 STEPPING STONES (LP) . . . 18
69 Transatlantic TRASAM 10 THE BERT JANSCH SAMPLER (LP) . . . 18
71 Transatlantic TRA 235 ROSEMARY LANE (LP) . . . 22
72 Transatlantic TRASAM 27 BOX OF LOVE — THE BERT JANSCH SAMPLER VOL. 2 (LP) . . . 15
73 Reprise K 44225 MOONSHINE (LP, with lyric insert) . . . 15
74 Charisma CAS 1090 L.A. TURNAROUND (LP, with lyric insert) . . . 12
75 Charisma CAS 1107 SANTA BARBARA HONEYMOON (LP) . . . 12
77 Charisma CAS 1127 A RARE CONUNDRUM (LP) . . . 12
79 Charisma CLASS 6 AVOCET (LP) . . . 12
80 Kicking Mule SNKF 162 THIRTEEN DOWN (LP, as Bert Jansch Conundrum) . . . 12
85 Konexion KOMA 788006 FROM THE OUTSIDE (LP, 500 only) . . . 15

BERT JANSCH & JOHN RENBOURN

66 Transatlantic TRA 144 BERT AND JOHN (LP) . . . 25
(see also Conundrum, Pentangle, John Renbourn)

JAPAN

78 Ariola Hansa AHA 510 Don't Rain On My Parade/Stateline (solid or press-out centre, no p/s) . . . 15
78 Ariola Hansa AHA 525 The Unconventional/Adolescent Sex (some with p/s) . . . 20/6
78 Ariola Hansa AHA 529 Sometimes I Feel So Low/Love Is Infectious (p/s, initially on blue vinyl) . . . 10/8
79 Ariola Hansa AHA 540 Life In Tokyo (Short Version)/Life In Tokyo Pt 2 (p/s, red vinyl) . . . 8
79 Ariola Hansa AHAD 540 Life In Tokyo (Long Version)/(Short Version) (12", p/s, red vinyl) . . . 12
80 Ariola Hansa AHA 559 I Second That Emotion/Quiet Life (dull red vinyl, card or paper p/s) . . . 8/6
80 Virgin VS 379 Gentlemen Take Polaroids/The Experience of Swimming (fully autographed by band, p/s) . . . 75
80 Virgin VS 379 Gentlemen Take Polaroids/The Experience of Swimming//The Width Of A Room/Burning Bridges (double pack, gatefold p/s) . . . 6
82 Virgin VSY 472 Ghosts/The Art Of Parties (Version) (picture disc, stickered PVC cover) . . . 5
88 Virgin CDT 11 Ghosts/The Art Of Parties (Version)/Visions Of China (3" CD, card sleeve) . . . 10
88 Virgin CDT 32 Gentlemen Take Polaroids/Cantonese Boy (12" Version)/Methods Of Dance (12" Version) (3" CD, gatefold card sleeve) . . . 10
80 Virgin V 2180 GENTLEMEN TAKE POLAROIDS (LP, with misprinted sleeve with sticker, "Some Kind Of Fool" listed instead of "Burning Bridges") . . . 12
(see also David Sylvian)

JOHNNY JAPES & HIS JESTICLES

87 Viz VIZ 1 Bags Of Fun With Buster/Scrotal Scratch Mix (p/s) . . . 5
(see also XTC, John Otway, Mr. Partridge)

JIMMY JAQUES

58 Fontana H 100 Come Walking/Baby, Don't You Cry (78) . . . 8
58 Fontana H 131 In My Life/Never Let You Go. . . . 12
58 Fontana H 131 In My Life/Never Let You Go (78) . . . 8
58 Fontana H 161 Barb'ry Ann/For A Lifetime . . . 8
58 Fontana H 161 Barb'ry Ann/For A Lifetime (78). . . . 8
60 Parlophone R 4710 Do Me A Favour/Not To Worry . . . 5

JARMELS

61 Top Rank JAR 560 She Loves To DanceLittle Lonely One. . . . 25
61 Top Rank JAR 580 A Little Bit Of Soap/The Way You Look Tonight. . . . 50

COOK E. JARR

69 RCA RCA 1820 Pledging My Love/If I Were A Carpenter . . . 6

JEAN-MICHEL JARRE

SINGLES

78 Polydor POSP 20 Equinoxe 5/Equinoxe 1 (p/s, with etched autograph on run-off) . . . 8
79 Polydor 2001 896 Equinoxe 4 (Remix)/Equinoxe 3 (p/s) . . . 6
80 Polydor 2001 968 Jarre At The Concorde: Equinoxe 7 (live)/Equinoxe 8 (live) (p/s). . . . 10
81 Polydor POSP 292 Magnetic Fields 2 (Remix)/Magnetic Fields 1 (Excerpt) (p/s) . . . 5
81 Polydor POSP 363 Magnetic Fields 4 (Remix)/Magnetic Fields 1 (Excerpt) (p/s) . . . 10
82 Polydor POSP 430 Orient Express/Fishing Junks At Sunset (p/s) . . . 8
84 Polydor POSPX 718 Zoolook (Remix)/Wooloomooloo/Zoolook (Extended)/Zoolook (Effects) (12", p/s) 18
85 Polydor POSP 740 Zoolookologie (Remix)/Ethnicolor 2 (p/s) . . . 8
85 Polydor POSPG 740 Zoolookologie (Remix)/Ethnicolor 2//Oxygene 4/Oxygene 6 (double pack). . . . 12
85 Polydor POSPX 740 Zoolookologie (Extended Remix)/(Remix)/Ethnicolor 2 (12", p/s) . . . 15
86 Polydor POSPX 788 Rendezvous 4 (Special Remix)/Rendezvous 4/Moon Machine
(12", 'face' or 'city skyline' p/s) . . . each 20
88 Polydor PZ 25 Revolutions (Ext'd Mix)/Revolutions (LP Mix)/Industrial Revolution 2 (12", p/s) . . . 8
88 Polydor PZCD 25 Revolutions (Extended Mix)/Revolutions/Revolutions (Single Remix)
(CD, jewel case) . . . 20
88 Polydor PZCD 32 London Kid (Full Version) (featuring Hank Marvin)/
Industrial Revolution 3/Revolutions (Remix) (CD, card sleeve) . . . 20
89 Polydor PZCD 55 Oxygene IV (Single Version)/Industrial Revolution Overture/
Oxygene IV (live)/September (CD, card sleeve). . . . 15
90 Polydor PZ 84 Calypso (Extended)/Calypso/Calypso Pt 2 (12", p/s) . . . 10
90 Polydor PZCD 84 Calypso (Extended)/Calypso/Calypso Pt 2 (CD) . . . 10

PROMOS

78 Polydor JM1 Equinoxe Part 4/Part 5 (12", company sleeve) . . . 35
93 Polydor CHRONO 1 Chronologie (Black Girl Rock)/(Sunscreem 2)/(Sunscreem) (12", white p/s). . . . 15
93 Polydor CHRONO 2 Chronologie (Praga Kahn Dream Time Mix)/(Praga Kahn Atomium Mix)
(12", black 'clock' p/s) . . . 15
94 Polydor PZ 307DJ Chronologie 6 (Slam Mix 1)/(Slam Mix 2) (12", pink marbled vinyl,
stickered PVC sleeve) . . . 25
94 Polydor PZ 307DJ2 Chronologie 6: Gatdecor Mixes (Main Mix)/(7" Edit Mix)/(Alternate Mix)/
(Original Mix) (12", blue marbled vinyl, stickered PVC sleeve). . . . 20
97 Sony XPR 3117 Oxygene 8 (Sunday Club Remix)/(Sunday Club Edit) (12", stickered title p/s) . . . 8
97 Sony SAMPMS 3984 Oxygene 8 (Hani Oxygene 101)/(Dado's Club Remix)/(Dado's Ethnic Remix)/
(Dado's FM Remix)/(Hani's Oxygene 303)/(Hani's 303 Reprise)
(12", double pack, die-cut gatefold stickered sleeve). . . . 8
97 Sony XPCD 2166 Oxygene 10 (Sash Edit 2)/Oxygene 10 (Original Edit) (CD) . . . 8
98 Sony XPR 3235 Rendezvous 98 (@ 440 Remix) (12", 1-sided, p/s). . . . 10
98 Sony XPR 3228 ODYSSEY 0_2: Oxygene 10 (Trancengenics 1)/Oxygene 7
(DJ Cam Remix)/Oxygene 8 (Trans Mix)/Oxygene 12
(Claude Monnet Remix) (12", title sleeve) . . . 18
99 Sony XPR 3371 C'est La Vie (10", 1-sided, white label, 500 only). . . . 20

ALBUMS

87 Polydor 833 737-2 THE JEAN-MICHEL JARRE 10TH ANNIVERSARY CD BOX SET
(7-CD, 5,000 only) . . . 40
88 Polydor C88 1-3 OXYGENE (LP, HMV-only box set with booklet, 3,300 only) . . . 15
88 Polydor C88-1-3 OXYGENE (CD, HMV-only box set with booklet, 3,500 only). . . . 20

MAURICE JARRE

63 Pye Intl. NPL 28023 LAWRENCE OF ARABIA (LP, soundtrack) . . . 12
65 Fontana (S)TL 5259 THE COLLECTOR (LP, soundtrack). . . . 25
66 MGM MGM-CS 8037 GRAND PRIX (LP, soundtrack). . . . 15
66 CBS (S)BPG 62843 IS PARIS BURNING? (LP, soundtrack). . . . 25
67 RCA RD 7848 NIGHT OF THE GENERALS (LP, soundtrack) . . . 20
67 RCA Victor RD/SF 7876 THE PROFESSIONALS (LP, soundtrack) . . . 50
68 Dot (S)LPD 515 VILLA RIDES (LP, soundtrack). . . . 20
71 MGM 2315 028 RYAN'S DAUGHTER (LP, soundtrack, gatefold sleeve). . . . 12
76 EMI SLCW 1033 THE MESSAGE (LP, soundtrack, gatefold sleeve). . . . 12
77 Pye NSPH 28504 JESUS OF NAZARETH (LP, soundtrack, gatefold sleeve). . . . 15

MARIAN JARVIS

75 Chelsea 2005 038 A Penny For Your Thoughts/A Good Man To Wake Up To . . . 6

JASON & THE SCORCHERS

85 EMI EA 200 Shop It Around/Change The Tune (p/s) . . . 5
85 EMI 12EA 200 Shop It Around/Absolutely Sweet Marie/Change The Tune (12", p/s). . . . 8

JASON CREST

68 Philips BF 1633 Turquoise Tandem Cycle/Good Life (some in export p/s) . . . 160/60
68 Philips BF 1650 Juliano The Bull/Two By The Sea. . . . 40
68 Philips BF 1687 (Here We Go Round) The Lemon Tree/Patricia's Dream . . . 50
69 Philips BF 1752 Waterloo Road/Education . . . 22
69 Philips BF 1809 A Place In The Sun/Black Mass . . . 140

(see also Holy Mackerel, High Broom)

JASON'S GENERATIONS
66 Polydor BM 56042 It's Up To You/Insurance Co.'s Are Very Unfair 40

JASPER
69 Spark SRLP 103 LIBERATION (LP) 220

JAVELLS
77 Pye Disco Demand BD 2003 Goodbye Nothin' To Say/Nothin' To Say 8

JAWBONE
70 Carnaby CNS 4007 How's Ya Pa?/Mister Custer 15
70 Carnaby CNS 4020 Way Way Down/Bulldog Goes West 15
72 B&C CB 190 Gotta Go/Automobile Blues 6
70 Carnaby CNLS 6004 JAWBONE (LP) 100
(see also Mirage, Portobello Explosion)

BOB JAXON (& HI-TONES)
55 London HL 8156 Ali Baba/Why Does A Woman Cry (as Bob Jaxon & Hi-Tones) 45
55 London HL 8156 Ali Baba/Why Does A Woman Cry (as Bob Jaxon & Hi-Tones) (78) 15
57 RCA RCA 1019 Beach Party/(Gotta Have Something In The) Bank Frank 80
57 RCA RCA 1019 Beach Party/(Gotta Have Something In The) Bank Frank (78) 25

FRANKIE JAXON/HOUNDHEAD HENRY
60 Jazz Collector JEL 10 THE MALE BLUES VOLUME 6 (EP) 18

JAY (Black)
64 Coral Q 72471 I Rise, I Fall/How Sweet It Is 25
67 United Artists UP 1174 What Will My Mary Say/Return To Me (as Jay Black) 10
(see also Jay & The Americans)

ABNER JAY
63 London HLN 9791 Cleo/Thresher 12

DAVID JAY
(see under David J.)

ERIC JAY
59 London HL 9004 The Little Drummer Boy/Blue Champagne Cha Cha 8
59 London HL 9004 The Little Drummer Boy/Blue Champagne Cha Cha (78) 12

LAURIE JAY COMBO
62 Ember JBS 710 Shades Of Red/Nevada Sunsets 10
63 HMV POP 1234 Teenage Idol/Think Of Me 12
64 HMV POP 1300 Love In My Heart/'Til You're Mine 8
64 HMV POP 1335 Maybe/Be Good To Me 8
65 Decca F 12083 A Song Called Soul/Just A Little Bit 25
(see also Nero & Gladiators)

LONNIE JAY & JAYNES
63 Stateside SS 197 Around And Around We Go/Somewhere 10

PETER JAY (& BLUE MEN)
60 Triumph RGM 1000 Just Too Late/Friendship (as Peter Jay & Blue Men) 40
60 Pye 7N 15290 Paradise Garden/Who's The Girl? 40
(see also Blue Men)

PETER JAY & JAYWALKERS
62 Decca F 11531 Can Can '62/Redskins 8
63 Decca F 11593 Totem Pole/Jaywalker 7
63 Decca F 11659 Poet And Peasant/Oo La La 10
63 Decca F 11757 Kansas City/The Parade Of Tin Soldiers 10
64 Decca F 11840 You Girl/If You Love Me 10
64 Piccadilly 7N 35199 Where Did Our Love Go/Caroline 12
64 Piccadilly 7N 35212 Tonight You're Gonna Fall In Love/Red Cabbage 10
65 Piccadilly 7N 35220 Parchman Farm/What's Easy For Two Is So Hard For One 20
65 Piccadilly 7N 35259 Before The Beginning/Solitaire 18
(see also Terry Reid, Miller, Big Boy Pete)

JAY & THE AMERICANS
62 HMV POP 1009 She Cried/Dawning 40
63 United Artists UP 1002 This Is It/It's My Turn To Cry 8
63 United Artists UP 1018 What's The Use/Strangers Tomorrow 8
64 United Artists UP 1039 Come Dance With Me/Look Into My Eyes Maria 12
64 United Artists UP 1069 Come A Little Bit Closer/Goodbye Boys Goodbye 8
65 United Artists UP 1075 Let's Lock The Door (And Throw Away The Key)/I'll Remember You 10
65 United Artists UP 1088 Think Of The Good Times/If You Were Mine Girl 8
65 United Artists UP 1094 Cara Mia/When It's All Over 10
65 United Artists UP 1108 Some Enchanted Evening/Girl 8
66 United Artists UP 1119 Sunday And Me/Through This Doorway 8
66 United Artists UP 1129 Why Can't You Bring Me Home/Baby Stop Your Crying 10
66 United Artists UP 1132 Crying/I Don't Need A Friend 8
66 United Artists UP 1142 Livin' Above Your Head/She's The Girl (That's Messing Up My Mind) 40
66 United Artists UP 1162 (He's) Raining In My Sunshine/Reason For Living 7
67 United Artists UP 1178 You Ain't As Hip As All That Baby/Nature Boy 8
67 United Artists UP 1191 (We'll Meet In The) Yellow Forest/Got Hung Up Along The Way 50
68 United Artists UP 2211 French Provincial/Shanghai Noodle Factory 7
69 United Artists UP 2268 This Magic Moment/Since I Don't Have You 7
69 United Artists UP 35008 When You Dance/So Much In Love 6
69 United Artists UP 35026 Hushabye/No I Don't Know Her 6
70 United Artists UP 35074 Walkin' In The Rain/For The Love Of A Lady 8
65 United Artists UEP 1003 COME A LITTLE BIT CLOSER (EP) 40
66 United Artists UEP 1017 LIVING WITH JAY AND THE AMERICANS (EP) 40
66 United Artists (S)ULP 1117 JAY AND THE AMERICANS (LP) 35

MINT VALUE £

Year	Label/Cat. No.	Title	Value £
66	United Artists (S)ULP 1128	SUNDAY AND ME (LP)	35
67	United Artists (S)ULP 1150	LIVIN' ABOVE YOUR HEAD (LP)	40
67	United Artists (S)ULP 1164	TRY SOME OF THIS (LP)	35

(see also Jay, Chapter Four)

JAY (John Holt) & JOYA (Landis)

Year	Label/Cat. No.	Title	Value £
68	Trojan TR 633	I'll Be Lonely/SUPERSONICS: Second Fiddle	10

(see also John Holt, Joya Landis)

JAY & TECHNIQUES

Year	Label/Cat. No.	Title	Value £
67	Philips PB 1597	Apples, Peaches, Pumpkin Pie/Stronger Than Dirt	12
67	Philips PB 1618	Keep The Ball Rollin'/Here We Go Again	10
67	Mercury 6052 302	Apples, Peaches, Pumpkin Pie/Contact	5
68	Philips PB 1644	Strawberry Shortcake/Still (In Love With You)	10
68	Mercury MF 1034	Baby Make Your Own Sweet Music/Help Yourself To All My Lovin'	12
75	Polydor 2066 473	I Feel Love Comin' On/This World Of Mine	6
71	Mercury MCF 127360	Baby Make Your Own Sweet Music/Help Yourself To All My Lovin' (reissue)	5
67	Philips (S)BL 7834	APPLES, PEACHES, PUMPKIN PIE (LP)	35

JAYBIRDS (U.K.)

Year	Label/Cat. No.	Title	Value £
64	Embassy WB 621	Not Fade Away/Over You	5
64	Embassy WB 624	Tell Me When/You Can't Do That	5
64	Embassy WB 625	Can't Buy Me Love/DEL MARTIN: I Love You Because	5
64	Embassy WB 626	Good Golly Miss Molly/	5
64	Embassy WB 628	Mockin' Bird Hill/Hubble Bubble (Toil And Trouble)	5
64	Embassy WB 632	Baby Let Me Take You Home/BUD ASHTON & HIS GROUP: Rise And Fall Of Fingel Blunt	5
64	Embassy WB 635	Juliet/Here I Go Again	5
64	Embassy WB 651	She's Not There/PAUL RICH: I Wouldn't Trade You For The World	5
64	Embassy WB 663	All Day And All Of The Night/Google Eye	8
64	Embassy WB 672	What Have They Done To The Rain/BUD ASHTON & HIS GROUP: Genie With The Light Brown Lamp	5
65	Embassy WB 673	Go Now/TERRY BRANDON: Ferry 'Cross The Mersey	5

(see also Ray Pilgrim & Beatmen)

JAYBIRDS (U.S.)

Year	Label/Cat. No.	Title	Value £
66	Sue WI 4013	Somebody Help Me/The Right Kind	35

JAY BOYS

Year	Label/Cat. No.	Title	Value £
69	Trojan TR 665	Splendour Splash/TREVOR SHIELD: Please	10
70	Harry J. HJ 6602	The Dog (Parts 1 & 2)	8
70	Harry J. HJ 6607	Jack The Ripper/Don't Let Me Down	8
70	Harry J. HJ 6609	Jay Moon Walk/Elcong	6
70	Harry J. HJ 6610	Je T'Aime/It Ain't Me Babe	6
70	Harry J. HJ 6617	Del Gago/Killer Version	7
70	Harry J. HJ 6618	Can't Get Next To You/(Part 2) (both actually by Charmers)	8
71	Harry J. HJ 6628	The Arcade Walk/The Arcade Walk Vers. II	6
72	Harry J. HJ 6644	African People/HARRY J. ALL STARS: African (Version)	6
72	Ashanti AHS 407	Rough Road/TREVOR SHIELD: Rough Road	7

(see also Roy Panton, Bob & Marcia, Cables)

JERRY JAYE

Year	Label/Cat. No.	Title	Value £
67	London HLU 10128	My Girl Josephine/Five Miles From Home	35

JAYE SISTERS

Year	Label/Cat. No.	Title	Value £
59	London HLT 9011	Sure Fire Love/G-3	60
59	London HLT 9011	Sure Fire Love/G-3 (78)	100

JAYHAWKS

Year	Label/Cat. No.	Title	Value £
56	Parlophone R 4228	Stranded In The Jungle/My Only Darling	600
56	Parlophone R 4228	Stranded In The Jungle/My Only Darling (78)	125

JAYLADS

Year	Label/Cat. No.	Title	Value £
71	Punch PH 95	Royal Chord (actually by Melodians)/Version (actually "In The Spirit" by Lloyd Charmers)	12

(see also Melodians)

JAYNETTS

Year	Label/Cat. No.	Title	Value £
63	Stateside SS 227	Sally Go Round The Roses/Sally Go Round The Roses (Instrumental)	15

JAYS

Year	Label/Cat. No.	Title	Value £
63	Parlophone R 4764	Shock A Boom/Across The Sea	12

JAYWALKERS

Year	Label/Cat. No.	Title	Value £
76	Cream CRM 5003	Can't Live Without You/Heartbroken Memories	6

JAZZATEERS

Year	Label/Cat. No.	Title	Value £
83	Rough Trade RT 138	Sixteen Reasons/Show Me The Door (p/s)	5
84	Rough Trade ROUGH 46	JAZZATEERS (LP, with insert)	12

JAZZ BUTCHER

Year	Label/Cat. No.	Title	Value £
83	Glass GLASS 027	Southern Mark Smith/Jazz Butcher Meets Count Dracula (p/s)	20
85	Glass GLASS 12041	Real Men/The Jazz Butcher V The Prime Minister/ Southern Mark Smith (Original) (12", p/s)	20
86	Glass HMMM 001	Christmas With The Pygmies (p/s, promo freebie, given away at gigs)	10

JAZZ COMPOSERS ORCHESTRA

Year	Label/Cat. No.	Title	Value £
74	JCOA/Virgin JDA 311	JAZZ COMPOSERS ORCHESTRA (2-LP, gatefold sleeve)	18

(see also Carla Bley, Mike Mantler, Don Cherry, Larry Coryell)

JAZZ COURIERS

Year	Label/Cat. No.	Title	Value £
57	Tempo EXA 75	JAZZ COURIERS (EP)	50
59	Tempo EXA 87	JAZZ COURIERS (EP)	50
58	Tempo TAP 22	IN CONCERT (LP)	400

MINT VALUE £

59 Tempo TAP 26 THE LAST WORD (LP) 500
60 London Jazz LTZ-L 15188 THE COURIERS OF JAZZ! (LP) 400
67 M. For Pleasure MFP 1072 IN CONCERT (LP) 20
(see also Tubby Hayes, Ronnie Scott)

JAZZ CRUSADERS
66 Fontana 688 149 ZL THE THING (LP) 20
66 Fontana 688 117 ZL LOOKING AHEAD (LP) 18
(see also Crusaders)

JAZZ FIVE
61 Tempo TAP 32 THE FIVE OF US (LP) 50
(see also Vic Ash Quartet, Harry Klein Quartet)

JAZZ HIP TRIO
67 Major Minor MMLP 8 JAZZ IN RELIEF (LP) 75

JAZZ MAKERS
66 Ember FA 2023 SWINGIN' SOUNDS (LP) 20

JAZZ MODES
60 London Jazz LTZ-K 15191 THE MOST HAPPY FELLA (LP) 20

JAZZ ROCK EXPERIENCE
70 Deram Nova SDN 19 JAZZ ROCK EXPERIENCE (LP) 40

J & B
66 Polydor 56095 Wow Wow Wow/There She Goes 50
(see also State Of Micky & Tommy, Foreigner)

J.B.'s
71 Mojo 2001 155 These Are The J.B.'s (Parts 1 & 2) 12
71 Mojo 2027 002 The Grunt (Parts 1 & 2) 12
72 Mojo 2093 007 Gimme Some More/The Rabbit Got The Gun 12
72 Mojo 2093 016 Hot Pants Road/Pass The Peas 12
72 Mojo 2093 021 Givin' Up Food For Funk (Parts 1 & 2) 12
72 Mojo 2918 004 PASS THE PEAS (LP) 50
72 Polydor 2391 034 FOOD FOR THOUGHT (LP) 50
74 Polydor 2391 087 DOING IT TO DEATH (LP) 50
75 Polydor 2391 194 HUSTLE WITH SPEED (LP) 50
76 Polydor 2391 204 GIVIN' UP FOOD FOR FUNK — THE BEST OF THE JB's (LP) 40
(see also Fred Wesley & JB's, James Brown, Bobby Byrd)

J.D. (THE ROC)
72 Sioux SI 008 Superbad/MONTEGO MELON: Lucky Dip 12
(see also Jeff Dixon)

BOBBI JEAN
65 Mercury MF 921 Dry Your Tears/Pity The Man 12

CATHY JEAN & ROOMATES
61 Parlophone R 4764 Please Love Me Forever/Canadian Sunset 60

LANA JEAN
63 Pye International 7N 25214 It Hurts To Be Sixteen/Bad Boy 25

JEAN & GAYTONES
71 Trojan TR 7817 I Shall Sing (actually by Judy Mowatt & Gaytones)/GAYTONES: Target 12

JEAN & STATESIDES
64 Columbia DB 7287 Putty In Your Hands/One Fine Day 40
64 Columbia DB 7439 You Won't Forget Me/Cold, Cold Winter 30
65 Columbia DB 7651 Mama Didn't Lie/Just Let Me Cry 30

JEAN-ETTES
59 Pye 7N 15185 May You Always/I Saw A Light 12
59 Pye N 15185 May You Always/I Saw A Light (78) 10

JEAN-JACQUES
69 Pye International 7N 25489 Maman/Les Beaux Dimanches 5

JEANNE & JANIE
60 Capitol CL 15146 Journey Of Love/JEANNE BLACK: Lisa 10
60 Capitol CL 15165 Sleep Walkin'/JEANNE BLACK: You'll Find Out 10
(see also Jeanne Black)

JEANNIE (& BIG GUYS)
63 Piccadilly 7N 35147 Don't Lie To Me/Boys (as Jeannie & Big Guys) 12
64 Piccadilly 7N 35164 I Want You/Sticks And Stones (as Jeannie & Big Guys) 12
65 Parlophone R 5343 I Love Him/With Any Other Girl 8
(see also Cindy Cole)

JEANNIE & REDHEADS
64 Decca F 11829 Animal Duds/ANDREW OLDHAM GROUP: Funky And Fleopatra 30
(see also Andrew Oldham Orchestra)

AUDREY JEANS
56 Decca F 10768 Ticky Ticky Tick (I'm Gonna Tell On You)/Will You, Willyum 18
56 Decca F 10788 It's Better In The Dark/The Bus Stop Song (A Paper Of Pins) 7
58 Decca F 11035 Send A Letter To Jeanette — Yet!/Bad Pianna Rag 7
58 Decca F 11035 Send A Letter To Jeanette — Yet!/Bad Pianna Rag (78) 8
61 HMV POP 876 How Lovely To Be A Woman/What Did I See In Him 6

JEDDAH
83 Death RIP 2001 Eleanor Rigby (with poster, no p/s) 20

MINT VALUE £

JEDI KNIGHTS

95 Clear CLR 406 MAY THE FUNK BE WITH YOU (12" EP, p/s) ... 30
95 Clear CLR 406X MAY THE FUNK BE WITH YOU (12" EP, clear vinyl, embossed sleeve) ... 50
(see also Global Communications)

JEEPS

66 Strike JH 308 He Saw Eesaw/The Music Goes Round ... 12
66 Strike JH 315 Ain't It A Great Big Laugh/I Put On My Shoes ... 12

JEFFERSON

68 Pye 7N 17634 Montage/Did You Hear A Heartbreak Last Night ... 10
69 Pye 7N 17706 The Colour Of My Love/Look No Further ... 8
69 Pye 7N 17810 Baby Take Me In Your Arms/I Fell Flat On My Face ... 8
69 Pye 7N 17855 Love And All The World/I've Got To Tell Her ... 8
69 Pye NSPL 18316 THE COLOUR OF MY LOVE (LP) ... 30
(see also Rockin' Berries, Sight & Sound)

BLIND LEMON JEFFERSON

50 Tempo R 38 Weary Dog Blues/Change My Luck Blues (78) ... 25
50 Tempo R 39 Lock Step Blues/Hangman's Blues (78) ... 25
51 Tempo R 46 Shuckin' Sugar Blues/Rabbit Foot Blues (78) ... 25
52 Tempo R 54 Gone Dead On You Blues/One Dime Blues (78) ... 25
53 Jazz Collector L 91 Shuckin' Sugar Blues/Rabbit Foot Blues (78) ... 20
53 Jazz Collector L 103 Jack O'Diamonds Blues/Clock House Blues (78) ... 20
54 Jazz Collector L 126 Gone Dead On You Blues/One Dime Blues (78) ... 20
50s Poydras 99 BLIND LEMON JEFFERSON (10" EP) ... 45
53 London Jazz AL 3508 FOLK BLUES OF BLIND LEMON JEFFERSON (10" LP) ... 55
55 London Jazz AL 3546 PENITENTIARY BLUES (10" LP) ... 55
57 London Jazz AL 3564 SINGS THE BLUES (10" LP) ... 55
69 CBS 63738 THE IMMORTAL (LP) ... 18
70s Roots Matchbox RL 301 BLIND LEMON JEFFERSON VOLUME 1 (LP) ... 15
70s Roots Matchbox RL 306 BLIND LEMON JEFFERSON VOLUME 2 (LP) ... 15
70s Roots Matchbox RL 331 BLIND LEMON JEFFERSON VOLUME 3 (LP) ... 15
(see also Paramount Allstars)

BLIND LEMON JEFFERSON/ED BELL

60 Jazz Collector JEL 13 THE MALE BLUES VOLUME 7 (EP) ... 22

BLIND LEMON JEFFERSON/BUDDY BOY HAWKINS

59 Jazz Collector JEL 8 THE MALE BLUES VOLUME 5 (EP) ... 22

BLIND LEMON JEFFERSON/LEADBELLY

61 Jazz Collector JEL 24 THE MALE BLUES VOLUME 8 (EP) ... 20

BLIND LEMON JEFFERSON & RAMBLING THOMAS

50s Heritage HLP 1007 BLIND LEMON JEFFERSON AND RAMBLING THOMAS (LP, 99 only) ... 100

EDDIE JEFFERSON

67 Stateside SS 591 Some Other Time/When You Look In The Mirror ... 12

GEORGE PAUL JEFFERSON

68 Fontana TF 923 Looking For My Mind/Out Of Place ... 12

MARSHALL JEFFERSON

88 ffrr FFRX 18 Open Your Eyes (Celestial Mix)/(Spiritual Mix)/
(Marshall's Elevated Dub) (12", p/s) ... 15

JEFFERSON AIRPLANE

67 RCA Victor RCA 1594 Somebody To Love/She Has Funny Cars ... 12
67 RCA Victor RCA 1631 White Rabbit/Plastic Fantastic Lover ... 15
67 RCA Victor RCA 1647 Ballad Of You And Me and Pooneil/Two Heads ... 10
68 RCA Victor RCA 1711 Greasy Heart/Share A Little Joke (With The World) ... 15
68 RCA Victor RCA 1736 If You Feel Like China Breaking/Triad ... 10
70 RCA RCA 1933 Volunteers/We Can Be Together ... 6
70 RCA RCA 1964 Somebody To Love/White Rabbit ... 6
70 RCA RCA 1989 Mexico/Have You Seen The Saucers? ... 6
72 Grunt 65-0500 Pretty As You Feel/Wild Turkey ... 7
72 Grunt 65-0506 Long John Silver/Milk Train ... 6
67 RCA Victor RD/SF 7889 SURREALISTIC PILLOW (LP, black label, mono/stereo) ... 40/30
68 RCA Victor RD/SF 7926 AFTER BATHING AT BAXTERS (LP, black label, mono/stereo) ... 40/30
68 RCA Victor RD/SF 7976 CROWN OF CREATION (LP, black label, mono/stereo) ... 20/18
69 RCA RD/SF 8019 BLESS ITS POINTED LITTLE HEAD (LP) ... 18
69 RCA Victor SF 7889 SURREALISTIC PILLOW (LP, repressing, orange label) ... 15
69 RCA Victor SF 7926 AFTER BATHING AT BAXTERS (LP, repressing, orange label) ... 15
69 RCA Victor SF 7976 CROWN OF CREATION (LP, repressing, orange label) ... 15
70 RCA SF 8076 VOLUNTEERS (LP, gatefold sleeve) ... 18
71 RCA SF 8164 THE WORST OF JEFFERSON AIRPLANE (LP, matt sleeve) ... 15
71 Grunt FTR 1001 BARK (LP, bag cover with lyric sheet & brown inner sleeve) ... 18
71 RCA SF 8195 JEFFERSON AIRPLANE TAKES OFF (LP) ... 15
72 Grunt FTR 1007 LONG JOHN SILVER (LP, open-out box cover with inner lyric sleeve) ... 18
73 Grunt FTR 0147 30 SECONDS OVER WINTERLAND (LP, with inner sleeve) ... 15
(see also Jefferson Starship, Great Society, Paul Kantner, Grace Slick, Papa John Creach, Hot Tuna)

FRAN JEFFRIES

67 Monument MON 1006 My Lonely Corner/Life Goes On ... 5

JEGA

96 Skam SKA 6 Phlax/Nortom Midgate/Bluette/Ionic/Evil Lee Kirtcele/
Steel Drum/In With The In (12", custom sleeve) ... 50
97 Skam SKA 9 Card Hore/Oak Hanger/Nausicaa/Stainless Steel Drum/Star Houdini (12", p/s) ... 50

JELLYBEAN

84 EMI America 12EAX 210 Sidewalk Talk (featuring Madonna)/Was Dog A Doughnut/Sidewalk Talk (featuring Madonna)/Was Dog A Doughnut (12" remix, p/s) ... 10

(see also Madonna)

JELLY BEANS

64 Pye International 7N 25252 I Wanna Love Him So Bad/So Long ... 25
64 Red Bird RB 10011 The Kind Of Boy You Can't Forget/Baby Be Mine ... 25
75 Right On R 102 You Don't Mean Me No Good/I'm Hip To You ... 15

JELLYBREAD

69 Blue Horizon 57-3162 Chairman Mao's Boogaloo/No One Else ... 15
70 Blue Horizon 57-3169 Comment/Funky Wasp ... 15
70 Blue Horizon 57-3174 Rockin' Pneumonia And The Boogie-Woogie Flu/Readin' The Meters ... 15
70 Blue Horizon 57-3180 Old Man Hank/Faded Grace ... 15
71 Blue Horizon 2096 001 Creepin' And Crawlin'/The Loser/The Clergyman's Daughter ... 12
72 Blue Horizon 2096 006 Down Along The Cove/Sister Lucy ... 15
60s Liphook 1 JELLYBREAD (mini-LP) ... 70
69 Blue Horizon 7-63853 FIRST SLICE (LP) ... 50
71 Blue Horizon 2431 002 65 PARKWAY (LP) ... 50
72 Blue Horizon 2931 004 BACK TO THE BEGINNING AGAIN (LP) ... 75

JELLYFISH

90 Charisma CUSS 2 Baby's Coming Back/All I Want Is Everything (Live) (p/s) ... 6
90 Charisma CUSCX 2 Baby's Coming Back (CD) ... 8
91 Charisma CUST 1 The King Is Half Undressed (12", p/s) ... 8
91 Charisma CUST 3 Now She Knows She's Wrong (12", p/s) ... 8
91 Charisma CUSCD 3 Now She Knows She's Wrong/Bedspring Kiss, Let 'Em In/That Is Why (Live)/ The King Is Half Undressed (Live) (CD) ... 8
91 Charisma CUSLP 3 BELLYBUTTON (LP) ... 12

DIANNE JENKINS

76 Crystal CR 7025 Tow-A-Way-Zone/Anniversary ... 10

GORDON JENKINS ORCHESTRA

60 London HLR 9089 The Clock Song/Romantica ... 8

(see also Ella Fitzgerald)

JOHNNY JENKINS

69 Atco 226 009 The Voodoo In You/Backside Blues ... 10
71 Atco 2400 033 TON-TON MACOUTE (LP) ... 25

JENNIFER (WARNES)

69 London HLU 10278 Let The Sun Shine In/Easy To Be Hard ... 7
70 London HLU 10312 Cajun Train/Old Folks (Les Vieux) ... 8

JENNIFERS

92 Nude NUD 2T Just Got Back Today/Rocks And Boulders/Danny's Song/ Tomorrow's Rain (12") ... 70
92 Nude NUD 2CD Just Got Back Today/Rocks And Boulders/Danny's Song/ Tomorrow's Rain (CD) ... 100

(see also Supergrass)

BILL JENNINGS

55 Parlophone MSP 6146 Stuffy/Solitude (as Bill Jennings-Leo Parker Quintet) ... 6
55 Parlophone MSP 6156 Soft Winds/What's New? (as Bill Jennings Quartet) ... 6

WAYLON JENNINGS

69 RCA RCA 1866 The Days Of Sand And Shovels/Delia's Gone ... 6
80 RCA PB 9561 The Dukes Of Hazzard Theme/Storms Never Last (p/s) ... 5
68 RCA SF 8003 ONLY THE GREATEST (LP) ... 15
70 A&M Mayfair AMLB 1006 THE COUNTRY SIDE OF WAYLON JENNINGS (LP) ... 12
70 RCA Victor LSA 3000 BEST OF WAYLON JENNINGS (LP) ... 12
72 RCA Victor LSA 3053 CEDARTOWN, GEORGIA (LP) ... 12
74 RCA AFL1-0240 HONKY TONK HEROES (LP) ... 12
74 RCA AFL1-0539 THIS TIME (LP) ... 12

JENNORS

67 Coxsone CS 7024 Pressure And Slide (actually by Tennors)/SOUL BROTHERS: One Stop ... 30

(see also Tennors)

KRIS JENSEN

62 Fontana 267 241 TF Torture/Let's Sit Down ... 15
63 Fontana 267 267 TF Don't Take Her From Me/Claudette ... 15
64 Hickory 45-1224 Donna Donna/Big As I Can Dream ... 15
64 Hickory 45-1243 Lookin' For Love/In Time ... 10
64 Hickory 45-1256 Come Back To Me/You've Only Got Me To Lose ... 10
65 Hickory 45-1285 The Little Wind-Up Doll/Somebody's Smiling While I'm Crying ... 10
65 Hickory 45-1311 What Should I Do/That's A Whole Lotta Love ... 10

KRIS JENSEN/SUE THOMPSON

65 Hickory LPE 1507 INTRODUCING KRIS JENSEN AND SUE THOMPSON (EP, 2 tracks each) ... 22

(see also Sue Thompson)

PAUL JENSEN & CAR THIEVES

78 Albatross TIT 3 Holiday In Spain/Always Arrive On Time (p/s) ... 6

JENSENS

68 Philips BF 1686 Deep Thinking/Marguerite ... 12

(see also Tempus Fugit)

BILL JENTIES

70 Smash SMA 2307 Stop Them (actually by Bill Gentles)/MAXINE: I Don't Care ... 10

(see also Bill Gentles/Bill Jentles)

MINT VALUE £

BILL JENTLES

70	Pama PM 809	True True Train/JEFF BARNES: Give And Take	15

(see also Bill Jenties)

JERICHO (JONES)

71	A&M AMS 833	Time Is Now/Freedom	5
72	A&M AMS 883	Don't Let Me Down/Mona Mona	10
72	A&M AMS 7017	Hey Man/Champs	10
72	A&M AMS 7037	Mama's Gonna Take You Home/So Come On	10
71	A&M AMLH 68050	JUNKIES, MONKEYS & DONKEYS (LP, as Jericho Jones)	100
72	A&M AMLS 68079	JERICHO (LP, beware of counterfeits with slightly thicker sleeves)	80

JERKS

78	Underground URA 1	Get Your Woofing Dog Off Me/Hold My Hand (p/s)	35
78	Lightning GIL 549	Cool/Jerkin' (p/s)	20
80	Laser LAS 25	Come Back Bogart (I Wish You Would)/Are You Strong Enough?/ The Strangest Man Of All (p/s)	15

JERMZ

78	One Way EFP 1	Power Cut/Me And My Baby (p/s)	200

JERRY JEROME

55	MGM SP 1118	Honey/In A Little Spanish Town	5

JERRY & FREEDOM SINGERS

70	Banana BA 308	It's All In The Game (pseudonym for Winston Francis)/ IM: The Way To My Heart (pseudonym for Cedric Brooks)	15

(see also Winston Francis)

JERRY O

67	London HLZ 10162	Karate Boo-ga-loo/The Pearl	10
71	Jay Boy BOY 33	Karate Boo-ga-loo/The Pearl (reissue)	8
72	Jay Boy BOY 62	Dance What 'Cha Wanna/Afro-Twist Time	8

JERUSALEM

72	Deram DM 358	Kamakazi Moth/Frustration	40
72	Deram SDL 6	JERUSALEM (LP, gatefold sleeve)	100

(see also Pussy, Ian Gillan)

JERUSALEM

79	Praise PLP 4	JERUSALEM (LP, with insert)	30
80	Myrrh MYR 1097	VOLUME 2 (LP, with insert)	25
82	Myrrh MYR 1113	WARRIOR (LP)	30

JESS & JAMES

68	MGM MGM 1389	Move/What Was I Born For	20
68	MGM MGM 1420	Something For Nothing/I Let The Day Go By (with J.J. Band)	20
68	MGM MGM 1454	Thank You Show Biz/Motherless Child	12

JESTERS

62	R&L RL 15/16	Little Girl/Casa Pedro (early labels blue and white)	30

JESTERS

73	Jam JAM 35	Fool For A Day/Can't Live Without You	18

JESUS & MARY CHAIN

84	Creation CRE 012	Upside Down/Vegetable Man (black & white wraparound p/s in poly bag with address on rear & name in red)	25
84	Creation CRE 012	Upside Down/Vegetable Man (red & white wraparound p/s in poly bag with address on rear & name in black)	20
84	Creation CRE 012	Upside Down/Vegetable Man (pink, blue or yellow wraparound p/s in poly bag; some with small T-shirt offer insert)	8
86	Creation CRE 012	Upside Down/Vegetable Man (reissue, different printed p/s)	5
86	Creation CRE 012T	Upside Down/Vegetable Man/Upside Down (demo) (12" white label, no sleeve)	35
85	Blanco Y Negro NEG 008	Never Understand/Suck (p/s)	5
85	Blanco Y Negro NEG 17F	Just Like Honey/Head//Inside Me/Just Like Honey (Demo Oct 84) (double pack, gatefold p/s)	15
86	Blanco Y Negro NEG 19F	Some Candy Talking/Psycho Candy/Hit//Cut Dead/You Trip Me Up/ Some Candy Talking/Psycho Candy (double pack, gatefold p/s, 2nd 7" all acoustic)	6
87	WEA NEG 24T	April Skies (Long Version) (12", p/s)	8
87	Blanco Y Negro NEGB 25	Happy When It Rains/Everything Is Alright When You're Down (box set with postcards)	7
87	WEA NEG 29F	Darklands/Rider/On The Wall (Demo) (gatefold p/s)	5
87	WEA NEG 29FTE	Darklands/Rider/On The Wall (Demo) (10", p/s)	7
89	Blanco Y Negro NEG 41	Blues From A Gun (p/s)	5
89	Blanco Y Negro NEG 41TE	Blues From A Gun/Shimmer/Penetration/Break Me Down (10", gatefold p/s)	25
89	Blanco Y Negro NEG 42/XB/Y/Z	Head On/Terminal Beach//Head On/Deviant Slice//Head On/ I'm Glad I Never//Head On/In The Black (4 x 7" box set; each single sold separately)	12
90	Blanco Y Negro NEG 45	Rollercoaster (p/s)	5
92	Blanco Y Negro NEG 57T	Almost Gold	5
92	Blanco Y Negro NEG 57T	Almost Gold (12")	8
94	Blanco Y Negro NEG 73CD1	Come On (CD)	8
85	Fierce FRIGHT 004	RIOT (EP, with 'LSD bar' & badge; 2 different sleeves)	25
87	WEA NEG 29TE	DARKLANDS EP: Darklands/Rider/Here It Comes Again/On The Wall (Demo) (10", p/s)	7
95	Blanco Y Negro NEG 81TEX	I HATE ROCK 'N' ROLL EP (10")	7

(see also Acid Angels, Primal Scream, Meat Whiplash)

JESUS IS

70s	Myrrh MYR 1049	JESUS IS (LP)	15

JESUS LIZARD

92	own label	Gladiator (Marquee gig freebie)	8
93	Touch & Go TG 83	Puss/NIRVANA: Oh, The Guilt (p/s, blue vinyl, some with poster)	25/12
93	Touch & Go TG 83	Puss/NIRVANA: Oh, The Guilt (p/s, black vinyl)	18
93	Touch & Go TG 83CD	Puss/NIRVANA: Oh, The Guilt (CD)	20
93	Touch & Go TG 128	Fly On The Wall/White Hole (green vinyl)	5

(see also Nirvana)

JESUS LOVES YOU

89	More Protein PRTOX 12	After The Love (Fon Force Remix)/After The Love (Dub) (12", p/s)	8
89	More Protein PROCD 2	After The Love (10 Glorious Years Edit)/After The Love (10 Glorious Years Mix)/ After The Love (Orbital House Mix) (3" CD, card sleeve)	8
91	More Protein PROT 1312DJ	After The Love (Prophets Of Doom Mix)/(Naughty Norman Normal's Nightie Mix)/Generations Of Love (Absolutely Queer Remix) (12", p/s, promo only)	15
92	Virgin VSCDX 1449	Sweet Toxic Love (Deliverance Mix)/(Hootenanny Mix)/ Am I Losing Control (Disco Mix)/Am I Losing Control (Dizzy Tequila Mix) (CD, plastic clip-shut pack with booklet)	12

(see also Boy George, Culture Club)

JET

75	CBS 80699	JET (LP)	15

(see also Andy Ellison, Nice, Radio Stars, Sparks)

JET (Australia)

03	Warner Bros 7559-62866-1	Are You Gonna Be My Girl (Album Version)/Hey Kids/That's Alright Mama (12", gatefold p/s)	8
03	Warner Bros 7559 628861	DIRTY SWEET EP: Take It Or Leave It/Cold Hard Bitch/Move On/Rollover DJ (12", p/s)	10

JETHRO TULL

SINGLES

68	MGM MGM 1384	Sunshine Day/Aeroplane (miscredited to 'Jethro Toe'; counterfeits credit 'Jethro Tull')	225
68	Island WIP 6043	A Song For Jeffrey/One For John Gee	60
68	Island WIP 6048	Love Story/A Christmas Song (2 different pink label designs)	each 8
68	Island WIP 6048	Love Story/A Christmas Song (mispressing, B-side or both sides credited to Ian Henderson)	each 12
69	Island WIP 6056	Living In The Past/Driving Song (2 different pink labels)	each 15
69	Chrysalis WIP 6070	Sweet Dream/17 (push-out or large centre hole)	7
70	Chrysalis WIP 6077	The Witch's Promise/Teacher (some in p/s)	20/15
70	Chrysalis WIP 6081	Inside/Alive And Well And Living In	10
71	Chrysalis WIP 6098	Lick Your Fingers Clean/Up To Me (unissued)	
71	Chrysalis WIP 6106	Life Is A Long Song/Up The 'Pool/Dr. Bogenbroom/From Later/Nursie (EP, p/s)	8
74	Chrysalis CHS 2054	Bungle In The Jungle/Back Door Angels	6
75	Chrysalis CHS 2075	Minstrel In The Gallery/Summerday Sands	5
76	Chrysalis CHS 2086	Too Old To Rock'n'Roll: Too Young To Die/Rainbow Blues	5
76	Chrysalis CXP 2275	Ring Out Solstice Bells/March The Mad Scientist/A Christmas Song/ Pan Dance (EP)	8
77	Chrysalis CHS 2135	The Whistler/Strip Cartoon (some in p/s)	25/8
78	Chrysalis CHS 2214	Moths/Life Is A Long Song (p/s)	10
78	Chrysalis CHS 2260	A Stitch In Time (3.30 Version)/Sweet Dream (p/s, white or black vinyl)	12/8
78	Chrysalis CHS 2260	A Stitch In Time (4.20 Version)/Sweet Dream (p/s, white or black vinyl)	12/8
79	Chrysalis CHS 2378	North Sea Oil/Elegy (p/s)	10
79	Chrysalis CHS 2394	Home/King Henry's Madrigal (Theme From Mainstream)/Warm Sporran (p/s)	12
79	Chrysalis CHS 2443	Ring Out Solstice Bells/March The Mad Scientist/A Christmas Song/ Pan Dance (EP, reissue)	7
79	Chrysalis CHS 2468	Working John, Working Joe/Flyingdale Flyer (p/s)	8
80	Chrysalis CHS 2619	Broadsword/Fallen On Hard Times (p/s)	6
80	Chrysalis CHSP 2619	Broadsword/Fallen On Hard Times (picture disc)	12
84	Chrysalis TULLD 1	Lap Of Luxury/Astronomy//Automotive Engineering/Tundra (double pack, gatefold p/s)	10
84	Chrysalis TULL X 1	Lap Of Luxury/Astronomy/Automotive Engineering/Tundra (12", p/s)	10
86	Chrysalis TULL 2	Coronach (with David Palmer)/Jack Frost And The Hooded Crow (p/s)	7
86	Chrysalis TULLX 2	Coronach (with David Palmer)/Jack Frost And The Hooded Crow/ Living In The Past/Elegy (12", p/s)	40
87	Chrysalis TULLP 3	Steel Monkey/Down At The End Of Your Road (die-cut picture disc)	20
87	Chrysalis ZTULL 3	Steel Monkey/Down At The End Of Your Road/Too Many Too/I'm Your Gun (cassette, numbered edition of 3,000 with competition pack & badge)	15
87	Chrysalis TULLX 3	Steel Monkey (12", p/s)	10
88	Chrysalis TULLX 4	Said She Was A Dancer/Dogs In The Midwinter (p/s)	6
88	Chrysalis TULLP 4	Said She Was A Dancer/Dogs In The Midwinter (shaped picture disc)	10
88	Chrysalis TULLX 4	Said She Was A Dancer/Dogs In The Midwinter (12", p/s)	8
88	Chrysalis TULLCD 4	Said She Was A Dancer/Dogs In The Midwinter/ Down At The End Of The Road/Too Many Too (CD, picture disc, limited issue)	25
88	Chrysalis TULPCD 1	Part Of The Machine (Edit)/Stormy Monday Blues (live)/Lick Your Fingers Clean/ Minstrel In The Gallery (live)/Farm On The Freeway (live) (CD, picture disc)	15
89	Chrysalis TULL 5	Another Christmas Song (p/s)	10
89	Chrysalis TULLCD 5	Another Christmas Song/Intro — A Christmas Song (live)/Cheap Day Return — Mother Goose (live)/Outro — Locomotive Breath (live) (CD)	10
91	Chrysalis TULLX 6	This Is Not Love (12", p/s)	10
92	Chrysalis TULLCD 7	Rocks On The Road/Jack-A-Lynn (Home Demo)/Tall Thin Girl (live)/Fat Man (live)/Rocks On The Road/Bouree (live)/Mother Goose-Jack-A-Lynn (live)/ Aqualung — Locomotive Breath (live) (2-CD, boxed)	8
92	Chrysalis TULLX 7	Rocks On The Road/Jack-A-Lynn (home demo)/ Aqualung-Locomotive Breath (live) (12", picture disc)	10
93	Chrysalis 12CHS 3970	Living In The Past (12", p/s)	10

MINT VALUE £

Year	Label/Cat. No.	Title	Value
93	Chrysalis 23970/1	Living In The (Slightly More Recent) Past (live)/Silver River Turning/Rosa On The Factory Floor/I Don't Want To Be Me/Living In The Past/Truck Stop Runner/Piece Of Cake/Man Of Principle (2-CD set)	8
99	Papillon BTFLYS 0001	Bends Like A Willow (edit)/Dot Com (edit)/It All Trickles Down (CD)	15

ORIGINAL LPs

Year	Label/Cat. No.	Title	Value
68	Island ILP 985	THIS WAS (1st pressing, pink label/black & orange 'circle' logo, mono)	100
68	Island ILPS 9085	THIS WAS (1st pressing, pink label/black & orange 'circle' logo, stereo, flipback sleeve, some sleeves as mono issues with stereo stickers)	40
69	Island ILPS 9103	STAND UP (1st pressing, pop-up sleeve, pink label/black & orange 'circle' logo)	40
70	Chrysalis ILPS 9123	BENEFIT (green Chrysalis or Island pink rim label/'palm tree' logo)	20
71	Island ILPS 9145	AQUALUNG (with gatefold sleeve & inner bag)	20
72	Chrysalis CHR 1003	THICK AS A BRICK (fold-out newspaper sleeve)	20
72	Chrysalis CJT 1	LIVING IN THE PAST (2-LP, with hard sleeve & booklet)	25
73	Chrysalis CHR 1040	A PASSION PLAY (with theatre booklet)	15
74	Chrysalis CHR 1067	WARCHILD (with lyric inner sleeve)	12
75	Chrysalis CHR 1082	MINSTREL IN THE GALLERY (with lyric inner sleeve)	12
76	Chrysalis CHR 1111	TOO OLD TO ROCK 'N' ROLL	12
77	Chrysalis CJT 4	LIVE — BURSTING OUT (2-LP, gatefold sleeve with inners)	15

(First pressings of all above Chrysalis LPs have a white 'I' logo on the label. Second pressings without this are worth slightly less)

Year	Label/Cat. No.	Title	Value
84	Chrysalis CDLP 1461	UNDER WRAPS (picture disc)	15
84	Chrysalis CHR 1078	MU — THE BEST OF (stickered sleeve, with poster)	15

LP REPRESSINGS

Year	Label/Cat. No.	Title	Value
68	Island ILP 985	THIS WAS (pink label/'i' logo, mono)	45
69	Island ILPS 9085	THIS WAS (pink label/black 'block' logo, 1st mix)	20
70	Island ILPS 9085	THIS WAS (pink label/'i' logo)	20
70	Chrysalis ILPS 9103	STAND UP (pop-up sleeve, pink label/black 'block' logo or pink label/'i' logo)	15/12

(see also Mick Abrahams, Blodwyn Pig, Wild Turkey, The John Even Band)

JETLINERS

Year	Label/Cat. No.	Title	Value
66	Blue Beat BB 367	Meditation (actually by Sugar & Dandy)/GIRL SATCHMO: Nature Of Love (actually with Jetliners)	25

JETS

Year	Label/Cat. No.	Title	Value
78	Soho SH 3	Rockabilly Baby/James Dean	5

JET SET

Year	Label/Cat. No.	Title	Value
62	Delta DW 5001	VC 10/Cruising 600 (some in p/s)	15

JET SET

Year	Label/Cat. No.	Title	Value
64	Parlophone R 5199	You Got Me Hooked/True To You	25

(see also Liza & Jet Set, Soulmates)

JETSET

Year	Label/Cat. No.	Title	Value
80s	Shadows And Reflections	What Can I Say (Demo)/Christmas Greeting (flexidisc free with fanzine)	6/5
84	Dance Network NET 1	BEST OF THE JETSET (EP)	10
85	Dance Network NET 3	APRIL, MAY, JUNE AND THE JETSET (12" EP)	12
85	Dance Network WORK 1	THERE GOES THE NEIGHBOURHOOD (LP, pink sleeve)	20
86	Dance Network WORK 4	4 GO BANANAS (LP, with lyric insert)	20

(see also Paul Bevoir)

JETSTREAMS

Year	Label/Cat. No.	Title	Value
59	Decca F 11149	Bongo Rock/Tiger	22
59	Decca F 11149	Bongo Rock/Tiger (78)	25

JEWELS

Year	Label/Cat. No.	Title	Value
64	Colpix PX 11034	Opportunity/Gotta Find A Way	18
65	Colpix PX 11048	But I Do/Smokey Joe	15

JIGSAW

Year	Label/Cat. No.	Title	Value
68	Polydor 56241	I Need Your Love/I've Gotta Get Me Some Money (as Jig-Saw Band)	8
68	Music Factory CUB 4	Mister Job/Great Idea	12
68	Music Factory CUB 6	Let Me Go Home/Tumblin'	75
68	MGM MGM 1410	One Way Street/Then I Found You	50
70	Philips 6006 112	One Way Street/Coffucious Confusion	40
70	Fontana 6007 017	Lollipop And Goody Man/Seven Fishes	50
71	Philips 6006 131	Jesu Joy Of Man's Desiring/No Questions Asked	7
71	Philips 6006 182	Keeping My Head Above Water/It's Nice But It's Wrong	7
73	U.K. UK 45	That's What It's All About/And I Like You	5
74	BASF BA 1002	I've Seen The Film, I've Read The Book/Mention My Name	5
74	BASF BA 1010	You're Not The Only Girl/Face The Music	5
71	Philips 6308 033	LETHERSLADE FARM (LP)	75
72	Philips 6308 072	AURORA BOREALIS (LP)	60
73	BASF 29106-5	BROKEN HEARTED (LP, gatefold sleeve)	30
74	BASF BAP 5051	I'VE SEEN THE FILM, I'VE READ THE BOOK (LP)	22

JIH

Year	Label/Cat. No.	Title	Value
88	Jungle JUNG 32T/BOV 3	Take Me To The Girl/Come Summer Come Winter/Wake Up (12", unissued, Mayking test pressings only, white proof p/s)	20
88	Jungle JUNG 32T/BOV 3	Take Me To The Girl/Come Summer Come Winter/Wake Up (12", 'small photos' p/s, later blue art p/s)	10/7

(see also Associates)

JILL & BOULEVARDS

Year	Label/Cat. No.	Title	Value
62	Columbia DB 4823	And Now I Cry/Eugene	22

JILL & Y'VERNS

Year	Label/Cat. No.	Title	Value
60s	Oak RGJ 503	My Soulful Dress/Anything He Wants Me To Do	90

JILTED JOHN

78 Rabid TOSH 105 — Jilted John/Going Steady (p/s) — 12
78 EMI International INT 567 — Jilted John/Going Steady (p/s, reissue) — 6
78 EMI International INT 577 — True Love/I Was A Pre-Pubescent (p/s) — 7
78 EMI International INT 587 — The Birthday Kiss/Baz's Party (p/s) — 7
78 EMI Intl. INS 3024 — TRUE LOVE STORIES (LP, some with board game insert) — 18/12
(see also Going Red?)

JIMBILIN

71 Bamboo BAM 68 — Human Race/Let Love In (both actually by Herman Chin-Loy & Aquarians) — 15

JIM & JOE

64 London HL 9831 — Fireball Mail/Daisy Mae — 20
(see also James Burton)

JIM & MONICA

64 Stateside SS 266 — Slippin' And Slidin'/Sing Along Without Jim & Monica — 20
(see also Jimmy Gilmer & Fireballs)

JIMMIE & NIGHT HOPPERS

59 London HLP 8830 — Cruisin'/Night Hop — 30
59 London HLP 8830 — Cruisin'/Night Hop (78) — 40

JIVA

75 Dark Horse AMLH 22003 — JIVA (LP, with inner sleeve) — 12

JIV-A-TONES

58 Felsted AF 101 — Flirty Gertie/Fire Engine Baby — 275
58 Felsted AF 101 — Flirty Gertie/Fire Engine Baby (78) — 150

JIVE FIVE

61 Parlophone R 4822 — My True Story/When I Was Single — 150
62 Stateside SS 133 — What Time Is It?/Begging You Please — 80
65 United Artists UP 1106 — I'm A Happy Man/Kiss Kiss KIss — 25

JIVERS (U.S.)

56 Vogue V 9060 — Little Mama/Cherie — 675
56 Vogue V 9060 — Little Mama/Cherie (78) — 150
57 Vogue V 9068 — Ray Pearl/Dear Little One — 625
57 Vogue V 9068 — Ray Pearl/Dear Little One (78) — 125

JIVERS (Jamaica)

68 Trojan TR 604 — Wear My Crown/Down On The Beach — 8
(see also Brother Dan Allstars)

JIVING JUNIORS

60 Blue Beat BB 4 — Lollipop Girl/Dearest Darling — 75
60 Blue Beat BB 5 — My Heart's Desire/I Love You — 75
60 Starlite ST45 028 — Lovers Line/Tu-Woo-Up-Tu-Woo — 70
61 Starlite ST45 049 — Slop & Mash/My Sweet Angel — 60
61 Blue Beat BB 36 — Over The River/Hip Rub (with Hersan & His City Slickers) — 50
62 Island WI 003 — Sugar Dandy/Valerie — 30
62 Island WI 027 — Andrea/Don't Leave Me — 50
63 Island WI 129 — Sugar Dandy/Valerie (reissue) — 30
73 United Artists UP 35494 — Stay/Call Me — 6
(see also Duke Reid)

J.J. ALLSTARS

68 Duke DU 3 — One Dollar Of Music/CARL DAWKINS: I'll Make It Up — 20
69 Trojan TR 691 — Memphis Underground (Parts 1 & 2) — 18
70 Duke DU 94 — Collecting Coins/Cabbage Leaf — 12
70 Duke DU 95 — This Land (actually by Carl Dawkins)/Land Version — 12
70 Escort ES 821 — Mango Tree/The Removers (both actually by Winston Wright & J.J. All Stars) — 12
71 Big Shot BI 570 — Perseverence Version/CARL DAWKINS: Perseverance — 12
71 Explosion EX 2051 — I Feel Good (Version 2)/CARL DAWKINS: I Feel Good — 10
(see also Lloyd Young, Bleechers, Ethiopians)

JJ72

IRISH PRESSING

99 JJ 72 CD 01 — Pillows (Oxygen)/Undercover Angel/Surrender (CD demo, some with handwritten note) — 150/125

UK PRESSINGS

99 Lakota LAK 0011 CD — October Swimmer/Improv/Gherkin (CD, 500 only) — 60
00 Lakota LAK 7 0014 — Snow/Willow/Fresh Water (7", p/s, 1000 only) — 30
00 Lakota LAK 0014 CD — Snow/Willow/Fresh Water (CD, 2000 only) — 25
00 Lakota 7 0015 — Long Way South/Snow (Acoustic)/Earthly Delights (7") — 5
00 Lakota LAK 12 0016 — Oxygen/Algeria (12", promo-only) — 15
00 Lakota 0016 CDP 01 — Oxygen (CD, promo-only single, custom card sleeve) — 10
00 Lakota 70020P — Algeria (white label 7", promo-only) — 15
01 Lakota 0020 CDP — Algeria (Flood Mix, Radio Edit)/It's A Sin/Algeria (Flood Mix) (CD, promo-only, custom card sleeve) — 15
00 Lakota LAKLP 017 — JJ72 (LP) — 12

JJ'S POWERHOUSE

83 Sillysybin COX 1657 — Running For The Line/Blackrods (no p/s) — 250

DAMITA JO

(see under 'D')

MARCY JO & EDDIE RAMBEAU

63 Stateside SS 235 — Lover's Medley/When You Wore A Tulip — 10
(see also Eddie Rambeau)

MINT VALUE £

ANTONIO CARLOS JOBIM

70	Paramount SPFL 260	THE ADVENTURERS (LP, soundtrack)	12
72	CTI CTL 3	STONE FLOWER (LP)	12

JOBRIATH

73	Elektra K 12129	Take Me I'm Yours/Earthling	6
74	Elektra K 12156	Ooh La La/Gone Tomorrow (demos £25)	6
73	Elektra EKS 75070	JOBRIATH (LP)	15
74	Elektra K 42163	CREATURES OF THE STREET (LP)	12

JO'BURG HAWK

72	Charisma CB 194	Orang Utang/Dark Side Of The Moon	5
73	Charisma CAS 1064	JO'BURG HAWK (LP, gatefold sleeve)	12

JOCK TAMSON'S BAIRNS

80	Temple TP 002	JOCK TAMSON'S BAIRNS (LP, with lyric insert)	12

JODIMARS

56	Capitol CL 14518	Well Now, Dig This/Let's All Rock Together	75
56	Capitol CL 14518	Well Now, Dig This/Let's All Rock Together (78)	25
56	Capitol CL 14627	Rattle My Bones/Lotsa Love	75
56	Capitol CL 14627	Rattle My Bones/Lotsa Love (78)	20
56	Capitol CL 14641	Rattle Shakin' Daddy/Eat Your Heart Out Annie	75
56	Capitol CL 14641	Rattle Shakin' Daddy/Eat Your Heart Out Annie (78)	20
56	Capitol CL 14642	Dance The Bop/Boom, Boom My Bayou Baby	75
56	Capitol CL 14642	Dance The Bop/Boom, Boom My Bayou Baby (78)	20
56	Capitol CL 14663	Midnight/Clarabella	80
56	Capitol CL 14663	Midnight/Clarabella (78)	20
57	Capitol CL 14700	Cloud 99/Later	80
57	Capitol CL 14700	Cloud 99/Later (78)	25
70s	Bulldog BD 16	Well Now, Dig This/Dance The Bop	5
72	Specialty SPE 6608	WELL NOW DIG THIS (LP)	20

(see also Bill Haley & Comets)

JODY GRIND

69	Transatlantic TRA 210	ONE STEP ON (LP)	55
70	Transatlantic TRA 221	FAR CANAL (LP)	55

AL T. JOE (& CELESTIALS)

62	Dice CC 9	Rise Jamaica/I'm On My Own	30
62	Blue Beat BB 126	You Cheated On Me/This Heart Of Mine (as Al T. Joe & Celestials)	30
63	Blue Beat BB 166	Goodbye Dreamboat/Please Forgive Me	30
63	Blue Beat BB 169	Fatso/Slow Boat	30
70	Duke DU 70	It's A Shame/Desertion	10
72	Duke DU 148	Vision/Young And Unlearned	8
72	Dynamic DYN 429	Oh What A Price/The Prisoners Song	8

(see also Jamaica Fats)

JOE & ANN

65	Black Swan WI 468	Gee Baby/Wherever You May Be	30

CALYPSO JOE

69	Escort ES 801	Adults Only/Calalue	8

BILLY JOE & CHECKMATES

61	London HLU 9502	Percolator/Round & Round & Round & Round	18

JOE COOL (& THE KILLERS)

77	Ariola ARO 105	I Just Don't Care/My Way (p/s)	25

JOE & EDDIE

59	Capitol CL 15038	Green Grass/And I Believed	7
64	Vocalion V 9215	There's A Meetin' Here Tonight/Lonesome Traveller	10
65	Vocalion V 9238	Gabrielle/He's Got The Whole World In His Hands	10
65	Vocalion V 9242	Depend On Yourself/With You In Mind	10
65	Vocalion V-N 9246	Farewell/Hey Nelly Nelly	10
65	Vocalion V-P 9250	Walkin' Down The Line/It Ain't Me Babe	15

BILLY JOEL

72	Philips 6078 001	She's Got A Way/Everybody Loves You Now	7
74	Philips 6078 018	The Ballad Of Billy The Kid/If I Only Had The Words (To Tell You) (some in p/s)	35/25
78	CBS SCBS 6821	My Life/She's Always A Woman	5
79	CBS 7150	Honesty/Root Beer Rag (withdrawn)	20
80	CBS SCBS 8753	It's Still Rock And Roll To Me/Through The Long Night (p/s)	5
83	CBS A 3655	Tell Her About It/Easy Money (p/s)	5
83	CBS A 4280	The Longest Time/Captain Jack (p/s)	5
83	CBS TA 4521	Leave A Tender Moment Alone/Goodnight Saigon/You May Be Right/Movin' Out/ Big Shot (12", p/s)	10
83	CBS A 4884	This Night/I'll Cry Instead (p/s; some in gatefold p/s [GA 4884])	7/5
86	CBS A 7247	Modern Woman/Sleep With The Television On (p/s)	5
86	CBS DA 7247	Modern Woman/Sleep With The Television On//Up Town/All For Love (double pack)	15
86	CBS 6500 577	A Matter Of Trust/Better Than Nothing (p/s)	5
89	CBS JOEL 1	We Didn't Start The Fire/House Of Blue Light (p/s)	5
89	CBS CDJOEL 1	We Didn't Start The Fire/House Of Blue Light/Just The Way You Are (CD, card sleeve)	12
89	CBS JOEL 3	Leningrad/The Times They Are A-Changin' (live) (p/s)	5
89	CBS CDJOEL 5	THAT'S NOT HER STYLE EP (CD, card sleeve)	15
90	CBS JOELC 2	I GO TO EXTREMES EP (CD)	10
72	Philips 6369 150	COLD SPRING HARBOR (LP)	18
73	Philips 6369 160	PIANO MAN (LP, withdrawn)	25

MINT VALUE £

73	Philips 6078 018	BALLAD OF BILLY THE KID (LP)	15
78	CBS H 82311	THE STRANGER (LP, half-speed master version)	15
79	CBS 66352	BILLY JOEL (3-LP box set)	18
81	CBS 85273	SONGS IN THE ATTIC (LP, gatefold sleeve)	12

(see also Hassles)

JOE 9T & THUNDERBIRDS

80s	Gemme JOE 9T/LYN 6526	Joe 9T Theme/THEY MUST BE RUSSIANS: Psycho Analysis (no p/s, stamped white label)	7

(see also They Must Be Russians)

JOE PUBLIC

70s	Wavelength HURT 3	Herman's Back/Travelling With Raymond/Like It (p/s)	8

JOE PUBLIC

85	Capital CLA 55	Anti CND	25

(see also Long Tall Shorty)

JOE'S ALLSTARS

69	Joe/Duke DU 24	Hey Jude/Musical Feet	12
69	Joe/Duke DU 28	Battle Cry Of Biafra/Funky Reggae Part 1	12
69	Joe/Duke DU 50	Brixton Cat/Solitude	15
70	Joe JRS 9	Tony B's Theme/JOE THE BOSS: Skinhead Revolt	40
72	Sioux SI 012	Tony B's Theme/RAY MARTELL: She Caught The Train	20
70	Trojan TBL 106	BRIXTON CAT (LP)	35

(see also Joe The Boss, Dice The Boss, King Horror, Pattie La Donne)

JOE SOAP

73	Polydor 2383 233	KEEP IT CLEAN (LP)	15

JOE (Mansano) THE BOSS

70	Joe JRS 6	Son Of Al Capone/All My Enemies	20
70	Joe JRS 10	If Life Was A Thing/LLOYD KINGPIN: Daisy Bothering	18

(see also Joe's Allstars, Joe Mansano, Dice The Boss, Pama Dice)

JOEY & CONTINENTALS

70	Polydor 56520	She Rides With Me/Rudy Vadoo	35

(see also G.T.O.'s)

JOEY & GENTLEMEN

64	Fontana TF 444	Like I Love You/I'll Never Let You Go	12
64	Fontana TF 485	Dummy Dum Song/Goodbye Little Girl	6

HENRIK JOHANSEN'S JAZZ BAND

55	Tempo EXA 23	THE TRADITIONAL DANES (EP)	8
57	Tempo EXA 64	HENRIK JOHANSEN'S JAZZ BAND (EP)	8

(see also City Ramblers Skiffle Group, Al Fairweather)

ALEXSANDER JOHN

70s	Myrrh MYR 1010	DAYS GO BY (LP)	18

ANDREW JOHN

71	CBS 7017	Streets Of London/Rick Rack	5
72	CBS 64835	THE MACHINE STOPS (LP)	12

BASIL JOHN

60s	Planetone RC 12	Drink And Drive/MIKE ELLIOTT: J.K. Shuffle	15

CLIVE JOHN

75	United Artists UAS 29733	YOU ALWAYS KNOW WHERE YOU STAND WITH A BUZZARD (LP)	12

(see also Man)

DAVID JOHN & MOOD

64	Vocalion V 9220	To Catch That Man/Pretty Thing	225
65	Parlophone R 5255	Bring It To Jerome/I Love To See You Strut	200
65	Parlophone R 5301	Diggin' For Gold/She's Fine	200

(these singles do NOT feature David Bowie; see also Gagalactyca, Astral Navigations, Little Free Rock)

ELTON JOHN

PHILIPS SINGLES

68	Philips BF 1643	I've Been Loving You/Here's To The Next Time	250
69	Philips BF 1739	Lady Samantha/All Across The Havens	75

DJM SINGLES

69	DJM DJS 205	It's Me That You Need/Just Like Strange Rain (some in p/s)	80/40
70	DJM DJS 217	Border Song/Bad Side Of The Moon	22
70	DJM DJS 222	Rock And Roll Madonna/Grey Seal	22
71	DJM DJS 233	Your Song/Into The Old Man's Shoes	7
71	DJM DJS 244	Friends/Honey Roll	8
72	DJM DJX 501	Rocket Man/Holiday Inn/Goodbye (gatefold p/s)	20
72	DJM DJX 501	Rocket Man/Holiday Inn/Goodbye (plain p/s)	7
72	DJM DJS 269	Honky Cat/Lady Samantha/It's Me That You Need	8
72	DJM DJS 271	Crocodile Rock/Elderberry Wine	7
73	DJM DJS 275	Daniel/Skyline Pigeon (some in p/s)	10/7
73	DJM DJX 502	Saturday Night's Alright For Fighting/Jack Rabbit/Whenever You're Ready (We'll Go Steady Again) (p/s)	7
73	DJM DJS 285	Goodbye Yellow Brick Road/Screw You	7
73	DJM DJS 290	Step Into Christmas/Ho! Ho! Ho! (Who'd Be A Turkey At Christmas)	8
73	DJM DJS 10705	Benny And The Jets/Rock 'N' Roll Madonna	7
74	DJM DJS 297	Candle In The Wind/Benny And The Jets	7
74	DJM DJS 302	Don't Let The Sun Go Down On Me/Sick City	7
74	DJM DJS 322	The Bitch Is Back/Cold Highway	7
74	DJM DJS 340	Lucy In The Sky With Diamonds (featuring Dr. Winston O'Boogie [John Lennon] & His Reggae Guitars)/One Day At A Time	7

MINT VALUE £

75	DJM DJS 354	Philadelphia Freedom/I Saw Her Standing There (as Elton John Band; B-side featuring John Lennon with Muscle Shoals Horns) (p/s)	18
75	DJM DJS 385	Someone Saved My Life Tonight/House Of Cards	5
75	DJM DJS 610	Island Girl/Sugar On The Floor (p/s)	6
76	DJM DJS 629	Grow Some Funk Of Your Own/I Feel Like A Bullet (In The Gun Of Robert Ford)	5
76	DJM DJS 652	Pinball Wizard/Harmony	5
77	DJM DJR 18001	FOUR FROM FOUR EYES (EP)	10
78	DJM DJS 10902	Your Song/Border Song (p/s)	15
78	DJM DJS 10903	Honky Cat/Sixty Years On (p/s)	10
78	DJM DJS 10904	Country Comfort/Crocodile Rock (p/s)	10
78	DJM DJS 10905	Rocket Man/Daniel (p/s)	10
78	DJM DJS 10908	Candle In The Wind/I Feel Like A Bullet (In The Gun Of Robert Ford) (p/s, limited edition)	15
78	DJM DJS 10910	Island Girl/Saturday Night's Alright For Fighting (p/s, limited edition)	15
78	DJM DJS 10911	Philadelphia Freedom/Lucy In The Sky With Diamonds (reissue)	15
78	DJM DJS 10912	Pinball Wizard/Benny And The Jets (p/s)	10
78	DJM EJ 12	THE ELTON JOHN SINGLES COLLECTION (12 x 7" box set [DJS 10901-12])	45
78	DJM DJT 15000	FUNERAL FOR A FRIEND (12" EP)	12
80	DJM DJS 10961	Harmony/Mona Lisas And Mad Hatters (glossy p/s)	5
81	DJM DJS 10965	I Saw Her Standing There/Whatever Gets You Thru The Night/Lucy In The Sky With Diamonds (EP, p/s, featuring John Lennon & Muscle Shoals Horns)	7

ROCKET SINGLES

76	Rocket ROKN 512	Don't Go Breaking My Heart/Snow Queen (with Kiki Dee, p/s)	5
76	Rocket ROKN 517	Sorry Seems To Be The Hardest Word/Shoulder Holster (some in p/s)	7/5
77	Rocket ROKN 521	Crazy Water/Chameleon	5
77	Rocket GOALD 1	The Goaldigger Song/Jimmy, Brian, Elton, Eric (mail-order, signed, 500 only)	300
77	Rocket ROKN 526	Bite Your Lip (Get Up And Dance) (Remix)/KIKI DEE: Chicago	5
77	Rocket RU 1	Bite Your Lip (Get Up And Dance) (Remix)/KIKI DEE: Chicago (12", p/s)	10
78	Rocket ROKN 538	Ego/Flintstone Boy (p/s)	10
78	Rocket XPRES 1	Part Time Love/I Cry At Night (p/s)	10
78	Rocket XPRES 5	Song For Guy/Lovesick	5
78	Rocket DJS 10909	The Bitch Is Back/Grow Some Funk Of Your Own (p/s)	15
79	Rocket XPRES 13	Are You Ready For Love Pts 1& 2	10
79	Rocket XPRES 1312	Are You Ready For Love Pts 1& 2 (12", p/s)	15
79	Rocket XPRES 20	Mama Can't Buy You Love/Strangers (p/s; withdrawn, misspelt "Mamma")	250
79	Rocket XPRES 21	The Victim Of Love/Strangers (p/s)	10
79	Rocket XPRES 24	Johnny B. Goode/Thunder In The Night (p/s)	5
79	Rocket XPRES 2412	Johnny B. Goode/Thunder In The Night (12", p/s)	8
80	Rocket XPRES 41	Sartorial Eloquence/White Man Danger/Cartier (p/s)	8
80	Rocket XPRES 45	Dear God/Tactics (company sleeve)	25
80	Rocket ELTON 1	Dear God/Tactics//Steal Away Child/Love So Cold (double pack, p/s)	10
81	Rocket XPRES 54	Nobody Wins/Fools In Fashions (p/s)	5
81	Rocket XPRES 59	Just Like Belgium/Can't Get Over Getting Over Losing You (company sleeve)	5
82	Rocket XPRES 77	Empty Garden/Take Me Down To The Ocean (p/s)	5
82	Rocket XPPIC 77	Empty Garden/Take Me Down To The Ocean (picture disc)	8
82	Rocket XPRES 85	Princess/The Retreat (p/s)	5
82	Rocket XPRES 88	All Quiet On The Western Front/Where Have All The Good Times Gone (p/s)	7
82	Rocket XPRPO 88	All Quiet On The Western Front/Where Have All The Good Times Gone (poster p/s)	15
83	Rocket XPRES 91	That's Why They Call It The Blues/Lord Choc Ice Goes Mental ('raised musical note' sleeve with shorter A-side title)	18
83	Rocket XPRES 91	I Guess That's Why They Call It The Blues/Lord Choc Ice Goes Mental ('raised musical note' sleeve)	5
83	Rocket EJPIC 1	I'm Still Standing/Earn While You Learn (piano-shaped picture disc)	15
83	Rocket EJS 112	I'm Still Standing (Extended Mix)/Earn While You Learn (12", p/s)	10
83	Rocket EJS 2/FREEJ 2	Kiss The Bride/Dreamboat//Ego/Song For Guy (double pack, p/s)	15
83	Rocket EJS 212	Kiss The Bride (Full Version)/Dreamboat (12", p/s)	8
83	Rocket EJS 3/2	Cold As Christmas/Crystal//Don't Go Breaking My Heart/Snow Queen (double pack, gatefold p/s, 2nd 45 with Kiki Dee)	25
83	Rocket EJS 312	Cold As Christmas/Crystal/J'Veux De La Tendresse (12", p/s)	8
84	Rocket PHPIC 7	Sad Songs (Say So Much) /Simple Man (hat-shaped picture disc)	15
84	Rocket EJS 512	Passengers/Lonely Boy (12", p/s)	10
85	Rocket EJS 7	Breaking Hearts (Ain't what It Used To Be)/Neon (p/s)	5
85	Rocket EJS 8	Act Of War (Part 1)/(Part 2) (with Millie Jackson, 'concertina pack' of video stills)	7
85	Rocket EJSR 8	Act Of War (Part 5) (1-sided promo, p/s lists 2 tracks & 12" cat. no.)	15
85	Rocket EJSR 812	Act Of War (Part 5)/Act Of War (Part 6) (Instrumental) (12", p/s)	15
85	Rocket EJSD 9	Nikita/The Man Who Never Died//Sorry Seems To Be The Hardest Word (live)/ I'm Still Standing (live) (double pack, gatefold p/s, some pop-up)	10/6
85	Rocket EJS 10/EJS 9	Wrap Her Up/Restless (live)//Nikita/The Man Who Never Died (double pack, stickered gatefold PVC wallet with 2 separate p/s's)	7
85	Rocket EJSC 10	Wrap Her Up/Restless (live) (with George Michael, open-out 'cube' p/s)	8
85	Rocket EJSC 10	Wrap Her Up/Restless (live) (with George Michael, open-out 'cube' p/s)	8
85	Rocket EJPIC 10	Wrap Her Up/Restless (live) (with George Michael, oblong-shaped picture disc)	12
85	Rocket EJSP 10	Wrap Her Up/Restless (live) (with George Michael, oblong-shaped picture disc, with pictures on wrong sides)	25
85	Rocket EJS 1012/ELTON 1	Wrap Her Up (Extended Remix) (with George Michael)/Restless (live)/ Nikita/Cold As Christmas (12", double pack in stickered PVC sleeve)	12
85	Rocket EJS 1112	Cry To Heaven/Candy By The Pound/Your Song (12", p/s)	10
86	Rocket EJSD 11	Cry To Heaven/Candy By The Pound//Rock'n'Roll Medley/Your Song (double pack, gatefold p/s)	6
86	Rocket EJSD 12	Heartache All Over The World/Highlander//Passengers/I'm Still Standing (double pack, gatefold p/s)	5
86	Rocket EJSP 13	Slow Rivers (with Cliff Richard)/Billy & The Kids (picture disc)	12
86	Rocket EJSM13	Slow Rivers (with Cliff Richard)/Billy & The Kids/Nikita/Blue Eyes I Guess That's Why They Call It The Blues (cassette)	6

Year	Label / Cat. No.	Title	£
86	Rocket EJS 13-12	Slow Rivers (with Cliff Richard)/Billy & The Kids/Lord Of The Flies (12", p/s)	10
87	Rocket EJS 14	Your Song (live)/Don't Let The Sun Go Down On Me (live) (p/s)	5
87	Rocket EJSM 14	Your Song/Need You To Turn To/Greatest Discovery/Don't Let The Sun Go Down On Me (all tracks live in Australia) (cassette)	5
87	Rocket EJS 1412	Your Song/Need You To Turn To/Greatest Discovery/Don't Let The Sun Go Down On Me (all tracks live in Australia) (12", p/s)	8
88	Rocket EJSP 15	Candle In The Wind (live)/Sorry Seems To Be The Hardest Word (live) (picture disc)	10
88	Rocket EJSM 15	Candle In The Wind (live)/Sorry Seems To Be The Hardest Word (live)/ Your Song (live)/Don't Let The Sun Go Down On Me (live) (cassette)	5
88	Rocket EJS 1512	Candle In The Wind (live)/Sorry Seems To Be The Hardest Word (live)/ Your Song (live)/Don't Let The Sun Go Down On Me (live) (12", p/s)	8
88	Rocket EJSCD 15	Candle In The Wind (live)/Sorry Seems To Be The Hardest Word (live)/ Your Song (live)/Don't Let The Sun Go Down On Me (live) (CD, card sleeve)	12
88	Rocket EJSIP 16	I Don't Wanna Go On With You Like That/Rope Around A Fool/ (Radio 1 interview) (33rpm, poster sleeve)	5
88	Rocket EJS 1612	I Don't Wanna Go On With You Like That (Remix)/(7" Version)/ Rope Around A Fool (12", blue vinyl factory custom pressing, no p/s)	80
88	Rocket EJSCD 16	I Don't Wanna Go On With You Like That/Rope Around A Fool/ I Don't Wanna Go On With You Like That (Extended Mix) (CD, card p/s)	10
88	Rocket EJSLB 17	Town Of Plenty (with Pete Townshend)/Whipping Boy ('look back' pack in box with 4 photos)	7
88	Rocket EJSCD 17	Town Of Plenty (with Pete Townshend)/Whipping Boy/My Baby's A Saint/ I Guess That's Why They Call It The Blues (CD, card p/s)	8
88	Rocket EJSCD 18	A Word In Spanish/Heavy Traffic/Live Medley (Song For You/Blue Eyes/ I Guess That's Why They Call It The Blues)/Daniel (live) (CD, card p/s)	8
88	Rocket 080 524 2	I Don't Wanna Go On With You Like That (CD Video)	12
88	Rocket 080 272 2	Nikita (CD Video)	12
89	Rocket EJSCD 19	Healing Hands/Sad Songs (Say So Much) (live)/Dancing In The End Zone (CD)	8
89	Rocket EJSCD 20	Sacrifice/Love Is A Cannibal/Durban Deep (CD)	15
90	Rocket EJS 21	Club At The End Of The Street/Give Peace A Chance (p/s, withdrawn)	500
90	Rocket EJSCD 21	Club At The End Of The Street/Give Peace A Chance/ I Don't Wanna Go On With You Like That (Live in Verona) (CD, withdrawn, with "Made In England" credit)	20
90	Rocket EJS 2312	Club At The End Of The Street/Whispers/I Don't Wanna Go On With You Like That (Live in Verona) (12", p/s)	8
90	Rocket EJSCD 22	Sacrifice/Healing Hands (CD)	12
90	Rocket EJSG 24	You Gotta Love Someone/Sacrifice (gatefold p/s with discography, dbl A-side)	5
90	Rocket EJS 2412	You Gotta Love Someone/Medicine Man (12", p/s)	8
90	Rocket EJSX 25	Step Into Xmas/Cold As Christmas/Easier To Walk Away/ I Swear I Heard The Night Talking ('Xmas EP', 33rpm, gatefold p/s)	5
90	Rocket EJS 2512	Easier Way To Walk (12", p/s)	10
94	Rocket EJCD 34	Can You Feel The Love Tonight/Hakuna Matata/Under The Stars (CD)	10
94	Rocket EJSJB 35	Circle Of Life (Elton's Version)/(Soundtrack Version) (jukebox issue, no p/s)	5
94	Rocket EJSMX 35	Circle Of Life (Elton's Version)/(Soundtrack Version) (cassette in heavy card box with hinged lid, with 4 mini-postcards)	6
95	Rocket EJSJB 36	Believe/The One (live) (jukebox 7", no p/s)	5
95	Rocket EJSDD 36	Believe/The One/Sorry Seems To Be The Hardest Word (CD)	10
95	Rocket EJSDD 36	Believe/The One/Sorry Seems To Be The Hardest Word//Last Song (live)/ Believe (live) (2-CD, in box)	15
95	Rocket EJSCD 38	Blessed/Made In England (Junior's Sound Factory Mix)/ Made In England (Junior's Joyous Mix) (CD, Part 1 of a 2-CD set, withdrawn)	20
95	Rocket EJSDD 38	Blessed/Honky Cat (live)/Take Me To The Pilot (live)/ The Bitch Is Back (live) (CD, withdrawn)	25
96	Rocket LLHJB 1	Live Like Horses (Studio Version)/(Live Finale Version) (jukebox issue, no p/s)	5
97	Rocket EJSCD 41	Something About The Way You Look Tonight (Edited Version)/ I Know Why I'm In Love/No Valentines/Something About The Way You Look Tonight (Album Version) (CD, jewel case, unreleased)	30
97	Rocket EJSCX 41	Something About The Way You Look Tonight (Edited Version)/ I Know Why I'm In Love/You Can Make History (Young Again)/ Something About The Way You Look Tonight (Album Version) (CD, digipak, unreleased)	30

OTHER SINGLES

Year	Label / Cat. No.	Title	£
81	Ariola ARO 269	Loving You Is Sweeter Than Ever/Twenty Four Hours (p/s, with Kiki Dee)	7
91	Epic 657 646-2	Don't Let The Sun Go Down On Me/I Believe (When I Fall In Love It Will Be Forever [with George Michael]) (live)/If You Were My Woman/Fantasy (CD)	8

DJM LPs

Year	Label / Cat. No.	Title	£
69	DJM DJLP 403	EMPTY SKY (gatefold sleeve, mono)	90
69	DJM DJLPS 403	EMPTY SKY (gatefold sleeve, stereo, with 'stereo' sticker on sleeve)	25
70	DJM DJLPS 406	ELTON JOHN (textured gatefold sleeve, later smooth)	15/12
70	DJM DJLPS 410	TUMBLEWEED CONNECTION (gatefold sleeve with stapled booklet)	12
71	DJM DJLPS 414	17.11.70	12
71	DJM DJLPH 420	MADMAN ACROSS THE WATER (gatefold sleeve)	12
72	DJM DJLPH 427	DON'T SHOOT ME, I'M ONLY THE PIANO PLAYER (gatefold sleeve, with booklet)	12
72	DJM DJLPH 423	HONKY CHATEAU (gatefold sleeve, with foldover flap & pasted photo on cover)	20
74	DJM DJLPH 439	CARIBOU (with inner)	12
75	DJM DJLPH 464	ROCK OF THE WESTIES (with inner & insert)	12
76	DJM DJLPH 473	HERE AND THERE (with inner)	12
76	DJM DJE 29001	GOODBYE YELLOW BRICK ROAD (2-LP, yellow vinyl, triplefold sleeve)	20
77	DJM DJLPH 20473	GREATEST HITS VOLUME TWO (with inner sleeve & lyric booklet)	12
78	DJM DJV 2300	CAPTAIN FANTASTIC AND THE BROWN DIRT COWBOY (picture disc)	20
78	DJM LSP 14512	ELTON JOHN (5-LP, box set)	35
80	DJM DJS 22085	LADY SAMANTHA	12

MINT VALUE £

OTHER LPs

70 Warlock Music WMM 101/2 WARLOCK MUSIC SAMPLER (untitled publishing sampler, 7 tracks by Elton, 4 by Linda Peters) 1,000
71 Paramount SPFL 269 FRIENDS (soundtrack) 12
78 St. Michael 2094 0102 CANDLE IN THE WIND (Marks & Spencer issue) 35
84 Cambra CR 130 SEASONS: THE EARLY LOVE SONGS (2-cassette set, withdrawn, includes unique track, "The Tide Will Turn For Rebecca") 15
87 Rocket EJBXL 1 LIVE IN AUSTRALIA WITH THE MELBOURNE SYMPHONY ORCHESTRA (2-LP box set, numbered banded sleeve, 3,000 only) 20

CDs

87 Rocket EJBXD 1 LIVE IN AUSTRALIA WITH THE MELBOURNE SYMPHONY ORCHESTRA (2-CD box set, 3,000 only) 25
83 DJM CD 4/8100 622 THE SUPERIOR SOUND OF ELTON JOHN 1970-1975 18
91 Rocket 848 236-2 TO BE CONTINUED ... THE VERY BEST OF ELTON JOHN (4-CD, 12" x 8" box set with large colour booklet) 90
93 Happenstance HAPP 001 PLAYS THE SIRAN (private pressing, 50 only) . . . . 500+
93 Happenstance HAPP 002 THE FISHING TRIP (4-CD set, private pressing, 100 only, existence unconfirmed) . . . . 700+
97 Rocket ELTON 50 CELEBRATING ELTON JOHN'S 50TH BIRTHDAY (promo only) 50
99 Mercury ADV 1999/1 AIDA (with Sir Tim Rice) (box set with wallet, plinth stand, interview CD, booklet and calender cards, promo only) 75
99 Mercury ADV 1999/1 AIDA PRESS KIT (card box set with wallet, plinth stand, interview CD, booklet, calender cards, scented candle and broadcast CD-R, promo only) 50
99 Rocket STAR 3 ELTON JOHN'S AIDA (export CD, card p/s, promo only) 30

SESSION RECORDINGS

69 Avenue AVE 80 untitled EP (includes Elton on "Don't Forget To Remember") 8
70 Avenue AVE 93 untitled EP (includes Elton on "I Can't Tell The Bottom From The Top" & "Travellin' Band") 8
70 Avenue AVE 94 untitled EP (includes Elton on "Cottonfields") 8
70 Avenue AVE 97 untitled EP (includes Elton on "Signed Sealed Delivered" & "Natural Sinner") 8
69 Hallmark GM 635 TOP OF THE POPS (LP, includes Elton on "Snake In The Grass") 12
70 Avenue AVE 031 12 TOP HITS (LP, includes Elton on "Don't Forget To Remember") 12
70 Avenue AVE 042 ENGLAND'S 12 TOP HITS (LP, includes Elton on "I Can't Tell The Bottom From The Top" & "Young, Gifted & Black") 12
70 Avenue AVE 055 12 TOP HITS (LP, includes Elton on "Signed Sealed Delivered" & "Natural Sinner") 12
70 Marble Arch MALS 1273 CHARTBUSTERS BOOMIN' (LP, includes Elton on "She Sold Me Magic") 12
70 Marble Arch MALS 1326 CHARTBUSTERS RISIN' (LP, includes Elton on "Young, Gifted & Black") 12
70 Marble Arch MALS 1347 CHARTBUSTERS AGAIN' (LP, includes Elton on "Cottonfields" & "Down The Dustpipe") 12
70 Marble Arch MALS 1357 CHARTBUSTERS TODAY (LP, includes Elton on "Signed Sealed Delivered", "Natural Sinner", "Up Around The Bend", "Rainbow" & "Neanderthal Man") 12
70 Marble Arch MALS 1397 SOUL SPECTACULAR VOL. 3 (LP, includes Elton on "Signed Sealed Delivered") 12
70 Deacon DEA 1015 PICK OF THE POPS (LP, includes Elton on "Spirit In The Sky", "I Can't Tell The Bottom From The Top", "Good Morning Freedom", "Travellin' Band") 12
70 Deacon DEA 1015 PICK OF THE POPS VOL. 4 (LP, includes Elton on "In The Summertime", "Yellow River" & "Natural Sinner") 12
70 Gallery GDEA 1015 PICK OF THE POPS VOL. 4 (LP, reissue of DEA 1015) 12
70 Gallery GDEA 1040 TOP HITS 1970 (LP, includes Elton on "In The Summertime", "Yellow River" & "Spirit In The Sky") 12
70 MFP MFP 1383 HITS 70 (LP, includes Elton on "United We Stand" & "My Baby Loves Lovin') 12
70 Boulevard BLVD 4060 1970 TOP 12 (LP, includes Elton on "In The Summertime", "Love Of The Common People", "Lady D'Arbanville", "Yellow River") 12
70 Stereo Gold Award MER 324 CHART TOPPERS (LP, includes Elton on "Natural Sinner" & "Signed Sealed Delivered") 12
70 Windmill WMD 188 CHARTBUSTING MOTORTOWN (LP, incl. Elton on "Signed Sealed Delivered") 12

(see also [Stu Brown &] Bluesology, Bread & Beer Band, Neil Sedaka, Kiki Dee, Aretha Franklin, Jennifer Rush, Dionne Warwick, Radio Heart)

LITTLE WILLIE JOHN

56 Parlophone DP 510 All Around The World/Don't Leave Me Dear (78, export issue) 50
56 Parlophone R 4209 Fever/Letter From My Darling 125
56 Parlophone R 4209 Fever/Letter From My Darling (78) 40
58 Parlophone R 4396 Uh, Uh, Baby/Dinner Date (With His Girl Friend) 50
58 Parlophone R 4396 Uh, Uh, Baby/Dinner Date (With His Girl Friend) (78) 45
58 Parlophone R 4432 Talk To Me, Talk To Me/Spasms 50
58 Parlophone R 4432 Talk To Me, Talk To Me/Spasms (78) 40
58 Parlophone R 4472 Let's Rock While The Rockin's Good/You're A Sweetheart 70
58 Parlophone R 4472 Let's Rock While The Rockin's Good/You're A Sweetheart (78) 50
59 Parlophone R 4571 Leave My Kitten Alone/Let Nobody Love You 50
60 Parlophone R 4674 Heartbreak (It's Hurtin' Me)/Do You Love Me 30
60 Parlophone R 4699 Sleep/There's A Difference 35
61 Parlophone R 4728 Walk Slow/HANK BALLARD: The Hoochie Coochie Coo 40
59 Parlophone PMC 1163 SURE THINGS (LP) 175
64 London HA 8126 COME ON AND JOIN LITTLE WILLIE JOHN (LP) 100

MABLE JOHN

66 Atlantic 584 022 It's Catching/Your Good Thing (Is About To End) 12
67 Stax 601 010 Same Time Same Place/Bigger And Better (dark blue or light blue label) 15/10
68 Stax 601 034 Able Mable/Don't Get Caught 10

ROBERT JOHN

68 CBS 3436 If You Don't Want My Love/Don't 12
68 CBS 3730 Don't Leave Me/Children 5
68 A&M AMS 835 Raindrops Love And Sunshine/When The Party Is Over 8

SAMMIE JOHN
67 Stateside SS 585 — Little John/Boss Bag 10

JOHN & JOHNNY
63 Decca F 11719 — I Want You To Be My Girl/It's You 6

JOHN & PAUL
65 London HLU 9997 — People Say/I'm Walkin' 15

JOHN LEE'S GROUNDHOGS
66 Planet PLF 104 — Over You Baby/I'll Never Fall In Love Again 150
(see also Groundhogs, Tony McPhee)

JOHNNY & JACK
54 HMV 7MC 21 — Honey, I Need You/Goodnight, Well It's Time To Go (export issue) 22
55 HMV JO 440 — Beware Of "It"/Kiss Crazy Baby (78, export) 12
56 HMV JO 456 — Weary Moments/S.O.S. (78, export) 12
59 RCA RCA 1145 — Sailor Man/Wild And Wicked World 6
59 RCA RCA 1145 — Sailor Man/Wild And Wicked World (78) 20
59 RCA RCX 176 — COUNTRY GUITAR VOL. 10 (EP) 12

JOHNNIE & JOE
58 London HLM 8682 — Over The Mountain, Across The Sea/My Baby's Gone, On, On 350
58 London HLM 8682 — Over The Mountain, Across The Sea/My Baby's Gone, On, On (78) 75

JOHNNY (Osborne) & ATTRACTIONS
67 Doctor Bird DB 1118 — Young Wings Can Fly/DUDLEY WILLIAMSON: I'm Moving On 30

JOHNNY (STEVENS) & THE BLUE BEATS
64 Blue Beat BB 229 — Shame/Ball And Chain 15

JOHNNY & CHAZ & GUNNERS
61 Decca F 11365 — Bobby/Out Of Luck 22

JOHNNY & THE COPYCATS
64 Norco AB 102 — I'm A Hog For You Baby/I Can Never See You 60
(see also My Dear Watson)

JOHNNY & THE HURRICANES
59 London HL 8899 — Crossfire/Lazy (initially triangular-centre, later round centre) 30/22
59 London HL 8899 — Crossfire/Lazy (78) 90
59 London HL 8948 — Red River Rock/Buckeye (initially triangular-centre, later round centre) 12/6
59 London HL 8948 — Red River Rock/Buckeye (78) 70
59 London HL 9017 — Reveille Rock/Time Bomb (initially triangular-centre, later round centre) 15/6
59 London HL 9017 — Reveille Rock/Time Bomb (78) 95
60 London HLI 9072 — Beatnick Fly/Sand Storm 7
60 London HLI 9072 — Beatnick Fly/Sand Storm (78) 105
60 London HLX 9134 — Down Yonder/Sheba 7
60 London HLX 9134 — Down Yonder/Sheba (78) 170
60 London HLX 9190 — Rocking Goose/Revival 7
60 London HLX 9190 — Rocking Goose/Revival (78) 240
60 London HL 7099 — The Hep Canary/Catnip (export issue) 45
61 London HLX 9289 — Ja-Da/Mr. Lonely 7
61 London HLX 9378 — High Voltage/Old Smokie 7
62 London HLX 9491 — Farewell, Farewell/Traffic Jam 7
62 London HLX 7116 — You Are My Sunshine/Farewell, Farewell (export issue) 30
62 London HLX 9536 — Salvation/Misirlou 18
62 London HLX 9617 — Minnesota Fats/Come On Train 8
63 London HLX 9660 — Whatever Happened To Baby Jane/Greens And Beans 8
68 London HLX 10199 — Rocking Goose/Beatnik Fly (reissue) 6
64 Stateside SS 347 — Money Honey/That's All 18
76 United Artists UPS 401 — Red River Rock/Sheba/Reveille Rock/Beatnik Fly (p/s) 6
61 London REX 1284 — ROCKING GOOSE (EP) 35
62 London REX 1347 — JOHNNY AND THE HURRICANES (EP) 35
64 London REX 1414 — JOHNNY AND THE HURRICANES VOL. 2 (EP) 40
60 London HA 2227 — RED RIVER ROCK (LP, plum label; reissues on black label £18) 50
60 London HA-I 2269 — STORMSVILLE (LP) 40
61 London HA-X 2322 — THE BIG SOUND OF JOHNNY AND THE HURRICANES (LP) 50

JOHNNY & JAMMERS
79 Big Beat NS 55 — School Day Blues/You Know I Love You (p/s) 5
(see also Johnny Winter)

JOHNNY & JOHN
66 Polydor 56087 — Bumper To Bumper/Scrape My Boot 15
(see also Johnny Gustafson, Big Three)

JOHNNY & JUDY
59 Vogue Pop V 9128 — Bother Me Baby/Who's To Say 650
59 Vogue Pop V 9128 — Bother Me Baby/Who's To Say (78) 150
(see also John Walker)

JOHNNY & THE SELF ABUSERS
77 Chiswick NS 22 — Saints And Sinners/Dead Vandals (p/s) 25
(see also Simple Minds)

JOHNNY & VIBRATONES
63 Warner Bros WB 107 — Bird Stompin'/Movin' The Bird 12

JOHNNY MOPED
76 Chiswick PROMO 3 — BASICALLY, THE ORIGINAL JOHNNY MOPED TAPE (33rpm, no p/s) 15
77 Chiswick S 15 — No-One/Incendiary Device (p/s) 7
78 Chiswick NS 27 — Darling, Let's Have Another Baby/Something Else/It Really Digs (p/s) 6
78 Chiswick NS 41 — Little Queenie/Hard Lovin' Man (p/s) 6
78 Chiswick WIK 8 — CYCLEDELIC (LP, some with free single [PROMO 3]) 30/12
(see also Slime, Maxim's Trash)

MINT VALUE £

JOHNNY'S BOYS

59	Decca F 11156	Sleep Walk/Ciao Ciao Bambina	12
59	Decca F 11156	Sleep Walk/Ciao Ciao Bambina (78)	8

JOHNNY'S JAZZ

56	Decca FJ 10663	R.J. Boogie/Get Happy (featuring Johnny Hawksworth)	6

(see also Johnny Hawksworth)

BARRY JOHNS

58	HMV POP 472	Locked In The Arms Of Love/Are You Sincere	6

GLYN JOHNS

62	Decca F 11478	January Blues/Sioux Indian	6
63	Decca F 11753	Old Deceiver Time/Dancing With You	6
65	Immediate IM 013	Mary Anne/Like Grains Of Yellow Sand	18
65	Pye 7N 15818	I'll Follow The Sun/I'll Take You Dancing	6
60s	Westcot LYN 827/828	Today You're Gone/Such Stuff Of Dreams (freebie with jeans offer)	6

GLYNIS JOHNS

54	Columbia SCM 5149	I Can't Resist Men/Always You	8

LYNDON JOHNS (& ISRAELITES)

69	Downtown DT 444	Don't Gamble With Love/Song Bird	6
69	Downtown DT 451	Oh Mama Oh Papa/Bring Back The Night (with The Israelites)	6

JOHN'S CHILDREN

66	Columbia DB 8030	The Love I Thought I'd Found/Strange Affair (very few in p/s)	275/150
67	Columbia DB 8124	Just What You Want — Just What You'll Get/But She's Mine	150
67	Track 604 003	Desdemona/Remember Thomas A'Beckett (some in p/s)	125/50
67	Track 604 005	Midsummer Night's Scene/Sara Crazy Child (withdrawn)	3,000+
67	Track 604 005	Come And Play With Me In The Garden/Sara Crazy Child (some in p/s)	150/80
67	Track 604 010	Go Go Girl/Jagged Time Lapse	40
87	Bam Caruso KIRI 095	MIDSUMMER NIGHT'S SCENE (LP)	20

(see also Marc Bolan, Andy Ellison, Radio Stars, Jook, Tyrannosaurus Rex)

AL JOHNSON & JEAN CARN

80	CBS 8545	I'm Back For More/You Are My Personal Angel	6

(see also Jean Carn)

ALEC JOHNSON

79	RFP RFP 001	Busman's Holiday (no p/s)	12

(see also Nightwing)

BARRY JOHNSON

58	HMV POP 472	Locked In The Arms Of Love/Are You Sincere (78)	12

BETTY JOHNSON

56	London HLU 8307	I'll Wait/Please Tell Me Why	55
56	London HLU 8307	I'll Wait/Please Tell Me Why (78)	15
56	London HLU 8326	Honky Tonk Rock/Say It Isn't So, Joe	175
56	London HLU 8326	Honky Tonk Rock/Say It Isn't So, Joe (78)	30
57	London HLU 8365	I Dreamed/If It's Wrong To Love You	50
57	London HLU 8365	I Dreamed/If It's Wrong To Love You (78)	15
57	London HLU 8432	1492/Little White Lies	35
57	London HLU 8432	1492/Little White Lies (78)	15
58	London HLE 8557	Little Blue Man/Song You Heard When You Fell In Love	35
58	London HLE 8557	Little Blue Man/Song You Heard When You Fell In Love (78)	15
58	London HLE 8678	Dream/How Much	22
58	London HLE 8678	Dream/How Much (78)	20
58	London HLE 8701	There's Never Been A Night/Mr. Brown Is Out Of Town	40
58	London HLE 8701	There's Never Been A Night/Mr. Brown Is Out Of Town (78)	25
58	London HLE 8725	Hoopa Hoola/One More Time	35
58	London HLE 8725	Hoopa Hoola/One More Time (78)	25
59	London HLE 8839	Does Your Heart Beat For Me?/You And Only You	30
59	London HLE 8839	Does Your Heart Beat For Me?/You And Only You (78)	30
59	London RE-E 1221	DREAM (EP)	75
59	London HA-E 2163	THE SONG YOU HEARD WHEN YOU FELL IN LOVE (LP)	80

BLIND WILLIE JOHNSON

50s	Square M1	Dark Was The Night, Cold Was The Ground/Lord I Just Can't Keep From Crying (78)	10
58	Fontana TFE 17052	TREASURES OF NORTH AMERICAN NEGRO MUSIC NO. 2 (EP)	20
70	Xtra XTRA 1098	BLIND WILLIE JOHNSON (LP)	20

BOB JOHNSON & PETE KNIGHT

77	Chrysalis CHR 1137	THE KING OF ELFLAND'S DAUGHTER (LP)	12

(see also Steeleye Span, Mary Hopkin)

BOBBY JOHNSON & ATOMS

67	Ember EMB S 245	Do It Again A Little Bit Slower/Tramp (some in p/s)	20/10

BROWNIE JOHNSON

62	Longhorn BLH 0004	Best Dressed Beggar/Just Pretending	25

BRYAN JOHNSON

60	Decca F 11213	Looking High, High, High/Each Tomorrow	6
60	Decca F 11213	Looking High, High, High/Each Tomorrow (78)	15
61	Decca DFE 6664	LOOKING HIGH (EP)	18

BUBBER JOHNSON

56	Parlophone R 4161	Keep A Light In The Window For Me/A Wonderful Thing Happens (78)	7
57	Parlophone R 4259	Confidential/Have A Little Faith In Me	35
57	Parlophone R 4259	Confidential/Have A Little Faith In Me (78)	9

MINT VALUE £

BUDDY JOHNSON

55 Mercury MB 3231 Upside Your Head/ELLA JOHNSON: Crazy About A Saxophone (78) 15
59 Mercury ZEP 10009 BUDDY JOHNSON WAILS (EP, with Ella Johnson) 80
57 Mercury MPT 7515 ROCK AND ROLL (10" LP, with Ella Johnson) 165

BUNK JOHNSON (& HIS NEW ORLEANS BAND)

55 HMV 7M 141 When The Saints Go Marching In/Darktown Strutters' Ball 5
50s Melodisc EPM7 52 ONE YOU LOVE (EP) 10
52 Jazz Man no cat. no. MANDADISC (LP, with the Original Superior Band) 15
54 Goodtime Jazz LDG 110 BUNK JOHNSON AND THE YERBA BUENA JAZZ BAND (10" LP) 15
54 Columbia 33SX 1015 BUNK JOHNSON AND HIS NEW ORLEANS BAND (LP) 12
59 Melodisc MLP 12-112 BUNK JOHNSON AND HIS NEW ORLEANS JAZZ BAND (LP, w/ George Lewis) .. 15
50s Goodtime Jazz SPIRITUALS AND JAZZ (10" LP) 12
62 Storyville SLP 152 BUNK JOHNSON'S BAND 1944 (LP) 12
63 Goodtime Jazz LAG 545 BUNK JOHNSON AND HIS SUPERIOR JAZZ BAND (LP) 10
70s Nola LP 3 BUNK JOHNSON AND HIS BAND (LP) 40

CAREY JOHNSON

72 Banana BA 369 Correction Train/SOUL DEFENDERS: Version 12

DANIEL JOHNSON

65 Island WI 250 Come On My People/Brother Nathan 25

DOMINO JOHNSON

72 Green Door GD 4045 Summertime/SWANS: Grazing 8

DOMINO JOHNSON & CHAMPIONS

70 Duke DU 89 You Broke My Heart/TONY & CHAMPIONS: Tell Me The Reason 12

GENERAL JOHNSON

73 Invictus INV 531 Only Time Will Tell/Only Time Will Tell (Instrumental Version) 6
76 Arista ARIST 45 All In The Family/Ready, Willing And Able 6
73 Invictus SVT 1008 GENERALLY SPEAKING (LP) 15

(see also Norman Johnson, Showmen, Chairmen Of The Board)

GINGER JOHNSON AND HIS AFRICAN MESSENGERS

67 Masquerade SM 02001 AFRICAN PARTY (LP) 250

HOLLY JOHNSON

89 MCA DMCA 1306 Love Train (12" Mix)/Love Train (7" Mix)/Murder In Paradise (CD, card sleeve, featuring Brian May) 8
89 MCA DMCAT 1306 Love Train (Ride The 'A' Train Mix)/Love Train (Stoke It Up Mix)/Love Train (7" Mix)/Murder In Paradise (3" CD, featuring Brian May) 8

(see also Holly, Frankie Goes To Hollywood, Big In Japan)

HOWARD JOHNSON

71 Jay Boy BOY 47 The Slide/That Magic Touch Can Send You Flying 12

JAMES P. JOHNSON

54 Columbia SCM 5127 Feeling Blues/Riffs 8
56 HMV 7EG 8164 JAMES P. JOHNSON (EP) 10
57 HMV 7EG 8215 LOUISIANA SUGAR BABIES (EP, with Fats Waller) 12
57 Tempo EXA 65 JAMES P. JOHNSON (EP) 10
52 Brunswick LA 8548 DADDY OF THE PIANO (10" LP) 15
53 Brunswick LA 8622 FATS WALLER FAVOURITES (10" LP) 15
54 London AL 3511 EARLY HARLEM PIANO (10" LP) 20
55 London AL 3540 EARLY HARLEM PIANO VOLUME 2 (10" LP) 20

JAMES P. JOHNSON/LUCKEY ROBERTS

56 London HB-U 1057 HARLEM PARTY PIANO (10" LP, 1 side each) 20

JIMMY JOHNSON

65 Sue WI 387 Don't Answer The Door Parts 1 & 2 12

J.J. JOHNSON

50 Melodisc MEL 1121 Teapot/Spider's Web (78) 8
51 Jazz Parade B 14 Foxhunt/Ulysses (78, as Jay Jay Johnson's Boppers) 8
55 Vogue LDE 124 J.J. JOHNSON SEXTET (10" LP) 15
55 Vogue LDE 162 J.J. JOHNSON QUINTET (10" LP) 15
60 Fontana TFL 5041 J.J. IN PERSON (LP) 12
61 Fontana TFL 5137 BLUE TROMBONE (LP, also stereo STFL 559) 12/15
63 Verve VLP 9056 J.J.'s BROADWAY (LP) 12
65 RCA RD/SF 7721 J.J.! (LP) 12
73 United Artists UAS 29451 ACROSS 110TH STREET (LP, soundtrack, with Bobby Womack) 25

(see also Sonny Stitt)

(JOHNNY JOHNSON &) THE BANDWAGON

68 Direction 58-3520 Baby Make Your Own Sweet Music/ On The Day We Fall In Love (as Bandwagon) 6
68 Direction 58-3670 Breaking Down The Walls Of Heartache/Dancin' Master (as Bandwagon) 6
69 Direction 58-3923 You/You Blew Your Cool And Lost Your Fool 6
69 Direction 58-4180 Let's Hang On/I Ain't Lying (withdrawn) 12
69 Direction 58-4180 Let's Hang On/Don't Let It In 6
72 Stateside SS 2207 Honey Bee/I Don't Know Why 10
69 Direction 8-63500 JOHNNY JOHNSON AND THE BANDWAGON (LP) 25
70 Bell SBLL 138 SOUL SURVIVOR (LP) 25

JOHNSON FAMILY

91 Camden Town GNAR 001 Motorcycle/Big Bang (p/s) 5
94 Camden Town GNAR 005 Be My Rose/Kennington Vigilante (p/s) 5

JUDI JOHNSON (& PERFECTIONS)

64 HMV POP 1371 My Baby's Face/Make The Most Of It (solo) 15
65 HMV POP 1399 How Many Times/A Way Out (as Judi Johnson & Perfections) 15

MINT VALUE £

LARRY JOHNSON

70	Blue Horizon 7-63851	PRESENTING THE COUNTRY BLUES (LP)	70

LAURIE JOHNSON ORCHESTRA

56	HMV 7MC 47	Buttercup/Lullaby Of The Leaves (export issue)	12
57	HMV POP 404	The Moonraker/Call Of The Casbah	7
57	HMV POP 404	The Moonraker/Call Of The Casbah (78)	10
60	Pye 7N 15251	No Hiding Place/The Deputy	6
64	Pye 7N 15599	Dr Strangelove Theme/Nevada	6
64	Pye 7N 15715	Call Me Irresponsible/The Beauty Jungle	6
65	Pye 7N 15933	Latin Quarter/M1 (some in p/s)	7/5
65	Pye 7N 17015	The Avengers/Minor Bossa Nova (some in p/s)	50/18
69	MGM MGM 1457	There Is Another Song/Caesar Smith	12
71	Columbia DB 8826	The Jason King Theme/There Comes A Time	50
76	EMI EMI 2562	The New Avengers Theme/A Flavour Of The Avengers (some in p/s)	10/5
80	Unicorn Kachana MCPS 5	The Professionals Main Title/On Target/The New Avengers Main Title (p/s, by Laurie Johnson & London Studio Orchestra)	6
57	Parlophone GEP 8604	THE GOOD COMPANIONS (EP)	15
58	Pye Nixa NPL 18017	SONGS OF THREE SEASONS (LP)	15
62	Golden Guinea GGL 0108	TOP SECRET (LP)	12
63	Pye NPL 18088	THE NEW BIG SOUND OF THE LAURIE JOHNSON ORCHESTRA (LP)	15
65	Pye NPL 18103	THE BIG NEW SOUND STRIKES AGAIN (LP)	18
67	Marble Arch MAL 695	THE AVENGERS AND OTHER FAVOURITES (LP)	30
68	Columbia S(C)X 6206	SOMETHING'S COMING (LP, mono/stereo)	15
69	MGM C(S) 8104	THEMES AND ... (LP)	25
70	Columbia SCX 6412	LAURIE JOHNSON/LONDON JAZZ ORCHESTRA — SYNTHESIS (LP, with Joe Harriott, Tubby Hayes, Stan Tracey & Tony Coe)	55
71	Columbia SCX 6464	CONQUISTADORS (LP)	15
73	Ronco RR 2006	THE BELSTONE FOX (LP, soundtrack, gatefold sleeve)	15
80	Unicorn Kachana KPM 7009	MUSIC FROM THE AVENGERS, THE NEW AVENGERS AND THE PROFESSIONALS (LP, gatefold sleeve, with London Studio Orchestra)	20

(see also Polka Dots)

LINTON KWESI JOHNSON

79	Island WIP 6494	Want Fi Goh Rave/Reality Poem (p/s)	5

LONNIE JOHNSON

51	Vogue V 2015	Drunk Again/Jelly Roll Baker (78)	30
51	Vogue V 2079	Happy New Year/Little Rockin' Chair (78)	30
51	Melodisc MEL 1138	Rocks In My Bed/Solid Blues (78)	35
51	Melodisc MEL 1186	Blues For Everybody/In Love Again (78)	35
52	Melodisc MEL 1221	Blues In My Soul/Keep What You Got (78)	35
57	Parlophone GEP 8635	LONESOME ROAD (EP)	50
57	Parlophone GEP 8663	LONNIE'S BLUES (EP)	45
58	Parlophone GEP 8693	LONNIE'S BLUES NO. 2 (EP)	45
64	Storyville SLP 162	PORTRAITS IN BLUES VOL. 6 (LP)	30
64	Storyville 616 010	SEE SEE RIDER (LP, with Otis Spann)	35
60s	Xtra XTRA 1037	LONNIE JOHNSON (LP)	30

(see also Eddie Lang & Lonnie Johnson)

LOU JOHNSON

63	London HLX 9805	Reach Out For Me/Magic Potion	50
64	London HLX 9917	(There's) Always Something There To Remind Me/Wouldn't That Be Something	25
64	London HLX 9929	A Message To Martha (Kentucky Bluebird)/The Last One To Be Loved	15
65	London HLX 9965	Please Stop The Wedding/Park Avenue	15
65	London HLX 9994	A Time To Love, A Time To Cry/Unsatisfied	75
69	London HLX 10269	(There's) Always Something There To Remind Me/Message To Martha	10
64	London REX 1438	THE MAGIC POTION OF LOU JOHNSON (EP)	125

LUTHER 'GEORGIA BOY SNAKE' JOHNSON

69	Transatlantic TRA 188	THE MUDDY WATERS BLUES BAND (LP, credits Muddy Waters on label)	30

MARGARET JOHNSON

52	Parlophone R 3506	Cushion Foot Stomp/Take Your Black Bottom Outside (78)	12
50s	Jazz Collector L 105	Death String Blues/Mistreating Man Blues (78)	8

MARV JOHNSON

59	London HLT 8856	Come To Me/Whisper	110
59	London HLT 8856	Come To Me/Whisper (78)	70
59	London HLT 9013	You Got What It Takes/Don't Leave Me	18
59	London HLT 9013	You Got What It Takes/Don't Leave Me (78)	65
60	London HLT 9109	I Love The Way You Love/Let Me Love You	22
60	London HL 7095	I Love The Way You Love/Let Me Love You (export issue)	35
60	London HLT 9165	Ain't Gonna Be That Way/All The Love I've Got	22
60	London HLT 9187	(You've Got To) Move Two Mountains/I Need You	22
61	London HLT 9265	Happy Days/Baby, Baby	22
61	London HLT 9311	Merry-Go-Round/Tell Me That You Love Me	45
65	Tamla Motown TMG 525	Why Do You Want To Let Me Go/I'm Not A Plaything	80
69	United Artists UP 35010	I Love The Way You Love/You Got What It Takes	6
68	Tamla Motown TMG 680	I'll Pick A Rose For My Rose/You Got The Love I Love	6
69	Tamla Motown TMG 713	I Miss You Baby (How I Miss You)/Bad Girl	7
70	Tamla Motown TMG 737	So Glad You Chose Me/I'm Not A Plaything	7
60	London HA-T 2271	MARVELLOUS MARV JOHNSON (LP)	140
69	T. Motown (S)TML 11111	I'LL PICK A ROSE FOR MY ROSE (LP)	40

MATT JOHNSON

81	4AD CAD 113	BURNING BLUE SOUL (LP, original 'psychedelic eye' cover)	25

(see also Gadgets, The The)

MIRRIAM JOHNSON

61	London HLW 9337	Lonesome Road/Young And Innocent	15

MINT VALUE £

NORMAN JOHNSON (& SHOWMEN)
69 Action ACT 4529 You're Everything/Our Love Will Grow . . . 40
69 Action ACT 4545 Take It Baby/In Paradise. . . . 45
71 Action ACT 4601 You're Everything/Our Love Will Grow (reissue). . . . 12
(see also General Johnson, Chairmen Of The Board, Showmen)

PETE JOHNSON
51 Vogue V 2007 J.J. Boogie/Yancey Special (78, red or orange label). . . . 15/18
51 Vogue V 2008 Swanee River Boogie/St. Louis Boogie (78, red or orange label) 15/18
51 Vogue V 2019 Hollywood Boogie/Central Avenue Drag (78, orange label) 18
56 Vogue V 2007 J.J. Boogie/Yancey Special 35
56 Vogue V 2008 Swanee River Boogie/St. Louis Boogie. . . . 35
55 Vogue EPV 1039 PETE JOHNSON (EP). . . . 35
59 Top Rank JKR 8009 ROLL 'EM BOY (EP). . . . 22
55 London AL 3549 JUMPIN' WITH PETE JOHNSON (10" LP) 55
55 Vogue Coral LRA 10016 BOOGIE WOOGIE MOOD (LP) 35
(see also Joe Turner & Pete Johnson, Albert Ammons & Meade Lux Lewis)

PLAS JOHNSON (ORCHESTRA)
57 Capitol CL 14772 The Big Twist/Come Rain Or Come Shine. . . . 18
57 Capitol CL 14816 Swanee River Rock/You Send Me 18
58 Capitol CL 14836 Popcorn/Hoppin' Mad. . . . 22
58 Capitol CL 14903 Little Rockin' Deacon/Dinah. . . . 22
59 Capitol CL 14973 Robbins Nest Cha Cha/Plaz Jazz 10
57 London HB-U 1078 BOP ME DADDY (10" LP). . . . 60

PROFESSOR JOHNSON & HIS GOSPEL SINGERS
51 Vocalion V 1013 Give Me That Old Time Religion/Where Shall I Be (78) 20
58 Brunswick OE 9352 PROFESSOR JOHNSON AND HIS GOSPEL SINGERS (EP) 22

RAY JOHNSON
57 Vogue V 9073 If You Don't Want Me Baby/Calypso Joe 55
57 Vogue V 9073 If You Don't Want Me Baby/Calypso Joe (78). . . . 20
58 Vogue V 9093 Calypso Blues/Are You There. . . . 45
58 Vogue V 9093 Calypso Blues/Are You There (78) 20

ROBERT JOHNSON
62 Philips BBL 7539 ROBERT JOHNSON 1936-1937 (LP) 110
65 CBS BPG 62456 KING OF THE DELTA BLUES SINGERS (LP). . . . 45
67 Kokomo K 1000 ROBERT JOHNSON (LP) 65
60s Smokestack SS/LP 1 BLUES LEGEND 1936-1937 (LP) 50
70 CBS 64102 KING OF THE DELTA BLUES SINGERS VOL. 2 (LP) 30

ROY LEE JOHNSON
69 Action ACT 4518 So Anna Just Love Me/Boogaloo No. 3. . . . 25

RUBY JOHNSON
67 Stax 601 020 If I Ever Needed Love (I Sure Do Need It Now)/Keep On Keeping On 15

SPIDER JOHNSON & POPEYE BAND
63 Riverside RIF 106904 Doin' The Popeye/The Gospel Truth. . . . 5

SYL JOHNSON
73 London HL 10403 We Did It/Anyway The Wind Blows 8
73 London HL 10438 Back For A Taste Of Your Love/Wind Blow Her Back My Way 7
75 London HL 10476 Let Yourself Go/Please Don't Give Up On Me 7

TEDDY JOHNSON & PEARL CARR
57 Pye 7N 15110 Tomorrow Tomorrow/Mandolin Serenade 5
58 Pye 7N 15123 Sweet Elizabeth/Never Let Me Go 5
59 Columbia DB 4260 Petite Fleur/Missouri Waltz 5
59 Columbia DB 4275 Sing Little Birdie/If Only I Could Live My Life Again. . . . 5
59 Columbia DB 4275 Sing Little Birdie/If Only I Could Live My Life Again (78) 5
59 Columbia DB 4318 Tell Me, Tell Me/Viva Viva Amor 5
59 Columbia DB 4318 Tell Me, Tell Me/Viva Viva Amor (78) 5
60 Columbia DB 4397 Pazzo Pazzo (Crazy Crazy)/The Five Pennies 5
59 HMV POP 697 Pickin' Petals/When The Tide Turns 5
59 Pye NEP 24112 MEET TEDDY AND PEARL (EP). . . . 5

THEO JOHNSON
65 Aladdin WI 604 Masters Of War/The Water Is Wide. . . . 12

TOMMY JOHNSON
60s Saydisc SDM 224 THE LEGACY OF TOMMY JOHNSON (LP). . . . 20

TONY JOHNSON
55 Melodisc 1331 Man Smart Woman Smarter/Give Her Banana (78) 15
50s Parlophone MP 121 Mattie Rag/Linstead Market (78, export issue) 15
50s Parlophone MP 123 Don't Fence Her In/Wheel And Turn Me (78, export issue) 15

WILKO JOHNSON & SOLID SENDERS
78 Virgin VS 214 Walking On The Edge/Dr. Dupree (p/s) 5
78 Virgin V 2105 SOLID SENDERS (LP, with free LP "Live" [VDJ 26]) 12
(see also Dr. Feelgood, Solid Senders, Ian Dury & Blockheads)

ADRIENNE JOHNSTON
75 RCA SF 8416 ADRIENNE JOHNSTON OF THE JOHNSTONS (LP). . . . 12
(see also Johnstons)

BRUCE JOHNSTON COMBO
63 London HL 9780 Original Surfer Stomp/Pajama Party 40
(see also Beach Boys, California Music, Fantastic Baggys, Sagittarius)

DANIEL JOHNSTON
92 Seminal Twang TWANG 13 Laurie/The Monster Inside Of Me/Whiz Kid/The Lennon Song (p/s). . . . 10

MINT VALUE £

JOHNSTON BROTHERS

54	Decca F 10234	The Creep/Crystal Ball	15
54	Decca F 10286	Oh Baby Mine I Get So Lonely/My Love, My Life, My Own	12
54	Decca F 10302	The Bandit/KEYNOTES: A Dime And A Dollar	22
54	Decca F 10364	Sh-Boom (Life Could Be A Dream)/Crazy 'Bout Ya Baby	18
54	Decca F 10401	Mambo In The Moonlight/Papa Loves Mambo (with Ted Heath Music)	7
54	Decca F 10414	"Join In And Sing" Medley (both sides)	7
55	Decca F 10451	Majorca/Heartbroken	7
55	Decca F 10490	The Right To Be Wrong/Hot Potato Mambo	7
55	Decca F 10513	Chee Chee-Oo Chee (Sang The Little Bird)Hubble Bubble	7
55	Decca F 10526	Dreamboat/Jim, Johnny And Jonas	7
55	Decca F 10608	Hernando's Hideaway/Hey There	25
55	Decca F 10636	"Join In And Sing Again" Medley (both sides)	10
56	Decca F 10721	No Other Love/Flowers Mean Forgiveness	10
56	Decca F 10747	How Little We Know/The Street Musician	7
56	Decca F 10781	In The Middle Of The House (with Keynotes)/Stranded In The Jungle	12
56	Decca F 10814	"Join In And Sing, No. 3" Medley (both sides)	10
56	Decca F 10828	Give Her My Love (When You Meet Her)/A Rose And A Candy Bar	10
57	Decca F 10860	Whatever Lola Wants (Lola Gets)/Heart	8
57	Decca F 10915	All Star Hit Parade No. 2 (with other artists)	5
57	Decca F 10939	I Like Music — You Like Music/Seven Bar Blues	7
57	Decca F 10962	"Join In And Sing, No. 4" Medley (both sides)	6
58	Decca F 10996	A Very Precious Love/Yours, Yours, Yours	5
58	Decca F 11021	Scratch, Scratch/Little Serenade	5
58	Decca F 11083	Love Is All We Need/Clementine Cha-Cha	5
58	Decca F 11083	Love Is All We Need/Clementine Cha-Cha (78)	7
56	Decca DFE 6249	JOIN THE JOHNSTON BROTHERS (EP)	10
56	Decca DFE 6311	JOIN IN AND SING WITH THE JOHNSTON BROTHERS (EP)	10
57	Decca DFE 6458	JOIN AND SING AGAIN (EP)	10
58	Decca DFE 6503	EASY NO. 1 (EP)	10
58	Decca LK 4266	EASY (LP)	18

(see also Dennis Lotis, Vera Lynn, Edmundo Ros, Joan Regan, Lita Roza, Suzi Miller, Ted Heath, Keynotes)

JOHNSTONS

66	Pye 7N 17144	Going Home/Travelling People	5
66	Pye 7N 17205	The Alamo/Life Of A Rover	5
67	Pye 7N 17205	The Curragh Of Kildare/Leaving London	5
67	Pye 7N 17430	I Never Will Marry/Banks Of Claudy	5
67	Transatlantic TRASP 17	They'll Never Get Their Man/Dublin Jack Of All Trades	5
68	Big T BIG 113	Both Sides Now/Urge For Going	5
68	Big T BIG 116	Give A Damn/Walking Out On Foggy Mornings	5
69	Big T BIG 121	My House/The Wherefore And The Why	5
70	Big T BIG 132	Streets Of London/The Spanish Lady	5
68	Transatlantic TRA 169	THE JOHNSTONS (LP)	18
68	Transatlantic TRA 184	GIVE A DAMN (LP)	15
68	Transatlantic TRA 185	THE BARLEYCORN (LP)	15
69	Marble Arch MAL 808	THE TRAVELLING PEOPLE (LP)	12
70	Transatlantic TRA 211	BITTER GREEN (LP)	12
70	Transatlantic TRASAM 16	THE JOHNSTONS SAMPLER (LP)	12
71	Transatlantic TRA 231	COLOURS OF THE DAWN (LP)	12
72	Transatlantic TRA 251	IF I SANG MY SONG (LP, gatefold sleeve)	12

(see also Adrienne Johnston)

JOHN THE POSTMAN

78	Bent BIG BENT 2	PUERILE (12" EP, some in stamped brown paper bag p/s, with inserts)	20/15
78	Bent BIG BENT 4	PSYCHEDELIC ROCK'N'ROLL FIVE SKINNERS (12" EP, white label, foldover p/s in bag)	15

JOINER, ARKANSAS, JUNIOR HIGH SCHOOL BAND

60	London HLG 9147	Big Ben/National City	8

JO JO GUNNE (U.K.)

68	Decca F 12807	Every Story Has An End/Should Live Like That	7
69	Decca F 12906	Beggin' You Baby/Bad Penny	7

JO JO GUNNE (U.S.)

72	Asylum AYM 501	Run Run Run/Shake That Fat (withdrawn)	10
72	Asylum AYM 507	Shake That Fat/I Make Love	5
73	Asylum AYM 518	Ready Freddy/Wait A Lifetime	5
74	Asylum AYM 528	I Wanna Love You/Neon City	5
74	Asylum AYM 534	Where Is The Show/Single Man	5

(see also Spirit)

JOKER

84	Lost Moment LM 018	Back On The Road/Pusher (p/s)	6

JOKERS

62	Salvo SLO 1806	Blue Moonbeam/Dog Fight (99 only)	35

JOKER'S WILD

66	Regent Sound RSR 0031	Don't Ask Me/Why Do Fools Fall In Love (handwritten labels, 50 only)	500+
66	Regent Sound RSLP 007	JOKER'S WILD: Don't Ask Me/Why Do Fools Fall In Love/You Don't Know What I Know/That's How Strong My Love Is (12", 1-sided, 50 copies only)	1,000+

(see also Dave Gilmour, Pink Floyd)

JOLLIVER ARKANSAS

69	Bell SBLL 119	HOME (LP)	35

(see also Leslie West, Mountain)

JOLLY BOYS

70	Moodisc MU 3504	On The Water/MUDIES ALL STARS: Cash Register	15

AL JOLSON

54	Brunswick OE 9011	SONGS HE MADE FAMOUS VOL. 1 (EP)	8
55	Brunswick OE 9159	AL JOLSON MEMORIAL (EP)	8
57	Brunswick OE 9336	SONGS HE MADE FAMOUS PT. 1 (EP)	8
57	Brunswick OE 9337	SONGS HE MADE FAMOUS PT. 2 (EP)	8
58	Brunswick OE 9364	AMONG MY SOUVENIRS PT. 2 (EP)	8
59	Brunswick OE 9418	THEY SOLD A MILLION NO. 2 (EP)	8
59	Brunswick OE 9419	THEY SOLD A MILLION NO. 3 (EP)	8
58	Fontana TFE 17024	AL JOLSON (EP)	8
50	Brunswick LA 8502	JOLSON SINGS AGAIN (10" LP)	15
50	Brunswick LA 8509	AL JOLSON SOUVENIR (10" LP)	15
51	Brunswick LA 8512	JOLSON MEMORIES (10" LP)	15
53	Brunswick LA 8554	STEPHEN FOSTER SONGS (10" LP)	15
53	Brunswick LA 8575	AL JOLSON SOUVENIR ALBUM VOLUME 3 (10" LP)	15
53	Brunswick LA 8570	AL JOLSON SOUVENIR ALBUM VOLUME 4 (10" LP)	15
54	Brunswick LA 8655	AL JOLSON SOUVENIR ALBUM VOLUME 6 (10" LP)	15
57	Brunswick LAT 8220	THE JOLSON STORY — AMONG MY SOUVENIRS (LP)	12
58	Brunswick LAT 8267	THE IMMORTAL AL JOLSON (LP)	12
59	Brunswick LAT 8294	AL JOLSON OVERSEAS (LP)	12
60	Brunswick LAT 8322	THE WORLD'S GREATEST ENTERTAINER (LP)	12
61	Brunswick LAT 8387	OSCAR LEVANT (LP)	12
61	Brunswick LAT 8403	YOU MADE ME LOVE YOU (LP, 2 tracks with Bing Crosby)	12

JOLT

77	Polydor 2058 936	You're Cold/All I Can Do (p/s)	20
78	Polydor 2059 008	What'cha Gonna Do About It/Again And Again (die-cut p/s)	20
78	Polydor 2059 039	I Can't Wait/Route 66 (p/s)	20
79	Polydor 2229 215	Maybe Tonight/I'm In Tears/See Saw/Stop Look (p/s)	20
79	Polydor 2229 215DJ	Maybe Tonight/See Saw (promo only, no p/s)	20
78	Polydor 2383 504	THE JOLT (LP)	30

JON

67	Parlophone R 5604	So Much For Mary/Polly Sunday (some in p/s)	30/12
67	Columbia DB 8249	Is It Love/Sing Out	50

(see also Titus Groan, Still Life)

JON & ALUN

63	Decca LK/SKL 4547	RELAX YOUR MIND (LP, mono/stereo)	22/30

JON & DAVE

97	Earworm SS 1	Land Beyond The Sun/Instrumental For Silence (p/s, pale green vinyl, 500 copies only)	8

JON & JEANNIE

68	Beacon 3-105	Lover's Holiday/Something You Got	5
69	Beacon BEA 113	Don't Sign The Papers/We Got Lovin'	5

JON & ROBIN & IN-CROWD

67	Stateside SS 2027	Do It Again A Little Bit Slower/If I Need Someone It's You	10

JON & VANGELIS

81	Polydor POSP 258	The Friends Of Mr. Cairo/Beside (p/s)	5
81	Polydor POSP 323	State Of Independence/Beside (p/s)	5
81	Polydor POSPX 323	State Of Independence/Beside (12", in blue plastic film canister, promo only)	80+
83	Polydor JV 3	And When The Night Comes/Song Is (p/s)	5
83	Polydor JV 4	He Is Sailing/Polonaise (p/s)	5
84	Polydor JV 5/POSP 246	State Of Independence/The Friends Of Mr. Cairo/Chariots Of Fire/ Eric's Theme (p/s doublepack, stickered shrinkwrapped p/s)	6
91	Arista 114 063	Wisdom Chain/Page Of Life (with Irene Papas, p/s)	5
91	Arista 664 063	Wisdom Chain (Edit)/Wisdom Chain (Album Version)/Page Of Life/ Sing With Your Eyes (CD, with Irene Papas)	10
81	Polydor POLD 5039	THE FRIENDS OF MR. CAIRO (LP, promo issue with b&w sleeve, raised figures & logo in left corner)	35

(see also Jon Anderson, Vangelis)

JONATHAN & CHARLES

69	Herald LLR 566	ANOTHER WEEK TO GO (LP)	150

JONATHAN *FIRE*EATER

96	Deceptive BLUFF 037	The Search For Cherry Red (p/s)	5
97	Deceptive BLUFF 048	When The Curtain Calls For You/Night In The Nursery (p/s)	5

JONCUNO(O)

(see Juncuno)

AL JONES

58	HMV POP 451	Mad, Mad, World/Lonely Traveller	275
58	HMV POP 451	Mad, Mad, World/Lonely Traveller (78)	75

AL JONES

69	Parlophone PMC/PCS 7081	ALUN ASHWORTH JONES (LP)	40
72	Village Thing VTS 19	JONESVILLE (LP)	20

(see also Anderson, Jones, Jackson)

ALLAN JONES

53	HMV 7M 111	Why Do I Love You/Make Believe	10
53	HMV 7M 135	I Believe/I Talk To The Trees	10
53	HMV 7M 161	Poppa Piccolino/Why?	10

BARBARA JONES

72	Bullet BU 516	Sad Movies/SIR HARRY: Deejay Version	12
74	Count Shelley CS 045	Baby I'm Yours/Don't Turn Your Back On Me	12
75	Dip DL 5085	Where Do I Turn/G.G. ALL STARS: Version	10

MINT VALUE £

BETTY HALL JONES

50 Capitol CL 13266 This Joint's Too Hip For Me/You've Got To Have What It Takes (78) . . . 25

BEVERLEY JONES (& PRESTONS)

63 HMV POP 1109 The Boy I Saw With You/When It Comes To Love . . . 12
63 HMV POP 1140 Why Do Lovers Break Each Other's Heart/I'm Just An In-Between . . . 15
63 HMV POP 1201 Wait 'Til My Bobby Gets Home/A Boy Like You . . . 12
64 Parlophone R 5189 Heatwave/Hear You Talking (with Prestons) . . . 18

B-LOU JONES & HIS JUPITERS

61 London HLU 9373 Anchors Aweigh (Parts 1 & 2) . . . 10

BRENDA LEE JONES

75 UK USA 8 You're The Love Of My Life/Thread Your Needle . . . 5
(see also Dean & Jean)

BRIAN JONES

(see under Pipes Of Pan, Rolling Stones)

CAROL JONES

60 Triumph RGM 1012 The Boy With The Eyes Of Blue/I Gave Him Back His Ring . . . 125

CASEY JONES & THE ENGINEERS

63 Columbia DB 7083 One Way Ticket/I'm Gonna Love . . . 35

CASEY JONES & THE GOVERNERS

64 Golden 12LP 106 DON'T HA HA (LP) . . . 50
(see also Casey Jones & The Engineers)

CURTIS JONES

66 RCA RCX 7184 R.C.A. VICTOR RACE SERIES VOL. 9 (EP) . . . 20
64 Decca LK 4587 CURTIS JONES IN LONDON (LP) . . . 65
68 Blue Horizon 7-63207 NOW RESIDENT IN EUROPE (LP) . . . 80

DAVEY JONES

65 Philips BF 1410 For Your Love/Love Bug . . . 10

DAVIE JONES & THE KING BEES

64 Vocalion Pop V 9221 Liza Jane/Louie, Louie Go Home (beware of counterfeits without centres) . . . 1,250
78 Decca F 13807 Liza Jane/Louie, Louie Go Home (reissue) . . . 12
(see also David Bowie, Davy Jones, Manish Boys, Calvin James)

DAVY JONES (U.K.)

65 Parlophone R 5315 You've Got A Habit Of Leaving/Baby Loves That Way . . . 500
(see also David Bowie)

DAVY JONES (U.K.) & THE LOWER THIRD/MANISH BOYS

79 EMI EMI 2925 You've Got A Habit Of Leaving/Baby Loves That Way/MANISH BOYS: I Pity The Fool/Take My Tip (p/s) . . . 12
82 Charly CYM 1 You've Got A Habit Of Leaving/Baby Loves That Way/MANISH BOYS: I Pity The Fool/Take My Tip (10", p/s) . . . 18
(see also David Bowie, Davie Jones & King Bees, Manish Boys, Calvin James)

DAVY JONES (U.K.)

65 Colpix PX 784 What Are We Going To Do/This Bouquet . . . 8
67 Pye 7N 17302 It Ain't Me Babe/Baby It's Me (some in p/s) . . . 12/7
67 Pye 7N 17380 Theme For A New Love/Dream Girl (some in p/s) . . . 12/7
67 Pye International 7N 25432 Theme For A New Love/Dream Girl (reissue, withdrawn) . . . 20+
71 Bell BLL 1163 Rainy Jane/Welcome To My Love . . . 8
77 MCA MCA 348 Life Line/It's A Jungle Out There/Gotta Get Up (from 'The Point') (p/s, last track with Micky Dolenz) . . . 8
78 Warner Bros K 17161 (Hey Ra Ra) Happy Birthday Mickey Mouse/You Don't Have To Be A Country Boy To Sing A Country Song (p/s) . . . 8
83 J.J. 2001 I'll Love You Forever/When I Look Back On Christmas . . . 12
67 Pye NPL 18178 DAVY JONES (LP) . . . 22
(see also Davy Jones & Micky Dolenz, Monkees)

DAVY JONES (U.K.) & MICKY DOLENZ

71 Bell BLL 986 Do It In The Name Of Love/Lady Jane . . . 18
(see also Monkees, Davey Jones)

DAVY JONES (U.S.)

60 Pye 7N 15254 Amapola/Mighty Man . . . 10
61 Pye 7N 15318 Shenandoah/Scenery . . . 8
61 Pye International 7N 25072 Model Girl/Scarlet Woman . . . 12
61 Pye International 7N 25095 Bonnie Banks/Baby Baby . . . 10
62 Piccadilly 7N 35038 Jezebel/Don't Come Crying To Me . . . 8
(see also Thelonious Monk)

DILL JONES TRIO

58 Pye Jazz 7NJ 2021 Little Rock Getaway/Carolina Shout . . . 5
56 Jazz Today JTE 104 PIANO MOODS VOL. 2 (EP) . . . 15
56 Pye Jazz NJE 1024 PIANO MOODS VOL. 5 (EP) . . . 20
57 Columbia SEG 7764 TOP OF THE POLL (EP) . . . 10
59 Columbia SEG 7893 DILL JONES PLUS FOUR (EP) . . . 8
60 Columbia 33SX 1336 JONES THE JAZZ (LP) . . . 60

DORIS JONES

76 NEMS NES 9 He's So Irreplaceable/Never Gonna Give Him Up . . . 6
76 NEMS NES 15 Stranded In The Wilderness/(Pt. 2) . . . 6

DOROTHY JONES

61 Philips 322 794 BF Takin' That Long Walk Home/It's Unbearable . . . 25
(see also Cookies)

FLOYD JONES/EDDIE TAYLOR

60s XX MIN 712 FLOYD JONES AND EDDIE TAYLOR (EP, 2 tracks each) 15

GEORGE JONES

59 Mercury AMT 1021 The Treasure Of Love/If I Don't Love You (Grits Ain't Groceries) 22
59 Mercury AMT 1021 The Treasure Of Love/If I Don't Love You (Grits Ain't Groceries) (78) 25
59 Mercury AMT 1036 White Lightning/Long Time To Forget 50
59 Mercury AMT 1058 Who Shot Sam/Into My Arms Again 25
59 Mercury AMT 1078 Big Harlan Taylor/Money To Burn 15
60 Mercury AMT 1100 Sparkling Brown Eyes/Accidentally On Purpose 15
61 Mercury AMT 1124 Candy Hearts/The Window Up Above 15
62 United Artists POP 1037 She Thinks I Still Care/Geronimo 15
63 United Artists UP 1015 I Saw Me/Not What I Had In Mind (as George Jones with Jones Boys) 12
64 United Artists UP 1044 Your Heart Turned Left (And I Was On The Right)/My Tears Are Overdue 12
65 United Artists UP 1080 The Race Is On/She's So Lonesome Again 15
69 Stateside SS 2145 If My Heart Had Windows/Taggin' Along 8
71 Pye International 7N 25547 It's Been A Good Year For The Roses/Let A Little Come In 6
80 Epic EPC 8560 Stranger In The House (with Elvis Costello)/A Drunk Can't Be A Man (p/s) 5
59 Mercury ZEP 10036 GEORGE JONES (EP) 90
60s Melodisc EPM7 109 COUNTRY SONG HITS (EP) 40
64 Mercury 10009 MCE C & W ACES (EP) 20
64 Ember EMB 4548 THE BEST OF AMERICAN COUNTRY MUSIC VOL. 4 (EP) 15
62 United Artists ULP 1007 THE NEW FAVOURITES OF GEORGE JONES (LP) 25
63 United Artists ULP 1014 MY FAVOURITES OF HANK WILLIAMS (LP) 25
63 Ember CW 101 THE CROWN PRINCE OF COUNTRY MUSIC (LP, original pressings have grey & orange label) 15
63 United Artists ULP 1037 HITS OF HIS COUNTRY COUSINS (LP) 22
64 United Artists ULP 1050 I WISH TONIGHT WOULD NEVER END (LP) 22
64 London HA-B 8125 GEORGE JONES SINGS HIS GREATEST HITS (LP) 20
64 United Artists ULP 1070 WHAT'S IN OUR HEARTS (LP, with Melba Montgomery) 18
64 Ember CW 109 THE FABULOUS COUNTRY MUSIC SOUND OF JONES (LP, original pressings have grey & orange label) 15
64 Wing WL 1175 COUNTRY & WESTERN NO. 1 MALE SINGER (LP) 12
64 United Artists ULP 1074 MORE NEW FAVOURITES (LP) 20
65 United Artists ULP 1077 BLUE GRASS HOOTENANNY (LP, with Melba Montgomery) 18
65 United Artists ULP 1091 I GET LONELY IN A HURRY (LP) 20
65 United Artists ULP 1082 JONES SINGS LIKE THE DICKENS (LP) 20
65 United Artists ULP 1101 TROUBLE IN MIND (LP) 20
65 Stateside SL 10147 GEORGE JONES AND GENE PITNEY (LP, with Gene Pitney) 25
65 Stateside SL 10157 MR. COUNTRY AND WESTERN MUSIC (LP) 18
66 London HA-B 8259 GEORGE JONES (LP, with Tommy Hill's Band) 25
66 United Artists (S)ULP 1136 THE GREAT GEORGE JONES (LP) 18
66 United Artists (S)ULP 1137 BLUE MOON OF KENTUCKY (LP, with Melba Montgomery) 18
66 Stateside SL 10173 IT'S COUNTRY TIME AGAIN (LP, with Gene Pitney) 25
66 Stateside S(S)L 10184 LOVE BUG (LP) 18
67 Stateside S(S)L 10195 WE FOUND HEAVEN RIGHT HERE ON EARTH AT '4033' (LP) 18
67 Mercury SMCL 20107 GREATEST HITS (LP) 18
67 London HA-B 8340 THE GEORGE JONES SONG BOOK (LP) 22
67 Stateside S(S)L 10215 VARIETY IS THE SPICE OF ... (LP) 18
68 Stateside S(S)L 10236 SINGS THE SONGS OF DALLAS FRAZIER (LP) 18
68 Mercury SMWL 21003 THE GREAT GEORGE JONES (LP) 20
69 Stateside S(S)L 10256 IF MY HEART HAD WINDOWS (LP) 15
69 Stateside S(S)L 10283 MY COUNTRY (LP) 15
70 Stateside SSL 10308 I'LL SHARE MY WORLD WITH YOU (LP) 15
72 Pye PKL 4412 THE BLUE SIDE OF LONESOME & OTHER COUNTRY FAVOURITES (LP) 12
72 Pye Intl. NSPL 28160 COUNTRY MUSIC '72 (LP) 12
72 CBS EQ 30802 WE GO TOGETHER (LP, with Tammy Wynette, quadrophonic) 12
73 Pye Intl. NSPL 28176 WRAPPED AROUND HER FINGERS (LP) 12

(see also Gene Pitney, Elvis Costello)

GEORGE JONES/JIMMIE SKINNER

59 Mercury ZEP 10012 COUNTRY AND WESTERN (EP, 2 tracks each) 45

GLORIA JONES

66 Capitol CL 15429 Heartbeat (Parts 1 & 2) 30
66 Stateside SS 555 Finders Keepers/Run One Flight Of Stairs 60
74 Tamla Motown TMG 910 Tin Can People/So Tired 6
76 EMI EMI 2437 Get It On/Get It On (Version) 6
76 EMI EMI 2522 I Ain't Going Nowhere/Simplicity Blues 6
77 EMI EMI 2570 Go Now/Drive Me Crazy 6
77 EMI EMI 2720 Bring On The Love/Cry Baby 6
74 Tamla Motown STML 11254 SHARE MY LOVE (LP) 22
76 EMI EMC 3159 VIXEN (LP) 15

(see also Marc Bolan & Gloria Jones)

GRACE JONES

86 Island 12IS 240 Pull Up To The Bumper/La Vie En Rose (12") 8

GRANDPA JONES

57 Brunswick 05676 Eight More Miles To Louisville/Dark As A Dungeon 25
59 Brunswick OE 9455 MOUNTAIN MUSIC VOL. 3 (EP) 30
57 Parlophone GEP 8666 MEET GRANDPA JONES (EP) 30
58 Parlophone GEP 8766 COUNTRY AND WESTERN (EP) 35
59 Parlophone GEP 8781 COUNTRY ROUND UP (EP) 30
64 London RE-U 1417 GRANDPA SINGS JIMMIE RODGERS (EP) 30
62 London HA-U/SH-U 8010 MAKES THE RAFTERS RING (LP) 35
64 London HA-U/SH-U 8119 YODELLING HITS (LP) 35

(see also Brown's Ferry Four)

MINT VALUE £

JACK JONES

Year	Label/Cat. No.	Title	£
65	London HLR 9939	Dear Heart/Where Love Has Gone	6
65	London HLR 9956	The Race Is On/I Can't Believe I'm Losing You	10
66	London HLR 10088	Impossible Dream/A Day In The Life Of A Fool	6
67	London HLR 10108	Lady/Afraid Of Love	6
63	London RER 1374	JACK JONES (EP)	8
64	London RER 1433	FOUR GREAT SONGS FROM FOUR GREAT SHOWS (EP)	8
64	London HA-R 8167	WIVES AND LOVERS (LP)	12
64	London HA-R/SH-R 8191	SHE LOVES ME (LP)	12
65	London HA-R 8202	BEWITCHED (LP)	12
65	London HA-R/SH-R 8209	WHERE LOVE HAS GONE (LP)	12
65	London HA-R/SH-R 8222	SONGS OF LOVE (LP)	12
65	London HA-R/SH-R 8236	MY KIND OF TOWN (LP)	12
65	London HA-R/SH-R 8246	THE JACK JONES CHRISTMAS ALBUM (LP)	12
66	London HA-R/SH-R 8254	AND THERE'S LOVE (LP)	12

JANET JONES

Year	Label/Cat. No.	Title	£
74	Midas MR 005	SING TO ME LADY (LP)	80

JANIE JONES (& LASH)

Year	Label/Cat. No.	Title	£
65	HMV POP 1495	Witches Brew/Take-A My Tip	15
66	HMV POP 1514	Gunning For You/Go Go Away From Me	15
67	Columbia DB 8173	Tickle Me Tootsie Wootsies/High And Dry	10
68	Pye 7N 17550	Charlie Smith/Nobody's Perfect	10
68	Major Minor MM 577	The Girl's Song/I've Never Met A Boy Like You	10
70	President PT 309	Back On My Feet Again/Psycho	7
83	Big Beat NS 91	House Of The Ju-Ju Queen/Sex Machine (as Janie Jones & Lash, p/s)	7

(see also The Clash)

JERRY JONES

Year	Label/Cat. No.	Title	£
70	Banana BA 316	Still Waters (Love)/SOUND DIMENSION: Wig Wam	18
71	Bamboo BAM 65	Still Waters (Love)/SOUND DIMENSION: Wig Wam (reissue)	12
71	Bamboo BALPS 213	LIVE AT THE KINGSTON HOTEL, JAMAICA (LP)	50

JIMMY JONES

Year	Label/Cat. No.	Title	£
60	MGM MGM 1051	Handy Man/The Search Is Over	6
60	MGM MGM 1051	Handy Man/The Search Is Over (78)	100
60	MGM MGM 1078	Good Timin'/Too Long Will Be Too Late	6
60	MGM MGM 1078	Good Timin'/Too Long Will Be Too Late (78)	100
60	MGM MGM 1091	I Just Go For You/That's When I Cried	12
60	MGM MGM 1103	Ready For Love/For You	12
61	MGM MGM 1123	I Told You So/You Got It	12
61	MGM MGM 1133	Dear One/I Say Love	12
61	MGM MGM 1146	Mr Music Man/Holler Hey	12
62	MGM MGM 1168	You're Much Too Young/Nights Of Mexico	12
65	Columbia DB 7592	Walkin'/Pardon Me	35
65	Cameo Parkway P 988	Don't You Just Know It	15
67	Stateside SS 2041	39-21-46/Personal Property	15
68	MGM MGM 1405	Good Timin'/Handy Man	8
60	MGM MGM-EP 745	JIMMY HANDYMAN JONES (EP)	60
61	MGM MGM-EP 787	ORIGINAL HITS (EP)	40
60	MGM MGM-C 832	GOOD TIMIN' (LP)	75

JO JONES TRIO

Year	Label/Cat. No.	Title	£
59	Top Rank 25/039	JO JONES (LP)	12

JOE JONES

Year	Label/Cat. No.	Title	£
60	Columbia DB 4533	You Talk Too Much/I Love You Still	12

JOHN PAUL JONES

Year	Label/Cat. No.	Title	£
64	Pye 7N 15637	Baja/A Foggy Day In Vietnam (B-side actually by Andrew Oldham Orchestra)	80

(see also Led Zeppelin, Tony Meehan, Andrew Oldham Orchestra)

JOHNNY JONES & KING CASUALS

Year	Label/Cat. No.	Title	£
68	MCA MU 1031	Soul Poppin'/Blues For The Brothers	12
76	Cream CRM 5004	Purple Haze/Horsing Around	10
76	Brunswick BR 37	Purple Haze/FRED HUGHES: Baby Boy	10
80	Sonet SNTF 821	JOHNNY JONES WITH BILLY BOY ARNOLD (LP)	12

JONAH JONES (QUARTET)

Year	Label/Cat. No.	Title	£
59	Mercury AMT 15085	I Dig Chicks/Cherry	5
62	Ember JBS 704	Down By The Riverside/Stars Fell On Alabama	7
65	Brunswick LAT 8633	ON THE SUNNY SIDE OF THE STREET (LP, as Jonah Jones Quartet)	12

JUGGY JONES

Year	Label/Cat. No.	Title	£
76	Contempo CS 2080	Inside America (Parts 1 & 2)	7

JUSTIN JONES

Year	Label/Cat. No.	Title	£
61	London HLU 9463	Dance By Yourself/Love	75

KEN JONES (& HIS ROCK'N'ROLLERS)

Year	Label/Cat. No.	Title	£
60	Parlophone R 4628	Two Way Stretch/Paper Chase	6
61	Parlophone R 4763	Bluesville/On The Rebound	7
61	Parlophone R 4788	Joxville/Just Rollin'	6
58	Embassy WEP 1004	ROCK'N'ROLL TIME (EP, as Ken Jones & His Rock'n'Rollers)	12

KENNEY JONES

Year	Label/Cat. No.	Title	£
74	GM GMS 027	Ready Or Not/Woman Trouble	7

(see also Small Faces, Faces, Who)

LESLIE JONES

Year	Label/Cat. No.	Title	£
59	Pye NSEP 85004	FOUR FARNON FAVOURITES (EP, stereo)	8
59	Pye NSPL 83008/9	THE MUSIC OF ROBERT FARNON (LP)	15

LINDA JONES

67 Warner Bros WB 2070 Hypnotised/I Can't Stop Lovin' My Baby . . . 40
72 London HLU 10368 For Your Precious Love/Don't Go . . . 12
75 Warner Bros WB 16621 I Just Can't Live My Life/My Heart Will Understand . . . 15

LINDA JONES/J.J. JACKSON

77 Loma/Warners K 56271 THIS IS LOMA — VOL. 7 (LP, 1 side each) . . . 15

LITTLE JOHNNY JONES

73 Pressure Beat PB 5515 More Dub/More Dub — Chapter Two . . . 8
(see also Johnny Lover)

LLOYD JONES

70 Bullet BU 429 Rome/RHYTHM RULERS: Version . . . 15

LOUIS JONES ROCK & ROLL BAND

50s Vogue VE1 70111 ROCK AND ROLL (EP) . . . 90

MAE JONES ENSEMBLE with MARGARET BOND

55 Decca F 10486 I Walked Into The Garden/Tenderly He Watches . . . 7

MAGGIE JONES

70 VJM VLP 23 COLUMBIA RECORDINGS IN CHRONOLOGICAL ORDER VOL. 1 (LP) . . . 15
70 VJM VLP 25 COLUMBIA RECORDINGS IN CHRONOLOGICAL ORDER VOL. 2 (LP) . . . 15

NIC JONES

70 Trailer LER 2014 BALLADS AND SONGS (LP, red label, later with 'highway' label) . . . 20/12
71 Trailer LER 2027 NIC JONES (LP, red label) . . . 15
78 Transatlantic LTRA 507 FROM THE DEVIL TO A STRANGER (LP) . . . 12
(see also Jon Raven, Halliard)

NIGEL MAZLYN JONES

76 Isle Of Light IOL 666/1 SHIP TO SHORE (LP) . . . 45
78 Avada AVA 105 SENTINEL (LP) . . . 15
82 Isle Of Light IOL 0230 BREAKING COVER (LP) . . . 15

PALMER JONES

68 Direction 58-3603 The Great Magic Of Love/Dancing Master . . . 7

PAUL JONES

66 HMV POP 1554 High Time/I Can't Hold On Much Longer . . . 7
67 HMV POP 1576 I've Been A Bad Bad Boy/Sonny Boy Williamson . . . 7
67 HMV POP 1602 Thinkin' Ain't For Me/Softly (La Vita) . . . 7
67 HMV PSR 5307 Privilege (1-sided demo) . . . 15
67 Columbia DB 8303 Sons And Lovers/Three Sisters . . . 8
68 Columbia DB 8379 And The Sun Will Shine/The Dog Presides . . . 25
68 Columbia DB 8417 When I Was Six Years Old/You Have No Idea . . . 10
68 Columbia DB 8514 Aquarius/Pisces . . . 6
69 Columbia DB 8567 It's Getting Better/Not Before Time . . . 8
71 Vertigo 6059 053 Life After Death/The Mighty Ship . . . 8
73 Philips 6006 282 Perfect Roadie/Mouth Organ . . . 6
78 RSO RSO 003 Sheena Is A Punk Rocker/Pretty Vacant (p/s) . . . 5
67 HMV 7EG 8974 PRIVILEGE (EP) . . . 18
66 HMV CLP/CSD 3586 MY WAY (LP, mono/stereo) . . . 20/25
67 HMV CLP/CSD 3602 LOVE ME, LOVE MY FRIENDS (LP, mono/stereo) . . . 20/25
67 HMV CLP/CSD 3623 PRIVILEGE (LP, soundtrack, with George Bean Group & Mike Leander) . . . 18
69 Columbia SX/SCX 6347 COME INTO MY MUSIC BOX (LP, mono/stereo) . . . 25
71 Vertigo 6360 059 CRUCIFIX IN A HORSESHOE (LP, gatefold sleeve, swirl label) . . . 50
70 President PTLS 1068 DRAKE'S DREAM (LP, soundtrack) . . . 20
(see also Manfred Mann, Blues Band)

QUINCY JONES

59 Mercury AMT 1037 Tuxedo Junction/The Syncopated Clock . . . 5
60 Mercury AMT 1111 Love Is Here To Stay/Moonglow . . . 5
62 Mercury AMT 1195 Soul Bossa Nova/On The Street Where You Live . . . 25
65 Mercury MF 844 Seaweed/Golden Boy Theme . . . 5
69 RCA RCA 1850 MacKenna's Gold/Soul Full Of Gold . . . 5
70 A&M AMS 781 Killer Joe/Oh Happy Day . . . 5
72 A&M AMS 888 Ironside/Cast Your Fate To The Wind . . . 5
72 Reprise K 14150 Money Runned . . . 8
72 Atlantic K 10172 Listen To The Melody/Hot Rock Theme . . . 5
97 EMI 7 BIGDJ 001 They Call Me Mr.Tibbs/LYN COLLINS: Mama Feelgood (promo only, some free with 'The Big Score' LP) . . . 5
60 Mercury ZEP 10047 BIG BAND BASH (EP) . . . 12
61 Mercury ZEP 10109 THE BIRTH OF A BAND (EP, also stereo SEZ 19017) . . . 10/15
61 Columbia SEG 8088 DOUBLE SIX MEET QUINCY JONES (EP) . . . 12
61 Mercury ZEP 10119 THE BIRTH OF A BAND PT. 2 (EP, also stereo SEZ 19021) . . . 10/12
60 Mercury MMC 14038 THE BIRTH OF A BAND (LP, also stereo CMS 18026) . . . 20/25
60 Mercury MMC 14046 THE GREAT WORLD OF QUINCY JONES (LP, also stereo CMS 18031) . . . 20/25
61 Mercury MMC 14080 I DIG DANCERS (LP, also stereo CMS 18055) . . . 18/22
62 HMV CLP 1581 THE QUINTESSENCE (LP, also stereo CSD 1452) . . . 18/22
62 Mercury MMC 14098 AROUND THE WORLD (LP, also stereo CMS 18064) . . . 18/22
63 Mercury MMC 14125 BIG BAND BOSSA NOVA (LP, also stereo CMS 18080) . . . 18/22
63 Mercury MMC 14128 PLAYS HIP HITS (LP) . . . 15
64 Mercury MCL 20016 EXPLORES THE MUSIC OF HENRY MANCINI (LP, also stereo SMCL 20016) . . . 18/22
65 Columbia 33SX 1637 QUINCY'S HOME AGAIN (LP) . . . 18
65 Mercury 20047 MCL GOLDEN BOY (LP) . . . 18
65 Mercury 20063 SMCL THE PAWNBROKER (LP, soundtrack) . . . 25
66 Mercury 20072 (S)MCL "MIRAGE" (LP, soundtrack) . . . 30
66 Mercury 20073 (S)MCL PLAYS FOR PUSSYCATS (LP) . . . 18
66 Mercury 20078 (S)MCL QUINCY'S GOT A BRAND NEW BAG (LP) . . . 20
66 Fontana FJL 127 FAB! (LP) . . . 18

			MINT VALUE £
67	Mercury SMWL 30003	TRAVELLIN' ON THE QUINCY JONES BANDWAGON (LP)	15
68	RCA Victor RD/SF 7931	IN COLD BLOOD (LP, soundtrack)	45
68	United Artists (S)ULP 1181	IN THE HEAT OF THE NIGHT (LP, soundtrack, with Ray Charles)	50
69	Uni UNLS 103	LOST MAN (LP, soundtrack)	22
69	Paramount SPFL 256	THE ITALIAN JOB (LP, soundtrack, with Matt Monro)	125
69	RCA Victor SF 8017	MACKENNA'S GOLD (LP, soundtrack, with Jose Feliciano)	25
70	United Artists UAS 29128	THEY CALL ME MISTER TIBBS (LP, soundtrack)	55
70	A&M AMLS 961	WALKING IN SPACE (LP; reissued as AMLH 68050)	12
71	A&M AMLS 992	GULA MATIRA (LP)	12
71	A&M AMLS 63037	SMACKWATER JACK (LP)	15
72	WEA K 44168	THE HEIST (LP, soundtrack, with Little Richard)	35
72	Atlantic K 40371	HOW TO STEAL A DIAMOND IN FOUR UNEASY LESSONS (LP, soundtrack)	18
73	A&M AMLS 63041	YOU'VE GOT IT BAD GIRL (LP)	12
75	A&M AMLH 64526	MELLOW MADNESS (LP)	12
75	A&M AMLP 8005	IRONSIDE (LP)	12

(see also Annie Ross, Eddie Barclay & Quincy Jones, Diana Ross & Quincy Jones, John & Joan Shakespeare)

RICK JONES

73	Argo ZDA 156	HIYA MAYA (LP)	12

RONNIE JONES

64	Decca F 12012	Let's Pin A Rose On You/I Need Your Loving (B-side with Night Timers)	18
65	Decca F 12066	My Love/It's All Over	18
65	Decca F 12146	Anyone Who Knows What Love Is/Nobody But You	18
65	Parlophone R 5326	You're Lookin' Good/I'm So Clean (with Blue Jays)	40
67	CBS 2699	Little Bitty Pretty One/Put Your Tears Away	18
67	Polydor 56222	In My Love Mind/Mama Come On Home	12
68	CBS 3304	Without Love (There Is Nothing)/Little Bitty Pretty One	12

(see also Night-Timers)

SALENA JONES

66	Columbia DB 7818	A Walk In The Black Forest (Our Walk Of Love)/As Long As I Live	7
66	Columbia DB 7991	I Am Yours/I Only Know I Love You	7
67	Columbia DB 8212	When I Tell You (That I Love You)/Respect	6
73	Indigo GOPOP	Live And Let Die/Some Other World (some in p/s)	15/6
69	CBS 63613	THE MOMENT OF TRUTH (LP)	35
70	CBS 63650	EVERYBODY'S TALKIN' ABOUT SALENA JONES (LP)	35
73	RCA Victor SF 8335	ALONE & TOGETHER (LP)	22
74	RCA LPL 1 5025	THIS'N'THAT (LP)	22
71	CBS 64435	PLATINUM (LP)	25

SALINA JONES

65	Polydor 56012	Longing/Too Late	7

SAMANTHA JONES

65	United Artists UP 1072	It's All Because Of You/I Woke Up Crying	10
65	United Artists UP 1087	Don't Come Any Closer/Just Call And I'll Be There	12
65	United Artists UP 1105	Chained To A Memory/Just For Him	10
66	United Artists UP 1139	That Special Way/Somebody Else's Baby	10
67	United Artists UP 1185	Surrounded By A Ray Of Sunshine/How Do You Say Goodbye	45
67	United Artists UP 1200	Why Can't I Remember/Live For Life	8
68	United Artists UP 2248	Lonely Lonely Man/Doll On A Music Box	10
68	United Artists UP 2258	And Suddenly/Go Ahead And Love Me	20
68	Ford	Ford Leads The Way/Go Ahead And Love Me (p/s, Ford cars promo disc)	25
69	Penny Farthing PEN 703	Today (Without You)/The Feelin' That I Get	6
69	Penny Farthing PEN 708	Do I Still Figure In Your Life?/I'm Sorry, But I Think I Love You	6
70	Penny Farthing PEN 734	My Way/Darling Be Home Soon	5
70	Penny Farthing PEN 746	Best Of Both Worlds/Guilty Of Loving You	5
68	United Artists	CALL IT SAMANTHA (LP)	12
70	Contour 2870 003	MY WAY (LP)	12

(see also Vernons Girls, Krimson Kake)

SAMMY JONES

70	Gas GAS 123	You're My Girl/HONEYBOY MARTIN: Unchained Melody	6
72	Sioux SI 002	Mendicino/RUM RUNNERS: Sugar Brown	6
72	Sioux SI 003	Little Caesar/TWINKLE BROTHERS: Happy Song	6
72	Sioux SI 011	You're My Girl/HONEY BOY MARTIN: Unchained Melody	6

SANDIE JONES

72	Polydor 2058 223	Music Of Love/Ceol An Ghra	12

SOLOMON JONES

70	Bullet BU 452	Be Strong/Version	10
70	Pama PM 812	Here Comes The Night/RECO RODRIQUEZ: Jaded Ramble	15

SPIKE JONES

53	HMV 7M 121	Hot Lips/Hotter Than A Pistol (as Spike Jones & His Country Cousins)	12
53	HMV 7M 160	I Saw Mommy Kissing Santa Claus/Winter (as Spike Jones & His City Slickers)	12
54	HMV 7MC 3	Deep Purple/Dragnet (as Spike Jones & His City Slickers, export issue)	10
54	HMV 7MC 17	I Wanna Go Back To West Virginia/Little Bo-Beep Has Lost Her Sheep (as Spike Jones & His City Slickers, export issue)	10
55	HMV 7M 324	Secret Love/I'm In The Mood For Love (as Spike Jones & His City Slickers)	10
61	Warner Bros WB 34	Monster Movie Babe/Teenage Brain Surgeon	5
57	HMV 7EG 8286	FUN IN HI FI (EP)	10
59	RCA RCX 1030	SPIKE JONES NO. 1 (EP)	10
59	RCA RCX 1037	SPIKE JONES NO. 2 (EP)	10
61	Warners W(S) EP 6044	SPIKE JONES IN HI FI (EP, mono/stereo)	10/12
60	Warner Bros WM 4004	THE BAND THAT PLAYS FOR FUN (LP, also stereo WS 8004)	12/15
60	London HA-G 2270	OMNIBUST — T.V. SCHEDULE (LP, also stereo SAH-G 6090)	12/15
61	London HA-G 2298	SIXTY YEARS OF MUSIC AMERICA HATES BEST (LP, stereo SAH-G 6106)	12/15

MINT VALUE £

STAN JONES

58 Pye Disneyland DPL 39000 CREAKIN' LEATHER (LP) . . . 20

STEVE JONES

87 MCA MCA 1184 Mercy/Through The Night (p/s) . . . 7
89 MCA MCAT 1371 Freedom Fighter/Gimme Love/Suffragette City (12", p/s) . . . 8
89 MCA DMCAT 1371 Freedom Fighter/Gimme Love/Suffragette City (CD, card sleeve) . . . 8
87 MCA MCF 3384 MERCY (LP) . . . 15
90 MCA CD45 18179 STEVE JONES LIVE (CD sampler, promo only from uniss. LP, clear PVC sleeve). 15
(see also Sex Pistols, Professionals)

TAMIKO JONES

75 Arista ARIST 6 Touch Me Baby/Creepin' On My Dreams . . . 6
76 Contempo CS 2079 I'm Spellbound/T.J.'s Magic . . . 8
76 Contempo CX 15 Let It Flow/DORIS DUKE: Woman Of The Ghetto . . . 15

THAD JONES

58 Nixa Jazz NJL 13 LEONARD FEATHER PRESENTS MAD THAD (LP, with others) . . . 15

THELMA JONES

68 Sue WI 4047 Stronger/Never Leave Me . . . 35
69 Soul City SC 110 The House That Jack Built/Give It To Me Straight . . . 30
76 CBS 4711 Salty Tears/You're The Song . . . 8

THUNDERCLAP JONES

56 Oriole CB 1320 Hurricane Boogie/The Laughing Rag (78) . . . 10
56 Oriole CB 1328 Sound Barrier Boogie/Ask For Joe (78) . . . 10

TOM JONES

64 Decca F 11966 Chills And Fever/Breathless . . . 55
65 Decca F 12062 It's Not Unusual/To Wait For Love (Is To Waste Your Life Away) . . . 5
65 Decca F 12121 Once Upon A Time/I Tell The Sea . . . 6
65 Columbia DB 7566 Little Lonely One/That's What We'll All Do . . . 25
65 Decca F 12191 With These Hands/Untrue . . . 6
65 Decca F 12203 What's New Pussycat?/Rose . . . 7
65 Columbia DB 7733 Lonely Joe/I Was A Fool . . . 30
65 Decca F 12292 Thunderball/Key To My Heart . . . 10
66 Decca F 12315 To Make A Big Man Cry/I'll Never Let You Go (export issue) . . . 15
66 Decca F 12349 Stop Breaking My Heart/Never Give Away Love . . . 8
66 Decca F 12390 Once There Was A Time/Not Responsible . . . 12
66 Decca F 12461 This And That/City Girl . . . 7
66 Decca F 12516 Green, Green Grass Of Home/If I Had You (export issue) . . . 15
67 Decca F 22555 Detroit City/If I Had You . . . 6
67 Decca F 22563 Detroit City/Ten Guitars (export issue) . . . 15
68 Decca F 12854 A Minute Of Your Time/Looking Out My Window . . . 10
71 Decca FR 13236 Till/The Sun Died (export issue) . . . 15
71 Decca FR 13237 Till/One Day Soon (export issue) . . . 15
73 Decca F 13434 Today I Started Loving You Again/I Still Love You Enough . . . 6
73 Decca F 13471 Golden Days/Goodbye, God Bless You Baby . . . 6
74 Decca F 13490 La La La (Just Having You Here)/Love Love Love . . . 6
74 Decca F 13564 Pledging My Love/I'm Too Far Gone (To Turn Away) . . . 6
75 Decca F 13575 Ain't No Love/When The Band Goes Home . . . 6
75 Decca F 13590 I Got Your Number/The Pain Of Love . . . 6
75 Decca F 13598 Memories Don't Leave Like People Do/My Helping Hand . . . 6
70s Decca F 12747/12062 Delilah/It's Not Unusual (double-A-side with different number each side) . . . 6
82 Decca JONES 1 I'll Be Here Where The Heart Is/My Last Goodbye (p/s) . . . 6
87 Epic OLE Q1 A Boy From Nowhere/I'll Dress You In Mourning (poster p/s) . . . 6
65 Decca DFE 8617 ON STAGE (EP) . . . 15
65 Columbia SEG 8464 TOM JONES (EP) . . . 45
65 Decca DFE 8668 WHAT A PARTY (EP) . . . 15
65 Decca LK 4693 ALONG CAME JONES (LP) . . . 12
65 Decca LK/SKL 4743 A-TOM-IC JONES (LP, mono/stereo) . . . 12/15
66 Decca LK 4814 FROM THE HEART (LP) . . . 12
67 Decca SKL 4855 GREEN, GREEN GRASS OF HOME (LP, stereo) . . . 12
67 Decca SKL 4874 LIVE! AT THE TALK OF THE TOWN (LP, stereo) . . . 12
67 Decca SKL 4909 13 SMASH HITS (LP, stereo) . . . 12
(Mono copies of the above three albums are worth around £8 each)
68 Decca LK 4946 DELILAH (LP, mono) . . . 12
68 Decca LK 4982 HELP YOURSELF (LP, mono) . . . 20
69 Decca LK 5007 THIS IS TOM JONES (LP, mono) . . . 15
69 Decca LK 5032 LIVE IN LAS VEGAS — AT THE FLAMINGO (LP, mono) . . . 12
(All the above LPs were issued with unboxed Decca logos on the labels; later boxed label logo copies are worth £8 each)
70 Decca LK 5045 TOM (LP, mono) . . . 12
70 Decca LK 5072 I, WHO HAVE NOTHING (LP, mono) . . . 12
(Stereo copies of the above two albums are worth £10 each)

U.K. JONES

69 Deram DM 231 Let Me Tell Ya/And The Rains Came Down . . . 8
70 Ember EMB S 298 Take Me For What I Am/Love Is Here To Stay . . . 6
(see also Mike Berry)

WINSTON JONES

73 Gayfeet GS 208 You Make Me Cry/Version . . . 6

WIZZ JONES

69 United Artists (S)ULP 1029 WIZZ JONES (LP) . . . 120
70 Village Thing VTS 4 LEGENDARY ME (LP) . . . 22
72 CBS 64809 RIGHT NOW (LP) . . . 55
74 Village Thing VTS 24 WHEN I LEAVE BERLIN (LP) . . . 20
77 Plant Life PLR 009 MAGICAL FLIGHT (LP, with insert) . . . 15
(see also Pete Stanley & Wizz Jones, Accolade)

MINT VALUE £

JONES BOYS

57 Columbia DB 4046 Cool Baby/Rock-A-Hula Baby (Ukulele Lady) 15
58 Columbia DB 4170 A Certain Smile/Kathy-O 7
58 Columbia DB 4217 The Day The Rains Came/Hideaway 7
59 Columbia DB 4278 Dream Girl/Straight As An Arrow 6
(see also Four Jones Boys)

JONES GIRLS

82 Philadelphia Intl. PIR 2031 Nights Over Egypt/Love Don't Ever Say Goodbye 6
82 Phil. Intl. PIR 12-2031 Nights Over Egypt/Love Don't Ever Say Goodbye (12") 10
79 Phil. Intl. PIR 83831 THE JONES GIRLS (LP) 12

JONESY

73 Dawn DNS 1030 Ricochet/Every Day's The Same 6
72 Dawn DNLS 3042 NO ALTERNATIVE (LP, gatefold sleeve) 25
73 Dawn DNLS 3048 KEEPING UP (LP) 25
73 Dawn DNLS 3055 GROWING (LP, gatefold sleeve) 25
(see also Alan Bown)

JON-MARK

65 Brunswick 05929 Baby I Got A Long Way To Go/Night Comes Down 6
66 Brunswick 05952 Paris Bells/Little Town Girl 6

HARLEM JONNS RESHUFFLE

68 Fontana TF 970 You Are The One I Love/Good Lovin' 18
69 Fontana TF 1004 Everything Under The Sun/Let Love Come Between Us 15
69 Fontana (S)TL 5509 HARLEM JONNS RESHUFFLE (LP) 30

JONSTON McPHILBRY

66 Fontana TF 663 She's Gone/Woke Up At Eight 80

JOOK

72 RCA RCA 2279 Alright With Me/Do What You Can 6
73 RCA RCA 2344 Shame/City And Suburban Blues 5
73 RCA RCA 2368 Oo-Oo-Rudi/Jook's On You 5
73 RCA RCA 2431 King Capp/Rumble 5
74 RCA RCA 5024 Bish Bash Bosh/Crazy Kids 5
78 Chiswick SW 30 Watch Your Step/La La Girl/Aggravation Place/Everything I Do (EP) 6
(see also John's Children)

JANIS JOPLIN

69 CBS 3683 Turtle Blues/Piece Of My Heart (withdrawn) 30+
71 CBS 7019 Me And Bobby McGee/Half Moon 6
71 CBS 7217 Cry Baby/Mercedes Benz 6
71 CBS 9136 Move Over/Cry Baby/Try/Piece Of My Heart (maxi-single) 8
72 CBS 8241 Down On Me/Bye Bye Baby 6
76 CBS 3960 Piece Of My Heart/Kozmic Blues (p/s) 7
69 CBS 63546 I GOT DEM OL' KOZMIC BLUES AGAIN, MAMA! (LP) 25
74 CBS CQ 30322/Q 64188 PEARL (LP, quadrophonic) 25
(see also Big Brother & Holding Company)

DANNY JORDAN

61 Mercury AMT 1159 Jeannie/Boom Ditty Boom 10

DICK JORDAN

60 Embassy WB 384 Let It Be Me/Running Bear (78) 8
60 Embassy WB 394 Cathy's Clown/Don't Throw All Those Teardrops (78) 8
60 Oriole CB 1534 Hallelujah, I Love Her So/Sandy 20
60 Oriole CB 1534 Hallelujah, I Love Her So/Sandy (78) 30
60 Oriole CB 1548 Little Christine/I'll Love You Forever 18
60 Oriole CB 1548 Little Christine/I'll Love You Forever (78) 30
60 Oriole CB 1566 Garden Of Eden/Alive, Alive Oh! 8
60 Oriole CB 1591 Angel On My Shoulder/The Next Train Home 15
61 Piccadilly 7N 35035 Some Of These Days/I Want Her Back 10
62 Piccadilly 7N 35057 Fortune Teller/My Angel 10
63 Columbia DB 7016 Stop The Music/Dream Chaser 10
(see also Don Duke)

FRED JORDAN

66 Topic 12T 150 SONGS OF A SHROPSHIRE FARM WORKER (LP, blue label) 15

JOHNNY JORDAN

57 HMV POP 349 It's Grand To Be In Love/Home At Last 5

LOUIS JORDAN (& HIS TYMPANY FIVE)

54 Melodisc 1031 Dad Gum Ya Hide Boy/Whiskey Do Your Stuff (78) 15
56 Melodisc 1349 Messy Bessy/I Seen What'cha Done (78) 20
60 Downbeat CHA 3 Ooo-Wee/I'll Die Happy 20
50s Melodisc EPM7 66 LOUIS JORDAN (EP, as Louis Jordan Tympany Five, 3 different covers) each 90
57 Mercury MPT 7521 SOMEBODY UP THERE DIGS ME (10" LP, with Tympany Five) 140
58 Mercury MPL 6541 MAN, WE'RE WAILIN' (LP, with Tympany Five) 60
64 HMV CLP 1809 HALLELUJAH, LOUIS JORDAN IS BACK (LP) 45
65 Ace Of Hearts AH 85 LET THE GOOD TIMES ROLL (LP) 18
(see also Louis Armstrong)

LOUIS JORDAN & CHRIS BARBER'S BAND

63 Melodisc 45-1616 Is She Is Or Is She Ain't Your Baby/Fifty Cents 18
(see also Chris Barber)

JORDANAIRES

57 Capitol CL 14687 Sugaree/Baby, Won't You Please Come Home? 80
57 Capitol CL 14687 Sugaree/Baby, Won't You Please Come Home? (78) 20
57 Capitol CL 14773 Summer Vacation/Each Day 20
57 Capitol CL 14773 Summer Vacation/Each Day (78) 15

MINT VALUE £

58	Capitol CL 14921	Little Miss Ruby/All I Need Is You	25
63	Capitol CL 15281	Don't Be Cruel/Don't Worry	18
71	Ember EMB S 313	Kentucky/Teach The World To Sing	6
62	Capitol T 1742	SPOTLIGHT ON THE JORDANAIRES (LP)	65

(see also Elvis Presley, Patsy Cline, Don Gibson, Marty Robbins)

JORDAN BROTHERS

59	London HLW 8908	Never, Never/Please Tell Me Now	30
59	London HLW 8908	Never, Never/Please Tell Me Now (78)	35
60	London HLW 9235	Things I Didn't Say/Polly Plays Her Kettle Drum	15
61	London HLW 9308	No Wings On My Angel/Living For The Day	10

JOSEF K

79	Absolute ABS 1	Chance Meeting/Romance (p/s, 1,000 only)	25
80	Postcard 80-3	Radio Drill Time/Crazy To Exist (live) (hand-coloured foldaround p/s, blue labels)	25
80	Postcard 80-3	Radio Drill Time/Crazy To Exist (live) (brown or cream/yellow sleeve & labels)	8/7
80	Postcard 80-5	It's Kinda Funny/Final Request (p/s in poly bag, some with picture insert)	15/8
81	Postcard 81-5	Chance Meeting/Pictures (die-cut sleeve, some with postcard)	8/6
81	Postcard 81-4/TWI 023	Sorry For Laughing/Revelation (p/s)	12
87	Supreme Intl. Edit. 87-7	Heaven Sent/Radio Drill Time/Heads Watch/Fun'n'Frenzy (12", p/s)	12
90	Supreme Intl. Edit.	Young And Stupid (CD)	12
81	Postcard 81-1	SORRY FOR LAUGHING (LP, unreleased, a few with proof sleeve)	
81	Postcard 81-7	THE ONLY FUN IN TOWN (LP, with inner sleeve)	15
87	Supreme Intl. Edit. 87-6	YOUNG AND STUPID (LP)	15

(see also Orange Juice, Paul Haig, Happy Family, Rhythm Of Life)

IRVING JOSEPH

60	London HLT 9027	I Left My Love/Lorena	8

MARGIE JOSEPH (& BLUE MAGIC)

72	Stax 2025 052	Medicine Bend/Same Thing	8
74	Atlantic K 10460	Sweet Surrender/My Love	6
75	Atlantic K 10649	What's Come Over Me/You And Me (as Margie Joseph & Blue Magic)	6
72	Stax 2362 008	MAKES A NEW IMPRESSION (LP)	25
73	Atlantic K 40462	MARGIE JOSEPH (LP)	20

(see also Blue Magic)

JOSH

69	Duke DU 41	Judge/RON: Soul Of Joemel	6

(see also Girlie)

JOSH & HERBIE

60s	Kalypso AB 107	I'm Nobody's Child/How Can I Believe In You	6

JOSHUA

73	Key KL 014	JOSHUA (LP)	140

MARVA JOSIE

66	Polydor 56711	Crazy Stockings/I'll Get By	15

JOURNEY

82	CBS CBS 11A 1728	Don't Stop Believin'/Natural Thing (12", picture disc)	8
92	Columbia 4728102	TIME3 (3-CD)	25

JOURNEYMEN

67	Ember EMB 3382	INTRODUCING THE JOURNEYMEN (LP)	12

RODDIE JOY

65	Red Bird RB 10021	Come Back Baby/Love Hit Me With A Wallop	45

JOY & DAVID/DAVE

58	Parlophone R 4477	Whoopee!/My Oh My! (as Joy & David)	45
58	Parlophone R 4477	Whoopee!/My Oh My! (78, as Joy & David)	40
59	Decca F 11123	Rocking Away The Blues/If You Pass Me By (as Joy & David)	45
59	Decca F 11123	Rocking Away The Blues/If You Pass Me By (78, as Joy & David)	50
60	Triumph RGM 1002	Let's Go See Gran'ma/Believe Me (as Joy & Dave)	45
60	Decca F 11291	My Very Good Friend The Milkman/Doopey Darling (as Joy & Dave)	35
61	Parlophone R 4855	Joe's Been A-Gittin' There/They Tell Us Not To Love (as Joy & Dave)	30
61	Parlophone R 4855	Joe's Been A-Gittin' There/They Tell Us Not To Love (demo copies with alternate take of B-side)	45

JOHNNY JOYCE

76	Freedom FLP 99003	JOYCE'S CHOICE MIXTURE (LP)	22

(see also Velvet Opera, Levee Breakers)

JOYCE'S ANGELS

67	Major Minor MM 526	Flowers For My Friends/Rodney Reginald Smithfield Harvey Jo	8

(see also Chris White)

JOY DE VIVRE

81	Crass CR & SS ENVY 1	Our Wedding (flexidisc, white vinyl, no p/s, some with mailer)	18/12

(see also Crass)

JOY DIVISION

78	Enigma PSS 139	AN IDEAL FOR LIVING (Warsaw/No Love Lost/Leaders Of Men/Failures) (EP, 1,000 only, foldout p/s; beware of counterfeits)	600
78	Anonymous ANON 1	AN IDEAL FOR LIVING (Warsaw/No Love Lost/Leaders Of Men/Failures) (12" EP reissue, 1,200 only)	400
79	Factory FAC 13	Transmission/Novelty (p/s)	6
80	Factory FAC 28	Komakino/Incubation/(As You Said) (flexidisc, 10,000 only)	5
88	Factory FACD 213	Atmosphere/Love Will Tear Us Apart/Transmission (live) (CD)	8
79	Factory FACT 10	UNKNOWN PLEASURES (LP with inner sleeve, textured sleeve)	18
81	Factory FACT 40	STILL (2-LP, hessian sleeve, card inners & white ribbon)	40

(see also New Order)

MINT VALUE £

COL JOYE & JOYBOYS

59 Brunswick 05806 (Rockin' Rollin') Clementine/Bye Bye Baby Goodbye 25
59 Brunswick 05806 (Rockin' Rollin') Clementine/Bye Bye Baby Goodbye (78) 20
60 Top Rank JAR 529 Be My Girl/Yes Sir, That's My Baby 10

JOYFUL SINGERS with Lynn Tait on organ

67 Master Time MT 001 Jesus Christ Is Risen/BELIEVERS: Honey In The Rock 6
67 Master Time MT 002 Happy Days/He Watches Over Me 6
(see also Lyn[n] Tait)

JOY GUESSING

70 Crimson N 034 The Blue Midget/Officer Bud Babe 6

JOY OF COOKING

72 Capitol E-ST 11050 CASTLES (LP) 12

JOY OF LIFE

85 New European BADVC 62 ENJOY (12" EP) 8

JOYRIDE

69 RCA SF 8027 FRIEND SOUND (LP) 25

JOY UNLIMITED

69 Page One POF 147 Daytime Night Time/Mister Pseudonym 12
69 Page One POF 160 Oh Darlin'/Feeling 10
70 Page One POLS 028 TURBULENCE (LP) 60

J.S.D. BAND

73 Cube BUG 29 Sarah Jane/Paddy Stacks (p/s) 6
71 Regal Zono. SRLZ 1018 COUNTRY OF THE BLIND (LP) 40
72 Cube HIFLY 11 J.S.D. BAND (LP) 15
73 Cube HIFLY 14 TRAVELLING DAYS (LP) 15

JUAN & JUNIOR

67 CBS 2949 The Chase/Nothing 6
68 CBS 3223 To Girls/Andurina 15

JUBILEE STOMPERS

70 Trojan TR 7725 Luciana/I Really Like It 6

JUDAS JUMP

70 Parlophone R 5828 Run For Your Life/Beer Drinking Woman 7
70 Parlophone R 5838 This Feelin' We Feel/Hangman's Playing 8
70 Parlophone R 5873 Beer Drinking Woman/I Have The Right 6
70 Parlophone PAS 10001 SCORCH (LP) 30
(see also Herd, Amen Corner, Andy Bown)

JUDAS PRIEST

74 Gull GULS 6 Rocka-Rolla/Never Satisfied 12
76 Gull GULS 31 The Ripper/Island Of Domination 12
77 CBS S CBS 5222 Diamonds And Rust/Dissident Aggressor 7
78 CBS S CBS 6077 Better By You, Better Than Me/Invader 5
78 CBS S CBS 6719 Evening Star/Starbreaker 5
78 CBS S CBS 6794 Before The Dawn/Rock Forever 5
79 CBS S CBS 6915 Take On The World/Starbreaker 5
79 CBS S CBS 12-6915 Take On The World/Starbreaker/White Heat Red Hot (12", p/s) 8
79 CBS S CBS 7312 Evening Star/Beyond The Realms Of Death 5
79 CBS 12-7312 Evening Star/The Green Manalishi/Beyond The Realms Of Death (12", clear vinyl with picture insert) 8
79 Gull GULS 71 The Ripper/Victims Of Change 8
79 Gull GULS 7112 The Ripper/Never Satisfied/Victim Of Changes (12", p/s) 12
80 CBS TA 4298 United/Grinder (poster p/s) 10
81 CBS A12 1153 Hot Rockin'/Steeler/You Don't Have To Be Old To Be Wise (12", no p/s) 8
82 CBS A 112611 You've Got Another Thing Comin'/Exciter (live) (picture disc) 6
82 CBS A 2822 (Take These) Chains/Judas Priest Audio File (p/s) 5
83 Gull GULS 7612 Tyrant/Rocka-Rolla/Genocide (12", p/s, white vinyl) 12
84 CBS TA 4298 Some Heads Are Gonna Roll/Green Manalishi (Live)/Jawbreaker (12", p/s) 8
86 CBS QTA 7144 Locked In (Extended)/Reckless/Desert Plains (live)/ Freewheel Burning (live) (12", poster p/s) 10
88 Atlantic A 9114CD Johnny B. Goode/Rock You All Around The World (live)/Turbo Lover (live)/ Living After Midnight (live) (3" CD, with 5" adaptor in 5" case) 8
90 Columbia 656273 6 Painkiller/United/Better By You, Better Than Me (12" red vinyl, p/s) 8
91 Columbia 656589 0 A Touch Of Evil/Between The Hammer And The Anvil (shaped disc) 10
91 Columbia 656589 6 A Touch Of Evil/Between The Hammer And The Anvil/ You've Got Another Thing Coming (Live) (12", p/s, with giant poster) 8
74 Gull GULP 1005 ROCKA ROLLA (LP, original issue, 'bottle top' sleeve) 15
76 Gull PGULP 1015 SAD WINGS OF DESTINY (LP, picture disc) 15
78 Gull PGULP 1026 THE BEST OF JUDAS PRIEST (LP, picture disc) 12
78 CBS 83135 KILLING MACHINE (LP, red vinyl) 15
79 CBS 83852 UNLEASHED IN THE EAST (LP, with free single "Rock Forever"/ "Hell Bent For Leather"/"Beyond The Realms Of Death" [SJP 1]) 12
79 CBS 66357 BOX SET (3-LP, reissue of "Sin After Sin"/"Stained Class"/"Killing Machine") 20
86 Shanghai PGLP 1026 JUDAS PRIEST (LP, picture disc) 12
93 CBS 473050 METAL WORKS (3-LP) 22
98 SPV 0891 8542 98 LIVE MELTDOWN (LP) 12
(see also Trapeze, Fancy)

JUDD

70 Penny Farthing PEN 709 Snarlin' Mumma Lion/Stronger Than A Man 6
70 Penny Farthing PEL 504 JUDD (LP) 40
(see also Kris Ife)

MINT VALUE £

TERRY JUDGE & THE BARRISTERS

63 Oriole CB 1896 Hey Look At Her/Kind Of Girl You Can't Forget ... 18
64 Oriole CB 1938 I Don't Care/Try To Forget ... 18
65 Fontana TF 599 Come With Me And Love Me/Waitin' For The Night To Come ... 15

JUDGE DREAD

72 Big Shot BI 608 Big Six/One-Armed Bandit (no p/s) ... 5
74 Horse HOSS 62 Hey There Lonely Girl/The Planet Of The Apes (as J.D. Alex, no p/s) ... 5
73 Trojan TRLS 60 DREADMANIA: IT'S ALL IN THE MIND (LP) ... 15
74 Trojan TRLS 100 WORKING CLASS 'ERO (LP) ... 15
75 Cactus CTLP 113 BEDTIME STORIES (LP) ... 15
76 Cactus CTLP 123 LAST OF THE SKINHEADS (LP) ... 25
76 Klik KLP 9008 THE BEST OF JUDGE DREAD (LP) ... 12
78 Cactus CTLP 126 THE BEST WORST OF JUDGE DREAD (LP) ... 12
81 Creole CRX 3 RUB-A-DUB (LP) ... 12

JUDGE HAPPINESS

85 Mynah SCS 8501 Hey Judge/Pig In Pink (very few with p/s) ... 25/10
(see also Mock Turtles)

JUGGERNAUTS

84 Supreme Int. Editions 84-2 Come Throw Yourself/My First Million (p/s) ... 10
(see also Paul Haig)

JUICE ON THE LOOSE

81 Juice JJOS 1 JUICE ON THE LOOSE (LP) ... 12

JUICY LUCY

70 Fontana TF 1068 Who Do You Love/Walking Down The Highway (unissued)
70 Vertigo V1/6059 001 Who Do You Love/Walking Down The Highway ... 10
70 Vertigo 6059 015 Pretty Woman/I'm A Thief ... 18
72 Polydor 2001 279 It Ain't Easy/Promised Land ... 12
69 Vertigo VO 2 JUICY LUCY (LP, swirl label, gatefold sleeve) ... 40
70 Vertigo 6360 014 LIE BACK AND ENJOY IT (LP, swirl label, gatefold poster sleeve) ... 40
71 Bronze ILPS 9157 GET A WHIFF OF THIS (LP) ... 15
72 Polydor 2310 160 PIECES (LP) ... 12
(see also Misunderstood, Van Der Graaf Generator, Ray Owen, Paul Williams' Big Roll Band)

JULIAN (Judy Mowatt) & CHOSEN FEW

71 High Note HS 054 Joy To The World/Joyful Version ... 8

JULIAN (Judy Mowatt) & GAYTONES

72 High Note HS 059 She Kept On Talking/Version ... 15

JULIAN (Scott)

59 Pye 7N 15236 Sue Saturday/Can't Wait ... 35
59 Pye N 15236 Sue Saturday/Can't Wait (78) ... 40
(see also Brian Bennett)

JULIAN KIRSCH

69 Columbia DB 8541 Clever Little Man/The Adventures Of A Young Cuckoo ... 15

JULIAN'S TREATMENT

70 Young Blood YB 1009 Phantom City/Alda, Dark Lady Of The Outer Worlds ... 15
70 Young Blood SYB 2 A TIME BEFORE THIS (2-LP) ... 125
(see also Julian Jay Savarin)

JULY

68 Major Minor MM 568 My Clown/Dandelion Seeds ... 175
68 Major Minor MM 580 Hello, Who's There?/The Way ... 100
68 Major Minor MMLP 29 JULY (LP) ... 500
87 Bam Caruso KIRI 097 DANDELION SEEDS (LP, reissue of above LP with extra tracks & different sleeve) ... 22
95 Essex 1011LP JULY (LP, reissue with bonus 7": "Hello Who's There?"/"The Way" [p/s, 10117]) . 20
(see also Jade Warrior, Tom Newman, Tomcats)

JUMBLE LANE

71 Holyground HG 115 JUMBLE LANE (LP, 99 copies only) ... 500

JUMP

80 Caveman CLUB 1 Shake Up/All In Vain (p/s) ... 25

JUMPIN' JACKS

58 HMV POP 440 My Girl, My Girl/Tried And Tested ... 25
58 HMV POP 440 My Girl, My Girl/Tried And Tested (78) ... 15

JUMPLEADS

82 Ock OC 001 THE STAG MUST DIE (LP, with insert) ... 30

JUMP SQUAD

81 101 UR 2 Lord Of The Dance/Debt (p/s) ... 20
(see also Embryo)

JUNCO PARTNERS

65 Columbia DB 7665 As Long As I Have You/Take This Hammer ... 60
79 Rigid JUNK 1028 Swinging Sixties Boys/Peepin' And Hidin' ... 6
81 Energy NRG 4 Tall Windows/Noizez In My Head (p/s) ... 5
81 Energy NRGX 4 Tall Windows (Extended)/Noizez In My Head (Extended) (12", stickered white label, plain sleeve, promo only) ... 10
71 Philips 6308 032 JUNCO PARTNERS (LP) ... 45

JUNCTION 32

75 Holyground HGS 119 JUNCTION 32 (LP, 100 copies only) ... 500

MINT VALUE £

JUNCUNO

71	Banana BA 361	The End (as Joncuno)/HORACE ANDY: See A Man's Face	20
72	Bamboo BA 69	Love Is A Stranger/When We Were Children	12

(see also Juncuno Singers)

JUNCUNO SINGERS

71	Bamboo BAM 69	Love Is Strange/When We Were Children	8
72	Banana BA 366	I'd Like To Teach The World To Sing/Rope Of Sand	7

ROSANNE JUNE

56	London HLU 8352	The Charge Of The Light Brigade/Broken Windows	30
56	London HLU 8352	The Charge Of The Light Brigade/Broken Windows (78)	12
58	Oriole CB 1430	When A Woman Cries/The Great Chicago Fire	8
58	Oriole CB 1430	When A Woman Cries/The Great Chicago Fire (78)	8

ROSEMARY JUNE

58	Fontana H 141	I'll Always Be In Love With You/Person To Person	10
58	Fontana H 141	I'll Always Be In Love With You/Person To Person (78)	8
59	Pye International 7N 25005	I'll Be With You In Apple Blossom Time/Always A Bridesmaid	6
59	Pye International N 25005	I'll Be With You In Apple Blossom Time/Always A Bridesmaid (78)	10
59	Pye International 7N 25015	With You Beside Me/I Used To Love You, But It's All Over Now	5
59	Pye International N 25015	With You Beside Me/I Used To Love You, But It's All Over Now (78)	12
59	London HLT 9014	The Village Of St. Bernadette/But Not For Me	10
59	London HLT 9014	The Village Of St. Bernadette/But Not For Me (78)	15

JUNE BRIDES

84	Pink PINKY 1	In The Rain/Sunday To Saturday (p/s)	10
84	Pink PINKY 2	Every Conversation/Disneyland (die-cut sleeve, some with insert)	8/7

(see also Phil Wilson)

JUNG COLLECTIVE

02	Nanny Tango NT 1	Injustice/Street Preacher (Plaid Mix) (clear vinyl, poly sleeve w/sticker insert)	20

JUNGLE JUICE

74	Bradley's BRAD 7407	The Zoo Gang/Monkey Business	5

HUGH ROY JUNIOR

71	Big BG 329	Papcito/RUPIE EDWARDS: I'm Gonna Live Some Life	10
71	Supreme SUP 211	Double Attack/MURPHY'S ALL STARS: Puzzle	10
72	Ashanti ASH 405	King Of The Road/ROOSEVELT ALL STARS: Version	10
72	Jackpot JP 806	Two Ton Guletto/Version	10

(see also U Roy Junior)

U ROY JUNIOR

72	Attack ATT 8030	This Is A Pepper/JOHN HOLT: Justice	10
72	Sioux SI 024	The Wedding/LLOYD'S ALL STARS: Buttercup	10
73	Randy's RAN 532	Froggie/RHYTHM RULERS: Version	10
73	Techniques TE 928	Aunt Kereba/DON RECO: Waterloo Rock (B-side actually by Reco Rodriquez)	10

(see also Hugh Roy Junior)

JUNIOR (Simpson)

68	Giant GN 18	I'm Gonna Leave You Girl/I Love You I Love You	15
68	Giant GN 25	Come Cure Me/I Want Your Loving	15

JUNIORS

64	Columbia DB 7339	There's A Pretty Girl/Pocket Size	50

JUNIOR'S EYES

69	Regal Zonophone RZ 3009	Mr. Golden Trumpet Player/Black Snake	20
69	Regal Zonophone RZ 3018	Woman Love/White Light Part 2 (withdrawn B-side)	25
69	Regal Zonophone RZ 3018	Woman Love/Circus Days	20
69	Regal Zonophone RZ 3023	Star Child/Sink Or Swim	20
69	Regal Zono. SLRZ 1008	BATTERSEA POWER STATION (LP)	55

(see also David Bowie, Tickle, Bunch Of Fives, Outsiders)

JUNIPER GREEN

71	Columbia DB 8809	Dreams In The Sky/Cascade Of Ice	25

LENA JUNOFF

68	Olga OLE 8	Yesterday Has Gone/Good Kind Of Hurt	30

ERIC JUPP & HIS ORCHESTRA

53	Columbia SCM 5070	Jog Trot/Doina Voda	8
54	Columbia SCM 5081	Ooop De Ooh (Lazy Mambo)/Footsteps In The Fog	8
54	Columbia SCM 5140	They Were Doin' The Mambo/Skokiian (with Coronets)	8
56	Columbia DB 3817	Theme From 'East Of Eden'/When The Lilac Blooms Again	8
57	Columbia DB 4030	Bleep! Bleep!/Three-Two-One-Zero!	10
55	Columbia SEG 7589	ERIC JUPP AND HIS ORCHESTRA (EP)	12
56	Columbia SEG 7603	RHYTHM AND BLUES (EP)	12
56	Columbia SEG 7621	THE PERFECT COMBINATION (EP)	8
56	Columbia 33S 1097	LET'S DANCE (10" LP)	15
58	Columbia 33SX 1072	MUSIC FOR SWEETHEARTS (LP)	12

(see also Coronets, Rockin' Strings)

MICKEY JUPP

83	A&M AM 128	Stormy Sunday Lunchtime/Reading Glasses	5
83	A&M AM 145	Boxes And Tins/Reading Glasses (p/s)	5
83	A&M AMLH 68559	SHAMPOO, HAIRCUT AND SHAVE (LP)	12

(see also Rossi & Frost)

CURT JURGENS

59	Top Rank JAR 151	Ferry To Hong Kong/Live For Love	8
59	Top Rank JAR 151	Ferry To Hong Kong/Live For Love (78)	15

SAMANTHA JUSTE

66	Go AJ 11402	No One Needs My Love Today/If Trees Could Talk	18

JUST FOUR MEN

64 Parlophone R 5186 That's My Baby/Things Will Never Be The Same (withdrawn, as Four Just Men) . 75
64 Parlophone R 5208 That's My Baby/Things Will Never Be The Same. 60
65 Parlophone R 5241 There's Not One Thing/Don't Come Any Closer 60
(see also Wimple Winch, Four Just Men, Pacific Drift)

JUST FRANK

80 Rok ROK III/IV You/SPLIT SCREENS: Just Don't Try (die-cut company sleeve). 35

JIMMY JUSTICE

60 Pye 7N 15301 I Understand Just How You Feel/Bloodshot Eyes (as Jimmy Justice & Jury) 20
61 Pye 7N 15351 When Love Has Left You/The Teacher 18
61 Pye 7N 15376 A Little Bit Of Soap/Little Lonely One 15
62 Pye 7N 15421 When My Little Girl Is Smiling/If I Lost Your Love. 6
62 Pye 7N 15443 Ain't That Funny/One (some with p/s) 18/7
62 Pye 7N 15457 Spanish Harlem/Write Me A Letter 6
62 Pye 7N 15469 Parade Of Broken Hearts/Dawning 7
63 Pye 7N 15502 The World Of Lonely People/I Wake Up Crying 7
63 Pye 7N 15509 Little Cracked Bell/Lighted Windows. 7
63 Pye 7N 15528 The Guitar Player/Don't Let The Stars Get In Your Eyes. 7
63 Pye 7N 15558 You're Gonna Need My Lovin'/Since You've Been Gone (with Exchequers) 7
63 Pye 7N 15601 Don't Say That Again/Green Leaves Of Summer 7
69 Decca F 12899 Running Out Of Time/There Goes My World 7
65 Pye 7N 15963 Only Heartbreak For Me/Everything In The Garden 7
68 RCA Victor RCA 1681 I'm Past Forgetting You/Walking Away With My Heart 25
63 Pye NEP 24159 HIT PARADE (EP) 40
62 Pye NPL 18080 TWO SIDES OF JIMMY JUSTICE (LP) 50
62 Pye NPL 18085 SMASH HITS (LP). 50

JUSTIFIED ANCIENTS OF MU MU (J.A.M.s)

87 KLF Comm. JAMS 23 All You Need Is Love (Original) (12", white label, 1-sided, 500 only) 50
87 KLF Comm. JAMS 23(s) All You Need Is Love (Me Ru Con Mix)/(Ibo Version) (1,000 only, plain sleeve) . . . 10
87 KLF Comm. JAMS 23T All You Need Is Love/Ivum Naya/Rap, Rhyme And Scratch Yourself (12", 'James Anderton' p/s, 5,000 only) 15
87 KLF Comm. JAMS 24T Whitney Joins The JAMs (120 bpm) (12", 1-sided, 'Scottish' issue, 500 only) 15
87 KLF Comm. JAMS 25T 1987 — The 45 Edits (12", p/s). 12
87 KLF Comm. JAMS 26T BURN THE BEAT (12" EP, 5,000 for export only). 10
87 KLF Comm. JAMS 27 Down Town/118 BPM 27 (p/s). 8
87 KLF Comm. JAMS 27 Down Town (A-side Mix) (12", 1-sided, white label, 500 only). 12
87 KLF Comm. JAMS 27 Down Town (B-side Mix) (12", 1-sided, white label, 500 only). 12
87 KLF Comm. JAMS 27 Down Town (A-side Mix)/(B-side Mix) (12", white label) 12
87 KLF Comm. JAMS 27T Down Town (118 bpm)/Down Town (12", JAMs or mispressed 'album' label, generic sleeve) 10/15
88 KLF Comm. JAMS 28T It's Grim Up North (Original Vocal Mix) (12", grey vinyl, 1-sided, 350 only) 50
87 KLF Comm. JAMS DS 1 Deep Shit (flexidisc, unreleased). 150
91 KLF Comm. JAMS 028R It's Grim Up North (Original Vocal Mix) (12", black vinyl, 1-sided promo) 8
88 Fierce FRIGHT 34(T) 20 GREATEST HITS (12" EP; not actually by J.A.M.s!). 12
87 KLF Comm. JAMS LP 1 1987 (WHAT THE FUCK IS GOING ON?) (LP, withdrawn) 50
87 KLF Comm. JAMS LP 1 1987 (WHAT THE FUCK IS GOING ON?) (cassette, withdrawn) 20
88 KLF Comm. JAMS LP 2 WHO KILLED THE JAMS? (LP, stickered sleeve with insert) 25
89 KLF Comm. JAMS DLP 3 SHAG TIMES (2-LP) 20
89 KLF Comm. JAMS CD 3 SHAG TIMES (CD). 20
(see also KLF, Timelords, Disco 2000, Space, Orb, Bill Drummond)

JAY JUSTIN

60 HMV POP 801 Nobody's Darlin' But Mine/Sweet Sensation 7
63 HMV POP 1183 Proud Of You/Love, Love Me, Baby Darling. 6
68 Columbia DB 8439 I Sell Summertime/Time (withdrawn). 8

JUSTINS

71 Punch PH 65 Cholera/LLOYD ALL STARS: Black Bird 6

JUSTIN CASE

80 Rok ROK XIX TV/STRAIGHT UP: One Out All Out (die-cut company sleeve). 40

JUSTINE

69 Dot DOT 121 Leave Me Be/Clown 10
69 Buffalo BFS 1001 Right Now/Place Where Sorrow Hides. 20
70 Uni UNS 528 She Brings Back The Morning With Her/Back To Boulder 10
70 Uni UNLS 111 JUSTINE (LP) 25

BILL JUSTIS & HIS ORCHESTRA

57 London HLS 8517 Raunchy/The Midnight Man. 20
57 London HLS 8517 Raunchy/The Midnight Man (78) 10
58 London HLS 8614 College Man/The Stranger (B-side with Spinners) 25
58 London HLS 8614 College Man/The Stranger (B-side with Spinners) (78). 15
63 Mercury AMT 1201 I'm Gonna Learn To Dance/Tamoure 10

JUST PLAIN JONES

71 CBS CBS 7480 Crazy, Crazy/Should Have Stayed With Mary 7
(see also Just Plain Smith, Micky Manchester, Dave Ballantyne, Esprit De Corps)

JUST PLAIN SMITH

69 Sunshine SUN 7702 February's Child/Don't Open Your Mind (p/s) 135
(see also Just Plain Jones, Micky Manchester, Esprit De Corps)

JUST US

66 CBS 202068 I Can't Grow Peaches On A Cherry Tree/I Can Save You 7

JUVENILES

66 Pye International 7N 25349 Bo Diddley/Yes I Believe 100

JYNX

64 Columbia DB 7304 How/Do What They Don't Say 60

CAROLINE K
87 Earthly Delights EARTH 1 NOW WAIT FOR LAST YEAR (LP, 1,500 only) . . . 20

KRISSIE K
74 People PEO 110 Stick Up/Who Do You Think You Are . . . 5

JOHNNY K & SINGIN' SWINGIN' 8
63 Fontana H 408 Lemonade/Come Closer Melinda . . . 15

MOSES K & PROPHETS
65 Decca F 12244 I Went Out With My Baby Tonight/So Long . . . 20
(see also Them)

KADDO STRINGS
80 Grapevine GRP 146 Nothing But Love/Crying Over You . . . 8
(see also Duke Browner, Tartans)

KADETTES
82 Blank GET 1 Fireball XL5/Mission Impossible . . . 8

BERT KAEMPFERT
65 Polydor BM 56504 Bye Bye Blues/Remember When . . . 5
66 Brunswick LAT/STA 8651 A MAN COULD GET KILLED (LP, soundtrack) . . . 20

KAINE & ABEL
66 Philips BF 1472 Then You Must Know My Love/Crying In The Rain . . . 8

KAKKO
90 CBS 656023 What Kind Of Fool (mixes)/I Pledge You My Heart (12", p/s) . . . 40
90 CBS 655 710 6 We Should Be Dancing (mixes) (12", p/s) . . . 30
90 CBS 655 710 8 We Should Be Dancing (mixes) (12", p/s) . . . 35
90 CBS 655 710 2 We Should Be Dancing (mixes) (CD) . . . 40

KALA
73 Bradleys BRAD 302 Travelling Home/Still Got Time . . . 5
73 Bradleys BRADL 1002 KALA (LP) . . . 15
(see also Quintessence)

ALAN KALANI
59 Vogue V 9147 A Touch Of Pink/SURFERS: Mambo Jambo . . . 18
59 Vogue V 9147 A Touch Of Pink/SURFERS: Mambo Jambo (78) . . . 20

KALASANDRO!
60 Warner Bros WB 13 Chi Chi/Forbidden City . . . 15

KALEIDOSCOPE (U.K.)
67 Fontana TF 863 Flight From Ashiya/Holidaymaker (some in p/s) . . . 90/40
68 Fontana TF 895 A Dream For Julie/Please Excuse My Face . . . 50
68 Fontana TF 964 Jenny Artichoke/Just How Much Are You . . . 35
69 Fontana TF 1002 Do It Again For Jeffrey/Poem . . . 40
69 Fontana TF 1048 Balloon/If You So Wish . . . 90
67 Fontana (S)TL 5448 TANGERINE DREAM (LP) . . . 200
69 Fontana STL 5491 FAINTLY BLOWING (LP, gatefold sleeve; most copies with watermark on beginning of each side) . . . 200/150
87 5 Hours Back TOCK 005 TANGERINE DREAM (LP, stereo reissue) . . . 25
87 5 Hours Back TOCK 006 FAINTLY BLOWING (LP, reissue, single sleeve) . . . 25
(see also Fairfield Parlour, I Luv Wight)

KALEIDOSCOPE (U.S.)
70 CBS 64005 BERNICE (LP, as American Kaleidoscope) . . . 15
76 Island ILPS 9462 WHEN SCOPES COLLIDE (LP) . . . 12

KALIN TWINS
58 Brunswick 05751 When/Three O'Clock Thrill . . . 8
58 Brunswick 05759 Forget Me Not/Dream Of Me (some B-side labels list "Dream Of You") . . . 10
58 Brunswick 05759 Forget Me Not/Dream Of Me (78, some B-side labels list "Dream Of You") . . . 8
59 Brunswick 05775 Oh! My Goodness/It's Only The Beginning . . . 12
59 Brunswick 05775 Oh! My Goodness/It's Only The Beginning (78) . . . 7
59 Brunswick 05797 Cool/When I Look In The Mirror . . . 10
59 Brunswick 05797 Cool/When I Look In The Mirror (78) . . . 15
59 Brunswick 05803 Moody/Sweet Sugar Lips . . . 8
59 Brunswick 05803 Moody/Sweet Sugar Lips (78) . . . 20
59 Brunswick 05814 The Meaning Of The Blues/Why Don't You Believe Me? . . . 10
59 Brunswick 05814 The Meaning Of The Blues/Why Don't You Believe Me? (78) . . . 20
60 Brunswick 05826 Chicken Thief/Loneliness . . . 12
60 Brunswick 05844 Zing! Went The Strings Of My Heart/No Money Can Buy . . . 10
61 Brunswick 05848 Momma Poppa/You Mean The World To Me . . . 12
61 Brunswick 05862 One More Time/I'm Forever Blowing Bubbles . . . 10
58 Brunswick OE 9383 WHEN (EP) . . . 50
59 Brunswick OE 9449 THE KALIN TWINS (EP) . . . 50

MINT VALUE £

KITTY KALLEN

54	Brunswick 05261	Are You Looking For A Sweetheart/In The Chapel In The Moonlight	20
54	Brunswick 05287	Little Things Mean A Lot/I Don't Think You Love Me Anymore	55
54	Brunswick 05357	Heartless Heart/The Spirit Of Christmas	20
54	Brunswick 05359	I Want You All To Myself/(Don't Let The) Kiddy Geddin'	15
55	Brunswick 05394	A Little Lie/Take Everything But You	12
55	Brunswick 05402	Polly Pigtails/I'm A Lonely Little Petunia (In A Potato Patch)	10
55	Brunswick 05431	Kitty Who?/By Bayou Bay	10
55	Brunswick 05447	Forgive Me/Lonely	12
55	Brunswick 05475	Let's Make The Most Of Tonight/Just Between Friends	12
55	Brunswick 05494	How Lonely Can I Get?/Sweet Kentucky Rose	10
56	Brunswick 05536	Go On With The Wedding (with Georgie Shaw)/Only Forever	12
56	Brunswick 05612	True Love/Will I Always Be Your Sweetheart?	8
57	Brunswick 05705	Long Lonely Nights/Lasting Love	8
58	Brunswick 05734	Crying Roses/I Never Was The One	6
59	Philips PB 971	If I Give My Heart To You/The Door That Won't Open	5
59	Philips PB 971	If I Give My Heart To You/The Door That Won't Open (78)	10
60	Philips PB 1028	Make Love To Me/Heaven Help Me	5
62	RCA RCA 1324	Call Me A Fool/My Colouring Book	5

(see also Georgie Shaw)

DICK KALLMAN

56	Brunswick 05608	Two Different Worlds/Love Me As Though There Were No Tomorrow	6
60	Vogue V 9162	Born To Be Loved/Just Squeeze Me But Don't Teeze Me	10
63	HMV POP 1118	Say It Isn't So/From This Day On (A-side with John Barry & His Orchestra)	5
63	HMV CLP 1642	SPEAK SOFTLY (LP)	20

GUNTER KALLMAN CHOIR

64	Polydor NH 24678	Elisabeth Serenade/Musik Zum	5

BOBBY KALPHAT

68	Nu Beat NB 007	Rhythm And Soul/BUNNY & RUDDY: True Romance	8
70s	Faith FA 008	Zion Hill/Dub Hill	5

KAMARAS

69	CBS 4199	Let This Moment Pass Away/I Just Can't Break Away From This Lovin'	6

AMORY KANE

68	MCA MU 1036	Reflections Of Your Face/Four Ravens	6
70	UNI UNS 518	You Were On My Mind/All The Best Songs And Marches	6
70	CBS 5111	Him Or Me/Forever Waiting	6
68	MCA MUP(S) 348	MEMORIES OF TIME UNWOUND (LP)	45
70	CBS 63849	JUST TO BE THERE (LP)	40

(see also Ron Geesin)

EDEN KANE

60	Pye 7N 15284	Hot Chocolate Crazy/You Make Love So Well	25
61	Decca F 11353	Well I Ask You/Before I Lose My Mind	6
61	Decca F 11381	Get Lost/I'm Telling You	7
62	Decca F 11418	Forget Me Not/A New Kind Of Lovin'	6
62	Decca F 11460	I Don't Know Why/Music For Strings	8
62	Decca F 11504	House To Let/I Told You	10
63	Decca F 11568	Sounds Funny To Me/Someone Wants To Know	10
63	Fontana TF 398	Tomorrow Night/I Won't Believe You (some in p/s)	12/7
63	Fontana TF 413	Like I Love You/Come Back (with Earl Preston's TTs)	10
64	Fontana TF 438	Boys Cry/Don't Come Cryin' To Me	6
64	Fontana TF 462	Rain Rain Go Away/Guess Who It Is	7
64	Fontana TF 508	Hangin' Around/Gonna Do Something About You	10
65	Fontana TF 582	If You Want This Love/Have I Done Something Wrong	10
66	Decca F 12342	Magic Town/The Whole World Was Crying	20
69	Fontana TF 1023	Boys Cry/Don't Come Cryin' To Me (p/s, reissue)	6
70	Bell BLL 1102	Reason To Believe/I Played It Like A Fool	6
62	Decca DFE 6696	WELL I ASK YOU! (EP)	35
62	Decca DFE 8503	HITS (EP)	30
64	Decca DFE 8567	SIX GREAT NEW SWINGERS (EP)	40
64	Fontana TFE 17424	IT'S EDEN (EP)	30
62	Ace Of Clubs ACL 1133	EDEN KANE (LP)	45
64	Fontana TL 5211	IT'S EDEN (LP)	40
64	Wing WL 1218	SMOKE GETS IN YOUR EYES (LP)	20

(see also Brothers Kane, Sarstedt Brothers)

GARY KANE

67	Pye 7N 17334	Too Good To Miss/Guilty Of Dreaming	5

HELEN KANE

55	MGM EP 549	The Boop-boop-a-doup Girl (EP)	25

LEE KANE

55	Capitol CL 14297	Ev'ry Day/How Would You Have Me?	10
55	Capitol CL 14328	Around And Around/Merci Beaucoup	10

MARIA KANE

65	Decca F 12184	Love Is Slipping Away/Love Is Strange	8

PAUL KANTNER

71	RCA Victor SF 8163	BLOWS AGAINST THE EMPIRE (LP, gatefold sleeve with booklet, as Paul Kantner & Jefferson Starship)	15
71	Grunt FTR 1002	SUNFIGHTER (LP, gatefold sleeve with booklet & inner sleeve; as Paul Kantner, Grace Slick & Jefferson Starship)	12
73	Grunt BFL 1 0148	BARON VON TOLBOOTH (LP, with Grace Slick & David Freiberg)	12

(see also Jefferson Airplane/Starship)

MINT VALUE £

KAPLAN

68	Philips BF 1636	Do You Believe In Magic/I Like	6
68	Philips BF 1699	I Love It/Trousers Down	6

KAPT. KOPTER & FABULOUS TWIRLY BIRDS

73	Epic EPC 65381	KAPT. KOPTER & THE FABULOUS TWIRLY BIRDS (LP)	15

(see also Spirit)

ANTON KARAS

60	Decca F 9235	The "Harry Lime" Theme/The Cafe Mozart Waltz	8
55	Decca DFE 6035	ANTON KARAS ZITHER SOLOS (EP)	10
51	Decca LF 1053	ANTON KARAS (10" LP)	15

KARINA

68	Hispavox HXS 305	Romeo Y Julieta/Fortuna Y Le Poder	5
71	United Artists UP 35205	Tomorrow I'm Coming Your Way/Something	10

MIRIAM KARLIN

67	Columbia DB 8220	Celebration/Nose For Trouble	6

KARLINS

66	Parlophone R 5457	You Mean Nothing To Me/Walkin' Away	6
66	Parlophone R 5550	The Spinning Wheel/It's Good To Be Around	6
67	Parlophone R 5607	The Hawkmoth And The Flame/Water Or The Wine	6
68	Columbia DB 8394	Everybody Wants To Go To Heaven/Stay On The Island	5

BILLY KARLOFF (& EXTREMES)

78	Wanted CULT-45-001	Back Street Billy/Crazy Paving (p/s)	8
81	Warner Bros K 17753	Headbangers/Don't Keep Me Down (p/s)	5

(see also Tom Robinson Band, Stiff Little Fingers)

BORIS KARLOFF

60	Caedmon CAL 102/1	HANS CHRISTIAN ANDERSEN (LP)	15
67	Brunswick LAT 8678	AN EVENING WITH BORIS KARLOFF AND FRIENDS (LP)	50

STEVE KARMEN BIG BAND

75	United Artists UP 35770	Breakaway/Breakaway (Vocal Version) (featuring Jimmy Radcliffe)	6

(see also Jimmy Radcliffe)

KAROO

65	Oak RGJ 193	Mamma's Out Of Town/Lonely Weekend	175

KARRIER

84	Unit TRANS 101	I'm Back/Dreaming (no p/s)	30
85	Unit	WAY BEYOND THE NIGHT (LP)	15

KARYN KARSH

68	RCA Victor RCA 1740	I Wasn't Born To Follow/Musty Dusty	5

KARYOBIN

(see under Spontaneous Music Ensemble)

KASENETZ-KATZ SINGING ORCHESTRAL CIRCUS

68	Pye International 7N 25472	Down In Tennessee/Mrs. Green	6
68	Pye International 7N 25476	Quick Joey Small (Run Joey Run)/Rumble '69 (unreleased)	
69	Pye International 7N 25480	We Can Work It Out/Latin Shake	5
68	Pye Int. NSPL 28119	KASENETZ-KATZ SINGING ORCHESTRAL CIRCUS (LP)	15
69	Buddah 203 018	QUICK JOEY SMALL — I'M IN LOVE WITH YOU (LP, as Kasenetz-Katz Super Circus)	12

AL KASHA

60	Coral Q 72410	Teardrops Are Falling/No Matter Where You Are	5

KATCH-22

66	Fontana TF 768	Major Catastrophe/Hold Me	30
67	Fontana TF 874	Makin' Up My Mind/While We're Friends	12
68	Fontana TF 930	The World's Gettin' Smaller/Don't Bother	12
68	Fontana TF 984	Pumpkin Mini/100,000 Years	12
69	Fontana TF 1005	Out Of My Life/Baby Love	12
69	CBS 4644	It's The Sunshine/Mrs. Jones	12
68	Saga EROS 8047	IT'S SOFT ROCK & ALLSORTS (LP, with insert)	30

KATCH 22

91	Kold Sweat KSLP 01	DIARY OF A BLACKMAN LIVING IN THE LAND OF THE LOST (LP)	12

KATE

68	CBS 3631	Strange Girl/I Don't Make A Sound	25
68	CBS 3815	Hold Me Now/Empty World	25
69	CBS 4123	Shout It/Sweet Little Thing	25

(see also Viv Prince, Pretty Things)

KATHY

69	Morgan MR 14	Bonjour Monsieur/Long Night	5

KATMANDU

86	Nightflite NTFL 2001	A CASE FOR THE BLUES (LP)	12

(see also Peter Green, Ray Dorset, Crane/Farlowe)

KATZ

60s	Tetlow TET 118	LIVE AT THE RUM RUNNER (EP)	75

DICK KATZ

60	Top Rank JAR 379	The Surrey With The Fringe On Top/Dreamride	6

MICKEY KATZ & HIS ORCHESTRA

56	Capitol CL 14579	David Crockett (The Ballad Of Davy Crockett)/Keneh Hora	8
58	Capitol CL 14926	The Poiple Kishke Eater/Knish Doctor	7

MINT VALUE £

ARTHUR KAY'S ORIGINALS

80	Red Admiral NYMPH 1	Ska-Wars/Warska (p/s)	20
80	Red Admiral NYMPH 2	Sooty Is A Rudie/Play My Record (p/s)	25
88	Skank MLP 105	RARE 'N' TASTY (mini-LP)	15

BARBARA KAY

65	Columbia DB 8009	The Power And The Glory/I Wanna Walk In Your Sun	8
65	Pye 7N 15774	That's What Angels Are For/What's The Good Of Loving	10
65	Pye 7N 15914	Yes I'm Ready/Someone Has To Cry	15
66	Pye 7N 15997	Chips With Everything/A Lot About Love	8

JOHN KAY

72	Probe PRO 558	I'm Movin' On/Walk Beside Me	5
73	Probe PRO 593	Moonshine/Nobody Lives Here Anymore	5
73	Probe PRO 601	Easy Evil/Dance To My Song	5
72	Probe SPB 1054	FORGOTTEN SONGS AND UNSUNG HEROES (LP)	15
73	Probe SPBA 6274	MY SPORTIN' LIFE (LP)	15

(see also Steppenwolf)

KATHIE KAY(E)

55	HMV 7M 335	Suddenly There's A Valley/Teddy Bear	12
56	HMV 7M 363	Jimmy Unknown/Dreams Can Tell A Lie	12
56	HMV POP 265	A House With Love In It/To Be Sure	8
57	HMV POP 315	From The First Hello — To The Last/Every Day Is Mother's Day	6
57	HMV POP 352	We Will Make Love/Wind In The Willow	8
57	HMV POP 385	Tammy/Away From You	6
57	HMV POP 410	Be Content/My Last Love	7
59	HMV POP 625	Goodbye Jimmy, Goodbye/Come Home To Loch Lomond And Me	5
59	HMV POP 625	Goodbye Jimmy, Goodbye/Come Home To Loch Lomond And Me (78)	10
61	HMV POP 878	In The Wee Small Hours Of The Morning/Come Home, My Darling	5

KATHIE KAY & BILLY COTTON

62	Columbia DB 4896	Til Tomorrow/Someone Nice Like You	5

CAB KAYE

50	Esquire 5-061	Everything I Have Is Yours/Don't Never Stop Looking (78, with Gary Moore Trio)	8
50	Esquire 5-079	Pennies From Heaven/More Than You Know (78, with Norman Burns)	8
61	Melodisc MEL 1584	Everything Is Go/Don't You Go Away	6

DANNY KAYE

51	Brunswick 04794	Blackstrap Molasses/How D'Ye Do And Shake Hands (78, with Jane Wyman, Jimmy Durante, Groucho Marx)	8
52	Brunswick 05023	Wonderful Copenhagen/Anywhere I Wander (78)	8
52	Decca A 73013	Wonderful Copenhagen/Anywhere I Wonder (export issue)	25
54	Brunswick 05296	Knock On Wood/All About You	12
54	Brunswick 05344	The Best Things Happen While You're Dancing/Choreography (with Skylarks)	12
55	Brunswick 05414	Night Of My Nights/Not Since Ninevah (with Sonny Burke Orchestra)	10
55	Brunswick 05424	In My Neck O' The Woods/Manhattan Mambo	8
55	Brunswick 05499	I Love You Fair Dinkum (Dinky Di I Do)/Happy Ending	8
56	Brunswick 05524	Life Could Not Be Better/I'll Take You Dreaming	8
56	Brunswick 05525	Outfox The Fox/Pass The Bucket	8
56	Brunswick 05532	Little Child/Laugh It Off Upsy Daisy (as Danny & Dena Kaye)	7
56	Brunswick 05559	Delilah Jones/Molly-O	7
57	Capitol CL 14672	Love Me Do/Ciu Ciu Bella	6
58	Capitol CL 14907	The Square On The Hypotenuse/Everything Is Ticketty-Boo	6
59	Capitol CL 15061	Mommy, Gimme A Drinka Water!/Crazy Barbara	6
59	Brunswick 05023	Wonderful Copenhagen/Anywhere I Wander (reissue, tri or round centre)	12/7
59	Brunswick 05031	The Ugly Duckling/The King's New Clothes	6
60	London HL 7091	The Five Pennies/Lullaby In Ragtime (B-side with Eileen Wilson, export issue)	10
51	Brunswick LA 8507	DANNY KAYE (10" LP)	20
53	Brunswick LA 8572	HANS CHRISTIAN ANDERSEN (10" LP)	20
54	Brunswick LA 8660	DANNY KAYE AT THE PALACE (10" LP)	20
54	Brunswick LA 8668	KNOCK ON WOOD (10" LP, soundtrack)	20
56	Brunswick LAT 8097	THE COURT JESTER (LP)	18
58	Fontana TFR 6008	PURE DELIGHT (10" LP)	20
58	Capitol T 937	MOMMY, GIMME A DRINKA WATER! (LP)	15
60	Brunswick LAT 8350	FOR CHILDREN (LP)	12

(see also Bing Crosby, Groucho Marx)

DANNY KAYE & LOUIS ARMSTRONG

60	London HLU 9346	The Five Pennies Saints/Bill Bailey Won't You Please Come Home	7
60	London HL 7092	The Five Pennies Saints/Bill Bailey Won't You Please Come Home (export issue)	10

(see also Louis Armstrong)

DAVE KAYE (& DYKONS)

64	Decca F 11866	A Fool Such As I/It's Nice Isn't It (as Davy Kaye)	35
65	Decca F 12073	In My Way/All The Stars In Heaven (as Dave Kaye)	25
69	Major Minor MM 641	Yesterday When I Was Young/Say You Love Me (as Dave Kaye & Dykons)	12

LINDA KAYE

66	Columbia DB 7915	I Can't Stop Thinking About You/When We Meet Again	20

PETER KAYE

60s	Aral PS 116	Do Me A Favour/You Doll (some in p/s)	10/5

SHIRLEY KAYE

68	Trojan TR 015	Make Me Yours/We Have Happiness	15

MINT VALUE £

STUBBY KAYE
53 Brunswick 05098 — Sit Down, You're Rocking The Boat/ The Oldest Established Permanent Floating Crap-Game In New York (78) 7
61 Polydor NH 66527 — My Wife's A Striptease Dancer/Lydia The Tattooed Lady 6
63 Parlophone R 4996 — More Humane Mikado/Cool Mikado 6

THOMAS JEFFERSON KAYE
73 Probe SPB 1074 — THOMAS JEFFERSON KAYE (LP) 12

TONY KAYE & HEARTBEATS
67 Pye International 7N 25412 — Hey, Hey Little Orphan Annie/Dream World 8

KAYES
67 Major Minor MM 515 — It's No Secret/Remember Me 8
(see also Kaye Sisters)

KAYE SISTERS
58 Philips PB 806 — Are You Ready, Freddy?/The Pansy 15
58 Philips PB 832 — Stroll Me/Torero 10
58 Philips PB 877 — Calla, Calla (The Bride, The Bride)/Oho-Aha 6
59 Philips PB 892 — Jerri-Lee (I Love Him So)/Deeply Devoted 8
59 Philips PB 892 — Jerri-Lee (I Love Him So)/Deeply Devoted (78) 8
59 Philips PB 925 — Goodbye Jimmy, Goodbye/Dancing With My Shadow 6
59 Philips PB 925 — Goodbye Jimmy, Goodbye/Dancing With My Shadow (78) 10
59 Philips PB 970 — True Love, True Love/Too Young To Marry 6
60 Philips PB 1024 — Paper Roses/If Only You'd Be Mine (some in p/s) 8/5
60 Philips PB 1088 — Come To Me/A Whole Lot Of Lovin' (some in p/s) 8/5
61 Philips PB 1156 — Palma De Majorca/I Just Wanna Be With You 5
61 Philips PB 1189 — Little Soldier/Mistletoe Kisses 6
61 Philips PB 1208 — If Only Tomorrow/Mistakes 5
63 Philips PB 1273 — Nine Girls Out Of Ten Girls/I Forgot More Than You'll Never Know 5
64 Philips PB 1340 — Keep On Loving Me/That Little Touch Of Magic 6
66 Philips PB 1468 — Life Goes On/I Should Never Know 5
62 Philips 326 541 BF — We Won't Say Goodbye/Seven Roses 5
63 Philips 326 569 BF — Big Wide World/I'm Forever Blowing Bubbles 5
57 Philips BBE 12166 — PRESENTING THE KAYE SISTERS (EP) 18
59 Philips BBE 12256 — THE KAYES AT THE COLONY (EP) 25
60 Philips BBE 12392 — KAYE SISTERS FAVOURITES (EP) 20
(see also Three Kayes/Three Kaye Sisters, Kayes, Frankie Vaughan)

KAY GEES
76 Polydor 2310 467 — HUSTLE WIT' EVERY MUSCLE (LP) 12

KITZA KAZACOS
56 MGM SP 1156 — You Should Know/There's Always A First Time 5

ERNIE K-DOE
61 London HLU 9330 — Mother-In-Law/Wanted, $10,000.00 Reward 18
61 London HLU 9390 — Te-Ta-Te-Ta-Ta/Real Man 18
62 London HLU 9487 — I Cried My Last Tear/A Certain Girl 18
65 Vocalion VP 9233 — My Mother In Law (Is In My Hair Again)/Looking Into The Future 18
68 Action ACT 4502 — Dancing Man/Later For Tomorrow 15
68 Action ACT 4512 — Gotta Pack My Bags/How Sweet You Are 15

PHIL KEAGGY BAND
70s Myrrh MYR 1046 — WHAT A DAY (LP) 15
70s Myrrh MYR 1066 — EMERGING (LP) 15

SHAKE KEANE
55 HMV 7MC 38 — Akinla/Fire, Fire (export issue) 7
62 Columbia SEG 8140 — IN MY CONDITION (EP) 40
65 Decca SKL 4720 — SHAKE KEANE WITH THE KEATING SOUND (LP) 22
66 Ace Of Clubs ACL 1219 — THAT'S THE NOISE (LP) 25
69 Phase 4 Stereo PFS 4154 — DIG IT (LP, with Ivor Raymonde Orchestra) 40
(see also Marie Bryant)

JOHNNY KEATING ORCHESTRA
62 Piccadilly 7N 35032 — Theme From Z-Cars (Johnny Todd)/The Lost Patrol 6
62 Piccadilly 7N 35071 — We Three Kings/Three Beats To The Casbah 5
63 Piccadilly 7N 35113 — The Preacher/Whoop Up (as Johnny Keating & Z Men) 5
63 Piccadilly 7N 35125 — Getaway/A Little Waltzing 5
71 Fly BUG 17 — Theme From The Onedin Line/Taransay Lullaby 5
62 Piccadilly NEP 34011 — Z-CARS (EP, with Z-Men) 12
57 Oriole MG 20011 — BRITISH JAZZ (LP) 75
58 London LTZ-15122 — SWINGIN' SCOTS (LP) 25
64 Decca PFS 4038 — SWING REVISITED (LP) 25
64 Decca PFS 4078 — STRAIGHT AHEAD (LP) 30
64 Phase 4 Stereo PFS 4060 — THE KEATING SOUND (LP, as Johnny Keating & 27 Men) 12
72 Studio Two TWO 393 — SPACE EXPERIENCE (LP) 20
72 Studio Two Q4 TWO 393 — SPACE EXPERIENCE (LP, quadrophonic) 25
74 Studio Two TWOX 1018 — HITS IN HI-FI 1 (LP) 12
75 Studio Two TWOX 1044 — SPACE EXPERIENCE 2 (LP) 15

KEEFERS KIDS
67 King KG 1068 — Millions Of Hearts/KEEFERS: Lonely Hill 6

HOWARD KEEL
57 Columbia DB 3969 — Love, Wonderful Love/Parisienne 6
(see also Kathryn Grayson & Howard Keel, Vic Damone, Doris Day)

SUSAN KEELEY
69 Parlophone R 5761 — Mulberry Down/I'd Fall In Love With The World 5

JOHN KEEN

72 Track 2094 103 — Old Fashioned Girl/That's The Way It Is — 8
73 Track 2094 108 — Let Us In/Keep On The Grass — 8
(see also Speedy Keen, Thunderclap Newman)

SPEEDY KEEN

71 Track 2406 105 — PREVIOUS CONVICTIONS (LP) — 15
(see also John Keen, Thunderclap Newman)

MARION KEENE

56 HMV 7M 395 — Fortune Teller/A Dangerous Age — 8
57 HMV POP 375 — In The Middle Of An Island/It's Not For Me To Say — 7

NELSON KEENE

60 HMV POP 771 — Image Of A Girl/Ocean Of Love — 15
60 HMV POP 814 — Keep Loving Me/Teenage Troubles — 12
61 HMV POP 916 — Miracles Are Happening To Me/Poor Little Rich Boy — 12
(see also Guv'ners)

REX KEENE

56 Columbia DB 3831 — Rebel In Town/Happy Texas Ranger — 10

ACE KEFFORD STAND

69 Atlantic 584 260 — For Your Love/Gravy Booby Jam (small or large centre hole) — 40/35
(see also Move, Cozy Powell, Young Blood, Big Bertha, Bedlam, Carl Wayne)

KEITH

66 Mercury MF 940 — Ain't Gonna Lie/It Started All Over Again — 7
67 Mercury MF 955 — 98.6/The Teeny Bopper Song — 10
67 Mercury MF 968 — Tell Me To My Face/I Can't Go Wrong — 7
67 Mercury MF 989 — Daylight Savin' Time/Happy Walking Around — 8
67 Mercury MF 1002 — Sugar Man/Easy As Pie (some in p/s) — 12/6
67 Mercury MCL 20103 — 98.6/AIN'T GONNA LIE (LP) — 35

KEITH (Poppin) & IMPACT ALL STARS

71 Randy's RAN 515 — Down By The Riverside/IMPACT ALL STARS: Version Two — 6

BRIAN KEITH

68 Page One POF 072 — The Shelter Of Your Arms/C'est La Vie — 7
68 Page One POF 103 — When The First Tear Shows/When My Baby Smiles At Me — 10
69 Page One POF 152 — Till We Meet Again/Lady Butterfly — 7
(see also Plastic Penny)

BRYAN KEITH

63 London HLU 9707 — Sad Sad Song/Mean Woman — 20

RON KEITH

76 A&M AMS 7217 — Party Music/Gotta Go By What You Tell Me — 65

KEITH & BILLIE

(see under Keith Powell & Billie Davis; see also Keith Powell, Billie Davis)

KEITH (Stewart) & ENID (Cumberland)

60 Blue Beat BB 6 — Worried Over You/Everything Will Be Alright — 20
60 Blue Beat BB 11 — Send Me/TRENTON SPENCE GROUP: People Will Say We're In Love — 20
61 Starlite ST45 047 — Never Leave My Throne/Only A Pity (as Keith & Enid with Caribs) — 18
61 Starlite ST45 067 — You're Gonna Break My Heart/What Have I Done — 18
62 Blue Beat BB 125 — When It's Spring/True Love (with Sonny Bradshaw Orchestra) — 15
63 Dice CC 14 — Sacred Vow/My Dreams — 15
63 Dice CC 20 — Just A Closer Walk/Don't Yield To Temptation — 15
64 Black Swan WI 429 — Lost My Love/I Cried — 22
63 Island ILP 901 — KEITH & ENID SING (LP) — 80
70 Trojan TTL 37 — KEITH & ENID SING (LP, reissue) — 30
70 Trojan TBL 154 — KEITH & ENID SING (LP, 2nd reissue) — 15

KEITH (Lyn) & KEN (Lazarus)

65 London HA-R/SH-R 8229 — YOU'LL LOVE JAMAICA (LP) — 60

KEITH (Rowe) & TEX (Dixon)

67 Island WI 3085 — Tonight/LYN TAIT & JETS: You Have Caught Me — 60
68 Island WI 3091 — Stop That Train/BOBBY ELLIS: Feeling Peckish (with Desmond Miles Seven) — 50
68 Island WI 3137 — Hypnotizing Eyes/Lonely Man — 25
70 Explosion EX 2008 — Tighten Up Your Gird/Look To The Sky — 12

JERRY KELLER

59 London HLR 8890 — Here Comes Summer/Time Has A Way (triangular or round centre) — 12/8
59 London HLR 8890 — Here Comes Summer/Time Has A Way (78) — 30
59 London HLR 8980 — If I Had A Girl/Lovable — 8
59 London HLR 8980 — If I Had A Girl/Lovable (78) — 35
60 London HLR 9106 — Now, Now, Now/Lonesome Lullaby — 10
60 London HA-R 2261 — HERE COMES JERRY KELLER (LP, also stereo SAH-R 6083) — 60/90

PAT KELL(E)Y

68 Giant GN 37 — Little Boy Blue/You Are Not Mine (as Pat Kelley & Uniques) — 20
68 Island WI 3121 — Somebodies Baby (as Pat Kelly)/BEVERLY SIMMONS: Please Don't Leave Me — 40
69 Gas GAS 110 — The Workman Song/Never Give Up (as Pat Kelly) — 7
69 Gas GAS 115 — How Long/Try To Remember (as Pat Kelly) — 8
69 Gas GAS 124 — Festival Time (Parts 1 & 2) (as Pat Kelley) — 8
69 Gas GAS 125 — If It Don't Work Out/I Am Coming Home (as Pat Kelley) — 7
70 Gas GAS 144 — Tammy/I Am Not Your Guy (as Pat Kelley) — 7
70 Gas GAS 145 — Striving For The Right/When A Boy Fall In Love (as Pat Kelley) — 7
70 Gas GAS 157 — I Just Don't Know What To Do With Myself/What's He Got That I Ain't Got (B-side actually titled 'Lorna') (as Pat Kelley) — 10
70 Jackpot JP 734 — I Just Don't Know What To Do With Myself/Lorna (as Pat Kelley) — 10

MINT VALUE £

71 Camel CA 65 — Talk About Love (as Pat Kelley)/PHIL PRATT ALL STARS: Version ... 10
71 Gas GAS 171 — Love/With All Your Heart (as Pat Kelley) ... 6
71 Punch PH 88 — Soulful Love (as Pat Kelly)/HUGH ROY & PARAGONS: One For All ... 10
72 Pama Supreme PS 353 — I'm Gonna Give Her All The Love I've Got (as Pat Kelley)/ MAYTONES: As Long As You Love Me ... 6
73 Pama Supreme PS 379 — Twelfth Of Never (as Pat Kelley)/JERRY LEWIS: 5000 Watts ... 5
73 Pama Supreme PS 384 — I Wish It Could Rain (as Pat Kelley)/PAT KELLY SINGERS: Hallelujah ... 5
77 Rainbow Stepper RK 231 — Carefree Girl/Version ... 8
69 Pama PMLP 12 — PAT KELLEY SINGS (LP) ... 60
71 Pama PMP 2013 — COOL BREEZING (LP) ... 70
(see also Wonder Boy)

MURRAY KELLUM
64 London HLU 9830 — Long Tall Texan/GLEN SUTTON: I Gotta Leave This Town ... 15

KELLY
66 RCA RCA 1507 — Be My Man/Here Comes My Baby ... 7

CHARLIE KELLY
68 Island WI 3155 — So Nice Like Rice/STRANGER & GLADDY: Over Again ... 22

DAVE KELLY
69 Mercury 20151 SMCL — KEEPS IT IN THE FAMILY (LP) ... 100
71 Mercury 6310 001 — DAVE KELLY (LP, with Jo-Ann Kelly & Brunning-Hall Sunflower Band) ... 150
(see also John Dummer Blues Band, Brunning-Hall Sunflower Blues Band)

FRANK KELLY & HUNTERS
62 Fontana 267 242 TF — Send Me The Pillow That You Dream On/'Cept Me ... 12
63 Fontana 267 261 TF — I Saw Linda Yesterday/Good And True ... 12
63 Fontana 267 277 TF — What Do You Wanna Do/She Loves Me So ... 15
64 Fontana TF 454 — Some Other Time/Why Baby Why ... 15
(this is not the same group as [Dave Sampson &] Hunters, also on Fontana)

GENE KELLY
51 MGM MGM 424 — I Got Rhythm/Love Is Here To Stay (78) ... 8
52 MGM MGM 493 — Good Morning (with Debbie Reynolds, etc.)/DEBBIE REYNOLDS: All I Do Is Dream Of You (78) ... 8
53 MGM SP 1012 — Singin' In The Rain/All I Do Is Dream Of You ... 18
53 MGM SP 1015 — 'S Wonderful (with Georges Guetary)/I Got Rhythm (with Children's Choir) ... 7
55 MGM MGM 829 — Almost Like Being In Love/I'll Go Home With Bonnie Jean (78) ... 8
57 MGM MGM 965 — The Happy Road (Ca Ca C'est La Vie)/My Baby Just Cares For Me ... 6
58 RCA RCA 1068 — A Very Precious Love/Uncle Samson ... 6
57 MGM MGM-EP 580 — AN AMERICAN IN PARIS (EP, with George Guetary) ... 10
57 MGM MGM-EP 671 — SINGING IN THE RAIN EXCERPTS (EP, with Donald O'Connor/Debbie Reynolds) ... 15
53 MGM MGM-D 117 — SONG AND DANCE MAN (10" LP) ... 20
55 MGM MGM-D 133 — S'WONDERFUL (10" LP) ... 20

JO-ANN KELLY
64 GW EP 1 — BLUES AND GOSPEL (EP, live at the Bridge House Club) ... 110
66 Harlequin HAL 1/HW 349 — NEW SOUNDS IN FOLK (LP, with other artists) ... 65
69 CBS 63841 — JO-ANN KELLY (LP) ... 130
76 Red Rag RRR 006 — DO IT (LP, with Peter Emery) ... 30
(see also Chilli Willi & Red Hot Peppers, Dave Kelly, Tramp)

JO-ANN KELLY & TONY McPHEE
72 Sunset SLS 50209 — THE SAME THING ON THEIR MINDS (LP) ... 30
(see also Tony McPhee, Dave Kelly)

JONATHAN KELLY
69 Parlophone R 5805 — Denver/Son John ... 6
70 Parlophone R 5830 — Make A Stranger Your Friend/Daddy Don't Take Me Down Fishing No More ... 6
70 Parlophone R 5851 — Don't You Believe It?/Billy ... 7
70 Parlophone PCS 7114 — JONATHAN KELLY (LP) ... 40
72 RCA SF 8262 — TWICE AROUND THE HOUSES (LP) ... 15
73 RCA SF 8353 — WAIT TILL THEY CHANGE THE BACKDROP (LP) ... 15
(see also John Ledingham)

KEITH KELLY
60 Parlophone R 4640 — (Must You Always) Tease Me/Ooh-La-La ... 18
60 Parlophone R 4676 — Listen Little Girl/Uh-Huh ... 15
60 Parlophone R 4713 — With You/You'll Break My Heart ... 10
61 Parlophone R 4797 — Cold White And Beautiful/When You First Fall In Love ... 10
65 CBS 201794 — Laurie/Save Your Love For Me ... 8

MONTE KELLY ORCHESTRA
59 London HLL 8777 — Willingly (Melodie Perdue)/The Blue Cha Cha ... 7
60 London HLL 9085 — Summer Set/Amalia ... 7

PAT KELLY
(see under Pat Kelley)

PAUL KELLY
65 Atlantic AT 4053 — Chills And Fever/Only Your Love ... 25
67 Philips BF 1591 — Sweet Sweet Lovin'/Cryin' For My Baby ... 18
72 Atlantic K 10272 — Chills And Fever/Only Your Love (reissue) ... 8

PETE KELLY'S SOULUTION
68 Decca F 12755 — Midnight Confessions/If Your Love Don't Swing ... 22
68 Decca F 22829 — Midnight Confessions/BERNIE & BUZZ BAND: The House That Jack Built (export issue) ... 15
(see also Bernie & Buzz Band, Rhythm & Blues Inc.)

PETER KELLY
71 Polydor 2310 119 DEALIN' BLUES (LP) . . . 35

SALLY KELLY
59 Decca F 11175 Little Cutie/Come Back To Me . . . 12
60 Decca F 11238 He'll Have To Stay/Honey That's Alright. . . . 10
60s Hit HIT 15 Believe In The Rain/So Much . . . 6

STAN KELLY
60s Transatlantic TRASP 21 The Ballad Of Armagh Jail/Kelly The Boy From Killang . . . 6
60 Topic TOP 27 LIVERPOOL PACKET (EP) . . . 10
60 Topic TOP 60 SONGS FOR SWINGING LANDLORDS TO (EP). . . . 10

WYNTON KELLY TRIO
65 Verve VLP 9103 UNDILUTED (LP) . . . 15

KELLY BROTHERS
67 Sue WI 4034 Falling In Love Again/Crying Days Are Over. . . . 70
68 President PT 143 You Put Your Touch On Me/Hanging In There . . . 22
70 Blue Horizon 57-3177 That's What You Mean To Me/Comin' On In . . . 35
68 President PTL 1019 SWEET SOUL (LP). . . . 80

REV. (Samuel) KELSEY (& CONGREGATION)
52 Vocalion V 1014 The Wedding Ceremony Of Sister Rosetta Tharpe And Russell Morrison (Parts 1 & 2) (78) . . . 20
52 Vocalion V 1020 Little Boy/Low Down The Chariot (78). . . . 20
53 Vocalion V 1028 I'm A Royal Child/Where Is The Lion In The Tribes Of Judea (78). . . . 20
56 Brunswick OE 9256 REV. KELSEY (EP) . . . 25
(see also Sister Rosetta Tharpe)

WAYNE KEMP
66 Atlantic 584 006 Watch That First Step/Little Home Wrecker. . . . 7

KEMPION
77 Broadside BRO 123 KEMPION (LP) . . . 15
77 Sweet Folk & C. SFA 044 CAM YE O'ER FRAE FRANCE (LP) . . . 15

KEN & NEW ESTABLISHMENT
73 Fab FAB 264 Soul Mood/Golden Locks . . . 8

BARRY KENDALL
59 Embassy WB 364 Seven Little Girls (Sitting In The Back Seat)/JOHNNY WORTH: What Do You Want To Make Those Eyes At Me For (78) . . . 8
(see also Johnny Worth)

JOHNNY KENDALL & HERALDS
64 RCA RCA 1416 St. James Infirmary/Little Girl . . . 22

KENDALL SISTERS
58 London HLM 8622 Won't You Be My Baby/Yea, Yea . . . 40
58 London HLM 8622 Won't You Be My Baby/Yea, Yea (78) . . . 20

GRAHAM KENDRICK
73 Key KL 011 FOOTSTEPS ON THE SEA (LP) . . . 22
73 Key KL 016 BRIGHT SIDE UP (LP) . . . 18
74 Key KL 024 PAID ON THE NAIL (LP) . . . 15

LINDA KENDRICK
66 Polydor 56076 It's The Little Things/When Your Love Is Warm . . . 22
66 Polydor 56146 I Fall Apart/Friend Of Mine. . . . 10
68 Philips BF 1660 Grey Sunny Day/In Need Of A Friend . . . 7
69 Philips BF 1750 I Will See You There/Inside My Heart . . . 7
69 Philips BF 1818 Hold On/Fah La La . . . 7
70 Philips SBL 7921 LINDA KENDRICK (LP). . . . 22

NAT KENDRICK & SWANS
60 Top Rank JAR 351 (Do The) Mashed Potatoes Parts 1 & 2 . . . 18
60 Top Rank JAR 387 Dish Rag Parts 1 & 2 . . . 18
(see also James Brown)

EDDIE KENDRICKS
73 Tamla Motown TMG 845 If You Let Me/Just Memories . . . 5
74 Tamla Motown TMG 916 Girl You Need A Change Of Mind Parts 1 & 2 . . . 5
75 Tamla Motown TMG 947 Shoe Shine Boy/Hooked On Your Love . . . 5
71 Tamla Motown STML 11186 ALL BY MYSELF (LP). . . . 18
73 Tamla Motown STML 11213 PEOPLE ... HOLD ON (LP). . . . 12
73 Tamla Motown STML 12245 EDDIE KENDRICKS (LP) . . . 12
(see also Temptations)

KENICKIE
95 Slampt U.O. SLAMPT 1 CATSUIT CITY EP. . . . 75
96 Fierce Panda NING 16 Come Out 2nite/How I Was Made (p/s) . . . 15
96 Fierce Panda NING 16CD THE SKILLEX EP (CD) . . . 10
96 Premier EMI DISC 001 Punka/Cowboy Song (p/s) . . . 5
96 Premier EMI 002 Millionaire Sweeper/Girl's Best Friend (p/s) . . . 5
97 Premier EMI 007 Punka/Brighter Shade Of Blue (picture disc in p/s) . . . 5
96 EMI CDDISC 001 PUNKA (EP, picture CD). . . . 8
97 EMI CDDISCS 007 PUNKA EP (2-CD, with postcards). . . . 10
97 EMI DISC 006 Millionaire Sweeper (picture disc). . . . 5

MINT VALUE £

CHERYL KENNEDY

67 Columbia DB 8271	Thoroughly Modern Millie/Cradle Song	5
68 Columbia DB 8347	Love Is Blue/I Could Be Happy With You	5

DOUG KENNEDY

65 Columbia DB 7707	Julie/Jailbreak Man	6

GENE KENNEDY

65 Hickory 45-1314	You Better Take Home/Stand In Line	6

JOHN F. KENNEDY

64 Stateside SL 10064	THE PRESIDENTIAL YEARS 1960-1963 (LP)	15

LOU KENNEDY

55 Columbia SCM 5198	Stars Shine In Your Eyes/The Kentuckian Song	10
56 Columbia SCM 5216	Whisper/Sincerely Yours	10

MIKE KENNEDY

69 Major Minor MM 614	I'll Never Forget/I'll Never Get You	6
69 Major Minor MM 629	Johnny Rebel/Golden Memories	6

(see also Los Bravos)

CHRIS KENNER

61 London HLU 9410	I Like It Like That Parts 1 & 2	22
65 Sue WI 351	Land Of 1,000 Dances/That's My Girl	30
66 Atlantic 587 008	LAND OF 1000 DANCES (LP)	30

JAMES KENNEY

58 Pye 7N 15150	The Shrine On The Second Floor/Expresso Party	10

TONY KENNY & SANDS SHOWBAND

67 Major Minor MM 555	Help Me Rhonda/Some Enchanted Evening	5
68 Major Minor MM 573	Yummy Yummy Yummy/Peanuts	5
71 Hit HIT 1	Knock Three Times/See You In September	5

(see also Sands)

KENNY (Everett) & (Dave) CASH

65 Decca F 12283	Knees/The B Side	15

(see also Kenny Everett)

KENNY & CORKY

59 London HLX 9002	Nuttin' For Christmas/Suzy Snowflake	10
59 London HLX 9002	Nuttin' For Christmas/Suzy Snowflake (78)	15

KENNY & DENY

65 Decca F 12138	Try To Forget Me/Little Surfer Girl	50

KENNY & WRANGLERS

64 Parlophone R 5224	Somebody Help Me/Who Do You Think I Am?	18
65 Parlophone R 5275	Doobie Doo/Moonshine	18

(see also Kenny Bernard & Wranglers)

JERRI BO KENO

75 Phil Spector Intl. 2010 001	Here It Comes (And Here I Go)/I Don't Know Why	12

KENT

00s RCA 560632	If You Were Here/Point Blank/The One To Blame (CD)	15
00s BMG 645912	747 (Radio Version)/What It Feels Like/Unprofessional (Live Radio Session Version) (CD)	15
00s Victor 74321812632	Heavenly Junkies (1-track CD)	12
00s BMG 748507	Music Non Stop/Insects (clear vinyl, withdrawn)	10

AL KENT

67 Track 604 016	You Got To Pay The Price/Where Do I Go From Here	45
71 Mojo 2092 015	You Got To Pay The Price/Where Do I Go From Here (unissued)	

BILL KENT

58 Decca F 10975	The Prettiest Girl In School/Hasty Words	8
58 Decca F 10997	Oh-Oh, I'm Falling In Love/In Love	8

ENOCH KENT

59 Top Rank JAR 238	The Ballad Of Johnny Ramensky/The Bonny Lass Of Fyvie	6
60 Top Rank JAR 386	The Smashing Of The Van/Sean South Of Garryowen	5
62 Topic TOP 81	SINGS THE BUTCHER BOY AND OTHER BALLADS (EP)	8

KLARK KENT

78 Kryptone KK 1	Don't Care/Thrills/Office Girls (p/s, green or rarer black vinyl)	each 5
78 Kryptone KMS 7390	Too Kool To Kalypso/Theme For Kinetic Ritual (p/s, green vinyl)	5

(pseudonym for Stewart Copeland; see also Police, Curved Air)

PAUL KENT

71 B&C CB 165	Do You/Helpless Harry	6
70 RCA SF 8083	P.C. KENT (LP)	30
71 B&C CAS 1044	PAUL KENT (LP)	25

RICHARD KENT STYLE

66 Columbia DB 7964	No Matter What You Do/Go, Go Children	110
66 Columbia DB 8051	You Can't Put Me Down/All Good Things	60
67 Columbia DB 8182	Marching Off To War/I'm Out	55
68 MCA MU 1032	Love Will Shake The World Awake/Crocodile Tears	35
69 Mercury MF 1090	A Little Bit O' Soul/Don't Tell Lies	35

SONIA KENT

66 Parlophone R 5401	This Is My Wonderful Day/Somebody Must Care	7

(see also Diamond Twins)

MINT VALUE £

SHIRLEY KENT

80	Tadpole TAD 001	My Dad/Marianne	6
66	Keele University 103	THE MASTER SINGERS AND SHIRLEY KENT SING FOR CHAREC 67 (EP)	30
89	Magic Spell 0001	FOREVER A WILLOW (LP)	12

(see also Ghost, Virginia Tree)

KENT (Brown) & DIMPLE (Hinds)

63	Island WI 046	Day Is Done/Linger A While	18

KENT (Brown) & JEANNIE with City Slickers

62	Blue Beat BB 98	Daddy/Hello Love	18

(see also Kent Brown & Rainbows)

RIK KENTON

74	Island WIP 6214	Bungalow Love/Lay It On You (no p/s)	5

(see also Roxy Music)

STAN KENTON & HIS ORCHESTRA

50	Capitol CL 11002	Theme For Sunday/Cuban Episode (12" 78)	7
50	Capitol CL 11005	Mirage/Conflict (12" 78, with June Christy)	7
50	Capitol CL 11008	June Christy/Maynard Ferguson (12" 78)	7
51	Capitol CL 11010	Art Pepper/Shelly Manne (12" 78)	7
51	Esquire 10-113	Turmoil/Jumping For Jane (78, with His Poll Cats)	8
54	Capitol CL 14191	The Lady In Red/Skoot	7
55	Capitol CL 14247	Alone Too Long/Don't Take Your Love From Me	7
55	Capitol CL 14259	A-Ting-A-Ling/Malaguena (with Ann Richards)	10
55	Capitol CL 14269	23 Degrees North, 82 Degrees West/Falling (B-side with Ann Richards)	7
55	Capitol CL 14287	Lover Man/I've Got You Under My Skin	7
55	Capitol CL 14301	Casanova/Dark Eyes (with Ann Richards)	7
55	Capitol CL 14319	Freddy/The Handwriting's On The Wall	7
56	Capitol CL 14537	Winter In Madrid (with Ann Richards)/Baa-Too-Kee	5
56	Capitol CL 14539	Sunset Tower/Opus In Chartreuse	5
56	Capitol CL 14540	My Lady/Frank Speaking	5
56	Capitol CL 14541	Portrait Of A Count/Invention For Guitar And Trumpet	5
56	Capitol CL 14542	Cherokee/Limelight	6
57	Capitol CL 14707	His Feet Too Big For De Bed (with June Christy)/Stardust — Boogie	6
57	Capitol CL 14707	His Feet Too Big For De Bed (with June Christy)/Stardust — Boogie (78)	8
57	Capitol CL 14806	Lemon Twist/Baby You're Tough	5
58	Capitol CL 14847	Tequila/Cuban Mumble	5
58	Capitol CL 14866	Reverie/More Love Than Your Love	5
59	Capitol CL 15029	Whistle Walk/Tamer-Lane	5
51	Capitol LC 6517	STAN KENTON'S MILESTONES (10" LP)	15
51	Capitol LC 6523	ENCORES (10" LP)	15
52	Capitol LC 6545	ARTISTRY IN RHYTHM (10" LP)	15
52	Capitol LC 6546	A CONCERT IN PROGRESSIVE JAZZ (10" LP)	15
52	Capitol LC 6548	PRESENTS (10" LP)	15
52	Capitol LCT 6006	INNOVATIONS IN MODERN MUSIC (LP)	12
53	Capitol LC 6577	CITY OF GLASS (10" LP)	15
53	Capitol LC 6595	NEW CONCEPTS OF ARTISTRY IN RHYTHM (10" LP)	15
53	Capitol LC 6602	SKETCHES ON STANDARDS (10" LP)	15
54	Capitol LC 6667	THIS MODERN WORLD (10" LP)	15
54	Capitol LC 6676	CLASSICS (10" LP)	15
54	Capitol LCT 6009	KENTON SHOWCASE (LP)	12
55	Capitol LC 6697	PORTRAITS ON STANDARDS (10" LP)	15
56	Capitol LCT 6109	IN HI-FI (LP)	12
56	Capitol LCT 6118	CUBAN FIRE (LP)	12
56	Brunswick LAT 8122	THE FORMATIVE YEARS (LP)	12
57	Capitol LCT 6138	KENTON WITH VOICES (LP)	12
58	Capitol LCT 6157	THE KENTON ERA VOLUME ONE — PROLOGUE (LP)	12
58	Capitol LCT 6158	THE KENTON ERA VOLUME TWO — GROWING PAINS (LP)	12
58	Capitol LCT 6159	THE KENTON ERA VOLUME THREE — PROGRESSIVE JAZZ (LP)	12
58	Capitol LCT 6160	THE KENTON ERA VOLUME FOUR — CONTEMPORARY (LP)	12
58	Capitol (S)T 932	RENDEZVOUS WITH KENTON (LP)	12
58	Capitol T 995	BACK TO BALBOA (LP)	12
59	Capitol (S)T 1068	BALLAD STYLE OF STAN KENTON (LP)	12
59	Capitol T 1130	LUSH INTERLUDE (LP)	12
59	Capitol (S)T 1166	THE STAGE DOOR SWINGS (LP)	12
60	Capitol W 1305	VIVA KENTON (LP)	12

(see also June Christy)

KEN-TONES

56	Parlophone MSP 6229	Get With It/In Port Afrique	12
57	Parlophone R 4257	I Saw Esau/Yaller, Yaller Gold	8

(see also Benny Lee)

KENTUCKY BOYS

55	HMV 7M 312	Don't Fetch It/A Little Fella Like Me	12

KENTUCKY COLONELS

74	United Artists UAS 29514	THE KENTUCKY COLONELS (LP)	18

(see also Byrds)

BILL KENWRIGHT (& RUNAWAYS)

67	Columbia DB 8239	I Want To Go Back There Again/Walk Through Dreams (with Runaways)	7
68	MGM MGM 1430	Giving Up/Love's Black And White (solo)	6
69	MGM MGM 1463	Tiggy/House That Fell On Its Face	5
69	MGM MGM 1478	Baby I Could Be So Good At Loving You/A Boy And A Girl	5
69	Fontana TF 1065	Sugar Man/Epitaph (When Times Were Good)	5

MINT VALUE £

KERBDOG

93 Vertigo VER 80 — End Of Green (p/s) — 8
93 Vertigo DOG 1 — Earthworks/Cleaver/Scram (die-cut sleeve, PVC outer with sticker) — 7
94 Vertigo VERR 83 — Dry Riser/Xena Phobia/Self Inflicted (p/s, clear vinyl) — 8
94 Vertigo VER 86 — Dummy Crusher/Too Much Too Young (p/s) — 6
94 Vertigo VERX 86 — Dummy Crusher/Mr. Clean/Don't Stand In Line (12", picture disc) — 10
96 Fontana KER 1 — J.J.'s Song/Don't Even Try (clear vinyl) — 7

MOIRA KERR

69 Beltona MBE 102 — FOLK WARM AND GENTLE (LP, also stereo [SBE 102]) — 20
71 Beltona SBE 118 — SHADOWS OF MY CHILDHOOD (LP) — 20

PATRICK KERR

65 Decca F 12069 — Magic Potion/It's No Trouble To Love You — 25

RICHARD KERR

66 Decca F 12468 — Concrete Jungle/You Got Nothing To Lose — 5
66 Decca F 12538 — Hard Lovin'/Auntie's Insurance Policy — 5
67 Deram DM 138 — Happy Birthday Blues/Mother's Blue Eyed Angel — 5
73 Warner Bros K 46206 — FROM NOW UNTIL THEN (LP) — 18

KERRIES

67 Major Minor MM 541 — Coulters Candy/Gallon Of Whisky And A Barrel Of Beer — 5
67 Major Minor MMLP/SMLP 9 — THE KERRIES (LP) — 15

CHRIS KERRY

65 Mercury MF 957 — Seven Deadly Sins/The Place — 18
66 Mercury MF 985 — Watermelon Man/I've Got My Pride — 20

DOUG KERSHAW

69 Warner Bros WB 7304 — Feed It To The Fish/You Fight Your Fight (I'll Fight Mine) — 6
70 Warner Bros WB 7413 — Orange Blossom Special/Swamp Rat — 6
71 Warner Bros WS 1906 — DOUG KERSHAW (LP) — 15
73 Warner Bros K 46196 — DEVIL'S ELBOW (LP) — 15
(see also Rusty & Doug)

MARY & HARVEY KERSHAW

76 Topic 12TS 302 — LANCASHIRE SINGS AGAIN! (LP) — 12

NIK KERSHAW

86 MCA DMCG 6016 — RADIO MUSICOLA (CD) — 18
(see also Fusion)

KEN KESEY

83 Psycho PSYCHO 4 — THE ACID TEST (LP, 300 only) — 30

BARNEY KESSEL

69 Polydor 56765 — Frank Mills/Quail Bait — 5
54 Vogue LDE 085 — BARNEY KESSEL (10" LP) — 18
55 Contemporary LDC 153 — BARNEY KESSEL VOLUME 2 (10" LP) — 18
59 Contemporary LAC 12206 — SOME LIKE IT HOT (LP) — 12
59 Contemorary LAC 12214 — BARNEY KESSEL PLAYS CARMEN (LP) — 12
77 Phil Spector Intl. 2307 011 — SLOW BURN (LP) — 15
(see also Rick Nelson)

LARRY KESSLER

96 Lissey's LISS 5S — Radar Eyes/Godz Mix (p/s) — 10

KESTREL

75 Cube HIFLY 19 — KESTREL (LP) — 110

KATE KESTREL & THE TERRAHAWKS

83 Anderburr HX 1020 — S.O.S./It's So Easy (p/s) — 5

KESTRELS

59 Pye 7N 15234 — There Comes A Time/In The Chapel In The Moonlight — 12
59 Pye 7N 15234 — There Comes A Time/In The Chapel In The Moonlight (78) — 10
60 Pye 7N 15248 — I Can't Say Goodbye/We Were Wrong — 12
61 Decca F 11391 — All These Things/That's It — 8
62 Piccadilly 7N 35056 — Wolverton Mountain/Little Sacka Sugar — 8
62 Piccadilly 7N 35079 — Don't Want To Cry/Love Me With All Your Heart — 8
63 Piccadilly 7N 35104 — Walk Right In/Moving Up The King's Highway — 8
63 Piccadilly 7N 35126 — There's A Place/Little Star — 10
63 Piccadilly 7N 35144 — Love Me With All Your Heart/Lazy River — 8
60s Donegal MAU 500 — THE KESTRELS (EP) — 45
63 Piccadilly NPL 38009 — SMASH HITS (LP) — 40
(see also Ivy League, Flowerpot Men, White Plains)

KEY CHAINS

66 London HLU 10055 — Morgan's Song/Scruggs — 6

BERT KEYES

54 London HL 8034 — Don't Break My Heart Again/Lonely (78) — 8

EBONY KEYES

66 Piccadilly 7N 35358 — Sitting In The Ring/If You Knew — 12
67 Piccadilly 7N 35375 — Cupid's House/If Our Love Should End — 7
67 Piccadilly 7N 35390 — Country Girl/How Many Times — 7
67 Picadilly 7N 35407 — Don't/Sweet Mary (Sweeter Than A Rose) — 8

KAROL KEYES

64 Fontana TF 517 — You Beat Me To The Punch/No-One Can Take Your Place (some in p/s) — 25/15
67 Fontana TF 846 — Can't You Hear The Music/The Sweetest Touch — 12
66 Columbia DB 7899 — A Fool In Love/The Good Love, The Bad Love — 15
66 Columbia DB 8001 — One In A Million/Don't Jump — 30
(see also Volunteers)

TROY KEYES
68 Stateside SS 2087 — Love Explosions/I'm Crying (Inside) — 25
69 Stateside SS 2149 — Love Explosions/I'm Crying (Inside) (reissue) — 12

KEY LARGO
71 Blue Horizon 57-3178 — Voodoo Rhythm/As The Years Go Passing By — 20
70 Blue Horizon 7-63859 — KEY LARGO (LP) — 40

KEYMEN
59 HMV POP 584 — Gazackstahagen/Miss You — 15
59 HMV POP 584 — Gazackstahagen/Miss You (78) — 12
62 Columbia DB 4902 — Five Weeks In A Balloon/Secretly — 8
57 Vogue Coral LVA 9048 — THE VOCAL SOUNDS OF THE KEYMEN (LP) — 22

KEYNOTES
50s Kingsway no cat. no. — Kingsway Beat (78, p/s, 1-sided promo) — 25
54 Decca F 10302 — A Dime And A Dollar/JOHNSTON BROTHERS: Bandit — 22
55 Decca F 10643 — Relax-Ay-Voo/Steam Heat — 12
56 Decca F 10693 — Scotland The Brave/Lewis Bridal Song — 6
56 Decca F 10745 — Let's Go Steady/Chincherinchee — 6
(see also Bobbie Britton, Johnston Brothers, Dave King, Suzi Miller)

KEYS
64 Oriole CB 1968 — Sleep Sleep My Baby/Colour Slide — 25
65 CBS 201804 — Go Get Her/My Everything — 8

K.G.B.
76 MCA MCF 2749 — K.G.B. (LP) — 12
(see also Barry Goldberg, Mike Bloomfield)

KHAN
72 Deram SDL 11 — SPACE SHANTY (LP, later copies in stickered sleeve) — 45
(see also Steve Hillage, Egg, Nick Greenwood, Arzachel, Hatfield & The North)

ASHISH KHAN
68 Liberty LBL 83083E — ASHISH KHAN (LP) — 15
73 Elektra K 42129 — JUGAL BANDI (LP, with John Barham) — 12

USTAD ALI AKBAR KHAN
69 HMV ASD 2367 — MUSIC FROM INDIA NO. 5 (LP) — 12
69 Transatlantic TRA 183 — DHUN PALAS KAFI (LP) — 12
71 Mushroom 100 MR 14 — THE PEACEFUL MUSIC OF USTAD ALI AKBAR KHAN (LP) — 20
(see also Ravi Shankar)

USTAD VILAYET KHAN
69 RCA SF 8025 — THE GURU (LP, soundtrack) — 18
70 Transatlantic TRA 239 — RAGA TILAKKAMOD (LP) — 15

KHANDARS
65 Blue Beat BB 332 — Don't Dig A Hole For Me/BUSTER'S ALL STARS: Skara — 30

KHANS
62 London HLU 9555 — New Orleans, 2 AM/Blue Mist — 15

KHARTOMB
83 Whaam! WHAAM 14 — Swahili Lullaby/Teekon Warriors — 6

KICK
84 Footwear FWR 01 — Let's Get Back Together/A Shot In The Dark/Don't Ever Change (p/s) — 6
86 Sponge SPONGE 01 — Scapegoat/Flingle Bunt (live)/Leavin' Here (live) (p/s) — 5
86 Countdown VAIN 03 — I Can't Let Go/Armchair Politician (p/s) — 8

KICKS
81 Blue Chip BC 102 — If Looks Could Kill/Don't She Look Fab — 40

KID GUNGO
69 Escort ES 801 — Hold The Pussy/KING CANNON: Wha Pen (B-side actually by Carl Bryan) — 7

EDDIE KIDD
77 Decca FR 13722 — Motorbike Kid/Big Jump At Picket's Lock — 8

JOHNNY KIDD (& PIRATES)
59 HMV POP 615 — Please Don't Touch/Growl — 30
59 HMV POP 674 — Feelin'/If You Were The Only Girl In The World (solo) — 20
60 HMV POP 698 — You Got What It Takes/Longin' Lips — 18
60 HMV POP 753 — Shakin' All Over/Yes Sir, That's My Baby — 10
60 HMV POP 790 — Restless/Magic Of Love — 15
61 HMV POP 853 — Linda Lu/Let's Talk About Us — 20
61 HMV POP 919 — Please Don't Bring Me Down/So What — 25
62 HMV POP 978 — Hurry On Back To Love/I Want That (with The Mike Sammes Singers) — 25
62 HMV POP 1088 — A Shot Of Rhythm And Blues/I Can Tell — 20
63 HMV POP 1173 — I'll Never Get Over You/Then I Got Everything — 10
63 HMV POP 1228 — Hungry For Love/Ecstasy — 15
64 HMV POP 1269 — Always And Ever/Dr. Feelgood — 15
64 HMV POP 1309 — Jealous Girl/Shop Around — 15
64 HMV POP 1353 — Whole Lotta Woman/Your Cheatin' Heart — 18
65 HMV POP 1397 — The Birds And The Bees/Don't Make The Same Mistake As I Did — 18
65 HMV POP 1424 — Shakin' All Over '65/Gotta Travel On — 22
65 HMV POP 1520 — It's Got To Be You/I Hate To Get Up In The Morning (solo) — 22
66 HMV POP 1559 — Send For That Girl/The Fool — 25
60s HMV JO 674 — Feelin'/If You Were The Only Girl In The World (export issue, black label) — 40
97 Cruisin' 50 CASB 005 — Shakin' All Over/Please Don't Touch (78rpm, 300 only) — 50
60 HMV 7EG 8628 — SHAKIN' ALL OVER (EP) — 55
64 HMV 7EG 8834 — JOHNNY KIDD AND THE PIRATES (EP) — 70
71 Regal Starline SRS 5100 — SHAKIN' ALL OVER (LP) — 15
78 EMI Nut NUTM 12 — THE BEST OF JOHNNY KIDD AND THE PIRATES (LP) — 12
(see also Pirates)

MINT VALUE £

KIDS
75 Atlantic K 50143 — ANVIL CHORUS (LP, with inner, stickered sleeve) . . . 12
(see also Heavy Metal Kids, Gary Holton)

KIDS NEXT DOOR
65 London HLR 9993 — Inky Dinky Spider/Goodbye Don't Cry . . . 10

KIDZ NEXT DOOR
79 Warner Bros K 17492 — What's It All About?/The Kidz Next Door (p/s) . . . 35

KILBURN & HIGH ROADS
74 Dawn DNS 1090 — Rough Kids/Billy Bentley . . . 12
75 Dawn DNS 1102 — Crippled With Nerves/Huffety Puff . . . 12
78 Warner Bros K 17225 — Bentley/Pam's Moods . . . 8
75 Dawn DNLS 3065 — HANDSOME (LP) . . . 25
(see also Ian Dury & Blockheads, 999, Nine Days Wonder)

ROY KILDARE
64 Blue Beat BB 226 — I Won't Leave/What About It . . . 18

JUDY KILEEN
56 London HLU 8328 — Just Walking In The Rain/A Heart Without A Sweetheart . . . 40
56 London HLU 8328 — Just Walking In The Rain/A Heart Without A Sweetheart (78) . . . 12

KILFENORA CEILI BAND
74 Transatlantic TRS 108 — KILFENORA CEILI BAND (LP) . . . 15

MERLE KILGORE
54 London HL 8103 — Seeing Double, Feeling Single/It Can't Rain All The Time . . . 200
54 London HL 8103 — Seeing Double, Feeling Single/It Can't Rain All The Time (78) . . . 40
57 London HLP 8392 — Ernie/Trying To Find (Someone Like You) . . . 350
57 London HLP 8392 — Ernie/Trying To Find (Someone Like You) (78) . . . 75
60 Melodisc MEL 1545 — Dear Mama/Jimmie Bring Sunshine . . . 15
62 Mercury AMT 1193 — 42 In Chicago/A Girl Named Liz . . . 15
65 London HA-B 8244 — THERE'S GOLD IN THEM THAR HILLS (LP) . . . 25

THEOLA KILGORE
67 Sue WI 4035 — I'll Keep Trying/He's Coming Back To Me . . . 35

LOUIS KILLEN
62 Topic TOP 75 — NORTHUMBRIAN GARLAND (EP) . . . 10
66 Topic 12T 126 — BALLADS AND BROADSIDES (LP, blue label) . . . 20

LOUIS KILLEN & JOHNNY HANDLE
62 Topic TOP 74 — THE COLLIER'S RANT (EP) . . . 10
65 Topic 12T 122 — TOMMY ARMSTRONG OF TYNESIDE (LP, with Colin Ross & Tom Gilfellon, blue label with booklet) . . . 18
68 Topic 12T 189 — ALONG THE COALY TYNE (LP, with Colin Ross, blue label with booklet) . . . 22
(see also Johnny Handle)

KILLERMETERS
79 Psycho P 2620 — Why Should It Happen To Me/Cardiac Arrest (some in p/s) . . . 80/30
80 Gem GEMS 22 — Twisted Wheel/SX 225 (p/s, demo copies £50) . . . 90

KILLER
77 Ariola ARL 5003 — KILLER (LP) . . . 30

KILLERS
78 Satril SAT 129 — Killer (On The Dancefloor) (no p/s) . . . 5
(see also Joe Cool & The Killers)

JOHN KILLIGREW
71 Penny Farthing PELS 513 — JOHN KILLIGREW (LP, with Pete Dello) . . . 18
(see also Pete Dello)

KILLING FLOOR
70 Penny Farthing PEN 745 — Call For The Politicians/Acid Bean . . . 20
69 Spark (S)RLP 102 — KILLING FLOOR (LP) . . . 130
70 Penny Farthing PELS 511 — OUT OF URANUS (LP, gatefold sleeve) . . . 120
73 Spark Replay SRLM 2004 — ORIGINAL KILLING FLOOR (LP, reissue) . . . 30
(see also Rory Gallagher)

KILLING JOKE
79 Malicious Damage MD 410 — Nervous System/Turn To Red/Are You Receiving (10" EP in bag, some with picture & 4 cards) . . . 15/10
80 Island WIP 6550 — Turn To Red/Nervous System (p/s) . . . 5
80 Island 12 WIP 6550 — Almost Red/Nervous System/Are You Receiving/Turn To Red (12", p/s) . . . 10
80 Malicious Damage MD 540 — Wardance/Psyche (p/s, some with 'call up paper' insert) . . . 10/7
80 E.G. EGMD 1.00 — Requiem/Change (p/s) . . . 5
80 E.G. EGMX 1.00 — Requiem/Change/Change/Requiem (12", stamped sleeve, later in p/s) . . . 10/8
81 E.G. EGMDX 1.01 — Follow The Leaders/Follow The Leaders — Dub/Tension (10", p/s) . . . 7
82 E.G. EGOX 10 — Birds Of A Feather/Flock The B-Side (12", p/s) . . . 8
83 E.G. EGOD 14/KILL 1/2 — Me Or You/Wilful Days//Feast Of Blaze (double pack, gatefold p/s) . . . 5
83 E.G. EGOXD 14 — Me Or You/Feast Of Blaze/Wilful Days//Let's All Go (To The Fire Dances)/The Fall Of Because (live)/Dominator (Version) (12", sealed double pack) . . . 15
84 E.G. EGOX 16 — Eighties (Serious Dance Mix)/Eighties/Eighties (Coming Mix) (12", p/s) . . . 8
85 E.G. EGOY 20 — Love Like Blood (Gestalt Mix)/Love Like Blood/Blue Feather (12", p/s) . . . 10
85 E.G. EGOY 21 — Kings And Queens (Knave Mix) (12", p/s) . . . 10
85 E.G. EGOX 21 — Kings And Queens (The Right Royal Mix)/The Madding Crowd/Kings And Queens (12", different withdrawn p/s) . . . 10
86 E.G. EGOD 27 — Adorations/Exile//Ecstasy/Adorations (Instrumental Mix) (double pack) . . . 5
86 E.G. EGO 30 — Sanity/Goodbye To The Village (stickered p/s & "Wardance [Remix]" cassette) . . 10

MINT VALUE £

88 E.G. EGOCD 40 America/Jihad (Beyrouth Edit)/America (Extended Mix)/ Change (Original 1980 Mix) (CD) . . . 8
88 E.G. EGOT 43 My Love Of This Land/Follow The Leaders (Dub)/Sun Goes Down (10", p/s, B-side matrix no. EGOT 43B; last track plays "The Gathering") . . . 7
(see also Youth, Peyr, Heavy Duty Breaks)

KILLJOYS
77 Raw RAW 3 Johnny Won't Get To Heaven/Naive (p/s, 4 different label designs) . . . 125
91 Dam. Goods FNARR LP10 NAIVE (LP, green vinyl) . . . 12
(see also Girlschool)

KILLS
02 Rug RUG 158 Fuck The People (1-sided, stamped card sleeve, 500 only) . . . 30
00s Domino RUG 144CD BLACK ROOSTER EP: Cat Claw/Wait/Dropout Boogie/Gum (CD) . . . 8

KILOWATTS
68 Doctor Bird DB 1140 Bring It On Home/What A Wonderful World . . . 25
(see also West Indians)

KILTIES
56 Beltona BL 2666 Teach You To Rock/Giddy-Up-A Ding Dong . . . 20
56 Beltona BL 2666 Teach You To Rock/Giddy-Up-A Ding Dong (78) . . . 12

KIM & KINETICS
60s Mortonsound 3032/3033 Without A Song/Stormy Monday . . . 40
60s Mortonsound 3036/3033 Wee Wee Hours/Stormy Monday . . . 40
(see also Kim Davis)

WILLIAM KIMBER
56 EFDSS LP 1001 WILLIAM KIMBER (LP, with booklet) . . . 15
74 Topic 12T 249 THE ART OF WILLIAM KIMBER (LP, with booklet) . . . 15

WILLIAM E. KIMBER
68 Parlophone R 5735 Kilburn Towers/Goodbye (withdrawn) . . . 8
(see also Couriers)

STEVIE KIMBLE
66 Decca F 12378 Some Things Take A Little Time/All The Time In The World . . . 18

MAX KIMINSKY
59 Melodisc MLP 12-126 DIXIELAND HORN (LP) . . . 20

KINESPHERE
76 Kinesphere KIN 5001 ALL AROUND YOU (LP) . . . 100

AL KING
68 Sue WI 4045 Think Twice Before You Speak/The Winner . . . 35

ALAN KING
73 Duke DU 151 Africa Wants Us All/JOE GIBBS: Liberation (B-side actually by Joe Gibbs' All Stars) . . . 6

ALBERT KING
67 Atlantic 584 099 Crosscut Saw/Down Don't Bother Me . . . 15
67 Stax 601 015 Born Under A Bad Sign/Personal Manager . . . 8
68 Stax 601 029 Cold Feet/You Sure Drive A Hard Bargain . . . 10
68 Stax 601 042 (I Love) Lucy/You're Gonna Need Me . . . 7
73 Stax 2025 162 Breaking Up Somebody's Home/Little Brother (Make A Way) . . . 6
67 Polydor 2343 026 TRAVELLIN' TO CALIFORNIA (LP) . . . 35
68 Stax (S)XATS 1002 LIVE WIRE — BLUES POWER (LP) . . . 30
69 Atlantic 588 173 KING OF THE BLUES GUITAR (LP) . . . 30
69 Stax SXATS 1017 KING DOES THE KING'S THINGS (LP) . . . 22
69 Stax SXATS 1022 YEARS GONE BY (LP) . . . 22
71 Stax 2363 003 LIVE WIRE — BLUES POWER (LP, reissue) . . . 15
71 Stax 2325 042 LOVEJOY (LP) . . . 18
73 Stax 2325 089 I'LL PLAY THE BLUES FOR YOU (LP) . . . 15
74 Stax STX 1003 I WANNA GET FUNKY (LP) . . . 15
(se also Steve Cropper & Albert King)

ANNA KING
65 Philips BF 1402 If Somebody Told You/Baby, Baby, Baby (as Anna King & Bobby Byrd) . . . 12
65 Philips BBE 12584 BACK TO SOUL (EP) . . . 40
65 Philips (S)BL 7655 BACK TO SOUL (LP) . . . 75
(see also Bobby Byrd)

ANTHONY KING
70s Peer Intl. ELECTRICAL BAZAAR — SYNTHESIZERS UNLIMITED (LP, library issue) . . . 25

B.B. KING
62 HMV POP 1101 Tomorrow Night/Mother's Love . . . 20
64 Ember EMB S 196 Rock Me Baby/I Can't Lose . . . 20
65 Sue WI 358 The Letter/You Never Know . . . 25
66 HMV POP 1568 Don't Answer The Door Parts 1 & 2 . . . 10
67 HMV POP 1580 Night Life/Waitin' On You . . . 12
67 HMV POP 1594 I Don't Want You Cuttin' Your Hair/Think It Over . . . 8
67 Polydor 56735 Jungle/Long Gone Baby . . . 7
68 Stateside SS 2112 Paying The Cost To Be The Boss/Having My Say . . . 6
68 Blue Horizon 57-3144 The Woman I Love/Blues For Me . . . 22
68 Speciality SPE 1006 Woke Up This Morning (possibly unissued) . . . 20+
69 Stateside SS 2141 Don't Waste My Time/Get Myself Somebody . . . 6
69 Blue Horizon 57-3161 Everyday I Have The Blues/Five Long Years . . . 22
70 Stateside SS 2161 The Thrill Is Gone/You're Mean . . . 6
70 Stateside SS 2169 So Excited/Confessin' The Blues . . . 5
70 Stateside SS 2176 Hummingbird/Ask Me No Questions . . . 5

			MINT VALUE £
71	Probe PRO 516	Chains And Things/King's Special	5
71	Probe PRO 528	Ask Me No Questions/Help The Poor/Humming Bird	5
71	Probe PRO 546	Ain't Nobody Home/Alexis' Boogie (with Alexis Korner)	10
72	Probe PRO 573	Summer In The City/Found What I Need	5
65	HMV CLP 1870	LIVE AT THE REGAL (LP)	40
66	HMV CLP 3514	CONFESSIN' THE BLUES (LP)	35
67	HMV CLP 3608	BLUES IS KING (LP)	35
67	Ember EMB 3379	THE R&B AND SOUL OF B.B. KING (LP)	20
68	Stateside (S)SL 10238	BLUES ON TOP OF BLUES (LP)	30
68	Blue Horizon 7-63216	THE B.B. KING STORY CHAPTER 1 (LP)	65
69	Stateside (S)SL 10272	LUCILLE (LP)	20
69	Stateside SSL 10284	HIS BEST — THE ELECTRIC B.B. KING (LP)	20
69	Blue Horizon 7-63226	THE B.B. KING STORY CHAPTER 2 — BEALE STREET BLUES (LP)	65
70	Stateside SSL 10297	LIVE AND WELL (LP)	20
70	Stateside SSL 10299	COMPLETELY WELL (LP)	20
70	Probe SPBA 6255	INDIANOLA MISSISSIPPI SEEDS (LP)	12
71	Blue Horizon 2431 004	TAKE A SWING WITH ME (LP)	75
71	Probe SPB 1032	LIVE IN COOK COUNTY JAIL (LP)	15
71	Probe SPB 1041	IN LONDON (LP)	15
72	Probe SPB 1051	L.A. MIDNIGHT (LP)	12
72	Probe SPB 1063	GUESS WHO (LP)	12
73	Probe SPB 1069	THE BEST OF B.B. KING (LP)	12
73	Probe SPB 1083	TO KNOW YOU IS TO LOVE YOU (LP)	12

(see also U2)

B.B. KING & BOBBY BLAND

74	ABC ABCD 605	TOGETHER FOR THE FIRST TIME (2-LP)	22

(see also Bobby Bland)

KING BEE

90	Big One RUFF6X	Back By Dope Demand/Oral Excitement (12")	15

BEN E. KING

61	London HLK 9258	Spanish Harlem/First Taste Of Love	15
61	London HLK 9358	Stand By Me/On The Horizon	18
61	London HLK 9416	Amor, Amor/Souvenir Of Mexico	10
61	London HLK 9457	Here Comes The Night/Young Boy Blues	15
62	London HLK 9517	Ecstasy/Yes	12
62	London HLK 9544	Don't Play That Song (You Lied)/The Hermit Of Misty Mountain (later copies have Atlantic labels instead of *London* Atlantic)	each 12
62	London HLK 9586	Too Bad/My Heart Cries For You	15
63	London HLK 9631	I'm Standing By/Walking In The Footsteps Of A Fool	15
63	London HLK 9691	How Can I Forget/Gloria, Gloria	12
63	London HLK 9778	I (Who Have Nothing)/The Beginning Of Time	12
63	London HLK 9819	I Could Have Danced All Night/Gypsy	12
64	London HLK 9840	Around The Corner/Groovin'	15
64	Atlantic AT 4007	It's All Over/Let The Water Run Down	15
65	Atlantic AT 4018	Seven Letters/River Of Tears	15
65	Atlantic AT 4025	The Record (Baby I Love You)/The Way You Shake It	18
65	Atlantic AT 4043	Cry No More/(There's) No Place To Hide	20
66	Atlantic AT 4065	Goodnight My Love, Pleasant Dreams/Tell Daddy	12
66	Atlantic AT 4065	Goodnight My Love, Pleasant Dreams/I Can't Break The News To Myself (demos with blank label on different B-side)	350
66	Atlantic 584 008	So Much Love/Don't Drive Me Away	10
66	Atlantic 584 046	I Swear By The Stars Above/Get In A Hurry	10
67	Atlantic 584 069	What Is Soul?/They Don't Give Medals To Yesterday's Heroes	12
67	Atlantic 584 090	Save The Last Dance For Me (as Ben E. King & Drifters)/Stand By Me	10
67	Atlantic 584 106	Tears, Tears, Tears/A Man Without A Dream	10
68	Atlantic 584 149	Seven Letters/Goodnight My Love	10
68	Atlantic 584 184	Don't Take Your Love From Me/Forgive This Fool	18
68	Atlantic 584 205	It's Amazing/Where's The Girl	10
69	Atlantic 584 238	'Till I Can't Take It Any More/It Ain't Fair	10
70	Crewe CRW 2	Goodbye My Old Gal/I Can't Take It Like A Man	5
71	Atlantic 2091 100	It's Amazing/Tears, Tears, Tears	10
71	CBS 7397	White Moon/All Of Your Sorrows	5
72	CBS 7785	Take Me To The Pilot/I Guess It's Goodbye	5
75	Atlantic K 10565	Supernatural Things (Parts 1 & 2)	12
75	Atlantic K 10618	Happiness Is Where You Find It/Drop My Heart Off	5
63	London REK 1361	BEN E. KING (EP)	40
63	London REK 1386	I'M STANDING BY (EP)	40
64	Atlantic AET 6004	WHAT NOW MY LOVE (EP)	35
61	London HA-K 2395	SPANISH HARLEM (LP, also stereo SAH-K 6195)	50/70
62	London HA-K 8012	DON'T PLAY THAT SONG! (LP)	50
63	London HA-K/SH-K 8026	SONGS FOR SOULFUL LOVERS (LP, cover credits "*Sings* For Soulful Lovers"; mono/stereo)	50/70
65	Atlantic ATL 5016	GREATEST HITS (LP, plum label)	45
65	Atlantic ATL 5024	SEVEN LETTERS (LP)	55
66	Atlantic 587/588 055	SONGS FOR SOULFUL LOVERS (LP, cover credits "*Sings* For Soulful Lovers"; reissue)	18
67	Atlantic 590 001	SPANISH HARLEM (LP, reissue)	18
67	Atlantic 587 072	WHAT IS SOUL? (LP)	25
68	Atlantic 588 125	SEVEN LETTERS (LP, reissue)	15
70	Crewe CRWS 203	ROUGH EDGES (LP)	12
71	CBS 64570	THE BEGINNING OF IT ALL (LP)	12
75	Atlantic K 50118	SUPERNATURAL THING (LP)	12

(see also Drifters, Soul Clan)

BRENTON KING

73	Downtown DT 505	Why Do People Have To Cry/Version	6

MINT VALUE £

BOB KING & THE COUNTRY KINGS

59	Oriole CB 1497	My Petite Marie/Hey Honey	100
59	Oriole CB 1497	My Petite Marie/Hey Honey (78)	30

BUZZY KING

60	Top Rank JAR 278	Schoolboy Blues/Your Picture	20

CANNON BALL KING

69	Camel CA 14	Danny Boy/Reggae Happiness	10
70s	Junior JR 103	Reggay Got Soul/Land Of Love (actually by Soul Cats)	10

(see also Carl Bryan, King Cannon, Cannon Ball & Johnny Melody)

CARL KING

66	CBS 202407	Out Of My Depth/Keep It Coming	20
67	CBS 202553	You And Me/Satin Doll	8

CAROLE KING

62	London HLU 9591	It Might As Well Rain Until September/Nobody's Perfect	7
66	London HLU 10036	Road To Nowhere/Some Of Your Lovin'	25
72	Ode ODS 66031	Been To Canaan/Bitter With The Sweet	5
71	A&M AMLS 996	WRITER — CAROLE KING (LP)	18
72	Ode ODE 77016	RHYMES AND REASONS (LP)	15
80	Capitol EA-ST 12073	PEARLS (LP, picture card inner)	12

CLAUDE KING

61	Philips PB 1173	Big River Big Man/Sweet Loving	10
61	Philips PB 1199	The Comancheros/I Can't Get Over The Way You Got Over Me	10
62	CBS AAG 108	Wolverton Mountain/Little Bitty Heart	12
62	CBS AAG 119	Burning Of Atlanta/Don't That Moon Look Lonesome	10
65	CBS EP 6067	TIGER WOMAN (EP)	35
62	CBS BPG 62114	MEET CLAUDE KING (LP)	45

CLYDIE KING

69	Minit MLF 11014	One Part, Two Part/Love Now Pay Later	10
75	UK USA 11	Punish Me/Punish Me (Instrumental Version)	5

(see also Jimmy Holiday & Clydie King, Raelets)

DANNY KING('S MAYFAIR SET)

64	Columbia DB 7276	Tossin' And Turnin'/Young Blood	35
65	Columbia DB 7456	Pretty Things/Outside Of My Room	40
65	Columbia DB 7792	Amen (My Teenage Prayer)/It's Such A Shame (as Danny King's Mayfair Set)	25

(see also Trevor Burton, Lemon Tree, Roy Wood)

DAVE KING

56	Decca F 10684	Memories Are Made Of This (& Keynotes)/I've Changed My Mind A 1000 Times	18
56	Decca F 10720	You Can't Be True To Two/A Little Bit Independent	15
56	Decca F 10741	The Birds And The Bees/Hot Chocolatta (with Keynotes)	15
56	Decca F 10791	Christmas And You/You Make Nice	18
57	Decca F 10865	Love Is A Golden Ring/If Your Heart Wants To Dance	7
57	Decca F 10910	With All My Heart/Red Shutters	7
57	Decca F 10947	Shake Me I Rattle/Chances Are	7
58	Decca F 10973	The Story Of My Life/I'll Buy You A Star	12
58	Decca F 11012	I Suddenly/There's Only One Of You	6
58	Decca F 11061	The Story/Home	6
59	Pye International 7N 25032	High Hopes/Night And Day	8
59	Pye International N 25032	High Hopes/Night And Day (78)	12
60	Pye 7N 15283	Many A Wonderful Moment/Goody Goody	6
61	Pye International 7N 25076	Young In Love/C'est La Vie, C'est L'amour	5
56	Decca DFE 6385	A DAVE KING SELECTION (EP)	18
58	Decca DFE 6514	DAVE KING NO. 2 (EP)	20
62	Ace Of Hearts ACL 1095	MEMORIES ARE MADE OF THIS (LP)	20

DAVE KING REGGAE BAND

70	Attack ATT 8014	Hey Little Girl/Why Don't You Try Me	7

DEE KING

66	Piccadilly 7N 35316	Sally Go Round The Roses/It's So Fine	8

DENNIS KING

77	EMI EMI 2578	Regan's Theme From The Film 'Sweeney'/F.J.'s Tune	20

(see also King Brothers)

EARL (CONNELLY) KING

56	Parlophone DP 511	Gratefully/Don't Take It So Hard (78, export issue)	20

EDDIE KING

65	Columbia DB 7572	Always At A Distance/If You Wish	8
65	Columbia DB 7654	I Wanna Love Her So Bad/If All You Need	10

FREDDY/FREDDIE KING

61	Parlophone R 4777	Hideaway/I Love The Woman	40
65	Sue WI 349	Driving Sideways/Hideaway	35
69	Atlantic 584 235	Play It Cool/Funky	10
73	A&M AMS 7076	Woman Across The River/Help Me Through The Day	5
69	Atlantic 588 186	FREDDIE IS A BLUES MASTER (LP)	30
69	Polydor 2343 009	KING OF R&B VOL. 2 (LP)	15
69	Python PLP-KM 5	FREDDY KING VOLUME 1 (LP, 99 copies only)	40
69	Python PLP-KM 7	FREDDY KING VOLUME 2 (LP, 99 copies only)	40
69	Python PLP-KM 11	FREDDY KING VOLUME 3 (LP, 99 copies only)	40

(Pre-1970 releases are usually credited to Freddy King, post-1970 releases to Freddie King.)

71	A&M AMLS 65004	GETTING READY (LP)	18
72	Polydor 2343 047	HIS EARLY YEARS VOLUME 1 (LP)	12
72	A&M AMLS 68113	TEXAS CANNONBALL (LP)	12

MINT VALUE £

72 Black Bear 904 LIVE PERFORMANCES VOLUME 1 (LP) 22
72 Black Bear 905 LIVE PERFORMANCES VOLUME 2 (LP) 22
73 A&M AMLS 68919 WOMAN ACROSS THE RIVER (LP) 12
73 Atlantic K 40496 FREDDIE IS A BLUES MASTER (LP, reissue) 12
73 Atlantic K 40497 MY FEELING FOR THE BLUES (LP) 12
75 RSO 2394 163 LARGER THAN LIFE (LP) 12
77 RSO 2394 192 FREDDIE KING (1934-1976) (LP) 12
(see also Lula Reed & Freddy King)

HAMILTON KING

64 HMV POP 1289 Not Until/I Wanna Live 10
64 HMV POP 1356 Ain't It Time/Money, Money 15
65 HMV POP 1425 Bird Without Wings/Shoppin' 15
60s Toast TT 511 This Love Of Mine/The Cup Is Fuller 6

HANK KING

63 Starlite STEP 41 COUNTRY AND WESTERN (EP) 25
66 Starlite GRK 510 COUNTRY AND WESTERN (EP, reissue) 10

JAY W. KING

66 Stateside SS 505 I'm So Afraid/I Don't Have To Worry (Not Anymore) 22

JONATHAN KING

67 Decca LK/SKL 4908 OR THEN AGAIN... (LP) 25
72 Decca SKL 5127 TRY SOMETHING DIFFERENT (LP) 15
75 UK UKAL 1010 A ROSE IN A FISTED GLOVE (LP) 12
76 UK UKAL 1024 J.K. ALL THE WAY (LP) 12
(see also Weathermen, Hedgehoppers Anonymous, Pleasure Garden)

DR. MARTIN LUTHER KING

68 Pama PM 732 I Have A Dream/Top Of The Mountain 15
68 Tamla Motown TML 11076 THE GREAT MARCH TO FREEDOM (LP) 100
60s Hallmark CHM 631 IN THE STRUGGLE FOR FREEDOM (LP) 12

P. KING

83 Red Bus RBUS 79 Hey Rosalyn/Lyin' Again 6
(see also Paul King)

PAUL KING

72 Dawn DNS 1023 Whoa Buck/Zoe 7
72 Dawn DNLS 3035 BEEN IN THE PEN TOO LONG (LP, with lyric insert) 22
(see also Mungo Jerry, P. King, P. Rufus King, King Earl Boogie Band, D'Jurann Jurran, Jigilo Jug Band, Russian Roulette)

KING ADORA

00s SQR RQS 007 Bionic/The Law (numbered wraparound sleeve, stickered plastic outer sleeve, 500 only, with promo postcard) 25
00s SQR RQS 008 Big Isn't Beautiful/Scream And Shout (numbered wraparound sleeve, 1000 only) 10

PEE WEE KING & HIS BAND

52 HMV B 10229 Bull Fiddle Boogie (with Golden West Cowboys)/Silver And Gold (78) 10
52 HMV B 10275 Busybody (with Redd Stewart)/I Don't Mind (with Golden West Trio) (78) 10
53 HMV B 10415 Tennessee Tango/The Crazy Waltz (78) 10
54 HMV 7MC 14 Bimbo/Changing Partners (export issue) 22
(see also Hank Snow)

PETE KING CHORALE & ORCHESTRA

61 London HLR 9437 Hey! Look Me Over/Tall Hope 7

PETER KING

68 Crab CRAB 3 Reggae Limbo/DERRICK MORGAN: River To The Bank 6

P. RUFUS KING

73 Dawn DNS 1031 Look At Me Now/Nobody Knows 6
(see also Paul King, Mungo Jerry)

RAMONA KING

64 Warner Bros WB 125 It's In His Kiss/It Couldn't Happen To A Nicer Guy 18

RAY KING SOUL BAND

67 Piccadilly 7N 35394 Behold/Soon You'll Be Gone 12

REG KING

71 United Artists UP 35204 Little Boy/10,000 Miles (as Reg King & B.B. Blunder) 7
71 United Artists UAG 29157 REG KING (LP) 35
(see also Action, Andy Leigh, B.B. Blunder, Mark Charig, Elton Dean, Mighty Baby)

SAMMY KING (& VOLTAIRS)

64 HMV POP 1285 What's The Secret/Great Balls Of Fire (as Sammy King & Voltairs) 12
64 HMV POP 1330 Rag Doll/We're Through 8
65 HMV POP 1384 Only You (And You Alone)/A Kiss, A Promise 12
66 HMV POP 1540 If You Can Find Someone To Love You/Past Caring (with Voltairs) 8

SID KING & FIVE STRINGS

56 Philips PB 589 Booger Red/Oobie-Doobie (78) 100

SOLOMON KING

67 Columbia DB 8306 She Wears My Ring/Try Try (withdrawn B-side) 10
68 Columbia DB 8402 When We Were Young/Those Gentle Hands 5
68 Columbia DB 8454 Somewhere In The Crowd/Hava Nagila 5
68 Columbia DB 8508 Goodbye My Old Gal/Hundred Years Or More 5
69 Columbia DB 8554 Cry Softly/Time Alone Will Tell 6
69 Columbia DB 8586 For Each Question/If I Had Three Wishes 6
70 Columbia DB 8676 Say A Prayer/This Beautiful Day (demos more common) 150/100
70 Columbia DB 8739 November Snow/Echoes Of A Million Kisses 6

MINT VALUE £

71	Columbia DB 8771	Answer Me/Don't You Be A Sinner	6
68	Columbia S(C)X 6250	SHE WEARS MY RING (LP)	18
71	Columbia SCX 6458	YOU'LL NEVER WALK ALONE (LP)	15

(see also Levi Jackson)

SONNY KING

60	Pye Intl. NPL 28001	FOR LOSERS ONLY (LP)	22

TEDDI KING

56	Vogue Coral Q 72142	My Funny Little Lover/I'll Never Be The Same	8
50s	Vogue EPV 1204	STORYVILLE PRESENTS MISS TEDDI KING (EP)	12
55	Vogue LDE 142	MISS TEDDI KING WITH RUBY BRAFF (10" LP)	22
57	Vogue VA 160109	NOW IN VOGUE (LP)	15

(see also George Shearing)

TEDDY KING & BUSTER'S ALLSTARS

67	Fab FAB 27	Mexican Divorce/SOUL TOPS: Baby I Got News	18

TONY KING (& HIPPY BOYS)

69	Trojan TR 667	Proud Mary/My Devotion (as Tony King & Hippy Boys)	6
70	Gas GAS 156	Daddy, Daddy Don't Cry/I Like It	7

(see also Maytals)

KINGBEES

66	Tempo TPO 103	I'm A Kingbee/My Little Red Book (Irish-only, some in p/s)	350/250

KING BISCUIT BOY

70	Paramount SPFL 270	OFFICIAL MUSIC (LP)	20
71	Paramount SPFA 7001	GOODUNS (LP)	20

(see also Bobby Bland)

KING BROTHERS

57	Conquest CP 104	The Cradle Rock/Crazy Little Palace (78)	10
57	Conquest CP 109	Steamboat Railroad/Heart (78)	8
57	Parlophone R 4288	Marianne/Little By Little	10
57	Parlophone R 4310	A White Sport Coat (And A Pink Carnation)/Minne-Minnehaha!	10
57	Parlophone R 4338	In The Middle Of An Island/Rockin' Shoes	7
57	Parlophone R 4367	Wake Up Little Susie/Winter Wonderland	8
57	Parlophone R 4389	Put A Light In The Window/Miss Otis Regrets	7
58	Parlophone R 4410	Hand Me Down My Walking Cane/6-5 Jive	12
58	Parlophone R 4438	Torero/Moonlight And Roses	6
58	Parlophone R 4469	Sitting In A Tree House/Father Time	5
59	Parlophone R 4513	Leaning On A Lamp-Post/Thank Heaven For Little Girls	5
59	Parlophone R 4554	Hop, Skip And Jump/Civilization (Bongo, Bongo, Bongo)	10
59	Parlophone R 4554	Hop, Skip And Jump/Civilization (Bongo, Bongo, Bongo) (78)	8
59	Parlophone R 4577	Makin' Love/Caribbean	5
60	Parlophone R 4639	The Waiter And The Porter And The Upstairs Maid/Standing On The Corner	5
60	Parlophone R 4672	Mais Oui/Gotta Feeling	5
60	Parlophone R 4715	Doll House/Si Si Si	5
61	Parlophone R 4737	Seventy-Six Trombones/I Like Everybody	5
61	Parlophone R 4778	Goodbye Little Darling/Tuxedo Junction	5
61	Parlophone R 4825	The Next Train Out Of Town/Sabre Dance	5
61	Parlophone R 4861	The Language Of Love/Go Tell Her For Me	5
64	Oriole CB 1978	Real Live Girl/Everytime It Rains	6
66	CBS 202030	Everytime I See You/Remember When	6
66	Page One POF 009	Symphony For Susan/My Time	8
67	Page One POF 033	My Mammy/Some Of These Days	8
57	Parlophone GEP 8638	HARMONY KINGS (EP)	10
57	Parlophone GEP 8651	SING AL JOLSON (EP)	10
57	Parlophone GEP 8665	LULLABIES OF BROADWAY (EP)	10
58	Parlophone GEP 8726	THAT'S ENTERTAINMENT (EP)	10
58	Parlophone GEP 8760	KINGS OF SONG (EP)	12
61	Parlophone GEP 8838	KING SIZE HITS (EP)	12
61	Encore ENC 106	KINGS OF SONG (EP)	12
67	Tupperware 7ES 25	THERE'S NO BUSINESS — LIKE OUR BUSINESS (EP)	8
58	Parlophone PMC 1060	THREE KINGS AND AN ACE (LP)	25

(see also Jim Dale, Dennis King)

KING CANNON

69	Trojan TR 663	Soul Scorcher/GLEN & DAVE: Lucky Boy	10
69	Trojan TR 644	Soul Special/TREVOR SHIELD: Moon Is Playing Tricks On Me	10
69	Crab CRAB 6	Mellow Trumpet/VAL BENNETT: Reggae City	10
71	Hillcrest HCT 2	Reggay Got Soul/SOUL CATS: Land Of Love	7
71	Moodisc HME 109	Raw Deal (as King Cannon Allout; actually by Carl Bryan)/ MUDIE'S ALL STARS: Shirley's Hide Out	6

(see also Cannon Ball & Johnny Melody, Carl Bryan, Max Romeo, Lester Sterling, Kid Gungo, Erroll Dunkley)

KING CANNON (BALL)

68	Trojan TR 636	Thunderstorm/BURT WALTERS: Honey Love	15

KING CHUBBY

70	Pama Supreme PS 297	What's The World Coming To/Live As One	10
70	Supreme PS 297	What's The World Coming To/Live As One (reissue)	10

(see also Junior Byles)

KING COLE TRIO

(see under Nat 'King' Cole)

MINT VALUE £

KING CRIMSON

69	Island WIP 6071	The Court Of The Crimson King (Parts 1 & 2)	15
70	Island WIP 6080	Cat Food/Groon (some in p/s)	20/6
74	Island WIP 6189	The Night Watch/The Great Deceiver	5
76	Island WIP 6274	21st Century Schizoid Man/Epitaph (some in p/s)	25/7
91	Caroline 1467	THE ABBREVIATED KING CRIMSON: HEARTBEAT (CD EP, digipak)	20
69	Island ILPS 9111	IN THE COURT OF THE CRIMSON KING (LP, 1st pressing, pink label/'i' logo)	40
70	Island ILPS 9111	IN THE COURT OF THE CRIMSON KING (LP, 2nd pressing, pink rim label/'palm tree' logo)	15
70	Island ILPS 9127	IN THE WAKE OF POSEIDON (LP, 1st pressing, pink label/'i' logo)	25
70	Island ILPS 9127	IN THE WAKE OF POSEIDON (LP, 2nd pressing, pink rim label/'palm tree' logo)	15
70	Island ILPS 9141	LIZARD (LP, pink rim label/'palm tree' logo)	20
71	Island ILPS 9175	ISLANDS (LP, pink rim label/'palm tree' logo, gatefold sleeve with inner)	15
72	Island HELP 6	EARTHBOUND (LP, black/pink label)	12
73	Island ILPS 9230	LARKS' TONGUES IN ASPIC (LP, pink rim label/'palm tree' logo, with inner)	12
74	Island ILPS 9275	STARLESS AND BIBLE BLACK (LP, pink rim label/'palm tree' logo, with inner)	12
74	Island ILPS 9308	RED (LP, pink rim label/'palm tree' logo, with inner sleeve)	12
75	Island ILPS 9316	U.S.A. (LP, pink rim label/'palm tree' logo, with inner)	12
76	Island ISLP 7	A YOUNG PERSON'S GUIDE (2-LP, with booklet)	18
90s	EG/Virgin CDVKCX 13	THRAK (CD, in metal box, with tour programme)	20

(see also Giles Giles & Fripp, Fripp & Eno, Andy Summers & Robert Fripp, Gordon Haskell, Shame, McDonald & Giles, Emerson Lake & Palmer, Uriah Heep, Boz, Trendsetters Ltd., Pete Sinfield)

KING CRY CRY (Prince Far I)

71	Banana BA 356	I Had A Talk/BURNING SPEAR: Zion Higher	25

KING CURTIS

62	London HLU 9547	Soul Twist/Twistin' Time (as King Curtis & Noble Knights)	18
64	Capitol CL 15346	Soul Serenade/More Soul	18
67	Atlantic 584 109	Good To Me/Hold On I'm Comin'	8
67	Atlantic 584 134	Memphis Soul Stew/Blue Nocturne	12
68	Speciality SPE 1000	Wiggle Wobble/Night Train	6
69	Atlantic 584 287	Little Green Apples/La Jeanne	6
70	Atco 2091 012	Teasin'/Soulin' (as King Curtis & Delaney Bramlett, Eric Clapton & Friends)	15
60	London RE-K 1307	HAVE TENOR SAX, WILL BLOW (EP)	45
60	London HA-K 2247	HAVE TENOR SAX, WILL BLOW (LP)	65
62	RCA RD 27252	ARTHUR MURRAY'S MUSIC FOR DANCING — THE TWIST (LP)	30
62	Esquire 32-161	THE NEW SCENE OF KING CURTIS (LP)	35
67	Atlantic 587 067	PLAYS THE GREAT MEMPHIS HITS (LP)	22
68	Ember SPE/LP 6600	SOUL SERENADE (LP)	18
68	Atlantic 587 093	KINGSIZE SOUL (LP, as King Curtis & Kingpins)	18
68	Atlantic 587/588 115	SWEET SOUL (LP)	18
69	Atco 228 002	BEST OF KING CURTIS (LP)	15
69	Atco 228 027	INSTANT GROOVE (LP)	15
70	Wand WNS 4	ETERNALLY SOUL (LP, as King Curtis & Shirelles)	12
71	Atlantic K 40214	LIVE AT FILLMORE WEST (LP)	15
72	Atlantic K 40360	EVERYBODY'S TALKIN' (LP)	12
72	Speciality SPE 6600	SOUL SERENADE (LP, reissue)	12
72	Speciality SPE 6607	MISTER SOUL (LP, reissue)	12
73	Atlantic K 40434	BLUES AT MONTREUX (LP, with Champion Jack Dupree)	12

(see also Champion Jack Dupree, Eric Clapton)

KING CURTIS, OLIVER NELSON & JIMMY FORREST

63	Esquire 32-189	SOUL BATTLE (LP)	35

KING DIAMOND

89	Road Runner RR 94616	CONSPIRACY (LP, picture disc)	20

BOBBY KINGDOM/BLUE BEATS

62	Blue Beat 45/BB/77	Spanish Town Twist/Brand New Automobile	40

KINGDOM COME (U.K.)

71	Polydor 2001 234	Eternal Messenger/I D Side To B Side The C Side	5
72	Polydor 2001 416	Spirit Of Joy/Come Alive	5
72	Polydor 2310 130	GALACTIC ZOO DOSSIER (LP, gatefold sleeve, some with poster)	40/20
72	Polydor 2310 178	KINGDOM COME (LP)	15
73	Polydor 2310 254	JOURNEY (LP)	15

(see also Arthur Brown)

KING-EARL BOOGIE BAND

72	Dawn DNS 1024	Plastic Jesus/If The Lord Don't Get You	6
72	Dawn DNS 1028	Starlight/Goin' To Germany	6
72	Dawn DNLS 3040	TROUBLE AT MILL (LP, with poster)	18

(see also Mungo Jerry, Paul King, Skeleton Crew)

KING FIGHTER

60s	Jump Up JU 518	People Will Talk/Same Thing	8

KINGFISH

76	United Artists UAG 29922	KINGFISH (LP)	12
77	United Artists UAG 30080	LIVE AND KICKIN' (LP)	12

(see also Grateful Dead, Bob Weir)

KING GEORGE

67	RCA RCA 1573	Drive On James/I'm Gonna Be Somebody Someday	18

KING HARVEST

73	Pye NSPL 28174	DANCING IN THE MOONLIGHT (LP)	12

KING HORROR

69	Joe/Duke DU 34	Dracula Prince Of Darkness/JOE'S ALL STARS: Honky	40
69	Grape GR 3003	Cutting Blade/Vampire	40
69	Grape GR 3006	The Hole/WINSTON GROOVY: Lover Come Back	60
69	Grape GR 3007	Lochness Monster/VISIONS: Zion I	40
69	Jackpot JP 713	Wood In The Fire/The Naked City	30
69	Jackpot JP 714	Police/PAMA DICE: Honky Tonk Popcorn	30
70	Nu Beat NB 051	Frankenstein/WINSTON GROOVY: I Can't Stand It	30

(see also Laurel Aitken)

KINGLY BAND

69	Decca F 12926	The Bitter And The Sweet/Standing At The Crossroads	7

KING MIGUEL

73	Bullet BU 524	The Word Is Black/Town Talk	8

KING OLIVER

53	London AL 3510	PLAYS THE BLUES (10" LP)	20
53	Columbia 33S 1065	KING JOE (10" LP)	15
55	Vogue/Coral LRA 10020	DIXIE SYNCOPATORS (10" LP)	15

KINGPINS (U.S.)

58	London HLU 8658	Ungaua Parts 1 & 2	18
58	London HLU 8658	Ungaua Parts 1 & 2 (78)	25

KINGPINS (U.K.)

65	Oriole CB 1986	Two Right Feet/That's The Way It Should Be	22

KINGPINS (U.K.)

67	Columbia DB 8146	Summer's Come And Gone/Another Tear Falls	7

KING ROCK & WILLOWS

67	Caltone TONE 111	You Are The One/ALVA LEWIS: Return Home	40

KING ROCKY

68	Studio One SO 2045	The King Is Back/THREE TOPS: Vex Till Yuh Buss	22

(see also Leroy & Rocky, Clancy Eccles, Heptones)

KINGS IV

59	London HLT 8914	Some Like It Hot/The World Goes On	18
59	London HLT 8914	Some Like It Hot/The World Goes On (78)	18

KING'S HENCHMEN

59	Coral FEP 2025	ALAN FREED PRESENTS VOL. 1 (EP)	180

KING SCRATCH

70s	Ethnic ETH 16	Spiritual Whip/Version	6
70s	Ethnic ETH 30	Mash Finger/Version	6

(see also Lee Perry/Upsetters, Skatalites)

KING SISTERS

57	Capitol CL 14711	While The Lights Are Low/In Hamburg (When The Nights Are Long)	8
57	Capitol CL 14729	Imagination/You're My Thrill	8
57	Capitol CL 14777	Easy To Love/That Old Feeling	8
58	Capitol CL 14865	Deep Purple/Unbelievable	8
58	Capitol CL 14893	What's New?/The Thrill Was New	7
58	Capitol CL 14934	Autumn In Pleasant Grove/The Guy In The Foreign Sports Car	7
59	Capitol CL 15012	Keep Smiling (Keep Laughin', Be Happy)/The Maids Of Cadiz	7
59	Capitol CL 15069	Lovin' Up A Storm/What Would I Do Without You	7
59	Capitol CL 15096	Over The River (And Through The Woods)/ Holiday Of Love (with Their Family)	7
57	Capitol EAP1 919	IMAGINATION (EP)	10
57	Capitol T 808	ALOHA (LP)	18

CHARLES KINGSLEY CREATION

65	Columbia DB 7758	Summer Without Sun/Still In Love With You	70

EVELYN KINGSLEY & TOWERS

58	Capitol CL 14944	To Know Him Is To Love Him/FRANK PERRY & TOWERS: Let Me Be The One	25

(see also Towers)

KINGSMEN

58	London HLE 8735	Better Believe It/Week-End	30
58	London HLE 8735	Better Believe It/Week-End (78)	25
59	London HLE 8812	Conga Rock/The Cat Walk	35
59	London HLE 8812	Conga Rock/The Cat Walk (78)	30
59	London REE 1211	THE KINGSMEN (EP)	90

(see also Bill Haley & Comets)

KINGSMEN

63	Pye International 7N 25231	Louie Louie/Haunted Castle	30
64	Pye International 7N 25262	Little Latin Lupe Lu/David's Mood	8
64	Pye International 7N 25273	Death Of An Angel/Searching For Love	15
65	Pye International 7N 25292	The Jolly Green Giant/Long Green	8
65	Pye International 7N 25311	The Climb/Waiting	7
65	Pye International 7N 25322	Annie Fanny/Something's Got A Hold On Me	7
66	Pye International 7N 25366	Little Latin Lupe Lu/Louie Louie	6
66	Pye International 7N 25370	Killer Joe/Little Green Thing	12
67	Pye International 7N 25406	Daytime Shadows/Trouble	8
71	Wand WN 14	Louie Louie/If I Needed Someone	15
64	Pye Intl. NEP 44023	THE KINGSMEN (EP)	30
65	Pye Intl. NEP 44040	MOJO WORKOUT (EP)	30
66	Pye Intl. NEP 44063	FEVER (EP)	25

MINT VALUE £

63	Pye Intl. NPL 28050	THE KINGSMEN IN PERSON (LP, live)	25
64	Pye Intl. NPL 28054	THE KINGSMEN VOLUME II (LP)	25
65	Pye Intl. NPL 28068	THE KINGSMEN ON CAMPUS (LP)	25
66	Pye Intl. NPL 28085	15 GREAT HITS (LP)	25
68	Marble Arch MAL 829	THE KINGSMEN'S GREATEST HITS (LP)	15
71	Wand WNS 6	UP AND AWAY (LP)	12

KING SPARROW

58	Melodisc MEL 1447	Leading Calypsonians/BILLY MOORE: Love Is Everywhere	7
58	Melodisc MEL 1447	Leading Calypsonians/BILLY MOORE: Love Is Everywhere (78)	7
58	Melodisc MEL 1475	Familysize Cokes/Clara Honey Bunch	7
58	Melodisc MEL 1475	Familysize Cokes/Clara Honey Bunch (78)	7
59	Melodisc MEL 1491	Goaty/I Confess	7
59	Melodisc MEL 1491	Goaty/I Confess (78)	10
66	Island WI 285	Beggars Have No Choice (actually by Laurence Dillon & Wailers)/ MARCIA GRIFFITHS: Funny	30
69	Trojan TRLS 8	SPARROW MEETS THE DRAGON (LP)	18
70s	Trojan TRLS 77	SPARROW POWER (LP)	15

(see also Mighty Sparrow, Sparrow)

KING SPORTY

70	Banana BA 321	Inspiration/Choice Of Music	12
70	Banana BA 322	Lover's Version (as Sporty & Wilson)/DUDLEY SIBLEY: Having A Party	12
70	Punch PH 44	For Our Desire/WINSTON WRIGHT: Version	15
71	Banana BA 323	D.J. Special/RICHARD & MAD: Creation Version	12
73	Green Door GD 4063	Yearful Of Sundays/Version	6

KING STITT

(see under 'S')

KINGSTON ALLSTARS

66	Dice CC 25	Happy Hunter/LITTLE NORMA: Ten Commandments Of Woman	18

KINGSTONIANS

67	Rio R 140	Winey Winey/I Don't Care	18
68	Coxsone CS 7066	Mother Miserable/I Make A Woman	25
68	Doctor Bird DB 1120	Put Down Your Fire/Girls Like Dirt	20
68	Doctor Bird DB 1123	Mummy And Daddy/False Witness	20
68	Doctor Bird DB 1126	Fun Galore/Crime Don't Pay	20
68	Trojan TR 627	Mix It Up/I'll Be Around	18
69	Big Shot BI 508	Sufferer/Kiss A Little Finger	12
69	Big Shot BI 526	Nice Nice/I'll Be Around	12
69	Crab CRAB 19	Hold Down/BARRY YORK: Who Will She Be	12
69	Bullet BU 409	I Am Just A Minstrel/Yesterday	6
69	Songbird SB 1011	The Clip/BRUCE ANTHONY: Little Miss Muffett	10
70	Songbird SB 1019	Singer Man/CRYSTALITES: Version	10
70	Songbird SB 1041	Rumble Rumble/CRYSTALITES: Version	10
70	Songbird SB 1045	Out There/CRYSTALITES: Out There Version II	12
70	Trojan TR 7708	I'll Need You Tomorrow/I'm Gonna Make It	5
70	Duke DU 88	You Can't Wine/RUPIE EDWARDS ALLSTARS: Bee Sting	8
72	Duke DU 126	Lion's Den/Version	6
70	Trojan TBL 113	SUFFERER (LP)	30

(see also Jack (Bernard) & Beanstalks, Gregory Isaacs)

KINGS OF LEON

03	Handmedown HMD 28	Molly's Chambers/Holy Roller Novocaine (10", limited issue, numbered p/s)	8
03	Handmedown HMD 31	Wasted Time/Molly's Hangover (10", silver vinyl, numbered p/s)	8
03	Handmedown HMD 20	HOLY ROLLER NOVOCAINE EP: Molly's Chambers/California Waiting/ Holy Roller Novocaine (10", clear red vinyl, numbered p/s, 1000 only)	30
03	Handmedown HMD 21	HOLY ROLLER NOVOCAINE EP (CD, digipak, 1000 only)	12
03	Handmedown HMD 22	WHAT I SAW EP: Red Morning Light/Wicker Chair (10", blue vinyl, numbered p/s)	12
03	Handmedown HMD	YOUTH & YOUNG MANHOOD (2 x 10", p/s with picture inners)	12

KINGSTON JOE

64	Blue Beat BB 253	Time Is On My Friend (actually by Lloyd Barnes)/Wear And Tear (B-side actually by Lascelles Perkins)	20

KINGSTON PETE & BUSTER'S ALL STARS

67	Blue Beat BB 403	Little Boy Blue/I'm A Lover Try Me (actually by Larry Marshall)	45

(see also Larry Marshall)

KINGSTON TRIO

78s

59	Capitol CL 14985	Raspberries, Strawberries/Sally	10
59	Capitol CL 15040	M.T.A./All My Sorrows	15
59	Capitol CL 15073	San Miguel/A Worried Man	20

SINGLES

58	Capitol CL 14918	Scarlet Ribbons/Three Jolly Coachmen	6
58	Capitol CL 14951	Tom Dooley/Ruby Red	6
59	Capitol CL 14985	Raspberries, Strawberries/Sally	8
59	Capitol CL 15002	The Tijuana Jail/Oh Cindy	6
59	Capitol CL 15040	M.T.A./All My Sorrows	6
59	Capitol CL 15073	San Miguel/A Worried Man	6
60	Capitol CL 15113	Green Grasses/Coo Coo U	6
60	Capitol CL 15199	El Matador/Home From The Hill	6
60	Capitol CL 15138	Bad Man's Blunder/The Escape Of Old John Webb	6
60	Capitol CL 15161	Everglades/This Mornin', This Evenin', So Soon	6
63	Capitol CL 15298	Reverend Mr. Black/One More Round	6

EPs

59	Capitol EAP1 1119	M.T.A.	12
59	Capitol EAP1 1136	TOM DOOLEY	10
59	Capitol EAP1 1182	RASPBERRIES STRAWBERRIES	10
60	Capitol EAP1 1258	HERE WE GO AGAIN (also stereo SEP1 1258)	10/15
60	Capitol EAP2 1258	HERE WE GO AGAIN (also stereo SEP2 1258)	10/15
60	Capitol EAP3 1258	HERE WE GO AGAIN (also stereo SEP3 1258)	10/15
60	Capitol EAP1 1322	A WORRIED MAN	10
62	Capitol EAP4 2011	TIME TO THINK	10
63	Capitol EAP1 20460	GREENBACK DOLLAR	10
64	Capitol EAP1 20655	LEMON TREE	10
65	Brunswick OE 9511	THE KINGSTON TRIO	12

LPs

58	Capitol T 996	THE KINGSTON TRIO	15
59	Capitol T 1107	FROM THE HUNGRY I	12
59	Capitol T 1199	AT LARGE	12
60	Capitol (S)T 1258	HERE WE GO AGAIN	12
60	Capitol (S)T 1352	SOLD OUT	12
60	Capitol (S)T 1407	STRING ALONG	12
60	Capitol ST 1183	STEREO CONCERT	12
60	Capitol (S)T 1446	LAST MONTH OF THE YEAR	12
61	Capitol (S)T 1474	MAKE WAY!	12
61	Capitol (S)T 1564	GOIN' PLACES	12
61	Capitol (S)T 1612	ENCORES	12
61	Capitol (S)T 1642	CLOSE UP	12
62	Capitol (S)T 1658	COLLEGE CONCERT	12
62	Capitol (S)T 1747	SOMETHING SPECIAL	12
63	Capitol (S)T 1809	NEW FRONTIER	12
63	Capitol (S)T 1871	NUMBER SIXTEEN	15
63	Capitol (S)T 1935	SUNNY SIDE	12
64	Capitol (S)T 2011	TIME TO THINK	12
64	Capitol (S)T 2081	BACK IN TOWN	12
64	Capitol (S)T 2180	FOLK ERA	12
64	Brunswick LAT 8597	NICK — BOB — JOHN	12
65	Brunswick LAT 8613	STAY AWHILE	12
65	Brunswick LAT/STA 8628	SOMETHIN' ELSE (mono/stereo)	12/15
66	Brunswick LAT 8654	CHILDREN OF THE MORNING	12

(see also John Stewart)

KING TIMOTH

53	Melodisc 1247	Gerrard Street/Nylon (78)	7

KING TRUMAN

89	Acid Jazz JAZID 9T	Like A Gun (Safe Sax Mix)/(Dub Version)/(Radio Edit) (12", p/s)	150

(see also Style Council, Paul Weller)

KING TUBBY

75	Klik KLP 9002	SHALOM DUB (LP, with Aggrovators)	35

KING TUBBY & LEE PERRY

77	Fay Music FMLP 304	KING TUBBY MEETS THE UPSETTER AT THE GRASS ROOTS OF DUB (LP)	22

KINKS

PYE SINGLES

64	Pye 7N 15611	Long Tall Sally/I Took My Baby Home	100
64	Pye 7N 15636	You Still Want Me/You Do Something To Me	150
64	Pye 7N 15673	You Really Got Me/It's All Right	10
64	Pye 7N 15714	All Day And All Of The Night/I Gotta Move	7
65	Pye 7N 15759	Tired Of Waiting For You/Come On Now	7
65	Pye 7N 15813	Everybody's Gonna Be Happy/Who'll Be The Next In Line	10
65	Pye 7N 15854	Set Me Free/I Need You	7
65	Pye 7N 15919	See My Friend/Never Met A Girl Like You Before	8
65	Pye 7N 15981	Till The End Of The Day/Where Have All The Good Times Gone	8
66	Pye 7N 17064	Dedicated Follower Of Fashion/Sittin' On My Sofa	8
66	Pye 7N 17125	Sunny Afternoon/I'm Not Like Everybody Else	8
66	Pye 7N 17222	Dead End Street/Big Black Smoke (some labels list "Deadend")	each 7
67	Pye 7N 17321	Waterloo Sunset/Act Nice And Gentle	7
67	Pye 7N 17400	Autumn Almanac/Mr. Pleasant	8
68	Pye 7N 17468	Wonderboy/Polly	10
68	Pye 7N 17573	Days/She's Got Everything	12
69	Pye 7N 17724	Plastic Man/King Kong	12
69	Pye 7N 17776	Drivin'/Mindless Child Of Motherhood	22
69	Pye 7N 17812	Shangri-La/Last Of The Steam-Powered Trains (unissued, acetates only)	
69	Pye 7N 17812	Shangri-La/This Man He Weeps Tonight	22
69	Pye 7N 17865	Victoria/Mr Churchill Says	12
70	Pye 7N 17961	Lola/Berkeley Mews	7
70	Pye 7N 45016	Apeman/Rats	7
71	Pye PMM 100	You Really Got Me/Set Me Free/Wonder Boy/Long Tall Shorty (maxi-single, p/s)	7
71	Pye 7NX 8001	PERCY (33rpm 4-track maxi-single, p/s)	12
74	Pye 7N 45313	Where Have All The Good Times Gone/Lola (p/s)	20
83	PRT KPD 1	You Really Got Me/Misty Water (picture disc)	6
84	PRT KIS 003	All Day And All Of The Night/I Gotta Move (picture disc)	7

EXPORT SINGLES

65	Pye 7N 15981	Till The End Of The Day/Where Have All The Good Times Gone (export p/s)	130
66	Pye 7N 17100	Well Respected Man/Milk Cow Blues	90
67	Pye 7N 17314	Mr. Pleasant/This Is Where I Belong	60
67	Pye 7N 17405	Autumn Almanac/David Watts	60
71	Pye 7N 8001	God's Children/Moments (some in p/s)	55/30

MINT VALUE £

RCA SINGLES

72	RCA RCA 2211	Supersonic Rocket Ship/You Don't Know My Name	8
72	RCA RCA 2299	Celluloid Heroes/Hot Potatoes	8
73	RCA RCA 2387	Sitting In The Midday Sun/One Of The Survivors	8
73	RCA RCA 2418	Sweet Lady Genevieve/Sitting In My Hotel	8
74	RCA RCA 5015	Mirror Of Love/Cricket	10
74	RCA RCA 5042	Mirror Of Love/He's Evil	10
74	RCA RCA 2478	Holiday Romance/Shepherds Of The Nation	8
75	RCA RCA 2546	Ducks On The Wall/Rush Hour Blues	8
75	RCA RCA 2567	You Can't Stop The Music/Have Another Drink	8
76	RCA RCM 1	No More Looking Back/Jack The Idiot Dunce/The Hard Way (p/s)	10

ARISTA SINGLES

77	Arista ARIST 153	Father Christmas/Prince Of The Punks (p/s)	8
78	Arista ARIST 189	A Rock'n'Roll Fantasy/Artificial Light	8
78	Arista ARIST 210	Black Messiah/Misfits (p/s)	7
79	Arista ARIST 300	Moving Pictures/In A Space	7
80	Arista ARIST 404	Lola (live)/Celluloid Heroes (live) (export only)	10
81	Arista ARIST 415	Better Things/Massive Reductions (p/s)	9
81	Arista ARIST 415/KINKS 1	Better Things/Massive Reductions//Lola (live)/David Watts (live) (double pack, gatefold p/s)	7
81	Arista ARIPD 426	Predictable/Back To Front (picture disc)	5
83	Arista ARIST 524	Don't Forget To Dance/Bernadette (p/s)	7
83	Arista ARIST 524	Don't Forget To Dance/Bernadette//Predictable/Back To Front (shrinkwrapped with free picture disc)	12

OTHER SINGLES

84	Music Week	How Are You (freebie with *Music Week* magazine)	7
87	London LONX 132	Lost And Found/Killing Time (p/s, shrinkwrapped with bonus 7" "The Official Ray Davies Interview"/"Extracts From The LP 'Think Visual' ")	10
88	London LON 165	The Road (7" Edit)/Art Lover (p/s)	6
89	London LONCD 239	Down All The Days (Til 1992)/You Really Got Me (live)/Entertainment (CD)	12
90	London LONCD 250	How Do I Get Close/War Is Over (CD, card sleeve)	12
91	Columbia COL 657593-2	Did Ya/Gotta Move (live)/New World/Days (1991) (CD)	12
94	Konk Grapevine KNKD 2	Waterloo Sunset 94/You Really Got Me (live)/Elevator Man/On The Outside (CD)	7

EPs

64	Pye NEP 24200	KINKSIZE SESSION	35
64	Pye NEP 24203	KINKSIZE HITS	20
64	Pye NEP 5039	THE KINKS (unreleased in U.K., Swedish only)	
65	Pye NEP 24221	KWYET KINKS	35
66	Pye NEP 24258	DEDICATED KINKS	100
68	Pye NEP 24296	THE KINKS	250
75	Pye AMEP 1001	THE KINKS ('Yesteryear' export issue, red or blue vinyl)	20

PYE LPs

64	Pye NPL 18096	THE KINKS (mono)	80
64	Pye NSPL 83021	THE KINKS (stereo, export only)	200
60s	Pye NSPL 15096	THE KINKS (stereo, export only, reissue)	250
65	Pye NPL 18112	KINDA KINKS	80
65	Pye NPL 18131	THE KINK KONTROVERSY	70
65	Pye NSPL 18131	THE KINK KONTROVERSY (reprocessed stereo with stickered catalogue number, export only)	250
66	Pye NPL 18149	FACE TO FACE (mono)	80
66	Pye NSPL 18149	FACE TO FACE (stereo, stickered sleeve)	150
66	Pye ZCP 18149	FACE TO FACE (cassette, original issue)	12
67	Golden Guinea GGL 0357	THE KINKS (reissue, also stereo GSGL 10357)	12/15
67	Pye N(S)PL 18191	LIVE AT KELVIN HALL (mono/stereo)	80/125

(The above Pye LPs were originally issued with laminated flipback sleeves, pink labels & light blue labels)

67	Pye N(S)PL 18193	SOMETHING ELSE BY THE KINKS (mono/stereo)	180/100
68	Pye N(S)PL 18233	THE KINKS ARE THE VILLAGE GREEN PRESERVATION SOCIETY (unissued, 12-track version, 2 test pressings only)	600+
68	Pye N(S)PL 18233	THE KINKS ARE THE VILLAGE GREEN PRESERVATION SOCIETY (15-track version, mono/stereo)	125/80
69	Pye N(S)PL 18317	ARTHUR (mono/stereo)	60/35
70	Pye NPL 18326	THE KINKS (2-LP, gatefold sleeve)	20
70	Pye NSPL 18359	THE KINKS PT 1 — LOLA VS POWERMAN & THE MONEY-GO-ROUND (gatefold sleeve)	20
71	Pye NSPL 18365	SOUNDTRACK FROM THE FILM 'PERCY' (soundtrack)	30
73	Pye 11PP 100	ALL THE GOOD TIMES (4-LP, box set)	50
83	PRT KINK 1	GREATEST HITS (with bonus 10" EP of unreleased material)	30

OTHER LPs

71	RCA SF 8243	MUSWELL HILLBILLIES (gatefold sleeve)	20
72	RCA DPS 2035	EVERYBODY'S IN SHOWBIZ, EVERYBODY'S A STAR (2-LP, gatefold sleeve)	20
73	RCA SF 8392	PRESERVATION ACT 1	20
74	RCA LPL2 5040	PRESERVATION ACT 2 (2-LP, gatefold sleeve)	25
75	RCA SF 8411	SOAP OPERA	15
75	RCA RS 1028	SCHOOLBOYS IN DISGRACE	15
76	RCA RS 1059	CELLULOID HEROES	15
93	Sony 472489-1	PHOBIA (omits 2 tracks from CD)	50
94	Konk Grapevine KNK LP 1	TO THE BONE	15

(see also Dave Davies, Ray Davies, Maple Oak, Leapy Lee, Phoenix)

TONY KINSEY (QUARTET)

55	Decca F 10548	She's Funny That Way/Fascinatin' Rhythm	20
55	Decca F 10606	Close Your Eyes/Pierrot	10
55	Decca F 10648	Hey! There/Ballet	25
56	Decca F 10708	Stompin' At The Savoy/China Boy (with Dill Jones)	6
56	Decca F 10709	Moonglow/One O'Clock Jump	6
56	Decca FJ 10725	Starboard Bow/Body And Soul	6

56 Decca FJ 10760 Lullaby Of The Leaves/Isolation . . . 12
56 Decca FJ 10773 In A Ditch/A Smooth One . . . 5
57 Decca FJ 10851 Mean To Me/Supper Party . . . 12
57 Decca F 10952 The Midgets/Blue Eyes . . . 5
62 Ember JBS 707 Girl In Blue/Weber The Great . . . 20
56 Decca DFE 6282 PRESENTING THE TONY KINSEY QUARTET NO. 1 (EP) . . . 40
56 Decca DFE 6285 PRESENTING THE TONY KINSEY QUARTET NO. 2 (EP) . . . 40
58 Decca DFE 6461 MY FAIR LADY (EP) . . . 15
59 Parlophone SGE 2004 RED BIRD — JAZZ AND POETRY (EP, mono [GEP 8765]/stereo, with Christopher Logue) . . . each 25
59 Parlophone SGE 2008 FOURSOME (EP, stereo) . . . 10
57 Decca LK 4186 INTRODUCING THE QUINTET (LP) . . . 100
57 Decca LK 4207 JAZZ AT THE FLAMINGO (LP) . . . 75
58 Decca LK 4274 TIME GENTLEMEN PLEASE (LP) . . . 90
61 Ember EMB 3337 AN EVENING WITH ... (LP) . . . 50
63 Decca LK 4534 HOW TO SUCCEED (LP, with Gordon Beck) . . . 50

TONY KINSEY TRIO & JOE HARRIOTT

54 Esquire EP 36 TONY KINSEY TRIO & JOE HARRIOTT (EP) . . . 35
54 Esquire EP 52 TONY KINSEY TRIO & JOE HARRIOTT (EP) . . . 35
54 Esquire EP 82 TONY KINSEY TRIO & JOE HARRIOTT (EP) . . . 35
(see also Joe Harriott)

KINSMEN

68 Decca F 22724 Glasshouse Green, Splinter Red/It's Started To Rain Again . . . 30
68 Decca F 22777 It's Good To See You/Always The Loser . . . 10
(see also Four Kinsmen)

KIPPER FAMILY

84 Dambuster DAM 005 SINCE TIME IMMORAL (LP) . . . 18

KIPPINGTON LODGE

67 Parlophone R 5645 Shy Boy/Lady On A Bicycle . . . 35
68 Parlophone R 5677 Rumours/And She Cried . . . 35
68 Parlophone R 5717 Tell Me A Story/Understand A Woman . . . 40
68 Parlophone R 5750 Tomorrow Today/Turn Out The Light . . . 35
69 Parlophone R 5776 In My Life/I Can See Her Face . . . 50
78 EMI NUT 2894 KIPPINGTON LODGE (EP) . . . 12
(see also Brinsley Schwarz, Nick Lowe)

KIRBY

76 Anchor ANC 1031 Love Letters/Flasher . . . 12
78 Hot Wax WAX 1/ANCHO 1 Bottom Line/That's Some Dream . . . 10
78 Hot Wax HW 2 COMPOSITION (LP) . . . 75
(see also Curved Air, Stretch)

KATHY KIRBY

60 Pye 7N 15313 Love Can Be/Crush Me . . . 22
61 Pye 7N 15342 Danny/Now You're Crying . . . 20
62 Decca F 11506 Big Man/Slowly . . . 8
63 Decca F 11682 Dance On/Playboy . . . 6
63 Decca F 11759 Secret Love/You Have To Want To Touch Him . . . 6
64 Decca F 11832 Let Me Go, Lover!/The Sweetest Sounds . . . 6
64 Decca F 11892 You're The One/Love Me Baby . . . 6
64 Decca F 11992 Don't Walk Away/No Regrets . . . 6
65 Decca F 12087 I Belong/I'll Try Not To Cry . . . 6
65 Decca F 12177 The Way Of Love/Oh Darling, How I Miss You . . . 7
65 Decca F 12280 Where In The World?/That Wonderful Feeling Of Love . . . 7
66 Decca F 12338 Spanish Flea/Till The End Of Time . . . 7
66 Decca F 12432 The Adam Adamant Theme/Will I Never Learn? . . . 35
67 Columbia DB 8139 No One's Gonna Hurt You Anymore/My Yiddishe Momme . . . 8
67 Columbia DB 8192 In All The World/Time . . . 8
67 Columbia DB 8302 Turn Around/Golden Days . . . 7
68 Columbia DB 8400 I Almost Called Your Name/Let The Music Start . . . 10
68 Columbia DB 8521 Come Back Here With My Heart/Antonio . . . 10
69 Columbia DB 8559 I'll Catch The Sun/Please Help Me I'm Falling . . . 10
69 Columbia DB 8634 Is That All There Is?/Knowing When To Leave . . . 10
70 Columbia DB 8682 Wheel Of Fortune/Lucky . . . 8
70 Columbia DB 8721 My Way/Little Green Apples . . . 8
71 Columbia DB 8795 So Here I Go/Yes — I've Got (A-side titled "Here I Go Again" on demos) . . . 10
71 Decca F 13228 Bill/Can't Help Lovin' Dat Man . . . 10
72 Columbia DB 8910 Do You Really Have A Heart/Dream On, Dreamer . . . 12
73 Columbia DB 8965 Little Song For You/Here, There And Everywhere . . . 12
73 Orange OAS 216 Singer With The Band/Hello Morning . . . 75
76 President PT 455 My Prayer/Nobody Loves Me Like You Do . . . 6
63 Decca DFE 8547 KATHY KIRBY (EP) . . . 15
65 Decca DFE 8596 KATHY KIRBY VOL. 2 (EP) . . . 15
65 Decca DFE 8611 A SONG FOR EUROPE (EP) . . . 15
65 Decca LK 4575 16 HITS FROM STARS AND GARTERS (LP) . . . 22
67 Decca LK 4746 MAKE SOMEONE HAPPY (LP) . . . 22
68 Ace Of Clubs ACL 1235 THE BEST OF KATHY KIRBY (LP) . . . 15
68 Columbia S(C)X 6259 MY THANKS TO YOU (LP) . . . 100
70 Decca PA/SPA 84 THE WORLD OF KATHY KIRBY (LP) . . . 12

LARRY KIRBY & ENCORES

59 Top Rank JAR 143 My Baby Don't Love Me/My Rose Of Kentucky . . . 20

MINT VALUE £

PAT KIRBY

56 Brunswick 05560 Happiness Is A Thing Called Joe/Don't Tell Me Not To . . . 10
56 Brunswick 05575 What A Heavenly Night For Love/Greensleeves . . . 6
57 Brunswick 05697 Tammy/Don't Keep Silent. . . . 5
58 Brunswick 05731 Sayonara/Please Be Gentle With Me . . . 5

BASIL KIRCHIN (BAND)

57 Parlophone R 4344 White Silver Sands/Waiting For The Robert E. Lee. . . . 5
58 Parlophone R 4511 Cha Cha Bells/Oh Dear What Can The Cha Cha Be (with Rock-A-Cha Cha Band) . 5
58 Parlophone R 4511 Cha Cha Bells/Oh Dear What Can The Cha Cha Be (with Rock-A-Cha Cha Band) (78) . . . 7
59 Parlophone R 4527 Rock-A-Conga/Skin Tight (as Basil Kirchin Band) . . . 7
71 Columbia SCX 6463 A WORLD WITHIN WORLDS (LP) . . . 200
(see also Shani Wallis)

(IVOR & BASIL) KIRCHIN BAND

54 Parlophone MSP 6144 Mambo Macoco/Tangerine (as Kirchin Band) . . . 8
55 Decca F 10434 Minor Mambo/Mother Goose Jumps (as Kirchin Band) . . . 12
56 Parlophone R 4222 The Roller/St. Louis Blues (as Ivor & Basil Kirchin) . . . 6
56 Parlophone R 4237 Rockin' & Rollin' Thru The Darktown Strutters' Ball/Ambush . . . 20
57 Parlophone R 4266 "Rock Around The World Medley" (with Shani Wallis) . . . 18
57 Parlophone R 4284 Calypso!!/Jungle Fire Dance (as Ivor & Basil Kirchin with Wendy Windows) . . . 5
57 Parlophone R 4335 Teenage World/So Rare (as Kirchin Band & Bandits) . . . 12
55 Parlophone GEP 8531 KIRCHIN BANDBOX (EP) . . . 12
56 Parlophone GEP 8569 THE IVOR AND BASIL KIRCHIN BAND (EP) . . . 30
(see also Basil Kirchin, London Studio Group)

DEE KIRK

62 Salvo SLO 1809 I'll Cry/My Used To Be . . . 25

KEVIN KIRK

62 Columbia DB 4909 Sweet/Don't Waste Your Tears On Him . . . 6
62 Columbia DB 4863 Teenage Heartache/Midnight . . . 6

RICHARD H. KIRK

81 Industrial IRC 34 DISPOSABLE HALF TRUTHS (cassette) . . . 8
(see also Cabaret Voltaire, Peter Hope & Richard H. Kirk)

(RAHSAAN) ROLAND KIRK

64 Mercury 10015 MCE THE KIRK QUARTET MEETS THE BENNY GOLSON ORCHESTRA (EP) . . . 8
65 Mercury 10016 MCE ROLAND SPEAKS (EP, with Benny Golson Orchestra) . . . 8
62 Esquire 32-164 KIRK'S WORK (LP, with Jack McDuff) . . . 18
63 Mercury MMC 14126 WE FREE KINGS (LP) . . . 18
64 Mercury MCL 20002 THE KIRK QUARTET MEETS THE BENNY GOLSON ORCHESTRA (LP) . . . 18
64 Mercury MCL 20021 KIRK IN COPENHAGEN (LP) . . . 18
65 Mercury MCL 20037 WE FREE KINGS (LP, reissue) . . . 12
65 Mercury MCL 20045 DOMINO (LP) . . . 18
65 Fontana FJL 114 HIP! (LP) . . . 18
66 Mercury (S)LML 4005 I TALK WITH THE SPIRITS (LP) . . . 15
66 Mercury (S)LML 4015 RIP, RIG AND PANIC (LP) . . . 15
67 Mercury (S)LML 4019 SLIGHTLY LATIN (LP) . . . 15
71 Atlantic 2400 110 RAHSAAN, RAHSAAN (LP, as Rahsaan Roland Kirk) . . . 12
72 Atlantic K 40358 BLACKNUSS (LP) . . . 12
73 Atlantic K 40457 MEETING OF THE TIMES (LP, with Al Hibbler) . . . 12

KIRKBYS

66 RCA RCA 1542 It's A Crime/I've Never Been So Much In Love . . . 125
(see also 23rd Turnoff, Jimmy Campbell, Rockin' Horse, Merseybeats)

KEN KIRKHAM

56 Columbia SCM 5244 It's Almost Tomorrow/No Not Much . . . 8
58 Columbia DB 4116 Now And For Always/Cathy . . . 7

JOHN KIRKPATRICK (& SUE HARRIS)

72 Trailer LER 2033 JUMP AT THE SUN (LP, with Sue Harris) . . . 15
76 Topic 12TS 295 AMONG THE MANY ATTRACTIONS AT THE SHOW WILL BE A REALLY HIGH-CLASS BAND (LP, with Sue Harris) . . . 12
76 Free Reed FRR 010 PLAIN CAPERS (LP, with booklet) . . . 12
77 Topic 12TS 355 SHREDS AND PATCHES (LP, with Sue Harris) . . . 15
78 Free Reed FRR 030 GOING SPARE (LP) . . . 12
84 Squeezer SXZ 123 THREE IN A ROW: THE ENGLISH MELODEON (LP) . . . 12
(see also Jon Raven)

JULIAN KIRSCH

(see under 'J')

DANNY KIRWAN

75 DJM DJS 396 Ram Jam City/Hot Summer's Day . . . 5
76 DJM DJS 666 Misty River/Rolling Hills . . . 5
76 DJM DJS 10709 Angel's Delight . . . 5
77 DJM DJS 10783 Hot Summer's Day/Love Can Always Bring You Happiness . . . 5
79 DJM DJS 10896 Only You/Caroline . . . 5
75 DJM DJLPS 454 SECOND CHAPTER (LP) . . . 12
(see also Fleetwood Mac, Tramp)

KISS

SINGLES

75 Casablanca CBX 503 Nothin' To Lose/Love Theme From Kiss . . . 25
75 Casablanca CBX 510 Rock And Roll All Nite/Anything For My Baby . . . 20
76 Casablanca CBX 516 Shout It Out Loud/Sweet Pain . . . 15
76 Casablanca CBX 519 Beth/God Of Thunder . . . 18

Year	Label / Cat. No.	Title	MINT VALUE £
77	Casablanca CAN 102	Hard Luck Woman/Calling Dr Love/Beth (initially in p/s)	35/10
77	Casablanca CAN 110	Then She Kissed Me/Hooligan/Flaming Youth	15
77	Casablanca CANL 110	Then She Kissed Me/Hooligan/Flaming Youth (12", company sleeve, some stickered)	15/12
78	Casablanca CAN 117	Rocket Ride/Love Gun (live)	8
78	Casablanca CANL 117	Rocket Ride/Detroit Rock City (live)/Love Gun (live) (12", company sleeve)	12
78	Casablanca CAN 126	Rock And Roll All Nite/C'Mon And Love Me (initially in p/s)	25/8
79	Casablanca CAN 152	I Was Made For Lovin' You/Hard Times	8
79	Casablanca CANL 152	I Was Made For Lovin' You (extended)/Charisma (12", p/s)	18
79	Casablanca CAN 163	Sure Know Something/Dirty Livin' (no p/s)	6
80	Casablanca NB 1001	2000 Man/I Was Made For Lovin' You/Sure Know Something (p/s)	15
80	Casablanca NBL 1001	2000 Man/I Was Made For Lovin' You/Sure Know Something (12", co. sleeve)	12
80	Casablanca MER 19	Talk To Me/She's So European (p/s)	10
80	Casablanca KISS 1	What Makes The World Go 'Round/Naked City (p/s)	10
81	Casablanca KISS 2	A World Without Heroes/Mr Blackwell (p/s)	7
81	Casablanca KISSP 002	A World Without Heroes/Mr Blackwell (picture disc)	12
82	Casablanca KISS 3	Killer/I Love It Loud (pull-out tongue p/s)	12
82	Casablanca KISS 312	Killer/I Love It Loud/I Was Made For Lovin' You (12", p/s)	15
82	Casablanca KISS 4	Creatures Of The Night/Rock And Roll All Nite (live) (p/s, pic or silver label)	10/8
82	Casablanca KISS 412	Creatures Of The Night/War Machine/Rock And Roll All Nite (live) (12", p/s)	15
82	Casablanca KISSD 4	Creatures Of The Night/Rock And Roll All Nite (live) (12", double groove, autographs engraved on 1 side)	20
83	Vertigo KISS 5	Lick It Up/Not For The Innocent (p/s)	5
83	Vertigo KISSP 5	Lick It Up/Not For The Innocent (poster p/s)	12
83	Vertigo KPIC 5	Lick It Up/Not For The Innocent (tank-shaped picture disc)	25
83	Vertigo KISS 512	Lick It Up/Not For The Innocent/I Still Love You (12", p/s)	8
84	Vertigo VER 12	Heaven's On Fire/Lonely Is The Hunter (p/s)	5
84	Vertigo VERX 12	Heaven's On Fire/Lonely Is The Hunter/All Hell's Breakin' Loose (12", p/s with poster)	10/8
85	Vertigo KISS 6	Tears Are Falling/Heaven's On Fire (live) (p/s)	5
87	Vertigo KISSP 7	Crazy Crazy Nights/No No No (poster p/s)	7
87	Vertigo KISSP 712	Crazy Crazy Nights/No No No/Heaven's On Fire/Tears Are Falling (12", picture disc)	8
87	Vertigo KISS 8	Reason To Live/Thief In The Night (p/s, with patch)	7
87	Vertigo KISSP 812	Reason To Live/Thief In The Night/Who Wants To Be Lonely/ Secretly Cruel (12", picture disc)	8
87	Vertigo KISCD 8	Reason To Live/Thief In The Night/Tears Are Falling/Crazy Crazy Nights (CD, card sleeve)	8
87	Vertigo KISSP 9	Turn On The Night/Hell Or High Water (poster p/s)	5
87	Vertigo KISSP 912	Turn On The Night/Hell Or High Water/King Of The Mountain/ Any Way You Slice It (12", picture disc)	8
87	Vertigo KISCD 9	Turn On The Night/Hell Or High Water/Heaven's On Fire/I Love It Loud (CD, card sleeve)	8
88	Vertigo 080 232-2	Crazy Crazy Nights/No, No, No/When Your Walls Come Down/ Thief In The Night (CD Video)	15
88	Mercury 080 100-1	EXPOSED (12" CD Video)	25
89	Mercury 080 044-2	Lick It Up/Dance All Over Your Face/Gimme More/Fits Like A Glove (CD Video)	15
89	Vertigo 080 059-2	Tears Are Falling/Anyway You Slice It/Who Want To Be Lonely/Secretly Cruel (CD Video)	15
89	Vertigo KISP 1010	Hide Your Heart/Lick It Up/Heaven's On Fire (10", picture disc)	8
89	Vertigo KISCD 10	Hide Your Heart/Betrayed/Boomerang (CD)	8
90	Vertigo KISXG 11	Forever (Remix)/The Street Giveth And The Street Taketh Away/ Deuce (Demo)/Strutter (Demo) (12", gatefold p/s)	8
90	Vertigo KISCD 11	Forever (Remix)/Creatures Of The Night/Lick It Up/Heaven's On Fire (CD)	8
92	Mercury KISS 1212	Unholy/Partners In Crime/Deuce (Demo)/Strutter (Demo) (12", picture sleeve, white vinyl)	8
92	Mercury KISCD 12	Unholy/God Gave Rock'N'Roll II You Too/Deuce (Demo)/Strutter (Demo) (CD, digipak, Part 1 of 2-part pack [Part 2 unreleased])	8
90s	East West SAM 886	God Gave Rock'n'Roll To You (LP Version)/(Edit Version) (12", no p/s, promo only)	12

LPs

Year	Label / Cat. No.	Title	MINT VALUE £
75	Casablanca CBC 4003	KISS (blue 'Bogart' label)	20
75	Casablanca CBC 4004	DRESSED TO KILL (blue 'Bogart' label, embossed sleeve)	20
76	Casablanca CBC 4008	DESTROYER (blue 'Bogart' label with inner sleeve)	20
76	Casablanca CBC 4011/2	ALIVE! (2-LP, blue 'Bogart' label, gatefold sleeve with insert, sleeve also lists CBSP 401)	20
77	Casablanca CALH 2001	ROCK AND ROLL OVER ('lovegun' label, red vinyl)	40
77	Casablanca CAL 2006	KISS (reissue, 'lovegun' label, red vinyl)	40
77	Casablanca CAL 2007	HOTTER THAN HELL ('lovegun' label, red vinyl)	40
77	Casablanca CAL 2008	DRESSED TO KILL (reissue, 'lovegun' label, red vinyl)	40
77	Casablanca CAL 2009	DESTROYER (reissue, different sleeve, 'lovegun' label, red vinyl)	40
77	Casablanca CALD 5001	ALIVE! (2-LP, reissue, 'lovegun' label, red vinyl)	50
77	Casablanca CALH 2017	LOVE GUN ('lovegun' label, with picture inner sleeve)	12
77	Casablanca CALH 2017	LOVE GUN ('lovegun' label, red vinyl with picture inner sleeve)	40
77	Casablanca CALD 5004	KISS ALIVE II (2-LP, 'lovegun' label, with colour booklet & transfer sheet)	25
77	Casablanca CALD 5004	KISS ALIVE II (2-LP, 'lovegun' label, red vinyl with colour booklet)	50
78	Casablanca CALD 5005	DOUBLE PLATINUM (2-LP, 'lovegun' label, silver foil embossed sleeve & insert; sleeve & insert pressed in U.S. with U.K. cat. no. sticker)	18
79	Casablanca CALH 2051	DYNASTY ('lovegun' label, black vinyl, colour inner sleeve & poster)	12
80	Mercury 6302 032	UNMASKED (with poster)	12
81	Casablanca 6302 163	(MUSIC FROM) THE ELDER (single sleeve)	12
82	Casa. CANL 4/6302 219	CREATURES OF THE NIGHT ('make-up' sleeve)	12
87	Vertigo 832 903-1	CRAZY NIGHTS (picture disc in stickered PVC wallet)	12

(see also Gene Simmons, Ace Frehley, Peter Criss, Paul Stanley)

MINT VALUE £

KISSING SPELL
93 Essex DELUJO 1001LP — LOS PAJAROS (LP, reissue of Chilean LP, 500 only) 12

KISSING THE PINK
83 Magnet KTP 36/KTP 0 — Last Film/Shine//Water In My Eye (Instrumental)/Garden Parties (double pack) 5

KATIE KISSOON
69 Columbia DB 8525 — Don't Let It Rain/Will I Never See The Sun 6
(see also Peanut, Marionettes, Rag Dolls [U.K.])

MAC KISSOON
60s Boulevard (no cat. no.) — Wear It On Your Face/In A Dream 10
69 Youngblood YB 1005 — Wear It On Your Face/In A Dream (reissue) 6
(see also Marionettes, Rag Dolls [U.K.])

KITCHENS OF DISTINCTION
87 Gold Rush GRR 3 — Escape/The Last Gasp Death Shuffle (p/s) 6

KIT KATS
66 London HLW 10075 — Won't Find Better Than Me/That's The Way 12
(see also New Hope)

EARTHA KITT
53 HMV JO 387 — C'est Si Bon (with Henri René)/African Lullaby (78, export issue) 7
53 HMV JO 404 — C'est Si Bon/Oh! Those Turks (78, export issue) 7
54 HMV 7M 191 — Under The Bridges Of Paris/Lovin' Spree 18
54 HMV 7M 198 — Somebody Bad Stole De Wedding Bell/Sandy's Tune 15
54 HMV 7M 234 — Santa Baby/Let's Do It (Let's Fall In Love) 15
54 HMV 7M 246 — Easy Does It/Mink Shmink 15
55 HMV 7M 282 — Monotonous/African Lullaby 15
55 HMV 7M 288 — C'est Si Bon (with Henri René)/Senor 15
56 HMV 7M 422 — Honolulu Rock-A-Roll-A/Je Cherche Un Homme (I Want A Man) 25
56 MGM SP 1153 — Please Do It/Lady Loves 10
56 MGM SP 1178 — Diamonds Are A Girl's Best Friend/Good Little Girls 12
57 HMV POP 309 — Just An Old-Fashioned Girl/If I Can't Take It With Me When I Go (gold or silver label) 15/10
57 HMV POP 346 — There Is No Cure For L'Amour/Hey Jacque 10
58 RCA RCA 1037 — Take My Love/Proceed With Caution 6
58 RCA RCA 1087 — Just An Old-Fashioned Girl/If I Can't Take It With Me When I Go (reissue) 7
58 RCA RCA 1093 — I Want To Be Evil/Oh John! 8
59 London HLR 8969 — Love Is A Gamble/Sholem 10
59 London HLR 8969 — Love Is A Gamble/Sholem (78) 12
60 RCA RCA 1180 — There's No Cure For L'Amour/Let's Do It 6
63 London HL 7119 — Shango/In The Evening (When The Sun Goes Down) (export issue) 18
70 Spark SRL 1039 — Hurdy Gurdy Man/Catch The Wind 6
71 CBS 7626 — A Knight For My Nights/Summer Storm 6
55 HMV 7EG 8079 — EARTHA KITT (EP) 10
57 HMV 7EG 8258 — EARTHA KITT (EP) 10
58 RCA SRC 7009 — SAINT LOUIS BLUES (EP, stereo) 15
58 RCA SRC 7015 — THAT BLUE EARTHA (EP, stereo) 15
63 MGM MGM-EP 772 — BAD BUT BEAUTIFUL NO. 1 (EP) 10
63 MGM MGM-EP 774 — BAD BUT BEAUTIFUL NO. 2 (EP) 10
63 MGM MGM-EP 777 — BAD BUT BEAUTIFUL NO. 3 (EP) 10
55 HMV DLP 1067 — THAT BAD EARTHA (10" LP) 20
55 HMV DLP 1087 — DOWN TO EARTHA (10" LP) 20
58 RCA RD 27067 — THAT BAD EARTHA (LP, reissue) 12
58 RCA RD 27076 — ST. LOUIS BLUES (LP) 20
58 RCA RD 27084 — DOWN TO EARTHA (LP, reissue) 12
59 RCA RD 27099 — THURSDAY'S CHILD (LP, reissue) 12
60 London HA-R 2207 — THE FABULOUS EARTHA KITT (LP, also stereo SAH-R 6058) 18/22
60 London HA-R 2296 — EARTHA KITT REVISITED (LP, also stereo SAH-R 6107) 18/22
62 MGM MGM-C 878/CS 6050 — BAD BUT BEAUTIFUL (LP, mono/stereo) 18/22

KITTENS
64 Decca F 12036 — Round About Way/Don't Stop Now 10

KLAN
67 Palette PG 9052 — Fifi The Fly/Already Mine 8

SUSIE KLEE
66 Polydor BM 56082 — Mr Zero/Punch And Judy Girl 10

KLEEER
84 Atlantic 7801451 — INTIMATE CONNECTION (LP) 12

KLEENEX
79 Rough Trade/Sunrise RT 9 — Ain't You/Hedi's Head (poster p/s) 5
79 Rough Trade RT 014 — You/U (p/s) 5

ALAN KLEIN
62 Oriole CB 1719 — Striped Purple Shirt/You Gave Me The Blues 30
62 Oriole CB 1737 — Three Coins In The Sewer/Danger Ahead 30
65 Parlophone R 5292 — It Ain't Worth The Lonely Road Back/I've Cried So Many Tears 6
65 Parlophone R 5370 — Age Of Corruption/I'm Counting On You 6
69 Page One POF 119 — Honey Pie/You Turned A Nightmare Into A Dream 6
70 Decca F 13033 — Dinner's In The Ice Box/Here I Am, There You Are 6
64 Decca LK 4621 — WELL, AT LEAST IT'S BRITISH (LP) 18
(see also New Vaudeville Band)

MINT VALUE £

HARRY KLEIN QUARTET

56 Jazz Today JTE 105 BRASH BARITONE (EP) . . . 25
56 Nixa NJE 1009 NEW SOUND (EP) . . . 25
56 Nixa NJE 1022 HARRY KLEIN QUARTET (EP) . . . 25
57 Columbia SEG 7647 BARITONE SAX (EP) . . . 15
(see also Jazz Five)

KLF

88 KLF Comms. KLF 002 Burn The Beat (II)/The Porpoise Song (p/s) . . . 10
88 KLF Comms. KLF 002T Burn The Bastards (LP Edit)/Burn The Beat (II) (12", p/s) . . . 15
89 KLF Comms. KLF 004T What Time Is Love? (Trance Mix)/What Time Is Love? (Mix 2) (12", 'Pure Trance 1', original issue with black/green p/s) . . . 20
89 KLF Comms. KLF 004R What Time Is Love? ('89 Primal Remix)/What Time Is Love? (Techno Slam)/ What Time Is Love? (Trance Mix 1) (12", p/s) . . . 35
89 KLF Comms. KLF 004M What Time Is Love? (Monster Attack Mix) (12", unissued, 1-sided acetate only, 3 pressed!) . . . 500
90 KLF Comms. KLF 004Y What Time Is Love? (Moody Boys Vs The KLF)/What Time Is Love? (Echo And The Bunnymen Mix)/What Time Is Love? (Virtual Reality Mix) (12", p/s) . . . 10
90 KLF Comms. KLF 004P What Time Is Love? (Live At Trancentral)/Wandafull Mix (12", w/l, 1,500 only) . . . 10
90 KLF Comms. KLF 004X What Time Is Love? (Live At Trancentral)/Techno Gate Mix (12", p/s, mispressing, B-side actually plays "Wandafull Mix", matrix no.: KLF 004X-B) . . . 40
90 KLF Comms. KLF 004CD What Time Is Love? (Radio)/(Live At Trancentral)/(Trance Mix 1) (CD, mispressing playing part of Knebworth '90 live CD) . . . 15
90 KLF Comms. KLF 005R 3AM Eternal 'Single Edit'/Blue Danube Orbital Mix/Moody Boys Version/ 3PM Electro (12", original issue with stickered p/s) . . . 20
91 KLF Comms. KLF 005S 3AM Eternal (Live At The S.S.L.) (Radio Freedom Edit) (white label, 500 only) . . . 12
91 KLF Comms. KLF 005X 3AM Eternal (mixes) (12", white label, promo only) . . . 10
91 KLF Comms. KLF 005Y 3AM Eternal (Moody Boys mixes) (12", white label, promo only) . . . 15
92 KLF Comms. KLF 5 TOTP 3AM Eternal (Xmas Top Of The Pops Version) (1-sided, w/Extreme Noise Terror, mail-order only, some with insert & mailing envelope; beware of bootlegs!) . . 50/10
89 KLF Comms. KLF 008R Last Train To Trancentral (Remixes 1 & 2) (12", p/s, 'Pure Trance 5', 2,000 pressed, some warped) . . . 50/8
91 KLF Comms. KLF 008X Last Train To Trancentral (Live From The Lost Continent) (12", white label) . . . 8
91 KLF Comms. KLF 008CD Last Train To Trancentral (Live From The Lost Continent)/(The Iron Horse)/ (The 1989 Pure Trance Original) (CD) . . . 8
89 KLF PROMO 2 Kylie Said To Jason (Full Length)/Kylie Said Trance (12", promo & press sheet) . 15
89 KLF Comms. KLF 010(S) Kylie Said To Jason (Edit)/Kylie Said Trance (p/s) . . . 10
89 KLF Comms. KLF 010P Kylie Said To Jason (Full Length)/Kylie Said Trance (12", stickered p/s & pstr) . . 25
89 KLF Comms. KLF 010R Kylie Said To Jason (Trance Kylie Express)/Kylie In A Trance/ Kylie Said Harder (12" remix, p/s, export issue) . . . 20
89 KLF Comms. KLF 010RR Kylie In A Trance/Kylie Said Mu (12", p/s, export edition, 500 only, some shrinkwrapped with KLF 010R) . . . 100/50
89 KLF Comms. KLF 010CD Kylie Said To Jason (Full Length)/Madrugada Eterna/Kylie Said Trance (CD) . . . 50
89 KLF Comms. KLF 006T Love Trance/What Time Is Love (12", p/s, 3 copies known) . . . 500
90 KLF Comms. KLF 011T Madrugada Eterna (Club Mix)/Madrugada Eterna (Edit)/Madrugada Eterna (Ambient House Mix) (12", 20 only, beware of counterfeits!) . . . 150
90 KLF Comms. ETERNA 1 Madrugada Eterna (Club Mix) (12", 1-sided, white label, 6 pressed, beware of counterfeits!) . . . 120/10
91 KLF Comms. CHOC ICE 1 Justified And Ancient (All Bound For Mu Mu Land)/Justified And Ancient (Make Mine A '99') (12", white label promo) . . . 15
91 KLF Comms. CHOC ICE 2 Justified And Ancient (Stand By The J.A.M.s)/Justified And Ancient (Let Them Eat Ice Cream) (12", white label promo) . . . 12
91 KLF Comms. CHOC ICE 3 Justified And Ancient (Anti-Acapella Version) (12", 1-sided, w/l, 200 only) . . . 30
91 KLF Comms. LP PROMO 1 Make It Rain/No More Tears (12", promo only, 1,729 pressed) . . . 25
91 KLF Comms. 92PROMO 1 America: What Time Is Love/America No More (12", white label) . . . 8
91 KLF Comms. 92PROMO 2 America: What Time Is January? (12", 1-sided, white label promo, 250 only) . . . 45
91 KLF Comms. 3AM 1 3AM Eternal (feat. Extreme Noise Terror) (p/s, mail order only) . . . 20
92 KLF Comms. 92PROMO 3 What Time Is Love (Acid Mix) (12", 1-sided, w/l promo, perhaps 20 only) . . . 120
92 KLF Comms. USA 4X/ CHOC ICE 2 Justified And Ancient/America: What Time Is Love? (12", 'longboat' picture disc, export edition, 4,000 only) . . . 20
92 KLF Comms. PUB 1 Justified And Ancient/America: What Time Is Love? (jukebox ed., 5,000 only) . . . 8
97 KLF Comms. Fuck The Millennium (4-track CD, in white carrier bag "Fuck The Millennium" kit, with T-shirt, window sticker, certificate) . . . 50
89 KLF Comms. JAMS LP 4 THE WHAT TIME IS LOVE STORY (LP) . . . 40
89 KLF Comms. JAMS CD 4 THE WHAT TIME IS LOVE STORY (CD) . . . 60
89 KLF Comms. JAMS LP 5 CHILL OUT (LP) . . . 40
89 KLF Comms. JAMS CD 5 CHILL OUT (CD) . . . 25
89 KLF Comms. JAMS LP 6 (TUNES FROM) THE WHITE ROOM (LP, 9-track white label, unreleased, promo only, beware of counterfeits!) . . . 50+
89 KLF Comms. JAMS MC 6 (TUNES FROM) THE WHITE ROOM (cassette, 10-track promo, beware of counterfeits!) . . . 40
(see also J.A.M.s, Timelords, Disco 2000, Bill Drummond, Space, Orb)

TONY KLINGER & MICHAEL LYONS

72 Deram SML 1095 EXTREEMS (LP, soundtrack) . . . 30

PETER KLINT (QUINTET)

66 Mercury MF 997 Walkin' Proud/Shake . . . 15
68 Atlantic 584 208 Hey Diddle Diddle/Just Holding On (solo) . . . 6

ANNETTE KLOOGER

56 Decca F 10701 The Rock And Roll Waltz/Rock Around The Island (with Ted Heath Music) . . . 18
56 Decca F 10733 The Magic Touch/We'll Love Again (with Four Jones Boys) . . . 15
56 Decca F 10738 Why Do Fools Fall In Love?/Lovely One (with Four Jones Boys) . . . 18
56 Decca F 10776 Mama, Teach Me To Dance/Mama, I Long For A Sweetheart (with Edmundo Ros Orchestra) . . . 10
57 Decca F 10844 The Wisdom Of A Fool/Tra La La . . . 10
(see also Four Jones Boys, Edmundo Ros, Ted Heath Orchestra)

MINT VALUE £

KLUBS

68 Cam CAM 681 I Found The Sun/Ever Needed Someone . . . 500+

KNACK (U.K.)

65 Decca F 12234 She Ain't No Good/Who'll Be The Next In Line . . . 35
65 Decca F 12278 It's Love Baby (24 Hours A Day)/Time Time Time . . . 35
66 Piccadilly 7N 35315 Did You Ever Have To Make Up Your Mind?/Red Hearts . . . 12
66 Piccadilly 7N 35322 Stop! (Before You Get Me Going)/Younger Girl . . . 12
66 Piccadilly 7N 35347 Save All My Love For Joey/Take Your Love . . . 12
67 Piccadilly 7N 35367 (Man From The) Marriage Guidance And Advice Bureau/ Dolly Catch Her Man . . . 12
(see also Gun, Sky)

KNACK (U.S.)

79 Capitol E-ST 11948 GET THE KNACK (LP, limited white cover, unissued) . . . 12

BERNIE KNEE QUARTETTE

55 HMV 7M 306 Chocolate Whiskey And Vanilla Gin/Scrape Off De Bark . . . 7
(see also Bernie Nee)

KNEES

74 United Artists UP 35773 Day Tripper/Slow Down . . . 20
(see also Brinsley Schwarz)

KNICKERBOCKERS

66 London HLH 10013 Lies/The Coming Generation . . . 18
66 London HLH 10035 One Track Mind/I Must Be Doing Something Right . . . 15
66 London HLH 10061 High On Love/Stick With Me . . . 15
66 London HLH 10093 Rumours, Gossip, Words Untrue/Love Is A Bird . . . 15
67 London HLH 10102 Can You Help Me/Please Don't Love Him . . . 15
73 Elektra K 12102 Lies/ELECTRIC PRUNES: I Had Too Much To Dream (Last Night) . . . 5
66 London HA-H 8294 THE FABULOUS KNICKERBOCKERS (LP) . . . 50

BAKER KNIGHT

66 Reprise RS 20465 Would You Believe It/Tomorrow's Good Time Girl . . . 12

CURTIS KNIGHT (& ZEUS)

69 RCA RCA 1888 Fancy Meeting You Here/Love In . . . 10
70 RCA RCA 1950 Down In The Village/No Point Of View . . . 8
74 Dawn DNS 1049 Devil Made Me Do It/Oh Rainbow . . . 7
74 Dawn DNS 1065 People Places And Things/Mysterious Lady . . . 7
74 Dawn DNLS 3060 ZEUS, THE SECOND COMING (LP) . . . 35
(see also Jimi Hendrix, Blue Goose)

GLADYS KNIGHT (& PIPS)

SINGLES

64 Stateside SS 318 Giving Up/Maybe Maybe Baby . . . 22
64 Stateside SS 352 Lovers Always Forgive/Another Love . . . 22
65 Sue WI 394 Letter Full Of Tears/You Broke Your Promise . . . 30
66 Tamla Motown TMG 576 Just Walk In My Shoes/Stepping Closer To Your Heart . . . 50
67 Tamla Motown TMG 604 Take Me In Your Arms And Love Me/Do You Love Me Just A Little Honey . . . 12
67 Tamla Motown TMG 619 Everybody Needs Love/Stepping Closer To Your Heart (demo-only B-side) . . . 80
67 Tamla Motown TMG 619 Everybody Needs Love/Since I've Lost You . . . 15
67 Tamla Motown TMG 629 I Heard It Through The Grapevine/It's Time To Go Now . . . 18
68 Tamla Motown TMG 645 The End Of Our Road/Don't Let Her Take Your Love From Me . . . 12
68 Tamla Motown TMG 660 It Should Have Been Me/You Don't Love Me No More . . . 15
68 Tamla Motown TMG 674 I Wish It Would Rain/It's Summer . . . 12
69 Tamla Motown TMG 714 The Nitty Gritty/Got Myself A Good Man . . . 8
70 Tamla Motown TMG 728 Didn't You Know (You'd Have To Cry Sometime)/Keep An Eye . . . 10
70 Tamla Motown TMG 756 Friendship Train/You Need Love Like I Do (Don't You) . . . 6
71 Tamla Motown TMG 765 If I Were Your Woman/The Tracks Of My Tears . . . 6
72 Tamla Motown TMG 805 Make Me The Woman That You Go Home To/I Don't Want To Do Wrong . . . 18
72 Tamla Motown TMG 813 Just Walk In My Shoes/I'm Losing You . . . 5
73 Ember EMB S 326 Every Beat Of My Heart/Room In Your Heart . . . 5
73 Tamla Motown TMG 844 The Look Of Love/You're My Everything . . . 5
73 Tamla Motown TMG 864 Take Me In Your Arms And Love Me/No One Could Love You More . . . 45
74 Contempo CS 2021 Why Don't You Leave Me/Maybe Baby . . . 6
75 Tamla Motown TMG 945 You've Lost That Loving Feeling/This Child Needs A Father . . . 5
89 MCA MCASP 1339 Licence To Kill/MICHAEL KAMEN: Pain (p/s with postcards & lyric sheet) . . . 6
89 MCA MCAT 1339 Licence To Kill (Extended Version)/MICHAEL KAMEN: Pain (12", picture sleeve) . . . 8
89 MCA DMCA 1339 Licence To Kill/MICHAEL KAMEN: Pain/Licence To Kill (Extended Version) (3" CD, card sleeve) . . . 10

LPs

67 Music F. Pleasure MFP 1187 GLADYS KNIGHT AND THE PIPS . . . 15
67 T. Motown (S)TML 11058 EVERYBODY NEEDS LOVE . . . 35
68 Bell MBLL 103 TASTIEST HITS . . . 30
68 T. Motown (S)TML 11080 FEELIN' BLUES . . . 35
69 T. Motown (S)TML 11100 SILK'N'SOUL . . . 35
69 T. Motown (S)TML 11135 THE NITTY GRITTY (mono/stereo) . . . 22/20
70 Tamla Motown STML 11148 GREATEST HITS (original with flipback sleeve) . . . 15
71 Tamla Motown STML 11187 IF YOU WERE A WOMAN . . . 12
75 Buddah BDLP 4038 2ND ANNIVERSARY . . . 12
77 Buddah BDLP 5014 STILL TOGETHER . . . 12
78 Buddah 11PP 602 COLLECTION (4-LP, box set) . . . 30
79 Buddah BDLP 4056 MISS GLADYS KNIGHT (solo) . . . 12
(see also Pips, Dionne Warwick)

JASON KNIGHT

67 Pye 7N 17399 Love Is Getting Stronger/Standing In My Shoes . . . 30
73 Pye 7N 45287 Love Is Getting Stronger/Standing In My Shoes (reissue) . . . 8

JEAN KNIGHT

71 Stax 2025 049 Mr Big Stuff/Why Do I Keep Living These Memories . . . 10
72 Stax 2025 103 Carry On/Do You Think You're Hot Stuff . . . 6
73 Stax 2025 161 Do Me/Save The Last Kiss For Me. . . . 6
72 Stax 2362 022 MR. BIG STUFF (LP). . . . 30

MARIE KNIGHT

61 Fontana H 354 Nothing/Come Tomorrow . . . 15
65 Stateside SS 419 Cry Me A River/Comes The Knight . . . 15
85 Kent TOWN 102 That's No Way To Treat A Girl/JACK MONTGOMERY: Dearly Beloved . . . 12
90s Soul CITY 125 You Lie So Well/That's No Way To Treat A Girl. . . . 12
57 Brunswick OE 9283 GOSPEL SONGS VOL. 1 (EP, with Sam Price Trio) . . . 18
64 Mercury 10001 MCE THE STORM IS PASSING OVER (EP). . . . 18
64 Mercury 10034 MCE SONGS OF THE GOSPEL (EP). . . . 15
58 Mercury MPL 6546 SONGS OF THE GOSPEL (LP). . . . 30
(see also Sister Rosetta Tharpe & Sister Marie Knight)

PETER KNIGHT ORCHESTRA/SINGERS

55 Parlophone MSP 6183 Twenty Minutes South (Medley) (both sides, as Peter Knight Singers) . . . 10
62 Pye 7N 15472 Camel Train/Scarlett . . . 6
67 Mercury SML 30023 SGT. PEPPER'S LONELY HEARTS CLUB BAND (LP) . . . 15

PETER KNIGHT & KNIGHT RIDERS

61 Pye 7N 15388 Lucky Stars/Double Trouble. . . . 7
64 Pye 7N 15687 Wonderful Day Like Today/It Isn't Enough . . . 8

ROBERT KNIGHT

62 London HLD 9496 Free Me/The Other Half Of Man . . . 15
68 Monument MON 1008 Everlasting Love/Somebody's Baby . . . 6
68 Monument MON 1016 Blessed Are The Lonely/It's Been Worth It All. . . . 5
68 Monument MON 1017 The Power Of Love/Love On A Mountain Top . . . 6
68 Bell BLL 1029 Isn't It Lonely Together/We'd Better Stop . . . 5
68 Monument LMO/SMO 5015 EVERLASTING LOVE (LP) . . . 22
71 Monument MNT 65956 LOVE ON A MOUNTAIN TOP (LP) . . . 20

SONNY KNIGHT

57 London HLD 8362 Confidential/Jail Bird (gold or silver label print) . . . 350/180
57 London HLD 8362 Confidential/Jail Bird (78) . . . 60
57 London HL 7016 Confidential/Jail Bird (export issue) . . . 120
59 Vogue Pop V 9134 But Officer/Dear Wonderful God . . . 220
59 Vogue Pop V 9134 But Officer/Dear Wonderful God (78). . . . 110

TERRY KNIGHT & PACK

66 Cameo Parkway C 102 I (Who Have Nothing)/Numbers . . . 70

TONY KNIGHT

64 Decca F 11989 Did You Ever Hear The Sound?/I Feel So Blue (as Tony Knight & Live Wires). . . . 35
65 Decca F 12109 How Sweet/Surfer Street (as Tony Knight's Chessmen) . . . 30

KNIGHT BROTHERS

65 Chess CRS 8015 Sinking Low/Temptation 'Bout To Get Me . . . 20
66 Chess CRS 8046 That'll Get It/She's A1. . . . 15

KNIGHTRIDER

87 Omega KS 1299 Shout Out Loud . . . 25

KNIGHTSBRIDGE STRINGS/BRASS CHORALE

59 Top Rank JAR 170 Cry/The Windows Of Paris. . . . 6
59 Top Rank JAR 216 Wheel Of Fortune/Cow-Cow Boogie . . . 6
59 Top Rank JAR 216 Wheel Of Fortune/Cow-Cow Boogie (78). . . . 8
59 Top Rank JAR 220 Eton Boating Song/In A Shanty In Old Shanty Town . . . 5
60 Top Rank JAR 314 Two-Way Stretch/The Glad Hand . . . 10
60 Top Rank JAR 364 The Executioner Theme/The Sioux March. . . . 6
60s Top Rank JKR 8040 ROCKING STRINGS (EP) . . . 8

KNIGHTS OF THE ROUND TABLE

68 Pama PM 734 Lament To Bobby Kennedy/If You Were My Girl . . . 7

K9's

79 Dog Breath WOOF 1 The K9 Hassle/Idi Amin/Sweeney Todd (1st issue in numbered blue p/s, with insert, 1000 only; reissue in white p/s with insert, 500 only). . . . each 20

KNOCKER JUNGLE

70 Ember EMB S 293 I Don't Know Why/Reality (p/s) . . . 6
71 Ember NR 5052 KNOCKER JUNGLE (LP, gatefold sleeve) . . . 25

KNOCKOUTS

60 Top Rank JAR 279 Riot In Room 3C/Darling Lorraine . . . 30

DAVID KNOPFLER

83 Peach River BBPR 7 Soul Kissing/Come To Me (p/s) . . . 8
83 Peach River BBPR 712 Soul Kissing/Come To Me/The Great Divide (12", p/s) . . . 8
84 Fast Alley FAR 701 Madonna's Daughter/Hey Henry (p/s) . . . 5
(see also Dire Straits)

MARK KNOPFLER

83 Vertigo DSTR 4 Going Home (Theme Of 'Local Hero')/Smooching (p/s) . . . 5
83 Vertigo DSFM 4 Going Home (Theme Of 'Local Hero') (Cinema Version) (promo only). . . . 12
83 Vertigo DSTR 5 Themes From Local Hero: Wild Theme/Going Home (p/s) . . . 5
84 Vertigo DSDJ 7 Joy (from 'Comfort And Joy') (unissued, 1-sided promo only) . . . 20
84 Vertigo DSTR 712 Joy (from 'Comfort And Joy')/Fistful Of Ice Cream (12", p/s). . . . 25
84 Vertigo MARK ONE Comfort And Joy (12", 1-sided promo) . . . 40
84 Vertigo DSTR 8 The Long Road (Theme From 'Cal')/Irish Boy (p/s). . . . 5
86 Vertigo DSTR 14 Going Home/Wild Theme (reissue, p/s). . . . 5

MINT VALUE £

88	Vertigo VERCD 37	Theme From 'The Princess Bride': Storybook Love (with Willy DeVille)/ The Friends' Song (with Guy Fletcher)/Once Upon A Time ... Storybook Love (CD, card sleeve)	12
90	CBS 656377	Poor Boy Blues/There'll Be Some Changes Made (with Chet Atkins) (p/s)	5
90	CBS 656373	Poor Boy Blues/There'll Be Some Changes Made/So Soft Your Goodbye (CD, with Chet Atkins)	10

(see also Dire Straits, Randy Newman, Chet Atkins)

KNOPOV'S POLITICAL PACKAGE

80	white label	Misadventure/You're In The Army Now	6

(see also Mission)

KNOTT SISTERS

58	London HLX 8713	Undivided Attention/SHADES with KNOTT SISTERS: Sun Glasses	45
58	London HLX 8713	Undivided Attention/SHADES with KNOTT SISTERS: Sun Glasses (78)	20

BUDDY KNOX

57	Columbia DB 3914	Party Doll/My Baby's Gone (gold label print)	140
57	Columbia DB 3914	Party Doll/My Baby's Gone (78)	18
57	Columbia DB 3952	Rock Your Little Baby To Sleep/Don't Make Me Cry (as Lieutenant Buddy Knox, gold label print)	100
57	Columbia DB 3952	Rock Your Little Baby To Sleep/Don't Make Me Cry (as Lieutenant Buddy Knox) (78)	25
57	Columbia DB 4014	Hula Love/Devil Woman	40
57	Columbia DB 4014	Hula Love/Devil Woman (78)	20
58	Columbia DB 4077	Swingin' Daddy/Whenever I'm Lonely	40
58	Columbia DB 4077	Swingin' Daddy/Whenever I'm Lonely (78)	25
58	Columbia DB 4180	Somebody Touched Me/C'mon Baby	25
58	Columbia DB 4180	Somebody Touched Me/C'mon Baby (78)	25
59	Columbia DB 4302	To Be With You/I Think I'm Gonna Kill Myself	22
61	London HLG 9268	Lovey Dovey/I Got You	15
61	London HLG 9331	Ling Ting Tong/The Kisses (They're All Mine)	15
61	London HLG 9472	Three-Eyed Man/All By Myself	15
62	Liberty LIB 55411	Chi-Hua-Hua/Open Your Loving Arms	12
62	Liberty LIB 55473	She's Gone/Now There's Only Me	12
63	Liberty LIB 55592	Shadaroom/Tomorrow Is Coming	10
64	Liberty LIB 55694	All Time Loser/Good Loving	10
69	United Artists UP 35019	God Knows I Love You/Night Runners	8
70	United Artists UP 35100	Party Doll/God Knows I Love You	6
57	Columbia SEG 7732	ROCK-A-BUDDY KNOX (EP)	125
62	Liberty LBY 1114	GOLDEN HITS (LP)	50
71	Sunset SLS 50206	ROCK REFLECTIONS (LP)	12

KNUCKLEHEAD

93	Saucerman ART 01	Red Eye, Dead Eye/Spirit Matter (p/s, hand-painted label, 150 copies only)	15

KOCK

83	Hard ON 11	One-Eyed Giant/Hickory Dickory Kock (p/s)	6

KODIAKS

69	Decca F 12942	All Because You Wanna See Me Cry/Tell Me Rhonda	10

(SPIDER) JOHN KOERNER

67	Elektra EKSN 45005	Won't You Give Me Some Love/Don't Stop	12
69	Elektra EKSN 45063	Friends And Lovers/Magazine Lady (with Willie Murphy)	10
65	Elektra EKL 290	SPIDER BLUES (LP)	35
68	Elek. EKL 4041/EKS 74041	RUNNING JUMPING STANDING STILL (LP, with Willie Murphy)	25
71	Elektra K 42026	RUNNING JUMPING STANDING STILL (LP, reissue)	12

KOLETTES

64	Pye International 7N 25278	Who's That Guy?/Just How Much	25
73	Chess 6145 021	Who's That Guy?/Just How Much (reissue)	8

BONNIE KOLOC

72	London HLO 10377	Jazz Man/Got To Get What You Can	6
72	London HLO 10392	Burgundy Wine/We Are Ships	6
72	London SHO 8432	AFTER ALL THIS TIME (LP)	25
72	London SHO 8440	HOLD ON TO ME (LP)	20

JIMMIE KOMACK

54	Vogue Coral Q 2031	Cold Summer Blues/The Nic-Name Song	12
55	Vogue Coral Q 72061	Wabash 4-7473/An Old Beer Bottle	10
55	Vogue Coral Q 72087	Rock-A-Bye Your Baby With A Dixie Melody/This Is The Place	8

CHRISTOPHER KOMEDA

66	Polydor 580001	CUL DE SAC (soundtrack EP)	300
68	Dot (S)LPD 519	ROSEMARY'S BABY (LP, as Kryzstophe Komeda)	35

JOHN (T.) KONGOS

66	Piccadilly 7N 35341	I Love Mary/Goodtime Party Companion (as John T. Kongos)	6
69	Dawn DNS 1002	Flim Flam Pharisee/Blood	6
71	Fly BUG 8	He's Gonna Step On You Again/Sometimes It's Not Enough (purple or black label, p/s)	6
71	Fly BUG 14	Tokoloshe Man/Can Someone Please Direct Me Back To Earth	5
72	Cube BUG 22	Great White Lady/Shamarack	5
73	Cube BUG 32	Higher Than God's Hat/Would You Follow Me	5
69	Dawn DNLS 3002	CONFUSIONS ABOUT A GOLDFISH (LP)	20
72	Fly HIFLY 7	KONGOS (LP)	12

(see also Scrugg, Floribunda Rose)

KONRADS

65	CBS 201812	Baby It's Too Late Now/I'm Over You	15

KONSTRUKTIVITS

80s Third Mind TM 02 PSYKO GENETIKA (LP) . . . 20
86 Sterile SR 10 GLENACAUL (LP) . . . 20
(see also Whitehouse)

KOOBAS

65 Pye 7N 17012 Take Me For A Little While/Somewhere In The Night . . . 50
66 Pye 7N 17087 You'd Better Make Up Your Mind/A Place I Know . . . 60
66 Columbia DB 7988 Sweet Music/Face . . . 50
67 Columbia DB 8103 Sally/Champagne And Caviar . . . 40
67 Columbia DB 8187 Gypsy Fred/City Girl . . . 40
68 Columbia DB 8419 The First Cut Is The Deepest/Walking Out . . . 60
69 Columbia S(C)X 6271 THE KOOBAS (LP) . . . 600
88 Bam Caruso KIRI 047 BARRICADES (LP) . . . 20
(see also Kubas, Van Der Graaf Generator, Gary & Stu, March Hare)

KOOGA

88 Kooga KO 001 Don't Break My Heart (p/s, private pressing) . . . 8
(see also Skin)

KOOL

67 CBS 203003 Look At Me, Look At Me/Room At The Top . . . 10
69 CBS 2865 Step Out Of Your Mind/Funny (What A Fool A Man Can Be) . . . 20
69 MCA MU 1085 Lovin'/Baby's Out Of Reach . . . 12

KOOL KEITH/PHAROE MONCH/AKINYELLE

95 Liberty Grooves LIB 008/DOLO 002 Freestyle Frenzy/Gotta Go Down (7") . . . 15

KOOL & THE GANG

70 London HLZ 10308 Kool And The Gang/Raw Hamburgers . . . 8
71 Mojo 2027 005 Funky Man/Kool And The Gang/Let The Music Take Your Mind . . . 6
71 Mojo 2027 006 Love The Life You Live/The Penguin . . . 6
72 Mojo 2027 009 Music Is The Message (Parts 1 & 2) . . . 6
73 Polydor 2001 474 Funky Stuff/More Funky Stuff . . . 6
74 Polydor 2001 500 Jungle Boogie/North, South, East, West . . . 6
74 Polydor 2001 530 Hollywood Swinging/Dujii . . . 6
74 Polydor 2001 541 Higher Plane/Wild Is Love . . . 6
75 Polydor 2001 558 Rhyme Tyme People/Father, Father . . . 6
75 Polydor 2001 566 Spirit Of The Boogie/Jungle Jazz . . . 6
76 Polydor 2058 645 Love And Understanding/Sunshine And Love . . . 6
77 Contempo CS 1001 Super Band/Open Sesame . . . 6
77 Contempo 12 CS 1001 Super Band/Open Sesame (12") . . . 8
81 De-Lite GANG 11 Jones Vs Jones/Summer Madness// Funky Stuff/Hollywood Swinging (double pack) . . . 5
81 De-Lite KOOL 11-12 Jones Vs Jones/Funky Stuff/Summer Madness (live)/ Hollywood Swinging (12") . . . 8
71 Mojo 2347 001 LIVE AT P.J.'S (LP) . . . 55
71 Mojo 2347 002 THE BEST OF KOOL AND THE GANG (LP) . . . 45
72 Mojo 2347 003 LIVE AT THE SEX MACHINE (LP) . . . 25
73 Mojo 2347 004 MUSIC IS THE MESSAGE (LP) . . . 30
74 Polydor 2310 299 WILD AND PEACEFUL (LP) . . . 15
74 Polydor 2310 357 LIGHT OF WORLDS (LP) . . . 12
75 Polydor 2310 416 SPIRIT OF THE BOOGIE (LP) . . . 12
76 Polydor 2343 083 LIVE AT THE SEX MACHINE (LP, reissue) . . . 12

AL KOOPER

65 Mercury MF 885 Parchman Farm/You're The Lovin' End (as Alan Kooper) . . . 12
69 CBS 4011 You Never Know Who Your Friends Are/Soft Landing On The Moon . . . 6
69 CBS 4160 Hey Western Union Man/I Stand Alone . . . 8
71 CBS 5146 Brand New Lady/The Landlord (Love Theme) . . . 5
71 CBS 7376 John The Baptist/Back On My Feet . . . 5
72 CBS 8084 Monkey Time/Bended Knees (Please Don't Let Me Down) . . . 6
69 CBS 63538 I STAND ALONE (LP, orange label) . . . 20
69 CBS 63651 YOU NEVER KNOW WHO YOUR FRIENDS ARE (LP, orange label) . . . 18
70 CBS 63797 KOOPER SESSION — WITH SHUGGIE OTIS (LP, orange label) . . . 18
70 CBS 66252 EASY DOES IT (2-LP, orange label) . . . 20
71 United Artists UAS 29120 THE LANDLORD (LP, soundtrack, with Staple Singers & Lorraine Ellison) . . . 20
71 CBS 64340 NEW YORK CITY (YOU'RE A WOMAN) (LP, gatefold sleeve, orange label) . . . 12
72 CBS 64208 A POSSIBLE PROJECTION OF THE FUTURE/CHILDHOOD'S END (LP, orange label) . . . 12
73 CBS 65193 NAKED SONGS (LP) . . . 12
(see also Blues Project, Blood Sweat & Tears, Shuggie Otis)

AL KOOPER, MIKE BLOOMFIELD & STEPHEN STILLS

68 CBS 3770 Season Of The Witch/Albert's Shuffle . . . 12
68 CBS 63396 SUPER SESSION (LP) . . . 20
73 CBS CQ 30991 SUPER SESSION (LP, quadrophonic) . . . 20
(see also Mike Bloomfield & Al Kooper, Stephen Stills)

KOPPYKATS

68 Fontana SFT 13052/3 BEATLES' BEST (2-LP) . . . 40
(see also Ian [Edward] & Zodiacs)

TAMARA KORAN WITH PERCEPTION

68 Domain D 7 Veils Of Mourning Lace/Don't Throw Our Love Away . . . 70

TOMMY KÖRBERG

69 Sonet SON 2005 Dear Mrs. Jones/Bird You Must Fly . . . 8

MINT VALUE £

PAUL KORDA

66 Columbia DB 7994 — Go On Home/Just Come Closer To Me . . . 18
69 Parlophone R 5778 — Seagull (West Coast Oil Tragedy Of '68)/Night Of The Next Day. . . 5
71 MAM MAM 20 — Between The Road/English Country Garden. . . 5
71 MAM AS 1003 — PASSING STRANGER (LP). . . 30
(see also Tim Andrews & Paul Korda, Dada, Fresh)

ALEXIS KORNER (BLUES INCORPORATED)

58 Tempo A 166 — I Ain't Gonna Worry No More/County Jail (as Alexis Korner Skiffle Group). . . 100
58 Tempo A 166 — I Ain't Gonna Worry No More/County Jail (78) . . . 80
63 Lyntone LYN 299 — Blaydon Races/Up-Town (as Blues Incorporated With Alexis Korner, free with women's magazine *Trio*) . . . 130
63 Parlophone R 5206 — I Need Your Loving/Please Please Please (as Alexis Korner's Blues Inc.). . . 25
65 Parlophone R 5247 — Little Baby/Roberta (as Alexis Korner's Blues Inc.) . . . 25
65 King KG 1017 — See See Rider/Blues A La King(as Alexis Korner's All Stars) . . . 45
66 Fontana TF 706 — River's Invitation/Everyday (I Have The Blues) . . . 22
67 Fontana TF 817 — Rosie/Rock Me . . . 25
75 CBS 3520 — Get Off My Cloud/Strange'n'Deranged . . . 8
76 CBS 3877 — Ain't That Peculiar/Tree Top Fever . . . 6
58 Tempo EXA 76 — BLUES FROM THE ROUNDHOUSE VOL. 1 (EP, as Alexis Korner Skiffle Group) . 180
59 Tempo EXA 102 — BLUES FROM THE ROUNDHOUSE VOL. 2 (EP, as Alexis Korner's Blues Inc.) . . 260
62 Topic TOP 70 — 3/4 A.D. (EP, with Davy Graham, first pressing in mauve sleeve with cream label; later pressings with lilac or bronze sleeve and blue label) . . . 260/150/120
57 '77' LP/2 — BLUES FROM THE ROUNDHOUSE (10" LP, 99 only, as Alexis Korner Breakdown Group). . . 900+
62 Ace of Clubs ACL 1130 — R&B FROM THE MARQUEE (LP, claret labels, with Long John Baldry). . . 120
64 Transatlantic TRA 117 — RED HOT FROM ALEX (LP, with Herbie Goins). . . 150
64 Oriole PS 40058 — AT THE CAVERN (LP, live, with Herbie Goins). . . 350
65 Ace of Clubs ACL 1187 — ALEXIS KORNER'S BLUES INCORPORATED (LP) . . . 170
65 Spot JW 551 — SKY HIGH (LP, featuring Duffy Power) . . . 400
67 Fontana (S)TL 5381 — I WONDER WHO (LP, black & grey label, mono/stereo) . . . 160/170
67 Polydor Special 236 206 — BLUES INCORPORATED (LP, reissue of Spot LP with fewer tracks). . . 90
68 Liberty LBL/LBS 83147 — A NEW GENERATION OF BLUES (LP) . . . 85
69 Transatlantic TRASAM 7 — ALEXIS KORNER'S ALL STAR BLUES INCORPORATED (LP, reissue of "Red Hot From Alex", different cover). . . 40
71 Rak SRAK 501 — ALEXIS (LP) . . . 80
72 Rak SRAKSP 51 — BOOTLEG HIM! (2-LP, with booklet) . . . 105
73 Transatlantic TRA 269 — ACCIDENTALLY BORN IN NEW ORLEANS (LP, as Snape). . . 50
75 CBS 69155 — GET OFF MY CLOUD (LP) . . . 50
(see also Cyril Davies, C.C.S., Bob Hall & Alexis Korner, Herbie Goins, Duffy Power, Long John Baldry, Rocket 88, Davy Graham, Beryl Bryden, Jimmy Cotton, Ken Colyer, Jack Bruce, Snape & Little Brother Montgomery)

ARTIE KORNFELD'S TREE

72 Neighbourhood NBH 3 — Island Song/Feel . . . 5
70 Probe SPB 1022 — A TIME TO REMEMBER (LP) . . . 20

KOSMIC KOMMANDO

94 Rephlex CAT 007EP — Cat 007 (I)/Cat 007 (II)/Cat 007 (III)/Cat 007 (IV) (12", clear vinyl) . . . 15
(see also Aphex Twin)

PAUL KOSSOFF

73 Island ILPS 9264 — BACK STREET CRAWLER (LP). . . 18
83 St. Tunes SDLP 0012PD — MR. BIG/BLUE SOUL (LP, picture disc). . . 12
(see also Free, Kossoff Kirke Tetsu & Rabbit, Creepy John Thomas)

KOSSOFF, KIRKE, TETSU & RABBIT

71 Island ILPS 9188 — KOSSOFF, KIRKE, TETSU AND RABBIT (LP) . . . 35
(see also Paul Kossoff, Rabbit, Free)

CHIM KOTHARI

66 Deram DM 108 — Sitar'N'Spice/Indian Bat. . . 12
66 Deram DML 1002 — SOUND OF THE SITAR (LP). . . 30

LEO KOTTKE

72 Sonet SNTF 629 — LEO KOTTKE & HIS 6 & 12-STRING GUITAR (LP). . . 12
(see also John Fahey)

KRACKER

73 Rolling Stones RS 19106 — A Song For Polly/Medicated Goo . . . 5
74 Rolling Stones COC 49102 — KRACKER BRAND (LP, gatefold sleeve) . . . 12

KRAFTWERK

SINGLES

75 Vertigo 6147 012 — Autobahn/Kometenmelodie 1 . . . 15
75 Vertigo 6147 015 — Comet Melody 2/Kristallo. . . 12
76 Capitol CL 15853 — Radio Activity/Antenna (some in p/s). . . 12/5
77 Capitol CL 104 — Showroom Dummies/Europe Endless. . . 6
77 Capitol CLX 104 — Showroom Dummies/Europe Endless (12", 'train station' p/s). . . 15
77 Capitol CL 15917 — Trans-Europe Express/Franz Schubert . . . 6
78 Capitol CL 15981 — The Robots/Spacelab (foldout p/s) . . . 15
78 Capitol CL 15981 — The Robots (alternative mix)/Spacelab (foldout p/s). . . 30
78 Capitol CL 15998 — Neon Lights/Trans-Europe Express/The Model. . . 10
78 Capitol 12CL 15998 — Neon Lights/Trans-Europe Express/The Model (12", luminous vinyl, dayglo sleeve) . . . 15
78 Capitol 12CL 16098 — Showroom Dummies/Spacelab/Europe Endless (12", reissue, 'red shirts' p/s). . . 15
81 EMI EMI 5175 — Pocket Calculator/Dentaku (p/s) . . . 5
81 EMI TCEMI 5175 — Pocket Calculator/Numbers/Dentaku (cassette, 'cigarette'-pack style box). . . 35
81 EMI 12EMI 5175 — Pocket Calculator/Numbers/Dentaku (12", p/s). . . 12
81 Vertigo VER 3 — Kometenmelodie 2/Vom Himmel Hoch (p/s) . . . 12
81 EMI EMI 5207 — Computer Love/The Model (p/s, original issue) . . . 6
81 EMI 12EMI 5207 — Computer Love/The Model (12", p/s, original issue). . . 15

82	EMI EMI 5272	Showroom Dummies/Numbers (p/s, some with mispressed B-side "The Model")	8/5
82	EMI 12EMI 5272	Showroom Dummies/Numbers/Pocket Calculator (12", p/s)	12
83	EMI EMI 5413	Tour De France/Tour De France (Instrumental) (p/s, red or yellow labels)	6
83	EMI TCEMI 5413	Tour De France/Tour De France (Short Version)/ Tour De France (2" Etape) (cassette)	35
83	EMI 12EMI 5413	Tour De France (Long Version)/(7" Version)/(2" Etape) (12", p/s, red or yellow labels)	20
84	EMI EMI 5413	Tour De France (Kevorkian Remix)/Tour De France (Original 7" Version) (reissue, 'Breakdance' p/s)	7
84	EMI 12EMI 5413	Tour De France (Kevorkian Remix)/Tour De France (Different Extended Version)/Tour De France (Original 7" Version) (12", reissue, 'Breakdance' p/s)	18
86	EMI EMI 5588	Musique Non-Stop/Musique Non-Stop (Different Version) (p/s)	5
86	EMI 12EMI 5588	Musique Non-Stop (6.15)/Musique Non-Stop (7" Version) (12", p/s)	15
87	EMI EMI 5602	The Telephone Call/Der Telefon Anruf (p/s)	6
87	EMI 12EMI 5602	The Telephone Call (Remix)/House Phone/Der Telefon Anruf (12", p/s)	20
91	EMI EM 192	The Robots (re-recorded version)/Robotronik (p/s, red/black or white/black song title box)	5
91	EMI 12EM 192	Robotronik/The Robots (Single Mix)/The Robots (Album Version) (12", p/s, red/black or white/black song title box)	8
91	EMI CDEM 192	Robotronik/Robotnik/The Robots (Single Edit) (CD, mispressing, plays 'Robotronik [mix]' in place of 'The Robots', red/black song title box)	18
91	EMI CDEM 192	Robotronik/Robotnik/The Robots (Single Edit) (CD, white/black song title box)	18
91	EMI EM 201	Radioactivity (Francois Kevorkian Remix)/(William Orbit Mix) (p/s)	6
91	EMI TCEM 201	Radioactivity (Francois Kevorkian Remix)/(William Orbit Mix) (cassette)	5
91	EMI 12EM 201	Radioactivity (Francois Kevorkian 12" Remix)/ (Francois Kevorkian 7" Remix)/(William Orbit 12" Remix) (12", p/s)	8
91	EMI CDEM 201	Radioactivity (Francois Kevorkian 7" Remix)/ (Francois Kevorkian 12" Remix)/(William Orbit 12" Remix) (CD)	18
97	EMI KLANG DJ 101	Trans Europe Express/Trans Europe Express (Inst.) (12", p/s, promo only)	40
97	EMI KLANG DJ 102	Numbers/Numbers (12", p/s, same track both sides, promo only)	40
97	EMI KLANG DJ 103	Musique Non Stop/Musique Non Stop (12", p/s, same track both sides, promo only)	40
97	EMI KLANG DJ 104	Homecomputer/It's More Fun To Compute (12", p/s, promo only)	40
97	EMI KLANG BOX 101	KRAFTWERK (4 x 12" box set, including "Trans Europe Express", "Numbers", "Musique Non Stop" & "Homecomputer"; *without* T-shirt, promo only)	350
97	EMI KLANG BOX 101	KRAFTWERK (4 x 12" box set, including "Trans Europe Express", "Numbers", "Musique Non Stop" & "Homecomputer"; *with* separate white or black T-shirt, promo only)	500

LPs

72	Vertigo 6641 077	KRAFTWERK (2-LP, gatefold sleeve, 'swirl' or 'spacecraft' labels)	140/50
74	Vertigo 6360 616	RALF AND FLORIAN (gatefold sleeve, 'spacecraft' label)	110/45
74	Vertigo 6360 620	AUTOBAHN (embossed blue sleeve)	30
75	Vertigo 6360 629	EXCELLER 8 (some with stickered sleeve)	22
75	Vertigo 6360 629	EXCELLER 8 (cassette)	15
76	Capitol EST 11457	RADIOACTIVITY (with insert)	15
81	Vertigo 6449 006	ELEKTROKINETIK	25
81	Vertigo 6449 006	ELEKTROKINETIK (cassette)	15
83	EMI EMC 3407	TECHNOPOP (unissued, sleeves only)	
91	EMI EM 1408	THE MIX (2-LP, with inner sleeves)	20
03	EMI EMI 591 708 1	TOUR DE FRANCE SOUNDTRACKS (2-LP, single stickered sleeve with inners)	15
04	EMI KLANG BOX 001	THE CATALOGUE (8-CD, in card box, 1,000 only)	450+

(see also Organisation, Elektric Music)

KRAKEN

81	Knave EJSP 9370	FANTASY REALITY (EP, no p/s)	50

BILLY J. KRAMER & THE DAKOTAS

63	Parlophone R 5023	Do You Want To Know A Secret/I'll Be On My Way	7
63	Parlophone R 5049	Bad To Me/I Call Your Name	5
63	Parlophone R 5073	I'll Keep You Satisfied/I Know	6
64	Parlophone R 5105	Little Children/They Remind Me Of You	5
64	Parlophone R 5156	From A Window/Second To None	5
65	Parlophone R 5234	It's Gotta Last Forever/Don't Do It No More	8
65	Parlophone R 5285	Trains And Boats And Planes/That's The Way I Feel	7
65	Parlophone R 5362	Neon City/I'll Be Doggone	12
66	Parlophone R 5408	We're Doing Fine/Forgive Me	18
63	Parlophone GEP 8885	THE BILLY J. KRAMER HITS (EP)	30
63	Parlophone GEP 8895	I'LL KEEP YOU SATISFIED (EP)	30
64	Parlophone GEP 8907	LITTLE CHILDREN (EP)	30
64	Parlophone GEP 8921	FROM A WINDOW (EP)	40
65	Parlophone GEP 8928	BILLY J. PLAYS THE STATES (EP)	50
63	Parlophone PMC 1209	LISTEN (LP, also stereo PCS 3047)	30/45
65	Regal REG 1057	BILLY J (LP, export only)	45
66	MFP MFP 1134	BILLY BOY (LP)	12

(see also Dakotas)

BILLY J. KRAMER

66	Parlophone R 5482	You Make Me Feel Like Someone/Take My Hand	8
67	Parlophone R 5552	Sorry/Going Going Gone	10
67	Reaction 591 014	Town Of Tuxley Toymakers/Chinese Girl	30
68	CBS 56-3396	1941/His Love Is Just A Lie	7
68	NEMS 56-3635	A World Without Love/Going Through It	7
69	MGM MGM 1474	The Colour Of My Love/I'm Running Away	10
73	Decca F 13426	A Fool Like You/I'll Keep You Satisfied	6
73	Decca F 13442	Darlin' Come To Me/Walking	6
74	BASF BA 1006	Stayin' Power/Blue Jean Queen	6

MINT VALUE £

77 EMI EMI 2661 San Diego/Warm Summer Rain . . . 5
78 EMI EMI 2740 Ships That Pass In The Night/Is There Anymore At Home Like You . . . 5
79 Hobo HOS 010 Blue Christmas/Little Love (p/s, blue vinyl) . . . 7
80 JM JM 1005 Silver Dream/Lonely Lady . . . 6
82 Runaway BJK 1 Rock It/Dum Dum . . . 6
83 Rak RAK 359 You Can't Live On Memories/Stood Up (p/s) . . . 6

WAYNE KRAMER

78 Stiffwick DEA/SUK 1 Ramblin' Rose/Get Some (numbered p/s) . . . 8
79 Radar ADA 41 The Harder They Come/East Side Girl (p/s) . . . 6
(see also MC5)

KRAY CHERUBS

88 Fierce FRIGHT 014 No (p/s, 1-sided) . . . 20
89 Snakeskin SS 002 Rot In Hell Mom/SAUCERMAN: Motor Drag (numbered black p/s, 300 only; later reissued in purple p/s) . . . 12/8
89 Forced Exposure FE 18 Teen Camel/I Hate My Job (p/s) . . . 15
(see also Art Attacks, Savage Pencil)

BILL KRENZ & HIS RAGTIMERS

56 London HLU 8258 There'll Be No New Tunes On This Old Piano/Goofus . . . 35
56 London HLU 8258 There'll Be No New Tunes On This Old Piano/Goofus (78) . . . 12

KREW KATS

61 HMV POP 840 Trambone/Peak Hour . . . 20
61 HMV POP 894 Samovar/Jack's Good . . . 20
(see also Shadows, Brian Bennett)

KRIMSON KAKE

69 Penny Farthing PEN 707 Feelin' Better/Waiter . . . 8
(see also Samantha Jones, Vernons Girls)

KRISPY 3

90 K3 K 3001 Coming Thru Clear/ Natch It Up . . . 5

DAVE KRISS

80s private pressing EMIGRATING (2-LP) . . . 15

SONJA KRISTINA

68 Polydor 56299 Let The Sunshine In/Frank Mills . . . 15
80 Chopper CHOP 101 St Tropez/Mr Skin (p/s) . . . 10
80 Chopper CHOPE 5 SONJA KRISTINA (LP) . . . 30
(see also Curved Air)

KRIS KRISTOFFERSON

70 Monument SMO 5042 KRISTOFFERSON (LP) . . . 15
71 Monument MNT 64636 THE SILVER TONGUED DEVIL AND ME (LP) . . . 12
72 Monument MNT 64963 BORDER LORD (LP) . . . 12
73 Monument MNT 64631 ME AND BOBBY McGEE (LP, reissue of "Kristofferson") . . . 12
73 Monument MNT 65391 JESUS WAS A CAPRICORN (LP) . . . 12
73 Monument ZQ 31909 JESUS WAS A CAPRICORN (LP, quadrophonic) . . . 15
74 Monument MNT 69074 SPOOKY LADY'S SIDESHOW (LP) . . . 12
75 Monument MNT 69158 WHO'S TO BLESS AND WHO'S TO BLAME (LP) . . . 12

KRIS KRISTOFFERSON & RITA COOLIDGE

73 A&M AMLH 64403 FULL MOON (LP) . . . 12
75 Monument MNT 80547 BREAKAWAY (LP) . . . 12

KROKODIL

69 Liberty LBS 83306 KROKODIL (LP) . . . 30
70 Liberty LBS 83417 SWAMP (LP) . . . 30

KRONSTADT UPRISING

80s Spider SDL 12 The Unknown Revolution (p/s) . . . 5
85 Dog Rock SD 108 Part Of The Game/The Horseman (p/s) . . . 5

HARDY KRUGER

59 Top Rank TR 5005 Blind Date (I'm A Lonely Man)/PINEWOOD ORCHESTRA: Blind Date (p/s) . . . 12

GENE KRUPA (& HIS ORCHESTRA)

55 Columbia LB 10000 Payin' Them Dues Blues/Jungle Drums (78) . . . 7
60 HMV POP 750 Cherokee/Indiana "Montage" . . . 5
54 Columbia/Clef SEB 10007 THE GENE KRUPA SEXTET (EP) . . . 8
55 Columbia/Clef SEB 10029 THE GENE KRUPA QUARTET (EP) . . . 8
59 HMV 7EG 8557 THE DRIVING GENE KRUPA (EP) . . . 8
59 HMV 7EG 8595 DRUM BOOGIE (EP) . . . 10
55 Columbia 33S 1051 DRUMMIN' MAN (10" LP) . . . 12
55 Columbia 33S 1064 RHYTHM PARADE (10" LP) . . . 12
55 Columbia Clef 33C 9000 THE GENE KRUPA TRIO COLLATES (10" LP) . . . 12
57 Columbia Clef 33C 9032 THE ROCKIN' MR. KRUPA (10" LP) . . . 18
58 Columbia/Clef CX 10133 KRUPA ROCKS (LP) . . . 20
61 Verve VLP/SVLP 9005 PERCUSSION KING (LP) . . . 15

GENE KRUPA & BUDDY RICH

64 Verve VS 503 Perdida/Night Train . . . 5
62 Verve SVLP 9014 BURNIN' BEAT (LP) . . . 12

KRYPTON TUNES

78 Black & Red FIRE 1 Behind Your Smile/Coming To See You (p/s) . . . 7
78 Lightning GIL 546 Limited Vision/All In Jail . . . 5
79 Secret SR 009 EXTENDED PLAY (EP) . . . 5

KRYSIA (Kocjan)

74 RCA LPL1 5052 KRYSIA (LP) . . . 15
(see also Natural Acoustic Band, Fairport Convention)

MINT VALUE £

KRYSTAL GENERATION

72 Mercury 6052 120 Wanted Dead Or Alive/Every Man Seems To Be For Himself . . . 7

BOB KUBAN & INMEN

66 Stateside SS 488 The Cheater/Try Me Baby . . . 40
66 Stateside SS 514 The Teaser/All I Want . . . 15
68 Bell BLL 1027 The Cheater/Try Me Baby (reissue) . . . 10

KUBAS

65 Columbia DB 7451 I Love Her/Magic Potion . . . 30
(see also Koobas)

KUF-LINX

58 London HLU 8583 So Tough/What'cha Gonna Do . . . 175
58 London HLU 8583 So Tough/What'cha Gonna Do (78) . . . 60

LENNY KUHR

69 Philips BF 1777 The Troubadour/Oh No Monsieur . . . 15

KUKL

84 Crass 1984/1 THE EYE (LP, foldout sleeve) . . . 18
85 Crass No. 4 HOLIDAYS IN EUROPE (LP, with inner sleeve) . . . 15
(see also Sugarcubes)

KULA SHAKER

95 Columbia KULA 71 Tattva (Lucky 13 Mix)/Hollow Man Part 2 (thick card p/s, mail-order only, 2,000 numbered copies) . . . 12
96 Columbia KULA 72 Grateful When You're Dead – Jerry Was There/Another Life (p/s) . . . 6
96 Columbia KULACD 72 Grateful When You're Dead – Jerry Was There/Another Life/ Under The Hammer (CD) . . . 8
96 Columbia XPCD 797 Tattva/Tattva On St. George's Day (CD, stickered 'Kevin Keegan' p/s) . . . 8
96 Columbia KULA 75 Govinda (Radio Mix)/Gokula/Temple Of Everlasting Light (p/s, states 45rpm but plays 33rpm, 5,000 only) . . . 20
96 Columbia KULA 75 Govinda (Radio Mix)/Gokula/Temple O (fan club issue, 'clock face' label p/s) . . . 20
96 Columbia XPR 2324 Govinda (Monkey Mafia Pigsy's Mix)/(Monkey Mafia Ten To Ten Mix) (12", p/s, sealed with sticker, promo only) . . . 10

KULT

69 CBS 4276 No Home Today/Mister Number One . . . 120

PRAMOD KUMAR

72 Philips 6460 854 THIS IS THE MUSIC OF INDIA (LP) . . . 12

CHARLIE KUNZ

54 Decca F 10419 Charlie Kunz Piano Medley, No. 114 . . . 15
54 Decca F 10441 Charlie Kunz Piano Medley, No. 115 . . . 5
54 Decca F 10481 Charlie Kunz Piano Medley, No. 116 . . . 5

KURASS

70 Escort ES 825 Stampede/KING STITT: You Were Meant For Me (B-side actually by Lee Perry) . . 10

FELA (RANSOME) KUTI (& AFRICA '70)

72 Regal Zonophone RZ 3052 Chop And Quench/Egbe Mi O (with Africa '70 & Ginger Baker) . . . 5
72 Regal Zono. SLRZ 1023 FELI RANSOME-KUTI & THE AFRICA '70 WITH GINGER BAKER LIVE! (LP) . . . 18
75 Creole CRLP 501 SHAKARA (LP, with Africa '70) . . . 15
77 Creole CRLP 511 ZOMBIE (LP, with Africa '70) . . . 12
78 Phase 4 Stereo PFS 4412 YELLOW FEVER (LP) . . . 12
79 Creole CRLP 502 GENTLEMEN (LP) . . . 12
79 Creole CRLP 509 EVERYTHING SCATTER (LP) . . . 12
81 Arista SPART 1167 BLACK PRESIDENT (LP) . . . 12
(see also Ginger Baker)

JIM KWESKIN JUG BAND

65 Fontana TFL 6036 JIM KWESKIN JUG BAND (LP) . . . 18
67 Fontana (S)TFL 6080 SEE REVERSE SIDE FOR TITLE (LP) . . . 15
68 Vanguard SVRL 19046 WHATEVER HAPPENED TO THOSE GOOD OLD DAYS AT CLUB 47 (LP) . . . 15

KYND

96 Go Go Girl GOGO 001 Egotripper (numbered p/s) . . . 5
97 Go Go Girl GOGO 002 World's Finest (clear vinyl) . . . 5

KYTES

66 Pye 7N 17136 Blessed/Call Me Darling . . . 10
66 Pye 7N 17179 Frosted Panes/I'll Give You Better Love . . . 35
68 Island WI 6027 Running In The Water/The End Of The Day . . . 45

KYTTOCK KYND

70 Decca SKL 4782 KYTTOCK KYND (LP) . . . 80

MINT VALUE £

L.A.

70	CBS 5017	Speak Of Peace, Sing Of Joy/Brings My Whole World Tumbling Down	7
70	CBS 64109	NEW DAY (LP)	22

(see also Love Affair)

PATTI LABELLE (& BLUE BELLES)

64	Sue WI 324	Down The Aisle/C'est La Vie	35
65	Cameo Parkway P 935	Danny Boy/I Believe	18
65	Atlantic AT 4055	All Or Nothing/You Forgot How To Love (as Patty LaBelle & Her Belles)	22
66	Atlantic AT 4064	Over The Rainbow/Groovy Kind Of Love (as Patty LaBelle & Her Belles)	10
66	Atlantic 584 007	Patti's Prayer/Family Man (as Patti LaBelle & Her Belles)	7
67	Atlantic 584 072	Take Me For A Little While/I Don't Want To Go On Without You (solo)	10
66	Atlantic 587 001	OVER THE RAINBOW (LP)	45

(see also Blue-Belles)

LACE

68	Columbia DB 8499	People People/The Nun	20
69	Page One POF 135	I'm A Gambler/Go Away	10

(see also Universals, Pete Dello, Honeybus, Red Herring, Gary Walker & Rain)

DAVE LACEY & CORVETTES

65	Philips BF 1419	That's What They All Say/I've Had Enough	10

LACKEY & SWEENEY

73	Village Thing VTS 23	JUNK STORE SONGS FOR SALE (LP)	15

STEVE LACY

72	Emanem 301	SOLO (LP)	30
73	Emanem 304	THE CRUST (LP)	30

STEVE LACY & DEREK BAILEY

76	Incus 26	COMPANY 4 (LP)	25

(see also Derek Bailey)

LADDERS

83	Statik TAK 2	Gotta See Jane/Krugerrands (p/s)	6
83	Statik TAK 2-12	Gotta See Jane/Krugerrands (12", p/s)	10

LADD'S BLACK ACES

56	London AL 3556	LADD'S BLACK ACES (10" LP)	15

LA-DE-DA BAND

69	Parlophone R 5810	Come Together/Here Is Love	10

LADIES

80s	Music Of Life MOLIS 6	Turned On To You/I Knew That Love (12")	15

TOMMY LADNIER

54	London AL 3524	BLUES AND STOMPS VOLUME ONE — TOMMY LADNIER (10" LP)	35
55	London AL 3548	PLAYS THE BLUES WITH MA RAINEY & EDMONIA HENDERSON (10" LP)	35

(see also Ma Rainey)

PATTIE LA DONNE

69	Joe/Duke DU 23	Friends And Lovers/JOE'S ALLSTARS: Hot Line	10

LA DüSSELDORF

78	Radar ADA 5	La Düsseldorf/Silver Cloud (unissued, white label promos only, no p/s)	25
80	Teldec	Dampfrieman/Individuellos (12", p/s)	10

(see also Neu!)

LADYBIRDS

64	Columbia DB 7197	Lady Bird/I Don't Care Any More	12
64	Columbia DB 7250	The White Cliffs Of Dover/It's Not The Same Without A Boy	10
64	Columbia DB 7351	Memories/Try A Little Love	12
65	Columbia DB 7523	I Wanna Fly/O.K. Fred	12

(see also Sharades, Russ Loader, Marion Davies, De Laine Sisters)

LADY JANE & VERITY

59	Pye International 7N 25036	The Slow Look/Cry Baby	8
59	Pye International N 25036	The Slow Look/Cry Baby (78)	12

LADY JUNE

74	Caroline C 1509	LADY JUNE'S LINGUISTIC LEPROSY (LP, with perforated lyric sheet)	20

(see also Kevin Ayers, Eno)

LADY LEE

64	Decca F 11961	I'm Into Something Good/When Love Comes Along	10
65	Decca F 12147	99 Times Out Of 100/I Can Feel It	6
65	Columbia DB 7121	My Whole World (Seems To Be Tumbling Down)/Girl	10

LADY LUCK & LULLABIES

62	Philips PB 1245	Young Stranger/Dance	7

LADYTRON

01	Invicta LIQ 008CD	Play Girl/Commodore Rock/Took Her To A Movie (Bertrand Mix) (CD, digipak)	10
01	Invicta Hi-Fi LIQO 12	The Way That I Found You/Holiday 601 (p/s)	5
00s	Telstar 7STAS 3311	Blue Jeans (Single Version)/Blue Jeans (Interpol Remix) (p/s, 1000 only)	7

LAFAYETTES

62	RCA RCA 1299	Life's Too Short/Nobody But You	10
62	RCA RCA 1308	Caravan Of Lonely Men/I Still Do	12

LA FUNK MOB

95	Mo' Wax MW 023R	Ravers Suck Our Sound (Carl Craig Mix)/Motor Bass Get Phunked Up (Electofunk Remix)/Ravers Suck Our Sound (Mystic Mix)/Ravers Suck Our Sound (Gangbang Mix)/Ravers Suck Our Sound (New Mix) (2 x 10")	25
96	Mo' Wax MW 017	Tribulations Extra Sensorielles (2 x 12")	10
96	Mo' Wax MW 017	Tribulations Extra Sensorielles (CD)	10
96	Mo' Wax MW 023	Breaking Boundaries Messing Up Heads/(mixes) (2 x 12")	10
96	Mo' Wax MWCD 023	Breaking Boundaries Messing Up Heads/(mixes) (CD, stickered card sleeve)	10

FRANCIS LAI

67	United Artists SULP 1155	A MAN AND A WOMAN (LP, soundtrack)	15
67	United Artists (S)ULP 1185	VIVRE POUR VIVRE (LIFE FOR LIFE) (LP, soundtrack)	15
67	Brunswick LAT/STA 8689	I'LL NEVER FORGET WHAT'S 'ISNAME (LP, soundtrack)	30
69	United Artists SULP 1231	HANNIBAL BROOKS (LP)	15
69	Philips SBL 7876	MAYERLING (Francis Lai)	60
70	United Artists UAS 29137	RIDER IN THE RAIN (LP)	20
71	M. F. Pleasure MFP 50034	THE LEGEND OF FRENCHIE KING (LP)	15
76	Warner Bros K 56231	EMMANUELLE 2 (LP)	15
77	Warner Bros K 56375	BILITIS (LP, gatefold sleeve)	15

LAIBACH

84	L.A.Y.L.A.H. LAY 002	Boji/Sila/Brat Moj (12", p/s)	12
84	East West 12 EWS 3	Panarama/Decree (12", p/s)	10
85	Cherry Red 12CHERRY 91	Die Liebe/Die Liebe Ist Grösste Kraft, Die Alles Schafft (12", p/s)	10
88	Mute PMUTE 80T	SYMPATHY FOR THE DEVIL (12" EP, picture disc)	10
86	Side Effects SER 08	OCCUPIED EUROPE TOUR '85 (LP)	15
92	Mute STUMM 82	KAPITAL (LP)	12
94	NSK NSK 2CDX	OCCUPIED EUROPE NATO TOUR (EPK, in numbered box, with CD, video & booklet)	25
96	Mute STUMM 136	JESUS CHRIST SUPERSTARS (LP)	15
98	Mute STUMM 121	MCMXCIV (LP, with poster and inner)	15

CLEO LAINE

54	Parlophone MSP 6107	I Got Rhythm/I Know You're Mine (with Johnny Dankworth Orchestra)	7
55	Parlophone MSP 6147	Ain't Misbehavin'/I Got It Bad, And That Ain't Good (with Johnny Dankworth Orchestra)	7
57	Pye Jazz 7NJ 2013	I'm Beginning To See The Light/Jeepers Creepers	5
58	Pye 7N 15143	Hand Me Down Love/They Were Right	5
60	Fontana H 269	Let's Slip Away/Thieving Boy	8
61	Columbia DB 4723	It Was A Lover And His Lass/O Mistress Mine	5
61	Fontana H 326	You'll Answer To Me/I Only Have Eyes For You	5
62	Fontana TF 267257	You Gotta Have Love/I Can Dream, Can't I?	6
65	Fontana TF 532	Little Boat/The Exciting Mr. Fitch	5
65	Fontana TF 622	If We Live On The Top Of A Mountain/Don't You Pass Me By	5
66	Fontana TF 759	There Is Nothing Left To Say/Life Is A Wheel	5
70	Philips 6006 016	It Will Soon Be Spring/Feeling Good	5
71	Philips 6006 077	Model City's Programme/Night Owl	20
57	Parlophone GEP 8613	I GOT RHYTHM (EP)	15
57	Pye Nixa Jazz NJE 1010	CLEO LAINE (EP)	15
57	Pye Nixa Jazz NJE 1026	THE APRIL AGE (EP, as Cleo Laine & Dave Lee Quintet)	25
57	Esquire EP 102	CLEO LAINE (EP, as Cleo Laine & Keith Christie Quintet)	25
57	Esquire EP 122	CLEO LAINE (EP, as Cleo Laine & Keith Christie Quintet)	25
59	Columbia SEG 7938	CLEO SINGS ELIZABETHAN (EP)	10
61	Fontana TFE 17381	THE FABULOUS CLEO (EP)	10
64	Fontana TFE 17404	CLEO (EP)	15
55	Esquire 15-007	CLEO LAINE (10" LP)	75
58	Pye Nixa NPT 19024	CLEO'S CHOICE (10" LP)	50
58	MGM MGM-C 765	SHE'S THE TOPS (LP)	25
62	Fontana 680 992 TL	ALL ABOUT ME (LP, also stereo 886 159 TY)	20
64	Fontana (S)TL 5209	SHAKESPEARE & ALL THAT JAZZ (LP)	18
66	Fontana (S)TL 5316	WOMAN TALK (LP)	20
68	Fontana STL 5483	SOLILOQUY (LP)	25
69	Fontana SFL 13006	ALL ABOUT ME (LP, reissue)	12

(see also Johnny Dankworth, Tubby Hayes & Cleo Laine)

DENNY LAINE

67	Deram DM 122	Say You Don't Mind/Ask The People	18
68	Deram DM 171	Too Much In Love/Catherine's Wheel	15
69	Deram DM 227	Say You Don't Mind/Ask The People (reissue)	10
73	Wizard WIZ 104	Find A Way Somehow/Move Me To Another Place	6
77	Palladin PAL 5014	Caroline/Blues	6

(see also Moody Blues, Paul McCartney/Wings, Balls, Trevor Burton, Magic Christians, Ginger Baker's Airforce, BL&G)

FRANKIE LAINE

78s

56	Philips PB 607	Champion The Wonder Horse/Ticky Ticky Tick (I'm Gonna Tell On You)	8
57	Philips PB 691	Lonely Man/Without Him	8
57	Philips PB 760	The Greater Sin/East Is East	8
58	Philips PB 797	Shine/Annabel Lee	8
58	Philips PB 821	The Lonesome Road/My Gal And A Prayer	8

MINT VALUE £

58	Philips PB 836	Lovin' Up A Storm/A Kiss Can Change The World	8
58	Philips PB 848	Choombala Bay/I Have To Cry	10
58	Philips PB 886	When I Speak Your Name/Cottage For Sale	15
59	Philips PB 905	That's My Desire/In My Wildest Dreams	25
59	Philips PB 965	Rawhide/Journey's End	25

SINGLES

53	Columbia SCM 5016	The Ruby And The Pearl/The Mermaid	40
53	Columbia SCM 5017	Jealousy/The Gandy Dancers' Ball	45
53	Columbia SCM 5031	I'm Just A Poor Bachelor/Tonight You Belong To Me	40
53	Columbia SCM 5064	September In The Rain/Chow Willy	35
53	Columbia SCM 5073	The Swan Song/My Ohio Home	35
54	Columbia SCM 5085	Tomorrow Mountain/I'd Give My Life	35
56	Philips JK 1000	Moonlight Gambler/Only If We Love (jukebox issue)	25
57	Philips JK 1009	Love Is A Golden Ring (with Easy Riders)/There's Not A Moment To Spare	25
57	Philips JK 1017	Lonely Man/Without Him (jukebox issue)	25
57	Philips JK 1032	The Greater Sin/East Is East (jukebox issue)	25
58	Philips PB 797	Shine/Annabel Lee	10
58	Philips PB 821	The Lonesome Road/My Gal And A Prayer	10
58	Philips PB 836	Lovin' Up A Storm/A Kiss Can Change The World	10
58	Philips PB 848	Choombala Bay/I Have To Cry	10
58	Philips PB 886	When I Speak Your Name/Cottage For Sale	7
59	Philips PB 905	That's My Desire/In My Wildest Dreams	7
59	Philips PB 965	Rawhide/Journey's End	6
60	Philips PB 997	Jelly Coal Man/Rocks And Gravel	7
60	Philips PB 1011	St. James Infirmary/Et Voila!	7
60	Philips PB 1064	And Doesn't She Roll/Seven Women	7
61	Philips PB 1135	Gunslinger/Wanted Man	6
63	CBS AAG 144	Don't Make My Baby Blue/The Moment Of Truth	6
63	CBS AAG 167	And Doesn't She Roll/I'm Gonna Be Strong	6
65	Capitol CL 15373	Go On With Your Dancing/Halfway	6
67	HMV POP 1573	Ev'ry Street's A Boulevard (In Old New York)/I'll Take Care Of Your Cares	6
67	HMV POP 1590	Making Memories/The Moment Of Truth	6
67	HMV POP 1597	You Wanted Someone To Play With/The Real True Meaning Of Love	6
67	HMV POP 1606	Laura/Sometimes	6
68	Stateside SS 2091	To Each His Own/I'm Happy To Hear You're Sorry	6
69	Stateside SS 2144	You Gave Me A Mountain/The Secret Of Happiness	6
73	CBS 1156	High Noon/Cool Water (p/s)	5
74	Warner Bros K 16414	Blazing Saddles/MADELINEKAHN: I'm Tired	5
70s	Bulldog BD 24	Jezebel/Answer Me	5

EPs

54	Columbia SEG 7505	JEZEBEL (company die-cut sleeve)	15
54	Philips BBE 12005	FRANKIE LAINE (I BELIEVE)	15
56	Mercury MEP 9000	FRANKIE LAINE SINGS	15
56	Mercury MEP 9500	MORE HITS BY FRANKIE LAINE	15
56	Philips BBE 12087	FRANKIE LAINE NO. 2	15
56	Philips BBE 12103	JUBA JUBA JUBALEE (as Frankie Laine & Four Lads)	12
57	Philips BBE 12130	FRANKIE LAINE NO. 3	15
57	Mercury MEP 9520	FRANKIE LAINE SINGS VOL. 2	15
58	Philips BBE 12216	FRANKIE LAINE (PHILIPS TV SERIES)	15
60	Mercury ZEP 10062	FRANKIE LAINE'S ALL TIME HITS	15
61	Philips BBE 12447	WESTERN FAVOURITES	15
62	CBS AGG 20003	DEUCES WILD NO. 1	15
62	CBS AGG 20007	DEUCES WILD NO. 2	15
62	CBS AGG 20011	DEUCES WILD NO. 3	15
64	CBS AGG 20036	SONG OF THE OPEN ROAD	15

LPs

52	Oriole/Mercury MG 10001	MR RHYTHM SINGS (10", stickered U.S. "Mr Rhythm" sleeve)	50
52	Oriole/Mercury MG 10002	SONGS BY FRANKIE LAINE (10")	50
54	Mercury MG 25097	MR. RHYTHM SINGS (10", reissue)	40
54	Mercury MG 25098	SONGS BY FRANKIE LAINE (10", reissue)	40
54	Columbia 33S 1047	ONE FOR MY BABY (10")	45
54	Philips BBR 8014	THE VOICE OF YOUR CHOICE (10")	40
55	Philips BBR 8068	MR. RHYTHM (10")	35
56	Mercury MPT 7007	CRY OF THE WILD GOOSE (10")	50
56	Philips BBL 7080	JAZZ SPECTACULAR (with Buck Clayton & His Orchestra)	20
56	Philips BBL 7111	JUBA JUBA JUBILEE (with Four Lads)	20
57	Philips BBL 7155	ROCKIN'	30
57	Mercury MPT 7513	THAT'S MY DESIRE (10")	35
58	Philips BBL 7238	FOREIGN AFFAIR	22
58	Philips BBL 7260	TORCHING	22
58	Philips BBL 7263	SHOWCASE OF HITS (flipback or non-flipback sleeve)	25/20
59	Philips BBL 7294	REUNION IN RHYTHM (with Michel Legrand, also stereo SBBL 541)	18/22
60	Philips BBL 7357	FRANKIE LAINE BALLADEER	18
61	Philips BBL 7468	HELL BENT FOR LEATHER (also stereo SBBL 616)	15/20
61	Ember EMB 3334	FRANKIE LAINE SINGS	15
62	Philips BBL 7535	DEUCES WILD (also stereo SBBL 663)	18/22
62	CBS (S)BPG 62052	HELL BENT FOR LEATHER (reissue)	12
62	CBS (S)BPG 62082	CALL OF THE WILD (mono/stereo)	18
63	CBS (S)BPG 62126	WANDERLUST	18
60s	World Records SM 531/536	THE FRANKIE LAINE SONGBOOK (6-LP box set)	25

(see also Jo Stafford & Frankie Laine, Four Lads, Doris Day, Easy Riders)

FRANKIE LAINE & JOHNNIE RAY

57 Philips JK 1026 Up Above My Head, I Hear Music In The Air/Good Evening Friends (jukebox issue) . . . 25
57 Philips PB 708 Up Above My Head, I Hear Music In The Air/Good Evening Friends (78) . . . 8
57 Philips BBE 12153 FRANKIE AND JOHNNIE (EP, 1 track each, 2 together) . . . 20
(see also Johnnie Ray)

LINDA LAINE (& SINNERS)

64 Columbia DB 7204 Doncha Know, Doncha Know, Doncha Know/Ain't That Fun . . . 15
64 Columbia DB 7370 Low Grades And High Fever/After Today . . . 15
65 Columbia DB 7549 Don't Do It Baby/All I Want To Do Is Run . . . 15
(see also Sinners)

SCOTT LAINE

63 Windsor WB 114 Tearaway Johnnie/John Silver . . . 25

DENZIL LAING

71 Songbird SB 1054 Medicine Stick/CRYSTALITES: Short Cut . . . 10
(see also Soul Vendors, Dennis Alcapone)

ALAN LAKE

70 Ember EMB S 278 Good Times/Got To Have Tenderness (p/s) . . . 15

BONNIE LAKE & HER BEAUX

56 Brunswick 05622 Thirteen Black Cats/The Miracle Of Love . . . 22
56 Brunswick 05622 Thirteen Black Cats/The Miracle Of Love (78) . . . 10
(see also Jack Pleis)

GREG LAKE

75 Manticore K 13511 I Believe In Father Christmas/Humbug (p/s) . . . 6
77 Atlantic K 10990 C'est La Vie/EMERSON, LAKE & PALMER: Jeremy Bender (p/s) . . . 5
78 Atlantic K 11061 Watching Over You/EMERSON, LAKE & PALMER: Hallowed Be Thy Name (p/s) . . . 5
81 Chrysalis CHS 2553 Love You Too Much/Someone (p/s) . . . 6
82 Chrysalis CHS 2567 It Hurts/Retribution Drive . . . 5
81 Chrysalis CHR 1357 GREG LAKE (LP, with inner sleeve) . . . 12
83 Chrysalis CHR 1392 MANOEUVRES (LP) . . . 12
(see also Emerson Lake & Palmer, King Crimson, Asia, Pete Sinfield, Gary Moore)

LEE LAMAR & HIS ORCHESTRA

57 London HLB 8508 Teenage Pedal Pushers/Sophia . . . 75
57 London HLB 8508 Teenage Pedal Pushers/Sophia (78) . . . 35

CHRIS LAMB & UNIVERSALS

65 Decca F 12176 Mysterious Land/If You Ask Me . . . 8
(see also Universals, Gidian)

KEVIN LAMB

70 Concord CON 23 Who Is The Hero?/The Road To Antibes . . . 6
73 Birth RAB 1004 Who Is The Hero?/Who Stole The Ice . . . 5
72 Birth RAB 4 WHO IS THE HERO? (LP) . . . 12

LAMBCHOP

00 City Slang 20174-2 THE QUEEN'S ROYAL TRIMMA (CD EP, sold at gigs) . . . 10

JEANNIE LAMBE

67 CBS 202636 Miss Disc/Montano Blues (with Gordon Beck Orchestra) . . . 20
67 CBS 2731 Day After Day After Day/City At Night . . . 10
67 CBS 3000 This Is My Love/Where Have All The Endings Gone (as Jeanne Lam) . . . 8

DAVE LAMBERT, JON HENDRICKS & ANNIE ROSS

60 Philips BBL 7368 DAVE LAMBERT, JON HENDRICKS & ANNIE ROSS (LP, stereo SBBL 562) . . . 15
(see also Jon Hendricks, Annie Ross)

DAVE LAMBERT & BUDDY STEWART

51 Vogue V 2039 Bopelbaby/Bopelground (78, with Al Haig) . . . 8

TREVOR LAMBERT

72 Duke DU 132 Bald Head Teacher (act. by Max Romeo)/HEADMASTERS: Bald Head Version . . . 7

LAMB LANCE

95 Long LENGTH 8 THE JOY OF JOUSTING (LP) . . . 12

LAMBRETTAS

79 Rocket XPRES 23 Go Steady/Listen Listen/Cortinas (p/s; later in art sleeve) . . . 7
80 Rocket XPRES 25 Poison Ivy/Runaround (with '2-Stroke' die-cut sleeve & label) . . . 5
80 Rocket XPRES 333 Da-a-a-ance/(Can't You) Feel The Beat (picture disc; 2 different shades, red, white & blue or pink, white & blue) . . . 5/8
80 Rocket XPRES 36 Page 3/Steppin' Out (Of Line) (withdrawn; copies rumoured to exist, some in p/s) . . . 500/300
80 Rocket XPRES 36 Another Day (Another Girl)/Steppin' Out (Of Line) ('emergency' p/s) . . . 10
81 Rocket XPRES 62 Decent Town/Da-a-a-ance (p/s) . . . 10
81 Rocket XPRES 6212 Decent Town/Da-a-a-ance/Total Strangers/Young Girls (12", p/s) . . . 12
82 Rocket XPRES 74 Somebody To Love/Nobody's Watching Me (p/s) . . . 8
82 Rocket XPRES 74 Somebody To Love/Nobody's Watching Me (p/s, mispressing, crediting "Leap Before You Look" on label & sleeve) . . . 8

TONI LAMOND

68 Philips BF 1722 Silent Voices/They Don't Give Medals (To Yesterday's Heroes) . . . 15

DUNCAN LAMONT

67 Studio Two TWO 159 LATIN A LA LAMONT (LP) . . . 12
68 Morgan MRSAM 2 THIS GUY (LP) . . . 15

LAMPLIGHTERS

55 Parlophone DP 416 Salty Dog/Ride Jockey Ride (78, export issue) . . . 120
(see also Thurston Harris)

MINT VALUE £

LAMP SISTERS

68 Sue WI 4048 A Woman With The Blues/I Thought It Was All Over . . . 40

LANA SISTERS

58 Fontana H 148 Ring-A My Phone/Chimes Of Arcady . . . 35
58 Fontana H 148 Ring-A My Phone/Chimes Of Arcady (78) . . . 20
59 Fontana H 176 Buzzin'/Cry, Cry, Baby . . . 30
59 Fontana H 176 Buzzin'/Cry, Cry, Baby (78) . . . 15
59 Fontana H 190 Mister Dee-Jay/Tell Him No . . . 30
59 Fontana H 190 Mister Dee-Jay/Tell Him No (78) . . . 20
59 Fontana H 221 (Seven Little Girls) Sitting In The Back Seat (with Al Saxon)/ Sitting On The Sidewalk . . . 20
59 Fontana H 221 (Seven Little Girls) Sitting In The Back Seat (with Al Saxon)/ Sitting On The Sidewalk (78) . . . 30
60 Fontana H 235 My Mother's Eyes/You've Got What It Takes . . . 20
60 Fontana H 235 My Mother's Eyes/You've Got What It Takes (78) . . . 30
60 Fontana H 252 Someone Loves You, Joe/Tinatarella Di Luna . . . 15
60 Fontana H 283 Two-some/Down South . . . 15

(see also Al Saxon, Dusty Springfield, Chantelles)

CYNTHIA LANAGAN

54 Columbia SCMC 8 Body And Soul/I Can't Believe You're In Love With Me (export issue) . . . 15
57 Parlophone R 4316 Jamie Boy/Silent Lips (as Cynthia Lanigan) . . . 12
57 Parlophone R 4383 I'm Available/(Don't Stop, Don't Stop) Tell Me More . . . 10

LANCASHIRE FAYRE

80 Folk Heritage FHR 113 LANCASHIRE FAYRE (LP) . . . 20

STEVE LANCASTER

67 Polydor 56215 San Francisco Street/Miguel Fernando San Sebastian Brown . . . 6

ALAN LANCASTER'S BOMBERS

96 P.J. Rocks PJR002CD THE MATCHSTICKMEN EP (CD, 4 tracks, card p/s) . . . 15

(see also Status Quo)

LANCASTRIANS

64 Pye 7N 15732 We'll Sing In The Sunshine/Was She Tall . . . 15
65 Pye 7N 15791 Let's Lock The Door (And Throw Away The Key)/If You're Goin' To Leave Me . . . 8
65 Pye 7N 15846 There'll Be No More Goodbyes/Never Gonna Come On Home . . . 8
65 Pye 7N 15927 Lonely Man/I Can't Stand The Pain . . . 8
66 Pye 7N 17043 The World Keeps Going Round/Not The Same Anymore . . . 15
66 Pye 7N 17072 The Ballad Of The Green Berets/My Little Rose . . . 6

MAJOR LANCE

63 Columbia DB 7099 The Monkey Time/Mama Didn't Know . . . 25
63 Columbia DB 7168 Hey Little Girl/Crying In The Rain . . . 18
64 Columbia DB 7205 Um, Um, Um, Um, Um, Um/Sweet Music . . . 15
64 Columbia DB 7271 The Matador/Gonna Get Married . . . 25
64 Columbia DB 7365 Rhythm/Please Don't Say No More . . . 20
65 Columbia DB 7463 I'm So Lost/Sometimes I Wonder . . . 18
65 Columbia DB 7527 Come See/You Belong To Me, My Love . . . 22
65 Columbia DB 7609 Pride And Joy/I'm The One . . . 30
65 Columbia DB 7688 Too Hot To Hold/Dark And Lonely . . . 25
65 Columbia DB 7787 Everybody Loves A Good Time/I Just Can't Help It . . . 25
66 Columbia DB 7967 Investigate/Little Young Lover . . . 50
67 Columbia DB 8122 Ain't No Soul (Left In These Ole Shoes)/You'll Want Me Back . . . 60
69 Atlantic 584 277 Follow The Leader/Since You've Been Gone . . . 12
69 Atlantic 584 302 Sweeter As The Days Go By/Shadows Of A Memory . . . 12
69 Soul City SC 114 The Beat/You'll Want Me Back . . . 18
70 Buddah 2011 046 Gypsy Woman/Stay Away From Me . . . 15
72 Stax 2025 124 I Wanna Make Up/That's The Story Of My Life . . . 12
72 Epic EPC 8404 Um, Um, Um, Um, Um, Um/Sweet Music (reissue) . . . 5
73 Contempo C 1 The Right Track/Um, Um, Um, Um, Um, Um . . . 5
73 Contempo C 9 Ain't No Soul (Left In These Ole Shoes)/Investigate . . . 5
73 Contempo C 26 Dark And Lonely/My Girl . . . 8
73 Warner Bros K 16334 Sweeter/Wild & Free . . . 10
74 Warner Bros K 16385 Without A Doubt/Open The Door To Your Heart . . . 10
74 Contempo CS 2017 Gimme Little Sign/How Can You Say Goodbye . . . 5
74 Contempo CS 9015 The Right Track/Ain't No Soul (Left In These Ole Shoes) . . . 5
75 Contempo CS 2045 Don't You Know I Love You (Parts 1 & 2) . . . 5
75 Pye 7N 45487 You're Everything I Need (Parts 1 & 2) . . . 5
76 Pye International 7N 25705 Nothing Can Stop Me/Follow The Leader . . . 5
64 Columbia SEG 8318 UM UM UM UM UM UM (EP) . . . 80
65 Columbia 33SX 1728 THE RHYTHM OF MAJOR LANCE (LP) . . . 160
73 Contempo COLP 1001 GREATEST HITS LIVE AT THE TORCH (LP) . . . 18
76 Epic EPC 81519 THE BEST OF MAJOR LANCE (LP) . . . 15
78 Tamla Motown STML 12094 NOW ARRIVING (LP) . . . 15
84 Edsel ED 124 MONKEY TIME (LP) . . . 12

RICK LANCELOT & SEVEN KNIGHTS

66 RCA RCA 1502 Say Girl/Live Like A Lion . . . 6

LANCERS

54 London HL 8002 Sweet Mama Tree Top Tall/Were You Ever Mine To Lose (78) . . . 8
54 London HL 8108 Live And Let Live/I Should Have Never Let You Go (78) . . . 8
54 London HL 8027 Stop Chasin' Me Baby/Peggy O'Neil . . . 65
54 London HL 8027 Stop Chasin' Me Baby/Peggy O'Neil (78) . . . 12
54 London HL 8079 So High, So Low, So Wide/It's You, It's You I Love . . . 65
54 London HL 8079 So High, So Low, So Wide/It's You, It's You I Love (78) . . . 12
54 Vogue Coral Q 2038 Mister Sandman/The Little White Light . . . 25

MINT VALUE £

54	Vogue Coral Q 2038	Mister Sandman/The Little White Light (78)	8
55	Vogue Coral Q 72062	Timberjack/C-r-a-z-y Music	20
55	Vogue Coral Q 72081	Get Out Of The Car (as Lancers & Georgie Auld)/Close Your Eyes	20
55	Vogue Coral Q 72081	Get Out Of The Car (as Lancers & Georgie Auld)/Close Your Eyes (78)	10
55	Vogue Coral Q 72100	Jo-Ann/The Bonnie Banks Of Loch Lomon'	12
56	Vogue Coral Q 72128	Alphabet Rock/Rock Around The Island	40
56	Vogue Coral Q 72128	Alphabet Rock/Rock Around The Island (78)	20
56	Vogue Coral Q 72157	Little Fool/A Man Is As Good As His Word	10
56	Vogue Coral Q 72157	Little Fool/A Man Is As Good As His Word (78)	10
56	Vogue Coral Q 72183	The First Travelling Saleslady/Free	8
57	Vogue Coral Q 72220	Never Leave Me/I Came Back To Say I'm Sorry	8
57	Vogue Coral Q 72254	It Happened In Monterey/Ramona/Freckled-Face Sara Jane	7
57	Vogue Coral Q 72282	Charm Bracelet/And It Don't Feel Bad	8
57	Vogue Coral Q 72282	Charm Bracelet/And It Don't Feel Bad (78)	10
58	Coral Q 72300	The Stroll/Don't Go Near The Water	12
58	Coral Q 72300	The Stroll/Don't Go Near The Water (78)	12
60	Coral Q 72398	Joey, Joey, Joey/JOHNNY DESMOND: The Most Happy Fella	5
61	Warner Bros WB 39	Young In Love/Lonesome Town	5
55	London REP 1027	PRESENTING THE LANCERS (EP)	35
54	London H-APB 1029	OH SWEET MAMA (10" LP)	50
61	London HA-P 2307	CONCERT IN CONTRASTS (LP)	15

ELSA LANCHESTER

58	Vogue VA 160126	SONGS FOR A SMOKE-FILLED ROOM (LP, with Charles Laughton)	18
59	Vogue VA 160139	SONGS FOR A SHUTTERED PARLOUR (LP, with Charles Laughton)	18

BILLY LAND

62	Oriole CB 1750	I Go Walking/You're Too Much	12

HAROLD LAND

58	Contemporary LAC 12178	HAROLD IN THE LAND OF JAZZ (LP)	20

BOB LANDER & SPOTNICKS

62	Oriole CB 1756	My Old Kentucky Home/Home On The Range (possibly unreleased)	15+
62	Oriole CB 1784	Midnight Special/My Old Kentucky Home	12

(see also Spotnicks)

BILL & BRETT LANDIS

59	Parlophone R 4516	Since You've Gone/Bright Eyes	15
59	Parlophone R 4516	Since You've Gone/Bright Eyes (78)	10
59	Parlophone R 4551	By You, By You/Forgive Me	12
59	Parlophone R 4570	Baby Talk/Love Me True	15

JERRY LANDIS

62	Oriole CB 1930	Carlos Dominquez/He Was My Brother	30

(see also Paul Simon)

JOYA LANDIS

68	Trojan TR 620	Kansas City/Out The Light	8
69	Trojan TR 641	Moonlight Lover/I Love You True	10

(see also Jay & Joya, Hugh Roy)

LANDSCAPE

79	RCA RCA T 22	Einstein A Go-Go/Japan (12", stickered company sleeve)	8

NEIL LANDSTRUMM

95	Mosquito MSQ 02	PASCAL EP (12", custom sleeve)	20

(see also Blue Arsed Fly)

HOAGY LANDS

67	Stateside SS 2030	The Next In Line/Please Don't Talk About Me When I'm Gone	200
68	Stateside SS 2085	I'm Yours/Only You	25
72	Action ACT 4605	Why Didn't You Let Me Know/Do You Know What Life Is All About	25
75	UK USA 13	Friends And Lovers Don't Go Together/True Love At Last	6
75	UK USA 14	The Next In Line/I'm Yours	8

DES(MOND) LANE

56	Decca F 10821	Penny-Whistle Rock/Penny-Whistle Polka	12
57	Decca F 10847	Rock Mister Piper/Plymouth Rock	15
59	Top Rank JAR 203	Moonbird/The Clanger March (as Des Lane Orchestra, with John Barry)	10
59	Top Rank JAR 203	Moonbird/The Clanger March (as Des Lane Orchestra, with John Barry) (78)	15
68	Pye 7N 17546	Sadie/No More Wild Oats (as Des Lane)	5

(see also Cyril Stapleton, John Barry)

GARY LANE & GARRISONS

61	Fontana H 338	Start Walking Boy/How Wrong Can You Be	18
62	Fontana 267221 TF	I'm A Lucky Boy/A Love Like You	15

LOIS LANE

67	RCA RCA 1570	One Little Voice/Sing To Me	7
68	Mercury MF 1042	Punky's Dilemma/Lazy Summer Day	7
69	Mercury MF 1092	Brontasaurus Named Bert/Windmills Of Your Mind	7
69	Mercury MF 1115	Lovin' Time/Winds Of Heaven	7
70	Philips BF 1829	Putting My Baby To Sleep/Far From The Madding Crowd	6
70	DJM DJS 2280	Day By Day/Cloud Of Blue	6
68	Mercury SMCL 20125	LOIS LANE (LP)	25

(see also Caravelles)

MICKEY LEE LANE

64	Stateside SS 354	Shaggy Dog/Oo Oo	10
65	Stateside SS 456	Hey Sah-Lo-Ney/Of Yesterday	50

MINT VALUE £

PENNY LANE

68 Columbia DB 8377 Loving Or Losing You/Deep Down Inside . . . 10
68 CBS 3718 The Boy Who Never Grew Up/I'm Going Back . . . 6
70 CBS 4749 Bouzouki/Make Up Or Break Up . . . 6
70 CBS 4905 Heartbreak House/He's Got A Hold Of My Heart. . . . 6
70 CBS 5311 Rock Me In The Cradle (Of Your Loving Arms)/I'm Free . . . 7

RONNIE LANE & SLIM CHANCE

73 GM GMS 011 How Come/Tell Everyone/Done This One Before (p/s) . . . 6
77 Polydor 2058 944 Street In The City/Annie (with Pete Townshend) . . . 6
77 Polydor 2058 944 Street In The City/Annie (12", with Pete Townshend) . . . 8
79 Gem GEMS 12 Kuschty Rye/You're So Right (p/s) . . . 5
74 GM GMS 1024 ANYMORE FOR ANYMORE (LP) . . . 18
75 Island ILPS 9321 RONNIE LANE AND SLIM CHANCE (LP) . . . 15
75 Island ILPS 9366 ONE FOR THE ROAD (LP) . . . 15
76 Atlantic K 50308 MAHONEY'S LAST STAND (LP, with Ron Wood, soundtrack) . . . 18
77 Polydor 2442 147 ROUGH MIX (LP, with Pete Townshend) . . . 12
80 Gem GEMLP 107 SEE ME (LP, with insert) . . . 12
88 Thunderbolt THBL 067P MAHONEY'S LAST STAND (LP, reissue, picture disc) . . . 12
(see also Small Faces, Faces, Pete Townshend & Ronnie Lane)

ROSEMARY LANE

60 Philips PB 1041 Down By The River/My First Love Letter. . . . 7
61 Philips BF 1127 Lyin' Kisses/The Nightingale Who Sang Off Key . . . 7
61 Philips BF 1172 Who Does He Think He Is/What Is The Age. . . . 7
63 Oriole CB 1871 Like You Should/Baby Please Be Kind . . . 8

TONY LANE & DELTONES

64 Sabre SA-45-5 It's Great/Now She's Mine . . . 15

LANE BROTHERS

60 London HLR 9150 Mimi/Two Dozen And A Half . . . 18

LANE SISTERS

61 Columbia DB 4671 Peek A Boo Moon/Birmingham Rag . . . 15

DON LANG (& HIS "FRANTIC" FIVE)

78s

56 HMV POP 178 Rock Around The Island/Jumpin' To Conclusions (solo) . . . 7
56 HMV POP 224 Rock And Roll Blues/Stop The World I Wanna Get Off (solo). . . . 8
56 HMV POP 260 Sweet Sue — Just You/Lazy Latin (solo). . . . 9
57 HMV POP 289 Rock Around The Cookhouse/Rock Mister Piper . . . 10
57 HMV POP 335 Rock-A-Billy/Come Go With Me (B-side with Skifflers). . . . 10
57 HMV POP 350 School Day (Ring! Ring! Goes The Bell)/Six-Five Special . . . 12
57 HMV POP 414 Red Planet Rock/Texas Tambourine . . . 12
58 HMV POP 434 Ramshackle Daddy/6-5 Hand Jive. . . . 12
58 HMV POP 465 Tequila/Junior Hand Jive. . . . 15
58 HMV POP 510 Hey Daddy!/The Bird On My Head. . . . 12
58 HMV POP 547 Queen Of The Hop/La-Do-Da-Da (solo) . . . 18
59 HMV POP 585 Wiggle Wiggle/(You Were Only) Teasin' (solo). . . . 30
59 HMV POP 623 Percy Green/Phineas McCoy (solo). . . . 35
59 HMV POP 649 A Hoot An' A Holler/See You Friday. . . . 40

SINGLES

56 HMV 7M 354 Four Brothers/I Want You To Be My Baby (solo) . . . 35
56 HMV 7M 381 Rock Around The Island/Jumpin' To Conclusions (solo) . . . 35
56 HMV 7M 416 Rock And Roll Blues/Stop The World I Wanna Get Off (solo). . . . 30
56 HMV POP 260 Sweet Sue — Just You/Lazy Latin (solo). . . . 20
57 HMV POP 289 Rock Around The Cookhouse/Rock Mister Piper . . . 35
57 HMV POP 335 Rock-A-Billy/Come Go With Me (B-side with Skifflers). . . . 30
57 HMV POP 350 School Day (Ring! Ring! Goes The Bell)/Six-Five Special . . . 25
57 HMV POP 382 White Silver Sands/Again 'N' Again 'N' Again. . . . 15
57 HMV POP 414 Red Planet Rock/Texas Tambourine . . . 35
58 HMV POP 434 Ramshackle Daddy/6-5 Hand Jive. . . . 25
58 HMV POP 465 Tequila/Junior Hand Jive. . . . 22
58 HMV POP 488 Witch Doctor/Cool Baby Cool . . . 12
58 HMV POP 510 Hey Daddy!/The Bird On My Head. . . . 12
58 HMV POP 547 Queen Of The Hop/La-Do-Da-Da (solo) . . . 15
59 HMV POP 585 Wiggle Wiggle/(You Were Only) Teasin' (solo). . . . 12
59 HMV POP 623 Percy Green/Phineas McCoy (solo). . . . 15
59 HMV POP 649 A Hoot An' A Holler/See You Friday. . . . 10
59 HMV POP 682 Reveille Rock/Frankie And Johnny . . . 15
60 HMV POP 714 Sink The Bismarck!/They Call Him Cliff (solo) . . . 25
60 HMV POP 805 Time Machine/Don't Open That Door. . . . 15
62 Decca F 11483 Wicked Women/Play Money (as Don Lang & Boulder Rollers). . . . 10

EP

57 HMV 7EG 8208 ROCK 'N' ROLL . . . 125

LPs

57 HMV DLP 1151 SKIFFLE SPECIAL (10", by Don Lang & His Skiffle Group) . . . 130
58 HMV DLP 1179 INTRODUCING THE HAND JIVE (10") . . . 125
62 Ace Of Clubs ACL 1111 TWENTY TOP-TWENTY TWISTS . . . 15
(see also Gordon Langhorn)

EDDIE LANG & LONNIE JOHNSON

67 Parlophone PMC 7019 BLUE GUITARS (LP). . . . 35
70 Parlophone PMC 7106 BLUE GUITARS VOLUME 2 (LP) . . . 35
(see also Blind Willie Dunn's Gin Bottle Four)

k.d. lang

87 Sire W 8465 — Rose Garden/High Time For A Detour (unissued in U.K.)
88 Sire W 7841 — Sugar Moon/Honky Tonk Medley (p/s) . . . 25
88 Sire W 7841T — Sugar Moon/Honky Tonk Medley/I'm Down To My Last Cigarette (12", p/s) . . . 50
88 Sire W 7697 — Our Day Will Come/Three Cigarettes In An Ashtray (live) (p/s) . . . 25
88 Sire W 7697T — Our Day Will Come/Three Cigarettes In An Ashtray (live)/ Johnny Get Angry (live) (12", p/s) . . . 50
90 Warner Brothers W 9535 — Ridin' The Rails (with Take Six)/DARLENE LOVE: Mr Fix-It (some with p/s) . . . 20/15
92 Sire W 0100 — Constant Craving (Edit)/Barefoot (Rhythmic Version) (p/s) . . . 5
92 Sire W 0100T — Constant Craving (Edit)/Barefoot (Rhythmic Version)/ Season Of Hollow Soul (12", p/s) . . . 10
92 Sire W 0100CD — Constant Craving (Edit)/Barefoot (Rhythmic Version)/ Season Of Hollow Soul (CD) . . . 18
92 Sire W 0135TW — Miss Chatelaine (St Tropez Mix)/Miss Chatelaine (St Tropez Edit)/Miss Chatelaine/Miss Chatelaine (Single Edit) (12", p/s with poster) . . . 10
92 Sire W 0135CD — Miss Chatelaine (Single Version)/Miss Chatelaine (St Tropez Edit)/ Wash Me Clean (live)/The Mind Of Love (live) (CD) . . . 10
93 Sire W 0157CD — Constant Craving (Edit)/Wash Me Clean (live)/The Mind Of Love (live) (CD) . . . 8
93 Sire W 0157CDX — Constant Craving (live)/Miss Chatelaine (live)/Big Boned Gal (live)/ Outside Myself (live) (CD) . . . 8

RAY LANG & JAMAICAN ROOM ORCHESTRA

57 Brunswick 05683 — Last Train (Biddi-Biddi Bum-Bum)/Keetch (Hey! Bernice) . . . 10
57 Brunswick 05683 — Last Train (Biddi-Biddi Bum-Bum)/Keetch (Hey! Bernice) (78) . . . 8

STEVIE LANGE

81 RCA RCA 152 — Remember My Name/I Don't Want To Know (1st issue, p/s) . . . 8
81 RCA LIM 1 — Remember My Name/I Don't Want To Know (2nd issue, p/s) . . . 6

LANGFORDS

60s Torino TSP 341 — Send Me An Angel/Candy (label credits to Langford Boys, some with p/s) . . . 10/6

GORDON LANGHORN

55 Decca F 10591 — Give A Fool A Chance/Don't Stay Away Too Long . . . 20
(see also Don Lang, Cyril Stapleton)

JERRY LANGLEY

65 Parlophone R 5325 — Little Grey Man/Bitter Sweets . . . 5
67 CBS 2935 — Joanna Jones/How Long . . . 5
(see also Langleys)

MARY LANGLEY

67 CBS 2862 — Stay In My World/Summer Love . . . 6
67 CBS 3032 — It Always Rains On Sunday/All My Life Is You . . . 5
(see also Perpetual Langley, Langleys)

PERPETUAL LANGLEY

66 Planet PLF 110 — We Wanna Stay Home/So Sad . . . 20
66 Planet PLF 115 — Surrender/Two By Two . . . 20
(see also Mary Langley, Langleys)

LANGLEYS

64 Fontana TF 483 — Snakes And Ladders/I Wander Everywhere . . . 5
65 Fontana TF 544 — Green Island/You Know I Love You . . . 5
(see also Jerry Langley, Mary Langley, Perpetual Langley)

(HUW) LLOYD LANGTON (GROUP)

83 Flicknife FLS 021 — Wind Of Change/Outside The Law (as Lloyd Langton Group, p/s) . . . 5
83 Flicknife SHARP 015 — OUTSIDE THE LAW (LP, 1,000 only with bonus 7": "Working Time"/ "I See You" [FREE 001], as Huw Lloyd Langton) . . . 15/12
86 Gas GAS 4014 — LIKE AN ARROW (THROUGH THE HEART) (LP) . . . 12
(see also Hawkwind, Widowmaker)

PHIL LANGTON TRIO

60s Holyground — PHIL LANGTON TRIO (LP) . . . 18

CYNTHIA LANIGAN

57 Parlophone R 4316 — Silent Lips/Jamie Boy (78) . . . 12

LESTER LANIN & HIS ORCHESTRA

62 Columbia 33SX 1442 — TWISTIN' IN HIGH SOCIETY! (LP) . . . 12

SNOOKY LANSON

50 London L 555 — The Old Master Painter/Did You Ever See A Dream Walking? (78) . . . 12
50 London L 682 — Roses/Where Are You Gonna Be When The Moon Shines (78) . . . 12
56 London HLD 8223 — It's Almost Tomorrow/Why Don't You Write . . . 120
56 London HLD 8223 — It's Almost Tomorrow/Why Don't You Write (78) . . . 12
56 London HLD 8236 — Stop (Let Me Off The Bus)/Last Minute Love . . . 200
56 London HLD 8236 — Stop (Let Me Off The Bus)/Last Minute Love (78) . . . 25
56 London HLD 8249 — Seven Days/Tippity Top . . . 200
56 London HLD 8249 — Seven Days/Tippity Top (78) . . . 20
56 London HL 7005 — Seven Days/Tippity Top (export issue) . . . 85
(see also Eve Young & Snooky Lanson, Teresa Brewer)

MARIO LANZA

53 HMV 7R 128 — The First Noel/Silent Night . . . 8
53 HMV 7R 129 — Questa O Quello (Verdi)/Recondita Armonia (Puccini) . . . 8
53 HMV 7R 130 — Be My Love/The Bayou Lullaby . . . 8
53 HMV 7R 131 — Serenade (Troselli)/Serenade (Drigo) . . . 8
53 HMV 7R 139 — Because/For You Alone . . . 8
53 HMV 7R 144 — Because You're Mine/The Song Angels Sing . . . 8
53 HMV 7R 145 — Lee-Ah-Loo/You Do Something To Me . . . 8
53 HMV 7R 146 — Mi Batte Il Cor ... O Paradiso!/Mamma, Quel Vino E Generoso . . . 8

MINT VALUE £

53	HMV 7R 147	O Come, All Ye Faithful/Oh! Little Town Of Bethlehem	8
53	HMV 7R 157	Granada/Lolita	8
53	HMV 7R 168	M'Appari Tutt' Amor (Flotow)/Libiamo, Libiamo Ne' Lieti Calici (B-side with Elaine Malbin)	8
53	HMV 7R 178	Valencia/Besame Mucho	8
57	RCA RCA 1026	A Night To Remember/Behold!	5
58	RCA RCA 1045	Seven Hills Of Rome/Come Dance With Me	5
58	RCA RCA 1059	On The Street Where You Live/Younger Than Springtime	5
58	RCA RCA 1080	Love In A Home/Do You Wonder	5
58	RCA RCA 1090	Drinking Song/Serenade (Romberg)	5
58	RCA RCA 1094	I'll Walk With God/The Lord's Prayer	5
60	RCA RCA 1155	O Come All Ye Faithful/Silent Night, Holy Night (78)	12
60	RCA RCA 1166	Because You're Mine/The Donkey Serenade	5
60	RCA RCA 1166	Because You're Mine/The Donkey Serenade (78)	15
53	HMV ALP 1071	THE GREAT CARUSO (LP, soundtrack)	12
54	HMV ALP 1202	OPERATIC ARIAS (LP)	18
55	HMV BLP 1071	SONGS OF ROMANCE (10" LP)	12
56	HMV ALP 1365	SERENADE (LP, soundtrack)	12
57	HMV BLP 1091	LANZA ON BROADWAY (10" LP)	12
57	HMV BLP 1094	THE TOUCH OF YOUR HAND (10" LP)	12
57	RCA RB 16002	IN A CAVALCADE OF SHOW TUNES (LP)	12
58	RCA RA 13001	THE SEVEN HILLS OF ROME (10" LP)	20
59	RCA RB 16085	SINGS A KISS AND OTHER LOVE SONGS (LP)	12
59	RCA RB 16113	THE STUDENT PRINCE (LP, soundtrack)	12
59	RCA RB 16158	FOR THE FIRST TIME (LP, soundtrack)	15
59	RCA RB 16167	LANZA ON BROADWAY (LP, soundtrack)	12
59	RCA RB 16171/SB 2054	LANZA SINGS CHRISTMAS CAROLS (LP, stereo)	15

LARKS

64	Pye International 7N 25284	The Jerk/Forget Me	30

SAM LARNER

61	Folkways FG 3507	NOW IS THE TIME FOR FISHING (LP)	18
74	Topic 12T 244	A GARLAND FOR SAM (LP, blue label)	15

LARO

60s	Kalypso XX 21	Jamaican Referendum Calypso/Wrong Impressions Of A Soldier	8

WINSTON LARO

70	Downtown DT 461	Goodnight My Love/BOYSIE: I Don't Want To Be Hurt	7

JULIUS LA ROSA

55	London HL 8154	Mobile/Pass It On	45
55	London HL 8154	Mobile/Pass It On (78)	8
55	London HLA 8170	Domani/Mama Rosa	40
55	London HLA 8193	Suddenly There's A Valley/Everytime I Kiss Carrie	45
56	HMV 7M 384	Lipstick And Candy And Rubber-Sole Shoe/Winter In New England	10
56	London HLA 8272	No Other Love/Rosanne	35
56	London HLA 8353	Jingle Bells (Campanelle)/Jingle Dingle	20
58	RCA RCA 1063	Torero/Milano	6
58	Columbia DB 4218	Let Nature Take Its Course/Until He Gets A Girl	6
59	Columbia DB 4287	Where's The Girl/Protect Me	6
60	London HLR 9092	Green Fields/Caress Me	7
64	London HLA 9901	Je/Gonna Build A Mountain	6
54	London RE-P 1005	SINGS (EP)	35
57	London HA-A 2031	JULIUS LA ROSA (LP)	60

LARRY'S ALL STARS

71	Ackee ACK 130	Pre-Fight/The Prayer	8

(see also Larry Lawrence, Delroy Wilson, Hugh Roy, Sensations)

LARRY (Marshall) & ALVIN

68	Studio One SO 2065	Nanny Goat/Smell You Crep	20
68	Studio One SO 2067	Can't You Understand/Hush Up	40
69	Studio One SO 2080	Lonely Room (No One To Give Me Love)/You Mean To Me	30
69	Coxsone CS 7081	Love Got Me/BOB ANDY: Lady With The Bright Light (both sides actually by Glen [Brown] & Dave [Barker])	25

(see also Larry Marshall, Sound Dimension, Vincent Gordon)

LARRY & JOHNNY

65	Outasite 45 501	Beatle Time Parts 1 & 2 (99 copies only)	120

(see also Larry Williams & Johnny 'Guitar' Watson)

LARRY & TOMMY

68	Polydor 56741	You've Gotta Bend A Little/Yo-Yo	8

JACK LARSON

61	Top Rank JAR 573	I Love The Way She Laughs/The Hammer Bell Song	8

LA'S

87	Go! Discs GOLAS 1	Way Out/Endless (p/s)	20
87	Go! Discs GOLAS 112	Way Out/Knock Me Down/Endless (12", red & silver p/s)	22
87	Go! Discs GOLAR 112	Way Out/Knock Me Down/Endless/Liberty Ship (Demo)/Freedom Song (Demo) (12", blue & silver stickered p/s listing 4 tracks)	22
87	Go! Discs GOLAR 112	Way Out/Knock Me Down/Endless/Liberty Ship (Demo)/Freedom Song (Demo) (12", blue & silver stickered p/s listing 5 tracks)	22
88	Go! Discs GOLAS 2	There She Goes/Come In Come Out (red p/s)	18
88	Go! Discs LASEP 2	There She Goes/Way Out/Who Knows/Come In Come Out (EP, blue p/s, 5,000 only)	25

88	Go! Discs GOLAS 212	There She Goes/Come In Come Out/Who Knows/ Man I'm Only Human (12", red sleeve)	20
88	Go! Discs LASCD 2	There She Goes/Come In Come Out/Who Knows/Man I'm Only Human (CD)	18
89	Go! Discs GOLAS 3	Timeless Melody/Clean Prophet (p/s, unissued; 10 test pressings only)	60+
89	Go! Discs LASEP 3	Timeless Melody (10", unissued)	
89	Go! Discs LASDJ 312	Timeless Melody/Clean Prophet/All By Myself/Rider Yer Camel (12", promo, 500 only)	50+
89	Go! Discs LASCD 3	Timeless Melody/Clean Prophet/All By Myself/Rider Yer Camel (CD, unissued)	
89	Go! Discs GOLAS 4	Timeless Melody/Clean Prophet (blue p/s)	8
89	Go! Discs LASMC 4	Timeless Melody/Clean Prophet (cassette, green inlay)	5
89	Go! Discs GOLAS 412	Timeless Melody/Clean Prophet/Knock Me Down/Over (12", purple p/s)	12
89	Go! Discs LASCD 4	Timeless Melody/Clean Prophet/Knock Me Down/Over (CD, orange card p/s)	18
90	Go! Discs GOLAS 5	There She Goes/Freedom Song (p/s)	5
90	Go! Discs GOLAB 5	There She Goes/Freedom Song (numbered box set with badge & 3 stickers)	10
90	Go! Discs GOLAS 5	There She Goes/Freedom Song (reissue, white sleeve)	7
90	Go! Discs GOLAS 512	There She Goes/Freedom Song/All By Myself (12", reissue, white p/s)	12
90	Go! Discs LASCD 5	There She Goes/Freedom Song/All By Myself (CD)	18
91	Go! Discs GOLAS 6	Feelin'/Doledrum (p/s)	6
91	Go! Discs LASMC 6	Feelin'/Doledrum (cassette)	5
91	Go! Discs GOLAB 6	Feelin'/IOU (Alternate Version)/Feelin' (Alternate Version)/Doledrum (numbered box set with badge & 3 stickers)	18
91	Go! Discs GOLAS 612	Feelin'/Liberty Ship/Doledrum/IOU (12", p/s)	8
91	Go! Discs GOLAR 612	Feelin'/IOU (Alternate Version)/Feelin' (Alternate Version)/Doledrum (12")	8
91	Go! Discs LASCD 6	Feelin'/Doledrum/IOU (Alternate Version)/Liberty Ship (CD)	8
90	Go! Discs LASCD 1	THE LA'S SOUND SAMPLER (CD, promo, 1,000 only)	15
91	Go! Discs 828 202-1	THE LA'S (LP)	35

(see also Cast)

COUNT LASHER

60s	Kalypso 100 AB	Calypso Cha Cha Cha/Perseverance	5
60s	Kalypso 105 AB	Slide Mongoose/Miss Constance	5

LASSIES & RAY CHARLES SINGERS

56	Brunswick 05571	Sleepy Head/This I Offer You	7

JAMES LAST

72	Polydor 2371 235	VOODOO PARTY (LP)	15

LAST BANDITS

80s	Solid ROK 722	The Angels Are Calling/The Dalkey Rake (p/s)	5

(see also Swell Maps, Nikki Sudden)

LAST CHANT

81	Chicken Jazz JAZZ 4	Run Of The Dove/Strength Alone/Tradition (p/s)	8

(see also Waterboys)

LAST EXIT

75	Wudwink WUD 01	Whispering Voices/Evensong (no p/s)	35
75	Wudwink WUD.C.101	FIRST FROM LAST EXIT (cassette only, pink card insert, sold at gigs, only 3 copies known to exist)	100+

(see also Newcastle Big Band, Police, Sting)

LAST FLIGHT

81	Heavy Metal HEAVY 5	Dance To The Music/I'm Ready (p/s)	8

LAST MAN IN EUROPE

85	Cocteau CO 22	A Certain Bridge/TV Addict (p/s)	15

LAST POETS

72	Douglas DGL 69012	THIS IS MADNESS (LP)	20

LAST RESORT

78	Red Meat RMRS 01	Having Fun?/F.U.2 (die-cut printed paper sleeve)	20

LAST RESORT

81	own label	Violence In Our Minds/Help Hostage/Soul Boys (cassette; 4-track issue)	20
81	own label	Violence In Our Minds/Help Hostage (cassette; 3-track issue)	20
82	Last Resort LR 1	SKINHEAD ANTHEMS (LP, red vinyl; also white, blue & black vinyl)	20-25

LAST RITES

83	Flicknife FLS 219	We Don't Care/Step Down (p/s)	5
84	Essential 004	FASCISM MEANS WAR (EP, gatefold p/s)	5

LAST ROUGH CAUSE

86	L.R.C. LRC 1	THE VIOLENT FEW (EP)	7

LAST STAND

81	Silly Symbol SJP 825	Just A Number/Caviare (p/s)	15

LAST STRAW

78	Solent SS 049	Oh Lady/Fly By Night (p/s)	50

LAST WORD

74	Polydor 2066 429	Keep On Bumping Before You Run Out Of Gas/Funky And Some	8

LAST WORDS

79	Rough Trade RT 022	Animal World/No Music In The World Today (p/s)	8
79	Remand REMAND 2	Todays Kidz/There's Something Wrong (p/s)	6
81	Armageddon ARM 2	THE LAST WORDS (LP)	12

LATE SHOW

78	Decca F 13777	Drop Dead/Ain't Gonna Stamp On His Face (p/s)	15
79	Decca F 13822	BRISTOL STOMP EP (p/s)	10

MINT VALUE £

YUSEF LATEEF
58 Esquire 32-069 THE SOUNDS OF YUSEF (LP) . . . 25
58 Columbia Clef 33CX 10124 BEFORE DAWN (LP) . . . 22
72 Atlantic K 40359 GENTLE GIANT (LP) . . . 12
73 Prestige PR 24007 YUSEF LATEEF (LP) . . . 15
74 Atlantic K 50041 PART OF THE SEARCH (LP) . . . 12
74 Milestone ML 47009 THE MANY FACES OF YUSEF LATEEF (LP) . . . 12
75 Atlantic K 60102 10 YEARS HENCE (LP) . . . 12

GENE LATTER
66 Decca F 12364 Just A Minute Or Two/Dream Lover . . . 10
66 Decca F 12397 Mother's Little Helper/Please Come Back To Me Again . . . 15
67 CBS 202483 Something Inside Me Died/Don't Go . . . 8
67 CBS 202655 Always/A Woman Called Sorrow . . . 8
67 CBS 2843 A Little Piece Of Leather/Funny Face Girl . . . 18
67 CBS 2986 With A Child's Heart/Ways . . . 15
68 Direction 58-3245 A Tribute To Otis/Bring Your Love Home . . . 8
68 Spark SRL 1015 My Life Ain't Easy/Angie (as Gene Latter & Detours) . . . 6
69 Spark SRL 1022 Sign On The Dotted Line/I Love You . . . 10
69 Spark SRL 1031 The Old Iron Bell/Holding A Dream . . . 6
69 Parlophone R 5800 Help Me Judy, Help Me/On The Highway . . . 7
69 Parlophone R 5815 Tiger Bay/We Can Make Out . . . 7
70 Parlophone R 5853 Someday You'll Need My Love/Come On Home . . . 6
71 Parlophone R 5896 Catch My Soul/Happiness . . . 6
71 Parlophone R 5913 Sing A Song Of Freedom/Too Busy Thinking About My Baby . . . 5
72 Spark SRL 1063 Sign On The Dotted Line/I Love You (reissue) . . . 6
70s Youngblood YB 1069 All Over Now/Annie's Place . . . 5
(see also Detours)

STANLEY LAUDAN
58 Oriole CB 1434 Two Guitars/Blue Shawl . . . 12
58 Oriole CB 1434 Two Guitars/Blue Shawl (78) . . . 8

THE LAUGHING APPLE
81 Autonomy AUT 001 HA HA HEE HEE (EP) . . . 8
81 Autonomy AUT 002 Participate!/Wouldn't You? (foldover p/s) . . . 6
82 Essential ESS 001 Precious Feeling/Celebration (p/s) . . . 8
83 Creation Artefact LYN 12903 Wouldn't You?/THE PASTELS: I Wonder Why! (live) (33rpm flexidisc, initially free with The Legend! 7" "'73 In '83" [CRE 001]) . . . 8/5
(see also Biff Bang Pow!, Revolving Paint Dream)

LAUGHING GAS
70 RCA RCA 2006 All Shapes And Sizes/Opus No. 1 . . . 8

CYNDI LAUPER
84 Portrait WA 4290 Time After Time/I'll Kiss You (picture disc) . . . 6
84 Portrait WA 4620 She Bop/Witness (Cyndi-shaped picture disc) . . . 8
86 Portrait CYNDI 1P Change Of Heart/What A Thrill (picture disc) . . . 5
87 Epic CYNP 1 What's Going On/What's Going On (Version) (picture disc) . . . 5
89 Epic CYNC 5 My First Night Without You/Unabbreviated Love/Iko Iko/ When You Were Mine (CD, picture disc) . . . 8
89 Epic 655 091-1 My First Night Without You (Edited Remix)/Unabbreviated Love (3" CD, gatefold card sleeve) . . . 8
89 Epic CYNC 6 Heading West/What's Going On (live)/She Bop (live)/ Money Changes Everything (live) (CD, picture disc) . . . 8
(see also Blue Angel)

LAUREL (Aitken) & OWEN (Gray)
62 Blue Beat BB 149 She's Going To Napoli/Have Mercy Mr Percy . . . 15
(see also Laurel Aitken, Owen Gray)

LAURELS
68 RCA Victor RCA 1741 Sunshine Thursday/Threepence A Tune . . . 6
69 RCA Victor RCA 1836 Making It Groovy/Rainmaker . . . 6

ROD LAUREN
59 RCA RCA 1165 If I Had A Girl/No Wonder . . . 10
59 RCA RCA 1165 If I Had A Girl/No Wonder (78) . . . 8

ZACK LAURENCE (ORCHESTRA)
61 Parlophone R 4802 Teenage Concerto/Saratoga . . . 6
63 Parlophone R 5000 Tempo Seven/Sleeve Shaker . . . 6
66 HMV 7EG 8968 BEATLE CONCERTO (EP) . . . 8

JOHN LAURENZ
55 London HL 8138 Goodbye, Stranger, Goodbye/Red Roses . . . 45
55 London HL 8138 Goodbye, Stranger, Goodbye/Red Roses (78) . . . 12
65 Decca F 12147 99 Times Out Of 100/I Can Feel It . . . 6

LAURIE
66 Decca F 12347 He Understands Me/Fools Never Learn . . . 6
66 Decca F 12424 I Love Onions/I Want Him . . . 7

CY LAURIE JAZZ BAND
60s Melodisc M 1479 You Make Me Love You/Dippermouth . . . 5
61 Storyville A 45045 Don't Go Away Nobody/There'll Come A Day . . . 5
55 Esquire EP 29 CY LAURIE BAND (EP) . . . 20
55 Esquire EP 39 CY LAURIE BAND (EP) . . . 10
56 Esquire EP 89 CY LAURIE BAND (EP) . . . 10
56 Esquire EP 120 CY LAURIE BAND (EP) . . . 20
56 Tempo EXA 32 JAZZ IN DENMARK (EP) . . . 12
57 Esquire EP 124 CY LAURIE BAND (EP) . . . 15

MINT VALUE £

57 Esquire EP 140 CY PLAYS LIL (EP) . . . 10
57 Melodisc EPM 7-71 CY LAURIE'S JAZZ BAND (EP) . . . 10
58 Esquire EP 200 YOU'RE NEXT (EP) . . . 10
59 Esquire EP 210 CY LAURIE BAND (EP) . . . 15
60 Esquire EP 234 CY LAURIE BAND (EP) . . . 15
58 Parlophone GEP 8710 JUNGLE JAZZ (EP) . . . 10
60s Storyville SEP 395 CY LAURIE BAND VOL. 5 (EP) . . . 8
55 Esquire 20-037 CY LAURIE JAZZ BAND (10" LP) . . . 30
50s Esquire 32-008 CY LAURIE JAZZ BAND (LP) . . . 30

LINDA LAURIE

59 London HL 8807 Ambrose/Ooh, What A Lover . . . 15
59 London HL 8807 Ambrose/Ooh, What A Lover (78) . . . 10
60 Top Rank JAR 277 Stay With Me/All Winter Long . . . 8

LAURIE SISTERS

60 MGM MGM 1083 Don't Forget (To Sign Your Name With A Kiss)/I Surrender Dear . . . 8
61 MGM MGM 1128 Live It Up/Lonesome And Sorry . . . 8

MISS LAVELL

65 Vocalion VP 9236 Everybody's Got Somebody/The Best Part Of Me . . . 25

DALIAH LAVI

70 Pye Intl. 7N 25533 Won't You Join Me/Karriere . . . 5
71 Pye Intl. 7N 25582 I'm Leaving/Here's To You . . . 6
70 Pye Intl. NSPL 28141 DALIAH LAVI (LP) . . . 15

JUNE LAVERICK

60 Oriole CB 1537 Stop/JOHNNY WEBB: Concertino . . . 8
60 Oriole CB 1537 Stop/JOHNNY WEBB: Concertino (78) . . . 15

(see also Dickie Henderson & June Laverick, Johnny Webb)

ROGER La VERN & MICRONS

63 Decca F 11791 Christmas Stocking/Reindeer Ride . . . 40
75 SRT SRTS/CUS/042 Sing-A-Long Piano Party Parts 1 & 2 (maxi-single, p/s) . . . 8

(see also Tornados)

BETTY LAVETTE

67 Stateside SS 2015 I Feel Good All Over/Only Your Love Can Save Me . . . 40
68 Pama PM 748 Only Your Love Can Save Me/I Feel Good All Over (reissue) . . . 25
70 Polydor 56786 He Made A Woman Out Of Me/Nearer To You . . . 10
72 Mojo 2092 030 Let Me Down Easy/I Feel Good All Over/What I Don't Know Won't Hurt Me . . . 8
73 Atlantic K 10299 Your Turn To Cry/Soul Tambourine . . . 12
78 Atlantic K 11198 Doin' The Best I Can Parts 1 & 2 . . . 5

AZIE LAWRENCE

59 Mezzotone ME 7001/7002 West Indians In England/Jump Up . . . 7
59 Mezzotone ME 7004 Love In Every Land/No Dice . . . 7
60 Starlite ST45 022 West Indians In England/Jump Up (with Carib Serenaders) . . . 7
61 Starlite ST45 041 No Dice/Love In Every Land . . . 7
61 Melodisc M 1563 Jamaica Blues/Come Rumble & Tumble With Me . . . 7
61 Melodisc M 1572 You Didn't Want To Know . . . 6
61 Blue Beat BB 71 So Far Apart/Palms Of Victory (with Melobeats) . . . 15
64 Blue Beat BB 222 Pempelem/Lovers Understand . . . 15

DIANE LAWRENCE

67 Doctor Bird DB 1075 I Won't Hang Around Like A Hound Dog/Read It Over . . . 25
68 Jolly JY 005 Treat Me Nice/I'll Be Loving You . . . 10

EDDIE LAWRENCE

59 Coral Q 72361 The Salesman's Philosopher/Mother Philosopher . . . 6

ELLIOTT LAWRENCE BAND

51 Vogue V 9024 Sixty-Minute Man/Quick (78) . . . 10
58 Vogue LAE 12057 PLAYS GERRY MULLIGAN ARRANGEMENTS (LP) . . . 15

GENE LAWRENCE

67 Jump Up JU 505 Longest Day Meringue/Bachelor Boy . . . 6
67 Jump Up JU 510 Meringue Triniana/Devil Woman . . . 6

LARRY LAWRENCE (Jamaica)

63 Island WI 091 Garden Of Eden/DERRICK MORGAN: Sendin' This Message . . . 20

(see also Larry's Allstars, McBean Scott & Champions)

LARRY LAWRENCE (U.S.)

59 Pye International 7N 25042 Goofin' Off/Bongo Boogie (as Larry Lawrence & Band Of Gold) . . . 8
59 Pye International N 25042 Goofin' Off/Bongo Boogie (as Larry Lawrence & Band Of Gold) (78) . . . 10
60 Ember EMB S 106 Squad Car Theme/Jug-A-Roo (with Beatniks, some in art p/s) . . . 12/7

LEE LAWRENCE (& CORONETS)

53 Decca F 10177 Crying In The Chapel/To Live My Life With You (78) . . . 8
54 Decca F 10285 The Little Mustard Seed/My Love For You . . . 15
54 Decca F 10367 The Story Of Tina/For You My Love . . . 15
54 Decca F 10408 The Things I Didn't Do/You Still Mean The Same To Me . . . 12
55 Decca F 10422 My Own True Love (Tara's Theme)/Beware Now! . . . 12
55 Decca F 10438 Lights Of Paris/A Love Like Ours . . . 10
55 Decca F 10485 Wedding Bells And Silver Horse-Shoes/Will You Be Mine Alone? . . . 10
55 Columbia SCM 5175 Beyond The Stars/Give Me Your Word . . . 12
55 Columbia SCM 5181 My World Stood Still/Don't Worry . . . 12
55 Columbia SCM 5190 More Than A Millionaire/Overnight . . . 10
55 Columbia SCM 5201 Suddenly There's A Valley/Mi Muchacha (Little Girl) . . . 18
56 Columbia SCM 5228 Young And Foolish/Don't Tell Me Not To Love You . . . 12
56 Columbia SCM 5254 We Believe In Love/Welcome To My Heart . . . 10
56 Columbia SCM 5283 Come Back, My Love/Valley Valparaiso . . . 10

MINT VALUE £

56	Columbia DB 3830	From The Candy Store On The Corner/High Upon A Mountain	18
57	Columbia DB 3855	Rock 'n' Roll Opera/Don't Nobody Move	25
57	Columbia DB 3855	Rock 'n' Roll Opera/Don't Nobody Move (78)	12
57	Columbia DB 3885	Your Love Is My Love/By You, By You, By You	10
57	Columbia DB 3922	Sold To The Man With The Broken Heart/Chapel Of The Roses	10
57	Columbia DB 3981	His Servant/Lonely Ballerina	8
59	Top Rank JAR 175	The Man I Could Be/Be My Love	7
58	Columbia SEG 7780	LEE LAWRENCE (EP)	22
53	Decca LF 1132	PRESENTING LEE LAWRENCE (10" LP)	35

STEVE LAWRENCE

78s

56	Vogue Coral Q 72133	Speedo/The Chicken And The Hawk	15
57	Vogue Coral Q 72243	Party Doll/Pum-Pa-Lum (The Bad Donkey)	10
57	Vogue Coral Q 72264	Fabulous/Can't Wait For The Summer (with Dick Jacobs Band)	8
57	Vogue Coral Q 72281	Fraulein/Blue Rememberin' You	8
58	Coral Q 72335	Those Nights At The Round Table (with Guinevere)/Stranger In Mexico	8
59	Coral Q 72353	These Things Are Free/I Only Have Eyes For You	20
60	HMV POP 689	Pretty Blue Eyes/You're Nearer	50
60	HMV POP 726	Footsteps/You Don't Know	60

SINGLES

53	Parlophone MSP 6038	Say It Isn't True/This Night (Madalena) (as Steve & Bernie Lawrence)	22
54	Parlophone MSP 6080	Remember Me (You Taught Me To Love)/Too Little Time	22
54	Parlophone MSP 6106	You Can't Hold A Memory In Your Arms/King For A Day	22
55	Vogue Coral Q 72114	Open Up The Gates Of Mercy/My Impression Of Janie	15
56	Vogue Coral Q 72133	Speedo/The Chicken And The Hawk	22
57	Vogue Coral Q 72228	The Banana Boat Song/If You Would Say You're Mine	12
57	Vogue Coral Q 72243	Party Doll/Pum-Pa-Lum (The Bad Donkey)	18
57	Vogue Coral Q 72264	Fabulous/Can't Wait For The Summer (with Dick Jacobs Band)	18
57	Vogue Coral Q 72281	Fraulein/Blue Rememberin' You	12
57	Vogue Coral Q 72286	Never Mind/Long Before I Knew You	12
58	Coral Q 72304	Geisha Girl/I Don't Know	6
58	Coral Q 72335	Those Nights At The Round Table (with Guinevere)/Stranger In Mexico	6
59	Coral Q 72353	These Things Are Free/I Only Have Eyes For You	7
59	HMV POP 604	Only Love Me (Angelina)/Loving Is A Way Of Living	6
60	HMV POP 689	Pretty Blue Eyes/You're Nearer	10
60	HMV POP 726	Footsteps/You Don't Know	8
60	Top Rank JAR 416	Say It Isn't True/My Shawl	6
60	HMV POP 763	Why, Why, Why/You're Everything Wonderful	6
60	London HLT 9166	Girls, Girls, Girls/Little Boy Blue	8
60	HMV POP 795	Going Steady/Come Back, Silly Girl	6
61	HMV POP 914	In Time/Oh How You Lied	6
61	HMV POP 950	Somewhere Along The Way/While There's Still Time	6
62	CBS AAG 101	The Lady Wants To Twist/Tell Her I Said Hello	6
62	CBS AAG 127	Go Away Little Girl/If You Love Her	7
62	CBS AAG 139	Don't Be Afraid Little Darlin'/Don't Come Running Back	6
63	CBS AAG 150	Poor Little Rich Girl/More	6
63	CBS AAG 166	Walking Proud/House Without Windows	6
65	CBS 201786	Last Night I Made A Little Girl Cry/Where Can I Go	7

EPs

59	Coral FEP 2010	HERE'S STEVE LAWRENCE NO. 1	18
59	Coral FEP 2012	HERE'S STEVE LAWRENCE NO. 2	18

LPs

60	HMV CLP 1326	SWING SOFTLY WITH ME	22
60	Top Rank BUY 033	STEVE LAWRENCE	20
61	HMV CLP 1462	THE STEVE LAWRENCE SOUND (also stereo CSD 1374)	18/22
62	HMV CLP 1504	PORTRAIT OF MY LOVE (also stereo CSD 1404)	18/22
63	CBS (S)BPG 62088	COME WALTZ WITH ME	12
63	United Artists (S)ULP 1022	LAWRENCE GOES LATIN	12
63	CBS BPG 62124	WINNERS	12
64	Coral LVA 9219	SONGS EVERYBODY KNOWS	15

STEVE LAWRENCE & EYDIE GORMÉ

55	Vogue Coral Q 72044	Make Yourself Comfortable/EYDIE GORMÉ: Chain Reaction	10
55	Vogue Coral Q 72085	Besame Mucho/Take A Deep Breath	10
61	London HLT 9290	The Facts Of Life/I'm A Girl, You're A Boy	8
63	CBS AAG 163	I Want To Stay Here/Ain't Love (some in p/s)	8/5
63	CBS AAG 178	I Can't Stop Talking About You/To The Movies We Go	5
59	Vogue Coral FEP 2017	STEVE LAWRENCE AND EYDIE GORMÉ (EP)	12
63	CBS AGG 20035	STEVE AND EYDIE (EP)	10
60	HMV CLP 1372/CSD 1310	STEVE AND EYDIE — WE GOT US (LP)	15
61	HMV CLP 1404/CSD 1329	THE GOLDEN HITS (LP)	15
61	HMV CLP 1463	COZY (LP)	15
62	HMV CLP 1517	COME SING WITH ME (LP)	15

(see also Eydie Gormé)

BILLY (M.) LAWRIE

69	Polydor 56363	Roll Over Beethoven/Come Back Joanna (as Billy M. Lawrie)	10
73	RCA RCA 2439	Rock And Roller/Shalee Shala	6
73	RCA SF 8395	SHIP IMAGINATION (LP)	25

ELOISE LAWS

69	CBS 4056	I'd Do It All Again/To Know Him Is To Love Him	6
70	CBS 4990	You Make Me Feel Like Someone/The Only Boy In My Life	6
77	Invictus INV 5247	Love Goes Deeper Than That/Camouflage	5

RONNIE LAWS

76 Blue Note BNXW 7004 Always There/Tidal Wave . . . 6
79 Blue Note UP 36497 Always There/Tidal Wave (reissue) . . . 5
79 Blue Note 12UP 36497 Always There/Tidal Wave (12") . . . 8
75 Blue Note BNLA 452 PRESSURE SENSITIVE (LP) . . . 12
76 Blue Note UAG 20007 FEVER (LP) . . . 12
77 Blue Note UAG 30079 FRIENDS AND STRANGERS (LP) . . . 12
78 Blue Note UAG 30204 FLAME (LP) . . . 12

LAWSON-HAGGART ROCKIN' BAND

59 Brunswick OE 9451 BOPPING AT THE HOP (EP) . . . 70
53 Brunswick LA 8576 JELLY ROLL'S JAZZ (10" LP) . . . 15
53 Brunswick LA 8580 BLUES ON THE RIVER (10" LP) . . . 18
53 Brunswick LA 8593 KING OLIVER'S JAZZ (10" LP) . . . 15
54 Brunswick LA 8635 RAGTIME JAMBOREE (10" LP) . . . 15
54 Brunswick LA 8639 WINDY CITY JAZZ (10" LP) . . . 15
55 Brunswick LA 8703 SOUTH OF THE MASON-DIXON LINE (10" LP) . . . 15
59 Brunswick STA 3010 BOPPING AT THE HOP (LP) . . . 90

JULIET LAWSON

72 Sovereign SOV 111 Only A Week Away/Weeds In The Yard . . . 7
72 Sovereign SVNA 7257 BOO (LP) . . . 35
(see also Trees)

SHIRLEY LAWSON

68 Soul City SC 108 The Star/One More Chance . . . 45

JOHN LAWTON featuring Roger Glover & Guests

75 Purple PUR 128 Little Chalk Blue/RONNIE DIO: Sitting In A Dream . . . 10
(see also Roger Glover, Ronnie Dio, Deep Purple, Uriah Heep, Lucifer's Friend)

LOU LAWTON

67 Ember EMB S 232 Doin' The Philly Dog/I Am Searching . . . 25
68 Speciality SPE 1005 I'm Just A Fool/Wrapped In A Dream . . . 22

LAXTON & OLIVER

69 Blue Cat BS 168 Wickeder/Stay In My Arms . . . 15

LAY-A-BAHTS

60 Parlophone R 4641 Fings Ain't Wot They Used T'be/Layin' Abaht/The Ceiling . . . 5

OSSIE LAYNE

65 R&B MRB 5006 Come Back/Never Answer That 'Phone . . . 30

EDDIE LAYTON

58 Mercury 7MT 221 Over The Waves/Bright Lights Over Brussels . . . 6
59 Mercury AMT 1064 Duck Walk/Doodles . . . 10

TEDDY LAYTON JAZZ BAND

58 Parlophone R 4411 Down By The Riverside/Wooden Joe's Weary Blues . . . 6

KEN LAZ(A)RUS (& CREW)

65 Island WI 220 Funny (as Ken Lazrus & Byron Lee Orchestra)/
BYRON LEE ORCHESTRA: Walk Like A Dragon . . . 22
70 London HLJ 10301 Monkey Man/Bongo Nyah . . . 7
71 Explosion EX 2056 Girl/TOMORROW'S CHILDREN: Sister Big Stuff . . . 10
72 Explosion EX 2064 Hail The Man/Where Do I Go . . . 6
72 London HLH 10379 Hail The Man/Where I Go . . . 5
70 London HA-J 8412 REGGAE SCORCHER (LP, unissued)
70 London LGJ/ZGJ 102 REGGAE SCORCHER (LP) . . . 22
70 London ZGJ 107 REGGAE — GREATEST HITS VOL. 1 (LP) . . . 15
70 London ZGJ 108 REGGAE — GREATEST HITS VOL. 2 (LP) . . . 15

LAZY LATINS

67 Morgan MR 110 P LAZY LATIN (LP) . . . 12

LAZY SMOKE

80s Heyoka CORRIDOR OF FACES (LP, reissue of U.S. LP) . . . 15

BARBARA LEA

56 London HB-U 1058 A WOMAN IN LOVE (10" LP) . . . 30
56 Esquire 32/043 NOBODY ELSE BUT ME (LP) . . . 22
57 Esquire 32/063 IN LOVE (LP) . . . 22

JIMMY LEA

85 Trojan KANE 001 Citizen Kane/Poland (p/s) . . . 15
(see also Slade)

LEADBELLY (HUDDIE LEDBETTER)

78s

50 Capitol CL 13282 Eagle Rock Rag/Backwater Blues . . . 15
51 Melodisc 1140 How Long/Good Morning Blues . . . 20
51 Melodisc 1151 Goodnight Irene/Ain't You Glad . . . 20
51 Melodisc 1187 On A Monday/John Henry . . . 20
54 Jazz Collector L 108 New Black Snake Moan/Fore Day Worry Blues . . . 20
55 Jazz Collector L 124 Pig Meat Papa/Becky Beem . . . 20
55 HMV MH 190 Alabama Bound/Pick A Bale Of Cotton . . . 30

EPs

56 Melodisc EPM7 63 HOW LONG BLUES . . . 20
58 Melodisc EPM7 77 LEADBELLY . . . 20
58 Melodisc EPM7 82 SEE SEE RIDER . . . 20
59 Melodisc EPM7 87 PARTY PLAYS AND SONGS . . . 18
59 RCA RCX 146 ROCK ISLAND LINE . . . 15
61 Capitol EAP1 1821 HUDDIE LEDBETTER'S BEST NO. 1 . . . 15

			MINT VALUE £
61	Capitol EAP4 1821	HUDDIE LEDBETTER'S BEST NO. 2	15
61	Capitol EAP1 20111	LEADBELLY	15
61	Storyville SEP 337	LEADBELLY	15
62	Storyville SEP 387	STORYVILLE BLUES ANTHOLOGY VOL. 7	15

LPs

53	Capitol LC 6597	LEADBELLY SINGS CLASSICS IN JAZZ (10")	35
57	Melodisc MLP 511	LEADBELLY VOL. 1 (10", green & silver labels)	25
57	Melodisc MLP 512	LEADBELLY VOL. 2 (10", green & silver labels)	25
58	Melodisc MLP 515	LEADBELLY VOL. 3 (10", green & silver labels)	25
58	Melodisc MLP 517	PLAYS PARTY SONGS (10", green & silver labels)	25
58	Melodisc MLP 12-107	THE SAGA OF LEADBELLY (green & silver or blue & black labels)	25
59	Melodisc MLP 12-113	LEADBELLY'S LAST SESSIONS VOLUME 2 PART 1	25
59	Melodisc MLP 12-114	LEADBELLY'S LAST SESSIONS VOLUME 2 PART 2	25
62	Storyville SLP 124	A DEMON OF A MAN — BLUES ANTHOLOGY	20
63	Storyville SLP 139	LEADBELLY 2 — T.B. BLUES	20
63	Capitol T 1821	HIS GUITAR, HIS VOICE, HIS PIANO: HUDDIE LEDBETTER'S BEST	15
63	RCA Victor RD 7567	GOOD MORNING BLUES	18
65	Verve (S)VLP 5002	TAKE THIS HAMMER	18
65	Society SOC 994	LEADBELLY PLAYS AND SINGS	15
66	Elektra EKL 301/2	THE LIBRARY OF CONGRESS RECORDINGS (3-LP)	25
67	Verve (S)VLP 5011	KEEP YOUR HANDS OFF HER	18
69	Xtra XTRA 1046	LEADBELLY SINGS FOLK SONGS	22
69	Xtra XTRA 1126	SHOUT ON	22
69	Storyville 616 003	IN THE EVENING WHEN THE SUN GOES DOWN	15
69	Storyville 616 004	GOODNIGHT IRENE	15
70	CBS 64103	LEADBELLY	15
72	Ember CW 132	LEADBELLY	12
70s	Xtra XTRAD 1017	THE LEADBELLY BOX SET (2-LP)	18

LEADBELLY & BLIND LEMON JEFFERSON

61	Jazz Collector JEL 124	THE MALE BLUES VOLUME 8 (EP)	18

(see also Blind Lemon Jefferson)

HARRY LEADER BAND

65	Parlophone R 5386	Dragon Fly/Rush Hour	5

LEADERBEATS

60	Top Rank JAR 405	Dance, Dance, Dance/Washington Square	12

LEADERS (Jamaica)

68	Amalgamated AMG 804	Tit For Tat (actually by Lynn Taitt & Jets)/MARVETTS: You Take Too Long	22

(see also Pioneers, Stranger Cole, Versatiles)

LEADERS (U.K.)

65	Fontana TF 602	Night People/Love Will Find A Way	10

ANN LEAF

50s	Parlophone DP 348	Rio Coco/Prom Rag (78, export issue)	8
50s	Parlophone DP 357	Tambo/In A Little Spanish Town (78, export issue)	8

LEADING FIGURES

67	Deram DML/SML 1006	OSCILLATION 67! (LP)	22
67	Ace Of Clubs SCL 1225	SOUND AND MOVEMENT (LP)	35

(see also Jon Lord, Deep Purple)

LEAF HOUND

71	Decca SKL-R 5094	GROWERS OF MUSHROOM (LP)	550

(see also Brunning Sunflower Blues Band, Black Cat Bones, Atomic Rooster, Cactus, Headbangers)

LEAGUE OF GENTLEMEN

65	Columbia DB 7666	Each Little Falling Tear/And I Do Now	60
66	Planet PLF 109	How Can You Tell/How Do They Know (with Planet company sleeve)	60
80	EG/Virgin EGEDS 1	Heptaparaparshinokh/Marriagemuzic	6

(see also Giles Giles & Fripp, Brain)

LEAH

73	GM GMS 10	Arise Sir Henry/Uptight Basil	5

(see also Pete Dello, Red Herring)

JOE LEAHY (ORCHESTRA)

55	Parlophone MSP 6149	Desiree/Milano	6
55	Parlophone MSP 6168	Green Fire/Secretly Mine	6
57	London HBZ 1072	LOVELY LADY (10" LP)	15

MIKE LEANDER ORCHESTRA

64	Decca F 11849	The Heroes/Rang A Tang	5
69	MCA MU 1095	Ride The Wild Wild Country/Here There And Everywhere	6
69	MCA MUPS 383	MIGRATION (LP)	12

VICKY LEANDROS

72	Philips 6000 025	I Am/Love Tell Me Where Is Your Home	10
72	Philips 6000 049	Come What May (Apres Toi)/Take A Little Time	5
72	Philips 6000 066	Country Freedom/Mouth Organ Boy	6
72	Philips 6000 081	The Love In Your Eyes/You Answered My Prayer	5
73	Philips 6000 111	When Bouzoukis Played/Jacques	5
74	Philips 6000 129	Dreams Are Good Friends/Lovin' And Tenderness	6
74	Philips 6000 408	Danny, Teach Me To Dance/Love Me Tender	5
75	Philips 6000 169	More Than That/Papa's Knee	8
72	Philips 6303 019	I AM (LP)	12
72	Philips 6303 062	VICKY LEANDROS (LP)	12

(see also Vicky)

BOB LEAPER
65 Pye 7N 15700 High Wire (Theme From 'Danger Man')/The Lost World ... 40
64 Decca LK 4639 BIG BAND, BEATLE SONGS (LP) ... 20

LEAPERS CREEPERS SLEEPERS
66 Island WI 275 Precious Words/Ba Boo ... 25

KEVIN 'KING' LEAR
67 Polydor 56203 Count Me Out/Pretty Woman ... 22
68 Page One POF 087 Power Of Love/Mr. Pearly ... 10
68 Page One POF 109 Cry Me A River/Shoe Shine Sam ... 18
69 Page One POF 132 The Snake/Man In The Funnies ... 15

ERNEST LEARDEE
50 Felstead SDL 86015 CARNIVAL IN MARTINIQUE (10" LP) ... 20

TIMOTHY LEARY MEETS THE GRID
90 Evolution EVO 1 Origins Of Dance (Electronic Future Mix)/(Hi-Tec Pagan Mix) (12") ... 10
(see also Grid)

LEATHERCOATED MINDS
67 Fontana (S)TL 5412 A TRIP DOWN THE SUNSET STRIP (LP) ... 60
(see also J.J. Cale)

LEATHERHEAD
74 Philips 6006 371 Gimme Your Money Please/Epitaph (die-cut 'Leatherhead' sleeve) ... 6

LEATHER NUN
79 Industrial IR 0006 Slow Death (EP) ... 10
84 Subterranean SUB 40 Prime Mover/F.F.A. (p/s) ... 5
79 Industrial IRC 27 THE LEATHER NUN AT THE SCALA CINEMA (cassette) ... 12

BILL LEATHERWOOD
60 Top Rank JAR 506 The Long Walk/My Foolish Heart ... 7

LEA VALLEY SKIFFLE GROUP
57 Esquire 10-508 Streamline Train/Railroad Bill (78) ... 22
58 Esquire 10-518 I'm Gonna Walk And Talk With Jesus/Oh Mary, Don't You Weep (78) ... 22
58 Esquire EP 163 LEA VALLEY SKIFFLE GROUP (EP) ... 60

LEAVES
66 Fontana TF 713 Hey Joe/Funny Little World ... 35

OTIS LEAVILL(E)
70 Atlantic 2091 015 I Love You/I Need You ... 10
70 Atlantic 2091 035 Love Uprising/Glad I Met You ... 8
71 Atlantic 2091 160 There's Nothing Better/I'm So Jealous ... 10

LE CHEILE
78 Inchecronin INC 7423 AIRIS (LP) ... 12
78 Inchecronin INC 7424 LORD MAYO (LP) ... 12

LECUONDA CUBAN BOYS
55 Columbia 33S 1075 BENEATH THE CUBAN MOON (10" LP) ... 25

JOHN LEDINGHAM
68 Pye 7N 17488 Love Is A Toy/Thank You Mrs. Gilbert ... 6
(see also Jonathan Kelly)

LED ZEPPELIN

SINGLES
69 Atlantic 584 268 Good Times, Bad Times (unissued, 1-sided acetates only) ... 400
69 Atlantic 584 269 Communication Breakdown/Good Times, Bad Times (unissued, promo only) .. 500
69 Atlantic 584 309 Whole Lotta Love (Edit)/Livin' Lovin' Maid (She's A Woman) (withdrawn, large centre hole) ... 500
69 Atlantic 584 309 Whole Lotta Love (Edit)/Livin' Lovin' Maid (She's A Woman) (withdrawn, solid centre with small centre hole, 1 copy known) ... 1,500
73 Atlantic K 10296 D'Yer Mak'er/Over The Hills And Far Away (unreleased, promo only) ... 250
75 Swan Song DC 1 Trampled Underfoot/Black Country Woman (freebie, die-cut title sleeve) ... 20
75 Swan Song DC 1 Trampled Underfoot/Black Country Woman (test pressing, white labels) ... 350
75 Swan Song SSK 19403 Trampled Underfoot/Black Country Woman (mispressed cat. no.) ... 100
79 Swan Song SSK 19421 Wearing And Tearing/Darlene (cancelled Knebworth 45, existence unconfirmed)
90 Atlantic LZ 2 Stairway To Heaven/Immigrant Song/Whole Lotta Love/ Good Times Bad Times (10", p/s, promo only) ... 25
90 Atlantic LZ 2 Stairway To Heaven/Immigrant Song/Whole Lotta Love/ Good Times Bad Times (10", test pressing, white labels) ... 350
90 Atlantic CD LZ 1 Stairway To Heaven/Immigrant Song/Whole Lotta Love/ Good Times Bad Times (CD, promo only, in Zeppelin-design long box) ... 30
90 Atlantic LZ 3 Stairway To Heaven/Whole Lotta Love (with memo, 150 copies only, promo) ... 100
90 Atlantic LZ 3 LC Stairway To Heaven/Whole Lotta Love (jukebox single, push-out centre) ... 25
97 Atlantic PRCD 923 BBC SESSIONS SAMPLER: The Girl I Love/Whole Lotta Love/ Communication Breakdown (CD, promo only) ... 20
97 Atlantic AT 0031CD Whole Lotta Love (Edit)/Baby Come On Home/Travelling Riverside Blues (CD, numbered digipak) ... 10
97 Atlantic AT 0031LC Whole Lotta Love (Edit)/Whole Lotta Love (Edit) (jukebox issue, with pushout centre) ... 10
03 Warner Vision PR 03945 What Is And What Should Never Be/In My Time Of Dying/Rock And Roll (DVD, promo sampler) ... 20

ALBUMS
69 Atlantic 588 171 LED ZEPPELIN (LP, 1st pressing, red/maroon label, turquoise sleeve lettering, "Superhype" publishing credit) ... 500
69 Atlantic 588 171 LED ZEPPELIN (LP, 2nd pressing, red/maroon label, orange sleeve lettering, "Warner Bros" or "Superhype" publishing credit) ... 40/25

MINT VALUE £

69	Atlantic 588 198	LED ZEPPELIN II (LP, 1st pressing, red/maroon label, with "Living Loving Wreck" miscredit, light brown gatefold sleeve with blue-green edge)	100
69	Atlantic 588 198	LED ZEPPELIN II (LP, 1st pressing, red/maroon label, with "The Lemon Song" credit, light brown gatefold sleeve with blue-green edge)	30
70	Atlantic 588 198	LED ZEPPELIN II (LP, light brown sleeve, 2nd pressing, credits "Killing Floor" instead of "The Lemon Song" on label)	20
70	Atlantic Deluxe 2401 002	LED ZEPPELIN III (LP, red/maroon label, gatefold rotating-wheel sleeve, "Do What Thou Wilt" in run-off)	35
71	Atlantic Deluxe 2401 012	LED ZEPPELIN IV (FOUR SYMBOLS) (LP, red/maroon label)	25
73	Atlantic K 50014	HOUSES OF THE HOLY (LP; original pressings have an 'obi' around the sleeve)	12
76	Swan Song SSK 59402	PRESENCE (LP, shrinkwrapped gatefold sleeve)	12
78	Atlantic K 50008	LED ZEPPELIN IV (FOUR SYMBOLS) (LP, lilac vinyl reissue)	40
79	Swan Song SSK 59410	IN THROUGH THE OUT DOOR (LP, 6 different covers with inner sleeves; set labelled 'A' to 'F', each in individual paper outer; available separately with paper outer £10 each)	250
88	Atlantic K 50008/C 88 1-4	FOUR SYMBOLS (LP, HMV 'Classic Collection' box set, with booklet, no'd)	25
88	Atlantic 250008/C 88 1-4	FOUR SYMBOLS (CD, HMV 'Classic Collection' box set, with booklet, no'd)	25
90	Atlantic ZEP 1	REMASTERS (3-LP, triple gatefold sleeve)	18
90	Atlantic 7567 82144-1	LED ZEPPELIN (5-LP, box set)	50
97	Atlantic 83061-1	BBC SESSIONS (4-LP, box set)	50

(see also Jimmy Page, Robert Plant, John Paul Jones, Listen, Family Dogg, Ian Whitcomb, P.J. Proby, Lord Sutch)

ALVIN LEE

74	Chrysalis CHS 2020	The World Is Changing/Riffin' (with Myron Le Fevre)	6
73	Chrysalis CHR 1054	ON THE ROAD TO FREEDOM (LP, with Myron Le Fevre)	15
75	Chrysalis CHR 1094	PUMP IRON! (LP)	15
78	Chrysalis CHR 1190	LET IT ROCK (LP)	15

(see also Ten Years After)

ARTHUR LEE

72	A&M AMLS 64356	VINDICATOR (LP)	18
81	Beggars Banquet BEGA 26	ARTHUR LEE (LP)	12

(see also Love)

BENNY LEE (& KEN-TONES)

56	Parlophone MSP 6214	Love Plays The Strings Of My Banjo (with Ken-Tones)/Born To Sing The Blues	7
56	Parlophone MSP 6252	Sweet Heartaches/How Long Has This Been Going On?	7
56	Parlophone R 4245	Rock 'N' Rollin' Santa Claus/Life Was Made For Livin' (with Ken-Tones)	22
57	Nestles NR 08	Last Train To San Fernando (as Benny Lee & Jackson Boys) (1-sided card flexi, 78rpm)	7

(see also Ken-Tones)

BRENDA LEE

78s

56	Brunswick 05628	I'm Gonna Lasso Santa Claus/Christy Christmas (as Little Brenda Lee)	80
57	Brunswick 05685	Dynamite/Love You Til I Die	60
57	Brunswick 05720	Ain't That Love/One Teenager To Another	50
58	Brunswick 05755	Ring-A-My-Phone/Little Jonah (Rock On Your Little Steel Guitar)	70
59	Brunswick 05780	Bill Bailey, Won't You Please Come Home/Hummin' The Blues Over You	70
60	Brunswick 05819	Sweet Nuthin's/Weep No More My Baby	150

SINGLES

56	Brunswick 05628	I'm Gonna Lasso Santa Claus/Christy Christmas (triangular centre)	200
57	Brunswick 05685	Dynamite/Love You Til I Die (with Anita Kerr Singers, triangular centre)	140
57	Brunswick 05720	Ain't That Love/One Teenager To Another (w/ Anita Kerr Singers, tri-centre)	125
58	Brunswick 05755	Ring-A-My-Phone/Little Jonah (Rock On Your Little Steel Guitar) (tri-centre)	140
58	Decca BM 31186	Fairyland/One Step At A Time (export issue, triangular centre)	75
59	Brunswick 05780	Bill Bailey, Won't You Please Come Home/Hummin' The Blues Over You (triangular or round centre)	20/15
60	Brunswick 05819	Sweet Nuthin's/Weep No More My Baby (triangular or round centre)	20/8
60	Brunswick 05823	Let's Jump The Broomstick/Rock-A-Bye Baby Blues	10
60	Brunswick 05833	I'm Sorry/That's All You Gotta Do	8
60	Brunswick 05839	I Want To Be Wanted/Just A Little	6
61	Brunswick 05847	Emotions/I'm Learning About Love	7
61	Brunswick 05849	You Can Depend On Me/It's Never Too Late	7
61	Brunswick 05854	Dum Dum/Eventually	8
61	Brunswick 05860	Fool No. 1/Anybody But Me	6
62	Brunswick 05864	Break It To Me Gently/So Deep	6
62	Brunswick 05867	Speak To Me Pretty/Lover, Come Back To Me	6
62	Brunswick 05871	Here Comes That Feeling/Everybody Loves Me But You	6
62	Brunswick 05876	It Started All Over Again/Heart In Hand	6
62	Brunswick 05880	Rockin' Around The Christmas Tree/Papa Noel	7
63	Brunswick 05882	All Alone Am I/Save All Your Lovin' For Me	6
63	Brunswick 05886	Losing You/He's So Heavenly	6
63	Brunswick 05891	I Wonder/My Whole World Is Falling Down	6
63	Brunswick 05896	Sweet Impossible You/The Grass Is Greener	6
64	Brunswick 05899	As Usual/Lonely Lonely Lonely Me	6
64	Brunswick 05903	Think/The Waiting Game	6
64	Brunswick 05911	Alone With You/My Dreams	6
64	Brunswick 05915	Is It True/What'd I Say	12
64	Brunswick 05921	Christmas Will Be Just Another Lonely Day/Winter Wonderland	6
65	Brunswick 05927	Thanks A Lot/Just Behind The Rainbow	5
65	Brunswick 05933	Truly, Truly True/I Still Miss Someone	5
65	Brunswick 05936	Too Many Rivers/No One	5
65	Brunswick 05943	Rusty Bells/If You Don't	7
66	Brunswick 05957	Too Little Time/Time And Time Again	6
66	Brunswick 05963	Ain't Gonna Cry No More/It Takes One To Know One	6
66	Brunswick 05967	Coming On Strong/You Keep Coming Back To Me	6

MINT VALUE £

67	Brunswick 05970	Ride, Ride, Ride/Lonely People Do Foolish Things	6
67	Brunswick 05976	Where's The Melody?/Born To Be By Your Side	10
68	Decca AD 1003	That's All Right/Baby, Won't You Please Come Home (export issue)	15
68	MCA MU 1001	That's All Right/Baby, Won't You Please Come Home	5
68	MCA MU 1021	Let's Jump The Broomstick/All Alone Am I	5
69	MCA MU 1063	Johnny One Time/I Must Have Been Out Of My Mind	5
70	MCA MU 1115	Johnny One Time/Bring Me Sunshine	5
72	MCA MU 1155	Everybody's Reaching Out For Someone/If This Is Our Last Time	5
73	MCA MUS 1189	Nobody Wins/We Had A Good Thing Going	5
73	MCA MUS 1219	Sunday Sunrise/Must I Believe	5
EPs			
59	Brunswick OE 9462	ROCK THE BOP (green p/s & tri-centre or blue p/s & round centre)	90/60
62	Brunswick OE 9482	PRETEND	45
62	Brunswick OE 9488	SPEAK TO ME PRETTY	35
63	Brunswick OE 9492	ALL ALONE AM I	30
64	Brunswick OE 9499	BRENDA LEE'S TRIBUTE TO AL JOLSON	40
65	Brunswick OE 9510	FOUR FROM '64	40
LPs			
59	Brunswick LAT 8319	GRANDMA WHAT GREAT SONGS YOU SANG	50
60	Brunswick LAT 8347	MISS DYNAMITE	40
61	Brunswick LAT 8360	THIS IS BRENDA	35
61	Brunswick LAT 8376	EMOTIONS (also stereo STA 3044)	20/30
61	Brunswick LAT 8383	ALL THE WAY (also stereo STA 3048)	20/30
61	Brunswick LAT 8396	SINCERELY (also stereo STA 3056)	20/30
62	Brunswick LAT/STA 8516	BRENDA, THAT'S ALL (mono/stereo)	20/30
62	Brunswick LAT/STA 8530	ALL ALONE AM I (mono/stereo)	15/20
63	Ace of Hearts AH 59	LOVE YOU	25
63	Brunswick LAT/STA 8548	LET ME SING (mono/stereo)	18/25
64	Brunswick LAT/STA 8576	BY REQUEST (mono/stereo)	18/25
64	Brunswick LAT/STA 8590	MERRY CHRISTMAS FROM BRENDA (mono/stereo)	25/30
65	Brunswick LAT/STA 8603	TOP TEEN HITS (mono/stereo)	18/25
65	Brunswick LAT 8614	THE VERSATILE BRENDA LEE	18
65	Brunswick LAT/STA 8622	TOO MANY RIVERS (mono/stereo)	18/25
66	Brunswick LAT/STA 8649	BYE BYE BLUES (mono/stereo)	18/25
67	Brunswick LAT/STA 8672	COMING ON STRONG (mono/stereo)	18/25
68	MCA MUP(S) 306	REFLECTIONS IN BLUE	15
68	MCA MUP(S) 321	CALL ME	15
68	MCA MUP(S) 322	THE GOOD LIFE	12
68	MCA MUP(S) 330	MERRY CHRISTMAS FROM BRENDA LEE	12
68	MCA MUP(S) 332	BRENDA AND PETE — FOR THE FIRST TIME (with Pete Fountain)	12
70	MCA MUP(S) 396	JOHNNY ONE TIME	12
71	MCA MUPS 423	MEMPHIS PORTRAIT	12
72	MCA MUPS 460	A WHOLE LOTTA BRENDA LEE	12
73	MCA MUPS 485	BRENDA	12

BUNNY LEE ALLSTARS

70	Pama PM 803	Annie Pama/Mr Magoo	10
71	Smash SMA 2304	Stanley (Parts 1 & 2) (as Bunnie Lee Allstars)	8

(see also Lloyd Charmers, Sonny Binns & Rudies, Copy Cats, John Holt, Lloyd & Doreen, Delroy Wilson)

BYRON LEE & DRAGONAIR(E)S

60	Blue Beat B 2	Dumplin's/Kissin' Gal (vocal: Buddy Davidson) (white label, blue print)	22
60	Blue Beat BB 2	Dumplin's/Kissin' Gal (vocal: Buddy Davidson) (2nd pressing, blue label, silver print)	20
61	Blue Beat BB 28	Mash! Mr. Lee/Help Me Forget (vocal: Keith Lyn)	18
61	Starlite ST45 045	Joy Ride/Over The Rainbow	15
64	Parlophone R 5124	River Bank/Musical Communion	12
64	Parlophone R 5125	Sour Apples/Hanging Up My Heart	12
64	Parlophone R 5140	Sammy Dead/Say Bye Bye (both actually by Eric Morris with Byron Lee)	12
64	Parlophone R 5177	Beautiful Garden/Too Late	12
64	Parlophone R 5182	Come Back/Jamaica Ska	15
64	MGM MGM 1256	Night Train From Jamaica/Ska Dee Wah (with Danny Davis)	30
66	Doctor Bird DB 1003	Sloopy/Gold Finger	20
67	Pyramid PYR 6015	Sloopy/Gold Finger (reissue)	12
68	Trojan TR 624	Soul Limbo/The Whistling Song	7
68	Trojan TR 631	Mr Walker/Sunset Jump Up	7
69	Major Minor MM 615	Every Day Will Be Like A Holiday/Oh What A Feeling	5
70	Trojan TR 7731	Squeeze Up (Parts 1 & 2)	6
70	Trojan TR 7736	Birth Control/Love At First Sight	6
70	Trojan TR 7747	Bond In Bliss/Musical Scorcher	6
70	Trojan TR 7761	Julianne/We Five	5
70	Duke DU 39	Elizabethan Reggae/Soul Serenade	6
70	Duke DU 91	Cashbox/WINSTON WRIGHT: Strolling Thru' The Park	6
71	Dynamic DYN 405	Hitching A Ride/Hitching A Ride Version	6
71	Dynamic DYN 409	My Sweet Lord/Shock Attack	7
71	Dynamic DYN 414	Way Back Home/Version	6
72	Dynamic DYN 435	Make It Reggae/DENNIS ALCAPONE: Go Johnny Go	18
73	Dragon DRA 1008	In The Mood/Black On	5
65	Atlantic AET 6014	SKA TIME (EP, as Byron Lee Ska Kings)	50
64	Island ILP 905	CARIBBEAN JOY RIDE (LP)	60
69	Trojan TTL 5	ROCKSTEADY EXPLOSION (LP)	40
69	Major Minor Sm 53	BYRON LEE & THE DRAGONAIRES (LP)	25
70	Trojan TRLS 18	REGGAE WITH BYRON LEE (LP)	12
70	Trojan TBL 110	REGGAE BLAST OFF (LP)	12
71	Trojan TRL 26	REGGAY SPLASHDOWN (LP)	15
72	Trojan TRL 40	REGGAY HOT COOL AND EASY (LP)	15

(see also Mighty Avengers, Ken Lazarus, Hopeton Lewis, Danny Davis Orchestra, Good Guys, Neville Hinds, Hubcaps & Wheels, Mighty Sparrow, Blues Busters)

MINT VALUE £

CHRISTOPHER LEE

74	Studio Two TWOA 5001	HAMMER PRESENTS DRACULA (LP, gatefold sleeve)	12
74	Studio Two TWOA Q4 5001	HAMMER PRESENTS DRACULA (LP, gatefold sleeve, quadrophonic)	15

C.P. LEE

80	New Hormones	RADIO SWEAT (cassette, with booklet & stickers in plastic 'radio' bag)	12

(see also Alberto Y Lost Trios Paranoias)

CURTIS LEE

60	Top Rank JAR 317	With All My Heart (I Love You)/Pure Love	60
61	London HLX 9313	Pledge Of Love/Then I'll Know	25
61	London HLX 9397	Pretty Little Angel Eyes/Gee How I Wish You Were Here	22
61	London HLX 9445	Under The Moon Of Love/Beverly Jean	22
62	London HLX 9533	A Night At Daddy Gee's/Just Another Fool	20
67	CBS 2717	Get My Bag/Everybody's Going Wild (as Curtis Lee & K.C.P.s)	35
72	Stateside SS 2208	Under The Moon Of Love/Beverly Jean (reissue)	6

DAVE LEE (& STAGGERLEES)

63	Decca F 11600	Take Four/Five To Four On	7
63	Oriole CB 1864	Dance Dance Dance/Love Me (as Dave Lee & Staggerlees)	7
63	Oriole CB 1907	Sweet & Lovely/Forever And Always (as Dave Lee & Staggerlees)	7
66	Fontana TF 723	Adam Adamant/Georgie's Theme (as Dave Lee & His Orchestra)	12

DAVE LEE

66	Colpix PXL 550	OUR MAN CRICHTON (LP, with Tubby Hayes)	90

(see also Tubby Hayes)

DAVID H. LEE

65	Pye 7N 15809	Heaven With No Angel	8
69	Morgan MR 1	Johnny's Eyes/You're The Only One	7

DEREK LEE

66	Parlophone R 5468	Girl/You've Done Something To My Heart	10

DICK LEE

53	Columbia SCM 5066	All I Want Is A Chance/The Show Is Ended	8
53	Columbia SCM 5078	I Thought You Might Be Lonely/Happy Bells	8
54	Columbia SCM 5094	Book/Stay In My Arms Cinderella	10

DICKIE/DICKEY LEE

59	MGM MGM 1013	A Penny A Kiss — A Penny A Hug/Bermuda (as Dick Lee)	25
62	Mercury AMT 1190	Patches/More Or Less	15
62	Mercury AMT 1196	I Saw Linda Yesterday/The Girl I Can't Forget	12
62	Mercury AMT 1200	Don't Wanna Think About Paula/Just A Friend	10
65	Stateside SS 433	Laurie (Strange Things Happen)/Party Doll (as Dickey Lee)	8
65	Stateside SS 464	The Girl From Peyton Place/A Girl I Used To Know (as Dickey Lee)	8

DINAH LEE

65	Brit WI 1005	I Can't Believe What You Say/Pushin' A Good Thing Too Far (unissued)	
65	Aladdin WI 606	I'll Forgive You Then Forget You/Nitty Gritty	25
65	Aladdin WI 608	I Can't Believe What You Say/Pushin' A Good Thing Too Far	35

DON (TONY) LEE

68	Big Shot BI 504	It's Reggae Time (as Don Tony Lee)/ERROL DUNKLEY: The Clamp Is On	18
68	Doctor Bird DB 1106	Lee's Special (as Don Tony Lee)/LLOYD & GROOVERS: My Heart And Soul	20
68	Island WI 3160	It's Reggae Time (as D. Tony Lee)/ERROL DUNKLEY: The Clamp Is On	22
69	Unity UN 519	Peyton Place/Red Gal In The Ring (as Don Tony Lee)	12

EDNA LEE

68	President PT 175	I Really Think I'm Crying 'Cause I Love You/ Don't Let My Friends See What You Do	7

(Freddie) 'FINGERS' LEE (& UPPER HAND)

65	Fontana TF 619	The Friendly Undertaker/Little Bit More (as 'Fingers' Lee)	22
66	Fontana TF 655	I'm Gonna Buy Me A Dog/I Can't Drive (as 'Fingers' Lee)	20
66	Columbia DB 8002	Bossy Boss/Don't Run Away (as Fingers Lee & Upper Hand)	15

(see also At Last The 1958 Rock & Roll Show)

GEORGE LEE (& MUSIC DOCTORS)

69	Downtown DT 443	Talking Boss/Jungle Fever (solo)	8
70	J-Dan JDN 4407	Johnny Dollar/Tough Of Poison (with Music Doctors)	8

(see also Desmond Riley)

HUBERT LEE

73	Ackee ACK 504	I Love Verona/Version	5
73	Downtown DT 498	Something On Your Mind/IMPACT ALL STARS: Mind Version	8
73	Green Door GD 4050	High School Dance/PRINCE TONY'S ALL STARS: Version	5
74	Ackee ACK 524	Tonight Will You Still Love Me/IMPACT ALL STARS: Version	5

JACKIE LEE (U.K.)

55	Decca F 10550	I Was Wrong/For As Long As I Live	8
65	Decca F 12068	I Cry Alone/Cause I Love Him	10
65	Columbia DB 7685	Lonely Clown/Love Is Gone	10
66	Columbia DB 7860	I Know, Know, Know I'll Never Love/So Love Me	8
66	Columbia DB 8052	The Town I Live In/You Too	10
67	Decca F 12663	Born To Lose/Saying Goodbye	8
69	Pye 7N 17829	Love Is a Gamble/Something Borrowed, Something Blue	7
71	Pye PKL 5503	JACKIE'S JUNIOR CHOICE (LP)	15

(see also Jacky, Jackie Lee & Raindrops, Emma Rede)

JACKIE LEE & RAINDROPS (U.K.)

62	Oriole CB 1702	I Was The Last One To Know/There's No One In The Whole World	12
62	Oriole CB 1727	There Goes The Lucky One/I Built My Whole World Around You	15
62	Oriole CB 1757	Party Lights/Midnight	12

MINT VALUE £

63 Oriole CB 1800 The End Of The World/Goodbye Is Such A Lonely Word 12
63 Philips BF 1283 Down Our Street/My Heart Is Your Heart (as Jackie & Raindrops) 15
64 Philips BF 1328 Here I Go Again/Come On Dream Come On (as Jackie & Raindrops) 12
(see also Jacky, Jackie Lee [U.K.], Raindrops [U.K], Emma Rede)

JACKIE LEE (U.S.)
60 Top Rank JAR 286 Rancho/Like Sunset 10

JACKIE LEE (U.S.)
65 Fontana TF 646 The Duck/Let Your Conscience Be Your Guide 20
66 Jay Boy BOY 28 Would You Believe/You're Everything 8
68 London HLM 10233 The Duck/Dancing In The Street 8
70 Jay Boy BOY 26 Do The Temptation Walk/The Shotgun And The Duck 12
72 Jay Boy BOY 66 Oh! My Darlin'/Don't Be Ashamed 6
72 Jay Boy BOY 76 African Boo-Ga-Loo/Bring It Home 6
73 Contempo CR 5 The Duck (Parts 1 & 2) 5
85 Kent TOWN 107 Darkest Days/EDDIE BISHOP: Call Me 8
67 London HA-M 8336 THE DUCK (LP) 35
71 Joy JOYS 192 THE DUCK (LP, reissue) 20
(see also Bob & Earl, Earl Nelson, Jackie Lee & Delores Hall)

JACKIE LEE & DELORES HALL
69 B&C CB 105 Whether It's Right Or Wrong/Baby I'm Satisfied 10
72 Jay Boy BOY 52 Whether It's Right Or Wrong/Baby I'm Satisfied (reissue) 6
(see also Jackie Lee [U.S.], Delores Hall)

JAMIE LEE & ATLANTICS
63 Decca F 11571 In The Night/Little Girl In Blue 40

JIMMY LEE
61 Starlite ST45 059 All My Life/Chicago Jump 35

JOHN LEE'S GROUNDHOGS
(see under 'J')

JOHN LEE
72 Explosion EX 2060 Stagger Lee/Musical Version (both sides actually by John Holt) 5

JOHNNIE LEE
59 Pye 7N 15201 Echo/It's-A Me, It's-A Me, It's-A Me My Love 10
59 Pye N 15201 Echo/It's-A Me, It's-A Me, It's-A Me My Love (78) 15
59 Pye 7N 15233 I'm Finally Free/I Fell (with The King's Men) 10
59 Pye N 15233 I'm Finally Free/I Fell (78, with the King's Men) 20
60 Fontana H 257 They're Wrong/Cindy Lou 8
60 Fontana H 280 Poetry In Motion/Let It Come True 8
61 Fontana H 306 Lonely Joe/Nobody 8
67 CBS 202591 Kiss Tomorrow Goodbye/Love No Longer Sounds 8
67 CBS 2802 I Forgot What It Was Like/Lonely Is The Willow 6
67 CBS 3112 Because You're Mine/I'll Not Forget 6

JULIA LEE (& HER BOYFRIENDS)
50 Capitol CL 13321 Nobody Knows You When You're Down And Out/Decent Woman Blues (78) 20
50 Capitol CL 13323 Cold Hearted Daddy/Snatch And Grab It (78) 20
51 Capitol LC 6535 PARTY TIME (10" LP, 2 different sleeves) 90

LAURA LEE (U.K.)
60 Triumph RGM 1030 Tell Tommy I Miss Him/I'm Sending Back Your Roses 40
62 Decca F 11513 Too Young To Be In Love/Brand New Heartbeat 15
68 Columbia DB 8495 Love In Every Room/Master Jack 12
71 Columbia DB 8770 Someone To Love Me/Look Left-Look Right 8

LAURA LEE (U.S.)
67 Chess CRS 8062 Dirty Man/It's Mighty Hard 10
68 Chess CRS 8070 As Long As I Got You/A Man With Some Backbone 10
72 Tamla Motown TMG 831 To Win Your Heart/So Will I 15
72 Hot Wax HWX 115 Rip Off/Two Lovely Pillows 6
73 Hot Wax HWX 118 Wedlock Is A Padlock/Since I Fell For You 6
73 Hot Wax HWX 119 You've Got The Love To Save Me/Crumbs Off The Table 6
74 Invictus INV 2654 I Need It Just As Bad As You/If I'm Good Enough To Love 6
71 Hot Wax SHW 5006 WOMEN'S LOVE RIGHTS (LP) 18
73 Hot Wax SHW 5009 TWO SIDES OF LAURA LEE (LP) 20

LEAPY LEE
65 Pye 7N 17001 It's All Happening/In The Meantime 8
66 Decca F 12369 King Of The Whole Wide World/Shake Hands (featuring the Kinks) 60
67 CBS 202550 The Man On The Flying Trapeze/My Mixed-Up Mind 7
68 Pye 7N 17619 It's All Happening/It's Great 5
69 MCA MK 5021 Good Morning/Teresa 5

LITTLE MR. LEE & CHEROKEES
66 Vocalion VP 9268 Young Lover/I Don't Want To Go 35

MANDY LEE
50s Poydras 76 I'm A Harmony Baby/If Your Man Is Like My Man 8

MANDY LEE
69 Dandelion S 4494 Bottle Up And Go (Parts 1 & 2) 6

MARILYN LEE
64 Embassy WB 636 My Guy/DAVE CHARLES: Hello, Dolly 5

MARILYN LEE & LES CARLE
62 Embassy WB 540 Keep Your Hands Off My Baby/Up On The Roof 5

MICHELLE LEE
68 CBS 3350 L. David Sloan/Everybody Loves My Baby 6

MINT VALUE £

MICKEY LEE

73	Smash SMA 2332	Hello My Little Queen/AUGUSTUS PABLO: African Queen	15

NICKIE LEE

69	Deep Soul DS 9103	And Black Is Beautiful/Faith Within	20

NORMA LEE

67	CBM CBM 002	Hurt/Rollin' On	6

PEGGY LEE

78s

54	Brunswick 05286	Johnny Guitar/I Didn't Know What Time It Was	8
57	Capitol CL 14741	Baby, Baby Wait For Me/Every Night	8
57	Capitol CL 14795	Uninvited Dreams/Listen To The Rockin' Bird	8
58	Capitol CL 14902	Fever/You Don't Know	20
58	Capitol CL 14955	Light Of Love/Sweetheart	15
59	Brunswick 05798	It Ain't Necessarily So/Swing Low, Sweet Chariot	10

SINGLES

54	Brunswick 05286	Johnny Guitar/I Didn't Know What Time It Was	20
54	Brunswick 05345	Love, You Didn't Do Right By Me/Sisters	15
55	Brunswick 05360	Let Me Go, Lover/Bouquet Of Blues	18
55	Brunswick 05368	Straight Ahead/It Must Be So (with Mills Brothers)	15
55	Brunswick 05421	Baubles, Bangles And Beads/Summer Vacation	15
55	Brunswick 05435	I Belong To You/How Bitter, My Sweet	15
55	Brunswick 05461	Ooh That Kiss/Oh! No! (Please Don't Go)	15
55	Brunswick 05471	Sugar/What Can I Say After I Say I'm Sorry	15
55	Brunswick 05472	He Needs Me/Sing A Rainbow	15
55	Brunswick 05482	He's A Tramp (with Pound Hounds)/The Siamese Cat Song (with Oliver Wallace)	20
55	Brunswick 05483	Bella Notte/La La Lu	15

(The above 45s were originally issued with gold label lettering; silver reissues are worth two-thirds these values.)

56	Brunswick 05549	Three Cheers For Mister Magoo/Mister Magoo Does The Cha Cha Cha (with Jim Backus)	15
56	Brunswick 05554	The Come Back/You've Got To See Mama Every Night	5
56	Brunswick 05593	That's All Right Honey/Love You So	5
56	Brunswick 05625	We Laughed At Love/They Can't Take That Away From Me	5
57	Brunswick 05671	Mr. Wonderful/The Gypsy With Fire In His Shoes	6
57	Brunswick 05714	I Don't Know Enough About You/Where Flamingo's Fly	5
57	Capitol CL 14741	Baby, Baby Wait For Me/Every Night	8
57	Capitol CL 14795	Uninvited Dreams/Listen To The Rockin' Bird	8
58	Capitol CL 14902	Fever/You Don't Know	8
58	Capitol CL 14955	Light Of Love/Sweetheart	5
59	Capitol CL 14984	Alright, Okay, You Win/My Man	5
59	Brunswick 05798	It Ain't Necessarily So/Swing Low, Sweet Chariot	5
59	Capitol CL 15025	Hallelujah, I Love Him So/I'm Lookin' Out The Window	5
59	Capitol CL 15058	You Came A Long Way From St. Louis/I Lost My Sugar In Salt Lake City (with George Shearing Quintet)	5
59	Capitol CL 15103	You Deserve/Things Are Swingin'	8
61	Capitol CL 15184	Till There Was You/Bucket Of Tears	5
61	Capitol CL 15214	Mañana/The Folks Who Live On The Hill	5
65	Capitol CL 15376	Pass Me By/That's What It Takes	10
65	Capitol CL 15413	I Go To Sleep/Stop Living In The Past	8
69	Capitol CL 15614	Is That All There Is?/I'm A Woman (2nd pressing with different A-side)	10
74	Warner Bros K 10527	Let's Love/Always	5

EPs

55	Brunswick OE 9153	PETE KELLY'S BLUES NO. 1	12
55	Brunswick OE 9154	PETE KELLY'S BLUES NO. 2	12
56	Brunswick OE 9282	PRESENTING PEGGY LEE	10
58	Brunswick OE 9400	SEA SHELLS PT. 1	10
58	Brunswick OE 9401	SEA SHELLS PT. 2	10
58	Philips BBE 12172	PEGGY WITH BENNY (with Benny Goodman)	8
59	Capitol EAP1 1052	FEVER	15
59	Capitol EAP1 1213	ALRIGHT OKAY YOU WIN	8
63	Capitol EAP1 1857	I'M A WOMAN	10

LPs

53	Capitol LC 6584	CAPITOL PRESENTS PEGGY LEE (10")	30
53	Brunswick LA 8629	BLACK COFFEE (10")	25
55	Brunswick LA 8717	SONGS IN AN INTIMATE STYLE (10")	25
55	Brunswick LAT 8078	PETE KELLY'S BLUES (with Ella Fitzgerald)	22
56	Brunswick LA 8731	SONGS FROM 'LADY AND THE TRAMP' (10")	40
56	Capitol LC 6817	MY BEST TO YOU (10")	25
56	Capitol T 864	THE MAN I LOVE	20
57	Brunswick LAT 8171	DREAM STREET	20
58	Capitol (S)T 979	JUMP FOR JOY	15
58	Brunswick LAT 8266	SEA SHELLS	15
59	Capitol T 1049	THINGS ARE SWINGIN'	15
59	Capitol (S)T 1131	I LIKE MEN!	15
59	Brunswick LAT 8287	MISS WONDERFUL	15
60	Capitol (S)T 1219	BEAUTY AND THE BEAT! (with George Shearing Quintet, mono/stereo)	10/12
60	Capitol (S)T 1401	PRETTY EYES (mono/stereo)	12/15
61	Capitol T 1366	ALL AGLOW AGAIN!	12
61	Capitol (S)T 1423	CHRISTMAS CAROUSEL	12
62	Capitol (S)T 1520	BASIN STREET EAST PRESENTS PEGGY LEE (mono/stereo)	12/15
62	Capitol (S)T 1630	IF YOU GO (mono/stereo)	12/15
62	Ace Of Hearts AH 26	PEGGY LEE	12
62	Capitol (S)T1 1671	BLUES CROSS COUNTRY (mono/stereo)	12/15
63	Capitol T 1743	BEWITCHING-LEE!	12
63	Capitol (S)T 1857	I'M A WOMAN (mono/stereo)	12/15

64 Capitol (S)T 1850 MINK JAZZ (mono/stereo) . . . 12/15
64 Capitol (S)T 1969 IN LOVE AGAIN (mono/stereo) . . . 12/15
64 Capitol (S)T 2096 IN THE NAME OF LOVE (mono/stereo) . . . 12/15
65 Capitol (S)T 2320 PASS ME BY . . . 12
66 Capitol (S)T 1475 OLE A LA LEE! . . . 12
66 Ace Of Hearts AH 107 THE FABULOUS PEGGY LEE . . . 12
66 Capitol (S)T 2388 THEN WAS THEN, NOW IS NOW! . . . 12
67 Capitol (S)T 2469 GUITARS A LA LEE . . . 15
67 Capitol (S)T 2475 BIG SPENDER . . . 15
69 Capitol (S)T 21141 IS THAT ALL THERE IS? . . . 15
(see also Bing Crosby, George Shearing)

ROBERTA LEE
52 Brunswick 04876 The Little White Cloud That Cried/Tell Me Why (78, with Grady Martin) . . . 10
53 Brunswick 05076 Sixty Minute Man (with Hardrock Gunter)/RED FOLEY: Hot Toddy (78) . . . 12
53 Brunswick 05116 Say It Isn't So/Dear Joe (78) . . . 8
53 Brunswick 05123 Don't Call My Name/Hey Mister Cottonpicker (78, with Tex Williams) . . . 8
53 Brunswick 05134 Ill Wind (You're Blowing Me No Good)/Fare-Thee-Well (78) . . . 8
53 Brunswick 05205 Caribbean/Let's Go Home (78) . . . 8
54 HMV 7M 261 True Love And Tender Care/When The Organ Played At Twilight . . . 10
55 Brunswick 05388 Ridin' To Tennessee/I'll Be There If Ever You Want Me . . . 15
(see also Red Foley, Hardrock Gunter)

ROBIN LEE
62 Reprise R 20068 Gamblin' Man/An Angel With A Broken Wing . . . 18

ROY LEE
61 Decca F 11406 Two Initials/Honey Lies . . . 6

TONY LEE
68 Doctor Bird DB 1106 Lee's Special/LLOYD & GROOVERS: My Heart My Soul . . . 30

VINNY LEE & RIDERS
61 HMV POP 856 Mule Train/Gambler's Guitar . . . 15

WARREN LEE
69 Pama PM 762 Underdog Backstreet/Come Put My Life In Order . . . 15

WILMA LEE & STONEY COOPER
64 Hickory 45-1257 Big John's Wife/Pirate King . . . 6

LEE & CLARENDONIANS
72 Green Door GD 4038 Night Owl/Night Owl Version . . . 8

LEE (Perry) & JIMMY (Riley)
75 Dip DL 5075 Rasta Train/Yagga Yagga . . . 25

LEE (Perry) & JUNIOR (Byles)
75 Dip DL 5060 Dreader Locks/Militant Rock . . . 7

LEE & PAUL
59 Philips PB 912 The Chick/Valentina, My Valentina . . . 6

BRAD LEEDS
60 Pye International 7N 25050 A Teenage Love Is Born/I'm Walking Behind You . . . 8

PHIL LEEDS
66 London HLR 10044 Would You Believe It?/FRANK GALLOP: The Ballad Of Irving . . . 8

MARK LEEMAN FIVE
65 Columbia DB 7452 Portland Town/Gotta Get Myself Together . . . 22
65 Columbia DB 7648 Blow My Blues Away/On The Horizon . . . 25
66 Columbia DB 7812 Forbidden Fruit/Goin' To Bluesville . . . 25
66 Columbia DB 7955 Follow Me/Gather Up The Pieces . . . 22
(see also Cheynes)

THOMAS LEER
78 Oblique ER 101 Private Plane/International (folded photocopied p/s, hand-stamped labels) . . . 10
78 Company/Oblique OBCO 1 Private Plane/International (reissue, printed p/s) . . . 6
82 Cherry Red CHERRY 52 All About You/Saving Grace (p/s) . . . 5
82 Cherry Red 12CHERRY 52 All About You/Saving Grace (12", p/s) . . . 8
82 Cherry Red ERED 26 CONTRADICTIONS EP (12", double pack) . . . 8
79 Industrial IR 0007 THE BRIDGE (LP, with Robert Rental) . . . 15
(see also Act, Robert Rental)

JOHN LEES
74 Polydor 2058 513 Best Of My Love/You Can't Get It . . . 15
77 Harvest HAR 5132 Child Of The Universe/Kes (A Major Fancy) . . . 5
73 Harvest SHVL 811 A MAJOR FANCY (LP) . . . 15
(see also Barclay James Harvest)

JACK LE FORGE
65 Stateside SS 444 Our Crazy Affair/Bossa Bossa Nova (withdrawn) . . . 18

LEFT BANKE
66 Philips BF 1517 Walk Away Renee/I Haven't Got The Nerve . . . 10
67 Philips BF 1540 Pretty Ballerina/Lazy Day . . . 10
67 Philips BF 1575 Ivy Ivy/And Suddenly . . . 10
67 Philips BF 1614 Desiree/I've Got Something On My Mind . . . 7
87 Bam Caruso OPRA 023 Walk Away Renee/Ivy Ivy (DJ/jukebox issue) . . . 6
67 Philips (S)BL 7773 WALK AWAY RENEE/PRETTY BALLERINA (LP) . . . 45

MINT VALUE £

LEFTFIELD

90 Outer Rhythm FOOT 9R — More Than I Know (10K Remix)/(More Mix)/(Even More Mix) (12") . . . 15•
91 Outer Rhythm FOOT 009 — More Than I Know (12" Mix)/Not Forgotten (Hard Hands Mix) (12") . . . 20
92 Hard Hands HAND 001T — Release The Pressure/Release The Pressure (Instrumental)/ Release The Pressure (with Earl Sixteen) (12") . . . 10•
92 Hard Hands HAND 001R — Release The Dubs (Dub 1)/(Dub 2)/(Dub 3)/(Dub 4) (12") . . . 15
92 Hard Hands HAND 002T — Song Of Life/Song Of Life (Dub Of Life)/Song Of Life (Fanfare Of Life) (12") . . . 10
92 Hard Hands HAND 002R — Song Of Life (Underworld Remix)/Release The Pressure (Release The Horns Mix)/Release The Pressure (Lemon Interrupt Mix) (12") . . . 15
94 Hard Hands LEFT EP1 — LEFTISM (12", 4-track sampler, promo only) . . . 10
95 Hard Hands LEFT EP2 — Original/Original (Jam)/Filter Fish/Original (Drift) (12", double pack, as Leftfield & Halliday, promo only) . . . 12
95 Hard Hands HAND 29P — RELEASE THE PRESSURE (12", double pack, promo only) . . . 10
95 Hard Hands AFRO EP — AFRO-LEFT EP (12", with Djum Djum, double pack, promo only) . . . 12

(see also A Man Called Adam, Curve)

LEFT-HANDED MARRIAGE

67 private pressing — ON THE RIGHT SIDE OF THE LEFT-HANDED MARRIAGE (LP) . . . 400
96 Tenth Planet TP 022 — ON THE RIGHT SIDE OF THE LEFT-HANDED MARRIAGE (LP, reissue, gatefold sleeve) . . . 15

LEFT HAND DRIVE

79 Bancrupt BAN 012 — Who Said Rock & Roll Is Dead/I Know Where I Am (p/s) . . . 5

LEFT SIDE

69 Columbia DB 8575 — Welcome To My House/This Little Village . . . 6

LANCE LE GAULT

68 United Artists UP 2255 — Billie/Louisiana Swamp Fox . . . 5

LEGAY

69 Fontana TF 904 — No-One/The Fantastic Story Of The Steam Driven Banana . . . 140

(see also Gypsy)

LEGEND

69 Bell BLL 1048 — National Gas/Wouldn't You . . . 12
69 Bell BLL 1082 — Georgia George Part 1/July . . . 10
70 Vertigo 6059 021 — Life/Late Last Night . . . 10
71 Vertigo 6059 036 — Don't You Know/Someday . . . 10
69 Bell MBLL/SBLL 115 — LEGEND (LP) . . . 55
71 Vertigo 6360 019 — LEGEND ('RED BOOT') (LP, gatefold sleeve, swirl label) . . . 50
72 Vertigo 6360 063 — MOONSHINE (LP, gatefold sleeve, swirl label) . . . 55

(see also Procol Harum, Fingers)

LEGEND

81 Legend LEG 1 — Hideaway/Heaven Sent (p/s) . . . 70

LEGEND

82 Workshop WR 3478 — FRONTLINE EP (Frontline/Sabre & Chatila/ Stormers Of Heaven/Open The Skies (12") . . . 25
81 Workshop WR 2007 — LEGEND (LP) . . . 90
82 Workshop WR 3477 — DEATH IN THE NURSERY (LP, with insert) . . . 20

LEGEND!

83 Creation CRE 001/ Lyntone LYN 12903 — '73 In '83/You (Chunka Chunka) Were Glamorous (foldaround p/s in poly bag, some with 33rpm flexidisc "I Wonder Why! (live)" by The Pastels/"Wouldn't You?" by The Laughing Apple) . . . 15/12
84 Creation CRE 010 — The Legend Destroys The Blues/Arrogant Bastards (foldaround p/s in poly bag) . 6

TOBI LEGEND

78 RK RK 1004 — Time Will Pass You By/DEAN PARRISH: I'm On My Way/ JIMMY RADCLIFFE: Long After Tonight Is All Over (p/s) . . . 12

LEGENDARY LONNIE

81 Nervous NER 002 — Constipation Shake/Devil's Guitar (p/s) . . . 6

LEGENDARY MASKED SURFERS

73 United Artists UP 35542 — Gonna Hustle You/Summertime, Summertime . . . 12

(see also Beach Boys, Jan & Dean)

LEGENDARY PINK DOTS

82 In Phaze IPNER 1 — THE TOWER (LP) . . . 18
82 In Phaze — BRIGHTER NOW (cassette) . . . 12
83 Third Mind TMT 08 — THE BASILISK (cassette) . . . 12
83 In Phaze PHA 2 — CURSE (LP) . . . 15
84 In Phaze PHA 3 — LEGENDARY PINK DOTS (LP) . . . 15

LEGENDS

65 Pye 7N 15904 — I've Found Her/Something's Gonna Happen . . . 15
67 Parlophone R 5581 — Tomorrow's Gonna Be Another Day/Nobody Laughs Anymore . . . 35
67 Parlophone R 5613 — Under The Sky/Twenty-Four Hours A Day . . . 20

(see also First Impressions)

B. LEGGS

71 Green Door GD 4004 — Drums Of Passion/Love And Emotion (Version) . . . 6

(see also Morgan's All Stars)

LEGO FEET

91 Skam SKAM 1 — Untitled1/Untitled 2 (12", die cut sleeve) . . . 120

MICHEL LEGRAND

54 Philips PB 261 — Me Que/Viens (78) . . . 8
69 United Artists UP 2259 — Play Dirty Theme/Jazz Theme . . . 6
71 Columbia DB 8803 — The Go Between/La Lettre . . . 5
73 Tamla Motown TMG 848 — Love Theme From "Lady Sings The Blues"/Any Happy Home (with Gil Askey) . . . 6

MINT VALUE £

73	Tamla Motown TMG 848	Love Theme From "Lady Sings The Blues"/Any Happy Home (demo in p/s)	15
58	Philips SBBL 510	LEGRAND JAZZ (LP)	12
64	Philips BL 7605	PLAYS RICHARD ROGERS (LP)	12
64	Mercury SML 30020	VIOLENT VIOLINS (LP)	25
66	Philips (S)BL 7792	THE YOUNG GIRLS OF ROCHEFORT (LP, soundtrack)	25
68	United Artists SULP 1218	THE THOMAS CROWN AFFAIR (LP, soundtrack)	35
68	Sunset SLS 50519	THE THOMAS CROWN AFFAIR (LP, reissue)	12
68	CBS (S)BPG 63276	HOW TO SAVE A MARRIAGE AND RUIN YOUR LIFE (LP, soundtrack)	18
69	MGM MGM-C(S) 8101	ICE STATION ZEBRA (LP, soundtrack)	20
70	United Artists UAS 29084	THE HAPPY ENDING (LP, soundtrack)	20
71	Warner Bros K 46098	SUMMER OF '42 (LP, soundtrack)	12
73	Bell BELLS 235	THE THREE MUSKETEERS (LP, soundtrack)	18
72	RCA SF 8253	TIME FOR LOVING (LP, soundtrack)	12

LE GRIFFE

83	Bullet BOL 1	Fast Bikes/Where Are You? (p/s)	8
83	Bullet BOLT 1	Fast Bikes/Where Are You?/The Actor (12", p/s)	15
84	Bullet BOL 7	You're Killing Me (p/s)	8
83	Bullet BOLT 7	You're Killing Me/E.T.A. (12", p/s)	20
84	Bullet BULP 2	BREAKING STRAIN (mini-LP)	20

LEGS

74	Warner Bros K 16317	So Many Faces/You Bet You Have	5

(see also Curved Air, Stretch)

TOM LEHRER

60	Decca F 11243	Poisoning Pigeons In The Park/The Masochism Tango (some in p/s)	10/6
66	Reprise RS 23049	Pollution/Folk Song Army	6
58	Decca LF 1311	SONGS BY TOM LEHRER (10" LP)	15
59	Decca LF 1323	MORE OF TOM LEHRER (10" LP)	15
59	Decca LK 4332/SKL 4097	AN EVENING WASTED WITH... (LP)	12
60	Decca LK 4375	TOM LEHRER REVISITED (LP)	12
65	Reprise R 6179	THAT WAS THE YEAR THAT WAS (LP)	12

LEIBER-STOLLER ORCHESTRA

62	HMV POP 1050	Cafe Expresso/Blue Baion	18

LEIBSTANDARTE SS MB

81	Come Organisation	TRIUMPH OF THE WILL (LP, 500 only)	60
80s	Come Organisation	WELTANSCHAUUNG (LP)	40

ADELE LEIGH

59	Philips PB 887	O My Beloved Father/Voi Che Sapete (78)	10

ANDREW LEIGH

70	Polydor 2343 034	MAGICIAN (LP)	25

(see also Reg King)

BERNIE LEIGHTON

63	Pye International 7N 25177	Lawrence Of Arabia Theme/The Wonderful World We Live In (some in p/s)	8/5

GARY LeMEL

67	London HLM 7124	Beautiful People/Take Me With You (export issue)	18

LEMMINGS

65	Pye 7N 15837	Out Of My Mind/My Little Girl	18
65	Pye 7N 15899	You Can't Blame Me For Trying/Bring Your Heart With You	18

(see also Honeycombs, Martin Murray)

JACK LEMMON

60	Fontana H 262	Theme From "The Apartment"/Lemmon-Flavoured Blues	8

LEMMY & UPSETTERS with MICK GREEN

90	Sunnyside STYLE 777	Blue Suede Shoes/Paradise (p/s)	6

(see also Motörhead, Rockin' Vickers, Sam Gopal)

LEMON DIPS

69	De Wolfe DW/LP 3114	WHO'S GONNA BUY? (LP, library issue)	75

LEMONHEADS

91	Atlantic A 7709	Gonna Get Along Without Ya Now/Half The Time (p/s, withdrawn)	10
96	Warner Bros	CAR BUTTON CLOTH (CD, includes track 'Purple Parallelagram', promo-only)	60

LEMON INTERRUPT

93	Jnr. Boys Own JBO 12002	Eclipse/Bigmouth (12")	15
93	Junior Boys Own JBO 712	Dirty/Minneapolis/Minneapolis (Airwaves) (12")	15

(see also Underworld)

LEMON JELLY

01	Soft Rock SOFTROCK 001	Soft/Rock (blue vinyl, denim sleeve with condom, 1000 only)	40
02	XL IFXLT 147P	Space Walk/Return To Patagonia (10", leather title sleeve, 3000 only)	20
03	Rolled Oats RO 01	Rolled/Oats (gold vinyl, hessian sleeve, 1200 only)	8
98	Impotent Fury IF 001	THE BATH EP: In The Bath/Nervous Tension/A Tune For Jack (10", 1000 only, stickered cardboard sleeve, 1st 250 in hand-printed p/s)	120/40
99	Impotent Fury IF 002	THE YELLOW EP: His Majesty King Raam/The Staunton Lick/ Homage To Patagonia (10", 1000 only, stickered cardboard sleeve, 1st 240 in hand-printed p/s)	100/40
00	Impotent Fury IF 003	THE MIDNIGHT EP: Kneel Before Your God/Page One/Come (10", 1000 only, stickered cardboard sleeve, 1st 350 in hand-printed p/s)	50/20
02	XL IFXLLP 160	LOST HORIZONS (2-LP, gatefold sleeve, with booklet)	20

MINT VALUE £

LEMON KITTENS

79 Step Forward SF 10 SPOONFED AND WRITHING (EP) 25
81 United Dairies UD 07 CAKE BEAST (12" EP, with inner sleeve & insert) 30
80 United Dairies UD 02 WE BUY A HAMMER FOR DADDY (LP, with inner sheet) 40
83 Illuminated JAMS 131 THE BIG DENTIST (LP) 30
(see also Danielle Dax, Shock Headed Peters, Underneath, Gland Shrouds, Karl Blake, Fur Fur)

LEMON LINE

67 Decca F 12688 For Your Precious Love/You Made Me See The Light 6

LEMON MEN

69 Polydor 56365 I've Seen You Cut Lemons/Lemon Strip/Lemon Walk 5

LEMON PIPERS

68 Pye International 7N 25444 Green Tambourine/No Help From Me 7
68 Pye International 7N 25454 Rice Is Nice/Blueberry Blue 7
68 Pye International 7N 25464 Jelly Jungle (Of Orange Marmalade)/Shoeshine Boy 7
68 Pye Intl. NPL 28112 GREEN TAMBOURINE (LP) 30
68 Pye Intl. NSPL 28118 JUNGLE MARMALADE (LP) 18
69 Marble Arch MAL 1120 THE LEMON PIPERS (LP) 12
(see also Ram Jam)

LEMON PIPERS/1910 FRUITGUM CO.

68 Pye Intl. NEP 44091 PRESENTING ... (EP, 1 side each) 15
(see also 1910 Fruitgum Co.)

LEMON TREE

68 Parlophone R 5671 I Can Touch A Rainbow/William Chalker's Time Machine 55
68 Parlophone R 5739 It's So Nice To Come Home/Come On Girl 25
(see also Idle Race, Uglys, Danny King's Mayfair Set, Balls)

LEN & HONEYSUCKERS

66 Rio R 75 One More River/Emergency Ward 22

FREDDIE LENNON

66 Piccadilly 7N 35290 That's My Life (My Love And My Home)/The Next Time You Feel Important 75
(see also Loving Kind)

JIMMY LENNON & ATLANTICS

64 Decca F 11825 Louisiana Mama/I Learned To Yodel 35

JOHN LENNON/PLASTIC ONO BAND

SINGLES

69 Apple APPLE 13/R 5795 Give Peace A Chance/Remember Love (p/s, as Plastic Ono Band; some with Parlophone catalogue number, dark green label) 18/10
69 Apple APPLES 1001 Cold Turkey/Don't Worry Kyoko (Mummy's Only Looking For A Hand In The Snow) (p/s, as Plastic Ono Band) 15
69 Apple APPLES 1002 You Know My Name (Look Up The Number)/What's The New Mary Jane? (as Plastic Ono Band, unreleased; vinyl test pressings only with typed Apple 'Custom Recording' labels & handwritten catalogue number) 2,000+
70 Apple APPLES 1003 Instant Karma!/Who Has Seen The Wind? (p/s, as Lennon/Ono with Plastic Ono Band) 12
71 Apple R 5892 Power To The People/YOKO ONO & PLASTIC ONO BAND: Open Your Box (p/s, full apple label both sides or full/half apple label) 15
72 Apple R 5970 Happy Xmas (War Is Over) (as John & Yoko/Plastic Ono Band with Harlem Community Choir)/YOKO ONO & PLASTIC ONO BAND: Listen, The Snow Is Falling (p/s, green vinyl) 15
72 Apple R 5953 Woman Is The Nigger Of The World/Sisters O Sisters (unreleased, test pressings only) 1,000+
73 Apple R 5994 Mind Games/Meat City (p/s) 6
74 EMI PSR 369 Interview With John Lennon By Bob Mercer And Message To The Salesmen/ Whatever Gets You Thru' The Night (promo only) 500
75 Apple R 6003 9 Dream (Edited Version)/What You Got (demo only) 50
75 Apple R 6009 Imagine/Working Class Hero (p/s) 12
84 Polydor PODJ 701 Borrowed Time (Edited Version)/YOKO ONO: Your Hands (promo only) 20
84 Polydor POSP 712 Every Man Has A Woman Who Loves Him/SEAN ONO LENNON: It's Alright (p/s, some with poster) 10/5
88 Parlophone RP 6199 Imagine/Jealous Guy (picture disc) 15
97 Parlophone IMAGINE 001 Imagine (CD, 1-track, card p/s, promo only) 10
97 Parlophone IMAGINE 002 Happy Xmas (War Is Over) (CD, 1-track, card p/s, promo only) 10
98 Parlophone LENNON 002 Happy Xmas (War Is Over) (rough mix)/Be Bop A Lula (CD, card p/s, promo only) 15

LPs

68 Apple APCOR 2 UNFINISHED MUSIC NO. 1: TWO VIRGINS (with Yoko Ono, mono; black inner, no track listing, with "Merrie In England..." blurb on *front* sleeve) 3,000
68 Apple SAPCOR 2/ Track 613 012 UNFINISHED MUSIC NO. 1: TWO VIRGINS (with Yoko Ono, stereo; black inner, with track listing & "Merrie In England..." blurb on *back* sleeve & Track Records logo on label) 500
69 Zapple ZAPPLE 01 UNFINISHED MUSIC NO. 2: LIFE WITH THE LIONS (with Yoko Ono, with inner sleeve) 200
69 Apple SAPCOR 11 WEDDING ALBUM (with Yoko Ono; gatefold sleeve in box set, includes wedding certificate glued to inside box lid, press booklet, poster, white 'Bagism' bag, passport photographs, postcard & picture of wedding cake) 300
69 Apple CORE 2001 LIVE PEACE IN TORONTO 1969 (as Plastic Ono Band, with stapled calendar, some sealed) 125/60
72 Apple PAS 10004 IMAGINE (LP, with inner sleeve, poster & postcard) 50
72 Apple Q4PAS 10004 IMAGINE (LP, quadrophonic, with inner sleeve, poster & postcard) 125
81 Parlophone JLB 8 THE JOHN LENNON BOX (9-LP set, with insert) 100
84 Polydor POLH P5 MILK AND HONEY (picture disc, original pressing, thin vinyl, 2,000 only) 40

84	Polydor POLH P5	MILK AND HONEY (picture disc, 2nd pressing, thicker vinyl, 1,000 only)	50
98	Parlophone 8306142	ANTHOLOGY (4-CDR, jewel cases with Abbey Road studio inlays, incorrect track listing and missing "Grow Old With Me" from CD4, promo only)	80

(see also Beatles, Yoko Ono, Bill Elliott/Elastic Oz Band, Elephant's Memory, Musketeer Gripweed, Elton John)

JOHN LENNON & BLEECHERS (Jamaica)

70 Punch PH 23 — Ram You Hard/UPSETTERS: Soul Stew — 20

LENNON SISTERS

56	Vogue Coral Q 72176	Graduation Day/Toy Tiger	15
57	Vogue Coral Q 72259	Young And In Love/Teenage Waltz	15
57	Vogue Coral Q 72285	Shake Me I Rattle/Pocohontas	18
61	London HLD 9417	Sad Movies/I Don't Know Why	15
64	London HA-D/SH-D 8154	GREAT FOLK SONGS (LP, as Lennon Sisters & Cousins)	30

LENNY THE LION (with Terry Hall)

59 Parlophone R 4609 — I Wish That I Could Be Father Christmas/ I Want A Hippopotamus For Christmas — 6

J.B. LENOIR (& AFRICAN HUNCH RHYTHM)

65	Sue WI 339	I Sing Um The Way I Feel/I Feel So Good (with His African Hunch Rhythm)	40
65	Bootleg 503	Man Watch Your Woman/Mama Talk To Your Daughter (99 copies only)	60
66	Blue Horizon 45-1004	Mojo Boogie/I Don't Care What Nobody Say (99 copies only)	110
68	Python PLP 25	J.B. LENOIR (LP, 99 copies only)	75
70	Polydor 2482 014	CRUSADE (LP)	20
75	Rarity LP 2	J.B. LENOIR (LP)	20
70s	CBS 62593	ALABAMA BLUES (LP)	30

ROBIN LENT

71 Nepentha 6347 002 — SCARECROW'S JOURNEY (LP, gatefold sleeve, with Focus) — 35

(see also Focus, Jan Akkerman)

VAL LENTON

65 Immediate IM 008 — Gotta Get Away/You Don't Care — 30

CHRIS LEON

72 Dynamic DYN 450 — (Last Night) I Didn't Get To Sleep At All/DYNAMITES: Instrumental Version — 6

LEON (Silvera) & OWEN (Gray)

62 Blue Beat BB 117 — Murder (with Drumbago All Stars)/ROY PANTON: Forty Four — 20

(see also Owen & Leon, Owen & Millie)

DEKE LEONARD

73	United Artists UP 35494	Diamond Road/Turning In Circles	5
73	United Artists UP 35556	Nothing Is Happening/Sixty Minute Man (unissued)	
73	United Artists UP 35556	Nothing Is Happening/She's A Cow (unissued, demo only)	12
73	United Artists UP 35556	A Hard Way To Live/The Aching Is So Sweet	5
74	United Artists UP 35668	Louisiana Hoedown/She's A Cow	5
79	United Artists UP 36488	Map Of India/Hey There! (Lady In The Black Tuxedo) (gatefold p/s)	5
73	United Artists UAS 29464	ICEBERG (LP)	15
74	United Artists UAG 29544	KAMIKAZE (LP)	15

(see also Man, Marty Wilde, Help Yourself, Pete Brown's Piblokto, Gary Pickford-Hopkins & Friends)

ANN LEONARDO

57	Capitol CL 14723	Straws In The Wind/Travelling Stranger	10
57	Capitol CL 14755	Lottery/One And Only	10
57	Capitol CL 14797	Three Time Loser/I'll Wait Till Monday	6

TOMMY LEONETTI

54	Capitol CL 14199	That's What You Made Me/I Love My Mama	8
55	Capitol CL 14272	Ever Since You Went Away/Untied	8
56	Capitol CL 14556	Heartless/Sometime	5
56	Capitol CL 14598	It's Wild/Free	5
56	Capitol CL 14654	Too Proud/Wrong	5
58	RCA RCA 1107	Dream Lover/Moonlight Serenade	6
58	RCA RCA 1107	Dream Lover/Moonlight Serenade (78)	10

LEONIE & JOE NOLAN BAND

68 Jolly JY 015 — Move And Groove/Don't Let Me Do It — 6

LE ORME

(see under 'O')

LEO'S SUNSHIPP

79	Grapevine RED 3	Give Me The Sunshine/I'm Back For More	6
79	Grapevine REDC 3	Give Me The Sunshine/I'm Back For More (12")	10

LEPRECHAUN

81 Excalibur EXC 508 — Loc It Up/Party Freaks (12") — 8

LE RITZ

77 Breaker BS 2001 — Punker/What A Sucker (p/s) — 35

LEROY & ROCKY (Ellis)

68 Studio One SO 2042 — Love Me Girl/WRIGGLERS: Reel Up — 25

(see also King Rocky)

LE ROYS

64	Give A Disc LYN 504/505	Money/Swinging On A Star (flexidisc)	10
64	HMV POP 1274	Gotta Lotta Love (Ciribiribin)/Don't Cry Baby	12
64	HMV POP 1312	Chills/Lost Out On Love	15
64	HMV POP 1368	I Come Smiling On Through/California GL 903	12

(see also Mike Sarne, Simon Scott, John Leyton, Mike Berry, Grazina, Billie Davis, Billy Boyle, Don Spencer)

MINT VALUE £

LEROYS & INNOCENTS

64 Regal Zonophone RZ 502 HOT SIX: Don't Throw Your Love Away; My Girl Lollipop; I Love You Because; Not Fade Away (maxi-single, plain sleeve) ... 12

(see also Innocents [U.K])

BILL LE SAGE

60s World Records PRESENTING THE BILL LESAGE/RONNIE ROSS QUARTET (LP) ... 20

(see also Ronnie Ross)

BONGO LES (Chen) & BUNNY (Herman)

72 Attack ATT 8041 Feel Nice (Version)/WINSTON SCOTLAND: Quick And Slick ... 7

(see also Bongo Herman)

LES & SILKIE

70 Torpedo TOR 13 I Don't Want To Tell You/DENZIL DENNIS: Come On In ... 6

LORNE LESLEY

59 Parlophone R 4518 Some Of These Days/When Love Has Let You Down ... 7
59 Parlophone R 4518 Some Of These Days/When Love Has Let You Down (78) ... 10
59 Parlophone R 4567 Warm/You Ought To Be Mine ... 8
59 Parlophone R 4581 So High, So Low/I Don't Know ... 10
60 Polydor NH 66928 Take All My Love/Ritroviamoci (Till We Meet Again) ... 10
60 Polydor NH 66956 Bloodshot Eyes/We're Gonna Dance ... 12
65 Philips BF 1403 Someone Like You/Where My Heart Never Wandered ... 6
65 Philips BF 1434 Rainy Days Were Made For Lonely People/Fire Down Below ... 6
66 Philips BF 1487 Somebody's Gonna Be Sorry/(I'm Afraid) The Masquerade Is Over ... 8
66 Parlophone R 5538 Little Snowflakes/Would You ... 6

MICHAEL LESLEY

65 Pye 7N 15835 Momma Didn't Know/I Don't Wanna Know ... 6
65 Pye 7N 15908 Penny Arcade/Bye Bye Baby ... 10
65 Pye 7N 15959 Make Up Or Break Up/She Can't See Me ... 10
66 Decca F 12531 Right Or Wrong/Office Girl (credited to Michael Leslie) ... 5

JOHN & CHRIS LESLIE

76 Cottage COT 901 THE SHIP OF TIME (LP) ... 15

LES RITA MITSOUKO

(see under 'R')

LES SAUTERELLES

(see under 'S')

HEDDY LESTER

77 Sonet SON 2013 The World Keeps Turning/Never Saw Him Laughing (p/s) ... 6

KETTY LESTER

62 London HLN 9527 Love Letters/I'm A Fool To Want You ... 8
62 London HLN 9574 But Not For Me/Moscow Nights ... 7
62 London HLN 9608 You Can't Lie To A Liar/River Of Salt ... 7
62 London HLN 9635 This Land Is Your Land/Love Belongs To Everyone ... 7
63 London HLN 9698 A Warm Summer Day/I'll Never Stop Loving You ... 7
64 RCA Victor RCA 1394 Some Things Are Better Left Unsaid/The House Is Haunted ... 80
64 RCA Victor RCA 1403 Roses Grow With Thorns/Please Don't Cry Anymore ... 40
64 RCA Victor RCA 1421 I Trust You Baby/Theme From "The Luck Of Ginger Coffey" ... 7
65 RCA Victor RCA 1460 Looking For A Better World/Pretty Eyes ... 7
65 Capitol CL 15427 West Coast/I'll Be Looking Back ... 18
66 Capitol CL 15447 When A Man Loves A Woman/We'll Be Together Again ... 7
62 London RE-N 1348 KETTY LESTER (EP) ... 40
63 London HA-N 2455 LOVE LETTERS (LP) ... 55
64 RCA Victor RD 7669 THE SOUL OF ME (LP) ... 30
65 RCA Victor RD 7712 WHERE IS LOVE (LP) ... 30
67 Stateside S(S)L 10196 WHEN A MAN LOVES A WOMAN (LP) ... 25

LAZY LESTER

64 Stateside SS 277 I'm A Lover Not A Fighter/Sugar Coated Love ... 30
71 Blue Horizon 2431 007 MADE UP MY MIND (LP) ... 110
77 Flyright FLYLP 526 THEY CALL ME LAZY (LP) ... 15
79 Flyright FLYLP 544 POOR BOY BLUES (LP) ... 15

ROBIE LESTER

62 Polydor NH 66963 Ballad Of Cheating John/Miracle Of Love ... 5

LES YPER SOUND

67 Fontana TF 880 Too Fortiche/Psyche Rock ... 75

JOE LETHAL

78 Lethal CI 200526 Don't Come Back (no p/s) ... 35

LETTERMEN

61 Capitol CL 15222 The Way You Look Tonight/That's My Desire ... 6
65 Capitol CL 15405 Theme From A Summer Place/Sealed With A Kiss ... 5
68 Capitol CL 15526 Goin' Out Of My Head/Can't Take My Eyes Off You — I Believe ... 5
69 Capitol CL 15609 Hurt So Bad/Traces ... 5
61 Capitol EAP 41669 THE LETTERMEN (EP) ... 12
62 Capitol (S)T 1669 A SONG FOR YOUNG LOVE (LP) ... 15
62 Capitol (S)T 1711 ONCE UPON A TIME (LP) ... 15
62 Capitol (S)T 1761 THE LETTERMEN (LP) ... 15
63 Capitol (S)T 1829 COLLEGE STANDARDS (LP) ... 15
63 Capitol (S)T 1936 IN CONCERT (LP) ... 15
64 Capitol (S)T 2083 LOOK AT LOVE (LP) ... 15
64 Capitol (S)T 2142 SHE CRIED (LP) ... 15
65 Capitol T 2270 PORTRAIT OF MY LOVE (LP) ... 15

LETTERMEN

74 Stag SG 10075 — FIRST CLASS (LP, private pressing) 90

LETTERS

79 Heartbeat PULSE 9 — Nobody Loves Me/Don't Want You Back (p/s) 100

DON LETTS & JAH WOBBLE

79 Virgin VS 239 — Steel Leg: Stratetime & The Wide Man/Electric Dread: Haile Unlikely (p/s) 10
79 Virgin VS 239-12 — Steel Leg: Stratetime & The Wide Man/Electric Dread: Haile Unlikely (12", p/s) .. 12
(see also Jah Wobble, PiL)

LEVEE BREAKERS

65 Parlophone R 5291 — Babe I'm Leaving You/Wild About My Loving 25
(see also Beverley, Johnny Joyce)

LEVEE CAMP MOAN

69 County — LEVEE CAMP MOAN (LP, private pressing) 600
69 County — PEACOCK FARM (LP, private pressing) 600

LEVEL 42

79 Elite DAZZ 4 — Sandstorm/ATMOSFEAR: Journey To The Powerline (Remix) (12", white label test pressing, no p/s) 25
80 Elite DAZZ 5 — Love Meeting Love/Instrumental Love (7", unreleased)
80 Elite DAZZ 5 — Love Meeting Love/Instrumental Love (12", company die-cut stickered sleeve) ... 8
81 Elite LEVLP 1 — STRATEGY (LP, unreleased, 6 white label test pressings only) 200
91 Polydor 511 635-2 — THE COMPLETE LEVEL 42 (9-CD box set) 40

LEVELLERS

89 Hag HAG 005 — Carry Me/What's In The Way/The Last Days Of Winter/England My Home (12" EP; first 1,000 copies with Brighton contact address on p/s) .... each 10
89 Hag HAG 006 — Outside Inside/I Have No Answers (500 promo copies only, no p/s) 6
91 On The Fiddle OTF EP 1 — Police On My Back/Where The Hell Are We Going To Love?/Travelogue (4am Mix) (12", fan club issue, p/s) 12
92 On The Fiddle OTF LP 2 — LIVE 1992 (LP, fan club issue, 2,000 only) 15

GERRY LEVENE (& AVENGERS)

64 Decca F 11815 — It's Driving Me Wild (solo)/Dr. Feelgood 55
(see also Moody Blues)

ANNABEL LEVENTON

69 Morgan MR 20 — Easy To Be Hard/My Dear Friend 6

LEVIATHAN

68 Elektra EKSN 45052 — Remember The Times/Second Production 50
69 Elektra EKSN 45057 — The War Machine/Time 45
69 Elektra EKSN 45052/45057 — (WAY IN) THE FOUR FACES OF LEVIATHAN (Remember The Times/ Second Production/The War Machine/Time)(2 x 7" press pack, A4 folder sleeve, some overprinted with "Harrods" logo, with biog & photo, promo, some commercial) 150
69 Elektra EKSN 45075 — Flames/Just Forget Tomorrow 40
90s (no cat.no.) — ELEKTRA DAZE (CD EP, private pressing) 25
69 Elektra EKS 74046 — LEVIATHAN (2-LP, unissued, acetates only, 1 copy known) .... 1000+
(see also Mike Stuart Span, High Broom)

HANK LEVINE ORCHESTRA

61 HMV POP 947 — Image (Parts 1 & 2) 15
65 HMV POP 1390 — Image (Parts 1 & 2) (reissue) 6

LEVITTS

69 ESP Disk/Fontana STL 5518 — WE ARE THE LEVITTS (LP) 25

LEVON & HAWKS

65 Atlantic AT 4054 — The Stones I Throw/He Don't Love You 40
(see also Band)

BARRINGTON LEVY

80s Time TR 009 — HERE I COME EP: Trouble Mixed/Run Come Dub/Rub A Dub 8
80s Jah Life JL 008 — Murderer/Tell Them A Ready (12") 8

BEN LEVY

66 Ska Beat JB 245 — Doren/Never Knew Love 15
66 Ska Beat JB 255 — I'll Make You Glad/Keep Smiling 15

CARL LEV(E)Y & CIMARRONS

70 Hot Rod HR 100 — Walk The Hot Street/PEGGY & CIMARRONS: You Say You Don't Love Me 10
70 Hot Rod HR 101 — Remember Easter Monday/PEGGY & JIMMY: Pum Pum Lover 10
(see also Hot Rod Allstars, Rita Alston, Peggy)

JONA LEWIE

74 Sonet SON 2048 — Piggy Back Sue/Papa Don't Go 5
75 Sonet SON 2056 — The Swan/Custer's Last Stand 5
76 Sonet SON 2081 — Hallelujah Europe Parts 1 & 2 5
77 Sonet SON 2117 — Rocking Yobs/After We Swum 5
(see also Brett Marvin & Thunderbolts)

CARL LEWIN

71 Bullet BU 456 — Knock Three Times/SIDNEY ALL STARS: The Whealing Mouse 7
71 Punch PH 98 — Nobody Told Me/WING: Don't Play That Song Again (version) 6

ALVA (REGGIE) LEWIS

67 Caltone TONE 111 — Return Home/KING ROCK & WILLOWS: You Are The One 40
67 Island WI 3080 — I'm Indebted/GROOVERS: You've Got To Cry 30
72 Upsetter US 391 — Natty Natty (as Alva Reggie Lewis)/UPSETTERS: Version 12
(see also Reggae Boys, Webber Sisters, Lester Sterling, Cool Cats)

MINT VALUE £

ANDY LEWIS & KEN BURKE

90s Acid Jazz AJX 147S (Love Is Alive) In Your Heart (pink vinyl, p/s) . . . 10

BARBARA LEWIS

63 London HLK 9724 Hello Stranger/Think A Little Sugar . . . 25
63 London HLK 9779 Straighten Up Your Heart/If You Love Her . . . 25
64 London HLK 9832 Snap Your Fingers/Puppy Love . . . 25
64 Atlantic AT 4013 Pushin' A Good Thing Too Far/Come Home . . . 25
65 Atlantic AT 4031 Baby I'm Yours/Hello Stranger . . . 15
65 Atlantic AT 4041 Make Me Your Baby/Love To Be Loved . . . 15
66 Atlantic AT 4068 Don't Forget About Me/It's Magic . . . 15
66 Atlantic 584 037 Make Me Belong To You/Girls Need Loving Care . . . 12
67 Atlantic 584 061 Baby What Do You Want Me To Do/I Remember The Feeling . . . 35
68 Atlantic 584 153 Hello Stranger/Baby I'm Yours (reissue) . . . 7
68 Atlantic 584 174 Sho Nuff (It's Got To Be Your Love)/Thankful For What I Got . . . 10
71 Atlantic 2091 143 Someday We're Gonna Love Again/Baby I'm Yours . . . 10
72 Atlantic K 10128 Someday We're Gonne Love Again/Baby I'm Yours (reissue) . . . 5
65 Atlantic AET 6015 SNAP YOUR FINGERS (EP) . . . 75
66 Atlantic ATL 5042 BABY I'M YOURS (LP) . . . 70
66 Atlantic 587 002 IT'S MAGIC (LP) . . . 45
70 Stax SXATS 1035 THE MANY GROOVES OF BARBARA LEWIS (LP) . . . 30

BOB LEWIS

57 Parlophone R 4309 Far Away/The Mayflower Song . . . 5

BOBBY LEWIS

61 Parlophone R 4794 Tossin' And Turnin'/Oh Yes, I Love You . . . 25
61 Parlophone R 4831 One Track Mind/Are You Ready . . . 20
62 Stateside SS 126 I'm Tossin' And Turnin' Again/Nothin' But The Blues . . . 20

CAPPY LEWIS

61 Vogue V 9184 Bullfight/OLYMPICS: Little Pedro . . . 20
(see also Olympics)

DAVE LEWIS

66 Pye Intl. NEP 44057 GIVIN' GAS (EP) . . . 35

DAVID LEWIS

70 AX 1 SONGS OF DAVID LEWIS (LP, private pressing, paste-on sleeve) . . . 300+
(see also Andwella['s Dream], David Baxter)

FURRY LEWIS

69 Blue Horizon 7-63228 PRESENTING THE COUNTRY BLUES (LP) . . . 80
70 Matchbox SDR 190 IN MEMPHIS (LP) . . . 25
71 Xtra XTRA 1116 FURRY LEWIS (LP) . . . 20
71 Spokane SPL 1004 THE EARLY YEARS 1927-1929 (LP) . . . 50
(see also John Estes)

GARY LEWIS & PLAYBOYS

65 Liberty LIB 10187 This Diamond Ring/Tijuana Wedding . . . 15
65 Liberty LIB 55778 Count Me In/Little Miss Go-Go . . . 18
65 Liberty LIB 55809 Save Your Heart For Me/Without A Word Of Warning . . . 7
65 Liberty LIB 55818 Everybody Loves A Clown/Time Stands Still . . . 7
66 Liberty LIB 55846 She's Just My Style/I Won't Make That Mistake Again . . . 10
66 Liberty LIB 55865 Sure Gonna Miss Her/I Don't Wanna Say Goodnight . . . 8
66 Liberty LIB 55880 Green Grass/I Can Read Between The Lines . . . 8
66 Liberty LIB 55898 My Heart's Symphony/Tina . . . 12
66 Liberty LIB 55914 (You Don't Have To) Paint Me A Picture/Looking For The Stars . . . 12
67 Liberty LIB 55933 Where Will The Words Come From/The Best Man . . . 7
67 Liberty LIB 55949 Loser (With A Broken Heart)/Ice Melts In The Sun . . . 7
67 Liberty LIB 55971 Girls In Love/Let's Be More Than Friends . . . 7
67 Liberty LBF 15025 Jill/Needles And Pins . . . 12
68 Liberty LBF 15131 Sealed With A Kiss/Pretty Thing . . . 7
70 Liberty LBF 15335 Orangutan/Something Is Wrong . . . 6
75 United Artists UP 35780 My Heart's Symphony/Tina (reissue) . . . 8
65 Liberty LBY 1259 THIS DIAMOND RING (LP) . . . 45
66 Liberty LBY 1322 JUST OUR STYLE (LP) . . . 30

GEORGE LEWIS & HIS NEW ORLEANS STOMPERS/BAND

78

51 Tempo AA 100 2.19 Blues/Jerusalem Blues
(12", as George Lewis & His New Orleans Music) . . . 7

SINGLES

56 Vogue V 2051 Climax Rag/Deep Bayou Blues . . . 7
56 Vogue V 2052 Millenberg Joys/Two Jim Blues . . . 7
56 Vogue V 2053 Just A Closer Walk With Thee/Just A Little While To Stay Here . . . 7
56 Vogue V 2054 Fidgety Feet/Dauphine Street Blues . . . 7
56 Vogue V 2055 Don't Go 'Way Nobody/Careless Love Blues . . . 7
60 HMV POP 707 South Rampart Street Parade/Chinatown My Chinatown (with Band) . . . 10

EPs

55 Vogue EPV 1066 GEORGE LEWIS AND HIS NEW ORLEANS STOMPERS . . . 15
55 Vogue EPV 1081 GEORGE LEWIS AND HIS NEW ORLEANS STOMPERS . . . 10
55 Tempo EXA 15 GEORGE LEWIS AND HIS NEW ORLEANS STOMPERS . . . 12
57 Tempo EXA 62 GEORGE LEWIS (as George Lewis' Ragtime Band) . . . 8
57 Tempo EXA 66 GEORGE LEWIS (as George Lewis' Ragtime Band) . . . 8
57 Tempo EXA 70 GEORGE LEWIS' RAGTIME BAND . . . 10
59 Tempo EXA 97 GEORGE LEWIS (as George Lewis & His New Orleans Rhythm Boys) . . . 8
59 Tempo EXA 101 GEORGE LEWIS . . . 8
59 Vogue EPV 1220 GEORGE LEWIS IN HI-FI . . . 10
59 Vogue EPV 1252 GEORGE LEWIS IN HI-FI . . . 10

50s	Esquire EP 125	NEW ORLEANS RAGTIME BAND VOL. 1	12
50s	Esquire EP 135	NEW ORLEANS RAGTIME BAND VOL. 2	12
50s	Esquire EP 155	NEW ORLEANS RAGTIME BAND VOL. 3	12
50s	Esquire EP 175	NEW ORLEANS RAGTIME BAND VOL. 4	12
50s	Esquire EP 209	NEW ORLEANS RAGTIME BAND VOL. 5	10
60s	Esquire EP 211	NEW ORLEANS RAGTIME BAND VOL. 6	10
60s	Esquire EP 215	NEW ORLEANS RAGTIME BAND VOL. 7	10
60s	Esquire EP 219	NEW ORLEANS RAGTIME BAND VOL. 8	10
60	Esquire EP 225	NEW ORLEANS RAGTIME BAND VOL. 9	12
60	HMV 7EG 8540	SOUNDS OF NEW ORLEANS	8
50s	Storyville SEP 315	ICE CREAM	8
50s	Storyville SEP 321	PANAMA	8
50s	Storyville SEP 322	LOUISIANA	8
50s	Storyville SEP 325	WILLIE THE WEEPER	8
60	Storyville SEP 349	JAZZ FROM NEW ORLEANS	8
61	Storyville SEP 361	TILL WE MEET AGAIN	8
61	Storyville SEP 365	ISLE OF CAPRI	8
61	Storyville SEP 369	MUSKRAT RUMBLE	8
60s	Storyville SEP 503	HIGH SOCIETY	8
60s	Storyville SEP 504	DALLAS BLUES	8

LPs

52	Vogue LDE 012	GEORGE LEWIS AND HIS NEW ORLEANS ALLSTARS (10")	20
54	Vogue LDE 082	GEORGE LEWIS JAM SESSION (10")	20
55	Vogue LAE 12005	GEORGE LEWIS AND HIS NEW ORLEANS STOMPERS	50
55	London H-APB 1041	VOL. 1 JAZZ BAND (10", with New Orleans Jazz Band & Quartet)	25
56	London HB-U 1045	VOL. 2 ALL STARS (10", with New Orleans All Stars & Quartet)	25
57	Tempo TAP 13	GEORGE LEWIS RAGTIME BAND	60
57	Melodisc MLP 12-101	NEW ORLEANS PARADE	15
50s	Esquire 20-067	GEORGE LEWIS RAGTIME BAND (10")	15
50s	Esquire 20-073	GEORGE LEWIS RAGTIME BAND (10")	15
50s	'77' LA 12/28	SMILE, DARN YA, SMILE (as George Lewis with Barry Martyn's Band)	20
59	Columbia Clef 33C 9042	RAGGIN' AND STOMPIN' (10")	15
60	HMV CLP 1371/CSD 1309	BLUES FROM THE BAYOU (mono/stereo)	25/30
61	HMV CLP 1413/CSD 1337	DOCTOR JAZZ (mono/stereo)	25/30
64	London HA-K/SH-K 8165	JAZZ AT PRESERVATION HALL VOL. 4 (with Band Of New Orleans)	20

GEORGE LEWIS/FREDDIE KOHLMAN

53	Brunswick LA 8627	NEW ORLEANS JAZZ CONCERT (10" LP)	25

HOPETON LEWIS

67	Island WI 3054	Rock Steady/Cool Collie	30
67	Island WI 3055	Finder's Keepers/ROLAND ALPHONSO: Shanty Town Curfew	25
67	Island WI 3056	Let Me Come On Home/Hardships Of Life (with Merritone All Stars)	25
67	Island WI 3057	Run Down/Pick Yourself Up	25
67	Island WI 3059	Let The Little Girl Dance/This Music Got Soul	30
67	Island WI 3068	Rock A Shacka/I Don't Want Trouble	75
68	Island WI 3076	Everybody Rocking/Stars Shining So Bright	30
68	Fab FAB 43	Skinny Leg Girl/Live Like A King (as Hopetown Lewis & Glenmore Brown)	22
70	Duke Reid DR 2505	Boom Shaka Lacka/TOMMY McCOOK QUINTET: Dynamite	22
70	Duke Reid DR 2516	Testify/TOMMY McCOOK: Super Soul	15
71	Duke DU 112	Grooving Out Of Life (with Byron Lee & Dragonaires) (actually titled "Grooving Out On Life")/BYRON LEE & DRAGONAIRES: Fire Fire	7
71	Treasure Isle TI 7060	To The Other Man/TOMMY McCOOK: Stampede	10
72	Treasure Isle TI 7071	Judgement Day (actually by Hopeton Lewis & Dennis Alcapone)/ EARL LINDO: Version Day	10
72	Attack ATT 8035	Starting All Over Again/DYNAMITES: Instrumental Version	5
72	Dynamic DYN 436	Come Together/Going Back To My Hometown	5
72	Dynamic DYN 447	Good Together/Version	5
73	Dragon DRA 1001	City Of New Orleans/The Wind Cries Mary	5
73	Dragon DRA 1011	Groovin' Out On Life/God Bless Whoever Sent You	5
67	Island ILP 957	TAKE IT EASY: ROCKSTEADY WITH HOPETON LEWIS (LP)	170
71	Trojan TRL 36	GROOVING OUT ON LIFE (LP)	25

(see also Glenmore Brown & Hopeton Lewis)

HUGH X. LEWIS

66	London HLR 10032	Looking In The Future/Too Late	6
66	London HA-R 8293	THE HUGH X. LEWIS ALBUM (LP)	15
67	London HA-R 8303	JUST BEFORE DAWN (LP)	15

JENNIFER LEWIS & ANGELA STRANGE

65	Columbia DB 7662	Bring It To Me/You Know	10
66	Columbia DB 7814	I've Heard It All Before/Bad Storm Coming	12

JERRY LEWIS

56	Capitol CL 14559	I Keep Her Picture Hanging Upside Down/I Love A Murder Mystery	7
56	Capitol CL 14626	Buckskin Beauty/Pardners (with Dean Martin)	7
57	Brunswick 05636	Rock-a-Bye Your Baby With A Dixie Melody/Come Rain Or Come Shine	15
57	Brunswick 05672	Let Me Sing And I'm Happy/It All Depends On You	7
57	Brunswick 05693	With These Hands/My Mammy	6
57	Brunswick 05710	By Myself/No One	6
58	Brunswick 05727	Sad Sack/Shine On Your Shoes	6
58	Brunswick 05756	Dormi, Dormi, Dormi/Love Is A Lonely Thing	6
58	Brunswick 05756	Dormi, Dormi, Dormi/Love Is A Lonely Thing (78)	8
59	Brunswick 05777	Song From "The Geisha Boy"/The More I See You	6
59	Brunswick 05777	Song From "The Geisha Boy"/The More I See You (78)	8
53	Capitol LC 6591	CAPITOL PRESENTS JERRY LEWIS (10" LP)	30

(see also Dean Martin)

MINT VALUE £

JERRY LEWIS (Jamaica)

72	Pama PM 862	The Godfather/ALTON ELLIS: Some Day	12
73	Explosion EX 2077	Rhythm Pleasure/AGGROVATORS: Doctor Seaton	12

(see also I Roy)

JERRY LEE LEWIS

78s

57	London HLS 8457	Whole Lotta Shakin' Goin' On/It'll Be Me	15
57	London HLS 8529	Great Balls Of Fire/Mean Woman Blues	15
58	London HLS 8559	You Win Again/I'm Feelin' Sorry	30
58	London HLS 8592	Breathless/Down The Line	35
58	London HLS 8700	Break-Up/I'll Make It All Up To You	40
59	London HLS 8780	High School Confidential/Fools Like Me	45
59	London HLS 8840	Lovin' Up A Storm/Big Blon' Baby	60
59	London HLS 8941	Let's Talk About Us/The Ballad Of Billy Joe	90
59	London HLS 8993	Little Queenie/I Could Never Be Ashamed Of You	150
96	Cruisin' The 50s CASB 002	Wild One/Old Black Joe (numbered, 300 only)	30

SINGLES

57	London HLS 8457	Whole Lotta Shakin' Goin' On/It'll Be Me	35
57	London HLS 8529	Great Balls Of Fire/Mean Woman Blues	22
58	London HLS 8559	You Win Again/I'm Feelin' Sorry	35
58	London HLS 8592	Breathless/Down The Line	20
58	London HLS 8700	Break-Up/I'll Make It All Up To You	18
59	London HLS 8780	High School Confidential/Fools Like Me	18
59	London HLS 8840	Lovin' Up A Storm/Big Blon' Baby	22
59	London HLS 8941	Let's Talk About Us/The Ballad Of Billy Joe	18
59	London HLS 8993	Little Queenie/I Could Never Be Ashamed Of You	18

(The above 45s were originally issued with triangular centres; round-centre pressings are worth two-thirds of these values.)

60	London HLS 9083	I'll Sail My Ship Alone/It Hurt Me So	15
60	London HLS 9131	Baby, Baby, Bye Bye/Old Black Joe	15
60	London HLS 9202	John Henry/Hang Up My Rock And Roll Shoes	18
61	London HLS 9335	What'd I Say?/Livin' Lovin' Wreck	10
61	London HLS 9414	It Won't Happen With Me/Cold Cold Heart	12
61	London HLS 9446	As Long As I Live/When I Get Paid	10
62	London HLS 9526	I've Been Twistin'/Ramblin' Rose	8
62	London HLS 9584	Sweet Little Sixteen/How's My Ex Treating You	8
63	London HLS 9688	Good Golly Miss Molly/I Can't Trust Me (In Your Arms Anymore)	8
63	London HLS 9722	Teenage Letter/Seasons Of My Heart (B-side with Linda Gail Lewis)	10
63	Mercury AMT 1216	Hit The Road Jack/Pen And Paper	7
64	Philips BF 1324	I'm On Fire/Bread And Butter Man	10
64	London HLS 9867	Lewis Boogie/Bonnie B	15
65	Philips BF 1371	Hi-Heel Sneakers/You Went Back On Your Word	7
65	Philips BF 1407	Baby Hold Me Close/I Believe In You	8
65	Philips BF 1425	Rockin' Pneumonia And The Boogie Woogie Flu/This Must Be The Place	8
65	London HLS 9980	Carry Me Back To Old Virginia/I Know What It Means	10
66	Philips BF 1521	Memphis Beat/If I Had It All To Do Over	8
67	Philips BF 1594	It's A Hang-Up Baby/Holdin' On	8
67	Philips BF 1615	Turn On Your Love Light/Shotgun Man	8
68	Mercury MF 1020	Another Place, Another Time/Walking The Floor Over You	6
69	Mercury MF 1088	To Make Love Sweeter For You/Let's Talk About Us	5
69	Mercury MF 1105	Long Tall Sally/Jenny, Jenny (some in p/s)	10/6
69	Mercury MF 1110	Great Balls Of Fire/Whole Lotta Shakin' Goin' On (some in p/s)	10/6
73	Mercury 6052 378	(Taking My) Music To The Man/Jack Daniels (Old No. 7) (some in p/s)	8/6
79	Elektra K 12374	Rocking My Life Away/Rita May (p/s)	8
80	Elektra K 12399	Everyday I Have To Cry/Who Will The Next Fool Be	5
80	Elektra K 12432	Rockin' Jerry Lee/Good Time Charles Got The Blues	5

EXPORT SINGLES

58	London HL 7050	High School Confidential/Fools Like Me	30
62	London HL 7117	Save The Last Dance For Me/Hello Josephine	40
63	London HL 7120	Good Golly Miss Molly/I Can't Trust Me (In Your Arms Anymore)	25
63	London HL 7123	In The Mood/I'm Feelin' Sorry	40
70s	Bulldog BD 17	Bonnie B./Down The Line/Baby Baby/I'm Feeling Sorry	5

EPs

58	London RE-S 1140	JERRY LEE LEWIS — NO. 1 (initially with triangular centre)	60/35
59	London RE-S 1186	JERRY LEE LEWIS — NO. 2 (initially with triangular centre)	60/35
59	London RE-S 1187	JERRY LEE LEWIS — NO. 3 (initially with triangular centre)	60/35
61	London RE-S 1296	JERRY LEE LEWIS — NO. 4	45
62	London RE-S 1336	JERRY LEE LEWIS — NO. 5	40
63	London RE-S 1351	JERRY LEE LEWIS — NO. 6	40
63	London RE-S 1378	FOUR MORE FROM JERRY LEE LEWIS	45
66	Philips BE 12599	COUNTRY STYLE	30
84	Sun JLL EP 001	THE FABULOUS JERRY LEE LEWIS VOL. 1 (Fan Club issue)	15
84	Sun JLL EP 002	THE FABULOUS JERRY LEE LEWIS VOL. 2 (Fan Club issue)	15

LPs

59	London HA-S 2138	JERRY LEE LEWIS	100
62	London HA-S 2440	JERRY LEE'S GREATEST	65
64	Philips (S)BL 7622	GOLDEN HITS	15
65	Philips (S)BL 7646	LIVE AT THE STAR CLUB, HAMBURG (with Nashville Teens)	20
65	Philips BL 7650	THE GREATEST LIVE SHOW ON EARTH	15
65	Philips BL 7668	THE RETURN OF ROCK	20
65	London HA-S 8251	WHOLE LOTTA SHAKIN' GOIN' ON	65
66	Philips BL 7688	COUNTRY SONGS FOR CITY FOLKS	18
66	Philips (S)BL 7706	MEMPHIS BEAT	15
66	Ember NR 5038	SUNSTROKE (shared with Carl Perkins)	12
67	Philips (S)BL 7746	BY REQUEST — MORE GREATEST LIVE SHOW ON EARTH (mono/stereo)	15/18
67	London HA-S 8323	BREATHLESS	75

(The above London LPs were originally issued with plum labels; later black label reissues are worth £15-£20.)

68 Mercury 20117 (S)MCL SOUL MY WAY . . . 16
68 Fontana SFJL 964 GOT YOU ON MY MIND . . . 18
69 Mercury 21011 SMWL ANOTHER PLACE, ANOTHER TIME . . . 15
69 Mercury 21047 SMCL SHE STILL COMES AROUND (TO WHAT'S LEFT OF ME) (stereo only) . . . 15
69 Mercury 20156 SMCL I'M ON FIRE . . . 15
69 Mercury 20157 SMCL SINGS THE COUNTRY MUSIC HALL OF FAME HITS VOL. 1 . . . 12
69 Mercury 20158 SMCL SINGS THE COUNTRY MUSIC HALL OF FAME HITS VOL. 2 . . . 12
70 Mercury 20172 SMCL TOGETHER (with Linda Gail Lewis) . . . 15
70 Mercury 6338 010 SHE EVEN WOKE ME UP TO SAY GOODBYE . . . 12
71 Mercury 6338 045 THERE MUST BE MORE TO LOVE THAN THIS . . . 12
72 Mercury 6338 071 WOULD YOU TAKE ANOTHER CHANCE ON ME? . . . 12
72 Mercury 6336 300 ROCKIN' WITH JERRY LEE LEWIS . . . 12
72 Mercury 6338 088 THE KILLER ROCKS ON . . . 12
73 Mercury 6672 008 THE SESSION (2-LP) . . . 18
73 Mercury 6338 148 LIVE AT THE INTERNATIONAL HOTEL, LAS VEGAS . . . 12
74 Mercury 6338 452 SOUTHERN ROOTS . . . 12
74 Mercury 6338 496 FAN CLUB CHOICE . . . 12
84 Sun SUN 102 THE SUN YEARS (12-LP, box set with booklet) . . . 70
(see also Nashville Teens)

JIMMY LEWIS

68 Minit MLF 11002 The Girls From Texas/Let Me Know . . . 30

JOE 'CANNONBALL' LEWIS

51 MGM MGM 430 Train Whistle Nightmare/Trust Me Again (78) . . . 12

JOHN LEWIS

60 London Jazz LTZ-K 15186 IMPROVISED MEDITATIONS AND EXCURSIONS (LP) . . . 15
61 London Jazz LTZ-K 15218 THE GOLDEN STRIKER (LP, also stereo SAH-K 6152) . . . 15
(see also Modern Jazz Quartet)

LEW LEWIS (REFORMER)

76 Stiff BUY 5 Caravan Man/Boogie On The Street (p/s, with Dr. Feelgood) . . . 5
77 United Artists UP 36217 Out For A Lark/Watch Yourself . . . 5
78 Lew Lewis LEW 1 Lucky Seven/Night Talk (500 only, plain white sleeve) . . . 8
(see also Oil City Sheiks, Dr. Feelgood, Eddie & the Hot Rods)

LINDA LEWIS

67 Polydor 56173 You Turned My Bitter Into Sweet/Do You Believe In Love . . . 80
71 Reprise K 14096 We Can Win/Hampstead Way . . . 6
72 Reprise K 14209 Old Smokey/It's The Frame . . . 6
75 Arista ARIST 17 It's In His Kiss/Walk About (p/s) . . . 6
73 Raft RA 18502 Rock A Doodle Doo/Reach For The Truth . . . 6
72 Reprise K 44208 LARK (LP) . . . 20
73 Raft RA 48501 FATHOMS DEEP (LP) . . . 12
79 Ariola ARL 5033 HACIENDA VIEW (LP) . . . 12
(see also Ferris Wheel)

MARGARET LEWIS

62 Starlite ST45 081 Sometin's Wrong Baby/John De Lee . . . 22

MEADE 'LUX' LEWIS

50 Melodisc 1006 Boogie Woogie At The Philharmonic — Fast/(Medium) (78) . . . 7
50 Melodisc 1007 Boogie Woogie At The Philharmonic — Slow/Honky Tonk Train (78) . . . 7
50 Melodisc 1130 Boogie Tidal/Yancey's Pride (78) . . . 12
50 Melodisc 1136 Glendale Glide/Denapas Parade (78) . . . 12
51 Melodisc 1153 Randini's Boogie/Lux's Boogie (78) . . . 12
52 Vogue V 2123 Blues Whistle/Chicago Flyer (78) . . . 12
54 Vogue V 2229 Six Wheel Chaser Boogie/Bass On Top Boogie (78) . . . 12
55 Vogue EPV 1065 MEADE 'LUX' LEWIS (EP) . . . 35
56 Melodisc EPM7 107 BOOGIE WOOGIE AND BLUES (EP) . . . 35
56 Columbia Clef SEB 10030 BOOGIE WOOGIE PIANO AND DRUMS NO. 1 (EP) . . . 20
56 Columbia Clef SEB 10052 BOOGIE WOOGIE PIANO AND DRUMS NO. 2 (EP) . . . 20
57 Columbia Clef 33CX 10094 YANCEY'S LAST RIDE (LP) . . . 20
57 HMV DLP 1176 OUT OF THE ROARING TWENTIES (10" LP) . . . 20
60s Philips 652 014 BL HOUSE PARTY (LP) . . . 20
(see also Albert Ammons, [Big] Joe Turner)

MEADE 'LUX' LEWIS & SLIM GAILLARD

56 Columbia Clef 33C 9021 JAZZ AT THE PHILHARMONIC (10" LP) . . . 20
(see also Slim Gaillard)

MIA LEWIS

65 Decca F 12117 Wish I Didn't Love Him/This Is The End . . . 12
65 Decca F 12240 It's Goodbye Now/The Luckiest Girl . . . 12
66 Parlophone R 5526 Nothing Lasts Forever/(Baby) I'm Feeling Good . . . 12
67 Parlophone R 5585 No Time For Lovin'/Onion . . . 7
67 Parlophone R 5617 Woman's Love/You Won't Get Away . . . 7

MICHAEL LEWIS

73 United Artists UP 35569 Theatre Of Blood Theme/Edwina's Theme . . . 22

MONICA LEWIS

56 Parlophone R 4224 I Wish You Love/Stay After School . . . 8

NIGEL LEWIS

86 Media Burn MB10 WHAT I FEEL NOW (LP) . . . 20

PATTI LEWIS

56 Columbia DB 3825 Earthbound/Happiness Street (Corner Sunshine Square) . . . 10
57 Columbia DB 3923 Your Wild Heart/A Poor Man's Roses (Or A Rich Man's Gold) . . . 8
57 Columbia DB 3967 Pull Down De Shade/Speak For Yourself John . . . 8

MINT VALUE £

PHILLIPPA LEWIS
65 Decca F 12152 Just Like In The Movies/Get Along Without You . . . 10

RAMSEY LEWIS (TRIO)
65 Chess CRS 8020 The 'In' Crowd/Since I Fell For You (as Ramsey Lewis Trio) . . . 10
65 Chess CRS 8024 Hang On Sloopy/Movin' Easy (as Ramsey Lewis Trio) . . . 7
66 Chess CRS 8029 A Hard Day's Night/'Tout A Doubt (as Ramsey Lewis Trio) . . . 7
66 Chess CRS 8031 Hi-Heel Sneakers (Parts 1 & 2) (as Ramsey Lewis Trio) . . . 10
66 Chess CRS 8041 Wade In The Water/Ain't That Peculiar (as Ramsey Lewis Trio) . . . 15
66 Chess CRS 8044 Uptight (Everything's Alright)/Money In The Pocket . . . 10
67 Chess CRS 8051 Day Tripper/Hurt So Bad . . . 12
67 Chess CRS 8055 1-2-3/Down By The Riverside . . . 7
67 Chess CRS 8058 Function At The Junction/Hey Mrs. Jones . . . 10
67 Chess CRS 8060 Saturday Night After The Movies/China Gate . . . 7
67 Chess CRS 8061 Girl Talk/Dancing In The Street . . . 7
67 Chess CRS 8064 Soul Man/Struttin' Lightly . . . 7
69 Chess CRS 8096 Cry Baby Cry/Wade In The Water . . . 7
70 Chess CRS 8104 Julia/Do What You Wanna . . . 10
72 Chess 6145 004 Wade In The Water/Ain't That Peculiar (silver label) . . . 10
72 Chess 6145 013 The 'In' Crowd/Soul Man . . . 5
72 CBS 8280 Slipping Into Darkness/Collage . . . 6
66 Chess CRE 6019 A HARD DAY'S NIGHT (EP, as Ramsey Lewis Trio) . . . 20
65 Pye Jazz NJL 55 AT THE BOHEMIAN CAVERNS (LP) . . . 18
65 Chess CRL 4511 THE 'IN' CROWD (LP) . . . 18
65 Chess CRL 4518 CHOICE! THE BEST OF RAMSEY LEWIS (LP) . . . 18
66 Chess CRL 4520 HANG ON RAMSEY! (LP) . . . 18
66 Chess CRL 4522 WADE IN THE WATER (LP) . . . 20
67 Chess CRL 4528 GOIN' LATIN (LP) . . . 18
67 Chess CRL 4531 THE MOVIE ALBUM (LP) . . . 15
68 Chess CRL(S) 4533 DANCIN' IN THE STREET (LP) . . . 18
68 Chess CRLS 4535 UP POPS RAMSEY LEWIS (LP) . . . 20
68 Chess CRLS 4539 MAIDEN VOYAGE (LP) . . . 20
69 Chess CRLS 4545 MOTHER NATURE'S SON (LP) . . . 20
60s Fontana SFJL 962 DOWN TO EARTH (LP) . . . 20
72 Chess 6310 106 BACK TO THE ROOTS (LP) . . . 12
72 Chess 6310 114 THE BEST OF RAMSEY LEWIS (LP) . . . 12
72 Chess 6310 124 TOBACCO ROAD (LP) . . . 12
72 CBS 64718 UPENDO NI PAMOJA (LP) . . . 12
73 CBS 65307 FUNKY SERENITY (LP) . . . 18
73 CBS CQ 31096 UPENDO NI PAMOJA (LP, quadrophonic) . . . 12
(see also Young-Holt Unlimited)

RICHARD LEWIS & HIS BAND
60 Downbeat CHA 1 Hey, Little Girl/Hey, Little Boy . . . 35

SMILEY LEWIS
53 London L 1189 Big Mamou/Play Girl (78, some copies miscredited to Smiley Davis) . . . 150
56 London HLU 8312 One Night/Ain't Gonna Do It . . . 800
56 London HLU 8312 One Night/Ain't Gonna Do It (78) . . . 125
56 London HLU 8337 Down Yonder We Go Ballin'/Don't Be That Way (Please Listen To Me) . . . 800
56 London HLU 8337 Down Yonder We Go Ballin'/Don't Be That Way (Please Listen To Me) (78) . . . 125
57 London HLP 8367 Shame, Shame, Shame/No, No (gold or silver label lettering) . . . 675/275
57 London HLP 8367 Shame, Shame, Shame/No, No (78) . . . 100
70 Liberty LBF 15337 I Hear You Knocking/Play Girl . . . 8
70 Liberty LBS 83308 SHAME, SHAME, SHAME (LP) . . . 25

STEVIE LEWIS
65 Mercury MF 871 Take Me For A Little While/My Whole World Seems To Be Tumbling Down . . . 10
65 Mercury MF 919 Sometimes When You're Lonely/Under The Smile Of Love . . . 6
65 Polydor 56003 Heard It All Before/Wild . . . 7
69 RCA RCA 1840 Take A Little Warning/I Can Try . . . 6

TAMALA LEWIS
79 Destiny DS 1010 You Won't Say Nothing/If You Can Stand Me . . . 5

TINY LEWIS
60 Parlophone R 4617 Too Much Rockin'/I Get Weak . . . 150

VIC LEWIS
55 Philips PB 503 Scramble/Walk, Don't Run (78) . . . 8
55 Philips PB 411 Barwick Green ("The Archers" Theme Tune)/Don't Say Goodbye (78) . . . 8
63 HMV POP 1127 Bossa Nova Scotia/Vic's Tune . . . 5
62 Columbia SEG 8202 SWINGS NELSON RIDDLE (EP) . . . 15
55 Decca LF 1216 PROGRESSIVE JAZZ (10" LP) . . . 20
62 HMV CLP 1641 PLAY BOSSA NOVA HOME AND AWAY (LP) . . . 40
60s Ember CJS 807 AT THE BEAULIEU FESTIVAL (LP) . . . 40
60s Ember SE 8018 BIG BAND EXPLOSION (LP) . . . 60
70s DJM SPECB 103 MY LIFE MY WAY (LP) . . . 30

LEWIS & CLARKE EXPEDITION
67 RCA Victor RCA 1633 I Feel Good/Blue Revelations . . . 6

LEWIS SISTERS
65 Tamla Motown TMG 536 You Need Me/Moonlight On The Beach . . . 80

DAVE LEWRY
72 Westwood WRS 019 ALL I WANT TO DO IS PLAY GUITAR (LP) . . . 35

MONIQUE LEYRAC
68 SNB 55-3309 Time Time/Love Is Blue . . . 5

JOHN LEYTON

60	Top Rank JAR 426	Tell Laura I Love Her/Goodbye To Teenage Love	60
60	HMV POP 798	The Girl On The Floor Above/Terry Brown's In Love With Mary Dee	100
61	Top Rank JAR 577	Johnny Remember Me/There Must Be	6
61	Top Rank JAR 585	Wild Wind/You Took My Love For Granted	7
61	HMV POP 956	Son This Is She/Six White Horses	8
62	HMV POP 992	Lone Rider/Heart Of Stone	15
62	HMV POP 1014	Lonely City/It Would Be Easy	8
62	HMV POP 1054	Down The River Nile/I Think I'm Falling In Love	10
62	HMV POP 1076	Lonely Johnny/Keep On Loving You	10
63	HMV POP 1122	Cupboard Love/Land Of Love	6
63	HMV POP 1175	I'll Cut Your Tail Off/The Great Escape	8
63	HMV POP 1204	On Lover's Hill/Lovers Lane	8
63	HMV POP 1230	I Guess You Are Always On My Mind/Beautiful Dreamer	8
64	HMV POP 1264	Make Love To Me/Missing You (as John Leyton & Le Roys)	15
64	HMV POP 1338	Don't Let Her Go Away/I Want A Love I Can See	12
64	HMV POP 1374	All I Want Is You/Every Day Is A Holiday (with Grazina Frame & Mike Sarne)	10
73	York SYK 551	Dancing In The Graveyard/Riversong	8
74	York YR 210	Rock 'N' Roll/Highway Song	10
62	Top Rank JKP 3016	JOHN LEYTON (EP)	45
62	HMV 7EG 8747	HIT PARADE (EP)	40
64	HMV 7EG 8843	BEAUTIFUL DREAMER (EP)	45
64	HMV 7EG 8854	TELL LAURA I LOVE HER (EP)	50
61	HMV CLP 1497	THE TWO SIDES OF JOHN LEYTON (LP)	60
62	HMV CLP 1664	ALWAYS YOURS (LP, with Charles Blackwell's Orchestra)	80
73	York FYK 416	JOHN LEYTON (LP)	40

(see also Le Roys)

LEYTON BUZZARDS

78	Small Wonder SMALL 7	19 And Mad/Villain/Youthanasia (p/s)	6
79	Chrysalis CHS 2288	Saturday Night Beneath The Plastic Palm Trees/Trough With You (p/s)	5
79	Chrysalis CHS 2328	I'm Hanging Around/I Don't Want To Go/No Dry Ice (p/s, green vinyl)	5
79	Chrysalis CHR 1213	JELLIED EELS TO RECORD DEALS (LP, as Buzzards)	12

L.F.O.

90	Warp WAP 5	L.F.O. (The Leeds Warehouse Mix)/L.F.O. (Track 4)/Probe (The Cuba Edit) (12")	15

LIAISON

82	Catweazle CR 001	Play It With A Passion/Caught In A ... (some in grey or yellow p/s)	35/10
83	Liaison LIC 101	LOOKING AFTER NUMBER ONE (EP)	5
84	Liaison LSN 0020	Only Heaven Knows/Ease The Pain Away (p/s)	5

LIAR

79	Bearsville K 55524	SET THE WORLD ON FIRE (LP, picture disc)	12

LIBERACE

56	Columbia DB 3834	I Don't Care (As Long As You Care For Me)/As Time Goes By	6

LIBERATION SUITE

70s	Myrrh MYR 1027	LIBERATION SUITE (LP)	18

LIBERATORS

65	Stateside SS 424	It Hurts So Much/You Look So Fine	10

(see also Pinkerton's Assorted Colours)

EVE LIBERTINE & CRASS

84	Crass 1984/4	ACTS OF LOVE (LP, with book)	12

(see also Crass)

LIBERTINES

02	Rough Trade RTRADES 054	What A Waster/I Get Along (p/s, 2000 only)	20
02	Rough Trade RTRADESCD 054	What A Waster/I Get Along (CD)	8
02	Rough Trade RTRADES 064	Up The Bracket/Boys In The Band (p/s)	8
03	Rough Trade RTRADES 119	Don't Look Back Into The Sun/Death On The Stairs (blue vinyl, fold-out poster sleeve in PVC slipcase, 3000 only)	20
03	Rough Trade RTRADES 074	Time For Heroes/The 7 Deadly Sins (demo version) (p/s)	12
02	Rough Trade RTRADELP 065	UP THE BRACKET (LP)	12

LIBERTY BELLES

71	Jay Boy BOY 40	Shing-A-Ling Time/Just Try Me	10

LICKS

79	Stortbeat BEAT 8	1970S EP	15

(see also Epileptics, Flux Of Pink Indians)

JAMIE LIDELL

97	Mosquito MSQ 08	FREAKIN' THE FRAME (12" EP)	20

LIEUTENANT BUDDY KNOX

(see under 'K')

LIEUTENANT PIGEON

73	Decca SKL 5154	MOULDY OLD MUSIC (LP)	12
74	Decca SKL 5174	PIGEON PIE (LP)	12
75	Decca SKL 5196	PIGEON PARTY (LP)	12
76	Decca SPA 414	THE WORLD OF LIEUTENANT PIGEON (LP, unreleased, test pressings only)	15

(see also Shel Naylor, Stavely Makepeace, Heavy Cochran)

LIFE

69	Polydor 56778	Hands Of The Clock/Ain't I Told You Before	12
74	Polydor 2058 500	Woman/Bless My Soul	6
74	Polydor 2383 295	LIFE AFTER DEATH (LP)	40

MINT VALUE £

LIFE
73 Philips 6006 280 — Cats Eyes/Death In The Family (paper or moulded label) — 7/5

LIFE AFTER LIFE
85 Timetrack SRTSKL 453 — LIFE AFTER LIFE (LP, private pressing) — 120

KEALOHA LIFE & HIS ROYAL SAMOANS
57 Lambda BB 3003 — The Beauty Hula/HARMONY HAWAIIANS: Auwei (78) — 10

LIFE 'N' SOUL
67 Decca F 12659 — Ode To Billy Joe/Peacefully Asleep — 30
68 Decca F 12851 — Here Comes Yesterday Again/Dear Paul — 15

LIFE SUPPORT
79 Slug SLUG 1 — Leader Deceiver/Confusion (p/s, white labels) — 6

LIFETIME
70 Polydor 2066 050 — One Word/Two Worlds — 7
(see also Tony Williams [Lifetime], Jack Bruce, John McLaughlin)

JOE LIGES
63 Blue Beat BB 172 — Spit In The Sky/Tell Me What (both actually by Delroy Wilson) — 35
(see also Delroy Wilson)

JOE LIGGINS & HONEYDRIPPERS
50 Parlophone R 3309 — I've Got The Right To Cry/Blue Moods (78) — 30
76 Specialty SDN 5006 — Pink Champagne/Honey Dripper — 6

LIGHT
78 Mint MINT 11 — LIGHT (LP, Irish-only) — 75
(see also Them)

BEN LIGHT
56 HMV 7M 350 — Bring Me A Bluebird/You — 8

ENOCH LIGHT
59 Top Rank JAR 134 — With My Eyes Wide Open/I Cried For You (as Enoch Light & Light Brigade) — 6
59 Top Rank JAR 134 — With My Eyes Wide Open/I Cried For You (78, as Enoch Light & Light Brigade) — 12
59 Top Rank JAR 234 — Scarlet Ribbons/Greensleeves (as Enoch Light & His Vibrant Strings) — 6
69 Studio Two TWO 312 — SPACED OUT (LP) — 25
70 Project 3 — PERMISSIVE POLYPHONICS (LP) — 25

LIGHT FANTASTIC
73 RCA RCA 2331 — Jeanie/You Don't Care — 20

GORDON LIGHTFOOT
62 Decca F 11527 — (Remember Me) I'm The One/Daisy-Doo (as Gord Lightfoot) — 30
63 Fontana 267 275TF — Negotiations/It's Too Late, He Wins (as Gordie Lightfoot) — 7
63 Fontana TF 405 — The Day Before Yesterday/Take Care Of Yourself (as Gordie Lightfoot) — 7
65 United Artists UP 1109 — Just Like Tom Thumb's Blues/Ribbon Of Darkness — 7
66 Warner Bros WB 5621 — I'm Not Sayin'/For Lovin' Me — 5
68 President PT 138 — Adios Adios/Is My Baby Blue Tonight (as Gordie Lightfoot) — 6
68 United Artists UP 2216 — Black Day In July/Pussy Willow's Cat Tails — 5
69 United Artists UP 2272 — The Circle Is Small/Does Your Mother Know — 5
69 United Artists UP 35020 — Bitter Green/May I — 5
69 United Artists UP 35036 — Early Morning Rain/The Gypsy — 5
72 Reprise K 14210 — If You Could Read My Mind/Me And Bobby McGee/Summer Side/Talking In Your Sleep (p/s) — 5
68 United Artists SULP 1199 — DID SHE MENTION MY NAME (LP) — 12
69 United Artists SULP 1239 — BACK HERE ON EARTH (LP) — 12
69 Utd. Artists UAL/UAS 29012 — EARLY LIGHTFOOT (LP) — 12
71 Reprise RSLP 6392 — IF YOU COULD READ MY MIND (LP) — 12

PADDY LIGHTFOOT
50s Melodisc EPM7 100 — PADDY LIGHTFOOT (EP) — 8

PAPA (GEORGE) LIGHTFOOT
69 Liberty LBF 15176 — Wine Whiskey And Woman/SLIM HARPO: Something Inside Me — 20
60s Jan & Dil JR 451 — MORE DOWN HOME BLUES (EP) — 35
71 Liberty LBS 83353 — NATCHEZ TRACE (LP, as Papa George Lightfoot) — 30

TERRY LIGHTFOOT'S (NEW ORLEANS) JAZZMEN
57 Columbia DB 4032 — I Saw Mommy Kissing Santa Claus/Winter Wonderland — 6
58 Pye Jazz 7NJ 2018 — My Bucket's Got A Hole In It/Good Time Swing — 5
60 Columbia DB 4519 — The Preacher/The Onions — 5
61 Columbia DB 4696 — True Love/Black Bottom Stomp — 7
61 Columbia SCD 2165 — King Kong/Riverside Blues (some with p/s) — 8/5
65 Columbia DB 7534 — Alley Cat/Petite Fleur — 5
56 Nixa NJE 1027 — TERRY LIGHTFOOT'S JAZZMEN (EP) — 12
58 Columbia SEG 7851 — PLAYS TRAD (EP) — 20
59 Columbia SEG 7917 — MORE TRAD (EP) — 10
60 Columbia SEG 7976 — TRAD AGAIN (EP) — 10
56 Nixa Jazz NJT 503 — JAZZ GUMBO VOLUME ONE (10" LP) — 22
58 Columbia 33SX 1073 — TRADITION IN COLOUR (LP) — 15
61 Columbia 33SX 1290 — TRAD PARADE (LP, with New Orleans Jazzmen, also stereo SCX 3354) — 15/18
61 Columbia 33SX 1353 — WORLD OF TRAD (LP) — 30
62 Columbia 33SX 1449 — LIGHTFOOT AT LANSDOWNE (LP) — 20
63 Columbia 33SX 1551 — TERRY (LP) — 18
65 Columbia 33SX 1721 — ALLEYCAT (LP, as Terry Lightfoot's Jazzmen) — 20

LIGHTHOUSE
69 RCA RCA 1884 — Eight Miles High/If There Ever Was A Time — 7
71 Vertigo 6073 150 — Hats Off (To The Strangers)/Sing Sing Sing — 7
72 Philips 6073 152 — One Fine Morning/Little Kind Words — 6

MINT VALUE £

72	Philips 6073 153	Take It Slow/Sweet Lullaby	6
70	RCA SF 8103	SUITE FEELING (LP)	18
70	RCA SF 8121	PEACING IT ALL TOGETHER (LP)	15
71	Vertigo 6342 010	ONE FINE MORNING (LP, gatefold sleeve, swirl label)	35
71	Vertigo 6342 011	THOUGHTS OF MOVIN' ON (LP, gatefold sleeve, swirl label)	35

LIGHTNIN' SLIM

72	Blue Horizon 2096 013	Just A Little Bit/You're Old Enough To Understand/Mind Your Own Business	30
65	Stateside SL 10135	A LONG DRINK OF BLUES (LP, with Slim Harpo)	65
69	Python PLP 8	THE DOWNHOME BLUES PART 1 (LP, 99 copies only)	55
70	Blue Horizon 7-63863	ROOSTER BLUES (LP)	90
72	Blue Horizon 2931 005	LONDON GUMBO (LP)	90
78	Flyright FLYLP 533	TRIP TO CHICAGO (LP)	15
79	Flyright FLYLP 583	THE FEATURE SIDES 1954 (LP)	15
80	Flyright FLYLP 612	WE GOTTA ROCK TONIGHT (LP)	15

(see also Slim Harpo)

LIGHTNING LEON

60s	Jan & Dil JR 450	DOWN HOME BLUES — SIXTIES STYLE (EP)	35

LIGHTNING RAIDERS

80	Arista ARIST 341	Psychedelik Musik ('adult' version)/Views (p/s)	20
80	Arista ARIST 341DJ	Psychedelik Musik ('censored' version)/Views (promo only, no p/s)	35
81	Revenge REVS 200	Criminal World/Citizens (p/s)	25
81	Revenge RSS 39	Sweet Revenge/Rowdies/Addiction/Soul Rescue (12", promo only)	45

(see also Pink Fairies, Professionals)

LIGHTNING SEEDS

89	Ghetto CDGTG 4	Pure/Fools/God Help Them/All I Want (CD, card sleeve)	10
89	Ghetto CDGTG 6	Joy/Frenzy/Control The Flame (CD, card sleeve)	8
92	Virgin VSCDG 1402	The Life Of Riley/Something In The Air/Marooned (CD, digipak)	8
92	Virgin VST 1414	Sense/Flaming Sword/Hang On To A Dream/The Life Of Riley (Remix) (12", heat sensitive p/s)	8
92	Virgin VSCDT 1414	Sense/Flaming Sword/Hang On To A Dream/The Life Of Riley (Riley) (CD, digipak)	8
95	Epic 6625192	Lucky You/Life Of Riley/Pure/Here Today (CD)	10

(see also Big In Japan, Care)

LIGHT OF THE WORLD

80	Ensign ENY 43	London Town/Pete's Crusade	5
80	Ensign ENY 4312	London Town/Pete's Crusade (12")	12
82	EMI EMI 5319	No. 1 Girl/Don't Run	10
82	EMI 12EMI 5319	No. 1 Girl/Don't Run (12")	15
79	Ensign ENVY 7	LIGHT OF THE WORLD (LP)	12
80	Ensign ENVY 14	ROUND TRIP (LP)	12
82	EMI EMC 3410	CHECK US OUT (LP)	15

LIKE A SONG

73	De Wolfe DW/LP 3273	LIKE A SONG (LP, library issue)	18

LILAC TIME

88	Swordfish LILAC 1	Return To Yesterday/Trumpets From Montparnasse (no p/s)	8
88	Swordfish 12 LILAC 1	Return To Yesterday/Railway Bazaar/Trumpets From Montparnasse/ Reunion Ball (12", p/s)	15
88	Fontana LILCD 2	Return To Yesterday/Rooftrees/Gone For A Burton/ Reunion Ball (CD, card sleeve)	10
88	Fontana LILCD 3	You've Got To Love/Railway Bazaar/Trumpets From Montparnasse (CD, card sleeve)	8
88	Fontana LILAC 4	Black Velvet/Black Dawn (p/s in Xmas card folder)	5
88	Fontana LILCD 4	Black Velvet/Tiger Tea/Street Corner/Black Dawn (CD)	8
89	Fontana LILCD 5	American Eyes/Shepherd's Plaid/The World In Her Arms/ Crossing The Line (CD)	8
89	Fontana LILCD 6	The Days Of The Week/The Queen Of Heartless/Spin A Cavalu (CD)	8
89	Fontana LILCD 7	The Girl Who Waves At Trains/If The Stars Shine Tonight (Acoustic Version)/ Ounce Of Nails/American Eyes (Acoustic Version) (CD)	8
90	Caff CAFF 12	Madresfield/Bird On The Wire (p/s, with insert)	20
88	Swordfish SWF LP 6	THE LILAC TIME (LP, original issue)	15
88	Swordfish SWF CD 6	THE LILAC TIME (CD, original issue)	30
88	Fontana 836 744-2	THE LILAC TIME (LP, reissue, with inner sleeve)	12
89	Fontana 838 641-2	PARADISE CIRCUS (CD)	20

(see also Hawks, Stephen Duffy)

LIL & RENEE

63	Reprise R 20206	Tennessee Waltz/Keep A Lite	6

LILYS

96	Ché CHE 51	Returns Every Morning/Touch The Water (white vinyl, p/s, 500 only)	6
96	Ché CHE 65	A Nanny In Manhattan/More Than Is Deserved (coffee-coloured vinyl, p/s, 500 only)	6

LIMELIGHT

75	United Artists UP 35779	I Should Have Known Better/Tell Me Why	12

(see also Brinsley Schwarz)

LIMELIGHT

80	Future Earth FER 006	Metal Man/Hold Me Touch Me (p/s)	12
82	Future Earth FER 010	Ashes To Ashes/Knife In Your Back (p/s, some with insert)	12/10
80	Future Earth FER 008	LIMELIGHT (LP)	30
81	Avatar AALP 5005	LIMITED LIMELIGHT (LP, some with bonus single)	35/20

MINT VALUE £

LIMELITERS
63 RCA RCX 7126 FUN FOLK (EP) 8
64 RCA RCX 7151 FOUR FOLK SONGS (EP) 8
60 Elektra EKL 180 FOLK SONGS FOR MODERNS (LP) 12
61 RCA RD 27254 SLIGHTLY FABULOUS LIMELITERS (LP) 15
63 RCA Victor RD/SF 7581 FOURTEEN 14K FOLK SONGS (LP) 12

ALISON LIMERICK
90 Arista 113509 Where Love Lives/Where Love Lives (Classic Mix) (p/s) 5
90 Arista 613509 Where Love Lives/Where Love Lives (Classic Mix)/
Where Love Lives (Zone)/Where Love Lives (Cut To The Bone) (12", p/s) 10

LIMEYS
65 Pye 7N 15820 I Can't Find My Way Through/Don't Cry (My Love) 8
65 Pye 7N 15909 Some Tears Fall Dry/Half Glass Of Wine 8
66 Decca F 12382 Cara-Lin/Feel So Blue 35
66 Decca F 12466 The Mountain's High/Lovin' Yourself 7

LIMIT
78 Private Stock PVT 156 Please Please Me/My World At Night (company sleeve) 90

PETER LINCOLN
67 Major Minor MM 520 In The Day Of My Youth/My Monkey Is A Junkie 10
(see also Peter Sarstedt, Sarstedt Brothers, Brothers Kane)

PHILAMORE LINCOLN
68 NEMS 56-3711 Running By The River/Rainy Day 35

LINCOLNS
66 Parlophone R 5418 Mister Loneliness/Only Love Will Break Your Heart 6

LINCOLN X
63 Oriole CB 1823 Heartaches And Happiness/Stand In For Her Past 8

BOB LIND
66 Fontana TF 670 Elusive Butterfly/Cheryl's Goin' Home 8
66 Fontana TF 702 Remember The Rain/Truly Julie's Blues (I'll Be There) 6
66 Fontana TF 750 San Francisco Woman/Oh Babe Take Me Home 6
67 Verve VS 1501 Hey Nellie Nellie/Wandering 6
66 Fontana (S)TL 5340 DON'T BE CONCERNED (LP) 25
66 Verve F'ways (S)VLP 5015 THE ELUSIVE BOB LIND (LP) 20
67 Fontana (S)TL 5395 PHOTOGRAPHS OF FEELINGS (LP) 18

ROSA LINDA
53 London L 1215 Flight 88/Taboo (78) 12

LINDA & FUNKY BOYS
76 Spark SRL 1149 Climbing The Steps Of Love/Baby Are You Satisfied 8

DADDY LINDBERG
67 Columbia DB 8138 Shirl/Wade In The Shade 15
(see also Crocheted Doughnut Ring, Fingers)

ANITA LINDBLOM
62 Fontana 267223 TF Uptown/Mr Big Wheel 8

DENNIS LINDE
73 Elektra K 42149 DENNIS LINDE (LP) 12
74 Elektra K 52013 TRAPPED IN THE SUBURBS (LP) 12

KATHY LINDEN
58 Felsted AF 102 Billy/If I Could Hold You In My Arms 12
58 Felsted AF 102 Billy/If I Could Hold You In My Arms (78) 15
58 Felsted AF 105 You'd Be Surprised/Why Oh Why 12
58 Felsted AF 105 You'd Be Surprised/Why Oh Why (78) 15
58 Felsted AF 108 Oh! Johnny, Oh! Johnny Oh!/Georgie 8
58 Felsted AF 108 Oh! Johnny, Oh! Johnny Oh!/Georgie (78) 15
58 Felsted AF 111 Kissin' Conversation/Just A Sandy Haired Boy Called Sandy 12
58 Felsted AF 111 Kissin' Conversation/Just A Sandy Haired Boy Called Sandy (78) 20
59 Felsted AF 122 Goodbye Jimmy, Goodbye/Heartaches At Sweet Sixteen 8
59 Felsted AF 122 Goodbye Jimmy, Goodbye/Heartaches At Sweet Sixteen (78) 12
59 Felsted AF 124 So Close To My Heart/You Don't Know Girls 12
59 Felsted AF 124 So Close To My Heart/You Don't Know Girls (78) 20
60 Felsted AF 130 Think Love/Mary Lou Wilson And Johnny Brown 12
59 Felsted GEP 1001 KATHY (EP) 35
59 Felsted GEP 1002 KATHY'S IN LOVE VOLUME ONE (EP) 30
59 Felsted GEP 1004 KATHY'S IN LOVE VOLUME TWO (EP) 30

LINDISFARNE
SINGLES
70 Charisma CB 137 Clear White Light Part II/Knackers Yard Blues 12
71 Charisma CB 153 Lady Eleanor/Nothing But The Marvellous Is Beautiful (some with p/s) 8/5
72 Charisma CB 173 Meet Me On The Corner/Scotch Mist/No Time To Lose (p/s) 6
72 Charisma CB 191 All Fall Down/We Can Swing Together (live) (p/s) 6
72 Charisma CB 199 Court In The Act/Don't Ask Me 5
74 Charisma CB 228 Taking Care Of Business/North Country Boy 6
74 Charisma CB 232 Fog On The Tyne/Mandolin King 6
75 Warner Brothers K 16489 Tonight/No Need To Tell Me 6
75 Charisma CB 266 Lady Eleanor/Fog On The Tyne 5
78 Mercury 6007 177 Run For Home/Stick Together (p/s) 5
78 Mercury 6007 195 Brand New Day/Winter Song 5
79 Mercury 6007 205 Warm Feeling/Clear White Light (live) (p/s) 5
79 Mercury NEWS 1 Easy And Free/When Friday Comes Along (p/s) 5

MINT VALUE £

79	Mercury 6007 241	Call Of The Wild/Dedicated Hound	5
81	Hangover HANG 9	I Must Stop Going To Parties/See How They Run (p/s)	5
82	LMP LM 1	Sunderland Boys/Cruising To Disaster	5
82	LMP FOG 1	Nights/Dog Ruff (p/s)	5
83	LMP FOG 2	Do What I Want/Same Way Down (p/s)	5
85	LMP FOG 3	I Remember The Lights (Acappella Version)/Day Of The Jackal (p/s)	6
85	LMP FOG 4	CHRISTMAS (EP, sold at Christmas concerts)	6
86	River City LIND 1	Shine On/Heroes/Dance Your Live Away (Gogo Mix) (p/s)	5
87	River City LIND 2	Love On The Run/One Hundred Miles To Liverpool (p/s)	5
88	River City LIND 2A	Save Our Ales/Save Our Ales (Sub Mix) (p/s)	6
90	Best ZA 44207	Fog On The Tyne (Revisited)/Fog On The Tyne (Revisited) (Instrumental) (picture disc, by Gazza [Paul Gascoigne] & Lindisfarne)	5

LPs

70	Charisma CAS 1025	NICELY OUT OF TUNE (pink or 'mad hatter' label)	15/12
71	Charisma CAS 1050	FOG ON THE TYNE (gatefold sleeve)	12
72	Charisma CAS 1057	DINGLY DELL (with inner sleeve & poster)	12
73	Charisma CLASS 2	LINDISFARNE LIVE	12
73	Charisma CAS 1076	ROLL ON RUBY (gatefold sleeve & poster)	12
74	Warner Brothers K 56070	HAPPY DAZE (with lyric sheet)	12
78	Mercury 9109 609	BACK AND FOURTH (gatefold sleeve)	12
79	Mercury 9109 626	THE NEWS (with lyric inner sleeve)	12
81	Charisma BG 5	REPEAT PERFORMANCE: THE LINDISFARNE SINGLES ALBUM	12

(see also Alan Hull, Jack The Lad, Chosen Few, Radiator, Ray Jackson)

MARK LINDSAY

69	CBS 4699	Arizona/Man From Houston	6
70	CBS 5055	Silver Bird/So Hard To Leave You	6
70	CBS 5219	And The Grass Won't Pay No Mind/Funny How Little Men Care	6
71	CBS 5408	Problem Child/Bookends	6
71	CBS 7330	Been Too Long On The Road/All I Really See Is You	6
71	CBS 7551	Are You Old Enough/Don't You Know	6
71	CBS 7690	Something Big/Pretty Pretty	6

(see also Paul Revere & Raiders)

TERRY LINDSEY

69	President PT 232	It's Over/One Day Up, Next Day Down	6

DAVID LINDUP ORCHESTRA

66	Columbia DB 7979	Informer Theme/Blue Mountain	8
66	Polydor 56106	Survival Theme/New Forest	20
70	Aristocrat AR 1021	WHEN THE SAINTS GO (LP)	25

LINDYS

60	Decca F 11253	The Train Of Love/You Know How Things Get Around	15
60	Decca F 11272	Boy With The Eyes Of Blue/Someone Else's Roses	18

LING FAMILY

77	Topic 12TS 292	SINGING TRADITIONS OF A SUFFOLK FAMILY (LP)	15

LINES

78	Linear SJP 782	White Night/Barbican (p/s)	7
79	Illegal ILS 0011	White Night/Barbican (p/s, reissue)	5
80	Red Linear RL 007	Nerve Pylon/Over The Brow (screen-printed p/s)	5
80s	Red Linear RL12 005	COOL SNAP EP (12")	15

BUZZY LINHART

69	Philips SBL 7885	BUZZY (LP)	12

LINK

92	Evolution EVO 05	THE FIRST LINK EP (12", plain sleeve)	50
93	Symbiotic SYM 001	THE LINK EP (12", plain sleeve, no credits on label)	50
95	Warp WAP 59	ANTACID EP (12", p/s)	15
95	Warp WAP 59R	ANTACID REMIXES EP (12", p/s)	15

(see also Reload, Global Communications, Mystic Institute)

LINKERS

71	Big Shot BI 567	Bongo Man/FUD CHRISTIAN ALLSTARS: Creation Version	6

(see also Links)

ANSEL LINKERS & FUD CHRISTIAN ALL STARS

73	Summit SUM 8540	Memories By The Score/FUD CHRISTIAN ALL STARS: Scorer	5

(see also Links)

LINKS

72	Tropical AL 0010	Sing A Song Of Freedom/TROPICAL ALL STARS: Love Rhythm (A-side actually by Linkers)	6

ELMO LINN

63	Starlite ST45 101	Another Man's Arms/Sam Houston	15

LINN COUNTY

68	Mercury SMCL 20142	PROUD FLESH SOOTHSEER (LP)	15
69	Mercury SMCL 20165	FEVER SHOT (LP)	15
70	Philips SBL 7923	TILL THE BREAK OF DAWN (LP)	15

LINOLEUM

96	Lino Vinyl LINO 001	Dissent/Twisted (lino sleeve, some sealed, 1,000 only)	10/7
96	Lino Vinyl LINO 002	Smear/Tired (lino sleeve, some sealed, 2,000 only)	7/5

JOE LINTHECOME

50s	Poydras 87	Pretty Mama Blues/Hummingbird Blues	15

LINUS & LITTLE PEOPLE

70	Evolution	Lovin' La La	10

MINT VALUE £

LION (& His Calypso Cubs)

51 Sagomes SG 117 Ugly Woman/The Lost Watch (78) 12
52 Parlophone MP 114 Mary Ann/Little Mary Had No Lamb (export 78) 12
52 Parlophone MP 115 Tick! Tick!/Ugly Woman (export 78) 12
53 Melodisc 1236 Coronation Of Elizabeth 2/Crosby Cavalcade (78, with Caribbean Rhythm) 10
54 Parlophone MP 129 The Royal Tour/The Weather Man (export 78) 12
54 Parlophone MP 132 I Ain't Gonna Do It No More/Trinidad, The Land Of Calypso (export 78) 12
55 Parlophone MP 135 Bananas/The Devil Fly (export 78, with His Calypso Cubs) 12
55 Parlophone MP 140 Go Away Miss Tina/Love Thy Neighbour (export 78, with His Calypso Cubs) 12
56 Parlophone MP 146 Merry Merry Christmas/Christmas Prayer Meeting (export 78, with His Calypso Cubs) 12
56 Parlophone MP 147 Money, Money, Money/Kalenda March (J'ouvert Barriot) (export 78, with His Calypso Cubs) 12

LIONHEART

85 Epic A 5001 Die For Love/Dangerous Games (p/s) 7
(see also Iron Maiden)

LIONROCK

92 M.E.R.C. 002 Roots'n'Culture (Part One)/Lionrock (12", original issue) 10
92 De Construc. 74321124381 Lionrock — The Remixes: (Most Excellent Mix)/(Roots 'n' Culture)/(A Trumpet Jamboree In Edinburgh)/(A Dubtastic Jamboree In Edinburgh) (12") 10
93 De Construc. 74321144371 Packet Of Peace (Prankster Sound System Mix)/(Instrumental)/(No More Fucking Trumpets) (12") 8
93 De Construc. 74321144372 Packet Of Peace (Dust Brothers Mix)/(Jeff Mills Mix) (12", promo only) 15
93 Distort & Cavort Dub Plate No. 1 (12") 10
94 De Construc. DUB PLATE 1 The Guide/Don't Be Foolish (12") 8
98 Concrete HARD 3112 Rude Boy Rock/Best Foot Forward/Push Button Cocktail (p/s) 8

LIONS

69 Polydor 56757 Twisted Nerve/My Friend The Blackbird 35

LIONS OF JUDAH

69 Fontana TF 1016 Our Love's A Growin' Thing/Katja 10

JOE LIPMAN ORCHESTRA

54 MGM SP 1108 Looking Back To See/Stop 6

LIP MOVES

79 Tichonderoga HP 1 Guest/What Is (p/s with insert, stickered white labels, some signed) 35/30

LIQUID SMOKE

75 Pye Int. 7N 25677 Dance Dance Dance/Where Is Our Love 6
70 Avco Embassy 646 6003 LIQUID SMOKE (LP) 50

LISTEN

65 CBS 202456 You'd Better Run/Everybody's Gonna Say 275
(see also Robert Plant, Led Zeppelin)

LITTER

69 Probe CLPS 4504 EMERGE (LP) 60

'BIG' TINY LITTLE

57 Vogue Coral Q 72263 School Day/That's The Only Way To Live 35
57 Vogue Coral Q 72263 School Day/That's The Only Way To Live (78) 25
60 Coral FEP 2058 HONKY TONK PIANO VOL. 1 (EP) 15
60 Coral FEP 2059 HONKY TONK PIANO VOL. 2 (EP) 15

KENNY LITTLE & LITTLE PEOPLE

65 United Artists UP 1074 A Shot In The Dark/Never On A Sunday 6

MARIE LITTLE

71 Argo ZFB 19 FACTORY GIRL (LP) 110
73 Trailer LER 2084 MARIE LITTLE (LP) 55
87 private pressing MY ELDORADO (LP) 12

LITTLE ABNER

57 Oriole CB 1380 Not Here, Not There/You Mean Everything To Me (78) 15

LITTLE ANGELS

88 Polydor LTLD 1 90 Degrees In The Shade/England Rocks (live) (poster p/s) 10
88 Polydor LTLXP 1 90 Degrees In The Shade/England Rocks (live) (shaped picture disc) 18
89 Polydor LTLXV 3 Do You Wanna Riot/Move In Slow/Some Kind Of Alien (live) (10", red vinyl) 15
89 Polydor LTLX 3 Do You Wanna Riot/Move In Slow/Some Kind Of Alien (live) (12", p/s) 12
89 Polydor LTLCD 3 Do You Wanna Riot/Move In Slow/Some Kind Of Alien (live) (CD) 20
89 Polydor LTL 4 Don't Pray For Me (7" Edit)/Radical Your Lover (p/s) 6
89 Polydor LTLS 4 Don't Pray For Me (7" Edit)/Radical Your Lover (p/s, sealed with patch) 10
89 Polydor LTLXP 4 Don't Pray For Me (7" Edit)/Radical Your Lover/What Do You Want/Don't Pray For Me (Extended Bob Clearmountain Mix) (12", poster p/s) 20
89 Polydor LTLCD 4 Don't Pray For Me (7" Edit)/Radical Your Lover/What Do You Want/Don't Pray For Me (Extended Bob Clearmountain Mix) (CD) 12
90 Polydor LTL 5 Kickin' Up Dust/Kickin' Up Dust (live) (p/s) 5
90 Polydor LTLP 5 Kickin' Up Dust/Kickin' Up Dust (live) (picture disc, die cut sleeve) 12
90 Polydor LTLXP 5 Kickin' Up Dust/Kickin' Up Dust (live)/Pleasure Pyre (live)/Kick Hard (live) (12", picture disc, numbered) 10
90 Polydor LTLCD 5 Kickin' Up Dust/Kickin' Up Dust (live)/Pleasure Pyre (live)/Kick Hard (live) (CD) 10
91 Polydor LTLX 11 I Ain't Gonna Cry/Babylon's Burning (12", picture disc, gatefold sleeve) 10
91 Polydor LTLXG 11 I Ain't Gonna Cry/Babylon's Burning (12", in tin, numbered) 8
87 Little Angels LAN 001 LITTLE ANGELS '87 (12" EP) 50
89 Polydor LTLCD 2 THE BIG BAD EP (CD) 12
90 Polydor LTLXP 6 GET RADICAL EP (picture disc) 8
91 Polydor LTLXB 10 YOUNG GODS EP (in box) 8
87 Powerstation AMP 14 TOO POSH TO MOSH (mini-LP) 25

MINT VALUE £

LITTLE ANN

98	Kent TOWN 111	What Should I Do/O.C. TALBOT: I'm Shooting High (I Reach For The Sky)	15

LITTLE ANTHONY & IMPERIALS

58	London HLH 8704	Tears On My Pillow/Two People In The World	50
58	London HLH 8704	Tears On My Pillow/Two People In The World (78)	35
59	London HL 8848	So Much/Oh Yeah	40
59	London HL 8848	So Much/Oh Yeah (78)	70
59	Top Rank JAR 256	Shimmy, Shimmy, Ko-Ko Bop/I'm Still In Love With You	22
60	Top Rank JAR 366	My Empty Room/Bayou, Bayou, Baby	22
64	United Artists UP 1065	I'm On The Outside Looking In/Please Go	15
64	United Artists UP 1073	Goin' Out Of My Head/Make It Easy On Yourself	20
65	United Artists UP 1083	Hurt So Bad/Reputation	20
65	United Artists UP 1098	Take Me Back/Our Song	10
65	United Artists UP 1112	I Miss You/Get Out Of My Life	10
66	United Artists UP 1126	Hurt/Never Again	25
66	United Artists UP 1137	Better Use Your Head/The Wonder Of It All	60
66	United Artists UP 1151	Gonna Fix You Good (Every Time You're Bad)/You Better Take It Easy Baby	70
67	United Artists UP 1189	My Love Is A Rainbow/You Only Live Twice	8
68	United Artists UP 2260	Let The Sunshine In/The Gentle Rain (as Anthony & Imperials)	10
69	United Artists UP 35017	Anthem/Goodbye Goodtimes (as Anthony & Imperials)	7
72	United Artists UP 35345	Gonna Fix You Good (Every Time You're Bad)/You Better Take It Easy Baby (reissue)	7
76	United Artists UP 36118	Better Use Your Head/Gonna Fix You Good (Every Time You're Bad)	5
76	United Artists REM 405	Goin' Out Of My Head/I'm On The Outside Looking In/Hurt So Bad/ Gonna Fix You Good (Every Time You're Bad)	5
65	United Artists UEP 1004	LITTLE ANTHONY AND THE IMPERIALS (EP)	100
64	United Artists ULP 1089	I'M ON THE OUTSIDE LOOKING IN (LP)	140
66	United Artists ULP 1100	GOIN' OUT OF MY HEAD (LP)	100

(see also Anthony & Imperials)

LITTLE ARCHIE

68	Atlantic 584 209	I Need You/I Am A Carpet	6

LITTLE BEAVER

72	President PTLS 1060	JOEY (LP)	12

LITTLE BEVERLEY

68	Pama PM 731	What A Guy/You're Mine	12

(see also Beverley Simmons)

LITTLE BILL & BLUE NOTES

59	Top Rank JAR 176	I Love An Angel/Bye, Bye Baby	25
59	Top Rank JAR 176	I Love An Angel/Bye, Bye Baby (78)	20

(see also Blue Notes)

LITTLE BIRD

84	Magus MGB 1	Zola/Reaching Out For Gold (p/s)	5

LITTLE BO BITCH

79	Cobra COB 1	It's Only Love/I'm Confused (p/s)	5
80	Cobra COB 4	Take It Easy (Lights Out Over London)/Lorraine, Lorraine (p/s)	5
79	Cobra CBR 1002	LITTLE BO BITCH (LP)	12

LITTLE BROTHER

(see under Little Brother Grant)

LITTLE DARLING

65	Blue Beat BB 325	No One/BUSTER'S ALL STARS: Congo Revolution	30

LITTLE DARLINGS

65	Fontana TF 539	Little Bit O' Soul/Easy To Cry	65

LITTLE DES

70	J-Dan JDN 4400	Somebody's Baby/Spy Man	7

LITTLE DIANA DAY

54	Melodisc P 219	I'm Goin' To Hang Up Mummy's Stocking/Funny Little Snowman (78)	7

LITTLE DIPPERS

60	Pye International 7N 25051	Forever/Two By Four	12
61	London HLG 9269	Lonely/I Wonder, I Wonder, I Wonder	25

LITTLE ESTHER

(see under Little Esther Phillips)

LITTLE EVA

62	London HL 9581	The Locomotion/He Is The Boy	10
62	London HLU 9633	Keep Your Hands Off My Baby/Where Do I Go	10
63	London HLU 9687	Let's Turkey Trot/Old Smokey Locomotion	10
63	Colpix PX 11013	The Trouble With Boys/What I Gotta Do (To Make You Jealous)	12
63	Colpix PX 11019	Please Hurt Me/Let's Start The Party Again	12
64	Colpix PX 11035	Run To Her/Making With The Magilla	10
65	Stateside SS 477	Stand By Me/That's My Man	20
63	London HA-U 8036	L-L-L-L-LOCO-MOTION (LP, original with plum label & laminated sleeve)	55
72	London SH-U 8437	L-L-L-L-LOCO-MOTION (LP, stereo reissue, plum label, boxed label logo)	15

(see also Big Dee Irwin & Little Eva)

LITTLE FOLK

71	Studio Republic CR 1001	LEAVE THEM A FLOWER (LP)	18

LITTLE FRANKIE (& COUNTRY GENTLEMEN)

65	Columbia DB 7490	The Kind Of Boy You Can't Forget/I'm Not Gonna Do It	15
65	Columbia DB 7578	Make-A-Love/Love Is Just A Game (with Country Gentlemen)	18
65	Columbia DB 7681	It Doesn't Matter Anymore/Happy, That's Me.	15

(see also Chimes featuring Denise)

MINT VALUE £

LITTLE FREDDY (McGregor)

70 Unity UN 551 — Why Did My Little Girl Cry/PETER AUSTIN: Change Partners 8
(see also Freddie McGregor, Ernest Wilson)

LITTLE FREE ROCK

69 Transatlantic TRA 608 — LITTLE FREE ROCK (LP) 80
(see also David John & Mood)

LITTLE GEORGE

64 Rio R 45 — Mary Anne/EDWARDS ALLSTARS: Blue Night 18

LITTLE GRANTS & EDDIE (Grant)

67 President PT 159 — Rudy's Dead/Everything's Alright 7
67 President PT 172 — Rock Steady '67/Bingo 7
(see also Equals, Pyramids)

LITTLE HANK

66 London HLU 10090 — Mr. Bang Bang Man/Don't You Know (withdrawn) 150
70 Monument MON 1045 — Mr. Bang Bang Man/Don't You Know (reissue) 12

LITTLE JOE (& THRILLERS)

57 Philips PB 759 — Peanuts/Lilly Lou (78) 20
60 Fontana H 281 — Stay (as Little Joe & Thrillers)/Cherry 25
63 Reprise R 20142 — Peanuts/No No I Can't Stop 20

LITTLE JOE (Jamaica)

70 Torpedo TOR 15 — Bad Blood/Maxi-Mini War 6
(see also Sexy Girls)

LITTLE JOEY & FLIPS

62 Pye International 7N 25152 — Bongo Stomp/Lost Love 12

LITTLE JOHN

67 Pama PM 702 — Let's Get Married/Around The World 10
70 Unity UN 561 — No Love/A Little Tear (both sides actually by John Holt) 10
(see also John Holt)

LITTLE JOHNNY & THREE TEENAGERS

58 Decca F 10990 — Baby Lover/Rickety Rackety Rendezvous 18
58 Decca F 10990 — Baby Lover/Rickety Rackety Rendezvous (78) 12

LITTLE LEMMY & BIG JOE

58 Decca F 11054 — Little Lemmy Kwela/Kwela No. 5 5
58 Decca F 11054 — Little Lemmy Kwela/Kwela No. 5 (78) 8

LITTLE LUMAN

64 Rio R 44 — Hurry Harry/R. ALPHONSE: Hucklebuck (B-side actually by Roland Alphonso) 20

LITTLE LUTHER

64 Pye International 7N 25266 — Eenie Meenie Minie Moe/Twirl 60

LITTLE MACK & BOSS SOUNDS

66 Atlantic 584 031 — In The Midnight Hour/You Can't Love Me (In The Midnight Hour) 15

LITTLE MILTON

65 Pye International 7N 25289 — Blind Man/Blues In The Night 18
65 Chess CRS 8013 — We're Gonna Make It/Can't Hold Back The Tears 18
65 Chess CRS 8018 — Who's Cheating Who?/Ain't No Big Deal On You 20
66 Sue WI 4021 — Early In The Morning/Bless Your Heart (actually by Roy Milton) 35
69 Chess CRS 8087 — Grits Ain't Groceries/I Can't Quit You Baby 18
69 Chess CRS 8100 — Let's Get Together/I'll Always Love You 15
72 Stax 2025 095 — That's What Love Will Make You Do/I'm Living Off The Love You Give 7
74 Stax STXS 2003 — Behind Closed Doors/Bet You I Win 6
75 Stax STA 100 — If That Ain't A Reason/Mr. Mailman 5
69 Chess CRLS 4552 — GRITS AIN'T GROCERIES (LP) 35
72 Chess 6310 120 — GOLDEN DECADE (LP) 15
74 Stax STX 1013 — BLUES 'N' SOUL (LP) 15

LITTLE NELL

76 A&M AMS 7374 — Fever/See You Round Like A Record (yellow vinyl) 7

LITTLE NORA

54 Melodisc MEL 1261 — Tomato/Nora's Blues (78) 8

LITTLE RED SCHOOLHOUSE

80s Waterfall WFL 3 — Aged Bee/HURT: Take My Breath (free with *Jump Away* fanzine) 5/4

LITTLE RED WALTERS

60s XX MIN 706 — DARK MUDDY BOTTOM (EP) 18

LITTLE RICHARD

78s

56 London HLO 8336 — Rip It Up/Ready Teddy 18
57 London HLO 8366 — Long Tall Sally/Tutti Frutti 18
57 London HLO 8382 — The Girl Can't Help It/She's Got It 15
57 London HLO 8446 — Lucille/Send Me Some Lovin' (as Little Richard & His Band) 18
57 London HLO 8470 — Jenny, Jenny/Miss Ann (as Little Richard & His Band) 18
57 London HLO 8509 — Keep A Knockin'/Can't Believe You Wanna Leave 20
58 London HLU 8560 — Good Golly Miss Molly/Hey-Hey-Hey-Hey 35
58 London HLO 8647 — Ooh! My Soul/True, Fine Mama 35
58 London HLU 8770 — Baby Face/I'll Never Let You Go 40
59 London HLU 8831 — By The Light Of The Silvery Moon/Early One Morning 50
59 London HLU 8868 — Kansas City/She Knows How To Rock 100
60 London HLU 9065 — Baby/I Got It 175

MINT VALUE £

SINGLES

56 London HLO 8336 Rip It Up/Ready Teddy (gold label print, later silver) . . . 140/50
50s London HLO 8336 Rip It Up/Ready Teddy (repressing, silver-top label, round centre) . . . 18
57 London HLO 8366 Long Tall Sally/Tutti Frutti (gold label print, later silver) . . . 140/50
50s London HLO 8366 Long Tall Sally/Tutti Frutti (repressing, silver-top label, round centre) . . . 18
57 London HLO 8382 The Girl Can't Help It/She's Got It (gold label print, later silver) . . . 160/55
50s London HLO 8382 The Girl Can't Help It/She's Got It (repressing, silver-top label, round centre) . . . 20
57 London HLO 8446 Lucille/Send Me Some Lovin' (as Little Richard & His Band) . . . 30
57 London HLO 8470 Jenny, Jenny/Miss Ann (as Little Richard & His Band) . . . 30
57 London HLO 8509 Keep A Knockin'/Can't Believe You Wanna Leave . . . 30
58 London HLU 8560 Good Golly Miss Molly/Hey-Hey-Hey-Hey . . . 30
58 London HLO 8647 Ooh! My Soul/True, Fine Mama . . . 15
58 London HLU 8770 Baby Face/I'll Never Let You Go . . . 8
59 London HLU 8831 By The Light Of The Silvery Moon/Early One Morning . . . 10
59 London HLU 8868 Kansas City/She Knows How To Rock . . . 15

(The above 45s were originally issued with triangular centres; later round-centres are worth around half to two-thirds these values.)

60 London HLU 9065 Baby/I Got It . . . 18
61 Mercury AMT 1165 Joy Joy Joy (Down In My Heart)/He's Not Just A Soldier . . . 7
62 Mercury AMT 1189 He Got What He Wanted (But He Lost What He Had)/ Why Don't You Change Your Ways? . . . 12
63 London HLK 9708 Crying In The Chapel/Hole In The Wall . . . 12
63 London HLK 9756 Travelin' Shoes/It Is No Secret . . . 12
64 London HL 9896 Bama Lama Bama Loo/Annie's Back . . . 12
64 Fontana TF 519 Blueberry Hill/Cherry Red . . . 12
64 Stateside SS 340 Whole Lotta Shakin' Goin' On/Goodnight Irene . . . 12
64 Mercury MF 841 Joy, Joy, Joy (Down In My Heart)/Peace In The Valley . . . 7
66 Fontana TF 652 I Don't Know What You've Got But It's Got Me (Parts 1 & 2) . . . 30
66 Stateside SS 508 Holy Mackeral/Baby, Don'tcha Want A Man Like Me? . . . 12
66 Sue WI 4001 Without Love/Dance What You Wanna . . . 35
66 Sue WI 4015 It Ain't Watcha Do (It's The Way How You Do It)/Crossover . . . 35
66 Columbia DB 7974 Poor Dog/Well . . . 20
66 Columbia DB 8058 I Need Love/The Commandments Of Love . . . 18
67 Columbia DB 8116 Get Down With It/Rose Mary . . . 20
67 Columbia DB 8240 A Little Bit Of Something/Money . . . 35
67 Columbia DB 8263 I Don't Want To Discuss It/Hurry Sundown . . . 35
68 MCA MU 1006 She's Together/Try Some Of Mine . . . 10
68 London HLU 10194 Good Golly Miss Molly/Lucille . . . 6
68 President PT 201 Whole Lotta Shakin' Goin' On/Lawdy Miss Clawdy . . . 6
69 Action ACT 4528 Baby What Do You Want Me To Do (Parts 1 & 2) . . . 12
70 Reprise RS 20907 Dew Drop In/Freedom Blues . . . 6
71 President PT 329 Without Love/Talkin' 'Bout Soul . . . 5
71 Reprise K 14124 Green Power/Dancing In The Street . . . 6
72 Reprise K 14150 Money Is/Money Runner . . . 5

EXPORT SINGLES

57 London HL 7022 Jenny, Jenny/Miss Ann (as Little Richard & His Band) . . . 35
58 London HL 7049 Ooh! My Soul/True, Fine Mama . . . 30
58 London HL 7056 Baby Face/I'll Never Let You Go . . . 30
59 London HL 7074 She Knows How To Rock/Early One Morning . . . 35
59 London HL 7079 By The Light Of The Silvery Moon/Kansas City . . . 30
59 London HL 7085 Whole Lotta Shakin' Goin' On/All Around The World . . . 70
68 Decca AD 1006 She's Together/Try Some Of Mine . . . 40

EPs

57 London RE-O 1071 LITTLE RICHARD AND HIS BAND VOL. 1 (gold tri-centre, later silver) . . . 60/35
57 London RE-O 1074 LITTLE RICHARD AND HIS BAND VOL. 2 (gold tri-centre, later silver) . . . 60/35
57 London RE-O 1103 LITTLE RICHARD AND HIS BAND VOL. 3 . . . 45
57 London RE-O 1106 LITTLE RICHARD AND HIS BAND VOL. 4 . . . 45
59 London RE-U 1208 LITTLE RICHARD AND HIS BAND VOL. 5 . . . 45
60 London RE-U 1234 LITTLE RICHARD AND HIS BAND VOL. 6 . . . 45
60 London RE-U 1235 LITTLE RICHARD AND HIS BAND VOL. 7 . . . 65

(The above EPs were originally issued with triangular centres; later round-centre pressings are worth two-thirds of silver values.)

62 Summit LSE 2049 FOUR DYNAMIC NUMBERS (2 each by Little Richard & Brock Peters) . . . 15
63 London REK 1400 HE'S BACK . . . 40
64 Vocalion VEP 170155 MEMPHIS SLIM AND LITTLE RICHARD . . . 75
66 Stateside SE 1042 DO YOU FEEL IT . . . 35

LPs

57 London HA-O 2055 HERE'S LITTLE RICHARD (flipback, rear sleeve initially in gloss red) . . . 125/70
57 London HA-O 2055 HERE'S LITTLE RICHARD (small flipback or non-flipback sleeve) . . . 75/40
58 London HA-U 2126 LITTLE RICHARD VOL. 2 (flipback or non-flipback sleeve) . . . 75/40
59 RCA Camden CDN 125 LITTLE RICHARD (8 tracks only; others by Buck Ram Orchestra) . . . 22
59 London HA-U 2193 THE FABULOUS LITTLE RICHARD (flipback or non-flipback sleeve) . . . 75/40
60 Top Rank 25/025 PRAY ALONG WITH LITTLE RICHARD VOL. 1: A CLOSER WALK WITH THEE (plain white sleeve, mail-order only) . . . 50
60 Top Rank 25/026 PRAY ALONG WITH LITTLE RICHARD VOL. 2: I'M QUITTING SHOW BUSINESS (plain white sleeve, mail-order only) . . . 100
62 Egmont EGM 9207 SINGS FREEDOM SONGS (reissue of Top Rank 25/025) . . . 15
63 Egmont EGM 9270 PRAY ALONG WITH LITTLE RICHARD (reissue of Top Rank 25/026) . . . 15
64 Stateside SL 10054 SINGS GOSPEL . . . 25
64 Coral LVA 9220 COMING HOME . . . 25
65 Fidelio ATL 4124 SINGS GOSPEL (4 tracks by Brock Peters but credited to Little Richard) . . . 12
65 Summit ATL 4124 SINGS GOSPEL (4 tracks by Brock Peters, overprinted front cover) . . . 12
65 Dial DLP 4124 SINGS GOSPEL (4 tracks by Brock Peters, correctly credited) . . . 12
65 Mercury MCL 20036 IT'S REAL . . . 15
65 Fontana TL 5235 IS BACK! . . . 25
65 Ember NR 5022 REALLY MOVIN' GOSPEL (3 tracks by Sister Rosetta Tharpe) . . . 12

MINT VALUE £

66	Fontana TL 5314	GREAT HITS	15
67	Columbia SX/SCX 6136	THE EXPLOSIVE LITTLE RICHARD	45
67	Polydor 236 202	THE INCREDIBLE LITTLE RICHARD (live)	12
68	Fontana SFL 13010	KING OF THE GOSPEL SINGERS	15
70	Reprise RSLP 6406	THE RILL THING	12
70	Union Pacific UP 003	YOU CAN'T KEEP A GOOD MAN DOWN	20
71	Epic EPC 66285	CAST A LONG SHADOW	12
71	Reprise K 44156	THE KING OF ROCK AND ROLL	15
73	Reprise K 44204	SECOND COMING	15
75	Rhapsody RHAS 9013	KEEP A KNOCKIN'	15

(see also Canned Heat, Sister Rosetta Tharpe, Buck Ram's Ramrocks)

LITTLE ROOSTERS

79	Pye 7P 152	She Cat Sister Floozie/Roostering With Intent (p/s)	6
80	Ami AIS 101	That's How Strong My Love Is/Suspicious (p/s)	6
80	Ami AIS 107	I Need A Witness/The Age Of Reason (p/s)	6

(see also Cocksparrer, Alison Moyet)

LITTLE ROYS

69	Camel CA 36	Bongonyah/CREATIONS: Dad Name (B-side actually "Bad Name")	8
70	Camel CA 42	Gold Digger (actually by Wailing Soul)/MATADORS: The Mine	8
70	Camel CA 57	Selassie Want Us Back/ROY AND JOY: Make It With You	8

(see also Little Roy, Hippy Boys)

LITTLE SAL with DANDY & SUPERBOYS

68	Giant GN 19	I'm In The Mood/I'm A Lover	8

(see also Dandy & Superboys, Superboys)

LITTLE SISTERS

63	MGM MGM 1192	Goin' To Boston/Where Does It Lead	6

LITTLE SONNY

71	Stax 2363 005	NEW KING OF THE BLUES HARMONICA (LP)	18

LITTLE SUZIE

61	Warner Bros WB 35	Young Love/The Boy I Left Behind	12

LITTLE TONY & HIS BROTHERS

59	Durium DC 16639	Who's That Knockin'/The Beat	25
59	Durium DC 16639	Who's That Knockin'/The Beat (78)	120
59	Durium DC 16657	Four An' Twenty Thousand Kisses/Bella Marie	20
59	Decca F 11164	I Can't Help It/Arrivederci Baby	10
59	Decca F 11164	I Can't Help It/Arrivederci Baby (78)	100
59	Decca F 11169	The Hippy Hippy Shake/Hey Little Girl	10
59	Decca F 11169	The Hippy Hippy Shake/Hey Little Girl (78)	125
59	Decca F 11190	Too Good/Foxy Little Mama	8
59	Decca F 11190	Too Good/Foxy Little Mama (78)	100
60	Decca F 21218	I Love You/The Magic Of Love	7
60	Decca F 21223	Princess/I Love You	7
60	Decca F 21247	Teddy Girl/Kiss Me, Kiss Me	10
66	Durium DRS 54008	Let Her Go/What Did I Do	8
67	Durium DRS 54012	Long Is The Lonely Night/People Talk To Me About You (as Little Tony)	8
58	Durium U 20058	PRESENTING LITTLE TONY AND HIS BROTHERS (EP)	60
65	Durium DRL 50006	I SUCCESSI DI LITTLE TONY (LP)	30
66	Durium DRL 50020	LET HER GO (LP)	25

LITTLE WALTER

60	London HLM 9175	My Babe/Blue Midnight	40
64	Pye International 7N 25263	My Babe/You Better Watch Yourself	18
56	London RE-U 1061	LITTLE WALTER AND HIS JUKES (EP)	175
64	Pye Intl. NPL 28043	LITTLE WALTER (LP)	50
67	Chess CRL 4529	SUPER BLUES (LP, with Bo Diddley & Muddy Waters)	45
68	Marble Arch MAL 815	LITTLE WALTER (LP, reissue)	12
69	Python PLP-KM 20	LITTLE WALTER AND HIS DUKES (LP, 99 copies only)	40
71	Syndicate Chapter SC 004	THUNDERBIRD (LP)	15

LITTLE WILBUR (& PLEASERS)

57	Vogue V 9091	Plaything/I Don't Care	650
57	Vogue V 9091	Plaything/I Don't Care (78)	150
58	Vogue V 9097	Heart To Heart/Alone In The Night (solo)	800
58	Vogue V 9097	Heart To Heart/Alone In The Night (solo) (78)	175

(see also Wilbur Whitfield)

LITTLE WILLIE (Francis)

63	Blue Beat BB 151	Settle Down/I'm Ashamed	20

(see also Wilbert Francis & Vibrators)

LIVE HUMAN

98	Fat Cat 12FAT 005	IMPROVISESSIONS (12" EP, custom sleeve)	8
99	Fat Cat 12FAT 019	ORANGEBUSHMONKEYFLOWER (12" EP, custom sleeve)	8

LIVELY ONES

63	London HA 8082	SURF DRUMS (LP)	50
63	London HA/SH 8107	SURF RIDER (LP, mono/stereo)	50/70

LIVELY SET

65	Pye 7N 15880	Don't Call My Name/What Kind Of Love	6
66	Capitol CL 15472	Let The Trumpets Sound/The Green Years	6

LIVERPOOL ECHO

73	Spark	LIVERPOOL ECHO (LP)	12

(see also Mandrake Paddle Steamers)

MINT VALUE £

LIVERPOOL F.C.
77 State STAT 50 — We Can Do It/Liverpool Lou/We Shall Not Be Moved/You'll Never Walk Alone (EP) . . 6
78 Logo GO 339 — Hail To The Kop/We Are Liverpool (p/s) . . . 5
80 no label — Liverpool's FA Cup Finals (gold flexi) . . . 10
83 Mean MEAN 102 — Liverpool We're Never Gonna Stop/Liverpool Anthem (red vinyl) . . . 5
65 Seddon SED 100 — EE AYE ADDIO: SEVENTY YEARS WAITING (LP) . . . 50
84 Extra-Terrestrial KOP 1 — CONQUERING LIONS OF ANFIELD (LP, picture disc, gatefold sleeve, with booklet, stickers & photographs) . . . 25

LIVERPOOL F.C. & LIVERPOOL SUPPORTERS
72 Penny Farthing PEN 794 — Sing A Song For Liverpool/Liverpool, Liverpool . . . 8

LIVERPOOL FISHERMEN
71 Mushroom 150 MR 9 — SWALLOW THE ANCHOR (LP) . . . 100

LIVERPOOL SCENE
68 RCA RCA 1762 — Son Son/Baby . . . 6
69 RCA RCA 1816 — The Woo-Woo/Love Is . . . 6
67 CBS 63045 — THE INCREDIBLE NEW LIVERPOOL SCENE (LP) . . . 20
68 RCA SF 7995 — THE AMAZING ADVENTURES OF THE LIVERPOOL SCENE (LP) . . . 15
69 RCA SF 8057 — BREAD ON THE NIGHT (LP) . . . 15
70 RCA SF 8100 — ST. ADRIAN AND CO. BROADWAY & 3RD (LP) . . . 15
70 RCA SF 8134 — HEIRLOON (LP) . . . 15
72 Charisma CS 3 — RECOLLECTIONS (LP) . . . 12
(see also Clayton Squares, Adrian Henri, Brian Patten, Mike Hart, Andy Roberts, Grimms)

LIVERPOOL SPINNERS
61 Topic TOP 69 — SONGS SPUN IN LIVERPOOL (EP) . . . 10
(see also Spinners [U.K.])

RICKY LIVID & TONE DEAFS
64 Parlophone R 5136 — Tomorrow/Nuts And Bolts . . . 15
(see also Bill Oddie)

LIVING DAYLIGHTS
67 Philips BF 1561 — Let's Live For Today/I'm Real (B-side actually titled "It's Real") . . . 20
67 Philips BF 1613 — Always With Him/Baila Maria . . . 30
(see also Greatest Show On Earth, Naturals)

LIVING DAYLIGHTS
79 E.S.R. S/79/CUS 523 — HEARTSTOP EP (Personality Changes/Outdoor Girl/Don't Fit/Let Me Know (33⅓, die-cut p/s, also listed as ESR 3) . . . 45

LIZA & JET SET
65 Parlophone R 5248 — How Can I Know?/Dancing Yet . . . 15
(see also Liza Strike, Jet Set)

LIZZIE & DELROY WILSON
71 Jackpot JP 771 — Double Attack/AGGRAVATORS: The Sniper . . . 7

LIZZY
70 Harry J HJ 6625 — More Heartaches/HARRY J ALL STARS: Version . . . 6
70 Pressure Beat PB 5508 — Ten Feet Tall (actually "Wear You From The Ball"/JOE GIBBS & DESTROYERS: Chapter (actually "Harmony Hall" by Mr Nigel) . . . 6
73 Duke DU 161 — Love Is A Treasure/FREDDIE McKAY: Love Is A Treasure . . . 7

LIZZY & DENNIS (Alcapone)
70 Ackee ACK 114 — Happy Go Lucky Girl/BOBBY & DAVE: Sammy . . . 10

LIZZY & PARAGONS
71 Ackee ACK 118 — On The Beach/DAVE BARKER: Maria . . . 15

LJ IV
69 CBS 63512 — AN ELIZABETHAN SONGBOOK (LP) . . . 75
(see also London Jazz Four)

LLAN
66 CBS 202405 — Realise/Anytime . . . 35
(see also Vogues)

BARRY LLEWELLYN
73 Downtown DT 515 — Meaning Of Life/MORWELL ESQ: Version Of Life . . . 12
(see also Heptones, Sound Dimension)

A.L. LLOYD
53 HMV B 10593 — The Shooting Of His Dear/Lord Bateman (78) . . . 8
53 HMV B 10594 — Down In The Forest/The Bitter Withy (78) . . . 8
60 Topic 12T 51 — OUTBACK BALLADS (LP, blue label) . . . 40
64 Topic 12T 103 — ENGLISH AND SCOTTISH FOLK BALLADS (LP, with Ewan MacColl, initially with blue label & booklet) . . . 30/20
65 Topic 12T 135 — BIRD IN THE BUSH (LP, with Anne Briggs & Frankie Armstrong, blue label) . . . 60
66 Topic 12T 118 — FIRST PERSON (LP, blue label) . . . 30
67 Topic 12T 174 — LEVIATHAN! (LP, blue label with booklet) . . . 30
(see also Frankie Armstrong, Anne Briggs)

A.L. LLOYD & MARTYN WYNDHAM-READ
71 Topic 12TS 203 — THE GREAT AUSTRALIAN LEGEND (LP, blue label with booklet) . . . 65
(see also Ewan MacColl, Peggy Seeger, Martin Wyndham-Read)

CHARLES LLOYD (QUARTET)
67 Atlantic 584 125 — Sombrero Sam (Parts 1 & 2) . . . 6
67 Atlantic 587/588 077 — LOVE-IN (LP) . . . 15
68 Atlantic 587/588 101 — JOURNEY WITHIN (LP) . . . 15
68 Atlantic 588 108 — IN EUROPE (LP) . . . 12
71 Atlantic 2400 108 — IN THE SOVIET UNION (LP) . . . 12

MINT VALUE £

FRED LLOYD

65 Polydor BM 56055 Girl From Chelsea/You Kissed Him . . . 6

JERRY LLOYD

60 Top Rank JAR 411 Be Faithful, Be True/Sooner Or Later . . . 7

JIMMY LLOYD

58 Philips PB 827 Witch Doctor/For Your Love . . . 8
58 Philips PB 827 Witch Doctor/For Your Love (78) . . . 8
58 Philips PB 871 The End/Street In The Rain . . . 6
58 Philips PB 871 The End/Street In The Rain (78) . . . 10
59 Philips PB 909 I Kneel At Your Throne/Sapphire . . . 6
59 Philips PB 909 I Kneel At Your Throne/Sapphire (78) . . . 15
60 Philips PB 1010 Teenage Sonata/Falling . . . 7
60 Philips PB 1055 I Double Dare You/Just For A Thrill . . . 6
61 Philips PB 1120 Pony Time/Three Handed Woman . . . 6
61 Philips PB 1157 Yellow Bird/Without The Sun . . . 6
61 Philips PB 1201 I'm Coming Home/You Are My Sunshine . . . 6
62 Philips 326 527 BF True Love/Mother Nature And Father Time . . . 5
63 Philips 326 568 BF Call On Me/Humma Humma Humma Humming Bird . . . 6
59 Philips BBE 12186 FOCUS ON JIMMY LLOYD (EP) . . . 15
62 Philips BBE 12509 YOU ARE MY SUNSHINE (EP) . . . 15
(see also Jimmy Logsdon)

KATHY LLOYD

54 Decca F 10386 It Worries Me/Tomorrow Night . . . 10
54 Decca F 10418 Teach Me Tonight/It's A Woman's World . . . 10
55 Decca F 10464 Our Future Has Only Begun/Unsuspecting Heart . . . 10
55 Decca F 10567 Experience Unnecessary/This Must Be Wrong (with Ted Heath Music) . . . 8

PEGGY LLOYD

55 London RE-P 1017 DIXIELAND HONKY-TONK (EP, with Bill Stegmeyer & His Orchestra) . . . 20

RUE LLOYD

72 Green Door GD 4033 Loving You/Version . . . 7
72 Green Door GD 4036 Cheer Up/Version . . . 7
(see also Joe White)

TREVOR LLOYD

70 Explosion EX 2018 Chinee Brush/DICE & CUMMIE: Real Colley . . . 8
70 Explosion EX 2019 Give Me Back Your Love/Hold Me . . . 5

LLOYD & BARBARA

73 Grape GR 3045 Dear Lonely Hearts/LLOYD BANTAM: I Tried To Love You . . . 5

LLOYD & CAREY WITH G.G. ALL STARS

72 Attack ATT 8029 Scorpion/MAYTONES: Hands And Feet . . . 7
(see also Carey & Lloyd, Pat Satchmo)

LLOYD & CLAUDETTE

70 Big Shot BI 546 Queen Of The World/PROPHETS: Top Of The World . . . 12

LLOYD (Robinson) & DEVON (Russell)

69 Punch PH 14 Love Is The Key/VIRTUES: High Tide . . . 12
69 Blue Cat BS 151 Out Of The Fire/Can't Understand (B-side actually by Austin Faithful) . . . 18
(see also Cobbs, Derrick Morgan)

LLOYD & DOREEN

71 Jackpot JP 762 Midnight/BUNNY LEE'S ALL STARS: Midnight — Version . . . 7
(see also Lloyd Clarke/Doreen Shaeffer)

LLOYD (Robinson) & GLEN (Brown)

67 Coxsone CS 7011 That Girl/You Got Me Wrong . . . 30
67 Doctor Bird DB 1058 Jezebel/TOMMY McCOOK & SUPERSONICS: Jam Session . . . 30
67 Doctor Bird DB 1071 Keep On Pushing/BOBBY AITKEN & CARIBBEATS: You Won't Regret (B-side actually by Lloyd & Glen) . . . 30

LLOYD (Jackson) & GROOVERS

67 Caltone TONE 108 Do It To Me Baby/DIPLOMATS: Meet Me At The Corner . . . 22
68 Caltone TONE 109 My Heart My Soul/DIPLOMATS with TOMMY McCOOK & SUPERSONICS: Going Along . . . 22
68 Caltone TONE 112 Listen To The Music/DIPLOMATS: Strong Man . . . 22
(see also Groovers, Don Lett, Tony Lee)

LLOYD & JOHNNY

68 Island WI 3158 My Argument (actually by Lloyd Terrell)/JOHNNY MELODY: Foey Man (actually by George Dekker) . . . 30
(see also Lloyd Terrell)

LLOYD & JOY

71 Explosion EX 2047 Back To Africa (actually by Alton Ellis)/Born To Lose . . . 12

LLOYD & KEN

72 Punch PH 110 Have I Sinned/Version . . . 6
(see also Lloyd Charmers/Ken Boothe)

LLOYD & LARRY

70s New Beat NB 080 Monkey Spanner/LLOYD & LARRY'S ALL STARS: Version . . . 6

LLOYD & THE PROPHETS

70 Big Shot BI 553 Bush Beat/PATRICK & PROPHETS: Please Come Come . . . 8
70 Big Shot BI 556 Jaco/Soul Reggae . . . 8
(see also Prophets [Jamaica], Patrick & Lloyd)

LLOYD, DICE & HIS MUM

70 Joe JRS 5 Trial Of Pama Dice/NYAH SHUFFLE: Jughead Returns Version 1 . . . 12

MINT VALUE £

LLOYD, DICE & THE BARRISTER
70 Joe JRS 14 — Appeal Of Pama Dice/BOSS ALL STARS: Young And Strong Version 2 12

LLOYD'S ALLSTARS
69 Doctor Bird DB 1178 — Love Kiss Blue/UNIQUES: Secretly 40
(see also Justins, U Roy Junior, Jimmy Green, Victors)

LLOYDIE & LOWBITES
73 Harry J HJ 6660 — Pussy Cat/Skanky Pussy 6
71 Lowbite LOW 001 — CENSORED! (LP, green/silver label) 30
(see also Lloyd Tyrell/Charmers)

LLOYD (Campbell) THE MATADOR
72 Sioux SI 010 — The Train/Julia Sees Me (Exodus) 8

LLYGOD FFYRNIG
78 Pwdwr PWDWR 1 — N.C.B./Sais/Cariad Y Bus Stop (p/s, stamped or printed white labels) 100/130

LOADED FORTY-FOURS
81 X-S TL 44/1 — Thunderbirds (Are Go!)/T.V. Child (p/s) 5

DICKIE LOADER
61 Palette PG 9015 — Heatwave/Happiness 20

RUSS LOADER
65 Columbia DB 7522 — When Your Heart Is Broken/That Girl Of Mine (with Breakaways Orchestra) 10
65 Columbia DB 7643 — Just Lies/Mona Lisa 8
65 Columbia DB 7696 — Count The Stars/Triyng Too Hard (with Ladybirds) 8
66 Columbia DB 7839 — Too Soon/Just A Little Step To Heaven 8
69 Conquest CXT 2 — Just Lies/Take Me Tonight 7
(see also Mark Wirtz)

JOSEF LOCKE
53 Columbia SCM 5008 — My Heart And I/Goodbye 10
53 Columbia SCM 5009 — Hear My Song, Violetta/The Soldier's Dream 10
92 EMI 78EM 231 — Hear My Song, Violetta/Charmaine/Count Your Blessings/Goodbye (12" 78) 8

LOCKETS
63 Pye International 7N 25232 — Don't Cha Know/Little Boy 30

LOCKJAW
77 Raw RAW 8 — Radio Call Sign/The Young Ones (p/s) 20
78 Raw RAW 19 — Journalist Jive/I'm A Virgin/A Doonga Doonga (p/s, beware of counterfeits) 80
(see also the Cure)

HANK LOCKLIN
60 RCA RCA 1188 — Please Help Me, I'm Falling/My Old Home Town 7
60 RCA RCA 1188 — Please Help Me, I'm Falling/My Old Home Town (78) 20
61 RCA RCA 1252 — You're The Reason/Happy Birthday To Me 7
62 RCA RCA 1273 — From Here To There To You/This Song Is Just for You 7
62 RCA RCA 1305 — We're Gonna Go Fishin'/Welcome Home, Mr. Blues 7
63 RCA RCA 1336 — Flyin' South/Behind The Footlights 6
63 RCA RCA 1370 — Wooden Soldier/Kiss On The Door 6
64 RCA RCA 1391 — You Never Want To Love Me/Followed Closely By My Teardrops 6
65 RCA RCA 1458 — Faith And Truth/Forty Nine, Fifty One 6
66 RCA RCA 1510 — I Feel A Cry Coming On/Insurance 6
66 RCA RCA 1548 — The Last Thing On My Mind/The Best Part Of Loving You 6
67 RCA RCA 1575 — It Is Love/The Upper Room 6
67 RCA RCA 1610 — Wishing On A Star/Hasta Luego 6
67 RCA RCA 1641 — The Country Hall Of Fame/Evergreen 6
68 RCA RCA 1678 — Love Song For You/Little Geisha Girl 6
68 RCA RCA 1729 — Everlasting Love/I'm Slowly Going Out Of Your Mind 6
58 RCA RCX 115 — COUNTRY GUITAR VOL. 3 (EP) 15
62 RCA RCX 217 — SEVEN DAYS (EP) 15
63 Parlophone GEP 8875 — ENCORES (EP) 20
63 RCA RCX 7116 — WALTZ OF THE WIND (EP) 15
64 RCA RCX 7150 — IRISH SONGS COUNTRY STYLE (EP) 15
61 RCA RD 27201 — PLEASE HELP ME, I'M FALLING (LP) 20
64 RCA RD 7623 — IRISH SONGS COUNTRY STYLE (LP) 15
65 Fontana FJL 305 — BORN TO RAMBLE (LP) 12

GERRY LOCKRAN
69 Decca F 12873 — Hey Jude/This Train 6
69 Decca F 12919 — Standing On Your Own/You're Not There 6
67 Planet PLL 1002 — HOLD ON, I'M COMING (LP) 85
68 Waverley ZLP 2091 — BLUES VENDETTA (LP) 35
69 Spark SRLP 104 — THE ESSENTIAL GERRY LOCKRAN (LP) 20
72 Polydor 2383 122 — WUN (LP) 12
76 Decca SKL-R 5257 — RAGS TO GLADRAGS (LP) 12

GERRY LOCKRAN, REDD SULLIVAN, DAVE TRAVIS
69 Fidelity FID 2165 — BLUES AT SUNRISE (LP) 18

ANNA LOCKWOOD
70 Tangent TGS 104 — THE GLASS WORLD OF ANNA LOCKWOOD (LP) 22

MALCOLM LOCKYER ORCHESTRA
54 Polygon P 1097 — Fiddler's Boogie/Pizzicato Rag (78) 7
54 Decca F 10304 — I'm Gonna Rock, Rock, Rock/Changing Partners (78, as Malcolm Lockyer & His Strict Tempo Music For Dancing) 10
61 HMV POP 929 — "The Pursuers" T.V. Theme/Stranger Than Fiction 7
65 Columbia DB 7552 — The Intelligence Men/Brighton Run 15
65 Columbia DB 7663 — The Eccentric Dr. Who/Daleks And Thals 50
75 Contour 2870 439 — TOP TV THEMES (LP) 12

MINT VALUE £

LOCOMOTIVE

67 Direction 58-3814 Rudy A Message To You/Broken Heart . . . 15
68 Parlophone R 5718 Rudi's In Love/Never Set Me Free . . . 15
69 Parlophone R 5758 Mr. Armageddon/There's Got To Be A Way (some in promos p/s) . . . 60/30
69 Parlophone R 5801 I'm Never Gonna Let You Go/You Must Be Joking . . . 18
70 Parlophone R 5835 Movin' Down The Line/Roll Over Mary . . . 10
71 Parlophone R 5915 Rudi's In Love/You Must Be Joking . . . 8
69 Parlophone PCS 7093 WE ARE EVERYTHING YOU SEE (LP) . . . 200
(see also Norman Haines Band, Dog That Bit People, Steam-Shovel)

NILS LOFGREN

76 CBS 4339 Soft Fun/Slippery Fingers (actually by Grin) . . . 5
79 A&M AMS 7455 Shine Silently/Kool Skool (p/s, coloured or black vinyl) . . . 5
(see also Grin, Crazy Horse, Bruce Springsteen)

LOFT

84 Creation CRE 009 Why Does The Rain/Like (foldaround p/s in poly bag) . . . 10
85 Creation CRE 015 Up The Hill And Down The Slope/Lonely Street (foldaround p/s in poly bag) . . . 10
85 Creation CRE 015T Up The Hill And Down The Slope/Lonely Street (12", p/s) . . . 8
(see also Weather Prophets, Wishing Stones)

CRIPPLE CLARENCE LOFTON

59 Vogue EPV 1209 CRIPPLE CLARENCE LOFTON (EP) . . . 60
54 London AL 3531 A LOST RECORDING DATE (10" LP) . . . 50
55 Vogue LDE 122 JAZZ IMMORTALS NO. 1 (10" LP) . . . 50

JIMMY LOGSDON

54 Brunswick 05226 Pa-Paya Mama/In The Mission Of St. Augustine (78) . . . 15

L.O.K.

79 Fetish FET 001 Fun House/Starlet Love/Tell Me (p/s) . . . 5

LOLITA

60 Polydor NH 66818 Sailor (Your Home Is The Sea)/La Luna (Quanda La Luna) . . . 7

LOLITA STORM

99 Rabid Badger NANG 09 Goodbye America/Get Back (I'm Evil) (p/s) . . . 5

LOLLIPOPS

71 Atlantic 2091 114 Nothing's Gonna Stop Our Love/I Believe In Love . . . 12

LAURIE LOMAN

54 London HL 8101 Whither Thou Goest/I Was The Last One To Know . . . 50
54 London HL 8101 Whither Thou Goest/I Was The Last One To Know (78) . . . 15

ALAN LOMAX (& RAMBLERS)

56 Decca F 10787 Dirty Old Town/Hard Case (as Alan Lomax & Ramblers) . . . 8
56 Decca DFE 6367 OH LULA (EP) . . . 10
58 Pye Jazz NJE 1055 SINGS (EP, with Dave Lee's Bandits) . . . 15
58 Pye Jazz NJE 1062 MURDERER'S HOME PT. 1 (EP) . . . 15
58 Pye Jazz NJE 1063 MURDERER'S HOME PT. 2 (EP) . . . 15
58 Pye Jazz NJE 1064 MURDERER'S HOME PT. 3 (EP) . . . 15
58 Pye Jazz NJE 1065 MURDERER'S HOME PT. 4 (EP) . . . 15
59 Melodisc EPM7 88 SONGS FROM TEXAS (EP) . . . 12
57 Nixa Jazz NJL 8 PRESENTS BLUES IN THE MISSISSIPPI NIGHT (LP, with others) . . . 15
57 Nixa Jazz NJL 11 MURDERER'S HOME (LP) . . . 15
58 Pye Nixa NPL 18013 PRESENTS AMERICAN SONG TRAIN VOLUME ONE (LP) . . . 12
58 HMV CLP 1192 GREAT AMERICAN BALLADS (LP, with Alexis Korner & Guy Carawan) . . . 25

JACKIE LOMAX

68 CBS 2554 Genuine Imitation Life/One Minute Woman . . . 20
68 Apple APPLE 3 Sour Milk Sea/The Eagle Laughs At You . . . 15
69 Apple APPLE 11 New Day/I Fall Inside Your Eyes . . . 15
70 Apple APPLE 23 How The Web Was Woven/Thumbin' A Ride (some in p/s) . . . 25/10
69 Apple (S)APCOR 6 IS THIS WHAT YOU WANT (LP, with inner sleeve, mono/stereo) . . . 75/40
91 Apple SAPCOR 6 IS THIS WHAT YOU WANT (LP, reissue, gatefold sleeve with bonus 12" [SAPCOR 62]) . . . 25
91 Apple SAPCOR 6 IS THIS WHAT YOU WANT (CD) . . . 35
(see also Lomax Alliance, Undertakers, Takers, Heavy Jelly, Badger)

LOMAX ALLIANCE

67 CBS 2729 Try As You May/See The People . . . 20
(see also Jackie Lomax)

GUY LOMBARDO (& ROYAL CANADIANS)

55 Brunswick 05372 No More/Pupalina . . . 8
55 Brunswick 05412 Softly Softly/(I'm Always Hearing) Wedding Bells . . . 8
55 Brunswick 05413 Hey, Mr. Banjo/Blue Mirage . . . 8
55 Brunswick 05443 Cherry Pink And Apple Blossom White/Marty . . . 8
56 Capitol CL 14585 Charleston Parisien/Rinka Tinka Man . . . 8

AL LOMBARDY & HIS ORCHESTRA

54 London HL 8076 The Blues/The Boogie . . . 60
54 London HL 8076 The Blues/The Boogie (78) . . . 12
55 London HL 8127 In A Little Spanish Town/Flying Home . . . 50
55 London HL 8127 In A Little Spanish Town/Flying Home (78) . . . 12

LONDON

77 MCA MCA 305 Everyone's A Winner/Handcuffed . . . 5
77 MCA MCA 336 Animal Games/Us Kids Cold . . . 5
77 MCA MCA 319 SUMMER OF LOVE (EP, p/s) . . . 6
77 MCA 12 MCA 319 SUMMER OF LOVE (12" EP, p/s) . . . 10
78 MCA MCF 2823 ANIMAL GAMES (LP) . . . 15

MINT VALUE £

EDDIE LONDON & CHIMES

57	Decca F 10859	Song Of The Moonlight/I'll Thank You	6

FRANCO LONDON ORCHESTRA

66	Philips BF 1470	Theme From Robinson Crusoe/Adrift	15

JIMMY LONDON

71	Randy's RAN 514	Shake A Hand/CARL MURPHY: Lick I Pipe	6
71	Randy's RAN 517	Bridge Over Troubled Waters/RANDY'S ALLSTARS: War	6
71	Randy's RAN 518	Hip Hip Hooray/IMPACT ALLSTARS: Version	6
71	Randy's RAN 520	A Little Love/IMPACT ALLSTARS: Version	6
72	Randy's RAN 521	It's Now Or Never/IMPACT ALLSTARS: Version	6
72	Randy's RAN 527	Jamaica Festival '72 (with Rocking Horse)/IMPACT ALLSTARS: Version	5
73	Explosion EX 2080	I'll Never Find Another You/IMPACT ALLSTARS: Version	6
73	Dragon DRA 1010	Jennie/I Wonder If I Care As Much (as Jimmi London)	5
74	Dragon DRA 1019	No Letter Today/The Road Is Rough	5
74	Ackee ACK 531	Till I Kiss You/Version	5
72	Trojan TRL 39	BRIDGE OVER TROUBLED WATERS (LP)	18

(see also Jimmy Green, The Inspirations)

JOE LONDON

59	London HLW 9008	Lonesome Whistle/It Might Have Been	12
59	London HLW 9008	Lonesome Whistle/It Might Have Been (78)	20

JULIE LONDON

78s

56	London HLU 8240	Cry Me A River/S'Wonderful	10
56	London HLU 8279	Baby, Baby All The Time/Shadow Woman	10
57	London HLU 8394	The Meaning Of The Blues/Now! Baby, Now!	10
57	London HLU 8414	The Boy On A Dolphin/Tall Boy	10
58	London HLU 8602	Saddle The Wind/It Had To Be You	10
58	London HLU 8657	My Strange Affair/It's Easy	10
58	London HLU 8769	Man Of The West/Blue Moon	20
59	London HLU 8891	Come On-A My House/Must Be Catchin'	40

SINGLES

56	London HLU 8240	Cry Me A River/S'Wonderful (gold label print, later silver)	75/35
56	London HLU 8279	Baby, Baby All The Time/Shadow Woman (gold label print)	45
57	London HLU 8394	The Meaning Of The Blues/Now! Baby, Now! (gold label print, later silver)	45/20
57	London HLU 8414	The Boy On A Dolphin/Tall Boy	20
58	London HLU 8602	Saddle The Wind/It Had To Be You	15
58	London HLU 8657	My Strange Affair/It's Easy	15
58	London HLU 8769	Man Of The West/Blue Moon	15
59	London HLU 8891	Come On-A My House/Must Be Catchin'	20
61	London HLG 9360	Sanctuary/Every Chance I Get	8
63	Liberty LIB 10078	There'll Be Some Changes Made/Love On The Rocks	7
63	Liberty LIB 55605	I'm Coming Back To You/When Snowflakes Fall In The Summer	10
64	Liberty LIB 55666	I Want To Find Out For Myself/Guilty Heart	7
65	Liberty LIB 10189	Send For Me/Bye Bye Blackbird	7
65	Liberty LIB 10205	Charade/Wives And Lovers	7
67	Liberty LIB 10274	Girl Talk/The Mickey Mouse March	7
83	Edsel PE 5004	Cry Me A River/February Brings The Rain (picture disc)	6

EPs

57	London RE-U 1076	JULIE SINGS FILM SONGS (gold label print, silver print labels £10)	20
57	London RE-N 1092	LONDON'S GIRL FRIENDS VOL. 1	22
58	London RE-U 1151	MAKE LOVE TO ME — PART ONE	25
58	London RE-U 1152	MAKE LOVE TO ME — PART TWO	25
58	London RE-U 1153	MAKE LOVE TO ME — PART THREE	25
59	London RE-U 1180	JULIE — PART ONE	20
59	London RE-U 1181	JULIE — PART TWO	20
59	London RE-U 1182	JULIE — PART THREE	20
63	Liberty LEP 2103	DESAFINADO	20
66	Liberty LEP 2260	ALL THROUGH THE NIGHT	20

LPs

56	London HA-U 2005	JULIE IS HER NAME	55
57	London HA-U 2038	CALENDAR GIRL	40
58	London HA-U 2083	MAKE LOVE TO ME	45
58	London HA-U 2091	ABOUT THE BLUES	45
58	London HA-U 2112	JULIE	45
59	London HA-U 2171	LONDON BY NIGHT	40
59	London HA-U 2186	JULIE IS HER NAME VOL. 2 (also stereo SAH-U 6042)	35/45
60	London HA-W 2225	SWING ME AN OLD SONG	35
60	London HA-W 2229	YOUR NUMBER PLEASE	35
60	London HA-G 2280	JULIE AT HOME (also stereo SAH-G 6097)	35/45
61	London HA-G 2299	AROUND MIDNIGHT	35
61	London HA-G 2353	SEND FOR ME (also stereo SAH-G 6154)	35/45
62	London HA-G 2405	WHATEVER JULIE WANTS (aso stereo SAH-G 6205)	35/45
62	Liberty LBY 1023	THE BEST OF JULIE LONDON	15
62	Liberty (S)LBY 1083	LOVE LETTERS	25
63	Liberty (S)LBY 1113	LOVE ON THE ROCKS	25
63	Liberty (S)LBY 1136	SINGS LATIN IN A SATIN MOOD	22
64	Liberty (S)LBY 1185	THE WONDERFUL WORLD OF JULIE LONDON	22
65	Liberty LBY 1222	IN PERSON AT THE AMERICANA	25
65	Liberty (S)LBY 1251	OUR FAIR LADY	22
66	Liberty (S)LBY 1281	FEELING GOOD (with Gerald Wilson Big Band)	25

			MINT VALUE £
66	Liberty (S)LBY 1300	ALL THROUGH THE NIGHT	22
67	Liberty (S)LBY 1334	FOR THE NIGHT PEOPLE	22
67	Liberty (S)LBY 1364	NICE GIRLS DON'T STAY FOR BREAKFAST	22
68	Liberty LBL/LBS 83049	GREAT PERFORMANCES	22
69	Liberty LBL/LBS 83183E	YUMMY, YUMMY, YUMMY	22

LAURIE LONDON

57	Parlophone R 4359	He's Got The Whole World In His Hands/The Cradle Rock	7
57	Parlophone R 4388	Handed Down/She Sells Sea Shells	7
58	Parlophone R 4408	The Gospel Train/Boomerang	8
58	Parlophone R 4408	The Gospel Train/Boomerang (78)	10
58	Parlophone R 4426	I Gotta Robe/Casey Jones	7
58	Parlophone R 4426	I Gotta Robe/Casey Jones (78)	10
58	Parlophone R 4450	Basin Street Blues/Joshua (Fit The Battle Of Jericho)	7
58	Parlophone R 4450	Basin Street Blues/Joshua (Fit The Battle Of Jericho) (78)	10
58	Parlophone R 4474	My Mother/Darktown Strutters' Ball	7
58	Parlophone R 4474	My Mother/Darktown Strutters' Ball (78)	10
58	Parlophone R 4499	Up Above My Head/Three O'Clock	7
58	Parlophone R 4499	Up Above My Head/Three O'Clock (78)	15
59	Parlophone R 4557	Pretty-Eyed Baby (with Gitte)/Boom-Ladda-Boom-Boom	10
59	Parlophone R 4557	Pretty-Eyed Baby (with Gitte)/Boom-Ladda-Boom-Boom (78)	20
59	Parlophone R 4601	Old Time Religion/God's Little Acre	6
60	Parlophone R 4635	I'm Afraid/Roll On Spring	6
60	Parlophone R 4662	Hear Them Bells/Banjo Boy	6
61	Parlophone R 4747	Today's Teardrops/Darling Sue	6
61	Parlophone R 4801	Down By The Riverside/I'll Make Her Forget Him	6
67	CBS 202461	The Bells Of St. Mary's/Sad Songs	6
57	Parlophone GEP 8664	LAURIE LONDON (EP)	40
58	Parlophone GEP 8689	LITTLE LAURIE LONDON No. 2 (EP)	40

MARK LONDON

65	Pye 7N 15825	Stranger In The World/Moanin'	10

MICHAEL LONDON

62	HMV POP 1026	Miracles Sometimes Happen/Stranger On The Shore (with Acker Bilk)	8
62	HMV POP 1085	Mutiny On The Bounty Love Song/For The Very Young	6

PETER LONDON

65	Pye 7N 15957	Bless You/Baby I Like The Look Of You	45

(see also Peter Cook)

LONDON & BRIDGES

66	CBS 202056	It Just Ain't Right/Leave Her Alone	35

LONDON BALALAIKA ENSEMBLE

68	Deram DML/SML 712	LONDON BALALAIKA ENSEMBLE (LP)	15

LONDON JAZZ CHAMBER GROUP

72	Ember CJS 823	ADAM'S RIB SUITE (LP)	20

(see also Ken Moule's London Jazz Chamber Group, Ken Moule Seven)

LONDON JAZZ FOUR

67	Polydor 56214	It Strikes A Chord/Song For Hilary	20
67	Polydor 582 005	TAKE A NEW LOOK AT THE BEATLES (LP)	80

(see also London Jazz Quartet, LJ IV)

LONDON JAZZ QUARTET

66	Polydor 56092	Norwegian Wood/I Feel Fine	6
60	Tempo TAP 28	LONDON JAZZ QUARTET (LP, with Tubby Hayes & Tony Crombie)	375
60s	Ember EMB 3306	LONDON JAZZ QUARTET (LP)	150

(see also London Jazz Four, Tubby Hayes, Tony Crombie)

LONDON POPS ORCHESTRA

68	Pye 7N 17630	Eleanor Rigby/If I Only Had Time	6
68	Pye NSPL 18241	THE LONDON POPS ORCHESTRA (LP)	12

LONDON POSSE

87	Bullett BULT3	Here Comes The Rugged One/Supermodel (12")	12
87	Big Life BLRT2	London Posse (12")	10
89	Mango Street 12IS447	Live Like The Other Half Do/Money Mad Remix (12")	10
90	Mango 12MNG752DJ	Tell Me Something/The Original London Style (12")	10
91	Mango MNG774	Jump Around/Gangster Chronical	12
91	Mango/ Island MLPS1066	Gangster Chronicle (12")	20
93	Bullett BULT2	How Is Life In London/Shut The Fuck Up/How I Make The Papers (12")	10

(see also Rodney P & Skitz)

LONDON PX

80	New Puritan NP 1	Orders/Eviction (p/s)	20
82	Terrapyn SYD 1	Arnold Layne/Indian Summer (1-sided flexidisc)	12

LONDON STUDIO GROUP

66	De Wolfe DW/LP 2974	THE WILD ONE (10" LP, tricolour label)	25

(see also Ivor & Basil Kirchen Band)

LONDON UNDERGROUND

82	On-U Sound ON-U 4	WATCHING WEST INDIANS IN THE COLD (10" EP)	7
83	On-U Sound ON-U 5	STRANGE (10" EP)	7

LONDON WAITS

66	Immediate IM 030	Softly Softly/Serenadio	25

LONDON ZOO
80 Gramaphone STB 80 — Who's Driving This Car?/You And Your Great Ideas (stamped white labels, no p/s) . . . 6
80 Zoom ZUM 12 — Receiving End/London Zoo (p/s) . . . 5

LONDONAIRES
66 Decca F12379 — Dearest Emma/Blues A Go-Go . . . 10

LONELY HEARTS
84 Tenacity TROIA — FM Fantasy/Young Girl (p/s) . . . 10

LONE PIGEON
00s Bad Jazz/Fence BEBOP 31 — TOUCHED BY TOMOKO EP: Summertime Beeswing/Touched By Tomoko/Empty Town/The Mean Old Mind Of Man/Waterfall . . . 10
(see also Beta Band)

JOHNNY LONESOME
61 HMV POP 837 — Marie Marie/Doctor Heartache . . . 18

LONESOME PINE FIDDLERS
64 London HA-B 8143 — MORE BLUEGRASS (LP) . . . 15

LONESOME STONE
73 Reflection RL 306 — LONESOME STONE (LP, stage production recording) . . . 22
(see also Sheep)

LONESOME SUNDOWN
71 Blue Horizon 7-63864 — LONESOME LONELY BLUES (LP) . . . 80
70s Flyright LP 529 — BOUGHT ME A TICKET (LP) . . . 15
70s Flyright LP 587 — LONESOME WHISTLER (LP) . . . 15

LONESOME TRAVELLERS
70 Tradition TSR 004 — THE LONESOME TRAVELLERS (LP) . . . 25
70s Nebula NEB 100 — THE LOST CHILDREN (LP) . . . 15

LONE WOLF
81 Kai KR 02 — Fighting For Sommerlund/Vonotar The Traitor (p/s) . . . 15

FITZROY D. LONG & BUSTER ALL STARS
68 Fab FAB 32 — Get A New Girl/BUSTER'S ALL STARS: Come And Do It With Me . . . 20
(see also Larry Marshall)

JOHNNY LONG ORCHESTRA
55 Parlophone MSP 6176 — Silver Dollar/We'll Build A Bungalow . . . 10

SHORTY LONG
65 Tamla Motown TMG 512 — Out To Get You/It's A Crying Shame . . . 80
66 Tamla Motown TMG 573 — Function At The Junction/Call On Me (narrow label print, later w/ wider print) . . . 25
67 Tamla Motown TMG 600 — Chantilly Lace/Your Love Is Amazing (narrow label print, later w/ wider print) . . . 15
68 Tamla Motown TMG 644 — Night Fo' Last (Vocal)/Night Fo' Last (Instrumental) . . . 10
68 Tamla Motown TMG 663 — Here Comes The Judge/Sing What You Wanna . . . 12
68 T. Motown (S)TML 11086 — HERE COMES THE JUDGE (LP) . . . 50
70 T. Motown STML 11144 — THE PRIME OF SHORTY LONG (LP) . . . 40
(see also Art Mooney)

LONG & SHORT
64 Decca F 11964 — The Letter/Love Is A Funny Thing . . . 25
64 Decca F 12043 — Choc Ice/Here Comes The Fool . . . 25

LONGBOATMEN
66 Polydor 56115 — Take Her Any Time/Only In Her Home Town . . . 500

LONG COLD STARE
90 Rise Above RISE 3 — TIRED EYES (LP) . . . 12

LONGDANCER
73 Rocket PIG 1 — If It Was So Simple/Silent Emotions . . . 5
74 Rocket PIG 11 — Puppet Man/Cold Love . . . 5
73 Rocket PIGL 1 — IF IT WAS SO SIMPLE (LP, gatefold sleeve) . . . 12
74 Rocket PIGL 6 — TRAILER FOR A GOOD LIFE (LP, die-cut gatefold sleeve) . . . 12
(see also Eurythmics, Dave Stewart & Harrison)

CLAUDINE LONGET
67 A&M AMS 708 — Good Day Sunshine/The Look Of Love . . . 6
67 A&M AML 903 — Claudine . . . 18

LONG HELLO
73 private pressing — THE LONG HELLO (LP, mail-order only, numbered white sleeve) . . . 20
(see also Van Der Graaf Generator)

LONG TALL SHORTY
79 Warner Bros K 17491 — By Your Love/1970's Boy (p/s, withdrawn) . . . 100
81 Dr Creation LYN 9904 — If I Was You/That's What I Want (flexidisc) . . . 12
81 Ramkup CAC 007 — Win Or Lose/Ain't Done Wrong (p/s) . . . 100
85 Diamond DIA 002 — On The Streets Again/I Fought The Law/Promises (p/s, some with poster) . . . 25/12
86 Diamond DIA 005 — What's Going On/Steppin' Stone/Win Or Lose/England (p/s) . . . 15
88 no label or cat. no. — ROCKIN' AT THE SAVOY (LP, official bootleg, some with poster) . . . 18/15
(see also Case, Joe Public, Rage, Charlie Harper)

LOOKING GLASS
72 Epic 65041 — LOOKING GLASS (LP) . . . 20

LOOP
86 Head HEAD 5 — 16 Dreams/Head On/Burning World (12", p/s) . . . 25
87 Head HEAD 7L — Spinning Parts 1 & 2 (large centre, plain black die-cut sleeve) . . . 20
87 Head HEAD 7 — Spinning/Deep Hit/I'll Take You There (12", p/s) . . . 25
88 Chapter 22 CAT 065 — Torched (flexidisc, with/without *The Catalogue* magazine no. 65) . . . 12/7

MINT VALUE £

89	Situation 2 SIT 64T	ARC LITE EP (12", p/s)	8
89	Situation 2 SIT 64CD	ARC LITE EP (CD)	8
88	Chapter 22 CHAPLLP 34	FADE OUT (LP, 2 x 45rpm 12", gold stickered gatefold sleeve, some signed)	15/12
91	Reactor REACTORLP 3	WOLF FLOW — JOHN PEEL SESSIONS 1987-90 (2-LP)	15

LOOSE ENDS

66	Decca F 12437	Send The People Away/I Ain't Gonna Eat My Heart Out Anymore	20
66	Decca F 12476	Taxman/That's It	40

LOOT

66	Page One POF 013	Baby Come Closer/Baby	12
67	Page One POF 026	I've Just Gotta Love You/You Need Someone To Love	20
67	CBS 2938	Whenever You're Ready/I Got What You Want	18
68	Page One POF 095	She's A Winner/Radio City (withdrawn B-side)	35
68	Page One POF 095	She's A Winner/Save Me	22
68	CBS 3231	Don't Turn Around/You Are My Sunshine Girl	12
69	Page One POF 115	Try To Keep It A Secret/Radio City	30

(see also Soul Agents, Hookfoot5

LINDA LOPEZ MAMBO ORCHESTRA

55	Parlophone MSP 6179	Limehouse Blues Mambo/Nursery Mambo	8

TRINI LOPEZ

63	London HL 9808	Jeanie Marie/Love Me Tonight	10
63	Reprise R 20198	If I Had A Hammer/Unchain My Heart	6
63	Reprise R 20236	Kansas City/Lonesome Traveller	5
63	Reprise R 20260	Jailer Bring Me Water/You Can't Say Goodbye	5
63	Reprise R 20276	Ya Ya/What Have I Got Of My Own	5
65	Reprise R 20238	Sad Tomorrows/I've Lost My Love For You	5
66	Reprise R 20455	I'm Coming Home Cindy/The 32nd Of May	5
66	Reprise R 20480	La Bamba/Trini's Tune	5
67	Columbia DB 4822	Gonna Get Along Without Ya Now/Love Letters	6
72	Reprise K 14205	America/If I Had A Hammer (p/s)	5
63	Reprise R(9) 6093	LOPEZ AT P.J.'s (LP, mono/stereo)	12
64	London HA 8132	TEENAGE LOVE SONGS (LP)	35
64	London HA 8160	MORE OF TRINI LOPEZ (LP)	30
64	Reprise R 6147	THE FOLK ALBUM (LP)	12

DENISE LOR

54	Parlophone MSP 6120	If I Give My Heart To You/Hallo Darling	15
55	Parlophone MSP 6148	Every Day Of My Life/And One To Grow On	12

KENNY LORAN

59	Capitol CL 15081	Mama's Little Baby/Magic Star	50

L'ORANGE MECHANIK

86	Art Pop POP 44	Symphony/Intermezzo (Sprechstimme)/Scherzo (p/s)	15

(see also Times)

BOBBY LORD

64	Hickory 45-1232	Life Can Have Meaning/Pickin' White Gold	7
64	Hickory 45-1259	Take The Bucket To The Well/A Man Needs A Woman	7
65	Hickory 45-1310	That Room In The Corner Of The House/I'm Going Home Next Summer	7

BOBBY LORD/BOB LUMAN

64	Hickory LPE 1501	HICKORY SHOWCASE VOL. 2 (EP, 1 side each)	20
64	Hickory LPE 1504	HICKORY SHOWCASE VOL. 3 (EP, 1 side each)	20
64	Hickory LPM 121	CAN'T TAKE THE COUNTRY FROM THE BOYS (LP, 1 side each)	18

(see also Bob Luman)

JON LORD

76	Purple PUR 131	Bourée/Aria	7
82	Harvest HAR 5220	Bach Onto This/Going Home (p/s)	6
71	Purple TPSA 7501	GEMINI SUITE (LP)	15
74	Purple TPSA 7513	WINDOWS (LP)	15
76	Purple TPSA 7516	SARABANDE (LP, die-cut sleeve)	15
82	Harvest SHSP 4123	BEFORE I FORGET (LP)	12

(see also Artwoods, Deep Purple, [Paice] Ashton & Lord, Bernie Marsden, Wizard's Convention, Episode Six, Leading Figures, Whitesnake, Cozy Powell)

TONY LORD

66	Planet PLF 102	World's Champion/It Makes Me Sad (with Planet company sleeve)	25/20

JERRY LORDAN

59	Parlophone R 4588	I'll Stay Single/Can We Kiss	8
60	Parlophone R 4627	Who Could Be Bluer?/Do I Worry?	8
60	Parlophone R 4653	Sing Like An Angel/Ev'ry Time	10
60	Parlophone R 4695	Ring, Write Or Call/I've Still Got You	12
61	Parlophone R 4748	You Came A Long Way From St. Louis/Let's Try Again	12
62	Parlophone R 4903	One Good Solid 24 Carat Reason/Second Hand Dress	18
70	CBS 5057	The Old Man And The Sea/Harlequin Melodies	20
61	Parlophone PMC 1133	ALL MY OWN WORK (LP, also stereo PCS 3014)	90/120

(see also Lee & Jay Elvin)

LORD BEGINNER

50	Melodisc 1131	Joe Louis Calypso/Trinidad Blues (78)	10
50	Melodisc 1133	Victory Test Match — Calypso/Sergeant Brown (78)	10
50	Melodisc 1134	Straight Hair Girl/Calinda (78)	10
51	Melodisc 1164	Gold Coast Victory/Family Scandal (78)	10
51	Melodisc 1167	Family Scandal/Gold Coast Champion (78)	10
51	Melodisc 1183	Jamaica Hurricane/Pretty Woman (78)	12
51	Melodisc 1193	John Goddard Calypso/Some Girl (78)	10
51	Parlophone MP 112	Federation/Rum, More Rum (78, export)	12

MINT VALUE £

51	Melodisc 1211	Australia V. West Indies/One Morning (78)	10
51	Esquire 5-034	Randolph Turpin's Victory/West Indians And The Steel Band (78, with Kenny Graham's Afro-Cubists)	15
51	Esquire 5-041	Fifty Women To One Man/1951 Festival Of Britain (78, with Kenny Graham's Afro-Cubists)	15
53	Esquire 5-091	England Regains The Ashes/Nobody Wants To Grow Old (78)	15
54	Melodisc 1333	Sir Winston Churchill Calypso/Rhythm Dance (78)	15
54	Melodisc 1334	She Walks Like You/Tambourine (78)	12
50s	Parlophone MP 144	Africa/Syncopation (export 78)	12
60s	Melodisc CAL 1	Victory Test Match — Calypso/Sergeant Brown (reissue)	10

(see also Lord Kitchener)

LORD BRISCO(E)

64	Black Swan WI 447	Spiritual Mambo/BABA BROOKS: Fly Right	25
64	Black Swan WI 450	My Love Has Come/BABA BROOKS: Sweet Eileen	25
64	Black Swan WI 454	Trojan/I Am The Least	25
64	Island WI 131	Praise For I/Tell You The Story	22
65	Island WI 187	Jonah (The Master)/Mr. Cleveland	22

LORD BRYNNER & SHEIKS

66	Island WI 266	Congo War/Teach Me To Ska	18

(see also Roland Alphonso)

LORD BUCKLEY

62	Fontana 688 010ZL	IN CONCERT (LP)	20
67	Fontana TL 5396	BLOWING HIS MIND (AND YOURS, TOO) (LP)	20
70	Elektra 2410 002	THE BEST OF LORD BUCKLEY (LP)	15

LORD BURGESS & HIS SUN ISLANDERS

67	Pye Intl. NPL 28109	CALYPSO GO-GO (LP)	15

LORD CHARLES & HIS BAND

70s	Sound Of Jamaica JA 1	Jamaican Bits And Pieces/JA Island Soul	18

LORD COMIC

70	Bamboo BAM 66	Rhythm Rebellion/ROY RICHARDS: Reggae Children	18
70	Pressure Beat PR 5507	Jack Of My Trade/CYNTHIA RICHARDS: United We Stand	18

(see also Sir Lord Comic)

LORD COMPOSER & HIS SILVER SEAS HOTEL ORCHESTRA

51	Queenophone KIN 501	Hill & Gully Ride/Mandeville Road/Gal A Gully/Matilda (78)	10

LORD CREATOR

62	Island WI 001	Independant [sic] Jamaica Calypso/Remember (B-side is actually "Remember Your Mother And Father")	22
63	Kalypso XX 24	Peeping Tom/Second Hand Piano	8
64	Port-O-Jam PJ 4005	Rhythm Of the Blues/Simple Things	12
64	Port-O-Jam PJ 4119	Jamaica's Anniversary/Mother's Love	10
64	National Calypso NC 2001	Drive With Care/Sweet Jamaica	7
65	Blue Beat BB 292	Evening News/Good For Creator	18
65	Black Swan WI 463	Wicked Lady/MAYTALS: My Little Ruby	25
66	Doctor Bird DB 1029	Obeah Wedding/BERTRAM ENNIS COMBO: Part Two	8
67	Jump Up JU 503	Jamaica Jump Up/Laziest Man	8
67	Jump Up JU 524	Big Bamboo/Marjorie And Harry	8
76	Island WIP 6344	Big Pussy Sally/UPSETTERS: Big Pussy Dub	6

(see also Kentrick Patrick, Fabulous Flames)

LORD CRISTO

55	Calypsotime CG 702	Jumbee Jamboree/Mabel Break-up Me Table (78)	7
67	Jump Up JU 515	Dumb Boy And The Parrot/General Hospital	8
67	Jump Up JU 517	Election War Zone/Bad Luck Man	8

LORD DANIEL

60s	Kalypso XX 26	Small Island Gal	6

LORD FLEA & HIS CALYPSONIANS

57	Capitol CL 14704	The Naughty Little Flea/Shake Shake Senora	6
57	Capitol CL 14704	The Naughty Little Flea/Shake Shake Senora (78)	12

LORD FLY & HIS ORCHESTRA

54	Motta's 25	Mabel/The Little Fly (78)	7

LORD GANDA

57	Melodisc MEL 1417	Everybody Is Rockin' & Rollin'/Landlady Don't Steal My Clothes (78)	12

LORD INVADER & HIS CALYPSO RHYTHM BOYS

59	Pye N 15162	Teddy Boy Calypso/Reincarnation (The Bed Bug) (78)	7

(see also Fitzroy Alexander Melody)

LORD KITCHENER

50	Parlophone MP 102	Nora/LORD BEGINNER: The Dollar And The Pound (export 78)	12
50	Parlophone MP 103	Underground Train/LORD BEGINNER: I Will Die A Bachelor (export 78)	12
52	Melodisc MEL 1160	Kitch/Food From The West Indies (78)	10
52	Melodisc MEL 1222	Two Timing Josephine/The Tongue Mopsie (78)	10
53	Lyragon J 717	Alec Bedser Calypso/Mistress Jacob (78)	10
55	Melodisc MEL 1325	My Wife's Nightie/Sweet Home (78)	10
56	Melodisc MEL 1400	Rock 'n' Roll Calypso/Life Begins At Forty (78)	10
56	Melodisc MEL 1401	Romeo/Kitch's Calypso Medley (78)	10
59	Melodisc MEL 1498	Black Puddin'/Piccadilly Folk	7
59	Melodisc MEL 1538	If You're Brown/Come Back In The Morning	7
60	Melodisc MEL 1577	Jamaica Turkey/Edna What You Want	7
63	Melodisc CAL 2	Kitch/Rebound Wife	6
63	Melodisc CAL 3	Muriel And The Bug/Nora And The Yankee	6

MINT VALUE £

63 Melodisc CAL 4 Kitch Take It Easy/Redhead . . . 6
63 Melodisc CAL 5 Drink A Rum/Your Wife . . . 6
63 Melodisc CAL 6 Too Late Kitch/Saxophone Number Two . . . 6
63 Melodisc CAL 7 Wife And Mother/Mango Tree . . . 6
64 Melodisc CAL 10 Kitch Mambo Calypso/Ghana . . . 6
64 Melodisc CAL 11 Life Begins At Forty/Short Skirts . . . 6
64 Melodisc CAL 12 Romeo/Kitch Calypso Medley . . . 6
64 Melodisc CAL 14 Federation/Alfonso In Town . . . 6
64 Melodisc CAL 19 Black Puddin'/Piccadilly Folk . . . 6
64 Melodisc CAL 21 Come Back In The Morning/If You're Brown . . . 6
64 Melodisc CAL 22 Jamaica Turkey/Edna What You Want . . . 6
64 Melodisc CAL 23 Carnival/More Rice . . . 6
60s Jump Up JU 504 Love In The Cemetery/Jamaica Woman . . . 6
60s Jump Up JU 506 Road/Neighbour . . . 6
64 Jump Up JU 511 Dr. Kitch/Come Back Home Meh Boy . . . 5
65 Jump Up JU 530 Kitch You So Sweet/Ain't That Fun . . . 6
65 Aladdin WI 612 Dr. Kitch/Come Back Home Meh Boy (reissue) . . . 8
71 Duke DU 115 Dr. Kitch/Love In The Cemetary . . . 5
55 Melodisc MLP 500 KITCH — KING OF CALYPSO (10" LP) . . . 20
57 Melodisc MLP 510 KING OF CALYPSO VOL. 2 (10" LP) . . . 20
60s Melodisc 12-129 CALYPSOS TOO HOT TO HANDLE (LP) . . . 20
60s Melodisc 12-130 CALYPSOS TOO HOT TO HANDLE VOL. 2 (LP) . . . 20
60s Melodisc 12-199 CALYPSOS TOO HOT TO HANDLE (LP, reissue with extra tracks) . . . 20
60s Melodisc 12-200 CALYPSOS TOO HOT TO HANDLE VOL. 2 (LP, reissue with extra tracks) . . . 20
(see also Lord Beginner)

LORD KITCHENER/FITZROY COLEMAN BAND

56 no label City And United 1956/The Manchester Football Double (78) . . . 60

LORD LEBBY

58 Kalypso XX 05 Sweet Jamaica/Mama Want No Rice No Peas . . . 12
58 Kalypso XX 05 Sweet Jamaica/Mama Want No Rice No Peas (78) . . . 12
60 Starlite ST45 018 Caldonia/One Kiss For My Baby . . . 60

LORD MELODY

58 Melodisc MEL 1440 The Devil/No, No . . . 6
58 Melodisc MEL 1440 The Devil/No, No (78) . . . 10
58 Melodisc MEL 1449 Robbery/Men Company . . . 8
58 Melodisc MEL 1449 Robbery/Men Company (78) . . . 10
58 Melodisc MEL 1474 Do Able/Happy Holiday . . . 6
58 Melodisc MEL 1474 Do Able/Happy Holiday (78) . . . 12
59 Melodisc MEL 1491 I Confess/MIGHTY SPARROW: Goaty . . . 8
59 Melodisc MEL 1491 I Confess/MIGHTY SPARROW: Goaty (78) . . . 12
59 Melodisc MEL 1503 Tom Dooley/Jealous Woman . . . 6
59 Melodisc MEL 1504 Romeo/Knock On Any Door . . . 6
60 Kalypso XX 14 Rock 'N' Roll Calypso/Bo Bo Man . . . 5
60s Melodisc CAL 16 Happy Holiday/Do Able . . . 5

LORD NELSON

63 Stateside SS 189 I Got An Itch/Problems On My Mind . . . 12
64 Stateside SS 281 It's Delinquency/Proud West Indian . . . 12
68 Direction 58-3909 Michael/No Hot Summer . . . 6
64 Stateside SE 1024 PROUD WEST INDIAN (EP) . . . 30

LORD POWER

57 Kalypso XX 02 Chambolina/Penny Reel (78) . . . 12
58 Maracas M 20001 Special Amber Calypso/Mambo La-La (78) . . . 12
69 Coxsone CS 7079 Temptation/AL & VIBRATORS: Change Everything . . . 22

LORD RIGBY

60s Kalypso XX 29 The Milkman/Old Veterans . . . 6

LORD ROCKINGHAM'S XI

58 Decca F 11024 The Squelch/Fried Onions . . . 15
58 Decca F 11024 The Squelch/Fried Onions (78) . . . 12
58 Decca F 11059 Hoots Mon/Blue Train . . . 8
58 Decca F 11059 Hoots Mon/Blue Train (78) . . . 8
59 Decca F 11104 Wee Tom/Lady Rockingham, I Presume? . . . 15
59 Decca F 11104 Wee Tom/Lady Rockingham, I Presume? (78) . . . 12
59 Decca F 11139 Ra-Ra Rockingham/Farewell To Rockingham . . . 10
59 Decca F 11139 Ra-Ra Rockingham/Farewell To Rockingham (78) . . . 18
62 Decca F 11426 Newcastle Twist/Rockingham Twist . . . 10
58 Decca DFE 6555 OH BOY! (EP) . . . 45
68 Columbia S(C)X 6291 THE RETURN OF LORD ROCKINGHAM'S XI (LP, mono/stereo) . . . 40
(see also Robinson Crew, Harry Robinson)

LORD ROSE

60s Kalypso XX 25 Independent Jamaica/Twistin' Uncle . . . 5

LORDS

67 Columbia DB 8121 Don't Mince Matters/No One Knows . . . 80
68 Columbia DB 8367 Gloryland/Gypsy Boy . . . 18

LORD SITAR

68 Columbia SX/SCX 6256 LORD SITAR (LP) . . . 45

LORD SPOON

70 Escort ERT 839 Woman A Love In The Night Time/World On A Wheel . . . 6

LORD TANAMO

60 Kalypso XX 20 Blues Have Got Me Down/Sweet Dreaming . . . 12
64 Rio R 21 I Had A Dream/OSBOURNE GRAHAM: Be There . . . 18

64 Ska Beat JB 177 — Night Food Ska/My Business . . . 20
65 Ska Beat JB 217 — Mattie Rag/BABA BROOKS BAND: Mattie Rag . . . 20
65 Ska Beat JB 224 — I'm In The Mood For Ska/You Never Know . . . 40
66 Ska Beat JB 243 — Mother's Love/Downtown Gal . . . 18
60s Caribou CRC 3 — I Love You Truly/If You Were Only Mine . . . 20
71 Banana BA 319 — Keep On Moving/JACKIE MITTOO: Totaly [sic] Together . . . 15

LORELEI

74 CBS 2048 — S.T.O.P. (Stop)/I'll Never Let You Down . . . 7

SOPHIA LOREN

58 Philips PB 857 — Love Song From "Houseboat"/Bing! Bang! Bong! . . . 10
71 Warner Bros WB 8126 — Anyone/There Is A Star . . . 8
(see also Peter Sellers & Sophia Loren)

LORENZO

71 New Beat NB 094 — I Will Never Let You Down/This Magic Moment . . . 6
(see also Laurel Aitken)

LORI & CHAMELEONS

78 Zoo CAGE 006 — Touch/Love On The Ganges (p/s) . . . 7
79 Sire SIR 4025 — Touch/Love On The Ganges (p/s, reissue) . . . 5
80 Korova KOW 5 — The Lonely Spy/Peru (p/s) . . . 5
81 Korova KOW 20 — Touch/The Lonely Spy (p/s) . . . 5
81 Korova KOW 20T — Touch/The Lonely Spy/Love On The Ganges (12", p/s) . . . 8
(see also Teardrop Explodes, Bill Drummond)

NASH LORRAINE

59 Pye N 15235 — I'm New In The Ways Of Love/Belle From Barcelona (78) . . . 8

MYRNA LORRIE

55 London HLU 8187 — Underway/I'm Your Man, I'm Your Gal (B-side with Buddy DeVal) . . . 50
55 London HLU 8187 — Underway/I'm Your Man, I'm Your Gal (B-side with Buddy DeVal) (78) . . . 15
56 London HLU 8294 — Life's Changing Scene/Listen To My Heartstrings . . . 55
56 London HLU 8294 — Life's Changing Scene/Listen To My Heartstrings (78) . . . 15

LORRIES

79 Redball RR 016 — The Night/Steal You Anyway/Pushover/Idiot Dances (p/s) . . . 6

DICK LORY

56 London HLD 8348 — Cool It Baby/Ball Room Baby . . . 650
56 London HLD 8348 — Cool It Baby/Ball Room Baby (78) . . . 150
61 London HLG 9284 — My Last Date/Broken Hearted . . . 40
62 Liberty LIB 55415 — Handsome Guy/The Pain Is Here . . . 10
63 Liberty LIB 55529 — Welcome Home Again/I Got Over You . . . 10

LOS BRAVOS

(see under 'B')

JOE LOSS (& HIS ORCHESTRA)

61 HMV POP 959 — Twistin' The Mood/Everybody Twist . . . 6
61 HMV POP 995 — The Maigret Theme/Along The Bouvelard . . . 6
63 HMV POP 1192 — Steptoe And Son/Phase Four . . . 6
64 HMV POP 1351 — March Of The Mods/Tango '65 . . . 6
65 HMV POP 1389 — A Shot In The Dark/Drum Diddley . . . 5
65 HMV POP 1470 — Let's Kick/Just For Kicks . . . 5
66 HMV POP 1500 — "Thunderbirds" Theme/"The Avengers" Theme . . . 22
66 HMV POP 1517 — The England World Cup March/Auld Lang Syne (March) . . . 30
62 HMV 7EG 8749 — TWISTING AT THE PALAIS (EP) . . . 8
62 HMV CLP 1636/CSD 1490 — MUST BE MADISON – MUST BE TWIST (LP) . . . 12

LOST CHEREES

83 Riot RIOT 3 — No Fighting No War (EP) . . . 5
84 Mortarhate MORT 3 — A MAN'S DUTY ... A WOMAN'S PLACE (EP) . . . 5
85 Mortarhate MORT 12 — UNWANTED CHILDREN (12" EP, with inner) . . . 8
84 Fight Back FIGHT 6 — ALL PART OF GROWING UP (LP, with lyric inner) . . . 12

LOST JOCKEY

82 Operation Twilight OPT 11 — Professor Slack/Rise And Fall/Animal/Behaviour And Crude Din (p/s) . . . 8

LOTHAR & THE HAND PEOPLE

69 Capitol CL 15610 — Sdrawkcab (Backwards)/Today Is Only Yesterday's Tomorrow . . . 15
69 Capitol E-ST 247 — SPACE HYMN (LP) . . . 45

DENNIS LOTIS

54 Decca F 10287 — Such A Night/Cuddle Me (with Ted Heath Music & Johnston Brothers) . . . 20
54 Decca F 10392 — Honey Love/Manhattan Mambo (with Ted Heath Music) . . . 18
55 Decca F 10469 — Face Of An Angel, Heart Of A Devil/The Golden Ring . . . 15
55 Decca F 10471 — Chain Reaction/Go, Go, Go (with Ted Heath Music) . . . 15
56 Pye 7N 15053 — Green Grows The Grass/No Other Love Can Take Your Place . . . 8
57 Columbia DB 3993 — Tammy/I Complain . . . 7
57 Columbia DB 4056 — Valentina/Good Mornin' Life . . . 7
58 Columbia DB 4090 — I May Never Pass This Way Again/Gretna Green . . . 5
58 Columbia DB 4158 — The Only Man On The Island/Guessing What The Neighbours'll Say . . . 5
58 Columbia DB 4182 — Safe In The Arms Of My Darling/Belonging To Someone . . . 5
59 Columbia DB 4277 — Moonlight Serenade/Danger Within . . . 5
59 Columbia DB 4277 — Moonlight Serenade/Danger Within (78) . . . 10
59 Columbia DB 4339 — Who Is? You Are!/Too Much . . . 5
60 Columbia DB 4432 — I Wish It Were You/Love Me A Little . . . 5
60 Columbia DB 4507 — Strangers When We Meet/Two Wrongs Don't Make A Right . . . 5
61 Columbia DB 4626 — Where Are You/Love's A Secret Game . . . 5
69 Polydor 56346 — One Woman Man/The Finger Points At You . . . 5
56 Pye NEP 24017 — PRESENTING DENNIS LOTIS (EP) . . . 18

MINT VALUE £

57	Pye NEP 24043	LET'S BE HAPPY (EP)	15
57	Pye NEP 24046	HOW ABOUT YOU (EP)	18
57	Pye NEP 24053	HOW ABOUT YOU PT. 2 (EP)	18
57	Pye NEP 24055	HOW ABOUT YOU PT. 3 (EP)	18
59	Columbia SEG 7955	HALLELUJAH IT'S DENNIS LOTIS (EP)	15
57	Nixa NPL 18002	HOW ABOUT YOU (LP)	40
58	Columbia 33SX 1089	BIDIN' MY TIME (LP)	30

(see also Johnstone Brothers)

PETER LOTIS

60	Ember EMB S 110	Doo-Dah/You're Singing Our Love Song To Somebody Else (some with p/s)	10/6

LOT 39 (STRANGERS)

60s	Eyemark EMS 1004	I'll Get Over You/I Still Love You	6

LOTUS EATERS

84	Sylvan SYL 2	You Don't Need Someone New/Two Virgins Tender (picture disc)	5
84	Sylvan SYL 4	Out Of Your Own/Endless (picture disc)	5
85	Arista FS 5	It Hurts/Evidence//The Soul In Sparks/Church At Llanbadrig (double pack)	5
84	Sylvan 206 263	NO SENSE OF SIN (LP)	12

(see also Wild Swans, Care)

BONNIE LOU

53	Parlophone MSP 6021	Seven Lonely Days/Dancin' With Someone	45
53	Parlophone MSP 6036	Hand-Me-Down Heart/Scrap Of Paper	45
53	Parlophone MSP 6048	Tennessee Wig Walk/Just Out Of Reach	70
53	Parlophone MSP 6051	Pa-Paya Mama/Since You Said Goodbye	40
54	Parlophone MSP 6072	The Texas Polka/No Heart At All	35
54	Parlophone MSP 6095	Don't Stop Kissing Me Goodnight/The Welcome Mat	35
54	Parlophone MSP 6108	No One/Huckleberry Pie	35
54	Parlophone MSP 6117	Blue Tennessee Rain/Wait For Me, Darling	35
54	Parlophone R 3895	Blue Tennessee Rain/Wait For Me, Darling (78)	12
54	Parlophone MSP 6132	Two Step — Side Step/Please Don't Laugh When I Cry	30
54	Parlophone R 3931	Two Step — Side Step/Please Don't Laugh When I Cry (78)	12
55	Parlophone MSP 6151	Tennessee Mambo/Train Whistle Blues	35
55	Parlophone R 3975	Tennessee Mambo/Train Whistle Blues (78)	12
55	Parlophone MSP 6157	Tweedle Dee/The Finger Of Suspicion Points At You	40
55	Parlophone R 3989	Tweedle Dee/The Finger Of Suspicion Points At You (78)	15
55	Parlophone R 4012	A Rusty Old Halo/Danger! Heartbreak Ahead (78)	15
55	Parlophone MSP 6173	Drop Me A Line/Old Faithful And True Love	22
55	Parlophone R 4037	Drop Me A Line/Old Faithful And True Love (78)	10
55	Parlophone MSP 6178	The Barnyard Hop/Tell The World	20
55	Parlophone R 4054	The Barnyard Hop/Tell The World (78)	10
55	Parlophone MSP 6188	Dancin' In My Socks/Daddy-O	40
55	Parlophone R 4096	Dancin' In My Socks/Daddy-O (78)	18
56	Parlophone MSP 6223	Darlin' Why/Miss The Love (That I've Been Dreaming Of)	20
56	Parlophone R 4146	Darlin' Why/Miss The Love (That I've Been Dreaming Of) (78)	10
56	Parlophone MSP 6234	Bo Weevil (A Country Song)/Chaperon	35
56	Parlophone R 4168	Bo Weevil (A Country Song)/Chaperon (78)	18
56	Parlophone MSP 6253	Lonesome Lover/Little Miss Bobby Sox	25
56	Parlophone R 4194	Lonesome Lover/Little Miss Bobby Sox (78)	15
56	Parlophone R 4215	No Rock 'N' Roll Tonight/One Track Love	22
56	Parlophone R 4215	No Rock 'N' Roll Tonight/One Track Love (78)	15
57	Parlophone R 4350	Teenage Wedding/Runnin' Away	22
57	Parlophone R 4350	Teenage Wedding/Runnin' Away (78)	18
58	Parlophone DP 545	I'm Available/Waiting In Vain (export issue)	35

BONNIE LOU & RUSTY YORK

58	Parlophone R 4409	Let The School Bell Ring Ding-A-Ling/La Dee Dah	80
58	Parlophone R 4409	Let The School Bell Ring Ding-A-Ling/La Dee Dah (78)	35

(see also Rusty York)

JOHN D. LOUDERMILK

61	RCA RCA 1269	The Language Of Love/Darling Jane	8
62	RCA RCA 1287	Thou Shalt Not Steal/Mister Jones	7
62	RCA RCA 1323	Angela Jones/Road Hog	10
68	RCA RCA 1761	Sidewalks/The Odd Folks Of Okracoke	8
62	RCA RD 27248/SF 5123	THE LANGUAGE OF LOVE (LP)	40
62	RCA Victor RD/SF 7515	TWELVE SIDES OF JOHN D. LOUDERMILK (LP)	35
67	RCA Victor RD/SF 7890	SINGS A BIZARRE COLLECTION OF SONGS (LP)	22
70	RCA LSA 3159	THE BEST OF JOHN D. LOUDERMILK (LP)	12
75	RCA LSA 3220	ENCORES (LP)	12

(see also Johnny Dee)

LOUDEST WHISPER

74	Polydor	CHILDREN OF LIR (LP, Ireland-only)	700-750
81	Polydor 2908 043	LOUDEST WHISPER (LP, Ireland-only)	250
83	Fiona 011	HARD TIMES (LP, with insert, Ireland-only)	250

LOUDNESS

84	Music For Nations MFN 22	DISILLUSION (LP)	12

JOE HILL LOUIS

65	Bootleg 502	Heartache Baby/I Feel Like A Million (99 copies only)	40
60s	Advent LP 2803	MEMPHIS BLUES AND BREAKDOWNS (LP)	60

JOE HILL LOUIS

74	Polydor 2383 214	BLUE IN THE MORNING (LP)	30

(see also Willie Nix)

LOUISE

96	EMI EMLH 397	Light Of My Life/Real Love (jukebox only, no p/s)	6
96	EMI CDEM 454	Light Of My Life/Real Love (Tin Tin Out Remix)/Real Love (Stonebridge Remix)/Interview with Louise (CD, with 3 prints)	8
97	EMI LOUPREM 101	SOFT & GENTLE: One Kiss From Louise Pop Megamix/Naked (Tony De Vit Mix)/Real Love (CD, promo/freebie)	10
97	EMI EMLH 490	Arms Around The World (Radio Mix)/Naked (Radio Mix) (jukebox only, no p/s)	5
97	EMI 12EMDJ 490	Arms Around The World (Rated PG Club Mix)/Arms Around The World (Rated PG Dub Mix) (12", p/s, promo only)	8
97	EMI 12DJD 490	Arms Around The World (Farley & Heller's Fire Island Vocal Mix)/ Arms Around The World (Farley & Heller's Roach Motel Dub)/ ArmsAround The World (T-Empo Club Mix)/Arms Around The World (T-Empo Dub Mix) (12", doublepack, p/s promo only)	8
97	EMI 12EMDJ 500	Let's Go Round Again (Colour Systems Inc. Gold Mix)/Let's Go Round Again (Rated PG Club Mix)/(Rated PG Mr. G Dub) (12", p/s, promo only)	8
97	EMI 12EMDJD 500	Let's Go Round Again (Colour Systems Inc. Amber Vox Mix)/ (187 Lockdown Dub Mix)/(Paul Gotel's Peaceful Warrior Mix)/ (187 Lockdown Vocal Mix)/(Colour Systems Inc. Amber Dub)/ (Paul Gotel's Warrior Dub) (12", double pack, p/s, promo only)	10
98	EMI 12EMDJD 506	All That Matters (DJ Tonka Mix)/All That Matters (Cas Roc Vocal Mix)/ All That Matters (Hex Hector Dub Revisited Mix)/All That Matters (Cas Roc Vocal Mix) (12" double pack, p/s, promo only)	10

LOUISIANA RED

64	Columbia DB 7270	Keep Your Hands Off My Woman/Don't Cry	35
64	Sue WI 337	I Done Woke Up/I Had A Feeling	35
64	Columbia 33SX 1612	LOWDOWN BACK PORCH BLUES (LP)	55
72	Atlantic K 40436	SINGS THE BLUES (LP)	20
72	Carnival 2941 002	THE SEVENTH SON (LP)	20

LOUISIANA SUGAR BABIES

57	HMV 7EG 8215	LOUISIANA SUGAR BABIES (EP, with Fats Waller & James P. Johnson)	15

JACQUES LOUSSIER

66	Decca F 22383	Air On A G String/Prelude No. 16 (Bach)	10
69	Decca F 22876	Air On A G String/Prelude No. 16 (Bach) (reissue)	6

LOUVIN BROTHERS

59	Capitol CL 14989	Knoxville Girl/I Wish It Had Been A Dream	20
59	Capitol CL 15078	You're Learning/My Curly Headed Baby	6
56	Capitol EAP1 769	TRAGIC SONGS OF LIFE (EP)	25
58	Capitol EAP1 910	IRA AND CHARLIE (EP)	25
59	Capitol EAP1 1106	COUNTRY LOVE BALLADS (EP)	20

LOVABLES

68	Stateside SS 2108	You're The Cause Of It/Beautiful Idea	20

LOVE

SINGLES

66	London HLZ 10053	My Little Red Book/Hey Joe	25
66	London HLZ 10073	7 And 7 Is/No. Fourteen	30
67	Elektra EKSN 45010	She Comes In Colours/Orange Skies	25
67	Elektra EKSN 45016	Softly To Me/The Castle	20
68	Elektra EKSN 45024	Alone Again Or/Bummer In The Summer	15
68	Elektra EKSN 45026	The Daily Planet/Andmoreagain	18
68	Elektra EKSN 45038	Laughing Stock/Your Mind And We Belong Together	30
70	Elektra EKSN 45086	I'm With You/Robert Montgomery	10
70	Harvest HAR 5014	Stand Out/Doggone	8
70	Harvest HAR 5030	The Everlasting First/Keep On Shining	12
70	Elektra 2101 019	Alone Again Or/Bummer In The Summer (reissue)	5
73	Elektra K 12113	Alone Again Or/Andmoreagain	5
75	RSO 2090 151	Time Is Like A River/You Said You Would	5

ORIGINAL LPs

66	Elek. EKL 4001/EKS 74001	LOVE (LP, gold label, U.K disc in U.S. sleeve)	60
67	Elek. EKL 4005/EKS 74005	DA CAPO (LP, orange label, with U.K. or U.S. sleeve)	55
67	Elek. EKL 4013/EKS 74013	FOREVER CHANGES (LP, orange label)	50
69	Elektra EKL 4049	FOUR SAIL (LP, orange label, mono, existence unconfirmed)	40+
69	Elektra EKS 74049	FOUR SAIL (LP, orange label, stereo)	40
70	Harvest SHDW 3/4	OUT HERE (2-LP, gatefold sleeve)	35
71	Harvest SHVL 787	FALSE START (LP, gatefold sleeve)	25
71	Elektra 2469 009	LOVE REVISITED (LP, gatefold sleeve)	15
73	Elektra K 32002	LOVE MASTERS (LP)	12
74	RSO 2394 145	REEL TO REAL (LP)	15

RE-PRESSINGS

67	Elek. EKL 4001/EKS 74001	LOVE (LP, orange label, with U.K. or U.S. sleeve)	35
72	Elektra K 42068	LOVE (LP, 'butterfly' label)	12
71	Elektra EKS 74005	DA CAPO (LP, 'butterfly' label)	15
72	Elektra K 42011	DA CAPO (LP, 'butterfly' label)	12
72	Elektra K 42015	FOREVER CHANGES (LP, 'butterfly' label)	12
72	Elektra K 42030	FOUR SAIL (LP, 'butterfly' label)	12

(see also Arthur Lee)

LOVE

90	Fierce FRIGHT 036	Welsh Girl (1-sided, p/s in bag, hand-finished labels, mail-order only)	20

CHRISTOPHER LOVE

69	London HLU 10263	The Curse Goes On/You May Be The Next	10

MINT VALUE £

DARLENE LOVE

63	London HLU 9725	(Today I Met) The Boy I'm Gonna Marry/Playing For Keeps	35
63	London HLU 9765	Wait 'Til My Bobby Gets Home/Take It From Me	35
63	London HLU 9815	A Fine Fine Boy/Marshmallow World	30
69	London HLU 10244	Wait 'Til My Bobby Gets Home/(Today I Met) The Boy I'm Gonna Marry	15
74	Warner Bros/Spector K 19011	Christmas (Baby Please Come Home)/Wait Till My Bobby Comes Home (blue vinyl)	5
77	Phil Spector Intl. 2010 019	Lord If You're A Woman/Johnny Baby	5
77	Phil Spector Intl. 2010 019	Lord If You're A Woman/Johnny Baby (12", some copies 1-sided)	15
88	CBS 6529357	He's Sure The Man I Love (New Version)/Everybody Needs (p/s)	5
90	Warner Brothers W 9535	Mr Fix-It/k.d. lang with TAKE SIX: Ridin' The Rails (some with p/s)	20/15
64	London RE-U 1411	WAIT TILL MY BOBBY GETS HOME (EP)	200

(see also Bob B. Soxx & Blue Jeans, Crystals, Phil Spector, Blossoms, Allisons [U.S.], Date With Soul, Cinders)

GARFIELD LOVE & JIMMY SPRUILL

69	Blue Horizon 57-3150	Next Time You See Me/Part Time Love	35

LOVE AND WAR

80s	SRT SRT9KS 2323	Touch Of Class (p/s)	125

GEOFF LOVE ORCHESTRA

57	Conquest CP 105	Baffi/Dancing Thru' (78)	7
61	Columbia DB 4627	Coronation Street Theme/Sophia	5
62	Columbia DB 4881	Steptoe And Son/Over The Backyard Fence	6
70	Columbia DB 8707	Coronation Street Theme/ALIRIO DIAZ: Aranjuez Mon Amour (Rodgigo)	5
74	EMI EMI 2105	Match Of The Day/Bless This House	6

(see also Mandingo, Manuel & Music Of The Mountains)

JILL BABY LOVE

76	Black Magic BM 116	My Way Or Hit The Highway (Parts 1 & 2)	5

MARY LOVE

65	King KG 1024	You Turned My Bitter Into Sweet/I'm In Your Hands	100
67	Stateside SS 2009	Lay This Burden Down/Think It Over Baby	40
68	Stateside SS 2135	The Hurt Is Just Beginning/If You Change Your Mind	25
82	Kent TOWN 501	You Turned My Bitter Into Sweet/SWEETHEARTS: This Couldn't Be Me	5

MIKE LOVE

83	Creole CR 61	Jingle Bell Rock/Let's Party (p/s)	5

(see also Beach Boys)

RONNIE LOVE

61	London HLD 9272	Chills And Fever/Pledging My Love	25
78	Grapevine GRP 108	Let's Make Love/Nothing To It	8

WILLIE LOVE/WILLIE NIX

66	Highway 51 H 700	THE TWO WILLIES FROM MEMPHIS (LP, 99 copies only)	75

(see also Willie Nix)

LOVE AFFAIR

67	Decca F 12558	She Smiled Sweetly/Satisfaction Guaranteed	65
67	CBS 3125	Everlasting Love/Gone Are The Songs Of Yesterday	6
68	CBS 3366	Rainbow Valley/Someone Like Us (some in p/s)	20/8
68	CBS 3674	A Day Without Love/I'm Happy	6
69	CBS 3994	One Road/Let Me Know	6
69	CBS 4300	Bringing On Back The Good Times/Another Day	6
69	CBS 4631	Baby I Know/Accept Me For What I Am	7
70	CBS 4780	Lincoln County/Sea Of Tranquility	6
70	Pye 7N 45218	Let Me Dance/Love's Looking Out At You	8
71	Parlophone R 5887	Wake Me I Am Dreaming/That's My Home	12
71	Parlophone R 5918	Help (Get Me Some Help)/Long Way Home	12
73	CBS 1144	Everlasting Love/Bringing On Back The Good Times (p/s, 'Hall Of Fame Hits' series)	5
77	Creole CR 146	Private Lives/Let A Little Love Come In	5
68	CBS 63416	THE EVERLASTING LOVE AFFAIR (LP, mono/stereo)	25

(see also L.A., Ellis, Steve Ellis, Elastic Band, Widowmaker, Morgan, Phillip Goodhand-Tait, English Rose, Rainbow Ffolly)

LOVE CHILDREN

69	Deram DM 268	Easy Squeezy/Every Little Step	15
70	Deram DM 303	Paper Chase/My Turkey Snuffed It	10

LOVE COMMITTEE

76	Ariola AA 105	Can't Win For Losing/Love Wins Every Time	5

LOVECUT D.B.

91	Suburbs Of Hell SOH 009EP	Heartspin/Heartspin (Dripping Clock Mix)/(Marisco Disco Mix)/ (Porn Cable Mix) (12", p/s)	10

(see also Sarah Cracknell, St. Etienne)

LOVE GENERATION (Jamaica)

73	Grape GR 3046	Money Raper/HEPTONES: The Magnificent Heptones 3 In One	5
73	Grape GR 3041	Warrika Hill/Battlefield (Third And Fourth Generation)	5

LOVE GENERATION (U.S.)

67	Liberty LBF 15018	She Touched Me/The Love In Me	10
68	Liberty LBL/LBS 83121E	LOVE GENERATION (LP)	20

JOY LOVEJOY

72	Chess 6145 010	In Orbit/Uh! Hum	6

LOVELITES

78	Grapevine GRP 107	Get It Off My Conscience/Oh, What A Day	15

TONY LOVELLO

59 Top Rank JAR 200 — Amore Mio/Dreamy Serenade 6
59 Top Rank JAR 200 — Amore Mio/Dreamy Serenade (78) 10

LOVE OF LIFE ORCHESTRA

80 Infidelity JMB 227 — EXTENDED NICETIES (12" EP) 8
(see also David Byrne)

JOHNNY LOVER

70 Amalgamated AMG 871 — Pumpkin Eater/Version 20
70 Amalgamated AMG 873 — Two Edged Sword/Version 20
(see also Little Johnny Jones, Heptones)

LOVERS

58 Vogue Pop V 9111 — Let's Elope/I Wanna Be Loved 700
58 Vogue Pop V 9111 — Let's Elope/I Wanna Be Loved (78) 175

LOVE SCULPTURE

68 Parlophone R 5664 — River To Another Day/Brand New Woman 30
68 Parlophone R 5731 — Wang-Dang-Doodle/The Stumble 20
68 Parlophone R 5744 — Sabre Dance/Think Of Love 6
69 Parlophone R 5807 — Seagull/Farandole 15
70 Parlophone R 5831 — In The Land Of The Few/People People 18
68 Parlophone PMC/PCS 7059 — BLUES HELPING (LP, 1st pressing, yellow/black label, mono/stereo) 40/30
69 Parlophone PCS 7090 — FORMS AND FEELINGS (LP, 1st pressing, yellow/black label) 30
70 Parlophone PCS 7059 — BLUES HELPING (LP, 2nd pressing, silver/black label) 12
70 Parlophone PCS 7090 — FORMS AND FEELINGS (LP, 2nd pressing, silver/black label) 12
(see also Human Beans, Dave Edmunds)

EDDIE LOVETTE

69 Big Shot BI 519 — You're My Girl/Let Them Say 10
70 London HLU 10298 — Boomerang/Together 10
70 London HLJ 10311 — Too Experienced/Little Blue Bird 10
70 London HA-J 8413 — TOO EXPERIENCED (LP, unissued)
70 London LGJ/ZGJ 103 — TOO EXPERIENCED (LP) 20

LOVE UNLIMITED

72 Uni UNLS 124 — FROM A GIRL'S POINT OF VIEW — LOVE UNLIMITED (LP) 12
73 Pye NSPL 28179 — UNDER THE INFLUENCE OF LOVE UNLIMITED (LP) 12
74 20th Century BT 443 — IN HEAT (LP) 12

LOVEY AUSTIN BLUE SERENADERS/STATE STREET RAMBLERS

60s Collector JE 123 — SMALL JAZZ BANDS VOL. 1 (EP) 8

LENE LOVICH

76 Polydor 2058 812 — I Saw Mommy Kissing Santa Claus/The Christmas Song (Merry Christmas To You)/Happy Christmas 10
78 Stiff BUYJ 32 — I Think We're Alone Now (Japanese)/Lucky Number (mail-order promo only) 10

LOVIN'

67 Page One POF 035 — Keep On Believing/I'm In Command 35
67 Page One POF 041 — All I've Got/Do It Again 50
(see also Nerve)

LOVING AWARENESS

76 More Love ML 001 — LOVING AWARENESS (LP, gatefold sleeve with 2 posters) 15
(see also Glencoe, Skip Bifferty, Ian Dury)

LOVING KIND

66 Piccadilly 7N 35299 — Accidental Love/Nothing Can Change This Love 15
66 Piccadilly 7N 35318 — I Love The Things You Do/Treat Me Nice 18
66 Piccadilly 7N 35342 — Ain't That Peculiar/With Rhyme And Reason 20
(see also Noel Redding Band, Freddie Lennon)

LOVIN' SPOONFUL

65 Pye International 7N 25327 — Do You Believe In Magic?/On The Road Again 12
66 Pye International 7N 25344 — You Didn't Have To Be So Nice/My Gal 12
66 Pye International 7N 25361 — Daydream/Night Owl Blues 6
66 Kama Sutra KAS 200 — Summer In The City/Bald Headed Lena 7
66 Kama Sutra KAS 201 — Rain On The Roof/Warm Baby 6
67 Kama Sutra KAS 204 — Nashville Cats/Full Measure 7
67 Kama Sutra KAS 207 — Darling Be Home Soon/Darlin' Companion 7
67 Kama Sutra KAS 208 — Six O'Clock/The Finale 7
67 Kama Sutra KAS 210 — She Is Still A Mystery/Only Pretty, What A Pity 8
67 Kama Sutra KAS 211 — Money/Close Your Eyes 8
68 Kama Sutra KAS 213 — Never Going Back/Forever 10
66 Kama Sutra KEP 300 — DID YOU EVER HAVE TO MAKE UP YOUR MIND (EP) 22
66 Kama Sutra KEP 301 — JUG BAND MUSIC (EP) 30
66 Kama Sutra KEP 302 — SUMMER IN THE CITY (EP) 30
67 Kama Sutra KEP 303 — DAY BLUES (EP) 30
67 Kama Sutra KEP 304 — NASHVILLE CATS (EP) 35
67 Kama Sutra KEP 305 — LOVIN' YOU (EP) 35
67 Kama Sutra KEP 306 — SOMETHING IN THE NIGHT (EP) 35
65 Pye Intl. NPL 28069 — DO YOU BELIEVE IN MAGIC? (LP) 30
66 Pye Intl. NPL 28078 — DAYDREAM (LP) 30
67 Kama Sutra KLP 401 — HUMS OF THE LOVIN' SPOONFUL (LP) 30
67 Kama Sutra KLP 402 — YOU'RE A BIG BOY NOW (LP, soundtrack) 30
67 Kama Sutra KLP 403 — THE BEST OF THE LOVIN' SPOONFUL (LP) 15
68 Kama Sutra KLP 404 — EVERYTHING PLAYING (LP) 20
68 Kama Sutra K(S)LP 405 — THE BEST OF THE LOVIN' SPOONFUL VOL. 2 (LP) 15
69 Kama Sutra 602 009 — REVELATION: REVOLUTION '69 (LP) 15
(see also John Sebastian, Mugwumps, Zalman Yanovsky, Even Dozen Jug Band)

MINT VALUE £

BRUCE LOW
56 HMV JO 464 — Just Walking In The Rain/Cindy Oh Cindy (export issue) . . . 20

LOWBITES
70 Black Swan BW 1403 — I Got It/I Got It (Version) . . . 12

ARTHUR LOWE
72 Columbia DB 8956 — My Little Girl, My Little Boy/How I Won The War . . . 6
69 World Record Club ST 1008 — BLESS 'EM ALL! (LP) . . . 12

DENNIS LOWE
70 Downtown DT 465 — What's Your Name/MUSIC DOCTORS: Mr Locabe . . . 10
70 Downtown DT 468 — Stand Up For The Sound/OWEN & DENNIS: Old Man Trouble . . . 10

JEZ LOWE & THE BAD PENNIES
90 Fellside FE 079 — BRIEFLY ON THE STREET (LP) . . . 12

JIM LOWE
55 London HLD 8171 — Close The Door/Nueva Laredo (gold label print) . . . 60
55 London HLD 8171 — Close The Door/Nueva Laredo (78) . . . 15
56 London HLD 8276 — Blue Suede Shoes/Maybellene (silver label print) . . . 100
56 London HLD 8276 — Blue Suede Shoes/Maybellene (78) . . . 30
56 London HLD 8288 — Love Is The $64,000 Dollar Question/Rene La Rue (gold label print) . . . 75
56 London HLD 8288 — Love Is The $64,000 Dollar Question/Rene La Rue (78) . . . 15
56 London HLD 8317 — The Green Door/The Little Man In Chinatown (as Jim Lowe & High Fives, gold label print, later silver) . . . 55/30
56 London HLD 8317 — The Green Door/The Little Man In Chinatown (78) . . . 10
57 London HLD 8368 — I Feel The Beat/By You, By You, By You (gold label print, later silver) . . . 45/30
57 London HLD 8368 — I Feel The Beat/By You, By You, By You (78) . . . 12
57 London HLD 8431 — Four Walls/Talkin' To The Blues . . . 30
57 London HLD 8431 — Four Walls/Talkin' To The Blues (78) . . . 15
58 London HLD 8538 — Roc-A-Chicka/The Bright Light (with Billy Vaughan's Orchestra) . . . 125
58 London HLD 8538 — Roc-A-Chicka/The Bright Light (with Billy Vaughan's Orchestra) (78) . . . 40
60 London HLD 9043 — He'll Have To Go/(This Life Is Just A) Dress Rehearsal . . . 15
65 United Artists UP 1096 — Mr Moses/Make Your Back Strong . . . 6
58 London HA-D 2108 — SONGS THEY SING BEHIND THE GREEN DOOR (LP) . . . 50
59 London HA-D 2146 — WICKED WOMEN (LP) . . . 35

(see also John Barry Seven)

PETER LOWE
57 Parlophone R 4270 — The Banana Boat Song/The Wisdom Of A Fool . . . 6

SAMMY LOWE
61 RCA RCA 1239 — Hey Lawdy Lawdy Mary . . . 20

LOWLIFE
88 LOLIF DEMO 1 — THE DEMOS (LP, white label test pressings only, hand-written white sleeve) . . . 25

LOW NOISE
81 Happy Birthday UR 5 — Jungle Line/Urban Tribal/Jungle Line (Instrumental) (12", p/s) . . . 8

LOW NUMBERS
79 Warner Brothers K 17493 — Keep In Touch/Nine All Out (p/s) . . . 40

PHILIP LOWRIE
63 Ember EMB S 179 — I Might Have Known (Before)/I Might Have Known (After) . . . 10

ART LOWRY
54 Columbia SCMC 1 — The Curse Of An Aching Heart/Heart Of My Heart (export issue) . . . 10

HENRY LOWTHER BAND
70 Deram SML 1070 — CHILD SONG (LP) . . . 85

(see also Manfred Mann, John Mayall & Bluesbreakers, Keef Hartley Band, Ricotti & Albuquerque)

MARK LOYD
65 Parlophone R 5277 — I Keep Thinking About You/Will It Be The Same . . . 7
65 Parlophone R 5332 — Everybody Tries/She Said No . . . 12
66 Parlophone R 5423 — When Evening Falls/When I'm Gonna Find Her . . . 160

L7
92 Slash LASH34 — Pretend We're Dead/Shit List . . . 6
92 Slash LASHX34 — Pretend We're Dead/Shit List/Lopsided Head/Mr Integrity (12", p/disc, w/insert) . 10
92 Slash LASCD34 — Pretend We're Dead/Shit List/Lopsided Head/Mr Integrity (CD p/disc, no'd slv.) . . . 8
92 Slash LASH 36 — Everglade/Freak Magnet (green vinyl, numbered) . . . 5
92 Slash LASHX 36 — Everglade/Freak Magnet (12", picture disc, numbered) . . . 10
92 Slash LASXP 36 — Everglade/Freak Magnet/Scrap (12", 33rpm etched disc) . . . 8
92 Slash LASH 38 — Monster/Used To Love Him (numbered green vinyl) . . . 6
92 Slash LASHX 38 — Monster/Used To Love Him/Diet Pill (12", picture disc, numbered card insert) . . . 10
92 Slash LASCD 38 — Monster/Used To Love Him/Diet Pill (CD picture disc, numbered sleeve) . . . 10
92 Slash LACDP42 — PRETEND WE'RE DEAD (CD EP gatefold digipak) . . . 10
92 Slash LASCD42 — PRETEND WE'RE DEAD (CD EPpicture disc, unnumbered sleeve) . . . 10
94 Slash LASH 48 — Andres/The Bomb (poster sleeve, numbered green vinyl) . . . 5
94 Slash 8576531 — Andres/The Bomb/interview (12", poly sleeve, green vinyl, no'd card insert) . . . 10

JEREMY LUBBOCK
58 Parlophone R 4399 — Catch A Falling Star/The Man Who Invented Love . . . 6
58 Parlophone R 4399 — Catch A Falling Star/The Man Who Invented Love (78) . . . 8
58 Parlophone R 4421 — Lemon Twist/Tonight . . . 6
58 Parlophone R 4421 — Lemon Twist/Tonight (78) . . . 8
58 Parlophone R 4473 — Odd Man Out/Too Bad You're Not Around . . . 6
58 Parlophone R 4473 — Odd Man Out/Too Bad You're Not Around (78) . . . 8
58 Parlophone GEP 8745 — JUST FOR THE FUN OF IT (EP) . . . 15

LUCAS (& MIKE COTTON SOUND)
66 Polydor 56114 I Saw Pity In The Face Of A Friend/Dance Children Dance (solo) . . . 20
67 Pye 7N 17313 Step Out Of Line/Ain't Love Good, Ain't Love Proud . . . 50
68 MGM MGM 1398 Soul Serenade/We Got A Thing Going Baby . . . 35
68 MGM MGM 1427 Jack And The Beanstalk/Mother-In-Law . . . 20
(see also Mike Cotton Sound, Artwoods)

BUDDY LUCAS BAND
53 London L 1181 Organ Grinder's Swing/Laura (78, as Buddy Lucas & His Orchestra) . . . 40
60 Pye International 7N 25045 I Want To Know/Deacon John . . . 12
60 Pye International N 25045 I Want To Know/Deacon John (78) . . . 20

TREVOR LUCAS
66 Reality RE 505 Waltzing Matilda/It's On . . . 30
66 Reality RY 1002 OVERLANDER (LP) . . . 300
(see also Eclection, Fotheringay, Fairport Convention, Bronco, Bunch, Sandy Denny)

LUCID DREAM
91 Euphoric E 9999T DRIPPY EP (12", p/s) . . . 8

LUCIFER
71 Lucifer L 001 Don't Care/Hypnosis . . . 8
72 Lucifer L 003/004 Fuck You/Bad . . . 8
72 Lucifer L 005/006 Prick/Want It . . . 8
72 Lucifer L 005/006/L 003/004 Prick/Want It//Fuck You/Bad (double pack, black box set) . . . 40
72 Lucifer LLP 1 BIG GUN (LP, private pressing, with poster/inserts, sold via *Oz* mag) . . . 60
72 Lucifer LLP 2 EXIT (LP, private pressing, with poster, sold via *Oz* magazine) . . . 80

LUCIFER'S FRIEND
71 Philips 6003 092 Ride The Sky/Horla . . . 15
71 Philips 6305 068 LUCIFER'S FRIEND (LP) . . . 18
(see also John Lawton, Uriah Heep)

JOHNNY LUCK
58 Fontana H 110 Play Rough/Buzz, Buzz, Buzz (78) . . . 15

LUCY
77 Lightning GIL 516 Never Never/Feel So Good (p/s) . . . 20
78 B&C BCS 8 Really Got Me Goin'/Oy (p/s) . . . 10
(see also Def Leppard)

TOM LUCY
82 Bridgehouse BHS 15 Paris, France/Man Found Dead In Graveyard (no p/s) . . . 6
(see also Wasted Youth)

LUCY SHOW
83 Shout XS 007 Leonardo Da Vinci/Kill The Beast (p/s) . . . 12

LUDDITES
83 Xcentric Noise SECOND 1 STRENGTH OF YOUR CRY (EP, black or pink foldout p/s) . . . 15/10

LUDLOWS
65 Pye 7N 15946 The Last Thing On My Mind/Kisses Sweeter Than Wine . . . 5
66 Pye 7N 17050 The Sea Around Us/The Butcher Boys . . . 5
66 Pye 7N 17123 The Winds Thro' The Rafters/That's My Song . . . 5
66 Pye 7N 17221 Johnny Lad/Pack Up Your Sorrows . . . 5
67 Pye 7N 17319 Enniskillen Dragoons/Foggy Dew . . . 5
67 Pye 7N 17384 Plaisir D'Amour/Yesterday's Dream . . . 5
66 Pye NPL 18150 THE WIND AND THE SEA (LP) . . . 15
(see also Jim McCann)

LUDUS
80 New Hormones ORG 4 The Visit/Lullaby Cheat/Unveil (12", p/s with insert) . . . 8
81 New Hormones ORG 8 My Cherry Is In Sherry/Anatomy Is Not Destiny (p/s) . . . 5
81 New Hormones CAT 1 PICKPOCKET (C-30 cassette pack with A4 book & button in PVC bag) . . . 12
81 New Hormones ORG 12 Mother's Hour/Patient (p/s, with poster) . . . 5
81 New Hormones ORG 16 THE SEDUCTION (2 x 12" EP, each in p/s; whole package in poly bag) . . . 12
80s New Hormones LINDER SINGS BARDOT (cassette) . . . 12
82 New Hormones ORG 20 DANGER CAME SMILING (LP) . . . 12

LUGWORM
97 Guided Missile GUIDE 11 Rococo Negro/BIS: Pop Song (p/s) . . . 5

LUKE & BLAKE
66 CBS 202467 Just You/Wandering Man . . . 8

ROBIN LUKE
58 London HLD 8676 Susie Darlin'/Living's Loving You . . . 18
58 London HLD 8676 Susie Darlin'/Living's Loving You (78) . . . 20
58 London HLD 8771 Chicka Chicka Honey/My Girl . . . 30
58 London HLD 8771 Chicka Chicka Honey/My Girl (78) . . . 40
59 London RED 1222 ROBIN LUKE (EP) . . . 125

LULU (& LUVVERS)
64 Decca F 11884 Shout/Forget Me Baby (as Lulu & Luvers) . . . 10
64 Decca F 11965 Can't Hear You No More/I Am In Love . . . 10
64 Decca F 12017 Here Comes The Night/That's Really Some Good . . . 10
65 Decca F 12128 Satisfied/Surprise Surprise (as Lulu & Luvers) . . . 15
65 Decca F 12169 Leave A Little Love/He Don't Want Your Love Anymore . . . 10
65 Decca F 12214 Try To Understand/Not In This Whole World . . . 10
65 Decca F 12254 Tell Me Like It Is/Stop Fooling Around . . . 10
66 Decca F 12326 Call Me/After You . . . 10
66 Decca F 12491 What A Wonderful Feeling/Tossin' And Turnin' . . . 10
67 Columbia DB 8169 The Boat That I Row/Dreary Days And Nights . . . 10

MINT VALUE £

67	Columbia DB 8221	Let's Pretend/To Sir With Love	10
67	Columbia DB 8295	Love Loves To Love/You And I	15
68	Columbia DB 8358	Me, The Peaceful Heart/Lookout	10
68	Columbia DB 8425	Boy/Sad Memories	10
68	Columbia DB 8500	I'm A Tiger/Without Him	10
69	Columbia DB 8550	Boom Bang-A-Bang/March!	5
69	Atco 226 008	Oh Me, Oh My (I'm A Fool For You Baby)/Sweep Around Your Own Backyard	5
70	Atco 2091 014	Hum A Song (From Your Heart)/Mr. Bojangles (with Dixie Flyers)	5
71	Atco 2091 049	Got To Believe In Love/Move To My Rhythm	8
71	Atlantic 2091 083	Everybody Clap/After The Feeling Is Gone	6
72	Atlantic K 10185	Even If I Could Change/You Ain't Wrong You Just Ain't Right	5
74	Polydor 2001 490	The Man Who Sold The World/Watch That Man	8
74	Chelsea 2005 015	The Man With The Golden Gun/A Boy Like You	10
75	Chelsea 2005 022	Take Your Mama For A Ride (Parts 1 & 2)	5
75	Chelsea 2005 031	Boy Meets Girl/Mama's Little Corner Of The World	5
75	Chelsea 2001 048	Heaven And Earth And The Stars/A Boy Like You	5
79	Alfa ALF 1700	I Could Never Miss You (More Than I Do)/Dance To The Feeling In Your Heart (p/s)	5
86	Jive LULU 2	My Boy Lollipop/It's Only Love (p/s)	5
65	Decca DFE 8597	LULU (EP)	50
65	Decca LK 4719	SOMETHING TO SHOUT ABOUT (LP)	75
67	Ace Of Clubs ACL 1232	LULU! (LP)	25
67	Fontana (S)TL 5446	TO SIR, WITH LOVE (LP, soundtrack, with Ron Grainer & Mindbenders)	60
67	Columbia S(C)X 6201	LOVE LOVES TO LOVE LULU (LP)	35
69	Columbia S(C)X 6365	LULU'S ALBUM (LP)	25
69	Atco 228 031	NEW ROUTES (LP)	25
70	Atco 2400 017	MELODY FAIR (LP)	12

(see also Luvvers, Scotland World Cup Squad)

LULU BELLE & SCOTTY

50	London L 833	Have I Told You Lately That I Love You/Schrudle Du (78)	10
65	London HA-B 8277	SWEETHEART STILL (LP)	18

BOB LUMAN

60	Warner Bros WB 12	Dreamy Doll/Buttercup	20
60	Warner Bros WB 18	Let's Think About Livin'/You've Got Everything	8
60	Warner Bros WB 28	Why, Why, Bye, Bye/Oh, Lonesome Me	10
61	Warner Bros WB 37	The Great Snow Man/The Pig Latin Song	10
61	Warner Bros WB 49	Private Eye/You Turned Down The Lights	10
62	Warner Bros WB 60	Louisiana Man/Rocks Of Reno (unissued)	
62	Warner Bros WB 75	Hey Joe/The Fool	10
64	Hickory 45-1238	The File/Bigger Men Than I	10
64	Hickory 45-1266	(Empty Walls) A Lonely Room/Run On Home Baby Brother	8
64	Hickory 45-1277	Old George Dickel/Fire Engine Red	8
65	Hickory 45-1289	Bad Bad Day/Tears From Out Of Nowhere	12
65	Hickory 45-1410	Come On And Sing/It's A Sin	8
68	CBS 3602	Ain't Got Time To Be Unhappy/I Can't Remember To Forget	15
61	Warner Bros WEP 6046	LET'S THINK ABOUT LIVIN' (EP, also stereo WSEP 2046)	45/60
62	Warner Bros WEP 6055	LET'S THINK ABOUT LIVIN' NO. 2 (EP, also stereo WSEP 2055)	45/60
62	Warner Bros WEP 6102	LET'S THINK ABOUT LIVIN' NO. 3 (EP, also stereo WSEP 2102)	45/60
60	Warner Bros WM 4025	LET'S THINK ABOUT LIVIN' (LP, also stereo WS 8025)	70/90
64	Hickory LPM 124	LIVIN' LOVIN' SOUNDS (LP)	35
71	London ZGE 115	LIVIN' LOVIN' SOUNDS (LP, reissue)	12

(see also Sue Thompson & Bob Luman)

BOB LUMAN/BOBBY LORD

64	Hickory LPE 1501	HICKORY SHOWCASE VOL. 2 (EP, 1 side each)	20
64	Hickory LPE 1504	HICKORY SHOWCASE VOL. 3 (EP, 1 side each)	20
64	Hickory LPM 121	CAN'T TAKE THE COUNTRY FROM THE BOYS (LP, 1 side each)	18

(see also Bobby Lord)

RUFUS LUMLEY

66	Stateside SS 516	I'm Standing/Let's Hide Away (Me And You)	130
78	EMI International INT 556	I'm Standing/Let's Hide Away (Me And You) (reissue)	12

LUNACHICKS

89	Blast First BFFP 44	SUGAR LUV EP (7" double pack)	10

LUNAR TWO

60s	Spot JWS 551	Get It Take It/Don't Ever Leave Me	10

JIMMIE LUNCEFORD

63	Capitol T/ST 1581	THE GREAT JIMMIE LUNCEFORD (LP)	18

LYDIA LUNCH

91	UFO UFOPF 1	Spooky (mono)/Spooky (stereo) (no p/s, promo only)	6
93	Clawfist X-PIG 19	Unearthly Delights/Busted (p/s)	10
82	Situation 2 SITU 6	13.13 (LP, with inner sleeve)	20
84	Doublevision DVR 5	IN LIMBO (LP, red vinyl with inner sleeve)	20
86	Widowspeak SWP 01/07	THE INTIMATE DIARIES OF THE SEXUALLY INSANE (cassette, box set with book, signed)	25
87	Widowspeak WSP 8	HYSTERIE (2-LP, with inners and poster)	20

(see also Eight-Eyed Spy, Roland S. Howard, No Trend)

ART LUND

53	MGM SP 1042	If I Were A Bell/JOHNNY DESMOND: A Bushel And A Peck	8
65	United Artists UP 1100	Branded/Gonna Have A Little Talk	6
57	Vogue Coral LVA 9056	THIS IS ART (LP)	30

TED LUNE

60	Philips PB 1068	Mr Custer/Time Machine	8

(see also Michael Medwin 8 Army Game Cast)

LARRY LUREX

73 EMI EMI 2030 — I Can Hear Music/Goin' Back (demo) . . . 300
73 EMI EMI 2030 — I Can Hear Music/Goin' Back (press-out centre; beware of solid-centered counterfeits) . . . 200
(see also Queen)

LURKERS

77 Beggars Banquet BEG 1 — Free Admission Single: Shadow/Love Story (p/s, black vinyl; reissued on red, blue or white vinyl) . . . 5/8
77 Beggars Banquet BEG 2 — Freak Show/Mass Media Believer (p/s) . . . 5
78 Beggars Banquet BEG 6 — Ain't Got A Clue/Ooh Ooh I Love You (p/s, 15,000 with gold flexidisc, 'Chaos Brothers Fulham Fallout Firty Free' [BEG 61/2]) . . . 6/4
78 Beggars Banquet BEG 6 — Ain't Got A Clue/Ooh Ooh I Love You (reissue, different p/s, with clear vinyl picture flexidisc) . . . 5
79 Beggars Banquet BACK 1 — Shadow/Love Story//Freak Show/Mass Media Believer (reissue double pack) . . . 5
79 Beggars Banquet BACK 3 — I Don't Need To Tell Her/Pills//Just Thirteen/Countdown (double pack) . . . 5
82 Clay CLAY 17P — Drag You Out/Heroin (It's All Over) (picture disc) . . . 5
78 Beggars Banquet BEGA 2 — FULHAM FALLOUT (LP, gatefold sleeve, some with picture disc flexi 'Chaos Brothers Fulham Fallout Firty Free' [BEG 6 1/2] & stickered sleeve) . . . 20/12
(see also Pete Stride & John Plain, Fulham Furies, Rowdies)

DON LUSHER BAND

55 Decca F 10560 — Rock 'n' Roll/On With The Don . . . 18
56 Decca F 10740 — Fast And Furious/Let's Do It . . . 7

LUSTMØRD

82 Sterile SR 3 — LUSTMØRD (LP, with odorous label) . . . 35

NELLIE LUTCHER (& HER RHYTHM)

50 Capitol CL 13223 — Kiss Me Sweet/The Pig-Latin Song (78) . . . 8
50 Capitol CL 13234 — Fine And Mellow/Lake Charles Boogie (78) . . . 8
50 Capitol CL 13254 — There's Another Mule In Your Stall/Glad Rag Doll (78) . . . 8
50 Capitol CL 13274 — That's A Plenty/Princess Poo-Poo-Ly Has Plenty Papaya (78) . . . 8
50 Capitol CL 13275 — Can I Come In For A Second/For You My Love (78, with Nat 'King' Cole) . . . 8
50 Capitol CL 13366 — Lovable/A Maid's Prayer (78) . . . 8
50 Capitol CL 13399 — Only You/Ditto From Me To You (78) . . . 8
50 Capitol CL 13421 — Let Me Love You Tonight/Lutcher's Leap (78) . . . 8
51 Capitol CL 13493 — Chi-Chi-Chi-Chicago/Do You Or Don't You Love Me? (78) . . . 8
51 Capitol CL 13502 — Reaching For The Moon/That'll Just 'Bout Knock Me Out (78) . . . 8
51 Capitol CL 13509 — Pa's Not Home, Ma's Upstairs/I Really Couldn't Love You (78) . . . 8
51 Capitol CL 13606 — The Birth Of The Blues/I Want To Be Near You (78) . . . 8
52 Capitol CL 13738 — What A Difference A Day Made/Mean To Me (78) . . . 8
52 Capitol CL 13770 — That's How It Goes/The Heart Of A Clown (78) . . . 8
54 Brunswick 05352 — Blues In The Night/Breezin' Along With The Breeze . . . 15
54 Brunswick 05352 — Blues In The Night/Breezin' Along With The Breeze (78) . . . 8
55 Brunswick 05437 — It's Been Said/Please Come Back . . . 18
55 Brunswick 05437 — It's Been Said/Please Come Back (78) . . . 8
55 Brunswick 05497 — Whose Honey Are You?/If I Didn't Love You Like I Do . . . 10
55 Brunswick 05497 — Whose Honey Are You?/If I Didn't Love You Like I Do (78) . . . 8
60 Capitol CL 15106 — My Mother's Eyes/The Heart Of A Clown . . . 8
60 Capitol EAP 20066 — REAL GONE (EP) . . . 50
56 Philips BBE 12045 — NELLIE LUTCHER (EP) . . . 35
51 Capitol LC 6500 — REAL GONE! (10" LP) . . . 80
57 London HA-U 2036 — OUR NEW NELLIE (LP) . . . 60
66 M. For Pleasure MFP 1038 — REAL GONE (LP) . . . 15

CLAUDE LUTER ORCHESTRA

59 Vogue V 9132 — The Day That The Rains Came/La Grande Coco . . . 10
59 Vogue V 9132 — The Day That The Rains Came/La Grande Coco (78) . . . 12

LUTHER

76 Cotillion K 10781 — It's Good For The Soul (Parts 1 & 2) . . . 15

FRANK LUTHER

53 Brunswick 05124 — I'll Ring You Up/Jig A Jig Jig (78) . . . 8
60 Decca F 9050 — The Little Red Hen (Song Story) (both sides) . . . 5
60 Decca F 9051 — The Three Billy Goats Gruff (Song Story) (both sides) . . . 5

LUTHER & LITTLE EVA

57 Parlophone R 4292 — Love Is Strange/Ain't Got No Home . . . 550
57 Parlophone R 4292 — Love Is Strange/Ain't Got No Home (78) . . . 150
(do not see also Little Eva)

LUV BUG

86 Roxy!-Ritz TEASE 2 — You Can Count On Me/You Can't Have It (p/s) . . . 7

LUV MACHINE

71 Polydor 2058 080 — Witches Wand/In The Early Hours . . . 12
71 Polydor 2460 102 — LUV MACHINE (LP) . . . 110

LUVVERS

66 Parlophone R 5459 — The House On The Hill/Most Unlovely . . . 30
(see also Lulu, Peter Ross Oliver)

MICK LUVZIT

66 Decca F 12421 — Long Time Between Lovers/Though I Still Love You . . . 8

GARY LUX

85 Global LUX 2 — Children Of The World/Movies (p/s) . . . 10

MINT VALUE £

L-VOAG

79	Sesame Songs MOVE 1	MOVE (EP, p/s with handmade labels & insert)	15
81	Axis No. 9	THE WAY OUT (LP, with booklet & poster)	30

(see also Homosexuals)

LYLE McGUINNESS BAND

83	Cool King CKLP 03	ACTING ON IMPULSE (LP)	12

(see also McGuinness Flint, Gallagher & Lyle)

ARTHUR LYMAN GROUP

59	Vogue V 9153	Taboo/Dahil Sayo	5
59	Vogue V 9153	Taboo/Dahil Sayo (78)	20
61	Vogue Pop V 9183	Yellow Bird/Havali Nagilali	6
62	Vogue Pop V 9195	I Talk To The Trees/Never On Sunday	6
62	Vogue Pop V 9199	Exodus/Aloha No Honolulu	6
63	Vogue Pop V 9208	Love For Sale/It's So Right To Love	6
66	Vogue Pop V 9265	Lemon Tree/The (Jungle) Cat	5
59	Vogue VEH 70166	GREATEST HITS VOL. 1 (EP)	12
59	Vogue VEH 70167	GREATEST HITS VOL. 2 (EP)	12
59	Vogue VEH 70168	GREATEST HITS VOL. 3 (EP)	12
59	Vogue VA 160142	TABOO VOL. 1 (LP, also stereo SAV 8002)	15/18
59	Vogue VA 160149	MORE EXOTIC SOUNDS — BWANA A (LP)	15
60	Vogue VA 160166	BAHIA (LP)	15
61	Vogue VA 160171	HAWAIIAN SUNSET (LP)	15
61	Vogue VA 160174	TABOO VOL. 2 (LP, also stereo SAV 8003)	15
63	Vogue SAVH 8030	LOVE FOR SALE (LP)	15

FRANKIE LYMON (& TEENAGERS)

56	Columbia SCM 5265	Why Do Fools Fall In Love?/Please Be Mine (as Teenagers featuring Frankie Lymon)	60
56	Columbia DB 3772	Why Do Fools Fall In Love?/Please Be Mine (78)	10
56	Columbia SCM 5285	I Want You To Be My Girl/I'm Not A Know It All	55
56	Columbia DB 3797	I Want You To Be My Girl/I'm Not A Know It All (78)	15
56	Columbia DB 3819	Who Can Explain?/I Promise To Remember	50
56	Columbia DB 3819	Who Can Explain?/I Promise To Remember (78)	15
56	Columbia DB 3858	Share/The A.B.C.'s Of Love	50
56	Columbia DB 3858	Share/The A.B.C.'s Of Love (78)	15
57	Columbia DB 3878	I'm Not A Juvenile Delinquent/Baby, Baby	35
57	Columbia DB 3878	I'm Not A Juvenile Delinquent/Baby, Baby (78)	10
57	Columbia DB 3910	Teenage Love/Paper Castles	45
57	Columbia DB 3910	Teenage Love/Paper Castles (78)	15
57	Columbia DB 3942	Miracle In The Rain/Out In The Cold Again	50
57	Columbia DB 3942	Miracle In The Rain/Out In The Cold Again (78)	15
57	Columbia DB 3983	Goody Goody/Creation Of Love	18
57	Columbia DB 3983	Goody Goody/Creation Of Love (78)	15
57	Columbia DB 4028	My Girl/So Goes My Love	30
57	Columbia DB 4028	My Girl/So Goes My Love (78)	20
58	Columbia DB 4073	Thumb Thumb/Footsteps (solo)	25
58	Columbia DB 4073	Thumb Thumb/Footsteps (78)	20
58	Columbia DB 4134	Mama Don't Allow It/Portable On My Shoulder (solo)	20
58	Columbia DB 4134	Mama Don't Allow It/Portable On My Shoulder (78)	25
59	Columbia DB 4245	Melinda/The Only Way To Love (solo)	20
59	Columbia DB 4245	Melinda/The Only Way To Love (78)	40
59	Columbia DB 4295	Up Jumped A Rabbit/No Matter What You've Done (solo)	22
60	Columbia DB 4499	Little Bitty Pretty One/Creation Of Love (solo)	30
66	King KG 1042	Why Do Fools Fall In Love?/I'm Not A Juvenile Delinquent	8
57	Columbia SEG 7662	TEENAGE ROCK (EP)	60
57	Columbia SEG 7694	THE TEENAGERS FEATURING FRANKIE LYMON (EP)	75
57	Columbia SEG 7734	FRANKIE LYMON AND THE TEENAGERS (EP)	80
58	Columbia 33S 1127	FRANKIE LYMON IN LONDON (10" LP, solo)	190
58	Columbia 33S 1134	ROCKIN' WITH FRANKIE LYMON (10" LP, solo)	500

LEWIS LYMON & TEENCHORDS

58	Oriole 45-CB 1419	Too Young/Your Last Chance	500
58	Oriole CB 1419	Too Young/Your Last Chance (78)	100

DERMOTT LYNCH

68	Blue Cat BS 101	Hot Shot/I've Got Your Number	30
68	Blue Cat BS 122	I Got Everything/Echo	30
68	Doctor Bird DB 1115	Adults Only/Cool It	30

(see also Trevor, Carl Dawkins, Joe White)

JOE LYNCH

56	Beltona BE 2668	Davy Crockett Is Helping Santa Claus/There's A Little Bit Of Irish (78)	7
69	Spectrum SP 107	King Child/Johnny Appleseed	5

KENNY LYNCH

60	HMV POP 751	Mountain Of Love/Why Do You Treat Me This Way?	15
60	HMV POP 786	Slowcoach/You Make Love So Well	10
61	HMV POP 841	So/Love Me	10
61	HMV POP 900	The Story Behind My Tears/Steady Kind	10
61	HMV POP 985	There's Never Been A Girl/Doll Face	10
62	HMV POP 1005	It Would Take A Miracle/Strolling Blues	10
62	HMV POP 1057	Puff/Happy That's Me	10
62	HMV POP 1090	Up On The Roof/Jump On Your Broomstick	7
63	HMV POP 1136	Misery/Shut The Door	10
63	HMV POP 1165	You Can Never Stop Me Loving You/Crazy Crazes	6
63	HMV POP 1229	For You (There's Not A Thing I Wouldn't Do)/With Somebody	8
63	HMV POP 1260	Shake And Scream/Harlem Library	8

64	HMV POP 1280	Stand By Me/Baby It's True	7
64	HMV POP 1321	That's What Little Girls Are Made For/What Am I To You?	7
64	HMV POP 1367	My Own Two Feet/So Much To Love You For	15
65	HMV POP 1430	I'll Stay By You/For Loving You Baby	7
65	HMV POP 1476	Nothing But The Real Thing/Don't Ask Me To Stop Loving You	7
65	HMV POP 1496	Get Out Of My Way/One Look At You	10
66	HMV POP 1534	The World I Used To Know/Come On Come On	7
67	HMV POP 1577	I Just Wanna Love You/It's Too Late	8
67	HMV POP 1604	Movin' Away/Could I Count On You	50
68	Columbia DB 8329	Mister Moonlight/The Other Side Of Dreamland	15
68	Columbia DB 8498	Along Comes Love/Sweet Situation	15
69	Columbia DB 8599	The Drifter/Did I Stay Too Long?	18
70	Columbia DB 8703	In Old Kentucky/Loving You Is Sweeter Than Ever	15
63	HMV 7EG 8820	HEY GIRL (EP)	35
64	HMV 7EG 8855	KENNY LYNCH (EP)	45
65	HMV 7EG 8881	WHAT AM I TO YOU (EP)	40
63	HMV CLP 1635	UP ON THE ROOF (LP, also stereo CSD 1489)	50/65
66	Music F. Pleasure MFP 1022	WE LIKE KENNY (LP)	12

LEE LYNCH (& BLUE ANGELS)

66	Decca F 12375	You Won't See Me/You Know There's Me (as Lee Lynch & Blue Angels)	10
69	Ember EMB S 262	Stay Awhile/Bad Time To Stop Loving Me (p/s)	10
70	Ember EMB S 271	Sweet Woman/Can't Take My Eyes Off You (p/s)	10
70	Ember EMB S 282	Joe Poor Loves Daphne Elizabeth Rich/It's Love (p/s)	10

LINDA LYNDELL

68	Stax 601 041	Bring Your Love Back To Me/Here I Am	30

BARBARA LYNN

64	London HLW 9918	Oh! Baby (We Got A Good Thing Goin')/Unfair	30
65	Immediate IM 011	You Can't Buy My Love/That's What A Friend Will Do	40
66	London HLU 10094	You Left The Water Running/Until I'm Free	25
67	Sue WI 4028	Letter To Mommy And Daddy/Second Fiddle Girl	35
67	Sue WI 4038	You'll Lose A Good Thing/Lonely Heartaches	40
71	Atlantic 2091 133	Take Your Love And Run/(Until Then) I'll Suffer	15
75	Oval OVAL 1006	Letter To Mommy And Daddy/You'll Lose A Good Thing	8
67	Sue ILP 949	THE BARBARA LYNN STORY (LP)	150

BOBBI LYNN

68	Stateside SS 2088	Earthquake/Opportunity Street	40
71	Bell BLL 1168	Earthquake/Opportunity Street (reissue)	7

CHERYL LYNN

84	Streetwave KHAN 23	Encore/Got To Be Real	5
84	Streetwave MKHAN 23	Encore/Got To Be Real (12")	8

KARI LYNN

61	Oriole CB 1632	Yo Yo/Summer Day	15
61	Oriole CB 1644	You've Got To See Mamma Every Night/Lonesome And Sorry	15

LORETTA LYNN

68	MCA MUP 338	LORETTA LYNN (LP)	15
69	MCA MUP(S) 385	GREATEST HITS (LP)	12
70	MCA MUP(S) 407	HERE'S LORETTA LYNN SINGING WINGS UPON YOUR HORNS (LP)	15
70	MCA MUPS 411	YOUR SQUAW IS ON THE WARPATH (LP)	15
71	MCA MUPS 417	WRITES 'EM AND SINGS 'EM (LP)	12
71	MCA MUPS 427	COAL MINER'S DAUGHTER (LP)	12
72	MCA MUPS 447	YOU'RE LOOKING AT COUNTRY (LP)	12

(see also Conway Twitty)

PATTI LYNN

62	Fontana H 370	I See It All Now/Someone Else's Valentine	15
62	Fontana H 391	Johnny Angel/Tonight You Belong To Me	15
62	Fontana 267 247 TF	Tell Me Telstar/Big Big Love	18
62	Fontana TFE 17392	PATTI (EP)	50

TAM(M)I LYNN

66	Atlantic AT 4071	I'm Gonna Run Away From You/The Boy Next Door	50
71	Mojo 2092 001	I'm Gonna Run Away From You/The Boy Next Door (reissue)	8
71	Mojo 2092 012	That's Understanding/Never No More	6
75	Contempo CS 9026	I'm Gonna Run Away From You/The Boy Next Door (2nd reissue)	8
71	Mojo 2916 007	LOVE IS HERE AND NOW YOU'RE GONE (LP)	35

VERA LYNN

52	Decca F 9927	Auf Wiederseh'n, Sweetheart/From The Time You Say Goodbye	7
54	Decca F 10253	Two Easter Sunday Sweethearts/Du Bist Mein Liebeshoen	7
54	Decca F 10290	The Homecoming Waltz/Humble People	7
54	Decca F 10372	My Son, My Son/Our Heaven On Earth (with Frank Weir & His Saxophone)	35
55	MGM SP 1142	From Tomorrow/Each Moment I Live	5
56	Decca F 10715	Who Are We?/I'll Be True To You	8
56	Decca F 10799	A House With Love In It/Little Lost Dog	8
57	Decca F 10846	The Faithful Hussar (Don't Cry My Love)/The One Beside You	7
57	Decca F 10903	Travellin' Home/Dear To Me	7
59	Decca F 11112	Glory Of Love/Walk With Faith In Your Heart (78)	8
59	Decca F 11129	Have I Told You Lately That I Love You/I'm A Fool To Forgive You (78)	8
59	Decca F 11157	Morgen/Time Marches On (78)	8
52	Decca LF 1022	SINCERELY YOURS, VERA LYNN (10" LP)	12
53	Decca LF 1102	SINCERELY YOURS, VERA LYNN VOL. 2 (10" LP)	12
53	Decca LF 1183	SINCERELY YOURS, VERA LYNN VOL. 3 (10" LP)	12

(see also Johnstone Brothers, Frank Weir & His Orchestra)

MINT VALUE £

GLORIA LYNNE

64	London HLY 9846	I Wish You Love/Through A Long And Sleeping Night	8
64	London HLY 9888	I Should Care/Indian Love Call	8
59	Top Rank JKP 2024	MEET GLORIA LYNNE (EP, with Wild Bill Davis)	20
60	Top Rank BUY 031	LONELY AND SENTIMENTAL (LP)	20
64	London HA-Y 8112	AT THE LAS VEGAS THUNDERBIRD (LP, with Herman Foster Trio)	20
72	Mojo 2916 016	HAPPY AND IN LOVE (LP)	25

JEFF LYNNE

77	Jet UP 36281	Doin' That Crazy Thing/Goin' Down To Rio (p/s)	5

(see also Nightriders, Idle Race, Move, E.L.O., Traveling Wilburys)

SUE LYNNE

68	RCA Victor RCA 1724	Reach For The Moon/All Alone	10
69	RCA Victor RCA 1822	You/Don't Pity Me	150
69	RCA Victor RCA 1874	Baby Baby Baby/You Lose Again	7

PHIL LYNOTT

80	Vertigo LYN 1	King's Call/Yellow Pearl (p/s)	5
80	Vertigo LYNT 1	King's Call/Yellow Pearl (12", p/s)	10
80	Vertigo SOLO 1	Dear Miss Lonely Hearts/Solo In Soho (p/s)	5
80	Vertigo SOLO 112	Dear Miss Lonely Hearts/Solo In Soho (12", p/s)	8
80	Vertigo SOLO 2	King's Call/Ode To A Black Man (p/s)	5
81	Vertigo SOLO 3	Yellow Pearl/Girls (p/s, clear vinyl)	5
85	Vertigo SOLO 5	Old Town/Beat Of The Drum (p/s)	6
85	Polydor POSPD 777	19/19 (Dub Version)//THIN LIZZY: Whiskey In The Jar (live) (double pack, 2nd disc 1-sided)	10
80	Vertigo PHIL 1	SOLO IN SOHO (LP, with inner sleeve)	12
80	Vertigo PHIL 1	SOLO IN SOHO (LP, picture disc, die-cut sleeve)	15

(see also Thin Lizzy, Gary Moore & Phil Lynott, John Sykes, Rockers)

JACKIE LYNTON

61	Piccadilly 7N 35012	Over The Rainbow/High In The Sky	10
62	Piccadilly 7N 35055	Don't Take Away Your Love/Wishful Thinking	10
62	Piccadilly 7N 35064	All Of Me/I'd Steal	15
63	Piccadilly 7N 35107	I Believe/The Girl In The Wood	8
63	Piccadilly 7N 35140	Jeannie With The Light Brown Hair/Teddy Bear's Picnic	8
63	Piccadilly 7N 35156	I'm Talkin' About You/Lawdy Miss Clawdy	8
64	Piccadilly 7N 35177	Little Child/Never A Mention	8
64	Piccadilly 7N 35190	Laura/Ebb Tide	8
65	Decca F 12052	Three Blind Mice/Corrina Corrine	8
67	Columbia DB 8097	He'll Have To Go/Only You	12
67	Columbia DB 8180	Decision/Sporting Life	12
67	Columbia DB 8224	Answer Me/I Never Loved A Girl Like You	12
79	Thumb TR003	Dan (The Hedgehog Song)/Farting With The Famous	8
74	WWA WWA 012	THE JACKIE LYNTON ALBUM (LP)	18

(see also Savoy Brown Blues Band)

LYNYRD SKYNYRD

74	MCA MCA 136	Don't Ask Me No Questions/Take Your Time	6
74	MCA MCA 160	Sweet Home Alabama/Take Your Time	5
75	MCA MCA 199	Saturday Night Special/Made In The Shade	5
76	MCA MCA 229	Double Trouble/Roll Gypsy Roll	5
76	MCA MCA 251	Free Bird/Sweet Home Alabama/Double Trouble (p/s)	8
76	MCA MCA 275	Free Bird (Edit)/Gimme Three Steps (p/s)	8
78	MCA MCEP 101	DOWN SOUTH JUKIN' (EP, p/s)	7
78	MCA MCA 342	What's Your Name/I Know A Little	5
82	MCA MCA 799	I've Been Your Fool/Gotta Go (p/s)	5
82	MCA MCAT 251	Free Bird/Sweet Home Alabama/Double Trouble (12", p/s)	8
82	MCA MCATP 251	Free Bird/Sweet Home Alabama/Double Trouble (12", picture disc)	12
89	MCA DMCA 251	Free Bird/Sweet Home Alabama/Double Trouble (3" CD, card sleeve)	8
74	MCA MCG 3502	PRONOUNCED LEH-NERD SKIN-NERD (LP, gatefold sleeve)	18
77	MCA MCG 3525	STREET SURVIVORS (LP, gatefold sleeve with tour dates on inner sleeve)	15

(see also Blackfoot)

BARBARA LYON

55	Columbia SCM 5186	I Love To Dance With You/Yes You Are	15
55	Columbia SCM 5207	Whisper/Where You Are	15
56	Columbia SCM 5232	Band Of Gold/Such A Day	15
56	Columbia SCM 5276	Puppy Love/The Birds And The Bees	15
56	Columbia DB 3786	Puppy Love/The Birds And The Bees (78)	8
56	Columbia DB 3826	It's Better In The Dark/A Heart Without A Sweetheart	6
56	Columbia DB 3865	Falling In Love/Letter To A Soldier	15
56	Columbia DB 3865	Falling In Love/Letter To A Soldier (78)	8
57	Columbia DB 3931	C'est La Vie/Fire Down Below	5
57	Columbia DB 4026	Thanks For The Loan Of A Dream/Third Finger — Left Hand	5
58	Columbia DB 4137	Red Was The Moon/Ring On A Ribbon	5
60	Triumph RGM 1027	My Charlie/Tell Me	40
56	Columbia SEG 7640	MY FOUR FRIENDS (EP)	25
55	Columbia DB 3619	Stowaway	15

PATTI LYON

62	Fontana H 370	I See It All Now/Someone Else's Valentine	12

RICHARD LYON

59	Fontana H 206	All My Own/Private Eye	20
59	Fontana H 206	All My Own/Private Eye (78)	12

LYONS & MALONE

69	Jay Boy BOY 9	Doctor Gentle/She's Alright	5

MINT VALUE £

LYON ST.

(see under Associates)

LYRICS

Year	Label / Cat. No.	Title	£
67	Coxsone CS 7003	A Get It/KEN PARKER: How Strong	30
68	Coxsone CS 7067	Music Like Dirt/TONETTES: I Give It To You	30
70	Randy's RAN 504	Give Thanks And Praises/TOMMY McCOOK: Get Ready	20
71	Randy's RAN 511	Give Thanks/RANDY'S ALL STARS: Give — Version	15

(see also Randy's All Stars, Viceroys, Jackie Mittoo)

JIMMY LYTELL

Year	Label / Cat. No.	Title	£
59	London HL 8873	Hot Cargo/A Blues Serenade	15

JOHNNY LYTLE

Year	Label / Cat. No.	Title	£
68	Minit MLF 11006	Gonna Get That Boat (Parts 1 & 2)	12

HUMPHREY LYTTELTON (& HIS BAND)

78s

Year	Label / Cat. No.	Title	£
51	Saturn EGX 105	When The Saints Go Marching In/Careless Love (78, picture disc)	85
56	Esquire 10-491	The Thin Red Line/Melancholy Blues (78)	8
56	Esquire 10-494	First Of Many/Blues For Two (78)	8
57	Esquire 10-501	Elizabeth/Blue For Waterloo (78)	8
57	Esquire 10-511	Cake Walkin' Babies/If You See Me Comin' (78)	8
57	Parlophone R 4277	Baby Doll/Red Beans And Rice (78)	8
58	Parlophone R 4428	Hand Me Down Love/Here And Gone (Blues In 1890) (78)	8
58	Decca F 11058	La Paloma/Bodega (78)	8
59	Parlophone R 4519	Saturday Jump/The Bear Steps Out (78)	10

SINGLES

Year	Label / Cat. No.	Title	£
53	Parlophone MSP 6001	Out Of The Gallion/The Old Grey Mare	10
53	Parlophone MSP 6023	Muskrat Ramble/Mamzelle Josephine (as Lyttelton Paseo Band, B-side with George Brown)	10
53	Parlophone MSP 6033	Maryland, My Maryland/Blue For Waterloo	10
53	Parlophone MSP 6034	Shake It And Break It/Jail Break	10
53	Parlophone MSP 6045	Red For Piccadilly/Kater Street Rag	10
54	Parlophone MSP 6061	Martiniquen Song (Last Year)/Ain't Cha Got Music	8
54	Parlophone MSP 6076	East Coast Trot/Breeze	8
54	Parlophone MSP 6093	Just Once For All Time/Joshua, Fit The Battle Of Jericho	8
54	Parlophone MSP 6097	Mainly Traditional/Oh! Dad (with 'Melody Maker' All Stars)	8
54	Parlophone MSP 6128	Mezzy's Tune/Jelly Bean Blues	8
56	Tempo A 10	When The Saints Go Marching In/Careless Love	7
56	Parlophone R 4212	Love, Love, Love/Echoing The Blues	6
57	Parlophone R 4262	It's Mardi Gras/Sweet And Sour	7
57	Parlophone R 4277	Baby Doll/Red Beans And Rice	7
57	Parlophone R 4333	Early Call (Bermondsey Bounce)/Creole Serenade	5
57	Parlophone R 4368	Dixie Theme/Blues At Dawn	5
58	Parlophone CMSP 41	Bad Penny Blues/Baby Doll (export issue)	30
58	Parlophone R 4392	Buona Sera/Blues In The Afternoon	5
58	Parlophone R 4428	Hand Me Down Love/Here And Gone (Blues In 1890)	5
58	Decca F 11058	La Paloma/Bodega	8
59	Parlophone R 4519	Saturday Jump/The Bear Steps Out	5
59	Parlophone R 4578	Summertime/Manhunt	5
50s	Storyville A 45041	The Thin Red Line/Ole Miss	5
60s	Summer County LYN 254	Swingin' On The Gate/Jeanie With The Light Brown Hair (flexidisc, some in p/s)	10/5
86	Calligraph CLGS 701	Bad Penny Blues/Feline Stomp (p/s)	6

EPs

Year	Label / Cat. No.	Title	£
55	Parlophone GEP 8503	HUMPHREY LYTTELTON & HIS BAND (EP)	10
55	Parlophone GEP 8514	HUMPHREY LYTTELTON & HIS BAND (EP)	15
55	Parlophone GEP 8546	JAZZ WITH LYTTELTON – 1 (EP)	8
56	Parlophone GEP 8572	JAZZ WITH LYTTELTON – 2 (EP)	12
56	Parlophone GEP 8580	LIGHTLY & POLITELY (EP)	10
56	Parlophone GEP 8584	HUMPH'S BLUES (EP)	12
55	Tempo EXA 1	HUMPHREY LYTTELTON & HIS BAND (EP)	20
56	Esquire EP 111	HUMPHREY LYTTELTON & HIS BAND (EP)	18
57	Esquire EP 141	HUMPHREY LYTTELTON & HIS BAND (EP)	18
57	Esquire EP 153	VINTAGE '49 (EP)	18
57	Parlophone GEP 8599	JAZZ WITH LYTTELTON – 4 (EP)	10
57	Parlophone GEP 8645	HUMPH'S BLUES NO. 2 (EP)	12
57	Parlophone GEP 8668	IT'S MARDI GRAS (EP)	8
58	Parlophone GEP 8700	COLOURFUL HUMPH (EP)	10
58	Parlophone GEP 8724	BLUE HUMPH (EP)	8
58	Parlophone GEP 8734	HUMPH'S JAZZ (EP)	15
58	Esquire EP 171	THAT REVIVAL SOUND (EP)	18
62	Columbia SEG 8163	DO THE BEAULIEU (EP)	15

LPs

Year	Label / Cat. No.	Title	£
53	Parlophone PMD 1006	JAZZ CONCERT (10" LP)	20
54	Parlophone PMC 1012	HUMPH AT THE CONWAY (LP)	25
55	Parlophone PMD 1032	JAZZ AT THE ROYAL FESTIVAL HALL (10" LP)	25
56	Parlophone PMD 1035	JAZZ SESSION WITH HUMPH (10" LP)	20
56	Parlophone PMD 1044	HUMPH SWINGS OUT (10" LP)	30
57	Parlophone PMD 1049	HERE'S HUMPH (10" LP)	20
58	Parlophone PMD 1052	KATH MEETS HUMPH (10" LP, with Kathy Stobart)	30
58	Parlophone PMC 1070	HUMPH IN PERSPECTIVE (LP)	30
58	Decca LK 4276	I PLAY AS I PLEASE (LP)	25
59	Parlophone PMC 1110	TRIPLE EXPOSURE (LP)	40
50s	Esquire 32-007	HUMPHREY LYTTELTON AND HIS BAND (LP)	25
60	Columbia 33SX 1239	BLUES IN THE NIGHT (LP)	30
60	Columbia 33SX 1305	HUMPH PLAYS STANDARDS (LP)	30

MINT VALUE £

60	Columbia 33SX 1364	HUMPH MEETS CAB (LP)	50
61	Columbia 33SX 3382	HUMPH RETURNS TO THE CONWAY (LP)	25
61	Columbia SEG 8130	BIG H (EP)	10
62	Columbia 33SX 1484	LATE NIGHT FINAL (LP)	25
65	Society SOC 1003	HUMPHREY LYTTELTON AND HIS BAND (LP)	20
69	Polydor 2460 140	DUKE ELLINGTON CLASSICS (LP)	35
69	Polydor 2661 001	21 YEARS ON (LP)	25
72	Parlophone PMC 7147	BEST OF 1949-1956 (LP)	15
73	Polydor 2460 233	SOUTH BANK SWING SESSION (LP)	25
74	Black Lion BLP 12149	ONCE IN A WHILE (LP)	20
78	Black Lion BLP 12173	SPREADIN' JOY (LP)	20
79	Black Lion BLP 12188	SIR HUMPH'S DELIGHT (LP)	20
79	Magnus 1	HUMPHREY'S ABOUT (LP)	20
80	Black Lion BLP 12199	ONE DAY I MET AN AFRICAN (LP)	20
82	Black Lion BLM 51011	ECHOES OF HARLEM (LP)	20

(see also Shirley Abicair, Sidney Bechet, George Brown, Buck Clayton, Radiohead)

M

79	MCA MCAT 413	Pop Musik/M Factor (12", p/s, double groove)	8

(see also Robin Scott)

MABEL

78	Sonet SON 2147	Boom Boom/FBI On The Nail (p/s)	6

MABEL JOY

75	Real RR 2004	MABEL JOY (LP)	35

MOMS MABLEY

69	Mercury MF 1127	Abraham, Martin And John/Sunny	8
71	Mercury 6052 109	That's Pops/I Surrender Dear	6

WILLIE MABON

64	Sue WI 320	Got To Have Some/Why Did It Happen To Me	25
65	Sue WI 331	Just Got Some/That's No Big Thing	25
65	Sue WI 382	I'm The Fixer/Some More	25

SPENCER MAC

70	Penny Farthing PEN 742	Commuter/Better By You — Better By Me	30

DAN MacARTHUR

79	Virgin VS 275	DAN MacARTHUR (EP)	5
79	Virgin VS 275-12	DAN MacARTHUR (12" EP)	8

(see also Jah Wobble, PiL)

NEIL MacARTHUR

69	Deram DM 225	She's Not There/World Of Glass	20
69	Deram DM 262	Don't Try To Explain/Without Her	12
69	Deram DM 275	It's Not Easy/12.29	12

(see also Colin Blunstone, Zombies)

GLO MACARI

65	Piccadilly 7N 35218	He Knows I Love Him Too Much/I've Lost You	15

MACARTHUR PARK

70	Columbia DB 8683	Taffeta Rose/Sammy	12
71	Philips 6006 086	Lottie Lottie/Love Is Coming	6

(see also Shadows)

DAVID MACBETH

59	Pye Nixa 7N 15231	Mr. Blue/Here's A Heart	8
59	Pye Nixa 7N 15231	Mr. Blue/Here's A Heart (78)	10
60	Pye 7N 15250	Tell Her From Me/Livin' Dangerously	8
60	Pye 7N 15274	Unhappy/Once Upon A Star	8
60	Pye 7N 15291	Blue Blue Blue/Pigtails In Paris	8
61	Pye 7N 15325	The Puppet Song/Angel On My Shoulder	8
61	Pye 7N 15364	Keep A-Walking/You're Free	8
61	Decca F 11402	Just A Twinkle/While I'm Away	6
62	Piccadilly 7N 35062	Roses Are Red (My Love)/Little Heart	7
62	Piccadilly 7N 35072	Have I Told You Lately That I Love You/A Brother Like You	7
63	Piccadilly 7N 35092	A Very Good Year For Girls/Broken Hearts	6
63	Piccadilly 7N 35114	My Golden Chance/Like A Falling Star	6
69	Pye 7N 17744	Does Anybody Miss Me/The Small Exception Of Me	6

MACATTACK

86	Baad! Records 12HIP1AZ	ART OF DRUMS (12" EP)	15

MACC LADS

89	Renegade RS 1	Jingle Bells/Even Uglier Women (p/s)	5
90	FM Revolver VHF 42	Barrels Round/Jingle Bells (p/s)	5
86	Hectic House HHS 1	EH UP! MACC LADS (EP)	5
85	FM Revolver FMLP 56	BEER AND SEX AND CHIPS'N'GRAVY (LP, white vinyl)	12
88	FM Revolver WKFMLP 115	LIVE AT LEEDS (LP, blue vinyl)	12

MINT VALUE £

EWAN MacCOLL

52	HMV B 10259	Lord Randall/Van Dieman's Land (78)	8
52	HMV B 10260	Sir Patrick Spens/Eppie Morrie (78)	8
58	Topic 10T 26	BARRACK ROOM BALLADS (10" LP)	30
58	Topic 10T 36	BOLD SPORTSMEN ALL (10" LP, with A.L. Lloyd)	30
58	Topic 10T 50	STILL I LOVE HIM (10" LP with booklet, with Isla Cameron)	35
60	Topic 12T 41	STREETS OF SONG (LP, with Dominic Behan, with booklet, originally with blue label)	20/12
61	PRE 13004	THE BEST OF EWAN MacCOLL (LP)	12
62	Topic 12T 79	THE JACOBITE REBELLIONS (LP, originally with blue label)	18/12
64	Topic 12T 103	ENGLISH AND SCOTTISH FOLK BALLADS (LP, with A.L. Lloyd, initially with blue label & booklet)	25/15
67	Topic 12T 130	BUNDOOK BALLADS (LP, originally with blue label)	18/12
67	Argo ZFB 12	SOLO FLIGHT (LP; reissued 1972)	30
67	Xtra 1052	BLOW BOYS BLOW – SONGS OF THE SEA (LP, with A.L. Lloyd)	12
68	Argo (Z)DA 85	THE WANTON MUSE (LP, with booklet)	30
72	Argo (Z)DA 85	THE WANTON MUSE (LP, reissue)	15

(see also A.L. Lloyd)

EWAN MacCOLL & PEGGY SEEGER (& CHARLES PARKER)

60s	AUEW AUEW 1	We Are The Engineers/I'm Gonna Be An Engineer (p/s)	6
57	Topic 10T 13	SHUTTLE AND CAGE (10" LP)	35
61	Topic 12T 16	CHORUS FROM THE GALLOWS (LP, originally with blue label)	18/12
64	Topic 12T 104	STEAM WHISTLE BALLADS (LP, blue label, later reissued with booklet)	18/12
65	Argo RG 474	THE BALLAD OF JOHN AXON (LP, by Ewan MacColl & Charles Parker)	25
67	Topic 12T 147	THE MANCHESTER ANGEL (LP, originally with blue label)	18/12
67	Argo DA 140	THE BIG HEWER — A RADIO BALLAD BY EWAN MacCOLL, PEGGY SEEGER, CHARLES PARKER (LP, documentary with music)	25
67	Argo (Z)DA 66	LONG HARVEST 1 (LP)	15
67	Argo (Z)DA 67	LONG HARVEST 2 (LP)	15
67	Argo (Z)DA 68	LONG HARVEST 3 (LP)	15
67	Argo (Z)DA 69	LONG HARVEST 4 (LP)	15
67	Argo RG 502	SINGING THE FISHING (LP, with Charles Parker)	25
67	Argo DA 142	SINGING THE FISHING (LP, reissue, with Charles Parker)	18
68	Argo (Z)DA 70	LONG HARVEST 5 (LP)	15
68	Argo (Z)DA 71	LONG HARVEST 6 (LP)	15
68	Argo (Z)DA 72	LONG HARVEST 7 (LP)	15
68	Argo (Z)DA 73	LONG HARVEST 8 (LP)	15
68	Argo (Z)DA 74	LONG HARVEST 9 (LP)	15
68	Argo (Z)DA 75	LONG HARVEST 10 (LP)	15
68	Argo (Z)DA 84	THE AMOROUS MUSE (LP)	15
68	Argo (Z)DA	THE ANGRY MUSE (LP)	15
69	Argo (Z)DA 98	THE PAPER STAGE 1 (LP, with booklet)	15
69	Argo (Z)DA 99	THE PAPER STAGE 2 (LP)	15
70	Argo SPA-A 102	THE WORLD OF EWAN MacCOLL & PEGGY SEEGER (LP)	20
70	Argo SPA-A 216	THE WORLD OF EWAN MacCOLL & PEGGY SEEGER VOL. 2 — SONGS FROM THE RADIO BALLADS (LP)	15
70	Argo DA 133	THE TRAVELLING PEOPLE (LP, with Charles Parker)	25
71	Argo DA 136	ON THE EDGE (LP)	15
72	Argo ZFB 65	THE ANGRY MUSE (LP, reissue)	12
72	Argo ZFB 66	THE AMOROUS MUSE (LP, reissue)	12

(see also Peggy Seeger, A.L. Lloyd, Isla Cameron)

KIRSTY MacCOLL

79	Stiff BUY 47	They Don't Know/Motor On (p/s)	8
79	Stiff PBUY 47	They Don't Know/Motor On (picture disc)	6
79	Stiff BUY 57	You Caught Me Out/Boys (with Boomtown Rats, unreleased, demos only)	6
81	Polydor POSP 225	Keep Your Hands Off My Baby/I Don't Need You (p/s)	7
81	Polydor POSP 368	You Still Believe In Me/Queen Of The High Teas (p/s)	10

(see also Drug Addix)

FINN MacCUILL

79	Radio Edinburgh REL 460	SINK YE — SWIM YE (LP)	300

AIMI MacDONALD

67	Polydor 56191	Thoroughly Modern Millie/Jimmy	6
70	Philips 6308 011	WHAT'S LOVE ALL ABOUT (LP)	15

BIG MACEO

62	RCA RCX 203	KINGS OF THE BLUES (EP)	20

MACEO & ALL THE KING'S MEN

72	Pye International 7N 25571	Got To Get 'Cha/Thank You For Letting Me Be Myself Again (Part 1)	7
72	Mojo 2916 017	FUNKY MUSIC MACHINE (LP)	60
75	Contempo CRM 114	FUNKY MUSIC MACHINE (LP, reissue)	20

MACEO & THE MACKS

87	Urban URB 1	Cross The Tracks (We Better Go Back)/Soul Power (printed die-cut sleeve)	5
87	Urban URBX 1	Cross The Tracks (We Better Go Back) (Extended Version)/Party Part 1/ Soul Power (12", printed die-cut sleeve)	12
74	Polydor 2391 122	US (LP)	30
88	Urban URBLP 8	US (LP, reissue)	15

(see also Maceo & All The King's Men, James Brown)

MACHINE

67	Granta GR 7STD	Stupidity/Please Stay (private pressing)	20

MACHINE

69	Polydor 56760	Spooky's Day Off/Nobody Wants You	6

(see also Swinging Soul Machine)

MINT VALUE £

MACHINES

78 Wax EAR 1 — True Life/Everything's Technical/You Better Hear/Evening Radio (stamped p/s, white labels) 50

MACHITO

50s Columbia — AFRO CUBAN JAZZ (10" LP) 20

ALURA MACK

50s Poydras 84 — Everybody's Man Is Mine/Monkey Blues 8

JOHNNY MACK

70 Columbia Blue Beat DB 116 — Reggae All Night Long/A Million Marvellous Feelings 12

LONNIE MACK

63 Stateside SS 207 — Memphis/Down In The Dumps 18
63 Stateside SS 226 — Wham!/Susie-Q 18
64 Stateside SS 312 — Lonnie On The Move/Say Something Nice To Me 15
65 Stateside SS 393 — Sa-Ba-Hoola/Chickin' Pickin' 20
67 President PT 127 — Where There's A Will/Baby What's Wrong? 7
67 President PT 142 — Save Your Money/Snow On The Mountain 7
68 President PT 198 — Soul Express/I Found A Love 8
69 Elektra EKSN 45044 — Memphis/Why (Edited Version) 10
69 Elektra EKSN 45060 — Save Your Money/In The Band 8
71 Elektra EK 45715 — Lay It Down/She Even Woke Me Up To Say Goodbye 6
79 Old Gold OG 9011 — Memphis/CHRIS MONTEZ: Let's Dance (picture disc) 5
67 President PTL 1004 — THE WHAM OF THAT MEMPHIS MAN (LP) 30
69 Elektra EKL 4040 — GLAD I'M IN THE BAND (LP, orange label, also stereo EKS 74040) 30
69 Elektra EKS 74050 — WHATEVER'S RIGHT (LP, orange label) 30
70 Elektra 2410 007 — FOR COLLECTORS ONLY (LP, reissue of "The Wham Of That Memphis Man") .. 15
72 Elektra K 42097 — THE HILLS OF INDIANA (LP) 15

WARNER MACK

58 Brunswick 05728 — Roc-A-Chicka/Since I Lost You (with Anita Kerr Quartet) 175
58 Brunswick 05728 — Roc-A-Chicka/Since I Lost You (with Anita Kerr Quartet) (78) 75
58 Decca — Roc-A-Chicka/Since I Lost You (export issue, with Anita Kerr Quartet) 90
62 London HA-R/SH-R 8002 — GOLDEN COUNTRY HITS (LP) 25
63 London HA-R/SH-R 8025 — GOLDEN COUNTRY HITS VOL. 2 (LP) 25
66 Brunswick LAT 8658 — COUNTRY TOUCH (LP) 18
67 Brunswick LAT 8684 — DRIFTING APART (LP) 18

ANDY MACKAY

74 Island WIP 6197 — Ride Of The Valkyries/Time Regained 5
75 Island WIP 6243 — Wild Weekend/Walking The Whippet (some in promo p/s) 10/5
78 Bronze BRO 64 — A Song Of Friendship/Skill And Sweat 5
74 Island ILPS 9278 — IN SEARCH OF EDDIE RIFF (LP, 2 different versions) 12
(see also Roxy Music, Rock Follies)

MAHNA MACKAY

69 Parlophone R 5808 — Mah Na Mah Na/Daydream 6

RABBIT MacKAY

68 MCA MU 1041 — Hard Time Woman/Candy 5
68 MCA MUPS 351 — BUG CLOTH (LP) 12

BILLY MacKENZIE

82 WEA MAK 1 — Ice Cream Factory/Cream Of Ice Cream Factory (p/s, as MacKenzie Sings Orbidöig) 5
82 WEA MAK 1T — Ice Cream Factory/Cream Of Ice Cream Factory (12", p/s, as MacKenzie Sings Orbidöig) 8
92 Circa YRCD 86 — Baby/Sacrifice And Be Sacrificed (CH 8032 Mix)/Grooveature (D 1000 Mix)/ Colours Will Come (US 60659 Mix) (CD, solo) 8
92 Circa YRCD 91 — Colours Will Come/Opal Krusch/Look What You've Done/ Feels Like The Richtergroove (CD) 15
01 Rhythm Of Life ROL 006 — Wild Is The Wind/Mother Earth/Baltimore/Give Me Time (Version) (CD, internet-only release) 75
92 Circa CIRCD 22 — OUTERNATIONAL (CD) 75
(see also Associates, Orbidöig, Yello, B.E.F., Sweden Through The Ages)

BILLY MacKENZIE with STEVE AUNGLE

01 Rhythm Of Life ROL 005 — EUROCENTRIC (CD) 25

BILLY MacKENZIE with PAUL HAIG

00 Rhythm Of Life ROL 003 — MEMORY PALACE (CD) 25

GISELE MacKENZIE

53 Capitol CL 13920 — Seven Lonely Days/Till I Waltz With You Again (78) 7
55 HMV 7M 318 — Hard To Get/Boston Fancy 7
56 Capitol Junior CJ 131 — Sings Children's Songs From France Parts 1 & 2 (78, p/s) 7

JUDY MacKENZIE

70 Key KL 005 — JUDY (LP) 30
71 Key KL 009 — PEACE AND LOVE AND FREEDOM (LP, with poster) 30

MACKENZIE JET COMBO

70 Torpedo TOR 18 — Milkman's Theme/Capadulah Recipe 8

MACKERAL

66 Columbia DB 8013 — Funny Fish/This Is Mine 5
68 Columbia DB 8388 — Trying Again/White Man's Burden 5

KEN MACKINTOSH (& HIS ORCHESTRA)

56 HMV 7M 343 — Creeping Tom/Lovers In The Dark 10
56 HMV 7M 359 — Start Walking/Curtain Call 10
56 HMV 7M 379 — Blues In The Night/Come Next Spring (B-side with Kenny Bardell) 10

MINT VALUE £

56 HMV 7M 403 Sleepwalker/The Berkeley Hunt 10
56 HMV 7M 417 Dizzy Fingers/The Policeman's Holiday 10
56 HMV POP 270 Soft Summer Breeze/Highway Patrol 7
57 HMV POP 287 The Buccaneers/Regimental Rock 12
57 HMV POP 300 Apple-Jack/Slow Walk 18
57 HMV POP 327 Almost Paradise/Rock Man Rock 18
57 HMV POP 358 Poni Tail/Keep It Movin' 8
57 HMV POP 396 Marching Along To The Blues/Six-Five Blues 8
57 HMV POP 426 Raunchy/Mojo 8
58 HMV POP 441 The Stroll/The Swingin' Shepherd Blues 8
58 HMV POP 464 Big Guitar/Squatty 8
58 HMV POP 506 The Swivel/Muchacha 7
58 HMV POP 543 Ulterior Motive/That Old Cha Cha Feeling 5
59 HMV POP 592 Rock-A-Conga/Hampden Park 7
59 HMV POP 592 Rock-A-Conga/Hampden Park (78) 8
59 HMV POP 656 Sleep Walk/Morgen (One More Sunrise) 7
60 HMV POP 713 No Hiding Place/Tally Ho! 8
56 HMV 7EG 8170 TEENAGER'S SPECIAL (EP) 22
58 HMV 7EG 8468 DANCING TO THE ROARING TWENTIES (EP) 10
55 HMV DLP 1093 KEN MACKINTOSH (10" LP) 18
58 HMV DLP 1178 ONE NIGHT STAND (10" LP) 25

MACK SISTERS
56 London HLU 8331 Long Range Love/Stop What You're Doing 50

PETE MacLAINE & CLAN
63 Decca F 11699 Yes I Do/U.S. Mail 15

SHIRLEY MacLAINE
69 MCA MU 1062 My Personal Property/Where Am I Going 5

DOUGIE MacLEAN
80 Plant Life PLR 022 SNAIGOW (LP, with lyric insert) 12
88 Dunkeld DUN 008 REAL ESTATE (LP) 20
(see also Alan Roberts)

DOLINA MACLENNAN & ROBIN GRAY
61 Topic TOP 68 BY MORMOND BRAES (EP) 8

JOHN MacLEOD'S FIRST XI
66 Fontana TF 696 Don't Shoot The Ref/Tomato Crisps 6

JOHN MacLEOD SOUND
60s Transatlantic TRASP 12 Russian Roulette/West Wind 6

ANGUS MacLISE
87 Fierce FRIGHT 010 Trance (1-sided, with 'Dopechoc' & badge) 10

PATRICK MacNEE & HONOR BLACKMAN
64 Decca F 11843 Kinky Boots/Let's Keep It Friendly 40
(see also Honor Blackman)

FLORA MacNEIL
77 Tangent TGS 124 CROABH NAN UBHAL (LP, with insert) 12

MADELINE MacNEIL
60s Skyline DD 103 PATCHWORK (LP) 25

UNCLE DAVE MACON
63 RCA RCX 7112 UNCLE DAVE MACON NO. 1 (EP) 22
63 RCA RCX 7113 UNCLE DAVE MACON NO. 2 (EP) 22
66 Ace Of Hearts AH 135 UNCLE DAVE MACON (LP) 15

MACON JUG
70 Saga FID 8157 IN THE SUMMERTIME (LP, with tracks by Good Earth) 15
72 Boulevard BLVD 4078 RAY DORSET'S BEST (LP, 4 tracks by Good Earth, 6 tracks by Macon Jug) 12
(see also Ray Dorset, Mungo Jerry)

GORDON MacRAE
54 Capitol CL 14168 How Do You Speak To An Angel?/C'est Magnifique 12
54 Capitol CL 14193 Count Your Blessings Instead Of Sheep/Never In A Million Years 12
55 Capitol CL 14222 Here's What I'm Here For/Love Can Change The Stars 7
55 Capitol CL 14276 Stranger In Paradise/High On A Windy Hill 12
55 Capitol CL 14293 You Forget (To Tell Me That You Love Me)/Tik-A-Tee, Tik-A-Tay 7
55 Capitol CL 14334 Jim Bowie/Why Break The Heart That Loves You 12
55 Capitol CL 14361 Bella Notte/Blame It On My Youth 12
56 Capitol CL 14526 Follow Your Heart/Fate 6
56 Capitol CL 14548 Never Before And Never Again/Don't Blame Me 6
56 Capitol CL 14576 Who Are We/There's A Lull In My Life 6
56 Capitol CL 14606 One Misty Morning/I Asked The Lord 5
56 Capitol CL 14613 People Will Say We're In Love/The Surrey With The Fringe On Top (with Ray Anthony) 6
56 Capitol CL 14622 Woman In Love/I Don't Want To Walk Without You 6
58 Capitol CL 14818 Lonely/Sayonora 6
58 Capitol CL 14864 I've Grown Accustomed To Her Face/Never Till Now 6
58 Capitol CL 14920 The Secret/A Man Once Said 6
58 Capitol CL 14920 The Secret/A Man Once Said (78) 10
59 Capitol CL 14983 Fly Little Bluebird/Little Do You Know 6
59 Capitol CL 15021 Palace Of Love/The Stranger 6
62 Capitol CL 15256 Sail Away/Face To Face 6
63 Capitol CL 15315 Lovely/Warmer Than A Whisper 6
52 Capitol LC 6564 THE MERRY WIDOW (10" LP, with Lucille Norman) 15
53 Capitol LC 6592 CAPITOL PRESENTS GORDON MACRAE (10" LP) 15

MINT VALUE £

53 Capitol LC 6599 BY THE LIGHT OF THE SILVERY MOON (10" LP, with June Hutton) 15
53 Capitol LC 6606 THE DESERT SONG (10" LP, with Lucille Norman). 15
53 Capitol LC 6613 THE STUDENT PRINCE (10" LP, with Dorothy Warenskjold) 15
54 Capitol LC 6663 NAUGHTY MARIETTA (10" LP, with Lucille Norman) 15
54 Capitol LC 6666 ROBERTA (10" LP, with Lucille Norman). 15
56 Capitol LC 6805 ROMANTIC BALLADS (10" LP) 15
60 Capitol (S)T 1251 SONGS FOR AN EVENING AT HOME (LP) 12
60 Top Rank 25/006 GORDON MACRAE (LP). 12
(see also Jo Stafford, Ray Anthony, Jonathan & Darlene Edwards)

JOSH MACRAE

60 Top Rank JAR 290 Talkin' Army Blues/Talkin' Guitar Blues. 12
60 Pye 7N 15306 Original Talkin' Blues (Talkin' Southern Blues)/Talkin' Thro' The Mill 7
60 Pye 7N 15307 Let Ramensky Go/Sky High Joe 7
60 Pye 7N 15308 Wild Side Of Life/Dear John 8
61 Pye 7N 15319 Messing About On The River/High Class Feeling 8
61 Pye 7N 15360 Arkansas Rambler/Never Never Man. 6
61 Pye 7N 15384 Do It Yourself/Special Place Of Yorn 6
60 Pye NEP 24131 WALKIN', TALKIN', SINGIN' (EP) 18
60 Top Rank JKP 2061 JOSH MACRAE (EP). 18
66 Transatlantic TRA 150 JOSH MACRAE (LP). 22
66 Golden Guinea GGL 0335 MESSING ABOUT ON THE RIVER (LP) 15

JOHNNY MADARA

57 HMV POP 389 Be My Girl/Lovesick 10

MADCAPS

50 London L 786 Nightingale/Sleighride (78) 8
51 Brunswick 04787 Josephine/Casa Loma Stomp 6
53 Brunswick LA 8631 HARMONICATERS (10" LP) 15

MADCAPS & HARMONICATS

54 London H-APB 1016 HARMONICA RHYTHMS (10" LP, 1 side each) 15

MAD DOG

74 Chappell LPC 1053 POP SOUNDS (LP, library edition). 30

MAD DOG

85 Brainy CUTN 1 Sheriff (p/s). 50

JOHNNY MADDOX (& HIS ORCHESTRA)

53 Vogue V 9047 Johnny Maddox Boogie/Little Grass Shack (78). 8
55 London MSD 1503/1504 Nickelodeon Tango/Solitude (unissued, demos only). 50
55 London HL 8056 I Don't Love Nobody/There's A Star-Spangled Banner (78) 12
55 London HL 8134 The Crazy Otto — Medley/Humoresque 30
55 London HL 8134 The Crazy Otto — Medley/Humoresque (78). 7
55 London HLD 8203 Do, Do, Do/When You Wore A Tulip (And I Wore A Big Red Rose) 30
56 London HLD 8277 Hop Scotch Boogie/Hands Off. 40
56 London HLD 8277 Hop Scotch Boogie/Hands Off (78) 12
56 London HLD 8347 Heart And Soul/Dixieland Band. 20
58 London HLD 8540 Yellow Dog Blues/Sugar Train 18
59 London HLD 8826 The Hurdy Gurdy Song/Old Fashioned Love 12
59 London HLD 8826 The Hurdy Gurdy Song/Old Fashioned Love (78) 10
55 London RE-P 1020 PRESENTING JOHNNY MADDOX AND THE RHYTHMASTERS (EP). 25
55 London RE-P 1040 PRESENTING JOHNNY MADDOX AND THE RHYTHMASTERS NO. 2 (EP). 18
58 London RE-D 1150 HONKY TONK JAZZ (EP) 12
61 London RE-D 1270 OLD FASHIONED LOVE (EP) 12
56 London HB-D 1060 JOHNNY MADDOX PLAYS (10" LP, with His Rhythmasters). 20
58 London HA-D 2101 MY OLD FLAMES (LP) 12

ROSE MADDOX

59 Capitol CL 15023 Gambler's Love/What Makes Me Hang Around. 7

MADE IN ENGLAND

86 Red Bus RBUS 2208 Prospects/Stay Sharp (A-side with Ray Dorset, p/s). 6
(see also Ray Dorset)

MADE IN SHEFFIELD

67 Fontana TF 871 Amelia Jane/Right Satisfied. 20
(see also Joe Cocker, Grease Band, Chris Stainton)

MADE IN SWEDEN

69 Sonet SLP 71 MADE IN SWEDEN (LP) 15
69 Sonet SLP 2504 SNAKES IN A HOLE (LP) 15
70 Sonet SLP 2506 LIVE AT THE GOLDEN CIRCLE (LP) 15
70 Sonet SLP 2512 MADE IN ENGLAND (LP) 20
71 Sonet SNTF 621 MAD RIVER (LP). 55

BETTY MADIGAN

54 MGM SP 1109 Always You/That Was My Heart You Heard! 8
55 MGM SP 1119 And So I Walked Home/Be A Little Darlin'. 8
55 MGM SP 1131 Salute/The Wheels Of Love 8
55 MGM SP 1137 I Had A Heart/Wonderful Words. 8
55 MGM SP 1138 Teddy Bear/Strangers 8
69 MGM MGM 1482 I'm Gonna Make You Love Me/Goodnight 6
58 Coral FEP 2009 JEROME KERN SONGBOOK VOL. 1 (EP) 12
59 Coral FEP 2011 JEROME KERN SONGBOOK VOL. 2 (EP) 12

MAD JOCKS & ENGLISHMEN

80 Wild Dog DOGLP 18 TONGUE IN CHEEK (LP) 15
80s Wild Dog DOGLP 50 THUD & BLUNDER (LP). 15

MINT VALUE £

MAD LADS (U.S.)

65 Atlantic AT 4051 Don't Have To Shop Around/Tear Maker . . . 12
66 Atlantic AT 4083 I Want Someone/Nothing Can Break Through . . . 15
66 Atlantic 584 038 Sugar Sugar/Get Out Of My Life Woman . . . 8

MAD LADS (Jamaica)

69 Coxsone CS 7099 Losing You/WINSTON JARRETT: Peck Up A Pagan . . . 20

MADNESS

SINGLES

79 2-Tone TT 3 The Prince/Madness (paper label, later plastic, company sleeve) . . . 15/10
79 Stiff BUY IT 56 One Step Beyond/Mistakes/Nutty Theme (12", p/s) . . . 10
79 Stiff MAD 1 Don't Quote Me On That/Swan Lake (12", promo only) . . . 50
81 Stiff BUY IT 108 The Return Of The Los Palmas 7/My Girl (Demo)/That's The Way To Do It/ Swan Lake (live) (12", p/s, with comic) . . . 10
81 Stiff BUY IT 112 Grey Day/Baggy Trousers/Take It Or Leave It/Un Paso Adelante (12", p/s) . . . 20
82 Stiff BUY IT 134 It Must Be Love/Mrs. Hutchinson/Shadow On The House (12", p/s credits "Limited Edition Special 12" Dance Mix", record plays standard mix) . . . 8
82 Stiff PBUY 146 House Of Fun/Don't Look Back (picture disc) . . . 5
82 Stiff BUY 153 Driving In My Car/Animal Farm (poster p/s) . . . 5
82 Stiff PBUY 153 Driving In My Car/Animal Farm (picture disc) . . . 5
82 Stiff GRAB 1 THE MADNESS PACK (6 x 7" in clear plastic folder) . . . 20
83 Stiff PBUY 169 Tomorrow's (Just Another Day)/Madness (Is All In The Mind) (picture disc) . . . 5
83 Stiff BUY IT 169 Tomorrow's (Just Another Day) (Warped Mix)/Blue Skinned Beast (warped mix)/Tomorrow's (Just Another Day) (Elvis Costello vocal) (12", p/s) . . . 8
83 Stiff BUY 169 Tomorrow's Just Another Day/Madness Is All In The Mind (test pressing, pink & blue vinyl, 1 copy known) . . . 350
84 Stiff BUY IT 196 Michael Caine (extended version)/Michael Caine/ If You Think There's Something (12", p/s) . . . 8
85 Zarjazz JAZZ D5 Yesterday's Men/All I Knew (square picture disc)//Yesterday's Men (Harmonica Mix)/It Must Be Love (live) (double pack, gold PVC wallet) . . . 6
85 Zarjazz JAZZY 7 Uncle Sam/Please Don't Go/Insanity Over Christmas (picture disc) . . . 5
86 Zarjazz JAZZ B9-12 (Waiting For) The Ghost-Train/Maybe In Another Life/ Seven Year Scratch (12", p/s with 8-page booklet) . . . 8
88 Virgin VSX 1054 I Pronounce You/4BF/Patience/11th Hour (as The Madness, box with badge, 2 cards & sticker) . . . 5
88 Virgin VSCD 1054 I Pronounce You/4BF/Patience/11th Hour (CD, as The Madness) . . . 8

FLEXIDISCS

80 Stiff/Lyntone LYN 8680 Patches Brings You A Few Minutes Of Madness (with *Patches* mag) . . . 10/7
81 Lyntone LYN 10208 Take It or Leave It (free with *Take It Or Leave It* magazine) . . . 12/8
81 Lyn. LYN 10353/EVENT 2 Event — The Madness (free with *Event* magazine) . . . 10/7
82 Lyntone LYN 11546 My Girl (Ballad) (green or white vinyl, with *Flexipop* mag issue 19; with/without magazine) . . . 8/6
82 Lyntone LYN 11546 My Girl (Ballad) (hard vinyl test pressing of above) . . . 25
82 Lyntone LYN 10719 Carols On 45 (fan club disc) . . . 8
84 Lyntone LYN 15280/1 Insanity Over Christmas/Visit To Castle Dracstein (fan club disc) . . . 7
85 Lyntone LYN 16676 From Us ... To You (Mad Not Mad tour disc, some with tour programme) . . . 10/6
85 Lyntone LYN 16981 Live From The Mad Not Mad Tour . . . 6
86 Lyntone LYN 18251 Ghost Train (The Demo)/The Final Goodbye (fan club disc) . . . 6

ALBUMS

80 Stiff SEEZ 29 ABSOLUTELY (LP, some in first-issue sleeve) . . . 30/20
84 Stiff PSEEZ 53 KEEP MOVING (LP, picture disc, U.S. running order) . . . 15
82 Madness Info Service (no cat. no.) THE M.I.S. RADIO PLAYERS PRESENT 30 MINUTES OF CULTURE (fan club cassette) . . . 12
86 Madness Info Service MADNESS LIVE (fan club cassette) . . . 20

(see also Suggs, Argonauts, Voice Of The Beehive)

MADONNA

SIRE SINGLES

82 Sire W 9899 Everybody/Everybody (Dub Version) (no p/s) . . . 125
82 Sire W 9899T Everybody/Everybody (Dub Version) (12", no p/s) . . . 100
83 Sire W 9522 Lucky Star (Edit)/I Know It ('sunglasses' p/s, Irish only) . . . 250
83 Sire W 9522T Lucky Star (Full Length Version)/I Know It (12", 'sunglasses' p/s; some rumoured to come with stickered p/s & poster different to reissue) . . . 90/65
83 Sire W 9522TV Lucky Star (U.S Remix)/I Know It (12", stickered plain white die-cut sleeve) . . . 60
83 Sire W 9405 Holiday (Edit)/Think Of Me ('train' p/s) . . . 12
83 Sire W 9405T Holiday (Full Length Version 6.08)/Think Of Me (12", 'train' p/s, some with 'Copyright Control' wording on label) . . . 10
84 Sire W 9522 Lucky Star (Edit)/I Know It (reissue, 'bangles & stars' p/s) . . . 5
84 Sire W 9522T Lucky Star (Full Length Version)/I Know It (12" reissue, stickered 'TV screen' p/s, some with poster) . . . 35/15
84 Sire W 9260 Borderline (Edit)/Physical Attraction (p/s, large 'A' on paper A-side label) . . . 5
84 Sire W 9260F Borderline (Edit)/Physical Attraction//Holiday (Edit)/Think Of Me ('map' p/s, double pack with European p/s, copies of "Holiday", shrinkwrapped & stickered; beware of counterfeits with less-than-Mint picture sleeves!) . . . 100
84 Sire W 9260T Borderline (U.S. Remix)/Borderline (Dub Remix)/Physical Attraction (12", p/s, with '9-' LP catalogue numbers on rear of sleeve) . . . 10
84 Sire W 9210T Like A Virgin (U.S. Dance Remix)/Stay (12", p/s, some with poster & sticker) . . 35/8
85 Sire W 9083 Material Girl/Pretender (p/s) . . . 5
85 Sire W 9083T Material Girl (Jellybean Dance Mix)/Pretender (12", p/s, some with poster) . . . 35/8
85 Sire W 8934P Into The Groove/Shoo-Be-Doo (heart-shaped picture disc with 2 stickers) . . . 35
85 Sire W 8934P Into The Groove/Shoo-Be-Doo (12" *uncut* heart-shaped picture disc, very few copies) . . . 500+
85 Sire W 8934T Into The Groove/Everybody/Shoo-Be-Doo (12", p/s, initially with poster) . . . 30/8
85 Sire W 9405 Holiday (Edit)/Think Of Me (reissue, 'train' p/s) . . . 12
85 Sire W 9405T Holiday (Full Length Version 6.08)/Think Of Me (12", 'cross earring' p/s reissue) . . . 15

MINT VALUE £

85	Sire W 9405P	Holiday (Full Length Version 6.08)/Think Of Me (12", picture disc)	30
85	Sire W 8881P	Angel (Edit)/Burning Up (shaped pic disc, some with cardboard plinth)	45/35
85	Sire W 8881T	Angel (Extended Dance Mix)/Burning Up (12", p/s)	8
85	Sire W 8848T	Dress You Up (12" Formal Mix)/(Casual Instrumental)/I Know It (12", p/s)	8
85	Sire W 8848TF	Dress You Up (12" Formal Mix)/(Casual Instrumental) /I Know It (12", poster p/s, '4 Track Studio' or 'Live Like A Virgin Tour' rear video advert)	each 30
85	Sire W 8848P	Dress You Up/I Know It ('Xmas tree star'-shaped picture disc)	30
86	Sire W 9260P	Borderline/Physical Attraction (Madonna-shaped picture disc)	50
86	Sire W 9260T	Borderline (U.S. Remix)/Borderline (Dub Remix)/Physical Attraction (12", p/s, reissue, with 'WX' LP catalogue numbers on rear of sleeve)	10
86	Sire W 8717T(W)	Live To Tell (LP Version)/(Edit)/(Instrumental) (12", p/s, some with poster)	15/8
86	Sire W 8636T(W)	Papa Don't Preach (Extended Version)/Papa Don't Preach (LP Version)/ Ain't No Big Deal (12", p/s, initially with free poster)	15/8
86	Sire W 8636TP	Papa Don't Preach (Extended Remix)/Ain't No Big Deal (LP Version)/ Papa Don't Preach (LP version) (12", picture disc; some copies play last 2 tracks in wrong order)	each 30
86	Sire W 8550	True Blue (Extended Dance Version)/Holiday (Extended Dance Mix) (12", p/s)	8
86	Sire W 8550P	True Blue (Extended Dance Version)/Holiday (Extended Dance Mix) (12", picture disc)	25
86	Sire W 8480	Open Your Heart (Extended Version)/Open Your Heart (Dub Mix)/ Lucky Star (Full Length Version) (12", p/s)	8
86	Sire W 8480P	Open Your Heart (Extended Version)/Open Your Heart (Dub Mix)/ Lucky Star (Full Length Version) (12", picture disc)	22
87	Sire W 8378	La Isla Bonita (Extended Remix)/(Extended Instrumental) (12", p/s)	8
87	Sire W 8378P	La Isla Bonita (Extended Remix)/(Extended Instrumental) (12", picture disc)	25
87	Sire W 8341T	Who's That Girl (Extended Remix)/White Heat (12" Remix) (12", p/s)	8
87	Sire W 8341TX	Who's That Girl (Extended Version)/Who's That Girl (Dub Mix)/ White Heat (12" Remix) (12", p/s)	20
87	Sire W 8341TP	Who's That Girl (Extended Version)/White Heat (12", picture disc; beware of original decaying PVC sleeves)	50
87	Sire W 8224	Causing A Commotion (Silver Screen Single Mix)/Jimmy Jimmy (p/s, with badge shrinkwrapped to p/s)	45
87	Sire W 8224TP	Causing A Commotion (Silver Screen Mix)/Causing A Commotion (Movie House Mix)/Jimmy Jimmy (Fade) (12", picture disc)	20
87	Sire W 8115T	The Look Of Love/Love Don't Live Here Anymore/I Know It (12", p/s & poster)	15
87	Sire W 8115TP	The Look Of Love/Love Don't Live Here Anymore/I Know It (12", picture disc)	25
89	Sire W 7539	Like A Prayer/Act Of Contrition (p/s, with free Virgin Megastore poster)	6
89	Sire W 7539TX	Like A Prayer (12" Dance Mix)/(Churchapella Mix)/(7"Remix Edit) (12", p/s)	12
89	Sire W 7539TP	Like A Prayer (12" Extended Remix)/(12" Club Version)/ Act Of Contrition (12", picture disc)	25
89	Sire W 7539CD	Like A Prayer/(12" Extended Remix)/(12" Club Version) (3" CD)	12
89	Sire W 2948X	Express Yourself (7" Remix)/The Look Of Love (LP) (poster p/s)	12
89	Sire W 2948W	Express Yourself (7" Remix)/The Look Of Love (LP) ('jeans zipper' p/s)	35
89	Sire W 2948CX	Express Yourself (Non-Stop Express Mix)/(Stop + Go Dubs) (cassette)	65
89	Sire W 2948TP	Express Yourself/(Non-Stop Express Mix)/(Stop + Go Dubs) (12", 'nude' picture disc)	25
89	Sire W 2948 CD	Express Yourself/(Non-Stop Express Mix)/(Stop + Go Dubs) (3" CD)	15
89	Sire W 2883TP	Cherish (Extended Version)/(7" Version)/Supernatural (12", picture disc)	25
89	Sire W 2883TP	Cherish (Extended Version)/(7" Version)/Supernatural (12", mispressed picture disc, plays "Cherish" but pictures feature Fish's "State Of Mind")	40
89	Sire W 2883 CD	Cherish (extended)/Cherish/Supernatural (3" CD)	15
89	Sire W 2668P	Dear Jessie/Till Death Do Us Part (picture disc)	10
89	Sire W 2668TW	Dear Jessie/Till Death Do Us Part/Holiday (12" Version) (12", poster p/s)	15
89	Sire W 2268CD	Dear Jessie/Till Death Do Us Part/Holiday (12" Version) (CD)	8
89	Sire W 2268CDX	Dear Jessie/Till Death Do Us Part/Holiday (12" Version) (CD, picture disc)	60
89	Sire 925 681-2	Papa Don't Preach (7" Version)/(12" Version)/Pretender (LP Version)/ Papa Don't Preach (CD Video)	65
90	Sire W 9851	Vogue/Keep It Together (Single Remix) (p/s, mispress with B-side twice)	15
90	Sire W 9851P	Vogue/Keep It Together (Single Remix) (picture disc)	10
90	Sire W 9851TW	Vogue (12" Version)/Keep It Together (12" Remix) (12", p/s, with 'Face of the 80s' poster)	12
90	Sire W 9851TX	Vogue (12" Version)/Vogue (Strike-A-Pose Dub) (12", p/s, with 'X-rated' 30" x 20" poster)	15
90	Sire W 9851TP	Vogue (12" Version)/Keep It Together (12" Remix) (12", picture disc)	25
90	Sire W 9789TP	Hanky Panky (Bare Bottom 12" Mix)/(Bare Bones Single Mix)/More (LP Version) (12", picture disc with gatefold insert & foldout poster)	15
90	Sire W 9000TP	Justify My Love (William Orbit Remix)/Justify My Love/Express Yourself (Shep's 'Spressin' Himself Remix) (12", picture disc with insert)	15
91	Sire W 0008P	Crazy For You (Remix)/Keep It Together (Single Remix) (shaped picture disc with plinth & insert)	15
91	Sire W 0008CD	Crazy For You (Remix)/Keep It Together (Shep Pettibone Remix)/ Into The Groove (Shep Pettibone Remix) (CD, picture disc)	10
91	Sire W 0037TP	Holiday/True Blue (12", clear vinyl picture disc with insert in PVC sleeve)	12
91	Sire W 0037CD	THE HOLIDAY COLLECTION (Holiday/True Blue/Who's That Girl/ Causing A Commotion) (CD)	8

MAVERICK SINGLES

92	Maverick W 0138TP	Erotica (Album Version 5.12)/Erotica (Instrumental 5.12)/Erotica (Radio Edit 4.31) (12", picture disc with gold insert, withdrawn, 138 only)	700
92	Maverick W 0146TP	Deeper And Deeper (Shep's Classic 12")/(Shep's Deep Makeover Mix)/ (Shep's Deep Beats)/(David's Klub Mix)/(David's Deep Mix)/ (Shep's Deeper Dub) (12", picture disc)	15
93	Maverick W 0168P	Fever (Edit)/Fever (Radio Edit Remix) (picture disc with numbered insert)	12
94	Maverick W 0268P	Secret (Edit)/Let Down Your Guard (Rough Mix Edit) (picture disc w/insert)	12

MINT VALUE £

95	Maverick W 0278P	Take A Bow (Edit)/Take A Bow (picture disc with insert)	7
95	Maverick W 0285CDX	Bedtime Story (Junior's Single Mix)/Secret (Allstar Mix)/Secret (Some Bizarre Mix)/Secret (Some Bizarre Single Mix) (CD, booklet sleeve)	10

OTHER SINGLES

85	Geffen A 6323	Crazy For You/SAMMY HAGAR: I'll Fall In Love Again (p/s)	5
85	Geffen WA 6323	Crazy For You/SAMMY HAGAR: I'll Fall In Love Again (Madonna-shaped picture disc)	65
85	Geffen A 6585	Gambler/BLACK 'N BLUE: Nature Of The Beast (p/s)	5
85	Geffen QA 6585	Gambler/BLACK 'N BLUE: Nature Of The Beast (poster p/s)	25
85	Geffen TA 6585	Gambler (Extended Dance Mix)/Gambler (Instrumental Remix)/ BLACK 'N BLUE: Nature Of The Beast (12", p/s)	20
92	Receiver RRSP 1007	Shine A Light/On The Ground (picture disc, withdrawn)	12
92	Receiver RRSPT 1007	Shine A Light/On The Ground/Little Boy (12", p/s, withdrawn)	8
92	Reciever RRSPT 1007	Shine A Light/On The Ground/Little Boy (12", picture disc)	15

PROMOS

89	Sire SAM 641	Keep It Together (12" Remix)/(Dub)/(Extended Remix)/(12" Mix)/ (Bonus Beats)/(Instrumental) (12")	25
90	Sire SAM 659	Vogue (12" Version)/Vogue (Strike A Pose Dub) (12")	25
94	Warner Bros SAM 1526	Bedtime Story (Junior's Sound Factory Mix)/(Mixes) (12")	20
94	Warner Bros SAM 1653	Human Nature/(Mixes) (12", stickered title sleeve)	30
94	Warner Bros W0300CDDJ	Human Nature (4'30" Radio Edit) (CD)	20
96	Sire SAM 1880	Love Don't Live Here Anymore (Mark!s It's A Girl Dub)/(Mark!s It's A Boy Dub)/(Mark!s Full On Vocal) (12")	35
96	Warner Bros SAM 1982	Don't Cry For Me Argentina (Miami Mix)/(Mixes) (12", title sleeve)	25
96	Warner Bros W0384CDDJ	Don't Cry For Me Argentina/(Radio Edit) (CD)	15
96	Warner Bros W0388CDDJ	Another Suitcase In Another Hall (CD, title inlay)	15
96	Warner Bros W0337CDDJ	One More Chance (CD, some with p/s)	15/10
98	Warner Bros 3331000037	Drowned World/Substitute For Love (BT & Sasha's Bucklodge Ashram Remix)/ Sky Fits Heaven (Sasha Remix)/Substitute For Love (Victor Calderone Remix Edit) (12")	25
98	Sire SAM 3173	Frozen (Extended Club Mix)/(Stereo MC's Mix)/(Meltdown Mix — Long Version) (12")	20
98	Sire SAM 3173	Frozen (Extended Club Mix)/(Stereo MC's Mix)/(Meltdown Mix — Long Version) (12", mispress, sleeve & labels credit "Dive Boogie" but play tracks from "Frozen" 12" promo)	15
90s	Warner Bros SAM 00061	Nothing Really Matters (mixes) (12")	20
90s	Warner Bros W 471CDDJ	Nothing Really Matters (Album Version)/Nothing Really Matters (Club 69 Radio Mix) (CD, slimline jewel case)	15
90s	Warner Bros (no cat. no.)	Buenos Aires (mixes) (CD-R, title sleeve)	150
00	Warner Bros PR01802	American Pie (Album Version)/(Richard 'Humpty' Vission Radio Mix) (CD)	15
00	Maverick PRO 261270	American Pie (Pie Mix)/(Orbit Sugar Free Mix) (CD, tin case)	35
00	Warner Bros PRO 6584	Music (mixes) (12" doublepack, title-stickered sleeve)	15
00	Warner Bros PR02054	Music (Album Version) (CD)	10
00	Warner Bros PR02055	Music (Groove Armada's 7" Edit)/(mixes) (CD)	15
01	Warner Bros PR02296	Don't Tell Me (Thunderpuss Radio Mix)/(mixes) (CD)	15
01	Warner Bros PR02461	What It Feels Like For A Girl (Edit)/(7 mixes) (CD-R, title sleeve)	30
01	Warner Bros (no cat. no.)	Don't Tell Me (7 different mixes) (CD-R, title sleeve)	35
01	Warner Bros (no cat. no.)	Impressive Instant (Rauhoffers Universal Club Mix)/Impressive Instant (Rauhoffers Drowned World Dub) (CD-R, paper title-sleeve)	35
01	Warner Bros (no cat. no.)	Thunderpuss GHV2 Megamix (Long Edit)/Thunderpuss GHV2 Megamix (Short Edit) (CD-R, paper title-sleeve)	35
01	Warner Bros PROP 05247	GHV2 (CD, slimline jewel case, 'collage' insert)	25
01	Warner Bros SAM 00586	GHV2 (CD, 10" x 10" gatefold p/s)	80
02	Warner Bros SAM 00721	Die Another Day (Dirty Vegas Main Mix)/(mixes) (12" double pack, stickered title sleeve)	20
02	Warner Bros (no cat. no.)	Die Another Day (9 mixes) (CD-R, title sleeve)	45
03	Warner Bros (no cat. no.)	American Life (Missy Elliott American Dream Remix)/(mixes)/Die Another Day (Richard Humpty Vission Electrofried Mix) (CD-R, card sleeve)	25
03	Warner Bros (no cat. no.)	Hollywood (4 mixes) (CD-R, title sleeve)	30
03	Warner Bros (no cat. no.)	Love Profusion (4 mixes) (CD-R, title sleeve)	30

ALBUMS

83	Sire 923 867-1	MADONNA (LP, with inner sleeve)	15
84	Sire 925 157-1	LIKE A VIRGIN (LP, without "Into The Groove", with inner sleeve)	15
85	Sire WX 20P	LIKE A VIRGIN (LP, picture disc in die-cut sleeve)	50
86	Sire WX 54	TRUE BLUE (LP, with tour poster)	12
87	Sire WX 76	YOU CAN DANCE (LP, with poster & gold 'obi')	12
90	Sire 7599 264932	ROYAL BOX (box set with "Immaculate Collection" CD in satin digipak, video, poster & postcards)	85

(see also Jellybean)

MADRIGAL

73	Madrigal MAD 100	BENEATH THE GREENWOOD TREE (LP, private pressing)	80

MAD RIVER

69	Capitol (S)T 2985	MAD RIVER (LP)	30

JOHNNY MAESTRO

61	HMV POP 875	What A Surprise/The Warning Voice	40
61	HMV POP 909	Mr. Happiness/Test Of Love	40
64	United Artists UP 1004	Before I Love Her/Fifty Million Heartbeats	30
71	Buddah 2011 061	Rain Came/Never Knew This Kind Of Hurt Before	6

(see also Crests, Brooklyn Bridge)

MAGAZINE

78	Virgin VS 200	Shot By Both Sides/My Mind Ain't So Open (card or paper p/s)	6/5
78	Virgin VS 207	Touch And Go/Goldfinger (p/s)	5

MINT VALUE £

78	Virgin VS 237	Give Me Everything/I Love You, You Big Dummy (p/s)	5
79	Virgin VS 251	Rhythm Of Cruelty/T.V. Baby (p/s)	5
80	Virgin VS 368	Sweetheart Contract/Feed The Enemy//Twenty Years Ago/ Shot By Both Sides (stickered, shrinkwrapped double pack)	8

(see also Buzzcocks)

MAGENTA

78	Cottage COT 821	CANTERBURY MOON (LP, with insert)	90
80	Little Stan LSP 811	RECOLLECTIONS (2-LP, gatefold sleeve with insert)	100
81	Little Stan LSP 831	WOT'S NEXT THEN (LP, with insert)	90

MAGGIE

68	Columbia DB 8389	L. David Sloane/Too Young To Get Married	6

MAGIC CARPET

72	Mushroom 200 MR 20	MAGIC CARPET (LP)	120

(see also Clem Alford)

MAGIC CHRISTIANS

69	Major Minor MM 673	If You Want It/Nuts	7
69	Major Minor MM 673	Come And Get It/Nuts (2nd pressing with correct title)	10
70	Major Minor SMLP 71	THE MAGIC CHRISTIANS (LP)	35

(see also Trevor Burton, Gary Wright, Denny Laine, Steve Gibbons)

MAGICIANS

66	Decca F 12361	Wet Your Whistle/Take The A Train	5
66	Decca F 12374	The Liars/Poggy Goes Pop	6
67	Decca F 12602	The Tarzan March/What A Day For A Metamorphosis	7
68	MCA MU 1046	Painting On Wood/Slow Motion	5

MAGIC LANTERNS

66	CBS 202094	Excuse Me Baby/Greedy Girl	8
66	CBS 202250	Rumplestiltskin/I Stumbled	50
67	CBS 202459	Knight In Rusty Armour/Simple Things	12
67	CBS 202637	Auntie Grizelda/Time Will Tell (If I'm A Loser)	12
67	CBS 2750	We'll Meet Again/What Else Can It Be But Love?	12
68	Camp 602 007	Shame Shame/Baby I Gotta Go Now	12
69	Camp 602 009	Melt All Your Troubles Away/Bossa Nova 1940 — Hello You Lovers	12
67	CBS (S) 62935	LIT UP WITH THE MAGIC LANTERNS (LP)	30
71	Polydor 2460 113	ONE NIGHT STAND (LP)	15

MAGIC MICHAEL

80	Atomic MAGIC 1	Millionaire/My Friend And I (p/s)	5

(see also Damned, Captain Sensible)

MAGIC MIXTURE

68	Saga FID 2125	THIS IS MAGIC MIXTURE (LP)	85

MAGIC MUSCLE

88	Five Hours Back TOCK 009	THE PIPE, THE ROAR, THE GRID (LP, with booklet)	15
90	Pilgrim (no cat. no.)	LIVING WEEDS FROM ANCIENT SEEDS (cassette, box set, autographed with booklet, posters & postcard)	15
91	Woronzow WOO 17	GULP! (LP)	20

(see also Keith Christmas, Hawkwind, High Tide, Twink)

MAGIC MUSHROOM BAND

85	Magick Eye MUSH 001	THE MAGIC MUSHROOM BAND (cassette EP)	12
85	Magick Eye MUSH 002	FEED YOUR HEAD (cassette)	12
86	Pagan PM 003	THE POLITICS OF ECSTASY (LP, 100 with A1 poster, 500 with A3 insert)	40/22
87	Aftermath AFT 3	BOMSHAMKAR (LP)	12
90	Fungus FUN 003	PROCESS OF ILLUMINATION (LP, signed with insert & foldaround sleeve & comic in printed PVC sleeve)	12
91	Fungus FUN 005	SPACED OUT (LP, foldout sleeve with A4 booklet)	15

MAGIC NIGHT

75	Pye 7N 25698	If You And I Had Never Met/(version)	8

MAGIC NOTES

60	Blue Beat BB 9	Album Of Memory/Why Did You Leave Me	25
61	Blue Beat BB 51	Rosabel/I'm Not Worthy2	25

MAGIC SAM

69	Python PEN 701	Twenty One Days In Jail/Easy Baby (99 copies only)	50
69	Rooster 707	MEAN MISTREATER (EP)	18
70	Blue Horizon 7-63223	MAGIC SAM: 1937-1969 (LP)	60
70	Delmark DS 615	WEST SIDE SOUL (LP, blue label)	25
71	Delmark DS 620	BLACK MAGIC (LP, blue label)	25

MAGIC SHOP

87	Sha La La Ba Ba 8	It's Time/VISITORS: Goldmining (flexidisc with various fanzines)	7/5

MAGIC SLIM & TEARDROPS

81	Rooster R 707	THREE THUNDERIN' TRACKS (EP)	7

MAGIC VALLEY

69	Penny Farthing PEN 701	Taking The Heart Out Of Love/Uptight Basil	10

(see also Pete Dello, Honeybus)

MAGISTRATES

68	MGM MGM 1425	Here Comes The Judge/Girl	8
68	MGM MGM 1437	After The Fox/Tear Down The Walls (with Jean Hillary)	8

(see also Jane Hillery)

MAGITS

79	Outer H. SRTS/79/CUS/401	Fragmented/Disconnected/Disjointed/Detached (p/s)	15

(see also Rudimentary Peni)

MAGMA

74	A&M AMS 7119	Mekanik Machine/Mekanik Machine (Version)	8
70	Philips 6359 051/2	MAGMA (2-LP)	18
71	Philips 6397 031	1001 CENTIGRADE (LP)	12
74	A&M AMLH 64397	MEKANIK DESTRUCTIW KOMMANDOH (LP)	12
74	A&M AMLH 68260	KOHN TARKOSZ (LP)	12

MAGNA CARTA

69	Fontana TF 1060	Romeo Jack/7 O'Clock Hymn	15
69	Mercury MF 1096	Mid-Winter/Spinning Wheels Of Time	15
70	Vertigo 6059 013	Airport Song/Elizabethan	10
71	Vertigo 6059 043	Time For The Leaving/Wayfarin'	8
72	Vertigo 6059 073	All My Life/Falkland Green	12
73	Vertigo 6059 092	Give Me Luv/Song Of Evening	10
70s	London Borough of Camden	When You're Young (charity issue for RoSPA)	5
69	Mercury SMCL 20166	MAGNA CARTA (LP)	45
70	Vertigo 6360 003	SEASONS (LP, gatefold sleeve, swirl label)	25
71	Vertigo 6360 040	SONGS FROM WASTIES ORCHARD (LP, gatefold sleeve, swirl label)	30
72	Vertigo 6360 068	IN CONCERT (LP, gatefold sleeve, swirl label)	30
73	Vertigo 6360 093	LORD OF THE AGES (LP, gatefold sleeve, spaceship label)	20
76	GTO GTLP 012	PUTTING IT BACK TOGETHER (LP)	18
77	GTO GTLP 112	TOOK A LONG TIME (LP)	15

MAGNA JAZZ BAND

57	Parlophone R 4387	Buddy's Habits/Flat Foot	7

(see also Brian White & Magna Jazz Band)

MAGNAPOP

96	Play It Again Sam BIAS 321LP	RUBBING DOESN'T HELP (LP, red vinyl, with inner)	12

MAGNETOPHONE

98	Earworm WORM 26	You Should Write Music/Monitor Rocket Science (p/s, red vinyl)	5

MAGNETS

86	Hurricane FIRE 1	Who's The Fool (Me Or You)/Best	25

MAGNIFICENT MEN

66	Capitol CL 15462	Peace Of Mind/All Your Lovin's Gone To My Head	22
68	Capitol CL 15530	Sweet Soul Medley Parts 1 & 2	6
68	Capitol CL 15570	Save The Country/So Much Love Waiting	6

MAGNIFICENT MERCURY BROTHERS

74	Transatlantic BIG 532	New Girl In School/What About Us	6
74	Transatlantic BIG 536	Why Do Fools Fall In Love/(I'm Not A) Juvenile Delinquent	6

(see also Decameron)

MAGNOG

90s	Enraptured RAPT 4508	Mist Waves Riding The Hills/Moving Ahead Again/Ghost States (p/s)	6

MAGNUM

75	CBS S CBS 2959	Sweets For My Sweet/Movin' On (no p/s)	40
78	Jet SJET 116	Kingdom Of Madness/In The Beginning	5
78	Jet SJET 128	Invasion/Universe	5
79	Jet JET 155	Changes/Lonesome Star (silver p/s, some with sew-on patch)	10/8
79	Jet JET 163	Foolish Heart/Baby Rock Me (p/s)	6
80	Jet JET 175	Magnum Live [All Of My Life (live)/Great Adventure (live)//Invasion (live)/ Kingdom Of Madness (live)] (double pack, stickered p/s)	6
80	Jet JET 188	Changes (live Remix)/Everybody Needs/Changes (live) (black p/s)	7
81	Jet JET 7007	Black Nights (possibly promo only)	10+
82	Jet JET 7020	The Lights Burned Out/Long Days Black Nights (p/s)	6
82	Jet JET 7027	Back To Earth (live)/Hold Back Your Love (live)//Soldier Of The Line (live)/ Sacred Hour (live) (double pack)	8
86	Polydor POSP 798	Lonely Night/Les Morts Dansant (live) (p/s)	5
86	Polydor POSPG 798	Lonely Night/Les Morts Dansant (live)//All England's Eyes (live)/ Hit And Run (live) (double pack)	7
86	Polydor POSPP 833	Midnight (Remix)/Back Street Kid/Kingdom Of Madness (live) (12", picture disc)	10
87	Polydor POSP 850	When The World Comes Down (Edit)/Vigilante (live) (p/s)	5
88	Polydor POSPG 910	Days Of No Trust/Maybe Tonight ('oct-o-pack', gatefold p/s)	8
88	Polydor POSPP 910	Days Of No Trust/Maybe Tonight (p/s, with sew-on patch)	7
88	Polydor POCD 910	Days Of No Trust/Maybe Tonight/Days Of No Trust (Extended Version/ How Far Jerusalem (live) (CD, card p/s)	8
88	Polydor POSPG 920	Start Talking Love/C'est La Vie (gatefold pop-up p/s)	5
88	Polydor POSPP 920	Start Talking Love/Days Of No Trust (10", shaped picture disc)	7
88	Polydor POCD 920	Start Talking Love (7" Version)/C'est La Vie/Start Talking Love (Extended Remix)/Sacred Hour (CD, p/s)	8
88	Polydor POSPG 930	It Must Have Been Love/Crying Time ('prismatic' pack)	5
88	Polydor POCD 930	It Must Have Been Love (Edit)/Crying Time/Lonely Night (live)/ Lights Burned Out (live) (CD, card sleeve)	8
88	Polydor 080 406-2	Start Talking Love (Extended Remix)/C'est La Vie/Back To Earth (live)/ On A Storyteller's Night (live) (CD Video)	12
78	Jet JETLP 210	KINGDOM OF MADNESS (LP, original 'king' sleeve)	18
83	FM WKFMPD 111	THE ELEVENTH HOUR (LP, picture disc)	15
85	FM WKFM LP 34	ON A STORYTELLER'S NIGHT (LP, with bonus single)	15
85	FM WKFM G/C LP 34	ON A STORYTELLER'S NIGHT (LP, gold or clear vinyl)	15
85	FM WKFM PD 34	ON A STORYTELLER'S NIGHT (LP, picture disc, with poster)	15
86	Polydor POLD 5198	VIGILANTE (LP)	12
88	Polydor POLDP 5221	WINGS OF HEAVEN (LP, picture disc with extra track, die-cut sleeve)	12
88	FM Revolver WKFMPD 110	MAGNUM II (LP, reissue, picture disc)	15
90	FM Revolver WKFMBX 145	FOUNDATION (6-LP box set)	40

MINT VALUE £

TEDDY MAGNUS
71 Green Door GD 4008 — Flying Machine/VERSION BOYS: Machine Version . . . 6

MAGOO
95 Noisebox NBX 013 — MUDSHARK EP: Tom, Lou And Me/Elsie's Skinny Arms/Hop Your Mouth (orange vinyl, numbered p/s, 500 only) . . . 8
95 Noisebox NBX 016 — ROBOT CARNIVAL EP: Robot Carnival/Sampa Calmida (Land Of Joy)/ Candle Buddah/Rocket To Spector City (blue vinyl, p/s) . . . 5
96 Noisebox NBX 020 — EYESPY EP: Eye Spy/Motel Mining/Soaterama/Polka Party No.2/ Silver Screen/Word Is Out/Diving Bell (lemon yellow vinyl, p/s, 500 only) . . . 5
98 Fierce Panda NING 47 — Black Sabbath/MOGWAI: Sweet Leaf (p/s) . . . 5

MAGPIES
68 Doctor Bird DB 1129 — Lulu/Must I Be Lonely . . . 20
68 Doctor Bird DB 1132 — Blue Boy/I Guess I'm Crazy . . . 20

ALEX MAGUIRE
87 Incus INCUS 52 — LIVE AT OSCARS (LP) . . . 50

JOHN MAGUIRE
73 Leader LEE 4062 — COME DAY, GO DAY, GOD SEND SUNDAY (LP, gatefold sleeve with booklet) . . . 12

LEO MAGUIRE
62 Parlophone R 4917 — Crying For The Moon/Small World . . . 6

MAGUS
80 Northern Sound NSR 200 — BREEZIN' AWAY (LP, private pressing) . . . 60
(see also Blue Epitaph)

TAJ MAHAL
68 Direction 58-3547 — Everybody's Got To Change Sometime/Statesboro Blues . . . 6
69 Direction 58-4044 — Ee Zee Rider/You Don't Miss Your Water . . . 6
70 Direction 58-4586 — Give Your Woman What She Wants/Further On Down The Road . . . 6
71 CBS 7413 — Diving Duck Blues/Fishin' Blues . . . 6
67 Direction 8-63279 — TAJ MAHAL (LP) . . . 20
69 Direction 8-63397 — THE NATCH'L BLUES (LP) . . . 20
69 Direction 8-66226 — GIANT STEP/DE OLE FOLKS AT HOME (2-LP) . . . 20
71 CBS 66288 — THE REAL THING (2-LP) . . . 20
72 CBS 64447 — HAPPY JUST TO BE LIKE I AM (LP) . . . 12
73 CBS 65090 — RECYCLING THE BLUES AND OTHER RELATED STUFF (LP) . . . 12
73 CBS 65814 — OOOH SO GOOD 'N BLUES (LP) . . . 12
73 CBS 70123 — SOUNDER (LP, soundtrack) . . . 12

MAHAVISHNU ORCHESTRA
75 CBS 3007 — Can't Stand Your Funk/Eternity's Breath Part 1 . . . 6
72 CBS 64717 — THE INNER MOUNTING FLAME (LP, with insert) . . . 12
74 CBS CQ 31996 — BIRDS OF FIRE (LP, quadrophonic) . . . 20
75 CBS 69108 — VISIONS OF THE EMERALD BEYOND (LP, with insert) . . . 12
(see also John McLaughlin)

MITCH MAHON & EDITIONS
69 Pye 7N 17844 — You've Got What I Need/I've Thrown Our Love Away . . . 5

SKIP MAHONEY & CASUALS
76 Contempo CLP 539 — LAND OF LOVE (LP) . . . 15

MAIL
71 Parlophone R 5916 — Omnibus/Life Goes On . . . 6

MAINFRAME
84 YYY — INTO TROUBLE WITH THE NOISE OF ART (12", 7-track EP) . . . 10

MAINHORSE
71 Polydor 2383 049 — MAINHORSE (LP) . . . 20

MAIN INGREDIENT
74 RCA PB 0305 — Happiness Is Just Around The Bend/Why Can't We All Unite . . . 6
71 RCA LSA 3020 — TASTEFUL SOUL (LP) . . . 15

MAINLAND
79 Christy ACML 0200 — EXPOSURE (LP) . . . 15

JULIE MAIRS & CHRIS STOWELL
77 Cottage COT 211 — SOFT SEA BLUE (LP) . . . 20

MAISON ROUGE
85 Red Barn RBR 0001 — Questions (p/s) . . . 5

DEXTER MAITLAND
69 United Artists UP 35006 — Take Ten Terrific Girls (But Only Nine Costumes)/ RUDY VALLEE: The Night They Raided Minsky's . . . 5

MAJAMOOD
66 Doc. Bird/W.I.R.L. DB 1052 — Two Hundred Million Red Ants/Faces Amassed . . . 30

MAJOR ACCIDENT
82 M. Melodies MAME 1001 — Warboots/Terrorist Gang (unissued, test pressings only) . . . 40
83 Step Forward SF 23 — Mr. Nobody/That's You (p/s) . . . 12
83 Flicknife FLS 216 — Fight To Win/Free Man (p/s) . . . 12
83 Flicknife FLS 023 — Leaders Of Tomorrow/Dayo/Breakaway (p/s) . . . 12
84 Flicknife FLS 026 — Respectable/Man On The Wall (p/s) . . . 12
83 Step Forward SFLP 9 — MASSACRED MELODIES (LP) . . . 20
84 Syndicate SYNLP 9 — TORTURED TUNES LIVE (LP) . . . 20
(see also Accident)

MAJORETTES
63 Lyntone LYN 982 — White Levi's (flexidisc) . . . 12

MINT VALUE £

MAJOR FORCE

94 Mo' Wax — Return Of The Original Artform/(mixes) (12") . . . 8
(see also Major Force West)

MAJOR FORCE WEST

94 Mo' Wax MWMFWLP 001 — HEADTURNER (LP, with obi) . . . 15
94 Mo' Wax MWMFWCD 001 — HEADTURNER (CD) . . . 35
(see also Major Force)

MAJORITY

65 Decca F 12186 — Pretty Little Girl/I Don't Wanna Be Hurt No More . . . 12
65 Decca F 12271 — A Little Bit Of Sunlight/Shut 'Em Down In London Town . . . 15
66 Decca F 12313 — We Kiss In A Shadow/Ring The Bells . . . 12
66 Decca F 12453 — Simplified/One Third . . . 70
66 Decca F 12504 — To Make Me A Man/Tears Won't Help . . . 12
67 Decca F 12573 — I Hear A Rhapsody/Wait By The Fire . . . 12
67 Decca F 12638 — Running Away With My Baby/Let The Joybells Ring . . . 18
68 Decca F 12727 — All Our Christmases/People . . . 12

MAJORS

62 London HLP 9602 — A Wonderful Dream/Time Will Tell . . . 20
62 London HLP 9627 — She's A Troublemaker/A Little Bit Now . . . 22
63 London HLP 9693 — What In The World/Tra La La . . . 20
64 Liberty LBF 66009 — Ooh Wee Baby/I'll Be There . . . 22
63 London RE-P 1358 — MEET THE MAJORS (EP) . . . 140
63 London HA-P 8068 — MEET THE MAJORS (LP) . . . 200

MAKADOPOULOS & HIS GREEK SERENADERS

60 Palette PG 9002 — In The Streets Of Athens/Festival A La Greca . . . 6
61 Palette PG 9005 — Never On Sunday/Yasou (some in p/s) . . . 12/7

PETER MAKANA & HIS RHYTHM BOYS

58 Oriole CB 1445 — Baboon Shepherd (with Black Duke)/Black John . . . 6
58 Oriole CB 1446 — Cool Mood/Sweet Baby . . . 6
58 Oriole CB 1446 — Cool Mood/Sweet Baby (78) . . . 8

TOMMY MAKEM

70 CBS 64001 — THE BARD OF ARMAGH (LP) . . . 12

MAKIN' TIME

85 Countdown VAIN 1 — Here Is My Number/Nothing Else (p/s) . . . 8
86 Countdown TVAIN 1 — Here Is My Number/Nothing Else (picture disc) . . . 8
86 Countdown VAIN 5 — Pump It Up/Walk A Thin Line (p/s) . . . 8
86 Countdown 12 VAIN 5 — PUMP IT UP EP: Once Again/Walk A Thin Line/Eating Up The Cold . . . 8
85 Countdown DOWN 1 — RHYTHM 'N' SOUL (LP) . . . 18
86 Ready To Eat READY 1 — NO LUMPS OF FAT OR GRISTLE GUARANTEED (LP) . . . 18
87 Re-Elect/President ELECT 1 — TIME, TROUBLE AND MONEY (LP) . . . 18
(see also Charlatans)

MALAGON SISTERS & CHA CHA RHYTHM BOYS

59 Pye International 7N 25008 — In A Little Spanish Town/Lessons In Cha-Cha-Cha . . . 6
59 Pye International 7N 25008 — In A Little Spanish Town/Lessons In Cha-Cha-Cha (78) . . . 8

MAL & PRIMITIVES

65 Pye 7N 15915 — Every Minute Of Every Day/Pretty Little Face . . . 125
(see also Primitives, Mal Ryder & Spirits)

MALARIA!

82 Jungle JUNG 3 — NEW YORK PASSAGE (12" EP) . . . 8

CARLOS MALCOLM & AFRO CARIBS

65 Island WI 173 — Bonanza Ska/Papa Luiga . . . 25

GEORGE MALCOLM

53 Parlophone MSP 6058 — Bach Goes To Town/Bach Before The Mast . . . 12

HUGH MALCOLM

68 Amalgamated AMG 827 — Good Time Rock/LYNN TAITT & JETS: Sleepy Ludy . . . 20
68 Amalgamated AMG 829 — Mortgage/CANNONBALL BRYAN TRIO: Man About Town . . . 20

MALCOLM & ALWYN

73 Pye NSPL 18404 — FOOL'S WISDOM (LP, with poster) . . . 12
74 Key KL 022 — WILDWALL (LP) . . . 12

MALLARD

77 Virgin VS 168 — Harvest/Green Coyote . . . 10
76 Virgin V 2045 — MALLARD (LP) . . . 12
77 Virgin V 2077 — IN A DIFFERENT CLIMATE (LP) . . . 12
(see also Captain Beefheart & His Magic Band)

STEPHEN MALLINDER

81 Fetish FE 12 — Temperature Drop/Cool Down (12", p/s) . . . 8
82 Fetish FM 2010 — POW-WOW (LP) . . . 12
(see also Cabaret Voltaire)

SIW MALMKVIST

59 Oriole CB 1486 — Sermonette/The Preacher . . . 6
61 Parlophone R 4765 — Wedding Cake/Red Roses And Little White Lies . . . 6
64 Columbia DB 7411 — Sole Sole Sole/Sabato Sera (as Siw Malmkvist & Umberto Marcato) . . . 5
68 Atlantic 584 229 — The Man Who Took The Valise Off The Floor/Sadie The Cleaning Lady . . . 5

CINDY MALONE

61 RCA RCA 1254 — Weird Beard/Young Marriage . . . 7

WIL MALONE

70 Fontana STL 5541 — WIL MALONE (LP) . . . 130
(see also Barnaby Rudge, Motherlight, Wilson Malone Voiceband)

MINT VALUE £

WILSON MALONE VOICEBAND

68 Morgan MR 112P FUNNY SAD MUSIC (LP) . . . 25
(see also Motherlight, Wil Malone)

RICHARD MALTBY

56 HMV 7M 393 "Man With The Golden Arm" Theme/Heart Of Paris . . . 8
59 Philips PB 955 Theme From The FBI Story/Morgen (78) . . . 10
61 Columbia DB 4606 The Rat Race/Walkie Talkie . . . 12

MAMAS & PAPAS

66 RCA Victor RCA 1503 California Dreamin'/Somebody Groovy . . . 5
66 RCA Victor RCA 1516 Monday, Monday/Got A Feelin' . . . 5
66 RCA Victor RCA 1533 I Saw Her Again/Even If I Could . . . 5
66 RCA Victor RCA 1551 Look Through My Window/Once There Was I Time I Thought . . . 6
67 RCA Victor RCA 1564 Words Of Love/I Can't Wait . . . 6
67 RCA Victor RCA 1576 Dedicated To The One I Love/Free Advice . . . 6
67 RCA Victor RCA 1613 Creeque Alley/No Salt On Her Tail . . . 6
67 RCA Victor RCA 1630 12.30/Straight Shooter . . . 6
67 RCA Victor RCA 1649 Glad To Be Unhappy/Hey Girl . . . 6
68 RCA Victor RCA 1710 Safe In My Garden/Too Late . . . 5
68 RCA Victor RCA 1726 Dream A Little Dream Of Me/Midnight Voyage . . . 6
68 RCA Victor RCA 1744 For The Love Of Ivy/Strange Young Girls . . . 6
69 Stateside SS 8009 You Baby/My Girl . . . 5
70 Stateside SS 8058 Go Where You Wanna Go/No Salt On Her Tail . . . 5
72 Probe PRO 552 Shooting Star/No Dough . . . 5
66 RCA Victor RD 7803 IF YOU CAN BELIEVE YOUR EYES AND EARS (LP) . . . 22
66 RCA Victor RD/SF 7834 CASS, JOHN, MICHELLE, DENNY (LP) . . . 20
67 RCA Victor RD/SF 7880 DELIVER (LP) . . . 20
68 RCA Victor RD/SF 7960 THE PAPAS AND THE MAMAS (LP) . . . 20
68 Stateside (S)SL 5002 THE MAMAS AND THE PAPAS GOLDEN ERA VOL. 2 (LP) . . . 15
68 Stateside TA-SL 5002 THE MAMAS AND THE PAPAS GOLDEN ERA VOL. 2 (reel-to-reel tape, mono) . . . 12
68 Stateside TA-SL 5007 HITS OF GOLD (reel-to-reel tape, mono) . . . 12
70 Probe SPB 1013/14 A GATHERING OF FLOWERS (2-LP) . . . 20
71 Probe SPB 1048 PEOPLE LIKE US (LP) . . . 15
78 St. Michael MO 101225 CALIFORNIA DREAMIN' (LP, exclusive to Marks & Spencer) . . . 25
(see also Mama Cass [Elliot], John Phillips, Michelle Phillips, Scott McKenzie, Barry McGuire, Mugwumps, Big Three [U.S], Spanky & Our Gang)

MAMA'S BOYS

81 Pussy Silence Is Out Of Fashion (Irish pressing, p/s) . . . 10
82 Scoff DT 015 Belfast City Blues/Reach For The Top (p/s; Ireland only) . . . 15
83 Spartan 12SP 6 Too Little Of You To Love/Freedom Fighters (12", p/s, with free "Official Bootleg" LP) . . . 15
84 Jive JIVEG 71 Mama We're All Crazee Now/Runaway Dreams//Crazy Daisy's House Of Dreams/Gentleman Rogues (double pack, p/s) . . . 8
84 Jive JIVET 71 Mama We're All Crazee Now/Crazy Daisy's House Of Dreams/Runaway Rogues (12", p/s) . . . 10
84 Spartan SP 11 Midnight Promises (p/s) . . . 8
84 Spartan 12SP 11 MIDNIGHT PROMISES (12" EP) . . . 12
85 Jive JIVEP 96 Needle In The Groove/Don't Tell Mama (shaped picture disc) . . . 8
85 Jive JIVET 110 Hard 'N' Loud (12", p/s) . . . 10
87 Jive MBOYD 1 Higher Ground/Last Thing At Night/Needle In The Groove (double pack, gatefold p/s) . . . 5
87 Jive MBOYCD 1 Higher Ground (Captain Love Mix)/Last Thing At Night/Needle In The Groove (Album Version) (CD) . . . 8
80 Pussy PU 004 OFFICIAL BOOTLEG (LP, Irish pressing) . . . 12
82 Pussy PU 010 PLUG IT IN (LP, Irish pressing) . . . 15
82 Ultra Noise ULTRA 1 PLUG IT IN (LP) . . . 15
85 Jive HIP 24 POWER AND PASSION (LP, with 12" interview picture disc) . . . 15

MAMMATH

84 Neat NEAT 42 Rock Me/Rough 'N' Ready (p/s) . . . 7

MAMMOTH

87 Jive MOTHCD 1 Fatman (Admiral Amour Mix)/Political Animal/Bad Times/Fatman (7" Version) (CD) . . . 8
89 Jive MOTHX 4 All The Days/Fatman/Bet You Wish (12", picture disc, PVC sleeve, withdrawn) . . . 20
(see also John McCoy, Gillan, Samson, Tiger, Nicky Moore Band, Hackensack)

MAN

69 Pye 7N 17684 Sudden Life/Love . . . 18
71 Liberty LBF 15448 Daughter Of The Fireplace/Country Girl . . . 15
74 United Artists UP 35643 Don't Go Away (possibly unissued) . . . 15+
74 United Artists UP 35703 Taking The Easy Way Out Again/California Silks And Satins . . . 6
74 United Artists UP 35739 Day And Night/A Hard Way To Live . . . 5
76 MCA MCA 236 Out Of Your Head/I'm A Love Taker . . . 5
76 United Artists REM 408 BANANAS (EP) . . . 8
69 Pye N(S)PL 18275 REVELATION (LP, mono/stereo, originals have sky blue label with black at top; reissues have black on the *side*) . . . 30/15/12
69 Dawn DNLS 3003 2 OZ'S OF PLASTIC WITH A HOLE IN THE MIDDLE (LP, orange label, g/f sleeve) . . . 30
69 Dawn DNLS 3003 2 OZ'S OF PLASTIC WITH A HOLE IN THE MIDDLE (LP, later pressings with red & blue or purple labels, gatefold sleeve) . . . 15
70 Liberty LBG 83464 MAN (LP, gatefold sleeve) . . . 25
72 United Artists UAS 29236 DO YOU LIKE IT HERE NOW, ARE YOU SETTLING IN? (LP) . . . 22
72 United Artists USP 100 LIVE AT THE PADGET ROOMS, PENARTH (LP) . . . 30
72 United Artists UAG 29417 BE GOOD TO YOURSELF AT LEAST ONCE A DAY (LP, 'map' sleeve with 'family tree' inner) . . . 20

73 United Artists UDX 205/6 CHRISTMAS AT THE PATTI (LP, 2 x 10", with other artists) . . . 25
73 Utd Artists UAD 60053/4 BACK INTO THE FUTURE (2-LP) . . . 18
74 United Artists UAG 29631 RHINOS, WINOS & LUNATICS (LP, gatefold sleeve) . . . 12
74 United Artists UAG 29675 SLOW MOTION (LP, with inner sleeve) . . . 12
75 United Artists UAG 29872 MAXIMUM DARKNESS (LP, gatefold sleeve, with poster) . . . 15
76 MCA MCF 2753 THE WELSH CONNECTION (LP) . . . 12
77 MCA MCF 2815 ALL'S WELL THAT ENDS WELL (LP, initially with History Of Man booklet) . . . 18/12
(see also Bystanders, Eyes Of Blue, Ancient Grease, Big Sleep, Clive John, Alkatraz, Help Yourself, Deke Leonard, Neutrons, Gary Pickford–Hopkins & Friends, Wild Turkey)

T. MAN & T. BONES

72 Sioux SI 007 True Born African (actually by Winston Jarrett & Righteous Flames)/ Tropical Chief . . . 5

(STEPHEN STILLS') MANASSAS

72 Atlantic K 60021 MANASSAS (2-LP, with 2 inner sleeves & lyric poster) . . . 18
73 Atlantic K 40440 DOWN THE ROAD (LP, with inner sleeve) . . . 12
(see also Stephen Stills, Crosby Stills & Nash, Flying Burrito Brothers)

MANASSEH

77 Genesis 12 MANASSEH (LP, with insert) . . . 20

JUNIOR MANCE

60 HMV CLP 1342 JUNIOR (LP) . . . 18
71 Atlantic 2400 028 WITH A LOTTA HELP FROM MY FRIENDS (LP) . . . 15

STEVE MANCHA/J.J. BARNES

69 Stax SXATS 1012 RARE STAMPS (LP) . . . 20
(see also J.J. Barnes)

MICKY MANCHESTER

75 Rainbow RBW 2001 Have You Seen Your Daughter Mrs. Jones/Chamberlain Said . . . 5
(see also Just Plain Smith, Just Plain Jones)

MANCHESTER CITY SQUAD

72 RCA Victor 2200 The Boys In Blue/Funky City . . . 5

MANCHESTER MEKON

79 Newmarket NEW 102 No Forgetting/Have A Go-Go/Jonathan Livingstone Seafood (hand-painted p/s with insert, 1,000 only) . . . 25

MANCHESTER MOB

67 Parlophone R 5552 Bony Maronie At The Hop/Afro Asian . . . 35
(see also Graham Gouldman, High Society, 10cc, Friday Browne)

MANCHESTERS

66 Ember TRIBUTE TO THE BEATLES (LP) . . . 25

MANCHESTER'S PLAYBOYS

66 Fontana TF 745 I Feel So Good/I Close My Eyes . . . 75

MANCHESTER UNITED FOOTBALL SQUAD

76 Decca F 13633 Manchester United/MARTIN BUCHAN: Old Trafford Blues . . . 8
79 RCA MAN 1 Onward Sexton's Soldiers/Come On You Reds (red vinyl) . . . 8
94 PolyGram TV MANUP 12 Come On You Reds/(Instrumental) (12" picture disc, with insert) . . . 20
(see also Status Quo)

HENRY MANCINI & HIS ORCHESTRA

59 RCA RCA 1134 Peter Gunn Theme/The Brothers Go To Mother's . . . 10
59 RCA RCA 1134 Peter Gunn Theme/The Brothers Go To Mother's (78) . . . 5
61 RCA RCA 1256 Moon River/Breakfast At Tiffanys . . . 5
62 RCA RCA 1285 Experiment In Terror/Tooty Twist . . . 12
62 RCA RCA 1312 Man Of The World Theme/Fluter's Ball . . . 8
64 RCA RCA 1414 How Soon/The Tiber Twist . . . 5
64 RCA RCA 1431 Dear Heart/A Shot In The Dark . . . 6
65 RCA RCA 1498 Soldier In The Rain/Moment To Moment . . . 5
68 RCA RCA 1689 Wait Until Dark/Norma De Guadalajara . . . 10
70 RCA RCA 1934 Z-Theme/Midnight Cowboy . . . 5
61 RCA RCX 205 BREAKFAST AT TIFFANY'S (EP) . . . 20
62 RCA RCX 7107 HATARI! (EP) . . . 10
64 RCA RCX 7136 THE PINK PANTHER (EP) . . . 15
57 Brunswick LAT 8162 ROCK, PRETTY BABY (LP, soundtrack, with Rod McKuen) . . . 100
59 RCA RD 27123/SF 5033 PETER GUNN (LP, soundtrack) . . . 15
63 RCA SF 7620 CHARADE (LP, soundtrack) . . . 30
64 RCA RD 7667 THE BEST OF MANCINI (LP) . . . 12
65 RCA RD 7759 THE GREAT RACE (LP, soundtrack) . . . 30
66 RCA SF 7818 WHAT DID YOU DO IN THE WAR, DADDY? (LP, soundtrack) . . . 20
66 RCA RD 7817 ARABESQUE (LP, soundtrack) . . . 15
67 RCA RD/SF 7891 TWO FOR THE ROAD (LP, soundtrack) . . . 20
67 RCA RD/SF 7899 GUNN (LP, soundtrack) . . . 20
69 United Artists UAS 29049 CHICAGO, CHICAGO (LP, soundtrack) . . . 18
70 CBS 70061 ME, NATALIE (LP, soundtrack, with Rod McKuen) . . . 18
70 Avco Embassy 6466 002 SUNFLOWER (LP, soundtrack) . . . 18
70 United Artists UAS 29122 MASTER OF THE ISLANDS (LP, soundtrack) . . . 18
70 RCA SF 8138 DARLIN' LILI (LP, soundtrack, gatefold sleeve) . . . 15
70 Paramount SPFL 259 THE MOLLY MAGUIRES (LP, soundtrack) . . . 12
72 RCA Victor SF 8127 FILM THEMES A TO Z (LP) . . . 15
73 RCA Victor SF 8366 OKLAHOMA CRUDE (LP, soundtrack) . . . 18
73 RCA Victor SF 8379 VISIONS OF EIGHT (LP, soundtrack) . . . 18
73 Elektra K 46239 THE THIEF WHO CAME TO DINNER (LP, soundtrack) . . . 18
74 RCA Victor APL 1 0270 COUNTRY GENTLEMEN (LP, soundtrack) . . . 18
75 RCA Red Seal RS 1010 THE RETURN OF THE PINK PANTHER (LP, soundtrack) . . . 18

MINT VALUE £

75 MCA MCF 2707 THE GREAT WALDO PEPPER (LP, soundtrack) . . . 18
76 United Artists UAS 30012 THE PINK PANTHER STRIKES AGAIN (LP, soundtrack) . . . 18
77 RCA PL 12290 MANCINI'S ANGELS (LP) . . . 15
82 MGM 2315 437 VICTOR, VICTORIA (LP, soundtrack) . . . 15

MANDALA BAND
75 Chrysalis CHR 1095 MANDALA BAND (LP) . . . 15
78 Chrysalis CHR 1181 THE EYE OF WENDOR: PROPHECIES (LP, with booklet) . . . 12

HARVEY MANDEL
74 Janus 6146 024 Uno Ino/Shangrenade . . . 6
68 Philips SBL 7873 CRISTO REDENTOR (LP) . . . 22
69 Philips SBL 7904 RIGHTEOUS (LP) . . . 18
70 Philips SBL 7915 GAMES GUITARS PLAY (LP) . . . 15
71 Dawn DNLS 3015 BABY BATTER (LP) . . . 15
71 Philips 6336 009 CRISTO REDENTOR (LP, reissue) . . . 12
72 London SH-O 8426 GET OFF IN CHICAGO (LP) . . . 12
72 Janus 6310 210 THE SNAKE (LP) . . . 12
73 Janus 6499 831 SHANGRENADE (LP) . . . 12
(see also Canned Heat, Dewey Terry)

NELSON MANDELA
64 Ember CEL 905 WHY I'M READY TO DIE (LP, spoken word, narrated by Peter Finch) . . . 25

MANDINGO
73 EMI EMI 2014 Medicine Man/Black Rite . . . 20
73 EMI EMC 3010 MANDINGO 1: SACRIFICE (LP) . . . 30
73 Studio Two TWO 400 MANDINGO 2: PRIMEVAL RHYTHM OF LIFE (LP) . . . 40
73 Studio Two Q4TWO 400 MANDINGO 2: PRIMEVAL RHYTHM OF LIFE (LP, quadrophonic) . . . 30
75 EMI EMC 3038 MANDINGO 3: STORY OF SURVIVAL (LP) . . . 30
77 EMI EMC 3217 MANDINGO 4: SAVAGE RITE (LP) . . . 30
(see also Geoff Love, Manuel & Music Of The Mountains)

MANDRAGORA
86 SAB 01 OVER THE MOON (LP) . . . 30
91 Resonance 33-9133 HEAD FIRST (LP) . . . 12

MANDRAKE
60 Philips PB 1093 Mandrake/The Witch's Twist . . . 12
61 Philips BF 1153 Thank Goodness It's Friday/Queen Of Sheba . . . 6

MANDRAKE MEMORIAL
69 RCA SF 8028 MEDIUM (LP) . . . 35
70 RCA/Poppy PYS 11003 PUZZLE (LP) . . . 40

MANDRAKE PADDLE STEAMERS
69 Parlophone R 5780 Strange Walking Man/Steam . . . 80
88 Bam Caruso NRIC 033 Strange Walking Man/Steam (reissue, gatefold p/s) . . . 12
(see also Liverpool Echo)

MANDRILL
73 Polydor 2066 320 Mandrill/Hang Loose . . . 5
73 Polydor 2066 357 Fencewalk/Polk Street Carnival . . . 5
70 Polydor 2489 028 MANDRILL (LP) . . . 12
72 Polydor 2391 030 MANDRILL IS (LP) . . . 12
73 Polydor 2391 061 COMPOSITE TRUTH (LP) . . . 12
73 Polydor 2391 092 JUST OUTSIDE OF TOWN (LP) . . . 12

MANDY (SMITH)
87 PWL PWLP 1 I Just Can't Wait/Instrumental/You're Never Alone (12" picture disc) . . . 15
88 PWL PWCD 11 Boys & Girls/Mandy's Theme (I Just Can't Wait) (The Cool & Breezy Jazz Mix)/ He's My Boy (3" CD) . . . 20
88 PWL PWCD 18 Victim Of Pleasure (Red Rooster Mix)/Say It's Love/Victim Of Pleasure (Instrumental) (3" CD) . . . 20
88 PWL HFCD 2 MANDY (CD) . . . 35

MANEATERS
82 Editions EG EGO 8 Nine To Five/SUZI PINNS: Jerusalem (withdrawn 'Adam & Toyah' p/s) . . . 100
82 Editions EG EGO 8 Nine To Five/SUZI PINNS: Jerusalem (title p/s) . . . 5
(see also Adam & The Ants)

MAN FRIDAY & JIVE JUNIOR
83 Malaco MAL 011 Picking Up Sounds/Picking Up Sounds (Radio Mix) (p/s, features John Deacon) 30
83 Malaco MAL 1211 Picking Up Sounds (Extended)/Picking Up Sounds (Radio Mix) (12", p/s, features John Deacon) . . . 50
(see also Queen)

MAN FROM DELMONTE
87 Ugly Man UGLY 3 Drive Drive Drive/Twenty Two And Still In Love With You/Sun Serious (p/s) . . . 6
87 Ugly Man UGLY 5 Water In My Eyes/Bred By You (p/s) . . . 5
87 Ugly Man UGLY 5T Water In My Eyes/Bred By You (12", p/s) . . . 18
88 Ugly Man UGLY 7T Will Nobody Save Louise/Good Things In Life/Like A Millionaire (12", p/s) . . . 50
89 Bop Cassettes BIP 502 WAITING FOR ANN (12" EP) . . . 20

MANHATTANS
65 Sue WI 384 I Wanna Be (Your Everything)/Searchin' For My Baby . . . 35
66 Carnival CAR 100 Baby I Need You/Teach Me (The Philly Dog) . . . 15
66 Carnival CAR 101 That New Girl/Can I . . . 15
74 CBS 2117 Soul Train/I'm Not A Run Around . . . 6
73 London SHB 8449 A MILLION TO ONE (LP) . . . 18
76 CBS 81513 THE MANHATTANS (LP) . . . 12
78 CBS 81828 IT FEELS GOOD (LP) . . . 12
79 CBS 35693 LOVE TALK (LP) . . . 12

MANIACS

77 United Artists UP 36327 Chelsea 1977/Ain't No Legend (p/s) 25
(see also Rings, Physicals)

MANIAX

66 White Label WLR 101/102 Out Of Reach/The Devil's Home 12

MANIC JABS

81 Waldo's MS 009 Autophagus/The Injuns Are Comin'/Thing Wild (p/s) 6

MANIC STREET PREACHERS

SINGLES

88 SBS SBS 002 Suicide Alley/Tennessee (I Get Low) (hand-made p/s with press-cuttings glued to plain card cover) 600
88 SBS SBS 002 Suicide Alley/Tennessee (I Get Low) (blue p/s, 200 only) 500
88 SBS SBS 002 Suicide Alley/Tennessee (I Get Low) (no p/s, 100 only) 300
90 Hopelessly Devoted 1 UK Channel Boredom/LAURENS: I Don't Know What The Trouble Is (p/s flexidisc, some free with *Hopelessly Devoted* fanzine; later 're-pressed') 60/45
90 Damaged Goods YUBB 4 NEW ART RIOT EP: New Art Riot/Strip It Down/ Last Exit On Yesterday/Teenage 20/20 (12", white label, 100 copies, plain sleeves rubber-stamped with "Made In Wales") 35
90 Damaged Goods YUBB 4 NEW ART RIOT EP: New Art Riot/Strip It Down/Last Exit On Yesterday/ Teenage 20/20 (12" EP, p/s, 1st 1,000 black & white label, 2nd 1,000 black-on-yellow; later red, orange & silver & green) 18/15/12
91 Damaged Goods YUBB 004P NEW ART RIOT EP: New Art Riot/Strip It Down/Last Exit On Yesterday/ Teenage 20/20 (12" EP, p/s, reissue on pink vinyl) 25
91 Heavenly HVN 812 Motown Junk/Sorrow 16/We Her Majesty's Prisoners (12", withdrawn p/s) 40
91 Heavenly HVN 8CD Motown Junk/Sorrow 16/We Her Majesty's Prisoners (CD, withdrawn sleeve) 80
91 Heavenly HVN 10 You Love Us/Spectators Of Suicide (p/s) 20
91 Heavenly HVN 1012 You Love Us/Spectators Of Suicide/Starlover/Strip It Down (live) (12", p/s) 30
91 Heavenly HVN 10CD You Love Us/Spectators Of Suicide/Starlover/Strip It Down (live) (CD) 40
91 Columbia 657337 7 Stay Beautiful/R.P. McMurphy (p/s) 8
91 Columbia 657337 6 Stay Beautiful/R.P. McMurphy/Soul Contamination (12", p/s) 15
91 Columbia 657337 8 Stay Beautiful/R.P. McMurphy/Soul Contamination (12", stickered poster p/s) 18
91 Columbia 657337 2 Stay Beautiful/Soul Contamination (CD, original issue) 12
91 Columbia 657582 7 Love's Sweet Exile/Repeat (p/s) 10
91 Columbia 657582 6 Repeat (U.K.)/Love's Sweet Exile/Democracy Coma (12", p/s) 12
91 Columbia 657582 8 Repeat/Democracy Coma/Love's Sweet Exile/Stay Beautiful (live) (12", gatefold, stickered p/s) 12
91 Columbia 657582 2 Love's Sweet Exile/Repeat/Democracy Coma/Stay Beautiful (live) (CD, original issue) 12
91 Caff CAFF 15 FEMININE IS BEAUTIFUL: Repeat After Me/New Art Riot (p/s, 500 only) 125
92 Columbia 657724 7 You Love Us/A Vision Of Dead Desire (p/s) 10
92 Columbia 657724 6 You Love Us/A Vision Of Dead Desire/It's So Easy (live) (12" gatefold p/s) 20
92 Columbia 657724 2 You Love Us/A Vision Of Dead Desire/We Her Majesty's Prisoners/ It's So Easy (live) (CD, original issue) 15
92 Columbia 657873 7 Slash'N'Burn/Motown Junk (poster p/s) 6
92 Columbia 657873 4 Slash'N'Burn/Motown Junk (cassette) 6
92 Columbia 657873 6 Slash'N'Burn/Motown Junk/Ain't Goin' Down (12", with print, stickered p/s) 12
92 Columbia 657873 2 Slash'N'Burn/Motown Junk/Ain't Goin' Down (gold CD, digipak) 15
92 Columbia 657724 2 You Love Us/A Vision Of Dead Desire/We Her Majesty's Prisoners/ It's So Easy (live) (CD, reissue) 8
92 Columbia 658083 7 Motorcycle Emptiness/Bored Out Of My Mind (p/s) 6
92 Columbia 658083 4 Motorcycle Emptiness/Bored Out Of My Mind (cassette) 6
92 Columbia 658083 6 Motorcycle Emptiness/Bored Out Of My Mind/Under My Wheels (12", picture disc, stickered PVC sleeve) 30
92 Columbia 658083 2 Motorcycle Emptiness/Bored Out Of My Mind/Under My Wheels (CD, digipak) 15
92 Damaged Goods YUBB 4CD New Art Riot/Strip It Down/Last Exit On Yesterday/Teenage 20/20 (CD, picture disc, reissue, 3,000 only) 15
92 Columbia 658382 7 Theme From M*A*S*H EP (Suicide Is Painless)/FATIMA MANSIONS: "Everything I Do (I Do It For You)" (poster p/s) 6
92 Columbia 658382 4 Theme From M*A*S*H EP (Suicide Is Painless)/FATIMA MANSIONS: "Everything I Do (I Do It For You)" (cassette) 5
92 Columbia 658382 6 Theme From M*A*S*H EP (Suicide Is Painless)/FATIMA MANSIONS/ "Everything I Do (I Do It For You)"/Sleeping With The NME (12", p/s) 10
92 Columbia 658382 2 Theme From M*A*S*H EP (Suicide Is Painless)/FATIMA MANSIONS: "Everything I Do (I Do It For You)"/Sleeping With The NME (CD) 20
92 Columbia 658796 7 Little Baby Nothing (7" Version)/Never Want Again/Suicide Alley (p/s) 5
92 Columbia 658796 Little Baby Nothing (7" Version)/Never Want Again/Suicide Alley (cassette) 5
92 Columbia 658796 7 Little Baby Nothing (7" Version)/Never Want Again/Dead Yankee Drawl/ Suicide Alley (CD, original issue) 8
92 Columbia 658796 5 Little Baby Nothing (7" Version)/R.P. McMurphy/Tennessee (live)/ You Love Us (live) (CD) 15
93 Columbia 659727 6 From Despair To Where/Hibernation/Spectators Of Suicide (Heavenly Version) (12", p/s) 8
93 Columbia 659727 7 From Despair To Where/Hibernation/Spectators Of Suicide (Heavenly Version)/Starlover (Heavenly Version) (CD) 18
93 Columbia 659477 6 La Tristesse Durera/Patrick Bateman/Repeat (live)/Tennessee (12", poster p/s) 8
93 Columbia 659477 2 La Tristesse Durera/Patrick Bateman/What's My Name (live)/ Slash'N'Burn (CD, digipak) 15
93 Columbia 659727 7 Roses In The Hospital/Us Against You/Donkeys (pink vinyl) 6
93 Columbia 659727 6 Roses In The Hospital (OG Psychovocal Mix)/ (OC Psychmental Mix)/(51 Funk Salute Mix)/(Fillet-O-Gang Mix)/ (ECG Mix)/(Album Version) (12", p/s) 8

MINT VALUE £

93 Columbia 659727 2 Roses In The Hospital/Us Against You/Donkeys/Wrote For Luck (CD) . . . 15
94 Columbia 660070 2 Life Becoming A Landslide/Comfort Comes/Are Mothers Saints/ Charles Windsor (CD) . . . 15
94 Columbia 660447 0 PCP/Faster/Sculpture Of Man (10", p/s) . . . 15
94 Columbia 660447 2 Faster/PCP/Sculpture Of Man/New Art Riot (In E Minor) (CD) . . . 15
94 Columbia 660686 0 Revol/Too Cold Here/You Love Us/Life Becoming A Landslide (Live in Bangkok) (10", p/s) . . . 7
94 Columbia 660686 2 Revol/Too Cold Here/You Love Us/Life's Sweet Exile (CD) . . . 10
94 Columbia 660686 5 Revol/Drug Drug Druggy (Live at Glastonbury)/Roses In The Hospital (Live Glastonbury)/You Love Us (Live at Glastonbury) (CD) . . . 15
94 Columbia 660895 0 She Is Suffering/The Drowners (live)/Stay With Me (live) (10", p/s) . . . 10
96 Columbia 663070 A Design For Life/Bright Eyes (jukebox issue, no p/s) . . . 8
96 Columbia 663468 Everything Must Go/Raindrops Keep Falling On My Head (Live Acoustic Version) (jukebox issue, no p/s) . . . 8
96 Columbia 664044 Australia/A Design For Life (Live City Hall Sheffield) (jukebox issue, no p/s) . . . 8
97 Columbia MANIC 1-6CD SIX SINGLES FROM GENERATION TERRORISTS (6-CD box set) . . . 90

PROMOS & MISC. RELEASES

91 Heavenly HVN 10P You Love Us (Radio Edit) (promo-only, some with stickered p/s, 1-sided white label, 500 only) . . . 30
92 Columbia XPCD 171 GENERATION TERRORISTS (CD, 5-track sampler, digipak) . . . 15
92 Columbia XPCD 185 Motorcycle Emptiness/Motorcycle Emptiness (Radio Edit) (CD) . . . 18
93 Columbia XPCD 285 GOLD AGAINST THE SOUL (CD, 4-track sampler, digipak) . . . 20
93 Columbia/Damont XPS 272 Symphony Of Tourette (1-sided, white label, no p/s) . . . 70
94 Columbia DONE AND DUSTED (12", Chemical Brothers remixes) . . . 20
94 Lyntone MAN 1C VERSES FROM THE HOLY BIBLE (flexidisc sampler, given away with NME [27/8/94]) . . . 10
96 Columbia XPR 3043 A Design For Life (Stealth Sonic Orchestra Remix)/(Instrumental) (12") . . . 20
96 Columbia XPR 3049 Kevin Carter (Stealth Sonic Orchestra Remix) (12", white label, 1-sided, stickered card sleeve, 30 only) . . . 30
96 Columbia XPR 3094 Australia (Lionrock Remix) (12", white label, 1-sided, stickered card sleeve, 20 only) . . . 60
99 Epic XPR 3320 Tsunami (Cornelius Remix)/(Electron Ray Tube Mix by Stereolab) (12", p/s, sealed with sticker, promo only) . . . 10

ALBUMS

92 Columbia 471060 9 GENERATION TERRORISTS (2-LP, picture discs, inner sleeves, 5,000 only) . . . 30
92 Columbia 471060 0 GENERATION TERRORISTS (CD, picture disc, 5,000 only) . . . 40
93 Columbia 4740649 1 GOLD AGAINST THE SOUL (LP, picture disc, inner sleeve, in custom carrier-bag) . . . 15
93 Columbia 4740649 2 GOLD AGAINST THE SOUL (gold CD) . . . 20
94 Epic 477421 9 THE HOLY BIBLE (LP, picture disc) . . . 20
94 Epic 4774212 THE HOLY BIBLE (CD, picture disc) . . . 20
98 Epic 4917031 THIS IS MY TRUTH TELL ME YOURS (LP, picture disc) . . . 18

MANICURED NOISE

80 Pre PRE 003 Metronome/Moscow (die-cut p/s with postcard) . . . 5
80 Pre PRE 006 Faith/Free Time (p/s) . . . 5
(see also Weatherman & Friends)

MANIFESTO

80s Fire BLAZE 66055 Pattern 26 (1-sided white/label in bag with biography) . . . 6

MANISH BOYS

65 Parlophone R 5250 I Pity The Fool/Take My Tip . . . 600+
(see also David Bowie)

MANISH BOYS/DAVY JONES & LOWER THIRD

79 EMI EMI 2925 I Pity The Fool/Take My Tip/DAVY JONES & LOWER THIRD: You've Got A Habit Of Leaving/Baby Loves That Way (p/s) . . . 10
82 Charly CYM 1 I Pity The Fool/Take My Tip/DAVY JONES & LOWER THIRD: You've Got A Habit Of Leaving/Baby Loves That Way (10", p/s, reissue) . . . 7
(see also David Bowie, Davy Jones, Davie Jones & King Bees)

MANITOBA

70 RCA 2016 You'll Never Get Back/Something In You . . . 5

EARLE MANKEY

78 Bronze BRO 53 Mau Mau/Crazy . . . 7

MAN MACHINE

90 Outer Rhythm MMAN 2T ZEN EP (12") . . . 10
91 Outer Rhythm MMAN 3T Animal (Primeaval Interface)/Shout (The Communicator)/ Shout (Primary Contact) (12") . . . 10

BARRY MANN

61 HMV POP 911 Who Put The Bomp/Love True Love . . . 30
61 HMV POP 949 Little Miss U.S.A./Find Another Fool . . . 18
62 HMV POP 1084 Hey Baby I'm Dancin'/Like I Don't Love You . . . 18
63 HMV POP 1108 Bless You/Teenage Has Been . . . 18
64 Colpix PX 776 Talk To Me Baby/Amy . . . 15
66 Capitol CL 15463 Angelica/Looking At Tomorrow . . . 10
68 Capitol CL 15538 The Young Electric Psychedelic Hippy Flippy Folk And Funky Philosophic Turned On Groovy 12 String Band/Take Your Love . . . 10
72 CBS S 7897 Ain't No Way To Go Home/You've Lost That Lovin' Feelin' . . . 5
79 Warner Bros K 17335 Almost Gone/For No Reason At All . . . 5
63 HMV CLP 1559 WHO PUT THE BOMP IN THE BOMP BOMP BOMP? (LP . . .)200

CARL MANN

59 London HLS 8935 Mona Lisa/Foolish One . . . 30
59 London HLS 8935 Mona Lisa/Foolish One (78) . . . 105
59 London HLS 9006 Pretend/Rockin' Love . . . 30

59	London HLS 9006	Pretend/Rockin' Love (78)	170
60	London HLS 9170	South Of The Border/I'm Comin' Home	25
60	London HA-S 2277	LIKE MANN — CARL MANN SINGS (LP)	325

CHARLES MANN

73	Probe PRO 585	Say You Love Me Too/I Can Feel It	5

GARY MANN ORCHESTRA

73	Penny Farthing PEN 820	The Original 'Big Match' Theme/Newscoop (The Original 'Grandstand' Theme)	6

GEOFF MANN

84	private pressing GM 001	CHANTS WOULD BE A FINE THING (cassette)	10
84	Food For Thought GRUB 4	I MAY SING GRACE (LP)	12
85	Wobbly WOB 1	PSALM ENCHANTED EVENING (LP)	12

GLORIA MANN

56	Brunswick 05569	Why Do Fools Fall In Love/Partners For Life	20
56	Brunswick 05569	Why Do Fools Fall In Love/Partners For Life (78)	8
56	Brunswick 05610	It Happened Again/My Secret Sin	15

HERBIE MANN

66	Atlantic 584 052	Philly Dog/DAVE PIKE: Sunny	10
66	Atlantic 584 058	Love Theme From Paris Burning/Happy Brass	5
67	Atlantic 584 112	And The Beat Goes On/Free For All	5
68	A&M AMS 719	Unchain My Heart/Glory Of Love	6
69	Atlantic 584 297	Memphis Underground/New Orleans	5
72	Atlantic K 10179	Philly Dog/Memphis Underground/It's A Funky Thing	5
75	Atlantic K 10580	Hijack/Orient Express	5
56	London EZN 19006	EAST COAST JAZZ NO. 4 PT. 1 (EP)	8
58	Fontana TFE 17113	HERBIE MANN (EP)	10
59	Columbia Clef SEB 10102	MAGIC FLUTE OF HERBIE MANN (EP)	10
58	Fontana TFL 5013	SALUTE TO THE FLUTE (LP)	15
60	Top Rank 25/015	FLUTE FOR ETERNITY (10" LP, with Buddy Collette)	15
63	London HA-K/SH-K 8043	RIGHT NOW (LP)	15
64	Atlantic ATL 5008	HERBIE MANN AT NEWPORT (LP)	15
65	Atlantic ATL/SAL 5035	THE ROAR OF THE GREASE PAINT (LP)	15
66	CBS (S)BPG 62585	LATIN MANN (LP)	12
66	Atlantic ATL/SAL 5038	STANDING OVATION AT NEWPORT (LP)	15
66	Atlantic 587/588 003	MONDAY NIGHT AT THE VILLAGE GATE (LP)	15
66	Atlantic 587/588 028	NIRVANA (LP, with Bill Evans)	15
67	Atlantic 1471	NEW MANN AT NEWPORT (LP)	12
67	Atlantic 587/588 054	HERBIE MANN AT THE VILLAGE GATE (LP)	12
67	Atlantic Special 590 013	FREE FOR ALL (LP)	12
68	Atlantic 1475	IMPRESSIONS OF THE MIDDLE EAST (LP)	15
68	Atlantic 1490	THE HERBIE MANN STRING ALBUM (LP)	12
69	Solid State USS 7007	ST. THOMAS (LP)	15
69	Atlantic 588 156	INSPIRATION I FEEL (LP)	12
69	A&M AMLS 944	GLORY OF LOVE (LP)	12
69	Atlantic 588 200	MEMPHIS UNDERGROUND (LP)	12
69	SRCP 3002	AFRO-JAZZIAC (LP)	12
70	Polydor 2465 005	CONCERTO GROSSO IN D BLUES (LP)	12
70	Polydor 2465 008	STONE FLUTE (LP)	12
71	Atco 2400 022	MUSCLE SHOALS NITTY GRITTY (LP)	12
71	Atco 2400 121	MEMPHIS TWO-STEP (LP)	12
72	Atco 2400 191	PUSH, PUSH (LP, with Duane Allman)	15
72	Atlantic K 40385	MISSISSIPPI GAMBLER (LP)	12
73	Atlantic K 40467	HOLD ON, I'M COMIN' (LP)	12
74	Atlantic K 50020	TURTLE BAY (LP)	12
74	Atlantic K 50032	LONDON UNDERGROUND (LP)	12
75	Atlantic K 50053	REGGAE (LP)	12
75	Atlantic K 50128	DISCOTHEQUE (LP)	12
75	Atlantic K 50174	WATER BED (LP)	12

LORIE MANN

59	Top Rank JAR 116	A Penny A Kiss, A Penny A Hug/Dream Lover	7
59	Top Rank JAR 116	A Penny A Kiss, A Penny A Hug/Dream Lover (78)	5
59	Top Rank JAR 148	Just Keep It Up/You Made Me Care	10
59	Top Rank JAR 148	Just Keep It Up/You Made Me Care (78)	5
59	Top Rank JAR 237	So Many Ways/I Wonder	7

MANFRED MANN

63	HMV POP 1189	Why Should We Not/Brother Jack	20
63	HMV POP 1225	Cock-A-Hoop/Now You're Needing Me	18
64	HMV POP 1252	5-4-3-2-1/Without You	8
64	HMV POP 1282	Hubble Bubble (Toil And Trouble)/I'm Your Kingpin	8
64	HMV POP 1320	Do Wah Diddy Diddy/What You Gonna Do?	6
64	HMV POP 1346	Sha La La/John Hardy	6
65	HMV POP 1381	Come Tomorrow/What Did I Do Wrong?	6
65	HMV POP 1413	Oh No Not My Baby/What Am I Doing Wrong	6
65	HMV POP 1466	If You Gotta Go, Go Now/Stay Around	6
66	HMV POP 1523	Pretty Flamingo/You're Standing By	6
66	HMV POP 1541	You Gave Me Somebody To Love/Poison Ivy	12
65	HMV 7TEA 2124	There's No Living Without Your Loving/Tired Of Trying, Bored With Lying, Scared Of Dying (demo-only EP sampler)	30
66	Fontana TF 730	Just Like A Woman/I Wanna Be Rich	6
66	Fontana TF 757	Semi-Detached, Suburban Mr. James/Morning After The Party	6
67	Fontana TF 812	Ha! Ha! Said The Clown/Feeling So Good (some in p/s)	15/6
67	Fontana TF 828	Sweet Pea/One Way	7
67	Fontana TF 862	So Long, Dad/Funniest Gig	7

MINT VALUE £

68 Fontana TF 897 Mighty Quinn/By Request — Edwin Garvey . . . 6
68 Fontana TF 908 Up The Junction/Sleepy Hollow (some in p/s) . . . 15/6
68 Fontana TF 943 My Name Is Jack/There Is A Man . . . 6
68 Fontana TF 985 Fox On The Run/Too Many People . . . 6
69 Fontana TF 1013 Ragamuffin Man/A 'B' Side . . . 6
64 HMV 7EG 8848 MANFRED MANN'S COCK-A-HOOP WITH 54321 (EP) . . . 25
65 HMV 7EG 8876 GROOVIN' WITH MANFRED MANN (EP) . . . 20
65 HMV 7EG 8908 THE ONE IN THE MIDDLE (EP) . . . 20
65 HMV 7EG 8922 NO LIVING WITHOUT LOVING (EP) . . . 20
66 HMV 7EG 8942 MACHINES (EP) . . . 25
66 HMV 7EG 8949 INSTRUMENTAL ASYLUM (EP, with Jack Bruce) . . . 30
66 HMV 7EG 8962 AS WAS (EP) . . . 25
66 Fontana TE 17483 INSTRUMENTAL ASSASSINATION (EP) . . . 12
68 Philips MCF 5002 THE HITS OF MANFRED MANN (cassette EP) . . . 12
68 Philips MCF 5005 THE HITS OF MANFRED MANN AND DDDBM&T (cassette EP) . . . 12
64 HMV CLP 1731 THE FIVE FACES OF MANFRED MANN (LP) . . . 40
65 HMV CLP 1911/CSD 1628 MANN MADE (LP, mono/stereo) . . . 30/40
66 HMV CLP 3559 MANN MADE HITS (LP) . . . 30
66 HMV TA-CLP 3559 MANN MADE HITS (reel-to-reel tape, mono) . . . 12
66 Fontana (S)TL 5377 AS IS (LP, 'alcove' cover, mono/stereo) . . . 20/30
66 Fontana (S)TL 5377 AS IS (LP, 'locomotive' cover, mono/stereo) . . . 35/45
67 HMV CLP/CSD 3594 SOUL OF MANN (LP, mono/stereo) . . . 40/55
67 HMV TA-CLP 3594 SOUL OF MANN (reel-to-reel tape, mono) . . . 12
68 Fontana (S)TL 5460 UP THE JUNCTION — ORIGINAL SOUNDTRACK RECORDING (LP) . . . 30
68 Fontana SFL 13003 WHAT A MANN (LP) . . . 30
68 Fontana (S)TL 5470 MIGHTY GARVEY! (LP, mono/stereo) . . . 20/15
70 Fontana 6852 005 UP THE JUNCTION — ORIGINAL SOUNDTRACK RECORDING (LP, reissue) . . . 12
(see also Paul Jones, Blues Band, Mike Hugg, Henry Lowther, Mike D'Abo, McGuinness Flint, Jack Bruce, Coulson & Dean, Lyn Dobson, Paddy Klaus & Gibson)

MANFRED MANN & MIKE HUG(G)

71 Ski SKI 1 Ski 'Full-Of-Fitness' Theme/Baby Jane (some in p/s) . . . 15/7
71 Michelin MIC+01 The Michelin Theme (Go Radial, Go Michelin) (1-sided, gatefold p/s) . . . 15

MANFRED MANN'S CHAPTER III

70 Vertigo 6059 012 Happy Being Me/Devil Woman . . . 10
69 Vertigo VO 3 MANFRED MANN CHAPTER III (LP, gatefold sleeve, swirl label) . . . 35
70 Vertigo 6360 012 MANFRED MANN CHAPTER III VOL. 2 (LP, gatefold sleeve, swirl label) . . . 45

MANFRED MANN'S EARTH BAND

70 Lyntone LYN 1981 The Maxwell House Shake (1-sided flexidisc) . . . 7
71 Philips 6006 122 Living Without You/Tribute (as Manfred Mann) . . . 5
71 Philips 6006 159 Mrs Henry/Prayer (as Manfred Mann) . . . 5
72 Philips 6006 251 Meat/Glorified Magnified (as Earth Band) . . . 5
73 Vertigo 6059 078 Get Your Rocks Off/Sadjoy (as Earth Band) . . . 6
79 Bronze BPO 77 Don't Kill It Carol/Blinded By The Light (picture disc) . . . 6
71 Philips 6308 062 STEPPING SIDEWAYS (LP, unissued)
72 Philips 6308 086 MANFRED MANN'S EARTH BAND (LP) . . . 15
72 Philips 6308 125 GLORIFIED MAGNIFIED (LP) . . . 15
73 Vertigo 6360 087 MESSIN' (LP) . . . 20
(see also Skeleton Crew)

SHADOW MANN

69 Roulette RO 504 Come Live With Me/One By One . . . 12

SHELLY MANNE

68 Atlantic 584 180 Daktari/Out On A Limb . . . 8
54 Vogue LDE 072 SHELLY MANNE AND HIS MEN VOL. 1 (10" LP) . . . 15
55 Contemporary LDC 143 SHELLY MANNE VOL. 2 (10" LP, with Andre Previn & Leroy Vinegar) . . . 15
56 Contemporary LDC 190 SHELLY MANNE, SHORTY ROGERS AND JIMMY GIUFFRE — THE THREE (10" LP) . . . 15
56 Contemporary LDC 192 SHELLY MANNE AND RUSS FREEMAN (10" LP) . . . 15
56 Contemporary LAC 12075 SHELLY MANNE AND HIS FRIENDS (LP, with Andre Previn & Leroy Vinegar) . . . 15
56 Contemporary LAC 12100 MY FAIR LADY (LP) . . . 15
57 Contemporary LAC 12148 SHELLY MANNE AND HIS MEN VOL. 5 (LP) . . . 12
57 Contemporary LAC 12232 SHELLY MANNE AND HIS MEN VOL. 6 (LP) . . . 12
61 Contemporary LAC 12250 AT THE BLACK HAWK VOL. 1 (LP, also stereo SCA 5015) . . . 12
61 Contemporary LAC 12255 AT THE BLACK HAWK VOL. 2 (LP, also stereo SCA 5016) . . . 12
61 Contemporary LAC 12260 AT THE BLACK HAWK VOL. 3 (LP, also stereo SCA 5017) . . . 12
61 Contemporary LAC 12265 AT THE BLACK HAWK VOL. 4 (LP, also stereo SCA 5018) . . . 12
61 Contemporary LAC 12293 THE PROPER TIME (LP, soundtrack) . . . 15
61 Contemporary LAC 12305/6 AT THE MANNE HOLE (2-LP) . . . 18
65 Stateside SL 10125 SHELLY MANNE AND CO. (LP) . . . 12
(see also Gerry Mulligan & Shelly Manne, Shorty Rogers & His Orchestra)

MANNIN FOLK

76 Kelly MAN 2 KING OF THE SEA (LP) . . . 35
70s Kelly KEP 1 MANNIN FOLK SING (LP) . . . 20

BOB MANNING

54 Capitol CL 14190 I'm A Fool For You/It's All Right With Me . . . 10
55 Capitol CL 14220 The Very Thought Of You/Just For Laughs . . . 10
55 Capitol CL 14256 Majorca (Isle Of Love)/It's My Life . . . 10
55 Capitol CL 14234 My Love Song To You/After My Laughter Came Tears . . . 10
55 Capitol CL 14288 The Mission San Michel/You Are There . . . 10
55 Capitol CL 14318 What A Wonderful Way To Die/Why Didn't You Tell Me? . . . 10

LINDA MANNING

66 King KG 1039 Buy Me Something Pretty, Joey/Downtown Lonely Girl Blues . . . 7

MINT VALUE £

MARTY MANNING & CHEETAHS

67 CBS 2721 Tarzan March/Sunny. . . . 12

MICHAEL MANNING

03 Ai AI 007 THE LOST ABERRANT DRAGONFLY EP (12", p/s). . . . 8

EDDIE MANNION

60 HMV POP 804 Just Driftin'/Quiet Girl 50

WINGY MANONE ORCHESTRA

57 Brunswick 05655 Party Doll/Real Gone 20
57 Brunswick 05655 Party Doll/Real Gone (78) 8

MAN ON THE MOON

69 Philips 88457 DE MAN ON THE MOON (EP, spoken word, 2-part tri-foldout p/s with insert, 'historic souvenir' available via *News Of The World* newspaper). . . . 8

MAN OR ASTROMAN

96 One Louder LOUDER 12 EXPERIMENTAL ZERO (LP, yellow vinyl, with poster) 15

MANOWAR

83 M. F. Nations 12 KUT 102 Defender (featuring Orson Welles)/Gloves Of Metal (12", p/s) 15
84 10 TEN 3012 All Men Play On 10/Mountains (12", p/s, some gatefold). . . . 18/12
87 Atlantic B 9463 Blow Your Speakers/Violence And Bloodshed (p/s) 7
87 Atlantic BT 9463 Blow Your Speakers/Violence And Bloodshed (12", embossed p/s, some with poster) 12/8

(see also Orson Welles)

JOE MANSANO

69 Blue Cat BS 150 Life On Reggae Planet/RECO & RHYTHM ACES: Z.Z. Beat 40
72 Sioux SI 022 The Trial Of Pama Dice/JACKIE ROWLAND: Lonely Man 20
70 Trojan TBL 106 BRIXTON CAT (LP). . . . 40

(see also Joe The Boss, Joe's Allstars, Dice The Boss)

TONY MANSELL

54 Parlophone MSP 6130 The High And The Mighty/Hold My Hand (with Johnny Dankworth Orchestra). . . . 8
56 Parlophone MSP 6222 Zambesi (Sweet African)/11th Hour Melody (with Johnny Dankworth Orchestra). . 8
58 Parlophone R 4471 Impossible/Who Are They To Say 6

(see also Johnny Dankworth)

KEITH MANSFIELD ORCHESTRA

68 CBS 3895 Beautiful//Soul Thing 15
68 CBS 63426 ALL YOU NEED IS KEITH MANSFIELD (LP) 35
69 CBS 64666 RACE ON THE WIND (LP). . . . 12
70 CBS 70073 LOOT (LP, soundtrack, with Steve Ellis) 60

JAYNE MANSFIELD

67 London HL 10147 As The Clouds Drift By/Suey (with Jimi Hendrix, demos more common, £20) . . . 45

(see also Jimi Hendrix)

CHARLES MANSON

86 Fierce FRIGHT 006 Rise/Sick City (p/s, 1 side etched, handwritten labels). . . . 25
88 Fierce FRIGHT 012 It's Comin' Down Fast (Helter Skelter) (p/s, 1 side etched, hand-made labels) . . . 25
86 Fierce FRIGHT 001 LOVE AND TERROR CULT (LP) 40

EDDY MANSON

55 HMV 7M 325 Oh! No!/The Lovers 10

JEANE MANSON

79 CBS S CBS 7222 I've Already Seen It In Your Eyes/J'ai Deja Vu Ca Dans Tes Yeux 15

MARILYN MANSON

97 Interscope INVP 95541 The Horrible People/The Not So Beautiful People (10" picture disc). . . . 10
97 Interscope INDX 95541 The Beautiful People/The Not So Beautiful People/Snake Eyes And Sissies/ Deformography (CD) 8
97 Interscope INVP 95552 Tourniquet/(remix) (10" picture disc). . . . 18
97 Interscope INDX 95552 Tourniquet/Lunchbox/Next MF (CD) 8
98 Nothing INVP 95610 The Dope Show/The Dope Show (10" picture disc, same track on both sides). . . 20
99 Interscope SAM 175 CD I Don't Like Drugs (But The Drugs Like Me) (radio edit)/(album version) (CD, card sleeve, promo only) 20
00 Nothing/Universe 4974581 Disposable Teens/Five To One/Diamonds & Pollen (12" picture disc, PVC sl.) . . . 20
01 Universal 4974911 The Fight Song/(Slipknot Remix)/(Love Song Remix) (12" picture disc, stickered sleeve) 15
03 Universal 9807728 Mobscene/Paranoiac (poster p/s) 5
03 Universal 9810794 This Is The New Shit/(Goldfrapp Version) (10" picture disc). . . . 15
95 Simply Vinyl SVLP 208 SMELLS LIKE CHILDREN (LP, 180 gm vinyl) 18
96 Interscope IND 90086 ANTICHRIST SUPERSTAR (CD, in slipcase) 18
98 Simply Vinyl SVLP 195 MECHANICAL ANIMALS (2-LP, 180 gm vinyl). . . . 20
98 Interscope IND 90273 MECHANICAL ANIMALS (CD, in slipcase) 18
99 Interscope ADV 490 394-2 MECHANICAL ANIMALS (CD, promo, no'd, card sl., with comic, PVC slipcase) . . 40
02 Simply Vinyl SVLP 055 ANTICHRIST SUPERSTAR (2-LP, 180 gm vinyl, gatefold sleeve) 20

MANSUN

95 Polygram no cat. no. Take It Easy Chicken (Demo)/Naked Twister/Drastic Sturgeon (cassette, promo only, with title inlay) 70
95 Sci Fi Hi Fi MANSON 1 Take It Easy Chicken/Take It Easy Chicken (as Manson, same track both sides, die-cut sleeve, 500 only; promos with "Manson Promo" on label £75). . . . 65
95 Regal REG 3 Skin Up Pin Up/Flourella (white vinyl). . . . 18
95 Regal REG 3CD Skin Up Pin Up/Flourella (CD, PVC sleeve with barcode sticker). . . . 25
96 Parlophone R 6447 Stripper Vicar/No One Knows Us (clear vinyl, p/s) 10
96 Parlophone CDRS 6447 Stripper Vicar/The Edge/Duchess (CD, card p/s with poster). . . . 12
96 Parlophone CDR 6447 Stripper Vicar/An Open Letter/No One Knows Us/Things Keep Falling Off (CD). . 15
96 Parlophone R 6453 Wide Open Space/Rebel Without A Quilt (white vinyl, foldout p/s in PVC sleeve). 10

MINT VALUE £

96	Parlophone CDR 6453	Wide Open Space/Rebel Without A Quilt/Vision Impaired/ Skin Up, Pin Up (CD, digipak)	20
96	Parlophone CDRS 6453	Wide Open Space/The Gods Of Not Very Much/Moronica (Acoustic Version)/ Lemonade Secret Drinker (Acoustic Version) (CD, fold-out card p/s)	25
97	Parlophone R 6458	She Makes My Nose Bleed/The Holy Blood And The Holy Grail (red vinyl, fold out sleeve)	7
97	Parlophone R 6482	Closed For Business/Egg Shaped Fred (Acoustic Version) (clear vinyl, p/s, with insert)	7
98	EMI R 6497	Legacy/GSOH/Can't Afford To Die (p/s)	7
99	fan club MANSUN 001	Taxloss/Everyone Must Win (live) (fanclub-only release)	30
98	Parlophone R 6508	Negative/Mansun's Only Live Song (clear vinyl, PVC sleeve, picture insert)	5
96	Parlophone R 6430	ONE EP (p/s)	18
96	Parlophone CDRS 6430	ONE EP (CD)	22
96	Parlophone R 6437	TWO EP (p/s)	15
96	Parlophone CDR 6437	TWO EP (CD)	15
97	Parlophone CDRS 6482	SEVEN EP (CD, digipak with poster)	10
98	Parlophone R 6487	EIGHT EP (p/s, red vinyl)	8
99	Parlophone R 6511	SIX EP (clear vinyl, p/s)	7
97	Parlophone CPCS 7387	ATTACK OF THE GREY LANTERN (2-LP, gatefold sleeve, with inners and poster)	30

JOHN MANTELL

65	CBS 201783	Remember Child/I'll See You Around	25

MIKE MANTLER

75	Watt WATT 3	13¾ (LP, with Carla Bley; with insert)	12

(see also Carla Bley, Jazz Composers Orchestra)

BOB MANTON

81	Mainstreet MS 101	No Trees In Brixton Prison/Brixton Walkabout (p/s)	8

(see also Purple Hearts)

MANTOVANI (ORCHESTRA)

51	Decca F 9696	Charmaine/Diane	5
53	Decca F 10168	Swedish Rhapsody/Jamaican Rumba (gold or silver label lettering)	15/8
54	Decca F 10233	Luxembourg Polka/Music Box Tango	6
54	Decca F 10250	Shadow Waltz/Moonlight Serenade	6
54	Decca F 10292	Bewitched/Dream, Dream, Dream	6
54	Decca F 10395	Lonely Ballerina/Lazy Gondolier	7
67	Decca F 12630	You Only Live Twice/Puppet On A String (as Mantovani Orchestra)	6

MANUEL & MUSIC OF THE MOUNTAINS

78	EMI EMI 2743	Princess Leia's Theme From Star Wars/Mountain Fire	5

(see also Geoff Love, Mandingo)

MANUFACTURED ROMANCE

81	Fresh FRESH 16	The Time Of My Life/Room To Breathe (various colours of p/s)	5

PHIL MANZANERA (& 801)

77	Polydor 2001 733	Flight 19/Car Rhumba	5
78	Polydor 2001 800	Island/Diamond Head	5
78	Polydor 2001 835	Remote Control/K Scope (1st issue)	5
78	Polydor PB 10	Remote Control/K Scope (2nd issue)	5

(see also Roxy Music, Quiet Sun, 801)

RAY MANZAREK

83	A&M AM 156	Wounds Of Fate/Roasted Swan (p/s)	5
84	A&M AM 173	Wheel Of Fortune/A Young Girl (p/s)	5
74	Mercury SRM 1703	THE WHOLE THING STARTED WITH ROCK'N'ROLL (LP)	15
83	A&M AMLX 64945	CARMINA BURANA (LP, with Philip Glass)	12

(see also Doors, Philip Glass)

MAPLEOAK

70	Decca F 13008	Son Of A Gun/Hurt Me So Much	20
71	Decca SKL 5085	MAPLEOAK (LP)	200

LUCILLE MAPP

57	Columbia DB 3916	Mangos/On Treasure Island	10
57	Columbia DB 3949	Jamie Boy/Moonlight In Vermont	8
57	Columbia DB 4040	I'm Available/Lovin' Ya, Lovin' Ya, Lovin' Ya	10
58	Columbia DB 4071	Love Is/The Early Birdie	7
58	Columbia DB 4168	Remember When/I'm A Dreamer, Aren't We All?	6
59	Columbia DB 4261	Chinchilla/Follow Me	15
57	Columbia SEG 7726	STREET OF DREAMS (EP)	15
57	Columbia SEG 7773	LUCILLE MAPP (EP)	15

TOMMY MARA

55	MGM SP 1128	Pledging My Love/Honey Bunch	10
55	MGM MGM 821	Pledging My Love/Honey Bunch (78)	8
58	Felsted AF 109	Where The Blues Of The Night/What Makes You So Lonely	12
59	Felsted AF 116	You Don't Know/Marie	7
59	Felsted AF 116	You Don't Know/Marie (78)	8
59	Felsted AF 123	Until I Hear From You/Now Is The Hour	7
59	Felsted AF 123	Until I Hear From You/Now Is The Hour (78)	8
58	Felsted GEP 1003	PRESENTING TOMMY MARA (EP)	22

MARABAR CAVES

85	Tiki MBAR 1	Sally's Place Crew/Seeds That Never Grew	15

(JOSEPH) MARAIS & MIRANDA

53	Columbia SCM 5025	Old Johnnie Goggabie/The Zulu Warrior	5
59	Fontana H 225	I-Ha-She/The Queen Bee (as Marais & Miranda)	5
59	Fontana H 225	I-Ha-She/The Queen Bee (as Marais & Miranda) (78)	8

MINT VALUE £

MARATHONS

61	Pye International 7N 25088	Peanut Butter/Down In New Orleans	25
61	Vogue V 9185	Peanut Butter/Talkin' Trash	25

MARAUDERS

63	Decca F 11695	That's What I Want/Hey What'd You Say	18
63	Decca F 11748	Always On My Mind/Heart Full Of Tears	12
64	Decca F 11836	Lucille/Little Egypt	15
65	Fontana TF 609	Baby I Wanna Be Loved/Somebody Told My Girl	12

(see also Danny Davis)

MARBLES

68	Polydor 56272	Only One Woman/By The Light Of A Burning Candle	7
69	Polydor 56310	The Walls Fell Down/Love You	8
70	Polydor 56378	Breaking Up Is Hard To Do/I Can't See Nobody	6

(see also Graham Bonnet, Fut)

MARBLE STAIRCASE

83	Whaam! WHAAM 11	Still Dreaming/Dark Ages (p/s)	12

MARC & MAMBAS

82	Some Bizzare BZS 512	Fun City/Sleaze (Take It, Shake It)/Taking It And Shaking It (12", p/s, fan club issue, mail-order only)	20
82	Lyntone LYN 12505	Discipline (*Flexipop* flexidisc, clear or black vinyl, as Marc & Friends)	10/6
82	Some Bizzare BZS 15	Big Louise/Empty Eyes (unreleased, artwork only)	
82	Some Bizzare BZS 1512	Big Louise/Empty Eyes/The Dirt Behind The Neon (Sleaze Revisited) (12", unreleased, artwork only)	
83	Some Bizzare BZS 19	Black Heart/Your Aura (p/s, with postcard insert)	7
83	Some Bizzare BZS 1912	Black Heart/Your Aura/Mamba (12", p/s)	8
83	Some Bizzare BZSDJ 21	Torment/You'll Never See On Sunday (promo)	15
83	Some Bizzare BZS 2112	Torment/First Time/You'll Never See Me On A Sunday/ Megamillionmania — Multimaniamix (12", p/s)	10
82	Some Bizzare B2A 4	UNTITLED (2-LP, gatefold sleeve)	15
83	Some Bizzare BZA 13	TORMENTS & TOREROS (2-LP)	15
84	Gutterhearts GH 1	BITE BLACK AND BLUES — RAOUL & THE RUINED LIVE (LP, fan club issue)	30

(see also Soft Cell, Marc Almond)

LYDIA MARCELLE

66	Sue WI 4025	Another Kind Of Fellow/I've Never Been Hurt Like This Before	40

MUZZY MARCELLINO

56	London HLU 8355	Mary Lou/MR. FORD & MR. GOON-BONES: Ain't She Sweet	40
56	London HLU 8355	Mary Lou/MR. FORD & MR. GOON-BONES: Ain't She Sweet (78)	8

MARCELS

61	Pye International 7N 25073	Blue Moon/Goodbye To Love	12
61	Pye International 7N 25083	Summertime/Teeter Totter Love	12
61	Pye International 7N 25105	You Are My Sunshine/Find Another Fool	15
61	Pye International 7N 25114	Heartaches/My Love For You	18
62	Pye International 7N 25124	My Melancholy Baby/Really Need Your Love	15
63	Pye International 7N 25201	I Wanna Be The Leader/Give Me Back Your Love	20
61	Pye Intl. NPL 28016	BLUE MOON (LP)	160

GLORIA MARCH

58	London HLB 8568	Baby Of Mine/Nippon Wishing Well	25
58	London HLB 8568	Baby Of Mine/Nippon Wishing Well (78)	12

HAL MARCH

58	London HLD 8534	Hear Me Good/One Dozen Roses	25
58	London HLD 8534	Hear Me Good/One Dozen Roses (78)	15

JO MARCH

58	London HLR 8696	Dormi, Dormi, Dormi (Sleep, Sleep, Sleep)/Fare Thee Well, Oh Honey	12
58	London HLR 8696	Dormi, Dormi, Dormi (Sleep, Sleep, Sleep)/Fare Thee Well, Oh Honey (78)	12
58	London HLR 8763	The Virgin Mary Had One Son/I, Said The Donkey	10
58	London HLR 8763	The Virgin Mary Had One Son/I, Said The Donkey (78)	10

(LITTLE) PEGGY MARCH

63	RCA RCA 1338	I Will Follow Him/Wind Up Doll (as Little Peggy March)	7
63	RCA RCA 1350	My Teenage Castle/I Wish I Were A Princess (as Little Peggy March)	7
63	RCA RCA 1362	Hello Heartache, Goodbye Love/Boy Crazy (as Little Peggy March)	7
64	RCA RCA 1426	Watch What You Do With My Baby/Can't Stop (as Little Peggy March)	8
65	RCA RCA 1472	Let Her Go/Your Girl	7
68	RCA RCA 1687	If You Loved Me/Thinking Through My Tears	22
68	RCA RCA 1752	I've Been Here Before/Time And Time Again	6
69	RCA RCA 1809	What Am I Going To Do Without You/Lilac Skies	6
65	RCA	IN OUR FASHION (LP, existence unconfirmed)	

BOBBY MARCHAN

68	Atlantic 584 155	Get Down With It/Half A Mind	7
69	Action ACT 4533	Ain't No Reason For Girls To Be Lonely Parts 1 & 2	12

(see also Huey 'Piano' Smith & Clowns)

VICTOR MARCHESE

53	MGM SP 1018	Fandango/Flamingo	8

MARCH HARE

68	Chapter One CH 101	Cry My Heart/With My Eyes Closed	10
69	Deram DM 258	I Could Make It There With You/Have We Got News For You	7

(see also Gary & Stu, Koobas)

MARCHING GIRLS

81	Pop:Aural POP 011	True Love/First In Line (p/s)	10

MINT VALUE £

MARCH VIOLETS

82	Merciful Release MR 013	Religious As Hell/Fodder/Children On Stun/Bon Bon Babies (p/s)	12
83	Merciful Release MR 017	Grooving In Green/Stream (p/s)	10
84	Rebirth RB 21	Snake Dance/Slow Drip Lizard (snakeskin-embossed stickered p/s with insert)	5

MARCIA & JEFF

68	Studio One SO 2047	Words/SHARKS: How Could I Live	30

MARCUS

76	United Artists UAS 30000	MARCUS (LP)	22

GUY MARDEL

65	Vogue VRS 7000	V'Avoue Jamais (actually "N'Avoue Jamais")/Si Tu N'y Crois Pas	5

JANIE MARDEN

55	Decca F 10600	Soldier Boy/Hard To Get	12
55	Decca F 10605	I'll Come When You Call/Thank You For The Waltz (with Frank Weir & His Saxophone)	10
55	Decca F 10673	You Are My Love/A Teen Age Prayer	12
56	Decca F 10765	Allegheny Moon/Magic Melody	8
63	Piccadilly 7N 35128	Make The Night A Little Longer/Walk Alone	8
65	Decca F 12101	They Long To Be Close To You/This Empty Place	10
65	Decca F 12155	You Really Didn't Mean It/Only The One You Love	6

MARDEN HILL

93	Mo Wax MW 004	Come On/(Mixes) (12", die-cut stickered sleeve)	8

ARIF MARDIN

69	Atlantic 584 295	Glass Onion/How Can I Be Sure	7

ERNIE MARESCA

62	London HLU 9531	Shout Shout/Crying Like A Baby Over You	12
62	London HLU 9579	Mary Jane/Down On The Beach	22
63	London HLU 9720	Love Express/Lorelei	15
64	London HLU 9834	Rovin' Kind/Please Be Fair	12
65	London HLU 10008	It's Their World/I Can't Dance	7
66	Stateside SS 560	Rockin' Boulevard Street/Am I Better Off Than Them	18

MARGO, Franck Oliver, Diane Solomon, Malcolm Roberts, etc.

85	Sonet SON 2281	Children, Kinder, Enfants (English)/(International)/(French)	5

MARGO & MARVETTES

64	Parlophone R 5154	Say You Will/Cherry Pie	18
64	Parlophone R 5227	Copper Kettle/So Fine	15
67	Piccadilly 7N 35387	Seven Letters/That's How Love Goes	12
67	Pye 7N 17423	When Love Slips Away/I'll Be Home (When You Call)	50

(see also Liza Dulittle)

MARGUERITA

64	Black Swan WI 431	Woman Come/ERIC MORRIS: Number One	25

CHARLES MARGULIS

59	London HLL 8774	Gigi/Malaguena	10
59	London HLL 8774	Gigi/Malaguena (78)	8

MARIANNE

68	Columbia DB 8420	As For Marionettes/You Know My Name	8
68	Columbia DB 8456	You Had Better Change Your Evil Ways/Like A See Saw	6

MARIANNE & MIKE

64	Vocalion V 9218	As He Once Was Mine/MARIANNE: Go On	12
64	Vocalion V 9225	You're The Only One/One Good Turn Deserves Another	12

(see also Friday Brown. These records do not feature Mick Jagger or Marianne Faithfull)

MARIAS & MIRANDA

59	Fontana TF 225	I He She/The Queen Bee	6

MARIBELLE

84	Ariola 106 235	In Love With You/Ik Hou Van Jou	5

ANNE MARIE

65	Fontana TF 523	Runaround/There Must Be A Reason	10

MARIE CELESTE

71	private pressing	AND THEN PERHAPS (LP)	300

MARIETTA

82	Polydor POSP 305	You're Only Lonely/Making Up My Mind (p/s, with Rick Parfitt & Andy Bown)	8
82	Polydor POSP 483	Do You Wanna Dance/Only In Your Eyes (p/s, with Rick Parfitt & Andy Bown)	8

(see also Status Quo)

MARILLION

82	EMI EMI 5351	Market Square Heroes/Three Boats Down From The Candy (p/s)	5
82	EMI 12 EMI 5351	Market Square Heroes/Three Boats Down From The Candy/Grendel (12", p/s)	8
82	EMI 12 EMIP 5351	Market Square Heroes/Three Boats Down From The Candy/Grendel (12", picture disc, 3,000 only)	40
83	EMI EMI 5362	He Knows, You Know/Charting The Single (p/s, originally with blue plastic label & paper sleeve)	5
83	EMI 12 EMI 5362	He Knows, You Know/Charting The Single/He Knows, You Know (Full Length Version) (12", p/s)	8
83	EMI 12 EMIP 5362	He Knows, You Know/Charting The Single/He Knows, You Know (Full Length Version) (12", picture disc, unreleased)	
83	EMI EMI 5393	Garden Party/Margaret (live) (p/s)	5
83	EMI EMIP 5393	Garden Party/Margaret (live) ('jester'-shaped picture disc)	18
83	EMI 12 EMIS 5393	Garden Party (Extended Version)/Charting The Single (live)/ Margaret (Extended Live Version) (12", p/s with poster)	15

MINT VALUE £

Year	Label / Cat. No.	Title	Value
83	EMI 12 EMI 5393	Garden Party (Extended Version)/Charting The Single (live)/ Margaret (Extended Live Version) (12", p/s)	8
84	EMI MARIL 1	Punch And Judy/Market Square Heroes (New Version) (p/s)	5
84	EMI 12 MARIL 1	Punch And Judy/Market Square Heroes (New Version)/ Three Boats Down From The Candy (New Version) (12", p/s)	8
84	EMI 12 MARILP 1	Punch And Judy/Market Square Heroes (New Version)/ Three Boats Down From The Candy (New Version) (12", picture disc)	15
84	EMI MARIL 2	Assassing/Cinderella Search (p/s)	5
84	EMI 12 MARIL 2	Assassing (Full Length Version)/Cinderella Search (Full Length Version) (12", p/s)	15
84	EMI 12 MARILP 2	Assassing (Full Length Version)/Cinderella Search (Full Length Version) (12", picture disc)	15
85	EMI MARILP 3	Kayleigh/Lady Nina (picture disc)	10
85	EMI 12 MARILP 3	Kayleigh (Alternative Mix)/Kayleigh (Extended Version)/ Lady Nina (Extended Version) (12", picture disc)	12
85	EMI 12 MARILP 4	Lavender (Remix)/Freaks/Lavender (12", picture disc)	12
85	EMI 12 MARILP 5	Heart Of Lothian (Full Length Version)/Chelsea Monday (live)/ Heart Of Lothian (7" Version) (12", picture disc)	12
87	EMI 12MARILP 6	Incommunicado (LP Version)/(Alternative Mix)/Going Under (12", picture disc)	8
87	EMI CD MARIL 6	Incommunicado (LP Version)/(Alternative Mix)/Going Under (CD, gatefold p/s)	8
87	EMI MARILP 7	Sugar Mice (Radio Edit)/Tux On (picture disc with poster)	8
87	EMI 12MARILP 7	Sugar Mice (Extended Version)/(Album Version)/Tux On (12", picture disc)	12
87	EMI CD MARIL 7	Sugar Mice (Radio Edit)/Tux On/Sugar Mice (Radio Edit)/ (CD, card p/s, 3,000 only, withdrawn)	18
87	EMI 12MARILP 8	Warm Wet Circles (Full Version)/White Russian (live at Loreley)/ Incommunicado (live at Loreley) (12", picture disc)	10
87	EMI CD MARIL 8	Warm Wet Circles (7" Version)/White Russian (live at Loreley)/ Incommunicado (live at Loreley)/Up On Top Of A Rainbow (CD)	8
88	EMI MARIL 9	Freaks (live)/Kayleigh (live) (p/s)	5
88	EMI MARILP 9	Freaks (live)/Kayleigh (live) ('jester'-shaped picture disc)	8
88	EMI CDMARIL 9	Freaks (live)/Kayleigh (live)/Childhoods End? (live)/White Feather (live) (CD)	8
89	EMI 12MARIL 10P	Hooks In You (Meaty Mix)/Hooks In You/After Me (12", p/s with poster)	8
89	EMI CDMARIL 10	Hooks In You (Meaty Mix)/Hooks In You (Seven Mix)/After Me (CD)	8
89	EMI MARIL PD 11	Uninvited Guests/The Bell In The Sea (shaped picture disc)	6
89	EMI CDMARIL 11	Uninvited Guests (7" Version)/Uninvited Guests (12" Version)/ The Bell In The Sea (CD)	8
90	EMI MARILP 12	Easter/The Release (picture disc)	8
91	EMI MARILS 14	No One Can/A Collection (box set with 4 colour pictures & badge)	5
99	Raw Power RAWP 2144	MARILLION.COM (CD, 3–track sampler, card p/s, promo only)	12
84	EMI EMCP 3429	SCRIPT FOR A JESTER'S TEAR (LP, picture disc)	35
84	EMI MRLP 1	FUGAZI (LP, picture disc)	25
85	EMI JESTP 1	REAL TO REEL (LP, picture disc)	15
85	EMI MRLP 2	MISPLACED CHILDHOOD (LP, picture disc)	20
87	EMI EMDP 1002	CLUTCHING AT STRAWS (LP, picture disc, die-cut sleeve)	12
89	EMI EMDPD 1011	SEASON'S END (LP, picture disc, with insert)	12

(see also Fish, Chemical Alice)

MARILYN SISTERS

Year	Label / Cat. No.	Title	Value
55	Decca F 10518	Bubbles/No Chance	10
55	Decca F 10552	Genuine Love/Everything Is Big Way Down In Texas	10
55	Decca F 10604	D-a-r-l-i-n'/The Kinkajou	10

(see also Suzi Miller)

MARINE GIRLS

Year	Label / Cat. No.	Title	Value
82	In Phaze COD 2	On My Mind/The Lure Of The Rockpools (p/s, with insert)	25
82	Cherry Red CHERRY 40	On My Mind/The Lure Of The Rockpools (reissue, different p/s)	10
83	Cherry Red CHERRY 54	Don't Come Back/You Must Be Mad (p/s)	8
80	private release	A DAY BY THE SEA (cassette, 50 copies only)	20
81	In Phaze Tapes 002	BEACH PARTY (cassette, with photocopied drawings, game & handmade sl.)	20
81	Whaam!/In Phaze COD 1	BEACH PARTY (LP, black & white sleeve & labels, with 2 inserts)	20
83	Cherry Red BRED 44	LAZY WAYS (LP, textured sleeve)	15

(see also Tracey Thorn, Everything But The Girl, Jane, Grab Grab The Haddock)

MARINERS

Year	Label / Cat. No.	Title	Value
55	London HLA 8201	I Love You Fair Dinkum/(At The) Steamboat River Ball	30
55	London HLA 8201	I Love You Fair Dinkum/(At The) Steamboat River Ball (78)	7
55	Philips PB 467	Chee-Chee-Oo-Chee/I Didn't Come To Say Hello (78)	8
58	Fontana H 127	I Heard Ya The First Time/I Live For You	6
56	London HA-A 2007	SPIRITUALS (LP)	18

MARINO MARINI & HIS QUARTET

Year	Label / Cat. No.	Title	Value
57	Durium DC 16629	With All My Heart/The Pansy	6
58	Durium DC 16631	Guitar Boogie/Armen's Theme	7
58	Durium DC 16632	Volare (Nel Blu Dipinto Di Blu)/Come Prima	6
58	Durium DC 16634	Saunabad/I Could Have Danced All Night	6
58	Durium DC 16635	Stella Stella (Star Of Love)/Lazzarella	6
59	Durium DC 16636	Ciao Ciao Bambina/Avevamo La Stessa Eta'	6
59	Durium DC 16636	Ciao Ciao Bambina/Avevamo La Stessa Eta' (78)	8
59	Durium DC 16637	Li Per Li/Io Sono Il Vento	6
59	Durium DC 16642	Guarda Che Luna/Sapra' Chi Sa'	6
59	Durium DC 16642	Guarda Che Luna/Sapra' Chi Sa' (78)	8
58	Durium U 20007	MARINO MARINI AND HIS HAPPY MUSIC (EP)	8
58	Durium U 20020	MARINO MARINI AND HIS HAPPY MUSIC VOLUME 2 (EP)	8
58	Durium U 20027	THE MARINO MARINI QUARTET (EP)	8
58	Durium U 20028	HAPPY MUSIC VOLUME 3 (EP)	8
58	Durium U 20030	THAT CRAZY QUARTET (EP)	8
58	Durium U 20031	THE MARINO MARINI QUARTET VOLUME 2 (EP)	8
58	Durium U 20036	MARINO MARINI VOLUME 3 (EP)	8

MINT VALUE £

58	Durium U 20047	MARINO AT SAN REMO (EP)	8
55	Durium DLU 96012	HAPPY MUSIC FROM ITALY (10" LP)	12
59	Durium DLU 96034	COME PRIMA (10" LP)	12
59	Durium DLU 96039	IN SOHO (10" LP)	15
50s	Durium DLU 96028	HAPPY MUSIC FROM ITALY VOLUME 2 (10" LP)	12
60	Durium TLU 97028	MARINO MARINI QUARTET (LP)	12

MARION (U.K.)

67	Page One POF 042	I Go To Sleep/Abyssinian Secret	8

MARION (Finland)

73	Columbia DB 8987	Tom Tom Tom/My Son John	15

MARION (U.K.)

94	Rough Trade RT 3197	Violent Men/Toys For Boys (p/s)	12
94	Rough Trade RT 3193	Violent Men/Toys For Boys/Today And Tonight (CD)	7
95	London LON 360	Sleep/Father's Day (numbered p/s)	7
95	London LONCD 360	Sleep/Father's Day/Moving Fast (CD, digipak)	8
95	London LON10 366	Toys For Boys/Down The Middle With You (10", p/s, export only)	40
96	London 828 695-1	THIS WORLD AND BODY (LP, sealed, with 1-sided single "Violent Men")	12

MARIONETTES

65	Decca F 12056	Whirlpool Of Love/Nobody But You	7
65	Parlophone R 5300	Was It Me?/Under The Boardwalk	7
65	Parlophone R 5356	Raining It's Pouring/Pick Up Your Feet (withdrawn)	12
65	Parlophone R 5374	At The End Of The Day/Pick Up Your Feet	7
66	Parlophone R 5416	Like A Man/Tonight It's Going To Storm	8

(see also Rag Dolls [U.K.], Katie Kissoon, Mac Kissoon)

JON MARK

69	Philips BF 1772	All Neat In Black Stockings/Run To Me	7

(see also Johnny Almond Music Machine, John Mayall, Mark-Almond)

MARK-ALMOND

71	Harvest SHSP 4011	MARK-ALMOND (LP)	30
73	Harvest SHVL 809	RISING (LP)	30

(see also Johnny Almond Music Machine, Jon Mark)

MARK & JOHN

64	Decca F 12044	Walk Right Back/Karen	6

MARKETTS

62	Liberty LIB 55401	Surfer's Stomp/Start (as Mar-kets)	15
62	Liberty LIB 55443	Balboa Blue/Stompede	15
64	Warner Bros WB 120	Out Of Limits/Bella Delana	25
64	Warner Bros WB 130	Vanishing Point/Borealis	10
66	Warner Bros WB 5696	The Batman Theme/Richie's Theme (some with p/s)	35/15
67	Warner Bros WB 5847	Tarzan's March/Stirrin' Up Some Soul	40
63	Warner Bros WM 8140	THE MARKETTS TAKE TO WHEELS (LP)	40
64	Warner Bros WM 8147	OUT OF LIMITS (LP)	35
66	Warner Bros W 1642	BATMAN (LP)	55

MAR-KEYS

61	London HLK 9399	Last Night/Night Before	15
61	London HLK 9449	Morning After/Diana	12
62	London HLK 9510	Foxy/One Degree North	12
66	Atlantic AT 4079	Philly Dog/Honey Pot	15
67	Atlantic 584 074	Last Night/Night Before	7
69	Stax STAX 132	Black/Jive Man	6
62	London HA-K 8011	DO THE POP-EYE (LP)	65
66	Atlantic 587/588 024	THE GREAT MEMPHIS SOUND (LP)	25
68	Atlantic 587/588 135	MELLOW JELLY (LP)	25
69	Stax SXATS 1021	DAMNIFIKNOW! (LP)	20
69	Stax 2363 008	DAMNIFIKNOW! (LP, reissue)	12

(see also Booker T. & M.G.'s)

MARK FIVE

64	Fontana TF 513	Baby What's Wrong/Tango	50

(see also Nazareth)

MARK FOUR

64	Mercury MF 815	Rock Around The Clock/Slow Down	40
64	Mercury MF 825	Try It Baby/Crazy Country Hop	40
65	Decca F 12204	Hurt Me If You Will/I'm Leaving	70
66	Fontana TF 664	Work All Day (Sleep All Night)/Going Down Fast	90
85	Bam-Caruso OPRA 037	LIVE AT THE BEAT SCENE CLUB (EP, promo, 500 only)	12

(see also Creation)

MARK IV

59	Mercury AMT 1025	Aah-Oo-Gah/I Got A Wife	15
59	Mercury AMT 1025	Aah-Oo-Gah/I Got A Wife (78)	20
59	Mercury AMT 1045	Move Over Rover/Dante's Inferno	12
59	Mercury AMT 1060	Ring, Ring, Ring Those Bells/Mairzy Doats	8

MARK II

60	Columbia DB 4549	Night Theme/Confusion	10

PIGMEAT MARKHAM

68	Chess CRS 8077	Here Comes The Judge/The Trial	12
68	Chess CRS 8085	Sock It To 'Em Judge/The Hip Judge	12

ALFRED MARKS

68	RCA RCA 1777	My Young Visitors And Me/When I Wed Miss Ethel Montiche	6

MINT VALUE £

GUY MARKS

68 Stateside SS 2107 — Loving You Has Made Me Bananas/Forgive Me My Love 7

MARKSMEN

63 Parlophone R 5075 — Smersh/Orbit Three 18

(see also Mark Rogers & Marksmen, Houston Wells & Marksmen)

BOB MARLEY/WAILERS

SINGLES

63 Island WI 088 — Judge Not/Do You Still Love Me (as Robert Marley) 270
63 Island WI 128 — ERNEST RANGLIN: Exodus/R. MARLEY (as Bobby Martell): One Cup Of Coffee 200
65 Island WI 188 — It Hurts To Be Alone/Mr. Talkative 90
65 Island WI 206 — Play Boy/Your Love 90
65 Island WI 211 — Hoot Nanny Hoot (actually by Peter Tosh & Wailers)/ BOB MARLEY: Do You Remember (actually with Wailers) 100
65 Island WI 212 — Hooligan/Maga Dog (B-side actually by Peter Tosh & Wailers) 90
65 Island WI 215 — Shame And Scandal (as Peter Touch [Tosh] & Wailers)/The Jerk 80
65 Island WI 216 — Donna/Don't Ever Leave Me 75
65 Island WI 254 — What's New Pussycat/Where Will I Find 60
65 Ska Beat JB 186 — Simmer Down/I Don't Need Your Love 75
65 Ska Beat JB 211 — Lonesome Feelings/There She Goes 50
65 Ska Beat JB 226 — I Made A Mistake/SOUL BROTHERS: Train To Skaville 50
66 Ska Beat JB 228 — Love And Affection/Teenager In Love 70
66 Ska Beat JB 230 — And I Love Her/Do It Right 70
66 Ska Beat JB 249 — Lonesome Tracks/Zimmerman 75
66 Island WI 260 — Jumbie Jamboree/SKATALITES: Independent Anniversary Ska (I Should Have Known Better) 75
66 Island WI 268 — Put It On/Love Won't Be Mine 40
66 Island WI 3001 — He Who Feels It Knows It/Sunday Morning 70
66 Island WI 3009 — Let Him Go (Rude Boy Get Bail)/Sinner Man (B-side matrix: WI-3009B+) 70
66 Island WI 3009 — Let Him Go (Rude Boy Get Bail)/The Masher (actually by Beverley's All Stars, or Soul Brothers) (B-side matrix: WI-3009 B+2) 70
66 Rio R 116 — Dancing Shoes/Don't Look Back 50
66 Doctor Bird DB 1013 — Rude Boy/ROLANDO AL & SOUL BROTHERS: Ringo's Theme (This Boy) 60
66 Doctor Bird DB 1021 — Good Good Rudie (Jailhouse)/CITY SLICKERS: Oceans II 60
66 Doctor Bird DB 1039 — Rasta Put It On/ROLAND AL & SOUL BROTHERS: Ska With Ringo 60
67 Island WI 3035 — Baby I Need You (credited to Ken Boothe)/KEN BOOTHE: I Don't Want To See You Cry 60
67 Island WI 3042 — I Am The Toughest (by Peter Touch [Tosh] & Wailers)/ MARCIA GRIFFITHS: No Faith 60
67 Island WI 3043 — Bend Down Low/Freedom Time 70
67 Coxsone CS 7021 — Oh My Darling/HAMLINS: Trying To Keep A Good Man Down 60
67 Doctor Bird DB 1091 — Nice Time/Hypocrite 65
67 Studio One SO 2010 — Have Faith In The Lord (with Heavenly Sisters; actually by Peter Austin)/ JOE HIGGS: Dinah 35
67 Studio One SO 2024 — I Stand Predominate/NORMA FRAZER: Come By Here 70
68 Fab FAB 34 — Pound Get A Blow/Funeral (white label only) 100
68 Fab FAB 36 — Thank You Lord/Mellow Mood (white label only) 100
68 Fab FAB 37 — Nice Time/Hypocrites (white label only) 100
68 Fab FAB 41 — Burial/Bus Them Shut (existence unconfirmed)
68 Trojan TR 617 — Stir It Up/This Train 55
70 Bamboo BAM 55 — Jailhouse (Good Rudy)/JOHN HOLT: A Stranger In Love 50

(All the above singles are credited to Wailers unless stated.)

70 Trojan TR 7759 — Soul Shake Down Party/BEVERLY'S ALLSTARS: Version 20
70 Escort ERT 842 — Run For Cover/To The Rescue 70
70 Unity UN 562 — Duppy Conqueror/UPSETTERS: Duppy Conqueror (Version) 40
70 Jackpot JP 730 — Mr Chatterbox (as Wailing Wailers)/DOREEN SHAEFFER: Walk Thru' This World 35
70 Upsetter US 340 — My Cup (solo)/LEE PERRY & WAILERS: Son Of Thunder 35
70 Upsetter US 342 — Version Of Cup (solo)/UPSETTERS: Dreamland 40
70 Upsetter US 348 — Doppy Conqueror (song actually titled "Duppy Conqueror" but plays "Runaway Child" by Dave Barker)/UPSETTERS: Justice 20
70 Upsetter US 349 — UPSETTERS: Upsetting Station (actually plays "Dig Your Grave" by Bob Marley & Wailers/UPSETTERS: Justice (Instrumental) 35
71 Upsetter US 354 — Mr. Brown/UPSETTERS: Dracula 35
71 Upsetter US 356 — Kaya/UPSETTERS: Version 35
71 Upsetter US 357 — Small Axe/All In One 35
71 Upsetter US 368 — Picture On The Wall (as Rass Dawkins & Wailers)/UPSETTERS: Version 22
71 Upsetter US 369 — More Axe (as Bob Marley)/UPSETTERS: Axe Man 22
71 Upsetter US 371 — Dreamland (as Wailers)/UPSETTERS: Version 22
71 Upsetter US 372 — More Axe (as Bob Marley, different version)/UPSETTERS: Axe Man 22
71 Bullet BU 464 — Soultown/Let The Sun Shine On Me 50
71 Bullet BU 493 — Lick Samba/Samba 25
71 Punch PH 69 — Small Axe/DAVE BARKER: What A Confusion 30
71 Punch PH 77 — Down Presser (as Wailers)/JUNIOR BYLES: Got The Tip 40
71 Summit SUM 8526 — Stop The Train/Caution (as Wailers) 35
71 Green Door GD 4005 — Trench Town Rock/Grooving Kingston 12 25
71 Green Door GD 4022 — Lively Yourself Up/TOMMY McCOOK: Lively 22
72 Green Door GD 4025 — Guava Jelly/Redder Than Red 35
72 Upsetter US 392 — Keep On Moving/African Herbsman 22
72 CBS 8114 — Reggae On Broadway/Oh Lord, I Got To Get There (as Wailers) 18
73 Blue Mountain BM 1021 — Baby Baby We've Got A Date/Stop That Train 18
73 Punch PH 101 — Screw Face/Face Man 22
73 Punch PH 102 — Lively Up Yourself/TOMMY McCOOK: Version 22
73 Supreme SUP 216 — I Like It Like This (as Bob Marley)/(other artist) 45
73 Island WIP 6164 — Concrete Jungle/Reincarnated Soul 5

MINT VALUE £

73	Island WIP 6167	Get Up, Stand Up/Slave Driver (as Wailers)	5
73	Island IDJ 2	I Shot The Sheriff/Pass It On/Duppy Conqueror (promo only)	10
74	Island 12WIP 6244	No Woman No Cry/Jamming (12", p/s)	8
74	Trojan TR 7911	Soul Shake Down Party/Caution	5
74	Trojan TR 7926	Mr Brown/Version	5
75	Island WIP 6212	Natty Dread/So Jah Seh	5
76	Island WIP 6478	Stir It Up/Rat Race (withdrawn, demos only)	15
77	Island WIP 6390	Exodus/Exodus (dub)	5
77	Island WIP 6402	Waiting In Vain/Roots	5
77	Island WIP 6402 1DJ	Promotional Advert For "Exodus" (handwritten label, same track both sides, with Marley commentary)	30
77	Island WIP 6410	Jamming/Punky Reggae Party (p/s)	5
77	Island IPR 2000	Exodus (7:38) / Exodus (3:08, inst. version)(12", pre-release Island sleeve)	12
78	Island WIP 6420	Is This Love?/Crisis (Version) (p/s)	5
78	Island WIP 6440	Satisfy My Soul/Smile Jamaica (p/s)	5
78	Island IPR 2026	War/No More Trouble/Jamming (12", p/s)	10
83	Island ISP 180	Waiting In Vain/Blackman Redemption (picture disc)	8
84	Daddy Kool DK 12101	Rainbow Country (Vocal)/Rainbow Country (Dub)/ PABLO & UPSETTERS: Lama Lava (12", p/s)	10
84	Daddy Kool DK 12102	Natural Mystic/Natural Mystic Rhythm (12", p/s)	10
84	Island 12ISPX 169	One Love/One Love (Dub Version) (p/s)	7
84	Island 12ISP 169	One Love/One Love (Dub Version) (12", white label, p/s)	10
84	Island 12ISPP 169	One Love/One Love (Dub Version) (12", picture disc)	15
80s	Island 12 BMRM 1	Get Up Stand Up/Get Up Stand Up (live) ('Rasta' p/s, promo only)	10
99	Columbia XPR 2533	Turn Your Lights Down Low (with Lauryn Hill)/(original version) (die-cut p/s, promo only)	8

(Island singles with the words "DJ Copy" stamped in the middle are worth the same as regular issues. All the above singles are credited to Bob Marley & Wailers unless stated.)

LPs

71	Upsetter TBL 126	SOUL REBEL	70
71	Trojan TBL 126	SOUL REBEL (reissue)	30
72	Island ILPS 9241	CATCH A FIRE (original 'pink rim' label, 'zippo lighter' sleeve)	40
73	Island ILPS 9256	BURNIN' (original label, gatefold sleeve with photos on innner)	15
73	Trojan TRLS 62	AFRICAN HERBSMAN (original issue with "12 Neasden Lane" address and rough orange/white paper labels)	35
74	Trojan TRLS 89	RASTA REVOLUTION (reissue of TBL 126 with 2 extra tracks)	12
75	Island ISS 3	BOB MARLEY & THE WAILERS RADIO SAMPLER (some with photos & press release, promo only)	30/12
83	Island PILPS 97690	CONFRONTATION (picture disc)	15
84	Island PBMW 1	LEGEND — THE BEST OF BOB MARLEY (picture disc)	12

(see also Peter Tosh, Rita Marley, Ernest Ranglin, Interns, Skatalites, Rass Dawkins & Wailers, Family Man, Norma Frazer)

RITA MARLEY

67	Rio R 108	Pied Piper/It's Alright	30
67	Island WI 3052	Come To Me/SOUL BOYS: Blood Pressure	22

(see also Soulettes, Soul Brothers)

MICKI MARLO

54	Capitol CL 14086	I'm Gonna Rock-Rock-Rock/Loves Like That (78)	8
55	Capitol CL 14271	Prize Of Gold/Foolish Notion	15
57	London HL 8481	That's Right/What You've Done To Me (B-side with Paul Anka)	25

(see also Paul Anka)

MARLON

74	Purple PUR 120	Let's Go To The Disco/Broken Man	7

(see also Roger Glover, Ray Fenwick)

ROBERT MARLOW

83	Reset 7REST 1	Pictures Of Dorian Grey/The Tale Of Dorian Grey (p/s)	5
83	Reset 12REST 1	Pictures Of Dorian Grey/The Tale Of Dorian Grey (12", p/s)	10
83	Reset 7REST 3	I Just Want To Dance/No Heart (p/s)	5
83	Reset 7RESTP 3	I Just Want To Dance/No Heart (picture disc)	6
83	Reset 12REST 3	I Just Want To Dance/No Heart (12", p/s)	10
84	Reset 12REST 4	Claudette/This Happy World (12", p/s)	10
85	Reset 7REST 6	Calling All Destroyers/In Retrospect (p/s)	10
85	Reset 12REST 6	Calling All Destroyers/In Retrosepct (12", p/s, existence unconfirmed)	

(see also Vince Clarke, Erasure)

MARION MARLOWE

56	London HLA 8306	The Hands Of Time/Ring, Phone, Ring (withdrawn)	100
56	London HLA 8306	The Hands Of Time/Ring, Phone, Ring (78, withdrawn)	75

MARMALADE

66	CBS 202340	It's All Leading Up To Saturday Night/Wait A Minute Baby	10
67	CBS 202643	Can't Stop Now/There Ain't No Use In Hangin' On	10
67	CBS 2948	I See The Rain/Laughing Man	15
67	CBS 3088	Man In A Shop/Cry	8
68	CBS 3412	Lovin' Things/Hey Joe	7
68	CBS 3708	Wait For Me Marianne/Mess Around	7
68	CBS 3892	Ob-La-Di, Ob-La-Da/Chains	6
69	CBS 4287	Baby Make It Soon/Time Is On My Side	7
69	CBS 4615	Butterfly/I Shall Be Released	7
69	Decca F 12982	Reflections Of My Life/Rollin' My Thing	6
70	Decca F 13035	Rainbow/The Ballad Of Cherry Flavar	6
72	CBS 7200	Man In A Shop/Cry (reissue)	5
73	CBS 8205	Ob-La-Di, Ob-La-Da/Lovin' Things (p/s, 'Hall Of Fame Hits' series)	5
84	Just Songs JST 1	Heartbreaker/I Listen To My Heart (p/s)	5
68	CBS 63414	THERE'S A LOT OF IT ABOUT (LP)	25
70	CBS SPR 36	THE BEST OF THE MARMALADE (LP)	20

70 Decca SKL 5047 REFLECTIONS OF THE MARMALADE (LP) 20
71 Decca SKL 5111 SONGS (LP) 20
(see also Dean Ford [& Gaylords], Gaylords, Junior Campbell, Chris McClure Section)

MARQUIS DE SADE
82 Out Of Town HOOT 8 Crystal Grieff/Vampire Affair (p/s) 5

MARQUIS OF KENSINGTON
67 Immediate IM 052 Changing Of The Guard/Reverse Thrust 30

HANK MARR
60 Blue Beat BB 26 Tonk Game/Hob-Nobbin 22

A MARRIAGE OF CONVENIENCE
85 Stranglers Info Service SIS2 My Young Dreams/Two Sides To Every Story (no p/s, fan club issue) 5
(see also Stranglers)

STEVE MARRIOTT
63 Decca F 11619 Give Her My Regards/Imaginary Love 100
65 Decca Tell Me/Maybe (unissued)
76 A&M AMS 7230 Star In My Life/Midnight Rollin' 5
85 Aura AUS 145 Wha'cha Gonna Do About It/All Shook Up 5
76 A&M AMLH 64572 MARRIOTT (LP) 20
85 Aura AUL 792 PACKET OF THREE (LP) 12
(see also Small Faces, Humble Pie, Spectrum, Pollcats)

M/A/R/R/S
87 4AD BAD 707R Pump Up The Volume (Remix)/Anitina (The First Time I See She Dance) (Remix) (12", p/s) 8
87 4AD CAD 707R Pump Up The Volume (Remix)/Anitina/Pump Up The Volume (12" Version)/ Anitina (The First Time I See She Dance) (Remix) (CD, gatefold p/s) 15
(see also A.R. Kane, Colourbox)

BETTY MARS
72 Columbia DB 8879 Come-Comedie/Mon Café Russe 7

JOHNNY MARS
81 Ace NS 73 Born Under A Bad Sign/Horses And Places/Mighty Mars (p/s, withdrawn) 5
72 Polydor 2460 168 BLUES FROM MARS (LP) 15

BERNIE MARSDEN
81 Parlophone R 6047 Sad Clown/You And Me (p/s) 6
81 Parlophone R 6050 Look At Me Now/Always Love You So (p/s) 6
81 Parlophone R 6052 Shakey Ground/After All This Madness (p/s) 6
82 Parlophone R 6053 Thunder And Lightning/Bylbo's Shack (p/s) 6
79 Parlophone PCS 7215 AND ABOUT TIME TOO (LP, with inner sleeve) 12
81 Parlophone PCS 7217 LOOK AT ME NOW (LP, with inner sleeve) 12
(see also Jon Lord, Whitesnake, Cozy Powell, Jack Bruce, Babe Ruth, Bogdon)

BERYL MARSDEN
63 Decca F 11707 I Know/I Only Care About You 20
64 Decca F 11819 When The Lovelight Starts Shining Through His Eyes/ Love Is Going To Happen To Me 20
65 Columbia DB 7718 Who You Gonna Hurt?/Gonna Make Him My Baby 20
65 Columbia DB 7797 Music Talk/Break-A-Way 20
66 Columbia DB 7888 What's She Got/Let's Go Somewhere 20
(see also Shotgun Express, She Trinity)

GERRY MARSDEN
67 CBS 2784 Please Let Them Be/I'm Not Blue 10
67 CBS 2946 Gilbert Green/What Makes Me Love You 10
68 CBS 3575 Liverpool/Charlie Girl (as Gerry Marsden & Derek Nimmo) 10
68 NEMS 56-3831 In The Year Of April/Every Day 6
69 NEMS 56-4229 Every Little Minute/In Days Of Old 6
71 Decca F 13172 I've Got My Ukelele/What A Day 5
72 Phoenix NIX 129 Amo Credo/Come Break Bread 5
(see also Gerry & Pacemakers)

MARSEILLE
77 Varèse International VI 1001 Do It The French Way/Not Tonight Josephine/She Gives Me Hell (12", stickered plain sleeve, 1,000 only) 8
78 Mountain BON 1 The French Way/Cold Steel (p/s) 10
79 Mountain BON 2 Over And Over/You're A Woman/Can Can (p/s) 6
79 Mountain TOP 39 Kiss Like Rock'n'Roll/Can Can 15
79 Mountain TOP 49 Bring On The Dancing Girls/Rock Me Tonight 15
80 Mountain TOP 51 Kites/Some Like It Hot 15
84 Ultra Noise WALK 1 Walking On A Highwire/Too Late (p/s) 5
84 Ultra Noise WALK 1 Walking On A Highwire/Too Late (silver vinyl, no p/s) 6
78 Mountain TOPC 5012 RED WHITE AND SLIGHTLY BLUE (LP) 12
79 Mountain TOPS 125 MARSEILLE (LP) 12
84 Ultra Noise ULTRA 3 TOUCH THE NIGHT (LP, with inner sleeve) 20
(see also Paul Dale)

STEVIE MARSH
59 Decca F 11181 If You Were The Only Boy In The World/Leave Me Alone 8
59 Decca F 11181 If You Were The Only Boy In The World/Leave Me Alone (78) 20
60 Decca F 11209 You Don't Have To Tell Me (I Know)/Wish 10
60 Decca F 11244 A Girl In Love/Over And Done With 10
62 Ember EMB S 139 I Shouldn't Be Kissing You/Time And Time Again 7

GARY MARSHALL
61 Parlophone R 4758 One Twitchy Baby/Ev'ry Chance I Get 15

MINT VALUE £

JACK MARSHALL ORCHESTRA & CHORUS

58 Capitol CL 14888 Thunder Road Chase/Finger Poppin' . . . 15

JOY MARSHALL

64 Decca F 11863 Rain On Snow/When You Hold Me Tight . . . 6
65 Decca F 12222 My Love Come Home/When A Girl Really Loves You . . . 7
66 Decca F 12422 The More I See You/Taste Of Honey. . . . 10

LARRY MARSHALL

67 Blue Beat BB 374 Move Your Feet/Find A New Baby . . . 20
67 Blue Beat BB 380 Suspicion/Broken Heart. . . . 20
67 Doctor Bird DB 1008 Snake In The Grass/ROLAND ALPHONSO: V.C. 10 . . . 35
68 Caltone TONE 126 No One To Give Me Love/PHIL PRATT: Safe Travel. . . . 30
70 Bamboo BAM 22 Girl Of My Dreams/SOUND DIMENSON: Give It Away . . . 12
70 Bamboo BAM 52 Man From Galilee/Give It Away (as Larry Marshall & Enid Cumberland). . . . 8
70 Banana BA 300 Stay A Little Longer/MAYTALS: He'll Provide . . . 10
71 Banana BA 364 Maga Dog/OSSIE ROBINSON: Economical Heatwave . . . 8
73 Pama PM 873 True Believer/FLAMES: Water Your Garden. . . . 6

(see also Larry & Alvin, Irving Brown, Fitzroy D. Long, Kingston Pete & Buster's Allstars, Max Romeo, Jackie Mittoo)

LOIS MARSHALL

59 HMV ALP 1671 BRITISH FOLK SONGS (LP). . . . 12

WILLIE MARSHALL

70 Torpedo TOR 20 Loosen Up Strong Man/Strong Man . . . 10

MARSHMALLOW WAY

69 United Artists UP 35031 C'mon Kitty Kitty/Michigan Mints . . . 7

MARSHMELLOW HIGHWAY

68 London HLR 10204 I Don't Wanna Live This Way/Loving You Makes Everything Alright . . . 8

MARSUPILAMI

70 Transatlantic TRA 213 MARSUPILAMI (LP) . . . 55
71 Transatlantic TRA 230 ARENA (LP) . . . 55

PIERA MARTELL

74 CBS S CBS 2293 My Ship Of Love/Mein Ruf Nach Dir . . . 12

RAY MARTELL

70 Joe JRS 3 She Caught The Train/PAMA DICE: Tea House From Emperor Rosko . . . 10
70 Attack ATT 8015 Loving Lover/Cora . . . 6
70 Doctor Bird DB 1503 This Little Light/Lover . . . 6
70 Trojan TR 7787 This Little Light/Lover . . . 6
72 Sioux SI 012 She Caught The Train/JOE'S ALLSTARS: Tony B.'s Theme. . . . 6

MARTELLS

66 Decca F 12463 Time To Say Goodnight/The Cherry Song. . . . 7

RALPH MARTERIE & HIS ORCHESTRA

57 Mercury 7MT 138 Guaglione/Carla . . . 6
57 Mercury 7MT 158 Tricky/Shish-Kebab . . . 6
58 Mercury MT 204 Tequila/Pop Corn . . . 6
58 Mercury 7MT 213 Night Stroll/Trombone Blues . . . 6
58 Mercury 7MT 232 Cha-Hua-Hua/Torero. . . . 6
58 Mercury AMT 1009 Pretend Cha Cha/Flighty . . . 5
58 Mercury AMT 1009 Pretend Cha Cha/Flighty (78). . . . 10
59 Mercury AMT 1042 Compulsion/Words Of Love. . . . 5
59 Mercury AMT 1056 Wampum/Cleopatra's Dream . . . 5
59 Mercury AMT 1074 In The Mood/Bwana . . . 5
57 Mercury MEP 9517 PRESENTING RALPH MARTERIE (EP) . . . 18
60 Mercury ZEP 10040 SWINGING SOUND OF MARTERIE (EP) . . . 10
60 Mercury ZEP 10068 MUSIC FOR A PRIVATE EYE (EP) . . . 10

MARTHA & THE MUFFINS

80 DinDisc DID 5 TRANCE & DANCE (LP, with bonus 7" [WAS E 20]) . . . 12

MARTHA (REEVES) & VANDELLAS

63 Oriole CBA 1814 I'll Have To Let Him Go/My Baby Won't Come Back . . . 350
63 Oriole CBA 1819 Come And Get These Memories/Jealous Lover . . . 150
63 Stateside SS 228 Heatwave/A Love Like Yours (Don't Come Knockin' Every Day) . . . 85
64 Stateside SS 250 Quicksand/Darling, I Hum Our Song . . . 45
64 Stateside SS 272 Live Wire/Old Love (Let's Try It Again) . . . 40
64 Stateside SS 305 In My Lonely Room/A Tear For The Girl. . . . 45
64 Stateside SS 345 Dancing In The Street/There He Is (At My Door) . . . 22
65 Stateside SS 383 Wild One/Dancing Slow . . . 35
65 Tamla Motown TMG 502 Nowhere To Run/Motoring . . . 18
65 Tamla Motown TMG 530 You've Been In Love Too Long/Love (Makes Me Do Foolish Things). . . . 22
66 Tamla Motown TMG 549 My Baby Loves Me/Never Leave Your Baby's Side . . . 30
66 Tamla Motown TMG 567 What Am I Going To Do Without Your Love/Go Ahead And Laugh. . . . 20
66 Tamla Motown TMG 582 I'm Ready For Love/He Doesn't Love Her Anymore . . . 12
67 Tamla Motown TMG 599 Jimmy Mack/Third Finger, Left Hand (original pressing, narrow print) . . . 8
72 Tamla Motown TMG 599 Jimmy Mack/Third Finger, Left Hand (reissue, fat print). . . . 6
67 Tamla Motown TMG 621 Love Bug Leave My Heart Alone/One Way Out. . . . 12
68 Tamla Motown TMG 636 Honey Chile/Show Me The Way . . . 12
68 Tamla Motown TMG 657 I Promise To Wait, My Love/Forget Me Not . . . 12
68 Tamla Motown TMG 669 I Can't Dance To That Music You're Playing/I Tried . . . 10
69 Tamla Motown TMG 684 Dancing In The Street/Quicksand . . . 5
69 Tamla Motown TMG 694 Nowhere To Run/Live Wire. . . . 6
71 Tamla Motown TMG 762 Forget Me Not/I Gotta Let You Go . . . 5
71 Tamla Motown TMG 794 Bless You/Hope I Don't Get My Heart Broke . . . 5
65 Tamla Motown TME 2009 MARTHA AND THE VANDELLAS (EP) . . . 125
66 Tamla Motown TME 2017 HITTIN' (EP) . . . 125

63	Oriole PS 40052	COME AND GET THESE MEMORIES (LP)	400
65	Tamla Motown TML 11005	HEATWAVE (LP)	80
65	Tamla Motown TML 11013	DANCE PARTY (LP)	90
67	T. Motown (S)TML 11040	GREATEST HITS (LP, original with flipback sleeve, mono/stereo)	25/30
67	T. Motown (S)TML 11040	GREATEST HITS (LP, re-pressing non-flipback sleeve)	12
67	T. Motown (S)TML 11051	WATCH OUT! (LP, mono/stereo)	40/50
68	T. Motown (S)TML 11078	RIDIN' HIGH (LP)	30
69	T. Motown (S)TML 11099	DANCING IN THE STREET (LP)	30
70	T. Motown (S)TML 11134	SUGAR N' SPICE (LP)	25
70	Tamla Motown STML 11166	NATURAL RESOURCES (LP)	25
72	Tamla Motown STML 11204	BLACK MAGIC (LP)	18

MARTIAN SCHOOLGIRLS

79	Red Planet RPR 1	Life In The 1980's/Lonely Nights (p/s)	10

PATRICK D. MARTIN

79	Deram DMR 432	I Like Electric Motors/Time (p/s)	5
80	Deram DM 433	Lucy 'Lectric/I Like Electric Motors/Mutant (p/s)	10
80	IRS/MCA ILS 0023	COMPUTER DATIN' EP	8

MARTIN

68	Coxsone CS 7056	I Second That Emotion (actually by Martin Riley)/ ROY TOMLINSON: I Stand For I	35

ALAN MARTIN

63	Rio R 3	The Party/Indeed	15
63	Rio R 6	You Came Late/Dreaming	15
63	Rio R 9	Secretly/Fame And Fortune	15
63	Rio R 10	Mother Brother/Tell Me	15
65	Rio R 66	Must Know I Love You/VIC BROWN'S COMBO: Rio Special	15
65	Rio R 67	Sweet Rosemarie/HONEY DUCKERS: Banjo Man	15
65	Rio R 68	Why Must I Cry/Shirley I Love You	15
65	Rio R 74	Since I Married Dorothy/You Promised Me	15
66	Rio R 94	Days Are Lonely/My Baby	15
66	Rio R 96	Rome Wasn't Built In A Day/I'm Hurt	15

BARRY MARTIN

61	RCA RCA 1234	Little Lonely One/Are You Sure	8

BENNY MARTIN

63	CBS Realm RM 174	COUNTRY MUSIC'S SENSATIONAL ENTERTAINER (LP)	12

BILL MARTIN

68	Page One POF 067	Private Scotty Grant/Singing Vietnam Blues	5

BOBBI MARTIN

64	Coral Q 72477	Don't Forget I Still Love You/On The Outside (Lookin' In)	10
65	Coral Q 72478	I Can't Stop Thinking About You/Million Thanks To You	8

CHRIS MARTIN

59	HMV POP 664	Lonely Street/Swing A Little Lover	10
60	HMV POP 692	Point Of No Return/I Don't Regret A Thing	6

DAVE MARTIN

64	Port-O-Jam PJ 4112	Let Them Fight/OSSIE IRVING SIX: Why I Love You	15
64	Port-O-Jam PJ 4115	All My Dreams/Take Your Belongings	15

DEAN MARTIN

78s

59	Capitol CL 14990	It Takes So Long (To Say Goodbye)/You Were Made For Love	10
59	Capitol CL 15039	On An Evening In Roma/You Can't Love 'Em All	15
59	Capitol CL 15064	Ain't Gonna Lead This Life/Maybe	20

SINGLES

54	Capitol CL 14123	Hey Brother, Pour The Wine/I'd Cry Like A Baby (green or purple labels)	40/25
54	Capitol CL 14138	Sway/Pretty As A Picture	35
54	Capitol CL 14150	How Do You Speak To An Angel?/Ev'ry Street's A Boulevard In Old New York (with Jerry Lewis)	22
54	Capitol CL 14170	The Peddlar Man (Ten I Loved)/Try Again	22
54	Capitol CL 14180	One More Time/If I Could Sing Like Bing	20
55	Capitol CL 14215	Open Up The Doghouse (Two Cats Are Trying To Get In) (with Nat 'King' Cole)/Long, Long Ago	22
55	Capitol CL 14226	Let Me Go, Lover/The Naughty Lady Of Shady Lane	35
55	Capitol CL 14227	Mambo Italiano/That's All I Want From You	35
55	Capitol CL 14253	Belle From Barcelona/Confused	22
55	Capitol CL 14255	What Could Be More Beautiful/Under The Bridges Of Paris	25
55	Capitol CL 14311	Chee Chee-Oo Chee (Sang The Little Bird)/Ridin' Into Love	22
55	Capitol CL 14356	Relax-Ay-Voo/Two Sleepy People (with Line Renaud)	22
55	Capitol CL 14367	Simpatico/Love Is All That Matters	22
55	Capitol CL 14370	In Napoli/I Like Them All	22

(The above 45s were originally issued with triangular centres; round-centre reissues are worth around half these values.)

56	Capitol CL 14505	When You Pretend/The Lucky Song	15
56	Capitol CL 14507	Inamorata/You Look So Familiar	18
56	Capitol CL 14519	Young And Foolish/Just One More Chance	18
56	Capitol CL 14523	Memories Are Made Of This/Change Of Heart	20
56	Capitol CL 14586	Watching The World Go By/The Lady With The Big Umbrella	12
56	Capitol CL 14624	The Test Of Time/I'm Gonna Steal You Away	8
56	Capitol CL 14625	Me 'N' You 'N' The Moon/The Wind, The Wind	8
56	Capitol CL 14626	Pardners (with Jerry Lewis)/Buckskin Beauty	10
56	Capitol CL 14656	Give Me A Sign/Mississippi Dreamboat	8
57	Capitol CL 14690	The Man Who Plays The Mandolino/I Know I Can't Forget	10
57	Capitol CL 14714	Bamboozled/Only Trust Your Heart	8

			MINT VALUE £
57	Capitol CL 14737	I Can't Give You Anything But Love/I Never Had A Chance	6
57	Capitol CL 14758	Beau James/Write To Me From Naples	10
57	Capitol CL 14782	The Triche Trache/Promise Her Anything	8
57	Capitol CL 14801	The Look/Just Kiss Me	7
57	Capitol CL 14813	Good Mornin' Life/Makin' Love Ukelele Style	8
58	Capitol CL 14844	Return To Me/Forgetting You	6
58	Capitol CL 14890	Angel Baby/I'll Gladly Make The Same Mistake Again	8
58	Capitol CL 14910	Volare (Nel Blu Dipinto Di Blu)/Outta My Mind	6
58	Capitol CL 14943	Once Upon A Time (It Happened)/The Magician	8
59	Capitol CL 14990	It Takes So Long (To Say Goodbye)/You Were Made For Love	8
59	Capitol CL 15015	Rio Bravo/My Rifle, My Pony And Me	20
59	Capitol CL 15039	On An Evening In Roma/You Can't Love 'Em All	6
59	Capitol CL 15064	Ain't Gonna Lead This Life/Maybe	8
59	Capitol CL 15102	(Love Is A) Career/For You	8
60	Capitol CL 15127	Who Was That Lady?/Love Me, My Love	10
60	Capitol CL 15145	Napoli/Buttercup A Golden Hair	6
60	Capitol CL 15155	Just In Time/Humdinger	6
60	Capitol CL 15172	Sogni D'Oro (Golden Dreams)/How Sweet It Is	8
61	Capitol CL 15188	Sparklin' Eyes/Tu Sei Bella, Signorina	8
61	Capitol CL 15198	All In A Night's Work/Bella Bella Bambina	10
61	Capitol CL 15209	Giuggiola/The Story Of Life	10
62	Reprise R 20058	Tik A Tee, Tik A Tay/Just Close Your Eyes	10
62	Reprise R 20076	C'est Si Bon!/The Poor People Of Paris	6
62	Reprise R 20082	Dame Su Amor/Baby O	10
63	Reprise R 20116	From The Bottom Of My Heart (Dammi, Dammi, Dammi)/ Who's Got The Action?	10
63	Reprise R 20128	Sam's Song (with Sammy Davis Jnr)/SAMMY DAVIS JNR. & FRANK SINATRA: Me And My Shadow	8
63	Capitol CL 15294	Cha Cha Cha D'Amour/I Wish You Love	6
63	Reprise R 20150	Face In A Crowd/Ain't Gonna Try Anymore	6
63	Reprise R 20215	Via Veneto/Mama Roma	12
64	Reprise R 20217	Fugue For Tin Horns/The Oldest Established (Permanent Crap Game In New York) (B-side with Frank Sinatra & Bing Crosby) (some in p/s)	10/6
64	Reprise R 20281	Everybody Loves Somebody Sometime/Little Voice	6
64	Reprise R 20307	The Door Is Still Open/Every Minute, Every Hour	6
64	Capitol CL 15363	Somebody Loves You/Hundred Years From Today	6
67	Pye DMA 1	I'm Not The Marrying Kind (Dean Martin Assoc. issue, 1-sided, promo only)	25
67	Reprise R 20538	Let The Good Times In/I'm Not The Marrying Kind	6
67	Reprise R 20601	In The Chapel In The Moonlight/Welcome To My World	6
67	Reprise R 20608	Little Ole Wine Drinker Me/I Can't Help Remembering You	7
67	Reprise R 20640	In The Misty Moonlight/Wallpaper Roses	5
68	Reprise RS 23259	Bumming Around/Home	8
68	Reprise R 20780	Not Enough Indians/Rainbows Are Back in Fashion	6
69	Reprise RS 23343	Gentle On My Mind/That Old Time Feelin'	6
69	Reprise RS 23387	By The Time I Get To Phoenix/Things	6
69	Reprise R 20841	I Take A Lot Of Pride/Drowning In My Tears	6
70	Reprise R 20893	Come On Down/Down Home	12
70	Reprise R 20973	Georgie Sunshine/For The Good TImes	6
75	Capitol CL 15821	Memories Are Made Of This/That's Amore (That's Love)	6
81	Reprise K 14512	Gentle On My Mind/King Of The Road (p/s)	6

EPs

55	Capitol EAP 1-9123	DEAN MARTIN	25
55	Capitol EAP 1-481	SUNNY ITALY	25
56	Capitol EAP 1007	SWINGIN' DOWN YONDER NO. 1	18*
56	Capitol EAP 1022	SWINGIN' DOWN YONDER NO. 2	18*
56	Capitol EAP 1033	DEAN MARTIN AND JERRY LEWIS: "PARDNERS" (with Jerry Lewis)	18*
56	Capitol EAP 1037	SWINGIN' DOWN YONDER NO. 3	18*
57	Capitol EAP 1-806	HOLLYWOOD OR BUST — FILM SELECTION	18*
57	Capitol EAP 1-840	TEN THOUSAND BEDROOMS — FILM SELECTION	22
57	Capitol EAP 1-939	RETURN TO ME	15
58	Capitol EAP 1-1027	VOLARE	12
60	Capitol EAP 1-1285	A WINTER ROMANCE PART 1	18
60	Capitol EAP 2-1285	A WINTER ROMANCE PART 2	18
60	Capitol EAP 3-1285	A WINTER ROMANCE PART 3	18
61	Capitol EAP 1-20072	RELAXIN' WITH DEAN MARTIN	18
61	Capitol EAP 1-20124	DEAN MARTIN IN MOVIELAND	20
61	Capitol EAP 1-20152	I'M YOURS	18
63	Reprise R 30005	FRENCH STYLE	15
64	Reprise R 20031	DINO LATINO	15
64	Capitol EAP 6-1702	SOMEBODY LOVES YOU	15
65	Capitol EAP 7-1702	CHA CHA DE AMOUR	15
64	Reprise R 30034	EVERYBODY LOVES SOMEBODY	10
65	Reprise R 30036	WE'LL SING IN THE SUNSHINE	12
65	Reprise R 30039	ROBIN AND THE SEVEN HOODS	15
65	Reprise R 30044	I'LL BE SEEING YOU	12
65	Reprise R 30051	SEND ME SOME LOVING	12
66	Reprise R 30059	THE BIRDS AND THE BEES	12
66	Reprise R 30066	RED ROSES FOR A BLUE LADY	12
66	Reprise R 30074	LOVE LOVE LOVE	12
67	Reprise R 30078	SINGS SONGS FROM 'THE SILENCERS': THE GLORY OF LOVE	15
67	Reprise R 30084	MR. HAPPINESS	12
67	Reprise R 30090	WINTER WONDERLAND	12

LPs

53	Capitol LC 6590	CAPITOL PRESENTS DEAN MARTIN (10")	75
56	Britone LP 1002	DEAN MARTIN SINGS, NICOLINI LUCCHESI PLAYS (10")	70
57	Capitol T 849	PRETTY BABY	25

58 Capitol T 1047 THIS IS DEAN MARTIN! . . . 25
59 Capitol (S)T 1150 SLEEP WARM (orchestra conducted by Frank Sinatra, mono/stereo) . . . 20/25
61 Capitol (S)T 1442 THIS TIME I'M SWINGIN'! (mono/stereo) . . . 20/25
62 Encore! ENC 103 DEAN GOES DIXIE . . . 22
62 Reprise R/R9 6021 FRENCH STYLE (mono/stereo) . . . 20/25
62 Capitol (S)T 1659 DINO (mono/stereo) . . . 22/30
63 Reprise R 6054 DINO LATINO . . . 20
63 Capitol (S)T 1702 CHA CHA DE AMOR (mono/stereo) . . . 18/20
63 Reprise R 6061 DEAN (TEX) MARTIN COUNTRY STYLE . . . 20
63 Reprise R 6085 DEAN (TEX) MARTIN RIDES AGAIN . . . 20
64 Regal REG 1010 DEAN MARTIN (export issue) . . . 22
64 Reprise R 6123 DREAM WITH DEAN . . . 20
64 Reprise R 6130 EVERYBODY LOVES SOMEBODY . . . 15
65 Reprise R 6140 THE DOOR IS STILL OPEN TO MY HEART . . . 15
65 Reprise R 6146 MARTIN HITS AGAIN . . . 15
65 Reprise R/R9 6168 HOUSTON (mono/stereo) . . . 12/15
65 Reprise R/R9 6170 (REMEMBER ME) I'M THE ONE WHO LOVES YOU (mono/stereo) . . . 12/15
66 Reprise R 6201 SOMEWHERE THERE'S SOMEONE . . . 12
66 Reprise R 6211 DEAN MARTIN SINGS SONGS FROM "THE SILENCERS" . . . 15
66 Reprise RLP/RSLP 6213 THE HIT SOUND OF DEAN MARTIN . . . 12
66 Reprise RLP 6222 THE DEAN MARTIN CHRISTMAS ALBUM . . . 15
67 Reprise RLP/RSLP 6233 AT EASE WITH DEAN . . . 15
67 Stateside SL/SSL 10201 LOVE IS A CAREER . . . 20
67 Reprise RLP/RSLP 6242 HAPPINESS IS . . . 12
67 Reprise RLP/RSLP 6250 WELCOME TO MY WORLD . . . 12
68 Reprise RLP/RSLP 6301 DEAN MARTIN'S GREATEST HITS VOL. 1 . . . 12
68 Reprise RLP/RSLP 6320 DEAN MARTIN'S GREATEST HITS VOL. 2 . . . 12
69 Reprise RLP/RSLP 6330 GENTLE ON MY MIND . . . 12
71 Reprise RSLP 6428 FOR THE GOOD TIME . . . 12
79 Capitol CAPS 1029 THE CLASSIC DINO . . . 12
(see also Jerry Lewis, Line Renaud & Dean Martin, Frank Sinatra)

DEREK MARTIN

64 Sue WI 308 Daddy Rolling Stone/Don't Put Me Down Like This (credited as Derak Martin) . . . 35
65 Columbia DB 7694 You Better Go/You Know . . . 35
68 Stax 601 039 Soul Power/Sly Girl . . . 22

DON MARTIN & DANDY (& SUPERBOYS)

67 Giant GN 6 Got A Feelin'/CONNECTIONS: At The Junction . . . 15
68 Giant GN 24 Keep On Fighting/Rock Steady Boogie (with Superboys) . . . 15
(see also Dandy & Superboys)

GEORGE MARTIN & HIS ORCHESTRA

64 Parlophone R 5135 I Saw Her Standing There/All My Loving . . . 10
64 Parlophone R 5166 And I Love Her/Ringo's Theme (This Boy) . . . 10
65 Parlophone R 5222 All Quiet On The Mersey Front/Out Of The Picture . . . 10
65 Parlophone R 5256 I Feel Fine/The Niagara Theme . . . 8
65 Parlophone R 5375 Yesterday/Another Girl . . . 15
66 United Artists UP 1154 By George! — It's The David Frost Theme/Double Scotch . . . 15
66 United Artists UP 1165 Love In The Open Air/Theme From "The Family Way" . . . 20
67 United Artists UP 1194 Theme One/Elephants And Castles . . . 15
72 United Artists UP 35423 Pulp — Theme/Pulp — Love Theme . . . 10
65 Parlophone GEP 8930 MUSIC FROM "A HARD DAY'S NIGHT" (EP) . . . 40
64 Parlophone PMC 1227 OFF THE BEATLE TRACK (LP, also stereo PCS 3057) . . . 30/35
65 Parlophone TA-PMC 1227 OFF THE BEATLE TRACK (reel-to-reel, mono only) . . . 12
65 Columbia SX 1775 PLAYS HELP! (LP, mono) . . . 20
65 Studio Two TWO 102 PLAYS HELP! (LP, stereo) . . . 20
66 United Artists (S)ULP 1157 INSTRUMENTALLY SALUTES THE BEATLES GIRLS (LP) . . . 30
66 Studio Two TWO 141 AND I LOVE HER (LP) . . . 25
67 Decca (S)KL 4847 THE FAMILY WAY (LP, soundtrack) . . . 100
68 United Artists (S)ULP 1196 BRITISH MAID (LP) . . . 22
70 Sunset SLS 50182 BY GEORGE! (LP) . . . 20
73 United Artists UAS 29475 LIVE AND LET DIE (LP, soundtrack, gatefold sleeve) . . . 25
74 Polydor Super 2383 304 BEATLES TO BOND AND BACH (LP) . . . 15
78 St. Michael IMP 105 BEATLES TO BOND AND BACH (LP, exclusive to Marks & Spencer) . . . 30
93 EMI RNB 1 THE BEATLES — GEORGE MARTIN INTERVIEW (CD, card sleeve, promo only) . 20
(see also Beatles, Ray Cathode)

GRADY MARTIN & THE SLEWFOOT FIVE

53 Brunswick 05201 Dragnet/The Velvet Glove (78) . . . 8
56 Brunswick 05535 Nashville/Don't Take Your Love From Me . . . 15
(see also Jane Turzy)

HONEYBOY MARTIN

67 Caltone TONE 103 Dreader Than Dread (and the Voices)/DANDY: In The Mood . . . 25
70 Gas GAS 123 Unchained Melody/SAMMY JONES: You're My Girl . . . 10
72 Sioux SI 011 Unchained Melody/SAMMY JONES: You're My Girl (reissue) . . . 10
72 Harry J HJ 6643 Have You Ever Seen The Rain/Spanish Harlem . . . 10
(see also Lynn Tait & Jets)

IRVING MARTIN

(see under Martin's Magic Sounds)

JANIS MARTIN

60 Palette PG 9000 Here Today And Gone Tomorrow Love/Hard Times Ahead . . . 40
80 RCA PL 43153 THE COMPLETE RCA JANIS MARTIN (2-LP) . . . 18

JEAN MARTIN

63 Decca F 11751 Ain't Gonna Kiss Ya/Three Times Three Is Love . . . 10
64 Decca F 11897 Save The Last Dance For Me/Will You Still Love Me Tomorrow . . . 10

MINT VALUE £

JERRY MARTIN
63	London HLU 9692	Shake-A Take-A/Exchange Student	15

KERRY MARTIN
58	Parlophone R 4449	Stroll Me/Cold Hands, Warm Heart	15

LUCIA MARTIN
62	Parlophone R 4915	Big Jim/Star From Heaven	12

MARK MARTIN
67	Page One POF 020	Extraordinary Girl/Love Could Be Like Hell	6

MARY MARTIN
64	London HLR 9938	A Spoonful Of Sugar/Feed The Birds	7

MILES MARTIN FOLK GROUP
71	Amber	MILES MARTIN FOLK GROUP (LP, private pressing)	90

MILLICENT MARTIN
58	Columbia DB 4171	Our Language Of Love/Seriously	5
60	Columbia DB 4466	Tintarella Di Luna/I Can Dream, Can't I?	5
63	Parlophone R 5033	Gravy Waltz/Get Lost My Love	5
64	Parlophone R 5096	In The Summer Of His Years/If I Can Help Somebody	6
64	Parlophone R 5120	Suspicion/Nothing But The Best	10

(see also Ronnie Carroll)

PAUL MARTIN
67	Sue WI 4041	Snake In The Grass/I've Got A New Love	35

RAY MARTIN (& HIS) CONCERT ORCHESTRA
53	Columbia SCM 5001	Blue Tango/Belle Of The Ball	8
53	Columbia SCM 5002	The Marching Strings/The Waltzing Cat	8
53	Columbia SCM 5020	Lady Of Spain/Ecstasy	8
53	Columbia SCM 5063	Swedish Rhapsody/Hi-Lili, Hi-Lo	8
56	Columbia SCM 5264	The Carousel Waltz/Port Au Prince	8
57	Columbia DB 4001	Manhattan Tango/Heladero	6
59	Columbia SCD 2123	The Carousel Waltz/Port Au Prince (reissue)	6
56	Columbia SEG 7639	IT'S GREAT TO BE YOUNG — FILM MUSIC (EP)	8
56	Pye Nixa NEP 24005	PRESENTING RAY MARTIN (EP)	8
53	Columbia 33S 1011	MUSIC IN THE RAY MARTIN MANNER VOL. 1 (10" LP)	15
54	Columbia 33S 1021	MUSIC IN THE RAY MARTIN MANNER VOL. 2 (10" LP)	15
64	Phase 4 Stereo PFS 4043	THE SOUND OF SIGHT (LP)	20

(see also Ray Burns)

RICKY MARTIN & TYME MACHINE
68	Olga OLE 4	Something Else/Blue Suede Shoes	12

RODGE MARTIN
67	Polydor 56725	When She Touches Me/Lovin' Machine	10

RON MARTIN & JUBILEE STOMPERS
68	Doctor Bird DB 1151	Give Your Love To Me/I Cry My Heart	25

RUPIE MARTIN('S ALLSTARS)
70	Torpedo TOR 24	Last Flight/Super Lotus	12
70	Torpedo TOR 26	Musical Container (Parts 1 & 2)	12
70	Punch PH 43	Death In The Arena (actually by Rupie Martin All Stars)/ MAN COMETH: Julia Caesar (actually by Charlie Ace)	12

SETH MARTIN
68	Page One POF 073	Another Day Goes By/Look At Me	6
69	Page One POF 134	What A Lovely Way To Spend Forever/Mystery Lady	5

SHANE MARTIN
68	CBS 2894	You're So Young/I Need You	200

SKIP MARTIN VIDEO ALL-STARS
60	Golden Guinea GGL 0060	TV JAZZ THEMES (LP, also stereo GGLS 10060)	12/15

STEVE MARTIN
56	Columbia DB 3703	Only You/Lola	8
56	Columbia SCM 5212	Only You/Lola (78)	8
58	Philips PB 820	Stairway Of Love/Chanson D'Amour	6
58	Philips PB 853	The Man Inside/Blue-Eyed Sue	6
58	Philips PB 853	The Man Inside/Blue-Eyed Sue (78)	7

TONY MARTIN
53	HMV 7M 105	Tenement Symphony (both sides)	10
53	HMV 7M 136	The Golden Years/April In Portugal	15
54	HMV 7M 203	Here/I Could Write A Book	8
54	HMV 7M 258	I Love Paris/Boulevard Of Nightingales	8
55	HMV 7M 302	Stranger In Paradise/Vera Cruz	18
55	HMV 7M 320	Domani/What's The Time In Nicaragua	8
56	HMV 7M 414	Walk Hand In Hand/Flamenco Love	15
56	HMV 7MC 41	Walk Hand In Hand/Flamenco Love (export issue)	15
57	HMV POP 282	All Of You/Moderation	8
57	RCA RCA 1002	The Man From Idaho/One Is A Lonely Number	5
59	RCA RCA 1101	She Is Not Thinking Of Me/GOGI GRANT: Say A Prayer For Me Tonight	6
59	RCA RCA 1101	She Is Not Thinking Of Me/GOGI GRANT: Say A Prayer For Me Tonight (78)	8
63	HMV 7P 314	Tenement Symphony (both sides, reissue)	6
65	Stateside SS 394	Talkin' To Your Picture/Our Rhapsody	85
65	Tamla Motown TMG 537	The Bigger Your Heart Is (The Harder You'll Fall)/The Two Of Us	75
67	RCA RCA 1582	This Year/Sand Pebbles	5
54	HMV 7EG 8006	TONY MARTIN (EP)	10

55 HMV 7EG 8124 TENEMENT SYMPHONY (EP) . . . 10
57 HMV 7EG 8205 THE DESERT SONG — SOUNDTRACK EXCERPTS (EP) . . . 8
58 RCA RCX 130 SONGS FROM CINDERELLA (EP) . . . 8
55 Brunswick LA 8713 TONY MARTIN SINGS VOL. 1 (10" LP) . . . 20
56 Mercury MPT 7005 TONY MARTIN FAVOURITES (10" LP) . . . 20
57 Mercury MPT 7516 DREAM MUSIC (10" LP) . . . 18
57 HMV DLP 1137 SPEAK TO ME OF LOVE (10" LP) . . . 18
57 RCA RD 27003 A NIGHT AT THE COPACABANA (LP) . . . 15
61 London HA-D 2341 TONY MARTIN'S GREATEST HITS (LP) . . . 15
65 Stateside SL 10113 AT CARNEGIE HALL (LP) . . . 15
(see also Gogi Grant)

TRADE MARTIN
63 London HL 9662 Hula Hula Dancin' Doll/Something In The Wind . . . 15

VINCE MARTIN
59 HMV POP 594 Old Grey Goose (Aunt Rhodie)/Goodnight, Irene . . . 10
59 HMV POP 594 Old Grey Goose (Aunt Rhodie)/Goodnight, Irene (78) . . . 15
(see also Tarriers)

MARTIN & THE BROWNSHIRTS
78 Lightning GIL 507 Taxi Driver/Boring . . . 35

MARTIN & DERRICK
61 Blue Beat BB 48 Times Are Going/I Love You Baby (with Cavaliers Combo) . . . 20
62 Island WI 024 Come On/MONTY & CYCLONES: Organisation . . . 22
(see also Derrick Morgan)

MARTIN & FINLEY
73 Tamla Motown TMG 867 It's Another Sunday/Best Friends (withdrawn, demo only) . . . 80

WINK MARTINDALE
59 London HLD 8962 Deck Of Cards/Now You Know How It Feels . . . 6
59 London HLD 8962 Deck Of Cards/Now You Know How It Feels (78) . . . 40
60 London HLD 9042 Life Gits Tee-Jus Don't It?/I Never See Maggie Alone . . . 8
61 London HLD 9419 Black Land Farmer/Make Him Happy . . . 8
67 Dot DS 26753 The Shifting Whispering Sands/Trees . . . 5
63 London RED 1370 DECK OF CARDS (EP) . . . 20
65 Dot DEP 20000 DECK OF CARDS (EP) . . . 12
60 London HA-D 2240 WINK MARTINDALE (LP) . . . 30
60s Golden Guinea GGL 0288 DECK OF CARDS (LP) . . . 15

RAY MARTINE
63 Piccadilly NPL 38007 EAST END — WEST END (LP) . . . 12

TONY MARTINEZ QUINTET
54 HMV 7M 264 Cucusa Tune Mambo/Bernie's Tune Mambo . . . 6

MIA MARTINI
77 CBS S CBS 5178 Freedom Is Today/Libera . . . 5

AL MARTINO
78s
59 Top Rank JAR 108 I Can't Get You Out Of My Heart/Two Hearts Are Better Than One . . . 12
SINGLES
54 Capitol CL 14128 Wanted/There'll Be No Teardrops Tonight . . . 30/25
54 Capitol CL 14148 On And On (In Love With You)/Give Me Something To Go With The Wine . . . 30/25
54 Capitol CL 14163 The Story Of Tina/Destiny (No One Can Change) . . . 30/25
(The first prices for the above 45s are for green labels with triangular centres, the second for later pressings with purple labels with triangular centres.)
54 Capitol CL 14192 I Still Believe/When? . . . 20
54 Capitol CL 14202 Not As A Stranger/No One But You . . . 20
55 Capitol CL 14224 Don't Go To Strangers/Say It Again . . . 20
55 Capitol CL 14284 The Snowy, Snowy Mountains/Love Is Eternal . . . 18
55 Capitol CL 14343 The Man From Laramie/To Please My Lady . . . 30
55 Capitol CL 14379 Come Close To Me/Small Talk . . . 15
(All the above 45s were originally issued with triangular centres; round-centre reissues are worth around half these values.)
56 Capitol CL 14550 Journey's End/Sound Advice . . . 15/8
56 Capitol CL 14614 The Girl I Left In Rome/Some Cloud Above . . . 15/8
57 Capitol CL 14680 I'm Sorry/A Love To Call My Own . . . 8
59 Top Rank JAR 108 I Can't Get You Out Of My Heart/Two Hearts Are Better Than One . . . 10
59 Top Rank JAR 187 Darling I Love You/The Memory Of You . . . 10
60 Top Rank JAR 312 Summertime/I Sold My Heart . . . 7
60 Top Rank JAR 337 Mama/Dearest (Cara) . . . 7
60 Top Rank JAR 418 Why Do I Love You/Sunday . . . 6
60 Ember EMB S 119 Our Concerto/It's All Over But The Crying . . . 6
61 Ember EMB S 122 My Side Of The Story/Little Boy Little Girl . . . 5
62 Ember EMB S 147 Darling I Love You/There's No Tomorrow . . . 6
62 Capitol CL 15260 Because You're Mine/Make Me Believe . . . 6
63 Capitol CL 15300 I Love You Because/Merry-Go-Round . . . 6
63 Capitol CL 15314 Painted, Tainted Rose/That's The Way It's Got To Be . . . 6
EPs
55 Capitol EAP1 405 AL MARTINO SINGS . . . 18
61 Capitol EAP1 20153 TO PLEASE MY LADY . . . 10
63 Ember EMB 4528 DARLING I LOVE YOU . . . 10
63 Capitol EAP4 2107 MARTINO SINGS OF LOVE . . . 8
64 Capitol EAP1 20590 LOSING YOU . . . 8

MINT VALUE £

LPs

60	Top Rank BUY 030	AL MARTINO	18
60	Top Rank 25/025	SWING ALONG WITH AL MARTINO	18
63	Capitol (S)T 1774	THE EXCITING VOICE OF AL MARTINO (mono/stereo)	15/18
63	Capitol (S)T 1914	I LOVE YOU BECAUSE (mono/stereo)	15/18
64	Capitol (S)T 1975	PAINTED, TAINTED ROSE (mono/stereo)	15/18
64	Capitol (S)T 2040	LIVING A LIE (mono/stereo)	15/18
64	Capitol (S)T 2107	AL MARTINO (mono/stereo)	15/18
65	Capitol (S)T 2200	WE COULD (mono/stereo)	15/18
65	Capitol (S)T 2312	SOMEBODY ELSE IS TAKING MY PLACE (mono/stereo)	15/18
66	Capitol (S)T 2362	MY CHERIE (mono/stereo)	15/18
66	Capitol (S)T 2435	SPANISH EYES (mono/stereo)	15/18

MARTIN'S MAGIC SOUNDS

67	Deram DM 141	Mon Amour, Mon Amour/Midem Melody	6
67	Deram DML/SML 1014	MARTIN'S MAGIC SOUNDS (LP)	18

JOHN MARTYN

71	Island WIP 6116	May You Never/Just Now	7
77	Island WIP 6385	Over The Hill/Head And Heart	6
78	Island WIP 6414	Dancing/Dealer (Version)	6
78	Island WIP	Dancing/Dealer (Version) (promo, 78 rpm)	8
80	Island WIP 6547	Johnny Too Bad/Johnny Too Bad (Version)	6
81	Island IPR 2046	Johnny Too Bad (Extended Dub Version)/Big Muff (Extended Mix) (12", promo)	10
82	WEA K 259987-7	Gun Money (US Remix)/Hiss On the Tape (live)	6
86	Island CID 265	Classic John Martyn: Angeline/Tight Connection To My Heart (Has Anybody Seen My Love)/May You Never/Solid Air/ Glistening Glyndebourne (CD, foldout sleeve)	25
92	Permanent CDPERM 6	Sweet Little Mystery (CD)	12
97	Blueprint BP 276CD	SNOOO... EP (She's A Lover/All In Your Favour/Step It Up/ Little Strange) (CD)	8
67	Island ILP 952	LONDON CONVERSATION (LP, 1st pressing, with black & orange 'circle' logo)	80
69	Island ILP 952	LONDON CONVERSATION (LP, 2nd pressing, 'pink rim' label, 'palm tree' logo)	18
68	Island ILP 991/ILPS 9091	THE TUMBLER (LP, 1st pressing, with black 'circle' logo, mono/stereo)	40/35
70	Island ILPS 9091	THE TUMBLER (LP, 2nd pressing, 'pink rim' label, 'palm tree' logo)	15
71	Island ILPS 9167	BLESS THE WEATHER (LP, 'pink rim' label, 'palm tree' logo)	15
73	Island ILPS 9226	SOLID AIR (LP, gatefold sleeve with lyric sheet 'pink rim' label, 'palm tree' logo)	15
73	Island ILPS 9253	INSIDE OUT (LP, gatefold sleeve with inner, 'pink rim' label, 'palm tree' logo)	15
75	Island ILPS 9296	SUNDAY'S CHILD (LP, with lyric inner sleeve, 'palm tree' label)	15
75	Island ILPS 9343	LIVE AT LEEDS (LP, mail-order, 10,000 only, numbered & signed)	25
86	Bodyswerve JMLP 001	PHILENTROPY (LP, red sleeve)	25
91	Permanent PERMLP 4	COOLTIDE (LP, with inner)	25

JOHN & BEVERLEY MARTYN

70	Island WIP 6076	John The Baptist/The Ocean	6
70	Island ILPS 9113	STORMBRINGER (LP, 1st pressing, pink label with 'i' logo)	30
70	Island ILPS 9113	STORMBRINGER (LP, 2nd pressing, 'pink rim' label, 'palm tree' logo)	12
70	Island ILPS 9133	THE ROAD TO RUIN (LP, 'pink rim' label, 'palm tree' logo)	15

(see also Beverley)

KID MARTYN

62	77 77LA 12/20	IN NEW ORLEANS WITH KID SHEIK'S BAND (LP)	15

MARVELETTES

61	Fontana H 355	Please Mr Postman/So Long Baby	50
62	Fontana H 386	Twistin' Postman/I Want A Guy	80
62	Oriole CBA 1764	Beechwood 4-5789/Someday Someway	120
63	Oriole CBA 1817	Locking Up My Heart/Forever	350
64	Stateside SS 251	As Long As I Know He's Mine/Little Girl Blue	55
64	Stateside SS 273	He's A Good Guy (Yes He Is)/Goddess Of Love	50
64	Stateside SS 334	You're My Remedy/A Little Bit Of Sympathy, A Little Bit Of Love	45
65	Stateside SS 369	Too Many Fish In The Sea/Need For Love	35
65	Tamla Motown TMG 518	I'll Keep Holding On/No Time For Tears	50
65	Tamla Motown TMG 535	Danger Heartbreak Dead Ahead/Your Cheating Ways	40
66	Tamla Motown TMG 546	Don't Mess With Bill/Anything You Wanna Do	40
66	Tamla Motown TMG 562	You're The One/Paper Boy	35
67	Tamla Motown TMG 594	The Hunter Gets Captured By The Game/I Think I Can Change You	18
67	Tamla Motown TMG 609	When You're Young And In Love/The Day You Take One, You Have To Take The Other	8
68	Tamla Motown TMG 639	My Baby Must Be A Magician/I Need Someone	10
68	Tamla Motown TMG 659	Here I Am Baby/Keep Off, No Trespassing	15
69	Tamla Motown TMG 701	Reachin' For Something I Can't Have/Destination Anywhere	12
73	Tamla Motown TMG 860	Reachin' For Something I Can't Have/Here I Am Baby	5
75	Tamla Motown TMG 1000	Finders Keepers, Losers Weepers/KIM WESTON: Do Like I Do	25
65	Tamla Motown TMG 2003	THE MARVELETTES (EP)	125
65	Tamla Motown TML 11008	THE MARVELLOUS MARVELETTES (LP)	225
67	T. Motown (S)TML 11052	THE MARVELETTES (LP, mono/stereo)	50/60
69	T. Motown (S)TML 11090	SOPHISTICATED SOUL (LP)	40
70	T. Motown STML 11145	IN FULL BLOOM (LP)	25
71	T. Motown STML 11177	THE RETURN OF THE MARVELETTES (LP, unissued)	

MARVELOWS

65	HMV POP 1433	I Do/My Heart	20

MINT VALUE £

MARVELS (Jamaica)

62 Dice CC 8 — Come To The Wedding/Angelo . . . 20
63 Blue Beat BB 191 — Sonia/The More We Are Together . . . 20
64 Blue Beat BB 221 — Millie/Saturday . . . 20
70 Pama PM 813 — Love One Another/Falling Rain . . . 10
70 Pama PM 817 — Don't Let Him Take Your Love From Me/A Little Smile . . . 10
70 Gas GAS 138 — Sail Away/Fight A Broke . . . 10
70 Gas GAS 139 — Someday We'll Be Together/MORGAN'S ALL STARS: Instrumental . . . 10
71 Pama PM 819 — Oh Lord Why Lord/NEVILLE HINDS: Love Letter . . . 10
71 Pama Supreme PS 338 — Rocksteady/ Be My Baby . . . 20
71 New Beat NB 081 — Co Co/Hey Girl Don't Bother Me . . . 10
72 Pama PM 832 — Do You Know You Have To Cry/Love Power . . . 10
72 Pama Supreme PS 348 — What A Hurricane/If You Love Her . . . 10

MARVELS (U.K.)

68 Columbia DB 8341 — Keep On Searching/Heartache . . . 15

MARVELS FIVE

65 HMV POP 1423 — Bye Bye Baby Bunting/In Front Of Her House . . . 7
65 HMV POP 1452 — Don't Play That Song/Forgive . . . 7

MARVETTE

68 Amalgamated AMG 804 — Tit For Tat (actually by Lyn Taitt & Jets)/You Take So Long To Know . . . 45
68 Sacred Sound SS 001 — We Are Not Divided/He Is So Real To Me . . . 8
68 Sacred Sound SS 002 — We Shall Have A Grand Time/Let The Power Fall On Me . . . 8
68 Sacred Sound SS 003 — I Was Once Lost In Sin/What A Wonderful Thing . . . 8
68 Tabernacle TS 1001 — I Want A Revival/Tell It . . . 7
68 Tabernacle TS 1003 — Sweet Jesus/When I Look Back . . . 7
60s Coxsone TLP 1002 — IT'S REVIVAL TIME (LP) . . . 100

BRETT MARVIN & THUNDERBOLTS

70 Sonet SON 2011 — Standing On The Platform/Too Many Hot Dogs . . . 5
71 Sonet SON 2015 — Thoughts Of You/Coming Back . . . 5
71 Sonet SON 2017 — Southbound Lane/Little Red Caboose . . . 5
70 Sonet SNTF 616 — BRETT MARVIN AND THE THUNDERBOLTS (LP) . . . 15
71 Sonet SNTF 619 — 12 INCHES OF BRETT MARVIN & THE THUNDERBOLTS (LP) . . . 12
71 Sonet SNTF 620 — BEST OF FRIENDS (LP) . . . 12
72 Sonet SNTF 630 — ALIAS TERRY DACTYL AND THE DINOSAURS (LP) . . . 12
73 Sonet SNTF 651 — TEN LEGGED FRIEND (LP) . . . 12

(see also Jona Lewie)

HANK (B.) MARVIN

68 Columbia DB 8326 — London's Not Too Far/SHADOWS: Running Out Of World . . . 15
69 Columbia DB 8552 — Goodnight Dick/Wahine . . . 12
69 Columbia DB 8601 — Sacha/Sunday For Seven Days . . . 12
69 Columbia DB 8628 — Midnight Cowboy/SHADOWS: Slaughter On Tenth Avenue . . . 18
70 Columbia DB 8693 — Break Another Dawn/Would You Believe It? (demo-only, unissued B-side) . . . 135
70 Columbia DB 8693 — Break Another Dawn/Morning Star . . . 15
78 EMI EMI 2744 — Flamingo/Syndicated (as Hank Marvin Guitar Syndicate) . . . 5
82 Polydor POSP 420 — Don't Talk/Life Line (p/s) . . . 5
83 Polydor POSP 618 — Invisible Man/All Alone With Friends (p/s) . . . 5
69 Columbia SCX 6352 — HANK MARVIN (LP, blue/black label, mono/stereo) . . . 30/25
70 Columbia SCX 6352 — HANK MARVIN (LP, silver/black label re-pressing) . . . 12

(see also Shadows, Marvin & Farrar, Marvin Welch & Farrar, Bruce Welch, Cliff Richard, Spaghetti Junction, Jean-Michel Jarre)

JOEL MARVIN

70 Explosion EX 2028 — Too Late/Each Day (both actually by Gregory Isaacs) . . . 15

(see also Gregory Isaacs)

MARVIN & FARRAR

73 EMI EMI 2044 — Music Makes My Day/Skin Deep (with Olivia Newton-John) . . . 10
75 EMI EMI 2335 — Small And Lonely Light/Galadriel (Spirit Of Starlight) . . . 7
73 EMI EMA 755 — HANK MARVIN AND JOHN FARRAR (LP, with Olivia Newton-John) . . . 25

(see also Shadows, Hank Marvin, Marvin Welch & Farrar)

MARVIN & JOHNNY

57 Vogue V 9074 — Yak Yak/Pretty Eyes . . . 550
57 Vogue V 9074 — Yak Yak/Pretty Eyes (78) . . . 150
58 Vogue V 9099 — Smack, Smack/You're In My Heart . . . 500
58 Vogue V 9099 — Smack, Smack/You're In My Heart (78) . . . 150
65 Black Swan WI 467 — Cherry Pie/Ain't That Right . . . 40

MARVIN, WELCH & FARR

71 Regal Zonophone RZ 3030 — Faithful/Mr. Sun . . . 8
71 Regal Zonophone RZ 3035 — Lady Of The Morning/Tiny Robin . . . 8
72 Regal Zonophone RZ 3048 — Marmaduke/Strike A Light . . . 12
71 Regal Zono. SRZA 8502 — MARVIN, WELCH AND FARRAR (LP) . . . 25
71 Regal Zono. SRZA 8504 — SECOND OPINION (LP) . . . 25
72 Regal Zono. Q4SRZA 8504 — SECOND OPINION (LP, quadrophonic) . . . 30

(see also Shadows, Marvin & Farrar, Bruce Welch [& Hank Marvin])

GROUCHO MARX

51 Brunswick 04794 — Blackstrap Molasses/How D'ye Do And Shake Hands (78, with Jimmy Durante & Danny Kaye) . . . 8
73 A&M AMS 7057 — Show Me A Rose/Lydia The Tattooed Lady . . . 6
72 A&M AMLS 6003 — AN EVENING WITH GROUCHO MARX (2-LP) . . . 30

(see also Danny Kaye, Jimmy Durante, Jerry Colonna & Groucho Marx)

GROUCHO & CHICO MARX

69 MCA MCA 758 — Ev'ryone Says I Love You/HARPO MARX: Ev'ryone Says I Love You (p/s) . . . 8

(see also Marx Brothers)

MINT VALUE £

MARX BROTHERS

70 MCA MCF 2533 ORIGINAL VOICE TRACKS FROM THEIR GREATEST MOVIES (LP) 15
(see also Groucho Marx)

MARY JANE with BARRY GRAY & SPACEMAKERS

63 Philips 326 587 BF Robot Man/Just The Same As I Do (some in p/s). 40/18
(see also Barry Gray)

MARZIPAN

70 Trend 6099 007 My Kind Of Music/Sweet Water Mary 6

MASAI

74 Contempo CS 2007 Across The Track (We Better Go Back) (Parts 1 & 2) 100

MASAI

82 Turbo TURB 01 Stranger To Myself/Lightning (p/s) 8

MASCOTS

63 Pye International 7N 25189 Hey Little Angel/Once Upon A Love 18

HUGH MASEKELA

68 Uni UN 504 Grazing In The Grass/Bajabula Bonke. 8
69 Uni UN 510 I Haven't Slept/Where Has All The Grass Gone? 6
68 Uni UNL(S) 101 ALIVE AND WELL AT THE WHISKEY (LP) 20
69 Fontana SFL 13056 HUGH MASEKELA (LP) 18
71 Rare Earth SRE 3002 HUGH MASEKELA AND THE UNION OF SOUTH AFRICA (LP). 15
72 Blue Thumb ICD 3 HOME IS WHERE THE MUSIC IS (LP) 25

SPOKES MASHIYANE

58 Oriole CB 1441 Jika Spokes (with Ben Nkosi)/Boys Of Jo'burg (with France Pilane). 6
58 Oriole CB 1441 Jika Spokes (with Ben Nkosi)/Boys Of Jo'burg (with France Pilane) (78) 8

MASKED PHANTOM

66 Parlophone R 5437 These Clogs Are Made For Waltzing/Fried Scampi. 5

MASKMAN & AGENTS

69 Direction 58-4059 One Eye Open/Y'awll 6

MASON

73 Dawn DNLS 3050 MASON (LP, export issue) 20

BARBARA MASON

65 London HL 9977 Yes, I'm Ready/Keep Him 25
68 Direction 58-3382 Oh How It Hurts/Ain't Got Nobody 18
69 Action ACT 4542 Slipping Away/Half A Love. 15
72 Buddah 2011 133 Bed And Board/Yes It's You 6
73 Buddah 2011 154 Give Me Your Love/You Can Be With The One You Don't Love 6
75 Buddah BDS 425 From His Woman To You/When You Wake Up In Georgia 5
69 Action ACLP 6002 OH HOW IT HURTS (LP). 70
75 Buddah BDLP 4027 TRANSITION (LP). 18
75 Buddah BDLP 4032 LOVE'S THE THING (LP). 18

BARRY MASON

66 Decca F 12401 Misty Morning Eyes/Take Your Time 8
66 Deram DM 104 Over The Hills And Far Away/A Collection Of Recollections 40
69 Decca F 12895 I'm In Love With You, Pom Pom/Mister D.J. Play Me A Sad Song. 7
(see also Sounds Of Les & Barry)

CURTISS MASON

71 Columbia DB 8800 Monkberry Moon Delight/Lot Of Lovin' 5

DAVE MASON

68 Island WIP 6032 Just For You/Little Woman 15
70 Harvest HAR 5017 World In Changes/Can't Stop Worrying, Can't Stop Lovin'. 6
70 Harvest HAR 5024 Only You Know And I Know/Sad And Deep As You 6
70 Harvest SHTC 251 ALONE TOGETHER (LP) 25
72 Blue Thumb ILPS 9203 HEAD KEEPER (LP) 20
72 Island ICD 5 SCRAPBOOK (2-LP). 20
73 CBS 65258 IT'S LIKE YOU NEVER LEFT (LP, gatefold sleeve) 12
(see also Hellions, Revolution, Traffic, Fox, Jaguars)

DAVE MASON & CASS ELLIOT

71 Probe PRO 513 Something To Make You Happy/Next To You
(as Mason & Cass, special sleeve) 6
71 Probe SPBA 6259 DAVE MASON AND CASS ELLIOT (LP). 20
(see also Dave Mason, Mama Cass [Elliot])

GLEN MASON

56 Parlophone MSP 6240 Hot Diggity (Dog Ziggity Boom)/Baby Girl Of Mine. 15
56 Parlophone R 4203 Love, Love, Love/Glendora 18
56 Parlophone R 4244 The Green Door/Why Must You Go, Go, Go. 18
57 Parlophone R 4271 Don't Forbid Me/Amore 10
57 Parlophone R 4291 Round And Round/Walking And Whistling 7
57 Parlophone R 4334 Crying My Heart Out For You/Why Don't They Understand 7
57 Parlophone R 4357 By My Side/By The Fireside. 6
58 Parlophone R 4390 What A Beautiful Combination/I'm Alone Because I Love You. 6
58 Parlophone R 4415 I May Never Pass This Way Again/A Moment Ago 8
58 Parlophone R 4451 I Know Where I'm Going/Autumn Souvenir. 7
58 Parlophone R 4485 The End/Fall In Love 7
59 Parlophone R 4562 The Battle Of New Orleans/I Don't Know 8
60 Parlophone R 4626 You Got What It Takes/If There's Someone 8
60 Parlophone R 4723 That's What I Want!/I Like It When It Rains 7
61 Parlophone R 4834 Don't Move/Shadrack. 7
62 Parlophone R 4900 St. Louis Blues/That's Life. 7

MINT VALUE £

MARLIN MASON
56 Vogue Coral Q 72168 Don't Throw My Love Away/The Mystery Of Love. . . . 10

NICK MASON (& RICK FENN)
85 Harvest HAR 5238 Lie For A Lie/And The Address (with Rick Fenn, p/s). . . . 5
85 Harvest 12 HAR 5238 Lie For A Lie (Extended 12" Version)/And The Address/ Mumbo Jumbo (with Rick Fenn) (12", p/s) 8
85 EMI MAF 1 PROFILES (LP, with Rick Fenn). . . . 12
81 Harvest SHSP 4116 FICTITIOUS SPORTS (LP, solo, with inner sleeve) 12
(see also Pink Floyd, 10cc)

SANDY MASON
80s Boot BOS 7234 ONLY LOVE (LP). . . . 12

SPENCER MASON
67 Parlophone R 5555 Flugel In Carnaby Street/Albuferia 8

MASQUERADERS
68 Bell BLL 1023 I Ain't Got To Love Nobody Else/I Got It 6
70 Now! NOW 1001 Love Peace And Understanding/Tell Me You Love Me 6
(see also Lester Tipton)

MASS
80 4AD AD 14 You And I/Cabbage (some with poster insert in die-cut sleeve) 12/8
81 4AD CAD 107 LABOUR OF LOVE (LP, with inner sleeve) 15
(see also Models, Rema-Rema, Wolfgang Press)

MASSED ALBERTS
64 Parlophone R 5159 Blaze Away/Goodbye Dolly (Gray). . . . 6

MASSIEL
68 Philips BF 1667 La La La/He Gives Me Love. . . . 7

MASSIVE ATTACK
90 Wild Bunch WBRT 1 Daydreaming (mixes) (12", p/s, with cards). . . . 15
91 Wild Bunch WBRT 2 Unfinished Sympathy/Instrumental (12", p/s) 25
91 Wild Bunch WBRR 2 Unfinished Sympathy (Nellee Hooper 12" Mix)/ (Nellee Hooper Instrumental Mix)/(Original) (12", p/s) 35
91 Wild Bunch WBRR 3 Safe From Harm (mixes) (12", p/s). . . . 8
98 Circa MASBOX 2 SINGLES 90/98 (11 x 12" singles in numbered heat sensitive box). . . . 30

MASTERBOY
91 Spaghetti CIAO 2 Shake It Up And Dance (Mini Live Version)/(Instrumental) (p/s). . . . 5
91 Spaghetti CIAOC 2 Shake It Up And Dance (Mini Live Version)/(Instrumental) (cassette) 6
91 Spaghetti CIAOX Shake It Up And Dance (Mini Live Version)/(Instrumental) (12", p/s). . . . 8
91 Spaghetti CIAOCD 2 Shake It Up And Dance (Mini Live Version)/(Remix '91)/ (Maxi Live Version) (CD). . . . 12

MASTERFLEET
73 Sussex LPSX 5 HIGH ON THE SEA (LP) 20

MASTERMINDS
65 Immediate IM 005 She Belongs To Me/Taken My Love 25
(see also Badfinger)

MASTERPLAN
78 Satril SAT 136 Love Crazy (Theme From 'Carry On Emmanuel')/ Since I've Been Away From My Love (p/s) 10

CARL MASTERS
72 Big Shot BI 604 Va Va Voom/GOD SONS: Rebel 15
(see also Max Romeo, Dennis Alcapone)

SAMMY MASTERS
60 Warner Bros WB 10 Rockin' Red Wing/Lonely Weekend 25
60 Warner Bros WB 10 Rockin' Red Wing/Lonely Weekend (78) 225
65 London HLR 9949 I Fought The Law (And The Law Won)/Big Man Cried 15

VALERIE MASTERS
58 Fontana H 132 Sharing/The Secret Of Happiness 10
58 Fontana H 145 (Well-a, Well-a) Ding-Dong/Merci Beaucoup 10
59 Fontana H 175 Dreams End At Dawn/Wonder 8
59 Fontana H 175 Dreams End At Dawn/Wonder (78) 8
59 Fontana H 195 Jack O' Diamonds/Say When 10
59 Fontana H 195 Jack O' Diamonds/Say When (78) 18
59 Fontana H 224 If There Are Stars In My Eyes/Just Squeeze Me 8
59 Fontana H 224 If There Are Stars In My Eyes/Just Squeeze Me (78). . . . 12
60 Fontana H 238 Oh, Gee/No One Understands 10
60 Fontana H 253 Banjo Boy/Cow Cow Boogie 10
60 Fontana H 268 Sweeter As The Day Goes By/Fools Fall In Love 8
61 Fontana H 293 Too Late For Tears/I Got Rhythm. . . . 8
61 Fontana H 322 Birmingham Rag/All The Days Of My Life 7
62 Fontana H 367 African Waltz/All Night Long 7
64 Columbia DB 7426 Christmas Calling/He Didn't Fool Me 75
65 Polydor 56056 It's Up To You/Next Train Out 6
66 Polydor 56135 Don't Ever Go/Say Hello 6
69 Columbia DB 8629 I Don't Wanna Play House/Just Wait A Little While. . . . 6

MASTER'S APPRENTICES
71 Regal Zonophone RZ 3031 I'm Your Satisfier/Because I Love Her 30
70 Regal Zono. SLRZ 1016 MASTER'S APPRENTICES (LP). . . . 160
71 Regal Zono. SLRZ 1022 A TOAST TO PANAMA RED (LP) 120

MASTERS AT WORK
96 Talkin' Loud 578795-1 NUYORICAN (6-LP box set) 50

MINT VALUE £

MASTER SINGERS

66	Parlophone R 5523	Weather Forecast/Roadilore	6
66	Parlophone GEP 8962	THE HIGHWAY CODE (EP)	8

MASTERS OF REALITY

88	Def American DEFA 1	The Candy Song/The Blue Garden	10
88	Def American 838 474-1	THE MASTERS OF REALITY (LP)	20
88	Def American 838 474-2	THE MASTERS OF REALITY (CD)	20

MATADOR

71	Big Shot BI 594	Nyah Festival (actually "What Am I Living For" by Derrick Morgan)/ Brixton Serenade	6

MATADORS

69	Crab CRAB 27	Death A Come (actually by Lloyd Robinson)/The Sword (actually "Zylon" by Lloyd Tyrell [Charmers])	12
70	Camel CA 45	Dark Of The Sun (actually by Jackie Mittoo)/Dreader Than Dread	12
71	Green Door GD 4017	I'm Sorry(actually by Tony Brevett)/JOE WHITE: I'm Sorry Version	10

(see also Emotions, Little Roys, Ethiopians)

MATATA (AIR-FIESTA)

72	President PT 380	I Wanna Do My Thing/Wild River	10
73	President PT 406	I Feel Funky/I Want You	12
74	President PT 417	Return To You/Something On My Mind	10
75	President PT 438	Good Good Understanding/Gimme Some Lovin'	10
72	President PTLS 1052	MATATA: AIR FIESTA (LP)	30
75	President PTLS 1057	INDEPENDENCE (LP)	80

MATCHING MOLE

72	CBS 8101	O Caroline/Signed Curtain	15
72	CBS 64850	MATCHING MOLE (LP)	25
72	CBS 65260	MATCHING MOLE'S LITTLE RED RECORD (LP, with inner sleeve)	20

(see also Robert Wyatt, Soft Machine, Caravan, Hatfield & The North)

MATCHMAKERS

71	Chapter One	BUBBLEGUM A GO GO (LP)	20

(see also Mark Wirtz, Philwit & Pegasus, Fickle Finger)

KAREN MATHESON

96	Survival SURCD 020B	THE DREAMING SEA (CD, limited edition in box, with 6 postcards)	20

(see also Capercaillie)

MATHETAI

77	Cavs CAV 017	KNOWING (LP)	50

MIREILLE MATHIEU

67	Columbia DB 8323	La Derniere Valse/Seuls Au Monde	5
68	Columbia DB 8375	Je Ne Suis Rien Sans Toi (I'm Coming Home)/J'ai Garde L'Accent	5
68	Columbia DB 8429	When You Return/Tonight's The Night (Ce Soir Ils Vont S'Aime)	5
68	Columbia DB 8457	Sweet Souvenirs Of Stefan/An Revoir Daniel	5
68	Columbia DB 8513	Les Bicyclettes De Belsize/Sometimes	5
69	Columbia DB 8621	Hold Me/Vivre Pour Toi	5
71	Columbia DB 8775	Can A Butterfly Cry/Nobody	5
67	Fontana TE 17492	MIREILLE MATHIEU (EP)	8
66	Fontana TL 5363	MIREILLE MATHIEU (LP)	15
67	Columbia SX/SCX 6210	MIREILLE MATHIEU (LP)	12
68	Columbia SX/SCX 6328	LES BICYCLETTES DE BELSIZE (LP)	12
68	Columbia SCX 6246	LIVE AT THE PARIS OLYMPIA (LP)	12
69	Columbia SCX 6391	OLYMPIA (LP, gatefold sleeve)	12
68	Columbia SCX 6369	MIREILLE MATHIEU'S CHRISTMAS (LP)	15

COUNTRY JOHNNY MATHIS

60	Top Rank JKP 2064	COUNTRY AND WESTERN EXPRESS NO. 5 (EP)	22

JODI MATHIS

75	Capitol CL 15827	Mama/Don't You Care Anymore	5

JOHNNY MATHIS

78s

57	Philips PB 713	Wonderful! Wonderful!/When Sunny Gets Blue	8
57	Philips PB 749	The Twelfth Of Never/Chances Are	8
58	Fontana H 117	Come To Me/When I Am With You	8
58	Fontana H 130	Teacher, Teacher/Easy To Love	8
58	Fontana H 165	Winter Wonderland/Sleigh Ride	10
59	Fontana H 186	Let's Love/You'd Be So Nice To Come Home To	10
59	Fontana H 199	Someone/They Say It's Wonderful	12
59	Fontana H 218	The Best Of Everything/Cherie	15
59	Fontana H 219	Misty/The Story Of Our Love	15
59	Fontana H 220	It's Not For Me to Say/Warm And Tender	15

SINGLES

57	Philips JK 1029	The Twelfth Of Never/Chances Are (jukebox issue)	20
57	Fontana H 103	Wild Is The Wind/No Love (But Your Love)	8
58	Fontana H 117	Come To Me/When I Am With You	6
58	Fontana H 130	Teacher, Teacher/Easy To Love	7
58	Fontana H 142	A Certain Smile/Let It Rain	7
58	Fontana H 163	Call Me/Stairway To The Sea	6
58	Fontana H 165	Winter Wonderland/Sleigh Ride	5
59	Fontana H 186	Let's Love/You'd Be So Nice To Come Home To	5
59	Fontana H 199	Someone/They Say It's Wonderful	5
59	Fontana H 218	The Best Of Everything/Cherie	6
59	Fontana H 219	Misty/The Story Of Our Love	6
59	Fontana H 220	It's Not For Me to Say/Warm And Tender	5

60	Fontana H 234	You Are Beautiful/Very Much In Love	5
60	Fontana H 248	The Twelfth Of Never/Get Me To The Church On Time	5
60	Fontana H 254	Starbright/All Is Well	5
60	Fontana H 267	My Love For You/Oh That Feeling (some in p/s)	7/5
61	Fontana H 272	Maria/Hey Love	5
61	Fontana H 316	You Set My Heart To Music/Jenny	5
61	Fontana H 328	Laurie, My Love/Should I Wait (Or Should I Run To Her)	5
61	Fontana H 335	Love Look Away/When My Sugar Walks Down The Street	5
62	Fontana H 372	Sweet Thursday/One Look	5
62	CBS AAG 117	Gina/I Love Her, That's Why (with picture insert)	7
63	CBS AAG 135	What Will Mary Say/Quiet Girl	5
63	HMV POP 1217	Your Teenage Dreams/Come Back (some in export p/s)	12/5
63	HMV POP 1267	Bye Bye Barbara/A Great Night For Crying	5
64	HMV POP 1294	The Fall Of Love/No More	5
64	HMV POP 1318	Taste Of Tears/White Roses From A Blue Valentine	5
64	HMV POP 1365	Listen Lonely Girl/All I Wanted	5
65	HMV POP 1467	Sweetheart Tree/Mirage	5
65	HMV POP 1491	Danny Boy/This Is Love	5
66	HMV POP 1503	On A Clear Day You Can See Forever/Come Back To Me	5
66	HMV POP 1527	Moment To Moment/The Glass Mountain	5
66	HMV POP 1550	The Impossible Dream/Hurry It's Lovely Up Here	5
EPs			
57	Philips BBE 12156	JOHNNY MATHIS	10
58	Fontana TFE 17011	JOHNNY MATHIS	8
58	Fontana TFE 17025	LET ME LOVE YOU	8
58	Fontana TFE 17039	COME TO ME	8
58	Fontana TFE 17047	WHILE WE'RE YOUNG	8
58	Fontana TFE 17056	THE TWELFTH OF NEVER	8
58	Fontana TFE 17064	AVE MARIA	8
58	Fontana TFE 17088	THERE GOES MY HEART	8
58	Fontana TFE 17089	SWING LOW	8
58	Fontana TFE 17091	A HANDFUL OF STARS	8
58	Fontana TFE 17162	CHRISTMAS WITH JOHNNY MATHIS	8
59	Fontana TFE 17177	MEET MISTER MATHIS	8
59	Fontana TFE 17194	IT'S DE LOVELY (also stereo STFE 8001)	8/12
60	Fontana TFE 17215	SO NICE (also stereo STFE 8000)	8/12
60	Fontana TFE 17275	FOUR HITS	8
60	Fontana TFE 17281	TENDERLY	8
60	Fontana TFE 17282	ELI ELI	8
60	Fontana TFE 17283	I'LL BE SEEING YOU	8
60	Fontana TFE 17285	LIKE SOMEONE IN LOVE (also stereo STFE 8018)	8/12
61	Fontana TFE 17316	MOONLIGHT AND MATHIS	8
61	Fontana TFE 17317	FOUR SHOW HITS	8
61	Fontana TFE 17318	CALL ME	8
61	Fontana TFE 17319	IT'S LOVE	8
61	Fontana TFE 17334	MY LOVE FOR YOU	8
61	Fontana TFE 17354	I AM IN LOVE	8
61	Fontana TFE 17355	LET'S DO IT	8
61	Fontana TFE 17356	SECRET LOVE	8
62	Fontana TFE 17393	RING THE BELL	8
62	Fontana TFE 17394	THE PARTY'S OVER	8
62	CBS AGG 20001	LIVE IT UP VOL. 1	8
62	CBS AGG 20006	LIVE IT UP VOL. 2	8
62	CBS AGG 20012	LIVE IT UP VOL. 3	8
63	CBS AGG 20028	RAPTURE	8
64	CBS AGG 20032	MATHIS ON BROADWAY	8
LPs			
57	Fontana TFL 5003	WONDERFUL, WONDERFUL	20
58	Fontana TFL 5011	JOHNNY MATHIS	20
58	Fontana TFL 5015	WARM (also stereo STFL 510)	15/18
58	Fontana TFL 5023	HEAVENLY	15
58	Fontana TFL 5031	MERRY CHRISTMAS (also stereo STFL 506)	15/18
59	Fontana TFL 5039	SWING SOFTLY (also stereo STFL 500)	15/18
59	Fontana TFL 5050	OPEN FIRE, TWO GUITARS (also stereo STFL 515)	15/18
59	Fontana TFL 5058	JOHNNY'S GREATEST HITS	15
60	Fontana TFL 5061	RIDE ON A RAINBOW (also stereo STFL 516)	15/18
60	Fontana TFL 5083	MORE OF JOHNNY'S GREATEST HITS (also stereo STFL 517)	15/18
60	Fontana TFL 5084	FAITHFULLY (lso stereo STFL 522)	15/18
60	Fontana SET(S) 101	THE RHYTHMS AND BALLADS OF BROADWAY (2-LP, mono/stereo)	18/22
61	Fontana TFL 5117	JOHNNY'S MOOD (also stereo STFL 545)	15/18
61	Fontana TFL 5134	I'LL BUY YOU A STAR (also stereo STFL 557)	15/18
61	Fontana TFL 5153	PORTRAIT OF JOHNNY (also stereo STFL 571)	15/18
62	Fontana TFL 5177	LIVE IT UP (also stereo STFL 589)	12/15
62	CBS (S)BPG 62077	PORTRAIT OF JOHNNY (reissue, mono/stereo)	12/15
62	CBS (S)BPG 62072	JOHNNY'S MOOD (reissue, mono/stereo)	12/15
63	CBS (S)BPG 62106	RAPTURE	12
63	CBS (S)BPG 62147	JOHNNY'S NEWEST HITS	12
63	CBS (S)BPG 62172	JOHNNY	12
63	HMV CLP 1696/CSD 1521	SOUNDS OF CHRISTMAS (mono/stereo)	12/15
64	CBS (S)BPG 62202	ROMANTICALLY	12
64	HMV CLP 1721	TENDER IS THE NIGHT (also stereo CSD 1535)	12/15
64	CBS (S)BPG 62270	I'LL SEARCH MY SECRET HEART & OTHER GREAT HITS	12
65	HMV CSD 1553	THE WONDERFUL WORLD OF MAKE BELIEVE (stereo only)	25
65	HMV CLP 1818/CSD 1578	OLÉ	50
65	HMV CLP 1859/CSD 1600	THIS IS LOVE (mono/stereo)	30/18

MINT VALUE £

66	HMV CLP 1926/CSD 1638	AWAY FROM HOME	40
66	CBS (S)BPG 62062	SWING SOFTLY (reissue, mono/stereo)	12/15
66	CBS (S)BPG 62569	JOHNNY'S GREATEST HITS (reissue)	12
66	CBS (S)BPG 62063	OPEN FIRE, TWO GUITARS (reissue, mono/stereo)	12/15
66	CBS (S)BPG 62064	RIDE ON A RAINBOW (reissue, mono/stereo)	12/15
66	CBS (S)BPG 62067	FAITHFULLY (reissue, mono/stereo)	12/15
66	CBS (S)BPG 62105	LIVE IT UP (reissue)	12
66	HMV CLP/CSD 3522	LOVE IS EVERYTHING	15
66	HMV CLP/CSD 3556	THE SHADOW OF YOUR SMILE	15
73	CBS CQ 30740	YOU'VE GOT A FRIEND — TODAY'S GREAT HITS (quadrophonic)	12
73	CBS GQ 30979	JOHNNY MATHIS IN PERSON (quadrophonic)	12
73	CBS CQ 31342	THE FIRST TIME EVER (I SAW YOUR FACE) (quadrophonic)	12
73	CBS CQ 31626	SONG SUNG BLUE (quadrophonic)	12
73	CBS CQ 32114	ME AND MRS JONES (quadrophonic)	12
74	CBS CQ 32435	I'M COMING HOME (quadrophonic)	12
75	CBS 66415	THE BEST OF JOHNNY MATHIS (3-LP box set, mail-order only)	20
79	CBS 66355	JOHNNY MATHIS (3-LP box set)	18
81	Readers Digest 034	THE BEST OF JOHNNY MATHIS (4-LP box set, mail-order only)	22
83	OPEN 1	THE ULTIMATE JOHNNY MATHIS (2-LP, mail-order only)	18

TONY MATOS

62	Salvo SLO 5520-LP	CHA CHA! WITH TONY MATOS (LP, issued with or without sleeve)	18/12

WALTER MATTHAU

73	MCA MU 1185	Love's The Only Game In Town/Pete 'N' Tillie — Love Theme	5

BRIAN MATTHEW

61	Pye 7N 15403	Trad Mad/Sing With Me, Mates	6

BRIAN MATTHEW & PETE MURRAY

60	Decca F 11305	What's It All About Eh?/Gee Ma, I Wanna Go Home	6

IAN MATTHEWS

71	Vertigo 6059 041	Hearts/Little Known	8
71	Vertigo 6059 048	Reno, Nevada/Desert Inn	8
72	Philips 6006 197	Da Doo Ron Ron/Never Again	10
73	Vertigo 6059 081	Devil In Disguise/Thro' My Eyes	5
73	Elektra K 12111	These Days/Same Old Man	5
71	Vertigo 6360 034	IF YOU SAW THRO' MY EYES (LP, gatefold sleeve, swirl label)	25
72	Vertigo 6360 056	TIGERS WILL SURVIVE (LP, gatefold sleeve, swirl label)	25
73	Elektra K 42144	VALLEY HI (LP, gatefold sleeve)	20
74	Elektra K 42160	SOME DAYS YOU EAT THE BEAR, SOME DAYS THE BEAR EATS YOU (LP)	20
76	CBS 81316	GO FOR BROKE (LP)	18
77	CBS 81936	HIT AND RUN (LP)	15

(see also Pyramid, Fairport Convention, Matthews Southern Comfort, Plainsong, Hi-Fi)

JOE MATTHEWS

68	Sue WI 4046	Sorry Ain't Good Enough/You Better Mend Your Ways	50

MILT MATTHEWS

75	London HLF 10479	All These Changes/When Kids Rule The World	10

RANDY MATTHEWS

70s	Myrrh MXX 1035	NOW DO YOU UNDERSTAND (LP, gatefold sleeve)	20

TOBIN MATTHEWS

63	Warner Brothers WB 117	Can't Stop Talking About You/When You Came Along	6

WINSTON MATTHEWS

71	Banana BA 329	Sun Is Shining/INN KEEPERS: My Friend (B-side actually "The Pressure Is On" by Purpleites)	15

MATTHEWS SOUTHERN COMFORT

70	Uni UNS 513	Colorado Springs Eternal/The Struggle	10
70	Uni UNS 521	Ballad Of Obray Ramsey/Parting	7
70	Uni UNS 526	Woodstock/Scion	5
70	Uni UNLS 108	MATTHEWS SOUTHERN COMFORT (LP)	25
70	Uni UNLS 112	SECOND SPRING (LP, with lyric insert)	22
70	Uni MKPS 2015	LATER THAT SAME YEAR... (LP)	18

(see also Ian Matthews, Marc Ellington, Southern Comfort)

MATUMBI

73	G.G. GG 4540	Brother Louie Parts 1 & 2	10

HARVEY MATUSOW'S JEWS HARP BAND

69	Head HDS 4004	Afghan Red/Wet Socks	8
69	Head HDLS 6001	WAR BETWEEN THE FATS & THE THINS (LP)	25

MAUDS

67	Mercury MF 1000	Hold On/C'mon And Move	10
68	Mercury MF 1062	Soul Drippin'/Forever Gone	10

SUSAN MAUGHAN

61	Philips BF 1216	Mama Do The Twist/Blue Night In Yokohama	15
62	Philips BF 1236	Baby Doll Twist/Some Of These Days	15
62	Philips 326 533BF	I've Got To Learn To Forget/I Didn't Mean What I Said	8
62	Philips 326 544BF	Bobby's Girl/Come A Little Closer	6
63	Philips 326 562BF	Hand A Handkerchief To Helen/I'm A Lonely One Too	6
63	Philips 326 586BF	She's New To You/Don't Get Carried Away	6
63	Philips BF 1266	The Verdict Is Guilty/Bachelor Girl	6
64	Philips BF 1301	Hey Lover/Stop Your Foolin'	6
64	Philips BF 1336	Kiss Me Sailor/Call On Me	6
64	Philips BF 1363	Little Things Mean A Lot/That Other Place	15
64	Philips BF 1382	Make Him Mine/South American Joe	7

MINT VALUE £

65	Philips BF 1399	You Can Never Get Away From You/Don't Be Afraid	6
65	Philips BF 1417	When She Walks Away/Come Along Down And See	6
65	Philips BF 1445	Poor Boy/Your Girl	6
66	Philips BF 1495	Come And Get Me/Don't Love Him Too Much	6
66	Philips BF 1518	Where The Bullets Fly/I'll Never Stop Loving You	6
67	Philips BF 1564	Don't Go Home (My Little Darlin')/Somebody To Love	6
68	Philips BF 1713	Cable Car For Two/Off My Mind	6
69	Philips BF 1824	We Really Go Together/I'll Never Forget You	5
71	Spark SRL 1049	I Can't Make You Love Me/I'm Gonna Get That Guy	8
71	Spark SRL 1054	I Saw A Rainbow/Love Of The Lonely	6
62	Philips BBE 12525	HI, I'M SUSAN MAUGHAN AND I SING (EP)	30
63	Philips BBE 12549	FOUR BEAUX AND A BELLE (EP)	30
62	Philips 433 621 BE	EFFERVESCENT MISS MAUGHAN (EP)	30
63	Philips 433 641 BE	MORE OF MAUGHAN (EP)	30
63	Philips 632 300 BL	I WANNA BE BOBBY'S GIRL BUT ... (LP)	55
64	Philips BL 7577	SWINGIN' SUSAN (LP)	35
65	Philips BL 7637	SENTIMENTAL SUSAN (LP)	35
67	Wing WL 1105	BOBBY'S GIRL (LP)	15
69	Fontana SFL 13135	HEY LOOK ME OVER (LP)	12

MAU-MAUS

82	Pax PAX 6	SOCIETY'S REJECTS (EP)	18
82	Pax PAX 8	No Concern/Clampdown/Why Do We Suffer (p/s)	6
83	Pax/Paragon PAX 12	FACTS OF WAR (EP)	15
85	Rebellion REBEL 01	TEAR DOWN THE WALLS (EP)	15
85	Rebellion REBEL 1202	SCARRED FOR LIFE (12" EP)	15
83	Pax PAX 16	LIVE AT THE MARPLES (LP)	20
84	Pax PAX 20	RUNNING WITH THE PACK (LP)	20

MAUREENY WISHFULL

68	Moonshine WO 2388	THE MAUREENY WISHFULL ALBUM (LP, 300 copies, beware of counterfeits)	85

(see also Jimmy Page, Big Jim Sullivan, John Williams)

PAUL MAURIAT

67	Philips BF 1637	Love Is Blue (L'Amour Est Bleu)/Une Petite Cantate	5

MAURICE & MAC

68	Chess CRS 8074	You Left The Water Running/You're The One	18
68	Chess CRS 8081	Why Don't You Try Me/Lean On Me	20

(see also Radiants)

MAX & ELAINE

73	Ackee ACK 516	I'm Leaving/Version	6

(see also Max Romeo)

MAX & GREGORY

73	Ackee ACK 525	My Jamaican Collie/Push It Down, Rub It Up	10

(see also Max Romeo)

SMILEY MAXEDON & HIS OKAW VALLEY BOYS

54	Columbia SCMC 3	Crazy To Care/In The Window Of My Heart (export issue)	25

JOE S. MAXEY

73	Action ACT 4607	Sign Of The Crab/May The Best Man Win (actually plays Packers' "Hole In The Wall"/"Go Ahead On")	12

MAX HEADROOM & CARPARKS

80	Parlophone R 6034	Don't Panic/Rhythm And Bluebeat (p/s)	30

MAX GROUP

69	Fab FAB 110	Abraham Vision/My Heart Was Breaking	10

MAXI

73	Decca F 13394	Do I Dream/Here Today And Gone Tomorrow	10

MAXI, DICK & TWINK

70	Columbia DB 8663	Things You Hear About Me/Catch The Bride's Bouquet	5

(This single does not feature Twink from Pink Fairies.)

MAXIE (Romeo) & GLEN

71	G.G. GG 4520	Jordan River (actually by Max Romeo & Glen Adams)/ GLEN ADAMS:Version Two	12

(see also Max Romeo, Ethiopians)

ERNST MAXIM

57	Parlophone R 4319	Four Walls/The Star You Wished Upon Last Night (78)	8

MAXIMILIAN

61	London HLX 9356	The Snake/The Wanderer	50

(see also Del Shannon)

MAXIM'S TRASH

79	Gimp GIMP 1	Disco Girls/Blu Shoes (plastic p/s & inner, hand-stamped white labels, tracks actually recorded in 1975)	40

(see also Sunset Boys, Captain Sensible, Johnny Moped)

MAXIMUM BAND

68	Fab FAB 51	Cupid/Hold Me Tight	6

MAXIMUM BREED

69	Revolution REV 1	Sitting In The Park/You've Got It	6

ERNEST MAXIN ORCHESTRA

57	Parlophone R 4319	Four Walls/The Star You Wished Upon Last Night	6
60	Top Rank JAR 267	On The Beach/Take A Giant Step	6
60	Top Rank JAR 335	Conspiracy Of Hearts/No Orchids For My Lady	6

MINT VALUE £

MAXINE

70 Smash SMA 2301 — My Boy Lollipop/Everybody Needs Love 6

BRIAN MAXINE

72 EMI Starline SRS 5140 — BRIAN MAXINE SINGS (LP) 12
(see also Fairport Convention)

MAX WEBSTER (BAND)

79 Capitol CLP 16079 — Paradise Skies/The Party (picture disc) 5
79 Capitol 12YCL 16079 — Paradise Skies/The Party/Let Your Man Fly (12") 10
81 Mercury MER 59 — Battlescar/April In Toledo (p/s) 10
78 Capitol EST 11776 — MEETING UP MY SLEEVE (LP) 12
79 Capitol EST 11937 — A MILLION VACATIONS (LP) 12
80 Mercury 6337 144 — UNIVERSAL JUVENILES (LP) 12
(see also Rush)

HOLLY MAXWELL

69 Buddah 201 056 — Suffer/No-One Else 6

BILLY MAY & HIS ORCHESTRA

55 Capitol CL 14210 — Loop-De-Loop Mambo/Rudolph The Red-Nosed Reindeer Mambo 6
55 Capitol CL 14266 — How Important Can It Be?/Let It Happen 6
55 Capitol CL 14353 — Hernando's Hideaway/Just Between Friends 6
56 Capitol CL 14551 — Main Title From "The Man With The Golden Arm"/Suzette 12
56 Capitol CL 14609 — Nightmare/The Beat 10
57 Capitol CL 14713 — Whatever Lola Wants/Mad About The Boy 5
56 Capitol EAP 1013 — IT'S BILLY MAY TIME (EP) 8
56 Capitol EAP3 677 — SWINGING DRUMS (EP) 8
55 Tempo EXA 4 — BILLY MAY'S DIXIELAND BAND (EP) 8
53 Capitol LC 6571 — CAPITOL PRESENTS BILLY MAY AND HIS ORCHESTRA (10" LP) 12
53 Capitol LC 6623 — BIG BAND BASH (10" LP) 12
54 Capitol LC 6644 — BACCHANALIA (10" LP) 12
54 Capitol LC 6659 — NAUGHTY OPERETTA (10" LP) 12
63 Capitol T/ST 2360 — BILL'S BAG (LP) 12
67 Capitol T/ST 2560 — TODAY (LP) 12

BRIAN MAY

83 EMI EMI 5436 — Starfleet (Single Version)/Son Of Starfleet (p/s) 20
91 Parlophone R 6304 — Driven By You (Single Version)/Just One Life (p/s) 5
91 Parlophone RDJ 6304 — Driven By You (Edited Version)/(Pollarded Version)/(Special Version)/(Proper Version) (promo only, no stars on p/s) 100
91 Parlophone 12R 6304 — Driven By You (Single Version)/Driven By You (Ford Advert Version)/Just One Life (Album Version)/Just One Life (Guitar Version) (12", p/s) 8
91 Parlophone CDR 6304 — Driven By You (Single Version)/Driven By You (Ford Advert Version)/Just One Life (Album Version)/Just One Life (Guitar Version) (CD) 10
91 Parlophone CDRDJ 6304 — Driven By You (Edited Version)/(Pollarded Version)/(Special Version)/(Proper Version) (CD, promo only, no stars on p/s) 125
92 Parlophone R 6320 — Too Much Love Will Kill You/I'm Scared (Single Version) (p/s) 6
92 Parlophone CDRS 6320 — Too Much Love Will Kill You (Album Version)/I'm Scared (Single Version)/Too Much Love Will Kill You (Guitar Version)/Driven By You (New Version) (CD, red circular gatefold card p/s) 8
92 Parlophone MAYDJ 1 — Too Much Love Will Kill You/Resurrection/Last Horizon/Driven By You (CD, promo only "Back To The Light" sampler, blue circular g/fold card p/s) 18
92 Parlophone RDJ 6329 — Back To The Light (Radio Version)/Nothin' But Blue (Guitar Version) (promo only, p/s) 100
92 Parlophone CDRX 6329 — Back To The Light/Starfleet/Let Me Out (CD) 8
92 Parlophone CDR 6329 — Back To The Light/Nothin' But Blue (Guitar Version)/Blues Breaker (CD) 8
92 Parlophone CDRDJ 6329 — Back To The Light (Radio Version)/Back To The Light (Album Version)/Nothin' But Blue (Guitar Version) (CD) 10
93 Parlophone 12RPF 6351 — Resurrection/Love Token/Too Much Love Will Kill You (Live Version) (12", with Cozy Powell, picture disc with insert in PVC sleeve) 8
93 Parlophone CDRS 6351 — Resurrection/Love Token/Too Much Love Will Kill You (Live Version) (CD) 8
93 Parlophone CDR 6351 — Resurrection/Driven By You Two/Back To The Light (live)/Tie Your Mother Down (live, with Slash) (CD) 8
93 Parlophone R 6371 — Last Horizon/39 (live)/Let Your Heart Rule Your Head (p/s) 5
93 Parlophone CDRS 6371 — Last Horizon (Radio Version)/(live)/(Album Version)/We Will Rock You (live slow version)/We Will Rock You (live fast version) (CD, pop-up p/s) 8
93 Parlophone HORIZON1 — Last Horizon (CD, 1-track, promo only) 50
83 EMI SFLT 1078061 — STARFLEET PROJECT (mini-LP) 15
93 Parlophone 0 7777 80400 19 — BACK TO THE LIGHT (LP, textured sleeve) 20
93 Parlophone CDPCSD X123 — BACK TO THE LIGHT (Commemorative Issue) (gold CD, 10,000 only, stickered jewel case) 30
(see also Queen, MC Spy-D & 'Friends', Eddie Howell, Holly Johnson, Bad News, D-Rok, Ian & Belinda, Rock Aid Armenia, Cozy Powell, Black Sabbath)

MARY MAY

64 Fontana TF 440 — Anyone Who Had A Heart/They Say It's Wonderful 12

JOHN MAYALL (& BLUESBREAKERS)

SINGLES

64 Decca F 11900 — Crawling Up A Hill/Mr. James (as John Mayall & Blues Breakers) 50
65 Decca F 12120 — Crocodile Walk/Blues City Shakedown 40
65 Immediate IM 012 — I'm Your Witchdoctor/Telephone Blues 40
66 Purdah 45-3502 — Lonely Years/Bernard Jenkins (as John Mayall & Eric Clapton, 500 copies only) 300
66 Decca F 12490 — Parchman Farm (solo)/Key To Love (B-side with Bluesbreakers) 25
66 Decca F 12506 — Looking Back/So Many Roads (as John Mayall's Bluesbreakers & Peter Green) 15
67 Decca F 12545 — Sitting In The Rain/Out Of Reach (as John Mayall's Bluesbreakers) 15
67 Decca F 12588 — Curly/Rubber Duck (as Bluesbreakers) 12
67 Decca F 12621 — Double Trouble/It Hurts Me Too (as John Mayall's Bluesbreakers) 15
67 Immediate IM 051 — I'm Your Witchdoctor/Telephone Blues (reissue,

		as John Mayall with Eric Clapton)	25
67	Decca F 12684	Suspicions (Parts 1 & 2) (as John Mayall's Bluesbreakers)	12
68	Decca F 12732	Picture On The Wall/Jenny (as John Mayall)	10
68	Decca F 12792	No Reply/She's Too Young (as John Mayall's Bluesbreakers)	10
68	Decca F 12846	The Bear/2401	8
69	Polydor 56544	Don't Waste My Time/Don't Pick A Flower	10
70	Polydor 2066 021	Thinking Of My Woman/Plan Your Revolution	10
79	DJM DJS 10918	Bottom Line/Dreamboat (p/s)	5

EP

67	Decca DFE-R 8673	THE BLUESBREAKERS WITH PAUL BUTTERFIELD	45

LPs

65	Decca LK 4680	PLAYS JOHN MAYALL — LIVE AT KLOOKS KLEEK!	70
66	Decca LK 4804	BLUES BREAKERS WITH ERIC CLAPTON (original label, mono)	50
67	Decca LK/SKL 4853	A HARD ROAD (as John Mayall & Bluesbreakers)	35
67	Decca LK/SKL 4890	CRUSADE (as John Mayall & Bluesbreakers)	35
67	Ace of Clubs ACL/SCL 1243	THE BLUES ALONE	22
68	Decca LK/SKL 4918	THE DIARY OF A BAND VOL. 1	22
68	Decca LK/SKL 4919	THE DIARY OF A BAND VOL. 2	22
68	Decca LK/SKL 4945	BARE WIRES (gatefold sleeve, as John Mayall & Blues Breakers)	22
68	Decca LK/SKL 4972	BLUES FROM LAUREL CANYON (gatefold sleeve)	22

(The above LPs were originally issued with unboxed Decca label logos. 1970s boxed-logo repressings are worth two-thirds these values.)

69	Polydor 583 571	THE TURNING POINT	22
69	Decca LK/SKL 5010	LOOKING BACK	22
69	Decca SKL 4804	BLUES BREAKERS WITH ERIC CLAPTON (reissue, original label, stereo)	35
70s	Decca LK/SKL 4804	BLUES BREAKERS WITH ERIC CLAPTON (reissue, boxed logo, mono/stereo)	18/15
70	Decca (S)PA 47	THE WORLD OF JOHN MAYALL	12
70	Polydor 583 580	EMPTY ROOMS (with lyric insert)	15
70	Polydor 2425 020	U.S.A. UNION	15
71	Decca SPA 138	THE WORLD OF JOHN MAYALL VOL. 2	12
71	Polydor 2657 005	BACK TO THE ROOTS (2-LP)	18
71	Polydor 2483 016	BEYOND THE TURNING POINT	15
71	Decca SKL 5086	THRU THE YEARS	15
71	Polydor 2425 085	MEMORIES	15
72	Polydor 2425 103	JAZZ-BLUES FUSION	15
73	Polydor 2391 047	MOVING ON	15
75	ABC ABCL 5115	NEW YEAR, NEW BAND, NEW COMPANY (gatefold sleeve)	12
76	Polydor 2482 272	JOHN MAYALL	12

(see also Paul Butterfield, Eric Clapton, Jack Bruce, Peter Green, McGuinness Flint, Johnny Almond Music Machine, Alan Skidmore, Mick Taylor, Dick Heckstall-Smith, Keef Hartley, Paul Williams, Ray Warleigh, Colosseum, Henry Lowther, Jon Mark, Aynsley Dunbar, Fleetwood Mac)

MAY BLITZ

70	Vertigo 6360 007	MAY BLITZ (LP, gatefold sleeve, swirl label)	40
71	Vertigo 6360 037	THE 2ND OF MAY (LP, gatefold sleeve, swirl label)	75

(see also Bakerloo)

MAYDAY

80	Reddingtons R.R. DAN 2	Day After Day/Love In The Spaceage (p/s)	8

JOHN MAYER (GROUP)

66	Columbia DB 8037	Acka Raga (as John Mayer's I-J-7)/Gana (as John Mayer & Joe Harriott)	8
60s	National Petrol W 1	"Music For People Who Go Your Own Way" Themes 1 & 2 (p/s, with Frank Cordell)	10
67	Columbia SX 6122	INDO-JAZZ FUSIONS (LP)	30
69	Sonet SNTF 603	ETUDES (LP, as John Mayer Indo-Jazz Fusions)	18

(see also Joe Harriott & John Mayer, Radha Krishna)

NATHANIEL MAYER & FABULOUS TWILIGHTS

62	HMV POP 1041	Village Of Love/I Want A Woman	80

CURTIS MAYFIELD

70	Buddah 2011 055	(Don't Worry) If There's A Hell Below We're All Going To Go (Edit)/ The Makings Of You	7
71	Buddah 2011 080	Move On Up/Give It Up/Beautiful Brother Of Mine (maxi-single)	6
71	Buddah 2011 101	We Got To Have Peace/People Get Ready	6
72	Buddah 2011 119	Keep On Keepin' On/Stone Junkie	6
72	Buddah 2011 141	Freddie's Dead (Theme From "Superfly")/Underground	6
72	Buddah 2011 156	Superfly/Give Me Your Love (Love Song)	6
73	Buddah 2011 187	Back To The World (edit)/The Other Side Of Town	6
74	Buddah BDS 402	Kung Fu/Right On For The Darkness	6
74	Buddah BDS 410	Move On Up/Give It Up	6
75	Buddah BDS 426	Mother's Son/Love Me Right In The Pocket	6
71	Buddah 2318 015	CURTIS (LP, gatefold sleeve)	22
71	Buddah 2659 004	CURTIS/LIVE (2-LP)	22
72	Buddah 2318 045	ROOTS (LP, gatefold sleeve)	15
72	Buddah 2318 065	SUPERFLY (LP, soundtrack, gatefold sleeve)	20
73	Buddah 2318 085	BACK TO THE WORLD (LP, gatefold sleeve)	12
73	Buddah 2318 091	CURTIS IN CHICAGO (LP, TV soundtrack, gatefold sleeve, with Impressions, Jerry Butler, Gene Chandler & Leroy Hutson)	15
74	Buddah 2318 099	SWEET EXORCIST (LP)	15
74	Buddah BDLP 2001	CURTIS/LIVE (2-LP, reissue)	18
74	Buddah BDLP 4010	CLAUDINE (LP, soundtrack, with Gladys Knight)	15
74	Buddah BDLH 5001	SWEET EXORCIST (LP, reissue)	12
74	Buddah BDLH 5005	CURTIS (LP, reissue)	12
74	Buddah BDLH 5006	ROOTS (LP, reissue)	12

MINT VALUE £

74	Buddah BDLP 4015	MOVE ON UP (THE BEST OF CURTIS MAYFIELD) (LP)	12
74	Buddah BDLP 4029	GOT TO FIND A WAY (LP)	12
75	Buddah BDLP 4033	THERE'S NO PLACE LIKE AMERICA TODAY (LP)	12
76	Buddah BDLP 4042	GIVE GET TAKE AND HAVE (LP)	12
76	Atlantic K 56248	SPARKLE (LP, soundtrack, with Aretha Franklin)	12

(see also Impressions, Blow Monkeys)

PERCY MAYFIELD

63	HMV POP 1185	The River's Invitation/Baby Please	10
76	Speciality SPE 5007	Please Send Me Someone To Love/The River's Invitation	6
67	HMV CLP/CSD 3572	MY JUG AND I (LP)	40

MAYFIELD'S MULE

69	Parlophone R 5817	Double Dealing Woman/(Drinking My) Moonshine (some in p/s)	30/15
70	Parlophone R 5843	I See A River/"Queen" Of Rock'n'Roll	20
70	Parlophone R 5858	We Go Rollin'/My Way Of Living	18

(see also Elastic Band, Sweet, Amen Corner, Andy Scott)

MAYHEM

82	Riot City RIOT 13	GENTLE MURDER (EP)	5
83	Riot City RIOT 24	PULLING PUPPET STRINGS (EP)	5

MAYHEM

85	Vigilante VIG 1	Bloodrush/Addictive Risk (p/s)	6
85	Vigilante VIG 1T	Bloodrush/Addictive Risk (12", p/s)	10

BILL MAYNARD

57	Decca F 10868	Hey Liley, Liley Lo/Who Needs You	8
57	Decca F 10868	Hey Liley, Liley Lo/Who Needs You (78)	10

JENNY MAYNARD

68	Inter-zel DR 001	He Gives Me Love/Something Here In My Heart	5

(TOOTS &) THE MAYTALS

63	Blue Beat BB 176	Hallelujah/Helping Ages Past	20
64	Blue Beat BB 215	He Is Real/Domino	20
64	Blue Beat BB 220	Pain In My Belly/BUSTER'S ALL STARS: City Riot	20
64	Blue Beat BB 231	Dog War/RECO & CREATORS: I'll Be Home	25
64	Blue Beat BB 245	Little Slea (song actually "Little Flea")/Don't Talk (song actually "Pain In My Belly") (both sides miscredited as V. Maytals)	22
64	Blue Beat BB 254	Sweet Love/PRINCE BUSTER: Wings Of A Dove	20
64	Blue Beat BB 255	Judgement Day/Goodbye Jane	20
64	Blue Beat BB 270	You've Got Me Spinning/Lovely Walking	20
64	R&B JB 130	Hurry Up/Love Divide	18
64	R&B JB 141	Another Chance/FRANKIE ANDERSON: Always On A Sunday	18
64	R&B JB 153	Give Me Your Love/He Will Provide	18
64	R&B JB 164	Hello Honey/ROLAND ALPHONSO: Crime Wave	35
64	R&B JB 174	Christmas Feelings/Let's Kiss	18
65	Blue Beat BB 281	Looking Down The Street/PRINCE BUSTER: Blues Market	20
65	Blue Beat BB 299	Light Of The World/Lovely Walking	25
65	Blue Beat BB 306	Ska War (song actually "Treating Me Bad")/SKATALITES: Perhaps	30
65	Ska Beat JB 202	Let's Jump/Joy And Jean	20
65	Island WI 200	Never You Change/What's On Your Mind	22
65	Island WI 213	My New Name/It's No Use	22
65	Black Swan WI 464	John James/THEO BECKFORD: Sailing On	22
66	Doctor Bird DB 1019	If You Act This Way/SIR LORD COMIC & HIS COWBOYS: Ska-ing West	40
66	Doctor Bird DB 1038	Bam Bam/So Mad In Love	20
68	Pyramid PYR 6030	54-46, That's My Number/ROLAND ALPHONSO: Dreamland	25
68	Pyramid PYR 6043	Struggle/ROLAND ALPHONSO: Stream Of Life	18
68	Pyramid PYR 6048	Just Tell Me/Reborn	18
68	Pyramid PYR 6050	Bim Today, Bam Tomorrow/Hold On	18
68	Pyramid PYR 6052	We Shall Overcome/DESMOND DEKKER & ACES: Fu Manchu	22
68	Pyramid PYR 6055	Schooldays/Big Man	15
68	Pyramid PYR 6057	Do The Reggay/BEVERLEY'S ALLSTARS: Motoring	22
68	Pyramid PYR 6064	Scare Him/In My Heart	15
69	Pyramid PYR 6066	Don't Trouble Trouble/BEVERLEY'S ALLSTARS: Double Action	18
69	Pyramid PYR 6070	Aldina/Hold On	18
69	Pyramid PYR 6073	Pressure Drop/BEVERLEY'S ALLSTARS: Express	12
69	Pyramid PYR 6074	Sweet And Dandy/Oh Yeah	12
69	Trojan TR 7709	Pressure Drop/BEVERLEY'S ALLSTARS: Smoke Screen	10
69	Nu Beat NB 031	My Testimony/JOHNSON BOYS: One Dollar Of Soul (actually by Ethiopians)	10
69	Trojan TR 7711	Monkey Man/Night And Day	10
70	Trojan TR 7726	Sweet And Dandy/54-46, That's My Number	8
70	Trojan TR 7741	Bla Bla Bla/Reborn	6
70	Trojan TR 7757	Water Melon/She's My Scorcher	6
70	Trojan TR 7786	Doctor Lester/Sun, Moon And Star	6
70	Summit SUM 8510	Peeping Tom/BEVERLEY'S ALLSTARS: Version	6
71	Trojan TR 7808	54-46 Was My Number/BEVERLEY'S ALLSTARS: 54-46 Instrumental	6
71	Trojan TR 7849	Johnny Cool Man/BEVERLEY's ALLSTARS: Version	5
71	Summit SUM 8513	Monkey Girl/BEVERLEY'S ALLSTARS: Version	6
71	Summit SUM 8520	One Eye Enos/BEVERLEY'S ALLSTARS: Enos Version	6
71	Summit SUM 8527	It's You/BEVERLEY'S ALLSTARS: Version	6
71	Summit SUM 8529	Walk With Love/BEVERLEY'S ALLSTARS: Version	6
71	Summit SUM 8533	Never You Change/BEVERLEY'S ALLSTARS: Version	6
72	Attack ATT 8042	It Was Written Down/Sweet And Dandy	5
72	Summit SUM 8536	Thy Kingdom Come/BEVERLEY'S ALLSTARS: Version	6
72	Summit SUM 8537	It Must Be True Love/BEVERLEY'S ALLSTARS: Version	6
72	Blue Mountain BM 1020	Christmas Song/I Can't Believe	6
72	Dynamic DYN 438	Redemption Song	6

72 Trojan TR 7865 Louie Louie/Pressure Drop '72 . . . 5
73 Dragon DRA 1007 Sit Right Down/Screwface Underground/Pomps & Pride (as Toots & Maytals) . . . 5
73 Dragon DRA 1013 Funky Kingston/Country Road (as Toots & Maytals) . . . 5
73 Dragon DRA 1016 In The Dark/Sailing On (as Toots & Maytals) . . . 5
74 Dragon DRA 1021 Fever/It Was Written Down . . . 5
74 Dragon DRA 1024 Time Tough/Time Tough Version . . . 5
74 Dragon DRA 1026 Sailing On/If You Act This Way (as Toots & Maytals) . . . 5
64 Ska Beat JBL 1113 PRESENTING THE MAYTALS (NEVER GROW OLD) (LP) . . . 150
66 Doctor Bird DLM 5003 THE SENSATIONAL MAYTALS (LP) . . . 150
70 Trojan TBL 107 MONKEY MAN (LP) . . . 30
73 Trojan TRLS 65 FROM THE ROOTS (LP) . . . 25
73 Dragon DRLS 5002 FUNKY KINGSTON (LP) . . . 18
74 Dragon DRLS 5004 IN THE DARK (LP) . . . 15
74 Prince Buster PB 11 ORIGINAL GOLDEN OLDIES VOLUME 3 (LP) . . . 22
(see also Vikings, Flames, Philip James & Blues Busters, Don Drummond, Stranger, Lord Creator, Larry Marshall, Derrick Morgan, Brentwood Road Allstars, Roland Alphonso, Charmers)

MAYTONES

68 Blue Cat BS 149 Billy Goat/Call You Up . . . 12
69 Blue Cat BS 152 Loving Reggae/Musical Beat . . . 12
69 Blue Cat BS 166 Copper Girl/Love . . . 12
69 Blue Cat BS 173 We Nah Tek You Lick/Dig Away De Money . . . 12
69 Camel CA 27 Sentimental Reason/Lover Girl . . . 8
69 Songbird SB 1009 I've Been Loving You/Memphis Reggae . . . 10
69 Songbird SB 1010 Gin Gan Goolie/I'm Thirsty . . . 7
70 Punch PH 35 Serious Love/CHARLIE ACE: Musical Combination . . . 8
70 Explosion EX 2012 Funny Man/G.G. ALLSTARS: Champion . . . 10
70 Explosion EX 2013 Sentimental Reason/Lover Girl . . . 7
70 Explosion EX 2014 Barrabus/G.G. ALLSTARS: Barrabus Part 2 (B-side actually "This Kind Of Life") . . . 12
70 Explosion EX 2027 Cecelia (actually by Keeling Beckford)/Chariot Without Horse (B-side actually "Willie My Darling") . . . 6
70 Explosion EX 2033 Another Festival/Happy Time . . . 6
70 Bullet BU 446 I Don't Like To Interfere/Preaching Love . . . 7
70 Camel CA 47 Black And White/GLORIA'S ALLSTARS: Jumbo Jet . . . 10
70 Camel CA 49 Since You Left/GLORIA'S ALL STARS: Bird Wing . . . 8
71 Duke DU 116 Babylon A Fall/TONY KING: Version Buggy . . . 10
71 Camel CA 61 Judas (actually by Gladstone Anderson & Followers)/Mi Nah Tek . . . 7
71 G.G. GG 4508 Cleanliness/G.G. ALL STARS: Cleanliness Version 2 . . . 7
71 G.G. GG 4511 Let The Version Play/Lonely Nights . . . 7
71 G.G. GG 4522 Black And White/TREVOR BROWN: Mr. Brown . . . 6
71 G.G. GG 4525 Bongo Man Rise/ROY & BIM: Remember . . . 6
72 G.G. GG 4530 Donkey Face/G.G. ALL STARS: Donkey Face – Version . . . 6
72 G.G. GG 4531 As Long As You Love Me (Side One)/As Long As You Love Me (Side Two) . . . 6
72 Attack ATT 8029 Hands And Feet/LLOYD & CAREY: Scorpion . . . 6
72 Grape GR 3028 If Loving You Was Wrong/FLOWERS & ALVIN: In De Pum Pum . . . 6
72 Pama PM 846 I'm Feeling Lonely/G.G. ALLSTARS: Version . . . 6
72 Explosion EX 2076 Brown Girl/SHORTY PERRY: Half-Way-Tree Rock . . . 6
73 Pama PM 871 All Over The World People Are Changing/Changing World (Dubwise) . . . 5
73 Bread BR 1114 All Over The World People Are Changing/Changing World (Dubwise) . . . 5
73 Bullet BU 528 People Get Funny/G.G. ALL STARS: Version . . . 5
(see also Vern & Alvin, Vern & Son, Roland Alphonso, G.G. Rhythm Section, Cynthia Richards, Max Romeo, Charlie Ace, Dennis Alcapone)

MAZE (U.K.)

66 Reaction 591 009 Hello Stranger/Telephone . . . 80
67 MGM MGM 1368 Catari Catari/Easy Street . . . 40
(see also M.I. Five, Deep Purple)

MAZE (U.S.)

82 Capitol 12CL 211 Joy And Pain/Happy (12") . . . 8
82 Capitol 12CL 244 Before I Let Go/Golden Time Of Day (12") . . . 8
77 Capitol E-ST 11607 MAZE FEATURING FRANKIE BEVERLY (LP) . . . 12

MAZZY STAR

93 R. T. Singles Club 45 rev 19 Five String Serenade/Under My Car (p/s) . . . 10
96 Capitol CL 781 FLOWERS IN DECEMBER (EP, blue vinyl) . . . 8
90 Rough Trade ROUGH 158 SHE HANGS BRIGHTLY (LP) . . . 30

JACKIE McAULEY

71 Dawn DNS 1011 Turning Green/It's Alright . . . 7
72 Dawn DNS 1020 Rocking Shoes/One Fine Day . . . 7
71 Dawn DNLS 3023 JACKIE McAULEY (LP) . . . 50
(see also Them, Belfast Gypsies, Trader Horne, Freaks Of Nature)

McAULEY SCHENKER GROUP

90 EMI EMPD 127 Anytime/What We Need/Anytime (Edit) (12", picture disc) . . . 8
90 EMI Electrola CDEM 127 Anytime (LP Version)/What We Need/Anytime (Single Edit) (CD) . . . 8
89 EMI CDP 518941 SAVE YOURSELF SPECIMEN DISC (CD, promo, interviews/album excerpts) . . . 18
(see also Michael Schenker, Michael Schenker Group)

GERRY McAVOY

79 Bridgehouse BHS 004 Street Talk/Many Rivers To Cross (p/s) . . . 10

JIMMY McBEATH

67 Topic 12T 173 WILD ROVER NO MORE (LP, blue label with booklet) . . . 12

MINT VALUE £

NICKO McBRAIN
91 EMI NICKO 1 — Rhythm Of The Beast/Beehive Boogie (p/s) 5
91 EMI NICKOPD 1 — Rhythm Of The Beast/McBrain Damage Interview (shaped picture disc with insert & plinth).... 8
(see also Iron Maiden, Pat Travers)

FRANKIE McBRIDE
67 Emerald MD 1081 — Five Little Fingers/Do You Mind If You Leave Me Sleeping.... 5

DAN McCAFFERTY
75 Mountain TOP 5 — Watcha Gonna Do About It/Nightingale 5
75 Mountain DAN 1 — Stay With Me Baby/Out Of Time/Watcha Gonna Do About It (p/s) 7
75 Mountain TOPS 102 — DAN McCAFFERTY (LP, with inner sleeve) 12
(see also Nazareth, Sensational Alex Harvey Band, Mitchell/Coe Mysteries, Roger Glover)

JERRY McCAIN
69 Python 02 — Homogenised Love/728 Texas (99 copies only) 45

CASH McCALL
63 Ember EMB S 173 — Anytime/From The Very First Rose 12
65 Ember EMB S 204 — Many Are The Words (I've Left Unspoken)/Buenos Noches 12

CASH McCALL
67 Chess CRS 8056 — It's Wonderful (To Be In Love)/Let's Try It Over.... 15

DARRELL McCALL
61 Capitol CL 15196 — My Kind Of Lovin'/Beyond Imagination.... 7
63 Philips 304 002 BF — Dear One/I've Been Known 10
63 Philips BF 1259 — Hud/No Place To Hide 7

TOUSSAINT McCALL
67 Pye International 7N 25420 — Nothing Takes The Place Of You/Shimmy 18
72 Mojo 2092 035 — Nothing Takes The Place Of You/Shimmy (reissue).... 6

NOEL McCALLA
80 Direction 58-8731 — Beggin'/Ain't That Peculiar/One More Heartache/Shake Me, Wake Me.... 5

DAVID McCALLUM
66 Capitol CL 15439 — Communication/My Carousel.... 7
66 Capitol CL 15474 — In The Garden/The House On Breckenridge Lane.... 5
66 Capitol (S)T 2432 — MUSIC ... A PART OF ME (LP).... 15
66 Capitol (S)T 2498 — MUSIC ... A BIT MORE OF ME (LP).... 15

McCALMANS
68 One Up OU 2161 — McCALMANS' FOLK (LP).... 15

JIM McCANN
72 Polydor 2489 053 — McCANNED! (LP) 25
(see also Ludlows)

LES McCANN (LTD)
60 Vogue V 2417 — Fish This Week/Vakushna (as Les McCann Ltd) 5
67 Mercury MF 973 — All/Bucket O'Grease.... 8
69 Atlantic 584 284 — With These Hands/Burnin' Coal.... 5
60 Vogue LAE 12238 — THE TRUTH (LP).... 12
66 Mercury LML 4026 — PLAYS THE HITS (LP, mono) 15
69 Atlantic 588 176 — MUCH LES (LP) 12
60s Fontana 688 150ZL — THE WAILERS! (with Gerald Wilson Orchestra) 12

McCARTHY
86 Wall Of Salmon MAC 001 — In Purgatory/The Comrade Era/Something Wrong Somewhere (foldover p/s in poly bag, white labels) 20
86 Pink PINKY 12 — Red Sleeping Beauty/From The Damned (stickered p/s) 8
86 Pink PINKY 12T — Red Sleeping Beauty/The Comrade Era/From The Damned/ For The Fat Lady (12", p/s with foldover insert) 8
87 Pink PINKY 17 — Frans Hals/The Fall (p/s) 5
87 Pink PINKY 17T — Frans Hals/The Fall (Remix)/Kill Kill Kill Kill/Frans Hals (Version) (12", p/s) 8
87 September SEPT 1 — The Well Of Loneliness/Antiamericancretin/Unfortunately (p/s).... 6
87 September SEPT 1T — The Well Of Loneliness/Bad Dreams/Someone Worse Off/ Antiamericancretin/Unfortunately (12", p/s) 8
88 September SEPTT 4 — This Nelson Rockefeller (p/s).... 10
(see also Stereolab)

KEITH McCARTHY
67 Coxsone CS 7014 — Everybody Rude Now/BASES: Beware 22

LYN & GRAHAM McCARTHY
65 Columbia DB 7584 — Seven Doves/Out After Ale 6
66 Columbia DB 7921 — I Can't Help But Wonder/There's Got To Be Love 6
66 Columbia DB 8087 — The Turkey's Trial/Bitter Withy 6
68 Columbia DB 8422 — I Think It's Going To Rain/Once I Was 7
68 RCA RCA 1759 — Scarborough Fair — Canticle/Wild Berries 5

MARY McCARTHY
67 CBS 2832 — The Folk I Love/You Know He Did.... 7
67 CBS 2987 — Happy Days And Lonely Night/Easy Kind Of Love.... 6

CECIL McCARTNEY
68 Columbia DB 8474 — Hey Aleuthia I Want You/Liquid Blue 10
69 Columbia DB 8595 — Orange And Green/Cloudy 7
68 Columbia S(C)X 6283 — OM (LP).... 22

LINDA McCARTNEY
(see under Suzy & The Red Stripes)

PAUL McCARTNEY/WINGS

SINGLES

Year	Label/Cat. No.	Title/Details	£
71	Apple R 5889	Another Day/Oh Woman, Oh Why	5
71	Apple R 5914	The Back Seat Of My Car/Heart Of The Country (as Paul & Linda McCartney)	5
72	Apple R 5932	Love Is Strange/I Am Your Singer (unreleased)	800
72	Apple R 5936	Give Ireland Back To The Irish/(Version) (as Wings, yellow 'Wings' die-cut sl.)	10
73	Apple R 5985	My Love/The Mess (as McCartney's Wings, later as Paul McCartney/Wings)	20/5
78	Parlophone R 6020	I've Had Enough/Deliver Your Children (p/s, as Wings)	6
80	Parlophone 12R 6039	Temporary Secretary/Secret Friend (12", p/s)	30
82	Parlophone R 6054	Ebony And Ivory/Rainclouds (unreleased sepia-toned 'studio photo' p/s; beware of clever counterfeits)	50
82	Epic A 11-2729	The Girl Is Mine (with Michael Jackson)/MICHAEL JACKSON: Can't Get Outta The Rain (picture disc)	25
84	Parlophone 12RP 6080	No More Lonely Nights (Extended Version)/Silly Love Songs/ No More Lonely Nights (Ballad) (12", picture disc)	20
84	Parlophone 12R(DJ) 6080	No More Lonely Nights (Extended Version)/Silly Love Songs/No More Lonely Nights (Ballad) (12", promo, blue 'Give My Regards To Broad Street' label, black die-cut sleeve)	100
84	Parlophone RP 6086	We All Stand Together/We All Stand Together (Humming Version) (with Frog Chorus, shaped picture disc, some in printed PVC sleeve)	25/8
85	Parlophone RP 6118	Spies Like Us/My Carnival (shaped picture disc)	25
85	Parlophone 12RP 6118	Spies Like Us (Party Mix)/Spies Like Us (Alternative Mix)/Spies Like Us (DJ Version)/My Carnival (Party Mix) (12", picture disc)	20
86	Parlophone 10R 6133	Press/It's Not True/Press (Video Edit) (10", circular foldout p/s)	10
87	Parlophone TCR 6145	Pretty Little Head/Write Away (cassette)	5
86	Parlophone R 6148/ R 6018	Only Love Remains/Tough On A Tightrope//Mull Of Kintyre/Girls' School (p/s, stickered double pack in PVC sleeve, no p/s on R 6018)	10
87	Parlophone CDR 6170	Once Upon A Long Ago/Back On My Feet/Don't Get Around Much Anymore/ Kansas City (CD, card sleeve with anti-static inner)	15
87	A&M FREE 21	Long Tall Sally (live)/I Saw Her Standing There (live) (p/s, free with "The Prince's Trust 10th Anniversary Birthday Party" LP [AMA 3906])	6
89	Parlophone RX 6223	This One/The Long And Winding Road (p/s, envelope pack with 6 postcards)	10

CONTRACT PRESSINGS

Year	Label/Cat. No.	Title/Details	£
71	Apple R 5914	The Back Seat Of My Car/Heart Of The Country (Decca)	35
73	Apple R 5987	Live & Let Die/Mess Around (Decca)	35
70s	Capitol R 5985	My Love/The Mess	35
70s	Capitol R 5997	Band On The Run (Edited Version)/(Full Version)	50

PROMO SINGLES

Year	Label/Cat. No.	Title/Details	£
74	EMI R 5997	Band On The Run (Edited Version)/(Full Version) (demo)	90
74	Apple R 5999	Junior's Farm (Edited Version)/Junior's Farm (Full Version) (demo)	80
75	Apple R 5999	Sally G/Junior's Farm (reversed sides, demo)	120
76	Parlophone R 6014	Silly Love Songs (Edited Version)/Silly Love Songs (Full Version) (demo)	50
76	Parlophone R 6015	Let 'Em In (Edited Version)/Let 'Em In (Full Version) (demo)	50
77	Capitol R 6018	Mull Of Kintyre (Edited Version)/Girls' School (Edited Version) (demo)	50
77	MPL Publishing MPL 1	We've Moved! (music publishing sampler with excerpts by Wings, Peggy Lee, Gene Vincent, Frank Sinatra, etc.; some with press pack & insert)	250/200
78	Parlophone R 6019	With A Little Luck (Edited Version)/Backwards Traveller-Cuff Link (demo)	40
80	Parlophone R 6037DJ	Waterfalls (3.22) (edit)/Check My Machine (demo)	40
80	Parlophone R 6039	Temporary Secretary (1-sided demo, no p/s)	75
84	Parlophone 12RDJ 6080T	No More Lonely Nights (Mole Mix) (12", 1-sided, plain white numbered sleeve with plain white inner sleeve & insert, 250 only; beware of counterfeits with scratched [not stamped] matrix)	250
85	Parlophone RDJ 6118	Spies Like Us (DJ Version 3.46)/My Carnival (demo, white printed die-cut sleeve)	35
89	Parl. 12R LOVE 6223	This One (Lovejoy's Remix) (12", 1-sided, plain label, black die-cut sleeve)	35
89	Parlophone GOOD 1	Good Sign (6.51)/Good Sign (Groove Mix) (7.22) (12", black die-cut sleeve)	45
89	Parlophone RDJ 6235	Figure Of Eight (Edited Version 3.59)/Ou Est Le Soleil? (Edited Version 3.57) (demo, standard p/s)	30
89	Parlophone RDJ 6238	Party (Remix By Bruce Forest)/Party (different remix) (12", some copies listed as 'Party Party', some with insert)	50/35
90	Parlophone 12 SOL 1	Où Est Le Soleil? (Tub Dub Mix)/Où Est Le Soleil? (Instrumental Mix) (12", black die-cut stickered sleeve, some with insert)	45/20
93	Parlophone 12 DELIVDJ 1	Deliverance/Deliverance (Dub Mix) (12", green label, plain black die-cut sleeve)	25
93	Parlophone CDRDJ 6338	C'mon People (Radio Edit)/C'mon People (CD)	30
93	Parlophone CDRS 6347	Biker Like An Icon/Things We Said Today/Mean Woman Blues/ Midnight Special (CD, unissued)	
93	Parlophone CDRDJ 6347	Biker Like An Icon/Things We Said Today/Mean Woman Blues/ Midnight Special (CD, no inlay, jewel case with large sticker; beware of counterfeits with thicker, blurred label print & small sticker on case)	70
93	Parlophone PM LIVE 1	PAUL IS LIVE! (CD, 5-track sampler)	30
99	Parlophone PROMO WC	WORKING CLASSICAL (CD, 4-track sampler, gatefold card sleeve, promo only)	30
99	EMI RDR 004	RUN DEVIL RUN (CD, 2-track sampler, card sleeve, promo only)	18

ALBUM

Year	Label/Cat. No.	Title/Details	£
70	Apple TA/TD-PCS 7102	McCARTNEY (reel-to-reel tape, jewel case, mono/stereo)	100/50

PROMO ALBUMS

Year	Label/Cat. No.	Title/Details	£
79	Parlophone PCTCP 257	BACK TO THE EGG (LP, as Wings, MPL in-house picture disc; die-cut sleeve, matrix numbers YEX 987-2 & YEX 988-4 or -1; beware counterfeits)	1000+
79	Parlophone PCTC 257	BACK TO THE EGG (LP, box set with badge, booklet, sticker, postcard & 5 cigarette cards; with or without T-shirt; beware of counterfeits with blurred printing)	300/250
79	Capitol (no cat. no.)	MPL PRESENTS (6-LP, box set, hand-numbered, 25 only)	700

MINT VALUE £

88	Parlophone PMBOX 11-19	ALL THE BEST! ('Special Edition') (9 x 7" box set, in black die-cut sleeves, with signed 7" print; some with genuine signatures)	200/75
93	Parlophone CDPMCOLDJ 1	PAUL McCARTNEY COLLECTION (CD, 18-track sampler)	25

(see also Beatles, Country Hams, Percy 'Thrills' Thrillington, Fireman, Mike McGear, Suzy & The Red Stripes, George Martin, Spirit Of Play, Ferry Aid, Michael Jackson)

DAVE McCLAREN

71	Big BG 323	Love Is What I Bring (actually by Dave Barker & Uniques)/ RUPIE EDWARDS ALL STARS: Love Version (with U Roy Junior)	15

TOMMY McCLENNAN

75	Flyright LP 112	TRAVELIN' HIGHWAY MAN (LP)	15

DELBERT McCLINTON

62	Decca F 11541	Hully Gully/Baby Heartbreak	12

BOBBY McCLURE

(see under Bobby McLure)

CHRIS McCLURE (SECTION)

66	Decca F 12346	The Dying Swan/The Land Of The Golden Tree	10
68	Polydor 56227	Hazy People/I'm Just A Country Boy	15
68	Polydor 56259	Answer To Everything/Meditation	7
69	RCA RCA 1849	Our Song Of Love/Weather Vane	7
69	CBS 7646	You're Only Passing Time/Sing Our Song (as Chris McClure Section)	7

(see also Marmalade)

McCLUSKY BROTHERS

88	DDT DISP 15T	She Said To The Driver/Upstreet Downfall/Silent Journey (12", p/s)	8

(see also Bluebells)

BRIAN McCOLLOM FOLK GROUP

66	Pye 7N 17198	This Dusty Road/Henry Joy McCraken	5

TOMMY McCOOK & BOBBY ELLIS

75	Grove Music GMLP 002	BLAZING HORNS (LP)	30

TOMMY McCOOK (& SUPERSONICS)

63	Island WI 102	Adam's Apple/MAYTALS: Every Time (B-side actually by Tonettes)	25
63	Island WI 118	Below Zero/LEE PERRY: Never Get Weary	35
63	Island WI 124	Junior Jive/HORACE SEATON: Power	22
64	R&B JB 139	Sampson/ROY & ANNETTE: My Arms Are Waiting	35
64	R&B JB 163	Bridge View/NAOMI & CO: What Can I Do (B-side actually by Naomi & Clive)	35
64	Port-O-Jam PJ 4001	Exodus (& His Group)/LEE PERRY: Help The Weak	30
64	Port-O-Jam PJ 4003	Jam Rock/LEE PERRY: Band Minded People	35
64	Port-O-Jam PJ 4010	Road Bloack/LEE PERRY: Chatty Chatty Woman	35
64	Black Swan WI 422	Two For One/LASCELLES PERKINS: I Don't Know	25
65	Island WI 232	Rocket Ship/JUSTIN HINDS & DOMINOES: Turn Them Back	35
66	Rio R 100	Jerk Time (with Supersonics)/UNIQUES: The Journey	22
66	Rio R 101	Out Of Space (with Supersonics)/UNIQUES: Do Me Good	22
66	Rio R 103	Ska Jam/Smooth Sailing (with Supersonics)	22
66	Rio R 104	Riverton City/HEPTONES: Gunmen Coming To Town	45
66	Doctor Bird DB 1028	More Love/SILVERTONES: True Confession	22
66	Doctor Bird DB 1032	Naked City (with Supersonics)/NORMA FRASER: Heartaches	20
66	Doctor Bird DB 1047	Spanish Eyes (with Lynn Taitt)/STRANGER & HORTENSE: Loving Wine	20
66	Doctor Bird DB 1051	A Little Bit Of Heaven (& His Band)/LLOYD WILLIAMS: Sad World	22
66	Doctor Bird DB 1053	Indian Love Call (with Supersonics)/OWEN & LEON: How Would You Feel	22
66	Doctor Bird DB 1056	Danger Man (with Supersonics)/ERIC MORRIS: If I Didn't Love You	25
66	Doctor Bird DB 1061	What Now/Don't Stay Away	22
67	Doctor Bird DB 1058	Jam Session (with Supersonics)/LLOYD & GLEN: Jezebel	22
67	Island WI 3047	One Two Three Kick/TREASURE ISLE BOYS: What A Fool (B-side actually by Silvertones)	40
67	Island WI 3049	Saboo (with Supersonics)/MOVING BROTHERS: Darling I Love You	22
67	Treasure Isle TI 7017	Persian Cat/JUSTIN HINDS: Once A Man	18
67	Treasure Isle TI 7018	Saboo (with Supersonics)/MOVING BROTHERS: Darling I Love You (reissue)	20
67	Treasure Isle TI 7020	Shadow Of Your Smile/SILVERTONES: Cool Down	20
68	Treasure Isle TI 7027	Soul For Sale/SILVERTONES: In The Midnight Hour	18
68	Treasure Isle TI 7032	Venus/Music Is My Occupation (with Supersonics)	18
68	Treasure Isle TI 7039	Our Man Flint (with Supersonics)/SILVERTONES: Old Man River	18
68	Treasure Isle TI 7042	Moving (with Supersonics)/SILVERTONES: Slow And Easy	18
68	Doctor Bird DB 1135	Mad Mad World/Wonderful World (with Lloyd Williams)	22
68	Unity UN 501	Last Flight To Reggie (Reggae) City (with Stranger Cole)/Watch Dem Go	8
69	Trojan TR 642	Breaking Up/Party Time (with Supersonics) (both actually by Alton Ellis)	10
69	Trojan TR 652	Third Figure/You Should've Known Better	12
69	Trojan TR 657	When The Saints Go Marching In/SOUL OFROUS: Ease Me Up Officer (B-side actually by Righteous Flames)	12
69	Trojan TR 671	Moonshot/PHYLLIS DILLON: The Right Shot	15
69	Trojan TR 686	Tribute To Rameses/PHYLLIS DILLION: Lipstick On Your Collar	12
69	Trojan TR 7706	Black Coffee (with Supersonics)/VIC TAYLOR: Heartaches	12
69	Unity UN 506	The Avengers/LAUREL AITKEN: Donkey Man	12
69	Unity UN 534	Dream Boat/Tommy's Dream	12
69	Unity UN 535	Peanut Vendor/100,000 Tons Of Rock	12
70	Duke DU 76	The Rooster (with Supersonics) (actually by Jeff Barnes)/ PHYLLIS DILLON: Walk Through This World	10
70	Duke DU 77	Open Jaw (with Supersonics)/JOHN HOLT: The Working Kind	10
70	Duke DU 78	Key To The City (with Supersonics)/DOROTHY REID: Give It To Me	10
71	Treasure Isle TI 7058	My Best Dress/PHYLISS DILLON: One Life To Live	15
71	Treasure Isle TI 7061	Testify Version/JOHN HOLT: Let's Build Our Dreams	18
71	Treasure Isle TI 7065	Black River/JOHN HOLT: Sister Big Stuff	18
71	Treasure Isle TI 7066	Paragon's Medley Version/JOHN HOLT: Paragon's Medley	18

71	Treasure Isle TI 7070	Midnight Confession Version/PHYLLIS DILLON: Midnight Confession	15
71	Big Shot BI 585	Psalm Nine To Keep In Mind (with Observers)/Psalm Nine (Version)	10
71	Spinning Wheel SW 109	Crying Everynight (with Supersonics) (actually by Stranger Cole)/ HERMAN MARQUIS: Tom's Version	30
71	Spinning Wheel SW 110	Stupid Doctor (with Supersonics)/ROB WALKER: Grooving In Style (B-side actually by Ken Parker)	30
73	Technique TE 927	Rub It Down/Rub It Down (Version) (as Tommy McCook Stars)	6
73	G.G. GG 4539	Bad Cow Skank (with Bobby Ellis)/ GLADSTONE ANDERSON: Drummer Roach	5
70	Trojan TBL 111	GREATER JAMAICA (MOONWALK REGGAE) (LP, actually by various artists)	35
74	Attack ATLP 1007	TOMMY McCOOK (LP)	22

(see also Denis Alcapone, Dave Barker, Dennis Brown, Chuck & Joe White, Shenley Duffas, Dennis & Lizzy, Dobby Dobson, Dynamics, Alton Ellis, Ethiopians, Eagles, Emotions, Herman, Heptones, Jamaicans, Hopeton Lewis, Lloyd & Glen, Lloyd & Groovers, Bob Marley, Maytals, Melodians, Mellodities, Millions, Paragons, Hugh Roy, Karl Walker & Allstars)

JASON McCORD

65	Pye 7N 15925	It Was A Very Good Year/Song Of The Pine Tree	20

GEORGE McCORMICK

55	MGM SPC 6	Don't Fix Up The Doghouse/Gold Wedding Band (export issue)	18

McCORMICK BROTHERS

63	Polydor NH 66986	Red Hen Boogie/Blue Grass Express	50
66	Hickory LPE 1509	AUTHENTIC BLUEGRASS HITS (EP)	22

BUDD McCOY

58	RCA RCA 1106	Hiawatha/The Midnight Ride Of Paul Revere	7
58	RCA RCA 1106	Hiawatha/The Midnight Ride Of Paul Revere (78)	15

CLYDE McCOY

57	Mercury MEP 9513	DANCING TO THE BLUES (EP)	20

JOE McCOY

59	Collector JDL 81	One In A Hundred/One More Greasing	30

(JOHN) McCOY

83	Legacy LGY 9	Oh Well! (Edit)/Because You Lied (p/s)	5
83	Legacy LLM 109	MINI ALBUM (mini-LP)	10
84	Mausoleum SKULL 8373	THINK HARD (LP, with inner sleeve)	12

(see also Gillan, Samson, Mammoth, Zzebra, Split Knee Loons)

VIOLA McCOY

50s	Ristic LP 27	VIOLA McCOY 1923-1927 (10" LP)	60

McCOYS

65	Immediate IM 001	Hang On Sloopy/I Can't Explain It	7
65	Immediate IM 021	Fever/Sorrow	10
66	Immediate IM 028	Don't Worry Mother, Your Son's Heart Is Pure/Ko-Ko	10
66	Immediate IM 029	Up And Down/If You Tell A Lie	10
66	Immediate IM 034	Runaway/Come On Let's Go	10
66	Immediate IM 037	(You Make Me Feel) So Good/Every Day I Have To Cry	8
67	Immediate IM 046	I Got To Go Back/Dynamite	15
67	London HLZ 10154	Say Those Magic Words/I Wonder If She Remembers Me	22
68	Mercury MF 1067	Jesse Brady/Resurrection	8
69	Immediate IM 076	Hang On Sloopy/This Is Where We Came In	5
66	Immediate IMEP 002	HITS VOL. 1 (EP)	40
66	Immediate IMEP 003	HITS VOL. 2 (EP)	40
65	Immediate IMLP 001	HANG ON SLOOPY (LP)	50
68	Mercury (S)MCL 20128	THE INFINITE McCOYS (LP)	22
71	Joy JOYS 196	HANG ON SLOOPY (LP, reissue)	12

JIMMY McCRACKLIN

58	London HLM 8598	The Walk/I'm To Blame (as Jimmy McCracklin & His Band)	45
58	London HLM 8598	The Walk/I'm To Blame (as Jimmy McCracklin & His Band) (78)	25
58	London HL 7035	The Walk/I'm To Blame (export issue, as Jimmy McCracklin & His Band)	35
62	Top Rank JAR 617	Just Got To Know/The Drag	22
65	R&B MRB 5001	I Got Eyes For You/I'm Gonna Tell Your Mother	25
66	Outasite 45 120	Christmas Time (Parts 1 & 2) (99 copies only)	60
65	Liberty LIB 66094	Every Night, Every Day/Can't Raise Me	12
66	Liberty LIB 66129	Think/Steppin' Up In Class	12
68	Minit MLF 11003	How Do You Like Your Love/Get Together	10
68	Minit MLF 11009	Pretty Little Sweet Thing/A And I	10
65	Vocalion VEP 170160	JIMMY McCRACKLIN (EP)	120
68	Minit MLL/MLS 40003	A PIECE OF JIMMY McCRACKLIN (LP)	45

GWEN McCRAE

74	President PT 416	It's Worth The Hurt/90% Of Me Is You	6
82	Atlantic FLAM 1	Keep The Fire Burning/Funky Sensation	5
82	Atlantic FLAM 1T	Keep The Fire Burning/Funky Sensation (12")	8
75	President	GWEN McCRAE (LP)	15

GWEN & GEORGE McCRAE

75	President PTLS 1070	TOGETHER (LP)	15

DANNY McCULLOCH

69	Capitol CL 15607	Blackbird/Time Of Man	6
70	Pye Intl./Festival 7N 25514	Colour Of The Sunset/Smokeless Zone	6
69	Capitol E-(S)T 174	WINGS OF A MAN (LP)	15

(see also Animals)

IAN McCULLOCH

64	Decca F11855	Come On Home/Down By The River	12

MINT VALUE £

IAN McCULLOCH

84	Korowa KOW 40	September Song/Cockles & Mussels (p/s)	5
84	Korowa KOW 40L	September Song/Cockles & Mussels (10", A-side plays at 78rpm)	8

(see also Echo & The Bunnymen)

HENRY McCULLOUGH

75	Dark Horse AMLH 22005	MIND YOUR OWN BUSINESS! (LP, some with inner sleeve)	20/15

(see also Grease Band, Eire Apparent, Paul McCartney & Wings)

GEORGE McCURN

63	London HLH 9705	I'm Just A Country Boy/In My Little Corner Of The World	12

LUKE McDANIEL

55	Parlophone CMSP 29	The Automobile Song/I Can't Steal Another's Bride (export issue)	40
55	Parlophone DP 407	The Automobile Song/I Can't Steal Another's Bride (78)	12

MAISIE McDANIEL

61	Beltona BE 2744	Christmastime In Ireland/The Old Pigsty	6
63	Fontana TF 400	Something Special/This Song Is Just For You	6
63	Fontana TE 17397	MEET MAISIE McDANIEL! (EP, with The Hunters)	15
63	Fontana TE 17398	COUNTRY STYLE (EP, with The Hunters)	12
65	Fontana TL 5215	ARE YOU LONESOME TONIGHT (LP)	12

(see also Hunters)

EUGENE McDANIELS

71	Atlantic 2465 022	OUTLAW (LP)	30

GENE McDANIELS

61	London HLG 9319	A Hundred Pounds Of Clay/Take A Chance On Love	15
61	London HLG 9396	A Tear/She's Come Back	15
61	London HLG 9448	Tower Of Strength/Secret	15
62	Liberty LIB 55405	Chip Chip/Another Tear Falls	10
62	Liberty LIB 55480	Point Of No Return/Warmer Than A Whisper	15
63	Liberty LIB 55510	Spanish Lace/Somebody's Waiting	8
63	Liberty LIB 55541	The Puzzle/Cry Baby Cry	8
63	Liberty LIB 55597	It's A Lonely Town/False Friends	25
63	Liberty LIB 10130	Anyone Else/New Love In Old Mexico	8
64	Liberty LIB 55723	In Times Like These/Make Me A Present Of You	15
65	Liberty LIB 55752	(There Goes The) Forgotten Man	18
65	Liberty LIB 55805	Walk With A Winner/A Miracle	175
61	London REG 1298	GENE McDANIELS (EP)	65
62	Liberty LEP 2054	A CHANGE OF MOOD (EP)	45
61	London HA-G 2384	A HUNDRED POUNDS OF CLAY (LP, also stereo SAH-G 6184)	80/100
62	Liberty LBY 1003	... SOMETIMES I'M HAPPY (LP)	45
62	Liberty LBY 1021	TOWER OF STRENGTH (LP)	45
63	Liberty (S)LBY 1128	SPANISH LACE (LP)	45
63	Liberty LBY 1179	THE WONDERFUL WORLD OF GENE McDANIELS (LP)	45
68	Sunset SLS 50017E	FACTS OF LIFE (LP)	15

BILL McDAVID

61	Starlite ST45 63	Kiss Me For Christmas/Little Shepherd Boy	8

McDERMOTTS

89	Hag HAGLP 2	THE ENEMY WITHIN (LP)	12

CHAS McDEVITT (SKIFFLE GROUP)

57	Oriole CB 1352	Freight Train (with Nancy Whiskey)/The Cotton Song	25
57	Oriole CB 1357	It Takes A Worried Man/The House Of The Rising Sun	18
57	Oriole CB 1371	Green Back Dollar (with Nancy Whiskey)/I'm Satisfied	18
57	Oriole CB 1386	Face In The Rain (with Nancy Whiskey)/Sporting Life (with Tony Kohn)	15
57	Oriole CB 1386	Face In The Rain (with Nancy Whiskey)/Sporting Life (with Tony Kohn) (78)	8
57	Oriole CB 1395	Sing, Sing, Sing/My Old Man	15
57	Oriole CB 1395	Sing, Sing, Sing/My Old Man (78)	12
58	Oriole CB 1403	Johnny-O (with Nancy Whiskey)/Bad Man Stack-O-Lee	15
58	Oriole CB 1403	Johnny-O (with Nancy Whiskey)/Bad Man Stack-O-Lee (78)	10
58	Oriole CB 1405	Across The Bridge (with Shirley Douglas)/Deep Down	15
58	Oriole CB 1405	Across The Bridge (with Shirley Douglas)/Deep Down (78)	8
58	Oriole CB 1457	Real Love (with Shirley Douglas)/Juke-Box Jumble	15
58	Oriole CB 1457	Real Love (with Shirley Douglas)/Juke-Box Jumble (78)	15
59	Oriole CB 1511	Teenage Letter (with Shirley Douglas)/SHIRLEY DOUGLAS: Sad Little Girl	12
59	Oriole CB 1511	Teenage Letter/SHIRLEY DOUGLAS: Sad Little Girl (78)	20
60	Top Rank JAR 338	Dream Talk/Forever (with Shirley Douglas)	8
61	HMV POP 845	One Love/Can It Be Love (with Shirley Douglas)	7
61	HMV POP 928	Mommy Out De Light/I've Got A Thing About You (with Shirley Douglas)	6
62	HMV POP 999	Happy Family/Throwing Pebbles In A Pool (with Shirley Douglas)	6
65	Columbia DB 7595	The Most Of What Is Least/Don't Blame Me (with Shirley Douglas)	6
68	Fontana TF 957	City Smoke/One Man Band	6
57	Oriole EP 7002	CHAS AND NANCY (EP, with Nancy Whiskey)	30
57	Oriole MG 10018	THE INTOXICATING MISS WHISKEY (10" LP, with Nancy Whiskey)	60
65	Columbia 33SX 1738	SIXTEEN BIG FOLK HITS (LP, with Shirley Douglas)	15

(see also Nancy Whiskey, Cranes Skiffle Group, Coffee Bar Skifflers)

ALISTAIR McDONALD

69	Major Minor MMLP 51	BATTLE BALLADS (LP)	15

GAVIN McDONALD

72	Regal Zono. SLRZ 1027	LINES (LP)	20

(COUNTRY) JOE McDONALD

71	Vanguard 6076 252	Hold On It's Coming Parts 1 & 2	6
70	Vanguard (S)VRL 19057	THINKING OF WOODY GUTHRIE (LP)	20
71	Vanguard 6359 004	TONIGHT I'M SINGING JUST FOR YOU (LP)	15

71 Sonet SNTF 622 QUIET DAYS IN CLICHY (LP, soundtrack) 18
71 Vanguard VSD 79314 HOLD ON — IT'S COMING (LP) 15
71 Vanguard VSD 79315 WAR WAR WAR (LP) 12
72 Vanguard VSD 79316 INCREDIBLE! LIVE! (LP) 12
73 Vanguard VSD 79328 PARIS SESSIONS (LP) 12
(see also Country Joe & Fish)

LARRY McDONALD & DENZIL LAING

71 Clandisc CLA 228 Name Of The Game/FABULOUS FLAMES: Holly Version 6

RITCHIE McDONALD & GLEN BROWN

72 Duke DU 141 Boat To Progress/Boat To Progress — Version 8

SHELAGH McDONALD

70 B&C CAS 1019 THE SHELAGH McDONALD ALBUM (LP) 22
71 B&C CAS 1043 STAR GAZER (LP, with inner sleeve) 22

SKEETS McDONALD

56 Capitol CL 14566 Fallen Angel/It'll Take Me A Long, Long Time 30
59 Capitol EAP1 1040 GOING STEADY WITH THE BLUES (EP) 90

TESFA McDONALD

72 Dynamic DYN 455 Life Is The Highest/Recarnate (Re-Incarnate) (actually by Bobby Ellis and Tommy McCook) 18

McDONALD & GILES

70 Island ILPS 9126 McDONALD AND GILES (LP, 1st pressing, pink label, with 'i' logo) 35
70 Island ILPS 9126 McDONALD AND GILES (LP, 2nd pressing, 'pink rim' label, 'palm tree' logo) 12
70 Polydor 2302 070 McDONALD AND GILES (LP) 15
(see also King Crimson; Giles, Giles & Fripp)

ROSE McDOWALL

88 Rio Digital 7RDS 3 Don't Fear The Reaper/Crystal Days (p/s) 5
88 Rio Digital 12RDS 3 Don't Fear The Reaper/Crystal Days (12", p/s) 8
(see also Strawberry Switchblade, Ornamental, Psychic TV, Current 93, Death In June)

(MISSISSIPPI) FRED McDOWELL

66 Bounty BY 6022 MY HOME IS IN THE DELTA (LP) 30
66 Fontana 688 806 ZL MISSISSIPPI DELTA BLUES (LP) 25
69 CBS 63735 LONG WAY FROM HOME (LP) 25
69 Polydor 236 278 GOING DOWN SOUTH (LP) 22
70 Capitol E-ST 409 I DO NOT PLAY NO ROCK & ROLL (LP) 20
70 Transatlantic TRA 194 LONDON 1 (LP) 18
71 Transatlantic TRA 203 LONDON 2 (LP) 18
71 Revival RVS 1001 EIGHT YEARS RAMBLIN' (LP, with Johnny Woods) 18
73 Black Lion 2460 193 MISSISSIPPI DELTA BLUES (LP) 12
74 Xtra XTRA 1136 MISSISSIPPI FRED McDOWELL 1904-1972 (LP) 15

FRED & ANNIE MAE McDOWELL

64 Polydor 236 570 GOING DOWN SOUTH (LP) 18

PAUL McDOWELL

62 Fontana 267228 TF Frankie/Be A Man 6

(BROTHER) JACK McDUFF

64 Stateside SS 275 Sanctified Samba/Whistle While You Work 10
64 Stateside SS 302 Rock Candy/Real Good 'Un 10
64 Stateside SS 328 Carpetbaggers (Main Theme)/The Pink Panther (Theme) 10
66 Atlantic 584 036 Down In The Valley/A Change Is Gonna Come 6
64 Stateside SL 10060 BROTHER JACK McDUFF LIVE! (LP) 20
64 Stateside SL 10101 THE DYNAMIC JACK McDUFF (LP, as Brother Jack McDuff Quartet) 20
65 Stateside SL 10121 BROTHER JACK McDUFF QUARTET LIVE! AT THE JAZZ WORKSHOP (LP) 20
65 Stateside SL 10142 PRELUDE (LP) 20
66 Stateside SL 10165 THE CONCERT McDUFF (LP) 18
66 Atlantic 587 030 A CHANGE IS GONNA COME (LP) 18
67 Transatlantic PR 7404 SILK AND SOUL (LP) 18
67 Transatlantic PR 7476 WALK ON BY (LP) 18
68 Transatlantic DYNAMIC JACK McDUFF (LP) 18
69 Blue Note BST 84322 DOWN HOME STYLE (LP) 15
70 Blue Note BST 84334 MOON RAPPIN' (LP) 12
71 Blue Note BST 84348 TO SEEK A NEW HOME (LP) 12
72 Blue Note BST 84353 WHO KNOWS WHAT TOMORROW'S (LP) 12
72 York FYK 407 IF THE CAP FITS ... WEAR IT (LP, as Jack McDuff Band) 12
72 Prestige PR 24013 ROCK CANDY (LP) 12
(see also Roland Kirk, Kenny Burrell, Jimmy Witherspoon)

MC DUKE

89 Music Of Life NOTE 025DJ I'm Riffin (English Rasta) (12") 8

McENROE & CASH With The FULL METAL RACKETS

91 M. For Nations KUT 141 Rock'N'Roll (7" Version)/(Instrumental) (p/s) 5
91 M. For Nations 12KUT 141 Rock'N'Roll (Dance Mix)/(7" Version)/(Instrumental) (12", p/s) 10
(see also Iron Maiden, Roger Daltrey)

JOHNNY McEVOY

73 Hawk HALPX 112 JOHNNY McEVOY (LP) 15
74 Hawk HALPX 117 SOUNDS LIKE JOHNNY McEVOY (LP) 20
(see also Rambler)

BOB McFADDEN & DOR

59 Coral Q 72378 The Mummy/The Beat Generation 18
59 Coral Q 72378 The Mummy/The Beat Generation (78) 15
(see also Rod McKuen)

MINT VALUE £

MC5

69	Elektra EKSN 45056	Kick Out The Jams/Motor City Is Burning	25
69	Elektra EKSN 45067	Ramblin' Rose/Borderline	22
69	Elek. EKL 4042/EKS 74042	KICK OUT THE JAMS (LP, red label, gatefold sleeve, mono/stereo)	70/50
70	Atlantic 2400 016	BACK IN THE U.S.A. (LP)	25
71	Atlantic 2400 135	HIGH TIME (LP)	22

(see also Wayne Kramer, Destroy All Monsters, Rob Tyner & Hot Rods)

MIKE McGEAR

72	Island WIP 6131	Woman/Kill	8
74	Warner Bros K 16446	Leave It/Sweet Baby (p/s)	12/8
75	Warner Bros K 16520	Sea Breezes/Givin' Grease A Ride	8
75	Warner Bros K 16573	Dance The Do/Norton	10
75	Warner Bros K 16658	Simply Love You/What Do We Really Know (some in p/s)	15/8
76	EMI EMI 2485	Doing Nothing All Day/A To Z	6
80	Carrere CAR 144	All The Whales In The Ocean/I Juz Want What You Got — Money! (some in p/s)	30/15
81	Conn SRTS/81/CUS 1112	No Lardidar/God Save The Gracious Queen (some in p/s)	55/35
72	Island ILPS 9191	WOMAN (LP)	15
74	Warner Bros K 56051	*McGEAR (LP, gatefold sleeve with insert)	15
74	Warner Bros KMG 1	McGEAR'S LIMITED EDITION (7-track white label sampler & press kit)	35
80s	Centre Labs	*McGEAR (LP, 6-track reissue, 500 only, numbered & signed)	30

(see also Grimms, Scaffold, McGough & McGear, Paul McCartney)

PAT McGEEGAN

68	Emerald MD 1096	Chance Of A Lifetime/Don't Laugh At Me (If I Cry)	7

BROWNIE McGHEE

51	Melodisc 1127	Secret Mojo Blues/Me And My Dog (78)	30
63	Columbia SEG 8226	BLUES ON PARADE NO. 1 (EP)	35
60s	Xtra 1021	BROWNIE McGHEE (LP)	25
78	Magpie PY 1805	LET'S HAVE A BALL (LP)	12

BROWNIE McGHEE & DAVE LEE

57	Pye Jazz NJE 1060	THE BLUEST (EP)	22

(see also Sonny Terry & Brownie McGhee)

HOWARD McGHEE SEXTET

50	Jazz Parade B1	Dimitar/Al's Tune (78)	7

(Roger) McGOUGH & (Mike) McGEAR

68	Parlophone PMC/PCS 7047	McGOUGH AND McGEAR (LP, with phasing on "So Much"; beware of counterfeits)	150
89	Parlophone PCS 7332	McGOUGH AND McGEAR (LP, stereo reissue with inner sleeve, without phasing on "So Much")	15
89	Parlophone CDP 7 91877-2	McGOUGH AND McGEAR (CD, without phasing on "So Much")	60

(see also Scaffold, Adrian Henri, Mike McGear, Jimi Hendrix, Grimms)

ROGER McGOUGH & BRIAN PATTEN

75	Argo ZPL 1190	READ THEIR OWN VERSE — BRITISH POETS OF OUR TIME (LP)	15

MAUREEN McGOVERN

73	Pye Intl. 7N 25603	The Morning After/Midnight Storm (p/s)	8

CHRIS McGREGOR('S BROTHERHOOD OF BREATH)

68	Polydor 184 137	VERY URGENT (LP, as Chris McGregor Group)	60
68	Polydor 583 072	UP TO EARTH (LP, unreleased, test pressings only)	150+
70	RCA Neon NE 2	CHRIS McGREGOR'S BROTHERHOOD OF BREATH (LP, gatefold sleeve)	50
72	RCA SF 8260	BROTHERHOOD (LP, gatefold sleeve, as Chris McGregor's Brotherhood Of Breath)	45
74	Ogun OG 100	LIVE, WILLISAU (LP)	15
77	Ogun OG 521	IN HIS OWN TIME (LP)	18
78	Ogun OG 524	PROCESSION (LP)	15

(see also Brotherhood Of Breath, Tunji)

FREDDIE McGREGOR

73	Fab FAB 261	Wise Words/NEW ESTABLISHMENT: Version	15
79	Jackal JALP 7000	FREDDIE McGREGOR (LP)	20

(see also Soul Brothers, Young Freddie)

JIMMY McGRIFF

64	Sue WI 303	All About My Girl/M.G. Blues	35
64	Sue WI 310	Last Minute (Parts 1 & 2)	25
64	Sue WI 317	I've Got A Woman (Parts 1 & 2)	25
64	Sue WI 333	'Round Midnight/Lonely Avenue	30
66	United Artists UP 1170	See See Rider/Hallelujah	8
70	United Artists UP 35025	The Worm/What's That	10
64	Sue ILP 907	I'VE GOT A WOMAN (LP)	90
64	Sue ILP 908	GOSPEL TIME (LP)	90
65	London HA-C 8247	BLUES FOR MISTER JIMMY (LP)	50
66	London HA-C 8242	AT THE APOLLO (LP)	50
66	United Artists (S)ULP 1158	A BAG FULL OF SOUL (LP)	30
68	United Artists (S)ULP 1170	THE BIG BAND (LP)	25
69	Solid State USS 7012	I'VE GOT A NEW WOMAN (LP)	12
72	Groove Merchant GM 503	GROOVE GREASE (LP)	15
73	Groove Merchant GM 2205	GOOD THINGS DON'T HAPPEN EVERY DAY (LP, with Junior Parker)	12
74	People PLEO 14	FLY DUDE (LP)	15
74	People PLEO 19	LET'S STAY TOGETHER (LP)	15

BILL McGUFFIE (TRIO)

53	Parlophone MSP 6040	Concerto For Boogie/Begin The Beguine (as Bill McGuffie Trio)	7
59	Philips PB 922	Elmer's Tune/Simple Simon (78)	8

67	Philips BF 1550	Fugue For Thought (from the film 'Dalek Invasion Earth 2150AD')/Fair's Fair	35
55	Philips BBR 8054	JAZZ WITH McGUFFIE (LP)	15
56	Philips BBR 8087	McGUFFIE MAGIC (LP)	30
56	Philips BBL 7072	MORE JAZZ WITH McGUFFIE (LP)	30
58	Philips BBL 7261	CONTINENTAL TOUR (LP)	30
61	Philips BBL 7450	PLAYING FOR PLEASURE (LP)	15
68	Philips LPS 16001	LATIN OVERTONES (LP)	20
71	Rediffusion ZS 48	AN ALTO AND SOME BRASS (LP)	12
72	Rediffusion ZS 130	BILL McGUFFIE BIG BAND (LP)	12

ROGER McGUINN

74	CBS 2649	Peace On You/Without You	6
77	CBS 5231	American Girl/Russian Hill	6
73	CBS 65274	ROGER McGUINN (LP)	15
74	CBS 81071	PEACE ON YOU (LP)	12
75	CBS 80877	ROGER McGUINN AND BAND (LP)	12
76	CBS 81369	CARDIFF ROSE (LP)	12

(see also Byrds)

McGUINNESS FLINT

70	Capitol CL 15662	When I'm Dead And Gone/Lazy Afternoon	5
71	Capitol CL 15682	Malt And Barley Blues/Rock On	5
70	Capitol EA-ST 22625	McGUINNESS FLINT (LP, gatefold sleeve)	15
71	Capitol ST 22794	HAPPY BIRTHDAY, RUTHY BABY (LP)	15
73	Bronze ILPS 9244	RAINBOW (LP, gatefold sleeve with inner)	12
74	Bronze ILPS 9302	C'EST LA VIE (LP, with inner sleeve)	12

(see also Manfred Mann, Blues Band, John Mayall, Coulson Dean McGuinness Flint, Gallagher & Lyle, Paladin)

BARRY McGUIRE

65	Ember EMB S 208	So Long Stay Well/Far Side Of The Hill	8
65	Ember EMB S 224	Greenback Dollar/One By One	8
65	RCA Victor RCA 1469	Eve Of Destruction/What Exactly Is The Matter With Me	6
65	RCA Victor RCA 1493	Child Of Our Times/Upon A Painted Ocean	8
66	RCA Victor RCA 1497	This Precious Time/Don't You Wonder Where It's At	8
66	RCA Victor RCA 1508	Walking My Cat Named Dog/I'd Have To Be Outta My Mind	7
66	RCA Victor RCA 1525	Cloudy Summer Afternoon/You've Got To Hide Your Love Away (B-side with Mamas & Papas)	18
67	RCA Victor RCA 1638	Masters Of War/Why Not Stop And Dig It While You Can	7
65	Envoy VOY 9153	HERE AND NOW (LP, with New Christy Minstrels)	15
65	RCA Victor RD 7751	SINGS EVE OF DESTRUCTION (LP)	35
66	Ember EMB 3362	THE EVE OF DESTRUCTION MAN (LP, with New Christy Minstrels)	25
71	A&M AMLS 2008	BARRY McGUIRE AND THE DOCTOR (LP, with Eric Hord)	15
70s	Sparrow BIRD 105	C'MON ALONG (LP)	20
70s	Sparrow BIRD 111	HAVE YOU HEARD? (LP)	20

(see also Mamas & Papas, New Christy Minstrels)

McGUIRE SISTERS

54	Vogue Coral Q 2028	Lonesome Polecat/Muskrat Ramble	18
55	Vogue Coral Q 72050	Sincerely/No More	25
55	Vogue Coral Q 72052	Melody Of Love/Open Up Your Heart	15
55	Vogue Coral Q 72082	Something's Gotta Give/It May Sound Silly	15
55	Vogue Coral Q 72108	Christmas Alphabet/He	18
56	Vogue Coral Q 72117	Young And Foolish/Doesn't Anybody Love Me?	15
56	Vogue Coral Q 72145	Missing/Be Good To Me (Baby, Baby)	15
56	Vogue Coral Q 72161	Delilah Jones/Picnic	18
56	Vogue Coral Q 72188	Weary Blues/In The Alps	15
56	Vogue Coral Q 72201	My Baby's Got Such Lovin' Ways/Endless	12
56	Vogue Coral Q 72209	Tip Toe Through The Tulips With Me/Do You Remember When?	12
56	Vogue Coral Q 72216	Goodnight My Love, Pleasant Dreams/Mommy	12
57	Vogue Coral Q 72238	Heart/Sometimes I'm Happy	12
57	Vogue Coral Q 72249	Kid Stuff/Without Him	12
57	Vogue Coral Q 72265	Rock Bottom/Beginning To Miss You	15
57	Vogue Coral Q 72265	Rock Bottom/Beginning To Miss You (78)	8
57	Vogue Coral Q 72272	He's Got Time/Interlude	8
57	Vogue Coral Q 72296	Forgive Me/Kiss Them For Me	8
58	Coral Q 72305	Sugartime/Banana Split	6
58	Coral Q 72327	Ding Dong/Since You Went Away To School	6
58	Coral Q 72327	Ding Dong/Since You Went Away To School (78)	8
58	Coral Q 72334	Volare/Do You Love Me Like You Kiss Me?	5
58	Coral Q 72334	Volare/Do You Love Me Like You Kiss Me? (78)	8
59	Coral Q 72356	May You Always/Achoo-Cha-Cha	5
59	Coral Q 72356	May You Always/Achoo-Cha-Cha (78)	8
59	Coral Q 72370	Summer Dreams/Peace (withdrawn)	10+
59	Coral Q 72370	Summer Dreams/Peace (78, withdrawn)	12+
59	Coral Q 72379	Red River Valley/Compromise	5
59	Coral Q 72379	Red River Valley/Compromise (78)	10
60	Coral Q 72387	Lovers' Lullaby/Livin' Dangerously	5
60	Coral Q 72399	"The Unforgiven" Theme (The Need For Love)/I Give Thanks	6
60	Coral Q 72406	Nine O'Clock/The Last Dance	5
60	Coral Q 72415	I Don't Know Why/To Be Loved	5
61	Coral Q 72427	Really Neat/Just For Old Time's Sake	6
61	Coral Q 72435	Will There Be Space In The Spaceship/Tears On My Pillow	8
61	Coral Q 72441	Just Because/I Do, I Do, I Do	6
62	Coral Q 72446	I Can Dream, Can't I/Old Devil Moon	5
62	Coral Q 72452	Sugartime Twist/More Hearts Are Broken That Way	5
64	Reprise R 20338	I'll Walk Alone/Ticket To Anywhere	5
58	Coral FEP 2001	THE McGUIRE SISTERS (EP)	20

MINT VALUE £

58	Coral FEP 2006	VOLARE (EP)	20
59	Coral FEP 2033	MAY YOU ALWAYS (EP)	20
56	Vogue Coral LVA 9024	DO YOU REMEMBER WHEN? (LP)	30
57	Vogue Coral LVA 9072	CHILDREN'S HOLIDAY (LP)	25
58	Coral LVA 9073	TEENAGE PARTY (LP)	25
58	Coral LVA 9082	WHILE THE LIGHTS ARE LOW (LP)	25
59	Coral LVA 9115	MAY YOU ALWAYS (LP)	25
60	Coral LVA 9133	GOLDEN FAVORITES (LP)	25
61	Coral LVA 9140	HIS AND HERS (LP)	25

JIM McHARG'S SCOTSVILLE JAZZ BAND

62	Pye Jazz 7NJ 2053	Forgotten Dreams/St Thomas	6
62	Pye Jazz 7NJ 2055	Look For A Sky Of Blue/Once In A Blue Moon	6

JOHN McHUGH

65	Columbia SCD 2245	When The Stars/Strange Harmony	5
65	Columbia SCD 2252	Goldsmith Of Toledo Serenade/O Vision Entrancing	5

FREDDIE McKAY

71	Banana BA 348	Picture On The Wall/SOUND DIMENSION: Version	15
71	Banana BA 358	Sweet You, Sour You/High School Dance	15
71	Moodisc HM 110	Old Joe/Too Much Fire	10
72	Banana BA 370	Drunken Sailor/SOUND DIMENSION: Version	10
73	Bullet BU 525	Go On This Way/SANTIC ALL STARS: Santic Dub	10
73	Dragon DRA 1012	Our Rendezvous/Black Beauty	10
73	Grape GR 3060	Our Rendezvous/SOUL DYMAMITES: Version	10
74	Dragon DRA 1022	Dream My Life Over/YOUTH STARS: Version	10
71	Banana BALPS 01	PICTURE ON THE WALL (LP)	40
73	Attack ATLP 1013	PICTURE ON THE WALL (LP, reissue)	15
74	Dragon DRLS 5005	LONELY MAN (LP)	15

(see also Lizzy)

SCOTT McKAY

67	Columbia DB 8147	I Can't Make Your Way/Take A Giant Step	30

SCOTTY McKAY

64	London HLU 9885	Cold Cold Heart/What You Wanna	10

TONY McKAY

66	Polydor BM 56513	Nobody's Perfect/Detroit	6

LONETTE McKEE

75	Sussex SXX 4	Save It/Do It To Me	5

KENNETH McKELLAR

66	Decca F 12341	A Man Without Love/As Long As The Sun Shines	6
66	Decca DFE 8645	SONGS FOR EUROPE (EP)	10

McKENDREE SPRING

69	MCA MUPS 277	McKENDREE SPRING (LP)	15
71	MCA MUPS 433	SECOND THOUGHTS (LP)	12
72	MCA MUPS 454	THREE (LP)	15
73	MCA MUPS 476	TRACKS (LP)	12
75	Dawn DNLS 3067	GET ME TO THE COUNTRY (LP)	12

MAE McKENNA

75	Transatlantic TRA 297	MAE McKENNA (LP)	12

(see also Contraband)

VAL McKENNA

65	Piccadilly 7N 35237	Baby Do It/I Believe In Love	12
65	Piccadilly 7N 35256	Mixed Up Shook Up Girl/Now That You've Made Up Your Mind	25
66	Piccadilly 7N 35286	I Can't Believe What You Say/Don't Hesitate	12
69	Spark SRL 1005	House For Sale/I'll Be Satisfied	10
69	Spark SRL 1023	It's All In My Imagination/Sweet Sweet Lovin'	7
70	Spark SRL 1038	Love Feeling/It's All In My Imagination	5

McKENNA MENDELSON MAINLINE

69	Liberty LBF 15235	You Better Watch Out/She's Alright	8
69	Liberty LBF 15276	Don't Give Me No Goose For Christmas/Beltmaker	7
69	Liberty LBS 83251	STINK (LP)	45

MARLENE McKENZIE

68	Double D DD 106	Left Me For Another/BOBBY AITKEN & CARIBBEATS: Cell Block Eleven	20

SCOTT McKENZIE

67	CBS 2816	San Francisco (Be Sure To Wear Some Flowers In Your Hair)/ What's The Difference	5
67	Capitol CL 15509	Look In Your Eyes/All I Want Is You	7
67	CBS 3009	Like An Old-Time Movie/What's The Difference Chapter II	7
68	CBS 3393	Holy Man/What's The Difference (Chapter 3)	6
73	CBS 1168	San Francisco (Be Sure To Wear Some Flowers In Your Hair)/ Reason To Believe ("Hall Of Fame Hits" series, p/s)	5
67	CBS (S)BPG 63157	THE VOICE OF SCOTT McKENZIE (LP)	20

(see also Mamas & Papas)

TOMMY McKENZIE

68	Pama PM 720	Fiddlesticks/Please Stay	12
71	Pama Supreme PS 327	Eastern Promise/Fiddlesticks (as Tommy McKenzie Orchestra)	7

MINT VALUE £

McKENZIE, DOUG & BOB

82 Mercury HOSER 1 — Take Off/Elron McKenzie (p/s) 20
(see also Rush)

McKINLEYS

64 Columbia DB 7230 — Someone Cares For Me/Million Miles Away 20
64 Columbia DB 7310 — When He Comes Along/Then I'll Know It's Love 12
64 Parlophone R 5211 — Sweet And Tender Romance/That Lonely Feeling 15
65 Columbia DB 7583 — Give Him My Love/Once More 18

ROD McKUEN

57 London HLU 8390 — Happy Is A Boy Named Me/Jaydee 45
60 Brunswick 05828 — Two Brothers/Time After Time 15
64 Capitol CL 15348 — The World I Used To Know/Someplace Green 5
66 Ember EMB 223 — Soldiers Who Want To Be Heroes/Wayfarin' Stranger 5
68 RCA Victor RCA 1734 — Cat Named Sloopy/Where Are We Now 5
71 Buena Vista DF 482 — Pastures Green/Theme From Scandalous John/Train To Quivira (p/s) 5
67 RCA Victor RD 7897 — THROUGH EUROPEAN WINDOWS (LP) 12
69 Warner Bros — LONESOME CITIES (LP) 15
69 Stateside (S)SL 10264 — JOANNA (LP, soundtrack, with Mike Sarne) 15
69 Stateside (S)SL 10278 — THE PRIME OF MISS JEAN BRODIE (LP, soundtrack, with Mike Redway) 15
69 Warner Bros WS 1705 — THE EARTH (LP) 12
70 Warner Bros WS 1720 — THE SKY (LP) 12
70 Warner Bros WS 1764 — HOME TO THE SEA (LP) 12
70 Warner Bros WS 1837 — NEW BALLADS (LP) 12
71 Warner Bros WS 3015 — THE ROD McKUEN SHOW (LP) 12
71 CBS 70078 — THE BOY NAMED CHARLIE BROWN (LP, soundtrack) 15
(see also Bob McFadden & Dor, Mike Redway, Mike Sarne, Henri Mancini)

HAL McKUSICK SEXTET/QUINTET

57 Vogue Coral Q 72258 — Kelly And Me (as Sextet)/When I Fall In Love (as Quintet) 6

ALTON McLAIN & DESTINY

78 Polydor 2391 370 — IT MUST BE LOVE (LP) 12

TOMMY McLAIN

66 London HL 10065 — Sweet Dreams/I Need You So 15
66 London HL 10091 — Think It Over/I Can't Take No More 12

JACKIE McLEAN QUINTET

56 Esquire 32-111 — JACKIE'S PAL (LP) 15

(MAHAVISHNU) JOHN McLAUGHLIN

69 Marmalade 608 007 — EXTRAPOLATION (LP) 40
70 Marmalade 2343 012 — EXTRAPOLATION (LP, reissue) 15
71 Douglas DGL 65075 — DEVOTION (LP, gatefold sleeve) 18
71 Douglas DGL 69014 — MY GOAL'S BEYOND (LP, as Mahavishnu John McLaughlin, gatefold sleeve) 18
73 CBS 69037 — LOVE, DEVOTION, SURRENDER (LP, by Mahavishnu John McLaughlin & Carlos Santana) 12
74 CBS Q 69037 — LOVE, DEVOTION, SURRENDER (LP, quadrophonic issue) 18
(see also Lifetime, Tony Williams [Lifetime], Mahavishnu Orchestra, John Surman, Santana)

DON McLEAN

72 United Artists UP 35359 — Vincent/Castles In The Air (p/s) 5

NANA McLEAN

71 Banana BA 355 — A Little Love/SOUND DIMENSION: Heavy Beat 22

PHIL McLEAN

61 Top Rank JAR 597 — Small Sad Sam/Chicken 8
62 Top Rank JAR 613 — Big Mouth Bill/Come With Us 8

GERALD McLEASH

71 G.G. GG 4516 — False Reaper/G.G. ALL STARS: Reaping Version 10

LARIS McLENNON

67 CBM 04 — Confusion/Turn Me Loose 6

ENOS McLEOD

68 Blue Cat BS 135 — You Can Never Get Away/ENOS & SHEILA: La La La Bamba 25
(see also Enos & Sheila)

VINCENT McLEOD

69 Jackpot JP 711 — Too Late/SIR COLLINS: Late Night 12

OSCAR McLOLLIE & HIS HONEYJUMPERS

55 London HL 8130 — Take Your Shoes Off, Pop/Love Me Tonight 260
55 London HL 8130 — Take Your Shoes Off, Pop/Love Me Tonight (78) 60

EDDIE McLOYD

75 Brunswick BR 27 — Once You Fall In Love/Baby Get Down 10

BOBBY McLURE

66 Chess CRS 8048 — Peak Of Love/You Got Me Baby 30
75 Island USA 006 — You Bring Out The Love In Me/SURVIVAL KIT: Daybreak 10
(see also Fontella Bass)

McLYNNS

70 CBS 63836 — OLD MARKET ST. (LP) 20

ROSS McMANUS

64 HMV POP 1279 — Patsy Girl/I'm The Greatest 8
66 HMV POP 1543 — Stop Your Playing Around/Girlie Girlie 6
67 Decca F 12618 — Can't Take My Eyes Off Of You/If I Were A Rich Man 6
60s Golden Guinea — SINGS ELVIS PRESLEY'S GOLDEN HITS (LP) 12
(see also Day Costello)

MINT VALUE £

MC MELLO

90	Republic LICT 033	Open Up Your Mind/Words Spoken (12")	8
99	Jazz Fudge JFR 018	Melloizdaman/Hedz Don't Know (EP)	8
90	Republic LIC LP 015	THOUGHTS RELEASED (LP)	12

MARGARET McMILLAN

65	Decca F 12272	You Can't Be True Dear/The Love Of My Man	6

BARBARA McNAIR

66	Tamla Motown TMG 544	You're Gonna Love My Baby/The Touch Of Time	200
59	Coral FEP 2021	FRONT ROW CENTRE VOL. 1 (EP)	40
64	Warner Bros WEP 6129	I ENJOY BEING A GIRL (EP)	40

(see also Billy Williams & Barbara McNair)

CHARLIE McNAIR'S JAZZ BAND

60	Waverly SLP 504	Big House Blues/Fish Man	6

HAROLD McNAIR

68	RCA Victor RCA 1742	The Hipster/Indecision	50
65	Island ILP 926	AFFECTIONATE FiNK (LP, with Ornette Coleman's Sidemen)	350
68	RCA SF 7969	HAROLD McNAIR (LP)	150
70	RCA Intl. INTS 1096	FLUTE AND NUT (LP)	40
70	B&C CAS 1016	THE FENCE (LP)	20
72	B&C CAS 1045	HAROLD McNAIR (LP)	20

(see also Ginger Baker's Airforce)

JOSEPH McNALLY

56	Oriole CB 1325	The March Hare/I'm A Sentimental One	6

JOHN McNALLY

69	CBS 4517	Mary In The Morning/My Love Forgive Me	5

(this is NOT John McNally of the Searchers)

TREVOR McNAUGHTON

72	Hillcrest HCT 5	No Sins At All/No Sins At All Version	5

(see also The Melodians)

BIG JAY McNEELY

59	Top Rank JAR 169	There Is Something On Your Mind/...Back...Shac...Track ('vocal: Little Sonny')	50
59	Top Rank JAR 169	There Is Something On Your Mind/...Back...Shac...Track (78)	25
65	Sue WI 373	There Is Something On Your Mind/...Back...Shac...Track ('vocal: Little Sonny') (reissue)	40
64	Warner Bros WM 8143	BIG JAY'S PARTY (LP)	40

AARON McNEIL

73	Action ACT 4619	Soul Of A Black Man/Reap What You Sow	12

DAVID McNEIL

68	President PT 212	Don't Let Your Chance Go By/Space Plane	15

PAUL McNEILL

66	Decca LK 4803	TRADITIONALLY AT THE TROUBADOUR (LP)	50

PAUL McNEILL & LINDA PETERS

68	MGM MGM 1408	You Ain't Goin' Nowhere/I'll Show You How To Sing	6

(see also Linda Peters, Richard & Linda Thompson)

McPEAKE FAMILY/FOLK GROUP

64	Fontana TL 5214	IRISH FOLK! (LP, as McPeake Family)	30
65	Fontana TL 5358	AT HOME WITH THE McPEAKES (LP)	25
67	Fontana TL 5433	PLEASANT AND DELIGHTFUL (LP, as McPeake Family)	20
69	Evolution Z 1002	WELCOME HOME (LP, as McPeake Folk Group)	40
72	Windmill WMD 151	IRISH TO BE SURE (LP, as McPeake Family)	25

CLYDE McPHATTER

78s

56	London HLE 8250	Seven Days/I'm Not Worthy Of You	35
56	London HLE 8293	Treasure Of Love/When You're Sincere	8
57	London HLE 8462	Just To Hold My Hand/No Matter What	30
57	London HLE 8476	Long Lonely Nights/Heartaches	30
57	London HLE 8525	Rock And Cry/You'll Be There	35
58	London HLE 8707	Come What May/Let Me Know	35
58	London HLE 8755	A Lover's Question/I Can't Stand Up Alone	40
59	London HLE 8878	Lovey Dovey/My Island Of Dreams	55
59	London HLE 8906	Since You've Been Gone/Try Try Baby	60
59	London HLE 9000	You Went Back On Your Word/There You Go	90

SINGLES

56	London HLE 8250	Seven Days/I'm Not Worthy Of You	400
56	London HL 7006	Seven Days/I'm Not Worthy Of You (export issue)	125
56	London HLE 8293	Treasure Of Love/When You're Sincere (gold or silver label lettering)	165/80
57	London HLE 8462	Just To Hold My Hand/No Matter What (triangular centre)	150
57	London HLE 8476	Long Lonely Nights/Heartaches (triangular centre)	110
57	London HLE 8525	Rock And Cry/You'll Be There (triangular centre, later round)	90/35
58	London HLE 8707	Come What May/Let Me Know (triangular centre)	65
58	London HLE 8755	A Lover's Question/I Can't Stand Up Alone (triangular centre)	30
59	MGM MGM 1014	I Told Myself A Lie/(I'm Afraid) The Masquerade Is Over	20
59	London HLE 8878	Lovey Dovey/My Island Of Dreams (triangular centre)	40
59	London HLE 8906	Since You've Been Gone/Try Try Baby (triangular centre)	40
59	MGM MGM 1040	Twice As Nice/Where Did I Make My Mistake	18
59	London HLE 9000	You Went Back On Your Word/There You Go	55
59	MGM MGM 1048	Bless You/Let's Try Again	18
60	London HLE 9079	Just Give Me A Ring/Don't Dog Me	55

MINT VALUE £

60	MGM MGM 1061	Think Me A Kiss/When The Right Time Comes Along	18
60	Mercury AMT 1108	I Ain't Givin' Up Nothin' (If I Can't Get Something)/Ta Ta	15
60	Mercury AMT 1120	You're For Me/I Just Want To Love You	15
61	Mercury AMT 1136	Tomorrow Is A-Comin'/I'll Love You Till The Cows Come Home	15
62	Mercury AMT 1174	Lover Please/Let's Forget About The Past	18
62	Mercury AMT 1181	Little Bitty Pretty One/Next To Me	15
66	Stateside SS 487	Everybody's Somebody's Fool/I Belong To You	18
66	Stateside SS 567	A Shot Of Rhythm And Blues/I'm Not Going To Work Today	18
67	Stateside SS 592	Lavender Lace/Sweet And Innocent	18
68	Deram DM 202	Only A Fool/Thank You Love	12
69	Deram DM 223	Baby I Could Be So Good At Loving You/Baby You've Got It	12
69	Pama PM 775	A Shot Of Rhythm And Blues/I'm Not Going To Work Today (reissue)	10
69	B&C CB 106	Denver/Tell Me	6
EPs			
59	London RE-E 1202	CLYDE McPHATTER	340
60	London RE-E 1240	CLYDE McPHATTER NO. 2 (unissued)	
59	MGM MGM-EP 705	TWICE AS NICE	175
60	MGM MGM-EP 739	THIS IS NOT GOODBYE	175
LPs			
63	Mercury MMC 14120	LOVER PLEASE	175
64	Atlantic ATL 5001	THE BEST OF CLYDE McPHATTER	120
71	MCA MUPS 418	WELCOME HOME	20
73	Atlantic K 30033	A TRIBUTE TO CLYDE McPHATTER	20

(see also Drifters, Jackie Wilson, Dominoes, Billy Ward & Dominoes, Jackie Wilson/Clyde McPhatter)

TONY (T.S.) McPHEE

66	Purdah 45-3501	Someone To Love Me/Ain't Gonna Cry No Mo' (as T.S. McPhee)	240
80s	TS 001	Time Of Action/Born To Be With You (sold at gigs)	10
68	Liberty LBL/LBS 83190	ME AND THE DEVIL (LP)	50
71	Sunset SLS 50209	THE SAME THING ON THEIR MINDS (LP, with Jo-Ann Kelly)	25
73	World Wide Artists WWA 1	THE TWO SIDES OF TONY (T.S.) McPHEE (LP, with insert)	20

(see also Groundhogs, Champion Jack Dupree, Jo-Ann Kelly, John Dummer Blues Band, Hapshash & Coloured Coat, Herbal Mixture)

CHARLES McPHERSON

65	Stateside SL 10151	BEBOP REVISITED (LP)	15
73	Mainstream MSL 1004	SIKU YA BIBI (LP)	12

GILLIAN McPHERSON

71	RCA Victor RCA 2089	It's My Own Way/Is Somebody In Tune With My Song	5
71	RCA Victor SF 8220	POETS AND PAINTERS AND PERFORMERS OF THE BLUES (LP)	20

KEVIN McQUINN

62	Top Rank JAR 598	Every Step Of The Way/Keep Me On Your Mind	8

CARMEN McRAE

55	Brunswick 05502	Love Is Here To Stay/This Will Make You Laugh	8
56	Brunswick 05588	You Don't Know Me/Never Loved Him Anyhow	7
56	Brunswick 05632	Star Eyes/I'm A Dreamer (Aren't We All)	7
57	Brunswick 05652	Whatever Lola Wants (Lola Gets)/Ooh (What 'Cha Doin' To Me) (with Dave Lambert Quartet)	10
57	Brunswick 05723	It's Like Getting A Donkey To Gallop/The Party's Over	7
58	Brunswick 05738	As I Love You/Passing Fancy	5
58	Brunswick 05761	Namely You/I'll Love You (Till I Die)	5
59	Brunswick 05789	Come On, Come In/I Love The Ground You Walk On	5
59	London HLR 8837	Play For Keeps/Which Way Is Love	15
59	London HLR 8837	Play For Keeps/Which Way Is Love (78)	12
60	Mercury AMT 1122	The Very Thought Of You/Oh! Look At Me Now	5
75	Blue Note BNXW 7002	Who Gave You Permission/The Trouble With Hello Is Goodbye	5
57	London RE-N 1094	LONDON'S GIRL FRIENDS (EP)	20
56	Brunswick LAT 8104	BY SPECIAL REQUEST (LP)	25
56	Brunswick LAT 8133	TORCHY (LP)	22
56	Brunswick LAT 8147	BLUE MOON (LP)	22
58	Brunswick LAT 8257	AFTER GLOW (LP)	22
59	London HA-R 2185	BOOK OF BALLADS (LP)	22
66	Ember CJS 819	IN LONDON (LP)	15

(see also Sammy Davis Jnr.)

CARMEN McRAE & DAVE BRUBECK FIVE

62	Fontana H 379	Take Five/It's A Raggy Waltz	8

(see also Dave Brubeck)

IAN McSHANE

62	Columbia DB 4932	The Tinker/Harry Brown	6

JAY McSHANN

55	Brunswick LA 8735	KANSAS CITY MEMORIES (10" LP)	25
73	Black Lion 2460 201	THE BAND THAT JUMPS THE BLUES (LP)	10

MC SPY-D & 'FRIENDS'

95	Parlophone 12RPD 6404	The Amazing Spider-Man (Mastermix)/(Sad Bit)/(The White Trouser Mix) (12", picture disc, with insert)	8
95	Parlophone 12RDJ 6404	The Amazing Spider-Man (Solution Mix)/(Solution Chilled Mix)/(B&J White Trouser Mix) (12", no p/s, promo only)	30

(see also Brian May)

BLIND WILLIE McTELL

66	Transatlantic PR 1040	LAST SESSION (LP)	40
67	Storyville 670 816	BLIND WILLIE McTELL 1940 (LP)	25
60s	Roots RL 324	BLIND WILLIE McTELL 1929-1935 (LP)	25
73	Atlantic K 40400	ATLANTA TWELVE STRING GUITAR (LP)	18

MINT VALUE £

RALPH McTELL

69	Big T BIG 125	Summer Comes Along	5
70	Big T BIG 131	Kew Gardens/Father Forgive Them	5
70	Big T BIG 134	Spiral Staircase/Terminus	5
71	Famous FAM 105	First And Last Man/In Some Way I Loved You	5
72	Famous FAM 111	Teacher, Teacher/Truckin' Little Baby	5
72	Reprise K 14225	Zimmerman Blues	5
74	Reprise K 14380	Streets Of London/Summer Lightning (p/s)	5
68	Transatlantic TRA 165	8 FRAMES A SECOND (LP)	20
69	Transatlantic TRA 177	SPIRAL STAIRCASE (LP, with insert)	18
69	Transatlantic TRA 209	MY SIDE OF YOUR WINDOW (LP)	15
70	Transatlantic TRA 227	REVISITED (LP)	15
71	Famous SFMA 5753	YOU, WELL MEANING, BROUGHT ME HERE (LP, gatefold sleeve)	15
77	Warner Bros K2 56296	RIGHT SIDE UP (LP, quadrophonic)	12

McTELLS

87	Frank TRUFFAUT 303	Jesse Man Rae/If Only/Rotten/M.T.B. (p/s in bag)	10

RAY McVAY SOUND

65	Pye 7N 15777	Raunchy/Revenge	35
65	Pye 7N 15816	Kinda Kinky/Kinkdom Come	30
66	Parlophone R 5460	Genesis/House Of Clowns (as Ray MacVay Band)	10
69	Mercury MF 1121	Destination Moon/Mexican Scavenger	7
71	Philips 6006 083	They Call Me Mr. Tibbs (as Ray McVay & Orchestra)	18

CHRISTINE McVIE

84	Warner Bros W 9372T	Got A Hold On Me/Who's Dreaming This Dream (12", p/s)	8
84	Warner Bros W 9372PT	Got A Hold On Me/Who's Dreaming This Dream (12", picture disc)	10

(see also Christine Perfect, Fleetwood Mac, Chicken Shack)

CARL McVOY

58	London HLU 8617	Tootsie/You Are My Sunshine	275
58	London HLU 8617	Tootsie/You Are My Sunshine (78)	75

DAVID McWILLIAMS

66	CBS 202348	God And My Country/Blue Eyes	10
67	Major Minor MM 533	The Days Of Pearly Spencer/Harlem Lady	12
68	Major Minor MM 561	This Side Of Heaven/Mister Satisfied	8
69	Major Minor MM 592	The Stranger/Follow Me	10
69	Major Minor MM 616	Oh Mama Are You My Friend?/I Love Susie In The Summer	8
71	Parlophone R 5886	The Days Of Pearly Spencer/Harlem Lady (reissue)	6
72	CBS 7782	Maggie's Coming Home/Margie	5
73	Mother MOT 101	Gold/Go On Back To Momma	5
73	Dawn DNS 1044	Love Like A Lady/Down By The Dockyard	5
74	Dawn DNS 1064	You've Only Been A Stranger/Ships In The Night	5
67	Major Minor MMLP 2	SINGING SONGS BY DAVID McWILLIAMS (LP, also stereo SMLP 2)	25
67	Major Minor MMLP 10	DAVID McWILLIAMS VOL. 2 (LP, also stereo SMLP 10)	25
68	Major Minor MMLP 11	VOLUME III (LP, also stereo SMLP 11)	22
69	Major Minor MCP 5026	THE DAYS OF DAVID McWILLIAMS (LP)	22
72	Dawn DNLS 3039	LORD OFFALY (LP)	18
73	Dawn DNLS 3047	THE BEGGAR AND THE PRIEST (LP)	18
74	Dawn DNLS 3059	LIVING'S JUST A STATE OF MIND (LP)	18

M.D.C.

83	Crass 121984/5	MULTI DEATH CORPORATION (EP)	8

(see also Millions Of Dead Children)

VAUGHN MEADER

63	MGM MGM 1239	No Hiding Place/The Elephant Song	6

ME & THEM

64	Pye 7N 15596	Feels So Good/I Think I'm Gonna Kill Myself	18
64	Pye 7N 15631	Everything I Do Is Wrong/Show You Mean It Too	15
64	Pye 7N 15683	Get Away/Tell Me Why	15

MEANIES

79	Vendetta VD 002	Waiting For You/It's True (p/s)	65

MEAN STREET DEALERS

79	Graduate GRAD 5	Japanese Motorbikes/Tight (p/s)	20
79	Mean St. Dealers MSD 001	BENT NEEDLES (LP)	30
79	Graduate GRADLP 1	BENT NEEDLES (LP, reissue)	18

MEANWHILE BACK IN COMMUNIST RUSSIA...

00	Jitter JTR 1SP	No Cigar/Morning After Pill (p/s, 300 only)	7

MEASLES

65	Columbia DB 7531	Casting My Spell/Bye Birdie Fly	40
65	Columbia DB 7673	Night People/Dog Rough Dan	25
66	Columbia DB 7875	Kicks/No Baby At All	35
66	Columbia DB 8029	Walkin' In/Looking For Love	25

MEAT LOAF

75	Ode ODS 66304	Clap Your Hands, Stamp Your Feet/Stand By Me (withdrawn)	25
78	Epic S EPC 5980	You Took The Words Right Out Of My Mouth/For Crying Out Loud (no p/s)	5
78	Epic S EPC 6281	Two Out Of Three Ain't Bad/For Crying Out Loud (no p/s)	5
78	Epic S EPC 6797	All Revved Up With No Place To Go/Paradise By The Dashboard Light (no p/s)	5
79	Epic S EPC 12-7018	Bat Out Of Hell/Heaven Can Wait (12", p/s, red vinyl)	8
81	Epic EPCA 1580	I'm Gonna Love Her For The Both Of Us/Everything Is Permitted (p/s)	5
81	Epic EPCA 11-1697	Dead Ringer For Love/More Than You Deserve (picture disc)	5
82	Epic EPCA 12-2251	MEAT LOAF IN EUROPE '82 (12" EP)	8
82	Epic EPCA 12-2251	MEAT LOAF IN EUROPE '82 (12" EP, clear vinyl, p/s, Irish issue)	30
83	Epic EPCA 2621	GREATEST ORIGINAL HITS (EP, p/s)	5

MINT VALUE £

83	Epic EPCA WA 3748	Midnight At The Lost And Found (Remix)/Fallen Angel/Bat Out Of Hell (live)/ Dead Ringer For Love (Long Version) (picture disc)	5
83	Epic EPCA A 4080	Razor's Edge (Remix)/Paradise By The Dashboard Light (p/s, with competition insert)	5
84	Arista ARISDP 585	Modern Girl/Take A Number (bike-shaped picture disc, some with poster & plinth)	6/5
84	Arista ARIST 12585D/ ARIPD 12585	Modern Girl (Freeway Mix)/Take A Number (Extended)//Modern Girl (Freeway Mix)/Take A Number (Extended) (12", double pack, 2nd 12" as picture disc)	12
85	Arista ARIPU 600	Nowhere Fast/Clap Your Hands (gatefold pop-up p/s)	5
85	Arista ARISG 600	Nowhere Fast/Clap Your Hands (gatefold p/s with booklet, some signed)	6/5
85	Arista ARISD 600	Nowhere Fast/Clap Your Hands (bike-shaped picture disc)	6
85	Arista ARISD 603	Piece Of The Action/Sailor To A Siren (jaw-shaped picture disc)	6
86	Arista ARIST 666P	Rock'N'Roll Mercenaries/RPM (w/ John Parr, black guitar-shaped picture disc)	5
86	Arista ARIST 666XP	Rock'N'Roll Mercenaries/RPM (w/ John Parr, white guitar-shaped picture disc)	5
86	Arista ARIST 683P	Getting Away With Murder/Rock'n'Roll Hero (camera-slide shaped picture disc)	5
86	Arista ARIST 10683	Getting Away With Murder/Rock'n'Roll Hero (10", circular p/s)	7
98	Virgin (no cat. no.)	No Matter What (single edit)/A Kiss Is A Terrible Thing To Waste (single edit) (CD-R, unreleased versions, custom printed disc and folded card inlay)	15
98	Virgin VSCDJX 1718	A Kiss Is A Terrible Thing To Waste (radio edit)/(soft radio edit) (CD, promo only, unreleased versions, card sleeve)	8
82	Epic EPC 11 82419	BAT OUT OF HELL (LP, picture disc)	15
82	Epic EPC 82419	BAT OUT OF HELL (LP, half-speed mastered audiophile pressing with inserts)	12

(see also Stoney & Meat Loaf, Jim Steinman, Rocky Horror Show)

MEAT WHIPLASH

85	Creation CRE 020	Don't Slip Up/Here It Comes (foldaround p/s in poly bag; 1st pressing has photo of band by fence, 2nd pressing has band in field)	15/8

(see also Jesus & Mary Chain)

MECHANICAL HORSETROUGH

70s	Kap KAPS 96	Dogshit On Your Shoes/Jeremy Germoline/Horsetrough Hoedown (p/s)	5
75	Sonet SON 2068	When Santa Lost His Trousers/The Ballad Of Big Bruce	5

MECKENBURG ZINC

70	Orange OAS 205	Hard Working Woman/I'd Like To Help You	5

MEDALLION STRINGS

60	London HLR 9218	Green Leaves Of Summer/Spellbound	6
60	London HLR 9242	Gloria's Theme (From "Butterfield 8")/Suzie Wong	6
61	London HA-R 2331	THE SOUND OF HOLLYWOOD (LP, also stereo SAH-R 6130)	12/15

MEDDY EVILS

65	Pye 7N 15941	Find Somebody To Love/A Place Called Love	125
66	Pye 7M 17091	It's All For You/Ma's Place	125

MEDIA

79	Takeaway TA 001	TV Kids/Don't Sit Back/Just For You/Rose And Crown (p/s)	12

MEDIA

80	Brain Booster Music 4	Back On The Beach Again/South Coast City Rockers (p/s)	5

MEDIATORS

70	Supreme SUP 210	When You Go To A Party (actually by Meditators)/ RUPIE EDWARDS ALLSTARS: Stop The Party	12

(see also Meditators)

MEDICINE HEAD

69	Dandelion S 4661	His Guiding Hand/This Love Of Old	18
70	Dandelion S 5075	Coast To Coast/All For Tomorrow	12
71	Dandelion DAN 7003	(And The) Pictures In The Sky/Natural Sight (also listed as K 19002) (some in p/s)	10/6
72	Dandelion 2001 276	Kum On/On The Land	6
72	Dandelion 2001 325	Only To Do What Is True/Sittin' In The Sun	6
72	Dandelion 2001 383	How Does It Feel/Morning Light	6
69	Dandelion 63757	NEW BOTTLES, OLD MEDICINE (LP)	40
71	Dandelion DAN 8005	HEAVY ON THE DRUM (LP, gatefold sleeve, also listed as K 49005; some with lyric insert)	60/45
71	Dandelion 2310 166	DARK SIDE OF THE MOON (LP, with insert)	30
73	Polydor 2310 248	ONE & ONE IS ONE (LP, gatefold sleeve)	15
74	Polydor 2383 272	THRU' A FIVE (LP)	15
76	Barn 2314 102	TWO MAN BAND (LP)	15

(see also Ashton Gardner & Dyke, British Lions)

MEDITATIONS

68	Liberty LBF 15045	Transcendental Meditation/Beautiful Experience	7

MEDITATORS

69	Bullet BU 403	Duba Duba/CECIL NICKY THOMAS: Running Alone	10
70	Big BG 302	When You Go To A Party/Good Morning Mother Cuba	10
71	Big BG 305	Music Alone Shall Live/RUPIE EDWARDS AND ALL STARS: Music Alone — Version	10
73	Pyramid PYR 7010	Great Messiah/Nana Nana	10
73	Smash SMA 2331	Things Not Easy/BONGO HERMAN & BINGY BUNNY: Ration	10

(see also Busty Brown, Pat Satchmo)

MEDIUM

68	CBS 3404	Edward Never Lies/Colours Of The Rainbow	25

MINT VALUE £

MEDIUM MEDIUM

80 APT SAP-01 — Them Or Me/Freeze (p/s) 7
81 Cherry Red CHEER 18 — Hungry, So Angry/Nadsat Dream (p/s) 7
81 Cherry Red BRED 19 — THE GLITTERHOUSE (LP) 14

BILL MEDLEY

67 Verve VS 564 — That Lucky Old Sun/My Darling Clementine 10
68 MGM MGM 1418 — I Can't Make It Alone/One Day Girl 7
68 MGM MGM 1432 — Brown Eyed Woman/Let The Good Times Roll 7
68 MGM MGM 1456 — Peace Brother Peace/Winter Won't Come This Year 10
69 MGM MGM 1475 — This Is A Love Song/Something's So Wrong 6
69 MGM MGM 1491 — Someone Is Standing Outside/Reaching Back 6
71 A&M AMS 898 — You've Lost That Lovin' Feelin'/We've Only Just Begun 6
69 MGM MGM-C(S) 8091 — BILL MEDLEY 100% (LP) 22
(see also Righteous Brothers, Garnet Mimms)

JOE MEDLIN

59 Mercury AMT 1032 — I Kneel At Your Throne/Out Of Sight, Out Of Mind 25
59 Mercury AMT 1032 — I Kneel At Your Throne/Out Of Sight, Out Of Mind (78) 10

MICHAEL MEDWIN

58 HMV POP 490 — The Army Game/What Do We Do In The Army? (with Bernard Bresslaw, Alfie Bass & Leslie Fyson) 7
58 HMV POP 490 — The Army Game/What Do We Do In The Army? (78, with Bernard Bresslaw, Alfie Bass & Leslie Fyson) 8
59 HMV POP 645 — Blankety-Blankety-Blank/Do It Yourself (with Norman Rossington) 5

KEITH MEEHAN

69 Marmalade 598 016 — Darkness Of My Life/TONY MEEHAN: Hooker Street 25

TONY MEEHAN

64 Decca F 11801 — Song Of Mexico/Kings Go Fifth 8
(see also Shadows, Jet Harris & Tony Meehan, Keith Meehan, John Paul Jones)

JOE MEEK ORCHESTRA

63 Decca F 11796 — The Kennedy March/The Theme Of Freedom 55
(see also Blue Men)

MEGADETH

87 Capitol CL 476 — Wake Up Dead/Black Friday (live) (p/s) 8
87 Capitol CLP 476 — Wake Up Dead/Black Friday (live) (skull-shaped picture disc with insert) 15
87 Capitol 12CL 476 — Wake Up Dead/Black Friday (live)/Devil's Island (live)/Wake Up Dead/ Black Friday (live) (12", p/s, some allegedly shrink-wrapped with 7" picture disc) 20/8
87 Capitol 12CL 476 — Wake Up Dead/Black Friday (Tommy Vance Show)/Devil's Island (Tommy Vance Show) (12", stickered p/s, with 'Deth' certificate) 12
88 Capitol CL 480 — Anarchy In The U.K./Liar (p/s) 8
88 Capitol CLP 480 — Anarchy In The U.K./Liar (U.K.-shaped picture disc) 10
88 Capitol CLP 489 — Mary Jane/Hook In Mouth (picture disc) 7
90 SBK SBKPD 4 — No More Mr. Nice Guy/DEAD ON: "Different Breed" (chair-shaped pic disc) 7
90 SBK 12 SBKP 4 — No More Mr. Nice Guy/DEAD ON: "Different Breed"/DANGEROUS TOYS: "Demon Bell [The Ballad Of Horace Pinker]" (12", poster p/s) 8
90 SBK CDSBK 4 — No More Mr. Nice Guy/(DEAD ON: "Different Breed")/(DANGEROUS TOYS: "Demon Bell [The Ballad Of Horace Pinker]") (CD) 8
91 Capitol CLS 604 — Hangar 18 (MJ 12 Edit)/The Conjuring (live) (p/s, shrinkwrapped with patch) 8
91 Capitol CLPD 604 — Hangar 18 (MJ 12 Edit)/The Conjuring (live) (Vic-shaped picture disc) 12
91 Capitol CDCL 604 — Hangar 18/Conjuring/Hangar 18 (version)/Hangar 18 (Live)/Hook In Mouth (CD) . 15
92 Capitol 12CLS 662 — Symphony Of Destruction/Breakpoint/Go To Hell (12", p/s, clear vinyl with giant autographed poster) 8
92 Capitol CLP 669 — Skin O' My Teeth (LP Version)/Holy Wars... The Punishment Due (The General Schwarzkopf Mix)/High Speed Dirt (live)/The Passes (Mustaine Remarks On Game) (10" bronze Megadeth box with passes & game rules) 10
88 Capitol ESTP 2053 — SO FAR, SO GOOD ... SO WHAT (LP, picture disc with insert) 18
88 M. For Nations MFN 46P — KILLING IS MY BUSINESS ... AND BUSINESS IS GOOD (LP, picture disc with insert) 18
88 Capitol ESTP 2022 — PEACE SELLS ... BUT WHO'S BUYING? (LP, picture disc with insert) 18
90 Capitol ESTPD 2132 — RUST IN PEACE (LP, picture disc, die cut sleeve) 18
94 Capitol ESTPD 2244 — YOUTHANASIA (LP, picture disc) 15
95 Capitol CDESTS 2244 — YOUTHANASIA/HIDDEN TREASURES (2-CD, card sleeve, 2,000 only) 30
(see also Marty Friedman, Cacophony)

MEGATON

71 Deram DM-R 331 — Out Of Your Own Little World/Niagara 40
71 Deram SML-R 1086 — MEGATON (LP) 320
(see also Hackensack)

MEGATON

81 Hot Metal HMM 69 — Aluminium Lady/Diehard (p/s) 40

MEGATONS (Jamaica)

70 Downtown DT 464 — Take It Easy/Funk The Beat 10
70 Downtown DT 469 — Militant Man/MUSIC DOCTORS: Reggae Jeggae Version 10
(see also Revelation)

MEGATONS (U.S.)

65 Sue WI 325 — Shimmy Shimmy Walk (Parts 1 & 2) 40
(see also Billy Lee Riley)

MEGATRONS

59 Top Rank JAR 146 Velvet Waters/The Merry Piper. . . . 8
59 Top Rank JAR 146 Velvet Waters/The Merry Piper (78) . . . 8
59 Top Rank JAR 236 Tootie Flootie/Whispering Winds. . . . 8

GEORGE MEGGIE

72 Bullet BU 504 Hard To Believe/MAX ROMEO: Softie . . . 7
72 Punch PH 112 People Like People/MAX ROMEO: Softie . . . 7

JOHN MEHEGAN TRIO

56 London EZC 19005 THE FIRST MEHEGAN VOLUME ONE (EP) . . . 8
56 London EZC 19015 THE FIRST MEHEGAN VOLUME TWO (EP) . . . 8

MEKONS

78 Fast Products FAST 1 Never Been In A Riot/32 Weeks/Heart And Soul (p/s). . . . 10
78 Fast Products FAST 7 Where Were You?/I'll Have To Dance Then (On My Own) (p/s) . . . 5
80 Virgin SV 101 Teeth/Guardian//Kill/Stay Cool (double pack, gatefold p/s) . . . 5
82 CNT CNT 1 This Sporting Life (6.12)/Frustration (6.21)/(mystery live track) (12", p/s) . . . 8
82 CNT CNT 008 This Sporting Life/Fight The Cuts (p/s) . . . 5
82 CNT CNT 014 THE ENGLISH DANCING MASTER (12" EP) . . . 8
80s Catalogue CAT 075/3 Amnesia (square flexidisc with *The Catalogue* magazine). . . . 5
(see also Batfish Boys, Sally Timms & Drifting Cowgirls, Ut)

(George) MELACHRINO ORCHESTRA

56 HMV B 10958 Autumn Concerto/A Woman In Love . . . 8
57 HMV 7 EG 8206 PARIS PROMENADE (EP) . . . 8
59 HMV GES 5762 THE MAGIC OF MELACHRINO STRINGS (EP, stereo). . . . 8

MEL & DAVE

70 Upsetter US 330 Spinning Wheel/Version. . . . 15

MEL & KIM

86 Supreme SUPETX 107 Showing Out (The Mortgage Mix)/System (House Mix) (12", p/s). . . . 12
86 Supreme SUPETZ 107 Showing Out (Freehold Mix)/System (House Mix) (12", p/s). . . . 12
87 Supreme SUPETX 111 Respectable (The Shop Mix)/Respectable (7" Version)/Respectable (Extra Beats Version) (12"). . . . 15
87 Supreme SUPETP 111 Respectable (The Tabloid Mix)/Respectable (7" Version)/Respectable (Extra Beats Version) (12", picture disc in PVC sleeve) . . . 10
87 Supreme SUPETX 113 F.L.M. (Two Grooves Under One Nation Remix)/F.L.M. (Dub Mix – Version 2) (12", p/s) . . . 12
87 Supreme SUPETP 113 F.L.M. (mixes) (12" picture disc) . . . 12
88 Supreme SUPETX 117 That's The Way It Is (House Remix)/I'm The One Who Really Loves You (US Remix)/You Changed My Life (12", p/s, initially with poster) . . . 15/12
88 Supreme SUPETZ 117 That's The Way It Is (Acid House Remix)/ That's The Way It Is (Acid Dub)/ You Changed My Life (12") . . . 12
88 Supreme SUPETP 117 That's The Way It Is (Acid House Remix)/ That's The Way It Is (Acid Dub)/ You Changed My Life (12" picture disc) . . . 12
88 Supreme SUPECD 117 That's The Way It Is/I'm The One Who Really Loves You (US Remix)/ You Changed My Life (CD). . . . 20

MEL & TIM

70 Concord CON 004 Backfield In Motion/Do Right Baby (pink label, later brown). . . . 6/5
73 Stax 2025 125 Starting All Over Again/It Hurts To Want You So Bad . . . 5
73 Stax 2025 171 What's Your Name/Free For All . . . 5
73 Stax 2325 090 STARTING ALL OVER AGAIN (LP). . . . 18

MELANIE

68 Buddah 201 027 Mr. Tambourine Man/Christopher Robin . . . 6
69 Buddah 201 028 Bobo's Party/I'm Back In Town . . . 6
69 Buddah 201 063 Tuning My Guitar/Beautiful People (withdrawn, demos may exist) . . . 10+
69 Buddah 201 066 Beautiful People/Uptown And Down . . . 6
70 Buddah 2011 013 Lay Down (Candles In The Rain)/Animal Crackers . . . 6
70 Buddah 2011 039 Peace Will Come (According To Plan)/Close To It All . . . 6
71 Buddah 2011 064 Stop! I Don't Wanna Hear It Any More/Beautiful People. . . . 6
71 Buddah 2011 071 The Good Book/Nickel Song . . . 6
72 Buddah 2011 093 Alexander Beetle/Christopher Robin/Animal Crackers. . . . 6
72 Buddah 2011 115 Ring The Living Bell/Railroad . . . 6
72 Buddah 2011 136 Some Day I'll Be A Farmer/Lay Lady Lay . . . 6
72 Neighbourhood NBH 1 Together Alone/Summer Weaving . . . 6
73 Neighbourhood NBH 5 Do You Believe/Stoneground Words . . . 6
73 Neighbourhood NBH 6 Bitter Bad/Do You Believe . . . 6
73 Neighbourhood NBH 8 Seeds/Some Say (I Got Devil) . . . 6
73 Neighbourhood NBH 9 Will You Love Me Tomorrow/Here I Am . . . 6
73 Lyntone LYN 2673/4 A Gift From Honey October 1973 (flexidisc, p/s). . . . 7
75 N'hood SNBH 3789 Almost Like Being In Love/Beautiful People. . . . 5
83 Neighbourhood NBP 1 Every Breath Of The Way/Lover's Lullaby (picture disc). . . . 5
69 Buddah 203 019 BORN TO BE (LP, gatefold sleeve). . . . 25
69 Buddah 203 028 AFFECTIONATELY MELANIE (LP, with inner lyric sheet) . . . 20
70 Buddah 2318 009 CANDLES IN THE RAIN (LP, gatefold sleeve) . . . 20
70 Buddah 2318 011 LEFTOVER WINE (LP, gatefold sleeve) . . . 20
71 Buddah 2318 034 ALL THE RIGHT NOISES (LP, soundtrack) . . . 20
71 Buddah 2322 001 THE GOOD BOOK (LP, gatefold sleeve, with booklet) . . . 15
71 Buddah 2322 002 GATHER ME (LP, gatefold sleeve) . . . 15
72 Buddah 2318 054 GARDEN IN THE CITY (LP, scratch'n'sniff sleeve) . . . 15
72 Buddah 2659 013 THE FOUR SIDES OF MELANIE (2-LP) . . . 18
73 Neighbourhood NHTC 251 STONEGROUND WORDS (LP, gatefold sleeve, with lyric inner & poster) . . . 12

TERRY MELCHER

68 Rex R 11039 Indian Lake/Be My Girl. . . . 7
60s Reprise K 54016 MEMORIES (LP) . . . 12

MINT VALUE £

GIL MELLE (QUINTET)
55 Vogue LDE 141 GIL MELLE QUINTET (10" LP) . . . 20

SUSAN MELLEN
75 MAM MAMAS 1014 THE MELLEN BIRD (LP, with insert) . . . 30

JOHN COUGAR MELLENCAMP
86 Riva JCMDP 5 Small Town/(Version)//Hurts So Good/The Kind Of Fella I Am (p/s, double pack) . . 5
89 Mercury 080 212-2 Paper In Fire/Never Too Old/Under The Boardwalk/Cold Sweat/ Paper In Fire (CD Video) . . . 12
89 Mercury 080 200-2 Pop Singer/J.M.'s Question/Check It Out (live)/Pop Singer (live)/ Pop Singer (CD Video) . . . 12
(see also John Cougar)

MELLODITIES
64 R&B JB 179 Vacation/TOMMY McCOOK: Music Is My Occupation . . . 30

MELLOTONES
57 Beltona BE 2673 Norah/If I Knocked The L Out Of Kelly (78) . . . 8

MELL(O)TONES
68 Amalgamated AMG 812 Fat Girl In Red/VERSATILES: Trust The Book . . . 18
68 Amalgamated AMG 817 Feel Good (actually maybe by Bleechers)/Soulful Mood (actually by Tommy McCook & Supersonics) . . . 22
68 Doctor Bird DB 1136 None Such/VAL BENNETT: Popeye On The Shore . . . 20
68 Trojan TR 612 Uncle Charlie/What A Botheration . . . 12
68 Pyramid PYR 6060 Let's Join Together/BEVERLEY'S ALLSTARS: I Don't Know . . . 12
69 Camel CA 18 Facts Of Life/TERMITES: I'll Be Waiting . . . 8
70 Escort ERT 844 Work It/SOUL MAN: Good Lover . . . 7
(see also Sexy Girls)

MELLO & MELLOTONES
72 Summit SUM 8538 Haile Selasie/Old Man River . . . 6
(see also Mellotones)

MELLOW CANDLE
68 SNB 55-3645 Feeling High/Tea With The Sun . . . 60
72 Deram DM 357 Dan The Wing/Silversong . . . 45
72 Deram SDL 7 SWADDLING SONGS (LP) . . . 475

MELLOW CATS with Count Ossie & Warrickas
61 Blue Beat BB 68 Rock A Man Soul/MONTO & CYCLONES: Lazy Lou (B-side actually by Monty [Alexander] & Cyclones) . . . 30
(see also Melo Cats)

MELLOW FRUITFULNESS
67 Columbia S(C)X 6242 MEDITATION (LP, mono/stereo) . . . 25

MELLOW LARKS
60 Blue Beat BB 16 Time To Pray (Alleluia)/Love You Baby . . . 25
61 Blue Beat BB 38 No More Wedding/Lite Of My Life . . . 25
(see also Basil Gabbidon)

GEORGE MELLY (& MICK MULLIGAN BAND)
51 Tempo A 96 Rock Island Line/Send Me To The 'Lectric Chair (78, as The George Melly Trio) . . 20
52 Tempo A 104 Kitchen Man/Jazzbo Brown From Memphis Town (78) . . . 10
55 Decca F 10457 Frankie And Johnny/I'm Down In The Dumps . . . 10
55 Decca F 10457 Frankie And Johnny/I'm Down In The Dumps (78) . . . 10
56 Tempo A 144 Jenny's Ball/Muddy Water . . . 10
56 Tempo A 144 Jenny's Ball/Muddy Water (78) . . . 10
56 Tempo A 147 Death Letter/Cemetery Blues . . . 10
56 Tempo A 147 Death Letter/Cemetery Blues (78) . . . 10
56 Decca F 10763 Kingdom Coming/I'm A Ding Dong Daddy . . . 10
56 Decca F 10763 Kingdom Coming/I'm A Ding Dong Daddy (78) . . . 10
56 Decca FJ 10779 Waiting For A Train/Railroadin' Man . . . 8
56 Decca FJ 10779 Waiting For A Train/Railroadin' Man (78) . . . 8
56 Decca FJ 10806 My Canary Has Circles Under His Eyes/Heebie Jeebies . . . 8
56 Decca FJ 10806 My Canary Has Circles Under His Eyes/Heebie Jeebies (78) . . . 8
57 Decca FJ 10840 Black Bottom/Magnolia . . . 8
57 Decca FJ 10840 Black Bottom/Magnolia (78) . . . 8
59 Decca F 11115 Abdul Abulbul Amir/Get Away, Old Man, Get Away . . . 5
59 Decca F 11115 Abdul Abulbul Amir/Get Away, Old Man, Get Away (78) . . . 8
60 Pye 7N 15253 Ise A Muggin'/Run Come See Jerusalem . . . 5
75 Warner Bros WB 16532 Ain't Misbehavin'/My Canary Has Circles Under His Eyes (p/s) . . . 5
56 Tempo EXA 41 GEORGE MELLY WITH MICK MULLIGAN'S JAZZ BAND (EP) . . . 12
56 Tempo EXA 47 GEORGE MELLY SINGS DOOM (EP, with Mick Mulligan's Jazz Band) . . . 18
58 Decca DFE 6552 MICHIGAN WATER BLUES (EP) . . . 10
58 Decca DFE 6557 ABDUL ABULBUL AMIR (EP) . . . 10
61 Columbia SEG 8093 THE PSYCHOLOGICAL SIGNIFICANCE OF ANIMAL SYMBOLISM IN AMERICAN NEGRO FOLK MUSIC AND ALL THAT JAZZ (EP) . . . 8
(see also Mick Mulligan Band)

MELO CATS
61 Blue Beat BB 54 Another Moses/ROLAND ALPHONSO & ALLEY CATS: Hully Gully Rock . . . 35
(see also Mellow Cats)

MELODIANS
66 Island WI 3014 Lay It On/Meet Me . . . 30
67 Coxsone CS 7004 I Should Have Made It Up/JOE HIGGS: Neighbour Neighbour . . . 30
67 Treasure Isle TI 7006 You Don't Need Me/I Will Get Along . . . 30
67 Treasure Isle TI 7022 You Have Caught Me/I Know Just How She Feels . . . 30
67 Treasure Isle TI 7023 Last Train To Expo. '67/TOMMY McCOOK & SUPERSONICS: Expo . . . 30
68 Treasure Isle TI 7028 Come On, Little Girl/TOMMY McCOOK & SUPERSONICS: Got Your Soul . . . 30

68 Doctor Bird DB 1125 Little Nut Tree/You Are My Only Love . . . 25
68 Doctor Bird DB 1139 Swing And Dine/I Could Be King . . . 25
68 Fab FAB 61 Sweet Rose/It Comes And Goes . . . 18
69 Gas GAS 108 Ring Of Gold/You've Got It . . . 8
69 Gas GAS 116 Personally Speaking/LLOYD ROBINSON: Trouble Trouble . . . 8
69 Crab CRAB 15 When There Is You/UNIQUES: My Woman's Love . . . 7
69 Trojan TR 660 Everybody Bawlin'/TOMMY McCOOK: Kilowatt . . . 8
69 Trojan TR 695 Sweet Sensation/It's My Delight . . . 5
70 Trojan TR 7720 A Day Seems So Long/BEVERLEY'S ALLSTARS: Project . . . 6
70 Trojan TR 7764 Say Darling Say/Come Rock It To Me . . . 8
70 High Note HS 044 Love Is A Good Thing/No Nola . . . 6
70 Summit SUM 8505 Walking In The Rain/Rivers Of Babylon . . . 7
70 Summit SUM 8508 Rivers Of Babylon/BEVERLEY'S ALL STARS: Babylon Version . . . 5
71 Duke DU 128 The Sensational Melodians (Parts 1 & 2) . . . 6
71 Summit SUM 8512 It Took A Miracle/BEVERLEY'S ALLSTARS: Miraculous Version . . . 5
71 Summit SUM 8522 Come Ethiopians, Come/BEVERLEY'S ALL STARS: Version Two . . . 7
71 Summit SUM 8532 My Love, My Life/My Love, My Life – Version . . . 6
72 Summit SUM 8534 The Time Has Come/BEVERLEY'S ALL STARS: McIntosh
(B-side actually "No Sins At All" by Melodians) . . . 6
72 Bullet BU 496 Tropical Land/HUGH ROY & SLIM SMITH: Love I Bring . . . 6
72 Duke DU 130 The Mighty Melodians (Adapted) (Parts 1 & 2) . . . 6
72 Attack ATT 8025 This Beautiful Land/MELODIOUS RHYTHMS: Version . . . 6
72 Attack ATT 8031 Without You (What Would I Do)/DYNAMITES: Instrumental . . . 6
72 Punch PH 111 Round And Round/UPSETTERS: Round Version . . . 6
73 Randy's RAN 530 Passion Love/Love Makes The World Go Round . . . 6
(see also Gentiles, Tony Brevett, Brent Dowe, Jaylads, Trevor McNaughton, Gaylads, Joe Grinne)

FITZROY ALEXANDER MELODY

50s Sagomes SG 107 One Gone/LORD INVADER: The Sport Pool (78) . . . 7

JOHNNY MELODY

67 Pyramid PYR 6023 Govern Your Mouth (actually by George Dekker)/
ROLAND ALPHONSO: Peace And Love . . . 20
(see also Lloyd & Johnny Melody under 'L', Lloyd Terrell)

MELODY ENCHANTERS

63 Island WI 049 Enchanter's Ball/I'll Be True . . . 25
63 R&B JB 117 Gone Gone/Blueberry Hill . . . 25

MELODY FAIR

68 Decca F 12801 Something Happened To Me/Sittin', Watchin', Waitin' . . . 5

'MELODY MAKER' ALLSTARS

(see under Humphrey Lyttelton)

MELO'S MARITIME

67 Philips BF 1602 Blow The Man Up/Maneater . . . 5

KANSAS CITY MELROSE/CASINO SIMPSON

72 Chicago Piano 12-001 KANSAS CITY MELROSE/CASINO SIMPSON (LP) . . . 15

MONIQUE MELSEN

71 Decca F 23170 The Love Beat/Pomme Pomme Pomme . . . 12

JOE MELSON

61 Polydor NH 66959 Oh Yeah!/What's The Use I Still Love You . . . 50
61 Polydor NH 66961 Hey Mister Cupid/No One Really Cares . . . 50
64 Hickory 45-1229 Stay Away From Her/His Girl . . . 7

MELTING BEAR

85 Beggars Banquet BEG 144 It Makes No Difference/Nature's Way/Sea Song (unreleased,
white label test pressings only) . . . 6
(see also Icicle Works)

MELTON CONSTABLE

70s SIS private pressing MELTON CONSTABLE (LP) . . . 200

HAROLD MELVIN & BLUE NOTES

72 CBS 8291 I Miss You (Parts 1 & 2) . . . 5
72 CBS 8496 If You Don't Know Me By Now/Let Me Into Your World . . . 5
75 Route RT 06 Get Out/You May Not Love Me . . . 10
77 ABC 4161 Reaching For The World/Stay Together . . . 5
73 CBS 65350 HAROLD MELVIN & THE BLUES NOTES (LP) . . . 12
73 CBS Q 65859 BLACK AND BLUE (LP, quadrophonic) . . . 12

MELVINS

90 Tupelo TUPEP 10 Sweet Young Thing Ain't Sweet No More/STEEL POLE BATH TUB:
I Dreamed I Dream (12", p/s, green vinyl, 600 only) . . . 12
92 Tupelo TUP 392 King Buzzo (CD) . . . 8
92 Tupelo TUP 412 Joe Preston (CD) . . . 8
92 Tupelo TUP 422 Lysol (CD) . . . 8
99 Ipecac IPC 2 The Maggot (CD) . . . 8

MEMBERS

78 Stiff/One Off OFF 3 Solitary Confinement/Rat Up A Drainpipe (p/s) . . . 15
79 Virgin VS 242 The Sound Of The Suburbs/Handling The Big Jets (clear vinyl, window p/s) . . . 5
80 Virgin VS 352 Flying Again/Disco Oui Oui//Live In A Lift/Rat Up A Drainpipe
(double pack, gatefold p/s) . . . 5

MEMOS

59 Parlophone R 4616 The Biddy Leg/My Type Of Girl . . . 90

MINT VALUE £

MEMPHIS BEND

76	United Artists UP 36132	Ubangi Stomp/Tennessee	8
77	United Artists UAS 30036	GOOD ROCKIN' TONITE (LP)	15

MEMPHIS HORNS

71	Atlantic 2091 080	Woolly Bully/I Can't Turn You Loose	6
77	RCA PB 0836	Get Up And Dance/Don't Abuse It	6
71	Mojo 2466 010	THE MEMPHIS HORNS (LP)	30

MEMPHIS JUG BAND

55	HMV 7EG 8073	MEMPHIS JUG BAND (EP, withdrawn)	100
70s	Saydisc Matchbox RL 33	MEMPHIS JUG BAND (LP)	18
71	Saydisc Matchbox RL 337	MEMPHIS JUG BAND VOLUME 2 (LP)	18

MEMPHIS MINNIE

64	Heritage H 103	MEMPHIS MINNIE (EP)	75
69	Limited Edition (no cat. no.)	MEMPHIS MINNIE 1934-1936 (LP)	40
69	Limited Edition (no cat. no.)	MEMPHIS MINNIE 1934-1941 (LP)	40
69	Sunflower ET 1400	MEMPHIS MINNIE 1941-1949 (LP, 99 copies only)	50
74	Flyright LP 108	MEMPHIS MINNIE 1934-1941 (LP, reissue)	12
74	Flyright LP 109	MEMPHIS MINNIE 1941-1949 (LP, reissue)	12

MEMPHIS SLIM

53	Esquire 10-319	Harlem Bound/ST. LOUIS JIMMY R&B BAND: Holiday For Boogie (78)	35
60	Collector JDN 102	Pinetop's Blues/How Long	18
62	Storyville A 45055	Big City Girl/El Capitan	15
61	Collector JEN 5	GOING TO KANSAS CITY (EP)	30
62	Storyville SEP 385	STORYVILLE BLUES ANTHOLOGY VOL. 5 — BOOGIE WOOGIE AND THE BLUES (EP)	22
63	Vocalion VEP 170155	MEMPHIS SLIM AND LITTLE RICHARD (EP)	75
63	Summit LSE 2041	WORLD'S FOREMOST BLUES SINGERS (EP)	12
61	Collector JGN 1004	MEMPHIS SLIM U.S.A. (LP)	45
61	Collector JGN 1005	MEMPHIS SLIM U.S.A. (VOL. 2) (LP)	45
62	Bluesville BV 1018	JUST BLUES (LP)	25
62	Storyville SLP 118	MEMPHIS SLIM (LP)	25
62	Storyville SLP 138	THIS IS A GOOD TIME TO WRITE A SONG (LP)	25
62	Fontana 688 302 ZL	NO STRAIN (LP)	22
63	United Artists ULP 1042	BROKEN SOUL BLUES (LP)	22
64	Storyville SLP 118	TRAVELLIN' WITH THE BLUES (LP)	22
64	Xtra XTRA 1008	MEMPHIS SLIM (LP)	18
64	Fidelio ATL 4115	THE WORLD'S FOREMOST BLUES SINGER (LP)	12
64	Fontana 688 701	ALONE WITH MY FRIENDS (LP)	30
65	Fontana TL 5254	CLAP YOUR HANDS (LP)	25
65	Melodisc MLPS 12-149	FATTENIN' FROGS FOR SNAKES (LP)	35
66	Fontana 688 315 ZL	FRISCO BAY BLUES (LP)	30
67	Polydor 623 211	PINETOP'S BLUES (LP)	20
68	Polydor 623 263	BLUESINGLY YOURS (LP, with Mickey Baker)	20
68	Xtra XTRA 5060	ALL KINDS OF BLUES (LP)	18
69	Xtra XTRA 1085	CHICAGO BLUES (LP)	18
69	Joy JOYS 143	AT THE GATE OF HORN (LP)	12
69	Beacon BEAS 6	LEGEND OF THE BLUES VOL. 2 (LP)	12
72	Barclay 920 214	BLUE MEMPHIS (LP, with Peter Green)	60
72	Barclay 920 332-3	OLD TIMES, NEW TIMES (2-LP)	20
72	Polydor 2460 155	ROCK ME BABY (LP)	12
73	Sonet SNTF 647	LEGACY OF THE BLUES: 7 (LP)	12
73	Ember EMB 3422	SOUL BLUES (LP)	12
74	Barclay 920 407	CLASSIC ALL AMERICAN MUSIC (LP)	12
75	Barclay 90 034	GOING BACK TO TENNESSEE (LP)	12
76	Black Lion BLP 30196	CHICAGO BOOGIE (LP)	12
70s	Xtra XTRA 5063	ALL KINDS OF BLUES (LP)	15

(see also Washboard Sam, Ivory Joe Hunter, Otis Spann)

MEMPHIS THREE

68	Page One POF 070	Wild Thing/She's A Yum Yum	7

MEN

79	Virgin VS 269	I Don't Depend On You/Cruel (p/s)	10
79	Virgin VS 269-12	I Don't Depend On You/Cruel (12", p/s)	15

(see also Human League, Philip Oakey & Giorgio Moroder)

MENACE

77	Illegal IL 004	Screwed Up/Insane Society (p/s)	15
77	Illegal IL 004	Screwed Up/Insane Society (12", p/s)	20
77	Small Wonder SMALL 5	G.L.C./I'm Civilized (p/s)	15
78	Illegal IL 008	I Need Nothing/Electrocutioner (p/s)	15
78	Fresh FRESH 14	The Young Ones/Tomorrow's World/Live For Today (p/s)	15
79	Small Wonder SMALL 16	Final Vinyl: Last Year's Youth/Carry No Banners (p/s)	12

(see also Aces, Vermilion & Aces)

CARLOS MENDES

72	Pye International 7N 25581	Shadows/Glow-Worm	8

SERGIO MENDES & BRASIL '66

68	A&M AMS 739	Scarborough Fair — Canticle/Canto Triste (p/s)	5
70	A&M AMS 774	Ye-me-le/Easy To Be Hard	6
66	Pye NPL 28089	HERB ALPERT PRESENTS SERGIO MENDES AND BRASIL '66 (LP)	14
67	A&M AML(S) 902	EQUINOX (LP)	12
68	A&M AML 911	LOOK AROUND (LP)	12
69	A&M AMLS 922	FOOL ON THE HILL (LP)	12
69	A&M AMLS 948	CRYSTAL ILLUSIONS (LP)	12
70	A&M AMLS 989	LIVE AT EXPO 70 (LP)	25

MINT VALUE £

70 A&M AMLS 2000 — STILLNESS (LP) 18
72 A&M AMLS 64353 — PRIMAL ROOTS (LP) 12
74 Bell BELLS 240 — VINTAGE '74 (LP, as Sergio Mendes & Brazil '74) 12

MENDES PREY

83 MP AM 076 — On To The Borderline/Runnin' For You (p/s) 20
86 Wag WAG 2 — Wonderland/Can You Believe It (p/s) 25
86 Wag 12 WAG 2 — Wonderland/Can You Believe It (12", p/s) 25

ENOCH & CHRISTY MENSAH

60s Melodisc M 1569 — Rebecca/Dakuku Dum 5

E.T. MENSAH & HIS TEMPO'S BAND

55 Decca WAL 1001 — DECCA PRESENTS (10" LP) 22

MENSWE@R

95 Laurel LAU 4 — I'll Manage Somehow/Secondhand (p/s, 2,500 only) 8
95 Laurel LAUCD 4 — I'll Manage Somehow/Secondhand (CD, 2,500 only) 10
95 Laurel LAUXDJ 5 — Daydreamer (Radio Mix)/(Student Union Mix) (10", no'd white sl., 5,000 only) 8

MENTATZ

81 Naff N 001 — Never Trust A Russian/Dead To The World (p/s) 5

MEN WITHOUT HATS

82 Statik STAT 13 — Antarctic/Modern Dancing (p/s) 6
82 Statik STAT 14 — I Got The Message/Utter Space (p/s) 5
85 Statik CDST — Folk Of The 80's Part 3 (CD) 8
87 Mercury MERCD 257 — Pop Goes The World/The End (Of The World)/ Pop Goes The World (Dance Mix) (CD) 8
85 Statik CDST 10 — RHYTHM OF YOUTH (CD) 75

IAN MENZIES

58 Pye Jazz 7NJ 2027 — Polly Wolly Doodle/In A Persian Market (with His New Stompers) 6
58 Pye Jazz 7NJ 2028 — Bill Bailey Won't You Please Come Home/Hot Time In The Old Town Tonight (as Ian Menzies & Clyde Valley Stompers) 6
58 Pye Jazz NJ 2028 — Bill Bailey Won't You Please Come Home/Hot Time In The Old Town Tonight (as Ian Menzies & Clyde Valley Stompers) (78) 8
59 Pye Jazz 7NJ 2031 — The Fish Man/Salty Dog (as Ian Menzies & Clyde Valley Stompers) 5
61 Pye Jazz 7NJ 2046 — Auf Wiedersehn/Taboo 10
58 Pye Jazz NJE 1049 — MELODY MAKER ALL STARS (EP) 12
60 Pye Nixa NJE 1071 — SWINGIN' SEAMUS (EP) 15
60 Pye Jazz NJL 26 — IAN MENZIES AND THE CLYDE VALLEY STOMPERS (LP) 15

(see also Clyde Valley Stompers)

JOHNNY MERCER

53 Capitol LC 6633 — CAPITOL PRESENTS JOHNNY MERCER (10" LP) 12
54 Capitol LC 6640 — CAPITOL PRESENTS JOHNNY MERCER VOL. 2 (10" LP) 12
54 Capitol LC 6648 — CAPITOL PRESENTS JOHNNY MERCER VOL. 3 (10" LP) 12
54 Capitol LC 6655 — CAPITOL PRESENTS JOHNNY MERCER VOL. 4 (10" LP) 12

MARY MAE MERCER

65 Decca DFE 8599 — MARY MAE MERCER (EP) 60

FREDDIE MERCURY

84 CBS A 4735 — Love Kills/GEORGIO MORODER: Rotwang's Party (p/s) 6
84 CBS WA 4735 — Love Kills/GEORGIO MORODER: Rotwang's Party (picture disc) 50
84 CBS TA 4375 — Love Kills (Extended)/GEORGIO MORODER: Rotwang's Party (12", p/s) 12
85 CBS A 6019 — I Was Born To Love You/Stop All The Fighting (p/s) 6
85 CBS DA 6019 — I Was Born To Love You/Stop All The Fighting//Love Kills (Extended)/ Stop All The Fighting (Extended) (double pack) 30
85 CBS TA 6019 — I Was Born To Love You (7.03)/Stop All The Fighting (12", p/s) 20
85 CBS A 6413 — Made In Heaven (Remix 3.59)/She Blows Hot And Cold (p/s) 10
85 CBS WA 6413 — Made In Heaven (Remix)/She Blows Hot And Cold (shaped picture disc) 50
85 CBS WA 6413 — Made In Heaven (Remix)/She Blows Hot And Cold (uncut shaped picture disc). 800
85 CBS TA 6413 — Made In Heaven (Extended Remix 4.43)/Made In Heaven (Remix 3.59)/ She Blows Hot And Cold (Extended Version) (12", p/s) 20
85 CBS A 6555 — Living On My Own/My Love Is Dangerous (p/s) 6
85 CBS TA 6555 — Living On My Own (Extended 6.38)/My Love Is Dangerous (Extended 6.25) (12", p/s) 18
85 CBS GTA 6555 — Living On My Own (Extended 6.38)/My Love Is Dangerous (Extended 6.25) (12", gatefold p/s) 30
85 CBS A 6725 — Love Me Like There's No Tomorrow/Let's Turn It On (p/s) 25
85 CBS TA 6725 — Love Me Like There's No Tomorrow (Extended Version)/Let's Turn It On (Extended Version) (12", p/s) 45
85 CBS DTA 6725 — Love Me Like There's No Tomorrow (Extended Version)/Let's Turn It On (Extended Version)//Living On My Own (Extended 6.38)/My Love Is Dangerous (Extended 6.25) (12", double pack, shrinkwrapped with stickers) 150
85 CBS TA 6725 — Love Me Like There's No Tomorrow (Extended Version)/Let's Turn It On (Extended Version) (12", promo, white card sleeve, with sticker) 75
86 EMI EMI 5559 — Time (From The Musical)/Time (Instrumental) (p/s, some with inner sleeve) ... 18/8
86 EMI 12EMI 5559 — Time (From The Musical) (Extended)/Time/Time (Instrumental) (12", p/s) 15
87 Parlophone R 6151 — The Great Pretender/Exercises In Free Love (Mercury Vocal) (p/s) 5
87 Parlophone RP 6151 — The Great Pretender/Exercises In Free Love (Mercury Vocal) (shaped picture disc) 50
87 Parlophone RP 6151 — The Great Pretender/Exercises In Free Love (Mercury Vocal) (shaped picture disc, with unfolded or folded plinth) 90/70
87 Parlophone RP 6151 — The Great Pretender/Exercises In Free Love (Mercury Vocal) (uncut shaped picture disc) 500
87 Parlophone 10R 6151 — The Great Pretender (Extended Version)/(7" Version)/Exercises In Free Love (7" Version) (10", 1-sided, printed white label, plain black die-cut sleeve, promo only) 40

MINT VALUE £

87 Parlophone 12R 6151 The Great Pretender (Extended)/(The Great Pretender 7")/ Exercises In Free Love (12", p/s) . . . 12
87 Polydor POSP 887 Barcelona/Exercises In Free Love (Caballé Vocal) (with Montserrat Caballé, some with gatefold p/s) . . . 8/5
87 Polydor POSPX 887 Barcelona (Single Version)/Exercises In Free Love (Caballé Vocal) (12" Version)/Barcelona (Extended) (12", some with gatefold p/s) . . . 18/12
87 Polydor POSPP 887 Barcelona (7" Version)/Exercises In Free Love (Caballé Vocal) (7" Version)/ Barcelona (Extended Version) (12", picture disc) . . . 50
87 Polydor POCD 887 Barcelona (7" Version)/Exercises In Free Love (Caballé Vocal) (7" Version)/ Barcelona (Extended Version) (CD, card p/s) . . . 20
87 Polydor POCD 887 Barcelona/Exercises In Free Love (Version 2) (Caballé Vocal)/ Barcelona (Extended) (CD, autographed card p/s, promo only) . . . 300+
87 Polydor PO 23 DJ The Golden Boy (with Montserrat Caballé) (radio edit) (1-sided DJ sampler, p/s, with sticker) . . . 250
88 Polydor POSP 23 The Golden Boy (with Montserrat Caballé)/The Fallen Priest (p/s) . . . 10
88 Polydor POSPX 23 The Golden Boy/The Fallen Priest/The Golden Boy (Instrumental) (12", p/s) . . . 20
88 Polydor POCD 23 The Golden Boy/The Fallen Priest/The Golden Boy (Instrumental) (CD) . . . 35
88 Polydor POSP 29 How Can I Go On/Overture Piccante (with Montserrat Caballe) (p/s) . . . 15
88 Polydor POSX 29 How Can I Go On/Overture Piccante (with Montserrat Caballe) (picture disc) . . . 45
89 Polydor PZ 29 How Can I Go On/Guide Me Home/Overture Piccante (12", p/s) . . . 25
89 Polydor PZCD 29 How Can I Go On/Guide Me Home/Overture Piccante (CD, picture disc) . . . 35
88 Polydor CD 3 125 211 The Golden Boy/La Japanese/Barcelona (CD promo, unreleased p/s, jewel case) . . . 100
89 Polydor 0805 548-2 Ensueno/Barcelona (Edit 4.24)/Exercises In Free Love/Barcelona (Extended Version 7.02)/Barcelona (Video) (CD Video) . . . 60
89 Polydor 0805 580-2 The Fallen Priest/The Golden Boy (Album Version)/The Golden Boy (Instrumental Version)/The Golden Boy (Video) (CD Video) . . . 60
92 Polydor PZCD 221 Barcelona (Single Version)/Exercises In Free Love (Caballé Vocal)/ Barcelona (Edit)/Barcelona/The Fallen Priest (TV Version) (CD) . . . 8
92 Polydor PO 234 How Can I Go On/The Golden Boy (yellow p/s) . . . 8
92 Polydor PZCD 234 How Can I Go On/The Golden Boy/The Fallen Priest (CD, yellow p/s) . . . 10
92 Parlophone R 6331 In My Defence/Love Kills (Wolf Euro Mix) (p/s) . . . 6
92 Parlophone CDR 6331 In My Defence (Original Version)/Love Kills (Wolf Euro Mix)/Mr. Bad Guy (Original Version)/Living On My Own (Underground Solutions Mix) (CD) . . . 8
92 Parlophone CDRS 6331 In My Defence (Album Version)/In My Defence (Original Version)/Love Kills (Wolf Euro Mix)/She Blows Hot And Cold (CD) . . . 8
93 Parlophone R 6336 The Great Pretender/Stop All The Fighting (p/s) . . . 5
93 Parlophone CDRS 6336 The Great Pretender (Single Version)/The Great Pretender (Album Version)/ Stop All The Fighting/Exercises In Free Love (Mercury Vocal) (CD, digipak) . . . 8
94 Parlophone R 6355 Living On My Own (Radio Version)/Living On My Own (Album Version) (p/s) . . . 5
94 Parlophone 12R 6355 Living On My Own (Extended Version)/Living On My Own (Club Version)/ Living On My Own (Dub Version)/Living On My Own (L.A. Version) (12", p/s) . . . 8
85 CBS 40-86312 MR. BAD GUY (cassette, with extra remix) . . . 20
85 CBS CD 86312 MR. BAD GUY (CD, with 3 extended mixes; beware of counterfeits) . . . 40
94 Parlophone 7234 8 2814 10 FREDDIE MERCURY REMIXES (LP, unreleased) . . . 150
(see also Queen, Larry Lurex, Eddie Howell, Billy Squier)

MERCURY REV

91 Mint Film MINT 5 Car Wash Hair/Coney Island Cyclone (4 track demo) (200 copies only, p/s) . . . 6
91 Mint Film MINT 5 T Car Wash Hair/Chasing A Bee (4 track demo)/Coney Island Cyclone (12", p/s) . . 10
91 Mint Film MINT 5 CD Car Wash Hair/Chasing A Bee (4 track demo)/Coney Island Cyclone (CD) . . . 12
92 Rough Trade 45REV 6 If You Want Me To Stay/Left Handed Raygun of Paul Sharits (Retirement Just Like That) (p/s, with insert) . . . 15
92 Beggars Banquet BBQ 1 CD Chasing A Bee/If You Want Me To Stay/Coney Island Cyclone (Peel Session) Frittering (Peel Session)/Syringe Mouth (Peel Session)/Chasing A Girl (Inside A Car) (Peel Session) (2-CD) . . . 10
93 Beggars Banquet BBQ 5 T The Hum Is Coming From Her (as Mercury Theremin Sextet)/So There (as Mercury Rev Orchestra with Robert Creely) (10", p/s) . . . 10
93 Beggars Banquet BBQ 5 CD The Hum Is Coming From Her (as Mercury Theremin Sextet)/So There (as Mercury Rev Orchestra with Robert Creely) (CD) . . . 12
93 Beggars Banquet BBQ 14 Something For Joey/There's Spiders Eggs In Bubbla Yhum (blue vinyl, two different p/s) . . . 6
99 V2 VVR 5006967 Opus 40/Motion Pictures . . . 6
01 V2 VVR 5017727 Nite And Fog/Nite And Fog (4 track demo) (p/s) . . . 6
91 Mint Film MINTLP 4 YERSELF IS STEAM (LP, with bonus LP 'Lego My Ego') . . . 20
93 Beggars Banquet BBQLP 140 BOCES (LP, clear red vinyl) . . . 15
95 B. Banquet BBQLP 176 P SEE YOU ON THE OTHER SIDE (LP, picture disc) . . . 12
98 V2 VVR 1002772 DESERTER'S SONGS (CD, with cardboard sleeve and stamps) . . . 20
(see also Shady)

MERCY

69 London HLZ 10273 Love (Can Make You Happy)/Fireball . . . 8

BURGESS MEREDITH

63 Colpix PX 690 Home In The Meadow/No Goodbye . . . 8

LOTTIE MERLE

72 Flyright 001 Howling In The Moonlight/Catfish . . . 5

ETHEL MERMAN

54 Brunswick 05346 A Husband — A Wife (with Jimmy Durante)/The Lake Song (with Ray Bolger) . . . 10
55 Brunswick 05381 (There's No Business Like) Show Business/Play A Simple Melody (B-side with Dan Dailey) . . . 10
58 RCA RCA 1039 A New-Fangled Tango/Mutual Admiration Society (with Virginia Gibson) . . . 6
58 RCA RCA 1039 A New-Fangled Tango/Mutual Admiration Society (with Virginia Gibson) (78) . . . 8
52 Brunswick LAT 8016 SONGS FROM "CALL ME MADAM" (LP) . . . 15
52 Brunswick LA 8539 CALL ME MADAM (LP, with Dick Haymes) . . . 15
54 Brunswick LA 8636 SONGS SHE HAS MADE FAMOUS (10" LP) . . . 18
54 Brunswick LA 8638 DUET FROM FORD 50TH ANNIVERSARY TV SHOW (LP, with Mary Martin) . . . 15
(see also Jimmy Durante)

MINT VALUE £

RAY MERRELL

60	Ember EMB S 113	Why Did You Leave Me?/Teenage Love (p/s)	10
60s	Aral PS 115	Battle Of Waterloo/Not Any More (p/s)	10
64	Pye 7N 15709	Where In The World/Share A Dream With Me	5
65	Pye 7N 15793	Almost There/Only In A Dream	5
67	Columbia DB 8204	Chiquita Mia/Lazy Miss Hazy	5
69	Columbia DB 8643	Memories/Red Summer Roses	5
70	Jay Boy BOY 22	Tears Of Joy/Searchin' (withdrawn)	180

TONY MERRICK

66	Columbia DB 7913	Lady Jane/Michelle	10
66	Columbia DB 7995	Wake Up/It's For You	6

BOB MERRILL

58	Columbia DB 4086	Nairobi/Jump When I Say Frog	15

BUDDY MERRILL

66	Vocalion VN 9261	Sweet September/Sherk	12

ROBERT MERRILL

59	RCA RCA 1109	À Toujours/Gigi	5

MERRITTS

70	Hot Rod HR 113	I Don't Want To (Part 1)/HOT ROD ALL STARS: Version	12

MERRYMEN

66	Doctor Bird DB 1004	Big Bamboo/Island Woman	15
69	Trojan TR 7707	Little Drummer Boy/Mary's Boy Child	6
71	Duke DU 113	Big Bamboo/King Ja-Ja (both sides actually with Emille Straker)	6
68	Island ILP 984	CARIBBEAN TREASURE CHEST (LP)	40

(see also Soul Brothers)

JASON MERRYWEATHER

69	Crystal CR 001	My Summer Love/Abigail	7

(see also Ricky Valance)

MERSEYBEATS

63	Fontana TF 412	It's Love That Really Counts/The Fortune Teller	12
64	Fontana TF 431	I Think Of You/Mister Moonlight	6
64	Fontana TF 459	Don't Turn Around/Really Mystified	6
64	Fontana TF 482	Wishin' And Hopin'/Milkman	6
64	Fontana TF 504	Last Night/See Me Back	8
65	Fontana TF 568	Don't Let It Happen To Us/It Would Take A Long Long Time	10
65	Fontana TF 607	I Love You, Yes I Do/Good Good Lovin'	7
65	Fontana TF 645	I Stand Accused/All My Life	8
69	Fontana TF 1025	I Think Of You/Wishin' And Hopin' (p/s)	10
81	Tudor CR 23	This Is Merseybeat (both sides) (p/s)	6
64	Fontana TE 17422	ON STAGE (EP)	40
64	Fontana TE 17423	I THINK OF YOU (EP)	35
64	Fontana TE 17432	THE MERSEYBEATS (EP)	35
64	Fontana TL 5210	THE MERSEYBEATS (LP)	80
65	Wing WL 1163	THE MERSEYBEATS (LP, reissue)	20
77	Look LKLP 6160	GREATEST HITS (LP)	12

(see also Merseys, Rockin' Horse, Tony Crane, Kirkbys, Quotations, Johnny Gustavson)

MERSEYBOYS

64	Ace Of Clubs ACL 1169	15 GREAT SONGS BY JOHN, PAUL AND GEORGE (LP)	20

MERSEYS

66	Fontana TF 694	Sorrow/Some Other Day	8
66	Fontana TF 732	So Sad About Us/Love Will Continue	10
66	Fontana TF 776	Rhythm Of Love/Is It Love?	10
67	Fontana TF 845	The Cat/Change Of Heart	15
68	Fontana TF 916	Penny In My Pocket/I Hope You're Happy	12
68	Fontana TF 955	Lovely Loretta/Dreaming	12
73	Philips 6006 258	Sorrow/MERSEYBEATS: I Think Of You	6

(see also Merseybeats, Crackers)

MERSEYSIPPI JAZZ BAND

55	Decca DFE 6251	AT THE ROYAL FESTIVAL HALL (EP)	10
55	Esquire EP 30	THE MERSEYSIPPI JAZZ BAND (EP)	15
55	Esquire EP 60	THE MERSEYSIPPI JAZZ BAND (EP)	15
56	Esquire EP 90	THE MERSEYSIPPI JAZZ BAND (EP)	15
56	Esquire EP 118	THE MERSEYSIPPI JAZZ BAND (EP)	15
57	Esquire EP 130	THE MERSEYSIPPI JAZZ BAND (EP)	15
54	Esquire 20-063	WEST COAST SHOUT (LP)	20
55	Esquire 20-083	ALL THE GIRLS (LP)	30
55	Esquire 20-088	MERSEY TUNNEL JAZZ (LP)	20
56	Esquire 20-093	ANY OLD RAGS (LP)	20

TEDDY MERTENS

63	Oriole CB 1904	Autumn Love/Try To Love Me Again	5
63	Oriole CB 1925	This Is My Prayer/My River Of Memories (as Teddy Mertens' Trumpet)	5

MERTON PARKAS

79	Beggars Banquet BEG 22	You Need Wheels/I Don't Want To Know You (coloured p/s with patch)	8/6
79	Beggars Banquet BEG 25	Plastic Smile/The Man With The Disguise (p/s)	5
79	Beggars Banquet BEG 30	Give It To Me Now/Gi's It (p/s)	5
80	Beggars Banquet BEG 43	Put Me In The Picture/In The Midnight Hour (p/s)	5
83	Well Suspect BLAM 002	Flat 19/Band Of Gold (p/s)	8
80s	Beggars Banquet BEG 22	You Need Wheels/I Don't Want To Know You (reissue, black & white p/s)	7
79	Beggars Banquet BEGA 11	FACE IN THE CROWD (LP)	20

(see also Style Council)

MINT VALUE £

JUNIOR MERVIN

69 Big Shot BI 527 — Hustler/Magic Touch. 10

MESCALINE UNITED

92 R&S RS 92019 — We Have Arrived (Aphex Twin QQT Reconstruction Mix)/We Have Arrived (Aphex Twin TTQ Reconstruction Mix) (limited issue 12", also known as "PCP Remixed", plain paper sleeve). 80

MESS

80s Reasonable MEP 1 — Tried And Trusted/I'm Falling (p/s). 5

MESSAGE

70 Songbird SB 1503 — Rum-Bum-A-Loo/Drummer Boy. 8

(see also Boris Gardner)

MESSENGERS

64 Columbia DB 7344 — I'm Stealin' Back/This Little Light Of Mine 10
65 Columbia DB 7495 — When Did You Leave Heaven/More Pretty Girls Than One 8

MESSENGERS (Jamaica)

73 Attack ATT 8057 — Crowded City/Thula Thula 6
73 Bread BR 1116 — Cherry Baby/B.B. SEATON: Summertime 6

METABOLISTS

79 Drömm DRO 1 — Drömm/Slaves/Eulam's Beat (p/s, rough screen-printed & folded p/s) 12
79 Drömm DRO 1 — Drömm/Slaves/Eulam's Beat (p/s, smooth printed & stapled p/s) 10
79 Drömm DRO 3 — Identity/Tiz Hoz Nam (p/s) 8
70s Metabolists — GOATMANAUT (cassette). 12
70s Drömm D 1 — GOATMANAUT (LP) 15
70s Drömm DRO 2 — HANSTEN KLORD (LP) 12

METAL BOYS

79 Rough Trade RT 016 — Sweet Marilyn/Fugue For A Darkening Island (p/s) 5

(see also Metal Urbain)

METAL GURUS

90 Phonogram GURU 112 — Merry Xmas Everybody/Metal Guru/Mama Weer All Crazee Now/ Gudbuy T'Jane (12", p/s) 8
90 Phonogram GURCD 1 — Merry Xmas Everybody/Metal Guru/Mama Weer All Crazee Now/ Gudbuy T'Jane (CD). 8

(see also Mission, Slade)

METALLICA

SINGLES

84 Music For Nations 12 KUT 105 — Jump In The Fire/Seek And Destroy (live)/Phantom Lord (live) (12", p/s, initially with beige labels [later red/yellow]) 18/15
84 Music For Nations CV12 KUT 105 — Jump In The Fire/Seek And Destroy (live)/Phantom Lord (live) (12", red vinyl, p/s). 28
84 Music For Nations 12 KUT 105XP — Jump In The Fire/Seek And Destroy (live)/Phantom Lord (live) (12", stickered sleeve with sew-on patch). 22
84 Music For Nations T 12 KUT 105 — Jump In The Fire/Seek And Destroy (live)/Phantom Lord (live) (cassette) 8
84 M. F. N. T 12 KUT 112 — Creeping Death/Am I Evil?/Blitzkrieg (cassette). 8
84 Music For Nations 12 KUT 112 — Creeping Death/Am I Evil?/Blitzkrieg (12", p/s, initially with beige label, later red/yellow). 12/10
84 M. F. N. CV12 KUT 112 — Creeping Death/Am I Evil?/Blitzkrieg (12", p/s, blue vinyl, red/yellow or 'Special Anniversary Edition' labels). 30
84 Music For Nations GV12 KUT 112 — Creeping Death/Am I Evil?/Blitzkrieg (12", no p/s, 'Anniversary Gold Edition', gold vinyl, 3000 only; some mispressed with 1 side gold, 1 side black vinyl) . 50/40
84 Music For Nations P12 KUT 112 — Creeping Death/Am I Evil?/Blitzkrieg (12", picture disc, initially without barcode). 30
84 Music For Nations CD12 KUT 112 — Creeping Death/Am I Evil?/Blitzkrieg Jump In The Fire/ Seek And Destroy (live)/Phantom Lord (live) (CD) 50
86 Music For Nations PKUT 105 — Jump In The Fire/Phantom Lord (live) (shaped picture disc, initially without barcode). 20/18
87 Vertigo METAL 112 — $5.98 EP — GARAGE DAYS RE-REVISITED: Helpless/Crash Course In Brain Surgery/The Small Hours/Last Caress - Green Hell (medley) (12", p/s, later copies allegedly add "The Wait") 25
88 Vertigo METAL 212 — Harvester Of Sorrow/Breadfan/The Prince (12", p/s, some with 'skull' label). 15
88 Vertigo METAL CD 2 — Harvester Of Sorrow/Breadfan/The Prince (CD, card sleeve) 18
89 Vertigo METAL 312 — Jump In The Fire/Seek And Destroy (live)/Phantom Lord (live) (12", p/s, reissue) 8
89 Vertigo METAL 412 — Creeping Death/Am I Evil?/Blitzkrieg (12", p/s, reissue). 8
89 Vertigo 842-219-2 — Creeping Death/Am I Evil?/Blitzkrieg/Jump In The Fire/ Seek And Destroy (live)/Phantom Lord (live) (CD) 40
89 Vertigo METAL 5 — One/Seek And Destroy (live) (silver/black labels, paper p/s) 6
89 Vertigo METAP 5 — One/Seek And Destroy (live) (card p/s, some stickered, with rolled poster) 12
89 Vertigo METDJ 5 — One/One (Edit) (unique blue cover, plus insert) 50
89 Vertigo METPD 510 — One/Seek And Destroy (live) (10", picture disc with card) 20
89 Vertigo METAL 512 — One (Demo Version)/For Whom The Bell Tolls (live)/Welcome Home (Sanitarium) (live) (12", p/s initially with white labels, later yellow) 12/8
89 Vertigo METAL 512 — One (Demo Version)/For Whom The Bell Tolls (live)/Welcome Home (Sanitarium) (live) (12", p/s mis-labelled as "Seek and Destroy" [live]) 10
89 Vertigo METG 512 — One (Demo Version)/For Whom The Bell Tolls (live)/Welcome Home (Sanitarium) (live) (12", gatefold p/s, with booklet, some mispressed with B-side label both sides). 18
89 Vertigo METCD 5 — One/For Whom The Bell Tolls (live)/Welcome Home (Sanitarium) (live) (CD). 18
90 Vertigo 875 487 1 — THE GOOD, THE BAD AND THE LIVE — THE 6½ YEARS ANNIVERSARY COLLECTION (6 x 12", with live 4-track EP [METAL 612]) 50
91 Vertigo METAL 7 — Enter Sandman/Stone Cold Crazy (p/s). 5
91 Vertigo METAL 7 — Enter Sandman/Stone Cold Crazy (picture disc in p/s, stickered) 12

			MINT VALUE £
91	Vertigo METAL 712	Enter Sandman/Stone Cold Crazy/Holier Than Thou (Demo)/ Enter Sandman (Demo) (12", p/s, with stickered sleeve)	8
91	Vertigo METBX 712	Enter Sandman/Stone Cold Crazy/Enter Sandman (Demo) (12", box with 4 photo prints)	18
91	Vertigo METCD 7	Enter Sandman/Stone Cold Crazy/Enter Sandman (Demo) (CD, picture disc in box with room for 3 more CDs)	30
91	Vertigo METAP 812	The Unforgiven/Killing Time /The Unforgiven (Demo) (picture disc, card insert)	8
91	Vertigo METAL 812	The Unforgiven/Killing Time/So What/The Unforgiven (Demo) (12", p/s, some stickered)	8
91	Vertigo METCD 8	The Unforgiven/Killing Time/The Unforgiven (Demo) (CD)	8
92	Vertigo METCB 9	Wherever I May Roam/Last Caress–Am I Evil?–Battery (Live Medley) (digipak CD)	8
92	Vertigo METAL 10	Nothing Else Matters/Enter Sandman (live) (p/s, black & white label)	6
92	Vertigo METCD 10	Nothing Else Matters/Enter Sandman (live)/Harvester Of Sorrow (live)/ Nothing Else Matters (Demo) (picture CD)	8
92	Vertigo METCL 10	Nothing Else Matters — Live At Wembley 20/4/92: Enter Sandman/ Sad But True/Nothing Else Matters (CD)	20
93	Vertigo METAL 11	Sad But True/Nothing Else Matters (p/s, stickered, no labels)	5
93	Vertigo METAL 1112	Sad But True/Nothing Else Matters (Elevator Version)/Creeping Death (live)/ Sad But True (Demo) (12" picture disc with insert)	20
93	Vertigo METCH 11	Sad But True/Nothing Else Matters (live)/Sad But True (Demo) (CD, picture disc)	8
96	Vertigo METJB 12	Until It Sleeps/Until It Sleeps (jukebox issue, no p/s)	8
96	Vertigo METAL 12	Until It Sleeps/2x4 (live)/Until It Sleeps (Moby Remix) (10" red vinyl, stickered)	7
96	Vertigo METCX 12	Until It Sleeps/Kill-Ride (Medley)/Until It Sleeps (Moby Remix) (digipak CD)	10
97	Vertigo METJB 13	Hero Of The Day/Hero Of The Day (jukebox issue, no p/s)	8
96	Vertigo METCY 13	Hero Of The Day/Overkill/Damage Case/Stone Dead Forever/Too Late Too Late (CD, with poster in card cover)	10
96	Vertigo METAL 14	Mama Said/Ain't My Bitch (live) (picture disc with insert)	5
ALBUMS			
83	M. For Nations MFN 7	KILL 'EM ALL (LP, 1st issue with beige labels [later red/yellow])	25/18
84	M. For Nations MFN 27	RIDE THE LIGHTNING (LP, with inner sleeve, initially with beige labels & without barcode)	18
86	M. For Nations MFN 27P	RIDE THE LIGHTNING (LP, picture disc, initially lacking barcode)	22/20
86	M. For Nations MFN 7P	KILL 'EM ALL (LP, picture disc, some lacking picture on 1 side, initially lacking barcode)	22/20
86	M. For Nations MFN 60	MASTER OF PUPPETS (LP, with inner sleeve & insert)	15
86	M. For Nations MFN 60	MASTER OF PUPPETS (LP, mispressing, Side 1 label on both sides)	18
86	M. For Nations MFN 60P	MASTER OF PUPPETS (LP, picture disc, initially lacking barcode)	22/18
87	M. For Nations MFN 7DM	KILL 'EM ALL (2-LP, 'direct metal mastered' reissue, gatefold sleeve)	35
87	M. For Nations MFN 60DM	MASTER OF PUPPETS (2-LP, 'direct metal mastered' reissue, gatefold sleeve with poster)	22
87	M. For Nations MFN 27DM	RIDE THE LIGHTNING (2-LP, 'direct metal mastered' reissue, gatefold sleeve with insert)	22
89	Vertigo 838-140-1	RIDE THE LIGHTNING (LP, reissue, mispressing, Side 1 lists "Master Of Puppets" tracks)	15
90	Vertigo 888 788-1	GARAGE DAYS RE-REVISITED (mini-LP)	20
84	M. For Nations MFNCD 7	KILL 'EM ALL (CD)	28
84	M. For Nations MFN 27P	RIDE THE LIGHTNING (CD)	25
86	M. For Nations MFNCD 60	MASTER OF PUPPETS (CD)	22
91	Vertigo MECAN 1/510-022-0	THE METALLICAN (CD, gold disc in metal 'paint can' with video & T-shirt; 35,000 only)	70
93	Vertigo 518-725-0	LIVE SHIT, BINGE & PURGE (3-CD box set with 3 videos & 72-page book)	70
PROMOS			
88	Vertigo MET CD 100	THE WHIPLASH SAMPLER (CD)	40
88	Vertigo METDJ 2	Harvester Of Sorrow/Harvester Of Sorrow (unique p/s)	50
89	Vertigo METDJ 512	One (Demo Version)/For Whom The Bell Tolls (live)/Welcome Home (Sanitarium) (live) (12", unissued, promo-only p/s)	50
91	Vertigo METDJ 7	Enter Sandman (Radio Edit)/Stone Cold Crazy (B-side actually silent)	8
96	Vertigo MET INT 1	LOAD — THE INTERVIEW (CD, with cue booklet)	50
96	Mercury MM CJ-1	MANDATORY METALLICA (CD, 7-track sampler)	30
97	Vertigo MMCJ-2	MANDATORY METALLICA 2 (2-CD, 17-track sampler)	40

METAL MIRROR

80	M&M MM 001	Rock 'N Roll Ain't Never Gonna Leave Us/English Booze (some in p/s)	150/50

METAL URBAIN

78	Radar ADA 20	Hysterie Connective/Pas Poubelle	7
79	Rough Trade RT 001	Paris Maquis/Cle De Contact (p/s)	6

METEORS

64	Polydor NH 52263	Get A Load Of This/Ruby Ann	5

METEORS

79	EMI EMI 5000	My Balls Ache/Action (p/s)	6

METEORS

81	Ace SW 65	METEOR MADNESS (EP, some on blue vinyl)	15/10
81	Ace SWT 65	METEOR MADNESS (10" EP, white label test pressings only, custom p/s)	80
81	Chiswick CHIS 147	Radioactive Kid/Graveyard Stomp (p/s)	10
81	Lost Soul LOST 101	The Crazed/Attack Of The Zorch Men (p/s)	6
81	Ace NS 74	Radioactive Kid/Graveyard Stomp (p/s, reissue, some clear or blue vinyl; most on black vinyl)	10/5
82	WXYZ ABCD 5	Mutant Rock/The Hills Have Eyes (p/s)	8
82	I.D. EYE 1	Johnny Remember Me/Fear Of The Dark/Wreckin' Crew (p/s)	8
82	I.D. EYE 1P	Johnny Remember Me/Fear Of The Dark/Wreckin' Crew (picture disc)	10

MINT VALUE £

82 Lyntone LYN 12647 METEORS: Mutant Rock (Instrumental)/ANTI NOWHERE LEAGUE: World War Three/DEFECTS: Dance (red flexidisc with *Flexipop* magazine, issue 26) 7/5
84 Mad Pig PORK 1 I'm Just A Dog/Electro Rock (p/s) 6
85 Mad Pig PORK 1T I'm Just A Dog (Wild Hog Mix Down)/Hoover Rock/Electro (12", p/s) 8
85 Mad Pig PORK 2 Fire, Fire/Little Red Riding Hood (p/s) 5
85 Mad Pig PORK 2T Fire, Fire/Little Red Riding Hood/Stampede (King Ray Bat Scalator In The Dark Mix) (12", p/s) 8
85 Mad Pig PORK 3 Bad Moon Rising/Rhythm Of The Bell (p/s) 5
85 Mad Pig PORK 3T Hogs And Cuties /Bad Moon Rising/Rhythm Of The Bell (What? Another Cover Mix) (12", p/s) 15
86 I.D. EYE 10 MUTANT ROCK (EP, green vinyl) 8
86 I.D. EYET 10 MUTANT ROCK (12" EP, green or blue vinyl) 12
86 Anagram ANA 31 Surf City/The Edge (p/s) 8
86 Anagram 12ANA 31 Surf City (Has Beens From Outer Space Mix)/The Edge/Johnny's Here (12", p/s) 15
87 Anagram ANA 35 Go Buddy Go/Wildkat Ways (p/s) 5
87 Anagram 12ANA 35 Go Buddy Go (The Wonkey Donkey Mix)/Wildkat Ways/You Crack Me Up (p/s) . . . 7
81 Ace MAD 1 THE METEORS MEET SCREAMIN' LORD SUTCH (mini-LP, 1 side each, 1,000 only, stickered cartoon print on plain card sleeve) 125
81 Lost Soul LOSTLP 3001 IN HEAVEN (LP) 20
86 Big Beat WIKA 47 TEENAGERS FROM OUTER SPACE (LP) 25
86 Big Beat WIKA 47CD TEENAGERS FROM OUTER SPACE (CD) 22
87 Dojo LP56P NIGHT OF THE WEREWOLF (LP, picture disc) 12
(see also Tall Boys, Clapham South Escalators, [Screamin'] Lord Sutch, Deadbeats)

METERS

69 Stateside SS 2140 Sophisticated Cissy/Sehorn's Farm 12
70 Direction 58-4751 Look-Ka-Py-Py/This Is My Last Affair 10
74 Reprise K 14367 People Say/Africa 6
75 Reprise K 14405 Fire On The Bayou/They All Ask'd For You 6
72 Reprise K 44242 CABBAGE ALLEY (LP) 25
74 Reprise K 54027 REJUVENATION (LP) 30
74 Island ILPS 9250 CISSY STRUT (LP) 30
75 Reprise K 54044 FIRE ON THE BAYOU (LP) 22
76 Reprise K 54076 BEST OF THE METERS (LP) 15
76 Reprise K 54078 TRICK BAG (LP) 22
77 Reprise K 56378 NEW DIRECTIONS (LP) 12
79 Pye PKL 5578 GOOD OLD FUNKY MUSIC (LP) 12

METHOD ACTORS

80 Armageddon AS 6 The Method/Can't Act (p/s) 7
81 Armageddon AS 11 Round World/Eye (p/s) 7

FRANK METIS ORCHESTRA

56 London REN 1048 SONGS FROM IRVING BERLIN'S 'SHOW BUSINESS' (EP) 10

METRONOME ALL STARS

51 Capitol CL 13545 Local 802 Blues/Early Spring (78, with Stan Getz & Miles Davis) 12

METROPAK

80 Metropak PAK 001 You're A Rebel/OK Let's Go/Run Run Run (numbered p/s) 6
80 Metropak PAK 002 Here's Looking At You/Walking (foldout card p/s) 5

METROPHASE

79 Neo London MS 01 In Black/Neo Beauty/Cold Rebellion (photocopied p/s with lyric insert) 8
79 Neo London MS 02 New Age/Frames Of Life (foldout p/s, stamped white labels) 8
81 Fresh FRESH 6 In Black/Neo Beauty/Cold Rebellion (reissue, better quality p/s with insert) 6
(see also Swell Maps)

METROPOLITAN POLICE BAND

66 Columbia DB 8095 Thunderbirds March/P.C. ALEXANDER MORGAN: Sussex By The Sea 10

METROTONE

97 Wurlitzer Jukebox WJ 40 Kiss Me Awake/Byddant Fel Y Ser/Four Continuous Tones (p/s, 1,000 only) 5
98 Earworm WORM 21 THE LESS YOU HAVE THE MORE YOU ARE (LP, 4 copies only on black vinyl) . . . 25

PAUL METSERS

81 Highway SHY 7014 CAUTION TO THE WIND (LP) 12

M.E.V.

69 Polydor 583 769 MUSICA ELETTRONICA VIVA (LP) 15

AUGIE MEYERS

70s Sonet SNTF 883 STILL GROWIN' (LP, with Doug Sahm) 12
(see also Sir Douglas Quintet, Doug Sahm)

ANTHONY MEYNELL

82 Hi-Lo LO 01 HITS FROM 3000 YEARS AGO (LP, purple sleeve) 15
(see also Squire)

LEE MEZA

67 Stateside SS 589 If It Happens/One Good Thing Leads To Another 25

MEZZ MEZZROW

62 Storyville SEP 394 KING JAZZ STORY (EP) 10
55 Vogue LAE 12007 PLEYEL CONCERT (LP) 12
(see also Mezzrow–Bechet Quartet)

MEZZROW–BECHET QUINTET

50 King Jazz KJ 2 Bowin' The Blues/Old School (78) 8
50 King Jazz KJ 3 Where Am I/Funky Butt (12" 78) 8
50 King Jazz KJ 5 Chicago Function Parts 1 & 2 (10" or 12" 78) 7/8
50 King Jazz KJ 7 Tommy's Blues/I'm Going Away From Here (12" 78) 8
50 King Jazz KJ 8 I Want Some/I'm Speaking My Mind (12" 78) 8
51 King Jazz KJ 9 Really The Blues Parts 1 & 2 (78) 8

MINT VALUE £

51 King Jazz KJ 11 — Kaiser's Last Break/Delta Mood (12" 78) — 8
51 Vogue KJ 1 — Ole Miss/Out Of The Galleon — 7
56 Vogue LAE 12017 — THE MEZZROW-BECHET QUINTET (LP) — 12
(see also Sidney Bechet)

M.F.Q.

(see under Modern Folk Quartet)

M.F.S.B.

81 Phil. Intl. PIR 12-9501 — Mysteries Of The World/Manhattan Skyline (12", no p/s) — 8
81 Phil. Intl. PIR 84251 — MYSTERIES OF THE WORLD (LP) — 12

M-G-M STUDIO ORCHESTRA

54 MGM SP 1099 — Peddler Song/Antonia/Fisherman's Song — 6
55 MGM SP 1144 — Rock Around The Clock/"Blackboard Jungle" Love Theme — 25

MIAMI

74 Jay Boy BOY 81 — Party Freaks/(Part 2) — 6
75 Jay Boy BOY 86 — Hey Y'all We're Miami/Chicken Yellow — 6
75 Jay Boy BOY 96 — Funk It Up/Freak On Down My Way — 6
76 Jay Boy BOY 111 — Kill That Roach/Mr Notorious — 7

MIAMI SOUND MACHINE

84 Epic TX 4800 — Prisoner Of Love/Toda Tuya (Toda Dia Eva Dia De Indio)/ Prisoner Of Love (Instrumental) (12", p/s) — 8
85 Epic DA 6537 — Bad Boy (Shep Pettibone Remix)/Movies//Dr. Beat/When Someone Comes (double pack, p/s) — 10
85 Epic QTA 6537 — Bad Boy (Club Mix)/Bad Boy (Rubber-Club-Dub Mix)/Movies (12", p/s) — 8
85 Epic TA 6361 — Conga! (Dance Mix)/Conga! (Instrumental) (12", p/s) — 8
86 Epic DTA 6956 — Falling In Love (Uh-Oh)/Conga (The Stronga-Conga Remix)/ Surrender Paradise//Bad Boy (Shep Pettibone Remix)/Bad Boy (Dub Version) (12", shrinkwrapped double pack) — 20
86 Epic TA 6956 — Falling In Love (Uh-Oh)/Conga (The Stronga-Conga Remix)/ Surrender Paradise (12", p/s) — 8
84 Epic EPC 26167 — EYES OF INNOCENCE (LP) — 12
84 Epic CDEPC 26167 — EYES OF INNOCENCE (CD) — 20
85 Epic EPC 26491 — PRIMITIVE LOVE (LP) — 12
85 Epic CDEPC 26491 — PRIMITIVE LOVE (CD) — 20
(see also Gloria Estefan [& Miami Sound Machine])

MIAOW

85 Venus VENUS 1 — Belle Vue/Fate (p/s) — 6
86 Venus VENUST 1 — Belle Vue/Fate/Grocer's Devil Daughter (12", p/s) — 10
87 Factory FAC 189 — Break The Code/Stolen Ears (p/s) — 10

MICHA

65 Pye 7N 15982 — Protest Singer/Serpent — 8

GEORGE MICHAEL

84 Epic A 4603 — Careless Whisper/Careless Whisper (Instrumental) (poster p/s) — 30
84 Epic QTA 4603 — Careless Whisper (Extended Mix)/Careless Whisper (Special Version Wexler)/Careless Whisper (Instrumental) (12", title p/s) — 30
84 Epic WA 4603 — Careless Whisper (Extended Mix)/Careless Whisper (Instrumental) (12", picture disc, clear or black rim) — each 30
87 Epic LUST QT 1 — I Want Your Sex (Monogamy Mix: Rhythm 1 Lust, Rhythm 2 Brass In Love, Rhythm 3 A Last Request)/Hard Day (12", gatefold envelope p/s) — 8
87 Epic CDLUST 1 — I Want Your Sex (Monogamy Mix: Rhythm 1 Lust, Rhythm 2 Brass In Love, Rhythm 3 A Last Request) (CD, gatefold gard p/s) — 8
87 Epic EMU C3 — Faith/Faith (Instrumental)/Hand To Mouth (cassette) — 6
87 Epic EMUP 3 — Faith/Faith (Instrumental)/Hand To Mouth (12", picture disc) — 20
87 Epic EMU 4 — Father Figure/Love's In Need Of Love Today (with calendar & stickered p/s) — 8
87 Epic EMUT 4 — Father Figure/Love's In Need Of Love Today/Father Figure (Instrumental) (12", stickered p/s with poster) — 8
88 Epic EMUP 4 — Father Figure/Love's In Need Of Love Today (square picture disc in wallet) — 15
88 Epic CD EMU 4 — Father Figure/Love's In Need Of Love Today/Father Figure (Instrumental) (CD) — 12
88 Epic CD EMU 3 — Faith/Hand To Mouth/Hard Day (Remix) (CD) — 12
88 Epic EMU B5 — One More Try/Look At Your Hands (p/s, shrinkwrapped with badge) — 12
88 Epic EMU T5 — One More Try/Look At Your Hands (12", p/s with poster) — 8
88 Epic EPC 651 5322 — One More Try/Look At Your Hands (3" CD, 5" case with adaptor) — 8
88 Epic CD EMU 5 — One More Try/Look At Your Hands (CD, picture disc) — 15
88 Epic EMU G6 — Monkey/Monkey (A Capella) (gatefold p/s, with photo insert) — 7
88 Epic CD EMU 6 — Monkey (Extended Version)/(A'Capella)/(Extra Bits)/(7" Edit) (CD) — 12
88 Epic CD EMU 7 — Kissing A Fool/(Instr.)/A Last Request (I Want Your Sex Part 3) (CD, card p/s) — 8
89 Epic Solid Gold 654 601-3 — I Want Your Sex (Parts 1 & 2)/A Different Corner/Careless Whisper (3" CD) — 8
90 Epic GEOC 1 — Praying For Time/If You Were My Woman/Waiting (Reprise) (CD, no'd p/s) — 10
90 Epic GEO C2 — Waiting For That Day/Fantasy/Father Figure/Kissing A Fool (CD, picture disc) — 8
90 Epic GEOC 3 — Freedom '90/Mother's Pride/Freedom (Back To Reality Mix) (CD) — 10
91 Epic 656 647 5 — Heal The Pain/Soul Free/Hand To Mouth (CD, gatefold card p/s) — 8
91 Epic XPC 4060 — WEMBLEY: I Believe/Freedom (Back To Reality Mix)/If You Were My Woman/ Fantasy (cassette, concert freebie) — 25
91 Epic 657 646-5 — Don't Let The Sun Go Down On Me/I Believe (When I Fall In Love It Will Be Forever [with Elton John]) (live)/WHAM!: Last Christmas (12", foldout poster p/s) — 8
91 Epic 657 646-2 — Don't Let The Sun Go Down On Me/I Believe (When I Fall In Love It Will Be Forever [with Elton John]) (live)/If You Were My Woman/Fantasy (CD) — 8
92 Epic 658 058-2 — Toofunky/Crazy Man Dance/Toofunky (Extended) (CD, picture disc) — 10
96 Virgin VSLH 1571 — Jesus To A Child/One More Try (Live Gospel Version) (jukebox issue, no p/s) — 8
96 Virgin VSLH 1579 — Fastlove/I'm Your Man (jukebox issue, no p/s) — 5
96 Virgin VSLH 1595 — Spinning The Wheel (Radio Edit)/You Know That I Want To (jukebox issue, no p/s) — 6

MINT VALUE £

97	Virgin VSLH 1626	Older (Radio Edit)/I Can't Make You Love Me (jukebox issue, no p/s)	5
97	Virgin VSLH 1641	Star People '97/Everything She Wants (jukebox issue, no p/s)	7
97	Virgin VSLH 1663	You Have Been LovedThe Strangest Thing '97 (Radio Edit) (jukebox issue, no p/s)	5
87	Epic 460000 9	FAITH (CD, extra tracks, picture disc, PVC box, some sealed)	50/40
90	Epic 467295 2	LISTEN WITHOUT PREJUDICE VOLUME 1 (CD, picture disc, stickered case)	40

PROMOS

99	Virgin GM 99	Roxanne (CD, 1 track, card p/s, promo only)	12
99	Virgin GMX 99	Miss Sarajevo (CD, 1 track, card p/s, promo only)	12
99	Epic XPR 3291	Outside (Hex Hector Mix)/(Dub Mix) (12", white sleeve and sticker, promo only)	20
02	Polydor GM 02	Freeek! (Jim Skreech Vocal Mix)/Freeek! (Octave Mix) (12" promo, title-stickered sleeve)	45
02	Polydor no cat. no.	Freeek! (Radio Version)/Freeek! (Slynus Mix)/Freeek! (Scumfrog Mix)/Freeek! (Moogymen Mix)/Freeek! (Max Reich Mix) (CD-R, title sleeve)	60
99	Epic GMCD 1	LADIES AND GENTLEMEN — THE BEST OF (CD, sampler, card case, promo only)	30

(see also Wham!, Deon Estus, High, Elton John, Queen)

RAS MICHAEL & THE SONS OF NEGUS

75	Vulcan VUL 005	RASTAFARI (LP)	20
75	Grounation GROL 505	RASTAFARI (LP)	20

CODY MICHAELS

79	Grapevine GRP 121	7 Days — 52 Weeks/VIRTUE ORCHESTRA: Don't Look Back (Instrumental)	8

LEE MICHAELS

68	A&M AMS 763	Heighty Hi/Want My Baby	5
71	A&M AMS 863	Do You Know What I Mean/Keep The Circle Turning	5
72	A&M AMS 882	Can I Get A Witness/You Are What You Do	6
69	A&M AML(S) 928	RECITAL (LP)	12
69	A&M AML(S) 956	LEE MICHAELS (LP)	12

MARILYN MICHAELS

60	RCA RCA 1208	Tell Tommy I Miss Him/Everyone Was There But You	12

MICHAEL SCHENKER GROUP

80	Chrysalis CHS 2455	Armed And Ready/Bijou Pleasurette (p/s, clear vinyl)	6
80	Chrysalis CHS 2471	Cry For The Nations/Into The Arena (live) (p/s, clear vinyl)	5
81	Chrysalis CHS 2541	Ready To Rock/Attack Of The Mad Axeman (p/s, clear vinyl)	5
81	Sounds FREEBIE No. 1	Let Sleeping Dogs Lie/PAT BENATAR: Promises In The Dark (Edit) (flexidisc in red printed sleeve, free with *Sounds*)	6/5
82	Chrysalis CHS 2636	Dancer/Girl From Uptown (picture disc)	5
82	Chrysalis CHS 2636	Dancer/Girl From Uptown (p/s, clear vinyl)	5
82	Chysalis PCHR 1393	ASSAULT ATTACK (LP, picture disc)	12
83	Chysalis CHRP 1441	BUILT TO DESTROY (LP, picture disc, U.S. remixes)	12

(see also McAuley Schenker Group, Michael Schenker, Scorpions, UFO, Cozy Powell, Graham Bonnet, Alex Harvey Band)

MICHELLE

66	Polydor BM 56070	Sally Fool/I Don't Know Your Name	7

MICHIGAN RAG

72	Blue Horizon 2096 009	Don't Run Away/She's Looking Good	18

MICHIGANS

63	Vogue V 9207	Intermission Riff/Tea For Two	15

MICKEY (Baker) & KITTY (Noble)

60	London HLE 9054	Buttercup/My Reverie	35

MICKEY (Baker) & SYLVIA

57	HMV POP 331	Love Is Strange/I'm Going Home	325
57	HMV POP 331	Love Is Strange/I'm Going Home (78)	100
58	RCA RCA 1064	Rock And Stroll Room/Bewildered	45
58	RCA RCA 1064	Rock And Stroll Room/Bewildered (78)	60
60	RCA RCA 1206	Sweeter As The Day Goes By/Mommy Out De Light	18
65	RCA Victor RCA 1487	Love Is Strange/Dearest	30
65	RCA Camden CDN 5133	LOVE IS STRANGE (LP)	200

(see also Sylvia [Robbins])

MICKEY FINN

64	Blue Beat BB 203	Tom Hark/Please Love Me (as 'Mickey Finn & the Blue Men')	35
64	Oriole CB 1927	Pills/Hush Your Mouth (as 'Mickey Finn & the Blue Men')	50
64	Oriole CB 1940	Reelin' & A'Rockin'/I Still Want You (as 'Mickey Finn')	50
65	Columbia DB 7510	The Sporting Life/Night Comes Down (as 'The Mickey Finn')	65
66	Polydor 56719	I Do Love You/If I Had You Baby (as 'The Mickey Finn')	40
67	Direction 58-3086	Garden Of My Mind/Time To Start Loving You (as 'The Mickey Finn')	55
95	Noiseburger 3	Ain't Necessarily So/God Bless The Child (foldaround p/s in poly bag, 1,000 only, 1st 500 signed)	10/5

BOBBY "BOBCATS" MICKLEBURGH

53	Esquire 10-327	Tin Roof Blues/Jazz Me Blues (78)	10
54	Esquire 10-337	Mahogany Hall Stomp/Basin Street Blues (78)	10
55	Esquire EP 40	MICKLEBURGH'S BOBCATS (EP)	15
56	Esquire EP 73	MICKLEBURGH'S BOBCATS (EP)	15

MICROBE

69	CBS 4158	Groovy Baby/MICROBOP ENSEMBLE: Your Turn Now	7

MICRODISNEY

82	Kabuki KAMD 2	Hello Rascals/The Helicopter Of The Holy Ghost (p/s)	6
83	Kabuki KAMD 4	Pink Skinned Man/Fiction Land (p/s)	5
80s	Virgin V2505	39 MINUTES (LP)	18

MINT VALUE £

80s Rough Trade ROUGH 75 EVERYBODY IS FANTASTIC (LP) . . . 15
80s Rough Trade ROUGH 85 THE CLOCK COMES DOWN THE STAIRS (LP) . . . 12
88 Rough Trade RTM 155 WE HATE YOU SOUTH AFRICAN BASTARDS (LP) . . . 20

TONY MIDDLETON

65 London HLR 9983 My Little Red Book (as Burt Bacharach Orchestra with Tony Middleton)/
BURT BACHARACH ORCHESTRA: What's New Pussycat . . . 30
66 Polydor BM 56704 To The Ends Of The Earth/Don't Ever Leave Me . . . 400
78 Grapevine GRP 115 Paris Blues/Out Of This World . . . 8
(see also Willows, Burt Bacharach)

MIDNIGHT CRUISER

77 It IT 2 Rich Bitch/Striker (p/s) . . . 10

MIDNIGHTERS

55 Parlophone DP 399 Work With Me Annie/Sexy Ways (78, export issue) . . . 70
55 Parlophone DP 422 Annie Had A Baby/THUNDERBIRDS: Pledging My Love (78, export issue) . . . 70
(see also Hank Ballard)

MIDNIGHT MOVERS

72 Mojo 2092 038 Why Can't We Do It In The Road Parts 1 & 2 . . . 7
73 Contempo C 7 Follow The Wind Parts 1 & 2 . . . 7

MIDNIGHT RAGS

80 Ace ACE 005 Public Enemy/Alcatraz/Mamma Said (p/s) . . . 8
80 Velvet Moon VM 1 The Cars That Ate New York/Oscar Automobile (p/s, withdrawn) . . . 8
(see also Paul Roland, Weird Strings)

MIDNIGHTS

66 Ember EMB S 220 (Won'tcha) Show Me Around/Only Two Can Play . . . 12
63 MEP 101/MN 1/EAG-EP-134 MIDNIGHTS (EP, private pressing) . . . 120

MIDNIGHT SHIFT

66 Decca F 12487 Saturday Jump/Living Fast . . . 20

MIDNIGHT SUN

72 MCA MKPS 2019 MIDNIGHT SUN (LP) . . . 20
72 MCA MKPS 2024 WALKING CIRCLES (LP) . . . 20
73 MCA MCF 2687 MIDNIGHT SUN (LP, reissue) . . . 15
73 MCA MCF 2691 WALKING CIRCLES (LP, reissue) . . . 15

M.I. FIVE

66 Parlophone R 5486 You'll Never Stop Me Loving You/Only Time Will Tell . . . 70
(see also Maze, Deep Purple)

MIGHT OF COINCIDENCE

72 Entropia BM 0001 WHY COULDN'T PEOPLE WAIT (LP) . . . 100

MIGHTY AVENGERS (U.K.)

64 Decca F 11891 Hide Your Pride/Hey Senorita . . . 18
64 Decca F 11962 So Much In Love/Sometime They Say . . . 18
65 Decca F 12085 Blue Turns To Grey/I'm Lost Without You . . . 22
65 Decca F 12198 (Walkin' Thru The) Sleepy City/Sir Edward And Lady Jane . . . 35
(see also Andrew Oldham)

MIGHTY AVENGERS (Jamaica)

66 Rymska RA 101 Scatter Shot (actually by Byron Lee & Dragonaires)/BYRON LEE:
Like You Do (B-side actually "No One" by Techniques) . . . 20

MIGHTY BABY

71 Blue Horizon 2096 003 Devil's Whisper/Virgin Spring . . . 25
69 Head HDLS 6002 MIGHTY BABY (LP, gatefold sleeve) . . . 140
71 Blue Horizon 2931 001 A JUG OF LOVE (LP, with lyric insert) . . . 140
84 Psycho PSYCHO 31 EGYPTIAN TOMB (LP, reissue of "Mighty Baby" in different sleeve) . . . 15
(see also Action, Robin Scott, Habibiyya, Keith Christmas, Gary Farr, Stone's Masonry)

THEE MIGHTY CAESARS

86 Empire LWC 604 Ten Bears Of The Comanches/Baby What's Wrong (p/s) . . . 6
86 Media Burn MB 5 Little By Little/The Swag/What You've Got/Cyclonic (12", p/s) . . . 7
88 Swag SWG 001 She's Just Fifteen Years Old/The Swag (flexi with *Pandora's Box* fanzine) . . . 10/7
(see also Milkshakes, Prisoners, Billy Childish, Thee Headcoats)

MIGHTY DIAMONDS

79 Virgin Frontline FLD 6001 DEEPER ROOTS (LP, with bonus dub LP) . . . 12

MIGHTY DOUGLAS

60s Jump Up JU 501 Laziest Man/Dance Me Lover . . . 8
60s Jump Up JU 508 Teacher Teacher/Split Me In Two . . . 8
60s Jump Up JU 509 Ugliness/My Wicked Boy Child . . . 8

MIGHTY FLEA & MICKEY BAKER

72 Polydor 2058 328 Bloodshot Eyes/Charley Stone . . . 6
73 Polydor 2460 185 LET THE GOOD TIMES ROLL (LP) . . . 22

MIGHTY FLYERS

74 Myrrh MYR 1016 LOW FLYING ANGELS (LP, with insert) . . . 20
(see also Mick Abrahams)

MIGHTY MEN

62 Salvo SLO 1804 No Way Out/You Too Much (99 copies only) . . . 35

MIGHTY MO

72 Columbia DB 8851 Ape Call/Heavy Bear . . . 8

MIGHTY POWER

67 Jump Up JU 513 You're Wasting Your Time/Smart Barbarian . . . 8

MINT VALUE £

MIGHTY SAM

66 Stateside SS 534 Sweet Dreams/Good Humor Man ... 18
66 Stateside SS 544 Fannie Mae/Badmouthin' ... 18
68 Stateside SS 2076 When She Touches Me/Just Like Old Times ... 18
70 Soul City SC 115 Papa True Love/I Need A Lot Of Lovin' ... 20
70 Soul City SCM 004 MIGHTY SOUL (LP) ... 75

MIGHTY SPARROW

59 Melodisc 1491 Goaty/LORD MELODY: I Confess (78) ... 12
60 Kalypso XX 22 Mr. Herbert/Simpson ... 6
68 NEMS 56-3558 Mr. Walker/Carnival In '68 ... 6
60s Jump Up JU 523 Village Ram/Pull Pistle Gang ... 6
69 Fab FAB 116 Mr. Walker/Jane ... 6
70 Fab FAB 147 I Don't Wanna Lose You/The Truth ... 6
71 Duke DU 114 Maria/Only A Fool ... 5
71 Jump Up JU 541 Mr Walker/Mae Mae ... 5
60 Kalypso XXEP 1 THIS IS SPARROW (EP) ... 10
60 Kalypso XXEP 2 MAN, DIG THIS SPARROW (EP) ... 10
60 Kalypso XXEP 3 A PARTY WITH SPARROW (EP) ... 10
61 Kalypso XXEP 4 THIS IS THE SPARROW AGAIN (EP) ... 10
61 Kalypso XXEP 5 GREETINGS FROM SPARROW (EP) ... 10
62 Kalypso XXEP 6 SPARROW THE CONQUEROR (EP) ... 10
63 Island ILP 902 THE SLAVE (LP) ... 30
66 RCA RD 7516 SPARROW COME BACK (LP) ... 15
72 Trojan TRL 49 HOTTER THAN EVER (LP) ... 12
(see also Sparrow, King Sparrow, Lord Melody)

MIGHTY SPARROW/BYRON LEE & DRAGONAIRES

69 Trojan TRL 8 THE SPARROW MEETS THE DRAGON (LP, gatefold sleeve) ... 12
(see also Byron Lee & Dragonaires)

MIGHTY TERROR & HIS CALYPSONIANS

50 Melodisc 1033 The Queen Is In/Chinese Children (78) ... 10
59 Pye N 15177 Women Police In England/Patricia Gone With Millicent (78) ... 12
59 Pye N 15178 Brown Skin Gal/Kitch Cavalcade (78) ... 12

MIGHTY VIKINGS

67 Island WI 3060 Do Re Mi/The Sound Of Music ... 18
67 Island WI 3074 Rockitty Fockitty/Give Me Back My Gal (both actually with Sammy Ismay) ... 18

MIGIL FIVE

64 Pye 7N 15597 Mockingbird Hill/Long Ago And Far Away ... 6
64 Pye 7N 15645 Near You/Don't Wanna Go On Shaking ... 6
64 Pye 7N 15677 Boys And Girls/I Saw Your Picture ... 7
65 Pye 7N 15757 Just Behind The Rainbow/Seven Lonely Days ... 7
65 Pye 7N 15874 One Hundred Years/I'm In Love Again ... 7
66 Pye 7N 17023 Pencil And Paper/Nevertheless (I'm In Love With You) ... 7
67 Columbia DB 8196 Together/Superstition ... 22
68 Jay Boy BOY 4 If I Had My Way/Somebody's Stolen The Moon ... 6
64 Pye NEP 24191 MEET THE MIGIL FIVE (EP) ... 22
64 Pye NPL 18093 MOCKING BIRD HILL (LP) ... 45
(see also Migil Four)

MIGIL FOUR

63 Pye 7N 15572 Maybe/Can't I? ... 10
(see also Migil Five)

MIKE & MECHANICS

85 WEA U 8908P Silent Running/I Get The Feeling (engine-shaped picture disc) ... 8
85 WEA U 8765TP All I Need Is A Miracle/You Are The One/A Call To Arms (12", picture disc) ... 10
88 WEA U 7789CD Nobody's Perfect/Nobody's Perfect (Extended)/Nobody Knows (3" CD) ... 8
89 WEA U 7717CD The Living Years/Too Many Friends/I Get The Feeling (live) (3" CD) ... 8
89 WEA U 7602CD Nobody Knows (Remix)/Why Me/Nobody Knows (Album Version) (3" CD, 5" jewel case or 3" card sleeve) ... 8
91 Virgin VSCDX 1351 A Time And Place/Yesterday Tomorrow/Word Of Mouth (East West Mix) (CD, in photo wallet with 5 prints) ... 8
91 Virgin VS 1359 Get Up/I Think I Got The Message (p/s, withdrawn) ... 6
91 Virgin VSCDG 1359 Get Up/I Think I Got The Message/Before The Next Heartache Falls (CD, withdrawn) ... 10
92 Virgin VSCDX 1396 Everybody Gets A Second Chance/The Way You Look At Me/At The End Of The Day (CD, with sheet music & lyrics) ... 8
(see also Mike Rutherford, Genesis, Paul Carrack)

MIKE & MODIFIERS

62 Oriole CB 1775 I Found Myself A Brand New Baby/It's Too Bad ... 600

MIKE STUART SPAN

66 Columbia DB 8066 Come On Over To Our Place/Still Nights ... 35
67 Columbia DB 8206 Dear/Invitation ... 45
68 Jewel JL 01 Children Of Tomorrow/Concerto Of Thoughts ... 250
68 Fontana TF 959 You Can Understand Me/Baubles And Bangles ... 25
93 117 CPAT 1171 EXSPANSIONS: Second Production/Rescue Me/Remember The Times/World In My Head (EP) ... 15
95 Tenth Planet TP 014 TIMESPAN (LP, gatefold sleeve, numbered, 1,000 copies only) ... 25
(see also Leviathan, High Defenders, Tony's Defenders, High Broom)

MIKI & GRIFF

59 Pye-Nixa 7N 15213 Hold Back Tomorrow/Deedle Dum Doo Die Day ... 5
60 Pye 7N 15266 Long Time To Forget/Someday You'll Call My Name ... 5
64 Pye 7N 15614 Here Today Gone Tomorrow/Changing Partners (p/s) ... 5

MINT VALUE £

BOBBY MILANO

55	Capitol CL 14252	A King Or A Slave/If You Cared	10
55	Capitol CL 14309	If Tears Could Bring You Back/Make Me A Present Of You	10

AMOS MILBURN

57	Vogue V 9064	Every Day Of The Week/Girl Of My Dreams (triangular or round centre)	150/75
57	Vogue V 9064	Every Day Of The Week/Girl Of My Dreams (78)	45
57	Vogue V 9069	Rum And Coca Cola/Soft Pillow (triangular centre)	225
57	Vogue V 9069	Rum And Coca Cola/Soft Pillow (78)	90
57	Vogue V 9080	Thinking Of You Baby/If I Could Be With You (One Hour Tonight) (triangular centre)	225
57	Vogue V 9080	Thinking Of You Baby/If I Could Be With You (One Hour Tonight) (78)	90
60	Vogue V 9163	One Scotch, One Bourbon, One Beer/Bad, Bad Whiskey	150
57	Vogue VE 1-70102	ROCK AND ROLL (EP)	275
78	United Artists UAS 30203	CHICKEN SHACK BOOGIE (LP)	12

AMOS MILBURN JNR

63	London HLU 9795	Gloria/Look At Me Fool	20

PERCY MILEM

66	Stateside SS 566	Crying Baby, Baby, Baby/Call On Me	22

BARRY MILES

60	Egmont AJS 14	MILES OF GENIUS (LP)	15

BERNARD MILES

57	Decca DFE 6415	BERNARD MILES (EP)	10
59	Decca DFE 6559	THE RACE FOR THE RHINEGOLD STAKES (EP)	12
60	HMV 7EG 8629	OLD ENGLISH FAIRY TALES (EP)	10
61	HMV 7EG 8716	OVER THE GATE (EP)	12

BUDDY MILES (EXPRESS)

68	Mercury MF 1065	Train (Parts 1 & 2)	8
69	Mercury MF 1098	Miss Lady/'69 Freedom Special	5
71	Mercury 6052 036	Them Changes/Your Feeling Is Mine (solo)	5
71	Mercury 6052 077	Wholesale Love/That's The Way Life Is	5
72	Mercury 6052 127	Give Away None Of My Love/Take It Off Him And Put It On Me (solo)	5
69	Mercury 20137 SMCL	EXPRESSWAY TO YOUR SKULL (LP)	15
69	Mercury 20163 SMCL	ELECTRIC CHURCH (LP)	15
70	Mercury 6338 016	THEM CHANGES (LP)	12
71	Mercury 6338 028	WE GOT TO LIVE TOGETHER (LP)	12
71	Mercury 6338 048	A MESSAGE TO THE PEOPLE (LP)	12
72	Mercury 6641 033	LIVE (2-LP)	18
73	CBS 65406	CHAPTER VII (LP)	12
74	CBS 80349	ALL THE FACES (LP)	12

(see also Electric Flag, Jimi Hendrix, Carlos Santana & Buddy Miles)

DICK & SUE MILES

70s	Sweet Folk & Country SFA 106	THE DUNMOW FLITCH (LP)	15

GARRY MILES

60	London HLG 9155	Look For A Star/Afraid Of Love	15
60	London REG 1264	LOOK FOR A STAR (EP)	50

JOHN MILES

70	Orange OAS 508	Why Don't You Love Me?/If I Could See Through	6
71	Decca F 13196	Jose/You Make It So Hard	5
72	Orange OAS 207	Come Away Melinda/Walking With My Head Held High	6
72	Orange OAS 208	Yesterday (Was Just The Beginning)/Road To Freedom	6
73	Orange OAS 209	Hard Road/You're Telling Me Lies	6
73	Orange OAS 211	Jacqueline/Keep On Tryin'	6
73	Orange OAS 213	One Minute Every Hour/Hollywood Queen	7
74	Orange OAS 220	Fright Of My Life/Good Time Woman	6
74	Orange OAS 223	What's On Your Mind/Rock'n'Roll Band	6
74	Orange OAS 224	What's On Your Mind/To Be Grateful	6
83	EMI EMI 5386	The Right To Sing/Back To The Magic (picture disc)	5

(see also Influence)

JOSIE MILES

60s	Poydras 103	JOSIE MILES (EP)	8

LENNY MILES

61	Top Rank JAR 546	Don't Believe Him Donna/Invisible	18

LIZZIE MILES

56	HMV 7EG 8178	THE BLUES THEY SANG (EP, 1 side by Billy Young, both with Jelly Roll Morton)	25
59	Columbia Clef SEB 10088	SCINTILLATING LIZZIE (EP, with Bob Scobey's Band)	10
50s	Melodisc EPM7 55	NEW ORLEANS BOYS (EP, with New Orleans Boys)	20
57	Capitol T 792	A NIGHT IN NEW ORLEANS (LP)	25

SARAH MILES

65	Fontana TF 552	Where Am I/Here Of All Places	7

MILESTONES & BUTCH BAKER

75	Black Magic BM 111	The Joker Parts 1 & 2	6

MILKSHAKES

82	Bilko BILK-O	Please Don't Tell My Baby/It's You (p/s)	8
83	Upright UP 6	Soldiers Of Love/Shimmy Shimmy (p/s)	6
84	Big Beat NS 94	Brand New Cadillac/Commanche/Jezebel/Jaguar And Thunderbird (p/s)	5
84	Big Beat SW 105	The Ambassadors Of Love/No More/Gringles And Groyles Again/Remarkable (p/s)	5

MINT VALUE £

86	Empire UXF 228	Let Me Love You/She Tells Me She Loves Me (p/s)	5
83	Big Beat NED 4	14 RHYTHM AND BEAT GREATS (LP)	18
83	Upright UPLP 1	AFTER SCHOOL SESSIONS (LP)	18
84	Milkshake HARP-O	NOTHING CAN STOP THESE MEN (LP)	18
85	Big Beat WIK 30	THEY CAME, THEY SAW, THEY CONQUERED (LP)	15
86	Milkshake MILK-O	TALKING 'BOUT MILKSHAKES (LP)	15

(see also Thee Mighty Caesars, Prisoners/Milkshakes, Pop Rivits, Len Bright Combo, Billy Childish, Thee Headcoats)

MILLER

65	Oak RGJ 190	Baby I've Got News For You/The Girl With The Castle	275
65	Columbia DB 7735	Baby I Got News For You/The Girl With The Castle	300

(see also Big Boy Pete, Peter Jay & Jaywalkers, Pete Miller, News)

ANN MILLER

54	MGM SP 1076	Too Darn Hot/KATHRYN GRAYSON & HOWARD KEEL: So In Love	10

ANN MILLER & KATHRYN GRAYSON

54	MGM SP 1078	Always True To You In My Fashion/I Hate Men	10

(see also Kathryn Grayson & Howard Keel)

BETTY MILLER

59	Top Rank JAR 115	Pearly Gates/Old Time Religion	8
59	Top Rank JAR 127	Jack O' Diamonds/(It Took) One Kiss	10
59	Top Rank JAR 127	Jack O' Diamonds/(It Took) One Kiss (78)	5

BOB MILLER & MILLERMEN

57	Columbia DB 4017	The Scamp/The Sack Line (as Bob Miller Music)	8
58	Columbia DB 4140	Square Bash/Muchacha (as Bob Miller Music)	8
59	Fontana H 181	Dig This!/The Poacher	10
59	Fontana H 192	Little Dipper/The Keel Row	7
59	Fontana H 192	Little Dipper/The Keel Row (78)	8
59	Fontana H 228	In The Mood/Joey's Song	7
59	Fontana H 228	In The Mood/Joey's Song (78)	12
60	Fontana H 236	The Busker's Tune/My Guy's Come Back	7
60	Fontana H 245	77 Sunset Strip/Manhunt	7
60	Fontana H 284	Night Theme/Last Date	7
61	Parlophone R 4779	Trouble Shooter/Hootin'	7
61	Parlophone R 4854	The "Oliver" Twist/That's It	6
65	Mercury MF 947	Uptown And Downtown/Carnaby Street Parade	10
65	Polydor 56005	6-5 Special/Dick Van Dyke Theme	12
66	Columbia DB 7877	Get Smart/Bony's Blues (as Bob Miller & His Millermen)	10

BOBBIE MILLER

65	Decca F 12064	What A Guy/You Went Away	40
65	Decca F 12252	Every Beat Of My Heart/Tomorrow	15
66	Decca F 12354	Everywhere I Go/IAN STEWART & RAILROADERS: Stu-Ball	80

(see also Mongrels, Rolling Stones)

CHUCK MILLER

56	Capitol CL 14543	Rogue River Valley/No Baby Like You	18
57	Mercury 7MT 153	The Auctioneer/Me Head's In De Barrel	25
57	Mercury MT 153	The Auctioneer/Me Head's In De Barrel (78)	10
57	Mercury MT 157	Bye, Bye Love/Rang Tang Ding Dong (78)	8
57	Mercury MT 181	Plaything/After Yesterday (78)	10
58	Mercury 7MT 215	Down The Road A-Piece/Mad About Her Blues	100
58	Mercury MT 215	Down The Road A-Piece/Mad About Her Blues (78)	10
59	Mercury AMT 1026	The Auctioneer/Baby Doll	12
59	Mercury AMT 1026	The Auctioneer/Baby Doll (78)	20
60	Mercury ZEP 10058	GOING GOING GONE (EP)	60

COUNT PRINCE (MILLER)

70	Downtown DT 460	I'm Gonna Keep On Trying/Girl I Need You (as Count Prince)	6
70	MCA MK 5042	Mule Train/Lucille (p/s)	5
72	Penny Farthing PEN 799	Rupert The Bear/When We Were Children	5

(see also Jimmy James & The Vagabonds)

FRANKIE MILLER

59	Melodisc MEL 1519	True Blue/Black Land Farmer	20
59	Melodisc MEL 1519	True Blue/Black Land Farmer (78)	15
59	Melodisc MEL 1529	Poppin' Johnnie/Family Man	20
59	Melodisc MEL 1529	Poppin' Johnnie/Family Man (78)	15
60	Melodisc MEL 1552	Rain, Rain/Baby Rocked Her Dolly	20
62	Top Rank JKP 3013	COUNTRY MUSIC (EP)	40
64	Ember CW 107	THE TRUE COUNTRY STYLE OF FRANKIE MILLER (LP)	30

GARY MILLER

58	Pye 7N 15120	The Story Of My Life/Put A Light In The Window	6
58	Pye 7N 15136	Lollipop/Dancing With My Shadow	8
58	Pye 7N 15140	On The Street Where You Live/That's For Me (with Kenny Ball & His Jazz Band)	6
58	Pye 7N 15151	A Couple Of Crazy Kids (with Marion Ryan)/Ivanhoe Of England	8
58	Pye 7N 15164	The First Christmas Day/Nearest And Dearest	7
59	Pye 7N 15188	Jezebel/The Railroad Song	7
59	Pye 7N 15207	Sing Along/Someone To Come Home To	7
59	Pye 7N 15239	Marina/Hold Me, Thrill Me, Kiss Me	7
61	Pye 7N 15404	There Goes That Song Again/The Night Is Young	6
64	Pye 7N 15698	Aqua Marina/Stingray	18
56	Pye NEP 24013	YELLOW ROSE OF TEXAS (EP, 2 different sleeves)	each 30
57	Pye NEP 24047	HIT PARADE VOL. 1 (EP)	22
57	Pye NEP 24057	MEET MISTER MILLER PT. 1 — ON STAGE (EP)	22
57	Pye NEP 24058	MEET MISTER MILLER PT. 2 — FOR THE YOUNG IN LOVE (EP)	22
57	Pye NEP 24059	MEET MISTER MILLER PT. 3 — FOR THE YOUNG IN LOVE (EP)	22

58	Pye NEP 24072	HIT PARADE VOL. 2 (EP)	25
60	Pye NEP 24123	FLOWER DRUM SONG (EP)	12
57	Nixa NPL 18008	MEET MISTER MILLER (LP)	45
61	Pye NPL 18059	GARY ON THE BALL (LP)	30

(see also Kenny Ball)

GLEN MILLER

67	Doctor Bird DB 1089	Where Is The Love/Funky Broadway	100
68	Doctor Bird DB 1128	Rocksteady Party/Book Of Memories	25

GLENN MILLER & HIS ORCHESTRA

54	Columbia SCM 5086	I Got Rhythm/Sleepy Time Gal	15
54	HMV 7M 195	Little Brown Jug/Don't Sit Under The Apple Tree	18
58	RCA RCA 1034	Falling Leaves/So Sweet (as Glenn Miller New Orchestra)	5
58	RCA RCA 1096	American Patrol/Little Brown Jug	7
59	Top Rank JAR 114	Boom Shot/You Say The Sweetest Things, Baby	6
59	Top Rank TR 5003	Chattanooga Choo Choo/Serenade In Blue	7
65	Columbia DB 7550	Pennsylvania 6-5000/The Girl From Ipanema	6
54	HMV 7EG 8031	GLENN MILLER AND HIS ORCHESTRA (EP)	8
54	HMV 7EG 8043	GLENN MILLER AND HIS ORCHESTRA (EP)	8
54	HMV 7EG 8055	GLENN MILLER AND HIS ORCHESTRA (EP)	8
55	HMV 7EG 8067	GLENN MILLER AND HIS ORCHESTRA (EP)	8
55	HMV 7EG 8077	GLENN MILLER AND HIS ORCHESTRA (EP)	8
55	HMV 7EG 8097	THAT MILLER MUSIC (EP)	8
55	Brunswick OE 9169	COLLECTOR'S ITEMS (EP)	8
57	HMV 7EG 8204	GLENN MILLER SPECIAL (EP)	8
59	Top Rank JKR 8019	GOLDEN MILLER (EP)	8
53	HMV DLP 1012	GLENN MILLER CONCERT VOL. 1 (10" LP)	15
53	HMV DLP 1013	GLENN MILLER CONCERT VOL. 2 (10" LP)	15
53	HMV DLP 1021	GLENN MILLER CONCERT VOL. 3 (10" LP)	15
54	HMV DLP 1024	THE GLENN MILLER STORY (10" LP)	15
54	HMV DLP 1049	TIME FOR MELODY (10" LP)	15
54	HMV DLP 1059	ORCHESTRA WIVES (10" LP)	15
54	HMV RLS 599	GLENN MILLER LIMITED EDITION (5-LP, presentation set, 'snakeskin' cover)	50
55	HMV DLP 1062	SUNRISE SERENADE (10" LP)	15
55	HMV DLP 1081	GLENN MILLER CONCERT VOL. 4 (10" LP)	15
55	HMV DLP 1104	SUN VALLEY SERENADE (10" LP)	15
55	Philips BBR 8072	GLENN MILLER (10" LP)	15
56	HMV CLPC 6-10/RLS 598	GLENN MILLER LIMITED EDITION VOL. 2 (5-LP, in presentation album)	50
56	HMV RLS 637	GLENN MILLER & THE ARMY AIRFORCE BAND (5-LP, presentation box, [CLP 1077-CLP 1081])	30
56	HMV DLP 1122	MILLER MAGIC (10" LP)	15
56	Philips BBR 8092	GLENN MILLER (10" LP)	15
57	HMV DLP 1145	POLKA DOTS AND MOONBEAMS (10" LP)	15
58	RCA RD 27057	THE GLENN MILLER CARNEGIE HALL CONCERT (LP)	12
58	RCA RD 27068	THE GLENN MILLER STORY (LP)	12
58	RCA RD 27090	THE MARVELLOUS MILLER MEDLEYS (LP)	12
58	RCA RD 27096	MARVELLOUS MILLER MOODS (LP)	12
58	RCA RD 27135	GLENN MILLER ARMY AIRFORCE BAND VOL. 1 (LP)	12
59	Top Rank RX 3004	GLENN MILLER AND HIS ORCHESTRA VOL. 1 (LP)	12
59	Top Rank 35/023	GLENN MILLER AND HIS ORCHESTRA VOL. 2 (LP)	12
60	RCA RD 27146/RD 27147	FOR THE VERY FIRST TIME (2-LP)	18

JAMES MILLER

70	Trojan TR 7804	You Got To Me/2001	5

JIMMY MILLER & (NEW) BARBECUES

57	Columbia DB 4006	Sizzlin' Hot/Free Wheelin' Baby (as Jimmy Miller & Barbecues)	80
57	Columbia DB 4006	Sizzlin' Hot/Free Wheelin' Baby (as Jimmy Miller & Barbecues) (78)	15
58	Columbia DB 4081	Jelly Baby/Cry, Baby, Cry (as Jimmy Miller & New Barbecues)	65
58	Columbia DB 4081	Jelly Baby/Cry, Baby, Cry (as Jimmy Miller & New Barbecues) (78)	30

(see also Station Skiffle Group)

JODY MILLER

64	Capitol CL 15335	He Walks Like A Man/Looking At The World Through A Tear	7
64	Capitol CL 15356	The Fever/In My Room	15
65	Capitol CL 15393	Queen Of The House/The Greatest Actor	7
65	Capitol CL 15404	Silver Threads And Golden Needles/Melody For Robin	6
65	Capitol CL 15415	Home Of The Brave/This Is The Life	10
66	Capitol CL 15482	If You Were A Carpenter/Let Me Walk With You	6
65	Capitol (S) T 2416	HOME OF THE BRAVE (LP)	20/25
66	Capitol (S) T 2446	JODY MILLER SINGS THE GREAT HITS OF BUCK OWENS (LP)	20/25

KENNY MILLER

65	Stateside SS 405	Restless/Take My Tip	40

MANDY MILLER

56	Parlophone R 4219	Nellie The Elephant/It's Time To Dream	12
58	Parlophone GEP 8776	CHILDREN'S CHOICE (EP)	8

MAX MILLER

54	Philips PB 236	Mary From The Dairy/Voulez Vous Promenade (78)	8
55	Philips PB 518	Ain't It Ni–Ice/The Budgie Song (78)	10
58	Pye 7N 15141	With A Little Bit Of Luck/Be Sincere	5
59	HMV 7EG 8558	THE CHEEKY CHAPPIE (EP)	8
61	Pye NEP 25154	MAX AT THE MET (EP)	8
62	Pye NEP 25162	MAX AT THE MET VOL. 2 (EP)	8
58	Pye NPT 19026	MAX AT THE MET (10" LP)	20

(see also Lonnie Donegan)

MINT VALUE £

MITCH MILLER ORCHESTRA

53	Columbia SCM 5058	Just Dreaming/Without My Lover	6
62	CBS AAG 118	The Longest Day/The Longest Day (Version) (p/s)	5
56	Philips BBE 12043	LISBON ANTIGUA (EP)	8

(see also Guy Mitchell)

MRS MILLER

66	Capitol CL 15444	Downtown/A Lover's Concerto	7
66	Capitol T 2494	MRS. MILLER'S GREATEST HITS (LP)	18
66	Capitol T 2579	WILL SUCCESS SPOIL MRS. MILLER (LP)	18

MRS MILLER

69	Jackpot JP 707	Feel It/LYN BECKFORD: Kiss Me Quick (actually by Keeling Beckford)	7

(see also Lloyd Terrell)

NED MILLER

63	Capitol CL 15301	Go On Back You Fool/Dark Moon	10
63	London HL 9658	From A Jack To A King/Parade Of Broken Hearts	5
63	London HL 9728	Just Before Dawn/Mona Lisa	6
63	London HL 9766	Another Fool Like Me/Magic Moon	6
64	London HL 9838	Big Love/Sunday Morning Tears	6
64	London HL 9873	Invisible Tears/Old Restless Ocean	6
64	London HL 9937	Do What You Do Do Well/Dusty Guitar	7
63	Capitol EAP1 20492	NED MILLER (EP)	25
63	London RE 1382	NED MILLER (EP)	30
63	London HA 8072	FROM A JACK TO A KING (LP)	30
66	Capitol T 2414	THE BEST OF NED MILLER (LP)	30
69	Capitol ST 2914	IIN THE NAME OF LOVE (LP)	25

PETE MILLER

97	Tenth Planet TP 030	SUMMERLAND (LP, numbered, 1000 only)	15

(see also Miller, Big Boy Pete)

ROGER MILLER

64	Philips BF 1354	Dang Me/Got 2 Again	6
64	Philips BF 1365	Chug-A-Lug/Reincarnation	6
65	Philips BF 1390	Do-Wacka-Do/Love Is Not For Me	6
65	Philips BF 1397	King Of The Road/Atta Boy Girl	6
65	Philips BF 1416	Engine Engine No. 9/The Last Word In Lonesome Is Me	6
65	Philips BF 1437	Kansas City Star/One Dyin' And Buryin'	6
65	Philips BF 1456	England Swings/The Good Old Days	6
66	Philips BF 1475	Husbands And Wives/I've Been A Long Time Leavin'	6
66	Philips BF 1498	You Can't Roller Skate In A Buffalo Herd/Train Of Life	6
66	Philips BF 1516	My Uncle Used To Love Me But She Died/You're My Kingdom	6
67	Philips BF 1560	Walkin' In The Sunshine/Home	6
68	Mercury MF 1021	Little Green Apples/Our Little Love	6
69	Mercury MF 1108	England Swings/King Of The Road (p/s)	6
65	Philips BE 12578	ROGER MILLER (EP)	12
65	Camden CDN 5121	SONGS I HAVE WRITTEN (LP)	15
65	Philips BL 7667	ROGER AND OUT! (LP)	15
66	Philips BL 7669	THE RETURN OF ROGER MILLER (LP)	15
66	Philips BL 7676	THE 3RD TIME AROUND (LP)	15
66	Philips BL 7748	WORDS AND MUSIC (LP)	15
67	Philips (S)BL 7822	WALKING IN THE SUNSHINE (LP)	15
67	Philips (S)BL 7833	SINGS THE MUSIC & TELLS THE TALE OF WATERHOLE 3 (LP)	15

RUSS MILLER

57	HMV POP 391	I Sit In My Window/Wait For Me, My Love	55
57	HMV POP 391	I Sit In My Window/Wait For Me, My Love (78)	15

STEPHEN MILLER & LOL COXHILL

73	Caroline C 1503	COXHILL MILLER (LP)	50
74	Caroline C 1507	THE STORY SO FAR ... OH REALLY? (LP)	50

(see also Lol Coxhill)

STEVE MILLER BAND

68	Capitol CL 15539	Sittin' In Circles/Roll With It	15
68	Capitol CL 15564	Living In The U.S.A./Quicksilver Girl	15
69	Capitol CL 15604	My Dark Hour/Song For Our Ancestors	15
69	Capitol CL 15618	Little Girl/Don't Let Nobody Turn You Around	7
70	Capitol CL 15656	Going To The Country/Never Kill Another Man	6
72	Capitol CL 15712	My Dark Hour/The Gangster Is Back/Song For Our Ancestors (33rpm)	5
73	Capitol CL 15765	The Joker/Something To Believe In	5
74	Capitol CL 15786	Living In The U.S.A./Kow Kow Calqulator	5
68	Capitol (S)T 2920	CHILDREN OF THE FUTURE (LP, 'rainbow rim' label)	30
69	Capitol (S)T 2984	SAILOR (LP, 'rainbow rim' label)	25
70	Capitol E-(S)T 184	BRAVE NEW WORLD (LP)	15
70	Capitol E-ST 331	YOUR SAVING GRACE (LP)	12
70	Capitol EA-ST 436	NUMBER 5 (LP)	10
82	Mercury HS 9919 916	GREATEST HITS 1974-1978 (LP, half-speed audiophile pressing)	12

(see also Boz Scaggs)

SUZI MILLER

54	Decca F 10264	The Tennessee Wig Walk/Bimbo (B-side with Johnston Brothers) (78)	10
54	Decca F 10389	Happy Days And Lonely Nights/Tell Me, Tell Me (with Johnston Brothers)	25
54	Decca F 10423	Two Step, Side Step (with Johnston Brothers)/ Hang My Heart On A Christmas Tree (with Keynotes)	18
55	Decca F 10475	Tweedlee-Dee (with Johnston Brothers)/That's All I Want From You	20
55	Decca F 10512	Dance With Me Henry (Wallflower) (with Johnston Brothers)/ Butterfingers (with Marilyn Sisters)	15
55	Decca F 10593	The Banjo's Back In Town/Go On By	10

56	Decca F 10677	Ay-Ay-Senores/Reckless	10
56	Decca F 10722	Get Up! Get Up! (You Sleepy Head)/The Key To My Heart	10
57	Decca F 10848	I Love My Baby/The Money Tree	8

(see also Marilyn Sisters, Johnston Brothers)

MILLIE (SMALL)

63	Fontana TF 425	Don't You Know/Until You're Mine	10
64	Fontana TF 449	My Boy Lollipop/Something's Gotta Be Done	6
64	Fontana TF 479	Sweet William/Oh Henry	8
64	Fontana TF 502	I Love The Way You Love/Bring It On Home To Me	8
64	Cadbury's BNVT 01F	The Bournvita Song/Three Nights A Week (p/s)	20
65	Fontana TF 515	I've Fallen In Love With A Snowman/What Am I Living For	7
65	Fontana TF 529	See You Later Alligator/Chilly Kisses	7
65	Fontana TF 591	My Street/It's Too Late	7
65	Fontana TF 617	Bloodshot Eyes/Tongue Tied	10
65	Brit WI 1002	My Street/A Mixed Up, Fickle, Moody, Self-Centred, Spoiled Kind Of Boy	15
66	Fontana TF 740	Killer Joe/Carry Go Bring Come (as Millie Small)	8
67	Fontana TF 796	Chicken Feed/Wings Of A Dove (as Millie Small)	8
67	Island WIP 6021	You Better Forget/I Am In Love	6
68	Fontana TF 948	When I Dance With You/Hey Mr. Love	6
69	Decca F 12948	Readin' Writin' Arithmetic/I Want You Never To Stop	12
70	Pyramid PYR 6080	My Love And I/Tell Me About Yourself	6
70	Trojan TR 7744	Enoch Power/Mayfair	6
70	President PT 306	We're All In A Zoo/Piccaninny Man	5
70	Trojan TR 7801	Honey Hush/Sunday Morning	5
61	Blue Beat BBEP 302	MILLIE (EP, with Little Roy & Owen Gray; most without sleeve)	200/50
64	Fontana TE 17425	MY BOY LOLLIPOP (EP)	45
66	Island IEP 705	MILLIE AND HER BOYFRIENDS (EP)	75
64	Fontana (S)TL 5220	MORE MILLIE (LP, mono/stereo)	45/50
65	Fontana TL 5276	MILLIE SINGS FATS DOMINO (LP)	80
67	Island ILP 953	THE BEST OF MILLIE SMALL (LP)	60
69	Trojan TTL 17	MILLIE AND HER BOYFRIENDS (LP)	18
69	Trojan TTL 49	THE BEST OF MILLIE SMALL (LP, reissue)	15
70	Trojan TBL 108	TIME WILL TELL (LP)	20

(see also Jackie & Millie, Roy & Millie, Owen & Millie)

SPIKE MILLIGAN

58	Parlophone R 4406	Wish I Knew/Will I Find My Love Today?	10
58	Parlophone R 4406	Wish I Knew/Will I Find My Love Today? (78)	15
61	Parlophone R 4839	I'm Walking Out With A Mountain/The Sewers Of The Strand	10
62	Parlophone R 4891	Wormwood Scrubs Tango/Postman's Knock	10
64	Pye 7N 15720	The Olympic Team/Epilogue (with John Bluthal)	8
66	Parlophone R 5513	Purple Aeroplane/Nothing At All	10
66	Parlophone R 5543	Tower Bridge/Silent Night	10
69	Parlophone R 5771	The Q.5 Piano Tune/Ning, Nang, Nong	10
73	Warner Bros. K 16240	Girl On A Pony/Old Man's Protest Song	7
61	Parlophone PMC 1148	MILLIGAN PRESERVED (LP, also in stereo [PCS 18])	20/25
65	Decca LK 4701	MUSES WITH MILLIGAN (LP)	18
68	Pye NPL 18271	THE WORLD OF THE BEACHCOMBER (LP)	18
75	Polydor 2460 235	BADJELLY THE WITCH AND OTHER GOODIES (LP)	15

(see also Goons, Famous Eccles, Peter Sellers)

LUCKY MILLINDER & HIS ORCHESTRA

51	Vogue V 9007	I'm Waiting Just For You/Bongo Boogie (78)	12
51	Vogue V 9021	No One Else Could Be/The Grape Vine (78)	12
52	Vogue V 2138	Ram-Bunk-Shush/Let It Roll Again (78)	12

(see also Wynonie "Mr Blues" Harris)

JEB MILLION

86	WEA YZ 82	Speed Up My Heartbeat/Who Sent You (p/s)	6
86	WEA YZ 82T	Speed Up My Heartbeat (Extended Mix)/Speed Up My Heartbeat/ Who Sent You (12", p/s)	12

MILLIONAIRES (Ireland)

66	Decca F 12468	Wishing Well/Chatterbox	60

MILLIONAIRES (U.S.)

73	Mercury 6052 301	Never For Me/If I Had You Babe (paper or plastic label)	10/8

MILLIONS

73	Duke DU 154	Murmuring/TOMMY McCOOK & BOBBY ELLIS: Murmuring — Version	6
73	Downtown DT 516	Love Of Jah Jah Children/Jah Jah Version	6

MILLIONS OF DEAD CHILDREN

85	Radical MDC 3	CHICKENSQUAWK EP (poster p/s)	15

(see also M.D.C.)

BARBARA MILLS

65	Hickory 45-1323	Queen Of Fools/Make It Last, Take Your Time	100
65	Hickory 45-1392	Try/Let's Make A Memory	20
75	London HLE 10491	Queen Of Fools/Make It Last, Take Your Time (reissue)	8

FREDDIE MILLS

57	Parlophone R 4374	"One For The Road" Medley (both sides)	8

GARRY MILLS

59	Top Rank JAR 119	Hey Baby (You're Pretty)/You Alone	15
59	Top Rank JAR 119	Hey Baby (You're Pretty)/You Alone (78)	15
59	Top Rank JAR 219	Seven Little Girls Sitting In The Back Seat/The Night You Became 17	8
59	Top Rank JAR 219	Seven Little Girls Sitting In The Back Seat/The Night You Became 17 (78)	15
59	Oriole CB 1529	Living Lord/Big Story Breaking	6

MINT VALUE £

59	Oriole CB 1530	I Am The Great I Am/Rhythm In Religion	6
60	Top Rank JAR 301	Running Bear/Teen Angel	12
60	Top Rank JAR 336	Look For A Star/Footsteps	7
60	Top Rank JAR 393	Comin' Down With Love/I'm Gonna Find Out	8
60	Top Rank JAR 500	Top Teen Baby/Don't Cheat Me Again (some in p/s)	15/8
61	Top Rank JAR 542	Who's Gonna Take You Home Tonight?/Christina	10
61	Decca F 11358	I'll Step Down/Your Way Is My Way	12
61	Decca F 11383	Bless You/Footprints In The Sand	10
61	Decca F 11415	Treasure Island/Sad Little Girl	10
62	Decca F 11471	Never Believed In Love/Save A Dream For Me	10
61	Top Rank JKP 3001	LOOK FOR A STAR (EP)	60

(see also Gary & Ariels)

GORDON MILLS

65	Ace Of Clubs ACL 1191	DO IT YOURSELF (LP)	12

(see also Viscounts)

HAYLEY MILLS

61	Decca F 21396	Let's Get Together/Cobbler Cobbler	5
62	Decca F 21442	Jeepers Creepers/Johnny Jingo	5
62	Decca LK 4426	LET'S GET TOGETHER (LP)	15

HAYLEY MILLS & EDDIE HODGES

63	HMV POP 1179	Flitterin'/Beautiful Beulah	6

(see also Eddie Hodges)

JEFF MILLS

61	Ember EMB S 133	Daddy's Home/TIMMY REYNOLDS: Lullaby Of Love	12

MAUDE MILLS

60s	Vintage Jazz VEP 34	MAUDE MILLS (EP)	12

RUDY MILLS

67	Island WI 3092	A Long Story/BOBBY ELLIS: Now We Know (actually. with Desmond Miles Seven)	22
68	Island WI 3136	I'm Trapped/BOBBY ELLIS & CRYSTALLITES: Dollar A Head	22
69	Big Shot BI 509	John Jones/A Place Called Happiness	15
69	Explosion EX 2007	Lemi Li/Goody Goody	10
69	Crab CRAB 20	Tears On My Pillow/I'm Trapped	7
69	Crab CRAB 24	A Heavy Load/Wholesale Love	12
69	Pama SECO 12	REGGAE HITS (LP)	60

STEPHANIE MILLS

74	Paramount PARA 3050	I Knew It Was Love/The Passion And The Pain	5
76	Tamla Motown TMG 1020	This Empty Place/I See You For The First Time (unissued, demo only)	25
76	T. Motown STML 12017	FOR THE FIRST TIME (LP)	12

MILLS BROTHERS

54	Brunswick 05325	How Blue?/Why Do I Keep Lovin' You?	12
55	Brunswick 05390	Paper Valentine/The Urge	10
55	Brunswick 05439	Smack Dab In The Middle/Opus One	15
55	Brunswick 05452	You're Nobody Till Somebody Loves You/Yes You Are	10
55	Brunswick 05487	Mi Muchacha (Little Girl)/Gum Drop	20
55	Brunswick 05488	Suddenly There's A Valley/That's All I Ask Of You	10
56	Brunswick 05522	I've Changed My Mind A Thousand Times/All The Way 'Round The World	10
56	Brunswick 05550	Dream Of You/In A Mellow Tone	7
56	Brunswick 05600	Ninety-Eight Cents/King Porter Stomp	6
56	Brunswick 05606	That's Right/Don't Get Caught (Short On Love)	8
56	Brunswick 05631	That's All I Need/Tell Me More	5
57	Brunswick 05664	In De Banana Tree/The Knocked Out Nightingale	5
57	Brunswick 05680	My Troubled Mind/Queen Of The Senior Prom	5
57	Brunswick 05680	My Troubled Mind/Queen Of The Senior Prom (78)	8
58	London HLD 8553	Get A Job/I Found A Million Dollar Baby	30
58	London HLD 8553	Get A Job/I Found A Million Dollar Baby (78)	15
60	London HLD 9169	I Got You/Highways Are Happy Ways	5
54	Brunswick OE 9014	PRESENTING THE MILLS BROTHERS (EP)	12
55	Brunswick OE 9060	THE MILLS BROTHERS NO. 2 (EP)	8
56	Brunswick OE 9239	SINGING AND SWINGING PT. 1 (EP)	8
59	London RED 1215	THE MILLS BROTHERS (EP)	15
54	Brunswick LA 8664	MEET THE MILLS BROTHERS (10" LP)	22
55	Brunswick LA 8702	FOUR BOYS AND A GUITAR (10" LP)	20
59	London HA-D 2192	THE MILLS BROTHERS' GREATEST HITS (LP, also stereo SAH-D 6046)	15
60	London HA-D 2250	THE MILLS BROTHERS SING (LP, also stereo SAH-D 6074)	15
61	London HA-D 2319	THE MILLS BROTHERS' GREATEST HITS VOLUME 2 (LP)	15
61	London HA-D 2383	SAN ANTONIO ROSE (LP, also stereo SAH-D 6183)	15
63	London HA-D/SH-D 8058	BEER BARREL POLKA (LP)	15
63	London HA-D/SH-D 8092	THE END OF THE WORLD (LP)	15

(see also Louis Armstrong)

MILLWALL F.C.

72	Decca F1 3350	Millwall/The Ballad Of Harry Cripps	8

RONNIE MILSAP

66	Pye International 7N 25392	Ain't No Soul (Left In These Old Shoes)/ Another Branch From The Same Old Tree	22
69	Pye International 7N 25490	Denver/Nothing Is As Good As It Used To Be	6
72	Wand WN 26	Ain't No Soul (Left In These Old Shoes)/ Another Branch From The Same Old Tree (reissue)	6

RONNIE MILSAP/ROSCOE ROBINSON

66	Pye Intl. NEP 44078	SOUL SENSATIONS (EP)	22

MINT VALUE £

JOHNNY MILTON & CONDORS

61 Oriole CB 1588 — Charleston Cocktail (medley) (as Johnny Milton Band) . . . 6
64 Decca F 11862 — A Girl Named Sue/Somethin' Else (as Johnny Milton & Condors) . . . 10
64 Fontana TF 488 — Cry Baby/Hurt . . . 7
(see also Symbols)

MILVA

63 Oriole CB 1899 — I Can't Believe You're Leaving Me/Loneliness Of Autumn . . . 8
64 Oriole CB 1952 — I'll Set My Love To Music/Come Sempre . . . 8
67 Major Minor MM 510 — Love Is A Feeling/Seasons Of Love . . . 5

MILWAUKEE COASTERS

68 Pama PM 733 — Treat Me Nice/Sick And Tired (Oh Babe) . . . 5
68 Pama PMLP 2 — WEST COAST ROCK'N'ROLL 1968 (LP) . . . 15
69 Pama PSP 10 — BEST PARTY ALBUM (LP, reissue of PMLP 2) . . . 12

GARNET MIMMS (& ENCHANTERS)

63 United Artists UP 1033 — Cry Baby/Don't Change Your Heart (with Enchanters) . . . 25
63 United Artists UP 1038 — Baby Don't You Weep/For Your Precious Love (with Enchanters) . . . 18
64 United Artists UP 1048 — Tell Me Baby/Anytime You Want Me (with Enchanters) . . . 18
65 United Artists UP 1090 — It Was Easier To Hurt Her/So Close . . . 22
66 United Artists UP 1130 — I'll Take Good Care Of You/Looking For You . . . 60
66 United Artists UP 1147 — It's Been Such A Long Way Home/Thinkin' . . . 18
66 United Artists UP 1153 — My Baby/It Won't Hurt Half As Much . . . 15
66 United Artists UP 1172 — All About Love/The Truth Hurts . . . 15
67 United Artists UP 1181 — Roll With The Punches/Only Your Love . . . 18
67 United Artists UP 1186 — As Long As I Have You/Yesterday . . . 15
68 Verve VS 569 — I Can Hear My Baby Crying/Stop And Think It Over . . . 10
68 Verve VS 569 — I Can Hear My Baby Crying/BILL MEDLEY: That Lucky Old Sun (mispress) . . . 10
68 Verve VS 574 — We Can Find That Love/Can You Top This . . . 10
76 United Artists REM 403 — REMEMBER GARNET MIMMS (EP) . . . 8
63 United Artists ULP 1067 — CRY BABY AND 11 OTHER HITS (LP, with Enchanters) . . . 120
66 United Artists (S)ULP 1145 — WARM AND SOULFUL (LP) . . . 90
67 United Artists (S)ULP 1174 — LIVE (LP, as Garnet Mimms & Senate) . . . 80

MINDBENDERS

66 Fontana TF 644 — A Groovy Kind Of Love/Love Is Good . . . 7
66 Fontana TF 697 — Can't Live With You, Can't Live Without You/One Fine Day . . . 7
66 Fontana TF 731 — Ashes To Ashes/You Don't Know About Love . . . 7
66 Fontana TF 780 — I Want Her, She Wants Me/The Morning After . . . 8
67 Fontana TF 806 — We'll Talk About It Tomorrow/Far Across Town . . . 10
67 Fontana TF 869 — The Letter/My New Day And Age . . . 10
67 Fontana TF 877 — Schoolgirl/Coming Back . . . 18
68 Fontana TF 910 — Blessed Are The Lonely/Yellow Brick Road . . . 10
68 Fontana TF 961 — Uncle Joe, The Ice Cream Man/The Man Who Loved Trees . . . 12
69 Fontana H 1026 — A Groovy Kind Of Love/Ashes To Ashes (p/s) . . . 10
66 Fontana (S)TL 5324 — THE MINDBENDERS (LP, mono/stereo) . . . 50/60
67 Fontana (S)TL 5403 — WITH WOMAN IN MIND (LP) . . . 55
68 Fontana SFL 13045 — THE MINDBENDERS (LP, reissue) . . . 15
(see also Wayne Fontana & Mindbenders, Hotlegs, Lulu)

SAL MINEO

57 Philips JK 1024 — Start Movin' (In My Direction)/Love Affair (jukebox issue) . . . 40
57 Philips PB 733 — Lasting Love/You Shouldn't Do That (78) . . . 12
57 Philips PB 764 — Party Time/The Words That I Whisper (78) . . . 12
58 Fontana H 118 — Little Pigeon/Cuttin' In . . . 55
58 Fontana H 118 — Little Pigeon/Cuttin' In (78) . . . 20
58 Fontana H 135 — Seven Steps To Love/A Couple Of Crazy Kids . . . 35
58 Fontana H 135 — Seven Steps To Love/A Couple Of Crazy Kids (78) . . . 20
58 Fontana TFL 5004 — SAL (LP) . . . 80

CORINA MINETTE

60 HMV POP 752 — He'll Have To Stay/TOMMY THOMAS ORCHESTRA: Young At Cha Cha . . . 7

SEXTON MING (& HIS DIAMOND GUSSETS)

96 D. Goods DAMGOOD 71 — I'm In Love With Danny Edwards/Break His Spirit/Son Of Tractor Nits (p/s) . . . 5

CHARLES/CHARLIE MINGUS

60 Philips BBE 12399 — CHARLES MINGUS (EP) . . . 8
61 Philips BBE 12451 — MINGUS DYNASTY (EP, as Charles Mingus Jazz Groups, also stereo SBBE 9050) . . . 8/10
61 Philips BBE 12453 — THINGS AIN'T WHAT THEY USED TO BE (EP, as Charles Mingus Jazz Groups, also stereo SBBE 9052) . . . 8/10
63 Parlophone GEP 8786 — SCENES IN THE CITY (EP) . . . 10
65 Mercury 10021 MCE — JAZZ MAKERS (EP, as Charlie Mingus Orchestra) . . . 8
56 Vogue LDE 178 — CHARLIE MINGUS PRESENTS JAZZ WORKSHOP VOL. 2 (10" LP) . . . 18
59 Parlophone PMC 1092 — EAST COASTING (LP) . . . 20
60 London Jazz LTZ-K 15194 — BLUES AND ROOTS (LP, also stereo SAH-K 6087) . . . 15
62 Atlantic SD 8005 — CHARLES MINGUS PRESENTS CHARLES MINGUS (LP, U.K. issue of U.S. LP) . . 15
62 United Artists ULP 1004 — JAZZ PORTRAITS (LP) . . . 15
62 London HA-K/SH-K 8007 — OH YEAH (LP, by Charlie Mingus & Jazz Group) . . . 25
63 RCA RD/SF 7514 — TIJUANA MOODS (LP) . . . 25
63 Vocalion LAE 543 — CHAZZ (LP) . . . 15
64 HMV CLP 1694 — THE BLACK SAINT AND THE SINNER LADY (LP) . . . 20
65 United Artists ULP 1068 — TOWN HALL CONCERT (LP) . . . 15
65 Vocalion LAEF/SEAF 591 — CHARLIE MINGUS QUINTET WITH MAX ROACH (LP) . . . 15
65 HMV CLP 1742 — MINGUS, MINGUS, MINGUS (LP, also stereo CSD 1545) . . . 15
65 HMV CLP 1796 — MINGUS PLAYS PIANO (LP) . . . 15
65 Atlantic ATL/SAL 5019 — CHARLIE MINGUS (LP) . . . 15
66 Realm RM 211 — JAZZ COMPOSERS WORKSHOP (NO. 1) (LP) . . . 12

MINT VALUE £

66	CBS (S)BPG 62261	MINGUS DYNASTY (LP)	20
68	Polydor 623 215	CHARLIE MINGUS (LP)	12
68	Atlantic 587 131	PITHECANTHROPUS ERECTUS (LP, as Charlie Mingus Jazz Workshop)	20
69	CBS 52346	MINGUS AH-UM! (LP)	12
69	Atlantic 587 166	REINCARNATION OF A LOVEBIRD (LP, as Charlie Mingus Jazz Workshop)	15
69	Mercury SMWL 21056	MINGUS REVISITED (LP)	12
70	Atlantic 545 111	DUKE'S CHOICE (LP, as Charlie Mingus Jazz Workshop)	12
70	Liberty LBS 83346	MY FAVOURITE QUINTET (LP)	12
72	Ember CJS 832	INTRUSIONS (LP)	12
72	CBS 24010	CHARLES MINGUS (2-LP)	18
72	CBS 64715	LET MY CHILDREN HEAR MUSIC (LP)	12
72	RCA LSA 3117	TIJUANA MOODS (LP, reissue)	12
72	Prestige PR 24010	CHARLES MINGUS (LP)	12
73	Atlantic K 60039	THE ART OF CHARLIE MINGUS: THE ATLANTIC YEARS (2-LP)	18

MINIM

67	Polydor 582 011	WRAPPED IN A UNION JACK (LP)	22

MINISTRY

92	Sire W 0096	Jesus Built My Hotrod/T.V. Song (p/s)	10

MINISTRY OF SOUND

66	Decca F 12449	White Collar Worker/Back Seat Driver	12

LIZA MINNELLI

66	Capitol CL 15483	The Middle Of The Street/I (Who Have Nothing)	8
89	Epic ZEE C1	Losing My Mind (Remix)/(Extended Remix)/Tonight Is Forever (CD, card p/s)	8
89	Epic ZEE 2	Don't Drop Bombs (Extended Remix)/(Dub Mix)/(Acappella) (12", p/s)	10
89	Epic ZEE C2	Don't Drop Bombs (7" Version)/(Extended Remix)/(Acappella) (CD, card p/s)	8
89	Epic ZEE G3	So Sorry, I Said/I Can't Say Goodnight (gatefold p/s)	7
89	Epic ZEE C3	So Sorry, I Said/I Can't Say Goodnight/Losing My Mind (Ultimix)/ Losing My Mind (Ultimix Dub) (CD, card sleeve)	8
89	Epic CP ZEE 3	So Sorry, I Said/I Can't Say Goodnight/Losing My Mind (Ultimix)/Losing My Mind (Ultimix Dub) (CD, 'Xmas' pack in pouch with gatefold card & envelope)	12
90	Epic ZEE 4	Love Pains/Love Pains (Steve "Silk" Hurley's Radio Edit) (p/s)	5
90	Epic ZEEQT 4	Love Pains (Deep House Pains)/Love Pains (Steve "Silk" Hurley's Radio Edit)/ PET SHOP BOYS: Rent (12", gatefold sleeve)	8
90	Epic CD ZEE 4	Love Pains/Love Pains (Steve "Silk" Hurley's Remix)/PET SHOP BOYS: Rent (CD, card sleeve)	8
02	Columbia (no cat. no.)	Losing My Mind (Almighty Mix)/(Almighty Dub) (CD-R, title sleeve, with the Pet Shop Boys)	65

(see also Pet Shop Boys)

MINNY POPS

80s	Factory FAC 31	MINNY POPS EP: Goddess/Dolphin Spurt	8

DANNII MINOGUE

91	MCA MCSR 1529	Love And Kisses (7" Mix)/(Instrumental) (poster p/s, some signed)	25/5
97	Warner Bros SAM 3009	All I Wanna Do (Trouser Enthusiasts' Toys Of Desperation Mix)/ (Trouser Enthusiasts' Ultra Sensitive Dub)/(Quatara Mix)/ (Dizzy's Mix) (12", double pack, blue title sleeve, promo only)	15
97	Warner Bros SAM 3022	All I Wanna Do (12" Extended Mix)/(7" Mix)/(Xenomania Dream House Mix)/ (Tiny Tim & The Mekon Dream Dub)/(D-Bop's Innocent Girl Mix)/ (Trouser Enthusiasts' Toys Of Desperation Mix) (12", double pack, gold title sleeve, promo only)	20
97	Warner Bros SAM 3106	Everything I Wanted (Jupiter 6 — Soul Surround Mix)/Heaven Can Wait (D'Bop's Melt & Sparkle Mix) (10", promo only)	15
97	Warner Bros SAM 3108	Everything I Wanted (Xenomania 12" Mix)/(Radio Edit)/ (Trouser Enthusiasts' Golden Delicious Mix)/(Metro's 7" Edit) (12", metallic green title sleeve,promo only)	12
97	Warner Bros SAM 3105	Everything I Wanted (Xenomania 12" Mix)/(Radio Edit)/ (Trouser Enthusiasts' Golden Delicious Mix)/(Hell Fire Club Dub)/ (Cloud Nine Mix)/(Liquid Silk Dub) (12" double pack, metallic pink title sleeve, promo only)	15

KYLIE MINOGUE

87	PWL PWLT 8R	I Should Be So Lucky (Bicentennial Mix)/(Instrumental) (12", stickered p/s)	12
88	PWL PWLT 12R	Got To Be Certain (Extra Beat Boys Mix)/Got To Be Certain (7" Mix)/ Got To Be Certain (Out For A Duck Bill Platter Plus Dub Mix) (12", stickered p/s)	15
88	PWL PWCD 12	Got To Be Certain (Extended Mix)/Got To Be Certain (Instrumental)/ I Should Be So Lucky (Extended Mix 6.03) (CD)	20
88	PWL PWLT 14R	The Loco-Motion (Sankie Mix)/I'll Still Be Loving You (12", stickered p/s)	18
88	PWL PWCD 14	The Loco-Motion/I'll Still Be Loving You (CD)	20
88	PWL PWLP 21	Je Ne Sais Pas Pourquoi/Made In Heaven (poster p/s)	35
88	PWL PWLT 21R	Je Ne Sais Pas Pourquoi (Revolutionary Mix)/Made In Heaven (Maid In England Mix) (12", stickered p/s)	15
88	PWL PWCD 21	Je Ne Sais Pas Pourquoi (Moi Non Plus Mix)/Made In Heaven (Maid In England Mix)/The Loco-Motion (Sankie Mix) (CD)	20
88	PWL PWCD 24	Especially For You (7" Mix)/Especially For You (Extended)/ All I Wanna Do Is Make You Mine (Extended) (with Jason Donovan) (CD)	15
89	PWL PWMC 35	Hand On Your Heart (7" Mix)/Hand On Your Heart (Great Aorta Mix)/ Just Wanna Love You (cassette)	8
89	PWL PWLT 35R	Hand On Your Heart (Heartache Mix)/Hand On Your Heart (Dub mix) Just Wanna Love You (12", with stickered p/s)	35
89	PWL PWCD 35	Hand On Your Heart (Great Aorta Mix)/Just Wanna Love You/ It's No Secret (Extended Mix) (CD)	15
89	PWL PWMC 42	Wouldn't Change A Thing/It's No Secret (Album Version) (cassette)	8
89	PWL PWLT 42R	Wouldn't Change A Thing (Espagna Mix)/Wouldn't Change A Thing (7" Mix)/ It's No Secret (Extended) (12", stickered p/s)	25

MINT VALUE £

89	PWL PWCD 42	Wouldn't Change A Thing (7" Mix)/Wouldn't Change A Thing (Your Thang Mix)/ Je Ne Sais Pas Pourquoi (Revolutionary Mix) (CD)	15
89	PWL PWCD 45	Never Too Late (7" Mix)/(Extended)/(Kylie Smiley Extended Mix) (6.17) (CD)	15
90	PWL PWMC47	Tears On My Pillow (7" Mix)/We Know The Meaning Of Love (7" mix) (cassette)	8
90	PWL PWCD47	Tears On My Pillow (7" Mix)/Tears On My Pillow (Extended Mix)/ We Know The Meaning Of Love (Extended Mix) (CD)	12
90	PWL PWMC 56	Better The Devil You Know (7" Mix)/I'm Over Dreaming Over You (7" Remix)/ (cassette, orange casing)	5
90	PWL PWCD 56	Better The Devil You Know (Mad March Hare Mix)/ I'm Over Dreaming Over You (7" Remix) (CD)	15
90	PWL PWMC 64	Step Back In Time (7" Mix)/Step Back In Time (Instrumental) (cassette, green casing)	5
90	PWL PWCD 64	Step Back In Time (7" Mix)/Step Back In Time (Walkin' Rhythm Mix)/ Step Back In Time (Extended instrumental) (CD)	15
91	PWL PWLP 72	What Do I Have To Do (New Mix)/What Do I Have To Do (Instrumental) (stickered p/s, with postcards)	15
91	PWL PWMC 72	What Do I Have To Do (New Mix)/What Do I Have To Do (Instrumental) (cassette)	5
91	PWL PWLT 72R	What Do I Have To Do (Between The Sheets Mix) (12", withdrawn, no p/s)	80
91	PWL PWCD 72	What Do I Have To Do (New Mix)/What Do I Have To Do (Pumpin Polly Mix)/ What Do I Have To Do (Extended Instrumental) (CD)	15
91	PWL PWL P81	Shocked (DNA 7" Mix)/Shocked (Harding & Curnow 7" Mix) (picture disc)	15
91	PWL PWCD 81	Shocked (DNA 7" Mix)/Shocked (DNA Extended Mix)/Shocked (Harding & Curnow Extended Mix) (CD)	15
91	PWL PWLT 204R	Word Is Out (Summer Breeze Mix) (12", p/s, 1-sided, B-side etched autograph)	15
91	PWL PWCD 204	Word Is Out (Extended Mix)/Word Is Out (Instrumental)/ Say The Word — I'll Be There (CD)	12
91	PWL PWL 207	Keep On Pumpin' It (Angelic Remix Edit)/(Astral Flight Mix Edit) (with Vision Masters) (p/s)	5
91	PWL PWMC 207	Keep On Pumpin' It (Angelic Remix Edit)/(Astral Flight Mix Edit) (with Vision Masters) (cassette)	5
91	PWL PWLT 207	Keep On Pumpin' It (Angelic Remix)/(Astral Flight Mix) (with Vision Masters) (12", p/s)	10
91	PWL PWCD 207	Keep On Pumpin' It (Angelic Remix Edit)/(Angelic Remix)/ (Astral Flight Mix) (with Vision Masters) (CD)	20
91	PWL PWCD 508	If You Were With Me Now (with Keith Washington) (7" Mix)/(Extended)/ I Guess I Like It Like That (Full Length Version) (CD)	8
92	PWL PWCD 212	Give Me Just A Little More Time (7" Mix)/(Extended)/ Do You Dare (NRG Mix)/(New Rave Mix) (CD)	8
94	Polygram PSPMC 344	Hand On Your Heart/Give Me Just A Little More Time (Woolworths giveaway cassette)	10
94	DeCon. 7432 1227477 JB	Confide In Me (Radio Mix)/(Truth Mix) 21227477 JB (jukebox issue, no p/s)	10
94	DeConstruction 278482-0	Confide In Me (Master Mix)/Nothing Can Stop Us/ If You Don't Love Me (CD)	12
97	DeCon. 7432 1517257	Some Kind Of Bliss/Love Takes Over Me (p/s)	6
98	Arthrob ART021 CD1	GBI/(The Sharp Boys Deee-Liteful Dub)/Boldline (with Towa Tei) (CD)	8
98	Arthrob ART021 CD2	GBI/(Rekut)/(Ebony Boogie Down Mix) (with Towa Tei) (CD)	8
00	Parlophone 12R 6542 A/B	Spinning Around (Sharp Vocal Mix)/(Sharp Double Dub)/ (7th Spinnin' Dizzy Dub)/(7th District Club Mix) (12" double-pack)	10
03	Parlophone 5533626	Slow (Extended Mix)/Slow (Radio Slave Remix)/Slow (Medicine 8 Remix) (12" picture disc, PVC title sleeve, sealed with sticker)	15
88	PWL HFD 4	KYLIE (DAT)	60
90	PWL HF 18	RHYTHM OF LOVE (LP, with free poster)	12
90	PWL HFL 18	RHYTHM OF LOVE (LP, gold leaf sleeve, 100 only)	250
91	PWL HFCL 18	RHYTHM OF LOVE (cassette, with 3 bonus tracks, gold case)	15
91	PWL HFCDL 18	RHYTHM OF LOVE (CD, with 3 bonus tracks, gold case)	20

PROMOS & TEST PRESSINGS

91	PWL PWLT 72R	What Do I Have To Do (Between The Sheets Mix) (12", promo, die-cut sleeve)	65
92	PWL PWLT 257	Celebration (Have A Party Mix)/Let's Get To It (Album Version) (12", Christmas "leaving PWL" promo p/s)	30
95	DeConstruction no cat. no.	Where Is The Feeling (Da Klubb Feelin' Mix)/(Aphroheadz Powerlite Mix)/(Three Rad Vid Clash Mix) (12", promo, no p/s)	80
98	DeConstruction TOOFAR 1	Too Far (Brothers In Rhythm Mix)/(Junior Vasquez Remix) (12", promo, no p/s)	20
00	Parlophone 12MIND JY 001	Spinning Around (7th District Dub Like This Mix)/Spinning Around (7th District Club-Mental Mix) (12" promo, p/s)	15
00	Parlophone 12MIND JX 001	Spinning Around (Sharp Vocal Mix)/Spinning Around (Sharp Double Dub Mix) (12" promo, p/s)	15
00	Parlophone CDMIND J 001	Spinning Around (CD promo, card insert)	10
00	Parlophone 12MINWL 002	Butterfly (Trisco Mix)/Butterfly (Sandstorm Dub) (12" test pressing, white label)	50
00	Parlophone NLT 001	On A Night Like This (Rob Searle Mix) (12" 1-sided test pressing, white label)	30
00	Parlophone 12MINWLS 002	On A Night Like This (Bini & Martini Club Mix)/On A Night Like This (Bini & Martini Dub Mix) (12" test pressing, white label)	30
00	Parlophone 12MINDJ 002	On A Night Like This (Motiv8 Nocturnal Vocal Mix)/On A Night Like This (Bini & Martini Vocal Mix)/On A Night Like This (Rob Searle Mix)/ Your Disco Needs You (Almighty Mix) (12" promo doublepack, p/s)	25
00	Parlophone CMINDJ 002	On A Night Like This (CD promo, card & paper inners)	10
00	Parlophone 12RDJ 6551	Please Stay (Metro Mix)/Please Stay (7th District Club Flava Mix)/ Please Stay (7th District Club Dub) (12" promo, p/s, with inner sleeve)	15
00	Parlophone 12MINWL 004	Please Stay (7th District Club Dub)/Please Stay (Hatiras Dreamy Dub)/ Please Stay (7th District Club Hava Mix) (12" promo, title-stickered sleeve)	15
01	Parlophone 12RDJ 6562	Can't Get Into My Head (Plastika Mix)/Can't Get Into My Head (Tim Deluxe Inst.)/Can't Get Into My Head (Time Deluxe Dub) (12" promo, no p/s)	20
01	Parlophone 12RDJY 6562	Can't Get Out Of My Head (Superchumbo Todo Mamado Mix)/ Can't Get Out Of My Head (Superchumbo Leadhead Dub)/ Can't Get Out Of My Head (Superchumbo Voltapella Mix) (12" promo)	20

MINT VALUE £

01	Parlophone 12RDJX 6562	Can't Get You Out Of My Head (K&M Mindprint Mix)/Can't Get You Out Of My Head (Nick Faber Mix) (12" promo, p/s, frosted PVC outer title sleeve)	25
01	Parlophone KBLUE1	Can't Get Blue Monday Out Of My Head (1-sided 12" promo, pink die-cut sl.)	40
01	Parlophone FEVER 01	Fever (CD-R promo, in DVD case)	60
02	Parlophone 12RDJ 6569	In Your Eyes (Powder's Spaced Dub)/In Your Eyes (Powder's 12" Dub)/ In Your Eyes (Saeed & Palash Mix)/In Your Eyes (Saeed & Palash Nightmare Dub) (12" test pressing,white label, title-stickered sleeve)	25
02	Parlophone 12RDJX 6569	In Your Eyes (The S Man's Release Mix)/In Your Eyes (Roger Sanchez Release The Dub Mix)/In Your Eyes (Jean Jacques Smoothie Dub) (12" promo, white sl. With title sticker)	18
02	Tripoli Trax 12RDJY 6569	In Your Eyes (Knuckleheadz Mix)/In Your Eyes (Mr. Bishi Mix) (12" promo, stickered title sleeve)	35
02	Parlophone 12RDJ 6577	Love At First Sight (The Scumfrog's Beauty & The Beast Vocal)/Love At First Sight (The Scumfrog's Beauty & The Beast Dub)/Love At First Sight (The Scum Frog's Beauty & The Beast Acappella) (12" promo, p/s)	18
02	Parlophone 12RDJX 6577	Love At First Sight (Twin Master Plan Mix)/(mixes) (12" promo, p/s)	18
02	Parlophone RDJ 6590	Come Into My World (Fischerspooner Mix)/Come Into My World (Ashtrax Mix) (promo, die-cut title sleeve)	40
02	Parlophone 12RDJ 6590	Come Into My World (Robbie Rivera's Hard & Sexy Mix)/(Robbie Rivera's NYC Dub) (12" promo, title sleeve)	15
03	Parlophone 12MINDJ 006	Slow (Remix)/Slow (Medicine 8 Remix) (12" promo)	15
03	Parlophone 12MINDJX 006	Slow (Extended Mix)/Slow (Extended Instrumental)/Slow (Acappella) (12" promo)	15
03	Parlophone 12MINDJY 006	Slow (Chemical Brothers Remix) (1-sided 12", yellow vinyl promo, 200 only)	45
03	Parlophone (no cat. no.)	Slow (CD promo, in black card fold-out sleeve)	45
03	Parlophone MININT 02	Body Language (CD interview promo)	30
94	DeConstruction KM 100	KYLIE MINOGUE (CD, promo, gatefold sl. in lilac slipcase with silver lettering)	100
97	DeConstruction KYLIE 1	IMPOSSIBLE PRINCESS (CD, promo, with insert, withdrawn)	120
97	DeConstruction KM 002	IMPOSSIBLE PRINCESS INTERVIEW DISC (CD, promo)	50
00	Parlophone LIGHT 001	LIGHT YEARS (CD promo, foldout 22" x 8" pack)	60
01	Parlophone FEVER 01	FEVER (CD-Rom promo, DVD-style picture case)	60
01	Parlophone FEVER 02	FEVER (CD promo, card sleeve, frosted PVC outer title sleeve)	40

MINORBOPS

58	Vogue V 9110	Need You Tonight/Want You For My Own	800
58	Vogue V 9110	Need You Tonight/Want You For My Own (78)	250

MINOR THREAT

85	Discord DISCORD 15	Salad Days/Stumped/Good Guys (p/s)	6

MINSTRELS

67	Studio One SO 2036	People Get Ready/HAMLINS: Everyone's Got To Be There	22
68	Studio One SO 2050	Miss Highty Tighty/WESTMORELITES: Let Me Be Yours Until Tomorrow	22

MINTS

57	London HLP 8423	Night Air/KEN COPELAND: Pledge Of Love	250
57	London HLP 8423	Night Air/KEN COPELAND: Pledge Of Love (78)	70

MINUTE MEN

61	Capitol CL 15206	Yankee Diddle/Blue Pearl	6

MINUTEMEN

83	SST SST 002	PARANOID TIME (8-track EP)	18
84	SST SST 016	BUZZ OR HOWL UNDER THE INFLUENCE OF THE HEAT (12" EP)	20
85	Homestead REFLEX-L	TOUR SPIEL (EP, live 4-track)	10

(SMOKEY ROBINSON &) MIRACLES

61	London HL 9276	Shop Around/Who's Lovin' You	60
61	London HL 9366	Ain't It Baby/The Only One I Love	100
62	Fontana H 384	What's So Good About Goodbye/I've Been So Good To You	200
63	Oriole CBA 1795	You've Really Got A Hold On Me/Happy Landing	100
63	Oriole CBA 1863	Mickey's Monkey/Whatever Makes You Happy	80
64	Stateside SS 263	I Gotta Dance To Keep From Crying/Such Is Love, Such Is Life	40
64	Stateside SS 282	The Man In You/Heartbreak Road	35
64	Stateside SS 324	I Like It Like That/You're So Fine And Sweet	30
64	Stateside SS 353	That's What Love Is Made Of/Would I Love You	25
65	Stateside SS 377	Come On Do The Jerk/Baby Don't You Go	30
65	Tamla Motown TMG 503	Ooo Baby Baby/All That's Good	25
65	Tamla Motown TMG 522	The Tracks Of My Tears/A Fork In The Road	30
65	Tamla Motown TMG 540	My Girl Has Gone/Since You Won My Heart	25
66	Tamla Motown TMG 547	Going To A Go-Go/Choosey Beggar	18
66	Tamla Motown TMG 569	Whole Lotta Shakin' In My Heart/Oh Be My Love	22
66	Tamla Motown TMG 584	(Come 'Round Here) I'm The One You Need/Save Me	15

(The above singles are credited to The Miracles.)

67	Tamla Motown TMG 598	The Love I Saw In You Was Just A Mirage/Swept For You Baby	15
67	Tamla Motown TMG 614	More Love/Swept For You Baby (withdrawn B-side)	100+
67	Tamla Motown TMG 614	More Love/Come Spy With Me	22
67	Tamla Motown TMG 631	I Second That Emotion/You Must Be Love	7
68	Tamla Motown TMG 648	If You Can Want/When The Words From Your Heart Get Caught Up In Your Throat	15
68	Tamla Motown TMG 661	Yester-Love/Much Better Off	8
68	Tamla Motown TMG 673	Special Occasion/Give Her Up	8
69	Tamla Motown TMG 687	Baby, Baby Don't Cry/Your Mother's Only Daughter	10
69	Tamla Motown TMG 696	The Tracks Of My Tears/Come On Do The Jerk	7
70	Tamla Motown TMG 745	The Tears Of A Clown/You Must Be Love (with withdrawn B-side)	40+
70	Tamla Motown TMG 745	The Tears Of A Clown/Who's Gonna Take The Blame	6

MINT VALUE £

Year	Label / Cat. No.	Title	£
71	Tamla Motown TMG 761	(Come Round Here) I'm The One You Need/We Can Make It, We Can	6
71	Tamla Motown TMG 774	I Don't Blame You At All/That Girl	6
72	Tamla Motown TMG 811	My Girl Has Gone/Crazy 'Bout The La-La-La	6
73	Tamla Motown TMG 853	Going To A Go-Go/Whole Lotta Shakin' In My Heart/Yester-Love	6
(The above singles are credited to Smokey Robinson & The Miracles.)			
76	Tamla Motown TMG 1023	Nightlife/The Miracle Workers: Overture (as The Miracles)	6
87	Motown ZB 41147 D	Just To See Her/Te Queiro Como Si No Hubiera Um Manana//Being With You/ What's In Your Life For Me? (solo, double pack)	5
61	London RE 1295	SHOP AROUND (EP, as The Miracles)	150
83	Tamla Motown CTME 2028	TEARS OF A CLOWN (cassette EP, as Smokey Robinson & The Miracles)	7
63	Oriole PS 40044	HI! WE'RE THE MIRACLES (LP)	275
64	Stateside SL 10099	THE FABULOUS MIRACLES (LP)	190
65	Tamla Motown TML 11003	I LIKE IT LIKE THAT (LP)	80
66	Tamla Motown TML 11024	GOIN' TO A GO-GO (LP, as Smokey Robinson & The Miracles, mono/stereo)	55/75
66	T. Motown (S)TML 11031	THE MIRACLES FROM THE BEGINNING (LP, mono/stereo)	55/65
67	T. Motown (S)TML 11044	AWAY WE A-GO-GO (LP, mono/stereo)	50/60
(The above albums are credited to The Miracles unless otherwise stated.)			
68	T. Motown (S)TML 11067	MAKE IT HAPPEN (LP)	45
68	T. Motown (S)TML 11072	GREATEST HITS (LP)	18
69	T. Motown (S)TML 11089	SPECIAL OCCASION (LP)	30
69	T. Motown (S)TML 11107	SMOKEY ROBINSON & THE MIRACLES LIVE! (LP)	22
70	T. Motown (S)TML 11129	TIME OUT FOR SMOKEY ROBINSON & THE MIRACLES (LP)	20
70	T. Motown STML 11151	FOUR IN BLUE (LP)	20
70	T. Motown STML 11163	WHAT LOVE HAS JOINED TOGETHER (LP, unissued)	
71	T. Motown STML 11172	POCKETFUL OF MIRACLES (LP)	15
73	T. Motown STMA 8008	1957-1972 (LP, gatefold sleeve)	12
73	Motown STMA 8012	SMOKEY (LP, solo)	12

MIRAGE

Year	Label / Cat. No.	Title	£
65	CBS 201772	It's In Her Kiss/What Ye Gonna Do 'Bout It	20
65	CBS 202007	Go Away/Just A Face	20
66	Philips BF 1534	Tomorrow Never Knows/You Can't Be Serious	35
67	Philips BF 1554	Hold On/Can You Hear Me	15
67	Philips BF 1571	The Wedding Of Ramona Blair/Lazy Man	85
68	Page One POF 078	Mystery Lady/Chicago Cottage	12
68	Page One POF 111	Carolyn/World Goes On Around You	12

(see also Yellow Payges, Caleb, Jawbone, Spencer Davis Group, Portobello Explosion)

MIRETTES

Year	Label / Cat. No.	Title	£
68	Uni UN 501	In The Midnight Hour/To Love Somebody	8
68	Uni UN 505	The Real Thing/Take Me For A Little While	8
69	MCA Soul Bag BAG 8	Whirlpool/Ain't You Trying To Cross Over	8
72	Jay Boy BOY 65	Now That I've Found You Baby/He's Alright With Me	6
69	MCA MUP(S) 344	IN THE MIDNIGHT HOUR (LP)	25

(see also Ikettes)

MIRK

Year	Label / Cat. No.	Title	£
79	Mother Earth MUM 1205	MODDANS BOWER (LP)	200
82	Spring Thyme SPR 1009	TAK A DRAM AFOR YE GO (LP)	25

MIRKWOOD

Year	Label / Cat. No.	Title	£
71	Flams Ltd PR 1067	MIRKWOOD (LP)	450+
93	Tenth Planet TP 003	MIRKWOOD (LP, reissue, numbered with insert, 500 only)	20

MIRO

Year	Label / Cat. No.	Title	£
90	Secret Heart SH 30008	GREETINGS FROM THE GOLBORNE RD (EP, handmade col'd p/s, 1,000 only)	6
90	Secret Heart SH 4008	The World In Maps/Great Dominions (handmade p/s & mini-booklet, 1,000 only)	5

STEVE MIRO & EYES

Year	Label / Cat. No.	Title	£
78	Object Music OM 03	Up And About/Smiling In Reverse (p/s)	6
79	Object Music OM 10	Dreams Of Desire/Queens Of The Sea (p/s)	5
80	Object Music OBF 008	RUDE INTRUSIONS (LP)	15
81	Object Music OBJ 015	SECOND SENTENCE (LP)	15

(see also Eyes, Noyes Bros)

MIRROR

Year	Label / Cat. No.	Title	£
68	Philips BF 1666	Gingerbread Man/Faster Than Light	60

MIRRORS

Year	Label / Cat. No.	Title	£
78	Lightning GIL 503	Cure For Cancer/Nice Vice (p/s)	15
79	Lightning GIL 540	Dark Glasses/999 (p/s)	15

MISFITS (U.K.)

Year	Label / Cat. No.	Title	£
66	A.S.C.C. PRI 101	You Won't See Me/Hanging Around (Aberdeen Students Charities Campaign)	10

(see also Complex)

MISFITS (U.S.)

Year	Label / Cat. No.	Title	£
81	Plan 9/Cherry Red PLP 9	BEWARE (12" EP)	120

MISSING PRESUMED DEAD

Year	Label / Cat. No.	Title	£
79	Sequel PART 2	Say It With Flowers/Double Life/Driving Home/Family Tree (p/s)	5
80s	Sequel PART 4	MISSING PRESUMED DEAD (LP)	12
80s	Sequel PART 5	REVENGE (LP)	12

MISSING SCIENTISTS

Year	Label / Cat. No.	Title	£
80	Rough Trade RT 057	Big City, Bright Lights/Discotheque X (p/s)	10

(see also Television Personalities, Slaughter)

MISSION

Year	Label / Cat. No.	Title	£
86	Chapter 22 CHAP 6/7	Serpent's Kiss/Wake (p/s)	5
86	Chapter 22 CHAP 7	Garden Of Delight/Like A Hurricane (p/s)	5
86	Chapter 22 L12 CHAP 7	Like A Hurricane/Garden Of Delight/Dancing Barefoot/The Crystal Ocean (12", autographed p/s)	8

86 Mercury MYSG 1 — Stay With Me/Blood Brother (autographed, gatefold p/s) . . . 5
88 Mercury MYTH 6 — Beyond The Pale (p/s) . . . 5
88 Mercury MYTHCD 6 — Beyond The Pale/Tower Of Strength/Tadeusz (CD, card sleeve, numbered) . . . 12
80s Mercury MYCDB 8 — Butterfly On A Wheel (CD, in box) . . . 15
80s Mercury MYCDB 8 — Butterfly On A Wheel (2-CD, in limited box) . . . 20
80s Flexi FLEX 1 — Crazy (1-track flexidisc) . . . 12
90 Mercury MYTH 11 — Hands Across The Ocean/Amelia/Love (p/s) . . . 5
90 Phonogram MYTH 910 — Deliverance/METAL GURUS: Virginia Plain (10", p/s) . . . 7
90 Phonogram MYTHB 912 — Deliverance/(Sorceror's Mix)/METAL GURUS: Virginia Plain (12", in box with poster) . . . 8
90 Mercury MTHCD 9 — Deliverance (CD) . . . 8
92 Vertigo MYTH 1310 — Like A Child Again/All Tangled Up In You (1-sided 10", etched, numbered p/s) . . . 7
00 Phonogram MYTHB 2 — IV: Wasteland/Shelter From The Storm (Live)//Serpent's Kiss (Live)/1969 (Live) (doublepack, in box, with insert and photo's) . . . 12
01 Playground PGND 001 — Evangeline/Anyone But You//Melt/Swoon (Reprise) (doublepack, pink & blue vinyl, gatefold p/s) . . . 8

(see also Sisters Of Mercy, Dead Or Alive, Pauline Murray, Artery, Red Lorry Yellow Lorry, Expelaires, Knopov's Political Package, TV Product)

MISSION BELLES

65 Decca F 12154 — Sincerely/When A Girl Really Loves You . . . 15

MISSISSIPPI

70 Fox FOX 1 — Mr. Union Railway Man/Main Street . . . 10

MISS JANE

68 Pama PM 704 — Bad Mind People/My Heart Is Aching (B-side act. "Witch Doctor" by Coolers) . . . 10

MISS X (Joyce Blair)

63 Ember EMB S 175 — Christine/S-E-X . . . 10

MISTER MOST

69 Downtown DT 409 — Reggae Train/Pushwood . . . 8

MISTER VERSATILE

69 Jackpot JP 701 — Apple Blossom/LITTLE BOY BLUE: Dark End Of The Street (act. by Pat Kelly) . . 10
69 Jackpot JP 702 — Devil's Disciples/ERROL DUNKLEY: Having A Party . . . 10

(see also Lester Sterling)

MISTURA feat. LLOYD MICHAELS

76 Route RT 30 — The Flasher/Life Is A Song Worth Singing . . . 5

MISTY

77 Cottage COT 511 — MISTY (LP) . . . 20

MISUNDERSTOOD

66 Fontana TF 777 — I Can Take You To The Sun/Who Do You Love . . . 55
69 Fontana TF 998 — Children Of The Sun/I Unseen (small or large centre hole) . . . 55/45
69 Fontana TF 1028 — You're Tuff Enough/Little Red Rooster (as Misunderstood featuring Glenn "Fernando" Campbell, some in p/s) . . . 60/35
69 Fontana TF 1041 — Never Had A Girl (Like You Before)/Golden Glass (as Misunderstood featuring Glenn "Fernando" Campbell) . . . 45
81 Cherry Red CHERRY 22 — Children Of The Sun/Who Do You Love/I'll Take You To The Sun (p/s) . . . 5
80s Bucketfull Of Brains BOB 2 — You're My Girl (flexidisc with *Bucketfull Of Brains* magazine) . . . 8/5

(see also Juicy Lucy, High Tide, Van Der Graaf Generator, Answers)

MITCH

52 Stardom LA 1005 — Cry Of The Wild Goose/Waltzing Matilda (78) . . . 7

BLUE MITCHELL

69 Blue Note BST 84300 — COLLISION IN BLACK (LP) . . . 15
73 Mainstream MSL 1002 — BLUE'S BLUES (LP) . . . 12

CHAD MITCHELL

62 London HLR 9509 — Lizzie Borden/Super Skier . . . 7

DENNY MITCHELL SOUNDSATIONS

64 Decca F 11848 — I've Been Crying/For Your Love . . . 8

(see also Preachers, Moon's Train)

GROVER MITCHELL

68 London HLU 10221 — Turned On/Blue Over You . . . 10
76 Vanguard VS 5003 — What Hurts/Super Hero . . . 40

GUY MITCHELL

78s

51 Columbia DB 2800 — My Heart Cries For You/Me And My Imagination . . . 8
51 Columbia DB 2816 — The Roving Kind/You're Not In My Arms Tonight . . . 8
51 Columbia DB 2831 — Sparrow In The Treetop/Christopher Columbus . . . 8
51 Columbia DB 2871 — A Beggar In Love/Unless . . . 10
51 Columbia DB 2885 — My Truly Truly Fair/Who Knows Love . . . 8
51 Columbia DB 2908 — Belle, Belle, My Liberty Belle/Sweetheart Of Yesterday . . . 8
51 Columbia DB 2969 — There's Always Room At Our House/Giddy-Ap . . . 8
52 Columbia DB 3001 — Wimmin/I Can't Help It . . . 8
52 Columbia DB 3018 — We Won't Live In A Castle/You're Just In Love (with Rosemary Clooney) . . . 8
52 Columbia DB 3056 — Pittsburgh Pennsylvania/The Girl With The Sawdust Heart . . . 8
52 Columbia DB 3074 — Gently Johnny/A Little Kiss Goodnight (both sides with Doris Day) . . . 10
52 Columbia DB 3087 — Don't Rob Another Man's Castle/Where In The World . . . 8
52 Vogue V 9033 — Cabaret (with Satisfiers)/I've Got A Frame Without A Picture . . . 20
52 Columbia DB 3104 — The Day Of Jubilo/You'll Never Be Mine . . . 8
52 Columbia DB 3151 — Feet Up/Angels Cry . . . 8
52 Columbia DB 3180 — Jenny Kissed Me/To Me You're A Song . . . 8
52 Columbia DB 3203 — That's A-Why/Train Of Love (both sides with Mindy Carson) . . . 8

			MINT VALUE £
53	Columbia DB 3238	She Wears Red Feathers/Why Should I Go Home?	8
53	Columbia DB 3255	Pretty Little Black-Eyed Susie/MITCH MILLER ORCHESTRA: Horn Belt Boogie	8
53	Columbia DB 3311	The House Of Singing Bamboo/The Place Where I Worship (both with Rosemary Clooney)	8
53	Philips PB 124	Walkin' And Wond'rin'/I Want You For A Sunbeam (with Mindy Carson)	8
53	Philips PB 136	So Am I/Tell Us Where The Good Times Are (with Mindy Carson)	8
53	Philips PB 162	Look At That Girl/Wise Man Or A Fool	8
53	Philips PB 178	Chicka Boom/Hannah Lee	8
53	Philips PB 210	Cloud Lucky Seven/Sippin' Soda	8
54	Philips PB 225	The Cuff Of My Shirt/Strollin' Blues	8
54	Philips PB 248	A Dime And A Dollar/Tear Down The Mountains	8
54	Philips PB 249	Meet A Happy Guy/ROSEMARY CLOONEY: Brave Man	8
54	Philips PB 255	Man And A Woman (with Rosemary Clooney)/Good Intentions	8
54	Philips PB 293	Bob's Yer Uncle/Got A Hole In My Sweater	8
54	Philips PB 330	What Am I Doing In Kansas City/My Heaven And Earth	8
54	Philips PB 387	I Met The Cutest Little Eyeful/Gee But Ya Gotta Come Home	8
55	Philips PB 452	Man Overboard/Zoo Baby	8
55	Philips PB 487	Too Late/Let Us Be Sweethearts Over Again	8
55	Philips PB 506	When Blinky Blows/Belonging	8
56	Philips PB 450	Green Grows the Grass/Solo	8
56	Philips PB 556	Perfume Candy And Flowers/Ninety Nine Years	8
56	Philips PB 610	Give Me A Carriage And Eight White Horses/I Used To Yate Ya	8
56	Philips PB 635	I'd Like To Say A Few Words About Texas/Finders Keepers	8
56	Philips PB 650	Singing The Blues/Crazy With Love	7
57	Philips PB 669	Knee Deep In The Blues/Take Me Back, Baby	7
57	Philips PB 685	Rock-A-Billy/Got A Feeling	8
57	Philips PB 712	Sweet Stuff/In The Middle Of A Dark, Dark Night	8
57	Philips PB 743	Call Rosie On The Phone/Cure For The Blues	8
58	Philips PB 766	C'mon Let's Go/The Unbeliever	10
58	Philips PB 798	Wonderin' And Worryin'/If Ya Don't Like It, Don't Knock It	12
58	Philips PB 830	Hangin' Around/Honey Brown Eyes	12
58	Philips PB 858	Let It Shine, Let It Shine/Butterfly Doll	15
58	Philips PB 885	My Heart Cries For You (2nd Version)/Till We're Engaged	18
59	Philips PB 915	Alias Jesse James/Pride O' Dixie	22
59	Philips PB 964	Heartaches By The Number/Two	40

45s

53	Columbia SCM 5018	Feet Up (Pat Him On The Po-Po)/Jenny Kissed Me	45
53	Columbia SCM 5022	'Cause I Love Ya, That's A-Why/Train Of Love (both with Mindy Carson)	40
53	Columbia SCM 5032	She Wears Red Feathers/Why Should I Go Home?	45
53	Columbia SCM 5037	Pretty Little Black-Eyed Susie/MITCH MILLER HORNS: Horn Belt Boogie	40
56	Philips JK 1001	Singing The Blues/Crazy With Love (jukebox issue)	65
57	Philips JK 1005	Knee Deep In The Blues/Take Me Back Baby (jukebox issue)	30
57	Philips JK 1015	Rock-A-Billy/Got A Feeling (jukebox issue)	30
57	Philips JK 1023	Sweet Stuff/In The Middle Of A Dark, Dark Night (jukebox issue)	30
57	Philips JK 1027	Call Rosie On The Phone/Cure For The Blues (jukebox issue)	30
58	Philips PB 766	C'mon Let's Go/The Unbeliever	15
58	Philips PB 798	Wond'rin' And Worryin'/If Ya Don't Like It, Don't Knock It	10
58	Philips PB 830	Hangin' Around/Honey Brown Eyes	12
58	Philips PB 858	Let It Shine, Let It Shine/Butterfly Doll	12
58	Philips PB 885	My Heart Cries For You (2nd Version)/Till We're Engaged	8
59	Philips PB 915	Alias Jesse James/Pride O' Dixie	8
59	Philips PB 964	Heartaches By The Number/Two (some with triangular centre)	12/6
60	Philips PB 998	The Same Old Me/Build My Gallows High (2nd version)	8
60	Philips PB 1026	Cry Hurtin' Heart/Symphony Of Spring	8
60	Philips PB 1050	Silver Moon Upon The Golden Sands/My Shoes Keep Walking Back To You	8
60	Philips PB 1084	Sunshine Guitar/One Way Street	8
61	Philips PB 1131	Your Goodnight Kiss/Follow Me	8
61	Philips PB 1183	Divorce/I'll Just Pretend	8
62	Philips PB 1202	Soft Rain/Big Big Change	8
63	Pye International 7N 25179	Go, Tiger, Go/If You Ever Go Away (unreleased)	
63	Pye International 7N 25185	Have I Told You Lately That I Love You/Blue Violet	8
66	CBS 202238	Singing The Blues/Rock-A-Billy	15
67	London HLB 10173	Traveling Shoes/Every Night Is A Lifetime	7*
68	London HLB 10190	Alabam/Goodbye Road, Hello Home	7*
68	London HLB 10218	Before You Take Your Love From Me/Singing The Blues	7*
68	London HLB 10234	Just Wish You'd Maybe Change Your Mind/If You Could Cry Me My Tears	7*

EPs

54	Columbia SEG 7513	PRETTY LITTLE BLACK EYED SUSIE plain sleeve)	15
55	Columbia SEG 7581	MY TRULY TRULY FAIR (plain sleeve)	15
55	Columbia SEG 7598	JENNY KISSED ME (plain sleeve)	15
55	Philips BBE 12008	GUY MITCHELL	20
56	Philips BBE 12093	GUY MITCHELL NO. 2	22
57	Philips BBE 12112	SINGING THE BLUES WITH GUY MITCHELL	20
58	Philips BBE 12215	GUY MITCHELL PHILIPS TV SERIES	25

LPs

54	Columbia 33S 1028	GUY MITCHELL SINGS (10")	60
55	Philips BBR 8031	THE VOICE OF YOUR CHOICE (10")	40
58	Philips BBL 7246	A GUY IN LOVE	40
58	Philips BBL 7265	SHOWCASE OF HITS	30
61	Philips BBL 7465	SUNSHINE GUITAR	40
66	CBS Realm RM 52336	THE BEST OF GUY MITCHELL	18
68	London HA-B 8364	TRAVELING SHOES (also stereo SH-B 8364)	22/25
77	CBS Embassy 31459	AMERICAN LEGEND	12
79	CBS Warwick PR 5066	20 GOLDEN GREATS	12
81	CBS 22109	THE HIT SINGLES 1950-1960 (2-LP)	18

MINT VALUE £

84	CBS Cameo 32519	GUY'S GREATEST HITS	12
85	President PRCV 129	A GARDEN IN THE RAIN	12
89	Harmony HARLP 106	PORTRAIT OF A SONG STYLIST	12

(see also Mindy Carson)

JONI MITCHELL

68	Reprise RS 20694	Night In The City/I Had A King	6
69	Reprise RS 23402	Chelsea Morning/Both Sides Now	7
70	Reprise RS 20906	Big Yellow Taxi/Woodstock	5
72	Asylum AYM 511	You Turn Me On, I'm A Radio/Urge For Going	5
83	Geffen DA 3122	Chinese Cafe/Ladies Man (double pack, with bonus interview 7")	5
88	Geffen GEF 37CD	My Secret Place (with Peter Gabriel)/Number One/Chinese Cafe-Unchained Melody/Good Friends (3" CD, 5" case)	8
68	Reprise RSLP 6293	JONI MITCHELL (LP, gatefold sleeve, 'steamboat' label)	20
69	Reprise RSLP 6341	CLOUDS (LP, textured single sleeve, 'steamboat' label)	20
69	Reprise RSLP 6341	CLOUDS (LP, 2nd pressing, stickered U.S. gatefold sleeve, 'steamboat' label)	20
70	Reprise RSLP 6376	LADIES OF THE CANYON (LP, gatefold sleeve, 'steamboat' label)	20
71	Reprise K 44128	BLUE (LP, gatefold sleeve, some with blue inner sleeve)	15/12
73	Asylum SYLA 8753	FOR THE ROSES (LP, gatefold sleeve)	12
74	Asylum SYLA 8756	COURT AND SPARK (LP, gatefold sleeve)	15
75	Asylum SYSP 902	MILES OF AISLES (2-LP, gatefold sleeve with inner flap)	20
79	Asylum K 53091	MINGUS (LP, gatefold sleeve)	12
70s	Asylum AS 53002	COURT AND SPARK (LP, reissue)	12
70s	Asylum AS 53007	FOR THE ROSES (LP, reissue)	12
70s	Asylum K 53053	HEJIRA (LP, gatefold sleeve)	15
70s	Reprise REP 44085	LADIES OF THE CANYON (LP, reissue)	12
80	Asylum K 62030	SHADOWS AND LIGHT (2-LP, gatefold sleeve with inners)	18
82	Asylum/Nimbus K 53018	THE HISSING OF SUMMER LAWNS (LP, audiophile pressing, mail order issue)	15
80s	Geffen GEF 26455	DOG EAT DOG (LP)	15

KEITH MITCHELL

70s	Spark SRLP 109	WORDS WORDS WORDS (LP)	12

MALCOLM MITCHELL

54	Parlophone MSP 6084	The Jones Boy/Granada	10

McKINLEY 'SOUL' MITCHELL

68	President PT 125	The Town I Live In/No Love Like Your Love	7
68	President PTL 1005	McKINLEY 'SOUL' MITCHELL (LP)	15

PHILIP MITCHELL

71	Jay Boy BOY 37	I'm Gonna Build California From All Over The World/The World Needs More People Like You	7
72	Jay Boy BOY 57	Free For All/Flower Child	7

RED MITCHELL

62	London LZ-N1 4017	HAPPY MINORS (10" LP)	15
63	London SH-K 8027	HEAR YE!! HEAR YE!! (LP)	12

RONNIE MITCHELL

60	London HLU 9220	How Many Times/The Only Love	8

SINX MITCHELL

64	Hickory 45-1248	Weird Sensation/Love Is All I'm Asking For	20

(see also Crickets, Earl Sinks)

VALERIE MITCHELL

65	Oak RGJ 160	There Goes My Heart Again/If I Didn't Love You (p/s)	60
65	HMV POP 1422	Bitter Tears/Forbidden	7
65	HMV POP 1462	There Goes My Heart Again/If I Didn't Love You	8
65	HMV POP 1490	Go My Way/Green Eyes	8
66	HMV POP 1509	Play With Me/Never Let It Be Said	8
66	HMV POP 1529	You Can Go/The Windmill Girls	7
67	Columbia DB 8186	Love Can Be The Sweetest Thing/I'm Sorry	6
67	Columbia DB 8265	Sunshine/You Belong To Me	6

WILLIE MITCHELL

64	London HLU 9926	20-75/Secret Home	18
65	London HLU 10004	Everything Is Gonna Be Alright/That Driving Beat	20
66	London HLU 10039	Bad Eye/Sugar T.	10
66	London HLU 10085	Mercy/Sticks And Stones	10
68	London HLU 10186	Soul Serenade/Buster Browne	25
68	London HLU 10215	Prayer Meetin'/Rum Daddy	6
68	London HLU 10224	Up Hard/Beale Street Mood	8
69	London HLU 10246	Everything Is Gonna Be Alright/Mercy	5
69	London HLU 10282	Young People/Kitten Korner	5
70	London HLU 10313	Robbin's Nest/Six To Go	5
73	London HLU 10407	Last Tango In Paris/Six To Go	5
74	London HLU 10545	The Champion (2 parts)	10
67	London HA-U 8319	THE HIT SOUND OF WILLIE MITCHELL (LP)	25
68	London HA-U/SH-U 8365	SOUL SERENADE (LP)	20
68	London HA-U/SH-U 8368	LIVE (LP)	18
69	London HA-U/SH-U 8372	SOLID SOUL (LP)	20
70	London HA-U/SH-U 8388	ON TOP (LP)	15
70	London HA-U/SH-U 8408	SOUL BAG (LP)	15

MITCHELL/COE MYSTERIES

80	RCA PL 25297	EXILED (LP, with inner sleeve, initially with gatefold sleeve)	15/12

(see also Colin Blunstone, Lesley Duncan, Dan McCafferty, Francis Rossi & Berni Frost, Ray Russell, Joe Jammer, Complex, Monsoon)

ROBERT MITCHUM
57	Capitol CL 14701	What Is This Generation Coming To?/Mama Looka Boo Boo	15
57	Capitol CL 14701	What Is This Generation Coming To?/Mama Looka Boo Boo (78)	8
62	Capitol CL 15251	The Ballad Of Thunder Road/My Honey's Lovin' Arms	12
67	Monument MON 1007	Little Ole Wine Drinker Me/Walker's Woods	7
55	Brunswick OE 9197	RACHEL AND THE STRANGER (EP)	20
67	Monument LMO 5011	THAT MAN (LP)	30

MITHRANDIR
82	New Leaf SVC 01	MAGICK EP (p/s)	75
82	New Leaf SVC 570	Dreamers Of Fortune (p/s)	50

JACKIE MITTO(O)
66	Island WI 293	Killer Diller (as Jackie Mitto & Soul Brothers)/PATRICK HYTTON: Oh Lady	22
67	Rio R 114	Home Made/ETHIOPIANS: I'm Gonna Take Over Now	25
67	Rio R 123	Got My Buglaoo/ETHIOPIANS: What To Do	40
67	Coxsone CS 7002	Somebody Help Me/GAYLADS & SOUL VENDORS: The Sound Of Silence	22
67	Coxsone CS 7009	Ba Ba Boom/SLIM SMITH & FREEDOM SINGERS: Mercy Mercy	22
67	Coxsone CS 7019	Ram Jam/SUMMERTAIRES: You're Gonna Leave	20
67	Coxsone CS 7026	Something Stupid/LYRICS: Money Lover	22
68	Coxsone CS 7040	Norwegian Wood/GAYLADS: Most Peculiar Man	22
68	Coxsone CS 7042	Sure Shot/OCTAVES: The Bottle	22
68	Coxsone CS 7046	Man Pon Shot/BOP & BELTONES: Not For A Moment	22
68	Coxsone CS 7050	Napoleon Solo/CANNON BALL BRYAN: You're My Everything	22
68	Coxsone CS 7075	Mission Impossible/HEPTONES: Giddy Up (B-side actually by Actions)	22
68	Studio One SO 2043	Put It One/SOUL VENDORS: Chinese Chicken	25
68	Studio One SO 2056	Race Track/BASES: I Don't Mind	30
69	Studio One SO 2082	Hi-Jack/TREVOR CLARKE: Sufferer	30
69	Doctor Bird DB 1177	Dark Of The Sun/MATADOR ALL STARS: Bridge View	30
69	Bamboo BAM 6	Our Thing (with Sound Dimension)/C. MARSHALL: Tra La La Sweet '69	18
69	Bamboo BAM 15	Clean Up/Spring Time (as Jackie Mittoo & Sound Dimension)	18
70	Bamboo BAM 17	Dark Of The Moon/Moon Walk (as Jackie Mittoo & Sound Dimension)	18
70	Bamboo BAM 20	Gold Dust/SUPERTONES: Real Gone Loser	18
70	Bamboo BAM 31	Can I Change My Mind/BRENTFORD ALLSTARS: Early Duckling	18
70	Bamboo BAM 38	Baby Why/ETHIOPIANS: You'll Want To Come Back	12
70	Bamboo BAM 51	Dancing Groove/BLACK & GEORGE: Peanut Butter	22
70	Banana BA 315	Holly Holy/LARRY MARSHALL: I've Got To Make It	15
71	Banana BA 320	Peenie Wallie/ROY RICHARDS: Can't Go On	10
72	London HLU 10357	Wishbone/Soul Bird (as Jackie Mittoo — The Reggae Beat)	7
67	Coxsone CSL 8009	IN LONDON (LP)	130
68	Coxsone CSL 8014	EVENING TIME (LP, with Soul Vendors)	130
69	Coxsone CSL 8020	KEEP ON DANCING (LP)	140
70	Bamboo BDLP 209	NOW (LP)	70
72	London SHU 8436	WISHBONE (LP)	25

(see also Lord Tanamo, Jamaican Actions, Matadors, Jackie Opel, Soul Vendors, Winston Francis, Donna & Freedom Singers, Skatalites)

MIX BLOOD
80	Creole CR 201	Last Train To Skaville/Move And Move (p/s)	10

MIXED BAG
69	Decca F 12880	Potiphar (with Ramases III Orchestra)/Million Dollar Bash	5
69	Decca F 12907	Round And Round/Have You Ever Been In Love	5

MIXMAN
90	Citizen Kane 12KANE 2	Bright Child (Manmix)/Bright Child (Dancemix) (12", p/s)	8

MIXTURE
65	Fontana TF 640	One By One/Monkey Jazz	8
69	Parlophone R 5755	Sad Old Song/Never Trust In Tomorrow	7

BILLY MIZE ORCHESTRA
60	Top Rank JAR 391	Little Coco Palm/The Windward Castle	6

JOHN MIZAROLLI
82	Carrere CAL 142	MESSAGE FROM THE 5TH STONE (LP)	18

VIC MIZZY, HIS ORCHESTRA & CHORUS
65	RCA RCA 1440	Addams Family Main Theme/Kentucky James Main Theme	20

M.J.6
60	Decca F 11212	Tracy's Theme/Private Eye	6

M.J.Q.
(see under Modern Jazz Quartet)

MO & STEVE
66	Pye 7N 17175	Oh What A Day It's Going To Be/Reach Out For Your Lovin' Touch	5

MOB
68	Mercury MF 1026	Disappear/I Wish You Would Leave Me Alone	6
71	Polydor 2001 127	I Dig Everything About You/Love's Got A Hold On Me	6
71	Polydor 2001 169	Give It To Me/I'd Like To See More Of You	5
71	Polydor 2001 200	Money/Once A Man Twice A Child	5
73	MGM 2006 278	Tear The House Down/One Way Ticket To Nowhere	5
74	UK USA 4	Give It To Me/I'd LIke To See More Of You	8
75	Private Stock PVT 32	I Can't Stop This Love Song/Hot Music	12
71	Polydor 2344 001	MOB (LP)	12

MOB
80	Kalida AKB 1/2	Send Me To Coventry/Mobbed (p/s)	8

MINT VALUE £

MOB

80	All The Madmen MAD 1	Youth/Crying Again (p/s)	7
80	All The Madmen MAD 002	Witch Hunt/Shuffling Souls/What's Going On (EP, handwritten white labels with sticker & foldout, stapled, gatefold p/s)	6
82	Crass 321984/7	No Doves Fly Here/I Hear You Laughing (foldout p/s)	5
83	All The Madmen MAD 6	The Mirror Breaks/Stay (screen-printed p/s, with lyric insert)	5
80s	All/Madmen MADPACK 1	MAD PACK 1 (3 x 7" in 12" pack)	12

HANK MOBLEY

61	Blue Note BLP 4031	HANK MOBLEY'S SOUL STATION (LP)	20

(see also Wynton Kelly, Art Blakey)

JOHN MOBLEY

62	Stateside SS 136	Tunnel Of Love/Work Out	10

MOBSTER

80	Ensign ENY 41	The Mobster Shuffle/Simmer Down (p/s)	6
81	Ensign ENY 209	Perfect Man/Trinidad (p/s)	5

MOBY DICK

82	Ebony EBON 5	Nothing To Fear/Can't Have My Body Tonight	6

MOBY GRAPE

67	CBS 2953	Omaha/Hey Grandma	25
68	CBS 3555	Can't Be So Bad/Murder In My Heart For The Judge	7
69	CBS 3945	Trucking Man/Ooh Mama Ooh	8
67	CBS (S)BPG 63090	MOBY GRAPE (LP)	35
68	CBS 63271	WOW (LP, mono & stereo)	22
69	CBS 63430	'69 (LP, mono & stereo)	22
69	CBS 63698	TRULY FINE CITIZEN (LP, mono & stereo)	22
72	Reprise K 44152	20 GRANITE CREEK (LP)	15
74	CBS 64743	GREAT GRAPE (LP)	15

MOCEDADES

73	Bell BELL 1303	Touch The Wind/Eres Tu	6

MOCKINGBIRDS

65	Columbia DB 7480	That's How It's Gonna Stay/I Never Should Have Kissed You	50
65	Columbia DB 7565	I Can Feel We're Parting/The Flight Of The Mockingbird	50
65	Immediate IM 015	You Stole My Love/Skit Skat	110
66	Decca F 12434	One By One/Lovingly Yours	45
66	Decca F 12510	How To Find A Lover/My Story	45

(see also 10cc, Graham Gouldman, Whirlwinds, Doctor Father, Hotlegs, Godley & Greme)

MOCK TURTLES

87	Imaginary MIRAGE 003	POMONA (12" EP, with press sheets & photos)	15
89	Imaginary MIRAGE 009	Wicker Man/The Willow Song/Another Jesus Walks On Water/ Fionnuala (12", p/s)	8
90	Imaginary MIRAGE 017	Lay Me Down/Can You Dig It? (fully autographed, sold at gigs)	5
91	Imaginary FREE 001	Pale Blue Eyes/ECHO & BUNNYMEN: Foggy Notion (promo only, no p/s)	8
89	Bucketfull Of Brains BOB 26	Croppies Lie Down/SAINTS: I Dreamed Of Marie Antoinette (free with ***Bucketfull Of Brains*** magazine, issue 32)	6/4

(see also Judge Happiness)

M.O.D.

79	Vertigo 6059 233	M.O.D./M.O.D. (2) (p/s, some allegedly mispressed on 2-Tone label)	30/7

(see also David Essex)

MODE

66	private pressing	THE MODE (EP, white labels, no p/s)	260

MODELS

77	Step Forward SF 3	Freeze/Man Of The Year (p/s)	20

(see also Adam & The Ants, Mass, Rema Rema, Wolfgang Press)

MODERATES

80	Open Eye OEEP 1001	FETISHES (12" EP)	8

MODERNAIRES (U.K.)

80	Illuminated ILL 2	Life In Our Times/Barbed Up (p/s)	5
81	Illuminated ILL 4	We Did It Again/And Again (p/s, red vinyl)	5

MODERNAIRES (U.S.)

54	Vogue Coral Q 2024	Teach Me Tonight/Mood Indigo (with Georgie Auld)	10
54	Vogue Coral Q 2035	New Juke Box Saturday Night/Bugle Call Rag	10
55	Vogue Coral Q 72069	Birds And Puppies And Tropical Fish/Mine! Mine! Mine!	10
55	Vogue Coral Q 72084	Wine, Women And Gold/Sluefoot (with Bob Crosby Bob Cats)	10
55	Vogue Coral Q 72112	At My Front Door/Alright, Okay, You Win	10
56	Vogue Coral Q 72135	"Let's Dance" Medley (Benny Goodman Story)	6
56	Vogue Coral Q 72158	Go On With The Wedding/Ain't She Sweet	6
56	Vogue Coral Q 72169	April In Paris/Hi-Diddlee-I-Dee	5
60	Coral FEP 2056	THE FORMER GLENN MILLER SINGERS — REUNION IN HI-FI (EP, with Tex Beneke, Marion Hutton & Ray Eberle)	8
55	Vogue Coral LVC 10012	STOP, LOOK AND LISTEN (10" LP)	25
58	Coral LVA 9080	HERE COME THE MODERNAIRES (LP)	15

(see also Four Guys, Georgie Auld, Bing Crosby)

MODERN ART

84	Color Disc COLORS 1	Dreams To Live/Beautiful Truth (p/s)	25
86	Color Disc COLORS 5	Penny Valentine/One Way Ticket (1-sided, clear vinyl flexidisc, 1,000 only)	12
87	Color Disc COLOR 3	STEREOLAND (LP, hand-stencilled with insert, 300 only)	60
94	Acme 8007 LP	ALL ABOARD THE MIND TRAIN (LP, 500 only, numbered)	12

(see also Sun Dial)

MODERN ENGLISH

79 Limp LMP 2 — Drowning Man/Silent World (p/s) 15
80 4AD AD 6 — Swans On Glass/Incident (p/s) 7
80 4AD AD 15 — Gathering Dust/Tranquility Of A Summer Moment (p/s) 6
81 4AD AD 110 — Smiles And Laughter/Mesh And Lace (p/s) 5
82 4AD BAD 208 — Life In The Gladhouse/The Choicest View (12", p/s) 8
82 4AD AD 212 — I Melt With You/The Prize (p/s) 5
83 4AD AD 309 — Someone's Calling/Life In The Gladhouse (p/s) 5
84 4AD AD 401 — Chapter 12/Ringing In The Change (p/s) 5

(see also This Mortal Coil)

MODERN EON

80 Modern Eon EON 001 — PIECES (EP) 20
80 Inevitable INEV 3 — Euthenics/Waiting For The Cavalry (p/s) 8
81 Dinsales 2 — Euthenics/Choreography/Waiting For The Cavalry/The Real Hymn (12", white label LP sampler) 30
81 DinDisc DIN 30 — Euthenics (New Version)/Cardinal Signs (tri-gatefold folder p/s) 5
81 DinDisc DID 11 — FICTION TALES (LP) 12

MODERN FOLK QUARTET (M.F.Q.)

64 Warner Bros WB 147 — The Love Of A Clown/If You All Think 15
66 RCA RCA 1514 — Night Time Girl/Lifetime (as M.F.Q.) 20
63 Warner Bros WM/WS 8135 — THE MODERN FOLK QUARTET (LP) 15

MODERN JAZZ QUARTET (M.J.Q.)

50s Esquire EP 106 — MODERN JAZZ QUARTET (EP) 8
50s Esquire EP 109 — MODERN JAZZ QUARTET (EP) 8
50s Esquire EP 116 — GERSHWIN BALLAD MEDLEY (EP) 8
50s Esquire EP 166 — FIVE WAYS OF PLAYING LA RONDE (EP) 8
50s Fontana 469 204TE — ALL OF YOU (EP) 8
57 London Jazz EZ-C 19019 — THE QUARTET (EP, as The Quartet) 8
59 London Jazz EZ-K 19046 — ONE NEVER KNOWS (EP) 8
59 London Jazz EZ-K 19047 — THE MODERN JAZZ QUARTET (EP) 8
61 London Jazz RE-K 1314 — MODERN JAZZ QUARTET (EP) 8
61 London Jazz RE-K 1320 — MODERN JAZZ QUARTET AT MUSIC INN (EP) 10
62 London Jazz RE-K 1319 — MODERN JAZZ QUARTET — EUROPEAN CONCERT (EP) 10
55 Esquire 20-069 — MODERN JAZZ QUARTET (10" LP) 18
55 Esquire 20-038 — MODERN JAZZ QUARTET VOL. 2 (10" LP) 18
55 Esquire 20-090 — THE CLASSICAL PERFORMANCES OF... (10" LP) 20
57 London Jazz LTZK 15022 — FONTESSA (LP) 15
58 London Jazz LTZK 15085 — AT THE MUSIC INN (LP) 12
58 London Jazz LTZ 15136 — MODERN JAZZ QUARTET (LP) 12
59 London Jazz LTZ-K 15140 — PLAYS ONE NEVER KNOWS (LP, also stereo SAH-K 6029) 15/18
59 London Jazz LTZK 15181 — ODDS AGAINST TOMORROW (LP) 15
59 Columbia Clef 33CX 11028 — MODERN JAZZ QUARTET & OSCAR PETERSON AT THE OPERA HOUSE (LP) .. 12
60 London Jazz LTZ-K 15193 — PYRAMID (LP, also stereo SAH-K 6086) 15
61 London Jazz LTZ-K 15207 — THIRD STREAM MUSIC (LP, with Beaux Arts String Quartet & Jimmy Giuffre Three) 15
61 London Jazz LTZK 15222 — EUROPEAN CONCERT (LP) 12
61 Esquire 32-124 — LOOKING BACK AT THE MODERN JAZZ QUARTET (LP) 12
63 London HA-K/SH-K 8016 — LONELY WOMAN (LP) 15
63 London HA-K/SH-K 8046 — THE COMEDY SUITE (LP) 15
64 London HA-K/SH-K 8161 — THE SHERIFF (LP) 15
65 Stateside SL 10141 — THE BEST OF THE MODERN JAZZ QUARTET (LP) 15
66 Atlantic 587 044 — A QUARTET IS A QUARTET IS A QUARTET (LP) 12
68 Atlantic 590 012 — STOCKHOLM CONCERT (LP) 12
68 Apple (S)APCOR 4 — UNDER THE JASMINE TREE (LP, mono/stereo) 75/50
69 Apple SAPCOR 10 — SPACE (LP, gatefold sleeve, dark green label, black inner) 50
70s Apple SAPCOR 10 — SPACE (LP, later pressing, light green label, single sl., white 'Apple' inner) 150
93 Apple SAPCOR 4 — UNDER THE JASMINE TREE (LP, reissue, gatefold sleeve with inner) 30
93 Apple SAPCOR 4 — UNDER THE JASMINE TREE (CD) 20
93 Apple SAPCOR 10 — SPACE (LP, reissue) 30
93 Apple SAPCOR 10 — SPACE (CD) 20

(see also John Lewis, Milt Jackson, Sonny Rollins)

MODERN JAZZ SEXTET

56 Columbia Clef 33CX 10048 — MODERN JAZZ SEXTET (LP) 15

MODERN JAZZ SOCIETY

56 Columbia Clef 33CX 10038 — A CONCERT OF CONTEMPORARY MUSIC (LP) 12

MODERN TALKING

86 RCA PD 71133 — READY FOR ROMANCE (CD) 50

MO-DETTES

79 Mode/Rough Trade MODE 1 — White Mice/Masochistic Opposite (pink [card or paper] or white p/s) 4/6
80 S.F.I. SFI 550/MODE 1½ — Twist And Shout (gig freebie flexidisc, different label design to later issue) 5
80 Deram DET-R-1/MODE 1½ — Paint It Black/Bitta Truth (with free flexidisc "Twist And Shout" & insert, black & white or blue & white p/s) .... each 6
81 Deram DET 3 — Tonight/Waltz In Blue Minor (p/s) 5
81 Human HUM 10 — White Mice/Kray Twins (live) (p/s) 5
80 Deram SML 1120 — THE STORY SO FAR (LP, with insert & free colour sticker) 15

MODIFIES

70 Punch PH 45 — Bye Bye Happyness/Sufferation We Must Bear 6

MODS

64 RCA RCA 1399 — Something On My Mind/You're Making Me Blue 50

MODS

80 Bootlegged Records 007 — LOST TOUCH (LP; sold only in Portobello Market, London) 25

MINT VALUE £

MOD '79

79	Casino Classics CC 13	Green Onions/High On Your Love	10

DOMENICO MODUGNO

58	Oriole ICB 5000	Volare (Nel Blu Dipinto Di Blu)/Nisciuno Po' Sape'	6
58	Oriole ICB 5001	Strada 'Nfosa/Lazzarella	6
58	Oriole ICB 5001	Strada 'Nfosa/Lazzarella (78)	8
58	Oriole CB 1460	Volare (Nel Blu Dipinto Di Blu)/Nisciuno Po' Sape'	6
59	Oriole CB 1475	Come Prima (More Than Ever)/Mariti In Citta	5
59	Oriole CB 1475	Come Prima (More Than Ever)/Mariti In Citta (78)	8
59	Oriole CB 1479	Resta Cu'mme/Io Mammeta Et Tu	5
59	Oriole CB 1479	Resta Cu'mme/Io Mammeta Et Tu (78)	8
59	Oriole CB 1482	Strada 'Nfosa/Lazzarella	5
59	Oriole CB 1482	Strada 'Nfosa/Lazzarella (78)	8
59	Oriole CB 1489	Ciao, Ciao Bambina (Piove)/Resta Cu 'Mme	6
59	Oriole CB 1489	Ciao, Ciao Bambina (Piove)/Resta Cu 'Mme (78)	8
59	Oriole CB 1513	Notte, Lunga Notte/Sole, Sole, Sole	5
59	Oriole CB 1513	Notte, Lunga Notte/Sole, Sole, Sole (78)	10
60	Oriole CB 1543	Libero/Nuda	5
60	Oriole CB 1543	Libero/Nuda (78)	15
60	Oriole CB 1547	Hello Amore/Olimpia	5
60	Oriole CB 1547	Hello Amore/Olimpia (78)	15
57	Felsted ESD 3047	FROM THE PALERMO TO PARIS (EP)	8
59	Oriole MG 10023	DOMENICO MODUGNO (10" LP)	15

MODULATIONS

74	Buddah BDS 406	I Can't Fight Your Love/Your Love Has Locked Me Up	6
70s	Buddah	THE MODULATIONS (LP)	22

MOE

88	Times Five T5 01	There Were Four Other Guys/One Man Went To Moe (12", p/s)	8

PETER MOESSER'S MUSIC

70	Stateside SS 2182	Hello/Bye Bye (withdrawn)	5

MOFFAT ALL STARS

70	Jackpot JP 719	Riot/IMPERSONATORS: Girls And Boys	7

MOGUL THRASH

70	RCA RCA 2030	Sleeping In The Kitchen/St. Peter	22
71	RCA SF 8156	MOGUL THRASH (LP)	45

(see also Colosseum, Eclection, Family, King Crimson)

MOGWAI

96	Rock Action RAR 01	Tuner/Lower (p/s, 500 only)	35
96	Ché CHE 059	4 TRACK 3 BAND TOUR EP (with Urusei Yatsura & Backwater, p/s, 50 only)	25
96	Ché CHE 61	Angels Vs Aliens/DWEEB: Buzzsong (p/s, 1st 500 on green vinyl)	12/6
96	Love Train PUBE 014	Summer/Ithica 27*9 (p/s, 1,500 only)	20
97	Wurlitzer Jukebox WJ 22	New Paths To Helicon (Parts 1 & 2) (foldover p/s in polythene bag, 1,000 only)	25
97	Flotsam/Jetsam SHAG13.04	Stereo Dee/PH FAMILY: Club Beatroot Part 4 (p/s, 400 only)	40
	Chemikal Underground CHEM 015	4 SATIN EP	7
98	Eye EYEUK 032	FEAR SATAN REMIXES: My Bloody Valentine Remix/μ-ziq Remix/Surgeon Remix (12", p/s)	12
01	Chrysalis 9460013221	FIVE TRACK TOUR SINGLE: Close Encounters/Drum Machine/D To E/You Don't Know Jesus/Helicon (tour CD, card sleeve)	45
98	Eye Q EYEUKLP 019	KICKING A DEAD PIG (2-LP)	18

(see also Magoo)

ESSRA MOHAWK

75	Mooncrest CREST 24	ESSRA MOHAWK (LP, with insert)	25
77	Private Stock PVLP 1016	ESSRA (LP)	15

MOHAWKS

68	Pama PM 719	The Champ/Sound Of The Witchdoctors	20
68	Pama PM 739	Baby Hold On (Parts 1 & 2)	12
68	Pama PM 751	Sweet Soul Music/Hip Jigger	15
68	Pama PM 757	Mony Mony/Pepsi	25
69	Pama PM 758	Ride Your Pony/Western Promise	12
69	Pama PM 798	Skinhead Shuffle/RICO: Red Cow	25
70	Supreme SUP 204	Let It Be/Looking Back	8
86	Pama PM (T) 1	The Champ/Landscape (12", p/s)	15
68	Pama PMLP 5	THE CHAMP (LP)	100

MOIST

86	Debris DEB 9/LYN 19589	The Cut Up 1/KING OF THE SLUMS: Haemophiliacs On Tacks (33rpm flexidisc free with *Debris* magazine)	8/6
95	Chrysalis 12CHSS 5019	SILVER (12" EP, clear vinyl)	10

MOJO HANNAH

73	Kingdom KV 8008	Six Days On The Road/Moon Dog's Gonna Howl Tonight	6
73	Kingdom KVL 9001	SIX DAYS ON THE ROAD (LP)	20

MOJO MEN

65	Pye International 7N 25336	Dance With Me/The Loneliest Boy In Town	30
66	Reprise RS 20486	Hanky Panky/She's My Baby	40
67	Reprise RS 20539	Sit Down I Think I Love You/Don't Leave Me Crying Like Before	15
67	Reprise RS 20580	Me About You/When You're In Love	15

MOJOS

63	Decca F 11732	They Say/Forever	15
64	Decca F 11853	Everything's Alright/Give Your Lovin' To Me	12
64	Decca F 11918	Why Not Tonight/Don/t Do It Any More	7

MINT VALUE £

64 Decca F 11959 Seven Daffodils/Nothin' At All . . . 8
65 Decca F 12127 Comin' On To Cry/That's The Way It Goes . . . 15
67 Decca F 12557 Goodbye Dolly Gray/I Just Can't Let Her Go. . . . 18
68 Liberty LBF 15097 Until My Baby Comes Home/Seven Park Avenue . . . 50
64 Decca DFE 8591 THE MOJOS (EP) . . . 70
(see also Stu James & Mojos, Faron's Flamingos)

MOLES

68 Parlophone R 5743 We Are The Moles (Parts 1 & 2). . . . 40
(see also Simon Dupree & Big Sound)

MOLESTERS

79 Small Wonder SMALL 14 Disco Love/Commuter Man (p/s) . . . 5
79 Small Wonder SMALL 18 End Of Civilisation/Girl Behind The Curtain (p/s) . . . 5

MOMENT

85 Diamond DIA 004 In This Town/Just Once . . . 8
85 Diamond DIA 008 One, Two, They Fly/Karl's New Haircut . . . 5
80s Tenth Floor Poor Mr. Diamond (Parts 1 & 2). . . . 10
89 Big Stuff Ready To Fall (promo only) . . . 8
86 Rave RAVE UP 1 THE WORK GETS DONE (LP, coloured vinyl) . . . 12

MOMENT OF TRUTH

75 Pye Int. 7N 25679 Helplessly/(Part 2) . . . 5
77 Salsoul SZ 2025 You've Got Me Hummin'/At Long Last . . . 5

MOMENTS

63 London HLN 9656 Walk Right In/Walk Right In (Instrumental) . . . 15

MOMENTS

72 London HLU 10378 Love On A Two Way Street/I Won't Do Anything . . . 6
74 London HL 10449 Sexy Mama/Where Can I Find Her. . . . 6
75 All Platinum 6146 309 Look At Me/French Version . . . 5
75 All Platinum 9109 302 SHARP (LP) . . . 12
(see also Fabulous Impact)

MOMUS

86 Él GPO 9T Nicky/Don't Leave/See A Friend In Tears (12") . . . 20
87 Creation CRE 037 T Murderers, The Hope Of Women (12", p/s). . . . 12
90 Creation CRELP 052 DON'T STOP THE NIGHT (LP) . . . 15
91 Creation CRELP 059 MONSTERS OF LOVE (LP). . . . 12
91 Creation CRELP 097 HIPPOPOTAMOMUS (LP, with "Michelin Man" track & Michelin Man style inlay, withdrawn). . . . 20
91 Creation CRECD 097 HIPPOPOTAMOMUS (CD, with "Michelin Man" track & Michelin Man style inlay, withdrawn). . . . 30
92 Creation SPACEWALK EP (CD) . . . 20
93 Creation CRECD 151 TIMELORD (CD) . . . 18
94 Creation CRECD 052 DON'T STOP THE NIGHT (CD) . . . 18
94 Creation CRECD 059 MONSTERS OF LOVE (CD) . . . 18
03 Analogue Baroque FORBIDDEN SOFTWARE TIMEMACHINE: THE BEST OF THE CREATION YEARS 1987-1993 (CD). . . . 18
88 Creation CRECD 036 TENDER PERVERT (CD) . . . 18
(see also Happy Family)

MONARCHS

64 London HLU 9862 Look Homeward Angel/What's Made You Change Your Mind . . . 45

JULIE MONDAY

66 London HLU 10080 Come Share The Good Times With Me/Time Is Running Out For Me. . . . 8

MONDO KANE

86 Lisson DOLEQ 2 New York Afternoon (mixes)/Manhattan Morning (12", p/s) . . . 10
(see also Georgie Fame)

MONEY

69 Major Minor MM 620 Come Laughing Home/Power Of The Rainbow . . . 5
69 Major Minor MM 669 Welcome Me Love/Breaking Of Her Heart. . . . 5

MONEY

79 Gull GULL 64 Aren't We All Searching/Where Have All The Dancers Gone . . . 8
80 Hobo HOS 011 FAST WORLD (EP, p/s) . . . 80
79 Gull GULP 1031 FIRST INVESTMENT (LP). . . . 25
(see also Iron Maiden)

ZOOT MONEY('S BIG ROLL BAND)

64 Decca F 11954 The Uncle Willie/Zoot's Suit (solo). . . . 40
65 Columbia DB 7518 Good/Bring It Home To Me. . . . 25
65 Columbia DB 7600 Please Stay/You Know You'll Cry. . . . 30
65 Columbia DB 7697 Something Is Worrying Me/Stubborn Kind Of Fellow . . . 25
65 Columbia DB 7768 The Many Faces Of Love/Jump Back (as Paul Williams & Zoot Money Band). . . . 30
66 Columbia DB 7876 Let's Run For Cover/Self-Discipline . . . 25
66 Columbia DB 7975 Big Time Operator/Zoot's Sermon . . . 18
66 Columbia DB 8090 The Star Of The Show (The La La Song)/The Mound Moves . . . 22
67 Columbia DB 8172 Nick Knack/I Really Learnt How To Cry . . . 22
70 Polydor 2058 020 No One But You/Prisoner . . . 8
80 Magic Moon/MPL MACH 3 Your Feet's Too Big/Ain't Nothin' Shakin' But The Bacon (solo). . . . 12
80 Magic Moon/MPL MACH 6 The Two Of Us/Ain't Nothin' Shakin' But The Bacon (solo). . . . 30
66 Columbia SEG 8519 BIG TIME OPERATOR (EP). . . . 250
66 Columbia S(C)X 6075 ZOOT! — LIVE AT KLOOK'S KLEEK (LP, mono/stereo). . . . 70/80
65 Columbia 33SX 1734 IT SHOULD'VE BEEN ME (LP) . . . 70

MINT VALUE £

68 Direction 8-63231 TRANSITION (LP) 55
70 Polydor 2482 019 ZOOT MONEY (LP) 22
80 Magic Moon/MPL LUNE 1 MR. MONEY (LP, solo) 18
(see also Paul Williams & Big Roll Band, Dantalian's Chariot, Eric Burdon & Animals, Grimms, Centipede, Ellis, Johnny Almond Music Machine)

MONEY MARK

94 Mo' Wax MW 032 Cry/Insects Are All Around Us (p/s) 6
95 Mo' Wax MW 036CD Cry/(mixes)/Never Stop/Invitation (CD, card sleeve) 10
95 Mo' Wax MW 044 LEGITIMATE POP SONGS?: Untitled Instrumental/Sometimes You Gotta Make It Alone/Untitled Instrumental (EP, die-cut sleeve) 6
98 Mo' Wax MW 089 Maybe I'm Dead/(mixes) (12", die-cut picture disc) 8
(see also Beastie Boys)

MONGREL

73 Polydor 2058 318 Lonely Street/Sing A Little Song 5
73 Polydor 2058 347 Last Night/Twist Her Hand 5
73 Polydor 2383 182 GET YOUR TEETH INTO THIS (LP) 20

MONGRELS

64 Decca F 12003 I Long To Hear/Everywhere 30
65 Decca F 12086 My Love For You/Stewball 30
(see also Bobbie Miller)

MONITORS

69 T. Motown (S)TML 11108 GREETINGS WE'RE THE MONITORS (LP) 90

THELONIOUS MONK

63 CBS AAG 172 Hackensack/Bye Ya 5
56 Vogue EPV 1115 THELONIOUS MONK (EP) 10
50s Esquire EP 75 THELONIOUS MONK TRIO (EP) 8
50s Esquire EP 148 SONNY ROLLINS AND THELONIOUS MONK (EP) 8
61 Esquire EP 236 NUTTY MONK (EP) 8
62 Esquire EP 246 BLUE MONK (EP) 8
60s Riverside REP 3214 NUTTY (EP, as Thelonious Monk & John Coltrane) 8
60s Riverside REP 3217 RUBY MY DEAR (EP, as Thelonious Monk & John Coltrane) 8
55 Esquire 20-039 THELONIOUS MONK QUINTET (10" LP) 18
55 Esquire 20-049 THELONIOUS MONK (10" LP) 18
56 Esquire 20-075 THELONIOUS MONK PLAYS (10" LP) 18
60 Esquire 32-109 THELONIOUS MONK QUINTETS (LP) 15
61 Esquire 32-115 WORK! (LP, with Art Blakey & Sonny Rollins) 15
61 Esquire 32-119 MONK'S MOODS (LP) 15
61 Riverside RLP 12-201 MONK PLAYS ELLINGTON (LP) 15
61 Philips BBL 1510 THELONIOUS MONK VOL. 1 (LP) 15
61 Riverside RLP 12-226 BRILLIANT CORNERS (LP) 15
61 Riverside RLP 12-262 MONK IN ACTION (LP) 15
62 Riverside RLP 12-300 AT THE TOWN HALL (LP, also stereo RLP 1138) 15/20
62 Riverside RLP 12-323 AT THE BLACK HAWK (LP, also stereo RLP 1171) 15
62 Philips BBL 1511 THELONIOUS MONK VOL. 2 (LP) 15
62 Riverside RLP 12-242 MONK'S MUSIC (LP) 15
63 Riverside RLP 201 MONK PLAYS ELLINGTON (LP, reissue) 10
63 CBS (S)BPG 62135 MONK'S DREAM (LP) 15
63 Riverside RLP 12-235 THELONIOUS HIMSELF (LP) 15
63 Riverside JLP (9)46 THELONIOUS MONK AND JOHN COLTRANE (LP) 15
64 Riverside RLP 002 IN EUROPE (VOL. 1) 15
64 CBS (S)BPG 62173 CRISS-CROSS (LP) 15
64 Blue Note (B)BLP 1510 THE GENIUS OF MODERN MUSIC (VOL. 1) (LP) 15
64 Blue Note (B)BLP 1511 THE GENIUS OF MODERN MUSIC (VOL. 2) (LP) 15
64 Riverside RLP 279 MISTERIOSO (LP) 15
64 CBS (S)BPG 62248 BIG BAND AND QUARTET IN CONCERT (LP) 15
65 CBS (S)BPG 62391 IT'S MONK'S TIME (LP) 15
65 Riverside RLP 305 FIVE BY MONK BY FIVE (LP) 15
65 Riverside RLP 003 IN EUROPE (VOL. 2) (LP) 15
65 CBS (S)BPG 62497 MONK (LP) 15
65 Riverside RLP 312 ALONE IN SAN FRANCISCO (LP) 15
65 Fontana FJL 113 WAY OUT! (LP) 15
65 Realm RM 52223 NICA'S TEMPO (LP, with Gigi Gryce) 12
65 CBS (S)BPG 62549 SOLO (LP) 15
65 Stateside SL 10152 THE GOLDEN MONK (LP) 15
66 Riverside RLP 004 IN EUROPE (VOL. 3) 12
66 CBS (S)BPG 62620 MISTERIOSO (LP, reissue) 12
67 CBS (S)BPG 63009 STRAIGHT, NO CHASER (LP) 12
67 Transatlantic PR 7169 WORK (LP) 12
69 CBS 63609 MONK'S BLUES (LP) 12
69 Storyville 673 014 THELONIOUS MONK PLAYS DUKE (LP) 12
69 Storyville 673 022 IN CONCERT (LP) 12
70 Storyville 673 024 *THE* THELONIOUS MONK (LP) 12
72 Polydor 2460 152 SOMETHING IN BLUE (LP) 12
72 Prestige PR 24006 THELONIOUS MONK (2-LP) 18
73 Black Lion 2460 197 THE MAN I LOVE (LP) 12
75 DJM DJSLM 2017 PURE MONK (LP) 12
75 CBS 88034 WHO'S AFRAID OF BIG BAD MONK (LP) 12
(see also John Coltrane, Sonny Rollins, Art Blakey, Miles Davis)

MONKEES

SINGLES

66 RCA Victor RCA 1547 Last Train To Clarksville/Take A Giant Step 8
66 RCA Victor RCA 1560 I'm A Believer/(I'm Not Your) Stepping Stone 6
67 RCA Victor RCA 1580 A Little Bit Me, A Little Bit You/The Girl I Knew Somewhere 7
67 RCA Victor RCA 1604 Alternate Title/Forget That Girl 7

MINT VALUE £

67 RCA Victor RCA 1620 Pleasant Valley Sunday/Words . . . 7
67 RCA Victor RCA 1645 Daydream Believer/Goin' Down . . . 7
68 RCA Victor RCA 1673 Valleri/Tapioca Tundra . . . 8
68 RCA Victor RCA 1706 D.W. Washburn/It's Nice To Be With You . . . 8
69 RCA RCA 1802 Teardrop City/Man Without A Dream . . . 8
69 RCA RCA 1824 Someday Man/Listen To The Band . . . 8
69 RCA RCA 1862 Daddy's Song/The Porpoise Song . . . 10
69 RCA RCA 1887 Mommy And Daddy/Good Clean Fun . . . 10
70 RCA RCA 1958 Oh My My/Love You Better . . . 12
74 Bell BLL 1354 Monkees Theme/I'm A Believer . . . 6
80 Arista ARIST 326 THE MONKEES (EP, p/s) . . . 8
81 Arista ARIST 402 THE MONKEES VOL. 2 (EP, p/s) . . . 8
82 Arista ARIST 487 I'M A BELIEVER (EP, p/s) . . . 8
84 Scoop 7SR 5035 6 TRACK HITS (EP, p/s) . . . 15
84 Scoop 7SC 5035 6 TRACK HITS (EP, cassette) . . . 12
86 Arista ARIST 673 That Was Then, This Is Now/(Theme From) The Monkees (p/s) . . . 6
86 Arista ARIST 1673 That Was Then, This Is Now/(Theme From) The Monkees ('Dolenz' picture disc) . . 8
86 Arista ARIST 2673 That Was Then, This Is Now/(Theme From) The Monkees ('Tork' picture disc) . . . 8
86 Arista ARIST 3673 That Was Then, This Is Now/(Theme From) The Monkees ('Jones' picture disc) . . 8
86 Arista ARIST 4673 That Was Then, This Is Now/(Theme From) The Monkees ('group' picture disc) . . 12
86 Arista ARIST 12673 That Was Then, This Is Now/Pleasant Valley Sunday/
(Theme From) The Monkees/Last Train To Clarksville (12", p/s) . . . 15
89 Arista 112 157 THE MONKEES (EP, p/s) . . . 8
89 Arista 112 157 THE MONKEES (EP, box set, with booklet & sew-on patch) . . . 15
89 Arista 112 157 THE MONKEES (10" EP, promo only, no p/s) . . . 22
89 Arista 662 157 THE MONKEES (CD EP) . . . 12
89 Arista 112 158 THE MONKEES VOL. 2 (EP, p/s) . . . 8
89 Arista 112 158 THE MONKEES VOL. 2 (10" EP, promo only, no p/s) . . . 22
89 Arista 662 158 THE MONKEES VOL. 2 (CD EP, card sleeve with anti-static inner) . . . 15
89 Arista 162 053 Last Train To Clarksville/Take A Giant Step/I'm A Believer/
(I'm Not Your) Stepping Stone (3" CD, gatefold card sleeve in blister pack) . . . 12
97 Telstar MON 2894 Daydream Believer (promo CD single) . . . 15

LPs

67 RCA Victor RD/SF 7844 THE MONKEES (LP, mono/stereo) . . . 18/20
67 RCA Victor RD/SF 7868 MORE OF THE MONKEES (LP, mono/stereo) . . . 18/20
67 RCA Victor RD/SF 7886 HEADQUARTERS (LP, mono/stereo) . . . 20/22
67 RCA Victor RD/SF 7886 HEADQUARTERS (LP, with different 'beard' photo on back, mono/stereo) . . . 25/30
67 RCA Victor RD/SF 7912 PISCES, AQUARIUS, CAPRICORN AND JONES LTD. (LP) . . . 25
68 RCA Victor RD/SF 7948 THE BIRDS, THE BEES & THE MONKEES (LP) . . . 25
(The above albums were originally issued with black labels; later orange label copies are worth the same value.)
69 RCA RD/SF 8016 INSTANT REPLAY (LP, mono/stereo) . . . 35/30
69 RCA RD/SF 8051 HEAD (LP, soundtrack, mono/stereo) . . . 80/55
73 M.F. Pleasure SPR 90032 THE MONKEES (LP, 'Sounds Superb' series, black 'circus' sleeve) . . . 12
79 Arista MONK-1 1/2 MONKEEMANIA (LP) . . . 25
81 Arista DARTY 12 THE MONKEES (2-LP) . . . 18
83 Arista RS 10063 HERE COME THE MONKEES (LP, part of *Reader's Digest* v/a box set) . . . 15
89 Circus BOY 1 IDOLISED, PLASTICISED, PSYCHOANYLYSED, STERILISED
(LP, spoken-word convention issue, white vinyl) . . . 18
89 Circus BOY 1 IDOLISED, PLASTICISED, PSYCHOANYLYSED, STERILISED
(LP, spoken-word convention issue, picture disc) . . . 20

CDs

88 Platinum PLATCD 05 HEY-HEY IT'S THE MONKEES — 20 SMASH HITS (CD) . . . 20
92 Arista 262 507 THE COLLECTION (CD) . . . 18
93 Arista EMD 018 THE BEST OF THE MONKEES (CD, exclusive via Avon Cosmetics) . . . 25
(see also Micky Dolenz, Davy Jones, Michael Nesmith, Tommy Boyce & Bobby Hart)

BOB MONKHOUSE

69 CBS 3958 I Remember Natalie/In My Dream World . . . 7
69 CBS 4607 Another Time, Another Place, Another World/When I Found You . . . 6
(see also Derek Roy)

MONKS

79 EMI EMI 2999 Johnny B. Rotten/Drugs In My Pocket (p/s) . . . 5
(see also Hudson-Ford)

MONOCHROME SET

79 Rough Trade RT 005 Alphaville/He's Frank (p/s) . . . 8
79 Rough Trade RT 019 Eine Symphonie Des Grauens/Lester Leaps In (1st 1,000 with labels
on wrong sides with explanatory insert, p/s) . . . 7/5
79 Rough Trade RT 028 The Monochrome Set/Mr Bizarro (p/s) . . . 6
79 Disquo Bleu BL 1 He's Frank (Slight Return)/Silicon Carne/Fallout (all cuts live) (no p/s) . . . 6
80 DinDisc DID 8 LOVE ZOMBIES (LP, with lithograph) . . . 12
(see also Art Attacks)

MONOGRAMS

59 Parlophone R 4515 Juke Box Cha Cha/The Greatest Mistake Of My Life . . . 10
59 Parlophone R 4515 Juke Box Cha Cha/The Greatest Mistake Of My Life (78) . . . 5
59 Parlophone R 4545 Crystal/Teach Me . . . 7

MONOPOLY

67 Polydor 56164 House Of Lords/Magic Carpet . . . 6
67 Polydor 56188 We're All Going To The Seaside/It Isn't Easy . . . 6
70 Pye 7N 17940 We Belong Together/Gone Tomorrow . . . 6
(see also Raymond Froggatt)

MONOTONES (U.K.)

64 Pye 7N 15608 What Would I Do/Is It Right . . . 10
64 Pye 7N 15640 It's Great/Anymore . . . 10
65 Pye 7N 15761 No Waiting/Like A Lover Should . . . 10
65 Pye 7N 15814 Something's Hurting Me/A Girl Like That . . . 10

MINT VALUE £

MONOTONES (U.S.)

58 London HLM 8625 Book Of Love/You Never Loved Me . . . 75
58 London HLM 8625 Book Of Love/You Never Loved Me (78) . . . 25

MATT MONRO

56 Decca F 10816 Ev'rybody Falls In Love With Someone/Out Of Sight, Out Of Mind . . . 20
57 Decca F 10839 Gone With The Wind/My Old Flame (unreleased)
57 Decca F 10845 The Garden Of Eden/Love Me Do . . . 20
57 Decca F 10870 My House Is Your House/The Bean Song . . . 20
58 Fontana H 122 The Story Of Ireland/Another Time Another Place . . . 18
58 Fontana H 167 Prisoner Of Love/Have Guitar, Will Travel . . . 18
58 Fontana H 167 Prisoner Of Love/Have Guitar, Will Travel (78) . . . 8
60 Parlophone R 4638 Love Walked In/I'll Know Her (as Matt Munro) . . . 6
60 Parlophone R 4714 Portrait Of My Love/You're The Top Of My Hit Parade . . . 6
61 Ember EMB S 120 The Ghost Of Your Past/Quite Suddenly . . . 12
61 Parlophone R 4755 My Kind Of Girl/This Time . . . 5
61 Parlophone R 4775 Why Not Now/Can This Be Love . . . 5
61 Parlophone R 4819 Gonna Build A Mountain/I'll Dream Of You . . . 5
62 Parlophone R 4868 Softly As I Leave You/Is There Anything I Can Do . . . 6
62 Parlophone R 4911 When Love Comes Along/Tahiti . . . 5
62 Parlophone R 4954 My Love And Devotion/By The Way . . . 5
63 Parlophone R 5068 From Russia With Love/Here And Now . . . 6
64 Parlophone R 5171 Walk Away/Around The World . . . 6
64 Parlophone R 5215 For Mama/Going Places . . . 5
65 Parlophone R 5251 Without You/Start Living . . . 5
65 Parlophone R 5348 Yesterday/Just Yesterday (Mine You Your Love Was Mine) . . . 6
66 Capitol CL 15436 Born Free/Other People . . . 6
66 Capitol CL 15477 Wednesday's Child/When You Become A Man . . . 6
69 Capitol CL 15603 On Days Like These/On A Clear Day I Can See Forever . . . 6
72 Columbia DB 8936 Curiouser/The Me I Never Knew . . . 8
73 Columbia DB 9060 If I Never Sing Another Song/We're Gonna Change The World . . . 8
63 Parlophone GEP 8889 SINGS THE THEME FROM THE FILM 'FROM RUSSIA FROM LOVE' (EP) . . . 15
64 Parlophone GEP 8898 A SONG FOR EUROPE (EP) . . . 8
57 Decca LF 1276 BLUE AND SENTIMENTAL (10" LP) . . . 70
61 Ace Of Clubs ACL 1069 PORTRAIT (LP) . . . 12
61 Parlophone PMC 1151 LOVE IS THE SAME ANYWHERE (LP, gold/black label, also stereo) . . . 12/18
62 Parl. PMC 1185/PCS 3034 MATT MONRO SINGS HOAGY CARMICHAEL (LP, gold/black label) . . . 18
65 Parlophone PMC 1250 I HAVE DREAMED (LP, yellow/black label, also stereo PCS 3067) . . . 12/15
66 Parlophone PMC 1265 HITS OF YESTERDAY (LP, yellow/black label) . . . 12
66 Capitol (S)T 2540 THIS IS THE LIFE! (LP) . . . 12
67 Capitol (S)T 2608 HERE'S TO MY LADY (LP) . . . 12
67 Capitol (S)T 2683 INVITATION TO BROADWAY (LP) . . . 12
67 Capitol (S)T 2730 INVITATION TO THE MOVIES (LP) . . . 12
68 Capitol (S)T 2801 THESE YEARS (LP) . . . 12
68 Capitol (S)T 2919 THE LATE, LATE SHOW (LP) . . . 12
69 Fontana SFL 13161 TONY BLACKBURN MEETS MATT MONRO (LP) . . . 12
69 RCA Victor SF 8024 THE SOUTHERN STAR (LP, soundtrack, with Georges Garvarentz) . . . 22
70 Capitol ST 22546 WE'RE GONNA CHANGE THE WORLD (LP) . . . 12
71 World Record Club ST 1024 SOFTLY AS I LEAVE YOU (LP) . . . 12
73 Columbia SCX 6525 FOR THE PRESENT (LP) . . . 15
75 Columbia SCX 6578 THE OTHER SIDE OF THE STARS (LP) . . . 15
(see also John Barry)

BARRY MONROE

66 Polydor 56088 World Of Broken Hearts/Never Again . . . 6

BILL MONROE (& HIS BLUE GRASS BOYS)

56 Brunswick 05567 New John Henry Blues/Put My Little Shoes Away . . . 15
56 Brunswick 05567 New John Henry Blues/Put My Little Shoes Away (78) . . . 10
57 Brunswick 05681 Four Walls/A Fallen Star . . . 12
57 Brunswick 05681 Four Walls/A Fallen Star (78) . . . 10
59 Brunswick 05776 Gotta Travel On/No One But My Darlin' . . . 10
59 Brunswick 05776 Gotta Travel On/No One But My Darlin' (78) . . . 20
66 Brunswick 05960 Blue Ridge Mountain Blues/John Hardy (solo) . . . 6
55 Brunswick OE 9160 COUNTRY DATE (EP) . . . 20
55 Brunswick OE 9195 COUNTRY WALTZ (EP) . . . 20
63 RCA RCX 7105 COUNTRY GUITAR VOL. 16 (EP, 2 tracks by Monroe Brothers) . . . 12
61 Brunswick LAT 8338 I SAW THE LIGHT (LP) . . . 20
63 Brunswick LAT/STA 8511 BLUEGRASS RAMBLE (LP, mono/stereo) . . . 18/22
65 Brunswick LAT/STA 8579 BLUEGRASS SPECIAL (LP) . . . 15
(see also Monroe Brothers)

GERRY MONROE

73 Chapter 1 SCH 187 Goodbye Bobby Boy/I've Got This Feeling . . . 10

MARILYN MONROE

53 MGM MGM 663 Diamonds Are A Girl's Best Friend/Bye Bye Baby (78) . . . 25
54 HMV 7M 232 The River Of No Return/I'm Gonna File My Claim . . . 60
54 HMV B 10723 The River Of No Return/I'm Gonna File My Claim (78) . . . 30
55 HMV B 10847 After You Get What You Want/Heat Wave (78) . . . 40
59 London HLT 8862 I Wanna Be Loved By You/I'm Thru' With Love . . . 40
59 London HLT 8862 I Wanna Be Loved By You/I'm Thru' With Love (78) . . . 75
78 United Artists UP 36484 I Wanna Be Loved By You/Running Wild/I'm Thru With Love (gatefold p/s) . . . 6
87 Zuma ZOOMP 6 When I Fall In Love/Heat Wave (picture disc) . . . 5
55 HMV 7EG 8090 THERE'S NO BUSINESS LIKE SHOW BUSINESS — SOUNDTRACK EXCERPTS (EP, company sleeve) . . . 40
59 London RET 1231 SOME LIKE IT HOT (EP, soundtrack; triangular centre, later round) . . . 80/50
60 Philips BBE 12414 LET'S MAKE LOVE — FILM SOUNDTRACK (EP, with Yves Montand & Frankie Vaughan; also stereo SBBE 9031) . . . 40/55

53 MGM MGM-D 116 GENTLEMEN PREFER BLONDES (10" LP, soundtrack with other artists). 100
59 London HA-T 2176 SOME LIKE IT HOT (LP, s/track with other artists, stereo SAH-T 6040). 90/110
60 Philips BBL 7414/SBBL 592 LET'S MAKE LOVE (LP, soundtrack, with Yves Montand & Frankie Vaughan; mono/stereo) 60/75
63 Stateside S(S)L 10048 MARILYN (LP, soundtrack, mono/stereo) 40/50
83 Liberty UASP 30226 SOME LIKE IT HOT (LP, picture disc) 15
(see also Frankie Vaughan)

VAUGHN MONROE (& HIS ORCHESTRA)

53 HMV 7M 144 Less Than Tomorrow (But More Than Yesterday)/Ruby. 8
54 HMV 7M 247 They Were Doin' The Mambo/Mister Sandman 10
56 HMV 7M 332 Black Denim Trousers And Motorcycle Boots/All By Myself 22
57 HMV POP 354 Wringle Wrangle/Westward Ho The Wagons! 7
59 RCA RCA 1124 The Battle Of New Orleans/Hercules. 7
59 RCA RCA 1124 The Battle Of New Orleans/Hercules (78) 15
60 London HLT 9123 Ballerina/Love Me Forever. 7
59 RCA RCX 1043 VAUGHAN MONROE'S GREATEST HITS (EP). 12
57 RCA RD 27049 FAMILY SING-SONG (LP) 15

MONROE BROTHERS

63 RCA RCX 7103 COUNTRY GUITAR VOL. 14 (EP) 15
63 RCA RCX 7104 COUNTRY GUITAR VOL. 15 (EP) 15
63 RCA RCX 7105 COUNTRY GUITAR VOL. 16 (EP, 2 tracks by Bill Monroe & Bluegrass Boys) 12
(see also Bill Monroe)

MONSOON

71 Trojan TR 7831 Hot Honolulu Night/Come Back Jane 6

MONSOON

81 Indipop IND 1 Ever So Lonely/Sunset Over The Ganges/The Mirror Of Your Mind/ Shout! (Till You're Heard) (in plastic sleeve with insert). 8
83 Mobile Suit Dist. MOBIL 1 THIRD EYE (LP) 12
(see also Complex)

MONSTER MAGNET

98 A&M 582822-7 Powertrip (1-sided picture disc) 5
98 A&M 563 274-7 Space Lord/The Game (picture disc). 5

MONTAG

03 Ai AI 006 OBJETS PERDUS EP (12", p/s). 8

MONTANAS

65 Piccadilly 7N 35262 All That Is Mine Can Be Yours/How Can I Tell 12
66 Pye 7N 17183 That's When Happiness Began/Goodbye Little Girl 45
67 Pye 7N 17282 Ciao Baby/Anyone There 7
67 Pye 7N 17338 Take My Hand/Top Hat. 10
67 Pye 7N 17394 You've Got To Be Loved/Difference Of Opinion 10
68 Pye 7N 17499 A Step In The Right Direction/Someday (You'll Be Breaking My Heart Again) . . . 10
68 Pye 7N 17597 You're Making A Big Mistake/Run To Me. 10
69 Pye 7N 17697 Roundabout/Mystery 10
69 Pye 7N 17729 Ciao Baby/Someday (You'll Be Breaking My Heart Again). 6
70 MCA MK 5036 Let's Get A Little Sentimental/Hey-Diddle-Diddle 5
(see also Trapeze)

MONTANA SEXTET

83 Virgin VS 600 Who Needs Enemies With A Friend Like You/Friendly Vibes (12"). 15
87 10 TENT 204 Heavy Vibes pts. 1 & 2 (12"). 8

MONTCLAIRS

74 Contempo CS 2008 Make Up For Lost Time/How Can One Man Live. 6
75 Contempo CS 2036 Hung Up On Your Love/I Need You More Than Ever 7
74 Contempo CLP 503 DREAMING OF A SEASON (LP). 15

LOU MONTE

54 HMV 7M 176 A Baby Cried/One Moment More. 12
54 HMV 7M 190 Darktown Strutters' Ball/I Know How You Feel 15
54 HMV 7M 249 Chain Reaction/Vera's Veranda 10
58 RCA RCA 1048 Lazy Mary (Luna Mezzo Mare)/Angelique-o 7
59 RCA RCA 1161 Santa Nicola/All Because It's Christmas. 6
59 RCA RCA 1161 Santa Nicola/All Because It's Christmas (78) 10
60 Columbia DB 4500 Oh! Oh! Rosie/(The New) Darktown Strutters' Ball. 6

VINNIE MONTE

59 London HL 8947 Summer Spree/I'll Walk You Home. 12
59 London HL 8947 Summer Spree/I'll Walk You Home (78) 20
63 Stateside SS 156 Joanie Don't Be Angry/Take Good Care Of Her 12

MONTEGO JOE

72 London HLP 10374 Stand Up And Be Counted/Glooey (with Seeds Of Life). 5
66 Stateside SL 10159 JARRIBA! CON MONTEGO JOE (LP). 12

MONTEGO MELON

72 Sioux SI 004 Swan Lake/HONG GANG: Reggae Mento 5

HUGO MONTENEGRO ORCHESTRA

62 Oriole CB 1765 Palm Canyon Drive/Dark Eyes. 7
63 Oriole CB 1792 Get Off The Moon/Sherry. 18
68 RCA Victor RCA 1727 The Good, The Bad And The Ugly/Fistful Of Dollars. 5
68 RCA Victor RCA 1771 Hang 'Em High/Tomorrow's Love 6
69 RCA RCA 1807 Tony's Theme/Good Vibrations 8
65 RCA Victor RD 7758 THE MAN FROM U.N.C.L.E. (LP, soundtrack) 45
66 RCA Victor RD 7832 MORE MUSIC FROM THE MAN FROM U.N.C.L.E. (LP, soundtrack) 45
67 RCA Victor RD/SF 7877 HURRY SUNDOWN (LP, soundtrack). 30

MINT VALUE £

68	RCA Victor RD 7994	A FISTFUL OF DOLLARS/FOR A FEW DOLLARS MORE/ THE GOOD, THE BAD AND THE UGLY (LP, soundtrack)	12
69	RCA SF 8053	MOOG POWER (LP)	30
69	Stateside S(S)L 10267	LADY IN CEMENT (LP, soundtrack)	45
70	Pye Intl. NSPL 28136	DAWN OF DYLAN (LP)	12
74	RCA APL1 0413	HUGO IN WONDERLAND (LP)	12

BOBBY MONTEZ

60	Vogue V 9165	Holiday In Havana/Jungle Stars	8

CHRIS MONTEZ

62	London HLU 9596	Let's Dance/You're The One	7
63	London HLU 9650	Some Kinda Fun/Tell Me	8
63	London HLU 9764	My Baby Loves To Dance/In An English Towne	10
66	Pye International 7N 25348	Call Me/Go 'Head On	8
66	Pye International 7N 25369	The More I See You/You, I Love You	5
66	Pye International 7N 25381	There Will Never Be Another You/You Can Hurt The One You Love	7
66	Pye International 7N 23599	Time After Time/Keep Talkin'	7
67	Pye International 7N 25415	Because Of You/Elena	6
68	London HLU 10205	Let's Dance/Some Kinda Fun	5
73	CBS S CBS 1291	Come On, Let's Go/Somebody Loves You	6
73	CBS S CBS 8343	Dolores, Dolores (I Told You I'd Be Back)/When Your Heart Is Full Of Love (Your Eyes Begin To Overflow)	6
79	Old Gold OG 9011	Let's Dance/LONNIE MACK: Memphis (picture disc)	6
63	London REU 1392	LET'S DANCE (EP)	50
66	Pye Intl. NEP 44071	THE MORE I SEE YOU (EP)	25
66	Pye Intl. NEP 44080	CHRIS MONTEZ (EP)	25
63	London HA-U 8079	LET'S DANCE AND HAVE SOME KINDA FUN!!! (LP)	65
66	Pye Intl. NPL 28080	THE MORE I SEE YOU (LP)	25
67	Pye Intl. N(S)PL 28087	TIME AFTER TIME (LP)	20
68	A&M AML 906	FOOLIN' AROUND (LP)	15
68	A&M AML(S) 925	WATCH WHAT HAPPENS (LP)	12
72	CBS 65408	LET'S DANCE (LP)	15

JACK MONTGOMERY

85	Kent TOWN 102	Dearly Beloved/MARIE KNIGHT: That's No Way To Treat A Girl	10
80s	Soul City 124	My Dear Beloved/Do You Believe It	8

LITTLE BROTHER MONTGOMERY

50	Jazz Collector L 44	No Special Rider Blues/Vicksburg Blues (78)	8
61	Columbia DB 4595	Pinetop's Boogie Woogie/Cow Cow Blues	20
61	Columbia 33SX 1289	LITTLE BROTHER MONTGOMERY (LP, with Alexis Korner)	70
62	'77' 77LA 12/21	LITTLE BROTHER MONTGOMERY/SUNNYLAND SLIM (LP)	25
65	Decca LK 4664	LITTLE BROTHER MONTGOMERY (LP)	25
66	Xtra XTRA 1018	LITTLE BROTHER MONTGOMERY (LP)	15
71	Xtra XTRA 1115	FARRO ST. JIVE (LP)	15
71	Saydisc SDR 213	LITTLE BROTHER MONTGOMERY 1930-1969 (LP)	18
72	Saydisc SDM 223	HOME AGAIN (LP)	20

MARIAN MONTGOMERY

65	Capitol CL 15375	When Sunny Gets Blue/Teach Me Tonight	6
67	Reaction 591 018	Love Makes Two People Sing/Monday Thru Saturday	15
68	Pye 7N 17533	Why Say Goodbye/Love Today — Cry Tomorrow	6

ROY MONTGOMERY

97	Enraptured RAPT 4510	Trajectory One/Trajectory Two (p/s, 27 in handmade p/s, 280 clear vinyl)	15/8

STUART MONTGOMERY

69	private pressing	CERTAIN SEA WORDS (LP, with insert)	15

WES MONTGOMERY

60	Fontana FJL 109	GO! (LP)	15
60	Riverside RLP 12-320	THE INCREDIBLE JAZZ GUITAR OF WES MONTGOMERY (LP, mono/stereo)	15/20

MONTROSE

74	Warner Brothers K 16382	Bad Motor Scooter/One Thing On My Mind	5
74	Warner Brothers K 16428	Rock The Nation/One Thing On My Mind	5
74	Warner Brothers/Sound For Industry SFI 175	Rock The Nation/Space Station No. 5/Good Rockin' Tonight (flexidisc)	7

(see also Sammy Hagar)

MONTY, DERRICK & PATSY

65	Blue Beat BB 280	Stir The Pot/Mercy	20

(see also Monty Morris, Derrick Morgan)

MONTY (Morris) & ROY

61	Blue Beat BB 61	In And Out The Window/Tra La La Boogie (with Dumbago's Orchestra)	12
61	Blue Beat BB 63	Sweetie Pie/ROLAND ALPHONSO'S GROUP: Green Door	18

(see also Monty Morris)

MONTY PYTHON('S FLYING CIRCUS)

70	BBC	Flying Sheep/Man With Three Buttocks (unissued)	
72	Charisma CB 192	Spam Song/The Concert (as Monty Python's Flying Circus, p/s)	6
72	Charisma CB 200	Eric The Half A Bee/The Yangtse Song (Extended) (as Monty Python with Niel [sic] Innes)	5
72	Python Productions	Teach Yourself Heath (flexidisc free with *Zig Zag* magazine)	12/5
74	Charisma CB 268	Lumberjack Song/Spam Song (p/s)	5
74	NME/Charisma SFI 1259	Monty Python's Tiny Black Round Thing (D.P. Gumby Presents "Election '74"/ The Lumberjack Song) (live flexidisc free with *NME*)	10/6
75	Charisma MP PROMO 1	In Store Commercial (promo only, jukebox single)	5
79	Warner Bros K 17495	Always Look On The Bright Side Of Life/Brian (p/s)	15
80	Charisma CB 374	I Like Chinese/I Bet You They Won't Play This Song On The Radio/Finland (p/s)	15

83	CBS WA 3495	Galaxy Song/Every Sperm Is Sacred (goldfish bowl-shaped picture disc)	8
88	Warner Bros W 7653	Always Look On The Bright Side Of Life/Brian (p/s, reissue)	10
91	Virgin PYTH 2	Galaxy Song/Every Sperm Is Sacred (p/s, reissue)	5
76	Charisma MP 001	PYTHON ON SONG (EP, double pack [CBS 268/PY 2])	10
70	BBC REB 73M	MONTY PYTHON'S FLYING CIRCUS (LP, mono, pink label)	15
73	Charisma CAS 1063	MONTY PYTHON'S PREVIOUS RECORD (LP, with free flexidisc in p/s, "Teach Yourself Heath" & inner sleeve)	12
73	Charisma CAS 1080	MATCHING TIE AND HANDKERCHIEF (LP, parallel grooves on side 2, die-cut sleeve, 2 inserts)	15
74	Charisma CLASS 4	LIVE AT THE THEATRE ROYAL DRURY LANE (LP)	12
77	Charisma CAS 1134	THE MONTY PYTHON INSTANT RECORD COLLECTION (LP, foldout sleeve)	12
79	Warner Bros K 56751	LIFE OF BRIAN (LP, soundtrack, with inner sleeve)	15
70s	Charisma	INSTANT RECORD COLLECTION (LP, fold out sleeve, with inner)	12

(see also John Cleese, Rutles, Barry Booth)

MONUMENT

71	Beacon BEAS 15	THE FIRST MONUMENT (LP)	90

(see also Zior)

MOOCHE

69	Pye 7N 17735	Hot Smoke And Sasafrass/Seen Through A Light	25

AMEIL MOODIE

69	Blue Cat BS 143	Mello Reggae/Lifeline	12
69	Blue Cat BS 164	Ratchet Knife/Bend The Tree	12

MOOD MOSAIC

66	Columbia DB 7801	A Touch Of Velvet, A Sting Of Brass/Bond Street P.M.	25
67	Columbia DB 8149	Chinese Chequers/The Real Mr. Smith	18
68	Parlophone R 5716	The Yellow Spotted Capricorn/ELMER HOCKETT'S HURDY GURDY: Fantastic Fair	8
69	Columbia DB 8618	A Touch Of Velvet, A Sting Of Brass/Bond Street P.M. (reissue)	10
67	Columbia SX 6153	MOOD MOSAIC (LP, mono)	30
67	Studio Two TWO 160	MOOD MOSAIC (LP, stereo)	25

(see also Mark Wirtz Orchestra & Chorus, Keith West)

MOOD OF HAMILTON

67	Columbia DB 8304	Why Can't There Be More Love?/King's Message	15

MOOD REACTION

70	Pama PSP 1007	LIVE AT THE CUMBERLAND (LP)	25

MOODS

63	Starlite ST45 098	Duckwalk/Easy Going	22

MOOD SIX

82	EMI EMI 5300	Hanging Around/Mood Music (p/s)	5
82	EMI EMI 5336	She's Too Far/Venus (unreleased; white label copies exist with p/s)	30
85	Psycho PSYCHO 2001	Plastic Flowers/It's Your Life (p/s)	5
85	Psycho PSYCHO 4001	PLASTIC FLOWERS (12" EP)	10
85	Psycho PSYCHO 33	THE DIFFERENCE IS... (LP)	12

(see also V.I.P.s)

JAMES MOODY

55	Esquire 20-071	MOODY HI FI (10" LP)	25

RON MOODY

61	Decca F 11371	You've Gotta Pick A Pocket Or Two/Reviewing The Situation	10
64	Parlophone R 5205	Rinkety Tink/Bringing Home My Darling	7

MOODY BLUES

SINGLES

64	Decca F 11971	Steal Your Heart Away/Lose Your Money (But Don't Lose Your Mind) (as Moodyblues)	40
64	Decca F 12022	Go Now!/It's Easy Child	6
65	Decca F 12095	I Don't Want To Go On Without You/Time Is On My Side	7
65	Decca F 12166	From The Bottom Of My Heart (I Love You)/And My Baby's Gone	7
65	Decca F 12266	Everyday/You Don't (All The Time)	8
66	Decca F 12498	Boulevard De La Madelaine/This Is My House (But Nobody Calls)	12
67	Decca F 12543	Life's Not Life/He Can't Win (withdrawn)	50
67	Decca F 12607	Fly Me High/Really Haven't Got The Time	18
67	Decca F 12670	Love And Beauty/Leave This Man Alone	18
67	Deram DM 161	Nights In White Satin/Cities (1st issue, darker labels than later copies)	6
68	Deram DM 196	Voices In The Sky/Doctor Livingstone, I Presume	7
68	Deram DM 213	Ride My See-Saw/A Simple Game	8
69	Deram DM 247	Never Comes The Day/So Deep Within You	7
69	Threshold TH 1	Watching And Waiting/Out And In	8
70	Threshold TH 4	Question/Candle Of Life	5
71	Threshold TH 7	Story In Your Eyes/Melancholy Man (unissued)	
72	Threshold TH 9	Isn't Life Strange/After You Came (p/s)	6
81	Threshold THPD 29	Talking Out Of Turn/Veteran Cosmic Rocker (picture disc)	7
83	Threshold TH 30	Blue World/Going Nowhere (p/s, with free T-shirt)	6
88	Polydor 080 409-2	Miracle/Vintage Wine/Deep/I Know You're Out There Somewhere/ I Know You're Out There Somewhere (Video) (CD Video)	12
88	Polydor 080 022-2	Your Wildest Dreams/Talkin' Talkin'/It May Be Fire/Rock'n'Roll Over You/ Your Wildest Dreams (Video) (CD Video)	12

EP

65	Decca DFE 8622	THE MOODY BLUES (EP, original label or reissue with boxed Decca logo)	30/10

MINT VALUE £

LPs

65 Decca LK 4711 THE MAGNIFICENT MOODIES (LP, unboxed or boxed Decca label logo) 40/15
67 Deram DML/SML 707 DAYS OF FUTURE PASSED (LP, originally with white band on sleeve & 'DSS' labels, mono/stereo) 25/12
68 Deram DML/SML 711 IN SEARCH OF THE LOST CHORD (LP, gatefold sleeve, mono/stereo) 25/12
69 Deram DML/SML 1035 ON THE THRESHOLD OF A DREAM (LP, gatefold sleeve with stapled booklet, mono/stereo) 25/12
69 Threshold THM/THS 1 TO OUR CHILDREN'S CHILDREN'S CHILDREN (LP, with insert, mono) 15
70 Threshold THS 3 A QUESTION OF BALANCE ('flap' gatefold sleeve with lyric sheet) 12
78 Decca TXS 129 OCTAVE (LP, blue vinyl) 12
(see also Justin Hayward, Denny Laine, Gerry Levene & Avengers, Ray Thomas)

MOOG MACHINE
69 CBS 63807 SWITCHED ON ROCK (LP) 15

MOON
68 Liberty LBF 15076 Someday Girl/Mothers And Fathers 10
70 Liberty LBF 15333 Pirate/Not To Know 10
68 Liberty LBL/LBS 83146 WITHOUT EARTH (LP) 30
(see also Beach Boys)

KEITH MOON
75 Polydor 2058 584 Don't Worry Baby/Together 18
75 Polydor 2442 134 TWO SIDES OF THE MOON (LP) 30
(see also Who)

LARRY MOON
63 Ember EMB 171 Tia Juana Ball/Bouquet Of Roses 22

PERRY MOON
63 Sway SW 002 Nine Five Baby/PLANTES: Water Front 12

TERRY MOON
63 Planetone RC 11 Moon Man/MIKE ELLIOT: This Love Of Mine 12

MOON BOYS
69 Amalgamated AMG 846 Apollo 11/PIONEERS: Love Love Everyday 12
(see also Hippy Boys)

MOONCHILD
75 Look LKSP 5010 War Orphan/Hour Glass 5

MOONDANCE
70 A&M AMS 792 Lazy River/Anna St Claire 5

MOONDOG
54 London REP 1010 ON THE STREETS OF NEW YORK (EP) 40
69 CBS 63906 MOONDOG (LP, gatefold sleeve) 75

MOONDOGS
78 Lyntone LT 002 Heads I Win/Two's A Crowd (p/s) 5

MOONDOGS
79 Good Vibrations GOT 10 She's Nineteen/Ya Don't Do Ya (foldout p/s) 10
80 Real ARE 13 Who's Gonna Tell Mary/Overcaring Parents (p/s) 10
81 Real ARE 14 Talking In The Canteen/Make Her Love Me (p/s, some with neckerchief) 35/10
81 Real ARE 16 Imposter/Baby Snatcher (p/s) 15

ART MOONEY (& HIS ORCHESTRA)
53 MGM SP 1037 I Played The Fool/I Just Couldn't Take It, Baby (with Cathy Ryan) 8
53 MGM SP 1045 Baby Don't Do It/Believe In Me (with Cathy Ryan) 8
54 MGM SP 1088 Oh Boy What Joy We Had/Silhouette D'Amour 6
55 MGM SP 1134 No Regrets/Honey Babe 6
56 MGM SP 1166 Memories Of You/I'm Looking Over 7
56 MGM MGM 899 Tutti Frutti/OCIE SMITH & CLOVERLEAFS: Our Melody (78) 10
57 MGM MGM 923 "Rebel Without A Cause" Theme/"East Of Eden" Theme 15
57 MGM MGM 943 Giant/There's Never Been Anyone Else But You 15
57 MGM MGM 943 Giant/There's Never Been Anyone Else But You (78) 8
57 MGM MGM 951 Rock And Roll Tumbleweed/Is There A Teenager In The House (with Ocie Smith) 22
57 MGM MGM 951 Rock And Roll Tumbleweed/Is There A Teenager In The House (78, with Ocie Smith) 15
(see also Ocie Smith, Shorty Long, Cloverleafs, Cathy Ryan)

HAL MOONEY ORCHESTRA
62 Oriole CB 1782 Small World/Let Us Entertain You 6

MOONGLOWS
57 London HLN 8374 I Knew From The Start/Over And Over Again 650
57 London HLN 8374 I Knew From The Start/Over And Over Again (78) 55
(see also Harvey & Moonglows, Etta & Harvey)

MOONKYTE
71 Mother SMOT 1 COUNT ME OUT (LP, with insert, spiral sleeve) 140

MOONLIGHTERS
63 Island WI 043 Going Out/Hold My Hands 25

MOONLIGHTERS
65 Columbia DB 7602 Come On Home/It's Too Late 7
66 Columbia DB 7910 We'll See It Through/Too Late To Come Home 7

MICKY MOONSHINE
74 Decca F 13555 Baby Blue/Name It You Got It 8
75 Decca F 13555 Baby Blue/Name It You Got It (reissue, with inverted matrix number) 5

MOONSHINERS

65	Stateside SL 10137	THE MOONSHINERS BREAKOUT! (LP)	18
67	Page One POLS 004	HOLD UP (LP)	22

MOONSTONES

65	Parlophone R 5331	Heaven Fell Last Night/Little Roses	6
66	Parlophone R 5497	Violets Of Dawn/Power Of Decision	6
67	Mercury MF 1011	How Many Times/Louisville	6

MOON'S TRAIN

67	MGM MGM 1333	Deed I Do/It's In My Mind	20

(see also Peter Frampton, Denny Mitchell, Preachers)

MOONTREKKERS

61	Parlophone R 4814	Night Of The Vampire/Melodie D'Amour	22
62	Parlophone R 4888	There's Something At The Bottom Of The Well/Hatashiai	35
63	Decca F 11714	Moondust/The Bogey Man	22

MICHAEL MOORCOCK('S DEEP FIX)

80	Flicknife FLS 200	Dodgem Dude/Star Cruiser (p/s)	10
82	Flicknife EJS P9831	Brothel In Rosenstrasse/Time Centre (numbered, 500 only, with autographed lyric sheet)	30
92	Cyborg (no cat. no.)	The Brothel In Rosenstrasse (cassette only)	20
75	United Artists UAG 29732	NEW WORLD'S FAIR (LP, with inner sleeve)	35

(see also Hawkwind)

ALEXANDER MOORE

60	77 77LA 12-7	WHISTLING ALEX MOORE (LP)	15

ALICE MOORE

50s	Poydras MC 66	Prison Blues/My Man Blues	15

ANTHONY MOORE

76	Virgin VS 144	Catch A Falling Star/Back To The Top	5
71	Polydor 2310 062	PIECES FROM THE CLOUDLAND BALLROOM (LP)	35
72	Polydor 2310 079	SECRETS OF THE BLUE BAG (LP)	35
79	Quango HMS 98	FLYING DOESN'T HELP (LP)	12
81	Do It RIDE 7	WORLD SERVICE (LP, with inner)	12

(see also Slapp Happy)

BOB MOORE & ORCHESTRA

61	London HLU 9409	Mexico/Hot Spot	7
62	London HLU 9538	Ooh La La/Aufwiedersehn Marlene	7
63	London HLU 9736	Kentucky/Flowers Of Florence	7
62	London HAU 2439	MEXICO (LP, also stereo [SAHU 6230])	12/15

BOBBY MOORE (& RHYTHM ACES)

66	Chess CRS 8033	Searching For My Love/Hey Mr D.J.	15
75	Pye International 7N 25691	Call Me Your Anything Man/Call Me Your Anything Man (Disco Version) (solo)	6
66	Chess CRL 4521	SEARCHIN' FOR MY LOVE (LP)	60

BUTCH MOORE

65	Pye 7N 15832	Walking The Streets In The Rain/I Stand Still	8

CHRISTY MOORE

69	Mercury 20170 SMCL	PADDY ON THE ROAD (LP)	250
75	Polydor 2383 344	WHATEVER TICKLES YOUR FANCY (LP)	25
76	Polydor 2383 426	CHRISTY MOORE (LP)	25
70s	WEA WX 286	VOYAGE (LP)	15

DUDLEY MOORE (TRIO)

61	Parlophone R 4772	Strictly For The Birds (solo)/Duddly Dell (B-side as Dudley Moore Trio)	70
68	Decca F 12850	30 Is A Dangerous Age, Cynthia/The Real Stuff (solo)	60
69	Decca F 12882	Keep It Up/Gently (as Dudley Moore Trio)	60
65	Decca LK 4732	THE OTHER SIDE OF DUDLEY MOORE (LP)	80
66	Decca LK 4788	GENUINE DUD (LP, as Dudley Moore Trio)	80
68	Decca LK/SKL 4923	BEDAZZLED (LP, soundtrack)	200+
69	Decca LK/SKL 4976	THE DUDLEY MOORE TRIO (LP)	50
69	Decca SKL 4980	THE MUSIC OF DUDLEY MOORE (LP)	50
70	Decca SPA 106	THE WORLD OF DUDLEY MOORE (LP)	30
70	Atlantic 2465 017	FROM BEYOND THE FRINGE (LP)	50
72	Atlantic K 40397	TODAY (LP)	40
73	Decca SPA 286	THE WORLD OF DUDLEY MOORE VOL. 2 (LP)	25
74	Black Lion BLP 12151	AT THE WAVENDON FESTIVAL (LP)	35

(see also Peter Cook & Dudley Moore)

GARY MOORE

78	MCA MCA 386	Back On The Streets/Track Nine (some in p/s)	30/5
79	MCA MCA 419	Parisienne Walkways/Fanatical Fascists (p/s)	8
79	MCA MCA 534	Spanish Guitar/Spanish Guitar (instrumental) (p/s)	12
81	Jet JET 12016	Nuclear Attack/Don't Let Me Be Misunderstood/Run To Your Mama (12", company sleeve, as Gary Moore & Friends)	10
82	Kerrang!	Wishing Well/GILLAN: Purple Sky/TELEPHONE: Squeeze (flexidisc with *Kerrang!* magazine)	8/6
82	Virgin VS 528	Always Gonna Love You/Cold Hearted (p/s)	8
82	Virgin VSY 528	Always Gonna Love You/Cold Hearted (picture disc)	8
83	Virgin VSY 564	Falling In Love With You/Falling In Love With You (Instrumental) (picture disc)	15
83	Virgin VS 564	Falling In Love With You/(Instrumental) (p/s, with comic)	10
83	Virgin VS 56412	Falling In Love With You/(Instrumental) (12", p/s)	20
84	10 TEN 13	Hold On To Love/Devil In Her Heart (poster p/s)	7
84	10 TENS 13	Hold On To Love/Devil In Her Heart (plectrum-shaped picture disc)	20
84	10 TEN 1312	Hold On To Love/Devil In Her Heart/Law Of The Jungle (12", p/s)	12
84	10 TEN 19	Shapes Of Things/Blinder (p/s, with patch)	15

MINT VALUE £

84	10 TENS 19	Shapes Of Things/Blinder (explosion-shaped picture disc)	22
84	10 TEN 1912	Shapes Of Things/Blinder/(Interview) (12", p/s)	10
84	10 TEN 25	Empty Rooms/Nuclear Attack (live) (some in poster p/s)	12/6
84	10 TEN 25-12	Empty Rooms (Ext. Mix)/Empty Rooms//Nuclear Attack (live)/ Empty Rooms (live)/Rockin' Every Night (live) (12", double pack, gatefold p/s with poster)	12
85	10 TEN 58	Empty Rooms (Summer 85 Version)/Out Of My System (p/s)	7
86	10 TENG 134	Over The Hills And Far Away/Crying In The Shadows (gatefold p/s)	5
86	10 TENS 134	Over The Hills And Far Away/Crying In The Shadows (guitar-shaped pic disc)	15
86	10 TEND 134	Over The Hills And Far Away/Crying In The Shadows//Out In The Fields (live with Phil Lynott)/All Messed Up (live) (double pack, gatefold p/s)	5
86	10 TENG 134	Over The Hills And Far Away (Extended Mix)/Over The Hills And Far Away (7" Version)/Crying In The Shadows/All Messed Up (live) (12", gatefold p/s)	8
87	10 TEND 159	Wild Frontier/Run For Cover (live)//Wild Frontier (live)/Murder In The Skies (live) (double pack, gatefold p/s)	5
87	10 KERRY 159	Wild Frontier/Run For Cover (live)/Over The Hills And Far Away/ Empty Rooms/Shapes Of Things (CD, gatefold card sleeve)	8
87	10 TENP 164	Friday On My Mind/Reach For The Sky (live) (picture disc)	5
87	10 KERRY 164	Friday On My Mind (12" Version)/Reach For The Sky (live)/Parisienne Walkways (live)/Friday On My Mind (Kool Rap Version) (CD, g/fold card sleeve)	15
87	10 TENC 178	The Loner (Extended Version)/(Edit)/Johnny Boy (PVC sleeve with patch)	5
87	10 TENT 178	The Loner/Johnny Boy/The Loner (Extended Version)/The Loner (Live At Hammersmith Odeon (12", p/s)	12
87	10 TEND 190	Take A Little Time/Out In The Fields//All Messed Up (live)/Thunder Rising (live) (double pack, gatefold p/s)	5
88	Virgin CDT 16	Over The Hills And Far Away (Extended Version)/Crying In The Shadows/ All Messed Up (3" CD, card sleeve)	8
88	Castle CD3 4	Don't Let Me Be Misunderstood/Parisienne Walkways (live)/White Knuckles/ Rockin' & Rollin' (3" CD, with 5" adaptor, 5,000 only)	8
88	Virgin CDT 35	Empty Rooms (Long Version)/Parisienne Walkways (live)/Empty Rooms (Summer 1985 Version) (3" CD, gatefold card sleeve)	8
88	Virgin GMSG 1	After The War/This Thing Called Love (gatefold p/s)	5
88	Virgin GMSY 1	After The War/This Thing Called Love (picture disc, stickered PVC sleeve)	6
88	Virgin GMSTW 1	After The War/Over The Hills And Far Away (live)/This Thing Called Love (12", p/s with patch)	10
88	Virgin GMSCD 1	After The War/This Thing Called Love/Emerald/Thunder Rising (live) (3" CD, in tin with sew-on patch)	10
89	Virgin GMSTG 2	Ready For Love (12" Version)/The Loner (live)/Wild Frontier (live) (12", gatefold p/s)	8
89	Virgin GMSCDX 2	Ready For Love (Edit)/Wild Frontier (live)/Military Man (live) (3" CD, card sleeve in 4" x 4" box with badge)	8
90	Virgin VS 1233	Oh Pretty Woman/King Of The Blues (p/s, black label)	5
90	Virgin VST 1233	Oh Pretty Woman/King Of The Blues/The Stumble (12", poster p/s)	8
97	Virgin VSTDJ 1674	Rhythm Of Our Lives(Stretch Mix)/(Gary's Mix)/Always There For You (New Version) (12", white label, promo only)	10
73	CBS 65527	GRINDING STONE (LP, as Gary Moore Band)	15
78	MCA MCF 2853	BACK ON THE STREETS (LP)	15
81	Jet JETLP 245	LIVE AT THE MARQUEE (LP, withdrawn test pressing, white sleeve with Jet Info sticker)	100
82	Virgin V 2245	CORRIDORS OF POWER (LP, with free live EP [VDJ 34])	12
84	EMI OVED 206	VICTIMS OF THE FUTURE (LP, with inner & poster)	20
84	Jet JETLP 241	DIRTY FINGERS (LP)	12
86	10 DIXP 16	RUN FOR COVER (LP, picture disc, die-cut sleeve)	30
87	10 DIXG 56	WILD FRONTIER (2-LP, gatefold sleeve)	18

(see also Granny's Intentions, Dr. Strangely Strange, Skid Row, Thin Lizzy, Gary Moore & Phil Lynott, Greg Lake, Eddie Howell, G-Force, Cozy Powell)

GARY MOORE & PHIL LYNOTT

85	10 TENS 49	Out In The Fields/Military Man (2 1-sided interlocking shaped picture-disc set, stickered gatefold PVC sleeve)	25
85	10 TEND 49	Out In The Fields/Military Man//Still In Love With You/ Stop Messin' Around (live) (double pack)	7
85	10 TEN 49-12	Out In The Fields/Military Man/Still In Love With You (12", gatefold p/s, with poster)	10
85	10 TENC 49-12	Military Man (12", 1-sided, B-side etched with signatures, promo only)	12

(see also Gary Moore, Phil Lynott, Thin Lizzy)

JACKIE MOORE

71	Jay Boy BOY 35	Dear John/Here Am I	6
71	Atlantic 2091 054	Precious Precious/Will Power	6
71	Atlantic 2091 095	Sometimes It's Got To Rain (In Your Love Life)/Wonderful, Marvellous (with Dixie Flyers)	6
74	Atlantic K 10481	Both Ends Against The Middle/Willpower	6

JOHNNY MOORE

67	Caltone TONE 101	Sound And Soul/ROY SHIRLEY: Get On The Ball	22
69	Doctor Bird DB 1180	Big Big Boss/CARL CANNONBALL BRYON: Reggae This Reggae	18

(see also Cannonball & Johnny Melody, Alton Ellis)

MATTHEW MOORE

66	Capitol CL 15467	A Face In The Crowd/St. James Infirmary	7

MERRILL E. MOORE

54	Capitol CL 14057	Bell Bottom Boogie/The House Of Blue Lights (78)	12
54	Capitol CL 14130	Nola/Fly Right Boogie (78)	12
55	Capitol CL 14369	Five Foot Two, Eyes Of Blue/Hard Top Race (as Merrill Moore)	200
55	Capitol CL 14369	Five Foot Two, Eyes Of Blue/Hard Top Race (as Merrill Moore) (78)	20
56	Capitol F 3397	King Porter Stomp/Rock Island Line (export only)	150

68	Ember EMB S 253	Down The Road A-Piece/Buttermilk Baby	15
69	B&C CB 100	Sweet Mama Tree Top Tall/Little Green Apples	7
70	Bulldog BD 20	House Of Blue Lights/Red Light	7
67	Ember EMB 3392	BELLYFUL OF BLUE-THUNDER (LP)	30
68	Ember EMB 3394	ROUGH-HOUSE 88 (LP; repressed 1973)	25
69	B&C CAS 1001	TREE TOP TALL (LP)	18

NICKY MOORE BAND

81	Street Tunes STS 006	Year Of The Lie	10
81	Street Tunes	7 YEARS OF THE LIE (LP)	12

(see also Tiger, Samson, Hackensack)

PETE MOORE ORCHESTRA

70	Fontana 6438 004	EXCITING SOUNDS OF TOMORROW (LP)	15

PETE MOORE'S SOLID ROCKIN' BRASS

74	Gold Star 1500 009	PETE MOORE'S SOLID ROCKIN' BRASS (LP)	15

OSCAR MOORE TRIO

55	London H-APB 1035	KENYA (10" LP)	15

ROGER MOORE

65	CBS 202014	Where Does Love Go/Tomorrow After Tomorrow (some in p/s)	25/10

SCOTTY MOORE

64	Columbia 33SX 1680	THE GUITAR THAT CHANGED THE WORLD! (LP)	75

(see also Elvis Presley)

SHELLEY MOORE (& MOORE SESSIONEERS)

55	Columbia SCM 5197	In The Wee Small Hours Of The Morning/ When You Lose The One You Love (solo)	5
58	Starlite ST45 002	You've Tied Me Up/Gone On The Guy	7
58	Starlite ST45 003	Where Is The Bluebird?/Everything Is Gonna Be All Right	7
57	Starlite ST EP 1	PORTRAIT OF SHELLEY (EP)	8
58	Starlite ST EP 7	KOOOL KANARY (EP)	8

THURSTON MOORE & DON FLEMING

97	Via Satellite V.SAT 6	Telstar/E.A.R.: Sputnik	20

WHISTLING ALEXANDER MOORE

63	'77' LA 12-6	WHISTLING ALEXANDER MOORE (LP)	25

ALAN MOORHOUSE ORCHESTRA

66	Pye 7N 17073	(The Ballad Of) The Green Berets/London Bridge	6
68	Page One POF 104	Stop Press/Chloe	7
70	Columbia DB 8674	Haunting Me/Soul Bossa	6

MOOSE

70	Escort ERT 840	Engine No. 9/KURASS: Do It	7

BIG MOOSE (Walker)

68	Python PKM 1	Puppy Howl Blues/Rambling Woman	30

MOPEDS

68	Col. Blue Beat DB 108	Whiskey And Soda/Do It	10

(see also Cindy Starr & Mopeds)

MOQUETTES

64	Columbia DB 7315	Right String, But The Wrong Yo-Yo/You Came Along	75

SANTOS MORADOS

68	Island WIP 6034	Tonopah/Anytime	6

NONO MORALES & HIS ORCHESTRA

54	HMV 7MC 5	Istanbul (Not Constantinople)/Am I Blue (export single)	5

MIKE MORAN

70s	Alba TAR 053	PENNY WHISTLES OF ROBERT LOUIS STEVENSON (LP)	20

MORBID ANGEL

94	Earache MOSH 112	LAIBACH REMIXES EP (God Of Emptiness/Sworn To The Black/Sworn To The Black [Laibach Remix]/God Of Emptiness [Laibach Remix]) (12", p/s)	8
89	Earache MOSH11	ALTARS OF MADNESS (LP, picture disc)	25

MORE

80	Atlantic K 11561	We Are The Band/Atomic Rock (some with p/s)	8/5
80	Atlantic K 11561T	We Are The Band/Atomic Rock (12", p/s, some with patch)	10/8
82	Atlantic K 11744	Trickster/Hey Joe (p/s)	18
81	Atlantic K 50775	WARHEAD (LP)	15
81	Atlantic K 50875	BLOOD & THUNDER (LP)	15

A. MORE

80	Quango HMGS 10	Judy/Lucia (p/s)	5

(see also Anthony Moore)

MORECAMBE & WISE

61	HMV POP 957	We're The Guys/Me And My Shadow	7
63	HMV POP 1240	Boom Oo Yatta Ta Ta/Why Did I Let You Go	8
64	HMV POP 1373	A-Wassailing/The Happiest Christmas Of All	6
66	HMV POP 1518	Now That You're Here/That Riviera Touch	10
67	Pye 7N 17436	Twelve Days Of Christmas/Bingle Jells	5
69	Columbia DB 8646	Bring Me Sunshine/Just Around The Corner	7
70	Philips 6006 069	Following You Around/Eric & Ernie's Theme	5
71	Columbia DB 8753	Bring Me Sunshine/Just Around The Corner (reissue)	5
74	Lyntone	Happy Birthday Record (flexidisc, promotion for Maltesers/Treets, etc, p/s)	10

MINT VALUE £

76	EMI EMI 2475	(We Get Along So Easily) Don't You Agree/Positive Thinking	5
78	(no cat. no.)	Morecambe & Wise & Cockram Talk Trio (p/s, promo)	8
64	HMV CLP 1682	MR. MORECAMBE MEETS MR. WISE (LP, also stereo CSD 1522)	12
66	Philips BL 7750	AN EVENING WITH MORECAMBE & WISE (LP)	15
71	BBC RED 128	IT'S MORECAMBE AND WISE (LP)	12

JOE MORELLO

62	RCA LSP 2486	IT'S ABOUT TIME (LP, also stereo [SF 7502])	12

MORGAN

73	RCA SF 8321	NOVA SOLIS (LP, with insert)	30
78	Cherry Red ARED 1	THE SLEEPER WAKES (LP)	12

(see also Mott The Hoople, Love Affair, Humpy Bong)

MORGAN & MARK SEVEN

66	Polydor BM 56083	I'm Gonna Turn My Life Around/Undercover Man	7

AL MORGAN

52	Brunswick 04913	Mistakes/My Castle In Spain Is A Shack In The Lane (with Frankie Froba & His Boys) (78)	8
58	London HLU 8741	Jealous Heart/Foolish Tears	10
50s	London BEP 6043	AL MORGAN (EP, export issue)	12
51	London H-APB 1001	JEALOUS HEART (10" LP)	20
51	London H-APB 1003	LITTLE RED BOOK (10" LP)	20

P.C. ALEXANDER MORGAN

66	Columbia DB 8095	Sussex By The Sea/METROPOLITAN POLICE BAND: Thunderbirds March	10

DAVID/DAVY MORGAN

65	Columbia DB 7624	Tomorrow I'll Be Gone/Ain't Got Much More To See (as Davy Morgan)	45
68	Parlophone R 5692	True To Life/Dawning (as David Morgan)	12

(see also Wishful Thinking)

DERRICK MORGAN

60	Blue Beat BB 7	Fat Man/I'm Gonna Leave You	25
60	Blue Beat BB 12	Don't Cry/I Pray For You (as Derrick Morgan & Ebonies)	25
60	Blue Beat BB 18	Lover Boy/Oh My!	22
61	Blue Beat BB 31	Now We Know/Nights Are Lonely (with Trenton Spence Orchestra)	20
61	Blue Beat BB 35	Leave Earth/Wigger Wee Shuffle (with Clue J. & His Blues Busters)	20
61	Blue Beat BB 62	Shake A Leg/Golden Rule (as Derrick & Drumbago All Stars)	18
62	Blue Beat BB 76	Sunday, Monday/Be Still	18
62	Blue Beat BB 82	Don't You Know Little Girl (actually by Derrick & Basil)/ B. GABBIDON: Hully Gully Miss Molly	18
62	Blue Beat BB 85	Come On Over/Come Back My Darling (with Buster's Group)	18
62	Blue Beat BB 91	Headache/OWEN GRAY: Millie Girl	20
62	Blue Beat BB 94	Meekly Wait/Day In And Day Out (both sides with Yvonne [Sterling])	18
62	Blue Beat BB 100	In My Heart/BELL'S GROUP: Kingston 13	20
62	Blue Beat BB 110	Are You Going To Marry Me?/Troubles (as Derrick Morgan & Patsy)	18
62	Blue Beat BB 130	Should Be Ashamed/Marjorie (with Buster's Group)	18
62	Blue Beat BB 141	Joybells (with Duke Reid Group)/Going Down To Canaan (with Denzil Dennis)	20
62	Island WI 004	Travel On/Teach Me Baby	20
62	Island WI 006	The Hop/Tell It To Me	20
62	Island WI 011	Forward March/Please Don't Talk About Me (B-side actually with Eric Morris)	20
62	Island WI 013	Cherry Home/See And Blind	20
63	Blue Beat BB 148	Jezebell/Burnette	20
63	Blue Beat BB 177	Patricia My Dear/The Girl I Left Behind	20
63	Blue Beat BB 187	Tears On My Pillow/You Should Have Known	18
63	Blue Beat BB 196	Telephone/Life Is Tough (B-side actually "Tough Man Tough")	22
63	Island WI 037	Dorothy/Leave Her Alone	25
63	Island WI 051	Blazing Fire/DERRICK & PATSY: I'm In A Jam	22
63	Island WI 053	No Raise, No Praise/Loving Baby	20
63	Island WI 080	Angel With Blue Eyes/Corner Stone	20
63	Rio R 1	Blazing Fire/Edmarine	18
64	Black Swan WI 402	Street Girl/Edmarine	25
64	Black Swan WI 425	Cherry Pie (actually by Frederick Hibbert)/BOB WALLS: Beware	25
64	Blue Beat BB 233	Let Them Talk/Sleeping	18
64	Blue Beat BB 239	Miss Lulu/DERRICK & PALOY: She's So Young (B-side act. by Derrick & Patsy)	18
64	Blue Beat BB 261	The Soldier Man/BUSTER'S ALL STARS: Jet 707	25
64	Blue Beat BB 268	Katy Katy/Call On Me	18
65	Blue Beat BB 276	Weep No More/I Want A Girl	18
65	Blue Beat BB 283	Johnny Grave/BUSTER'S ALL STARS: Yeah Yeah	20
65	Blue Beat BB 311	Throw Them Away/Baby Face	18
65	Blue Beat BB 329	Sweeter Than Honey/You Never Know (with Prince Buster)	18
65	Ska Beat JB 185	Heart Of Stone/Let Me Go (with Baba Brooks Group)	18
65	Ska Beat JB 218	Don't Call Me Daddy/BABA BROOK'S BAND: Girl's Town Ska	25
65	Island WI 193	Two Of A Kind/I Want A Lover (both actually with Naomi)	22
65	Island WI 225	Starvation/I Am A Blackhead Again	20
66	Island WI 277	It's Alright/I Need Someone (both sides actually with Blenders)	22
66	Island WI 289	Ameletia (actually by Frank Cosmo)/Don't You Worry (B-side with Patsy Todd)	18
66	Island WI 3010	Gather Together Now (Jamaican Independence Song)/Soft Hand (actually "So Hard") (both sides actually with Blenders)	22
66	Rio R 122	Cool Off Rudies/Take It Easy	20
67	Island WI 3079	Someone (actually Derrick & Pauline Morgan)/Do You Love Me (with Pauline)	18
67	Pyramid PYR 6010	Tougher Than Tough/ROLAND ALPHONSO: Song For My Father	20
67	Pyramid PYR 6013	Greedy Gal/SOUL BROTHERS: Marcus Junior	20
67	Pyramid PYR 6014	Court Dismiss/FREDERICK McCLEAN: Fine Fine Fine	20
67	Pyramid PYR 6019	Judge Dread In Court/Last Chance	125
67	Pyramid PYR 6021	Kill Me Dead/Don't Be A Fool	15
67	Pyramid PYR 6024	No Dice/I Mean It	15

MINT VALUE £

67 Pyramid PYR 6025 Do The Bang Bang/Revenge 15
68 Island WI 3094 Conquering Ruler/LLOYD & DEVON: Red Rum Ball 20
68 Island WI 3101 Gimme Back/VICEROYS: Send Requests 25
68 Island WI 3159 Hold You Jack/One Morning In May 18
68 Pyramid PYR 6029 I Am The Ruler/I Mean It 15
68 Pyramid PYR 6039 Woman A Grumble/Don't Be A Fool 15
68 Pyramid PYR 6040 Want More/ROLAND ALPHONSO: Goodnight My Love 15
68 Pyramid PYR 6045 Try Me/I'm Leaving (B-side with Pauline) 15
68 Pyramid PYR 6046 King For Tonight (with Pauline)/Last Chance 15
68 Pyramid PYR 6053 Me Naw Give Up/BEVERLEY'S ALLSTARS: Dreadnaught 15
68 Pyramid PYR 6056 Ben Johnson Day/MAYTALS: Ain't Got No Tip 18
68 Pyramid PYR 6061 What's Your Grouse/BEVERLEY'S ALLSTARS: I Don't Know 15
68 Pyramid PYR 6063 Johnny Pram Pram/Don't Say (B-side with Pauline Morgan) 15
68 Amalgamated AMG 824 I Want To Go Home/JACKIE ROBINSON: Let The Little Girl Dance 12
68 Crab CRAB 3 River To The Bank/PETER KING: Reggae Limbo 12
68 Trojan TR 626 Fat Man/VAL BENNETT: South Parkway Rock 12
68 Nu Beat NB 016 I Love You/JUNIOR SMITH: Searching 15
68 Big Shot BI 506 Shower Of Rain/VAL BENNETT: It Might As Well Be Spring 12
69 Crab CRAB 8 Seven Letters/TARTANS: Lonely Heartaches (B-side act. by Clarendonians) 12
69 Crab CRAB 11 My First Taste Of Love/TARTANS: Dance All Night 12
69 Crab CRAB 18 Don't Play That Song/How Can I Forget You? 10
69 Crab CRAB 23 Send Me Some Loving/Come What May 7
69 Crab CRAB 22 Mek It Tan Deah/Gimme Back 8
69 Crab CRAB 28 Hard Time/ROY RICHARDS: Death Rides A Horse 12
69 Crab CRAB 30 Man Pon Spot/What A Thing 12
69 Crab CRAB 32 Moon Hop/Harris Wheel 10
69 Jackpot JP 700 Seven Letters/Too Bad 8
69 Unity UN 507 Belly Woman/PAULETT & LOVERS: Please Stay 6
69 Unity UN 540 Derrick – Top The Pop/GLEN ADAMS: Capone's Revenge 8
70 Unity UN 546 Return Of Jack Slade/Fat Man 8
70 Unity UN 569 The Conquering Ruler/Bedweight 8
70 Crab CRAB 44 A Night Of Sin/Telephone 7
70 Crab CRAB 51 I Wish I Was An Apple/The Story 5
70 Crab CRAB 52 Take A Letter Maria/OWEN GRAY: Just A Little Loving 5
70 Crab CRAB 57 My Dickie/Brixton Hop 5
70 Crab CRAB 58 I Can't Stand It No Longer/Beyond The Wall 5
70 Crab CRAB 59 Endlessly/Who's Making Love 5
70 Crab CRAB 62 Hurt/Julia 5
70 Pama PM 822 Love Bug/My Dickie 5
71 Bullet BU 467 Nobody's Business/Standing By 5
71 Camel CA 84 I Am Just A Sufferer/We Want To Know 5
71 Crab CRAB 67 Searching So Long/MORGAN'S ALL STARS: Drums Of Passion 5
72 Grape GR 3032 Send A Little Rain/DERRICK MORGAN ALL STARS: A Little Rain (Version) 6
72 Jackpot JP 793 Let Them Talk/Bringing In the Guns 6
72 Jackpot JP 794 Won't Be This Way/Ain't No Love 6
72 Jackpot JP 797 Me Naw Run/All Night Long 6
72 Jackpot JP 802 Festival 10/Festival 10 – Version 6
72 Punch PH 107 Forward March/Plenty Of One 6
72 Buster PB 60 Tears On My Pillow/KEITH REID: Worried Over You (actually by Keith & Enid) 7
73 Attack ATT 8048 Derrick's Big Eleven/My Ding A Ling 5
73 Big Shot BI 617 Housewives Choice/Don't You Worry (both sides with Hortense Ellis) 5
73 Bread BR 1119 I Who Have Nothing/I'm Not Home 5
73 Downtown DT 520 Hey Little Girl/Don't Blame The Man 5
73 Pama Supreme PS 387 I'll Never Give Up/I Who Have Nothing 5
75 Klik KL 603 Wet Dreams Part 1/Wet Dreams Part 2 8
63 Island ILP 903 FORWARD MARCH (LP) 180
69 Doctor Bird DLMB 5014 BEST OF DERRICK MORGAN (LP) 120
69 Island ILP 990 DERRICK MORGAN AND HIS FRIENDS (LP) 120
69 Pama ECO 10 DERRICK MORGAN IN LONDON (LP) 70
69 Pama PSP 1006 MOON HOP (LP) 70
69 Trojan TTL 5 SEVEN LETTERS (LP) 30
70 Trojan TTL 38 FORWARD MARCH (LP, reissue) 22
70s Magnet MGT 004 IN THE MOOD (LP) 22

(see also Roland Alphonso; Frank Cosmo; Copy Cats, Derrick & Lloyd; Derrick, Morris & Patsy; Derrick & Patsy; Derrick & Naomi; Derrick & Paulette; Derrick & Pauline; Morgan's All Stars; Martin & Derrick; Larry Lawrence; Matador, Jackie Robinson)

FREDDY MORGAN

59 London HL 7077 Side Saddle/64 Rue Blondell (export issue) 18

GEORGE MORGAN

68 London HLB 10197 Barbara/Sad Bird 6
57 Philips BBE 12149 COUNTRY AND WESTERN SPECTACULAR (EP) 20
68 London HAB 8353 COUNTRY HITS BY CANDLELIGHT (LP) 20

JANE MORGAN (& TROUBADORS)

55 London HL 8148 Why — Oh Why/The Heart You Break (May Be Your Own) 45
55 London HL 8148 Why — Oh Why/The Heart You Break (May Be Your Own) (78) 8
57 London HLR 8395 From The First Hello To The Last Goodbye/
Come Home, Come Home, Come Home 40
57 London HLR 8436 Around The World/It's Not For Me To Say 25
57 London HLR 8436 Around The World/It's Not For Me To Say (78) 8
57 London HLR 8468 Fascination (with Troubadors)/Why Don't They Leave Us Alone 25
58 London HLR 8539 I'm New At The Game Of Romance/It's Been A Long Long Time
(with Troubadors) 20
58 London HLR 8611 I've Got Bells On My Heart/Only One Love 15
58 London HLR 8649 Enchanted Island/Once More, My Love, Once More 12

MINT VALUE £

58	London HLR 8751	The Day The Rains Came/Le Jour Ou La Pluie Viendra	7
58	London HL 7064	The Day The Rains Came/I May Never Pass This Way Again (export issue)	18
59	London HLR 8810	If I Could Only Live My Life Again/To Love And Be Loved	7
59	London HLR 8810	If I Could Only Live My Life Again/To Love And Be Loved (78)	10
59	London HLR 8925	With Open Arms/I Can't Begin To Tell You	7
59	London HLR 8925	With Open Arms/I Can't Begin To Tell You (78)	20
59	London HLR 8999	Happy Anniversary/C'est La Vie, C'est L'Amour	7
59	London HLR 8999	Happy Anniversary/C'est La Vie, C'est L'Amour (78)	30
60	London HLR 9087	My Love Doesn't Love Me At All/The Bells Of St. Mary's	7
60	London HLR 9120	Romantica/I Am A Heart	8
60	London HLR 9210	Lord And Master/Where's The Boy (I Never Met)	10
60	London HLR 9249	Somebody/The Angry Sea	8
61	London HLR 9421	It Takes Love/Homesick For Old England	7
62	London HLR 9528	What Now My Love/Forever My Love	7
63	London HLR 9683	Theme From Carnival (Love Makes The World Go 'Round)/ The Second Time Around	7
63	Colpix PX 700	Red Sails In The Sunset/My Special Dream	6
64	Colpix PX 713	Bless 'Em All/Does Goodnight Mean Goodbye	6
67	Columbia DB 7645	Maybe/Walking The Streets In The Rain	8
67	Columbia DB 8177	The Three Bells (Jimmy Brown Song)/I Want To Be With You	7
67	HMV POP 1608	This Is My World Without You/Somebody, Someplace	8
68	Stateside SS 2082	Masquerade/Smile	6
58	London RE-R 1161	ALL THE WAY PART 1 (EP, with Troubadours)	20
58	London RE-R 1162	ALL THE WAY PART 2 (EP, with Troubadours)	20
59	London RE-R 1204	THE DAY THAT THE RAINS CAME (EP, triangular or round centre)	22/15
61	London RE-R 1331	JANE MORGAN (EP)	22
57	London HA-R 2086	FASCINATION (LP)	40
58	London HA-R 2110	ALL THE WAY (LP, with Troubadors)	25
58	London HA-R 2133	SOMETHING OLD, SOMETHING NEW, SOMETHING BORROWED, SOMETHING BLUE (LP)	25
59	London HA-R 2136	GREAT SONGS FROM THE GREAT SHOWS OF THE CENTURY VOL. 1 (LP)	25
59	London HA-R 2137	GREAT SONGS FROM THE GREAT SHOWS OF THE CENTURY VOL. 2 (LP)	25
59	London HA-R 2158	THE DAY THE RAINS CAME (LP)	25
60	London HA-R 2244	JANE IN SPAIN (LP)	25
60	London HA-R 2316	THE BALLADS OF LADY JANE (LP)	25
61	London HA-R 2371	JANE MORGAN TIME (LP)	25
61	London HA-R 2377	THE SECOND TIME AROUND (LP, also stereo SAH-R 6177)	22/30
62	London HA-R 2430	AT THE COCONUT GROVE (LP, also stereo SAH-R 6226)	22/30
62	London HA-R/SH-R 8042	WHAT NOW MY LOVE (LP, mono/stereo)	22/30
63	London HA-R/SH-R 8069	LOVE MAKES THE WORLD GO ROUND (LP, mono/stereo)	20/25
63	Colpix PXL 460	JANE MORGAN SERENADES THE VICTORS (LP)	18
65	Columbia SX 6010	IN MY STYLE... (LP)	18

(see also Troubadors, Roger Williams)

JAYE P. MORGAN

54	London HL 8009	Life Is Just A Bowl Of Cherries/Operator 299 (78)	8
55	HMV 7M 327	The Longest Walk/Swanee	15
56	HMV 7M 348	If You Don't Want My Love/Pepper Hot Baby	25
56	HMV POP 144	If You Don't Want My Love/Pepper Hot Baby (78)	8
56	HMV 7M 365	Not One Goodbye/My Bewildered Heart	10
56	Brunswick 05519	Have You Ever Been Lonely?/Baby Don't Do It	10
57	RCA RCA 1014	You, You Romeo/Graduation Ring	8
57	RCA RCA 1014	You, You Romeo/Graduation Ring (78)	8
59	MGM MGM 1005	Are You Lonesome Tonight?/Miss You	10
59	MGM MGM 1005	Are You Lonesome Tonight?/Miss You (78)	18
59	MGM MGM 1021	(It Took) One Kiss/My Reputation	6
59	MGM MGM 1039	Somebody Loses, Somebody Wins/Somebody Else Is Taking My Place	6
60	MGM MGM 1093	I Walk The Line/Wondering Where You Are	6
62	MGM MGM 1182	Heartache Named Johnny/He Thinks I Still Ache	6
62	MGM MGM 1190	Brotherhood Of Man/Nobody's Sweetheart	6
54	London RE-P 1013	JAYE P. SINGS (EP)	22
59	MGM MGM-C 793	SLOW AND EASY (LP)	25
50s	RCA	JUST YOU, JUST ME (LP)	22

JOHN MORGAN

72	Carnaby 6302 010	KALEIDOSCOPE (LP)	55
70s	SWP 1007	LIVE AT DURRANT HOUSE (LP, private pressing)	90

(see also Spirit Of John Morgan)

LEE MORGAN

61	Columbia 33SX 1399	THE BIRDLAND STORY VOL. 1 (LP)	15
62	Stateside SL 10016	EXPOOBIDENT (LP)	15
65	Blue Note (B)BLP 4157	THE SIDEWINDER (LP)	15
65	Blue Note (B)BLP 4034	LEEWAY (LP)	15
66	Blue Note BLP 4199	THE RUMPROLLER (LP, also stereo BST 84199)	15
66	Blue Note BLP 4169	SEARCH FOR THE NEW LAND (LP, also stereo BST 84169)	15
69	Blue Note BST 84289	CARAMBA (LP)	12
69	Blue Note BST 84312	CHARISMA (LP)	12

MACE MORGAN THUNDERBIRDS

63	Starlite STEP 36	SHAKE AND SWING (EP)	60

MARY MORGAN

56	Parlophone MSP 6204	Jimmy Unknown/You Are My Love	12
56	Parlophone R 4227	From The Candy Store On The Corner/No-One Was There But You	10
57	Parlophone R 4348	A Call To Arms/One For Sorrow, Two For Joy	7

MINT VALUE £

RUSS MORGAN ORCHESTRA

55 Brunswick 05464 Alabamy Bound/SCRANTON 7: The Popcorn Song . . . 6
55 Brunswick 05493 Dog Face Soldier/Don't Cry Sweetheart . . . 6
56 Brunswick 05537 The Poor People Of Paris (Poor John)/Silver Moon . . . 6
56 Brunswick 05602 Lay Down Your Arms/My Best You You . . . 6
55 Brunswick OE 9068 MOONLIGHT MUSIC (EP) . . . 8

SAMMY MORGAN

70 Bullet BU 455 Get Out Of This Land/SYDNEY ALL STARS: Landmark . . . 6
70 Punch PH 57 Get Out Of This Land/SYDNEY ALL STARS: Landmark . . . 6

MORGAN BROTHERS

59 MGM MGM 1007 Nola/Guiding Star . . . 8
59 MGM MGM 1007 Nola/Guiding Star (78) . . . 5
59 MGM MGM 1026 Kissin' On The Red Light/Milk From The Coconut . . . 6

MORGAN TWINS

58 RCA RCA 1083 T.V. Hop/Let's Get Going . . . 120
58 RCA RCA 1083 T.V. Hop/Let's Get Going (78) . . . 50

MORGAN'S ALL STARS

71 Camel CA 76 I Love You The Most (actually by Lloyd Clarke)/I Love You The Most – Version . . . 7
(see also B. Leggs, Derrick Morgan, Marvels)

(Ron Paul) MORIN & (Luke P.) WILSON

72 Sovereign SVNA 7252 PEACEFUL COMPANY (LP) . . . 20

JOHNNY MORISETTE

62 Stateside SS 107 Meet Me At The Twistin' Place/Any Time Any Day Any Where . . . 12

MORNING

70 Liberty LBS 83463 MORNING (LP) . . . 22
72 United Artists UAS 29337 STRUCK LIKE SILVER (LP) . . . 22

MORNING AFTER

71 Sky SKYLP 71014 BLUE BLOOD (LP) . . . 80

MORNING GLORY

73 Island ILPS 9237 MORNING GLORY (LP) . . . 18
(see also John Surman)

GIORGIO MORODER

66 Page One POF 003 Full Stop/Believe Me . . . 15
67 Page One POF 028 How Much Longer Must I Wait/Bla Bla Diddley . . . 15
(see also Phil Oakey & Giorgio Moroder, Freddie Mercury, Giorgio)

ENNIO MORRICONE ORCHESTRA

67 RCA Victor RCA 1596 A Fistful Of Dollars/The Man With No Name . . . 6
67 RCA Victor RCA 1634 For A Few Dollars More/La Resi Dei Conti . . . 6
69 RCA RCA 1892 Once Upon A Time In The West (Jill's Theme)/Finale . . . 8
67 RCA Victor RD/SF 7875 A FISTFUL OF DOLLARS (LP, soundtrack) . . . 20
68 RCA Victor RD 7994 A FISTFUL OF DOLLARS/FOR A FEW DOLLARS MORE/ THE GOOD, THE BAD AND THE UGLY (LP, soundtrack) . . . 15
68 United Artists (S)ULP 1197 THE GOOD, THE BAD AND THE UGLY (LP, soundtrack) . . . 18
69 United Artists (S)ULP 1228 THE BIG GUNDOWN (LP, soundtrack) . . . 15
69 United Artists UAS 29005 A PROFESSIONAL GUN (LP, soundtrack) . . . 30
70 Stateside SSL 10307 THE SICILIAN CLAN (LP, soundtrack) . . . 20
70 CBS 70067 LOVE CIRCLE (LP, soundtrack) . . . 60
70 MCA MKPS 2013 TWO MULES FOR SISTER SARA (LP, soundtrack) . . . 15
72 United Artists UAS 29345 A FISTFUL OF DYNAMITE (LP, soundtrack) . . . 40
72 Bell BELLS 209 THE BURGLARS (LP, soundtrack) . . . 15
72 Paramount SPFL 275 THE RED TENT (LP, soundtrack) . . . 12

CHRIS MORRIS

91 Flexi FLOP 1 THE SELECT FLOPPY DISC (EP, 33rpm, poly sleeve, some with magazine) . . 18/15

ERIC MORRIS

61 Starlite ST45 052 Search The World/Buster's Shack . . . 25
61 Blue Beat BB 53 Humpty Dumpty/Corn Bread And Butter (as Eric 'Humpty Dumpty' Morris & Drumbago All Stars; [B-side actually by Drumbago All Stars]) . . . 20
62 Blue Beat BB 74 My Forty-Five/I've Tried Everybody (as Eric 'Humpty Dumpty' Morris & Drumbago All Stars) . . . 20
62 Blue Beat BB 81 Sinners Repent And Pray/Now And Forever More (B-side act. by Alton Ellis) . . . 22
62 Blue Beat BB 83 Money Can't Buy Life (with Buster's Group)/A. ELLIS: True Love . . . 20
62 Blue Beat BB 105 Pack Up Your Troubles/Oh What A Smile Can Do (with D. Cosmo & Drumbago's All Stars) . . . 18
62 Blue Beat BB 115 G.I. Lady/Going To The River . . . 18
62 Blue Beat BB 128 Over The Hills/Lazy Woman (with Buster's Group) . . . 18
62 Blue Beat BB 137 Miss Peggy's Grandmother/BUSTER'S GROUP: Megaton . . . 20
62 Blue Beat BB 140 Seven Long Years/For Your Love . . . 18
63 Blue Beat BB 153 Lonely Blue Boy/PRINCE BUSTER: Oh We . . . 20
63 Blue Beat BB 184 Sweet Love/BUSTER, DEREK, ERIC: Country Girl . . . 20
64 Blue Beat BB 218 Love Can Break A Man/Worried People . . . 18
64 Blue Beat BB 273 Stitch In Time/For Ever . . . 18
64 Black Swan WI 412 Sampson/BABA BROOKS: Jelly Beans . . . 25
64 Black Swan WI 414 Solomon Grundie/BABA BROOKS: Key To The City . . . 25
64 Black Swan WI 433 Supper In The Gutter/Words Of My Mouth . . . 25
64 Black Swan WI 439 River Come Down/Seek And You'll Find . . . 25
64 Black Swan WI 445 Home Sweet Home/LESTER STERLING: '64 Special . . . 25
64 Island WI 142 Penny-Reel/DUKE REID'S GROUP: Darling When (B-side act. Dotty & Bonnie) . . 22
64 Island WI 147 Mama No Fret/FRANKIE ANDERSON: Santa Lucia (B-side w/Roland Alphonso) . 22
64 Island WI 150 Drop Your Sword/Catch A Fire (B-side actually by Roland Alphonso) . . . 22

MINT VALUE £

64	Island WI 151	What A Man Doeth/DUKE REID'S GROUP: Rude Boy (B-side actually by Baba Brooks)	22
64	Port-O-Jam PJ 4006	Oh My Dear/Lena Belle	15
64	Rio R 39	Little District/True And Just	18
64	Rio R 48	Live As A Man/Man Will Rule	18
65	Rio R 72	By The Sea/I Wasn't Around	18
65	Island WI 183	Love Can Make A Mansion (actually "Love Can Break A Man")/ Ungodly People	25
65	Island WI 185	Suddenly/Many Long Years	25
65	Island WI 199	Fast Mouth/The Harder They Come	22
65	Island WI 234	Children Of Today/BABA BROOKS: Greenfield Ska	22
65	Blue Beat BB 298	Those Teardrops/DON DRUMMOND: Ska Town	25
66	Blue Beat BB 349	I'm The Greatest/BUSTER'S ALL STARS: Picket Line	25
60s	Fab BB 30	Humpty Dumpty (as Eric 'Humpty Dumpty' Morris & Buster All Stars)/ FOLKS BROTHERS: Carolina	7

(see also Monty Morris, Byron Lee & Dragonaires, Cool Sticky, Tommy McCook, Zoot Simms, Marguerita, Cool Cats)

HELMSLEY MORRIS

67	Caltone TONE 104	Love Is Strange/DON D. JUNIOR: Sir Pratt Special	20
68	Pama PM 720	Stay Loose Mama/You Think I'm A Fool (as Hainsley Morris)	7

JOE MORRIS & ORCHESTRA

54	London HL 8088	I Had A Notion/Just Your Way Baby (78)	60
54	London HL 8098	Travelin' Man/No, It Can't Be Done (78)	35

LIBBY MORRIS

56	Parlophone R 4225	When Liberace Winked At Me/None Of That Now	12
65	RCA RCA 1499	One Of Those Songs/The Phoenix Love Theme (Senza Fine)	6
67	Polydor 56206	Ballad Of Yesterday's Idol/Bye, Yum, Pum, Pum	5

MILTON MORRIS

69	Upsetter US 318	No Bread And Butter/UPSETTERS: Soulful I	10

MONTY MORRIS

67	Doctor Bird DB 1067	Play It Cool/BABA BROOKS' BAND: Open The Door	22
67	Doctor Bird DB 1081	Put On Your Red Dress/BABA BROOKS' BAND: Faberge	22
68	Doctor Bird DB 1162	Last Laugh/You Really Got A Hold On Me	30
68	Pama PM 721	Say What You're Saying/Tears In Your Eyes	15
68	Nu Beat NB 007	True Romance/BUNNY & RUDDY: Rhythm And Soul	15
68	Nu Beat NB 011	Simple Simon/BUNNY & RUDDY: On The Town	15
69	Doctor Bird DB 1176	Same Face/A Little Bit Of This	18
69	Big Shot BI 513	Deportation/Say I'm Back	8
69	Camel CA 12	Can't Get No Peace/UPSETTERS: For A Few Dollars More	12
69	Camel CA 28	No More Teardrops/Love Me Or Leave Me (as Monty Morris & Maples)	7
70	Unity UN 557	Do It My Way/Where In The World (Are You Going)	6
70	Explosion EX 2016	Higher Than The Highest Mountain/G.G. ALL STARS: Musical Shot	12
73	Ackee ACK 527	I'm Ready To Go/TOMMY McCOOK: Flower Pot	5

(see also Eric Morris, Monty, Derrick & Patsy, Monty & Roy, Alton Ellis)

ROGER MORRIS

72	Regal Zono. SRZA 8509	FIRST ALBUM (LP)	22

RUSSELL MORRIS

69	Decca F 22964	The Real Thing (Parts I & II)/It's Only A Matter Of Time	40
70	Decca F 23066	Rachel/Slow Joey	5

VICTOR MORRIS

68	Amalgamated AMG 813	Now I'm Alone/Rise And Fall	8

MORRIS & MINORS

80	Round MOR 1	STATE THE OBVIOUS (EP, p/s in poly bag)	10

MORRIS & MITCH

57	Decca F 10900	Cumberland Gap/I'm Not A Juvenile Delinquent	12
57	Decca F 10900	Cumberland Gap/I'm Not A Juvenile Delinquent (78)	8
57	Decca F 10929	What Is A Skiffler?/The Tommy Rot Story	12
58	Decca F 11086	Highway Patrol/Bird Dog	12
58	Decca F 11086	Highway Patrol/Bird Dog (78)	8
68	Trend TRE 1010	The Magical Musherishi Tourists/Mister D.J. Man	6
58	Decca DFE 6486	SIX FIVE NOTHING SPECIAL (EP)	25

MORRIS FAMILY & GOSPEL JUBILEERS

60	Top Rank JAR 322	Wake Up Jonah/He Never Complained	7

CURLEY JIM MORRISON

61	Starlite ST45 065	Air Force Blues/Didn't I Tell You	175

DOROTHY MORRISON

69	Elektra EKSN 45070	All God's Children Got Soul/Put A Little Love In Your Heart	8

HAROLD MORRISON

65	Brunswick LAT 8639	HOSS HE'S THE BOSS (LP)	12

JAMES MORRISON & TOM ENNIS

80	Topic 12T 390	JAMES MORRISON & TOM ENNIS (LP)	12

PROFESSOR MORRISON'S LOLLIPOP

68	London HLU 10228	You Got The Love/Gypsy Lady	6
69	London HLU 10254	Oo-Poo-Pah Susie/You Take It	6

TOM MORRISON

60	MGM MGM-EP 709	THE ADVENTURES OF MIGHTY MOUSE AND HIS PALS (EP)	8

MINT VALUE £

VAN MORRISON

Year	Label/Cat. No.	Title	Value
67	London HLZ 10150	Brown-Eyed Girl/Goodbye Baby (Baby Goodbye)	45
70	Warner Brothers WB 7383	Come Running/Crazy Love	6
70	Warner Brothers WB 7434	Domino/Sweet Jannie	6
70	President PT 328	Brown-Eyed Girl/Goodbye Baby (Baby Goodbye) (reissue)	15
72	Warner Brothers K 16210	Jackie Wilson Said/You've Got The Power	7
74	London HLM 10453	Brown-Eyed Girl/Goodbye Baby (Baby Goodbye) (2nd reissue)	10
74	Warner Brothers K 16392	Caldonia/What's Up, Crazy Pup	10
77	Warner Brothers K 16939	The Eternal Kansas City/Joyous Sound	5
77	Warner Brothers K 16986	Joyous Sound/Mechanical Bliss	6
79	Mercury 6001 121	Bright Side Of The Road/Rolling Hills (p/s)	5
89	Polydor VANX 2	Whenever God Shines His Light (Album Version) (with Cliff Richard)/ Cry For Home/I'd Love To Write Another Song (12", p/s)	8
89	Polydor VANCD 2	Whenever God Shines His Light (7" Version) (with Cliff Richard)/ I'd Love To Write Another Song/Cry For Home/Whenever God Shines His Light (Album Version) (CD)	8
68	London HA-Z 8346	BLOWIN' YOUR MIND (LP)	60
69	Warner Brothers WS 1768	ASTRAL WEEKS (LP, orange or green label)	25/15
70	Warner Brothers WS 1835	MOONDANCE (LP, orange or green label)	25/15
71	Warner Brothers WS 1884	HIS BAND AND STREET CHOIR (LP, green label)	15
71	President PTLS 1045	THE BEST OF VAN MORRISON (LP)	15
71	Warner Brothers K 46114	TUPELO HONEY (LP, gatefold sleeve, green label)	12
72	Warner Brothers K 46172	SAINT DOMINIC'S PREVIEW (LP, with insert, 'Burbank' label)	12
73	Warner Brothers K 46024	ASTRAL WEEKS (LP, reissue, 'Burbank' label)	12
73	Warner Brothers K 46040	MOONDANCE (LP, reissue, 'Burbank' label)	12
73	Warner Brothers K 46066	HIS BAND AND STREET CHOIR (LP, reissue, 'Burbank' label)	12
73	Warner Brothers K 46242	HARD NOSE THE HIGHWAY (LP, gatefold sleeve, 'Burbank' label)	12
74	London HSM 5008	T.B. SHEETS (LP)	12
74	Warner Brothers K 86007	IT'S TOO LATE TO STOP NOW (2-LP, gatefold sleeve, 'Burbank' label)	18
74	Warner Brothers K 56068	VEEDON FLEECE (LP, 'Burbank' label)	12
77	Bang 6467 625	THIS IS WHERE I CAME IN (LP)	12
77	Warner Brothers K 56322	A PERIOD OF TRANSITION (LP)	12
84	Mercury MERH 54	A SENSE OF WONDER (LP, white label test pressings with "Crazy Jane On God")	25
84	Mercury MERH 54	A SENSE OF WONDER (LP, credits but doesn't play "Crazy Jane On God")	12
99	Virgin VPBCDJ 50	BACK ON TOP (CD in A4 folder, with 1-sided 7", photo and biography, promo only)	50

(see also Them)

MORRISSEY

SINGLES

Year	Label/Cat. No.	Title	Value
88	HMV POP 1618	Suedehead/I Know Very Well How I Got My Name (p/s)	5
88	HMV TCPOP 1618	Suedehead/I Know Very Well How I Got My Name/ Hairdresser On Fire/Oh Well, I'll Never Learn (cassette)	20
88	HMV TCPOP 1618	Suedehead/I Know Very Well How I Got My Name/Oh Well, I'll Never Learn (mispressed cassette, plays "Ordinary Boys" instead of "I Know Very Well...", withdrawn)	12
88	HMV 12 POP 1618	Suedehead/I Know Very Well How I Got My Name/Hairdresser On Fire (12", 1st pressings in brown p/s)	12
88	HMV CDPOP 1618	Suedehead/I Know Very Well How I Got My Name/Hairdresser On Fire/ Oh Well, I'll Never Learn (CD)	18
88	HMV POP 1619	Everyday Is Like Sunday/Disappointed (p/s)	7
88	HMV TCPOP 1619	Everyday Is Like Sunday/Sister I'm A Poet/Disappointed (cassette)	8
88	HMV 12 POP 1619	Everyday Is Like Sunday/Sister I'm A Poet/Disappointed/ Will Never Marry (12", p/s)	10
88	HMV CDPOP 1619	Everyday Is Like Sunday/Sister I'm A Poet/Disappointed/ Will Never Marry (CD)	18
89	HMV TCPOP 1620	The Last Of The Famous International Playboys/Lucky Lisp/ Michaels Bones (cassette)	10
89	HMV CDPOP 1620	The Last Of The Famous International Playboys/Lucky Lisp/ Michaels Bones (CD)	15
89	HMV POP 1621	Interesting Drug/Such A Little Thing Makes Such A Big Difference (p/s)	8
89	HMV TCPOP 1621	Interesting Drug/Such A Little Thing Makes Such A Big Difference (cassette)	10
89	HMV 12 POP 1621	Interesting Drug/Such A Little Thing Makes Such A Big Difference/ Sweet And Tender Hooligan (live) (12", p/s)	8
89	HMV 12 POPS 1621	Interesting Drug/Such A Little Thing Makes Such A Big Difference (12", p/s, 1 side etched)	10
89	HMV CDPOP 1621	Interesting Drug/Such A Little Thing Makes Such A Big Difference/ Sweet And Tender Hooligan (live) (CD)	12
90	HMV POP 1622	Ouija Board, Ouija Board/Yes, I Am Blind (p/s)	5
90	HMV CDPOP 1622	Ouija Board, Ouija Board/Yes, I Am Blind/East West (CD)	10
90	HMV POP 1623	November Spawned A Monster/He Knows I'd Love To See Him (p/s)	5
90	HMV TCPOP 1623	November Spawned A Monster/He Knows I'd Love To See Him (cassette, card slip case)	10
90	HMV 12 POP 1623	November Spawned A Monster/Girl Least Likely To/ He Knows I'd Love To See Him (12", p/s)	10
90	HMV CDPOP 1623	November Spawned A Monster/He Knows I'd Love To See Him/ Girl Least Likely To (CD)	8
90	HMV POP 1624	Piccadilly Palare/Get Off The Stage (p/s)	5
90	HMV TCPOP 1624	Piccadilly Palare/Get Off The Stage (cassette)	10
90	HMV 12 POP 1624	Piccadilly Palare/At Amber/Get Off The Stage (12, p/s)	15
90	HMV CDPOP 1624	Piccadilly Palare/At Amber/Get Off The Stage (CD)	12
91	HMV POP 1625	Our Frank/Journalists Who Lie (p/s)	6
91	HMV TCPOP 1625	Our Frank/Journalists Who Lie (cassette)	10
91	HMV 12 POP 1625	Our Frank/Journalists Who Lie/Tony The Pony (12", p/s)	8
91	HMV CDPOP 1625	Our Frank/Journalists Who Lie/Tony The Pony (CD)	12

MINT VALUE £

91 HMV POP 1626 Sing Your Life/That's Entertainment (p/s) . . . 5
91 HMV TCPOP 1626 Sing Your Life/That's Entertainment (cassette) . . . 10
91 HMV CDPOP 1626 Sing Your Life/That's Entertainment/The Loop (CD) . . . 10
91 HMV POP 1627 Pregnant For The Last Time/Skin Storm (p/s) . . . 5
91 HMV TCPOP 1627 Pregnant For The Last Time/Skin Storm (cassette) . . . 10
91 HMV 12 POP 1627 Pregnant For The Last Time/Skin Storm/Cosmic Dancer (live)/ Disappointed (live) (12", p/s) . . . 8
91 HMV CDPOP 1627 Pregnant For The Last Time/Skin Storm/Cosmic Dancer (live)/ Disappointed (live) (CD) . . . 12
91 HMV CDPOP 1628 My Love Life/I've Changed My Plea To Guilty/There's A Place In Hell For Me And My Friends (live) (CD) . . . 10
92 HMV 12POP 1629 We Hate It When Our Friends Become Successful/Suedehead/I've Changed My Plea To Guilty/Pregnant For The Last Time (12", p/s) . . . 10
92 HMV CDPOP 1629 We Hate It When Our Friends Become Successful/Suedehead/I've Changed My Plea To Guilty/Alsatian Cousin (12", p/s) . . . 10
92 HMV CDPOP 1629 Certain People I Know/You've Had Her/Jack The Ripper (CD) . . . 15
94 Parlophone R 6372 The More You Ignore Me, The Closer I Get/Used To Be A Sweet Boy/ I'd Love To (numbered p/s) . . . 5
94 Parlophone CDR 6383 Hold On To Your Friends/Moon River (CD) . . . 8
95 RCA 74321332947 Boy Racer/London (Live Version) (p/s) . . . 7
95 RCA 74321332952 Boy Racer/Spring Heeled Jim/Why Don't You Find Out For Yourself (CD) . . . 15
95 RCA Victor LC 0316 Dagenham Dave/Nobody Loves Us (p/s) . . . 5
97 Island IS 667 Alma Matters/Heir Apparent (p/s) . . . 5
97 Island IS 671 Roy's Keen/Lost (p/s) . . . 5
97 Island IS 686 Satan Rejected My Soul/Now I Am A Was (p/s) . . . 5
00 EMI EMI 8872932 SINGLES 88-91 (10 x CDs, card sleeves, in box) . . . 25
01 EMI EMI 8797452 SINGLES 91-95 (9 X CDs, card sleeves, in box) . . . 25

PROMOS

92 HMV POP DJ 1629 We Hate It When Our Friends Become Successful/We Hate It When Our Friends Become Sucessful (10", A-side plays at 45rpm, B-side at 78rpm, die-cut sleeve) . . . 30
92 HMV POP DJ 1630 You're The One For Me, Fatty/You're The One For Me, Fatty (10", A-side plays at 45rpm, B-side at 78rpm, die-cut sleeve) . . . 30
93 HMV POPDJ 1631 Certain People I Know/Jack The Ripper (die-cut 'Moz' p/s) . . . 12
93 HMV POPDJ 1632 Jack The Ripper/Sister I'm A Poet (p/s) . . . 10
95 Parlophone CDRDJ 6243 Sunny/Black-Eyed Susan/A Swallow On My Neck (CD) . . . 15
94 Parlophone RDJ 6372 The More You Ignore, Me The Closer I Get/Used To Be A Sweet Boy (yellow p/s) . 12
94 Parlophone CDRDJ 6372 The More You Ignore, Me The Closer I Get/Used To Be A Sweet Boy/ I'd Love To (CD, yellow card p/s) . . . 12
94 Parlophone CDRDJ 6372 The More You Ignore, Me The Closer I Get (CD, with "45rpm" logo on disc, withdrawn) . . . 20
94 Parlophone CDRDJ 6383 Hold On To Your Friends/Moonriver (CD, card p/s) . . . 10
95 Parlophone RDJ 6400 Have-A-Go Merchant/Whatever Happens, I Love You (p/s) . . . 25
95 Parlophone CDRDJ 6400 Have-A-Go Merchant/Whatever Happens, I Love You (CD, 'skinhead' card p/s) . . . 20
95 Parlophone CDRDJX 6400 Boxers/Have-A-Go Merchant/Whatever Happens I Love You (CD) . . . 10

(see also Smiths, Durutti Column)

DICK MORRISSEY

61 '77' LEU 12/8 HAVE YOU HEARD? (LP) . . . 225
61 Fontana TFL 5149 IT'S MORRISSEY MAN! (LP) . . . 225
67 Mercury 20093 HERE AND NOW AND SOUNDING GOOD (LP) . . . 200
67 Mercury 20077MCL STORM WARNING (LP) . . . 200

(see also If, Morrissey-Mullen)

MORRISSEY-MULLEN

79 Harvest SHSP 4098 CAPE WRATH (LP) . . . 20

(see also Dick Morrissey)

BUDDY MORROW & HIS ORCHESTRA

53 HMV 7M 145 Heap Big Beat/I Can't Get Started . . . 6
53 HMV 7M 151 I Can't Get Started/Heap Big Beat (reissue) . . . 6
53 HMV 7M 162 Dragnet/Your Mouth's Got A Hole In It . . . 8
54 HMV 7M 216 Knock On Wood (with Shaye Cogan)/All Night Long . . . 10
60 RCA RCA 1167 Staccato's Theme/Scrauunchy . . . 6
60 RCA RCA 1167 Staccato's Theme/Scrauunchy (78) . . . 15
56 Mercury MPT 7003 SHALL WE DANCE (10" LP) . . . 15

ELLA MAE MORSE

52 Capitol CL 13666 Tennessee Saturday Night/A Little Further Down The Road (78) . . . 8
52 Capitol CL 13727 Blacksmith Blues/Love Me Or Leave Me (78) . . . 8
52 Capitol CL 13754 Oakie Boogie/Love Ya' Like Mad (78) . . . 8
52 Capitol CL 13798 Male Call/Sleepin' At The Foot Of The Bed (78) . . . 8
53 Capitol CL 13853 Jump Back Honey/Greyhound (78) . . . 10
53 Capitol CL 13930 Big Mamou/Is It Any Wonder (78) . . . 10
53 Capitol CL 13960 Forty Cups Of Coffee/Oh! You Crazy Moon (78) . . . 12
54 Capitol CL 14037 T'Ain't What You Do, It's The Way That You Do It/ It Ain't Necessarily So (78) . . . 8
54 Capitol CL 14044 The Guy Who Invented Kissin'/Good (78) . . . 8
54 Capitol CL 14116 Goodnight, Well It's Time To Go/Sensational (78) . . . 8
54 Capitol CL 14176 (We've Reached) The Point Of No Return/Give A Little Time (78) . . . 10
55 Capitol CL 14223 Bring Back My Baby To Me/Lovey Dovey . . . 65
55 Capitol CL 14223 Bring Back My Baby To Me/Lovey Dovey (78) . . . 8
55 Capitol CL 14303 Smack Dab In The Middle/Yes, Yes I Do . . . 55
55 Capitol CL 14303 Smack Dab In The Middle/Yes, Yes I Do (78) . . . 10
55 Capitol CL 14332 Livin', Livin', Livin'/Heart Full Of Hope . . . 45
55 Capitol CL 14332 Livin', Livin', Livin'/Heart Full Of Hope (78) . . . 8
55 Capitol CL 14341 Razzle-Dazzle/Ain't That A Shame (with Big Dave & His Music) . . . 100

55 Capitol CL 14341 Razzle-Dazzle/Ain't That A Shame (with Big Dave & His Music) (78) . . . 20
55 Capitol CL 14362 Seventeen/Piddily Patter Song (with Big Dave & His Music) . . . 100
55 Capitol CL 14362 Seventeen/Piddily Patter Song (with Big Dave & His Music) (78) . . . 15
55 Capitol CL 14376 Birmin'ham/An Occasional Man . . . 50
55 Capitol CL 14376 Birmin'ham/An Occasional Man (78) . . . 10
(The above 45s were originally issued with triangular centres; later round-centres are worth around two-thirds these values.)
56 Capitol CL 14508 When Boy Kiss Girl (It's Love)/Sing-Ing-Ing-Ing . . . 30
56 Capitol CL 14508 When Boy Kiss Girl (It's Love)/Sing-Ing-Ing-Ing (78) . . . 10
56 Capitol CL 14572 Rock And Roll Wedding/Down In Mexico . . . 40
56 Capitol CL 14572 Rock And Roll Wedding/Down In Mexico (78) . . . 12
57 Capitol CL 14726 What Good'll It Do Me/Mister Money Maker . . . 22
57 Capitol CL 14726 What Good'll It Do Me/Mister Money Maker (78) . . . 12
57 Capitol CL 14760 I'm Gone/Sway Me . . . 22
57 Capitol CL 14760 I'm Gone/Sway Me (78) . . . 15
55 Capitol EAP1 513 BARRELHOUSE BOOGIE AND THE BLUES (EP) . . . 65
54 Capitol LC 6687 BARRELHOUSE BOOGIE AND THE BLUES (10" LP) . . . 110
(see also 'Tennessee' Ernie Ford)

ELLA MAE MORSE & FREDDIE SLACK
67 Ember SPE 6605 ROCKIN' BREW (LP) . . . 25

AZIE MORTIMER
60 London HLX 9237 Lips/Wrapped Up In A Dream . . . 10

JELLY ROLL MORTON('S RED HOT PEPPERS)
53 HMV 7M 132 The Chant/Tank Town Bump . . . 12
54 HMV 7M 178 Fat Frances/Pep (solo) . . . 12
54 HMV 7M 187 Wild Man Blues/Smoke-House Blues . . . 12
54 HMV 7M 207 Harmony Blues/Jungle Blues . . . 12
54 HMV 7M 256 Fussy Mabel/Burnin' The Iceberg . . . 12
57 Vogue EPV 1126 JELLY ROLL MORTON (EP) . . . 15
55 HMV 7EG 8178 THE BLUES THEY SANG (EP) . . . 15
59 RCA RCX 168 JELLY ROLL MORTON (EP) . . . 10
50s Collector JE 120 JAZZ ORIGINATORS VOL. 3 (EP) . . . 12
60 RCA RCX 207 JELLY ROLL MORTON NO. 2 (EP) . . . 10
60 Fontana TFE 17263 TREASURES OF NORTH AMERICAN NEGRO MUSIC VOL. 4 (EP) . . . 10
61 Storyville SEP 379 JELLY ROLL MORTON (EP) . . . 10
53 HMV DLP 1016 JELLY ROLL MORTON AND HIS RED HOT PEPPERS (10" LP) . . . 22
54 HMV DLP 1044 MORTON'S RED HOT PEPPERS VOLUME 2(10" LP) . . . 22
54 Vogue LDE 080 NEW ORLEANS MEMORIES (10" LP) . . . 18
54 London AL 3519 JELLY ROLL MORTON SOLOS (10" LP) . . . 18
54 London AL 3520 JELLY ROLL MORTON'S KINGS OF JAZZ (10" LP) . . . 18
54 London AL 3534 CLASSIC JAZZ PIANO VOL. 1 (10" LP) . . . 18
55 HMV DLP 1071 MORTON'S RED HOT PEPPERS NO. 3 (10" LP) . . . 20
56 London AL 3559 CLASSIC JAZZ PIANO VOL. 2 (10" LP) . . . 18
59 RCA RD 27113 THE KING OF NEW ORLEANS JAZZ (LP) . . . 12
61 RCA RD 27184 THE KING OF NEW ORLEANS JAZZ VOL. 2 (LP) . . . 12
61 Riverside RLP 12-132 MR. JELLY LORD (LP) . . . 12
62 Riverside RLP 12-111 CLASSIC PIANO SOLOS (LP) . . . 12
65 Fontana TL 5261 JELLY ROLL MORTON (LP) . . . 12
67 Fontana TL 5415 MORTON SIXES AND SEVENS (LP) . . . 12
69 RCA RD 8048 I THOUGHT I HEARD BUDDY BOLDEN SAY (LP) . . . 12

LIONEL MORTON
67 Philips BF 1578 What To Do With Laurie/I'll Just . . . 7
67 Philips BF 1607 First Love Never Dies/Try Not To Cry . . . 7
69 RCA RCA 1875 Waterloo Road/Floral Street . . . 7
(see also Four Pennies)

MANDY MORTON (BAND)
79 Banshee BANS 791 Song For Me (Music Prince)/Little Inbetween (with Spriguns) . . . 15
80 Polydor 2382 101 Ghost Of Christmas Past/Black Nights (p/s) . . . 6
78 Banshee BAN 1011 MAGIC LADY (LP, with lyric insert, 1,000 only) . . . 175
78 Banshee BAN 1011 MAGIC LADY (LP, with lyric insert, blue vinyl, 20 only) . . . 400
80 Polydor 2382 101 SEA OF STORMS (LP, solo, with insert) . . . 20
83 Banshee VALLEY OF LIGHT (LP, private pressing) . . . 40
(see also Spriguns [Of Tolgus])

MOSAICS
66 Columbia DB 7990 Let's Go Drag Racing/Now That You're Here . . . 22

PABLO MOSES
77 Klik KLP 9026 REVOLUTIONARY DREAM (LP) . . . 12
78 Different GETL 104 REVOLUTIONARY DREAM (LP) . . . 12

MOSES & JOSHUA
(see under Moses & Joshua Dillard)

MOSKOW
78 Moskow SRS 2103 Man From U.N.C.L.E./White Black (p/s) . . . 25
81 T.W. HIT 103 Man From U.N.C.L.E./White Black (reissue in different p/s) . . . 8

BILL MOSS
69 Pama PM 765 Sock It To 'Em Soul Brother (Parts 1 & 2) . . . 6
70 Pama PM 796 Number One . . . 6

BUDDY MOSS
60s Kokomo K 1003 GEORGIA BLUES VOLUME 2 (LP) . . . 60

JENNY MOSS
63 Columbia DB 7061 Hobbies/Big Boys . . . 65

MINT VALUE £

STIRLING MOSS

61 Redemption RLP 5004 THE STIRLING MOSS STORY (LP) . . . 15

TEDDY MOSS/JOSH WHITE

62 Jazz Collector JEL 5 THE MALE BLUES (EP) . . . 18
(see also Josh White)

MOST

79 SRT SRTS/CUS/570 Carefree/In And Out (stamped lyric insert) . . . 8

MOST

94 Detour DR 012 Days, Days, Days/Take You There/Six Fifteen/Our Time (p/s, white vinyl) . . . 6

ABE MOST OCTET

55 London RE-P 1028 PRESENTING THE ABE MOST OCTET (EP) . . . 15

MICKIE MOST (& GEAR)

63 Decca F 11664 Mr. Porter/Yes Indeed I Do . . . 30
63 Columbia DB 7117 The Feminine Look/Shame On You Boy . . . 18
63 Columbia DB 7180 Sea Cruise/It's A Little Bit Hot . . . 20
64 Columbia DB 7245 Money Honey/That's Alright (as Mickey Most & Gear) . . . 25
(see also Most Brothers)

MR MOST

69 Downtown DT 408 Push Wood/Reggae Train . . . 12

MOST BROTHERS

57 Decca F 10968 Whistle Bait/I'm Comin' Home . . . 20
57 Decca F 10968 Whistle Bait/I'm Comin' Home (78) . . . 10
58 Decca F 10998 Whole Lotta Woman/Teen Angel . . . 20
58 Decca F 10998 Whole Lotta Woman/Teen Angel (78) . . . 10
58 Decca F 11040 Don't Go Home/Dottie . . . 18
58 Decca F 11040 Don't Go Home/Dottie (78) . . . 10
(see also Mickie Most, Alex Murray)

BENNY MOTEN('S KANSAS CITY ORCHESTRA)

54 HMV DLP 1057 BENNIE MOTEN PLAYS KAY-CEE JAZZ (10" LP) . . . 15
64 RCA Victor RD 7660 K.C. JAZZ (LP) . . . 12

MOTHER EARTH

69 Mercury MF 1081 Goodnight Melda Grebe The Telephone Company Has Cut Us Off/
I Did My Part . . . 8
71 Reprise K 14089 Temptation Took Control Of Me/I'll Be Long Gone . . . 5
68 Mercury SMCL 20143 LIVING WITH THE ANIMALS (LP) . . . 20
69 Mercury SMCL 20173 MAKE A JOYFUL NOISE (LP) . . . 20
69 Mercury SMCL 20179 TRACY NELSON COUNTRY (LP) . . . 20
71 Mercury 6338 023 SATISFIED (LP) . . . 20
71 Reprise K 44133 BRING ME HOME (LP) . . . 15

MOTHER EARTH

90s Acid Jazz JAZID 100 Jesse (Live) (company sleeve) . . . 25
90s Acid Jazz JAZID LP 48 STONED WOMAN (LP) . . . 18

MOTHER GONG

81 Butt BUTT 003 ROBOT WOMEN (LP) . . . 12
82 Shanghai HAI 100 ROBOT WOMEN 2 (LP) . . . 12
83 Shanghai HAI 109 ROBOT WOMEN 3 (LP) . . . 12
(see also Gong)

MOTHERLIGHT

69 Morgan Bluetown BT 5003 BOBAK, JONS, MALONE (LP) . . . 150
(see also Will Malone [Voice Band], Orange Bicycle)

MOTHERLODE

69 Buddah 201 064 When I Die/Hard Life . . . 6
69 Buddah 2318 043 WHEN I DIE (LP) . . . 15

MOTHERS OF INVENTION

(see under Frank Zappa/Mothers Of Invention)

MOTHER'S RUIN

81 Spectra SPC 1 Streetfighters/Leaving You (some in p/s) . . . 55/40
82 Spectra SPC 6 Street Lights/Turn A Corner (p/s) . . . 20
82 Spectra SPC 7 Say It's Not True/It's Illogical (p/s) . . . 35
81 Off Course G33303 WANT MORE (LP) . . . 12
82 Spectra SPA 1 ROAD TO RUIN (LP) . . . 12

MOTHER'S SONS

70 J-Dan JDN 4415 I Want To Tell The World/Underground Man . . . 6

MOTHER YOD

97 Prescription DRUG 1 MOTHER YOD (LP, 99 copies only) . . . 25

MOTHMEN

79 Absurd ABSURD 6 Does It Matter Irene?/Please Let Go (p/s) . . . 10
81 Do It DUN 12 Show Me Your House And Car/People People (p/s, deleted after 1 day) . . . 10
81 Do It DUNIT 12 Show Me Your House And Car/People People (12", p/s, deleted after 1 day) . . . 12
81 Do It DUN 14 Temptation/People People (p/s) . . . 8
82 Do It DUN 19 Wadada/As They Are (p/s) . . . 10
82 Do It RIDE 9 ONE BLACK DOT (LP) . . . 15
80s On-U-Sound LP 2 PAY ATTENTION (LP) . . . 12
(see also Alberto Y Lost Trios Paranoias)

MOTHS

69 Deroy MOTHS (LP, private pressing in plain white sleeve) . . . 600

MINT VALUE £

MOTIFFE

Year	Label / Cat. No.	Title	Value
72	Deroy 777	MOTIFFE (LP, private pressing in hand-illustrated white sleeve)	1,200

MOTIONS

Year	Label / Cat. No.	Title	Value
66	Pye International 7N 25390	Stop Your Crying/Every Step I Take	12

MOTIVATION

Year	Label / Cat. No.	Title	Value
68	Direction 58-3248	Come On Down/Little Man	35

FRANK MOTLEY & BRIDGE CROSSINGS

Year	Label / Cat. No.	Title	Value
98	Jazzman JM 002	Ya Ya/Ooga Boogaloo (no p/s, large centre hole)	5

MÖTLEY CRÜE

Year	Label / Cat. No.	Title	Value
84	Elektra E 9756	Looks That Kill/Piece Of The Action (p/s)	10
84	Elektra E 9756T	Looks That Kill/Piece Of The Action/Live Wire (12", p/s with free tattoo)	15
84	Elektra E 9756TP	Looks That Kill/Piece Of The Action/Live Wire (12", picture disc)	40
84	Elektra E 9732	Too Young To Fall In Love/Take Me To The Top (p/s)	7
84	Elektra E 9732T	Too Young To Fall In Love/Take Me To The Top (12", p/s, some with poster)	12/7
85	Elektra EKR 33T	Smokin' In The Boys' Room/Use It Or Lose It/Shout At The Devil (12", p/s)	10
86	Elektra EKR 16TP	Smokin' In The Boys' Room/Use It Or Lose It (mask-shaped pic disc & sticker)	20
86	Elektra EKR 33P	Smokin' In The Boys' Room/Home Sweet Home (2 different interlocking mask-shaped picture disc set)	30
86	Elektra EKR 33T	Smokin' In The Boys' Room/Home Sweet Home/Shout At The Devil (12", p/s with poster)	10
87	Elektra EKR 59P	Girls, Girls, Girls/Sumthin' For Nuthin' (poster p/s)	7
87	Elektra EKR 59V	Girls, Girls, Girls/Sumthin' For Nuthin' ('X-rated' stickered p/s, 3,000 only)	15
87	Elektra EKR 59T	Girls, Girls, Girls/Sumthin' For Nuthin'/Smokin' In The Boys' Room (12", p/s with patch)	8
87	Elektra EKR 59B	Girls, Girls, Girls/Sumthin' For Nuthin'/Smokin' In The Boys' Room (12", box set with patch)	12
87	Elektra EKR 59TP	Girls, Girls, Girls/Sumthin' For Nuthin'/Smokin' In The Boys' Room (12", picture disc)	12
88	Elektra EKR 65TP	You're All I Need/Wild Side/Home Sweet Home/Looks That Kill (12", picture disc)	12
88	Elektra EKR 65TB	You're All I Need/Wild Side/Home Sweet Home/Looks That Kill (12", box set with poster, tour pass & patch)	20
89	Elektra EKR 97	Dr Feelgood/Sticky Sweet (p/s)	5
89	Elektra EKR 97P	Dr Feelgood/Sticky Sweet (shaped picture disc)	10
89	Elektra EKR 97CD	Dr Feelgood/Sticky Sweet/All In The Name Of . . . (3" CD, gatefold card sleeve)	8
89	Elektra EKR 109P	Without You/Live Wire (die-cut picture disc)	15
91	Elektra EKR 136TG	Home Sweet Home (12", gatefold sleeve)	10
91	Elektra EKR 136TP	Home Sweet Home (12" picture disc)	8
94	Elektra EKR 180	Hooligan's Holiday/(mixes) (yellow vinyl, numbered p/s)	6
94	Elektra EKR 180T	Hooligan's Holiday/(mixes) (12", numbered, stickered)	10
83	Elektra 9602 89-1	SHOUT AT THE DEVIL (LP, with bonus 12" picture disc & poster)	20
83	Elektra 9602 89-1	SHOUT AT THE DEVIL (LP, gatefold 'pentagram' black sleeve & inner)	10

MOTÖRHEAD

SINGLES

Year	Label / Cat. No.	Title	Value
77	Stiff BUY 9	White Line Fever/Leaving Here (p/s, "Stiff Boxed Set" 45, later mail-order)	20
77	Chiswick S 13	Motörhead/City Kids (p/s)	8
77	Chiswick NS 13	Motörhead/City Kids (12", p/s)	10
78	Bronze BRO 60	Louie Louie/Tear Ya Down (p/s)	6
79	Bronze BRO 67	Overkill/Too Late, Too Late (p/s, initially with 'Overkill' badge)	10/5
79	Bronze 12 BRO 67	Overkill/Too Late, Too Late (12", p/s)	10
79	Bronze BRO 78	No Class/Like A Nightmare (3 different sleeves)	each 6
79	Bronze BRO 85	Bomber/Over The Top (p/s, some on blue vinyl)	8/5
79	Big Beat NS 13	Motörhead/City Kids (p/s, black, pink, blue, orange or white vinyl)	6-8
80	Big Beat NSP 13	Motörhead/City Kids (p/s, black & white or blue & white picture disc)	8/10
80	Bronze BRO 106	Ace Of Spades/Dirty Love (p/s)	5
80	Bronze BROX 106	Ace Of Spades/Dirty Love (12", 'Xmas' sleeve)	10
81	Lyntone LYN 9661	The Train Kept-A Rollin' (live) (blue flexi free with *Flexipop* mag, issue 7)	10/6
81	Bronze BROP 124	Motörhead (live)/Over The Top (live) (picture disc)	6
82	Bronze BRO 146	Iron Fist/Remember Me I'm Gone (p/s, blue, red or black vinyl)	12/5/5
82	Bronze BRO 151	Stand By Your Man/No Class/Masterplan (p/s, as Lemmy & Wendy O. Williams)	7
83	Bronze BRO 165	I Got Mine/Turn You Round Again (p/s)	5
83	Bronze BROX 165	I Got Mine/Turn You Round Again (12", p/s)	8
83	Bronze BRO 167	Shine/Hoochie Coochie Man (live) (p/s)	5
83	Bronze BROX 167	Shine/Hoochie Coochie Man (live)/Don't Need Religion (live) (12", p/s)	8
83	Bronze BROX 167/ BROX 92	Shine/Hoochie Coochie Man (live)/Don't Need Religion (live)/ THE GOLDEN YEARS (12", p/s, stickered, shrinkwrapped double pack)	18
83	Lyntone LYN 4383	In Their Own Words/BRONZ: Taken By Storm (flexi free with *Kerrang!* mag)	10/5
84	Bronze BRO 185	Killed By Death/Under The Knife (p/s)	5
84	Bronze BROP 185	Killed By Death/Under The Knife (logo skull-shaped picture disc)	15
84	Bronze BROX 185	Killed By Death (Full Length Version)/Under The Knife/Under The Knife (12", stickered p/s, some with poster)	12/8
86	GWR GWR 2	Deaf Forever/On The Road (live) (p/s, some with competition form)	6/5
87	GWR GWR 6	Eat The Rich/Cradle To The Grave (p/s)	5
88	Sounds WAVES 1	Killed By Death (live) (p/s, with others, free with *Sounds* magazine)	8/5
88	GWR GWR 15	Ace Of Spades/Dogs/Traitor (sold at concerts & through fan club, no p/s)	12
90	Epic 656578 0	The One To Sing The Blues/Dead Man's Hand (shaped picture disc)	8
80	Bronze BRO 92	THE GOLDEN YEARS (EP)	5
80	Bronze 12 BRO 92	THE GOLDEN YEARS (12" EP)	8
80	Big Beat SWT 61	BEER DRINKERS EP (12", p/s, black, blue or scarcer pink or orange vinyl)	7-10
80	Big Beat SWT 61	BEER DRINKERS EP (12", p/s, brown vinyl)	15
81	Bronze BROX 116	ST. VALENTINES DAY MASSACRE (10" EP, with Girlschool)	12

MINT VALUE £

ALBUMS

77	Chiswick WIK 2	MOTÖRHEAD (LP, black & silver sleeve with inner, 600 only)	60
77	Chiswick WIK 2	MOTÖRHEAD (LP, black & white laminated sleeve with inner)	12
77	Chiswick CWK 3008	MOTÖRHEAD (LP, white vinyl)	15
79	Bronze BRON 515	OVERKILL (LP, green vinyl)	20
79	Bronze BRON 523	BOMBER (LP, 3 different shades of blue vinyl)	each 15
80	Bronze BRONG 531	ACE OF SPADES (LP, gold vinyl, stickered sleeve)	15
80	Big Beat WIK 2	MOTÖRHEAD (LP, reissue, red or clear vinyl with inner sleeve)	15
81	Bronze BRONG 535	NO SLEEP 'TIL HAMMERSMITH (LP, gold vinyl, stickered sleeve)	15
84	Bronze/Pro MOTOR 1	NO REMORSE (2-LP, leather sleeve with inners)	18
84	Bronze/Pro MOTOC 1	NO REMORSE (cassette, in leather case)	12
86	Castle CLACD 121	NO REMORSE (CD, leather sleeve)	18
86	GWR GWRLP 1	ORGASMATRON (LP, picture disc)	15
91	Epic 467481-0	1916 (LP, picture disc, stickered PVC sleeve)	15
91	Epic 467481 9	1916 (CD, 'tour' picture disc shrinkwrapped with booklet, stickered case)	18
93	Castle/Bronze CTVCD 125	ALL THE ACES (CD, numbered promo, in box with metal skull, 10 only)	400

(see also Lemmy & Upsetters, Sam Gopal, Hawkwind, Girlschool, Wild Horses, Filthy Phil & Fast Eddie, Young & Moody, Rocking Vickers, Blue Goose)

MOTORS

77	Virgin VS 194	Be What You Gotta Be/You Beat The Hell Outa Me (p/s)	5
78	Virgin VS 206	Sensation/The Day I Found A Fiver (p/s, some with £5 note offer)	7/5
78	Virgin VS 219	Airport/Cold Love (live)	5
78	Virgin VS 219-12	Airport/Cold Love (live) (12", blue vinyl, company sleeve)	8
78	Virgin VS 222-12	Forget About You/Picturama/The Middle Bit/Soul Surrender (12", red vinyl, stickered company die-cut sleeve)	8
79	Virgin VS 263	Love And Loneliness/Time For Make Up (10", red, green, blue or yellow vinyl, die-cut p/s)	each 8
78	Virgin V 2089	APPROVED BY THE MOTORS (LP, withdrawn group photo & inner sleeve)	12

(see also Ducks Deluxe, Heroes)

MOTOWN SPINNERS

(see under Detroit Spinners)

MOTT

75	CBS 3528	Monte Carlo/Shout It All Out	6
75	CBS 3741	I Can Show You How It Is/By Tonight	5
75	CBS 4005	It Takes One To Know One/I'll Tell You Something	5

(see also Mott The Hoople)

TONY MOTTOLA

61	London HAZ 2442	STRING BAND STRUM-ALONG (LP, also stereo SAHZ 6231)	10/12

MOTT THE HOOPLE

69	Island WIP 6072	Rock And Roll Queen/Road To Birmingham	25
71	Island WIP 6105	Midnight Lady/The Debt (some in p/s)	12/6
71	Island WIP 6112	Downtown/Home (Is Where I Want To Be)	10
74	CBS 2439	Foxy Foxy/Trudi's Song (cherry vinyl)	6
76	CBS 3963	All The Young Dudes/Roll Away The Stone (p/s)	5
89	CBS 654853 3	All The Young Dudes/Roll Away The Stone/All The Way From Memphis/ The Golden Age Of Rock'n'Roll (3" CD, gatefold card sleeve)	8
69	Island ILPS 9108	MOTT THE HOOPLE (LP, pink label; mispress with 5 alternate mixes & "Road To Birmingham" in place of "Backsliding Fearlessly" or 1 alternate mix with "Road To Birmingham", and "Rock And Roll Queen" correctly credited)	50
69	Island ILPS 9108	MOTT THE HOOPLE (LP, pink label; with "Backsliding Fearlessly" in correct order)	35
70	Island ILPS 9119	MAD SHADOWS (LP, pink label, gatefold sleeve)	22
71	Island ILPS 9144	WILD LIFE (LP, pink rim palm tree label)	22
71	Island ILPS 9178	BRAIN CAPERS (LP, pink rim palm tree label & inner sleeve, some with mask)	40/20
72	CBS 65184	ALL THE YOUNG DUDES (LP, with inner sleeve)	12
72	Island ILPS 9215	ROCK AND ROLL QUEEN (LP, 'pink rim palm tree' label)	12
73	CBS 69038	MOTT (LP, die-cut gatefold sleeve with inner)	12
80	Island IRSP 8	TWO MILES FROM HEAVEN (LP, early copies list "Moving On" on rear sleeve)	25/15

(see also Mott, Ian Hunter, At Last The 1958 Rock & Roll Show, Morgan, Mick Ronson, British Lions, Luther Grosvenor, Charlie Woolfe)

KEN MOULE'S LONDON JAZZ CHAMBER GROUP

70	Ember EMB S 275	Mae West/Zsa Zsa Gabor (some in p/s)	20/10
69	Ember CJS 823	ADAM'S RIB SUITE (LP)	50

(see also London Jazz Chamber Group, Ken Moule Seven)

KEN MOULE SEVEN

55	Esquire 10-417	Hallelujah/Bensonality (78)	8
57	Decca LK 4192	KEN MOULE ARRANGES FOR (LP)	25
58	Decca LK 4261	JAZZ AT TOAD HALL (LP)	30

(see also London Jazz Chamber Group)

MATTIE MOULTRIE

67	CBS 202547	That's How Strong My Love Is/The Saddest Story Ever Told	10

MOUND CITY BLUE BLOWERS

55	HMV 7EG 8096	MOUND CITY BLUE BLOWERS (EP)	8
60	Collector JEL 1	BLUES BLOWING JAZZ VOL. 1 (EP)	10

MOUNTAIN

70	Bell BLL 1112	Mississippi Queen/The Laird	15
70	Bell BLL 1125	Sittin' On A Rainbow/To My Friend	20
71	Island WIP 6119	Roll Over Beethoven/Crossroader	8

MINT VALUE £

70	Bell SBLL 133	MOUNTAIN CLIMBING! (LP)	22
71	Island ILPS 9148	NANTUCKET SLEIGHRIDE (LP, 'pink rim palm tree' label)	15
71	Island ILPS 9179	FLOWERS OF EVIL (LP, 'pink rim palm tree' label)	15
72	Island ILPS 9199	LIVE — THE ROAD GOES ON FOREVER (LP, 'pink rim' label, 'palm tree' logo)	12

(see also West Bruce & Laing, Leslie West, Jolliver Arkansas)

VALERIE MOUNTAIN

61	Columbia DB 4660	Go It Alone/Gentle Christ	7
62	Pye 7N 15450	Some People/Yes You Did	6
62	Pye NEP 24158	SOME PEOPLE — SOUNDTRACK (EP, some tracks by Eagles)	8

(see also Eagles)

MOUNTAIN ASH

75	Witches Bane LKLP 6036	THE HERMIT (LP, private pressing with insert)	165

MOUNTAIN LINE

74	Xtra XTRA 1140	MOUNTAIN LINE (LP)	12
75	Xtra XTRA 1147	HORSEPOWER (LP)	12

MOUNT RUSHMORE

68	Dot DOT 115	Stone Free/She's No Good To Me	5

MOURNING AFTER

94	Detour DR 017	Doin' Me In/Out For The Count (p/s, 100 blue vinyl)	6

MOURNING PHASE

71	Eden	MOURNING PHASE (LP, private pressing)	500
91	Eden EDEN 1	EDEN (LP, reissue of "Mourning Phase")	20

MOUSE

73	Sovereign SOV 122	We Can Make It/It's Happening To Me And You	12
74	Sovereign SOV 127	All The Fallen Teen Angels/Just Came Back	12
73	Sovereign SVNA 7262	LADY KILLER (LP)	125

(see also Ray Russell Quartet, Running Man)

MOUSE & TRAPS

68	President PT 174	L.O.V.E. Love/Beg Borrow And Steal	15
68	President PT 210	Sometimes You Just Can't Win/Crying Inside	12

MOUSEFOLK

88	Tea Time Surf's Up 01	Don't Let It Slip Away/Spinning Round (flexidisc, initially with p/s)	7/5
88	Tea Time Surf's Up 02	HAZY TAMBOURINE DAYS EP (p/s)	7
89	Flowerpot 001	Motorcycle Boy/RISK: This Year's Model (p/s flexi, foldaround p/s)	5

MOUSE ON MARS

97	Too Pure PURE 65S	Cache Coeur Naif/Schnick-Schnack (with Stereolab) (red vinyl, p/s)	6
94	Too Pure PURE 36	VULVALAND (LP, with bonus 4-track 12")	12

ALPHONSE MOUZON

76	United Artists UAG 20005	THE MAN INCOGNITO (LP)	12

ALPHONSE MOUZON & LARRY CORYELL

77	Atlantic K 50382	BACK TOGETHER AGAIN (LP)	12

(see also Larry Coryell)

MOVE

66	Deram DM 109	Night Of Fear/Disturbance	8
67	Deram DM 117	I Can Hear The Grass Grow/Wave The Flag And Stop The Train	8
67	Regal Zonophone RZ 3001	Flowers In The Rain/(Here We Go Round) The Lemon Tree	7
67	Regal Zonophone	Cherry Blossom Clinic/Vote For Me (unissued)	
68	Regal Zonophone RZ 3005	Fire Brigade/Walk Upon The Water	7
68	Regal Zonophone RZ 3012	Wild Tiger Woman/Omnibus	15
69	Regal Zonophone RZ 3015	Blackberry Way/Something	10
69	Regal Zonophone RZ 3021	Curly/This Time Tomorrow	10
70	Regal Zonophone RZ 3026	Brontosaurus/Lightnin' Never Strikes Twice	10
70	Fly BUG 2	When Alice Comes Back To The Farm/What?	6
71	Harvest HAR 5036	Ella James/No Time (unissued)	
71	Harvest HAR 5038	Tonight/Don't Mess Me Up	6
71	Harvest HAR 5043	Chinatown/Down On The Bay	6
72	MagniFly ECHO 104	Fire Brigade/I Can Hear The Grass Grow/Night Of Fear (p/s)	7
72	Harvest HAR 5050	California Man/Do Ya/Ella James	6
74	Harvest HAR 5086	Do Ya/No Time	5
68	Regal Zono. TRZ 2001	SOMETHING ELSE FROM THE MOVE (EP, 33rpm)	55
68	Regal Zono. (S)LRZ 1002	THE MOVE (LP, mono/stereo)	75/50
68	Regal Zono. TA-LRZ 1002	THE MOVE (reel-to-reel, mono only)	12
70	Regal Zono. SLRZ 1012	SHAZAM (LP)	50
70	Fly HIFLY 1	LOOKING ON (LP)	15
71	Harvest SHSP 4013	MESSAGE FROM THE COUNTRY (LP)	15
72	Fly TOOFA 5/6	THE MOVE/SHAZAM (2-LP reissue)	18
74	Harvest SHSP 4035	CALIFORNIA MAN (LP)	12

(see also Roy Wood, Jeff Lynne, ELO, Idle Race, Trevor Burton, Nicky James Movement, Ace Kefford Stand, Grunt Futtock, Rick Price, Uglys, Charlie Wayne)

MOVEMENT

68	Pye 7N 17443	Something You've Got/Tell Her	85
68	Target 7N 17443	Something You've Got/Tell Her (Irish issue)	85
68	Big T BIG 112	Head For The Sun/Mister Mann	85

MOVERS

65	Ska Beat JB 191	Jo-Anne/DON DRUMMOND: Don De Lion	30

MOVIES

75	A&M AMLH 33002	THE MOVIES (LP)	12

(see also Ora, Public Foot The Roman)

MINT VALUE £

MOVIETONE
94 Planet PUNK 003 She Smiled Mandarine Like/Orange Zero (p/s) . . . 6
94 Planet PUNK 009 Mono Valley/Under The 3000 Foot Red Ceiling (p/s, 1,000 only). . . . 5

MOVING BROTHERS
67 Island WI 3049 Darling I Love You/TOMMY McCOOK & SUPERSONICS: Saboo. . . . 22
67 Treasure Isle TI 7018 Darling I Love You/TOMMY McCOOK & SUPERSONICS: Saboo (reissue) . . . 15

MOVING FINGER
68 Mercury MF 1051 Jeremy The Lamp/Pain Of My Misfortune . . . 40
69 Mercury MF 1077 Higher And Higher/Shake And Fingerpop. . . . 10
73 Decca F 13406 So Many People/We're Just As Happy As We Are . . . 8
(see also Anglians)

JUDY MOWATT
73 Gayfeet GS 207 Emergency Call/Emergency Call – Version . . . 8
(see also Jean & Gaytones)

MOWREY JNR. & WATSON
76 Riverdale RRL 1000 BUSKER (LP, with insert). . . . 30

MOXY
77 Power Exchange PXL 011 MOXY II (LP) . . . 12
77 Power Exchange PXL 022 RIDING HIGH (LP) . . . 12
78 Polydor 2480 400 UNDER THE LIGHTS (LP). . . . 12

MOZABITES
80 Rock Steady MICK 010 Soul To Save/Ananta Snake Dance (p/s) . . . 5

MICKEY MOZART QUINTET
59 Columbia DB 4308 Little Dipper/Mexican Hop . . . 8

MP's
80 Moving Plastic WSP 006 Housewives' Choice/Life On The Dole. . . . 5

MR. BLOE
70 DJM DJS 216 Groovin' With Mr. Bloe/Sinful . . . 6
70 DJM DJLPS 409 GROOVIN' WITH MR. BLOE (LP) . . . 15
(see also Harry Pitch)

MR. CALYPSON
71 Jump Up JU 40 Mohammed Ali/SAMSON DE LARK: Undemocratic Rhodesia . . . 6

MR. DYNAMITE
67 Sue WI 4027 Sh'mon/DYNAMITE ORCHESTRA: Sh'mon (Part Two) . . . 40

MR. FLOOD'S PARTY
71 Ember EMB S 312 Compared To What/Unbreakable Toy . . . 10
75 Bulldog BD 6 Compared To What/Unbreakable Toy (reissue) . . . 5
(see also Mike Corbett & Jay Hirsch)

MR. FORD & MR. GOON-BONES
56 London HLU 8355 Ain't She Sweet/MUZZY MARCELLINO: Mary Lou . . . 25
56 London HLU 8355 Ain't She Sweet/MUZZY MARCELLINO: Mary Lou (78). . . . 10
(see also Mr. Goon-Bones & Cavaliers)

MR. FOUNDATION
67 Studio One SO 2001 Have A Good Time/KEN PARKER: See Them A Come . . . 30
67 Studio One SO 2003 All Rudies In Jail (actually by Zoot Simms)/ HORTENSE & ALTON: Easy Squeeze . . . 30
68 Studio One SO 2061 Time-Oh/DUDLEY SIBLEY & PETER AUSTIN: Hole In Your Soul . . . 30
68 Studio One SO 2069 Reggae Rumble/MARCIA GRIFFITHS: You Keep Me On The Move. . . . 30
69 Supreme SUP 201 Time To Pray (actually by Lloyd Robinson)/Young Budd (by Leonard Dillon) . . . 12
(see also Sound Dimension)

MR. FOX
70 Big T BIG 135 Little Woman/Join Us In Our Game . . . 8
70 Transatlantic TRA 226 MR FOX (LP). . . . 50
71 Transatlantic TRA 236 THE GIPSY (LP, gatefold sleeve) . . . 50
75 Transatlantic TRA 303 THE COMPLETE MR FOX (2-LP, reissue of "Mr Fox" & "The Gypsy") . . . 50
(see also Bob Pegg, Bob & Carol Pegg)

MR. MO'S MESSENGERS
67 Columbia DB 8133 Feelin' Good/The Handyman . . . 10

MR. REJECT
71 private pressing MR. REJECT (LP) . . . 40

MR. RUBBISH
93 M.P. MP 002 CHARLES MANSON MEETS CAPTAIN BEEFHEART!!! (LP, unissued)
(see also Breadwinner)

MR. TWISTER & TORNADOS
63 Starlite ST45 099 Big Twist (Parts 1 & 2) . . . 7

MU
74 United Artists UAG 29709 LEMURIAN MUSIC (LP) . . . 35
(see also Captain Beefheart, Fapardokly)

MUCKRAM WAKES
76 Trailer LER 2093 MUCKRAM WAKES (LP). . . . 20

MUD
67 CBS 203002 Flower Power/You're My Mother (some in p/s) . . . 35/22
68 CBS 3355 Up The Airy Mountain/Latter Days. . . . 15
69 Philips BF 1775 Shangri-La/House On The Hill . . . 15
70 Philips 6006 022 Jumping Jehosaphat/Won't Let It Go . . . 10

74	Rak RAK 187	Lonely This Christmas/I Can't Stand It (p/s)	7
75	Rak RAK 194	The Secrets That You Keep/Still Watching The Clock (p/s)	7
76	Rak RR 6	Tiger Feet/Oh Boy/Dynamite (p/s)	5
76	Private Stock PVT 65	Shake It Down/Laugh, Live, Love (p/s)	5
79	Carrere CAR 117	Drop Everything And Run/Taking The Easy Way Out (picture disc)	5

(see also Dum)

MARY MUDD

58	Columbia DB 4144	Stroll Me/Learning To Love (unreleased)	

(see also Mudlarks)

MUDHONEY

89	Blast First BFFP 46	Halloween/SONIC YOUTH: Touch Me I'm Sick (12")	8
92	Reprise WO 137	Suck You Dry/Version/Over The Top/Underide (12")	10
92	Reprise WO 137T	Suck You Dry (LP Version)/Deception Pass (12")	10
95	Reprise 9362 458401	MY BROTHER THE COW (LP, with 6-track EP, [PRO S 7492])	18

(see also Sonic Youth)

MUD HUTTERS

79	Defensive NATO ONE	INFORMATION (EP, foldout p/s, also listed as SRTS/79/CUS 263)	8
79	Defensive NATO TWO	THE DECLARATION (EP, also listed SRTS/79/CUS 496)	8
81	Defensive NATO 3	FACTORY FARMING (LP)	15

MUDIE'S ALL STARS

70	Moodisc HM 3503	Wha Who Wha – Version/G.G. RUSSELL: Wha Who Wha	8

(see also I Roy, Eternals, King Cannon, John Holt, Niney, Jolly Boys, Jo Jo Bennett)

MUDLARKS

58	Columbia DB 4064	Mutual Admiration Society/A New Love	12
58	Columbia DB 4099	Lollipop/Young Dove's Calling	7
58	Columbia DB 4133	Book Of Love/Yea, Yea	7
58	Columbia DB 4190	There's Never Been A Night/Lightnin' Never Strikes Twice	7
58	Columbia DB 4210	Which Witch Doctor/My Grandfather's Clock	8
58	Columbia DB 4210	Which Witch Doctor/My Grandfather's Clock (78)	8
59	Columbia DB 4250	Abdul The Bulbul Amer Cha Cha/The Love Game	7
59	Columbia DB 4250	Abdul The Bulbul Amer Cha Cha/The Love Game (78)	10
59	Columbia DB 4291	Time Flies/Tell Him No	7
59	Columbia DB 4331	Waterloo/Mary	7
59	Columbia DB 4331	Waterloo/Mary (78)	15
59	Columbia DB 4374	Tennessee/True Love, True Love	6
60	Columbia DB 4417	Never Marry A Fishmonger/Candy	6
60	Columbia DB 4513	(You've Got To) Move Two Mountains/You're Free To Go	6
61	Columbia DB 4636	When Mexico Gave Up The Rumba/Toy Balloon	6
61	Columbia DB 4708	The Mountain's High/Don't Gamble With Love	6
62	Columbia DB 4788	Them Twistin' Bones/Coney Island Washboard	6
62	Columbia DB 4861	Mañana Pasado Mañana/March Of The Broken Hearts	6
62	Decca F 11537	I've Been Everywhere/Just The Snap Of Your Fingers	6
63	Decca F 11601	The Little Cracked Bell Of San Raquel/La De Da	6
64	Fontana TF 495	Walk Around/Here's Another Day	6
58	Columbia SEG 7854	THE MUDLARKS! (EP)	50

(see also Mary Mudd)

MUGWUMPS

64	Warner Bros WB 144	I'll Remember Tonight/I Don't Wanna Know	10
67	Warner Bros W 1697	THE MUGWUMPS — AN HISTORICAL RECORDING (LP)	25
70	Valiant VS 134	THE MUGWUMPS — AN HISTORICAL RECORDING (LP, reissue)	15

(see also Mamas & Papas, Mama Cass Elliot, Lovin' Spoonful, Zalman Yanovsky)

BOBBY MUIR & BLUEBEATS

60	Blue Beat BB 20	Baby What You Done Me Wrong/Go Pretty Baby Go (as Blue Beats)	15
61	Blue Beat BB 44	Honey Please/That's My Girl (as Bobby Kingdom & Blue Beats)	15
62	Blue Beat BB 77	Brand New Automobile/Spanish Town Twist (as Bobby Kingdom & Blue Beats)	15

JAMIE MUIR & DEREK BAILEY

81	Incus INCUS 41	DART DRUG (LP)	50

(see also Derek Bailey)

LINDSAY MUIR'S UNTAMED

66	Planet PLF 113	Daddy Long Legs/Trust Yourself A Little Bit (initially with Planet company sleeve)	125/105

(see also Untamed)

MULCAYS

55	London HLF 8188	Harbour Lights/Dipsy Doodle	35
55	London HLF 8188	Harbour Lights/Dipsy Doodle (78)	10
54	London REP 1016	MERRY CHRISTMAS (EP)	15
56	London REF 1046	HARMONICS BY THE MULCAYS (EP)	15

MULDOONS

65	Decca F 12164	I'm Lost Without You/Come Back Now Baby	30

MULESKINNERS

65	Fontana TF 527	Back Door Man/Need Your Lovin'	140
65	Keepoint KEE-EP-7104	MULESKINNERS (EP, private pressing, no p/s)	750

(see also Small Faces, Faces)

MULL HISTORICAL SOCIETY

00s	Tugboat Records TUG 028	Barcode Bypass/Mull Historical Society (p/s, 2000 only)	10

MOON MULLICAN

51	Vogue V 9013	Cherokee Boogie/Love Is The Light That Leads Me Home (78)	50
56	Parlophone DP 503	Yearning (Just For You)/Put Your Arms Around Me, Honey (export 78)	30
56	Parlophone DP 512	San Antonio Rose/Cedarwood Blues (export 78)	30

MINT VALUE £

56	Parlophone MSP 6254	Seven Nights To Rock/Honolulu Rock-A Roll-A (with Boyd Bennett & His Rockets)	500
56	Parlophone R 4195	Seven Nights To Rock/Honolulu Rock-A Roll-A (with Boyd Bennett & His Rockets) (78)	75
59	Parlophone GEP 8794	COUNTRY ROUND UP (EP)	60
50s	Parlophone CGEP 13	MOON MULLICAN (EP, export issue)	45
50s	Parlophone CGEP 15	PIANO BREAKDOWN (EP, export issue, company sleeve)	45

(see also Boyd Bennett & His Rockets)

GERRY MULLIGAN

56	Vogue V 2157	Frenesi/Nights At The Turntable	6
56	Vogue V 2158	Bernie's Tune/Freeway	6
56	Vogue V 2159	Carioca/My Funny Valentine	6
56	Vogue V 2225	Lullaby Of The Leaves/Walkin' Shoes	6
56	Vogue V 2257	Darn That Dream/I'm Beginning To See The Light	6
56	Vogue V 2258	Swing House/I May Be Wrong	6
56	Vogue V 2259	Jeru/Love Or Leave Me	6
56	Vogue V 2260	Bark For Barksdale/Moonlight In Vermont	6
56	Vogue V 2304	Carson City Stage/Cherry	6
56	Vogue V 2305	I Can't Believe That You're In Love With Me/Lady Be Good (with Lee Konitz)	6
56	Vogue V 2306	Motel/Makin' Whopee	6
56	Vogue V 2324	Soft Shoe/Aren't You Glad You're You?	6
56	Vogue V 2337	Line For Lyons/Limelight	6
59	London HLT 8901	I Want To Live — Theme/Black Nightgown (as Gerry Mulligan Combo)	8
59	London HLT 8901	I Want To Live — Theme/Black Nightgown (as Gerry Mulligan Combo) (78)	20
60	HMV POP 734	Line For Lyons/Standstill (with Paul Desmond Quartet)	5
60	HMV POP 769	I'm Gonna Go Fishin' (both sides)	5
60	Philips JAZ 102	News From Blueport/Utter Chaos (p/s)	5
55	Capitol EAP1 439	PRESENTING GERRY MULLIGAN AND HIS TENTETTE (EP)	8
55	Capitol EAP2 439	PRESENTING GERRY MULLIGAN AND HIS TENTETTE (EP)	8
58	Emarcy ERE 1553	PRESENTING THE GERRY MULLIGAN SEXTET (EP)	8
58	Emarcy ERE 1556	PRESENTING THE GERRY MULLIGAN SEXTET VOL. 2 (EP)	8
58	Emarcy ERE 1560	PRESENTING THE GERRY MULLIGAN SEXTET VOL. 3 (EP)	8
58	Emarcy ERE 1574	MAINSTREAM VOL. 1 (EP)	8
58	Emarcy ERE 1575	MAINSTREAM VOL. 2 (EP)	8
60	Mercury ZEP 10071	MULLIGAN MANIA (EP)	8
53	Capitol LC 6621	THE GERRY MULLIGAN TENTETTE — ROCKER (10" LP)	22
53	Vogue LDE 029	THE GERRY MULLIGAN QUARTET VOL. 1 (10" LP)	22
53	Vogue LDE 030	THE GERRY MULLIGAN QUARTET VOL. 2 (10" LP)	22
53	Vogue LDE 031	THE GERRY MULLIGAN QUARTET VOL. 3 (10" LP)	22
54	Vogue LDE 075	THE GERRY MULLIGAN QUARTET (10" LP)	22
54	Vogue LDE 083	THE GERRY MULLIGAN QUARTET VOL. 4 (10" LP)	22
54	Esquire 20-032	GERRY MULLIGAN ALLSTARS — MULLIGAN'S TOO (10" LP)	25
55	Vogue LDE 156	GERRY MULLIGAN QUARTET WITH LEE KONITZ (10" LP)	22
56	Esquire 32-014	GERY MULLIGAN ALLSTARS (LP)	18
56	Vogue LAE 12006	THE GERRY MULLIGAN QUARTET (LP)	18
56	Vogue LAE 12015	THE GERRY MULLIGAN QUARTET (LP)	18
56	Emarcy EJL 101	PRESENTING THE GERRY MULLIGAN SEXTET (LP)	18
57	Emarcy EJL 1259	MAINSTREAM OF JAZZ (LP, by Gerry Mulligan Sextet)	18
58	Columbia Clef 33CX 10113	GERRY MULLIGAN AND PAUL DESMOND QUARTET (LP)	15
58	HMV CLP 1204	PHIL SUNKEL'S "JAZZ CONCERTO GROSSO" (LP, with Bob Brookmeyer)	15
59	Philips SBBL 552	WHAT IS THERE TO SAY? (LP, stereo)	15
59	Vogue SEA 5006	GERRY MULLIGAN SONGBOOK (LP, stereo)	15
59	Vogue SEA 5007	REUNION WITH CHET BAKER (LP, stereo, as Gerry Mulligan Quartet)	15
59	London Jazz LTZT 15161	I WANT TO LIVE (LP, with Shelly Manne)	12
60	HMV CLP 1373	GERRY MULLIGAN MEETS BEN WEBSTER (LP)	12
61	HMV CLP 1432	THE CONCERT JAZZ BAND (LP, also stereo CSD 1351)	12/15
61	Vocalion LAE 12268	THE GENIUS OF GERRY MULLIGAN (LP)	12
62	HMV CLP 1465	GERRY MULLIGAN MEETS JOHNNY HODGES (LP, also stereo CSD 1372)	12/15
62	HMV CLP 1488	AT THE VILLAGE VANGUARD (LP, also stereo CSD 1396)	12/15
62	Riverside RLP 12-247	MULLIGAN MEETS MONK (LP, with Thelonious Monk)	15
62	HMV CLP 1549	A CONCERT IN JAZZ (LP, also stereo CSD 1432)	12/15
62	HMV CLP 1585	ON TOUR (LP, with Zoot Sims)	12
60s	Fontana FJL 133	SAXY (LP)	12

(see also Gerry Mulligan, Chet Baker, Shelly Manne, Annie Ross)

MICK MULLIGAN'S JAZZ BAND

50	Tempo AA 66	Candy Lips/Savoy Blues (12" 78, as Mick Mulligan's Magnolia Jazz Band)	7
56	Tempo A 139	In A Shanty In Old Shanty Town/Snag It	6
56	Tempo A 143	Oriental Strut/Big House Blues	6
56	Tempo A 152	Beale Street Blues/Raver's Edge	6
57	Tempo A 155	St. James' Infirmary/After A While	6
57	Tempo A 164	Old Stack-O-Lee Blues/Double Dee	6
50s	Saga STP 7020	YOUNG AND HEALTHY (EP)	18
55	Tempo EXA 25	MICK MULLIGAN'S JAZZ BAND (EP)	10
56	Tempo EXA 37	MICK MULLIGAN'S JAZZ BAND (EP)	18
56	Tempo EXA 41	GEORGE MELLY WITH MICK MULLIGAN'S JAZZ BAND (EP)	20
56	Tempo EXA 47	DOOM (EP, with George Melly)	18
57	Tempo EXA 54	MICK MULLIGAN'S JAZZ BAND (EP)	15
58	Parlophone GEP 8750	MICK BLOWS (EP)	18
57	Tempo TAP 14	JAZZ AT THE RAILWAY ARMS (LP, with George Melly)	50
59	Pye Jazz NJL 21	MEET MICK MULLIGAN (LP)	30
59	Parlophone PMC 1103	THE SAINTS MEET THE SINNERS (LP, with George Melly & Saints Jazz Band)	20

(see also George Melly)

MUM

02	Fat Cat 7FAT 06	Green Grass Of Tunnel/In Through The Lamp (p/s)	5

MUM & DAD

99 Twisted Nerve TN 006 Donington/13th Chime/Monster Truck (p/s) . . . 15

GENE MUMFORD

58 Philips PB 862 More Than You Know/Please Give Me One More Chance . . . 8

MUNGO JERRY

70 Dawn DNX 2502 In The Summertime/Mighty Man/Dust Pneumonia Blues (p/s) . . . 8
70 Pye 7N 2502 In The Summertime/Mighty Man/Dust Pneumonia Blues (jukebox issue) . . . 18
71 Dawn DNX 2505 Baby Jump/The Man Behind The Piano/Live From Hollywood: Maggie/ Midnight Special/Mighty Man (p/s) . . . 7
71 Dawn DNX 2510 Lady Rose/Have A Whiff On Me/Milk Cow Blues/Little Louis (p/s, withdrawn) . . . 8
71 Dawn DNX 2510 Lady Rose/She Rowed/Milk Cow Blues/Little Louis (re-pressing with different track, p/s) . . . 8
71 Dawn 7N 2513 You Don't Have To Be In The Army To Fight In The War/We Shall Be Free (jukebox issue) . . . 6
71 Dawn DNX 2513 You Don't Have To Be In The Army To Fight In The War/The Sun Is Shining/ O'Reilly/We Shall Be Free (p/s) . . . 8
72 Dawn DNX 2514 Open Up/Going Back Home/I Don't Wanna Go Back To School/ No Girl Reaction (p/s) . . . 7
72 Dawn 7N 2514 Open Up/Going Back Home (jukebox issue) . . . 10
72 Dawn DNX 2515 My Girl And Me/Summer's Gone/46 And On/It's A Goodie Boogie Woogie (p/s) . . . 8
73 Dawn DNS 1037 Alright, Alright, Alright/Little Miss Hipshake . . . 5
73 Dawn DNS 1051 Wild Love/Glad I'm A Rocker . . . 5
74 Dawn DNS 1092 All Dressed Up And No Place To Go/Shake 'Til I Break/ Too Fast To Live And Too Young To Die/Burnin' Up (p/s) . . . 8
75 Dawn DNS 1113 In The Summertime/She Rowed . . . 6
75 Polydor 2058 603 Can't Get Over Loving You/Let's Go . . . 6
75 Polydor 2058 654 Hello Nadine/Bottle Of Beer . . . 6
76 Polydor 2058 759 Don't Let Go/Give Me Bop . . . 6
77 Polydor 2058 868 Heavy Foot Stomp/That's My Baby . . . 6
77 Polydor 2058 947 We're O.K./Let's Make It . . . 6
77 Pye Big Deal BD 114 In The Summertime/Mighty Man/Baby Jump/Lady Rose (12" EP) . . . 10
79 Pye Flashbacks FBS 7 In The Summertime/Baby Jump (yellow vinyl, p/s) . . . 8
80 Satellite SATS 1001 What's Her Name, What's Her Number?/Why D'You Lie To Me . . . 8
80 Satellite/Scratch HS 406 MUNGO'S SUMMER FUN PACKAGE (maxi-single, p/s) . . . 10
83 Mach 1 MAGIC 008 There Goes My Heart Again/Thinking Of You (featuring Ray Dorset & Tarts) . . . 8
85 Orbit TRIP 4 Sunshine Reggae/Nightlife (reissue of Horizon 45; as Mungo Jerry & Horizon) . . 10
87 Illegal MUNG 1 In The Summertime '87/Got A Job (as Mungo Jerry & Brothers Grimm, p/s) . . . 5
96 Fan Club 12/1 Sugar In The Bowl/In The Summertime (fan club only, white label, autographed) . . 5
70 Dawn DNLS 3008 MUNGO JERRY (LP, gatefold sleeve, with 3-D glasses) . . . 22
71 Dawn DNLS 3020 ELECTRONICALLY TESTED (LP, gatefold sleeve) . . . 18
71 Dawn DNLS 3028 YOU DON'T HAVE TO BE IN THE ARMY (LP, gatefold sleeve, with lyric insert) . . . 18
72 Dawn DNLS 3041 BOOT POWER (LP, with 'Dennis The Menace' or 'gun' gatefold sleeve) . . . 15/12
73 Dawn DNLS 3045 MUNGO JERRY'S GREATEST HITS (LP) . . . 12
74 Dawn DNLS 3501 LONG LEGGED WOMAN (LP) . . . 12
76 Polydor 2383 364 IMPALA SAGA (LP) . . . 12
77 Polydor 2383 435 LOVIN' IN THE ALLEYS, FIGHTIN' IN THE STREETS (LP) . . . 12
80 Satellite SATLP 1001 SIX-A-SIDE (LP) . . . 12

(see also Ray Dorset, Good Earth, King Earl Boogie Band, Horizon, Made In England, Jigilo Jug Band, P. King, Paul King, P. Rufus King, Russian Roulette, First Impression, Good Earth)

RAY MUNNINGS

79 Tammi TAM 102 It Could Happen To You/Let's Boogie . . . 12
79 Tammi TAM 103 Funky Nassau/Jump In The Water . . . 10

CAROLINE MUNRO

67 Columbia DB 8189 Tar And Cement/The Sporting Life . . . 12

CAROLINE MUNRO

85 Numa NU 5 Pump Me Up/The Picture (p/s) . . . 6
85 Numa NUM 5 Pump Me Up (Ext. 6.09)/The Picture/Pump Me Up (4.00 7" Version) (12", p/s) . . . 10

(see also Gary Numan)

HAL MUNRO

58 Embassy WB 284 Breathless/Wear My Ring Around Your Neck . . . 6
59 Embassy WB 336 C'mon Everybody/It's Late . . . 6
59 Embassy WB 340 Dream Lover/Where Were You . . . 5
59 Embassy WB 386 You Got What It Takes/California Here I Come . . . 5
60 Embassy WB 401 Good Timin'/I Wanna Go Home . . . 5
60 Embassy WB 401 Good Timin'/I Wanna Go Home (78) . . . 8

(see also Neville Taylor)

JANET MUNRO & SEAN CONNERY

59 Top Rank JAR 163 Pretty Irish Girl/Ballamaquilty's Band . . . 10
59 Top Rank JAR 163 Pretty Irish Girl/Ballamaquilty's Band (78) . . . 12

LEE MUNRO

86 Numa NU 20 Stereo Headphones/Give Me Your Love (p/s) . . . 6
86 Numa NUM 20 Stereo Headphones (Extended Version)/Give Me Your Love/ Stereo Headphones (7" Version) (12", p/s) . . . 10

PATRICE MUNSEL

53 HMV 7M 152 Is This The Beginning Of Love/The Melba Waltz . . . 7

ADRIAN MUNSEY

79 Virgin VS 266 C'Est Sheep (Part 1)/C'Est Sheep (Part 2) (p/s) . . . 6
79 Virgin VS 266-12 C'Est Sheep (Part 1)/C'Est Sheep (Part 2) (12", p/s) . . . 8

(see also Sparks)

MINT VALUE £

STEPHAN MUNSON & FRIENDS
82 Rhythmic RMNS 2 — And David Cried/And Dem Bahnhoff (fold-out photocopied p/s) ... 8

JERRY MURAD'S HARMONICATS
59 Mercury ZEP 10001 — IT'S CHA CHA TIME (EP) ... 8
67 CBS 63133 — GREATEST HITS (LP) ... 12

MURDER INC.
80 MIL MIL 1 — SOUNDS SO FALSE (EP) ... 8
(see also Business)

MURDER THE DISTURBED
79 Small Wonder SMALL 17 — GENETIC DISRUPTION (EP) ... 7

BILLY MURE (ORCHESTRA)
59 Felsted AF 120 — Tea & Trumpets/A String Of Trumpets ... 6
59 Felsted AF 120 — Tea & Trumpets/A String Of Trumpets (78) ... 12
60 Top Rank JAR 344 — Jambalaya/Kaw Liga (as Billy Mure Orchestra) ... 6
59 RCA RCX 158 — SUPERSONICS IN FLIGHT (EP, also stereo SRC 7032) ... 12/20
59 Felsted GEP 1006 — THE VERSATILE BILLY MURE (EP) ... 8
60 MGM MGM-C 800 — SUPERSONIC GUITARS (LP) ... 12
60 MGM MGM-C 835/CS 5011 — SUPERSONIC GUITARS VOL. 2 (LP, mono/stereo) ... 12/15
(see also Supersonics)

MURGATROYD BAND
71 Decca F 13256 — Magpie (Theme From The TV Series)/Twice A Week (some with p/s) ... 25/15
(see also Spencer Davis Group, Ray Fenwick)

MURMAIDS
63 Stateside SS 247 — Popsicles And Icicles/Comedy And Tragedy ... 20

MICHAEL MURPHEY
72 Regal Zonophone RZ 3062 — Boy From The Country/Geronimo's Cadillac ... 5
72 Regal Zono. SRZA 8512 — GERONIMO'S CADILLAC (LP) ... 12
73 EMI EMA 754 — COSMIC COWBOY SOUVENIR (LP) ... 12

ARTHUR MURPHY
59 Parlophone R 4523 — Sixteen Candles/Molly Malone ... 10
59 Parlophone R 4523 — Sixteen Candles/Molly Malone (78) ... 8

DELIA MURPHY
57 HMV 7EG 8295 — DELIGHTFUL DELIA (EP) ... 8

ELLIOT MURPHY
74 Polydor 2391 100 — AQUASHOW (LP) ... 12

LYLE MURPHY
58 Contemporary LAC 12135 — GONE WITH THE WOODWINDS (LP) ... 12

MARK MURPHY
57 Brunswick 05701 — Goodbye Baby Blues/The Right Kind Of Woman ... 6
58 Capitol CL 14962 — Belong To Me/Don't Cry My Love ... 5
60 Capitol CL 15117 — Send For Me/Come To Me ... 5
63 Riverside RIF 106905 — Like Love/Fly Away My Sadness ... 5
63 Riverside RIF 106908 — Fly Me To The Moon/Why Don't You Do Right ... 12
65 Fontana TF 572 — High On Windy Hill/Broken Heart ... 5
67 Fontana TF 803 — (Ain't That) Just Like A Woman/Do You Wonder If I Love You ... 5
69 Pye 7N 17661 — Come Back To Me/Dear Heart ... 5
57 Brunswick LAT 8172 — MEET MARK MURPHY (LP) ... 15
60 Capitol (S)T 5011 — HIT PARADE (LP) ... 12
64 Fontana (S)TL 5217 — MARK TIME! (LP) ... 12
66 Immediate IMLP/IMSP 004 — WHO CAN I TURN TO (LP) ... 40

NOEL MURPHY
67 Fontana TL 5450 — NYA-A-A-H! (LP) ... 12
73 Village Thing VTS 25 — MURF (LP) ... 12

ROSE MURPHY
52 Oriole/Mercury MG 10004 — SONGS BY ROSE MURPHY (10" LP) ... 18

TURK MURPHY & WALLY ROSE
56 Philips BBL 7051 — THE MUSIC OF JELLY ROLL MORTON (LP) ... 12

TURK MURPHY'S JAZZ BAND
52 Good Time Jazz 31 — By & By/St. James' Infirmary (78) ... 7

ALEX MURRAY
60 Decca F 11203 — Teen Angel/Paper Doll ... 15
60 Decca F 11225 — All On My Own/String Along ... 7
61 Decca F 11345 — When You Walked Out/Send For Me ... 7
(see also Most Brothers)

LADY MURRAY
66 Clan 597 002 — Mister Abercrombie Taught Me/In My Imagination ... 7
(see also Grazina, Mr & Mrs Murray)

MARTIN MURRAY
66 Pye 7N 17070 — I Know What I Want/Goodbye Baby ... 10
(see also Honeycombs, Lemmings)

MICKEY MURRAY
67 Polydor 56738 — Shout Bama Lama/Lonely Room ... 7

MISTER MURRAY
65 Fontana TF 623 — Down Came The Rain/Whatever Happened To Music? ... 12
66 Fontana TF 674 — I Drink To Your Memory/I Was A Good Song ... 6
(see also Mitch Murray Clan, Mr & Mrs Murray)

MITCH MURRAY CLAN

66 Clan 597 001 Skyliner/Cherokee . . . 12
(see also Mister Murray, Mr & Mrs Murray)

MR & MRS MURRAY

68 CBS 3633 You're Outa Your Mind/A Little Bit Of You . . . 6
(see also Mitch Murray Clan, Lady Murray, Grazina, Mister Murray)

PETE MURRAY

(see under Pascal Murray, Brian Matthew & Pete Murray)

RUBY MURRAY

55 Columbia SCM 5162 Softly, Softly/What Could Be More Beautiful . . . 25
55 Columbia SCM 5165 Spring, Spring, Spring/Goin' Co'tin (with Ray Burns, Diana Decker & Ronnie Harris) . . . 15
55 Columbia SCM 5169 If Anyone Finds This, I Love You (with Anne Warren)/Before We Know It . . . 20
55 Columbia SCM 5180 Evermore/Bambino . . . 20
56 Columbia SCM 5222 Two Rivers/Boy Meets Girl (with Norman Wisdom) . . . 18
56 Columbia SCM 5225 For Now, For Ever/Oh, Please Make Him Jealous . . . 18
56 Columbia DB 3810 Teddy O'Neil/It Only Hurts For A Little While . . . 18
57 Columbia DB 3849 Knock On Any Door/True Love . . . 18
57 Columbia DB 3852 In Love/O'Malley's Tango . . . 15
57 Columbia DB 3911 From The First Hello — To The Last Goodbye/Heart . . . 15
57 Columbia DB 3933 Mr. Wonderful/Pretty, Pretty . . . 15
57 Columbia DB 3955 Scarlet Ribbons/Macushla Mine . . . 12
57 Columbia DB 3994 Little White Lies/Passing Strangers . . . 8
57 Columbia DB 4042 Ain't That A Grand And Glorious Feeling/I'll Remember Today . . . 8
58 Columbia DB 4075 Forgive Me My Darling/Keep Smiling At Trouble . . . 8
58 Columbia DB 4108 In My Life/Nora Malone (Call Me By 'Phone) . . . 8
58 Columbia DB 4192 Real Love/Little One . . . 8
58 Columbia DB 4192 Real Love/Little One (78) . . . 8
59 Columbia DB 4266 Nevertheless (I'm In Love With You)/Who Knows . . . 7
59 Columbia DB 4305 Goodbye Jimmy, Goodbye/The Humour Is On Me Now . . . 8
55 Columbia SEG 7588 RUBY IS A GEM (EP) . . . 20
56 Columbia SEG 7620 EVERYBODY'S SWEETHEART NO. 1 (EP) . . . 18
56 Columbia SEG 7631 EVERYBODY'S SWEETHEART NO. 2 (EP) . . . 18
56 Columbia SEG 7636 EVERYBODY'S SWEETHEART NO. 3 (EP) . . . 18
57 Columbia SEG 7748 MUCUSHLA MINE (EP) . . . 18
59 Columbia SEG 7952 ENDEARING YOUNG CHARMS (EP) . . . 18
60 Columbia SEG 8052 LOVE'S OLD SWEET SONG (EP, also stereo ESG 7830) . . . 18/22
55 Columbia 33S 1079 WHEN IRISH EYES ARE SMILING (10" LP) . . . 22
58 Columbia 33S 1135 ENDEARING YOUNG CHARMS (10" LP) . . . 35
60 Columbia 33SX 1201 RUBY (LP, also stereo SCX 3289) . . . 22/30
(see also Norman Wisdom & Ruby Murray, Ray Burns, Ronnie Harris, Diana Decker)

MAC MURROUGH

72 Polydor SHADES OF MAC MURROUGH (LP, Ireland-only) . . . 250
74 Polydor 2908 014 MAC MURROUGH (LP, with insert, Ireland-only) . . . 300
77 Polydor 2908 030 MERRY AND FINE (LP, Ireland-only) . . . 150

JOHN MURTAUGH

70 Polydor 2482 015 BLUES CURRENT (LP) . . . 20

JUNIOR MURVIN

(see under Junior Soul)

MUSE

99 Mushroom MUSH 50S Uno/Agitated (p/s, clear vinyl) . . . 25
99 Mushroom MUSE 1 Uno/Jimmy Kane/Forced In/Agitated (minimax CD, with slipcase) . . . 10
99 Mushroom MUSH 50CDS Uno/Jimmy Kane/Forced In (CD) . . . 8
99 Mushroom MUSH 58 CDS Cave/Twin/Cave (Remix) (CD, part 1 of 2-CD set) . . . 8
99 Mushroom MUSH 58 CDX Cave/Host/Coma (CD, part 2 of 2-CD set) . . . 8
99 Mushroom MUSH 66S Muscle Museum/Escape (p/s) . . . 8
99 Mushroom MUSH 66S Muscle Museum/Minimum (clear vinyl, autographed p/s, 1000 only) . . . 25
99 Mushroom MUSH 68S Sunburn/(Live Acoustic Version) (stickered p/s, clear vinyl) . . . 8
00 Mushroom MUSH 72S Unintended/Sober (p/s, clear vinyl) . . . 8
01 Mushroom MUSH 89S Plug In Baby/Nature 1 (p/s) . . . 7
01 Mushroom MUSH 92S New Born/Shrinking Universe (p/s, limited issue) . . . 7
01 Mushroom MUSH 92T New Born/Sunburn (Timo Maas Sunstroke Remix)/(Breakz Again Mix (12", p/s) . 10
01 Taste/Mushroom MUSH 968 Bliss/Hyper Chondriac Music (p/s) . . . 8
01 Mushroom MUSH 104S Dead Star/In Your World (p/s) . . . 7
98 Dangerous DREX CDEP 103 MUSE EP (CD, 999 copies) . . . 110
98 Dangerous DREX CDEP 104 MUSCLE MUSEUM EP: Sober/Uno/Unintended/Instant Messenger/Muscle Museum # 2/Muscle Museum (CD, 999 copies) . . . 90
00 Mushroom MUSH 59LP SHOWBIZ (2-LP, clear vinyl, gatefold sleeve, with inners) . . . 20
01 Mushroom MUSH 93LP ORIGIN OF SYMMETRY (2-LP, gatefold sleeve, with lyric inner sleeves, 1500 only) . . . 18
01 Mushroom MUSH 105CDS HULLABALOO LIVE (CD, with bonus CD, limited issue) . . . 18

MUSHROOM

73 Hawk HASP 320 Devil Among The Tailors/Sun Ni Dhuibir/King Of Ireland's Daughter . . . 25
74 Hawk HASP 340 Kings And Queens/Met A Friend . . . 25
73 Hawk HALPX 116 EARLY ONE MORNING (LP, some with poster inner) . . . 375/300
(see also Joe O'Donnell)

MUSIC

01 Fierce Panda NING 107 Take The Long Road And Walk It/The Walls Get Smaller (p/s, 1,000 only) . . . 35
01 Fierce Panda NINGT 107 Take The Long Road And Walk It/The Walls Get Smaller (12", p/s, 250 only) . . . 50
01 Hut HUTT 145 THE MUSIC EP: You Might As Well Try To Fuck Me/Karma/Treat Me Right On/Too High (12", p/s, with inner) . . . 18

MINT VALUE £

02	Hut HUTT 152	THE PEOPLE EP: Let Love Be The Healer/Life/Jag Tune (12", p/s)	12
02	Hut HUT 158	Take The Long Road And Walk It/Alone (picture disc, stickered poly sleeve)	7
03	Hut HUT 164	The Truth Is No Words/What's It For (picture disc, stickered poly sleeve)	5

MUSICAL THEATRE

70	Pye Intl. NSPL 28128	A REVOLUTIONARY REVELATION (LP)	12

MUSIC BOX

72	Westwood MRS 013	SONGS OF SUNSHINE (LP)	110

MUSIC DOCTORS

69	Downtown DT 447	Music Doctor (Parts 1 & 2)	8
70	J-Dan JDN 4402	Electric Shock/KING DENNIS: Black Robin	8
70	J-Dan JDN 4403	Bush Doctor/Lick Your Stick	8
70	J-Dan JDN 4411	The Wild Bunch/ISRAELITES: Born To Be Strong	8
70	J-Dan JDN 4414	In The Summertime/Foundation	6
70	J-Dan JDN 4417	Discretion Version/Doctor Dan, Boy Friday And Friend	6
71	Downtown DT 479	The Pliers (Parts 1 & 2)	6
70	Trojan TBL 117	REGGAE IN THE SUMMERTIME (LP)	20

(see also Dennis Lowe, Audrey, Desmond Riley, Megatons, Prince Of Darkness, Gene Rondo)

MUSIC EMPORIUM

83	Psycho PSYCHO 11	MUSIC EMPORIUM (LP)	15

MUSIC EXPLOSION

67	Stateside SS 2028	A Little Bit O' Soul/I See The Light	18
67	Stateside SS 2054	Sunshine Games/Can't Stop Now	10
67	Philips BF 1547	Little Black Egg/Stay By My Side	7
69	London HLP 10272	A Little Bit O' Soul/Everybody	6
67	London HA-P/SH-P 8352	A LITTLE BIT O' SOUL (LP)	30

MUSICIANS

66	King KG 1055	Jaunty Joe/The Chelsea Set	7

MUSIC MACHINE

67	Pye International 7N 25407	Talk Talk/Come On In	50
67	Pye International 7N 25414	The People In Me/Masculine Intuition	40

MUSIC SPECIALISTS

70	London HLJ 10309	Dynamic Pressure/Flip	7

MUSIC TAPES

98	Earworm WORM 32	The Television Tells Us/Freeing Song By Reindeer (p/s, pop-up sleeve with 2 inserts, 1,500 copies only)	5

MUSIC THROUGH SIX

68	Domain D3	Riff Raff/ROY DOCKER: Mellow Moonlight	7

(see also Jason Sims & Music Through Six)

MUSKETEER GRIPWEED & THIRD TROOP

66	United Artists UP 1196	How I Won The War/Aftermath (stock copies or demos; stock are much rarer)	1000/120

(see also John Lennon)

MUSKETEERS

69	Philips BF 1773	Fight/Magnifico	5

CHARLIE MUSSELWHITE BLUES BAND

69	Vanguard SVRL 19012	STONE BLUES (LP)	22

VIDO MUSSO & HIS ORCHESTRA

54	London HL 8077	Vido's Boogie/Blue Night (78)	8

BOOTS MUSSULLI QUARTET

54	Capitol KC 65002	Diga Diga Doo/Lullaby In Rhythm	6
54	Capitol KC 65002	Diga Diga Doo/Lullaby In Rhythm (78)	8
55	Capitol KPL 106	THE BOOTS MUSSULLI QUARTET (10" LP)	12

(see also Stan Kenton)

MUSTANG

67	Parlophone R 5579	Why/Here, There And Everywhere	25

MUS-TWANGS

61	Mercury AMT 1140	Roch Lomond/Marie	12

MUTANTS

77	Rox ROX 002	Boss Man/Back Yard Boys (p/s)	6
78	Rox ROX 005	School Teacher/Hard Time/Lady (p/s, red vinyl)	6

MUTE DRIVERS

80s	Mute Drivers MD 001	MUTE DRIVERS (LP, with insert in handmade painted sleeve, 300 only)	15

(see also Anonymes)

MUTT 'N' JEFF

66	Decca F 12335	Don't Nag Me Ma/Strolling The Blues	12

µ-ZIQ

93	Rephlex CAT 018	Bluff Limbo (remixes) (2 x 12", 800 only)	40

(see also Rude Ass Tinker)

MY BLOODY VALENTINE

86	Fever FEV 5X	No Place To Go/Moonlight (p/s)	100
86	Fever FEV 5	GEEK! (12" EP)	30
86	Kaleid. Sound KS 101	THE NEW RECORD BY MY BLOODY VALENTINE (12" EP)	60
87	Lazy LAZY 04	Sunny Sundae Smile/Paint A Rainbow (p/s)	20
87	Lazy LAZY 04T	Sunny Sundae Smile/Paint A Rainbow/Kiss The Eclipse/ Sylvie's Head (12", p/s)	40

87	Lazy LAZY 07	Strawberry Wine/Never Say Goodbye/Can I Touch You (12", p/s)	50
88	Creation CRE 055	You Made Me Realise/Slow (die-cut company sleeve)	6
88	Creation CRE 055T	You Made Me Realise/Slow/Thorn/Cigarette/Drive It All Over Me (12", p/s)	22
88	Creation CRE 061	Feed Me With Your Kiss/Emptiness Inside (plays "I Believe") (die-cut company sleeve)	20
88	Creation CRE 061T	Feed Me With Your Kiss/I Believe/Emptiness Inside/I Need No Trust (12", p/s)	20
89	Creation CRE 085	Tremolo/To Hear Knows When (p/s)	8
89	Creation CRE 085T	Tremolo/To Hear Knows When (12", p/s)	12
89	Creation CRECD 085	Tremolo/To Hear Knows When (CD)	10
89	Lyntone CAT 067	Sugar/PACIFIC: December, With The Day (square flexidisc free with *The Catalogue* magazine, issue 67)	10/7
90	Creation CRE 073	Soon/Glider (p/s)	10
90	Creation CRE 073T	GLIDER EP (12", p/s)	15
90	Creation CRE 073T	GLIDER EP (12", remixed by Andy Weatherall, stickered die-cut sleeve)	15
87	Lazy LAZY 08	ECSTACY (mini-LP, 3,000 only)	60
88	Creation CRELP 040	ISN'T ANYTHING (LP, initial 3,000 copies with bonus 7", "Instrumental"/ "Instrumental" [CRE FRE 4, no p/s] & stickered sleeve)	22/12
89	Lazy LAZY 12	ECSTACY & WINE (LP, compilation of LAZY 07 & LAZY 08)	35
89	Lazy LAZY 12CD	ECSTACY & WINE (CD)	40
91	Creation CRELP 060	LOVELESS (LP)	12

MY CAPTAINS

81	4AD AD 103	Fall/Converse/History/Nothing (EP)	8

MY DEAR WATSON

68	Parlophone R 5687	Elusive Face/The Shame Just Drained	25
68	Parlophone R 5737	Make This Day Last/Stop, Stop, I'll Be There	25
70	DJM DJS 224	Have You Seen Your Saviour/White Line Road	10

(see also Johnny & Copycats)

MY DYING BRIDE

94	Peaceville CC5	Sexuality Of Bereavement/Crown Of Sympathy	25
94	Peaceville VILE 45	THE STORIES EP (box set, 1000 only)	75
95	Peaceville VILE 50	THE ANGEL AND THE DARK RIVER (LP, picture disc)	12

BILLY MYLES

57	HMV POP 423	The Joker (That's What They Call Me)/Honey Bee	65
57	HMV POP 423	The Joker (That's What They Call Me)/Honey Bee (78)	12

MEG MYLES

56	Capitol CL 14555	Sing On, Baby/Will You Shed A Tear For Me?	7

MY LIFE STORY

86	Think Tank CHAPTER 1	HOME SWEET ZOO EP (gatefold p/s, 500 only)	90
93	M. Tongue MOTHER 2MC	Girl A, Girl B, Boy C/You Don't Sparkle (In My Eyes)/Star Colliding/ You Don't Sparkle (Big Screen Soundtrack) (cassette)	5
93	M. Tongue MOTHER 2T	Girl A, Girl B, Boy C/You Don't Sparkle (In My Eyes)/Star Colliding/ You Don't Sparkle (Big Screen Soundtrack) (12", p/s)	12
93	M. Tongue MOTHER 2CD	Girl A, Girl B, Boy C/You Don't Sparkle (In My Eyes)/Star Colliding/ You Don't Sparkle (Big Screen Soundtrack) (CD)	15
94	M. Tongue MOTHER 3S	Funny Ha Ha/The Lady Is A Tramp (p/s)	5
94	M. Tongue MOTHER 3T	Funny Ha Ha/The Lady Is A Tramp/These Words Are Haunting/ Funny Peculiar (12", p/s)	12
94	M. Tongue MOTHER 3CD	Funny Ha Ha/The Lady Is A Tramp/These Words Are Haunting/ Funny Peculiar (CD)	12
94	M. Tongue MOTHER 004CD	You Don't Sparkle (In My Eyes) (Radio Edit)/First Person Singular/ Stood Amongst Friends/You Don't Sparkle (In My Eyes) (Quintet) (CD)	12
94	M. Tongue MOTHER 005CD	MORNINGTON CRESCENT COMPANION: Checkmate/Outdoor Miner/ Under The Ice/Forever (CD, 2,000 only)	22
97	Parlophone 12RDJ 6474	Duchess (John '00' Fleming Remix)/(Xenomania Remix) (12", title stickered sleeve, promo only)	12
95	M. Tongue MOTHERLP 1	MORNINGTON CRESCENT (LP)	12

MY LORDE SHERIFFE'S COMPLAINTE

79	Frog FROG 1	MY LORDE SHERIFFE'S COMPLAINTE (LP, private pressing)	15

MYND MUZIC

94	Poor Person Prod.	IMAGINE THIS (LP, handmade sleeve, 500 only)	20

ROWLAND MYRES

74	Deroy DER 1063	JUST FOR THE RECORD (LP, private pressing, also listed as Music Sound Enterprise MSE 1)	110

MYRTELLES

63	Oriole CB 1805	Don't Wanna Cry Again/Just Let Me Cry	35

(see also Sue & Sunshine, Sue & Sunny, Stockingtops)

MY RUIN

99	Snapper SMAS 106	Tainted Love/Blasphemous Girl (p/s, red vinyl, 1,000 only)	6

MYSTERE FIVE'S

80	Flicknife FLS 001	No Message/Shake Some Action (p/s)	10
81	Flicknife FLS 202	Never Say Thank You/Heart Rules The Head (p/s)	5

(see also Wayne County & Electric Chairs)

MYSTERIES

64	Decca F 11919	Give Me Rhythm And Blues/Teardrops	25

WILLIAM MYSTERIOUS

82	Mezzanine MEZ 1	Security Of Noise/Alright (p/s, with Fay Fife & Revettes)	6

(see also Rezillos, Revillos)

MINT VALUE £

MYSTERY GIRLS

80	Strange HAM 001	SOUNDS LIKE (EP)	5
81	Strange HAM 002	I'm A Believer/Modern Mystery Pop/Walking Backwards (p/s)	6

MYSTERY GUESTS

80	Boys Own/Heater Volume BO 1	Wurlitzer Junction/The Merry Shark You Are (handmade stickered white labels)	6
81	Boys Own BO 3	The Sparrow That Ate New York/The Nude (p/s)	5

MYSTERY MAKER

77	Caves UHC 3	MYSTERY MAKER (LP, private pressing with booklet)	120

MYSTIC INSTITUTE

92	Evolution EVO 06	CYBERDON EP (12")	50

(see also Global Communications, Reload, Link)

MYSTIC MOODS

73	Warner Bros K 16265	Cosmic Sea/Awakening	7
74	Warner Bros K 46250	AWAKENING (LP)	15

MYSTIC NUMBER NATIONAL BANK

69	Probe SPB 1001	THE MYSTIC NUMBER NATIONAL BANK (LP)	12

MYSTICS

59	HMV POP 646	Hushabye/Adam And Eve	50
59	Top Rank JAR 243	Don't Take The Stars/So Tenderly	65

MYSTICS (Jamaica)

75	Grounation GRO 2049	God Bless The Youths/Dub	5

MYTHRA

79	Guardian GRMA 16	DEATH & DESTINY: Death And Destiny/Killer/Overload/UFO (EP, no p/s)	8
80	Streetbeat LAMP 2	Death Or Destiny/Killer/U.F.O. (some with p/s)	90/10
80	Streetbeat 12 LAMP 2	Death Or Destiny/Killer/Overlord/U.F.O. (12", some with p/s)	125/20

NAAFI SANDWICH

80	Absurd ABSURD 8	Slice One/Slice Two (p/s)	5

NABAY

80	Grapevine GRP 143	Believe It Or Not/Believe It Or Not (Instrumental)	75

RICKY NADIR

79	Charisma CB 339	The Polaroid/PETER HAMMILL: The Old School Tie	10

(see also Peter Hammill)

NA FILI

74	Dolphin DOL 1008	CHANTER'S TUNE (LP)	12

NA H-ORGANAICH

73	Beltona SBE 145	THE GREAT GAELIC SOUND OF (LP)	15
74	Beltona SBE 160	GAEL FORCE 3 (LP)	15

NAKED LUNCH

81	Ramkup CAC 003	Rabies/Slipping Again (p/s)	7

NAKED TRUTH

70	Deram DM 287	Two Little Rooms/Rag Doll Boy	7

NAME

80	Din Disc DIN 14	Forget Art, Let's Dance/Misfits (p/s)	10

NAMES

80	Factory FAC 29	Nightshift/I Wish I Could Speak Your Language (p/s)	5

NANETTE

70	Columbia DB 8659	Flying Machine/You're Wasting Your Time	6
70	Columbia DB 8673	Every Night When I Cry Myself To Sleep/Jamie	5
70	Columbia DB 8733	Let Me Be The One/To Be Loved	5
71	Columbia DB 8751	Everybody's Singing Right Now/Could I Forget	5
70	Columbia SCX 6398	NANETTE (LP)	15

ED NANGLE

68	Blue Cat BS 120	Good Girl/ENFORCERS: Musical Fever	18
68	Coxsone CS 7038	Whipping The Prince (actually by Ed Nangle & Alton Ellis & Soul Vendors)/HEPTONES: If You Knew	30

NINO NANNI

58	London SAHD 6043	CHIC TO CHIC (LP)	12

NICK NANTOS & HIS FIREBALLERS

63	Summit LSE 2042	GUITARS ON FIRE (EP)	12
64	Summit ATL 4114	GUITARS ON FIRE (LP)	15

(see also Bill Haley & Comets)

NAOMI
70 Gayfeet GS 207 You're Not My Kind/GAYTONES: You're Not My Kind (Version II) . . . 8
70 High Note HS 047 Natural Woman/GAYTONES: Natural Woman – Version . . . 8
(see also Derrick Morgan, Tommy McCook)

NAPALM DEATH
89 Earache MOSH 014 MENTALLY MURDERED EP (Rise Above/The Missing Link/Mentally Murdered Walls Of Confinement/Cause And Effect/No Mental Effort) (12", p/s) . . . 10
90 Earache MOSH 024 Suffer The Children/Siege Of Power/Harmony Corruption (12", p/s) . . . 8
91 Earache MOSH 046 Mass Appeal Madness (12", p/s) . . . 8
92 Earache MOSH 065CD The World Keeps Turning/A Means To An End/Insanity Excursion (CD) . . . 8
95 Earache MOSH 146 GREED KILLING EP (Greed Kiling/My Own Worst Enemy/Self Betrayal/Finer Truths White Lies/Antibody/All Links Severed/Plague Rages [Live]) (10", p/s) . . . 8
90 Earache MOSH 19 HARMONY CORRUPTION (2-LP) . . . 25

NAPOLEON XIV
66 Warner Bros WB 5831 They're Coming To Take Me Away Ha-Haa!/ !Aah-Ah Yawa Em Ekat Ot Gnimoc Er'Yeht . . . 8
66 Warner Bros WB 5853 I'm In Love With My Little Red Tricycle/Doin' The Napoleon . . . 10
66 Warner Bros W 1661 THEY'RE COMING TO TAKE ME AWAY HA-HA-A! (LP) . . . 70
(see also Jerry Samuels, Kim Fowley)

MARTY NAPOLEON
56 London EZ-N 19001 MARTY NAPOLEON SWINGS AND SINGS (EP) . . . 8

PETER NARDINI
80s Kettle KS 701 I Think You're Great/Ma Maw's A Mod (some in p/s) . . . 15/8

NARNIA
74 Myrrh MYR 1007 NARNIA – ASLAN IS NOT A TAME LION (LP) . . . 130
(see also After The Fire, Pauline Filby)

BILLY NASH
61 Philips PB 1181 Sunset/Nobody Loves Me Like You (as Billy Nash Combo) . . . 5
63 Philips 370 406 BF The Madison Step/Madison Rhythm (as Billy Nash Rock Band) . . . 5

GENE NASH
59 Capitol CL 15042 I'm An Eskimo Too/Ja, Ja, Ja (Deutsche Rock 'N Roll) . . . 25

GRAHAM NASH
71 Atlantic 2091 096 Chicago/Simple Man . . . 5
71 Atlantic 2091 135 Military Madness/I Used To Be A King . . . 5
71 Atlantic 2401 011 SONGS FOR BEGINNERS (LP) . . . 15
(see also Hollies, Crosby Stills Nash & Young)

JOHNNY NASH
57 HMV POP 402 Ladder Of Love/I'll Walk Alone . . . 10
57 HMV POP 402 Ladder Of Love/I'll Walk Alone (78) . . . 12
58 HMV POP 435 Won't You Let Me Share My Love With You?/A Very Special Love . . . 8
58 HMV POP 435 Won't You Let Me Share My Love With You?/A Very Special Love (78) . . . 8
58 HMV POP 475 It's Easy To Say/My Pledge To You . . . 8
58 HMV POP 475 It's Easy To Say/My Pledge To You (78) . . . 10
58 HMV POP 553 Almost In Your Arms/Midnight Moonlight . . . 7
58 HMV POP 553 Almost In Your Arms/Midnight Moonlight (78) . . . 12
59 HMV POP 597 Walk With Faith In Your Heart/Roots Of Heaven . . . 7
59 HMV POP 597 Walk With Faith In Your Heart/Roots Of Heaven (78) . . . 20
59 HMV POP 620 As Time Goes By/Voice Of Love . . . 7
59 HMV POP 651 And The Angels Sing/Baby, Baby, Baby . . . 7
59 HMV POP 673 Take A Giant Step/Imagination . . . 7
60 HMV POP 746 A Place In The Sun/Goodbye . . . 7
60 HMV POP 822 Somebody/Kisses . . . 7
62 Warner Bros WB 65 Don't Take Away Your Love/Moment Of Weakness . . . 7
62 Warner Bros WB 76 Ol' Man River/My Dear Little Sweetheart . . . 7
63 Warner Bros WB 93 Cigareets, Whuskey And Wild, Wild Women/I'm Moving On . . . 6
64 Pye International 7N 25250 Love Ain't Nothin'/Talk To Me . . . 20
65 Chess CRS 8005 Strange Feelin'/Rainin' In My Heart . . . 18
66 Pye International 7N 25353 Let's Move And Groove (Together)/Understanding . . . 7
66 Pye International 7N 25363 One More Time/Tryin' To Find Her . . . 7
68 Regal Zono. RZ 3010 Hold Me Tight/Let's Move And Groove Together . . . 7
68 Major Minor MM 586 You Got Soul/Don't Cry . . . 7
69 Major Minor MM 603 Cupid/People In Love . . . 7
69 MGM MGM 1480 (I'm So) Glad You're My Baby/Stormy . . . 20
64 RCA Victor RCX 7163 PRESENTING JOHNNY NASH (EP) . . . 100
59 HMV CLP 1251 JOHNNY NASH (LP) . . . 40
59 HMV CLP 1299 QUIET HOUR WITH JOHNNY NASH (LP) . . . 25
60 HMV CLP 1325/CSD 1288 I GOT RHYTHM (LP, mono/stereo) . . . 30/40
62 Encore ENC 2005 LET'S GET LOST (LP) . . . 15
69 Major Minor MMLP/SMLP 47 YOU GOT SOUL (LP) . . . 18
69 Major Minor MMLP/SMLP 56 SOUL FOLK (LP) . . . 18
69 Major Minor MMLP/SMLP 63 PRINCE OF PEACE (LP) . . . 18
73 CBS Q 56449 MY MERRY GO ROUND (LP, quadrophonic) . . . 12

JOHNNY NASH & KIM WESTON
69 Major Minor SMLP 54 JOHNNY NASH AND KIM WESTON (LP) . . . 30
(see also Kim Weston)

TONY NASH
70 Hot Rod HR 110 Keep On Trying/WINSTON JAMES: Just Can't Do Without Your Love . . . 7

MINT VALUE £

NASH THE SLASH

81 Smash Hits (no cat. no.) Swing-Shift (Flexi-Version)/ORCHESTRAL MANOEUVRES IN THE DARK: Pretending To See The Future (live) (blue flexidisc with *Smash Hits* mag) 6/4
81 Dindisc DIN 28 Dead Man's Curve/Reactor No. 2 (p/s) 7

NASHVILLE FIVE

62 Decca F 11427 Stand Up And Say That/Like Nashville 7
62 Decca F 11484 Some Other Love/Brainwave 7
62 Decca DFE 6706 LIKE NASHVILLE (EP) 40

NASHVILLE TEENS

64 Decca F 11930 Tobacco Road/I Like It Like That 10
64 Decca F 12000 Google Eye (some misspelled "Goggle Eye" on label)/T.N.T. 8
65 Decca F 12089 Find My Way Back Home/Devil-In-Law 8
65 Decca F 12143 This Little Bird/Whatcha Gonna Do? 6
65 Decca F 12255 I Know How It Feels To Be Loved/Soon Forgotten 8
66 Decca F 12316 The Hard Way/Upside Down 15
66 Decca F 12458 Forbidden Fruit/Revived 45 Time 18
66 Decca F 12542 That's My Woman/Words 18
67 Decca F 12580 I'm Coming Home/Searching 10
67 Decca F 12657 The Biggest Night Of Her Life/Last Minute 10
68 Decca F 12754 All Along The Watchtower/Sun-Dog 10
69 Major Minor MM 599 The Lament Of The Cherokee Reservation Indian/Looking For You 18
69 Decca F 12929 Tobacco Road/All Along The Watchtower 6
71 Parlophone R 5925 Ella James/Tennessee Woman 15
72 Parlophone R 5961 You Shouldn't Have Been So Nice/Tell The People (unissued)
72 Enterprise ENT 001 Lawdy Miss Clawdy/Let It Rock: Break Up 6
77 Sky 1007 Tobacco Road/Chips And Peas 5
81 Go GO 2 Midnight/Live For The Summer (p/s) 5
82 Shanghai HAI 200 LIVE AT THE RED HOUSE (12" EP) 8
84 Butt FUNEP 4 Tobacco Road/Find My Way Back Home/Born To Be Wild (p/s) 5
65 Decca DFE 8600 THE NASHVILLE TEENS (EP) 60
75 New World NW 6002 THE NASHVILLE TEENS (LP) 30

(see also Arizona Swamp Company, Jerry Lee Lewis, Carl Perkins)

NASTY FACTS

81 5th Column FC 2 Drive My Car/Gotta Get To You/Crazy 'Bout You (p/s) 10

NASTY MEDIA

78 Lightning GIL 542 Spiked Copy/Winter (p/s) 10

NATCHBAND

78 Far In FARS 01 Cadillac (Made In USA)/Being From The Sky (p/s) 6

NATIONAL-ELLS

67 Parlophone R 5609 Mr. Moon/Dance, Dance 5

NATIONAL HEAD BAND

71 Warner Bros K 46094 ALBERT 1 (LP) 35

(see also Caravan, Gary Moore, Toe-Fat, Uriah Heep)

NATIONAL HEALTH

78 Affinity AFF 6 NATIONAL HEALTH (LP) 12
78 Charly CRL 5010 OF QUEUES AND CURES (LP) 12

(see also Hatfield & The North)

NATIONAL LAMPOON

78 Island HELP 8 RADIO DINNER (LP) 12

NATIONAL PINION POLE

66 Planet PLF 111 Make Your Mark Little Man/I Was The One You Came In With (some in Planet sleeve) 20/15

NATIONWIDE ENGLAND SUPPORTERS CLUB

86 Peak PRIDE 1 Oh Sweet England/England Supporter (picture disc, with rosette & beermat) . . . 10

NATURAL ACOUSTIC BAND

73 RCA RCA 2324 Echoes/Is It True Blue 5
72 RCA SF 8272 LEARNING TO LIVE (LP, gatefold sleeve) 22
72 RCA SF 8314 BRANCHING IN (LP) 18

(see also Krysia)

NATURAL BRIDGE BUNCH

69 Atlantic 584 231 Pig Snoots (Parts 1 & 2) 5

NATURAL FOUR

75 Atlantic K 56142 HEAVEN RIGHT HERE ON EARTH (LP) 25

NATURAL GAS

76 Private Stock PVT 71 The Right Time/Miracle Mile 5
76 Private Stock PSS 1 NATURAL GAS (EP, promo only) 8
76 Private Stock PVLP 1007 NATURAL GAS (LP, with inner sleeve) 12

(see also Badfinger, Blue Goose, Humble Pie, Uriah Heep, Quiver)

NATURAL MAGIC

75 Oyster OYR 102 Strawberry Fields Forever/Isolated Lady 10

(see also Roger Glover, Eddie Hardin)

NATURALS (U.K.)

64 Parlophone R 5116 Daisy Chain/That Girl 8
64 Parlophone R 5165 I Should Have Known Better/Didn't I? 12
64 Parlophone R 5202 It Was You/Look At Me Now 15
65 Parlophone R 5257 Blue Roses/Shame On You 15

(see also Living Daylights, Greatest Show On Earth)

MINT VALUE £

NATURALS (U.S.)

55 MGM SP 1123 The Finger Of Suspicion Points At You/You Forgot To Remember 12
57 MGM MGM 939 The Buccaneers/The Ballad Of Sir Lancelot 8
(see also Debbie Reynolds)

FATS NAVARRO

56 London LZ-C 14015 MEMORIAL (LP) 18

NAVIGATOR

96 Noisebox NBX 022 Kill Taker/Swing/We Will All Burn Together (spearmint coloured vinyl, p/s, 500 only) 8
96 Noisebox NBX 026 A Little Astronomy/At The End Of The Bay (blue vinyl, p/s, 500 only) 5
97 Noisebox NBX 027 When The Wires Fall/Impossible Without (cherry-coloured vinyl, 750 only) 5

JERRY NAYLOR

61 Top Rank JAR 591 Stop Your Crying/You're Thirteen 25
67 Stateside SS 2029 Sweet Violets/Temptation Leads Me 8
70 CBS 4882 But For Love/Angeline 6
70 CBS 5265 Marie/If I Promise 6
71 CBS 7093 Come On Love/Las Virgenese Road 6

SHEL NAYLOR

63 Decca F 11776 How Deep Is The Ocean/La Bamba 18
64 Decca F 11856 One Fine Day/It's Gonna Happen Soon 100
(see also Lieutenant Pigeon, Stavely Makepeace)

NAZARETH

72 Pegasus PGS 2 Dear John/Friends 15
72 Pegasus PGS 2 Dear John/Friends (2nd issue, PEG label, B-side lists 'Occasional Failure') 15
72 Pegasus BCP 3 Dear John/Witchdoctor Woman/Morning Dew (unreleased, promo only, stamped white labels and insert) 20
72 Pegasus PGS 4 Morning Dew/Spinning Top (PEG label) 20
72 Pegasus BCP 8 Fool About You/Woke Up This Morning/Morning Dew (unreleased, promo only, handwritten white labels) 50
72 Pegasus PGS 5 If You See My Baby/Hard Living (PEG label) 20
73 Mooncrest MOON 1 Broken Down Angel/Witchdoctor Woman (solid or push-out centre) .... each 5
73 Mooncrest MOON 9 Bad Bad Boy/Hard Living/Spinning Top (initially in p/s) 10/4
73 Mooncrest MOON 14 This Flight Tonight/Called Her Name 5
74 Mooncrest MOON 22 Shanghai'd In Shanghai/Love, Now You're Gone 5
74 Mooncrest MOON 37 Love Hurts/Down 5
75 Mooncrest MOON 44 Hair Of The Dog/Too Bad, Too Sad 5
75 Mooncrest MOON 47 My White Bicycle/Miss Misery 5
76 Mountain TOP 21 I Don't Want To Go On Without You/Good Love 5
77 Mountain TOP 22 Somebody To Roll/Vancouver Shakedown 5
78 Mountain NAZ 2 Gone Dead Train/Greens/Desolation Road (p/s) 5
78 Mountain TOP 37 Place In Your Heart/Kentucky Fried Blues (company sleeve) 5
78 Mountain TOP 37 Place In Your Heart/Kentucky Fried Blues (mispressing, B-side plays Bee Gees track, company sleeve) 20
79 Mountain NAZ 3 May The Sunshine/Expect No Mercy (p/s) 5
79 Mountain NAZ 4 Whatever You Want Babe/Telegram Parts 1, 2 & 3 (p/s, some purple vinyl) 10/5
79 Mountain TOP 45 Star/Born To Love (p/s) 5
81 NEMS BSD 1 LIVE (double pack, gatefold p/s) 6
81 NEMS NES 301 Dressed To Kill/Pop The Silo (p/s) 5
81 NEMS NES 302 Morning Dew (re-recording)/Juicy Lucy (no p/s) 5
83 NEMS Int. NIS 102 Games/You Love Another (p/s) 5
83 Mountain NEP 2 HOT TRACKS (EP, reissue, picture disc) 5
84 Vertigo VERX 13 Ruby Tuesday/Sweetheart Tree/This Month's Messiah/ Do You Think About It (12", p/s) 10
71 Pegasus PEG 10 NAZARETH (LP, 1st issue, Pegasus picture label/matt sleeve) 30
72 Pegasus PEG 10 NAZARETH (LP, 2nd issue, PEG label/glossy sleeve) 20
72 Pegasus PEG 14 EXERCISES (LP, gatefold sleeve) 20
74 Mooncrest CREST 10 NAZARETH (LP, reissue) 12
74 Mooncrest CREST 14 EXERCISES (LP, reissue, gatefold sleeve) 12
74 Mooncrest CREST 15 RAMPANT (LP, embossed sleeve with inner & dollar sticker insert) 12
85 Sahara SAH 130 SOUND ELIXIR (LP, Marimba label, withdrawn) 15
(see also Dan McCafferty, Mark Five, Sensational Alex Harvey Band, Tandoori Cassette, Billy Rankin)

NAZIS AGAINST FASCISM

79 Truth TRUTH 1 Sid Did It (Intelligible)/Sid Did It (Radio Version) (p/s, 2 different issues) .... each 10
(see also Vibrators)

NAZZ

68 Atlantic 584 224 Open My Eyes/Hello It's Me (unissued)
68 Screen Gems SGC 219001 Open My Eyes/Hello It's Me 12
69 Screen Gems SGC 219002 Hello It's Me/Crowded 12
69 Screen Gems SGC 219003 Not Wrong Long/Under The Ice 12
69 Screen Gems SGC 221001 NAZZ (LP) 40
(see also Todd Rundgren)

'N BETWEENS

66 Columbia DB 8080 You Better Run/Evil Witchman (demos credit In-Be-Tweens) 420
(see also Slade, Vendors)

YOUSSOU N'DOUR & PETER GABRIEL

89 Virgin VSCD 1207 The Lion (Gaiende)/Macoy/The Lion (Gaiende) (African Mix) (3" CD, card p/s) 8
(see also Peter Gabriel)

CHRIS NEAL

71 Fly BUG 15 Blame It All On Eve/All The Time In The World (p/s) 6

MINT VALUE £

JOHNNY NEAL & STARLINERS

65 Pye 7N 15388 And I Will Love You/Walk Baby Walk ... 75
70 Parlophone R 5870 Put Your Hand In The Hand/Now ... 7
(see also Storyteller)

TOMMY NEAL

68 Vocalion VL 9290 Goin' To A Happening/Tee Ta ... 25

NEARLY NORMAL

82 Insurrection Now! IN 1 Bedtime/Die Baby Die (p/s) ... 5

NEAT

80s Neatbeat LYN 6269 Hormones In Action/Take Your Chances (p/s) ... 60

NEAT CHANGE

68 Decca F 12809 I Lied To Auntie May/Sandman (some copies in foldout p/s) ... 30/15
(see also Peter Banks, English Rose)

NECROMANDUS

90 Reflection MM 09 QUICKSAND DREAM (LP, 500 only) ... 20

BERNIE NEE

58 Philips PB 794 Lend Me Your Comb/Medal Of Honour ... 22
58 Philips PB 794 Lend Me Your Comb/Medal Of Honour (78) ... 15
(see also Bernie Knee)

NEEDLES

80 Ellie Jay EJSP 9340 Gotta Know You/Jayneski (no p/s) ... 150

LOUIS NEEFS

69 Columbia DB 8561 Jennifer Jennings/I Love You ... 25

ELGIN NEELY

65 Vogue V 9240 Four Walls/I Could Be ... 10

NEGATIVES

78 Look LK/SP 6478 Stakeout (50 copies with p/s) ... 40/20

NEGATIVES

80 Aardvark STEAL 1 Electric Waltz/Money Talks (p/s) ... 25
81 Aardvark STEAL 3 Scene Of The Crime (p/s) ... 15

FRED NEIL

69 Elektra EKSN 45036 Candy Man/The Water Is Wide ... 8
69 Capitol CL 15616 Everybody's Talkin'/Badi-Da ... 10

DON NEILSON

60 Philips BF 1058 The House Is Haunted/For All We Know ... 6
63 Piccadilly 7N 35103 I Will Live My Life For You/How Do You Keep From Crying ... 5

NEKTAR

73 United Artists NEK 1 What Ya Gonna Do?/Day In The Life Of A Preacher Pt. One (Edit) (p/s) ... 15
74 United Artists UP 35706 Fidgety Queen/Little Boy ... 10
75 United Artists UP 35853 Astral Man/Nelly The Elephant ... 10
73 United Artists UAD 60041/2 SOUNDS LIKE THIS (2-LP) ... 30
74 United Artists UAS 29499 A TAB IN THE OCEAN (LP, gatefold sleeve) ... 25
74 United Artists UAS 29545 REMEMBER THE FUTURE (LP) ... 25
74 United Artists UAG 29680 DOWN TO EARTH (LP) ... 25
76 Decca SKL-R 5250 RECYCLED (LP) ... 20

BILL NELSON('S RED NOISE)

85 Les Disques Du Crépuscule TWI 013 Rooms With Brittle Views/Dada Guitare (p/s, at least 2 different designs) ... 5
85 Cocteau JEAN 1 PERMANENT FLAME SINGLES BOX (box set of 5 singles) ... 10
71 Smile LAF 2182/ HG 116 NORTHERN DREAM (LP, 250 only, numbered, in foldover gatefold sleeve with booklet; second pressings £20; reissues on the Butt label £15) ... 35
85 Cocteau JEAN 2 TRIAL BY INTIMACY (THE BOOK OF SPLENDOURS) (4-LP, box set, with book & postcards, initial copies misspelt as "The Book Splendours") ... 20
86 KPM/Themes TIM CHAMELEON — THE MUSIC OF BILL NELSON (LP, library issue) ... 12
(see also A — Austr, Astral Navigations, Gagalactyca, Be-Bop Deluxe)

CLARE NELSON

59 MGM MGM 1025 The Valley Of Love/You Are My Sunshine ... 7

DAVID NELSON

64 Philips BF 1321 Somebody Loves Me/Well I Have ... 8

EARL NELSON

59 London HLW 8950 No Time To Cry/Come On ... 25
59 London HLW 8950 No Time To Cry/Come On (78) ... 10

OZZIE & HARRIET NELSON

59 London HA-P 2145 OZZIE AND HARRIET NELSON (LP) ... 50

RICK(Y) NELSON

78s

57 HMV POP 355 I'm Walkin'/A Teenager's Romance ... 60
57 HMV POP 390 You're My One And Only Love/BARNEY KESSEL: Honey Rock ... 70
57 London HLP 8499 Be-Bop Baby/Have I Told You Lately That I Love You ... 30
58 London HLP 8542 Stood Up/Waitin' In School ... 30
58 London HLP 8594 Believe What You Say/My Bucket's Got A Hole In It ... 30
58 London HLP 8670 Poor Little Fool/Don't Leave Me This Way ... 20
58 London HLP 8732 Someday/I Got A Feeling ... 30
58 London HLP 8738 Lonesome Town/My Babe ... 20
59 London HLP 8817 It's Late/Never Be Anyone Else But You ... 35

MINT VALUE £

59 London HLP 8927 Just A Little Too Much/Sweeter Than You 45
60 London HLP 9021 I Wanna Be Loved/Mighty Good 80
60 London HLP 9121 Young Emotions/Right By My Side 100
60 London HLP 9188 Yes, Sir, That's My Baby/I'm Not Afraid 120
(All the above 78s were credited to Ricky Nelson.)

45s

57 HMV POP 355 I'm Walkin'/A Teenager's Romance (gold or silver label lettering) 160/90
57 HMV POP 390 You're My One And Only Love/BARNEY KESSEL: Honey Rock 100
57 London HLP 8499 Be-Bop Baby/Have I Told You Lately That I Love You 30
58 London HLP 8542 Stood Up/Waitin' In School 25
58 London HLP 8594 Believe What You Say/My Bucket's Got A Hole In It 25
58 London HLP 8670 Poor Little Fool/Don't Leave Me This Way 10
58 London HLP 8732 Someday/I Got A Feeling 10
58 London HLP 8738 Lonesome Town/My Babe 10
59 London HLP 8817 It's Late/Never Be Anyone Else But You (all black or silver-top label) 10
59 London HLP 8894 Just A Little Too Much/Sweeter Than You (unreleased)
59 London HLP 8927 Just A Little Too Much/Sweeter Than You (triangular centre) 12
(The above 45s were originally issued with triangular centres; later round-centre copies are worth half to two-thirds the value.)
59 London HL 7081 Just A Little Too Much/Sweeter Than You (export issue) 10
60 London HLP 9021 I Wanna Be Loved/Mighty Good 15
60 London HLP 9121 Young Emotions/Right By My Side 7
60 London HLP 9188 Yes, Sir, That's My Baby/I'm Not Afraid 7
61 London HLP 9260 You Are The Only One/Milk Cow Blues 20
61 London HLP 9260 You Are The One And Only/Milk Cow Blues (with different label credit) 10
61 London HLP 9347 Hello Mary Lou Goodbye Heart/Travelin' Man
(later copies as "Hello Marylou Goodbye Heart") 7
61 London HLP 9440 Everlovin'/A Wonder Like You 7
(The above singles were credited to Ricky Nelson; all subsequent singles were credited to Rick Nelson unless stated.)
62 London HLP 9524 Young World/Summertime 10
62 London HLP 9583 Teen Age Idol/I've Got My Eyes On You (And I Like What I See) 8
63 London HLP 9648 It's Up To You/I Need You 8
63 Brunswick 05885 I Got A Woman/You Don't Love Me Anymore 8
63 Brunswick 05889 String Along/Gypsy Woman 10
63 Brunswick 05895 Fools Rush In/Down Home 8
64 Brunswick 05900 For You/That's All She Wrote 8
64 Liberty LIB 66004 Today's Teardrops/Thank You Darling 10
64 Brunswick 05908 The Very Thought Of You/I Wonder 8
64 Brunswick 05918 Lonely Corner/There's Nothing I Can Say 8
64 Brunswick 05924 A Happy Guy/Don't Breathe A Word 8
65 Brunswick 05939 Come Out Dancin'/Yesterday's Love 15
66 Brunswick 05964 Louisiana Man/You Just Can't Quit (as Ricky Nelson) 18
66 Liberty LIB 12033 I Need You/Wonder Like You 10
69 MCA MU 1106 She Belongs To Me/Promises 6
70 MCA MU 1124 Red Balloon/I Shall Be Released 7
71 MCA MU 1135 Life/California (with Stone Canyon Band) 7
72 MCA MU 1147 Love Minus Zero: No Limit/Gypsy Pilot (with Stone Canyon Band) 6
72 MCA MU 1165 Garden Party/So Long Mama 7
73 MCA MUS 1181 Palace Guard/A Flower Opens Gently By Itself 6
73 MCA MUS 1225 Lifestream/Evil Woman Child 6
74 MCA MCA 126 Windfall/Legacy (with Stone Canyon Band) 6
74 MCA MCA 144 One Night Stand/Lifestream (with Stone Canyon Band) 6
75 MCA MCA 198 Try (Try To Fall In Love)/Louisiana Belle (with Stone Canyon Band) 6
77 Epic S EPC 5821 You Can't Dance/It's Another Day 5

EPs

58 London RE-P 1141 RICKY PART 1 40
58 London RE-P 1142 RICKY PART 2 40
58 London RE-P 1143 RICKY PART 3 40
58 London RE-P 1144 RICKY PART 4 40
59 London RE-P 1168 RICKY NELSON PART 1 35
59 London RE-P 1169 RICKY NELSON PART 2 35
59 London RE-P 1170 RICKY NELSON PART 3 35
59 London RE-P 1200 RICKY SINGS AGAIN PART 1 35
59 London RE-P 1201 RICKY SINGS AGAIN PART 2 35
60 London RE-P 1238 I GOT A FEELING 35
60 London RE-P 1249 RICKY SINGS SPIRITUALS 35
61 London RE-P 1300 RICKY NELSON PART 4 40
(The above EPs were credited to Ricky Nelson; all subsequent EPs were credited to Rick Nelson.)
62 London RE-P 1339 IT'S A YOUNG WORLD 35
63 London RE-P 1362 IT'S UP TO YOU 35
63 Brunswick OE 9502 ONE BOY TOO LATE 35
64 Liberty LEP 4001 SINGS FOR YOU 50
64 Liberty LEP 4019 THAT'S ALL 55
65 Liberty LEP 4028 I'M IN LOVE AGAIN 60
65 Brunswick OE 9512 HAPPY GUY 50

LPs

57 London HA-P 2080 RICKY 50
58 London HA-P 2119 RICKY NELSON 50
59 London HA-P 2159 RICKY SINGS AGAIN 50
59 London HA-P 2206 SONGS BY RICKY 50
60 London HA-P 2290 MORE SONGS BY RICKY (gatefold sleeve, also stereo SAH-P 6102) 40/50
61 London HA-P 2379 RICK IS 21 (also stereo SAH-P 6179) 40/50
(The above LPs were credited to Ricky Nelson; all subsequent LPs were credited to Rick Nelson.)
62 London HA-P 2445 ALBUM SEVEN (also stereo SAH-P 6236) 40/50
63 London HA-P 8066 IT'S UP TO YOU 40
63 Brunswick LAT 8545 FOR YOUR SWEET LOVE (also stereo STA 8545) 35/40

			MINT VALUE £
64	Brunswick LAT/STA 8562	RICKY SINGS "FOR YOU" (mono/stereo)	50/60
64	Liberty LBY 3027	MILLION SELLERS	45
64	Brunswick LAT/STA 8581	THE VERY THOUGHT OF YOU	50
64	Brunswick LAT/STA 8596	SPOTLIGHT ON RICK	50
65	Brunswick LAT/STA 8615	BEST ALWAYS	50
65	Brunswick LAT/STA 8630	LOVE AND KISSES	50
66	Brunswick LAT/STA 8657	BRIGHT LIGHTS, COUNTRY MUSIC	50
67	Brunswick LAT/STA 8680	COUNTRY FEVER	50
68	Liberty LBL 83020	MILLION SELLERS (reissue)	15
68	MCA MUP(S) 302	ANOTHER SIDE OF RICK	22
70	MCA MUPS 409	IN CONCERT (with Stone Canyon Band)	20
71	MCA MUPS 422	RICK SINGS NELSON (with Stone Canyon Band)	20
72	MCA MUPS 440	RUDY THE FIFTH (with Stone Canyon Band)	20
73	MCA MDKS 8009	GARDEN PARTY (gatefold sleeve, with Stone Canyon Band)	20
74	MCA MCG 3516	WINDFALL	20
77	Epic EPC 81102	INTAKES	18

SANDY NELSON

59	Top Rank JAR 197	Teen Beat/Big Jump	10
59	London HLP 9015	Drum Party/The Big Noise From Winnetka	12
59	London HLP 9015	Drum Party/The Big Noise From Winnetka (78)	50
60	London HLP 9214	I'm Walkin'/Bouncy (as Sandy Nelson & His Combo)	10
61	London HLP 9377	Get With It/Big Noise From The Jungle	10
61	London HLP 9466	Let There Be Drums/Quite A Beat (as Sandy Nelson On The Drums)	6
62	London HLP 9521	Drums Are My Beat/My Girl Josephine	7
62	London HLP 9558	Drummin' Up A Storm/Drum Stomp	10
62	London HLP 9612	...And Then There Were Drums/Live It Up	8
63	London HLP 9717	Ooh Poo Pah Doo/Feel So Good	8
64	Liberty LIB 66060	Teen Beat '65/Kitty's Theme	7
66	Liberty LIB 12062	Hey Joe/Come On Let's Go	7
70	President PT 294	Teen Beat/PRESTON EPPS: Bongo Rock	7
60	Top Rank JKP 2060	RUSHING FOR PERCUSSION (EP, 2 tracks by Preston Epps)	22
62	London REP 1337	LET THERE BE DRUMS (EP)	20
63	London REP 1371	IN THE MOOD (EP)	20
65	Liberty LEP 4033	SANDY NELSON PLAYS (EP)	18
60	London HA-P 2260	TEEN BEAT (LP, also stereo SAH-P 6082)	25/30
61	London HA-P 2425	LET THERE BE DRUMS (LP, also stereo SAH-P 6221)	25/30
62	London HA-P 2446	DRUMS ARE MY BEAT! (LP, also stereo SAH-P 6237)	25/30
62	London HA-P/SH-P 8009	DRUMMIN' UP A STORM (LP)	25/30
63	London HA-P/SH-P 8029	COMPELLING PERCUSSION (LP)	25
63	London HA-P/SH-P 8051	TEENAGE HOUSE PARTY (LP)	25
65	Liberty LBY 3007	SANDY NELSON PLAYS (LP)	18
65	Liberty LBY 3035	LIVE IN LAS VEGAS (LP)	18
66	Liberty LBY 3061	DRUMS A GO-GO (LP)	18
66	Liberty (S)LBY 3080	SUPERDRUMS (LP)	18
67	Liberty LBL/LBS 83043E	THE BEAT GOES ON (LP)	15
68	Liberty LBL/LBS 83094E	SOUL DRUMS (LP)	20
68	Liberty LBL/LBS 83110E	BOOGALOO BEAT (LP)	20
68	Liberty LBL/LBS 83131E	SUPERDRUMS (LP, reissue, different sleeve)	12
69	Liberty LBL/LBS 83165E	ROCK'N'ROLL REVIVAL (LP)	12
70	Liberty LBS 83302E	GROOVY (LP)	12

(see also Preston Epps)

TERRY NELSON (& FIREBALLS)

65	Dice CC 23	Run Run Baby/Bonita (as Terry Nelson & Fireballs)	10
65	Dice CC 25	Bulldog Push/Pretty Little Girl (as Terry Nelson & Fireballs)	10
65	Dice CC 27	Tomorrow Will Soon Be Here/My Blue Eyed Baby	10
65	Blue Beat BB 326	Help/PRINCE BUSTER: Johnny Dollar	25
66	Halagala HG 11	Take These Chains From My Heart/Let-Kiss	5
67	Halagala HG 19	That True Love Must Be Me/Bulldog Walk	6

WILLIE NELSON

63	Liberty LIB 55532	Half A Man/The Last Letter	10
64	Liberty LIB 55697	River Boy/Opportunity To Cry	10
69	RCA RCA 1867	My Own Peculiar Way/Natural To Be Gone	6
66	RCA Victor RD 7749	COUNTRY WILLIE (LP)	25
66	Liberty (S)LBY 1240	AND THEN I WROTE (LP)	22
69	RCA RD 7997	TEXAS IN MY SOUL (LP)	20

NELSON TRIO (U.K.)

57	Oriole CB 1360	Tear It Up/Roll The Carpet Up	12
57	Oriole CB 1360	Tear It Up/Roll The Carpet Up (78)	10

NELSON TRIO (U.S.)

60	London HLL 9019	All In Good Time/The Town Crier	15
60	London HLL 9019	All In Good Time/The Town Crier (78)	50

CHIITRA NEOGY

68	Gemini GMX 5030	THE PERFUMED GARDEN (LP)	20

NEO MAYA

67	Pye 7N 17371	I Won't Hurt You/U.F.O.	60

(see also Episode Six)

NEON BOYS

90	Overground OVER 11	TIME (EP, purple vinyl, 2,000 only)	6
90	Overground OVER 11	TIME (12" EP, 20 test pressings only)	20
91	Overground OVER 19	That's All I Know (Right Now)/Love Comes In Spurts/High Heeled Wheels/ Don't Die/Time (last 2 tracks credited to Richard Hell & Voidoids [Part III]) (12", p/s, 2,000 only, clear vinyl)	8

MINT VALUE £

91	Overground OVER 19	That's All I Know (Right Now)/Love Comes In Spurts/High Heeled Wheels/ Don't Die/Time (Last 2 tracks credited to Richard Hell & Voidoids [Part III]) (CD, 2,000 only)	8

(see also Richard Hell, Television)

NEON HEARTS

77	Neon Hearts NEON 1	Venus Eccentric/Regulations (8" p/s)	30
78	Satril SAT 133	Answers/Armchair Thriller (p/s)	8
79	Satril SAT 139	Popular Music/Pretty As A Picture (p/s)	8
79	Satril SATL 4012	POPULAR MUSIC (LP)	15

NEPTUNE'S EMPIRE

71	Polymax PXX 01	NEPTUNE'S EMPIRE (LP)	120

PETER NERO

69	CBS M 63589	I'VE GOTTA BE ME (LP)	12

NERO & GLADIATORS

61	Decca F 11329	Entry Of The Gladiators/Boots	12
61	Decca F 11367	In The Hall Of The Mountain King/The Trek To Rome	12
61	Decca F 11413	Czardas/That's A Long Time Ago	20

(see also Laurie Jay, Gladiators, Screaming Lord Sutch & Savages, State Of Mickey & Tommy)

PAUL NERO (SOUNDS)

68	Liberty LBL 83100	NERO'S SOUL PARTY (LP)	15

NERVE

67	Page One POF 019	No. 10 Downing Street/Georgie's March	12
68	Page One POF 055	Magic Spectacles/Come The Day	18
68	Page One POF 081	It Is/Mystery Lady	18
68	Page One POF 097	Piece By Piece/Satisfying Kind	15

(see also Lovin')

NERVES

78	Lightning GIL 520	TV Adverts/Sex Education (p/s)	35

NERVES

81	Good Vibrations BIG 3	NOTRE DEMO (LP, official bootleg, foldover sleeve with booklet [matrix A1])	15

NERVOUS CHOIR

89	Cathexis CRN 5407	O'David/Tonight We Start On Witches/Alsatians/Introducing (p/s, with inserts)	5

NERVOUS NORVUS

56	London HLD 8338	Ape Call/Wild Dog Of Kentucky (gold label print, later silver)	100/50
56	London HLD 8338	Ape Call/Wild Dog Of Kentucky (78)	8
57	London HLD 8383	Dig/Bullfrog Hop (gold label print, later silver)	125/60
57	London HLD 8383	Dig/Bullfrog Hop (78)	8
62	Salvo SLO 1812	Does A Chinese Chicken Have A Pigtail/ROD BARTON: Dear Old San Francisco	35

JIM NESBIT

65	Vocalion V 9241	Tiger In My Tank/I Can't Stand This Living Alone	25

MICHAEL NESMITH (& FIRST/SECOND NATIONAL BAND)

70	RCA RCA 2001	Joanne/The Crippled Lion (with First National Band)	10
71	RCA RCA 2053	Silver Moon/Lady Of The Valley (with First National Band)	10
71	RCA RCA 2086	Nevada Fighter/Here I Am (with First National Band)	10
76	RCA RCA 2692	Silver Moon/Lady Of The Valley (reissue)	6
76	Island IEP 4	I Fall To Pieces/Silver Moon/Some Of Shelley's Blues/Joanne (solo, p/s)	8
76	Island WIP 6373	Rio/Life, The Unsuspecting Captive (solo)	6
78	Island WIP 6398	Navajo Trail/Love's First Kiss (solo)	7
89	Awareness AWP 014	Rio/I'll Remember You (solo) (p/s)	6
70	RCA SF 8136	MAGNETIC SOUTH (LP, with First National Band)	25
71	RCA SF 8209	NEVADA FIGHTER (LP, with First National Band)	25
72	RCA SF 8276	TANTAMOUNT TO TREASON VOLUME ONE (LP, with Second National Band)	22
73	RCA APL1 0164	PRETTY MUCH YOUR STANDARD RANCH STASH (LP, solo)	15
75	Island ILPS 9428	THE PRISON (LP, boxed with book, unreleased in U.K.)	
76	RCA RS 1064	THE BEST OF MICHAEL NESMITH (LP)	15
77	Island ILPS 9439	AND THE HITS JUST KEEP ON COMIN' (LP, gatefold sleeve, solo)	12
77	Island ILPS 9486	FROM A RADIO ENGINE TO A PHOTON WING (LP, solo)	12

(see also Monkees, Wichita Train Whistle)

NEU!

73	United Artists UP 35485	Super/Neuschnee	8
75	United Artists UP 35874	Isi/After Eight	7
72	United Artists UAS 29396	NEU (LP)	60
73	United Artists UAS 29500	NEU II (LP, gatefold sleeve)	60
75	United Artists UAS 29782	NEU '75 (LP, gatefold sleeve)	30

(see also La Düsseldorf)

NEUTRONS

74	United Artists UP 35704	Dance Of The Psychedelic Lounge Lizard/Suzy And The Wonder Boy	5
74	United Artists UAG 29652	BLACK HOLE STAR (LP, with inner sleeve)	15
75	United Artists UAG 29726	TALES FROM THE BLUE COCOONS (LP)	15

(see also Man)

MIKE NEVARD'S MELODY MAKER ALL STARS

54	Atlantic Golden Bell ATL LP2	ACES ANONYMOUS (10" LP)	20

NEVILLE (Willoughby)

72	Explosion EX 2057	I Love Jamaica/Marry Me Marie	6

(see also Whistling Willie)

MINT VALUE £

AARON NEVILLE

67	Stateside SS 584	Tell It Like It Is/Why Worry	20
69	B&C CB 107	Tell It Like It Is/Why Worry (reissue)	6
67	Liberty LBY 3089	HERE 'TIS (LP)	45

DEREK NEW QUINTET

63	Ember JBS 711	Scandinavian Nocturne/Nearly Ready To Begin	5

NEW AGE STEPPERS

80	On-U Sound ONU 1	Fade Away/LONDON UNDERGROUND: Learn A Language (p/s)	7
80	On-U Sound ONULP 1	NEW AGE STEPPERS (LP)	10

NEWBEATS

64	Hickory 45-1269	Bread And Butter/Tough Little Buggy (pink or black/blue label)	each 7
64	Hickory 45-1282	Everything's Alright/Pink Dally Rue	8
65	Hickory 45-1290	Break Away/Hey O Daddy O	8
65	Hickory 45-1305	The Birds Are For The Bees/Better Watch Your Step	8
65	Hickory 45-1320	I Can't Hear You No More/Little Child	8
65	Hickory 45-1332	Run Baby Run/Mean Woolly Willie	12
66	Hickory 45-1366	Shake Hands (And Come Out Crying)/Too Sweet To Be Forgotten	12
66	Hickory 45-1387	Crying My Heart Out/Short Of Love	15
66	Hickory 45-1422	My Yesterday Love/Patent On Love	10
69	London HLE 10270	Bread And Butter/Pink Dally Rue	5
70	London HLE 10299	Groovin' (Out On Life)/Everything's Alright	5
71	London HLE 10341	Run Baby Run/Am I Not My Brother's Keeper	5
72	London HLE 10356	Thou Shalt Not Steal/Bad Dreams	5
65	Hickory LPE 1503	NEWBEATS (EP)	25
65	Hickory LPE 1506	AIN'T THAT LOVIN' YOU BABY (EP)	25
66	Hickory LPE 1510	OH! GIRLS GIRLS (EP)	35
65	Hickory LPM 120	BREAD AND BUTTER (LP)	40
72	London SHE 8428	RUN, BABY, RUN (LP)	15

(see also Dean & Mark, Larry Henley)

PHINEAS NEWBORN

61	Columbia 33SX 1311	I LOVE A PIANO (LP, also stereo SCX 3370)	12/15

(see also Roy Haines)

NEW BREED

65	Decca F 12295	Friends And Lovers Forever/Unto Us	35

MICKEY NEWBURY

72	Elektra K 12047	An American Trilogy/San Francisco Mabel Joy	6

NEWCASTLE BIG BAND

72	Impulse ISS NBB 106	NEWCASTLE BIG BAND (LP, white labels, 2,000 only)	185

(see also Last Exit, Police, Sting, Radio Actors)

NEW CENSATION

75	DJM DJS 10371	First Round Knockout/Everybody's Got A Story	7

NEW CHRISTY MINSTRELS

63	CBS AAG 160	Green, Green/The Banjo	7
63	AAG 175	Saturday Night/The Wheeler Dealers	6
64	CBS AAG 234	Down The Road I Go/Gotta Get A' Goin'	6
64	CBS 201328	Three Wheels On My Wagon/Mighty Mississippi	7
65	CBS 201758	The River/Se Piangi Se Ridi	6
65	CBS EP 6057	THREE WHEELS ON MY WAGON (EP)	12
66	CBS EP 6072	EVERYBODY LOVES SATURDAY NIGHT (EP)	10
63	CBS BPG 62268	TELL TALL TALES (LP)	12
63	CBS BPG 62269	RAMBLIN' (LP)	12
65	CBS BPG 62492	SING AND PLAY COWBOYS AND INDIANS (LP)	12
66	CBS 63338	ON TOUR THROUGH MOTORTOWN (LP)	15

(see also Barry McGuire)

NEW COLONY SIX

66	London HLZ 10033	I Confess/Dawn Is Breaking	50
66	Stateside SS 522	I Lie Awake/At The River's Edge	75
68	Mercury MF 1030	I Will Always Think About You/Hold Me With Your Eyes	8
69	Mercury MF 1086	Things I'd Like To Say/Come And Give Your Love To Me	8

NEWCOMERS

72	Stax 2025 063	Pin The Tail On The Donkey/Mannish Boy	6
75	Stax STXS 2023	Keep An Eye On Your Close Friends/(Instrumental Version)	8

NEW DAWN

69	private pressing	MAINLINE (LP)	120

NEW DEAL STRING BAND

69	Argo ZDA 104	DOWN IN THE WILLOW (LP, with insert)	35

NEW DEPARTURES QUARTET

60s	Transatlantic TRA 134	THE NEW DEPARTURES QUARTET (LP, with Stan Tracey)	40

(see also Stan Tracey)

NEW ENGLAND

79	Infinity INF 110	P.U.N.K./Shoot (green vinyl, 'lightning' PVC sleeve)	10

DENNIS NEWEY

61	Philips PB 1134	Checkpoint/Title Unknown	7
61	Philips PB 1198	Border Patrol/Yes Yes	6
62	Philips 326 588 BF	The Nightriders/The Pied Piper	6

MINT VALUE £

NEW FACES
65	Pye 7N 15842	So Small/Blue Mist	8
65	Pye 7N 15931	Never Gonna Love Again/You'll Be Too Late	8
66	Pye 7N 17029	Like A Man/Shake Up The Party (Myra)	12
67	Pye 7N 17335	Lace Covered Window/The Life That I Lead	8

NEW FORESTERS
65	Lyntone LYN 932/933	Travel/LIZARDS: My Love Goes On (Sheffield Students Rag record)	30

NEW FORMULA
67	Piccadilly 7N 35381	Do It Again A Little Bit Slower/I'm On The Outside Looking In	10
67	Piccadilly 7N 35401	I Want To Go Back There Again/Can't You See That She Loves Me	10
68	Pye 7N 17552	My Baby's Coming Home/Burning In The Background	8
69	Pye 7N 17818	Stay Indoors/Hare Krishna	25

NEW GENERATION
69	Spark SRL 1000	Sadie And Her Magic Mister Garland/Digger	6
69	Spark SRL 1007	Smokey Blues Away/She's A Soldier Boy	10
70	Spark SRL 1019	Police Is Here/Mister C.	5

BOB NEWHART
60	Warner Bros WM 4010	THE BUTTON-DOWN MIND OF BOB NEWHART (LP, also stereo WS 8010)	12
61	Warner Bros WM 4032	THE BUTTON-DOWN MIND STRIKES BACK (LP)	12
62	Warner Bros WM 4055	BEHIND THE BUTTON-DOWN MIND OF BOB NEWHART (LP)	12
63	Warner Bros WM/WS 8110	THE BUTTON-DOWN MIND ON TV (LP)	12
64	Warner Bros WM 8148	NEWHART FACES BOB NEWHART (LP)	12
65	Warner Bros W(W) 1588	THE WINDMILLS ARE WEAKENING (LP)	12

NEW HEARTS
77	CBS 5800	Just Another Teenage Anthem/Blood On The Knife (p/s)	10
78	CBS 6381	Plain Jane/My Young Teacher (p/s)	10

(see also Secret Affair)

NEW HERITAGE
73	Westwood WRS 028	ALL MANNER OF THINGS (LP)	50

NEW HOPE
69	London HL 10296	Won't Find Better Than Me/They Call It Love	10

(see also Kit Kats)

NEW JAZZ GROUP
56	Tempo EXA 39	MODERN JAZZ SCENE (EP)	20

NEW JAZZ ORCHESTRA
65	Decca LK 4690	WESTERN REUNION (LONDON 1965) (LP)	50

(see also Neil Ardley, Nucleus)

NEW JERSEY CONNECTION
82	Nitelife LIFE 1	Love Don't Come Easy/Love Don't Come Easy (Instrumental) (12")	8

NEW JERSEY KINGS
90s	Acid Jazz JAZIDLP 33	PARTY TO THE BUS STOP (LP)	20
90s	Acid Jazz JAZIDCD 33	PARTY TO THE BUS STOP (CD)	20

(see also James Taylor Quartet)

NEW JUMP BAND
68	Domain D 1	The Only Kind Of Girl/Seven Kinds Of Sweet Lovin'	8

ANTHONY NEWLEY
78s
59	Decca F 11127	I've Waited So Long/Sat'day Night Rock-A-Boogie	12
59	Decca F 11137	Idle On Parade/Idle Rock-A-Boogie	15
59	Decca F 11142	Personality/My Blue Angel	18
59	Decca F 11163	Someone To Love/It's All Over	18
60	Decca F 11194	Why/Anything You Wanna Do	20
60	Decca F 11220	Do You Mind/Girls Were Made To Love And Kiss	25
60	Decca F 11254	If She Should Come To You/Lifetime Of Happiness	30

SINGLES
59	Decca F 11127	I've Waited So Long/Sat'day Night Rock-A-Boogie	8
59	Decca F 11137	Idle On Parade/Idle Rock-A-Boogie	7
59	Decca F 11142	Personality/My Blue Angel	7
59	Decca F 11163	Someone To Love/It's All Over	6
60	Decca F 11194	Why/Anything You Wanna Do	5
60	Decca F 11220	Do You Mind/Girls Were Made To Love And Kiss	5
60	Decca F 11254	If She Should Come To You/Lifetime Of Happiness	5
60	Decca F 11295	Strawberry Fair/A Boy Without A Girl	5
61	Decca F 11331	And The Heavens Cried/Lonely Boy And Pretty Girl	5
61	Decca F 11362	Pop Goes The Weasel/Bee Bom	5
61	Decca F 11376	What Kind Of Fool Am I/Once In A Lifetime	5
62	Decca F 11419	D-Darling/I'll Walk Beside You	6
62	Decca F 11486	That Noise/The Little Golden Clown	6
63	Decca F 11636	There's No Such Thing As Love/She's Just Another Girl	6
63	Decca F 11767	The Father Of Girls/I Love Everything About You	6
64	Decca F 11818	Tribute/Lament To A Hero	12
66	RCA RCA 1518	Why Can't You Try To Didgeridoo/Is There A Way Back To Your Arms	8

EPs
59	Decca DFE 6566	SINGS FOUR SONGS FROM IDLE ON PARADE	12
60	Decca DFE 6629	TONY'S HITS	12
60	Decca DFE 6655	MORE HITS FROM TONY	12
61	Decca DFE 6687	THIS TIME THE DREAM'S ON ME	12

MINT VALUE £

LPs

60	Decca LK 4343	LOVE IS A NOW AND THEN THING	18
61	Decca LK 4406	TONY	18
64	Decca LK 4600	IN MY SOLITUDE	18
64	Decca LK 4654	NEWLEY DELIVERED	18
65	RCA Victor RD/SF 7737	WHO CAN I TURN TO (mono/stereo)	15/18
66	RCA Victor RD/SF 7837	NEWLEY RECORDED	15

ANDY NEWMAN

72	Track 2406 103	RAINBOW (LP)	18

(see also Thunderclap Newman)

BRAD NEWMAN

62	Fontana H 357	Somebody To Love/This Time It's Love	12
62	Fontana H 369	Get A Move On/Here And Now And Evermore	10
62	Fontana 267 220TF	Stay By Me/Candy Lips	10
62	Fontana 267 243TF	Point Of No Return/Now I've Lost You	10
63	Fontana 267 273TF	I'll Find You Another Baby/No Man Should Ever Be Alone	10
64	Piccadilly 7N 35174	Please Don't Cry/Every Hour Of Living	8

COLIN NEWMAN

80	Beggars Banquet BEG 48	B/Classic Remains/Alone On Piano (p/s)	5
81	Beggars Banquet BEG 52	Inventory/This Picture (p/s)	5
82	4AD AD 209	We Means We Starts/Not To (Remix) (p/s)	7
88	4AD CN 1	Not To (We Means We Starts)/Not To/You And Your Dog/ H.C.T.F.R./No Doubt/The Grace You Know (CD free with "Provisionally Entitled The Singing Fish" CD)	8

(see also Wire)

DEL NEWMAN SOUND

67	Columbia SCX 6181	FLOWER GARDEN (LP)	30

JIMMY (C.) NEWMAN

57	London HLD 8460	A Fallen Star/I Can't Go On This Way	30
57	London HLD 8460	A Fallen Star/I Can't Go On This Way (78)	10
59	MGM MGM 1009	What'cha Gonna Do/So Soon	15
59	MGM MGM 1009	What'cha Gonna Do/So Soon (78)	10
59	MGM MGM 1037	Grin And Bear It/The Ballad Of Baby Doe	10
60	MGM MGM 1085	A Lovely Work Of Art/What About Me	7
61	MGM MGM 1112	Now That You're Gone/Wanting You With Me Tonight	6
59	MGM MGM-EP 706	GRIN AND BEAR IT — COUNTRY AND WESTERN STYLE (EP)	45

JOE NEWMAN (SEXTET)

57	Vogue Coral Q 72244	Cocktails For Two/Later For The Happenings	6
57	Vogue Coral LVA 9052	HAPPY CATS (LP)	12
57	Pye/Vanguard PPT 12001	JOE NEWMAN (LP)	15

LIONEL NEWMAN ORCHESTRA

58	Columbia DB 4150	Hey! Eula/Two Butterflies	8

PAUL NEWMAN

66	Mercury MF 969	Ain't You Got A Heart/Tears On My Pillow	15

RANDY NEWMAN

68	Reprise RS 20692	Love Story/I Think It's Going To Rain Today	6
70	Reprise RS 20945	Gone Dead Train/JACK NITZSCHE: Harry Flowers	6
72	Reprise K 14155	Lonely At The Top/My Old Kentucky Home	5
72	Reprise K 14190	Sail Away/Political Science	5
89	Warner Bros 925 680-2	I Love L.A. (LP Version)/I'm Different (LP Version)/Miami (LP Version)/ I Love L.A. (Video) (CD Video)	8
68	Reprise R(S)LP 6286	RANDY NEWMAN CREATES SOMETHING NEW UNDER THE SUN (LP)	15
70	Reprise RSLP 6373	12 SONGS (LP)	12

(see also Harry Nilsson, Tom Petty & Heartbreakers)

TOM NEWMAN

74	Virgin VS 120	Sad Sing/Ali's Got A Broken Nose	5
75	Virgin VS 130	Don't Treat Your Woman Bad/Why Does Love Hurt So Bad	5
76	Virgin VS 133	Sleep/Darling Corey	5
76	Virgin VS 141	Ebony Eyes/Draught Guinness	5
77	Decca F 13735	Dance Of The Theena Shee (Daoine Sidhe)/The Unseelie Court (as Faerie Symphony [Tom Newman])	5
75	Virgin V 2022	FINE OLD TOM (LP, features Mike Oldfield)	15
75	Virgin V 2042	LIVE AT THE ARGONAUT (LP, unreleased, test pressings only)	80
77	Decca TXS 123	FAERIE SYMPHONY (LP, gatefold sleeve)	18
88	Oceandisc	OZYMANDIAS (LP, unissued, 20 test pressings only in proof sleeve)	30

(see also July, Mike Oldfield)

TONY NEWMAN

68	Decca F 12795	Soul Thing/Let The Good Times Roll	12
70	Decca F 13041	Soul Thing/Let The Good Times Roll (reissue)	7

(see also Sounds Incorporated, Flying Machine, Pinkerton['s Assorted Colours], May Blitz, Three Man Army)

NEW MODEL

83	Mr. Clean MERC 001	Chilean Warning/The World Thru Our Eyes/Totalitarian Terror (p/s, some in 7" x 10" folder)	12/8

NEW MODEL ARMY

83	Shout QS 002/QF 001	Bittersweet/Betcha/Tension (p/s, with flexi "Fashion"/"The Cause")	5

NEW MONITORS

72	Buddah 2011 118	Fence Around Your Heart/Have You Seen Her	8

NEW ORDER

Year	Label / Cat. No.	Title	Value £
81	Factory FAC 33	Ceremony/In A Lonely Place (p/s)	8
81	Factory FAC 3312	Ceremony (Re-recording)/In A Lonely Place (Extended) (12", cream & blue p/s)	10
81	Factory FAC 53	Procession/Everything's Gone Green (grey p/s, white writing; also other colours)	12
81	Factory Benelux FBNL 8	Everything's Gone Green/Mesh/Cries & Whispers (12", yellow sleeve)	15
82	Factory FAC 51B	Rocking Carol/Ode To Joy (flexidisc, given away at Hacienda, 4,000 only)	15
82	Factory FAC 63	Temptation/Hurt (p/s)	10
83	Factory FAC 7312	Blue Monday/The Beach (12", die-cut sleeve, silver insert)	12
83	Factory FAC 93	Confusion (Edit)/(same) (p/s, DJ promo only)	12
84	Factory FAC 103	Thieves Like Us/Lonesome Tonight (p/s)	8
84	Factory FAC 103	Thieves Like Us (Edit)/Lonesome Tonight (Edit) (p/s, DJ promo only)	12
87	Factory FACD 187	Touched By The Hand Of God (Twelve Inch Mix)/Confusion Dub 1987/ Temptation (Original Mix) (CD, gatefold card sleeve)	12
88	Factory FAC 73RD	Blue Monday 1988/Blue Monday (DJ-only mix) (12", p/s, DJ promo only)	10
88	Factory FACD 73R	Blue Monday 1988 (12 Inch)/Beach Buggy (12 Inch)/Blue Monday 1988 (7 Inch) (CD)	10
88	Factory FACDV 73R	Blue Monday 1988 (12 Inch)/Blue Monday 1988 (7 Inch)/Beach Buggy/ Blue Monday 1988 (Video) (CD Video)	50
88	Factory FACDV 183	True Faith (Remix 12 Inch)/Evil Dust/True Faith (7 Inch) (CD Video)/ True Faith (CD Video)	20
88	Factory FAC 223A	Fine Time/Don't Do It/Fine Line (12", 33rpm, 'capsule' sleeve)	12
89	Factory FAC 263DJ	Round & Round (Ben Grosse Mix)/(12" Mix)/(Detroit Mix) (12", p/s, DJ only)	10
89	Factory FAC 263R	Round & Remix (12", p/s with orange or green inner)	10
89	Factory FACD 263R	Round & Round (Seven Inch)/Vanishing Point (Instrumental Making Out Mix)/Round & Round (Twelve Inch)/ Best & Marsh (Seven Inch) (3" CD, g/f card p/s)	10
89	Factory FAC 273/7	Run 2 (Edit)/MTO (Edit) (DJ promo only, 500 pressed)	20
89	Factory FAC 273	Run 2/Run 2 (Extended Version)/MTO/MTO (Minus Mix) (12", p/s, with inner sleeve, 20,000 only)	15
85	Factory FACTUS 12C	POWER, CORRUPTION & LIES (cassette with 2 extra tracks)	12
86	Factory FACT 150SP	BROTHERHOOD (LP, limited metallic sleeve)	12
86	Factory FACD 150SP	BROTHERHOOD (CD, with "State Of The Nation" & metallic booklet)	20
87	Factory FACT 200	THE GATEFOLD SUBSTANCE (LP, numbered gatefold sleeve, 1,000 only)	35
87	Factory FACT 200C	SUBSTANCE (cassette, 200 only in box set with insert)	30

(see also Joy Division, Electronic, England/New Order, Revenge)

NEW ORDER

Year	Label / Cat. No.	Title	Value £
81	Come Org. CARA12	BRADFORD RED LIGHT DISTRICT (LP)	110

(see also Come)

NEW ORLEANS ALL STAR BAND

Year	Label / Cat. No.	Title	Value £
56	Vogue V 2380	Struttin' With Some Barbecue/Basin Street Blues	12
56	Vogue V 2368	Christopher Columbus/Bugle Call Rag	7

NEW ORLEANS BOOTBLACKS

Year	Label / Cat. No.	Title	Value £
54	Columbia SCM 5090	Flat Foot/Mad Dog	15

NEW ORLEANS WILD CATS

Year	Label / Cat. No.	Title	Value £
62	Storyville A 45048	Roll Along Prairie Moon/Well Well Well	5

NEWPORT JAZZ FESTIVAL ALL STARS

Year	Label / Cat. No.	Title	Value £
61	London Jazz LTZ-K 15202	NEWPORT JAZZ FESTIVAL ALL STARS (LP, also stereo SAH-K 6116)	10/12

NEW RELIGION

Year	Label / Cat. No.	Title	Value £
72	Bamboo BAM 70	In The Black Caribbean/Black Is Black	15
73	Ackee ACK 526	Walk Away Renee/What's It All About	6

NEWS

Year	Label / Cat. No.	Title	Value £
66	Decca F 12356	The Entertainer/I Count The Tears	15
66	Decca F 12477	This Is The Moment (from the TV series "Adam Adamant")/Ya Ya Da Da	12

(see also Patto, Glenn Hughes, Finders Keepers, Miller, Big Boy Pete)

NEWS FROM BABEL

Year	Label / Cat. No.	Title	Value £
86	Recommended RE 6116	NEWS FROM BABEL (LP, hand-screened sleeve)	12

BOBBY NEWSOME

Year	Label / Cat. No.	Title	Value £
72	Mojo 2093 018	Jody Come And Get Your Shoes/Post Office	6

WAYNE NEWTON

Year	Label / Cat. No.	Title	Value £
63	Capitol CL 15319	Danke Schoen/Better Now Than Later	8
65	Capitol CL 15380	Comin' On Too Strong/Red Roses For A Blue Lady	8
65	Capitol CL 15422	Keep The Lovin'/Remember When	5
68	MGM MGM 1426	Dreams Of The Everyday Housewife/The Tips Of My Fingers	5

OLIVIA NEWTON-JOHN

Year	Label / Cat. No.	Title	Value £
66	Decca F 12396	Till You Say You'll Be Mine/For Ever	200
71	Pye International 7N 25543	If Not For You/The Biggest Clown	12
76	EMI EMI 2519	Don't Stop Believin'/Greensleeves (p/s)	5
77	EMI EMI 2616	Sam/Changes (p/s)	5
77	EMI (no cat. no.)	Please Mr. Please/PILOT: Love Is (flexidisc free with *Record Mirror*)	6/5
80	Jet JET 185	Xanadu/Fool Country (gatefold p/s, with ELO)	6
80	Jet JET 10-185	Xanadu/Fool Country (10" pink vinyl, die-cut p/s, with ELO)	15
80	Jet JETP 196	Magic/Whenever You're Away From Me (picture disc)	15
88	Mercury MERCD 272	The Rumour/Winter Angel/The Rumour (12" Extended Mix) (CD, picture disc, card sleeve)	15
89	Mercury MERCD 313	When You Wish Upon A Star/Rocking/Rock A Bye Baby/ Twinkle Twinkle Little Star (CD)	15
78	EMI EMAP 789	TOTALLY HOT (LP, picture disc)	15
85	Mercury 826 169-2	SOUL KISS (CD)	20

(see also Toomorrow, Marvin & Farrar)

MINT VALUE £

OLIVIA NEWTON-JOHN & CLIFF RICHARD

80 Jet JET 7002 Suddenly/You Made Me Love You (p/s) 7
(see also Cliff Richard)

NEWTOWN NEUROTICS

79 No Wonder A 45 Hypocrite/You Said No (no p/s, some with insert & sticker) 25/30/35
80 No Wonder NOW 4 When The Oil Runs Out/Oh No (p/s) 30
82 CNT 4/No Wonder NOW 56 Kick Out The Tories!/Mindless Violence! (p/s) 20
82 CNT CNT 010 Licensing Hours/No Sanctuary (p/s) 15
83 Razor RZS 107 Blitzkrieg Bop/Hypocrite (New Version)/I Remember You (p/s) 10
84 No Wonder NOW 6T Suzi/Fools (p/s) 10
83 Razor RAZ 6 BEGGARS CAN BE CHOOSERS (LP) 28

NEW TRENDS

67 Columbia SX 6245 THE NEW TRENDS (LP) 15

NEW VAUDEVILLE BAND

66 Fontana TF 741 Winchester Cathedral/Wait For Me, Baby 6
67 Fontana TF 784 Peek-A-Boo/Amy 6
67 Fontana TF 824 Finchley Central/Rosie (some in p/s) 10/6
67 Fontana TF 853 Green Street Green/Fourteen Lovely Women 6
68 Fontana TF 909 The Bonnie And Clyde/Uncle Gabriel (some in p/s) 8/5
67 Fontana TFE 17497 THOROUGHLY MODERN MILLIE (EP) 8
67 Fontana (S)TL 5386 WINCHESTER CATHEDRAL (LP) 18
67 Fontana (S)TL 5430 FINCHLEY CENTRAL (LP) 15
(see also Bonzo Dog Doo Dah Band, Alberts, Alan Klein)

NEW VENTURES

76 United Artists UP 36101 Moonlight Serenade (Parts 1 & 2) 5

NEW VICTORY BAND

78 Topic 12TS 382 ONE MORE DANCE AND THEN (LP) 15

NEW WANDERERS

79 Grapevine GRP 144 This Man In Love/Adam And Eve 8

NEW YORK BLONDES featuring MADAME X

79 London/Bomp HLZ 10574 Little GTO/RODNEY & BRUNETTES: Holocaust On Sunset Boulevard (no p/s) .. 12

NEW YORK DOLLS

73 Mercury 6052 402 Jet Boy/Vietnamese Baby 10
74 Mercury 6052 615 Stranded In The Jungle/Who Are The Mystery Girls 8
77 Mercury 6160 008 Jet Boy/Babylon/Who Are The Mystery Girls 5
85 Antler DOLLS 1 Personality Crisis/Subway Train (picture disc) 8
85 Antler DOLLS 2 Looking For A Kiss/Bad Girl (picture disc) 8
73 Mercury 6338 270 NEW YORK DOLLS (LP) 25
74 Mercury 6338 498 TOO MUCH TOO SOON (LP) 25
(see also Johnny Thunders, Heartbreakers, Sylvain Sylvain, Idols)

NEW YORK PORT AUTHORITY

77 Invictus INV 5312 I Got It/I Got It (Version) 6
77 Invictus INV 5312 I Got It/I Got It (Version) (12") 8

NEW YORK PUBLIC LIBRARY

66 Columbia DB 7948 I Ain't Gonna Eat Out My Heart Anymore/Rejected 22
68 MCA MU 1025 Gotta Get Away/Time Wastin' 8
68 MCA MU 1045 Love Me Two Times/Which Way To Go 8

NEW YORK ROCK ENSEMBLE

71 CBS 5292 Running Down The Highway/Law And Order 5
69 Atco 228 932 FAITHFUL FRIENDS (LP) 12
71 CBS 64126 ROLL OVER (LP) 12
72 CBS 64324 FREEDOMBURGER (LP) 12

NIADEM'S GHOST

87 Hibination HIDE 002 THIRST (EP, cassette) 15
86 Hibination HIDE 001 IN SHELTERED WINDS (LP, with insert) 50
(see also IQ)

NICE

67 Immediate IM 059 The Thoughts Of Emerlist Davjack/Angel Of Death 8
68 Immediate IM 068 America/The Diamond Hard Blue Apples Of The Moon (pink label, some in p/s) 18/8
68 Immediate IM 072 Brandenburger/Happy Freuds 8
70 Charisma CB 132 Country Pie/One Of Those People 6
70s Immediate IM 068 America/The Diamond Hard Blue Apples Of The Moon (white label, reissue in p/s) 6
67 Immediate IMLP/IMSP 016 THE THOUGHTS OF EMERLIST DAVJACK (LP) 18
67 Immediate AS 2 ALBUM SAMPLER — THE THOUGHTS OF EMERLIST DAVJACK (1-sided LP, promo only) 30
68 Immediate IMSP 020 ARS LONGA VITA BREVIS (LP) 18
69 Immediate IMSP 026 THE NICE (LP) 18
70 Charisma CAS 1014 FIVE BRIDGES (LP, pink label, gatefold sleeve) 15
71 Charisma CAS 1030 ELEGY (LP, pink label) 15
72 Charisma CS 1 AUTUMN '67 AND SPRING '68 (LP) 12
(see also Keith Emerson, Emerson Lake & Palmer, Jackson Heights, Habits, Brian Davison, Refugee, Attack, Jet, P.P. Arnold)

NICK NICELY

80 Voxette VOX 1001 D.C.T. Dreams/Treeline (p/s, reissue copies £5) 8
81 EMI EMI 5256 Hillyfields (1892)/49 Cigars (p/s) 8

ALBERT NICHOLAS

56 Tempo A 129 How Long Blues (with Al Fairweather)/Rose Room (with Lise West) 10
(see also Al Fairweather)

PAUL NICHOLAS

68 Polydor 56285 Where Do I Go/Here Comes The Clown 5
69 Polydor 56322 Who Can I Turn To/Sing A Sad Song For Sammy 5
70 Polydor 56374 Freedom City/Run Shaker Life 5
(see also Oscar, Paul Dean)

BILLY NICHOLLS

68 Immediate IM 063 Would You Believe/Daytime Girl (features Small Faces) 40
73 Track 2094 109 Forever's No Time At All/This Song Is Green (with Pete Townshend) 12
68 Immediate IMCP 009 WOULD YOU BELIEVE (LP, withdrawn) .... 2,000+
74 GM GML 1011 LOVE SONGS (LP) 12

JANICE NICHOLLS

63 Decca F 11586 Oi'll Give It Foive/The Wednesbury Madison 5

SUE NICHOLLS

68 Pye 7N 17565 Where Will You Be/Every Day 5

JOY NICHOLS

53 Parlophone R 3684 Little Red Monkey/Me An' Johnny (78, with Dick Bentley and Jimmy Edwards) 10

MIKE NICHOLS & ELAINE MAY

62 Mercury AMT 1192 A Little More Gauze/Merry Christmas Doctor 6
59 Mercury MMC 14005 IMPROVISATIONS TO MUSIC (LP) 25
65 Mercury 20031 MCL THE BEST OF MIKE NICHOLS & ELAINE MAY (LP) 18

RED NICHOLS & HIS PENNY SYMPHONY

55 Capitol CL 14365 The Viennese Lantern (Lights Of Vienna)/While You're Away 10
56 Capitol CL 14544 Glory, Glory/Bugler's Lament 5
56 Capitol CL 14560 Corky/The Wail Of The Winds 5
56 Capitol CL 14596 The Beautiful Girls Of Vienna/Speak Easy 5
56 Capitol CL 14617 Cool Tango/Indiana 5
51 Capitol LC 6534 JAZZ TIME (10" LP) 12
(see also Kay Starr)

SAM NICHOLS (& MELODY RANGERS)

50 MGM MGM 225 Keep Your Motor Hot/Who Puts The Cat Out When Papa's Out Of Town? (78) 12

LEA NICHOLSON

72 Trailer LER 3010 HORSEMUSIC (LP) 15
80 Kicking Mule SNKF 165 THE CONCERTINA RECORD (LP, features Mike Oldfield) 12

ROGER NICHOLSON

74 Argo ZDA 204 THE GENTLE SOUND OF THE DULCIMER (LP) 12
76 Trailer LER 2094 TIMES & TRADITIONS FOR DULCIMER (LP, with Jake Walton & Andrew Cronshaw) 12

STEVIE NICKS

81 WEA K 79231 Stop Draggin' My Heart Around/Kind Of Woman (p/s, with Tom Petty & Heartbreakers) 6
81 WEA K 79265 Leather And Lace (edit)/Outside The Rain (p/s) 7
82 WEA K 79264 Edge Of Seventeen/Outside The Rain (p/s) 6
83 WEA U 9870 Stand Back/Garbo (p/s) 5
83 WEA U 9870T Stand Back/Garbo/Wild Heart (12", p/s) 10
83 WEA X 9590 If Anyone Falls/Gate & Garden (p/s) 6
84 WEA U 9690 Nightbird/Nothing Ever Changes (p/s) 18
86 Parlophone 12R 6110 I Can't Wait (Extended Mix)/Rock A Little (long)/I Can't Wait (7" Mix) (12", p/s) ... 10
86 Parlophone 12R 6124 Talk To Me/One More Big Time Rock'n'Roll Star/Imperial Hotel (12", p/s) 10
86 EMI EMI 5574 Has Anyone Ever Written Anything For You?/I Can't Wait (Dub Mix) (p/s) 5
86 EMI 12EMI 5574 Has Anyone Ever Written Anything For You?/No Spoken Word/ I Can't Wait (Dub Mix) (12", p/s) 12
89 EMI 12EM 90 Rooms On Fire (extended)/Alice/Has Anyone Ever Written Anything For You? (live) (12", p/s) 8
89 EMI 12EMP 90 Rooms On Fire (extended)/Alice/Has Anyone Ever Written Anything For You? (live) (12", poster p/s) 8
89 EMI TCEM 90 Rooms On Fire (extended)/Alice/Has Anyone Ever Written Anything For You? (live) (cassette) 5
89 EMI CDEM 90 Rooms On Fire (extended)/Alice/Has Anyone Ever Written Anything For You? (live) (CD) 8
89 EMI 12EM 97 Long Way To Go (Remix)/Long Way To Go (7" Version)/Real Tears (12", p/s) 8
89 EMI 12EMG 97 Long Way To Go (7" Version)/(Remix)/Real Tears (12", gatefold p/s) 10
89 EMI 12EMP 114 Whole Lotta Trouble (remix)/Edge Of Seventeen/Beauty And The Beast (live) (12", p/s with poster) 10
91 EMI 12EMS 214 I Can't Wait (Time Space Mix)/I Can't Wait (Dub Mix)/Sleeping Angel (12", p/s with 2 colour photos) 8
91 EMI CDEM 214 I Can't Wait (Time Space Mix)/Edge Of Seventeen (live)/ I Can't Wait (12" Version)/Sleeping Angel (CD) 8
81 WEA 499169 BELLA DONNA (LP) 10
83 WEA 2500 7100 THE WILD HEART (LP) 10
89 EMI EMD 1008 THE OTHER SIDE OF THE MIRROR (LP, early copies with hologram) 15
89 EMI CDEMC 1008 THE OTHER SIDE OF THE MIRROR (CD, early copies with hologram) 20
(see also Fleetwood Mac, Buckingham-Nicks, Tom Petty & Heartbreakers)

NICKY AND THE DOTS

78 Small Wonder SMALL 12 Never Been So Stuck/Linoleum Walk (p/s) 20

MINT VALUE £

NICO
65 Immediate IM 003 I'm Not Sayin'/The Last Mile . . . 40
81 Flicknife FLS 206 Vegas/Saeta (p/s) . . . 8
82 Immediate IMS 003 I'm Not Saying/The Last Mile (p/s, reissue) . . . 5
82 Half 1/2 1 Procession/All Tomorrow's Parties (p/s) . . . 5
68 Elektra EKL 4029 THE MARBLE INDEX (LP, orange label, also stereo EKS 74029) . . . 45/40
71 Reprise RSLP 6424 DESERTSHORE (LP, with John Cale) . . . 25
71 MGM Select 2353 025 CHELSEA GIRL (LP) . . . 25
74 Island ILPS 9311 THE END (LP) . . . 18
81 Aura AUL 715 DRAMA OF EXILE (LP, colour cover) . . . 12
(see also John Cale, Velvet Underground, Ayers Cale Nico & Eno)

JIMMY NICOL (& SHUBDUBS)
64 Pye 7N 15623 Humpty Dumpty/Night Train . . . 20
64 Pye 7N 15666 Husky/Don't Come Back (solo) . . . 18
64 Pye 7N 15699 Baby Please Don't Go/Shub Dubbery (possibly unissued) . . . 20+
(see also Sound Of Jimmy Nicol, Georgie Fame)

WATT NICOLL
71 Xtra XTRA 1122 NICE TO BE NICE (LP) . . . 12

NICRA
77 Ogun OG 010 LISTEN/HEAR (LP) . . . 18
(see also Keith Tippett)

NIE ELECTRIKK
80 Synesthesia SYN 1 Cover Girl/Practically Isolate (p/s) . . . 8

NIGGY HOI!
80s Deli K1Z Theme From Niggy Hoi!/Titanium Kedi (p/s) . . . 8

NIGHTBIRDS
59 Oriole CB 1490 Cat On A Hot Tin Roof/The Square . . . 12
59 Oriole CB 1490 Cat On A Hot Tin Roof/The Square (78) . . . 10

NIGHTBLOOMS
90 Fierce FRIGHT 041 Crystal Eyes/Never Dream At All (p/s) . . . 10

NIGHTCRAWLERS
67 London HLR 10109 The Little Black Egg/You're Running Wild . . . 40

ROBERT NIGHTHAWK
60s XX MIN 718 ROBERT NIGHTHAWK (EP) . . . 15

NIGHT-HAWKS
58 Fontana H 120 Cool For Cats/Time Will Tell (78) . . . 10

NIGHTIME FLYER
69 Pye 7N 17739 Talk To Me/Spinning Wheel . . . 6
69 Pye 7N 17798 Don't Push Me Baby/Thru' Loving You . . . 7
71 Pye 7N 45046 Love On Borrowed Time/It's A Hurtin' Thing . . . 6

NIGHTIME FLYER
81 Red Eye EYE 2 Out With A Vengeance/Heavy Metal Rules (p/s) . . . 15

NIGHTMARE
84 Ebony EBON 22 WAITING FOR THE TWILIGHT (LP) . . . 12

NIGHTMARES IN WAX
79 Inevitable INEV 0002 BIRTH OF A NATION (EP, with wraparound p/s) . . . 40
84 KY KY 9 Black Leather/Shangri-La (12", 'horror' p/s) . . . 35
85 KY KY 9 1/2 Black Leather/Shangri-La/Girls Song (12", different p/s, 3,000 only) . . . 40
(see also Dead Or Alive)

NIGHTRIDERS
66 Polydor BM 56066 Love Me Right Now/Your Friend (withdrawn, issue or promo) . . . 100/75
66 Polydor BM 56116 It's Only The Dog/Your Friend . . . 55
(see also Mike Sheridan & Nightriders, Mike Sheridan's Lot, Idle Race, Jeff Lynne)

NIGHTRIDERS
79 Stardust STR 1001 I Saw Her With Another Guy/London Town (picture insert) . . . 15

NIGHTSHIFT
65 Piccadilly 7N 35243 Corrine Corrina/Lavender Tree . . . 15
65 Piccadilly 7N 35264 That's My Story/Stormy Monday Blues . . . 18

NIGHT-TIMERS
65 Parlophone R 5355 The Music Played On/Yield Not To Temptation (featuring Herbie Goins) . . . 50
(see also Herbie Goins & Night-Timers, Ronnie Jones)

NIGHTWING
80 Ovation OVS 1209 Barrel Of Pain/Nightwing (p/s) . . . 12
84 Gull GULS 75 Treading Water/Call Your Name (p/s) . . . 8
84 Gull GULS 7512 Treading Water/Call Your Name/Barrel Of Pain (12", red vinyl, p/s) . . . 15
84 Gull GULS 77 Night Of Mystery/Dressed To Kill (p/s) . . . 15
84 Gull GULS 7712 Night Of Mystery/Dressed To Kill (12", p/s) . . . 20
85 Gull GULS 80 Strangers Are Welcome/Games To Play//The Devil Walks Behind You/ Cell 151 (double pack, gatefold p/s) . . . 7
79 Ovation OV 1757 SOMETHING IN THE AIR (LP) . . . 15
82 Gull GULP 1036 BLACK SUMMER (LP) . . . 12
83 Gull GULP 1038 STAND UP AND BE COUNTED (LP) . . . 12
83 Gull PGULP 1038 STAND UP AND BE COUNTED (LP, picture disc) . . . 15
85 Gull GULP 1043 NIGHT OF MYSTERY (LP) . . . 12
(see also Alec Johnson Band, Nutz)

NIHILIST SPASM BAND
85 United Dairies UD 016 1X - X = X (LP) . . . 15

MINT VALUE £

BILL NILE (& HIS GOODTIME BAND)

67 Decca F 12661 Pashionella Grundy/Bric A Brac Man . . . 5
70 Deram DM 290 I Try Not To Laugh/Nobody Knows The Trouble I've Seen . . . 6

WILLY NILLY

84 Ad Hoc AH 1 On The Spur Of The Moment/Half A Job (p/s, with 'time-table' insert) . . . 45

(HARRY) NILSSON

67 RCA Victor RCA 1632 You Can't Do That/Ten Little Indians . . . 6
68 RCA Victor RCA 1675 One/Sister Marie . . . 6
68 RCA RCA 1707 Everybody's Talkin'/Don't Leave Me . . . 6
68 RCA RCA 1764 Mourning Glory/Rainmaker . . . 6
69 RCA RCA 1864 Maybe/The Puppy Song . . . 6
69 RCA RCA 1876 Everybody's Talkin'/One . . . 6
70 RCA RCA 1913 I Guess The Lord Must Be In New York City/Good Old Desk . . . 5
70 RCA RCA 1935 I'll Be Home/Waiting . . . 5
70 RCA RCA 1987 Down To The Valley/Buy My Album . . . 5
71 RCA RCA 2080 Are You Sleeping? . . . 5
72 RCA RCA 2300 Me And My Arrow/Remember (Christmas)/The Lottery Song . . . 5
74 RCA RCA 2459 Many Rivers To Cross/Don't Forget Me . . . 5
75 RCA RCA 2504 Save The Last Dance For Me/All My Life . . . 5
79 RCA Record Year LB 2 Without You/Noel Edmonds Introduces Record Year (Lever Bros premium) . . . 5
84 Polydor POSP 703 Loneliness/Silver Horse (p/s) . . . 5
68 RCA Victor RD/SF 7928 PANDEMONIUM SHADOW SHOW (LP, mono/stereo) . . . 18/15
68 RCA RD/SF 7973 AERIAL BALLET (LP, mono/stereo) . . . 18/15
69 RCA SF 8010 SKIDOO (LP, soundtrack) . . . 20
69 RCA SF 8046 HARRY (LP) . . . 15
70 RCA SF 8091 NILSSON SINGS NEWMAN (LP, with Randy Newman) . . . 15
71 RCA SF 8166 THE POINT (LP, single sleeve or reissue with gatefold sleeve & book) . . . . each 15
73 RCA SF 8326 AERIAL PANDEMONIUM BALLET (LP) . . . 12
74 Rapple/RCA APL1-0220 SON OF DRACULA (LP, soundtrack, with Ringo Starr, fold-out sleeve) . . . 15

(see also Randy Newman, Ringo Starr, Cher)

NILSSON TWINS

57 Capitol CL 14698 Rain On My Window/I Dance When I Walk . . . 5

LEONARD NIMOY

68 Dot (S)LPD 511 MR. SPOCK PRESENTS MUSIC FROM OUTER SPACE (LP) . . . 25
72 Rediffusion ZS 156 MUSIC FROM OUTER SPACE (LP) . . . 15

NINA

69 CBS 4681 Do You Know How Christmas Trees Are Grown?/The More Things Change . . . 12

NINA & FREDERIK

59 Pye Intl. 7N 25021 Jamaica Farewell/Come Back Liza . . . 8
59 Pye Intl. N 25021 Jamaica Farewell/Come Back Liza (78) . . . 8
59 Pye Intl. 7N 25043 The Formula For Love (with Louis Armstrong)/LOUIS ARMSTRONG with VALMA MIDDLETON: Struttin' With Some Barbecue . . . 6
59 Columbia DB 4332 Listen To The Ocean/I Would Amor Her . . . 5
59 Pye Nixa NPT 19023 NINA & FREDERICK (10" LP) . . . 15

NINE BELOW ZERO

81 A&M AMS 8127 Ain't Comin' Back/Liquor Lover (p/s) . . . 8
81 A&M AMS 8110 Three Times Enough/Doghouse (p/s, yellow vinyl) . . . 6
82 A&M AMSX 8210 Wipe Away Your Kiss/True Life Is A Crime (12") . . . 10
81 A&M AMLH 68537 THIRD DEGREE (LP) . . . 12

NINE DAYS WONDER

71 Harvest SHSP 4014 NINE DAYS WONDER (LP) . . . 40

(see also Kilburn & High Roads)

NINE INCH NAILS

90 Island CID 482 DOWN IN IT (mixes) (CD EP, numbered case) . . . 20
90 Island CID 484 HEAD LIKE A HOLE (CD EP) . . . 10
91 Island ISDJ 508 Sin (Radio Edit)/(same) (promo only, stickered p/s) . . . 12
91 Island 9IS 508 Sin (Long)/Sin (Dub)/Get Down Make Love (9", p/s) . . . 15
92 Island IS 552DJ Wish (Radio Edit) (1-sided, stickered plain sleeve, promo only) . . . 12
92 Interscope IMCD 8004 BROKEN (CD EP, foldout digipak) . . . 8
94 Island ILPSD 8012 THE DOWNWARD SPIRAL (2-LP) . . . 18

NINE INCH WORMS

97 Martian BEER 05 A NIGHT ON THE TOWN WITH THE NINE INCH WORMS (9" LP) . . . 12

999

77 Labritain LAB 999 I'm Alive/Quite Disappointing (p/s) . . . 12
77 United Artists UP 36299 Nasty Nasty/No Pity (p/s, green or black vinyl) . . . 10/5
77 United Artists FREE 7 Nasty Nasty/No Pity (78rpm promo, 50 copies only) . . . 60
78 Labritain 12 FREE 10 Waiting/Action (12", mail-order freebie) . . . 8
78 United Artists UP 36399 Emergency/My Street Stinks (p/s) . . . 5
78 United Artists UP 36376 Me And My Desire/Crazy (p/s) . . . 5
78 United Artists UP 36435 Feelin' Alright With The Crew/Titanic (My Over) Reaction (p/s) . . . 8
78 United Artists UP 36467 Homicide/Soldier (p/s, green vinyl) . . . 5
81 Albion ION 1011 Obsessed/Change/Lie, Lie, Lie (live) (p/s, with laminated sleeve, shrinkwrapped with patch) . . . 7
81 Albion ION 1017 Li'l Red Riding Hood/Waiting For Your Number To Be Called/I Ain't Gonna Tell Ya (live) (p/s, with stencil; shrinkwrapped) . . . 7
81 Albion ION 1023 Indian Reservation/So Greedy (Remixed)/Taboo (Remix) (p/s, clear vinyl, with sticker) . . . 5
82 Albion ION 1033 Wild Sun/Scandal City/Bongos On The Nile (p/s, yellow vinyl) . . . 5
78 United Artists UAG 30199 999 (LP, with inner sleeve) . . . 15
78 United Artists UAG 30209 SEPARATES (LP, with inner sleeve) . . . 15

(see also Kilburn & High Roads)

MINT VALUE £

NINESENSE

76	Ogun OG 900	OH! FOR THE EDGE (LP)	12
77	Ogun OG 910	HAPPY DAZE (LP)	12

(see also Elton Dean, Julie Tippetts, Keith Tippett, Mark Charig, Harold Beckett, Alan Skidmore)

1910 FRUITGUM CO.

68	Pye International 7N 25447	Simon Says/Reflections From The Looking Glass	7
68	Pye International 7N 25458	May I Take A Giant Step (Into Your Heart)/(Poor Old) Mr. Jensen	6
68	Pye International 7N 25468	1, 2, 3, Red Light/Sticky, Sticky	6
68	Pye International 7N 25478	Pop Goes The Weasel/The Year 2001	6
69	Buddah 201 037	Indian Giver/Liza	5
69	Buddah 201 049	Special Delivery/No-Good Annie	5
68	Pye Intl. N(S)PL 28115	SIMON SAYS (LP)	25
69	Buddah 203 014	GOODY GOODY GUMDROPS (LP)	18
70	Buddah 2359 006	HARD RIDE (LP)	15

1910 FRUITGUM CO./LEMON PIPERS

68	Pye Intl. NEP 44091	PRESENTING... (EP, 1 side each)	15

1984

69	Big T BIG 117	This Little Boy/Rosalyn	6
69	Big T BIG 120	Got To Have Your Love/Here We Are	6

9.30 FLY

72	Ember NR 5062	9.30 FLY (LP)	90

NINEY (& DESTROYERS/OBSERVERS)

70	Amalgamated AMG 856	Niney Special/Danger Zone	15
70	Pressure Beat PR 5501	Honey No Money/INSPIRATIONS: This Message To You	10
71	Big BG 317	You Must Believe/You Must Believe Version	12
71	Big Shot BI 568	Blood And Fire/Mud And Water	15
71	Big Shot BI 586	Message To The Ungodly/Message To The Ungodly — Version	8
71	Gas GAS 167	Blood And Fire/ROLAND ALPHONSO: 33 66	12
71	Moodisc HME 111	People Let Love Shine/MUDIES ALL STARS: Too Much	6
72	Big Shot BI 607	Hiding By The Riverside/The Red Sea	6
72	Big Shot BI 609	Beg In The Gutter/Beg In The Gutter Version	6
72	Big Shot BI 610	Everyday Music (by The Observers)/Observing The Avenue	7
72	Bullet BU 503	Aily And Ailaloo (& Max)/Version	7
72	Downtown DT 494	Get Out My Life/Get Out My Life — Version	6
72	Downtown DT 495	Hi Diddle/Hi Diddle — Version	6

(see also Niney's All Stars, Observers)

NINEY'S ALL STARS

70	Unity UN 563	Skankee/Skankee — Version	10

(see also Niney, Observers)

NINJAMAN & FLOURGON

90	Sure Delight 23 SDT	ZIG IT UP — MAIN ATTRACTION: Zig It Up (Radio/Freestyle/Funke-Club/Funke-Instrumental Mixes) (12", p/s)	10

NINO & EBBTIDES

61	Top Rank JAR 572	Those Oldies But Goodies/Don't Run Away	60

NIPPLE ERECTORS

78	Soho SH 1/2	King Of The Bop/Nervous Wreck (50 only with glossy p/s, later matt p/s)	28/20

(see also Nips, Pogues)

NIPS

78	Soho SH 4	All The Time In The World/Private Eyes (foldover p/s)	25
80	Soho SH 9	Gabrielle/Vengeance	15
80	Soho SH 9	Gabrielle/Vengeance (tour copy with 'licensed to cool' stamp)	30
80	Chiswick CHIS 119	Gabrielle/Vengeance (reissue, p/s)	15
81	Test Pressing TP 5	Happy Song/Nobody To Love (p/s)	20
80	Soho HOHO 1	ONLY AT THE END OF THE BEGINNING (LP, with insert, white labels)	50

(see also Nipple Erectors, Pogues)

NIRVANA (U.K.)

67	Island WIP 6016	Tiny Goddess/I Believe In Magic	22
67	Island WIP 6020	Pentecost Hotel/Feelin' Shattered	15
68	Island WIP 6029	Rainbow Chaser/Flashbulb	18
68	Island WIP 6038	Girl In The Park/C Side In Ocho Rios	15
68	Island WIP 6045	All Of Us (The Touchables)/Trapeze	12
69	Island WIP 6052	Wings Of Love/Requiem To John Coltrane	22
69	Island WIP 6057	Oh! What A Performance/Darling Darlene	18
70	Pye International 7N 25525	The World Is Cold Without You/Christopher Lucifer	18
71	Vertigo 6059 035	The Saddest Day Of My Life/(I Wanna Go) Home	15
71	Philips 6006 127	Pentecost Hotel/Lazy Day Drift	12
72	Philips 6006 166	Stadium/Please Believe Me	8
76	Bradleys BRAD 7602	Two Of A Kind/Before Midnight	6
76	Island WIP 6180	Rainbow Chaser/Tiny Goddess (p/s)	7
78	Pepper UP 36461	Love Is/Pascale	5
79	Pepper UP 36538	Restless Wind/Thank You And Goodnight	5
81	Zilch ZILCH 8	The Picture Of Dorian Gray/No It Isn't	5
82	Zilch ZILCH 15	Black And White Or Colour/Tall Trees	5
88	Bam Caruso OPRA 45	Black Flower/WIMPLE WINCH: Save My Soul (jukebox issue, die-cut sleeve)	5
68	Island ILP 959/ILPS 9059	THE STORY OF SIMON SIMOPATH (LP, pink label, mono/stereo)	70
68	Island ILPS 9087	ALL OF US (LP, pink label)	70
70	Pye Intl. NSPL 28132	DEDICATED TO MARKOS III (LP)	125
71	Vertigo 6360 031	LOCAL ANAESTHETIC (LP, gatefold sleeve, swirl label)	60
72	Philips 6308 089	SONGS OF LOVE AND PRAISE (LP)	65
87	Bam-Caruso KIRI 061	BLACK FLOWER (LP)	12

(see also Patrick Campbell-Lyons, Ray Singer, Pica, Hat & Tie)

NIRVANA (U.S.)

Year	Label / Cat. No.	Title	Value
89	Tupelo TUP EP8	Blew/Love Buzz/Been A Son/Stain (12", p/s)	30
89	Tupelo TUP CD8	Blew/Love Buzz/Been A Son/Stain (CD)	40
90	Tupelo TUP 25	Sliver/Dive (gatefold p/s, green vinyl only, 2,000 pressed)	20
91	Tupelo TUP EP25	Sliver/Dive/About A Girl (live)/Dive (12", p/s)	40
91	Tupelo TUP EP25	Sliver/Dive/About A Girl (live)/Dive (12", repressing, blue vinyl, p/s)	50
91	Tupelo TUP CDEP25	Sliver/Dive/About A Girl (live)/Spank Thru (live) (CD)	20
91	Geffen DGCT 5	Smells Like Teen Spirit (Edit)/Even In His Youth/Aneurysm (12", p/s)	10
91	Geffen DGCTP 5	Smells Like Teen Spirit (Edit)/Drain You (LP Version)/Aneurysm (12", picture disc, die-cut p/s)	40
91	Geffen DGCCD 5	Smells Like Teen Spirit (Edit)/Drain You/Even In His Youth/Aneurysm (CD, digipak with tour dates)	15
92	Geffen DGCTP 7	Come As You Are/Endless, Nameless/School (live) (12", picture disc, die-cut p/s)	35
92	Geffen DGCTP 9	Lithium/Been A Son (live)/Curmudgeon (12", picture disc, die-cut p/s)	30
92	Geffen DGCTD 9	Lithium/Been A Son (live)/Curmudgeon (CD, digipak)	10
92	Geffen GFS 34	In Bloom/Sliver (live)/Polly (live) (p/s)	10
92	Geffen DGCTP 34	In Bloom/Sliver (live)/Polly (live) (12", picture disc, die-cut p/s)	15
93	Touch & Go TG 83	Oh, The Guilt/JESUS LIZARD: Puss (p/s, blue vinyl, some with poster)	18/10
93	Touch & Go TG 83	Oh, The Guilt/JESUS LIZARD: Puss (p/s, black vinyl)	30
93	Touch & Go TGCD 83	Oh, The Guilt/JESUS LIZARD: Puss (CD)	15
93	Geffen GFST 66	All Apologies/Rape Me (12", p/s with 2 art prints)	8
93	Geffen GFSC 66	All Apologies/Rape Me (cassette)	8
93	Geffen GFSTD 66	All Apologies/Rape Me (CD)	10
94	Geffen (no cat. no.)	Penny Royal Tea (Scott Litt Mix)/Where Did You Sleep Last Night (live) (unreleased, 10 test pressings only)	800+
94	Geffen NIRPRO (no cat. no.)	Penny Royal Tea (Scott Litt Mix) (CD, 1-track, no inlay, promo only)	800+
89	Tupelo TUP LP 6	BLEACH (LP, 300 on white vinyl, 2,000 on green vinyl)	250/100
89	Tupelo TUP LP 6	BLEACH (LP, black vinyl)	20
89	Tupelo TUP CD 6	BLEACH (CD, original issue with extra tracks "Love Buzz" & "Downer")	20
91	Geffen DGC 24425	NEVERMIND (LP, with inner sleeve)	15
91	Geffen DGCCD 24425	NEVERMIND (CD, without uncredited bonus track "Endless, Nameless")	20
94	Geffen GED 24727	UNPLUGGED IN NEW YORK (LP, white vinyl with inner sleeve)	15
02	Sub Pop 9878700341	BLEACH (LP, white vinyl, with inner)	15

(see also Foo Fighters)

NITE-LITERS

Year	Label / Cat. No.	Title	Value
72	RCA 2214	K-Jee/Tanga Boo Gonk	6
72	RCA SF 8282	INSTRUMENTAL DIRECTIONS (LP)	15

NITE PEOPLE

Year	Label / Cat. No.	Title	Value
66	Fontana TF 747	Sweet Tasting Wine/Nobody But You	18
67	Fontana TF 808	Trying To Find Another Man/Stay As Sweet As You Are	15
67	Fontana TF 885	Summertime Blues/In The Springtime	40
68	Fontana TF 919	Morning Sun/Where You There	18
69	Page One POF 149	Love, Love, Love/Hot Smoke And Sassafras (some with insert)	18/12
69	Page One POF 159	Is This A Dream/Cream Tea	12
70	Page One POF 174	Season Of The Rain/P.M.	12
69	Page One POLS 025	P.M. (LP)	190

(see also Banana Bunch)

NITE ROCKERS

Year	Label / Cat. No.	Title	Value
58	RCA RCA 1079	Nite Rock (Lonely Train)/Oh! Baby	100
58	RCA RCA 1079	Nite Rock (Lonely Train)/Oh! Baby (78)	70

NITESHADES

Year	Label / Cat. No.	Title	Value
65	CBS 201763	Be My Guest/I Must Reveal	10
65	CBS 201817	Fell So Fast/I'm Not Gonna Worry	10

NITRO FUNCTION

(see under Billy Cox)

NITTY GRITTY DIRT BAND

Year	Label / Cat. No.	Title	Value
67	Liberty LIB 55948	Buy Me For The Rain/Candy Man	10
68	Liberty LBF 15099	Collegiana/End Of Your Line	8
70	Liberty LBF 15358	Rave On/The Cure	6
71	United Artists UP 35253	House At Pool Corner/Travelin' Mood	6
71	United Artists UP 35282	Some Of Shelley's Blues/The Cure	6
72	United Artists UP 35357	Jambalaya/Hoping To Say	6
68	Liberty LBL/LBS 83122	PURE DIRT (LP)	25
69	Liberty LBL/LBS 83286	DEAD AND ALIVE (LP)	25
71	Liberty LBG 83345	UNCLE CHARLIE AND HIS DOG TEDDY (LP, gatefold sleeve)	22
72	United Artists UAS 29284	ALL THE GOOD TIMES (LP)	15
74	United Artists USD 307/8	STARS AND STRIPES FOREVER (2-LP)	18

NITZER EBB

Year	Label / Cat. No.	Title	Value
85	Power Of Voice NEP 1	Isn't It Funny How Your Body Works/The Way You Live/Crane/Cold War (12", p/s with insert)	8
85	own label	BASIC PAIN PROCEDURE (EP, cassette, given away at gig)	30
86	Power Of Voice NEB 3	Let Your Body Learn/Let Your Body Learn (Instrumental) (12", p/s)	10

JACK NITZSCHE

Year	Label / Cat. No.	Title	Value
63	Reprise R 20202	The Lonely Surfer/Song For A Summer Night	20
63	Reprise R 20237	Night Walker/Green Grass Of Texas	10
78	MCA MCA 366	Hard Workin' Man (featuring Captain Beefheart)/Coke Machine	10
74	Warner Bros K 41211	ST GILES CRIPPLEGATE (LP)	20

(see also Date With Soul, Mick Jagger, Captain Beefheart, Randy Newman, Crazy Horse)

MINT VALUE £

NIVENS

88 Woosh WOOSH 1 — Let Loose Of My Knee/HOLIDAYMAKERS: Everyday (flexidisc with *Woosh* fanzine, foldaround p/s in poly bag) . . . 8
89 Woosh WOOSH 5 — Yesterday/I Hope You'll Always Be My Friend (p/s) . . . 5

REVEREND A.W. NIX

51 Decca F 9720 — The Black Diamond Express To Hell (Parts 1 & 2) (78) . . . 7

WILLIE NIX

(see under Willie Love, Joe Hill Louis)

NIX-NOMADS

64 HMV POP 1354 — You're Nobody (Till Somebody Loves You)/She'll Be Sweeter Than You (demos miscredited to Nix-Nom*ands*) . . . 90

MEL NIXON

75 Alaska ALA 26 — Every Beat Of Your Heart/ASTRA NOVA ORCHESTRA: Soul Sleeper . . . 5

N-JOI

90 Deconstruction PT 44042 — Anthem/Manic/Techno Gangsters (12", original issue) . . . 15

RAB NOAKES

78 Ring O' 2017 115 — Waiting Here For You/Restless (some in p/s) . . . 18/12
78 Ring O' 2017 117 — I Won't Let You Down/Long After Dark (unreleased)
70 Decca SKL 5061 — DO YOU SEE THE LIGHTS (LP) . . . 22
72 A&M AMLS 68119 — RAB NOAKES (LP, with Stealers Wheel) . . . 15
78 Ring O' 2339 201 — RESTLESS (LP) . . . 20

NOBELMEN

59 Top Rank JAR 155 — Thunder Wagon/Dragon Walk . . . 25
59 Top Rank JAR 155 — Thunder Wagon/Dragon Walk (78) . . . 15

LISA NOBLE

58 Decca F 11006 — Maggie! — Yes Ma!/Who's Sorry Now . . . 5
58 Decca F 11051 — It's A Boy/The Saints . . . 5

NICK NOBLE

57 Mercury MT 165 — Fallen Star/Let Me Hold You In My Arms (78, with Dick Noel Singers) . . . 12
60 Coral Q 72403 — The Tip Of My Fingers/Sweet Love . . . 7
60 Coral Q 72413 — Island Farewell/Excuse Me (I Think I've Got A Heartache) . . . 6
(see also Dick Noel)

PATSY ANN NOBLE

61 HMV POP 980 — Good Looking Boy/The Guy Who Can Mend A Broken Heart . . . 20
63 Columbia DB 4956 — Don't You Ever Change Your Mind/Sour Grapes . . . 15
63 Columbia DB 7008 — Heartbreak Avenue/I'm Nobody's Baby . . . 12
63 Columbia DB 7060 — I Was Only Foolin' Myself/Ordinary Love . . . 12
63 Columbia DB 7088 — Accidents Will Happen/He Tells Me With His Eyes . . . 15
63 Columbia DB 7148 — It's Better To Cry Today/Don't Tell Him I Told You . . . 12
64 Columbia DB 7258 — I Did Nothing Wrong/Better Late Than Never . . . 12
64 Columbia DB 7318 — Private Property/Crack In The Door . . . 12
64 Columbia DB 7386 — Tied Up With Mary/Green Eyed People . . . 10
65 Columbia DB 7472 — Then You Can Tell Me Goodbye/If You Wanna Be More Than Friends . . . 10
65 Polydor BM 56054 — He Who Rides A Tiger/City Of Night . . . 18
(see also Trisha Noble)

TRISHA NOBLE

67 MGM MGM 1371 — Live For Life/The New Is Rarely Patchka . . . 15
(see also Patsy Ann Noble)

CLIFF NOBLES (& CO.)

68 Direction 58-3518 — The Horse/Love Is Alright . . . 8
68 Direction 58-3738 — Judge Baby, I'm Back/Horse Fever (solo) . . . 7
69 Direction 58-4205 — Switch It On/Burning Desire . . . 7
68 Direction 8-63477 — THE HORSE (LP) . . . 25

NO CHOICE

83 Riot City RIOT 20 — SADIST DREAM (EP) . . . 5

NO COVER

82 Guardian GRC 136 — 200 Voices/Seen Too Much . . . 5

NOCTURNAL EMISSIONS

81 Sterile ION 2 — FRUITING BODY (LP) . . . 50
84 Sterile SR 6 — NO SACRIFICE (12", p/s, 2,000 only) . . . 12
84 CFC LP 2 — CHAOS — LIVE AT THE RITZY (LP) . . . 25
84 Illuminated JAMS LP 33 — VIRAL SHEDDING (LP) . . . 25
84 Sterile EMISS 001 — TISSUE OF LIES (LP, 1st batch numbered, later in blue sleeve) . . . 50/25
84 Sterile SR 4 — DROWNING IN A SEA OF BLISS (LP) . . . 60
84 Sterile SR 5 — BEFEHLSNOTSTAND (LP) . . . 25
85 Sterile SRC 003 — DEATHDAY (cassette) . . . 10
85 Sterile SR 7 — SONGS OF LOVE AND REVOLUTION (LP) . . . 18
86 Sterile SR 9 — SHAKE THOSE CHAINS, RATTLE THOSE CAGES (LP) . . . 15
87 Earthly Delights EARTH 02 — THE WORLD IS MY WOMB (LP) . . . 20
88 Earhtly Delights EARTH 04 — SPIRITFLESH (LP) . . . 20
89 Earthly Delights EARTH 03 — STONEFACE (LP) . . . 12
89 Earthly Delights EARTH 05 — BEYOND LOGIC (LP, 250 signed) . . . 25/18
90 Earthly Delights EARTH 06 — MOUTH OF THE BABES (LP) . . . 30
93 Earthly Delights EARTH 08 — THE QUICKENING (LP, 250 signed) . . . 25/18
(see also Caroline K)

NOCTURNES

55 MGM SP 1120 — Whodat? (Buck Dance)/Hey Punchinello . . . 10
55 MGM SP 1148 — Birmin'ham/Toodle-oo Igaloo . . . 10

NOCTURNES

64 Solar SRP 102 — Troika/Rawhide . . . 18

NOCTURNES

67 Columbia DB 8158 — Wish You Would Show Me Your Mind/I Do, I Do . . . 8
67 Columbia DB 8219 — Why (Am I Treated So Bad?)/Save The Last Dance For Me . . . 8
68 Columbia DB 8332 — A New Man/Suddenly Free . . . 8
68 Columbia DB 8453 — Carpet Man/Look At Me . . . 7
68 Columbia DB 8493 — Montage/Fairground Man . . . 7
68 Columbia S(C)X 6223 — THE NOCTURNES (LP) . . . 22
68 Columbia S(C)X 6315 — WANTED ALIVE (LP) . . . 25
(see also Lyn Paul)

NOCTURNS

64 Decca F 12002 — Carryin' On/Three Cool Cats . . . 10

NO DOUBT

96 Interscope INSP 95515 — Don't Speak/Greener Pastures (picture disc, numbered p/s) . . . 6
97 Interscope INSJB 95515 — Don't Speak/Greener Pastures (jukebox issue) . . . 8
97 Interscope INSJB 95539 — Just A Girl/Open The Gate (jukebox issue) . . . 8

PROFESSOR ERNEST NODE & HIS MUG & JUG BAND

67 Columbia DB 8100 — The Egg Plant That Ate Chicago/I'm In The Doghouse . . . 10

NOËL

79 Virgin VS 258 — Dancing Is Dangerous/Dancing Is Dangerous (Long Version) (p/s) . . . 5
79 Virgin VS 286 — The Night They Invented Love/Au Revoir (p/s) . . . 5
79 Virgin V 2126 — IS THERE MORE TO LIFE THAN DANCING (LP, picture disc) . . . 12
(see also Sparks)

DICK NOEL

56 London HLH 8295 — (The Same Thing Happens With) The Birds And The Bees/Birth Of The Blues . . . 30
56 London HLH 8295 — (The Same Thing Happens With) The Birds And The Bees/ Birth Of The Blues (78) . . . 12
(see also Nick Nobel)

NO FAITH

81 No Faith NF 001 — Double Trouble/Only The Good Die Young (p/s, private pressing) . . . 160

NOIR

71 Dawn DNLS 3029 — WE HAD TO LET YOU HAVE IT (LP, with insert) . . . 25

NO KIDDING

74 Wave — NO KIDDING (LP) . . . 15

JOE NOLAN & HIS BAND

69 Jolly JY 013 — Cool It With Reggae/Reggae With Me . . . 7
69 Jolly JY 016 — Confidential/Poison Reggae . . . 7
(see also Bonnie Frankson)

TERRY NOLAND

58 Coral Q 72311 — Oh Baby! Look At Me/Puppy Love . . . 200
58 Coral Q 72311 — Oh Baby! Look At Me/Puppy Love (78) . . . 90

NOLAN SISTERS/NOLANS

72 Nevis NEVS 007 — Blackpool, Blackpool/Apple Pie . . . 10
72 Nevis NEVEP 005 — SILENT NIGHT (EP) . . . 6
74 EMI EMI 2209 — But I Do/Now I'm Stuck On You . . . 8
75 Target TGT 103 — Make A Little Sunshine Shine/Have Love Will Travel . . . 5
76 Target TGT 108 — Rain/Oh My Darling . . . 6
76 Target TGT 116 — Thanks For Calling/Oh My Darling . . . 5
76 Target TGT 121 — When You Are A King/Hey What A Day . . . 5
82 Epic EPCA 2625 — GREATEST ORIGINAL HITS (EP) . . . 5
82 Lyntone LYN 11763 — Konica Pop Flexi (p/s, 1-sided flexidisc, featuring edits of Nolan Sisters' "Attention To Me" + tracks by Abba & Stars On 45) . . . 5
72 Nevis NEVR 009 — THE SINGING NOLANS (LP) . . . 18
77 Hanover Grand HG 19751 — THE NOLAN SISTERS (LP, sold only at London Room Club, Drury Lane) . . . 25

PIERRE NOLES

63 Oriole CB 1791 — Jacqueline/Marilyn . . . 7

NAZ NOMAD & NIGHTMARES

84 Big Beat NS 93 — I Had Too Much To Dream (Last Night)/Cold Turkey (p/s) . . . 5
84 Big Beat WIK 21 — GIVE DADDY THE KNIFE CINDY (LP, purple vinyl) . . . 12
(see also Damned)

NOMADS

70 Pye 7N 17906 — The Singer Sang His Song/Lovin' Him . . . 6

NON

80 Mute MUTE 7 — I Can't Look Straight/SMEGMA: Flash Cards (p/s, with 2 centre holes) . . . 10
81 Mute MUTE 015 — NON EP (Rise/Out Out Out/Romance Fatal Dentro Deun Auto) (12", p/s) . . . 12
00 Mute MUTE 250 — Solitude/Receive The Flame (p/s, two centre holes, A-side plays at 45 rpm, B-side has closed grooves and plays at *any* speed, 700 copies only) . . . 8
(see also Boyd Rice)

NO NAMES

65 Polydor NH 59080 — All Because Of You/She Is Mine . . . 40

JIMMY NOONE

55 Vogue/Coral LRA 10026 — APEX CLUB ORCHESTRA (10" LP) . . . 15

MINT VALUE £

PETER NOONE
71 Rak RAK 114 — Oh You Pretty Things/Together Forever. . . . 5
71 Rak RAK 121 — Right On Mother/Walnut Whirl 7
72 Rak RAK 129 — Shoo Be Doo Wah/Because You Were There 6
72 Rak RAK 136 — Should I/Each And Every Minute. . . . 5
(see also Herman's Hermits)

NO OTHER NAME
79 Daylight LD 500 — DEATH INTO LIFE (LP, with insert) 25

NO QUARTER
83 Reel REEL 1 — Survivors/Time And Space/Racing For Home (12", foldout p/s). . . . 40
83 Bonzo Bear — BIRDS OF PREY EP (12"). . . . 30

NORA/BUNNY
72 Tropical AL 0015 — Butterfly/TROPICAL ALL STARS: Fly Version 5

KEN NORDINE
57 London RE-D 1091 — KEN NORDINE READS (EP, with Billy Vaughn Orchestra) 20
59 London Jazz EZ-D 19040 — WORD JAZZ (EP) 15
67 Philips BL 7785 — COLOURS (LP). . . . 50
(see also Billy Vaughn & His Orchestra)

NORFOLK & JOY
79 Dara MPA 031 — SCOTSOUNDS (LP) 30

NO RIGHT TURN
83 Chelful CHL 001 — NO (LP). . . . 25

NORMA & TONY
69 (No Cat. No.) — YOU ARE ALWAYS WELCOME AT OUR HOUSE (LP, private pressing, 100 only) . 80

NORMAL
78 Mute MUTE 001 — T.V.O.D./Warm Leatherette (p/s). . . . 6
(see also Robert Rental)

NORMAL
03 Ai AI 005 — GREEN FUELS EP (12", p/s) 8

GENE NORMAN (JUST JAZZ)
51 Vogue V 2022 — Hot House (Parts 1 & 2) (78, solo). . . . 8
51 Vogue V 2047 — Blue Lou (Parts 1 & 2) (78) 8
56 Vogue V 2047 — Blue Lou (Parts 1 & 2) 6
50s Vogue V 2022 — Hot House (Parts 1 & 2) (solo). . . . 6
50s Vogue V 2272 — Four O'Clock Jump/Three O'Clock Jump 6

LARRY NORMAN
69 Key KL 010/Dove DOVE 64 — UPON THIS ROCK (LP). . . . 15
73 MGM 2315 135 — I'M ONLY VISITING THIS PLANET (LP, with lyric sheet) 12
76 Solid Rock ROCKY 1 — IN ANOTHER LAND (LP, gatefold sleeve) 18

MONTY NORMAN
55 HMV 7M 349 — The Shifting, Whispering Sands/Bonnie Blue Gal. . . . 15
57 HMV POP 281 — The Garden Of Eden/Priscilla 15
63 United Artists UEP 1010 — DOCTOR NO SOUNDTRACK (EP) 25
63 United Artists (S)ULP 1097 — DOCTOR NO (LP, soundtrack, mono/stereo) 30/35

OLIVER NORMAN
67 Polydor 56176 — Down In The Basement/Drowning In My Own Despair 10
68 Polydor 56247 — People People/You'll Find It Will Come 6

NORMAN & HOOLIGANS
77 President PT 461 — I'm A Punk/Re-Entry. . . . 15

NORMAN & INVADERS
64 United Artists UP 1031 — Stacey/Our Wedding Day 10
64 United Artists UP 1058 — Our Wedding Day/Stacey (reissue) 6
65 United Artists UP 1077 — Night Train To Surbiton/Likely Lads. . . . 12

NORMAN CONQUEST
67 MGM MGM 1376 — Two People/Upside Down 60
(see also Factory, Peter & Wolves, John Pantry)

FREDDIE NORTH
72 Mojo 2092 043 — Sweeter Than Sweetness/I Did The Woman Wrong 6
72 Mojo 2916 012 — FRIEND (LP). . . . 25

ROY NORTH
63 Oak RGJ 107 — Blues In Three/Blues In Five 50

NORTH BANK
72 Polydor 2058225 — Arsenal We're On Your Side/Half Time. . . . 5

NORTHERN LIGHT
75 CBS 3370 — Minnesota/Minnesota (DJ Version) 12

NORTHERN LIGHTS
66 United Artists UP 1123 — No Time/Time To Move Along 40
66 United Artists UP 1161 — Through Darkness, Light/Baby Those Are The Rules 40
(see also Hooten[anny] Singers, Abba)

NORTHSIDE
91 Factory FACT 310 — CHICKEN RHYTHMS (LP, with inner sleeve). . . . 15
91 Factory FACTCD 310 — CHICKEN RHYTHMS (CD) 20

NORTH STARS
65 Fontana TF 581 — For My True Love/Nothing But The Best 8
66 Fontana TF 726 — She's So Far Out She's In/Eeenie Meenie Minee Mo. . . . 20

MINT VALUE £

NORTHWIND
71 Regal Zono. SLRZ 1020 — SISTER, BROTHER, LOVER (LP) 190
(see also Elastic Band)

NOSEBLEEDS
77 Rabid TOSH 12 — Ain't Bin To No Music School/Fascist Pigs (p/s) 30
(see also Durutti Column, Ed Banger, Blue Orchids)

NOSMO
74 Pye 7N 45382 — Teenage Love/Goodbye 8

NO SWEAT
79 Rip Off RIP 4 — Start All Over Again/You Should Be So Lucky (p/s) 8

NOTATIONS (U.K.)
72 Chapter One SCH 174 — Need Your Love/Just Nothing Left To Give 35

NOTATIONS (U.S.)
76 Curtom K 16696 — Think Before You Stop/I'm Losing 6
76 Curtom K 56212 — NOTATIONS (LP) 25

FREDDIE NOTES & RUDIES
69 Downtown DT 427 — I Don't Wanna Lose That Girl/Train From Vietnam 12
69 Grape GR 3010 — Guns Of Navarone/Yester-Me, Yester-You 8
69 Grape GR 3011 — Babylon Girl/Girl I've Got A Date 8
69 Trojan TR 7713 — Shanghai/Rome Wasn't Built In A Day 10
70 Bullet BU 421 — The Feeling Is Fine/Girl You're Killing Me 7
70 Trojan TR 7724 — Rocco/Don't Tell Your Mama 8
70 Trojan TR 7734 — Down On The Farm/Easy Street 10
70 Trojan TR 7791 — Montego Bay/RUDIES: Blue Mountain 5
70 Trojan TR 7810 — Walk A Mile In My Shoes/JOHNNY ARTHEY ORCHESTRA: Reggae Rouser 5
70 Duke DU 63 — The Bull/River Ben Come Up 7
70 Duke DU 68 — Chicken Inn/Chicken Scratch 7
70 B&C CB 125 — It Came Out The Sky/Well Oh Well (p/s) 5
70 Trojan TBL 109 — UNITY (LP) 35
70 Trojan TBL 152 — MONTEGO BAY (LP) 30

NOTHINGS
65 CBS 201779 — At Times Like This/Love So Sweet 8

NO TREND/LYDIA LUNCH
85 Widowspeak WSP 3 — HEART OF DARKNESS (12" EP) 8
(see also Lydia Lunch)

NOTSENSIBLES
79 Redball RR 02 — (I'm In Love With) Margaret Thatcher/Little Boxes/Gary Bushell's Band Of The Week (p/s) 15
80 Bent SMALL BENT 5 — Death To Disco/Coronation Street Hustle/Lying On The Sofa (p/s) 10
80 Snotty Snail NELCOL 1 — (I'm In Love With) Margaret Thatcher/Little Boxes/Gary Bushell's Band Of The Week (p/s, reissue) 10
80 Snotty Snail NELCOL 3 — I Thought You Were Dead/I Make A Balls Of Everything I Do/ Teenage Revolution (p/s) 10
81 Snotty Snail NELCOL 6 — I Am The Bishop/The Telephone Rings Again (p/s) 8
80 Bent — INSTANT CLASSICS (LP) 35
80 Snotty Snail SSLP 1 — INSTANT CLASSICS (LP, reissue) 25

NOTTS ALLIANCE
72 Tradition TSR 011 — THE CHEERFUL 'ORN (LP, with Roy Harris) 15

NOVAK
97 Enraptured WORM 2 — Silver Seas/Schmaltz (p/s in outer hand-sewn cloth sleeve with embroidered "Hand-knitted by Novak" label, 200 only, each different) 15
97 Enraptured WORM 2 — Silver Seas/Schmaltz (p/s, 800 only) 8
97 Kitty Kitty CHOOSY 007 — Rapunzel/Almost Chinook (hand crayoned p/s, 1,000 only) 8

NOVA LOCAL
69 MCA MUPS 377 — NOVA 1 (LP) 35

NOVAS
63 RCA RCA 1360 — Push A Little Harder/Oh, Gee Baby! 22

NOVAS
65 London HLU 9940 — The Crusher/Take 7 40

NOW
69 NEMS 56-4125 — Marcia/Hands On My Clock Stand Still 20

NOW
77 Ultimate ULT 401 — Development Corporations/Why (p/s, some on blue vinyl) 35/20
79 Raw RAW 31 — Into The 1980s/Nine O'Clock (p/s, 800 only) 40

NO WAY
78 Our Own IS/NW/1035 — Breaking Point/TV Pox/30 Seconds (p/s) 30

NOW GENERATION
73 Green Door GD 4055 — Alone Again, Naturally/MIND-BODY-SOUL: My Part (Version) 6
73 Pyramid PYR 7007 — Baby Don't Do It/You'll Never Know 6
(see also I Roy, B.B. Seaton, Audley Rollins)

NOYES BROTHERS
80 Object Music OBJ 009/010 — SHEEP FROM GOATS (2-LP) 40
(see also Steve Miro & Eyes, Spherical Objects)

NOYS OF US
60s KPS KPS 502 — He's Alright Jill/What Can I Do 30

MINT VALUE £

N.R.B.Q. (New Rhythm & Blues Quintet)

69	CBS 4290	Stomp/I Didn't Know Myself	6
69	CBS 4501	C'mon Everybody/Rocket Number 9	6
73	Kama Sutra 2013 056	Ain't It All Right/Only You	5
69	CBS 63653	N.R.B.Q. (LP)	20
72	Buddah 2319 018	SCRAPS (LP)	12

(see also Carl Perkins)

N.S.U.

69	Stable SLE 8002	TURN ON OR TURN ME DOWN (LP)	130

GUITAR NUBBIT

64	Bootleg 501	Georgia Chain Gang/Hard Road (99 copies only)	45
60s	XX MIN 705	GUITAR NUBBIT (EP)	20

NUCHA

90	CBS 655885 7	Together/Ha Sempre Alguem	5

NUCLEAR SOCKETTS

81	Subversive SUB 001	HONOR BEFORE GLORY (EP, folded p/s, 33rpm)	10
81	Subversive SUB 002	Play Loud/Shadow On The Map	10

(IAN CARR'S) NUCLEUS

70	Vertigo 6360 008	ELASTIC ROCK (LP, gatefold sleeve, swirl label, later 'spaceship' label)	45/15
71	Vertigo 6360 027	WE'LL TALK ABOUT IT LATER (LP, g/fold sl., swirl or 'spaceship' label)	55/15
71	Vertigo 6360 039	SOLAR PLEXUS (LP, as Ian Carr's Nucleus, gatefold sleeve, swirl or 'spaceship' label)	40/12
72	Vertigo 6360 076	BELLADONNA (LP, as Ian Carr's Nucleus, gatefold sleeve, swirl or 'spaceship' label)	50/12
73	Vertigo 6360 091	LABYRINTH (LP, 'spaceship' label)	20
73	Vertigo 6360 100	ROOTS (LP, 'spaceship' label)	20
74	Vertigo 6360 110	UNDER THE SUN (LP, 'spaceship' label)	12
75	Vertigo 6360 119	SNAKE HIPS ETCETERA (LP, 'spaceship' label)	20
75	Vertigo 6360 124	ALLEY CAT (LP, 'spaceship' label)	12
76	Vertigo 9286 019	DIRECT HITS (LP, 'spaceship' label)	12
80	Mood 24000	AWAKENING (LP)	30

(see also Don Rendell & Ian Carr Quintet, Neil Ardley, Centipede, Michael Garrick, New Jazz Orchestra, Linda Hoyle)

TED NUGENT (& AMBOY DUKES)

74	Discreet K 19200	Sweet Revenge/Ain't It The Truth (as Ted Nugent & Amboy Dukes)	8
75	Epic S EPC 3900	Stormtroopin'/Hey Baby (some in p/s, orange label)	5
76	Epic S EPC 4796	Dog Eat Dog/Love You So I Told You A Lie	5
77	Epic S EPC 5482	Cat Scratch Fever/A Thousand Nights	5
78	Epic S EPC 9545	Homebound/Death By Misadventure (p/s)	5
75	Discreet K 59203	CALL OF THE WILD (LP)	12

(see also [American] Amboy Dukes)

NUGGETS

55	Capitol CL 14216	Quirl Up In My Arms/So Help Me, I Love You	25
55	Capitol CL 14267	Shtiggy Boom/Anxious Heart	22

GARY NUMAN

SINGLES

79	Beggars Banquet BEG 23	Cars/Asylum (p/s,orange plastic labels)	6
79	Beggars Banquet BEG 23	Cars/Asylum (p/s, 'mispressed' on dark red vinyl)	10
79	Beggars Banquet BEG 29	Complex/Bombers (live) (p/s, 'mispressed' on dark red vinyl)	12
80	Beggars Banquet SPC 7	Cars/We Are Glass (cassette, cigarette-pack style box)	8
80	Beggars Banquet BEG 35	We Are Glass/Trois Gymnopedies (1st Movement) (p/s)	5
80	Beggars Banquet BEG 35	We Are Glass/Trois Gymnopedies (1st Movement) (p/s, 'mispressed' on dark red vinyl)	12
80	Beggars Banquet BEG 46	I Die, You Die/Down In The Park (Piano Version) (p/s, dark red vinyl 'mispress')	8
80	Beggars Banquet BEG 46	I Die, You Die/Down In The Park (Piano Version) (p/s, mispressing, plays "Remember I Was Vapour" & "On Broadway" [SAM 126])	12
81	Beggars Banquet BEG 62	She's Got Claws/I Sing Rain (p/s, mispressing, plays Dollar's "Hand Held In Black And White")	18
81	Beggars Banquet BEG 68	Love Needs No Disguise/Take Me Home (textured p/s, with Dramatis)	5
81	Beggars Banquet BEG 68T	Love Needs No Disguise/Take Me Home/Face To Face (12", with Dramatis)	8
83	Beggars Banquet BEG 95P	Warriors/My Car Slides (aeroplane-shaped picture disc)	15
84	Beggars Banquet TUB 1	This Is My Life (unissued promo for "The Plan", 300 white label test pressings only)	60
84	Numa NUP 4	Berserker/Empty Bed, Empty Heart (head shaped picture disc)	5
85	Strange Fruit ST 503	JOHN PEEL SESSION ONE (poster p/s)	6
85	Strange Fruit ST 503	JOHN PEEL SESSION TWO (poster p/s)	6
85	Numa NU 7	THE LIVE EP (p/s, blue, white or black vinyl)	5
85	Numa NUM 7	THE LIVE EP (12", p/s, blue, white vinyl or black vinyl)	8
85	Numa NUM 7	THE LIVE EP (12", p/s, mispressing on multicoloured vinyl)	80
85	Numa NUP 9	Your Fascination/We Need It (picture disc)	6
85	Numa NUMP 9	Your Fascination (Extended)/We Need It/Anthem (12", picture disc)	10
85	Numa NU 11	Call Out The Dogs/This Ship Comes Apart (p/s)	7
85	Numa NUM 13	Miracles/Fear (12", 'mispressed' p/s - no red ink)	15
85	Numa NUM 13	Miracles/Fear (12", p/s, red or white vinyl)	8
86	Numa NUMX 16	This Is Love/Survival//Call Out The Dogs (Extended)/No Shelter/This Ship Comes Apart (12", p/s, stickered double pack, shrinkwrapped)	12
86	Numa NUP 17	I Can't Stop/Faces (aeroplane-shaped picture disc)	8
86	Numa NUDJ 17	I Can't Stop/Faces (10", p/s, with preview flexidisc)	8
86	Numa NUM 17	I Can't Stop/(Extended Mix)/Faces (12", p/s, with interview flexidisc)	8
87	B. Banquet BEG 199P	Cars ('E' Reg Model)/Are 'Friends' Electric? (picture disc)	6
87	B. Banquet BEG 199C	Cars ('E' Reg Model)/Are 'Friends' Electric?/We Are Glass/ I Die, You Die (USA Mix) (cassette)	5

MINT VALUE £

Year	Label / Cat. No.	Title / Details	Value
87	Beggars Banquet BEG 199TR	Cars ('E' Reg Extended Model)/Are 'Friends' Electric?/Cars ('E' Reg Model 7" Mix)/Cars (Motorway Mix) (12", p/s)	8
88	Polydor POSPP 894	No More Lies (picture disc)	6
88	I.R.S. ILSP 1003	New Anger/I Don't Believe (poster p/s)	5
88	I.R.S. ILSCD 1003	New Anger/I Don't Believe/Creatures (live)/I Can't Stop (live) (CD)	15
88	Illegal ILS 1004	America/Respect (p/s)	5
88	I.R.S. ILSPD 1004	America/Respect (live) (picture disc)	5
88	I.R.S. ILSPD 1004	America/Respect (live) (mispressed picture disc, 'Gary' picture both sides)	30
88	I.R.S. ILSCD 1004	America (Remix)/Respect (live)/New Anger (live)/Call Out The Dogs (live) (CD)	15
89	B. Banquet BBP 5CD	SELECTION (CD EP, picture disc)	8
91	I.R.S. NUMAN 1	Heart/Icehouse (p/s, black vinyl)	5
91	I.R.S. NUMANCD 1	Heart/Icehouse/Tread Careful (CD)	8
91	Numa NUCD 22	Emotion/In A Glass House/Hanoi/Emotion (CD mix) (CD, 'mispressed' disc)	12
92	Numa NU 24DJ	Machine & Soul/Machine & Soul (fan club issue, white label, mail-order only)	8
92	Numa NUCD 224	Machine & Soul/(Mix 4)/(Promo Mix 2)/1999/The Hauntings (CD)	12
93	Beggars Banquet BEG 264T	Cars (Multivalve)/Cars (Endurance Model)/Cars (Top Gear Model) (12", black vinyl, promo only)	12
93	Beggars Banquet BEG 264	Cars ('93 Sprint)/Cars (Top Gear) (poster p/s)	5
93	Beggars Banquet BEG 264L	Cars ('93 Sprint)/Cars (Endurance) (McLaren F1-shaped picture disc)	8
93	Beggars Banquet BEG 264CD	Cars ('93 Sprint)/(Multivalve)/(Classic)/(Endurance)/(Top Gear)/(Motorway Mix)/('E' Reg Version) (CD, withdrawn, last track mispressed with 12" mix)	15
94	Salvation SACD 1	THE RADIAL PAIR (CD EP, fan club issue, mail order only)	12
94	Numa NU 26	A Question Of Faith/Whisper Of Truth (fan club issue, white label, mail-order only)	18
95	Numa NUMP 27	Absolution/Magic (Trick Mix)/Magic (extended mix) (12", picture disc)	8
95	Numa NUCDP 27	Absolution/Magic (Trick Mix)/Magic (extended mix) (CD, picture disc)	8
96	Polygram TV PRM 1	Cars (Premier Mix)/Are 'Friends' Electric? (live version) (picture disc, numbered, 5,000 only)	5
96	Polygram TV GNRAD 1	Cars (Premier Mix)/Are 'Friends' Electric? (live version)/We Are Glass (CD, promo only)	12
96	The Record Label SPIND 6	Radio (with N.R.G.)/Radio (extended mix) (CD, withdrawn)	60

ALBUMS

Year	Label / Cat. No.	Title / Details	Value
80	Beggars Banquet BEGA 19	TELEKON (LP, dark red vinyl 'mispressing', with stickered sl.; some with bonus single SAM 126 "Remember I Was Vapour [live]"/"On Broadway [live]")	20/15
81	Beggars Banquet BEGA 28	DANCE (LP, gatefold sleeve with poster)	12
82	Beggars Banquet BEGA 40	I, ASSASSIN (LP, initial copies at Woolworths with colour poster and merchandise sheet)	20
83	TV Records TVA 7	NEW MAN (LP, mail-order)	15
84	B. Banquet BEGA 55P	THE PLAN (LP, picture disc)	12
85	Numa NUMAD 1002	WHITE NOISE (2-LP, gatefold p/s)	20
85	Numa NUMAP 1003	THE FURY (LP, with mispress pink inner sleeve)	12
86	Numa NUMAP 1003	THE FURY (LP, mispress picture disc, "Your Fascination" 12" photo on A-side)	35
86	Numa GNFCDA 1	IMAGES 1 & 2 (2-LP, fan club issue with photo inserts, mail-order only)	25
86	Numa CDNUMA 1003	THE FURY (CD, with original mixes and artwork)	30
86	Numa CDNUMA 1005	STRANGE CHARM (CD)	30
87	Numa GNFCDA 2	IMAGES 3 & 4 (2-LP, fan club issue with photo inserts, mail-order only)	25
87	Numa GNFCDA 3	IMAGES 5 & 6 (2-LP, fan club issue with photo inserts, mail-order only)	20
87	Numa GNFCDA 4	IMAGES 7 & 8 (2-LP, fan club issue with photo inserts, mail-order only)	20
87	Numa NUMAD 1007	GHOST (2-LP, fan club issue, mail-order only)	18
88	I.R.S. ILPPD 035	METAL RHYTHM (LP, picture disc)	12
88	IRS ILPCD 035	METAL RHYTHM (CD)	30
89	IRS EIRSACD 1021	METAL RHYTHM (CD, reissue)	30
89	IRS EIRSACD 1019	THE SKIN MECHANIC — LIVE (CD)	20
89	Numa GNFCDA 5	IMAGES 9 & 10 (2-LP, fan club issue with photo inserts, mail-order only)	20
91	Numa NUMACD 1001	BERSERKER (CD, fan club issue, mail order only, blue text on CD & inlay)	30
91	Numa GNFCCD 11	IMAGES 11 (CD, fan club issue, mail order only)	20
92	Receiver RRLP 170	THE OTHER SIDE OF GARY NUMAN (LP, withdrawn)	12
93	Numa NUMACDX 1009	MACHINE & SOUL (CD, mispressed with 9 tracks instead of 13)	20
94	Numa NUMA 1010	DREAM CORROSION (3-LP, autographed gatefold sleeve; copies bought at HMV with signed 10" x 8" photo)	20
94	Numa NUMA 1011	SACRIFICE (LP, with lyric sheet, stickered sleeve & bonus single: "The Seed Of A Lie [5.26]"/"The Seed Of A Lie [7.07]")	15

(see also Tubeway Army, Sharpe & Numan, Paul Gardiner, Dramatis, Claire Hamill, Radio Heart, Nicky Robson, Paper Toys, Caroline Munro, Generator, Bauhaus, Bill Sharpe)

NUMBER NINE BREAD STREET

Year	Label / Cat. No.	Title / Details	Value
67	Holy Ground HG 112/1109	NUMBER NINE BREAD STREET (LP, 250 copies only)	400

NUMBERS

Year	Label / Cat. No.	Title / Details	Value
79	Blasto SRTS 79/CUS/358	ROCK STARS (EP, with insert)	30

NUMBERS

Year	Label / Cat. No.	Title / Details	Value
92	Homegrown HG 701	Here Today/Put 'Em All To Shame/Another Day/Tear You Down (photocopied or green & white sleeve; some with poster)	60/50

NU NOTES

Year	Label / Cat. No.	Title / Details	Value
63	HMV POP 1232	Hall Of Mirrors/Fury	22
64	HMV POP 1311	Kathy/Sunset	18

(see also Russ Sainty & Nu Notes)

NUNS

Year	Label / Cat. No.	Title / Details	Value
81	Butt FUN 2	Wild/Suicide Child (p/s)	5

NURSE WITH WOUND

Year	Label / Cat. No.	Title / Details	Value
83	L.A.Y.L.A.H. LAY 3	GYLLENSKÖLD, GEIJERSTAM AND I AT RYDBERG'S (12" EP)	40
84	L.A.Y.L.A.H. LAY 7	BRAINED BY FALLING MASONRY (12" EP)	12

MINT VALUE £

86	Torso 33016	SPIRAL INSANA (12" EP)	12
87	Crystal/Wisewound WW 01	Crank/TERMITE QUEEN: Wisecrack (numbered plain black sleeve with printed band, 500 only)	20
88	Yangki 002	FAITH'S FAVOURITES EP: Swamp Rat (with Current 93)/Ballad Of The Pale Girl (12", laminated p/s)	30
88	Idle Hole MIRROR 003	Cooloorta Moon/Great Empty Space (12", p/s)	20
90	Harbinger 001	The Burial Of The Stoned Sardine/CURRENT 93: No Hiding From The Blackbird	15
90	United Dairies UD 031	SORESUCKER EP: I Am The Poison/Journey Through Cheese (12", p/s, 2,000 only)	20
90	United Dairies UD 031CD	SORESUCKER EP: I Am The Poison/Journey Through Cheese (CD EP)	8
90	Shock SX 004	Sinister Senile: Human Human Human/Psychedelic Underground (45/33rpm, 1,000 only)	25
92	Clawfist 12	Steel Dream March Of The Metal Men/The Dadda's Intoxication ('singles club' release, 33rpm, foldover p/s in poly bag, 1,400 only)	15
93	Clawfist 20	CRUMB DUCK (10" EP, shared with Stereolab, 1,450 only; 50 with handmade p/s)	80/40
93	World Serpent WS 7003	Alien (1-sided, company sleeve 1,000 only)	25
95	WN 001	ALICE THE GOON (1-sided 12", p/s, 500 only)	75
79	United Dairies UD 01	CHANCE MEETING ON A DISSECTING TABLE OF A SEWING MACHINE AND AN UMBRELLA (LP, 500 only, originals have hand-painted numbers; beware of bootlegs with *printed* numbers)	115
80	United Dairies UD 03	TO THE QUIET MEN FROM A TINY GIRL (LP, numbered, 500 only, originals have hand-painted numbers; beware of bootlegs with *printed* numbers)	75
80	United Dairies UD 04	MERZBILD SCHWET (LP, numbered, 500 only, originals have hand-painted numbers; beware of bootlegs with *printed* numbers)	75
81	United Dairies UD 08	INSECT AND INDIVIDUAL SILENCED (LP, 1,000 only)	60
83	Mi Mort MI MORT iii	GYLLENSKÖLD, GEIJERSTAM & FRIENDS, LIVE AT BAR MALDOROR (LP, some with insert)	50
83	Third Mind TMR 03	OSTRANENIE 1913 (LP, 3,000 only)	45
85	L.A.Y.L.A.H. LAY 15	THE SYLVIE AND BABS HI-FI COMPANION (LP, gatefold sleeve)	25
85	United Dairies UD 110	DRUNK WITH THE OLD MAN OF THE MOUNTAINS (LP)	25
85	United Dairies UD 012	HOMOTOPY TO MARIE (LP, 5,000 only)	35
86	United Dairies UD 019	AUTOMATING VOL. 1 (LP, 3,000 only)	30
86	United Dairies UD 020	A MISSING SENSE (LP, 1 side only; other side by Organum; 2,000 only)	30
87	United Dairies UD 025	DRUNK WITH THE OLD MAN OF THE MOUNTAINS (LP, reissue, handmade custom sleeve, with insert, signed, 100 only)	125
88	United Dairies UD 027	ALAS THE MADONNA DOES NOT FUNCTION (mini-LP, 45/33rpm, 3,000 only)	25
88	Idle Hole MIRROR ONE	SOLILOQUY FOR LILITH (3-LP box set, 1,000 only)	60
88	Idle Hole MIRROR 1C	SOLILOQUY FOR LILITH PTS 5/6 (LP, with insert)	25
89	Idle Hole MIRROR TWO	PRESENTS THE SISTERS OF PATAPHYSICS (LP, 1,000 only)	25
89	United Dairies UD 030	AUTOMATING VOL. II (LP)	20
89	United Dairies UD 032	A SUCKED ORANGE (LP, some with full colour insert)	25/20
89	Yangki 003	LUMBS SISTER (LP)	30
90	United Dairies UD 134	PSILOTRIPITAKA (3-LP [UD 01, 03 & 04], with bonus LP "Registered Nurse" [UD 00], 1,000 only, some possibly in leather bag)	400/125
90	United Dairies UD 134CD	PSILOTRIPITAKA (3-CD [UD 01, 03 & 04], with bonus CD "Registered Nurse" [UD 00CD], 1,000 only, 30 in 'leather bondage bag')	400/60
90	L.A.Y.L.A.H. LAY 30	BRAINED/GYLLENSKÖLD (LP, withdrawn)	35
91	United Dairies UD 038	CREAKINESS (LP, with Spasm)	20
91	United Dairies UD 09	THE 150 MURDEROUS PASSIONS (LP)	25
91	United Dairies UD 09CD	THE 150 MURDEROUS PASSIONS (CD, sealed in black plastic, 500 only)	30
93	United Dairies UD 059	CRUMB DUCK (LP, shared with Stereolab, reissue of Clawfist EP, 50 copies on pink vinyl, 500 on fluorescent yellow vinyl)	50/25
94	United Dairies UD 043	SECOND PIRATE SESSION – ROCK'N'ROLL STATION – SPECIAL EDITION (LP, red vinyl, 500 only)	20
99	United Dairies UD 056	AN AWKWARD PAUSE (2-LP, translucent grey vinyl, 500 only, 1 side not available on CD)	30
01	United Durtro UDOR 8	BRIGHT YELLOW MOON (CD, with Current 93, first 1,000 with bonus CD)	30
02	United Durtro UD 102	MAN WITH THE WOMAN FACE (LP, ltd. edition clear vinyl, poly sleeve, 2 inserts)	15
00s	United Dairies UDX 092	SOLILOQUY FOR LILITH (3-CD box set)	25

(see also Current 93, Organum/New Blockaders, Diana Rogerson, Sol Invictus, Steven Stapleton & David Tibet, Tibet & Stapleton, Whitehouse)

NU-SOUND EXPRESS LTD.

72	Pye Int'l 7N 25580	One More Time Y'all/A Rose For A Lady	20

NUTHIN' FANCY

80s	Dynamic Cat DC 1001	Looking For A Good Time/Too Much Rock'n'Roll (p/s)	250

(see also Terraplane, Thunder)

NU TORNADOS

58	London HLU 8756	Philadelphia U .S.A./Magic Record	18
58	London HLU 8756	Philadelphia U.S.A./Magic Record (78)	12

NUTRONS

60s	Melodisc M 1593	The Very Best Things/Stop For The Music	18

NUTSHELL

70s	Myrrh MYR 1056	FLYAWAY (LP)	18

MAY'F NUTTER

66	Vocalion VL 1282	Head Shrinker/Don't Know What To Do	15
73	London HLL 10414	I Don't Care/Hitch Hike Nightmare	6

NUTTY SQUIRRELS

59	Pye International 7N 25044	Uh! Oh! Parts 1 & 2	6
59	Pye International N 25044	Uh! Oh! Parts 1 & 2 (78)	15

NUTZ

74 A&M AMS 7115 As Far As The Eye Can See/Just For The Crack . . . 5
74 A&M AMLS 68256 NUTZ (LP) . . . 12
75 A&M AMLS 68306 NUTZ TOO (LP) . . . 12
77 A&M AMLH 64623 HARD NUTZ (LP) . . . 12
77 A&M AMLH 68453 LIVE CUTZ (LP) . . . 12
(see also Rage, Nightwing)

NYAH EARTH

70 Attack ATT 8016 Nyah Bingy/Message . . . 5
70 Attack ATT 8017 Dual Heat/Night Of The Long Knives . . . 5

NYAH FEARTIES

86 Nya DOPLP 001 A TASTY HEIDFUL (LP) . . . 25

NYAH SHUFFLE

70 Grape GR 3021 Sting Ray/Paradise . . . 10

JUDY NYLON

82 On-U-Sound LP 16 PAL JUDY (LP) . . . 12
(see also John Cale, Snatch)

NYLONS

82 Attic NYLON 1 A Million Ways/Up On The Roof (p/s) . . . 6

LAURA NYRO

67 Verve Forecast VS 1502 Wedding Bell Blues/Stoney End . . . 10
68 CBS 3604 Eli's Coming/Sweet Blindness . . . 5
68 CBS 4031 Once It Was Alright Now (Farmer Joe)/Woman's Blues . . . 5
69 CBS 4719 Time And Love/The Man Who Sends Me Home . . . 5
68 CBS 63346 ELI AND THE THIRTEENTH CONFESSION (LP, gatefold sleeve, orange label) . . . 22
69 CBS 63510 NEW YORK TENDABERRY (LP, orange label) . . . 22
69 Verve Forecast SVLP 6022 THE FIRST SONGS (LP) . . . 22
70 CBS 64157 CHRISTMAS AND THE BEADS OF SWEAT (LP, orange label) . . . 12
71 CBS 64770 GONNA TAKE A MIRACLE (LP, orange label) . . . 12
73 CBS 64991 THE FIRST SONGS (LP, orange label) . . . 12
(see also Blondie, Debbie Harry)

OAK

71 Topic 12TS 212 WELCOME TO OUR FAIR (LP) . . . 40
(see also Peta Webb)

OAKENSHIELD

82 Acorn OAK 001 ACROSS THE NARROW SEAS (LP) . . . 18
85 Acorn OAK 002 AGAINST THE GRAIN (LP, with insert) . . . 18

PHILIP OAKEY & GIORGIO MORODER

84 Virgin VSY 713 Together In Electric Dreams/(Instrumental) (picture disc) . . . 6
(see also Human League, Men)

OASIS

SINGLES

94 Creation CRE 176 Supersonic/Take Me Away (p/s) . . . 25
94 Creation CRE 182 Shakermaker/D'Yer Wanna Be A Spaceman? (p/s) . . . 20
94 Creation CRESCD 182 Shakermaker/Alive (Demo Version)/Bring It On Down (Live) (CD) . . . 8
94 Creation CRE 185 Live Forever/Up In The Sky (Acoustic) (numbered foldover p/s in stickered poly bag) . . . 20
94 Creation CRE 190 Cigarettes & Alcohol/I Am The Walrus (live at Glasgow Cathouse June '94) (numbered foldover p/s in poly bag) . . . 15
94 Creation CRECS 190 Cigarettes & Alcohol/I Am The Walrus (live at Glasgow Cathouse June '94) (cassette, flip-top 'cigarette' pack) . . . 20
94 Creation CRE 195 Whatever/(It's Good) To Be Free (no'd foldover p/s in stickered poly bag) . . . 14
96 Creation CRE 221 Don't Look Back In Anger/Step Out (p/s, with poly outer) . . . 10
97 Creation CRE 278 Stand By Me/I Got The Fever (p/s) . . . 5
02 Big Brother RKID 23 The Hindu Times/Just Getting Older (p/s, limited edition) . . . 6

ALBUMS

94 Creation CRELP 169 DEFINITELY MAYBE (2-LP, gatefold sleeve) . . . 40
95 Creation CRELP 189 (WHAT'S THE STORY) MORNING GLORY? (2-LP, gatefold sleeve) . . . 40
98 Creation CRELP 241 THE MASTERPLAN (3-LP) . . . 40

PROMO SINGLES

93 Creation CTP 8 Columbia (Demo) (12", 1-sided, white label, 510 pressed) . . . 275
94 Creation CRE 176TP Supersonic/Take Me Away/I Will Believe (Live) (12", company sleeve) . . . 50
94 Creation CRESCD 176P Supersonic/Take Me Away/I Will Believe (Live)/ Columbia (White Label Demo) (CD) . . . 35
94 Creation CRE 182TP Shakermaker/D'Yer Wanna Be A Spaceman?/Alive (8 Track Demo) (12") . . . 100
94 Creation CRESCD 182P Shakermaker/D'Yer Wanna Be A Spaceman?/Alive (8 Track Demo)/ Bring It On Down (Live) (CD) . . . 30
94 Creation CRE 185TP Live Forever/Up In The Sky (Acoustic)/Cloudburst (12") . . . 70

OASIS

			MINT VALUE £
94	Creation CRESCD 185P	Live Forever/Up In The Sky (Acoustic)/Cloudburst/ Supersonic (Live April '94) (CD)	20
94	Creation CTP 190TP	I Am The Walrus (Live At Glasgow Cathouse June '94) (12", 250 only, co. sl.)	375
94	Creation CTP 190CL	Cigarettes & Alcohol (12", 1-sided)	90
94	Creation CTP 190CL	Cigarettes & Alcohol/I Am The Walrus (live Glasgow Cathouse June '94)/ Fade Away (12", 300 only)	80
94	Creation CRESCD 190P	Cigarettes & Alcohol/I Am The Walrus (live Glasgow Cathouse June '94)/ Listen Up/Fade Away (CD)	25
94	Creation CRE 195TP	Whatever (12", 1-sided, 560 only)	100
94	Creation CRESCD 195P	Whatever/(It's Good) To Be Free/Half The World Away/Slide Away (CD)	10
94	Creation CTP 195	(It's Good) To Be Free (12", 1-sided, 360 only)	60
94	Creation CREDM 001	DEFINITELY MAYBE (4 x 7" box set, in silver cigarette-pack-shaped plastic box, with booklet & interview CD)	35
95	Creation CREMG 001	(WHAT'S THE STORY) MORNING GLORY? (4 x 7" box set, in gold cigarette-pack-shaped plastic box,with booklet & interview CD)	35
95	Creation CCD 169	Slide Away (CD, 1-track Brits Awards issue, 1,000 only; beware of counterfeits)	45
95	Creation CCD 204	Some Might Say (CD, 1-track, 350 only)	125
95	Creation CRESCD 204P	Some Might Say/Talk Tonight/Acquiesce/Headshrinker (CD)	20
95	Creation CTP 204	Acquiesce (12", 1-sided, 570 only)	170
95	Creation CCD 204P	Acquiesce (CD, 1-track, 300 only)	170
95	Creation CTP 212	Roll With It (12", 1-sided)	85
95	Creation CRESCD 212P	Roll With It/Better People/Rockin' Chair/ Live Forever (Live at Glastonbury '95) (CD, 3,078 only)	10
95	Creation CRESCD 215P	Wonderwall/Round Are Way/The Swamp Song/The Masterplan (CD, 2,320 only)	10
95	Creation CTP 215	Round Are Way (12", 1-sided, 843 only)	60
96	Creation CTP 221X	Cum On Feel The Noize/Champagne Supernova (Lynchmob Beats Mix) (12", 1,203 pressed, plain die-cut sleeve; beware of counterfeits)	70
96	Creation CCD 221	Cum On Feel The Noize (CD, pic. disc, 1-track, with football motif, no inlay, 500 only)	175
96	Creation CRESCD 221P	Don't Look Back In Anger/Step Out/Underneath The Sky/ Cum On Feel The Noize (CD)	10
96	Creation P 96/1	OASIS (Fade Away/Half The World Away/Acquiesce/The Masterplan) (CD sampler for singles box set)	30
(N.B.: the 4-track 12" "In-Store Sampler" [OASIS 1-12] is a bootleg.)			
97	Creation CTP 256	D'You Know What I Mean?/Heroes (12")	30
97	Creation CRESCD 256P	D'You Know What I Mean/Stay Young/Angel Child/Heroes (CD, digipak)	20
97	Creation CCD 256	D'You Know What I Mean (CD, 1-track, black card p/s)	20
97	Creation CCD 256X	D'You Know What I Mean?/Heroes (CD, 2-track, white card title p/s)	25
97	Creation CCD 219PL	Be Here Now (live)/Be Here Now (live with DJ intro) (CD)	25
97	Creation CTP 278	Stand By Me/I Got The Fever (12")	35
97	Creation CCD 278	Stand By Me (CD, 1-track, black card p/s)	20
97	Creation CCD 278X	Stand By Me (CD, 2-track, white card p/s)	18
97	Creation CRESCD 278P	Stand By Me/(I Got) The Fever/My Sister Lover/Going Nowhere (CD, digipak)	12
97	Creation CTP 282	All Around The World/Street Fighting Man (12", black die-cut sleeve)	25
97	Creation CCD 282	All Around The World (Edit) (CD, 1-track, black card sleeve)	15
97	Creation CCD 282X	All Around The World/Street Fighting Man (CD, blue card sleeve)	20
97	Creation CRESCD 282	All Around The World/The Fame/Flashbax/Street Fighting Man (CD)	15
97	Creation (no cat. no.)	VOX BOX (9-CD, wooden guitar-amp-shaped box set in outer box, with booklets from "Silver" & "Gold" CD box sets; contains commerical issues of "Supersonic" through to "Don't Look Back In Anger"; in-house giveaway only)	800+
98	Creation CRELP 241P	THE MASTERPLAN SAMPLER (Acquiesce/Underneath The Sky/ I Am The Walrus/The Masterplan) (12" sampler)	25
98	Creation CCD 241	Acquiesce/Talk Tonight/Rockin' Chair/The Masterplan (CD sampler)	25
98	Sony SAMPMS 6032	Acquiesce/Underneath The Sky/I Am The Walrus/The Masterplan (CD sampler)	40
00	Creation CTP 327	Go Let It Out (12", 1-track, 1-sided, p/s)	45
00	Creation CCD 327	Go Let It Out (CD, 1-track, card sleeve)	15
00	Big Brother FITB 001	Fuckin' In The Bushes (12", 1-sided, white label)	65
00	Big Brother RKID 03TP	Who Feels Love? (12", 1-sided, laminated p/s)	25
00	Big Brother RKID 004TP	Sunday Morning Call (12", 1-sided, flipback laminated p/s)	30
00	Big Brother RKIDSCD 005P	FAMILIAR TO MILLIONS (Gas Panic/Supersonic/Helter Skelter) (live CD, promo-only)	15
01	own label OASIS 10	10 YEARS OF NOISE & CONFUSION (Columbia/Rock & Roll Star (Live)/ Acquiesce/Fuckin' In The Bushes) (10", promo-only, custom labels, die-cut sleeve, 200 only, some with press release)	85/80
02	Big Brother RKID 25TPX	Hung In A Bad Place (12", 1-track, 1-sided, in die-cut mauve/pink sleeve, some in brown sleeve)	30/40
02	Big Brother RKID 24TP	Stop Crying Your Heart Out (Spike Mix) (12", custom sleeve, 250 only)	22
02	Big Brother RKIDSCD 24PX	Stop Crying Your Heart Out (Spike Mix) (CD, custom sleeve, 250 only)	18
02	Big Brother RKID 23TP	The Hindu Times (Spike Mix) (12", promo-only, custom logo sleeve, 250 only)	22
PROMO ALBUMS			
94	Creation CRECD 169P	DEFINITELY MAYBE (CD)	75
95	Creation C-CRE 189PX	(WHAT'S THE STORY) MORNING GLORY? (cassette, 4-track sampler with "Hello"/"[What's The Story] Morning Glory"/ "Wonderwall"/"Don't Look Back In Anger")	18
95	Creation CRECD 189P	(WHAT'S THE STORY) MORNING GLORY? (CD, with "Step Out", black card p/s, withdrawn, beware of counterfeits)	75
95	Creation CRECD 189P	(WHAT'S THE STORY) MORNING GLORY? (CD, without "Step Out", black card p/s)	20
95	Creation C-CRE 189P	(WHAT'S THE STORY) MORNING GLORY? (cassette, with "Step Out", card p/s, withdrawn)	25
95	Creation C-CRE 189P	(WHAT'S THE STORY) MORNING GLORY? (cassette, without "Step Out", card p/s)	15
97	Creation (no cat. no.)	BE HERE NOW (LP, mail-order 12" box set, with "The Making Of Be Here Now" booklet, 1,000 only)	70

Year	Label / Cat. No.	Title	Value £
97	Creation (no cat. no.)	BE HERE NOW (CD, mail-order 12" box set, with "The Making Of Be Here Now" booklet, 1,000 only)	70
97	Creation C-CRE 219P	BE HERE NOW (cassette)	12
97	Creation C-CRE 219PX	BE HERE NOW (cassette, 4-track sampler with "D'You Know What I Mean?"/ "All Around The World"/"Stand By Me"/"It's Gettin' Better [Man!!]")	18
97	Creation CCD 219	BE HERE NOW (CD, black card sleeve, some in custom picture sleeve)	30/25
98	Sony SAMPCD 5859	THE MASTERPLAN (CD, slimline case, p/s)	35
98	Sony SAMPCD 6034	THE MASTERPLAN INTERVIEW (CD, slimline case, no p/s)	25
00	Big Brother RKIDCD 001P	STANDING ON THE SHOULDER OF GIANTS (cassette, flip-top card box)	25
00	Big Brother RKIDCD 002P	STANDING ON THE SHOULDER OF GIANTS (CD, g/fold card sl. with sticker)	30
02	Big Brother RKIDCD 25P	HEATHEN CHEMISTRY (CD, in promo-only hardback photobook, features hidden track)	30

*(see also Oas*s)*

OAS*S

Year	Label / Cat. No.	Title	Value £
95	Fierce Panda NING 12	WIBBLING RIVALRY (interview disc, stickered p/s, without barcode, 1000 only)	8
95	Fierce Panda CDNING 12	WIBBLING RIVALRY (CD)	12

(see also Oasis)

OBERON

Year	Label / Cat. No.	Title	Value £
71	Acorn (no cat. no.)	A MIDSUMMER NIGHT'S DREAM (LP, private pressing)	400+

HUGH O'BRIAN

Year	Label / Cat. No.	Title	Value £
58	HMV POP 539	Legend Of Wyatt Earp/Down In The Meadow	8
58	Oriole CB 1480	I'm Looking For A Girl/Ain't Got A Nickel	6
58	HMV DLP 1189	TV'S WYATT EARP SINGS (10" LP)	20

IAIN O'BRIEN

Year	Label / Cat. No.	Title	Value £
96	Ferox FER 020	INTELLIGENT DESERT EP (12")	10
96	Ferox FER 023	MONKEY JAZZ EP (12")	10
96	Ferox FERLP 3	DESERT SCORES (2-LP)	17

JIMMY O'BRYANT

Year	Label / Cat. No.	Title	Value £
60	Heritage RE-101	Famous Original Washboard Band, Vol. 1 (99 copies only) (EP)	30
60	Heritage RE-106	Famous Original Washboard Band, Vol. 2 (99 copies only) (EP)	30

OBSERVERS

Year	Label / Cat. No.	Title	Value £
71	Big Shot BI 575	Brimstone And Fire/Lightning And Thunder	5
71	Big Shot BI 588	Keep Pushing/Hot Tip	10
72	Big Shot BI 610	Everyday Music/NINEY: Observing The Av	5
72	Songbird SB 1083	International Pum/Reggaematic	6

(see also Niney)

OBTAINERS

Year	Label / Cat. No.	Title	Value £
79	Dance Fools Dance (no cat. no.)	Yeh Yeh Yeh/Pussy Wussy/MAG-SPYS: Lifeblood/Bombs (stickered plain sleeve, 100 only)	100

(see also Cure)

DIERDRE O'CALLAGHAN

Year	Label / Cat. No.	Title	Value £
59	Top Rank JAR 164	The Bridal Path/I'll Walk With My Love	6
59	Top Rank JAR 164	The Bridal Path/I'll Walk With My Love (78)	12

OCCASIONALLY DAVID

Year	Label / Cat. No.	Title	Value £
79	Oven Ready OD 77901	TWIST AND SHOUT (EP)	15
80	Oven Ready OD 1/98002	I Can't Get Used To Losing You (So I'm Coming Back)/ Will You Miss Me Tonight? (foldout p/s)	15
80	Oven Read (no cat. no)	FOREVER CHANGES (cassette)	10

OCCASIONAL WORD ENSEMBLE

Year	Label / Cat. No.	Title	Value £
69	Dandelion 63753	THE YEAR OF THE GREAT LEAP SIDEWAYS (LP)	18

OCCULT CHEMISTRY

Year	Label / Cat. No.	Title	Value £
80	Bikini Girl (no. cat. no.)	Water Earth Fire Air (Rough Version) (5" clear flexidisc in stamped envelope with *Bikini Girl* magazine)	40/35
81	Dining Out TUX 4	Water Earth Fire Air/Fire Air Water Earth (handmade p/s)	35

(see also Twilight Zonerz)

OCEAN COLOUR SCENE

Year	Label / Cat. No.	Title	Value £
90	!Phffft WAVE 1P	One Of These Days/Talk On (p/s, promo only)	50
90	!Phffft WAVE 1	One Of These Days/Talk On (12", p/s, promo only)	50
90	!Phffft FIT 001	Sway/Talk On (p/s)	18
90	!Phffft FITX 001	Sway (Extended)/Lullaby/Sway (7" Version)/One Of These Days (12", p/s)	20
90	!Phffft FITX 001	Sway (Extended)/Lullaby/Sway (7" Version)/One Of These Days (CD)	25
91	!Phffft FIT 002	Yesterday Today/Another Girl's Name/Fly Me (p/s, promos with sticker £20)	7
91	!Phffft FITX 002	Yesterday Today/Another Girl's Name/Fly Me/No One Says (12", p/s)	18
91	!Phffft FITCD 002	Yesterday Today/Another Girl's Name/Fly Me/No One Says (CD)	20
92	Fontana OCSS 1	Sway/My Brother Sarah (p/s)	7
92	Fontana OCS 112	Sway/My Brother Sarah/Mona Lisa Eyes/Bellechoux (12", p/s)	8
92	Fontana OCSCD 1	Sway/My Brother Sarah/Mona Lisa Eyes/Bellechoux (CD)	12
92	Fontana OCSS 2	Giving It All Away/Third Shade Of Green (p/s)	6
92	Fontana OCS 212	Giving It All Away/Flowers/Third Shade Of Green/Don't Play (12", p/s)	8
92	Fontana OCSCD 2	Giving It All Away/Flowers/Third Shade Of Green/Don't Play (CD)	10
92	Fontana OCSS 3	Do Yourself A Favour/The Seventh Floor (p/s)	7
92	Fontana OCS 312	Do Yourself A Favour/The Seventh Floor/Patsy In Green/ Suspended Motion (12", p/s)	8
92	Fontana OCSCD 3	Do Yourself A Favour/The Seventh Floor/Patsy In Green/ Suspended Motion (CD)	12
95	MCA OCS 1	You've Got It Bad/You've Got It Bad (p/s, promo only)	18
96	MCA OCS 2	You've Got It Bad (Full Length Demo Version)/Mona Lisa Eyes (featuring Jimmy Miller) (p/s, mail-order only)	15
97	MCA MCS 40144	Traveller's Tune/Song For The Front Row (gatefold p/s)	7
03	Sanctuary SANSE 159	I Just Need Myself/I Wanna See The Bright Nights Tonight (die-cut p/s)	5

MINT VALUE £

97 MCA MCD 60034 B-SIDES, SEASIDES AND FREE RIDES (2-LP, with lyric booklet) 25
97 MCA MCD 60034 B-SIDES, SEASIDES AND FREE RIDES (CD, with booklet, in slipcase)......... 25
92 Fontana 512 269-1 OCEAN COLOUR SCENE (LP, with inner sleeve) 12
92 Fontana 512 269-2 OCEAN COLOUR SCENE (CD) 18
97 MCA MCA 60048 MARCHIN' ALREADY (2-LP, with booklet) 25
(see also Boys, Fanatics, Echo Base)

PHIL OCHS
66 Elektra EKSN 45002 I Ain't Marching Any More/That Was The President 15
68 A&M AMS 716 Outside Of A Small Circle Of Friends/Miranda 7
65 Elektra EKL 269 ALL THE NEWS THAT'S FIT TO SING (LP) 40
65 Elektra EKL 287 I AIN'T MARCHIN' ANYMORE (LP) 40
66 Elektra EKL 310 PHIL OCHS IN CONCERT (LP, gold label) 35
67 A&M AML(S) 913 PLEASURES OF THE HARBOR (LP) 20
68 A&M AMLS 919 TAPE FROM CALIFORNIA (LP) 20
69 A&M AMLS 934 REHEARSALS FOR RETIREMENT (LP) 20
70 A&M AMLS 973 GREATEST HITS (LP) 20

DES O'CONNOR
57 Columbia DB 4011 Moonlight Swim/Sailing Down The Chesapeake Bay 8
57 Columbia DB 4011 Moonlight Swim/Sailing Down The Chesapeake Bay (78) 8
62 Piccadilly 7N 35023 Thin Chow Min/Twist Drive 7

JOHNNY O'CONNOR
53 London L 1171 Fickle Fingers/GUY NELSON: When The World Was Young (78) 10

JOHNNY OCTOBER
59 Capitol CL 15070 Growin' Prettier/Young And In Love 15
60 Capitol CL 15121 So Mean/There'll Always Be A Feeling 15

OCTOPUS
69 Penny Farthing PEN 705 Laugh At The Poor Man/Girl Friend 18
70 Penny Farthing PEN 716 The River/Thief 18
73 Mooncrest MOON 7 Hey Na Na/Future Feelings 6
70 Penny Farthing PELS 508 RESTLESS NIGHT (LP, gatefold sleeve) 140
96 Essex ESSEX 1013LP RESTLESS NIGHT (LP, reissue, gatefold sleeve) 12
(see also Cortinas)

MARTIN O'CUTHBERT
78 Esoteric EE 1 BEMS (Bug Eyed Monsters)/Fragments Of A Possessed Ego (p/s) 5
79 Esoteric EE 2 Serene Machines/Space Shall Weave Our Destiny (foldover p/s) 5

RAY O'DANIEL
62 Longhorn BLH 0001 What Goes Up Always Comes Down/You're The Only Love For Me 8

ANITA O'DAY
51 London L 867 Tennessee Waltz/Yea Boo (78) 8
56 HMV POP 245 You're The Top/Honeysuckle Rose 6
60 HMV POP 821 Tea For Two/Sweet Georgia Brown 6
55 Columbia Clef SEB 10042 ANITA O'DAY (EP) 8
56 HMV CLP 1085 ANITA (LP) 15
56 Columbia Clef 33C 9020 ANITA O'DAY COLLATES (10" LP) 18
57 Columbia Clef 33CX 10068 AN EVENING WITH ANITA O'DAY (LP) 15
58 Columbia Clef 33CX 10125 ANITA SINGS THE MOST (LP) 15
58 HMV DLP 1169 PICK YOURSELF UP (10" LP) 18
59 HMV DLP 1203 ANITA AT MISTER KELLY'S (10" LP) 18
60 HMV CLP 1332 ANITA O'DAY SWINGS COLE PORTER WITH BILLY MAY (LP) 12
63 Verve VLP 9125 THE JAZZ STYLINGS OF (LP) 15

PAT O'DAY
55 MGM SP 1129 Earth Angel (Will You Be Mine?)/A Rusty Old Halo 18
55 MGM SP 1142 Soldier Boy/Annie Oakley 15
60 Pye International 7N 25048 I'll Build A Stairway To Your Paradise/No One Understands 6

ODD
84 OK OK 007 Last Time I Saw You/Look Into My Eyes (p/s) 15

BILL ODDIE
64 Parlophone R 5153 Nothing Better To Do/Traffic Island 7
65 Parlophone R 5346 Knitting Song/Ain't Got Rhythm 6
66 Parlophone R 5433 I Can't Get Through/Because She Is My Love 6
69 Decca F 12903 We Love Jimmy Young/Irish Get Out (as Bill Oddie & Average Mothers) 6
70 Dandelion S 4786 On Ilkla Moor Baht'at/Harry Krishna 6
(see also Ricky Livid)

ODDS
80 Double R RED 001 Saturday Night/Not Another Love Song (p/s) 18
81 JSO EAT 1 Yesterday Man/So You Think (p/s) 25
81 JSO EAT 7 Dread In My Bed/Spare Rib (with press release) 12

ODDSOCKS
75 Sweet Folk & C. SFA 030 MEN OF THE MOMENT (LP) 18
(see also Bevis Frond)

ANN ODELL
73 DJM DJS 10280 Swing Song/Everything's Fine Sunshine 6
73 DJM DJLPS 434 A LITTLE TASTE (LP) 30
(see also Chopyn, Blue Mink)

DOYE O'DELL
57 London HAP-B 1073 DOYE (10" LP) 12

MAC ODELL

54 Parlophone DP 387 What Then/One Day Religion (78, export issue) . . . 10
54 Parlophone CMSP 25 The Stone Was Rolled Away/Heaven-Bound Gospel Train (export issue) . . . 22
54 Parlophone DP 397 The Stone Was Rolled Away/Heaven-Bound Gospel Train (78) . . . 10
56 Parlophone DP 507 A Crown He Wore/Are You Practicing His Love? (78, export issue) . . . 10

RONNIE O'DELL & HIS ORCHESTRA

57 London HLD 8439 Melody Of Napoli/Struttin' Down Jane Street . . . 25

ODIN'S PEOPLE

67 Major Minor MM 501 From A Distance/I Need You . . . 7
67 Major Minor MM 506 Tommy Jones/I Need Your Hand In Mine . . . 7

JOE ODOM

69 Capitol CL 15600 Big Love/It's In Your Power . . . 10

AL O'DONNELL

72 Trailer LER 2073 AL O'DONNELL (LP, red label) . . . 20
78 Transatlantic LTRA 501 AL O'DONNELL 2 (LP) . . . 12

JOE O'DONNELL

77 EMI International INT 540 Golden Earrings/Omega . . . 5
77 Polydor 2058 930 Poets And Story Tellers/The Great Banqueting Hall . . . 5
77 Polydor 2383 465 GAODHAL'S VISION (LP) . . . 25
(see also Mushroom, Rory Gallagher, Jade Warrior)

ROCK O'DOODLE

73 Decca F 13450 Queen Of Rock & Roll/Woman . . . 5
(see also Patrick Campbell-Lyons)

ODYSSEY (U.K.)

66 Strike JH 312 How Long Is Time/Beware . . . 20
(see also Sons Of Fred)

ODYSSEY (U.S.)

73 Mowest MWS 7002 ODYSSEY (LP) . . . 25

OEDIPUS COMPLEX

68 Philips BF 1716 Holding My Hands Out/Brought Me Such Confusion . . . 7
69 Philips BF 1771 Up Down Round And Round/Empty Highway . . . 7

OFFSIDE

70 Pye Intl. 25534 Match Of The Day/Small Deal (p/s) . . . 8

OFFSPRING

94 Epitaph EPUK 001 Come Out And Play/Session/Come Out And Play (12", p/s) . . . 8
95 Epitaph 12HOLE 001 Self Esteem/Burn It Up/Jennifer Lost The War (12", p/s) . . . 8

JAMES O'GWYNN

59 Mercury AMT 1052 How Can I Think Of Tomorrow/Were You Ever A Stranger . . . 12

JOHN O'HARA

77 President PT 465 Starsky And Hutch/Sister Rae . . . 5

MARY O'HARA

70s Images IMG 0001 COLOURS (LP) . . . 12

MAUREEN O'HARA

66 Realm RM 52320 SINGS HER FAVOURITE IRISH SONGS (LP) . . . 12

O'HARA'S PLAYBOYS

66 Fontana TF 763 Start All Over/I've Been Wondering . . . 6
68 Fontana TF 924 In The Shelter Of My Heart/Goodnight Mr. Nightfall . . . 6
68 Fontana TF 974 I Started A Joke/Show Me . . . 10
68 Fontana (S)TL 5461 GET READY (LP) . . . 35

OHIO EXPRESS

69 Pye Intl. NSPL 28117 OHIO EXPRESS (LP) . . . 18
69 Buddah 203 015 CHEWY CHEWY (LP) . . . 15
(see also Joey Vine)

OHIO KNOX

71 Reprise RSLP 6435 OHIO KNOX (LP) . . . 15
(see also Fifth Avenue Band)

OHIO PLAYERS

69 Capitol CL 15587 Here Today And Gone Tomorrow/Bad Bargain . . . 7
72 Janus 6146 009 Pain (Parts 1 & 2) . . . 5
72 Janus 6146 017 Got Pleasure/I Wanna Hear From You . . . 5
73 Westbound 6146 100 Funky Worm/Paint Me . . . 5
74 Mercury 6167 012 Skin Tight/Heaven Must Be Like This . . . 6
75 Mercury 6167 058 Fire/Together . . . 6
74 Mercury 6338 497 SKIN TIGHT (LP) . . . 15

OHR MUSIK

97 Prescription DRUG 2 OHR MUSIK (LP, 99 copies only) . . . 25
(see also Spiral Sky)

OIL CITY SHEIKS

79 United Artists UP 36514 Don't Take But A Few Minutes/Blues Jam (p/s) . . . 7
(see also Dr. Feelgood, Lew Lewis)

OI POLLOI

80s Wonderful World WOW 17 OMNICIDE (EP) . . . 8
87 Oi! OIR 011 UNITE AND WIN (LP, with lyric sheet) . . . 12

MINT VALUE £

OISIN

80	Tara 2012	OVER THE MOOR TO MAGGIE (LP)	15
82	Tara 2013	THE JEANNIE C (LP)	15

O'JAYS

65	Liberty LIB 66102	Lipstick Traces/Think It Over Baby	45
66	Liberty LIB 66197	Stand In For Love/Friday Night	22
67	Stateside SS 2073	I'll Be Sweeter Tomorrow/I Dig Your Act	60
68	Bell BLL 1020	Look Over Your Shoulder/I'm So Glad I Found You	18
68	Bell BLL 1033	The Choice/Going Going Gone	8
70	Now! NOW 1002	Don't You Know A True Love/That's Alright	8
72	United Artists UP 35337	Working On Your Case/Hold On	7
73	CBS 1181	Love Train/Who Am I?	6
73	Mojo 2092 052	I Dig Your Act/I'll Be Sweeter Tomorrow (reissue)	6
73	CBS 1546	Time To Get Down/Shifty Shadey Jealous Kind Of People	5
74	Power Exchange PX 101	Peace/Little Brother	5
74	Philadelphia PIR 2186	For The Love Of Money/People Keep Telling Me	6
75	Philadelphia PIR 3297	Give The People What They Want/What Am I Waiting For	6
77	Philadelphia PIR 4834	Darlin' Darlin Baby/Prayer	6
69	Sunset SLS 50038	FULL OF SOUL (LP)	15
72	CBS 65257	BACKSTABBERS (LP)	15
73	Epic EPC 65469	IN PHILADELPHIA (LP)	12

O'KAYSIONS

68	Stateside SS 2126	Girl Watcher/Deal Me In	35

JOHNNY O'KEEFE (& DEE JAYS)

58	Coral Q 72330	Shake Baby Shake/Real Wild Child (as Johnny O'Keefe & Dee Jays)	180
58	Coral Q 72330	Shake Baby Shake/Real Wild Child (as Johnny O'Keefe & Dee Jays) (78)	80
60s	Zodiac ZR 0016	Sing/Tell The Blues So Long	20

(ROGER) EARL OKIN

67	Parlophone R 5644	Yellow Petals/I Can't Face The Animals (as Roger Earl Okin)	6
69	CBS 4495	Stop And You'll Become Aware/You're Not There At All (as Earl Okin)	10

OLA (& JANGLERS)

67	Decca F 12646	I Can Wait/Eeny Meeny Miney Moe	8
68	Big T BIG 108	What A Way To Die/That's Why I Cry (solo)	6
69	Sonet SON 2004	Let's Dance/Bird, Bird	5

BABATUNDE OLATUNJI

73	Paramount PARA 3038	Soul Makossa (Parts 1 & 2)	5
73	Paramount SPFL 289	SOUL MAKOSSA (LP)	12

OLD AND IN THE WAY

75	Round RX 103	OLD AND IN THE WAY (LP)	12

(see also Jerry Garcia, Seatrain, Rowan Brothers)

MIKE OLDFIELD

SINGLES

74	Virgin VS 101	Mike Oldfield's Single ("Tubular Bells" Theme)/ Froggy Went A-Courtin' (some in p/s)	20/5
75	Virgin VS 117	Don Alfonso (with David Bedford)/In Dulci Jubilo (For Maureen) (p/s rumoured to exist)	100+/15
75	Virgin VS 131	In Dulci Jubilo/On Horseback	5
76	Virgin VS 163	Portsmouth/Speak (Tho' You Only Say Farewell) (Roger Dean or blue/red label; reissued in brown wraparound p/s)	6/5/20
77	Virgin VS 167	The William Tell Overture/Argiers	5
77	Virgin VS 198	The Cuckoo Song/Pipe Tune	6
78	Virgin VS 238	Take 4 (EP, p/s)	8
78	Virgin VS 238-12	Take 4 (12", white vinyl, stickered p/s)	12
79	Virgin VS 245	Guilty/Excerpt From Incantations (p/s, red/green or white/blue label)	8/7
79	Virgin VS 245-12	Guilty (Extended Mix)/Guilty/Excerpt From Incantations (12", blue vinyl, p/s)	20
79	Virgin VS 317	Blue Peter/Woodhenge (p/s, sudden or 'refined' ending (A7 matrix))	each 6
80	Virgin VS 374	Arrival/Polka (live) (p/s)	5
80	Virgin VS 389	Wonderful Land/Sheba (p/s)	7
82	Virgin VSY 464	Five Miles Out/Live Punkadiddle (picture disc)	20
82	Virgin VSY 489	Family Man/Mount Teidi (picture disc)	15
82	Virgin VSY 541	Mistake/Waldberg (The Peak) (picture disc)	6
83	Virgin VS 586	Moonlight Shadow/Rite Of Man (p/s abrupt or faded ending for Rite of Man)	6
83	Virgin VSY 586	Moonlight Shadow/Rite Of Man (picture disc)	7
84	Virgin VS 648-12	Crime Of Passion (Extended)/Jungle Gardenia (12", p/s)	8
84	Virgin VS 701-12	Tricks Of The Light/Tricks Of The Light (Instrumental)/Afghan (12", p/s)	8
84	Virgin VS 1328	Etude (12", p/s)	12
85	Virgin VSD 836	Pictures In The Dark/Legend//Moonlight Shadow/Rite Of Man (double pack in PVC gatefold stickered p/s)	35
86	Virgin VSS 863	Shine (with Jon Anderson)/The Path (shaped picture disc, some uncut)	60/12
87	Virgin VS 955	In High Places (with Jon Anderson)/Poison Arrows (p/s)	6
87	Virgin VS 955-12	In High Places (with Jon Anderson)/Poison Arrows/Jungle Gardenia (12", p/s)	12
87	Virgin VSC 99012	Islands (with Bonnie Tyler)/When The Night's On Fire/ The Wind Chimes Part 1 (cassette)	6
88	Virgin CDT 7	Moonlight Shadow (Extended Version)/Rite Of Man/To France/ Jungle Gardenia (3" CD, card p/s)	12
89	Virgin VSCD 1189	Earth Moving (7" Version)/(Disco Mix)/Bridge To Paradise (3" CD, card p/s)	15
89	Virgin VST 1214	Innocent (7" Version)/(12" Mix)/(Club Version) (12", p/s)	10
89	Virgin VSCD 1214	Innocent (7" Version)/(12" Mix)/(Club Version) (3" CD, card p/s)	12
90	Virgin VS 1328	Etude (The Theme Music For The "Nurofen" TV Commercial)/ ONO GAGAKU KAÏ SOCIETY ORCHESTRA: Gakkain (p/s)	10
90	Virgin VSC 1328	Etude (The Theme Music For The "Nurofen" TV Commercial)/ ONO GAGAKU KAÏ SOCIETY ORCHESTRA: Gakkain (cassette)	6

			MINT VALUE £
90	Virgin AMACD 1	AMAROK X-TRAX 3 extracts from the Amarok album (3" CD EP, 'discount voucher CD' free with W.H. Smith's Insight magazine)	30/25
92	WEA YZ 698 CDX	Sentinel (Total Overhaul)/Sentinel (Nobel Prize Mix)/Orbular Bells/Seven Inch Mix (CD)	8
92	WEA YZ 698 CD	Sentinel(Single Restructure)/The Orb 7" Mix/Early Stages (CD)	10
92	WEA YZ 708 CD	Tattoo (Edit)/Silent Night/Sentinel (Live) (5" CD)	8
92	WEA YZ 708 CDX	Tattoo (Live)/Maya Gold (Live)/Moonshine (Live)/Reprise(Live) (CD, hologram sleeve)	15
92	WEA YZ 708	Tattoo (Edit)/Silent Night (p/s)	6
93	WEA YZ 737	The Bell (MC Viv Stanshall)/Sentinel Restructure (Trance Mix) (p/s)	6
93	WEA YZ 737 CD	The Bell (MC Viv Stanshall)/Sentinel Restructure (Trance Mix, Global Lust Mix and Satoshi Tomii Interpretation) (with 3 photocards) (CD)	8
93	WEA YZ 737 CD	The Bell Live (MC John Gordon Sinclair)/The Bell (MC Billy Connolly/The Bell (MC Otto, German Version)/The Bell (MC Strolling Player)/The Bell (Instrumental Version) (CD)	8
94	WEA YZ 871 CDX	HIBERNACULUM (CD EP, with hologram sleeve)	10
97	WEA WEA 093T	Women of Ireland: System 7 12" Mix, Lurker Mix, Lurker Edit (12", p/s)	10
99	WEA WEA 206T	Far Above The Clouds: Jam And Spoon Mix, Timewriter's Big Bag Of Secrets (12", p/s)	10
ALBUMS			
73	Virgin V 2001	TUBULAR BELLS (LP, White label)	15
74	Virgin QV 2001	TUBULAR BELLS (LP, quadrophonic, with model plane noise at the end of side 2, stickered sleeve)	20
75	Virgin QVQS 2043	OMMADAWN (LP, quadrophonic, stickered sleeve)	20
75	Virgin VD 2502	V (2-LP, compilation, includes long version of 'Don Alfonso')	30
76	Virgin 2043	OMMADAWN (LP, blue Virgin label)	15
76	Virgin QV 2043	OMMADAWN (LP, different quadrophonic mix, stickered sleeve)	20
76	Virgin VBOX 1	BOXED (4-LP box set, with booklet)	25
78	Virgin VDT 101	INCANTATIONS (2-LP, some with 7" red vinyl of Julie Covington, & poster)	35/30
78	Virgin VP 2001	TUBULAR BELLS (LP, picture disc, die-cut sleeve, stereo remix of 1976 "Boxed" quadrophonic mix; with or without model plane noise)	each 15
78	Virgin VD 2511	EXPOSED (2-LP live, with '100,000 Limited Edition' sticker, and black inners)	12
79	Virgin V 2141	PLATINUM (LP, with inner sleeve & "Sally"; matrix reads "V 2141 B1" or "B2", 30,000 copies, withdrawn)	100
79	Tellydisc TELLY 4	IMPRESSIONS (LP, mail-order only)	25
79	Tellydisc TELLYC 4	IMPRESSIONS (cassette, mail-order only)	30
82	Virgin V 2222	FIVE MILES OUT (LP, gatefold sleeve)	12
83	Virgin V 2262	CRISES (LP, with bonus 7" 'Moonlight Shadow')	15
83	Virgin V 2001	TUBULAR BELLS (LP, reissue at 1973 price, with sticker)	15
84	Virgin V 2328	THE KILLING FIELDS (LP, with 20 page film booklet)	25
85	Virgin MOC 1	THE COMPLETE MIKE OLDFIELD (2-LP with bonus 7" 'Pictures in the Dark')	18
93	Virgin CD BOX 2	ELEMENTS (4-CD, remastered best of in special plastic box with 64pp booklet)	60
94	WEA 4509-98581-1	THE SONGS OF DISTANT EARTH (LP, rumoured 1000 copies only, German pressing)	20
97	Virgin LPCENT 18	TUBULAR BELLS (LP, coloured Dean label, audiophile pressing)	20
01	Simply Vinyl SVLP 322	OMMADAWN (LP, Audiophile pressing on 180g vinyl, with 2 stickers)	18
01	Virgin CD BOXY 2	ELEMENTS (4-CD remastered best of, revised "book" sleeve, 64pp booklet)	40
PROMOS			
74	Virgin VS 112	Hergest Ridge (1-sided white label)	75
75	Virgin VDJ 1	Extract from The Orchestral Tubular Bells/Extract from The Orchestral Tubular Bells	25
75	Virgin VS 117	Don Alfonso ('A' label)	25
75	Virgin VDJ 9	An Extract From Ommadawn Part 1/An Extract From Ommadawn Part 2 (On Horseback) (12")	50
75	Virgin VS 131	In Dulci Jubilo/On Horseback ('A' label)	10
76	Virgin VS 163	Portsmouth/Speak (Tho' You Only Say Farewell) (Roger Dean label)	8
77	Virgin VS 167	The William Tell Overture/Argiers (blue Virgin 'A' label)	10
78	Virgin VS 238-12	Take 4 EP (12", red vinyl test pressing)	100
79	Virgin VS 245-12	Guilty (Extended Mix)/Guilty/Excerpt From Incantations (12", black vinyl test pressing)	25
79	Virgin VSDJ 317	Blue Peter (1-sided)	25
82	Virgin VS 464	Five Miles Out/Live Punkadiddle (white label test pressing)	20
82	Virgin VSY 541	Mistake/Waldberg (The Peak) (white label test pressing)	20
85	Virgin SWALLOW 1	Etude/Moonlight Shadow/Portsmouth/In Dulci Jubilo (p/s, promo-only for "The Complete Mike Oldfield")	30
85	Virgin	Pictures in the Dark (1-sided Abbey Road acetate)	50
87	Virgin VST 990	Islands (Extended Version)/When The Night's On Fire/The Wind Chimes (Part One) (white label test pressing)	20
87	Virgin CDEP 6	Islands/When The Night's On Fire/The Wind Chimes(Part One)/ Islands (Extended Version) (white gatefold stickered card p/s)	25
94	WEA YZ 880 T	Let There Be Light: BT's Pure Luminescence Remix/Hardfloor Remix/ Hardfloor Dub (12" p/s, some with 'promo not for sale' sticker)	12/10
89	Virgin VST 1214	Innocent (12" Mix)/7" Mix/Earth Moving (Club Mix) (white label test pressing)	20
90	Virgin AMACD 1DJ	Mike Oldfield Album Sampler (CD, 5 Extracts From Amarok)	30
92	WEA SAM 1085	Sentinel (Single Restructure) (CD, stickered p/s)	15
92	WEA SAM 1094	OLDFIELD V THE ORB: Sentinel (Total Overhaul/Sentinel Nobel Prize Mix/ Sentinel Orbular Bells/Sentinel 7" Mix (12")	15
92	WEA SAM 1150	SENTINEL RESTRUCTURE MIXES: Satoshi Tomii Interpretation/ Global Lust Mix/TranceMix/Tubular Beats (12", title stickered red sleeve)	20
92	WEA SAM 1470	A SHOT OF MOONSHINE: Jungle Mix (Featuring Rankin' Sean & Peter Lee)/ A Shot Of Moonshine (Jungle Instrumental)/A Shot of Moonshine (Solution Hoedown Mix) (12", lists artist as MOT2)	15
92	WEA YZ 708CDDJ	Tattoo (stickered p/s)	15
76	Virgin QVQS 2043	OMMADAWN (LP, unreleased different quadrophonic mix, promo stickered sleeve)	50

MINT VALUE £

76	Virgin V BOX 1	COLLABORATIONS (LP, green/yellow label in stamped white sleeve)	30
79	(no cat. no.)	THE SPACE MOVIE (4 x 1-sided acetates of unreleased LP containing music from soundtrack to the 'Space Movie' video; includes Orchestral Hergest Ridge, Orchestral Tubular Bells, Incantations, Ommadawn and Portsmouth, some extracts otherwise unreleased)	600+
80	Virgin V 2181	QE2 (LP, white label test pressing in white sleeve)	30
83	Virgin V 2262	CRISES (LP, 2 x 1-sided acetates)	100
90	Virgin CDV 2640 WL	AMAROK (CD, test pressing)	30
92	WEA 4509-90618-2	TUBULAR BELLS 2 (CD, with unique back sleeve)	25
92	WEA WX 2002	TUBULAR BELLS 2 (LP, stickered sleeve)	20
94	WEA SAM 1477	THE SONGS OF DISTANT EARTH (CD in film can, with 2 inserts)	75
94	WEA 4509-98581-1	THE SONGS OF DISTANT EARTH (LP, 2-sided acetate)	100
94	WEA 4509-98581-1	THE SONGS OF DISTANT EARTH (LP, white label test pressing)	60
98	WEA 3331000043	TUBULAR BELLS III (CD, in special 'Waterside Inn' card sleeve)	30
98	WEA 3331000043	TUBULAR BELLS III (CD, in card sleeve, some with bag, TB III tag, press releases and premiere concert details)	50/20
99	WEA (no cat. no.)	MILLENNIUM BELL (CD-R, some tracks with different samples to released album)	75/60
01	Simply Vinyl SVLP 322	OMMADAWN (LP, white label promo of Audiophile pressing on 180g vinyl)	25

(see also Sallyangie, David Bedford, Kevin Ayers & Whole World, Pekka, Lea Nicholson, Tom Newman)

ANDREW OLDHAM (ORCHESTRA)

64	Decca F 11878	365 Rolling Stones/Oh I Do Like To See Me On The 'B' Side	25
64	Decca F 11987	We Don't All Wear D'Same Size Boots/Right Of Way	25
64	Ace Of Clubs ACL 1180	16 HIP HITS (LP)	45
64	Decca LK 4636	LIONEL BART'S MAGGIE MAY (LP)	25
66	Decca LK/SKL 4796	THE ROLLING STONES SONGBOOK (LP)	80
82	Decca 820 186-1	THE ROLLING STONES SONGBOOK (LP, reissue)	12

(see also Aranbee Pop Symphony, Rolling Stones, Cleo, Bo & Peep, Jeannie & Her Redheads, Gulliver's Travels, Mighty Avengers, John Paul Jones)

OLDHAM TINKERS

74	Topic 12TS 237	BEST O' T' BUNCH (LP, blue label)	18
75	Topic 12TS 276	FOR OLD TIMES SAKE (LP)	15
77	Topic 12TS 323	SIT THEE DOWN (LP)	15
79	Topic 12TS 399	THAT LANCASHIRE BAND (LP)	15

OLD SWAN BAND

71	Dingles DIN 322	GAMESTERS, PICKPOCKETS AND HARLOTS (LP)	15
80	Free Reed 028	OLD SWAN BAND (LP)	15
81	Free Reed FRR 011	NO REELS (LP)	15

OLD TIMERS SKIFFLE GROUP

58	Fontana H 105	The Woman Who Loved A Swine/The Lynching Of Jeff Buckner (78)	15

JOHNNY OLENN & HIS BAND

57	London HLU 8388	I Ain't Gonna Cry No More/My Idea Of Love	380
57	London HLU 8388	I Ain't Gonna Cry No More/My Idea Of Love (78)	90
59	Mercury AMT 1050	Born Reckless/You Lovable You (as Johnny Olenn & Blockbusters)	100

O-LEVEL

78	Psycho PSYCHO 2	East Sheen/Pseudo Punk ('map' or 'schoolboy' p/s)	30/35
78	Kings Road KR 002	THE MALCOLM EP (photocopied wraparound or printed p/s)	25/15

(see also Teenage Filmstars, Times, Television Personalities)

OLIVER

69	CBS 4435	Good Morning Starshine/Can't You See	5
70	Crewe CRW 1	Jean/Good Morning Starshine (Arrangement) (p/s)	5

OLIVER

74	Oliv OL 1	STANDING STONE (LP, private pressing, withdrawn blue sleeve, later in green sleeve)	350/250
92	Tenth Planet TP 001	STANDING STONE (LP, reissue, numbered, 500 only)	20

JANE OLIVER

60s	Columbia 35437	STAY THE NIGHT (LP)	25

(see also Johnny Mathis)

JOHNNY OLIVER

56	MGM SP 1165	Chain Gang/These Hands	22
60	Mercury AMT 1095	What A Kiss Won't Do/That's All I'm Living For	12

SY OLIVER & HIS ORCHESTRA

58	London HL 7067	The Mardi Gras March/One More Time (export issue)	12
59	London HLJ 8776	In A Little Spanish Town Cha-Cha/The Mardi Gras March	10
59	London HLJ 8776	In A Little Spanish Town Cha-Cha/The Mardi Gras March (78)	8
53	Brunswick LA 8586	FOR DANCERS ONLY (10" LP)	12

OLIVER & TWISTERS

64	Pye Intl. NPL 28018	LOOK WHO'S TWISTIN' (LP)	25

OLIVERS

57	Columbia DB 3995	Ma Curly Headed Baby/Beautiful Dreamer	6

(see also Russ Conway)

OLLIE & NIGHTINGALES

69	Stax STAX 109	You're Leaving Me/Showered With Love	18

OLYMPICS

58	HMV POP 528	Western Movies/Well!	15
58	HMV POP 528	Western Movies/Well! (78)	10
58	HMV POP 564	(I Wanna) Dance With The Teacher/Everybody Needs Love	20
58	HMV POP 564	(I Wanna) Dance With The Teacher/Everybody Needs Love (78)	10

59	Columbia DB 4346	Private Eye/(Baby) Hully Gully	22
60	Vogue Pop V 9174	I Wish I Could Shimmy Like My Sister Kate/Workin' Hard	20
61	Vogue Pop V 9181	Dance With A Dolly/Dodge City	18
61	Vogue Pop V 9184	Little Pedro/CAPPY LEWIS: Bullfight	20
62	Vogue Pop V 9196	The Twist/Everybody Likes To Cha Cha Cha	15
62	Vogue Pop V 9198	The Stomp/Mash Them 'Taters	18
62	Vogue Pop V 9204	Baby It's Hot/The Scotch	18
63	HMV POP 1155	Sidewalk Serenade/Nothing	12
64	Sue WI 348	The Bounce/Fireworks	22
65	Warner Bros WB 157	Good Lovin'/Olympic Shuffle	15
66	Fontana TF 678	We Go Together (Pretty Baby)/Secret Agents	18
66	Fontana TF 778	Baby, Do The Philly Dog/Western Movies	15
69	Action ACT 4539	Baby, Do The Philly Dog/Mine Exclusively	15
70	Action ACT 4556	I'll Do A Little Bit More/Same Old Thing	15
71	Jay Boy BOY 27	Hully Gully/Big Boy Pete	8
72	Jay Boy BOY 56	Baby, Do The Philly Dog/Secret Agents	8
72	Jay Boy BOY 74	I'll Do A Little Bit More/Same Old Thing (reissue)	8
61	Vocalion VAH 8059	DANCE BY THE LIGHT OF THE MOON (LP)	75
67	London HA-M 8327	SOMETHING OLD, SOMETHING NEW (LP, unissued)	
67	Fontana TL 5407	SOMETHING OLD, SOMETHING NEW (LP)	60
72	Jay Boy JSX 2008	THE OLYMPICS (LP)	20

(see also Cappy Lewis)

PATRICK O'MAGICK

74	Chrysalis CHS 2041	You're A Winner/The Proposal	5

(see also Patrick Campbell-Lyons)

MICHAEL O'MARTIAN

76	Myrrh MYRA 1048	WHITE HORSE (LP, gatefold sleeve, with Larry Carlton)	12
77	Myrrh MYR 1073	SEASONS OF THE SOUL (LP, with Stormie)	18
78	Sparrow BIRD 141	MAINSTREAM (LP)	18

O.M.D.

(see under Orchestral Manoeuvres In The Dark)

OMEGA

76	Decca SKL-R 5219	HALL OF FLOATERS IN THE SKY (LP)	25
76	Decca SKL-R 5243	TIME ROBBER (LP)	25

OMEGA

85	Rock Machine MACH 1	THE PROPHET (LP)	40

OMEGA RED STAR

69	Decca LK/SKL 4974	OMEGA RED STAR (LP)	50

OMEGA TRIBE

83	Crass 221984/10	ANGRY SONGS (EP)	5

(see also Pete Fender)

OMEN SEARCHER

82	OCS 001	Too Much/Teacher Of Sin (p/s)	75
82	OCS 002	Teacher Of Sin/Too Much (p/s)	75

ONDIOLINE BAND

66	London HL 10022	Last Bicycle To Brussels/Lovers Of Cologne	6

ONE

69	Fontana STL 5539	ONE (LP)	55

ONE & ONE

64	Decca F 11948	I'll Give You Lovin'/It's Me	10

(see also Ivy League, Flowerpot Men)

ONE EYED JACKS

78	Pennine PSS 154	TAKE AWAY (LP, some in "One Eyed Jacks" brown paper carrier bag)	28/25

101'ERS

76	Chiswick (N)S 3	Keys To Your Heart/5 Star Rock & Rock Petrol (some with p/s)	20/8
79	Big Beat NS 3	Keys To Your Heart/5 Star Rock & Rock Petrol (reissue, some with p/s)	10/8
80	Big Beat NS 63	Sweet Revenge/Rabies (From The Dogs Of Love) (p/s)	5
81	Andalucia AND 101	ELGIN AVENUE BREAKDOWN (LP)	30

(see also Clash, Alvaro)

100% PROOF

80	Smile SR 929	NEW WAY OF LIVIN' (EP)	25
81	Myrrh MYR 1107	100% PROOF (LP, with insert)	50

100% PROOF AGED IN SOUL

71	Hot Wax HWX 102	Somebody's Been Sleeping/I've Come To Save You	5
71	Hot Wax HWX 108	Somebody's Been Sleeping/I've Come To Save You (reissue)	5
72	Hot Wax HWX 113	Everything Good Is Bad/I'd Rather Fight Than Switch	5
72	Hot Wax HWX 120	Never My Love/Since You've Been Gone	5
71	Hot Wax SHW 5003	SOMEBODY'S BEEN SLEEPING IN MY BED (LP)	15

100% PURE POISON

77	EMI Intl. INS 3001	COMING RIGHT AT YOU (LP)	300+

MATTY O'NEIL

54	London L 1037	Don't Sell Daddy Any More Whiskey/Little Rusty (gold label, tri-centre)	45
54	London L 1037	Don't Sell Daddy Any More Whiskey/Little Rusty (silver label, tri-centre)	25
54	London L 1037	Don't Sell Daddy Any More Whiskey/Little Rusty (silver top, round centre)	12

JOHNNY O'NEILL

59	RCA RCA 1114	Wagon Train/Somebody, Just Like You	8

MINT VALUE £

ONE IN A MILLION

67	CBS 202513	Use Your Imagination/Hold On	110
67	MGM MGM 1370	Fredereek Hernando/Double Sight	300

(see also Thunderclap Newman)

ONE MILLION FUZZTONE GUITARS

82	Monsters In Orbit TVEYE 3	Heaven/Annuese (foldover p/s, at least 2 different designs)	6
83	Monsters In Orbit TVEYE 10	26 (LP)	12

ONENESS OF JUJU

79	Buddah BDS 497	Everyway But Loose/Make A Change	5
79	Buddah BDS 497	Everyway But Loose/Make A Change (12")	8

1,000 MEXICANS

83	Whaam! WHAAM 12	The Art Of Love/News For You (p/s, 1,500 only)	6

1,000 VIOLINS

85	Dreamworld DREAM 2	Halcyon Days/I Remember When Everybody Used To Ride Bikes ... Now We All Drive Cars (12", p/s, 1,000 only)	35
86	Dreamworld DREAM 8	Please Don't Sandblast My House/Time I Broke Down (p/s, 2,000 only)	12
86	Dreamworld DREAM 8T	Please Don't Sandblast My House/You Ungrateful Bastard/Though It Poured The Next Day, I Never Noticed The Rain (12", p/s)	15
86	Lyntone	You Ungrateful Bastard (fanzine flexidisc)	6
87	Dreamworld DREAM 14	Locked Out Of The Love-In (p/s)	15
88	Immaculate	If I Were A Bullet (Then For Sure I'd Find A Way To Your Heart) (p/s)	8
88	Immaculate	HEY MAN, THAT'S BEAUTIFUL (LP)	50

(see also Page Boys)

ONE TWO & THREE

65	Decca F 12093	Black Pearl/Bahama Lullaby	15
65	Decca LK 4682	BLACK PEARLS AND GREEN DIAMONDS (LP)	100

ONE WAY SYSTEM

82	Lightbeat WAY 1	Stab The Judge/Riot Torn City/Me And You (p/s)	8
82	Anagram ANA 1	Give Us A Future/Just Another Hero (p/s)	5
83	Anagram ANA 5	Jerusalem/Jackie Was A Jackie (p/s)	10
83	Anagram ANA 9	Cum On Feel The Noise/Breakin' In (p/s)	6
83	Anagram ANA 14	This Is The Age/Into Fires (p/s)	5
84	Anagram ANA 19	Visions Of Angels/Shine Again (p/s)	5
80s	Anagram	ALL SYSTEMS GO (LP, with lyric inner)	15
83	Anagram GRAM 008	WRITING ON THE WALL (LP, with lyric inner)	12

ONE WAY TICKET

78	President PTLS 1069	TIME IS RIGHT (LP, featuring tracks from "Five Day Rain" LP)	90

(see also Five Day Rain)

ONLOOKERS

82	Demon D 1012	You And I/Understand/Julia (p/s)	15

ONLY ONES

77	Vengeance VEN 001	Lovers Of Today/Peter And The Pets (p/s)	12
77	Vengeance VEN 001	Lovers Of Today/Peter And The Pets (12", with 7" x 7" sticker)	12
78	CBS S CBS 6228	Another Girl, Another Planet/Special View (p/s)	10
78	CBS S CBS 6576	Another Girl, Another Planet/As My Wife Says	6
78	CBS S CBS 12-6576	Another Girl, Another Planet/As My Wife Says (12", p/s)	10
79	CBS S CBS 7086	You've Got To Pay/This Ain't All (It's Made Out To Be) (p/s)	6
79	CBS S CBS 7285	Out There In The Night/Lovers Of Today	5
79	CBS S CBS 12-7285	Out There In The Night/Lovers Of Today/Peter And The Pets (12", p/s, blue vinyl, 2 slight sleeve variations)	10
79	CBS S CBS 7963	Trouble In The World/Your Chosen Life (withdrawn 'group' black & red p/s)	350
79	CBS S CBS 7963	Trouble In The World/Your Chosen Life (standard p/s)	5
80	CBS S CBS 8535	Fools/Castle Built On Sand (p/s, with Pauline Murray)	5
83	Vengeance VEN 002	Baby's Got A Gun/PETER PERRETT: Silent Night	5
78	CBS 82830	THE ONLY ONES (LP, orange label)	12
79	CBS 83451	EVEN SERPENTS SHINE (LP, orange label)	12
80	CBS 84089	BABY'S GOT A GUN (LP, orange label)	12

(see also England's Glory)

YOKO ONO

71	Apple APPLE 38	Mrs. Lennon/Midsummer New York	18
72	Apple APPLE 41	Mind Train/Listen, The Snow Is Falling (p/s)	22
73	Apple APPLE 47	Death Of Samantha/Yang Yang	20
73	Apple APPLE 48	Run Run Run/Men Men Men	25
70	Apple SAPCOR 17	YOKO ONO/PLASTIC ONO BAND (LP, with inner sleeve)	55
71	Apple SAPTU 101/2	FLY (2-LP, with inner sleeves, poster & postcard)	60
73	Apple SAPDO 1001	APPROXIMATELY INFINITE UNIVERSE (2-LP, with inner sleeves)	35
73	Apple SAPCOR 26	FEELING THE SPACE (LP)	45

(see also John Lennon, Bill Elliott & Elastic Oz Band)

ONSLAUGHT

83	Complete Control TROL 1	First Strike/State Control/No More (p/s)	8

ONYX

68	Pye 7N 17477	You've Gotta Be With Me/It's All Put On	20
68	Pye 7N 17622	My Son John/Step By Step	20
69	Pye 7N 17768	Tamaris Khan/So Sad Inside	75
69	CBS 4635	Time Off/Movin' In	22
71	Parlophone R 5888	Air/Our House	12
71	Parlophone R 5906	The Next Stop Is Mine/What's That You Say	12

(see also Salamander)

OOBERMAN

98	Transcopic TRAN 002	Sugarbum/Tears From A Willow (p/s, 1,000 copies only)	10
98	Tugboat TUGS 003	SHORLEY WALL EP (12", clear vinyl, 500 copies only)	15

OPAL BUTTERFLY

68 CBS 3576 Beautiful Beige/Speak Up 35
69 CBS 3921 Mary Anne With The Shakey Hand/My Gration Or? 60
70 Polydor 2058 041 You're A Groupie Girl/Gigging Song 60
(see also Hawkwind, Motorhead, Mott The Hoople)

JACKIE OPEL

63 Jump Up JU 512 TV In Jamaica/Worrell's Captaincy 18
64 Black Swan WI 421 You're No Good/King Liges 25
64 R&B JB 138 Stand By Me (as Jackie Opel & Hortense Ellis)/Solid Rock 25
64 R&B JB 160 Pity The Fool/The Day Will Come 25
65 King KG 1011 Cry Me A River/Eternal Love 18
65 Island WI 203 Wipe Those Tears/Don't Take Your Love 22
65 Island WI 209 Go Whey/Shelter The Storm 20
65 Island WI 227 Old Rockin' Chair/SKATALITES: Song Of Love (B-side is actually "Ska In Vienna Woods") 175
65 Ska Beat JB 190 Done With A Friend/More Wood In The Fire 22
65 Ska Beat JB 227 The Lord Is With Thee/A Little More 22
66 Island WI 264 A Love To Share/ROLAND ALPHONSO: Devoted To You 22
66 Rio R 117 I Am What I Am/JACKIE MITTOO & SKATALITES: Devil's Bug 35
66 Rio R120 I Don't Want Her/SOUL BOYS: Rudie Get Wise 30
(see also Jackie & Doreen, Doreen & Jackie, Hortense & Jackie)

OPEN MIND

69 Philips BF 1790 Horses And Chariots/Before My Time 60
69 Philips BF 1805 Magic Potion/Cast A Spell 240
69 Philips SBL 7893 OPEN MIND (LP) 475
86 Antar ANTAR 2 OPEN MIND (LP, reissue) 15
(see also Drag Set)

OPEN ROAD

72 Greenwich GSS 102 Swamp Fever/Lost And Found 6
71 Greenwich GSLP 1001 WINDY HAZE (LP) 30
(see also Warm Sounds, Denny Gerrard, Donovan)

OPERATING THEATRE

86 Mother MUM 4 Queen Of No Heart/Spring Is Coming With A Strawberry In The Mouth (p/s) 5
86 Mother 12MUM 4 Queen Of No Heart/Spring Is Coming With A Strawberry In The Mouth/Part Of My Make-Up/Atlantean Satanosa (12", p/s) 8

OPPRESSED

83 Firm NICK 1 NEVER SAY DIE (EP) 15
83 Oppressed OPPO 1 Work Together/Victims (p/s) 30
84 Oppressed OPLP 1 OI! OI! MUSIC (LP) 20
85 Skinhead CREW 1 FATAL BLOW (LP) 20

OPTIC EYE

92 Mystic Stones RUNE LP 3 TRANCE (LP) 12
94 Jump/Pumping LPTOT 17 LIGHT SIDE OF THE SUN (LP, coloured vinyl) 12

OPTIMISTS

81 Armageddon AS 018 Mull Of Kintyre/The Plumbers Song (p/s) 12

OPUS

70 Columbia DB 8675 Baby, Come On/Angela Grey 12

ORA

69 Tangerine OPLOP 0025 ORA (LP) 230
(see also Byzantium, Movies)

ORANGE ALABASTER MUSHROOM

98 Earworm WORM 36 The Slug/Ethel Tripped A Mean Gloss (p/s, with sticker) 8

ORANGE BICYCLE

67 Columbia DB 8259 Hyacinth Threads/Amy Peate 20
67 Columbia DB 8311 Laura's Garden/Lavender Girl 20
68 Columbia DB 8352 Early Pearly Morning/Go With Goldie 20
68 Columbia DB 8413 Jenskadajka/Nicely 20
68 Columbia DB 8483 Sing This All Together/Trip On An Orange Bicycle 20
69 Parlophone R 5789 Tonight I'll Be Staying Here With You/Last Cloud Home 12*
69 Parlophone R 5811 Carry That Weight/You Never Give Me Your Money/Want To B Side 12*
70 Parlophone R 5827 Take Me To The Pilot/It's Not My World 12*
70 Parlophone R 5854 Jelly On The Bread/Make It Rain 12*
71 Regal Zonophone RZ 3029 Goodbye Stranger/Country Comforts 15
70 Parlophone PCS 7108 ORANGE BICYCLE (LP) 80
88 M'n Blue Town MBT 5003 LET'S TAKE A TRIP ON ON AN ORANGE BICYCLE (LP) 15
(see also Motherlight)

ORANGE BLOSSOM

74 Westwood WRS 038 KEEP ON PUSHING (LP) 100

ORANGE BUFFOON

98 own label BUFF 2 I Tattooed Myself Orange For A Laugh/InGod's Name, What Have I Done? 5

ORANGE DISASTER

80s Neuter OD 1 Something's Got To Give/Out Of The Room/Hiding From Frank 6
(see also Varicose Veins)

ORANGE JUICE

80 Postcard 80-1 Falling And Laughing/Moscow Olympics/Moscow (foldover p/s in poly bag, some with postcard; with or without flexidisc "Felicity (live)" [I Wish I Was A Postcard 1], 963 only) 70
80 I Wish I Was A Postcard 1 Felicity (live) (freebie flexidisc, also given away with fanzines) 15

ORANGE JUICE

			MINT VALUE £
80	Postcard 80-2	Blue Boy/Lovesick (hand-coloured p/s in poly bag, blue labels)	18
80	Postcard 80-2	Blue Boy/Lovesick (brown labels & co. sleeve or yellow labels/cream co. sl.)	4/8
80	Postcard 80-6	Simply Thrilled Honey/Breakfast Time (p/s, with picture insert in poly bag)	12
81	Postcard 81-2	Poor Old Soul/Poor Old Soul Pt. 2 (die-cut co. sleeve, some with postcard)	8/5
81	Postcard 81-6	Wan Light/You Old Eccentric (unreleased)	
83	Polydor POSP 547	Rip It Up/Snake Charmer (p/s, with free live 21/4/79 cassette)	6
84	Polydor OJ 5/JUICE 1	Bridge/Out For The Count (stickered p/s, with free flexidisc "Poor Old Soul [live]")	6
84	Polydor OJ 6/OJC 6	What Presence?!/A Place In My Heart (Dub) (p/s, with free cassette "The Felicity Flexi Session: The Formative Years")	6
92	Postcard DUBH 922	OSTRICH CHURCHYARD (LP, 1,000 with bonus 10" "Irritation Disc" [922TEN])	12

(see also Edwyn Collins, Paul Quinn & Edwyn Collins, Fun Four, Josef K)

ORANGE MACHINE

68	Pye 7N 17559	Three Jolly Little Dwarfs/Real Life Permanent Dream	130
69	Pye 7N 17680	You Can All Join In/Dr. Crippen's Waiting Room	60

(see also Danny Hughes)

ORANGE PEEL

71	Reflection HRS 5	I Got No Time/Searching For A Place To Hide	18

ORANGE SEAWEED

68	Pye 7N 17515	Stay Awhile/Pictures In The Sky	40

(see also Fadin' Colours)

ORB

SINGLES

89	Wau! Mr Modo MWS 010T	KISS (12" EP, 949 only, die-cut company sleeve)	40
90	Wau! Mr Modo MWS 017T	A Huge Ever Growing Pulsating Brain That Rules From The Centre Of The Ultraworld: Loving You (Orbital Mix)/(Bucket And Spade Mix)/Why Is 6 Scared Of 7? (12" p/s, B-side matrix states 'MWS 016T')	25
90	Big Life BLR 270T	A Huge Ever-Growing Pulsating Brain That Rules From The Centre Of The Ultraworld : Loving You (edited)/(Bucket And Spade Mix)/ Why Is 6 Scared Of 7? (12", p/s, 8,000 only, B-side matrix: 'MWS 016T')	20
90	Big Life BLR 270CD	A Huge Ever-Growing Pulsating Brain That Rules From The Centre Of The Ultraworld : Loving You (Original Ambient House Mix) (CD)	20
90	Big Life BLR 27T	A Huge Ever-Growing Pulsating Remix (Orbital Dance Mix)/ (9am Radio Mix)/(Aubrey Mix I) (12", p/s, 8,000 only)	20
90	Big Life BLR 27CD	A Huge Ever-Growing Pulsating Remix (Orbital Dance Mix)/ (9am Radio Mix)/(Aubrey Mix I) (CD)	20
90	Big Life BLR 33T	Little Fluffy Clouds (Dance Mk 2)/Into The Fourth Dimension (Essenes Beyond Control)/Little Fluffy Clouds (Ambient Mk 1) (12", p/s)	10
90	Big Life BLR 33CD	Little Fluffy Clouds (Dance Mk 2)/Into The Fourth Dimension (Essenes Beyond Control)/Little Fluffy Clouds (Ambient Mk 1) (CD)	12
90	Big Life BLR 33R	Little Fluffy Clouds (Drum & Vox Version)/(Seven Inch Mk 1)/ Into The Fourth Dimension (12" remix, p/s)	12
91	Big Life BLR 46	Perpetual Dawn: Solar Youth/Star 6 & 789 (Phase II) (p/s)	10
91	Big Life BLRT 46	Perpetual Dawn: Solar Flare Extended Mix/Star 6 & 789 (Phase II)/ Perpetual Dawn: Ultrabass (12", p/s)	10
91	Big Life BLR 46CD	Perpetual Dawn: Solar Youth/Star 6 & 789 (Phase II)/ Perpetual Dawn: Solar Flare (CD)	10
91	Big Life BLR R46	Orb In Dub: Towers Of Dub (Ambient Mix)/Perpetual Dawn (Ultrabass II) (12" remix, stickered p/s, with Jah Wobble)	15

PROMOS

90	Wau! Mr Modo MWS 017T	A Huge Ever-Growing Pulsating Remix/From One Ear To Another/ Why Is 6 Scared Of 7? (12", white label, 100 only)	35
90	Wau! Mr Modo MWS 017R	A Huge Ever-Growing Pulsating Brain That Rules From The Centre Of The Ultraworld (Orbital Dance Mix)/(Orbital Radio Mix)/(Aubrey Mix Mk II) (12", stamped white label, 1,000 only)	20
90	Big Life ORB PROMO 1	A Huge Ever-Growing Pulsating Remix (Orbital Dance Mix)/ (9am Radio Mix)/(Aubrey Mix Mk 1) (12")	15
90	Big Life ORB PROMO 2	Little Fluffy Clouds (Dance Mk 1)/Into The Fourth Dimension/ Little Fluffy Clouds (Ambient Mk 1) (12")	12
91	Big Life ORB PROMO 3	Perpetual Dawn: Ultrabass/Perpetual Dawn: Solar Flare (12")	12
91	Big Life ORB PICTURE 3	Perpetual Dawn: Ultrabass II (12", 1-sided picture disc, 400 only, stickered PVC sleeve; later 'reissued' without sticker, 4,000 only)	25/15
91	Big Life ORB PICTURE 3	Perpetual Dawn: Ultrabass II (12", 1-sided picture disc, mispressing, plays "Towers Of Dub (Ambient)", 400 pressed but 300 allegedly destroyed)	25
91	Big Life	THE ORB SAMPLER (CD, 4-track)	10
92	Big Life ORB PROMO 4	Blue Room (Part One)/(Part Two) (12")	10
92	Big Life BLR 81D	Blue Room (Radio 7)/Assassin (Radio 7) (jukebox 7", 1,000 only)	8
92	Big Life ORB PROMO 5	Assassin (The Oasis Of Rhythms Mix)/(Another Live Version) (12", turquoise vinyl)	10
92	Big Life ORB PROMO CD 5	Assassin (Radio 7 Edit)/(Another Live Version)/ (Chocolate Hills Of Bohol Mix) (CD)	10
95	Island 12ISD 609DJ	Oxbow Lakes (12" double pack, yellow vinyl)	12

ALBUMS

91	Big Life BLRDLP 5	THE ORB'S ADVENTURES BEYOND THE UNDERWORLD (2-LP, with inner sleeve, 'classical pressing' sticker on sleeve)	20
91	Big Life BLRLP 14	THE ORB AUBREY MIXES: THE ULTRAWORLD EXCURSIONS (LP, with inner sleeve, deleted on day of release)	15
92	Big Life BLV 2	ADVENTURES BEYOND THE ULTRAWORLD: PATTERNS AND TEXTURES VERSION (video with 7-track live CD from Brixton Academy)	20

(see also System 7, KLF, J.A.M.s, Jah Wobble, Apollo XI, Space)

ORBIDÖIG

81	Situation 2 SIT 15	Nocturnal Operation/Down Periscope (p/s)	25

(see also Billy MacKenzie, Sensational Creed)

MINT VALUE £

ROY ORBISON

SINGLES

Year	Label / Cat. No.	Title	Value £
60	London HLU 9149	Only The Lonely (Know How I Feel)/Here Comes That Song Again	10
60	London HLU 9149	Only The Lonely (Know How I Feel)/Here Comes That Song Again (78)	550
60	London HLU 9207	Blue Angel/Today's Teardrops	15
61	London HLU 9307	I'm Hurtin'/I Can't Stop Loving You	10
61	London HLU 7108	I'm Hurtin'/I Can't Stop Loving You (export issue)	30
61	London HLU 9342	Runnin' Scared/Love Hurts	10
61	London HLU 9405	Cryin'/Candy Man	10
62	London HLU 9511	Dream Baby/The Actress	10
62	London HLU 9561	The Crowd/Mama	10
62	London HLU 9607	Workin' For The Man/Leah	10
63	London HLU 9676	In Dreams/Shahdaroba	7
63	London HLU 9727	Falling/Distant Drums	7
63	London HLU 9777	Blue Bayou/Mean Woman Blues	7
64	London HLU 9845	Borne On The Wind/What'd I Say	6
64	London HLU 9882	It's Over/Indian Wedding	5
64	Ember EMB S 197	Rock House/You're My Baby	20
64	Ember EMB S 200	This Kind Of Love/I Never Knew (some in p/s)	20/10
64	London HLU 9919	Oh, Pretty Woman/Yo Te Amo Maria	5
64	London HLU 9930	Pretty Paper/Summersong	5
65	London HLU 9951	Goodnight/Only With You	6
65	Ember EMB S 209	Sweet And Easy To Love/You're Gonna Cry (some in p/s)	20/10
65	London HLU 9978	(Say) You're My Girl/Sleepy Hollow	6
65	London HLU 9986	Ride Away/Wondering	7
65	London HLU 10000	Crawling Back/If You Can't Say Something Nice	5
66	London HLU 10015	Breakin' Up Is Breakin' My Heart/Wait	7
66	London HLU 10034	Twinkle Toes/Where Is Tomorrow	7
66	London HLU 10051	Lana/House Without Windows	6

(London 45s from HLU 9676 to HLU 9978, and HLU 10051, were originally issued on the London Monument label, as were later pressings of HLU 9149, 9405, 9511, and 9607)

Year	Label / Cat. No.	Title	Value £
66	London HLU 10067	Too Soon To Know/You'll Never Be Sixteen Again	5
66	London HLU 10096	There Won't Be Many Coming Home/Going Back To Gloria	6
67	London HLU 10113	So Good/Memories	7
67	London HLU 10143	Cry Softly Lonely One/Pistolero	8
67	London HLU 10159	She/Here Comes The Rain Baby	8
68	London HLU 10176	Born To Be Loved By You/Shy Away	8
68	London HLU 10206	Walk On/Flowers	8
68	London HLU 10222	Heartache/Sugar Man	8
69	London HLU 10261	My Friend/Southbound Jerico Parkway	12
69	London HLU 10285	Penny Arcade/Tennessee Owns My Soul	18
69	London HLU 10294	Break My Mind (by Roy Orbison & Art Movement)/How Do You Start Over	12
70	London HLU 10310	So Young/If I Had A Woman Like You	12
71	London HLU 10339	(Love Me Like You Did It) Last Night/Close Again	12
72	Sun 6094 001	Ooby Dooby/Devil Doll	5
72	London HLU 10358	God Love You/Changes	15
72	London HLU 10388	Memphis Tennessee/I Can Read Between The Lines	15
72	London HLU 10388	Memphis Tennessee/I Can Read Between The Lines (export issue with alternate take of A-side: matrix no. MSC-8474-T2-IL)	20
74	Mercury 6167 014	Sweet Mama Blue/Heartache	7
75	Mercury 6167 067	Hung Up On You/Spanish Nights	7
76	Monument S MNT3965	Only The Lonely/It's Over (p/s)	6
76	Monument S MNT 4247	Belinda/No Chain At All	5
76	Monument S MNT 4797	(I'm A) Southern Man/Born To Love Me	5
77	Monument S MNT 5151	Drifting Away/Under Suspicion	5
79	Asylum K 13153	Easy Way Out/Tears (p/s)	5
79	Asylum K 12391	Lay It Down/Warm Hot Spot (p/s)	5
80	WEA K 17649	That Lovin' You Feelin' Again (with Emmylou Harris)/Craig Hundley:Lola (p/s)	5
81	WEA K 18432	Until The Night Is Over/Long Way Back To Love (p/s)	5
85	ZTT ZTAS 9	Wild Hearts (...Time)/Wild Hearts (Voiceless) (p/s)	5
85	ZTT DZTAS 9	Wild Hearts (...Time)/Wild Hearts (Voiceless)//Ooby Dooby/ Crying (double pack, p/s)	30
85	ZTT 12 ZTAS 9	Wild Hearts (And Time Again)/Wild Hearts (Voiceless)/Wild Hearts (...Time)/Ooby Dooby (12", p/s)	7
89	Virgin VSG 1166	You Got It/The Only One (gatefold p/s)	5
89	Virgin VST 1166	You Got It/The Only One/Crying (with k.d. lang) (12", p/s)	15
89	Virgin VSCD 1166	You Got It/The Only One/Crying (with k.d. lang) (CD)	20
89	Virgin VS 1173	She's A Mystery To Me/Crying (with k.d. lang) (p/s)	7
89	Virgin VS T1173	She's A Mystery To Me/Crying (with k.d. lang)/Dream Baby (12", p/s)	10
89	Virgin VS CD 1173	She's A Mystery To Me/Crying (with k.d. lang)/Dream Baby (CD)	15
89	Virgin VS 1193	California Blue/Blue Bayou (live, with k.d. lang) (p/s)	7
89	Virgin VSC 1193	California Blue/Blue Bayou (live, with k.d. lang) (cassette)	6
89	Virgin VST 1193	California Blue/Blue Bayou (live, with k.d. lang)/Leah (12", p/s)	10
89	Virgin VS 1193	California Blue/Blue Bayou (live, with k.d. lang)/Leah/In Dreams (live) (CD)	15
89	Virgin VST 1224	Oh, Pretty Woman/Oh, Pretty Woman (edit)/Claudette (12", p/s, as Roy Orbison & Friends [including Jackson Browne, Elvis Costello, k.d. lang, Bonnie Raitt, Bruce Springsteen & Tom Waits])	7
89	Virgin VSCD 1224	Oh Pretty Woman (Edit) (live)/Claudette/Oh Pretty Woman (LP Version) (3" CD, card sleeve, as Roy Orbison & Friends [including Jackson Browne, Elvis Costello, k.d. lang, Bonnie Raitt, Bruce Springsteen & Tom Waits])	7
92	Virgin America VUS 63	Crying (with k.d. lang)/Falling (p/s)	5
92	Virgin America VUSC 63	Crying (with k.d. lang)/Falling (Cassette)	5
92	Virgin America VUSCD 63	Crying (with k.d. lang)/Falling/Oh, Pretty Woman (Edit)/ She's A Mystery To Me (CD)	7
92	Virgin America VUSCX 63	Crying (with k.d. Lang)/Falling/Only The Lonely/It's Over (CD)	10
92	Virgin America VUS 68	Heartbreak Radio/Crying (with k.d. lang) (p/s)	5
92	Virgin America VUSC 68	Heartbreak Radio/Crying (with k.d. lang) (cassette)	5

MINT VALUE £

EPs

Year	Label/Cat. No.	Title	Value
57	London RE-S 1089	HILLBILLY ROCK (orange p/s, mauve/silver label, triangular centre)	150
57	London RE-S 1089	HILLBILLY ROCK (orange p/s, mauve/silver label, round centre)	115
60	London RE-U 1274	ONLY THE LONELY	30
63	London RE-S 1089	HILLBILLY ROCK (re-pressing, yellow p/s, silver-top, round centre)	85
63	London RE-U 1354	ROY ORBISON	25

(The London EPs listed below were issued on London Monument, as were the later pressings of RE-U 1274 and RE-U 1354)

Year	Label/Cat. No.	Title	Value
63	London RE-U 1373	IN DREAMS	25
64	Ember EP 4546	SWEET AND EASY TO LOVE	75
64	Ember EP 4563	TRYIN' TO GET TO YOU	75
64	London RE-U 1435	IT'S OVER	25
64	London RE-U 1437	OH PRETTY WOMAN	25
65	London RE-U 1439	ROY ORBISON'S STAGE SHOW HITS	35
65	Ember EP 4570	DEVIL DOLL	70
65	London RE-U 1440	LOVE HURTS	40

LONDON LPs

Year	Label/Cat. No.	Title	Value
61	London HA-U 2342	LONELY AND BLUE	45
62	London HA-U 2437	CRYIN' (also stereo SAH-U 6229)	35/45
63	London HA-U/SH-U 8108	IN DREAMS (mono/stereo)	30/35
64	London HA-U 8207	OH, PRETTY WOMAN	25
65	London HA-U/SH-U 8252	THERE IS ONLY ONE ROY ORBISON (mono/stereo)	35/45
66	London HA-U/SH-U 8279	THE ORBISON WAY (mono/stereo)	35/45
66	London HA-U 8297	THE CLASSIC ROY ORBISON (mono)	30
66	London HA-U/SH-U 8297	THE CLASSIC ROY ORBISON (black label mono/blue label stereo)	35/45
67	London HA-U/SH-U 8318	SINGS DON GIBSON (black label mono/blue label stereo)	35/45

(Unless stated, the above London LPs were originally issued with plum labels [mono] or blue labels [stereo]. Later copies were re-pressed with black labels [mono] or plum labels [stereo] with a boxed London logo. These are worth around two-thirds these values.)

Year	Label/Cat. No.	Title	Value
68	London HA-U/SH-U 8357	CRY SOFTLY, LONELY ONE	30
68	London HA-U/SH-U 8358	SONGS FROM "THE FASTEST GUITAR ALIVE" FILM SOUNDTRACK	35
70	London HA-U/SH-U 8406	THE BIG "O" (mono/stereo)	35/30
72	London SH-U 8435	ROY ORBISON SINGS	35
73	London SH-U 8445	MEMPHIS	40

OTHER LPs

Year	Label/Cat. No.	Title	Value
64	Ember NR 5013	THE EXCITING SOUNDS OF ROY ORBISON (original copies list 'Great Newport Street' address on cover; reissued 1972)	25/18
65	Allegro ALL 778	ROY ORBISON SINGS (some tracks by Jerry Lee Lewis, Tommy Roe; black or blue label)	12
65	Ember FA 2005	ROY ORBISON AND OTHERS (with 4 tracks by Orbison)	15

(Copies of the above LP are rumoured to exist with all tracks solely by Orbison)

Year	Label/Cat. No.	Title	Value
67	Monument LMO/SMO 5007	ROY ORBISON'S GREATEST HITS	18
67	Monument LMO/SMO 5004	ORBISONGS	20
68	Monument LMO/SMO 5013	EARLY ORBISON	20
68	Monument LMO/SMO 5014	MORE OF ROY ORBISON'S GREATEST HITS	18
69	RCA Camden CDN 5118	SPECIAL DELIVERY (with other tracks by Bobby Bare & Joey Powers)	12
70	RCA Camden CDS 1077	LITTLE RICHARD AND ROY ORBISON	12
77	Monument SMNT 81808	REGENERATION	20
79	Asylum K 53092	LAMINAR FLOW	20
70s	Fan Club	ROY ORBISON RETURNS (10")	12
70s	Lone Star	THE CONNOISSEURS' ROY ORBISON VOL. 1 (fan club issue)	20
70s	Lone Star	THE CONNOISSEURS' ROY ORBISON VOL. 2 (fan club issue)	20
70s	Fan Club	BIG 'O' LIVE AT THE SNCO (fan club issue)	20

(see also Traveling Wilburys)

WILLIAM ORBIT

Year	Label/Cat. No.	Title	Value
93	Virgin VSCDT 1465	WATER FROM A VINE LEAF (CD)	20

ORBITAL

SINGLES

Year	Label/Cat. No.	Title	Value
89	Oh Zone ZONE 1	Chime/Deeper (12", p/s)	25
90	ffrr FRRF 135	Chime (Edit)/Deeper (Edit) (p/s)	7
90	ffrr FRRFX 135	Chime/Deeper (12", reissue, p/s)	15
90	ffrr FRRFXR 135	Chime (JZJ Remix)/Deeper (Bacardi Mix) (12", p/s)	15
90	ffrr FRRCD 135	Chime/Chime (Edit)/Deeper (Edit) (CD)	20
90	ffrr FRR 145	Omen/2 Deep (p/s)	7
90	ffrr FRRX 145	Omen/2 Deep/Open Mind (12", p/s)	15
90	ffrr FRRXR 145	The Chariot/Wheel Of Fortune/The Fool (12", p/s)	15
90	ffrr FRRCD 145	Omen (7" Version)/Omen (12" Version)/Open Mind (CD)	15
91	ffrr FRR 147	Satan/Belfast (p/s)	7
91	ffrr FRRX 149	Satan/LC1/Belfast (12", p/s)	15
91	ffrr FRRXR 149	Satan (The Rhyme & Reason Vocal Mix)/LC2 (Outer Limits Mix)/Chime (12", p/s)	15
91	ffrr FRRCD 149	Satan/LC1/Belfast (CD)	15
92	ffrr FRRCD 181	MUTATIONS: Chime Crime/Oolaa (Betram Mix)/Farenheit 3D3/ Speed Freak (Moby Mix) (CD)	10
92	Internal LIARX 1	Halcyon/The Naked And The Dub (12", p/s)	8
92	Internal LIAXR 1	The Naked And The Dead/Sunday (12", p/s)	8
92	Internal LIECD 1	Halcyon/The Naked And The Dead/Sunday (CD)	10
93	Internal LIECD 7	Lush 3 — 1/Lush 3 — 2/Lush 3 — 3/Lush 3 — 4/Lush 3 — 5 (CD)	7
94	Internal LIARX 12	PEEL SESSIONS: Lush (Euro Tunnel Disaster '94)/Walk About/ Semi Detached/Attached (12", p/s)	8
94	Internal LIECD 12	PEEL SESSIONS: Lush (Euro Tunnel Disaster '94)/Walk About/ Semi Detached/Attached (CD)	10
95	Internal LIE 23	Times Fly (Slow)/Sad But New/Times Fly (Fast)/The Tranquiliser (double pack, p/s)	6

PROMOS

90	ffrr FRRXDJ 145	Omen (7")/Omen (12")/2 Deep/Open Mind (12")	15
91	ffrr FRRXDJ 149	Satan (2 mixes)/LC1/Belfast (12")	15
91	ffrr FRRDJ 163	Midnight (Radio Edit)/Choice (Radio Edit)	10
91	ffrr FRRXDJ 163	Midnight/Midnight (Sasha Mix)/Choice/Choice Remix (12")	15
91	ffrr FRRX 163	Midnight/Choice (12", p/s)	15
91	ffrr FRRXR 163	Midnight (Sasha Mix)/Choice (Remix) (12", p/s)	15
91	ffrr FRRCD 163	Midnight (Sasha Mix)/Choice/Analogue Test Feb '90 (CD)	18
97	ffrr FRR GUARD 1	Belfast/Impact USA/Sad But New/The Girl With The Sun In Her Head (CD, free with The Guardian inside 'M25 orbital')	12
97	ffrr FRR F 296	The Saint/The Sinner (Industry Standard) (jukebox issue, no p/s)	7
97	ffrr FRR FXDJ 296	The Saint/The Sinner	7
97	ffrr FRR FXXDJ 296	The Sinner (1-sided, withdrawn)	8
97	ffrr FRR FCD 296	The Saint/The Sinner (CD, custom p/s)	8
96	Internal ORB CD3	EVIL SANTA (3-CD set, including LIECD 37, LICDP 37 & LICDD 37, silver box)	20
96	Internal PromoBox TRUCD 10/LIECD 30	IN SIDES (2-CD, 245mm x 175mm burgundy box with "The Box" video)	30
97	ffrr FRR PromoBox TRCDR10/FCD 296	IN SIDES (2-CD, in 245mm x 175mm burgundy box with gold Orbital logo & "The Saint" second promo video by Activate, custom sleeve)	25

ALBUMS

91	ffrr FRR 828248 - 2	ORBITAL (CD, green sleeve, with bonus track)	18

ORBIT FIVE

68	Decca F 12799	I Wanna Go To Heaven/Walking (some in p/s)	35/15

ORBITONES

73	Explosion EX 207	Memories Of Love/SONNY EARLE: In Peace	6

ORCHESTRAL MANOEUVRES IN THE DARK (O.M.D.)

79	Factory FAC 6	Electricity/Almost (black 'braille' p/s)	35
79	Din Disc DIN 2	Electricity (Re-Recorded Version)/Almost (p/s, reissue)	8
79	Din Disc DIN 2	Electricity (LP Version)/Almost (2nd reissue, diff. production details on rear sl.)	8
80	Din Disc DIN 6	Red Frame-White Light/I Betray My Friends (p/s)	7
80	Din Disc DIN 6/12	Red Frame-White Light/I Betray My Friends (12", p/s)	10
80	Din Disc DIN 15-10	Messages (Extended)/Waiting For The Man/Taking Sides Again (10", p/s)	8
80	Din Disc DIN 22-12	Enola Gay (Extended)/Annex (p/s)	15
80	Din Disc DIN 24-10	Souvenir (Extended)/Motion And Heart (Amazon Version)/Sacred Heart (10", p/s)	8
81	Flexi/Smash Hits (no cat. no.)	Pretending To See The Future (Live Version)/NASH THE SLASH: Swing-Shift (Flexi-Version) (blue 33rpm 1-sided flexidisc free with *Smash Hits* mag)	12/6
82	Din Disc DIN 40-12	Maid Of Orleans (The Waltz Joan Of Arc)/Navigation/Of All The Things We've Made (12", 'coin' cover; incorrectly lists "Experiments In Vertical Take-Off")	15
82	Din Disc DIN 40-12	Maid Of Orleans (The Waltz Joan Of Arc)/Navigation/Of All The Things We've Made (12", 'stained glass' cover, some metallic; incorrectly lists "Experiments In Vertical Take-Off"or "Of All Things We've Done")	12/8
82	Virgin VSY 527	Genetic Engineering/4-Neu (picture disc)	6
83	Virgin VSY 580	Telegraph/66 And Fading (picture disc)	6
83	Virgin VS 580-12	Telegraph (Extended)/66 And Fading (12", p/s)	12
84	Virgin VSX 660	Locomotion/Her Body In My Soul ('competition' p/s)	15
84	Virgin VSS 660	Locomotion/Her Body In My Soul (train-shaped picture disc)	15
84	Virgin VSY 685	Talking Loud And Clear/Julia's Song (picture disc)	6
84	Virgin TVS 70512	Tesla Girls (Remix)/Garden City/Telegraph (live)/Tesla Girls (cassette)	10
84	Virgin VSY 727	Never Turn Away/Wrappup (picture disc)	6
85	Virgin VS 766	So In Love/Concrete Hands//Maria Gallante/White Trash (live) (double pack, stickered gatefold p/s)	6
85	Virgin VSY 766-14	So In Love (Extended Remix)/Concrete Hands (Extended)/ Maria Gallante (12", picture disc)	8
85	Virgin VS 796	Secret/Drift (poster p/s)	8
85	Virgin VS 796-12	Secret (Extended)/Drift//Red Frame-White Light/I Betray My Friends (12", double pack)	12
85	Virgin VSS 811	La Femme Accident/Firegun (shaped picture disc)	10
85	Virgin VSD 811-12	La Femme Accident/Firegun/La Femme Accident (12" Mix)/ Locomotion (live)/Enola Gay (12", double pack)	10
86	Virgin VSD 911	We Love You/(Dub)//If You Leave/88 Seconds In Greensboro' (double pack)	6
86	Virgin VSC 911	We Love You/We Love You (Dub) (shrinkwrapped with cassette: "Souvenir"/ "Electricity"/"Enola Gay"/"Joan Of Arc"/"We Love You"/"We Love You [Dub]")	10
87	Virgin MIKE 938-12	Shame (Extended Re-recorded Version)/Goddess Of Love/(Forever) Live And Die (12" Mix)/Messages (10" Mix) (CD, gatefold card p/s)	12
88	Virgin VS 987-10	Dreaming (The William Orbit Remix)/Dreaming/Messages/Secret (10", numbered p/s)	8
88	Virgin VSY 987-12	Dreaming (Extended Mix)/Satellite/Gravity Never Failed (12", picture disc with poster, gatefold PVC sleeve)	8
88	Virgin VSCD 987	Dreaming (Extended Mix)/Satellite/Gravity Never Failed/Dreaming (CD)	15
88	Virgin VSCDX 987	Dreaming (Extended Mix)/Satellite/Gravity Never Failed/Dreaming (CD, trifold card digipak)	18
88	Virgin TRICD 4	Dreaming/Satellite/Gravity Never Failed (3" CD, with adaptor, no inlay)	10
88	Virgin CDT 12	Locomotion/Her Body In My Soul/The Avenue (3" CD, card sleeve)	12
88	Virgin CDT 27	Maid Of Orleans (The Waltz Joan Of Arc) (12" Version)/Joan Of Arc (12" Version)/Navigation/Of All The Things We've Made (3" CD, card sleeve)	12
91	Virgin VSCDX 1310	Sailing On The Seven Seas (Extended)/Burning/Dancing On The Seven Seas/Big Town (CD, in foldout box)	20
91	Virgin VSCDX 1331	Pandora's Box/Pandora's Box (Lost Girl Mix)/Pandora's Box (Abstract Mix)/ Pandora's Box (American Venus 7" Mix) (CD, in wooden box)	15
91	Virgin VSCDG 1368	Then You Turn Away/Sailing On The Seven Seas/Then You Turn Away (Infinite Repeat Mix)/Vox Humana (CD, in felt box with scented postcard)	15
80	Din Disc DID 2	ORCHESTRAL MANOEUVRES IN THE DARK (LP, 12" x 12" grid sleeve, black, blue or grey outer sleeves with orange, pink or red inner)	each 10
80	Din Disc DID 6	ORGANISATION (LP, stickered sleeve, with insert & 7": "Introducing Radios"/ "Distance Fades Between Us"/"Progress"/"Once When I Was Six" [DEP 2])	15

MINT VALUE £

84 Virgin V 2310 — JUNK CULTURE (LP, stickered sleeve, with free 7": "[Angels Keep Turning] The Wheels Of The Universe" [JUNK 1]) . . . 15
91 Virgin V 2648 — SUGAR TAX (LP, mispressing with extra track "All She Wants Is Everything" instead of "Neon Lights") . . . 15

ORCHIDS
63 Decca F 11743 — Gonna Make Him Mine/Stay At Home . . . 20
63 Decca F 11785 — Love Hit Me/Don't Make Me Mad . . . 15
64 Decca F 11861 — I've Got That Feeling/Larry . . . 20
(see also Exceptions)

ORCHIDS
88 Sarah SARAH 002 — I've Got A Habit/Give Me Some Peppermint Freedom/Apologies (foldover p/s with poster, 1,000 only) . . . 20
88 Sarah SARAH 011 — UNDERNEATH THE WINDOW, UNDERNEATH THE SINK EP (p/s) . . . 10
89 Sarah SARAH 023 — WHAT WILL WE DO NEXT? EP (p/s) . . . 12
88 Sha La La BaBaBaBaBa 5 — From This Day/SEA URCHINS: Summertime (flexi, 2,500 only, 1,000 in p/s) . . . 10/8
90 Sarah SARAH 029 — Something For The Longing/Farewell Dear Bonnie/On A Sunday (p/s, with inserts) . . . 10
90 Caff CAFF 11 — An Ill Wind That Blows/All Those Things (p/s, with insert) . . . 20
91 Sarah SARAH 042 — PENETRATION EP (12", p/s with insert) . . . 12
95 Sarah SARAH 401 — LYCEUM (10" mini-LP) . . . 12
95 Sarah SARAH 611LP — EPICUREAN: A SOUNDTRACK (2-LP) . . . 18

ORE
82 Bandit BR 003 — Your Time Will Come/Yellow River (p/s) . . . 250

CHARLES ORGANAIRE
64 Blue Beat BB 241 — How Did Moses Cross The Red Sea/You May Not Believe (as Big Charlie) . . . 18
64 R&B JB 149 — Little Village/It Happens On A Holiday . . . 25
64 Rio R 28 — Little Village/It Happens On A Holiday (reissue) . . . 20

ORGANISATION
70 RCA SF 8111 — TONE FLOAT (LP) . . . 190
(see also Kraftwerk)

ORGANISERS
66 Pye 7N 17022 — Lonesome Road/The Organiser . . . 130

ORGANUM/NEW BLOCKADERS
80s Aeroplane AR 7 — Pulp Parts 1 & 2 (gatefold p/s) . . . 30
85 Laylah/Antirecords LAY 19 — IN EXTREMIS (LP) . . . 20
88 Laylah LAY 012 — TOWER OF SILENCE (LP) . . . 15
(see also Current 93, Nurse With Wound, Eddie Prevost Band)

ORIGINAL BARNSTORMERS SPASM BAND
59 Tempo A 168 — That's All There Is/Stormin' The Barn . . . 7
59 Tempo A 168 — That's All There Is/Stormin' The Barn (78) . . . 20
59 Tempo EXA 95 — ORIGINAL BARNSTORMERS SPASM BAND (EP) . . . 18
(see also Barnstormers Spasm Band)

ORIGINAL BLIND BOYS OF ALABAMA
65 Fontana 688 520 ZL — OLD TIME RELIGION (LP) . . . 20

ORIGINAL CHECKMATES
62 Pye 7N 15428 — Hot Toddy/Tuxedo Junction . . . 18
62 Pye 7N 15442 — Checkmate Stomp/Begin The Beguine . . . 20
63 Decca F 11688 — Union Pacific/The Spy . . . 35
(see also Checkmates)

ORIGINAL DIXIELAND JAZZ BAND
56 HMV DLP 1065 — HISTORIC RECORDS OF THE FIRST RECORDED JAZZ (10" LP) . . . 20
56 Columbia 33S 1087 — ORIGINAL DIXIELAND JAZZ BAND IN ENGLAND (1919) (10" LP) . . . 20
56 Columbia 33S 1133 — ORIGINAL DIXIELAND JAZZ BAND IN ENGLAND NO. 2 (1919-20) (10" LP) . . . 20

ORIGINAL DOWNTOWN SYNCOPATORS
62 VJM VEP 14 — ORIGINAL DOWNTOWN SYNCOPATORS (EP) . . . 10
64 Columbia SEG 8293 — IT'S JASS (EP) . . . 10
63 J.R.T. Davies DAVLP 301/2 — THE ORIGINAL DOWNTOWN SYNCOPATORS (10" LP, white labels only) . . . 35
(see also Ron Geesin)

ORIGINAL DYAKS
67 Columbia DB 8184 — Got To Get A Good Thing Going/Would You Love Me Too . . . 10

ORIGINAL NEW ORLEANS RHYTHM KINGS
54 Columbia SCM 5113 — Golden Leaf Strut/She's Crying For Me . . . 10

ORIGINALS
59 London HL 8783 — Sleepless Nights/Anna (unissued)
62 Top Rank JAR 600 — Gimme A Little Kiss, Will Ya, Huh/At Times Like This . . . 35

ORIGINALS
67 Tamla Motown TMG 592 — Goodnight Irene/Need Your Lovin', Want You Back . . . 70
69 Tamla Motown TMG 702 — Green Grow The Lilacs/You're The One . . . 18
70 Tamla Motown TMG 733 — Baby I'm For Real/The Moment Of Truth . . . 15
72 Tamla Motown TMG 822 — God Bless Whoever Sent You/I Like Your Style/Baby I'm For Real . . . 6
76 T. Motown TMGT 1038 — Down To Love Town/Just To Be Closer To You (12") . . . 8
76 Tamla Motown TMG 1066 — Six Million Dollar Man/Mother Nature's Best (unreleased)
69 T. Motown (S)TML 11116 — GREEN GROW THE LILACS (LP) . . . 45

ORIGINAL SIN
84 Sin S1N — The Shadow/Salvation (12", p/s, private pressing) . . . 25

ORIGINAL TORNADOS
75 SRT SRTS 75350 — Telstar/Red Rocket . . . 10
(see also Tornados)

ORIGINELLS 4
64 Columbia DB 7259 My Girl/Kathy (as Origenells) 20
64 Columbia DB 7388 Nights/I Can Make You Mine 18

ORIOLES
53 London L 1180 Hold Me, Thrill Me, Kiss Me/Teardrops On My Pillow (78) 50
53 London L 1201 Crying In The Chapel/Don't You Think I Ought To Know (78) 50
54 London HL 8001 In The Mission Of St. Augustine/Write And Tell Me Why (78) 50

ORION
84 Lost Moment LM 02 Insane In Another World/Storm (p/s) 8

ORION
87 Gypsy GYP 001 JACK ORION (LP) 30

ORION THE HUNTER
84 Portrait PRT 25906 ORION THE HUNTER (LP) 12
(see also Boston)

ORLANDO
69 NEMS 56-4159 Am I The Same Guy/Poor Little Me 6

ORLANDO
96 Blanco Y Negro 0630-19718-2 PASSIVE SOUL (CD) 30

TONY ORLANDO
61 Fontana H 308 Halfway To Paradise/Lonely Tomorrows 20
61 Fontana H 330 Bless You/Am I The Guy 8
61 Fontana H 350 Happy Times (Are Here To Stay)/Lonely Am I 10
62 Fontana H 366 Talkin' About You/My Baby's A Stranger 8
62 Columbia DB 4871 Chills/At The Edge Of Tears 12
63 Columbia DB 4954 Beautiful Dreamer/The Loneliest 10
63 Columbia DB 4991 Shirley/Joanie 8
64 Columbia DB 7288 Tell Me What Can I Do/She Doesn't Know It 8
63 Columbia SEG 8238 BLESS YOU (EP) 90
63 Fontana TFL 5167 BLESS YOU (LP, also stereo STFL 582) 60/75

ORLONS
62 Columbia DB 4865 The Wah Watusi/Holiday Hill 20
62 Cameo Parkway C 231 Don't Hang Up/The Conservative 15
63 Cameo Parkway C 243 South Street/Them Terrible Boots 15
63 Cameo Parkway C 257 Not Me/My Best Friend 12
63 Cameo Parkway C 273 Crossfire/It's No Big Thing 12
63 Cameo Parkway C 287 Bon Doo Wah/Don't Throw Your Love Away 15
63 Cameo Parkway C 295 Shimmy Shimmy/Everything Nice 12
64 Cameo Parkway C 319 Rules Of Love/Heartbreak Hotel 15
64 Cameo Parkway C 332 Knock Knock (Who's There)/Goin' Places 15
66 Planet PLF 117 Spinnin' Top/Anyone Who Had A Heart 80
72 Mojo 2092 029 Spinnin' Top/Anyone Who Had A Heart (reissue) 8
62 Cameo Parkway C 1033 ALL THE HITS (LP) 60
63 Cameo Parkway C 1061 BIGGEST HITS (LP) 55
78 London HA-U 8504 CAMEO PARKWAY SESSIONS (LP) 22
(see also Rosetta Hightower)

LE ORME
73 Charisma CAS 1072 FELONA AND SORONA (LP) 20
(see also Peter Hammill)

ORNAMENTAL
88 One Little Indian 18TP 7 Crystal Nights/Yonilingaphonics (p/s) 5
(see also Sugarcubes, Rose McDowall)

CYRIL ORNADEL (ORCHESTRA)
55 MGM SP 1141 King Of Kings (Theme From)/El Cid (Theme From) 7

ORNATE TRAMP
95 Pointed Remark PORE 012 Suit Of Piss/Early Warning (p/s) 12

OROONIES
91 Demi Monde DMLP 1027 OF HOOF AND HORN (LP) 12

ORPHAN
85 Swoop RTLS 013 Nervous/Little England (p/s) 15

ORPHEUS
66 Red Bird RB 10-041 My Life/Music Minus Orpheus 25

ORPHEUS
68 MGM MGM 1413 I've Never Seen Love Like This/Lesley's World 6
68 MGM MGM-C(S) 8072 ORPHEUS (LP) 18

ORSON FAMILY
83 Orson Enterprises OE 1 Heartbeat/(Be My) Ball And Chain/You Shake My Soul (gatefold p/s) 5

RIZ ORTOLANI
71 United Artists UP 35278 The Hunting Party/CAROL CARMICHAEL: Where's Poppa? 8

BETH ORTON
96 Heavenly HVN 56A I Wish I Never Saw The Sunshine (p/s, 1-sided limited edition, 500 only) 25
96 Heavenly HVN 6010 She Cries Your Name/Tangent/Safety/It's Not The Spotlight (10", p/s) 10
96 Heavenly HVN 60CD She Cries Your Name/Tangent/Safety/It's Not The Spotlight (CD, original issue) 8
96 Heavenly HVN 6410 Touch Me With Your Love/Galaxy Of Emptiness/Pedestal/Touch Me With Your Love (Instrumental) (10" EP, p/s with insert) 10
96 Heavenly HVN 64CD Touch Me With Your Love/Galaxy Of Emptiness/Pedestal/Touch Me With Your Love (Instrumental) (CD, digipak) 8

MINT VALUE £

97 Heavenly HVN 6510 — Someone's Daughter/I Wish I Never Saw The Sunshine/It's This I Am I Find (10" EP, p/s) . . . 10
97 Heavenly HVN 65CD — Someone's Daughter/I Wish I Never Saw The Sunshine/It's This I Am I Find (CD, digipak) . . . 8
97 Heavenly HVN 6810 — She Cries Your Name/Bullet/Best Bit/It's Not The Spotlight (10", reissue, p/s) . . . 8
97 Heavenly HVN 7212 — Best Bit (Version)/Skimming Stones/Dolphins/Lean On Me (12", p/s) . . . 8
96 Heavenly HVNLP 17 — TRAILER PARK (LP, 100 copies only) . . . 40
99 Heavenly HVNLP 22 — CENTRAL RESERVATION (2-LP, gatefold sleeve, 1000 copies only) . . . 30
02 Heavenly HVNLP 37 — DAYBREAKER (LP) . . . 15
(see also Spill)

KID ORY & HIS CREOLE JAZZ/DIXIELAND BAND

50 Jazz Collector N1 — High Society/Panama Rag (78, as Kid Ory's Creole Jazz Band) . . . 7
51 Jazz Man 21 — South/Creole Song (78) . . . 8
51 Jazz Man 22 — Get Out Of Here/Blues For Jimmy (78) . . . 8
52 Good Time Jazz 65 — Oh! Didn't He Ramble/Maryland, My Maryland (78) . . . 7
52 Tempo A 106 — Dippermouth Blues/Savoy Blues (78) . . . 8
52 Tempo A 107 — High Society/Ballin' The Jack (78) . . . 8
52 Vocalion V 1012 — Muskrat Ramble/High Society (78) . . . 8
53 Columbia SCM 5047 — Mahogany Hall Stomp/At A Georgia Camp Meeting . . . 5
53 Columbia SCM 5069 — Tiger Rag/The World's Jazz Crazy, Lawdy So Am I . . . 5
53 Columbia DB 3351 — Tiger Rag/The World's Jazz Crazy, Lawdy So Am I (78) . . . 8
56 Tempo A 106 — Dippermouth Blues/Savoy Blues . . . 5
56 Tempo A 107 — High Society/Ballin' The Jack . . . 5
56 Vogue V 2011 — Tiger Rag/Eh, La-Bas . . . 5
56 Vogue V 2012 — 12th Street Rag/Savoy Blues . . . 5
50s Storyville SEP 317 — KID ORY (EP) . . . 8
55 Tempo EXA 5 — KID ORY'S CREOLE JAZZ BAND (EP) . . . 8
55 Vogue EPV 1035 — KID ORY'S CREOLE JAZZ BAND (EP) . . . 8
59 Philips BBE 12275 — KID ORY (EP) . . . 8
60 Collector JE 117 — IN THE BEGINNING (EP) . . . 8
54 Goodtime Jazz LDG 055 — KID ORY'S CREOLE JAZZ BAND 1944-1945 (10" LP) . . . 15
54 Goodtime Jazz LDG 093 — KID ORY'S CREOLE JAZZ BAND 1944-1945 VOL. 2 (10" LP) . . . 20
56 Goodtime Jazz LDG 184 — KID ORY'S CREOLE JAZZ BAND 1944-1945 VOL. 3 (10" LP) . . . 15
56 Capitol T 389 — SONG OF THE WANDERER (LP) . . . 12
58 Columbia Clef 33CX 10116 — KID ORY IN EUROPE (LP) . . . 15
59 Columbia Clef 33CX 10134 — SONG OF THE WANDERER (LP) . . . 15
59 HMV CLP 1303 — A KID FROM NEW ORLEANS — ORY, THAT IS (LP) . . . 25
60 HMV CLP 1329 — IN THE MOOD (LP) . . . 15
60 HMV CLP 1364 — KID ORY PLAYS W.C. HANDY (LP) . . . 18
60 HMV CLP 1395/CSD 1325 — DANCE WITH KID ORY — OR JUST LISTEN (LP) . . . 25
61 HMV CLP 1422 — WE'VE GOT RHYTHM (LP, with Red Allen) . . . 20
64 World Record Club T 389 — SONG OF THE WANDERER (LP, reissue) . . . 12
(see also Roberta Dudley)

EILEEN OSBORNE

75 Seagull SG1 — SINGING SHORES (LP) . . . 15

MIKE OSBORNE

71 Turtle TUR 300 — OUTBACK (LP) . . . 50
73 Cadillac SGC 1002 — ORIGINAL (LP, as Mike Osborne & Stan Tracey) . . . 20
77 Ogun OG 210 — TANDEM — LIVE AT BRACKNELL FESTIVAL (LP, with Stan Tracey) . . . 18
70s Ogun OG 300 — BORDER CROSSING (LP) . . . 15
70s Ogun OG 700 — ALL NIGHT LONG (LP) . . . 20
70s Ogun OG 810 — MARCEL'S MUSE (LP) . . . 15
(see also Stan Tracey)

OSBORNE BROTHERS

62 MGM MGM 1184 — The Banjo Boys/Poor Old Cora . . . 8
59 MGM MGM-EP 691 — COUNTRY PICKING AND HILLSIDE SINGING (EP) . . . 25
62 MGM MGM-C 914 — BLUE GRASS MUSIC (LP) . . . 20
63 Brunswick LAT 8620 — VOICES IN BLUE GRASS (LP) . . . 15
66 Brunswick LAT 8662 — UP THIS HILL AND DOWN (LP) . . . 15

OZZY OSBOURNE

80 Jet JET 197 — Crazy Train/You Looking At Me Looking At You (p/s) . . . 7
80 Jet JET 7003 — Mr. Crowley (live)/You Said It All (live) (p/s) . . . 8
80 Jet JET 12003 — Mr. Crowley (live)/You Said It All (live)/Suicide Solution (live) (12", p/s) . . . 10
80 Jet JETP 12003 — Mr. Crowley (live)/You Said It All (live)/Suicide Solution (live) (12", picture disc) . 15
81 Jet JET 7017 — Over The Mountain/I Don't Know (p/s) . . . 5
81 Jet JET 12017 — Over The Mountain/I Don't Know (12", p/s) . . . 8
82 Jet JET 7030 — Symptom Of The Universe/N.I.B. (p/s) . . . 6
82 Jet JETP 7030 — Symptom Of The Universe/N.I.B. (picture disc) . . . 10
82 Jet JET 12030 — Symptom Of The Universe/N.I.B./Children Of The Grave (12", p/s) . . . 8
83 Epic TA 3915 — Bark At The Moon/One Up The B-Side (12", p/s, silver vinyl) . . . 15
83 Epic WA 3915 — Bark At The Moon/One Up The B-Side (12", picture disc, unreleased)
84 Epic DA 4452 — So Tired/Bark At The Moon (live)//Waiting For Darkness/ Paranoid (live) (double pack) . . . 8
84 Epic TA 4452 — So Tired/Bark At The Moon (live)/Waiting For Darkness/ Suicide Solution/Paranoid (live) (12", p/s with free patch) . . . 8
84 Epic WA 4452 — So Tired/Bark At The Moon (live)/Waiting For Darkness/ Suicide Solution/Paranoid (live) (12", p/s, gold vinyl) . . . 12
86 Epic A 6859 — Shot In The Dark/Rock'n'Roll Rebel (p/s, with signature card) . . . 6
86 Epic QA 6859 — Shot In The Dark/Rock'n'Roll Rebel (poster p/s) . . . 8
86 Epic A 7311 — The Ultimate Sin/Lightning Strikes (p/s, with free patch) . . . 5
88 Epic 652 875-2 — Back To Ozz (The Ultimate Sin)/Bark At The Moon/Mr. Crowley/ Diary Of A Madman (CD, gatefold card sleeve with family tree) . . . 8
88 Epic 653 063-9 — Miracle Man/Crazy Babies (head-shaped picture disc) . . . 8
88 Epic 653 063-2 — Miracle Man/The Liar/Crazy Babies (CD) . . . 8

MINT VALUE £

88	Spiral Scratch 2/Ozzy 1	An Interview With... (no p/s, free with Spiral Scratch, issue 2, 5,000 only)	5
90	Adventure ADV TS 102	The Urpney Song/Whirlypad Launch (p/s, some with poster, with Frank Bruno/Billy Connolly)	6/5
91	Epic 657 4406	No More Tears (extended version)/S.I.N./Party With The Animals (12" pic. disc)	8
93	Epic 659 3406	Changes/Changes (extended version)/No More Tears (extended version)/ Desire (12" picture disc)	8
96	Epic 662 6391	Perry Mason/Living With The Enemy (picture disc)	6
86	Epic EPC 11-26404	THE ULTIMATE SIN (LP, picture disc)	12
89	Epic 463 0862	DIARY OF A MADMAN (CD, promo-only, with diary)	20
91	Epic 467 8592	NO MORE TEARS (CD in embossed wallet)	18
95	Epic XP CD 2007	THE BALLADS OF OZ (CD, promo-only compilation)	40

(see also Black Sabbath, Lita Ford & Ozzy Osbourne)

JOHNNY OSBOURNE (& SENSATIONS)

70	Big Shot BI 549	See And Blind (solo)/THE TECHNIQUES: Scar Face	12
72	Techniques TE 916	See And Blind/TECHNIQUES ALL STARS: Rema Skank	10
70	Trojan TTL 29	COME BACK DARLING (LP, with Sensations)	30

TONY OSBOURNE ORCHESTRA

61	HMV POP 827	Man From Madrid/Let's Take A Spin	5
62	HMV POP 967	Turkish Coffee/Tony's Tune	5
59	HMV GES 5764	THE LATIN TOUCH (EP, stereo)	10
73	Philips 6382 069	GREAT TV THEMES (LP, as Tony Osbourne Sound)	12

BOB OSBURN

64	London HLD 9869	Bound To Happen/Think Of Me	15

OSCAR

66	Reaction 591 003	Club Of Lights/Waking Up	20
66	Reaction 591 006	Join My Gang/Days Gone By	30
67	Reaction 591 012	Over The Wall We Go/Every Day Of My Life	30
67	Reaction 591 016	Holiday/Give Her All She Wants	20
68	Polydor 56257	Open Up The Skies/Wild Ones	18

(see also Paul Dean, Paul Nicholas)

OSCAR

74	Buk BULP 2001	OSCAR (LP)	12

OSCAR BICYCLE

68	CBS 3237	On A Quiet Night/The Room Revolves Around Me	40

PETER OSGOOD

70	Penny Farthing PEN 715	Chelsea/Stamford Bridge	10

OSIBISA

71	Smoke SS 1001	Black Ant/Kotoko	5
72	MCA MKS 5079	Music For Gong Gong/Woyaya	5
72	MCA MKS 5093	Wango, Wango/Ana-Bo	5
73	Buddah 2011 179	Superfly Man/Prophets	5
71	MCA MDKS 8001	OSIBISA (LP)	12
72	MCA MDKS 8005	WOYOYA (LP)	12
72	MCA MDKS 8007	HEADS (LP)	12
73	Buddah 2318 087	SUPER FLY T.N.T. (LP, soundtrack)	15

OSMOND BROTHERS

63	MGM MGM 1208	Be My Little Baby Bumble Bee/I Wouldn't Know	25
63	MGM MGM 1245	Travels Of Jamie McPheeters/Aura Lee	18
63	MGM MGM-C 1011	NEW SOUND OF THE BROTHERS (LP)	45

OSMONDS

71	MGM 2006 075	Yo Yo/Keep On My Side	10
74	MGM 2315 312	LOVE ME FOR A REASON (LP)	12

OSSIAN

77	Spring Thyme SPR 1004	OSSIAN (LP)	12
79	Iona IR 001	ST. KILDA WEDDING (LP, with lyric insert)	12
81	Iona IR 002	SEAL SONG (LP, with lyric insert)	12

OSSIE & SWEET BOYS

67	Polydor 56167	Nothing Takes The Place Of You/Brixton Boo-Ga-Loo	6

OSSIE & UPSETTERS

66	Doctor Bird DB 1018	Turn Me On/True Love	22

(see also Upsetters, Desmond Dekkar)

AL OSTER

60s	Dominion LP 1321	ECHO OF THE YUKON (LP)	20

GILBERT O'SULLIVAN

71	Columbia DB 8779	I Wish I Could Cry/Mr Moody's Garden	8
73	Columbia DB 8967	I Wish I Could Cry/Mr Moody's Garden (reissue)	5
73	MAM MAMSS 505	I'M A WRITER, NOT A FIGHTER (LP)	12

(see also Gilbert)

PETER O'SULLIVAN

70s	Charisma CAS 1160	PETER O'SULLIVAN TALKS TURF (LP)	15

BASHFUL BROTHER OSWALD

64	London HA-B/SH-B 8104	BASHFUL BROTHER OSWALD (LP, mono/stereo)	12/15

OTHER BROTHERS

69	Pama PM 785	Let's Get Together/Little Girl	7

OTHERS

64	Fontana TF 501	Oh Yeah/I'm Taking Her Home	75

(see also Sands, Sundragon; this single does not feature Brian May)

MINT VALUE £

OTHER TWO

64	Decca F 11911	I Wanna Be With You/Grumbling Guitar	12
65	RCA RCA 1465	Don't You Wanna Love Me Baby/Hold Back The Light Of Dawn	10
66	RCA RCA 1531	I'll Never Let You Go/Hot At Night	12

(see also Storyteller, J.J. Jackson)

CLYDE OTIS ORCHESTRA

61	Mercury AMT 1143	Jungle Drums/Peanut Vendor	6

JOHNNY OTIS SHOW

50	Parlophone R 3291	Harlem Nocturne (solo)/SLIM GAILLARD: Jam Man (78)	30
57	Capitol CL 14794	Ma (He's Makin' Eyes At Me)/Romance In The Dark	12
58	Capitol CL 14817	Bye Bye Baby (as Johnny Otis Show with Marie Adams)/Good Golly	25
58	Capitol CL 14817	Bye Bye Baby (as Johnny Otis Show with Marie Adams)/Good Golly (78)	8
58	Capitol CL 14837	The Light Still Shines In My Window/All I Want Is Your Love (with Marie Adams)	25
58	Capitol CL 14837	The Light Still Shines In My Window/All I Want Is Your Love (78, with Marie Adams)	18
58	Capitol CL 14854	Well, Well, Well, Well!/You Just Kissed Me Goodbye (with Mel Williams)	25
58	Capitol CL 14854	Well, Well, Well, Well!/You Just Kissed Me Goodbye (78, with Mel Williams)	12
58	Capitol CL 14875	Ring-A-Ling/The Johnny Otis Hand Jive	22
58	Capitol CL 14875	Ring-A-Ling/The Johnny Otis Hand Jive (78)	20
58	Capitol CL 14941	Crazy Country Hop/Willie Did The Cha Cha	22
59	Capitol CL 15008	You/My Dear (as Johnny Otis Show with Mel Williams)	18
59	Capitol CL 15018	Castin' My Spell/Telephone Baby (as Johnny Otis Show with Marci Lee)	25
59	Capitol CL 15057	Three Girls Named Molly Doin' The Hully Gully/I'll Do The Same Thing For You	20
60	Capitol CL 15112	Mumblin' Mosie/Hey Baby, Don't You Know?	15
64	Ember EMB S 192	Hand Jive One More Time/Baby I Got News For You	12
69	Sonet SON 608	Country Girl/Signifyin' Monkey	5
72	Epic EPC 7896	The Watts Breakaway/You Can Depend On Me	6
72	Epic EPC 8071	The Watts Breakaway/Willie And The Hand Jive	6
75	Ember EMB S 345	Jaws/Good To The Last Drop	5
70s	Bulldog BD 2	Willie And The Hand Jive/Harlem Nocturne	5
59	Capitol EAP1 1134	THE JOHNNY OTIS SHOW (EP)	90
65	Vocalion VEP 170162	JOHNNY OTIS (EP)	110
58	Capitol T 940	THE JOHNNY OTIS SHOW (LP)	110
69	Sonet SNTF 613	COLD SHOT (LP)	15
72	Ember SPE 6604	FORMIDABLE (LP)	20
73	Starline SRS 5129	PIONEERS OF ROCK VOLUME 3 (LP)	12

(see also Marie Adams)

SHUGGIE OTIS

70	CBS 63996	HERE COMES SHUGGIE OTIS (LP)	15

(see also Al Kooper & Shuggie Otis)

NOIT OTNI & PITS

79	Automotive AERS 107	A Heart Can Only Be Broken Once/Moving Target (some in p/s)	35/25

JOHN OTWAY

72	County COUN 215	Gypsy/Misty Mountain (private pressing, with duplicated lyric sheet)	25
76	Viking YRS CF 01	Louisa On A Horse/Beware Of The Flowers (private pressing)	15
78	Polydor 2059 001	Geneve/It's A Long Time Since I Heard Homestead On The Farm (p/s)	5
78	Polydor 2059 060	Baby's In The Club/Julie Julie Julie (p/s)	5
79	Polydor 2059 105	Frightened And Scared (instrumental)/Are You On My Side? (p/s, only 3 copies pressed!)	80+
80	Stiff BUY 101	Green Green Grass Of Home/Wednesday Club (p/s)	5
82	Empire HAM 3	In Dreams/You Ain't Seen Nothing Yet (as John Otway Sweat, p/s)	5
86	'Warner Bros' OTWEAY 1	The New Jerusalem/The Tyger (private pressing)	20
82	Empire HAMLP 1	JOHN OTWAY (ALL BALLS AND NO WILLY) (LP, with Europeans)	12

JOHN OTWAY & WILD WILLY BARRETT

73	Track 2094 111	Murder Man/If I Did	8
76	Track 2094 133	Louisa On A Horse/Misty Mountain	5
77	Polydor 2058 916	Racing Cars (Jet Spotter Of The Track)/Running From The Law (p/s)	10
77	Polydor 2058 951	Really Free/Beware Of The Flowers (Cos I'm Sure They're Going To Get You Yeh) (p/s or die-cut 'review' sleeve)	6/5
82	Stiff Indie STIN 1	Headbutts/Live Version Headbutts (p/s)	6
82	Empire HAM 5T	12 STITCH EP (12" EP in polythene bag with jay-card)	15
87	VM VMS 6	The Last Of The Mohicans/Fashion (brown paper bag sleeve)	5
77	Extracted EXLP 1	JOHN OTWAY AND WILD WILLY BARRETT (LP, handmade stickered sleeve)	20
77	white label OBL 1	OTWAY AND BARRETT LIVE AT THE ROUNDHOUSE (private pressing LP, freebie, handwritten labels, plain sleeve, 250 numbered copies only)	35
81	Polydor POLS 1039	GONE WITH THE BIN (THE BEST OF OTWAY-BARRETT) (LP)	12
87	VM VM 7	THE WIMP AND THE WILD (LP, 1,000 only)	12

(see also Wild Willy Barrett)

OUR PLASTIC DREAM

67	Go AJ 11411	A Little Bit Of Shangrila/Encapsulated Marigold	100

OUT

79	Rabid TOSH 113	Who Is Innocent/Linda's Just A Statue (p/s)	7

OUTCASTS

78	It IT 4	Frustration/Don't Want To Be No Adult/You're A Disease (p/s)	30
78	Good Vibrations GOT 3	Just Another Teenage Rebel/Love Is For Sops (poster p/s, various colours; 'band' p/s or 'type' p/s)	12/10
79	Good Vibrations GOT 17	Self Conscious Over You/Love You For Never (p/s)	10
81	GBH GBH 001	Magnum Force/Gangland Warfare (p/s)	6
81	Outcasts Only 0001	Programme Love/Beating And Screaming (Parts 1 & 2)/Mania (p/s)	5
79	Good Vibrations BIG 1	SELF CONSCIOUS OVER YOU (LP)	25

OUTER LIMITS

60s	Teldisc TD 154	Paradise For Two/Don't Ever Change	20

OUTER LIMITS

67	Elephant LUR 100	When The Work Is Thru'/5 MAN CARGO: What A Wonderful Feeling (Leeds Students Charity Rag record)	55
67	Deram DM 125	Just One More Chance/Help Me Please	20
68	Immediate IM 067	Great Train Robbery/Sweet Freedom (demo only)	70
68	Instant IN 001	Great Train Robbery/Sweet Freedom	22
71	Decca F 13176	The Dark Side Of The Moon/Black Boots	10

(see also Christie, Acid Gallery)

OUTER LIMITS

70s	Snow/Deroy 1049	(I'm Not) Your Stepping Stone/Great Balls Of Fire	40

OUTLAW BLUES BAND

69	Stateside SSL 10290	BREAKING IN (LP)	18

OUTLAWS

61	HMV POP 844	Swingin' Low/Spring Is Near	18
61	HMV POP 877	Ambush/Indian Brave	18
61	HMV POP 927	Valley Of The Sioux/Crazy Drums	18
62	HMV POP 990	Ku-pow!/Last Stage West	18
62	HMV POP 1074	Sioux Serenade/Fort Knox	18
63	HMV POP 1124	The Return Of The Outlaws/Texan Spiritual	12
63	HMV POP 1195	That Set The Wild West Free/Hobo	18
63	HMV POP 1241	Law And Order/Do-Da-Day	18
64	HMV POP 1277	Keep-A-Knockin'/Shake With Me	40
61	HMV CLP 1489	DREAM OF THE WEST (LP, mauve label, later black)	120/60

(see also Mike Berry, Ritchie Blackmore, Bobbie Graham, Chaps, Rally Rounders, Houston Wells [& Marksmen])

OUT OF DARKNESS

70	Key KL 006	OUT OF DARKNESS (LP)	200

OUTRAGE

70	Kama Sutra 618 027	The Letter/The Way I See It	5

OUTSIDERS (U.K.)

65	Decca F 12213	Keep On Doing It/Songs We Sang Last Summer	18

(see also Bunch Of FIves, Junior's Eyes, Tickle)

OUTSIDERS (U.S.)

66	Capitol CL 15435	Time Won't Let Me/Was It Really Real?	30
66	Capitol CL 15450	Girl In Love/What Makes You So Bad, You Weren't Brought Up That Way	15
66	Capitol CL 15468	Respectable/Lost In My World	15
66	Capitol CL 15480	Help Me Girl/You Gotta Look	10
67	Capitol CL 15495	I'll Give You Time/I'm Not Tryin' To Hurt You	12

OUTSIDERS (U.K.)

77	Raw Edge RER 002	ONE TO INFINITY (EP)	25
78	Xciting Plastic	Vital Hours/Take Up (unissued)	
77	Raw Edge RER 001	CALLING ON YOUTH (LP)	25
78	Raw Edge RER 003	CLOSE UP (LP, with insert)	25

(see also Second Layer, Sound)

OUTSKIRTS OF INFINITY

87	Woronzow WOO 7	LORD OF THE DARK SKIES (LP)	20
89	Infinity INF 001	SCENES FROM THE DREAMS OF ANGELS (LP)	12
89	Infinity INF 002	STONED CRAZY (LP)	12
94	Dark Skies DSKLP 2	INCIDENT AT PILATUS (2-LP)	18

OVALTINEES

83	BAA 021	BRITISH JUSTICE EP (p/s)	30

OVARY LODGE

73	RCA SF 8372	OVARY LODGE (LP)	60
76	Ogun OG 600	OVARY LODGE (LP)	30

(see also Keith Tippett)

OVERDRIVE

81	Boring Grantham BGR 1	ON THE RUN (EP)	80
90	Boring Grantham BGR 11	DISHONEST WORDS (LP)	20

OVERLANDERS

63	Pye 7N 15544	Summer Skies And Golden Sands/Call Of The Wild	12
63	Pye 7N 15568	Movin'/Rainbow	7
64	Pye 7N 15619	Yesterday's Gone/Gone In The Rainbow	6
64	Pye 7N 15678	Don't It Make You Feel Good/Sing A Song Of Sadness	6
64	Pye 7N 15712	If I Gave You/I Wonder Why	6
64	Pye 7N 15719	The Leaves Are Falling/Delia's Gone	6
65	Pye 7N 15804	Along Came Jones/Walking The Soles Off My Shoes	6
65	Pye 7N 15883	Freight Train/Take The Bucket To The Well	6
65	Pye 7N 15967	Room Enough For You And Me/January	6
66	Pye 7N 17034	Michelle/Cradle Of Love	7
66	Pye 7N 17068	My Life/The Girl From Indiana	6
66	Pye 7N 17159	Go Where You Wanna Go/Don't Let It Happen Again	6
66	Pye NEP 24245	MICHELLE (EP)	35
66	Pye NPL 18138	MICHELLE (LP)	40

(see also Paul Arnold, Cuppa T)

OVERLOAD

80	MCA MCA 618	Into Overload/Follow The Lines (p/s)	7
81	MCA MCA 656	Who Are You/Drift Away	7

OVERLORD

78	Airebeat ABT 3	Lucy (p/s)	25

MINT VALUE £

RUNE OVERMAN

63 Decca F 11605 Big Bass Boogie/Madison Piano . . . 10

OVERTAKERS

68 Amalgamated AMG 803 That's The Way You Like It/The Big Take-Over . . . 15
68 Amalgamated AMG 809 Girl You Ruff/KEITH BLAKE: Woo Oh Oh . . . 18

OWEN (Da Silvera) & LEON

64 Island WI 146 Nextdoor Neighbour/ROLAND ALPHONSO: Feeling Fine . . . 22
64 Island WI 163 My Love For You/How Many Times . . . 22
64 Island WI 164 The Fits Is On Me/SKATALITES: Good News . . . 22
64 Island WI 165 Running Around/SKATALITES: Around The World . . . 22
65 Ska Beat JB 189 Woman/BABA BROOKS with DON DRUMMOND: Doctor Decker . . . 25
(see also Leon & Owen, Tommy McCook)

OWEN (Gray) & DANDY (Livingstone)

69 Downtown DT 428 Lovey Dovey/HERBIE GRAY & RUDIES: Kitty Wait . . . 7

OWEN (Gray) & MILLIE

62 Blue Beat BB 96 Sit And Cry/Do You Know (with City Slickers Orchestra) . . . 15
62 Island WI 014 Sugar Plum/OWEN GRAY: Jezebel . . . 15
(see also Owen Gray, Millie, Owen & Leon, Leon & Owen)

RAY OWEN('S MOON)

69 Fontana TF 1045 Tonight I'll Be Staying Here With You/Down, Don't Bother Me (solo) . . . 5
71 Polydor 2058 095 Hey Sweety/Free Man (as Ray Owen's Moon) . . . 5
71 Polydor 2325 061 RAY OWEN'S MOON (LP) . . . 20
(see also Juicy Lucy)

REG OWEN & HIS ORCHESTRA

56 Parlophone R 4217 Comin' Thru' The Rye Bread/Harlem Swing . . . 6
57 Parlophone R 4303 Easy Now/Sweeping The Floor . . . 7
59 Pye International 7N 25009 Manhattan Spiritual/Ritual Blues . . . 7
59 Pye International 7N 25040 Ginchy/Kazoo . . . 6
59 Pye International N 25040 Ginchy/Kazoo (78) . . . 7
60 Palette PG 9004 Obsession/Sunday Morn . . . 12
61 Palette PG 9013 Payroll/Swing A Ling-Ling . . . 7
61 Palette PG 9022 Teen Dreams/Bye Bye Blackbird (as Reg Owen Strings) . . . 7
62 Palette PG 9030 Hula Twist/Gonna High Life . . . 7
56 Parlophone PMD 1045 SWING ME HIGH (10" LP) . . . 20
59 Pye Intl. NPL 28000 MANHATTAN SPIRITUAL (LP, also stereo NSPL 93000) . . . 18/35

BUCK OWENS (& BUCKAROOS)

59 Capitol CL 15009 Everlasting Love/Second Fiddle . . . 10
60 Capitol CL 15123 Above And Beyond/Til These Dreams Come True . . . 10
60 Capitol CL 15162 Excuse Me (I Think I've Got A Heartache)/I've Got A Right To Know . . . 10
61 Capitol CL 15187 Foolin' Around/High As The Mountain . . . 7
62 Longhorn BLH 0006 Down On The Corner Of Love/Right After The Dance . . . 8
63 Capitol CL 15321 Love's Gonna Live Here/Getting Used To Losing You . . . 6
64 Capitol CL 15364 Together Again/Ain't It Amazin' Gracie (as Buck Owens & Buckaroos) . . . 6
65 Capitol CL 15379 I've Got A Tiger By The Tail/Cryin' Time . . . 7
65 Capitol CL 15402 Before You Go/(I Want) No One But You . . . 6
66 Capitol CL 15437 Waitin' In Your Welfare Line/In The Palm Of Your Hand . . . 6
66 Capitol CL 15452 Think Of Me/Heart Of Glass (as Buck Owens & Buckaroos) . . . 6
67 Capitol CL 15501 Sam's Place/Don't Ever Tell Me Goodbye (as Buck Owens & Buckaroos) . . . 7
69 Capitol CL 15593 Johnny B. Goode/Maybe If I Close My Eyes (It'll Go Away) . . . 5
63 Capitol EAP1 1550 FOOLIN' AROUND (EP) . . . 22
65 Capitol EAP1 20602 ACT NATURALLY (EP) . . . 22
64 Capitol (S)T 2105 THE BEST OF BUCK OWENS (LP) . . . 15
65 Capitol T 2135 TOGETHER AGAIN/MY HEART SKIPS A BEAT (LP) . . . 15
66 Capitol (S)T 2353 BEFORE YOU GO/NO ONE BUT YOU (LP) . . . 15
66 Capitol (S)T 2443 ROLL OUT THE RED CARPET (LP) . . . 15
66 Fontana FJL 307 BUCK OWENS WITH FERLIN HUSKY & FARON YOUNG (LP) . . . 15
66 Capitol (S)T 2283 I'VE GOT A TIGER BY THE TAIL (LP) . . . 15
66 Capitol (S)T 20861 YOURS, COUNTRY STYLE (LP) . . . 18
67 Capitol (S)T 2556 CARNEGIE HALL CONCERT (LP) . . . 15
68 Capitol (S)T 2760 YOUR TENDER LOVING CARE (LP, with His Buckaroos) . . . 15
68 Capitol (S)T 2841 IT TAKES PEOPLE LIKE YOU TO MAKE PEOPLE LIKE ME (LP) . . . 15
68 Capitol (S)T 2897 THE BEST OF BUCK OWENS VOL. 2 (LP) . . . 12
69 Capitol (S)T 2994 THE GUITAR PLAYER (LP) . . . 12
69 Capitol E-(S)T 131 I'VE GOT YOU ON MY MIND AGAIN (LP) . . . 12
69 Capitol E-(S)T 232 BUCK OWENS IN LONDON (LP) . . . 12
70 Capitol E-ST 212 TALL DARK STRANGER (LP) . . . 12
71 Capitol E-ST 628 I WOULDN'T LIVE IN NEW YORK CITY (LP) . . . 12
71 Capitol E-ST 685 BRIDGE OVER TROUBLED WATER (LP) . . . 12
72 Capitol E-ST 795 BUCK OWENS' RUBY (LP) . . . 12
72 Capitol E-ST 11039 BUCK OWENS LIVE AT THE NUGGET (LP) . . . 12
73 Capitol E-ST 11136 IN THE PALM OF YOUR HAND (LP) . . . 12
73 Capitol E-ST 11180 AIN'T IT AMAZING, GRACIE (LP) . . . 12

DONNIE OWENS

58 London HLU 8747 Need You/If I'm Wrong . . . 25
58 London HLU 8747 Need You/If I'm Wrong (78) . . . 25
59 London HLW 8897 Ask Me Anything/Between Midnight And Dawn (unissued)

OWL

68 United Artists UP 2240 Run To The Sun/Shades Of Blue And Green Water Flies . . . 20

O.W.L.

70s Shebazz SHE 002 — Shady Tree/4th STREET ORCHESTRA: Sun Hot . . . 8

TONY OXLEY (QUARTET)

69 CBS 52664 — THE BAPTISED TRAVELLER (LP) . . . 100
70 CBS 64071 — 4 COMPOSITIONS FOR SEXTET (LP, with Derek Bailey) . . . 100
71 RCA SF 8215 — ICHNOS (LP) . . . 60
70s Incus INCUS 8 — TONY OXLEY (LP, with Derek Bailey, et al.) . . . 100
70s Incus INCUS 18 — FEBRUARY PAPERS (LP) . . . 50
80s Bead BEAD 25 — THE GLIDER & THE GRINDER (LP) . . . 40
(see also Derek Bailey, Howard Riley)

OXY & MORONS

81 Music For The Deaf MFD 1 — Dirty Harry In The Falls Road/Nice To Be Back (printed brown paper bag p/s) . . . 6
82 Music For The Deaf MFD 2 — Work/The Good Life . . . 5

OXYM

80 Cargo CRS 003 — Music Power/Mind Key (p/s) . . . 30

OYSTER BAND

89 Cooking Vinyl FRYX 012 — Love Vigilantes/Polish Plain/I Fought The Law (Live)/Between The Wars (Live) (10", pink vinyl, poster sleeve) . . . 10
82 Pukka YOP 01 — ENGLISH ROCK 'N' ROLL, 1800-1850 (LP) . . . 50
85 Pukka YOP 04 — LIE BACK AND THINK OF ENGLAND (LP) . . . 50
85 Pukka YOP 07 — LIBERTY HALL (LP) . . . 40

OYSTER CEILIDH BAND

80 Dingles DIN 309 — JACK'S ALIVE (LP) . . . 30

OZRIC TENTACLES

94 Dovetail DOVEBOX 1 — VITAMIN ENHANCED (6-CD box set) . . . 30
98 Snapper SMALP 410 — CURIOUS CORN (LP) . . . 12

OZZ II

83 Streamline — EXPLOITED (LP, red vinyl) . . . 12
84 Zebra ZEB 2 — THE ASSASSIN (LP) . . . 12

P

AUGUSTUS PABLO

71 Big Shot BI 578 — The Mood/HERMAN CHIN-LOY: New Love . . . 22
71 Big Shot BI 579 — East Of The River Nile/HERMAN CHIN-LOY: East Of River Nile Version (B-side actually by Aquarians) . . . 30
71 Creole CR 1004 — 405 (actually "The Mood" by Tommy McCook)/Duck It Up (actually "Confidential Version" by Charmers) . . . 18
71 Ackee ACK 134 — Still Yet/AQUARIANS: Version . . . 18
71 Ackee ACK 138 — Snowball And Pudding/AQUARIANS: Version . . . 15
71 Duke DU 122 — Reggae In The Fields/TOMMY McCOOK: Love Brother . . . 18
73 Randy's RAN 536 — Bedroom Mazurka (as Augustus Pablo & Fay)/Melodica Version . . . 20
75 Island WIP 6226 — King Tubby Meets The Rockers Uptown/Baby I Love You So . . . 10
75 Island 12 WIP 6226 — King Tubby Meets The Rockers Uptown/Baby I Love You So (12") . . . 15
78 Rough Trade RT 002 — Pablo Meets Mr. Bassie/Mr. Bassie Special (with Rockers All Stars) (with colour sticker) . . . 12
74 Tropical TROPS 101 — THIS IS (LP) . . . 35
75 Trojan TRLS 115 — ITAL DUB (LP, original issue with "12 Neasden Lane" address on sleeve and rough orange/white paper labels) . . . 25
75 Nationwide NW 03 — THRILLER (LP) . . . 20
(see also Mickey Lee, I Roy)

PACESETTERS

70 Big Chief BC 101 — Cool Coffee/Israelites . . . 15
70 Escort ERT 829 — Bits And Pieces/Nimrod Leap . . . 10
74 Saga SAGA 8154 — REGGAE MEETS POP (LP) . . . 25

PACIFIC DRIFT

70 Deram DM 304 — Water Woman/Yes You Do . . . 15
70 Deram Nova (S)DN 13 — FEELIN' FREE (LP) . . . 50
(see also Wimple Winch, Just Four Men)

PACIFIC GAS & ELECTRIC (P.G. & E.)

70 CBS 5039 — Are You Ready?/Staggolee . . . 6
70 CBS 5204 — Father Come On Home/Elvira . . . 5
69 B&C CAS 1003 — GET IT ON (LP) . . . 20
69 CBS 63822 — PACIFIC GAS & ELECTRIC (LP, orange label) . . . 18
70 CBS 64026 — ARE YOU READY (LP, orange label) . . . 18
71 CBS 64295 — HARD BURN (LP, orange label) . . . 18

PACK

65 Columbia DB 7702 — Do You Believe In Magic?/Things Bring Me Down . . . 40

MINT VALUE £

PACK

79 SS PAK 1 — Brave New Soldiers/Heathen (p/s, 2,500 only) . . . 12
79 Rough Trade RT 025 — King Of Kings/Number 12 (p/s) . . . 8
80 SS SS 1N2/SS 2N1 — KIRK BRANDON AND THE PACK OF LIES (EP, with printed inner sleeve) . . . 12
82 Cyclops CYCLOPS 1 — LONG LIVE THE PAST (EP) . . . 8
82 Donut DONUT 2 — THE PACK LIVE, 1979 (cassette) . . . 15
(see also Theatre Of Hate, Spear Of Destiny, Senate)

PACKABEATS

61 Parlophone R 4729 — Gypsy Beat/Big Man . . . 20
62 Pye 7N 15480 — Evening In Paris/The Traitors . . . 22
63 Pye 7N 15549 — Dream Lover/Packabeat . . . 30

PACKERS

66 Pye International 7N 25343 — Hole In The Wall/Go 'Head On . . . 20
69 Soul City SC 111 — Hole In The Wall/Go 'Head On (reissue) . . . 12
70 Soul City SCM 003 — HOLE IN THE WALL (LP) . . . 40

PAC-KEYS

68 Speciality SPE 1003 — Stone Fox/Diggin' . . . 15

PADDY, KLAUS & GIBSON

65 Pye 7N 15906 — I Wanna Know/I Tried . . . 22
66 Pye 7N 17060 — No Good Without You Baby/Rejected . . . 40
66 Pye 7N 17112 — Teresa/Quick Before They Catch Us . . . 25
(see also Manfred Mann, Big Three, Rory Storm & Hurricanes, Kingsize Taylor)

BILLY PAGE

65 London HLU 10006 — It's Pop/American Girl . . . 8

CHRIS PAGE

66 Cameo Parkway CP 751 — Wait And See/Mine Mine Mine . . . 10

HOT LIPS PAGE & HIS ORCHESTRA

55 Parlophone MSP 6172 — Ain't Nothing Wrong With That Boy/The Cadillac Song . . . 30

JIMMY PAGE

65 Fontana TF 533 — She Just Satisfies/Keep Moving . . . 600
88 Geffen GEF 41 — Wasting My Time/Writes Of Winter (p/s, withdrawn) . . . 8
91 Fontana TFCD 533 — She Just Satisfies/Keep Moving (CD, in 'Led Zeppelin, A Celebration' pack) . . . 10
(see also Led Zeppelin, Page & Plant, Firm, Yardbirds, Paul, Carter-Lewis & Southerners, Neil Christian & Crusaders, Bobby Graham, Robert Plant, Honeydrippers, Brian Auger, Cartoone, Maureeny Wishfull)

LARRY PAGE (ORCHESTRA)

57 Columbia DB 3965 — Cool Shake/Start Movin' (In My Direction) . . . 22
57 Columbia DB 3965 — Cool Shake/Start Movin' (In My Direction) (78) . . . 15
58 Columbia DB 4012 — That'll Be The Day/Please Don't Blame Me . . . 22
58 Columbia DB 4012 — That'll Be The Day/Please Don't Blame Me (78) . . . 15
58 Columbia DB 4080 — Under Control/This Is My Life . . . 20
58 Columbia DB 4080 — Under Control/This Is My Life (78) . . . 15
59 Saga SAG 45-2902 — Big Blon' Baby/I Vibrate . . . 20
60 Saga SAG 45-2903 — How'm I Doing, Hey Hey/Throw All Your Lovin' My Way . . . 10
60 Saga SAG 45-2904 — Little Old Fashioned You/Marylin . . . 8
66 Decca F 12320 — Waltzing To Jazz/Jo Jo (as Larry Page Orchestra) . . . 5
66 Decca F 12368 — Peyton Place Theme/Leanda's Theme (as Larry Page Orchestra) . . . 5
68 Page One POF 068 — Take Five/Michelle . . . 6
68 Page One POF 096 — Hey Jude/Those Were The Days (as Larry Page Orchestra) . . . 6
60 Saga STP 1024 — SINGS HIS PERSONAL CHOICE (EP) . . . 10
65 Decca LK 4692 — KINKY MUSIC (LP, as Larry Page Orchestra) . . . 75
68 Page One POL(S) 002 — EXECUTIVE SUITE (LP, as Larry Page Orchestra) . . . 30
68 Page One POLS 004 — FROM LARRY, WITH LOVE (LP) . . . 12
69 Page One POLS 601 — LARRY PAGE ORCHESTRA (LP) . . . 12

MALLY PAGE

66 Pye 7N 17105 — The Life And Soul Of The Party/You Can Be Wrong About Boys . . . 6

PATTI PAGE

78s

58 Mercury AMT 1000 — Fibbin'/You Will Find Your Love (In Paris) . . . 8
59 Mercury AMT 1022 — Trust In Me/Under The Sun Valley Moon . . . 12
59 Mercury AMT 1054 — My Mother's Eyes/With My Eyes Wide Open I'm Dreaming . . . 20

45s

58 Mercury 7MT 184 — I'll Remember Today/My, How The Time Goes . . . 10
58 Mercury 7MT 200 — Bring Us Together/Belonging To Someone . . . 10
58 Mercury 7MT 206 — These Worldly Wonders/Another Time, Another Place . . . 10
58 Mercury 7MT 223 — Left Right Out Of Your Heart/Longing To Hold You Again . . . 12
58 Mercury AMT 1000 — Fibbin'/You Will Find Your Love (In Paris) . . . 7
59 Mercury AMT 1022 — Trust In Me/Under The Sun Valley Moon . . . 7
59 Mercury AMT 1038 — The Walls Have Ears/My Promise . . . 7
59 Mercury AMT 1054 — My Mother's Eyes/With My Eyes Wide Open I'm Dreaming . . . 7
60 Mercury AMT 1089 — Promise Me Thomas/Two Thousand, Two Hundred And Twenty-Three Miles . . . 7
60 Mercury AMT 1102 — One Of Us (Will Weep Tonight)/What Will My Future Be . . . 7
60 Mercury AMT 1112 — I Wish I'd Never Been Born/I Need You . . . 6
61 Mercury AMT 1160 — Broken Heart And A Pillow Full Of Tears/Dark Moon . . . 6
63 CBS AAG 136 — Just A Simple Melody/Pretty Lonely Boy . . . 6

EPs

56 Mercury MEP 9502 — PATTI PAGE . . . 20
59 Mercury ZEP 10006 — PATTI PAGE ONE . . . 20
59 Mercury ZEP 10017 — PATTI PAGE TWO . . . 20
59 Mercury ZEP 10032 — PATTI PAGE THREE . . . 20
59 Mercury ZEP 10045 — PATTI PAGE FOUR . . . 20

60 Mercury ZEP 10073 PATTI PAGE FIVE . . . 20
61 Mercury ZEP 10092 THIS LADY IS NO TRAMP (also stereo [SEZ 19008], with Pete Rugolo All Stars) . . . 15/20
61 Mercury ZEP 10114 MY KINDA LOVE (also stereo [SEZ 19020]) . . . 15/20

LPs

54 Mercury MG 25101 FOLK SONG FAVOURITES (10") . . . 35
55 Mercury MG 25197 PATTI'S SONGS (10") . . . 35
56 Mercury MPT 7510 CHRISTMAS WITH PATTI PAGE (10") . . . 35
57 Mercury MPT 7531 I'M GETTING SENTIMENTAL OVER YOU (10") . . . 35
57 Mercury MPT 7535 PATTI'S SONGS (10", reissue) . . . 20
57 Emarcy EJL 1252 PATTI PAGE IN THE LAND OF HI-FI . . . 15
57 Mercury MPL 6506 MANHATTAN TOWER . . . 18
58 Mercury MPL 6521 YOU GO TO MY HEAD . . . 18
58 Mercury MPL 6524 PAGE 1 — A COLLECTION OF HER MOST FAMOUS SONGS . . . 18
59 Mercury MMC 14000 LET'S GET AWAY FROM IT ALL . . . 18
59 Mercury MMC 14007 I'VE HEARD THAT SONG BEFORE . . . 18
59 Mercury MMC 14013 I'LL REMEMBER APRIL . . . 18
59 Mercury MMC 14017 INDISCRETION . . . 18
59 Mercury CMS 18004 PATTI PAGE IN THE LAND OF HI-FI (stereo reissue) . . . 18
60 Mercury MMC 14036 THREE LITTLE WORDS . . . 18
61 Mercury MMC 14064 ROMANCE IN RHYTHM . . . 18

(see also Pete Rugolo)

PATTI PAGE & REX ALLEN

54 Oriole CB 1253 Broken-Down Merry-Go-Round/I Want To Be A Cowboy's Sweetheart (78) . . . 8

PAGE & PLANT

94 Fontana PRCDJ 1 Gallows Pole (CD, in special brown or red sleeve, promo only) . . . each 10
94 Fontana PPCD 2 Gallows Pole/City Don't Cry/The Rain Song (CD, pic. disc, part 1 of 2-CD set) . . . 8
94 Fontana PPDD 2 Gallows Pole/Four Sticks/What Is And What Should Never Be (CD, picture disc, part 2 of 2-CD set) . . . 10
95 Fontana PPCDJ 3 Kashmir (CD promo, withdrawn) . . . 30
95 Fontana PPCDJ 4 The Battle Of Evermore (CD promo) . . . 15
98 Mercury 558 324 2 Walking Into Clarksdale (CD, limited issue digipak) . . . 15
98 Mercury ADV 1998 Walking Into Clarksdale (CD promo, card sleeve) . . . 50
94 Fontana PP ID 1 NO QUARTER UNLEDDED (CD, radio-promo only, with 'question' booklet) . . . 50
98 Mercury PPTIC 1 WALKING INTO CLARKSDALE AN INTERVIEW (CD radio promo) . . . 50

(see also Jimmy Page, Robert Plant)

PAGE BOYS (U.K.)

83 Whaam! WHAAM 10 You're My Kind Of Girl/In Love With You (p/s, 1,000 only) . . . 20

(see also 1,000 Violins)

PAGEBOYS (U.S.)

65 London HLU 9948 When I Meet A Girl Like You/I Have Love . . . 8

PAGE FIVE

66 Parlophone R 5426 Let Sleeping Dogs Lie/I Know All About Her . . . 30

PAGE TEN

65 Decca F 12248 Boutique/Colour Talk . . . 12

CARLOS PAIAO

81 EMI EMI 5174 Playback (English)/Playback (Portuguese) . . . 7

PAICE, ASHTON & LORD

77 Polydor/Oyster 2391 269 MALICE IN WONDERLAND (LP, with inner sleeve) . . . 12

(see also Deep Purple, Jon Lord, Ashton & Lord, Ashton Gardner & Dyke, Elf, Bernie Marsden)

HAL PAIGE & WHALERS

60 Melodisc MEL 1553 Going Back To My Home Town/After Hours Blues . . . 50

JOEY PAIGE

65 Fontana TF 554 Cause I'm In Love With You/Yeah Yeah Yeah . . . 20

ROSALIND PAIGE

55 London HL 8120 When The Saints Go Marching In/Nobody's Sweetheart Now . . . 30
55 London HL 8120 When The Saints Go Marching In/Nobody's Sweetheart Now (78) . . . 7
57 MGM MGM 937 Love, Oh Careless Love/That Funny Melody . . . 10

PAINTBOX

70 Young Blood YB 1013 Get Ready For Love/Can I Get To Know You . . . 7
71 Young Blood YB 1029 Get Ready For Love/Can I Get To Know You (reissue) . . . 5

(see also Easybeats, Haffy's Whiskey Sour)

PAINTED SHIP

67 Mercury MF 988 Frustration/I Told Those Little White Lies . . . 70

PAISLEYS

83 Psycho PSYCHO 7 COSMIC MIND AT PLAY (LP, reissue) . . . 20

PALACE COURT BRIGADE

69 CBS 4643 Whistlin' In The Sunshine/Girls Grow Up . . . 5

PALADIN

71 Bronze WIP 6108 Anyway/Giving All My Love . . . 5
73 Bronze BRO 3 Sweet Sweet Music/Get One Together . . . 5
71 Bronze ILPS 9150 PALADIN (LP) . . . 20
72 Bronze ILPS 9190 CHARGE (LP, gatefold sleeve) . . . 25

(see also Glass Menagerie, McGuinness Flint)

MINT VALUE £

PALE FOUNTAINS

82 Operation Twilight OPT 09 (There's Always) Something On My Mind/Just A Girl (p/s) . . . 30
82 Virgin VS 557 Thank You/Meadow Of Love (picture disc, stickered PVC sleeve) . . . 8
82 Virgin VS 557-12 Thank You/Meadow Of Love/(There's Always) Something On My Mind (12", p/s) . 25
83 Virgin VS 568 Palm Of My Hand/(Instrumental)/Love's A Beautiful Place (p/s) . . . 10
83 Virgin VS 568-12 Palm Of My Hand/(Instrumental)/Love's A Beautiful Place (12", p/s) . . . 25
85 Virgin VS 750 From Across The Kitchen Table/Bicycle Thieves//Thank You/ Just A Girl (double pack) . . . 12
84 Virgin V 2274 PACIFIC STREET (LP) . . . 20
85 Virgin V 2333 FROM ACROSS THE KITCHEN TABLE (LP, with inner sleeve) . . . 25
(see also Shack)

PALE SAINTS

88 Panic PANIC FIRST Children Break/SAVLONS: ...And What's More/KERRY FIDDLES: Shiver Me Timbers (33rpm flexidisc, stickered card sleeve, some with postcard) . . . 8
92 4AD PS 2CD EXTRACTS FROM IN RIBBONS: Throwing Back The Apple/Featherframe/ Babymaker/A Thousand Stars Burst Open (CD, card sleeve) . . . 12
90 4AD CAD 0002 COMFORTS OF MADNESS (LP, with postcards) . . . 12
92 4AD CAD 2004 IN RIBBONS (LP, with free 7" "A Thousand Stars Burst Open"/ "A Revelation" [RIB 1]) . . . 12

TOM PALEY

69 Argo ZFB 3 SUE COW (LP) . . . 12

PALEY BROTHERS

78 Sire SRE 4005 Come On Let's Go/Magic Power (p/s) . . . 10
78 Sire 6078 613 Ecstacy/Rendezvous/Hide N' Seek/Come Out And Play (12", p/s) . . . 10
(see also Ramones)

PALI GAP

82 Sinister SYN 001 Under The Sun/The Knives Are Out (p/s, with insert) . . . 20

MORTY PALITZ & ACES

59 London HLJ 8778 The Grocer's Cha Cha Cha/Eso Es El Amor (This Is Love) . . . 8
59 London HLJ 8778 The Grocer's Cha Cha Cha/Eso Es El Amor (This Is Love) (78) . . . 12

PALLAS

78 Sue-i-cide PAL/101 THE PALLAS EP (stamped plain die-cut sleeve) . . . 50
82 Granite Wax GWS 1 Arrive Alive/Stranger (On The Edge Of Time) (two different p/s, some w/insert) . . . 50/40
83 Cool King CK 010 Paris Is Burning/The Hammer Falls (p/s) . . . 6
83 Cool King 12 CK 010 Paris Is Burning/The Hammer Falls/Stranger At The Edge Of Time (12", p/s) . . . 15
84 EMI Harvest PLS 1 Eyes In The Night (Arrive Alive)/East West (p/s) . . . 5
84 EMI Harvest PLSP 1 Eyes In The Night (Arrive Alive)/East West (picture disc) . . . 10
84 EMI Harvest 12 PLS 1 Eyes In The Night (Arrive Alive)/East West/Crown Of Thorns (12", p/s) . . . 10
84 EMI Harvest 12 PLSP 1 Eyes In The Night (Arrive Alive)/East West/Crown Of Thorns (12", picture disc, unreleased)
84 EMI Harvest PLS 2 Shock Treatment/March On Atlantis (poster p/s) . . . 10
84 EMI Harvest 12 PLS 2 Shock Treatment/March On Atlantis/Heart Attack (12", p/s) . . . 10
85 Harvest PLS 3 Strangers/Nightmare/Sanctuary (p/s) . . . 6
85 Harvest 12 PLS 3 THE KNIGHTMOVES EP (Strangers/Nightmare/Sanctuary) (12", p/s) . . . 8
85 Harvest 12 PLSP 3 THE KNIGHTMOVES EP (12", picture disc) . . . 18
85 Harvest 12 PLSD 3 THE KNIGHTMOVES EP (12", with free 7" "Mad Machine"/"Stitch In Time" in sealed plastic sleeve) . . . 20
86 Harvest PLS 4 Throwing Stones At The Wind/Cut And Run (live) (p/s) . . . 5
86 Harvest 12 PLS 4 Throwing Stones At The Wind/Cut And Run (live)/Crown Of Thorns (live) (12", p/s) . . . 8
83 Cool King CKLP 002 ARRIVE ALIVE (LP) . . . 18
84 Harvest SHSP 2400 121 THE SENTINEL (LP, gatefold sleeve, some with poster and sticker) . . . 20/12
86 Harvest SHVL 850 THE WEDGE (LP, with inner) . . . 12

EARL PALMER & HIS TEN PIECE ROCKIN' BAND

58 Capitol CL 14859 Drum Village (Parts 1 & 2) . . . 10
61 Liberty LBY 1008 DRUMSVILLE (LP) . . . 18

EDDIE PALMER

57 Decca F 10873 The Sky/The Twilight Theme . . . 8

JACK PALMER

50 London L 605 Sweet Jennie Lee/All My Baby's Got To Wear Is Minks (78) . . . 8

RICK PALMER

59 London HLL 8900 You Threw A Heart/My Greatest Wish (unreleased)

ROBERT PALMER

75 Island WIP 6250 Which Of Us Is The Fool/Get Outside (some in p/s) . . . 5
76 Island WIP 6272 Gimme An Inch Girl/Pressure Drop . . . 5
76 Island WIP 6345 Man Smart, Woman Smarter/From a Whisper To A Scream . . . 5
78 Island WIP 6425 Every Kinda People/Keep In Touch . . . 5
78 Island WIP 6445 Best Of Both Worlds/Where Can It Go . . . 5
79 Island WIP 6481 Bad Case Of Loving You (Doctor Doctor)/Love Can Run Faster (p/s) . . . 5
81 Island WIP 6678 Not A Second Time/Woke Up Laughing (p/s) . . . 5
82 Island PWIP 6754 Some Guys Have All The Luck/Too Good To Be True (picture disc) . . . 5
82 Island 12PWIP 6754 Some Guys Have All The Luck/Style Kills/Si Chatouillieux/ What Do You Care (12", picture disc) . . . 8
82 Island PWIP 6833 Pride/Pride (Instrumental) (picture disc) . . . 5
83 Island ISP 121 You Can Have It (Take My Heart)/The Silver Gun (picture disc) . . . 5
85 Island ISD 256 Riptide/Johnny And Mary//Trick Bag/No Not Much/Back In My Arms (double pack) . . . 5
86 Island ISP 270 Addicted To Love/More (shaped picture disc) . . . 5
86 Island CID 283 I Didn't Mean To Turn You On/Addicted To Love/Get It Through Your Heart/ You Are in My System (Remix)/Johnny And Mary (CD, g/f card p/s, withdrawn) . . 20
88 Island CIDX 352 Sweet Lies/Want You More/Riptide (3" CD, with adaptor in 5" case) . . . 8
(see also Alan Bown [Set], Dada, Vinegar Joe)

ROY PALMER & STATE STREET RAMBLERS
54 London AL 3518 A CHICAGO SKIFFLE SESSION (10" LP) 30

PALMETTO KINGS
60 Starlite ST45 021 Ten Rum Bottles/Home Cookin' Mama 10

PALM SKIN PRODUCTIONS
93 Mo' Wax MW 003 Getting Out Of Hell/Like Brothers/A Little Skin (12", die-cut sleeve) 8
93 Mo' Wax MW 013 In A Silent Way/Sunlight On The Garden (12", p/s) 18
93 Mo' Wax MW 009 TIME AND SPACE EP: I/Just Trying To Live/Moon Base Alpha/Spock With A Beard (12") 25

PAMA DICE
69 Jackpot JP 715 Bongo Man/Bear De Pussy 20
69 Jackpot JP 716 Sin, Sun And Sex/Reggae Pop-Corn 15
70 Reggae REG 3001 Brixton Fight/OPENING: Tea House 20
(see also Winston Groovy, King Horror, Ray Martell)

PAN
93 Big Cat ABB 49 HANGIN' OUT FOR JUNE (LP) 15

PANACHE
83 Mach 1 MAGIC 004 I Wanna Dance/Crazy For Your Love (with Ray Dorset) 7
(see also Ray Dorset)

PANAMA FRANCIS BLUES BAND
64 Stateside SL 10070 TOUGH TALK!! (LP) 25

PANAMA LIMITED (JUG BAND)
69 Harvest HAR 5010 Lady Of Shallot/Future Blues 25
70 Harvest HAR 5022 Round And Round/Rotting Wooden In A White Collar's Grave 25
69 Harvest SHVL 753 PANAMA LIMITED JUG BAND (LP) 70
70 Harvest SHVL 779 INDIAN SUMMER (LP, as Panama Limited) 70

GENE PANCHO
68 Giant GN 21 I Like Sweet Music/Seven Days (with Sandy & Superboys) 10
(see also Gene Rondo)

PANDEMONIUM
67 CBS 202462 Season Of The Witch/Today I'm Happy 45
67 CBS 2664 No Presents For Me/The Sun Shines From His Eyes 150
68 CBS 3451 Chocolate Buster Dam/Fly With Me Forever 45

PANDIT PRANNATH
69 Transatlantic TRA 193 EARTH GROOVE (LP) 20

PANHANDLE
72 Decca SKL 5105 PANHANDLE (LP) 22
(see also Chris Spedding)

PANIK
77 Rainy City SHOT 1 IT WON'T SELL (EP) 15

PANKOW
89 Contempo TEMPO 130 ART & MADNESS EP (12") 8

BILL PANNELL
50 London L 623 A Heart Of Stone/I Miss My Miss From Mississippi (78) 10

GARY PANTER & JAY COTTON
90 Blast First FU 7 ONE HELL SOUNDWICH (LP, picture disc) 20

JAN PANTER
65 Oriole CB 1938 My Two Arms Minus You Equals Tears/Does My Heart Show 22
65 CBS 201810 Let It Be Now/Stand By And Cry 20
66 Pye 7N 17097 Scratch My Back/Put Yourself In My Place 150
69 President PT 241 Si Si Senor/Stella In Lights 8

PANTHER BURNS
81 Rough Trade RT 077 Train Kept A Rollin'/Red Headed Woman (p/s) 10
(see also Tav Falco's Panther Burns, Alex Chilton)

ROY PANTON
63 Blue Beat BB 182 Mighty Ruler/Run Old Man 20
64 Blue Beat BB 219 Good From The Bad/Hell Gate 25
64 Rio R 19 Cherita/Seek And You Shall Find 20
64 Rio R 33 You Don't Know Me/KING EDWARD'S ALLSTARS: Doctor No 20
64 Island WI 137 Goodbye Peggy Darling (actually "Goodbye Peggy" by Stranger Cole)/ BABA BROOKS: Portrait Of My Love 25
70 Harry J HJ 6624 The Same Old Life/JAYBOYS: Life Version 10
(see also Roy & Annette, Roy & Millie, Roy & Paulette, Roy & Yvonne, Roy & Duke Allstars, Roy & Patsy, Derrick Harriot, Leon & Owen, Charmers)

JOHN PANTRY
72 Philips 6006 250 Net Of Concern/Words 8
72 Philips 6308 129 JOHN PANTRY (LP) 18
73 Philips 6308 138 LONG WHITE TRAIL (LP) 18
80s Tenth Planet TP 040 THE UPSIDE DOWN WORLD OF JOHN PANTRY (LP, limited edition, 1,000 only) 30
(see also Factory, Peter & Wolves, Norman Conquest, Sounds Around, Bunch)

PAPA DOO RUN RUN
75 RCA RCA 2620 Be True To Your School/Disney Girls 8

NIKKI PAPAS
59 Parlophone R 4590 49 State Rock/Try Again 45
60 Parlophone R 4652 By The River/Don't Leave Me Alone 18

MINT VALUE £

PAPER BLITZ TISSUE

67 RCA Victor RCA 1652 Boy Meets Girl/Grey Man 150
(see also Cupid's Inspiration)

PAPER BUBBLE

70 Deram DML/SML 1059 SCENERY (LP) 40

PAPER DOLLS

68 Pye 7N 17456 Something Here In My Heart/All The Time In The World 7
68 Pye 7N 17547 My Life Is In Your Hands/There's Nobody I'd Sooner Love 7
68 Pye 7N 17655 Someday/Any Old Time You're Lonely And Sad 6
70 RCA RCA 1919 My Boyfriend's Back/Mister Good Time Friday 6
70 RCA RCA 2007 Remember December/Same Old Story 6
68 Pye N(S)PL 18226 PAPER DOLLS HOUSE (LP) 30

PAPERHOUSE

91 Mystic Stones RUNE LP 11 SPONGY COMESTIBLES (LP) 20

PAPERTOYS

90 Armada ARMAP 003 Cold Surrender (Winston Club Mix)/Cold Surrender (D-Day 7" Radio Mix)/ Cold Surrender (Outland Mix) (12", numbered p/s, 500 only) 10
(see also Gary Numan)

PARADE

67 A&M AMS 701 Sunshine Girl/This Old Melody 12
67 A&M AMS 720 Radio Song/I Can See Love 10

VANESSA PARADIS

87 Polydor POSPG 902 Joe Le Taxi/Varvara Pavlovna (poster p/s) 25
87 Polydor POSPX 902 Joe Le Taxi (Version Longue)/Joe Le Taxi/Varvara Pavlovna (12", p/s) 7
88 Polydor 080 466-2 Joe Le Taxi/Manolo Manolete/Joe Le Taxi (Version Espagnole)/ Joe Le Taxi (Version Longue)/Joe Le Taxi (Video) (CD Video) 35
88 Polydor PO 16 Marilyn And John (English Version)/(French Version) (p/s) 7
88 Polydor PZ 16 Marilyn And John (English Version)/(French Version)/Soldat (12", p/s) 12
88 Polydor 080 468-2 Marilyn And John (Version Français) (4.40)/Soldat/Marilyn And John (Version Anglais)/Marilyn And John (Version Français) (5.44)/ Marilyn And John (Version Français) (Video) (CD Video) 30
88 Polydor 081 312-2 Coup Coup (Remix)/Maxou/Marilyn And John/Coup Coup (Remix) (Video) (CD Video) 40
88 Polydor PO 38 Maxou (Remix)/Le Bon Dieu Est Un Marin (p/s) 6
88 Polydor PZ 38 Maxou (Remix)/Soldat/Le Bon Dieu Est Un Marin (12", p/s) 12
89 Polydor 871 225-2 Maxou (Remix)/Soldat/Le Bon Dieu Est Un Marin (CD) 15
92 Polydor PZCDD 235 Be My Baby/The Future Song/Joe Le Taxi (CD, with video picture insert) 6
88 Polydor POLD 5232 M + J (LP) 12
92 Polydor 513 954-1 VANESSA PARADIS (LP) 12

JOE PARADIS

59 Top Rank JAR 195 From The French/CLAUDE DAUPHON: From The French 6

PARADONS

60 Top Rank JAR 514 Diamonds And Pearls/I Want Love 150

PARADOX

68 Polydor 56275 The Wednesday Theme/Ring The Changes 100
(see also David Walker)

PARADOX

90 Ronin RDP10 Revolutionary/Dedicated (12") 8

PARAFFIN JACK FLASH LTD

68 Pye NSPL 18252 MOVERS AND GROOVERS (LP) 15

PARAGONS

66 Doctor Bird DB 1060 Happy-Go-Lucky Girl/Love Brings Pain 30
67 Island WI 3045 On The Beach/CAROL & TOMMY McCOOK: Sweet And Gentle (B-side actually by Tommy McCook & Supersonics) 30
67 Island WI 3067 Talking Love/If I Were You 30
67 Treasure Isle TI 7009 Only A Smile/The Tide Is High 25
67 Treasure Isle TI 7011 Mercy, Mercy, Mercy/Riding On A High And Windy Day 25
67 Treasure Isle TI 7013 The Same Song/TOMMY McCOOK & SUPERSONICS: Soul Serenade 25
67 Treasure Isle TI 7025 Wear You To The Ball/You Mean The World To Me 30
68 Treasure Isle TI 7034 Silver Bird/My Best Girl 25
68 Island WI 3138 Memories By The Score/The Number One For Me 25
69 Studio One SO 2081 Have You Ever Been In Love/Change Your Style 25
69 Duke DU 7 Left With A Broken Heart/I've Got To Get Away 18
67 Doctor Bird DLM 5010 ON THE BEACH (LP) 150
(see also Rosalyn Sweat & Paragons, John Holt, Lester Sterling)

PARALEX

80 Reddingtons R.R. DAN 4 White Lightning/Travelling Man/Black Widow, (12", p/s, green vinyl) 55

PARAMETER

70 Deroy GALACTIC RAMBLE (LP) 1,500

NORRIE PARAMOR & HIS ORCHESTRA

53 Columbia SCM 5023 Cotton Reel/Pink Plank Plonk 8
53 Columbia SCM 5034 Fandango/Penny Whistle 8
53 Columbia SCM 5051 April In Portugal/The Song From Moulin Rouge (Where Is Your Heart) 8
53 Columbia SCM 5068 Man Between/Callaghan's Monkey 8
54 Columbia SCM 5126 Johnny Guitar/Paramambo 8
54 Columbia SCM 5136 High And Mighty/Rip Van Twinkle 7
56 Columbia SCM 5251 Theme From The Threepenny Opera/Poor John 7
60 Columbia DB 4419 Summer Place (Theme)/Half Pint 7
62 Columbia DB 4789 Z Cars (Theme)/Ballad Of A Soldier (Theme) 7

MINT VALUE £

65 Columbia DB 7446 — Dance Of The Warriors/Dragon Dance . . . 6
70 Polydor 56375 — Randall And Hopkirk (Deceased)/A Summer Palace . . . 65
74 BBC RESL 63 — Ricochet/Dial M For Murder (as Norrie Paramor & The Midlands Radio Orchestra) . . . 5
57 Columbia SEG 7720 — A KING IN NEW YORK (EP) . . . 10
55 Columbia 33S 1076 — JUST WE TWO (10" LP) . . . 15
66 Columbia SX 6012 — SHADOWS IN LATIN (LP, also stereo [Studio Two TWO 107]) . . . 12/15
67 Studio Two TWO 172 — PLAYS THE HITS OF CLIFF RICHARD (LP) . . . 20
74 Contour 2870 369 — LAW BEAT (LP) . . . 12
(see also Harry Gold)

PARAMOUNT ALL-STARS

50 Tempo R 20 — Hometown Skiffle (Parts 1 & 2) (78) . . . 30
(see also Blind Blake, Will Ezell, Georgia Tom, Alex Hill, Papa Charlie Jackson, Blind Lemon Jefferson, Charlie Spand)

PARAMOUNTS

63 Parlophone R 5093 — Poison Ivy/I Feel Good All Over . . . 15
64 Parlophone R 5107 — Little Bitty Pretty One/A Certain Girl . . . 20
64 Parlophone R 5155 — I'm The One Who Loves You/It Won't Be Long . . . 20
64 Parlophone R 5187 — Bad Blood/Do I . . . 18
65 Parlophone R 5272 — Blue Ribbons/Cuttin' In . . . 18
65 Parlophone R 5351 — You Never Had It So Good/Don't Ya Like My Love . . . 18
64 Parlophone GEP 8908 — THE PARAMOUNTS (EP) . . . 235
(see also Procol Harum)

PARANOIA

84 Rot ASS 8 — Dead Man's Dreams/Man In Black (p/s) . . . 5
84 Rot ASS 11 — SHATTERED GLASS (LP) . . . 15

PARANOIDS

79 Hurricane FIRE 8 — Stupid Guy/Road To Ruin (p/s) . . . 10
80 Hurricane FIRE 14 — The Love Job/Theme From Gravity's Rainbow (p/s) . . . 10

PARCEL OF ROGUES

(see under Villagers)

PARCHMENT

72 Pye 7N 45178 — Light Up The Fire/Let There Be Light (p/s) . . . 6
72 Pye 7N 45214 — Where Can I Find You/Working Man . . . 5
73 Pye 7N 45233 — You Were On My Mind/Rock'n'Roll Part Time . . . 5
73 Pye 7N 45261 — You Are My Morning/Getting Out Of This Town . . . 5
72 Pye NSPL 18388 — LIGHT UP THE FIRE (LP, with poster insert) . . . 15
73 Pye NSPL 18409 — HOLLYWOOD SUNSET (LP) . . . 12
75 Myrrh MYR 1028 — SHAMBLEJAM (LP) . . . 20
77 Pilgrim GRAPEVINE 106 — REHEARSAL FOR A REUNION (LP) . . . 15

WALTER PARDON

75 Leader LED 2063 — A PROPER SORT (LP) . . . 20

TONY PARENTI

50 Esquire 10-048 — The Entertainer's Rag/Cataract Rag (78) . . . 8
52 Vogue V 2115 — Hysteric's Rag/Sunflower Slow Drag (78, With Ralph Sutton) . . . 8
57 London EZ V 19022 — RAGTIME (EP) . . . 10
57 London LTZU 15072 — RAGTIME (LP) . . . 22

PAULA PARFITT

69 Beacon BEA 135 — I'm Gonna Give You Back Your Ring/Love Is Wonderful . . . 75

RICK PARFITT JNR.

00 peoplesound.com ART0413-CD01-00 — RICK PARFITT JNR. (CD-R, 4-track EP, title-stickered generic peoplesound.com digipak, mail-order only) . . . 10

TINY PARHAM

50s Audubon AAC — TINY PARHAM (10" LP) . . . 25

PARIS

72 Avalanche AV 67312 — I've Lost The Way/Long Time . . . 8
76 Thunderbird THE 114 — Circles/Liar . . . 5
84 Bluebird BR 9 — I Choose You/Punkin' Funkin' (p/s) . . . 5
84 Bluebird BRT 9 — I Choose You/Punkin' Funkin' (12", p/s) . . . 8

PARIS

82 RCA RCA 222 — No Getting Over You/Fighting For The Country (p/s) . . . 5

BOBBY PARIS

68 Polydor 56747 — Per So Nal Ly/Tragedy . . . 75
69 Polydor 56762 — Let The Sun Shine In/You . . . 20
77 London HLU 10553 — Night Owl/YVONNE BAKER: You Didn't Say A Word . . . 15

PRISCILLA PARIS

74 Rak RAK 184 — I Love How You Love Me/Over You . . . 10
(see also Paris Sisters)

PARIS SISTERS

61 Top Rank JAR 588 — I Love How You Love Me/I'll Be Crying Tomorrow . . . 100
64 MGM MGM 1240 — Dream Lover/Lonely Girl . . . 45
(see also Date With Soul, Priscilla Paris)

JOHN PARISH & POLLY JEAN HARVEY

96 Island IS 648 — That Was My Veil/Losing Ground (p/s) . . . 12
96 Island CIDX 8051 — DANCE HALL AT LOUSE POINT (CD, 5,000 in digipak with insert) . . . 20
(see also P.J. Harvey)

PARISH HALL

70 Liberty LBS 83374 — PARISH HALL (LP) . . . 15

MINT VALUE £

ALAN PARKER

70	Aristocrat AR 1022	GUITAR FANTASY (LP)	18
73	MCA MUPS 471	BAND OF ANGELS (LP)	12

(see also Hungry Wolf, Ugly Custard)

BENNY PARKER & DYNAMICS

64	Decca F 11944	Boys And Girls/You'll Be On Your Way	45

BILLY PARKER

63	Decca F 11668	Thanks A Lot/Out Of Your Heart	7

BOBBY PARKER

61	London HLU 9393	Watch Your Step/Steal Your Heart Away	50
64	Sue WI 340	Watch Your Step/Steal Your Heart Away (reissue)	35
69	Blue Horizon 57-3151	It's Hard But It's Fair/I Couldn't Quit My Baby	40

CHARLIE PARKER

78s

50	Savoy 939	Ah-Leu-Cha/Constellation (78, as Charlie Parker's All Stars)	7
51	Savoy 977	Chasing The Bird (as Charlie Parker's All Stars)/MILES DAVIS ALL STARS: Little Willie Leaps (78)	7

SINGLES

50	Savoy 928	Buzzy/Donna Lee (78)	8
60	HMV POP 747	Kim/Cosmic Eyes (as Charlie Parker Quartet)	5

EPs

55	Vogue EPV 1011	CHARLIE PARKER PLAYS	25
55	Columbia Clef SEB 10002	THE MAGNIFICENT CHARLIE PARKER NO. 1	8
56	Columbia Clef SEB 10026	NOW'S THE TIME	12
56	Columbia Clef SEB 10032	PLAYS SOUTH OF THE BORDER	8
56	Columbia Clef SEB 10038	THE MAGNIFICENT CHARLIE PARKER NO. 2 (as Charlie Parker Group)	10
57	Columbia Clef SEB 10053	THE MAGNIFICENT CHARLIE PARKER NO. 3	8
50s	Esquire EP 57	CHARLIE PARKER QUINTET	20
60	Vogue EPV 1264	ALL STARNTET/SEXTET	20
60	HMV 7EG 8626	CHARLIE PARKER BIG BAND	8
64	Realm REP 4008	PARKER'S MOOD (as Charlie Parker All Stars)	8

LPs

52	Vogue LDE 004	CHARLIE PARKER VOLUME ONE (10")	60
53	Vogue LDE 016	CHARLIE PARKER VOLUME TWO (10")	60
50s	Vogue LAE 12002	CHARLIE PARKER MEMORIAL ALBUM (gatefold sleeve w/ 2 inserts)	18
55	Melodisc MLP 12-105	BIRD AT ST. NICK'S	35
55	Columbia Clef 33CX 10004	CHARLIE PARKER BIG BAND	75
56	Columbia Clef 33C 9026	BIRD AND DIZ (10", with Dizzy Gillespie)	75
57	Columbia Clef 33CX 10081	APRIL IN PARIS (as Charlie Parker With Strings)	40
57	Columbia Clef 33CX 10090	CHARLIE PARKER PLAYS COLE PORTER	35
58	Columbia Clef 33CX 10117	CHARLIE PARKER JAZZ PERENNIAL	20
58	London Jazz LTZ-C 15104	THE IMMORTAL CHARLIE PARKER VOL. 1	20
58	London Jazz LTZ-C 15105	THE IMMORTAL CHARLIE PARKER VOL. 2	20
58	London Jazz LTZ-C 15106	THE IMMORTAL CHARLIE PARKER VOL. 3	20
58	London Jazz LTZ-C 15107	THE IMMORTAL CHARLIE PARKER VOL. 4	20
58	Mercury MPL 12-105	BIRD AT NICK'S	15
60	Collector JGN 1002	CHARLIE PARKER IN SWEDEN	50
61	HMV CLP 1538	THE ESSENTIAL CHARLIE PARKER	15
62	Verve VLP 9105	"BIRD" SYMBOLS (with insert for Egmont AJS 3)	15
62	Storyville SLP 27	IN SWEDEN 1950	18
62	Esquire 32-157	'BIRD' IS FREE	22
62	Eros ERL 50054	MEMORIAL VOL. 1	12
62	Eros ERL 50057	MEMORIAL VOL. 2	12
62	Eros ERL 50060	MEMORIAL VOL. 3	12
62	Eros ERL 50065	MEMORIAL VOL. 4	12
63	Realm RM 131	MEMORIAL VOL. 5	12
63	Columbia 33SX 1555	PORTRAIT OF THE BIRD	12
64	MGM MGM-C 986	HISTORICAL MASTERPIECES VOL. 1	12
64	MGM MGM-C 987	HISTORICAL MASTERPIECES VOL. 2	12
64	MGM MGM-C 988	HISTORICAL MASTERPIECES VOL. 3	12
65	Realm RM 214	MEMORIAL VOL. 6	12
71	Xtra XTRA 1118	CHARLIE PARKER VOL. 2	12

(see also Dizzy Gillespie & Charlie Parker, Sir Charles Thompson)

DAVID PARKER

71	Polydor 2460 101	DAVID PARKER (LP)	45

(see also Andwella's Dream)

DEAN PARKER & REDCAPS

62	Decca F 11555	Stormy Evening/Blue Eyes And Golden Hair	45

EDDIE PARKER

55	Columbia SCM 5211	Far Away From Everybody/Bella Notte	10
56	Columbia DB 3804	Love Me As Though There Were No Tomorrow/Rich In Love	10

EDDIE PARKER (U.S.)

79	Grapevine GRP 119	Love You Baby (Parts 1 & 2) (some in p/s)	15/10

EULA PARKER

58	Oriole CB 1411	Silhouettes/Hedgehopper	22
58	Oriole CB 1411	Silhouettes/Hedgehopper (78)	12

(see also Frank Weir)

EVAN PARKER

75	Incus INCUS 19	SAXOPHONE SOLOS (LP)	50
78	Incus INCUS 27	MONOCEROS (LP)	50
80	Incus INCUS 39	SIX OF ONE (LP)	50
86	Incus INCUS 49	THE SNAKE DECIDES (LP)	50

MINT VALUE £

EVAN PARKER, BARRY GUY & PAUL LYTTON
83 Incus INCUS 42 — TRACKS (LP) . . . 50

EVAN PARKER & GEORGE LEWIS
80 Incus INCUS 35 — FROM SAXOPHONE & TROMBONE (LP) . . . 50

EVAN PARKER, GEORGE LEWIS, BARRY GUY & PAUL LYTTON
83 Incus INCUS 45 — HOOK, DRIFT & SHUFFLE (LP) . . . 50

EVAN PARKER & PAUL LYTTON
72 Incus INCUS 5 — COLLECTIVE CALLS (URBAN) (TWO MICROPHONES) (LP) . . . 50
75 Incus INCUS 14 — AT THE UNITY THEATRE (LP) . . . 50

(see also Derek Bailey & Evan Parker, Derek Bailey Evan Parker & Han Bennink)

FESS PARKER
57 Oriole CB 1378 — Wringle Wrangle/Ballad Of John Colter . . . 15

JIMMY PARKER
62 Top Rank JAR 608 — We Gonna/No Word From Betty . . . 18

(LITTLE) JUNIOR PARKER
61 Vogue V 9179 — Stand By Me/I'll Forget About You (as Little Junior Parker) . . . 30
62 Vogue V 9193 — Mary Jo/Annie Get Your Yo-Yo (as Little Junior Parker) . . . 30
66 Vocalion VP 9256 — These Kind Of Blues (Parts 1 & 2) . . . 30
66 Vocalion VP 9275 — Goodbye Little Girl/Walking The Floor Over You . . . 25
67 Mercury SMCL 20097 — LIKE IT IS (LP) . . . 35
72 Groove Merchant GM 502 — BLUE SHADOWS FALLING (LP) . . . 12
73 Groove Merchant GM 2205 — GOOD THINGS DON'T HAPPEN EVERY DAY (LP, with Jimmy McGriff) . . . 12
73 Vogue LDM 30163 — MEMORIAL (LP) . . . 15
73 People PLEO 4 — YOU DON'T HAVE TO BE BLACK TO LOVE THE BLUES (LP) . . . 15

(see also Howlin' Wolf, Bobby Bland)

KEN PARKER
67 Island WI 3082 — How Could I/SONNY BURKE: Choo Choo Train . . . 30
67 Studio One SO 2001 — See Them A-Come/MR FOUNDATION: Have A Good Time . . . 30
68 Island WI 3096 — Down Low/Sad Mood . . . 30
68 Island WI 3105 — Lonely Man/ERROL DUNKLEY: I Am Going Home . . . 30
68 Giant GN 34 — Change Is Gonna Come/VAL BENNETT: Jumping With Val . . . 20
69 Bamboo BAM 1 — My Whole World Is Falling Down/The Chokin' Kind . . . 20
69 Amalgamated AMG 847 — It's Alright/COBBS: One One . . . 20
69 Amalgamated AMG 853 — Only Yesterday/COBBS: Joe Gibbs Mood . . . 20
70 Duke DU 79 — I Can't Hide/TOMMY McCOOK: Kansas City . . . 10
70 Unity UN 553 — When You Were Mine/CLAREDONIANS: The Angels (song actually "The Angels Listened In") . . . 10
71 Duke Reid DR 2504 — Sugar Pantie (as Ken Parker & Tommy McCook; actually by Andy Capp)/ TOMMY McCOOK: All Afire . . . 10
71 Duke Reid DR 2521 — Jimmy Brown/Version . . . 8
71 Big BG 332 — Ain't Misbehaving/Genuine Love . . . 8
72 Jackpot JP 805 — Guilty/AGGROVATORS: Guilty (Version) . . . 8
72 Pama PM 844 — Shake It Loose/TOMMY McCOOK: Shake It Loose — Version (actually titled "Help Me Make It Through The Night") . . . 8
72 Treasure Isle TI 7073 — Help Me Make It Through The Night/ TOMMY McCOOK & ALLSTARS (Version) . . . 8
73 Dragon DRA 1003 — Will The Circle Be Unbroken/DYNAMITES: Instrumental . . . 8
73 Dragon DRA 1015 — Say Wonderful Things/It's True . . . 8
74 Attack ATT 8063 — Kiss An Angel/TOMMY McCOOK: Inez . . . 8
74 Attack ATT 8073 — Count Your Blessings/Count Your Blessings (Version) . . . 8
74 Trojan TRLS 80 — JIMMY BROWN (LP) . . . 20

(see also Lyrics, Scotty)

RAYMOND PARKER
66 Sue WI 4024 — Ring Around The Roses/She's Coming Home . . . 30

ROBERT PARKER
66 Island WI 286 — Barefootin'/Let's Go Baby . . . 15
66 Island WI 3008 — Happy Feet/The Scratch . . . 20
74 Island USA 991 — Get Ta Steppin'/Get Right On Down . . . 8
74 Contemporaries CS 9010 — Barefootin'/I Caught You In A Lie . . . 12
66 Island ILP 942 — BAREFOOTIN' (LP) . . . 80

(see also Huey 'Piano' Smith & Clowns)

SONNY PARKER
56 Vogue V 2392 — My Soul's On Fire/Disgusted Blues . . . 425
56 Vogue V 2392 — My Soul's On Fire/Disgusted Blues (78) . . . 100

(see also Lionel Hampton)

WILLIE PARKER
67 President PT 171 — You Got Your Finger In My Eye/I Love The Life I Live . . . 10

WINFIELD PARKER
72 Mojo 2093 019 — Stop Her On Sight/I'm On My Way . . . 10

JOHNNY PARKER WASHBOARD BAND
55 Pye Nixa NJE 1000 — JOHNNY PARKER WASHBOARD BAND (EP) . . . 8
56 Metronome MEP 1092 — BARRELHOUSE (EP) . . . 8
57 Storyville SEP 366 — JOHNNY PARKER (EP, solo) . . . 8

PARKING LOT
69 Parlophone R 5779 — Carpet Man/World Spinning Sadly . . . 35

JIMMY PARKINSON
56 Columbia SCM 5236 — The Great Pretender/Hand In Hand . . . 30
56 Columbia SCM 5267 — Walk Hand In Hand/Cry Baby . . . 25
56 Columbia DB 3808 — Gina/A Lover's Quarrel . . . 15

MINT VALUE £

56	Columbia DB 3833	In The Middle Of The House/You To Me	20
57	Columbia DB 3876	But You/Together (You And I)	10
57	Columbia DB 3912	Round And Round/Whatever Lola Wants (Lola Gets)	12
57	Columbia 33S 1109	SOLO (10" LP)	50

BERNICE PARKS

55	Coral Q 72056	Lovin' Machine/Only Love Me	15

LLOYD PARKS

70	Harry J. HJ 6603	Feel A Little Better/I'll Be Your Man	15
72	Randy's RAN 524	Stars/Stars – Version	12
74	Fab FAB 273	Schooldays/Version	7

(see also L. Sparks)

SONNY PARKS

63	Warner Bros WB 100	New Boy In Town/Us Kids Have Got To Make Up Our Minds	7

VAN DYKE PARKS

66	MGM MGM 1301	Number Nine/Do What You Wanta	12
69	Warner Bros W(S) 1727	SONG CYCLE (LP)	20

PARLET

79	Casablanca CAL 2052	INVASION OF THE BOOTY SNATCHERS (LP)	15

(see also Parliament)

PARLIAMENT

71	Invictus INV 513	The Silent Boatman/Livin' The Life	18
72	Invictus INV 522	Come In Out Of The Rain/Little Ole Country Boy	15
75	Casablanca CBX 505	Up On The Down Stroke/Presence Of A Brain	8
76	Casablanca CBX 518	Tear The Roof Off The Sucker (Give Up The Funk)/P. Funk	8
77	Casablanca CAN 103	Tear The Roof Off The Sucker (Give Up The Funk)/Dr. Funkenstein/P. Funk	8
78	Casablanca CAN 115	Bop Gun/I've Been Watching You	8
78	Casablanca CANL 115	Bop Gun/I've Been Watching You (12")	8
78	Casablanca CAN 136	Aqua Boogie/Water Sign	5
79	Casablanca CAN 154	Deep/Flashlight	5
79	Casablanca CANL 154	Deep/Flashlight (12")	8
80	Casablanca CANL 188	Theme From Black Hole/Big Bang Theory (12")	8
81	Casablanca CAN 223	Agony Of De Feet/The Freeze	4
81	Casablanca CANL 223	Agony Of De Feet/The Freeze (12")	7
71	Invictus SVT 1004	OSMIUM (LP)	80
74	Casablanca NBLP 7002	UP ON THE DOWN STROKE (LP)	20
75	Casablanca NBLP 7014	CHOCOLATE CITY (LP)	15
76	Casablanca CBC 4009	MOTHERSHIP CONNECTION (LP)	15
76	Casablanca CAL 2003	THE CLONES OF DR. FUNKENSTEIN (LP)	12
74	Casablanca CAL 2011	UP ON THE DOWN STROKE (LP, reissue)	12
75	Casablanca CAL 2012	CHOCOLATE CITY (LP, reissue)	12
77	Casablanca CAL 2013	MOTHERSHIP CONNECTION (LP, reissue)	12
77	Casablanca CALD 5002	PARLIAMENT LIVE — P. FUNK EARTH TOUR (2-LP, with poster & transfer)	15
78	Casablanca CALH 2021	FUNKENTELECHY VS. THE PLACEBO SYNDROME (LP, with poster)	12
79	Casablanca CALN 2044	MOTOR BOOTY AFFAIR (LP)	12
79	Casablanca CALN 2044	MOTOR BOOTY AFFAIR (LP, picture disc)	12

(see also Parliaments, Funkadelic, Parlet, Brides Of Funkenstein, Bootsy's Rubber Band, P-Funk Allstars)

PARLIAMENTS

67	Track 604 013	I Wanna Testify/I Can Feel The Ice Melting	30
69	Track 604 032	I Wanna Testify/I Can Feel The Ice Melting (reissue)	15

(see also Parliament, Funkadelic)

PARLOPHONE POPS ORCHESTRA

56	Parlophone R 4250	Giddy Up A Ding Dong/(We're Gonna) Rock Around The Clock	12

(see also Ron Goodwin)

PARLOUR BAND

72	Deram SDL 10	IS A FRIEND? (LP)	120

CHRIS PARMENTER ORCHESTRA

66	Polydor 56107	Cul De Sac/Donkey	25

JACK PARNELL (ORCHESTRA)

53	Parlophone MSP 6009	Waltzing The Blues/Catherine Wheel (as Jack Parnell Band)	10
53	Parlophone MSP 6031	Night Train/Hawk Talks (as Jack Parnell & His Music Makers)	10
53	Parlophone MSP 6046	Cotton Tail/April In Paris	10
53	Parlophone MSP 6054	Dragnet/Fuller Bounce (as Jack Parnell & His Music Makers)	12
54	Parlophone MSP 6066	Route 66/The Creep	12
54	Parlophone MSP 6078	Skin Deep/Devil's Eyes (B-side with Dennis Hale)	20
54	Parlophone MSP 6094	Knock Out/Blowin' Wild (B-side with Dennis Hale)	12
54	Parlophone MSP 6102	The Bandit (with Dennis Hale)/Annie's Blues (with Annie Ross)	15
54	Parlophone MSP 6138	Sky Blue Shirt And Rainbow Tie/Trip To Mars	12
58	Parlophone R 4500	Topsy/Cha Cha Rock	5
59	HMV POP 630	Kansas City/The Golden Stalker	12
60	Philips PB 1005	77 Sunset Strip/Teen Ride	6
74	Bradley BRAD 7420	Spy Glass/Razor's Edge	5
76	EMI EMI 2480	Gotham City Municipal Swing Band/The Kiss	5
55	Parlophone GEP 8532	JACK PARNELL AND HIS ORCHESTRA (EP)	8
55	Parlophone GEP 8564	PARNELL ON PARADE (EP)	8
52	Decca LF 1065	THE JACK PARNELL QUARTET (10" LP)	20
58	Parlophone PMD 1053	TRIP TO MARS (10" LP)	60
70s	Sounds Superb SPR 90082	MUSIC OF THE GIANTS (LP)	12

(see also Dennis Hale)

CATHERINE PARR

65	Decca F 12210	You Belong To Me/He's My Guy	10

MINT VALUE £

DEAN PARRISH

66	Stateside SS 531	Tell Her/Fall On Me	40
66	Stateside SS 550	Turn On Your Lovelight/Determination	70
67	Stateside SS 580	Skate (Parts 1 & 2)	40
75	UK USA 2	I'm On My Way/Watch Out	10
90s	Soul City SC 126	Bricks Broken Bottles & Sticks/JOHNNY MAESTRO: I'm Stepping Out Of The Picture	5

PARRISH & GURVITZ

71	Regal Zono. SRZA 8506	PARRISH & GURVITZ (LP)	25

(see also Baker Gurvitz Army, Three Man Army, Frampton's Camel)

SAM PARRY

73	Argo ZDA 155	IF SADNESS COULD SING (LP)	140

ALAN PARSONS PROJECT

76	Charisma CB 293	(The System Of) Doctor Tarr And Professor Fether/ A Dream Within A Dream	5
76	Charisma CB 298	The One In Paradise/The Cask Of Amontillado	5
84	Arista ARISD 553	Don't Answer Me/You Don't Believe (shaped picture disc)	5

BILL PARSONS & HIS ORCHESTRA

59	London HL 8798	The All American Boy/Rubber Dolly	18
59	London HL 8798	The All American Boy/Rubber Dolly (78)	40

(see also Bobby Bare)

GENE PARSONS

74	Warner Bros K 46257	KINDLING (LP)	18

(see also Byrds, Flying Burrito Brothers)

GRAM PARSONS

73	Reprise K 14245	The New Soft Shoe/She	6
73	Reprise K 44228	GP (LP, gatefold sleeve)	25
74	Reprise K 54018	GRIEVOUS ANGEL (LP, with Emmylou Harris)	25
76	A&M AMLH 65478	SLEEPLESS NIGHTS (LP, with Flying Burrito Brothers & Emmylou Harris)	20
82	Sundown SDLP 003	GRAM PARSONS AND THE FALLEN ANGELS (LP, featuring Emmylou Harris)	15

(see also Byrds, Flying Burrito Brothers)

PARTICULAR PEOPLE

68	Big T BIG 105	Boys Cry/What's The Matter With Juliet	6

PARTISANS

63	E.R.S. EP 63:33	THE PARTISANS (EP, private pressing)	60

PARTISANS

82	No Future OI 2	Police Story/Killing Machine (p/s, with lyric insert)	15
82	No Future OI 12	17 Years Of Hell/The Power And The Greed/Bastards In Blue (p/s)	15
83	Cloak & Dagger PART 1	Blind Ambition/Come Clean (p/s)	15
83	No Future PUNK 4	PARTISANS (LP)	20
84	Cloak & Dagger PARTLP 1	THE TIME WAS RIGHT (LP)	20

PARTISANS

88	Hotwire HWS 863	Open Your Eyes/Partisan (p/s)	8

(see also Blades)

PARTNERS IN CRIME

84	Epic A 4803	Hold On/She's Got Eyes For You (p/s)	6
84	Epic TX 4803	Hold On (Extended)/She's Got Eyes For You (12", p/s)	8
85	Epic A 5040	Miracles/What You Gonna Do? (p/s)	6
85	Epic TX 5040	Miracles (Extended)/What You Gonna Do? (12", p/s)	8
85	Epic A 6170	Hollywood Dreams/She's Got Eyes For You (p/s)	7
85	Epic TX 6170	Hollywood Dreams (Extended)/She's Got Eyes For You (12", p/s)	10
85	Epic EPC 26356	ORGANISED CRIME (LP)	12

(see also Status Quo)

MR. PARTRIDGE

80	Virgin V 2145	TAKEAWAY — THE LURE OF THE SALVAGE (LP)	12

(see also XTC, Three Wise Men, Dukes Of Stratosphere, Colonel)

DON PARTRIDGE

68	Columbia DB 8330	Rosie/Going Back To London	6
68	Columbia DB 8416	Blue Eyes/I've Got Something For You	6
68	Columbia DB 8484	Top Man/We Have Ways Of Making You Laugh	7
69	Columbia DB 8538	Breakfast On Pluto/Stealin'	7
69	Columbia DB 8583	Colour My World/Homeless Bones	7
69	Columbia DB 8617	Going To Germany/Ask Me Why	7
60s	CFP CFP 001/002	SINGING SOHO STYLE (EP)	18
68	Columbia S(C)X 6280	DON PARTRIDGE (LP)	22

(see also Accolades)

PARTRIDGE FAMILY

71	Bell BELL 1150	Doesn't Somebody Want To Be Wanted/You Are Always On My Mind	5
72	Bell MABEL 1	Breaking Up Is Hard To Do/I Think I Love You/I'll Meet You Halfway (p/s, maxi-single)	5

(see also David Cassidy)

PARTY BOYS

87	Epic 651230 7	He's Gonna Step On You Again/She's A Mystery (p/s)	5
87	Epic 651230 0	He's Gonna Step On You Again/She's A Mystery (shaped picture disc)	12
87	Epic 651230 6	He's Gonna Step On You Again (Stomp Mix)/She's A Mystery (12", p/s)	8

(see also Status Quo)

PASADENA ROOF ORCHESTRA

78	CBS CBS 12-637	Pennies From Heaven/Back In Your Own Back Yard/Pennies From Heaven (p/s, last track plays at 78rpm)	15

MINT VALUE £

JEAN CLAUDE PASCAL
61 HMV POP 861 Nous Les Amoureux/Les Oubliettes 7

PASHA
69 Liberty LBF 15199 Someone Shot The Lollipop Man/Pussy Willow Dragon 110
(see also Searchers)

PASSAGE
78 Object Music OM 02 NEW LOVE SONGS (EP) 5
79 Object Music OM 08 ABOUT TIME (EP) 5
82 Lyntone LYN 1183/84 Born Every Minute/BLANCMANGE: Living On The Ceiling/Sad Day (excerpt) (black 33rpm flexidisc free with *Melody Maker* magazine) 10/5
80 Object Music OBJ 11 PINDROP (LP) 12
(see also Contact)

PASSENGERS
95 Island IS 625 Miss Sarajevo/One (live) (7", with poster in 12" card in PVC p/s) 6
95 Island CID 625 Miss Sarajevo/One (live)/Bottoms (Zoo Station Remix)/ Via Davidoff (CD, with shrinkwrapped poster, withdrawn) 30
96 Island OST 3 Your Blue Room (CD, 1-track promo, card sleeve, export issue) 45
95 Island OST 2 ORIGINAL SOUNDCHAT 1 (2-CD, music & interview disc, fold-out digipaks, with cue sheet, promo only) 80
(see also U2, Brian Eno)

PASSIONS
58 Capitol CL 14874 My Aching Heart/Jackie Brown 50

PASSIONS
59 Top Rank JAR 224 Just To Be With You/Oh Melancholy Me 65
60 Top Rank JAR 313 I Only Want You/This Is My Love 75

PAST AND PRESENT
79 Rook CUS 423 FIRST TIME OUT (LP, private pressing) 30

PAST PRESENT ORGANISATION
90s Acid Jazz AJX 107T Itchy Feet (12", p/s) 10

PAST SEVEN DAYS
86 4AD AD 102 Raindance/So Many Others/Nothing (p/s) 10

PASTELS
82 Whaam! WHAAM 005 Songs For Children: Heavens Above!/Tea Time Tales (p/s) 22
83 Rough Trade RT 137 I Wonder Why/Supposed To Understand (p/s) 18
83 Creation Artefact/Lyntone LYN 12903 I Wonder Why! (live)/THE LAUGHING APPLE: Wouldn't You? (33rpm flexidisc, initially free with The Legend! 7" "'73 In '83" [CRE 001]) 6/4
84 Creation CRE 005 Something Going On/Stay With Me Till Morning (foldaround p/s in poly bag) 18
84 Creation CRE 011T A Million Tears/Baby Honey/Surprise Me (12", p/s) 8
85 Villa 21 VILLA 3 Heavens Above!/Tea Time Tales/I Wonder Why (live)/Tea Time Tales (live) (p/s) 25
87 Glass PASTEL 001 Truck Train Tractor/Truck Train Tractor (2)/Breaking Lines//Crawl Babies/ Empty House/The Day I Got Certified (12", double pack) 8
90 Overground OVER 06 Heavens Above!/Tea Time Tales/Something Going On (demo)/ Until Morning Comes (demo) (p/s; 200 clear vinyl, 157 green vinyl) 5/6
(see also Buba & Shop Assistants, Jad Fair, Vaselines)

PASTEL SIX
63 London HLU 9651 The Cinnamon Cinder/Bandido 15

PASTORAL SYMPHONY
68 President PT 202 Love Machine/Spread A Little Love Around 6

PAT
71 Gas GAS 158 Teach Me (actually "Words Of Temptation" by Earl Lawrence)/ RHYTHM RULERS: Sea Breeze (actually by Im & David) 10

PAT & MARIE
66 Ska Beat JB 234 I Try Not To Tell You/PAT RHODEN: Don't Blame It On Me 15
66 Ska Beat JB 235 You're Really Leaving/PAT RHODEN: Broken Heart 15
(see also Pat Rhoden)

PAT & MICK
89 PWL PWCD 33 I Haven't Stopped Dancing Yet (Extended Version)/You Better Not Fool Around (Instrumental)/Let's All Chant (Something For The Kids Mix) (CD) 8
89 PWL PWCD 55 Use It Up & Wear It Out/remix/Star Teaser (CD) 8
91 PWL PWCD 75 Gimme Some (7" Version)/Gimme Some (12" Version)/Arcadia (CD) 8

PAT & ROXIE
65 Caribou CRC 2 Sing To Me/Things I Used To Do 7

PATCHES
72 Warner Bros K 16201 Living In America/Quicksand 8

JOHNNY PATE ORCHESTRA
58 Parlophone R 4404 Swinging Shepherd Blues/The Elder (as Johnny Pate Quartet) 5
58 Parlophone R 4437 Muskeeta/Pretty One (as Johnny Pate Quintet) 5
59 Parlophone PMD 1057 JAZZ GOES IVY LEAGUE (10" LP) 12
59 Parlophone PMD 1072 SWINGIN' FLUTE (10" LP) 12
60s MGM OUTRAGEOUS (LP) 25
73 Probe SPB 1077 SHAFT IN AFRICA (LP, soundtrack, with Four Tops) 25
74 ABC ABCL 5035 SHAFT IN AFRICA (LP, soundtrack, reissue) 15

PAMELA PATERSON
72 Polydor 2001 278 Finally (Theme From 'Gumshoe')/OLYMPIC STUDIO CONCERT ORCHESTRA: Music From 'Gumshoe' (p/s) 20

PATHETIX
78 No Records NO 001 Aleister Crowley/Don't Touch My Machine/Snuffed It (p/s, with insert) 70
79 TJM TJM 12 THE PATHETIX EP (no p/s) 50

PATHFINDERS
64 Decca F 12038 — I Love You Caroline/Something I Can Always Do — 18

PATHFINDERS
64 Hayton SP 138/139 — What Do You Do/What'd I Say (private pressing) — 20

PATHFINDERS
65 Parlophone R 5372 — Don't You Believe It/Castle Of Love — 18

(see also [White] Trash, Poets)

PATHWAY TO YOUR MIND
68 Major Minor SMLP 19 — PREPARING THE MIND AND BODY FOR MEDITATION (LP, spoken word) — 40

PATIENCE & PRUDENCE
56 London HLU 8321 — Tonight You Belong To Me/A Smile And A Ribbon (Gold/Silver) — 45/30

57 London HLU 8369 — Gonna Get Along Without Ya Now/The Money Tree (Gold/Silver) — 45/30

57 London HL 7017 — Gonna Get Along Without Ya Now/The Money Tree (export issue) — 30

57 London HLU 8425 — Dreamer's Bay/We Can't Sing Rhythm And Blues — 25

57 London HLU 8425 — Dreamer's Bay/We Can't Sing Rhythm And Blues (78) — 10

57 London HLU 8493 — You Tattletale/Very Nice Is Bali Bali — 22

57 London HLU 8493 — You Tattletale/Very Nice Is Bali Bali (78) — 10

58 London HLU 8773 — Tom Thumb's Tune/Golly Oh Gee — 22

58 London HLU 8773 — Tom Thumb's Tune/Golly Oh Gee (78) — 18

57 London REU 1087 — A SMILE AND A SONG (EP) — 70

LEON PATILLO
70s Maranatha MM 0049 — DANCE CHILDREN, DANCE (LP) — 18

70s Myrrh MYR 1136 — LIVE EXPERIENCE (LP) — 18

SANDY & CAROLINE PATON
60 Topic TOP 57 — HUSH LITTLE BABY (EP) — 10

BOBBY PATRICK BIG SIX
64 Decca F 11898 — Shake It Easy Baby/Wildwood Days — 30

64 Decca F 12030 — Monkey Time/Sweet Talk Me Baby — 30

64 Decca DFE 8570 — TEENBEAT 3 (FROM STAR CLUB, HAMBURG) (EP) — 125

(see also Beat Brothers, Tony Sheridan & Beat Brothers)

DAN PATRICK
67 Stateside SS 2004 — Tiger Lee/Call Of The Wild — 7

KENTRICK PATRICK
63 Island WI 066 — Man To Man/ROLAND ALFONSO: Blockade (B-side actually "Hit And Run") — 30

63 Island WI 079 — Don't Stay Out Late/Forever And Ever — 25

63 Island WI 104 — The End Of The World/Little Princess — 25

63 Island WI 119 — Golden Love/Beyond — 25

64 Island WI 132 — Take Me To The Party/I'm Sorry — 25

64 Island WI 140 — I Am Wasting Time/RANDY'S GROUP: Royal Charley — 30

(see also Lord Creator)

PATRICK & LLOYD
70 Big Shot BI 550 — Return Of The Pollock/PROPHETS: Concorde — 12

(see also Lloyd & Prophets)

PATRIOTS
66 Fontana TF 650 — Prophet/I'll Be There — 12

PATRON OF THE ARTS
66 Page One POF 012 — The True Patron Of The Arts/Eleanor Rigby (B-side actually by Queen City Show Band) — 50

PATSY
68 Doctor Bird DB 1122 — Little Flea/The Retreat Song — 20

(see also Patsy Todd, Derrick & Patsy, Stranger & Patsy, Emotions)

PATSY & PEGGY
70 Hot Rod HR 107 — Dog Your Woman/HOT ROD ALLSTARS: Strictly Invitation — 10

BRIAN PATTEN
70 Caedmon TC 1300 — BRIAN PATTEN (LP) — 15

76 Tangent TGS 116 — VANISHING TRICK (LP) — 30

77 Argo ZSW 607 — SLY CORMORANT (LP) — 12

(see also Liverpool Scene, Roger McGough & Brian Patten)

PATTERN PEOPLE
68 MGM MGM 1429 — Love Is A Lover/Loving To Be Loved — 6

BOBBY PATTERSON (& MUSTANGS)
68 Pama PM 735 — Broadway Ain't Funky No More/I Met My Match (with Mustangs) — 18

68 Pama PM 743 — The Good Ol' Days/Don't Be So Mean — 10

68 Pama PM 754 — Busy Busy Bee/Sweet Taste Of Love (with Mustangs) — 10

69 Pama PM 763 — T.C.B. Or T.Y.A./What A Wonderful Night For Love (with Mustangs) — 10

69 Pama PM 773 — My Thing Is Your Thing/Keep It In The Family — 10

72 Action ACT 4604 — I'm In Love With You/Married Lady — 60

72 Mojo 2092 037 — How Do You Spell Love/She Don't Have To See You — 10

DON PATTERSON
64 Transatlantic PR 733 — THE EXCITING NEW ORGAN SOUND OF (LP) — 12

67 Transatlantic PR 7430 — SATISFACTION! (LP) — 12

MANLEY PATTERSON
72 Pama Supreme PS 337 — I Stayed Away Too Long/Country Boy — 6

OTTILIE PATTERSON
55 Decca F 10472 — I Hate A Man Like You/Reckless Blues (with Chris Barber's Jazz Band) — 10

55 Decca F 10472 — I Hate A Man Like You/Reckless Blues (78, with Chris Barber's Jazz Band) — 8

55 Decca F 10621 — Weeping Willow Blues/Nobody Knows You When You're Down And Out — 10

MINT VALUE £

55 Decca F 10621 Weeping Willow Blues/Nobody Knows You When You're Down And Out (78) 8
57 Pye 7N 15109 Kay-Cee Rider/I Love You Baby 7
58 Pye Jazz 7NJ 2015 Jailhouse Blues/Beale Street Blues 10
58 Pye Jazz 7NJ 2025 Trombone Cholly/Lawdy, Lawdy Blues 6
61 Columbia DB 4760 Blueberry Hill/I'm Crazy 'Bout My Baby 15
62 Columbia DB 4834 I Hate Myself/Come On Baby 10
63 Columbia DB 7140 Jealous Heart/Won't Be Long 6
63 Columbia DB 7208 Baby Please Don't Go/I Feel So Good (with Sonny Boy Williamson) 30
65 Columbia DB 7332 Tell Me Where Is Fancy/Oh Me What Eyes 10
69 Marmalade 598 016 Spring Song/Sound Of The Door As It Closes 7
69 Marmalade 598 020 Bitterness Of Death/Spring Song 6
55 Jazz Today JTE 102 THAT PATTERSON GIRL (EP) 20
56 Decca DFE 6303 BLUES (EP) 20
56 Pye Jazz Today NJE 1012 THAT PATTERSON GIRL (EP, reissue) 15
56 Pye Jazz Today NJE 1023 THAT PATTERSON GIRL VOL. 2 (EP) 15
59 Columbia SEG 7915 OTTILIE (EP) 15
60 Columbia SEG 7998 SWINGS THE IRISH (EP) 10
59 Pye NPL 18028 OTTILIE'S IRISH NIGHT (LP) 20
69 Marmalade 608 011 3000 YEARS WITH OTTILIE (LP) 18
69 Polydor 2384 031 SPRING SONG (LP) 50
(see also Chris Barber)

PATTERSONS

70s CBS 63522 AGAIN (LP) 15
70s CBS 63335 TRAVELLING PEOPLE (LP) 12

ROBERT PATTERSON SINGERS

60s United Artists UAS 2903 THE SOUL OF GOSPEL (LP) 25
65 Fontana 688 516 ZL I'M SAVED (LP) 18

PATTERSON'S PEOPLE

66 Mercury MF 913 Shake Hands With The Devil/Deadly Nightshade 18

PATTI & PATETTES

75 Dart ART 2053 Bill/It's My Party 6
76 United Artists UP 36077 Summer Heartbreak/Too Much 6

HUBERT PATTISON

66 Pye 7N 17207 Bare Back Rider/The Baby 1 & 2 Problem 5
67 Fontana TF 859 My Home's In My Pocket/Saturday Morning Bride 5

LITTLE JOHN PATTISON

64 Giv-A-Disc LYN 510 Needles And Pins/All My Loving (flexidisc free with *Giv-A-Disc* booklet) 8/6

(MIKE) PATTO

66 Columbia DB 8091 Can't Stop Talking About My Baby/Love (as Mike Patto) 60
74 Goodear EAR 106 Sitting In The Park/Get Up And Dig It (as Mike Patto) 7
70 Vertigo 6360 016 PATTO (LP, gatefold sleeve, swirl label) 60
71 Vertigo 6360 032 HOLD YOUR FIRE (LP, swirl label, foldout sleeve) 125
72 Island ILPS 9210 ROLL 'EM SMOKE 'EM PUT ANOTHER LINE OUT (LP) 35
(see also Bo Street Runners, Breakaways, Boxer, News, Chicago Line, Timebox, Felder's Orioles, Steve York, Centipede, Grimms, V.I.P.s)

ALEXANDER PATTON

66 Capitol CL 15461 A Lil Lovin' Sometimes/No More Dreams (demos more common) 125/180

CHARLIE PATTON

50s Heritage REU 4 CHARLIE PATTON (EP, 99 only) 65

JOHN PATTON

64 Blue Note 45-1889 I'll Never Be Free/Along Came John 8

PATTY & EMBLEMS

64 Stateside SS 322 Mixed Up Shook Up Girl/Ordinary Guy 45

PATTY FLABBIE'S COUGHED ENGINE

69 Stateside SS 2136 Billy's Got A Goat/Tin Can Eater 6

PAUL

65 Polydor BM 56045 Will You Follow Me/Head Death 75
(see also Jimmy Page)

ANDY PAUL

84 Proto ENA 117 Anna Mari-Elena (Greek)/Anna Mari-Elena (English)/Bistepsememe (p/s, all copies mispressed with Greek version of A-side included twice) 12

BILLY PAUL

73 Epic EPC 1055 Me And Mrs. Jones/Your Song 5
73 Epic EPC 65351 360 DEGREES OF BILLY PAUL (LP) 15
73 Epic EPC 65456 EBONY WOMAN (LP) 15
74 Phil. Intl. PIR 65861 WAR OF THE GODS (LP, gatefold sleeve) 15

BUNNY PAUL

54 London HL 8008 Magic Guitar/Never Let me Go (78) 7
54 Columbia SCM 5102 New Love/You'll Never Leave My Side 15
54 Columbia SCM 5112 Such A Night/I'm Gonna Have Some Fun 18
54 Columbia DB 3469 Such A Night/I'm Gonna Have Some Fun (78) 7
54 Columbia SCM 5131 Lovey Dovey/Answer The Call 22
54 Columbia DB 3510 Lovey Dovey/Answer The Call (78) 7
54 Columbia SCM 5151 You Came A Long Way From St. Louis/You Are Always In My Heart 12
55 Capitol CL 14279 Please Have Mercy (On A Fool)/These Are The Things We'll Share 12
55 Capitol CL 14304 Leave My Heart Alone/Two Castanets 12
55 Capitol CL 14368 Song Of The Dreamer/For The Very First Time 12

MINT VALUE £

CLARENCE PAUL
75 London HLU 10492 — I'm In Love Again/Blue Tuesday . . . 6

DARLENE PAUL
64 Capitol CL 15344 — Act Like Nothing Happened/Little Bit Of Heaven . . . 25

EUGENE PAUL
70 Pama Supreme PS 303 — Don't Let The Tears Fall/Another Saturday Night . . . 10
70 Pama Supreme PS 305 — I Found A Man In My Bed/So Many Things . . . 10
71 Pama Supreme PS 317 — Farewell My Darling/Whole Lot Of Woman . . . 10
71 Pama Supreme PS 329 — Somebody's Changing My Sweet Baby's Mind/Hard Minded Neighbour . . . 10
72 Pama PM 838 — Beautiful Sunday/Take Care Son . . . 10
72 Pama Supreme PS 357 — I'll Take You There/Beautiful Baby . . . 10
73 Pama Supreme PS 382 — Power To All Our Friends/RANNY WILLIAMS ALLSTARS: Wicked And Dreadful . . 10

EUGENE PAUL & PILOTS
70 Torpedo TOR 17 — Sugar Dumpling/I May Dwell . . . 5

JASON PAUL
69 Pye 7N 17710 — Shine A Little Light Into My Room/Paradise Pudding . . . 6
(see also Svensk)

JOHN E. PAUL
67 Decca F 12685 — Prince Of Players/I Wanna Know . . . 40

LES PAUL (& MARY FORD)
78s
53 Capitol CL 13943 — Vaya Con Dios/ Johnny . . . 10
58 Philips PB 873 — Put A Ring On My Finger/Fantasy . . . 8
58 Philips PB 882 — Jealous Heart/Big Eyed Girl . . . 8

45s
54 Capitol CL 14185 — Mandolino/Whither Thou Goest . . . 20
55 Capitol CL 14212 — Mister Sandman/That's What I Like . . . 22
55 Capitol CL 14233 — Someday Sweetheart/Song In Blue . . . 20
55 Capitol CL 14300 — No Letter Today/Genuine Love . . . 20
55 Capitol CL 14342 — Goodbye My Love/Hummingbird . . . 20
56 Capitol CL 14502 — Alabamy Bound/Texas Lady . . . 12
56 Capitol CL 14521 — Magic Melody/Amukiriki (The Lord Willing) . . . 12
56 Capitol CL 14534 — Theme From "The Threepenny Opera" (Moritat) (as Les Paul)/Nuevo Laredo . . . 12
56 Capitol CL 14577 — Send Me Some Money/Say The Words I Love To Hear . . . 10
56 Capitol CL 14593 — San Antonio Rose/Cimarron (Roll On) . . . 10
56 Capitol CL 14665 — Runnin' Wild/Blow The Smoke Away . . . 8
57 Capitol CL 14710 — Cinco Robles (Five Oaks)/Ro-Ro-Robinson . . . 7
57 Capitol CL 14738 — Hummin' And Waltzin'/Tuxedos And Flowers . . . 6
57 Capitol CL 14776 — Strollin' Blues/I Don't Want You No More . . . 8
57 Capitol CL 14809 — (I'm Keeping My Heart Away From) Fire/A Pair Of Fools . . . 8
58 Capitol CL 14839 — Bewitched/The Night Of The Fourth (as Les Paul solo) . . . 7
58 Capitol CL 14858 — More And More Each Day/Small Island . . . 6
58 Philips PB 873 — Put A Ring On My Finger/Fantasy . . . 10
58 Philips PB 882 — Jealous Heart/Big Eyed Girl . . . 7
59 Philips PB 906 — At The Sav-A-Penny Super Store/All I Need Is You . . . 7
61 Philips PB 1155 — Jura/It's Been A Long Long Time . . . 5
83 Capitol 10CL 282 — How High The Moon/Vaya Con Dios/How High The Moon (last track plays at 78rpm) . . . 7

EPs
55 Capitol EAP1 9121 — PRESENTING LES PAUL AND MARY FORD . . . 12
55 Capitol EAP1 540 — SITTING ON TOP OF THE WORLD . . . 15
60 Capitol EAP1 20048 — MR AND MRS MUSIC . . . 15
61 Capitol EAP1 20145 — NOLA . . . 10
65 Capitol EAP1 20540 — JAZZ ME BLUES . . . 12

LPs
51 Capitol LC 6514 — THE NEW SOUND (10") . . . 25
53 Capitol LC 6581 — THE NEW SOUND VOL. 2 (10") . . . 25
54 Capitol T 416 — HIT MAKERS . . . 15
55 Capitol LC 6701 — LES AND MARY (10") . . . 25
55 Capitol LC 6704 — LES AND MARY PART 2 (10") . . . 25
56 Capitol LC 6806 — BYE BYE BLUES! (10") . . . 25
57 Capitol T 802 — TIME TO DREAM . . . 15
59 Capitol T 1276 — LOVER . . . 15
59 Philips BBL 7306 — LOVER'S LUAU . . . 15
61 Capitol T 1476 — HITS OF LES AND MARY . . . 12
68 Decca LK 4924 — LES PAUL NOW (also stereo [Phase 4 PFS 4138]) . . . 12

LYN PAUL
74 Polydor 2058 472 — Sail The Summer Winds/Lay Me Down (with John Barry) . . . 7
75 Polydor 2383 340 — GIVE ME LOVE (LP) . . . 15
(see also Nocturnes)

RIM D. PAUL
68 Philips BF 1737 — Thousand Hours/Downstairs To Meet Her . . . 5

SHELLEY PAUL
69 Jay Boy BOY 10 — Clowns Are Coming In/Take Me To Your Heart . . . 6

PAUL & LINDA
69 Page One POF 140 — You're Taking My Bag/When I Hear Your Name . . . 6
(this single is not by Paul & Linda McCartney)

MINT VALUE £

PAUL & PAULA

63 Philips 304 012 BF — Hey Paula/Bobby Is The One 10
63 Philips 304 016 BF — Young Lovers/Ba-hey-be 10
63 Philips BF 1256 — First Quarrel/School Is Thru 10
63 Philips BF 1269 — Something Old, Something New/Flipped Over You 10
63 Philips BF 1281 — First Day Back At School/A Perfect Pair 10
64 Philips BF 1380 — No Other Baby/Too Dark To See 10
63 Philips BBE 12639 — YOUNG LOVERS (EP) 35
63 Philips 652 026BL — SING FOR YOUNG LOVERS (LP) 40
63 Philips BL 7573 — WE GO TOGETHER (LP) 40
63 Philips BL 7587 — HOLIDAY FOR TEENS (LP) 35

PAUL RITCHIE & CRYING SHAMES

66 Decca F 12483 — September In The Rain/Come On Back (demos more common, £100) 150
(see also Cryin' Shames, Gary Walker & Rain)

PAULA & JETLINERS

66 Rainbow RAI 102 — The Great Pretender/The Legend Of The Man From U.N.C.L.E. 15
66 Rainbow RAI 105 — I Know Someday/Something On My Mind (B-side with Carols) 8

PAULETTE (Williams)

68 Major Minor MM 565 — One Love In My Heart/Must We Say Goodbye 6
73 Summit SUM 8543 — Every Day Is The Same Kind Of Thing/ SHORTY PERRY: The Sweat Of Your Brow 6
(see also Paulette & Gee)

PAULETTE & DELROY

63 Island WI 120 — Little Lover/Lovin' Baby 22
(see also Paulette, Paulette & Gee)

PAULETTE & GEE

70 G.G. GG 4506 — Hold On Tight/G.G. ALL STARS: Tight Version 7
(see also Paulette, Sister, Winston Wright)

PAULETTE SISTERS

55 Capitol CL 14294 — Dream Boat/Leave My Honey Be 20
55 Capitol CL 14310 — Ring-A-Dang-A-Doo/Lonely One 20
55 Capitol CL 14347 — You Win Again/Mama, El Baion 20

PAUL'S DISCIPLES

65 Decca F 12081 — See That My Grave Is Kept Clean/Sixteen Tons 10

PAUL'S TROUBLES

67 Ember EMB S 233 — You'll Find Out/You've Got Something 22

PAUPERS

68 Verve Forecast VS 1514 — Think I Care/White Song 15
69 Verve Forecast VS 1520 — Southdown Road/Numbers 15
68 Verve Forecast (S)VLP 6017 — ELLIS ISLAND (LP, mono/stereo) 22

PAVEMENT

92 Ablaze 8 — My First Mine/FLUFF: "Us" (flexi, free with *Ablaze* magazine) 10/7
92 Big Cat ABB 35S — Trigger Cut/Sue Me Jack/So Stark (You're A Skyscraper) (p/s) 8
92 Big Cat ABB 35T — Trigger Cut/Sue Me Jack/So Stark (You're A Skyscraper) (12", p/s) 8
92 Big Cat ABB 38 — WATERY, DOMESTIC: Texas Never Whispers/Frontwards/Feed Them To The Lions (Linden)/Shoot The Singer (1 Sick Verse) (12" EP) 8
92 Big Cat ABB 38P — WATERY, DOMESTIC (12" EP, picture disc, stickered poly sleeve) 15
92 Big Cat ABB 38CD — WATERY, DOMESTIC: Texas Never Whispers/Frontwards/Feed Them To The Lions (Linden)/Shoot The Singer (1 Sick Verse) (CD EP) 8
94 Big Cat ABB 55S — Cut Your Hair/Camera Stare (p/s) 8
94 Big Cat ABB 70T — GOLD SOUNDZ: Kneeling Bus/Strings Of Nashville/Exit Theory (12", p/s) 10
95 Big Cat ABB 86S — Rattled By La Rush/False Skorpion/Easily Fooled (p/s) 8
95 Big Cat ABB 91S — Father To A Sister Of Thought/Kris Kraft/Mussle Rock Is A Horse In Transition (p/s) 8
96 Big Cat ABB 110S — Give It A Day/Gangsters And Pranksters/Saganaw/I Love Perth (p/s, transparent orange vinyl) 5
97 Domino RUG 53 — Shady Lane (Krossfader)/Unseen Power Of The Picket Fence (p/s) 5
94 Big Cat ABB 56L — CROOKED RAIN CROOKED RAIN (LP, with inner sleeve, some with free 7": "Haunt You Down"/"Jam Kids") 20/15

PAVLOV'S DOG

75 CBS S CBS 3671 — Julia/Episode 5
(see also Hi-Fi)

RITA PAVONE

64 RCA RCA 1415 — Remember Me/Just Once More 6
66 RCA RCA 1553 — Heart/The Man Who Made Music 10
66 RCA RCA 1561 — You Only You/Before You Go 7
73 Decca F 13462 — He (Didn't Remember My Name)/(Vado Via) Last Summer 6
64 RCA RD/ SF 7657 — RITA PAVONE (mono/stereo) 20/25

PAX EXTERNAL

71 Decca F 13167 — A Second Chance Mr. Jones/You See Him As Your Brother 6

GARY PAXTON

62 Liberty LIB 55485 — Stop Twistin' Baby/Alley Oop Was A Two Dab Man 15
(see also Skip & Flip)

TOM PAXTON

66 Elektra EKSN 45001 — The Last Thing On My Mind/Goin' To The Zoo 8
66 Elektra EKSN 45003 — One Time And One Time Only/Bottle Of Wine 10
67 Elektra EKSN 45006 — Leaving London/All The Way Home 8
69 Elektra EKSN 45021 — Jennifer's Rabbit/The Marvellous Toy 10
69 Elektra EKSN 45049 — Victoria Dines Alone/Clarissa Jones 7

69 Elektra EKSN 45064 Crazy John/Things I Notice Now . . . 7
67 Elektra EPK 802 TOM PAXTON (EP) . . . 20
66 Elektra EKL 277/EKS 7277 RAMBLIN' BOY (LP, U.K. pressing in U.S. sleeve) . . . 25
66 Elektra EKL 298/EKS 7298 AIN'T THAT NEWS (LP, U.K. pressing in U.S. sleeve) . . . 25
66 Elektra EKL 317/EKS 7317 OUTWARD BOUND (LP) . . . 18
68 Elek. EKL 4019/EKS 74019 MORNING AGAIN (LP, red label) . . . 18
69 Elektra EKS 74043 THINGS I NOTICE NOW (LP, red label) . . . 15
70 Elektra EKS 74066 TOM PAXTON 6 (LP; also listed as 2469 003) . . . 12
71 Reprise K 44129 HOW COME THE SUN (LP) . . . 12
75 EMI MAM AS-R 1012 SOMETHING IN MY LIFE (LP) . . . 12

DAVEY PAYNE & MEDIUM WAVE

69 Ember EMB S 265 Walk In The Sunshine/Looking Towards The Sky (p/s) . . . 6

FREDA PAYNE

62 HMV POP 1091 He Who Laughs Last/Slightly Out Of Tune . . . 20
70 Invictus INV 502 Band Of Gold/The Easiest Way To Fall . . . 6
70 Invictus INV 505 Deeper And Deeper/Unhooked Generation . . . 5
71 Invictus INV 509 Cherish What Is Dear To You (While It's Near To You)/
The World Don't Owe You A Thing . . . 5
71 Invictus INV 512 Rock Me In The Cradle (Of Your Lovin' Arms)/
Now Is The Time To Say Goodbye . . . 5
71 Invictus INV 515 Bring Home The Boys/Odds And Ends . . . 5
71 Invictus INV 518 You've Got To Love Somebody/Mama's Gone . . . 5
72 Invictus INV 520 You Brought Me Joy/Suddenly It's Yesterday . . . 5
72 Invictus INV 526 Unhooked Generation/Come Back . . . 5
73 Invictus INV 529 I Shall Not Be Moved/Thru' The Memory Of My Mind . . . 5
73 Invictus INV 533 Band Of Gold/The Easiest Way To Fall (reissue, withdrawn) . . . 10
75 ABC ABC 4087 You/Lost In Love . . . 5
78 Capitol 12CL 15959 Love Magnet/Bring Back The Joy (12", promo only) . . . 8
83 Inferno FIRE 14 Band Of Gold (Original Version)/(Extended Version Alternate Take)
(12", gold vinyl) . . . 8
70 Invictus SVT 1001 BAND OF GOLD (LP) . . . 30
71 Invictus SVT 1005 CONTACT (LP) . . . 25
72 Invictus SVT 1007 THE BEST OF FREDA PAYNE (LP) . . . 15
78 Capitol E-ST 11864 SUPERNATURAL HIGH (LP) . . . 12
70s MGM 2351 004 FREDA PAYNE (LP) . . . 12

LEON PAYNE

51 Capitol CL 13474 I Love You Because/KEN MARVIN: Why Don't You Haul Off And Love Me? (78) . . . 7
64 London HA-B 8136 AMERICANA (LP) . . . 12

PAZ

79 Magnus 2 PAZ AT CHICHESTER (LP) . . . 25
83 Spotlight SPJ 507 KANDEEN LOVE SONG (LP) . . . 12
83 Spotlight SPJ 518 PAZ ARE BACH (LP) . . . 10
83 Paladin PALP 001 LOOK INSIDE (LP) . . . 10

EDDIE PEABODY

55 London RE-D 1034 THE MAN WITH THE BANJO (EP) . . . 12

DAVE PEACE QUARTET

69 Saga FID 2155 GOOD MORNING MR. BLUES (LP) . . . 22
(see also Birmingham)

PEACEFUL COMPANY

(see under Morin & Wilson)

PEACHES & HERB

67 CBS 202509 Let's Fall In Love/We're In This Thing Together . . . 15
67 CBS 2711 Close Your Eyes/I Will Watch Over You . . . 8
67 CBS 2866 For Your Love/I Need Your Love So Desperately . . . 18
67 Direction 58-3096 Love Is Strange/Two Little Kids . . . 7
68 Direction 58-3415 Let It Be Me/I Need Your Love So Despeartely . . . 7
68 Direction 58-3548 United/Thank You . . . 6
68 Direction 58-3829 Let's Make A Promise/Me And You . . . 6
69 Direction 58-4085 When He Touches Me/Thank You . . . 6
70 Direction 58-4909 Satisfy My Hunger/It's Just A Game, Love . . . 6
70 Direction 58-5249 Soothe Me With Your Love/We're So Much In Love . . . 6
71 CBS 5249 Soothe Me With Your Love/We're So Much In Love (reissue) . . . 6
77 Epic EPC 4903 Soothe Me With Your Love/Satisy My Hunger (coloured vinyl) . . . 6
67 CBS 62966 LET'S FALL IN LOVE (LP) . . . 35
67 CBS 63119 FOR YOUR LOVE (LP) . . . 35
68 Direction 8-63263 GOLDEN DUETS (LP) . . . 30

ANNETTE PEACOCK

72 RCA SF 8255 I'M THE ONE (LP) . . . 12
78 Aura AUL 702 X DREAMS (LP) . . . 12
79 Aura AUL 707 THE PERFECT RELEASE (LP) . . . 15
70s Aura LIVE IN PARIS (LP) . . . 25
83 Aura AUL 722 THE COLLECTION (LP) . . . 12

ANNETTE PEACOCK & PAUL BLEY

73 Freedom 2383 105 DUAL UNITY (LP) . . . 20
(see also Paul Bley, Bley-Peacock Synthesiser Show, Annette Peacock)

BERNIE PEACOCK

53 Vogue V 2168 Dog Days/My Blue Heaven (78) . . . 8

TREVOR PEACOCK

61 Decca F 11414 I Didn't Figure On Him To Come Back/Can I Walk You Home . . . 18

MINT VALUE £

PEANUT

65	Pye 7N 15901	Thank Goodness For The Rain/I'm Not Sad	8
65	Pye 7N 15963	Home Of The Brave/I Wanna Hear It Again	15
66	Columbia DB 8032	I'm Waiting For The Day/Someone's Gonna Be Sorry	18
67	Columbia DB 8104	I Didn't Love Him Anyway/Come Tomorrow	18

(see also Katie Kissoon, Ragdolls U.K.)

PEANUT BUTTER CONSPIRACY

67	CBS 2981	It's A Happening Thing/Twice Is Life	8
68	CBS 3543	Turn On A Friend/Captain Sandwich	7
69	London HLH 10290	Back In L.A./Have A Little Faith	8
68	CBS 63277	THE GREAT CONSPIRACY (LP)	35
80s	Drop Out DO 2000	TURN ON A FRIEND (LP)	12

BOB PEARCE BLUES BAND

74	Westwood WRS 040	LET'S GET DRUNK AGAIN (LP)	18
79	Forest Tracks FT 3015	COLOUR BLIND (LP)	12

(see also Brother Bung)

PEARL JAM

92	Epic 657 572-7	Alive/Once (white vinyl p/s)	10
92	Epic 657 572-6	Alive/Once/Wash (12", poster p/s)	15
92	Epic 657 857-8	Even Flow/Dirty Frank/Oceans (12", white vinyl, p/s)	15
92	Epic 658 258-7	Jeremy/Alive (live) (white vinyl, p/s)	8
92	Epic 658 258-4	Jeremy/Alive (live) (cassette, jewel case with outer card sleeve)	5
92	Epic 658 258-6	Jeremy/Alive (live)/Footsteps (12", picture disc, with card insert)	25
92	Epic 658 258-2	Jeremy/Yellow Ledbetter/Alive (live) (CD, picture disc)	15
93	Epic 660 020-6	Daughter/Blood (Live)/Yellow Ledbetter (Live) (12", ltd. ed. poster sleeve)	15
94	Epic 660 441-2	Dissident/Release/Even Flow (CD, 1 of 2-part set, numbered)	10
94	Epic 660 441-5	Dissident/Deep/Even Flow (CD, 2 of 2-part set)	10
92	Epic 657 857-8	Even Flow/Oceans/Dirty Frank (12", white vinyl)	15
93	Epic 659 795-6	Go/Alone/Elderly Woman Behind The Counter In A Small Town (Acoustic) (12", with free cassette [plays 'Animal' (Live)])	15
92	Epic 468 884-0	TEN (LP, picture disc)	18
92	Epic 468 884-5	TEN (CD, with 3 bonus tracks, in metallic yellow digipak)	20

(see also Temple Of The Dog)

PEARLS

62	Embassy EMB 564	He's So Fine/BUD ASHTON: Scarlett O'Hara	5

(see also Bud Ashton)

PEARLS BEFORE SWINE

68	Fontana STL 5503	BALAKLAVA (LP)	30
68	Fontana STL 5505	ONE NATION UNDERGROUND (LP)	25
69	Reprise RSLP 6364	THESE THINGS TOO (LP)	20
70	Reprise RSLP 6405	THE USE OF ASHES (LP)	20
71	Reprise RSLP 6442	CITY OF GOLD (LP)	20
71	Reprise RSLP 6467	BEAUTIFUL LIES YOU COULD LIVE (LP)	15

PEARLY GATES

70	MCA MU 1109	Free/Carole's Epic Song	8

BUSTER PEARSON BAND

73	Action ACT 4612	Big Funky/Pretty Woman	25

DUKE PEARSON

60s	Polydor	ANGEL EYES (LP)	70

JOHNNY PEARSON

66	Columbia DB 7851	Rat Catcher's Theme/Weaver's Green Theme	18
73	BBC RESL 6	Spy Trap/Playgirl (with Quator)	10
75	Pye 7N 45537	Red Alert/Midland Parade	5
78	Rampage RAM 2	All Creatures Great And Small/Love Dream (p/s)	6

(see also John Barry Seven)

KEITH PEARSON'S RIGHT HAND BAND

76	Eron ER 014	KEITH PEARSON'S RIGHT HAND BAND (LP)	12

RONNIE PEARSON

58	HMV POP 489	Flippin' Over You/Teen-Age Fancy	800
58	HMV POP 489	Flippin' Over You/Teen-Age Fancy (78)	175

PEASANTS

65	Columbia DB 7642	Got Some Lovin' For You Baby/Let's Get Together	125

PEBBLES

68	Major Minor MM 574	40 Miles Inside Your Heart/Get Around	6
69	Decca F 22944	Incredible George/Playing Chess	8
70	Deram DM 305	Stand Up And Be Counted/May In The Morning	6
71	Parlophone R 5900	Goodnight Ma/Sadness Of A Summer's Afternoon	7
71	Parlophone R 5921	First Time Loving/Party	7

PEDDLERS

64	Philips BF 1375	Let The Sunshine In/True Girl	6
65	Philips BF 1404	Whatever Happened To The Good Times/Song For The Blues	6
65	Philips BF 1455	Over The Rainbow/You Must Be Having Me On	6
66	Philips BF 1506	Adam's Apple/Anybody's Fool	6
66	Philips BF 1530	I've Got To Hold On/Gassin'	6
67	Philips BF 1557	What'll I Do/Delicious Lady	6
73	Philips 6006 283	Sing Me An Old Song/It's So Easy	6
66	Philips BE 12954	SWINGING SCENE (EP)	20
67	Philips (S)BL 7768	LIVE AT THE PICKWICK (LP)	20
67	CBS (S)BPG 63183	FREE WHEELERS (LP)	15

MINT VALUE £

68 CBS 63411 THREE IN A CELL (LP) 20
68 Fontana SFL 13016 THE FANTASTIC PEDDLERS (LP) 15
70 CBS 63682 BIRTHDAY (LP) 12
70 Philips 6308 028 THREE FOR ALL (LP) 12
71 Philips 6386 066 GEORGIA ON MY MIND (LP) 12

MIKE PEDICIN QUINTET

62 HMV POP 1001 When Cats Come Twistin' In/Gotta Twist 15

BOBBY PEDRICK

58 London HLX 8740 White Bucks And Saddle Shoes/Stranded 40
58 London HLX 8740 White Bucks And Saddle Shoes/Stranded (78) 15

ANN PEEBLES

70 London HLU 10322 Part Time Love/I Still Love You 5
71 London HLU 10328 I Pity The Fool/Heartaches, Heartaches 5
71 London HLU 10346 Slipped, Tripped And Fell In Love/99 lbs 5
72 London HLU 10361 Breaking Up Somebody's Home/Troubles, Heartaches And Sadness 5
72 London HLU 10385 Somebody's On Your Case/I've Been There Before 5
73 London HLU 10405 I'm Gonna Tear Your Playhouse Down/One Way Street 5
74 London HLU 10428 I Can't Stand The Rain/I've Been There Before 5
74 London HLU 10468 (You Keep Me)/Hangin' On/Run Run Run 5
75 London HLU 10484 Beware/You Got To Feed The Fire 5
75 London HLU 10508 Come On Mama/I'm Leaving You 5
72 London SHU 8434 STRAIGHT FROM THE HEART (LP) 15
74 London SHU 8468 I CAN'T STAND THE RAIN (LP) 12
76 London SHU 8490 TELLIN' IT (LP) 12

PAUL PEEK

61 Pye International 7N 25102 Brother In Law/Through The Teenage Years 18
66 CBS 202073 Pin The Tail On The Donkey/Rockin' Pneumonia 12
(see also Gene Vincent & Blue Caps)

DAVID PEEL (& LOWER EAST SIDE)

68 Elektra EKL 4032 HAVE A MARIJUANA (LP, red label, also stereo EKS 74032) 20/22
70 Elektra 2401 001 AMERICAN REVOLUTION (LP) 15

PEELERS

72 Polydor Folk Mill 2460 165 BANISHED MISFORTUNE (LP) 135

PEELS

66 Stateside SS 513 Juanita Banana/Fun 8
66 Audio Fidelity AFSP 527 Scrooey Mooey/Time Marches On 30

PEENUTS

67 Ember EMB S 242 The Theme For "The Monkees"/The World's Been Good To Me Tonight (some in p/s) 20/10

PEEPS

65 Philips BF 1421 Now Is The Time/Got Plenty Of Love 12
65 Philips BF 1443 What Can I Say?/Don't Talk About Love 15
66 Philips BF 1478 Gotta Get A Move On/I Told You Before 10
66 Philips BF 1509 Tra La La/Loser Wins 10
(see also Martin Cure & Peeps, Sabres, Rainbows)

PEEP SHOW

67 Polydor 56196 Your Servant, Stephen/Mazy 100
68 Polydor 52226 Esprit De Corps/Mino In A Mix Up 25

BEV PEGG (& HIS GOIN' NOWHERE BAND)

70s Beaujangle DB 0007 NOSTALGIA IS A THING OF THE PAST (LP, private pressing, with booklet, 100 only; as Bev Pegg & His Goin' Nowhere Band) 100
70s Beaujangle DB 0008 THE FOUNDRY DITTY AND THE INDUSTRIAL AIR (LP, private pressing, 500 only) 25
(see also David Cartwright, Away From The Sand, Brindley Brae)

BOB PEGG

74 Transatlantic TRA 280 THE SHIPBUILDER (LP, with Nick Strutt) 18
75 Transatlantic TRA 299 ANCIENT MAPS (LP, with insert) 18

BOB & CAROL PEGG

71 Trailer LER 3016 HE CAME FROM THE MOUNTAIN (LP, red label) 25
72 Galliard GAL 4017 AND NOW IT IS SO EARLY — THE SONGS OF SYDNEY CARTER (LP) 35
(see also Carol Pegg, Mr. Fox)

BOB PEGG & NICK STRUTT

73 Transatlantic TRA 265 BOB PEGG & NICK STRUTT (LP) 18

CAROL PEGG

73 Transatlantic TRA 266 CAROL PEGG (LP, gatefold sleeve) 45
(see also Bob & Carol Pegg)

PEGGY

70 Trojan TR 7752 All Kinds Of Everything Part 1/CARL LEVEY: Instrumental Version 6
70 Hot Rod HR 103 I Shall Follow The Star/CARL LEVEY: Gifted At The Top 6

PEGGY & JIMMY

70 Hot Rod HR 101 Pum Pum Lover/CARL LEVY: Remember Easter Monday 8

PEGGY'S LEG

73 Bunch William Tell Overture 30
73 Bunch BAN 2001 GRINILLA (LP, with insert) 400
(see also Skid Row, Jimi Slevin)

PEG LEG SAM

74 Flyright LP 507/8 THE LAST MEDICINE SHOW (2-LP) 15

MINT VALUE £

BERNARD PEIFFER

54	Felsted ED 82010	Strip Tease/Who Is Me? (78)	10

PEKKA

77	Virgin V 2084	THE MATHEMATICIANS AIR DISPLAY (LP, features Mike Oldfield)	18

LANA PELLAY

86	Sublime LIMET 101	Pistol In My Pocket/Dirty Harry Version (12", p/s)	12

DAVE PELL OCTET

54	London RE-P 1008	IRVING BERLIN GALLERY VOL. 1 (EP)	12
55	London RE-P 1018	RODGERS AND HART (EP)	12

TRACY PENDARVIS

60	London HLS 9059	A Thousand Guitars/Is It Too Late	30
60	London HLS 9213	Is It Me/South Bound Line	30

MIKE PENDER

86	Sierra FED 23	It's Over/Brothers And Sisters (p/s)	6
86	Sierra FED 23T	It's Over/Brothers And Sisters (12", p/s)	8

(see also Searchers)

PENDLEFOLK

70	Folk Heritage FHR 007	PENDLEFOLK (LP)	20

PENDRAGON

82	private pressing	VICTIMS OF LIFE (demo cassette)	8
83	private pressing	ALASKA (demo cassette)	8
87	Awareness AWS 101	Red Shoes/Searching/Contact (p/s)	5
87	Awareness AWSX 101	Red Shoes/Searching/Contact (12", p/s)	7
89	Toff PENDS 7S	Saved By You/Lady Luck (p/s)	8
89	Toff PENDS 12S	Saved By You/Lady Luck/Elephants Never Grow Old (12", p/s)	8
84	Elusive ARRMP 001	FLY HIGH FALL FAR (12" mini-LP)	8
85	Elusive ARRLP 100	FIRE IN HARMONY (LP)	12
85	Elusive ARRLP 101	THE JEWEL (LP)	12

PENETRATION

77	Virgin VS 192	Don't Dictate/Money Talks (p/s)	8
78	Virgin VS 213	Firing Squad/Never (p/s)	8
78	Virgin VS 226	Life's A Gamble/V.I.P. (p/s)	5
79	Virgin VS 257	Danger Signs/Stone Heroes (live) (p/s)	5
79	Virgin VS 268	Come Into The Open/Lifeline (p/s)	5
78	Virgin V 2109	MOVING TARGETS (LP, 15,000 on luminous vinyl)	12
79	Virgin V 2131	COMING UP FOR AIR (LP)	10
79	Virgin/Clifdayn PEN 1	RACE AGAINST TIME (LP, official bootleg)	15

PENGUINS

55	London HL 8114	Earth Angel/Hey Senorita (gold label print, triangular centre)	1,800+
55	London HL 8114	Earth Angel/Hey Senorita (silver label print, tri-centre, existence unconfirmed)	
55	London HL 8114	Earth Angel/Hey Senorita (large centre hole, export issue)	900
55	London HL 8114	Earth Angel/Hey Senorita (78)	175

DAWN PENN

66	Rio R 113	Long Days Short Night/Are You There	45
67	Studio One SO 2030	You Don't Love Me/SOUL VENDORS: Portobello Road	40
68	Island WI 3097	I'll Never Let You Go/MARK BROWN: Brown Low Special	30

(see also Max Romeo, Viceroys)

TONY PENN

62	Starlite ST45 083	That's What I Like/I Won't Cry Anymore	40

LEONARD PENNARIO

54	Capitol CL 14173	Midnight On The Cliffs/Dream Rhapsody (with Les Baxter Orchestra)	10

(see also Les Baxter)

BARBARA PENNINGTON

76	United Artists UP 36170	24 Hours A Day/I Can't Erase The Thoughts Of You	6

PENNSYLVANIA SIXPENCE

67	Pye 7N 17326	Love Of The Common People/Midweek Excursion	7

PENNY

61	Piccadilly 7N 35009	Who Does He Think He Is/Sparks	8
62	Piccadilly 7N 35045	Shall I Take My Heart And Go/What'd I Do?	8

GEORGE A. PENNY

68	Trojan TR 625	Win Your Love/VAL BENNETT: All In The Game	12

HANK PENNY

56	Parlophone MSP 6202	Bloodshot Eyes/Wham! Bam! Thank You Ma'am	100
56	Parlophone R 4120	Bloodshot Eyes/Wham! Bam! Thank You Ma'am (78)	15

PENNY PEEPS

68	Liberty LBF 15053	Little Man With A Stick/Model Village	75
68	Liberty LBF 15114	I See The Morning/Curly, The Knight Of The Road	25

CHARLES PENROSE

57	COLUMBIA SEG 7743	ADVENTURES OF THE LAUGHING POLICEMAN (EP)	12

LYDIA PENSE & COLD BLOOD

70s	ABC ABC 4109	I Get Off On You/We Came Down Here/Cold Blood Smoking	6

PENTAD

65	Parlophone R 5288	Silver Dagger/Nothing But Love	18
65	Parlophone R 5368	Don't Throw It All Away/Too Many Ways	12
66	Parlophone R 5424	Something Other People Call Love/It Better Be Me	12

PENTAGONS

61 London HLU 9333 To Be Loved Forever/Down At The Beach . . . 90

PENTAGRAM

85 own label DEVIL 4 PENTAGRAM (LP) . . . 12
92 Peaceville 1972-1979 (LP) . . . 12
93 Peaceville VILE 38 RELENTLESS (LP) . . . 12

PENTANGLE

68 Big T BIG 109 Travellin' Song/Mirage (some in title die-cut sleeve) . . . 10/6
69 Big T BIG 124 Once I Had A Sweetheart/I Saw An Angel . . . 6
70 Big T BIG 128 Light Flight/Cold Mountain . . . 6
73 Big T BIG 567 Light Flight/Market Song/The Time Has Come . . . 6
68 Transatlantic TRA 162 THE PENTANGLE (LP) . . . 22
68 Transatlantic TRA 178 SWEET CHILD (2-LP) . . . 22
69 Transatlantic TRA 205 BASKET OF LIGHT (LP, gatefold sleeve) . . . 22
70 Transatlantic TRA 228 CRUEL SISTER (LP, gatefold sleeve) . . . 22
71 Transatlantic TRA 240 REFLECTION (LP, gatefold sleeve with inner sleeve) . . . 20
72 Reprise K 44197 SOLOMON'S SEAL (LP, with lyric insert) . . . 30
72 Transatlantic TRASAM 23 HISTORY BOOK (LP) . . . 15
73 Transatlantic TRASAM 29 PENTANGLING (LP) . . . 15
(see also Bert Jansch, John Renbourn, Duffy's Nucleus)

PEOPLE

69 Capitol CL 15553 I Love You/Somebody Tell Me My Name . . . 20
69 Capitol CL 15599 Ulla/Turnin' Me In . . . 20
70 RCA RCA 2028 I Am (The Preacher)/September's Son . . . 10
71 Deram DM 346 In Ancient Times/Glastonbury . . . 15
70 Paramount SPFL 261 THERE ARE PEOPLE AND THERE ARE PEOPLE (LP) . . . 20

PEOPLE BAND

70 Transatlantic TRA 214 THE PEOPLE BAND (LP, with Charlie Watts) . . . 50
(see also Charlie Watts, Battered Ornaments)

PEOPLE'S CHOICE

71 Mojo 2092 024 I Like To Do It/Big Ladies Man . . . 6
73 London HLU 10404 Let Me Do My Thing/On A Cloudy Day . . . 5
77 Philadelphia Int. PIR 5891 Jam Jam Jam (All Night Long)/Cold Blooded & Downright Funky . . . 5

PEPPER

68 Pye 7N 17569 We'll Make It Together/I'm On The Way Down . . . 12

ART PEPPER

54 Vogue LDE 067 ART PEPPER QUARTET (10" LP) . . . 15
50s London HLZ V 14038 ART PEPPER QUARTET (10" LP) . . . 60
60 Contemporary LAC 12229 MODERN JAZZ CLASSICS (LP, as Art Pepper Eleven) . . . 12
(see also Chet Baker)

JIM PEPPER

71 Atlantic 2400 149 PEPPER'S POW WOW (LP) . . . 20

KEN PEPPER

61 Top Rank JAR 535 Just A Little At A Time/I Get The Blues When It Rains . . . 7

DANNY PEPPERMINT (& JUMPING JACKS)

61 London HLL 9478 The Peppermint Twist/Somebody Else Is Taking My Place
(with Jumping Jacks) . . . 10
62 London HLL 9516 One More Time/La Dee Dah . . . 10
62 London HLL 9614 Maybe Tomorrow But Not Today/Passing Parade . . . 10
62 London HA-L 2438 TWIST WITH DANNY PEPPERMINT (LP) . . . 65

PEPPERMINT CIRCUS

67 Olga OLE 007 All The King's Horses/It Didn't Take Long . . . 10
68 Polydor 56288 I Won't Be There/Keeping My Head Above Water . . . 6
69 Polydor 56312 Please Be Patient/Take My Love . . . 6
69 A&M AMS 765 One Thing Can Lead To Another/It's So Easy . . . 5
70 A&M AMS 778 Let Me Go/School Days . . . 5

PEPPERMINT RAINBOW

68 MCA MU 1034 Walking In Different Circles/Pink Lemonade . . . 5
69 MCA MU 1076 Will You Be Staying After Sunday/And I'll Be There . . . 10
69 MCA MU 1091 Don't Wake Up In The Morning, Michael/Rosemary . . . 5

PEPPERMINT TROLLEY COMPANY

68 Dot DOT 110 Baby You Come Rolling 'Cross My Mind/Nine O'Clock Business Man . . . 8

PEPPERS

73 Spark SRL 1100 Pepper Box/Pinch Of Salt . . . 5

PEPPI

62 Decca F 11520 Stories/When I Think Of You . . . 6
63 Decca F 11638 Can You Waddle/I Never Danced Before . . . 10
64 Decca F 11991 Pistol Packin' Mama/Roll On Baby . . . 8
64 Fontana TF 446 So Used To Loving You/Don't Trust My Friend . . . 7
65 Decca F 12055 The Skip/Do The Skip . . . 10

PERCELLS

63 HMV POP 1154 What Are Boys Made Of?/Cheek To Cheek . . . 15

LANCE PERCIVAL

63 Parlophone R 5032 Riviera Cafe/You're Joking Of Course . . . 7
63 Parlophone R 5071 Dancing In The Streets Tonight/The Beetroot Song . . . 7
65 Parlophone R 5335 Shame And Scandal In The Family/There's Another One Behind . . . 7
66 Parlophone R 5517 End Of The Season/Our Jim . . . 7
67 Parlophone R 5587 The Maharajah Of Brum/Taking The Maharajah Apart . . . 10

MINT VALUE £

NORMAN PERCIVAL
67 United Artists UP 1197 Theme From "Billion Dollar Brain"/Shades Of Green 10

PERCY PAVILION
83 Pavil. In Splendour PIS 1 CRICKET (EP) 7
84 Dead Good Dolly P. DMS 2 Gower Power/You're An Extra Baby (p/s) 5
(see also Captain Sensible)

PEREGRINE
72 Westwood WRS 016 SONGS OF MINE (LP) 100

RAY PEREIRA
70 Baf BAF 5 Don't Mess With Cupid/CATS: Falling In Love 6
70 Baf BAF 6 On Broadway/Hey Chick 6

PERERIN
80 Gwerin SYWM 215 HAUL AR YR EIRA (LP, with insert) 180

PERE UBU
79 Chrysalis CHS 2372 The Fabulous Sequel (Have Shoes Will Walk)/Humour Me (live)/ The Book Is On The Table (p/s) 8
80 Rough Trade RT 049 Final Solution/My Dark Ages (p/s) 8
81 Rough Trade RT 066 Not Happy/Lonesome Cowboy Dave (p/s) 8
78 Radar RDR 1 DATAPANIK IN THE YEAR ZERO (12" EP) 10
78 Blank BLANK 001 THE MODERN DANCE (LP) 15
78 Rough Trade ROUGHUS 14 DUB HOUSING (LP) 15
79 Rough Trade ROUGHUS 20 NEW PICNIC TIME (LP) 15
80 Rough Trade ROUGH 14 THE ART OF WALKING (LP, original with "Miles" & "Arabia") 15
81 Rough Trade ROUGH 23 390° OF SIMULATED STEREO — UBU LIVE: VOLUME 1 (LP) 12
(see also David Thomas)

CHRISTINE PERFECT
69 Blue Horizon 57-3165 When You Say/No Road Is The Right Road 20
70 Blue Horizon 57-3172 I'm Too Far Gone (To Turn Around)/Close To Me 25
70 Blue Horizon 7-63860 CHRISTINE PERFECT (LP) 60
82 CBS 32198 CHRISTINE PERFECT (LP, reissue) 12
(see also Christine McVie, Fleetwood Mac, Illusive Dream, Chicken Shack, Rick Hayward)

PERFECT PEOPLE
69 MCA MU 1079 House In The Country/Polyanna 10

PERFORMANCE
73 Polydor 2058 324 Funny Little Things/Rejoice 6

PERFORMERS
69 Action ACT 4552 I Can't Stop You/L.A. Stomp 15

EMILIO PERICOLI
58 Parlophone DP 536 Chella Lla!/La Più Bella Del Mondo (78, export issue) 8
62 Warner Brothers WB 69 Al Di La/Sassi 8

PERISHERS
68 Fontana TF 965 How Does It Feel/Bye Bye Baby 25
(see also Seftones)

NICK PERITO ORCHESTRA
60 London HLT 9221 Green Leaves Of Summer/Jennifer 8
62 HMV POP 1032 Jessica/Gina 6

CARL PERKINS
78s
56 London HLU 8271 Blue Suede Shoes/Honey Don't 35
57 London HLS 8408 Matchbox/Your True Love 50
57 London HLS 8527 Glad All Over/Forever Yours 65
58 London HLS 8608 Lend Me Your Comb/That's Right 85
59 Philips PB 983 I Don't See Me In Your Eyes Anymore/One Ticket To Loneliness 115
45s
56 London HLU 8271 Blue Suede Shoes/Honey Don't 220
57 London HLS 8408 Matchbox/Your True Love 160
57 London HLS 8527 Glad All Over/Forever Yours 115
58 London HLS 8608 Lend Me Your Comb/That's Right 115
59 Philips PB 983 I Don't See Me In Your Eyes Anymore/One Ticket To Loneliness 18
61 Philips PB 1179 Anyway The Wind Blows/The Unhappy Girls 18
64 Brunswick 05905 Help Me Find My Baby/I Wouldn't Have You 12
64 Brunswick 05909 Big Bad Blues/Lonely Heart (with Nashville Teens) 12
64 Brunswick 05923 The Monkey Shine/Let My Baby Be 15
67 Stateside SS 599 A Country Boy's Dream/If I Could Come Back 12
68 London HLP 7125 A Country Boy's Dream/Shine Shine Shine (export issue) 22
68 Spark SRL 1009 Lake County, Cotton Country/It's You 10
68 London HLS 10192 Blue Suede Shoes/Dixie Fried (unissued)
68 London HLS 10192 Blue Suede Shoes/Matchbox 8
69 CBS 3932 Restless/11.43 7
70 CBS 4991 All Mama's Children/Step Aside (with N.R.B.Q.) 6
77 Mercury ELV 15 The E.P. Express/Big Bad Blues (p/s) 7
78 Jet UP 36365 Blue Suede Shoes/That's All Right/Rock On Around The World (p/s) 5
78 Jet SJET 117 Mustang Wine/The Whole World Misses You (p/s) 5
80 Jet JET 182 Love Sick Blues/Turn Around/Miss Misunderstood/Blue Suede Shoes (p/s) 5
LPs
59 London HA-S 2202 THE DANCE ALBUM OF CARL PERKINS (flipback/non-flipback sleeve) 130/90
66 Ember NR 5038 SUNSTROKE (shared with Jerry Lee Lewis) 18
66 CBS Realm 52305 WHOLE LOTTA CARL PERKINS (boxed square logo on originals) 50/25
68 CBS 63309 KING OF ROCK 20

68 London HA-P/SH-P 8366 COUNTRY BOY'S DREAM ... 30
69 CBS 63676 CARL PERKINS' GREATEST HITS ... 15
70 CBS 63826 BOPPIN' THE BLUES (with N.R.B.Q.) ... 15
74 Mercury 6338 475 MY KIND OF COUNTRY ... 12
78 Jet JETLP 208/UATV 30146 OL' BLUE SUEDE'S BACK (record & spine list UATV cat. no.) ... 12
82 Sun BOX 101 THE SUN YEARS (3-LP, box set with booklet) ... 30
(see also N.R.B.Q.)

JOE PERKINS
63 London HLU 9794 Little Eeefin Annie/Encle Eeef ... 8
72 Mojo 2092 047 Wrapped Up In Your Love/Looking For A Woman ... 6

LASCELLES PERKINS
61 Blue Beat BB 41 Creation/Lonely Robin ... 25
63 Island WI 038 Tango Lips (with Yvonne)/DENNIS SINDREY: Rub Up (B-side actually plays "Jamaica's Song") ... 25
64 R&B JB 175 I Am So Grateful/When I Survey ... 25
70 Escort ES 814 Please Stay/MATADORS: Voyage From The Moon ... 12
71 Banana BA 317 Tell It All Brothers/SOUND DIMENSION: Polkadots ... 15
(see also Tommy McCook)

POLLY PERKINS
63 Decca F 11583 I Reckon You (as Polly Perkins & Bill)/The Girls Are At It Again ... 8
63 Oriole CB 1869 Sweet As Honey/I've Gotta Tell You ... 8
63 Oriole CB 1929 Young Lover/You Too Can Be A Beatle ... 8
63 Oriole CB 1979 Faling In Love Again/I Went By Your House Today ... 8
73 Chapter One CMS 1018 LIBERATED WOMAN (LP) ... 12
(see also Academy)

TONY PERKINS
57 RCA RCA 1018 Moonlight Swim/First Romance ... 12
57 RCA RCA 1018 Moonlight Swim/First Romance (78) ... 10

PERMANENTS
63 London HLU 9803 Oh Dear, What Can The Matter Be/Let Me Be Baby ... 12

JEAN-JACQUES PERREY
72 Vanguard VAN 1005 Gossipo Perpetuo/Moog Indigo ... 8
73 Vanguard VAN 1008 Minuet Of The Robots/Porcupine Rock ... 8
71 Vanguard VSD 6525 KALEIDOSCOPIC VIBRATIONS — SPOTLIGHT ON THE MOOG (LP, 'kaleidoscope' sleeve, with Gershon Kingsley) ... 20
72 Vanguard VSD 6549 MOOG INDIGO (LP, title sleeve) ... 40
73 Vanguard VSD 79222 THE IN SOUND FROM WAY OUT! (LP, green/black 'starburst' sleeve, with Gershon Kingsley) ... 20
73 Vanguard VSD 79286 THE AMAZING NEW ELECTRONIC POP SOUND OF... (LP) ... 15
74 Vanguard DPS 2051 THE BEST OF THE MOOG (2-LP) ... 25
96 Beat Goes Public BGPZ 1103 MOOG INDIGO (LP, mono vinyl reissue, 3,000 only) ... 12

PAT PERRIN
68 Island WI 3115 Over You/LLOYD TERRELL: Lost Without You ... 22

PERRI'S
59 Oriole CB 1481 Jerri-Lee/Ballad Of A Happy Heart ... 15
59 Oriole CB 1481 Jerri-Lee/Ballad Of A Happy Heart (78) ... 15

BARBARA PERRY
70 Pama PM 795 Say You Need Me/Unloved ... 20

JEFF PERRY
76 Arista ARIST 51 Love Don't Come No Stronger/I've Got To See You Right Away ... 5

JOHN PERRY
73 Philips 6006 319 Nancy Sing Me A Song/Crying Eyes ... 5
(see also Summer Wine)

KING PERRY
(see under Lee Perry)

LEE 'SCRATCH' PERRY (& UPSETTERS)
63 R&B JB 102 Prince In The Black/Don't Copy ... 40
63 R&B JB 104 Old For New/Prince And Duke ... 40
63 R&B JB 106 Mad Head/Man And Wife ... 40
63 R&B JB 135 Royalty/Can't Be Wrong ... 40
63 Island WI 118 Never Get Weary/TOMMY McCOOK: Below Zero ... 35
64 Port-O-Jam PJ 4001 Help The Weak/TOMMY McCOOK: Exodus ... 40
64 Port-O-Jam PJ 4003 Bad Minded People/TOMMY McCOOK & HIS GROUP: Jam Rock ... 40
64 Port-O-Jam PJ 4010 Chatty Chatty Woman/TOMMY McCOOK & HIS GROUP: Road Block ... 40
65 Island WI 210 Please Don't Go/Bye, St. Peter (both sides with Soulettes) ... 35
65 Island WI 223 Country Girl/Strange Country (as Upsetters; both act. by Ossie & Upsetters) ... 35
65 Ska Beat JB 201 Roast Duck/Hand To Hand, Man To Man ... 35
65 Ska Beat JB 203 Trail And Crosses/Jon Tom ... 35
65 Ska Beat JB 212 Wishes Of The Wicked/Hold Down ... 35
65 Ska Beat JB 215 Open Up/ROLAND ALPHONSO: Twin Double ... 35
66 Ska Beat JB 251 The Woodman/Give Me Justice ... 35
66 Island WI 259 Just Keep It Up/ROLAND ALPHONSO: James Bond ... 35
66 Island WI 292 Doctor Dick (as King Perry)/SOUL BROTHERS: Magic Star ... 35
66 Island WI 298 Rub And Squeeze (as King Perry & Soulettes)/SOUL BROTHERS: Here Comes The Minx ... 35
67 Doctor Bird DB 1073 Run For Cover/Something You've Got (as Lee 'King' Perry & Sensations) ... 25
67 Doctor Bird DB 1098 Whop Whop Man/Wind-Up Doll (with Dynamites) ... 25
68 Amalgamated AMG 808 The Upsetter/Thank You Baby ... 45

			MINT VALUE £
68	Doctor Bird DB 1146	People Funny Boy/BURT WALTERS: Blowing In The Wind	25
68	Trojan TR 644	Uncle Desmond/Bronco (with Upsetters)	20
69	Upsetter US 303	People Funny Fi True/UPSETTERS: Ten To Twelve	20
69	Upsetter US 324	Yakety Yak/Tackio (with Upsetters)	20
70	Upsetter US 325	Kill Them All/Soul Walk (with Upsetters)	20
71	Bullet BU 461	All Combine Pts 1& 2 (as Lee Perry & Upsetters)	18
72	Upsetter US 385	French Connection (with Upsetters)/UPSETTERS: Version	15
72	Upsetter US 389	Back Biter (with Dennis Alcapone)/UPSETTERS: Version	18
73	Upsetter US 397	Jungle Lion/Freakout Skank	18
73	Upsetter US 398	Cow Thief Skank (actually by Lee Perry & Charlie Ace)/ Seven And Three Quarters Skank	20
73	Bread BR 1111	Station Underground/CARLTON & SHOES: Better Days	25
73	Downtown DT 513	Bucky Skank/Mid East Rock	25
73	Jackpot JP 812	Justice To The People/UPSETTERS: Version	12
74	Dip DL 5037	Dub A Pum Pum (with Silvertones)/Version	12
74	Dip DL 5060	Dreader Locks (& Junior Byles)/Militant Rock	12
73	SRNO 8002	CLOAK & DAGGER (LP, as Scratch The Upsetter)	120
75	Cactus CTLP 112	REVOLUTION DUB (LP)	40
75	DIP DLPD 6002	KUNG FU MEETS THE DRAGON (LP, as The Mighty Upsetter)	50

(see also Upsetters, Defenders, Roland Alphonso, Bob Marley/Wailers, King Scratch, Punchers, Roy Shirley, Pioneers, Desmond Dekker)

MAL PERRY

58	Fontana H 125	Lollipop/Love Me Again (78)	8
58	Fontana H 133	That's When Your Heartaches Begin/Make Me A Miracle	12
58	Fontana H 133	That's When Your Heartaches Begin/Make Me A Miracle (78)	8
58	Fontana H 149	Too Young To Love/Who Are They To Say	12
58	Fontana H 149	Too Young To Love/Who Are They To Say (78)	8
58	Fontana H 157	Things I Didn't Say/The Girl Next Door	12
58	Fontana H 157	Things I Didn't Say/The Girl Next Door (78)	8
59	Fontana H 172	Richer Than I/Willingly	12
59	Fontana H 172	Richer Than I/Willingly (78)	12

MARK PERRY

80	Deptford Fun City DFC 09	You Cry Your Tears/Music Death? (with Dennis Burns, unissued)	
80	NB NB 7	You Cry Your Tears/Music Death? (with Dennis Burns, p/s in poly bag)	5
80	Deptford Fun City DFC 12	Whole World's Down On Me/I Live — He Dies (p/s)	5
80	Deptford Fun City DLP 06	SNAPPY TURNS (LP)	12

SHORT(L)Y PERRY

72	Attack ATT 8043	Musical Goat/WINSTON GRENNON & J. JACKSON: Stinging Dub	7
72	Explosion EX 2067	Sprinkle Some Water/FLOWERS & ALVIN: Howdy And Tenky	6
72	Bullet BU 512	Sprinkle Some Water/FLOWERS & ALVIN: Howdy And Tenky	6
73	Bullet BU 529	Yama Skank/U ROY JUNIOR: Doctor Run Come Quick	8
73	Downtown DT 517	Dedicated To Illiteracy/G.G. ALL STARS: Illiteracy Dub	7
73	Grape GR 3052	Abusing And Assaulting (by Flowers & Alvin)/Food Control	7
73	Green Door GD 4043	President Mash Up The Resident/President Mash Up The Resident Part Two	7

(see also Shorty, Cornell Campbell, Maytones, Paulette Williams)

STEVE PERRY

60	HMV POP 745	Step By Step/Because They're Young	15
62	Decca F 11462	Ginny Come Lately/Two Of A Kind	10
62	Decca F 11526	Young And In Love/Let It Come True	7
63	Decca F 11656	Find Me A Girl/My Dad	6
64	Decca F 11895	Crooked Little Man/Day Dreams	6

PERRY SISTERS

59	Brunswick 05802	Fabian/Willie Boy	25
59	Brunswick 05802	Fabian/Willie Boy (78)	15

PERSIAN RISK

81	SRT SRTS/81/CUS/1146	Calling For You/Chasing The Dragon (p/s)	175
83	Neat NEAT 24	Ridin' High/Hurt You (p/s)	18
86	Metal Masters METALLP 2	RISE UP (LP)	12

PERSIANS

69	Pama PM 772	I Only Have Eyes For You	12
72	Capitol CL 15726	Baby Come Back Home/I Want To Go Home	6

PERSIMMON'S PECULIAR SHADES

68	Major Minor MM 554	Watchmaker/Coplington	20

PERSONALITIES

65	Dice CC 30	I Remember/Suffering	15
66	Blue Beat BB 354	Push It Down/BUSTER'S ALL STARS: Blues Market	20

PERSONALITY CRISIS

90	Overground OVER 09	Twilight's Last Gleaming/The Jam (live) (p/s, 1,000 only)	5

PERSUADERS

93	Detour DR 001	Finished Forever/In The Night (p/s, 300 only)	15
94	Detour DR 011	Waiting For The Nowhere Express/Girl/The Paperchase (p/s, 100 on red vinyl)	8/5

PERSUADERS (U.S.)

72	Atlantic K 40370	THE THIN LINE BETWEEN LOVE AND HATE (LP)	20
73	Atlantic K 40476	THE PERSUADERS (LP)	12

PERSUASIONS

65	Columbia DB 7560	I'll Go Crazy/Try Me	25
65	Columbia DB 7700	Big Brother/Deep Down Love	25
66	Columbia DB 7859	La, La, La, La, La/Opportunity	25

PERSUASIONS (U.S.)

69	Minit MLF 11017	Party In The Woods/It's Better To Have Loved And Lost	7
73	MCA MUS 1222	Good Old Acappella/You Must Believe Me	5
70	Straight STS 1062	A CAPPELLA (LP)	35
72	Island ILPS 9201	STREET CORNER SYMPHONY (LP)	18

MORRIS PERT

75	Chantry ABM 21	LUMINOS/CHROMOSPHERE/4 JAPANESE VERSES (LP)	40
80	Chantry CHT 001	LUMINOS/CHROMOSPHERE/4 JAPANESE VERSES (LP, reissue)	30
82	Chantry CHT 007	BOOK OF LOVE/FRAGMENTI I/ULTIMATE DECAY (LP)	30

JON PERTWEE

72	Purple PUR 111	Who Is The Doctor/Pure Mystery	15
85	Safari DOCTOR 1	Who Is The Doctor/Doctor Blood Donor (p/s)	5
62	Phillips BBL 7558	SONGS FOR VULGAR BOATMEN (LP)	20

(see also Rupert Hine, Derek Roy, BBC Radiophonic Workshop)

PESKY GEE!

69	Pye 7N 17708	Where Is My Mind/A Place Of Heart Break	30
69	Pye N(S)PL 18293	EXCLAMATION MARK (LP)	50

(see also Black Widow, Agony Bag)

PETALS

63	Decca F 11650	Let's Do The Tamoure/Look At Me	8

PETER & GORDON

64	Columbia DB 7225	A World Without Love/If I Were You	5
64	Columbia DB 7292	Nobody I Know/You Don't Have To Tell Me	5
64	Columbia DB 7356	I Don't Want To See You Again/I Would Buy	6
64	Columbia DB 7407	I Go To Pieces/Love Me Baby	6
65	Columbia DB 7524	True Love Ways/If You Wish	5
65	Columbia DB 7617	To Know You Is To Love You/I Told You So	5
65	Columbia DB 7729	Baby I'm Yours/When The Black Of Your Eyes Turns To Grey	5
66	Columbia DB 7834	Woman/Wrong From The Start	7
66	Columbia DB 7951	Don't Pity Me/To Show I Love You	7
66	Columbia DB 8003	Lady Godiva/Morning's Calling	7
66	Columbia DB 8075	Knight In Rusty Armour/The Flower Lady	7
67	Columbia DB 8159	Sunday For Tea/Start Trying Someone Else	7
67	Columbia DB 8198	The Jokers/Red, Cream And Velvet	7
68	Columbia DB 8398	I Feel Like Going Out/The Quest For The Holy Grail	7
68	Columbia DB 8451	You've Had Better Times/Sipping My Wine	7
69	Columbia DB 8585	I Can Remember (Not Too Long Ago)/Hard Time, Rainy Day	7
64	Columbia SEG 8337	JUST FOR YOU (EP)	20
64	Columbia SEG 8348	NOBODY I KNOW (EP)	30
64	Columbia 33SX 1630	PETER AND GORDON (LP, also stereo SCX 3518)	22/35
64	Columbia 33SX 1660	IN TOUCH WITH PETER AND GORDON (LP, also stereo SCX 3532)	22/35
65	Columbia 33SX 1761	HURTIN 'N' LOVIN' (LP, also stereo SCX 3565)	22/35
66	Columbia S(C)X 6045	PETER AND GORDON (LP, mono/stereo)	35/50
66	Columbia S(C)X 6097	SOMEWHERE... (LP, mono/stereo)	22/35
65	Columbia SCXC 25	I GO TO PIECES (LP, export issue)	60
66	Columbia SCXC 29	WOMAN (LP, export issue)	60
66	Columbia SCXC 33	LADY GODIVA (LP, export issue)	70

(see also Gordon Waller)

PETER & HEADLINES

64	Decca F 11980	Don't Cry Little Girl/It Was Love	18
64	Decca F 12035	Tears And Kisses/I've Got My Reasons	18

(see also Count Downe & Zeros)

PETER & MARY

54	Columbia SCMC 6	Crazy Mix Up Song/What Shall We Do With The Lonesome Lover (export issue)	6

(see also Peter Lind Hayes)

PETER & PAUL

66	Blue Beat BB 364	Hosana/Schoolgirl	20

PETER & PERSUADERS

65	Oak RGJ 197	The Wanderer/Wine Glass Rock/Oh My Soul/Cross My Heart (EP)	50

(see Legendary Lonnie)

PETER & TEST TUBE BABIES

81	No Future OI 4	Banned From The Pubs/Moped Lads/Peacehaven Wild Lads (p/s)	10
82	No Future OI 15	Run Like Hell/Up Yer Bum (p/s)	10
83	Trapper EARS 1	Zombie Creeping Flesh/No Invitation/Smash And Grab (p/s)	8
83	Trapper 12 EARS 1	Zombie Creeping Flesh/No Invitation/Smash And Grab (12", p/s)	8
83	Trapper EARS 2	The Jinx/Trapper Ain't Got A Bird (p/s)	8
83	Trapper 12 EARS 2	The Jinx/Trapper Ain't Got A Bird (12", p/s)	8
84	Trapper EARFIT 1	Pressed For Cash/Blown Out Again (Blender Version)/FITS: Peace And Quiet But Never Dreamed It Was Going To Be Like This (12", p/s)	8
85	Jungle JUNG 21T	ROTTING IN THE FART-SACK (12" EP, white vinyl)	10
82	No Future Punk 3	PISSED AND PROUD (LP)	15
83	Trapper THIN 1	MATING SOUNDS OF SOUTH AMERICAN FROGS (LP, with lyric inner)	15

PETER & WOLVES

67	MGM MGM 1352	Little Girl Lost And Found/Is Me	18
68	MGM MGM 1374	Lanternlight/Break Up-Break Down	15
68	MGM MGM 1397	Julie/Birthday	12
68	MGM MGM 1452	Woman On My Mind/Old & The New	30
70	UPC UPC 104	Something In The Way She Moves/The Lady And Me	6

(see also Factory, Norman Conquest, John Pantry, Sounds Around, Bunch)

MINT VALUE £

PETER B's

66 Columbia DB 7862 — If You Wanna Be Happy/Jodrell Blues . . . 65
(see also Tony Colton, Peter Bardens, Peter Green, Cheynes, Shotgun Express)

PETER, PAUL & MARY

63 Warner Bros WB 95 — Puff (The Magic Dragon)/Pretty Mary . . . 5
63 Warner Bros WB 104 — Blowing In The Wind/Flora . . . 6
64 Warner Bros WB 127 — Tell It On The Mountain/Old Coat . . . 5
64 Warner Bros WB 142 — The Times They Are A-Changin'/Blue . . . 5
63 Warner Bros WSE 6119 — MOVING (EP, stereo) . . . 10
63 Warner Bros WSE 6122 — PETER, PAUL AND MARY (EP, stereo) . . . 10
63 Warner Bros WM 4064 — PETER, PAUL AND MARY (LP, also stereo WS 9064) . . . 15
63 Warner Bros WM/WS 8124 — MOVING (LP) . . . 15
64 Warner Bros WM/WS 8142 — IN THE WIND (LP) . . . 15
65 Warner Bros WM/WS 8158 — IN CONCERT VOL. 1 (LP) . . . 15
65 Warner Bros WM/WS 8159 — IN CONCERT VOL. 2 (LP) . . . 15
65 Warner Bros (W)S 1589 — A SONG WILL RISE (LP) . . . 15
66 Warner Bros (W)S 1615 — SEE WHAT TOMORROW BRINGS (LP) . . . 15
66 Warner Bros W(S) 1648 — PETER, PAUL & MARY ALBUM (LP) . . . 15
67 Warner Bros W(S) 1700 — ALBUM 1700 (LP) . . . 15
68 Warner Bros W(S) 1751 — LATE AGAIN (LP) . . . 15
60s Warner Bros WB BSK 3231 — REUNION (LP) . . . 12
60s Warner Bros WB 1507 — IN THE WIND (LP) . . . 12

PETER ROSS OLIVER

68 Pro PRO 101 — THREE'S COMPANY (LP, private pressing) . . . 10
(see also Luvvers)

PETER'S FACES

64 Piccadilly 7N 35178 — Why Did You Bring Him To The Dance/She's In Love . . . 12
64 Piccadilly 7N 35196 — Try A Little Love My Friend/I Don't Care . . . 12
64 Piccadilly 7N 35205 — Just Like Romeo And Juliet/Wait . . . 25
65 Piccadilly 7N 35225 — De-Boom-Lay-Boom/Suzie Q . . . 10
(see also Flowerpot Men, White Plains)

JANICE PETERS & PLAYBOYS

58 Columbia DB 4222 — This Little Girl's Gone Rockin'/Kiss Cha Cha . . . 40
58 Columbia DB 4222 — This Little Girl's Gone Rockin'/Kiss Cha Cha (78) . . . 20
59 Columbia DB 4276 — A Girl Likes/You're The One . . . 35
59 Columbia DB 4276 — A Girl Likes/You're The One (78) . . . 20

LENNIE PETERS

63 Oriole CB 1887 — And My Heart Cried/For A Lifetime . . . 7
64 Oriole CB 1956 — Let The Tears Begin/Love Me, Love Me . . . 7

LINDA PETERS

70 Warlock Music WMM 101/2 — WARLOCK MUSIC SAMPLER (LP, sampler, 7 tracks by Elton John) . . . 1,000
(see also Paul McNeill & Linda Peters, Richard & Linda Thompson)

MARK PETERS & SILHOUETTES

63 Oriole CB 1836 — Fragile (Handle With Care)/Janie . . . 30
64 Oriole CB 1909 — Cindy's Gonna Cry/Show Her . . . 30
64 Piccadilly 7N 35207 — Don't Cry For Me/I Told You So . . . 15
(see also Rats)

WENDY PETERS

68 Saga OPP 1 — Morning Dew/I Don't Understand . . . 12

PAUL PETERSEN

62 Pye International 7N 25153 — Keep Your Love Locked/Be Everything To Anyone You Love . . . 7
62 Pye International 7N 25163 — Lollipops And Roses/Please Mr Sun . . . 7
63 Pye International 7N 25173 — My Dad/Little Boy Sad . . . 7
63 Pye International 7N 25196 — Amy/Goody Goody . . . 7
68 Tamla Motown TMG 670 — A Little Bit For Sandy/Your Love's Got Me Burnin' Alive . . . 25

PAUL PETERSEN & SHELLEY FABARES

62 Pye International 7N 25133 — She Can't Find Her Keys/Very Unlikely . . . 10
(see also Shelley Fabares)

BOBBY PETERSON (QUINTET)

59 Top Rank JAR 232 — The Hunch/Love You Pretty Baby (as Bobby Peterson Quintet) . . . 22
64 Sue WI 342 — Rockin' Charlie (Parts 1 & 2) (solo) . . . 25
65 Sue WI 346 — Piano Rock/One Day (solo) . . . 25

OSCAR PETERSON

57 HMV POP 366 — Soft Sands/Echoes . . . 5
60 HMV POP 706 — Jive At Five/Blues For Basie . . . 5
61 HMV POP 850 — Woody 'N' You/Liza . . . 5
55 Columbia Clef SEB 10005 — OSCAR PETERSON (EP) . . . 8
56 Columbia Clef SEB 10022 — OSCAR PETERSON NO. 2 (EP) . . . 8
55 Columbia 33C 1037 — PLAYS PRETTY (10" LP) . . . 40
55 Columbia Clef 33C 9012 — PLAYS PRETTY (10" LP, reissue) . . . 15
55 Columbia 33C 1038 — THE OSCAR PETERSON QUARTET (10" LP) . . . 15
55 Columbia Clef 33C 9013 — THE OSCAR PETERSON QUARTET (10" LP, reissue) . . . 15
55 Columbia 33C 1039 — OSCAR PETERSON SINGS (10" LP) . . . 15
55 Columbia Clef 33C 9014 — OSCAR PETERSON SINGS (10" LP, reissue) . . . 12
55 Columbia Clef 33CX 10012 — PLAYS DUKE ELLINGTON (LP) . . . 18
55 Columbia Clef 33CX 10016 — PLAYS COLE PORTER (LP) . . . 12
55 Columbia Clef 33CX 10028 — PLAYS RICHARD RODGERS (LP) . . . 20
55 Columbia Clef 33CX 10039 — PLAYS COUNT BASIE (LP) . . . 12
56 Columbia Clef 33C 9025 — O LADY BE GOOD (10" LP) . . . 25
56 HMV CLP 1086 — IN ROMANTIC MOOD (LP) . . . 12

MINT VALUE £

57	Columbia Clef 33CX 10062	KEYBOARD (LP)	12
57	Columbia Clef 33CX 10073	PLAYS HAROLD ARLEN (LP)	12
58	Columbia Clef 33CX 10096	STRATFORD (CANADA SHAKESPEAREAN FESTIVAL) (LP)	12
59	Columbia Clef 33CX 10135	A NIGHT ON THE TOWN (LP)	12
59	HMV CLP 1278	THE OSCAR PETERSON TRIO SWINGS "MY FAIR LADY" (LP)	12
59	HMV CLP 1317	OSCAR PETERSON AT THE CONCERTGEBOUW (LP)	12
60	HMV CLP 1355	JAZZ PORTRAIT OF SINATRA (LP)	12
60	HMV CLP 1403/CSD 1326	SWINGING BRASS (LP)	12
61	HMV CLP 1429	THE JAZZ SOUL OF OSCAR PETERSON (LP)	12
62	HMV CLP 1563	WEST SIDE STORY (LP)	12
63	Verve (S)VLP 9052	NIGHT TRAIN (LP)	12

(see also Louis Armstrong, Lester Young, Ella Fitzgerald, Sonny Stitt)

RAY PETERSON

59	RCA RCA 1131	The Wonder Of You/I'm Gone	20
59	RCA RCA 1131	The Wonder Of You/I'm Gone (78)	30
59	RCA RCA 1154	Shirley Purley/Come And Get It	20
59	RCA RCA 1154	Shirley Purley/Come And Get It (78)	60
60	RCA RCA 1175	Answer Me/Goodnight My Love, Pleasant Dreams	15
60	RCA RCA 1195	Tell Laura I Love Her/Wedding Day	12
60	London HLX 9246	Corrine, Corrina/Be My Girl	15
61	London HLX 9332	Sweet Little Kathy/You Didn't Care	12
61	London HLX 9379	Missing You/You Thrill Me	10
62	London HLX 9489	I Could Have Loved You So Well/Why Don't You Write Me	15
62	London HLX 9569	You Didn't Care/You Know Me Much Too Well	10
63	London HLX 9746	Without Love/Give Us Your Blessing	10
64	MGM MGM 1249	Oh No/If You Were Here	6
64	MGM MGM 1258	Across The Street/When I Stop Dreaming	6
65	MGM MGM 1273	House Without Windows/Wish I Could Say No To You	6
65	MGM MGM 1288	I'm Only Human/One Lonesome Rose	6
66	MGM MGM 1303	Everybody/Love Hurts	6
61	London REX 1293	CORRINE CORRINA (EP)	90

PETER, SUE & MARC & PFURI, GORPS & KNIRL

79	EMI EMI 2940	Second Hand Company/Troedler & Co.	6

PETEY, PATTY, PEGGY & BRUCE

59	Top Rank JAR 250	The Happy Penguins/IRVING KRASE ORCHESTRA: The Happy Penguin Waltz	5

PET HATE

83	FM 12VHF 2	Roll Away The Stone/Caught/Playing With My Heart (12", p/s)	12
84	Heavy Metal HMRLP 23W	BAD PUBLICITY (LP, white vinyl)	12

(see also Silverwing)

PETITES

60	Philips PB 1035	Get Your Daddy's Car Tonight/Sun Showers	10

MARY PETTI

61	RCA RCA 1239	Hey! Lawdy Lawdy/Gee, But It Hurts	60

PETS

58	London HL 8652	Cha-Hua-Hua/Cha-Kow-Ski	30
58	London HL 8652	Cha-Hua-Hua/Cha-Kow-Ski (78)	20
59	Pye International 7N 25004	(You Wandered) Beyond The Sea/Wow-ee!!!	10
59	Pye International N 25004	(You Wandered) Beyond The Sea/Wow-ee!!! (78)	10

(see also Seph Acre & Pets)

PET SHOP BOYS

SINGLES

84	Epic A 4292	West End Girls/Pet Shop Boys (p/s)	40
84	Epic TA 4292	West End Girls (Extended)/Pet Shop Boys (12", p/s)	60
85	Parlophone R 6097	Opportunities (Let's Make Lots of Money)/In The Night (matrix: A-3-1-2) (1st mix, white p/s)	25
85	Parlophone 12R 6097	Opportunities (Let's Make Lots of Money) (Dance Mix)/In The Night (Extended) (12", white p/s)	40
85	Parlophone 12RA 6097	Opportunities (Let's Make Lots of Money) (Version Latina)/(Dub For Money Remix)/In The Night (Extended Mix) (12", large picture labels, die-cut p/s)	80
85	Parlophone 12R 6097	Opportunities (Let's Make Lots of Money) (Dance Mix)/ In The Night (Extended) (12", p/s, mispressing, B-side plays "Opportunities [Dub For Money Remix]")	50
85	Parlophone 12R 6097	Opportunities (Let's Make Lots of Money) (Dance Mix)/ In The Night (Extended) (12", p/s, 2nd mispressing, A-side plays "Opportunities [Version Latina]")	50
85	Parlophone R 6115	West End Girls/A Man Could Get Arrested (4.36 Mix) (glossy p/s)	6
85	Parlophone 10R 6115	West End Girls (Untitled Mix)/A Man Could Get Arrested (4.09 Mix)/ West End Girls (7" Mix) (10", round foldout p/s; some sealed, some stickered)	75/65/60
85	Parlophone 12R 6115	West End Girls (Dance Mix)/A Man Could Get Arrested (4.36 Mix)/ West End Girls (7" Mix) (12", standard p/s, standard labels)	10
85	Parlophone 12R 6115	West End Girls (Dance Mix)/A Man Could Get Arrested (4.09 Mix)/ West End Girls (7" Mix) (12", 4" die-cut hole in front or front & back of p/s, 4" picture labels)	10
85	Parlophone 12R 6115	West End Girls (Dance Mix)/A Man Could Get Arrested (4.09 Mix)/ West End Girls (7" Mix) (12", with 6" die-cut holes in p/s, 6" picture labels)	12
86	Parlophone 12RA 6115	West End Girls (Shep Pettibone Mastermix)/West End Dub/A Man Could Get Arrested (4.09 Mix) (12", black/blue/red p/s, standard labels)	18
86	Parlophone 12RA 6115	West End Girls (Shep Pettibone Mastermix)/West End Dub/A Man Could Get Arrested (4.09 Mix) (12", same as above with 6" yellow circle on sleeve)	18

			MINT VALUE £
86	Parlophone 12RA 6115	West End Girls (Shep Pettibone Mastermix)/West End Dub/A Man Could Get Arrested (4.09 Mix) (12", stickered black/blue/red p/s with 6" die-cut hole & 6" yellow picture labels)	18
86	Parlophone R 6116	Love Comes Quickly/That's My Impression (glossy p/s)	5
86	Parlophone 10R 6116	Love Comes Quickly (Dance Mix)/That's My Impression (Disco Mix) (10", PVC sleeve with poster)	80
86	Parlophone 12R 6116	Love Comes Quickly (Dance Mix)/That's My Impression (Disco Mix) (12", standard p/s)	12
86	Parlophone 12R 6116	Love Comes Quickly (Dance Mix)/That's My Impression (Disco Mix) (12", large picture labels, die-cut white sleeve)	20
86	Parlophone 12R 6129	Opportunities (Let's Make Lots of Money) (7.18 Shep Pettibone Mastermix)/ Opportunities (4.27 Reprise)/Opportunities (6.44 Original Dance Mix)/ Was That What It Was (12", stickered silver title sleeve)	15
86	Parlophone RD 6140	Suburbia/Paninaro//Love Comes Quickly (Shep Pettibone Remix)/Jack The Lad/Suburbia Part Two (double pack, gatefold p/s)	18
86	Parlophone TR 6140	Suburbia/Paninaro/Jack The Lad/Love Comes Quickly (Shep Pettibone Remix) (cassette)	12
86	Parlophone TR 6140	Suburbia/Paninaro/Jack The Lad/Love Comes Quickly (Shep Pettibone Remix) (cassette, mispressed with TCR 6140 tracks)	15
86	Parlophone TCR 6140	Suburbia (The Full Horror)/Paninaro/Jack The Lad/Love Comes Quickly (Shep Pettibone Remix) (cassette)	12
86	Parlophone 12R 6140	Suburbia (The Full Horror)/Paninaro/Jack The Lad (12", p/s, some with inner sleeve)	10/8
87	Parlophone RS 6158	It's A Sin/You Know Where You Went Wrong (p/s, with inner sleeve)	8
87	Parlophone TCR 6158	It's A Sin (7" version)/You Know Where You Went Wrong/It's A Sin (Disco Mix) (cassette)	8
87	Parlophone 12R 6158	It's A Sin (Disco Mix)/You Know Where You Went Wrong (7" Version) (12", p/s with inner sleeve)	15
87	Parlophone 12RX 6158	It's A Sin (Ian Levine Remix)/You Know Where You Went Wrong (Rough Mix) (12", 'video still' p/s)	15
87	Parlophone CDR 6158	It's A Sin (7" Version)/You Know Where You Went Wrong/ It's A Sin (Disco Mix) (CD, card sleeve)	18
87	Parlophone TCR 6163	What Have I Done To Deserve This? (Extended Mix) (with Dusty Springfield)/ A New Life/What Have I Done To Deserve This? (Disco Mix) (cassette)	8
87	Parlophone CDR 6163	What Have I Done To Deserve This? (Extended Mix) (with Dusty Springfield)/ A New Life/What Have I Done To Deserve This? (Disco Mix) (CD, card sleeve)	18
87	Parlophone TCR 6168	Rent (Extended Mix)/Rent (Dub)/I Want A Dog (cassette)	8
87	Parlophone 12R 6168	Rent (Extended Mix)/Rent (Dub)/I Want A Dog (12", p/s)	10
87	Parlophone CDR 6168	Rent (Extended Mix)/Rent (Dub)/I Want A Dog (CD, card sleeve)	18
87	Parlophone RS 6171	Always On My Mind/Do I Have To? (p/s, with inner sleeve)	7
87	Parlophone TCR 6171	Always On My Mind (Extended Dance Mix)/Do I Have To?/ Always On My Mind (Edit) (cassette)	8
87	Parlophone 12RS 6171	Always On My Mind (Extended Dance Mix)/Do I Have To?/ Always On My Mind (Edit) (12", p/s with inner sleeve)	15
87	Parlophone 12RX 6171	Always On My Mind (Phil Harding Remix)/Do I Have To?/ Always On My Mind (Dub) (12", title sleeve)	15
87	Parlophone CDR 6171	Always On My Mind (Extended Dance Version)/Do I Have To?/ Always On My Mind (Edit) (CD)	20
88	Parlophone TCR 6177	Heart (Disco Mix)/I Get Excited (You Get Excited Too)/Heart (Dance Mix) (cassette)	8
88	Parlophone 12R 6177	Heart (Disco Mix)/I Get Excited (You Get Excited Too)/Heart (Dance Mix) (12", 'Neil' or 'Chris' p/s)	each 8
88	Parlophone 12RX 6177	Heart (Julian Mendelssohn Remix)/Heart (Dub Mix)/I Get Excited (You Get Excited Too) (12", p/s)	12
88	Parlophone CDR 6177	Heart (Disco Mix)/I Get Excited (You Get Excited Too)/Heart (Dance Mix) (CD, card sleeve)	18
88	Parlophone TCR 6190	Domino Dancing (Disco Mix)/Don Juan (Disco Mix)/Domino Dancing (Alternative Mix) (cassette)	8
88	Parlophone 12RS 6190	Domino Dancing (Disco Mix)/Don Juan (Disco Mix)/Domino Dancing (Alternative Mix) (12", 'van' p/s with inner sleeve)	8
88	Parlophone 12RX 6190	Domino Dancing (Remix)/Don Juan (Demo)/Domino Dancing (Demo) (12", 'hotel' p/s)	20
88	Parlophone CDR 6190	Domino Dancing (Disco Mix)/Don Juan (Disco Mix)/Domino Dancing (Alternative Mix) (CD, card sleeve with inner)	20
88	Parlophone TCR 6198	Left To My Own Devices/Left To My Own Devices (The Disco Mix)/ The Sound Of The Atom Splitting (cassette, with outer slip case)	8
88	Parlophone 12RS 6198	Left To My Own Devices (The Disco Mix)/Left To My Own Devices/ The Sound Of The Atom Splitting (12", p/s with inner sleeve)	10
88	Parlophone CDR 6198	Left To My Own Devices/Left To My Own Devices (The Disco Mix)/ The Sound Of The Atom Splitting (CD, yellow card p/s, some with inner)	20/15
89	Parlophone TCR 6220	It's Alright/One Of The Crowd/Your Funny Uncle (cassette)	5
89	Parlophone 10R 6220	It's Alright (Alternative Mix)/It's Alright (Extended Dance Mix) (10", black title sleeve with poster)	15
89	Parlophone 12RS 6220	It's Alright (Extended)/One Of The Crowd/Your Funny Uncle (12", p/s, with obi)	8
89	Parlophone 12RX 6220	It's Alright (The Tyree Mix)/It's Alright (The Sterling Void Mix) (12", p/s)	12
89	Parlophone CDR 6220	It's Alright (Seven Inch Vocal)/One Of The Crowd/Your Funny Uncle/ It's Alright (Extended Version) (CD, card sleeve)	12
90	Parlophone 12RX 6269	So Hard (KLF Vs Pet Shop Boys Mix)/It Must Be Obvious (U.F.O. Mix) (12", p/s)	12
90	Parlophone CDR 6269	So Hard (7" Mix)/It Must Be Obvious/So Hard (Extended Dance Mix) (CD, card sleeve)	8
90	Parlophone CDR 6275	Being Boring/We All Feel Better In The Dark/Being Boring (Extended Mix) (CD)	15
90	Parlophone 12RX 6275	Being Remixed/We All Feel Better In The Dark (After Hours Climax)/ (Ambient Mix) (12", title sleeve)	12
91	Parlophone CDR 6283	Jealousy (7" Version)/Lose My Mind (Disco Mix)/Jealousy (Extened Mix) (CD)	12
91	Parlophone CDRS 6283	Jealousy (Extended Version)/This Must Be The Place I Waited Years To Leave (Extended Mix)/So Hard (Eclipse Mix) (CD, gatefold digipak)	22

MINT VALUE £

91	Parlophone TCRX 6301	DJ Culturemix (Grid Remix)/Music For Boys Part 3/ Overture To Performance (cassette)	5
91	Parlophone CDRX 6301	DJ Culturemix (Grid Remix)/Music For Boys Part 3/ Overture To Performance (CD)	20
93	Parlophone R 6348	Can You Forgive Her? (7" Version)/Hey Headmaster (red vinyl, factory custom pressing, p/s)	500
93	Parlophone 12R 6348	Can You Forgive Her? (MK Remix)/Can You Forgive Her? (MK Dub) (12", p/s)	10
93	Parlophone CDRS 6348	Can You Forgive Her? (MK Remix)/I Want To Wake Up (1993 Remix)/ What Keeps Mankind Alive/Can You Forgive Her? (MK Dub) (CD, with wallet)	15
93	Parlophone CDRS 6370	I Wouldn't Normally Do This Kind Of Thing (LP Version)/Too Many People/ Violence (Hacienda Version)/West End Girls (Sasha Remix) (CD, PVC pack)	12
93	Parlophone CDRS 6386	Yesterday When I Was Mad (Coconut 1 Remix)/If Love Were All)/ Can You Forgive Her? (Swing Version)/Yesterday When I Was Mad (Jam & Spoon Mix) (CD, card sleeve)	12
93	Parlophone CDR 6386	Yesterday When I Was Mad (Coconut 1 Remix)/(Junior Vasquez Factory Dub)/ (R.A.F. Zone Dub)/Some Speculation (CD, card sleeve)	15
95	Parlophone 12RX 6614	Paninaro '95 — The Remixes Part 1 (Tracy's 12" Mix)/ (Sharon's Sexy Boyz Dub)/(Tin Tin Out Mix)/(Pet Shop Boys Extended Mix) (12", 'Neil' p/s)	15
95	Parlophone 12R 6614	Paninaro '95 — The Remixes Part 2 (Angel Morales Dub Dance Mix)/ (Angel Morales Girls Boys In Dub)/(Angel Morales The Hot 'N' Spycy Dub) (12", 'Chris' p/s)	15
96	Parlophone 12RX 6431	Before (Underground Mix)/(Bonus Dub)/(Underground Instrumental)/ (Bonus Beats)/(Classic Paradise Mix)/(Afrodisiac Mix)/(Hedboys Mix)/ (Hedboys Dub)/(Joey Negro Extended Mix) (3 x 12", each in p/s, box set)	25
96	Parlophone 12RD 6443	Se A Vida É (That's The Way Life Is) (Mark's Deep And Dark Vocal)/ (Mark's Deep And Dark Instrumental)/(Mark's Shelter Dub)/ (Deep Dish Liquid Remix)/(Pink Noise Mix)/(Deep Dish Dub)/(7" Version) (12", double pack, yellow & green vinyl, p/s, 2 inner sleeves)	15
97	Parlophone Fan Club	It Doesn't Often Snow At Christmas (CD, fan club issue, in sealed silver bubble wrap)	200
02	Protein	You Only Tell Me You Love Me When You're Drunk/Break 4 Love (USA Radio Mix)/So Hard (D Morales Red Zone Mix)/You Only Tell Me You Love Me When You're Drunk (CD-Rom video) (CD, free with *Daily Mirror*, card sleeve)	10
03	Parlophone 12R 6620	Miracles (Lemon Jelly Remix)/Miracles (Eric Prydz Remix)/Miracles (Extended Mix) (12", white vinyl, die-cut p/s, sealed with title sticker)	12

ALBUMS

87	Parlophone PCSDX 104	ACTUALLY (LP, with U.S. import "Always On My Mind" 12", stickered sleeve)	12
87	Parlophone PCSDX 104	ACTUALLY (cassette, with U.S. import "Always On My Mind" cassette)	10
87	Parlophone CDPCSDX 104	ACTUALLY (CD, with U.S. import "Always On My Mind" CD single)	35
88	Parlophone PCSX 7325	INTROSPECTIVE (LP, 3 x clear vinyl 12" factory custom pressing, picture labels, with wraparound paper obi strip, 10 copies only)	1500+
93	Parlophone CDPSDX 143	VERY (CD, with 6-track bonus CD "Relentless" in foldout 'bubble' wallet)	45
96	Parlophone	BILINGUAL (LP)	15
00	Parlophone 724352185719	NIGHTLIFE (LP)	15
02	Parlophone	RELEASE (LP, white vinyl)	20

PROMOS

85	Parlophone R 12R 6097	Opportunities (Let's Make Lots of Money)/In The Night (12", "photocopy" sl.)	50
85	Parlophone R 6097 (matrix: A-1U-1-1-1)	Opportunities (Let's Make Lots of Money) (New Mix)/In The Night (2nd mix, stickered plain sleeve)	100
86	Parlophone R 6116	Love Comes Quickly (1-sided, p/s)	75
86	Parlophone 12R 6129	Opportunities (Let's Make Lots of Money) (7.18 Shep Pettibone Mastermix)/ Opportunities (4.27 Reprise)/Opportunities (6.44 Original Dance Mix)/ Was That What It Was (12", autographed black die-cut sleeve, some with press release)	45/40
86	Parlophone 12R 6140	Suburbia (The Full Horror)/Paninaro/Jack The Lad (12", blank red labels)	20
88	Parlophone 12RDJ 6198	Left To My Own Devices (The Disco Mix)/Left To My Own Devices/ The Sound Of The Atom Splitting (12", unique title sleeve)	25
90	Parlophone 12RXDJ 6275	Being Boring (Remix)/We All Feel Better In The Dark (After Hours Climax)/ We All Feel Better In The Dark (Ambient) (12", black die-cut sleeve)	15
91	Parlophone 12R 6283A	Lose My Mind (Disco Version) (12", 1-sided)	15
91	Parlophone 12RDJ 6301A	D.J. Culture (12", 1-sided)	15
91	Parlophone MFB 1	Music For Boys (12", 3 untitled mixes, hand-stamped white label)	45
91	Parlophone 12MFBX 1	Music For Boys (12", 2 untitled mixes, white label)	25
92	Parlophone CDRX 6332	Go West (7" Version)/West End Girls (Sacha Mix)/Forever/Go West (Extended Dance Mix) (cassette, title sleeve)	250
93	Parlophone 12RXDJ 6348	Can You Forgive Her? (MK Remix)/(MK Bicycle Dub)/I Want To Wake Up (Johnny Marr 1993 Remix)/(Johnny Marr Groove Mix) (12")	40
93	Parlophone 12RDJ 6348	Can You Forgive Her (Rollo Remix)/(Rollo Dub) (12")	12
93	Abbey Road	COMPILED EP (CD-R, Abbey Road title sleeve; autographed by The Boys, 20 only)	1000
94	Parlophone 12RDJ 6386	Yesterday When I Was Mad (Jam & Spoon Mix)/(Junior Vasquez Factory Dub)/ (Junior Vasquez Fabulous Dub)/(Junior Vasquez Body Dub)/(Coconut 12" Mix)/ (RAF Zone Mix)/(RAF Zone Dub)/Euroboy/Some Speculation (12", double pack, unique p/s)	30
95	Parlophone RLH 6414	Paninaro '95/In The Night (jukebox issue)	10
95	Parlophone 12RDJX 6614	Paninaro '95 — The Remixes Part 1 (Tracy's 12" Mix)/ (Sharon's Sexy Boyz Dub)/(Tin Tin Out Mix)/(Pet Shop Boys Extended Mix) (12", 'close-ups' p/s)	12
95	Parlophone 12RDJ 6614	Paninaro '95 — The Remixes Part 2 (Angel Morales Dub Dance Mix)/ (Angel Morales Girls Boys In Dub)/(Angel Morales The Hot 'N' Spycy Dub) (12", different 'close-ups' p/s)	12
96	Parlophone RLH 6431	Before/The Truck Driver & His Mate (jukebox issue)	10
96	Parlophone 12RDJD 6431	Before (Classic Paradise Mix)/(Afrodisiac Mix)/(Hedboys Mix)/ (Dub)/(Extended Mix) (2 x 12", blue 'penis' p/s)	45

			MINT VALUE £
96	Parlophone 12RJD 6431	Before (Underground Mix)/(Bonus Dub)/(Underground Instrumental)/ (Bonus Beats) (12", red 'penis' p/s)	35
96	Parlophone CDRDJ 6431	Before/The Truck Driver & His Mate/Hit & Miss/In The Night 1995 (CD, slimline jewel case)	10
96	Parlophone 12RDJS 6443	Se A Vida É (That's The Way Life Is) (Mark Picchiotti's Deep And Dark Vocal)/ (Mark Picchiotti's Shelter Deep And Dark Instrumental)/ (Mark Picchiotti's Shelter Dub) (12", purple p/s)	12
96	Parlophone 12RDJ 6443	Se A Vida É (That's The Way Life Is) (Deep Dish Liquid Remix)/ (Pink Noise Mix)/(Deep Dish Dub)/(Radio Mix) (12", yellow vinyl, p/s)	15
96	Parlophone CDIN 103	BILINGUAL THE INTERVIEW (CD)	45
97	Parlophone 12 BARDJ 2	The Truck Driver & His Mate/Before (Love To Infinity Classic Paradise Mix) (12", 'two knobs' p/s, 150 copies)	125
97	Parlophone 12RDJ 6460	A Red Letter Day (Trouser Enthusiasts Autoerotic Decapitation Mix)/ (Trouser Enthusiasts Congo Dongo Dubstramental) (12")	10
97	Parlophone 12RDJX 6460	A Red Letter Day (Basement Jaxx Vocal Mix)/(Motiv8 Cyber Dub Mix)/ The Boy Who Couldn't Keep His Clothes On (On Stage At Twilo) (12")	10
97	Parlophone 12RDJZ 6460	A Red Letter Day (Motiv8 Twelve-Inch Master Mix)/(Basement Jaxx Nite Dub)/ (PSB Extended Edit)/The Boy Who Couldn't Keep His Clothes On (The Far & Away Dub) (12")	10
97	Parlophone 12BOYDJ 101	The Boy Who Couldn't Keep His Clothes On (Main Vocal)/(INT... Club Mix)/ (Banji Girlfriend Beats)/(On Stage At Twilo)/(Radio Edit) (12", die-cut sleeve)	65
97	Parlophone CDRDJ 6460	A Red Letter Day/The Boy Who Couldn't Keep His Clothes On (CD, card p/s)	10
97	Parlophone 12RDJX 6452	Discoteca (Baby Doc Mix)/Single-Bilingual (Baby Doc Mix)/ Single-Bilingual (Baby Doc Mix) (Original Baby Doc Mix) (12", yellow title p/s)	15
97	Parlophone 12RDJ 6452	Discoteca (Pet Shop Boys Extended Mix)/Discoteca (Trouser Enthusiasts Adventures Beyond The Stellar Empire Mix) (12", green title p/s)	12
97	Parlophone 12RDJD 6470	Somewhere (Forthright Club Mix)/(Trouser Enthusiasts Mix)/To Step Aside (Brutal Bill Mix)/Somewhere (Forthright Dub)/To Step Aside (Ralphi's Old School Dub)/To Step Aside (Davidson Ospina Dub) (12" double pack, title p/s)	25
97	PSB 97	PET SHOP BOYS TALK (interview CD, promo-only)	30
99	Parlophone 12 RDJX 6523	I Don't Know What You Want (6 mixes) (2 x 12", gatefold p/s)	20
99	Parlophone 12 CDRDJX 6523	I Don't Know What You Want (7 mixes) (CD, double card sleeve)	75
99	Parlophone 12 RDJD 6533	You Only Tell Me You Love Me When You're Drunk (Brother Brown's Mix)/ (Attaboy Mix)/(T-Total Mix)/(Brother Brown's Dub) (12", p/s)	20
99	Parlophone 12 CDRDJ 6533	You Only Tell Me You Love Me When You're Drunk (1-track CD, card sleeve)	10
99	Parlophone 12 CDRDJ Y6533	You Only Tell Me You Love Me When You're Drunk (Brother Brown's Newt Mix) (1-track CD, card sleeve)	55
99	Parlophone 12 CDRDJX 6533	You Only Tell Me You Love Me When You're Drunk (5 Mixes) (CD, card sleeve)	50
99	Parlophone 12 RDJ 6525	New York City Boy (Superchumbo's Uptown Mix)/ (Superchumbo's Downtown Dub) (12", p/s)	10
99	Parlophone 12 RDJX 6525	New York City Boy (Almighty Definitive Mix)/(Man On A Mission Mix) (12", p/s)	10
99	Parlophone 12 RDJY 6525	New York City Boy (Morales Mix)/(Thunderpuss 2000 Mix) (12", p/s)	10
99	Parlophone 12 RDYZ 6525	New York City Boy (Lange Mix) (1-sided 12", p/s)	10
99	Parlophone 12 RDJS 6525	NEW YORK CITY BOY (all the mixes) (4 x 12", in slip case)	45
99	Parlophone 12 CDRDJ 6525	New York City Boy (CD, card slipcase)	10
99	Parl. 12 CDRDJX 6525	NEW YORK CITY BOY (6 mixes) (CD, double card sleeve)	45
99	Parlophone (no cat. no.)	New York City Boy (Almighty Definitive Mix 8:54) (CD-R, title sleeve)	125
99	Parlophone (no cat. no.)	NIGHTLIFE (10" x 10" box in PVC slip case, contains interview CD, music CD, book, EPK & 3 photographs)	175
01	Parlophone CTH 1	SONGS FROM THE MUSICAL CLOSER TO HEAVEN: Closer To Heaven (Slow Version)/Friendly Fire/Shameless/Closer To Heaven (CD, Daily Telegraph freebie, card p/s)	10
01	10th Planet/PSBP/RUG	FIVE TITLES FROM CLOSER TO HEAVEN: Positive Role Model/Friendly Fire/ Shameless/K-Hole/For All Of Us (CD-R, title sleeve, all sung by Neil Tennant)	280
03	Parlophone 12RDJ 6620	Miracles (Extended Version) (12", 1-sided white label test pressing)	75
03	Parlophone 12RDJX 6620	Miracles (Lemon Jelly Remix) (12", 1-sided white label test pressing)	75
03	Parlophone POPART 03	POPART (EP, 12", white label sampler in white die-cut sleeve)	30
03	Parlophone LONDON 001	London/(Remix) (12", white label)	20
88	Parlophone (no cat. no.)	INTROSPECTIVE (cassette, video-style case, with lyric booklet)	75
89	Parlophone CDPCSD 113	BEHAVIOUR (CD, commercial issue, different inlay, in white monogrammed pouch, with full-album cassette & chronology)	90
91	Parlophone CDPSBDJ 1	DISCOGRAPHY (CD, with Mark Goodyear spoken-word introductions)	30
93	Parlophone DF 118	RELENTLESS (3 x 12", on pink/yellow/blue vinyl)	90
96	Parlophone BILING 1	BILINGUAL (A4 yellow box set, including "A Taste Of Bilingual" CD: [Discoteca/Electricity/A Red Letter Day/It Always Comes As A Surprise/ Se A Vida É], with 2 photos & insert)	150
96	Parlophone PSBCDDJ 1	BILINGUAL (A4 pale blue launch party promo box set including "A Taste Of Bilingual" CD [Before/Se A Vida É], & album cassette, unique inlay)	250
99	Parlophone CDIN 126	INTERVIEW (CD, slipcase)	25
01	Parlophone PSB 001	SAMPLER (CD, 13-track sampler, includes six previously unreleased versions, part-laminated card sleeve)	40
01	Really Useful Group	CLOSER TO HEAVEN (CD-R, title sleeve; 19 tracks, all sung by Neil Tennant)	450
02	Parlophone RELEASE 01	RELEASE (CD, white card sleeve sealed with title sticker)	30
02	Parlophone RELEASE 02	RE-RELEASE (interview CD, white card sleeve sealed with title sticker, with cue sheet)	45
03	Parlophone POPART 01	POPART (2-CD, card sleeve, with outer sleeve)	25
03	Parlophone POPART 02	THE INTERVIEW (interview CD for 'PopArt', with cue sheet)	45

(see also Eighth Wonder, Dusty Springfield, Absolutely Fabulous, Cicero, Electronic, Liza Minnelli, Ian Wright, Peter Rauhofer)

MINT VALUE £

FRANK PETTY TRIO
53 MGM SP 1010 St. Louis Blues (Boogie Woogie)/Somebody Stole My Girl 20
53 MGM SP 1033 Side By Side/Who's Sorry Now 10
53 MGM SP 1038 Sugar/Sioux City Sue 10
53 MGM SP 1053 Sweet Jenny Lee/Yes Sir That's My Baby 8
54 MGM SP 1092 Loch Lomond/Pino Pantaloni 8
54 MGM SP 1112 Mr Pogo/Sunday 8

NORMAN PETTY TRIO
54 HMV 7M 274 Mood Indigo/Petty's Little Polka 22

TOM PETTY (& HEARTBREAKERS)
77 Shelter WIP 6377 American Girl/Wild One Forever (some in p/s) 5
77 Shleter WIP 12-6396 Anything That's Rock'n'Roll/Fooled Again (I Don't Like It) (live) (12") 10
77 Shelter WIP 12-6403 American Girl/Luna (live) (12") 10
80 MCA Backstreet MCA 596/ MSAM 4 Don't Do Me Like That/Century City//Something Else (live)/ Stories We Could Tell (live) (double pack) 6
82 MCA MCAP 778 Refugee/Insider (picture disc) 5
85 MCA MCAT 1047 Refugee (live)/Don't Do Me Like That (live)/Here Comes My Girl/ The Waiting (12", p/s) 10
(The above releases are by Tom Petty & the Heartbreakers. Those listed below are solo releases.)
89 MCA MCA 1334 I Won't Back Down/The Apartment Song (numbered pack with 4 postcards) 5
89 MCA DMCAX 1334 I Won't Back Down/The Apartment Song/Don't Treat Me Like A Stranger (CD, in 6" black embossed plastic pouch) 8
89 MCA MCA 1359 Runnin' Down A Dream/Alright For Now (numbered pack with 4 postcards) 6
89 MCA DMCAX 1359 Runnin' Down A Dream/Alright For Now/Down The Line (CD, numbered envelope-shaped card pack with square polystyrene insert) 8
89 MCA MCA 1381 Free Fallin'/Love Is A Long Road (numbered gatefold p/s) 6
89 MCA DMCAX 1381 Free Fallin'/Love Is A Long Road/Free Fallin' (live) (CD, 6" gatefold hardback book sleeve with 8-page biography) 8
76 Shelter 1DJ 24A OFFICIAL LIVE BOOTLEG (LP, with Heartbreakers, 1-sided 5-track, promo only). 35
(see also Stevie Nicks, Randy Newman, Traveling Wilburys, k.d. lang & Roy Orbison)

PEYR
(see under Theyr)

P.F.M.
73 Manticore K 43502 PHOTOS OF GHOSTS (LP, gatefold sleeve) 20
74 Manticore K 53502 THE WORLD BECAME THE WORLD (LP) 20
75 Manticore K 53506 COOK (LP) 20
76 Manticore K 53508 CHOCOLATE KINGS (LP, gatefold sleeve with lyric sheet) 18
77 Manticore K 53511 JET LAG (LP) 15

PHANTOM
78 Cool Ghoul COOL 1 Lazy Fascist/Power Dub 6
(see also Tom Robinson, Blazing Sons)

PHANTOM CHORDS
92 Camden Town GNAR 003 Town Without Pity/She's A Bad Motorcycle (p/s, 2,000 only) 5
(see also Damned)

PHANTOMS
61 Palette PG 9014 Phantom Guitar/Cachina 18
60s Arc ARC GREAT GUITAR HITS (LP) 30

PHARAOHS
58 Decca DFE 6522 THE PHARAOHS (EP) 1,100
86 Ace SW 116 THE PHARAOHS (EP, reissue) 5

RORY PHARE
88 Parlophone RP 1 Laughing Inside/Laughing Inside (actually by Roy Harper; p/s, promo only) 7
(see also Roy Harper)

PHASE 4
66 Decca F 12327 What Do You Say About That/Think I'll Sit Down And Cry (1st issue) 18
66 Fab FAB 1 What Do You Say About That/I'm Gonna Sit Down And Cry (2nd issue) 12
67 Fab FAB 6 Man Am I Worried?/Listen To The Blues 45
(see also Mike Batt)

PHASE 5
70 Polydor 2058 063 Star Trek/Enterprise 40

JAMES PHELPS
72 Paramount PARA 3019 Check Yourself/My Lover's Prayer 10

PHENOMENA
85 Bronze BRO 193 Dance With The Devil/Hell On Wings (p/s) 7
85 Bronze BROX 193 Dance With The Devil (MIdnight Mix)/Hell On Wings (12", p/s with poster) 10
87 Arista RIS 42 Did It All For Love/Double 6, 55, 44... (box set with insert) 5
91 Parachute PAR 002 INNERVERSIONS (LP) 12
(see also Trapeze, Whitesnake, Cozy Powell, Black Sabbath, Thin Lizzy, Budgie, A-Ha)

PHILADELPHIA SOCIETY
75 Gull GULS 21 100 South Of Broadway (Parts 1 & 2) 5

PHIL & FLINTSTONES
64 Bedrock PR 5371 Love Potion No. 9/Honey Don't (private pressing) 50

PHILIP & HIS FOETUS VIBRATIONS
82 Self Immol. WOMB KX 07 Tell Me, What Is The Bane Of Your Life/Mother I've Killed The Cat (p/s) 25
(see also You've Got Foetus On Your Breath, Foetus Art Terrorism, Foetus Über Frisco, Foetus Under Glass, Scraping Foetus Off The Wheel)

LOUIS PHILIPPE
86 él GPO 15 Like Nobody Do/Twangy Twangy (p/s) 10

MINT VALUE £

ANTHONY PHILLIPS

78 Arista ARIST 192 We're All As We Lie/Squirrel/Sitars And Nebulous 10
79 Arista ARIST 252 Um & Aargh/Souvenir (p/s) 10
81 RCA RCA 102 Prelude '84/Anthem '84 (p/s) 8
84 Street Tunes JJ 102-12 Sally/Exocet/Women Were Watching (12", p/s) 8
88 PRT PYS 18 The Anthem From Tarka/The Rising Spring (p/s) 10
88 PRT PYD 18 The Anthem From Tarka (Single Mix)/The Rising Spring/Excerpt From Tarka (Movement 1)/(Movement 3)/The Anthem From Tarka (Ext. Single Mix) (CD) 15
79 Arista SPART 1085/AFLP 1 SIDES (LP, 1st 500 copies sealed with free LP "Private Parts & Pieces") 35
85 Cherry Red BRED 66 HARVEST OF THE HEART (LP) 12
89 Occasional (no cat. no.) FINGER PAINTING — MISSING LINKS VOL. 1 (cassette, 1,000 copies, mail order only) 12

(see also Genesis)

CONFREY PHILLIPS (TRIO)

56 Columbia SCM 5223 Love And Marriage/The Others I Like 5
57 Decca F 10835 Am I Going Out Of My Mind?/Afterglow 5
57 Decca F 10866 Shotgun Rock 'n' Roll/Hokey-Kokey Rock 'n' Roll (as Confrey Phillips Trio) 20
57 Decca F 10866 Shotgun Rock 'n' Roll/Hokey-Kokey Rock 'n' Roll (as Confrey Phillips Trio) (78) . 10
58 Decca DFE 6518 SWINGING DOWN BROADWAY (EP) 8

EDDY/EDWIN PHILLIPS

76 Charisma CB 283 Limbo Jimbo/Change My Ways (as Eddy Phillips) 5
85 T-Mac UEZT 003 Life On Earth/(Radio Mix)/(Instrumental) (12", as Edwin Phillips) 8

(see also Creation, Mark Four, Spectrum)

(LITTLE) ESTHER (PHILLIPS)

62 Stateside SS 140 Release Me/Don't Feel Rained On 15
63 Ember EMB S 174 Am I That Easy To Forget/I Really Don't Want To Know (as Little Esther Phillips). 10
65 Sue WI 395 The Chains/Feel Like I Wanna Cry (as Esther Philips) 25
65 Atlantic AT 4028 And I Love Him/Shangri-La 15
65 Atlantic AT 4048 Let Me Know When It's Over/I Saw Me 15
66 Atlantic AT 4077 I Could Have Told You/Just Say Goodbye 75
66 Ember EMBS 221 Release Me/Be Honest With Me (as Little Esther Phillips) 8
66 Atlantic 584 013 When A Woman Loves A Man/Ups And Downs 7
67 Atlantic 584 062 Someone Else Is Taking My Place/When Love Comes To The Human Race 7
67 Atlantic 584 103 And I Love Him/Shangri-La (reissue) 6
67 Atlantic 584 126 I'm Sorry/Cheater Man 7
69 Roulette RO 505 Too Late To Worry, Too Blue To Cry/I'm In The Mood For Love (Moody's Mood For Love) 6
69 Roulette RO 508 Tonight I'll Be Staying Here With You/Sweet Dreams 6
72 Atlantic K 10168 Catch Me I'm Falling/Release Me. 6
72 Kudu KUS 4000 Home Is Where The Hatred Is/Til My Back Ain't Got No Bone 8
73 Kudu KUS 4002 I've Never Found A Man/Cherry Red 7
63 Ember CW 103 REFLECTIONS OF GREAT COUNTRY AND WESTERN STANDARDS (LP) 60
65 Atlantic ATL 5030 AND I LOVE HIM (LP) 65
67 Atlantic 587/588 010 ESTHER PHILLIPS SINGS (LP) 40
72 Kudu KUL 2 FROM A WHISPER TO A SCREAM (LP) 25
73 Kudu KUL 6 ALONE AGAIN, NATURALLY (LP) 15
75 Kudu KU 18 PERFORMANCE (LP) 15
76 Atlantic K 50521 CONFESSIN' THE BLUES (LP, gatefold sleeve) 15

FLIP PHILLIPS

50s Columbia/Clef 33C 9003 FLIP PHILLIPS QUARTET (10" LP) 22

GLENN PHILLIPS

75 Caroline C 1519 LOST AT SEA (LP) 12

GREGORY PHILLIPS

63 Pye 7N 15546 Angie/Please Believe Me 12
64 Pye 7N 15593 Everybody Knows/Closer To Me (with Remo Four) 10
64 Pye 7N 15633 Don't Bother Me/Make Sure That You're Mine 10
65 Immediate IM 004 Down In The Boondocks/That's The One 20

(see also Remo Four)

JOHN PHILLIPS

70 Stateside SS 8046 Mississippi/April Anne 6
70 Stateside-Dunhill SSL 5027 JOHN PHILLIPS: THE WOLFKING OF L.A. (LP) 25

(see also Mamas & Papas)

LESLIE PHILLIPS

59 Parlophone R 4610 The Navy Lark/The Disc 8
62 Parlophone R 4912 I Must Resist Temptation/Jolly Old Spring 6
69 Columbia DB 8562 The Man Most Likely To/Marigold 6

MICHELLE PHILLIPS

76 A&M AMS 7250 No Love Today/Aloha Louie 5
77 A&M AMS 7340 Victim Of Romance/Lady Of Fantasy 10
77 A&M AMLS 64651 VICTIM OF ROMANCE (LP) 20

(see also Mamas & Papas)

PHIL PHILLIPS & TWILIGHTS

59 Mercury AMT 1059 Sea Of Love/Juella 35
60 Mercury AMT 1072 Take This Heart/Verdi Mae 30
60 Mercury AMT 1093 Your True Love Once More/What Will I Tell My Heart 25
61 Mercury AMT 1139 I Love To Love You/No One Else But You. 25

SHAWN PHILLIPS

65 Columbia DB 7611 Hey Nelly Nelly/Solitude. 12
65 Columbia DB 7699 Doesn't Anybody Know My Name?/Nobody Listens 12
65 Columbia DB 7789 Little Tin Soldier/London Town 8
66 Columbia DB 7956 Summer Came/Storms. 8

MINT VALUE £

67	Parlophone R 5606	Stargazer/Woman Mine	50
70	A&M AMS 819	Christmas Song/Lovely Lady	6
65	Columbia 33SX 1748	I'M A LONER (LP)	80
66	Columbia S(C)X 6006	SHAWN (LP)	70
70	A&M AMLS 978	CONTRIBUTION (LP)	12
71	A&M AMLS 2006	SECOND CONTRIBUTION (LP, with insert)	12
72	A&M AMLS 64324	COLLABORATION (LP)	12
73	A&M AMLS 64363	FACES (LP)	12
74	A&M AMLH 68278	FURTHERMORE (LP)	12
74	A&M AMLH 64402	BRIGHT WHITE (LP)	12
75	A&M AMLH 64539	DO YOU WONDER (LP)	12
76	A&M AMLH 64582	RUMPLESTILTSKIN'S RESOLVE (LP)	12
77	A&M AMLH 64650	SPACED (LP, with inner sleeve)	15

SID PHILLIPS BAND

56	HMV 7M 372	Bugle Call Rag/Memories Of You	8
56	HMV 7M 396	Rockin' Thru' The Rye/Everybody Step	8
56	HMV 7M 406	Juke Box Baby/My Honey's Lovin' Arms	8
56	HMV 7M 418	Mamma Don't Allow/Glad Rag Doll	8
56	HMV POP 269	Farewell Blues (Rock 'N' Roll Style)/It Goes Like This	7
57	HMV POP 416	The Midgets/Tropical Twilight	7
59	HMV POP 549	Weekend/Enchiladas-Cha-Cha	6
57	HMV 7EG 8253	DIXIELAND RAMBLINGS (EP)	18
58	HMV 7EG 8363	SID PHILIPS BAND (EP)	8
59	HMV 7EG 8425	DIXIE SPECIAL (EP)	12
59	HMV 7EG 8461	DIXIE BEAT (EP)	12
61	HMV 7EG 8645	DIXIELAND EXPRESS (EP)	12
55	HMV DLP 1102	HORS D'OEUVRES (10" LP)	20
57	HMV DLP 1164	DOWN DIXIELAND HIGHWAY (10" LP)	18
58	HMV DLP 1194	CRUISING DOWN TO DIXIE (10" LP)	15
58	HMV DLP 1212	FLYING DOWN TO DIXIE (10" LP)	15
70	Fontana 6438 026	RHYTHM IS OUR BUSINESS (LP)	12

STU PHILLIPS

58	London HL 8673	The Champlain And St. Lawrence Line/The Priest Who Slept 100 Years	12
58	London HL 8673	The Champlain And St. Lawrence Line/The Priest Who Slept 100 Years (78)	15
60	Pye International 7N 25062	Strangers When We Meet/BOB MERSEY ORCHESTRA: Song Of India	6
67	RCA RCA 1601	Angel Of Love/The Great El Tigre	5
59	Pye Intl. NEP 44001	STU PHILLIPS (EP)	12

TEDDY PHILLIPS & HIS ORCHESTRA

54	London HL 8032	Ridin' To Tennessee/Alone Tonight	60
54	London HL 8032	Ridin' To Tennessee/Alone Tonight (78)	12
54	Parlophone CMSP 4	Down Boy/Meet "Miss Pippin" (export issue)	15
54	Parlophone CMSP 12	The Old Red Barn/JIMMY BLUE CREW: The Old Shoe Cobbler (export issue)	15
54	Parlophone CMSP 28	Life Is Like A Slice Of Cake/One-Sided Love Affair (export issue)	15

WARREN PHILLIPS & THE ROCKETS

69	Decca (S)PA 43	THE WORLD OF ROCK 'N' ROLL (LP)	20

(see also Savoy Brown, Foghat)

WOOLF PHILLIPS & HIS ORCHESTRA

54	Decca F 10416	Count Your Blessings Instead Of Sheep/Your Heart, My Heart (B-side with Dennis Morley — Vocal)	6

VINCE PHILPOTT & DRAGS

64	Decca F 11997	The Cramp/Eenie Meenie Miny Mo	20

PHILWIT & PEGASUS

70	Chapter One CHR 130	And She Came — Final Thought/Pauper's Son	8
70	Chapter One CHR 131	And I Try/Pauper's Son	8
70	Chapter One CHR 137	The Elephant Song/Pseudo Phoney Mixed Up Croney	8
70	Chapter One CHSR 805	PHILWIT AND PEGASUS (LP)	35

(see also Mark Wirtz)

PHOENIX

69	President PT 246	Tour De France/Time To Go	6

PHOENIX

76	CBS 81621	PHOENIX (LP)	12
80	Charisma CAS 1150	IN FULL VIEW (LP)	12

(see also Argent, Kinks, Michael Des Barres)

PHOENIX

81	Rising PR 433032	PHOENIX RISING EP (Lonely Attack/The Minstrel/Understanding/Phoenix Rising 'av an 'am) (12" EP)	35

PAT PHOENIX

62	HMV POP 1030	The Rovers Chorus/Coronation Street Monologue	12

PHONES SPORTSMAN BAND

81	Rather GEAR 9	I REALLY LIKE YOU (EP)	8

(see also Swell Maps)

PHOTOGRAPHED BY LIGHTNING

86	Fierce FRIGHT 008	Sleep's Terminator/Winter Trees (foldaround p/s, hand-coloured labels)	30

PHUTURE PHANTASY

88	Low Fat Vinyl LFV 1	SLAM (12")	15

PHYSICALS

78	Physical PR 001	ALL SEXED UP (EP)	6
79	Big Beat NS 58	Be Like Me/Pain In Love (p/s)	6

(see also Maniacs)

MINT VALUE £

EDITH PIAF

53 Columbia DCF 152 Soeur Anne/Misericorde (78) . . . 15
60 Columbia DC 754 Milord/Je Sais Comment (export issue) . . . 5
61 Columbia DB 4596 Non, Je Ne Regrette Rien/Les Amants D'Un Jour . . . 5
61 Columbia DB 4642 Exodus/No Regrets . . . 5
63 Columbia DB 7149 Polichinelle/Le Billiard Electrique . . . 5
63 Columbia SEG 8220 GREAT PIAF (EP) . . . 8
64 Columbia SEG 8308 NON, JE NE REGRETTE RIEN (EP) . . . 8
65 Columbia SEG 8387 QU'IL ETAIT TRISTE (EP) . . . 8
57 Columbia SCX 5 MEA CULPA (LP) . . . 18
60 Columbia 33SX 1276 SINCERELY ... EDITH PIAF (LP) . . . 15
61 Columbia 33SX 1330 PIAF AT THE PARIS OLYMPIA (LP) . . . 15

PIANO MAGIC

97 Wurlitzer Jukebox WJ 26 For Engineers A/For Engineers AA (p/s) . . . 7
98 Lissy's LISS 32 Music For Rolex/Matmos (p/s) . . . 6
98 Darla DRL 074 A Trick Of The Sea/Halloween Boat (CD) . . . 12
98 Debut DEBT 001SP French Mittens/Icebreaker: Melody For Nato (p/s) . . . 9
98 Bad Jazz BEBOP 9 Music For Annahbird/Music For Wasps/Me At 19 (p/s) . . . 8
99 Acetone Solve 010 Amongst The Books, An Angel/C'est Un Mauvais Presage Lorsque Ton Aureole A Tombe (1st 20 copies with interlocking p/s) . . . 10/6
00 Morr MUSIC 008 Panic Amigo — Piano Magic Remixed (12" EP) . . . 10
97 i/Che IRE 2102 POPULAR MECHANICS (LP) . . . 12

PIANO RED

52 HMV B 10244 Rockin' With Red/Red's Boogie (78) . . . 15
52 HMV B 10246 Just Right Bounce/Hey, Good Lookin' (78) . . . 15
52 HMV B 10316 Count The Days I'm Gone/Bouncin' With Red (78) . . . 15
52 HMV JO 244 Rockin' With Red/Red's Boogie (78, export issue) . . . 15
52 HMV JO 276 Layin' The Boogie/Baby What's Wrong (78, export issue) . . . 15
52 HMV JO 296 My Gal Jo/Let's Have A Good Time (78, export issue) . . . 15
53 HMV JO 334 Voo Doopee Doo/Everybody's Boogie (78, export issue) . . . 15
53 HMV 7M 108 Rockin' With Red/Red's Boogie . . . 200
64 RCA RCX 7138 RHYTHM AND BLUES VOL. 2 (EP) . . . 40
(see also Dr. Feelgood [U.S.])

PIBLOKTO

(see under Pete Brown & Piblokto)

PICA

70 Polydor 2058 056 Take The Barriers Down/Insurance Man . . . 6
71 Philips 6006 129 Rainbow Chaser/Ad Lib . . . 6
(see also Nirvana [UK])

PIC & BILL

67 Page One POF 024 All I Want Is You/It's Not You . . . 12
67 Page One POF 037 This Is It/Nobody But My Baby . . . 12
68 Page One POF 052 Sad World Without You/Just A Tear . . . 12

PICADILLY LINE

67 CBS 2785 At The Third Stroke/How Could You Say You're Leaving Me . . . 12
67 CBS 2958 Emily Small (The Huge World Thereof)/Gone Gone Gone . . . 15
68 CBS 3595 Yellow Rainbow/Evenings With Corrina . . . 7
68 CBS 3595 Yellow Rainbow/I Know, She Believes (reissue with different B-side) . . . 12
68 CBS 3743 Evenings With Corrina/My Best Friend . . . 7
67 CBS (S)BPG 63129 THE HUGE WORLD OF EMILY SMALL (LP, some with promo insert) . . . 70
(see also Edwards Hand)

PICCADILLY STRINGS

61 Piccadilly 7N 35013 Sir Francis Drake Theme/Our House . . . 6

PIERO PICCIONI

67 Fontana TF 898 Main Theme From 'The Tenth Victim'/Part 2 (mono) . . . 12

BUSTER PICKENS

60s Heritage HLP 1008 TEXAS PIANO (LP, 99 only) . . . 60

J.B. PICKERS

71 London HLU 10334 Super Soul Sounds/KIM & DAVE: Nobody Knows . . . 15

BOBBY (BORIS) PICKETT & CRYPT-KICKERS

62 London HLU 9597 Monster Mash/Monsters' Mash Party . . . 10
73 London ZGU 133 MONSTER MASH (LP) . . . 30

DAN PICKETT

60s XX MIN 710 DAN PICKETT (EP) . . . 15

NICK PICKETT

72 Warner Bros K 14156 America/Lady Luck . . . 5
72 Warner Bros K 44172 SILVERSLEEVES (LP) . . . 15
(see also John Dummer Blues Band)

WILSON PICKETT

63 Liberty LIB 10115 It's Too Late/I'm Gonna Love You . . . 22
65 Atlantic AT 4036 In The Midnight Hour/I'm Not Tired . . . 18
65 MGM MGM 1286 Let Me Be Your Boy/My Heart Belongs To You (DJ copies £80) . . . 55
65 Atlantic AT 4052 Don't Fight It/It's All Over . . . 15
66 Atlantic AT 4072 634-5789/That's A Man's Way . . . 15
66 Atlantic 584 023 99 And A Half (Won't Do)/Danger Zone . . . 10
66 Atlantic 584 039 Land Of 1000 Dances/You're So Fine . . . 10
66 Atlantic 584 066 Mustang Sally/Three Time Loser . . . 10
67 Atlantic 584 101 Everybody Needs Somebody To Love/Nothing You Can Do . . . 10
67 Atlantic 584 107 New Orleans/Soul Dance III . . . 10

MINT VALUE £

67 London HLU 10146 Billy The Kid/I Don't Want No Part-Time Love (with Falcons) . . . 10
67 Atlantic 584 130 Funky Broadway/I'm Sorry About That . . . 10
67 Atlantic 584 142 Stag-O-Lee/I'm In Love . . . 10
68 Atlantic 584 150 In The Midnight Hour/Danger Zone . . . 7
68 Atlantic 584 173 That Kind Of Love/I've Come A Long Way . . . 7
68 Atlantic 584 183 She's Looking Good/We've Got To Have Love . . . 7
68 Atlantic 584 203 I'm A Midnight Mover/Deborah . . . 7
68 Atlantic 584 221 I Found A True Love/For Better Or Worse . . . 7
69 Atlantic 584 236 Hey Jude/Night Owl . . . 6
69 Atlantic 584 261 Mini-Skirt Minnie/Back In Your Arms . . . 6
69 Atlantic 584 281 Hey Joe/Born To Be Wild . . . 6
70 Atlantic 584 313 You Keep Me Hangin' On/Now You See Me, Now You Don't . . . 6
70 Atlantic 2091 005 Sugar, Sugar/Cole, Cooke And Redding . . . 6
70 Atlantic 2091 032 (Get Me Back On Time) Engine No. 9/International Playboy . . . 7
71 Atlantic 2091 086 Fire And Water/Don't Let The Green Grass Fool You . . . 6
71 Atlantic 2091 124 Don't Know My Love (Parts 1 & 2) . . . 6
72 Atlantic K 10166 Don't Let The Green Grass Fool You/Covering The Same Old Ground . . . 6
72 Atlantic K 10181 Funk Factory/One Step Away . . . 6
72 President PT 319 If You Need Me/I'm Gonna Love You . . . 6
73 President PT 322 I Can't Stop/Down To My Last Heartbreak . . . 7
65 Atlantic ATL 5037 IN THE MIDNIGHT HOUR (LP) . . . 65
66 Atlantic 587/588 029 THE EXCITING WILSON PICKETT (LP) . . . 35
66 Atlantic 587 032 IN THE MIDNIGHT HOUR (LP, reissue) . . . 18
67 Atlantic 587/588 057 THE WICKED PICKETT (LP) . . . 25
67 Atlantic 587/588 080 THE SOUND OF WILSON PICKETT (LP) . . . 25
68 Atlantic 587/588 092 THE BEST OF WILSON PICKETT (LP) . . . 18
68 Atlantic 587/588 107 I'M IN LOVE (LP) . . . 25
68 Atlantic 587/588 111 MIDNIGHT MOVER (LP) . . . 22
69 Atlantic 588 170 HEY JUDE (LP) . . . 20
70 Atlantic 2465 002 RIGHT ON (LP) . . . 20
70 Joy JOYS 181 IF YOU NEED ME (LP) . . . 18
71 Atlantic 2400 026 ENGINE NO. 9 — IN PHILADELPHIA (LP) . . . 20
72 Atlantic K 40319 DON'T KNOCK MY LOVE (LP) . . . 12
75 RCA APL 2 0669 LIVE IN JAPAN (LP) . . . 12
(see also Falcons)

PICKETTYWITCH

70 Pye NSPL 18357 PICKETTYWITCH (LP) . . . 12
(see also Polly Brown)

GARY PICKFORD-HOPKINS & FRIENDS

83 Spartan SP 143 Why? (The Song)/Why? (The Story) (p/s) . . . 8
83 Spartan SP 143T Why? (The Song)/Why? (The Story) (12", p/s) . . . 10
(see also Deke Leonard, Man, Andy Fairweather-Low, Alan Ross, Big Sleep, Eyes Of Blue, Wild Turkey)

PICKWICKS

64 Decca F 11901 Apple Blossom Time/I Don't Wanna Tell You Again . . . 15
64 Decca F 11957 You're Old Enough/Hello Lady . . . 15
65 Warner Bros WB 151 Little By Little/I Took My Baby Home . . . 60

PICTURES FROM THE GREAT EXHIBITION

80s Recommended RE/ARC The Housewife's Nightmare (silkscreened, 1-sided, gatefold p/s) . . . 6

PIED PIPERS

54 Parlophone CMSP 21 Kissin' Drive Rock/Please Understand (export issue) . . . 18

PIED PIPERS

66 Columbia DB 7883 Ragamuffin/Fat Marie . . . 6

BILLY & DEDE PIERCE/JIM ROBINSON

64 London HA-K/SH-K 8163 JAZZ AT PRESERVATION HALL VOL. 2 (LP) . . . 12

WEBB PIERCE

50s Decca BM 311368 We'll Find A Way/Any Old Time (export issue) . . . 30
56 Brunswick 05630 Teenage Boogie/Any Old Time . . . 180
56 Brunswick 05630 Teenage Boogie/Any Old Time (78) . . . 25
57 Brunswick 05682 Bye, Bye Love/Honky Tonk Song . . . 40
57 Brunswick 05682 Bye, Bye Love/Honky Tonk Song (78) . . . 20
59 Brunswick 05809 I Ain't Never/Shanghaied . . . 15
59 Brunswick 05809 I Ain't Never/Shanghaied (78) . . . 18
60 Brunswick 05820 No Love Have I/Whirlpool Of Love . . . 10
60 Brunswick 05842 Drifting Texas Sand/All I Need Is You . . . 10
56 Brunswick OE 9253 WEBB PIERCE PT. 1 (EP) . . . 22
56 Brunswick OE 9254 WEBB PIERCE PT. 2 (EP) . . . 22
56 Brunswick OE 9255 WEBB PIERCE PT. 3 (EP) . . . 22
62 Ember EMB 4520 COUNTRY AND WESTERN FAVOURITES VOL. 1 (EP) . . . 18
59 Parlophone GEP 8792 COUNTRY ROUND UP (EP) . . . 40
55 Brunswick LA 8716 THE WONDERING BOY (10" LP) . . . 40
60 Brunswick LAT 8324 WEBB! (LP) . . . 25
65 Brunswick LAT 8540 HIDEAWAY HEART (LP) . . . 22
65 Brunswick LAT 8551 CROSS COUNTRY (LP) . . . 18
69 MCA MUPS 364 IN THE JAILHOUSE NOW (LP) . . . 12
(see also Red Sovine & Webb Pierce)

CLIVE PIG & THE HOPEFUL CHINAMEN

79 Pinnacle PIN 21 Happy Birthday Sweet Sixteen/Our Movement (p/s) . . . 10
(see also Trixie's Big Red Motorbike)

PIGEON FLYERS

68 Columbia DB 8449 The Heaven We Shared Together/Keep On Sayin' . . . 5

MINT VALUE £

BILLY PIGG
71 Leader LEA 4006 THE BORDER MINSTREL (LP, gatefold sleeve with booklet) . . . 12

PIGGLESWICK FOLK
77 Acorn CF 256 PIG IN THE MIDDLE (LP) . . . 12

PIGS
77 Bristol Recorder NBR 01 Youthenasia/They Say/Psychopath/National Front (p/s) . . . 8

PIGSTY HILL LIGHT ORCHESTRA
70 Village Thing VTS 1 PHLOP! (LP) . . . 15
72 Village Thing VTS 8 PIGGERY JOKERY (LP) . . . 15

DAVE PIKE
63 Starlite ST45 094 Melvalita/Ginha . . . 5
66 Atlantic 584 052 Sunny/HERBIE MANN: Philly Dog . . . 10
66 Atlantic 588 005 JAZZ FOR THE JET SET (LP) . . . 15

PiL
(see under Public Image Ltd)

RAY PILGRIM (& BEATMEN)
60 Oriole CB 1557 Baby Doll/Gambler's Guitar (solo) . . . 15
61 Oriole CB 1616 Little Miss Makebelieve/Granada (solo) . . . 15
64 Embassy WB 645 Kissin' Cousins (with Beatmen)/ JAYBIRDS: Some Day We're Gonna Love Again . . . 8
(see also Bud Ashton, Jaybirds, Typhoons)

PILTDOWN MEN
60 Capitol CL 15149 McDonald's Cave/Brontosaurus Stomp . . . 10
61 Capitol CL 15175 Piltdown Rides Again/Bubbles In The Tar . . . 10
61 Capitol CL 15186 Goodnight Mrs Flintstone/The Great Imposter . . . 10
61 Capitol CL 15211 Gargantua/Fossil Rock . . . 15
62 Capitol CL 15245 A Pretty Girl Is Like A Melody/Big Lizard . . . 15
61 Capitol EAP1 20155 GOODNIGHT MRS. FLINTSTONE (EP) . . . 50

SIR HUBERT PIMM
55 London HL 8155 Goodnight And Cheerio/Honky Tonk Train Blues . . . 35
55 London RE-U 1032 PIMM'S PARTY (EP, with Ellen Sutton) . . . 20
(see also Duke & Duchess)

COURTNEY PINE
88 Island 10ISB 301 CHILDREN OF THE GHETTO (LP, 2 x 10", with 4 prints) . . . 20

PINEAPPLE CHUNKS
65 Mercury MF 922 Drive My Car/Dream About . . . 12

PINEWOOD STUDIO ORCHESTRA with PHILIP GREEN
59 Top Rank TR 5005 Blind Date/HARDY KRUGER: Blind Date . . . 6
59 Top Rank JAR 112 Sapphire (featuring Johnny Dankworth)/Tiger Bay . . . 5
60 Top Rank JAR 355 'League Of Gentlemen' March/'Golden Fleece' Theme . . . 10
60 Top Rank JAR 361 French Horn Blues (Augie's Theme)/Elevator Ride . . . 5
(see also Johnny Dankworth Orchestra)

PINEWOOD TOM/TOM TALL
59 Jazz Collector JEL 5 THE MALE BLUES VOLUME 4 (EP) . . . 18

'PING PING' & AL VERLANE
60 Oriole CB 1589 Sucu Sucu/Maria Della Montagna . . . 15

PINKERTON'S ('ASSORTED' COLOURS)
65 Decca F 12307 Mirror Mirror/She Don't Care (as Pinkerton's 'Assorted' Colours) . . . 8
66 Decca F 12377 Don't Stop Loving Me Baby/Will Ya? (as Pinkerton's 'Assorted' Colours) . . . 10
66 Decca F 12493 Magic Rocking Horse/It Ain't Right (as Pinkerton's Colours) . . . 25
67 Pye 7N 17327 Mum And Dad/On A Street Car (as Pinkerton's Colours) . . . 12
67 Pye 7N 17414 There's Nobody I'd Sooner Love/Look At Me (as Pinkerton's) . . . 12
68 Pye 7N 17574 Kentucky Woman/Behind The Mirror (as Pinkerton's) . . . 12
(see also Flying Machine, Liberators, Tony Newman)

PINK FAIRIES
71 Polydor 2058 089 The Snake/Do It . . . 20
72 Polydor 2059 302 Well Well Well/Hold On . . . 25
76 Stiff BUY 2 Between The Lines/Spoiling For A Fight (p/s) . . . 12
71 Polydor 2383 045 NEVERNEVERLAND (LP, printed PVC outer & gatefold card inner, in white bag, some allegedly with photos & notes) . . . 60
71 Polydor 2383 045 NEVERNEVERLAND (LP, printed PVC outer & gatefold card inner, pink vinyl & "pink plastic" in text on rear sleeve, around 100 pressed) . . . 350+
71 Polydor 2383 045 NEVERNEVERLAND (LP, black vinyl, standard sleeve) . . . 20
72 Polydor 2383 132 WHAT A BUNCH OF SWEETIES (LP) . . . 25
73 Polydor 2383 212 KINGS OF OBLIVION (LP, with poster) . . . 40
75 Polydor 2384 071 FLASHBACK (LP) . . . 20
84 Big Beat WIK 14 LIVE AT THE ROUNDHOUSE '75 (LP, pink vinyl, with inner sleeve) . . . 20
(see also Twink, Larry Wallis, Deviants, Lightning Raiders, Shagrat)

PINK FLOYD
SINGLES
67 Columbia DB 8156 Arnold Layne/Candy And A Currant Bun . . . 90
67 Columbia DB 8214 See Emily Play/Scarecrow . . . 60
67 Columbia DB 8310 Apples And Oranges/Paintbox . . . 150
68 Columbia DB 8401 It Would Be So Nice/Julia Dream . . . 100
68 Columbia DB 8511 Point Me At The Sky/Careful With That Axe, Eugene . . . 80
79 Harvest HAR 5194 Another Brick In The Wall (Part 2)/One Of My Turns (initial pressing, plain B-side label without 'window' picture) . . . 6

81	Harvest HAR 5217	Money (Edit)/Let There Be More Light (unreleased)	
81	Harvest 12HAR 5217	Money (Full Length)/Let There Be More Light (12", unreleased)	
82	Harvest HAR 5222	When The Tigers Broke Free/Bring The Boys Back Home (gatefold p/s)	7
82	Harvest HAR 5222	When The Tigers Broke Free/Bring The Boys Back Home (standard p/s)	8
87	EMI EMDJ 26	Learning To Fly (Edited Version)/One Slip (Edited Version)/Terminal Frost (no p/s, mispressing without "One Slip", 1,000 only on pink vinyl, 50 on black)	12/20
87	EMI EM 26	Learning To Fly (Edited Version)/One Slip (Edited Version)/Terminal Frost (p/s)	5
87	EMI 12EM 26	Learning To Fly (Edited Version)/One Slip (Edited Version)/ Terminal Frost (DYOL Version) (12", p/s)	8
87	EMI CDEM 26	Learning To Fly (Edited Version)/One Slip (Edited Version)/Terminal Frost (Album Version)/Terminal Frost (DYOL Version) (CD, card sleeve & inner)	15
87	EMI EM 34	On The Turning Away (Album)/Run Like Hell (Live Version) (p/s)	5
87	EMI EMP 34	On The Turning Away (Album)/Run Like Hell (Live Version) (p/s, pink vinyl, 1000 only)	8
87	EMI 12EMP 34	On The Turning Away (Album)/Run Like Hell (Live Version)/ On The Turning Away (Live Version) (12", poster p/s)	12
87	EMI CDEM 34	On The Turning Away/Run Like Hell (Live Version)/ On The Turning Away (Live Version) (CD)	15
88	EMI EM 52	One Slip/Terminal Frost (p/s)	5
88	EMI EMG 52	One Slip/Terminal Frost (pink vinyl, gatefold p/s with ticket application)	8
88	EMI 12EMP 52	One Slip/Terminal Frost/The Dogs Of War (live) (12", poster p/s)	8
88	EMI CDEM 52	One Slip/Terminal Frost/The Dogs Of War (live) (CD)	12
94	EMI EM 309	Take It Back (Edit)/Astronomy Domine (live) (jukebox issue, black vinyl)	8
94	EMI EM 309	Take It Back (Edit)/Astronomy Domine (live) (red vinyl, p/s)	7
94	EMI CDEMS 309	Take It Back (Album Version)/Astronomy Domine (live)/Take It Back (Edit) (CD, picture disc, with poster)	8
94	EMI EM 342	High Hopes (Radio Edit)/Keep Talking (Radio Edit) (clear vinyl, poster p/s)	5
94	EMI 12EM 342	High Hopes (Album Version)/Keep Talking (Album Version)/ One Of These Days (live) (12", 1-sided, laser-etched blue vinyl, p/s in outer gatefold p/s with 7 postcards)	8
94	EMI CDEM 342	High Hopes (Radio Edit)/Keep Talking (Radio Edit)/One Of These Days (live) (CD, with 7 postcards)	8

ALBUMS

67	Columbia S(C)X 6157	THE PIPER AT THE GATES OF DAWN (LP, blue/black label, mono/stereo)	180/110

(second pressings of the above LP have "File Under Pop" on the right of the flipback; first pressings do not *have this. Second pressings are worth half to a third less.)*

68	Columbia S(C)X 6258	A SAUCERFUL OF SECRETS (LP, blue/black label, mono/stereo)	200/110
70	Columbia SCX 6157	THE PIPER AT THE GATES OF DAWN (LP, re-pressing, silver & black label)	20
70	Columbia SCX 6258	A SAUCERFUL OF SECRETS (LP, re-pressing, silver & black label)	25
69	Columbia SCX 6346	SOUNDTRACK FROM THE FILM 'MORE' (LP, laminated flipback sleeve, 'couple facing west' photo on green-tinted rear sleeve)	35
70s	Columbia SCX 6346	SOUNDTRACK FROM THE FILM 'MORE' (LP, laminated non-flipback sleeve, 'couple facing west' photo on black-tinted rear sleeve)	25
70s	Columbia SCX 6346	SOUNDTRACK FROM THE FILM 'MORE' (LP, laminated non-flipback sleeve, 'couple facing east' photo on black-tinted rear sleeve)	35
69	Harvest SHDW 1/2	UMMAGUMMA (2-LP, laminated gatefold sleeve)	22
70	MGM 2315 002	ZABRISKIE POINT (LP, soundtrack, with Jerry Garcia/Kaleidoscope, et al.)	20
70	Harvest SHVL 781	ATOM HEART MOTHER (LP, gatefold sleeve)	18

(first pressings of the above Harvest LPs have "The Gramophone..." text on label rim and "Harvest" on the left side of the label; second pressings have "The Gramophone..." text with a boxed EMI logo above "Harvest". Second pressings are worth a little less)

71	Harvest SHVL 795	MEDDLE (LP, gatefold sleeve)	15
71	Starline SRS 5071	RELICS (LP, white textured sleeve)	15
72	Harvest SHSP 4020	OBSCURED BY CLOUDS (LP, rounded sleeve)	20
73	Harvest SHVL 804	THE DARK SIDE OF THE MOON (LP, first pressing, solid light blue triangle label, black inner, 2 posters & 2 stickers, gatefold sleeve, only one side opening)	400
73	Harvest SHVL 804	THE DARK SIDE OF THE MOON (LP, blue & black label, gatefold sleeve with black inner, 2 posters & 2 stickers, some with stickered sleeve)	20/15
70s	Harvest SHVL 804	THE DARK SIDE OF THE MOON (LP, repressing, blue & silver label, gatefold sleeve with black inner, 2 posters & 2 stickers)	12
73	Harvest Q4 SHVL 781	ATOM HEART MOTHER (LP, quadrophonic, gatefold sleeve, initially with 'quadrophonic' logo on front sleeve, later inside)	30/25
73	Harvest Q4 SHVL 804	THE DARK SIDE OF THE MOON (LP, quadrophonic, gatefold sleeve, no inserts)	30
73	Harvest SHDW 403	A NICE PAIR (2-LP, gatefold sleeve, with 2 inner sleeves; early copies with 'Mr Phang' dentist cover)	20/15
75	Harvest SHVL 814	WISH YOU WERE HERE (LP, with inner sleeve, postcard & black cellophane wraparound with sticker)	15
76	Harvest Q4 SHVL 814	WISH YOU WERE HERE (LP, quadrophonic, with inner sleeve)	35
77	Harvest SHVL 815	ANIMALS (LP, picture labels, non-barcode gatefold sleeve with inner)	12
78	Harvest SHDW 411	THE WALL (2-LP, plastic stickered gatefold sleeve, with inners)	15
79	Harvest PF 11	THE FIRST XI (11-LP set, original sleeves, plus exclusive "Dark Side Of The Moon" & "Wish You Were Here" picture discs, 1,000 only)	200
83	Harvest SHPF 1983	THE FINAL CUT (LP, gatefold sleeve with title sticker)	12
87	EMI EMD 1003	A MOMENTARY LAPSE OF REASON (LP, gatefold sleeve with inner)	12
92	EMI CDS 7805572	SHINE ON (9-CD box set, with book and postcards)	100
93	EMI CDDSOM 20	THE DARK SIDE OF THE MOON (CD, 20th anniversary box set with booklet & 5 art cards)	18
94	EMI EMD 1055	THE DIVISION BELL (LP, gatefold sleeve, with inner)	12
95	EMI EMD 578	PULSE (4-LP box set in slipcase with hardback book)	35
97	EMI 859 857-1	THE PIPER AT THE GATES OF DAWN (LP, reissue, gatefold sleeve with inner, mono)	12
97	EMI CDEMD 1110	THE PIPER AT THE GATES OF DAWN (CD, mono, 30th anniversary box set with prints)	18

MINT VALUE £

97 EMI SIGMA 630 — '97 VINYL COLLECTION
(7-LP set, die-cut box, includes "The Piper At The Gates Of Dawn" [EMD 1110], "The Wall" [EMD 1111], "Atom Heart Mother" [EMD 1112]", "Relics" [EMD 1113], "The Dark Side Of The Moon" [EMD 1114], "Wish You Were Here" [EMD 1115], each in stickered gatefold sleeve & inner [no inner on EMD 1111], withdrawn) . . 80
97 EMI CDEMD 1118 — THE FIRST THREE SINGLES (CD, mono, mini album in card gatefold sleeve) . . . 20

PROMOS

67 Columbia DB 8156 — Arnold Layne/Candy And A Currant Bun (demo copy in promo-only p/s) 2,000
67 Columbia DB 8214 — See Emily Play/Scarecrow (demo copy in promo-only p/s) 2,000
67 Columbia DB 8310 — Apples And Oranges/Paintbox (demo copy in promo-only p/s) 2,000
68 Columbia DB 8401 — It Would Be So Nice/Julia dream (demo copy in promo p/s) 2,000
68 Columbia DB 8401 — It Would Be So Nice (1-sided demo, plain white sleeve, with typed insert). . . . 1,000
68 Columbia DB 8511 — Point Me At The Sky/Careful With That Axe, Eugene (demo in promo p/s) 1,200
69 Emidisc no cat. no. — The Narrow Way (acetate, different version, 1 copy only). . . . 150
81 Harvest HAR 5217 — Money (Edited Version) (1-sided, pink vinyl, 200 only) 35
81 Harvest HAR 5217 — Money (Edited Version) (1-sided, pink vinyl, mispressing with "Let There Be More Light" label on B-side). . . . 50
87 EMI EMDJ 34 — On The Turning Away (edit)/On The Turning Away (album) (stickered p/s). . . . 8
88 EMI 12PF 1 — Delicate Sound Of Thunder Sampler: Another Brick In The Wall Part 2/ One Of These Days/Run Like Hell (12", black & pink sleeve) 20
88 EMI PSLP 1026 — Pink Floyd In Europe '88: Money/Shine On/Another Brick In The Wall Part 2/ One Slip/On The Turning Away/Learning To Fly (12", with "Another Brick . . . Part 1" miscredit on back p/s) 20
88 EMI CDPINK 1 — Wish You Were Here/Learning To Fly/Run Like Hell (CD) 20
92 EMI SHINE 1 — SELECTED TRACKS FROM "SHINE ON" (CD, card sleeve) 18

(see also Syd Barrett, Roger Waters, Dave Gilmour, Rick Wright, Nick Mason, Joker's Wild, Ron Geesin)

PINK INDUSTRY

82 Zulu ZULU 1 — Is This The End?/47/Don't Let Go/Final Cry (12", p/s). . . . 8
85 Zulu ZULU RA 8 — What I Wouldn't Give 6
83 Zulu ZULU 2 — LOW TECHNOLOGY (LP) 12
83 Zulu ZULU 4 — WHO TOLD YOU — YOU WERE NAKED (LP) 12

(see also Pink Military, Big In Japan)

PINK MILITARY

79 Last Trumpet LT 001 — BUDDHA WALKING DISNEY SLEEPING (EP, foldout sleeve) 8
79 Eric's ERIC'S 002 — BLOOD AND LIPSTICK (12" EP, die-cut p/s) 8
80 Eric's ERIC'S 005 — Did You See Her/Everyday (p/s) 5
80 Virgin/Eric's ERIC'S 004 — DO ANIMALS BELIEVE IN GOD? (LP) 12

(see also Pink Industry, Big In Japan, Ambrose Reynolds)

PINK PEOPLE

64 Philips BF 1355 — Psychologically Unsound/Cow Catcher 25
64 Philips BF 1356 — Indian Hate Call/I Dreamt I Dwelt In Marble Halls 20

(see also Four Squares)

PINKY (& FELLAS)

65 Polydor BM 56009 — All Cried Out/Back Where I Belong 6
68 Decca F 12748 — Manchester And Liverpool/Come Back Again (as Pinky & Fellas). . . . 5
69 Polydor BM 56338 — Let The Music Start/Oh, A Beautiful Day (as Pinky & Fellas) 5

PINKY & PERKY

58 Decca F 11095 — Tom Dooley/The Velvet Glove (Pinky & Perky Theme) (some in p/s). . . . 8/5
58 Decca F 11095 — Tom Dooley/The Velvet Glove (Pinky & Perky Theme) (78, some in 10" p/s). . . 20/12
59 Decca F 11116 — The Little Mountaineer/Does Your Chewing Gum Lose Its Flavour (some in p/s) 25/15
59 Decca F 11116 — The Little Mountaineer/Does Your Chewing Gum Lose Its Flavour (78, some in 10" p/s) 20/12
59 Decca F 11174 — Pinky And Perky's Sing Song Medley (both sides). . . . 5
59 Decca F 11174 — Pinky And Perky's Sing Song Medley (both sides) (78) 20
60 Columbia DB 4538 — Eeny Meeney Miney Mo/The Ugly Duckling 5
61 Columbia DB 4710 — What's New At The Zoo?/Dream Your Tears Away. . . . 5
65 Columbia DB 7548 — Hole In My Bucket/Glow Worm 5
60 Columbia SEG 8058 — CHILDREN'S CHOICE (EP) 8
61 Columbia SEG 8122 — CHRISTMAS WITH PINKY & PERKY (EP) 8
62 Columbia SEG 8152 — PINKY & PERKY OUT WEST (EP) 8
63 Columbia SEG 8261 — DOWN ON THE FARM (EP). . . . 8
63 Columbia SEG 8344 — NURSERY ROMP (EP) 8
68 MFP MFP 1282 — HIT PARADE (LP) 12

PINNACLE

74 Stag HP 125 — ASSASSIN (LP, later pressings on Little Wing worth £25) 150

PIONEERS

66 Rio R 102 — Good Nannie/Doreen Girl. . . . 25
66 Rio R 106 — Too Late/Give Up 25
68 Blue Cat BS 100 — Shake It Up/Rudies Are The Greatest 25
68 Blue Cat BS 103 — Give It To Me/LEADERS: Someday Someway 25
68 Blue Cat BS 105 — Whip Them/Having A Bawl. . . . 25
68 Blue Cat BS 139 — Reggae Beat/Miss Eva 25
68 Caltone TONE 119 — I Love No Other Girl/MILTON BOOTHE: I Used To Be A Fool 30
68 Amalgamated AMG 811 — Give Me A Little Loving/This Is Soul (B-side actually by Lyn Tait & Jets) 18
68 Amalgamated AMG 814 — Long Shot/Dip And Fall Back. . . . 18
68 Amalgamated AMG 821 — Jackpot/CREATORS: Kimble (B-side actually by Lee Perry) 35
68 Amalgamated AMG 823 — No Dope Me Pony/LORD SALMONS: Great — Great In '68 15
68 Amalgamated AMG 826 — Tickle Me For Days/VERSATILES: The Time Has Come 15
68 Amalgamated AMG 828 — Catch The Beat/SIR GIBB'S ALLSTARS: Jana (B-side actually Immortals' "Jane Anne") 18
68 Amalgamated AMG 830 — Sweet Dreams/DON DRUMMOND JUNIOR: Caterpillar Rock 18

68	Pyramid PYR 6062	Easy Come, Easy Go/BEVERLEY'S ALLSTARS: Only A Smile (B-side actually by Lyn Tait & Jets)	15
69	Pyramid PYR 6065	Pee Pee Cluck Cluck/BEVERLEY'S ALLSTARS: Exclusively	15
69	Amalgamated AMG 833	Don't You Know/Me Naw Go A Believe	15
69	Amalgamated AMG 835	Mama Look Deh/BLENDERS: Decimal Currency	15
69	Amalgamated AMG 840	Who The Cap Fits/I'm Moving On	12
69	Amalgamated AMG 850	Alli Button/HIPPY BOYS: Death Rides	15
69	Trojan TR 672	Long Shot Kick The Bucket/RICO: Jumping The Gun	6
69	Trojan TR 685	Black Bud/Too Late	7
69	Trojan TR 698	Poor Rameses/BEVERLEY'S ALLSTARS: In Orbit	6
70	Trojan TR 7781	Money Day/BEVERLEY ALL STARS: Ska Ba Do	8
71	Summit SUM 8511	Starvation/BEVERLEY'S ALLSTARS: Version	7
72	Summit SUM 8535	Story Book Children/SIDNEY, GEORGE AND JACKIE: Gorgeous, Marvellous	7
77	Mercury 6007147	My Good Friend James/Secrets Of You	35
78	Ice GUY 14	My Good Friend James/Secrets Of You (reissue)	30
68	Amalgam. AMGLP 2003	GREETINGS FROM THE PIONEERS (LP)	80
70	Trojan TBL 103	LONGSHOT (LP)	25
70	Trojan TBL 139	BATTLE OF THE GIANTS (LP)	20
71	Trojan TRL 24	YEAH! (LP)	15

(see also Sir Gibbs, Rebels [Jamaica], Jackey Robinson, Moonboys, Sidney George & Jackie)

PIPES OF PAN

67	Page One POF 038	Monday Morning Rain/Monday Morning Rain (Instrumental Mix)	10

PIPES OF PAN

71	Rolling Stones COC 49100	BRIAN JONES PLAYS WITH THE PIPES OF PAN AT JOUJOUKA (LP, gatefold sleeve with foldout insert; front cover with misprinted title)	90
71	Rolling Stones COC 49100	BRIAN JONES PRESENTS THE PIPES OF PAN AT JOUJOUKA (LP, gatefold sleeve with foldout insert; "Presents" sticker on misprinted cover)	70
71	Rolling Stones COC 49100	BRIAN JONES PRESENTS THE PIPES OF PAN AT JOUJOUKA (LP, gatefold sleeve with foldout insert; corrected title on front cover)	65

(see also Rolling Stones)

PIPKINS

(see under Sweet)

PIPS

61	Top Rank JAR 574	Every Beat Of My Heart/Room In Your Heart	55

(see also Gladys Knight & Pips)

PI-R-SQUARE

00	Jazzman JM 017	Fantasy/Fantasy (Pt 2)	5

PIRATES

64	HMV POP 1250	My Babe/Casting My Spell	35
66	Polydor BM 56712	Shades Of Blue/Can't Understand	25
77	Warner Bros K 17002	Sweet Love On My Mind/You Don't Own Me (p/s)	12
78	Warner Bros K 17113	All In It Together/Dr. Feelgood (p/s)	10
78	Warner Bros K 17231	Shakin' All Over/Saturday Night Shoot Out	5
79	Sound For Industry SFI 431	All By Myself/Cat Clothes (1-sided fan club flexidisc, gold vinyl)	5
79	Cube Hi Fly 33	HAPPY BIRTHDAY ROCK N' ROLL (LP, with flexidisc [PIR 2])	12

(see also Johnny Kidd & Pirates, [Billy J. Kramer &] Dakotas)

PISCES

71	Trailer LER 2025	PISCES (LP)	30

HARRY PITCH

68	MOR MR 101P	HARMONICA JEWEL BOX (LP)	20

(see also Mr. Bloe)

PITCH PIKES

57	Mercury MT 171	Come Back To Me/How Will I Know (78)	8

PITCH SHIFTER

92	Earache MOSH 66	SUBMIT EP (12")	8

GENE PITNEY

SINGLES

61	London HL 9270	(I Wanna) Love My Life Away/I Laughed So Hard I Cried	18
61	HMV POP 933	Every Breath I Take/Mr Moon, Mr Cupid & I	25
61	United Artists POP 952	Town Without Pity/Air Mail Special	12
62	United Artists POP 1018	The Man Who Shot Liberty Valance/Take It Like A Man	12
62	United Artists UP 1005	If I Didn't Have A Dime/Only Love Can Break A Heart	8
63	United Artists UP 1012	Half Heaven, Half Heartache/Tower Tall	8
63	United Artists UP 1021	Mecca/Teardrop By Teardrop	8
63	United Artists UP 1030	True Love Never Runs Smooth/Donna Means Heartbreak	7
63	United Artists UP 1035	24 Hours From Tulsa/Lonely Night Dreams (blue or black label)	6
64	United Artists UP 1045	That Girl Belongs To Yesterday/Who Needs It?	7
64	United Artists UP 1055	I'm Gonna Find Myself A Girl/Lips Are Redder On You	12
64	United Artists UP 1063	It Hurts To Be In Love/Hawaii	8
64	Stateside SS 358	I'm Gonna Be Strong/Aladdin's Lamp	7
64	Stateside SS 365	It Hurts To Be In Love/Hawaii (reissue)	7
65	Stateside SS 390	I Must Be Seeing Things/Save Your Love	7
65	Stateside SS 420	Lookin' Thru The Eyes Of Love/Last Chance To Turn Around	7
65	Stateside SS 471	Princess In Rags/Amore Mio	7
66	Stateside SS 490	Backstage/In Love Again	7
66	Stateside SS 518	Nobody Needs Your Love/Dream World	7
66	Stateside SS 558	Just One Smile/The Boss's Daughter	7
67	Stateside SS 597	(In The) Cold Light Of Day/Flower Girl	7
67	Stateside SS 2060	Something's Gotten Hold Of My Heart/Where Did The Magic Go	6

MINT VALUE £

68	Stateside SS 2103	Somewhere In The Country/Lonely Drifter	6
68	Stateside SS 2118	Love Grows/Conquistador	6
68	Stateside SS 2131	Yours Until Tomorrow/She's A Heartbreaker	10
69	Stateside SS 2142	Maria Elena/The French Horn	6
70	Stateside SS 2177	Shady Lady/Billy, You're My Friend	6
71	Pye International 7N 25564	Run Run Road Runner/Rain Maker	6
72	Pye International 7N 25579	I Just Can't Help Myself/Beautiful Sounds	6
EPs			
63	HMV 7EG 8832	TOWN WITHOUT PITY	65
64	United Artists UEP 1001	TWENTY FOUR HOURS FROM TULSA	15
64	United Artists UEP 1002	THAT GIRL BELONGS TO YESTERDAY	12
65	Stateside SE 1027	TWENTY FOUR HOURS FROM TULSA (reissue)	15
65	Stateside SE 1028	THAT GIRL BELONGS TO YESTERDAY (reissue)	12
65	Stateside SE 1030	I MUST BE SEEING THINGS	15
65	Stateside SE 1032	GENE ITALIANO	18
66	Stateside SE 1036	GENE PITNEY SINGS JUST FOR YOU	12
66	Stateside SE 1040	BACKSTAGE	15
66	Stateside SE 1041	SAN REMO WINNERS AND OTHERS	18
67	Stateside SE 1045	THERE'S NO LIVING WITHOUT YOUR LOVING	15
66	Bravo BR 375	GENE PITNEY	10
LPs			
62	HMV CLP 1566	THE MANY SIDES OF GENE PITNEY	50
63	United Artists (S)ULP 1028	ONLY LOVE CAN BREAK A HEART (mono/stereo)	30/40
63	United Artists ULP 1043	GENE PITNEY SINGS JUST FOR YOU	22
64	United Artists ULP 1061	BLUE GENE	22
64	United Artists ULP 1064	GENE PITNEY MEETS THE FAIR YOUNG LADIES OF FOLKLAND	22
64	United Artists ULP 1073	GENE PITNEY'S BIG SIXTEEN	20
65	Stateside SL 10118	GENE PITNEY'S BIG SIXTEEN (reissue)	15
65	Stateside SL 10119	BLUE GENE (reissue)	15
65	Stateside SL 10120	I'M GONNA BE STRONG	18
65	Stateside SL 10132	GENE PITNEY'S MORE BIG SIXTEEN (VOL. 2)	20
65	Stateside SL 10147	GEORGE JONES AND GENE PITNEY (with George Jones)	20
65	Stateside SL 10148	LOOKING THRU THE EYES OF LOVE	18
65	Stateside SL 10156	SINGS THE GREAT SONGS OF OUR TIME	20
66	Stateside SL 10173	IT'S COUNTRY TIME AGAIN (with George Jones)	20
66	Stateside S(S)L 10181	BEING TOGETHER (with Melba Montgomery)	18
66	Stateside S(S)L 10183	NOBODY NEEDS YOUR LOVE	18
67	Stateside S(S)L 10194	YOUNG, WARM AND WONDERFUL	18
67	Stateside S(S)L 10199	GENE PITNEY'S BIG SIXTEEN (VOL. 3)	20
67	Stateside S(S)L 10212	JUST ONE SMILE	18
67	Stateside S(S)L 10216	GOLDEN GREATS	15
68	Stateside S(S)L 10242	PITNEY TODAY	18
69	Stateside S(S)L 10286	THE BEST OF GENE PITNEY	15
71	Pye Intl. NSPL 28148	TEN YEARS LATER	15
72	Pye Intl. NSPL 28165	THE NEW SOUNDS OF GENE PITNEY	15

(see also Marc Almond & Gene Pitney, George Jones)

PETE PITTERSON

52	Esquire 5-058	West Indian Folk Music/Bali Game (78)	10

PIXIES

88	4AD BAD 805	Gigantic/River Euphrates/Vamos (live)/In Heaven (Lady In The Radiator Song) (live) (12", p/s)	8
88	4AD BAD 805CD	Gigantic/River Euphrates/Vamos (live)/In Heaven (Lady In The Radiator Song) (live) (CD)	10
89	4AD AD 904	Monkey Gone To Heaven/Manta Ray (p/s)	5
89	4AD BAD 904CD	Monkey Gone To Heaven/Manta Ray/Weird At My School/ Dancing The Manta Ray (CD)	12
90	4AD C 0009	Velouria/Make Believe (cassette)	5
89	4AD PIX ONE	DOOLITTLE SAMPLER: Debaser/Wave Of Mutilation/I Bleed/Gouge Away (12", 1-sided, title sleeve, promo only)	20
89	4AD PIX 2	Into The White/Wave Of Mutilation (U.K. Surf) (12", 1-sided, promo only)	10
90	4AD PIX 3	EXTRACTS FROM BOSSANOVA: Allison/Rock Music/Down To The Well/ The Happening (12", 1-sided, promo only)	15
90	4AD AD 0014	Dig For Fire (p/s)	6
91	4AD PIX 4	EXTRACTS FROM TROMPE LE MONDE: U-Mass/Letter To Memphis/ Subbacultcha (10", same track both sides, promo only)	15
04	4AD PIX 2004CD	BEST OF PIXIES (CD, 5-track sampler, promo only)	20
87	4AD MAD 709	COME ON PILGRIM (mini-LP)	15
88	4AD CAD 803	SURFER ROSA (LP, with inner)	20
89	4AD CAD 905	DOOLITTLE (LP, with lyric booklet & postcard, some in carrier bag)	30/25
90	4AD CAD 0010	BOSSANOVA (LP, with booklet)	20

(see also Breeders, Frank Black)

PIXIES THREE

63	Mercury AMT 1214	Birthday Party/Our Love	20

PIZZICATO 5

97	Matador OLE 289-7	Mon Amour Tokyo/Trailer Music (p/s)	5

P.J. HARVEY

(see under 'H')

PLACEBO

95	Fierce Panda NING 13	Bruise Pristine/SOUP: M.E.L.T.D.O.W.N. (foldover p/s, 1500 only)	40
96	Deceptive BLUFF 024	Come Home/Drowning By Numbers (p/s)	15
96	Deceptive BLUFF 024	Come Home/Drowning By Numbers (CD)	25
96	Hut FLOOR 3	Teenage Angst/Hug Bubble/Been Smoking Too Long (p/s)	10
96	Hut FLOORCD 3	Teenage Angst/Hug Bubble/Been Smoking Too Long (CD, card sleeve)	12

96	Hut FLOOR 4	Nancy Boy (Sex Mix)/Slackerbitch (p/s)	12
97	Hut FLOOR 5	Bruise Pristine/(One Punch Remix) (p/s)	12
98	Hut SILVER 1	THE ORIGINAL DEMOS: Nancy Boy/Teenage Angst/36 Degrees/ Bruise Pristine (CD, fan club issue, card sleeve)	18
99	Hut FLOOR TP 10	Without You I'm Nothing (with David Bowie) (UNKLE Remix)/ (Flexirol Mix)/(Brothers In Rhythm Club Mix) (12" promo, 500 only, stickered die-cut sleeve)	20
99	Hut FLOOR CD 10	Without You I'm Nothing (Single Mix)/(UNKLE Remix)/(Flexirol Mix)/ (Brothers In Rhythm Club Mix) (multimedia CD, gatefold card sleeve)	15
99	Elevator SILVER 2	I Feel You (1-track cassette, fan club issue)	50
96	Hut LPFLOORY 2	PLACEBO (LP)	35
96	Hut CD FLOOR 2	PLACEBO (CD, digipak, 5000 only)	30

PLAGUE

68	Decca F 12730	Looking For The Sun/Here Today, Gone Tomorrow	100

PLAGUE

80	Evolution EV 1	In Love/Wimpey Bar Song (some in p/s)	250/200

PLAID

92	GPR GENP(X) 7	Scoobs In Columbia (remixes) (12", custom sleeve)	40
94	Clear CLR 409	ANDROID (12" EP, p/s, clear or black vinyl)	40/30
95	Rumble RUMBLE 01	MIND OVER RHYTHM MEET THE MEN FROM PLAID (3 x 10" in p/s)	25
92	Black Dog Prods. LP 1	MBUKI MVUKI (LP)	125

(see also Black Dog)

PLAIN CHARACTERS

(see under Gadgets)

PLAINSONG

72	Elektra K 12976	Even The Guiding Light/Yoko Man/Call The Tune	5
72	Elektra K 42120	IN SEARCH OF AMELIA EARHART (LP, gatefold sleeve with lyric insert)	18
73	Elektra K 42136	PLAINSONG II (LP, white label, promo only)	100

(see also Andy Roberts, Ian Matthews)

PLANET GONG

77	Affinity AF 5101	Opium For The People/Poet For Sale (p/s)	8
78	Charly CYX 202	Opium For The People/Stoned Innocent Frankenstein (10", p/s)	18
78	Charly	FLOATING ANARCHY — LIVE 1977 (LP)	18

(see also Daevid Allen, Gong)

PLANET P PROJECT

83	Geffen A 3204	Why Me?/Only You And Me (p/s)	6
83	Geffen GEF 25367	PLANET P PROJECT (LP, with inner sleeve)	12
85	MCA MCSP 311	PINK WORLD (2-LP, gatefold sleeve)	18

(see also Tony Carey, Rainbow)

PLANETS

60	Palette PG 9008	Like Party/Ippy Yippy Beatnik (some in p/s)	20/15

PLANETS

60	HMV POP 818	Chunky/Screwball	15
61	HMV POP 832	Jam Roll/Delaney's Theme	20
61	HMV POP 895	Jungle Street/The Grasshopper	20

ROBERT PLANT

67	CBS 202656	Our Song/Laughin', Cryin', Laughin'	300
67	CBS 202656	Our Song/Laughin' Cryin' Laughin' ('A' label demo)	250
67	CBS 202858	Long Time Coming/I've Got A Secret	300
67	CBS 202858	Long Time Coming/I've Got A Secret ('A' label demo)	250
82	Swan Song SSK 19429T	Burning Down One Side/Far Post (12", p/s)	10
83	WEA B 9848	Big Log/Messin' With The Mekon (p/s)	5
85	Es Paranza B 9621 F	Little By Little (Remix)/Doo Doo A Do Do//Easily Lead (live)/ Rockin' At Midnight (live) (double pack)	8
88	Es Paranza A 9373 TB	Heaven Knows (Extended Remix)/Walking Towards Paradise/Heaven Knows (Astral Mix) (12", stickered sealed box set with colour poster & 2 prints)	8
88	Es Paranza A 9373 CD	Heaven Knows/Walking Towards Paradise/Big Log (3" CD & adaptor, 5" case)	8
88	Es Paranza A 9348 CD	Tall Cool One/White, Clean And Neat/Tall Cool One (Extended Version)/ Little By Little (3" CD, with adaptor, 5" case)	8
88	Es Paranza A 9281 CDB	Ship Of Fools/Helen Of Troy (live)/Dimples (live) (3" CD, with adaptor & 5" case, inside 5" box set with card, foldout lyric sheet & 2-page biography)	8
90	Es Paranza A 8985P	Hurting Kind (I've Got My Eyes On You)/I Cried (shaped picture disc)	5
90	Es Paranza A 8985	Hurting Kind (I've Got my Eyes On You)/Don't Look Back/Oompah (Watery Bint)/One Love (CD)	8
93	Fontana FATE 212	I Believe/Hey Jane/Great Spirit (Acoustic)/Whole Lotta Love (You Need Love) (12" limited edition picture disc)	10
93	Fontana FATEX 4	If I Were A Carpenter/I Believe (live)/Tall Cool One (live) (limited issue, clear plastic sleeve)	8
93	Fontana/Es Paranza FATE 1	Fate Of Nations/Interview (radio promo)	20
03	Mercury LASTCJ 1	Last Time I Saw Her (Remix) (CD, radio promo)	8
90	Es Paranza WX 339X	MANIC NIRVANA (LP, gatefold sleeve)	12
02	Mercury (no cat. no.)	HEAD FIRST (LP, promo)	25
02	Mercury 063 4652	DREAMLAND COLLECTORS EDITION (CD, limited issue, with bonus CD)	18
02	Mercury (no cat. no.)	DREAMLAND (LP, promo)	20
02	Mercury PLANT CJ 1	DREAMLAND (CD, card sleeve)	18
02	Mercury DREAMINT 1	DREAMLAND INTERVIEW DISC (CD, radio promo)	18
03	Mercury PLANT 1/2	66 TO TIMBUKTU (3-CD, promo, with bonus album sampler CD, in folder with press release)	30

(see also Led Zeppelin, Listen, Jimmy Page, Page & Plant, Honeydrippers)

MINT VALUE £

PLANXTY

73	Polydor 2383 186	PLANXTY (LP)	12
73	Polydor 2383 232	THE WELL BELOW THE VALLEY (LP)	12
74	Polydor 2383 301	COLD BLOW AND RAINY NIGHT (LP)	12
76	Polydor 2389 387	THE PLANXTY COLLECTION (LP, gatefold sleeve)	12
79	Tara 3001	AFTER THE BREAK (LP, with poster & lyric insert)	12
80	Tara 3005	THE WOMAN I LOVED SO WELL (LP)	12

PLASTIC GANGSTERS

83	Secret SHH 144	Plastic Gangsters/Sretsgnag Citsalp (7", 12", no p/s, unissued, DJ copies only)	each 200

(see also 4 Skins)

PLASTIC ONO BAND

(see under John Lennon, Yoko Ono)

PLASTIC PENNY

67	Page One POF 051	Everything I Am/No Pleasure Without Pain My Love	7
68	Page One POF 062	Nobody Knows It/Just Happy To Be With You	8
68	Page One POF 079	Your Way To Tell Me Go/Baby You're Not To Blame	15
69	Page One POF 107	Hound Dog/Currency	22
69	Page One POF 146	She Does/Genevieve	8
68	Page One POL(S) 005	TWO SIDES OF THE PENNY (LP)	50
69	Page One POLS 014	CURRENCY (LP)	50
70	Page One POLS 611	HEADS YOU WIN, TAILS I LOSE (LP)	45

(see also Universals, Circles, Brian Keith, Mick Grabham)

PLASTIKMAN

94	NovaMute L NO MU 37	MUSIK (2-LP, with bonus 1-sided etched 12")	15

PLATFORM SIX

65	Piccadilly 7N 35255	Money Will Not Mean A Thing/Girl Down Town	20

EDDIE PLATT

58	Columbia DB 4101	Tequila/Pop Corn	25
58	Columbia DB 4101	Tequila/Pop Corn (78)	8

PLATTERS

78s

55	Parlophone DP 433	Voo-Vee-Ah-Bee/STRANGERS: Just Don't Care (export issue)	40
56	Parlophone DP 506	Beer Barrel Boogie/Roses Of Picardy (export issue)	40
56	Mercury MT 107	(You've Got) The Magic Touch/Winner Takes All	15
58	Mercury MT 197	Helpless/Indiff'rent	10
58	Mercury MT 205	Don't Let Go/Are You Sincere?	10
58	Mercury MT 214	Twilight Time/Out Of My Mind	7
58	Mercury MT 227	You're Making A Mistake (featuring Tony Williams)/My Old Flame	12
58	Mercury AMT 1001	I Wish/It's Raining Outside	15
58	Mercury AMT 1016	Smoke Gets In Your Eyes/No Matter What You Are	20
59	Mercury AMT 1039	Enchanted/The Sound And The Fury	30
59	Mercury AMT 1053	Remember When/Love Of A Lifetime (featuring Tony Williams)	35
60	Mercury AMT 1081	Harbour Lights/(By The) Sleepy Lagoon	45

45s

56	Mercury MT 117	The Great Pretender/Only You (And You Alone) (export issue)	35
58	Mercury 7MT 197	Helpless/Indiff'rent	40
58	Mercury 7MT 205	Don't Let Go/Are You Sincere?	30
58	Mercury 7MT 214	Twilight Time/Out Of My Mind	12
58	Mercury 7MT 227	You're Making A Mistake (featuring Tony Williams)/My Old Flame	20
58	Mercury AMT 1001	I Wish/It's Raining Outside	18
58	Mercury AMT 1016	Smoke Gets In Your Eyes/No Matter What You Are	8
59	Mercury AMT 1039	Enchanted/The Sound And The Fury	6
59	Mercury AMT 1053	Remember When/Love Of A Lifetime (featuring Tony Williams)	6
59	Mercury AMT 1066	My Blue Heaven/Wish It Were Me	7
60	Mercury AMT 1076	My Secret/What Does It Matter	6
60	Mercury AMT 1081	Harbour Lights/(By The) Sleepy Lagoon	6
60	Mercury AMT 1098	Ebb Tide/(I'll Be With You In) Apple Blossom Time (featuring Tony Williams)	6
60	Mercury AMT 1106	Red Sails In The Sunset/Sad River (featuring Tony Williams)	6
60	Mercury AMT 1118	To Each His Own/Down The River Of Golden Dreams	6
61	Mercury AMT 1128	If I Didn't Care/True Lover	6
61	Mercury AMT 1154	I'll Never Smile Again/You Don't Say	6
62	Ember JBS 701	Only You/Tell The World	200
66	Stateside SS 511	I Love You 1000 Times/Hear No Evil, Speak No Evil, See No Evil	18
66	Stateside SS 568	I'll Be Home/(You've Got) The Magic Touch	8
67	Stateside SS 2007	With This Ring/If I Had A Love	12
67	Stateside SS 2042	Washed Ashore (On A Lonely Island In The Sea)/ What Name Shall I Give You My Love	12
67	Stateside SS 2067	Sweet Sweet Lovin'/Sonata	12
69	Stateside SS 2150	With This Ring/If I Had A Love (reissue)	7
71	Pye Intl. 7N 25559	Sweet Sweet Lovin'/Going Back To Detroit	7
71	Pye Intl. 7N 25569	With This Ring/I Washed Ashore (On A Lonely Island In The Sea)	8

EPs

56	Mercury MEP 9504	THE FABULOUS PLATTERS	15
57	Mercury MEP 9514	THE FABULOUS PLATTERS VOL. II	18
57	Mercury MEP 9524	THE FABULOUS PLATTERS VOL. III	20
58	Mercury MEP 9526	THE FLYING PLATTERS VOL. I	22
58	Mercury MEP 9528	THE FLYING PLATTERS VOL. II	22
58	Mercury MEP 9537	THE PLATTERS	25
59	Mercury ZEP 10000	PICK OF THE PLATTERS NO. 1	20
59	Mercury ZEP 10008	PICK OF THE PLATTERS NO. 2	20
59	Mercury ZEP 10025	PICK OF THE PLATTERS NO. 3	20

59	Mercury ZEP 10031	PICK OF THE PLATTERS NO. 4	25
59	Mercury ZEP 10042	PICK OF THE PLATTERS NO. 5	25
60	Mercury ZEP 10056	PICK OF THE PLATTERS NO. 6	22
60	Mercury ZEP 10070	PICK OF THE PLATTERS NO. 7	22
61	Mercury ZEP 10112	HARBOUR LIGHTS	25
62	Mercury ZEP 10126	THE PLATTERS ON A PLATTER	35

LPs

57	Mercury MPL 6504	THE PLATTERS	45
57	Mercury MPL 6511	THE PLATTERS VOL. 2	45
58	Mercury MPL 6528	THE FLYING PLATTERS	35
58	Parlophone PMD 1058	THE PLATTERS (10")	325
59	Mercury MMC 14009	AROUND THE WORLD WITH THE FLYING PLATTERS	35
59	Mercury MMC 14010	THE PLATTERS ON PARADE	35
59	Mercury MMC 14014	REMEMBER WHEN?	30
60	Mercury MMC 14045	REFLECTIONS	25
61	Mercury MMC 14072	LIFE IS JUST A BOWL OF CHERRIES	25
62	Ember EMB 3339	THE BEST OF THE PLATTERS	12
62	Mercury MMC 14091	GOLDEN HITS	15
64	Mercury MCL 20000	THE PLATTERS SING LATINO	15
64	Concert Hall CJ 1255	THE PLATTERS	12
66	Wing WL 1044	REFLECTIONS (reissue)	12
67	Stateside S(S)L 10208	GOING BACK TO DETROIT	15
67	Wing WL 1174	TENTH ANNIVERSARY ALBUM	12
68	Stateside S(S)L 10227	THE NEW GOLDEN HITS OF THE PLATTERS	12
68	Stateside S(S)L 10245	SWEET, SWEET LOVIN'	15
68	Polydor Special 236 223	ONLY YOU	12
68	Fontana SFL 13040	THE PLATTERS SING LATINO (reissue)	12
71	Pye Intl. NSPL 28149	OUR WAY	12

(see also Buck Ram's Ramrocks, Linda Hayes)

PLAYBOY CLUB BUNNIES

68	Decca F 12832	Keep The Ball Rollin'/I Only Want To Be With You	6

PLAYBOYS

60s	Lyntone LYN 549/550	THE PLAYBOYS FOR CHARITY (EP, flexidisc, no p/s)	15

PLAYBOYS (Jamaica)

71	Tropical AL 007	Change Change/TROPICAL ALL STARS: Version 2	6

PLAYBOYS (U.S.)

58	London HLU 8681	Over The Weekend/Double Talk	40
58	London HLU 8681	Over The Weekend/Double Talk (78)	20

PLAYBOYS (U.S.)

69	Capitol CL 15621	Let's Get Back To Rock And Roll/Homemade Cookin'	6

(see also Rad Bryan)

PLAY DEAD

81	Fresh FRESH 29	Poison Takes A Hold/Introduction (p/s)	12
81	Fresh FRESH 38	T.V. Eye/Final Epitaph (p/s)	12

PLAYERS

63	Oriole CB 1861	Mockingbird/Bizet As It May	18

PLAYGIRLS (Jamaica)

65	Black Swan WI 456	Looks Are Deceiving/BABA BROOKS: Dreadnaught	30

PLAYGIRLS (U.S.)

59	RCA RCA 1133	Hey Sport/Young Love Swings The World	22
59	RCA RCA 1133	Hey Sport/Young Love Swings The World (78)	20

PLAYGROUND

67	MGM MGM 1351	At The Zoo/Yellow Balloon	12
69	NEMS 56-4019	I Could Be So Good/The Girl Behind The Smile	6
69	NEMS 56-4442	Things I Do For You/Lazy Days	6

PLAYMATES

53	London L 1198	My Love Was Wasted On You/You Never Get Too Old To Fall In Love (78)	10
57	Columbia DB 3941	Pretty Woman/Barefoot Girl	15
57	Columbia DB 4033	Island Girl/Darling, It's Wonderful	15
58	Columbia DB 4084	Jo-Ann/You Can't Stop Me From Dreaming	12
58	Columbia DB 4127	Let's Be Lovers/Give Me Another Chance	10
58	Columbia DB 4151	Can't You Get It Through Your Head/Don't Go Home	8
58	Columbia DB 4207	While The Record Goes Around/The Day I Died	8
58	Columbia DB 4224	Beep Beep/Your Love	8
58	Columbia DB 4224	Beep Beep/Your Love (78)	8
59	Columbia DB 4288	Star Love/The Thing-A-Ma-Jig	6
59	Columbia DB 4338	What Is Love?/I Am	8
59	Columbia DB 4389	On The Beach/First Love	6
60	Columbia DB 4468	Parade Of Pretty Girls/Jubilation T. Cornpone	6
60	Columbia DB 4551	Wait For Me/Eyes Of An Angel	6
61	Columbia DB 4628	Little Miss Stuck Up/Real Life	6
59	Columbia SEG 7949	PARTY PLAYMATES NO. 1 (EP)	12
59	Columbia SEG 7966	PARTY PLAYMATES NO. 2 (EP)	12
60	Columbia 33SX 1215	BROADWAY SHOW STOPPERS (LP, also stereo SCX 3300)	12/15

PLAYMATES (Ireland)

70	Emerald MD 1150	Don't Fight It/Jodi	10

PLAYTHINGS

70	Pye 7N 45212	Stop What You're Doing To Me/Sad Songs (re-pressed 1973)	8
73	Pye 7N 45399	Surrounded By A Ray Of Sunshine/Dance The Night Away	5

MINT VALUE £

BOBBY PLEASE
57 London HLB 8507 — Your Driver's Licence, Please (unissued, 1-sided demo only) . . . 300+
57 London HLB 8507 — Your Driver's Licence, Please/Heartache Street (78) . . . 100

PLEASERS
77 Solid Gold SGR 104 — You Know What I'm Thinking/Hello Little Girl . . . 8
77 Arista ARIST 21 — Girl I Know/Don't Go Breaking My Heart (p/s) . . . 5
77 Arista ARIST 152 — You Keep Tellin' Lies/I'm In Love/Who Are You (p/s, silver or blue labels) . . . 5/8
78 Arista ARIST 180 — The Kids Are Alright/Stay With Me (p/s) . . . 10

PLEASURE
75 Fantasy FTC 115 — Dust Yourself Off/Midnight At The Oasis . . . 5
78 Fantasy FT 543 — GET TO THE FEELIN' (LP) . . . 12

PLEASURE BEACH
90s Acid Jazz AJX 124S — Rollercoaster/Smells Like Teen Spirit (p/s) . . . 15

PLEASURE FAIR
68 Uni UN 500 — Morning Glory Blues/Fade Out Fade In . . . 8
67 Uni UNL(S) 100 — PLEASURE FAIR (LP) . . . 20
(see also Bread)

PLEASURE GARDEN
68 Sound For Industry SFI 31H/32H — Permissive Paradise/EMPEROR ROSKO & JONATHAN KING: Young London (flexidisc, art sleeve) . . . 40
(see also Iveys)

PLEASURES
65 Sue WI 357 — Music City/If I Had A Little Money . . . 30

PLEBS
64 Decca F 12006 — Bad Blood/Babe I'm Gonna Leave You . . . 75
60s Oak — THE PLEBS (LP, 1-sided, private pressing) . . . 1000+

JACK PLEIS & HIS ORCHESTRA
56 Brunswick 05534 — The Trouble With Harry (with Bonnie Lake & Her Beaux)/Pauline . . . 6
57 Brunswick 05634 — Giant (with Ralph Young)/Lonesome Without You . . . 6
59 Brunswick 05795 — Theme From "Compulsion"/Romantico . . . 5
59 Brunswick 05795 — Theme From "Compulsion"/Romantico (78) . . . 8
61 Brunswick 05846 — Pepe/Theme From "The Sundowners" . . . 5
(see also Ralph Young, Bonnie Lake & Her Beaux)

PLEXUS
78 Look LKLP 6175 — PLEXUS (LP) . . . 65
79 Hill & Dale HD004 — LIFE UP THE CREEK (LP) . . . 55

PLONE
97 Wurlitzer Jukebox WJ 36 — Press A Key/Electronic Beauty Parlour (p/s, red vinyl, 300 only) . . . 6

PLUGS
79 Cathedral CATH 1 — Too Late/UFO/Sally (gatefold p/s) . . . 20

JEAN PLUM
76 London HLU 10514 — Look At The Boy/Back At You . . . 10

PLUM & YOUTH
80s Checkmount CHK 1 — I Got You Babe/Got To Be Moving On (p/s, withdrawn) . . . 15
(see also Cozy Powell, Rainbow, Bernie Marsden)

PLUMMERS
64 Blue Beat BB 260 — Johnny/Little Stars (actually by Plamers) . . . 22

PLUS
70 Probe SPB 1009 — SEVEN DEADLY SINS (LP) . . . 20

PLUTO
71 Dawn DNS 1017 — Rag A Bone Joe/Stealing My Thunder . . . 20
72 Dawn DNS 1026 — I Really Want It/Something That You Loved . . . 25
71 Dawn DNLS 3030 — PLUTO (LP) . . . 60
(see also Dry Ice, Foundations)

NICK PLYTAS & ANN PIGALLE
82 Illuminated ILL 1210 — HOT SAGAS (10" EP) . . . 7

PNEUMONIA
68 Oak RGJ 625 — I Can See Your Face . . . 200

PNEUMONIA
79 Plastic PLAS 001 — Exhibition/Coming Attack/U.K. DECAY: U.K. Decay/Carcrash (folded p/s) . . . 18
(see also U.K. Decay)

POCO
71 Epic EQ 30209 — DELIVERIN' (LP, quadrophonic) . . . 12
(see also Buffalo Springfield, Au Go-Go Singers)

POEMS
81 Polka DOT 1 — ACHIEVING UNITY (EP, initially with booklet) . . . 10
(see also Strawberry Switchblade)

POET & ONE MAN BAND
69 Verve Forecast SVLP 6012 — THE POET AND THE ONE MAN BAND (LP) . . . 45
(see also Tony Colton, Nicky Hopkins, Heads Hands & Feet)

POETS
64 Decca F 11995 — Now We're Thru/There Are Some . . . 20
65 Decca F 12074 — That's The Way It's Got To Be/I'll Cry With The Moon . . . 90
65 Decca F 12195 — I Am So Blue/I Love Her Still . . . 50
65 Immediate IM 006 — Call Again/Some Things I Can't Forget . . . 100

			MINT VALUE £
66	Immediate IM 024	Baby Don't You Do It/I'll Come Home	100
67	Decca F 12569	Wooden Spoon/In Your Tower	300
71	Strike Cola SC 1	Heyla Hola/Fun Buggy	60
88	Bam Caruso OPRA 088	I Love Her Still/GHOST: Time Is My Enemy (company sleeve, promo only)	12

(see also Pathfinders, [White] Trash, Blue)

POETS (Ireland)

68	Pye 7N 17668	Locked In A Room/Alone Am I	150
68	Target 7N 17668	Locked In A Room/Alone Am I (Irish issue, different label)	150

POETS (U.S.)

(see under American Poets)

POGUE MAHONE

84	Pogue Mahone PM 1	Dark Streets Of London/The Band Played Waltzing Mathilda	10
84	Pogue Mahone PM 1	Dark Streets Of London/The Band Played Waltzing Mathilda (white label tour copy with 'harp' stamp, 237 only)	50

(see also Pogues)

POGUES

84	Stiff BUY 207	Dark Streets Of London/The Band Played Waltzing Mathilda (reissue of Pogue Mahone)	10
84	Stiff BUY 212	Boys From The County Hell/Repealing Of The Licensing Laws (green-tinted p/s)	10
84	Stiff BUY 212	Boys From The County Hell/Repealing Of The Licensing Laws (A-label promos in blue-tinted p/s)	12
84	Stiff BUY 207/BUY 212	Dark Streets Of London/The Band Played Waltzing Mathilda//Boys From The County Hell/Repealing Of The Licensing Laws (shrinkwrapped double pack)	20
85	Stiff BUY 220	A Pair Of Brown Eyes/Whiskey You're The Devil (p/s)	6
85	Stiff DBUY 220	A Pair Of Brown Eyes/Whiskey You're The Devil (picture disc)	15
85	Stiff BUYIT 220	A Pair Of Brown Eyes/Whiskey You're The Devil/Muirshin Durkin (12", p/s)	15
85	Stiff BUY 212/BUY 220	Boys From The County Hell/Repealing Of The Licensing Laws//A Pair Of Brown Eyes/Whiskey You're The Devil (shrinkwrapped double pack)	15
85	Stiff BUY 224	Sally MacLennane/Wild Rover (wraparound poster p/s, some green vinyl)	10/7
85	Stiff BUY 224	Sally MacLennane/Wild Rover (standard p/s)	6
85	Stiff PBUY 224	Sally MacLennane/Wild Rover (shaped picture disc)	10
85	Stiff BUYIT 224	Sally MacLennane/Wild Rover/The Leaving Of Liverpool (12", p/s)	8
85	Stiff BUYC 224	Sally MacLennane/Wild Rover/The Leaving Of Liverpool/ Wild Cats Of Kilkenny (cassette)	12
85	Stiff PBUY 229	Dirty Old Town/A Pistol For Paddy Garcia (picture disc)	10
85	Stiff BUYIT 229	Dirty Old Town/A Pistol For Paddy Garcia/The Parting Glass (12", some with poster & stickered p/s)	20/15
85	Stiff MAIL 3	Dirty Old Town (live)/Sally MacLennane (live)/(interview) (12", mail-order)	12
86	Stiff PBUY 243	POGUETRY IN MOTION (EP, picture disc)	5
86	MCA MCAT 1084	Haunted/Junk Theme/Hot Dogs With Everything (12", p/s, with poster)	7
87	Stiff/Hell BLOOD 1	The Good, The Bad & The Ugly/Rake At The Gates Of Hell (unreleased)	
87	Stiff/Hell BLOODY 1	The Good, The Bad & The Ugly/Rake At The Gates Of Hell (12", unreleased)	
88	Pogue Mahone SGG 1-12	ST. PATRICK'S NIGHT EP (12" EP)	7
89	WEA SAM 553	Misty Morning Albert Bridge/(same track) (12" promo, green vinyl)	8

(see also Pogue Mahone, Nips, Nipple Erectors, Radiators From Space)

POGUES featuring KIRSTY MacCOLL

87	Pogue Mahone CDNY 7	A Fairytale Of New York/The Battle March Medley/Shane Bradley (CD)	8

POINDEXTER BROTHERS

66	Verve VS 550	(Git Your) Backfield In Motion/(Grandma) Give That Girl Some Slack	15

POINTED STICKS

79	Stiff BUY 59	Out Of Luck/What Do You Want Me To Do/Somebody's Mom (7" or 12", p/s)	8/10

POISON

87	M. F. Nations P12 KUT 125	Talk Dirty To Me/We Want Some Need Some/Interview (12", picture disc)	8
87	Music For Nations P12 KUT 127	Cry Tough/Cry Tough (U.S. Mix)/Look What The Cat Dragged In (12", picture disc)	8
88	Capitol CLP 486	Nothin' But A Good Time/Look But You Can't Touch (poster p/s)	5
88	Capitol CLP 486	Nothin' But A Good Time/Look But You Can't Touch (picture disc)	6
88	Capitol CL 500	Fallen Angel/Bad To Be Good (p/s)	5
88	Capitol CL 520	Every Rose Has Its Thorn/Back To The Rocking Horse (p/s)	6
89	Capitol CLP 520	Every Rose Has Its Thorn/Back To The Rocking Horse (shaped picture disc, with inner)	7
89	Capitol CLS 523	Your Mama Don't Dance/Tearin' Down The Walls (p/s, green vinyl)	6
90	Capitol CL 582	Swamp Juice (Soul-O)/Valley Of Lost Souls (p/s)	6
87	Baktabak BAK 2047	POISON: INTERVIEW PICTURE DISC (LP, picture disc, PVC sleeve)	12

POISON GIRLS

79	Small Wonder WEENY 4	HEX (12" EP, with lyric insert)	8
80	Crass/Xntrix 421984/1	Persons Unknown/CRASS: Bloody Revolutions (folded 21" x 14" poster p/s)	5
81	Crass 421984/10	Pretty Polly/Bully Boys (live) (square red or clear flexidisc free with *In The City* fanzine, with/without magazine)	6/4
81	Crass 421984/8	All Systems Go/Promenade Immortelle/Dirty Work (p/s with lyrics)	5
83	Illuminated ILL 23	One Good Reason/Cinnamon Gardens (p/s)	5
83	Illuminated ILL 25	Are You Happy Now?/Cream Dream (p/s)	5
80	Crass 421984/2	CHAPPAQUIDICK (LP, with free flexidisc "Statement" [421984/7])	12

(see also Crass, Fatal Microbes/Poison Girls)

POISON IDEA

91	Vinyl Solution VS 29	Plastic Bomb/We Got The Beat/Harder They Come/Lawdy Miss Clawdy (double pack, p/s)	8

POISON IVY

64	Granta GR 7EP 1011	CLINGING MEMORIES (EP)	110

POLECATS

81	Nervous NER 001	Rockabilly Guy/Chicken Shack (p/s)	6

MINT VALUE £

ROLO POLEY

69 Jackpot JP 704 — Zapatoo The Tiger/Music House (both sides actually by Lester Sterling) 12

POLICE

77 Illegal IL 001 — Fall Out/Nothing Achieving (black & white p/s, red & black label, various designs) 18
78 A&M AMS 7348 — Roxanne/Peanuts (2.52) ('telephone' p/s, typed matrix no., 'All Rights ...' on top half of label) 7
78 A&M AMS 7348 — Roxanne/Peanuts (12", 'telephone' p/s)............................ 15
78 A&M AMS 7381 — Can't Stand Losing You/Dead End Job (glossy p/s, original issue, label credited to 'Police', mid-blue or rarer black vinyl)................... 10/7
78 A&M AMS 7402 — So Lonely/Time This Time (p/s, miscredited flip, label credited to 'Police')....... 5
79 A&M AMS 7348 — Roxanne/Peanuts (3.54) (reissue, 'group' p/s, handwritten matrix number, blue or black vinyl) 6/4
79 A&M AMS 7348 — Roxanne/Peanuts (2.52) (reissue, 'group' p/s, typed matrix number, blue or black vinyl) 6/4
79 A&M AMSP 7348 — Roxanne/Peanuts (12", reissue, 'group' p/s) 10
79 A&M AMS 7381 — Can't Stand Losing You/Dead End Job (reissue, label credited to 'The Police'; dark blue or light blue vinyl) .... each 10
79 A&M AMS 7381 — Can't Stand Losing You/Dead End Job (p/s, reissue, red, yellow, green or white vinyl)... 10-12
79 A&M AMS 7381 — Can't Stand Losing You/Dead End Job (p/s, mispressed B-side, plays "No Time This Time") .... 20+
79 A&M AMS 7474 — Message In A Bottle/Landlord (p/s, green vinyl)............................. 5
79 Illegal IL 001 — Fall Out/Nothing Achieving (reissue, various label designs, green/black p/s)..... 8
79 Illegal IL 001 — Fall Out/Nothing Achieving (reissue, various label designs, purple/blue p/s).... 15
79 Illegal IL 001 — Fall Out/Nothing Achieving (reissue, various label designs, black & orange p/s). 30
80 A&M AMPP 6001 — POLICE PACK (6 x 7" printed foldout PVC pack [AMS 7348, 7381, 7402, 7474 & 7494] & "The Bed's Too Big Without You"/"Truth Hits Everybody" [AMPP 6001/E]; all on blue vinyl with 6 inserts) 25
80 A&M SAMP 5 — SIX-TRACK RADIO SAMPLER (custom p/s, promo radio sampler) 15
80 A&M AMS 7564 — Don't Stand So Close To Me/Friends (poster p/s)........................... 7
81 A&M AMS 8174 — Every Little Thing She Does Is Magic/Flexible Responses (p/s) 5
81 A&M AMS 8194 — Spirits (In The Material World)/Low Life (poster p/s, some with badge) 8/4
83 A&M AM 117 — Every Breath You Take/Murder By Numbers (p/s, with free badge) 5
83 A&M AM 117/AM 01 — Every Breath You Take/Murder By Numbers//Truth Hits Everybody/Man In A Suitcase (double pack, gatefold p/s) 12
83 A&M AMSP 117 — Every Breath You Take/Murder By Numbers (picture disc)................... 12
83 A&M AMP 127 — Wrapped Around Your Finger/Someone To Talk To (Sting picture disc).......... 10
83 A&M AMP 127 — Wrapped Around Your Finger/Someone To Talk To (Andy Summers or Stewart Copeland picture disc, 1,000 each)............................. each 12
86 A&M AMY 354 — Don't Stand So Close To Me/Don't Stand So Close To Me (Dance Mix) Friends (12", p/s) 10
95 A&M 581 036 7 A 581 036 7B — Can't Stand Losing You (Live In Boston)/Roxanne (uncut white vinyl test pressing, one copy only)... 1,500
88 A&M AMCD 905 — COMPACT HITS (CD EP) 20
78 A&M AMLN 68502 — OUTLANDOS D'AMOUR (LP, blue vinyl) 15

(see also Sting, Radio Actors, Zoot Money's Big Roll Band, Last Exit, Newcastle Big Band, Eberhard Schoener, Andy Summers & Robert Fripp)

POLIPHONY

73 Zella JHLPS 136 — POLIPHONY (LP, private pressing) 150

POLITICIANS

72 Hot Wax HWX 114 — Love Machine/Free Your Mind 5
72 Hot Wax SHW 5007 — THE POLITICIANS (LP) 18

FRANK POLK

65 Capitol CL 15389 — Trying To Keep Up With The Joneses/Welcome Home, Baby 40

POLKA DOTS

58 Pye Nixa 7N 15144 — Don't Make Small Talk Baby/There Will Never Be Another 6
58 Pye Nixa N 15144 — Don't Make Small Talk Baby/There Will Never Be Another (78) 6
59 Pye Nixa 7N 15194 — Hey Liley, Liley Lo/Go Chase A Moonbeam 6
59 Pye Nixa N 15194 — Hey Liley, Liley Lo/Go Chase A Moonbeam (78)........................ 8
59 Pye Nixa 7N 15211 — Girls In Arms/You've Done Something To My Heart (with Laurie Johnson Orch.). . 6
59 Pye Nixa N 15211 — Girls In Arms/You've Done Something To My Heart (78) 8
59 Columbia SEG 7894 — SINGIN' AND SWINGIN' (EP) 18
61 Philips BBE 12487 — THE POLKA DOTS (EP, also stereo SBBE 9074) 10/15
62 Philips BBE 12528 — STRICTLY FOR KICKS (EP).. 10
62 Philips BE 12534 — RELAX AWHILE (EP)... 10
62 Philips 433 625 BE — VOCAL SPECTACULAR (EP) 10
63 Philips BL 7576 — NICE WORK AND YOU CAN BUY IT (LP)................................... 15

(see also Teddy Johnson, Laurie Johnson)

RAY POLLARD

65 United Artists UP 1111 — The Drifter/Let Him Go (And Let Me Love You)....................... 190
66 United Artists UP 1133 — It's A Sad Thing/All The Things You Are.......................... 120

(see also Wanderers)

POLLCATS

90 Community Charge AXT 1 — Poll Tax Blues/Poll Tax Blues (same track both sides, p/s).................. 10

(see also Steve Marriott)

MICHAEL POLNAREFF

66 Vogue VRS 7012 — La Poupée Qui Fait Non/Beatnik 10
66 Vogue VRS 7013 — No No No No No No/Beatnik 10
66 Vogue VRS 7019 — Love Me Please Love Me/L'Amour Avec Toi 10

MINT VALUE £

POLYGON WINDOW

92 Warp WARP LP 7 SURFING ON SINE WAVES (2-LP) 30
93 Warp WARP 33 QUOTH (12" EP, clear vinyl) 25
92 Warp WARP LP 7LTD SURFING ON SINE WAVES (LP, clear vinyl) 50
(see also Aphex Twin)

POLYPHEMUS

92 Placebo PILL 001 GREAT VILLAGE TRIP EP (10") 8
95 Beggars Banquet BBQ 57CD Stonecutter (p/s) 8
95 Acme AC 8010LP SCRAPBOOK OF MADNESS (LP, reissue with insert, 500 only) 18
95 Acme AC 8016LP STONEHOUSE (LP, gatefold sleeve, 700 only) 18

POLYPHONIC SPREE

02 679 679LO14 ORCHESTRAL: Light And Day/Soldier Girl (p/s, 500 only) 20
03 679 679LO14X Soldier Girl/(Go! Team Remix) (gatefold p/s, with poster) 8

HERB POMEROY BIG BAND

57 Columbia SX 1091 LIFE IS A MANY SPLENDOURED GIG (LP) 12

POMPHEY

72 Green Door GD 4029 Jamaica Skank/JOHNNY MOORE: Bing Comes To Town 10

PONI-TAILS

58 HMV POP 516 Born Too Late/Come On Joey, Dance With Me (as Pony-Tails) 10
58 HMV POP 516 Born Too Late/Come On Joey, Dance With Me (as Pony-Tails) (78) 15
58 HMV POP 558 Close Friends/Seven Minutes In Heaven 15
58 HMV POP 558 Close Friends/Seven Minutes In Heaven (78) 10
59 HMV POP 596 Early To Bed/Father Time 15
59 HMV POP 596 Early To Bed/Father Time (78) 10
59 HMV POP 644 Moody/Oom Pah Polka 15
59 HMV POP 663 I'll Be Seeing You/I'll Keep Tryin' 15
58 HMV 7EG 8427 THE PONI-TAILS (EP) 150

JEAN-LUC PONTY

69 Liberty LBL/LBS 83262 ELECTRIC CONNECTION (LP) 12
70 Liberty LBL/LBS 83375 KING KONG (LP) 12

POOGY

74 EMI EMI 2136 She Looked Me In The Eye (I Gave Her My Life)/Morris And His Turtle 8

POOH STICKS

88 Fierce FRIGHT 011 On Tape (p/s, 1-sided, some with *un*etched B-side) 40/35
88 Fierce FRIGHT 021 1-2-3 Red Light (p/s, 1-sided) 20
88 Fierce FRIGHT 021-025 FIERCE BOX SET (5 x 1-sided etched discs, hand-coloured labels, with insert) . . 50
88 Fierce FRIGHT 026 ALAN McGEE (CD EP, with FRIGHT 021-025 tracks plus "On Tape"/ "Please Hue, Please", some in 7" box with booklet) 20/10
89 Fierce FRIGHT 034 Dying For It (p/s, sold at U.L.U. gig, 300 only, some signed) 25/15
89 Fierce FRIGHT 034 Dying For It (1-sided, different p/s to above) 15
89 Cheree CHEREE 3 Go Go Girl/Simon E (flexidisc with foldout *Cheree* fanzine/sleeve) 12
89 Woosh WOOSH 007/ WOOSH 6 Hard On Love (yellow flexi with Pooh Sticks fanzine)// GROOVE FARM: Heaven Is Blue/ESMERALDA'S KITE: Vampire Girl (red flexi) (with *Woosh* fanzine 3) 12
89 Anonymous ANON 2 ENCORES (EP, numbered box set, multi-coloured 1-sided 7" with sweet watch, badge, sticker & booklet) 25
92 Fierce/BMG FRIGHT 42 Million Seller (1-sided) 6
89 53rd & 3rd AGAMC 5 ORGASM (LP, a few on pink vinyl with insert for export) 30/15
89 Fierce FRIGHT 025 THE POOH STICKS (mini-LP, with inner, black & white sleeve, 1-sided, side 2 etched) 20
89 Fierce FRIGHT 035 TRADE MARK OF QUALITY (LP, mail-order only, plain stickered sleeve with insert, numbered) 35
(see also Dumb Angels)

BRIAN POOLE

66 Decca F 12402 Hey Girl/Please Be Mine 8
66 CBS 202349 Everything I Touch Turns To Tears/I Need Her Tonight 20
67 CBS 202661 That Reminds Me Baby/Tomorrow Never Comes 6
67 CBS 3005 Just How Loud/The Other Side Of The Sky 12
69 President PT 239 Send Her To Me/Pretty In The City (as Brian Poole & Seychelles) 5
69 President PT 264 What Do Women Most Desire/Treat Her Like A Woman (with Seychelles) 5
(see also Brian Poole & Tremeloes)

BRIAN POOLE & TREMELOES

62 Decca F 11455 Twist Little Sister/Lost Love 12
62 Decca F 11515 That Ain't Right/Blue 10
63 Decca F 11567 A Very Good Year For Girls/Meet Me Where We Used Meet 8
63 Decca F 11616 Keep On Dancing/Run Back Home 8
63 Decca F 11694 Twist And Shout/We Know 5
63 Decca F 11739 Do You Love Me?/Why Can't You Love Me? 5
63 Decca F 11771 I Can Dance/Are You Loving Me At All 6
64 Decca F 11823 Candy Man/I Wish I Could Dance 5
64 Decca F 11893 Someone, Someone/Till The End Of Time 5
64 Decca F 11951 Twelve Steps To Love/Don't Cry 6
64 Decca F 12037 Three Bells/Tell Me How To Care 5
65 Decca F 12124 After A While/You Know 7
65 Decca F 12197 I Want Candy/Love Me Baby 10
65 Decca F 12274 Good Lovin'/Could It Be You 7
64 Decca DFE 8566 BRIAN POOLE AND THE TREMELOES (EP) 40
65 Decca DFE 8610 BRIAN POOLE AND THE TREMELOES (EP) 35
63 Ace of Clubs ACL 1146 BIG BIG HITS OF '62 (LP) 25
63 Decca LK 4550 TWIST AND SHOUT WITH BRIAN POOLE AND THE TREMELOES (LP) 45
65 Decca LK 4685 IT'S ABOUT TIME (LP) 70
(see also Brian Poole, Tremeloes)

MINT VALUE £

LOU & LAURA POOLE
72 Jay Boy BOY 63 — Only You And I Know/Look At Me 8

POOR SOULS
65 Decca F 12183 — When My Baby Cries/My Baby She's Not There 18
66 Alp ALP 595 004 — Love Me/Please Don't Change Your Mind 45

GROOVY JOE POOVEY
70 Injun 100 — Ten Long Fingers On The 88 Keys/Thrill Of Love 12

IGGY POP
77 RCA PB 9093 — China Girl/Baby 5
77 RCA PB 9160 — Success/The Passenger 5
77 RCA PB 9160 — Some Weird Sin/The Passenger 5
78 RCA PB 9213 — Sixteen/I Got A Right 5
78 Radar ADA 4 — Kill City (with James Williamson)/I Got Nothin' 5
79 Arista ARISP 274 — Five Foot One/Pretty Flamingo (picture disc) 6
80 Arista ARIST 327 — Loco Mosquito/Take Care Of Me (p/s) 5
82 Chrysalis/Melody Maker — Extracts From "Zombie Birdhouse"/STIFF LITTLE FINGERS: Excerpts From "Now Then" (flexidisc, free with *Melody Maker*) 6/4
88 A&M AMCD 909 — COMPACT HITS (EP) 8
90 Virgin America VUSCD 18 — Livin' On The Edge Of The Night (Edit)/The Passenger/Nightclubbing/ China Girl (3" CD, card sleeve) 8
73 CBS 65586 — RAW POWER (LP, with inner, orange label, as Iggy & Stooges) 30
78 Radar RAD 2 — KILL CITY (LP, as Iggy Pop & James Williamson) 12
(see also Stooges)

POPCORNS
63 Columbia DB 4968 — Zero Zero/Chinese Twist 15

DAVE POPE
70s Myrrh MYR 1003 — TIME TO TAKE ACCOUNT (LP) 18

TIM POPE
84 Fiction FICS 21 — I Want To Be A Tree/The Double Crossing Of Two Faced Fred (p/s) 15
84 Fiction FICSX 21 — I Want To Be A Tree/(Elephant) Song/The Double Crossing Of Two Faced Fred (12", p/s) 25
(see also Cure)

POP GROUP
79 Radar ADA 29 — She Is Beyond Good And Evil/3.38 (p/s) 6
79 Radar ADA 1229 — She Is Beyond Good And Evil/3.38 (12", p/s) 10
79 Rough Trade RT 023 — We Are All Prostitutes/Amnesty International Report On British Army Torture Of Irish Prisoners (p/s) 5
80 Rough Trade RT 039/ Y Y1 — Where There's A Will There's A Way/SLITS: In The Beginning There Was Rhythm (p/s) 5
79 Radar RAD 20 — Y (LP, with foldout colour poster) 15
80 Rough Trade ROUGH 9 — FOR HOW MUCH LONGER DO WE TOLERATE MASS MURDER? (LP, with 4 black-and-white posters) 15
80 Y/Rough Trade ROUGH 12 — WE ARE TIME (LP, plain black sleeve) 12
(see also Slits)

POP GUNS
80s La Di Da LA-DI-DA 001 — Where Do You Go/HOW MANY BEANS MAKE FIVE: Another Friendly Face (flexidisc, 33rpm, p/s) 5
89 Medium Cool MC 019T — LANDSLIDE (12" EP) 8
(see also Wedding Present)

POPINJAYS
88 Big Cat BBA 02 — Don't Go Back/So Close/Move To Perish (12", p/s) 8

POPPIES
66 Columbia DB 7879 — Lullaby Of Love/I Wonder Why 25

KEITH POPPIN
73 Randy's RAN 531 — Kick The Bucket/I'm A Man Of My Word 6

POPPY FAMILY
70 Decca (S)KL-R 5022 — WHICH WAY YOU GOING BILLY? (LP, mono/stereo) 15/12
72 Decca SKL 5114 — POPPY SEEDS (LP) 12

POPPYHEADS
88 Sha La La Ba Ba Ba Ba 4 — POSTCARD FOR FLOSSY (EP, 1-sided flexidisc, p/s in poly bag) 8
88 Sarah SARAH 006 — Cremation Town/Pictures You Weave/Dreamboat (foldaround p/s with large poster in poly bag) 10

POP RIVETS
79 Hypocrite HEP 001 — POP RIVITS (EP, no p/s) 12
79 Hypocrite HEP 002 — Pop Rivits/Sulphate 15
79 Hypocrite JIM 1 — FUN IN THE U.K. (EP, no p/s, double pack) 30
79 Hypocrite HIP-O — EMPTY SOUNDS FROM ANARCHY RANCH (LP, coloured back, stamped labels) 30
80 Hypocrite HIP 007 — THE POP RIVETS GREATEST HITS (LP, screen-printed sleeve) 15
(see also Milkshakes)

POPSICLES
65 Vogue V 9243 — I Don't Want To Be Your Baby Anymore/Baby I Miss You 30
(see also Ellie Greenwich, Raindrops)

POPULAR 5
68 Minit MLF 11011 — I'm A Lovemaker/Little Bitty Pretty One 12

POP WILL EAT ITSELF
86 Desperate SRT 1 — POPPIES SAY GRRR! (EP, stamped white labels in brown paper bag) 15
86 Desperate DAN 1 — POPPIES SAY GRRR! (EP, reissue, orange sleeve) 5

MINT VALUE £

86	Chapter 22 CHAP 9	POPPIECOCK (EP)	5
87	Chapter 22 LCHAP 13	Love Missile F1-11(Designer Grebo Mix)/(Original Poppies Mix)/Orgone Accumulator (Original Version)/Everything That Rises (New Version) (p/s)	8
87	Chapter 22 LCHAP 16	Beaver Patrol/Bubbles (numbered p/s, clear vinyl in stickered PVC sleeve)	6
87	Chapter 22 LCHAP 16	Beaver Patrol/Bubbles (no'd p/s, signed, pink vinyl in stickered PVC sleeve)	8
88	Chapter 22 LCHAP 20	There Is No Love Between Us Anymore/Picnic in The Sky (picture disc)	5
88	Chapter 22 CLUB CHAP 20	There Is No Love Between Us Anymore (Speciality Extended High Mix)/ Hit The Hi-Tech Groove (The M & K Mix) (12", die-cut sleeve)	8
89	RCA PB 42729	Can U Dig It/Poison To The Mind (p/s, shrinkwrapped to 10" card with patch)	5
89	RCA PB 43021	VERY METAL NOISE POLLUTION (EP, pink or yellow gatefold p/s)	5/6
89	RCA PT 43022	VERY METAL NOISE POLLUTION (EP, shaped picture disc)	5
89	House Of Dolls HOD 009	Wake Up! Time To Die.../WILD POPPIES: The Last Thing/BLOW UP: Slip Into Something (Rough Mix)/GODSPEED: Radiate (freebie with *House Of Dolls*)	6/4

(see also Wild & Wandering)

POP WORKSHOP

68	Page One POF 091	Fairyland/When My Little Girl Is Happy	7
69	Page One POF 129	Punch And Judy Man/Love Is A One Way Highway	7

PORCUPINE TREE

94	Delerium DELEC EP 032	Stars Die/Moonloop (12", p/s)	10
00	Snapper SMAS 7111	4 Chords That Made A Million (p/s, 1,000 only)	8
92	Delerium DELEC EP 007	VOYAGE 34 (Astralasia Remix) (12" EP)	12
92	Delerium DELEC EP 010	VOYAGE 34 (12" EP)	18
92	Delerium DELECD EP 010	VOYAGE 34 (CD EP)	18
89	Delerium DELC 0002	TARQUIN'S SEAWEED FARM (cassette, 1st issue, around 50 only)	35
91	Delerium DELC 0002	TARQUIN'S SEAWEED FARM (cassette, 2nd issue, silver print, with A4 booklet, red/black text, 200 only)	25
91	Delerium DELC 0002	TARQUIN'S SEAWEED FARM (cassette, silver print, with photocopied A5 booklet, label on Side 1, 200 only)	22
91	Delerium DELC 0003	THE NOSTALGIA FACTORY (cassette, silver print, with A4 booklet, red/black text, 200 only)	22
91	Delerium DELC 0003	THE NOSTALGIA FACTORY (cassette, with photocopied A5 booklet, label on Side 1, 200 only)	22
92	Delerium DELEC 008	ON THE SUNDAY OF LIFE (2-LP, gatefold sleeve)	20
92	Delerium DELEC 008	ON THE SUNDAY OF LIFE (2-LP, gatefold sleeve)	20
92	Delerium DELEC CD 008	ON THE SUNDAY OF LIFE (CD)	20
94	Magic Gnome MG 4299325	YELLOW HEADGROW DREAMSCAPE (CD, 2,500 only)	50
95	Delerium DELEC LP 028	THE SKY MOVES SIDEWAYS (LP, 2,000 on blue vinyl w/poster)	15

PORK DUKES

77	Wood WOOD 9	Bend And Flush/Throbbing Gristle (p/s)	25
77	Wood BRANCH 9	Making Bacon/Tight Pussy (12", p/s, yellow vinyl)	25
78	Wood Standard WOOD 56	Telephone Masturbator/Melody Makers (p/s)	25
78	Wood PORK 001	THE PORK DUKES (LP, pink vinyl with warning sticker & postcard)	18
80	Wood PORK 2	PIG OUT OF HELL (LP)	15
82	Butt PORK 1	PIG IN A POKE (LP)	15

DAVID PORTER

70	Stax STAX 150	One Part — Two Parts/Can't I See You When I Want To	6
70	Stax SXATS 1034	GRITTY, GROOVY AND GETTIN' IT (LP)	15
71	Stax 2362 006	INTO A REAL THING (LP)	15

NOLAN PORTER

72	Probe PRO 580	If I Could Only Be Sure/Work It Out In The Morning	60
72	Probe SPB 1067	NOLAN (LP)	30

PORTER & CALYPSO STAR BAND

59	Kalypso XX 11	Cinemascope/Sally Brown (78)	8

PORTER CUNNINGHAM

72	Folk Heritage FHR 027	OBSERVATIONS (LP)	130

HUBERT PORTER & JAMAICAN CALYPSONIANS

50s	Times Record UD 1011	Ten Penny Nail/Mary's Lamb/Intro: The More We Are Together (78)	7

PORTION CONTROL

82	In Phaze POR CON 006	Surface And Be Seen/Spinola (Blotch)/Terror Leads To Better Days/ Simple As ABC/Monstrous Bulk/He Is A Barbarian (12", p/s, with plastic outer sleeve)	15
84	Illuminated ILL 2612	Raise The Pulse/Collapse/Bite My Head (12", p/s)	10
84	Illuminated ILL 3212	Rough Justice/The Man Who Did Backwards Somersaults (12", p/s with inner)	8
85	Illuminated ILL 4312	Go-Talk/Upside Down/Drag Down (12", p/s)	10
85	Rhythmic/Havoc 7RMIC 7	The Great Divide/Totall Recall (p/s)	5
85	Rhythmic/Havoc 12RMIC 7	The Great Divide/Divided/Bolt It Down (12", p/s)	8
85	Rhythmic/Havoc 12RMICX 7	The Great Divide (Julian Mendelsohn Remix)/Divided/Bolt It Down (12", p/s)	12
86	Dead Man's Curve DMC 1	PRESENT PURGE (12" EP)	8
87	Big Noise In Archgate BNIA 1	LIVE IN EUROPE (10" mini-LP)	10
83	In Phaze EZ 2	HIT THE PULSE (mini-LP, 45/33rpm)	18
84	Illuminated JAMS 44	STEP FORWARD (LP)	12
85	In Phaze PHA 5	SIMULATE SENSUAL (LP, clear vinyl, PVC sleeve with insert)	20
86	Dead Man's Curve DMC 8	PSYCHO-BOD SAVES THE WORLD (LP, with inner sleeve)	12

PORTISHEAD

94	Go Beat GODX 120	Glory Box/Toy Box/Scorn/Sheared Box (12", p/s)	8
97	Go Beat 571 597-1	All Mine/Cowboys/Cowboys (Instrumental) (12", p/s)	8
94	Go Beat GOLCD 116	SOUR TIMES EP (CD, limited edition, with postcards)	15
94	Go Beat GODCD 116	SOUR TIMES EP (CD, limited edition, blue sleeve, with postcards)	10
94	Go Beat 828 522	DUMMY (LP)	15
97	Go Beat 539189-1	PORTISHEAD (LP, gloss sleeve)	12

MINT VALUE £

PORTOBELLO EXPLOSION

69 Carnaby CNS 4001 We Can Fly/Hot Smoke And Sasafrass (label credits *Portebello Explosion*) 30
(see also Mirage, Jawbone, Spencer Davis Group)

PORTWAY PEDLARS

84 Greenwich Village GVR 229 IN GREENWOOD SHADES (LP) 15

SANDY POSEY

66 MGM MGM 1321 Born A Woman/Caution To The Wind 7
66 MGM MGM 1330 Single Girl/Blue Is My Best Colour 7
67 MGM MGM 1335 What A Woman In Love Won't Do/Shattered 7
67 MGM MGM 1342 I Take It Back/The Boy I Love 8
67 MGM MGM 1364 Are You Never Coming Home/I Can Show You How To Live 8
67 MGM MGM-C(S) 8035 BORN A WOMAN (LP) 25
67 MGM MGM-C(S) 8042 SINGLE GIRL (LP) 25
68 MGM MGM-C(S) 8051 SANDY POSEY (LP) 25
68 MGM MGM-C 8060 THE BEST OF SANDY POSEY (LP, original with blue label) 15
68 MGM MGM-C(S) 8073 LOOKING AT YOU (LP) 20

POSITIVE FORCE

79 Sugarhill SH 102 We Got The Funk/Tell Me What You See (12") 8

HOWIE POST & SWIFTIES

63 Fontana TF 421 Tom Swift/The Elephant 12

ADRIENNE POSTER/POSTA

63 Oriole CB 1890 Only Fifteen/There's Nothing You Can Do About That 20
63 Decca F 11797 Only Fifteen/There's Nothing You Can Do About That (reissue) 18
64 Decca F 11864 Shang A Doo Lang/When A Girl Really Loves You 20
65 Decca F 12079 He Doesn't Love Me/The Way You Do The Things You Do 18
65 Decca F 12181 The Winds That Blow/Back Street Girl 18
66 Decca F 12329 Something Beautiful/So Glad You're Mine 15
66 Decca F 12455 They Long To Be Close To You/How Can I Hurt You (as Adrienne Posta) 12
76 President PT 453 Cruisin Casanova/Sing Me 10

POST MORTEM

82 Regime RM 006 AGAINST ALL ODDS (EP) 5

POTATOES

66 Fontana TF 756 The Bend/Bend Ahead 7

KEITH POTGER

69 Mercury MF 1073 The World Would Never Turn Again/Santa Marie (some in p/s) 12/6
(see also Seekers, Judith Durham)

POTLIQUOR

72 Janus 6146 011 Cheer/Chatanooga 6
70 Dawn DNLS 3016 FIRST TASTE (LP, withdrawn) 90
72 Janus 6310 202 LEVEE BLUES (LP) 12
72 Janus 6310 203 FIRST TASTE (LP, reissue) 12

PHIL POTTER

76 Genesis GEN 10 MY SONG IS LOVE UNKNOWN (LP) 20
79 Dove DOVE 61 THE RESTORER (LP) 18
70s Kingsway KMR 321 LEAD ME ON (LP) 15

POTTERS

72 Trent JT 100 We'll Be With You/Theme For A Team 20

POUND HOUNDS

55 Brunswick 05484 Home Sweet Home/MELLOMEN: Lady 12
(see also Peggy Lee)

ALLEN POUND'S GET RICH

66 Parlophone R 5532 Searchin' In The Wilderness/Hey You (most copies are demos) ..... 500+

POWDER

95 Parkway PARK 001X 20th Century Gods/Dizco Girl (embossed p/s, numbered, 2,000 only) 7
95 Parkway PARK 002 Afrodiziak/Shave Me (p/s, 2,000 only) 5

BOBBY POWELL

72 Mojo 2092 034 Peace Begins Within/Question 10
75 Contempo CLP 516 THANK YOU (LP) 15

BUD POWELL (TRIO)

58 Columbia LB 10086 That Old Black Magic/Someone To Watch Over Me (78) 8
64 Blue Note 45-1712 Buster Rides Again/Dry Soul 7
55 Vogue EPV 1030 BUD POWELL TRIO (EP) 70
55 Vogue EPV 1033 BUD POWELL'S MODERNISTS (EP) 70
55 Vogue EPV 1036 BUD POWELL TRIO (EP) 60
55 Columbia Clef SEB 10013 BUD POWELL (EP) 70
57 Columbia Clef SEB 10074 GENIUS OF BUD POWELL (EP) 70
58 Columbia Clef SEB 10094 GENIUS OF BUD POWELL NO. 2 (EP) 60
52 Vogue LDE 010 THE BUD POWELL TRIO (10" LP) 30
54 Vogue LDE 053 JAZZ AT THE MASSEY HALL VOL. 2 (10" LP) 25
56 Columbia Clef 33C 9016 BUD POWELL TRIO (10" LP) 30
57 Columbia Clef 33CX 10069 JAZZ ORIGINAL (LP) 40
58 Columbia Clef 33CX 10123 BLUES FOR BUD (LP) 75
59 HMV CLP 1294 THE LONELY ONE (LP) 60
63 Blue Note (B)BLP 1503 THE AMAZING BUD POWELL VOL. 1 (LP) 15
63 Vogue LAE 558 THE BUD POWELL TRIO (LP) 15
63 Columbia 33SX 1575 THE BUD POWELL TRIO FEATURING MAX ROACH (LP) 60
64 Blue Note (B)BLP 1504 THE AMAZING BUD POWELL VOL. 2 (LP) 15
64 Fontana FJL 903 HOT HOUSE (LP) 100

65 Columbia 33SX 1701 THE RETURN OF POWELL (LP) . . . 12
65 Xtra XTRA 1011 BOUNCING WITH BUD (LP) . . . 12
65 Verve VLP 9075 THE VINTAGE YEARS (LP) . . . 12
68 Fontana SFJL 901 BLUES FOR BOUFFEMONT (LP) . . . 90
69 Fontana SFJL 924 AT THE BLUE NOTE CAFE, PARIS 1961 (LP) . . . 12

COZY POWELL

73 Rak RAK 164 Dance With The Devil/And Then There Was Skin . . . 5
73 Rak 4C 006 94962 Dance With The Devil/And Then There Was Skin (export issue, p/s, RAK 164 in run out groove, some on blue or yellow vinyl) . . . 35/15
74 Rak RAK 173 The Man In Black/After Dark . . . 5
74 Rak RAK 180 Na Na Na/Mistral (as Cozy Powell's Hammer) . . . 5
79 Ariola ARO 189 Theme One/Over The Top Part 1 (p/s, red vinyl) . . . 6
79 Ariola AROD 189 Theme One/Over The Top (full version) (12", company sleeve) . . . 10
79 Ariola ARO 205 The Loner/El Sid (p/s, blue vinyl) . . . 6
80 Ariola ARO 222 Heidi Goes To Town/Over The Top Part 2 (p/s, clear vinyl) . . . 6
81 Polydor POSP 328 Sooner Or Later/The Blister (p/s) . . . 5
80 Ariola ARL 5038 OVER THE TOP (LP) . . . 15
81 Polydor POLD 5047 TILT (LP, with inner sleeve) . . . 15

(see also Rainbow, Young Blood, Big Bertha, Ace Kefford Stand, Bedlam, Bernie Marsden, Phenomena, Black Sabbath, Jeff Beck, Whitesnake, Michael Schenker Group, Donovan, Gary Moore, Young & Moody, Brian May, Chick Churchill, Graham Bonnet, Forcefield, Emerson Lake & Powell, Jack Bruce, Plum & Youth)

JANE POWELL

53 MGM SP 1061 Something Wonderful/I Whistle A Happy Tune . . . 8
53 MGM SP 1062 Hello, Young Lovers/We Kiss In A Shadow . . . 8
56 HMV POP 267 True Love/Mind If I Make Love To You . . . 12
59 MGM MGM-EP 701 JANE POWELL SINGS (EP) . . . 22
54 Capitol LC 6665 THREE SAILORS AND A GIRL (10" LP) . . . 30
57 HMV CLP 1131 JANE POWELL (LP) . . . 30

*(see also Marilyn Monroe)**

JIMMY POWELL (& DIMENSIONS)

62 Decca F 11447 Sugar Babe (Parts 1 & 2) (solo) . . . 12
62 Decca F 11544 Tom Hark/Dance Her By Me (solo) . . . 12
63 Decca F 11570 Remember Them/Everyone But You (solo) . . . 8
64 Pye 7N 15663 That's Alright/I'm Looking For A Woman . . . 45
64 Pye 7N 15735 Sugar Babe/I've Been Watching You (as Jimmy Powell & 5 Dimensions) . . . 20
66 Strike JH 309 I Can Go Down/Love Me Right . . . 12
67 Decca F 12664 Unexpected Mirrors/Time Mends Broken Hearts (with Dimensions) . . . 10
68 Decca F 12751 I Just Can't Get Over You/Real Cool (with Dimensions) . . . 8
68 Decca F 12793 Sugar Babe (Parts 1 & 2) . . . 8
69 Young Blood YB 1002 I Can Go Down/Captain Man . . . 5
69 Young Blood YB 1006 House Of The Rising Sun/That's Love . . . 5
70 Young Blood YB 1019 Witness To A War/Strangers On A Train . . . 5

JUDITH POWELL

67 RCA RCA 1569 Greener Days/No Goodbyes . . . 6

KEITH POWELL (& VALETS)

63 Columbia DB 7116 The Answer Is No!/Come On And Join The Party (with Valets) . . . 15
64 Columbia DB 7229 Tore Up/You Better Let Him Go (with Valets) . . . 18
64 Columbia DB 7366 I Should Know Better (But I Don't)/Too Much Monkey Business (with Valets) . . . 35
65 Piccadilly 7N 35235 People Get Ready/Paradise . . . 8
65 Piccadilly 7N 35249 Come Home Baby/Beyond The Hill . . . 8
66 Piccadilly 7N 35275 Goodbye Girl/It Was Easier To Hurt Her . . . 8
66 Piccadilly 7N 35300 Victory/Some People Only . . . 8
66 Piccadilly 7N 35353 It Keeps Rainin'/Song of The Moon . . . 10

(see also Move, Carl Wayne & Vikings)

KEITH (POWELL) & BILLIE (DAVIES)

66 Piccadilly 7N 35288 When You Move, You Lose/Tastes Sour, Don't It? (as Keith & Billie) . . . 10
66 Piccadilly 7N 35321 You Don't Know Like I Know/Two Little People . . . 12
66 Piccadilly 7N 35340 Swingin' Tight/That's Really Some Good . . . 12

(see also Keith Powell, Billie Davis)

MARILYN POWELL

64 Fontana TF 448 All My Loving/After The Party . . . 12
65 Fontana TF 526 Please Go Away/Where Did I Go Wrong . . . 10
65 Fontana TF 557 As Long As You Come Back To Me/Go Away . . . 8
65 Fontana TF 687 Showdown/Came The Day . . . 10
68 CBS 2331 Something To Hold On To/Kiss Me Again . . . 8
69 CBS 4440 Have Another Dream On Me/Afraid To Love You . . . 5
70 CBS 5290 Dear Madame/Home . . . 5

DUFFY POWER

59 Fontana H 194 Dream Lover/That's My Little Suzie . . . 18
59 Fontana H 194 Dream Lover/That's My Little Suzie (78) . . . 20
59 Fontana H 214 Kissin' Time/Ain't She Sweet . . . 18
59 Fontana H 214 Kissin' Time/Ain't She Sweet (78) . . . 20
59 Fontana H 230 Starry-Eyed/Prettier Than You . . . 15
59 Fontana H 230 Starry-Eyed/Prettier Than You (78) . . . 30
60 Fontana H 279 Whole Lotta Shakin' Goin' On/If I Can Dream . . . 30
61 Fontana H 302 I've Got Nobody/When We're Walking Close . . . 20
61 Fontana H 344 No Other Love/What Now . . . 18
63 Parlophone R 4992 It Ain't Necessarily So/If I Get Lucky Someday . . . 18
63 Parlophone R 5024 I Saw Her Standing There (with Graham Bond Quartet)/Farewell Baby . . . 50
63 Parlophone R 5059 Hey Girl/Woman Made Trouble . . . 18
64 Parlophone R 5111 Parchman Farm/Tired, Broke And Busted (with Paramounts) . . . 30

MINT VALUE £

64	Parlophone R 5169	Where Am I?/I Don't Care	30
67	Parlophone R 5631	Davy O'Brien (Leave That Baby Alone)/July Tree	20
70	CBS 5176	Hell Hound/Hummingbird	12
71	Epic EPC 7139	Hummingbird/Hell Hound (reissue)	8
73	GSF GSZ 6	River/Little Soldiers	6
73	GSF GSZ 8	Liberation/Song About Jesus	6
71	Transatlantic TRA 229	INNOVATIONS (LP)	60
73	GSF GS 502	DUFFY POWER (LP)	22
73	Spark SRLM 2005	DUFFY POWER (LP)	22
76	Buk BULP 2010	POWERHOUSE (LP, revised reissue of GSF GS 502)	15

(see also Alexis Korner, John McLaughlin, Jack Bruce, Graham Bond, Duffy's Nucleus)

JIMMY POWER

76	Topic 12TS 306	IRISH FIDDLE PLAYER (LP)	12

POWERHOUSE

66	Decca F 12471	Chain Gang/Can You Hear Me?	15
66	Decca F 12507	Raindrops/La Bamba	8

POWERPACK

66	CBS 202335	It Hurts Me So/What You Gonna Do	40
67	CBS 202551	I'll Be Anything For You/The Lost Summer	18
69	Polydor 56319	Hannibal Brooks/Juliet Simkins	7
70	Polydor 2001 077	Oh Calcutta/Soul Searchin'	15
69	Polydor 583 057	SOUL CURE (LP)	25

(see also Procol Harum, Emperor Rosko & Power Pack)

POWERPILL

92	ffrreedom TABX 110	PAC MAN EP: Powerpill Mix/Ghost Mix/Choci's Hi Score Mix/Mickey Finn's Yum Yum Mix (12", some on limited edition yellow vinyl)	30/20
92	ffrreedom TABX 110	PAC MAN EP: Powerpill Mix/Ghost Mix/Choci's Hi Score Mix/Mickey Finn's Yum Yum Mix (CD)	30

(see also Aphex Twin)

JETT POWERS

70	Liberty LBS 83320	CALIFORNIA LICENCE (LP)	60

(see also P.J. Proby)

KID CONGO POWERS

89	Night Shift NISHI 208T	In The Heat Of The Night/Cat Tabu/La Historia Des Un Amour (12", p/s)	8

(see also Gun Club)

JOEY POWERS

63	Stateside SS 236	Midnight Mary/Where Do You Want The World Delivered	12

POWERS OF BLUE

67	CBS 62953	FLIP OUT! (LP)	15

POWER STATION

85	Parlophone 12 RP 6091	Some Like It Hot (Full Length Version)/The Heat Is On/ Some Like It Hot (12", picture disc)	8
85	Parlophone 12R 6114	Communication (Extended Remix)/Murderess (12", p/s)	8

(see also Duran Duran, Robert Palmer)

P.P. & PRIMES

96	Nice (no cat. no.)	Understanding/STEVIE'S BUZZ (i.e. Buzzcocks): Autumn Stone (promo only)	10

(see also Primal Scream, P.P. Arnold)

PEREZ 'PREZ' PRADO & HIS ORCHESTRA

54	HMV 7M 255	Skokiaan — Mambo/The High And The Mighty	10
54	HMV GV 203	April In Portugal/Mexicanita (78, export issue)	7
55	HMV 7M 295	Cherry Pink And Apple Blossom White/Maria Elena	15
55	HMV POP 102	Marilyn Monroe Mambo/C'est Si Bon (78)	12
55	HMV 7MC 29	Mambo De La Telefonista/En Las Calles De La Habana (export issue)	10
58	RCA RCA 1067	Patricia/Why Wait	7
58	RCA RCA 1067	Patricia/Why Wait (78)	6
58	RCA RCA 1082	Guaglione/Paris	8
58	RCA RCA 1082	Guaglione/Paris (78)	10
59	RCA RCA 1129	Tic Toc Polly Woc/My Roberta	6
59	RCA RCA 1129	Tic Toc Polly Woc/My Roberta (78)	8
60	RCA RCA 1199	Rockambo Baby/Oh, Oh, Rosie	6
55	HMV 7EG 8104	KING OF MAMBO (EP)	10
58	RCA SRC 7004	PREZ (EP)	10
59	RCA RCX 140	PRADO PLAYS PATRICIA (EP)	10
59	RCA RCX 1001	PEREZ PRADO (EP)	10
60	RCA RD 27046	LATIN SATIN (LP)	18
64	Parlophone PMC 1226	A CAT IN LATIN (LP)	20

PRAG VEC

78	Spec SP 001	Wolf/Cigarettes/Existential/Bits! (p/s)	10
79	Spec SP 002	Expert/The Follower! (p/s)	10
81	Spec RESPECT 1	NO COWBOYS (LP, with insert)	15

(see also Foetus etc.)

PRAMS

81	Product/Ltd. Edition TAKE 3	Nowhere's Safe/TV PRODUCT: Jumping Off Walls (foldout p/s)	15

PRAISE

76	No Seven 001	BLESSED QUIETNESS (LP)	40

PRATS

80	Rough Trade RT 42	Disco Pope/Nothing/TV Set/Nobody Noticed	6

MINT VALUE £

ANDY PRATT
69 Polydor 2489 003 RECORDS ARE LIKE LIFE (LP) 12

GRAHAM & EILEEN PRATT
85 Plant Life PLR 068 HEIROGLYPHICS (LP) 15

PHIL PRATT
69 Jolly JY 008 Sweet Song For My Baby/THRILLERS: I'm Restless 15
(see also Charlie Ace, Larry Marshall, Don Drummond)

PHIL PRATT ALL STARS
70 Jackpot JP 748 Cut Throat/KEN BOOTHE: You Left The Water Running 18
71 Punch PH 94 Winey Winey (actually "Kingstonians Medley" by Kingstonians)/
There Is A Place (actually by Barrington Spence) 7
(see also Dennis Alcapone, Horace Andy, Dennis Brown, Ken Boothe, Erroll Dunkley, John Holt, Delroy Wilson)

GRAHAM & EILEEN PRATT
80s Dingle's DIN 308 TO FRIEND & FOE (LP) 18

PRAYING MANTIS
79 Ripper/Harvest HAR 5201 THE SOUNDHOUSE TAPES PART 2: Captured City/Johnny Cool
(some in p/s) 70/18
79 Ripper/Harvest 12HAR 5201 THE SOUNDHOUSE TAPES PART 2 (12") 15
80 Gem GEMS 36 Praying Mantis/High Roller (p/s, some with transfer). 25/20
80 Arista ARIST 378 Cheated/Thirty Pieces Of Silver (gatefold p/s, with bonus single). 8
81 Arista ARIST 397 All Day And All Of The Night/Beads Of Ebony (p/s) 12
82 Jet JET 7026 Tell Me The Nightmare's Wrong/A Question Of Time/Turn The Tables (p/s) 50
81 Arista SPART 1153 TIME TELLS NO LIES (LP, with inner sleeve) 35
(see also Stratus, Grand Prix, Uriah Heep)

PREACHERS
65 Columbia DB 7680 Hole In My Soul/Too Old In The Head 75
(see also Herd, Peter Frampton, Denny Mitchel & Soundsations, Moon's Train)

PRECIOUS FEW
68 Pye 7N 17510 Young Girl/Little Children Sleep 7
68 Pye 7N 17641 Pleasure Of You/Little Children Sleep 7

PRECISIONS
67 Track 604 014 If This Is Love/You'll Soon Be Gone 30
79 Grapevine GRP 129 Such Misery/A Lovers Plea 15

PREDATOR
78 Bust! SOL 2 Punk Man/Paperboy Song (with insert). 40

PREDATOR
85 CTM C 001 Don't Stop/Shotdown (some in p/s) 80/30

PREDATORS
83 Ears And Eyes EER 012 SOCIAL DECAY (LP) 40

PREDATUR
82 Quicksilver QUICK 5 Take A Walk/Seen You Here (p/s) 125

PREFAB SPROUT
82 Candle CANDLE 1 Lions In My Own Garden (Exit Someone)/Radio Love 20
83 Kitchenware SK 4 Lions In My Own Garden (Exit Someone)/Radio Love (p/s, reissue, black labels) . 5
88 Kitchenware SKQ 35 Cars And Girls/Real Life (Just Around The Corner)/Vendetta (10", no'd p/s). 7
88 Kitchenware CDDSK 35 Cars And Girls/Faron Young (Truckin' Mix)/Real Life
(Just Around The Corner)/Vendetta (CD, picture disc) 8

PREGNANT INSOMNIA
67 Direction 58-3132 Wallpaper/You Intrigue Me. 50

PRELUDE
70s Crotchet CME 18A/B PRELUDE (LP, private pressing) 60

PRELUDE
73 Dawn DNLS 3052 HOW LONG IS FOREVER (LP, gatefold sleeve). 15
74 Dawn DNLS 3061 DUTCH COURAGE (LP) 15
75 Dawn DNLH 3 OWL CREEK INCIDENT (LP) 15

PREMIERS (U.K.)
64 Silver Phoenix 1002 Tears, Tears/Bye Bye Johnny. 35

PREMIERS (U.S.)
64 Warner Bros WB 134 Farmer John/Duffy's Blues 15
64 Warner Bros W 1565 FARMER JOHN "LIVE" (LP) 55

YVONNE PRENOSILOVA
65 Pye 7N 15775 When My Baby Cries/Come On Home. 8

PRESENCE
76 NC SLCW 1031 PRESENCE (LP). 35

PRESENCE
91 Reality LOL 1 In Wonder/Soft (p/s, withdrawn). 5
91 Reality LOLX 1 In Wonder/Soft/In Wonder (Didgeribdub Mix) (12", p/s, withdrawn) 8
91 Reality LOLCD 1 In Wonder/Soft/In Wonder (Didgeribdub Mix)/In Wonder (Millies Mix) (CD) 8
(see also Cure)

PRESIDENT REAGAN IS CLEVER
86 Hyena HAHA 001 FROM THIS TO THAT EP (12") 8

MINT VALUE £

PRESIDENTS

64	Decca F 11826	Candy Man/Let The Sunshine In	40

PRESIDENTS

72	A&M AMS 856	5-10-15-20 Years Of Love/Triangle Of Love	5
72	Sussex AMLS 65001	5-10-15-20-25-30 (LP)	15

ELVIS PRESLEY

HMV 78s

56	HMV POP 182	Heartbreak Hotel/I Was The One	20
56	HMV POP 213	Blue Suede Shoes/Tutti Frutti	25
56	HMV POP 235	I Want You, I Need You, I Love You/My Baby Left Me	25
56	HMV POP 249	Hound Dog/Don't Be Cruel	15
56	HMV POP 253	Love Me Tender/Anyway You Want Me (That's How I Will Be)	20
56	HMV POP 272	Blue Moon/I Don't Care If The Sun Don't Shine	20
57	HMV POP 295	Mystery Train/Love Me	45
57	HMV POP 305	Rip It Up/Baby, Let's Play House	40
57	HMV POP 330	Too Much/Playing For Keeps	30
57	HMV POP 359	All Shook Up/That's When Your Heartaches Begin	18
57	HMV POP 378	Paralyzed/When My Blue Moon Turns To Gold Again	30
57	HMV POP 408	Tryin' To Get To You/Lawdy, Miss Clawdy	30
58	HMV POP 428	I'm Left, You're Right, She's Gone/How Do You Think I Feel?	50

HMV 45s: PURPLE LABEL/GOLD PRINT

56	HMV 7M 385	Heartbreak Hotel/I Was The One ('removable/replaceable' or solid centre)	400/275
56	HMV 7M 405	Blue Suede Shoes/Tutti Frutti	300
56	HMV 7M 424	I Want You, I Need You, I Love You/My Baby Left Me	180
56	HMV POP 249	Hound Dog/Don't Be Cruel	110
56	HMV POP 253	Love Me Tender/Anyway You Want Me (That's How I Will Be)	110
56	HMV POP 272	Blue Moon/I Don't Care If The Sun Don't Shine ('removable/replaceable' centre or solid centre)	175/120
57	HMV POP 295	Mystery Train/Love Me ('removable/replaceable' centre or solid centre)	350/290
57	HMV 7MC 42	Mystery Train/I Forgot To Remember To Forget (U.K. issue of export single, gold label print only, smooth edge to labels)	325
57	HMV POP 305	Rip It Up/Baby, Let's Play House ('removable/replaceable' centre or solid centre)	275/210
57	HMV POP 330	Too Much/Playing For Keeps	120
57	HMV POP 359	All Shook Up/That's When Your Heartaches Begin (push-out centre or solid centre)	160/100
57	HMV POP 378	Paralyzed/When My Blue Moon Turns To Gold Again	90

HMV 45s: PURPLE LABEL/SILVER PRINT

56	HMV 7M 385	Heartbreak Hotel/I Was The One	240
56	HMV 7M 405	Blue Suede Shoes/Tutti Frutti	300
56	HMV 7M 424	I Want You, I Need You, I Love You/My Baby Left Me	180
56	HMV POP 249	Hound Dog/Don't Be Cruel	120
56	HMV POP 253	Love Me Tender/Anyway You Want Me (That's How I Will Be)	150
56	HMV POP 272	Blue Moon/I Don't Care If The Sun Don't Shine	150
57	HMV POP 295	Mystery Train/Love Me	300
57	HMV POP 305	Rip It Up/Baby, Let's Play House	220
57	HMV POP 330	Too Much/Playing For Keeps	150
57	HMV POP 359	All Shook Up/That's When Your Heartaches Begin ('removable/replaceable' centre or solid centre)	190/90
57	HMV POP 378	Paralyzed/When My Blue Moon Turns To Gold Again	90
57	HMV POP 408	Tryin' To Get To You/Lawdy, Miss Clawdy	70
58	HMV POP 428	I'm Left, You're Right, She's Gone/How Do You Think I Feel?	70

HMV EXPORT 45s

57	HMV 7MC 42	Mystery Train/I Forgot To Remember To Forget (gold label print, serrated edge to labels)	300
57	HMV 7MC 45	I Want You, I Need You, I Love You/My Baby Left Me (gold label print)	325
57	HMV 7MC 50	Hound Dog/Don't Be Cruel (gold label print)	325
57	HMV JO 465	Love Me Tender/Anyway You Want Me (That's How I'll Be) (gold label print)	325
57	HMV JO 466	Too Much/Playing For Keeps (gold label print)	275
57	HMV JO 473	All Shook Up/That's When Your Heartaches Begin (gold label print)	265

RCA 78s

57	RCA RCA 1013	(Let Me Be Your) Teddy Bear/Loving You	15
57	RCA RCA 1020	Party/Got A Lot O' Livin' To Do	15
57	RCA RCA 1025	Santa Bring My Baby Back (To Me)/Santa Claus Is Back In Town	25
58	RCA RCA 1028	Jailhouse Rock/Treat Me Nice	15
58	RCA RCA 1043	Don't/I Beg Of You	25
58	RCA RCA 1058	Wear My Ring Around Your Neck/Doncha' Think It's Time	30
58	RCA RCA 1070	Hard Headed Woman/Don't Ask Me Why	30
58	RCA RCA 1081	King Creole/Dixieland Rock	40
58	RCA RCA 1088	All Shook Up/Heartbreak Hotel	130
58	RCA RCA 1095	Hound Dog/Blue Suede Shoes	130
59	RCA RCA 1100	One Night/I Got Stung (composing credit: Bartholomew or Bartholemew)	50
59	RCA RCA 1113	(Now And Then There's) A Fool Such As I/I Need Your Love Tonight	80
59	RCA RCA 1136	A Big Hunk O' Love/My Wish Came True	95
60	RCA RCA 1187	Stuck On You/Fame And Fortune	1000+
60	RCA RCA 1194	A Mess Of Blues/The Girl Of My Best Friend	1000+

ORIGINAL RCA 45s: BLACK LABELS

57	RCA RCA 1013	(Let Me Be Your) Teddy Bear/Loving You	25
57	RCA RCA 1020	Party/Got A Lot O' Livin' To Do	20
57	RCA RCA 1025	Santa Bring My Baby Back (To Me)/Santa Claus Is Back In Town	25
58	RCA RCA 1028	Jailhouse Rock/Treat Me Nice	15
58	RCA RCA 1043	Don't/I Beg Of You	15
58	RCA RCA 1058	Wear My Ring Around Your Neck/Doncha' Think It's Time	15

			MINT VALUE £
58	RCA RCA 1070	Hard Headed Woman/Don't Ask Me Why	15
58	RCA RCA 1081	King Creole/Dixieland Rock	18
58	RCA RCA 1088	All Shook Up/Heartbreak Hotel	50
58	RCA RCA 1095	Hound Dog/Blue Suede Shoes	50
59	RCA RCA 1100	One Night/I Got Stung	12
59	RCA RCA 1113	(Now And Then There's) A Fool Such As I/I Need Your Love Tonight	15
59	RCA RCA 1136	A Big Hunk O' Love/My Wish Came True	15

(The above RCA 45s were issued with triangular centres, round-centre re-pressings are worth half to two-thirds these values.)

60	RCA RCA 1187	Stuck On You/Fame And Fortune	12
60	RCA RCA 1194	A Mess Of Blues/The Girl Of My Best Friend	8
60	RCA RCA 1207	It's Now Or Never (O Sole Mio)/Make Me Know It	6
61	RCA RCA 1216	Are You Lonesome Tonight?/I Gotta Know	7
61	RCA RCA 1226	Wooden Heart/Tonight Is So Right For Love	6
61	RCA RCA 1227	Surrender (Torna A Surriento)/Lonely Man	7
61	RCA RCA 1244	Wild In The Country/I Feel So Bad	7
61	RCA RCA 1258	(Marie's The Name) His Latest Flame/Little Sister	7
62	RCA RCA 1270	Rock-A-Hula Baby/Can't Help Falling In Love	6

ORIGINAL RCA VICTOR 45s: BLACK LABELS

63	RCA Victor RCA 1337	One Broken Heart For Sale/They Remind Me Too Much Of You	8
63	RCA Victor RCA 1355	(You're The) Devil In Disguise/Please Don't Drag That String Around	7
63	RCA Victor RCA 1374	Bossa Nova Baby/Witchcraft	7
63	RCA Victor RCA 1375	Kiss Me Quick/Something Blue	7
64	RCA Victor RCA 1390	Viva Las Vegas/What'd I Say	7
64	RCA Victor RCA 1404	Kissin' Cousins/It Hurts Me	6
64	RCA Victor RCA 1411	Such A Night/Never Ending	8
64	RCA Victor RCA 1422	Ain't That Loving You Baby/Ask Me	6
64	RCA Victor RCA 1430	Blue Christmas/White Christmas	6
65	RCA Victor RCA 1443	Do The Clam/You'll Be Gone	7
65	RCA Victor RCA 1455	Crying In The Chapel/I Believe In The Man In The Sky	8
65	RCA Victor RCA 1489	Tell Me Why/Puppet On A String	8
66	RCA Victor RCA 1504	Blue River/Do Not Disturb	7
66	RCA Victor RCA 1509	Frankie And Johnny/Please Don't Stop Loving Me	10
66	RCA Victor RCA 1526	Love Letters/Come What May	7
66	RCA Victor RCA 1545	All That I Am/Spinout	7
66	RCA Victor RCA 1557	If Every Day Was Like Christmas/How Would You Like To Be?	8
67	RCA Victor RCA 1565	Indescribably Blue/Fools Fall In Love	10
67	RCA Victor RCA 1593	The Love Machine/You Gotta Stop	12
67	RCA Victor RCA 1616	Long-Legged Girl (With The Short Dress On)/ That's Someone You Never Forget	20
67	RCA Victor RCA 1628	Judy/There's Always Me	55
67	RCA Victor RCA 1642	Big Boss Man/You Don't Know Me	12
68	RCA Victor RCA 1663	Guitar Man/Hi-Heel Sneakers	12
68	RCA Victor RCA 1688	U.S. Male/Stay Away	15
68	RCA Victor RCA 1714	Your Time Hasn't Come Yet Baby/Let Yourself Go	20
68	RCA Victor RCA 1747	You'll Never Walk Alone/We Call On Him	25
68	RCA Victor RCA 1768	A Little Less Conversation/Almost In Love	30
62	RCA Victor RCA 1280	Good Luck Charm/Anything That's Part Of You	6
62	RCA Victor RCA 1303	She's Not You/Just Tell Her Jim Said Hello	6
62	RCA Victor RCA 1320	Return To Sender/Where Do You Come From	6

RCA VICTOR 45s: BLACK LABEL REISSUES

64	RCA Victor RCA 1020	Party/Got A Lot O' Livin' To Do	35
64	RCA Victor RCA 1025	Santa Bring My Baby Back (To Me)/Santa Claus Is Back In Town	35
64	RCA Victor RCA 1028	Jailhouse Rock/Treat Me Nice	30
64	RCA Victor RCA 1043	Don't/I Beg Of You	18
64	RCA Victor RCA 1058	Wear My Ring Around Your Neck/Doncha' Think It's Time	30
64	RCA Victor RCA 1070	Hard Headed Woman/Don't Ask Me Why	35
64	RCA Victor RCA 1081	King Creole/Dixieland Rock	35
64	RCA Victor RCA 1088	All Shook Up/Heartbreak Hotel	35
64	RCA Victor RCA 1095	Hound Dog/Blue Suede Shoes	35
64	RCA Victor RCA 1100	One Night/I Got Stung	18
64	RCA Victor RCA 1113	(Now And Then There's) A Fool Such As I/I Need Your Love Tonight	18
64	RCA Victor RCA 1136	A Big Hunk O' Love/My Wish Came True	18
64	RCA Victor RCA 1187	Stuck On You/Fame And Fortune	8
64	RCA Victor RCA 1194	A Mess Of Blues/The Girl Of My Best Friend	7
64	RCA Victor RCA 1207	It's Now Or Never (O Sole Mio)/Make Me Know It	6
64	RCA Victor RCA 1216	Are You Lonesome Tonight?/I Gotta Know	6
64	RCA Victor RCA 1226	Wooden Heart/Tonight Is So Right For Love	6
64	RCA Victor RCA 1227	Surrender (Torna A Surriento)/Lonely Man	6
64	RCA Victor RCA 1244	Wild In The Country/I Feel So Bad	6
64	RCA Victor RCA 1258	(Marie's The Name) His Latest Flame/Little Sister	6
64	RCA Victor RCA 1270	Rock-A-Hula Baby/Can't Help Falling In Love	7

RCA VICTOR 45s: ORANGE LABEL REISSUES

69	RCA Victor RCA 1088	All Shook Up/Heartbreak Hotel	35
69	RCA Victor RCA 1095	Hound Dog/Blue Suede Shoes	35
69	RCA Victor RCA 1207	It's Now Or Never (O Sole Mio)/Make Me Know It	35
69	RCA Victor RCA 1216	Are You Lonesome Tonight?/I Gotta Know	35
69	RCA Victor RCA 1226	Wooden Heart/Tonight Is So Right For Love	50
69	RCA Victor RCA 1688	U.S. Male/Stay Away	110
71	RCA MAXI 2104	Heartbreak Hotel/Hound Dog/Don't Be Cruel ('Maximillion' sleeve)	5
71	RCA MAXI 2153	Jailhouse Rock/Are You Lonesome Tonight?/(Let Me Be Your) Teddy Bear/ Steadfast, Loyal And True ('Maximillion' sleeve)	8
75	RCA MAXI 2601	Blue Moon/You're A Heartbreaker/I'm Left, You're Right, She's Gone ('Maximillion' sleeve)	8

MINT VALUE £

ORIGINAL RCA VICTOR ORANGE LABEL 45s

Year	Label / Cat. No.	Title	Mint Value £
69	RCA Victor RCA 1795	If I Can Dream/Memories	10
69	RCA Victor RCA 1831	In The Ghetto/Any Day Now	6
69	RCA Victor RCA 1869	Clean Up Your Own Backyard/The Fair's Moving On	6
69	RCA Victor RCA 1900	Suspicious Minds/You'll Think Of Me (p/s)	10
70	RCA Victor RCA 1916	Don't Cry Daddy/Rubberneckin' (p/s)	10
70	RCA Victor RCA 1949	Kentucky Rain/My Little Friend (p/s)	10
70	RCA Victor RCA 1999	I've Lost You/The Next Step Is Love	6
71	RCA Victor RCA 2060	There Goes My Everything/I Really Don't Want To Know (p/s)	10
71	RCA Victor RCA 2084	Rags To Riches/Where Did They Go, Lord (p/s)	10
71	RCA Victor RCA 2125	I'm Leavin'/Heart Of Rome	6
71	RCA Victor RCA 2158	I Just Can't Help Believin'/How The Web Was Woven	6
72	RCA Victor RCA 2188	Until It's Time For You To Go/We Can Make The Morning (p/s)	10
72	RCA Victor RCA 2229	American Trilogy/The First Time Ever I Saw Your Face	12
72	RCA Victor RCA 2267	Burning Love/It's A Matter Of Time	5
72	RCA Victor RCA 2304	Always On My Mind/Separate Ways	7
73	RCA Victor RCA 2359	Polk Salad Annie/See See Rider	7
73	RCA Victor RCA 2393	Fool/Steamroller Blues	7
73	RCA Victor RCA 2435	Raised On Rock/For Ol' Times Sake	7
74	RCA Victor APBO 0196	Take Good Care Of Her/I've Got A Thing About You Baby (solid centre, no p/s; most copies as U.S. imports with large centre hole in U.S. p/s)	220/15
74	RCA Victor APBO 0280	If You Talk In Your Sleep/Help Me	6
74	RCA Victor RCA 2458	My Boy/Loving Arms	5
74	RCA Victor PB 10074	Promised Land/It's Midnight (1st pressing)	5
74	RCA Victor PB 10074	Promised Land/It's Midnight And I Miss You (2nd pressing with correct B-side title)	15
75	RCA Victor RCA 2562	T-R-O-U-B-L-E/Mr. Songman	5
75	RCA Victor RCA 2635	Green Green Grass Of Home/Thinking About You	5
76	RCA Victor RCA 2674	Hurt/For The Heart	20

RETROSPECTIVE RCA BLUE LABEL 45s

Year	Label / Cat. No.	Title	Mint Value £
78	RCA PB 9265	Don't Be Cruel/Hound Dog (p/s)	5
78	RCA PB 9334	Old Shep/Paralysed (p/s)	5
80	RCA RCA 4	It's Only Love/Beyond The Reef (p/s)	5
80	RCA RCA 16	Santa Claus Is Back In Town/I Believe (p/s)	5
81	RCA RCA 43	Guitar Man/Faded Love (with matt U.K. p/s [cat. no. RCA 43])	30
81	RCA RCA 43	Guitar Man/Faded Love (with glossy U.S. p/s [cat. no. PB 12158])	5
82	RCA RCA 196	Are You Lonesome Tonight? (Laughing Version)/From A Jack To A King (p/s)	6

OTHER RCA 45s

Year	Label / Cat. No.	Title	Mint Value £
82	RCA RCAP 232	The Sound Of Your Cry/I'll Never Know (picture disc)	5
83	RCA RCAP 1028	Jailhouse Rock/The Elvis Medley (without "Hound Dog" credit on B-side) (reissue, picture disc)	5
83	RCA RCAP 1028	Jailhouse Rock/The Elvis Medley (with "Hound Dog" credit on B-side) (reissue, picture disc)	25
83	RCA RCAP 332	Baby, I Don't Care/One-Sided Love Affair/Tutti Frutti (picture disc)	5
83	RCA RCA 369	I Can Help/The Lady Loves Me (p/s)	5
83	RCA RCAT 369	I Can Help/If Every Day Was Like Christmas/The Lady Loves Me (10", p/s)	15
83	RCA RCAP 369	I Can Help/If Every Day Was Like Christmas/The Lady Loves Me (10", picture disc)	15
84	RCA RCA 405	Green Green Grass Of Home/Release Me (And Let Me Love Again)/ Solitaire (p/s, some with poster)	20/5
84	RCA RCA 459	The Last Farewell/It's Easy for You (p/s)	5
84	RCA RCAT 459	The Last Farewell/It's Easy for You (10", p/s)	15
85	RCA RCA 476	The Elvis Medley/Blue Suede Shoes (p/s)	5
85	RCA PB 49943	Always On My Mind (Alternate Version)/Tomorrow Night (p/s)	5
87	RCA ARON 1	Bossa Nova Baby/Ain't That Loving You Baby (p/s)	5
87	RCA ARONT 1	Bossa Nova Baby/Ain't That Loving You Baby (12", p/s)	15
87	RCA ARON 2	Love Me Tender/If I Can Dream (p/s)	5
87	RCA ARONT 2	Love Me Tender/If I Can Dream (p/s) (12", p/s)	15
88	RCA PB 49177	Are You Lonesome Tonight/Reconsider Baby (p/s)	5
88	RCA PB 49177	Are You Lonesome Tonight/Reconsider Baby (12", p/s)	8
88	RCA PB 49473	Mean Woman Blues/I Beg Of Of You (p/s)	10
88	RCA PT 49474	Mean Woman Blues/I Beg Of Of You (12", p/s)	15
88	RCA PB 49545	Stuck On You/Any Way You Want Me (p/s)	5
88	RCA PT 49546	Stuck On You/Any Way You Want Me (12", p/s)	15
88	RCA PB 49943	Always On My Mind/Tomorrow Night (p/s)	8
88	RCA PT 49944	Always On My Mind/Tomorrow Night (12", p/s)	20
89	RCA PD 49467	Heartbreak Hotel/I Was The One/Don't Be Cruel (To A Heart That's True)/ Hound Dog (3" CD, gatefold card sleeve)	8

SINGLES BOX SET

Year	Label / Cat. No.	Title	Mint Value £
77	RCA (no cat. no.)	PRESLEY GOLD — 16 NUMBER ONES (16 x 7", each in p/s, black box set)	40

OTHER SINGLES & FLEXIDISCS

Year	Label / Cat. No.	Title	Mint Value £
57	Weekend Mail (no cat. no.)	THE TRUTH ABOUT ME (1-sided 6" 78 rpm, mail-order only, some in mailer)	60/40
75	Reader's Digest/RCA RD ELV 785/65	Brian Matthew Introduces Excerpts From Elvis Presley's Greatest Hits (6" flexidisc, some with newsletter & advertising leaflet)	7/5
77	RCA Victor 2694-2709	"GOLD 16" SERIES (16 x p/s 7" in foldout cardboard carrier)	35
79	RCA LB 1	The Wonder Of You/Noel Edmonds Introduces Record Year (Lever Brothers premium)	15
81	Chiswick NS 71	Press Conference 1957/DEKE RIVERS: Elvis Presley Medley (picture disc)	6
83	Buttons BUT 3	A.F.N. RADIO INTERVIEW (p/s, fan club interview flexidisc)	5
83	Buttons BUT 4	NEW YORK PRESS CONFERENCE (orange vinyl fan club flexidisc, free with *Elvis Monthly Collector's Special*, issue 2)	5
83	Buttons BUT 5	INTERVIEW BETWEEN ELVIS, PETER NOONE AND TOM MOFFETT (fan club flexidisc free with *Elvis Monthly Collector's Special*, issue 4)	5

84	Buttons BUT 6	GERMAN RADIO INTERVIEW (fan club flexidisc free with *Elvis Monthly Collector's Special*, issue 6)	5
84	Buttons BUT 7	ELVIS' 1964 GREETING TO HIS BRITISH FANS/THE TRUTH ABOUT ME (fan club flexi with *Elvis Monthly Collector's Special*, issue 8)	5
85	Buttons BUT 8	1956 NEW ORLEANS INTERVIEW (fan club flexidisc free with *Elvis Monthly Collector's Special*, issue 10)	5
85	Buttons BUT 9	JACKSON, FLORIDA 1955 INTERVIEW/MEMPHIS 1957 INTERVIEW (fan club flexidisc free with *Elvis Monthly Collector's Special*, issue 10)	5

HMV EPs

57	HMV 7EG 8199	LOVE ME TENDER (soundtrack, round or removeable/replaceable centre)	150/175
57	HMV 7EG 8256	GOOD ROCKIN' TONIGHT (round centre only)	200

RCA EPs: TRIANGULAR CENTRES

57	RCA RCX 101	PEACE IN THE VALLEY	50
57	RCA RCX 104	ELVIS PRESLEY	35
58	RCA RCX 106	JAILHOUSE ROCK (soundtrack)	35
58	RCA RCX 117	KING CREOLE VOL. 1 (soundtrack, black label, cream or white rear p/s)	40
58	RCA RCX 118	KING CREOLE VOL. 2 (soundtrack, cream or white rear sleeve)	40
58	RCA RCX 121	ELVIS SINGS CHRISTMAS SONGS (1st issue, single sleeve)	90
58	RCA RCX 131	ELVIS SAILS (interview record, sleeve laminated front & back)	55
59	RCA RCX 135	ELVIS IN TENDER MOOD (with red print on rear sleeve)	60

*(The above RCA EPs were originally issued with **laminated front and back** sleeves; later copies with **front-only** laminate are worth three quarters of these values.)*

59	RCA RCX 1045	A TOUCH OF GOLD (laminated front sleeve only)	70
59	RCA RCX 175	STRICTLY ELVIS	55
60	RCA RCX 1048	A TOUCH OF GOLD VOL. 2	150

RCA EPs: ROUND CENTRE RE-PRESSINGS

60s	RCA RCX 101	PEACE IN THE VALLEY	20
60s	RCA RCX 104	ELVIS PRESLEY	15
60s	RCA RCX 106	JAILHOUSE ROCK (soundtrack)	15
60s	RCA RCX 117	KING CREOLE VOL. 1 (soundtrack)	18
60s	RCA RCX 118	KING CREOLE VOL. 2 (soundtrack)	15
60s	RCA RCX 121	ELVIS SINGS CHRISTMAS SONGS (gatefold p/s)	130
60s	RCA RCX 131	ELVIS SAILS (interview record)	25
60s	RCA RCX 135	ELVIS IN TENDER MOOD	20
60s	RCA RCX 1045	A TOUCH OF GOLD	25
60s	RCA RCX 175	STRICTLY ELVIS	12
60s	RCA RCX 1048	A TOUCH OF GOLD VOL. 2	50

ORIGINAL RCA EPs: ROUND CENTRES

60	RCA RCX 190	SUCH A NIGHT	25
62	RCA RCX 211	FOLLOW THAT DREAM (soundtrack)	10
62	RCA RCX 211	FOLLOW THAT DREAM (mispressing, 2nd side features Jim Reeves)	100
62	RCA RCX 7109	KID GALAHAD (soundtrack)	14
64	RCA Victor RCX 7141	LOVE IN LAS VEGAS (soundtrack)	20
64	RCA Victor RCX 7142	ELVIS FOR YOU VOL. 1	60
64	RCA Victor RCX 7143	ELVIS FOR YOU VOL. 2	60
65	RCA Victor RCX 7173	TICKLE ME (soundtrack)	45
65	RCA Victor RCX 7174	TICKLE ME VOL. 2 (soundtrack)	45
67	RCA Victor RCX 7187	EASY COME, EASY GO (soundtrack)	50

RCA VICTOR EPs: BLACK LABEL RE-PRESSINGS

64	RCA Victor RCX 101	PEACE IN THE VALLEY	20
64	RCA Victor RCX 104	ELVIS PRESLEY	15
64	RCA Victor RCX 106	JAILHOUSE ROCK (soundtrack)	25
64	RCA Victor RCX 117	KING CREOLE VOL. 1 (soundtrack)	15
64	RCA Victor RCX 118	KING CREOLE VOL. 2 (soundtrack)	15
64	RCA Victor RCX 121	ELVIS SINGS CHRISTMAS SONGS (single p/s)	45
64	RCA Victor RCX 131	ELVIS SAILS (interview record)	40
64	RCA Victor RCX 135	ELVIS IN TENDER MOOD	30
64	RCA Victor RCX 1045	A TOUCH OF GOLD	25
64	RCA Victor RCX 175	STRICTLY ELVIS	15
64	RCA Victor RCX 1048	A TOUCH OF GOLD VOL. 2	40
64	RCA Victor RCX 190	SUCH A NIGHT	10
64	RCA Victor RCX 211	FOLLOW THAT DREAM (soundtrack)	10
64	RCA Victor RCX 7109	KID GALAHAD (soundtrack)	10

RCA VICTOR EPs: ORANGE LABEL RE-PRESSINGS

69	RCA Victor RCX 101	PEACE IN THE VALLEY (push-out or solid centre)	15/30
69	RCA Victor RCX 104	ELVIS PRESLEY (push-out or solid centre)	18/12
69	RCA Victor RCX 106	JAILHOUSE ROCK (soundtrack, push-out or solid centre)	8/12
69	RCA Victor RCX 117	KING CREOLE VOL. 1 (soundtrack, push-out or solid centre)	18/12
69	RCA Victor RCX 118	KING CREOLE VOL. 2 (soundtrack, push-out or solid centre)	18/12
69	RCA Victor RCX 131	ELVIS SAILS (interview record, push-out or solid centre)	each 18
69	RCA Victor RCX 135	ELVIS IN TENDER MOOD (push-out or solid centre, with different take of "Lover Doll")	each 18
69	RCA Victor RCX 1045	A TOUCH OF GOLD (push-out or solid centre)	22/18
69	RCA Victor RCX 175	STRICTLY ELVIS (push-out or solid centre)	each 18
69	RCA Victor RCX 1048	A TOUCH OF GOLD VOL. 2 (push-out or solid centre)	22/18
69	RCA Victor RCX 190	SUCH A NIGHT (push-out or solid centre)	18/12

EP BOX SETS

82	RCA EP 1	THE EP COLLECTION (11-EP box set, reissues, with booklet)	60
83	RCA EP 2	THE EP COLLECTION VOL. 2 (11-EP box set, reissues, with booklet)	80

LPs: HMV ISSUES

56	HMV CLP 1093	ROCK 'N' ROLL	550
57	HMV CLP 1105	ROCK 'N' ROLL NO. 2	625
57	HMV DLP 1159	THE BEST OF ELVIS (10")	375

MINT VALUE £

LPs: ORIGINAL BLACK/SILVER SPOT RCA ISSUES

57	RCA RC 24001	LOVING YOU (10", soundtrack)	110
57	RCA RD 27052	ELVIS' CHRISTMAS ALBUM (laminated front & back covers with 4 pictures on back cover)	100
58	RCA RD 27088	KING CREOLE (soundtrack)	50
59	RCA RD 27120	ELVIS	75
59	RCA RD 27128	A DATE WITH ELVIS	45
60	RCA RD 27159	ELVIS' GOLDEN RECORDS VOL. 2	30
60	RCA RD 27171/SF 5060	ELVIS IS BACK! (gatefold sleeve, mono/stereo)	40/60
60	RCA RD 27192/SF 5078	G.I. BLUES (soundtrack, mono/stereo)	18/45
61	RCA RD 27211/SF 5094	HIS HAND IN MINE (mono/stereo)	25/45
61	RCA RD 27224/SF 5106	SOMETHING FOR EVERYBODY (mono/stereo)	22/45
61	RCA RD 27238/SF 5115	BLUE HAWAII (soundtrack, mono/stereo)	25/40
62	RCA RD 27265/SF 5135	POT LUCK (mono/stereo)	20/40

LPs: SILVER SPOT/'RED SEAL' RCA ISSUES

58	RCA RB 16069	ELVIS' GOLDEN RECORDS (maroon 'silver spot' label, gatefold sleeve with stapled-in 4-page photo booklet)	100
60	RCA RB 16069	ELVIS' GOLDEN RECORDS ('Red Seal'/'silver spot' label, gatefold sleeve with stapled-in 2-page photo booklet)	35
63	RCA RB 16069	ELVIS' GOLDEN RECORDS ('Red Seal'/'black spot' label, no booklet, gatefold sleeve)	25
67	RCA RB 16069	ELVIS' GOLDEN RECORDS ('Red Seal'/'black spot' label, no booklet, single sleeve)	18

LPs: ORIGINAL BLACK/SILVER SPOT RCA VICTOR ISSUES

63	RCA Victor RD/SF 7534	GIRLS! GIRLS! GIRLS! (soundtrack, mono/stereo)	20/45
63	RCA Victor RD/SF 7565	IT HAPPENED AT THE WORLD'S FAIR (soundtrack, mono/stereo)	20/45
63	RCA Victor RD/SF 7609	FUN IN ACAPULCO (soundtrack, mono/stereo)	20/45

LPs: ORIGINAL BLACK/RED SPOT RCA VICTOR ISSUES

64	RCA Victor RD/SF 7630	ELVIS' GOLDEN RECORDS VOL. 3 (mono/stereo)	18/35
64	RCA Victor RD/SF 7645	KISSIN' COUSINS (soundtrack, mono/stereo)	18/40
64	RCA Victor RD/SF 7678	ROUSTABOUT (soundtrack, mono/stereo)	16/40
65	RCA Victor RD/SF 7714	GIRL HAPPY (soundtrack, mono/stereo)	18/40
65	RCA Victor RD 7723	FLAMING STAR AND SUMMER KISSES (soundtrack, mono only, black label)	100
65	RCA Victor RD/SF 7752	ELVIS FOR EVERYONE (mono/stereo, 'orange shirt' sleeve)	35/55
65	RCA Victor RD/SF 7767	HAREM HOLIDAY (soundtrack, mono/stereo)	20/30
66	RCA Victor RD/SF 7793	FRANKIE AND JOHNNY (soundtrack, mono/stereo)	25/40
66	RCA Victor RD/SF 7810	PARADISE, HAWAIIAN STYLE (soundtrack, mono/stereo)	25/40
66	RCA Victor RD/SF 7820	CALIFORNIA HOLIDAY (soundtrack, mono/stereo)	25/40
67	RCA Victor RD/SF 7867	HOW GREAT THOU ART (mono/stereo)	25/40
67	RCA Victor RD/SF 7892	DOUBLE TROUBLE (soundtrack, mono/stereo)	20/30
68	RCA Victor RD/SF 7917	CLAMBAKE (soundtrack, black/red dot labels, mono/stereo)	20/30
68	RCA Victor RD/SF 7924	ELVIS' GOLD RECORDS VOLUME 4 (with "Never Ending" listed on sleeve instead of "Love Letters"; mono/stereo)	40/60
68	RCA Victor RD/SF 7924	ELVIS' GOLD RECORDS VOLUME 4 (corrected sleeve, mono/stereo)	25/30
68	RCA Victor RD/SF 7957	SPEEDWAY (soundtrack, with Nancy Sinatra, mono/stereo)	25/30

LPs: ORIGINAL ORANGE RCA VICTOR ISSUES

69	RCA Victor RD 8011	ELVIS ("TV Special" Soundtrack)	15
69	RCA Victor RD/SF 8029	FROM ELVIS IN MEMPHIS (mono/stereo)	15/12
70	RCA Victor SF 8080/1	FROM MEMPHIS TO VEGAS — FROM VEGAS TO MEMPHIS (2-LP, with 2 x 10" x 8" photos, glossy or matt cover)	30/25
70	RCA SF 8128	ON STAGE, FEBRUARY 1970 (with 30" x 20" colour poster; glossy or matt cover)	15/12
70	RCA LPM 6401	WORLDWIDE 50 GOLD AWARD HITS VOL. 1 — A TOUCH OF GOLD (4-LP, box set with 20-page photo book)	40
71	RCA LPM 6402	THE OTHER SIDES — WORLDWIDE 50 GOLD AWARD HITS VOL. 2 (4-LP, box with material patch & colour portrait)	40
71	RCA Victor SF 8162	THAT'S THE WAY IT IS (glossy or matt cover)	15/12
71	RCA Victor SF 8172	I'M 10,000 YEARS OLD — ELVIS COUNTRY (with colour print, glossy or matt cover)	15/10
71	RCA Victor SF 8202	LOVE LETTERS FROM ELVIS	18
71	RCA Victor SF 8221	ELVIS SINGS THE WONDERFUL WORLD OF CHRISTMAS	25
72	RCA Victor SF 8266	ELVIS NOW	22
72	RCA Victor SF 8275	HE TOUCHED ME	22
72	RCA Victor SF 8296	ELVIS AS RECORDED AT MADISON SQUARE GARDEN	15
73	RCA Victor SF 8378	ELVIS (with "Fool" sticker)	30
73	RCA DPS 2040	ALOHA FROM HAWAII VIA SATELLITE (2-LP)	20
73	RCA APL1 0388	RAISED ON ROCK/FOR OL' TIMES SAKE (U.K. disc in U.K. sleeve)	220
74	RCA CPL1 0341	ELVIS — A LEGENDARY PERFORMER VOL. 1	15
74	RCA APL1 0475	GOOD TIMES (back cover credits "Loving Arms" or "Lovin' Arms")	18
74	RCA APL1 0606	ELVIS AS RECORDED ON STAGE IN MEMPHIS	15
74	RCA LPL1 7527	HITS OF THE 70s	15
75	RCA APL1 0873	PROMISED LAND	15
75	RCA APM1 0818	HAVING FUN WITH ELVIS ON STAGE	40
75	RCA RS 1011	TODAY	18
76	RCA CPL1 1349	ELVIS — A LEGENDARY PERFORMER VOL. 2	25
76	RCA RS 1060	FROM ELVIS PRESLEY BOULEVARD, MEMPHIS, TENNESSEE	15
77	RCA LP 3021	MOODY BLUE	12
77	RCA PL 02587	ELVIS IN CONCERT	18
77	RCA PL 12274	WELCOME TO MY WORLD	15
77	RCA PL 12772	HE WALKS BESIDE ME	15
77	RCA PL 42003	ELVIS IN DEMAND	15
80	RCA CPL8 3699	ELVIS ARON PRESLEY (8-LP, box set)	60
83	RCA RCALPP 9020	JAILHOUSE ROCK/LOVE IN LAS VEGAS (picture disc)	12
84	RCA PLP 89287	I CAN HELP (picture disc)	12
84	RCA PL 85172	A GOLDEN CELEBRATION (6-LP box set with inserts)	25

LPs: BLACK/SILVER SPOT RCA VICTOR RE-PRESSINGS

64 RCA Victor RC 24001 LOVING YOU (10" LP, mono only) 75
64 RCA Victor RD 27052 ELVIS' CHRISTMAS ALBUM (laminated front & back covers, no pictures on back cover, mono only) 60
64 RCA Victor RD/SF 7528 ROCK 'N' ROLL NO. 2 (reissue of HMV LP, mono/stereo) 18/25
64 RCA Victor RD 27088 KING CREOLE (soundtrack, mono only) 50
64 RCA Victor RD 27120 ELVIS (mono only) 35
64 RCA Victor RD 27128 A DATE WITH ELVIS (mono only) 20
64 RCA Victor RD 27159 ELVIS' GOLDEN RECORDS VOL. 2 (mono only) 15
64 RCA Victor RD 27171 ELVIS IS BACK! (gatefold sleeve, mono) 30
64 RCA Victor SF 5060 ELVIS IS BACK! (gatefold sleeve, stereo) 40
64 RCA Victor RD 27192 G.I. BLUES (soundtrack, mono) 15
64 RCA Victor SF 5078 G.I. BLUES (soundtrack, stereo) 30
64 RCA Victor RD 27211 HIS HAND IN MINE (mono) 25
64 RCA Victor SF 5094 HIS HAND IN MINE (stereo) 30
64 RCA Victor RD 27224 SOMETHING FOR EVERYBODY (mono) 18
64 RCA Victor SF 5106 SOMETHING FOR EVERYBODY (stereo) 30
64 RCA Victor RD 27238 BLUE HAWAII (soundtrack, mono) 18
64 RCA Victor SF 5115 BLUE HAWAII (soundtrack, stereo) 25
64 RCA Victor RD 27265 POT LUCK (mono) 15
64 RCA Victor SF 5135 POT LUCK (stereo) 30

LPs: BLACK/RED SPOT RCA VICTOR RE-PRESSING

64 RCA Victor RD/SF 7528 ROCK 'N' ROLL NO. 2 (reissue of HMV LP, mono/stereo) 18/25

LPs: 'SMALL' ORANGE RCA VICTOR MONO RE-PRESSINGS

69 RCA Victor RD 27052 ELVIS' CHRISTMAS ALBUM 40
69 RCA Victor RD 27088 KING CREOLE (soundtrack) 30
69 RCA Victor RD 27120 ELVIS 30
69 RCA Victor RD 27128 A DATE WITH ELVIS 30
69 RCA Victor RD 27159 ELVIS' GOLDEN RECORDS VOL. 2 30
69 RCA Victor RD 27171 ELVIS IS BACK! (gatefold sleeve) 30
69 RCA Victor RD 27192 G.I. BLUES (soundtrack) 30
69 RCA Victor RD 27211 HIS HAND IN MINE 30
69 RCA Victor RD 27224 SOMETHING FOR EVERYBODY 30
69 RCA Victor RD 27238 BLUE HAWAII (soundtrack) 30
69 RCA Victor RD 7528 ROCK 'N' ROLL NO. 2 30
69 RCA Victor RD 7630 ELVIS' GOLDEN RECORDS VOL. 3 30
69 RCA Victor RD 7723 FLAMING STAR AND SUMMER KISSES (soundtrack) 350
69 RCA Victor RD 7810 PARADISE, HAWAIIAN STYLE (soundtrack) 30
69 RCA Victor RD 7867 HOW GREAT THOU ART 30
69 RCA Victor RD 7917 CLAMBAKE (soundtrack) 40
69 RCA Victor RD 7924 ELVIS' GOLD RECORDS VOLUME 4 30
69 RCA Victor RD 7957 SPEEDWAY (soundtrack, with Nancy Sinatra) 30

LPs: 'LARGE' ORANGE RCA VICTOR STEREO RE-PRESSINGS

72 RCA Victor SF 8232 ELVIS FOR EVERYONE ('blue shirt'/'TV Special' sleeve) 40

LPs: GREEN RCA INTERNATIONAL ISSUES

69 RCA Intl. INTS 1012 ELVIS SINGS FLAMING STAR 12
70 RCA Intl. INTS 1103 LET'S BE FRIENDS 12
70 RCA Intl. INTS 1206 ALMOST IN LOVE 15
72 RCA Intl. INTS 1414 BURNING LOVE AND HITS FROM HIS MOVIES (U.K. disc in U.K. sleeve) 40

OTHER LPs

78 St. Michael IMP 113 ELVIS (exclusive to Marks & Spencer) 55
78 St. Michael IMPD 204 THE WONDERFUL WORLD OF ELVIS PRESLEY (2-LP, via Marks & Spencer) 75
79 Hammer HMR 6002 THE KING SPEAKS (green sleeve) 30
84 Imperial Records DR 1124 AMERICAN TRILOGY (3-LP, box set) 25
86 RCA AREP 1 ACUFF-ROSE PRESENTS ELVIS (promo-only, 300 copies) 180

CDs

84 RCA PD 89061/2/3 THE LEGEND (3-CD, gold box set, with booklet, numbered, 5,000 only) 300
84 RCA PD 89061/2/3 THE LEGEND (3-CD, silver box set, 5,000 only, with booklet, numbered) 350

PROMO CDs

92 BMG ELVIS 58 Love Letters (1-track, plain PVC sleeve, no inlay) 200
94 BMG 74321 24079/2 SELECTIONS FROM AMAZING GRACE (sampler) 100
96 BMG 74321 36570/2 Twelfth Of Never/Walk A Mile In My Shoes ('live' picture disc, box set sampler) . 50
97 BMG ELVIS DJ 1/97 Always On My Mind (Orchestral Version)/Are You Lonesome Tonight (Laughing Version)/Moody Blue/Way Down (numbered digipak) 250
97 BMG 74321 46658/2 OFF CAMERA (compilation) 50
99 BMG/RCA 74321 68133 2 ARTIST OF THE CENTURY SAMPLER (10-track European sampler, digipak, promo only) 250

(see also Jordanaires, Scotty Moore, Bill Black's Combo)

REG PRESLEY

69 Page One POF 131 Lucinda Lee/Wichita Lineman 12
73 CBS 1478 'S Down To You Marianne/Hey Little Girl 10

(see also Troggs, Suzi Quatro)

PRESSGANG

89 Vox Pop VOX 022 ROGUES (LP) 15

RAY PRESSLEY

62 Longhorn BLH 0002 Living, Learning, Trying To Forget/Half A Love 8

PRESSURE CO.

82 Paradox SOLID 1 LIVE IN SHEFFIELD 19 JAN '82 (LP) 12

(see also Eric Random, Cabaret Voltaire)

MINT VALUE £

BILLY PRESTON

66	Sue WI 4012	Billy's Bag/Don't Let The Sun Catch You Cryin'	30
66	Capitol CL 15458	In The Midnight Hour/Advice	8
66	Capitol CL 15471	Sunny/Let The Music Play	7
69	President PT 263	Billy's Bag/Don't Let The Sun Catch You Crying (reissue)	6
69	President PT 263	Billy's Bag/Goldfinger (different B-side)	6
69	Apple APPLE 12	That's The Way God Planned It/What About You (p/s)	12
69	Apple APPLE 19	Everything's Alright/I Want To Thank You	15
70	Apple APPLE 21	All That I've Got/As I Get Older (some in p/s)	25/8
70	Apple APPLE 29	My Sweet Lord/Long As I Got My Baby (unreleased)	
70	President PT 298	If I Had A Hammer/Goldfinger (possibly unreleased)	
70	President PT 298	If I Had A Hammer/Ferry 'Cross The Mersey	5
70	Soul City SC 107	Greazee (Parts 1 & 2)	15
73	A&M AMS 7049	Will It Go Round In Circles/Blackbird	5
75	A&M AMS 7198	Fancy Lady/Song Of Joy	5
67	Capitol (S)T 2532	THE WILDEST ORGAN IN TOWN (LP)	20
67	Sue ILP 935	THE MOST EXCITING ORGAN EVER (LP)	50
69	President PTLS 1034	APPLE OF MY EYE (LP)	15
69	Apple SAPCOR 9	THAT'S THE WAY GOD PLANNED IT (LP)	30
70	Apple SAPCOR 14	ENCOURAGING WORDS (LP)	40
70	Soul City SCM 002	GREAZEE SOUL (LP)	35
72	A&M AMLH 63507	I WROTE A SIMPLE SONG (LP)	12
91	Apple SAPCOR 9	THAT'S THE WAY GOD PLANNED IT (LP, gatefold sleeve, with bonus 12" [SAPCOR 92])	15
93	Apple SAPCOR 14	ENCOURAGING WORDS (LP, gatefold sleeve with bonus 12" [SAPCOR 142])	15

(see also Beatles)

EARL PRESTON

63	Fontana TF 406	I Know Something/Watch Your Step (as Earl Preston & T.T.'s)	22
64	Fontana TF 481	Raindrops/That's For Sure (as Earl Preston & Realms)	22

(see also Realm)

JOHNNY PRESTON

60	Mercury AMT 1079	Running Bear/My Heart Knows	8
60	Mercury AMT 1079	Running Bear/My Heart Knows (78)	110
60	Mercury AMT 1092	Cradle Of Love/City Of Tears (some in p/s)	25/8
60	Mercury AMT 1104	Feel So Fine/I'm Starting To Go Steady	12
60	Mercury AMT 1114	Charming Billy/Up In The Air	15
61	Mercury AMT 1129	Leave My Kitten Alone/Do What You Did	15
61	Mercury AMT 1145	Big Chief Heartbreak/Madre De Dios (Mother Of God)	15
61	Mercury AMT 1164	New Baby For Christmas/Rock And Roll Guitar	15
61	Mercury AMT 1167	Free Me/Kissing Tree	15
60	Mercury ZEP 10078	RUNNING BEAR (EP)	90
60	Mercury ZEP 10098	RING TAIL TOOTER (EP)	120
61	Mercury ZEP 10116	TOKEN OF LOVE (EP)	150
60	Mercury MMC 14051	JOHNNY PRESTON — RUNNING BEAR (LP)	150

MIKE PRESTON

58	Decca F 11053	A House, A Car And A Wedding Ring/My Lucky Love	10
58	Decca F 11053	A House, A Car And A Wedding Ring/My Lucky Love (78)	6
58	Decca F 11087	Why, Why, Why/Whispering Grass	10
58	Decca F 11087	Why, Why, Why/Whispering Grass (78)	6
59	Decca F 11120	Dirty Old Town/In Surabaya	10
59	Decca F 11120	Dirty Old Town/In Surabaya (78)	6
59	Decca F 11167	Mr. Blue/Just Ask Your Heart	7
59	Decca F 11167	Mr. Blue/Just Ask Your Heart (78)	6
60	Decca F 11222	A Girl Like You/Too Old	7
60	Decca F 11222	A Girl Like You/Too Old (78)	12
60	Decca F 11255	I'd Do Anything/Where Is Love?	6
60	Decca F 11255	I'd Do Anything/Where Is Love? (78)	10
60	Decca F 11287	Togetherness/Farewell My Love	6
60	Decca F 11335	Marry Me/Girl Without A Heart	5
61	Decca F 11366	It's All Happening/Just As I Am	5
62	Decca F 11440	Innocent Eyes/I've Got All The Time In The World	5
62	Decca F 11498	It's A Sin To Tell A Lie/Careless Love	5
63	Decca F 11613	Punish Her/From The Very First Rose	5
66	Emerald MD 1028	Forgive Me/Our Love Will Go On	6
60	Decca DFE 6635	FOUR SONGS BY RAY NOBLE (EP)	30
61	Decca DFE 6679	MARRY ME (EP)	30

PRETENDERS

81	Lyntone LYN 9650	Whatcha Gonna Do About It/Stop Your Sobbin' (orange flexi with *Flexipop* 6)	6/4

(see also Jimmy Edwards)

PRETTY BOY FLOYD & GEMS

79	Rip Off RIP OFF 1	Spread The Word Around/Hold Tight (p/s)	40
79	Rip Off RIP 10	Sharon/The Instigator (p/s)	45

PRETTY THINGS

64	Fontana TF 469	Rosalyn/Big Boss Man	22
64	Fontana TF 503	Don't Bring Me Down/We'll Be Together	12
65	Fontana TF 537	Honey I Need/I Can Never Say	12
65	Fontana TF 585	Cry To Me/Get A Buzz	18
65	Fontana TF 647	Midnight To Six Man/Can't Stand The Pain	18
66	Fontana TF 688	Come See Me/£.s.d.	15
66	Fontana TF 722	A House In The Country/Me Needing You	18
66	Fontana TF 773	Progress/Buzz The Jerk	18
67	Fontana TF 829	Children/My Time	18
67	Columbia DB 8300	Defecting Grey/Mr. Evasion	55

MINT VALUE £

68	Columbia DB 8353	Talkin' About The Good Times/Walking Through My Dreams	40
68	Columbia DB 8494	Private Sorrow/Balloon Burning	40
69	Fontana TF 1024	Rosalyn/Don't Bring Me Down (p/s)	12
70	Harvest HAR 5016	The Good Mr. Square/Blue Serge Blues	8
70	Harvest HAR 5031	October 26/Cold Stone	8
71	Harvest HAR 5037	Stone-Hearted Mama/Summertime/Circus Mind	8
72	Warner Bros K 16225	Over The Moon/Havana Bound	5
64	Fontana TE 17434	THE PRETTY THINGS (EP)	60
65	Fontana TE 17442	RAININ' IN MY HEART (EP)	55
66	Fontana TE 17472	ON FILM (EP)	150
65	Fontana TL 5239	THE PRETTY THINGS (LP)	60
65	Fontana TL 5280	GET THE PICTURE (LP)	110
67	Wing WL 1164	BEST OF THE PRETTY THINGS (LP)	25
67	Fontana (S)TL 5425	EMOTIONS (LP, mono/stereo)	55
67	Wing WL 1167	THE PRETTY THINGS (LP, stereo reissue)	18
68	Columbia S(C)X 6306	S.F. SORROW (LP, gatefold sleeve, blue/black label, mono/stereo)	160/80
70	Columbia SCX 6306	S.F. SORROW (LP, gatefold sleeve; silver/black label re-pressing, stereo)	30
70	Harvest SHVL 774	PARACHUTE (LP, gatefold sleeve)	25
72	Fontana Special SFL 13140	EMOTIONS (LP, reissue)	15
72	Warner Bros K 46190	FREEWAY MADNESS (LP, gatefold sleeve)	15
74	Swan Song SSK 59400	SILK TORPEDO (LP, gatefold sleeve with insert)	15
75	Harvest SHDW 406	S.F. SORROW/PARACHUTE (2-LP)	18
75	Swan Song SSL 59401	SAVAGE EYE (LP, gatefold sleeve with inner)	15
77	Harvest SHSM 2022	THE SINGLES A's & B's (LP)	12
82	G.I. WAX 6	PARACHUTE (LP, reissue, 1,000 only)	12

(see also Electric Banana, Twink, Viv Prince, Sunshine, Fenmen, Kate, Zac Zolar & Electric Banana)

DORY PREVIN

70	United Artists UAG 29176	ON MY WAY TO WHERE (LP)	15
71	United Artists UAG 29186	MYTHICAL KINGS & IGUANAS (LP, gatefold sleeve)	15
71	United Artists UAG 29346	REFLECTIONS IN A MUD PUDDLE (LP, stickered sleeve with poster)	15
72	United Artists UAG 29435	MARY C. BROWN & THE HOLLYWOOD SIGN (LP, gatefold sleeve)	15
72	Sunset SLS 50385	ON MY WAY TO WHERE (LP, reissue)	12
73	United Artists UAD 60045/6	LIVE AT CARNEGIE HALL (2-LP, gatefold sleeve)	18
74	Warner Bros K 56066	DORY PREVIN (LP)	12
76	Warner Bros K 56213	WE'RE CHILDREN OF COINCIDENCE AND HARPO MARX (LP, with insert)	12
77	United Artists UAS 30070	ONE A.M. PHONECALLS (LP)	12

EDDIE PREVOST BAND

78	Matchless MR 1	LIVE VOLUME 1 (LP, private pressing)	15

(see also Amm, Organum)

JOEL PREVOST

78	CBS SCBS 6300	Somewhere Sometime/Il Y Aura Toujours Des Violins	10

ALAN PRICE (SET)

65	Decca F 12217	Any Day Now (My Wild Beautiful Baby)/Never Be Sick On Sunday	7
66	Decca F 12367	I Put A Spell On You/Iechyd-Da	7
66	Decca F 12442	Hi-Lili, Hi-Lo/Take Me Home	6
66	Decca F 12518	Willow Weep For Me/Yours Until Tomorrow	6
67	Decca F 12570	Simon Smith And His Amazing Dancing Bear/Tickle Me	6
67	Decca F 12641	The House That Jack Built/Who Cares	6
67	Decca F 12691	Shame/Don't Do That Again	6
68	Decca F 12731	Don't Stop The Carnival/The Time Has Come	6
68	Decca F 12774	When I Was A Cowboy/Tappy Turquoise (export issue)	20
68	Decca F 12808	Love Story/My Old Kentucky Home	6
69	Deram DM 263	Trimdon Grange Explosion/Falling In Love Again	6
70	Decca F 13017	Sunshine And Rain (The Name Of The Game)/ Is There Anybody Out There? (solo)	6
73	Warner Bros K 16266	O Lucky Man!/Pastoral	6
78	Jet UP 36358	Just For You/I'm A Gambler (p/s, heart-shaped disc, red vinyl; solo)	6
67	Decca DFE 8677	THE AMAZING ALAN PRICE (EP)	30
66	Decca LK 4839	THE PRICE TO PLAY (LP)	30
67	Decca LK/SKL 4907	A PRICE ON HIS HEAD (LP)	18
73	Warner Bros K 46227	O LUCKY MAN! (LP, soundtrack)	20

(see also Animals, Paul Williams Set, Johnny Almond Music Machine, Dave Greenslade)

BILL PRICE

72	Folk Heritage FHR 038	THE FINE OLD YORKSHIRE GENTLEMAN (LP)	22

KENNY PRICE

66	Stateside SS 554	Walking On New Grass/Wasting My Time	8

LLOYD PRICE

78s

57	London HL 8438	Just Because/Why	30
59	HMV POP 580	Stagger Lee/You Need Love	50
59	HMV POP 598	Where Were You (On Our Wedding Day)?/Is It Really Love?	55
59	HMV POP 626	Personality/Have You Ever Had The Blues?	60
59	HMV POP 650	I'm Gonna Get Married/Three Little Pigs	75
59	HMV POP 672	Won'tcha Come Home/Come Into My Heart	80
60	HMV POP 712	Lady Luck/Never Let Me Go	100
60	HMV POP 772	Question/If I Look A Little Blue (as Lloyd Price Orchestra)	120

45s

57	London HL 8438	Just Because/Why (triangular or round centre)	140/75
59	HMV POP 580	Stagger Lee/You Need Love	20
59	HMV POP 598	Where Were You (On Our Wedding Day)?/Is It Really Love?	10
59	HMV POP 626	Personality/Have You Ever Had The Blues?	10
59	HMV POP 650	I'm Gonna Get Married/Three Little Pigs	10

MINT VALUE £

60 HMV POP 712 — Lady Luck/Never Let Me Go — 10
60 HMV POP 741 — For Love/No If's — No And's — 10
60 HMV POP 772 — Question/If I Look A Little Blue (as Lloyd Price Orchestra) — 10
60 HMV POP 799 — Just Call Me (And I'll Understand)/Who Coulda' Told You (They Lied) — 10
61 HMV POP 826 — Know What You're Doin'/That's Why Tears Come And Go (as Lloyd Price Orchestra) — 10
61 HMV POP 926 — Boo Hoo/I Made You Cry — 10
62 HMV POP 983 — Be A Leader/'Nother Fairy Tale — 10
62 HMV POP 1100 — Under Your Spell, Again/Happy Birthday Mama — 10
71 Wand WN 17 — Hooked On A Feeling/If You Really Love Him — 5
71 Wand WN 21 — Natural Sinner/Mr & Mrs Untrue — 5
73 GSF GSZ 5 — Love Music/Just For Baby — 7
73 GSF GSZ 11 — Trying To Slip Away/They Get Down — 5

EP

59 HMV 7EG 8538/GES 5784 — THE EXCITING LLOYD PRICE (mono/stereo) — 65/85

LPs

59 HMV CLP 1285 — THE EXCITING LLOYD PRICE — 70
59 HMV CLP 1314 — MR. PERSONALITY — 60
60 London HA-U 2213 — LLOYD PRICE — 80
60 HMV CLP 1361 — MR. PERSONALITY SINGS THE BLUES — 55
60 HMV CLP 1393 — THE FANTASTIC LLOYD PRICE (also stereo CSD 1323) — 55/75
62 HMV CLP 1519 — COOKIN' (also stereo CSD 1413) — 55/75
63 Encore ENC 2004 — PRICE SINGS THE MILLION DOLLAR SELLERS — 25
69 Major Minor SMLP 57 — LLOYD PRICE NOW — 22
70 Regal Starline SRS 5025 — THE BEST OF LLOYD PRICE — 12
71 Joy JOYS 202 — STAGGER LEE — 12

MALCOLM PRICE (TRIO)

61 Oak RGJ 106 — PICKIN' ON THE COUNTRY STRINGS! (EP) — 20
64 Decca LK 4627 — COUNTRY SESSION (LP, as Malcolm Price Trio) — 15
65 Decca LK 4665 — WAY DOWN TOWN (LP) — 15
69 Saga FID 2156 — HIS SONGS, HIS GUITARS (LP) — 12
75 Sweet Folk & C. SFA 017 — THEN WE ALL GOT UP AND WALKED AWAY (LP) — 12

RAY PRICE

52 Columbia MC 342 — Weary Blues (From Waiting)/I Made A Mistake And I'm Sorry (export 78) — 12
57 Philips BBE 12137 — RAY PRICE (EP) — 35

(ROCKIN') RED PRICE

56 Decca F 10822 — Rocky Mountain Gal/Rock O' The North (as Red Price & His Rockin' Rhythm) — 15
56 Decca F 10822 — Rocky Mountain Gal/Rock O' The North (78) — 12
57 Woodbine — Woodbine Rock (78, some in p/s, promo only) — 25/15
58 Pye 7N 15169 — Weekend/The Sneeze — 12
58 Pye N 15169 — Weekend/The Sneeze (78) — 25
60 Pye 7N 15262 — Wow!/My Baby's Door — 12
61 Parlophone R 4789 — Theme From "Danger Man"/Blackjack (as Red Price Combo) — 30

(see also Cherry Wainer)

RED PRICE & BLUE BEATS

64 Blue Beat BB 209 — Blue Beats Over (The White Cliffs Of Dover)/Kiss The Baby (When You Grow Too Old To Dream) — 10

RICK PRICE

70 Gemini GMS 012 — Davey Has No Dad/Bitter Sweet — 8
71 Gemini GMS 017 — Top Ten Record/Beautiful Sally — 7
70 Gemini GME 1002 — THIS IS TO CERTIFY THAT (LP, as Rick Price & Gemini) — 25
71 Gemini GME 1017 — TALKING TO THE FLOWERS (LP) — 22

(see also Move, Sheridan-Price, Sight & Sound)

RIKKI PRICE

58 Fontana H 162 — Tom Dooley/(It Looks Like Rain In) Cherry Blossom Lane — 7
58 Fontana H 162 — Tom Dooley/(It Looks Like Rain In) Cherry Blossom Lane (78) — 6
59 Fontana H 171 — Honey, Honey/The Very Thought Of You — 10
59 Fontana H 171 — Honey, Honey/The Very Thought Of You (78) — 6
59 Fontana H 217 — Mr. Blue/Man On My Trail — 7
59 Fontana H 217 — Mr. Blue/Man On My Trail (78) — 8
62 Fontana H 371 — You're For Real/When You Pass By — 6
58 Fontana TFE 17100 — RIKKI PRICE (EP) — 22

(see also Sheridan-Price)

SAMMY PRICE

63 Storyville A 45 068 — Boogieing With Big Sid/133 Street Boogie (some with p/s) — 30/20
57 Columbia SEG 7679 — ORIGINAL SAMMY BLUES (EP) — 20
58 Vogue EPV 1146 — SAMMY PRICE (EP) — 65
58 Vogue EPV 1151 — SAMMY PRICE'S BLUESICIANS (EP) — 65
58 Vogue LAE 12027 — SWINGIN' PARIS STYLE (LP) — 40
62 London Jazz LTZ-R 15240 — THE BLUES AIN'T NOTHIN' (LP, also stereo SAH-R 6234) — 30/40

(see also SIster Rosetta Tharpe)

VINCENT PRICE

77 EMI EMI 2659 — The Monster Mash/The Bard's Own Recipe — 15
59 Columbia 33SX 1141 — VINCENT PRICE (LP) — 45

DICKIE PRIDE

59 Columbia DB 4283 — Slippin' 'N' Slidin'/Don't Make Me Love You — 35
59 Columbia DB 4296 — Fabulous Cure/Midnight Oil — 30
59 Columbia DB 4340 — Frantic/Primrose Lane — 30
60 Columbia DB 4403 — Betty, Betty (Go Steady With Me)/No John — 25
60 Columbia DB 4451 — You're Singin' Our Love Song To Somebody Else/Bye Bye Blackbird — 8

59	Columbia SEG 7937	SHEIK OF SHAKE (EP)	250
61	Columbia 33SX 1307	PRIDE WITHOUT PREJUDICE (LP, also stereo SCX 3369)	110/130

(see also Guvners)

LOUIS PRIMA (& HIS ORCHESTRA)

52	Columbia DB 3070	Ooh–Dahdily–Dah/Eleanor (with Keely Smith) (78)	18
53	Columbia DC 604	Chili Sauce/One Mint Julep (78, export issue)	20
53	Columbia DC 609	Bigger The Figure/Honey Bones (78, export issue)	18
56	Capitol CL 14669	5 Months, 2 Weeks, 2 Days/Banana Split For My Baby	25
56	Capitol CL 14669	5 Months, 2 Weeks, 2 Days/Banana Split For My Baby (78)	10
58	Capitol CL 14821	Buona Sera/Beep! Beep!	15
58	Capitol CL 14821	Buona Sera/Beep! Beep! (78)	10
60	London HLD 9230	Ol' Man Moses (with Sam Butera's Witnesses)/Wonderland By Night	10
64	Prima PR 1000	Robin Hood/Angelina (with Gia Maione)	5
64	Prima PR 1001	Fee Fie Fo O (Parts 1 & 2)	5
64	Prima PR 1006	Spoonful Of Sugar/Stay Awake	5
64	Prima PR 1009	Robin Hood/Angelina	5
59	Capitol EAP1 1132	STRICTLY PRIMA (EP)	12
57	Capitol T 755	THE WILDEST (LP)	45
58	Capitol T 836	THE CALL OF THE WILDEST (LP)	30
58	Capitol T 1010	LAS VEGAS PRIMA STYLE (LP)	20
62	Ember EMB 3348	LOUIS PRIMA SWINGS (LP)	15
60s	Dot GTL 0287	HIS GREATEST HITS (LP)	12

(see also Sam Butera's Witnesses)

LOUIS PRIMA & KEELY SMITH

50	Polygon P 1001	Oh Babe!/LOUIS PRIMA: Piccolina Lena (78)	10
54	Columbia SCM 5092	Take A Little Walk Around The Block/LOUIS PRIMA: Oh! Cumari	20
54	Columbia DB 3431	Take A Little Walk Around The Block/LOUIS PRIMA: Oh! Cumari (78)	10
58	Capitol CL 14862	The Lip/KEELY SMITH: Foggy Day	6
58	Capitol CL 14862	The Lip/KEELY SMITH: Foggy Day (78)	20
58	Capitol CL 14948	That Old Black Magic/KEELY SMITH: You Are My Love	6
58	Capitol CL 14948	That Old Black Magic/KEELY SMITH: You Are My Love (78)	6
59	Capitol CL 14994	I've Got You Under My Skin/KEELY SMITH: Don't Take Your Love From Me	5
59	London HLD 8923	Bei Mir Bist Du Schon/I Don't Know Why	10
59	London HLD 8923	Bei Mir Bist Du Schon/I Don't Know Why (78)	30
60	London HLD 9084	I'm Confessin' (That I Love You)/Night And Day	8
59	Capitol T 1160	HEY BOY! HEY GIRL! (LP)	20
60	London HA-D 2243	LOUIS AND KEELY (LP)	25
61	London HA-D 2350	ON STAGE (LP, also stereo SAH-G 6149)	20/25
62	Capitol T 1531	THE HITS OF LOUIS & KEELY (LP)	15

(see also Keely Smith)

PRIMAL SCREAM

85	Creation CRE 017	All Fall Down/It Happens (foldaround p/s in poly bag)	25
86	Creation CRE 026	Crystal Crescent/Velocity Girl (p/s)	10
86	Creation CRE 026T	Crystal Crescent/Velocity Girl/Spirea X (12", p/s)	12
87	Elevation ACID 3	Gentle Tuesday/Black Star Carnival (p/s)	5
87	Elevation ACID 3T	Gentle Tuesday/Black Star Carnival/I'm Gonna Make You Mine (12", p/s)	10
87	Elevation ACID 5	Imperial/Star Fruit Surf Rider (p/s)	6
87	Elevation ACID 5T	Imperial/Star Fruit Surf Rider/So Sad About Us/Imperial (demo) (12", some in poster p/s with 'special price' sticker)	12/10
90	Creation CRE 070X	LOADED EP (12", black die-cut stickered sleeve, 5,000 only)	8
90	Creation CRE 078X	Come Together/(Hypnotone Brain Machine Mix)/(BBG Mix) (12", die-cut p/s)	15
91	Creation CRESCD 096	Higher Than The Sun (7" Edit)/Higher Than The Sun (12")/ Higher Than The Orb (CD)	8
94	Creation CTP 183X	Rockers Dub (Kris Needs Remix)/Give Out But Don't Give Up (Portishead Remix)/ Struttin' Back In Our Mind (Brendan Lynch Remix) (10", promo only)	15
97	Creation CRE 272	Burning Wheel/The Hammond Connection (p/s)	5
97	Creation CTP 263X	Star (1-sided 10", promo only)	10
98	Creation CRE 284	If They Move, Kill 'Em (My Bloody Valentine Arkestra)/Darklands (p/s, 2,000 only)	5
98	Creation CRESCD 284	If They Move, Kill 'Em (My Bloody Valentine Arkestra)/Darklands/If They Move, Kill 'Em (12" Disco Mix)/Badlands (CD)	8
99	Creation CX 239	Pills/(Instrumental Version)/Shoot Speed — Kill Light (12", p/s, promo only)	8
89	Creation CRELP 054	PRIMAL SCREAM (LP, with bonus 45 "Split Wide Open 1"/ "Lone Star Girl 1" [CREFRE 6, no p/s])	15
97	Creation CREL 7224	ECHO DEK (5 x 7", box set)	22
02	Simply Vinyl SVLP 344	SCREAMADELICA (2-LP, 180 gm vinyl)	20

(see also Jesus & Mary Chain, Revolving Paint Dream, P.P. & Primes, Death In Vegas)

PRIMETTES

68	Ember EMBS 3398	LOOKING BACK WITH THE PRIMETTES AND EDDIE FLOYD (LP, 1 side each)	45
73	Windmill WMD 192	LOOKING BACK WITH THE PRIMETTES AND EDDIE FLOYD (LP, reissue)	15

(see also Supremes, Eddie Floyd)

PRIME-MATES

69	Action ACT 4530	Hot Tamales (Versions 1 & 2)	15

PRIME MOVERS

89	Cyanide CND 001	SINS OF THE FOREFATHERS (LP)	20

PRIMITIVES

64	Pye 7N 15721	Help Me/Let Them Tell	220
65	Pye 7N 15755	You Said/How Do You Feel	250

(see also Mal & Primitives)

MINT VALUE £

PRIMITIVES

86	Head HEAD 010	Thru The Flowers/Across My Shoulder/Lazy/She Don't Need You (12", unreleased, white label test pressings only)	30
86	Lazy LAZY 01	Thru The Flowers/Across My Shoulder/She Don't Need You/Lazy (12", p/s)	10
86	Lazy LAZY 02	Really Stupid/We Found A Way To The Sun (p/s)	5
86	Lazy LAZY 02T	Really Stupid/We Found A Way To The Sun/Where The Wind Blows (12", p/s)	8
86	Lazy LAZY 03	Stop Killing Me/Buzz Buzz Buzz (p/s, with postcard, sleeves printed back-to-front; also a very few with badge)	5/4
87	Lazy LAZY 05	Ocean Blue/Shadow (2,000 only, given away free at London Astoria gig)	6
88	RCA PB 41761X	Crash/I'll Stick With You/Crash (Live In Studio) (10", 1,500 signed, gatefold p/s)	5

PRIMO & HOPETON

67	Rio R 139	Your Safekeep/Loving And Kind	20
68	Pama PM 753	Peace On Earth/SCHOOL BOYS: Love Is A Message	12

PRIMROSE

69	NEMS 56-4129	Just For You/Nine Till Five	25

PRIMROSE CIRCUS

70	President PT 314	P.S. Call Me Lulu/In My Mind	10

PRINCE (& REVOLUTION)

SINGLES

79	Warner Bros K 17537	I Wanna Be Your Lover/Just As Long As We're Together	10
79	Warner Bros K 17537T	I Wanna Be Your Lover/Just As Long As We're Together (12", company sleeve)	18
80	Warner Bros K 17590	Sexy Dancer/Bambi (die-cut company sleeve)	30
80	Warner Bros K 17590T	Sexy Dancer (Remix)/Bambi (12", die-cut company sleeve)	45
81	Warner Bros K 17768	Do It All Night/Head (die-cut company sleeve)	30
81	Warner Bros K 17768T	Do It All Night/Head (12", die-cut company sleeve)	60
81	Warner Bros K 17819	Gotta Stop (Messin' About)/Uptown (p/s)	75
81	Warner Bros K 17819	Gotta Stop (Messin' About)/I Wanna Be Your Lover (p/s)	75
81	Warner Bros LV 47	Gotta Stop (Messin' About)/Uptown/Head (12", stickered p/s)	180
81	Warner Bros LV 47	Gotta Stop (Messin' About)/I Wanna Be Your Lover/Head (12", stickered, colour p/s)	200
81	Warner Bros K 17866	Controversy/When You Were Mine (p/s)	40
81	Warner Bros K 17866T	Controversy/When You Were Mine (12", p/s)	60
82	Warner Bros K 17922	Let's Work/Ronnie, Talk To Russia (p/s)	40
82	Warner Bros K 17922T	Let's Work (Extended)/Ronnie, Talk To Russia (12", p/s)	130
83	Warner Bros W 9896	1999/How Come U Don't Call Me Anymore (paper labels, p/s, some with free cassette mini-album in card p/s: "1999 (Edit)"/ "Uptown"/"Controversy"/"Dirty Minds"/"Sexuality")	45/15
83	Warner Bros W 9896T	1999/How Come U Don't Call Me Anymore/D.M.S.R. (12", p/s)	25
83	Warner Bros W 9688	Little Red Corvette/Lady Cab Driver (p/s)	10
83	Warner Bros W 9688T	Little Red Corvette (Full Length Version)/Automatic/International Lover (12", stickered p/s, some with poster insert)	60/25
83	Warner Bros W 9436	Little Red Corvette/Horny Toad (poster calendar p/s)	55
83	Warner Bros W 9436	Little Red Corvette/Horny Toad (standard p/s)	40
83	Warner Bros W 9436T	Little Red Corvette (Full Length Version)/Horny Toad/D.M.S.R. (12", p/s)	30
83	Warner Bros W 9436T	Little Red Corvette (Full Length Version)/Horny Toad/D.M.S.R. (12", p/s, with spiral-bound calendar or poster)	85/75
84	Warner Bros W 9286C	When Doves Cry/17 Days/1999/D.M.S.R. (cassette, some with paper labels)	10/8
84	Warner Bros W 9286T	When Doves Cry/17 Days (12", p/s)	8
84	Warner Bros W 9286T	When Doves Cry/17 Days//1999/D.M.S.R. (12", stickered shrinkwrapped double pack)	70
84	Warner Bros W 9174P	Purple Rain/God (motorbike-shaped picture disc)	70
84	Warner Bros W 9174T	Purple Rain/God (instrumental)/God (12", p/s, initially with poster)	20/8
84	Warner Bros W 9121	I Would Die 4 U/Another Lonely Christmas (paper labels, p/s)	5
84	Warner Bros W 9121T	I Would Die 4 U/Another Lonely Christmas (12", p/s)	10
84	Warner Bros W 9121TE	I Would Die 4 U (U.S. Remix)/Another Lonely Christmas (U.S. Remix) (12", p/s)	30
85	Warner Bros W 2000	Let's Go Crazy/Take Me With U (paper labels, p/s)	5
85	Warner Bros W 2000T	Let's Go Crazy (Extended)/Take Me With U/Erotic City (12", stickered p/s)	10
85	Paisley Park W 9052P	Paisley Park/She's Always In My Hair (shaped picture disc)	35
85	Paisley Park W 9052T	Paisley Park/She's Always In My Hair/Paisley Park (Remix) (12", p/s)	12
85	Paisley Park W 9052T	Paisley Park/She's Always In My Hair/Paisley Park (Remix) (12", mispressing with repeated 2nd track "She's Always In My Hair")	25
85	Paisley Park W 8929	Raspberry Beret/Hello (paper label, p/s)	5
85	Paisley Park W 8929T	Raspberry Beret (Extended Remix)/Hello (Extended Remix) (12", p/s)	12
85	Paisley Park W 8858	Pop Life/Girl (paper label, p/s)	5
85	Paisley Park W 8858T	Pop Life (Extended)/Girl (12", p/s)	15
86	Paisley Park W 8751P	Kiss/Love Or Money (shaped picture disc with plinth)	30
86	Paisley Park W 8751T	Kiss (Extended)/Love Or Money (12", p/s, some with poster)	15/8
86	Paisley Park W 8711TE	Mountains (Ext.)/Alexa De Paris (Extended) (10", white vinyl in PVC sleeve)	40
86	Paisley Park W 8711T	Mountains (Extended 9.56)/Alexa De Paris (12", p/s, some with poster)	20/10
86	Paisley Park W 8586F	Girls And Boys (Edit)/Under The Cherry Moon//She's Always In My Hair/ 17 Days (double pack, gatefold p/s)	15
86	Paisley Park W 8586P	Girls And Boys (Edit)/Under The Cherry Moon (shaped picture disc)	45
86	Paisley Park W 8586T	Girls And Boys/Under The Cherry Moon/Erotic City (12", p/s, some with poster advertising London gigs)	18/10
86	Paisley Park W 8521W	Anotherloverholenyohead/I Wanna Be Your Lover (paper or plastic labels, poster p/s)	15
86	Paisley Park W 8521T	Anotherloverholenyohead (Extended)/I Wanna Be Your Lover (12", p/s)	10
87	Paisley Park W 8399TP	Sign O' The Times (Extended)/La La La He He Hee (Extended) (12", picture disc)	30
87	Paisley Park W 8334W	If I Was Your Girlfriend/Shockadelica (poster p/s)	10
87	Paisley Park W 8334E	If I Was Your Girlfriend/Shockadelica (peach vinyl, PVC cover, with postcards & stickers)	15
87	Paisley Park W 8334TP	If I Was Your Girlfriend/Shockadelica (Extended) (12", picture disc)	25

			MINT VALUE £
87	Paisley Park W 8289TP	U Got The Look (Long Look)/Housequake (7 min MoQuake)/ U Got The Look (Single Cut) (12", picture disc)	25
87	Paisley Park W 8288TP	I Could Never Take The Place Of Your Man/Hot Thing (Remixed Edit)/ Hot Thing (Extended) (12", picture disc)	25
88	Paisley Park W 7900CD	Alphabet Street (Album Version)/This Is Not Music, This Is A Trip (Alphabet Street) (Extended) (3" CD, with adaptor, 5" case)	20
88	Paisley Park W 7806CD	Glam Slam (Edit)/Escape (Free Yo Mind) (Edit)/Glam Slam (Remix) (3" CD, with adaptor, 5" case)	20
88	Paisley Park W 7745	I Wish U Heaven (Edit)/Scarlet Pussy (Edit) (poster p/s)	10
88	Paisley Park W 7745TW	I Wish U Heaven (Parts 1/2/3)/CAMILLE: Scarlet Pussy (Edit) (12", p/s with poster)	15
88	Paisley Park W 7745CD	I Wish U Heaven (Parts 1/2/3)/CAMILLE: Scarlet Pussy (Edit) (3" CD, with adaptor, 5" case)	25
89	Paisley Park W 2924TP	Batdance (LP Version)/200 Balloons (12", picture disc, PVC sleeve)	12
89	Paisley Park W 2924CD	Batdance (LP Version)/200 Balloons (3" CD, card sleeve)	10
89	Paisley Park W 2924CDX	Batdance (LP Version)/200 Balloons (3" CD, oval card sleeve)	15
89	Paisley Park W 2814TP	Partyman (Video Mix)/Feel U Up (Long Stroke) (12", picture disc, PVC sleeve)	12
89	Paisley Park W 2814CD	Partyman (Video Mix)/Feel U Up (Long Stroke) (3" CD, gatefold card sleeve in outer plastic pouch)	8
89	Paisley Park W 2814CDX	Partyman (Video Mix)/Feel U Up (Long Stroke) (3" CD, octagonal foldout sleeve with film stills)	15
89	Paisley Park W 2814CDT	Partyman (The Purple Party Mix)/(Partyman Music Mix)/(The Video Mix)/ Feel U Up (Short Stroke) (3" CD, card sleeve)	8
89	Paisley Park W 2757TP	The Arms Of Orion (5.03)/I Love U In Me/The Arms Of Orion (3.52) (12", with Sheena Easton, picture disc, PVC sleeve)	10
89	Paisley Park W 2757CD	The Arms Of Orion (5.03)/I Love U In Me/The Arms Of Orion (3.52) (3" CD, with Sheena Easton, gatefold card sleeve)	8
89	Paisley Park W 2757CDX	The Arms Of Orion (5.03)/I Love U In Me/The Arms Of Orion (3.52) (CD, shrinkwrapped tri-fold stickered sleeve, some with sticker insert)	15/12
88	Paisley Park W 8751TP	Kiss/Love Or Money (shaped picture disc, 're-promoted' edition with longer, extended version of B-side & without plinth)	25
90	Paisley Park W 9751TP	Thieves In The Temple/Thieves In The Temple (Thieves In The House Mix)/ (Temple House Dub) (12", picture disc with insert)	8
90	Paisley Park W 9525TP	New Power Generation/New Power Generation (Melody Cool Extended Remix)/Part II (12", picture disc with insert)	8
92	Paisley Park W 0091TP	Money Don't Matter 2 Night/Push/Call The Law (12", picture disc with insert)	8
92	Paisley Park W 0113TP	Thunder/Violet The Organ Grinder/Gett Off (Thrust Dub) (12", 1-sided picture disc, with numbered insert)	10
92	Paisley Park W 0123TP	Sexy M.F./Strollin' (shaped picture disc with insert)	8
94	Paisley Park W 0260P	Let It Go/Solo (picture disc with numbered insert)	5
95	NPG 6104-0	Get Wild (including Prince Rap)/Beautiful Girl/Hallucination Rain (12", 33rpm, as NPG, plays from the inside out)	8
95	NPG 6104	Get Wild Remixes (Money Maker)/(Mix)/(Mix)/(In The House Remix)/(Funky Jazz) (12", p/s, as NPG)	10
95	NPG 6104	Get Wild Remixes (Money Maker)/(Mix)/(Mix)/(In The House Remix)/(Funky Jazz) (CD, as NPG)	10
95	NPG 615157	The Good Life (Platinum People Edit)/(Platinum People Mix)/(Dancing Divaz Mix)/ (Bullets Go Bang Remix)/(Big City Remix)/(Album Version) (CD, as NPG, UK issue has black car on disc, 'Edel' not credited on spine)	8
99	Warners W 467 T	1999/How Come You Don't Call Me Anymore/D.M.S.R. (12", p/s)	8

ALBUMS

83	Warner Bros 923 809-1	1999 (LP, original issue, single disc)	30
84	Warner Bros 925 110-1	PURPLE RAIN — MUSIC FROM THE MOTION PICTURE (LP, purple vinyl with poster)	25
85	Warner Bros 925 286-1	AROUND THE WORLD IN A DAY (LP, perforated gatefold sleeve, with lyric insert)	12
86	Paisley Park WX 39P	PARADE — MUSIC FROM "UNDER THE CHERRY MOON" (LP, pic. disc, die-cut sleeve)	50
89	Paisley Park WX 281P	BATMAN (LP, picture disc, die-cut sleeve)	15
89	Paisley Park 927 489-2	BATMAN (CD, picture disc)	20
89	Paisley Park 925 978-2	BATMAN (CD, picture disc in 'Bat' tin with booklet)	25
94	Edel NPG 6051-2	1-800-NEW FUNK (LP, with inner and sticker)	20
94	Warners 936245700-1	COME (LP, with inner)	18
94	Warners 936245793-1	BLACK ALBUM (LP, title sticker)	15
95	NPG 6103-1	EXODUS (LP, as NPG)	15
96	NPG EMI CDEMO 1102	EMANCIPATION (3-CD, as)	25
98	NPG BCT 9871	CRYSTAL BALL (4-CD, import only, as ⚥)	40

PROMOS

95	NPG 61225	Get Wild (Money Maker Radio Mix) (CD, as NPG, radio programmer's picture disc)	45
95	NPG 61047	Get Wild/Beautiful Girl (no p/s, as NPG)	6
96	NPG 60667	Lovesign/MARGIE COX: Standing At The altar (no p/s, as ⚥)	10
96	NPG 60600	Lovesign (Radio Edit Mix)/(1-800 New Funk Version)/(The Storyboard Video Mix) (12", as ⚥, most with title sticker)	35
96	NPG 60605	Lovesign (Radio Edit Mix)/(1-800 New Funk Version)/(The Storyboard Video Mix) (CD, as ⚥)	30
01	Warners PRO 2721	THE VERY BEST OF PRINCE: (When Doves Cry/Purple Rain/Kiss/Cream/1999/ Money Don't Matter) (CD, radio sampler)	20

(The Revolution are credited on all recordings from "Purple Rain" to "Anotherloverholenyohead")

VIV PRINCE

66	Columbia DB 7960	Light Of The Charge Brigade/Minuet For Ringo	40

(see also Pretty Things, Bunch Of Fives, Kate, Vamp, Chicago Line)

PRINCE & PRINCESS

65	Aladdin WI 609	Ready Steady Go/Take Me Serious	22

MINT VALUE £

PRINCE BUSTER (& ALL STARS)

Year	Label	Cat. No.	Title	Mint Value £
61	Starlite	ST45 052	Buster's Shack (as Buster's Group)/ERIC MORRIS: Search The World	40
62	Blue Beat	BB 101	My Sound That Goes Around/They Got To Go (with Torchlighters)	30
62	Blue Beat	BB 116	Independence Song (with Bluebeats)/RICO & BLUEBEATS: August 1962	30
62	Blue Beat	BB 133	Time Longer Than Rope/Fake King (with Voice Of The People)	30
62	Blue Beat	BB 138	One Hand Washes The Other/Cowboy Comes To Town	30
63	Blue Beat	BB 150	Run Man Run/Danny, Dane And Lorraine	30
63	Blue Beat	BB 158	Open Up, Bartender/Enjoy It (B-side actually "Enjoy Yourself")	30
63	Blue Beat	BB 162	Money/SCHOOL BOYS: Little Boy Blue	30
63	Blue Beat	BB 163	King, Duke, Sir/I See Them In My Sight	30
63	Blue Beat	BB 167	The Ten Commandments (with All Stars)/Buster's Welcome	20
63	Blue Beat	BB 170	Madness/PRINCE BUSTER ALL STARS: Toothache	20
63	Blue Beat	BB 173	Burning Creation/PRINCE BUSTER ALL STARS: Boop	30
63	Blue Beat	BB 180	Three More Rivers To Cross/RAYMOND HARPER & PRINCE BUSTER ALL STARS: African Blood	30
63	Blue Beat	BB 186	Fowl Thief/Remember Me	30
63	Blue Beat	BB 189	Watch It Blackhead/Hello My Dear	30
63	Blue Beat	BB 192	Rollin' Stone (with Charmers)/RICO & HIS BLUES BAND: This Day	30
63	Blue Beat	BB 197	Window Shopping/Sodom And Gomorrah	30
63	Blue Beat	BB 199	Spider And Fly/Three Blind Mice	30
63	Blue Beat	BB 200	Wash All Your Troubles Away/RICO & BLUE BEATS: Soul Of Africa	30
63	Dice	CC 6	They Got To Come/These Are The Times (with Voice Of The People)	30
63	Dice	CC 11	Blackhead Chinaman/You Ask (I Had A Girl)	30
63	Dice	CC 18	World Peace/The Lion Roars (as Prince Buster & Hazel)	30
64	Stateside	SS 335	30 Pieces Of Silver/Everybody Ska	35
64	Blue Beat	BB 210	Wash All Your Troubles Away/RICO & BLUE BEATS: Soul Of Africa (reissue)	30
64	Blue Beat	BB 211	Bluebeat Spirit/Beggars Are No Choosers	30
64	Blue Beat	BB 216	You're Mine/Tongue Will Tell	30
64	Blue Beat	BB 225	Three Blind Mice/I Know	30
64	Blue Beat	BB 232	Sheep On Top (song actually titled "She Pon Top")/Midnight	30
64	Blue Beat	BB 234	She Loves You/Healing	30
64	Blue Beat	BB 243	Jealous/Buster's Ska	30
64	Blue Beat	BB 248	Thirty Pieces Of Silver/The National Dance	30
64	Blue Beat	BB 254	Wings Of A Dove/MAYTALLS: Sweet Love	30
64	Blue Beat	BB 262	Old Lady/Dayo Ska	30
64	Blue Beat	BB 271	No Knowledge In College/In The Middle Of The Night	30
64	Blue Beat	BB 274	I May Never Love You Again/Hey Little Girl	30
65	Blue Beat	BB 278	Blood Pressure/Islam	90
65	Blue Beat	BB 281	Blues Market/MAYTALS: Looking Down The Street	30
65	Blue Beat	BB 282	Big Fight/Red Dress	30
65	Blue Beat	BB 293	Agua Fumar/Long Winter (with Charmers)	30
65	Blue Beat	BB 302	Ling Ting Tong/Walk Along	30
65	Blue Beat	BB 307	Bonanza/Wonderful Life	30
65	Blue Beat	BB 309	Here Comes The Bride (with Patsy Todd, as Jamaica's Greatest)/ BUSTER'S ALLSTARS: Burkes' Law	30
65	Blue Beat	BB 313	Everybody Yeah Yeah (as Jamaica's Greatest)/ BUSTER'S ALLSTARS: Gun The Man Down	30
65	Blue Beat	BB 314	Float Like A Butterfly/Haunted Room	30
65	Blue Beat	BB 316	Sugar Pop/Feel Up (as Prince & Jamaica's Greatest)	30
65	Blue Beat	BB 317	Come Home/I Thank You (as Jamaica's Greatest)	30
65	Blue Beat	BB 321	My Girl/BUSTER'S ALL STARS: The Fugitive	30
65	Blue Beat	BB 324	Al Capone/One Step Beyond (as Prince Buster's Allstars) (blue label or other label colours)	10/6
65	Blue Beat	BB 328	Ambition/BUSTER'S ALL STARS: Ryging	30
65	Blue Beat	BB 330	Rum And Coca Cola/I Love Her	30
65	Blue Beat	BB 334	The Ten Commandments/BUSTER'S ALL STARS: Sting Like A Bee (reissue)	30
65	Blue Beat	BB 335	Respect/BUSTER'S ALL STARS: Virginia (B-side actually "Dance Jamaica" by Val Bennett & Prince Buster's All Stars)	30
66	Blue Beat	BB 338	Big Fight (Prince Buster Versus Duke Reid)/Adios, Senorita	30
66	Blue Beat	BB 339	Under Arrest (But Officer)/PRINCE BUSTER'S ALLSTARS: Say Boss Man	30
66	Blue Beat	BB 343	Prince Of Peace/Don't Throw Stones	75
66	Blue Beat	BB 352	Day Of Light (song actually "Dayo")/It's Too Late	30
66	Blue Beat	BB 355	Sunshine With My Girl/Girl Answer Your Name	30
66	Blue Beat	BB 357	I Won't Let You Cry/Hard Man Fe Dead	30
66	Blue Beat	BB 359	The Prophet (actually "Feel The Spirit" with Slim Smith)/ BUSTER'S ALL STARS: Lion Of Judah	50
66	Blue Beat	BB 362	To Be Loved/BUSTER'S ALLSTARS: Set Me Free	30
66	Rainbow	RAI 107	Your Turn (Sad Song)/If You Leave Me (with Allstars)	18
67	Blue Beat	BB 370	Shanty Town (Get Scanty)/BUSTER'S ALL STARS: Duppy	30
67	Blue Beat	BB 373	Knock On Wood/And I Love Her	30
67	Blue Beat	BB 377	Dark End Of The Street/Love Oh Love	30
67	Blue Beat	BB 378	Drunkard's Psalm (Wise Man)/7 Wonders Of The World (as Prince Buster All Stars)	125
67	Blue Beat	BB 382	Sit And Wonder (with His All Stars)/ROLAND ALFONSO: Sunrise In Kingston	30
67	Blue Beat	BB 383	Sharing You/You'll Be Lonely On The Blue Train (as Prince Buster's Allstars; A-side actually by Prince Buster, B-side actually by Rico's Band)	30
67	Blue Beat	BB 384	Take It Easy/Why Must I Cry (2nd issue, B-side actually by Hopeton Lewis)	30
67	Blue Beat	BB 387	Judge Dread (Judge Four Hundred Years)/FITZROY CAMPBELL & PRINCE BUSTER ALL STARS: Waiting For My Rude Girl	30
67	Blue Beat	BB 388	Dance Cleopatra/All In My Mind	60
67	Blue Beat	BB 390	Soul Serenade/Too Hot	30*
67	Blue Beat	BB 391	Land Of Imagination/The Appeal (B-side actually "The Barrister Appeal")	30*
67	Blue Beat	BB 393	Johnny Dollar/Rude Boys Rule	30*
67	Blue Beat	BB 395	This Gun's For Hire/Yes, Daddy	30*
67	Blue Beat	BB 400	All In My Mind/Judge Dread Dance (The Pardon)	30*
67	Blue Beat	BB 402	Vagabond/PRINCE BUSTER ALL STARS: Come Get Me	30*

			MINT VALUE £
67	Philips BF 1552	The Ten Commandments/Don't Make Me Cry	15
67	Fab FAB 10	Shakin' Up Orange Street/Black Girl (with Allstars)	18
67	Fab FAB 11	Johnny Cool (Parts 1 & 2) (with Allstars)	20
67	Fab FAB 16	Bye Bye Baby/Human (with Allstars)	18
67	Fab FAB 25	Train To Girls Town/Give Love A Try (with Allstars)	18
67	Fab FAB 26	Going To The River (as Prince Buster & Allstars)/ PRINCE BUSTER'S ALLSTARS: Julie On My Mind	20
68	Fab FAB 31	Kings Of Old (My Ancestors)/Sweet Inspiration (with Allstars)	18
68	Fab FAB 35	Try A Little Tenderness/All My Loving (with Allstars)	40
68	Fab FAB 36	The Glory Of Love/Another Sad Nite	18
68	Fab FAB 37	This Is A Hold Up/Julie On My Mind (with Allstars)	12
68	Fab FAB 38	Free Love (with Allstars)/DALTONS: All Over The World	18
68	Fab FAB 40	Rough Rider (with Allstars)/PRINCE BUSTER: 127 Orange Street (B-side actually by Prince Buster Allstars)	12
68	Fab FAB 41	Shepherd Beng Beng (with Teddy King)/TENNORS: Ride Your Donkey	20
68	Fab FAB 47	Going To Ethiopia (as Prince Buster & Allstars)/ PRINCE BUSTER ALLSTARS: Shakin' Up Orange Street	15
68	Fab FAB 49	Glory Of Love/WAILERS: Mellow Mood (possibly white labels only)	100+
68	Fab FAB 56	Intensified Dirt/Don't You Know I Love You (with Allstars)	15
68	Fab FAB 57	Green Green Grass Of Home (as Prince Buster's Allstars; actually by Prince Buster & Allstars)/SOUL MAKERS: Girls Like You	12
68	Fab FAB 58	We Shall Overcome/Keep The Faith (as Prince Buster's Allstars; actually by Prince Buster & Allstars)	10
68	Fab FAB 64	Cool Stroker/It's You I Love (B-side actually by Little Roy)	15
68	Fab FAB 80	Hypocrite/New Dance (B-side actually by Little Roy)	15
68	Fab FAB 81	Wine And Grind/The Scorcher (with Allstars)	15
69	Unity UN 522	30 Pieces Of Silver/Everybody Ska (reissue)	15
69	Fab FAB 82	Dr. Rodney (Black Power)/Taxation	18
69	Fab FAB 92	Pharaoh House Crash/Ob-La-Di, Ob-La-Da	12
69	Fab FAB 93	Ob-La-Di, Ob-La-Da/Wreck A Pum Pum	8
69	Fab FAB 94	Hey Jude/Django Fever	12
69	Fab FAB 102	Black Soul/CALEDONIANS: Oh Baby (B-side actually by Claredonians)	12
69	Fab FAB 108	Wine And Grind/The Scorcher (with Allstars) (reissue)	12
69	Fab FAB 118	Bull Buck/ROLAND ALPHONSO: One Heart	12
69	Fab FAB 119	Let Her Go/Tie The Donkey's Tail	12
69	Fab FAB 122	Stand Up/Happy Reggae (with Allstars)	10
70	Fab FAB 127	Young Gifted And Black/PRINCE BUSTER'S ALLSTARS: The Rebel	10
70	Fab FAB 131	That's All/The Preaching (B-side actually titled "The Preacher")	10
70	Fab FAB 132	Ganja Plant/Creation	10
70	Fab FAB 140	Hit Me Back/Give Peace A Chance	15
70	Fab FAB 150	Big Five/Musical College	10
70	Prince Buster PB 1	Big Five/Musical College (reissue)	6
70	Prince Buster PB 2	Rat Trap/Black Organ (B-side with Allstars but actually by Ansell Collins & Prince Buster's Allstars)	8
71	Fab FAB 162	Baby Version (with Jan Fender)/Holly	8
71	Fab FAB 176	Police Trim Rasta (with Allstars)/Smooth (B-side actually by Ansell Collins & Prince Buster Allstars)	10
71	Prince Buster PB 4	Fishey/More Fishey	7
71	Prince Buster PB 7	I Wish Your Picture Was You/PRINCE BUSTER ALLSTARS: It Mash Up — Version (B-side actually by Dennis Alcapone)	7
71	Prince Buster PB 8	Sons Of Zion (actually by Dennis Alcapone)/ANSELL COLLINS: Short Circuit	7
71	Prince Buster PB 9	My Happiness/Human (with Allstars)	7
72	Prince Buster PB 14	Big Sister Stuff/Satta Massagana (with Allstars)	10
72	Prince Buster PB 15	Protection/Cool Operator (with Allstars)	7
72	Prince Buster PB 16	I Stand Accused/My Heart is Gone (with Allstars)	7
72	Prince Buster PB 19	Four In One Medley/Drums Drums (as Prince Buster & Allstars, B-side actually by Prince Buster Allstars)	7
72	Prince Buster PB 32	Still/Sister Big Stuff (with Allstars)	7
72	Prince Buster PB 36	South Of The Border/South Of The Border (Version) (with Allstars)	5
72	Fab FAB 36	South Of The Border/South Of The Border (Version) (with Allstars)	5
72	Prince Buster PB 47	Baldhead Pum Pum/Giver Her (with Allstars)	7
79	Blue Beat DDBB 324	Al Capone/One Step Beyond (12", p/s)	8
79	Blue Beat DDBB 334	THREE OF THE BEST (12" EP, p/s)	8
79	Blue Beat DDPB 1	Big Five/FOLK BROTHERS: Carolina/ PRINCE BUSTER: Shaking Up Orange Street (12", p/s)	8
79	Blue Beat DDPB 2	PICK OF THE PUNCH (12" EP, p/s, 2 tracks each by Tennors & Prince Buster)	8
79	Blue Beat DDPB 3	NAUGHTY BUT NICE (12" EP, p/s)	8
79	Blue Beat DDPB 4	BEHIND BARS (12" EP, p/s)	8
63	Blue Beat BBLP 802	I FEEL THE SPIRIT (LP)	110
65	Blue Beat BBLP 805	SKA-LIP-SOUL (LP, with His All Stars)	150
65	Blue Beat BBLP 806	IT'S BURKE'S LAW — JAMAICA SKA EXPLOSION! (LP, as Prince Buster All Stars; 2 different sleeves, laminated plain and unlaminated 'explosion')	175
67	Blue Beat BBLP 807	WHAT A HARD MAN FE DEAD — PRINCE BUSTER SINGS FOR THE PEOPLE (LP, with Baba Brooks)	200
67	Blue Beat BBLP 808	ON TOUR (LP)	90
67	Blue Beat BBLP 809	JUDGE DREAD (LP)	110
67	Blue Beat BBLP 820	SHE WAS A ROUGH RIDER (LP)	90
68	Fab BBLP 820	SHE WAS A ROUGH RIDER (LP, reissue on Fab label)	45
68	Fab BBLP 821	WRECK A PUM PUM (LP)	45
69	Fab BBLP 822	THE OUTLAW (LP, title listed as "Queen Of The Outlaws" on disc)	75
70	Fab MS 1	FABULOUS GREATEST HITS (LP, original issue with 'West Brothers Printers' credit on rear of sleeve)	20
70	Fab MS 2	I FEEL THE SPIRIT (LP)	55
70	Fab MS 6	TUTTI FRUTTI (LP)	45
72	Melodisc MLP 12-156	SISTER BIG STUFF (LP)	45

MINT VALUE £

72 Melodisc MLP 12-157 BIG FIVE (LP) 30
73 Prince Buster PB 9 ORIGINAL GOLDEN OLDIES VOLUME 1 (LP) 18
70s Fab MS 7 THE MESSAGE DUBWISE (LP) 40
(see also Buster's Allstars, Buster's Group, Dennis Alcapone, Jim Dakota, Hortense Ellis, Heptones, Eric Morris, Terry Nelson, Schoolboys, Protegue)

PRINCE CHARLIE

69 Coxsone CS 7101 Hit And Run/Darling, There I Stand 25

PRINCE HAROLD

66 Mercury MF 952 Forget About Me/Baby You've Got Me 10

PRINCE JAZZBO

73 Grape GR 3047 Free From Chains/LLOYD & PATSY: Papa Do It Sweet 10
73 Techniques TE 921 Mr. Harry Skank/GLEN BROWN: Telavid Drums 10
74 Ackee ACK 532 Kick Boy Face/Version 10
74 Dip DL 5036 Penny Reel/Good Things 10
(see also Earl George)

PRINCE OF DARKNESS

69 Downtown DT 441 Burial Of Long Shot/MUSIC DOCTORS: Burial Of Long Shot 12
69 Downtown DT 448 Meeting Over Yonder/MUSIC DOCTORS: Ghost Rider 12
71 Downtown DT 467 Sound Of Today/MUSIC DOCTORS: Red Red Wine Version 12

PRINCE FAR I

79 Virgin Frontline FLX 4002 CRY TUFF DUB ENCOUNTER PART 2 (LP) 15
79 HitRun APLP 9006 DUB TO AFRICA (LP, as Prince Far I & The Arabs) 20

PRINCE JAZZBO

76 Black Wax WAXLP 1 NATTY PASSING THRU' (LP) 40

PRINCE PATO EXPEDITION

70s Beacon BEAS 18 FIREBIRD (LP) 25

PRINCESS

85 Supreme SUPETX 101 Say I'm Your No. 1 (Remix Number 2)/Say I'm Your No. 1 (Alt. Version) (12", p/s) 8
85 Supreme SUPETZ 101 Say I'm Your No. 1 (HRH Mix Number 3)/Say I'm Your No. 1 (Short Version)/ Say I'm Your No. 1 (Senza Voce) (12", p/s) 8
85 Supreme SUPETX 103 After The Love Has Gone (PW Floater Mix)/After The Love Has Gone (DJ Bad Mix) (12", p/s) 8
85 Supreme SUPETG 103 After The Love Has Go-Go Gone (A PWL Remix)/After The Love Has Gone (After The Dub Has Gone) (12") 8
86 Supreme SUPETP 105 I'll Keep On Loving You (Extended)/I'll Keep On Loving You (US Remix) (12", picture disc) 10
86 Supreme SUPETX 105 I'll Keep On Loving You (mixes) (12", gatefold p/s) 12
86 Supreme SUPERX 106 Tell Me Tomorrow (Saturday DJ Edit)/Tell Me Tomorrow/Say I'm Your Number One (Original Demo Version) (10") 8
86 Supreme SU 1 PRINCESS (LP) 12
86 Supreme CDSU 1 PRINCESS (CD) 60

PRINCESS & SWINEHERD

68 Oak RGJ 633 PRINCESS AND THE SWINEHERD (LP, plain black sleeve) 100

PRINCIPAL EDWARDS MAGIC THEATRE

69 Dandelion S 4405 Ballad Of The Big Girl Now/Lament For The Earth 10
73 Deram DM 391 Captain Lifeboy/Nothing 5
73 Deram DM 398 Weekdaze/Whizzmore Kid 5
69 Dandelion 63752 SOUNDTRACK (LP) 35
71 Dandelion DAN 8002 THE ASOMOTO RUNNING BAND (LP, gatefold sleeve) 25
74 Deram SML 1108 ROUND ONE (LP) 25

JOHN PRINE

72 Atlantic K 40357 JOHN PRINE (LP) 12
72 Atlantic K 40427 DIAMONDS IN THE ROUGH (LP) 12
74 Atlantic K 40524 SWEET REVENGE (LP) 12
75 Atlantic K 50137 COMMON SENSE (LP) 12

MADDY PRIOR

78 Chrysalis CHS 2232 Baggy Pants/Woman In The Wings 6
80 EMI EMI 5903 Wake Up England/Paradise (p/s, as Maddy Prior Band) 6
82 Plant Life PLRS 001 Face To Face/Half Listening (p/s, as Maddy Prior Band) 6
83 RCA/Spindrift RCA 379 Deep In The Darkest Night/Western Movies (p/s) 6
85 Making Waves SURF 108 Stookie/Incidental Music From Stookie (p/s) 6
85 Making Waves SURF 109 Deep In The Darkest Night/Western Movies (p/s, reissue) 6
90 Parks PRKS 3 Happy Families/Who's Sorry Now (p/s, with Rick Kemp) 5
90 Parks PRKS 7 Who's Sorry Now/Happy Families (p/s, with Rick Kemp) 5
92 Park PRKCD 16 I Saw Three Ships (Dance Doctor's Christmas Remix)/The Boar's Head/ Poor Little Jesus/I Saw Three Ships (CD) 8
78 Chrysalis CHR 1185 WOMAN IN THE WINGS (LP, with insert) 18
87 Saydisc SDL 366 A TAPESTRY OF CAROLS (LP) 20
(see also Steelye Span, Tim Hart & Maddy Prior)

PRISONERS

83 Big Beat NS 90 Hurricane/Tomorrow (She Said) (p/s) 12
84 Big Beat SW 98 ELECTRIC FIT (EP) 12
82 Own Up OWN UP U2 A TASTE OF PINK (LP) 30
83 Big Beat WIK 19 THE WISERMISERDEMELZA (LP) 25
85 Own Up OWN UP U2 A TASTE OF PINK (LP, reissue in pink sleeve on pink vinyl) 30
85 Own Up OWN UP U3 THE LAST FOURFATHERS (LP) 20
86 Countdown DOWN 2 IN FROM THE COLD (LP) 20
89 Hangman HANG 23 UP RARE AND UNISSUED (LP) 20
(see also James Taylor Quartet)

MINT VALUE £

PRISONERS/MILKSHAKES

86 Empire MIC 001 THE LAST NIGHT AT THE MIC CLUB (LP, live, 1 side each) . . . 18
86 Media Burn MB 17 THEE MILKSHAKES VS. THE PRISONERS (LP, live, 1 side each) . . . 18
(see also Milkshakes, Thee Mighty Caesars)

PRIVATE DICKS

79 Heartbeat PULSE 6 She Said So/Private Dicks (p/s) . . . 20

PRIVATE SECTOR

78 TJM TJM 8 Just Just (Wanna) Stay Free/Things Get Worse (p/s) . . . 25

P.J. PROBY

62 Liberty LIB 55367 Try To Forget Her/There Stands The One . . . 12
64 Decca F 11904 Hold Me/The Tips Of My Fingers . . . 7
64 Decca F 11967 Together/Sweet And Tender Romance (some in p/s) . . . 25/7
64 Liberty LIB 10182 Somewhere/Just Like Him . . . 6
65 Liberty LIB 10188 I Apologise/What's On Your Mind . . . 7
65 Liberty LIB 10206 Let The Water Run Down/I Don't Want To Hear It Anymore . . . 10
65 Liberty LIB 10215 That Means A Lot/My Prayer . . . 12
65 Liberty LIB 10218 Maria/She Cried . . . 6
66 Liberty LIB 10223 You've Come Back/It Ain't Necessarily So . . . 7
66 Liberty LIB 10236 To Make A Big Man Cry/Wicked Woman . . . 7
66 Fab FAB 2 You've Got Me Cryin'/I Need Love (some in die-cut p/s) . . . 12/7
66 Liberty LIB 10250 I Can't Make It Alone/Sweet Summer Wine . . . 10
67 Liberty LIB 55936 Nicki Hoeky/Good Things Are Coming My Way . . . 12
67 Liberty LIB 55974 You Can't Come Home Again/Work With Me Annie . . . 15
68 Liberty LBF 15046 It's Your Day Today/I Apologise Baby . . . 7
68 Liberty LBF 15085 What's Wrong With My World/Why Baby Why . . . 8
68 Liberty LBF 15152 The Day That Lorraine Came Down/Mery Hopkins Never Had Days Like These (B-side features Led Zeppelin) . . . 15
69 Liberty LBF 15245 Hanging From Your Loving Tree/Empty Bottles . . . 15
70 Liberty LBF 15280 Today I Killed A Man/It's Too Good To Last . . . 15
70 Liberty LBF 15386 It's Goodbye/Gift Of Love . . . 15
72 Columbia DB 8874 We'll Meet Again/Clown Shoes . . . 10
73 Ember EMB S 328 Put Your Head On My Shoulder/Momma Married A Preacher . . . 7
74 Seven Sun SSUN 13 The Champ (Parts 1 & 2) . . . 8
81 Rooster RONS 101 You've Got It All/Starting All Over Again (with Polly Brown) . . . 5
87 Savoy PJS 6 M97002: Hardcore/Elvis Was Not The White Nigger — I Was (Hardcore Reprise) (12", p/s) . . . 8
64 Liberty LEP 2192 P. J. PROBY (EP) . . . 15
65 Liberty LEP 2229 SOMEWHERE (EP) . . . 15
65 Liberty LEP 2239 CHRISTMAS WITH P. J. (EP) . . . 18
66 Liberty LEP 2251 P. J.'s HITS (EP) . . . 25
67 Liberty LEP 2267 PROBY AGAIN (EP) . . . 35
65 Liberty LBY 1235 I AM P. J. PROBY (LP) . . . 30
65 Liberty LBY 1264 P. J. PROBY (LP) . . . 30
66 Liberty LBY 1291 P. J. PROBY IN TOWN (LP) . . . 22
67 Liberty LBY 1361 ENIGMA (LP) . . . 22
67 Liberty LBL/LBS 83018 P. J. PROBY IN TOWN (LP, blue label reissue) . . . 12
67 Liberty LBL/LBS 83032 ENIGMA (LP, blue label reissue) . . . 15
67 Liberty LBL/LBS 83045 PHENOMENON (LP) . . . 22
68 Liberty LBL/LBS 83087 BELIEVE IT OR NOT (LP) . . . 30
69 Liberty LBS 83219E THREE WEEK HERO (LP, featuring Led Zeppelin on "Jim's Blues") . . . 60
73 Ember NR 5069 I'M YOURS (LP) . . . 20
78 Astoria 1 ELVIS (LP; sold at theatres) . . . 30
(see also Jett Powers, Marc Almond)

PROCESSION

68 Mercury MF 1053 Every American Citizen/Essentially Susan (p/s) . . . 6
68 Mercury MF 1070 One Day In Every Week/Wigwam City . . . 5
69 Mercury SMCL 20132 PROCESSION (LP) . . . 12

PROCOL HARUM

67 Deram DM 126 A Whiter Shade Of Pale/Lime Street Blues (1st issue with darker labels) . . . 6
67 Regal Zonophone RZ 3003 Homburg/Good Captain Clack . . . 7
68 Regal Zonophone RZ 3007 Quite Rightly So/In The Wee Small Hours Of Sixpence . . . 8
69 Regal Zonophone RZ 3019 A Salty Dog/Long Gone Geek . . . 8
72 Fly Magni Fly ECHO 101 A Whiter Shade Of Pale/A Salty Dog/Homburg (p/s) . . . 7
79 RCA LB 6 A Whiter Shade Of Pale/Noel Edmonds Introduces Record Year (Lever Brothers premium) . . . 5
67 Regal Zono. LRZ 1001 PROCOL HARUM (LP) . . . 40
67 Regal Zono. TA-LRZ 1001 PROCOL HARUM (reel-to-reel, mono only) . . . 12
68 Regal Zono. (S)LRZ 1004 SHINE ON BRIGHTLY (LP, mono/stereo) . . . 30/18
69 Regal Zono. SLRZ 1009 A SALTY DOG (LP) . . . 30
70 Regal Zono. SLRZ 1014 HOME (LP, with lyric sheet) . . . 25
71 Chrysalis ILPS 9158 BROKEN BARRICADES (LP, gatefold sleeve, first pressings have a small white "i" at the top of the label) . . . 15/12
(see also Paramounts, Legend, Matthew Fisher, Robin Trower, Matthew Ellis, Freedom, Mick Grabham, Power Pack)

JUDD PROCTOR

61 Parlophone R 4769 Rio Grande/Plainsman . . . 12
61 Parlophone R 4809 Palamino/Nola . . . 12
61 Parlophone R 4841 Speakeasy/Clearway . . . 12
62 Parlophone R 4885 The Turk/Mad . . . 12
62 Parlophone R 4920 Backfire/It's Bluesy . . . 12
64 Parlophone R 5126 Better Late/Boots . . . 12
60s Morgan MR 103P GUITARS GALORE (LP) . . . 45
70s Gemini GMX 5004 GUITARS GALORE (LP, reissue) . . . 18

MINT VALUE £

MIKE PROCTOR

67	Columbia DB 8254	Mr. Commuter/Sunday, Sunday, Sunday	80

PRODIGY

91	XL XLT 17	WHAT EVIL LURKS EP (What Evil Lurks/We Gonna Rock/Android/ Everybody In The Place) (12", company sleeve)	100
91	XL XLS 21	Charly/Charly (Original Mix) (p/s)	10
91	XL XLS 26	Everybody In The Place (Fairground Edit)/G-Force (Energy Flow) (p/s)	10
92	XL XLS 30	Fire (Edit)/Jericho (Original Version) (p/s)	10
92	XL XLS 35	Out Of Space/Ruff In The Jungle Bizness (Uplifting Vibes Remix) (p/s)	10
93	XL XLS 39	Wind It Up (Rewound)/We Are The Ruffest (p/s)	10
95	XL SC 1	SCIENIDE (12", white label, 500 hand-stamped promos only)	50
96	XL XLT 70LC	Firestarter/Molotov Bitch (jukebox issue, 500 copies only)	10
96	XL XLT 70P	Firestarter/Firestarter (Instrumental)/Firestarter (Empirion Mix)/Molotov Bitch (12", 'photocopied' molotov cocktail sleeve, promo only)	20
96	XL 76 XLC 76	Minefields (Radio Edit)/Minefields (Monkey Mafia Mix)/ Minefields (Headrock Beats)/Minefields (Full Length) (cassette, promo only, 50 copies with photocopied inlay)	60
96	XL XLT 76	Minefields (Radio Edit)/(Monkey Mafia Mix)/(Headrock Beats) (Full Length Version) (12", unreleased, 10 test pressings only)	300+
96	XL XLS 76CD	Minefields (Radio Edit)/(Monkey Mafia Mix)/(Headrock Beats) (Full Length Version) (CD, unreleased, advance copy only)	80
97	XL XLS 80LC	Breathe (Edit)/The Trick (jukebox issue, no p/s)	10
98	XL XLT 98	Smack My Bitch Up (Slacker mix) (12", promo only)	40
92	XL XLLP 110	THE PRODIGY EXPERIENCE (2-LP)	18
94	XL XLLP 114	MUSIC FOR THE JILTED GENERATION (LP)	15
96	XL XLS 70CDP	FIRESTARTER (Firestarter/Charly/Everybody In The Place/Out Of Space/ Wind It Up/Firestarter/One Love/No Good/Voodoo People/Poison/Firestarter) (CD, no inlay, in-store promo only, 1000 only)	18

PROFESSIONALS

80	Virgin VS 353	Just Another Dream/Action Man (p/s)	5
80	Virgin VS 376	1-2-3/White Light White Heat/Baby I Don't Care (p/s, with giant foldout poster in stickered PVC sleeve)	6
80	Virgin VS 376	1-2-3/White Light White Heat/Baby I Don't Care (p/s, signed by Cook & Jones)	30
81	Sounds FREEBIE No. 2	Little Boys In Blue (extract)/GILLAN: I'll Rip Your Spine Out (extract) (33rpm 1-sided flexi, printed die-cut sleeve, free with Sounds)	8
81	Virgin VS 426	Join The Professionals/Has Anybody Got An Alibi? (gatefold p/s)	8
81	Virgin V 2220	I DIDN'T SEE IT COMING (LP)	18

(see also Sex Pistols, Greedies, Lightning Raiders, Steve Jones)

PROFESSOR LONGHAIR

65	Sue WI 397	Baby Let Me Hold Your Hand/Looka' No Hair	35
78	Harvest HAR 5154	Mess Around/Tipitina	15
60s	XX MIN 708	PROFESSOR LONGHAIR (EP)	18
72	Speakeasy 10-78	NEW ORLEANS 88 (10" LP)	45
72	Atlantic K 40402	NEW ORLEANS PIANO (LP)	30
78	Harvest SHSP 4086	LIVE ON THE QUEEN MARY (LP)	30
83	Stateside SSL 6004	LIVE ON THE QUEEN MARY (LP, reissue)	18

PROFESSOR LUDLOW & DR. SMITH

99	Fat Cat 12FAT 029	Professor's Saying Raas (12", custom sleeve)	8

PROFIL

80	CBS S CBS 8574	Hey Music Man/Jour De Chance (p/s)	10

PROFILE

65	Mercury MF 875	Haven't They Got Better Things To Do/Touch Of Your Hand	12
65	Mercury MF 981	Got To Find A Way/Don't Say Goodbye	12
69	Philips BF 1757	Politician Man/Where Is Love	6

(see also Karl Stuart & Profiles, Voice)

PROLES

79	Rock Against Racism RAR 1	Stereo Love/Thought Crime/CONDEMNED: Soldier Boys/ Endless Revolution (p/s)	40
79	Small Wonder SMALL 23	Softground/SMK (p/s)	12

PROPAGANDA

85	ZTT ZTAS 2	Dr. Mabuse/Dr. Mabuse Der Spieler ('white glove' p/s)	5
85	ZTT ZTAS 2 (matrix: 2A X1)	Dr. Mabuse (Instrumental Mix)/Dr. Mabuse Der Spieler ('dark photo' p/s)	6
85	ZTT CTIS 101	Das Testaments Des Mabuse/The Last Word/Dr. Mabuse (cassette, "Femme Fatale" is listed but doesn't appear)	10
85	ZTT 12 ZTAS 2	Das Testaments Des Mabuse/Femme Fatale (The Woman With The Orchid)/The 9th Life (Of Dr. Mabuse) (12", white p/s)	8
85	ZTT 12 ZTAS 2 (matrix: 2A 2U)	Das Testaments Des Mabuse/Femme Fatale/The 9th Life (Of Dr. Mabuse) (12", white p/s, title sticker reads "13th Life New Mix")	15
85	ZTT 12 ZTAS 2	Das Testaments Des Mabuse (The Third Side)/Femme Fatale (The Woman With The Orchid) The Fourth Side (12", 'dark photo' p/s)	10
85	ZTT P ZTAS 8	Duel/Jewel (Rough Cut) (ZTT logo-shaped picture disc, uncut or cut)	75/10
85	ZTT DUAL 1	Duel/Jewel//Lied/The Lesson (double pack, gatefold ZTT sleeve)	8
85	ZTT 12 ZTAS 8/12 ZTAS 2	Duel (Bittersweet)/Jewel (Cut Rough) (12", p/s, shrinkwrapped with "Dr. Mabuse" 12" [ZTT sleeve])	18
85	ZTT PROP 1	Bejewelled (12", 1-sided, white label, stickered title sleeve, promo only)	12
85	ZTT CTIS 108	DO WELL: The First Cut/Duel (7")/(Cut Rough)/Wonder/Bejewelled (cassette)	10
85	ZTT PZTAS 12	P-Machinery/Frozen Faces (clear vinyl, printed PVC sleeve)	5
85	ZTT 12X ZTAS 12	P-Machinery (Beta)/Complete Machinery/Frozen Faces (12", 'sofa' p/s)	10
85	ZTT 12 ZTAS 21/12 ZTAS 8	P-Machinery (Polish)/P-Machinery (Passive)/Frozen Faces (12", p/s, shrinkwrapped with "Duel" 12")	18

MINT VALUE £

85 ZTT 12P ZTAS 12 — P-Machinery (Polish)/P Machinery (Passive)/Frozen Faces (12", p/s, clear vinyl, printed PVC sleeve) . . . 8
85 ZTT 12X ZTAST 12 — P-Machinery (Beta)//Complete Machinery/Frozen Faces//P-Machinery (Polish)/ P-Machinery (Passive)/Frozen Faces (12", clear vinyl/black vinyl double pack, gatefold PVC sleeve with poster) . . . 30
85 ZTT CTIS 12 — COMPLETE MACHINERY: Introduction/P-Machinery (Connected)/ P-Machinery (Separation)/Frozen Faces (cassette) . . . 10
02 ZTT ZTT 180CDX — Outside World (CD, with bonus DVD, digipak, mail order only edition) . . . 30
(see also Act, Ralph Dorper, Claudia Brücken)

PROPHET
74 UK UK 64 — Have Love Will Travel/Blues In B Sharp . . . 40

ORVAL PROPHET
63 London HLL 9729 — Run Run Run/My Lois And Me . . . 12

REX PROPHET
55 Brunswick OE 9144 — CANADIAN PLOWBOY (EP) . . . 15

PROPHETS (Jamaica)
70 Big Shot BI 554 — Crystal Blue Persuasion (Parts 1 & 2) . . . 12
70 Big Shot BI 555 — Tumble Time (Parts 1 & 2) . . . 12
70 Big Shot BI 557 — Revenge Of Eastwood Version One/Version Two . . . 12
70 Jackpot JP 712 — Let's Fall In Love/Purple Moon . . . 12
(see also Lloyd & Prophets, Claudette, Lloyd & Claudette, Patrick & Lloyd)

PROPHETS (U.S.)
69 Mercury MF 1097 — I Got The Fever/Soul Control . . . 25
(see also Creation [U.S.])

PROS & CONS
66 CBS 202341 — Bend It/No Time . . . 7

PROTEGUE (& PRINCE BUSTER'S ALL STARS)
67 Blue Beat BB 398 — Foul Dance/PRINCE BUSTER'S ALL STARS: This Is It . . . 25

PROTEX
78 Good Vibrations GOT 6 — Don't Ring Me Up/(Just Want) Your Attention/Listening In (wraparound p/s) . . . 15
79 Rough Trade GOT 1 — Don't Ring Me Up/(Just Want) Your Attention/Listening In (reissue, p/s) . . . 10
79 Polydor 2059 124 — I Can't Cope/Popularity (p/s) . . . 15
79 Polydor 2059 167 — I Can Only Dream/Heartache (p/s) . . . 40
80 Polydor 2059 245 — A Place In Your Heart/Jeepster (p/s) . . . 15

PROTOS
82 Airship AP 391 — ONE DAY A NEW HORIZON (LP) . . . 250

PROVIDENCE
73 Threshold TH 14 — Fantasy Fugue/Island Of Light . . . 5
72 Threshold THS 9 — EVER SENCE THE DAWN (LP, gatefold sleeve with insert) . . . 15

DOROTHY PROVINE
61 Warner Bros WB 53 — Don't Bring Lulu/Whisper Song . . . 5
62 Warner Bros WB 70 — Crazy Words, Crazy Tune/Bye Bye Blackbird . . . 8

PROWLER
73 Parlophone R 5986 — Pale Green Hnmmmm Driving Man/Jaywick Cowboy . . . 10

PROWLER
85 SRT SRT5KS/368 — Alcatraz/So Lonely (p/s) . . . 60

PRUDES
89 Yo Yo PRU 1 — P.S. I'm Leaving/Lighthouse Keeper's Daughter (p/s, white vinyl) . . . 5

PRUNES
70 Songbird SB 1023 — Come A Little Closer/Come A Little Closer Version II . . . 8
(see also Eric Donaldson, West Indians)

SNOOKY PRYOR
70 Flyright LP 100 — SNOOKY PRYOR (LP) . . . 18

ARTHUR PRYSOCK
65 CBS 201820 — It's Too Late, Baby Too Late/My Special Prayer . . . 15
66 CBS EP 6076 — AGAIN (EP) . . . 25
67 Verve SVLP 9176 — MISTER PRYSOCK (LP) . . . 20
78 Polydor 2383 481 — DOES IT AGAIN (LP) . . . 15

RED PRYSOCK
54 Mercury MB 3158 — Blow Your Horn/Happy Feet (78) . . . 25
57 Mercury MT 154 — Teen-Age Rock/Paquino Walk (78) . . . 30
59 Mercury AMT 1028 — Chop Suey/Margie . . . 18
59 Mercury AMT 1028 — Chop Suey/Margie (78) . . . 10
58 Mercury MPL 6535 — THE BEAT (LP) . . . 50
58 Mercury MPL 6550 — FRUIT BOOTS (LP) . . . 45

PSEUDO EXISTORS
80 Dead Good DEAD 2 — Pseudo Existence/Coming Up For Air/New Modern Warfare (rubber-stamped folded p/s, pink/white label; later red/black label & stamped white sleeve) . . . 60/40

PSYCHEDELIC FURS
79 Epic EPC 8005 — We Love You/Pulse (green, pink or orange p/s) . . . 5
81 CBS A 1166 — Dumb Waiters/Dash (1st 5,000 with playable p/s) . . . 5
81 CBS A 13 1327 — Pretty In Pink/Mack The Knife/Soap Commercial (12", shrinkwrapped with free T-shirt) . . . 8
(see also Unwanted)

MINT VALUE £

PSYCHIC TV

Year	Label / Cat. No.	Title	Value
82	Some Bizzare PTV 1	Just Drifting/Breakthrough (p/s)	8
82	Some Bizzare PTV 1T	Just Drifting/Just Drifting (Midnight) (12", p/s)	15
84	Temple TOPY 001	Unclean/Mirrors (12", p/s)	10
86	Temple TOPYS 009	Godstar/Godstar (BJ Mix)/Discopravity/Yes It's The B Side (double pack, gatefold p/s)	8
86	Temple TOPIC 009	Godstar/Godstar (California Mix) (12", picture disc)	15
86	Temple TOPYD 023	Good Vibrations/Interzone/Roman P/Hex-Sex/Godstar (Ugly Mix)/Je T'Aime (double pack, gatefold p/s)	6
86	Temple TOPYT 023	Roman P (Fireball Mix)/Interzone/Good Vibrations (Kundalini Mix)/Hex-Sex (Voodoo Mix) (12", p/s)	10
88	Temple TOPY 037	Tune In (Turn On To Thee Acide House) (12", p/s, as (Psychic TV/Jack The Tab)	10
88	DC DC 23	Superman/Jack The Tab (12", p/s, no artist credit on label)	20
89	Temple TOPY 048	Love, War, Riot/Eve Of Destruction (Vocoder Mixes) (12", p/s, including sticker)	15
94	Tribal TOPY 077CD	Tribal (Four Versions) (CD)	8
82	Some Bizzare PSY 1	FORCE THE HAND OF CHANCE (LP, with bonus LP & double-sided poster, featuring Marc Almond)	35
83	CBS 25737	DREAMS LESS SWEET (LP, with inner sleeve, some with free 12" EP [XPR 1251])	25/20
84	Temple TOPY 003	PAGAN DAY (LP, picture disc, 999 copies)	50
84	Gramm GRAMM 23	THOSE WHO DO NOT (2-LP, 5000 copies)	30
85	Temple TOPY 004	THEMES 2 (LP)	15
85	Temple TOPY 008	THEMES 3 (LP)	15
85	Temple TOPY 010	MOUTH OF THE NIGHT (LP)	15
85	Temple TOPIC 010	MOUTH OF THE NIGHT (LP, picture disc)	20
86	Temple TOPIC 009	GODSTAR (LP, with picture disc)	15
86	Temple TOPY 014	LIVE IN PARIS (LP)	15
86	Temple TOPY 015	LIVE IN TOKYO	15
87	Temple TOPY 016	LIVE IN GLASGOW	15
87	Temple TOPY 018	LIVE IN HEAVEN (LP)	15
87	Temple TOPY 026	LIVE IN REYKJAUIK (LP)	15
87	Temple TOPY 027	LIVE EN SUISSE (LP)	15
87	Temple TOPY 028	LIVE IN TORONTO (LP)	15
87	Temple TOPY 029	LIVE IN GOTTINGEN (LP)	15
88	Temple TOPY 031	PSYCHIC TV (LP, picture disc)	15
88	Temple TOPY 032	ALBUM 10 (LP, picture disc)	15
88	Temple TOPY 038	ALLEGORY AND SELF (LP, blue vinyl)	20
88	Temple TOPY 036	LIVE AT MARDI GRAS	15
88	Temple TOPY 045	LIVE AT THEE CIRCUS	15
89	Temple TOPY 045	LIVE AT THEE RITZ	15
89	Temple TOPY 046	KONDOLE / COPYCAT (LP)	15
89	Temple TOPY 047	LIVE AT THE PYRAMID NYC (LP, picture disc)	18
91	Temple TOPY 020	LIVE IN BRENGENZ (LP)	18

(see also Throbbing Gristle, Coil, Monte Cazazza, Rose McDowall)

PSYCHOPATHS

Year	Label / Cat. No.	Title	Value
91	Elicit 12 ELIC 2	NIGHTMARES (12", no p/s)	8

PSYCHO'S MUM

Year	Label / Cat. No.	Title	Value
89	Woronzow W 011	A SIBILANT SIN (LP, with insert)	15

PSYKYK VOLTS

Year	Label / Cat. No.	Title	Value
79	Ellie Jay EJPS 9262	Totally Useless/Horror Story No. 5 (p/s)	50
79	MHG GHM 109	Totally Useless/Horror Story No. 5	35

PSYLONS

Year	Label / Cat. No.	Title	Value
86	E Type ETYPE 1	The Mockery Of Decline/Clear Sky	10

PUBLIC ENEMY

Year	Label / Cat. No.	Title	Value
87	Def Jam 651 245-0	Rebel Without A Pause (Vocal Mix)/(Instrumental) (picture disc)	8
88	Def Jam 652 833-0	Don't Believe The Hype/Prophets Of Rage (p/s, with patch)	5
88	Def Jam 653 089-7	Night Of The Living Baseheads/Terminator X To The Edge Of Panic (p/s, badge pack)	5

PUBLIC FOOT THE ROMAN

Year	Label / Cat. No.	Title	Value
73	Sovereign SVNA 7259	PUBLIC FOOT THE ROMAN (LP)	25

(see also Movies)

PUBLIC IMAGE LTD (PiL)

Year	Label / Cat. No.	Title	Value
78	Virgin VS 228	Public Image/The Cowboy Song (foldout 'newspaper' p/s)	8
79	Virgin VS 274-12	Death Disco/And No Bird Do Sing (1/2 Mix)/Death Disco Megamix (12", p/s, 5,000 only)	8
86	Virgin VSD 855	Home/Round//Rise/Rise (Instrumental) (double pack)	5
87	Virgin VS 988	Seattle/Selfish Rubbish (box set with 7", badge, postcard & sew-on patch)	6
88	Virgin CDT 14	This Is Not A Love Song/Blue Water/This Is Not A Love Song (Remixed Version)/Public Image (3" CD, card sleeve)	8
89	Virgin VSCD 1181	Disappointed/Same Old Story/Disappointed (12" Version) (3" CD, picture disc, card sleeve in 3" envelope-shaped plastic pouch)	8
89	Virgin VSCD 1195	Warrior (Edit)/U.S.L.S.I. (Extended Mix) (3" CD, card sleeve)	8
79	Virgin METAL 1	METAL BOX (LP, 3 x 12" with circular paper dividers & inner sheet in round tin)	20
90	Virgin TPAK 5	METAL BOX (CD, in round tin with insert)	18

(see also Sex Pistols, Jah Wobble, Don Letts & Jah Wobble, Vivien Goldman, Time Zone, Cowboys International)

GARY PUCKETT (& UNION GAP)

Year	Label / Cat. No.	Title	Value
68	CBS 3365	Young Girl/I'm Losing You (as Union Gap featuring Gary Puckett)	7
68	CBS 3551	Lady Willpower/Daylight Stranger	7
68	CBS 3713	Over You/If The Day Would Come	6
69	CBS 4505	This Girl Is A Woman Now/His Other Woman	6

			MINT VALUE £
69	CBS 4122	Don't Give In To Him/Could I	6
70	CBS 4885	Let's Give Adam & Eve Another Chance/Beggar	6
70	CBS 4345	I Just Don't Know What To Do With Myself/All That Matters (solo)	6
71	CBS 7021	Keep The Customer Satisfied/No-One Really Knows (solo)	6
73	CBS 8202	Young Girl/Woman, Woman (p/s, 'Hall Of Fame Hits' series)	6
68	CBS (S) 63342	YOUNG GIRL (LP)	30
68	CBS (S) 63429	INCREDIBLE (LP)	25
70	CBS 63794	THE NEW GARY PUCKETT AND THE UNION GAP ALBUM (LP)	20

PUDDING

67	Decca F 12603	The Magic Bus/It's Too Late	70

TITO PUENTE

54	Seeco SV 2249	Por Tu Amor/Plaza Stomp (78, as Tito Puente & His Conjunto)	7
57	RCA RD 27002	LET'S CHA-CHA WITH PUENTE (LP)	12
58	RCA SF 5008	MUCHO PUENTE (LP)	15

LEROY PULLINS

66	London HLR 10056	I'm A Nut/Knee Deep	18
79	Pulp Music PB 1	Low Flying Aircraft/Something Just Behind My Back/So Lo (blank labels, some numbered up to 2,000 & signed, some with handmade sleeve)	25/20

PULP

83	Red Rhino RED 32	My Lighthouse (Remix)/Looking For Life (p/s)	70
83	Red Rhino RED 37	Everybody's Problem/There Was (p/s)	70
85	Fire BLAZE 5	Little Girl (With Blue Eyes)/Simultaneous/Blue Glow/The Will To Power (12", p/s)	15
86	Fire BLAZE 10	Dogs Are Everywhere/The Mark Of The Devil/97 Lovers/Aborigine/ Goodnight (12", p/s)	12
87	Fire BLAZE 17	They Suffocate At Night (Edited Version)/Tunnel (Cut Up Version) (p/s)	10
87	Fire BLAZE 17T	They Suffocate At Night (Uncut Version)/Tunnel (Full Length Version) (12", p/s)	12
87	Fire BLAZE 21T	Masters Of The Universe (Sanitised Version)/Manon/Silence (12", p/s)	12
90	Fire BLAZE 44T	My Legendary Girlfriend/Is This House?/This House Is Condemned (12", p/s)	10
91	Fire BLAZE 51T	Countdown/Death Goes To The Disco/Countdown (Radio Edit) (12", p/s)	15
92	Gift GIF 1	O.U. (Gone Gone)/Space/O.U. (Gone Gone) (Radio Edit) (12", p/s)	10
92	Gift GIF 1CD	O.U. (Gone Gone) (Radio Edit)/Space/O.U. (Gone Gone) (CD)	15
92	Caff CAFF 17	My Legendary Girlfriend/Sickly Grin/Back In L.A. (foldover p/s with insert in poly bag, 500 only)	90
92	Fire BLAZE 44CD	My Legendary Girlfriend/Is This House?/This House Is Condemned (CD)	20
92	Gift GIF 3	Babies/Styloroc (Nites Of Suburbia)/Sheffield: Sex City (12", p/s)	8
92	Gift GIF 3CD	Babies/Styloroc (Nites Of Suburbia)/Sheffield: Sex City/ Sheffield: Sex City (Instrumental) (CD, card sleeve)	22
93	Gift GIF 6CD	Razzmatazz/Inside Susan: A Story In 3 Songs (Stacks/Inside Susan/ 59 Lyndhurst Grove) (CD)	15
93	Island IS 567	Lip Gloss/You're A Nightmare (p/s)	8
95	Island CIDX 613	Common People/Razzmatazz/Dogs Are Everywhere/Joyriders (CD, with sticker)	8
96	Island ISC 574	Do You Remember The First Time/Street Lites (reissue, brown vinyl, p/s)	5
94	Island 12IS 595	THE SISTERS EP (12", p/s with print)	12
84	Red Rhino REDLP 29	IT (mini-LP)	25
94	Cherry Red CDMRED 112	IT (CD, with extra tracks; withdrawn, 1,000 only)	20

PULSAR

76	Decca SKL-R 5228	POLLEN (LP)	18
77	Decca TXS 119	STRANDS OF THE FUTURE (LP)	15

PULSE

70	Major Minor SMLP 64	PULSE (LP)	50

PUMPHOUSE GANG

77	Kitsch FAD 1	Motorcity Fantasy/Cocaine (p/s)	7

PUNCHERS

70	Punch PH 46	Sons Of Thunder (actually by Lee Perry & The Upsetters)/ Only If You Understand	20

PUNCHIN' JUDY

73	Transatlantic TRA 272	PUNCHIN' JUDY (LP)	25

PUNCTURE

77	Small Wonder SMALL 1	Mucky Pup/Can't Rock'n'Roll (p/s)	10

PUNKETTES

77	Response SR 511	Going Out Wiv A Punk/Polythene	25

PUPILS

66	Wing WL 1150	A TRIBUTE TO THE ROLLING STONES (LP)	80
69	Fontana SFL 13087	A TRIBUTE TO THE ROLLING STONES (LP, reissue)	40

(see also Eyes)

PUPPETS

63	Pye 7N 15556	Poison Ivy/Everybody's Talking	45
64	Pye 7N 15625	Shake With Me/Three Boys Looking For Love (existence unconfirmed)	
64	Pye 7N 15634	Baby Don't Cry/Shake With Me	45

FRANK PURCELL

73	Paramount PAS 6064	JAMES BOND'S GREATEST HITS (LP)	20

DANNY PURCHES

55	Columbia SCM 5183	Mama/Just One More Time	15
58	Columbia DB 4129	The Shrine On The Second Floor/He	12
58	Columbia DB 4129	The Shrine On The Second Floor/He (78)	8

MINT VALUE £

(BERNARD) PRETTY PURDIE
68 Direction 58-3301 Funky Donkey/Caravan . . . 7
68 Direction 58-3628 Soul Clappin'/Blow Your Lid . . . 7
71 Philips 6073 708 Good Livin' Good Lovin'/Day Dreaming . . . 5
68 Direction 8-63290 SOUL DRUMS (LP) . . . 55
71 Philips 6369 421 SOUL IS ... (LP) . . . 25

PURE HELL
78 Golden Sphinx GSX 002 These Boots Are Made For Walking/No Rules (p/s) . . . 30

PURE LOVE & PLEASURE
70 Stateside SSL 5026 A RECORD OF PURE LOVE AND PLEASURE (LP) . . . 18

PURGE
69 Corn CP 101 The Mayor Of Simpleton Hall/The Knave (p/s) . . . 150

JAMES & BOBBY PURIFY
66 Stateside SS 547 I'm Your Puppet/So Many Reasons . . . 12
67 Stateside SS 595 Wish You Didn't Have To Go/You Can't Keep A Good Man Down . . . 12
67 Stateside SS 2016 Shake A Tail Feather/Goodness Gracious . . . 15
67 Stateside SS 2039 I Take What I Want/Sixteen Tons . . . 12
67 Stateside SS 2049 Let Love Come Between Us/I Don't Want To Have To Wait . . . 20
68 Stateside SS 2093 Do Unto Me/Everybody Needs Somebody . . . 12
68 Bell BLL 1008 I Can't Remember/I Was Born To Lose Out . . . 7
68 Bell BLL 1024 Help Yourself To All My Lovin'/Last Piece Of Love . . . 7
69 Bell BLL 1043 Untie Me/We're Finally Gonna Make It . . . 7
69 Bell BLL 1056 Let Love Come Between Us/Shake A Tail Feather . . . 10
69 Bell BLL 1067 Do Unto Me/Wish You Didn't Have To Go . . . 6
72 Mojo 2092 056 I'm Your Puppet/Wish You Didn't Have To Go . . . 6
67 Stateside SL 10206 JAMES AND BOBBY PURIFY (LP) . . . 50
67 Bell MBLL/SBLL 101 THE PURE SOUND OF THE PURIFYS (LP) . . . 40

ALTON PURNELL
70 Dixie DIX 4 TRAVELLING LIGHT (LP) . . . 30
(see also Bonnie Raitt)

PURPLE ALGAE
95 Poor Person Prod. PPPR 7 ADRIFT ON A SEA OF SOUND (LP, handmade sleeve & insert, no'd, 500 only) . . 20

PURPLE GANG
67 Big T BIG 101 Granny Takes A Trip/Bootleg Whisky . . . 12
68 Big T BIG 111 Kiss Me Goodnight Sally Green/Auntie Monica . . . 7
68 Transatlantic THE PURPLE GANG STRIKES (LP) . . . 40

PURPLE HAZE
85 S.R.S. SRS 6 Hear It On The Radio (p/s) . . . 55

PURPLE HEARTS
79 Fiction FICS 003 Millions Like Us/Beat That! (p/s) . . . 10
79 Fiction FICS 007 Frustration/Extraordinary Sensations (p/s) . . . 10
80 Fiction FICS 9 Jimmy/What Am I Gonna Do (p/s) . . . 10
80 Safari SAFE 30 My Life's A Jigsaw/The Guy Who Made Her A Star/Just To Please You (initially in foldout jigsaw p/s) . . . 18/12
82 Road Runner RR 1 Plane Crash/Scooby Doo/Gun Of Life (p/s) . . . 15
80 Fiction FIX 002/2383 568 BEAT THAT! (LP) . . . 20
85 Razor RAZS 13 HEAD ON COLLISION TIME (LP) . . . 12
85 Razor RAZS 19 POPISH FRENZY (LP) . . . 12
(see also Bob Manton, Rage)

GEOFF PURVIS
77 Fellside FE 003 THE BORDER FIDDLER (LP) . . . 15

PUSSY
72 Deram DM 368 Feline Woman/Ska Child . . . 22
(see also Jerusalem)

PUSSY
69 Morgan Bluetown BT 5002 PUSSY PLAYS (LP) . . . 330
(see also Angel Pavement, Fortes Mentum)

PUSSYFOOT
66 Decca F 12474 Freeloader/Things That Still Remind Me . . . 18
67 Decca F 12561 Mr Hyde/Hasty Words . . . 18
68 Pye 7N 17520 Good Times/Till You Don't Want Me Anymore . . . 15
(see also Rare Breed)

PUSSY GALORE
89 Product INCLP 1 DIAL M FOR MOTHERFUCKER (LP) . . . 18
(see also Jon Spencer Blues Explosion)

ASHA PUTHLI
73 CBS 65804 ASHA PUTHLI (LP) . . . 15
75 CBS 80978 SHE LOVES TO HEAR THE MUSIC (LP) . . . 15
76 CBS 81443 THE DEVIL IS LOOSE (LP) . . . 15

PUZZLE
69 Stateside SS 2146 Hey Medusa/Make The Children Happy . . . 7
69 Stateside SSL 10285 PUZZLE (LP) . . . 20

PVC 2
77 Zoom ZUM 2 Put You In The Picture/Pain/Deranged, Demented and Free (p/s) . . . 15
(see also Midge Ure, Zones)

NATASHA PYNE
66 Polydor 56713 It's All In Your Head/I'm A Dreamer . . . 8

MINT VALUE £

PYRAMID

67 Deram DM 111 — Summer Of Last Year/Summer Evening . . . 35
(see also Fairport Convention, Ian Matthews)

PYRAMIDS (Jamaica)

67 President PT 161 — Train Tour To Rainbow City/John Chewey . . . 7
68 President PT 177 — Wedding In Peyton Place/Girls Girls Girls . . . 7
68 President PT 195 — All Change On The Bakerloo Line/Playing Games . . . 7
68 President PT 206 — Mexican Moonlight/Mule . . . 6
68 President PT 225 — Tisko My Darling/Movement All Around . . . 7
69 President PT 243 — Do-Re-Mi/I'm Outnumbered . . . 7
69 President PT 274 — I'm A Man/Dragon Fly . . . 7
69 Doctor Bird DB 1307 — Stay With Him/Chicken Mary . . . 18
70 Duke DU 80 — Geronimo/Feel Alright . . . 10
70 Trojan TR 7755 — Feel Alright/Telstar . . . 7
70 Trojan TR 7770 — To Sir With Love/Reggae Shuffle . . . 7
71 Trojan TR 7803 — All For You/All For You Version . . . 6
71 Creole CR 1003 — Mosquito Bite/Mother's Bath . . . 7
68 President PTL 1021 — THE PYRAMIDS (LP) . . . 45

PYRAMIDS (U.K.)

65 Polydor BM 56028 — Baby's Gone Away/Kiss And Dance With You . . . 6

PYRAMIDS (U.S.)

64 London HLU 9847 — Penetration/Here Comes Marsha . . . 35
(see also Symarip, Equals, Little Grants & Eddie, Seven Letters, Bruce Ruffin)

PYTHAGORAS THEOREM

70 Pye 7N 17924 — Give A Damn/London Bridge . . . 8
70 Pye 7N 17990 — Our House/Free Like Me . . . 5

PYTHON LEE JACKSON

70 Young Blood YB 1017 — In A Broken Dream/Doing Fine . . . 6
76 Young Blood YB 1077 — The Blues/Cloud Nine . . . 5
80 Young Blood YB 0089 — In A Broken Dream/The Blues . . . 6
80 Young Blood YEP 89 — In A Broken Dream (mono)/In A Broken Dream (stereo)/The Blues/ Cloud Nine (EP, "Kelly Girl" Employment Agency advert on p/s) . . . 12
74 Young Blood YB 3001 — IN A BROKEN DREAM (LP, featuring Rod Stewart) . . . 18
(see also Rod Stewart)

PYEWACKET

81 Dingles DIN 312 — PYEWACKET (LP) . . . 15
83 Familiar FAM 43 — THE MAN IN THE MOON DRINKS CLARET (LP) . . . 15

Q-BERT

97 Mo' Wax MW 084 — Camel Bobsled Race/(mixes) (12") . . . 12
(see also DJ Shadow)

Q-CHASTIC

92 Rephlex 002EP — Q-CHASTIC EP (double pack) . . . 200
(see also Aphex Twin)

QUAD

97 Acme AC 8020LP — QUAD (LP, clear vinyl in printed clear PVC cover) . . . 15
97 Prescription DRUG 3 — QUAD (LP, 99 copies only, handmade sleeve, mail-order only) . . . 25
(see also Sun Dial)

CHRISTINE QUAITE

62 Oriole CB 1739 — Guilty Eyes/Oh My! . . . 20
62 Oriole CB 1772 — Your Nose Is Gonna Grow/Our Last Chance . . . 20
63 Oriole CB 1845 — Mister Heartache/Whisper Wonderful Words . . . 20
63 Oriole CB 1876 — In The Middle Of The Floor/Tell Me Mama . . . 20
63 Oriole CB 1921 — I Believe In Love/Here She Comes . . . 20
64 Oriole CB 1945 — Mister Stuck Up/Will You Be The Same Tomorrow . . . 20
65 Stateside SS 435 — If You've Got A Heart/So Near So Far . . . 20
66 Stateside SS 482 — Long After Tonight Is All Over/I'm Hoping . . . 35

QUAKER CITY BOYS

59 London HLU 8796 — Teasin'/Won't Y' Come Out, Mary Ann . . . 15
59 London HLU 8796 — Teasin'/Won't Y' Come Out, Mary Ann (78) . . . 15

QUAKERS

65 Oriole CB 1992 — I'm Ready/Down The Road A Piece . . . 110
65 Studio 36 KSP 109/110 — She's Alright/Talk To Me . . . 350

QUALITY DRIVEL

81 No Cure WHOOP 1 — SUBLIMINAL CUTS EP (p/s) . . . 30

MINT VALUE £

QUANDO QUANGO

84 Factory FAC 102 — Atom Rock (p/s) . . . 6
85 Factory FAC 137 — Genius/This Feeling (p/s) . . . 6
85 Factory FAC 137 — Genius/This Feeling (12", p/s) . . . 6
85 Factory FACT 110 — PIGS & BATTLESHIPS (LP) . . . 18
85 Factory FACT 110C — PIGS & BATTLESHIPS (cassette, with postcards) . . . 18

QUARRY MEN

58 'P.F. Phillips, Kensington' (no cat. no.) — That'll Be The Day/In Spite Of All The Danger (78rpm shellac acetate, handwritten labels, 1 copy only, owned by Paul McCartney, worth over £100,000 but priceless)
81 'P.F. Phillips, Kensington' (no cat. no.) — That'll Be The Day/In Spite Of All The Danger (78rpm, private pressing reproduction of 1958 demo disc, repro Parlophone co. sleeve, 25 only) . . . 10,000+
81 'P.F. Phillips, Kensington' (no cat. no.) — That'll Be The Day/In Spite Of All The Danger (45rpm, private pressing reproduction of 1958 demo disc, repro Parlophone co. sleeve, 25 only) . . . 10,000+
(see also Beatles, Trad Grads)

JOE QUARTERMAN & FREE SOUL

73 GSF GSZ 3 — So Much Trouble In My Mind (Parts 1 & 2) . . . 7
74 GSF GSZ 12 — Thanks Dad Parts 1 & 2 . . . 5
73 GSF GS 504 — JOE QUARTERMAN & FREE SOUL (LP) . . . 40

QUARTER NOTES

57 Parlophone R 4365 — My Fantasy/Ten Minutes To Midnight . . . 15
57 Parlophone R 4365 — My Fantasy/Ten Minutes To Midnight (78) . . . 8

QUARTZ

77 Jet UP 36290 — Sugar Rain/Street Fighting Lady/Mainline Riders . . . 15
77 Jet UP 36317 — Street Fighting Lady/Mainline Riders . . . 12
80 Reddingtons R.R. DAN 1 — Nantucket Sleighride/Wildfire (p/s, white or blue vinyl; also black vinyl) . . . 10/5
80 Jet SJET 189 — Street Fighting Lady/Mainline Riders (p/s, reissue, demos £15) . . . 10
80 Logo GO 387 — Satan's Serenade/Bloody Fool (p/s) . . . 5
80 Logo GOT 387 — Satan's Serenade/Bloody Fool/Roll Over Beethoven (live) (12", p/s, blue or red vinyl) . . . 30/12
80 Sound For Industry SFI 549 — Satan's Serenade (flexidisc) . . . 7
80 MCA MCA 642 — Stoking The Fires Of Hell/Circles (p/s) . . . 10
80 Logo MOGO 4007 — LIVE QUARTZ (12" EP) . . . 18
81 MCA MCA 661 — Stand Up And Fight/Charlie Snow (p/s) . . . 18
83 Heavy Metal HEAVY 17 — Tell Me Why/Streetwalker (p/s) . . . 7
77 Jet UAG 30081 — QUARTZ (LP, with inner sleeve) . . . 50
79 Jet JETLP 233 — DELETED (LP, in sealed brown paper bag) . . . 18
80 Reddingtons R.R. REDD 001 — QUARTZ LIVE — COUNT DRACULA (LP, some in b&w 'live' sleeve) . . . 15/12
80 Logo MOGO 4007 — LIVE QUARTZ (LP) . . . 12
80 MCA MCF 3080 — STAND UP AND FIGHT (LP, with lyric insert) . . . 25
83 Heavy Metal HMRLP 9 — AGAINST ALL ODDS (LP, with inner sleeve) . . . 12
83 Heavy Metal HMRPD 9 — AGAINST ALL ODDS (LP, picture disc) . . . 30
(see also Black Sabbath, Copperfield, Bandy Legs)

QUATERMASS

70 Harvest SVHL 775 — QUATERMASS (LP, gatefold sleeve) . . . 90
75 Harvest SHSM 2002 — QUATERMASS (LP, reissue, different sleeve) . . . 18
(see also Ian Gillan Band, Episode Six, Strapps)

QUATRAIN

69 Polydor 583 743 — QUATRAIN (LP) . . . 12

SUZI QUATRO

72 Rak RAK 134 — Rolling Stone/Brain Confusion (For All The Lonely People) . . . 20
75 Rak RAK 200 — I Bit Off More Than I Could Chew/Red Hot Rosie . . . 5
75 Rak RAK 215 — I May Be Too Young/Don't Mess Around . . . 5
75 Rak RAK 256 — Roxy Roller/I'll Grow On You . . . 5
73 Rak PSR 355 — Primitive Love/Shakin' All Over (promo only) . . . 40
78 Rak RAK 285 — Stumblin' In/Stranger With You (with Chris Norman) (p/s) . . . 5
79 Rak RAK 285 — Stumblin' In/Stranger With You (with Chris Norman) (clear vinyl, different p/s) . . . 5
79 Rak RAK 299 — She's In Love With You/Space Cadets (p/s) . . . 5
81 Dreamland DLSP 8 — Glad All Over/Ego In The Night (no p/s) . . . 5
81 Dreamland DLSP 10 — Lipstick/Woman Cry (p/s) . . . 5
83 Polydor PSOP 555 — Main Attraction/Transparent (red or silver label) . . . 5
84 Rak/Golden 45 G 45 35 — Can The Can/Devilgate Drive (Rak label, p/s) . . . 5
84 Rak RAK 372 — I Go Wild/I'm A Rocker (p/s) . . . 5
84 Rak 12RAK 372 — I Go Wild/I'm A Rocker (12", p/s) . . . 8
85 Rak RAK 384 — Tonight I Could Fall In Love/Good Girl (Looking For A Bad Time) (p/s) . . . 5
85 Rak 12RAK 384 — Tonight I Could Fall In Love (Extended Mix)/ Good Girl (Looking For A Bad Time) (12", p/s) . . . 8
86 First Night SCORE 3 — I Got Lost In His Arms/You Can't Get A Man With A Gun (p/s) . . . 5
86 PRT 7P 367 — Wild Thing/I Don't Want You (with Reg Presley) (p/s) . . . 5
86 PRT 12P 367 — Wild Thing (Extended)/I Don't Want You (with Reg Presley) (12", p/s) . . . 8
87 Rak/Golden 45 G 45 35 — Can The Can/Devilgate Drive (reissue, black label) . . . 5
87 Hackenbacker HACK 101 — Am I Dreaming/Who Needs Chairs/Will You Take This Woman (only available at pantomime show) . . . 10
89 Teldec 247 008-7/ WEA YZ 406 — Baby You're A Star/Baby You're A Star (Instrumental) (p/s, early pressings with German labels & sticker "U.K. Cat. No. YZ 406"; later WEA copies) . . . 6/5
89 WEA YZ 406T — Baby You're A Star/(Extended)/(Instrumental)/(Radio Version) (12", p/s) . . . 8
74 Rak SRAK 509 — QUATRO (LP, white label test pressing with longer intro on "The Wild One") . . . 18
80 Rak GMTV 24 — GREATEST HITS (LP, w/l test press., w/diff., slower version of "Tear Me Apart") . 20

IKE QUEBEC

64 Blue Note 45-1749 — Buzzard Lope/Blue Friday . . . 8
63 Blue Note (B)BLP 4098 — BLUE AND SENTIMENTAL (LP) . . . 20
64 Blue Note (B)BLP 4114 — BOSSA NOVA — SOUL SAMBA (LP) . . . 20
65 Blue Note BLP 4105 — IT MIGHT AS WELL BE STRING (LP) . . . 20

QUEEN

SINGLES

Year	Label / Cat. No.	Title	Value £
73	EMI EMI 2036	Keep Yourself Alive/Son And Daughter	25
74	EMI EMI 2121	Seven Seas Of Rhye/See What A Fool I've Been	8
74	EMI EMI 2229	Killer Queen/Flick Of The Wrist	6
75	EMI EMI 2256	Now I'm Here/Lily Of The Valley	10
75	EMI EMI 2375	Bohemian Rhapsody/I'm In Love With My Car (p/s; beware counterfeits with 'computer-scanned' logo)	30
76	EMI EMI 2565	Somebody To Love/White Man (p/s, beware of recent counterfeit sleeves)	15
77	EMI EMI 2593	Tie Your Mother Down/You And I	8
77	EMI EMI 2623	QUEEN'S FIRST EP: Good Old Fashioned Lover Boy/Death On Two Legs/ Tenement Funster/White Queen (As It Began) (p/s)	12
77	EMI EMI 2708	We Are The Champions/We Will Rock You (p/s)	7
78	EMI EMI 2575	Spread Your Wings/Sheer Heart Attack (p/s)	8
78	EMI EMI 2870	Bicycle Race/Fat Bottomed Girls (p/s)	8
78	EMI EMI 2870	Bicycle Race/Fat Bottomed Girls (different p/s for export to Belgium)	200
79	EMI EMI 2910	Don't Stop Me Now/In Only Seven Days (p/s)	7
79	EMI EMI 2959	Love Of My Life (live)/Now I'm Here (live)	20
79	EMI EMI 5001	Crazy Little Thing Called Love/We Will Rock You (live) (p/s)	5
80	EMI EMI 5022	Save Me/Let Me Entertain You (live) (p/s)	6
80	EMI EMI 5076	Play The Game/A Human Body (p/s, beige label with red 'EMI' logo or white label with large black 'Queen' logo)	each 8
80	EMI EMI 5102	Another One Bites The Dust/Dragon Attack (p/s)	7
82	EMI EMI 5293	Body Language/Life Is Real (Song For Lennon) (p/s)	5
82	EMI EMI 5316	Las Palabras De Amor (The Words Of Love)/Cool Cat (p/s)	6
82	EMI EMI 5325	Backchat/Staying Power (p/s)	8
82	EMI 12EMI 5325	Backchat (Extended)/Staying Power (12", p/s)	25
84	EMI 12QUEEN 1	Radio Ga Ga (Ext. Version)/Radio Ga Ga (Instrumental)/I Go Crazy (12", p/s)	10
84	EMI QUEEN 2	I Want To Break Free (Remix)/Machines (Back To Humans) ('Freddie' p/s, gold or white lettering)	15/8
84	EMI QUEEN 2	I Want To Break Free (Remix)/Machines (Back To Humans) ('Brian', 'Roger' or 'John' p/s, each with gold lettering)	12/18/20
84	EMI 12QUEEN 2	I Want To Break Free (Extended Remix)/Machines (Back To Humans) (12", p/s, with red background with gold or black lettering)	20/12
84	EMI 12QUEEN 2	I Want To Break Free (Extended Remix)/Machines (Back To Humans) (12", p/s, with white background)	10
84	EMI QUEEN 3	It's A Hard Life/Is This The World We Created...? (p/s)	6
84	EMI QUEEN 3	It's A Hard Life/Is This The World We Created...? ('Roger Taylor' overprinted photo p/s)	25
84	EMI 12QUEEN 3	It's A Hard Life (Extended)/It's A Hard Life/ Is This The World We Created...? (12")	35
84	EMI 12QUEENP 3	It's A Hard Life/Is This The World We Created...? (12", picture disc)	18
84	EMI QUEEN 4	Hammer To Fall (Edit)/Tear It Up ('live' p/s, withdrawn)	200
84	EMI QUEEN 4	Hammer To Fall (Edit)/Tear It Up (red p/s)	8
84	EMI 12 QUEEN 4	Hammer To Fall (The Headbangers Mix)/Tear It Up (12", 'live' p/s, withdrawn)	75
84	EMI 12 QUEEN 4	Hammer To Fall (The Headbangers Mix)/Tear It Up (12", red p/s)	12
84	EMI QUEEN 5	Man On The Prowl/Keep Passing The Open Windows (unreleased, white label test pressings only)	250
84	EMI QUEEN 5	Thank God It's Christmas/Man On The Prowl/ Keep Passing The Open Windows (p/s)	8
84	EMI 12QUEEN 5	Thank God It's Christmas/Man On The Prowl (Extended Version)/ Keep Passing The Open Windows (Extended Version) (12", p/s)	18
85	EMI QUEEN 6	One Vision (7" Mix)/Blurred Vision (p/s, some with red lyric inner sleeve)	7/5
85	EMI 12QUEEN 6	One Vision (Extended Vision)/Blurred Vision (12", p/s, some with red inner)	12/10
85	EMI 12QUEEN 6	One Vision (Extended Vision)/Blurred Vision (12", printed PVC sl. & red inner)	35
86	EMI 12QUEEN 7	A Kind Of Magic (Ext. Version)/A Dozen Red Roses For My Darling (12", p/s)	12
86	EMI 12QUEENP7	A Kind Of Magic (Extended Version)/Don't Lose Your Head (Instrumental Version) (12", picture disc)	40
86	EMI QUEEN 8	Friends Will Be Friends/Seven Seas Of Rhye (p/s)	6
86	EMI QUEEN P8	Friends Will Be Friends/Seven Seas Of Rhye (picture disc)	40
86	EMI 12QUEEN 8	Friends Will Be Friends (Extended Version)/Friends Will Be Friends (7" Version)/Seven Seas Of Rhye (12", p/s)	10
86	EMI QUEEN 9	Who Wants To Live Forever/Killer Queen (p/s)	8
86	EMI 12QUEEN 9	Who Wants To Live Forever (7" Version)/(Album Version)/Killer Queen/ Who Wants To Live Forever (Piano Version) (12", p/s)	15
89	Parlophone QUEEN C10	I Want It All/Hang On In There (cassette)	8
89	Parlophone 12QUEEN 10	I Want It All (Single Version)/Hang On In There/ I Want It All (Album Version) (12", p/s)	12
89	Parlophone CDQUEEN 10	I Want It All (Album Version)/Hang On In There/I Want It All (Single Version) (CD, picture disc)	20
89	Parlophone QUEEN PD 11	Breakthru' (7" Mix)/Stealin' (shaped picture disc, 12" PVC sleeve with insert)	20
89	Parlophone QUEEN PD 11	Breakthru' (7" Mix)/Stealin' (*uncut* picture disc, 12" PVC sleeve with insert)	75
89	Parlophone QUEEN C11	Breakthru' (7" Mix)/Stealin' (cassette)	5
89	Parlophone 12QUEEN 11	Breakthru' (12" Version)/Breakthru' (Single Version)/Stealin' (12", p/s)	12
89	Parlophone CD QUEEN 11	Breakthru' (12" Version)/Stealin'/Breakthru' (7" Mix) (CD)	25
89	Parlophone QUEEN 12	The Invisible Man/Hijack My Heart (black vinyl, p/s)	8
89	Parlophone QUEEN X12	The Invisible Man/Hijack My Heart (clear vinyl, p/s)	12
89	Parlophone QUEEN C12	The Invisible Man/Hijack My Heart (cassette)	8
89	Parlophone 12QUEEN 12	The Invisible Man (12" Version)/(7" Version)/Hijack My Heart (12", p/s)	12
89	Parlophone 12QUEENX12	The Invisible Man (12" Version)/The Invisible Man (7" Version)/ Hijack My Heart (12", clear vinyl, PVC sleeve with insert)	18
89	Parlophone CD QUEEN 12	The Invisible Man (12" Version)/Hijack My Heart/ The Invisible Man (Single Version) (CD)	30
89	Parlophone QUEEN 14	Scandal/My Life Has Been Saved (p/s)	8
89	Parlophone QUEEN P14	Scandal/My Life Has Been Saved (poster p/s)	15
89	Parlophone QUEEN C14	Scandal/My Life Has Been Saved (cassette, card sleeve)	8

MINT VALUE £

89	Parlophone 12QUEEN 14	Scandal (12" Version)/Scandal (7" Version)/My Life Has Been Saved (12", p/s)	10
89	Parlophone 12QUEENS 14	Scandal (12" Version)/My Life Has Been Saved/Scandal (7" Version)/ (12", p/s, 1-sided, B-side etched with group's signatures)	25
89	Parlophone CD QUEEN 14	Scandal (12" Version)/My Life Has Been Saved/Scandal (7" Version) (CD)	35
89	Parlophone QUEEN 15	The Miracle/Stone Cold Crazy (live) (p/s)	8
89	Parlophone QUEEN H15	The Miracle/Stone Cold Crazy (live) (orange hologram p/s)	12
89	Parlophone QUEEN H15	The Miracle/Stone Cold Crazy (live) (proof sleeve with negative hologram p/s)	450
89	Parlophone QUEEN C15	The Miracle/Stone Cold Crazy (live) (cassette)	8
89	Parlophone 12QUEEN 15	The Miracle/Stone Cold Crazy (live)/My Melancholy Blues (live) (12", yellow p/s)	15
89	Parlophone 12QUEENP 15	The Miracle/Stone Cold Crazy (live)/My Melancholy Blues (live) (12", turquoise p/s with insert print)	18
89	Parlophone QUEENCD 15	The Miracle/Stone Cold Crazy (live)/My Melancholy Blues (live) (CD)	25
91	Parlophone QUEEN 16	Innuendo/Bijou (p/s)	5
91	Parlophone 12QUEEN 16	Innuendo (Explosive Version)/Under Pressure/Bijou (12", p/s)	8
91	Parl. 12QUEEN PD16	Innuendo (Explosive Version)/Under Pressure/Bijou (12", picture disc, PVC sleeve with insert)	20
91	Parl. CDQUEEN PD16	Innuendo (Explosive Version)/Under Pressure/Bijou (CD)	8
91	Parlophone QUEEN 17	I'm Going Slightly Mad/The Hitman (p/s)	7
91	Parlophone QUEEN PD 17	I'm Going Slightly Mad/The Hitman (shaped picture disc with insert)	20
91	Parlophone QUEEN PD 17	I'm Going Slightly Mad/The Hitman (*uncut* picture disc with insert)	80
91	Parlophone QUEEN C17	I'm Going Slightly Mad/The Hitman (cassette)	6
91	Parlophone 12QUEENG 17	I'm Going Slightly Mad/The Hitman/Lost Opportunity (12", gatefold p/s)	15
91	Parlophone CDQUEEN 17	I'm Going Slightly Mad/The Hitman/Lost Opportunity (CD)	15
91	Parlophone 12QUEEN 18	Headlong/All God's People/Mad The Swine (12", p/s)	8
91	Parlophone 12QUEEN PD18	Headlong/All God's People/Mad The Swine (12", clear vinyl picture disc, with insert in PVC sleeve)	18
91	Parlophone CD QUEEN 18	Headlong/All God's People/Mad The Swine (CD)	15
91	Parlophone QUEEN 19	The Show Must Go On/Keep Yourself Alive (p/s)	5
91	Parlophone QUEEN C19	The Show Must Go On/Keep Yourself Alive (cassette)	25
91	Parlophone 12QUEENSG 19	The Show Must Go On/Keep Yourself Alive/Queen Talks (12", 1-sided, B-side etched with group's signatures, gatefold p/s)	18
91	Parlophone CDQUEEN 19	The Show Must Go On/Keep Yourself Alive/Queen Talks/Body Language (CD)	10
91	Parlophone CDQUEENS 19	The Show Must Go On/Now I'm Here/Fat Bottomed Girls/Las Palabras De Amor (The Words Of Love) (CD, in box with foldout poster, 10,000 only)	25
91	Parlophone QUEEN 19/20	The Show Must Go On/Bohemian Rhapsody (unissued, no p/s)	500
93	Parlophone CDR 6340	FIVE LIVE EP: Killer/Papa Was A Rolling Stone (PM Dawn Remix)/ Somebody To Love/These Are The Days Of Our Lives (as Queen featuring George Michael & Lisa Stansfield) (CD, picture disc, silver inlay)	10
95	Parlophone CDQUEENS 21	Heaven For Everyone (Single Version)/It's A Beautiful Day/Heaven For Everyone (Album Version) (CD)	8
95	Parlophone CDQUEENS 22	A Winter's Tale/Thank God It's Christmas/Rock In Rio Blues (CD, 'Merry Christmas' box)	8
96	Parlophone QUEEN 23	Too Much Love Will Kill You/We Will Rock You/We Are The Champions (p/s, pink vinyl)	5
96	Parlophone QUEENPD 24	Let Me Live/Fat Bottomed Girls/Bicycle Race (picture disc with poster)	5
97	Parlophone QUEEN 26	No-One But You (Only The Good Die Young)/Princes Of The Universe/ We Will Rock You (Rick Rubin 'Ruined' Remix)/ Gimme The Prize (Instrumental 'Eye' Remix) (unissued 7")	150
97	Parlophone QUEENPD 27	No-One But You (Only The Good Die Young)/We Will Rock You (Rick Rubin 'Ruined' Remix)/Tie Your Mother Down/Gimme The Prize (Instrumental 'Eye' Remix) (picture disc)	5

3" CD SINGLES

88	Parlophone QUECD 1	Seven Seas Of Rhye/See What A Fool I've Been/Funny How Love Is	15
88	Parlophone QUECD 2	Killer Queen/Flick Of The Wrist/Brighton Rock	15
88	Parlophone QUECD 3	Bohemian Rhapsody/I'm In Love With My Car/You're My Best Friend	15
88	Parlophone QUECD 4	Somebody To Love/White Man/Tie Your Mother Down	15
88	Parlophone QUECD 5	QUEEN'S FIRST EP: Good Old Fashioned Lover Boy/Death On Two Legs/ Tenement Funster/White Queen (As It Began)	15
88	Parlophone QUECD 6	We Are The Champions/We Will Rock You /Fat Bottomed Girls	15
88	Parlophone QUECD 7	Crazy Little Thing Called Love/Spread Your Wings/Flash	15
88	Parlophone QUECD 8	Another One Bites The Dust/Dragon Attack/Las Palabras De Amor	15
88	Parlophone QUECD 9	Under Pressure/Soul Brother/Body Language	20
88	Parlophone QUECD 10	Radio Ga Ga/I Go Crazy/Hammer To Fall	15
88	Parlophone QUECD 11	I Want To Break Free/Machines (Back To Humans)/It's A Hard Life	15
88	Parlophone QUECD 12	A Kind Of Magic/A Dozen Red Roses For My Darling/One Vision	15

(The above 3" CDs were all issued in card sleeves with generic plastic EMI outer packages.)

ALBUMS

78	EMI EMA 788	JAZZ (LP, gatefold sleeve with poster)	12
81	EMI EMTV 30	GREATEST HITS (LP, mispress, side 2 plays "Anne Murray's Greatest Hits")	15
85	EMI QB 1	THE COMPLETE WORKS (14-LP box set including "Complete Vision" LP of non-LP tracks, 2 booklets & map, numbered; 600 autographed)	1000+/100
86	EMI EU 3509	A KIND OF MAGIC ('Princes Of The Universe' proof sleeve; unreleased)	500
89	Band Of Joy BOJLP 001	QUEEN AT THE BEEB (LP)	15
91	Parlophone PMTV 2	GREATEST HITS 2 (2-LP, embossed gatefold sleeve)	35
91	Parlophone PCSD 115	INNUENDO (LP)	25
92	Parlophone PCSP 725	LIVE AT WEMBLEY (2-LP, gatefold sleeve)	45
92	Parlophone CDQTEL 0001	BOX OF TRIX (CD, box set, with video, book, poster, T-shirt, patch & badge)	60
92	Parlophone CQTEL 0001	BOX OF TRIX (cassette, box set, with video, book, poster, T-shirt, patch & badge)	45
95	Parlophone QUEEN BOX 20	ULTIMATE QUEEN (20 x CD set, in numbered glazed box and numbered cardboard outer box, with Freddie hologram and 2 booklets)	500

MINT VALUE £

PROMOS

Year	Label / Cat. No.	Title / Details	£
77	EMI SP SLP 241 A1U	We Will Rock You/We Are The Champions/Spread Your Wings (12", 1-sided)	400
78	EMI EMI 2375	Bohemian Rhapsody/I'm In Love With My Car (EMI 'Queen's Award For Export' in-house edition, blue vinyl, Queen crest label, hand-numbered, purple p/s)	3,500
78	EMI EMI 2375	Bohemian Rhapsody/I'm In Love With My Car (as above, with outer 'EMI International' carrying envelope)	3,800
78	EMI EMI 2375	Bohemian Rhapsody/I'm In Love With My Car (as above, with invites, matches, pen, ticket, menu, outer card sleeve, scarf & EMI goblets in card box)	5,000

(The blue vinyl "Bohemian Rhapsody" was limited to 200 numbered copies)

Year	Label / Cat. No.	Title / Details	£
84	EMI QUEEN 1	Radio Ga Ga (Edit)/I Go Crazy ('video shoot' p/s, unreleased, proofs only)	600
84	EMI QUEENDJ 5	Man On The Prowl/Thank God It's Christmas	150
84	Flexi Ltd. (no cat. no.)	Excerpts From Their New Album 'The Works' (flexidisc sampler, p/s)	15
86	Parlophone EMCDV 2	THE HIGHLANDER SELECTION (CD Video, 50 only)	450
86	(no label or cat. no.)	A Message From Queen (cassette, 1st Fan Club Convention issue)	20
89	Flexi Ltd. (no cat. no.)	A Message From Queen (flexidisc, 4th Fan Club Convention issue)	25
89	Parlophone TEASER 1	THE TEASER TAPE (cassette, edits sampler for "The Miracle")	15
95	EMI QUEEN DJ95	Bohemian Rhapsody/I'm In Love With My Car (purple vinyl, hand numbered, p/s, 10th anniversary Fan Club Convention issue, 2,000 only)	150
95	Parlophone QUEENLHDJ 21	Heaven For Everyone (Album Version)/Heaven For Everyone (Single Version) (jukebox issue, plain white sleeve, with poster, fold-out card & jukebox strip)	20
95	Parlophone QUEENDJ 22	A Winter's Tale/Thank God It's Christmas (jukebox issue, plain white sleeve, with jukebox strip)	10
96	Parlophone QUEENDJ 23	Too Much Love Will Kill You/We Are The Champions (jukebox issue, plain white sleeve, with jukebox strip)	8
96	Parlophone VIRGIN 1	Heaven For Everyone/Heaven For Everyone (12", white label, Virgin Radio 'Queen Day' competition prize, black 'Queen crest' p/s with handwritten details; mispressing with same track both sides, unreleased)	
96	Parlophone VIRGIN 2	Heaven For Everyone (12", 1-sided, white labels, Virgin Radio 'Queen Day' competition prize, 'Queen crest' p/s w/ handwritten details, 15 copies only)	600+
96	Parlophone VIRGIN 3	A Winter's Tale (12", 1-sided, white labels, Virgin Radio 'Queen Day' competition prize, 'Queen crest' p/s with handwritten details, 15 only)	600+
96	Parlophone VIRGIN 4	Mother Love (12", 1-sided, white labels, Virgin Radio 'Queen Day' competition prize, 'Queen crest' p/s with handwritten details, 15 only)	600+
96	Parlophone VIRGIN 5	Let Me Live (12", 1-sided, white labels, Virgin Radio 'Queen Day' competition prize, 'Queen crest' p/s with handwritten details, 15 only)	600+
96	Parlophone VIRGIN 6	You Don't Fool Me (12", 1-sided, white labels, Virgin Radio 'Queen Day' competition prize, 'Queen crest' p/s with handwritten details, 15 only)	600+
96	Parlophone VIRGIN 7	It's A Beautiful Day (12", 1-sided, white labels, Virgin Radio 'Queen Day' competition prize, 'Queen crest' p/s with handwritten details, 15 only)	600+
96	Parlophone VIRGIN 8	I Was Born To Love You (12", 1-sided, white labels, Virgin Radio 'Queen Day' competition prize, 'Queen crest' p/s with handwritten details, 15 only)	600+
99	EMI QUEENWL 28	Under Pressure (Remixes) (with David Bowie) (12", white label, unreleased mix, promo only)	60
99	EMI QUEEN DJ 28	Under Pressure (Rah Mix)/(Mike Spencer Mix)/The Show Must Go On (CD, card p/s, promo only)	15
73	EMI (no cat. no.)	QUEEN (LP, white label, EMI conference custom issue, die-cut sleeve, with/without outer envelope)	450/250
77	EMI (no cat. no.)	NEWS OF THE WORLD (LP, box set, with factory sample sticker, 5 photos, bio, badge & demo copy of "We Are The Champions"/ "We Will Rock You", 50 only)	400
91	Parlophone (no cat. no.)	HINTS OF INNUENDO (cassette, edits/out-takes sampler for "Innuendo")	30
91	Parlophone (no cat. no.)	EIGHT GOOD REASONS TO BUY GREATEST HITS 2 (cassette, segued excerpts)	30
91	Parlophone (no cat. no.)	A SAMPLE OF MAGIC (CD, segued excerpts from "Greatest Hits 2")	60
94	EMI CD DIG 1	DIGITAL MASTER SAMPLER (CD, picture disc)	45
97	Parlophone CDQT 1	QUEEN ROCKS (CD, Brian May interview)	75

MISPRESSINGS

Year	Label / Cat. No.	Title / Details	£
75	EMI EMI 2378	Bohemian Rhapsody/I'm In Love With My Car (2nd issue, with incorrect cat. no.)	12
78	EMI EMI 2870	Bicycle Race/Fat Bottomed Girls (p/s, B-side plays Crystal Gayle's "3 O'Clock In The Morning" or Dollar track)	each 10
79	EMI EMI 2975	CLIFF RICHARD: We Don't Talk Anymore/Count Me Out (A-side plays "Bohemian Rhapsody")	12
79	EMI EMI 5001	Crazy Little Thing Called Love/We Will Rock You (live) (p/s, both sides play "We Will Rock You")	15
80	EMI EMI 5076	Play The Game/A Human Body (p/s, both sides play "A Human Body")	12
86	Parlophone RP 5452	BEATLES: Paperback Writer/Rain (picture disc, A-side plays "Friends Will Be Friends")	75

(see also Freddie Mercury, Brian May, Roger Taylor, Larry Lurex, Cross, Immortals, Hilary Hilary, Eddie Howell, Man Friday & Jive Junior)

QUEENSRYCHE

Year	Label / Cat. No.	Title / Details	£
83	EMI America 12EA 162	Queens Of The Reich/Nightrider/Blinded/Lady Wore Black (12", p/s)	12
84	EMI America EA 183	Take Hold Of The Flame/Nightrider (p/s)	12
86	EMI America EA 22	Gonna Get Close To You/Prophecy (p/s)	12
86	EMI America EAD 22	Gonna Get Close To You/Prophecy//Queen Of The Reich (live)/ Deliverance (live) (double pack)	12
88	EMI Manhattan 10QR 1	OVERSEEING THE OPERATION (10" EP)	12
89	EMI USA MT 65	Eyes Of A Stranger/Queen Of The Reich (p/s)	5
89	EMI USA 12MT 65	Eyes Of A Stranger/Queen Of The Reich/Walk In The Shadows/ Take Hold Of The Flame (12", p/s)	8

MINT VALUE £

89 EMI USA 12MTG 65 Eyes Of A Stranger/Queen Of The Reich/Walk In The Shadows/ Take Hold Of The Flame (12", gatefold p/s) . . . 12
89 EMI USA CDMT 65 Eyes Of A Stranger/Take Hold Of The Flame/Queen Of The Reich/ Prophecy (CD) . . . 8
90 EMI USA MTPD 90 Empire/Scarborough Fair (shaped picture disc) . . . 8
91 EMI USA MTS 94 Silent Lucidity (LP Version)/The Mission (live) (box set, 5 portraits & 2 stencils) . . . 5
91 EMI USA 10MT 97 Best I Can/I Dream In Infrared (1991 Acoustic Remix)/Prophecy (10", box set with poster & badge) . . . 8
91 EMI USA MTPD 98B Jet City Woman/Empire (live) (shaped picture disc) . . . 5
91 EMI USA 12MTS 98 Jet City Woman/Walk In The Shadows (live)/Empire (live) (12", box set with tour laminate & poster) . . . 8

? & THE MYSTERIANS

66 Cameo Parkway C 428 96 Tears/Midnight Hour . . . 25
66 Cameo Parkway C 441 I Need Somebody/'8' Teen . . . 20
67 Cameo Parkway C 467 Can't Get Enough Of You, Baby/Smokes . . . 15
67 Cameo Parkway C 479 Girl (You Captivate Me)/Got To . . . 15
67 Cameo Parkway C 496 Do Something To Me/Love Me Baby . . . 15
76 London HLU 10534 96 Tears/'8' Teen . . . 10

QUESTIONS

68 Decca F 22740 We Got Love/Something Wonderful . . . 22

QUESTIONS

86 Respond KOBX 707 Tuesday Sunshine (Jock Mix)/Tuesday Sunshine(Sass Mix)/The House That Jack Built/No One (Long Version) (12" p/s) . . . 8

TOMMY QUICKLY (& REMO FOUR)

63 Piccadilly 7N 35137 Tip Of My Tongue/Heaven Only Knows (solo) . . . 35
63 Piccadilly 7N 35151 Kiss Me Now/No Other Love . . . 8
64 Piccadilly 7N 35167 Prove It/Haven't You Noticed . . . 8
64 Piccadilly 7N 35183 You Might As Well Forget Him/It's As Simple As That . . . 8
64 Pye 7N 15708 The Wild Side Of Life/Forget The Other Guy . . . 10
64 Pye 7N 15748 Humpty Dumpty/I'll Go Crazy . . . 18
(see also Remo Four)

QUICKSAND

70 Carnaby CNS 4015 Passing By/Cobblestones . . . 8
73 Dawn DNS 1046 Time To Live/Empty Street, Empty Heart . . . 6
74 Dawn DNLS 3056 HOME IS WHERE I BELONG (LP) . . . 40

QUICKSILVER MESSENGER SERVICE

76 Capitol CL 15859 Gypsy Lights/Witches' Moon . . . 5
68 Capitol (S)T 2904 QUICKSILVER MESSENGER SERVICE (LP, black label with rainbow rim) . . . 30
69 Capitol E-(S)T 120 HAPPY TRAILS (LP) . . . 25
70 Capitol E-ST 391 SHADY GROVE (LP) . . . 18
70 Capitol EA-ST 498 JUST FOR LOVE (LP) . . . 15
71 Capitol EA-ST 630 WHAT ABOUT ME? (LP) . . . 15
72 Capitol E-SW 819 QUICKSILVER (LP) . . . 12
72 Capitol EA-ST 11002 COMIN' THRU (LP) . . . 12
75 Capitol E-ST 11462 SOLID SILVER (LP) . . . 12
83 Psycho PSYCHO 10 MAIDEN OF THE CANCER MOON (2-LP) . . . 50
(see also Dino Valenti, Nicky Hopkins)

QUICKSPACE (SUPERSPORT)

94 Love Train PUBE 04 Found A Way/Do It My Own Way (12", p/s, 1,500 only) . . . 15
95 Kitty Kitty Corp. CHOOSY 1 Quickspace Happy Song (1)/Unique Slippy (as Quickspace Supersport, hand painted/stamped p/s, 1000 only) . . . 6
96 Kitty Kitty Corp. CHOOSY 4 Friend/Good Timez (as Quickspace, painted wallpaper sleeve, 500 only) . . . 6
97 Kitty Kitty Corp. CHOOSY 8 QUICKSPACE (LP, die-cut spray-painted sleeve, 1000 only) . . . 12

QUIET FIVE

65 Parlophone R 5273 When The Morning Sun Dries The Dew/Tomorrow I'll Be Gone (some in p/s) . . . 20/10
65 Parlophone R 5302 Honeysuckle Rose/Let's Talk It Over . . . 8
66 Parlophone R 5421 Homeward Bound/Ain't It Funny What Some Lovin' Can Do . . . 12
66 Parlophone R 5470 I Am Waiting/What About The Time For Me . . . 8
67 CBS 202586 Goodnight Sleep Tight/Just For Tonight . . . 6
(see also Kris Ife, Patrick Dane, Richard Barnes)

QUIET SUN

75 Island HELP 19 MAINSTREAM (LP) . . . 12
(see also Phil Manzanera, Roxy Music)

QUIET WORLD

69 Dawn DNS 1001 Miss Whittington/There Is A Mountain (as Quiet World Of Lea & John) . . . 25
70 Dawn DNS 1005 Children Of The World/Love Is Walking . . . 25
70 Pye 7N 45005 Rest Comfortably/Gemima . . . 10
71 Pye 7N 45074 Visitor/Sam . . . 8
70 Dawn DNLS 3007 THE ROAD (LP) . . . 65
(see also Steve Hackett, Genesis)

QUIK

67 Deram DM 121 Love Is A Beautiful Thing/Bert's Apple Crumble . . . 80
67 Deram DM 139 King Of The World/My Girl . . . 30
67 Deram DM 155 I Can't Sleep/Soul Full Of Sorrow . . . 75
98 Klooks Kleek 60 Bert's Apple Crumble/THE SONICS: The Witch . . . 5
(see also Meddy Evils)

QUILLER

75 BBC RESL 25 Quiller/General Direction . . . 5

QUINCICASM
73 Saydisc SDL 249 — QUINCICASM (LP) 20

ANTHONY QUINN
70 Capitol CL 15649 — I Love You And You Love Me/Sometimes (I Just Can't Stand You) 5

MIKE QUINN
66 Fontana TF 761 — Someone's Slipping Into My Mind/I Know What You Know 7
69 CBS 4506 — Apple Pie/There's A Time 6
69 Jay Boy BOY 7 — Toothbrush Nell/Fairy Cakes 5

PAUL QUINN & EDWYN COLLINS
84 Swamplands SWP 1 — Pale Blue Eyes (Edited Version)/Burro (p/s) 5
84 Swamplands SWX 1 — Pale Blue Eyes/Pale Blues Eyes (Western)/Burro (12", original with 'film' p/s, inner sleeve & yellow obi) 10/7
(see also Edwyn Collins, Orange Juice)

QUINTESSENCE
70 Island WIP 6075 — Notting Hill Gate/Move Into The Light 20
71 Neon NE 1003 — Sweet Jesus/You Never Stay The Same (some in p/s) 15/6
69 Island ILPS 9110 — IN BLISSFUL COMPANY (LP, pink label) 45
70 Island ILPS 9128 — QUINTESSENCE (LP, pink label) 45
70 Island ILPS 9143 — DIVE DEEP (LP) 20
72 RCA SF 8273 — SELF (LP) 18
72 RCA SF 8317 — INDWELLER (LP) 18
(see also Kala)

QUINTET OF HOT CLUB OF FRANCE
53 Decca LF 1139 — SWING FROM PARIS (10" LP) 15
(see also Django Reinhardt)

QUINTET OF THE YEAR
54 Vogue L.D.E. 087 — JAZZ AT THE MASSAY HALL VOL. 3 (10" LP) 18

QUIREBOYS
88 Survival SUR 043 — Mayfair/Misled (p/s) 5
88 Survival SURT 043 — Mayfair/Misled/Man On The Loose (12", p/s) 8
88 Survival SUR 46 — There She Goes Again/How Do Ya Feel (p/s) 5
88 Survival PDSUR 46 — There She Goes Again/How Do Ya Feel (picture disc) 8
88 Survival SURT 46 — There She Goes Again/How Do Ya Feel/Sex Party (12", p/s) 8
89 Parlophone CDR 6230 — Seven O'Clock/Pretty Girls/How Do You Feel? (CD, picture disc, with gatefold insert) 8
89 Parlophone CDR 6241 — Hey You/Sex Party/Hoochie Coochie Man (live) (CD, picture disc, with gatefold insert) 8
89 Parlophone CDR 6248 — I Don't Love You Anymore/Mayfair (Original Version)/Hey You (CD, picture disc, with gatefold insert) 8
90 Parlophone RPD 6248 — I Don't Love You Anymore/Mayfair (Original Version) (uncut shaped picture disc) 25
(see also Wildhearts)

DARYL QUIST
63 Pye 7N 15538 — Thanks To You/Keep Moving (some in p/s) 12/7
63 Pye 7N 15563 — Goodbye To Love/All Through The Night 7
64 Pye 7N 15605 — True To You/Above And Beyond 8
64 Pye 7N 15656 — See The Funny Little Clown/When She Comes To You 7
65 Decca F 12058 — Put Away Your Teardrops/Across The Street 7

QUIVER
72 Warner Bros K 16165 — Green Tree/I Might Stumble 6
71 Warner Bros K 46089 — QUIVER (LP) 18
72 Warner Bros K 46153 — GONE IN THE MORNING (LP) 18
(see also Bridget St. John, Natural Gas, Village)

QUODLING'S DELIGHT
76 Fanfare FR 2179 — AMONG THE LEAVES SO GREEN (LP) 25

QUOTATIONS (U.K.)
64 Decca F 11907 — Alright Baby/Love You All Over Again 18
68 CBS 3710 — Cool It/Mark Of Her Head 12
69 CBS 4378 — Hello Memories/Pretend 7
(see also Fleur De Lys, Johnny B. Great, Johnny Gustafson, Merseybeats, Johnny Goodison)

QUOTATIONS (U.S.)
61 HMV POP 975 — Imagination/Ala Men Say 100

QUOTING MARX
77 Full Stop PUNC 28 — Opening And Closing/66 And 99 12

QUO VARDIS
(see under Vardis)

RABBI JOSEPH GORDAN
85 Bam Caruso Intl. NRICO 30 Competition/Belief In Him (large centre hole, plain beige sleeve) ... 15
(see also Julian Cope)

RABBIT
73 Island WIP 6161 Broken Arrows/Blues My Guitar ... 5
73 Island ILPS 9238 BROKEN ARROWS (LP) ... 12
74 Island ILPS 9289 DARK SALOON (LP) ... 12
(see also Free; Kossoff, Kirke, Tetsu & Rabbit)

RABID
82 Fallout FALL 007 BLOODY ROAD TO GLORY (EP) ... 5

MIKE RABIN (& DEMONS)
64 Columbia DB 7350 Head Over Heels/Leaving You (as Mike Rabin & Demons) ... 60
65 Polydor BM 56007 If I Were You/What Do You Do ... 22

OSCAR RABIN & HIS BAND
53 Polygon P 1086 Crazy Man Crazy/Forgive Me (B-side with Mel Gaynor) (78) ... 8
(see also David Ede Band)

TREVOR RABIN
79 Chrysalis CHS 2282 Painted Picture/Stay With Me (p/s) ... 5
79 Chrysalis CHS 2362 Don't You Ever Lose/Stay With Me/Getting To Know You Better (p/s) ... 5
81 Chrysalis CHS 2508 Take Me To A Party/Looking For A Lady (p/s, coloured vinyl) ... 5
78 Chrysalis CHR 1196 TREVOR RABIN (LP) ... 12
79 Chrysalis CHR 1221 FACE TO FACE (LP) ... 12
(see also Yes)

JOSEPH RACAILLE
80s Recommended RRA 16.5 6 PETITES CHANSONS (EP, clear vinyl, foldaround p/s) ... 6

STEVE RACE
61 Parlophone R 4808 Crosstrap/Stop Look Listen ... 10
62 Parlophone R 4894 Nicola/Ring Ding ... 5
63 Parlophone R 4981 The Pied Piper/Here And Now ... 5
63 World Records TP 285 DANCE TO THE TV THEMES (LP) ... 15
65 World Records TP 453 TAKE ONE (LP) ... 12
65 World Records (S)TP 456 LATE RACE (LP, mono/stereo) ... 12
66 Studio Two TWO 137 STEVE RACE (LP, stereo) ... 15

RACE DANS
68 Trojan TR 610 Bookie Man/UNIQUES: More Love ... 10

YANK RACHELL TENNESSEE JUG BUSTERS
64 '77' LA 12-23 MANDOLIN BLUES (LP) ... 22

RADAR
83 House Of Wax WAX 1 Leave Her Alone/Reach For The Sky (p/s) ... 25

JIMMY RADCLIFFE
65 Stateside SS 374 Long After Tonight Is Over/What I Want I Can Never Have ... 60
73 Pye International 7N 25614 Long After Tonight Is Over/What I Want I Can Never Have (reissue) ... 12
77 DJM DJS 10772 Long After Tonight Is Over/What I Want I Can Never Have (2nd reissue) ... 8
(see also Steve Karmen Big Band)

RADHA KRISHNA
71 Columbia SCX 6462 RADHA KRISHNA (LP, composed & directed by John Mayer) ... 35
(see also John Mayer)

RADHA KRISHNA TEMPLE (LONDON)
69 Apple APPLE 15 Hare Krishna Mantra/Prayer To The Spiritual Masters (p/s, as Radha Krishna Temple [London], some with insert) ... 25/15
69 Apple APPLE 15 Hare Krishna Mantra/Prayer To The Spiritual Masters (no p/s, as Radha Krishna Temple [London]) ... 8
70 Apple APPLE 25 Govinda/Govinda Jai Jai (p/s) ... 35
70 Apple APPLE 25 Govinda/Govinda Jai Jai (some in company sleeve) ... 15/8
71 Apple SAPCOR 18 THE RADHA KRSNA TEMPLE (LP, gatefold sleeve, some with insert) ... 45/40
93 Apple SAPCOR 18 THE RADHA KRSNA TEMPLE (LP, reissue, gatefold sleeve with inner) ... 20
93 Apple SAPCOR 18 THE RADHA KRSNA TEMPLE (CD) ... 25

RADIANTS
64 Chess CRS 8002 Voice Your Choice/If I Only Had You ... 22
68 Chess CRS 8073 Hold On/I'm Glad I'm The Loser ... 18
(see also Maurice & Mac, Caston & Majors)

RADIATORS (FROM SPACE)
77 Chiswick S 10 Television Screen/Love Detective (p/s, original issue) ... 8
77 Chiswick NS 19 Enemies/Psychotic Reaction (p/s) ... 8
78 Chiswick NS 24 Prison Bars/(Why Can't I Be A) Teenager In Love (unreleased, promo only white label in stamped white sleeve & loose printed labels) ... 40
79 Chiswick NS 45 Walkin' Home Alone Again/Try And Stop Me/The Hucklebuck (unreleased; white label test pressings exist with loose labels; as Radiators) ... 30

79 Chiswick CHIS 115 Kitty Ricketts/Ballad Of The Faithful Departed (company sleeve) 12
79 Chiswick CHIS 144 Song Of The Faithful Departed/They're Looting In The Town (Irish-only). 8
79 CBS 5572 Sunday World/(Why Can't I Be A) Teenager In Love (p/s, Irish-only) 20
77 Chiswick WIK 4 TV TUBE HEART (LP). 20
(see also Pogues)

MARK RADICE

72 Paramount PARA 3024 Hey My Love/Your Love Is Like Fire 6
72 Paramount PARA 3025 New Day/Take Me To The Park 6
72 Paramount SPFA 7004 MARK RADICE (LP) 15

RADIO ACTORS

79 Charly CYS 1058 Nuclear Waste/Digital Love (p/s, reissue of Fast Breeder & Radio Actors single, 2 slightly different label designs) 8
79 DB DBS 5 Nuclear Waste/Digital Love (different p/s, 2nd reissue) 8
(see also Fast Breeder & Radio Actors, Sting, Newcastle Big Band, Police, Gilli Smyth, Inner City Unit, Steve Hillage, Sphynx)

RADIO BIRDMAN

78 Sire 6078 617 What Gives/Anglo Girl Desire 10
78 Sire 9103 332 RADIOS APPEAR (LP, with inner sleeve) 25
78 Sire SRK 6050 RADIOS APPEAR (LP, reissue) 12

RADIOHEAD

92 Parlophone TCR 6312 DRILL EP (Prove Yourself/Stupid Car/You/Thinking About You) (cassette, 3,000 only) 60
92 Parlophone 12R 6312 DRILL EP (Prove Yourself/Stupid Car/You/Thinking About You) (12", p/s, 3,000 only). 150
92 Parlophone CDR 6312 DRILL EP (Prove Yourself/Stupid Car/You/Thinking About You) (CD, 3,000 only) 250
92 Parlophone TCR 6078 Creep/Lurgee/Inside My Head/Million $ Question (cassette, 6,000 only) 15
92 Parlophone 12R 6078 Creep/Lurgee/Inside My Head/Million $ Question (12", p/s, 6,000 only). 30
92 Parlophone CDR 6078 Creep/Lurgee/Inside My Head/Million $ Question (CD, 6,000 only) 80
93 Parlophone TCR 6333 Anyone Can Play Guitar/Faithless, The Wonder Boy/Coke Babies (cassette) 10
93 Parlophone 12R 6333 Anyone Can Play Guitar/Faithless, The Wonder Boy/Coke Babies (12", p/s) 50
93 Parlophone CDR 6333 Anyone Can Play Guitar/Faithless, The Wonder Boy/Coke Babies (CD). 60
93 Parlophone TCR 6345 Pop Is Dead/Banana Co. (Acoustic)/Creep (live)/Ripcord (live) (cassette). 8
93 Parlophone 12R 6345 Pop Is Dead/Banana Co. (Acoustic)/Creep (live)/Ripcord (live) (12", g/fold p/s) . . 40
93 Parlophone CDR 6345 Pop Is Dead/Banana Co. (Acoustic)/Creep (live)/Ripcord (live) (CD) 70
93 Parlophone RS 6359 Creep/Yes I Am/Blow Out (Remix)/Inside My Head (live) (p/s, clear vinyl) 45
93 Parlophone TCR 6359 Creep/Yes I Am/Blow Out (Remix)/Inside My Head (live) (cassette). 8
93 Parlophone 12RG 6359 U.S. LIVE EP (Creep [Acoustic KROQ]/You [live]/Vegetable [live]/Killer Cars [live]) (12", numbered gatefold p/s) 25
93 Parlophone CDR 6359 Creep/Yes I Am/Blow Out (Remix)/Inside My Head (live) (CD, digipak) 50
94 Parlophone TCR 6394 My Iron Lung/The Trickster/Lewis (Mistreated)/Punchdrunk Lovesick Singalong (cassette) 8
94 Parlophone 12R 6394 My Iron Lung/Punchdrunk Lovesick Singalong/The Trickster/ Lewis (Mistreated) (12", numbered p/s). 15
94 Parlophone CDRS 6394 My Iron Lung/Punchdrunk Lovesick Singalong/Lozenge Of Love (CD). 22
94 Parlophone CDR 6394 My Iron Lung/The Trickster/Lewis (Mistreated)/Permanent Daylight/ You Never Wash Up After Yourself (CD) 25
95 Parlophone 12R 6405 Planet Telex/(remixes)/High & Dry (12", limited edition, numbered p/s). 30
95 Parlophone CDRS 6405 High & Dry/Planet Telex/Maquiladora/Planet Telex (Hexidecimal Mix) (CD) 12
95 Parlophone CDRS 6411 Fake Plastic Trees/India Rubber/How Can I Be Sure? (CD) 12
95 Parlophone CDR 6411 Fake Plastic Trees/Fake Plastic Trees (Acoustic)/Bulletproof (...I Wish I Was) (Acoustic)/Street Spirit (Fade Out) (Acoustic) (CD, with poster) 30
95 Parlophone CDR 6415 Just/Bones (live)/Planet Telex (live)/Anyone Can Play Guitar (live) (CD, box set with 2 prints) 25
95 Parlophone 8 83115 2 The Bends/My Iron Lung (Live At Forum)/Bones (Live At Forum) (CD, for export to Ireland, slimline jewel case) 30
95 Parlophone 8 83115 2 The Bends/My Iron Lung (Live At Forum)/Bones (Live At Forum) (CD, for export to Ireland, mispressed with "Planet Telex" instead of "The Bends", slimline jewel case). 30
96 Parlophone R 6419 Street Spirit (Fade Out)/Bishop's Robes (die-cut p/s, white vinyl) 10
96 Parlophone R 6419LH Street Spirit (Fade Out)/Bishop's Robes (jukebox issue, black vinyl) 15
96 Parlophone CDRS 6419 Street Spirit (Fade Out)/Talk Show Host/Bishop's Robes (CD, with poster). 20
97 Parlophone NODATA 01 Paranoid Android/Polyethelene (Parts 1 & 2) (blue vinyl, die-cut p/s) 30
97 Parlophone NODATALH 03 Karma Police (Album Version)/Lull (jukebox issue, black vinyl). 15
97 Parlophone 12NODATA 03 Karma Police/Meeting Up The Aisle/Climbing Up The Walls (Zero 7 Mix) (12", p/s) 18
97 Parlophone NODATALH 04 No Surprises/Palo Alto (jukebox issue, black vinyl) 12
98 Parlophone 12NODATA 04 No Surprises/Palo Alto (12", p/s). 15
93 Parlophone PCS 7360 PABLO HONEY (LP). 15
95 Parlophone PCS 7372 THE BENDS (2-LP). 15
97 Parlophone NODATA 02 OK COMPUTER (2-LP) 20
97 Parlophone NODATA 02 OK COMPUTER (EPK, with CD & video in polystyrene case in jiffy bag) 85
01 Parlophone 12FHEIT 45104 I MIGHT BE WRONG (mini-LP). 12
03 Parlophone 5848052 HAIL TO THE THIEF (CD, limited issue, with foldout map) 18

PROMOS

92 Parlophone 12RDJ 6078 Creep/Lurgee/Inside My Head/Million Dollar Question (12", die-cut sleeve) 100
92 Parlophone CDRDJ 6078 Creep (Radio Version)/Lurgee/Inside My Head/Million Dollar Question (CD). 80
93 Parlophone 12RDJ 6369 Ripcord/Prove Yourself/Faithless, The Wonderboy/ Stop Whispering (Album Version) (12", p/s) 100
93 Parlophone CDRDJ 6345 Pop Is Dead/Banana Co. (live)/Creep (live)/Ripcord (live) (CD) 75
93 Parlophone CDRDJ 6359 Creep (CD, picture disc). 50
93 Parlophone CDRDJ 6369 Stop Whispering (U.S. Version)/Prove Yourself/Lurgee (CD, promo only, card p/s & inner sleeve). 15
94 Parlophone (no cat. no.) PLANET TELEX: LFO & Hexidecimal mixes (12") 30

MINT VALUE £

94 Parlophone 12RSDJ 6394 | My Iron Lung/Lozenge Of Love/The Trickster/Punchdrunk Lovesick Singalong (12", die-cut red or blue sleeve) . . . 45/40
95 Parlophone 12RDJ 6411 | Fake Plastic Trees/India Rubber/How Can I Be Sure? (12", die-cut sleeve) . . . 30
95 Parlophone 12RDJ 6145 | Just/Planet Telex/Killer Cars (12", die-cut sleeve) . . . 25
95 Parlophone CDRDJ 6415 | Just (Album Version)/(Edit Version) (CD, custom sleeve) . . . 12
95 Parlophone HIGH-1 | High & Dry (1-track CD, custom sleeve) . . . 40
95 Parlophone RHEAD US 1 | JUST FOR COLLEGE: India Rubber/Maquiladora/ How Can I Be Sure?/Just (CD) . . . 100
96 Parlophone 12RDJ 6419 | Street Spirit (Fade Out)/Talk Show Host/Bishop's Robes (12", promo-only) . . . 25
97 Parlophone NODATADJ 01 | Paranoid Android (1-track CD, digipak) . . . 15
98 Parlophone 12DATADJO3 | Climbing Up The Walls (Zero 7 Mix)/(Fila Brazilia Mix) (1-sided 12", 200 only) . . . 60
98 12RDJ 6333 | Anyone Can Play Guitar/Faithless, The Wonder Boy/Coke Babies (12", die-cut sleeve) . . . 110
00 Parlophone 12KIDA 6 | Idioteque (12", white label test pressing, p/s) . . . 50
01 Parlophone AMNESIAC 01 | 4 SONGS FROM AMNESIAC: Pyramid Song/I Might Be Wrong/Packt Like Sardines In A Crushd Tin Box/Dollars & Cents (CD, card sleeve) . . . 25
03 Parlophone 12RDJWL 6623 | SKTTERBRAIN (Four Tet Mix)/REMYXOMOTOSIS (Super Collider Mix) (12", 100 only) . . . 100
97 Parlophone (no cat. no.) | OK COMPUTER (promo Aiwa personal stereo, glued-in cassette, two stickers) . 150
97 Parlophone CDPP 005 | OK COMPUTER (CD, numbered title sleeve) . . . 70
00 Parlophone CDKIDA 3 | KID A (CD, card title sleeve) . . . 22
01 Parlophone AMNESIAC 01 | AMNESIAC (CD, 4-track sampler in card p/s) . . . 25
01 Parlophone AMNESIAC 02 | AMNESIAC (CD, in facsmile library book, with press release & inserts) . . . 55
01 Parlophone CDKIDA 4 | KID A (CD, in 6"x 6" hardback book) . . . 55

(see also Headless Chickens)

RADIO HEART

87 GFM GFMP 109 | Radio Heart/Radio Heart (Instrumental) (picture disc) . . . 5
87 GFM GFMG 109 | Radio Heart/Radio Heart (Instrumental) (radio-shaped picture disc) . . . 6
87 GFM GFMP 112 | London Times/Rumour (picture disc) . . . 5
87 GFM GFMX 112 | London Times/Rumour (oblong picture disc) . . . 6
87 NBR CDNBR 1 | All Across The Nation (extended remix)/(radio mix)/(Instrumental)/River (CD, card sleeve) . . . 12
87 NBR NBRL 1 | RADIO HEART (LP, withdrawn) . . . 12

(see also Gary Numan)

RADIO MOSCOW

87 Status RM 100 | Hand Of Freedom (p/s) . . . 8
91 Status RMLP 103 | WORLD SERVICE (LP) . . . 15
92 Status RMLP 104 | GET A NEW LIFE (LP) . . . 15

RADIO 9

90s Enraptured RAPT 1031 | Motorik/Fluid/Moving In Two Directions/Pianosong (10", 9 only) . . . 15

RADIOPHONIC WORKSHOP

73 BBC RESL 13 | Moonbase 3/World Of Dr. Who . . . 18

(see also BBC Radiophonic Workshop)

RADIO STARS

78 Chiswick NS 36 | From A Rabbit/To A Beast (6" 'hip pocket' issue, p/s) . . . 5

(see also John's Children, Andy Ellison, Trevor White)

JACKIE RAE

58 Fontana H 155 | More Than Ever/Hello Ma Baby . . . 6
58 Fontana H 155 | More Than Ever/Hello Ma Baby (78) . . . 6
58 Fontana H 170 | Day By Day/Take A Deep Breath . . . 6
58 Fontana H 170 | Day By Day/Take A Deep Breath (78) . . . 6
60 Fontana H 242 | Summer Place/The Moon Got In My Eyes . . . 6
60 Fontana H 275 | Dreamy/Close . . . 6
67 Coral Q 72495 | Believe In Love/Lonely One . . . 6

(see also Janet Scott & Jackie Rae)

RAELET(T)S

67 HMV POP 1591 | One Hurt Deserves Another/One Room Paradise (as Raelets) . . . 15
71 Tangerine 6121 002 | Bad Water/That Goes To Show You . . . 6
71 Tangerine 6121 003 | Here I Go Again/Leave My Man (Woman) Alone . . . 6

(see also Ray Charles, Clydie King, Merry Clayton)

GERRY RAFFERTY

71 Transatlantic TRA 241 | CAN I HAVE MY MONEY BACK? (LP) . . . 15

(see also Humblebums, Fifth Column)

RAG DOLLS (U.K.)

67 Columbia DB 8289 | Never Had So Much Loving/Any Little Bit . . . 8
68 Columbia DB 8378 | My Old Man's A Groovy Old Man/They Didn't Believe Me . . . 8

(see also Marionettes, Peanut, Katie Kissoon, Mac Kissoon)

RAG DOLLS (U.S.)

64 Cameo Parkway P 921 | Society Girl/Ragen (with Caliente Combo) . . . 18
65 Stateside SS 398 | Dusty/Hey Hoagy . . . 25

RAGE

80 Carrere CAR 159 | Money/Thank That Woman (p/s) . . . 8
80 Carrere CAR 159CT | Money/Thank That Woman (10", red vinyl, stickered clear sleeve) . . . 12
81 Carrere CAR 182 | Out Of Control/Double Dealer (p/s) . . . 5
81 Carrere CAR 182CT | Out Of Control (Extended Version)/Double Dealer (12", yellow vinyl, PVC sleeve) . . . 15
83 Carrere CAR 304 | Cry From A Hill (p/s) . . . 10
81 Carrere CAL 124 | OUT OF CONTROL (LP) . . . 15
82 Carrere CAL 138 | NICE N' DIRTY (LP) . . . 15
83 Carrere CAL 149 | RUN FOR THE NIGHT (LP) . . . 12

(see also Nutz)

RAGE
86 Diamond RAGE 1 — Looking For You/Come On Now (p/s) 5
86 Diamond RAGE 112 — Looking For You/Come On Now/Great Balls Of Fire/Hallelujah I Love Her So (12", unissued, test pressings only) 25
(see also Case, Long Tall Shorty, Purple Hearts, Chords)

RAGE AGAINST THE MACHINE
96 Epic 663 152-7 — Bulls On Parade/Hadda Be Playing On The Jukebox (red vinyl) 7

RAGGAMUFFINS
67 London HLU 10134 — Four Days Of Rain/It Wasn't Happening At All 8

RAGGED HEROES
83 Celtic CM 013 — ANNUAL (LP) 25

RAGING STORMS
62 London HLU 9556 — The Dribble/Hound Dog 22

LOU RAGLAND
73 Warner Bros K 16312 — Since You Said You'd Be Mine/I Didn't Mean To Love You 20

RAGPICKERS
59 Saga SAG 45-2906 — Fifi/Cat On A Cool Tin Roof (p/s) 8
(see also Bert Weedon)

RAINBEAUS
60 Vogue V 9161 — That's All I'm Asking Of You/Maybe It's Wrong (triangular centre) 175

(RITCHIE BLACKMORE'S) RAINBOW
74 Oyster OYR 103 — Man On The Silver Mountain/Snake Charmer (as Ritchie Blackmore's Rainbow) 8
77 Polydor 2066 845 — Kill The King (live)/Man On The Silver Mountain (live)/Mistreated (live) (p/s) 6
78 Polydor 2066 913 — Long Live Rock'n'Roll/Sensitive To Light (p/s) 5
78 Polydor 2066 968 — L.A. Connection/Lady Of The Lake (p/s, initially on red vinyl) 10/5
82 Polydor POSPX 421 — Stone Cold/Rock Fever (12", some on blue vinyl) 10/8
83 Polydor POSP 631 — Street Of Dreams/Anybody There? (p/s) 5
83 Polydor POSPP 631 — Street Of Dreams/Anybody There? (picture disc, 2000 only) 20
83 Polydor POSPX 631 — Street Of Dreams/Anybody There?/Power (live) (12", p/s) 10
83 Polydor POSP 654 — Can't Let You Go/All Night Long (live) (p/s) 5
83 Polydor POSPP 654 — Can't Let You Go/All Night Long (live) (guitar-shaped picture disc) 15
83 Polydor POSPX 654 — Can't Let You Go/All Night Long (live)/Stranded (live) (12", p/s) 10
75 Oyster OYA 2001 — RITCHIE BLACKMORE'S RAINBOW (LP, gatefold sleeve, as Ritchie Blackmore's Rainbow) 12
77 Polydor 2808 010 010 — RAINBOW ON STAGE (LP, music & interview disc, with insert, promo only) 75
79 Polydor POLD 5023 — DOWN TO EARTH (LP, clear vinyl, with inner sleeve) 15
(see also Ritchie Blackmore, Deep Purple, Elf, Dio, Graham Bonnet, Cozy Powell, Roger Glover, Wild Horses, Tony Carey)

CHRIS RAINBOW
81 EMI 12EMI 5215 — Body Music/Girl In Collision (12", p/s) 10
75 Polydor 2383 338 — HOME OF THE BRAVE (LP, with lyric inner sleeve) 12
78 Polydor 2383 467 — LOOKING OVER MY SHOULDER (LP, with lyric inner sleeve) 15
79 EMI EMC 3305 — WHITE TRAILS (LP) 12

RAINBOW FAMILY
72 President PT 375 — Travellin' Lady/My Father 8

RAINBOW FFOLLY
68 Parlophone R 5701 — Go Girl/Drive My Car 50
67 Parlophone PMC/PCS 7050 — SALLIES FFORTH (LP) 200
(see also Love Affair)

RAINBOW PEOPLE
68 Pye 7N 17582 — Walk'll Do You Good/Dream Time 15
68 Pye 7N 17624 — The Sailing Song/Rainbows 8
69 Pye 7N 17759 — Living In A Dream World/Happy To See You Again 8

RAINBOWS
69 CBS 3995 — Rainbows/Nobody But You 12
69 CBS 4568 — New Day Dawning/Days And Nights 7
(see also Peeps, Martin Cure & Peeps)

RAINCOATS
79 Rough Trade ROUGH 3 — THE RAINCOATS (LP, with lyric booklet) 12
(see also Slits)

RAINCHECKS
64 Solar SRP 104 — Something About You/You're My Angel 18
65 R&B MRB 5002 — How Are You Boy/Bye Bye Baby 35

RAINDROPS (U.K.)
59 Parlophone R 4559 — Italian Style/Along Came Jones 10
60 Oriole CB 1544 — Let's Make A Foursome/If I Had My Life To Live Over 12
60 Oriole CB 1544 — Let's Make A Foursome/If I Had My Life To Live Over (78) 5
60 Oriole CB 1555 — Banjo Boy/Crazy Rhythm 8
61 Oriole CB 1595 — Will You Love Me Tomorrow/Raindrops 12
62 Oriole CB 1707 — Paintin' The Town With Teardrops/A Letter From Anne 10
67 CBS 202669 — Foolman/Got To Find A Reason (credited to *Raindrops '67*) 8
(see also Jackie & Raindrops, Jackie Lee, Jacky, Emma Rede, Vince Hill)

RAINDROPS (U.S.)
63 London HL 9718 — What A Guy/It's So Wonderful 18
63 London HL 9769 — The Kind Of Boy You Can't Forget/Even Though You Can't Dance 18
64 London HL 9825 — That Boy John/Hanky Panky 18
64 Fontana TF 463 — The Book Of Love/I Won't Cry 18
64 London RE 1415 — WHAT A GUY (EP) 100
64 London HA 8140 — THE RAINDROPS (LP) 80
(see also Ellie Greenwich, Popsicles)

MINT VALUE £

CLAIRE RAINE

68	Jolly JY 010	La-La-La/I Want You	8

LORRY RAINE

51	London L 899	Spin The Bottle/Who'll Take My Place When I'm Gone (78)	12
51	London L 1081	Sometime, Somewhere/Why Cry (78)	7
53	London L 1220	I've Gotta Have Love/A Wooin' We Will Go (78)	9
54	London HL 8043	You Broke My Broken Heart/I'm In Love With A Guy	25
54	London HL 8043	You Broke My Broken Heart/I'm In Love With A Guy (78)	9
55	London HL 8132	Love Me Tonight/What Would I Do	40
55	London HL 8132	Love Me Tonight/What Would I Do (78)	9

MA RAINEY

50	Jazz Collector L 16	Don't Fish My Sea/Soon This Morning (78)	8
50	Jazz Collector L 20	Jealous Hearted Blues/See See Rider Blues (78)	8
50	Jazz Collector L 35	Blues The World Forgot (Parts 1 & 2) (78)	8
50	Jazz Collector L 42	New Bo-Weavil Blues/Moonshine Blues (78)	8
50	Jazz Collector L 48	Barrel House Blues/Walking Blues (78)	8
50	Jazz Collector L 52	Misery Blues/Dead Drunk Blues (78)	8
50	Jazz Collector L 57	Morning Hour Blues/Weepin' Woman Blues (78)	8
50	Jazz Collector L 66	Moonshine Blues/Southern Blues (78)	8
51	Jazz Collector L 73	Stack O'Lee Blues/Yonder Come The Blues (78)	8
52	Jazz Collector L 78	Those Dogs Of Mine/Lucky Rock Blues (78)	8
52	Jazz Collector L 82	Honey Where Have You Been So Long/Ma Rainey's Mystery Record (78)	8
52	Jazz Collector L 87	Slave To The Blues/Oh My Babe Blues (78)	8
52	Jazz Collector L 98	Blues Oh Blues/Oh Papa Blues (78)	8
54	Jazz Collector L 107	Lawd Send Me A Man Blues/South Bound Blues (78)	8
55	Jazz Collector L 120	Gone Daddy Blues/Slow Driving Moan (78)	8
50s	Signature 908	Yonder Come The Blues/Stack O'Lee Blues (78)	8
53	London AL 3502	MA RAINEY VOLUME 1 (10" LP)	50
55	London AL 3538	MA RAINEY VOLUME 2 (10" LP)	50
56	London AL 3558	MA RAINEY VOLUME 3 (10" LP)	50
50s	Ristic LP 13	MA RAINEY (10" LP)	50
50s	Ristic LP 19	MA RAINEY (10" LP)	50
62	Riverside RL 12-108	MA RAINEY SINGS THE BLUES (LP)	25
64	Riverside RLP 8807	MOTHER OF THE BLUES (LP, gatefold sleeve with booklet)	25
70	CBS 52798	MA RAINEY AND THE CLASSIC BLUES SINGERS (LP)	15

MA RAINEY & IDA COX

60	Jazz Collector JEL 12	THE FEMALE BLUES VOL. 1 (EP)	20
64	Jazz Collector JEL 22	THE FEMALE BLUES VOL. 3 (EP, with Trixie Smith)	18

(see also Ida Cox, Tommy Ladnier)

MA RAINEY & PAPA CHARLIE JACKSON

50s	Poydras 11	Ma And Papa Poorhouse Blues/Big Feeling Blues	12

RAIN PARADE

83	Enigma BOB 4/LYN 15263	Sad Eyes Kill (3.16) (1-sided flexi with *Bucketfull Of Brains* mag, issue 10)	6/4
83	Enigma BOB 4/LYN 15263	Sad Eyes Kill (3.16) (hard vinyl white label test pressing)	12

MARVIN RAINWATER

55	MGM SP 1150	Tennessee Houn' Dog Yodel/Albino (Pink-Eyed) Stallion	65
55	MGM MGM 876	Tennessee Houn' Dog Yodel/Albino (Pink-Eyed) Stallion (78)	15
56	MGM MGM 929	What Am I Supposed To Do/Why Did You Have To Go And Leave Me	30
56	MGM MGM 929	What Am I Supposed To Do/Why Did You Have To Go And Leave Me (78)	10
57	MGM MGM 961	Gonna Find Me A Bluebird/So You Think You've Got	30
57	MGM MGM 961	Gonna Find Me A Bluebird/So You Think You've Got (78)	10
58	MGM MGM 974	Whole Lotta Woman/Baby, Don't Go	10
58	MGM MGM 980	I Dig You Baby/Two Fools In Love (B-side with Sister Patty)	8
58	MGM MGM 988	Dance Me Daddy/Because I'm A Dreamer (B-side with Sister Patty)	18
58	MGM MGM 988	Dance Me Daddy/Because I'm A Dreamer (B-side with Sister Patty) (78)	10
59	MGM MGM 1030	Half-Breed/A Song Of New Love	12
59	MGM MGM 1030	Half-Breed/A Song Of New Love (78)	20
60	MGM MGM 1052	Nothin' Needs Nothin' (Like I Need You)/The Valley Of The Moon	20
61	London HLU 9447	Boo Hoo/I Can't Forget	110
58	MGM MGM-EP 647	MEET MARVIN RAINWATER (EP)	60
58	MGM MGM-EP 662	WHOLE LOTTA MARVIN (EP)	75
59	MGM MGM-EP 685	MARVIN RAINWATER (EP)	70
63	Ember EMB 4521	COUNTRY AND WESTERN FAVOURITES VOL. 2 (EP)	30
58	MGM MGM-D 152	SONGS BY MARVIN RAINWATER (10" LP)	100
72	Philips 6414 110	MARVIN RAINWATER GETS COUNTRY FEVER (LP)	15

(see also Connie Francis & Marvin Rainwater)

RAINY DAY

84	EMI EMI 5472	Painting Pictures/Welche Farbe Hat Der Sonnenschein (p/s)	12

RAINY DAZE

67	CBS 3200	What Do You Think/Autumn Leaves	15
67	Polydor 56731	That Acapulco Gold/In My Mind Lives A Forest	12
68	Polydor 56737	Blood Of Oblivion/Stop Sign	18
68	CBS 56731	THAT ACAPULCO GOLD (LP, unissued in U.K.)	

RAISINS

68	Major Major MM 540	Ain't That Lovin' You Baby/Stranger Things Have Happened	8
69	Major Minor MM 602	I Thank You/Don't Leave Me Like This	6
68	Major Minor MMLP 20	THE RAISINS (LP, also stereo SMLP 20)	30

(see also Coloured Raisins)

BONNIE RAITT

72	Warner Bros K 16226	Too Long At The Fair/Under The Falling Sky	5
72	Warner Bros K 46189	GIVE IT UP (LP)	12
73	Warner Bros K 46261	TAKIN' MY TIME (LP)	12
74	Warner Bros K 56075	STREETLIGHTS (LP)	12
75	Warner Bros K 56160	HOME PLATE (LP)	12

(see also Roy Orbison, Alton Purnell)

DON RALKE ORCHESTRA

59	Vogue V 9152	Maverick/Travellin' West	10
59	Vogue V 9152	Maverick/Travellin' West (78)	12
60	Warner Brothers WB 2	77 Sunset Strip (as Big Sound Of Don Ralke)/ PETE CANDOLI & HIS ORCHESTRA: 77 Sunset Strip Cha-Cha	7
60	Warner Brothers WM 4014	DANCE CAPER IN HI-FI (LP)	25
60	Warner Brothers WS 8007	YOU'VE NEVER HEARD GERSHWIN WITH BONGOS (LP)	12

TOMMY RALL, ANN MILLER, BOBBY VAN & BOB FOSSE

54	MGM SP 1079	From This Moment On/So Kiss Me Kate (by Kathryn Grayson & Howard Keel)/ Brush Up Your Shakespeare (by Keenan Wynn & James Whitmore)	7

RALLY ROUNDERS

64	Lyntone LYN 573/574	Bike Beat Part 1/Bike Beat Part 2 (actually by the Outlaws) (p/s, flexidisc)	75

(see also Outlaws, Ritchie Blackmore)

RALPH & PONYTAILS

80	Pony Tunes RATP 1	James Bond/James Bond (Different Version) (p/s)	5

BUCK RAM'S RAMROCKS

63	London HLU 9677	Benfica/Odd Man Theme	15

(see also Little Richard, Platters)

RAMASES

71	Philips 6113 001	Ballroom/Muddy Water	7
71	Philips 6113 003	Jesus Come Back/Hello Mister	7
71	Vertigo 6360 046	SPACE HYMNS (LP, foldout sleeve, swirl label, later 'spaceship' label)	30/15
75	Vertigo 6360 115	GLASS TOP COFFIN (LP, gatefold sleeve)	15

(see also 10cc, Ramases & Seleka, Ramases & Selket)

RAMASES & SELEKA

70	Major Minor MM 704	Love You/Gold Is The Ring	50

(see also Ramases)

RAMASES & SELKET

68	CBS 3717	Crazy One/Mind's Eye	100

(see also Ramases)

RAMATAM

72	Atlantic K 40415	RAMATAM (LP)	12

(see also Iron Butterfly)

EDDIE RAMBEAU

62	Stateside SS 116	Summertime Guy/Last Night Was My Last Night	10
64	Stateside SS 301	Come Closer/She's Smilin' At Me	8
65	Stateside SS 448	My Name Is Mud/I Just Need Your Love	10
66	Stateside SS 486	The Train/Yesterday's Newspapers	10
66	Stateside SS 501	I'm The Sky/I Just Need Your Love	7
66	Stateside SS 561	The Clock/If I Were You	7

(see also Marcy Jo & Eddie Rambeau)

RAMBLER

66	Pye 7N 17164	Love Minus Zero No Limit/An Bonnan Bui	7

(see also Johnny McEvoy)

RAMBLERS

63	Decca F 11775	Dodge City/Just For Chicks	40

RAMBLERS TWO

65	Pye 7N 15989	Today Is The Highway/The Mountains And The Sea	5

RAMBLETTES

65	Brunswick 05932	Thinking Of You/On Back Street	20

RAMBLING SYD RUMPO

67	Parlophone R 5638	The Ballad Of The Wogglers Moulie/Green Grow My Nadgers Oh!	7
68	Parlophone GEP 8965	RAMBLING SYD RUMPO IN CONCERT VOL. 1 (EP)	12
68	Parlophone GEP 8966	RAMBLING SYD RUMPO IN CONCERT VOL. 2 (EP)	12
70	Starline SRS 5034	THE BEST OF RAMBLING SYD RUMPO (LP)	15

(see also Kenneth Williams)

RAMBLIN' JIMMY DOLAN

51	Capitol CL 13600	Wine, Women And Pink Elephants/GENE O'QUIN: Boogie Woogie Fever (78)	10
53	Capitol CL 13982	Playin' Dominoes And Shootin' Dice/The Wheel That Does The Squeekin' (78)	10

SID RAMIN

69	CBS 70062	STILETTO (LP, soundtrack)	30

CARLOS RAMIREZ

54	MGM SP 70062	I Had To Kiss You/Little More Of Your Armour	6

RAM JAM BAND

65	Columbia DB 7621	Shake Shake Senora/Akinla	18

(see also Geno Washington & Ram Jam Band, Ram John Holder, Ram Holder Brothers)

MINT VALUE £

RAMLEH

83	Broken Flag BF V4	THE HAND OF GLORY (EP)	15
91	Shock SX 013	Slammers/Black Moby Dick (p/s, numbered, 500 only)	8
92	Dying Earth DE 003	Loser Patrol/Tracers (p/s, numbered, 500 only, 1st 30 in red sleeve)	15/8
93	Dying Earth DE 007	Say Fuck/Slackjaw (wraparound p/s, numbered, 500 only)	8
94	Format Supremacy (no cat. no.)	Welcome/Pristine Womankind (cardboard p/s, 500 only)	8
94	Freek FRR 006	HOMELESS (CD-only EP)	15
95	Broken Flag BS 78	ADIEU ALL YOU JUDGES (CD-only live EP, features Skullflower, 500 only)	20
83	Broken Flag BF V2	A RETURN TO SLAVERY (LP, with Libertarian Recordings)	40
91	Shock Records SX D14	BLOWHOLE (LP)	12

(see also Skullflower)

RAMON & CRYSTALITES

71	Songbird SB 1053	Golden Chickens/Stranger Version	18

DEE DEE RAMONE

97	Blackout BLK 5000-7	I Am Seeing UFOs (featuring Joey Ramone)/Bad Horoscope (2,500 copies only)	5

DEE DEE RAMONE & ICLC

94	Rough Trade/World Service RDT 157.1757.2	Chinese Bitch/I Don't Want To Get Involved With You/ That's What Everybody Else Does/We're A Creepy Family (CD)	10

(see also Ramones)

RAMONES

76	Sire 6078 601	Blitzkrieg Bop/Havana Affair (some with p/s)	100/10
77	Sire 6078 603	I Remember You/California Sun (live)/I Don't Wanna Walk Around With You (live) (p/s)	20
77	Sire RAM 001 (6078 606)	Sheena Is A Punk Rocker/Commando/I Don't Care (no p/s)	5
77	Sire RAM 001 (6078 606)	Sheena Is A Punk Rocker/Commando/I Don't Care (12", with or without T-shirt offer on perforated centre of numbered p/s, 12,000 only)	20/15
77	Sire 6078 607	Swallow My Pride/Pinhead/Let's Dance (live) (p/s)	10
77	Sire 6078 611	Rockaway Beach/Teenage Lobotomy/Beat On The Brat (p/s)	10
77	Sire 6078 611	Rockaway Beach/Teenage Lobotomy/Beat On The Brat (12", p/s, some with poster)	35/10
78	Sire 6078 615	Do You Wanna Dance?/It's A Long Way Back To Germany/Cretin Hop (p/s)	10
78	Sire (no cat. no.)	Questioningly/Don't Come Close/Sedated/I Just Want To Have Something To Do (some with p/s, promo only, with spoken intros by Joey Ramone)	25/12
78	Sire SRE 1031	Don't Come Close/I Don't Want You (p/s, some on yellow vinyl)	10/5
78	Sire SRE 1031	Don't Come Close/I Don't Want You (12", p/s, yellow or red vinyl, red vinyl lacks p/s)	each 15
79	Sire SIR 4009	She's The One/I Wanna Be Sedated (p/s)	10
79	Sire SIR 4021	Rock'n'Roll High School/Rockaway Beach (live)/Sheena Is A Punk Rocker (live) (p/s)	8
80	Sire SIR 4031	Baby, I Love You/High Risk Insurance (p/s)	5
80	Sire SIR 4031	Baby, I Love You/High Risk Insurance (cassette)	8
80	Sire SIR 4037	Do You Remember Rock'n'Roll Radio/I Want You Around (p/s)	6
80	RSO RSO 70 (2090 512)	I Wanna Be Sedated/The Return Of Jackie And Judy (p/s)	15
80	Sire SREP 1	MELTDOWN WITH THE RAMONES: I Just Want To Have Something To Do/ Here Today Gone Tomorrow/I Wanna Be Your Boyfriend/Questioningly (EP)	20
81	Sire SIR 4051	We Want The Airwaves/You Sound Like You're Sick (p/s)	10
81	Sire SIR 4052	She's A Sensation/All Quiet On The Eastern Front (no p/s)	8
83	Sire W 9606	Time Has Come Today/Psycho Therapy (p/s)	15
83	Sire W 9606T	Time Has Come Today/Sheena Is A Punk Rocker/Teenage Lobotomy/ Rock'n'Roll Radio (12", p/s)	25
85	Beggars Banquet BEG 128	Chasing The Night/Howling At The Moon (p/s)	6
85	Beggars Banquet BEG 128D	Chasing The Night/Howling At The Moon//Smash You/Street Fighting Man (double pack, gatefold sleeve)	8
85	Beggars Banquet BEGTP 128	Chasing The Night/Howling At The Moon//Smash You/Street Fighting Man (12", p/s)	8
85	Beggars Banquet BEG 140	Bonzo Goes To Bitburg/Go Home Ann (p/s)	7
85	Beggars Banquet BEG 140T	Bonzo Goes To Bitburg/Go Home Ann/Daytime Dilemma (12", p/s)	8
86	Beggars Banquet BEG 157	Somebody Put Something In My Drink/Something To Believe In (p/s)	5
86	Beggars Banquet BEG 157T	Somebody Put Something In My Drink/(You) Can't Say Anything Nice/ Something To Believe In (12", p/s, some with promo poster)	15/8
87	Beggars Banquet BEG 198	Real Cool Time/Life Goes On (p/s)	6
87	Beggars Banquet BEG 198T	Real Cool Time/Life Goes On/Indian Giver (12", p/s)	8
87	Beggars Banquet BEG 201	I Wanna Live/Merry Christmas (I Don't Want To Fight Tonight) (p/s)	8
87	Beggars Banquet BEG 201T	I Wanna Live/Merry Christmas (I Don't Want To Fight Tonight) (12", p/s)	10
92	Chrysalis CHS 3917	Poison Heart/Censorshit (p/s)	5
92	Chrysalis 0946 3 23917 66	Poison Heart/Chinese Rocks/Sheena Is A Punk Rocker (live)/ Rockaway Beach (live) (12", yellow vinyl, p/s)	8
76	Sire 9103 253	RAMONES (LP, with insert)	20
77	Sire 9103 254	RAMONES LEAVE HOME (LP, with "Carbona Not Glue" or "Babysitter", both with inner sleeve)	25/15
77	Sire 9103 255	ROCKET TO RUSSIA (LP, with inner sleeve)	12
78	Sire SRK 6063	ROAD TO RUIN (LP, yellow vinyl)	18
80	Sire SRK 6077	END OF THE CENTURY (LP)	15
81	Sire SRK 3571	PLEASANT DREAMS (LP)	12
90	Beggar's Banquet (no cat. no.)	END OF THE DECADE (6 x 12" singles, box set with t-shirt, postcards & poster, 2,500 copies only)	50
91	Chysalis CHR 1901	LOCO LIVE (LP)	15
93	Chrysalis CHR 6052	ACID EATERS (LP)	15

(see also Paley Brothers & Ramones, Holly & Joey, Dee Dee Ramone)

RAM RAM KINO

85	Temple TOPY 006	Advantage — Tantric Routines 1-4 (3.23)/(Basket Mix) (4.00)/ Into The Bush (3.26)/Special (3.56) (12", p/s)	8

(see also Crispy Ambulance)

RAMRODS
65 United Artists UP 1113 — Overdrive/Stalker — 12

RAMRODS (U.S.)
61 London HLU 9282 — Riders In The Sky/Zig Zag — 10
61 London HLU 9355 — Loch Lomond Rock/Take Me Back To My Boots And Saddle — 18
61 London RE-U 1292 — RIDERS IN THE SKY (EP) — 125

BILL RAMSEY
62 Polydor NH 66812 — Go Man Go/Rocking Mountain — 12

RANCHERS
65 Cavern Sound IMSTL 2 — An American Sailor At The Cavern/Sidetracked — 20
(see also Phil Brady & Ranchers)

RANCID
94 Epitaph 86434-1 — LET'S GO (LP, 2 x 10", gatefold sleeve, white vinyl) — 12

ALAN RANDALL (& SHEP'S BANJO BOYS)
70 Domino 110 — The Coventry City Song/Football Football — 6

ELLIOTT RANDALL
71 Polydor 2489 004 — RANDALL'S ISLAND (LP) — 15

FREDDY RANDALL & HIS BAND
50 Tempo A 45 — Dark Night Blues/Washington And Lee Swing (78) — 8
50 Tempo A 49 — Riverside Blues/Jazz Club Stomp (78) — 8
50 Tempo A 55 — Georgia Cake Walk/Sugar Foot Strut (78) — 8
53 Parlophone MSP 6007 — Clarinet Marmalade/Original Dixieland One-Step — 6
53 Parlophone MSP 6030 — At The Jazz Band Ball/Way Down Yonder In New Orleans — 6
53 Parlophone MSP 6043 — Twelve For Six/Copenhagen — 6
54 Parlophone MSP 6087 — Carolina In The Morning/Tin Roof Blues — 6
54 Parlophone MSP 6098 — Muskrat Ramble/Shine — 6
54 Parlophone MSP 6137 — Someday Sweetheart/Hotter Than That — 6
58 Parlophone GEP 8715 — CHICAGO JAZZ (EP) — 12
58 Parlophone PMD 1046 — DR JAZZ (LP) — 18

TONY RANDALL & JACK KLUGMAN
72 Decca Phase Four PFS 4277 — THE ODD COUPLE SINGS (LP) — 20

TEDDY RANDAZZO (& DAZZLERS)
59 HMV POP 578 — It's Magic/Richer Than I — 10
59 HMV POP 578 — It's Magic/Richer Than I (78) — 6
60 HMV POP 806 — Journey To Love/Misery — 10
61 HMV POP 866 — Happy Ending/But You Broke My Heart — 10
61 HMV POP 925 — Let The Sunshine In/Broken Bell — 10
62 HMV POP 1067 — Dance To The Locomotion/Cottonfields (as Teddy Randazzo & Dazzlers) — 15
63 HMV POP 1119 — Echoes/It Wasn't A Dream — 8
63 Pye International 7N 25181 — Big Wide World/Be Sure, My Love — 8
62 HMV CLP 1527 — JOURNEY TO LOVE (LP, also stereo CSD 1421) — 6075
63 HMV CLP 1601 — TEDDY RANDAZZO TWISTS (LP, with Dazzlers) — 90
(see also Three Chuckles)

LYNNE RANDELL
67 CBS 2847 — Ciao Baby/Stranger In My Arms — 220
67 CBS 2927 — That's A Hoe Down/I Need You Boy — 20

RAN-DELLS
63 London HLU 9760 — The Martian Hop/Forgive Me Darling — 25
(see also Jeff Wayne)

DON RANDI
65 London HLU 9963 — Mexican Pearls/I Don't Wanna Be Kissed — 8

BARBARA RANDOLPH
67 Tamla Motown TMG 628 — I Got A Feelin'/You Got Me Hurtin' All Over — 50
71 Tamla Motown TMG 788 — I Got A Feelin'/You Got Me Hurtin' All Over (reissue) — 15
79 Tamla Motown TMG 1133 — Can I Get A Witness/You Got Me Hurtin' All Over — 10

BOOTS RANDOLPH
62 London HLU 9567 — Bluebird Of Happiness/Keep A Light In Your Window Tonight — 10
63 London HLU 9685 — Yakety Sax/I Really Don't Want To Know — 12
63 London HLU 9798 — Windy And Warm/Lonely Street — 10
64 London HLU 9891 — Hey, Mr. Sax Man/Baby Go To Sleep — 10
66 London HLU 10017 — Theme From A Dream/King Of The Road — 6
66 London HLU 10028 — These Boots Are Made For Walking/Honey In Your Heart — 6
67 Monument MON 1001 — The Shadow Of Your Smile/I'll Just Walk Away — 6
67 Monument MON 1011 — Big Daddy/Love Letters — 6
69 Monument MON 1028 — Games People Play/By The Time I Get To Phoenix — 6
63 London RE-U 1365 — THE YAKETY SAX OF BOOTS RANDOLPH (EP) — 40
63 London HA-U 8106 — YAKETY SAX (LP) — 40
66 London HA-U 8280 — MORE YAKETY SAX (LP, as Boots Randolph & His Combo) — 35
67 Monument LMO/SMO 5002 — HIP BOOTS (LP) — 18
67 Monument LMO/SMO 5003 — BOOTS WITH STRINGS (LP) — 18
68 Monument LMO/SMO 5012 — THE FANTASTIC BOOTS RANDOLPH (LP) — 18
69 Monument LMO/SMO 5022 — SAXSATIONAL (LP) — 18
70 Monument LMO/SMO 5040 — YAKETY REVISITED (LP) — 15

CHARLES RANDOLPH GREEN SOUND
69 London HLD 10283 — Quintin's Theme/Number One At The Blue Whale — 6

ERIC RANDOM
81 D. du Crepescule TW 1029 — 23 Skidoo/Subliminal (p/s) — 5
80 New Hormones CAT 4 — LIVE IN EUROPE (cassette) — 10
(see also Tiller Boys, Cabaret Voltaire, Free Agents, Pressure & Co.)

MINT VALUE £

RANDOM HARVEST
82 Random Harvest RH 501 — RANDOM HARVEST (LP) ... 12

RANDY & RAINBOWS
63 Stateside SS 214 — Denise/Come Back ... 60

RANDY'S ALLSTARS
70 Randy's RAN 500 — I'm The One, You're The One/End Us ... 7
70 Randy's RAN 501 — Pepper Pot (act. with Count Machuki)/Same Thing (B-side actually by Gaylads) . 10
70 Randy's RAN 502 — Dixie/Five Cents (B-side actually "A Lover's Question" by Winston Samuels) ... 7
70 Randy's RAN 505 — Emperor Waltz/War ... 8
70 Randy's RAN 506 — Blue Danube Waltz/Together (B-side actually by Delroy Wilson) ... 8
70 Randy's RAN 507 — Bridge Over Troubled Water (actually by Lyrics)/Waterfall ... 7
71 Explosion EX 2052 — Hold On Girl (actually by Lyrics)/Hold On Girl (Version) ... 7
(see also Impact Allstars, Lyrics, Dave Barker, Ethiopians, Jimmy London)

RANEE & RAJ
68 Fontana TF 920 — Feel Like A Clown/Rainbow Land ... 10
68 Fontana TF 941 — Don't Tell Me I Must Go/Razor Edge ... 7

SUE RANEY
57 Capitol CL 14757 — The Careless Years/What's The Good Word, Mr. Bluebird ... 7
57 Capitol CL 14792 — Please Hurry Home/Don't Take My Happiness ... 7
58 Capitol CL 14923 — My, My, How The Time Goes By/Periwinkle Blue ... 7
59 Capitol CL 14980 — Ever/The Restless Sea ... 7
59 Capitol CL 15045 — Swingin' In A Hammock/I Don't Look Right Without You ... 7
60 Capitol CL 15132 — Biology/I Stayed Too Long At The Fair ... 7
58 Capitol T 964 — WHEN YOUR LOVER HAS GONE (LP) ... 25

WAYNE RANEY (STRING BAND)
53 Parlophone DP 333 — If You Never Slip Around/The Child's Side Of Life (78, export issue) ... 10
54 Parlophone CSMP 20 — Adam/The Roosters Are Crowing (export issue) ... 25
54 Parlophone DP 380 — Adam/The Roosters Are Crowing (78, export issue) ... 8
55 Parlophone DP 413 — Mama (Don't You Remember When You Were Young)/Trying To Live Without You (78, export issue) ... 8
50s Parlophone DP 349 — Burning Your Love Letters/Falling (78, export issue) ... 10
58 Parlophone GEP 8746 — COUNTRY AND WESTERN (EP) ... 40

RANGLERS
68 Trend TRE 1007 — You Never Said Goodbye/Step Down ... 18

ERNEST RANGLIN
62 Island WI 015 — Harmonica Twist/Mitty Gritty (as Ernest Ranglin Orchestra) ... 25
63 Island WI 128 — Exodus/ROBERT MARLEY: One Cup Of Coffee ... 250
66 Black Swan IEP 704 — ERNEST RANGLIN & THE G.B.'s (EP, some with p/s) ... 180/5
64 Island ILP 909 — WRANGLIN' (LP) ... 125
64 Island ILP 915 — REFLECTIONS (LP) ... 100
60s Vista Sounds — FROM KINGSTON J.A. TO MIAMI U.S.A. (LP) ... 25
(see also Owen Gray, Graham Bond)

MASSIMO RANIERI
71 CBS 7207 — Goodbye My Love/The Sun Shining Down On Me ... 12

BILLY RANKIN
83 A&M AM 172 — Baby Come Back/Part Of The Scenery (p/s) ... 6
(see also Nazareth)

KENNY RANKIN
60 Brunswick 05845 — As Sure As You're Born/Teasin' Heart ... 10
73 Atlantic K 10275 — Comin' Down/Stringman ... 6

FELA RANSOME KUTI
(see under 'K')

RAOUL & RUINED
84 Gutter Hearts GH 1 — BITE BACK + BLUES (LP, fan-club only issue) ... 50
(see also Marc Almond)

RAPED
78 Parole KNIT 1 — PRETTY PAEDOPHILES (EP) ... 20
78 Parole PURL 1 — Cheap Night Out/Foreplay Playground (p/s, with ad sheet) ... 8
84 Iguana PILLAGED 1 — PHILES AND SMILES (LP, official bootleg, with booklet) ... 20
(see also Cuddly Toys)

RAPEMAN
88 Fierce FRIGHT 031 — Hated Chinee/Marmoset (p/s) ... 30
(see also Big Black)

JOHNNY RAPHAEL
58 Vogue V 9104 — We're Only Young Once/The Lonely Road To Nowhere ... 90
58 Vogue V 9104 — We're Only Young Once/The Lonely Road To Nowhere (78) ... 40

RAPIERS
60s Ilford Sound ILF 272 — The Phantom Stage/Valencia ... 12

RAPIERS
86 Off Beat NS 112A — The Closing Theme/Still I Cry ... 10
83 Red Door RA 001 — THE RAPIERS VOL. 1 (EP) ... 20
84 Twang RA 002 — THE RAPIERS VOL. 2 (EP) ... 15
85 Twang RA 003 — THE RAPIERS VOL. 3 (EP) ... 15
86 Twang RA 004 — THE RAPIERS VOL. 4 (EP) ... 12
85 Off Beat WIK 40 — STRAIGHT TO THE POINT (LP) ... 20
87 Off Beat WIK 67 — 1961 (LP) ... 20

BRIAN RAPKIN & KELVIN JONES

70s MSR DREAMS OF THE BEAST (LP) 20

MARIE RAPP

53 London L 1207 When A Man Loves A Woman/When I'm With You (78) 15

RAPTURE

03 Output OPRDFA 006 House Of Jealous Lovers/(Morgan Geist Version)/(Maurice Fulton Remix)/(Original Instrumental)/(A Capella) (12", p/s) 8

RARE AMBER

69 Polydor BM 56309 Malfunction Of The Engine/Blind Love 20
69 Polydor 583 046 RARE AMBER (LP) 80

RARE BIRD

70 Charisma CB 120 Sympathy/Devil's High Concern (some in p/s) 10/5
70 Charisma CB 138 What You Want To Know/Hammerhead 7
72 Charisma CB 179 Sympathy/Devil's High Concern/What Do You Want To Know/Hammerhead (p/s) 8
73 Polydor 2058 402 Virgina/Lonely Street 5
74 Polydor 2058 471 Body And Soul/Redman 5
74 Polydor SH 1041/2 Diamonds/BARCLAY JAMES HARVEST: Negative Earth (flexi, with *Sounds*) 10/5
75 Polydor 2058 591 Don't Be Afraid/Passin' Through 5
75 Charisma CB 262 Sympathy/Beautiful Scarlet 5
69 Charisma CAS 1005 RARE BIRD (LP) 22
70 Charisma CAS 1011 AS YOUR MIND FLIES BY (LP) 22
72 Polydor 2442 101 EPIC FOREST (LP & poster, some with bonus EP "Roadside Welcome"/"Four Grey Walls"/"You're Lost" [2814 011], p/s) 30/20
73 Polydor 2383 211 SOMEBODY'S WATCHING (LP) 12
74 Polydor 2383 274 BORN AGAIN (LP) 12
(see also Fields, Fruit Machine)

RARE BREED

66 Strike JH 316 Beg, Borrow And Steal/Jeri's Theme 25
(see also Pussyfoot)

RARE EARTH

70 Tamla Motown TMG 742 Get Ready/Magic Key 12
71 Rare Earth RES 102 I Just Want To Celebrate/The Seed 5
72 Rare Earth RES 104 Hey Brother/Under God's Light 5
72 Rare Earth RES 105 Born To Wander/Here Comes The Night 5
73 Rare Earth RES 109 Good Time Sally/Love Shines Down 5
70 T. Motown STML 11165 GET READY (LP) 25
71 T. Motown STML 11180 ECOLOGY (LP) 22
71 Rare Earth SREA 4001 ONE WORLD (LP) 15
72 Rare Earth SRESP 301 IN CONCERT (2-LP, satchel sleeve) 18
73 Rare Earth SRE 3008 WILLIE REMEMBERS (LP, gatefold sleeve) 12
73 Rare Earth SRE 3010 MA (LP) 12

RASCALS

68 Atlantic 584 182 A Beautiful Morning/Rainy Day 7
68 Atlantic 584 210 People Got To Be Free/My World 6
69 Atlantic 584 255 Heaven/Baby I'm Blue 6
69 Atlantic 584 274 See/Away Away 6
69 Atlantic 584 292 Carry Me Back/Real Thing 6
70 Atlantic 584 307 Hold On/I Believe 6
70 Atlantic 2091 029 Glory, Glory/You Don't Know 6
71 CBS 7363 Love Me/Happy Song 6
71 CBS 7672 Lucky Day/Love Letter 6
68 Atlantic 587/588 098 ONCE UPON A DREAM (LP) 22
68 Atlantic 587/588 120 TIME PEACE — RASCALS' GREATEST HITS (LP) 18
69 Atlantic 588 183 FREEDOM SUITE (LP) 18
70 Atlantic 588 210 SEE (LP) 15
71 Atlantic 2400 113 SEARCH AND NEARNESS (LP) 15
72 CBS 64756 THE ISLAND OF REAL (LP) 12
(see also Young Rascals)

RENATO RASCEL

60 RCA RCA 1177 Romantica/Dimmelo Con Un Fiore 10

RASPBERRIES

72 Capitol CL 15718 I Don't Want To Say Goodbye/Rock And Roll Mama 5
72 Capitol CL 15730 Go All The Way/With You In My Life 5
73 Capitol CL 15740 I Wanna Be With You/Goin' Nowhere Tonight 5
74 Capitol CL 15801 Overnight Sensation/Hands On You 5
72 Capitol E-ST 11036 THE RASPBERRIES (LP) 15
72 Capitol E-ST 11123 FRESH RASPBERRIES (LP) 15
73 Capitol E-ST 11220 SIDE THREE (LP) 15
74 Capitol E-ST 11329 STARTING OVER (LP) 12
(see also Choir)

RASTA TWINS

(see under Aggrovators)

THE RAT & THE WHALE

80 Rewind REWIND 5 Wheels On Fire/Wheels On Fire (Long Version) (p/s) 5
(see also Alternative TV, Rat Scabies)

BASIL RATHBONE

60s Caedmon TC 1028 EDGAR ALLAN POE (LP) 15

RATIO

70 Big Chief BC 102 Let There Be Peace In The World/Pharaoh's Walk 7

MINT VALUE £

RATIONAL ANTHEM

86	Radio Humberside/HLS 001	THE NORTHERN TRAWL (LP)	50

ARMAN RATIP

73	Regal Zono. SLRZ 1038	THE SPY FROM ISTANBUL (LP)	30

RATS

64	Oak RGJ 145	Spoonful (1-sided, some with foldout p/s)	350/200
65	Columbia DB 7483	Spoonful/I've Got My Eyes On You Baby	110
65	Columbia DB 7607	I Gotta See My Baby Everyday/Headin' Back (To New Orleans)	70
95	Tenth Planet TP	THE RISE AND FALL OF BERNIE GRIPPLESTONE & THE SPIDERS FROM HULL (LP, gatefold sleeve, 1,000 only)	15

(see also Beat Boys, Mark Peters; the above singles do not feature Mick Ronson)

RATS

64	Oriole CB 1967	Parchman Farm/Every Day I Have The Blues	110
65	CBS 201740	Sack Of Woe/Gimme That Wine	80

RATS

74	Goodear EARLH 5003	FIRST (LP)	18

(see also World of Oz)

RATT

85	Atlantic A 9546P	Lay It Down/Got Me On The Line (shaped picture disc)	6
86	Atlantic A 9502P	You're In Love/Between The Eyes (shaped picture disc)	8

RATTLES

63	Philips BF 1277	The Stomp/Zip A Dee Doo Dah	15
64	Decca F 11873	Bye Bye Johnny/Roll Over Beethoven	20
64	Decca F 11936	Tell Me What I Can Do/Sunbeam At The Sky	15
65	Fontana TF 618	Come On And Sing/Candy To Me	15
66	Fontana TF 724	Say All Right/Love Of My Life	15
70	Decca F 23058	The Witch/Geraldine	7
71	Decca F 23119	You Can't Have Sunshine Every Day/Where Is The Friend?	6
71	Decca F 13243	Devil's On The Loose/I Know You Don't Know	6
64	Decca DFE 8568	TEENBEAT FROM THE STAR CLUB HAMBURG (EP)	125
64	Philips BL 7614	TWIST AT THE STAR CLUB HAMBURG (LP)	100
67	Mercury MG 1127	GREATEST HITS (LP)	25
71	Decca SKL-R 5088	THE RATTLES (LP)	20

(see also Wonderland)

PETER RAUHOFER (& PET SHOP BOYS)

02	Parlophone 12RDJ 6574	Break 4 Love (Classic Club Mix)/Break 4 Love (Mike Monday Kit Kat Dub)/ Break 4 Love (Friburn & Urik Hi Pass Mix)/Break 4 Love (Friburn & Urik Tribal Mix)/Break 4 Love (Ralphie's Dub For Love)/Home & Dry (Acappella) (2 x 12", promo, p/s)	15

(see also Pet Shop Boys)

CARL RAVAZZA

51	HMV B 10202	Rock, Rock, Rock/Like A Dream (78)	10

CHRIS RAVEL & RAVERS

63	Decca F 11696	I Do/Don't You Dig This Kind Of Beat	18

(see also Chris Andrews)

RAVEN

80	Neat NEAT 06	Don't Need Your Money/Wiped Out (p/s)	10
81	Neat NEAT 11	Hard Ride/Crazy World (p/s)	7
82	Neat NEAT 15	Crash Bang Wallop/Rock Hard (no p/s)	5
82	Neat NEAT 1512	CRASH BANG WALLOP (Crash Bang Wallop/Firepower/Run Them Down/ Rock Hard) (12" EP, mauve splattered vinyl)	25
83	Neat NEAT 28	Break The Chain/Ballad Of Marshall Stack (p/s)	5
83	Neat NEAT 29P	Born To Be Wild/Inquisitor (with Udo Dirkschneider) (picture disc)	6
83	Neat NEAT 2912	Break The Chain/Born To Be Wild/Inquisitor (with Udo Dirkschneider) (12", p/s)	8
86	WEA A 9453	Gimme Some Lovin' (no p/s)	20
81	Neat NEAT 1001	ROCK UNTIL YOU DROP (LP, with lyric insert)	12
81	Neat NEAT 1004	WIPED OUT (LP, limited issue, with poster)	12
83	Neat NEATP 1001	ROCK UNTIL YOU DROP (LP, reissue, picture disc)	15
83	Neat NEAT 1011	ALL FOR ONE (LP)	15

JON RAVEN

70s	Broadside	HARVEST (LP, with book)	15
71	Argo ZFB 29	KATE OF COALBROOKDALE (LP, as Jon & Mike Raven with Jean Ward)	150
73	Trailer LER 2083	SONGS OF A CHANGING WORLD (LP, with Nic Jones & Tony Rose, red label with insert)	25
75	Tradition TSR 019	THE BOLD NAVIGATORS: THE STORY OF ENGLAND'S CANALS IN SONG (LP, with John Kirkpatrick, Sue Harris, & Gary & Vera Aspey)	20
76	Broadside BRO 118	THE ENGLISH CANALS (LP, with John Kirkpatrick & Sue Harris)	15
81	Dingles DIN 319	REGAL SLIP (LP)	30

(see also Halliard, Black Country Three, John Kirkpatrick)

SIMON RAVEN

66	Piccadilly 7N 35301	I Wonder If She Remembers Me/Sea Of Love	50

RAVENS

53	Oriole CB 1148	Rock Me All Night Long/Write Me One Sweet Letter (78)	25
53	Oriole CB 1149	Begin The Beguine/Looking For My Baby (78)	25
53	Oriole CB 1258	Who'll Be The Fool?/Rough Ridin' (78)	25

RAVENS

63	Oriole CB 1910	I Just Wanna Hear You Say/Send Me A Letter	18

RAVENS ROCK GROUP

61	Pye International 7N 25077	The Ghoul Friend/Career Girl	18

MINT VALUE £

RAVEONETTES

03 Sony RAVE 009 Heartbreak Stroll/The Christmas Song (limited edition green vinyl, p/s) . . . 5

RAVE ONS

60s Sounds Good MT 103 She's A Spoon/Keep Wrong . . . 80

RAVERS

69 Upsetter US 312 Badam Bam/UPSETTERS: Medical Operation . . . 20

RAW DEAL

81 White Witch WIT 701 Out Of My Head/In The Mood (no p/s) . . . 125
81 Neat NEAT 12 Lonewolf/Take The Sky (p/s) . . . 7

RAW DEAL

95 Mental Disorder MAD 666 THE LEGENDARY RAW DEAL (10" LP) . . . 12

PETER RAWES

87 Official OFFA 5 Why Should I Ask Her To Stay?/Theme From Shark/Theme From Forever (with Jet Harris) (p/s) . . . 6

(see also Jet Harris)

RAW MATERIAL

69 Evolution E 2441 Time And Illusion/Bobo's Party . . . 40
70 Evolution E 2445 Hi There Hallelujah/Days Of The Fighting Cock . . . 35
70 Evolution E 24495 Travelling Man (Part 1)/Part 2 . . . 30
71 RCA Neon NE 1002 Ride On Pony/Religion . . . 22
70 Evolution Z 1006 RAW MATERIAL (LP) . . . 200
71 RCA Neon NE 8 TIME IS (LP) . . . 160

(see also Shoot)

LOU RAWLS

65 Capitol CL 15398 Three O'Clock In The Morning/Nothing Really Feels The Same . . . 10
66 Capitol CL 15465 Love Is A Hurtin' Thing/Memory Lane . . . 10
67 Capitol CL 15488 You Can Bring Me All Your Heartaches/A Woman Who's A Woman . . . 10
67 Capitol CL 15499 Dead End Street/Yes It Hurts Doesn't It . . . 10
67 Capitol CL 15507 Show Business/When Loves Goes Wrong . . . 10
67 Capitol CL 15515 Hard To Get Thing Called Love/(How Do You Say) I Don't Love You Anymore . . . 10
67 Capitol CL 15522 Little Drummer Boy/Child With A Toy . . . 10
68 Capitol CL 15533 My Ancestors/Evil Woman . . . 10
68 Capitol CL 15548 You're Good For Me/Soul Serenade . . . 10
68 Capitol CL 15560 Down Here On The Ground/I'm Satisfied . . . 10
69 Capitol CL 15583 It's You/Sweet Charity . . . 10
69 Capitol CL 15611 Your Good Thing (Is About To End)/Season Of The Witch . . . 10
70 Capitol CL 15630 You've Made Me So Very Happy/Let's Burn Down The Cornfield . . . 10
74 Bell BLL 1390 She's Gone/Hourglass . . . 6
63 Capitol EAP-1 20646 LOST AND LOOKIN' (EP) . . . 50
65 Capitol T 1824 BLACK AND BLUE (LP) . . . 25
66 Capitol (S)T 2459 LIVE (LP) . . . 20
67 Capitol (S)T 2566 SOULIN' (LP) . . . 22
67 Capitol (S)T 2632 CARRYIN' ON! (LP) . . . 18
68 Capitol (S)T 2864 FEELIN' GOOD (LP) . . . 18
69 Capitol ST 2927 YOU'RE GOOD FOR ME (LP) . . . 18
71 MGM 2315 054 NATURAL MAN (LP) . . . 12

RAW STYLUS

93 Mo Wax MW 002 Many Ways/Many Ways (Jam Up The Vibe Mix)/Bright Lights, Big City (Dark Mix) (12", die-cut stickered sleeve) . . . 12

CLYDE RAY

57 Columbia DB 3875 Follow Me/Steady As A Rock . . . 7
57 Columbia DB 3875 Follow Me/Steady As A Rock (78) . . . 10
58 Columbia DB 4106 Locked In The Arms Of Love/I'm Not Afraid Anymore . . . 7
58 Columbia DB 4106 Locked In The Arms Of Love/I'm Not Afraid Anymore (78) . . . 8

DANNY RAY & FALCONS

70 MCA MK 5037 Scorpion/I Love You Girl . . . 10

DIANE RAY

63 Mercury AMT 1209 Please Don't Talk To The Lifeguard/That's All I Want From You . . . 20

FROGGIE RAY

71 Big BG 313 Uncle Charlie/Party Version . . . 12
71 Big BG 314 Half Moon/RUPIE EDWARDS ALL STARS: Full Moon . . . 7

JAMES RAY

62 Pye International 7N 25126 If You Gotta Make A Fool Of Somebody/It's Been A Drag . . . 18
62 Pye International 7N 25147 Itty Bitty Pieces/You Remember The Face . . . 15

JOHNNIE RAY

78s

58 Philips PB 849 Up Until Now/No Regrets . . . 8
58 Philips PB 884 What More Can I Say/You're The One Who Knows . . . 8
59 Philips PB 901 When's Your Birthday, Baby/One Man's Love Song Is Another Man's Blues . . . 15
59 Philips PB 918 Call Me Yours/Here And Now . . . 25
59 Philips PB 952 I'll Never Fall In Love Again/You're All That I Live For . . . 35

45s

53 Columbia SCM 5015 Walkin' My Baby Back Home/The Lady Drinks Champagne (B-side with the Four Lads) . . . 45
53 Columbia SCM 5033 Mama Says, Pa Says/A Full Time Job (with Doris Day) . . . 45
53 Columbia SCM 5041 Whiskey And Gin/Tell The Lady I Said Goodbye . . . 55
53 Columbia SCM 5074 Please Don't Talk About Me When I'm Gone/Coffee And Cigarettes (B-side with the Four Lads) . . . 45
54 Columbia SCM 5111 Nobody's Sweetheart/I Can't Escape From You . . . 40

MINT VALUE £

54	Columbia SCM 5122	She Didn't Say Nothin' At All/I'm Just A Shadow Of Myself	40
57	Philips JK 1004	You Don't Owe Me A Thing/Look Homeward, Angel (jukebox issue)	40
57	Philips JK 1011	So Long/I Miss You So (jukebox issue)	35
57	Philips JK 1016	Yes, Tonight, Josephine/No Wedding Today (jukebox issue)	35
57	Philips JK 1025	Build Your Love (On A Strong Foundation)/Street Of Memories (jukebox issue)	25
57	Philips JK 1026	Up Above My Head, I Hear Music On The Air/Good Evening Friends/ Memories (with Frankie Laine, jukebox issue only)	35
57	Philips JK 1033	Pink Sweater Angel/Texas Tambourine (jukebox issue)	35
58	Philips PB 785	Miss Me Just A Little/Soliloquy Of A Fool	12
58	Philips PB 808	Strollin' Girl/Plant A Little Seed	7
58	Philips PB 829	Lonely For A Letter/Endlessly	10
58	Philips PB 849	No Regrets/Up Until Now	12
58	Philips PB 884	What More Can I Say/You're The One Who Knows	10
59	Philips PB 901	When's Your Birthday, Baby/One Man's Love Song Is Another Man's Blues	10
59	Philips PB 918	Call Me Yours/Here And Now	7
59	Philips PB 952	You're All That I Live For/I'll Never Fall In Love Again	10
60	Philips PB 990	When It's Springtime In The Rockies/Wagon Wheels	10
60	Philips PB 1025	Before You/I'll Make You Mine	8
60	Philips PB 1047	Tell Me/Don't Leave Me Now	8
60	London HLA 9216	In The Heart Of A Fool/Let's Forget It Now	12
61	Philips PB 1126	An Ordinary Couple/Cool Water	6
61	United Artists POP 902	How Many Nights How Many Days/I'll Bring Along My Banjo	10
62	London HLG 9484	I Believe (with Timi Yuro)/TIMI YURO: Smile	15
63	Brunswick 05884	Lookout Chatanooga/After My Laughter Came Tears	8
69	Pye 7N 17691	Wise To The Ways Of The World/Since I Lost You Baby	8
69	Pye 7N 17760	Long And Lonely Nights/Brokenhearted Me, Evilhearted You	8
EPs			
54	Columbia SEG 7511	JOHNNIE RAY (company sleeve)	18
55	Philips BBE 12006	JOHNNIE RAY	20
57	Philips BBE 12115	WALKING AND CRYING	20
58	Philips BBE 12192	YES, TONIGHT, JOSEPHINE	25
58	Philips BBE 12217	T.V. SERIES	22
61	Philips BBE 12460	ON THE TRAIL	25
LPs			
54	Philips BBR 8001	AT THE LONDON PALLADIUM (10", red or blue sleeve)	40/30
55	Philips BBR 8062	THE VOICE OF YOUR CHOICE (10")	35
57	Philips BBL 7148	THE BIG BEAT	35
58	Philips BBL 7254	AT THE DESERT INN — LAS VEGAS	35
58	Philips BBL 7264	SHOWCASE OF HITS	30
59	Philips BBL 7285	'TIL MORNING (also stereo SBBL 555)	35/45
59	Philips BBL 7348	A SINNER AM I	40
60	Philips BBL 7363	ON THE TRAIL	35
62	Liberty LBY 1020	JOHNNIE RAY	25
66	CBS Realm 52317	THE BEST OF JOHNNIE RAY	12

(see also Four Lads, Frankie Laine & Johnnie Ray, Timi Yuro)

RICARDO RAY

68	Roulette RO 501	Nitty Gritty/Mony Mony	10

WADE RAY

63	London HL 9700	Burning Desire/Two Red Red Lips	18

RAY & COLLUNEY

71	Westwood WRS 001	TYRANTS OF ENGLAND (LP)	40

RAY & HIS COURT

00	Jazzman JM 014	Soul Freedom/RAY & HIS FAMILY: Cookie Crumbs	5

CHRIS(TINE) RAYBURN

63	Parlophone R 5098	Slow Loving Woman/Same Old Places	10
64	Parlophone R 5144	I've Cried My Last Tear/You Forgot To Say When	10
66	Parlophone R 5422	I Wanna Be In Love Again/Another Night Alone	10
68	Music Factory CUB 2	One Way Ticket/Photograph Of Love	8
69	Pye 7N 17679	Skip A Rope/Starlight (as Christine Rayburn)	8

MARGIE RAYBURN

56	Capitol CL 14532	The Wedding Song/That's The Chance I've Got To Take	10
57	London HLU 8515	I'm Available/If You Were	25
57	London HLU 8515	I'm Available/If You Were (78)	6
58	London HLU 8648	I Would/Alright, But It Won't Be Easy	20
58	London HLU 8648	I Would/Alright, But It Won't Be Easy (78)	6

ANTHONY RAYE

80	Grapevine GRP 147	Give Me One More Chance/Hold On To What You've Got	8

SOL RAYE

63	Oriole CB 1855	Dear Michelle/I Love You Because	10
67	Deram DM 154	While I'm Here/To Be With You	8

BILLY RAYMOND

58	HMV POP 503	Making Love/I Would	6
58	HMV POP 503	Making Love/I Would (78)	10
58	HMV POP 526	One In Particular/Seven Daughters	6
58	HMV POP 526	One In Particular/Seven Daughters (78)	10
59	HMV POP 614	Charlie Is Their Darling/Loch Lomond	6

DANNY RAYMOND

71	Big Shot BI 587	Sister Big Stuff/BOY FRIDAY: Free Man	7

LEE RAYMOND with COSTELLO SISTERS

55	Brunswick 05438	Foolishly Yours/Baby Darling	15

MINT VALUE £

MARK RAYMOND & CROWD

64 Columbia DB 7308 Girls/Remember Me To Julie ... 8

TONY RAYMOND

59 Fontana H 213 Broken-Hearted Melody/This Earth Is Mine... 8
59 Fontana H 213 Broken-Hearted Melody/This Earth Is Mine (78) ... 10
62 Oriole CB 1777 The Infant King/Because Of You ... 6

IVOR RAYMONDE & HIS ORCHESTRA

65 Mercury MF 866 Feelin' Fruggy/Grotty ... 6

JULIE RAYNE

59 HMV POP 665 Waltz Me Around/Love Where Can You Be? ... 12
60 HMV POP 785 Bim Bam Bom/One More Time... 12
61 HMV POP 868 Green With Envy Purple With Passion/My First Romance ... 15
63 Windsor WPS 123 Faithfully/Free To Love... 12
64 Windsor WPS 128 You Can't Come Back/Straight To Your Arms ... 12

LISA RAYNE

65 Fontana TF 563 Don't Ever Change/It Had To Be You ... 10

MARTIN RAYNOR & SECRETS

65 Columbia DB 7563 Candy To Me/You're A Wonderful One... 40
(see also Secrets, Simon's Secrets, Clifford T. Ward)

MIKE RAYNOR & CONDORS

67 Decca F 12605 Turn Your Head/Lazy Day... 8
67 Decca F 22690 Is She A Woman Now?/My Shy Serenade ... 7
68 Decca F 22790 Wonderful Day/On Top Of The World ... 7
69 Decca F 22864 Ob-La-Di, Ob-La-Da/I'm Goin' Down (as Mike Raynor & Sky; Danish export issue) ... 10

RAY O VACS

50 Brunswick 04511 Sentimental Me/Once Upon A Time (78) ... 10

RAYS

57 London HLU 8505 Silhouettes/Daddy Cool ... 50
57 London HLU 8505 Silhouettes/Daddy Cool (78) ... 25

RAZORCUTS

86 Subway Org. SUBWAY 5 Big Pink Cake/I'll Still Be There (foldover p/s with insert, poly bag, 2,000 only) ... 8
86 Subway Org. SUBWAY 8 Sorry To Embarrass You/Summer In Your Heart (p/s, with insert, 2,000 only) ... 5
87 Sha La La BaBaBaBaBa 02 Sad Kaleidoscope/TALULAH GOSH: I Told You So (flexidisc p/s, 2,500 only) ... 8
80s Caff CAFF 10 Sometimes I Worry About You/For Always/Sorry To Embarrass You/ Music From The Big Pink (foldaround p/s with insert, 500 only) ... 15
(see also Cinematics, Red Chair Fadeaway)

RAZORLIGHT

03 Mercury 9814044 Rip It Up/Here It Comes (numbered p/s)... 6
03 Mercury 9800413 Rock 'n' Roll Lies/Action/Yeah Yeah Yeah (CD, card sleeve)... 8
03 Mercury 9800414 Rock 'n' Roll Lies/In The City (some in numbered p/s) ... 12/8

RAZOR'S EDGE

66 Stateside SS 532 Let's Call It A Day, Girl/April ... 18

CHRIS REA

74 Magnet MAG 10 So Much Love/Born To Lose (no p/s) ... 25
79 Magnet MAGL 5028 DELTICS (LP, blue vinyl, stickered sleeve) ... 12

REACTA

79 Battery Operated WAC 1 Stop The World/SUS (p/s)... 40
(see also Television Personalities)

REACTION

68 President PT 208 That Man/Falling In Love With You... 15

REACTION

70 Columbia Blue Beat DB 119 Oh Me, Oh My/RECO: It's Love ... 15
70 Attack ATT 8022 You Yes You/CIMARONS: Be There ... 12
(see also Ezz Reco, Joe Higgs)

REACTION

78 Island WIP 6437 I Can't Resist/I Am A Case (p/s) ... 15
(see also Talk Talk)

AL READ

56 HMV POP 278 What Is A Home?/We Haven't Any Money... 12
59 HMV POP 575 That's Life/Our Maggie's Going To Get Married... 10
59 HMV POP 575 That's Life/Our Maggie's Going To Get Married (78) ... 10
59 HMV 7EG 8440 SUCH A LIFE (EP) ... 18

PAT READER

60 Triumph RGM 1024 Ricky/Dear Daddy... 40
62 Piccadilly 7N 35077 Cha Cha On The Moon/May Your Heart Stay Young Forever... 50
63 Oriole CB 1903 Helpless/Lover's Lane ... 15

BERTICE READING

55 Parlophone R 4045 My One Sin (In Life)/Frankie And Johnnie (78)... 6
55 Parlophone R 4057 Songs From "Jazz Train" Parts 1 & 2 (78, with Edric Connor) ... 6
55 Parlophone R 4058 Songs From "Jazz Train" Parts 3 & 4 (78) ... 6
55 Parlophone R 4064 Bessie Smith Blues/Everybody's Somebody's Fool (78) ... 6
57 Decca F 10965 No Flowers By Request/September In The Rain ... 12
58 Parlophone R 4462 Rock Baby Rock/It's A Boy ... 45
58 Parlophone R 4462 Rock Baby Rock/It's A Boy (78)... 25
58 Parlophone R 4487 My Big Best Shoes/No More In Life... 30
58 Parlophone R 4487 My Big Best Shoes/No More In Life (78) ... 10

MINT VALUE £

WILMA READING
74 Pye 7N 45380 — Play It Again/Two Can Have A Party — 6

REALITY FROM DREAM
75 (no label) CP 109 — REALITY FROM DREAM (LP, private pressing) — 150

REAL KIDS
78 Bronze BRO 54 — All Kindsa Girls/Common At Noon (p/s) — 8
78 Bronze BRON 509 — REAL KIDS (LP) — 15

REALM
66 CBS 202044 — Hard Time Loving You/Certain Kind Of Girl — 25
(see also Earl Preston & Realms)

REAL McCOY
67 Fontana TF 794 — Show Me How You Milk A Cow/I Paid For My Laughs — 8
68 Pye 7N 17618 — I Get So Excited/Somebody's Taken Maria Away — 7
69 Pye 7N 17669 — Quick Joey Small/Happiness Is Love — 7
69 Pye 7N 17704 — Round The Gum Tree/I Will — 7
69 Pye 7N 17772 — Gitarzan/Anytime You Need Me — 7
69 Pye 7N 17850 — Many The Memories/She's Different, She's Beautiful — 7
70 Marble Arch MAL 1251 — THIS IS THE REAL McCOY (LP) — 25
(see also Tony Colton)

REAL THING
72 Bell BLL 1232 — Vicious Circles Parts 1 & 2 — 5
(see also Chants)

REASONS
78 Island WIP 6467 — Hard Day At The Office/Baby Bright Eyes (no p/s) — 30

REBEL
81 Bridge House BHS 2 — Rocka Shocka/Drift Away (p/s) — 30
86 Flying Pig REBS 1 — Valentino/Lonely Traveller (p/s, with free single) — 12

REBEL ROUSERS
68 Fontana TF 973 — Should I?/As I Look — 35
(see also Cliff Bennett & Rebel Rousers, Soul Sounds)

REBELS (Jamaica)
70 Bullet BU 440 — Nice Grind/SIDNEY ALL STARS: Nice Grind — Version — 12
70 Trojan TR 7779 — It's All In The Game/Easy Come — 12
(see also The Pioneers)

REBELS (U.K.)
67 Page One POF 017 — Hard To Love You/Call Me — 20

REBELS
78 Rigid IS REB 1029 — Suicide — 175

REBOUNDS
64 Fontana TF 461 — Help Me/The World Is Mine — 20

REBS
58 Capitol CL 14932 — Bunky/Renegade — 12

RECO
69 Downtown DT 417 — Quando Quando/Reg 'A' Jeg (as Reco & Rudies) — 10
69 Jackpot JP 710 — Memory Of Don Drummond/THE TOBIES: Resting — 8
69 Treasure Isle TI 7052 — The Lion Speaks/ANDY CAPP: Pop A Top — 8
69 Pama ECO 14 — RECO IN REGGAE LAND (LP) — 60
(see also Reaction, Don Reco, Rico Rodriguez, Father Sketto, Joe Monsano, Slim Smith, Laurel Aitken)

DON RECO
71 Big Shot BI 597 — Waterloo Rock/LLOYD'S ALL STARS: Walls Soul — 12
(see also U Roy Junior)

EZZ RECO & LAUNCHERS
64 Columbia DB 7217 — King Of Kings/Blue Beat Dance — 8
64 Columbia DB 7222 — Little Girl/The Bluest Beat — 8
64 Columbia DB 7290 — Please Come Back/At A Party — 8
64 Columbia SEG 8326 — JAMAICAN BLUE BEAT (EP) — 35
(see also Reaction)

RECORD PLAYERS
78 Wreckord WRECK 001 — DOUBLE C SIDE (EP, label also listed as Aerco AERO 1104) — 8
80 Wreckord WRECK 002 — Give An Inch/Squirming In The Vermin By The Bonny Banks Of Clyde/ 67/Parasite (p/s) — 6

RECORDS
79 Virgin V 2122 — SHADES IN BED (LP, with bonus 12" EP "High Heels") — 20

RECTIFY
88 Taffcore TAFF 001 — 20TH CENTURY EP (foldout p/s) — 10

RED
83 Jigsaw SAW 2 — RED (LP, private pressing) — 25

RED ALERT
80 Guardian GM-RA/B 61 — BORDER GUARDS (EP) — 60
82 No Future OI 5 — In Britain/Screaming At The Nation/Murder Missile (p/s) — 10
82 No Future OI 13 — Take No Prisoners/Empire Of Crime/Sell Out (p/s) — 10
83 No Future OI 20 — City Invasion/Negative Reaction (p/s) — 8
83 No Future OI 27 — THERE'S A GUITAR BURNING (12" EP) — 15
83 No Future PUNK 5 — WE'VE GOT THE POWER (LP, with inner) — 15

RED ALERT
82 Steel City AJS7R — Run To Ground/Wild You (no p/s) — 10

MINT VALUE £

RED BALUNE
78 MCCB 001 Capitalist Kid/Spider In Love (p/s) ... 25

REDBEAT
80 Malicious Damage MD 440 Machines In Motion/More Or Less Cut (12", p/s) ... 8

REDBONE
70 CBS 5061 Crazy Cajun Cakewalk Band/Night Come Down ... 5
70 CBS 5326 Maggie/New Blue Sermonette ... 5
73 Epic EPC 1398 Hail/Condition Your Condition ... 5
73 Epic EPC 1154 Witch Queen Of New Orleans/Maggie (p/s, "Hall Of Fame Hits" series) ... 5
70 CBS 64069 REDBONE (LP) ... 15
70 CBS 64198 POTLATCH (LP) ... 12
71 Epic EPC 64709 WITCH QUEEN OF NEW ORLEANS (LP) ... 12
72 Epic EQ 30815 MESSAGE FROM A DRUM (LP, quadraphonic) ... 15

RED BOX
86 WEA 242-037-2 THE CIRCLE AND THE SQUARE (CD) ... 25
90 East West 9031-72614-2 MOTIVE (CD) ... 35

REDCAPS
63 Decca F 11716 Shout/Little Things You Do ... 15
63 Decca F 11789 Talkin' 'Bout You/Come On Girl ... 15
64 Decca F 11903 Mighty Fine Girl/Funny Things ... 12

REDCELL
92 B12 07 An Escape From Unpleasant Realities (12", black, red or blue vinyl) ... 18

RED CHAIR FADEAWAY
89 Cosmic Eng. M. CTA 103 Let It Happen/Myra/Dragonfly/Grasshopper (12", p/s, 500 only) ... 30
89 Cosmic Eng. M. CTA 105 Mr Jones/Chimney Pots/Faraway Lights/Out Of The Grey (12", p/s, 450 only) ... 30
91 Tangerine MM 10 CURIOUSER AND CURIOUSER (LP, foldaround sleeve with booklet, no'd) ... 20
93 Aural AUR 102 MESMERISED (LP, 500 only) ... 12
(see also Razorcuts)

RED CRAYOLA
78 Radar ADA 22 Wives In Orbit/Yik Yak (p/s, red vinyl) ... 5
78 Radar/Sound For Industry SFI 347 Hurricane Fighter Plane/13TH FLOOR ELEVATORS: Reverberation (flexidisc free with *Zig Zag* magazine, issue 88) ... 8/6
78 Radar/Sound For Industry SFI 347 Hurricane Fighter Plane/13TH FLOOR ELEVATORS: Reverberation (hard vinyl test pressing, blank labels) ... 15

FREDDIE REDD
58 Nixa NJL 19 GET HAPPY (LP) ... 50

GENE REDD & GLOBETROTTERS
59 Parlophone R 4584 Red River Valley Rock/Kentucky Home Rock ... 8

NOEL REDDING BAND
75 RCA RS 1030 CLONAKILTY COWBOYS (LP) ... 15
(see also Loving Kind, Jimi Hendrix, Fat Mattress, Lord Sutch)

OTIS REDDING
SINGLES
64 London HLK 9833 Pain In My Heart/Something Is Worrying Me ... 18
64 London HLK 9876 Come To Me/Don't Leave Me This Way ... 18
65 Atlantic AT 4024 Mr Pitiful/That's How Strong My Love Is ... 12
65 Sue WI 362 Shout Bamalama/Fat Girl ... 20
65 Atlantic AT 4029 I've Been Loving You Too Long/Winter Wonderland (unissued, demos only) ... 40+
65 Atlantic AT 4039 Respect/I've Been Loving You Too Long ... 10
65 Atlantic AT 4050 My Girl/Down In The Valley ... 8
66 Atlantic AT 4080 (I Can't Get No) Satisfaction/Any Ole Way ... 7
66 Atlantic 584 019 My Lover's Prayer/Don't Mess With Cupid ... 6
66 Atlantic 584 030 I Can't Turn You Loose/Just One More Day ... 6
66 Atlantic 584 049 Fa-Fa-Fa-Fa-Fa (Sad Song)/Good To Me ... 6
67 Atlantic 584 070 Try A Little Tenderness/I'm Sick Y'all ... 6
67 Atlantic 584 091 Respect/These Arms Of Mine ... 5
67 Atlantic 584 092 My Girl/Mr Pitiful ... 6
67 Stax 601 005 Day Tripper/Shake (dark blue labels, later copies with light blue labels) ... 10/6
67 Stax 601 007 Let Me Come On Home/I Love You More Than Words Can Say (dark blue labels, later copies with light blue labels) ... 10/6
67 Stax 601 011 Shake (live)/634-5789 (live) ... 8
67 Stax 601 017 The Glory Of Love/I'm Coming Home ... 7
67 Stax 601 027 (I Can't Get No) Satisfaction/I've Been Loving You Too Long ... 7
68 Stax 601 031 (Sittin' On) The Dock Of The Bay/My Sweet Lorene ... 7
68 Stax 601 040 The Happy Song/Open The Door ... 6
68 Pye International 7N 25463 She's All Right/Gama Lama ... 8
68 Atlantic 584 199 Hard To Handle/Amen ... 6
68 Atlantic 584 220 Champagne And Wine/I've Got Dreams To Remember ... 7
68 Atlantic 584 234 Papa's Got A Brand New Bag/Direct Me ... 7
69 Atlantic 584 249 A Lover's Question/You Made A Man Out Of Me ... 6
69 Atco 226 001 Love Man/That's How Strong My Love Is ... 7
69 Atco 226 002 Free Me/Higher And Higher ... 7
69 Evolution E 2442 She's All Right/Tuff Enuff ... 12
70 Atco 226 012 Look At That Girl/That's A Good Idea ... 5
70 Atco 2091 020 Wonderful World/Security ... 5
71 Atlantic 2091 062 I've Been Loving You Too Long/Try A Little Tenderness ... 5
71 Atlantic 2091 112 (Sittin' On) The Dock Of The Bay/Respect/Mr Pitiful (reissue) ... 5
72 Atlantic K 10206 White Christmas/Merry Christmas, Baby ... 5

MINT VALUE £

EP

66 Sue IEP 710 EARLY OTIS REDDING . . . 80

LPs

65 Atlantic ATL 5029 THE GREAT OTIS REDDING SINGS SOUL BALLADS . . . 45
66 Atlantic ATL 5041 OTIS BLUE: OTIS REDDING SINGS SOUL . . . 40
66 Atlantic 587 011 THE SOUL ALBUM . . . 25
66 Atlantic 587 035 THE GREAT OTIS REDDING SINGS SOUL BALLADS (reissue) . . . 18
66 Atlantic 587/588 036 OTIS BLUE: OTIS REDDING SINGS SOUL (reissue, mono/stereo) . . . 18
67 Atlantic 587/588 050 COMPLETE AND UNBELIEVABLE: THE OTIS REDDING DICTIONARY OF SOUL . 25
67 Atlantic 587 042 PAIN IN MY HEART . . . 18
67 Stax VOLT 418 THE HISTORY OF OTIS REDDING . . . 18
68 Stax 589 016 OTIS REDDING IN EUROPE . . . 18
68 Stax 230 001/231 001 THE DOCK OF THE BAY . . . 18
68 Atlantic 587/588 113 THE IMMORTAL OTIS REDDING . . . 18
68 Atlantic 587/588 148 OTIS REDDING AT THE WHISKEY A GO GO, LOS ANGELES . . . 18
69 Atco 228 001 THE HISTORY OF OTIS REDDING (reissue) . . . 15
69 Atco 228 022 THE DOCK OF THE BAY (reissue) . . . 15
69 Atco 228 017 OTIS REDDING IN EUROPE (reissue) . . . 12
69 Atco 228 025 LOVE MAN . . . 20
70 Atlantic 2464 003 REMEMBERING . . . 18
71 Atco 2400 018 TELL THE TRUTH . . . 18
71 Reprise K 40430 LIVE AT THE MONTEREY INTERNATIONAL POP FESTIVAL (shared with Jimi Hendrix) . . . 30
72 Atlantic K 60015 THE BEST OF OTIS REDDING . . . 12
93 Atlantic K 2411182 DOCK OF THE BAY: THE DEFINITIVE COLLECTION . . . 12

OTIS REDDING & CARLA THOMAS

67 Stax 601 012 Tramp/Oooh Carla, Oooh Otis (with Carla Thomas) . . . 10
67 Stax 601 021 Knock On Wood/Let Me Be Good To You . . . 5
68 Stax 601 033 Lovey Dovey/OTIS REDDING: New Year's Resolution . . . 5
67 Stax 589 007 THE KING AND QUEEN OF SOUL . . . 25
(see also Carla Thomas)

RED DIRT

70 Fontana STL 5540 RED DIRT (LP) . . . 500

EMMA REDE

67 Columbia DB 8136 Just Like A Man/I Gotta Be With You . . . 25
(see also Jacky, Jackie Lee, Jackie & Raindrops, Raindrops)

TEDDY REDELL

60 London HLK 9140 Judy/Can't You See . . . 60

MICHAEL REDGRAVE

50 Topic TRC 12 A New World Will Be Born/ALAN KANE: Me Without You (78) . . . 8

VANESSA REDGRAVE

64 Topic STOP 111 Hanging On A Tree/Where Have All The Flowers Gone (some in title sleeve) . . . 10/6

RED HOT CHILI PEPPERS

85 EMI America EA 205 Hollywood (Africa)/Never Mind (p/s) . . . 10
85 EMI America 12EA 205 Hollywood (Africa) (Remix)/Hollywood (Africa) (Dub Mix)/Never Mind (12", p/s) . . 12
88 EMI CDP 790 869-2 ABBEY ROAD EP (CD) . . . 15
89 EMI 12MT 70 KNOCK ME DOWN EP (12", p/s) . . . 15
89 EMI 12MT 75 Higher Ground/Catholic Schoolgirls Rule (p/s) . . . 10
90 EMI 12MTX 85 TASTE THE PAIN EP (12", push-out sleeve with inner) . . . 12
90 EMI 10MTX 85 TASTE THE PAIN EP (square disc, numbered) . . . 12
90 EMI 12MTG 88 Higher Ground/Catholic Schoolgirls Rule/None As Weird As Me (12", g/f slv.) . . . 15
90 EMI 12MTPD 88 Higher Ground/Catholic Schoolgirls Rule/None As Weird As Me (12", picture disc, card insert) . . . 12
92 Warner Bros. W0126CDX BREAKING THE GIRL EP (CD) . . . 8

RED LETTERS

70s Burning Bing CPS 025 SACRED VOICES EP (p/s) . . . 50

RED LIGHTS

78 Free Range PF 5 Never Wanna Leave/Seventeen (p/s) . . . 25

RED LONDON

83 Razor RZS 105 Sten Guns In Sunderland/This Is England/Soul Train/Revolution Times (p/s) 8

RED LORRY, YELLOW LORRY

80s Red Rhino RED 28 Take It All/Happy (p/s) . . . 6

ROY REDMOND

67 Warner Bros WB 2075 Good Day Sunshine/That Old Time Feeling . . . 6

RED ONION JAZZ BABIES

60 Collector JE 19 RED ONION JAZZ BABIES (EP) . . . 8
(see also Louis Armstrong)

JEAN REDPATH

66 Bounty BY 6004 LOVE LILT AND LAUGHTER (LP) . . . 20
77 Trailer LER 2106 THERE WERE MINSTRELS (LP) . . . 12

RED RAGE

80 Flicknife FLS 203 Total Control/I Give You This (p/s) . . . 40

RED RIVER BAND

70 Banana BA 35 I'm Gonna Use What I've Got/Shame Shame . . . 8

REDSKINS

82 CNT CNT 007 Lev Bronstein/The Peasant Army (p/s) . . . 25
83 CNT CNT 016 Lean On Me!/Unionize! (p/s) . . . 7

84	Decca FX 1	Keep On Keepin' On! (Die On Your Feet Mix)!/16 Tons (Coal Not Dole)/Reds Strike The Blues! (12", with inner, some shrinkwrapped with free 7")	10/8
85	Decca FDP 2	Bring It Down! (This Insane Thing)/You Want It They've Got It/Turnin' Loose (The Furious Flames)/Take No Heroes (live)/Go Get Organized (live) (double pack, stickered gatefold p/s)	5
86	Decca FXT 3	THE POWER IS YOURS ... THE BOOTLEG EXCERPTS PROPAGANDA EP (10", 33rpm, stickered plain black die-cut sleeve)	7
86	Decca FXT 4	It Can Be Done/Let's Make It Work! (live)/K.O.! K.O.! (live)/A Plateful Of Hateful (10" 'Russian Import', numbered stickered plain white die-cut sleeve)	7

RED SQUARES

67	Columbia DB 8160	Mountain's High/Pity Me	8
67	Columbia DB 8257	True Love Story/Lollipop	8

RED TELEVISION

71	Brecht Times	RED TELEVISION (LP, private pressing with insert)	150

REDUCERS

78	Vibes XP 1/VR 001	Things Go Wrong/We Are Normal (p/s)	50
79	Vibes VR 003	Man With A Gun/Vengeance/Can't Stop Now (p/s)	50

MIKE REDWAY

63	Embassy WB 549	That's What Love Will Do/TYPHOONS: Please Please Me	5
63	Embassy WB 579	Just Like Eddie/Bad To Me	5
63	Embassy WB 589	I Want To Stay Here/TYPHOONS: Surf City	5
63	Embassy WB 604	It's Almost Tomorrow/TYPHOONS: This Boy	5
64	Oriole CB 1948	Many People/It's So Funny I Could Cry	6
65	CBS 201755	Darling Take Me Back/That's The Way Love Goes	7
65	CBS 202017	Magic Rocking Chair/When You Go	6
66	CBS 202092	One Day/Let Me Be The Someone	6
67	Deram DM 124	Have No Fear, Bond Is Here (Casino Royale)/My Poem For You	12
67	Deram DM 157	Don't Speak Of Me/Sometimes I Remember	5

(see also Rod McKuen, Typhoons, Bud Ashton)

REDWOODS

62	Columbia DB 4859	Please Mr Scientist/Where You Used To Be	20

DIZZY REECE QUINTET

56	Tempo A 140	Chorus/Basie Line	6
58	Tempo EXA 84	A VARIATION ON MONK (EP)	150
59	Tempo EXA 86	NOWHERE TO GO (EP)	100
59	Tempo EXA 89	ON THE SCENE (EP)	40
55	Tempo LAP 3	A NEW STAR... (10" LP)	200
57	Tempo TAP 9	PROGRESS REPORT (LP)	400
58	Esquire 32 185	ASIA MINOR (LP)	120
80s	Jasmine JASM 2013	PROGRESS REPORT (LP, reissue)	18

(see also Victor Feldman, Ronnie Scott)

CHUCK REED

57	Brunswick 05646	Whispering Heart/Another Love Has Ended	15
57	Brunswick 05646	Whispering Heart/Another Love Has Ended (78)	6
58	Columbia DB 4113	No School Tomorrow/Let's Put Our Hearts Together	22
58	Columbia DB 4113	No School Tomorrow/Let's Put Our Hearts Together (78)	6
62	Stateside SS 108	Just Plain Hurt/Talking No Trash	15

DEAN REED

59	Capitol CL 14986	The Search/Annabelle	10
59	Capitol CL 15030	I Kissed A Queen/A Pair Of Scissors (And A Pot Of Glue)	10

DENNY REED

61	London HLK 9274	A Teenager Feels It Too/Hot Water	18

JERRY REED

58	Capitol CL 14851	Bessie Baby/Too Young To Be Blue	260
58	Capitol CL 14851	Bessie Baby/Too Young To Be Blue (78)	50
69	RCA RCA 1798	Oh What A Woman/Claw	6
70	RCA RCA 2025	Georgia Sunshine/Singing '69	6
71	RCA RCA 2063	Amos Moses/The Preacher And The Bear	6
69	RCA SF 8006	ALABAMA WILD MAN (LP)	15

JIMMY REED

60	Top Rank JAR 333	Baby What You Want Me To Do/Caress Me Baby	22
60	Top Rank JAR 394	Found Love/Where Can You Be	20
60	Top Rank JAR 533	Hush-Hush/Going By The River	20
63	Stateside SS 205	Shame Shame Shame/Let's Get Together	18
64	Stateside SS 330	Shame Shame Shame/Let's Get Together (reissue)	5
66	Sue WI 4004	Odds And Ends/Going By The River Pt. II (B-side actually Pt. I)	25
67	HMV POP 1579	Two Ways To Skin A Cat/Got Nowhere To Go	15
64	Stateside SE 1016	BLUES OF JIMMY REED (EP)	35
64	Stateside SE 1026	I'M JIMMY REED (EP)	35
62	Stateside SL 10012	JIMMY REED AT CARNEGIE HALL (LP)	45
64	Stateside SL 10055	JUST JIMMY REED (LP)	45
64	Stateside SL 10069	SINGS THE BEST OF THE BLUES (LP)	35
64	Stateside SL 10086	PLAYS 12-STRING GUITAR BLUES (LP)	35
64	Stateside SL 10091	THE BOSS MAN OF THE BLUES (LP)	30
65	Fontana 688 514 ZL	THINGS AIN'T WHAT THEY USED TO BE (LP)	25
67	HMV CLP/CSD 3611	THE NEW JIMMY REED (LP)	22
68	Stateside S(S)L 10221	SOULIN' (LP)	25
69	Action ACLP 6011	DOWN IN VIRGINIA (LP)	50
69	Joy JOY(S) 111	THE LEGEND — THE MAN (LP)	12
69	Joy JOY(S) 120	AT CARNEGIE HALL (LP, reissue)	12

			MINT VALUE £
69	Joy JOYS 127	AT SOUL CITY (LP)	12
69	Joy JOYS 132	PLAYS THE 12-STRING GUITAR BLUES (LP, reissue)	12
69	Joy JOYS 141	ROCKIN' WITH REED (LP)	12
69	Joy JOYS 146	JUST JIMMY REED (LP, reissue)	12
69	Joy JOYS 151	JIMMY REED SINGS THE BEST OF THE BLUES (LP)	12
69	Joy JOYS 155	THE BEST OF JIMMY REED (LP)	12

JIMMY REED & EDDIE TAYLOR

60s	XX MIN 704	JIMMY REED & EDDIE TAYLOR (EP)	18

JOE REED

71	Dawn DNS 1012	Ain't That A Shame/Follow Me	6

LES REED

62	Piccadilly 7N 35080	Theme From Dr. Finlay's Casebook/The Saint (as Les Reed Strings)	7
64	Fontana TF 455	Spanish Armada/Madrid (as Les Reed Combo)	8
70	Chapter One CH 126	Man Of Action/Madrid (as Les Reed Orchestra)	10
72	Chapter One SCH 189	Man Of Action/Lest We Forget (as Les Reed Orchestra)	6

LOU REED

72	RCA RCA 2240	I Can't Stand It (unissued)	
72	RCA RCA 2240	Walk And Talk It/Wild Child	8
73	RCA RCA 2318	Vicious/Satellite Of Love	5
73	MGM 2006 283	I'm Waiting For The Man/Run Run Run/Candy Says (with Velvet Underground)	8
74	RCA APBO 0221	Caroline Says (Parts 1 & 2)	5
74	RCA APBO 0238	Sweet Jane/Lady Day	5
74	RCA RCA 2467	Sally Can't Dance/Ennui	5
76	RCA RCA 2666	Charley's Girl/Nowhere At All	5
78	Arista ARIST 198	Street Hassle/VELVET UNDERGROUND: I'm Waiting For The Man Venus In Furs (12", p/s)	8
72	RCA SF 8281	LOU REED (LP, orange label)	12
73	RCA RS 1002	BERLIN (LP, orange label with insert)	12
75	RCA CPL 2 1101	METAL MACHINE MUSIC (2-LP, U.S. import with U.K. sticker)	30
88	RCA/HMV C 881-9	TRANSFORMER (CD, box set, limited edition of 2,500, no'd, with certificate)	20

(see also Velvet Underground)

LULA REED

55	Parlophone CMSP 34	Troubles On Your Mind/Bump On A Log (export issue)	60
55	Parlophone DP 408	Troubles On Your Mind/Bump On A Log (78, export issue)	15

LULA REED & SYL JOHNSON

63	Ember EMB EP 4535	RHYTHM & BLUES BLUE BEAT STYLE (EP)	65

LULA REED & FREDDIE KING

63	Ember EMB 4536	LULA REED AND FREDDIE KING (EP)	50

(see also Freddie King)

NANCY REED

53	London L 1179	You Never Tell Me You Love Me/It's Written All Over Your Face (78)	12

OLIVER REED

61	Decca F 11390	The Wild One/Lonely For A Girl	40
62	Piccadilly 7N 35037	Sometimes/Ecstasy	18

TAWNY REED

65	Pye 7N 15935	Needle In A Haystack/I've Got A Feeling	25
66	Pye 7N 17078	You Can't Take It Away/My Heart Cries	20

VIVIEN REED

68	Direction 58-3574	I Wanna Be Free/Yours Until Tomorrow	6

WINSTON REED

72	Pama Supreme PS 365	Breakfast In Bed/RANNY WILLIAMS: Guitar Shuffle	8
73	Pama PM 863	Big Eight/RANNY WILLIAMS & CLASSICS: Big Eight – Version	8

VALA REEGAN & VALARONS

66	Atlantic 584 009	Fireman/Living In The Past	200

DELLA REESE

57	London HL 7024	I Cried For You (Now It's Your Turn To Cry Over Me)/And That Reminds Me (export issue)	20
58	London HLJ 8687	You Gotta Love Everybody/I Wish	20
58	London HLJ 8687	You Gotta Love Everybody/I Wish (78)	12
59	London HLJ 8814	Sermonette/Dreams End At Dawn	15
59	London HLJ 8814	Sermonette/Dreams End At Dawn (78)	12
59	RCA RCA 1160	Not One Minute More/Soldier Won't You Marry Me	6
59	RCA RCA 1160	Not One Minute More/Soldier Won't You Marry Me (78)	20
60	RCA RCA 1185	Someday/Let's Get Away From It All	5
60	RCA RCA 1192	Everyday/There's No Two Ways About It	5
60	RCA RCA 1204	And Now/There's Nothing Like A Boy	5
64	RCA RCA 1407	Forbidden Games/If Ever I Would Leave You	5
66	HMV POP 1504	Home/Her Little Heart Went To Loveland	5
66	HMV POP 1553	It Was A Very Good Year/Solitary Woman	10
68	Stateside SS 2128	It Was A Very Good Year/I Had To Know My Way Around	5
72	Avco Embassy 6105 010	If It Feels Good, Do It/Good Lovin' (Makes It Right)	5
74	People PEO 106	Who Is She And What Is She To You/If Loving You Is Wrong	5
59	London LTZ-J 15163	THE HISTORY OF THE BLUES (LP)	30
60	RCA RD 27167/SF 5057	DELLA (LP)	18
61	RCA RD 27208/SF 5091	DELLA DELLA CHA-CHA-CHA (LP)	15
62	RCA RD 27234/SF 5112	SPECIAL DELIVERY (LP)	15
63	RCA Victor RD/SF 7508	ON STAGE (LP)	15
63	RCA Victor RD/SF 7584	WALTZ WITH ME, DELLA (LP)	12
64	RCA RD/SF 7628	AT BASIN STREET EAST (LP)	12

65	RCA RD 7695	MOODY (LP)	12
65	HMV CLP 1923	C'MON AND HEAR (LP, also stereo CSD 1636)	12
66	HMV CLP/CSD 3540	I LIKE IT LIKE DAT! (LP)	12
66	HMV CLP/CSD 3573	LIVE (LP, with Bill Doggett & others)	12
67	HMV CLP/CSD 3605	ONE MORE TIME! (LP)	12
68	Stateside S(S)L 10230	THE BEST OF DELLA REESE (LP)	12
68	Stateside S(S)L 10261	I GOTTA BE ME ... THIS TRIP OUT (LP)	12

TONY REESE

59	London HLJ 8987	Just About This Time Tomorrow/Lesson In Love	25
59	London HLJ 8987	Just About This Time Tomorrow/Lesson In Love (78)	10

DEL REEVES

65	United Artists UP 1092	Girl On The Billboard/Eyes Don't Come Crying To Me	7
66	United Artists UP 1122	Women Do Funny Things To Me/My Half Of Our Past	7
66	United Artists UP 1145	Gettin' Any Feed For Your Chickens/Plain As The Tears On My Face	7

EDDIE REEVES

62	London HL 9548	Cry Baby/Talk Talk	18

JIM REEVES

78s

54	London HL 8014	Bimbo/Gipsy Heart	30
54	London HL 8030	Mexican Joe/I Could Cry (with Circle O Ranch Boys)	30
54	London HL 8055	Butterfly Love/It's Hard To Love Just One (with String Band)	30
54	London HL 8064	Echo Bonita/Then I'll Stop Loving You (with Louisiana Hayride Band)	30
54	London HL 8105	Padre Of Old San Antone/Mother Went A-Walkin'	25
55	London HL 8118	Penny Candy/I'll Follow You (with Louisiana Hayride Band)	30
55	London HL 8159	Drinking Tequila/Red-Eyed And Rowdy	35
55	London HLU 8185	Tahiti/Give Me One More Kiss	30
56	London HLU 8351	The Wilder Your Heart Beats, The Sweeter You Love/ Where Does A Broken Heart Go	30
57	RCA RCA 1005	Four Walls/I Know And You Know	20
58	RCA RCA 1074	Blue Boy/Theme Of Love	25
59	RCA RCA 1144	Partners/I'm Beginning To Forget You	40
60	RCA RCA 1168	He'll Have To Go/In A Mansion Stands My Love	60

45s

54	London HL 8014	Bimbo/Gipsy Heart	225
54	London HL 8030	Mexican Joe/I Could Cry (with Circle O Ranch Boys)	225
54	London HL 8055	Butterfly Love/It's Hard To Love Just One (with String Band)	225
54	London HL 8064	Echo Bonita/Then I'll Stop Loving You (with Louisiana Hayride Band)	225
54	London HL 8105	Padre Of Old San Antone/Mother Went A-Walkin'	150
55	London HL 8118	Penny Candy/I'll Follow You (with Louisiana Hayride Band)	200
55	London HLU 8185	Tahiti/Give Me One More Kiss	200
55	London HL 8159	Drinking Tequila/Red-Eyed And Rowdy	275

(All the above 45s were issued with gold label print)

56	London HLU 8351	The Wilder Your Heart Beats, The Sweeter You Love/ Where Does A Broken Heart Go	200
57	RCA RCA 1005	Four Walls/I Know And You Know	35
58	RCA RCA 1074	Blue Boy/Theme Of Love	22
59	RCA RCA 1144	Partners/I'm Beginning To Forget You (triangular or round centre)	18/12
60	RCA RCA 1168	He'll Have To Go/In A Mansion Stands My Love	7
60	RCA RCA 1197	I'm Getting Better/I Know One	7
60	RCA RCA 1214	Am I Losing You/I Missed Me	7
61	RCA RCA 1223	Whispering Hope/I'd Like To Be	6
61	RCA RCA 1233	Danny Boy/The Blizzard	6
61	RCA RCA 1261	You're The Only Good Thing (That's Happened To Me)/ Oh, How I Miss You Tonight	6
62	RCA RCA 1293	Adios Amigo/Letter To My Heart	6
62	RCA RCA 1317	I'm Gonna Change Everything/Pride Goes Before A Fall	6
63	RCA RCA 1330	Missing Angel/Is This Me?	7
63	RCA RCA 1364	Guilty/Little Ole You	6
65	RCA RCA 1448	Don't Let Me Cross Over/The World You Left Behind	7
67	RCA RCA 1611	The Storm/Trying To Forget	5
67	RCA RCA 1750	How Can I Write On Paper (What I Feel In My Heart)?/When You Are Gone	5

EPs

54	London RE-P 1015	THE BIMBO BOY	90
55	London RE-P 1033	THE BIMBO VOL. 2	90

LPs

60	RCA RD 27176	HE'LL HAVE TO GO	22
61	RCA RD 27193	THE INTIMATE JIM REEVES (also stereo SF 5079)	18/22
62	London HA-U 8015	BIMBO	22

(All the above LPs were originally issued with black labels, later orange label reissues are worth around £6 each.)

MARTHA REEVES & VANDELLAS

(see under Martha & Vandellas)

REFLECTION

68	Reflection RL 3015	THE PRESENT TENSE: SONGS OF SYDNEY CARTER (LP)	20

(see also Sounds Of Salvation)

REFLECTIONS (U.K.)

74	Purple PUR 124	Love And Affection/No More	7
75	Purple PUR 127	Moon Power/Little Star	7

REFLECTIONS (U.S.)

64	Stateside SS 294	(Just Like) Romeo & Juliet/Can't You Tell By The Look In My Eyes	50
65	Stateside SS 406	Poor Man's Son/Comin' At You	20
74	Tamla Motown TMG 907	(Just Like) Romeo & Juliet/Can't You Tell By The Look In My Eyes (reissue)	10

		MINT VALUE £
77 ABC ABC 4181	Like Adam And Eve/AUGUST & DENEEN: We Go Together	10
65 Stateside SE 1034	POOR MAN'S SON (EP)	90

REFUGEE

74 Charisma CAS 1087 *(see also Nice, Yes)*	REFUGEE (LP, with inner sleeve)	15

REGAL DEWY

78 RCA XB 1032	Love Music/Where Would I Be Without Me	5

JOAN REGAN

54 Decca F 10362	Wait For Me, Darling (with Johnston Brothers)/Two Kinds Of Tears (gold or silver lettering)	40/30
54 Decca F 10373	If I Give My Heart To You/Faded Flowers	22
54 Decca F 10397	This Ole House/Can This Be Love?	20
55 Decca F 10432	Prize Of Gold/When You're In Love	22
55 Decca F 10474	Open Up Your Heart And Let The Love In (with Rusty Regan)/ If You Learn To Love Each Other	22
55 Decca F 10505	Danger! Heartbreak Ahead/Don't Be Afraid Of Love	15
55 Decca F 10521	Just Say You Love Her/Nobody Danced With Me	15
55 Decca F 10598	The Shepherd Boy/The Rose And The Flame	10
56 Decca F 10659	Love And Marriage/Cross Of Gold (Croce Di Oro)	15
56 Decca F 10710	Don't Take Me For Granted/The Boy With The Magic Guitar	8
56 Decca F 10742	Honestly/I'd Never Leave You Baby (B-side with Johnston Brothers)	8
56 Decca F 10757	Sweet Heartaches/Second Fiddle (with Ted Heath)	8
56 Decca F 10801	Gone/Make Me A Child Again	8
57 Decca F 10871	Nearer To Me/Cross My Ever-Loving Heart	7
57 Decca F 10911	Wonderful! Wonderful!/Speak For Yourself John	7
57 Decca F 10934	7½ Cents/Good Evening Friends (with Max Bygraves)	7
57 Decca F 10942	Soft Sands/Love Me To Pieces	7
58 Decca F 11009	I May Never Pass This Way Again/Breezing Along With The Breeze	7
58 HMV POP 555	Love Like Ours/Take Me In Your Arms	7
58 HMV POP 555	Love Like Ours/Take Me In Your Arms (78)	6
59 HMV POP 593	May You Always/Have You Ever Been Lonely?	6
59 HMV POP 593	May You Always/Have You Ever Been Lonely? (78)	8
59 Pye Nixa 7N 15238	Happy Anniversary/So Close To My Heart	6
59 Pye Nixa N 15238	Happy Anniversary/So Close To My Heart (78)	10
60 Pye 7N 15259	If Only You'd Be Mine/O Dio Mio	6
60 Pye 7N 15278	Papa Loves Mama/When You Know Someone Loves You	7
60 Pye 7N 15310	One Of The Lucky Ones/My Thanks To You	8
60 Pye 7N 15303	Must Be Santa/Will Santa Come To Shanty Town	6
61 Pye 7N 15367	We Who Are In Love/My Foolish Heart	6
61 Pye 7N 15400	Surprisin'/In The Arms Of My Love (some with p/s)	10/6
66 CBS 202100	Don't Talk To Me About Love/I'm No Toy	40
67 CBS 2657	No-One Beside Me/A Love So Fine	20
55 Decca DFE 6235	JOAN REGAN SUCCESSES (EP)	22
56 Decca DFE 6278	JOAN REGAN SUCCESSES VOL. 2 (EP)	22
54 Decca LF 1182	THE GIRL NEXT DOOR (10" LP)	60
56 Decca LK 4153	JUST JOAN (LP)	60

RUSS REGAN

59 Capitol CL 15084	Adults Only/Just The Two Of Us	10

TOMMY REGAN

64 Colpic PX 725	I'll Never Stop Loving You/This Time I'm Losing You	110

REGENTS (U.K.)

63 Oriole CB 1912 *(see also Buddy Britten)*	Bye Bye Johnny/Come Along	25

REGENTS (U.K.)

66 CBS 202247	Words/Worryin' Kind	35

REGENTS (U.K.)

79 Rialto TREB 111	7 Teen (Uncensored Version)/Hole In The Heart (p/s)	6

REGENTS (U.S.)

61 Columbia DB 4666	Barbara Ann/I'm So Lonely	25
61 Columbia DB 4694	Runaround/Laura My Darling	25

REGGAE BOYS

69 Amalgamated AMG 841	Me No Born Ya/The Wicked Must Survive	20
69 Amalgamated AMG 843	The Reggae Train/Dolly House On Fire	20
69 Gas GAS 135	Ba Ba/GLEN ADAMS: Power Cut	15
69 Unity UN 530	What You Gonna Do/HEDLEY BENNETT: Hot Coffee	15
70 Bullet BU 431	Pupa Live On Eye Top/Give Me Faith	15
70 Gas GAS 122	Phrases/Give Me Faith	12
70 Upsetter US 339	Hurry Up/Thanks We Get	20
70 Pressure Beat PR 5503	Walk By Day, Fly By Night/JOE GIBBS & DESTROYERS: Unknown Tongue	18

(see also Glen Adams, Alva Lewis, Upsetters)

REGGAE STRINGS

73 Trojan TRLS 54 *(see also Horace Faith)*	REGGAE STRINGS (LP)	15

REGULAR FRIES

97 Fierce Panda NING 41 *(see also Campag Velocet)*	Dust It, Don't Bust It/CAMPAG VELOCET: Drencrom [Velocet Synthemesc] (p/s, 1,500 only)	18

LOU REICHNER BAND

80 ESR Records S/80/CUS 733	Photograph/I Sit And Stare/The End Of The World/Out On The Streets (also listed as ESR 4, 300 only, some with insert)	55/25

AL REID

69 Blue Cat BS 161 Vietcong/MAX ROMEO: Me Want Man . . . 25
69 Blue Cat BS 163 Darling/MAX ROMEO: It's Not The Way . . . 25

ALTYMAN REID

72 Green Door GD 4026 A Sugar/A Sugar Part Two (with Roy Shirley) . . . 7
(see also Roy Shirley)

CARLTON REID

66 Ska Beat JB 254 Funny/Turn On The Lights . . . 25
69 Blue Cat BS 162 Leave Me To Cry/Warning . . . 25

CLARENCE REID

69 Atlantic 584 290 Nobody But You Babe/Send Me Back My Money . . . 6
69 Atlantic 584 301 I'm Gonna Tear You A New Heart/I'm A Man Of My Word . . . 6

DUKE REID (& HIS GROUP)

60 Blue Beat BB 24 Duke's Cookies (with His Group)/JIVING JUNIORS: I Wanna Love . . . 30
62 Blue Beat BB 119 Twelve Minutes To Go (actually by Don Drummond)/ HORTENSE ELLIS: Midnight Train . . . 30
63 Duke DK 1002 Pink Lane Shuffle (with His Group)/LAUREL AITKEN: Low Down Dirty Girl . . . 30
67 Master's Time MT 003 Religious Service At Bond Street Gospel Hall/Religious Service At Bond Street Gospel Hall (Continued) . . . 10
67 Trojan TR 001 Judge Sympathy (actually by Freedom Singers & Duke Reid All Stars)/ ROLAND ALPHONSO: Never To Be Mine . . . 30
72 Duke Reid DR 2522 Hurt Parts 1 & 2 (actually by Eagles [Jamaica]) . . . 10
(see also Chuck & Darby, Derrick Morris, Stranger)

LEYROY REID

68 Blue Cat BS 125 The Fiddler/LOVELETTES: Shook . . . 25
68 Blue Cat BS 127 Great Surprise/TEN(N)ORS: Khaki . . . 25
(see also Nehemiah Reed)

MARC REID

66 CBS 202244 For No One/Lonely City Blues . . . 8
67 CBS 202581 Magic Book/My World Turns Around . . . 8
67 CBS 2950 We Should Live Together/Sale By Auction . . . 7

NEHEMIAH REID('S ALL STARS)

68 Island WI 3102 Family War/Give Me That Love . . . 18
70 Hot Shot HS 03 Hot Pepper/Seawave (as Nehemiah Reid's All Stars) . . . 10
70s Torpedo TOR 23 Mafia/H.E.L.L. 5 (as Nehemiah Reid's All Stars) . . . 7
(see also Leyroy Reid, Cynthia Richards)

NORVELLE REID

57 Brunswick 05725 All The Way/The World Won't End (export issue) . . . 5

P. REID

65 Ska Beat JB 197 Redeemed/Goodbye World . . . 25

PATTI REID

87 Fellside FE 061 PATTI REID (LP) . . . 12

TERRY REID (& JAYWALKERS)

67 Columbia DB 8166 The Hand Don't Fit The Glove/This Time (as Terry Reid & Jaywalkers) . . . 18
68 Columbia DB 8409 Better By Far/Fires Alive . . . 20
69 Columbia PSRS 323 Superlungs (promo only, as "Terry Reid Is Superlungs") . . . 22
76 ABC 4137 Oooh Baby/Brave Awakening . . . 5
79 Capitol CL 16071 Ain't No Shadow/Bowangi . . . 5
69 Columbia SCX 6370 TERRY REID (LP) . . . 35
71 M. For Pleasure MFP 5220 THE MOST OF TERRY REID (LP) . . . 12
73 Atlantic K 40340 RIVER (LP, gatefold sleeve) . . . 15
76 ABC ABCL 5162 SEED OF MEMORY (LP) . . . 12
79 Capitol E-ST 11857 ROGUE WAVES (LP) . . . 12
(see also Peter Jay & Jaywalkers)

REIGN

70 Regal Zonophone RZ 3028 Line Of Least Resistance/Natural Lovin' Man . . . 40
(see also Yardbirds, Keith Relf, Renaissance, Armageddon, Illusion)

JOHN REILLY

78 Topic 12T 359 THE BONNY GREEN TREE (LP, with booklet) . . . 12

TOMMY REILLY & TRADESMEN

51 Hohner Minuet/Badinerie (78) . . . 7
63 Oriole CB 1833 Dakota/S.O.S. . . . 6

DJANGO REINHARDT

53 Decca F 10219 Le Soir/Deccaphonie (78) . . . 8
50s Collector JEN 6 SWING GUITARS (EP) . . . 10
50s Collector JEN 8 IMPROVISATION (EP) . . . 10
55 HMV 7EG 8132 DJANGO REINHARDT (EP) . . . 10
54 Oriole/Mercury MG 10019 DJANGO (10" LP) . . . 25
54 Vogue LDE 049 DJANGO REINHARDT VOL. 1 (10" LP) . . . 25
54 Vogue LDE 084 DJANGO REINHARDT VOL. 2 (10" LP) . . . 25
54 Vogue LDE 106 DJANGO REINHARDT VOL. 3 (10" LP, as Django Reinhardt Quintet) . . . 25
54 HMV DLP 1045 DJANGO REINHARDT (10" LP) . . . 22
54 Felsted EDL 87005 NUAGES (10" LP, as Django Reinhardt & His Rhythm) . . . 22
59 HMV CLP 1249 DJANGO (LP) . . . 18
60 HMV CLP 1340 THE ART OF DJANGO (LP) . . . 18
60 HMV CLP 1389 DJANGO — THE UNFORGETTABLE (LP) . . . 18
60s Ember CJS 810 REQUIEM FOR A JAZZMAN (LP) . . . 15
64 Realm RM 184 INCOMPARABLE (LP) . . . 12
71 Xtra XTRA 1117 DJANGO REINHARDT VOL. 2 (LP) . . . 12
(see also Quintet Of Hot Club Of France)

MINT VALUE £

JOE REISMAN ORCHESTRA

55 HMV B 10891 Bo Diddley/Bubble Boogie (78) ... 10
56 HMV 7M 364 Robin Hood/His Name Was Judas ... 8
60 Columbia DB 4553 The World Of Suzi Wong (Theme)/Melodie D'Amour ... 6
61 Pye International 7N 25087 The Guns Of Navarone/Yassu ... 7

REIVERS

59 Top Rank JAR 244 The Wee Magic Stane/The Wreck Of The John B ... 6
60 Top Rank JAR 283 Down In The Mines/Govan Is A Busy Place ... 7

REJOICE!

69 Stateside SS 8010 November Snow/Quick Draw Man ... 6
69 Stateside S(S)L 5009 REJOICE! (LP) ... 18

BOB RELF

75 Black Magic BM 101 Blowin' My Mind To Pieces/PAULA RUSSELL: Blowin' My Mind To Pieces ... 7
(see also Bob & Earl)

JANE RELF

71 Decca F 13231 Without A Song From You/Make My Time Pass By ... 22
(see also Stairway, Renaissance)

KEITH RELF

66 Columbia DB 7920 Mr. Zero/Knowing ... 40
66 Columbia DB 8084 Shapes In My Mind/Blue Sands ... 50
(see also Yardbirds, Jim McCarty, Renaissance, Reign, Together, Armageddon)

RELIGIOUS OVERDOSE

80 Glass GLASS 004 Control Addicts/25 Minutes (p/s, initially with green labels) ... 6/5
81 Glass GLASS 009 I Said Go/Alien To You (p/s) ... 5
82 Glass GLASS 018 In This Century/The Girl With The Disappearing Head (12", p/s) ... 8

RELOAD

92 Evolution EVO 01 RELOAD EP (12", plain sleeve) ... 50
92 Evolution EVO 02 AUTO RELOAD EP (12", with E 621) ... 50
92 Evolution EVO 03 RELOAD EP (12", 1-side credited to E 621) ... 40
93 Infonet INF 13 AURO RELOAD EP VOLUME 2 (12", p/s) ... 20
93 Infonet INF 04LP A COLLECTION OF SHORT STORIES (2-LP, some with colour booklet) ... 50/40
93 Infonet INF 04CD A COLLECTION OF SHORT STORIES (CD, some with colour booklet) ... 40/30
95 Warp WARPLP 29 THE THEORY OF EVOLUTION (2-LP, gatefold sleeve) ... 20
95 Surreal Sound TAPE 2 THE BIOSPHERE (cassette, free with initial copies of 'Surreal Sound' magazine) 15
(see also Global Communications, Link, Mystic Institute)

R.E.M.

I.R.S. SINGLES

83 I.R.S. PFP 1017 Radio Free Europe/There She Goes Again (p/s) ... 50
83 I.R.S. PFSX 1026 Talk About The Passion/Shaking Through/Carnival Of Sorts (Box Cars)/ 1,000,000 (12", p/s) ... 25
84 I.R.S. IRS 105 S. Central Rain (I'm Sorry)/King Of The Road (p/s) ... 15
84 I.R.S. IRSX 105 S. Central Rain (I'm Sorry)/Voice Of Harold/Pale Blue Eyes (12", p/s) ... 20
84 I.R.S. IRS 107 (Don't Go Back To) Rockville/Wolves (Lower) (p/s) ... 15
84 I.R.S. IRSX 107 (Don't Go Back To) Rockville/Wolves/9 - 9 (Live Version)/ Gardening At Night (live) (12", p/s) ... 20
85 I.R.S. IRM 102 Can't Get There From Here/Bandwagon (p/s) ... 12
85 I.R.S. IRT 102 Can't Get There From Here (sleeve states 'Extended Mix', label states 'LP Version', but actually 3.39 edit)/Bandwagon/Burning Hell (12", p/s, some with printed banner crediting unissued tracks) ... 25/10
85 I.R.S. IRM 105 Wendell Gee/Crazy (p/s) ... 20
85 I.R.S. IRMD 105 Wendell Gee/Crazy//Ages Of You/Burning Down (double pack) ... 25
85 I.R.S. IRT 105 Wendell Gee/Crazy/Driver 8 (live) (12", p/s) ... 15
86 I.R.S. IRM 121 Fall On Me/Rotary Ten (p/s, blue, gold or silver label) ... 15
86 I.R.S. IRMT 121 Fall On Me/Rotary Ten/Toys In The Attic (12", p/s) ... 15
86 I.R.S. IRM 128 Superman/White Tornado (p/s, gold or silver label) ... 15
86 I.R.S. IRMT 128 Superman/White Tornado/Femme Fatale (12", p/s) ... 15
86 I.R.S. DIRM 128 Superman/White Tornado/Femme Fatale (CD, unissued)
87 I.R.S. IRM 145 It's The End Of The World As We Know It (And I Feel Fine) (2.59 edit)/ This One Goes Out (live) (p/s, gold or metallic blue label) ... 15
87 I.R.S. IRMT 145 It's The End Of The World As We Know It (And I Feel Fine)/This One Goes Out (live)/Maps And Legends (live) (12", p/s) ... 12
87 I.R.S. IRM 146 The One I Love/Last Date (bronze label, glossy p/s; silver label, matt p/s) ... 15
87 I.R.S. IRMT 146 The One I Love/Last Date/Disturbance At The Heron House (live) (12", p/s) ... 12
87 I.R.S. DIRM 146 The One I Love/Last Date/Disturbance At The Heron House (live) (CD) ... 20
88 I.R.S. IRM 161 Finest Worksong/Time After Time, Etc. (live) (stickered p/s) ... 10
88 I.R.S. IRMT 161 Finest Worksong (Lengthy Club Mix)/Finest Worksong (Other Mix)/ Time After Time, Etc. (live) (12", stickered p/s) ... 12
88 I.R.S. DIRM 161 Finest Worksong (LP Version)/Time After Time, Etc. (live)/ It's The End Of The World As We Know It (And I Feel Fine) (CD, numbered stencilled 7" box, 5,000 only) ... 22
88 I.R.S. IRM 173 The One I Love/Fall On Me (p/s, reissue) ... 10
88 I.R.S. IRMT 173 The One I Love/Fall On Me/S. Central Rain (12", p/s, reissue) ... 12
88 I.R.S. DIRM 173 The One I Love/Fall On Me/S. Central Rain (CD, reissue) ... 15
91 I.R.S. IRM 178 The One I Love/Crazy (2nd reissue, jukebox pressing with black label) ... 7
91 I.R.S. DIRMT 178 The One I Love/This One Goes Out (live)/Maps And Legends (CD, with 10-page insert) ... 20
88 I.R.S. IRMC 178 The One I Love (cassette) ... 8
91 I.R.S. DIRMX 178 The One I Love/Driver 8 (live)/Disturbance At The Heron House (live)/Crazy (CD, with 4-page discography) ... 8

Year	Label / Cat. No.	Title	Value £
91	I.R.S. DIRMX 180	It's The End Of The World As We Know It (And I Feel Fine)/Radio Free Europe (Hib-Tone Version)/Last Date/White Tornado (CD, withdrawn)	12
92	I.R.S. DIRM 180	It's The End Of The World As We Know It (And I Feel Fine)/Radio Free Europe (Hib-Tone Version) (gold or silver labels, p/s, some copies have Album Version of 'Radio Free Europe')	10/5

WARNER BROS SINGLES

Year	Label / Cat. No.	Title	Value £
89	Warner Bros W 7577	Stand/Memphis Train Blues (p/s)	7
89	Warner Bros W 7577X	Stand/Memphis Train Blues (recycled paper p/s)	10
89	Warner Bros W 7577T	Stand/Memphis Train Blues/(The Eleventh Untitled Song) (12", p/s)	12
89	Warner Bros W 7577CD	Stand/Memphis Train Blues/(The Eleventh Untitled Song) (3" CD, card sleeve)	15
89	Warner Bros W 7577CDX	Stand/Memphis Train Blues/(The Eleventh Untitled Song) (3" CD, 'maple-leaf' pack)	25
89	Warner Bros W 2960	Orange Crush/Ghost Riders (p/s)	6
89	Warner Bros W 2960X	Orange Crush/Ghost Riders (recycled paper p/s)	10
89	Warner Bros W 2960B	Orange Crush/Ghost Riders ('The Green Package' box set with poster)	15
89	Warner Bros W 2960C	Orange Crush/Ghost Riders (cassette)	5
89	Warner Bros W 2960T	Orange Crush/Ghost Riders/Dark Globe (12", p/s)	12
89	Warner Bros W 2960CD	Orange Crush/Ghost Riders/Dark Globe (3" CD, gatefold card sleeve)	15
89	Warner Bros W 2833	Stand/Pop Song '89 (Acoustic) (reissue, p/s)	8
89	Warner Bros W 2833W	Stand/Pop Song '89 (Acoustic) (stencil die-cut p/s)	15
89	Warner Bros W 2833T	Stand/Pop Song '89 (Acoustic)/Skin Tight (live) (12", p/s)	12
89	Warner Bros W 2833CD	Stand/Pop Song '89 (Acoustic)/Skin Tight (live) (3" CD, gatefold card sleeve)	15
89	Warner Bros W 2833CDX	Stand/Pop Song '89 (Acoustic)/Skin Tight (live) (3" CD, black die-cut sleeve in Velcro seal envelope)	20
91	Warner Bros W 0015	Losing My Religion/Rotary Eleven (some with large centre, p/s)	6
91	Warner Bros W 0015T	Losing My Religion/Rotary Eleven/After Hours (live) (12", p/s)	8
91	Warner Bros W 0015CD	Losing My Religion/Rotary Eleven/After Hours (live) (CD)	10
91	Warner Bros W 0015CDX	Losing My Religion/Stand (live)/Turn You Inside-Out (live)/World Leader Pretend (live) (CD, with fold-out poster)	18
91	Warner Bros W 0027	Shiny Happy People/Forty Second Song (p/s)	7
91	Warner Bros W 0027T	Shiny Happy People/Forty Second Song (12", p/s)	12
91	Warner Bros W 0027CDX	Shiny Happy People/I Remember California (live)/Get Up (live)/ Pop Song '89 (live) (CD)	10
91	Warner Bros W 0055CDX	Near Wild Heaven/Tom's Diner (live)/Low (live)/Endgame (live) (CD)	8
91	Warner Bros W 0072	Radio Song/Love Is All Around (live) (p/s)	7
92	Warner Bros W 0136	Drive/World Leader Pretend (p/s)	5
92	Warner Bros W 0136CDX	Drive/World Leader Pretend (CD, limited issue)	15
92	Warner Bros W 0143	Man On The Moon (edit)/Turn You Inside-Out (p/s)	5
92	Warner Bros W 0143CDX	Man On The Moon/(mixes) (CD, limited issue)	15
93	Warner Bros W 0152	The Sidewinder Sleeps Tonite/Get Up (p/s)	5
93	Warner Bros W 0152CD1	The Sidewinder Sleeps Tonite/Get Up (CD, 1 of 2-CD set)	15
93	Warner Bros W 0152CD2	The Sidewinder Sleeps Tonite (CD, 2 of 2-CD set)	15
93	Warner Bros W 0169	Everybody Hurts (edit)/Pop Song '89 (p/s)	5
93	Warner Bros W 0211CD	Find The River (CD)	8
95	Warner Bros W 0281X	Crush With Eyeliner (Album Version)/(Instrumental Version) (orange vinyl, with calendar, numbered p/s)	5
95	Warner Bros W 0290X	Strange Currencies (Album Version)/(Instrumental Version) (yellow or green vinyl, with metal 'Monster' badge, numbered p/s)	10
95	Warner Bros W 0308X	Tongue (Album Version)/(Instrumental Version) (numbered p/s, with 14-page 'tour souvenir')	8
96	Warner Bros W 0369LC	E-Bow The Letter/Tricycle (jukebox pressing with black label)	7
96	Warner Bros W 0369CDX	E-Bow The Letter/Tricycle (CD, limited issue)	8
96	Warner Bros W 0377LC	Bittersweet Me/Undertow (live) (jukebox pressing with black label)	5
99	Warner Bros W 477CDX	At My Most Beautiful (3" CD, in long box)	10

OTHER RELEASES

Year	Label / Cat. No.	Title	Value £
85	Bucketfull Of Brains BOB 5	Tighten Up (flexidisc [LYN 15742] with *Bucketfull Of Brains* magazine)	15
85	Bucketfull Of Brains BOB 5	Tighten Up (hard vinyl test pressing, 50 only)	75
92	Lyntone BOB 32	Academy Fight Song (live)/COAL PORTERS: Watching Blue Grass Burn (p/s, free with *Bucketfull Of Brains* magazine, double issue 39/40)	15
92	Lyntone BOB 32	Academy Fight Song (live)/COAL PORTERS: Watching Blue Grass Burn (white label test pressing)	30

PROMOS

Year	Label / Cat. No.	Title	Value £
83	I.R.S. PFP 1026	Talk About The Passion/Talk About The Passion (plain sleeve, promo only)	30
88	I.R.S. WIRM(T) 161 DL	Finest Worksong (Lengthy Club Mix)/Finest Worksong (Other Mix)/Time After Time Etc. (12" in 'media' p/s)	40
92	I.R.S. CDREM 92	THE ALTERNATIVE RADIO SAMPLER (CD, 7-track promo, includes unreleased version of 'Gardening At Night')	135
92	B.O.B. BOB 32	Academy Flight Song (free with *Bucketfull Of Brains*)	20
95	Warner Bros WO 290CDDJ	Strange Currencies (1-track CD)	20
96	Warner Bros W 0377LC	Bittersweet Me (black label jukebox issue, no p/s)	10
96	Warner Bros W 0377CDDJ	Bittersweet Me (1-track CD)	20
98	Warner Bros PRO 1118	Lotus (1-track promo CD)	15
99	Warner Bros W 477CDDJ	At My Most Beautiful (1-track CD)	15
99	WEA (no cat. no.)	Suspicion (1-track CD-R)	30
94	Warner Bros REM 1	SAMPLER FROM THE BEST OF REM (CD, Brit Awards nomination issue)	70
95	Warner Bros SAM 1558	POP SONGS 89 — 95 (CD, 18-track sampler)	25
99	Warner Bros SAM 00132	POP SONGS 89 — 99 (CD, slimline case, promo only)	30
03	Warners PR 04359	THE BEST OF REM — IN TIME 1980-2003 (promo box set containing 18 1-trk CDs each housed in individual card sleeve in flip top box)	100

(see also Full Time Men, Syd Straw)

REMA-REMA

Year	Label / Cat. No.	Title	Value £
80	4AD BAD 5	WHEEL IN THE ROSES: Feedback Song/Rema-Ream/Instrumental/ Fond Affections (12" EP, original pressings have blue labels)	12/8

(see also Adam & The Ants, Mass, Models, Wolfgang Press)

MINT VALUE £

REMAYNS

85	Bam Caruso NRIC 029	FIRST (EP, coloured vinyl)	5

HERBIE REMINGTON

66	Fontana FJL 313	REMINGTON RIDES AGAIN (LP)	12

REMO FOUR

64	Piccadilly 7N 35175	I Wish I Could Shimmy Like My Sister Kate/Peter Gunn	20
64	Piccadilly 7N 35186	Sally Go Round The Roses/I Know A Girl	20
67	Fontana TF 787	Live Like A Lady/Sing Hallelujah	60

(see also Tommy Quickly, Johnny Sandon, Gregory Phillips, Ashton Gardner & Dyke, Mike Hurst, George Harrison)

REMOTE VIEWER

01	City Centre Offices BLOCK 9	Walsh Ambrose (plain sleeve with insert, 1000 only)	8

RENAISSANCE (U.S.)

68	Polydor BM 56736	Mary Jane (Get Off The Devil's Merry-Go-Round)/Daytime Lovers	35

RENAISSANCE (U.K.)

70	Island WIP 6079	Island/The Sea	15
78	Sire SRE 1022	Northern Lights/Opening Out (picture disc, export issue)	15
79	Sire SIR 4019	Jekyll And Hyde/Forever Changing (withdrawn)	15
69	Island ILPS 9114	RENAISSANCE (LP, pink label)	25
71	Island HELP 27	ILLUSION (LP, withdrawn, export only)	40
72	Sovereign SVNA 7253	PROLOGUE (LP)	12
73	Sovereign SVNA 7261	ASHES ARE BURNING (LP)	12
75	BTM BTM 1000	TURN OF THE CARDS (LP)	12
75	BTM BTM 1006	SCHEHERAZADE AND OTHER STORIES (LP)	12

(see also Jim McCarty, Keith Relf, Jane Relf, Yardbirds, Rupert's People, Reign, Stairway)

LINE RENAUD

53	Columbia SCM 5055	April In Portugal/The Song From Moulin Rouge	10
55	Capitol CL 14230	If I Love You /Pam-Pou-De (Pam-Poo-Day) (triangular centre)	15
56	Columbia SCM 5268	Flamenco Love/To You, My Love	10
56	Columbia DB 3824	Strange/You Can't Keep Running	6
58	Columbia DB 4193	Irma La Douce/Disc-Donc, Disc-Donc	5
60	Columbia DB 4485	Mon Coeur Au Portugal/Jeremy	5

LINE RENAUD & DEAN MARTIN

61	Capitol EAP1 20060	LINE AND DINO (EP)	20

(see also Dean Martin)

RENAULTS

60	Warner Bros WB 11	Meloncolie/Stella	6

DIANE RENAY

64	Stateside SS 270	Navy Blue/Unbelievable Guy	15
64	Stateside SS 290	Kiss Me Sailor/Soft Spoken Guy	15
64	MGM MGM 1262	Watch Out Sally/Billy Blue Eyes	25
65	MGM MGM 1274	Troublemaker/I Had A Dream	25

(see also Laura Greene)

JOHN RENBOURN

65	Transatlantic TRA 135	JOHN RENBOURN (LP)	25
66	Transatlantic TRA 149	ANOTHER MONDAY (LP)	25
68	Transatlantic TRA 167	SIR JOHN ALOT OF MERRIE ENGLANDE'S MUSICK THYNGE AND YE GREENE KNIGHT (LP)	22
70	Transatlantic TRA 224	THE LADY AND THE UNICORN (LP)	22
72	Transatlantic TRA 247	FARO ANNIE (LP)	22
73	Transatlantic TRA 336	THE HERMIT (LP)	22
73	Transatlantic TRASAM 20	THE JOHN RENBOURN SAMPLER (LP)	15
73	Transatlantic TRASAM 28	SO CLEAR — THE JOHN RENBOURN SAMPLER VOL. 2 (LP)	15

(see also Pentangle, Bert Jansch & John Renbourn, Steve Tilston, Dorris Henderson)

JOHN RENBOURN & STEFAN GROSSMAN

70s	Kicking Mule SNKF 139	JOHN RENBOURN & STEFAN GROSSMAN (LP)	12
70s	Kicking Mule SNKF 161	UNDER THE VOLCANO (LP)	12

(see also Stefan Grossman)

JOHN RENBOURN'S SHIP OF FOOLS

88	Run River 009	SHIP OF FOOLS (LP)	20

DON RENDELL

55	Tempo A 108	Muskrat Ramble/Thames Walk (78, as Don Rendell Sextet)	25
55	Tempo A 110	You Stepped Out Of A Dream/Slow Boat To China (78, as Don Rendell Quartet)	25
55	Tempo A 112	Didn't We/Dance Of The Ooblies (78, as Don Rendell Sextet)	25
55	Tempo A 114	From This Moment On/Blow Mr. Dexter (78, as Don Rendell Quartet)	25
54	Decca LK 4087	JAZZ AT THE FESTIVAL HALL (LP)	70
55	Tempo EXA 11	DON RENDELL QUARTET (EP)	50
55	Tempo EXA 12	DON RENDELL SEXTET (EP)	30
55	Tempo EXA 16	DON RENDELL SEXTET/DAMIAN ROBINSON TRIO (EP, 2 tracks each)	50
55	Tempo EXA 20	DON RENDELL QUINTET (EP)	55
57	Pye Jazz NJE 1044	DON RENDELL JAZZ SIX (EP)	30
58	Decca DFE 6501	PACKET OF BLUES (EP, as Don Rendell Jazz Six)	20
54	Vogue LDE 050	MUSIC IN THE MAKING (10" LP)	75
55	Vogue LDE 144	DON RENDELL IN PARIS (10" LP, with Bobby Jaspa)	75
55	Tempo LAP 1	MEET DON RENDELL (10" LP)	350
56	Nixa NJL 4	TENORAMA (LP)	70
57	Nixa Jazz Today NJL 7	DON RENDELL PRESENTS THE JAZZ SIX (LP)	100
58	Decca LK 4265	PLAYTIME (LP, as Don Rendell Jazz 6)	60
62	Jazzland JLP 51	ROARIN' (LP, as Don Rendell New Jazz Quintet [with Graham Bond])	100
72	Columbia SCX 6491	SPACEWALK (LP, as Don Rendell Quintet)	100

DON RENDELL & IAN CARR QUINTET

65 Columbia 33SX 1733 SHADES OF BLUE (LP) . . . 350
66 Columbia S(C)X 6064 DUSK FIRE (LP) . . . 350
68 Columbia S(C)X 6214 PHASE III (LP) . . . 200
69 Columbia S(C)X 6316 LIVE (LP) . . . 180
69 Columbia SCX 6368 CHANGE IS (LP) . . . 220
(see also Neil Ardley, Ian Carr, Nucleus)

DON RENDELL QUARTET/JOE HARRIOT QUARTET

57 MGM MGM-EP 615 JAZZ BRITANNIA (EP, 2 tracks each) . . . 25
(see also Joe Harriott)

GOOGIE RENE COMBO

60 London HLY 9056 Forever/Ez-zee . . . 18
66 Atlantic AT 4076 Smokey Joe's La La/Needing You . . . 50
66 Atlantic 584 015 Chica-Boo/Mercy Mercy (Too Much For The Soul) . . . 15

HENRI RENE

55 HMV 7M 308 Enchantment/Crystal Chandelier (with Hugo Winterhalter Orchestra) . . . 6
59 London HLP 8960 La Shabla (The Shovel)/Destiny (with His Orchestra & Chorus) . . . 10
59 London HLP 8960 La Shabla (The Shovel)/Destiny (with His Orchestra & Chorus) (78) . . . 15

RENE & HIS ALLIGATORS

66 Decca F 22324 She Broke My Heart/I Can Wait . . . 18

RENE & RENE

65 HMV POP 1468 Chantilly Lace/I'm Not The Only One . . . 8
67 Island WIP 6001 Loving You Could Hurt Me So Much/Little Diamonds . . . 7

RENEGADE

80 White Witch WIT 1 LONELY ROAD (12" EP, with insert) . . . 100

RENEGADES

66 Polydor BM 56508 Cadillac/Every Minute Of The Day . . . 30
66 President PT 106 Thirteen Women/Walking Down The Street . . . 75
67 Parlophone R 5592 Take A Message/Second Thoughts . . . 25
68 Columbia DB 8383 No Man's Land/Sugar Loaf Mountain . . . 25

RENIA

73 Transatlantic TRA 261 FIRST OFFENDERS (LP) . . . 20

JON RENNARD

70 Tradition TSR 003 BRIMBLEDON FAIR (LP) . . . 12
71 Tradition TSR 010 THE PARTING GLASS (LP) . . . 12

DON RENNIE

56 Parlophone MSP 6218 To Love, To Love Is Wonderful/One Girl — One Boy . . . 8
56 Parlophone MSP 6237 Who Are We?/Can You Find It In Your Heart? . . . 8

DON RENO & RED SMILEY

58 Parlophone GEP 8777 COUNTRY AND WESTERN (EP) . . . 30
61 Melodisc MLP 12-123 HYMNS SACRED GOSPEL SONGS (LP) . . . 15
64 Ember CW 104 SING SWEET BALLADS OF THE WEST (LP) . . . 15

GERRY RENO

62 Decca F 11477 Don't Ever Change/What Would You Do . . . 8
62 Decca F 11516 Who's Fooling You/Three Deadly Sins . . . 8
63 Decca F 11774 It Only Happens In The Movies/One Lonely Guy . . . 15

GINETTE RENO

69 Decca F 22972 Don't Let Me Be Misunderstood/Everything That I Am . . . 8

PAUL RENO

63 Oriole CB 1872 Lonely Little Girl/Angela . . . 10

TEDDY RENO

59 RCA RCA 1108 Ciao Ciao Bambino/Li Per Li (78) . . . 8

CHRIS RENSHAW & THE KEEPERS

73 Pye 7N 45285 Banksie (A Tribute To Gordon Banks)/National (Health) Anthem (p/s) . . . 8

ROBERT RENTAL

78 Regular ER 102 Paralysis/A.C.C. (photocopied black & white foldover p/s) . . . 30
78 Company/Regular RECO 2 Paralysis/A.C.C. (reissue, card gatefold p/s) . . . 20
80 Mute MUTE 010 On Location/Double Heart (p/s) . . . 15
79 Industrial IR 0007 THE BRIDGE (LP, with Thomas Leer) . . . 15
80 Rough Trade ROUGH 17 ROBERT RENTAL AND THE NORMAL (LP, 1-sided, plain red sleeve) . . . 18
(see also Thomas Leer, Normal)

R.E.O. SPEEDWAGON

72 Epic EPC 8044 157 Riverside Avenue/Five Men Were Killed Today . . . 5
72 Epic EPC 64813 R.E.O. SPEEDWAGON (LP) . . . 12
75 Epic EPC 80175 LOST IN A DREAM (LP) . . . 12

REPARATA & DELRONS

65 Stateside SS 382 Whenever A Teenager Cries/He's My Guy . . . 22
65 Stateside SS 414 Tommy/Momma Don't Allow . . . 18
68 Bell BLL 1002 Captain Of Your Ship/Toom Toom Is A Little Boy . . . 10
68 RCA Victor RCA 1691 I Can Hear The Rain/Always Waitin' . . . 18
68 Bell BLL 1014 Saturday Night Didn't Happen/Panic . . . 30
68 Bell BLL 1021 Weather Forecast/You Can't Change A Young Boy's Mind . . . 12
72 Bell BLL 1252 Captain Of Your Ship/Toom Toom Is A Little Boy (reissue) . . . 5
73 Dart ART 2006 Octopus's Garden/Your Life Is Gone . . . 5
76 Polydor 2058 688 Jesabee Lancer (The Belly Dancer)/We Need You . . . 5
76 Polydor 2066 562 Shoes/A Song For All . . . 5
72 Avco 6467 250 ROCK AND ROLL REVOLUTION (LP) . . . 30

MINT VALUE £

REPERCUSSIONS
92 Mo' Wax MW 001 — Promise/Promise (Dub)/Field Trippin' (12", die-cut stickered sleeve) . . . 15

REQUIEM
80 Sacrificial SAC 001 — Angel Of Sin/Sacrificial Wanderer (no p/s) . . . 220

REPERCUSSIONS
92 Mo'Wax MW 001 — Promise/(dub)/Field Trippin' (12") . . . 20

RESERVE
88 Sha La La Ba Ba Ba-Ba Ba 006 — Wherever You Go/SIDDELEYS: The Sun Slid Down/Behind The Tower (flexidisc, foldover p/s) . . . 10

RESIDENTS
80 Pre PRE 009 — THE COMMERCIAL SINGLE (p/s) . . . 10
84 Korova KOW 36 — It's A Man's Man's Man's World/I'll Go Crazy (p/s, 5,000 only) . . . 8
83 London RALPH 1 — INTERMISSION (12" EP) . . . 15
88 Torso TORSOCD 322 — KAW-LIGA (CD) . . . 8
89 Torso TORSOCD 355 — Double Shot/Loss Of Loved One (Extended Version)/ Kiss Of Flesh (Instrumental) (3" CD, picture disc) . . . 8
89 Torso TORSOCD 421 — Diskomo/Whoopy Snorp/Saint Nix/Diskomo Live (CD) . . . 8
79 Virgin VR 3 — NIBBLES (LP, 5,000 only) . . . 12
80 Pre PRE X2 — PICNIC BOY — THE COMMERCIAL ALBUM (LP, 5,000 only, with incorrect song order) . . . 15
84 Korova CODE 9 — GEORGE AND JAMES (cassette with extra track) . . . 10
84 Doublevision DV 9 — THE MOLE SHOW/WHATEVER HAPPENED TO VILENESS FATS (cassette) . . . 20
85 Doublevision DVR 17 — THE PAL TV LP (LP, red vinyl, 5,000 only) . . . 15

(see also Snakefinger)

RESISTANCE
81 Fontana KIT 1 — Survival Kit/Big Flame (p/s) . . .

RESISTANCE 77
82 Riot City RIOT 18 — NOWHERE TO PLAY (EP) . . . 7
84 Resistance RESIST 1 — You Reds/Young And Wrong (p/s) . . . 5

RESISTORS
80 Break SMASH 1 — For Jeanie/Takeaway Love/End Of The Line (p/s) . . . 10

RESPECT featuring PHIL OAKEY
90 Chrysalis CHS 123640 — What Comes After Goodbye (Extended Mix)/Ghostdance/What Comes After Goodbye (7" Version) (12", p/s) . . . 10
90 Chrysalis CHSCD 3640 — What Comes After Goodbye (7" Version)/ What Comes After Goodbye (Extended Mix)/The Girl Needs Respect/Ghostdance (CD) . . . 15

JOHNNY RESTIVO
59 RCA RCA 1143 — The Shape I'm In/Ya Ya (initially with triangular centre, later round) . . . 35/20
59 RCA RCA 1143 — The Shape I'm In/Ya Ya (78) . . . 50
59 RCA RCA 1159 — I Like Girls/Dear Someone . . . 15
59 RCA RCA 1159 — I Like Girls/Dear Someone (78) . . . 60
60 Ember EMB S 135 — Look Here Now/Sweet Sweet Lovin' . . . 18

RESTLESS ONES
65 Herald HSR 2521 — The Restless Ones/He's Everything To Me (p/s) . . . 8

RESTRICTED HOURS
79 Stevenage (no cat. no.) — Getting Things Done/Still Living Out The Car Crash/SYNDICATE: One Way Or Another/I Want To Be Somebody (white label, foldover p/s) . . . 10

(see also Astronauts)

RETREADS
81 Eddi Osmo EO 101 — Would You Listen Girl/One After 909/You Said You Knew (p/s, with mini-poster insert) . . . 55

RETURN TO FOREVER
74 Polydor 2310 283 — HYMN OF GALAXY (LP) . . . 12

(see also Chick Corea)

MARTIN REV
85 New Rose ROSE 52 — CLOUDS OF GLORY (LP, red vinyl) . . . 12

(see also Suicide)

REVELATION
80 Handshake HANDS 1 — Feel It/When I Fall In Love . . . 8
81 Handshake HANDS 3 — Feel It/When I Fall In Love (reissue) . . . 5

REVELATION (Jamaica)
70 Trojan TR 7727 — Suffering/MEGATONS: Crazy Elephant . . . 6

REVELLERS
66 Columbia DB 8093 — Believe, Believe/Love Is The Greatest Thing . . . 7
67 Spin LP 1703 — REVELLERS AGAIN (LP) . . . 35

REVELS
59 Top Rank JAR 235 — Midnight Stroll/Talking To My Heart . . . 75

REVELLS
71 CBS 7050 — Mind Party/Indian Ropeman . . . 25

DIGGER REVELL'S DENVERMEN
63 Decca F 11657 — Surfside/Lisa Marie . . . 18

REVENGE
76 Normal QS 000 — Go Away/Game . . . 12
70s Blood CUS 614 — Don't Tell Me Lies/Gimme The Good Times . . . 10

REVENGE

78	Loony LOO 1	Our Generation/I Love Her Way (counterfeits lack ridge around label)	300
78	Loony LOO 2	We're Not Gonna Take It/Pornography (glossy p/s, counterfeits have matt sleeve, and lack ridge around label)	200

PAUL REVERE & THE RAIDERS (featuring Mark Lindsay)

61	Top Rank JAR 557	Like Long Hair/Sharon	25
65	Sue WI 344	Like Long Hair/Sharon (reissue)	22
65	CBS 202003	Steppin' Out/Blue Fox	10
66	CBS 202027	Just Like Me/B F D R F Blues	20
66	CBS 202205	Kicks/Shake It Up	12
66	CBS 202253	Hungry/There She Goes	8
66	CBS 202411	The Great Airplane Strike/In My Community	12
67	CBS 202502	Good Thing/Undecided Man	12
67	CBS 202610	Ups And Downs/Leslie	10
67	CBS 2737	Him Or Me — What's It Gonna Be?/The Legend Of Paul Revere	12
67	CBS 2919	I Had A Dream/Upon Your Leaving	7
67	CBS 3186	Mo'reen/Oh! To Be A Man	7
68	CBS 3310	Too Much Talk/Happening '68 (featuring Mark Lindsay)	7
68	CBS 3586	Don't Take It So Hard/Observation From Flight 285 (featuring Mark Lindsay)	8
68	CBS 3757	Cinderella Sunshine/Theme From It's Happening (featuring Mark Lindsay)	7
69	CBS 4025	Mr. Sun, Mr. Moon/With You (featuring Mark Lindsay)	7
69	CBS 4260	Let Me/I Don't Know (featuring Mark Lindsay)	8
69	CBS 4504	We Gotta All Get Up Together/Frankfurt Side Street (featuring Mark Lindsay)	7
66	CBS (S)BPG 62406	JUST LIKE US (LP)	25
66	CBS (S)BPG 62797	MIDNIGHT RIDE (LP)	25
67	CBS (S)BPG 62963	GOOD THING (LP)	25
68	CBS (S)BPG 63095	REVOLUTION (LP)	25
69	CBS 63265	GOIN' TO MEMPHIS (LP, mono/stereo)	22
69	CBS 63649	HARD 'N' HEAVY (LP)	22

(see also Mark Lindsay)

REVILLOS

79	Snatzo/Dindisc DIN 1	Where's The Boy For Me/The Fiend (p/s)	6
79	Snatzo/Dindisc DIN 5	Motor Bike Beat/No Such Luck (p/s)	6
80	Snatzo/Dindisc DINZ 16	Scuba Scuba/Scuba Boy Bop (p/s)	6
80	Snatzo/Dindisc DINZ 20	Hungry For Love/Voodoo 2 (p/s, label also lists SP 703)	6
82	Superville SV 1001	She's Fallen In Love With A Monster Man/Mind Bending Cutie Doll (p/s)	6
82	Superville SV 2001	Bongo Brain/Hip City — You Were Meant For Me (p/s)	6
82	Aura AUS 135	Tell Him/Graveyard Groove (p/s)	6
83	EMI RVL 1	Bitten By A Love Bug/Cat Call	6
83	EMI 12 RVL 1	Bitten By A Love Bug (Extended Version)/Cat Call (12", p/s)	8
84	EMI RVL 2	Midnight/Z-X-7 (p/s)	5
84	EMI 12 RVL 2	Midnight (Extended Version)/Midnight (7" Version)/Z-X-7 (12", p/s)	8
80	Snatzo/Dindisc DID X 3	REV UP (LP, green or pink titles)	25
82	Superville SV 4001	ATTACK! (LP, withdrawn)	80

(see also Rezillos)

REVOLUTION

66	Piccadilly 7N 35289	Hallelujah/Shades Of Blue	50

(see also Hellions, Luther Grosvenor, Family, Traffic, Dave Mason & Cass Elliot, Spirit)

REVOLUTIONARIES

76	Sagittarius SULP 03	DAWN OF CREATION (LP)	12

REVOLUTIONARY ARMY OF INFANT JESUS

87	Probe Plus PROBE 12	THE GIFT OF TEARS (LP)	45

REVOLUTIONARY BLUES BAND

70	MCA MUP(S) 402	REVOLUTIONARY BLUES BAND (LP)	15

REVOLUTIONARY CORPS OF TEENAGE JESUS VS SUICIDE

96	Creeping Bent BENT 005	FRANKIE TEARDROP EP (Frankie Teardrop [126 b.p.m.]/U.S.A. '95/ Frankie Teardrop [114 b.p.m.]/Womb 17) (12", p/s, 1,000 only)	10

(see also Suicide, Future Pilot A.KA.)

REVOLVING PAINT DREAM

84	Creation CRE 002	Flowers In The Sky/In The Afternoon (foldaround p/s in poly bag)	25

(see also Laughing Apple, Primal Scream)

REVS

91	Vinyl Japan TASK 9	Just Ask Why/We're So Modern/Stay With Me/Julie Got A Raise (12", p/s)	8

KIMBERLEY REW

80	Armageddon AS 004	Stomping All Over The World/Nothing's Going To Change In Your Life/ Fighting Someone's War (p/s)	5
81	Armageddon AS 012	My Baby Does Her Hairdo Long/Fishing (p/s, with dB's)	5

(see also Soft Boys, Waves)

ROBERTA REX

68	Fontana TF 967	Joey/I Can Feel It	6

REX (Morris) & MINORS

60	Triumph RGM 1023	Chicken Sax/Snake Eyes	45

ALVINO REY

61	London HLD 9431	Original Mama Blues/Steel Guitar Rag	12
62	London HA-D 2414	ALVINO REY'S GREATEST HITS (LP)	25

LITTLE BOBBY REY & HIS BAND

60	Top Rank JAR 525	Rockin' "J" Bells/Dance Of The New Year	8

REYNARD

76	Pilgrim/Grapevine GRA 102	FRESH FROM THE EARTH (LP)	40

MINT VALUE £

AMBROSE REYNOLDS

83	Zulu ZULU 3	GREATEST HITS (LP)	12

(see also Pink Military)

DEBBIE REYNOLDS

55	MGM SP 1127	Carolina In The Morning/Never Mind The Noise In The Market (B-side as Debbie Reynolds' Naturals)	20
56	MGM SP 1155	(Love Is) The Tender Trap/Canoodlin' Rag	15
57	Vogue Coral Q 72274	Tammy/French Heels	10
58	MGM MGM 968	All Grown Up/Wall Flower	8
58	Coral Q 72297	A Very Special Love/I Saw A Country Boy	8
58	Coral Q 72324	This Happy Feeling/Hillside In Scotland	8
58	Coral Q 72345	Hungry Eyes/Faces There Are Fairer	8
59	MGM MGM 1019	The Mating Game/Right Away	6
59	MGM MGM 1019	The Mating Game/Right Away (78)	10
59	MGM MGM 1043	It Started With A Kiss/Love Is A Gamble	6
60	London HLD 9028	Am I That Easy To Forget?/Ask Me To Go Steady	7
60	London HLD 9128	City Lights/Just For A Touch Of Your Love	7
61	London HLD 9351	Lonely People/Just A Little Girl	7
58	MGM MGM-EP 670	DEBBIE REYNOLDS (EP)	25
58	MGM MGM-EP 671	SINGING IN THE RAIN (EP, with Gene Kelly & Donald O'Connor)	10
59	MGM MGM-EP 694	DELIGHTFUL DEBBIE REYNOLDS (EP)	18
60	MGM MGM-EP 725	FROM DEBBIE WITH LOVE (EP)	20
59	London HA-D 2200	DEBBIE (LP, also stereo SAH-D 6051)	45/60
60	London HA-D 2294	AM I THAT EASY TO FORGET? (LP, also stereo SAH-D 6106)	45/60
61	London HA-D 2326	FINE AND DANDY (LP)	45
63	London HA-D/SH-D 8075	GREAT FOLK HITS (LP, mono/stereo)	45/55

(see also Naturals [U.S.])

DONN REYNOLDS

57	HMV POP 314	Hasta Luego/Lorelei	6
58	MGM MGM 971	Rose Of Ol' Pawnee/All Alone (With No One By My Side)	6
58	MGM MGM 996	Blue Eyes Crying In The Rain/Bella Belinda	6
58	MGM MGM 996	Blue Eyes Crying In The Rain/Bella Belinda (78)	6
58	Pye 7N 15122	Swing Low Sweet Chariot/Ramona	6
58	Pye N 15122	Swing Low Sweet Chariot/Ramona (78)	6
59	Pye NEP 24098	THE DONN REYNOLDS SONGBAG (EP)	22

ELI REYNOLDS

70	Punch PH 37	Mr Car Man/Chiney Man	7

JODY REYNOLDS

58	London HL 8651	Endless Sleep/Tight Capris	25
58	London HL 8651	Endless Sleep/Tight Capris (78)	20

TIMMY REYNOLDS

62	Ember EMB S 133	Lullaby Of Love/JEFF MILLS: Daddy's Home	12

REZILLOS

77	Sensible FAB 1	Can't Stand My Baby/I Wanna Be Your Man (p/s, 15,000 only, 5,000 no'd)	12/7
77	Sensible FAB 2	Flying Saucer Attack/(My Baby Does) Good Sculptures (p/s, unissued)	
77	Sire 6078 612	Flying Saucer Attack/(My Baby Does) Good Sculptures (p/s)	8
78	Sire 6198 215	Cold Wars/William Mysterious Overture (unissued)	
78	Sire SIR 4001	Top Of The Pops/20,000 Rezillos Under The Sea (p/s)	8
78	Sire SIR 4008	Destination Venus/Mystery Action (p/s)	6
79	Sire SIR 4014	Cold Wars (live)/Flying Saucer Attack (live)/Twist & Shout (live) (p/s)	5
79	Sensible FAB 1 (Mark 2)	Can't Stand My Baby/I Wanna Be Your Man (reissue, new p/s, run out groove reads "Come Back John Lennon")	7
79	Sensible FAB 1 (Mark 2)	Can't Stand My Baby/I Wanna Be Your Man (reissue, p/s, mispressing, B-side plays "(My Baby Does) Good Sculptures (live)", run-off groove reads "De-sire-able product?", 4,000 only)	6
81	Sire SPC 3	Top Of The Pops/Destination Venus (cassette, flip-up box)	5
78	Sire K 56530	CAN'T STAND THE REZILLOS (LP, with inner sleeve & postcard insert)	25
78	Sire SRK 6069	MISSION ACCOMPLISHED ... BUT THE BEAT GOES ON (LP, live)	18

(see also Revillos, Shake, Jo Callis, William Mysterious)

RHABSTALLION

81	Rhab RHAB 001	Day To Day/Breadline (p/s, some with badge)	30/20

RHINOCEROS

69	Elektra EKSN 45051	You're My Girl (I Don't Want To Discuss It)/Apricot Brandy	8
69	Elektra EKSN 45058	I Will Serenade You/Belbuekul	7
70	Elektra EKSN 45080	Back Door/In A Little Room	6
70	Elektra 2101 009	Old Age/Let's Party	5
69	Elektra EKL 4030	RHINOCEROS (LP, orange label, also stereo EKS 74030)	25
69	Elektra EKL 4056	SATIN CHICKENS (LP, also stereo EKS 74056)	25
70	Elektra 2469 006	BETTER TIMES ARE COMING (LP)	15

RHODA with The SPECIAL A.K.A.

82	2-Tone CHS TT 18	The Boiler/Theme From The Boiler (p/s)	5
82	2-Tone CHS TT 1218	The Boiler/Theme From The Boiler (12", p/s)	8

(see also Special A.K.A.)

JAN RHODE & HIS COOL CATS

60	Qualiton Offbeat PSP 7128	Come Back Baby/So Shy	8

PAT RHODEN

68	Trojan TR 606	Woman Is Greedy/Endlessly	7
70	Pama PM 811	Maybe The Next Time/Got To See You	6
70	Pama Supreme PS 298	Do What You Gotta Do/Crying Won't Help You	6
70	Mary Lyn ML 101	Time Is Tight/MILTON & DENZIL: I Like It Like That	6
73	Pama Supreme PS 378	Out Of Time/Put A Little Rain Into My Life	6

(see also Pat Riden, Pat & Marie, Denzil & Pat)

MINT VALUE £

WINSTON RHODEN
66 Blue Beat BB 360 Send Your Love/Make Believe . . . 20

EMITT RHODES
71 Probe PRO 520 Fresh As A Daisy/You Take The Dark Out Of The Night . . . 6
71 Probe PRO 529 With My Face On The Floor/Somebody Made For Me . . . 6
71 A&M AMS 865 You're A Very Lovely Woman/Till The Day After . . . 6
72 Probe PRO 565 Tame The Lion/Golden Child Of God . . . 6
71 Probe SPBA 6256 EMITT RHODES (LP, gatefold sleeve) . . . 18
71 A&M AMLS 64254 AMERICAN DREAM (LP) . . . 18
71 Probe SPBA 6262 MIRROR (LP) . . . 15
72 Probe SPBA 6266 FAREWELL TO PARADISE (LP) . . . 15

TODD RHODES ORCHESTRA
55 Parlophone R 4029 Specks/Silver Sunset (78) . . . 8
55 Parlophone MSP 6171 Specks/Silver Sunset . . . 30

RHUBARB RHUBARB
68 President PT 229 Rainmaker/Moneylender . . . 35

RHYTHM ACES
55 Senafone FAO 1311 Wondzi Ndzi (Believe It)/Mercy (78) . . . 7
61 Starlite ST45 061 A Thousand Teardrops/Wherever You May Go . . . 22
61 Starlite ST45 066 Please Don't Go Away/Oh My Darling . . . 20
62 Blue Beat BB 134 I'll Be There/DON DRUMMOND: Dewdrops . . . 22
62 Island WI 032 C-H-R-I-S-T-M-A-S/TOP GRANT: A Christmas Drink . . . 22

RHYTHM & BLUES INC.
65 Fontana TF 524 Louie Louie/Honey Don't . . . 60

RHYTHMETTES
59 Coral Q 72358 Page From The Future/I'll Be With You In Apple Blossom Time . . . 10
59 Coral Q 72358 Page From The Future/I'll Be With You In Apple Blossom Time (78) . . . 8

RHYTHM FORCE
72 Tropical AL 0013 Satta Call/Satta Version . . . 6

RHYTHM HERITAGE
76 ABC 4095 Theme From S.W.A.T./I Wouldn't Treat A Dog . . . 5
76 ABC ABCL 5174 DISCO-FIED (LP) . . . 12

RHYTHM KINGS
63 Vocalion POP V 9212 Blue Soul/Exotic . . . 25

RHYTHM MAKERS
76 Polydor 2001 651 Zone/Prime Cut . . . 25

RHYTHM OF LIFE
81 Rational RATE 6 Soon/Summertime (p/s; label also lists Rhythm RHYTHM 1) . . . 6
82 Rational RATE 7 Uncle Sam/Portrait Of The Heart (p/s; label also lists Rhythm RHYTHM 2) . . . 5
(see also Josef K, Paul Haig)

RHYTHM RULERS
70 Bullet BU 447 Second Pressure/Sammy Dead . . . 10
(see also Lloyd Jones, U Roy Junior, Matadors, Winston Groovy, Pat, Winston Wright)

RIALTO
96 Jealous COUP 005 Skyscraper/DOGGER: Bitter Almonds (CD, stickered slimline green case) . . . 12
97 EastWest EW 107 TE Untouchable/Monday Morning 5:19 (10", p/s) . . . 8
98 EastWest 0630 19745-2 RIALTO (CD, withdrawn) . . . 18

RIBS
78 Aerco AERS 101 Man With No Brain/Long Time Coming (p/s) . . . 25

RICARDO
52 Melodisc MEL 1210 Grenada (Land Of Spice)/Banana Song (78) . . . 7

BOYD RICE & FRIENDS
90 New European BADVC 1969 MUSIC, MARTINIS AND MISANTHROPY (LP, with inner sleeve) . . . 25
(see also Non, Death In June, Current 93)

MACK RICE
69 Atlantic 584 250 Love's A Mother Brother/Coal Man . . . 6

MANDY RICE-DAVIES
64 Ember EMB 4537 MANDY (EP) . . . 60

TIM RICE & WEBBER GROUP
69 RCA RCA 1895 Come Back Richard (Your Country Needs You)/Roll On Over The Atlantic . . . 6
(see also Tales Of Justine, Nightshift)

BUDDY RICH
67 Fontana TF 836 Norwegian Wood/The Monitor Theme . . . 5
56 Columbia Clef SEB 10024 SING AND SWING WITH BUDDY RICH (EP) . . . 8
57 Columbia Clef SEB 10071 SWINGING BUDDY RICH (EP) . . . 8
56 HMV CLP 1092 BUDDY RICH SINGS JOHNNY MERCER (LP) . . . 15
56 Columbia Clef 33CX 10052 THE WAILING BUDDY RICH (LP) . . . 15
57 Columbia Clef 33CX 10071 THIS ONE'S FOR BASIE (LP) . . . 15
57 Columbia Clef 33CX 10080 BUDDY AND SWEETS (LP, with Harry 'Sweets' Edison) . . . 25
58 HMV CLP 1185 BUDDY RICH JUST SINGS (LP) . . . 12
59 Columbia Clef 33CX 10138 BUDDY RICH AT MIAMI (LP) . . . 12
67 Verve VLP 9151 THAT'S RICH (LP) . . . 12
68 Liberty LBL/LBS 83090 TAKE IT AWAY! (LP) . . . 12
80 Pye NSPL 18620 THE MAN FROM PLANET JAZZ (LP) . . . 15

MINT VALUE £

BUDDY RICH & MAX ROACH

60 Mercury MMC 14031 RICH VERSUS ROACH (LP, also stereo CMS 18021) . . . 12
(see also Max Roach)

CHARLIE RICH

60 London HLU 9107 Lonely Weekends/Everything I Do Is Wrong . . . 45
62 London HLS 9482 Just A Little Bit Sweet/It's Too Late . . . 40
65 RCA RCA 1433 Too Many Teardrops/It's All Over Now . . . 12
65 Philips BF 1432 Mohair Sam/I Washed My Hands In Muddy Water . . . 15
67 London HLU 10104 Love Is After Me/Pass On By (silver-top label, later boxed logo label) . . . 30/15
69 Mercury MF 1109 Mohair Sam/I Washed My Hands In Muddy Water (reissue) . . . 7
65 RCA RD 7719 THAT'S RICH (LP) . . . 45
66 Philips BL 7695 THE MANY NEW SIDES OF CHARLIE RICH (LP) . . . 30
73 Epic Q 65716 BEHIND CLOSED DOORS (LP, quadrophonic) . . . 12
75 London ZGU 136 CHARLIE RICH SINGS THE SONGS OF HANK WILLIAMS & OTHERS (LP) . . . 12

DAVE RICH

58 RCA RCA 1092 Burn On Love Fire/City Lights . . . 20
58 RCA RCA 1092 Burn On Love Fire/City Lights (78) . . . 15
66 Polydor BM 56113 Last Two People On Earth/I Just Wanna Dance . . . 6

JOHNNY RICH

64 Mercury MF 836 Dream On/Together . . . 6

LEWIS RICH

66 Parlophone R 5434 I Don't Want To Hear It Anymore/Shedding Tears . . . 10

PAUL RICH (& BEATMEN)

59 Embassy WB 322 Smoke Gets In Your Eyes/Problems . . . 5
59 Embassy WB 327 Does Your Chewing Gum Lose Its Flavour (On The Bedpost Overnight)/ Stagger Lee . . . 5
59 Embassy WB 330 Venus/Wonderful Secret Of Love . . . 5
59 Embassy WB 345 Battle Of New Orleans/BUD ASHTON: Peter Gunn . . . 5
59 Embassy WB 353 I'm Gonna Get Married/Mona Lisa . . . 5
59 Embassy WB 363 Makin' Love/GORDON FRANKS SEXTET: Red River Rock . . . 5
60 Embassy WB 374 Heartaches By The Number/BUD ASHTON: Some Kinda Earthquake . . . 5
60 Embassy WB 374 Heartaches By The Number/BUD ASHTON: Some Kinda Earthquake (78) . . . 6
60 Embassy WB 378 Little White Bull/Harbour Lights . . . 5
60 Embassy WB 378 Little White Bull/Harbour Lights (78) . . . 6
60 Embassy WB 387 My Old Man's A Dustman/Fings Ain't Wot They Used To Be . . . 5
60 Embassy WB 387 My Old Man's A Dustman/Fings Ain't Wot They Used To Be (78) . . . 8
60 Embassy WB 403 What A Mouth/Itsy Bitsy Teeny Weeny Yellow Polka Dot Bikini . . . 5
60 Embassy WB 403 What A Mouth/Itsy Bitsy Teeny Weeny Yellow Polka Dot Bikini (78) . . . 10
60 Embassy WB 411 Tell Laura I Love Her/Lorelei . . . 5
60 Embassy WB 411 Tell Laura I Love Her/Lorelei (78) . . . 12
61 Embassy WB 479 Tower Of Strength/Hit The Road Jack . . . 5
62 Embassy WB 548 Don't You Think It's Time/Little Town Flirt . . . 5
62 Embassy WB 567 Young Lovers (as Paul Rich & Kay Barry)/JOAN BAXTER: I Will Follow Him . . . 5
64 Embassy WB 637 No Particular Place To Go (as Paul Rich & Beatmen)/ TERRY BRANDON & BEATMEN: I Love You Baby . . . 5
65 Embassy WB 678 Keep Searchin' (as Paul Rich & Beatmen)/BURT SHANE: The Special Years . . . 5
(see also Bud Ashton, Jaybirds, Jean Campbell)

RICHIE RICH

89 ffrr FX 113 Salsa House (Silver On Black Mix)/(Original Mix)/(Orbital Mix) (12") . . . 15
89 ffrr FXR 156 You Used To Salsa/You Used To Hold Me (12", remix) . . . 25

SKETTO RICH

70 Pama PM 806 Hound Dog/Black Girl . . . 7
71 Big Shot BI 596 Know Your Friend/Know Your Friend — Version . . . 7
(see Buddy & Sketto, Ruddy & Sketto, Father Sketto, Owen Gray)

TONY RICH

66 Piccadilly 7N 35291 Save Your Love/Don't Mention Your Name . . . 8
66 Piccadilly 7N 35323 It's All Up To You Now/See Saw . . . 8
(see also Tony Sheveton)

RICHARD & GLEN

72 Duke DU 141 Boat To Progress (Parts 1 & 2) . . . 12

RICHARD & YOUNG LIONS

66 Philips BF 1520 Open Up Your Door/Once Upon Your Smile . . . 35

RICHARD BROTHERS

63 Island WI 060 I Need A Girl/Desperate Lover . . . 25
63 Island WI 109 I Shall Wear A Crown/BABA BROOKS: Robin Hood . . . 25
(see also Joe White)

CLIFF RICHARD (& DRIFTERS/SHADOWS)

78s

58 Columbia DB 4178 Move It!/Schoolboy Crush . . . 40
58 Columbia DB 4203 High Class Baby/My Feet Hit The Ground . . . 35
59 Columbia DB 4249 Livin' Lovin' Doll/Steady With You . . . 110
59 Columbia DB 4290 Mean Streak/Never Mind . . . 130
59 Columbia DB 4306 Living Doll/Apron Strings . . . 40
(The above 78s were credited to Cliff Richard & Drifters)
59 Columbia DB 4351 Travellin' Light/Dynamite . . . 50
60 Columbia DB 4398 A Voice In The Wilderness/Don't Be Mad At Me . . . 90
60 Columbia DB 4431 Fall In Love With You/Willie And The Hand Jive (existence unconfirmed)
(The above 78s were credited to Cliff Richard & Shadows)

MINT VALUE £

COLUMBIA 45s

58	Columbia DB 4178	Move It!/Schoolboy Crush (green label, later black)	25/35
58	Columbia DB 4203	High Class Baby/My Feet Hit The Ground (green label, later black)	25/35
59	Columbia DB 4249	Livin' Lovin' Doll/Steady With You (green label, later black)	40/40
59	Columbia DB 4290	Mean Streak/Never Mind (green label, later black)	20/35
59	Columbia DB 4306	Living Doll/Apron Strings (green label, later black)	10/30
(The above singles were credited to Cliff Richard & Drifters)			
59	Columbia DB 4351	Travellin' Light/Dynamite	10
60	Columbia DB 4398	A Voice In The Wilderness/Don't Be Mad At Me	6
60	Columbia DB 4431	Fall In Love With You/Willie And The Hand Jive	6
60	Columbia DB 4479	Please Don't Tease/Where Is My Heart	6
60	Columbia DB 4506	Nine Times Out Of Ten/Thinking Of Our Love	7
60	Columbia DB 4547	I Love You/"D" In Love	6
61	Columbia DB 4593	Theme For A Dream/Mumblin' Mosie	6
61	Columbia DB 4667	A Girl Like You/Now's The Time To Fall In Love	6
61	Columbia DB 4716	When The Girl In Your Arms Is The Girl In Your Heart/ Got A Funny Feeling (solo)	6
62	Columbia DB 4761	The Young Ones/We Say Yeah (green label, later black)	5/7
62	Columbia DB 4828	I'm Lookin' Out The Window/Do You Want To Dance?	6
62	Columbia DB 4886	It'll Be Me/Since I Lost You	6
(The above 45s were originally green labels; later black label copies are worth at least twice the listed values unless stated.)			
62	Columbia DB 4950	The Next Time/Bachelor Boy	6
63	Columbia DB 4977	Summer Holiday/Dancing Shoes	6
63	Columbia DB 7034	Lucky Lips/I Wonder	6
63	Columbia DB 7089	It's All In The Game/Your Eyes Tell On You (solo)	6
63	Columbia DB 7150	Don't Talk To Him/Say You're Mine	6
64	Columbia DB 7203	I'm The Lonely One/Watch What You Do With My Baby	6
64	Columbia DB 7272	Constantly (solo)/True True Lovin'	6
64	Columbia DB 7305	On The Beach/A Matter Of Moments	7
64	Columbia DB 7372	The Twelfth Of Never/I'm Afraid To Go Home (solo)	7
64	Columbia DB 7420	I Could Easily Fall (In Love With You)/I'm In Love With You	6
(The above singles were credited to Cliff Richard & Shadows unless stated; the singles listed below were solo unless stated.)			
64	Columbia DB 7435	This Was My Special Day/I'm Feeling Oh So Lovely (withdrawn, credited to Cliff Richard, Audrey Bayley, Joan Palethorpe & Faye Fisher)	50
65	Columbia DB 7496	The Minute You're Gone/Just Another Guy	6
65	Columbia DB 7596	On My Word/Just A Little Bit Too Late	7
65	Columbia DB 7660	The Time In Between/Look Before You Love (as Cliff Richard & Shadows)	8
65	Columbia DB 7745	Wind Me Up (Let Me Go)/The Night	6
66	Columbia DB 7866	Blue Turns To Grey/Somebody Loses (as Cliff Richard & Shadows)	8
66	Columbia DB 7968	Visions/What Would I Do (For The Love Of A Girl?)	6
66	Columbia DB 8017	Time Drags By/La La La Song (as Cliff Richard & Shadows)	6
66	Columbia DB 8094	In The Country/Finders Keepers (as Cliff Richard & Shadows)	6
66	Columbia PSRS 304	Finders Keepers (promo only, 1-sided, with spoken intro by Simon Dee)	90
67	Columbia DB 8150	It's All Over/Why Wasn't I Born Rich?	6
67	Columbia DB 8210	I'll Come Runnin'/I Get The Feelin'	12
67	Columbia DB 8245	The Day I Met Marie/Our Story Book	6
67	Columbia DB 8293	All My Love/Sweet Little Jesus Boy	6
68	Columbia DB 8376	Congratulations/High 'N' Dry	6
68	Columbia DB 8437	I'll Love You Forever Today/Girl, You'll Be A Woman Soon	12
68	Columbia DB 8476	Marianne/Mr Nice	8
68	Columbia DB 8503	Don't Forget To Catch Me/What's More (I Don't Need Her)	8
69	Columbia DB 8548	Good Times (Better Times)/Occasional Rain	7
69	Columbia DB 8581	Big Ship/She's Leaving You	10
69	Columbia DB 8615	Throw Down A Line (as Cliff & Hank)/Reflections	7
69	Columbia DB 8641	With The Eyes Of A Child/So Long	8
70	Columbia DB 8657	Joy Of Living (as Cliff & Hank)/CLIFF RICHARD: Leave My Woman Alone/ HANK MARVIN: Boogatoo	7
70	Columbia DB 8685	Goodbye Sam, Hello Samantha/You Never Can Tell	6
70	Columbia DB 8708	I Ain't Got Time Anymore/Monday Comes Too Soon	7
71	Columbia DB 8747	Sunny Honey Girl/Don't Move Away (with Olivia Newton-John)/ I Was Only Fooling Myself	12
71	Columbia DB 8774	Silvery Rain/Annabella Umbrella/Time Flies	12
71	Columbia DB 8797	Flying Machine/Pigeon	12
71	Columbia DB 8836	Sing A Song Of Freedom/A Thousand Conversations	6
72	Columbia DB 8864	Jesus/Mister Cloud	12
72	Columbia DB 8917	Living In Harmony/Empty Chairs	6
72	Columbia DB 8957	Brand New Song/The Old Accordion	20

EXPORT SINGLES

61	Columbia DC 756	Gee Whiz It's You/I Cannot Find A True Love	10
63	Columbia DC 758	What'd I Say/Blue Moon	300
65	Columbia DC 762	Angel/Razzle Dazzle	100

EMI SINGLES

73	EMI EMI 2012	Power To All Our Friends/Come Back Billie Joe	5
73	EMI EMI 2022	Help It Along/Tomorrow Rising/The Days Of Love/Ashes To Ashes (some in p/s)	12/6
73	EMI EMI 2088	Take Me High/Celestial Houses	5
74	EMI PSR 368	Nothing To Remind Me/The Learning (promo only)	60
74	EMI EMI 2150	(You Keep Me) Hangin' On/Love Is Here	5
75	EMI EMI 2279	It's Only Me You've Left Behind/You're The One	15
75	EMI EMI 2344	Honky Tonk Angel/(Wouldn't You Know It) Got Myself A Girl	20
76	EMI EMI 2376	Miss You Nights/Love Enough (later available with p/s in box set)	6/5
76	EMI EMI 2458	Devil Woman/Love On (Shine On)	5
76	EMI EMI 2499	I Can't Ask For Anything More Than You/Junior Cowboy	5
76	EMI EMI 2559	Hey Mr Dream Maker/No One Waits	5

MINT VALUE £

77	EMI EMI 2584	My Kinda Life/Nothing Left For Me To Say	5
77	EMI EMI 2633	When Two Worlds Drift Apart/That's Why I Love You	8
78	EMI EMI 2730	Yes! He Lives/Good On The Sally Army	15
78	EMI EMI 2832	Please Remember Me/Please Don't Tease	8
78	EMI EMI 2885	Can't Take The Hurt Anymore/Needing A Friend (p/s)	8
79	EMI EMI 2920	Green Light/Imagine Love (some in p/s)	30/5
79	EMI EMI 2975	We Don't Talk Anymore/Count Me Out (p/s)	5
79	EMI EMI 2975	We Don't Talk Anymore/Count Me Out (p/s, mispress, A-side plays Queen's "Bohemian Rhapsody")	12
79	EMI EMI 5003	Hot Shot/Walking In The Light (p/s)	5
80	EMI EMI 5006	Carrie/Moving In (p/s)	5
82	EMI EMI 5341	Where Do We Go From Here/Discovering (p/s)	6
82	EMI EMIP 5348	Little Town/Love And A Helping Hand/You Me And Jesus (picture disc)	6
83	EMI 12EMI 5415	Never Say Die (Give A Little Bit More)/Lucille (12", p/s)	10
83	EMI EMI 5437	Please Don't Fall In Love/Too Close To Heaven (p/s)	5
84	EMI EMI 5457	Ocean Deep/Baby You're Dynamite (different version) (blue p/s, A & B-sides reversed)	15
84	EMI 12EMI 5457	Baby You're Dynamite (Extended Mix)/Ocean Deep (12", p/s)	12
84	EMI RICHP 1	Shooting From The Heart/Small World (heart-shaped picture disc)	12
85	EMI RICHP 2/RICHP 1	Heart User/I Will Follow You//Shooting From The Heart/Small World (shrinkwrapped double pack, 2nd single as shaped picture disc)	12
85	EMI 12 RICH 2	Heart User (Extended)/I Will Follow You (12", poster p/s)	12
86	WEA YZ 65P	Living Doll (with Young Ones)/YOUNG ONES: (All The Little Flowers Are) Happy (picture disc)	8
85	EMI EMI 5531	She's So Beautiful/(Special Mix) (p/s, some with 'Time' inner sleeve)	6/4
85	EMI EMI 5537	It's In Every One Of Us/Alone (p/s, some with 'Time' inner sleeve)	6/4
86	EMI EMI 5545	Born To Rock And Roll/Law Of The Universe (p/s, some with 'Time' inner)	6/4
86	EMI 12EMI 5545	Born To Rock And Roll (Special Extended Mix)/Born To Rock And Roll/ Law Of The Universe (12", p/s)	12
87	EMI EMG 4	My Pretty One/Love Ya (gatefold p/s)	5
87	EMI EMG 18	Some People/One Time Lover Man (gatefold p/s with booklet)	5
87	EMI EMP 18	Some People/One Time Lover Man (Cliff-shaped picture disc)	10
87	EMI EM 31	Remember Me/Another Christmas Day (gold-embossed p/s)	6
87	EMI 12EMP 31	Remember Me/Another Christmas Day/Brave New World (12", gold embossed p/s)	12
87	EMI CDEM 31	Remember Me/Some People/Another Christmas Day/Remember Me (12" Version) (CD, card sleeve with inner)	10
87	EMI EMP 42	Two Hearts/Yesterday, Today, Forever (double heart-shaped picture disc)	10
87	EMI EMG 42	Two Hearts/Yesterday, Today, Forever (gatefold p/s)	8
87	EMI 12EMG 42	Two Hearts/Yesterday, Today, Forever/Wild Geese (12", gatefold p/s)	12
88	EMI CDEM 42	Two Hearts/Yesterday, Today, Forever/Two Hearts (Ext.)/Wild Geese (CD)	10
88	EMI EMS 78	Mistletoe And Wine/Marmaduke/True Love Ways (p/s)	5
88	EMI EMP 78	Mistletoe And Wine/Marmaduke (poster/calendar p/s)	5
88	EMI 12EMX 78	Mistletoe And Wine/Marmaduke/Little Town (12", Advent calendar p/s)	12
88	EMI CDEM 78	Mistletoe And Wine/Marmaduke/Little Town/La Gonave (CD, with Christmas card)	10
89	EMI EM 92	The Best Of Me/Move It/Lindsay Jane (gold '100th Single' p/s)	6
89	EMI 12EM 92	The Best Of Me/Move It/Lindsay Jane/High Class Baby (12", gold '100th Single' p/s)	10
89	EMI CDEM 92	The Best Of Me/Move It/Lindsay Jane/High Class Baby (CD)	8
89	EMI CDEMS 92	The Best Of Me/Move It/Lindsay Jane/High Class Baby (CD, gold '100th Single' card sleeve)	10
89	EMI 12EMX 101	I Just Don't Have The Heart (Remix)/Wide Open Space/ I Just Don't Have The Heart (Instrumental) (12", plain black sleeve)	10
89	EMI CDEM 101	I Just Don't Have The Heart/Wide Open Space/ I Just Don't Have The Heart (Instrumental) (CD)	10
89	EM EMPD 105	Lean On You/Hey Mister (Cliff-shaped picture disc)	8
89	EM CDEM 105	Lean On You (Extended Mix)/Lean On You/Hey Mister (CD)	10
89	EMI EM 129	Stronger Than That/Joanna (p/s, with 3 postcards pack)	7
89	EMI 12EM 129	Stronger Than That (Extended Version)/Joanna/Stronger Than That (12" p/s, some with 'signed' print)	8/7
89	EMI CDEM 129	Stronger Than That (Extended Version)/Joanna/Stronger Than That (CD)	10
89	EMI EMS 152	Silhouettes/The Winner ('photoframe' p/s with stand)	5
89	EMI CDEM 152	Silhouettes/The Winner/All The Time You Need (CD)	8
90	EMI EMPD 155	From A Distance/I Could Easily Fall (picture disc, PVC sleeve)	5
90	EMI 12EMP 155	From A Distance/Lindsay Jane II/Wired For Sound (12", poster p/s)	8
90	EMI CDEM 155	From A Distance/Lindsay Jane II/Wired For Sound (CD)	8
90	EMI CRTBX 31	Miss You Nights (Acappella version) (1-sided 7", p/s, with etched message and autograph on reverse)	8
90	EMI XMAS P90	Saviour's Day/Oh! Boy Medley ('Xmas' pack, envelope p/s with 5 photos)	7
90	EMI CDXMAS 90	Saviour's Day/Oh! Boy Medley/Where You Are (CD)	10
91	EMI CDEM 205	More To Life/Mo's Theme (Intrumental) (CD)	8
91	EMI XMAS G91/XMAS 91	We Should Be Together/Miss You Nights (live)//We Should Be Together/ Twelve Days Of Christmas/Mistletoe And Wine/The Holly And The Ivy (Acappella Version) (double pack, gatefold p/s, discs sold separately)	7
91	EMI CDXMAS 91	We Should Be Together/Miss You Nights (live)/Mistletoe And Wine (CD)	8
91	EMI EM 218	This New Year/Scarlet Ribbons (p/s, 1 side etched with autograph)	5
91	EMI CDEM 218	This New Year/I Love You/Scarlet Ribbons/We Don't Talk (CD)	8
92	EMI EM 255	I Still Believe In You/Boulange Downpour (p/s)	5
93	EMI EM 265	Peace In Our Time (Album Version)/Somebody Loves You (p/s)	5
93	EMI EM 267	Human Work Of Art (7" Version)/Ragged (p/s)	5
93	EMI EM 281	Never Let Go/Congratulations (p/s, with poster)	5
93	EMI EM 294	Healing Love/Yesterday's Memories/Carrie (p/s)	5
94	EMI EM 359	All I Have To Do Is Dream/Miss You Nights (p/s)	5
95	EMI EM 394	Misunderstood Man/Misunderstood Man (Instrumental) (p/s)	5

MINT VALUE £

FLEXIDISCS & OTHER RELEASES

60 Serenade Magazine/ Rainbow (no cat. no.) — *Serenade* Presents Cliff Richard's Personal Message To You (turquoise flexidisc free with magazine)........ 25/20
60s Serenade Magazine — Cliff's Rock Party (flexidisc with magazine)........ 30/20
60s Boyfriend Magazine — untitled flexidisc with magazine........ 30/20
60s Rainbow Magazine — Music From America (flexidisc with magazine)........ 35/25
60s New Spotlight — Star Souvenir Greetings (208 Radio Luxembourg flexidisc)........ 20
73 Lyntone LYN SF 1218 — The Cliff Richard Story (World Record Club 1-sided flexidisc)........ 6
73 Spree (no cat. no.) — Good News (plain black flexidisc with spoken/sung introduction from Cliff, other side by Johnny Cash)........ 20
70s Lyntone LYN 14745 — The Best Of Cliff Richard And The Shadows (preview flexidisc)........ 8
80s Weetabix — Children's Hospital Appeal (spoken-word cassette)........ 5
92 Balladeer — Access All Areas (interview flexidisc)........ 5
98 Cruisin' The 50's CASB 007 — Breathless/Lawdy Miss Clawdy (10" 78, p/s, with 6 inserts)........ 50

EPs

59 Columbia SEG 7895 — SERIOUS CHARGE (soundtrack)........ 35
59 Columbia SEG 7903 — CLIFF NO. 1 (also stereo ESG 7754)........ 35/60
59 Columbia SEG 7910 — CLIFF NO. 2 (also stereo ESG 7769)........ 35/60
59 Columbia SEG 7971 — EXPRESSO BONGO (soundtrack, also stereo ESG 7783)........ 25/45
60 Columbia SEG 7979 — CLIFF SINGS NO. 1 (also stereo ESG 7788)........ 35/65
60 Columbia SEG 7987 — CLIFF SINGS NO. 2 (also stereo ESG 7794)........ 35/65
60 Columbia SEG 8005 — CLIFF SINGS NO. 3 (also stereo ESG 7808)........ 35/65
60 Columbia SEG 8021 — CLIFF SINGS NO. 4 (also stereo ESG 7816)........ 35/65
60 Columbia SEG 8050 — CLIFF'S SILVER DISCS........ 22
60 Columbia SEG 8065 — ME AND MY SHADOWS NO. 1 (also stereo ESG 7837)........ 35/65
61 Columbia SEG 8071 — ME AND MY SHADOWS NO. 2 (also stereo ESG 7481)........ 35/65
61 Columbia SEG 8078 — ME AND MY SHADOWS NO. 3 (also stereo ESG 7843)........ 35/65
61 Columbia SEG 8105 — LISTEN TO CLIFF NO. 1 (also stereo ESG 7858)........ 35/65
61 Columbia SEG 8119 — DREAM (also stereo ESG 7867)........ 22/55
61 Columbia SEG 8126 — LISTEN TO CLIFF NO. 2 (also stereo ESG 7870)........ 35/65
62 Columbia SEG 8133 — CLIFF'S HIT PARADE........ 20
62 Columbia SEG 8151 — CLIFF RICHARD........ 40
62 Columbia SEG 8159 — HITS FROM 'THE YOUNG ONES'........ 18
62 Columbia SEG 8168 — CLIFF RICHARD NO. 2........ 40

(The above EPs were originally issued with turquoise labels, later blue/black label copies are worth two-thirds these values.)

62 Columbia SEG 8203 — CLIFF'S HITS........ 20
63 Columbia SEG 8228 — TIME FOR CLIFF AND THE SHADOWS (mono)........ 30
63 Columbia ESG 7887 — TIME FOR CLIFF AND THE SHADOWS (stereo, turquoise or blue/black)........ 65/50
63 Columbia SEG 8246 — HOLIDAY CARNIVAL (also stereo ESG 7892)........ 20/55
63 Columbia SEG 8250 — HITS FROM 'SUMMER HOLIDAY' (also stereo ESG 7896)........ 18/50
63 Columbia SEG 8263 — MORE HITS FROM 'SUMMER HOLIDAY' (also stereo ESG 7898)........ 30/55
63 Columbia SEG 8269 — CLIFF'S LUCKY LIPS........ 22
63 Columbia SEG 8272 — LOVE SONGS (also stereo ESG 7900)........ 22/65
64 Columbia SEG 8290 — WHEN IN FRANCE........ 30
64 Columbia SEG 8299 — CLIFF SINGS 'DON'T TALK TO HIM'........ 30
64 Columbia SEG 8320 — CLIFF'S PALLADIUM SUCCESSES........ 40
64 Columbia SEG 8338 — WONDERFUL LIFE (also stereo ESG 7902)........ 22/55
64 Columbia SEG 8347 — A FOREVER KIND OF LOVE........ 35
64 Columbia SEG 8354 — WONDERFUL LIFE NO. 2 (also stereo ESG 7903)........ 25/55
64 Columbia SEG 8376 — HITS FROM 'WONDERFUL LIFE' (also stereo ESG 7906)........ 25/55
65 Columbia SEG 8384 — WHY DON'T THEY UNDERSTAND?........ 30
65 Columbia SEG 8395 — CLIFF'S HITS FROM 'ALADDIN AND HIS WONDERFUL LAMP'........ 25
65 Columbia SEG 8405 — LOOK IN MY EYES, MARIA........ 35
65 Columbia SEG 8444 — ANGEL........ 40
65 Columbia SEG 8450 — TAKE FOUR........ 45
66 Columbia SEG 8474 — WIND ME UP........ 35
66 Columbia SEG 8478 — HITS FROM 'WHEN IN ROME'........ 70
66 Columbia SEG 8488 — LOVE IS FOREVER........ 50
66 Columbia SEG 8510 — THUNDERBIRDS ARE GO! (3 tracks by Cliff & Shadows, 1 solo)........ 70
66 Columbia SEG 8517 — LA LA LA LA LA (1 track by Bruce Welch & Hank Marvin)........ 45
67 Columbia SEG 8527 — CINDERELLA........ 125
67 Columbia SEG 8533 — CAROL SINGERS........ 40
68 Columbia SEG 8540 — CONGRATULATIONS........ 30
77 EMI PSR 410 — EVERY FACE TELLS A STORY (promo, issued to shops only)........ 22
77 EMI PSR 414/415 — 40 GOLDEN GREATS (double pack promo, issued to shops only)........ 40

COLUMBIA LPs

59 Columbia 33SX 1147 — CLIFF (green labels, later blue/black labels)........ 50/30
59 Columbia 33SX 1192 — CLIFF SINGS (green labels, later blue/black labels)........ 50/30
60 Columbia 33SX 1261 — ME AND MY SHADOWS (also stereo SCX 3330)........ 35/55
61 Columbia 33SX 1320 — LISTEN TO CLIFF! (also stereo SCX 3375)........ 30/65
61 Columbia 33SX 1368 — 21 TODAY (also stereo SCX 3409)........ 30/65
61 Columbia 33SX 1384 — THE YOUNG ONES (soundtrack with inner, also stereo SCX 3397)........ 20/40
62 Columbia 33SX 1431 — 32 MINUTES AND 17 SECONDS WITH... (also stereo SCX 3436)........ 30/65

(The above LPs were originally issued with green labels, later blue/black copies are worth two-thirds the value unless stated.)

63 Columbia 33SX 1472 — SUMMER HOLIDAY (soundtrack with inner sleeve, mono)........ 15
63 Columbia SCX 3462 — SUMMER HOLIDAY (stereo, initially green labels, later blue/black)........ 30/20
63 Columbia SX 1512 — CLIFF'S HIT ALBUM........ 15
63 Columbia SX 1541 — WHEN IN SPAIN (also stereo SCX 3488)........ 20/30
64 Columbia SX 1628 — WONDERFUL LIFE (soundtrack, mono, gatefold sleeve with inner sleeve)........ 15
64 Columbia SCX 3515 — WONDERFUL LIFE (soundtrack, stereo, gatefold sleeve with inner sleeve)........ 25
64 Columbia SX 1676/ SCX 3522 — ALADDIN AND HIS WONDERFUL LAMP (with stage cast, gatefold sleeve, mono/stereo)........ 18/25
65 Columbia SX 1709 — CLIFF RICHARD (also stereo SCX 3546)........ 35/40
65 Columbia SX 1737 — MORE HITS BY CLIFF (also stereo SCX 3555)........ 14/18
65 Columbia SX 1762 — WHEN IN ROME........ 35

MINT VALUE £

Year	Label	Title	Value
65	Columbia SX 1769	LOVE IS FOREVER (also stereo SCX 3569)	25
66	Columbia S(C)X 6039	KINDA LATIN (mono/stereo)	30/35
66	Columbia S(C)X 6079	FINDERS KEEPERS (soundtrack, with inner sleeve, mono/stereo)	15/20
67	Columbia S(C)X 6103	CINDERELLA (with stage cast)	35
67	Columbia S(C)X 6133	DON'T STOP ME NOW	30
67	Columbia S(C)X 6167	GOOD NEWS	18
67	Columbia JSX 6167	GOOD NEWS (export issue)	35
68	Columbia S(C)X 6244	CLIFF IN JAPAN (blue/black labels, later white/black labels)	30/20
68	Columbia S(C)X 6262	TWO A PENNY (blue/black labels, later white/black labels)	25/18
68	Columbia S(C)X 6282	ESTABLISHED 1958 (gatefold sleeve, half tracks by Shadows, mono/stereo)	18/15

(The above Columbia LPs were originally issued with blue/black labels; white/black copies are worth half the value unless stated)

Year	Label	Title	Value
69	Columbia S(C)X 6343	THE BEST OF CLIFF	15
69	Columbia S(C)X 6357	SINCERELY CLIFF RICHARD (mono/stereo)	25/20
70	Columbia SCX 6408	ABOUT THAT MAN (4 songs plus narration)	100
70	Columbia SCX 6435	TRACKS 'N' GROOVES	25
70	Columbia SCX 6443	HIS LAND (documentary soundtrack, with Cliff Barrows)	50
72	Columbia SCX 6519	THE BEST OF CLIFF VOLUME 2	15

EMI LPs

Year	Label	Title	Value
73	EMI EMC 3016	TAKE ME HIGH (soundtrack, some with poster)	25/15
74	EMI EMA 768	HELP IT ALONG (gatefold sleeve)	25
74	EMI EMC 3048	THE 31ST OF FEBRUARY STREET	30
74	EMI TC EXSP 1601	THE MUSIC AND LIFE OF CLIFF RICHARD (6-cassette box set, music & intervews, with Brian Bennett, Olivia Newton-John, Cilla Black etc.)	25
82	EMI PSLP 350	CLIFF (promo-only sampler)	40
83	EMI EMC 1077 871/881	SILVER/ROCK'N'ROLL SILVER (2-LP, box set, with booklet)	20
87	EMI EMDB 1004	ALWAYS GUARANTEED (box set, some in embossed sleeve with free 7" "Another Christmas Day")	15/12
89	EMI CR 1	THE 30TH ANNIVERSARY PICTURE RECORD COLLECTION (2-LP, picture discs, gatefold sleeve, mail-order only)	50
90	EMI CRTVB 31	FROM A DISTANCE ... THE EVENT (box set, includes 6 prints, engraved 7" "Miss You Nights (A Capella Version)" & lyric poster)	15
90	EMI CRTVBC 31	FROM A DISTANCE ... THE EVENT (cassette, box set, includes 6 prints, engraved 7" "Miss You Nights (A Capella Version)" & lyric poster)	12
91	EMI EMD 1028	TOGETHER WITH CLIFF (with lyric inner)	12
93	EMI EMD 1043	CLIFF RICHARD — THE ALBUM (with lyric inner)	12
97	EMI 7243	THE ROCK 'N' ROLL YEARS 1958-1963 (4-CD box set, with booklet)	35
98	EMI/Alliance 50285	YESTERDAY, TODAY, FOREVER (2-CD)	25
98	EMI Blacknight 4979	REAL AS I WANNA BE (40th anniversary limited edition, with postcards)	18
98	EMI CDCRDJ 40	40 YEARS OF HITS (CD, book sleeve)	50

OTHER LPs

Year	Label	Title	Value
63	Elstree Extra Range	SUMMER HOLIDAY (2-LP, full soundtrack recording, 80 copies only)	700+
64	Elstree Extra Range	WONDERFUL LIFE (2-LP, full soundtrack recording, 150 copies only)	700+
64	World Record Club (S)T 643	HOW WONDERFUL TO KNOW (mono/stereo)	20/25
64	EMI Regal SREG 1120	ME AND MY SHADOWS (export issue)	70
69	Regal Starline SRS 5011	IT'LL BE ME (reissue of "32 Minutes And 17 Seconds With Cliff Richard")	12
69	World R. Club STP 1051	CLIFF RICHARD	60
70	MFP MFP 1420	ALL MY LOVE	12
70	Regal Starline SRS 5031	CLIFF 'LIVE' AT THE TALK OF THE TOWN	12
72	World R. Club SM 255-260	THE CLIFF RICHARD STORY (6-LP box set with booklet)	30
72	World R. Club CSM 255-260	THE CLIFF RICHARD STORY (6-cassette box set with booklet)	30
73	Sounds Superb SPR 90018	IT'LL BE ME (2nd reissue, different cover)	12
75	Sounds Superb SPR 90070	EVERYONE NEEDS SOMEONE TO LOVE	12
70s	Readers Digest	THE BEST OF CLIFF RICHARD AND THE SHADOWS (8-LP box set)	50
80	World R. Club ALBUM 26	THE CLIFF RICHARD SONGBOOK (6-LP box set)	35
80	WRC CASSETTE 26	THE CLIFF RICHARD SONGBOOK (6-cassette box set)	25
85	Tellydisc TELLY 28	FROM THE HEART (2-LP, gatefold sleeve, mail-order only)	25
85	Myrrh MYR 1176	WALKING IN THE LIGHT (with insert)	15
85	Myrrh MYRCD 1176	WALKING IN THE LIGHT (CD)	20
86	Word WRD C 3017	HYMNS AND INSPIRATIONAL SONGS (cassette)	10
88	Myrrh MYR R 1209	IT'S A SMALL WORLD	30
88	Word WRD R 3034	CAROLS	20
88	Word WRD R 3036	SMALL CORNERS (reissue)	20

REEL-TO-REEL TAPE

Year	Label	Title	Value
64	EMI TA-SX 1628	WONDERFUL LIFE	12

(other reel-to-reel tapes may be worth up to a maximum of £12)
(see also Drifters [U.K.], Shadows, Olivia Newton-John, Sheila Walsh, Janet Jackson, Elton John, Phil Everly, Grazina)

WENDY RICHARD & DIANA BERRY

Year	Label	Title	Value
63	Decca F 11680	We Had A Dream/Keep 'Em Looking Around	15

(see also Mike Sarne)

BARRY RICHARDS

Year	Label	Title	Value
73	MAM R 198	Durango (parts 1 & 2)	5

CYNTHIA RICHARDS

Year	Label	Title	Value
69	Clandisc CLA 203	Foolish Fool/KING STITT: On The Street	12
70	Clandisc CLA 210	Conversation/DYNAMITES: Conversation Version II	10
70	Clandisc CLA 216	Can't Wait/Promises	7
70	Clandisc CLA 220	Foolish Fool/CLANCY & STITT: Dance Beat	12
71	Clandisc CLA 229	Stand By Your Man (actually by Merlene Webber)/DYNAMITES: Version 2	6
71	Big Shot BI 581	I'm Moving On/HIPPY BOYS: I'm Moving On – Version	7
71	Escort ERT 861	Love & Unity/MAYTONES: Wah Noh Dead	7
71	G.G. GG 4528	Place In My Heart/You've Got A Friend (act. Irving [Brown] & Cynthia Richards)	8
72	Pama Supreme PS 366	Mr Postman/SKIN, FLESH AND BONES: Version	10
73	Attack ATT 8047	Aily I/REID'S ALL STARS: Aily I – Version	6
70	Trojan TBL 123	FOOLISH FOOL (LP, actually Clancy Eccles productions compilation)	30

(see also Bobby Aitken, Lord Comic, Sir Lord Comic)

MINT VALUE £

JOHN RICHARDS

57 HMV POP 401 — Let Me Be Loved/By The Fireside ... 6
65 Oriole CB 312 — Folks Get Married In The Spring/Then I'll Be There ... 7
66 Polydor BM 56705 — I Will Go Again To Ireland/Midnight Sky ... 5

JOHNNY RICHARDS

59 Esquire 32-076 — THE RITES OF DIABLO (LP) ... 15

KEITH RICHARDS

79 Rolling Stones RSR 102 — Run Rudolph Run/The Harder They Come (p/s) ... 15
86 Arista ARIST 678P — Jumping Jack Flash/Integrity (with Aretha Franklin) (shaped pic disc & plinth) .. 12
88 Virign VS 1125 — Take It So Hard/I Could Have Stood You Up (p/s) ... 5
88 Virign VST 1125 — Take It So Hard/I Could Have Stood You Up/It Means A Lot (12", p/s) ... 8
88 Virign VSCD 1125 — Take It So Hard/I Could Have Stood You Up/It Means A Lot (3" CD, 4" x 4" gatefold card sleeve) ... 8
89 Virgin VS 1179 — Make No Mistake (Edit)/It Means A Lot (p/s) ... 6
89 Virgin VST 1179 — Make No Mistake (Extended Version)/(LP Version)/It Means A Lot (12", p/s) ... 8
89 Virgin VSCD 1179 — Make No Mistake/It Means A Lot/Make No Mistake (Extended Version) (3" CD, card sleeve) ... 10
88 Virgin KEITH 1234 — Make No Mistake/Locked Away/Struggle/Big Enough (4 x 1-sided 7", "Talk Is Cheap" sampler box set, promo only) ... 75
88 Virgin 2-91047 A/B/C — TALK IS CHEAP (3 x 3" CDs in tin) ... 40

(see also Rolling Stones, Aranbee Pop Symphony Orchestra, Dirty Strangers, Screamin' Jay Hawkins)

LISA RICHARDS

65 Vocalion VP 9244 — Mean Old World/Take A Chance ... 35

LLOYD RICHARDS

64 Port-O-Jam PJ 4004 — Be Good/I Need You ... 15

ROY RICHARDS

66 Doctor Bird DB 1012 — Contact/Maureen ... 25
66 Island WI 297 — Green Collie/MARCIA GRIFFITHS: You No Good ... 25
66 Island WI 283 — Double Trouble/FITSY & FREDDY: Why Did You Do It ... 30
66 Island WI 299 — Western Standard Time/(JA) EAGLES: What An Agony ... 50
66 Island WI 3000 — South Viet Nam/You Must Be Sorry (Vocal) ... 30
67 Island WI 3027 — Rub-A-Dub/SHARKS: Baby Come Home ... 25
67 Island WI 3037 — Hopeful Village Ska/DELROY WILSON: Ungrateful Baby ... 35
67 Island WI 3050 — Port-O-Jam/DELROY WILSON: Get Ready ... 35
67 Studio One SO 2020 — Hanky Panky/ALTON ELLIS: I Am Still In Love ... 40

(see also Roland Alphonso, Lord Comic, Soul Vendors, Jackie Mittoo, Derrick Morgan, Righteous Flames)

RUSTY RICHARDS

60 Top Rank JAR 297 — Middle Hand Road/Golden Moon (China Night) ... 7

TRUDY RICHARDS

57 Capitol CL 14728 — Wishbone/Hangin' Around ... 8
57 Capitol CL 14744 — Weaker Than Wise/I Want A Big Butter And Egg Man ... 6
58 Capitol CL 14857 — Somebody Just Like You/The Night When Love Was Born ... 6
57 Capitol EAP 1 1087 — CRAZY IN LOVE (EP) ... 12
57 Capitol T 838 — CRAZY IN LOVE (LP) ... 25

WINSTON RICHARDS

67 Rio R 124 — Studio Blitz/Don't Up ... 35

JOE 'GROUNDHOG' RICHARDSON

69 Major Minor MM 632 — Take It Off/Blues To Take It Off ... 8

MARK RICHARDSON

65 Stateside SS 440 — Baby, I'm Sorry/Blanket Fair ... 8
65 Stateside SS 467 — See It My Way/Think ... 8

RICH GYPSY

80 Splash SP 016 — What Hit Me (no p/s) ... 25

RICH KIDS

78 EMI EMI 2738 — Rich Kids/Empty Words (red vinyl, p/s) ... 7
78 EMI EMI 2803 — Marching Men/Here Comes The Nice (p/s) ... 6
78 EMI EMC 3263 — GHOSTS OF PRINCES IN TOWERS (LP) ... 15

(see also Sex Pistols, Ultravox, Spectres, Swingers, Visage)

JONATHAN RICHMAN & MODERN LOVERS

75 United Artists UP 36006 — Road Runner/It Will Stand ... 7
77 Beserkley BZZ 1 — Road Runner (Once)/Road Runner (Twice) (p/s) ... 5
77 Beserkley BSERK 9 — ROCK 'N' ROLL WITH THE MODERN LOVERS (LP) ... 12
77 Beserkley BSERK 2 — JONATHAN RICHMAN AND THE MODERN LOVERS (LP) ... 12
77 Beserkley BSERK 12 — MODERN LOVERS LIVE (LP) ... 12
77 Beserkley BSERK 17 — BACK IN YOUR LIFE (LP) ... 12

RICHMOND

73 Dart ART 2008 — Candy Dora/Willow Farm ... 5
73 Dart ART 2025 — Frightened/Breakfast ... 5
73 Dart ART 2031 — Raise Your Heads To The Wind/All I Really Need ... 5
74 Dart ART 2044 — Peaches/Work For My Baby ... 5
73 Dart ARTS 65371 — FRIGHTENED (LP) ... 20

BEN RICHMOND

63 Piccadilly 7N 35132 — You Gotta Have Love/I Don't Care ... 7

FIONA RICHMOND

73 Raymond PR 112 — FRANKLY FIONA (LP) ... 50

MINT VALUE £

JANET RICHMOND

60 Top Rank JAR 288 — You Got What It Takes/Not One Minute More . . . 10
60 Top Rank JAR 378 — June Bride/My One And Only Love . . . 7
61 Top Rank JAR 536 — Senora/I Need You . . . 7

RICHUS FLAMES

67 Fab FAB 17 — Need To Be Loved/I Am Going Home . . . 15
(see also Righteous Flames)

RICK & KEENS

61 Mercury AMT 1150 — Peanuts/I'll Be Home . . . 75

BERESFORD RICKETTS

60 Starlite ST45 025 — Cherry Baby/I Want To Know . . . 20
60 Starlite ST45 029 — Baby Baby/When I Woke Up . . . 20
61 Starlite ST45 048 — Hold Me Tight/Dream Girl (as Ricketts & Rowe) . . . 20
62 Starlite ST45 079 — I'm Going To Cry/Waiting For Me . . . 20
62 Blue Beat BB 107 — You Better Be Going/I've Been Walking (as Beresford Ricketts & Blue Beats) . . . 20
63 Dice CC 12 — Oh Jean/Rivers Of Tears (as Lauren Aitken's Group) . . . 20
66 Blue Beat BB 350 — Jailer Bring Me Water/Careless Love . . . 20

RICO (RODRIGUEZ)

61 Blue Beat BB 56 — Luke Lane Shuffle (as Rico Rodrigues & Buster's All Stars)/ BUSTER'S GROUP: Little Honey . . . 35
62 Island WI 022 — Rico Special (as Emanuel Rodrigues Orchestra; some copies may credit Reco & His Happy Orchestra)/BUNNY & SKITTER: A Little Mashin' . . . 35
62 Planetone RC 1 — London Here I Come/Midnight In Ethiopia . . . 25
62 Planetone RC 4 — Planet Rock/You Win . . . 15
62 Planetone RC 5 — Youth Boogie/Western Serenade (as Rico's Combo) . . . 15
67 Fab FAB 12 — Jingle Bells/Silent Night (with His Boys) . . . 10
68 Pama PM 706 — Soul Man/It's Not Unusual (as Reco Rodriguez) . . . 12
68 Pama PM 715 — Tender Foot Ska/Memories (as Reco Rodriguez) . . . 15
69 Blue Cat BS 160 — The Bullet/Rhythm In (as Reco Rodriguez & His Rhythm Aces) . . . 25
69 Doctor Bird DB 1302 — Baby Face (as Reco & Rudies)/RUDIES: News . . . 25
69 Bullet BU 407 — Tribute To Don Drummond/Japanese Invasion (as Rico Rodriquez) . . . 20
71 Duke DU 96 — Surprise Package (as Rico & Satch)/PETE JOHNSON: I'm Sorry . . . 20
70s Island IPR 2006 — Ska-Wars/Ramble (12") . . . 20
80 2-Tone CHS TT 15 — Sea Cruise/Carolina (p/s, paper label) . . . 8
82 2-Tone CHS TT 19 — Jungle Music/Rasta Call (paper label, 2-Tone sleeve, with Special A.K.A.) . . . 8
82 2-Tone CHS TT 1219 — Jungle Music/Rasta Call/You/Easter Island (12", p/s, with Special A.K.A.) . . . 15
69 Trojan TTL 12 — BLOW YOUR HORN (LP, as Rico & Rudies) . . . 40
69 Pama ECO 014 — IN REGGAE LAND (LP) . . . 50
78 Island ILPS 9485 — MAN FROM WARREIKA (LP) . . . 20
78 Ghetto Rockers PRE 1 — WARREIKA DUB (LP, white label, white sleeve) . . . 30
(see also Special A.K.A., Reco, Andy Capp, Don Reco, Prince Buster, Pioneers, Stranger)

RICOCHET

80s Heavy Rock HER 1 — Midas Light/Off The Rails (p/s) . . . 400

RICOTTI & ALBUQUERQUE

71 Pegasus PEG 2 — FIRST WIND (LP) . . . 12
(see also Frank Ricotti, Henry Lowther)

FRANK RICOTTI

69 CBS 52668 — OUR POINT OF VIEW (LP) . . . 18
(see also Ricotti & Albuquerque)

NELSON RIDDLE ORCHESTRA

55 Capitol CL 14241 — Vera Cruz/You Won't Forget Me . . . 12
55 Capitol CL 14262 — The Pendulum Song/Brother John . . . 12
55 Capitol CL 14305 — Run For Cover (with Bob Graham)/Make Believe That You're In Love With Me (with Pat Auld) . . . 12
56 Capitol CL 14510 — Robin Hood/In Old Lisbon (Lisboa Antigua) . . . 7
58 Capitol CL 14911 — Volare (Del Blu Dipinto Di Blu)/Walkin' . . . 5
59 Capitol CL 15016 — Blue Safari/De Guello (No Quarter) . . . 5
62 Capitol CL 15253 — Route 66 Theme/Lolita Ya Ya . . . 5
63 Capitol CL 15309 — Supercar/The Dick Van Dyke Theme . . . 15
66 Stateside SS 517 — Batman Theme (from the T.V. series)/Nelson's Riddler . . . 20
59 HMV GES 5792 — NELSON RIDDLE PLAYS GERSHWIN (EP, stereo) . . . 10
61 Capitol EAP4 1771 — ROUTE 66 AND OTHER T.V. THEMES (EP) . . . 12
57 Capitol T 893 — C'MON . . . GET HAPPY! (LP) . . . 12
58 Capitol ST 915 — SEA OF DREAMS (LP) . . . 12
59 Philips SBBL 565 — LI'L ABNER (LP, soundtrack) . . . 12
60 Capitol SW 1301 — CAN CAN (LP, soundtrack) . . . 12
62 Capitol (S)T 1771 — ROUTE 66 AND OTHER GREAT T.V. THEMES (LP) . . . 15
62 MGM MGM-C 896 — LOLITA (LP, soundtrack) . . . 25
64 Stateside SL 10090 — WHAT A WAY TO GO! (LP, soundtrack) . . . 12
64 Reprise R 2021 — ROBIN AND THE SEVEN HOODS (LP, soundtrack) . . . 30
64 Reprise R 6138 — GREAT MUSIC, GREAT FILMS, GREAT SOUNDS (LP) . . . 15
66 Stateside S(S)L 10179 — BATMAN (LP, TV soundtrack) . . . 60
67 Columbia S(C)X 6155 — EL DORADO (LP, soundtrack) . . . 30
69 Paramount SPFL 257 — PAINT YOUR WAGON (LP, gatefold sleeve) . . . 12
(se also Shirley Bassey)

RIDDLERS

66 Polydor BM 56716 — Batman Theme/Weegie Walk . . . 20

RIDE

94 Creation CRE 189T — I Don't Know Where It Comes From/Drive Blind/From Time To Time/How Does It Feel To Feel (p/s) . . . 8

PAT RIDEN & BROTHER LLOYD'S ALL STARS

69 Mercury MF 1072 I Need Help/Let The Red Wine Flow (actually by Pat Rhoden) . . . 6
(see also Pat Rhoden)

JACKIE RIDING & IMESON SOUND

66 Fab FAB 4 Don't Wanna Leave/The Wave . . . 8

NICOLE RIEU

75 Barclay BAR 31 Live For Love/Et Bonjour A Toi L'Artiste . . . 12

RIFF

64 Blue Beat BB 242 Oh What A Feeling/Primitive Man . . . 20

RIFF-RAFF

73 RCA RCA 2396 Copper Kettle/You Must Be Joking . . . 5
73 RCA SF 8351 RIFF-RAFF (LP) . . . 15
74 RCA LPL1 5023 ORIGINAL MAN (LP) . . . 15

RIFF RAFF

78 Chiswick SW 34 I WANNA BE A COSMONAUT (EP) . . . 8

RIFKIN

68 Page One POF 071 Continental Hesitation/We're Not Those People Any More . . . 70

ELEANOR RIGBY

85 Waterloo Sunset RUSS 101 I Want To Sleep With You/At The End Of The Day (p/s, first 1,000 with condom) . . . 12/10
87 Waterloo Sunset RUSS 103 Over And Over/Last Night In Soho (p/s) . . . 6
87 Waterloo Sunset RUSS 103 Over And Over/Last Night In Soho/See My Friends (12", p/s) . . . 8
87 Waterloo Sunset RUSS 104 Kiss Me Quickly It's Christmas/Mad Christmas (p/s) . . . 6
93 Future Legend FLER 1 You Only Live Twice/Think For Yourself (p/s) . . . 5
87 Waterloo Sunset WSR 001 CENSORSHIP (LP) . . . 15

BRAM RIGG SET

67 Stateside SS 2020 Take The Time Be Yourself/I Can Only Give You Everything . . . 70

DIANA RIGG

72 RCA RCA 2178 Forget Yourself/Sentimental Journey . . . 20

JACKIE RIGGS

56 London HLF 8244 The Great Pretender/His Gold Will Melt . . . 40
56 London HLF 8244 The Great Pretender/His Gold Will Melt (78) . . . 8

RIGHTEOUS BROTHERS

63 London HL 9743 Little Latin Lupe Lu/I'm So Lonely . . . 12
63 London HL 9814 My Babe/Fee-Fi-Fidily-I-Oh . . . 10
65 London HL 9943 You've Lost That Lovin' Feelin'/There's A Woman . . . 7
65 Pye International 7N 25297 Bring Your Love To Me/Try To Find Another Man . . . 12
65 Pye International 7N 25304 Something's Got A Hold On Me/Night Owl . . . 8
65 London HL 9962 Just Once In My Life/The Blues (withdrawn) . . . 50+
65 London HL 9975 Hung On You/Unchained Melody . . . 8
65 Pye International 7N 25323 Let The Good Times Roll/B Flat Blues . . . 8
65 Pye International 7N 25334 For Your Love/My Tears Will Go Away . . . 8
65 London HL 10011 Ebb Tide/(I Love You) For Sentimental Reasons . . . 8
66 Pye International 7N 25358 Georgia On My Mind/My Tears Will Go Away . . . 8
66 Verve VS 535 (You're My) Soul And Inspiration/B Side-Blues . . . 8
66 Verve VS 537 He/He Will Break Your Heart . . . 7
66 Sue WI 4018 You Can Have Her/Justine . . . 30
66 London HL 10066 Just Once In My Life/The Blues (reissue) . . . 7
66 Verve VS 542 Go Ahead And Cry/Things Didn't Go Your Way . . . 6
66 London HL 10086 The White Cliffs Of Dover/Baby She's Mine . . . 7
66 Verve VS 547 Island In The Sun/What Now My Love . . . 6
67 Verve VS 554 Melancholy Music Man/Don't Give Up On Me . . . 6
67 Verve VS 560 Stranded in The Middle Of No Place/Been So Nice . . . 6
69 London HL 10241 You've Lost That Lovin' Feelin'/Unchained Melody . . . 5
77 Phil Spector International 2010 022 You've Lost That Lovin' Feelin'/RIGHTEOUS BROTHERS BAND: Rat Race (Instrumental) . . . 7
65 Pye Intl. NEP 44043 THE RIGHTEOUS BROTHERS (EP) . . . 35
66 Verve VEP 5024 SOUL AND INSPIRATION (EP) . . . 30
66 Verve VEP 5025 THE RIGHTEOUS BROTHERS (EP, reissue) . . . 22
65 Pye Intl. NPL 28056 SOME BLUE-EYED SOUL (LP) . . . 35
65 London HA-U 8226 YOU'VE LOST THAT LOVIN' FEELIN' (LP) . . . 40
65 Pye Intl. NPL 28059 RIGHT NOW! (LP) . . . 22
65 London HA 8245 JUST ONCE IN MY LIFE (LP) . . . 40
66 London HA 8278 BACK TO BACK (LP) . . . 35
66 Verve (S)VLP 9131 SOUL AND INSPIRATION (LP) . . . 25
66 Sue ILP 937 IN ACTION! (LP) . . . 60
66 Verve (S)VLP 9140 GO AHEAD AND CRY (LP) . . . 18
67 Verve (S)VLP 9168 SAYIN' SOMETHIN' (LP) . . . 18
67 Verve (S)VLP 9183 THE RIGHTEOUS BROTHERS GREATEST HITS (LP) . . . 15
68 Verve (S)VLP 9190 SOULED OUT (LP) . . . 22
68 Verve (S)VLP 9204 THE RIGHTEOUS BROTHERS STANDARDS (LP) . . . 18
68 Verve (S)VLP 9228 ONE FOR THE ROAD (LP) . . . 18
69 Verve (S)VLP 9240 GREATEST HITS VOLUME 2 (LP) . . . 18
70 Verve (S)VLP 9249 RE-BIRTH (LP) . . . 18
(see also Bill Medley, Bobby Hatfield)

MINT VALUE £

RIGHTEOUS FLAMES

67	Fab FAB 18	Gimme Some Sign Girl/Let's Go To The Dance (B-side act. by Prince Buster)	18
67	Fab FAB 30	When A Girl Loves A Boy	15
68	Coxsone CS 7061	You Don't Know/ROY RICHARDS & SOUL VENDORS: Summertime	20
71	High Note HS 052	Run To The Rock/GAYTONES: Run To The Rock Version	10
71	Nu Beat NB 083	Love And Emotion/Version	10

(see also Richus Flames, Alton Ellis, Flames, Soul Vendors)

RIGHTEOUS HOMES (FLAMES)

68	Coxsone CS 7049	I Was Born To Be Loved/NORMA FRAZER: Heartaches	25
68	Blue Cat BS 112	Seven Letters (actually by Winston Jarrett)/SOUL VENDORS: To Sir With Love	25

RIGHTEOUS SOULS

71	Supreme SUP 217	Mount Zion/ECCLE & NEVILL: All Over	10

RIGHTEOUS TWINS

69	Blue Cat BS 174	If I Could Hear My Master/Satan Can't Prevail	20

RIGOR MORTIS

73	Track 2094 107	Made In Japan/Hound Dog	7
73	Track 2406 106	RIGOR MORTIS SETS IN (LP)	12

(see John Entwistle, Who)

RIKKI & CUFFLINKS

79	Different HAVE 17	Nervous Breakdown/Steamin' On	5

RIKKI & THE LAST DAYS OF EARTH

77	(own label)	Oundle 29/5/77 (1-sided)	25
77	DJM DJS 10814	City Of The Damned/Victimized (p/s)	10
77	DJM DJF 20526	FOUR MINUTE WARNING (LP)	12

BILLY LEE RILEY

65	King KG 1015	I've Been Searchin'/Everybody's Twistin'	15
69	Stax STAX 120	Going Back To Memphis/Family Portrait	15
72	CBS 8182	I Got A Thing About You Baby/You Don't Love Me	6

(see also Megatons)

BOB RILEY

58	MGM MGM 977	The Midnight Line/Wanda Jean	60
58	MGM MGM 977	The Midnight Line/Wanda Jean (78)	25

DESMOND RILEY

69	Downtown DT 432	Tear Them/GEORGE LEE & RUDIES: Chaka Ground	15
69	Downtown DT 435	Tears On My Pillow/RUDIES: Man Pon Spot	10
69	Downtown DT 436	If I Had Wings/AUDREY: You'll Lose A Good Thing	10
69	Downtown DT 438	Out Your Fire/No Return	12
69	Downtown DT 450	Skinhead, A Message To You/MUSIC DOCTORS: Going Strong	25
69	Downtown DT 454	If I Had Wings/AUDREY: You'll Lose A Good Thing (reissue)	6

HOWARD RILEY (TRIO)

68	Opportunity CP 2499	DISCUSSIONS (LP with insert, as Howard Riley Trio)	1,000+
69	CBS 52669	ANGLE (LP)	20
70	CBS 64077	THE DAY WILL COME (LP)	40
71	Turtle TUR 301	FLIGHT (LP, gatefold sleeve)	100
76	Incus INCUS 13	SYNOPSIS (LP, as Howard Riley Trio with Tony Oxley & Barry Guy)	100
79	Spotlite	THE OTHER SIDE (LP)	12

(see also Colosseum, Karyobin)

JEANNIE C. RILEY

68	Polydor 56748	Harper Valley P.T.A./Yesterday All Day Long Today	6
68	Polydor 56756	The Girl Most Likely/My Scrapbook	6
69	Polydor 56782	Things Go Better With Love/Back Side Of Dallas	5
69	Polydor 583 716	HARPER VALLEY P.T.A. (LP)	15
69	Polydor 583 733	YEARBOOKS AND YESTERDAYS (LP)	15
70	Polydor 583 753	THINGS GO BETTER WITH LOVE (LP)	15

JIMI/JIMMY RILEY

71	Supreme SUP 217	Mount Zion (actually by Jimi Riley & Stranger Cole)/ ECCLE & NEVIL: All Over	7
75	Dip DL 5067	Ram Goat Liver/OMAR & MARSHA PERRY: Ram Goat Dub	7

(see also Martin Riley, Sensations, Uniques)

MARTIN RILEY

69	Gas GAS 114	Walking Proud/LLOYD CHARMERS: Why Baby	10
69	Punch PH 7	Trying To Be Free/I've Got It Bad	10
70	Camel CA 53	Catch This Sound/Suspense	10
70	Escort ES 823	It Grows (actually "It's Growing")/We Had A Good Thing Going	10
71	Camel CA 77	When Will We Be Paid/WILLIE FRANCIS: He's Got The Whole World In His Hands	10

(see also Slim Smith, Slickers)

TERRY RILEY

71	CBS 64259	CHURCH OF ANTHRAX (LP, with John Cale)	15
71	CBS 64564	A RAINBOW IN CURVED AIR (LP)	15
71	CBS 64565	IN "C" (LP)	12
72	Shandar 83501/2	PERSIAN SURGERY DERVISHES (2-LP)	18

(see also John Cale)

WINSTON RILEY

73	Techniques TE 922	Woman Don't You Go Astray/Travelling Man	6

(see also Techniques)

MINT VALUE £

RILEY'S ALLSTARS
71 Banana BA 343 — Glory Of Love (actually "Mystic Blue" by Hugh Hendricks & Buccaneers)/ We'll Cry Together — Version 10
(see also Bobby Davis, Techniques)

SHANE RIMMER
59 Columbia DB 4293 — (Roll Along) Wagon Train/A Touch Of Pink 8
59 Columbia DB 4343 — The Three Bells (Jimmy Brown Song) (as Shane Rimmer & Spinners)/ I Want To Walk You Home 8

RINGS
77 Chiswick S 14 — I Wanna Be Free/Automobile (p/s) 10
(see also Maniacs, Twink)

RINGS & THINGS
68 Fontana TF 987 — Strange Things Are Happening/To Me: To Me: To Me 80

RINKY DINKS
58 London HLE 8679 — Early In The Morning/Now We're One (as Rinky-Dinks featuring Bobby Darin) 40
58 London HLE 8679 — Early In The Morning/Now We're One (78) 40
59 London HLE 8793 — Mighty Mighty Man/You're Mine (as Bobby Darin with Rinky Dinks) 30
59 London HLE 8793 — Mighty Mighty Man/You're Mine (78) 50
(see also Bobby Darin)

RINKY DINKS
59 Capitol CL 14999 — Catch A Little Moonbeam/Choo Choo Cha Cha 10

BOBBY RIO (U.S.)
63 Stateside SS 211 — Don Diddley/I Got You 18

BOBBY RIO (& REVELLES)
65 Pye 7N 15790 — Boy Meets Girl/Don't Break My Heart And Run Away 45
65 Pye 7N 15897 — Everything In The Garden/When Love Was Young 45
65 Pye 7N 15958 — Value For Love/I'm Not Made Of Clay 40
66 Piccadilly 7N 35303 — Ask The Lonely/Be Lonely Little Girl (solo) 12
66 Piccadilly 7N 35337 — Angelica/Lovin' You (solo) 12

RIO GRANDE
71 RCA SF 8208 — RIO GRANDE (LP) 15

RIO GRANDES
66 Pyramid PYR 6001 — Soldiers Take Over/Moses 15

RIOT
81 Elektra K 12565 — Outlaw (Remix)/Rock City (p/s) 6
81 Elektra K 12565T — Outlaw (Remix)/Rock City (12", p/s) 8
77 Ariola ARL 5007 — ROCK CITY (LP) 12
78 Capitol E-ST 12081 — NARITA (LP) 12

RIOT CLONE
82 Riot Clone RC 001 — THERE'S NO GOVERNMENT LIKE NO GOVERNMENT (EP) 5
82 Riot Clone RC 002 — DESTROY THE MYTH OF MUSICAL DESTRUCTION (EP) 5
84 Riot Clone RCR 004 — BLOOD ON YOUR HANDS (EP) 5

RIOTS
65 Island WI 176 — Telling Lies/Don't Leave Me (actually by Techniques) 30
65 Island WI 195 — You Don't Know (actually by Techniques)/DON DRUMMOND & DRUMBAGO: Treasure Island 30
65 Island WI 197 — I Am In Love/When You're Wrong (actually by Techniques) 30
65 Island WI 247 — Yeah Yeah/BABA BROOKS: Virginia Ska 30
(see also Techniques)

RIOT SQUAD
65 Pye 7N 15752 — Any Time/Jump 35
65 Pye 7N 15817 — I Wanna Talk About My Baby/Gonna Make You Mine 45
65 Pye 7N 15869 — Nevertheless/Not A Great Talker 40
66 Pye 7N 17041 — Cry Cry Cry/How Is It Done 45
66 Pye 7N 17092 — I Take It We're Through/Working Man 45
66 Pye 7N 17130 — It's Never Too Late To Forgive/Try To Realise 45
67 Pye 7N 17237 — Gotta Be A First Time/Bitter Sweet Love 50
(see also Graham Bonney, Jimi Hendrix Experience, Blue Aces)

RIOT SQUAD
82 The THE 001 — Total Onslaught (p/s) 7

RIOT SQUAD
82 Rondelet ROUND 23 — Fuck The Tories/Civil Destruction (p/s) 6
82 Rondelet ROUND 25 — Riot In The City/Religion (p/s) 5
83 Rot ASS 1 — DON'T BE DENIED (EP) 6
83 Rot ASS 2 — I'm OK Fuck You/In The Future/Friday Night (p/s) 6
84 Rot ASS 3 — THERE AIN'T NO SOLUTION (EP) 6
84 Rot ASS 13 — NO POTENTIAL THREAT (LP, with free single [ASS3], stickered sleeve) 12

RIP CHORDS
63 CBS AAG 143 — Here I Stand/Karen 12
63 CBS AAG 162 — Gone/She Thinks I Still Care 15
64 CBS AAG 181 — Hey Little Cobra/The Queen 22
64 CBS AAG 202 — Three Window Coupe/Hot Rod USA 25
64 CBS BPG 62228 — HEY LITTLE COBRA (LP) 75
(see also Terry Day, Terry Melcher, Bruce Johnston)

RIP CHORDS
78 Cells SELL 1 — Ringing In The Streets/Music's Peace Artist/Television Television (p/s) 18

RIPCORD
89 private pressing — HARVEST HARDCORE (EP, foldout sleeve) 8

MINT VALUE £

RIPLEY WAYFARERS
71 Tradition TSR 006 — CHIPS AND BROWN SAUCE (LP) 15
72 Tradition TSR 013 — FIVE WELLS (LP) 18
74 Tradition TSR 018 — GENTLEMEN OF HIGH RENOWN (LP) 15
78 MWM MWM 1017 — SONG AND DANCE TUNES (LP, as The Wayfarers) 15
85 Singabout SIN 001 — DOWN THE ROAD (LP) 15

RIP 'N' LAW
71 Crab CRAB 64 — In The Ghetto/Something Sweet 6

RIPPERS
68 Saga — HONESTLY (LP) 30

RIP SNORTER
79 Pye 7N 46159 — Standing In A Little 'Ole/Confidentially (p/s) 8

RISING MOON
74 Theatre Projects — RISING MOON (LP) 30

RISING SONS (U.K.)
68 Pye 7N 17554 — Hold Me Just A Little While Longer/Fountain Of Love 6

RISING SONS (U.S.)
65 Stateside SS 426 — You're My Girl/Try To Be A Man 18

RITA
69 Major Minor MM 653 — Erotica/Sexologie 35

RITA (Alston)
69 Jackpot JP 718 — Love Making/NAT COLE: My Love 7
(see also Rita Alston)

LES RITA MITSOUKO
89 Virgin VSCD 1163 — Singing In The Shower (with Sparks)/Smog/Hip Kit (3" CD) 10
(see also Sparks)

RITA & TIARAS
79 Destiny DS 1002 — Gone With The Wind Is My Love/Wild Times (p/s) 8

JEAN RITCHIE
53 Argo ARS 1009 — SONGS FROM KENTUCKY (10" LP) 20

TEX RITTER
54 Capitol CL 14175 — Is There A Santa Claus?/Old Tex Kringle 15
55 Capitol CL 14277 — A Whale Of A Tale/High On A Mountain Top 15
55 Capitol CL 14335 — Marshal Of Wichita/September Song 15
56 Capitol Junior CJ 144 — Animal Fair/I Was Born A Hundred Years Ago (78, p/s) 7
56 Capitol CL 14536 — The Last Frontier/These Hands 8
56 Capitol CL 14581 — The Wayward Wind/Gunsmoke 12
56 Capitol CL 14605 — The Searchers (Ride Away)/Remember The Alamo 10
56 Capitol CL 14660 — The Last Wagon/Paul Bunyan Love 8
57 Capitol CL 14684 — Green Grow The Lilacs/The Touch Of The Master's Hand 6
57 Capitol CL 14715 — Children And Fools/I Leaned On A Man 6
57 Capitol CL 14805 — Here Was A Man/It Came Upon The Midnight Clear 6
58 Capitol CL 14900 — Jealous Heart/Burning Sand 6
58 Capitol CL 14933 — I Look For A Love/The History Song 5
59 Capitol CL 15041 — Rye Whisky/Conversation With A Gun 5
60 Capitol EAP1-1323 — DECK OF CARDS (EP) 15
52 Capitol LC 6552 — COWBOY FAVOURITES (10" LP) 25
59 Capitol T 1100 — PSALMS (LP) 12
60 Capitol (S)T 1292 — BLOOD ON THE SADDLE (LP) 20

BOB RITTERBUSH
59 Top Rank JAR 118 — I Wish That You Were Mine/Darling Corey 7
59 Top Rank JAR 118 — I Wish That You Were Mine/Darling Corey (78) 6

RIVALS
78 Sound On Sound SOS 100 — Skateboarding In The UK/Top Of The Pops 12

RIVALS
80 Ace ACE 007 — Future Rights/Flowers (p/s) 20
80 Oakwood/Ace ACE 011 — Here Comes The Night/Both Sides (p/s) 20

HECTOR RIVERA
67 Polydor 65728 — At The Party/Do It To Me 65

ROYD RIVERS & CLIFF AUNGIER
65 Decca LK 4696 — WANDERIN' (LP) 30
(see also Cliff Aungier)

CLIFF RIVERS
63 London HLU 9739 — True Lips/Marsha 40
(pseudonym for Joey Castle)

DANNY RIVERS
60 Top Rank JAR 408 — Hawk/I Got 30
60 Decca F 11294 — Can't You Hear My Heart/I'm Waiting For Tomorrow 22
61 Decca F 11357 — Once Upon A Time/My Baby's Gone Away (with Alexander Combo) 35
64 Decca F 11865 — There Will Never Be Anyone Else/I Don't Think You Know How I Feel 15
62 HMV POP 1000 — We're Gonna Dance/Movin' In (as Danny Rivers & River Men) 45

DEKE RIVERS
62 Oriole CB 1735 — One Kiss/Outsider 18
81 Chiswick NS 71 — Elvis Presley Medley/ELVIS PRESLEY:
Press Conference Vancouver 1957 (picture disc) 6

MINT VALUE £

JOHNNY RIVERS

62	Pye International 7N 25118	Blue Skies/That Someone Should Be Me	10
64	Liberty LIB 66032	Memphis/It Wouldn't Happen With Me	10
64	Liberty LIB 66056	Maybellene/Walk Myself On Home	8
64	Liberty LIB 66075	Mountain Of Love/Moody Love	8
64	Liberty LIB 66087	Midnight Special/Cupid	8
65	Liberty LIB 66112	Seventh Son/Un-Square Dance	8
65	Liberty LIB 12021	He Don't Love You Like I Love You/Where Have All The Flowers Gone	6
66	Liberty LIB 66144	Under Your Spell Again/Long Time Man	6
66	Liberty LIB 12023	Secret Agent Man/Tom Dooley	12
66	Liberty LIB 66175	I Washed My Hands In Muddy Water/Roogalator	10
66	Liberty LIB 66205	The Poor Side Of Town/Baby She's Mine	12
67	Liberty LIB 66227	Baby I Need Your Lovin'/Getting Ready For Tomorrow	7
67	Liberty LIB 66244	The Tracks Of My Tears/Rosecrans Blvd.	8
68	Liberty LBF 15041	Summer Rain/Memory Of The Coming Good	7
68	Liberty LBF 15078	Look To Your Soul/Something Strange	6
68	Liberty LBF 15163	Right Relations/Better Life	6
69	Liberty LBF 15239	John Lee Hooker (Parts 1 & 2)	6
69	Liberty LBF 15241	Muddy River/Resurrection	6
70	Liberty LBF 15364	Into The Mystic/Jesus Is A Soul Man	6
74	Atlantic K 10469	Six Days On The Road/Artists And Poets	7
75	Atlantic K 10544	Sitting In Limbo/Geronimo's Cadillac	6
75	Epic EPC 3482	Help Me Rhonda/New Lovers And New Friends	6
66	Liberty LEP 4049	MORE JOHNNY RIVERS (EP)	25
64	Liberty LBY 3031	AT THE WHISKY A GO-GO (LP)	25
65	Liberty LBY 3036	HERE WE A GO-GO AGAIN (LP)	22
65	Liberty LBY 3056	MEANWHILE BACK AT THE WHISKY A GO-GO (LP)	22
66	Liberty LBY 3064	RIVERS ROCKS THE FOLK (LP)	22
67	Liberty (S)LBY 3087	CHANGES (LP)	18
67	Liberty LBL/LBS 83040	REWIND (LP)	18
68	Liberty LBL/LBS 83118	REALIZATION (LP)	15
69	Liberty LBS 83141	A TOUCH OF GOLD (LP)	15
70	Liberty LBS 83383	SLIM SLO RIDER (LP)	15
72	United Artists UAS 29253	HOME GROWN (LP)	12
75	Epic EPC 80987	HELP ME RHONDA (LP)	15

MAVIS RIVERS

60	Capitol CL 15120	So Rare/Longing, Longing, Longing	6
63	Reprise RS 20115	Slightly Out Of Tune/Footsteps Of A Fool	5

TONY RIVERS & THE CASTAWAYS

63	Columbia DB 7135	Shake Shake Shake/Row Row Row	18
64	Columbia DB 7224	I Love The Way You Walk/I Love You	12
64	Columbia DB 7336	Life's Too Short/Tell On Me	12
65	Columbia DB 7448	She/Till We Get Home	12
65	Columbia DB 7536	Come Back/What To Do	12
66	Columbia DB 7971	God Only Knows/Charade	15
66	Parlophone R 5400	Nowhere Man/The Girl From New York City	10
66	Immediate IM 027	Girl Don't Tell Me/The Girl From Salt Lake City	25
68	Polydor 56245	I Can Guarantee Your Love/Pantomime	7

(see also Capability Brown, Grapefruit, Harmony Grass, Senators, Sugarbeats)

RIVIERA

69	Pye 7N 17712	Baby Won't Leave Me Alone/The Love Story	5

RIVIERAS

60	HMV POP 773	Blessing Of Love/Moonlight Cocktails	100

RIVIERAS

64	Pye International 7N 25237	California Sun/H B Goose Step	35

RIVINGTON PIKE

72	Decca F 13329	Wish A Little Love/I'll Be There	5

RIVINGTONS

62	Liberty LIB 55427	Papa Oom Mow Mow/Deep Water	30
63	Liberty LIB 55553	The Bird's The Word/I'm Losing My Grip	40
66	CBS 202088	Rose Growing In The Ruins/Tend To Business	45

RIVVITS

79	Alien AUX 1	Saturday Night At The Dance/Girl Next Door (p/s, with flexi)	10

FREDDIE ROACH

67	Transatlantic PR 7490	THE SOUL BOOK (LP)	12

MAX ROACH (& CLIFFORD BROWN GROUP)

55	Vogue EPV 1074	MAX ROACH AND CLIFFORD BROWN (EP)	8
55	Vogue EPV 1083	MAX ROACH AND CLIFFORD BROWN (EP)	8
55	Vogue EPV 1091	MAX ROACH AND CLIFFORD BROWN (EP)	8
58	Emarcy ERE 1572	MAX ROACH AND CLIFFORD BROWN (EP, withdrawn)	15
55	Vogue LDE 117	MAX ROACH & CLIFFORD BROWN IN CONCERT VOL. 1 (10" LP)	18
55	Vogue LDE 128	MAX ROACH & CLIFFORD BROWN IN CONCERT VOL. 2 (10" LP)	18
58	Emarcy EJL 1282	JAZZ IN THREE-QUARTER TIME (LP)	15
59	Emarcy MMB 12005	MAX ROACH, NEWPORT (LP, by Max Roach)	15
59	Emarcy MMB 12009	THE MAX ROACH FOUR PLUS FOUR (LP, by Max Roach)	15
60	Mercury MMC 14041	I REMEMBER CLIFFORD (LP)	12
60	Mercury MMC 14054	QUIET AS IT'S KEPT (LP, by Max Roach)	12

(see also Clifford Brown, Buddy Rich)

ROAD

73	Rare Earth SRE 3006	ROAD (LP)	15

MINT VALUE £

ROADHOUSE

92	Vertigo VERP 57	Hell Can Wait/Loving You/Jackson High/More Than I Want (12", picture disc)	10

ROADRUNNERS

65	Cavern Sound 2BSNL 7	PANTOMANIA (EP, with tracks by Chris Edwards & Clive Wood)	35

ROADSTER

81	Mayhem SRTS 81	Fantasy/45 MPH (p/s)	100

ROADSTERS

64	Stateside SS 293	Joy Ride/Drag	25

ROARING SIXTIES

66	Marmalade 598 001	We Love The Pirates/I'm Leaving Town	45

(see also Family)

ROBAN'S SKIFFLE GROUP

61	Storyville A45 062	Careless Love/Frankie And Johnny (some with p/s)	35/18

E.G. ROBB

63	Columbia DB 7100	Stage To Cimarron/Jezebel	15

MARTY ROBBINS

78s

56	Philips PB 590	Long Tall Sally/Mr. Teardrop	25
57	Philips PB 696	A White Sport Coat (And A Pink Carnation)/Grown-Up Tears	25
57	Philips PB 741	Please Don't Blame Me/Teen-Age Dream	25
58	Fontana H 102	The Story Of My Life/Once-A-Week Date	20
58	Fontana H 128	Stairway Of Love/Just Married	25
58	Fontana H 150	Sittin' In A Tree House/She Was Only Seventeen	35
59	Fontana H 184	The Hanging Tree (from film)/The Blues Country Style	40
59	Fontana H 212	Cap And Gown/Last Night About This Time	40
59	Fontana H 229	Big Iron/Cool Water	50
59	Fontana H 233	El Paso/Running Gun	60

45s

57	Philips JK 1019	A White Sport Coat (And A Pink Carnation)/Grown-Up Tears (jukebox issue)	50
58	Fontana H 128	Stairway Of Love/Just Married	25
58	Fontana H 150	Sittin' In A Tree House/She Was Only Seventeen	18
59	Fontana H 184	The Hanging Tree (from film)/The Blues Country Style	12
59	Fontana H 212	Cap And Gown/Last Night About This Time	10
59	Fontana H 229	Big Iron/Cool Water	10
59	Fontana H 233	El Paso/Running Gun	6
60	Fontana H 263	I Told My Heart/Is There Any Chance	6
60	Fontana H 270	Ballad Of The Alamo/Five Brothers (some in p/s)	12/6
61	Fontana H 301	Don't Worry/Like All Other Times	6
61	Fontana H 324	Ghost Train/Jimmy Martinez	6
61	Fontana H 342	It's Your World/You Told Me So	6
62	CBS AAG 114	Devil Woman/April Fool's Day	7
63	CBS AAG 128	Ruby Ann/Won't You Forgive	8
63	CBS AAG 141	Cigarette And Coffee Blues/Teenager's Dad	10
63	CBS AAG 151	No Signs Of Loneliness Here/I'm Not Ready Yet	6
63	CBS AAG 164	Not So Long Ago/I Hope You Learn A Lot	5
65	CBS 201729	Whole Lot Easier/I Eish Tay Mah Su	5
65	CBS 201789	Ribbon Of Darkness/Little Robin	5
65	CBS 202012	While You're Dancing/Lonely Too	5
67	CBS 2955	Tonight Carmen/No Tears Milady	6
68	CBS 3585	Love Is In The Air/I've Been Leaving Every Day	5
68	CBS 3828	I Walk Alone/Lily Of The Valley	5

EPs

59	Fontana TFE 17161	MARTY'S BIG HITS	40
59	Fontana TFE 17168	WEDDING BELLS	15
60	Fontana TFE 17167	SONG OF THE ISLANDS	15
61	Fontana TFE 17224	GUNFIGHTER	15
61	CBS AGG 20004	JUST A LITTLE SENTIMENTAL	12
61	CBS AGG 20013	JUST A LITTLE SENTIMENTAL VOL. 2	12
66	CBS AGG 20049	MARTY ROBBINS	12

LPs

59	Fontana TFL 5063	GUNFIGHTER BALLADS AND TRAIL SONGS	35
60	Fontana TFL 5086	MARTY'S GREATEST HITS	18
61	Fontana TFL 5113	MORE GUNFIGHTER BALLADS AND TRAIL SONGS (stereo STFL 541)	30/35
61	Fontana TFL 5145	MORE GREATEST HITS (also stereo STFL 565)	18/25
61	Fontana TFL 5162	JUST A LITTLE SENTIMENTAL (with Jordanaires, also stereo STFL 579)	22/30
62	CBS (S)BPG 62041	MARTY AFTER MIDNIGHT	22
63	CBS (S)BPG 62113	DEVIL WOMAN (mono/stereo)	15/18
63	CBS BPG 62131	PORTRAIT OF MARTY (mono/stereo)	15/18
63	CBS (S)BPG 62169	HAWAII'S CALLING ME (mono/stereo)	15/18
64	CBS (S)BPG 62190	THE RETURN OF THE GUNFIGHTER (mono/stereo)	15/18
64	CBS (S)BPG 62297	ISLAND WOMAN (mono/stereo)	15/18
65	CBS (S)BPG 62437	R.F.D. (mono/stereo)	15/18
65	CBS (S)BPG 62499	TURN THE LIGHTS DOWN LOW	15
65	CBS (S)BPG 62359	GUNFIGHTER BALLADS AND TRAIL SONGS (reissue, mono/stereo)	12/15
66	CBS (S)BPG 62070	MORE GUNFIGHTER BALLADS AND TRAIL SONGS (reissue, m/s)	12/15
66	CBS (S)BPG 62075	MORE GREATEST HITS (reissue)	12
66	CBS (S)BPG 62689	WHAT GOD HAS DONE	15
66	CBS (S)BPG 62782	THE DRIFTER	20
67	CBS (S)BPG 62962	MY KIND OF COUNTRY	15
67	CBS (S)BPG 63116	TONIGHT CARMEN	15
68	CBS 63295	BY THE TIME I GET TO PHOENIX (mono/stereo)	12

MINT VALUE £

68 CBS 63354 — CHRISTMAS WITH MARTY ROBBINS (mono/stereo) . . . 18
69 CBS 63431 — I WALK ALONE (mono/stereo) . . . 12
70 CBS 64066 — MY WOMAN, MY WOMAN, MY WIFE . . . 15
72 CBS 64810 — TODAY . . . 12
(see also Jordanaires)

MEL ROBBINS
59 London HLM 8966 — Save It/To Know You (initially triangular centre, later round centre) . . . 600/320
59 London HLM 8966 — Save It/To Know You (78) . . . 150

SYLVIA ROBBINS
60 London HLJ 9118 — Frankie And Johnny/Come Home . . . 30
(see also Mickey & Sylvia)

ROBERT & REMOULDS
79 Black & White BW 1 — X No. 1/Do Eyes Ever Meet? (p/s) . . . 35

ANDY ROBERTS
73 Elektra K 12109 — Baby Baby/All Around My Grandmother's Floor . . . 5
70 RCA SF 8086 — HOME GROWN (LP) . . . 18
71 Charisma CAS 1034 — HOME GROWN (LP, reissue, different sleeve) . . . 12
71 B&C — HOME GROWN (LP, reissue) . . . 12
71 Pegasus PEG 5 — NINA AND THE DREAM TREE (LP) . . . 18
73 Elektra K 42139 — URBAN COWBOY (LP, with insert) . . . 12
73 Elektra K 42151 — ANDY ROBERTS AND THE GREAT STAMPEDE (LP, gatefold sleeve) . . . 12
(see also Clayton Squares, Liverpool Scene, Everyone, Plainsong)

ALAN ROBERTS
70s Plant Life PLR 012 — CALEDONIA (LP, with Dougie Maclean) . . . 12
(see also Dougie MacLean)

BOB ROBERTS
70 Explosion EX 2021 — Stick By Me/TOMMY McCOOK: The Designer . . . 7

BOB ROBERTS (U.K.)
81 Solent SS 054 — BREEZE FOR A BARGEMAN (LP) . . . 15

HUGH ROBERTS
70 Explosion EX 2041 — California Dreaming/One Woman (both sides actually by Lloyd Charmers) . . . 6

J. ROBERTS
70 Bamboo BAM 30 — Someday We'll Be Together/SOUND DIMENSION: Everyday People . . . 10

JOHN ROBERTS
68 Sue WI 4042 — Sockin' 1, 2, 3, 4/Sophisticated Funk . . . 25
68 Action ACT 4511 — I'll Forget You/Be My Baby . . . 18

KEITH ROBERTS
72 Trailer LER 3031 — PIER OF THE REALM (LP) . . . 20

KENNY ROBERTS
57 Brunswick 05638 — I'm Looking For The Bully Of The Town/Broken Teenage Heart . . . 12

KENNY ROBERTS
65 Pye 7N 15882 — Say, Do You Mean It/Since My Love Has Gone . . . 10
66 Pye 7N 17054 — Run Like The Devil/Where Goes My Heart . . . 30
(see also Kenny Damon)

KIM ROBERT
64 Decca F 11813 — I'll Prove It/For Loving Me This Way . . . 85

RENEE ROBERTS
62 Oriole CB 1731 — I Want To Love You/Aching Heart . . . 6

RICK ROBERTS
72 A&M AMLH 64372 — WINDMILLS (LP) . . . 12
(see also Flying Burrito Brothers)

ROCKY ROBERTS
67 Durium DRL 50026 — SABATO SERA (LP) . . . 45

DALE ROBERTSON
60 RCA SF 5064 — PRESENTS HIS ALBUM OF WESTERN CLASSICS (LP) . . . 20

DON ROBERTSON
50 London L 629 — Gamblin' Fever/On The Hudson Bay Line (78, with Lou) . . . 10
56 Capitol CL 14575 — The Happy Whistler/You're Free To Go (B-side with Lou Dinning) . . . 8
56 Capitol CL 14629 — Every Day That I Live (with Lou Dinning)/You . . . 6
59 Capitol CL 15088 — Fine Day/The Merry Men . . . 6
59 Capitol CL 15088 — Fine Day/The Merry Men (78) . . . 10

JEANNIE ROBERTSON
59 Topic 10T 52 — I KEN WHERE I'M GOING (10" LP) . . . 18
59 Topic 12T 96 — JEANNIE ROBERTSON (LP, blue label, with card insert) . . . 15
60 Collector JFS 4001 — LORD DONALD (LP) . . . 15

JIM ROBERTSON
55 MGM SPC 7 — Pride Of My Heart/Walkin' And Talkin' With The Lord (export issue) . . . 15

PAUL ROBESON
52 HMV 7P 113 — Ol' Man River/I Suits Me . . . 10
57 HMV DLP 1155 — THE INCOMPARABLE VOICE OF PAUL ROBESON (10" LP) . . . 12
57 HMV DLP 1165 — EMPEROR OF SONG (10" LP) . . . 12

DAVE ROBIN
65 Eyemark EMS 1003 — You I Don't Want To Share/Life's Too Short . . . 6

MINT VALUE £

EDE ROBIN
75 Crystal CR 7023 There Must Be A Love Somewhere/Soul Over Easy . . . 10

RICHIE ROBIN
60 Top Rank JAR 262 Strange Dream/GERRY GRANAHAN: It Hurts . . . 15

TINA ROBIN
57 Vogue Coral Q 72284 Over Somebody Else's Shoulder/Lady Fair . . . 20
57 Vogue Coral Q 72284 Over Somebody Else's Shoulder/Lady Fair (78) . . . 12
57 Vogue Coral Q 72294 Never In A Million Years/Ça C'est L'Amour . . . 15
57 Vogue Coral Q 72294 Never In A Million Years/Ça C'est L'Amour (78) . . . 10
58 Coral Q 72309 Everyday/Believe Me . . . 18
58 Coral Q 72309 Everyday/Believe Me (78) . . . 12
58 Coral Q 72323 No School Tomorrow/Sugar Blues . . . 18
58 Coral Q 72323 No School Tomorrow/Sugar Blues (78) . . . 15
62 Mercury AMT 1199 Get Out Of My Life/Why Did You Go . . . 8

ROBIN HOODS
65 Mercury MF 865 Wait For The Dawn/Love You So . . . 6

ROBINS
60 Vogue V 9168 Cherry Lips/Out Of The Picture . . . 160
60 Vogue V 9173 Just Like That/Whole Lot Imagination . . . 120
(see also H.B. Barnum)

JIMMY ROBINS
68 President PT 118 I Can't Please You/I Made It Over . . . 70

ALVIN ROBINSON
64 Pye International 7N 25248 Something You Got/Searchin' . . . 20
64 Red Bird RB 10010 Down Home Girl/Fever . . . 20
66 Strike JH 307 You Brought My Heart Right Down To My Knees/Whatever You Had . . . 18

BROTHER CLEOPHUS ROBINSON
57 Vogue EPV 1196 BROTHER CLEOPHUS ROBINSON (EP) . . . 25

EDDIE ROBINSON
71 Ember EMB S 301 Hey Blackman Parts 1 & 2 . . . 5
70s Myrrh MYR 1013 REFLECTIONS OF THE MAN INSIDE (LP) . . . 15

ELZADIE ROBINSON
50 Tempo R 33 The Santa Claus Crave/St. Louis Cyclone Blues (78) . . . 10
50 Tempo R 36 Arkansas Mill Blues/Gold Mansion Blues (78, with Will Ezell) . . . 10
50 Tempo R 37 Rowdy Man Blues/Going South Blues (78) . . . 10
(see also Will Ezell)

FLOYD ROBINSON
59 RCA RCA 1146 Makin' Love/My Girl (initially with triangular centre, later round) . . . 12/6
59 RCA RCA 1146 Makin' Love/My Girl (78) . . . 10
60 RCA RCA 1179 I Believe In Love/Tattletale . . . 7
60 RCA RD 27166 FLOYD ROBINSON (LP) . . . 60

FREDDY ROBINSON
72 Stax 2325 085 AT THE DRIVE-IN (LP) . . . 18

HARRY ROBINSON
60 Top Rank JAR 325 The Skirl/Wimoweh (as Harry Robinson "String Sound") . . . 7
61 Decca F 11319 Heavy Date/Sentimental Journey (as Harry Robinson's XV) . . . 6
(see also Lord Rockingham's XI)

JACKEY ROBINSON
70 Punch PH 50 Heart Made Of Stone (actually by Jackie Bernard)/BOB TAYLOR: I May Never See My Baby Anymore . . . 30
(see also Jackie Robinson, Pioneers)

JACKIE ROBINSON
68 Amalgamated AMG 819 Over And Over/Woman Of Samaria . . . 20
68 Amalgamated AMG 824 Let The Little Girl Dance/DERRICK MORGAN: I Want To Go Home . . . 20
74 Harry J. HJ 6695 My Love For You/R.D. Livingstone: Smokey Mountains . . . 8

JIM ROBINSON NEW ORLEANS BAND
61 Riverside RLP 369 NEW ORLEANS: THE LIVING LEGENDS (LP) . . . 15
64 Riverside RLP 393 PLAYS SPIRITUAL AND BLUES (LP) . . . 15

J.P. ROBINSON
72 Atlantic K 10149 George Jackson/Wall To Wall Love . . . 6
72 Atlantic K 10209 What Can I Tell Her/Please Accept My Call . . . 5

JUNE ROBINSON
56 Oriole CB 1319 45 Men In A Telephone Box/Oo-Shoo-Be-Doo-Be (78) . . . 10

LLOYD ROBINSON
62 Blue Beat BB 122 Give Me A Chance/When You Walk . . . 25
63 Blue Beat BB 159 I Need Your Love/You Told Me . . . 25
69 Duke DU 5 Cuss Cuss/Lavender Blue . . . 22
70 Camel CA 41 The Worm/NEVILLE HYNES: Afro (actually by Neville Hinds) . . . 12
72 Green Door GD 4028 I Can't Forget/LLOYD AND THE NOW GENERATION: I Can't Forget – Version . . . 6
(see also Lloyd Clarke, Lloyd Charmers, Harry J. Allstars, Matadors, Melodians)

M. ROBINSON
64 Port-O-Jam PJ 4114 Who Are You/Follow You . . . 20

ROSCO ROBINSON
66 Pye International 7N 25385 That's Enough/One More Time . . . 45
72 Wand WN 27 That's Enough/One More Time (reissue) . . . 10
73 Contempo C 16 We're Losing It Baby/We Got A Good Thing Going . . . 6

MINT VALUE £

SUGAR CHILE ROBINSON

50 Capitol CL 13393 Christmas Boogie/Rudolph The Red Nosed Reindeer (78) . . . 6
51 Capitol CL 13589 After School Blues/Caldonia (78) . . . 6
51 Capitol CL 13636 Green Grass/Baby Blues (78) . . . 6
52 Capitol CL 13796 Lazy Boy's Boogie/Whop Whop (78) . . . 8
53 Capitol LC 6586 CAPITOL PRESENTS SUGAR CHILE ROBINSON (10" LP) . . . 60

TOM ROBINSON (BAND)

75 Chebel SRT/CUS 015 GOOD TO BE GAY (EP, as Bradford Gay Liberation Front) . . . 15
79 EMI EMI 2946 All Right All Night/Black Angel (withdrawn, demo-only) . . . 8
(see also Cafe Society, Phantom, Billy Karloff [& Extremes])

ROBINSON CREW

63 Decca F 11706 Taxi (Theme From TV Series)/Stormalong . . . 8
(see also Lord Rockingham's XI)

CARSON ROBISON (& HIS PLEASANT VALLEY BOYS)

53 MGM SP 1004 Lady Round The Lady/Pokeberry Promenade . . . 10
53 MGM SP 1024 Square Dance Jitterbug/Keep On Circlin' 'Round . . . 15
58 MGM MGM-EP 669 LIFE GETS TEEJUS (EP) . . . 12
61 MGM MGM-EP 755 SQUARE DANCE — WITH CALLS (EP) . . . 10
52 MGM MGM-D 101 EIGHT SQUARE DANCES (10" LP) . . . 15

RALPH ROBLES

69 London HA/SH 8385 TAKING OVER (LP) . . . 20

ROBOTMAN & FRIENDS

86 Columbia DB 9126 I Wanna Be Your Robotman/Hi Tech Heart Touch (p/s) . . . 5

NICKY ROBSON

80 Scratch SCR 006 Stars/Eye To Eye (p/s) . . . 20
80 Scratch SCRT 006 Stars (Extended)/Eye To Eye (12") . . . 40
(see also Gary Numan)

ROCAMARS

65 King KG 1031 All In Black Woman/Give Me Time . . . 15

TONY ROCCO

62 Parlophone R 4886 Stalemate/Keep A Walking . . . 18
62 Parlophone R 4946 Torture/Competition . . . 12

HARRY ROCHE CONSTELLATION

67 CBS 202653 Casino Royale/In The Pad Of The Mountain King . . . 10
67 CBS SBPG 63013 CASINO ROYALE (LP) . . . 35
71 Studio Two TWO 340 SPINDRIFT (LP) . . . 20
73 Pye Intl. NSPL 41024 SPIRAL (LP) . . . 50
73 Pye QUAD 1022 SOMETIMES (LP, quadrophonic) . . . 25

ROCHEE & SARNOS

85 Nervous NERD 018 UNDERSTANDING SARNO (LP) . . . 12

JACKIE ROCHELLE

68 Olga OLE 011 Till The End/Grown Up Games . . . 5

ROCKABILLY PSYCHOSIS

84 Big Beat WIK 18 ROCKABILLY PSYCHOSIS AND THE GARAGE DISEASE (LP) . . . 15
89 Big Beat CDWIK 18 ROCKABILLY PSYCHOSIS AND THE GARAGE DISEASE (CD) . . . 18

DICKIE ROCK & MIAMI SHOWBAND

63 Piccadilly 7N 35154 Boys/There's Always Me . . . 6
64 Piccadilly 7N 35202 From The Candy Store/Twenty Flight Rock . . . 8
65 Pye 7N 15750 Round And Around/Little Baby . . . 5
65 Pye 7N 15855 Every Step Of The Way/Rock And Roll Music . . . 5
65 Pye 7N 17063 Come Back To Stay/Can't Make Up My Mind (p/s) . . . 12
65 Pye NEP 24251 COME BACK TO STAY (EP) . . . 15

ROCK AID ARMENIA

89 Life Aid Armenia ARMEN 01 Smoke On The Water/BLACK SABBATH: Paranoid (1970) (p/s) . . . 5
89 L. A. Armenia ARMEN T01 Smoke On The Water/BLACK SABBATH: Paranoid (1970) (12", blue or white p/s) . . . 8
89 Life Aid Armenia ARMENCD 01 Smoke On The Water (Radio Mix)/Smoke On The Water (Extended Mix)/ BLACK SABBATH: Paranoid (1970) (CD) . . . 10
90 L. A. Armenia ARMEN 002 Smoke On The Water '90 (Radio Edit)/BLACK SABBATH: Paranoid ('90) (p/s) . . . 5
(see also Brian May, Roger Taylor, Ritchie Blackmore, Dave Gilmour, Black Sabbath, Rush, Bruce Dickinson, Ian Gillan, Free, Firm, Yes, Keith Emerson, Eighth Wonder)

ROCK-A-TEENS

59 Columbia DB 4361 Woo-Hoo/Untrue . . . 40

ROCK BROTHERS

56 Parlophone MSP 6201 Dungaree Doll/Livin' It Up . . . 80
56 Parlophone R 4119 Dungaree Doll/Livin' It Up (78) . . . 35

ROCKERS

59 Oriole CB 1501 Get Cracking/Counter Melody . . . 20
59 Oriole CB 1501 Get Cracking/Counter Melody (78) . . . 6

ROCKERS

83 CBS A 3929 We Are The Boys (Who Make All The Noise)/Rockin' On Stage (p/s) . . . 8
83 CBS TA 3929 We Are The Boys (Who Make All The Noise) (Extended Version)/ Rockin' On Stage (12", p/s) . . . 12
(see also Phil Lynott, Roy Wood, Status Quo)

ROCKET 88

81 Atlantic K 50776 ROCKET 88 (LP) . . . 20
(see also Charlie Watts, Alexis Korner, Jack Bruce, Dick Heckstall-Smith)

MINT VALUE £

ROCKET FROM THE CRYPT

93 Southern Studios PUS 007 Glazed/Pressures/Cut It Loose (white label test pressing, 5-10 copies only) 30
95 Elemental ELM 32S Born in 69/Ciao Patsy (p/s) 5
96 Elemental ELM 33S Young Livers/Burning Army Men (p/s) 5
96 Dinked 1 Used/Lose Your Clown (in-store giveaway) 25
98 Elemental ELM 47PIC When In Rome/Tarzan/Tiger Feet Tonight (picture disc) 7
98 Elemental ELM 48S Lipstick/Hot Heart (p/s) 5
98 Elemental ELM 49S Break It Up/Turkish Revenge (p/s) 5
95 Elemental ELM 27LP HOT CHARITY (LP) 12

ROCKETS

60 Philips PB 982 Gibraltar Rock/Walkin' Home 20
60 Philips PB 982 Gibraltar Rock/Walkin' Home (78) 40
61 Zodiac ZR 0010 Warrior/Countdown 20

ROCKIN' BERRIES

63 Decca F 11698 Wah Wah Wah Woo/Rockin' Berry Stomp 25
63 Decca F 11760 Itty Bitty Pieces/The Twitch 20
64 Piccadilly 7N 35197 I Didn't Mean To Hurt You/You'd Better Come Home 6
64 Piccadilly 7N 35203 He's In Town/Flashback 5
64 Piccadilly 7N 35217 What In The World's Come Over You/You Don't Know What To Do 5
65 Piccadilly 7N 35236 Poor Man's Son/Follow Me 5
65 Piccadilly 7N 35254 You're My Girl/Brother Bill 7
65 Piccadilly 7N 35270 The Water Is Over My Head/Doesn't Time Fly 7
66 Piccadilly 7N 35304 I Could Make You Fall In Love/Land Of Love 6
66 Piccadilly 7N 35327 Midnight Mary/Money Grows On Trees 8
67 Piccadilly 7N 35373 Sometimes/Needs To Be 6
67 Piccadilly 7N 35400 Smile/Breakfast At Sam's 8
67 Pye 7N 17411 Dawn (Go Away)/She's Not Like Any Girl 8
68 Pye 7N 17519 When I Reach The Top/Pain 8
68 Pye 7N 17589 Mr. Blue/Land Of Love 6
73 Satril SAT 9 Day To Day/Big Louis' Birthday 5
74 Pye 7N 45394 Rock-A-Bye Nursery Rhyme/Long Time Ago 5
65 Piccadilly NEP 34039 I DIDN'T MEAN TO HURT YOU (EP) 35
65 Piccadilly NEP 34043 NEW FROM THE BERRIES (EP) 35
65 Piccadilly NEP 34045 HAPPY TO BE BLUE (EP) 50
64 Piccadilly NPL 38013 IN TOWN (LP) 80
65 Piccadilly NPL 38022 LIFE IS JUST A BOWL OF BERRIES (LP) 70
76 Satril SATL 4002 BLACK GOLD (LP) 12
(see also Jefferson)

ROCKIN' DUPSEE

70s Flyright FLY 592 ROCKIN' WITH DUPSEE (LP) 12

ROCKIN' FOO

70 Stateside SS 2168 Rochester River/Stranger In The Attic 6
70 Stateside SSL 10303 ROCKIN' FOO (LP) 20

ROCKIN' HENRI & HAYSEEDS

63 Decca F 11700 Sally/Sweet Adeline 8

ROCKIN' HORSE

71 Philips 6006 156 The Biggest Gossip In Town/You Say 12
72 Philips 6006 200 Julian The Hooligan/Stayed Out Late Last Night 12
70 Philips 6308 075 YES IT IS (LP) 30
(see also Jimmy Campbell, 23rd Turnoff, Kirkbys, Merseys)

ROCKING HORSE

71 Camel CA 75 Running Back Home/SOUL SYNDICATE BAND: Running Back — Version 6
72 Randy's RAN 522 Hard Time/Change Your Ways 6
73 Randy's RAN 535 I'm So Fed Up/I'm So Fed Up — Version 5
74 Pyramid PYR 7009 New Situation/New Version 5

ROCKIN' RAMRODS

66 Polydor BM 56512 Don't Fool With Fu Manchu/Tears Melt The Stone 18

ROCKIN' REBELS

63 Stateside SS 162 Wild Weekend/Wild Weekend Cha Cha 18
63 Stateside SS 187 Rockin' Crickets/Hully Gully Rock (both sides actually by Hot-Toddys) 18
(see also Hot-Toddys)

ROCKIN' R's

59 London HL 8872 The Beat/Crazy Baby 45
59 London HL 8872 The Beat/Crazy Baby (78) 25

ROCKIN' SAINTS

60 Brunswick 05843 Cheat On Me, Baby/Half And Half 110

ROCKIN' STRINGS

59 Columbia DB 4349 Red Sails In The Sunset/Autumn Leaves 7
(see also Eric Jupp)

ROCKIN' VICKERS

64 Decca F 11993 I Go Ape/Someone Like You (as Rocking Vickers) 30
66 CBS 202051 It's Alright/Stay By Me 50
66 CBS 202241 Dandy/I Don't Need Your Kind 40
(see also Sam Gopal, Motörhead)

ROCKITS

73 Mowest MW 3012 Livin' Without You/Love My Love 5

ROCK MACHINE

73 T.I.M. THEMES (LP) 50
(see also Ugly Custard)

MINT VALUE £

ROCK'N'ROLL REVIVAL SHOW
68 Decca F 12752 Midnight Train/Oh Boy (both sides featuring Tommy Bishop) 8
(see also Tommy Bishop's Ricochets)

ROCK-OLGA
60 Ember EMB S 105 Red Sails In The Sunset/My Dixieland Doll (some in p/s) 10/5

ROCKSTEADYS
67 Giant GN 2 Squeeze And Freeze/JUNIOR SMITH: I'm A Good Boy. 10

ROCKSTONES
70 Trojan TR 7762 A.B.C. Reggae/BEVERLEY'S ALLSTARS: Be Yours 6
70 Summit SUM 8501 Everything Is Beautiful/BEVERLEY'S ALLSTARS: Give Up 6
(see also Gaylads)

ROCK WORKSHOP
70 CBS 5046 You To Lose/Born In The City. 6
71 CBS 7252 Very Last Time/Light Is Light. 5
70 CBS 64075 ROCK WORKSHOP (LP, orange label). 30
71 CBS 64394 THE VERY LAST TIME (2-LP, orange label) 30
(see also Alex Harvey)

ROCKY & MUTATIONS
83 Cool Ghoul COOL 003 Thatcher Rap/Crisis! 5

ROCKY FELLERS
63 Stateside SS 175 Killer Joe/Lonely Treardrops 12
63 Stateside SS 212 Like The Big Guys Do/Great Big World 10
63 Pye International 7N 25225 Ching A Ling Baby/Hey Little Donkey 12

ROCKY HORROR SHOW
75 Ode ODS 66305 Science Fiction Double Feature/Time Warp 8
74 Ode ODE 77026 THE ROCKY HORROR SHOW (LP, original US Roxy cast). 15
75 UK UKAL 1015 THE ROCKY HORROR SHOW (LP, London cast) 15
75 Ode ODE 78332 THE ROCKY HORROR PICTURE SHOW ALBUM (LP, soundtrack). 15
83 Ode OSVP 78332 THE ROCKY HORROR PICTURE SHOW ALBUM (LP, soundtrack, picture disc) . . 20
86 Ode ODE 21653 THE ROCKY HORROR PICTURE SHOW ALBUM (LP, soundtrack, reissue). 12
87 Ode OSVP 21653 THE ROCKY HORROR PICTURE SHOW ALBUM (LP, soundtrack, reissue, picture disc) 20
87 Ode ODE 9009 THE ROCKY HORROR SHOW (LP, reissue of original U.S. cast, with inner sleeve). 15
87 Ode RHVX 1 ROCKY HORROR BOX SET (4-LP box, with inserts, numbered) 30
87 Ode RHBXLP 1 ROCKY HORROR BOX SET (4-LP box, with different inserts to above) 25
90 Ode RHBXCD 1 THE ROCKY HORROR PICTURE ALBUMS (15th ANNIVERSARY) (4-CD, with booklet) 45
(see also Meat Loaf, Original Soundtracks)

GENE RODDENBERRY
76 CBS 4692 Star Trek Theme/Star Trek Philosophy. 12

RODD-KEN & CAVALIERS
60 Triumph RGM 1001 Magic Wheel/Happy Valley 45
(see also Blue Men)

CLODA(GH) RODGERS
62 Decca F 11534 Believe Me I'm No Fool/End Of The Line. 8
63 Decca F 11607 Sometime Kind Of Love/I See More Of Him 8
63 Decca F 11667 To Give My Love To You/I Only Live To Love You 8
64 Decca F 11812 Mister Heartache/Time. 8
65 Columbia DB 7468 Wanting You/Johnny Come Home 8
66 Columbia DB 7926 Every Day Is Just The Same/You'll Come A Running 8
66 Columbia DB 8038 Stormy Weather/Lonely Room 8
68 RCA RCA 1684 Room Full Of Roses/Play The Drama To The End 7
68 RCA RCA 1748 Rhythm Of Love/River Of Tears. 6
69 RCA RCA 1792 Come Back And Shake Me/I Am A Fantasy 5
69 RCA RCA 1891 Biljo/Spider. 5
69 RCA SF 8033 CLODAGH RODGERS (LP). 18
69 RCA SF 8071 MIDNIGHT CLODAGH (LP). 18
71 RCA SF 8180 RODGERS AND HART (LP) 18
72 RCA SF 8271 IT'S DIFFERENT NOW (LP) 18
74 RCA SF 8394 YOU ARE MY MUSIC (LP) 18
77 Polydor 2383 473 SAVE ME (LP). 15

EILEEN RODGERS
58 Fontana H 136 Careful, Careful/I'm Alone Because I Love You. 12
58 Fontana H 136 Careful, Careful/I'm Alone Because I Love You (78) 8
58 Fontana H 156 Treasure Of Your Love/Little Bit Bluer. 12
58 Fontana H 156 Treasure Of Your Love/Little Bit Bluer (78) 10
61 London HLR 9271 Sailor/Wait Till Tomorrow 15

IKE RODGERS
(see under Henry Brown)

JEAN RODGERS
65 Columbia DB 7637 Take What I Have/Baby What You Gonna Do?. 6

JIMMIE RODGERS (The Blue Yodeller)
56 HMV MH 192 Blue Yodel No. 4/Waiting For A Train (78, export issue) 12
56 HMV MH 193 In The Jailhouse Now No. 2/Peach Picking Time Down In Georgia (78, export). . . 12
56 HMV MH 194 Blue Yodel No. 9/Jimmie The Kid (78, export issue) 12
58 HMV 7EG 8163 JIMMIE RODGERS (EP) 20
60 RCA RCX 1058 LEGENDARY JIMMIE RODGERS (EP) 15
59 RCA RD 27110 TRAIN WHISTLE BLUES (LP). 20

MINT VALUE £

59	RCA RD 27138	NEVER NO MO' BLUES (JIMMIE RODGERS MEMORIAL ALBUM) (LP)	20
61	RCA RD 27203	MY ROUGH AND ROWDY WAYS (LP)	20
61	RCA RD 27241	JIMMIE THE KID (LP)	20
62	RCA RD 7505	COUNTRY MUSIC HALL OF FAME (LP)	20
63	RCA RD 7562	THE SHORT BUT BRILLIANT LIFE OF JIMMIE RODGERS (LP)	20
64	RCA RD 7644	MY TIME AIN'T LONG (LP)	20

JIMMIE RODGERS

57	Columbia DB 3986	Honeycomb/Their Hearts Were Full Of Spring (as Jimmy Rodgers)	18
57	Columbia DB 4052	Kisses Sweeter Than Wine/Better Loved You'll Never Be	8
58	Columbia DB 4078	Oh-Oh, I'm Falling In Love Again/The Long Hot Summer	8
58	Columbia DB 4130	Secretly/Make Me A Miracle	8
58	Columbia DB 4175	Are You Really Mine/The Wizard	8
58	Columbia DB 4206	Woman From Liberia/Girl In The Wood	8
59	Columbia DB 4235	Bimbombey/You Understand Me	7
	Columbia DB 4281	Because You're Young/I'm Never Gonna Tell	7
59	Columbia DB 4327	Soldier, Won't You Marry Me?/Ring-A-Ling-A-Lario	7
59	Columbia DB 4327	Soldier, Won't You Marry Me?/Ring-A-Ling-A-Lario (78)	10
59	Columbia DB 4362	Tucumcari/The Night You Became Seventeen	6
60	Columbia DB 4401	Waltzing Matilda/T.L.C. — Tender Loving Care	6
60	Columbia DB 4447	Joshua Fit The Battle Of Jericho/Just A Closer Walk With Thee	6
61	Columbia DB 4617	Little Shepherd Of Kingdom Come/When Love Is Young	6
62	Columbia DB 4847	English Country Garden/Little Dog Cried	6
62	Columbia DB 4904	The Fox And The Goose/Soldier, Won't You Marry Me	6
62	London HLD 9582	No One Will Ever Know/Because	8
63	London HLD 9654	Rhumba Boogie/Rainbow At Midnight	7
63	London HLD 9697	Face In A Crowd/Lonely Tears	7
63	London HLD 9752	I'm Gonna Be The Winner/Poor Little Raggedy Ann	8
64	London HLD 9904	I Forgot More Than You'll Ever Know/The World I Used To Know (unissued)	
64	Pye International 7N 25253	I Forgot More Than You'll Ever Know/The World I Used To Know	7
58	Columbia SEG 7770	JIMMIE RODGERS (EP)	25
58	Columbia SEG 7811	JIMMIE RODGERS SINGS (EP)	20
59	Columbia SEG 7911	JIMMIE RODGERS NO. 2 (EP)	25
63	Columbia SEG 8253	ENGLISH COUNTRY GARDEN (EP)	8
65	Dot DEP 20007	JIMMIE RODGERS FAVOURITES (EP)	12
58	Columbia 33SX 1082	JIMMIE RODGERS (LP)	25
58	Columbia 33SX 1097	THE NUMBER ONE BALLADS (LP)	30
59	Columbia 33SX 1144	SINGS FOLK SONGS (LP)	20
59	Columbia 33SX 1176	JIMMIE RODGERS FAVOURITES (LP)	20
59	Columbia 33SX 1206	IT'S CHRISTMAS ONCE AGAIN (LP)	20
60	Columbia 33SX 1217	TWILIGHT ON THE TRAIL (LP, also stereo SCX 3302)	15/18
60	Columbia 33SX 1236	WHEN THE SPIRIT MOVES YOU (LP, also stereo SCX 3313)	15/18
61	Columbia 33SX 1292	AT HOME WITH JIMMIE RODGERS (LP, also stereo SCX 3355)	12/15
61	Columbia 33SX 1393	THE FOLK SONG WORLD OF . . . (LP, also stereo SCX 3425)	12/15
63	London HA-D 8040	NO ONE WILL EVER KNOW (LP)	30
65	London HA-D/SH-D 8116	HONEYCOMB (LP)	30
66	Dot DLP 3710	COUNTRY MUSIC 1966 (LP)	15

SIDNEY RODGERS

75	Ethnic Fight	DJs Party/Dub	5

RODNEY & BRUNETTES

79	London/Bomp HLZ 10574	Holocaust On Sunset Boulevard/NEW YORK BLONDES featuring MADAME X: Little GTO (no p/s)	8

(see also Blondie, Debbie Harry)

RODNEY P & SKITZ

99	Ronin RDP10	Revolutionary/Dedicated (12")	8

TOMMY ROE (& ROEMANS)

62	HMV POP 1060	Sheila/Save Your Kisses	6
62	HMV POP 1092	Susie Darlin'/Piddle De Pat	8
63	HMV POP 1117	Gonna Take A Chance/Don't Cry Donna	8
63	HMV POP 1138	The Folk Singer/Count On Me	7
63	HMV POP 1174	Kiss And Run/What Makes The Blues	7
63	HMV POP 1207	Everybody/There's A Day A Coming	7
64	HMV POP 1290	Be A Good Little Girl/Carol	10
63	HMV POP 1259	Come On/There Will Be Better Years	8
64	HMV POP 1364	Little Miss Heartbreak/You Might As Well Forget Him (with Roemans)	8
65	HMV POP 1386	Diane From Manchester Square/Party Girl (as Tommy Roe & Roemans)	8
65	HMV POP 1469	Doesn't Anybody Know My Name/I'm A Rambler, I'm A Gambler	8
66	HMV POP 1539	Sweet Pea/Much More Love	8
66	HMV POP 1556	Hooray For Hazel/Need For Love	8
67	HMV POP 1574	It's Now Winter's Day/Kick Me Charlie	7
67	HMV POP 1611	Melancholy Mood/Paisley Dreams	7
69	Stateside SS 2143	Dizzy/The You I Need	6
69	Stateside SS 2152	Heather Honey/Money Is My Pay	6
69	Stateside SS 2156	Jam Up Jelly Tight/Moontalk	6
70	Stateside SS 2165	Stir It Up And Serve It/Firefly	6
70	Stateside SS 2174	Pearl/A Dollar's Worth Of Pennies	6
71	Probe PRO 527	Greatest Love/King of Fools	6
71	Probe PRO 538	Stagger Lee/Back Streets And Alleys	6
72	Probe PRO 555	We Can Make Music/Gotta Keep Rolling Along	6
72	MGM 2006 134	Mean Little Woman, Rosalie/Skyline	7
63	HMV 7EG 8806	THE FOLK SINGER (EP)	35
63	HMV CLP 1614	SHEILA (LP)	75
64	HMV CLP 1704	EVERYBODY LIKES TOMMY ROE (LP)	45
65	HMV CLP 1860	BALLADS AND BEAT (LP)	35
69	Stateside S(S)L 10282	DIZZY (LP)	18

70	Stateside SSL 10296	TOMMY ROE'S GREATEST HITS (LP)	15
70	Probe SPB 1021	WE CAN MAKE MUSIC (LP)	15
72	Probe SPB 1046	BEGINNINGS (LP)	15

ROGER ROGER & HIS ORCHESTRA

63	Fontana 267 268TF	The Desperadoes/Song Of Mexico	5

BILL ROGERS

52	Melodisc 1230	Nice Woman, Ugly Man/B.G. BARGEE: Shanto (78)	8

CE CE ROGERS

89	WEA A 8852T	Forever/Someday (12", no p/s)	20

DANE ROGERS & NU BEATS

64	Pye 7N 15621	Mary Jane/Jeanette	10

DEAN ROGERS

60	Parlophone R 4732	End Of Time (as Dean Rogers & Hi-Fi's)/Keep The Miracle Going	10
61	Parlophone R 4835	Timber/High In A Misty Sky	10

(see also Sydney James)

ERIC ROGERS

59	Decca F 11151	Joanna/Lingering Lovers (78)	6
63	Decca F 11585	The Iron Maiden/Fly-Wheel	6

JULIE ROGERS

64	Mercury MF 809	It's Magic/Without Your Love	8
64	Mercury MF 820	The Wedding (La Novia)/The Love Of A Boy	6
65	Mercury MF 838	Like A Child/Our Day Will Come	6
65	Mercury MF 849	Hawaiian Wedding Song/Turn Around, Look At Me	7
65	Mercury MF 858	Sudden Love/Play The Music	7
65	Mercury MF 868	Day By Day/I'm Walking Behind You	7
65	Mercury MF 895	Another Year, Another Love, Another Heartache/ Don't Waste Young Years On Him	7
65	Mercury MF 901	In My Room/Three Unspoken Words	7
65	Mercury MF 917	I Love Him/Lullaby For Lovers	7
65	Mercury MF 950	While The Angel Was Ringing/Climb Every Mountain	7
66	Mercury MF 980	These Gentle Hands/When Two Worlds Collide	7
66	Mercury MF 993	Bless You/Go On Home	7
68	Mercury MF 1015	Let Me Belong To You/You Never Told Me	7
69	Ember EMB S 267	Almost Close To You (O Mio Angelo)/This Is Me (C'est Ton Nom) (p/s)	8
69	Ember EMB S 273	Which Way To Nowhere/Love Theme From The Motion Picture "Michael And Helga" (p/s)	8
70	Ember EMB S 287	Children Of My Mind/Once More With Feeling (p/s)	8
70	Ember EMB S 300	Baby Don't You Leave Me/Where Do You Go (p/s)	8
64	Mercury 10023 MCE	JULIE ROGERS (EP)	20
65	Mercury 10028 MCE	THE SOUND OF JULIE (EP)	20
65	Mercury 20048 (S)MCL	THE SOUND OF JULIE (LP, mono/stereo)	30/35
66	Mercury 20086 (S)MCL	CONTRASTS (LP, mono/stereo)	25/30
67	Mercury 20100 (S)MCL	SONGS OF INSPIRATION (LP, mono/stereo)	15/18

KENNY ROGERS (& FIRST EDITION)

69	Reprise RS 20829	Ruby Don't Take Your Love To Town/Girl Get A Hold Of Yourself	5
70	Reprise RS 20888	Something's Burning/Momma's Waiting	5
70	Reprise RS 20923	Tell It All Brother/Just Remember You Are My Sunshine	5
70	Reprise RS 20953	Heed The Call/Stranger In My Place	5
70	Reprise RS 20999	Someone Who Cares/Mission Of San Nohero	5
72	Reprise K 14009	Ruby Don't Take Your Love To Town/Girl Get A Hold Of Yourself (p/s)	5
72	Reprise K 14206	Ruby Don't Take Your Love To Town/Me And Bobby McGee/ Reuben James/Something's Burning (maxi-single)	5
69	Reprise RSLP 6352	RUBY DON'T TAKE YOUR LOVE TO TOWN (LP)	15
70	Reprise RSLP 6385	SOMETHING'S BURNING (LP)	12
70	Reprise RSLP 6412	TELL IT ALL BROTHER (LP)	12

(see also First Edition)

LINCOLN ROGERS

73	Phoenix NIX 137	Let Love Come Between Us/She Looked At Me With Love	10

LYNNE ROGERS

65	RCA RCA 1479	Sometimes/I Shouldn't Care	7

MARK ROGERS & MARKSMEN

63	Parlophone R 5045	Bubble Pop/Hold It!	18

(see also Marksmen, Mark Wirtz)

PAUL ROGERS

61	HMV POP 872	Four An' Twenty Thousand Kisses/Free To Love	10
63	HMV POP 1121	Always/Joanie Don't Be Angry	10

PAULINE ROGERS

54	Columbia SCM 5106	Spinnin' The Blues/But Good	15

PIERCE ROGERS & OVERLANDERS

61	Parlophone R 4838	Do You Still Love Me?/That Someone	12

ROY ROGERS

50	HMV MH 109	Oh Dem Golden Slippers/Lucky Leather Breeches (78, export issue)	10
51	HMV BD 1267	Me And My Teddy Bear/Buffalo Billy (78)	6
51	HMV BD 1286	A Four Legged Friend/There's A Cloud In My Valley Of Sunshine (78)	10
55	HMV 7EG 8145	KING OF THE COWBOYS (EP)	25
55	HMV 7EG 8182	HAPPY TRAILS (EP)	25

MINT VALUE £

ROY ROGERS & DALE EVANS

53 HMV MH 174 — Hazy Mountains/You've Got A Rope Around My Heart (78, export issue) 10
54 HMV 7MC6 — Old Rugged Cross/In The Garden (export issue) 10
60s Gala Goldentone GG 2 — Me And My Teddy Bear/Buffalo Billy (6", some in p/s, orange vinyl, 78rpm) ... 10/8
60s Gala Goldentone GG 3 — Happy Trails To You/A Cowboy Needs A Horse (6", some in p/s, orange vinyl, 78rpm) 10/8

SHORTY ROGERS & HIS ORCHESTRA

54 HMV 7M 267 — Tale Of An African Lobster/Sweetheart Of Sigmund Freud 5
54 HMV 7EG 8044 — THE WILD ONE (EP) 10
52 Capitol LC 6549 — MODERN SOUNDS (10" LP, as Shorty Rogers & His Giants) 15
54 HMV DLP 1030 — COOL AND CRAZY (10" LP, featuring Giants) 15
54 HMV DLP 1058 — EIGHT SHORTY ROGERS' NUMBERS (10" LP) 15
56 Contemporary LDC 190 — SHELLY MANNE, SHORTY ROGERS AND JIMMY GIUFFRE — THE THREE (10" LP, with Shelly Manne & Jimmy Giuffre) 15

(see also Boots Brown, Bud Shank, Shelly Manne, Jimmy Giuffre)

SIDNEY ROGERS

73 Techniques TE 923 — Don't Throw Stones/Toughness 10

TIMMIE ROGERS

53 Capitol CL 13991 — Nothin's Wrong With Nothin'/Oh, Yeah! (78) 6
57 London HLU 8510 — Back To School Again/I've Got A Dog Who Loves Me 80
57 London HLU 8510 — Back To School Again/I've Got A Dog Who Loves Me (78) 25
58 London HLU 8601 — Take Me To Your Leader/Fla-Ga-La-Pa 100
58 London HLU 8601 — Take Me To Your Leader/Fla-Ga-La-Pa (78) 30

TRACY ROGERS

65 Polydor 56029 — How Love Used To Be/When I Realise 6
65 Polydor 56037 — Love Story/I Remember When I Loved You (p/s) 10
66 Polydor 56077 — Baby/Through Thick And Thin 25
67 Polydor 56197 — Back With You Baby/In The Morning 10

VERN ROGERS & HI-FI'S

62 Oriole CB 1785 — That Ain't Right/Be Everything 10
63 Oriole CB 1826 — He's New To You/Can't Complain 7
63 Oriole CB 1885 — I Will/One Way Love Affair 10
63 Oriole CB 1923 — Anna/Pride 7

DIANA ROGERSON

85 United Dairies UD 017 — THE INEVITABLE CHRYSTAL BELLE SCRODD RECORD (LP) 30
86 United Dairies UD 021 — CHRYSTAL BELLE SCRODD: BELLE DE JOUR (LP) 30

(see also Nurse With Wound)

ROGUES (U.K.)

67 Decca F 12718 — Memories Of Missy/And You Let Her Pass By 7

ROGUES (U.S.)

65 CBS 201731 — Everyday/Rogers Reef 12

(see also Terry Day, Terry Melcher, Bruce Johnston)

ROKES

67 RCA RCA 1587 — Let's Live For Today/Ride On 20
67 RCA RCA 1646 — Hold My Hand/Regency Sue 40
68 RCA RCA 1694 — When The Wind Arises/The Works Of Bartholemew 55

ROKKA

80 Rock Trax RT 01 — Come Back 10

CHERRY ROLAND

63 Decca F 11579 — Handy Sandy/Stay As I Am 10
63 Decca F 11648 — What A Guy/Just For Fun 10

(see also Cherry Rowland)

PAUL ROLAND

82 Aristocrat ARC 1389 — Doctor Strange/Madelaine (p/s) 8
82 Scoff DT 020 — Doctor Strange/Madelaine (p/s, Irish-only) 10
83 Aftermath AEP 12011 — Blades Of Battenburg (Remix)/Captain Blood/Puppet Master/Cavalier (12", p/s) 10
85 Aftermath AEP 12012 — Death Or Glory (Revamped Version)/The Great Edwardian Air Raid/ Beau Brummel/The Curious Case Of Richard Fielding (12", p/s) 8
86 Aftermath AEP 12013 — Gabrielle/Berlin/Sword & Sorcery (p/s) 8
86 Imaginary MIRAGE 002 — Demon In A Glass Case/In The Opium Den (oversized p/s) 7
87 Bam Caruso PABL 094 — Alice's House/Go Down You Murderers/Happy Families/Jumbee (demo) (p/s) 8
87 Bucketfull Of Brains BOB 14 — Madhouse (Demo)/GIANT SAND: Wishing Well (flexidisc free with *Bucketfull Of Brains* magazine) 6/4
87 Bucketfull Of Brains — Madhouse (Demo)/GIANT SAND: Wishing Well (hard vinyl test pressing) 10
85 Aftermath SCOOP 2 — BURNT ORCHIDS (mini LP) 12
80 Ace ACE 013 — THE WEREWOLF OF LONDON (LP) 18
81 Armageddon ARM 9 — THE WEREWOLF OF LONDON (Revamped Version) (LP, different sleeve) 12

(see also Weird Strings, Midnight Rags)

WALTER ROLAND/GEORGIA SLIM

59 Jazz Collector JEL 2 — THE MALE BLUES VOL. 1 (EP) 18

ROLLER

95 Poor Person Prod. — LIFE IN THE DAY OF... (LP, handmade sleeve with insert, numbered, 500 only) 12

ROLLERS

61 London HLG 9340 — Continental Walk/I Want You So 18

ROLLING STONES

DECCA SINGLES

63	Decca F 11675	Come On/I Want To Be Loved (demo copies £150)	30
63	Decca F 11742	Fortune Teller/Poison Ivy (solid centre, withdrawn)	1,000+
63	Decca F 11764	I Wanna Be Your Man/Stones (B-side mis-spelled)	25
63	Decca F 11764	I Wanna Be Your Man/Stoned	18
64	Decca F 11845	Not Fade Away/Little By Little	10
64	Decca F 11934	It's All Over Now/Good Times, Bad Times	10
64	Decca F 12014	Little Red Rooster/Off The Hook	10

(The above singles were originally issued with 'Recording First Published ...' text & 'wide' label lettering.)

65	Decca F 12104	The Last Time/Play With Fire	10
65	Decca F 12220	(I Can't Get No) Satisfaction/The Spider And The Fly	10
65	Decca F 12263	Get Off Of My Cloud/The Singer Not The Song	10
66	Decca F 12331	19th Nervous Breakdown/As Tears Go By	8
66	Decca F 12395	Paint It, Black/Long Long While	10

(The above singles were originally issued with a round Decca logo; later boxed-logo pressings are worth £4 each.)

66	Decca F 12497	Have You Seen Your Mother, Baby, Standing In The Shadow?/ Who's Driving Your Plane	10
67	Decca F 12546	Let's Spend The Night Together/Ruby Tuesday	10
67	Decca F 12654	We Love You/Dandelion	10
68	Decca F 12782	Jumping Jack Flash/Child Of The Moon	8
69	Decca F 12952	Honky Tonk Women/You Can't Always Get What You Want (some in demo-only p/s)	50/5
71	Decca F 13195	Street Fighting Man/Surprise Surprise/Everybody Needs Somebody To Love (33rpm maxi-single)	7
71	Decca F 13203	Street Fighting Man/Surprise Surprise (jukebox edition)	20
73	Decca F 13404	Sad Day/You Can't Always Get What You Want	7
74	Decca F 13517	Paint It Black/It's All Over Now (release cancelled, demo-only)	200
75	Decca F 13584	I Don't Know Why I Love You (credited to either 'Jagger/Richard/Taylor' or 'Stevie Wonder')/Try A Little Harder	15/8
75	Decca F 13597	Out Of Time/Jiving Sister Fanny	6
76	Decca F 13635	Honky Tonk Women/Sympathy For The Devil	8
70s	Decca F 11934	It's All Over Now/Good Times, Bad Times (repressing, with stereo mix on A-side, [ZXDR instead of XDR matrix no.] boxed Decca logo)	6
87	Decca F 102	Jumping Jack Flash/Child Of The Moon (p/s, reissue)	6
87	Decca FX 102	Jumping Jack Flash/Child Of The Moon/Sympathy For The Devil (12", p/s, reissue)	10

EXPORT SINGLES

63	Decca AT 15005	I Wanna Be Your Man/Stoned	85
64	Decca AT 15006	Not Fade Away/Little By Little	85
64	Decca AT 15032	Come On/Tell Me (You're Coming Back)	120
64	Decca AT 15035	Empty Heart/Around And Around	120
65	Decca AT 15039	Time Is On My Side/Congratulations	120
65	Decca AT 15040	Little Red Rooster/Off The Hook	60
65	Decca AT 15043	(I Can't Get No) Satisfaction/The Under Assistant West Coast Promotional Man (p/s)	120
65	Decca F 12104	The Last Time/Play With Fire (with Dutch or Scandinavian p/s)	30
65	Decca F 22180	Heart Of Stone/What A Shame (some in p/s)	60/30
65	Decca F 12220	(I Can't Get No) Satisfaction/The Under Assistant West Coast Promotional Man (some with p/s)	40/18
65	Decca F 22265	Get Off My Cloud/I'm Free (some in p/s)	40/18
66	Decca F 12331	19th Nervous Breakdown/As Tears Go By (with Dutch p/s)	30
66	Decca F 12395	Paint It, Black/Long Long While (p/s)	30
67	Decca F 12546	Let's Spend The Night Together/Ruby Tuesday (p/s)	30
67	Decca F 12654	We Love You/Dandelion (p/s)	30
67	Decca F 22706	2,000 Light Years From Home/She's A Rainbow	35
68	Decca F 22825	Street Fighting Man (remix)/No Expectations (some in p/s)	30/30
69	Decca F 12952	Honky Tonk Women/You Can't Always Get What You Want (p/s)	50
71	Decca F 13126	Little Queenie/Love In Vain (some in p/s)	35/18
71	Decca F 13195	Street Fighting Man/Surprise Surprise/Everybody Needs Somebody To Love (33rpm maxi-single, p/s)	30
71	Decca F 13204	Street Fighting Man/Everybody Needs Somebody To Love (some in p/s)	30/18

SINGLES BOX SETS

80	Decca STONE 1-12	SINGLE STONES (12-single box set)	50
80	Decca BROWSE 1	SINGLE STONES (in-store, 3 x 12-single box set [STONE 1-12], with poster & badge, also available via mail-order)	150

ROLLING STONES LABEL SINGLES

71	Rolling Stones RS 19100	Brown Sugar/Bitch/Let It Rock (some in p/s)	22/6
74	Rolling Stones RS 19114	It's Only Rock 'N' Roll/Through The Lonely Nights	6
78	R. Stones 12EMI 2802	Miss You (8.26)/Faraway Eyes (12", p/s, pink vinyl)	8
81	Rolling Stones	Beast Of Burden/Everything Is Turning Gold (unreleased)	
82	Rolling Stones RSR 111	Time Is On My Side (live)/Twenty Flight Rock (live) (p/s)	5
82	Rolling Stones 12RSR 111	Time Is On My Side (live)/Twenty Flight Rock (live)/ Under My Thumb (live) (12", p/s)	10
84	Rolling Stones RSR 114	She Was Hot/I Think I'm Going Mad (p/s)	5
84	Rolling Stones RSRP 114	She Was Hot/I Think I'm Going Mad (shaped picture disc)	20
84	Rolling Stones SUGAR 1	Brown Sugar/Bitch (p/s, reissue)	6
84	Rolling Stones SUGARP 1	Brown Sugar/Bitch (shaped picture disc)	15
93	Rolling Stone RS LH 1	Brown Sugar/Start Me Up (jukebox issue, no p/s)	15
93	Rolling Stone ORDER LH 1	Gimme Shelter/TOM JONES: Gimme Shelter (jukebox issue, no p/s)	15

OTHER SINGLES

74	Atlantic K 19107	Brown Sugar/Happy/Rocks Off (possibly unissued)	75+
72	Sound For Industry 107	Mick Jagger Introduces 'Exile On Main Street' (flexidisc free with *NME*)	12/6

			MINT VALUE £
CBS SINGLES			
86	CBS QA 6864	Harlem Shuffle/Had It With You (poster p/s)	8
86	CBS TA 6864	Harlem Shuffle (N.Y. Mix)/(London Mix)/Had It With You (12", p/s)	10
86	CBS QTA 6864	Harlem Shuffle (N.Y. Mix)/(London Mix)/Had It With You (12", p/s)	15
86	CBS A 7160	One Hit (To The Body)/Fight (p/s)	5
86	CBS TA 7160	One Hit (To The Body) (London Mix)/Fight (12", p/s)	8
89	CBS 655 193-2	Mixed Emotions (7" Version)/Mixed Emotions (Chris Kimsey's 12")/ Fancyman Blues (CD, picture disc, card sleeve)	10
89	CBS 655 193-5	Mixed Emotions (7" Version)/Fancyman Blues/Tumbling Dice/Miss You (CD, picture disc, in circular tin with 'tongue' logo sticker)	30
89	CBS 655 193-6	Mixed Emotions (Chris Kimsey's 12")/Fancyman Blues (12", p/s)	10
89	CBS 655 193-6	Mixed Emotions (Chris Kimsey's 12")/Fancyman Blues/ Mixed Emotions (7" Version) (12", p/s)	10
89	CBS 655 214-2	Mixed Emotions (7" Version)/Fancyman Blues/Shattered/Waiting On A Friend (CD, picture disc, in circular tin with 'tongue' logo sticker)	30
89	CBS 655 422-7	Rock And A Hard Place/Cook Cook Blues (p/s)	5
89	CBS 655 422-6	Rock And A Hard Place (Dance Mix)/Emotional Rescue/Some Girls/ Rock And A Hard Place (Hard Dub Mix)/Cook Cook Blues (12", p/s)	8
89	CBS 655 422-5	Rock And A Hard Place (Michael Brauer Mix)/Rock And A Hard Place (Bonus Beats Mix)/Rock And A Hard Place (Edited 7" Version) (2nd 12", p/s)	10
89	CBS 655 422-8	Rock And A Hard Place (Dance Mix)/(Hard Dub Mix)/Cook Cook Blues (3rd 12", p/s)	10
89	CBS 655 422-2	Rock And A Hard Place (7" Version)/(Dance Mix)/(Bonus Beats Mix)/ Cook Cook Blues (CD, picture disc, card sleeve)	15
89	CBS 655 422-3	Rock And A Hard Place (Dance Mix)/Cook Cook Blues/Rock And A Hard Place (Hard Dub Mix) (2nd CD)	10
89	CBS 655 448-2	Rock And A Hard Place (7" Version)/Cook Cook Blues/It's Only Rock'n'Roll (But I Like It)/Rocks Off (3rd CD, picture disc, 7" box set with poster)	20
89	CBS 655 448-5	Rock And A Hard Place (7" Version)/Cook Cook Blues/Emotional Rescue/ Some Girls (CD, tongue-shaped card sleeve)	25
90	CBS 656 065-6	Almost Hear You Sigh/Beast Of Burden/Angie/Fool To Cry (12", gatefold p/s)	8
90	CBS 656 065-2	Almost Hear You Sigh/Beast Of Burden/Angie/Fool To Cry (CD, gold disc)	20
90	CBS 656 065-5	Almost Hear You Sigh/Miss You/Waiting On A Friend/Wish I'd Never Met You (CD, in tin with 'Urban Jungle' sticker)	30
90	CBS 656 122-6	Terrifying (12" Dance Remix)/Rock And A Hard Place (Dance Mix)/ Harlem Shuffle (London Mix) (12", p/s)	10
90	CBS 656 122-2	Terrifying (7" Remix Edit)/(12" Remix)/Rock And A Hard Place (7" Version)/ Harlem Shuffle (LP Version) (CD)	10
90	CBS 656 122-5	Terrifying (7" Remix Edit)/Start Me Up/Shattered/If You Can't Rock Me (2nd CD, card p/s)	10
91	CBS 656 756-6	Highwire/2,000 Light Years From Home (live)/Sympathy For The Devil (live)/ I Just Wanna Make Love To You (live) (12", gatefold p/s)	10
91	CBS 656 756-2	Highwire/2,000 Light Years From Home (live)/Sympathy For The Devil (live)/ I Just Wanna Make Love To You (live) (CD)	10
91	CBS 656 756-5	Highwire/Play With Fire (live)/Factory Girl (live) (CD)	12
91	CBS 656 892-6	Ruby Tuesday/Play With Fire (live)/You Can't Always Get What You Want (live)/Rock And A Hard Place (live) (12", p/s)	12
91	CBS 656 892-2	Ruby Tuesday/Play With Fire (live)/You Can't Always Get What You Want (live)/Undercover Of The Night (live) (CD)	10
91	CBS 656 892-5	Ruby Tuesday/Harlem Shuffle (live)/Winning Ugly (CD)	10
91	CBS 657 334-2	Sex Drive (single edit)/(Dirty Hands Mix)/(Club Version) (CD)	10
VIRGIN SINGLES			
94	Virgin VS 1503	Love Is Strong/The Storm (numbered p/s, 7,000 only)	10
94	Virgin VSCDT 1503	Love Is Strong/The Storm/So Young/Love Is Strong (Bob Clearmountain Mix) (CD)	10
94	Virgin VS 1518	You Got Me Rocking/Jump On Top Of Me (numbered p/s, 7,000 only)	8
94	Virgin VST 1518	You Got Me Rocking (Perfecto Mix)/(Sexy Disco Dub Mix)/(Trance Mix) (12", p/s)	12
94	Virgin VS 1524	Out Of Tears/I'm Gonna Drive (numbered p/s, 7,000 only)	8
94	Virgin VSCDX 1524	Out Of Tears (Don Was Edit)/I'm Gonna Drive/Sparks Will Fly (Radio Clean)/ Out Of Tears (Bob Clearmountain Remix Edit) (CD, tear-shaped card p/s)	10
94	Virgin VSCDG 1524	Out Of Tears (Don Was Edit)/I'm Gonna Drive/So Young/The Storm/ Jump On Top Of Me (CD, digipak, numbered, 4,000 only, withdrawn)	350
94	Virgin VSP 1539	I Go Wild/I Go Wild (live) (picture disc)	15
96	Virgin VS 1578	Wild Horses/Tumbling Dice/Gimme Shelter (unreleased)	
96	Virgin VSCDT 1578	Wild Horses/Tumbling Dice/Gimme Shelter (CD, unreleased)	
97	Virgin VS 1653	Anybody Seen My Baby? (LP Edit)/(Soul Solution Remix Edit) (numbered picture disc, p/s, 7,500 only)	15
97	Virgin VST 1653	Anybody Seen My Baby? (Armand's Rolling Steelo Mix)/(Soul Solution Remix)/ (Bonus Roll) (12", p/s)	30
98	Virgin VSY 1667	Saint Of Me (Radio Edit)/Anyway You Look At It (picture disc)	10
98	Virgin VSTX 1667	Saint Of Me (remixes)/Anybody Seen My Baby? (remixes) (12", double pack, stickered p/s)	15
98	Virgin VSTTDT 1667	Saint Of Me (remixes)/Anybody Seen My Baby? (remixes) (12", double pack, stickered p/s)	15
98	Virgin VSY 1700	Out Of Control (Album Radio Edit)/(In Hand With Fluke Radio Edit)	8
PROMO SINGLES			
83	R. Stones RSR 112 (DJ)	Let's Spend The Night Together (live)/Start Me Up (live)	18
91	CBS A 026/B 027	Highwire/Sympathy For The Devil (live) (12")	10
93	EMI ORDERLH 1	Gimme Shelter (live) (1-sided jukebox issue)	20
93	Virgin STONES 1	JUMP BACK (EP)	25
94	Virgin VSCDJ 1518	You Got Me Rocking (Original Version)/(Perfecto Mix) (CD)	15
95	Virgin VSCDJ 1539	I Go Wild (CD, 1-track)	25
95	Virgin VSCDJ 1562	Like A Rolling Stone (Edit)/(Album Version) (CD)	15
96	Virgin VSCDJ 1578	Wild Horses (Edit) (CD, 1-track)	25
97	Virgin VSCDJ 1653	Anybody Seen My Baby? (LP Edit)/(Don Was Radio Remix) (CD)	15

			MINT VALUE £
97	Virgin VSCDXJ 1653	Anybody Seen My Baby? (Armand's Rolling Steelo Mix)/(Soul Solution Remix)/ (Bonus Roll) (CD)	15
98	Virgin VSCDJ 1667	Saint Of Me (Radio Edit)/(Album Version) (CD)	15
98	Virgin VSCDJX 1667	Saint Of Me (Deep Dish Grunge Garage Remix Edit) (CD, 1-track)	8
98	Virgin VSTDJ 1667	Saint Of Me (Deep Dish Grunge Garage Remix) (Part 1)/(Part 2)/ (Grunge Garage Dub)/(Rolling Dub)/Anyone Seen My Baby? (Armand's Rolling Steelo Mix)/Anybody Seen My Baby? (Bonus Roll) (12", double pack, stickered sleeve)	15
98	Virgin VSP 1700	Out Of Control (Bi-Polar At The Controls)/(Bi-Polar Outer Version) (withdrawn brown label or silver label)	50/12
98	Virgin VSTDJ 1700	Out Of Control (In Hand With Fluke)/(In Hand Full Version)/ (Bi-Polar's Fat Controller Mix)/(Bi-Polar At The Controls) (12")	10
98	Virgin VSTDDJ 1700	Out Of Control (In Hand With Fluke Instrumental)/(In Hand Full Version)/ (Bi-Polar's Fat Controller Mix)/(Bi-Polar At The Controls) (12")	10
98	Virgin VSCDJ 1700	Out Of Control (Album Radio Edit)/(Album Version) (CD)	15
98	Virgin VSCDXJ 1700	Out Of Control (In Hand With Fluke Edit)/(In Hand With Fluke Instrumental)/ (Bi-Polar At The Controls)/(Bi-Polar's Fat Controller Mix) (CD)	18
98	Virgin VSCDF 1700	Out Of Control (Album Radio Edit)/(In Hand With Fluke)/ (In Hand With Fluke Instrumental)/(Bi-Polar At The Controls) (CD)	18
98	Virgin VSCDJ 1700	Out Of Control (Album Radio Edit)/(Saber Master With Fade)/ (In Hand With Fluke Radio Edit) (CD)	20
90s	Virgin VSCDY 1838	Don't Stop (1-track CD)	15
00s	Virgin DEVIL 666	Sympathy For The Devil (Fatboy Slim Remix)/(Neptunes Remix)//(Full Phat Remix)/ (Original Version) (2 x 12", with press sheet)	35

EPs

64	Decca DFE 8560	THE ROLLING STONES (with unboxed or later boxed Decca logo)	25/12
64	Decca DFE 8590	FIVE BY FIVE (with unboxed or later boxed Decca logo)	25/12
65	Decca DFE 8620	GOT LIVE IF YOU WANT IT! (with unboxed or later boxed Decca logo)	25/12
83	Decca DFEX 8560	THE ROLLING STONES (12", reissue)	10
83	Decca DFEX 8590	FIVE BY FIVE (12", reissue)	10
83	Decca DFEX 8620	GOT LIVE IF YOU WANT IT (12", reissue)	10

EXPORT EPs

64	Decca SDE 7260	ROLLING STONES	90
64	Decca SDE 7501	THE ROLLING STONES VOLUME 2	75
65	Decca SDE 7502	GOT LIVE IF YOU WANT IT!	90
65	Decca DFE 8620	GOT LIVE IF YOU WANT IT! (red label, some with yellow titles on p/s)	each 90
65	Decca SDE 7503	ROLLING STONES (with "Out Of Our Heads [U.K. version]" sleeve)	90

DECCA LPs

64	Decca LK 4605	ROLLING STONES (1st pressing, plays 2.52 version of "Tell Me"; Side 2 matrix: XARL 6272-1A)	800-1200
64	Decca LK 4605	ROLLING STONES (2nd pressing, plays 4.06 version of "Tell Me"; a few sleeves list "Mona", most list "I Need You, Baby" instead)	180/100
65	Decca LK 4661	ROLLING STONES NO. 2	90

*(The above LPs were simultaneously pressed with both **flipback** and **non-flipback** sleeves. Values are the same.)*

65	Decca LK/SKL 4733	OUT OF OUR HEADS (mono/stereo)	90/70
66	Decca TXL/TXS 101	COULD YOU WALK ON THE WATER (unreleased, proof sleeves exist)	
66	Decca LK/SKL 4786	AFTERMATH (mono/stereo)	90/70
66	Decca LK/SKL 4786	AFTERMATH (mono/stereo, front cover title is shadowed)	140/160
66	Decca LK 4786	AFTERMATH (mono, front cover title has purple shadow)	160
66	Decca TXL/TXS 101	BIG HITS (HIGH TIDE AND GREEN GRASS) (1st pressing, gatefold sleeve, with stapled 12" x 12" picture booklet, mono/stereo)	70/50
67	Decca TXL/TXS 101	BIG HITS (HIGH TIDE AND GREEN GRASS) (2nd pressing, gatefold sleeve, without booklet, mono/stereo)	40/30
67	Decca LK/SKL 4852	BETWEEN THE BUTTONS (mono/stereo)	100/70
67	Decca TXL/TXS 103	THEIR SATANIC MAJESTIES REQUEST (3-D gatefold sleeve with red inner, mono/stereo)	100/90
68	Decca LK/SKL 4955	BEGGARS BANQUET (gatefold sleeve, with Stones Decca label insert, mono/stereo)	100/60
69	Decca LK/SKL 5019	THROUGH THE PAST, DARKLY (BIG HITS VOL. 2) (octagonal gatefold sleeve, mono/stereo)	80/60
69	Decca LK 5025	LET IT BLEED (mono, red inner, with poster, with Stones Decca label insert, some with stickered sleeve; copies without poster or sticker £60)	120/90
69	Decca SKL 5025	LET IT BLEED (stereo, blue inner, with poster, some w/ stickered sleeve; copies without poster or sticker £30)	50/40
69	Decca TXL/TXS 103	THEIR SATANIC MAJESTIES REQUEST (2nd pressing, gatefold sleeve with red inner, mono/stereo, stereo disc in stickered mono sleeve)	each 50

*(The above LPs were originally issued with Decca labels with a large-print logo **without** a box surrounding it; later pressings with smaller print & boxed logo are worth between half the value for earlier LPs to two-thirds the value for later LPs and three-quarters for "Let It Bleed".)*

70	Decca SKL 5065	GET YER YA-YA'S OUT!	15
71	Decca SKL 5084	STONE AGE	15
71	Decca SKL 5101	GIMME SHELTER	12
72	Decca SKL 5098	MILESTONES	12
72	Decca SKL 5149	ROCK 'N' ROLLING STONES	12
73	Decca SKL 5165	GOLDEN B-SIDES (unreleased, test pressings only)	600
73	Decca SKL 5173	NO STONE UNTURNED	12

(Except where noted, the above Decca LPs were originally issued with dark blue labels & laminated sleeves; later copies are worth two-thirds the value.)

75	Decca SKL 5212	METAMORPHOSIS (dark blue label, matt sleeve)	12
70s	Decca TXS 101	BIG HITS (HIGH TIDE AND GREEN GRASS) (2nd pressing, gatefold sleeve, later issue with foldout insert & later Decca logo, stereo only)	12
75	Decca TXS 103	THEIR SATANIC MAJESTIES REQUEST (3rd pressing, 3-D matt gatefold sleeve, stereo only)	20
70s	Decca SKL 4733	OUT OF OUR HEADS (2nd pressing, light green sleeve, box Decca logo)	30

			MINT VALUE £
75	Decca (no cat. no.)	THE HISTORY OF THE ROLLING STONES (3-LP box set; 3x12" pink label test pressings exist, no sleeves, matrices read: ZAL 12996/7, ZAL 12998/9 & ZAL 13000/1; release cancelled in favour of "Rolled Gold" 2-LP)	800
75	Decca ROST 3/4	LIVE STONES (2-LP, compilation, pink label test pressings only, follow-up to "Rolled Gold", unreleased)	500
83	Decca ROLL 1	THE FIRST EIGHT STUDIO ALBUMS (8-LP set, with 192-page book; wraparound card box, each LP has star printed on rear sleeve)	275

EXPORT LPs

65	Decca LK/SKL 4725	OUT OF OUR HEADS (with U.S. track listing & cover design, unboxed Decca label logo, mono/stereo, withdrawn)	125/150
66	Decca LK/SKL 4838	HAVE YOU SEEN YOUR MOTHER, LIVE (laminated sleeve & unboxed Decca label logo, mono/stereo)	110/130
67	Decca LK/SKL 4888	FLOWERS (laminated sleeve, unboxed Decca label logo)	150
70s	Decca LK/SKL 4888	FLOWERS (later pressing, laminated sleeve, boxed Decca label logo)	90
70	Decca SKL 4786	AFTERMATH (white label, black print, supposedly for export)	18
70	Decca TXS 103	THEIR SATANIC MAJESTIES REQUEST (gatefold sleeve, white label, black print, supposedly for export)	18
70	Decca SKL 5065	GET YER YA-YA'S OUT! (white label, black print, supposedly for export)	18
70s	Decca LK/SKL 4838	HAVE YOU SEEN YOUR MOTHER, LIVE (later pressing, boxed logo, laminated sleeve)	75

ROLLING STONES LABEL LPs

71	Rolling Stones COC 59100	STICKY FINGERS (zip sleeve with insert)	20
72	Rolling Stones COC 69100	EXILE ON MAIN STREET (2-LP, with inners, some with postcard inserts)	35/15
73	Rolling Stones COC 59101	GOAT'S HEAD SOUP (gatefold sleeve, with insert)	12
78	Rolling Stones CUN 39108	SOME GIRLS (LP, with uncensored inner sleeve)	12
82	R. Stones CUNP 39115	STILL LIFE (AMERICAN CONCERT 1981) (LP, picture disc, a few mispressed with wrong tracks)	125/12

OTHER ALBUMS

83	R. Digest GROLA 119	THE GREAT YEARS (4-LP, box set)	25
89	ABKCO 820900-1	ROLLING STONES SINGLES COLLECTION/LONDON YEARS (4-LP set)	40
89	CBS 466 918 2	COLLECTION 1971-1989 (15-CD box set, with bonus CD, 'Collector's Edition')	120
91	Sony 468 135-9/468 135-2	FLASHPOINT/INTERVIEW 1990 (2-CD pack, shrinkwrapped with tongue logo sticker, numbered)	35

PROMO ALBUMS

67	Decca TXL/TXS 103	THEIR SATANIC MAJESTIES REQUEST (LP, padded silk sleeve)	1,000+
69	Decca RSM. 1	PROMOTIONAL ALBUM (LP, U.K. disc in U.S. sleeve [lists RSD-1], 200 copies pressed [100 each for U.K. & U.S.], U.K. issues include a letter from Decca)	800
86	CBS SAMP 1103	STONES ON CD — A RADIO SAMPLER (CD, poly sleeve)	250
89	CBS SAMPC 1347	SAY AHHH! (LP, promo-only compilation)	150
89	CBS (no catalogue no.)	STEEL WHEELS - THE ALBUM OF THE TOUR (box set, with LP, CD, cassette and "Terrifying" 12", European tour dates & sticker)	125
95	Virgin IVDG 2801	STRIPPED (2-CD, interview disc & album, fold-out digipak)	50
97	Virgin CDVDJ 2840	BRIDGES TO BABYLON (CD, with spoken word intros, 200 only)	60
97	Virgin IVDG 2840	BRIDGES TO BABYLON INTERVIEW (2-CD, interview disc & album, fold-out digipak)	50
97	Virgin (no catalogue no.)	BRIDGES TO BABYLON (CD in promo press box, with "Anybody Seen My Baby?" promo CD, press release, bottle opener, notebook and sheet of stamps, 200 only)	150
99	Virgin CDVDJ 2880	NO SECURITY ALBUM SAMPLER (CD, card p/s)	20
99	Virgin CDIDJ 2880	NO SECURITY (3-CD [2 interview discs], foldout digipak)	60
90s	Virgin CDVDY 2964	FORTY LICKS (CD)	40

(see also Mick Jagger, Keith Richards, Pipes Of Pan, Bill Wyman, Charlie Watts, Mick Taylor, Andrew Oldham, Bobbie Miller)

AUDLEY ROLLINS

72	Explosion EX 2062	Repatriation/HUGH ROY JUNIOR: Repatriation – Version	10
73	Attack ATT 8060	Without You In My World/It's Flowing (actually "It's Growing")	6
73	Harry J HJ 6654	What's Your Name/NOW GENERATION: What's Your Name – Version	6

(see also A. Boyne)

BIRD ROLLINS

72	Mojo 2092 049	Love Man From Carolina/She Needs Loving All The Time	10

(HENRY) ROLLINS BAND

91	Vinyl Solution VS 30	Let There Be Rock/Carry Me Down (12", p/s, as Henry Rollins & Hard-Ons)	18
91	Vinyl Solution VS 30CD	Let There Be Rock/Carry Me Down (CD, as Henry Rollins & Hard-Ons)	18
92	Imago 72787250187	TEARIN' (EP, poster p/s)	8
92	Imago 72787250181	TEARIN' (12" EP, poster p/s)	8
92	Imago 72787250187	TEARIN' (CD EP, poster p/s)	10
94	Imago 7432323057	LIAR (EP, poster p/s)	10
92	Quarter Stick QS 13CD	DEEP THROAT (4-CD box set, spoken-word)	45

SONNY ROLLINS

66	HMV (no cat. no.)	Alfie's Theme (1-sided promo)	20
56	Esquire EP 94	SONNY ROLLINS AND THE MODERN JAZZ QUARTET (EP)	10
57	Esquire EP 148	SONNY ROLLINS WITH THELONIUS MONK (EP)	10
58	Esquire EP 198	WAILING MISTER ROLLINS (EP)	20
60	Esquire EP 228	VALSE HOT (EP, as Sonny Rollins Plus Four)	10
61	Esquire EP 238	ROLLINS AND BROWNIE (EP, with Clifford Brown)	8
62	Esquire EP 248	SAINT THOMAS (EP)	10
56	Esquire 20-050	SONNY ROLLINS QUARTET (10" LP)	40
57	Esquire 20-080	SONNY ROLLINS QUINTET (10" LP)	25
57	Esquire 32-025	SONNY ROLLINS PLUS FOUR (LP)	35
57	Esquire 32-035	PERSPECTIVES (LP, with Modern Jazz Quartet)	40
58	Esquire 32-038	SONNY ROLLINS QUARTET (LP)	45
58	Esquire 32-045	SAXOPHONE COLOSSUS (LP, as Sonny Rollins Four)	70

58 Contemporary LAC 12118 WAY OUT WEST (LP) . . . 35
58 Esquire 32-058 TENOR MADNESS (LP) . . . 45
59 Esquire 32-075 SONNY ROLLINS QUINTET (LP) . . . 30
59 Esquire 32-085 TOUR-DE-FORCE (LP) . . . 22
59 MGM MGM-C 776 SONNY ROLLINS AND THE BIG BRASS (LP) . . . 15
60 Contemporary SCA 5013 SONNY ROLLINS AND THE CONTEMPORARY LEADERS (LP, stereo only) . . . 20
61 Riverside RLP 12-241 THE SOUND OF SONNY (LP) . . . 15
61 Blue Note BLP 1558 SONNY ROLLINS VOL. 2 (LP) . . . 20
62 Riverside RLP 12-258 FREEDOM SUITE (LP) . . . 15
62 Esquire 32-155 MOVIN' OUT (LP) . . . 35
62 RCA RD/SF 7504 THE BRIDGE (LP) . . . 15
63 Esquire 32-175 SONNY BOY (LP) . . . 30
63 RCA RD/SF 7524 WHAT'S NEW (LP) . . . 15
63 RCA RD/SF 7546 OUR MAN IN JAZZ (LP) . . . 15
64 RCA RD/SF 7593 SONNY MEETS HAWK (LP, with Coleman Hawkins) . . . 15
64 Blue Note (B)BLP 4001 NEWK'S TIME (LP) . . . 20
64 RCA RD/SF 7626 SONNY ROLLINS & CO. (LP) . . . 15
64 Blue Note (B)BLP 1581 A NIGHT AT THE VILLAGE VANGUARD (LP) . . . 20
65 RCA RD 7670 NOW'S THE TIME (LP) . . . 15
65 Blue Note (B)BLP 1542 THE SONNY ROLLINS QUARTET (LP) . . . 20
65 Fontana FJL 124 BLOW! (LP) . . . 25
66 HMV CLP 1915 ROLLINS ON IMPULSE (LP) . . . 15
66 Stateside SL 10164 SAXOPHONE COLOSSUS (LP, reissue) . . . 12
67 RCA RD/SF 7736 STANDARD SONNY ROLLINS (LP) . . . 15
67 HMV CLP/CSD 3529 SONNY PLAYS ALFIE (LP) . . . 20
67 HMV CLP/CSD 3610 EAST BROADWAY RUNDOWN (LP) . . . 15

(see also Modern Jazz Quartet, Thelonious Monk, Clifford Brown, Coleman Hawkins, Kenny Durham)

ROLL MOVEMENT

67 Go AJ 11410 I'm Out On My Own/Just One Thing . . . 25

ROLL-UPS

80 Bridgehouse BHS 6 Blackmail/Hold On (p/s) . . . 15
79 Bridgehouse BHLP 004 LOW DIVES FOR HIGHBALLS (LP) . . . 25

DICK ROMAN

59 MGM MGM 1004 Party Girl/My Greatest Mistake . . . 10
59 MGM MGM 1004 Party Girl/My Greatest Mistake (78) . . . 6
65 London HLU 10007 The Truth Hurts/What Good Does It Do Me . . . 7
66 Coral Q 72485 Green Years/Ivy . . . 6
63 Stateside SL 10023 TOUCH OF LOVE (LP) . . . 18

LYN ROMAN

74 Brunswick BR 11 Stop, I Don't Need No Sympathy/Where Do You Go . . . 6

MIMI ROMAN

61 Warner Bros WB 55 Johnny Will/Let It Be Me . . . 6

MURRAY ROMAN

69 Track 613 007 YOU CAN'T BEAT PEOPLE UP AND HAVE THEM SAY I LOVE YOU (LP) . . . 22
69 Track 613 015 A BLIND MAN'S MOVIE (LP) . . . 18
70 Track 2407 013 YOU CAN'T BEAT PEOPLE UP AND HAVE THEM SAY I LOVE YOU (LP, 'Backtrack' reissue) . . . 12

SANDY ROMAN

66 Columbia DB 7931 Dale Anne/Home Is Where The Heart Is . . . 5

TONY ROMAN

67 Stateside SS 2022 Shadows On A Foggy Day/Maggie . . . 6

MAX ROMEO

68 Island WI 3104 Put Me In The Mood/My One Girl . . . 25
68 Island WI 3111 Walk Into The Room/DAWN PENN: I'll Get You . . . 25
68 Island WI 3124 Twelfth Of Never (actually by Pat Kelly)/VAL BENNETT: Caledonia . . . 25
68 Unity UN 503 Wet Dream/She's But A Little Girl . . . 12
69 Blue Cat BS 161 We Want Man/AL REID: Vietcong . . . 25
69 Blue Cat BS 163 It's Not The Way/AL REID: Darling . . . 25
69 Nu Beat NB 022 Blowing In The Wind/LARRY MARSHALL: Money Girl . . . 12
69 Trojan TR 656 Sweet Chariot/Far Far Away (with Hippy Boys) . . . 10
69 Unity UN 507 Belly Woman (actually by Derrick Morgan)/PAULETT & LOVERS: Please Stay . . . 10
69 Unity UN 511 Twelfth Of Never (actually by Pat Kelly)/TARTONS: Solid As A Rock (actually by Tartans) . . . 10
69 Unity UN 516 Wine Her Goosie/KING CANNON: Fire Ball . . . 10
69 Unity UN 532 Mini-Skirt Vision/Far Far Away . . . 12
70 Unity UN 545 Clap Clap (with Hippy Boys)/Death Rides A Horse . . . 15
70 Unity UN 547 What A Cute Man/Buy You A Rainbow . . . 15
70 Unity UN 560 Fish In The Pot/Feel It . . . 10
71 Bullet BU 478 Mother Oh Mother/Dreams Of Passion (actually "Judgement Rock" by Charlie Ace) . . . 10
71 Pama Supreme PS 328 Ginal Ship/UPSETTERS: Version 2 . . . 15
71 Pama Supreme PS 306 Let The Power Fall On I/The Raid . . . 10
71 Pama Supreme PS 318 Don't You Weep/Weeping (Version) . . . 10
71 Punch PH 73 Chie Chie Bud/Version . . . 10
71 Unity UN 571 Macabee (Version)/SOUL SYNDICATE: Music Book . . . 8
71 Camel CA 82 The Coming Of Jah/Watch And Pray . . . 8
72 Camel CA 85 Rasta Bandwagon/When Jah Speaks . . . 8
72 Camel CA 86 Public Enemy Number One/How Long Must We Wait . . . 8
72 Big BG 334 Are You Sure/RUPIE EDWARDS ALL STARS: Are You Sure – Version . . . 8
72 Dynamic DYN 444 We Love America/SOUL RHYTHM: We Love Jamaica Version . . . 8
72 G.G. GG 4535 Is It Really Over?/MAYTONES: Born To Be Loved . . . 8

		MINT VALUE £
72 High Note Hs 058	Pray For Me (with Gaytones)/GAYTONES: Pray For Me — Version	8
72 Pama PM 836	Wet Dream/("Bang Bang Lulu" by Lloyd Tyrell)/("Birth Control" by Lloyd Tyrell)/ "Sex Education" by Classics) (Maxi-Single)	8
72 Pama Supreme PS 345	Pray For Me/Version	8
72 Pama Supreme PS 359	Are You Sure/CARL MASTERS: Va-Va-Voom	8
72 Prince Buster PB 11	River Jordan/Words Sound And Power	8
73 Dragon DRA 1028	No Joshua No/JOSHUA'S ALL STARS: No Joshua No (Version)	8
73 Magnet MA 032	Murder In The Place/Version	8
73 Magnet MA 032	I Woke Up In Love/Version	8
73 Pama PM 875	Pussy Watchman/You Are My Sunshine	8
73 Pama Supreme PS 383	Hide Away/SOUL SYNDICATE: Sweet And Gentle	8
73 Pama Supreme PS 385	Everyman Aught To Know/Version	8
73 Unity UN 572	Rent Crisis/Version	8
74 Ackee ACK 529	Sixpence/Eating Competition	8
69 Pama PMLP 11	A DREAM (LP)	60
71 Pama PMP 2010	LET THE POWER FALL (LP)	50
76 Island ILPS 9392	WAR INA BABYLON (LP)	25

(see also Max & Elaine, Maxie & Glen, Al Read, Henry & Lisa, Dennis Alcapone, George Meggie, David Isaacs)

ROMEO & EMOTIONS

67 Caltone TONE 106	Don't Want To Let You Go/I Can't Do No More	25

CHAN ROMERO

59 Columbia DB 4341	The Hippy Hippy Shake/If I Had A Way	75
60 Columbia DB 4405	My Little Ruby/I Don't Care Now	200

ROMI & JAZZ

90 Chrysalis CHSR 123545	One Love One World (Feel The Rhythm Mix)/One Love One World (Unity '90 Mix)/Love Crime (Sunrise Mix) (12", p/s)	12
90 Chrysalis CHSCD 123545	One Love One World/One Love One World (Unity '90 Mix)/ One Love One World (Instrumental) Love Crime (Indian Mix) (CD)	12

RONALD & LLOYD

74 Magnet MG 042	Back In My Arms/HEPTONES: Drifting Away	8

RONALD & RUBY

58 RCA RCA 1053	Lollipop/Fickle Baby	30
58 RCA RCA 1053	Lollipop/Fickle Baby (78)	15

RONNIE RONALDE

53 Columbia SCM 5006	Song Of The Mountains/If I Were A Blackbird	15
53 Columbia SCM 5007	In A Monastery Garden/Bells Across The Meadow	15
56 Columbia SCM 5214	Ballad Of Davy Crockett/Hair Of Gold	15
56 Columbia SCM 5241	Robin Hood/Happy Trails	15
56 Columbia SCM 5262	The Yarmouth Song/Macnamara's Band	8
55 Columbia SEG 7512	RONNIE RONALDE (EP)	8
56 Columbia SEG 7651	YODELLING, WHISTLING AND SINGING (EP)	8
57 Columbia SEG 7678	BEAUTIFUL DREAMER (EP)	8
58 Columbia SEG 7784	T.V. TOP FOUR (EP)	8
58 Columbia SEG 7838	STORY OF CHRISTMAS (EP)	8
59 Columbia SEG 7945	RONNIE (EP)	8
60 Columbia SEG 7990	LITTLE BOY BLEW (EP, also stereo ESG 7797)	8/10
61 Columbia SEG 8087	YODELLING (EP, also stereo ESG 7850)	8/10
63 Golden Guinea GGL 0193	THE INIMITABLE RONNIE RONALDE (LP)	12

RON & KEN

70s Ethnic Fight	Waiting For You/Dub	5

RONDELLS

58 London HLU 8716	Good Good/Dreamy (with Ned Jr.)	120
58 London HLU 8716	Good Good/Dreamy (with Ned Jr.) (78)	60

RONDELS

61 London HLU 9404	Back Beat No. 1/Shades Of Green	20

DON RONDO

56 Columbia DB 3854	Two Different Worlds/He Made You Mine	10
57 Columbia DB 3909	The Love I Never Had/Don't	10
57 London HLJ 8466	White Silver Sands/Stars Fell On Alabama	15
58 London HLJ 8567	What A Shame/Made For Each Other	18
58 London HLJ 8567	What A Shame/Made For Each Other (78)	7
58 London HLJ 8610	I've Got Bells On My Heart/School Dance	12
58 London HLJ 8610	I've Got Bells On My Heart/School Dance (78)	12
58 London HLJ 8641	Blonde Bombshell/Her Hair Was Yellow	20
58 London HLJ 8641	Blonde Bombshell/Her Hair Was Yellow (78)	12
58 London HLJ 8695	Dormi, Dormi, Dormi (Sleep, Sleep, Sleep)/In Chi Chi Chihuahua	8
58 London HLJ 8695	Dormi, Dormi, Dormi (Sleep, Sleep, Sleep)/In Chi Chi Chihuahua (78)	8
58 London HLJ 8749	City Lights/I Could Be A Mountain	8
58 London HLJ 8749	City Lights/I Could Be A Mountain (78)	15
59 London HLJ 8808	Song From "The Geisha Boy"/Gretna Green	8
59 London HLJ 8808	Song From "The Geisha Boy"/Gretna Green (78)	15
60 London HLL 9217	The King Of Holiday Island/Wanderlust	7
59 London RE-J 1154	RONDO PT. 1 (EP)	25
59 London RE-J 1155	RONDO PT. 2 (EP)	25

GENE RONDO

68 Giant GN 39	Ben Nevis/Grey Lies	12
68 Jolly JY 004	Mary, Mary/Baby, Baby	10
69 Downtown DT 422	A Lover's Question/HERBIE GRAY & RUDIES: Blue Moon	7
69 Downtown DT 431	Sentimental Reasons/Then You Can Tell Me Goodbye	7
70 Downtown DT 459	Spreading Peace/MUSIC DOCTORS: Guitar Riff	7

MINT VALUE £

72	Downtown DT 490	Wanna Be Like Daddy/STUDIO SOUND: A Little More	5
72	Count Shelly CS 005	Happy Birthday Sweet Sixteen/Meditation	5
73	Magnet MA 001	Prisoner Of Love/How Many Times Girl	6
73	Magnet MA 006	Each Moments/If You Do Want Me	5
73	Magnet MA 028	Oh Sweet Africa/This Is Love	6
73	Magnet MA 035	Valley Of Tears/He'll Break Your Heart	5

(see also Gene Pancho)

RONETTES

63	London HLU 9793	Be My Baby/Tedesco And Pitman	8
64	London HLU 9826	Baby I Love You/Miss Joan And Mr Sam	10
64	London HLU 9905	(The Best Part Of) Breakin' Up/Big Red	15
64	London HLU 9922	Do I Love You?/When I Saw You	15
64	London HLU 9931	(Walking) In The Rain/How Does It Feel?	12
65	London HLU 9952	Born To Be Together/Blues For Baby	18
65	London HLU 9976	Is This What I Get For Loving You?/You Baby	22
66	London HLU 10087	I Can Hear Music/When I Saw You (withdrawn)	100
69	London HLU 10240	Be My Baby/Baby I Love You	6
69	A&M AMS 748	You Came, You Saw, You Conquered/I Can Hear Music	8
75	Phil Spector Intl. 2010 009	I'm A Woman In Love/When I Saw You	12
77	Phil Spector Intl. 2010 017	I Wonder/Walking In The Rain	12
64	London HA-U 8212	PRESENTING THE FABULOUS RONETTES FEATURING VERONICA (LP, originally on plum label, later on black label)	130/75
65	Colpix PXL 486	THE RONETTES (LP)	120
75	Phil Spector Intl. 2307 003	SING THEIR GREATEST HITS (LP)	15

(see also Ronnie Spector, Joey Dee & Starlighters)

RONNIE & DEL AIRES

64	Coral Q 72473	Drag/Wigglin' 'N' Wobblin'	25

RONNIE & HI-LITES

62	Pye International 7N 25140	I Wish That We Were Married/Twistin' And Kissin'	25

RONNIE & RAINBOWS

61	London HL 9345	Loose Ends/Sombrero	18

RONNIE & ROBYN

80	Grapevine GRP 137	As Long As You Love Me/Sidra's Theme (unissued)	

RONNIE & ROY

59	Capitol CL 15028	Big Fat Sally/Here I Am	120

RONNO

71	Vertigo 6059 029	Fourth Hour Of My Sleep/Powers Of Darkness	80

(see also Mick Ronson, Rats)

RONNY

64	Decca F 21908	Oh! My Darling Caroline/Lu La Lu	10

RONNY & THE DAYTONAS

64	Stateside SS 333	G.T.O./Hot Rod Baby	20
64	Stateside SS 367	California Bound/Hey Little Girl	15
65	Stateside SS 391	Bucket T/Little Rail Job	22
65	Stateside SS 432	Beach Boy/No Wheels	22
66	Stateside SS 484	Sandy/Sandy (Instrumental)	18

(see also Buzz & Bucky)

MICK RONSON

74	RCA APBO 0212	Love Me Tender/Only After Dark	5
74	RCA 11474 XSP	Love Me Tender/Slaughter On 10th Avenue (1-sided red or black interview flexidisc, included in press kits)	10
74	RCA LPBO 5022	Slaughter On 10th Avenue/Leave My Heart Alone	5
75	RCA RCA 2482	Billy Porter/Seven Days	5
94	Epic EPC 474742 1	HEAVEN AND HULL (LP, picture disc)	20

(see also Ronno, David Bowie, Mott The Hoople, Slaughter & The Dogs, Ian Hunter)

LINDA RONSTADT

69	Capitol CL 15590	The Long Way Round/The Dolphins	5
69	Capitol CL 15612	Baby You've Been On My Mind/I'll Be Your Baby Tonight	5
79	Asylum K 13149	Alison/All That You Dream (picture disc)	5
87	MCA MCAP 1172	Somewhere Out There/(Fievel's Version)/(Instrumental) (with James Ingram) (picture disc)	5
69	Capitol E-ST 208	HOME SOWN, HOME GROWN (LP)	15
70	Capitol E-ST 407	SILK PURSE (LP)	12
72	Capitol EA-ST 635	LINDA RONSTADT (LP)	12
73	Asylum SYL 9012	DON'T CRY NOW (LP)	12
73	Capitol E-ST 11358	HEART LIKE A WHILE (LP)	12
73	Asylum SYL 8761	PRISONER IN DISGUISE (LP)	12
78	Asylum K 53085	LIVING IN THE USA (LP, red vinyl)	12

(see also Stone Poneys)

ROOFTOP SINGERS

63	Fontana 271 700 TF	Walk Right In/Cool Water	6
63	Fontana 271 702 TF	Tom Cat/Hey Boys	5
63	Fontana TF 411	Mama Don't Allow/It Don't Mean A Thing	5
63	Fontana 680 999 TL	WALK RIGHT IN (LP)	15
66	Fontana TFL 6065	RAINY RIVER (LP)	12

(see also Tarriers)

ROOM

70	Deram SML 1073	PRE-FLIGHT (LP)	400

MINT VALUE £

ROOM

80	Box BOX 001	Motion/Waiting Room (p/s)	6
81	Box BOX 003	In Sickness And Health/Bated Breath (p/s)	5

ROOM 10

65	Decca F 12249	I Love My Love/Going Back	6

ROOM 13

82	Woronzow W 002	Murder Mystery/Need Some Dub (12", p/s)	25

(see also Bevis Frond)

MICKEY ROONEY

57	RCA RD 27038	MICKEY ROONEY SINGS GEORGE M. COHAN (LP)	15

(see also Judy Garland)

MARY ROOS

72	CBS 7959	Wake Me Early In The Morning/When You're Singing (Don't Forget)	6

ROOSEVELT SINGERS

73	Sioux SI 025	Heavy Reggae/HONG GANG: Smoking Wild	10

ROOT BOYS

70	Columbia Blue Beat DB 115	Please Don't Stop The Wedding/Your Love, Your Love	15

ROOTS & JENNY JACKSON

70	Beacon BEA 164	Save Me/If I Didn't Love You	25

ROOTS MANUVA

95	Sound Of Money SNM006	Next Type Of Motion/Raw Uncut (12")	10
97	Wayward	Fever (12")	7
98	Big Dada BD022	Jungle Tings Proper (12")	8
98	Big Dada BD009	Motion 500 (12")	8
01	Big Dada BD022	Witness (1 Hope)/Son Of The Soil	8

RO RO

70	Parlophone R 5920	Here I Go Again/What You Gonna Do	12
72	Regal Zonophone RZ 3056	Goin' Round My Head/Down On The Road	12
73	Regal Zonophone RZ 3076	Blackbird/Feel It Coming	12
72	Regal Zono. SRZA 8510	MEET AT THE WATER (LP)	250

(see also Ross)

GEORGE ROPER & PIPEDREAM

70s	Goldspinners GOLD 1	Manchester United/Tribute To The Fans	5

EDMUNDO ROS (& HIS ORCHESTRA)

53	Decca F 10214	Blowin' Wind/Istanbul (B-side as Edmundo Ros & Johnston Brothers)	8
54	Decca F 10263	Somebody Bad Stole De Wedding Bell/Chili Sauce	8
55	Decca F 10480	Cherry Pink And Apple Blossom White/Ole Mambo	8
55	Decca F 10669	Sixteen Tons/Robin Hood	8
56	Decca F 10716	Mister Cuckoo/Don't Ringa Da Bell	6
57	Decca F 10834	I Saw Esau/Jamaica Farewell (Kingston Town)	6

(see also Johnston Brothers, Annette Klooger, Annie Ross)

ROSITA ROSANO

54	Melodisc M 1308	Down In The Indies/Admiral's Daughters (78)	8
55	Melodisc M 1320	Pull Down The Shade, Marie/Cutest Little Dinghy (78)	6
57	Melodisc M 1436	Queer Things/Little Boy	8
57	Melodisc M 1436	Queer Things/Little Boy (78)	10

ANDY ROSE

58	London HLU 8761	Lov-A Lov-A Love/Just Young	25
58	London HLU 8761	Lov-A Lov-A Love/Just Young (78)	6

DAVID ROSE ORCHESTRA

53	MGM SP 1009	Harlem Nocturne (with Woody Herman)/Vanessa	6
56	MGM SP 1181	Forbidden Planet/The Portuguese Washerwomen	10
60	MGM MGM1110	Bonanza/Gloria's Theme	8
62	MGM MGM 1158	The Stripper/Ebb Tide	8
63	MGM C/CS 961	VERY BEST OF DAVID ROSE (LP)	12
65	MGM MGM-C(S) 8002	THE VELVET BEAT (LP)	15
68	Studio Two TWO 216	HOLIDAY FOR STRINGS (LP)	12

(see also Woody Herman, Rush Adams)

DUSTY ROSE

55	London HLU 8162	The Birds And The Bees/It Makes Me So Mad	50
55	London HLU 8162	The Birds And The Bees/It Makes Me So Mad (78)	20
57	London RE-U 1078	COUNTRY SONGS (EP)	50

JOHNNY ROSE

60	Capitol CL 15166	Linda Lee/The Last One To Know	15

MARGARET ROSE

57	Nestles NR 03	In The Middle Of An Island (78, 1-sided card flexi)	7

TIM ROSE

67	CBS 202631	Morning Dew/You're Slipping Away From Me	7
68	CBS 3277	I Got A Loneliness/Long Time Man	22
68	CBS 3478	I Guess It's Over/Hello Sunshine	7
68	CBS 3598	Long-Haired Boy/Looking At A Baby	7
69	CBS 4209	Roanoke/Baby You Turn Me On	7
70	CBS 2631	Morning Dew/You're Slipping Away From Me (reissue)	6
70	Capitol CL 15664	I've Gotta Get A Message To You/Ode To An Old Ball	5
67	CBS (S)BPG 63168	TIM ROSE (LP)	25
69	CBS 63636	THROUGH ROSE COLOURED GLASSES (LP)	20

MINT VALUE £

71 Capitol ST 22673 LOVE — A KIND OF HATE STORY (LP) . . . 12
74 Dawn DNLS 3062 TIM ROSE (LP) . . . 15
75 Atlantic K 50183 MUSICIAN (LP, with lyric insert) . . . 12

TONY ROSE
70 Trailer LER 2013 YOUNG HUNTING (LP) . . . 12
72 Trailer LER 2024 UNDER THE GREENWOOD TREE (LP) . . . 12

ROSE GARDEN
68 Atlantic 584 163 Next Plane To London/Flower Town . . . 7

ROSEHIPS
87 Subway Organisation SUBWAY 10 Room In Your Heart/Thrilled To Bits/Dead End (foldaround p/s with insert in poly bag) . . . 10
87 Subway Organisation SUBWAY 10T Room In Your Heart/Middle Of Next Week/Thrilled To Bits/So Naive/ Just Another Girl/Dead End (12", p/s) . . . 15
87 Subway Organisation SUBWAY 16 I Shouldn't Have To Say/Loophole/Wastin' My Time/All Mine/ Sad As Sunday (p/s, with insert) . . . 10
87 Subway Organisation SUBWAY 16T I Shouldn't Have To Say/Loophole/Wastin' My Time/All Mine/ Sad As Sunday (12", p/s with insert) . . . 15
88 Sweet William BILLY 001 Ask Johnny Dee/FAT TULIPS: You Opened My Eyes (33rpm flexi, p/s w/insert) . . 12

JIMMY ROSELLI
62 Pye International 7N 25134 The Sheik Of Araby/A Fool In Love . . . 6
62 Pye International 7N 25156 I'm Gonna Sit Right Down And Write You A Letter/I Love You . . . 6

ROSEMARY'S CHILDREN
86 él GPO 012 Southern Fields/Whatever Happened To Alice . . . 15
87 Cherry Red MRED 077 KINGS AND PRINCES EP (12", p/s) . . . 15

LEONARD ROSENMAN ORCHESTRA
57 London HA-P 2040 A TRIBUTE TO JAMES DEAN (LP) . . . 20

ROSE OF VICTORY
83 No Future OI 24 Suffragette City/Overdrive (p/s) . . . 12
(see also Blitz)

ROSE TATTOO
78 Carrere CAL 125 Bad Boy For Love/Tramp (p/s) . . . 6
78 Carrere CAL 125 Bad Boy For Love/Tramp (12", p/s) . . . 8
78 Epic EPC 9411 Rock 'N' Roll Outlaw/One Of The Boys (p/s) . . . 5
80 Repeal PRS 2724 Release Legalise/COL PATERSON: Bong On Aussie (500 only) . . . 40
81 Mirage PR 405 Rock 'N' Roll Is King/Sidewalk Sally (12", promo only) . . . 10
81 Carrere CAR 200P Rock 'N' Roll Outlaw/Remedy (picture disc) . . . 5
81 Carrere CAR 220 Assault And Battery/Astra Wally//One Of The Boys/Manzil Madness (double pack, gatefold p/s) . . . 5
83 Carrere CARP 263 It's Gonna Work Itself Out/Fightin' Sons (picture disc) . . . 5
82 Albert Productions AP 854 We Can't Be Beaten/Fightin' Sons . . . 5
82 Albert Productions AP 898 Branded/Dead Set . . . 5
82 Albert Productions AP 1007 It's Gonna Work Itself Out/Sydney Girls . . . 6
84 Albert Productions AP 1299 I Wish/Wild One . . . 6
82 Albert Productions AP 1384 Freedom's Flame/Never Too Loud (p/s) . . . 6

ROSIE (& ORIGINALS)
61 London HLU 9266 Angel Baby/Give Me Love (as Rosie & Originals) . . . 40
61 Coral Q 72426 Lonely Blue Nights/We'll Have A Chance . . . 30

ROSKO
70 Trojan TR 7758 Al Capone/Kaiser Bill . . . 6
70 Philips 6009 070 Grab The Rabbit/Mohammed Ben Ali . . . 5
(see also Emperor Rosko & Power Pack)

EMPEROR ROSKO & POWER PACK
69 Polydor 56316 Opposite Lock Parts 1 & 2 . . . 10
71 B&C CB 148 The Customs Man/Take It In Your Stride . . . 5
(see also Rosko, Power Pack, Pleasure Garden)

FRANK ROSOLINO SEXTET
54 Capitol KC 65001 That Old Black Magic/Yo Yo . . . 5

ROSS
74 RSO 2394 127 ROSS (LP) . . . 12
75 RSO 2394 144 THE PIT AND THE PENDULUM (LP) . . . 12
(see also Indian Summer, Gary Pickford-Hopkins, Ro Ro)

ANNIE ROSS
54 Esquire 10-334 Annie's Lament/Twisted (78, with Teacho Wiltshire, Art Blakey) . . . 8
54 Esquire 10-344 Jackie/The Song Is You (78, with Quincy Jones) . . . 10
55 Decca F 10514 Mama (He Treats Your Daughter Mean)/The Fish . . . 12
55 Decca F 10637 I Want You To Be My Baby (with Tony Crombie)/TONY CROMBIE & HIS ORCHESTRA: Three Little Words . . . 10
55 Decca F 10637 I Want You To Be My Baby (with Tony Crombie)/TONY CROMBIE & HIS ORCHESTRA: Three Little Words (78) . . . 8
56 Decca F 10680 Cry Me A River/Only You . . . 8
63 Ember EMB S 182 Bye Bye Blues/A Lot Of Livin' To Do . . . 10
72 Columbia DB 8912 Straight On Till Morning/God Bless The Child . . . 10
57 Pye Jazz NJE 1035 NOCTURNE FOR VOCALIST (EP) . . . 20
50s Esquire EP 1 WITH THE TEACHO WILTSHIRE GROUP (EP) . . . 30
50s Pieces Of Eight PEP 604 WITH THE TONY CROMBIE FOURTET (EP) . . . 12
64 Transatlantic TRAEP 112 GO TO THE WALL (EP) . . . 15
57 Nixa Jazz NJT 504 ANNIE BY CANDLELIGHT (10" LP) . . . 175
59 Vogue LAE 12203 ANNIE ROSS (LP, with Gerry Mulligan Quintet) . . . 60
60 Vogue LAE 12233 A GASSER (LP, with Zoot Sims) . . . 60

MINT VALUE £

63 Ember NR 5008 — A HANDFULL OF SONGS (LP) — 75
63 Transatlantic TRA 107 — LOGUERRHYTHMS (LP) — 60
65 Golden Guinea GGL 0316 — ANNIE BY CANDLELIGHT (LP, reissue) — 100
66 Xtra XTRA 1049 — ANNIE ROSS WITH THE TONY KINSEY QUINTET (LP) — 60

(see also Tony Crombie, Dave Lambert, Gerry Mulligan, Zoot Sims, Jack Parnell, Teacho Wiltshire, Art Blakey, Quincy Jones)

DAVID ROSS

58 Oriole CB 1416 — Pit-A-Patter Boom Boom/Everybody's Got A Girl But Tino (as Dave Ross) — 6
58 Oriole CB 1416 — Pit-A-Patter Boom Boom/Everybody's Got A Girl But Tino (78, as Dave Ross) — 6

DIANA ROSS

70 Tamla Motown TMG 743 — Reach Out And Touch (Somebody's Hand)/Dark Side Of The World — 5
70 Tamla Motown TMG 751 — Ain't No Mountain High Enough/Can't It Wait Until Tomorrow — 5
71 Tamla Motown TMG 768 — Remember Me/How About You — 5
71 Tamla Motown TMG 781 — I'm Still Waiting/Reach Out I'll Be There — 5
71 Tamla Motown TMG 792 — Surrender/I'm A Winner (mono) — 5
79 Motown TMG 1136 — Pops, We Love You/Pops, We Love You (Instrumental) (p/s, with Smokey Robinson, Marvin Gaye & Stevie Wonder) — 5
79 Motown 12TMG 1136 — Pops, We Love You/Pops, We Love You (Instrumental) (12", p/s, with Smokey Robinson, Marvin Gaye & Stevie Wonder) — 8
81 Tamla Motown TMG 1248 — Tenderness/Supremes Medley (picture disc) — 5
82 Capitol CLP 247 — Work That Body/Two Can Make It (picture disc) — 5
83 Motown CTME 2021 — DIANA ROSS (cassette EP) — 5
84 Capitol CLP 337 — Touch By Touch/Fight For It (picture disc) — 5
85 Motown TMGT 1380 — Love Hangover/Remember Me (12") — 12
95 Azuli AZLP 03 — Love Hangover (Remix)/(mixes) (12") — 10
73 Tamla Motown TMSP 1131 — LADY SINGS THE BLUES (2-LP, soundtrack, brown inner sleeves) — 18

DIANA ROSS & MICHAEL JACKSON

78 MCA MCA 396 — Ease On Down The Road/QUINCY JONES: Poppy Girls (p/s) — 8
78 MCA MCAT 12-396 — Ease On Down The Road (U.S. Version)/THE WIZ: Poppy Girls (12", p/s) — 15
78 MCA MCA 898 — Ease On Down The Road/QUINCY JONES: Poppy Girls (p/s, reissue) — 6
78 MCA MCAT 12-898 — Ease On Down The Road (Extended Version)/THE WIZ: Poppy Girls (12", reissue, p/s) — 12

(see also [Diana Ross &] Supremes, Michael Jackson, Quincy Jones)

DOCTOR (Isaiah) ROSS

66 Blue Horizon LP 1 — THE FLYING EAGLE (LP, 99 copies only) — 800
66 Xtra XTRA 1038 — DOCTOR ROSS (LP, reissue of "The Flying Eagle") — 50
66 Bounty BY 6020 — CALL THE DOCTOR (LP) — 40
72 Polydor 2460 169 — LIVE AT MONTREUX (LP) — 22
75 Big Bear BEAR 2 — THE HARMONICA BOSS (LP) — 15

ERROL ROSS

80 Carrere CAR 149 — Round And Round In Circles/Reggae Music Of Today (p/s) — 6

GENE ROSS

58 Parlophone R 4434 — Endless Sleep/The Only One — 25
58 Parlophone R 4434 — Endless Sleep/The Only One (78) — 10

JACK ROSS

62 London HLD 9534 — Cinderella/Margarita — 6
62 London HLD 9485 — Happy Jose/Sweet Georgia Brown — 6

JACKIE ROSS

64 Pye International 7N 25259 — Selfish One/Everything But Love — 50
64 Chess CRS 8003 — Jerk And Twine/New Lover — 30

JOAN ROSS

70 Crab CRAB 61 — Band Of Gold/HAMMERS: Midnight Sunshine — 10

JOE E. ROSS

64 Columbia 335X1710 — LOVE SONGS FROM A COP (LP) — 18

RICKY ROSS

83 Sticky Music GUM 8 — SO LONG AGO (cassette only, existence unconfirmed)
93 Sticky Music GUM 8CD — SO LONG AGO (CD, reissue) — 20

(see also Deacon Blue)

RONNIE ROSS

58 Parlophone PMC 1079 — DOUBLE EVENT (LP) — 75
61 Ember EMB 3323 — STOMPIN' WITH (LP) — 80
65 Ember FA 2023 — THE SWINGIN' SOUNDS OF THE JAZZ MAKERS (LP, with Allan Ganley) — 60
69 Fontana SFJL 915 — CLEOPATRA'S NEEDLE (LP) — 150

(see also Bill Le Sage)

SONNY ROSS

71 Mojo 2093 001 — Alakazam/The Piper Must Be Paid — 6

SPENCER ROSS

60 Philips PB 992 — Tracy's Theme/Thanksgiving Day Parade — 6
60 London HLX 9141 — Theme Of A Lonely Evening/Bobby's Blues — 7

T.T. ROSS

75 Dip DL 5079 — Single Girl/Funny What Love Can Do — 5
76 Dip DL 5104 — Last Date/I Am Sorry — 5
76 Lucky LY 6000 — No Charge/When I Was A Little Girl — 5
76 Lucky LY 6014 — Baby Why/TOUGH GANG: Part 2 — 5
76 Lucky LY 6017 — Misty Blue/Version — 5
76 House Of Eve 001 — Let The World Go Away/Part 2 — 5
76 House Of Eve 002 — Piece Of My Heart/Part 2 — 5
77 Lovers Rock CJ 622 — I Will/I Will Dub — 5

MINT VALUE £

LEON ROSSELSON

70 Acorn CF 206 SONGS FOR SCEPTICAL CIRCLES. 18
71 Trailer LER 3015 THE WORD IS HUGGA MUGGA CHUGGA HUMBUGGA BOOM CHIT (LP, with Roy Bailey & Martin Carthy) 15
75 Acorn CF 249 PALACES OF GOLD (LP) 18
75 Acorn CF 251 THAT'S NOT THE WAY IT'S GOT TO BE (LP, with Roy Bailey) 18
(see also Three City Four, Roy Bailey)

NITA ROSSI

65 Piccadilly 7N 35258 Every Little Day Now/Untrue Unfaithful. 30
66 Piccadilly 7N 35307 Here I Go Again/Something To Give 30
66 Piccadilly 7N 35354 The Daddy Christmas Song/Our Love Was Meant To Be 8
67 Piccadilly 7N 35384 Misty Blue/Come Around. 12

(Francis) ROSSI & (Bernard) FROST

85 Vertigo VER 17/FROS 1 Modern Romance (I Want To Fall In Love Again)/I Wonder Why (p/s). 6
85 Vertigo VERX 17/FROSX 1 Modern Romance (I Want To Fall In Love Again) (Extended Remix)/ I Wonder Why (Extended Remix) (12", p/s) 15
85 Vertigo VER 24 Jealousy/Where Are You Now? (p/s) 8
85 Vertigo VERX 24 Jealousy/Where Are You Now?/That's Alright (12", p/s) 18
(see also Status Quo, Bernie Frost, Boz Frost, Mickey Jupp, Mitchell/Coe Mysteries, Demis Roussos, Tokyo Olympics)

JOHN HENRY ROSTILL

71 Columbia DB 8794 Funny Old World/Green Apples 60
(see also Shadows)

STEVE ROSTRON

74 Sweet Folk & Country SFA 009 NO STRANGER'S FACE (LP) 30

ROTARY CONNECTION

68 Chess CRS 8072 Soul Man/Ruby Tuesday. 8
69 Chess CRS 8103 The Weight/Respect 12
70 Chess CRS 8106 Want You To Know/Memory Band 7
68 Chess CRL 4538 ROTARY CONNECTION (LP) 35
69 Chess CRL(S) 4547 ALADDIN (LP). 35
69 Chess CRLS 4551 SONGS (LP) 25

DAVID LEE ROTH

86 Warner Bros W 8656P Yankee Rose/Shy Boy (pin-up shaped picture disc). 10
88 Warner Bros W 7753W Damn Good (Edit)/Stand Up (7" in 12" x 12" card p/s with poster) 5
88 Warner Bros W 7650 California Girls (LP Version)/Just A Gigolo/I Ain't Got Nobody (Medley)/ Yankee Rose (Spanish Version) (CD). 8
91 Warner Bros W 0016P Sensible Shoes/California Girls (5" 'backstage tour pass'-shaped picture disc) . . 8
85 Warner Bros 925 2221 CRAZY FROM THE HEAT (mini LP) 8
(see also Van Halen)

ROTHCHILDS

66 Decca F 12411 You've Made Your Choice/It's Love 8
66 Decca F 12488 Artificial City/I Let Her Go 10

ROTORIK

01 Mosquito MSQ 018 (Sending All Processes) The Term Signal (12" EP). 8

ROUGE

78 SRT SRTSCUS 78104 Have You Seen Gene (no p/s) 75

ROUGH DIAMOND

90 Bedrock BR 1 Woman's Touch (p/s) 12

ROUGH JUSTICE

80s Rough Justice RJ 001 MILLION TO ONE (EP, p/s) 200

ROUGH RIDERS

74 Rare Earth RES 118 Hot California Beach/Do You See Me. 10

ROULETTES

62 Pye 7N 15467 Hully Gully Slip 'N' Slide/La Bamba. 20
63 Parlophone R 5072 Soon You'll Be Leaving Me/Tell Tale Tit 15
64 Parlophone R 5110 Bad Time/Can You Go. 15
64 Parlophone R 5148 I'll Remember Tonight/You Don't Love Me. 15
64 Parlophone R 5218 Stubborn Kind Of Fellow/Melody. 20
65 Parlophone R 5278 I Hope He Breaks Your Heart/Find Out The Truth 15
65 Parlophone R 5382 The Long Cigarette/Junk 30
66 Parlophone R 5419 The Tracks Of My Tears/Jackpot 20
66 Oak RGJ 205 I Can't Stop (1-sided, some with p/s) 250/150
66 Parlophone R 5461 I Can't Stop/Yesterday, Today And Tomorrow 20
67 Fontana TF 822 Rhyme Boy, Rhyme/Airport People 20
67 Fontana TF 876 Help Me To Help Myself/To A Taxi Driver. 20
65 Parlophone PMC 1257 STAKES AND CHIPS (LP). 600
(see also Adam Faith, Unit 4 + 2, Argent)

ROUND ROBIN

64 London HLU 9908 Kick That Little Foot Sally Ann/Slauson Party 20

ROUNDTABLE

69 Jay Boy BOY 18 Saturday Gigue/Scarborough Fair. 20
69 Jay Boy JSL 2 SPINNING WHEEL (LP) 35

DEMIS ROUSSOS

80 Mercury MER 25 Sorry/Love Is The Answer (p/s, A-side written by & featuring Francis Rossi/ Bernie Frost) 8
(see also Aphrodite's Child, Forminx, Rossi & Frost)

MINT VALUE £

ROUTERS

62	Warner Bros WB 77	Let's Go/Mashy	10
63	Warner Bros WB 91	Make It Snappy/Half Time	10
63	Warner Bros WB 97	Stingray/Snap Happy	12
63	Warner Bros WB 108	Big Band/A Ooga	10
64	Warner Bros WB 139	Stamp And Shake/Ah Ya	10
73	Warner Bros K 16156	Let's Go/Mashy (reissue)	5
63	Warner Bros WM/WS 8126	LET'S GO! WITH THE ROUTERS (LP, features Scott Walker)	50
64	Warner Bros WM/WS 8144	PLAY 1963'S GREAT INSTRUMENTALS (LP)	30
65	Warner Bros WM/WS 8162	CHARGE! (LP)	30

(see also Scott Walker)

JONATHAN ROUTH

57	Nixa NPT 19016	CANDID MIKE (10" LP)	18
62	Pye NPL 18077	CANDID CAMERA (LP)	18

ROVERS

55	Capitol CL 14283	Ichi-Bon Tami, Dachi/Why Oh-h (Why Do You Lie To Me?)	400
55	Capitol CL 14283	Ichi-Bon Tami, Dachi/Why Oh-h (Why Do You Lie To Me?) (78)	90

ROVING KIND

65	Decca F 12264	Ain't It True/Don't Tell Me The Time	7
66	Decca F 12381	Lies A Million/How Many Times	7

ROWAN & MARTIN

69	CBS 63490	ROWAN AND MARTIN'S LAUGH-IN (LP)	12
69	Atlantic 588 151	ROWAN AND MARTIN AT WORK (LP)	15

ROWDIES

78	Birds Nest BN 109	A.C.A.B. (All Coppers Are Bastards)/Negative Malfunction/Freeze Out	25
79	Teenage Depression TD 1/2	She's No Angel/Had Me A Real Good Time (p/s)	8

(see also Boys, Lurkers, Steve Sharp & Cleancuts)

NORMIE ROWE

66	Polydor 56132	It's Not Easy/Mary Mary	6
66	Polydor 56144	Ain't Nobody Home/Ooh La La	5
67	Polydor 56159	Going Home/I Don't Care (Just Take Me There) (some in p/s)	8/5

MAJOR ROWELY

65	Stateside SS 438	There's A Riot Going On/Do It The Right Way	15

JEFF ROWENA GROUP

61	Pye 7N 15328	Peanut Vendor/Bullfight	6
61	Pye 7N 15365	Ambush/John Peel	5
62	Pye 7N 15423	La Cucuracha/Ten Ton Caroline	5
63	Oriole CB 1787	Dance Baby Dance/Diddle De Dum (as Jeff Rowena Five)	6
63	Oriole CB 1797	Dance Baby Dance/Love Me Once Again	6
63	Oriole CB 1810	Diddle De Dum/Lovely Water Melon	6
67	CBS 202460	Eleanor/Short Skirts (solo)	5

(see also Big Joe Smith)

CHERRY ROWLAND

63	Fontana TF 420	Nobody But Me/Boys	10
74	Decca F 13491	Here Is Where The Love Is/I Can Give You Back Yourself	12

(see also Cherry Roland)

JACKIE ROWLAND

72	Sioux SI 015	Indian Reservation/JUNIOR SMITH: I'm In A Dancing Mood	15
72	Sioux SI 022	Lonely Man/JOE MANSANO: The Trial Of Pama Dice	25

(see also Joe Higgs)

KEVIN ROWLAND

88	Mercury DEXYB 1412	Young Man/The Way You Look Tonight/Even When I Hold You/Walk Away (12", gatefold p/s)	8
88	Mercury ROW 112	Tonight (12" Dance Mix)/Tonight (New York Dub Mix)/Come On Eileen/Kevin Rowland's Band (12", p/s)	8

(see also Dexys Midnight Runners)

STEVE ROWLAND

67	Fontana TF 844	So Sad/I See Red	10

(see also Family Dogg)

JOHN ROWLES

68	MCA MU 1023	Hush Not A Word To Mary/The Night We Called It A Day	5
69	MCA MKPS 2001	THAT LOVIN' FEELING (LP)	15

ROX

82	Teenteeze ROX 100	HOT LOVE IN THE CITY (Hot Love In The City/Do Ya Feel Like Lovin'/Love Ya Like A Diamond (EP)	25
83	MFN 12KUT 103	KRAZY KUTZ (EP)	8

ROXETTE

89	EMI CDEM 87	The Look (Head Drum Mix)/The Look (7" Version)/Silver Blue (Demo Version)/Sleeping Single (Demo Version) (CD)	20
89	EMI EM 96	Dressed For Success/The Look (white p/s)	5
89	EMI 12EM 96	Dressed For Success (The Mark McGuire Mix)/The Look (Big Red Mix)/ Dressed For Success (7" Version) (12", white p/s)	12
89	EMI CDEM 96	Dressed For Success (7" Version)/The Look (7" Version)/Dressed For Success — The Remix/Dressed For Success — The Voice (CD, white inlay)	20
90	EMI CDEM 108	Listen To Your Heart (Single Mix)/Dressed For Success (New Radio Mix)/ (I Could Never) Give You Up/Never Ending Love (live) (CD)	18
90	EMI CDEM 141	It Must Have Been Love/Paint/Cry (live)/Surrender (live) (CD)	18
90	EMI CDEM 149	Listen To Your Heart (Swedish Single Mix)/Listen To Your Heart (U.S. Club Edit Mix)/Listen To Your Heart (Dangerous LP Mix) (CD)	18

91	EMI CDEM 162	Dressed For Success (Single Version)/(New Radio Mix)/ The Look (Big Red Mix)/The Voice (CD)	20
91	EMI CDEM 177	Joyride (7" Version)/Come Back (Before You Leave)/Joyride (Magicfriendmix) 12" Version/Joyride (U.S. Remix) (CD)	8
91	EMI CDEM 190	Fading Like A Flower (Every Time You Leave) (Gatica Remix)/The Look/ Physical Fascination (Guitar Solo Version)/I Remember You (CD)	10
91	EMI CDEM 204	The Big L (Album Version)/The Big L (The Bigger The Better Mix)/ One Is Such A Lonely Number (Demo)/It Must Have Been Love (CD)	10
91	EMI EM 215	Spending My Time/Listen To Your Heart (poster p/s)	6
91	EMI CDEM 215	Spending My Time (Single Version)/(Electric Dance Remix)/The Sweet Hello, The Sad Goodbye/Listen To Your Heart (7" Edit) (CD)	15
92	EMI CDEM 227	Church Of Your Heart/I Call Your Name/Come Back (Before You Leave) (Demo)/ Fading Like A Flower (Every Time You Leave) (3.54) (CD)	15
92	EMI CDEMS 227	Church Of Your Heart/I Call Your Name/Soul Deep (Tom Lord-alge Remix)/ The Roxette Megamix (CD, digipak)	15
92	EMI CDEM 241	How Do You Do/Fading Like A Flower(live)/Knockin' On Every Door (Bomkrash (12" Remix)/How Do You Do (Bomkrash 12" Remix) (CD)	10
92	EMI EM 253	It Must Have Been Love/It Must Have Been Love (p/s)	15
92	EMI CDEMS 253	Queen Of Rain (Radio Edit)/Pearls Of Passion/Interview With Roxette (CD)	12
92	EMI CDEM 253	Queen Of Rain/It Must Have Been Love/Paint/Dangerous (CD)	12
95	EMI 12EMDJ 406	The Look '95 (Rapino Club Mix)/(Rapino Dub Mix)/(Chaps Donna Bass Mix) (12", promo only)	12
98	EMI CDEMDJ 537	Wish I Could Fly (CD in box with photos and retrospective CD [ROXHITS 001], promo only)	80

ROXY MUSIC

72	Island WIP 6144	Virginia Plain/The Numberer (initially pink labels, later orange)	each 5
73	Island WIP 6159	Pyjamarama/The Pride And The Pain	5
74	Island WIP 6173	Street Life/Hula Kula	5
74	Island WIP 6208	All I Want Is You/Your Application's Failed	5
78	Polydor/EG 2001 756	Do The Strand/Editions Of You (12", p/s)	8
79	Polydor/EGPOSPX 67	Angel Eyes (Extended 6.39)/My Little Girl (12", p/s)	8
82	E.G. ROXYX 3	More Than This/India (12", p/s)	8
86	E.G. EGOX 26	Love Is The Drug/Let's Stick Together (12", p/s, promo only)	15
79	Polydor/E.G. EGPD 001	MANIFESTO (LP, picture disc)	12
79	Polydor/E.G. EGPD 001	MANIFESTO (LP, picture disc, mispress, 1 side plays Gordon Giltrap's "Fear Of The Dark" LP)	12
81	Polydor/E.G. EGBS 001	THE FIRST SEVEN ALBUMS (7-LP box set plus insert)	50
81	Polydor/E.G. EGBS 001	THE FIRST SEVEN ALBUMS (7-cassette box set)	35
83	E.G. 815 849-2	THE ATLANTIC YEARS 1973-1980 (CD)	18

(see also Brian Eno, Bryan Ferry, Andy Mackay, Phil Manzanera, Dumbelles, 801, Fripp & Eno)

ALVIN ROY & THE SARATOGA JAZZ BAND

61	Interdisc INT 45001	Yogi/Broken Promises	5

DEREK ROY

57	Oriole CB 1415	Derek Roy's All-Star Party (with Bob Monkhouse, Richard Murdoch, Jon Pertwee, Ted Ray & others)	12
57	Oriole CB 1415	Derek Roy's All-Star Party (78)	10

(see also Jon Pertwee, Bob Monkhouse)

HUGH ROY

70	Supreme SUP 211	Double Attack/Puzzle	12
70	Explosion EX 2040	Whisper A Little Prayer (actually by Audley Rollins)/ Rain A Fall (actually by Melanie)	12
70	Punch PH 34	Scandal/Son Of The Wise	12
70	Duke Reid DR 2509	Wake The Town/Big Boy And Teacher	15
70	Duke Reid DR 2510	Rule The Nation/NORA DEAN: Ay Ay Ay Ay	15
70	Duke Reid DR 2513	Wear You To The Ball (with John Holt)/EARL LINDO: The Ball	15
70	Duke Reid DR 2514	You'll Never Get Away/TOMMY McCOOK QUINTET: Rock Away	15
70	Duke Reid DR 2515	Version Galore/TOMMY McCOOK: Nehru	25
71	Duke Reid DR 2516	Testify/TOMMY McCOOK: Super Soul	15
71	Duke Reid DR 2517	Tom Drunk (with Hopeton Lewis)/TOMMY McCOOK: Wailing	15
71	Duke Reid DR 2518	True True/On The Beach	15
71	Duke Reid DR 2519	Flashing My Whip/Do It Right	15
71	Treasure Isle TI 7059	Drive Her Home (Parts 1 & 2) (with Hopeton Lewis)	15
71	Treasure Isle TI 7062	Behold/Way Back Home (with Tommy McCook)	15
71	Treasure Isle TI 7064	Everybody Bawlin'/Ain't That Loving You	15
71	Upsetter US 375	Earthquake/Suspicious Minds	12
71	Duke DU 105	Love I Tender/JOYA LANDIS: When The Lights Are Low	12
71	Duke Reid DR 2517	Tom Drunk/Wailing (as U Roy, B-side actually by Tommy McCook)	12
72	G.G. GG 4532	Way Down South/BILLY DYCE: Be My Guest	12
72	Duke DU 137	Live It Up/DENNIS BROWN: Baby Don't Do It	12
72	Jackpot JP 806	Two Ton Gulleto/Version	12
72	Dynamic DYN 448	Festival Wise/Festival Wise Part 2	12
72	Banana BA 367	Keep On Running/LARRY'S ALL STARS: Version	12
72	Grape GR 3026	On Top The Peak/TYPHOON ALLSTARS: Race Attack	12
72	Pama PM 835	Way Down South/BILLY DYCE: Be My Guest	12
72	Punch PH 104	Nannyscrank (title actually "Nanny Skank")/PITTSBURG ALLSTARS: Scank Version	12
72	Green Door GD 4034	Hudson Affair/KEITH HUDSON: Hot Stick — Version	15
72	Trojan TR 7884	Hat Trick/Wet Version	15
73	Green Door GD 4052	King Tubby's Special/Here Come The Heartaches	12
73	Gayfeet GS 210	Hard Feeling/Regular Style	12
73	Duke DU 157	Higher The Mountain/OLD BOYS INC.: Version	12

MINT VALUE £

73	Harry J. HJ 6651	Treasure Isle Skank/Words Of Wisdom	12
76	Soulfood SF 001	High Priest/London City Rock	15
71	Trojan TBL 161	VERSION GALORE (LP, as U Roy)	30
73	Attack ATLP 1006	U ROY (LP, as U Roy)	25

(see also U Roy, Jeff Barnes, Melodians, Delroy Wilson)

HUGH ROY JUNIOR

71	Big BG 329	Papacito/RUPIE EDWARDS: I'm Gonna Live Some Life	12
71	Supreme SUP 211	Double Attack/MURPHY'S ALL STARS: Puzzle	12
72	Ashanti ASH 405	King Of The Road/ROOSEVELT ALL STARS: Version	12
72	Jackpot JP 806	Two Ton Guletto/Version	12

I ROY

71	Moodisc MU 3509	Musical Pleasure/JO JO BENNETT: Hot Pop	12
71	Moodisc MU 3510	Heart Don't Leap (as I. Roy & Dennis Walks)/ DENNIS WALKS & MUDIE'S ALLSTARS: Snow Bird	12
71	Moodisc MU 3512	Let Me Tell You Boy (with Ebony Sisters)/MUDIE'S ALLSTARS: Version	12
71	Moodisc HM 104	The Drifter (with Dennis Walks)/JO JO BENNETT: Snowbird	12
72	Green Door GD 4030	Hot Bomb (with Jumpers)/JUMPERS: The Bomb	12
72	Green Door GD 4044	Make Love/STAGE: Tic Toc Bill	12
73	Pyramid PYR 7001	Tip From The Prince/Fat Beef Skank	12
73	Attack ATT 8050	Space Flight/JERRY LEWIS: Burning Wire	12
73	Downtown DT 503	Blackman's Time/High Jacking	12
73	Downtown DT 519	Clapper's Tail/Live And Learn	12
73	Duke DU 156	Buck And The Preacher/PETE WESTON ALLSTARS: Preacher — Version	12
73	Smash SMA 2337	The Magnificent Seven/Leggo Beast	12
73	Smash SMA 2338	Rose Of Sheron/Slip Out	12
73	Techniques TE 926	Pauper And The King/GREGORY ISAACS: Loving Pauper	12
73	Techniques TE 930	Monkey Fashion/Medley Mood	12
73	Ackee ACK 503	Great Great Great (with Ken Parker)/RUPIE EDWARDS ALLSTARS: Version	12
73	Ackee ACK 510	Sound Education/AUGUSTUS PABLO: Cinderella In Black	18
73	Harry J HJ-6655	Musical Drum Sound/NOW GENERATION: Musical Drum — Version	12
73	Pama PM 854	Cowtown Skank/AUGUSTUS PABLO: Cowtown Skank Version	12
74	Atra ATRA 017	Yah Ma Ride/SWEET HARMONY: Mexican Rockin'	12
74	Ashanti ASH 412	Mood For Love (Parts 1 & 2)	12
75	Bullet BU 551	Step Right Up/ANDY'S ALLSTARS: Banjo Serenade	12
75	Lucky DL 5098	I Man Time/Version	12
76	Dip DL 5107	Padlock/Lock And Key (copies also exist with Lucky label)	each 12
70s	Nationwide NW 005	Tea Pot/Tea Cup	12
73	Trojan TRLS 63	PRESENTING I ROY (LP, original issue with "12 Neasden Lane" address and rough orange/white paper labels)	30
74	Trojan TRLS 71	HELL AND SORROW (LP, original issue with "12 Neasden Lane" address and rough orange/white paper labels)	25
74	Trojan TRLS 91	THE MANY MOODS OF I ROY (LP, original issue with "12 Neasden Lane" address and rough orange/white paper labels)	25
75	Grounation GROL 504	TRUTH & RIGHTS (LP)	25
78	Third World TWS 930	THE GODFATHER (LP)	20

(see also Keith Hudson & I Roy)

LEE ROY

54	Philips PB 226	The Creep/B.O. Plenty (78)	6
65	Island WI 251	Oh Ee Baby/My Loving Baby Come Back	12

LITTLE ROY

69	Crab CRAB 39	Without My Love (actually by Roy & Joy)/WINSTON SAMUELS: Here I Come Again	12
70	Bullet BU 445	Keep Trying/THE MATADORS: Version II	12
70	Camel CA 43	Scrooge/In The Days Of Old	12
70	Camel CA 46	You Run Come/THE LITTLE ROYS: Skank King (actually "Skank Me" by Little Roy)	12
70	Camel CA 52	Fight Them/Dreadlock	12
71	Escort ERT 850	Yester-Me Yester-You Yesterday/MATADOR ALL-STARS: Yes Sir	12
71	Punch PH 75	Hard Fighter/COUNT OSSIE: Back To Africa Version	12

(see also Roy & Joy, Little Roys)

MAD ROY

70	Banana BA 324	Nanny Version (actually by Dennis Alcapone)/BIGGER D: Freedom Version	15
71	Banana BA 326	Home Version (actually by Dennis Alcapone)/SOUND DIMENSION: One Time	15
71	Banana BA 327	Universal Love/ROLAND ALPHONSO: Shelly Belly	15
71	Banana BA 328	Duppy Serenade/Sunshine Version (both sides actually by Dennis Alcapone)	15

(pseudonym for Leroy Wallace; see also Dennis Alcapone)

U ROY JUNIOR

72	Duke Reid DR 2520	Rock To The Beat/Love Is Not A Gamble (both actually by Dennis Alcapone)	12
72	Attack ATT 8030	This Is A Pepper (as U Roy Junior)/JOHN HOLT: Justice	12
72	Sioux SI 024	The Wedding (as U Roy Junior)/LLOYD'S ALL STARS: Buttercup	12
73	Randy's RAN 532	Froggie (as U Roy Junior)/RHYTHM RULERS: Version	12
73	Techniques TE 928	Aunt Kereba (as U Roy Junior)/DON RECO: Waterloo Rock (B-side actually by Reco Rodriquez)	12

(see also Hugh Roy, Dennis Alcapone, Sir Harry, Shorty Perry, Heptones, Herman Chin-Loy)

ROY & ANNETTE

63	R&B JB 107	My Baby/Go Your Ways	20

(see also Tommy McCook, Lester Sterling)

ROY & DUKE ALL STARS

68	Blue Cat BS 113	Pretty Blue Eyes Parts 1 & 2	25
68	Blue Cat BS 117	The Train Parts 1 & 2	25

(see also Roy Panton)

MINT VALUE £

ROY & ENID

68	Coxsone CS 7063	Rocking Time/RALPH BLAKE: High Blood Pressure	25
68	Coxsone CS 7069	He'll Have To Go/CARLTON & SHOES: Love Is A Treasure	30
69	Coxsone CS 7088	Reggae For Days/SOUND DIMENSION: Holy Moses	25

(Little) ROY & JOY

73	Camel CA 107	Rainy Weather/THE DEN BROTHERS: Version	8

(see also Little Roys)

ROY (Panton) & MILLIE

62	Island WI 005	We'll Meet/ROLAND ALPHONSO: Back Beat (B-side act. with City Slickers)	30
63	Island WI 050	This World/Never Say Goodbye	20
63	Island WI 090	There'll Come A Day/I Don't Want You	20
63	Blue Beat BB 154	Over And Over/I'll Go (with Prince Buster All Stars)	22
64	Black Swan WI 409	Cherry I Love You/You're The Only One	20
64	Black Swan WI 410	Oh Merna/DON DRUMMOND: Dog War Bossa Nova	20
64	Black Swan WI 427	Oh Shirley/Marie	20

(see also Roy Panton, Millie [Small])

ROY (Panton) & PATSY

62	Blue Beat BB 118	My Happy Home/In Your Arms Dear (with Hersang & His Combo)	20

(see also Roy Panton)

ROY (Richards) & PAULETTE

63	Island WI 067	Have You Seen My Baby/Since You're Gone	20

ROY (Panton) & YVONNE (Harrison)

64	Blue Beat BB 258	Little Girl/No More	20
64	Black Swan WI 436	Two Roads/Join Together	20

(see also Roy Panton)

BILLY JOE ROYAL

62	Oriole CB 1751	Never In A Hundred Years/We Haven't A Moment To Lose	18
65	CBS 201802	Down In The Boondocks/Oh! What A Night	10
65	CBS 201983	You Make Me Feel Like A Man/I've Got To Be Somebody	7
65	CBS 202009	I Knew You When/Steal Away	7
66	CBS 202052	It's A Good Time/Don't Wait Up For Me Mama	7
66	CBS 202087	Heart's Desire/Everbody's Gotta Cry	35
66	Atlantic 584 002	Never In A Hundred Years/We Haven't A Moment To Lose (reissue)	7
66	CBS 202400	High On A Hilltop/I'm Gonna Get Right Tonight	8
67	CBS 202548	Yo Yo/We Tried	8
67	CBS 2861	The Greatest Love/These Are Not My People	7
67	CBS 3044	Hush/Watching From The Bandstand	7
68	CBS 3402	Don't You Be Ashamed/Don't You Think It's Time	7
68	CBS 3644	Storybook Children/Just Between You And Me	7
68	CBS 3858	Gabriel/Movies In My Mind	7
69	CBS 4470	Cherry Hill Park/Helping Hand	7
66	CBS BPG 62590	INTRODUCING BILLY JOE ROYAL (LP)	35

BOBBY ROYAL

63	HMV POP 1253	Big Big Star/Little Word Of Love	10

JAMES ROYAL (& HAWKS)

65	Parlophone R 5290	She's About A Mover/Black Cloud (as James Royal & Hawks)	25
65	Parlophone R 5383	Work Song/I Can't Stand It	35
67	CBS 202525	Call My Name/When It Comes To My Baby	20
67	CBS 2739	It's All In The Game/Green Days	8
68	CBS 2959	Take Me Like I Am/Sitting In The Station	6
68	CBS 3232	I Can't Stand It/Little Bit Of Rain	7
68	CBS 3450	Hey Little Boy/Thru' The Love	15
68	CBS 3624	A Woman Called Sorrow/Fire	20
69	CBS 3797	Time Hangs On My Mind/Anna-Lee	7
69	CBS 3915	House Of Jack/Which Way To Nowhere	12
69	CBS 4139	I've Something Bad On My Mind/She's Independent	7
69	CBS 4463	Send Out Love/I've Lost You	15
70	CBS 5032	And Soon The Darkness/I'm Going Home	6
70	Carnaby CNS 4021	Carolina/Big Heat On The Loose	7
71	Carnaby 6151 002	Carolina/A Woman Called Sorrow	6
72	Carnaby 6151 006	Two Of Us/Who Are We (with Liz Christian)	6
69	CBS 63780	CALL MY NAME (LP)	30
70	Carnaby CNLS 6008	ONE WAY (LP)	40
72	Carnaby 6302 011	THE LIGHT AND SHADE OF JAMES ROYAL (LP)	40

ROBBIE ROYAL

65	Mercury MF 923	Only Me/I Don't Need You	8
65	Decca F 12097	Within My Lonely Heart/When I Found You	6

ROYAL AIR FORCE CENTRAL BAND

56	HMV B 10957	"Reach For The Sky" Theme/The Jolly Airman	5
57	Decca F 10932	High Flight/Out Of The Blue	5
61	HMV 7P 287	The Dambusters March/Lilliburlero	5
57	HMV 7EG 8265	R.A.F. CENTRAL BAND (EP)	8

ROYAL BLUES

69	Pye 7N 17670	Mountain Of Love/Wishful Thinking	6
69	Pye 7N 17732	Mendocino/Hi-Lili Hi-Lo	6
69	Pye 7N 17769	Proud Mary/Sunny Girl Friend	6
69	Pye 7N 17847	High As A Mountain/Wildwood Flower	6

ROYALETTES

65	MGM MGM 1272	Poor Boy/Watch What Happens	18
65	MGM MGM 1279	It's Gonna Take A Miracle/Out Of Sight Out Of Mind	25

MINT VALUE £

65	MGM MGM 1292	I Want To Meet Him/Never Again	22
66	MGM MGM 1302	You Bring Me Down/Only When You're Lonely	22
66	MGM MGM 1324	It's A Big Mistake/I Want To Meet Him	18
68	Big T BIG 106	River Of Tears/Something Wonderful	20
66	MGM MGM-C 8028	THE ELEGANT SOUND OF THE ROYALETTES (LP)	100

ROYAL GUARDSMEN

67	Stateside SS 574	Snoopy Vs The Red Baron/I Needed You	6
67	Stateside SS 2010	The Return Of The Red Baron/Sweetmeats Slide	6
67	Stateside SS 2035	Airplane Song/OM	6
67	Stateside SS 2051	Wednesday/So Right (To Be In Love)	8
67	London HLP 10171	Snoopy's Christmas/It Kinda Looks Like Christmas	6
68	London HLP 10211	Snoopy For President/Down Behind The Lines	6
68	London HLP 10235	Baby Let's Wait/So Right (To Be In Love)	5
68	London HLP 10182	I Say Love/I'm Not Gonna Stay	5
67	Stateside S(S)L 10202	SNOOPY VS THE RED BARON (LP)	30
68	London HA-P/SH-P 8351	THE RETURN OF THE RED BARON (LP)	30

ROYAL HOLIDAYS

58	London HLU 8722	Margaret/I'm Sorry (I Did You Wrong)	120
58	London HLU 8722	Margaret/I'm Sorry (I Did You Wrong) (78)	45

ROYAL ROCKERS

60	Top Rank JAR 326	Jet II/Swinging Mambo	18

ROYALS

64	Blue Beat BB 259	Save Mama/Out De Fire	20
68	Amalgamated AMG 831	Never See Come See/CANNONBALL BRYAN TRIO: Jumping Jack	18
69	Trojan TR 662	Pick Out Me Eye/Think You Too Bad	12
69	Duke DU 29	Never Gonna Give You Up/Don't Mix Me Up	10
73	Dip DL 5016	Promised Land/Every Jamaican Is A Rebel	6

ROYAL SHOWBAND, WATERFORD

64	HMV POP 1377	Huckle Buck/I Ran All The Way Home	6

ROYAL TEENS

58	HMV POP 454	Short Shorts/Planet Rock	40
58	HMV POP 454	Short Shorts/Planet Rock (78)	15
59	Capitol CL 15068	Little Cricket/Believe Me	25

ROYALTONES

58	London HLJ 8744	Poor Boy/Wail!	20
58	London HLJ 8744	Poor Boy/Wail! (78)	20
61	London HLU 9296	Flamingo Express/Tacos	18
64	Stateside SS 309	Our Faded Love/Holy Smokes	12

ROYALTY

69	CBS 4181	That Kind Of Girl/Will You Be Staying After Sunday	6

EARL ROYCE & OLYMPICS

64	Columbia DB 7433	Que Sera Sera/I Really Do	25
65	Parlophone R 5261	Guess Things Happen That Way/Sure To Fall	22

ROY'S BOYS

64	Columbia DB 7425	Do Wah Diddy Diddy—I'm Into Something Good—I Want To Hold Your Hand/ Oh! Pretty Woman—Have I The Right?—It's All Over Now	7

LITA ROZA

51	Decca F 9731	Allentown Jail/I Wish I Knew (78)	8
51	Decca F 9785	I'm Gonna Wash That Man Right Outta My Hair/A Wonderful Guy (78)	8
52	Decca F 9955	Oakie Boogie/Raminay (78)	10
53	Decca F 10070	(How Much Is) That Doggie In The Window/Tell Me We'll Meet Again (78)	20
53	Decca F 75082	(How Much Is) That Doggie In The Window/Tell Me We'll Meet Again (export issue)	100
53	Decca F 10128	Seven Lonely Days/No-One Will Ever Know (78)	8
53	Decca F 10144	Crazy Man, Crazy/Oo! What You Do To Me (78)	6
54	Decca F 10363	Skinnie Minnie (Fishtail)/My Kid Brother (78)	8
54	Decca F 10240	Changing Partners/Just A Dream Or Two Ago (B-side with Stargazers)	20
54	Decca F 10269	Bell Bottom Blues (with Johnston Brothers)/Make Love To Me (both with Ted Heath Orchestra)	15
54	Decca F 10277	Young At Heart/Secret Love	15
54	Decca F 10393	Call Off The Wedding/The "Mama-Doll" Song	15
55	Decca F 10427	Heartbeat/Leave Me Alone	15
55	Decca F 10431	Let Me Go, Lover!/Make Yourself Comfortable	15
55	Decca F 10479	Tomorrow/Foolishly	15
55	Decca F 10536	Two Hearts, Two Kisses (Make One Love)/Keep Me In Mind	15
55	Decca F 10541	The Man In The Raincoat/Today And Ev'ry Day	12
55	Decca F 10611	Hey There/Hernando's Hideaway	20
56	Decca F 10679	Jimmy Unknown/The Rose Tattoo	20
56	Decca F 10728	Too Young To Go Steady/You're Not Alone	12
56	Decca F 10761	No Time For Tears/But Love Me (Love But Me)	12
56	Decca F 10792	Innismore/The Last Waltz	12
56	Decca F 10830	Hey! Jealous Lover/Julie	12
57	Decca F 10861	Lucky Lips/Tears Don't Care Who Cries Them	15
57	Decca F 10884	Tonight My Heart She Is Crying/Five Oranges, Four Apples	10
57	Decca F 10921	I Need You/You've Changed	10
58	Pye 7N 15119	Pretend You Don't See Him/Ha-Ha-Ha!	7
58	Pye 7N 15133	I Need Somebody/You're The Greatest	7
58	Pye 7N 15139	I Could Have Danced All Night/The Wonderful Season Of Love	7
58	Pye 7N 15149	Sorry, Sorry, Sorry/Hillside In Scotland	7
58	Pye 7N 15155	Nel Blu Dipinto Di Blu (Volare)/It's A Boy	7

			MINT VALUE £
58	Pye N 15155	Nel Blu Dipinto Di Blu (Volare)/It's A Boy (78)	6
59	Pye 7N 15190	This Is My Town/Oh Dear What Can The Matter Be	7
59	Pye N 15190	This Is My Town/Oh Dear What Can The Matter Be (78)	6
59	Pye 7N 15204	Allentown Jail/Once In A While	7
59	Pye N 15204	Allentown Jail/Once In A While (78)	6
59	Pye 7N 15241	Let It Rain, Let It Rain/Maybe You'll Be There	7
59	Pye N 15241	Let It Rain, Let It Rain/Maybe You'll Be There (78)	8
63	Ember EMB S 168	Mama (He Treats Your Daughter Mean)/(He's My) Dreamboat (as Lisa Rosa)	12
65	Columbia DB 7785	What Am I Supposed To Do/Where Do I Go From Here	6
65	Columbia DB 7689	Keep Watch Over Him/Stranger Things Have Happened	7
57	Decca DFE 6386	LITA ROZA SELECTION (EP)	40
57	Decca DFE 6399	LITA ROZA (EP)	35
58	Decca DFE 6443	BETWEEN THE DEVIL AND THE DEEP BLUE SEA NO. 1 (EP)	35
54	Decca LF 1187	PRESENTING LITA ROZA (10" LP)	130
56	Decca LF 1243	LISTENING IN THE AFTER HOURS (10" LP)	120
57	Decca LK 4171	LOVE IS THE ANSWER (LP)	100
57	Decca LK 4218	BETWEEN THE DEVIL AND THE DEEP BLUE SEA (LP)	75
58	Pye Nixa NPL 18020	ME ON A CAROUSEL (LP, also stereo NSPL 83003)	45/50
60	Pye NPL 18047	DRINKA LITA ROZA DAY (LP)	80
64	Ember NR 5009	LOVE SONGS FOR NIGHT PEOPLE (LP)	40

(see also Stargazers, Johnston Brothers)

RPM

93	Mo' Wax MW 005	Food Of My D'Rhythm/(Version)/Take Me Out Of The Ordinary/(Version) (12", stickered sleeve)	8
94	Mo' Wax MW018	2,000/Sorti Des Ombres/(dub) (12", 3 different covers, full colour, green and purple or blue)	25/15/10

RUB-A-DUBS WITH DANDY

65	Blue Beat BB 304	Without Love/I Know	25

(see also Dandy)

RUBBER BAND

73	Youngblood YB 1052	Moonwalker/Wichita	6
69	Major Minor SMCP 5045	CREAM SONGBOOK (LP)	22
69	Major Minor SMCP 5048	HENDRIX SONGBOOK (LP)	22

RUBBER BOOTZ

67	Deram DM 134	Joy Ride/Chicano	25

JOHNNY RUBBISH

78	United Artists UP 36405	Living In NW3 4JR/Other Side (p/s)	10

RUBELLA BALLET

82	Xntrix XN 2005	The Ballet Dance/Something To Give/Unemployed/Krak Trak (p/s)	5
82	Xntrix ZN 2004	BALLET DOG (C-30 cassette with insert)	6
88	Ubiquitous DAY-GLO 6	THE BALLET'S BIRTHDAY (2-LP, box set, with book & 5 inserts)	15

RUBETTES

74	Polydor 2058 529	Juke Box Jive/When You're Falling In Love (p/s)	5
76	State STAT 27	Under One Roof/Sign Of The Times (p/s)	5
77	Polydor 2058 943	Come On Over/Let Him Bleed (p/s)	5
78	Polydor 2059 042	Goodbye Dolly Gray/Great Be The Nation (p/s)	5
78	Polydor 2059 059	Movin'/San Andreas (p/s)	5
79	Polydor 2059 100	Lola/Truth Of The Matter (p/s)	5
79	Polydor 2059 173	Kid Runaway/Southbound Train (p/s)	5
82	V-Tone VTONE 004	Don't Come Crying/Breakdown	5
74	Polydor 2489 090	WEAR IT'S AT (LP, gatefold sleeve, with paper hat insert)	12

(see also Baskin & Copperfield)

RUBIN

75	MCA MU 196	You've Been Away/Baby, You're My Everything	6

RUBAIYATS

68	Action ACT 4516	Omar Khayam/Tomorrow	18

RUBY & GLORIA

71	Big Shot BI 583	Worried Over You/Worried Over You – Version	10
71	Black Swan BW 1409	Talk To Me Baby/LLOYD'S ALL STARS: Talk To Me Baby — Version	10

RUBY & ROMANTICS

63	London HLR 9679	Our Day Will Come/Moonlight And Music	12
63	London HLR 9734	My Summer Love/Sweet Love And Sweet Forgiveness	15
63	London HLR 9771	Hey There Lonely Boy/Not A Moment Too Soon	15
63	London HLR 9801	Young Wings Can Fly/Day Dreaming	12
64	London HLR 9881	Our Everlasting Love/Much Better Off Than I've Ever Been	10
64	London HLR 9916	Baby Come Home/Every Day's A Holiday	15
64	London HLR 9935	When You're Young And In Love/I Cry Alone	15
65	London HLR 9972	Your Baby Doesn't Love Me Anymore/We'll Meet Again	15
69	A&M AMS 750	Hurting Each Other/Baby I Could Be So Good At Loving You	15
63	London RE-R 1389	OUR DAY WILL COME (EP)	80
64	London RE-R 1427	HEY THERE LONELY BOY (EP)	90
63	London HA-R 8078	OUR DAY WILL COME (LP)	90
66	London HA-R 8282	GREATEST HITS (LP)	90

(see also Danny Davis Orchestra)

RUDDY & SKETTO

71	Supreme SUP 218	Every Night/Ethiopia	8

(see also Sketto Rich)

MINT VALUE £

RUDE ASS TINKER
90s Deathchant DEATH 30 — Imperial Break/Silk Ties (12", limited issue) 18
(see also Mu-Ziq)

RUDE BOYS
67 Island WI 3088 — Rock Steady Massachusetts/Going Home 20

RUDI
78 Good Vibrations GOT 1 — Big Time/Number 1 (folded p/s, 3,000 only) 20
79 Good Vibrations GOT 12 — I Spy/Genuine Reply/Sometimes/Ripped In Two (p/s) 18
81 Jamming! CREATE 1 — When I Was Dead/The Pressure's On (p/s) 5
82 Jamming! CREATE 3 — Crimson/14 Steps (p/s) 5

RUDIES (FANATICS)
68 Blue Cat BS 107 — The 7-11 Go To The Go Go Club (Parts 1 & 2) 20
68 Blue Cat BS 109 — Cupid/RECO'S ALLSTARS: Wise Message 20
68 Nu Beat NB 001 — Train To Vietnam/Skaville To Rainbow City 15
68 Nu Beat NB 005 — Engine 59/My Girl 12
68 Fab FAB 46 — I Wanna Go Home/La Mer 10
68 Fab FAB 70 — Give Me The Rights/I Do Love You (as Rudies Fanatics) 10
68 Fab FAB 71 — Mighty Meaty/Go (as Rudies Fanatics) 10
69 Doctor Bird DB 1301 — Sin Thing/What's Your Name 15
69 Doctor Bird DB 1302 — Boss Sound/RECO & RUDIES: Peace 20
69 Fab FAB 104 — Brixton Market/Rudie's Joy 10
70 Pama PM 789 — Give Peace A Chance/Theme From She 10
70 Trojan TR 7798 — Patches/Split 10
71 Spinning Wheel SW 106 — My Sweet Lord/Devil's Lead Soup 10
(see also Freddie Notes, Sonny, Binns & Rudies, Rico, Dandy, Owen & Dandy, Downtown All Stars, Desmond Riley)

RUDIMENTARY PENI
81 Outer Himalayan OH 003 — RUDIMENTARY PENI (EP, A4 foldout p/s with booklet, later 14" x 7") 12/10
82 Crass 211984/2 — FARCE (EP, initially in 21" x 14" foldout black & white p/s) 10/7
83 Corpus Christi CHRISTITS 6 — DEATH CHURCH (LP) 14
80s Corpus Christi — CACOPHONY (LP, with booklet) 15
(see also Magits)

RUD(D)Y (Grant) & SKETTO (Rich)
62 Dice CC 5 — Summer Is Just Around The Corner/Nothing Like Time (as Ruddy & Sketto & Reco's All Stars) 20
62 Dice CC 7 — Little Schoolgirl/Hush Baby (as Ruddy & Sketto & Baron Twist & His Knights) 20
62 Dice CC 10 — Mr Postman/Christmas Blues (as Rudy & Sketto with Laurel's Group) 20
63 Dice CC 16 — Hold The Fire/Good Morning Mr Jones 20
63 Dice CC 19 — Never Set You Free/Brothers And Sisters 20
63 Blue Beat BB 198 — Was It Me/Minna Don't Deceive Me 20
64 Blue Beat BB 208 — Show Me The Way To Go Home/Let Me Dream 20
64 Blue Beat BB 230 — Ten Thousand Miles From Home/I Need Someone (as Ruddy & Sketto) 20
64 Blue Beat BB 252 — I Love You/If Only Tomorrow 20
65 Blue Beat BB 297 — See What You Done/Heart's Desire (as Ruddy & Sketto) 20
65 Blue Beat BB 310 — Oh Dolly/You're Mine (as Ruddy & Sketto) 20
(see also Ruddy & Sketto)

RUEFREX
80 Good Vibrations GOT 8 — One By One/Cross The Line/Don't Panic (foldover p/s, 2 different designs). each 12
83 Kabuki KAR 7 — Capital Letters/April Fool (p/s) 5

RAY RUFF & CHECKMATES
64 London HLU 9889 — I Took A Liking To You/A Fool Again 25

RUFFIANS
71 Banana BA 359 — Room Full Of Tears (actually by Sensations)/Black Soul (actually "Black And White — Version" by Riley's Allstars) 12
(see Al Brown, Sensations)

BRUCE RUFFIN
69 Songbird SB 1002 — Long About Now/Come See About Me (as Bruce Ruffin & Temptations) 15
69 Trojan TR 7704 — Dry Up Your Tears/BEVERLEY'S ALLSTARS: One Way Street 8
70 Trojan TR 7737 — I'm The One/Who's Gonna Be Your Man? 8
70 Trojan TR 7776 — Cecelia/BEVERLEY ALL STARS: Stand Up 8
70 Summit SUM 8509 — O-o-h Child/Bitterness Of Life 8
71 Summit SUM 8516 — Candida/Are You Ready 8
71 Trojan TR 7814 — Rain/THE PYRAMIDS: Geronimo (B-side actually by Pyramids) 8
71 Trojan TR 7814 — Rain/THE PYRAMIDS: Off Limits (B-side actually by Aquarians) 8
71 Trojan TR 7832 — One Big Happy Family (Parts 1 & 2) 8
72 Trojan TRM 9000 — Songs Of Peace/You Are The Best/We Can Make It 8
71 Trojan TRL 23 — RAIN (LP) 18
72 Rhino SRNO 8001 — BRUCE RUFFIN (LP) 12
(see also Bruce Downer)

DAVID RUFFIN
69 Tamla Motown TMG 689 — My Whole World Ended (The Moment You Left Me)/I've Got To Find Myself A Brand New Baby 8
69 Tamla Motown TMG 711 — I've Lost Everything I've Ever Loved/We'll Have A Good Thing Going On 7
76 Tamla Motown TMG 1022 — Heavy Love/Me And Rock And Roll Are Here To Stay 6
69 T. Motown (S)TML 11118 — MY WHOLE WORLD ENDED (LP) 40
70 T. Motown (S)TML 11139 — FEELIN' GOOD (LP) 35
73 Tamla Motown STML 11228 — DAVID RUFFIN (LP) 18
(see also Temptations)

JIMMY RUFFIN

66	Tamla Motown TMG 577	What Becomes Of The Broken-Hearted?/Baby I've Got It (small print, later large)	15/8
67	Tamla Motown TMG 593	I've Passed This Way Before/Tomorrow's Tears	15
67	Tamla Motown TMG 603	Gonna Give Her All The Love I Got/World So Wide, Nowhere To Hide	10
67	Tamla Motown TMG 617	Don't You Miss Me A Little Bit Baby/I Want Her Love	15
68	Tamla Motown TMG 649	I'll Say Forever My Love/Everybody Needs Love	10
68	Tamla Motown TMG 664	Don't Let Him Take Your Love From Me/Lonely Lonely Man Am I	10
69	Tamla Motown TMG 703	I've Passed This Way Before/Tomorrow's Tears	5
70	Tamla Motown TMG 726	Farewell Is A Lonely Sound/If You Let Me, I Know I Can	5
70	Tamla Motown TMG 740	I'll Say Forever My Love/Everybody Needs Love	5
70	Tamla Motown TMG 753	It's Wonderful (To Be Loved By You)/Maria (You Were The Only One)	5
71	Tamla Motown TMG 767	Let's Say Goodbye Tomorrow/Living In A World I Created For Myself	5
71	Tamla Motown TMG 784	On The Way Out (On The Way In)/Honey Come Back	6
73	Mojo 2092 060	Mother's Love/Waiting For You	5
74	Polydor 2058 433	Tell Me What You Want/Going Home (p/s)	5
67	T. Motown (S)TML 11048	THE JIMMY RUFFIN WAY (LP)	60
69	T. Motown (S)TML 11106	RUFF 'N' READY (LP)	40
70	T. Motown STML 11161	JIMMY RUFFIN ... FOREVER (LP)	30
73	Polydor 2383 240	JIMMY RUFFIN (LP)	15
70s	Sounds Superb SPR 90041	I'VE PASSED THIS WAY BEFORE (LP)	12

(see also Council Collective)

JIMMY & DAVID RUFFIN

71	Tamla Motown STML 11176	I AM MY BROTHER'S KEEPER (LP)	22

(see also David Ruffin, Temptations)

RUFUS

74	ABC ABC 4022	You Got The Love/Rags To Rufus	5
75	ABC ABC 4038	Stop On By/Rufusized	5
75	ABC ABC 4055	Once You Get Started/Right Is Right (p/s)	5
84	Warner Bros RCKT 1	Ain't Got You/Stop On By/Don't Go To Strangers (12", with Chaka Khan)	8
75	ABC ABCL 5151	RUFUS WITH CHAKA KHAN (LP)	12

RUGBYS

69	Polydor 56781	You And I/Stay With Me	50
70	Polydor 56789	Wendegahl The Warlock/Light	20

PETE RUGOLO (& DIAMONDS)

61	Mercury AMT 1147	Marie/Moonglow And Theme From Picnic (as Pete Rugolo & His Perfect Presence Sound Orchestra)	5
58	Emarcy ERE 1577	MUSIC FOR HI-FI BUGS VOL. 1 (EP)	8
58	Emarcy ERE 1578	MUSIC FOR HI-FI BUGS VOL. 2 (EP)	8
59	Mercury ZEP 10020	THE DIAMONDS MEET PETE RUGOLO (EP)	22
60	Mercury ZEP 10084	RUGOLO PLAYS KENTON (EP, also in stereo SEZ 19000)	7/8
61	Mercury ZEP 10097	PETE RUGOLO LEADS THE DIAMONDS (EP, also stereo SEZ 19012)	30/35
61	Mercury ZEP 10099	THE MASTERPIECES OF KENTON (EP, also stereo SEZ 19015)	7/8
54	Philips BBR 8024	PETE RUGOLO AND HIS ORCHESTRA (10" LP)	12
57	Mercury MPL 6517	BRASS IN HI-FI (LP)	12
57	Emarcy EJL 1254	FOR HI-FI BUGS (LP)	12
58	Emarcy EJL 1274	OUT ON A LIMB (LP)	12
59	Mercury MMC 14012	ADVENTURES IN SOUND — REEDS IN HI-FI (LP)	12
60	Mercury MMC 14034	"RICHARD DIAMOND" MUSIC (LP, also stereo CMS 18025)	12/15
60	Warner Bros WM 4001	BEHIND BRIGITTE BARDOT — COOL SOUNDS FROM HER HOT SCENES (LP, also stereo WS 8001)	25

(see also Diamonds, Patti Page)

RULERS

66	Rio R 105	Don't Be A Rude Boy/Be Good	25
66	Rio R 107	Copasetic/Too Late	35
67	Rio R 132	Wrong 'em Boyo/Why Don't You Change	25
67	Rio R 135	Well Covered/CARL DAWKINS: Help Time	25
67	Rio R 138	Be Mine/CARL DAWKINS: Hot And Sticky	25
69	Trojan TR 696	Got To Be Free/Situation	12

RUMBLE

70	Warner Bros WB 8011	Rich Man, Poor Man/Let Me Down	5

RUMBLERS

63	London HLD 9684	Boss/I Don't Need You No More	30
65	King KG 1021	Soulful Jerk/Hey Did A Da Da	50
63	London RE-D 1396	BOSSOUNDS (EP)	200
63	London HA-D/SH-D 8081	BOSSOUNDS (LP, mono/stereo)	100/120

RUMPLESTILTSKIN

70	Bell BLL 1101	Squadron Leader Johnson/Rumplestiltskin	8
71	Bell BLL 1157	Wimoweh/Through My Looking Glass	8
70	Bell SBLL 130	RUMPLESTILTSKIN (LP, gatefold sleeve)	45

(see also Clem Cattini)

RUNAWAYS

76	Mercury 6167 392	Cherry Bomb/Blackmail	10
77	Mercury 6167 493	Queens Of Noise/Born To Be Bad	6
77	Mercury 6167 587	School Days/Wasted (p/s)	8
79	Cherry Red CHERRY 8	Right Now/Black Leather (p/s)	12
76	Mercury 9100 029	THE RUNAWAYS (LP, with gatefold sleeve & lyric sheet; U.S. pressing, with cat. no. SRM 1 1090, in U.K. sleeve)	15
77	Mercury 9100 032	QUEENS OF NOISE (LP, with lyric sheet)	15
77	Mercury 9100 046	LIVE IN JAPAN (LP)	12

MINT VALUE £

77	Mercury 9100 047	WAITIN' FOR THE NIGHT (LP)	12
79	Cherry Red ARED 38	AND NOW ... THE RUNAWAYS (LP, 1,000 copies each in yellow, red, blue & orange vinyl)	each 25
80	Cherry Red BRED 9	FLAMING SCHOOLGIRLS (LP)	15

(see also Joan Jett, Lita Ford & Ozzy Osbourne)

TODD RUNDGREN

72	Bearsville K 15502	I Saw The Light/Marlene	5
76	Bearsville K 15524	Good Vibrations/Love Of The Common Man	5

(see also Nazz, Utopia, Runt)

RUNESTAFF

85	FM VHF 5	Road To Ruin/Last Chances (p/s)	7
85	FM VHF 17	Do It!/Runestaff (no p/s)	6
85	Heavy Metal HMRLP 26	RUNESTAFF (LP)	15

RUNNING MAN

72	RCA Neon NE 11	THE RUNNING MAN (LP)	110

(see also Ray Russell Quartet, Mouse)

RUNRIG

83	Ridge RRS 103	Loch Lomond/Tuireadh Iain Ruaida (p/s)	30
84	Simple SIM 4	Dance Called America/Na H Uain A's T-Earrach (p/s)	25
84	Simple 12 SIM 4	Dance Called America/Na H Uain A's T-Earrach/Ribhinn (12", p/s)	20
84	Simple SIM 8	Skye/Hey Mandu (p/s)	20
86	Ridge RRS 006	The Work Song/This Time Of Year (p/s)	20
86	Ridge RRS 007	Alba/Worker For The Wind (p/s)	12
88	Chrysalis CHS 3284	Protect And Survive/Hearts Of Olden Glory (live) (p/s)	15
88	Chrysalis CHS 12 3284	Protect And Survive/Hearts Of Olden Glory (live)/ Protect And Survive (live) (12", p/s)	18
88	Chrysalis CHSCD 3284	Protect And Survive/Hearts Of Olden Glory (live)/ Protect And Survive (live) (CD)	18
89	Chrysalis CHS 3404	News From Heaven/Chi Mi'n Tir (p/s)	5
89	Chrysalis CHS 12 3404	News From Heaven/Chi Mi'n Tir/The Times They Are A'Changing (12", p/s)	8
89	Chrysalis CHS 12T 3404	News From Heaven/Chi Mi'n Tir/The Times They Are A'Changing (12", picture disc)	20
89	Chrysalis CHSCD 3404	News From Heaven/Chi Mi'n Tir/The Times They Are A'Changing (CD)	20
89	Chrysalis CHS 3451	Every River/This Time Of Year (p/s)	15
89	Chrysalis CHS 12 3451	Every River/This Time Of Year/Our Earth Was Once Green (12", p/s)	15
89	Chrysalis CHSCD 3451	Every River/This Time Of Year/Our Earth Was Once Green (CD)	18
90	Chrysalis CHSCD 3594	CAPTURE THE HEART EP: Stepping Down The Glory Road/Satellite Flood/ Harvest Moon/The Apple Came Down (10", p/s)	15
90	Chrysalis CHSCD 1235941	CAPTURE THE HEART EP: Stepping Down The Glory Road/Satellite Flood/ Harvest Moon/The Apple Came Down (12", p/s)	15
90	Chrysalis CHSCD 3594	CAPTURE THE HEART EP: Stepping Down The Glory Road/Satellite Flood/ Harvest Moon/The Apple Came Down (CD)	15
90	Chrysalis CHSGCD 3754	HEARTHAMMER EP: Hearthammer/Pride Of The Summer (live)/ Loch Lomond (live)/Solus Na Madainn (CD, with booklet)	8
90	Chrysalis CHS 38051	Flower Of The West/Ravenscraig/Ch Mi'n Greamhradh (p/s)	10
90	Chrysalis CHSCD 3805	Flower Of The West/Ravenscraig/Ch Mi'n Greamhradh/ Harvest Moon (CD, digipak)	15
91	Chrysalis CHS 3754	HEARTHAMMER EP	8
91	Chrysalis CHSG 123754	HEARTHAMMER EP (12", gatefold p/s, with booklet)	12
91	Chrysalis CHS 123805	FLOWER OF THE WEST EP (12", numbered box set, with poster, discography & sticker)	12
93	Chrysalis CHSS 3952	Wonderful/April Come She Will (limited edition blue vinyl)	7
93	Chrysalis CHS 3975	THE GREATEST FLAME (EP, numbered postcard pack)	10
93	Chrysalis CDCHS 3975	THE GREATEST FLAME (CD EP, part 1 of double pack)	8
93	Chrysalis CDCHSS 3975	THE GREATEST FLAME (CD EP, part 2 of double pack)	8
94	Chrysalis CHS P 5018	THIS TIME OF YEAR EP (12", poster/calendar sleeve)	15
78	Neptune NA 105	RUNRIG PLAY GAELIC (LP)	18
79	Ridge RR 001	THE HIGHLAND CONNECTION (LP)	15
81	Ridge RR 002	RECOVERY (LP, with inner)	20
91	Chrysalis CHR 18582	BIG WHEEL (LP, with inner)	12
96	Chrysalis CDCHRS 6116	LONG DISTANCE (CD, with bonus CD)	20

RUNS

80	Carrere CAR 139	Bun In The Oven (no p/s)	40

RUNT

71	Bearsville K 44505	RUNT (LP)	15
71	Bearsville K 44506	RUNT — THE BALLAD OF TODD RUNDGREN (LP)	15

(see also Todd Rundgren, Utopia, Nazz)

R.U.1.2.

78	SRTS/78/CUS 131	She's Gone/Purely Physical/Teenage Girl (p/s)	20

RUN 229

80	MM JR 7040S	Soho/Dance/In This Day And Age	40

RUPERT'S PEOPLE

67	Columbia DB 8226	Reflections Of Charles Brown/Hold On	45
67	Columbia DB 8278	A Prologue To A Magic World/Dream In My Mind	70
68	Columbia DB 8362	I Can Show You/I've Got The Love	90

(see also Renaissance, Fleur-De-Lys, Gun, Sweet Feeling)

RUSH (Australia)

67	Decca F 12614	Happy/Once Again	7
67	Decca F 12635	Make Mine Music/Enjoy It	8

RUSH (Canada)

77	Mercury RUSH 7	Closer To The Heart/Bastille Day/Temples Of Syrinx (metallic blue or beige labels)	18/8
78	Mercury RUSH 12	Closer To The Heart/Anthem/Bastille Day/Temples Of Syrinx (12", p/s)	12
80	Mercury RADIO 7	Spirit Of Radio/The Trees (p/s)	12
80	Mercury RADIO 12	Spirit Of Radio/The Trees/Working Man (12", p/s)	12
81	Mercury VITAL 7	Vital Signs/In The Mood (p/s)	10
81	Mercury VITAL 12	Vital Signs/In The Mood/A Passage To Bangkok/Circumstances (12", p/s)	10
81	Mercury EXIT 7	Tom Sawyer (live)/A Passage To Bangkok (live) (p/s)	8
81	Mercury EXIT 12	Tom Sawyer (live)/A Passage To Bangkok (live)/Red Barchetta (live) (12", p/s)	10
81	Mercury RUSH 1	Closer To The Heart (live)/The Trees (live) (p/s)	6
82	Mercury RUSH 8	New World Man/Vital Signs (live) (p/s)	6
82	Mercury RUSH 812	New World Man/Vital Signs (live)/Freewill (live) (12", p/s)	15
82	Mercury RUSH 9	Subdivisions/Red Barchetta (live) (p/s)	5
82	Mercury RUSH P9	Subdivisions/Red Barchetta (live) (picture disc)	12
82	Mercury RUSH 912	Subdivisions/Red Barchetta (live)/Jacob's Ladder (live) (12", p/s)	8
82	Mercury RUSH 10	Countdown/New World Man (p/s)	5
82	Mercury RUSH 10 PD	Countdown/New World Man (shaped picture disc)	25
82	Mercury RUSH 1012	Countdown/New World Man/Spirit Of Radio (live)/Interview Excerpts (12", p/s)	10
84	Vertigo RUSH 11	The Body Electric/The Analog Kid (p/s)	6
84	Vertigo RUSH 1110	The Body Electric/The Analog Kid/Distant Early Warning (10", p/s, red vinyl)	15
84	Vertigo RUSH 1112	The Body Electric/The Analog Kid/Distant Early Warning (12", p/s)	50
85	Vertigo RUSH D12	The Big Money/Territories//Closer To The Heart/Spirit Of Radio (double pack)	20
85	Vertigo RUSH G12	The Big Money/Middletown Dreams (gatefold 'window' p/s)	10
87	Vertigo RUSH 13	Time Stand Still/Force Ten (p/s, red label)	10
87	Vertigo RUSH D13	Time Stand Still/Force Ten (cut-out p/s)	15
87	Vertigo RUSH P1312	Time Stand Still/Force Ten/The Enemy Within (live) (12", picture disc)	20
87	Vertigo RUSH CD 13	Time Stand Still/Force Ten/The Enemy Within (live)/Witch Hunt (live) (CD, card sleeve)	12
88	Vertigo RUSH 14	Prime Mover/Distant Early Warning (live) (p/s)	6
88	Vertigo RUSH R14	Prime Mover/Distant Early Warning (live) (p/s, white vinyl)	10
88	Vertigo RUSH R1412	Prime Mover/Tai Shan/Distant Early Warning (live)/New World Man (live) (12", 3-D p/s)	8
88	Vertigo RUSH 1412	Prime Mover/Tai Shan/Distant Early Warning (live)/New World Man (live) (12", p/s)	12
88	Vertigo RUSH CD 14	Prime Mover/Tai Shan/Distant Early Warning (live)/New World Man (live) (CD, numbered card sleeve)	12
88	Old Gold OG 9767	Spirit Of Radio/Closer To The Heart	6
89	Vertigo 080 084-2	The Big Money/Red Sector A (live)/Marathon/ The Big Money (video) (CD Video)	25
92	Atlantic A 7524	Roll The Bones/Dreamline (p/s)	6
92	Atlantic A 7524 CD	Roll The Bones/Anagram/Interview (CD, hologram sleeve)	8
92	Atlantic A 7491	Ghost Of A Chance/Dreamline (p/s)	6
92	Atlantic A 7491CD	Ghost Of A Chance/Dreamline/Chain Lightning/Red Tide (CD, slimline case)	8
74	Mercury 9100 011	RUSH (LP)	12
78	Mercury 9100 059	HEMISPHERES (LP, mispressing, both sides play Side 1)	100
80	Mercury 9100 071	PERMANENT WAVES (LP, with newspaper)	15
85	Vertigo VERHP 31	POWER WINDOWS (LP, picture disc, with discography on sleeve)	25

(see also McKenzie Doug & Bob, Max Webster Band)

MERRILEE RUSH & TURNABOUTS

68	Bell BLL 1013	Angel Of The Morning/Reap What You Sow	6
68	Bell BLL 1026	That Kind Of Woman/Sunshine And Roses	6
69	Bell BLL 1041	Reach Out I'll Be There/Love Street	10
68	Bell MBLL/SBLL 109	MERRILEE RUSH (LP)	20

OTIS RUSH

66	Vocalion V-P 9260	Homework/I Have To Laugh	30
69	Blue Horizon 57-3159	All Your Love/Double Trouble	25
68	Blue Horizon 7-63222	THIS ONE'S A GOOD UN (LP)	55
69	Atlantic 588 188	MOURNING IN THE MORNING (LP)	40
70s	Atlantic K 40495	MOURNING IN THE MORNING (LP, reissue)	15
70	Python KM 3	GROANING THE BLUES (LP)	45
76	Delmark DS 63?	COLD DAY IN HELL (LP)	15
78	Sonet SNTF756	TROUBLES, TROUBLES (LP)	15

TOM RUSH

67	Elektra EKSN 45004	Who Do You Love/On The Road Again	8
67	Elektra EKSN 45015	On The Road Again/Love's Made A Fool Of You	8
68	Elektra EKSN 45025	No Regrets/Shadow Dream Song	7
68	Elektra EKSN 45032	Something In The Way She Moves/Rockport Sunday	8
66	Xtra XTRA 5024	BLUES, SONGS & BALLADS (LP)	25
66	Xtra XTRA 5053	I GOT A MIND TO RAMBLE (LP)	25
67	Elektra EKL 308	TAKE A LITTLE WALK WITH ME (LP, also stereo EKS 7308)	35
68	Elektra EKL 4018	THE CIRCLE GAME (LP, red label, also stereo EKS 74018)	25
69	Elektra EKL 4062	CLASSIC RUSH (LP, red label, also stereo EKS 74062)	25
70	CBS 63940	TOM RUSH (LP)	15
70	CBS 64268	WRONG END OF A RAINBOW (LP)	15
71	Elektra EKS 74062	CLASSIC RUSH (LP, reissue, 'butterfly' label)	12
72	CBS 64887	MERRIMACK COUNTRY (LP)	12

JIMMY RUSHING (with ADA MOORE & BUCK CLAYTON)

57	Philips BBE 12150	CAT MEETS CHICK (EP, as Jimmy Rushing, Buck Clayton & Ada Moore)	20
57	Vanguard EPP 14003	LITTLE JIMMY ALL STAR BAND (EP)	15
57	Parlophone GEP 8597	JIMMY RUSHING (EP)	15
58	Parlophone GEP 8695	THE WAY I FEEL (EP)	15
63	Ember EMB 4523	JIMMY RUSHING (EP)	12

MINT VALUE £

55	Vanguard PPT 12002	SINGS THE BLUES (10" LP)	40
57	Vanguard PPT 12016	SHOWCASE (10" LP)	35
57	Philips BBL 7105	CAT MEETS CHICK (LP, with Ada Moore & Buck Clayton)	22
57	Philips BBL 7166	THE JAZZ ODYSSEY OF JAMES RUSHING ESQ (LP, with Buck Clayton)	22
58	Vanguard PPL 11008	IF THIS AIN'T THE BLUES (LP)	18
58	Philips BBL 7252	LITTLE JIMMY RUSHING AND THE BIG BRASS (LP, also stereo SBBL 524)	20
60	Philips BBL 7360	RUSHING LULLABIES (LP)	18
61	Philips BBL 7484	THE SMITH GIRLS — BESSIE, CLARA (LP, also stereo SBBL 631)	20/25
66	Ace Of Hearts AH 119	BLUES I LOVE TO SING (LP)	15
67	Golden Guinea GGL 0384	FIVE FEET OF SOUL (LP)	12
67	Fontana FJL 405	LISTEN TO THE BLUES (LP)	15
67	HMV CLP/CSD 3632	EVERYDAY I HAVE THE BLUES (LP)	15
71	Vanguard VRS 8513	IF THIS AIN'T THE BLUES (LP, reissue)	12
72	Vanguard VRS 8518	GOING TO CHICAGO (LP)	12

(see also Count Basie, Dave Brubeck, Buck Clayton)

JIMMY RUSHING/CHAMPION JACK DUPREE

64	Ember CJS 800	TWO SHADES OF BLUE (LP, 1 side each)	25

(see also Champion Jack Dupree)

BARBARA RUSKIN

65	Piccadilly 7N 35224	Halfway To Paradise/I Can't Believe In Miracles	10
65	Piccadilly 7N 35246	You Can't Blame A Girl For Trying/No More To Fall	12
66	Piccadilly 7N 35274	Well How Does It Feel/Wishing Your Life Away	10
66	Piccadilly 7N 35296	Song Without End/Love Came Too Late	10
66	Piccadilly 7N 35328	Light Of Love/At Times Like These Mama	10
67	Parlophone R 5571	Take It Easy/Sunshowers	8
67	Parlophone R 5593	Euston Station/Hear That Telephone	8
67	Parlophone R 5642	Come Into My Arms Again/Just A Little While Longer	12
68	Parlophone R 5685	Is This Another Way/The Night Of The Spanish Tightrope Walker	6
68	President PT 217	Pawnbroker Pawnbroker/Almost	25
69	President PT 238	Gentlemen Please/24th Of July	6
69	President PT 261	Hail Love/Lady Of Leisure	6
70	President PT 280	A Little Bit Of This (And A Little Bit Of That)/Where Are We	6

ROGER RUSKIN SPEAR

72	United Artists UAG 29381	ELECTRIC SHOCKS (LP)	20

(see also Bonzo Dog Doo-Dah Band, Topo D. Bill)

LONNIE RUSS

62	Fontana 267263 TF	Something Old Something New/My Wife Can't Cook	7

THANE RUSSAL (& THREE)

66	CBS 202049	Security/Your Love Is Burning Me (some with p/s)	250/125
66	CBS 202403	Drop Everything And Run/I Need You (solo)	125

ANDY RUSSELL

58	RCA RCA 1076	Seven Daughters/A Certain Smile	6
58	RCA RCA 1076	Seven Daughters/A Certain Smile (78)	8

BOBBY RUSSELL

68	Bell BLL 1019	Dusty/I Made You This Way	6
68	Bell BLL 1034	1432 Franklin Pike Circle Hero/Let's Talk About It	6
69	Bell BLL 1050	Carlie/Ain't Society Great?	6

BRENDA RUSSELL

79	A&M AMSP 7515	In The Thick Of It/So Good So Right (12", p/s)	12
88	Breakout USAT 647	Get Here/Le Restaurant (with David Sanborn)/A Little Bit Of Love/So Good So Right (12", p/s)	8
79	A&M AMLJ 739	BRENDA RUSSELL (LP)	12

CONNIE RUSSELL

54	Capitol CL 14171	No One But You/One Arabian Night	18
54	Capitol CL 14197	Love Me/Papa's Puttin' The Pressure On	15
55	Capitol CL 14214	Foggy Night In San Francisco/This Is My Love	15
55	Capitol CL 14236	Ayuh, Ayuh/I'm Making Believe	25
55	Capitol CL 14246	Snow Dreams/Green Fire	12
55	Capitol CL 14268	Farewell, Farewell/The Magnificent Matador	12
57	Capitol CL 14676	All Of You/This Is My Love	8

DAVE RUSSELL

66	Columbia DB 7828	When I Grow Too Old To Dream/All The Tears In The World	5

(see also Dave & Diamonds)

DOROTHY RUSSELL

71	Duke Reid DR 2524	You're The One I Love/Version	6

JANE RUSSELL

51	London L 956	Dear Dear Dear/I Can't Get Started With You (78)	10
51	London L 969	Five Little Miles From San Berdoo/You'll Know (78)	10
53	Columbia SCM 5043	Please Do It Again/Two Sleepy People (B-side with Bob Lowery)	22
53	Columbia DB 3293	Please Do It Again/Two Sleepy People (B-side with Bob Lowery) (78)	12
53	MGM MGM 662	A Little Girl From Little Rock/When Love Goes Wrong (78)	25
53	MGM MGM 664	Bye Bye Baby/Ain't There Anyone Here For Love? (78)	20
56	Capitol CL 14590	If You Wanna See Mamie Tonight/Keep Your Eyes On The Hands	10
59	MGM MGM-EP 702	JANE RUSSELL (EP)	35

JANET RUSSELL

88	Harbourtown HAR 003	GATHERING THE FRAGMENTS (LP)	20

JOHN RUSSELL/RICHARD COLDMAN

79	Incus INCUS 31	HOME COOKING/GUITAR SOLOS (LP, 1 side each)	50

JOHNNY RUSSELL

60	MGM MGM 1074	Lonesome Boy/Baby Won't You Tell Me So	10

MINT VALUE £

KEITH RUSSELL

65	Piccadilly 7N 35235	People Get Ready/Paradise	7

LEON RUSSELL

65	Dot DS 16771	Everybody's Talkin' 'Bout The Young/It's Alright With Me	12
70	A&M AMS 788	Roll Away The Stone/Hummingbird	5
71	A&M AMS 806	Delta Lady/Apple Pisces Lady	5
71	A&M AMS 841	Ballad Of Mad Dogs And Englishmen/CLAUDIA LINNEAR: Let It Be (p/s)	5
70	A&M AMLS 982	LEON RUSSELL (LP, with Shelter People)	12
71	A&M AMLS 65003	LEON RUSSELL AND THE SHELTER PEOPLE (LP)	12
72	A&M AMLS 68089	ASYLUM CHOIR II (LP, as Leon Russell & Asylum Choir, with Marc Benno)	12
72	A&M AMLS 68911	CARNEY (LP)	12

(see also Asylum Choir)

PEE WEE RUSSELL & RUBY BRAFF

50	Melodisc MEL 1137	Baby Won't You Please Come Home/Dinah (78)	6
57	London Jazz LTZ-C 15061	JAZZ AT STORYVILLE VOL. 2 (LP)	15

RAY RUSSELL QUARTET

68	CBS Realm 52586	TURN CIRCLE (LP)	20
69	CBS Realm 52663	DRAGON HILL (LP)	20
71	RCA SF 8214	JUNE 11TH 1971 (LP)	18
71	CBS 64271	RITES AND RITUALS (LP)	30
73	Black Lion BLP 12100	SECRET ASYLUM (LP)	12

(see also Running Man, Mouse, Chopyn)

ROLAND RUSSELL

68	Nu Beat NB 019	Rhythm Hips/RHYTHM FLAMES: Deltone Special	12

ROSALIND RUSSELL & EDITH ADAMS

55	Brunswick 05406	Ohio/Little Bit Of Love	5

RUSSELL FAMILY

75	Topic 12TS 251	OF DOOLIN COUNTY CLARE (LP, with insert)	12

RUSSIAN ROULETTE

84	Red Bus RBUS 86	Come Into My Room/Lyin' Again (p/s)	5

(see also Paul King, Mungo Jerry)

CHARLIE RUSSO

63	Stateside SS 165	Preacherman/Teresa	8

RUSTIKS

64	Decca F 11960	What A Memory Can Do/Hello Anne	10
65	Decca F 12059	I'm Not The Loving Kind/Can't You See	8

RUSTLERS

61	Pye 7N 15398	High Strung/Matter Of Who	12

RUSTY & DOUG (Kershaw)

59	Oriole CB 1510	Hey Mae!/Why Don't You Love Me	200
59	Oriole CB 1510	Hey Mae!/Why Don't You Love Me (78)	25
59	London HL 8972	I Like You (Like This)/Dancing Shoes	30
59	London HL 8972	I Like You (Like This)/Dancing Shoes (78)	50
62	Polydor NH 66970	Hey Mae!/Sweet Thing	45
62	Fontana 267 238 TF	Cajun Joe (The Ballad Of The Bayou)/Sweet Sweet Girl To Me	15

(see also Doug Kershaw)

RUSTY HARNESS

70	Ember EMB S 283	Ain't Gonna Get Married/Goodbye (some in p/s)	10/5
73	Ember SE 8024	DISCOTHEQUE EXPLOSION (LP)	12

RUSTY NAIL

60s	Hi-Fi MEP 3093	RUSTY NAIL (EP, some in p/s)	100/40

RUTH

67	Columbia DB 8216	Leaf In The Wind/Society's Child	7
68	Columbia DB 8386	Cherish/Until It's Time For You To Go	7

MIKE RUTHERFORD

80	Charisma CB 364	Time And Time Again/At The End Of The Day (p/s, correct B-side & label)	6
80	Charisma CB 364	Time And Time Again/Overnight Job (p/s, with new label on B-side, credits & plays "Overnight Job")	5

(see also Genesis, Mike & Mechanics)

RUTLES

78	Warner Bros K 17125	I Must Be In Love/Cheese And Onions/With A Girl Like You (p/s)	5
78	Warner Bros K 17180	Let's Be Natural/Piggy In The Middle	6

(see also Dirk & Stig, Neil Innes, Monty Python, Beach Boys, Patto)

RUTS (D.C.)

79	People Unite SJP 795	In A Rut/H-Eyes (1,000 only, black-ringed label)	20
79	People Unite RUT 1	In A Rut/H-Eyes (repressing)	10
79	Virgin VS 271	Babylon's Burning/Society (p/s)	8
79	Virgin VS 298	Jah War/I Ain't Sofisticated (p/s)	5
80	RSO RSO 71	Babylon's Burning/XTC: Take This Town (p/s)	6
81	Virgin VS 396	Different View/Formula Eyes (p/s, as Ruts D.C.)	5
82	Bohemian BO 2	Whatever We Do/Push Yourself — Make It Work (p/s, as Ruts D.C.)	5
83	Bohemian BO 3	Weak Heart/Militant (white label, with paper insert; as Ruts D.C., promo only)	15
83	Bohemian BO 4	Stepping Bondage/Lobotomy/Rich Bitch (p/s)	12
87	Strange Fruit SFPSC 011	PEEL SESSION 14.5.79 (EP, cassette)	5
88	Virgin OVED 80	THE CRACK (LP, stickered sleeve)	15

(see also Laurel Aitken, Typhoons, Pete Zear)

MINT VALUE £

BARRY RYAN (& MAJORITY)

68	MGM MGM 1423	Goodbye/I'm So Sad	10
68	MGM MGM 1442	Eloise/Love I Almost Found You (as Barry Ryan & Majority)	10
68	MGM MGM 1464	Love Is Love/I'll Be On My Way Dear	10
69	Polydor 56348	The Hunt/No Living Without Her	10
70	Polydor 56370	Magical Spiel/Caroline	10
70	Polydor 2001 035	Kitsch/Give Me A Sign	10
71	Polydor 2001 154	It Is Written/Annabella	10
72	Polydor 2001 335	From My Head To My Toes/Alimony Money Blues	10
69	MGM MGM-C(S) 8106	SINGS PAUL RYAN (LP)	35
69	Polydor 583 067	BARRY RYAN (LP)	22

(see also Paul & Barry Ryan)

CATHY RYAN

53	MGM SP 1051	Show Me The Way To Go Home/If I Had You	7

(see also Art Mooney)

KRIS RYAN (& QUESTIONS)

64	Mercury MF 818	Miss Ann/She Told Me Lies (as Kris Ryan & Questions)	10
64	Mercury MF 832	Don't Play That Song/If You Don't Come Back	12
64	Mercury MF 852	Marie Marie/I've Had Enough Of You Baby	10
65	Mercury MF 877	Tell Me How/She Belongs To Me	10
65	Mercury 10024 MCE	ON THE RIGHT TRACK (EP, as Kris Ryan & Questions)	50

MARION RYAN

57	Pye N 15105	Ding Dong Rock-A-Billy Wedding/That's Happiness (78)	6
58	Pye 7N 15121	Love Me Forever/Make The Man Love Me	8
58	Pye 7N 15130	Oh Oh, I'm Falling In Love Again/Always And Forever	8
58	Pye 7N 15138	Stairway Of Love/I Need You	8
58	Pye N 15138	Stairway Of Love/I Need You (78)	6
58	Pye 7N 15157	The World Goes Around And Around/Please Don't Say Goodnight	6
58	Pye 7NSR 15157	The World Goes Around And Around/Please Don't Say Goodnight (stereo)	18
59	Pye 7N 15184	Wait For Me/Jeepers Creepers	6
59	Pye N 15184	Wait For Me/Jeepers Creepers (78)	10
59	Pye 7N 15200	Jo-Jo The Dog-Faced Boy/Doin' What Comes Naturally	8
59	Pye N 15200	Jo-Jo The Dog-Faced Boy/Doin' What Comes Naturally (78)	8
59	Pye 7N 15216	Too Much/Promise Me	6
59	Pye N 15216	Too Much/Promise Me (78)	8
60	Columbia DB 4448	Sixteen Reasons/Mangos	8
60	Columbia DB 4550	It's You That I Love/Somebody	6
62	Columbia DB 4857	No Love But Your Love/An Occasional Man (A-side with John Barry & Orch.)	7
68	Philips BF 1721	Better Use Your Head/The Seasons Change	15
57	Pye Nixa NEP 24041	THAT RYAN GIRL! (EP)	30
58	Pye NEP 24079	MARION RYAN HIT PARADE (EP)	25
59	Pye N(S)PL 18030	A LADY LOVES! (LP, mono/stereo)	60/80

(see also Ray Ellington, Gary Miller)

PAT RYAN

77	Folk Heritage FHR 094	LEA BOY'S LASSIE (LP)	15

PAUL & BARRY RYAN

65	Decca F 12260	Don't Bring Me Your Heartaches/To Remind Me Of Your Love	10
66	Decca F 12319	Have Pity On The Boy/There You Go	10
66	Decca F 12391	I Love Her/Gotta Go Out To Work	10
66	Decca F 12445	I Love How You Love Me/Baby I'm Sorry	10
66	Decca F 12494	Have You Ever Loved Somebody?/I'll Tell You Later	10
66	Decca F 12520	Missy, Missy/Rainbow Weather	10
67	Decca F 12567	Keep It Out Of Sight/Who Told You?	10
67	Decca F 12633	Claire/I'll Make It Worth Your While	10
67	MGM MGM 1354	Heartbreaker/Night Time	10
68	MGM MGM 1385	Pictures Of Today/Madrigal	10
67	Decca LK 4878	THE RYANS — TWO OF A KIND (LP)	40
68	MGM MGM-C(S) 8081	PAUL AND BARRY RYAN (LP)	35

(see also Barry Ryan)

PHIL RYAN & CRESCENTS

64	Columbia DB 7406	Mary Don't You Weep/Yes I Will	8
65	Columbia DB 7574	Gypsy Woman/Be Honest With Yourself	18

BOBBY RYDELL

59	Top Rank JAR 181	Kissin' Time/You'll Never Tame Me	15
59	Top Rank JAR 181	Kissin' Time/You'll Never Tame Me (78)	80
59	Top Rank JAR 227	We Got Love/I Dig Girls	12
60	Columbia DB 4429	Wild One/Little Bitty Girl	8
60	Columbia DB 4471	Swingin' School/Ding-A-Ling	8
60	Columbia DB 4495	Volare/I'd Do It Again	10
60	Columbia DB 4545	Sway/Groovy Tonight	8
61	Columbia DB 4600	Good Time Baby/Cherie	7
61	Columbia DB 4651	Don't Be Afraid/That Old Black Magic	7
61	Columbia DB 4690	The Fish/The Third House	7
61	Columbia DB 4731	I Wanna Thank You/The Door To Paradise	7
62	Columbia DB 4785	I've Got Bonnie/Lose Her	7
62	Columbia DB 4858	I'll Never Dance Again/Gee, It's Wonderful	7
63	Cameo Parkway C 108	Forget Him/Hey Ev'rybody (some in p/s)	15/7
63	Cameo Parkway C 129	It's Time We Parted/Too Much Too Soon	7
63	Cameo Parkway C 228	Cha Cha Cha/The Best Man Cried	6
63	Cameo Parkway C 242	Butterfly Baby/Love Is Blind	7
63	Cameo Parkway C 272	Since We Fell In Love/Childhood Sweetheart	6
64	Cameo Parkway C 309	Make Me Forget/Darling Jennie	6

		MINT VALUE £
65 Capitol CL 15371	I Can't Say Goodbye/Two Is The Loneliest Number	7
65 Capitol CL 15424	When I See That Girl Of Mine/It Takes Two	10
66 Cameo Parkway CP 601	Until I Met You/New Love	7
60 Top Rank JKP 2059	LOVINGEST (EP)	50
63 Cameo Parkway CPE 551	SWAY WITH BOBBY RYDELL (EP)	30
63 Cameo Parkway CPE 553	BOBBY RYDELL (EP)	25
63 Summit LSE 2036	BEST OF BOBBY RYDELL (EP)	10
60 Columbia 33SX 1243	WILD ONE (LP)	60
61 Columbia 33SX 1308	SINGS AND SWINGS (LP)	22
61 Columbia 33SX 1352	SALUTES "THE GREAT ONES" (LP)	25
62 Columbia 33SX 1425	RYDELL AT THE COPA (LP)	50
62 Cameo Parkway C 1019	ALL THE HITS (LP)	25
63 Cameo Parkway C 1040	ALL THE HITS VOL. 2 (LP)	30
63 Cameo Parkway C 1043	BYE BYE BIRDIE (LP)	18
63 Cameo Parkway C 1055	WILD (WOOD) DAYS (LP)	30
65 Capitol T 2281	SOMEBODY LOVES YOU (LP)	22

(see also Chubby Checker & Bobby Rydell)

RUTH RYDELL

54 London HL 8016	On The Carousel/Someone Is Crying (78)	6

RUTHLESS RAP ASSASSINS

90 Sycopate 12SY35	Just Mellow/Here Today... Here Tomorrow (12")	8

FREDDIE RYDER

65 Mercury MF 864	To Get Your Love Back/A Little Thing Called Love	6
65 Mercury MF 879	Some Kind Of Wonderful/Slow Down	12
65 Mercury MF 935	Man Of The Moment/My Block	10
68 Columbia DB 8335	Shadows (I Can't See You)/Airport	6
68 Columbia DB 8427	Worst That Could Happen/World Of My Own	6

(see also Freddie Self, Trends)

MAL RYDER (& SPIRITS)

63 Decca F 11669	Cry Baby/Take Over (as Mal Ryder & Spirits)	20
64 Vocalion V 9219	See The Funny Little Clown/Slow Down	60
64 Piccadilly 7N 35209	Your Friend/Forget It (as Mal Ryder & Spirits)	30
65 Piccadilly 7N 35234	Lonely Room/Tell Your Friend	22

(see also Mal & Primitives)

MITCH RYDER (& DETROIT WHEELS)

66 Stateside SS 481	Jenny Take A Ride/Baby Jane	10
66 Stateside SS 498	Little Latin Lupe Lu/I Hope	10
66 Stateside SS 521	Breakout/I Need Help	35
66 Stateside SS 549	Devil With A Blue Dress On (Medley)/I Had It Made	10
67 Stateside SS 596	Sock It To Me Baby/I Never Had It Better	10
67 Stateside SS 2023	Too Many Fish In The Sea — Three Little Fishes/One Grain Of Sand	15
67 Stateside SS 2037	Joy/I'd Rather Go To Jail (solo)	8
67 Stateside SS 2063	What Now My Love/Blessing In Disguise (solo)	18
68 Stateside SS 2075	You Are My Sunshine/Wild Child (solo)	7
68 Stateside SS 2096	Personality/Chantilly Lace/I Make A Fool Of Myself (solo)	7
69 Dot DOT 129	Sugar Bee/I Believe (There Must Be Someone)	6
71 Avco 6105 001	Jenny Take A Ride/I Never Had It Better	6
72 Paramount PARA 3022	It Ain't Easy/Long Neck Goose	6
75 Pye Disco Demand DDS 113	You Get Your Kicks/Breakout	6
66 Stateside SE 1039	RIDIN' (EP)	50
66 Stateside S(S)L 10178	TAKE A RIDE ... (LP)	45
67 Stateside S(S)L 10189	BREAKOUT. . . !! (LP)	45
67 Stateside S(S)L 10204	SOCK IT TO ME (LP)	40
68 Stateside S(S)L 10229	WHAT NOW MY LOVE (LP, solo)	22
69 Bell MBLL/SBLL 114	ALL MITCH RYDER HITS (LP)	15

(see also Detroit)

TONY RYMOND

62 Oriole CB 1708	Handful Of Songs/She'll Have To Go	7

MINT VALUE £

PARK SABLE & JUNGLE 'N' BEATS
64 Fontana TF 457 Never Be Blue/Rave On ... 35

JEAN SABLON
53 HMV 7M 109 The Cab/Paris You Have Not Changed ... 8
55 HMV 7M 272 C'est Magnifique/Sur Les Pavements Of Paris ... 7

SABRE
83 Neat NEAT 23 Miracle Man/On The Loose (p/s) ... 8

SABRES
66 Decca F 12528 Roly Poly/Will You Always Love Me? ... 20
(see also Peeps)

SABRES OF PARADISE
93 Sabres Of Paradise PT 001 United (Andrew Weatherall Mix) (12", p/s, actually remix of Throbbing Gristle's "United", 800 only) ... 25
94 Sabres Of Paradise PT 009 Smokebelch II (Entry)/(Exit) (12", red p/s) ... 20
94 Sabres Of Paradise PT 009R Smokebelch II (David Holmes Mix)/(Flute Mix) (12", yellow p/s) ... 20
94 Sabres Of Paradise PT 014 Theme/Return Of Carter & Edge 6 (Original Mix) (12") ... 10
94 Sabres Of Paradise PT 014R Theme (Underdog Vs Sabres)/(Version) (10" remix) ... 10
94 Warp WAP 50 Wilmot/Rumble Summons (12") ... 15
94 Warp 10WAP 50 WILMOT II: Wilmot Meets Lord Scruffage/Wilmot's Last Skank (10", p/s) ... 8
95 Warp WARP 62 Tow Truck/(mixes) (12") ... 10
96 Emissions SEO 11 Ysaebud (PVC sleeve, 1-sided, etched B-side, 1,000 only) ... 10
90s Sabres Of Paradise 002 Internal/Internment/Internalized/The Creator Speaks (12", blue vinyl) ... 8
93 Warp LP 16 SABRESONIC (2-LP, with unreleased 7", 5,000 only) ... 20

SABRES OF PARADISE VS LFO AND NIGHTMARES ON WAX
95 Warp 10WAO 62 Duke Of Earlsfield (LFO Mix)/Bubble & Slide (Nightmares On Wax Mix) (10") ... 7

SABRINA
57 Conquest CP 102 Persuade Me/A Man Not A Mouse (78) ... 6

SACASAS AND HIS ORCHESTRA
55 Parlophone DP 501 Mamsaca/Mambo Jet (78, export issue) ... 8

JIMMY SACCA
54 London L 8028 You're All That I Need/Alone (78) ... 15
(see also Hilltoppers)

SACRED ALIEN
81 Greenwood GW 001 Spiritual Planet/Energy (stickered labels, some in p/s) ... 30/10
83 Heighway Robbery SAD 001 Legends/VIRGIN: Sittin' In Front Row (gatefold p/s) ... 30

SACRILEGE
85 C.O.T.R. GURT 4 BEHIND THE REALMS OF MADNESS (12" EP) ... 8

SADDAR BAZAAR
98 Earworm WORM 13/WJ37 Crystalline/ELECTROSCOPE: Circus Heights/TRANSPARENT THING: Ahh (p/s, 1,500 in hand painted sleeve, 1st 176 embossed) ... 10/5

SADDAR BAZAAR/AMP/3RD EYE FOUNDATION
90s Enraptured RAPT 4503 Arabesque (p/s) ... 5

SADIE'S EXPRESSION
69 Plexium PXM 4 Deep In My Heart/My Way Of Living ... 7

BARRINGTON SADLER
69 Clandisc CLA 204 Soul Power/Rub It Down ... 10

S. SGT. BARRY SADLER
66 RCA RCA 1506 Ballad Of The Green Berets/I'm A Lucky One ... 6
66 RCA RCA 1520 The A Team/An Empty Glass ... 6

JERRY SADOWITZ
88 Gobshite GOBSHITE 01 GOBSHITE (LP) ... 12

SAFARI PARTY
85 Pure & Vain 1 PAV Hope In Hell/Not There (p/s) ... 5

SAFARIS (& PHANTOM BAND)
60 Top Rank JAR 424 Image Of A Girl/Four Steps To Love ... 90
60 Top Rank JAR 528 The Girl With The Story In Her Eyes/Summer Nights (with Phantom Band) ... 60

SAFFRON SUMMERFIELD
74 Mother Earth MUM 1001 SALISBURY PLAIN (LP) ... 45
76 Mother Earth MUM 1202 FANCY MEETING YOU HERE (LP) ... 45
76 Spectator FANCY MEETING YOU HERE (LP, reissue) ... 20

SA 55
82 1966 EISP 9868 Compromise/Love Love Love Here I Come ... 80

SAGA
72 Westwood WRS 017 SAGA (LP) ... 80
73 Westwood WRS 036 SWEET PEG O'DERBY (LP) ... 100

MIKE SAGAR (& CRESTERS)

Year	Label / Cat. No.	Title	Value
60	HMV POP 819	Deep Feeling/You Know (as Mike Sagar & Cresters)	20
61	HMV POP 988	The Brothers Three/Set Me Free	18

(see also Cresters, Richard Harding)

SAGE

Year	Label / Cat. No.	Title	Value
80	Redball RR 032	GOING STRONG (LP)	45

SAGITTARIUS

Year	Label / Cat. No.	Title	Value
67	CBS 2867	My World Fell Down/Libra	18
68	CBS 3276	Another Time/Virgo	15

(see also Bruce Johnston, Glen Campbell)

SAGRAM

Year	Label / Cat. No.	Title	Value
72	Windmill WMD 118	POP EXPLOSION SITAR STYLE (LP)	15

(see also Clem Alford, Magic Carpet)

SAHARA

Year	Label / Cat. No.	Title	Value
73	Dawn DNLS 3068	SUNRISE (LP)	15

MORT SAHL

Year	Label / Cat. No.	Title	Value
59	HMV CLP 1252	THE FUTURE LIES AHEAD (LP)	15

DOUG SAHM

Year	Label / Cat. No.	Title	Value
73	Atlantic K 10293	Is Anybody Going To San Antoine/Don't Turn Around	5
73	Atlantic K 40466	DOUG SAHM AND BAND (LP)	12
70s	Warner Bros K 56067	GROOVERS PARADISE (LP)	12
70s	Chrysalis CHR 1249	HELL OF A SPELL (LP)	12

(see also Sir Douglas Quintet, Augie Meyers)

OLIVER SAIN (& SHIRLEY BROWN)

Year	Label / Cat. No.	Title	Value
72	Mojo 2092 031	St. Louis Breakdown/I Ain't Gonna Tell (with Shirley Brown)	10
74	Contempo CS 2026	Bus Stop/Nightime (solo)	8
75	Contempo CS 2057	London Express/Blowing For Love (solo)	8

(see also Shirley Brown, Fontella Bass)

ST. CHRISTOPHER

Year	Label / Cat. No.	Title	Value
84	Bluegrass GM 001	Crystal Clear/My Fond Farewell (p/s)	12
86	Bluegrass GM 003	Go Ahead Cry/Charmelle (p/s)	10
87	Veston VOD 001	Forevermore Stars Here/Remember Me To Her/Sinking Ships (flexidisc, p/s)	7
88	Clarity CLARITY 1	Josephine Why?/I Wish I Hadn't Hurt Her/Tell The World (flexidisc, foldaround p/s, 33rpm)	5
89	Sarah SARAH 015	You Deserve More Than A Maybe/The Kind Of Girl/The Summer Of Love (foldaround p/s with poster in poly bag)	12
89	Sarah SARAH 020	All Of A Tremble/My Fortune/The Hummingbird (foldaround p/s with poster in poly bag)	8

CHERYL ST. CLAIR

Year	Label / Cat. No.	Title	Value
66	CBS 202041	My Heart Is Not In It/We Want Love	15
66	Columbia DB 8077	What About Me/I'll Forget You Tonight	12

(see also Alison Wonder)

ISLA ST. CLAIR

Year	Label / Cat. No.	Title	Value
81	Clare ISLA 1	THE SONG AND THE STORY (LP)	20
85	Topic 12TS 436	SCOTCH MEASURE (LP)	15

SAINT ETIENNE

Year	Label / Cat. No.	Title	Value
90	Heavenly HVN 2	Only Love Can Break Your Heart/Only Love Can Break Your Heart (Version) (p/s)	6
90	Heavenly HVN 212	Only Love Can Break Your Heart/Only Love Can Break Your Heart (Original Version) (12", p/s)	10
90	Heavenly HVN 212R	Only Love Can Break Your Heart (A Mix Of Two Halves)/ The Official Saint Etienne World Cup Theme (12", die-cut p/s)	12
90	The Catalogue CAT 084	Only Love Can Break Your Heart (remixed by Flowered Up)/FLOWERED UP: It's On (The Posh Facker Mix) (square flexidisc with *The Catalogue* mag)	5/4
90	Heavenly HVN 4	Kiss And Make Up/Sky's Dead (p/s)	5
90	Heavenly HVN 412	Kiss And Make Up/Sky's Dead (12", p/s)	12
90	Heavenly HVN 412R	Kiss And Make Up (Midsummer Madness Remix)/Kiss And Make Up (Midsummer Dubness Mix) (12", p/s)	12
90	Heavenly HVN 4CD	Kiss And Make Up (7")/Kiss And Make Up (12")/Sky's Dead (CD)	18
91	Heavenly HVN 912R	Speedwell (Flying Mix)/Speedwell (Project Mix)/Nothing Can Stop Us (Instrumental)/3D Tiger (12", p/s)	8
91	Heavenly HVN 9CD	Nothing Can Stop Us/Speedwell/Nothing Can Stop Us (Instrumental) (CD)	15
92	Heavenly HVN 12CD	Only Love Can Break Your Heart/Only Love Can Break Your Heart (A Mix Of Two Halves)/Filthy (CD)	12
92	Heavenly HVN 22	Live — Paris '92 (clear flexidisc, gig freebie, 1,000 only)	10
93	Heavenly HVN 2912	Hobart Paving/Who Do You Think You Are (12", p/s, mispressed with "Hobart Paving" & "Your Head My Voice" on both sides)	15
93	Heavenly HVN 36CD	I Was Born On Christmas Day/My Christmas Prayer/Snowplough/Peterloo (CD, picture disc)	8
95	Heavenly HVN 41	XMAS '95: A Christmas Gift To You/Driving Home For Christmas/ A Message In A Bottle (CD, signed fan club edition)	75
98	Creation CRECS 279	Sylvie/(Trouser Enthusiast's Tintinnabulation Edit) (cassette)	6
03	Mantra MNT 78	Soft Like Me/Gimp Crisis (p/s, limited edition)	5
93	Heavenly HVNCDX 6	SO TOUGH/YOU NEED A MESS OF HELP TO STAND ALONE (2-CD)	20
95	Heavenly HVNLP 9CD	I LOVE TO PAINT (CD, fan club edition, 600 only)	180
95	Heavenly HVNCD 10	TOO YOUNG TO DIE (CD, with bonus CD "Too Young To Die — The Remix Album" [HVN LP 10CDR])	25
98	Fan Club SPCD 463	XMAS '98: I Don't Intend To Spend Christmas Without You/Kofi Annan (CD, fan club edition, in card sleeve)	50
98	Creation CRECD 225L	GOOD HUMOUR (CD, digipak with booklet and slipcase)	18
00	Mantra MNSTET 1	BUILT ON SAND: RARITIES 1994-1999 (CD, fan club edition)	130

(see also 50 Year Void, Sarah Cracknell, Lovecut D.B., Mike Vickers)

MINT VALUE £

SAINT ORCHESTRA

78	Pye 7N 46127	Return Of The Saint/Funko (p/s)	12

BARRY ST. JOHN

64	Decca F 11933	A Little Bit Of Soap/Thing Of The Past	15
64	Decca F 11975	Bread And Butter/Cry To Me	15
65	Decca F 12111	Mind How You Go/Don't You Feel Proud	18
65	Decca F 12145	Hey Boy/I've Been Crying	15
65	Columbia DB 7783	Come Away Melinda/Gotta Brand New Man	12
66	Columbia DB 7868	Everything I Touch Turns To Tears/Sounds Like My Baby	45
68	Major Minor MM 587	Cry Like A Baby/Long And Lonely Night	7
69	Major Minor MM 604	By The Time I Get To Phoenix/Turn On Your Light	7
69	M. Minor MMLP/SMLP 43	ACCORDING TO ST. JOHN (LP)	40

BRIDGET ST. JOHN

69	Dandelion K 4404	To B Without A Hitch/Autumn Lullaby	10
70	Warner Bros WB 8019	If You've Got Money/Yep	12
72	Polydor 2001 280	Fly High/There's A Place I Know/Suzanne (p/s)	12
72	Polydor 2001 361	Nice/Goodbye Baby Goodbye	8
73	MCA MUS 1203	Passing Thru'/The Road Was Lonely On My Own	10
69	Dandelion 63750	ASK ME NO QUESTIONS (LP, gatefold sleeve)	50
71	Dandelion DAN 8007	SONGS FOR THE GENTLE MAN (LP, gatefold sleeve, also listed as K 49007)	40
72	Dandelion 2310 193	THANK YOU FOR... (LP, gatefold sleeve)	40
74	Chrysalis CHR 1062	JUMBLE QUEEN (LP)	20

(see also Ron Geesin, Quiver)

TAMMY ST. JOHN

64	Pye 7N 15682	Boys/Hey Hey Hey Hey	10
65	Pye 7N 15762	He's The One For Me/I'm Tired Of Just Looking At You	10
65	Pye 7N 15948	Dark Shadows And Empty Hallways/I Mustn't Cry	10
66	Pye 7N 17042	Nobody Knows What's Goin' On (In My Mind But Me)/ Stay Together Young Lovers	45
69	Tangerine DP 0007	Concerning Love/Sound Of Love	8

(see also Trends)

ST. LOUIS JIMMY

53	Esquire 10-319	Holiday For Boogie/MEMPHIS SLIM: Harlem Bound (78)	35

ST. LOUIS UNION

66	Decca F 12318	Girl/Respect	20
66	Decca F 12386	Behind The Door/English Tea	25
66	Decca F 12508	East Side Story/Think About Me	80

OLIVER ST. PATRICK & DIAMONDS

67	Trojan TR 005	I Want To Be Loved By You/Tulips	12

CRISPIAN ST. PETERS

65	Decca F 12080	At This Moment/Goodbye, You'll Forget Me	15
65	Decca F 12207	No No No/Three Goodbyes	15
65	Decca F 12287	You Were On My Mind/What I'm Gonna Be	6
66	Decca F 12359	The Pied Piper/Sweet Dawn My True Love	6
66	Decca F 12480	Changes/My Little Brown Eyes	7
66	Decca F 12525	But She's Untrue/Your Ever Changin' Mind	6
67	Decca F 12596	Almost Persuaded/You Have Gone	6
67	Decca F 12677	Free Spirit/I'm Always Crying	7
68	Decca F 12761	That's The Time/The Silent Times	7
68	Decca F 12861	Carolina/That's Why We Are Through	7
69	Mencap MEN 002	Monumental Queen/Soft As A Rose	7
70	Decca F 13055	So Long/My Little Brown Eyes (withdrawn)	12+
70	Square SQ 2	Wandering Hobo/Love, Love, Love	6
74	Santa Ponsa PNS 17	Do Daddy Do/Every Time You Sinned	6
67	Decca DFE 8678	ALMOST PERSUADED (EP)	55
66	Decca LK 4805	FOLLOW ME... (LP)	55
70	Square SQA 102	SIMPLY... CRISPIAN ST. PETERS (LP)	25

KIRBY ST. ROMAIN

63	Stateside SS 199	Summer's Comin'/Miss You So	8

SAINT STEVEN

69	Probe SPB 1005	OVER THE HILLS/THE BASTICH (LP)	50

ST. VALENTINE'S DAY MASSACRE

67	Fontana TF 883	Brother Can You Spare A Dime/Al's Party (some with p/s)	175/75

(see also Artwoods)

BUFFY SAINTE-MARIE

65	Fontana TF 574	Until It's Time For You To Go/The Flower And The Apple Tree	7
65	Fontana TF 614	The Universal Soldier/Cripple Creek	7
66	Fontana TF 695	Timeless Love/Lady Margret	7
72	Vanguard VRS 35143	I'm Gonna Be A Country Girl Again/Piney Wood Hills	5
75	Vanguard VS 5002	I'm Gonna Be A Country Girl Again/Now That The Buffalo's Gone	5
65	Fontana TFL 6040	IT'S MY WAY! (LP)	25
65	Fontana TFL 6047	MANY A MILE (LP)	25
66	Fontana (S)TFL 6071	LITTLE WHEEL SPIN AND SPIN (LP)	25
71	Vanguard VSD 79311	SHE USED TO WANNA BE A BALLERINA (LP)	12
71	Vanguard VSD 79250	FIRE & FEET & CANDLELIGHT (LP)	12
71	Vanguard VSD 79300	ILLUMINATIONS (LP)	12
72	Vanguard VSD 79280	I'M GONNA BE A COUNTRY GIRL AGAIN (LP)	12
72	Vanguard VSD 79312	MOONSHOT (LP)	12
73	Vanguard VSD 79330	QUIET PLACES (LP)	12
74	Vanguard VSD 79340	NATIVE NORTH AMERICAN CHILD (LP)	12
76	ABC ABCL 5168	SWEET AMERICA (LP)	15

SAINTS (Australia)

76	Power Exchange PX 242	I'm Stranded/No Time (p/s)	10
77	Power Exchange PXE 101	I'm Stranded/(STANLEY FRANK: 2 tracks) (p/s)	8
77	Harvest HAR 5123	Erotic Neurotic/One Way Street	10
77	Harvest HAR 5130	This Perfect Day/L-I-E-S	6
77	Harvest 12 HAR 5130	This Perfect Day/L-I-E-S/Do The Robot (12", with 'disclaimer' stickered p/s)	10
77	Harvest HAR 5137	1, 2, 3, 4 (River Deep, Mountain High/Lipstick On Your Collar/One Way Street/ Demolition Girl) (EP, double pack, gatefold p/s)	30
77	Harvest HAR 5137	1, 2, 3, 4 (River Deep, Mountain High/Lipstick On Your Collar/One Way Street/ Demolition Girl) (EP, p/s)	5
78	Harvest HAR 5148	Know Your Product/Run Down (no p/s)	5
78	Harvest HAR 5166	Security/All Times Through Paradise (p/s)	12
89	Bucketfull Of Brains BOB 26	I Dreamed Of Marie Antoinette/MOCK TURTLES: Croppies Lie Down (free with *Bucketfull Of Brains* magazine, issue 32)	6/4
77	Harvest SHSP 4065	I'M STRANDED (LP)	25
78	Harvest SHSP 4078	ETERNALLY YOURS (LP, with inner sleeve)	20
78	Harvest SHSP 4094	PREHISTORIC SOUNDS (LP)	20

SAINTS (Jamaica)

66	Doctor Bird DB 1009	Brown Eyes/BABA BROOKS & HIS BAND: King Size	25
69	Big Shot BI 522	Windy Part One/Windy Part Two	12

SAINTS (Jamaica)

73	Count Shelley CS 043	How Long/Feeling Good	6

SAINTS (U.K.)

63	Pye 7N 15548	Wipe Out/Midgets	25
63	Pye 7N 15582	Husky Team/Pigtails	25

(see also Tornados, Heinz)

SAINTS (U.K.)

64	MJB BEV 73/4	SAINTS (10" LP, private pressing)	300
64	MJB BEVLP 127/8	SAINTS ALIVE! (LP, private pressing)	300

SAINTS JAZZ BAND

51	Decibel J 3	Old Stack O' Lee Blues/1919 March (78)	7
51	Parlophone R 3427	I Want A Girl Just Like The Girl That Married Dear Old Dad/ CRANE RIVER JAZZ BAND: I'm Travelling (78)	6
51	Parlophone R 3427	I Want A Girl Just Like The Girl That Married Dear Old Dad/ CRANE RIVER JAZZ BAND: I'm Travelling	12
53	Parlophone MSP 6042	Hey Lawdy Papa/Who Walks In When I Walk Out?	10
56	Parlophone R 4240	Mahogany Hall Stomp/Stack O' Lee Blues	8
57	Parlophone R 4260	Blue Turning Grey Over You/'Till We Meet Again	6
57	Parlophone R 4304	How Come You Do Me Like You Do/Willie The Weeper	6
58	Parlophone R 4417	Swingin' The Blues/I've Found A New Baby	7
58	Parlophone R 4417	Swingin' The Blues/I've Found A New Baby (78)	6
56	Parlophone GEP 8560	SAINTS PLAY JAZZ (EP)	12
56	Parlophone GEP 8577	SAINTS JAZZ BAND (EP)	10

RUSS SAINTY (& NU NOTES)

60	Top Rank JAR 381	Happy-Go-Lucky-Me/Standing Around	15
60	Decca F 11270	Race With The Devil/Too Shy (solo)	15
61	Decca F 11325	Don't Believe Him, Donna/Your Other Love (solo)	10
62	HMV POP 1055	Keep Your Love Locked/I've Got A Girl (as Russ Sainty & Nu Notes)	10
62	HMV POP 1069	Send Me The Pillow That You Dream On/ What Do You Know About That (solo)	10
63	HMV POP 1181	Unforgettable Love/The Twinkle In Your Eye (solo)	10
64	Parlophone R 5168	That's How I'm Gonna Love You/Lonesome Town (as Russ Sainty & Nu-Notes)	6
64	Columbia DB 7394	This Is My Lovely Day/Bless You, Girl (as Russ Sainty & Nu-Notes)	6
65	Columbia DB 7521	It Ain't That Easy/And Then (solo)	6
65	Columbia DB 7708	Saving My Tears (For A Rainy Day)/She (solo)	6
60s	Society SOC 1035	THE GENIUS OF LENNON AND McCARTNEY (LP)	15

(see also Nu Notes)

KYU SAKAMOTO

63	HMV POP 1171	Sukiyaki/Anoko No Namae Wa Nantenkana	8
63	HMV POP 1211	China Nights/Benkyo No Cha Cha Cha	8
64	HMV POP 1342	Rose Rose I Love You/Sayonara Tokyo	8
62	HMV CLP 1674	SUKIYAKI (LP)	90

RYUICHI SAKAMOTO

80	Island IPR 2048	Riot In Lagos/Iconic Storage (12", company sleeve)	8
82	Virgin VS 510	Bamboo Houses/Bamboo Music (p/s)	7
86	10 TEND 112	Field Work/Exhibition (double pack, gatefold p/s)	8
80	Island ILPS 9656	B-2 UNIT (LP)	18
90	Virgin VUSLP 14	BEAUTY (LP, with inner)	12

(see also David Sylvian, Yellow Magic Orchestra)

(BOB) SAKER

68	Polydor BM 56231	Still Got You/Imagination (as Bob Saker)	6
68	Parlophone R 5740	Foggy Tuesday/Ooh Nana Na (as Bob Saker)	10
69	Parlophone R 5752	Hey Joe!/Christianity	15
71	CBS 7010	What A Beautiful World/City Of The Angels	6
71	CBS 7399	Even Though We Ain't Got Money/Wild Winds Are Blowing	6

SALAMANDER

70	CBS 5102	Crystal Ball/Billy	25

(see also Onyx)

SALAMANDER

71	Youngblood SSYB 14	THE TEN COMMANDMENTS (LP, gatefold sleeve)	200

MINT VALUE £

SALEM

82	Hilton FMR 056	Cold As Steel/Reach To Eternity	50

SOUPY SALES

65	HMV POP 1432	The Mouse/Pachalfaka	6

SALFORD JETS

78	WEA K 18008	Lookin' At The Squares/Dancing School (no p/s)	5
79	EMI INT 590	Manchester Boys/Last Bus (p/s)	20

SALLY & ALLEY CATS

64	Parlophone R 5183	Is It Something I Said/You Forgot To Remember	12

SALLYANGIE

69	Big T BIG 126	Two Ships/Colours Of The World	18
72	Philips 6006 259	Child Of Allah/Lady Go Lightly	18
68	Transatlantic TRA 176	CHILDREN OF THE SUN (LP, gatefold sleeve)	50
78	Transatlantic TRA 176	CHILDREN OF THE SUN (LP, reissue, different single sleeve)	20

(see also Mike Oldfield)

DOUG SALMA & HIGHLANDERS

63	Philips BF 1279	Highland Fling/The Scavenger	10

SALMONTAILS

80	Oblivion OBL 001	SALMONTAILS (LP, with Dave Pegg)	18

SALOME

69	Page One POF 137	Vivo Cantando/Amigos Amigos	7

SALSOUL STRUT

96	Records Inc. no cat. no.	Better Days/(mixes)	12

SALT

78	Grapevine GRA 111	BEYOND A SONG (LP, with insert)	18

SALT & PEPPER

61	London HLU 9338	High Noon/Come Softly To Me	15

SAL SALVADOR

55	KPL 105	SAL SALVADOR QUARTET (10" LP)	12

SALVATION

69	United Artists UP 35048	Cinderella/The Village Shuck	8
69	United Artists UAS 29062	SALVATION (LP)	20

SALVATION

83	Merciful Release MR 025	Girlsoul/Evelyn (p/s)	12
83	Merciful Release MRX 025	Girlsoul/Evelyn/Dust Up (12", p/s)	15
86	Batfish Inc. BF 103	Jessica's Crime/The Shining (p/s)	12
86	Batfish Inc. USS 104	Jessica's Crime (Extended Mix)/The Shining/Shattered Sky (12", p/s)	8
86	Ediesta CALC 4	Seek: Strange Fruit/Lady Faith (p/s)	5

RINO SALVIATI

55	Durium DC 16579	Canto Nella Valle/Ersa Do Mare (78)	6

SAMMY SALVO

58	RCA RCA 1032	Oh Julie/Say Yeah	30
58	RCA RCA 1032	Oh Julie/Say Yeah (78)	20
59	London HLP 8997	Afraid/Marble Heart	15
59	London HLP 8997	Afraid/Marble Heart (78)	10
62	Polydor NH 66974	Billy Blue/French Poodle	10

SAM & BILL

66	Pye International 7N 25355	Fly Me To The Moon/Treat Me Right	12
67	Brunswick 05973	I Feel Like Cryin'/I'll Try	25

SAM & DAVE

66	King KG 1041	No More Pain/You Ain't No Big Thing Baby	20
66	Atlantic AT 4066	You Don't Know Like I Know/Blame Me, Don't Blame My Heart	15
66	Atlantic 584 003	Hold On I'm A Comin'/I Got Everything I Need	8
66	Atlantic 584 047	If You Got The Loving (I Got The Time)/Said I Wasn't Gonna Tell Nobody	7
67	Atlantic 584 064	You Got Me Hummin'/Sleep Good Tonight	8
67	Atlantic 584 086	You Don't Know Like I Know/Blame Me, Don't Blame My Heart (reissue)	7
67	Stax 601 004	Soothe Me/Sweet Pains (initially dark blue label, later light blue)	10/6
67	Stax 601 006	When Something Is Wrong With My Baby/A Small Portion Of Your Love (initially with dark blue labels, later light blue)	10/6
67	Stax 601 023	Soul Man/May I Baby	6
68	Stax 601 030	I Thank You/Wrap It Up	6
68	Atlantic 584 192	You Don't Know What You Mean To Me/This Is Your World	7
68	Atlantic 584 211	Can't You Find Another Way/Still Is The Night	7
68	Atlantic 584 228	Everybody's Got To Believe In Somebody/If I Didn't Have A Girl Like You	6
69	Atlantic 584 237	Soul Sister, Brown Sugar/Come On In	6
69	Atlantic 584 247	You Don't Know Like I Know/Hold On I'm A Comin'	6
69	Atlantic 584 303	Ooh, Ooh, Ooh/Holdin' On	6
70	Atlantic 584 324	Baby, Baby, Don't Stop Now/I'm Not An Indian Giver	6
66	King KGL 4001	SAM AND DAVE (LP)	60
66	Atlantic 587/588 045	HOLD ON, I'M A COMIN' (LP)	30
67	Stax 589 003	DOUBLE DYNAMITE (LP)	25
68	Stax 589 015	SOUL MEN (LP)	25
68	Major Minor MCP 5000	SAM AND DAVE (LP)	22
69	Atlantic 588 154	I THANK YOU (LP)	22
69	Atlantic 588 155	THE BEST OF SAM AND DAVE (LP)	15
69	Atlantic 587/588 181	DOUBLE TROUBLE (LP)	22
69	Atlantic 588 185	SOUL MEN (LP, reissue)	15

MINT VALUE £

SAM & KITTY

80 Grapevine GRP 132 — I've Got Something Good/Love Is The Greatest ... 8

SAM APPLE PIE

69 Decca F 22932 — Tiger Man (King Of The Jungle)/Sometime Girl ... 12
73 DJM DJS 274 — Call Me Boss/Old Tom ... 5
69 Decca LK-R/SKL-R 5005 — SAM APPLE PIE (LP) ... 100
73 DJM DJLPS 429 — EAST 17 (LP) ... 30

SAME

79 Wessex WEX 267 — Wild About You/Movements (p/s) ... 70
80 Blue Print BLU 2008 — Movements/Wild About You (reissue with reversed sides & blue print on p/s; some with no p/s) ... 50/40

SAM, ERV & TOM

68 Direction 58-3339 — Soul Teacher/Hard To Get ... 10
(see also Diplomats)

SAM GOPAL

(see under 'G')

MIKE SAMMES & HIS SINGERS

56 Bristol Cigarettes — Today's Cigarette Is A Bristol (promo 78, same track on both sides) ... 10
56 Bristol Cigarettes — The Bristol Bounce (1-sided 78, promo only) ... 10
58 Fontana H 159 — Heartaches/The Gang That Sang Heart Of My Heart (78) ... 6
59 Fontana H 232 — Little Drummer Boy/Comin' Through The Rye (78) ... 6
59 Top Rank JAR 166 — Upstairs And Downstairs/IVOR RAYMONDE: Mylene ... 6
62 Oriole CB 1738 — Oh My Twisted Bach/Al Of A Twist ... 8

SAMMY

72 Philips 6006 227 — Goo Ger Woogie/Big Lovin' Woman ... 5
72 Philips 6308 136 — SAMMY (LP) ... 15
(see also Ian Gillan)

SAMPLES

80 Sample — VENDETTA (Vendetta/ (EP) ... 20
84 No Future OI 14 — Dead Hero/Fire Around Round/Suspicion (p/s) ... 12

DAVE SAMPSON & HUNTERS

60 Columbia DB 4449 — Sweet Dreams/It's Lonesome ... 20
60 Columbia DB 4502 — If You Need Me/See You Around ... 20
61 Columbia DB 4597 — Why The Chicken?/1999 ... 15
61 Columbia DB 4625 — Easy To Dream/That's All ... 18
62 Fontana H 361 — Wide, Wide World/Since Sandy Moved Away (solo) ... 15
61 Columbia SEG 8095 — DAVE (EP, also stereo ESG 7853) ... 125/160
(see also Hunters [U.K.])

TOMMY SAMPSON

58 Melodisc MEL 1411 — Rockin'/Rock'n'Roll Those Big Brown Eyes (with His Strongmen) ... 25
58 Melodisc MEL 1411 — Rockin'/Rock'n'Roll Those Big Brown Eyes (with His Strongmen) (78) ... 20
58 Parlophone R 4458 — Lazy Train/Smooth Mood (as Tommy Sampson Orchestra) ... 7
58 Parlophone R 4458 — Lazy Train/Smooth Mood (as Tommy Sampson Orchestra) (78) ... 10

SAMSON

69 Instant INSP 004 — ARE YOU SAMSON (LP) ... 50
(see also Strider)

SAMSON

70 Parlophone R 5867 — Venus/Wool And Water ... 6

SAMSON

78 Lightning GIL 547 — Telephone/Leavin' You (p/s) ... 35
79 Lightning GIL 553 — Mr. Rock'n'Roll/Drivin' Music (p/s) ... 35
79 Laser LAS 6 — Mr. Rock'n'Roll (remix)/Primrose Shuffle ... 12
80 EMI EMI 5061 — Vice Versa (Edit)/Hammerhead (p/s, withdrawn, 1,000 demos only) ... 45
80 Gem GEMS 34 — Vice Versa (Edit)/Hammerhead (reissue, p/s, some with sticker) ... 8/5
80 Gem GEMS 38 — Hard Times (Remix)/Angel With A Machine Gun (p/s) ... 5
81 RCA RCA 67 — Riding With The Angels (Edit)/Little Big Man (no p/s) ... 12
81 RCA RCA 67 — Riding With The Angels (Edit)/Little Big Man (picture disc) ... 10
82 Polydor POSPP 471 — Losing My Grip/Pyramid To The Stars (picture disc) ... 6
82 Polydor POSPX 471 — Losing My Grip/Pyramid To The Stars/Mr. Rock'n'Roll (live)/Tomorrow Or Yesterday (live) (12" EP) ... 10
82 Polydor POSPG 519/SAM 1 — Life On The Run/Drivin' With ZZ!/Walking Out On You (live)/Bright Lights (live) (double pack, gatefold p/s) ... 7
82 Polydor SAM 2 — Red Skies/Young Idea (unissued, promo only) ... 18
83 Polydor PODJ 554 — Red Skies (DJ Edit) (1-sided promo) ... 12
83 Polydor POSPP 554 — Red Skies/Livin', Lovin', Lyin' (picture disc) ... 6
83 Polydor POSPX 554 — Red Skies/Livin', Lovin', Lyin'/Running Out Of Time (12", p/s) ... 10
84 Polydor POSP 670 — Are You Ready?/Front Page News (p/s) ... 7
84 Polydor POSPP 670 — Are You Ready?/Front Page News (picture disc) ... 8
84 Polydor POSPX 670 — Are You Ready?/Front Page News/La Grange (12", p/s) ... 8
84 Polydor POSP 680 — The Fight Goes On/Riding With The Angels (re-recording) (p/s) ... 5
84 Polydor POSPX 680 — The Fight Goes On (Long Version)/Riding With The Angels (re-recording)/Vice Versa (live) (12", p/s) ... 8
84 Thunderbolt THBE 1.003 — Mr Rock'n'Roll/Primrose Shuffle/Telephone/Leavin' You (12", p/s) ... 8
86 Capitol CL 395 — Vice Versa (Remix)/Losing My Grip (Remix) (p/s) ... 8
86 Capitol 12CLP 395 — Vice Versa (Remix)/Losing My Grip (Remix) (12", picture disc) ... 15
87 Metal Hammer METAL 1 — One Day's Heroes (as Paul Samson's Empire)/CHARIOT: Life On The Line/HEAVY PETTIN': Heaven Sent/STRANGEWAYS: Never Gonna Lose It (EP, with/without *Metal Hammer* magazine) ... 6/5
79 Laser LAP 1 — SURVIVORS (LP) ... 15

MINT VALUE £

80	Gem GEMLP 108	HEAD ON (LP, 2 different mixes, A1/B1 or A2/B2 in matrix; each with insert, some with free patch)	15/12
80	Gem GEMLP 108	HEAD ON (LP, mispress with A1/B2 matrix)	20
81	Gem GEMLP 113	SHOCK TACTICS (LP, release cancelled)	
81	RCA LP 5031	SHOCK TACTICS (LP, with insert)	15
82	Polydor POLS 1077	BEFORE THE STORM (LP, initially with poster, stickered sleeve)	20/12
84	Polydor POLD 5132	DON'T GET MAD, GET EVEN (LP)	15
84	Polydor POLD 5132	DON'T GET MAD, GET EVEN (2-LP, white labels, 2 different mixes of same album, promo only)	35

(see also Bruce Dickinson, Iron Maiden, John McCoy, Tiger, Colin Town[e]s, Thunderstick, Nicky Moore, Mammoth, Egypt)

SAM THE SHAM & THE PHARAOHS

65	MGM MGM 1269	Woolly Bully/Ain't Gonna Move	12
65	MGM MGM 1278	Ju Ju Hand/Big City Lights	10
65	MGM MGM 1285	Ring Dang Doo/Don't Try It	10
66	MGM MGM 1298	Red Hot/Long Long Way	15
66	MGM MGM 1315	Li'l Red Riding Hood/Love Me Like Before	10
66	MGM MGM 1326	The Hair On My Chinny Chin Chin/The Out Crowd	8
66	MGM MGM 1331	How Do You Catch A Girl/The Love You Left Behind	8
67	MGM MGM 1337	Oh That's Bad No That's Good/Take What You Can Get	8
67	MGM MGM 1343	Black Sheep/My Day's Gonna Come	15
68	MGM MGM 1379	Yakety Yak/Let Our Lovelight Shine	8
69	MGM MGM 1473	Woolly Bully/Ring Dang Doo	6
66	MGM MGM-EP 794	RED HOT (EP)	60
65	MGM MGM-C 1007	WOOLY BULLY (LP)	50
66	MGM MGM-C(S) 8032	LI'L RED RIDING HOOD (LP)	40
71	Atco 2400 146	SAM HARD AND HEAVY (LP, as Sam Samudio)	15

LEROY SAMUEL

72	Punch PH 113	Trying To Wreck My Life/JOHN HOLT: Pride And Joy	12

(Phillip) SAMUEL THE FIRST

71	Summit SUM 8515	Sounds Of Babylon/BEVERLEY'S ALL STARS: Second Babylon Version	8

JERRY SAMUELS

56	HMV 7M 411	Puppy Love/The Chosen Few	18
56	HMV POP 219	Puppy Love/The Chosen Few (78)	8

(see also Napoleon XIV)

WINSTON SAMUELS

64	Columbia DB 7405	You Are The One/Angela	25
64	Rio R 26	Follow/I'm So Glad	25
64	Black Swan WI 419	Luck Will Come My Way/LLOYD BREVITT: One More Time	25
64	Black Swan WI 426	You Are The One/Gloria Love (B-side actually by Beltones)	25
65	Ska Beat JB 196	Be Prepared/Jericho Wall	25
65	Ska Beat JB 213	My Bride To Be/LLOYD PREVITT: Wayward Ska	25
65	Ska Beat JB 214	Never Again/My Angel	25
66	Ska Beat JB 238	What Have I Done/Broken Hearted	25
66	Ska Beat JB 241	Ups And Downs/Come What May	25
66	Ska Beat JB 244	Time Will Tell/I'm Sorry	25
67	Island WI 3051	The Greatest/FREDDIE & FITZY: Truth Hurts	25
67	Island WI 3053	I Won't Be Discouraged/FREDDIE & FITZIE: Why Did My Little Girl Cry	25

SAMURAI

71	Greenwich GSLP 1003	SAMURAI (LP)	125

(see also Greenslade, Web)

SAMURAI

85	Ebony EBON 25	Fires Of Hell/Dreams Of The World (no p/s)	15

SANDALS

90s	Acid Jazz JAZID 47	A Profound Gas (p/s)	10

ALEX SANDERS

70	A&M AMLS 984	A WITCH IS BORN (LP, foldout sleeve with warning sticker, withdrawn)	150

GARY SANDERS

66	Warner Bros WB 5676	Ain't No Beatle/Ain't I Good To You	12

GEORGE SANDERS

58	HMV 7EG 8395	THE GEORGE SANDERS TOUCH (EP)	15

PHARAOH SANDERS

60s	Fontana SFJL 931	ON ESP (LP)	20
71	Probe SPB 1019	DEAF, DUMB AND BLIND (LP)	25
70s	Impulse AS 9138	TAUHID (LP)	20
70s	Impulse AS 9199	SUMMUN BUKMUN UMYUN (LP)	25
70s	Impulse AS 9219	BLACK UNITY (LP)	25
70s	Impulse AS 9227	LIVE AT THE EAST (LP)	25
70s	Impulse AS 9229	THE BEST OF PHARAOH SANDERS (2-LP)	20
70s	Impulse 9233	WISDOM THROUGH MUSIC (LP)	20
70s	Impulse 9254	VILLAGE OF PHARAOHS (LP)	20
70s	Impulse 9261	ELEVATION (LP)	20
70s	Impulse 9280	LOVE IN US ALL (LP)	20
82	Jasmine JAS 53	THEMBI (LP)	20

PHARAOH SANDERS QUINTET

66	ESP Disk/Fontana SFJL 931	PHARAOH SANDERS QUINTET (LP)	40

RAY SANDERS

60	London HLG 7106	A World So Full Of Love/A Little Bitty Tear (export issue)	12

TOMMY SANDERSON & SANDMEN
61 Ember EMB 131 — Deadline/Candelglow . . . 12
62 Ember EMB 152 — Ding Dong Rag/Piano A-Go Go . . . 10

CHRIS SANDFORD (& CORONETS)
63 Decca F 11778 — Not Too Little — Not Too Much/I'm Lookin' . . . 5
64 Decca F 11842 — You're Gonna Be My Girl/Don't Leave Me Now (with Coronets) . . . 7
65 Fontana TF 633 — I Wish They Wouldn't Always Say I Sound Like The Guy From The U.S.A. Blues/Little Man, Nobody Cares . . . 8

FLO SANDON
59 Durium DC 16641 — La Strada Dell Amore/Passion Flower (78) . . . 6

GERRY SANDON
96 Twangsville TW 001 — JUST GERRY (EP) . . . 10

JOHNNY SANDON (& REMO FOUR)
63 Pye 7N 15542 — Lies/On The Horizon (as Johnny Sandon & Remo Four) . . . 15
63 Pye 7N 15559 — Magic Potion/Yes (as Johnny Sandon & Remo Four) . . . 15
64 Pye 7N 15602 — Sixteen Tons/The Blizzard . . . 12
64 Pye 7N 15665 — Donna Means Heartbreak/Some Kinda Wonderful . . . 12
64 Pye 7N 15717 — The Blizzard/(I'd Be A) Legend In My Time . . . 10
(see also Remo Four)

SAND PEBBLES
67 Track 604 015 — Love Power/Because Of Love . . . 18
68 Toast TT 505 — If You Didn't Hear Me The First Time/Flower Power . . . 8
69 Track 604 028 — Love Power/Because Of Love (reissue) . . . 10

SANDPIPERS
66 Pye International 7N 25380 — Guantanamera/What Makes You Dream, Pretty Girl? . . . 5
66 Pye International 7N 25396 — Louie Louie/Things We Said Today . . . 8
60s A&M AML 918 — SOFTLY (LP) . . . 12
60s A&M AML 912 — MISTY ROSES (LP) . . . 12
60s A&M AMLS 935 — KUMBAYA (LP) . . . 12
60s A&M AMLS 975 — SOFTLY AS I LEAVE YOU (LP) . . . 12
60s A&M AMLB 1004 — GUANTANAMERA (LP) . . . 12
60s A&M AMLB 51030 — LA BAMBA (LP) . . . 12

SANDRA
86 10 TENY 78-12 — (I'll Never Be) Maria Magdalena/Party Games/Little Girl (12", picture disc) . . . 15
86 10 TEN 113-12/TENY 78-12 — In The Heat Of The Night/Heatwave (Instrumental)//(I'll Never Be) Maria Magdalena/Party Games/Little Girl (12", double pack, including picture disc, gatefold PVC sleeve) . . . 30
89 Siren SRNCD 85 — Everlasting Love/Stop For A Minute/Everlasting Love (Remix)/(I'll Never Be) Maria Magdalena (CD) . . . 70
89 Siren SRNCD 104 — Heaven Can Wait (Single Version 4.05)/(Dub Mix)/Heaven's Theme (Instrumental)/Heaven Can Wait (Extended Version) (3" CD, card sleeve) . . . 30

SANDROSE
73 Polydor 2480 137 — SANDROSE (LP) . . . 110

SANDS (Ireland)
70 Major Minor MM 681 — Venus/Cara Mia . . . 15

SANDS (U.K.)
67 Reaction 591 017 — Mrs. Gillespie's Refrigerator/Listen To The Sky . . . 280
(see also Others, Sundragon)

SANDS
69 Tribune TRS 122 — Dance Dance Dance/The Cheater . . . 10
69 Tribune — SAND DOIN'S (LP) . . . 50
(see also Tony Kenny & Sands)

CLIVE SANDS
69 CBS 3955 — Lo Mucho Que Te Quiro/Picture On The Wall . . . 6
69 S.N.B. 55-4058 — Hooked On A Feeling/Marie . . . 7
69 S.N.B. 55-4431 — Whitchi Tai Yo/In A Dream . . . 12
69 CBS 4672 — A Very Lonely Man/You Made Me What I Am . . . 6
(see also Brothers Kane, Sarstedt Brothers, Wes Sands)

DAVEY SANDS & ESSEX
65 Decca F 12170 — Please Me Mine/All The Time . . . 18
67 CBS 202620 — Advertising Girl/Without You I'm Nothing . . . 15

EVIE SANDS
65 Red Bird BC 118 — Take Me For A Little While/Run Home To Mama . . . 45
66 Cameo Parkway C 413 — Picture Me Gone/It Makes Me Laugh . . . 100
68 A&M AMS 736 — Shadow Of The Evening/Until It's Time For You To Go . . . 10
69 A&M AMS 748 — I'll Hold Out Of My Hand/One Fine Summer Morning . . . 10
69 A&M AMS 760 — Anyway That You Want Me/I'll Never Be Alone . . . 10
75 Capitol CL 15818 — You Brought The Woman Out In Me/Early Morning Sunshine . . . 7

JODI(E) SANDS
57 London HL 8456 — With All My Heart/More Than Only Friends (as Jodi Sands) . . . 20
57 London HL 8530 — Please Don't Tell Me (Sayonara)/If You're Not Completely Satisfied . . . 20
57 London HL 8530 — Please Don't Tell Me (Sayonara)/If You're Not Completely Satisfied (78) . . . 25
58 Starlite ST45 005 — All I Ask Of You/The Way I Love You . . . 12
58 HMV POP 533 — Someday (You'll Want Me To Want You)/Always In My Heart . . . 7
58 HMV POP 533 — Someday (You'll Want Me To Want You)/Always In My Heart (78) . . . 10

MINT VALUE £

TOMMY SANDS

78s

57	Capitol CL 14695	Teen-Age Crush/Hep Dee Hootie (Cutie Wootie)	6
57	Capitol CL 14724	Ring-A-Ding-A-Ding/My Love Song	6
57	Capitol CL 14745	Goin' Steady/Ring My 'Phone	8
57	Capitol CL 14781	Let Me Be Loved/Fantastically Foolish	6
57	Capitol CL 14811	Man, Like Wow!/A Swingin' Romance	10
58	Capitol CL 14834	Sing, Boy, Sing/Crazy 'Cause I Love You	10

45s

57	Capitol CL 14695	Teen-Age Crush/Hep Dee Hootie (Cutie Wootie)	25
57	Capitol CL 14724	Ring-A-Ding-A-Ding/My Love Song	20
57	Capitol CL 14745	Goin' Steady/Ring My 'Phone	25
57	Capitol CL 14781	Let Me Be Loved/Fantastically Foolish	12
57	Capitol CL 14811	Man, Like Wow!/A Swingin' Romance	18
58	Capitol CL 14834	Sing, Boy, Sing/Crazy 'Cause I Love You	18
58	Capitol CL 14872	Hawaiian Rock/Teen-Age Doll	25
58	Capitol CL 14889	After The Senior Prom/Big Date	20
58	Capitol CL 14925	Blue Ribbon Baby/I Love You Because (as Tommy Sands & Raiders)	30
59	Capitol CL 14971	The Worryin' Kind/Bigger Than Texas	30
59	Capitol CL 15013	Is It Ever Gonna Happen/I Ain't Gittin' Rid Of You	25
59	Capitol CL 15047	Sinner Man/Bring Me Your Love	10
59	Capitol CL 15071	That's The Way I Am/I'll Be Seeing You	10
60	Capitol CL 15109	I Gotta Have You/You Hold The Future	10
60	Capitol CL 15143	The Old Oaken Bucket/These Are The Things You Are	10
61	Capitol CL 15219	Love In A Goldfish Bowl/I Love My Baby	8
63	HMV POP 1193	Connie/Young Man's Fancy	8
63	HMV POP 1247	Only 'Cause I'm Lonely/Cinderella	8
66	Liberty LIB 55842	The Statue/Lolita	40

EPs

57	Capitol EAP1 848	STEADY DATE WITH TOMMY SANDS PT. 1	50
57	Capitol EAP2 848	STEADY DATE WITH TOMMY SANDS PT. 2	50
57	Capitol EAP3 848	STEADY DATE WITH TOMMY SANDS PT. 3	50
57	Capitol EAP1 851	TEENAGE CRUSH	50
59	Capitol EAP1 1081	SANDS STORM PART 1	50
59	Capitol EAP2 1081	SANDS STORM PART 2	50
59	Capitol EAP3 1081	SANDS STORM PART 3	50
59	Capitol EAP1 1123	THIS THING CALLED LOVE	40

LPs

57	Capitol T 848	STEADY DATE WITH TOMMY SANDS	65
58	Capitol T 929	SING, BOY, SING (soundtrack)	75
59	Capitol T 1081	SANDS STORM!	55
59	Capitol T 1123	THIS THING CALLED LOVE	40
60	Capitol (S)T 1239	WHEN I'M THINKING OF YOU (mono/stereo)	25/35
61	Capitol T 1426	A DREAM WITH TOMMY SANDS	25

TONY SANDS & DRUMBEATS

60s	Studio 36 NSRS EP 1/22	Shame Shame Shame/I Got A Feeling	250

WES SANDS

63	Columbia DB 4996	There's Lots More Where This Came From/Three Cups	45

(see also Brothers Kane, Sarstedt Brothers, Clive Sands)

SANDS OF TIME

66	Pye 7N 17140	Where Did We Go Wrong/When I Look Back	8
67	Pye 7N 17236	One Day/Ev'ry Time We Say Goodbye	8

PAT SANDY

69	Attack ATT 8000	Gentle On My Mind/BIG L: Soulful	6

SANDY & TEACHERS

64	Columbia DB 7244	Listen With Mammy/Real Sweet	5

(see also Sandy Brown)

SANDY COAST

71	Polydor 2121 046	True Love/That's A Wonder	7
73	Polydor 2001 457	Blackboard Jungle Lady/Don't Get Me Wrong	7
69	Page One POLS 020	FROM THE STEREO WORKSHOP (LP)	125
69	Page One MORS 201	SHIPWRECK (LP)	125
73	Polydor 2310 277	STONEWALL (LP)	18

SAN FRANCISCO EARTHQUAKE

68	Mercury MF 1036	Fairy Tales Can Come True/Su Su	10

CLAUDE SANG

70	Sugar SU 105	I'm In Love Again/You'll Never Fool Me Again	6
70	Sugar SUM 1	THE WORLD OF REGGAE VOL. 1 (LP)	15

SAN REMO STRINGS

71	Tamla Motown TMG 795	Festival Time/All Turned On	12
72	Tamla Motown TMG 807	Reach Out, I'll Be There/Hungry For Love	6
73	Tamla Motown STML 11216	SAN REMO STRINGS SWING (LP)	18

BOBBY SANSOM (& GIANTS)

63	Oriole CB 1837	There's A Place/Lucille (as Bobby Sansom & Giants)	18
63	Oriole CB 1888	Where Have You Been/Do You Promise (as Bobby Sansom & Giants)	15
70	Decca F 13104	Lady One And Only/Handbags And Gladrags	6
71	Decca F 13151	I Believe In Music/The Valley Of The Shadows Of Tears	6

MONGO SANTAMARIA

63	Riverside RIF 106909	Watermelon Man/Don't Bother Me No More	20
65	CBS 201766	El Pussycat/Black Eyed Peas And Rice	20

MINT VALUE £

69	Direction 58-4086	Cloud Nine/Son Of A Preacher Man	20
69	Direction 58-4430	Twenty Five Miles/El Tres	20
66	CBS SS 62123	HEY! LET'S PARTY (LP)	18
69	CBS S 233811	ALL STRUNG OUT (LP)	15
71	CBS 63904	WORKING ON A GROOVY THING (LP)	20
71	Atlantic 2400 140	MONGO'S WAY (LP)	18

SANTANA

69	CBS 4593	Persuasion/Savor	6
70	CBS 4940	Evil Ways/Jin-Go-Lo-Ba	6
70	CBS 5325	Black Magic Woman/Hope You're Feeling Better	6
71	CBS 7046	Oye Como Va/Samba Pa Ti	5
71	CBS 7546	Everybody's Everything/Guajira	5
73	CBS 1155	Oye Como Va/Black Magic Woman (p/s, 'Hall Of Fame Hits' series)	5
89	CBS 654 568-3	SOLID GOLD (3" CD EP, gatefold card sleeve)	8
99	Arista ASCD 3662	SANTANA (CD, 5-track album sampler, digipak, promo only)	12
69	CBS 63015	SANTANA (LP, laminated sleeve original, orange label)	18
70	CBS 63815	SANTANA (LP, non-laminated sleeve reissue, orange label)	12
70	CBS 64087	ABRAXAS (LP, orange label)	12
71	CBS 69015	SANTANA (III) (LP, gatefold sleeve, some stickered, orange label)	12
72	CBS CQ 30595	SANTANA (III) (LP, gatefold sleeve, quadrophonic)	18
72	CBS 65299	CARAVANSERAI (LP, gatefold sleeve, orange label)	12
73	CBS CQ 31610	CARAVANSERAI (LP, gatefold sleeve, quadrophonic)	18
73	CBS 69040	WELCOME (LP, embossed gatefold sleeve)	12
74	CBS CQ 32445	WELCOME (LP, embossed gatefold sleeve, quadrophonic)	15
75	CBS 66325	LOTUS (3-LP, triple-gatefold sleeve, with inners)	18
75	CBS CQ 30130	ABRAXAS (LP, gatefold sleeve, quadrophonic)	18
75	CBS Q 69081	GREATEST HITS (LP, quadrophonic)	18
75	CBS Q 69084	BORBOLETTA (LP, quadrophonic)	18
76	CBS Q 86005	AMIGOS (LP, quadrophonic)	18

CARLOS SANTANA & BUDDY MILES

72	CBS 8338	Evil Ways/Them Changes	5
83	CBS A 3359	They All Went To Mexico (with Willie Nelson)/BUDDY MILES: Mudbone (p/s)	5
72	CBS 65142	CARLOS SANTANA & BUDDY MILES LIVE (LP, gatefold sleeve)	12
73	CBS CQ 31308	CARLOS SANTANA & BUDDY MILES LIVE (LP, quadrophonic)	18

(see also Santana, Buddy Miles, Mahavishnu Orchestra, John McLaughlin, John Lee Hooker)

SANTELLS

66	Sue WI 4020	So Fine/These Are Love	25

DAVID SANTO

68	London HLK 10219	Jingle Down A Hill/Rising Of Scorpio	6

SANTO & JOHNNY

59	Pye International 7N 25037	Sleep Walk/All Night Diner	15
59	Pye International N 25037	Sleep Walk/All Night Diner (78)	15
60	Parlophone R 4619	Tear Drop/The Long Walk Home	10
60	Parlophone R 4644	Caravan/Summertime	10
61	Pye International 7N 25111	Theme From Come September/Hopscotch	10
61	Parlophone R 4844	Bullseye!/Twistin' Bells	10
62	Parlophone R 4865	Birmingham/The Mouse	10
62	Stateside SS 110	Spanish Harlem/Stage To Cimarron	10
64	Stateside SS 253	Three Cabelleros/Manhattan Spiritual	10
64	Stateside SS 292	In The Still Of The Night/Song For Rosemary	10
60	Parlophone GEP 8806	SANTO AND JOHNNY NO. 1 (EP)	35
60	Parlophone GEP 8813	SANTO AND JOHNNY NO. 2 (EP)	30
64	Stateside S(S)L 1008	HAWAII (LP)	20
67	Philips (S)BL 7759	PULCINELLA (LP)	15
67	Philips (S)BL 7760	MONA LISA (LP)	15

SAPODILLA PUNCH

69	Mercury MF 1112	Hold On I'm Coming/Bach To Minor	8

SAPPHIRE

72	SRT SRT 72226	SAPPHIRE (LP)	180

SAPPHIRE

82	Sapphire Rocks SRR 001	Jealousy (p/s)	150

SAPPHIRES

63	Stateside SS 223	Where Is Johnny Now/Your True Love	50
64	Stateside SS 267	Who Do You Love/Oh So Soon	60
65	HMV POP 1441	Gotta Have Your Love/Gee Baby I'm Sorry	140
65	HMV POP 1461	Evil One/How Could I Say Goodbye	150
72	Probe PRO 556	Gotta Have Your Love/Gee Baby I'm Sorry (reissue)	10
74	Probe PRO 609	Slow Fizz/Our Love Is Everywhere	10
78	ABC 4221	Gonna Be A Big Thing/EDDIE REGAN: Playin' Hide And Seek	8

SARABAND

73	Folk Heritage FHR 050	CLOSE TO IT ALL (LP)	25

SARACEN

82	Nucleus SAR 1	No More Lonely Nights/Rock Of Ages (p/s, some with patch)	8/6
83	Neat NEAT 30	We Have Arrived/Face In The Crowd (p/s)	7
82	Nucleus MPGR 492	HEROES, SAINTS AND FOOLS (LP)	15

SARAH JANE

66	Pye 7N 17114	Listen People/The World Is Round	7

DON SARGENT

60	Vogue Pop V 9160	St. James' Infirmary/Gypsy Boots (triangular centre)	500

MINT VALUE £

SARI & SHALIMARS

68	United Artists UP 2235	It's So Lonely (Being Together)/You Walked Out On Me Before	20

DEREK SARJEANT

61	Oak RGJ 101	FOLK SONGS SUNG BY DEREK SARJEANT (EP)	25
61	Oak RGJ 103	SONGS WE LIKE TO SING (EP, with tracks by Lisa Turner & Mick Wells)	20
61	Oak RGJ 105	FOLK SONGS SUNG BY DEREK SARJEANT VOL. 2 (EP)	20
63	Oak RGJ 117	MAN OF KENT (EP)	25

MIKE SARNE

62	Parlophone R 4902	Come Outside (with Wendy Richard)/Fountain Of Love	6
62	Parlophone R 4932	Will I What (with Billie Davis)/Bird, You Know I Love Ya	6
62	Parlophone R 4974	Just For Kicks/Don't You Phone Me, I'll Phone You	7
63	Parlophone R 5010	Code Of Love/Are You Satisfied	7
63	Parlophone R 5060	Please Don't Say/Now You've Moved	6
63	Parlophone R 5090	Hello Lover Boy/Baby I'm On My Way	6
64	Parlophone R 5129	Out And About/A Place To Go	7
64	Parlophone R 5170	Love Me Please/You've Got Something (as Mike Sarne & Le Roys)	6
63	Parlophone DP 558	Just Like Eddie/Slow Twistin' Round The Totem Pole (export issue)	80
63	Parlophone GEP 8879	MIKE SARNE HIT PARADE (EP)	50
62	Parlophone PMC 1187	COME OUTSIDE (LP)	50

(see also Wendy Richards, Le Roys, Billie Davis, Rod McKuen)

SAROFEEN & SMOKE

71	Pye International 7N 25556	Susan Jane/Tomorrow	5
71	Pye Intl. NSPL 28153	DO IT (LP)	15

SAROLTA

68	Island WIP 6035	Open Your Hands/L.O.V.E.	15

PETER SARSTEDT

68	Island WIP 6028	I Must Go On/Mary Jane	45
69	United Artists UP 2262	Morning Mountain/Step Into The Candelight (unissued)	
69	United Artists UP 35895	Frozen Orange Sea/Arethusa Loser	20
69	United Artists (S)ULP 1219	PETER SARSTEDT (LP)	20
69	United Artists UAL 29037	AS THOUGH IT WERE A MOVIE (LP)	20
71	United Artists UAS 29247	EVERY WORD YOU SAY (LP)	20

(see also Sarstedt Brothers, Brothers Kane, Peter Lincoln)

SARSTEDT BROTHERS

73	Regal Zonophone RZ 3081	Chinese Restaurant/Beloved Illusions	7
73	Regal Zono. SRZA 8516	WORLDS APART TOGETHER (LP, gatefold sleeve)	20

(see also Brothers Kane, Peter Sarstedt, Eden Kane, Clive Sands, Wes Sands)

SASPARELLA

69	Decca F 12892	Spooky/Come Inside	8

SASSAFRAS

74	Polydor 2058 497	Oh My (Don't It Make You Want To Cry)/Kansas City Wine	5
73	Polydor 2383 245	EXPECTING COMPANY (LP)	15

SASSENACHS

64	Fontana TF 518	That Don't Worry Me/All Over You	25

SATAN

82	Guardian GRC 145	Kiss Of Death/Heads Will Roll (some with p/s)	250/50
85	Neat NEAT 1012	COURT IN THE ACT (LP)	40

SATANIC RITES

81	Heavy Metal HEAVY 8	Live To Ride/Hit And Run (p/s)	12
85	Chub CHUBLP 001	WHICH WAY THE WIND BLOWS (LP)	25
87	Chub CHUBLP 002	NO USE CRYING (LP)	30

SATAN'S RATS

77	DJM DJS 10819	In My Love For You/Façade (p/s)	40
77	DJM DJS 10821	Year Of The Rats/Louise (p/s)	35
78	DJM DJS 10840	You Make Me Sick/Façade (p/s)	35
89	Overground OVER 01	Year Of The Rats/Louise (p/s, 600 yellow vinyl, 400 white vinyl, 25 gold vinyl, numbered test pressings)	6/7/15
89	Overground OVER 02	In My Love For You/Facade (p/s, 600 yellow vinyl, 400 white vinyl, 25 gold vinyl, numbered test pressings)	6/7/15
91	Overground OVER 14	You Make Me Sick/Louise (p/s, clear vinyl, 567 copies only)	7

YOUNG SATCH

70	Black Swan BW 1401	Bongo Bongo/BOYS: Ramba	12

GIRL SATCHMO

61	Blue Beat BB 45	Satchmo's Mash Potato/Darling	20
62	Blue Beat BB 79	Twist Around Town/My New Honey (with Karl Rowe & Bluebeats)	20
63	Blue Beat BB 156	Don't Be Sad/Brother Joe (with Les Dawson Combo)	20
64	Blue Beat BB 227	Rhythm Of The New Beat/Blue Beat Chariot	20
69	Fab FAB 111	Take You For A Ride/I'm Coming Home	12
69	Trojan TR 676	Taken For A Ride/I'm Coming Home	10

(see also Pat Satchmo, Sugar & Dandy)

PAT SATCHMO

69	Punch PH 9	Hello Dolly/ERIC DONALSON: Never Get Away	10
69	Upsetter US 316	Hello Dolly/King Of The Trombone	10
70	Punch PH 24	Wonderful World/MEDITATORS: Purple Mast	10
70	Songbird SB 1039	A Handful Of Friends/CRYSTALITES: Handful — Version	10
72	Attack ATT 8024	What's Going On/LLOYD & CAREY: Tubby's In Full Swing	10

(see also Girl Satchmo, Hortense Ellis)

MINT VALUE £

SATIN BELLS

68	Pye 7N 17531	Baby You're So Right For Me/When You're Ready	5
68	Pye 7N 17608	Da-Di-Da-Da/Oh No Oh Yes	5
69	Decca F 22937	I Stand Accused (Of Loving You)/Sweet Darlin'	10
70	Decca F 23044	The Power Of Love/Baby Come Back	5
71	CBS S 7220	The Belle Telephone Song/Losing You	5

(see also Three Bells)

SATISFACTION

71	Decca F 13129	Love It Is/Cold Summer	10
71	Decca F 13207	Don't Rag The Lady/Gregory Shan't	10
71	Decca SKL 5075	SATISFACTION (LP)	65

(see also Mike Cotton Sound)

SATISFIERS

57	Vogue Coral Q 72247	Where'll I Be Tomorrow Night?/Come Away, Love	15
57	Vogue Coral Q 72247	Where'll I Be Tomorrow Night?/Come Away, Love (78)	8
57	Vogue Coral LVA 9068	THE SATISFIERS (LP)	25

LONNIE SATTIN

56	Capitol CL 14552	Trapped (In The Web Of Love)/Your Home Can Be A Castle	8
56	Capitol CL 14638	High Steel/What Time Does The Sun Go Down?	7
57	Capitol CL 14771	I'll Never Stop Loving You/Whoo-Pie Shoo-Pie	7
57	Capitol CL 14771	I'll Never Stop Loving You/Whoo-Pie Shoo-Pie (78)	6
58	Capitol CL 14831	Ring Around The Moon/My Heart's Your Home	6
60	Warner Bros WB 15	I'll Fly Away/Any More Than I	6

SATURNALIA

71	Matrix TRIX 1	MAGICAL LOVE (LP, picture disc, with booklet & ticket)	100
71	Matrix TRIX 1	MAGICAL LOVE (LP, test pressing on black vinyl)	70
73	Matrix TRIX 1	MAGICAL LOVE (LP, picture disc, reissue)	15

(see also Horse)

SAUCERMAN

88	Fierce FRIGHT 029	Scatterbrain/Beyond Repair (12", p/s with inner, 1 side etched, 1,000 only)	8
88	Fierce FRIGHT 029P	Scatterbrain (Long Gone Rancid Mix) (acetate, 2 only)	25
89	Fierce FRIGHT 035	I Will Be King/Sid James Rules (withdrawn)	25
80s	Fierce	WRESTLING (12", sampler, withdrawn)	12

(see also Kray Cherubs)

JACK SAUNDERS & ROBERT FARNON ORCHESTRA

59	Top Rank 35/021	MIKE TODD'S BROADWAY (LP)	15

LARRY SAUNDERS

74	London HLU 10469	On The Real Side/Let Me Be The Special One	15

MAHALIA SAUNDERS

71	Moodisc HME 112	Down The Aisle/IAN ROBINSON: Three For One	10
71	Upsetter US 374	Pieces Of My Heart/UPSETTERS: Version	10

TUPPER SAUSSY

63	London HAU 8127	DISCOVER TUPPER SAUSSY (LP)	12

LES SAUTERELLES

68	Decca F 22824	Heavenly Club/Dream Machine	60

SAVAGE

82	Ebony EBON 10	Ain't No Fit Place/China Run	8
83	Ebony EBON 12	LOOSE 'N' LETHAL (LP)	25
85	Zebra ZEB 4	HYPERACTIVE (LP)	12

EDNA SAVAGE

55	Parlophone MSP 6175	Stars Shine In Your Eyes/A Star Is Born	20
55	Parlophone MSP 6181	Candlelight/In The Wee Small Hours Of The Morning	20
55	Parlophone MSP 6189	Arrivederci Darling/Bella Notte	20
56	Parlophone MSP 6217	Tell Me, Tell Me, Tell Me That You Love Me/Please Hurry Home	18
56	Parlophone R 4226	My Prayer/Me 'n' You 'n' The Moon	18
56	Parlophone R 4253	Never Leave Me/Don't Ever Go (I Need You)	10
57	Parlophone R 4301	Me Head's In De Barrel/Five Oranges, Four Apples	10
57	Parlophone R 4360	Let Me Love/Diano Marina	10
58	Parlophone R 4420	My Shining Star/Once	6
58	Parlophone R 4489	Why, Why, Why/Near You	6
59	Parlophone R 4572	Maybe This Year/Beautiful Love	6
60	Parlophone R 4648	All I Need/Everyday	6

(see also Michael Holliday)

JOAN SAVAGE

57	Columbia DB 3929	Five Oranges, Four Apples/Bamboozled	10
57	Columbia DB 3968	With All My Heart/Love Letters In The Sand	10
57	Columbia DB 4039	Shake Me, I Rattle/Lula Rock-A-Hula	18
57	Columbia DB 4039	Shake Me, I Rattle/Lula Rock-A-Hula (78)	6
58	Columbia DB 4159	Hello Happiness, Goodbye Blues/Left Right Out Of My Heart	10

SAVAGE PENCIL

88	Blast First FU 3LP	PRESENTS ANGEL DUST: MUSIC FOR MOVIE BIKERS (LP, picture disc, 1,000 only)	20

(see also Kray Cherubs)

SAVAGE RESURRECTION

68	Mercury MF 1027	Thing In E/Fox Is Sick	30
68	Mercury SMCL 20123	SAVAGE RESURRECTION (LP)	150

MINT VALUE £

SAVAGE ROSE

68	Polydor 184 144	SAVAGE ROSE (LP)	12
68	Polydor 184 206	IN THE PLAIN (LP)	12
69	Polydor 184 316	TRAVELLIN' (LP)	12
71	RCA SF 8169	YOUR DAILY GIFT (LP)	12

SAVAGES

63	Decca DFE 8546	EVERYBODY SURF! WITH THE SURFIN' SAVAGES (EP)	200

(see also Soul Sounds, Screaming Lord Sutch, Circles, Tony Dangerfield & Thrills)

JULIAN JAY SAVARIN

70s	Lyntone LYN 3426	I Am You/Kizeesh (Corgi Books sampler)	10
73	Birth RAB 2	WAITERS ON THE DANCE (LP, some with insert)	175/135
87	Five Hours Back TOCK 002	WAITERS ON THE DANCE (LP, reissue)	20

(see also Julian's Treatment)

JIMMY SAVILE

62	Decca F 11493	Ahab The Arab/Very Unlikely	10
63	Decca F 11576	The Bossa Nova/Don't Do Anything I Like	7

(see also Vernons Girls)

RONNIE SAVOY

61	MGM MGM 1122	And The Heavens Cried/Big Chain	8
61	MGM MGM 1131	Bewitched/It's Gotta Be Love	8

SAVOY BROWN (BLUES BAND)

66	Purdah 45-3503	I Tried/Can't Quit You Baby (as Savoy Brown's Blues Band)	250
67	Decca F 12702	Taste And Try, Before You Buy/Someday People (as Savoy Brown Blues Band)	18
68	Decca F 12797	Walking By Myself/Vicksburg Blues	12
69	Decca F 12843	Train To Nowhere/Tolling Bells	20
69	Decca F 12978	I'm Tired/Stay With Me Baby	18
70	Decca F 13019	A Hard Way To Go/Waiting In The Bamboo Grove	15
70	Decca F 13098	Poor Girl/Master Hare	12
71	Decca F 13247	Tell Mama/Let It Rock	10
73	Decca F 13372	So Tired/The Saddest Feeling	7
73	Decca F 13431	Coming Down Your Way/I Can't Find You	7
67	Decca LK/SKL 4883	SHAKE DOWN (LP, mono/stereo)	45/50
68	Decca LK/SKL 4925	GETTING TO THE POINT (LP, mono/stereo)	40/45
69	Decca LK/SKL 4994	BLUE MATTER (LP, mono/stereo)	35/30
69	Decca LK/SKL 5013	A STEP FURTHER (LP, mono/stereo)	35/30
70	Decca LK/SKL 5043	RAW SIENNA (LP, mono/stereo, gatefold sleeve)	35/30
70	Decca SKL 5066	LOOKING IN (LP, gatefold sleeve)	30
71	Decca TXS 104	STREET CORNER TALKING (LP, gatefold sleeve)	25
72	Decca TXS 107	HELLBOUND TRAIN (LP, gatefold sleeve)	20
73	Decca SKL 5152	LION'S SHARE (LP)	20
73	Decca TXS 112	JACK THE TOAD (LP)	15
74	Decca SKL 5186	BOOGIE BROTHERS (LP)	15

(see also Warren Philips & The Rockets, Chris Youlden, Stone's Masonry, Jackie Lynton, Foghat)

TOM SAWYER

69	CBS 4243	Cookbook/Gates	10

(see also Unit 4 + 2)

'ACE' DINNING SAX

59	Top Rank JAR 184	Mulholland Drive/My Love	15
59	Top Rank JAR 184	Mulholland Drive/My Love (78)	15

MIKE SAX & IDOLS

65	Mercury MF 886	My Little One/Come Back To Me	5

(see also Idols)

SAXON

79	Carrere SAM 109	Big Teaser/Stallions Of The Highway (12", promo only)	12
79	Carrere CAR 118	Big Teaser/Stallions Of The Highway (p/s)	10
79	Carrere CAR 129	Backs To The Wall/Militia Guard (p/s)	10
80	Carrere CAR 151	747 (Strangers In The Night)/See The Light Shining (p/s)	5
80	Carrere CAR 151	747 (Strangers In The Night)/See The Light Shining (12", p/s)	10
80	Carrere HM 5	Big Teaser/Stallions Of The Highway (p/s, reissue)	5
80	Carrere HM 6	Backs To The Wall/Militia Guard (p/s, reissue)	5
80	Carrere CAR 165	Suzie Hold On/Judgement Day (live) (p/s)	5
81	Carrere CAR 180P	And The Bands Played On/Hungry Years/Heavy Metal Thunder (picture disc)	8
81	Carrere CAR 204/ SAM 134	Never Surrender/20,000 Feet (Remix)//Bap-shoo-ap! (live)/ Street Fighting Gang (double pack)	5
83	Carrere CARP 284P	Nightmare/Midas Touch (picture disc)	10
83	Carrere CART 284	Nightmare/Midas Touch/747 (Strangers In The Night) (12", p/s, some with patch)	15/10
83	Carrere SAXON 1	The Power And The Glory/See The Light Shining (live) (poster p/s)	7
83	Carrere SAXON P 1	The Power And The Glory/See The Light Shining (live) (pic disc, 600 signed)	10/6
83	Carrere SAXON T 1	The Power And The Glory/See The Light Shining (live) (12", p/s)	8
84	Carrere CAR 323	Do It All For You/Just Let Me Rock (p/s)	5
84	Carrere CART 323	Do It All For You/Just Let Me Rock (12", p/s)	8
85	Parlophone RP 6103	Back On The Streets/Live Fast Die Young (shaped picture disc)	7
85	Parlophone 12RA 6103	Back On The Streets (Extended Version)/Back On The Streets/ Live Fast Die Young (12", p/s with poster & sticker)	8
85	Parlophone 12R 6103	Back On The Streets (Club Mix)/Back On The Streets/Live Fast Die Young (12", promo only)	15
86	Parlophone R 6112	Rock 'n' Roll Gypsy/Krakatoa (poster p/s)	5
86	Parlophone RP 6112	Rock 'n' Roll Gypsy/Krakatoa (picture disc)	7
86	EMI EMIP 5587	Rock The Nations/747/And The Bands Played On (shaped picture disc)	7
86	EMI 12EMI 5587	Rock The Nations/747/And The Bands Played On (12", clear vinyl, st'krd p/s)	10
88	EMI EMP 43	Ride Like The Wind/Red Alert (shaped picture disc)	10

MINT VALUE £

88	EMI CDEM 43	Ride Like The Wind/Red Alert/Rock The Nations (live)/ Back On The Streets (live) (CD)	10
88	EMI EMP 54	I Can't Wait Anymore/Broken Heroes (live) (pouch pack, with discography & poster)	7
80s	Din Disc DINSY 105	We Will Remember/Altar Of The Gods (shaped picture disc)	8
82	Carrere CAL 137	THE EAGLE HAS LANDED (LP, picture disc)	18
83	Carrere CAL 147	THE POWER AND THE GLORY (LP, picture disc)	12
84	Carrere CALP 200	CRUSADER (LP, picture disc)	15
85	Parlophone SAXONP 2	INNOCENCE IS NO EXCUSE (LP, picture disc)	18
87	EMI EMS 1163	DENIM AND LEATHER (LP, blue vinyl reissue)	12

(see also Son Of A Bitch)

AL SAXON

57	Fontana H 111	Dreamboy/You, All You (78)	6
58	Fontana H 138	Where The Black-Eyed Susans Grow/She Screamed	7
58	Fontana H 138	Where The Black-Eyed Susans Grow/She Screamed (78)	6
58	Fontana H 164	The Day The Rains Came (Le Jour Ou La Pluie Viendra)/You're The Top-Cha	10
58	Fontana H 164	The Day The Rains Came (Le Jour Ou La Pluie Viendra)/You're The Top-Cha (78)	8
59	Fontana H 188	Chattanooga Choo-Choo/Chip Off The Old Block	5
59	Fontana H 188	Chattanooga Choo-Choo/Chip Off The Old Block (78)	10
59	Fontana H 205	Only Sixteen/I'm All Right, Jack	8
59	Fontana H 205	Only Sixteen/I'm All Right, Jack (78)	8
59	Fontana H 222	Linda Lu/Heart Of Stone	8
59	Fontana H 222	Linda Lu/Heart Of Stone (78)	10
59	Fontana H 231	Marina/Me Without You	7
59	Fontana H 231	Marina/Me Without You (78)	10
60	Fontana H 244	The Piper Of Love/Believe Me	5
60	Fontana H 261	I've Heard That Song Before/Someone Like You	5
60	Fontana H 278	Blue-Eyed Boy/Don't Push Your Luck	5
61	Piccadilly 7N 35002	Can You Keep A Secret/Promises	5
61	Piccadilly 7N 35011	There, I've Said It Again/You Came A Long Way From St. Louis	5
62	Parlophone R 4966	But I Do/I Got A Girl	5
58	Fontana TFE 17014	THOSE YOU'VE NEVER HEARD (EP)	12
59	Fontana TFE 17202	BIG DEAL (EP)	12
60	Fontana TFE 17271	THE BATTLE OF THE SEXES (EP)	12

(see also Lana Sisters, Ella Stone & Moss)

SKY 'SUNLIGHT' SAXON

87	Fierce FRIGHT 009	Dog=God (p/s, with badge, piece of shirt, sugar 'skycubes' & inserts)	20
90s	Expression EXP 777	Beautiful Stars/Universal Stars (p/s)	5
84	Psycho PSYCHO 29	STARRY EYED (LP, some on clear vinyl)	20/12
90s	Water NOXAS 39	DRAGON SLAYER (LP, multicoloured vinyl)	12

(see also Seeds)

SKY SAXON & THE NEW SEEDS

90s	Expression EXP 777-3	In Love With Life/Starry Ride/Queen/Tired Of Being Poor	6

LINDA SAXONE

64	Pye 7N 15624	Love Is A Many Splendoured Thing/The Other Side Of The Street	10
65	Polydor BM 56015	I've Got To Say No/Another Day Another Night	7
65	Polydor BM 56032	Only Last Night/Lucky Girl	7

SAXONS

63	Ace Of Clubs ACL 1173	MEET THE SAXONS (LP)	110

SAXONS

65	Decca F 12179	Saxon War Cry/Click-Ete-Clack	55

(see also Tornados)

JOE SAYE & HIS SEXTET

54	Columbia SCMC 7	Have You Met Miss Jones/Cynthia's In Love (export)	6

JOHNNY SAYLES

66	Liberty LIB 12042	Deep Down In Your Heart/Anything For You	25

RAT SCABIES

84	Paradiddle Music HIT 1	Let There Be Rats/Wiped Out/Drums Drums Drums (mail-order only, no p/s)	8

(see also Damned, Rat & The Whale, Pete Zear)

SCABS

79	Clubland Records SJP 799	Amory Building/Leave Me Alone/Don't Just Sit There/U.R.E. (blue/black or red/black fold out 'envelope' p/s, 2 inserts)	each 40

SCAFFOLD

66	Parlophone R 5443	2 Day's Monday/3 Blind Jellyfish	8
66	Parlophone R 5548	Goodbat Nightman/A Long Strong Black Pudding	10
67	Parlophone R 5643	Thank U Very Much/Ide B The First	5
68	Parlophone R 5734	Lily The Pink/Buttons On Your Mind	5
68	Parlophone R 5679	Do You Remember?/Carry On Krow	6
68	Parlophone R 5703	1-2-3/Today	6
69	Parlophone R 5784	Charity Bubbles/Goose	6
69	Parlophone R 5812	Gin Gan Goolie/Liver Birds	8
70	Parlophone R 5847	All The Way Up/Please — Sorry	8
70	Parlophone R 5866	Busdreams/If I Could Start All Over Again	8
71	Parlophone R 5922	Do The Albert/Commercial Break	8
74	Warner Bros K 16400	Liverpool Lou/Ten Years On After Strawberry Jam	8
68	Parlophone PMC/PCS 7051	AN EVENING WITH ... — LIVE AT QUEEN ELIZABETH HALL (LP, black/yellow label)	18
69	Parlophone PMC/PCS 7077	L THE P (LP, black/yellow label)	15
73	Island ILPS 9234	FRESH LIVER (LP)	15

(see also McGough-McGear, Roger McGough, Mike McGear, Liverpool Scene, Grimms, John Gorman)

MINT VALUE £

BOZ SCAGGS

71	CBS 7219	We Were Always Sweethearts/Painted Bells	5
71	CBS 7401	Near You/Downright Woman	5
72	CBS 7803	Up To You/Runnin' Blue	5
69	Atlantic 588 205	BOZ SCAGGS (LP)	20
71	CBS 64248	MOMENTS (LP, plain orange label)	12

(see also Steve Miller Band, Steve York's Camelo Pardalis)

HARVEY SCALES & 7 SOUND

67	Atlantic 584 146	Get Down/Love It Is	7

SCAMPS

59	London HLW 8827	Petite Fleur/Naomi	12
62	Ace Of Clubs ACL 1116	TEEN DANCE AND SING ALONG PARTY (LP)	15

SCARAB

80	Inferno HEADBANGER 1	Rock Night/Wicked Woman	30
84	Pharaoh PR-001	Poltergeist/Hell On Wheels (p/s)	50

SCARECROW

78	Spilt Milk SMFM 11278	SCARECROW LIVE (LP, numbered foldout sleeve with insert; beware of watermarked unnumbered copies)	40

SCARLETS

64	Philips BF 1376	Let's Go/Tambourine Shake	5

CHARLES FRANCIS SCARRATT III

59	Felsted AF 113	Two Innocent Lovers/Lovemobile	6
59	Felsted AF 113	Two Innocent Lovers/Lovemobile (78)	8

SCARS

79	Fast Product FAST 8	Horrorshow/Adult-ery (p/s)	5
81	Pre PRE 014	All About You/Author Author (p/s)	7
80	Pre PRE 005	Love Song (p/s)	12
81	I.D. ID-1	Your Attention Please (gold vinyl flexidisc with *ID* magazine, issue 3)	8
81	Pre PREX 5	AUTHOR! AUTHOR! (LP)	12

SCENE

80	Inferno BEAT 2	I've Had Enough/Show 'Em Now (p/s)	12

SCENE

80	Hole In The Wall HS 1	Hey Girl/Reach The Top (p/s)	50

SCENE

83	Diamond DIA 001	Looking For A Love/Let Me Know (p/s)	8
85	Diamond DIA 003	Something That You Said/Stop-Go (p/s)	7
85	Diamond DIA 007	Good Lovin'/2 Plus 2 (some with p/s)	15/5

(see also Diplomats)

MIKE SCENE

71	Pye LBB 9050	For The Love Of Mike	7

SCEPTERS

69	Spark SRL 1006	What's The Matter With Juliet/Something's Coming Along	35

HAL SCHAEFER ORCHESTRA & CHORUS

58	London HLT 8692	March Of The Vikings/March Of The Parisian Bakers	10
58	London HLT 8692	March Of The Vikings/March Of The Parisian Bakers (78)	8

SCHEER

93	Son BUACD 293	Wish You Were Dead/Green Room Sex Kitten/Don't Know Why (p/s)	20

MICHAEL SCHENKER

94	EMI 724382861 1423	THE STORY OF MICHAEL SCHENKER (2-CD)	20

(see also McAuley Schenker Group, Michael Schenker Group, Scorpions, UFO)

LALO SCHIFRIN

68	Dot DOT 103	Mission: Impossible/Jim On The Move	20
74	20th Century BTC 2150	Ape Shuffle (Theme From 'Planet Of The Apes')/Escape From Tomorrow	20
76	CTI CTSP 5	Jaws Theme/Quiet Village	5
68	Dot (S)LPD 503	'MISSION: IMPOSSIBLE' — MUSIC FROM THE TV SERIES (LP, TV soundtrack)	40
69	Paramount SPFL 252	MORE 'MISSION: IMPOSSIBLE' (LP, TV soundtrack)	40
70s	Verve 2304 051	ROCK REQUIEM (LP)	12

SCHMETTERLINGE

77	Pye International 7N 25743	Boom Boom Boomerang/Mr Moneymaker's Music Show	10

TOBIAS SCHMIDT

96	Mosquito MSQ 06	THE FINGERPRINT EP (12", p/s)	15

ZAPPATA SCHMIDT

71	President PTLS 1041	IT'S GONNA GET YOU (LP)	25

(see also Equals)

OLIVER LINDSEY SCHMITT

72	private pressing	GRAFFENSTADDEN (LP)	40

ULRICH SCHNAUSS

90s	City Centre Offices TOWERBLOCK 005LP	FAR AWAY TRAINS PASSING BY (LP)	14

EBERHARD SCHOENER

79	Harvest HAR 5196	Video Magic/Code Word Elvis (p/s)	8

(see also Police)

SCHOLARS

64	Stagesound SDE 29370/1	THE SCHOLARS (EP, no p/s)	15

SCHOLARS
70s Unicorn 254 — VERSATILITY OF THE SCHOLARS (LP) . . . 12

SCHOOL BOYS
63 Blue Beat BB 162 — Little Boy Blue/PRINCE BUSTER: Money . . . 30
63 Blue Beat BB 174 — Little Dilly/The Joker (B-side actually by Prince Buster's Allstars) . . . 30
64 Port-O-Jam PJ 4000 — Dream Lover/I Want To Know . . . 30
(see also Bill Gentles)

SCHOOLERS
69 Doctor Bird DB 1170 — Ugly Man (actually by Scorchers)/Whip Cracker (actually by Vincent Gordon) . . . 25

SCHOOLGIRL BITCH
78 Garage!/Aerco AERS 102 — Abusing The Rules/Thinking For Yourself (no p/s) . . . 40
78 Garage!/Aerco AERS 102 — Abusing The Rules/Thinking For Yourself (spray-painted p/s) . . . 150
78 Garage!/Aerco AERS 102 — Abusing The Rules/Thinking For Yourself ('gasmask' p/s) . . . 80
78 Garage!/Aerco AERS 102 — Abusing The Rules/Thinking For Yourself ('queen' p/s) . . . 45

SCHOOL GIRLS
63 Blue Beat BB 168 — Love Another Love/Little Keithie . . . 20
63 Blue Beat BB 185 — Live Up To Justice/Give Up . . . 20
64 Blue Beat BB 214 — Sing And Shout/Last Time . . . 20
64 Blue Beat BB 263 — Never Let You Go/BUSTER'S ALL STARS: Supercharge . . . 25

SCHOOL TIES
81 School Ties SCF 01 — No Future . . . 45

DON SCHROEDER
62 Philips BF 3040033 — Quicksand/My Kind Of Woman . . . 6

JOHN SCHROEDER ORCHESTRA
65 Piccadilly 7N 35240 — The Fugitive Theme/Don't Break The Heart Of Kimble (some in p/s) . . . 12/6
65 Piccadilly 7N 35253 — You've Lost That Lovin' Feeling/Funny How Love Can Be . . . 6
66 Piccadilly 7N 35280 — Ave Maria No Morro/Peter Popgunn . . . 5
66 Piccadilly 7N 35285 — Hungry For Love/Soul Destroyer . . . 25
65 Piccadilly 7N 35271 — Agent 00 Soul/Night Rider . . . 25
66 Piccadilly 7N 35319 — On The Ball (Theme For The World)/The Britannia March . . . 15
67 Piccadilly 7N 35362 — Soul For Sale/Loving You Girl . . . 25
69 Pye 7N 17862 — The Virgin Soldiers' March/Sweet Soul Talk . . . 6
66 Piccadilly N(S)PL 38025 — JOHN SCHROEDER'S WORKING IN THE SOULMINE (LP) . . . 40
67 Piccadilly N(S)PL 38036 — THE DOLLY CATCHER! (LP) . . . 40
68 Marble Arch MAL 839 — WORKING IN THE SOULMINE (LP, reissue) . . . 25
71 Pye NSPL 18362 — WITCHI-TAI-TO (LP) . . . 12
71 Polydor 2460 134 — DYLAN VIBRATIONS (LP) . . . 12
72 Polydor 2460 149 — TV VIBRATIONS (LP) . . . 20
73 Polydor 2460 188 — WAR AND PEACE & OTHER TELEVISION THEMES (LP) . . . 20

IVY SCHULMAN & BOWTIES
57 London HLN 8372 — Rock, Pretty Baby/BOWTIES: Ever Since I Can Remember . . . 60
57 London HLN 8372 — Rock, Pretty Baby/BOWTIES: Ever Since I Can Remember (78) . . . 35

KLAUS SCHULZE
77 Island ZCI 9510 — BODYLOVE (cassette EP) . . . 12
75 Caroline CA 2003 — BLACK DANCE (LP) . . . 12
77 Island ILPS 9461 — MIRAGE (LP) . . . 15
(see also Tangerine Dream)

(Voices Of) WALTER SCHUMANN
54 HMV 7M 229 — Haunted House/I Only Have Eyes For You . . . 10
55 HMV 7M 323 — The Man From Laramie/Let Me Hear You Whisper . . . 10

SCHUNGE
72 Regal Zonophone RZ 3066 — Misty/Joseph Demanio . . . 7
73 Regal Zonophone RZ 3077 — Ballad Of A Simple Love/Enter The Violins . . . 7
72 Regal Zono. SLRZ 1033 — BALLAD OF A SIMPLE LOVE (LP) . . . 18

ARMANDO SCIASCIA ORCHESTRA
66 Ember EMB S 228 — Theme From 'The Liars'/World Tomorrow Theme . . . 5
66 Ember NR 5030 — THE PEACH THIEF & GREAT MUSIC FROM TV SHOWS (LP) . . . 15

SCIENCE POPTION
67 Columbia DB 8106 — You've Got Me High/Back In Town . . . 60

SCIENTIST
69 Amalgamated AMG 848 — Professor In Action/SUPERSONICS: Reflections Of Don D . . . 30
80 JB JBLP 004 — INTRODUCING (LP) . . . 30

SCIENTISTS
85 Karbon KAR 007 — You Only Live Twice/If It's The Last Thing I Do (p/s) . . . 25
85 Karbon KAR 101 L — YOU GET WHAT YOU DESERVE (LP) . . . 18
86 Karbon KAR 103 L — WEIRD LOVE (LP) . . . 22
87 Karbon KAR 105 L — THE HUMAN JUKEBOX (LP) . . . 22

SCI-FI SEX STARS
86 Who Am I WM 1001 7 — Rock It Miss U.S.A./Teenage Thunder (p/s) . . . 8
86 Who Am I WM 1001 — Rock It Miss U.S.A. (Death Wish IV)/Commercial Break/Teenage Thunder (Spitstyle)/Suicide (12", stickered p/s) . . . 10
(see also Sigue Sigue Sputnik)

SCISSOR FITS
79 Dubious DUB 1/SJP 793 — TAUT? TENSE? ANGULAR? AND OTHER BRITISH RAIL SANDWICHES (EP, gatefold sleeve) . . . 8
79 Tortch TOR 005 — SOON AFTER DARK (EP) . . . 6

MINT VALUE £

BOB SCOBEY'S FRISCO BAND
52 Good Time Jazz 50/V 2184 That's A Plenty/Beale Street Mama (78) 7

JOANNE SCOONI
59 Philips PB 936 Constantly/Scibidou (78) 8

SCOOP
80 Sharp POINT 1 You Can Do It/Disco/My Friend Tony/Anonymity (p/s) 15

SCORCHED EARTH
85 Carrere CAR 342 Tomorrow Never Comes/Questions (promo only) 35
85 Carrere CART 342 Tomorrow Never Comes/Questions/So Long/Where Do We Go From Here (12", initially black sleeve, later red sleeve with insert) 70/60

SCORCHERS
69 Camel CA 17 Hold On Tight/THE ROYALS: 100 Lbs Of Clay 15
69 Duke DU 26 Hear Ya/VIBRATORS: Live Life 12
(see also Neville Hinds)

SCORE
66 Decca F 12527 Please Please Me/Beg Me 175

SCORN
95 Earache SCORN 001 ELLIPSIS (5 x 12" box set) 18

SCORPION & BORIS GARDINER HAPPENING
73 Dragon DRA 1002 Deadly Sting/BORIS GARDINER HAPPENING: Boing Boing 6

SCORPIONS (Germany)
77 RCA PB 5556 He's A Woman, She's A Man/Suspender Love 8
79 Harvest HAR 5185 Is Anybody There?/Another Piece Of Meat (p/s, green vinyl, some on black vinyl) 6/7
79 Harvest HAR 5185 Is Anybody There?/Another Piece Of Meat (12", p/s) 10
79 Harvest HAR 5188 Love Drive/Coast To Coast (p/s) 6
79 Harvest 12HAR 5188 Love Drive/Coast To Coast (12", p/s) 10
79 RCA PC 9402 All Night Long/Fly To The Rainbow/Speedy's Coming/In Trance (12", p/s) 10
80 Harvest HAR 5206 Make It Real/Don't Make No Promises (p/s) 10
82 Harvest HAR 5219 No One Like You/The Zoo (p/s) 8
82 Harvest HARP 5219 No One Like You/The Zoo (picture disc) 10
84 Harvest 12HARP 5231 Big City Nights/Bad Boys Running Wild (12" picture disc, die-cut sleeve) 12
84 Harvest HAR 5225 Rock You Like A Hurricane/Coming Home (p/s) 6
85 Harvest 12HAR 5232 Still Loving You/Holiday/Big City Night (12", p/s) 8
85 Harvest 12HAR 5232 Still Loving You/Holiday/Big City Night (12", picture disc) 10
88 Harvest HARX 5240 Rhythm Of Love/We Let It Rock (box set with postcards) 8
88 Harvest HARP 5240 Rhythm Of Love/We Let It Rock (picture disc) 6
88 Harvest HARP 5242 Passion Rules The Game (die-cut picture disc) 6
91 Vertigo VER 54 Wind Of Change/Restless Nights (p/s, red vinyl) 5
91 Vertigo VERXP 54 Wind Of Change (12", etched red vinyl) 10
91 Vertigo VERXP 54 Wind Of Change/Restless Nights/Hit Between The Nights/Blackout (live) (12", picture disc) 8
91 Vertigo VERX 58 Wind Of Change (12", white vinyl, 3-D sleeve) 8
93 Mercury MERX 395 Under The Same Sun/Ship Of Fools/Partners In Crime (12", yellow vinyl) 8
79 Harvest LP SHSP 4097 LOVE DRIVE (LP) 12
80 Harvest SHSP 4113 ANIMAL MAGNETISM (LP) 12
82 H.M. Worldwide HMILP 2 LONESOME CROW (LP, clear vinyl) 12
82 H.M. Worldwide HMIPD 2 LONESOME CROW (LP, picture disc) 12
88 Harvest SHSPP 4125 SAVAGE AMUSEMENT (LP, picture disc, with lyric sheet) 15
97 Mercury 314 534 788 2 WORLD WIDE LIVE (CD, reissue) 18
(see also Michael Schenker, Michael Schenker Group)

SCORPIONS (Jamaica)
72 Green Door GD 4019 Breaking Your Heart/IN CROWD BAND: Breaking Your Heart Version 5
(see also Bill Gentles, Lloyd Jackson)

SCORPIONS (U.K.)
61 Parlophone R 4740 (Ghost) Riders In The Sky/Torquay 18
61 Parlophone R 4768 Rockin' At The Phil/Scorpio 18

COLIN SCOT
71 United Artists UP 35216 Hey! Sandy/Nite People 5
73 Warner Bros K 16330 Call Me Mr Blue/It's Gonna Be Alright 7
71 United Artists UAG 29154 COLIN SCOT WITH FRIENDS (LP, gatefold sleeve, with Peter Hammill & Peter Gabriel) 30
73 Warner Bros K 46281 OUT OF THE BLUE (LP) 12
(see also Peter Hammill, Peter Gabriel)

WINSTON SCOTLAND
72 Green Door GD 4027 My (Girl) Little Filly/BUNNY BROWN: My Girl 7
72 Punch PH 100 Butter Cup/RONALD WILSON: I Care 7
(see also Bunny Flip, Big Youth, Bongo Les, Lennox Brown, Dennis Alcapone)

SCOTLAND WORLD CUP SQUAD
74 Polydor 2383282 SCOTLAND, SCOTLAND (LP) 12

SCOTS OF ST. JAMES
66 Go AJ 111404 Gypsy/Tic Toc 125
67 Spot JW 1 Timothy/Eiderdown Clown 100
(see also Hopscotch, Forever More, Five Day Rain)

ANDY SCOTT
75 RCA RCA 2629 Lady Starlight/Where D'Ya Go (p/s) 12
83 Static TAK 10 Krugerrands/Face (p/s) 8
84 Static TAK 24 Let Her Dance/Suck It And See (p/s) 10

MINT VALUE £

84 Static TAK 24-12 Let Her Dance (Full Version)/(Instrumental)/Suck It And See (12", p/s) 10
84 Static TAK 31 Invisible/Never Too Young (clear vinyl, stickered PVC sleeve) 12
84 Statik TAK 31-12 Invisible (Single Version)/(Instrumental)/Invisible (Extended Version)/ Never Too Young (12", clear vinyl, stickered PVC sleeve). 15

(see also Sweet, Elastic Band, Mayfield's Mule)

ARTIE SCOTT ORCHESTRA

70 Major Minor MM 670 March Of The Skinheads/Love At First Sight 10

BILLY SCOTT

58 London HLU 8565 You're The Greatest/That's Why I Was Born 30
58 London HLU 8565 You're The Greatest/That's Why I Was Born (78) 12
60 Top Rank JAR 270 Carole/Stairway To The Stairs 7

BOBBY SCOTT

56 London HL 8254 Chain Gang/Shadrack 60
56 London HL 8254 Chain Gang/Shadrack (78). 12
55 London Jazz LZ-N 14001 BOBBY SCOTT TRIO (10" LP) 15

BRUCE SCOTT

65 Mercury MF 857 I Made An Angel Cry/Don't Say Goodbye To Me. 18
65 MGM MGM 1291 Once A Thief Twice A Thief/So Much To Live For 7

BUNNY SCOTT

75 KLIK KLP 9004 TO LOVE SOMEBODY (LP) 15

DEREK SCOTT ORCHESTRA

63 Pye 7N 15500 Hancock's Tune/Spying Tonight. 12
67 Philips BF 1568 Honey Lane/Song Without Words 6

FREDDIE SCOTT

63 Colpix PX 692 Hey Girl/The Slide 30
63 Colpix PX 709 I Got A Woman/Brand New World 30
67 London HLZ 10103 Are You Lonely For Me/Where Were You 12
67 London HLZ 10123 Cry To Me/No One Could Ever Love You 8
67 London HLZ 10139 Am I Grooving You?/Never You Mind. 8
67 London HLZ 10172 He Ain't Give You None/Run Joe 8
69 Roulette RO 509 Sugar Sunday/Johnny's Hill. 6
71 Jay Boy BOY 34 Just Like A Flower/Spanish Harlem 5
72 Jay Boy BOY 59 Are You Lonely For Me Baby/The Woman Of My Love 5
70s Upfront UP 1 The Great If/Deep In The Night 5
71 Joy JOYS 215 ARE YOU LONELY FOR ME (LP) 25

GERRY SCOTT

62 Parlophone R 4908 Stay With Me/Summer Love. 6

HAZEL SCOTT

53 Capitol LC 6607 LATE SHOW (10" LP) 25

JACK SCOTT (& CHANTONES)

78s

58 London HLU 8626 My True Love/Leroy 25
58 London HLL 8765 With Your Love/Geraldine (as Jack Scott with Chantones). 35
59 London HLL 8804 Goodbye Baby/Save My Soul (as Jack Scott with Chantones) 45
59 London HLL 8851 I Never Felt Like This/Bella 55
59 London HLL 8912 The Way I Walk/Midgie 75
59 London HLL 8970 There Comes A Time/Baby Marie. 105

45s

58 London HLU 8626 My True Love/Leroy 20
58 London HLL 8765 With Your Love/Geraldine (as Jack Scott with Chantones). 20
59 London HLL 8804 Goodbye Baby/Save My Soul (as Jack Scott with Chantones) 20
59 London HL 7069 Goodbye Baby/Save My Soul (export issue). 20
59 London HLL 8851 I Never Felt Like This/Bella 20
59 London HLL 8912 The Way I Walk/Midgie (triangular or round centre) 25/18
59 London HLL 8970 There Comes A Time/Baby Marie (triangular or round centre) 25/18
60 Top Rank JAR 280 What In The World's Come Over You/Baby, Baby 8
60 Top Rank JAR 375 Burning Bridges/Oh, Little One 10
60 Top Rank JAR 419 Cool Water/It Only Happened Yesterday 10
60 Top Rank JAR 524 Patsy/Old Time Religion. 10
61 Top Rank JAR 547 Is There Something On Your Mind/Found A Woman 10
61 Capitol CL 15200 A Little Feeling/Now That I. 10
61 Capitol CL 15216 Strange Desire/My Dream Come True 15
62 Capitol CL 15236 One Of These Days/Steps 1 And 2. 15
62 Capitol CL 15261 Sad Story/I Can't Hold Your Letters In My Arms 15
63 Capitol CL 15302 Meo Myo/All I See Is Blue 15

EPs

59 London RE-I 1205 MY TRUE LOVE (initially triangular centre, later round centre) 125/90
61 Top Rank JKP 3002 WHAT IN THE WORLD'S COME OVER YOU 75
61 Top Rank JKP 3011 I REMEMBER HANK WILLIAMS 60
64 Capitol EAP 20035 BURNING BRIDGES (existence unconfirmed). . . . . 250+

LPs

58 London HA-L 2156 JACK SCOTT 150
60 Top Rank BUY 034 I REMEMBER HANK WILLIAMS 40
60 Top Rank 25-024 WHAT IN THE WORLD'S COME OVER YOU 85
61 Top Rank 35-109 THE SPIRIT MOVES ME 75
64 Capitol (S)T 2035 BURNING BRIDGES (mono/stereo). 70/90

JANET SCOTT & JACKIE RAE

60 Fontana TFE 17203 SWEET TALK (EP, also stereo STFE 8009) 10/15
60 Fontana TFL 5102 WE LOVE LIFE! (LP, also stereo STFL 533) 15/18

(see also Jackie Rae)

MINT VALUE £

JIMMY SCOTT
69 Revolution REV 002 — Ob-La-Di, Ob-La-Da/Story Part 2 — Allulo & Doh ... 20

JOHN SCOTT
73 JSD JSD 100 — JOHN SCOTT DEMONSTRATION RECORD (LP, beware, many warped) ... 100

JOHN SCOTT
60 Parlophone R 4697 — Hi-Flutin' Boogie/Peace Pipe ... 6
65 Parlophone R 5380 — A Study In Terror/Punjab ... 6
67 Polydor 56184 — Rocket To The Moon Theme/The Long Duel Theme ... 10
(see also Johnny Scott)

JOHN(NY) SCOTT
60 Oriole CB 1542 — Darlin'/Why Don't You Write Me? (as Johnny Scott) ... 7
60 Philips PB 1056 — They Say/How About That (as John Scott) ... 6
(see also Johnny Scott Quintet)

JOHNNY SCOTT QUINTET
67 Columbia S(C)X 6149 — COMMUNICATION (LP) ... 15
70 Fontana 6383 002 — PURCELL VARIATIONS FOR FIVE (LP) ... 12

JUDI SCOTT
68 Page One POF 066 — Billy Sunshine/Happy Song ... 20

JUDY SCOTT
57 Brunswick 05687 — The Game Of Love (A-One And A-Two)/With All My Heart ... 10
57 Brunswick 05704 — Parlour Piano Theme/A Tender Word ... 8

JULIAN SCOTT
61 Columbia DB 4571 — My Steady Date/So Tired ... 7

KEVIN SCOTT
59 Parlophone R 4520 — Wait For Me/Love Of My Life ... 7
59 Parlophone R 4520 — Wait For Me/Love Of My Life (78) ... 6
59 Parlophone R 4540 — Ciao Ciao Bambina (Piove)/Broken-Hearted Clown ... 6
60 HMV POP 731 — You Are Beautiful/Love Look Away ... 6

LINDA SCOTT
60 Columbia DB 4638 — I've Told Every Little Star/Three Guesses ... 10
61 Columbia DB 4692 — Don't Bet Money, Honey/Starlight Starbright ... 10
61 Columbia DB 4748 — I Don't Know Why/It's All Because ... 10
61 Columbia DB 4829 — Count Every Star/Land Of Stars ... 10
62 Pye International 7N 25146 — Never In A Million Years/Through The Summer ... 15
63 London HLR 9802 — Let's Fall In Love/I Know It, You Know It ... 15
61 Columbia 33SX 1386 — STARLIGHT, STARBRIGHT (LP) ... 75

LINDA SCOTT
69 CBS 4528 — The Composer/You Made A Fool Out Of Me ... 10
69 CBS 4246 — First Of All/The Answer's In My Eyes ... 6

McBEAN SCOTT & CHAMPIONS
70 Jackpot JP 744 — Top Of The World/LARRY LAWRENCE & CHAMPIONS: Everybody Reggae ... 10

MIKE SCOTT
65 Mercury MF 906 — I Am A Rock/I'm Gonna Be Somebody Someday ... 6

NEIL SCOTT
61 Pye International 7N 25096 — Bobby/I Haven't Found It With Another ... 8

NICKY SCOTT
67 Immediate IM 044 — Big City/Everything's Gonna Be Alright ... 25
67 Immediate IM 045 — Backstreet Girl/Chain Reaction ... 35
69 Pye 7N 17688 — Honey Pie/No More Tomorrow ... 7
(see also Diane Ferraz & Nicky Scott)

PEGGY SCOTT
69 Polydor 56722 — Every Little Bit Hurts/You Can Never Get Something For Nothing ... 7
79 Pinnacle PIN 73 — You've Got It All/Let Me Unite You (p/s) ... 6
(see also Peggy Scott & Jo Jo Benson)

PEGGY SCOTT & JO JO BENSON
68 Polydor 56745 — Lover's Holiday/Here With Me ... 8
69 Polydor 56750 — Pickin' Wild Mountain Berries/Pure Love And Pleasure ... 7
69 Polydor 56761 — Soulshake/We Were Made For Each Other ... 7
69 Polydor 56773 — We Got Our Own Bag/I Want To Love You Babe ... 7
71 Atlantic 2091 066 — I Thank You/Spreadin' Love ... 6
69 Polydor 583 731 — SOULSHAKE (LP) ... 25
70 Polydor 583 756 — LOVER'S HEAVEN (LP) ... 25
(see also Peggy Scott)

RAMBLIN' TOMMY SCOTT
54 Parlophone CMSP 15 — Ain't Love Grand/What Do You Know — I Love Her (export issue) ... 20

RAYMOND SCOTT
54 London L 1229 — Naked City/Shadow Dance (78) ... 10

ROBIN SCOTT
69 Head HDS 4003 — The Sailor/Sound Of The Rain ... 35
69 Head HDLS 6003 — WOMAN FROM THE WARM GRASS (LP, with insert) ... 140
(see also Mighty Baby, M)

RONNIE SCOTT
51 Esquire 10-154 — Crazy Rhythm/El Sino (78) ... 6
51 Esquire 10-185 — Close Your Eyes/I Didn't Know What Time It Was (78, with Ronnie Ball) ... 6
53 Esquire 10-321 — Stomping At The Savoy/Body Beautiful (78) ... 6
54 Esquire 10-335 — Night And Day ... 10
56 Decca FJ 10712 — Basie Talks/Flying Home (as Ronnie Scott Orchestra) ... 10

			MINT VALUE £
57	Tempo A 153	I'll Take Romance/Speak Low (as Ronnie Scott New Quintet)	35
57	Tempo A 153	I'll Take Romance/Speak Low (as Ronnie Scott New Quintet) (78)	6
55	Esquire EP 31	RONNIE SCOTT ORCHESTRA (EP)	20
55	Esquire EP 51	RONNIE SCOTT QUARTET (EP)	20
55	Esquire EP 61	RONNIE SCOTT ORCHESTRA (EP)	20
55	Esquire EP 65	RONNIE SCOTT QUINTET (EP)	10
56	Esquire EP 81	RONNIE SCOTT ORCHESTRA (EP)	20
56	Esquire EP 85	RONNIE SCOTT ORCHESTRA (EP)	25
56	Esquire EP 95	RONNIE SCOTT ORCHESTRA (EP)	18
56	Tempo EXA 45	RONNIE SCOTT BLOWS WITH THE DIZZY REECE QUARTET (EP)	100
52	Esquire 20-006	RONNIE SCOTT QUARTET (10" LP)	100
54	Esquire 32-001	THE RONNIE SCOTT JAZZ CLUB VOLUME 1 (LP)	45
54	Esquire 32-002	THE RONNIE SCOTT JAZZ CLUB VOLUME 2 (LP)	45
54	Esquire 32-003	THE RONNIE SCOTT JAZZ CLUB VOLUME 3 (LP)	45
54	Esquire 32-006	THE RONNIE SCOTT JAZZ CLUB VOLUME 4 (LP)	45
56	Decca LF 1261	AT THE ROYAL FESTIVAL HALL (10" LP)	45
57	Philips BBL 7153	PRESENTING THE RONNIE SCOTT SEXTET (LP)	80
66	Fontana TL 5332	THE NIGHT IS SCOTT AND YOU'RE SO SWINGABLE (LP)	50
69	CBS Realm Jazz 523661	LIVE AT RONNIE SCOTT'S (LP)	30
74	RCA Victor LPL1	SCOTT AT RONNIE'S (LP)	30
77	Pye NSPL 18542	SERIOUS GOLD (LP)	20

(see also Jazz Couriers, Tubby Hayes, Dizzy Reece)

SHIRLEY SCOTT

66	Transatlantic PR 7205	HIP SOUL (LP)	25
69	Atlantic 588 175	SOUL SONG (LP)	15
71	Chess 6310 109	MYSTICAL LADY (LP)	15

SIMON SCOTT (& LE ROYS)

64	Parlophone R 5164	Move It Baby/What Kind Of Woman (with Le Roys)	12
64	Parlophone R 5207	My Baby's Got Soul/Midnight (with Le Roys)	10
65	Parlophone R 5298	Tell Him I'm Not Home (as Simon Scott & All Nite Workers)/Heart Cry	20
69	Polydor 56355	Brave New World/I'm The Universe	7

(see also Le Roys)

TERRY SCOTT

62	Parlophone R 4967	My Brother/Don't Light The Fire 'Til After	15
66	Pye 7N 17093	Juanita Banana/I Like Birds	7
76	DJM DJS 665	A Bed Full Of Foreigners/Nicholas The Circus Clown (with June Whitfield)	6

TOMMY SCOTT

62	Decca F 11474	Angela/Did You (as Jay & Tommy Scott)	7
64	Decca F 11839	Who Will It Be?/If It's Me That You Want	6
64	Decca F 11942	Wrap Your Troubles In Dreams/Blueberry Hill	6

TOM SCOTT

77	Epic EPC 5589	Gotcha (Theme From 'Starsky & Hutch')/Smoothin' On Down	12

TONY SCOTT

69	Escort ES 805	What Am I To Do/Bring Back That Smile	8
69	Escort ES 816	Darling If You Love Me/Saturday Night	6

SCOTT BROTHERS

61	Fontana H 317	Travellin' Home/Susie Black	8
63	Decca F 11539	Yuggi Duggi/Our Time	7

GIL SCOTT-HERON (& BRIAN JACKSON)

73	Philips 6073 705	Lady Day And John Coltrane/When You Are Who You Are (with Pretty Purdie & The Playboys)	15
75	Arista ARIST 23	(What's The Word) Johannesburg/Fell Together	5
78	Arista ARIST 169	The Bottle (live)/Hello Sunday, Hello Road	10
79	Inferno HEAT 23	The Bottle (Drunken Mix)/The Bottle (Sober Mix) (with Brian Jackson)	5
79	Inferno HEAT 23-12	The Bottle (Drunken Mix)/The Bottle (Sober Mix) (12", with Brian Jackson)	12
73	Philips 6369 415	PIECES OF A MAN (LP)	30
74	RCA SF 8428	THE REVOLUTION WILL NOT BE TELEVISED (LP)	25
75	Arista ARTY 106	FIRST MINUTES OF A NEW DAY (LP)	40
76	Arista DARTY 1	IT'S YOUR WORLD (LP, with Brian Jackson)	30

MICHELLE SCOTTI

64	Philips BF 1384	Little Drummer Boy/Lonely Lonely Lonely	5

SCOTT'S WASHBOARD BAND

60	Columbia 33SX 1232	HARLEM WASHBOARD (LP)	12

SCOTTY (David Scott)

70	Songbird SB 1044	Sesame Street/CRYSTALITES: Version	18
71	Duke DU 106	Donkey Skank (with Tennors)/MURPHY'S ALLSTARS: Version	12
71	Songbird SB 1049	Riddle I This/Musical Chariot	10
71	Songbird SB 1051	Jam Rock Style/Jam Rock Style Version (with Crystalites)	10
71	Songbird SB 1056	Penny For Your Song/CRYSTALITES: Version	7
72	Songbird SB 1080	Clean Race/CRYSTALITES: Version Train	7
72	Harry J. HJ 6642	Skank In Bed/BONGO HERMAN: African Breakfast	8
73	Count Shelley CS 036	Salvation Train/KEN PARKER: Message To Mary	8
71	Trojan TRL 33	SCHOOLDAYS (LP)	40

(see also Lloyd Charmers, Joe White)

SCRAPING FOETUS OFF THE WHEEL

80s	Womb 12	Ramrod/Boxhead/Smut	20
81	Womb WOMB-OYBL-2	HOLE (LP, gatefold sleeve with lyrics, also listed as FDL 3)	40

(see also Foetus, You've Got Foetus On Your Breath, Philip & His Foetus Vibrations, Foetus Corruptus, Foetus Inc, Foetus Uber Frisco)

MINT VALUE £

SCREAMING DEAD

82 Skull DEAD 1 Valley Of The Dead/Schoolgirl Junkie (p/s) . . . 5

SCRITTI POLITTI

78 St. Pancras SCRIT 1 Skank Bloc Bologna/Is And Ought Of The Western World/28.8.78 (photocopied stapled foldout p/s, hand-stamped white labels) . . . 6
79 Rough Trade RT 027T 4 A SIDES: Doubt Beat/Confidences/Bibbly O'Tek/P.A.s (12" EP) . . . 8
79 Rough Trade Songs To Remember/The Cassette Interview (cassette, with 12-page booklet & 2 photos, promo only) . . . 10
79 St. Pancras SCRIT 2/RT 034 WORK IN PROGRESS (Peel Session): (EP, with photocopied inserts) . . . 5

SCROTUM POLES

79 Scrotum Poles ERECT 1 Revelation: Why Don't You Come Out Tonight?/Night Train/ Pick The Cat's Eyes Out/Helicopter Honeymoon/Radio Tay (handwritten labels, 2 p/s designs, some with insert) . . . each 120/100
80s One-Tone ERECT 1 AUCHMITHY CALLING (cassette) . . . 15

SCRUBS

86 Anubis ANU 003 Battle (p/s) . . . 20
87 Flicknife FLS 035 Time For You (p/s) . . . 10

SCRUGG

68 Pye 7N 17451 I Wish I Was Five/Everyone Can See . . . 30
68 Pye 7N 17551 Lavender Popcorn/Sandwichboard Man . . . 45
69 Pye 7N 17656 Will The Real Geraldine Please Stand Up/Only George . . . 30
(see also Floribunda Rose, John T. Kongos)

EARL SCRUGGS

72 CBS 7877 Brand New Tennessee Waltz/Foggy Mountain Breakdown . . . 5
72 CBS 64777 EARL SCRUGGS: HIS FAMILY AND FRIENDS (LP, with Byrds, Joan Baez, Bob Dylan, etc.) . . . 15
(see also Flatt & Scruggs, Byrds)

IRENE SCRUGGS

50s Poydras 80 You've Got What I Want/My Back To The Wall . . . 8

CYRIL SCUTT & HIS BOOGIE PIANO

51 88 882 Delta Express/Steady Stomp Boogie (78) . . . 12

MR. JOHNNY SEA

60s Fontana FJL 315 EVERYBODY'S FAVOURITE (LP) . . . 15

SEA & CAKE

95 Lissy's LIS 1 Glad You're Right/Tiger Partner/Crimson Wing (p/s, 500 only) . . . 15
99 Hefty HEFTY 013 Window Light/JOHN McENTIRE: Setup For Bed (p/s) . . . 5
95 Thrill Jockey TKCD 70951 THE BIZ (CD) . . . 20
(see also Tortoise)

SEA-DERS

67 Decca F 22576 Thanks A Lot/Undecidedly . . . 50
67 Decca DFE-R 8674 THE SEA-DERS (EP, export issue) . . . 200+
(see also Cedars)

DAVE SEALEY

69 DJM DJS 210 Picking Up The Pieces/I Can't Go On Living Without You . . . 6

MILT SEALEY TRIO

60s Duc. Thompson DEP 95017 MILTON SEALEY AND KANSAS FIELDS (EP) . . . 8

PHIL SEAMAN

68 Verve (S)VLP 9220 PHIL SEAMAN NOW ... LIVE (LP) . . . 150
60s Decibel BSN 103 PHIL SEAMAN STORY (LP) . . . 40
60s Saga OPP 102 MEETS EDDIE GOMEZ (LP) . . . 100
74 77 Records 77 SEU 12/53 PHIL ON DRUMS (LP) . . . 35

SEARCHERS

SINGLES

63 Pye 7N 15533 Sweets For My Sweet/It's All Been A Dream . . . 6
63 Philips BF 1274 Sweet Nuthins/What'd I Say . . . 12
63 Pye 7N 15566 Sugar And Spice/Saints And Searchers (dark maroon or lighter pink label) . . . 12/6
64 Pye 7N 15594 Needles And Pins/Saturday Night Out . . . 6
64 Pye 7N 15630 Don't Throw Your Love Away/I Pretend I'm With You . . . 6
64 Pye 7N 15670 Someday We're Gonna Love Again/No One Else Could Love You . . . 6
64 Pye 7N 15694 When You Walk In The Room/I'll Be Missing You . . . 6
64 Pye 7N 15739 What Have They Done To The Rain/This Feeling Inside (maroon or lighter pink label) . . . 7/5
65 Pye 7N 15794 Goodbye My Love/Till I Met You . . . 6
65 Pye 7N 15878 He's Got No Love/So Far Away . . . 7
65 Pye 7N 15950 When I Get Home/I'm Never Coming Back . . . 6
65 Pye 7N 15992 Take Me For What I'm Worth/Too Many Miles (a few in export p/s) . . . 25/6
66 Pye 7N 17094 Take It Or Leave It/Don't Hide It Away . . . 7
66 Pye 7N 17170 Have You Ever Loved Somebody/It's Just The Way . . . 7
67 Pye 7N 17225 Popcorn, Double Feature/Lovers . . . 15
67 Pye 7N 17308 Western Union/I'll Cry Tomorrow . . . 15
67 Pye 7N 17424 Secondhand Dealer/Crazy Dreams . . . 50
68 Liberty LBF 15159 Umbrella Man/Over The Weekend . . . 50
69 Liberty LBF 15340 Kinky Kathy Abernathy/Suzanna . . . 55
71 RCA RCA 2057 Desdemona/The World Is Waiting For Tomorrow . . . 15
71 RCA RCA 2139 Love Is Everywhere/And A Button . . . 10
72 RCA RCA 2231 Sing Singer Sing/Come On Back To Me . . . 10
72 RCA RCA 2248 Needles And Pins/When You Walk In The Room/Come On Back To Me . . . 10
72 RCA RCA 2288 Vahevala/Madman . . . 15
73 RCA RCA 2330 Solitaire/Spicks And Specks . . . 6
79 Sire SIR 4029 Hearts In Her Eyes/Don't Hang On (p/s) . . . 10

MINT VALUE £

80	Sire SIR 4036	It's Too Late/This Kind Of Love Affair (p/s)	7
81	Sire SIR 4046	Love's Melody/Changing (p/s)	12
81	Sire SIR 4049	Another Night/Back To The War (p/s)	10
80s	private pressing	Don't Make Promises	10
80s	private pressing	Four Strong Winds	10

EPs

63	Pye NEP 24177	AIN'T GONNA KISS YA	10
63	Pye NEP 24183	SWEETS FOR MY SWEET (some copies with white & maroon label)	15
64	Pye NEP 24184	HUNGRY FOR LOVE	20
64	Pye NEP 24201	THE SEARCHERS PLAY THE SYSTEM	25
64	Pye NEP 24204	WHEN YOU WALK IN THE ROOM	22
65	Pye NEP 24218	BUMBLE BEE	22
65	Pye NEP 24222	SEARCHERS '65	30
65	Pye NEP 24228	FOUR BY FOUR	35
66	Pye NEP 24263	TAKE ME FOR WHAT I'M WORTH	100

LPs

62	private pressing	THE SEARCHERS (demo acetate)	200+
63	Pye NPL 18086	MEET THE SEARCHERS	25
63	Pye NPL 18089	SUGAR AND SPICE	22
64	Pye NPL 18092	IT'S THE SEARCHERS	22
65	Pye NPL 18111	SOUNDS LIKE SEARCHERS	22
65	Pye NPL 18120	TAKE ME FOR WHAT I'M WORTH	40
67	Marble Arch MAL 640	SMASH HITS VOL. 1	12
67	Marble Arch MAL(S) 673	SMASH HITS VOL. 2 (mono/stereo)	12
72	RCA SF 8289	SECOND TAKE	18
79	Sire SRK 6082	SEARCHERS	15
80	Sire SRK 6086	THE SEARCHERS	15
81	Sire SRK 3523	PLAY FOR TODAY	15
83	PRT DOW 11	LOVE LIES BLEEDING (10")	15

(see also Tony Jackson & Vibrations, Chris Curtis, Pasha)

SEARS

84	Bluurg FISH 9	IF ONLY... (LP)	15

AL SEARS

52	Vogue V 2142	Berry Wells/Steady Eddie (78)	10

SEA STONE

82	Plankton 02	AGAINST THE TIDE (EP, foldout sleeve)	40
78	Plankton PKN 101	MIRRORED DREAMS (LP, with insert)	80

SEATHROUGH

70s	private pressing	LALA LAPLA (LP)	30

B.B. SEATON

72	Big BG 336	I Want Justice/RUPIE EDWARD'S ALL STARS: Justice (Version)	8
72	Bullet BU 514	I Miss My Schooldays/CONSCIOUS MINDS: School Days — Version	8
72	Camel CA 100	Lean On Me/NOW GENERATION: Samba Pati	8
72	Pama PM 864	I Want Justice/RUPIE EDWARD'S ALL STARS: Justice — Version	8
72	Pama Supreme PS 374	Sweet Caroline/Eleanor Rigby	8
73	Trojan TRLS 59	THE THIN LINE BETWEEN LOVE AND HATE (LP)	25

(see also Bibby, Winston & Bibby, Gaylads, Messengers)

HORACE SEATON

63	Island WI 123	I'm So Glad/Tell Me	25
64	R&B JB 143	Hold On/LESTER STERLING: Peace And Love	25

(see also Bibby, B.B. Seaton, Tommy McCook)

SEA TRAIN

68	A&M AMS 737	Let The Duchess Know/As I Lay Losing	5
69	A&M AMLS 941	SEA TRAIN (LP)	20
71	Capitol EA-ST 659	SEA TRAIN (LP)	15
72	Capitol EA-ST 829	MARBLEHEAD MESSENGER (LP, gatefold sleeve)	12
73	Warner Bros K 46222	WATCH (LP)	12

(see also Blues Project, Old & In The Way)

SEA URCHINS

87	Kvatch KVATCH 001/ Lyntone LYN 18632	Clingfilm/GROOVE FARM: Baby Blue Marine (flexidisc, 1,000 only, 500 in p/s)	15/10
87	Sha La La Ba Ba Ba Ba 5	Summershine/ORCHIDS: From This Day (flexidisc, 2,500 only, 1,000 w/p/s)	12/6
87	Sarah SARAH 001	Pristine Christine/Sullen Eyes/Everglades (foldaround p/s with 14" x 10" poster in poly bag, 1,600 only)	60
88	Sarah SARAH 008	Solace/Please Rain Fall (foldaround p/s in poly bag)	20
89	Fierce FRIGHT 032	30.10.88 (live) (1-sided, p/s)	15
91	Cheree CHEREE 15	Please Don't Cry/Time Is All I've Seen (die-cut company sleeve)	10

JOHN SEBASTIAN

54	London HL 8029	Inca Dance/Foolish Waltz	30
54	London HL 8029	Inca Dance/Foolish Waltz (78)	6
55	London HL 8131	Stranger In Paradise/Autumn Leaves	25

JOHN (B.) SEBASTIAN

69	Kama Sutra 618 026	She's A Lady/The Room Nobody Lives In	6
70	Reprise RS 20902	Magical Connection/Fa-Fana-Fa	5
70	Reprise RSLP 6379	JOHN B. SEBASTIAN (LP, gatefold sleeve)	20
70	Buddah 2361 003	JOHN SEBASTIAN SONGBOOK VOLUME ONE (LP, with Lovin' Spoonful)	15
71	Reprise K 44149	THE FOUR OF US (LP, gatefold sleeve)	15

(see also Lovin' Spoonful, Even Dozen Jug Band)

MINT VALUE £

SECESSION

80s Siren SRN12 23	Michael (12", p/s)	12
88 Siren SRNLP 11	A DARK ENCHANTMENT (LP, with inner)	40

HARRY SECOMBE

60 Philips PB 974	Jerusalem/The Holy City (78)	6
(see also Goons)		

SECOND CITY SOUND

65 Decca F 12310	Tchaikovsky One/Shadows	8
66 Decca F 12366	Greig One/In A Mist	5
66 Decca F 12406	Love's Funny/Tell Me Where I'm Going	5
69 Major Minor MM 600	The Dream Of Olwyn/A Touch Of Velvet, A Sting of Brass	8

SECOND COMING

71 Mercury 6338 030	SECOND COMING (LP)	15

SECOND HAND

68 Polydor 583 045	REALITY (LP, labels on early copies credit band as Moving Finger)	125
72 Mushroom MR 2006	DEATH MAY BE YOUR SANTA CLAUS (LP, some copies omit "Funeral")	100+

(see also Andreas Thomopoulos, Fungus, Chillum, Vulcans, Seventh Wave)

SECOND LAYER

79 Tortch-r TOR 001	FLESH AS PROPERTY (EP, white p/s, black printed labels)	25
80 Tortch TOR 006	State Of Emergency/I Need Noise/The Cutting Motion (p/s)	20
81 Tortch/Fresh FRESH 5	FLESH AS PROPERTY (EP, reissue, yellow p/s & white labels)	20
81 Cherry Red CHERRY 21	FLESH AS PROPERTY (EP, 2nd reissue, unreleased)	
82 Cherry Red BRED 14	WORLD OF RUBBER (LP, with inner)	50
(see also Outsiders, Sound)		

SECRET

77 Arista ARIST 142	The Young Ones/Handel A Vandel	25
78 Arista ARIST 173	Do You Really Care?/I Wanna Car Like That	25

SECRET AFFAIR

79 I-Spy SEE 1	Time For Action/Soho Strut (brown p/s, black print or black p/s, white print)	10
79 I-Spy SEE 3	Let Your Heart Dance/Sorry Wrong Number (p/s)	5
80 I-Spy SEE 5	My World/So Cool (paper labels, some with badge)	8/6
80 I-Spy SEE 8	Sound Of Confusion/Take It Or Leave It (p/s)	5
81 I-Spy SEE 10	Do You Know?/Dance Master (keyhole company sleeve, paper labels)	10
82 I-Spy SEE 11	Lost In The Night (Mack The Knife)/The Big Beat (p/s)	10
79 I-Spy I SPY 1	GLORY BOYS (LP, with 2 inserts)	18
80 I-Spy I SPY 2	BEHIND CLOSED DOORS (LP, with inner sleeve)	15
82 I-Spy I SPY 3	BUSINESS AS USUAL (LP, stickered sleeve)	18
90s own label	CITY OF DREAMS (LP, handmade sleeve)	15

(see also New Hearts, Advertising, Innocents [U.K.])

SECRET KNOWLEDGE

90s Sabres Of Paradise	Sugar Daddy (mixes) (12")	10

SECRET OYSTER

74 CBS 80489	SEA SON (LP)	12

SECRETS (U.K.)

66 CBS 202466	I Suppose/Such A Pity	25
67 CBS 202585	Infatuation/She's Dangerous	25
67 CBS 2818	I Intend To Please/I Think I Need The Cash	25

(see also Simon's Secrets, Clifford T. Ward, Martin Raynor & Secrets)

SECRETS (U.S)

64 Philips BF 1298	The Boy Next Door/Learnin' To Forget	20
64 Philips BF 1318	Hey Big Boy/Other Side Of Town	20

SECT

81 Shoestring SHOE 1	This is Your Life/Private Eye (p/s)	5

SECTION 5

85 Oi OIR 002	WE WON'T CHANGE (LP)	22
80s OI	STREET ROCK 'N' ROLL (LP)	22

SECTION 25

80 Factory FAC 18	Girls Don't Count/New Noise/Up To You (tracing paper p/s)	5
81 Factory FACT 45	ALWAYS NOW (LP, in envelope/folder)	12
84 Factory FACT 90	FROM THE HIP (LP, with inner)	25

NEIL SEDAKA

59 RCA RCA 1099	The Diary/No Vacancy	25
59 RCA RCA 1099	The Diary/No Vacancy (78)	20
59 RCA RCA 1115	I Go Ape/Moon Of Gold	20
59 RCA RCA 1115	I Go Ape/Moon Of Gold (78)	20
59 RCA RCA 1130	You've Got To Learn Your Rhythm And Blues/Crying My Heart Out For You	25
59 RCA RCA 1130	You've Got To Learn Your Rhythm And Blues/Crying My Heart Out For You (78)	25
59 London HLW 8961	Ring A Rockin'/Fly Don't Fly On Me	40
59 London HLW 8961	Ring A Rockin'/Fly Don't Fly On Me (78)	120
(The above RCA 45s were originally issued with triangular centres; later round-centres are worth two-thirds these values.)		
59 RCA RCA 1152	Oh! Carol/One Way Ticket (triangular centre or round centre)	25/7
59 RCA RCA 1152	Oh! Carol/One Way Ticket (78)	200
60 RCA RCA 1178	Stairway To Heaven/Forty Winks Away	7
60 RCA RCA 1178	Stairway To Heaven/Forty Winks Away (78)	200
60 RCA RCA 1198	Run Samson Run/You Mean Everything To Me	7
60 RCA RCA 1198	Run Samson Run/You Mean Everything To Me (78)	200
61 RCA RCA 1220	Calendar Girl/The Same Old Fool	7
61 RCA RCA 1236	Little Devil/I Must Be Dreaming	7
61 RCA RCA 1250	Sweet Little You/I Found My World In You	7

MINT VALUE £

61	RCA RCA 1266	Happy Birthday, Sweet Sixteen/Don't Lead Me On	7
62	RCA RCA 1282	King Of Clowns/Walk With Me	7
62	Stateside SS 105	Oh Delilah/MARVELS: Neil's Twist	15
62	RCA RCA 1298	Breaking Up Is Hard To Do/As Long As I Live	7
62	RCA RCA 1319	Next Door To An Angel/I Belong To You	7
63	RCA RCA 1331	Circulate/Alice In Wonderland	7
63	RCA RCA 1343	Let's Go Steady Again/Waiting For Never	7
63	RCA RCA 1359	The Dreamer/Look Inside Your Heart	8
63	RCA RCA 1368	Bad Girl/Wait 'Til You See My Baby	15
65	RCA RCA 1475	World Through A Tear/High On A Mountain	12
74	Polydor 2058 532	Bad Blood/Hey Mister Sunshine (with Elton John)	5
59	RCA RCX 166	NEIL SEDAKA (EP)	45
60	RCA RCX 186	NEIL SEDAKA VOL. 2 (EP)	35
62	RCA RCX 212	NEIL SEDAKA VOL. 3 (EP)	35
59	RCA RD 27140	NEIL SEDAKA (LP)	90
60	RCA RD 27207/SF 5090	CIRCULATE (LP, mono/stereo)	50/65

(see also Sam Cooke, Paul Anka, 10cc)

MIKE SEDGEWICK

68	Parlophone R 5694	The Good Guys In The White Hats Never Lose/ Woman (She's Got To Be Treated Right)	5

(see also Adam Mike & Tim)

SEDUCER

83	Sticky SSR 0017	Call Your Name/Survivor	50
84	Thunderbolt THBE 1007	Indecent Exposure/Down Down/No No Baby/DTs/Wild Joker (12", p/s)	8
85	Thunderbolt THBL 016	CAUGHT IN THE ACT (LP)	15
86	Stud STUDLP 2	'EADS DOWN — SEE YOU AT THE END (LP)	15

RUDY SEEDORF

65	Island WI 189	One Million Stars/Mr. Blue	18

SEEDS

66	Vocalion VN 9277	Pushin' Too Hard/Try To Understand	40
67	Vocalion VN 9287	Can't Seem To Make You Mine/Daisy Mae	30
88	Bam Caruso OPRA 091	Pushin' Too Hard/Greener Day	12
67	Vocalion VAN 8062	A WEB OF SOUND (LP)	60
67	Vocalion VAN/SAVN 8070	FUTURE (LP, mono/stereo)	40/60
78	Sonet SNTF 746	THE SEEDS (LEGENDARY MASTER RECORDINGS) (LP)	15
88	Strange Things STRANGEP 1	EVIL HOODOO (LP, picture disc)	20

(see also Sky Saxon, Sky Saxon & The New Seeds, Ya Ho Wa 13)

SEEDS OF THE EARTH

75	Contempo CS 2052	Planting Seeds/Brother Bad	20
75	Contempo CS 2073	Zion Plus/Phire	15

MIKE SEEGER

65	Fontana TFL 6039	MIKE SEEGER (LP)	15

(see also Peggy & Mike Seeger)

PEGGY SEEGER

57	Topic TRC 107	Freight Train/Cumberland Gap (78)	30
58	Topic TRC 108	Pretty Little Baby/Child Of God (78)	10
65	Decca F 12282	Pretty Little Baby/My Love And I Are One	6
57	Pye Jazz NJE 1043	ORIGINS OF SKIFFLE (EP)	20
60	Topic TOP 38	SHINE LIKE A STAR (EP)	10
61	Topic TOP 72	TROUBLED LOVE (EP)	10
61	Topic TOP 73	EARLY IN THE SPRING (EP)	8
50s	Topic 10T 9	PEGGY SEEGER (10" LP)	15
61	PRE 13005	THE BEST OF PEGGY SEEGER (LP)	15
64	Topic 12T 113	WHO'S GOING TO SHOE... (LP, with Tom Paley)	18
69	Argo (Z)DA 63	PEGGY ALONE (LP)	18
72	Argo ZFB 63	PEGGY ALONE (LP, reissue)	12
72	Argo ZFB 64	FEMALE FROLIC (LP, with Frankie Armstrong & Sandra Kerr)	15
79	Blackthorne BR 1061	DIFFERENT THEREFORE EQUAL (LP)	15
86	Blackthorne BR 1067	ITEMS OF NEWS (LP, with Ewan MacColl)	12
86	Blackthorne BR 1069	FAMILIAR FACES (LP)	12

(see also Al Lloyd)

PEGGY SEEGER & GUY CARAWAN

58	HMV CLP 1174	AMERICA AT PLAY (LP)	18

(see also Guy Carawan)

PEGGY & MIKE SEEGER

68	Argo (Z)DA 80	PEGGY 'N' MIKE (LP)	18

(see also Ewan MacColl & Peggy Seeger, Mike Seeger)

PETE SEEGER

60	Top Rank TR 5020	Careless Love/LEON BIBB: Times Are Getting Hard (p/s)	12
63	CBS AAG 187	Little Boxes/Mail Myself To You	5
58	Melodisc EPM7 78	TRIBUTE TO LEADBELLY (EP)	12
58	Topic TOP 33	PETE AND FIVE STRINGS (EP)	10
59	Topic TOP 37	HOOTENANNY NEW YORK CITY (EP, with Sonny Terry)	15
64	CBS AGG 20055	IN CONCERT (EP)	8
65	CBS EP 6065	HEALING RIVER (EP)	8
66	Ember EP 4560	D-DAY DODGERS (EP)	8
61	Philips BBL 7507	PETE SEEGER STORY SONGS (LP)	12
63	Folklore F-LAUT 1	PETE SEEGER IN CONCERT (LP)	12
63	Folklore F-LAUT 2	PETE SEEGER IN CONCERT VOL. 2 (LP)	12
64	CBS (S)BPG 62209	WE SHALL OVERCOME (LP)	15

MINT VALUE £

65	Xtra XTRA 1005	SING WITH SEEGER (LP)	12
65	CBS (S)BPG 62462	I CAN SEE A NEW DAY (LP)	12
65	CBS (S)BPG 62528	STRANGERS AND COUSINS (LP)	12
66	Xtra XTRA 1016	BROADSIDES (LP)	12
66	Xtra XTRA 1034	FOLK SINGER'S GUITAR GUIDE (LP, with 16-page booklet)	12
66	Verve (S)VLP 5004	IN PERSON (LP)	12
68	Ember CW 130	PETE SEEGER (LP)	12
68	Xtra XTRA 1066	ABIYOYO AND OTHER SONGS (LP)	12

(see also Big Bill Broonzy, Sonny Terry [& Brownie McGhee], Weavers)

PETE SEEGER & BIG BILL BROONZY

64	Xtra XTRA 1006	IN CONCERT — PETE SEEGER & BIG BILL BROONZY (LP)	20
66	Verve Folkways VLP 5006	IN CONCERT (LP, reissue, also ST SVLP 506)	12/15

(see also Big Bill Broonzy)

SEEKERS

65	Oriole CB 1935	With A Swag On My Shoulder/Myra	15
65	Decca F 22167	Chilly Winds/Kumbaya	10
66	Columbia DB 7867	Someday, One Day/Nobody Knows The Trouble I've Seen	6
66	Columbia DB 8000	Walk With Me/We're Moving On	6
67	Columbia DB 8134	Georgy Girl/The Last Thing On My Mind	5
67	Columbia DB 8273	When Will The Good Apples Fall/Myra	5
67	Columbia DB 8313	Emerald City/Music Of The World A Turnin'	5
68	Columbia DB 8407	Days Of My Life/Study War No More (as Seekers with Judith Durham)	5
68	Columbia DB 8460	Love Is Kind, Love Is Wine/All I Can Remember	5
68	Columbia DB 8509	Island Of Dreams/Red Rubber Ball	5
69	Columbia DB 8609	Colours Of My Life/Rattler	5
81	Lyntone LYN 2359	A World Of Their Own (flexidisc sampler for World Record Club box set)	5
65	Columbia SEG 8425	THE SEEKERS (EP)	7
65	Columbia SEG 8465	THE SEEKERS (EP)	7
66	Columbia SEG 8496	HITS FROM THE SEEKERS (EP)	7
67	Columbia SEG 8522	MORNINGTOWN RIDE (EP)	7
65	Decca LK 4694	THE SEEKERS (LP)	12
67	Columbia S(C)X 6193	SEEN IN GREEN (LP, blue/black label, gatefold sleeve)	12

(see also Judith Durham, Keith Potger)

SEFTONS

66	CBS 202491	I Can See Through You/Here Today	30

(see also Perishers)

VIVIENNE SEGAL & HAROLD LANG

54	Columbia SCM 5114	Den Of Iniquity/BARBARA ASHLEY: That Terrific Rainbow	7

BOB SEGER (SYSTEM)

68	Capitol CL 15574	Ramblin' Gamblin' Man/Tales Of Lucy Blue (as Bob Seger System)	10
70	Capitol CL 15642	Lucifer/Big River (as Bob Seger System)	8
72	Reprise K 14208	If I Were A Carpenter/Jesse James	5
73	Reprise K 14243	Rosalie/Back In '72	5
74	Reprise K 14364	Get Out Of Denver/Long Song Comin'	5
78	Capitol CL 16004	Hollywood Nights/Brave Strangers (silver vinyl, special sleeve)	5
83	Capitol CLD 284	Even Now/Little Victories//We've Got Tonight/ Brave Strangers (double pack)	5
83	Capitol TC-CL 284	Even Now/We've Got Tonight (cassette)	5
86	Capitol CLD 396	American Storm/Fortunate Son//Hollywood Nights/ Hollywood Nights (live) (double pack)	5
72	Reprise K 44214	SMOKIN' O.P.'s (LP)	15
73	Reprise K 44227	BACK IN '72 (LP)	12
77	Capitol CAPS 1010	MONGREL (LP)	12

LLOYD SEIVRIGHT

70	Creole CR 1001	Mary's Boy Child/And Glory Walked Among Men	6

SEIZE

81	Why Not? NOT 001	Grovelands Road/Why? (p/s)	15
82	Why Not? NOT 002	EVERYBODY DIES EP (p/s)	15

RICHARD SELANO

69	Jolly JY 019	All Of The Time/Broken Romance	6

SELECTED FOUR

71	Banana BA 351	Selection Train/SOUND DIMENSION: Version Train	8

SELECTER

79	2-Tone CHS TT 4	On My Radio/Too Much Pressure (paper label, company sleeve)	5
80	2-Tone CHS TT 8	Three Minute Hero/James Bond (no labels, silver print middle, company sleeve)	6
80	2-Tone CHS TT 8	Three Minute Hero/James Bond (paper labels, company sleeve)	5
82	Flexipop 001/SFI 566	Ready Mix Radio (1-sided clear flexidisc with *Flexipop* mag, issue 1)	8/4
80	2-Tone TT 5002	TOO MUCH PRESSURE (LP)	12

(see also Special A.K.A.)

FREDDIE SELF

64	Mercury MF 839	Don't Cry/Why Should I?	7

(see also Freddie Ryder, Trends)

RONNIE SELF

58	Philips PB 810	Bop-A-Lena/Ain't I A Dog (78)	310

SELF ABUSE

84	Radical Change RC 5	SOLDIER (EP)	5

SELF DESTRUCT

91	Retch RR 12004	AFFRAY (12" EP)	8

MINT VALUE £

BROTHER JOHN SELLERS

56 Vanguard EPP 14002 BLUES AND SPIRITUALS (EP) . . . 15
57 Columbia SEG 7740 BLUES AND SPIRITUALS (EP) . . . 15
57 Decca DFE 6457 BROTHER JOHN SELLERS IN LONDON (EP) . . . 12
56 Vanguard PPT 12008 BROTHER JOHN SELLERS SINGS BLUES AND FOLK SONGS (10" LP) . . . 25
57 Vanguard PPT 12017 JACK OF DIAMONDS AND OTHER FOLK SONGS AND BLUES (10" LP) . . . 25

PETER SELLERS (& SOPHIA LOREN)

52 Parlophone R 3785 Jakka And The Flying Saucers (An Interplanetary Fairy Tale) (both sides) (78) . . . 8
54 HMV B 10724 Dipso-Calypso/Never Never Land (78) . . . 15
57 Parlophone R 4337 Any Old Iron/Boiled Bananas And Carrots . . . 7
58 Parlophone R 4491 I'm So Ashamed/A Drop Of The Hard Stuff . . . 6
58 Parlophone R 4491 I'm So Ashamed/A Drop Of The Hard Stuff (78) . . . 15
59 Parlophone R 4605 Puttin' On The Smile/My Old Dutch . . . 6
59 Parlophone R 4605 Puttin' On The Smile/My Old Dutch (78) . . . 20
60 Parlophone R 4702 Goodness Gracious Me! (with Sophia Loren)/Grandpa's Grave . . . 5
61 Parlophone R 4724 Bangers And Mash (with Sophia Loren)/SOPHIA LOREN: Zoo Be Zoo Be Zoo . . . 7
65 Parlophone R 5393 A Hard Day's Night/Help! . . . 6
66 United Artists UP 1152 After The Fox (as Peter Sellers & Hollies)/BURT BACHARACH: The Fox-Trot . . . 25
79 United Artists BP 335 There Are Camels Where The Taxis Used To Be/Night And Day . . . 5
59 Parlophone GEP 8770 BEST OF SELLERS NO. 1 (EP) . . . 10
59 Parlophone GEP 8784 BEST OF SELLERS NO. 2 (EP) . . . 10
59 Parlophone GEP 8809 BEST OF SELLERS NO. 3 (EP) . . . 10
59 Parlophone GEP 8822 SONGS FOR SWINGIN' SELLERS (EP, also stereo SGE 2013) . . . 10/15
59 Parlophone GEP 8827 SONGS FOR SWINGIN' SELLERS NO. 2 (EP, also stereo SGE 2016) . . . 10/15
61 Parlophone GEP 8832 SONGS FOR SWINGIN' SELLERS NO. 3 (EP, also stereo SGE 2019) . . . 10/15
61 Parlophone GEP 8835 SONGS FOR SWINGIN' SELLERS NO. 4 (EP, also stereo SGE 2020) . . . 10/15
61 Parlophone GEP 8843 PETER AND SOPHIA NO. 1 (EP, with Sophia Loren, also stereo SGE 2021) . . . 12/15
61 Parlophone GEP 8845 PETER AND SOPHIA NO. 2 (EP, with Sophia Loren, also stereo SGE 2022) . . . 12/15
61 Parlophone GEP 8848 PETER AND SOPHIA NO. 3 (EP, with Sophia Loren, also stereo SGE 2023) . . . 12/15
62 Parlophone GEP 8853 TWO PETERS (EP, with Peter Ustinov, 1 side each) . . . 10
58 Parlophone PMD 1069 THE BEST OF SELLERS (10" LP) . . . 15
59 Parlophone PMC 1111 SONGS FOR SWINGIN' SELLERS (LP, also stereo PCS 3003) . . . 12/15
60 Parlophone PMC 1131 PETER AND SOPHIA (LP, with Sophia Loren, also stereo PCS 3012) . . . 15/18
79 United Artists UAG 30266 SELLERS' MARKET (LP) . . . 15

PETER SELLERS, SPIKE MILLIGAN & HARRY SECOMBE

64 Philips AL 3464 HOW TO WIN AN ELECTION (LP) . . . 20
(see also Goons, Spike Milligan, Sophia Loren, Hollies, Harry Secombe, Peter Ustinov)

SELOFANE

68 CBS 3413 Girl Called Fantasy/Happiness Is Love . . . 8
68 CBS 3700 Shingle I.A.O./Chase The Face . . . 8

SEMA 4

79 Pollen PBM 022 4 FROM SEMA 4 (EP, 2 different coloured sleeves, 500 only, numbered) . . . 100
79 Pollen PBM 024 UP DOWN AROUND (EP, 1,000 only) . . . 75

ARCHIE SEMPLE

60 Columbia 33SX 1240 JAZZ FOR YOUNG LOVERS (LP) . . . 50
62 Columbia 33SX 1450 EASY LIVING (LP) . . . 50
63 Columbia 33SX 1580 THE TWILIGHT COMETH (LP) . . . 18
64 77 LEU 12/6 THE CLARINET OF ARCHIE SEMPLE (LP) . . . 30

SEMPRINI

53 HMV 7M 104 Variations On Boogie/Kitten On The Keys . . . 7

SENATE

67 Columbia DB 8110 I Can't Stop/Ain't As Sweet As You . . . 15
68 United Artists (S)ULP 1180 THE SENATE SOCK IT TO YOU ONE MORE TIME (LP) . . . 40
(see also Garnet Mimms)

SENATOR BOBBY

62 Cameo Parkway P 127 Wild Thing/SENATOR EVERETT McKINLAY: Wild Thing . . . 8

SENATORS

64 Dial DSP 7001 She's A Mod/Lot About You . . . 50
64 Oriole CB 1957 When Day Is Done/Breakdown . . . 30
65 CBS 201768 The Tables Are Turning/Stop Wasting Time . . . 25
(see also Tony Rivers & Castaways)

RAY SENDIT & HIS ROCKEY TEAM

57 Felsted SD 80052 Rocket 0869/Spike's Rock . . . 6

LOS SENORS

63 Cameo Parkway C 290 Amapola/Acapulco . . . 5

SENSATIONAL ALEX HARVEY BAND

(see under Alex Harvey)

SENSATIONAL CREED

84 Beggars Banquet BEG 125 Nocturnal Operation/Down Periscope (p/s, reissue of Orbidöig single) . . . 15
84 Beggars Banquet BEG 125T Nocturnal Operation/Down Periscope/Voyage Of The Titanic (12", p/s, reissue of Orbidöig single) . . . 25
(see also Orbidöig)

SENSATIONS (Jamaica)

67 Doctor Bird DB 1074 A Thing Called Soul/BOBBY LEE & SENSATIONS: I Was Born A Loser . . . 18
67 Doctor Bird DB 1100 Right On Time/Lonely Lover . . . 18
67 Doctor Bird DB 1102 Born To Love You/Your Sweet Love . . . 18
68 Duke DU 2 Those Guys/I'll Never Fall In Love . . . 15
68 Island WI 3110 Long Time Me No See You Girl/ROY SHIRLEY: Million Dollar Baby . . . 20

MINT VALUE £

69 Camel CA 31 The Warrior (actually by Johnny Osbourne & Sensations)/ JOHNNY ORGAN: Don Juan ... 10
70 Techniques TI 902 War Boat/Mr Blue ... 7
71 Duke DU 120 Remember/LARRY'S ALLSTARS: Madhouse ... 6
71 Duke DU 121 What Are You Doing Sunday/RUFFIANS: Sweet Dream ... 6
(see also Roy Shirley, Baba Dise, Winston Wright)

SENSATIONS (U.K.)
66 Decca F 12392 Look At My Baby/What A Wonderful Feeling ... 12
71 MCA MK 5078 Oh My Eli/Let's Get A Little Sentimental ... 6

SENSATIONS (featuring Yvonne) (U.S.)
61 Pye International 7N 25110 Music, Music, Music/A Part Of Me (as Sensations featuring Yvonne) ... 20
62 Pye International 7N 25128 Let Me In/Oh Yes I'll Be True ... 20
(see also Yvonne Baker)

SEONA DANCING
83 London LON 22 More To Lose (p/s) ... 18
83 London LONX 22 More To Lose (12", p/s) ... 10
83 London LON 32 Bitter Heart/Tell Her (p/s) ... 18
83 London LONX 32 Bitter Heart/Tell Her (12", p/s) ... 12

SEPTIC DEATH
85 Pusmort 0012-01D NOW THAT I HAVE THE ATTENTION... (LP, with inner sleeve, 18 tracks) ... 18

SEPULTURA
96 Roadrunner RR 23145 Ratamahatta/War/Slave New World (Live)/Amen/Inner Self (Live) (CD, digipak) ... 10
91 Roadracer RO 9328-8 ARISE (LP, picture disc) ... 18
94 Roadrunner RR 90000 0 CHAOS A.D. (CD, limited edition tin box; CD has embossed cover & different sleeve, Brazilian flag & 2 bonus tracks, "Policia" & "Inhuman Nature") ... 22

SERENA
95 Love This LUVTHIST 3 Ridin' High (mixes) (12", p/s, withdrawn) ... 10
95 Love This LUVTHISCD 3 Ridin' High (mixes) (CD, p/s, withdrawn) ... 15

SERENADERS
59 Top Rank JAR 111 Sudden Holiday/Tango Madeira ... 6
59 Top Rank JAR 111 Sudden Holiday/Tango Madeira (78) ... 8

SERENDIPITY
68 CBS 3733 Through With You/I'm Flying ... 80
69 CBS 4428 If I Could/Castles ... 55

SERENDIPITY SINGERS
64 Philips BF 1333 Don't Let The Rain Come Down (Crooked Little Man)/Freedom's Star ... 5

SERFS
69 Capitol E-ST 207 THE SERFS (LP) ... 15

WILL SERGEANT
82 WEA K 19238 Favourite Branches/RAVI SHANKAR & BILL LOVEDAY: Himalaya (p/s) ... 25
95 Ochre OCH 003 Cosmos/Venus In Flares (p/s, orange vinyl) ... 15
78 (no label or cat. no.) WEIRD AS FISH (cassette, 7 copies only, each with a different cover) ... 50+
83 92 Happy Cust. HAPLP 1 THEMES FOR "GRIND" (LP) ... 15
(see also Echo & Bunnymen)

SERGIO & ESTIBALIZ
75 Epic S EPC 3187 Love Come Home/Tu Volveras ... 12

SERIOUS DRINKING
80s Upright YOURS 4 Love On The Terraces/Hypocrite/Bobby Moore Was Innocent (p/s) ... 5

ROSITA SERRANO
51 HMV JO 226 Bibbidi-Bobbidi-Boo/Cinderella (78, export issue) ... 7

SESAME STREET
72 CBS 5366 Rubber Duckie (Ernie)/Sesame Street ... 5

NANCY SESAY & MELODAIRES
81 It's War Boys S 1 C'est Fab/The Ballad Of Hong Kong/National Honk (gatefold p/s) ... 6
(see also Homosexuals)

SETTERS
70 Duke DU 65 Paint Your Wagon/Organ Man (both sides actually by Hot Rod All Stars) ... 8
70 Trojan TR 7738 Virgin Soldier/Brixton Reggae Festival (both actually by Hot Rod All Stars) ... 7

SETTLERS
64 Decca F 11938 Settle Down/Sassafras ... 6
65 Decca F 12123 When's It Gonna Be My Turn?/Good News ... 6
65 Pye 7N 15965 A Woman Called Freedom/I Know I'm Right ... 5
66 Pye 7N 17065 Nowhere Man/Call Again ... 5
66 Pye 7N 17104 Early Morning Rain/Without You ... 5
66 Pye 7N 17171 'Til Winter Follows Spring/Do You Want To Know The Reason Why ... 5
66 Pye 7N 17213 On The Other Side/Can't Stop Following You ... 5
67 Pye 7N 17375 Major To Minor/I Love 'Oo Kazoo ... 5
68 Columbia DB 8424 As Long As There's Love/Penny To My Name ... 5
69 Columbia DB 8570 Keep Movin' On/Love Is More Than Words ... 5
70 Columbia DB 8695 Nessie The Monster/Jesus Met The Woman At The Well ... 5
71 York FYK 505 The Lightning Tree/Just This Side Of Nowhere ... 5
64 Decca LK 4645 SING OUT (LP) ... 12
67 Island ILP 947 EARLY SETTLERS (LP) ... 20
70 Columbia SCX 6381 SETTLERS ALIVE (LP) ... 12
72 York FYK 405 LIGHTNING TREE (LP) ... 12
70s Myrrh MST 6507 SING A NEW SONG (LP) ... 12

MINT VALUE £

SEVEN AGES OF MAN

72 Rediffusion ZS 115 SEVEN AGES OF MAN (LP) 15
(see also Madeline Bell, Gordon Beck)

SEVEN LETTERS/SYMARIP

69 Doctor Bird DB 1189 People Get Ready/The Fit (as Seven Letters) 15
69 Doctor Bird DB 1194 Please Stay/Special Beat (as Seven Letters) 15
69 Doctor Bird DB 1195 Flour Dumpling/Equality (as Seven Letters [Symarip]) 15
69 Doctor Bird DB 1206 Mama Me Want Girl/Sentry (as Seven Letters) 15
69 Doctor Bird DB 1207 Soul Crash/Throw Me Things (as Seven Letters) 15
69 Doctor Bird DB 1208 There Goes My Heart/Wish (as Seven Letters) 15
69 Doctor Bird DB 1209 Bam Bam Baji/Hold Him Joe (as Seven Letters [Symarip]) 15
69 Doctor Bird DB 1306 Fung Sure/Tomorrow At Sundown (as Symarip) 15
69 Treasure Isle TI 7050 Skinhead Moonstomp/Must Catch A Train (as Symarip) 10
70 Treasure Isle TI 7054 Parson's Corner/Redeem (as Symarip) 12
70 Treasure Isle TI 7055 La Bella Jig/Holidays By The Sea (as Symarip) 10
70 Attack ATT 8013 I'm A Puppet/Vindication (as Symarip) 6
70 Trojan TBL 102 SKINHEAD MOONSTOMP (LP, as Symarip) 25
(see also Pyramids, Equals, Laurel Aitken)

7 SECONDS

82 Alt. Tentacles VIRUS 15 SKIN, BRAINS AND GUTS (EP, with insert) 12

SEVENTEEN

80 Vendetta VD 001 Don't Let Go/Bank Holiday Weekend (p/s) 150
(see also Alarm)

SEVENTH SEAL

97 Acme ACLP 8018LP THE SEVENTH SEAL (LP) 12

SEVENTH SON

82 Rising Son FMR 067 Man In The Street/Immortal Hours (some in p/s) 75/20
84 Rising Son SRT4KS 282 Metal To The Moon/Sound And Fury (some in gatefold p/s) 60/30
87 Music Factory MF 0043 Northern Boots/The Harder You Rock (p/s) 18
89 Rising Son SRT9KLS What More Do You Want/Sister Strange/Bitter Ashes (12", p/s) 12

SEVENTH WAVE

75 Gull GULS 14 Manifestations/Only The Beginning (Part 1) 5
(see also Second Hand, Fungus)

SEVENTH WAVE

89 SRT SRT9KS 2018 Tonight (p/s) 20

SEVENTH WONDER

80 Grapevine GRP 130 Captain Of My Ship/Pharaoh 8

SEVERED HEAD

83 Plastic Canvas PC 002 Heavy Metal/Killin' The Kidz (p/s) 35

SEVERINE

71 CBS 7230 Chance In Time/Nothing Bad Can Be This Good 8
71 Philips 6009 135 Un Banc, Un Arbre, Une Rue/Viens 5
71 Philips 6009 151 La La Melodie/Je Ferme Les Yeux, Je Compte Dix 5

DAVID SEVILLE & HIS ORCHESTRA (& THE CHIPMUNKS)

57 London HLU 8359 Armen's Theme/Carousel In Rome (initially gold label print, later silver) 18/10
57 London HLU 8411 The Gift/The Donkey And The Schoolboy 12
57 London HLU 8411 The Gift/The Donkey And The Schoolboy (78) 12
57 London HLU 8485 Gotta Get To Your House/Camel Rock 12
57 London HLU 8485 Gotta Get To Your House/Camel Rock (78) 10
58 London HLU 8582 Bonjour Tristesse/Dance From "Bonjour Tristesse" 12
58 London HLU 8582 Bonjour Tristesse/Dance From "Bonjour Tristesse" (78) 6
58 London HLU 8619 Witch Doctor/Don't Whistle At Me Baby 10
58 London HLU 8619 Witch Doctor/Don't Whistle At Me Baby (78) 8
58 London HLU 8659 The Bird On My Head/Hey There Moon 10
58 London HLU 8659 The Bird On My Head/Hey There Moon (78) 8
58 London HLU 8736 Little Brass Band/Take Five 8
58 London HLU 8736 Little Brass Band/Take Five (78) 10
58 London HLG 8762 Almost Good/THE CHIPMUNKS: The Chipmunk Song 6
58 London HLG 8762 Almost Good/THE CHIPMUNKS: The Chipmunk Song (78) 6
59 London HLG 8823 Alvin's Harmonica (with The Chipmunks)/Mediocre 5
59 London HLG 8823 Alvin's Harmonica (with The Chipmunks)/Mediocre (78) 15
59 London HLU 8893 Judy/Maria From Madrid 7
59 London HLU 8893 Judy/Maria From Madrid (78) 15
59 London HLU 7083 Alvin's Harmonica/Ragtime Cowboy Joe 6
59 London HLG 8916 Ragtime Cowboy Joe (with The Chipmunks)/Flip Side 5
59 London HLG 8916 Ragtime Cowboy Joe (with Chipmunks)/Flip Side (78) 15
60 London HLG 9061 Alvin's Orchestra (with The Chipmunks)/Copyright 1960 (B-side as Music Of David Seville) 5
60 London HLG 9061 Alvin's Orchestra (with The Chipmunks)/Copyright 1960 (78) 20
60 London HLG 9125 Coming 'Round The Mountain/Sing A Goofy Tune (with Chipmunks) 5
60 London HLG 9193 Alvin For President (with The Chipmunks)/Sack Time 5
60 London HLG 9243 Rudolph The Red-Nosed Reindeer/Lilly Of Laguna (with The Chipmunks) 5
61 London HLU 9329 Oh Judge, Your Honour, Dear Sir/Freddy, Freddy 5
64 Liberty LIB 10170 All My Loving/Please Please Me (with The Chipmunks) 7
57 London RE-U 1085 DAVID SEVILLE & HIS ORCHESTRA (EP) 25
59 London RE-U 1219 WITCH DOCTOR AND FRIENDS (EP) 25
63 Liberty LEP 2057 SING ALONG WITH THE CHIPMUNKS (EP) 12
63 Liberty LEP 2117 SING AGAIN WITH THE CHIPMUNKS (EP) 12
59 London HA-U 2153 THE WITCH DOCTOR PRESENTS DAVID SEVILLE AND HIS FRIENDS (LP) 35
64 Liberty LBY 1218 THE CHIPMUNKS SING THE BEATLES (LP) 15
(see also Alfi & Harry)

MINT VALUE £

ALEC SEWARD
56 Vogue LDE 165 — CITY BLUES (10" LP) 40

SEX AIDS
83 Riot City RIOT 23 — BACK ON THE PISS AGAIN (EP) 5
(see also Vice Squad)

SEX BEATLES
79 Charly CYS 1061 — Well You Never/Fatal Fascination (p/s) 5

SEXHURT
98 Dobbstown BOB 23 — A ROMANTIC EVENING WITH BIG RED STRAPS (LP, with free straps) 12

SEX PISTOLS
76 EMI EMI 2566 — Anarchy In The U.K./I Wanna Be Me (black p/s, with Chris Thomas production credit on B-side) 30
76 EMI EMI 2566 — Anarchy In The U.K./I Wanna Be Me (Dave Goodman production credit on B-side) 25
77 A&M AMS 7284 — God Save The Queen/No Feelings (withdrawn, some in brown envelope with press release) 6,000/5,500
77 Virgin VS 181 — God Save The Queen/Did You No Wrong (p/s) 6
77 Virgin VS 184 — Pretty Vacant/No Fun (p/s, some with push-out centre) .... each 6/5
77 Virgin VS 191 — Holidays In The Sun/Satellite (withdrawn p/s) 15
77 Virgin/Lyntone LYN 3261 — Lentilmas — A Seasonal Offering To You From Virgin Records (flexidisc, Xmas freebie to journalists; some with Xmas card) 200/150
78 Virgin VS 220 — No-One Is Innocent (A Punk Prayer By Ronald Biggs)/SID VICIOUS: My Way (p/s) 5
78 Virgin VS 220 — No-One Is Innocent (mispress, plays Motors track)/SID VICIOUS: My Way (p/s) 10
78 Virgin VS 22012 — The Biggest Blow (A Punk Prayer By Ronald Biggs)/(Interview)/SID VICIOUS: My Way (12", p/s [matrix: VS 22012A3], some without interview [VS 22012 A1]) 20/10
79 Virgin VS 240 — Something Else/Friggin' In The Riggin' (p/s) 5
79 Virgin VS 240 — Something Else/Friggin' In The Riggin' (p/s, black & white labels) 12
79 Virgin VS 290 — The Great Rock 'n' Roll Swindle/Rock Around The Clock (vocals by Tenpole Tudor) (withdrawn 'American Express' p/s) 5
79 Virgin VS 290 — The Great Rock 'n' Roll Swindle (mispressing with 'lawyers' telephone conversation' track)/Rock Around The Clock ('American Express' p/s) 15
80 Virgin VS 339 — (I'm Not Your) Stepping Stone/Pistols Propaganda (p/s, mispressing, B-side plays "Substitute") 15
80 Virgin VS 339 — (I'm Not Your) Stepping Stone/Pistols Propaganda (p/s, mispressing, B-side plays Gillan track "No Laughing In Heaven") 12
80 Virgin SEX 1 — PISTOLS PACK (6 x 7" in p/s; all in plastic wallet) 25-30
81 Virgin VS 443 — Who Killed Bambi?/Rock Around The Clock (by Tenpole Tudor & Pistols, p/s) 5
85 Chaos DICK 1 — Submission/No Feelings (p/s, 5,000 only, blue, pink or yellow vinyl) 7/15/5
85 Chaos SUB 1 — Submission (12", 1-sided test pressing, die-cut sleeve, label has big red 'A') 15
85 Chaos — Pretty Vacant (unreleased, 20 copies only) 50
85 Chaos CARTEL 1 — Submission (12", 1-track promo, withdrawn) 60
86 Archive 4 TOF 104 — THE ORIGINAL SEX PISTOLS LIVE (4-track 12", p/s, 5,000 only) 8
86 Archive 4 TOF 104 — THE ORIGINAL SEX PISTOLS LIVE (4-track 12", p/s, blue vinyl) 15
88 Virgin CDT 3 — Anarchy In The U.K./No Fun/EMI (3" CD, card sleeve) 18
88 Virgin CDT 37 — God Save The Queen/Did You No Wrong/Don't Give Me No Lip Child (3" CD, gatefold card sleeve) 15
88 Spiral Scratch SCRATCH 4 — Pretty Vacant (Demo)/I Wanna Be Me (Demo) (with *Spiral Scratch* magazine, issue 4, B-side actually plays "Seventeen") 10/4
96 Virgin VUSCDJ 113 — Pretty Vacant (live) (CD, promo only, card sleeve) 20
77 Virgin V 2086/SPOTS 001 — NEVER MIND THE BOLLOCKS, HERE'S THE SEX PISTOLS (LP, pink rear sleeve, with no track listing, with poster & 1-sided single, "Submission" [VDJ 24], shrinkwrapped with sticker) 200
77 Virgin V 2086 — NEVER MIND THE BOLLOCKS, HERE'S THE SEX PISTOLS (LP, with track listing, no shrinkwrap) 20
78 Virgin V 2086 — NEVER MIND THE BOLLOCKS, HERE'S THE SEX PISTOLS (LP, pink rear sleeve with no track listing) 25
78 Virgin VP 2086 — NEVER MIND THE BOLLOCKS, HERE'S THE SEX PISTOLS (LP, picture disc) 40
79 Virgin VD 2510 — THE GREAT ROCK 'N' ROLL SWINDLE (2-LP, including "Watcha Gonna Do About It", with paper insert) 60
79 Virgin VD 2510 — THE GREAT ROCK 'N' ROLL SWINDLE (2-LP, "I Wanna Be Me" and "Who Killed Bambi?" replace "Watcha Gonna Do About It", with spoken overdubs on "God Save The Queen Symphony") 30
80 Factory FACT 30 — THE HEYDAY (gold interview cassette in satin pouch with Xmas card) 50
81 Factory FACT 30 — THE HEYDAY (cassette, in vinyl pouch without Xmas card) 25
86 Virgin CDV 2086 — NEVER MIND THE BOLLOCKS, HERE'S THE SEX PISTOLS (CD, mispressing, plays country music titles) 20
(see also Public Image Ltd, Professionals, Rich Kids, Steve Jones, Cash Pussies, Spectres (UK), Swingers)

SEXY GIRLS
69 Fab FAB 100 — Pom-Pom Song/LITTLE JOE & BUSTER'S ALLSTARS: Hy There (B-side actually by Melltones) 12
69 Dice CC 100 — Pom-Pom Song/LITTLE JOE & BUSTER'S ALLSTARS: Hy There (B-side actually by Melltones) (reissue) 12

DENNY SEYTON & SABRES
64 Mercury MF 800 — Tricky Dicky/Baby What You Want Me To Do 18
64 Mercury MF 814 — Short Fat Fanny/Give Me Back My Heart 20
64 Mercury MF 824 — The Way You Look Tonight/Hands Off 20
65 Parlophone R 5363 — Just A Kiss/In The Flowers By The Trees (as Denny Seyton Group) 28
65 Wing WL 1032 — IT'S THE GEAR (14 HITS) (LP) 40

SHACK

88	Ghetto GTG B 1	Emergency/Liberation (p/s)	10
88	Ghetto GTG T 1	Emergency/Liberation/Faith (12", p/s)	20
88	Ghetto GTG CD 1	Emergency/Liberation/Faith/What's It Like (CD)	15
89	Ghetto GTG B 2	High Rise Low Life/Who Killed Clayton Square? (p/s)	5
89	Ghetto GTG T 2	High Rise Low Life/Who Killed Clayton Square?/High Rise Low Life (Bert Hardy Mix) (12", p/s)	8
89	Ghetto GTG CD 2	High Rise Low Life/Who Killed Clayton Square?/High Rise Low Life (Bert Hardy Mix) (CD)	8
90	Ghetto GTG B 11	I Know You Well/I Feel No Way (p/s)	5
90	Ghetto GTG 11T	I Know You Well (Extended Mix)/I Feel No Way/(If You Want It Mix) (12", p/s)	8
90	Ghetto GTG CD 11	I Know You Well (7" Version)/(If You Want It Mix)Feel No Way/(Ext. Mix) (CD)	10
88	Ghetto GHETT 1	ZILCH (LP, distributed by Epic, or later independent issue)	10/12
88	Ghetto GHETT D 1	ZILCH (CD)	18

(see also Pale Fountains)

SHADE JOEY & NIGHTOWLS

64	Parlophone R 5180	Bluebirds Over The Mountain/That's When I Need You Baby	80

SHADER

81	Piston Broke REDASH 1	Bad News Blues (no p/s)	100

SHADES (U.S.)

58	London HLX 8713	Sun Glasses (with Knott Sisters)/KNOTT SISTERS: Undivided Attention	40
58	London HLX 8713	Sun Glasses (with Knott Sisters)/KNOTT SISTERS: Undivided Attention (78)	18

SHADES

62	Starlite ST45 074	Weird Walk/Joe's Shuffle	22

SHADES (Jamaica)

69	Gas GAS 119	Never Gonna Give You Up/Let Me Remind You (both actually by Techniques)	10

(see also Techniques)

SHADES OF BLUE (U.K.)

65	Parlophone R 5270	Voodoo Blues/Luceanne	45
65	Pye 7N 15988	Where Did All The Good Times Go/I Ain't No Use	12

(see also Toby Twirl)

SHADES OF BLUE (U.S.)

66	Sue WI 4022	Oh! How Happy/Little Orphan Boy	20

SHADES OF JOY

69	Fontana STL 5498	SHADES OF JOY (LP)	30

SHADES OF MORLEY BROWN

66	Mercury MF 896	In Time/Walking Proud	6
68	Mercury MF 1054	Silly Girl/Pretty Blue Bird	5

(see also Help Yourself)

JOHNNY SHADOW (& DANNY GAVIN)

63	Pye 7N 15506	Golli Golli/I'm Coming Home To You (with Danny Gavin) (some in p/s)	15/7
63	Pye 7N 15529	Golli Guitar/Week (with Danny Gavin)	7
65	Parlophone R 5286	Kiss Me Now/What Colour Is The Wind	7
65	Parlophone R 5308	Atom Bomb Song Part 3/Talented Man	7

(see also Ivy League)

SHADOWFAX

79	BFD SFX 100	Really Into You (p/s)	50
80	Risky Discs RISK 1	The Russians Are Coming/Calling The Shots	8

SHADOWS (U.S.)

58	HMV POP 563	Jungle Fever/Under Stars Of Love	85
58	HMV POP 563	Jungle Fever/Under Stars Of Love (78)	60

SHADOWS (U.K.)

SINGLES

59	Columbia DB 4387	Saturday Dance/Lonesome Fella	50
59	Columbia DB 4387	Saturday Dance/Lonesome Fella (78)	220
60	Columbia DB 4484	Apache/Quartermaster's Stores (green label, later black)	10/12
60	Columbia DB 4530	Man Of Mystery/The Stranger	7
61	Columbia DB 4580	F.B.I./Midnight	6
61	Columbia DB 4637	The Frightened City/Back Home	6
61	Columbia DB 4698	Kon-Tiki/36-24-36	6
61	Columbia DB 4726	The Savage/Peace Pipe	6
62	Columbia DB 4790	Wonderful Land/Stars Fell On Stockton	6
62	Columbia DB 4870	Guitar Tango/What A Lovely Tune	6

(The above singles were originally issued with green labels; later black label copies are worth £12-£15 unless otherwise stated.)

62	Columbia DB 4948	Dance On!/All Day	6
63	Columbia DB 4984	Foot Tapper/The Breeze And I	6
63	Columbia DB 7047	Atlantis/I Want You To Want Me	6
63	Columbia DB 7106	Shindig/It's Been A Blue Day	7
63	Columbia DB 7163	Geronimo/Shazam	6
64	Columbia DB 7231	Theme For Young Lovers/This Hammer	6
64	Columbia DB 7261	The Rise And Fall Of Flingel Bunt/It's A Man's World	6
64	Columbia DB 7261	The Rise And Fall Of Flingel Bunt/It's A Man's World (mispressing with A-side on both sides)	12
64	Columbia DB 7342	Rhythm 'n' Greens/The Miracle	7
64	Columbia DB 7416	Genie With The Light Brown Lamp/Little Princess	7
65	Columbia DB 7476	Mary Anne/Chu-Chi	7
65	Columbia DB 7588	Stingray/Alice In Sunderland (some in export p/s)	20/7
65	Columbia DB 7650	Don't Make My Baby Blue/My Grandfather's Clock (some in export p/s)	20/7
65	Columbia DB 7769	The War Lord/I Wish I Could Shimmy Like My Sister Arthur	7

MINT VALUE £

66	Columbia DB 7853	I Met A Girl/Late Night Set	8
66	Columbia DB 7952	A Place In The Sun/Will You Be There	8
66	Columbia DB 8034	The Dreams I Dream/Scotch On The Socks ('B' label demos worth £50)	30
67	Columbia PSR 305	Thunderbirds Are Go (1-sided advance promo)	60
67	Columbia DB 8170	Maroc 7/Bombay Duck	7
67	Columbia PSR 308	Maroc 7 (1-sided demo with spoken-word intro)	60
67	Columbia PSR 310	Chelsea Boot/Jigsaw (demo only)	80
67	Columbia DB 8264	Tomorrow's Cancelled/Somewhere	12
68	Columbia DB 8326	Running Out Of World/HANK MARVIN: London's Not Too Far	12
68	Columbia DB 8372	Dear Old Mrs. Bell/Trying To Forget The One You Love	12
69	Columbia DB 8628	Slaughter On Tenth Avenue/HANK MARVIN: Midnight Cowboy	15
72	Columbia DB 8958	Apache/Wonderful Land/F.B.I.	5
72	Lyntone LYN 10099	The Shadows (flexidisc sampler from World Record Club box set)	6
73	EMI EMI 2081	Turn Around And Touch Me/Jungle Jam	5
75	EMI EMI 2269	Let Me Be The One/Stand Up Like A Man	5
75	EMI EMI 2269	Stand Up Like A Man/Let Me Be The One (sides reversed)	7
75	EMI EMI 2310	Run Billy Run/Honourable Puff-Puff	6
76	EMI EMI 2461	It'll Be Me Babe/Like Strangers	7
77	EMI EMI 2573	Apache/Wonderful Land/F.B.I. (reissue)	5
77	EMI EMI 2660	Another Night/Cricket Bat Boogie	6
78	EMI EMI 2838	Love Deluxe/Sweet Saturday Night	6
78	EMI EMI 2890	Don't Cry For Me Argentina/Montezuma's Revenge (p/s)	5
79	EMI EMI 2939	Theme From "The Deer Hunter"/Bermuda Triangle (p/s)	5
79	EMI EMI 5004	Rodrigo's Guitar Concerto/Song For Duke (p/s)	5
80	EMI EMI 5083	Heart Of Glass/Return To The Alamo (p/s)	5
80	Polydor POSP 148	Equinoxe (Part V)/Fender Bender (p/s)	5
80	Polydor POSP 187	Mozart Forte/Midnight Creepin'	5
81	Polydor POSP 255	The Third Man/The Fourth Man	5
81	Polydor POSP 316	Telstar/Summer Love '59	5
81	Polydor POSP 376	Imagine — Woman (Medley)/Hats Off To Wally	5
82	Polydor POSP 439	Treat Me Nice/Spot The Ball (p/s)	6
82	Polydor POSP 485	The Theme From "Missing"/The Shady Lady (p/s)	5
83	Polydor POSP 629	Diamonds/Elevensis (p/s)	6
83	Polydor POSP 657	Going Home/Cat 'N' Mouse (p/s)	5
86	Polydor POSPX 808	Dancing In The Dark (12" Remix)/Dancing In The Dark (7" Version)/ Turning Point (12", p/s)	15
89	Polydor PZCD 47	Mountains Of The Moon/Stack-It/Turning Point (CD)	8

EPs

61	Columbia SEG 8061	THE SHADOWS (also stereo ESG 7834)	12/30
61	Columbia SEG 8094	THE SHADOWS TO THE FORE	12
62	Columbia SEG 8135	SPOTLIGHT ON THE SHADOWS	15
62	Columbia SEG 8148	THE SHADOWS NO. 2 (only some sleeves list "No. 2")	15
62	Columbia SEG 8166	THE SHADOWS NO. 3	15
62	Columbia SEG 8171	WONDERFUL LAND OF THE SHADOWS	15

(The above EPs were originally issued with turquoise labels; later blue/black label copies are worth two-thirds the values listed.)

62	Columbia SEG 8193	THE BOYS (mono)	12
62	Columbia ESG 7881	THE BOYS (stereo, turquoise labels, later black/blue labels)	40/35
63	Columbia SEG 8218	OUT OF THE SHADOWS (mono)	15
63	Columbia ESG 7883	OUT OF THE SHADOWS (stereo, turquoise or black/blue labels)	40/35
63	Columbia SEG 8233	DANCE ON WITH THE SHADOWS	18
63	Columbia SEG 8249	OUT OF THE SHADOWS NO. 2 (also stereo ESG 7895)	18/35
63	Columbia SEG 8268	FOOT TAPPING WITH THE SHADOWS	18
63	Columbia SEG 8278	LOS SHADOWS (2 different sleeves)	18
63	Columbia SEG 8286	SHINDIG WITH THE SHADOWS	20
64	Columbia SEG 8321	THOSE BRILLIANT SHADOWS	20
64	Columbia SEG 8342	DANCE WITH THE SHADOWS	20
64	Columbia SEG 8362	RHYTHM AND GREENS (also stereo ESG 7904)	18/35
64	Columbia SEG 8375	DANCE WITH THE SHADOWS NO. 2	20
65	Columbia SEG 8396	THEMES FROM "ALADDIN AND HIS WONDERFUL LAMP"	20
65	Columbia SEG 8408	DANCE WITH THE SHADOWS NO. 3	22
65	Columbia SEG 8445	ALICE IN SUNDERLAND	22
65	Columbia SEG 8459	THE SOUND OF THE SHADOWS	25
66	Columbia SEG 8473	THE SOUND OF THE SHADOWS NO. 2	25
66	Columbia SEG 8494	THE SOUND OF THE SHADOWS NO. 3	25
66	Columbia SEG 8500	THOSE TALENTED SHADOWS	22
66	Columbia SEG 8510	THUNDERBIRDS ARE GO! (with Cliff Richard)	65
67	Columbia SEG 8528	THE SHADOWS ON STAGE AND SCREEN	35

LPs

61	Columbia 33SX 1374	THE SHADOWS (also stereo SCX 3414)	18/45
62	Columbia 33SX 1458	OUT OF THE SHADOWS (also stereo SCX 3449)	18/30

(The above LPs were originally issued with green labels; later blue/black label copies are worth two-thirds the values listed.)

63	Columbia 33SX 1522	GREATEST HITS (also stereo SCX 1522)	12/15
64	Columbia 33SX 1619	DANCE WITH THE SHADOWS (also stereo SCX 3511)	18/22
65	Columbia 33SX 1736	THE SOUND OF THE SHADOWS (also stereo SCX 3554)	18/22
65	Columbia 33SX 1791	MORE HITS! (also stereo SCX 3578)	12/15
66	Columbia 33SX/SCX 6041	SHADOW MUSIC	15
67	Columbia S(C)X 6148	JIGSAW	18
67	Columbia S(C)X 6199	FROM HANK, BRUCE, BRIAN AND JOHN	18
68	Columbia S(C)X 6282	ESTABLISHED 1958 (half by Cliff Richard, mono/stereo)	18/15

(The above LPs were originally issued with blue/black labels; later silver/black label copies are worth half the values listed.)

MINT VALUE £

70	M. For Pleasure MFP 1388	WALKIN' WITH THE SHADOWS (royal blue sleeve & red lettering)	12
70	Columbia SCX 6420	SHADES OF ROCK	18
72	World Records ALBUM 72	THE SHADOWS (6-LP box set)	30
73	EMI EMA 762	ROCKIN' WITH CURLY LEADS	15
75	EMI EMC 3066	SPECS APPEAL	12
77	EMI EMTV 3	TWENTY GOLDEN GREATS (mispressing, side 2 plays Pink Floyd's "Animals")	12

(see also Cliff Richard, Drifters, Five Chesternuts, Hank Marvin, Marvin Welch & Farrar, Bruce Welch, John Henry Rostill, Brian Bennett, Jet Harris, Tony Meehan, Vipers Skiffle Group, Marty Wilde, Krew Kats, Interns, Strangers, Wasp, MacArthur Park, Thunder Company, Alan Hawkshaw)

SHADOWS OF KNIGHT

66	Atlantic AT 4085	Gloria/Dark Side	30
66	Atlantic 584 021	Oh Yeah/Light Bulb Blues	22
66	Atlantic 584 045	Bad Little Woman/Gospel Zone	22
67	Atlantic 584 136	Someone Like Me/Three For Love	22
69	Buddah 201 024	Shake/From Way Out To Way Under	15
79	Radar ADA 11	GLORIA (LP)	22

SHADROCKS

67	Island WI 3061	Go Go Special/Count Down	20
68	Jay Boy BOY 2	There Is/Jigsaw	6

SHADY

98	Narcotic Candy BBQ 41 TT	Narcotic Candy/Micro Bodi Dot Con (10", p/s)	8
98	Narcotic Candy BBQ 41 CD	Narcotic Candy/Micro Bodi Dot Con (CD)	8

(see also Mercury Rev)

DOREEN SHAFFER

69	Unity UN 536	No Matter What/Walk Through This World	8
69	Unity UN 538	How Much Is That Doggy In The Window/As Long As He Needs Me	6

(see also Bob Marley/Wailers, Lloyd Clarke, Doreen & Jackie)

JOHN SHAFT

72	Downtown DT 488	Forever Music/BLOSSOM JOHNSON: The Boy I Love	6

SHAFTESBURY

80	O.K. SRT CUS 025	Hit Man	5
80	O.K. OKA 001	THE LULL BEFORE THE STORM (LP, with insert)	50
81	O.K. OKA 002	WE ARE THE BOYS (LP)	25

BOBBY SHAFTO

62	Parlophone R 4870	Over And Over/I Want My Bed	8
62	Parlophone R 4958	Feel So Blue/I Haven't Got A Girl	10
64	Parlophone R 5130	She's My Girl/Wonderful You	10
64	Parlophone R 5167	Love, Love, Love (Don't Let Me Down)/I Don't Love You Anymore	10
64	Parlophone R 5184	Who Wouldn't Love A Girl Like That/I Remember	10
65	Parlophone R 5252	How Could You Do A Thing Like That To Me/Baby Then	10
66	Parlophone R 5403	Lonely Is As Lonely Does/The Same Old Room	10
66	Parlophone R 5481	A Little Like You/See Me Cry	10

SHAG NASTY

79	Shag Nasty SN 1	No Bullshit Just Rock 'n' Roll/Looking For A Love? (p/s)	30

SHAGRAT

90	Shagrat ORC 001	Amanda/Peppermint Flickstick (p/s, 500 only, some autographed)	5/7
91	Shagrat ENT 001	NOTHING EXCEEDS LIKE EXCESS (mini LP, as Steve Took's Shagrat, numbered, 400 only)	10

(see also Tyrannosaurus Rex, Pink Fairies, Larry Wallis, Tools You Can Trust)

SHAKE

79	Sire SIR 4016	Culture Shock/Dream On	10
79	Sire SIR 4016-10	Culture Shock/Glass House/Dream On/(But) Not Mine (10", p/s)	12

(see also Rezillos, Jo Callis, TV 21)

SHAKEOUTS

65	Columbia DB 7613	Every Little Once In A While/Well Who's That	45

SHAKERS (U.K.)

63	Polydor NH 52158	Money/Memphis Tennessee	20
63	Polydor NH 52213	Hippy Hippy Shake/Dr. Feelgood	20
63	Polydor NH 66991	Hippy Hippy Shake/Dr. Feelgood	20
63	Polydor NH 52258	Money/Hippy Hippy Shake	20
63	Polydor NH 52272	Whole Lotta Lovin'/I Can Tell	20
63	Polydor 237 139	LET'S DO THE SLOP, TWIST, MADISON, HULLY GULLY WITH THE SHAKERS (LP)	60

(see also Kingsize Taylor & Dominoes)

SHAKERS (U.S.)

73	Probe PRO 582	One Wonderful Moment/Love, Love, Love	6
74	ABC ABC 4018	One Wonderful Moment/Love, Love, Love (reissue)	5

JOHN & JOAN SHAKESPEARE

69	Decca F 12896	Number One Theme/Fade Out (p/s)	30

CHRIS SHAKESPEARE GLOBE SHOW

69	Page One POF 113	Ob-La-Di, Ob-La-Da/Tin Soldier	18

(see alslo Globe Show)

SHAKESPEARES

68	RCA Victor RCA 1695	Something To Believe In/Burning My Fingers	35

(see also Fynn McCool)

MINT VALUE £

SHAKEY JAKE
69 Liberty LBL 83217E — FURTHER ON UP THE ROAD (LP) 30

SHAKEY VICK
69 Pye N(S)PL 18276 — LITTLE WOMAN, YOU'RE SO SWEET (LP) 20

SAM SHAM
69 Blue Cat BS 157 — Drumbago's Dead/SPARTERS: Song Of The Year 8

SHAMANIC TRIBES ON ACID
93 Ambient Space Acid 1202 — SHAMANIC TRIBES ON ACID EP (12", blue vinyl) 8

SHAME
67 MGM MGM 1349 — Don't Go Away Little Girl/Dreams Don't Bother Me (125 with picture insert) .. 90/70

(see also Shy Limbs, King Crimson, Gods, Emerson Lake & Palmer)

SHAME
85 Fierce FRIGHT 003 — Real Tears (1-sided, hand-coloured p/s, possibly unissued) 50

SHAMEN
86 One Big Guitar OBG 003T — THEY MAY BE RIGHT ... BUT THEY'RE CERTAINLY WRONG (12" EP) 15

86 Skipping Kitten (no cat. no.) — WAYWARD WEDNESDAY IN MAY AFFAIR ("Four Letter Girl"/"Stay In Bed") (33rpm 1-sided flexidisc, with insert, free with *Skipping Kitten* fanzine) 5

88 Ediesta CALC CD 069 — Jesus Loves Amerika/Darkness In Zion/Do What You Will/Sub Knature Dub (CD) . 8

89 Moksha SOMA 6CD — You, Me And Everything (Evil Edit)/Reraptyouare (Evil Edit)/ Ed's Bonus Beats (CD, no inlay) 8

(see also Alone Again Or, Stretchheads)

SHAMES
66 CBS 202344 — Sugar And Spice/Ben Franklin's Almanac 30

66 CBS 202450 — I Wanna Meet You/We Could Be Happy 10

67 CBS 2704 — Mr Unreliable/Georgia 10

67 CBS 2929 — It Could Be We're In Love/I Was Lonely When 20

68 CBS 3820 — Greenburg, Glickstein, Charles, David, Smith And Jones/Warm 10

(see also Isaac Guillory)

SHAM 69
77 Step Forward SF 4 — I Don't Wanna/Ulster/Red London (black & white photo p/s) 15

77 Step Forward SF 412 — I Don't Wanna/Ulster/Red London (12", black & white photo p/s) 12

77 Polydor (no cat. no.) — Song Of The Streets/Fanx (1-sided concert freebie, red brick-wall label; white label copies are counterfeits) 25

78 Polydor 2058 966 — Borstal Breakout/Hey Little Rich Boy (p/s) 12

78 Polydor 2059 023 — Angels With Dirty Faces/The Cockney Kids Are Innocent (p/s) 8

78 Polydor 2059 050 — If The Kids Are United/Sunday Morning Nightmare (p/s) 8

79 Step Forward SF 412 — I Don't Wanna/Red London/Ulster (12" reissue, yellow p/s) 8

79 Polydor POSP 64 — Hersham Boys/I Don't Wanna (live)/Tell Us The Truth (live) (p/s) 5

79 Polydor POSPX 64 — Hersham Boys/I Don't Wanna (live)/Rip Off (live)/I'm A Man, I'm A Boy (live)/ Tell Us The Truth (live) (12", p/s) 8

79 Polydor POSP 82 — You're A Better Man Than I/Give A Dog A Bone (p/s) 5

87 Legacy LGY 70 — Ban The Gun/Ban The Gun (withdrawn) 15

79 Polydor POLD 5025 — THE ADVENTURES OF THE HERSHAM BOYS (LP, with 12" EP [2812 045], stickered sleeve) 12

80 Polydor 2383 596 — THE FIRST, THE BEST AND THE LAST (LP, with live EP [RIOT 1/2816 028]) 12

(see also Jimmy Edwards)

SHAMROCKS
65 Polydor BM 56503 — La La La La La/And I Need You 8

SHA NA NA
70 Kama Sutra 2013 010 — Little Darlin'/Teenager In Love 5

71 Kama Sutra 2013 022 — Only One Song/Yakety Yak/Jailhouse Rock 5

72 Kama Sutra 2013 042 — Rock'n'Roll Is Here To Stay/At The Hop/Duke Of Earl/FLAMIN' GROOVIES: Gonna Rock Tonite/Keep A-Knockin' 6

72 Kama Sutra 2013 045 — Sea Cruise/Vote Song 5

70 Buddah 2361 001 — ROCK AND ROLL IS HERE TO STAY (LP) 12

71 Buddah 2319 007 — SHA NA NA (LP) 12

72 Buddah 2319 019 — THE NIGHT IS STILL YOUNG (LP) 12

SHA NA NETTES
75 Disco Demand DDS 114 — Romeo And Juliet/Flint Nit Rock 5

WINSTON SHAN(D)
69 Bullet BU 399 — Throw Me Corn/Darling Remember (B-side actually by Pat Edwards) 7

69 Bullet BU 411 — Matilda (as Wilston Shan)/HARMONIANS: Come To Me 7

70 Moodisc MU 3505 — I'll Run Away/Time Is The Master 7

72 Camel CA 88 — Audrey (as Winston Shan)/So Nice (as Winston Shan) 7

DAVE SHAND & HIS ROCKIN' RHYTHM
56 Oriole CB 1321 — Rockin' The Boat/LIZZIE BORDEN: You Can't Chop Your Poppa Up In Massachusetts (actually by Derek Nimmo) (78) 10

SHANE & SHANE GANG
64 Pye 7N 15662 — Whistle Stop/Who Wrote That Song 15

JOHN SHANE
77 Full Moon — CROSS MY PALM WITH SILVER (LP) 12

VALERIE SHANE
58 Philips PB 833 — When The Boys Talk About The Girls/Careful, Careful 10

58 Philips PB 879 — Meet Me Tonight In Dreamland/One Billion Seven Million Thirty-Three 10

59 Philips PB 929 — Make Love To Me/Baisez-Moi (Kiss Me) 7

59 Philips PB 929 — Make Love To Me/Baisez-Moi (Kiss Me) (78) 5

SHANES
65 Columbia DB 7601 — I Don't Want Your Love/New Orleans 50

SHANGAANS

65 Columbia DB 7551 — Ngenzeni (What Have I Done)/Yeh Girl . . . 10

SHANGRI-LAS

64 Red Bird RB 10008 — Remember (Walking In The Sand)/It's Easier To Cry . . . 8
64 Red Bird RB 10014 — Leader Of The Pack/What Is Love? . . . 10
65 Red Bird RB 10018 — Give Him A Great Big Kiss/Twist And Shout . . . 12
65 Red Bird RB 10025 — Out In The Streets/The Boy . . . 12
65 Red Bird RB 10030 — Give Us Your Blessings/Heaven Only Knows . . . 15
65 Red Bird RB 10036 — Right Now And Not Later/Train From Kansas City . . . 20
66 Red Bird RB 10043 — I Can Never Go Home Anymore/Bulldog . . . 12
66 Red Bird RB 10048 — Long Live Our Love/Sophisticated Boom Boom . . . 15
66 Red Bird RB 10053 — He Cried/Dressed In Black . . . 15
66 Red Bird RB 10068 — Past, Present, And Future/Paradise . . . 18
67 Mercury MF 962 — The Sweet Sound Of Summer/I'll Never Learn . . . 8
67 Mercury MF 979 — Take The Time/Footsteps On The Roof . . . 8
73 Buddah 2011 164 — Give Him A Great Big Kiss/TRADEWINDS: New York Is A Lonely Town/ AD LIBS: The Boy From New York City . . . 5
73 Philips 6051 027 — Train From Kansas City/Past, Present & Future . . . 5
65 Red Bird RB 40 002 — THE SHANGRI-LAS (EP) . . . 75
66 Red Bird RB 40 004 — I CAN NEVER GO HOME ANYMORE (EP, unreleased)
65 Red Bird RB 20 101 — THE SHANGRI-LAS — LEADER OF THE PACK (LP) . . . 60
66 Mercury MCL 20096 — GOLDEN HITS OF THE SHANGRI-LAS (LP) . . . 15

BUD SHANK

56 Vogue V 2376 — Royal Garden Blues/It Had To Be You (with Bill Perkins Quintet) . . . 6
56 Vogue V 2383 — When Your Lover Has Gone/There's A Small Hotel (with Bob Brookmeyer) . . . 6
56 Vogue V 2385 — Shank's Pranks/Left Bank (with Shorty Rogers Quintet) . . . 6
59 Vogue LAE 12248 — LATIN CONTRASTS (LP) . . . 20
66 Fontana STL 5371 — CALIFORNIA DREAMIN' (LP) . . . 12

(see also Shorty Rogers)

ANANDA SHANKAR

69 Reprise RSLP 6398 — ANANDA SHANKAR (JUMPING JACK FLASH) (LP) . . . 200
60s EMI — ANANDA SHANKAR AND HIS MUSIC (LP) . . . 50
71 Reprise K 44092 — ANANDA SHANKAR (LP, reissue) . . . 180

RAVI SHANKAR

66 Fontana TF 712 — Song From The Hills/Dhun . . . 8
72 Apple APPLE 37 — Joi Bangla/Oh Bhaugowan/Raga Mishri-Jhinjhoti (p/s) . . . 18
74 Dark Horse AMS 7133 — I Am Missing You/Lust (as Shankar Family & Friends) . . . 5
59 Vogue VA 160156 — INDIA'S MASTER MUSICIAN (LP) . . . 20
62 HMV ASD 463 — MUSIC OF INDIA (LP) . . . 15
63 Melodisc MLP 12-151 — THE EXCITING MUSIC OF RAVI SHANKAR (LP) . . . 15
65 Fontana TF 5253 — INDIA'S MASTER MUSICIAN (LP, reissue) . . . 15
66 Fontana TL 5285 — PORTRAIT OF GENIUS (LP) . . . 15
66 Fontana TL 5357 — SOUND OF THE SITAR (LP) . . . 15
67 Fontana TL 5424 — IN NEW YORK (LP) . . . 15
67 HMV ASD 2304 — DUETS: RAVI SHANKAR & ALI AKBAR KHAN (LP) . . . 12
67 HMV ASD 2341 — MUSIC OF INDIA NO. 4 (LP) . . . 12
68 HMV ASD 2418 — MUSIC OF INDIA NO. 8 (LP) . . . 12
68 Liberty LBL/LBS 83076 — IMPROVISATIONS (LP) . . . 12
68 Liberty LBL/LBS 83077 — IN CONCERT (LP) . . . 12
68 Liberty LBL/LBS 83078 — INDIA'S MASTER MUSICIAN (LP, 2nd reissue) . . . 12
68 Liberty LBL/LBS 83079 — PORTRAIT OF GENIUS (LP, reissue) . . . 12
68 Liberty LBL/LBS 83080 — SOUND OF THE SITAR (LP, reissue) . . . 12
68 Liberty LBL/LBS 83081 — IN NEW YORK (LP, reissue) . . . 12
68 Columbia S(C)X 6273 — LIVE AT THE MONTEREY POP FESTIVAL (LP) . . . 15
69 Transatlantic TRA 182 — A SITAR RECITAL (LP) . . . 12
69 Transatlantic TRA 183 — DHUN PALAS KAFI (LP, with Ali Akbar Khan) . . . 12
70 Columbia SCX 6382 — RAVI SHANKAR IN SAN FRANCISCO (LP) . . . 12
71 Mushroom 300 MR 8 — FOUR RAGA MOODS (2-LP) . . . 30
72 United Artists UAG 29379 — AT THE WOODSTOCK FESTIVAL (LP) . . . 12
73 Apple SAPDO 1002 — IN CONCERT — 1972 (2-LP, with Ali Akbar Khan, gatefold sleeve) . . . 165
74 Dark Horse AMLH 22002 — SHANKAR FAMILY & FRIENDS (LP) . . . 15
76 Dark Horse AMLH 22007 — RAVI SHANKAR'S MUSIC FESTIVAL FROM INDIA (LP) . . . 20
96 Apple SAPDO 1002 — IN CONCERT — 1972 (2-LP, reissue) . . . 25
96 Apple SAPDO 1002 — IN CONCERT — 1972 (CD) . . . 20

(see also Ali Akbar Khan, Will Sergeant)

BILL SHANKLY

70s Technical TECLP 001A — SHANKS ON SOCCER (2-LP) . . . 30

JOHNNY SHANLY

60 Columbia DB 4425 — This Day I Promise/Makin' Love To You . . . 6
60 Columbia DB 4526 — I Wonder/It Happens That Way . . . 6

DEAN SHANNON

60 HMV POP 820 — Blinded With Love/Jezebel . . . 25
62 HMV POP 1103 — Ubangi Stomp/Blowing Wild . . . 35

DEL SHANNON

SINGLES

61 London HLX 9317 — Runaway/Jody . . . 10
61 London HLX 9317 — Runaway/Jody (mispressed B-side, plays "The Snake" by Maximilian) . . . 30
61 London HLX 9402 — Hats Off To Larry/Don't Gild The Lily, Lily . . . 10
61 London HLX 9462 — So Long Baby/The Answer To Everything . . . 10
62 London HLX 9515 — Hey! Little Girl/You Never Talked About Me . . . 10
62 London HLX 9587 — Cry Myself To Sleep/I'm Gonna Move On . . . 10

MINT VALUE £

62	London HLX 9609	The Swiss Maid/Ginny In The Mirror	7
63	London HLX 9653	Little Town Flirt/The Wamboo	10
63	London HLX 9710	Two Kinds Of Teardrops/Kelly	10
63	London HLX 9761	Two Silhouettes/My Wild One	10
63	London HLU 9800	Sue's Gonna Be Mine/Since She's Gone	10
64	London HLU 9858	That's The Way Love Is/Time Of The Day	10
64	Stateside SS 269	Mary Jane/Stains On My Letter	8
64	Stateside SS 317	Handy Man/Give Her Lots Of Lovin'	8
64	Stateside SS 349	Do You Want To Dance/This Is All I Have To Give	8
65	Stateside SS 368	Keep Searchin' (We'll Follow The Sun)/Broken Promises	7
65	Stateside SS 395	Stranger In Town/Over You	8
65	Stateside SS 430	Break Up/Why Don't You Tell Him	8
65	Stateside SS 452	Move It On Over/She Still Remembers Tony	15
66	Stateside SS 494	I Can't Believe My Ears/I Wish I Wasn't Me Tonight	15
66	Liberty LIB 55866	The Big Hurt/I Got It Bad	12
66	Liberty LIB 55889	For A Little While/Hey Little Star	15
67	Liberty LIB 55939	She/What Makes You Run	15
67	Liberty LIB 10277	Mind Over Matter/Led Along	12
67	Liberty LBF 15020	Runaway '67/Show Me	12
68	Liberty LBF 15061	Thinkin' It Over/Runnin' On Back	15
68	Liberty LBF 15079	Gemini/Magical Musical Box	15
69	Stateside SS 8025	Comin' Back To Me/Sweet Mary Lou	12
70	Stateside SS 8040	Sister Isabelle/Colorado Rain	12
72	United Artists UP 35460	What's A Matter, Baby/Early In The Morning	8
73	United Artists UP 35535	Kelly (live)/Coppersville Yodel	8
74	United Artists UP 35740	And The Music Plays On/In My Arms Again	7
83	Demon D 1017	Cheap Love/Distant Ghost (p/s)	6
83	Demon D 1019	Sea Of Love/Help Me (p/s)	6
EPs			
62	London RE-X 1332	RUNAWAY WITH DEL SHANNON	25
63	London RE-X 1346	DEL SHANNON NO. 2	25
63	London RE-X 1383	DEL'S OWN FAVOURITES	30
63	London RE-X 1387	FROM DEL TO YOU	35
65	Stateside SE 1029	DEL SHANNON'S HITS	35
67	Liberty LEP 2272	THE NEW DEL SHANNON	50
LPs			
61	London HA-X 2402	RUNAWAY WITH DEL SHANNON	50
63	London HA-X 8071	HATS OFF TO DEL SHANNON	40
63	London HA-X 8091	LITTLE TOWN FLIRT	45
65	Stateside SL 10115	HANDY MAN	45
65	Stateside SL 10130	DEL SHANNON SINGS HANK WILLIAMS	40
65	Stateside SL 10140	ONE THOUSAND SIX HUNDRED AND SIXTY-ONE SECONDS WITH DEL SHANNON	40
66	Liberty (S)LBY 1320	THIS IS MY BAG (mono/stereo)	25/30
66	Liberty (S)LBY 1335	TOTAL COMMITMENT (mono/stereo)	25/30
68	Liberty LBL/LBS 83114E	THE FURTHER ADVENTURES OF CHARLES WESTOVER	55
73	United Artists UAS 29474	LIVE IN ENGLAND	18

(see also Maximilian)

LINDA SHANNON

59	Parlophone R 4603	Goodbye Charlie/If You Only Knew	5

MIKE SHANNON & STRANGERS

(see under Strangers)

SHAPE OF THE RAIN

71	RCA Neon NE 1001	Woman/Wasting My Time	7
71	RCA RCA 2129	My Friend John/Yes	5
71	RCA Neon NE 7	RILEY, RILEY, WOOD & WAGGETT (LP, gatefold sleeve)	45

SHAPES

79	Sofa SEAT 1/FRR 004	THE SHAPES (WOT'S FOR LUNCH, MUM?) (EP, no p/s, with insert)	22
79	Good Vibrations GOT 13	Blast Off/Airline Disasters (p/s)	15

SHAPES & SIZES

66	Decca F 12441	A Little Lovin' Somethin'/Rain On My Face	7

HELEN SHAPIRO

SINGLES

61	Columbia DB 4589	Don't Treat Me Like A Child/When I'm With You	6
61	Columbia DB 4670	You Don't Know/Marvellous Lie	6
61	Columbia DB 4715	Walkin' Back To Happiness/Kiss 'N' Run	6
62	Columbia DB 4782	Tell Me What He Said/I Apologise	6
62	Columbia DB 4824	Let's Talk About Love/Sometime Yesterday	7
62	Columbia DB 4869	Little Miss Lonely/I Don't Care	7
62	Columbia DB 4908	Keep Away From Other Girls/Cry My Heart Out	7
63	Columbia DB 4966	Queen For Tonight/Daddy Couldn't Get Me One Of Those	20
63	Columbia DB 7026	Woe Is Me/I Walked Right In	8
63	Columbia DB 7072	Not Responsible/No Trespassing	8
63	Columbia DB 7130	Look Who It Is/Walking In My Dreams	10
64	Columbia DB 7190	Fever/Ole Father Time	15
64	Columbia DB 7266	Look Over Your Shoulder/You Won't Come Home	10
64	Columbia DB 7340	Shop Around/He Knows How To Love Me	60
64	Columbia DB 7395	I Wish I'd Never Loved You/I Was Only Kidding	10
65	Columbia DB 7517	Tomorrow Is Another Day/It's So Funny I Could Cry	10
65	Columbia DB 7587	Here In Your Arms/Only Once	10
65	Columbia DB 7690	Something Wonderful/Just A Line	10
66	Columbia DB 7810	Forget About The Bad Things/Wait A Little Longer	10
66	Columbia DB 8073	In My Calendar/Empty House	10

			MINT VALUE £
67	Columbia DB 8148	Make Me Belong To You/The Way Of The World	10
67	Columbia DB 8256	She Needs Company/Stop And You Will Become Aware	125
68	Pye 7N 17600	You'll Get Me Loving You/Silly Boy (I Love You)	10
69	Pye 7N 17714	Today Has Been Cancelled/Face The Music	10
69	Pye 7N 17785	You've Guessed/Take Me For A While	12
70	Pye 7N 17893	Take Down A Note Miss Smith/Couldn't You See	18
70	Pye 7N 17975	Waiting On The Shores Of Nowhere/A Glass Of Wine	12
83	Oval HELEN 25	Let Yourself Go/Funny (p/s)	5
83	Oval HELEN 25/10	Let Yourself Go/Cry Me A River/Funny (10", p/s)	6
84	Oval OVAL 26	Brickyard Blues/Just Another Weekend (p/s)	6

EPs

61	Columbia SEG 8128	HELEN (mono, 'smiling' or 'cross-armed' sleeve)	each 15
61	Columbia ESG 7872	HELEN (stereo, 'smiling' or 'cross-armed' sleeve)	each 20
61	Columbia SEG 8136	HELEN'S HIT PARADE	15
62	Columbia SEG 8170	A TEENAGER SINGS THE BLUES (also stereo ESG 7880)	20/25
62	Columbia SEG 8174	MORE HITS FROM HELEN	15
62	Columbia SEG 8209	EVEN MORE HITS FROM HELEN	18
63	Columbia SEG 8229	'TOPS' WITH ME NO. 1 (also stereo ESG 7888)	20/30
63	Columbia SEG 8243	'TOPS' WITH ME NO. 2 (also stereo ESG 7891)	20/30

LPs

62	Columbia 33SX 1397	'TOPS' WITH ME (also stereo SCX 3428)	20/40
63	Columbia 33SX 1494	HELEN'S SIXTEEN (also stereo SCX 3470)	35/60
63	Columbia 33SX 1561	HELEN IN NASHVILLE	30
64	Columbia 33SX 1661	HELEN HITS OUT (also stereo SCX 3533)	35/60
65	EMI Encore! ENC 209	12 HITS AND A MISS HELEN SHAPIRO	20
74	Columbia SCX 6565	THE VERY BEST OF HELEN SHAPIRO	12

(see also Ella Stone & Moss)

SHARADES

64	Decca F 11811	Dumb Head/Boy Trouble	75

(see also Ladybirds, Breakaways)

BILLY SHA RAE

71	Action ACT 4602	Do It/Crying Clown	15

(BILLY) SHARI

58	Decca F 11069	Going Home For Christmas/Count Every Star (as Shari)	6
68	United Artists UP 2235	It's So Lonely Being Together/You Walked Out On Me Before	5

SHARKEY & HIS KINGS OF DIXIELAND

57	Capitol CL 14767	Look Sharp, Be Sharp/Sharkey Strut	5
51	Capitol LC 6531	SHARKEY'S SOUTHERN COMFORT (10" LP)	12
53	Capitol LC 6600	MIDNIGHT ON BOURBON STREET (10" LP)	12
54	Melodisc MLP 503	SHARKEY'S KINGS OF DIXIELAND (10" LP)	12

SHARKS

68	RCA RCA 1776	Goodbye Lorene/Funkology	10

(see also Marcisa & Jeff, Roy Richards)

SHARKS

73	Island ILPS 9233	FIRST WATER (LP, 'pink rim palm tree' label with inner sleeve)	12
74	Island ILPS 9271	JAB IT IN YORE EYE (LP, 'palm tree' label with inner sleeve)	12

(see also Chris Spedding, Andy Fraser Band)

RALPH SHARON

53	Decca LF 1107	SPRING FEVER (10" LP)	12
53	Decca LF 1138	AUTUMN LEAVES (10" LP)	30
53	Lyragon AF 1	COCKTAIL TIME (10" LP)	15

(see also Tony Bennett)

SHARONS

70	Emblem JDR 325	SOMEONE TO TURN TO (LP, Irish only)	120

SHARP

86	Unicorn-Kanchana PHZ 5	Entertain Me/So Say Hurrah (The Emperor's New Clothes) (p/s)	5

(see also Jam)

BOBBY SHARP & OTHERS

65	Stateside SS 404	Blues For Mr. Charlie (Parts 1 & 2) (with Paul Sindap, Joe Lee Wilson & Little Butler)	10

DEE DEE SHARP

62	Columbia DB 4818	Mashed Potato Time/Set My Heart At Ease	15
62	Columbia DB 4874	Gravy (For My Mashed Potatoes)/Baby Cakes	15
62	Cameo Parkway C 230	Ride/Night	10
63	Cameo Parkway C 244	Do The Bird/Lover Boy	15
63	Cameo Parkway C 260	Rock Me In The Cradle Of Love/You'll Never Be Mine	20
63	Cameo Parkway C 274	Wild/Why Doncha Ask Me	10
65	Cameo Parkway C 375	I Really Love You/Standing In The Need Of Love	50
65	Cameo Parkway C 382	It's A Funny Situation/There Ain't Nothing I Wouldn't Do (demo-only)	110
66	Atlantic 584 056	My Best Friend's Man/Bye Bye Baby	15
69	Action ACT 4522	What Kind Of Lady/You're Gonna Miss Me	30
79	London HA-U 8514	CAMEO PARKWAY SESSIONS (LP)	20

(see also Chubby Checker & Dee Dee Sharp)

STEVE SHARP & THE CLEANCUTS

80	Happy Face MM 122	We Are The Mods/He Wants To Be A Mod	125

(see also Rowdies)

RAY SHARPE

59	London HLW 8932	Linda Lu/Red Sails In The Sunset (triangular or round centre)	50/40
59	London HLW 8932	Linda Lu/Red Sails In The Sunset (78)	25
63	United Artists UP 1032	Hey Little Girl/Day You Left Me	15

MINT VALUE £

ROCKY SHARPE & THE REPLAYS
82	Chiswick DICE 9	Heart/Mary (Won't You Marry Me) (withdrawn, approx. 100 only)	10

SHARPE & NUMAN
85	Polydor POSPP 722	Change Your Mind/Remix, Remake, Remodel (picture disc)	8
85	Polydor POSPX 722	Change Your Mind (Extended Mix)/Remix, Remake, Remodel/Fools In A World Of Fire (12", picture disc)	8
86	Numa NU 19	New Thing From London Town/Time To Die (p/s, 1,000 autographed)	6
86	Numa NUM 19	New Thing From London Town/Time To Die (12", picture disc)	8
88	Polydor POSP B/W/T 894	No More Lies/Voices (p/s, blue, white or clear vinyl)	5
88	Polydor POCD 894	No More Lies (Extended Mix)/Voices/Change Your Mind/ No More Lies (7" Version) (CD, card sleeve, some autographed)	12/10
89	Polydor POPB 43	I'm On Automatic/No More Lies ('89 Remix) (poster p/s)	5
89	Polydor POPD 43	I'm On Automatic/Love Like A Ghost (picture disc)	6
89	Polydor PZPD 43	I'm On Automatic (Extended Mix)/Love Like A Ghost (12", picture disc)	8
89	Polydor PZCD 43	I'm On Automatic (12" Remix)/Love Like A Ghost/Voices ('89 Remix) (CD)	10
89	Polydor 839 520-0	AUTOMATIC (CD, with bonus tracks "No More Lies" [12" Version] & "I'm On Automatic" [12" Version])	20

(see also Gary Numan)

SHARPEES
66	Stateside SS 495	Tired Of Being Lonely/Just To Please You	50
73	President PT 389	Do The 45/Make Up Your Mind	10
73	President PT 399	Tired Of Being Lonely/Just To Please You (reissue)	10

BOB SHARPLES & HIS (DANCE) MUSIC/ORCHESTRA
55	Decca F 10450	Capitano/Time Remembered	7
56	Decca F 10707	Hurricane Boogie/Concetta	6
56	Decca F 10748	The Portuguese Washerwoman/Sadie's Shawl	5

SHARPS
57	Vogue V 9086	Lock My Heart/Love Is Here To Stay	750
57	Vogue V 9086	Lock My Heart/Love Is Here To Stay (78)	110
58	Vogue V 9096	Shufflin'/What Will I Gain	750
58	Vogue V 9096	Shufflin'/What Will I Gain (78)	110

(see also Thurston Harris)

S-HATERS
81	Outer Himmilayan OHR 02	Death Of A Vampire/Research (p/s)	6
81	Outer Himmilayan OHR 05	STORIES AS COLD AS THE IRISH SEA (EP, foldover p/s)	5

SHAVED FISH
87	Antar ANTAR 4501	Two Minutes Silence/Two Minutes Silence (Demo Version) (p/s)	5

SHAVERS, GETZ, COLE, NORVO, BELLSON, MILLER, etc
52	Vogue V 2104	Charlie Got Rhythm Parts 1 & 2 (78)	10

ADRIAN SHAW
96	Woronzow W0027	TEA FOR THE HYDRA (LP, 299 copies only, in hand-finished sleeves)	15

(see also Hawkwind, Bevis Frond)

ARTIE SHAW
54	MGM EPC 3	ARTIE SHAW (EP, export issue)	8
54	Brunswick LA 8677	SPEAK TO ME OF LOVE (10" LP)	15
55	Columbia Clef 33C 9006	ARTIE SHAW AND HIS GRAMERCY FIVE (10" LP)	15
58	RCA RD 27065	ANY OLD TIME (LP)	12

GEORGIE SHAW
55	Brunswick 05356	Give Me The Right/Yearning (Just For You)	6
55	Brunswick 05362	Unsuspecting Heart/Let Me Go, Devil	6
55	Brunswick 05426	I'll Step Aside/The Water Tumbler Tune	6
55	Brunswick 05476	Banjo Woogie/I Can Tell	7

(see also Kitty Kallen)

MARLENA SHAW
67	Chess CRS 8054	Mercy Mercy Mercy/Go Away Little Boy	12
73	United Artists UP 35517	Last Tango In Paris/Save The Children	5
76	United Artists UP 36125	It's Better Than Walking Out/Be For Real	5
76	Blue Note UP 36163	Love Has Gone Away/No Hiding Place	5
77	CBS 5550	Go Away Little Boy/Look At Me Look At You	5

NINA SHAW
68	CBS 3239	Woven In My Soul/Love So Fine	7
68	CBS 3556	From Now Till Then/Window Of My Mind	5
69	CBS 3943	Stop The Music/Celebration Of The Year	5
69	CBS 4227	One Fine Day/Somewhere In The World	5
69	CBS 4673	In One Hour/I Will Come To You	5

RICKY SHAW
62	London HLU 9606	No Love But Your Love/Be Still, Be Still, My Own	10

ROLAND SHAW ORCHESTRA
54	Decca F 10407	No One But You (with Kim Bennett)/The High And The Mighty	8
55	Decca F 10449	Softly, Softly (with Kim Bennett)/A Trumpeter's Lullaby	8
50s	Decca F 10758	Trails End/You're Only Young Once	8
67	Decca F 12595	The Look Of Love/Have No Fear, Mr Bond Is Here	5
64	Decca DFE 8573	RIDERS IN THE SKY (EP)	10
66	Decca DFE 8657	THE IPCRESS FILE (EP, with the Ivor Raymond Orchestra)	8
66	Decca DFE 8670	I SPY (EP)	10
65	Decca LK 4730	JAMES BOND IN ACTION (LP)	25
66	Decca LK 4765	THEMES FOR SECRET AGENTS (LP, mono)	22
66	Phase 4 Stereo PFS 4094	THEMES FOR SECRET AGENTS (LP, stereo)	22
67	Phase 4 Stereo PFS 4125	MORE JAMES BOND IN ACTION (LP)	22

MINT VALUE £

60s London BSP — DIAMONDS ARE FOREVER (LP, gatefold sleeve) . . . 22
60s Decca — THE LOOK OF LOVE (LP) . . . 12
71 Decca Phase 4 SPA 158 — THE WORLD OF JAMES BOND ADVENTURE (LP) . . . 12
72 Decca Phase 4 SPA 213 — PHASE 4 WORLD OF SPY THRILLERS (LP) . . . 12

SANDIE SHAW

SINGLES

64 Pye 7N 15671 — As Long As You're Happy Baby/Ya-Ya-Da-Da . . . 30
64 Pye 7N 15704 — (There's) Always Something There To Remind Me/Don't You Know . . . 5
64 Pye 7N 15743 — I'd Be Far Better Off Without You/Girl Don't Come . . . 5
65 Pye 7N 15783 — I'll Stop At Nothing/You Can't Blame Him . . . 5
65 Pye 7N 15841 — Long Live Love/I've Heard About Him . . . 5
65 Pye 7N 15940 — Message Understood/Don't You Count On It . . . 5
65 Pye 7N 15987 — How Can You Tell/If Ever You Need Me . . . 6
66 Pye 7N 17036 — Tomorrow/Hurting You . . . 5
66 Pye 7N 17086 — Nothing Comes Easy/Stop Before You Start . . . 5
66 Pye 7N 17163 — Run/Long Walk Home . . . 6
66 Pye 7N 17212 — Think Sometimes About Me/Hide All Emotion . . . 6
67 Pye 7N 17239 — I Don't Need Anything/Keep In Touch . . . 6
67 Pye 7N 17272 — Puppet On A String/Tell The Boys (pink label, later blue) . . . 5/6
67 Pye 7N 17346 — Tonight In Tokyo/You've Been Seeing Her Again . . . 6
67 Pye 7N 17378 — You've Not Changed/Make Me Cry . . . 6
68 Pye 7N 17441 — Today/London (pink label, later blue) . . . each 6
68 Pye 7N 17504 — Don't Run Away/Stop . . . 6
68 Pye 7N 17564 — Show Me/One More Life . . . 6
68 Pye 7N 17587 — Together/Turn On The Sunshine . . . 6
68 Pye 7N 17611 — Those Were The Days/Make It Go . . . 6
69 Pye 7N 17675 — Monsieur Dupont/Voice In The Crowd . . . 5
69 Pye 7N 17726 — Think It All Over/Send Me A Letter . . . 6
69 Pye 7N 17821 — Heaven Knows I'm Missing Him Now/So Many Things To Do . . . 6
70 Pye 7N 17894 — By Tomorrow/Maple Village . . . 6
70 Pye 7N 17954 — Wight Is Wight/That's The Way He's Made . . . 6
71 Pye 7N 45040 — Rose Garden/Maybe I'm Amazed . . . 6
71 Pye 7N 45073 — The Power And The Glory/Dear Madame . . . 6
72 Pye 7N 45118 — Where Did They Go/Look At Me . . . 6
72 Pye 7N 45164 — Father And Son/Pity The Ship . . . 6
77 CBS 5371 — One More Night/Still So Young . . . 6
77 Epic EPC 5513 — Just A Disillusion/Your Mama Wouldn't Like It . . . 6
82 Virgin VS 484 — Anyone Who Had A Heart/Anyone Who Had A Heart (instrumental) (p/s) . . . 12
84 Rough Trade RTT 130 — Hand In Glove/I Don't Owe You Anything/Jeanne (12", p/s, with The Smiths) . . . 8
88 Rough RTT 220CD — Please Help The Cause Against Loneliness/Jeanne/Lover Of The Century/ I Will Remain (Alternative Mix) (CD) . . . 15
88 Rough RTT 230CD — Nothing Less Than Brilliant (Remix)/I Don't Owe You Anything/ Where Were You/I Love Peace (CD) . . . 15

EPs

64 Pye NEP 24208 — (THERE'S) ALWAYS SOMETHING THERE TO REMIND ME . . . 20
65 Pye NEP 24220 — LONG LIVE LOVE . . . 20
65 Pye NEP 24232 — TALK ABOUT LOVE . . . 20
65 Pye NEP 24234 — SANDIE . . . 20
66 Pye NEP 24236 — MESSAGE UNDERSTOOD . . . 20
66 Pye NEP 24247 — TOMORROW . . . 25
66 Pye NEP 24254 — NOTHING COMES EASY . . . 22
66 Pye NEP 24264 — RUN WITH SANDIE SHAW . . . 22
67 Pye NEP 24271 — SANDIE SHAW IN FRENCH . . . 40
67 Pye NEP 24273 — SANDIE SHAW IN ITALIAN . . . 40
67 Pye NEP 24281 — TELL THE BOYS . . . 25

LPs

65 Pye NPL 18110 — SANDIE SHAW . . . 25
65 Pye NPL 18122 — ME . . . 25
66 Golden Guinea GGL 0360 — THE GOLDEN HITS OF SANDIE SHAW . . . 15
67 Golden Guinea GGL 0378 — SANDIE SINGS . . . 15
67 Pye N(S)PL 18182 — PUPPET ON A STRING . . . 22
67 Pye N(S)PL 18205 — LOVE ME, PLEASE LOVE ME . . . 22
68 Marble Arch MAL(S) 781 — THE GOLDEN HITS OF SANDIE SHAW . . . 12
68 Pye N(S)PL 18232 — THE SANDIE SHAW SUPPLEMENT . . . 22
69 Pye N(S)PL 18323 — REVIEWING THE SITUATION . . . 35

SANDY SHAW

58 Starlite ST45 007 — Hello, Goodbye/TERRY TAYLOR: The Only Way . . . 6

THOMAS SHAW

72 Xtra XTRA 1132 — THOMAS SHAW (LP) . . . 15

TIMMY SHAW & STERNPHONES

64 Pye International 7N 25239 — Gonna Send You Back To Georgia/I'm A Lonely Guy . . . 25

TREVOR SHAW

81 CMS PR 26 — WHEELS IN MOTION (LP) . . . 20

DOROTHY SHAY

53 Capitol LC 6618 — THE PARK AVENUE HILLBILLIE (10" LP) . . . 12

SHE

85 Neat NEAT 50 — Never Surrender/Breaking Away (p/s) . . . 5
85 Neat NEAT 5012 — Never Surrender/Breaking Away/On My Way (12", p/s) . . . 8

LEE SHEARIN

50 London L 695 — Give A Broken Heart A Chance To Cry/I Need You (78) . . . 6

MINT VALUE £

GEORGE SHEARING (QUINTET)

53	MGM SP 1006	I'll Remember April/Jumping With Symphony Sid	5
53	MGM SP 1017	There's A Lull In My Life/Bassic English	5
53	MGM SP 1031	Night Flight/Love (Your Magic Spell Is Everywhere) (B-side with Teddi King)	5
53	MGM SP 1035	How High The Moon/So This Is Cuba	5
53	MGM SP 1046	Body And Soul/The Lady Is A Tramp	5
53	MGM SP 1047	Love Is Just Around The Corner/Point And Counterpoint	5
54	MGM SP 1066	Tiempo De Cencerro (both sides)	5
54	MGM SP 1080	Rap Your Troubles In Drums/Love Is Here To Stay	5
54	MGM SP 1090	Spring Is Here/Easy To Love	5
54	MGM SP 1103	Mambo Inn/I've Never Been In Love Before	5
56	MGM SP 1113	Lullaby Of Birdland/Get Off My Bach	6
56	MGM SP 1161	I'll Never Smile Again/If You Were The Only Girl In The World	5
56	MGM SP 1171	I Wished On The Moon/It's Easy To Remember (with Teddi King)	5
56	Vogue V 2043	Cherokee/Four Bars Short	5
62	Capitol CL 15269	Baubles, Bangles And Beads/Cocktails For Two	5
54	MGM EPC 4	GEORGE SHEARING (EP, export issue)	8
56	MGM EP 563	WHEN LIGHTS ARE LOW (EP)	8
50s	London BEP 6029	PIANOLOGY (EP, export issue)	8
50s	London BEP 6030	THE GEORGE SHEARING TRIO (EP, export issue)	8
50s	London BEP 6031	THE GEORGE SHEARING TRIO (EP, export issue)	8
57	Vogue EPV 1145	THE GEORGE SHEARING QUINTET (EP)	8
59	MGM MGM EP 708	I'LL BE AROUND (EP)	8
51	Decca LF 1036	THE NEARNESS OF YOU (10" LP, as George Shearing Trio)	12
52	MGM MGM-D 103	YOU'RE HEARING GEORGE SHEARING (10" LP)	12
53	MGM MGM-D 118	I HEAR MUSIC (10" LP)	12
54	MGM MGM-D 129	TOUCH OF GENIUS (10" LP)	12
56	Vogue LDE 188	THE VERY FIRST SESSION (10" LP)	12
56	Capitol LC 6803	THE SHEARING SPELL (10" LP)	12
59	Capitol T/ST 1275	LATIN AFFAIR (LP)	12
62	MGM C 912	SOFT AND SILKY (LP)	12
75	MPS/BASF BAP 5059	THE WAY WE ARE (LP)	15

(see also Peggy Lee)

SHEDS

85	John Wayne's S/bags 1	BIMBO EP (cassette, shrinkwrapped with free packet of tomato seeds)	7

(see also Super 8)

SHED SEVEN

94	Polydor YORKX 1	Mark/Casino Girl/Mobile 10 (12", p/s)	12
94	Polydor YORKCD 1	Mark/Casino Girl/Mobile 10 (CD)	8
94	Polydor YORKX 2	Dolphin/Immobilise/Dolphin (Remix) (12", p/s)	8
94	Polydor YORK 3	Speakeasy (p/s, blue vinyl)	5
94	Polydor YORK 4	Ocean Pie/Never Again (clear vinyl, p/s)	5
95	Polydor YORK 5	Where Have You Been Tonight/Swing My Wave (gatefold sleeve, green vinyl)	5
96	Polydor 576 214-7	Going For Gold/Making Waves (withdrawn 'nude' gatefold p/s, some without disc)	15/8
96	Polydor 5762147	Going For Gold/Making Waves (gold vinyl, numbered sleeve)	5
96	Polydor 5765967	BULLY BOY (EP, orange vinyl, gatefold sleeve, numbered)	5
98	Polydor 5695432	She Left Me On Friday/Mispent Youth/You (CD)	8

BOBBY SHEEN

66	Capitol CL 15455	Dr. Love/Sweet, Sweet Love (demos more common)	150/100
72	Capitol CL 15713	Dr. Love/Sweet, Sweet Love (reissue)	15

(see also Bob B. Soxx & Blue Jeans)

SHEEP (U.K.)

73	Myrrh MYR 1000	SHEEP (LP, with insert)	30

(see also Lonesome Stone)

SHEEP (U.S.)

66	Stateside SS 493	Hide And Seek/Twelve Months Later	25
69	Stateside SS 2147	Hide And Seek/HAWKS: The Grissle	12

IREEN SHEER

70	Bell BLL 1129	Hey Pleasure Man/You Walked Away	5
71	Parlophone R 5930	Many Rivers/Is It Me	5
74	Polydor 2041 533	Bye Bye I Love You/Roseberry Avenue	6

SHEER KHAN

84	SRT 4KS 140	Last Generation/Lady's Dance (p/s)	70
85	Mill	QUIET ENOUGH FOR LOVE (LP)	30

SHEFFIELDS

64	Pye 7N 15600	It Must Be Love/Say Girl	50
64	Pye 7N 15627	I Got My Mojo Working/Hey Hey Lover Boy	70
65	Pye 7N 15767	Bag's Groove (Skat Walking)/Plenty Of Love	75

SHEGUI

84	Highway SHP 105	IN THE WIND (LP, with lyric insert)	12

SHEIKS (U.K.)

66	Parlophone R 5500	Missing You/Tell Me Bird	8

SHEIKS (U.S.)

59	London HLW 9012	Très Chic/Little French Doll	15
59	London HLW 9012	Très Chic/Little French Doll (78)	40

SHEILA & JENNY

64	Ember EMB S 3202	When The Boy's Happy/Please Don't Break Her Heart (some in p/s)	10/6

ERNIE SHELBY

73	Mojo 2093 026	Bend Over Backwards/Punish Me	5

MINT VALUE £

ALLEN SHELDON

70 Plexium PXM 14 Mirror Of My Mind/Old Windmill Tree 20

DOUG SHELDON

61 Decca F 11368 The Book Of Love/Play Me The Blues 10
61 Decca F 11398 Runaround Sue/Come With Me 10
61 Decca F 11416 Your Ma Said You Cried In Your Sleep/You're Only Fooling Yourself 10
62 Decca F 11433 My Kingdom For A Girl/You Never Had It So Good 10
62 Decca F 11463 A Big Big Baby/If You'd Be Mine 10
62 Decca F 11514 Lollipops And Roses/One Way To Say Goodbye 10
62 Decca F 11529 Live Now Pay Later/Me 7
63 Decca F 11564 I Saw Linda Yesterday/My Billy 8
63 Decca F 11654 Let's Make A Habit Of This/I Was Alone 8
63 Decca F 11790 Mickey's Monkey/Falling In Love With Love 10
65 Sue WI 332 Take It Like A Man/Lonely Boy 18
65 Pye 7N 17011 It's Because Of You/How Can I Tell Her? 7
63 Decca DFE 8527 HERE I STAND (EP) 75

SANDI SHELDON

76 Epic EPC 4186 You're Gonna Make Me Love You/Baby You're Mine 12

SHELL

66 Columbia DB 8082 Goodbye Little Girl/Little Bit Of Lovin' 12

SHELLEY

64 Pye 7N 15711 I Will Be Wishing/Why Don't You Say You Love Me 12
65 Pye 7N 15773 Stairway To A Star/I Heard A Whisper 8
65 Pye 7N 15913 Where Has Your Smile Gone/Paradise 8

LIZ SHELLEY

65 Brunswick 05940 Make Me Your Baby/You Made Me Hurt 10
66 Brunswick 05953 No More Love/I Can't Find You 10

PETE SHELLEY

82 Lyntone 10952/53 Qu'est-Ce Que C'est, Qu'est Que Ça (Dub)/ANIMAL MAGNET: More (hard vinyl test pressing, numbered, some with info sheet/letter) 15/12
80 Groovy STP 2 SKY YEN (mini-LP) 18
(see also Buzzcocks, Free Agents, Tiller Boys)

SHELLS

61 London HLU 9288 Baby, Oh Baby/Angel Eyes 50
62 London HLU 9644 It's A Happy Holiday/Deep In My Heart 40

ALAN SHELLY & MANU DIBANGO'S BROTHERS

69 Philips BF 1709 Lady Black Wife/Give Me Time 12

ANNE SHELTON

78s

54 HMV B 10732 Juke Box Rag/Love Him So Much I Could Scream 8
58 Philips PB 852 Volare/Do You Love Me Like You Kiss Me? 8
58 Philips PB 878 Hurry Home/I.T.A.L.Y. (I Trust And Love You) 8
59 Philips PB 969 The Village Of St. Bernadette/You're Not Living In Vain 15

45s

53 HMV 7M 164 Answer Me (Mutterlein)/The Bridge Of Sighs 15
54 HMV 7M 186 The Book/Why Does It Have To Be Me 15
54 HMV 7M 197 Cross Over The Bridge/(O Baby Mine) I Get So Lonely 15
54 HMV 7M 240 Goodnight, Well It's Time To Go/If I Give My Heart To You 15
54 HMV 7M 279 My Gypsy Heart/Teach Me Tonight 15
57 Philips JK 1012 Absent Friends/Seven Ages Of Man (jukebox issue) 18
58 Philips PB 779 Until They Sail/Ha! Ha! Ha! 8
58 Philips PB 815 The Girl He Left Behind/Sail Along, Silv'ry Moon 8
58 Philips PB 852 Volare/Do You Love Me Like You Kiss Me? 8
58 Philips PB 878 Hurry Home/I.T.A.L.Y. (I Trust And Love You) 8
59 Philips PB 920 Just Love Me/Could I Love You More 7
59 Philips PB 956 Now Hear This!/To Love And Be Loved 7
59 Philips PB 969 The Village Of St. Bernadette/You're Not Living In Vain 7
60 Philips PB 994 The Angels' Lullaby/Where Can I Go 7
60 Philips PB 1042 Papa Loves Mama/Come Back Again 7
61 Philips PB 1096 Sailor/A Souvenir Of Ireland (some with p/s) 10/6
61 Philips PB 1165 Don't Forget/Aidios, My Love 5
66 Philips BF 1464 The Carnival Is Closed Today/The Sounds Of Summer 5

EPs

50s London BEP 6043 ANNE SHELTON WITH ORCHESTRAL ACCOMPANIMENT (export issue) 12
56 Decca DFE 6321 FOUR STANDARDS 15
56 Philips BBE 12090 ANNE SHELTON 12
58 Philips BBE 12169 THE SHELTON SOUND 12
58 Philips BBE 12205 ITALIAN TOUCH 12
58 Philips BBE 12218 ANNE SHELTON 12
59 Philips BBE 12292 JUST LOVE ME 12
60 Philips BBE 12344 SONGS OF FAITH 12
60 Philips BBE 12347 MY YIDDISHE MOMMA (also stereo SBBE 9003) 12/15
61 Philips BBE 12430 FAVOURITES 12
62 Philips BBE 12526 SPRING FEVER 12

LPs

52 Decca LF 1023 FAVOURITES (10") 35
53 Decca LF 1106 FAVOURITES VOL. 2 (10") 35
57 Philips BBL 7188 THE SHELTON SOUND 25
59 Philips BBL 7291 SONGS FROM THE HEART 22
60 Philips BBL 7393 ANNE SHELTON SHOWCASE 25
62 Philips BBL 7541 A SOUVENIR OF IRELAND (also stereo SBBL 664) 18/22
62 Ace Of Clubs ACL 1101 ANNE 15

MINT VALUE £

JO SHELTON

59	Top Rank JAR 124	Tread Softly (You're Stepping On My Heart)/More, More, More Romancing	8
59	Top Rank JAR 124	Tread Softly (You're Stepping On My Heart)/More, More, More Romancing (78)	8
59	Top Rank JAR 245	If There Are Stars In My Eyes/I Need Your Arms Around Me	8

ROSCOE SHELTON

65	Sue WI 354	Strain On My Heart/Question (A- & B-side labels reversed)	25

CAROL SHELYNE

65	Liberty LIB 55794	The Girl With The Horn Rim Glasses/Boys Do Make Passes At Girls Who Wear Glasses	7

DEANNA SHENDEREY

65	Decca F 12090	Comin' Home Baby/I've Got That Feeling	8

SHENLEY (Duffas) & ANNETTE

61	Blue Beat BB 72	Million Dollar Baby/The First Time I Met You	25

SHENLEY (Duffas) & HYACINTH (Brown)

66	Rio R 80	The World Is On A Wheel/ROY & CORNELL: Salvation	20

(see also Baba Brooks)

SHENLEY (Duffas) & (Little) LUNAN

65	Rio R 52	Something On Your Mind/The Rain Came Tumbling Down	20

(see also Shenley Duffas)

SHEP & LIMELITES

61	Pye International 7N 25090	Daddy's Home/This I Know	100
61	Pye International 7N 25112	Ready For Your Love/You'll Be Sorry	80

JEAN SHEPARD

53	Capitol CL 13986	A Dear John Letter/I'd Rather Die Young	6
59	Capitol CL 15031	Jeopardy/Better Love Next Time	6
56	Capitol EAP 1030	SONGS OF A LOVE AFFAIR NO. 1 (EP)	10
56	Capitol EAP2 728	SONGS OF A LOVE AFFAIR NO. 2 (EP)	10
60	Capitol T 1253	THIS IS JEAN SHEPARD (LP)	15

BILLY SHEPHARD

59	Felstad AF 117	You Call Everybody Darling/Somebody Stole My Gal	5
59	Felstad AF 117	You Call Everybody Darling/Somebody Stole My Gal (78)	10

BILL SHEPHERD ORCHESTRA

58	Pye Nixa 7N 15137	Big Guitar/Tequila	7
58	Pye Nixa N 15137	Big Guitar/Tequila (78)	8
59	Pye Nixa 7N 15180	"Inn Of The 6th Happiness" Theme/DR. BARNARDO'S CHILDREN: This Old Man	5
59	Pye Nixa N 15180	"Inn Of The 6th Happiness" Theme/DR. BARNARDO'S CHILDREN: This Old Man (78)	6

PAULINE SHEPHERD

57	Columbia DB 4010	Love Me To Pieces/Just Between You And Me	12

SHEPHERD BOYS (& GIRLS)

56	Columbia SCM 5282	Little Girls And Little Boys/Teenage Love (as Shepherd Boys & Girls)	8
56	Columbia DB 3793	Little Girls And Little Boys/Teenage Love (as Shepherd Boys & Girls) (78)	8
56	Columbia DB 3816	Summer Sweetheart/Song For A Summer Night	6

SHEPHERD/SHEPPARD SISTERS

57	HMV POP 411	Alone (Why Must I Be Alone)/Congratulations To Someone	10
57	HMV POP 411	Alone (Why Must I Be Alone)/Congratulations To Someone (78)	8
58	Mercury 7MT 196	Gettin' Ready For Freddy/Best Thing There Is (Is Love) (as Sheppard Sisters)	15
58	Mercury MT 196	Gettin' Ready For Freddy/Best Thing There Is (Is Love) (78)	10
58	Mercury 7MT 218	Eating Pizza/A Boy And A Girl (as Sheppard Sisters)	10
58	Mercury MT 218	Eating Pizza/A Boy And A Girl (as Sheppard Sisters) (78)	6
58	Mercury AMT 1005	Dancing Baby/Is It A Crime?	7
58	Mercury AMT 1005	Dancing Baby/Is It A Crime? (78)	6
63	London HLK 9681	Don't Mention My Name/What Makes Little Girls Cry	20
63	London HLK 9758	Talk Is Cheap/Greatest Lover	15

TOM SHEPLEY'S BAND

78	Tradition TSR 031	HOW DO YOU DO? (LP)	15

ARCHIE SHEPP

66	HMV CLP/CSD 3524	FOUR FOR TRANE (LP)	25
66	HMV CLP/CSD 3561	ON THIS NIGHT (LP)	20
67	HMV CLP/CSD 3600	LIVE IN SAN FRANCISCO (LP)	15
67	Polydor 623 235	ARCHIE SHEPP AND THE NEW YORK CONTEMPORARY FIVE (LP)	12
67	Fontana 681 014 ZL	RUFUS (LP, with John Tchicai)	12
68	Impulse MIPL/SIPL 508	MAMA TOO TIGHT (LP)	12
68	Polydor 623 267	NEW YORK CONTEMPORARY FIVE VOL. 2 (LP)	12
69	Impulse MILP/SIPL 512	THE MAGIC OF JU-JU (LP)	12
69	Impulse MIPL/SIPL 516	THE WAY AHEAD (LP)	12
69	Atlantic 583 732	ONE FOR THE TRANE (LP)	12
69	Impulse SIPL 520	THREE FOR A QUARTER, ONE FOR A DIME (LP)	12

(see also John Coltrane)

SHEPPARDS

71	Jay Boy BOY 30	How Do You Like It/Stubborn Heart	35

SHEPPERTON FLAMES

69	Deram DM 257	Take Me For What I Am/Goodbye	45

(see also Mike Berry)

SHERE KHAN

69	Tepee TPR 1007	Little Louise/No Reason	100+

MINT VALUE £

SHERIDAN
70 Gemini GMS 001 — Follow Me Follow/When Love Breaks Your Heart . . . 15
(see also Sheridan-Price, Mike Sheridan & Night Riders, Mike Sheridan's Lot)

DANI SHERIDAN
66 Planet PLF 106 — Guess I'm Dumb/Songs Of Love . . . 30

MIKE SHERIDAN & NIGHT RIDERS
63 Columbia DB 7141 — Tell Me What'cha Gonna Do/No Other Guy . . . 30
63 Columbia DB 7183 — Please Mr. Postman/In Love . . . 30
64 Columbia DB 7302 — What A Sweet Thing That Was/Fabulous . . . 20
65 Columbia DB 7462 — Here I Stand/Lonely Weekends . . . 20
84 Edsel ED 120 — BIRMINGHAM BEAT (LP) . . . 12
(see also Roy Wood, Idle Race, Mike Sheridan's Lot, Nightriders, Sheridan-Price, Sight & Sound)

MIKE SHERIDAN'S LOT
65 Columbia DB 7677 — Take My Hand/Make Them Understand . . . 30
66 Columbia DB 7798 — Don't Turn Your Back On Me, Babe/Stop, Look, Listen . . . 22
(see also Roy Wood, Idle Race, Mike Sheridan & Night Riders, Nightriders, Sheridan-Price, Sight & Sound)

TONY SHERIDAN & THE BEAT BROTHERS
64 Polydor NH 52315 — Jambalaya/Will You Still Love Me Tomorrow (with The Beat Brothers) . . . 15
64 Polydor NH 52927 — Skinny Minny/You'd Better Move On (with The Beat Brothers) . . . 15
75 Buk BU 3026 — Lonely/I Should Have Stayed (solo) . . . 5
(see also Bobby Patrick Big Six, Beat Brothers, Pete Best Four)

TONY SHERIDAN & THE BEATLES
(see under The Beatles)

SHERIDAN-PRICE
70 Gemini GMS 009 — Sometimes I Wonder (as Sheridan & Rick Price)/SHERIDAN: Lightning Never Strikes Twice . . . 20
70 Gemini GME 1002 — THIS IS TO CERTIFY THAT... (LP, gatefold sleeve) . . . 25
(see also Rick Price, Mike Sheridan & Nightriders, Mike Sheridan's Lot, Idle Race, Sight & Sound, Sheridan)

ROGER SHERLOCK
78 Inchecronin INC 7419 — MEMORIES OF SLIGO (LP) . . . 12

ALLAN SHERMAN
63 Warner Bros WB 106 — Hello Muddah Hello Faddah/Rat Fink . . . 5
64 Warner Bros WEP 6148 — YOUR MOTHER'S HERE TO STAY (EP) . . . 12

JOE SHERMAN
58 Fontana H 129 — Miraculous Music Box/Make Me Laugh . . . 7
58 Fontana H 129 — Miraculous Music Box/Make Me Laugh (78) . . . 6
58 Fontana H 147 — Buttermilk/Please Don't Say Goodnight . . . 7
58 Fontana H 147 — Buttermilk/Please Don't Say Goodnight (78) . . . 6

BILLY SHERRILL
61 Mercury AMT 1131 — Like Making Love/Rules Of The Game . . . 6

SHERRYS
62 London HLW 9625 — Pop Pop Pop-Pie/Your Hand In Mine . . . 20
63 London HL 9686 — Let's Stomp Again/Slop Time . . . 20
63 London RE 1363 — DO THE POPEYE (EP) . . . 100

SHERWOOD
86 Sherwood SRT6KL 901 — RIDING THE RAINBOW (12" EP) . . . 50

BOBBY SHERWOOD
55 Vogue Coral Q 72097 — The Kentuckian Song/Far Away Places . . . 6

HOLLY SHERWOOD
71 Bell BLL 1180 — Day By Day/Great Golden Day . . . 5

ROBERTA SHERWOOD
56 Brunswick 05572 — Lazy River/This Train . . . 10
57 Brunswick 05654 — Tears Don't Care Who Cries Them/You're Nobody Till Somebody Loves You . . . 7
57 Brunswick 05670 — Mary Lou/What Does It Matter . . . 7
57 Brunswick 05670 — Mary Lou/What Does It Matter (78) . . . 6
63 Stateside SS 154 — You Always Hurt The One You Love/In San Francisco . . . 6
63 Stateside SL 10039 — ON STAGE (LP) . . . 18

TONY SHERWOOD TRIO
60s Zodiac ZR 010 — Piano Boogie Twist/Tom Dooley . . . 15

SHERWOODS
61 Pye International 7N 25097 — Nanette/El Scorpion . . . 12

SHERWOODS
64 Solar SRP 105 — Memories/Some Other Time . . . 10

SHERWOODS
67 Major Minor MM 516 — Here's To You Sir Francis/Butcher Boy . . . 5

SHE TRINITY
66 Columbia DB 7874 — He Fought The Law/The Union Station Blues . . . 15
66 Columbia DB 7943 — Have I Sinned/Wild Flower . . . 8
66 Columbia DB 7959 — Wild Flower/The Man Who Took The Valise Off The Floor Of Grand Central Station At Noon . . . 8
66 Columbia DB 7992 — Yellow Submarine/Promise Me You'll Never Cry . . . 15
67 CBS 2819 — Across The Street/Over And Over Again . . . 7
70 President PT 283 — Hair/Climb That Tree . . . 35
(see also Shotgun Express, Beryl Marsden, Gilded Cage)

SHEVELLES
63 Oriole CB 1915 — Ooh Poo Pa Doo/Like I Love You . . . 20

MINT VALUE £

SHEVELLS

64	United Artists UP 1059	I Could Conquer The World/How Would You Like Me To Love You	20
65	United Artists UP 1076	Walking On The Edge Of The World/Not So Close	20
65	United Artists UP 1081	Watermelon Man/Taking Over Your Life	20
66	United Artists UP 1125	Come On Home/I Gotta Travel All Over	40
68	Polydor 56239	Big City Lights/Coffee Song	15

(see also Mike Stevens & Shevells)

TONY SHEVETON

62	Oriole CB 1705	Lullaby Of Love/I Have A Feeling	15
62	Oriole CB 1726	Lonely Heart/Foolish Doubts	15
62	Oriole CB 1766	Hey Little Girl/Kissing Date	22
63	Oriole CB 1788	Runaround Sue Is Getting Married/I Love The Girl Next Door	22
63	Oriole CB 1895	Million Drums/Dance With Me	15
64	Oriole CB 1975	Excuses/Is It Me, Is It You?	15

(see also Tony Rich)

SHIDE & ACORN

73	private pressing	UNDER THE TREE (LP)	400
94	Acme AC 8006LP	UNDER THE TREE (LP, reissue, 500 only, numbered)	15

(see also Jeremy Cahill)

SHIELA

71	Nu Beat NB 079	Only Heaven Knows/GRANT & RICHARDS: Freedom Psalm	6

TREVOR SHIELD

69	Trojan TR 664	The Moon Is Playing Tricks On Me/KING CANNON: Soul Special	8
69	Trojan TR 665	Please/JAY BOYS: Splendour Splash	8
72	Ashanti ASH 407	Rough Road/JAY BOYS: Rough The Road	6

(see also Beltones, Trevor)

SHIELDS

58	London HLD 8706	You Cheated/That's The Way It's Gonna Be	40
58	London HLD 8706	You Cheated/That's The Way It's Gonna Be (78)	20

KEITH SHIELDS

67	Decca F 12572	Hey Gyp (Dig The Slowness)/Deep Inside Your Mind	60
67	Decca F 12609	The Wonder Of You/Run, Run, Run	20
67	Decca F 12666	So Hard Livin' Without You/Baby Do You Love Me	20

(see also Marty Wilde [& Wildcats])

PETER SHILTON & RAY CLEMENCE

80	Polydor POSP 206	Side By Side/We're Gonna Win Again (p/s)	7

PETER SHILTON & JON SAMMELS

73	Sports Talk ST 102	SIMON SMITH INTERVIEWS.... 1973 (LP)	20

YASUKI SHIMIZU

88	Benelux Crammed MTM 12	MUSIC FOR COMMERCIALS (LP)	12

SHINDIGS

65	Parlophone R 5316	One Little Letter/What You Gonna Do	35
65	Parlophone R 5377	A Little While Back/Why Say Goodbye	35

SHINDOGS

67	Fontana TF 790	Who Do You Think You Are/Yes, I'm Going Home	10

(see also Delaney & Bonnie, James Burton)

JOHNNY SHINES

69	Blue Horizon 7-63212	LAST NIGHT'S DREAM (LP, with Otis Spann, mono or stereo)	80
74	Xtra XTRA 1142	COUNTRY BLUES (LP)	30

DON SHINN (& THE SOUL AGENTS)

66	Polydor BM 56075	A Minor Explosion/Pits Of Darkness (with The Soul Agents)	60
69	Columbia S(C)X 6319	TEMPLES WITH PROPHETS (LP)	50
69	Columbia SCX 6355	DEPARTURES (LP)	50

(see also The Soul Agents)

SHIP

72	Elektra K 42122	THE SHIP — A CONTEMPORARY FOLK JOURNEY (LP, gatefold sleeve)	20

SHIRALEE

67	Fontana TF 855	I'll Stay By Your Side/Penny Wren	12

SHIRELLES

SINGLES

58	Brunswick 05746	I Met Him On A Sunday/I Want You To Be My Boyfriend	70
58	Brunswick 05746	I Met Him On A Sunday/I Want You To Be My Boyfriend (78)	45
60	London HL 9233	Tonight's The Night/The Dance Is Over	20
60	Top Rank JAR 540	Will You Love Me Tomorrow/Boys	10
61	Top Rank JAR 549	Dedicated To The One I Love/Look-A-Here Baby	15
61	Top Rank JAR 567	Mama Said/Blue Holiday	15
61	Top Rank JAR 578	What A Sweet Thing That Was/A Thing Of The Past	12
61	Top Rank JAR 590	Big John/Twenty One	12
62	Top Rank JAR 601	Baby It's You/The Things I Want To Hear	15
62	HMV POP 1019	Soldier Boy/Love Is A Swingin' Thing	12
62	Stateside SS 119	Welcome Home Baby/Mama Here Comes The Bride	12
62	Stateside SS 129	Stop The Music/It's Love That Really Counts	12
63	Stateside SS 152	Everybody Loves A Lover/I Don't Think So	10
63	Stateside SS 181	Foolish Little Girl/Not For All The Money In The World	15
63	Stateside SS 213	Don't Say Goodnight And Mean Goodbye/I Didn't Mean To Hurt You	10
63	Stateside SS 232	What Does A Girl Do/Don't Let It Happen To Us	12
63	Pye International 7N 25229	It's A Mad, Mad, Mad, Mad World/31 Flavours	10
64	Pye International 7N 25233	Tonight You're Gonna Fall In Love With Me/20th Century Rock And Roll	12

MINT VALUE £

64 Pye International 7N 25240 Sha La La/His Lips Get In The Way . . . 10
64 Pye International 7N 25279 Maybe Tonight/Lost Love . . . 15
65 Pye International 7N 25288 Are You Still My Baby/I Saw A Tear . . . 8
66 Pye International 7N 25386 Shades Of Blue/When The Boys Talk About The Girls . . . 10
67 Pye International 7N 25425 Too Much Of A Good Thing/Bright Shiny Colours . . . 12
69 Mercury MF 1093 There's A Storm Going On In My Heart/Call Me (If You Want Me). . . . 15
71 United Artists UP 31592 Take Me/Dedicated To The One I Love . . . 6
75 Pye Disco Demand DDS 115 Last Minute Miracle/March . . . 5

EP

61 Top Rank JKP 3012 THE SHIRELLES SOUND FEATURING "WILL YOU LOVE ME TOMORROW" . . . 90

LP

61 Top Rank 35-115 THE SHIRELLES SING — TO TRUMPET AND STRINGS . . . 80
62 Stateside SL 10006 BABY IT'S YOU . . . 70
63 Stateside SL 10041 THE SHIRELLES' HITS . . . 60
70 Wand WNS 4 ETERNALLY SOUL (with King Curtis) . . . 15
71 Wand WCS 1001 TONIGHT'S THE NIGHT . . . 15
72 RCA Victor SF 8237 HAPPY AND IN LOVE . . . 15
72 RCA Victor SF 8279 THE SHIRELLES . . . 15
72 Wand WCS 1009 REMEMBER WHEN VOL. 1 . . . 18
72 Wand WCS 1010 REMEMBER WHEN VOL. 2 . . . 18

(see also Shirley & Shirelles, Shirley Alston)

DON SHIRLEY

61 London HLA 9391 Water Boy/Freedom, I'm On My Way . . . 6
62 London HLA 9503 Drown In My Own Tears/Lonesome Road . . . 6
56 London HA-A 2003 PIANO PERSPECTIVES (LP) . . . 15
56 London HA-A 2004 TONAL EXPRESSIONS (LP) . . . 15
62 London HAA 2448 DROWN IN MY OWN TEARS (LP, also stereo [SAHA 6238]) . . . 12/15
63 London HAA 8038 PIANIST EXTRAORDINARY (LP) . . . 12

ROY SHIRLEY

66 Ska Beat JB 253 Paradise/Calling . . . 20
66 Doctor Bird DB 1068 Hold Them/Be Good . . . 20
67 Doctor Bird DB 1079 I'm A Winner/Sleeping Beauty . . . 20
67 Doctor Bird DB 1088 Prophet/What To Do . . . 20
67 Doctor Bird DB 1093 Musical Field/LEE PERRY & DYNAMITES: Trial And Crosses . . . 25
67 Doctor Bird DB 1108 Thank You/Touch Them . . . 18
67 Caltone CAL 101 Get On The Ball/JOHNNY MOORE: Sound And Soul . . . 20
67 Island WI 3070 People Rock Steady/I'm Trying To Find A Home (actually by Uniques) . . . 22
67 Island WI 3071 Musical War/Soul Voice . . . 20
67 Island WI 3120 Girlie/GLEN ADAMS: She's So Fine . . . 20
68 Doctor Bird DB 1165 Hush A Bye/Musical Dinner . . . 15
68 Doctor Bird DB 1168 Dance The Reggae/The Agreement . . . 15
68 Giant GN 32 Dance Hall Arena/The Musical Train . . . 12
68 Giant GN 33 Warming Up The Scene/GLEN ADAMS: Lonely Girl . . . 12
68 Island WI 3098 Thank You/Touch Them . . . 18
68 Island WI 3108 Move All Day/Rollin' Rollin' . . . 18
68 Island WI 3110 Million Dollar Baby/SENSATIONS: Long Time No See You Girl . . . 18
68 Island WI 3118 Good Is Better Than Bad/Fantastic Lover . . . 18
68 Island WI 3119 Facts Of Life/Lead Us Not Into Temptation (as Roy Shirley & Uniques;
B-side actually by Roy Shirley & Slim Smith) . . . 18
68 Island WI 3125 If I Did Know/Good Ambition . . . 18
68 Amalgamated AMG 815 The World Needs Love/Dance The A . . . 12
68 Fab FAB 54 Think About The Future/Golden Festival . . . 8
69 Duke DU 18 Life/I Like Your Smile . . . 8
71 Nu Beat NB 090 Hold Them One/Two Three Four . . . 6
72 Punch PH 103 Don't Be A Loser/Jamaican Girl . . . 6
72 Punch PH 108 A Sugar/ALTYMAN REID: A Sugar — Version . . . 6
75 R&JJ 001 Heart Breaking Jepsey/Version . . . 5
80s Shirley SHIRLEY 1 For Everyone/Version (p/s) . . . 10

(see also Val Bennett, Glen Adams, Shirley & Charmers, Sensations, Denzil, Errol & His Group, Ronsig, Stranger & Glady, Untouchables)

SUSAN SHIRLEY

68 Mercury MF 1038 Sun Shines Out Of Your Shoes/Tomorrow Today . . . 5
69 Mercury MF 1087 Too Many Tears/Boy From Boston Massachusetts USA . . . 5
70 Philips 6006 037 Really Into Somethin'/My Friend The Clown . . . 12
71 Columbia DB 8835 Jealous Guy/Oh Yoko . . . 6
72 Columbia DB 8937 The Other Side Of Me/Imagine . . . 5

SHIRLEY & CHARMERS

72 Bullet BU 502 Rum Rhythm/LLOYD CHARMERS: Rhythm (Version) . . . 6

(see also Roy Shirley)

SHIRLEY & JOHNNY

64 Parlophone R 5149 It Must Me Love/I Don't Want To Know . . . 5
65 Parlophone R 5246 Only Once/Make Me An Offer . . . 5
65 Parlophone R 5319 Day Dreamin' Of You/Till You Say You'll Be Mine . . . 5
66 Parlophone R 5411 I'm Sorry/Breakaway . . . 5
67 Parlophone R 5630 And I Don't Want Your Love/There Go The Heartaches . . . 5
69 Mercury MF 1074 Don't Make Me Over/Baby Baby Baby . . . 5
69 Mercury MF 1114 Just Say Goodbye/The Sunshine After The Rain . . . 5

SHIRLEY & LEE

78s

56 Vogue V 9059 Let The Good Times Roll/Do You Mean To Hurt Me So . . . 40
57 Vogue V 9063 I Feel Good/Now That It's Over . . . 40
57 Vogue V 9067 That's What I Wanna Do/When I Saw You . . . 50

MINT VALUE £

57 Vogue V 9072 Rock All Nite/Don't You Know I Love You 50
57 Vogue V 9084 Rockin' With The Clock/The Flirt 50
57 Vogue V 9088 I Want To Dance/Marry Me 50
57 Vogue V 9094 Feel So Good/You'd Be Thinking Of Me. 50
58 Vogue V 9103 I'll Thrill You/Love No One But You 50
58 Vogue V 9118 Everybody's Rockin'/Don't Leave Me Here To Cry 70
59 Vogue V 9129 All I Want To Do Is Cry/Come On And Have Your Fun. 50
59 Vogue V 9135 A Little Word/That's What I'll Do 50
59 Vogue V 9137 I'll Do It/Lee's Dream 50
59 Vogue V 9156 True Love/When Day Is Done. 60

SINGLES

56 Vogue V 9059 Let The Good Times Roll/Do You Mean To Hurt Me So 140
57 Vogue V 9063 I Feel Good/Now That It's Over 90
57 Vogue V 9067 That's What I Wanna Do/When I Saw You 85
57 Vogue V 9072 Rock All Nite/Don't You Know I Love You 110
57 Vogue V 9084 Rockin' With The Clock/The Flirt 120
57 Vogue V 9088 I Want To Dance/Marry Me 80
57 Vogue V 9094 Feel So Good/You'd Be Thinking Of Me. 80
58 Vogue V 9103 I'll Thrill You/Love No One But You 85
58 Vogue V 9118 Everybody's Rockin'/Don't Leave Me Here To Cry 100
59 Vogue V 9129 All I Want To Do Is Cry/Come On And Have Your Fun. 80
59 Vogue V 9135 A Little Word/That's What I'll Do 80
59 Vogue V 9137 I'll Do It/Lee's Dream 80

(The above 45s were originally issued with triangular centres; later round-centre issues are worth two-thirds of these values.)

59 Vogue V 9156 True Love/When Day Is Done. 80

(Later Vocalion pressings of the above singles are worth two-thirds the values listed.)

60 London HLI 9186 I've Been Loved Before/Like You Used To Do 25
60 London HLI 9209 Let The Good Times Roll/Keep Loving Me 20
65 Island WI 257 Let The Good Times Roll/I'm Gone 18

EPs

57 Vogue VE 1-70101 ROCK 'N' ROLL (triangular centre, later round) 300/220
60 Vogue VE 1-70145 SHIRLEY AND LEE. 250

LP

71 Jay Boy JSX 2005 LET THE GOOD TIMES ROLL. 20

SHIRLEY & RUDE BOYS

67 Blue Beat BB 375 Gently Set Me Free/BUSTER'S ALL STARS: Rock Steady 25

SHIRLEY & SHIRELLES

69 Bell BLL 1049 Look What You've Done To My Heart/A Most Unusual Boy. 10
69 Bell BLL 1065 Plaything/Looking Glass 5
72 Bell BLL 1251 Look What You've Done To My Heart/A Most Unusual Boy (reissue). 5

(see also Shirelles)

SHIRTS

78 Harvest HAR 5170 Lonely Android/Running Through The Night (p/s) 5

SHIVA

82 Heavy Metal HEAVY 13 Rock Lives On/Sympathy For The Devil (p/s) 20
82 Heavy Metal HEAVY 16 Angel Of Mons/Stranger Lands (p/s). 10
82 Heavy Metal HMRLP 6 FIREDANCE (LP) 25

BUNNY SHIVEL

67 Capitol CL 15487 You'll Never Find A Love Like Mine/The Slide 8

JOYCE SHOCK

58 Philips PB 780 Pit A Patter Boom Boom/Bells In My Heart (78) 8
58 Philips PB 824 Take Your Foot From The Door!/I've Got Bells On My Heart. 10
58 Philips PB 824 Take Your Foot From The Door!/I've Got Bells On My Heart (78) 8
58 Philips PB 872 Hoopa Hoola/You're Not Losing A Daughter, Mama 10
58 Philips PB 872 Hoopa Hoola/You're Not Losing A Daughter, Mama (78) 6
59 Philips PB 934 Personality/I Can't Love You Anymore 10
59 Philips PB 934 Personality/I Can't Love You Anymore (78). 7
59 Philips PB 957 Cry, Baby, Cry/Dear Diary. 10
59 Philips PB 957 Cry, Baby, Cry/Dear Diary (78) 7

SHOCK ABSORBERS

69 Major Minor SMCP 5028 GUITAR PARTY (LP). 20

SHOCK HEADED PETERS

84 él EL 1 I, Blood Brother Be/Truth Has Come (p/s). 7
84 él ONET I, Blood Brother Be/Truth Has Come/Katabolism/Hate On Sight (12", p/s) 8

(see also Lemon Kittens, Underneath, Karl Blake, Sol Invictus)

SHOCKING BLUE

69 Olga OLE 015 Send Me A Postcard/Harley Davidson (demo only) 55
69 Penny Farthing PEN 702 Venus/Hot Sand 5
70 Penny Farthing PEN 713 Mighty Joe/Wild Wind 5
70 Penny Farthing PEN 721 Never Marry A Railroad Man/Roll Engine Roll 5
70 Penny Farthing PEN 744 Sally Was A Good Old Girl/Long And Lonesome Road 5
71 Penny Farthing PEN 758 Shocking You/Waterloo 5
72 Polydor 2001 266 Out Of Sight Out Of Mind/I Like You 5
72 Polydor 2001 298 Inkpot/Give Me Love In The Sunrise 5
70 Penny Farthing PELS 500 SHOCKING BLUE AT HOME (LP). 22
70 Penny Farthing PELS 510 SCORPIO'S DANCE (LP) 22

SHOES

67 Polydor 56739 Farewell In The Rain/What In The World Is Love 12

SHOGUN

86 Attack ATA 913 — High In The Sky/When The Lights Go Down (p/s) ... 30
87 Jet JET 12049 — Cloak And Dagger/Too Late For The Hunter/Tokyo Girl (12", p/s, red vinyl) ... 8
86 Attack ATA 006 — SHOGUN (LP) ... 75

TROY SHONDELL

61 London HLG 9432 — This Time/Girl After Girl ... 10
62 Liberty LIB 55398 — Island In The Sky/Tears From An Angel ... 15
63 London HL 9668 — I Got A Woman/Some People Never Learn ... 15
64 London HAY 8128 — MANY SIDES OF TROY SHONDELL (LP) ... 80

SHONDELLS

64 Ember EMB S 191 — My Love/Don't Cry My Soldier Boy ... 40

SHOOT

73 EMI EMI 2026 — On The Frontier/Ships And Sails ... 5
72 EMI EMA 73 — ON THE FRONTIER (LP) ... 12
(see also Yardbirds, Raw Material)

SHOOTER

78 EMI Intl. INS 3020 — SHOOTER (LP) ... 12

SHOOTING PARTY

88 Lisson DOLER 9 — Safe In The Arms Of Love (Phil's Extra Beat Update)/Safe In The Arms Of Love (Hot Power Mix) (12", p/s) ... 12

SHOP ASSISTANTS

85 Subway Organisation SUBWAY 1 — All Day Long/All That Ever Mattered/It's Up To You/Switzerland (red foldaround hand-coloured p/s in poly bag, later blue) ... 12/6
85 Subway Organisation GVP 007 — Home Again/CHESTERFIELDS: Nose Out Of Joint (33rpm flexidisc, with *The Underground* issue 4, *Screed* or *The Legend!* fanzine) ... 8/5
86 53rd & 3rd AGAAR 1 — Safety Net/Somewhere In China/Almost Made It (p/s) ... 5
86 53rd & 3rd AGAAR 112 — Safety Net/Somewhere In China/Almost Made It (12", p/s) ... 8
90 Avalanche AGAP 001C — Here It Comes/I'd Rather Be With You//You Trip Me Up/The Other One (with 33rpm Flexi Records flexidisc) ... 5
90 Avalanche AGAP 001B — Here It Comes/Look Out/I'd Rather Be With You/Adrenalin (12", box set with flexidisc, badge, postcard & lyric sheet, 1st 200 numbered) ... 8/5
(see also Buba & Shop Assistants)

DINAH SHORE

53 HMV 7M 119 — Keep It A Secret/Bella Musica ... 18
53 HMV 7M 139 — Sweet Thing/Three-Cornered Tune ... 15
54 HMV 7M 183 — Changing Partners/Think ... 15
54 HMV 7M 221 — This Must Be The Place/Come Back To My Arms ... 15
54 HMV 7M 236 — Three Coins In The Fountain/Pakistan ... 18
54 HMV 7M 250 — If I Give My Heart To You/Let Me Know ... 18
56 HMV 7M 352 — Love And Marriage/Compare ... 12
56 HMV POP 148 — Love And Marriage/Compare (78) ... 12
57 RCA RCA 1003 — The Cattle Call/Promises, Promises (Skip Redwine) ... 8
58 RCA RCA 1054 — Thirteen Men/I'll Never Say "Never Again" Again ... 6
58 RCA RD 27072 — HOLDING HANDS AT MIDNIGHT (LP) ... 25
59 Capitol (S)T 1247 — DINAH, YES INDEED! (LP) ... 18
60 Fontana Fortune Z 4026 — BUTTONS AND BOWS (LP) ... 15
60 Capitol (S)T 1296 — SOMEBODY LOVES ME (LP) ... 15
60 Capitol (S)T 1354 — DINAH SINGS SOME BLUES WITH RED (LP, with Red Norvo) ... 15
(see also Doris Day)

BRIAN SHORT

71 Transatlantic TRA 245 — ANYTHING FOR A LAUGH (LP, gatefold sleeve) ... 20
(see also Black Cat Bones)

J.D. SHORT

73 Sonet SNTF 648 — THE LEGACY OF THE BLUES VOL. 8 (LP) ... 12

KEVIN SHORT

79 EMI INT 574 — Punk Strut/Short Cut (no p/s, demos £60) ... 50

SHORT KUTS with Eddie Harrison

68 United Artists UP 2233 — Your Eyes May Shine/Letting The Tears Tumbling Down ... 15

SHORTWAVE (BAND)

75 RCA Victor SF 8400 — SHORTWAVE BAND (LP, with lyric sheet) ... 12
77 Crescent/Avada ARS 111 — GREATEST HATS (LP) ... 20
79 Pye 2CN 111 — SHORTWAVE (LP) ... 12

SHORTY (THE PRESIDENT)

73 Ackee ACK 509 — Aquarius Pressure/Halfway Tree Pressure (as Shorty The President) ... 8
73 Ackee ACK 517 — Jelly-Belly-Nelly/Message Of Love (as Shorty) ... 5
(see also Shorty Perry)

SHORTY & THEM

64 Fontana TF 460 — Pills Or Love's Labours Lost/Live Laugh And Love ... 35

SHOTGUN EXPRESS

66 Columbia DB 8025 — I Could Feel The Whole World Turn Round/Curtains ... 45
67 Columbia DB 8178 — Funny 'Cos Neither Could I/Indian Thing ... 50
83 See For Miles CYM 2 — I Could Feel The Whole World Turn Round/Curtains/Funny 'Cos Neither Could I/Indian Thing (10", p/s) ... 15
(see also Rod Stewart, Peter Bardens, Spencer Davis, Brian Auger, She Trinity, Beryl Marsden, Fleetwood Mac)

SHOTS

65 Columbia DB 7713 — Keep A Hold Of What You've Got/She's A Liar ... 35
(see also Smoke)

MINT VALUE £

SHOUT

72 Explosion 2058 — Life Is Rough/Life Is Rough – Version . . . 6

SHOUTS

64 React EA 001 — She Was My Baby/That's The Way It's Gonna Be . . . 35

SHOWBIZ KIDS

80s Top Secret CON 1 — She Goes To Finos/I Don't Want To Discuss That (p/s) . . . 35

(see also Toy Dolls)

SHOW BOYS

69 Gas GAS 129 — People Are Wondering/Long Time . . . 10

SHOWMEN

62 London HLP 9481 — It Will Stand/Country Fool . . . 65

62 London HLP 9571 — The Wrong Girl/I Love You Can't You See . . . 85

69 Pama PM 767 — Action/What Would It Take . . . 10

(see also Norman Johnson, General Johnson, Chairmen Of The Board)

SHOWSTOPPERS

68 Beacon 3-100 — Ain't Nothing But A House Party/What Can A Man Do (red swirly label) . . . 8

68 Beacon 3-106 — Shake Your Mini/Heartbreaker . . . 8

68 MGM MGM 1436 — Eeny Meeny/How Easy Your Heart Forgets Me . . . 5

69 Beacon BEA 110 — Don't Leave Me Standing In The Rain/Do You Need My Love . . . 5

69 Beacon BEA 130 — Just A Little Bit Of Lovin'/School Prom . . . 5

69 Beacon BEA 100 — Ain't Nothing But A House Party/What Can A Man Do (reissue, yellow label) . . . 5

70 Beacon BEA 100 — Ain't Nothing But A House Party/What Can A Man Do (reissue, green label) . . . 5

71 Beacon BEA 3-182 — Actions Speak Louder Than Words/ Pick Up Your Smile . . . 18

SHOWTIMERS

64 HMV POP 1328 — You Must Be Joking/Don't Say Goodbye . . . 10

SHOX

80 Axis AXIS 4 — No Turning Back/Lying Here (p/s) . . . 15

80 Beggars Banquet BEG 33 — No Turning Back/Lying Here (p/s, reissue) . . . 8

MARK SHREEVE

83 Uniton U 021 — ASSASSIN (LP) . . . 15

SHUBERT

68 Fontana TF 942 — Until The Rains Come/Let Your Love Go . . . 15

SHUDDER TO THINK

90s Dischord — Vacation Brain (p/s, with insert) . . . 12

MORT SHUMAN

59 Decca F 11184 — Turn Me Loose/I'm A Man (initially triangular centre, later round) . . . 50/40

59 Decca F 11184 — Turn Me Loose/I'm A Man (78) . . . 25

66 Fontana TF 685 — Cry A Little/She Ain't Nothing But A Little Child . . . 7

67 Immediate IM 048 — Monday Monday/Little Children . . . 15

SHUSHA

74 United Artists UP 35699 — Barun Baruneh/Wild Flowers . . . 5

74 United Artists UP 35759 — Ev'ry Time We Say Goodbye/Siren's Call . . . 5

71 Tangent TGS 108 — PERSIAN LOVE SONGS AND MYSTIC CHANTS (LP) . . . 20

72 Tangent TGS 114 — SONGS OF LONG TIME LOVERS (LP) . . . 15

74 United Artists UAS 29575 — SHUSHA (LP) . . . 12

74 United Artists UAS 29684 — THIS IS THE DAY (LP) . . . 12

75 United Artists UAS 29879 — BEFORE THE DELUGE (LP) . . . 12

78 Tangent TGS 138 — FROM EAST TO WEST (LP) . . . 15

83 Linnet LIN 1 — DURABLE FIRE: SONGS BY BRITISH POETS (LP) . . . 15

SHUTDOWNS

63 Colpix PX 11016 — Four In The Floor/Beach Buggy . . . 35

SHY

87 RCA PT 41180 — Break Down The Walls/Under Fire/Young Heart (12", gatefold p/s) . . . 8

87 FM 12VHF 43 — Just Love Me/Deep Water/Hold On To Your Love/Break Down The Walls (12", p/s) . . . 15

89 MCA MCATG 1369 — Give It All You've Got/She's Got What It Takes (12", gatefold p/s, with stencil) . . . 8

89 MCA MCATB 1391 — Money (12", metallic sleeve, limited issue) . . . 10

90 MCA MCATB 1399 — Broken Heart (12", numbered p/s) . . . 10

83 Ebony EBON 15 — ONCE BITTEN TWICE SHY (LP) . . . 40

SHY LIMBS

69 CBS 4190 — Reputation/Love . . . 70

69 CBS 4624 — Lady In Black/Trick Or Two . . . 70

(see also Shame)

SHY ONES

63 Oriole CB 1848 — Nightcap/Carry Me Back . . . 18

64 Oriole CB 1924 — La Route/Susanna . . . 15

(see also Spotnicks)

SHYSTER

68 Polydor 56202 — Tick Tock/That's A Hoe Down . . . 200

(see also Fleur-De-Lys)

SHYWOLF

82 MRS SW 001 — Lucretia/California Jam (p/s) . . . 40

LEROY SIBBLES & ROCKY ELLIS

68 Studio One SO 2042 — Love Me Girl/WRIGGLERS: Reel Up . . . 20

(see also John Holt, King Rocky)

DUDLEY SIBLEY

67 Coxsone CS 7010 — Run Boy Run/Message Of Old (B-side actually by Joe Higgs & Ken Boothe) 30
67 Island WI 3034 — Gun Man/Monkey Speaks His Mind (B-side actually by Dinsdell Thorpe) 20
(see also Delroy & Sporty, King Sporty, Mr. Foundation)

SICKIDZ

84 Big Beat SWT 97 — I COULD GO TO HELL FOR YOU (EP) 5

SICK THINGS

83 Chaos CH 3 — THE LEGENDARY SICK THINGS (EP) 10

SIDDELEYS

86 Sha La La Ba Ba Ba 006 — Wherever You Go/RESERVE: The Sun Slid Down (flexidisc with fanzines, p/s) . 12/8
87 Medium Cool MC 005 — What Went Wrong This Time? (p/s) 20
88 Sombrero THREE — Sunshine Thuggery/Are You Still Evil When You're Sleeping/Falling Off My Feet Again (12", p/s). 20

SIDEKICKS

66 RCA RCA 1538 — Suspicions/Up On The Roof. 12

ANN SIDNEY

65 HMV POP 1411 — The Boy In The Woolly Sweater/Lonely Doll 7

SIDNEY, GEORGE & JACKIE

71 Summit SUM 8528 — Lady Of My Complexion/No Sad Song 5
72 Summit SUM 8535 — Story Book Children/Gorgeous Marvellous 5
(see also Pioneers)

PAUL SIEBEL

70 Elektra EKSN 45085 — Bride 1945/Miss Cherry Lane. 5
70 Elektra EKS 74064 — WOODSMOKE AND ORANGES (LP) 18
71 Elektra EKS 74081 — JACK-KNIFE GYPSY (LP). 18

SIEGE

85 Siege THM 1 — Goddess Of Fire (no p/s) 18

SIEGEL-SCHWALL BAND

68 Vanguard SVRL 19044 — SHAKE (LP) 15
72 RCA SF 8246 — THE SIEGEL-SCHWALL BAND (LP). 12

CHRIS SIEVEY

79 Rabid TOSH 109 — Baiser/Last (p/s). 10
79 Razz RAZZXEP 1 — BAISER (33rpm EP, 2 tracks each by Sievey & Freshies, handwritten labels). . . . 35
80 Razz RAZZ 4 — My Tape's Gone/Moon Midsummer (some with True Life Revealing Confessions Of Romance And Love fanzine) 10/6
81 Razz RAZZ 5 — Hey/FRESHIES: We're Like You (p/s) 6
82 Razz RAZZ 8 — RED INDIAN MUSIC (EP) 8
82 Razz RAZZ 9 — Skip The Flight/Jim Baiser ("Baiser"/"Last" with new labels & sleeve). 8
83 Random RND 1 — Camouflage/(ZX 81 Programme "Camouflage")/Flying Train/F.T. (p/s, 'computer' single, B-side at 33rpm, 2,000 only) 5
75 Hey Boss (no. cat. no.) — GIRL IN MY BLUE JEANS (16-track cassette, 250 only) 20
76 Razz CS-1 — ALL SLEEPS SECRETS (cassette, 1,000 only) 12
80 Razz (no cat. no.) — NO GO DEMOS (cassette, with "Complete Book Of Rejection Slips" booklet, 400 only). 12
85 11.37 ETS-S — DENIGRATION NOW (cassette, reissue with 2 extra tracks, 250 only). 12
(see also Freshies, Going Red?)

LABI SIFFRE

70 Pye Intl. NSPL 28135 — LABI SIFFRE (LP). 15
71 Pye Intl. NSPL 28147 — THE SINGER AND THE SONG (LP, gatefold sleeve) 20
72 Pye Intl. NSPL 28163 — CRYING, LAUGHING, LOVING, LYING (LP, gatefold sleeve with lyric insert) 12
75 EMI EMC 3065 — REMEMBER MY SONG (LP). 125
98 EMI/Mr. Bongo MRBLP 011 — REMEMBER MY SONG (LP, reissue) 12

RON SIG

71 Camel CA 58 — 1970's/Version 6
71 Camel CA 59 — You Girl/ROY SHIRLEY & SLIM SMITH: Facts Of Life 6

SIGHT & SOUND

68 Fontana TF 927 — Ebenezer/Our Love (Is In The Pocket) 15
68 Fontana TF 982 — Alley Alley/Little Jack Monday. 15
(see also Jefferson, Sheridan & Price, Mike Sheridan)

BUNNY SIGLER

67 Cameo Parkway P 153 — Let The Good Times Roll — Feel So Good/There's No Love Left. 25
73 Epic S EPC 1177 — Tossin' And Turnin'/Picture Us. 5
76 London HLU 10518 — Let The Good Times Roll/Girl Don't Make Me Wait 15

SIGNS

66 Decca F 12522 — Ain't You Got A Heart/My Baby Comes To Me. 8

SIGUE SIGUE SPUTNIK

86 Parlophone 12 SSS 1 — Love Missile F1-11 (Bangkok Remix)/(Dance Mix)/Hack Attack (Dub Mix) (12", p/s, 'German' or 'Spanish' obi sleeve bands). . . . . each 15
86 Parlophone 12 SSSX 1 — Love Missile F1-11 (Trailer Mix): Love Missile F1-11 (Video Mix)/Love Missile F1-11 & Actuality Sound/Hack-Attack (12", p/s, with 6 poster inserts) . . . 12
86 Parlophone SSS 2 — 21st Century Boy/Buy EMI (foldout 'crucifix' p/s) 5
88 Parlophone 12 SSSW 3 — Success (Extended)/(Seven Inch) Frankenstein Cha-Cha-Cha (Extended) (12", 'Pete Waterman' p/s, withdrawn) 50
88 Parlophone 12 SSSP 3 — Success (Extended)/Frankenstein Cha-Cha-Cha (Extended)/Nightmare Of Neal X/Success Sputnik Style (12", picture disc, unissued)
88 Parlophone CD SSS 3 — Success (Seven Inch) Frankenstein Cha-Cha-Cha/Last Temptation Of Sputnik (CD). 15

MINT VALUE £

89 Parlophone CD SSS 4 Albinoni Vs Star Wars (Part 1 — 7" Version)/(Part 1 — Extended Version)/ (Part 2 — Extended Version) (Bonus Beats) (CD) . . . 15
89 Parlophone CD SSS 5 Dancerama (7" Mix)/(12" Extended)/(Album Mix Extended) (CD) . . . 18
89 Parlophone CD SSS 6 Rio Rocks (7 Inch)/Rio Rocks (Extended)/Rio Rocks (Samba) (CD) . . . 12
86 Parlophone PCSS 7305 FLAUNT IT (LP, box set with insert) . . . 15
(see also Bizet Boys, Sci Fi Sex Stars, Generation X, Sisters Of Mercy)

SIGUR RóS

99 Fat Cat 12FAT 036 Svefn-G-Englar (12" EP, custom sleeve) . . . 10
00 Fat Cat 12FAT 039 NY BATTERY (mini-LP) . . . 15
00 Fat Cat FATLP 11 AGAETIS BYRJUN (2-LP) . . . 15
03 Fat Cat FATLP 22 () (LP) . . . 12

SILENT MAJORITY

71 Hot Wax HWX 110 Frightened Girl/Colours Of My Love . . . 5

SILENT MOVIES

79 ESR Records ESR 1 Ain't No Van Gough/What Did Ya Say? (p/s) . . . 40

SILENT NOISE

79 Silent Noise/Easy ER 02 I've Been Hurt (Too Many Times Before)/Heart To Heart . . . 25

SILHOUETTES (Jamaica)

69 Sound System SSR 103 In Times Like These (act. by Lloyd Jackson & Groovers)/In Times Like These . . . 6

SILHOUETTES (U.S.)

58 Parlophone R 4407 Get A Job/I Am Lonely . . . 80
58 Parlophone R 4407 Get A Job/I Am Lonely (78) . . . 45
58 Parlophone R 4425 Headin' For The Poorhouse/Miss Thing . . . 150
58 Parlophone R 4425 Headin' For The Poorhouse/Miss Thing (78) . . . 70

SILICON TEENS

79 Mute MUTE 003 Memphis Tennessee/Let's Dance (p/s, some with poster) . . . 5/10

ERIC SILK (& His Southern Jazz Band)

56 Esquire EP 70 AND HIS SOUTHERN JAZZ BAND (EP) . . . 15
56 Esquire EP 100 AND HIS SOUTHERN JAZZ BAND (EP) . . . 10
57 Esquire EP 110 AND HIS SOUTHERN JAZZ BAND (EP) . . . 10
57 Esquire EP 128 AND HIS SOUTHERN JAZZ BAND (EP) . . . 15
57 Esquire EP 150 AND HIS SOUTHERN JAZZ BAND (EP) . . . 15
57 Esquire 20-065 SOUTHERN JAZZ (LP) . . . 30
58 Esquire 20-095 THE SILKEN TOUCH (LP) . . . 30
67 Polydor 582 002 OFF THE CUFF (LP) . . . 25

SILKIE

65 Fontana TF 556 Blood Red River/Close The Door Gently . . . 6
65 Fontana TF 603 You've Got To Hide Your Love Away/City Winds . . . 10
66 Fontana TF 659 Keys To My Soul/Leave Me To Cry . . . 10
66 Fontana TF 709 Born To Be With You/So Sorry Now . . . 6
65 Fontana TL 5256 THE SILKIE SING THE SONGS OF BOB DYLAN (LP) . . . 45

JUDEE SILL

72 Asylum AYM 502 Jesus Was A Cross Maker/The Phantom Cowboy . . . 5
72 Asylum AYM 509 Enchanted Sky Machines/My Man On Love . . . 5
73 Asylum AYM 513 The Kiss/Down Where The Valleys Are Low . . . 5
72 Asylum SYLA 8751 JUDEE SILL (LP, gatefold sleeve) . . . 15
73 Asylum SYL 9006 HEART FOOD (LP) . . . 15

SILLY SISTERS

76 Chrysalis CHR 1101 SILLY SISTERS (LP, with lyric insert) . . . 12
(see also Steeleye Span, Maddy Prior, June Tabor)

SILVER (Jamaica)

68 Jolly JY 006 Baby Oh Yeah/Rock Steady Is Here To Stay (as Silver & Magnets) . . . 20
68 Jolly JY 012 Things/Sweet Lovin' . . . 15
68 Jolly JY 017 I Need A Girl/Lost And Found . . . 15
70 Columbia Blue Beat DB 117 Love Me Forever/Sugar, Sugar (B-side as Silver & Noreen) . . . 10
71 Fab FAB 163 Change Has Got To Come/Magnet Stomp (as Silver & Magnets) . . . 6

SILVER (U.S.)

76 Arista ARIST 79 Musician (It's Not An Easy Life)/Right On Time . . . 6
76 Arista ARTY 144 SILVER (LP, U.S. disc & inner [AL 4076] in U.K. sleeve) . . . 12
(see also Grateful Dead)

ANDEE SILVER

64 HMV POP 1297 Too Young To Go Steady/Sleeping Beauty . . . 8
64 HMV POP 1344 The Boy I Used To Know/What Do You Do . . . 8
66 Fontana TF 666 Only Your Love Can Save Me/Window Shopping . . . 10
69 Decca F 22872 Go Now/You're Just What I Was Looking For Today . . . 7
69 Decca F 22953 With A Little Love/Te Quiero (unreleased)
70 Decca F 23071 Love Me/You're Breaking My Heart (export issue) . . . 10
70 Decca SKL-R 5059 A HANDFUL OF SILVER (LP) . . . 40

EDDIE SILVER

58 Parlophone R 4439 Seven Steps To Love/Put A Ring On Her Finger . . . 15
58 Parlophone R 4439 Seven Steps To Love/Put A Ring On Her Finger (78) . . . 10
58 Parlophone R 4483 Rockin' Robin/The Ways Of A Woman In Love . . . 20
58 Parlophone R 4483 Rockin' Robin/The Ways Of A Woman In Love (78) . . . 15

HORACE SILVER QUINTET/TRIO

61 Blue Note 45-1750 Sister Sadie/Break City . . . 8
63 Blue Note 45-1873 Too Much Sake (Parts 1 & 2) . . . 8
63 Blue Note 45-1902 Let's Get To The Nitty Gritty/Silver's Serenade . . . 8
64 Blue Note 45-1903 Sweet Sweetie Dee/Dragon Lady . . . 8

54 Vogue LDE 065 THE HORACE SILVER TRIO (10" LP) . . . 20
69 Blue Note BST 84277 SERENADE TO A SOUL SISTER (LP) . . . 15

LORRAINE SILVER
65 Pye 7N 15922 Lost Summer Love/I'll Know You'll Be There . . . 70
66 Pye 7N 17055 The Happy Faces/When The Love Light Starts Shining Thru His Eyes . . . 45

SILVER APPLES
90s Enraptured RAPT 4507 Fractal Flow/Love Fingers (p/s) . . . 5

SILVER BIRCH
73 Brayford BRO 2 SILVER BIRCH (LP, private pressing) . . . 240

SILVER BYKE
68 London HLZ 10200 Who Needs Tomorrow/I've Got Time . . . 10

SILVER EAGLE
67 MGM MGM 1345 Theodore/True As A Brand New Lie . . . 18

SILVERGINGER 5
01 Sanctuary SANCD 078 BLACK LEATHER MOJO (unreleased)
01 Infernal INFERNAL 13CD/X BLACK LEATHER MOJO (2-CD, in stickered leather-effect slipcase, 5000 only) . . 25
(see also Ginger, Super$hit666, Wildhearts)

SILVERHEAD
72 Purple PUR 104 Ace Supreme/Oh No No No . . . 7
72 Purple PUR 110 Rolling With My Baby/In Your Eyes . . . 7
73 Purple TPSA 7506 SILVERHEAD (LP) . . . 12
73 Purple TPSA 7511 SIXTEEN AND SAVAGED (LP) . . . 12
(see also Michael Des Barres, Blondie)

SILVER MOUNTAIN
83 Road Runner RR 9884 SHAKIN' BRAINS (LP) . . . 15

SILVERS
66 Polydor BM 56094 What A Way To Start A Day/Blue Blue Eyes . . . 6

PHIL SILVERS
57 Fontana Fortune Z 4040 BUGLE CALLS FOR BIG BAND (LP) . . . 15

SILVER SISTERS
60 Parlophone R 4669 Waiting For The Stars To Shine/When A Boy Meets A Girl . . . 10

DOOLEY SILVERSPOON
76 Seville SEV 1022 Game Players/Believe In Me . . . 8

SILVERSTARS
69 Trojan TR 646 Old Man Say/Promises . . . 8

SILVER STARS STEEL BAND
63 Island ILP 904 THE SILVER STARS STEEL BAND (LP) . . . 18
(see also Clancy Eccles)

SHEL SILVERSTEIN
73 CBS 65452 FREAKIN' AT THE FREAKER'S BALL (LP, with Dr. Hook) . . . 12
(see also Dr. Hook)

SILVERTONES
66 Doctor Bird DB 1028 True Confession (with Duke Reid)/TOMMY McCOOK & SUPERSONICS: More Love . . . 25
66 Doctor Bird DB 1041 It's Real (with Lynn Tait & Boys)/LYNN TAIT & BOYS: Storm Warning . . . 25
66 Rymska RA 105 True Confession/GRANVILLE WILLIAMS ORCHESTRA: Honky Tonk Ska . . . 30
67 Treasure Isle TI 7020 Cool Down/TOMMY McCOOK & SUPERSONICS: Shadow Of Your Smile . . . 18
68 Treasure Isle TI 7027 In The Midnight Hour/TOMMY McCOOK & SUPERSONICS: Soul For Sale . . . 15
68 Treasure Isle TI 7039 Old Man River/TOMMY McCOOK & SUPERSONICS: Our Man Flint . . . 15
68 Treasure Isle TI 7042 Slow And Easy/TOMMY McCOOK & SUPERSONICS: Moving . . . 15
69 Trojan TR 7705 Intensified Change/Marie . . . 12
71 Clandisc CLA 234 Tear Drops Will Fall/DYNAMITES: Tear Drops — Version . . . 6
73 Techniques TE 924 That's When It Hurts/I'll Take You Home . . . 6
71 Trojan TRLS 69 SILVER BULLETS (LP) . . . 30
(see also Valentines, Tommy McCook, Vincent Gordon, Alton Ellis, Carl Bryon, Charmers)

SILVERWING
80 Mayhem SILVER 1 Rock'n'Roll Are Four-Letter Words/High Class Woman . . . 6
82 Mayhem SILV 02 Sittin' Pretty/Teenage Love Affair (p/s) . . . 8
82 Mayhem SILV 212 Sittin' Pretty/Teenage Love Affair/Flashbomb Fever/Rock'n'Roll Mayhem (12") . . 15
82 Mayhem SILV 3 That's Entertainment/Flashbomb Fever (poster p/s) . . . 6
83 Bullet BULP 1 ALIVE AND KICKING (LP) . . . 18
(see also Pet Hate, Big Amongst Sheep)

VICTOR SILVESTER & HIS ROCK 'N' ROLL RHYTHM
57 Columbia DB 3888 Rockin' Rhythm Roll/Society Rock . . . 10
57 Columbia DB 3907 Alligator Roll/Off Beat Rock . . . 10

VICTOR SILVESTER ORCHESTRA
62 Columbia World Cup Cha Cha Cha Santiago . . . 10
66 Columbia DB 7900 The World Cup Waltz/The World Cup Cha Cha Cha . . . 30

SIMBA
71 Fire FIR 100 Louie Louie/Movin' . . . 5

HARRY SIMEONE CHORALE
59 Top Rank JAR 101 The Little Drummer Boy/JUNIOR CHORALE: Die Lorelei . . . 6
59 Top Rank JAR 101 The Little Drummer Boy/JUNIOR CHORALE: Die Lorelei (78) . . . 8
59 Top Rank JAR 109 In The Valley Of Love/The Beat O' My Heart . . . 5
59 Top Rank JAR 109 In The Valley Of Love/The Beat O' My Heart (78) . . . 6

		MINT VALUE £
59 Top Rank JAR 222	The Little Drummer Boy/The Toy Drum	5
59 Top Rank JAR 222	The Little Drummer Boy/The Toy Drum (78)	7
60 Top Rank JAR 397	Onward Christian Soldiers/Won't You Marry Me?	5

SIMIAN

02 Source SOUR 067	Never Be Alone/(Simian Mobile Disco Remix) (p/s)	5
03 Source SOUR 069	La Breeze/(Brian Eno Remix) (p/s)	5

BEVERLEY SIMMON(D)S

68 Pama PM 716	Mr. Pitiful/That's How Strong My Love Is	6
73 Pama Supreme PS 380	You're Mine/What A Guy (as Beverley Simmonds)	5
69 Pama PMLP/PMSP 9	REMEMBER OTIS (LP)	18
(see also Little Beverly)		

(JUMPIN') GENE SIMMONS

64 London HLU 9913	Haunted House/Hey, Hey Little Girl	20
64 London HLU 9933	The Jump/The Dodo	20

GENE SIMMONS

79 Casablanca CAN 134	Radioactive/When You Wish Upon A Star (p/s, red vinyl with mask, picture label)	20
79 Casablanca CAN 134	Radioactive/When You Wish Upon A Star (p/s, black vinyl)	12
(see also Kiss)		

JEFF SIMMONS

69 Straight STS 1057	LUCILLE HAS MESSED UP MY MIND (LP)	50
(see also Frank Zappa)		

LITTLE MAC SIMMONS

66 Outasite OSEP 1	BLUES FROM CHICAGO (EP, 99 copies only)	190

(Zoot) SIMMS & (Lloyd) ROBINSON

62 Blue Beat BB 143	White Christmas/Searching	12

JASON SIMMS & MUSIC THROUGH SIX

68 Domain D 5	It's Got To Be Mellow/MUSIC THROUGH SIX: Floppy Ears	15
(see also Music Through Six)		

ZOOT SIMMS (Jamaica)

63 Blue Beat BB 183	Press Along/PRINCE BUSTER ALLSTARS: 100 Ton Megaton (B-side actually "Mighty As A Rose" by Raymond Harper)	25
63 Blue Beat BB 193	Golden Pen/ERIC MORRIS: So You Shot Reds	25
64 Port-O-Jam PJ 4007	Please Don't Do It/Don't Do It (as Simms & [Lloyd] Robinson)	25
68 Blue Cat BS 118	Bye Bye Baby/AL & THRILLERS: Heart For Sale	25
69 Coxsone CS 7095	Tit For Tat/We Can Talk It Over (as Simms & Elmond)	30

SEIJA SIMOLA

78 Sonet SON 2145	Give Love A Chance/Little Smile (p/s)	12

SIMON

67 RCA Victor RCA 1609	I Like The Way/Little Tin Soldier	5
68 RCA Victor RCA 1668	Dream Seller/Sweet Reflections Of You	5
69 Plum PLS 002	Mrs Lillyco/There's No More You	25

JOE SIMON

66 London HLU 10057	Teenager's Prayer/Long Hot Summer	20
67 Monument MON 1004	My Special Prayer/Travelin' Man	8
68 Monument MON 1010	Nine Pound Steel/The Girl's Alright With Me	8
68 Monument MON 1014	No Sad Songs/Come On And Get It	8
68 Monument MON 1019	You Keep Me Hangin' On/What Makes A Man Feel Good	8
68 Monument MON 1025	Message From Maria/I Worry About You	8
69 Monument MON 1029	Looking Back/Standing In The Safety Zone	8
69 Monument MON 1032	The Chokin' Kind/Come On And Get It	8
69 Monument MON 1038	San Francisco Is A Lonely Town/It's Hard To Get Along	5
70 Monument MON 1042	Moon Walk (Parts 1 & 2)	6
70 Monument MON 1044	Further Down The Road/Wounded Man	5
70 Monument MON 1049	Yours Love/I Gotta Whole Lot Of Lovin'	8
70 Monument MON 1051	That's The Way I Want Our Love/When	10
71 Polydor 2066 066	Your Time To Cry/I Love You More (Than Anything)	7
71 Mojo 2006 098	Help Me Make It Through The Night/Most Of All	5
71 Mojo 2093 003	You Are The One/I Ain't Givin' Up	5
72 Mojo 2093 008	Drowning In A Sea Of Love/Let Me Be The One	5
72 Mojo 2093 014	You Are Everything/Pool Of Bad Luck	5
73 Mojo 2093 024	Trouble In My Home/I Found My Dad	5
74 Mojo 2093 030	Step By Step/Talk Don't Bother Me	7
75 Polydor 2006 551	Get Down Get Down/In My Baby's Arms	5
67 Monument LMO/SMO 5005	SIMON PURE SOUL (LP)	18
68 Monument LMO/SMO 5017	NO SAD SONGS (LP)	18
69 Monument LMO/SMO 5026	SIMON SINGS (LP)	18
70 Monument LMO/SMO 5030	THE CHOKIN' KIND (LP)	18
70 Monument LMO/SMO 5033	BETTER THAN EVER (LP)	18
71 Mojo 2918 001	THE SOUNDS OF SIMON (LP)	18
72 Mojo 2918 003	DROWNING IN THE SEA OF LOVE (LP)	18

PAUL SIMON

65 CBS 201797	I Am A Rock/Leaves That Are Green	22
73 CBS 1545	Kodachrome (withdrawn, any pressed?)	15+
65 CBS (S) 62579	THE PAUL SIMON SONGBOOK (LP, mono/stereo)	30/40
72 CBS CQ 30750/Q 69007	PAUL SIMON (LP, quadrophonic)	18
74 CBS CQ 32280/Q 69035	THERE GOES RHYMIN' SIMON (LP, quadrophonic)	18
75 CBS Q 86001	STILL CRAZY AFTER ALL THESE YEARS (LP, quadrophonic)	18
(see also Simon & Garfunkel, Jerry Landis, Tom & Jerry)		

TONY SIMON

67	Track 604 012	Gimme A Little Sign/Never Too Much To Love	18

SIMON & GARFUNKEL

SINGLES

65	CBS 201977	The Sound Of Silence/We've Got A Groovy Thing Goin'	7
66	CBS 202045	Homeward Bound/Leaves That Are Green	7
66	CBS 202303	I Am A Rock/Flowers Never Bend With The Rainfall	7
66	CBS 202285	The Dangling Conversation/The Big Bright Green Pleasure Machine	15
66	CBS 202378	A Hazy Shade Of Winter/For Emily, Whenever I May Find Her	7
67	CBS 202608	At The Zoo/The 59th Street Bridge Song (Feelin' Groovy)	10
67	CBS 2911	Fakin' It/You Don't Know Where Your Interest Lies	10
68	CBS Special Prods. WB 73	The Sound Of Silence/GEORGIE FAME: By The Time I Get To Phoenix (p/s)	5
68	CBS Special Prods. WB 728	The 59th Street Bridge Song (Feelin' Groovy)/TREMELOES: Here Comes My Baby (p/s, mail-order only with Pepsi Cola tokens)	7
69	CBS 4162	The Boxer/Baby Driver (p/s)	7
73	CBS 1159	Mrs. Robinson/Bookends Theme (p/s, 'Hall Of Fame Hits' series)	5

EPs

65	CBS EP 6053	WEDNESDAY MORNING 3AM	20
66	CBS EP 6074	I AM A ROCK	20
67	CBS EP 6360	FEELING GROOVY	20
68	CBS EP 6400	MRS ROBINSON	15

LPs

66	CBS (S)BPG 62690	THE SOUNDS OF SILENCE	18
66	CBS (S)BPG 62860	PARSLEY, SAGE, ROSEMARY AND THYME	15

(The above LPs were originally issued with flipback sleeves & textured orange labels.)

67	Allegro ALL 836	SIMON AND GARFUNKEL	25
68	CBS (S) 70042	THE GRADUATE (soundtrack, blue label, mono/stereo)	18/15
68	CBS (S) 63370	WEDNESDAY MORNING 3AM (flipback sleeve, textured orange label, mono/stereo)	18/15
72	CBS CQ 30995	BRIDGE OVER TROUBLED WATER (quadrophonic)	18

(see also Paul Simon, Art Garfunkel, Tom & Jerry)

NINA SIMONE

SINGLES

59	Parlophone R 4583	I Loves You Porgy/Love Me Or Leave Me	20
59	Pye International 7N 25029	Solitaire/Chilly Winds Don't Blow	6
59	Pye International N 25029	Solitaire/Chilly Winds Don't Blow (78)	15
63	Colpix PX 200	You Can Have Him/Return Home	6
64	Colpix PX 799	Exactly Like You/The Other Woman	6
65	Philips BF 1388	Don't Let Me Be Misunderstood/Monster	8
65	Philips BF 1415	I Put A Spell On You/Gimme Some	8
66	Philips BF 1465	Either Way I Lose/Break Down And Let It Out	8
67	RCA Victor RCA 1583	Do I Move You?/Day And Night	5
68	RCA Victor RCA 1697	Why? (The King Of Love Is Dead) Parts 1 & 2	5
68	RCA Victor RCA 1743	Ain't Go No — I Got Life/Do What You Gotta Do	5
68	RCA Victor RCA 1779	To Love Somebody/I Can't See Nobody	5
68	Pye International 7N 25466	The Other Woman/Exactly Like You	5
69	Philips BF 1736	I Put A Spell On You/Don't Let Me Be Misunderstood	6

EPs

61	Parlophone GEP 8844	MY BABY JUST CARES FOR ME	30
62	Parlophone GEP 8864	INTIMATE NINA SIMONE	22
64	Colpix PXE 303	FINE AND MELLOW	15
66	Colpix PXE 306	JUST SAY I LOVE HIM	15
66	Colpix PXE 307	I LOVE TO LOVE	15
65	Philips BE 12585	DON'T LET ME BE MISUNDERSTOOD	12
65	Philips BE 12589	STRANGE FRUIT	12

LPs

61	Pye Intl. NPL 28014	AT THE TOWN HALL	20
62	Pye Jazz NJL 36	FORBIDDEN FRUIT	20
64	Colpix PXL 419	FORBIDDEN FRUIT (reissue)	15
64	Colpix PXL 421	NINA AT THE VILLAGE GATE	22
65	Colpix PXL 465	FOLKSY NINA	22
65	Fontana SFJL 954	TELL ME MORE	15
65	Philips BL 7662	BROADWAY . . . BLUES . . . BALLADS	15
65	Philips BL 7671	I PUT A SPELL ON YOU	18
65	Philips BL 7678	IN CONCERT	15
66	Philips BL 7683	PASTEL BLUES	15
66	Philips (S)BL 7722	LET IT ALL OUT	15
66	Philips (S)BL 7726	WILD IS THE WIND	15
67	Philips (S)BL 7764	HIGH PRIESTESS OF SOUL	15
67	RCA RD/SF 7883	SINGS THE BLUES	15
68	RCA RD/SF 7967	SILK AND SOUL	12
69	RCA RD/SF 7979	NUFF SAID!	12
71	RCA	BLACK GOLD	12
71	RCA SF 8192	HERE COMES THE SUN	12
72	Mojo 2383 110	GIFTED AND BLACK	12
73	RCA SF 8304	EMERGENCY WARD	15

SUGAR SIMONE

66	Rainbow RAI 103	Is It Because/I Want To Know	12
67	Rainbow RAI 115	I Love My Baby/I'll Keep You Satisfied	10
67	Sue WI 4029	Suddenly/King Without A Throne	30
67	Go AJ 11409	It's Alright/Take It Easy	25
68	CBS 3250	The Vow/Spinning Wheel	15
69	Doctor Bird DB 1192	Black Is Gold/The Invitation	20

MINT VALUE £

69 Doctor Bird DB 1193 The Squeeze Is On/Tell Me 20
69 Doctor Bird DB 1201 Come And Try/Don't Listen To What They Say 20
69 Fab FAB 106 Boom Biddy Boom/RUDIES: What Can I Do 10
69 Fab FAB 107 I Need A Witness/Johnny Dollar 10
69 Upfront UPF 1 Turns On The Heatwave/Crying Blues 6
70 Beacon BEA 156 Keep On Trying/Only The Lonely 6
70 Beacon BEA 174 Why Can't I Touch You/Gotta Get It Off My Mind 6
(see also Sugar & Dandy, Les Foster, Larry Foster & Soul Explosion, Lance Hannibal)

SIMON PLUG & GRIMES

70 Deram DM 296 Is This A Dream?/I'm Going Home 12
70 President PT 310 Way In, Way Out/Long Long Summer 5
71 President PT 354 Pull Together/I'll Keep Smiling 5

SIMON'S SECRETS

68 CBS 3406 Naughty Boy/Sympathy 25
68 CBS 3856 I Know What Her Name Is/Keeping My Head Above Water 25
(see also Secrets, Clifford T. Ward, Martin Raynor & Secrets)

SIMON SISTERS

64 London HLR 9893 Winkin', Blinkin' And Nod/So Glad I'm Here 15
65 London HLR 9984 Cuddlebug/No One To Talk My Trouble To 15

NIC SIMPER'S FANDANGO

83 Paro PAR 0S4 Just Another Day (In The Life Of A Fool)/Wish I'd Never Woke Up 6
79 Gull GULP 1033 SLIPSTREAMING (LP) 20
(see also Deep Purple, Warhorse)

SIMPLE IMAGE

70 Carnaby CNS 4013 Spinning Spinning Spinning/Shy Boy 10

SIMPLE MINDS

79 Zoom ZUM 10 Life In A Day/Special View (p/s) 6
79 Zoom ZUM 11 Chelsea Girl/Garden Of Hate (p/s) 6
80 Arista ARIST 325 Changeling/Premonition (live) (p/s) 8
80 Arista ARIST 372 I Travel/New Warm Skin (p/s, some with blue vinyl flexidisc: "Kaleidoscope"/"Film Theme Dub") 10/4
80 Arista ARIST 12372 I Travel (Mix)/Film Theme (12", p/s) 8
81 Arista ARIST 394 Celebrate/Changeling (p/s) 7
81 Arista ARIST 12394 Celebrate (Mix)/Changeling/I Travel (12", stickered sleeve) 8
81 Virgin VS 451 Sweat In Bullet/20th Century Promised Land (non-gatefold p/s) 15
85 Virgin V 2364 ONCE UPON A TIME (LP, picture disc, gatefold sleeve) 12
89 Virgin SMBXC 1 STREET FIGHTING YEARS (box set w/ interview cassettes & songbook, no'd) 15
(see also Johnny & Self Abusers)

SIMPLICITY PEOPLE

73 Grape GR 3062 Murderer/BIG YOUTH: The Killer 12
73 Harry J HJ 6649 Time Is Getting Harder/HARRY J ALLSTARS: Time Is Getting Harder 5

SIMPLY RED

85 The Hit HOT 001 Every Bit Of Me (with *The Hit* magazine) 12
85 Lyntone LYN 15914 Something's Burning/10,000 MANIACS: Grey Victory (33rpm 1-sided clear flexidisc free with *Jamming!* magazine, issue 29) 15/10
85 Elektra EKR 9P Money's Too Tight (To Mention)/Open Up The Red Box (picture disc) 8
85 Elektra EKR 9TX Money's Too Tight (To Mention)/(Cutback Mix)/(Dub Version)/Open Up The Red Box (12", p/s) 8
85 Elektra EKR 19TX Come To My Aid (Survival Mix)/Granma's Hands/Come To My Aid (Heavy Dub Mix)/Valentine (12", p/s) 10
85 Elektra EKR 29 Holding Back The Years/I Won't Feel Bad (p/s) 5
85 Elektra EKR 29F Holding Back The Years/I Won't Feel Bad (gatefold p/s, with poster) 5
85 Elektra EKR 29P Holding Back The Years/I Won't Feel Bad (shaped picture disc) 22
85 Elektra EKR 29T Holding Back The Years (Extended)/I Won't Feel Bad/Drowning In My Own Tears (12", p/s) 15
86 WEA YZ 63R Jericho/Jericho The Musical (red vinyl in clear PVC sleeve) 8
86 WEA YZ 75B Open Up The Red Box (Remix)/Look At You Now (foldout box p/s) 8
86 WEA YZ 75F Open Up The Red Box (Remix)/Look At You Now//Holding Back The Years/I Won't Feel Bad (shrinkwrapped double pack) 7
86 WEA YZ 75TF Open Up The Red Box (Remix)/Look At You Now (live)/Heaven The Movie (live)//Holding Back The Years (Extended)/Drowning In My Own Tears/Picture Book In Dub (12", double pack) 12
87 WEA YZ 103F The Right Thing/There's A Light//Holding Back The Years/Drowning In My Own Tears (double pack) 8
87 WEA YZ 103TP The Right Thing/There's A Light/Ev'ry Time We Say Goodbye (12" picture disc) 8
87 WEA YZ 114T Infidelity (Stretch Mix)/Love Fire (Massive Red Mix)/Lady Godiva's Room (12", p/s) 8
87 WEA YZ 114TP Infidelity (Stretch Mix)/Love Fire (Massive Red Mix)/Lady Godiva's Room (12", picture disc) 15
87 WEA YZ 161TE Ev'ry Time We Say Goodbye/Love For Sale (live in studio)/Sad Old Red/Broken Man (10", stitched cardboard die-cut sleeve) 10
87 WEA YZ 161TW Ev'ry Time We Say Goodbye/Ev'ry Time We Say Goodbye (live in studio)/Love For Sale (live in studio) (12", envelope pack with sheet music & 4 postcards) 18
87 WEA YZ 161CD Ev'ry Time We Say Goodbye/Love For Sale (live in the studio)/Ev'ry Time We Say Goodbye (live)/Sad Old Red (CD, red or silver discs) 10/8
88 WEA YZ 172CD I Won't Feel Bad (Arthur Baker Remix)/The Right Thing/I Won't Feel Bad (Edit)/Lady Godiva's Room (Ellis Hucknall Mix) (3" CD, with adaptor, 5" case) 15
89 WEA YZ 349TE It's Only Love (Valentine Mix)/Turn It Up/I'm Gonna Lose You (10", numbered stitched cardboard die-cut sleeve) 8
89 WEA YZ 349 CDX It's Only Love (4.00 remix)/Turn It Up/X/The Right Thing (3" CD, 'criss-cross' box pack) 12

MINT VALUE £

89	WEA YZ 377TE	If You Don't Know Me By Now/Move On Out (live)/The Great Divide (S.H.T.G.) (10", stitched cardboard die-cut sleeve)	8
89	WEA YZ 377CD	If You Don't Know Me By Now/Move On Out (live)/Shine (live)/Sugar Daddy (3" CD)	8
89	WEA YZ 377CDX	If You Don't Know Me By Now/Move On Out (live)/Shine (live)/Sugar Daddy (3" CD, 'criss-cross' box pack)	12
89	WEA YZ 404TE	A New Flame/More/I Asked Her For Water (live)/Funk On Out (instrumental) (live) (10", numbered stitched cardboard die-cut sleeve)	7
89	WEA YZ 404CD	A New Flame/More/I Asked Her For Water (live)/Funk On Out (instrumental) (live) (CD, gatefold sleeve)	8
89	WEA YZ 424TE	You've Got It/Holding Back The Years (Live Acoustic Version)/I Wish/ I Know You Got Soul (live) (10", numbered stitched cardboard sleeve)	7
85	Elektra EKT 27P	PICTURE BOOK (LP, picture disc, die-cut sleeve)	20

(see also Frantic Elevators)

BILL SIMPSON

64	Piccadilly 7N 35179	I Love You For Sentimental Reasons/My Love Is Like A Red Red Rose (p/s)	8

DANNY SIMPSON

69	Trojan TR 653	Outa Sight/JOHN HOLT: I Want You Closer	12

DUDLEY SIMPSON ORCHESTRA

78	BBC RESL 58	Blake's 7/The Federation March (p/s)	8

HOKE SIMPSON

58	HMV POP 442	I Finally Found You/Gi-Gi	8

JEANETTE SIMPSON

67	Giant GN 16	Rain/Whatcha Gonna Do About It	10
68	Giant GN 29	My Baby Just Cares For Me/Don't Let Me Cry No More (with Superboys)	10
68	Giant GN 35	Through Loving You/Send Me Some Lovin' (with Missions)	10

LEO SIMPSON

65	Blue Beat BB 351	I Love Her So/Good To Be Seen (as Leo Simmo)	20
73	Pyramid PYR 7004	Waxy Doodle/Go Away	5

(see also Lionel Simpson)

LIONEL SIMPSON

65	Ska Beat JB 205	Tell Me What You Want/Love Is A Game	20
65	Ska Beat JB 221	Red River Valley/Eight People	20
66	Ska Beat JB 233	Give Over/Never Before	20

(see also Leo Simpson)

MARTIN SIMPSON

76	Trailer LER 2099	GOLDEN VANITY (LP)	12

RED SIMPSON

66	Capitol ST 2468	ROLL TRUCK ROLL (LP)	12

VALERIE SIMPSON

72	Tamla Motown STML 11194	EXPOSED (LP)	15

(see also Ashford & Simpson)

CHUCK SIMS

58	London HLR 8577	Little Pigeon/Life Isn't Long Enough	340
58	London HLR 8577	Little Pigeon/Life Isn't Long Enough (78)	50

FRANKIE LEE SIMS

71	Specialty SPE 5009	Married Woman Blues/Lucy Mae Blues	5
71	Specialty SNTF 5004	LUCY MAE BLUES (LP)	15

JOAN SIMS

63	Parlophone R 5021	Oh Not Again Ken/Hurry Up Gran	6
67	CBS 202635	Sweet Lovely Whatsisname/The Lass With The Delicate Hair	6

KELLY SIMS

60	Top Rank JAR 321	Betrayed By Love/A Girl In Love	6

ZOOT SIMS

51	Esquire 10-107	Yellow Duck/Boot It Zoot (78)	6
57	Esquire EP 183	ZOOT! (EP)	20
57	Esquire EP 204	ZOOT'S CASE (EP)	20
52	Esquire 20-002	ZOOT SIMS QUARTET/QUINTET (10" LP)	50
53	Esquire 20-010	ZOOT SIMS ALLSTARS (10" LP)	20
53	Esquire 20-018	ZOOT SIMS QUARTET/QUINTET (10" LP)	20
54	Vogue LDE 056	ZOOT SIMS GOES TO TOWN (10" LP)	250
55	Esquire 20-040	ZOOT SIMS QUARTET/QUINTET (10" LP)	60
50s	Esquire 32-040	ZOOT SIMS SEPTET (LP)	30
58	HMV CLP 1165	GEORGE HANDY COMPOSITIONS (LP)	18
58	HMV CLP 1188	PLAYS FOUR ALTOS (LP)	20
61	Vogue LAE 12309	CHOICE (LP)	20
61	Fontana TFL 5176	ZOOT AT RONNIE SCOTT'S (LP)	350
62	Fontana (S)TFL 588	ZOOT AT RONNIE SCOTT'S (LP, reissue)	150
62	Fontana 886 151 TY	SOLO FOR ZOOT (LP, also mono [680 982 TL], £20)	50
65	Fontana FJL 123	COOKIN'! (LP)	150
60s	Xtra XTRA 5001	TROTTING! (LP)	15

(see also Sims-Wheeler Vintage Jazz Band)

SIMS TWINS/VALENTINOS

68	Soul City SCM 001	THE VALENTINOS/THE SIMS TWINS (LP, 1 side each)	40

SIMS-WHEELER VINTAGE JAZZ BAND

60	Polydor NH 66638	Never On A Sunday/Ma Curly Headed Baby	5

(see also Zoot Sims)

MINT VALUE £

FRANK SINATRA

78s

50	Columbia DX 1666	Soliloquy (Parts 1 & 2) (12")	6
51	Columbia LB 104	If She'd Only Look My Way/London By Night	8
54	Philips PB 364	My Blue Heaven/Should I	6
55	Philips PB 363	It's Only A Paper Moon/When You're Smiling	8
57	Philips PB 734	Once In Love With Amy/I Am Loved	8
57	Philips PB 756	Full Moon And Empty Arms/Autumn In New York	8
57	Philips PB 763	White Christmas/Christmas Dreaming	8
58	Capitol CL 14863	Nothing In Common/How Are Ya Fixed For Love (with Keely Smith)	8
58	Capitol CL 14904	The Song From "Kings Go Forth" (Monique)/The Same Old Song And Dance	8
58	Fontana H 109	I Could Write A Book/Nevertheless (I'm In Love With You)	8
58	Fontana H 140	If I Forget You/I'm A Fool To Want You	10
59	Capitol CL 14997	Time After Time/French Foreign Legion	6
59	Capitol CL 15006	To Love And Be Loved/No-One Ever Tells You	10
59	Capitol CL 15052	High Hopes/All My Tomorrows	15
59	Capitol CL 15086	Talk To Me/They Came To Cordura	20

45s

53	Columbia SCM 5052	Birth Of The Blues/Why Try To Change Me Now?	35
53	Columbia SCM 5060	You Do Something To Me/Lover	35
53	Columbia SCM 5076	Santa Claus Is Comin' To Town/My Girl	35
54	Capitol CL 14064	Young-At-Heart/Take A Chance	20
54	Capitol CL 14120	Three Coins In The Fountain/I Could Have Told You	25
54	Capitol CL 14174	White Christmas/The Christmas Waltz	25
54	Capitol CL 14188	When I Stop Loving You/It Worries Me	18
55	Capitol CL 14221	Someone To Watch Over Me/The Gal That Got Away	18
55	Capitol CL 14238	Melody Of Love/I'm Gonna Live Till I Die	18
55	Columbia SCM 5167	S'posin'/How Deep Is The Ocean	30
55	Capitol CL 14240	You, My Love/Just One Of Those Things	18
55	Capitol CL 14270	Don't Change Your Mind About Me/Why Should I Cry Over You	18
55	Capitol CL 14292	Two Hearts, Two Kisses (Make One Love)/From The Bottom To The Top	18
55	Capitol CL 14296	Learnin' The Blues/If I Had Three Wishes	18
55	Capitol CL 14326	Not As A Stranger/How Could You Do A Thing Like That To Me	18
55	Capitol CL 14352	My Funny Valentine/I Get A Kick Out Of You	15
55	Capitol CL 14360	It Never Entered My Mind/In The Wee Small Hours Of The Morning	15
55	Capitol CL 14373	Fairy Tale/Same Old Saturday Night	15

(The above Capitol 45s were originally issued with triangular centres; later round-centre copies are worth half these values.)

56	Capitol CL 14503	Love And Marriage/Look To Your Heart	10
56	Capitol CL 14511	(Love Is) A Tender Trap/Weep They Will	8
56	Capitol CL 14564	You'll Get Yours/Flowers Mean Forgiveness	7
56	Capitol CL 14584	Five Hundred Guys/(How Little It Matters) How Little We Know	6
56	Capitol CL 14607	"Johnny Concho" Theme (Wait For Me)/Hey! Jealous Lover	6
56	Capitol CL 14620	The Impatient Years/Our Town	6
56	Capitol CL 14644	Who Wants To Be A Millionaire? (with Celeste Holm)/Mind If I Make Love To You?	7
56	Capitol CL 14646	You're Sensational/You Forgot All The Words	6
57	Capitol CL 14696	Can I Steal A Little Love?/Your Love For Me	6
57	Capitol CL 14719	So Long, My Love/Crazy Love	6
57	Capitol CL 14750	Something Wonderful Happens In Summer/You're Cheatin' Yourself	6
57	Capitol CL 14800	All The Way/Chicago	6
57	Capitol CL 14804	Mistletoe And Holly/Jingle Bells	6
58	Capitol CL 14819	Witchcraft/Tell Her You Love Her	7
58	Capitol CL 14863	Nothing In Common/How Are Ya Fixed For Love (with Keely Smith)	6
58	Capitol CL 14904	The Song From "Kings Go Forth" (Monique)/The Same Old Song And Dance	6
58	Fontana H 140	If I Forget You/I'm A Fool To Want You	12
58	Capitol CL 14956	Mr. Success/Sleep Warm	6
59	Capitol CL 14997	Time After Time/French Foreign Legion	6
59	Capitol CL 15006	To Love And Be Loved/No-One Ever Tells You	6
59	Capitol CL 15052	High Hopes/All My Tomorrows	6
59	Capitol CL 15086	Talk To Me/They Came To Cordura	6
60	Capitol CL 15116	It's Nice To Go Trav'ling/Brazil	5
60	Capitol CL 15135	River, Stay 'Way From My Door/It's Over, It's Over, It's Over	5
60	Capitol CL 15150	Nice 'n' Easy/This Was My Love	5
60	Capitol CL 15168	Ol' MacDonald/You'll Always Be The One I Love	5
61	Capitol CL 15193	My Blue Heaven/Sentimental Baby	5
61	Reprise R 20010	Granada/Have Yourself A Merry Little Xmas	5
61	Reprise R 20035	The Coffee Song/Foggy Day	5
62	Reprise RS 20063	Ev'rybody's Twistin'/Nothing But The Best	5
63	Reprise R 20148	My Kind Of Girl/Please Be Kind	5
64	Reprise R 20351	Hello Dolly/I Wish You Love	5
66	Reprise R 23052	Strangers In The Night/My Kind Of Town	5
66	Reprise RS 20509	Summer Wind/You Make Me Feel So Young	5
66	Reprise RS 20531	That's Life/I've Got You Under My Skin	5
67	Reprise RS 20610	The World We Knew (Over And Over)/You Are There	5
69	Reprise RS 20817	My Way/Blue Lace	5
69	Reprise RS 20852	Love's Been Good To Me/A Man Alone	5

EPs

54	HMV 7EG 8004	TOMMY DORSEY & HIS ORCHESTRA (plain sleeve, 2 tracks with Sinatra)	10
54	HMV 7EG 8070	FRANK SINATRA (plain sleeve)	8
54	Capitol EAP1-488	SONGS FOR YOUNG LOVERS NO. 1	8
55	HMV 7EG 8128	MOONLIGHT SINATRA	12
55	Columbia SEG 7565	FRANK SINATRA (plain sleeve)	10
55	Columbia SEG 7582	SINATRA SERENADE (plain sleeve)	10
55	Columbia SEG 7597	FRANKIE'S FAVOURITES (plain sleeve)	10
55	Capitol EAP 2-488	SONGS FOR YOUNG LOVERS NO. 2	8
55	Capitol EAP 1-571	SONGS FROM "YOUNG AT HEART"	8
56	Capitol EAP 1-590	MELODY OF LOVE	8

			MINT VALUE £
56	Capitol EAP 1-629	SESSION WITH SINATRA	8
56	Capitol EAP 1025	OUR TOWN	8
56	Capitol EAP 2-488	YOUNG AT HEART	8
60	Fontana TFE 17273	'BYE BABY	12
61	Capitol SEP1-221	NO ONE CARES (stereo)	15
61	Capitol SEP2-1221	NO ONE CARES NO. 2 (stereo)	15
61	Capitol SEP3-1221	NO ONE CARES NO. 3 (stereo)	15
CAPITOL LPs			
54	Capitol LC 6654	SONGS FOR YOUNG LOVERS (10")	30
54	Capitol LC 6689	SWING EASY (10") Decca Pressing/EMI	30
55	Capitol LC 6702	IN THE WEE SMALL HOURS VOL. 1 (10")	25
55	Capitol LC 6705	IN THE WEE SMALL HOURS VOL. 2 (10")	25
(The above LPs were originally pressed by Decca. Subsequent pressings were by EMI, and are worth 40% less)			
56	Capitol LCT 6106	SONGS FOR SWINGIN' LOVERS	15
56	Capitol LCT 6111	FRANK SINATRA CONDUCTS TONE POEMS OF COLOUR	18
57	Capitol LCT 6123	THIS IS SINATRA	15
57	Capitol LCT 6130	CLOSE TO YOU	15
57	Capitol LCT 6135	A SWINGIN' AFFAIR	15
57	Capitol LCT 6144	A JOLLY CHRISTMAS FROM FRANK SINATRA	15
58	Capitol (S)LCT 6152	WHERE ARE YOU? (mono/stereo)	15/18
58	Capitol LCT 6155	THIS IS SINATRA VOL. 2	15
58	Capitol (S)LCT 6168	FRANK SINATRA SINGS FOR ONLY THE LONELY (mono/stereo)	15/18
59	Capitol (S)LCT 6179	COME DANCE WITH ME	15
59	Capitol LCT 6181	LOOK TO YOUR HEART	15
59	Capitol (S)LCT 6185	NO ONE CARES	15
60	Capitol W 587	SWING EASY	15
61	Capitol W(S) 1417	NICE'N'EASY (mono/stereo)	15/18
61	Capitol W(S) 1491	SINATRA'S SWINGIN' SESSION! (mono/stereo)	15/18
62	Capitol W(S) 1594	COME SWING WITH ME! (mono/stereo)	15/18
62	Capitol W(S) 1676	POINT OF NO RETURN (mono/stereo)	15/18
62	Capitol T 20389	LONDON BY NIGHT	15
62	Capitol W(S) 1538	ALL THE WAY (mono/stereo)	15/18
63	Capitol W(S) 1729	SINATRA SINGS ... OF LOVE AND THINGS! (mono/stereo)	15/18
63	Capitol W 1/2/3-1762	THE GREAT YEARS (3-LP)	20
63	Capitol W 1825	FRANK SINATRA SINGS RODGERS AND HART	15
64	Capitol T 20577	MY FUNNY VALENTINE	15
65	Capitol W 20652	SINGING AND SWINGING	15
65	Capitol (S)T 1919	TELL HER YOU LOVE HER	15
65	Capitol T 20734	THE CONNOISSEUR'S SINATRA	15
66	Capitol T 20757	SINATRA FOR THE SOPHISTICATED	15
67	Capitol (S)T 2700	THE MOVIE SONGS	15
85	Capitol SINATRA 20	FRANK SINATRA: THE CAPITOL YEARS (20-LP, box set)	80
90	Capitol C1-94777	THE CAPITOL YEARS (5-LP, box set)	30
PHILIPS/FONTANA LPs			
54	Philips BBR 8003	SING AND DANCE WITH FRANK SINATRA (10")	30
55	Philips BBR 8038	FABULOUS FRANK (10")	25
55	Philips BBR 8040	YOUNG AT HEART (10", with Doris Day)	25
57	Philips BBR 8114	CHRISTMAS DREAMING (10")	30
57	Philips BBL 7137	DORIS AND FRANK (6 tracks each by Doris Day & Frank Sinatra)	25
57	Philips BBL 7168	FRANKIE	20
57	Philips BBL 7180	THAT OLD FEELING	20
58	Fontana TFL 5000	THE VOICE	25
58	Fontana TFL 5006	ADVENTURES OF THE HEART	20
58	Fontana TFL 5030	THE FRANK SINATRA STORY	18
59	Fontana TFL 5048	PUT YOUR DREAMS AWAY	25
59	Fontana TFL 5054	THE BROADWAY KICK	20
60	Fontana TFL 5074	LOVE IS A KICK	18
60	Fontana TFL 5082	COME BACK TO SORRENTO	18
60	Fontana TFL 5107	REFLECTIONS	15
61	Fontana TFL 5138	SINATRA SOUVENIR	15
61	Fontana SET 303	SINATRA PLUS (2-LP)	18
REPRISE LPs			
61	Reprise R 1001	RING-A-DING-DING!	15
61	Reprise R(9) 1002	SINATRA SWINGS (mono/stereo)	12/15
62	Reprise R(9) 1003	I REMEMBER TOMMY... (die-cut gatefold sleeve, mono/stereo)	12/15
62	Reprise R(9) 1004	SINATRA AND STRINGS (mono/stereo)	12/15
62	Reprise R(9) 1005	SINATRA AND SWINGIN' BRASS (mono/stereo)	12/15
62	Reprise R(9) 1006	SINATRA SINGS GREAT SONGS FROM GREAT BRITAIN (mono/stereo)	30/45
63	Reprise R 1007	ALL ALONE	12
63	Reprise R(9) 1008	SINATRA-BASIE	12
63	Reprise R(9) 1009	THE CONCERT SINATRA	12
63	Reprise R 1010	SINATRA'S SINATRA	12
64	Reprise R(9) 1011	FRANK SINATRA SINGS "DAYS OF WINE AND ROSES" & OTHER ACADEMY AWARD WINNERS	12
64	Reprise R(9) 1012	IT MIGHT AS WELL BE SWING (with Count Basie)	12
64	Reprise R 2022	TWELVE SONGS OF CHRISTMAS (with Bing Crosby, Fred Waring, etc)	12
65	Reprise R(9) 1013	SOFTLY AS I LEAVE YOU	12
65	Reprise R(9) 1014	SEPTEMBER OF MY YEARS	12
65	Reprise R(9) 6167	SINATRA '65	12
66	Reprise R(9) 1015	MY KIND OF BROADWAY	12
66	Reprise R(9) 1017	STRANGERS IN THE NIGHT	12
66	Reprise R(9) 1018	MOONLIGHT SINATRA	15
66	Reprise R(S)LP 1019	IN CONCERT: SINATRA AT 'THE SANDS' (2-LP, with Count Basie)	18
67	Reprise R(S)LP 1020	THAT'S LIFE	12
67	Reprise R(S)LP 1021	FRANCIS ALBERT SINATRA — ANTONIO CARLOS JOBIM	12

			MINT VALUE £
67	Reprise R(S)LP 1022	FRANK SINATRA	12
68	Reprise R(S)LP 1024	FRANCIS A. EDWARD K. (with Duke Ellington)	12
69	Reprise R(S)LP 1027	CYCLES	12
69	Reprise R(S)LP 1030	A MAN ALONE — THE WORDS AND MUSIC OF ROD McKUEN	12
70	Reprise R(S)LP 1031	WATERTOWN	15
71	Reprise RSLP 1033	SINATRA AND COMPANY	12
77	Reprise K 94003	SINATRA — THE REPRISE YEARS (4-LP, box set)	18

OTHER LPs

56	HMV DLP 1123	IT'S D-LOVELY (with Tommy Dorsey Orchestra)	25
58	RCA RD 27069	FRANKIE AND TOMMY (with Tommy Dorsey Orchestra)	20
61	Encore ENC 101	WHEN YOUR LOVER HAS GONE	12
61	World Record Club TP 81	LOOK OVER YOUR SHOULDER	12
66	World Record C. (S)T 545	CLOSE TO YOU (reissue)	12
67	World Record C. (S)T 635	SEPTEMBER SONG	12
68	CBS 63172	THE ESSENTIAL FRANK SINATRA VOL. 1	12
68	CBS 63173	THE ESSENTIAL FRANK SINATRA VOL. 2	12
68	CBS 63174	THE ESSENTIAL FRANK SINATRA VOL. 3	12
69	World Records SM 137-142	THE SINATRA TOUCH (6-LP, box set, mail-order only)	30
70	Valiant VS 144	FRANK SINATRA WITH COUNT BASIE (reissue)	12
81	World Records ALBUM 47	THE SINATRA TOUCH (4-LP, box set, mail-order only)	20
83	Mobile Fidelity SC 1	THE SINATRA COLLECTION (16-LPs in silver box, with *Swing Easy* LP unavailable elswhere)	500+

(see also Nancy Sinatra, Count Basie, Tommy Dorsey, Dean Martin, Doris Day)

FRANK & NANCY SINATRA

67	Reprise REP 30082	SOMETHING STUPID (EP)	10
69	Reprise R(S)LP 1026	THE SINATRA FAMILY WISH YOU A HAPPY CHRISTMAS (LP)	20

NANCY SINATRA

61	Reprise RS 20017	Cuff Links And Tie Clips/Not Just Your Friend (with p/s)	15/10
62	Reprise RS 20045	To Know Him Is To Love Him/Like I Do	12
63	Reprise RS 20144	I See The Moon/Put Your Head On My Shoulder	10
64	Reprise RS 20335	True Love/The Answer To Everything	8
65	Reprise RS 20407	So Long Babe/If He'd Loved Me	10
66	Reprise RS 20432	These Boots Are Made For Walkin'/The City Never Sleeps At Night	5
66	Reprise RS 20461	How Does That Grab You Darlin'/I Move Around	6
66	Reprise RS 20491	Friday's Child/Hutchinson Jail	6
66	Reprise RS 20514	In Our Time/Leave My Dog Alone	6
66	Reprise RS 20527	Sugar Town/Summer Wine	6
67	Reprise RS 20559	Love Eyes/Coastin'	6
67	Reprise RS 20595	You Only Live Twice/Jackson	6
67	Reprise RS 20620	Lightning's Girl/Until It's Time For You To Go	6
68	Reprise RS 20670	100 Years/See The Little Children	6
68	Reprise RS 20756	Happy/Nice 'N Easy	6
68	Reprise RS 20789	Good Time Girl/Old Devil Moon	6
69	Reprise RS 20813	God Knows I Love You/Just Being Plain Old Me	6
69	Reprise RS 20851	Drummer Man/Home	6
69	Reprise RS 20869	The Highway Song/Are You Growing Tired Of My Love	6
75	Private Stock PVT 27	Annabell Of Mobile/She Played Piano And He Beat The Drums	5
77	Private Stock PVT 114	It's For My Dad/A Gentle Man Like You	6
66	Reprise REP 30069	RUN FOR YOUR LIFE (EP)	18
66	Reprise REP 30072	I MOVE AROUND (EP)	18
67	Reprise REP 30080	SORRY 'BOUT THAT (EP)	18
67	Reprise REP 30086	NASHVILLE NANCY (EP)	15
66	Reprise R 6202	BOOTS (LP)	15
66	Reprise R 6207	HOW DOES THAT GRAB YOU? (LP)	15
66	Reprise R(S)LP 6221	NANCY IN LONDON (LP)	15
67	Reprise RLP 6239	SUGAR (LP)	15
67	Reprise R(S)LP 6251	COUNTRY, MY WAY (LP)	15
68	Reprise R(S)LP 6277	MOVIN' WITH NANCY (LP)	15
69	Reprise RSLP 6333	NANCY (LP)	15
72	RCA DPS 2037	THIS IS NANCY SINATRA (LP)	15
73	RCA SF 8331	WOMAN (LP)	15

(see also Elvis Presley)

NANCY SINATRA & LEE HAZLEWOOD

67	Reprise RS 20629	Lady Bird/Sand	6
67	Reprise RS 23215	Some Velvet Morning/Tony Rome	6
71	Reprise K 14093	Did You Ever?/Back On The Road Again	5
67	Reprise REP 30083	JACKSON (EP)	15
68	Reprise R(S)LP 6273	NANCY & LEE (LP)	15
72	RCA Victor SF 8240	DID YOU EVER? (LP)	15

(see also Lee Hazlewood, Frank Sinatra)

BETTY SINCLAIR

70	Torpedo TOR 19	Why Why Why/HOT ROD ALL STARS: Fistful Of Dollars	10

JIMMY SINCLAIR & TRENTON SPENCE ORCHESTRA

61	Blue Beat BB 47	Verona/To Prove My Love	12

STEPHEN SINCLAIR

62	HMV POP 1066	Mister Sandman/Part Lights	10

WINSTON SINCLAIR

69	Nu Beat NB 026	Another Heartache/Come On Little Girl	10

(see also Harmonisers)

SINDECUT

90	Virgin VSTX 1282	Live The Life Remix/Slow Down Remix (12")	7
90	Virgin VSTX 1288	Tell Me Why/Wisdom (12")	7
92	VST 1326DJ	Won't Change/Panic Stricken!!/Crack Business	8
90	Virgin V2635	CHANGING THE SCENERY (LP)	15

SINDELFINGEN

73	Medway	ODGIPIG (LP, private pressing, with insert)	800
90	Cenotaph CEN 111	ODGIPIG/TRIANGLE (2-LP, reissue with live album, 300 only)	25

TONY SINDEN, ALAN BAKER & THE INSECTS

79	Piano SING 001	Magnificent Cactus Trees/Cast Shadows	5

SINEWAVE

72	Chapter One SCH 172	Clochemerle/Star Trek	10

PETE SINFIELD

73	Manticore K 43501	STILL (LP, textured gatefold sleeve)	25

(see also Emerson Lake & Palmer, King Crimson, Greg Lake)

SINGAROUND

69	G. Guinea GSGL 10436	SINGAROUND (LP)	15

RAY SINGER

64	Ember EMB S 187	Tell Me Now/I'm Comin' Home	7
64	Ember EMB S 199	It's Gotta Be/Hey, Who?	7
65	Ember EMB S 215	I'm The Richest Man Alive/Pretty Little Rambling Rose (some in p/s)	12/7
65	Fontana TF 621	You'll Come Crying To Me/Who Can I Talk To About You	7
67	Ember EMB S 231	What's Done Has Been Done/Won't It Be Fine	8
60s	Ember NR	RAY SINGER (LP)	30

(see also Nirvana [U.K.])

SUSAN SINGER

62	Oriole CB 1703	Gee It's Great To Be Young/Hello First Love	15
62	Oriole CB 1741	Bobby's Loving Touch/Johnny Summertime	40
62	Oriole CB 1778	Love Me With All Your Heart/Autumn Leaves	15
63	Oriole CB 1802	Lock Your Heart Away/Answer To A Prayer	15
63	Oriole CB 1882	I Know/That Old Feeling	15

(see also Susan Holiday)

SINGING BELLES

60	Top Rank JAR 350	The Empty Mailbox/Someone Loves You, Joe	10

SINGING DOGS

57	Pye NEP 24029	SINGING DOGS (EP)	25

SINGING NUN

63	Philips BL 7593	SOEUR SOURIRE (LP)	12
63	Philips BL 7607	HER JOY — HER SONGS (LP)	12

SINGING POSTMAN

64	Ralph Tuck Promotions Ltd. BEV EP 153	Come Along A Me/Moind Yer Hid Boy/Hev Yew Gotta Loight Boy/ Miss From Diss (EP)	10
66	Parlophone GEP 8956	FIRST DELIVERY (EP)	8
72	Starline SRS 5063	THE BEST OF (LP)	15

SINGING PRINCIPAL

73	Action ACT 4608	Thank You Baby/Women's Lib	5

SINGING REINDEER

60	Capitol CL 15124	The Happy Birthday Song/I Wanna Be An Easter Bunny	5

(see also "Dancer, Prancer & Nervous")

MARGIE SINGLETON

60	Melodisc 45-1544	Angel Hands/The Eyes Of Love	15
62	Mercury AMT 1197	Magic Star/Only Your Shadow Knows	20
68	Fontana TL 5456	SINGS COUNTRY WITH SOUL (LP)	18

SINISTER DUCKS

83	Situation 2 SIT 25	Suicide: March Of The Sinister Ducks/ Homicide: Old Gangsters Never (foldout p/s)	10

(see also Bauhaus)

SINITTA

87	Fanfare 12FANX 12	Toy Boy (Pumped Up Megamix)/Toy Boy (Overextended Bicep Mix) (12", p/s)	10
88	Fanfare 12FANX 15	Cross My Broken Heart (Extra Pulsing Beat Mix)/Toy Boy (Brand New Megamix)/Cross My Broken Heart (Instrumental) (12", p/s)	10
88	Fanfare 12FANX 16	I Don't Believe In Miracles (Club Remix)/I Don't Believe In Miracles (Instrumental Club Remix) (12", p/s)	10
88	Fanfare CDFAN 16	I Don't Believe In Miracles (7" Radio Version)/I Don't Believe In Miracles (12" Extended Club Remix)/I Don't Believe In Miracles (Instrumental) (CD)	15
88	Fanfare CDFAN2 16	I Don't Believe In Miracles/Cross My Broken Heart/Toy Boy/I Don't Believe In Miracles (Instrumental) (CD)	18
89	Fanfare 12FANX 18	Right Back Where We Started From (Maxine's Night In A Gale Remix)/I Just Can't Help It (12", p/s)	10
89	Fanfare FANCD 18	Right Back Where We Started From/I Just Can't Help It/Right Back Where We Started From (Left Back On The Side Mix) (3" CD)	15
89	Fanfare 12FANX 21	Love On A Mountain Top (Extended Club)/Love On A Mountain Top (Bonus Beats Mix)/Don't Tell Me Not To Cry (12", p/s)	12
89	Fanfare no cat. no.	Fletcher/Madchester Rave On (12", mispressing, unissued)	
90	Fanfare 12FANX 24	Hitchin' A Ride/I'm On My Way (12", p/s)	12
90	Fanfare CDFAN 24	Hitchin' A Ride (Remix)/So Macho/Toy Boy/Right Back Where We Started From (12", p/s)	15
87	Fanfare CDBOY 1	SINITTA (CD)	25

MINT VALUE £

EARL SINK(S)

Year	Label	Title	Value
61	Warner Bros WB 38	Look For Me, I'll Be There/Super Market (as Earl Sink)	15
61	Warner Bros WB 51	Superstitious/Little Suzie Parker	20
63	Capitol CL 15310	Looking For Love/Raining On My Side Of Town (as Earl Sinks)	15

(see also Crickets, Sinx Mitchell)

SINNER

Year	Label	Title	Value
79	Whitetower AMC 705	Need Your Love/Beggar/God's In His Heaven (foldout p/s)	75

SINNERMAN & SARA

Year	Label	Title	Value
68	MGM MGM-C(S) 8099	SINNERMAN AND SARA (LP)	20

SINNERS

Year	Label	Title	Value
63	Columbia DB 7158	I Can't Stand It/If You Leave Me Now	8
64	Columbia DB 7295	It's So Exciting/Leave Him	10

(see also Linda Laine & Sinners)

SINS OF THE FLESH

Year	Label	Title	Value
90s	Plastic Head 014	In The Image Of Torture (12", p/s)	10

SIOUXSIE & BANSHEES

Year	Label	Title	Value
78	Polydor 2059 052	Hong Kong Garden/Voices (10,000 only in gatefold p/s; beige plastic, silver plastic, red plastic or red paper label)	each 20
78	Polydor 2059 052	Hong Kong Garden/Voices (p/s)	5
79	Polydor POSP 9	The Staircase (Mystery)/20th Century Boy (p/s)	5
79	Polydor POSP 59	Playground Twist/Pull To Bits (p/s, some with red paper label)	5/4
79	Polydor 2059 151	Mittageisen (Metal Postcard)/Love In A Void (p/s)	6
80	Polydor 2059 249	Christine/Eve White, Eve Black (with Nigel Gray credit on B-side, p/s)	5
80	Polydor POSPX 205	Israel (Extended)/Red Over White (Extended) (12", a few with 'Made In England' credit, most with 'Made In France' credit)	10/8
82	Polydor POSPG 450	Fireworks/Coal Mind (gatefold p/s)	7
82	Polydor POSP 510	Slowdive/Cannibal Roses (p/s, red paper label)	5
83	Wonderland SHEG 4	Dear Prudence/Tattoo (foldout p/s)	6
83	Fan Club FILE 1	Head Cut/Running Town (freebie, p/s)	40
84	Wonderland SHEX 6	Swimming Horses/Let Go/The Humming Wires (12", p/s with poster)	8
85	Wonderland SHE 7	Dazzle/I Promise (p/s)	5
85	Wonderland SHE 8	Overground/Placebo Effect (p/s)	5
85	Wonderland SHE 9	Cities In Dust/An Execution (poster p/s)	5
85	Wonderland SHEX 9	Cities In Dust/An Execution/Quarterdrawing Of The Dog (12", p/s, 'banned' picture label)	8
86	Wonderland SHEDP 10	Candyman/Lullaby (with free 2nd single, gatefold p/s, 2,000 only)	8
87	Wonderland SHEG 11	This Wheel's On Fire/Shooting Sun/Sleepwalking (On The High Wire)/She's Cracked (numbered double pack, gatefold p/s)	10
88	Spiral Scratch SCRATCH 2	An Interview With... (free with *Spiral Scratch* mag, 5,000 only)	6/4
88	Wonderland SHE 14	Peek A Boo/False Face (gatefold pop-up p/s)	8
88	Wonderland SHECD 15	Killing Jar/Something Wicked (This Way Comes) (CD)	20
88	Wonderland SHE 16	The Last Beat Of My Heart (numbered, gilded p/s)	6
88	Wonderland SHECD 16	The Last Beat Of My Heart (CD)	18
89	Wonderland SHEX 19	Kiss Them For Me (Snapper Mix)/Staring Back/Return (p/s) (12", gatefold p/s)	8
78	Polydor POLD 5009	THE SCREAM (LP, with inner sleeve; some with labels reversed)	12/10
87	Wonderland SHELP 4	THROUGH THE LOOKING GLASS (LP, mispressing, 1 side plays Jimi Hendrix's "War Heroes")	25
90s	Sioux 300	LOVE IN A VOID (LP)	40

(see also Creatures, Cure, Glove)

SIR ALEC & HIS BOYS

Year	Label	Title	Value
67	Deram DM 116	I'm A Believer/Green Green Grass Of Home	7

SIR ALICK & PHRASER

Year	Label	Title	Value
82	Recommended/Black Noise 7 NO 5	In Search Of The Perfect Baby/PROLIFIKURDS: Nursery Crymes (printed p/s in PVC sleeve or standard p/s)	10

(see also Homosexuals)

SIR CHAUNCEY AND HIS EXCITING STRINGS

Year	Label	Title	Value
60	Warner Bros. WB 9	Beautiful Obsession/Tenderfoot	6

(see also Ernie Freeman)

SIR (Clancy) COLLINS BAND

Year	Label	Title	Value
68	Collins Downbeat CR 005	Sock It Softly (with Bob Stackie)/LESTER STERLING, SIR COLLINS & BAND: Three Wise Men	30
68	Collins Downbeat CR 0011	Collins And The Boys/Bob Stackie In Soho (both with Bob Stackie)	30
68	Collins Downbeat CR 0017	Soul Feelings/SIR COLLINS: Hello Stella	30
69	Duke DU 46	Black Panther/I Want To Be Loved	10
69	Duke DU 47	Black Diamonds (with Diamonds)/DIAMONDS: I Remember	8
69	Duke DU 55	Brother Moses/Funny Familiar Feeling (both with Earthquakes)	8

(see also Bob Stackie, Earthquakes, Collins Band, Owen Gray)

SIRCONICAL

Year	Label	Title	Value
99	Twisted Nerve TN 004	CATALOGUE OF ERRORS EP: Frail/Moondance/Bimbo Quick (wraparound p/s)	8

SIR COXSONE SOUND

Year	Label	Title	Value
75	Safari SFA 100	KING OF DUB ROCK (LP)	30
76	Regal RLP 001	KING OF DUB ROCK PART 2 (LP)	25

SIR D's GROUP

Year	Label	Title	Value
61	Blue Beat BB 66	Hey Diddle Diddle (with K. Brown)/Pocket Money (with Mossman & Zeddze)	25

(see also Kent Brown & Rainbows)

SIR DOUGLAS QUINTET

Year	Label	Title	Value
65	London HLU 9964	She's About A Mover/We'll Take Our Last Walk Tonight	10
65	London HLU 9982	The Tracker/Blue Norther	10
65	London HLU 10001	The Story Of John Hardy/In Time	8
66	London HLU 10019	The Rains Came/Bacon Fat	8

MINT VALUE £

Year	Label	Title	£
69	London HLU 10248	She's About A Mover/The Rains Came	5
69	Mercury MF 1079	Mendocino/I Wanna Be Your Mama Again	8
69	Mercury MF 1129	Dynamite Woman/Too Many Dociled Minds	8
82	Sonet SON 2243	Who Were You Thinking Of/Village Girl	5
65	London RE-U 1441	SHE'S ABOUT A MOVER (EP, unissued)	
65	London HA-U 8311	THE SIR DOUGLAS QUINTET (LP)	80
69	Mercury SMCL 20160	MENDOCINO (LP)	25
69	Mercury SMCL 20186	TOGETHER AFTER FIVE (LP)	22
79	Sonet SNTF 804	WANTED VERY MUCH ALIVE (LP)	12
81	Chrysalis CHR 1330	BORDER WAVE (LP)	12
82	Sonet SNTF 881	QUINTESSENCE (LP)	12
83	Sonet SNTF 897	MIDNIGHT SUN (LP)	12
84	Sonet SNTF 912	RIO MEDINA (LP)	12
85	Sonet SNTF 936	LUV YA' EUROPE (LP)	12

(see also Doug Sahm, Augie Meyers)

SIREN

Year	Label	Title	£
71	Dandelion DAN 7002	Strange Locomotion/I'm All Aching (label also lists K 19004)	6
69	Dandelion 63755	SIREN (LP)	22
71	Dandelion DAN 8001	STRANGE LOCOMOTION (LP, gatefold sleeve, label also lists K 49001)	22

(see also Kevin Coyne, Clague)

SIR GIBBS

Year	Label	Title	£
68	Amalgamated AMG 822	People Grudgeful/Pan Ya Machet (both sides actually by Pioneers)	18

SIR HARRY

Year	Label	Title	£
71	Duke DU 127	Last Call/ORGAN D: Hot Organ	10
72	Duke DU 136	Apples To Apples/DRUM BEAT ALL STARS: Good Life	10
72	Bullet BU 519	Mr. Parker's Daughter/U.ROY: On Top Of The Peak	10
72	Downtown DT 493	Meet The Boss/Musical Light	10
73	Downtown DT 504	Apollo 17 (with Cables)/Uptown Rock	12

(see also Barbara Jones)

SIR HENRY (& HIS BUTLERS)

Year	Label	Title	£
68	Columbia DB 8351	Camp/Pretty Style (as Sir Henry & His Butlers)	18
68	Columbia DB 8497	The Rolo Sensation (Camp)/Pretty Style (reissue, as Sir Henry & His Butlers)	10
70	Columbia DB 8740	Annie Got A Date/Like A Rose	5

SIR HORATIO

Year	Label	Title	£
82	Rock Steady/666 Mix 1T	Abracadubra/Sommadub (12", plain sleeve)	15

(see also A Certain Ratio)

SIR LORD COMIC

Year	Label	Title	£
67	Doctor Bird DB 1070	The Great Wuga Wuga (with Cowboys)/THREE TOPS: Feel So Lonesome	40
70	Pressure Beat PR 5507	Jack Of My Trade/CYNTHIA RICHARDS: United We Stand	30

(see also Lord Comic)

SIR WASHINGTON

Year	Label	Title	£
69	Star ST 1	Apollo 12/When You Kiss Me	12
70	Big Chief BC 100	Apollo 13/Space	10

SIR WILLIAM

Year	Label	Title	£
67	Stateside SS 583	Shakespeare's Shrew/Patsy	5

SISTER

Year	Label	Title	£
70	Camel CA 55	Feel It/MAYTONES: Serious	8
73	Camel CA 106	Every Day Is The Same Kind Of Thing/Sweat Of Your Brow	5

(see also Paulette & Gee, Ebony Sisters)

SISTERHOOD

Year	Label	Title	£
86	Merciful Release SIS 010	Giving Ground (RSV)/Giving Ground (AV) (p/s)	5

(see also Sisters Of Mercy, James Ray & Performance)

SISTER SLEDGE

Year	Label	Title	£
73	Atlantic K 10375	Mama Never Told Me/Neither One Of Us	5
75	Atlantic K 10551	Love Don't You Go Through No Changes On Me/Don't You Miss Me	15
75	Atlantic K 10683	Love Has Found Me/Love Ain't Easy	5
77	Cotillion K 10876	Cream Of The Crop/Love Ain't Easy	5

SISTERS LOVE

Year	Label	Title	£
70	A&M AMS 772	Forget It, I've Got It/Eye To Eye	5
70	A&M AMS 808	The Bigger Your Love/Piece Of My Heart	6
72	Tamla Motown TMG 828	Mr. Fix It Man/You've Got To Make Your Choice	5
73	Mowest MW 3009	I'm Learning To Trust My Man/Try It You'll Like It	6
75	Tamla Motown TMG 1002	I'm Learning To Trust My Man/Try It You'll Like It (reissue)	5

SISTERS OF MERCY

Year	Label	Title	£
80	Merciful Release MR 7	The Damage Done/Watch/Home Of The Hitmen (p/s, 1,000 only; beware of counterfeits without 'MR 7' matrix number)	150
82	CNT CNT 002	Body Electric/Adrenochrome (p/s)	60
82	Merciful Release MR 015	Alice/Floorshow (white background p/s)	30
83	Merciful Release MR 019	Anaconda/Phantom (p/s)	5
83	Merciful Release MR 021	Alice/Floorshow/1969/Phantom (12", p/s)	8
83	Merciful Release MR 023	THE REPTILE HOUSE (12" EP, with lyric sheet)	10
83	Merciful Release MR 027	Temple Of Love/Heartland (p/s)	5
83	Merciful Release MRX 027	Temple Of Love (Extended)/Heartland/Gimme Shelter (12", without bardcode on p/s)	8
84	Merciful Release MR 029	Body And Soul/Train (p/s)	8
84	Merciful Release MR 029T	Body And Soul/Body Electric/Train/Afterhours (12", p/s)	10
84	Merciful Release/WEA	ALICE/TEMPLE OF LOVE/REPTILE HOUSE/BODY AND SOUL (4 x 12" box set, promo only)	150
84	Merciful Release MR 033	Walk Away/Poison Door (p/s, some with flexidisc "Long Train" [SAM 218])	15/8

MINT VALUE £

84	Merciful Release MR 033T	Walk Away/Poison Door/On The Wire (12", p/s, with flexi "Long Train")	15/8
85	Merciful Release MR 335	No Time To Cry/Blood Money (p/s)	8
85	Merciful Release MR 035T	No Time To Cry/Blood Money/Bury Me Deep (12", p/s)	10
87	Merciful Release MR 39	This Corrosion/Torch (box set, with 3 postcards, 5,000 only)	10
87	Merciful Release MR 39C	This Corrosion/Torch/Colours (cassette)	5
87	Merciful Release MR 39CD	This Corrosion (11.15)/Torch/Colours (CD, black disc, gatefold card sleeve with gauze inner, some without 'WEA' logo on back sleeve)	12
88	Merciful Release MR 43C	Dominion/Untitled/Sandstorm/Ozymandias (cassette in presentation box)	6
88	Merciful Release MR 43TB	Dominion (Extended)/Untitled/Sandstorm/Emma (12", box set with poster)	8
88	Merciful Release MR 43CD	Dominion (Extended)/Untitled/Sandstorm/Ozymandias (3" CD, black disc with adaptor, 5" case)	8
88	Merciful Release MR 44CD	Lucretia My Reflection (Extended 9.52)/Long Train (1984) (3" CD, with adaptor, 5" case)	8
90	Merciful Release MR 47CD	More/More (Extended)/You Could Be The One (CD)	8
90	Merciful Release MR 47CDX	More/More (Extended)/You Could Be The One (CD, 12" foldout p/s)	10
90	Merciful Release MR 51TX	Doctor Jeep (Extended)/Burn (live)/Amphetamine Logic (live) (12", p/s, 6,000 only)	8
92	Merciful Release MR 53CDX	Temple Of Love (1992) (Touched By The Hand Of Ofra Haza)/I Was Wrong (American Fade)/Vision Thing (Canadian Club Remix)/When You Don't See Me (German Release) (CD, box set with 4 postcards)	8
85	Merciful Release MR 337L	FIRST AND LAST AND ALWAYS (LP, gatefold sleeve, beware of copies with faked autographs!)	18
87	Merciful Release MR 441L	FLOODLAND (LP, numbered sleeve with lyric sheet)	12

(see also Mission, Sisterhood, Ghost Dance, Dead Or Alive)

SITUATION

66	CBS 202392	Situation Now/Time	10

SIVUCA

74	Vanguard VSD 79337	SIVUCA (LP)	12

SIX OF ONE

64	Mercury MF 812	He's The One You Love/I Love My Little Girl	10

SIXPENCE

67	London HLJ 10124	You're The Love/What To Do	6

SIX TEENS

56	London HLU 8345	A Casual Look/Teen Age Promise	425
56	London HLU 8345	A Casual Look/Teen Age Promise (78)	100

SIXTH COMM

87	Eyas Media EYAS 002	CONTENT WITH BLOOD/TURN OF THE WHEEL (LP, embossed, textured sleeve, 2,000 only)	20
87	Eyas Media EYAS 005	TASTE FOR FLESH (1st 2,000 in laminated, full-cover sleeve)	18/12
88	Eyas Media EYAS 006	FRUITS OF YGGDRASIL (LP, limited issue, 669 copies only)	25
90	Eyas Media EYAS 013	ASYLUM (LP)	15
90	Eyas Media EYAS 071	COMING OF SEVEN (LP)	12

64 SPOONS

78	Bushbaby	LADIES DON'T HAVE WILLIES (EP)	10

SIZE SEVEN GROUP

65	Mercury MF 845	Where Do We Go From Here/Till I Die	8
65	Mercury MF 854	In Time/Walking Proud	8
65	Mercury MF 896	It's Got To Be Love/I Met Her In The Rain	6

SKA CHAMPIONS

65	Blue Beat BB 305	My Tears/Yesterday's Dreams	25

SKA CITY ROCKERS

80	Inferno BEAT 1	Time Is Tight/Roadrunner/You Don't Know Like I Know (p/s)	6
80	Inferno BEAT 1	Time Is Tight/Roadrunner/You Don't Know Like I Know (12", p/s)	10

SKA-DOWS

80	Cheapskate CHEAP 1	Apache/The Tune That Time Forgot (p/s)	7
80	Cheapskate CHEAP 4	Telstar/Yes Yes Yes (p/s)	8
81	Cheapskate CHEAP 25	Yes Yes Yes/Twice (p/s)	8
81	Penthouse PENT 7	Ska's On 45/Rhapsody In Buh (plain stickered sleeve)	6
81	Penthouse PENT 127	Ska's On 45/The Ska-Dows Live (Let's Twist Again/Everybody Knows It's Shocking/Aye-Ho — Kinky Reggae) (12", p/s)	12
81	Cheapskate CHEAP 36	Ska's On 45/Rhapsody In Buh (p/s, reissue)	6
81	Cheapskate CHEAPT 36	Ska's On 45/The Ska-Dows Live (Let's Twist Again/Everybody Knows It's Shocking/Aye-Ho — Kinky Reggae) (12", p/s, reissue)	8
82	Cheapskate CHEAP 41	We Gotta Get Out Of This Place/Ska'd For Life	5
82	Cheapskate SKATE 3	SKA'D FOR LIFE (LP)	15

SKA KINGS

64	Atlantic AT 4003	Jamaica Ska (actually by Keith Lynn & Ken Lazarus, & Byron Lee/Dragonaires)/ Oil In My Lamp (actually by Eric Morris with Byron Lee & Dragonaires)	15
65	Parlophone R 5338	Bimbo/Ska'ville	12

SKATALITES (Jamaica)

65	Island WI 161	Trip To Mars/DOTTIE & BONNIE: Bunch Of Roses	30
65	Island WI 164	Good News/OWEN & LEON: The Fits Is On Me	20
65	Island WI 168	Guns Of Navarone (actually by Roland Alphonso & Studio One Orchestra)/ Marcus Garvey (actually "Where's Marcus Garvey" by Bongoman Byfield)	10
65	Island WI 175	Dragon Weapon/DESMOND DEKKER & FOUR ACES: It Was Only A Dream	22
65	Island WI 191	Dr. Kildare/Sucu Sucu	20
65	Island WI 207	Ball O' Fire/LINVAL SPENCER: Can't Go On	20
65	Island WI 226	Dick Tracy/RITA & SOULETTES: One More Chance	25
65	Island WI 228	Beardman Ska/BONNIE & RITA: Bless You	20

65 Island WI 244 — Lucky Seven/JUSTIN HINDS & DOMINOES: Never Too Young ... 20
66 Island WI 260 — Independent Anniversary Ska (I Should Have Known Better)/ WAILERS: Jumbie Jamboree ... 75
65 Ska Beat JB 177 — Latin Goes Ska/LORD TANAMO: Night Food Ska ... 35
65 Ska Beat JB 178 — Silver Dollar/My Business ... 20
65 Ska Beat JB 182 — Street Corner/DREAMLETS: Really Now ... 20
65 Ska Beat JB 206 — Timothy/KING SCRATCH & DYNAMITES: Gumma ... 40
73 Trojan Maxi TRM 9008 — Guns Of Navarone/Bonanza Ska/Napolean Solo ... 5
67 Studio One SOL 9006 — SKA AUTHENTIC (LP) ... 125

(see also Justin Hinds, Deltas, Four Aces, Maytals, Jackie Opel, Joe White, Jackie Mittoo)

SKATALITES (U.K.)

68 Decca F 12743 — Don't Knock It/I Know ... 6
69 Spark SRL 1034 — 'Cos You're The One I Love/Please Let Me Hide ... 8

SKAVENGERS

80 Identity Discs ID 001 — Party Girls/Go To Pieces/Happy ... 10

SK'BOO

70s Cuecumber CUE 1001 — It's A Hard Road/Music Is Life/Talking Pictures/God's Peace In Mind ... 5

(see also Them)

BOBBY SKEL

64 London HLU 9942 — Kiss And Run/Say It Now ... 15

SKELETAL FAMILY

83 Luggage RRP 00724 — Trees/Just A Friend (foldout p/s) ... 12

(see also Ghost Dance)

SKELETON CREW

87 B BS 1 — BOOGIE-WOOGIE, SKIFFLE & BLUES (12" EP, p/s) ... 15
88 B BS 2 — House Of The Rising Sun/Hurricane Janine (white label promo only) ... 15

(see also King Earl Boogie Band, Manfred Mann's Earth Band)

PETER SKELLERN

72 Decca SKL 5151 — PETER SKELLERN (LP) ... 12
74 Decca SKL 5178 — NOT WITHOUT A FRIEND (LP) ... 12

(see also Harlan County)

SKEPTIK

84 Zenon — RETURN TO HELL (12" EP) ... 8

SKEPTIX

82 Zenon SKEP 001 — Routine Machine/Curfew (p/s) ... 5
83 Zenon SKEP 002 — Scarred For Life/Born To Lose/Peaceforce (p/s) ... 5
83 Zenon SKEP 003 — RETURN TO HELL (EP) ... 5

SKERNE

81 Guardian GRC 81 — BETTER LATE THAN NEVER (LP, private pressing) ... 15

FATHER SKETTO

73 Pama PM 877 — Big Nine/RECO'S GROUP: Old Lady ... 6

(see also Sketto Rich, Ruddy & Sketto)

SKIDDY & DETROIT

72 Grape GR 3030 — The Exile Song/BUNNY GALE: In The Burning Sun Joh-Ho ... 6

ALAN SKIDMORE (QUINTET)

69 Deram Nova SDN 11 — ONCE UPON A TIME (LP) ... 110
71 Philips 6308 041 — T.C.B. (LP) ... 130

(see also John Mayall's Bluesbreakers, Brian Bennett, Centipede)

JIMMY SKIDMORE

72 DJM DJSL 026 — SKID MARKS (LP) ... 50

SKID ROW (Ireland)

70 Song 003 — Saturday Morning Man (Irish pressing) ... 25
70 CBS 4893 — Sandie's Gone (Parts 1 & 2) ... 15
71 CBS 7181 — Night Of The Warm Witch/Mr. Deluxe ... 10
70 CBS 63965 — SKID (LP, orange label, red & blue sleeve) ... 55
71 CBS 64411 — 34 HOURS (LP, orange label) ... 50

(see also Gary Moore, Thin Lizzy, Peggy's Leg, UFO)

SKID ROW (U.S.)

89 Atlantic A 8935W — Youth Gone Wild/Sweet Little Sister (poster p/s) ... 5
89 Atlantic A 8935B — Youth Gone Wild/Sweet Little Sister (box set) ... 5
89 Atlantic A 8935P — Youth Gone Wild/Rattlesnake Shake (Live) (guitar-shaped picture disc) ... 8
91 Atlantic A 7603TX — Slave To The Grind/C'mon And Love Me/Creepshow/Beggars Day (12", "rubberised" p/s) ... 8

SKIDS

78 No Bad NB 1 — Charles/Reasons/Test Tube Babies (p/s) ... 10
78 Virgin VS 227 — Sweet Suburbia/Open Sound (p/s, white vinyl) ... 5
78 Virgin VS 232-12 — WIDE OPEN (12" EP, red vinyl) ... 8
79 Virgin VS 262 — Masquerade/Out Of Town//Another Emotion/Aftermath Dub (double pack) ... 5
79 Virgin VS 306 — Working For The Yankee Dollar/Vanguard's Crusage//All The Young Dudes/ Hymns From A Haunted Ballroom (double pack) ... 5
92 Virgin VSCDT 1411 — THE SKIDS VS THE RUTS EP (EP, shared with The Ruts) ... 10
79 Smash Hits HIT 002 — The Olympian/XTC: Ten Feet Tall (33rpm red flexi with *Smash Hits* mag) ... 6/4
79 Virgin V 2116 — SCARED TO DANCE (LP, blue vinyl, withdrawn) ... 40
79 Virgin V 2138 — DAYS IN EUROPA (LP, with insert, 1st pressing with withdrawn cover featuring German 'gothic' lettering & 1936 Olympics picture) ... 12
80 Virgin V 2174 — THE ABSOLUTE GAME (LP, with free LP "Strength Through Joy" [VDJ 33]) ... 12

(see also Big Country)

MINT VALUE £

BJORN SKIFS
78 EMI EMI 2785 When The Night Comes/Don't Stop Now. 6
81 EMI EMI 5172 Haunted By A Dream/Fangad I En Drom 8

SKILLETS
70 Pantonic PAN 6303 BOTH SIDES NOW (LP) 15

SKIN
80s Product Inc. 12 PROD 6 Girl Come Out/(Version) (12", p/s). 8
80s Product Inc. 12 PROD 3 One Thousand Years (12", p/s). 8
80s Product Inc. 33 PROD 11 SHAME, HUMILITY, REVENGE (LP, with inner) 12

SKIN ALLEY
70 CBS 5045 Tell Me/Better Be Blind 10
72 Transatlantic BIG 506 You Got Me Danglin'/Skin Valley Serenade. 8
72 Transatlantic BIG 511 In The Midnight Hour/Broken Eggs 8
69 CBS 63847 SKIN ALLEY (LP) 50
70 CBS 64140 TO PAGHAM AND BEYOND (LP) 30
72 Transatlantic TRA 260 TWO QUID DEAL (LP, with inner sleeve & poster) 35
73 Transatlantic TRA 273 SKIN TIGHT (LP). 22

SKIN DEEP
85 Enemy ENEMY 1 FOOTBALL VIOLENCE (EP). 40

SKIN, FLESH & BONES
74 Pyramid PYR 7014 Butter Te Fish/Bammie And Fish. 5
(see also Vincent Gordon, Cynthia Richards)

JIMMIE SKINNER
59 Mercury AMT 1030 Walkin' My Blues Away/Dark Hollow 15
59 Mercury AMT 1030 Walkin' My Blues Away/Dark Hollow (78) 10
59 Mercury AMT 1062 John Wesley Hardin/Misery Loves Company 10
60 Mercury AMT 1088 Riverboat Gambler/Married To A Friend 5
60 Mercury AMT 1117 Reasons To Live/I'm A Lot More Lonesome Now 5
64 London RE-B 1421 KENTUCKY COLONEL VOL. 1 (EP) 20
64 London RE-B 1422 KENTUCKY COLONEL VOL. 2 (EP) 20
64 London RE-B 1423 KENTUCKY COLONEL VOL. 3 (EP) 20

JIMMIE SKINNER/GEORGE JONES
59 Mercury ZEP 10012 COUNTRY AND WESTERN (EP, 2 tracks each) 45

SKI PATROL
80 Clever Metal VIN 1 Everything Is Temporary/Silent Screams (p/s) 10
80 Malicious Damage MD 2 Agent Orange/Driving (p/s, with insert). 12
81 Malicious Damage MD 3 Cut/Faith In Transition (p/s) 10
(see also Wall)

SKIP & FLIP
59 Top Rank JAR 156 It Was I/Lunch Hour 10
59 Top Rank JAR 156 It Was I/Lunch Hour (78). 25
59 Top Rank JAR 248 Fancy Nancy/It Could Be 15
60 Top Rank JAR 358 Cherry Pie/(I'll Quit) Cryin' Over You 10
(see also Gary Paxton, Skip Battin, Hollywood Argyles)

SKIP BIFFERTY
67 RCA Victor RCA 1621 On Love/Cover Girl 35
67 RCA Victor RCA 1648 Happy Land/Reason To Live 35
68 RCA Victor RCA 1720 Man In Black/Mr. Money Man 50
68 RCA Victor RD/SF 7941 SKIP BIFFERTY (LP, black label, later orange). 90/45
(see also Chosen Few, Heavy Jelly, Griffin, Graham Bell, Arc, Bell & Arc, Every Which Way, Loving Awareness)

SKREWDRIVER
77 Chiswick S 11 You're So Dumb/Better Off Crazy (orange or green p/s). 45
77 Chiswick NS 18 Anti-Social/19th Nervous Breakdown (p/s) 30
78 Chiswick NS 28 Streetfight/Unbeliever (unissued, white label acetates only) . . . . . 100+
80 TJM TJM 4 Built Up, Knocked Down/A Case Of Pride/Breakout (p/s). 20
82 Skrewdriver SKREW 1T BACK WITH A BANG (12", p/s) 60
83 White Noise WN 1 White Power/Smash The I.R.A./Shove The Dove (p/s). 35
83 White Noise WN 2 Voice Of Britain/Sick Society (p/s). 35
77 Chiswick CH 3 ALL SKREWED UP (mini-LP, 12-track, 45rpm, 3 different colour sleeves). 50
77 Chiswick WIK 3 ALL SKREWED UP (LP, 15-track, 33rpm, unissued in U.K.; German-only)

SKROTEEZ
82 Skroteez SPILL 1 OVERSPILL (EP). 20

SKULLFLOWER
86 Broken Flag BF V9 BIRTHDEATH (12" EP) 30
89 Shock SX 001 (I Live) In The Bottomless Pit/Bo Diddley's Shitpump
(foldaround p/s in poly bag, 500 only, 75 copies in 'burns victim' sleeve) 20/12
90 Toe Jam Rotten Sun/Spook Rise (p/s, numbered, 500 only) 8
92 Dying Artefact DE 002 Bad Alchemy/Blues For H.M. (p/s in poly bag, numbered, 500 only) 8
94 Freak Records RR 001 White Fang 2/Glassy Essence (wraparound sleeve, stamped label). 7
89 Shock SX 008 XAMAN (LP) 12
89 Broken Flag BFV 10 FORM DESTROYER (LP) 20
(see also Ramleh)

SKULLS
89 Snake Skin SS 001 Graveyard Signal/Idols And Dolls (p/s, 300 only) 10

SKULLSNAPS
73 GSF GSZ 7 My Hang Up Is You/It's A New Day. 20

SKUNKS
78 Eel Pie EPS 001 Good From The Bad/Back Street Fightin' (2,000 only, die-cut 'swirl' sleeve) 12
(see also Craze, Hard Corps)

SKY

Year	Label / Cat. No.	Title	£
68	United Artists UP 2234	Air-O-Plane Ride/Weather Forecast	5
69	Decca F 12971	On Our Way/The Singer Is Singing His Song	5

(see also Knack)

SKY

Year	Label / Cat. No.	Title	£
71	RCA RCA 2070	Goodie Two Shoes/Make It On Time (as U.S. Sky)	5
71	RCA SF 8168	DON'T HOLD BACK (LP, as U.S. Sky)	12

PATRICK SKY

Year	Label / Cat. No.	Title	£
65	Vanguard VSD 79179	PATRICK SKY (LP)	20
70	Vanguard SVRL 19054	A HARVEST OF GENTLE CLANG (LP)	20

SKYBIRD

Year	Label / Cat. No.	Title	£
74	Holyground HGS 118	SUMMER OF '73 (LP, 250 copies only)	50

SKY BLUES

Year	Label / Cat. No.	Title	£
67	Centaur CPC 1003	PLAYERS AT EASE: COVENTRY CITY (LP)	12

SKY HIGH

Year	Label / Cat. No.	Title	£
80	Circus CIRC 5	Ghettos Of Your Own Kind/Passing By/Moving To The Music/Red Light (p/s)	5

SKYLARK

Year	Label / Cat. No.	Title	£
73	Capitol CL 15764	Wildflower/Writing On the Wall	5
72	Capitol E-ST 11048	SKYLARK (LP)	12

SKYLINERS

Year	Label / Cat. No.	Title	£
59	London HLB 8829	Since I Don't Have You/One Night, One Night	200
59	London HLB 8829	Since I Don't Have You/One Night, One Night (78)	50
59	London HLU 8924	This I Swear/Tomorrow	75
59	London HLU 8924	This I Swear/Tomorrow (78)	50
59	London HLU 8971	It Happened Today/Lonely Way	75
59	London HLU 8971	It Happened Today/Lonely Way (78)	50
60	Polydor NH 66951	Pennies From Heaven/I'll Be Seeing You	15
61	Pye International 7N 25091	I'll Close My Eyes/The Door Is Still Open	15

SKYSOUNDS

Year	Label / Cat. No.	Title	£
66	Anglo TPMA 101/102	Two Timer/No Matter Where I Wander (private pressing)	5

FREDDIE SLACK (& Orchestra)

Year	Label / Cat. No.	Title	£
50	Capitol 13340	Whatever Happened To Ol' Jack?/Is I Gotta Practice, Ma? (78)	8
50	Capitol 13379	Be-Bop Boogie/On The Road To Mandolin (78)	6
51	Capitol LC 6529	FREDDIE SLACK'S BOOGIE WOOGIE (10" LP)	35

(see also Ella Mae Morse & Freddie Slack)

SLACK ALICE

Year	Label / Cat. No.	Title	£
74	Fontana 6007 038	Motorcycle/Ridin' The Wind	5
74	Philips 6308 214	SLACK ALICE (LP)	18

(see also Sandra Alfred, Sandra Barry)

SLADE

SINGLES

Year	Label / Cat. No.	Title	£
69	Fontana TF 1056	Wild Winds Are Blowing/One Way Hotel (credited to *The* Slade)	150
70	Fontana TF 1079	Shape Of Things To Come/C'mon C'mon	150
70	Polydor 2058 054	Know Who You Are/Dapple Rose	150
71	Polydor 2058 112	Get Down With It/Do You Want Me/The Gospel According To Rasputin (with writing credit: Holder/Hill/Lea/Powell/Penniman; some copies repressed as "Get Down And Get With It")	8
72	Polydor 2058 195	Look What You Dun/Candidate	7
72	Polydor 2058 231	Tak Me Bak 'Ome/Wonderin'	7
73	Polydor 2058 377	Skweeze Me Pleeze Me/Kill 'Em At The Hot Club Tonite	6
73	Polydor 2058 407	My Friend Stan/My Town	6
74	Polydor 2058 453	Everyday/Good Time Gals	6
74	Polydor 2058 453	Everyday/Good Time Gals (mispressed with Hollies' "The Air That I Breathe" on A-side)	6
74	Polydor 2058 492	Bangin' Man/She Did It To Me	5
74	Polydor 2058 522	Far Far Away/O.K. Yesterday Was Yesterday (p/s)	5
75	Polydor 2058 547	How Does It Feel?/So Far So Good (p/s)	8
75	Polydor 2058 663	In For A Penny/Can You Just Imagine (some in p/s)	8/6
76	Polydor 2058 716	Nobody's Fool/L.A. Jinx	6
77	Barn 2014 105	Gypsy Roadhog/Forest Full Of Needles	7
77	Barn 2014 106	Burning In The Heat Of Love/Ready Steady Kids	18
77	Barn 2014 114	My Baby Left Me; That's Alright/O.H.M.S. (p/s)	6
78	Barn 2014 121	Give Us A Goal/Daddio	8
78	Barn 2014 127	Rock'n'Roll Bolero/It's Alright By Me	15
79	Barn BARN 002	Ginny Ginny/Dizzy Mama (yellow vinyl only, some with sticker)	10/8
79	Barn BARN 010	Sign Of The Times/Not Tonight Josephine	15
79	Barn BARN 011	Okey Cokey/My Baby's Got It	10
80	RSO RSO 051	Okey Cokey/My Baby's Got It (withdrawn reissue, existence unconfirmed)	
80	S.O.T.B. SUPER 45 3	SIX OF THE BEST — NIGHT STARVATION (12" EP, die-cut sleeve)	15
80	Cheapskate CHEAP 5	ALIVE AT READING '80 (EP, die-cut sleeve)	7
80	Cheapskate CHEAP 11	Merry Xmas Everybody/Okey Cokey/Get Down And Get With It (as Slade & Reading Choir, some in die-cut p/s)	8/5
80	Polydor 2058 422	Merry Xmas Everybody/Don't Blame Me (reissue, green background, 'holly leaf' design, colour group photo p/s)	5
81	Cheapskate CHEAP 16	We'll Bring The House Down/Hold On To Your Hats (p/s)	7
81	Cheapskate CHEAP 21	Wheels Ain't Comin' Down/Not Tonight Josephine (p/s)	7
81	Cheapskate CHEAP 24	Knuckle Sandwich Nancy/I'm Mad (p/s)	10
81	RCA	Tak Me Bak 'Ome/Gudbuy T'Jane) (12" EP, p/s)	10
82	RCA RCA 191	Ruby Red/Funk Punk And Junk (p/s)	10
82	RCA RCAD 191	Ruby Red/Funk Punk And Junk//Rock And Roll Preacher (live)/Take Me Bak 'Ome (live) (double pack, gatefold p/s)	5

		MINT VALUE £
82 RCA RCA 291	(And Now The Waltz) C'est La Vie/Merry Xmas Everybody (p/s)	5
82 Speed SPEED 201	Okey Cokey/Get Down And Get With It (no p/s)	8
82 Speed SPEEDP 201	Okey Cokey/Get Down And Get With It (picture disc)	5
83 RCA RCA 373	My Oh My/Merry Xmas Everybody (live)/Keep Your Hands Off My Power Supply (3-track edition, p/s)	7
83 RCA RCA 373	My Oh My/Merry Xmas Everybody (live)/Keep Your Hands Off My Power Supply (12", p/s)	8
83 RCA RCA 385	Run Runaway/Two Track Stereo One Track Mind (p/s)	6
84 RCA RCAT 455	All Join Hands/My Oh My/Here's To... (The New Year)/ Merry Xmas (Live & Kickin') (12", stickered p/s)	8
85 RCA PB 40027	Myzterious Mizster Jones/Mama Nature Is A Rocker (p/s)	7
85 RCA PB 40027	Myzterious Mizster Jones/Mama Nature Is A Rocker (picture disc, PVC sleeve)	10
85 RCA PT 40028	Myzterious Mizster Jones (Extended Version)/Mama Nature Is A Rocker/ My Oh My (Piano And Vocal Version) (12", p/s)	8
85 Polydor POSPX 780	Merry Xmas Everybody/Don't Blame Me (12", p/s)	8
85 RCA PB 40449	Do You Believe In Miracles/My Oh My (p/s)	5
85 RCA PB 40449/PB 40549	Do You Believe In Miracles/My Oh My (Swing Version)//Santa Claus Is Coming To Town/Auld Lang Syne/You'll Never Walk Alone (double pack, gatefold PVC sleeve, 2nd 45 without p/s)	30
85 RCA PT 40450D (PT 40450/PT 40550)	Do You Believe In Miracles/My Oh My (Swing Version)/Time To Rock/ Santa Claus Is Coming To Town/Auld Lang Syne/You'll Never Walk Alone (12", 'Slade Xmas' double pack, separate sleeves in gatefold PVC cover)	20
87 RCA PB 41147D	Still The Same/Gotta Go Home//The Roaring Silence/Don't Talk To Me About Love (21st anniversary double pack, gatefold p/s)	10
88 Cheapskate BOYZ 3	Let's Dance (1988 Remix)/Standing On The Corner (p/s)	7
88 Cheapskate BOYZCD 3	Let's Dance (1988 Remix)/Far Far Away/How Does It Feel/ Standing On The Corner (3" CD, with adaptor, 5" case)	8
88 Counterpoint CDEP 12 C	How Does It Feel/Far Far Away/(WIZZARD: 2 tracks) (CD)	10
89 RCA PD 42637	My Oh My/Keep Your Hands Off My Power Supply/Run Runaway/ Two Track Stereo, One Track Mind (CD)	8
89 Cheapskate CD BOYZ 4	Merry Xmas Everybody/Don't Blame Me/Far Far Away (CD)	8
80s Polydor 2058 422	Merry Xmas Everybody/Don't Blame Me (export p/s from various artist box set, green background, 4 individual photos)	25
80s SLADE 1	An Interview With Slade (picture disc, 2,000 only, PVC sleeve)	10
91 Polydor PZ 189	Universe/Red Hot/Gypsy Roadhog/Merry Xmas Everybody (12", stickered p/s)	8
91 Polydor PZCD 189	Universe/Red Hot/Merry Xmas Everybody (CD)	8
81 Polydor POSP 399	CUM ON FEEL THE NOIZE (EP)	6
81 Polydor POSPX 399	CUM ON FEEL THE NOIZE (Cum On Feel The Noize/Coz I Luv You/Tak Me Back 'Ome/Gudbye T'Jane)	6
FLEXIDISCS		
72 Polydor/Sound For Industry SFI 122	The Whole World's Going Crazee/MIKE HUGG: Bonnie Charlie (33rpm free with *Music Scene* magazine)	18/8
73 Lyntone LYN 2645	Slade talk to *Melanie* readers (with *Melanie* magazine)	15/8
74 Lyntone LYN 2797	Slade exclusive to all *19* readers (with *19* magazine)	15/8
75 Lyntone LYN 3156/7	Far Far Away/Thanks For The Memory (with Smith's Crisps offer)	8
75 Fan Club LYN 2645/2797	Slade talk to *Melanie* readers/Slade talk to *19* readers	10
PROMOS etc.		
72 Polydor 2814 008	Hear Me Calling/Get Down With It (33rpm sampler for "Slade Alive", 500 only)	125
74 Polydor 2058 492	The Bangin' Man/She Did It To Me (export p/s)	25
75 Polydor 2058 585	Thanks For The Memory (with altered lyrics)/Raining In My Champagne	25
77 Barn 2014 105	Gypsy Roadhog/Forest Full Of Needles (mono, DJ copy)	25
80 S.O.T.B. SUPER 3	Night Starvation/When I'm Dancing I Ain't Fightin'	45
91 Polydor PO 180 DJ	Radio Wall Of Sound /Radio Wall Of Sound	15
91 Polydor PZ 180 DJ	Radio Wall Of Sound /Lay Your Love On The Line/Cum On Feel The Noize (12", p/s)	10
ALBUMS		
70 Polydor 2383 026	PLAY IT LOUD (LP)	15
72 Polydor 2383 101	SLADE ALIVE (LP, gatefold sleeve)	12
73 Polydor 2383 261	OLD NEW BORROWED AND BLUE (LP, gatefold sleeve)	12
73 Polydor 2442 119	SLADEST (LP)	12
74 Polydor 2442 126	SLADE IN FLAME (LP, gatefold sleeve)	12
76 Polydor 2383 377	NOBODY'S FOOLS (LP, with inner sleeve)	12
77 Barn 2314 103	WHATEVER HAPPENED TO SLADE (LP, with lyric sheet)	20
78 Barn 2314 106	SLADE ALIVE VOLUME 2 (LP)	20
79 Barn NARB 003	RETURN TO BASE (LP)	40
83 Action Replay REPLAY 1000	SLADE IN FLAME (LP, reissue)	12
85 RCA PD 70604	ROGUES GALLERY (CD)	20
87 RCA PD 71260	YOU BOYS MAKE BIG NOIZE (CD)	18

(see also Ambrose Slade, Steve Brett, 'N Betweens, Vendors, Dummies, Jimmy Lea, Gary Holton, China Dolls, Clout, Gang Of Angels, Metal Gurus)

PRENTIS SLADE

61 Parlophone R 4850	I Can Tell/Looking For A Friend	7

SLADE BROTHERS

66 Pye 7N 17080	Peace In My Mind/Life's Great Race	70

SLAM CREEPERS

68 Olga OLE 009	Saturday/Hold It Baby	15
73 Sonet SON 2003	We Are Happy People/Yansbro Memories	5

SLANES

65 Blue Beat BB 300	It Takes Time/LIGES: Have Mercy Baby (B-side actually by Frank Cosmo)	25

MINT VALUE £

IVOR SLANEY ORCHESTRA

61 HMV POP 943 The Sir Francis Drake Theme/Midsummer Madness. . . . 6
63 HMV POP 1210 The Carlos Theme/Chant Espana 6
64 HMV POP 1347 High Wire/Sacramento 12
66 Columbia DB 8020 Long Weekend/Eleven Up (as Slaney Strings) 10

SLAPP HAPPY

74 Virgin VS 105 Casablanca Moon/Slow Moon's Rose 12
75 Virgin VS 124 Johnny's Dead/Mr. Rainbow (p/s) 12
83 Half Cat HC 001 Everybody's Slimmin' (Even Men And Women!)/Blue-Eyed Villain (p/s). . . . 12
72 Polydor 2310 204 SORT OF (LP, with insert) 140
74 Virgin V 2014 SLAPP HAPPY (LP) 12
74 Virgin V 2024 DESPERATE STRAIGHTS (LP, with Henry Cow) 12
86 Recommended RRS 5 SORT OF (LP, reissue) 15
(see also Henry Cow, Peter Blegvad, Anthony Moore, Art Bears)

FELIX SLATKIN ORCHESTRA

61 London HLG 9256 Sundowners (Theme)/Gaythers Gone 6

SLAUGHTER (& THE DOGS)

77 Rabid TOSH 101 Cranked Up Really High/The Bitch (p/s, blue, later cream plastic labels) 12
77 Rabid TOSH 101 Cranked Up Really High/The Bitch (p/s, repressings with b&w paper label). . . . 10
77 Decca FR 13723 Where Have All The Boot Boys Gone/You're A Bore (paper label). . . . 8
77 Decca LF 13723 Where Have All The Boot Boys Gone/You're A Bore (12", p/s, 10,000 only) 12
77 Decca FR 13743 Dame To Blame/Johnny T. 12
78 Decca FR 13758 Quick Joey Small/Come On Back (with Mick Ronson) 6
79 TJM TJM 3 It's Alright/Edgar Allen Poe/Twist & Turn/UFO (12", p/s). . . . 12
79 DJM DJS 10927 You're Ready Now/Runaway (p/s) 6
80 Decca FR Where Have All The Boot Boys Gone/You're A Bore (reissue, p/s) 10
80 DJM DJS 10936 East Side Of Town/One By One (p/s, as Slaughter) 6
80 DJM DJS 10945 I'm The One/What's Wrong Boy? (live)/Hell In New York (p/s, as Slaughter) 5
82 Thrush THRUSH 1 HALF ALIVE (12" EP) 10
88 Damaged Goods FNARR 1 Where Have All The Boot Boys Gone/You're A Bore/Johnny T. (p/s, 1,000 only: 500 on green vinyl, 500 on red vinyl) . . . . each 15
78 Decca SKL 5292 DO IT DOG STYLE (LP) 30
78 Rabid HAT 23 LIVE SLAUGHTER RABID DOGS (LP, plain white sleeve with large sticker) 12
80 DJM DJF 20566 BITE BACK (LP, as Slaughter) 12
89 Damaged Goods FNARRLP 2 DO IT DOG STYLE (LP, reissue, 1,000-only, multi-coloured vinyl, numbered, with 2 multi-coloured stickers) 12
(see also Studio Sweethearts, Ed Banger)

SLAUGHTER JOE

85 Creation CRE 019 I'll Follow You Down/Napalm Girl (foldaround p/s in poly bag) 6
87 Kaleidoscope S. KLSLP 003 ALL AROUND MY HOBBY HORSE'S HEAD (LP). . . . 12
(see also Television Personalities, Missing Scientists)

SLAVE

84 Cotillion BT 6955 Just A Touch Of Love/Wait For Me (12") 10
77 Cotillion K 50358 SLAVE (LP). . . . 15

MARTIN SLAVIN & HIS GANG

60 Oriole CB 1587 Rock-A-Charleston/The Charleston's Gonna Rock The Hop 8
(see also Martinas & His Music)

FRANK SLAY ORCHESTRA

62 Top Rank JAR 599 Flying Circle/Cincinnati 7

SLAYER

84 Roadrunner RR 2444 2 HAUNTING THE CHAPEL (12" EP). . . . 10
87 London LON 133 Criminally Insane/Aggressive Perfector (Remix) ('cross' p/s, some on red vinyl with patch) 20/6
87 London LONX 133 Criminally Insane/Postmortem/Aggressive Perfector (Remix) (12", red vinyl, no p/s) 25
89 Roadrunner RR 2444 2 Haunting The Chapel/Chemical Warfare/Captor Of Sin (CD, reissue). . . . 10
87 Enigma 720151 LIVE UNDEAD (LP, picture disc) 15
87 London LONPP 34 REIGN IN BLOOD (LP, picture disc). . . . 15

F. SLEDGE

67 Blue Beat BB 386 Red Eye Girl/Try To Love Again (actually by "Go On Girl"/"Giving You A Try Girl" by Freddie McKay & Buster's Group) 25

PERCY SLEDGE

66 Atlantic 584 001 When A Man Loves A Woman/Love Me Like You Mean It 7
66 Atlantic 584 034 Warm And Tender Love/Sugar Puddin' 7
66 Atlantic 584 055 Heart Of A Child/My Adorable One 8
67 Atlantic 584 071 It Tears Me Up/Oh, How Happy 7
67 Atlantic 584 080 Baby, Help Me/You've Lost That Something Wonderful 8
67 Atlantic 584 108 Out Of Left Field/It Can't Be Stopped 7
67 Atlantic 584 140 Pledging My Love/You Don't Miss Your Water. . . . 7
68 Atlantic 584 177 Take Time To Know Her/It's All Wrong But It's Alright 7
68 Atlantic 584 225 Come Softly To Me/You're All Around Me 6
69 Atlantic 584 264 Any Day Now/The Angels Listened In. . . . 8
69 Atlantic 584 286 Kind Woman/Woman Of The Night. . . . 6
69 Atlantic 584 300 True Love Travels On A Gravel Road/Faithful And True 6
72 Atlantic K 10144 Rainbow Road/Standing on The Mountain 6
72 Atlantic K 10165 Baby, Help Me/Warm And Tender Love/Take Time To Know Her. . . . 6
74 Capricorn 2089 009 I'll Be Your Everything/Walkin' In The Sun. . . . 6
67 Atlantic 587/588 048 WARM AND TENDER SOUL (LP) 30
67 Atlantic 587/588 081 THE PERCY SLEDGE WAY (LP). . . . 22
68 Atlantic 587/588 105 WHEN A MAN LOVES A WOMAN (LP). . . . 25
69 Atlantic 587/588 153 THE BEST OF PERCY SLEDGE (LP). . . . 15

MINT VALUE £

SLEDGEHAMMER
79 Slammer SRTS79CUS 395 Sledgehammer/Feel Good (some with p/s) 20/10
80 Slammer CELL 2 Living In Dreams/Fantasia (p/s) 10
80s Slammer MRSB 2 In The Middle Of The Night 10
80 Valiant STRONG 1 Sledgehammer/Feel Good (p/s, reissue) 10
80 Valiant ROUND 2 Sledgehammer/Feel Good (p/s, 2nd reissue) 6
85 Illuminated ILL 33 In The Queue/Oxford City (shaped picture disc) 25
83 Illuminated JAMS 32 BLOOD ON THEIR HANDS (LP, some with bonus 12") 30/25

SLEEPER
93 Indolent SLEEP 002 SWALLOW EP: Swallow/Twisted/One Girl Dreaming (p/s) 6
90s Indolent BUCKET & SPADE EP (numbered, die-cut sleeve) 10
90s (no cat. no.) Gorgeous & Fully Equipped (flexi, with fanzine) 6

SLEEPWALKERS
59 Parlophone R 4580 Sleep Walk/Golden Mile 15

SLEEPY
68 CBS 3592 Love's Immortal Fire/Is It Really The Same 22
68 CBS 3838 Rosie Can't Fly/Mrs. Bailey's Barbecue And Grill 22
(see also Grapefruit, Fynn McCool)

SLENDER PLENTY
67 Polydor BM 56189 Silver Tree Top School For Boys/I've Lost A Friend And Found A Lover 22

SLENDER THREAD
80 Rock MHMS 193 I See The Light/Where Is The Beat 80

JIMI SLEVIN
82 Claddagh CCF 7 FREEFLIGHT (LP) 25
(see also Peggy's Leg)

RICKY SLICK
72 Dynamic DYN 449 Family Man/Family Man — Version 6

SLICKERS
68 Blue Cat BS 133 Wala Wala/LESTER STERLING: Super Special 25
68 Blue Cat BS 134 Nana (actually by George Dekker)/MARTIN RILEY: I May Never See My Baby Anymore 25
69 Blue Cat BS 154 Frying Pan/RARFIELD WILLIAMS: Code It 25
69 Amalgamated AMG 852 Man Beware/Matty Matty 10
69 Amalgamated AMG 866 Money Reaper/Man Beware 10
70 Bullet BU 449 Coolie Girl/BIGGIE: Bawling Baby 6
70 Trojan TR 7718 Run Fattie/Hoola Bulla (song actually "Bulla Man") 8
71 G.G. GG 4524 Oh My Baby/WINSTON WRIGHT: Change Of Love Version 5
71 Punch PH 59 Johnny Too Bad/Johnny Too Bad — Version 6
71 Dynamic DYN 406 Johnny Too Bad/ROLAND ALFONSO: Saucy Horde (act. by Roland Alphonso) 8
71 Dynamic DYN 419 You Can't Win/Don't Fight The Law 5
72 Explosion EX 2061 Bounce Me Johnny/Bounce Me 'Version' (actually "Say You") 5
(see also G.G. Allstars, Clancy Eccles, Viceroys)

SLIM & FREEDOM SINGERS
70 Banana BA 304 Do Dang Do (actually by Leroy Sibbles)/JACKIE MITTOO & SOUND DIMENSION: Hot Milk 20

SLIME
78 Toadstool GOOD 1 Controversial/Loony (p/s) 8
(see also Johnny Moped)

SLIPKNOT
00 Roadrunner RR 8655-6 SLIPKNOT (LP, picture disc) 15

SLIPSTREAM
90s Enraptured RAPT 4522 NO. 2 IN THE STRESS FREE 7" SERIES: Everything & Anything/Midnight Train (p/s) 5

SLITS
79 Island WIP 6505 Typical Girls/I Heard It Through The Grapevine (p/s) 12
79 Island 12 WIP 6505 Typical Girls (Brink Style)/I Heard It Through The Grapevine/ Liebe And Romanze (12", p/s) 15
80 Rough Trade RT 039/Y Y 1 In The Beginning There Was Rhythm/POP GROUP: Where There's A Will There's A Way (p/s) 5
79 Island ILPS 9573 CUT (LP, with inner sleeve) 18
80 Rough Trade/Y Y 3 BOOTLEG RETROSPECTIVE (LP, plain sleeve) 30
81 CBS 85269 THE RETURN OF THE GIANT SLITS (LP, some with bonus 45 "American Radio Interview"/"Face Dub" [XPS 125]) 22/18
80 CBS Man Next Door/ Same Human (12", p/s) 15
81 CBS A1498 Earthbeat Begin Again Rhythm (7", p/s) 8
(see also Raincoats)

P.F. SLOAN
65 RCA Victor RCA 1482 Sins Of The Family/This Mornin' 12
67 RCA Victor RCA 1623 Sunflower Sunflower/The Man Behind The Red Balloon 8
72 Epic EPC 65179 RAISED ON RECORDS (LP) 18
80s Big Beat WIK 73 SONGS OF OTHER TIMES (LP, some tracks as Grass Roots) 20
(see also Grass Roots, Fantastic Baggys, Willie & Wheels)

SAMMI SLOAN
68 Columbia DB 8480 Yes I Would/Be His Girl 8

SLOWBONE
74 Rare Earth RES 119 Get What You're Given/Oh Man 6
(see also Roll Ups)

MINT VALUE £

SLOWBURNER

89 Burn BURN LP 001 — AN EMOTIONAL BUSINESS (LP) . . . 12

SLUSH

78 Ember EMB 5367 — White Christmas/Rich Man (no p/s) . . . 70

SLY & THE FAMILY STONE

(see under Sly [& Family] Stone)

SMACK

78 Asprin 001 — Edward Fox/Came Again (p/s, original issue) . . . 5

JOAN SMALL

56 Parlophone MSP 6219 — Change Of Heart/Come Next Spring . . . 10
56 Parlophone R 4211 — Love Is A Stranger/Autumn Concerto . . . 10
57 Parlophone R 4269 — Gonna Get Along Without You Now/You Can't Say I Love You To A Rock & Roll Tune . . . 15
57 Parlophone R 4269 — Gonna Get Along Without You Now/You Can't Say I Love You To A Rock & Roll Tune (78) . . . 6
58 Parlophone R 4431 — Afraid/How Many Times (Can I Fall In Love) . . . 15
58 Parlophone R 4431 — Afraid/How Many Times (Can I Fall In Love) (78) . . . 12
60 Parlophone R 4622 — The Big Hurt/Ask Me To Go Steady . . . 15

KAREN SMALL

66 Vocalion V 9281 — To Get You Back Again/That's Why I Cry . . . 25

MARY SMALL

56 Vogue Coral Q 72196 — None Of That Now/Dino . . . 5
56 Vogue Coral Q 72196 — None Of That Now/Dino (78) . . . 8

MILLIE SMALL

(see under Millie)

SMALL FACES

SINGLES

65 Decca F 12208 — Whatcha Gonna Do About It?/What's A Matter, Baby? . . . 12
65 Decca F 12276 — I've Got Mine/It's Too Late . . . 20
66 Decca F 12317 — Sha-La-La-La-Lee/Grow Your Own . . . 10
66 Decca F 12393 — Hey Girl/Almost Grown . . . 12
66 Decca F 12470 — All Or Nothing/Understanding (curved or boxed Decca logo) . . . 10
66 Decca F 12500 — My Mind's Eye (alternate demo mix, matrix no. ends T1-1C)/I Can't Dance With You (withdrawn) . . . 30
66 Decca F 12500 — My Mind's Eye (matrix no. ends T2-1C)/I Can't Dance With You . . . 7
67 Decca F 12565 — I Can't Make It/Just Passing . . . 15
67 Decca F 12619 — Patterns/E Too D (some with export p/s) . . . 125/50
67 Immediate AS 1 — Small Faces (1-sided sampler for "Small Faces", promo only) . . . 90
67 Immediate IM 050 — Here Comes The Nice/Talk To You . . . 8
67 Immediate IM 057 — Itchycoo Park/I'm Only Dreaming . . . 8
67 Immediate IM 062 — Tin Soldier/I Feel Much Better (some in p/s) . . . 50/15
68 Immediate IM 064 — Lazy Sunday/Rollin' Over . . . 8
68 Immediate IM 069 — The Universal/Donkey Rides, A Penny A Glass (lilac label, later pink) . . . 10/6
69 Immediate IM 077 — Afterglow (Of Your Love)/Wham Bam, Thank You Mam (demos [& perhaps some copies] have demo version of B-side) . . . 45/7
75 Immediate IM 064 — Lazy Sunday/Rollin' Over (p/s, reissue with white label) . . . 8
80 Virgin VS 367 — Tin Soldier/Tin Soldier (live)/Rene . . . 6
86 Archive 4 TOF 103 — Itchycoo Park/Lazy Sunday/Sha-La-La-La-Lee/Here Comes The Nice (12", p/s) . . . 8
88 Castle Comms. Special Edition CD 3-9 — THE SMALL FACES (Itchycoo Park/Lazy Sunday/All Or Nothing (live)/ Autumn Stone) (3" CD EP, with adaptor, 5" case, 5,000 only) . . . 8

LPs

66 Decca LK 4790 — SMALL FACES (original red label) . . . 90
67 Decca LK 4879 — FROM THE BEGINNING (original red label) . . . 90
67 Immediate IMLP/IMSP 008 — SMALL FACES (mono/stereo) . . . 120/140
68 Immediate IMLP/IMSP 012 — OGDENS' NUT GONE FLAKE (lilac label, circular foldout sleeve, mono/stereo) . . . 100/60
68 Immediate IMLP/IMSP 012 — OGDENS' NUT GONE FLAKE (pink label, circular foldout sleeve, m/s) . . . 80/50
69 Decca LK 4790 — SMALL FACES (boxed Decca label) . . . 35
69 Decca LK 4879 — FROM THE BEGINNING (boxed Decca label) . . . 35
69 Immediate IMLP/IMSP 022 — IN MEMORIAM (export issue [German copies more common, £55]) . . . 140
69 Immediate IMAL 01/02 — THE AUTUMN STONE (2-LP, gatefold sleeve) . . . 35
75 Immediate/NEMS IML 1001 — OGDENS' NUT GONE FLAKE (reissue, round sleeve, white label) . . . 15
76 NEMS AML 1008 — MAGIC MOMENTS . . . 15
77 Immediate/NEMS IML 2001 — OGDENS' NUT GONE FLAKE (reissue, square sleeve) . . . 12
77 Decca ROOTS 5 — ROCK ROOTS — THE DECCA SINGLES . . . 12
78 Charly CR 300005 — OGDENS' NUT GONE FLAKE (export release, square sleeve) . . . 12
78 Charly CR 300025 — THE SMALL FACES — LIVE U.K. 1969 (export release) . . . 12
80 Virgin/Immediate V 2166 — SMALL FACES: BIG HITS (gatefold sleeve) . . . 12
80 Virgin/Immediate V 2178 — FOR YOUR DELIGHT, THE DARLINGS OF WAPPING WHARF LAUNDERETTE . . . 20
97 Castle CLA 016 — OGDENS' NUT GONE FLAKE (reissue, round sleeve with obi) . . . 12
91 Castle CLACT 016 — OGDENS' NUT GONE FLAKE (CD, in round tin box with beer mats & booklet) . . . 50

(see also Faces, Steve Marriott, Humble Pie, Jimmy Winston & His Reflections, Winston's Fumbs, Billy Nicholls, Kenney Jones)

SMALL ADS

81 Bronze BRO 115 — Small Ads/Motorway Madness (p/s) . . . 7
81 Bronze BRO 125 — HP Man/Radio Love (p/s) . . . 7
81 Bronze BRO 135 — Friday Nite Cowboy/I Wanna Fly Concorde (p/s) . . . 7

SMALL HOURS

80 Automatic K 17708 — The Kid/Business In Town/Midnight To Six/End Of The Night (p/s) . . . 30
80 Automatic K 17708X — The Kid/Business In Town/Midnight To Six/End Of The Night (10", p/s) . . . 20

MINT VALUE £

SMALL WORLD

81 Whaam! WHAAM 003 — Love Is Dead/Liberty (p/s) 80
83 Valid VC 001 — First Impressions/Stupidity Street/Tomorrow Never Comes (p/s) 80

SMART

82 Complex CPX 001 — This Time (p/s) 35

SMART ALEC

79 B&C BCS 20 — Scooter Boys/Soho (p/s) 100

SMASHING PUMPKINS

91 Hut — I Am One (1-sided blue flexidisc) 65
91 Caroline SMASH 1 — Siva/Rhinoceros (no p/s, promo only) 65
91 Hut HUTT 6 — Siva/Window Paine (12", p/s, 5,000) 30
92 Hut HUTT 10 — LULL EP (Rhinoceros/Blue/Slunk/Bye June [Demo]) (12", p/s) 10
92 Hut CDHUT 10 — LULL EP (Rhinoceros/Blue/Slunk/Bye June [Demo]) (CD) 8
92 Hut HUTC 017 — PEEL SESSIONS: Siva/A Girl Named Sandoz/Smiley (cassette EP) 5
92 Hut HUTT 017 — PEEL SESSIONS: Siva/A Girl Named Sandoz/Smiley (12" EP, p/s) 12
92 Hut HUTEN 018 — I Am One/Terrapin (live)/Bullet Train To Osaka (10", p/s, 6,000 only) 20
92 Hut HUTT 18 — I Am One/Plume/Starla (12", p/s) 12
93 Sup Pop SP 90 — Tristessa/La Dolly Vita/Honeyspider (12", 5,000 only) 35
93 Hut HUT 31 — Cherub Rock/Purr Snickety (p/s, clear vinyl, numbered, 5,000 only) 20
93 Hut HUTT 31 — Cherub Rock/Pissant/French Movie Theme/(Star Spangled Banner) (12", p/s, last track uncredited) 8
93 Hut HUT 37 — Today/Apathy's Last Kiss (p/s, red vinyl, 5,000 only) 15
93 Hut HUTT 37 — Today/Hello Kitty Kat/Obscured (12", p/s) 8
94 Hut HUT 43 — Smile (Disarm/Siamese Dream) (stickered p/s, purple vinyl) 10
94 Hut HUTL 48 — Rocket/Never Let Me Down (box set, salmon pink vinyl, 1,500 only) 35
93 Hut HUTTDJ 73 — Zero (12", promo only) 12
94 Hut SPBOX 1 — SIAMESE SINGLES (Rocket/Never Let Me Down//Cherub Rock/Purr Snickety// Today/Apathy's Last Kiss/Smile [Disarm/Siamese Dream]) (4 x 7" box set, black vinyl, 6,000 only) 40
94 Hut HUTLPX 2 — GISH (LP, with inner) 18

ROY SMECK

54 Brunswick LA 8649 — SONGS OF THE RANGE (10" LP) 15
65 London (S)HAR 8273 — WIZARD OF THE STRINGS (LP) 12

PHILIP LLOYD SMEE & DONATO CINICOLO III

71 Deroy PLS 1 — DAS LUNE/SYNTHI-A (LP, private pressing, handmade sl., up to 5 copies only) 300

BRETT SMILEY

74 Anchor ANC 70 — Va Va Va Voom/Space Age (p/s) 5

K. SMILEY

72 Pressure Beat PB 5514 — Tipatone/Do It To Me 6

SMILEY

72 Philips 6006 206 — Penelope/I Know What I Want 5

(see also Creation)

SMILIN' JOE

54 London HL 8106 — A.B.C.'s Parts 1 & 2 (78) 100

SMITH

69 Stateside-Dunhill SS 8028 — Baby It's You/I Don't Believe 5
70 Stateside-Dunhill SS 8042 — Take A Look Around/Mojalesky Ridge 5
70 Stateside-Dunhill SS 8055 — What Am I Gonna Do/Born In Boston 5
69 Stateside-Dunhill SSL 5016 — A GROUP CALLED SMITH (LP) 15
70 Stateside-Dunhill SSL 5031 — MINUS-PLUS (LP) 15

SMITH (U.K.)

81 Rarn RARNS 1 — Here Comes My Baby/Just Another Line/Too Late (p/s) 70

ADAM (Eric) SMITH

62 Island WI 057 — I Wonder Why/My Prayer 20

ALEXANDER MURRAY SMITH & BLACK O'TOWN SYNCOPATORS

63 Decca F 11604 — "Steptoe And Son" Theme/Ragtime Tuba 6

A.S.A.P. (Adrian Smith & Project)

89 EMI 12 EMPD 107 — Silver And Gold/Blood Brothers (12", silver & gold vinyl) 7
90 EMI EMPD 131 — Down The Wire (Crossed Line Mix)/When She's Gone (shaped picture disc) 6

(see also Iron Maiden, Urchin)

ARTHUR 'GUITAR BOOGIE' SMITH (& HIS CRACKERJACKS)

50 MGM MGM 254 — Mule Train/ROY LEAR & BETTY SMITH: Dime A Dozen (78) 6
50 MGM MGM 329 — Guitar Boogie/Be Bop Rag (78) 8
51 MGM MGM 363 — Mandolin Boogie/The Memphis Blues (78) 6
52 MGM MGM 484 — Alabama Jubilee/Fiddle-Faddle (78, with Crackerjacks) 10
52 MGM MGM 518 — Guitar And Piano Boogie/Banjo Buster (78) 6
52 MGM MGM 555 — Express Train Boogie/River Rag (78) 7
53 MGM SP 1008 — Guitar Boogie/Be Bop Rag 30
53 MGM SP 1021 — Five String Banjo Boogie/South 20
53 MGM MGM 599 — Five String Banjo Boogie/South (78) 8
53 MGM SP 1039 — Express Train Boogie/River Rag 20
53 MGM MGM 630 — Recitation Sonny Smith: In Memory Of Hank Williams/HANK WILLIAMS & HIS DRIFTING COWBOYS: I Saw The Light (78) 8
53 MGM MGM 660 — Big Mountain Shuffle/KEN CURTIS: The Call Of The Faraway Hills (78) 6
53 MGM MGM 695 — Three D Boogie/He Went That-A-Way (78) 6
54 MGM SP 1096 — Oh, Baby Mine, I Get So Lonely/Outboard 20
54 MGM MGM 755 — Oh, Baby Mine, I Get So Lonely/Outboard (78) 8
54 MGM SP 1110 — Redheaded Stranger/Texas Hop 20
54 MGM MGM 779 — Redheaded Stranger/Texas Hop (78) 10

MINT VALUE £

54	MGM MGM 3011	Guitar Boogie/Boomerang (78)	10
55	MGM SP 1122	Hi Lo Boogie/Truck Stop Grill	20
55	MGM MGM 805	Hi Lo Boogie/Truck Stop Grill (78)	10
54	MGM MGM-EP 510	ARTHUR 'GUITAR BOOGIE' SMITH AND HIS CRACKERJACKS (EP)	25
54	MGM MGM EPC 5	ARTHUR 'GUITAR BOOGIE' SMITH (EP, export issue)	25
59	MGM MGM-EP 695	ARTHUR 'GUITAR BOOGIE' SMITH AND HIS CRACKERJACKS (EP)	22
63	Stateside SE 1005	MISTER GUITAR (EP)	20
53	MGM MGM-D 111	FINGERS ON FIRE (10" LP)	30
54	MGM MGM-D 131	FOOLISH QUESTIONS (10" LP)	30
71	MGM 2354 009	GUITAR BOOGIE (LP)	12

BARRY SMITH

74	People PEO 114	Hold On To It (Parts 1 & 2)	15

BEASLEY SMITH & HIS ORCHESTRA

56	London HLD 8235	Goodnight, Sweet Dreams/Parisian Rag	25
56	London HLD 8273	My Foolish Heart/Old Spinning Wheel	25

BESSIE SMITH

51	Columbia DB 2796	Empty Bed Blues (Parts 1 & 2) (78)	25
58	Philips BBE 12202	EMPRESS OF THE BLUES (EP)	18
59	Philips BBE 12231	EMPRESS OF THE BLUES NO. 2 (EP)	18
59	Philips BBE 12233	EMPRESS OF THE BLUES NO. 3 (EP)	18
60	Philips BBE 12360	BESSIE SMITH (EP)	15
55	Philips BBL 7019	THE BESSIE SMITH STORY VOLUME 1 (LP, with Louis Armstrong)	25
55	Philips BBL 7020	THE BESSIE SMITH STORY VOLUME 2 (LP)	25
55	Philips BBL 7042	THE BESSIE SMITH STORY VOLUME 3 (LP)	25
55	Philips BBL 7049	THE BESSIE SMITH STORY VOLUME 4 (LP)	25
62	Philips BBL 7513	BESSIE'S BLUES 1923-1924 (LP)	30
66	CBS BPG 62377	THE BESSIE SMITH STORY VOLUME 1 (LP)	12
66	CBS BPG 62378	THE BESSIE SMITH STORY VOLUME 2 (LP)	12
66	CBS BPG 62379	THE BESSIE SMITH STORY VOLUME 3 (LP)	12
66	CBS BPG 62380	THE BESSIE SMITH STORY VOLUME 4 (LP)	12
71	CBS 66258	THE WORLD'S GREATEST BLUES SINGER (2-LP, some with booklet)	20/15
71	CBS 66262	ANY WOMAN'S BLUES (2-LP)	15
71	CBS 66273	EMPTY BED BLUES (2-LP)	15
72	CBS 66264	THE EMPRESS (2-LP)	15
73	CBS 67232	NOBODY'S BLUES BUT MINE (2-LP)	15
70s	Empress 10006	THE COMPLETE ST. LOUIS BLUES SOUNDTRACK (10" LP)	12

BETTY SMITH SKIFFLE GROUP

57	Tempo A 162	There's A Blue Ridge Round My Heart, Virginia/Double Shuffle	15
57	Tempo A 162	There's A Blue Ridge Round My Heart, Virginia/Double Shuffle (78)	8

(see also Betty Smith Quintet)

BETTY SMITH QUINTET

57	Tempo A 163	Sweet Georgia Brown/Little White Lies	20
57	Tempo A 163	Sweet Georgia Brown/Little White Lies (78)	8
58	Decca F 10986	Hand Jive/Bewitched (as Betty Smith Group)	8
58	Decca F 10986	Hand Jive/Bewitched (as Betty Smith Group) (78)	6
58	Decca F 11031	Will The Angels Play Their Harps For Me/Betty's Blues	8
58	Decca F 11031	Will The Angels Play Their Harps For Me/Betty's Blues (78)	6
58	Decca F 11071	Begin The Beguine/Song Of The Boulevards	6
58	Decca F 11071	Begin The Beguine/Song Of The Boulevards (78)	10
59	Decca F 11124	Song Of India/Stormy Weather	6
59	Decca F 11124	Song Of India/Stormy Weather (78)	12
57	Tempo EXA 74	BETTY SMITH QUINTET (EP)	15
57	Decca DFE 6446	BETTY SMITH QUINTET (EP)	15

(see also Betty Smith Skiffle Group)
(see Jeff Rowena)

BUSTER SMITH

61	London Jazz LTZ-K 15206	THE LEGENDARY BUSTER SMITH (LP)	12

CARL SMITH

52	Columbia DB 3077	Let's Live A Little/Me And My Broken Heart (78)	6
53	Columbia DC 608	Our Honeymoon/Sing Her A Love Song (78, export issue)	7
56	Philips PB 572	Loose Talk/More Than Anything Else In The World (78)	8
59	Philips PB 943	Ten Thousand Drums/The Tall, Tall Gentlemen	10
59	Philips PB 943	Ten Thousand Drums/The Tall, Tall Gentlemen (78)	20
60	Philips BBL 7437	THE CARL SMITH TOUCH (LP)	15

CLARA SMITH

69	VJM VLP 15	CLARA SMITH VOLUME 1 (LP)	15
69	VJM VLP 16	CLARA SMITH VOLUME 2 (LP)	15
69	VJM VLP 17	CLARA SMITH VOLUME 3 (LP)	15

CLARA SMITH & FLETCHER HENDERSON

61	Philips BBE 12491	BLUES BY CLARA SMITH 1926-1928 (EP)	15

(see also Fletcher Henderson)

CONNIE SMITH

66	RCA Victor RD 7785	CUTE AND COUNTRY (LP)	15
71	RCA LSA 3042	WHERE IS MY CASTLE (LP)	12
73	RCA LSA 3150	IT AIN'T LOVE (LP)	12

COUNTY SMITH

68	Decca F 12818	Low Bad Hurting/No Longer Mine	5

DAVE SMITH & ASTRONAUTS

67	C'mbia Blue Beat DB 104	A Lover Like You/Cup Of Love	15

MINT VALUE £

DAVE SMITH & JUDY DINNING
83 Rubber RUB 043 WAITING FOR THE CHANGE (LP) 20

DICK SMITH BAND
79 Smile SR 012 Body Heat/Motorway Madness (p/s) 75
80 Hol-O-Gram HOL 001 Way Of The World/Giving The Game Away (some with p/s) 45/25

EDDIE SMITH
55 Parlophone MSP 6186 Silver Star Stomp/Stumbling (as Eddie Smith & Chiefs) 15
60 Top Rank JAR 285 Upturn/Border Beat (as Eddie Smith & Hornets) 25

EDGEWOOD SMITH & FABULOUS TAILFEATHERS
67 Sue WI 4037 Ain't That Lovin'/Yeah 45

EFFIE SMITH
66 Sue WI 4010 Dial That Telephone Parts 1 & 2 25

ELLIOTT SMITH
98 Domino RUG 074 Ballad Of Big Nothing/Some Song (p/s) 6
98 Dreamworks DRMS 22347 Waltz No. 2/Our Thing (p/s) 8
99 Dreamworks DRMS 7 Baby Britain/Waltz No. 1 (p/s) 6
98 Domino REWIGLP 001 ELLIOTT SMITH (LP) 50
98 Domino REWIGLP 002 ROMAN CANDLE (LP) 50
98 Domino REWIGLP EITHER/OR (LP) 50

ELSON SMITH
61 Fontana H 291 Flip Flop/Are You Ready For That 25

ERNIE SMITH
71 Duke DU 119 Bend Down/Heaven Help Us All 6
71 Horse HOSS 6 Sunday Morning/One Three 5
73 London SHS 8442 ERNIE SMITH (LP) 12

ETHEL SMITH
55 Brunswick 05470 Hernando's Hideaway/Lemon Merengue 8

(LITTLE) GEORGE (HARMONICA) SMITH
65 Blue Horizon 45-1002 Blues In The Dark/Telephone Blues (as Little George Smith) 80
70 Blue Horizon 57-3170 Someday You're Gonna Learn/Before You Do Your Thing (as George Smith) 18
69 Liberty LBL/LBS 83218E BLUES WITH FEELING — A TRIBUTE TO LITTLE WALTER (LP, with Chicago Blues Band) 35
70 Blue Horizon 7-63856 NO TIME TO JIVE (LP) 85
71 Deram SML 1082 ARKANSAS TRAP (LP) 50
(see also Bacon Fat)

GLORIA SMITH
59 London HLU 8903 Playmates/Don't Take Your Love From Me 18
59 London HLU 8903 Playmates/Don't Take Your Love From Me (78) 10

GORDON SMITH
69 Blue Horizon 57-3156 Too Long/Funk Pedal 20
69 Blue Horizon 7-63211 LONG OVERDUE (LP) 90
(see also Kevin Coyne)

HAROLD SMITH'S MAJESTIC CHOIR
69 Chess CRS 8100 We Can All Walk A Little Bit Prouder/Why Am I Treated So Bad 8

HARVEY SMITH
75 Hankerchief Hanky 3 True Love/ End Of The World (p/s) 7

HUEY 'PIANO' SMITH & THE CLOWNS
58 Columbia DB 4138 Don't You Just Know It/High Blood Pressure 60
58 Columbia DB 4138 Don't You Just Know It/High Blood Pressure (78) 40
60 Top Rank JAR 282 Don't You Just Know Kokomo/FRANKIE FORD: Cheatin' Woman 22
62 Top Rank JAR 614 Pop-Eye/Scald-Dog (as Huey Smith) 18
65 Sue WI 364 If It Ain't One Thing It's Another/Tu-Ber-Cu-Lucas And The Sinus Blues 25
65 Sue WI 380 Rockin' Pneumonia And The Boogie Woogie Flu (Parts 1 & 2) 25
78 Chiswick NS 43 Rockin' Pneumonia And The Boogie Woogie Flu (unissued)
65 Sue ILP 917 ROCKIN' PNEUMONIA AND THE BOOGIE WOOGIE FLU (LP, titled "Havin' A Good Time" on labels) 40
78 Chiswick CH 9 ROCKIN' PNEUMONIA AND THE BOOGIE WOOGIE FLU (LP) 10
(see also Frankie Ford, Lee Allen, Bobby Marchan, Robert Parker)

IAN SMITH & INNER MIND
71 Bullet BU 490 Devil Woman/Nenn Street Rub 6
(see also Smithy All Stars)

JENNIE SMITH
59 Philips PB 924 Huggin' My Pillow (Sweet Side)/Huggin' My Pillow (Sweet Beat Side) 5
59 Philips PB 924 Huggin' My Pillow (Sweet Side)/Huggin' My Pillow (Sweet Beat Side) (78) 20

JIMMY SMITH
SINGLES
62 HMV POP 1025 Walk On The Wild Side Parts 1 & 2 12
65 Verve VS 509 Hobo Flats Parts 1 & 2 5
65 Verve VS 521 Who's Afraid Of Virginia Woolf Parts 1 & 2 6
65 Verve VS 523 The Cat/Basin Street Blues 15
65 Verve VS 531 The Organ Grinder's Swing/I'll Close My Eyes 6
66 Verve VS 534 Slow Theme From "Where The Spies Are" Parts 1 & 2 6
66 Verve VS 536 Got My Mojo Working Parts 1 & 2 8
66 Verve VS 540 I'm Your Hoochie-Coochie Man Parts 1 & 2 7
67 Verve VS 551 Cat In A Tree Parts 1 & 2 6
67 Verve VS 562 Mickey Mouse Parts 1 & 2 6

MINT VALUE £

EPs

64	Verve VEP 5008	WALK ON THE WILD SIDE	15
64	Verve VEP 5017	A COOL YULE WITH...	8
65	Verve VEP 5021	CREEPER	15
65	Verve VEP 5016	PLAYS THE BLUES	15
65	Verve VEP 5022	SWINGING WITH THE INCREDIBLE JIMMY SMITH	15

LPs

62	Verve CLP 1596/CSD 1462	BASHIN' THE UNPREDICTABLE (Verve label with HMV number)	15
63	Verve (S)VLP 9039	HOBO FLATS	18
64	Verve VLP 9057	ANY NUMBER CAN WIN	15
64	Verve VLP 9068	WHO'S AFRAID OF VIRGINIA WOOLF	18
64	Verve (S)VLP 9079	THE CAT	25
65	Verve (S)VLP 9093	MONSTER	20
66	Verve (S)VLP 9108	ORGAN GRINDER SWING	20
66	Verve (S)VLP 9123	GOT MY MOJO WORKING	20
66	Verve (S)VLP 9142	HOOCHIE COOCHIE MAN	20
67	Verve (S)VLP 9159	PETER & THE WOLF	20
67	Verve (S)VLP 9160	THE DYNAMIC DUO (with Wes Montgomery)	15
67	Verve (S)VLP 9182	RESPECT	15
68	Verve (S)VLP 9218	STAY LOOSE	25
68	Verve (S)VLP 9227	LIVIN' IT UP	20
68	Verve (S)VLP 9231	CHRISTMAS COOKIN'	18
69	Verve (S)VLP 9241	FURTHER ADVENTURES OF JIMMY AND WES (with Wes Montgomery)	15
71	Verve 2304 020	I'M GON' GIT MYSELF TOGETHER	20
71	Verve 2304 021	OTHER SIDE	15
71	Verve 2304 033	THE BEST OF JIMMY SMITH	12
72	Verve 2304 044	THE BEST OF JIMMY SMITH VOL. 2	12
73	Decca SKL 5146	AT THE LOWERY ORGAN	15
74	Verve 2304 167	PORTUGUESE SOUL	20
75	DJM DJLPS 451	BLACK SMITH	15

(see also Kenny Burrell)

JOEY SMITH & BABA BROOKS BAND

64	R&B JB 131	Maybe Once/Tell Me You're Mine	25

JOHNNY SMITH & STAN GETZ

52	Vogue V 2137	Tabou/Moonlight In Vermont (78)	6

(see also Stan Getz)

JUDI SMITH

65	Decca F 12132	Leaves Come Tumbling Down/Come My Way	20

JUNIOR SMITH

67	Giant GN 1	Cool Down Your Temper/I'm Groovin'	15
68	Giant GN 18	I'm Gonna Leave You Girl/I Love You, I Love You	15
68	Giant GN 25	Come Cure Me/I Want Your Lovin'	15
68	Gas GAS 132	Gimme Little/Trip To War Land	12
69	Crystal CR 7002	Put On The Pressure/I Don't Know	10
72	Sioux SI 019	Saturday Child/JUMBO STERLING: Hot Dog	10
72	Sioux SI 023	You Don't Know/JUMBO STERLING: My Sugar Ain't Sweet	10

(see also Stranger Cole, Derrick Morgan, Rocksteadys)

KATHY SMITH

70	Polydor 2310 081	SOME SONGS I'VE SAVED (LP)	25

KEELY SMITH (& LOUIS PRIMA)

57	Capitol CL 14717	Hurt Me/High School Affair	8
57	Capitol CL 14739	Young And In Love/You Better Go Now	8
57	Capitol CL 14754	Good Behaviour/You'll Never Know	8
57	Capitol CL 14803	Autumn Leaves/I Keep Forgetting	7
57	Capitol CL 14803	Autumn Leaves/I Keep Forgetting (78)	6
58	Capitol CL 14862	Foggy Day/The Lip (B-side with Louis Prima)	6
58	Capitol CL 14885	The Whippoorwill/Sometimes	5
58	Capitol CL 14948	That Old Black Magic (with Louis Prima)/You Are My Love	6
58	Capitol CL 14948	That Old Black Magic (with Louis Prima)/You Are My Love (78)	20
59	Capitol CL 14994	I've Got You Under My Skin (with Louis Prima)/Don't Take Your Love From Me	6
59	London HLD 8984	If I Knew I'd Find You (I'd Climb The Highest Mountain)/ Don't Let The Stars Get In Your Eyes	12
59	London HLD 8984	If I Knew I'd Find You (I'd Climb The Highest Mountain)/ Don't Let The Stars Get In Your Eyes (78)	30
60	London HLD 9240	Here In My Heart/Close	8
64	Reprise R 20346	You're Breaking My Heart/Crazy	6
64	Reprise R 20356	If I Fell/Do You Want To Know A Secret	5
65	Reprise R 20402	Somethin' Wonderful Happened/Have You Ever Been Lonely	5
65	Reprise R 20482	If I Fell/Do You Want To Know A Secret (reissue)	5
65	Reprise R 23048	Standing In The Ruins/That Old Black Magic	5
65	Capitol CL 15385	S'posin'/The Song Is You	5
66	Reprise R 20482	The Wonder Of You/Who's Afraid	5
61	London RE-D 1269	YOU LOVERS (EP)	35
65	Capitol EAP 1-20629	IT'S MAGIC (EP)	12
65	Reprise R 30042	JOHN LENNON, PAUL McCARTNEY SONGBOOK VOL. 1 (EP)	12
65	Reprise R 30045	THE SUCCESS OF KEELY SMITH (EP)	10
65	Reprise R 30046	JOHN LENNON, PAUL McCARTNEY SONGBOOK VOL. 2 (EP)	12
66	Reprise R 30053	SOMEBODY LOVES ME (EP)	10
66	Reprise R 30062	I'VE GOT THE WORLD ON A STRING (EP)	10
58	Capitol (S)T 914	I WISH YOU LOVE (LP, mono/stereo)	15/18
59	Capitol T 1073	POLITELY (LP)	14
59	Capitol T 1145	SWINGIN' PRETTY (LP)	14
59	Capitol T 1160	HEY BOY! HEY GIRL! (LP, soundtrack, with Louis Prima)	20

			MINT VALUE £
64	Reprise R 6086	LITTLE GIRL BLUE, LITTLE GIRL NEW (LP)	15
65	Reprise R 6132	THE INTIMATE SMITH (LP)	15
65	Reprise R 6142	THE JOHN LENNON-PAUL McCARTNEY SONGBOOK (LP)	15
65	Reprise R 5012	YOU'RE BREAKING MY HEART (LP)	15
66	Reprise R 6175	THAT OLD BLACK MAGIC (LP)	12

(see also Louis Prima, Frank Sinatra)

LONNIE LISTON SMITH (& THE COSMIC ECHOES)

75	RCA RCA 2568	Expansions (Parts 1 & 2) (& Cosmic Echoes)	6
76	RCA RCA 2668	Chance For Peace/Sunset	5
76	RCA RCA 2727	Get Down Everybody/Inner Beauty	5
79	RCA PB 9450	Expansions/A Chance For Peace	5
79	RCA PC 9450	Expansions/A Chance For Peace (12", reissue)	10
75	RCA SF 8434	EXPANSIONS (LP, with Cosmic Echoes)	10
76	RCA SF 8461	VISIONS OF A NEW WORLD (LP)	20
76	RCA RS 1053	REFLECTIONS OF A GOLDEN DREAM (LP, with Cosmic Echoes)	20
77	RCA PL 11822	RENAISSANCE (LP, with Cosmic Echoes)	20

LONNIE SMITH

67	CBS 63146	FINGER LICKIN' GOOD (LP)	25
70s	Blue Note BST 84290	THINK (LP)	25
70s	Blue Note BST 84313	TURNING POINT (LP)	25
70s	Blue Note BST 84326	MOVE YOUR HAND (LP)	30
70s	Blue Note BST 84351	DRIVES (LP)	25

LORENZO SMITH

66	Outasite 45-503	(Too Much) Firewater/Count Down (99 copies only)	100

LOU SMITH

60	Top Rank JAR 520	Cruel Love/Close To My Heart	10

MARTHA SMITH

65	Pye 7N 15778	As I Watch You Walk Away/It Always Seems Like Summer	10
65	Pye 7N 15860	Love Means Nothing To You/The Song Is Love	7

MARVIN SMITH

66	Coral Q 72486	Time Stopped/Have More Time	40
74	Contempo CS 2034	Let The Good Times Roll/Ain't That A Shame	5

MEL SMITH

81	Mercury MEL 1	Mel Smith's Greatest Hits/Richard & Joey (p/s, with Roger Taylor)	22
91	Epic 657687 7	Another Blooming Christmas/Ho! Ho! Ho! Hoedown (p/s)	5

MELODY SMITH

71	CBS CBS 7561	You Never Hear A Teardrop Fall/Rastus Ravel	10

MICK SMITH

76	Midas MFHR 078	SOMEBODY NOBODY KNOWS (LP)	35
77	Alida Star AS 771	WORDS AND MUSIC (LP)	30
79	Repercussion RR 1000	RAINDANCE (LP, as Mike Smith)	25

MIKE SMITH

85	Proto ENA 130	Medley (7" version)/Bits And Pieces (some in p/s)	7/5
85	Proto ENAT 130	Medley (12" version)/Glad All Over (12", p/s)	12
90	Mooncrest MOON 1010	You Gotta Play Rock'N'Roll/Operator	6

(see also Dave Clark 5, Smith & D'Abo)

MURIEL SMITH & CARMEN JONES CHORUS

55	Brunswick 05370	Dat's Love/JUNE HAWKINS: Beat Out Dat Rhythm On A Drum	8

O.C. (OCIE) SMITH

57	London HLA 8480	Lighthouse/Too Many (as Ocie Smith)	65
57	London HLA 8480	Lighthouse/Too Many (as Ocie Smith) (78)	20
68	CBS 3343	The Son Of Hickory Holler's Tramp/On A Clear Day You Can See Forever	6
70	CBS 5203	Baby I Need Your Loving/San Francisco Is A Lonely Town	6
68	CBS (S) 63147	THE DYNAMIC O.C. SMITH (LP)	20
68	CBS (S) 63362	HICKORY HOLLER REVISITED (LP)	15
69	CBS 63805	AT HOME (LP)	15

(see also Art Mooney)

OTELLO SMITH & TOBAGO BAD BOYS

67	Direction 58-3082	My Home Town/Trouble	5
68	Direction 8-63242	THE BIG ONES GO SKA (LP)	40

PATTI SMITH (GROUP)

76	Arista ARIST 47	Gloria (In Excelsis Deo) (Edit)/My Generation (p/s)	5
77	Arista ARIST 12135	Gloria (In Excelsis Deo)/My Generation (live) (12", Rough Trade copies in brown paper bag with titles in felt pen)	10/7
78	Arista ARIST 181	Because The Night/God Speed (p/s)	10
78	Sire 6078 614	Hey Joe (Version)/Piss Factory (p/s)	15
78	Arista ARIST 197	Privilege (Set Me Free)/Ask The Angels (p/s)	5
78	Arista ARIST 12197	Privilege (Set Me Free)/Ask The Angels/25th Floor (Live Version)/ Babelfield (12", p/s)	10
79	Arista ARIST 264	Frederick/Fire Of Unknown Origin (p/s)	5
79	Arista ARIST 281	Dancing Barefoot/5-4-3-2-1 (live) (p/s)	5
79	Arista ARIST 291	So You Want To Be A Rock'n'Roll Star/Frederick (live) (p/s)	5
88	Fierce FRIGHT 017	Brian Jones/Stockinged Feet/Jesus Christ (1-sided, white label)	15
75	Arista ARTY 122	HORSES (LP, blue label)	12
76	Arista SPARTY 1001	RADIO ETHIOPIA (LP, as Patti Smith Group, with lyric insert)	12
78	Arista SPARTY 1043	EASTER (LP, as Patti Smith Group, with lyric insert)	12
79	Arista SPARTY 1086	WAVE (LP, as Patti Smith Group, with lyric insert)	12

PAUL SMITH

65	Columbia DB 7636	Piccadilly Paper Boy/Yakety Yak	7

MINT VALUE £

PETER SMITH

70s	Pilgrim JLPS 148P	FAITH, FOLK & CLARITY (LP, with Kinfolk)	18
70s	Galliard GAL 4016P	FAITH, FOLK & FESTIVITY (LP)	12

PHOEBE SMITH

70	Topic 12T 93	ONCE I HAD A TRUE LOVE (LP)	12

RAY SMITH

51	London L 857	When The Saints Go Marching Home/ You Gotta Walk The Straight & Narrow (78)	6
51	London L 1002	It's No Secret/All Alone Neath The Blue Grass (78)	6

RAY SMITH

60	London HL 9051	Rockin' Little Angel/That's All Right	75

ROY SMITH (Jamaica)

70	Grape GR 3013	See Through Craze/TERRY CARL & DERRICK: I'm The One	10
70	Jackpot JP 723	The Wedding/Air Balloon	10

ROY SMITH (& THE STARGAZERS) (U.K.)

55	Decca F 10529	Red Roses (For My Lady Fair)/The Devil's In Your Eyes	6
55	Decca F 10644	He/Glengarry (solo)	6

(see also Stargazers)

SLIM SMITH (& THE UNIQUES)

66	Island WI 3023	I've Got Your Number/The New Boss	35
67	Coxsone CS 7016	Hip Hug/FREEDOM SINGERS: I Want Money	30
67	Coxsone CS 7034	Rougher Yet/I'll Never Let Go	30
67	Coxsone CS 7009	Mercy Mercy/JACKIE MITTOO: Baba Boom	25
68	Trojan TR 619	Watch This Sound/Out Of Love (as Slim Smith & Uniques)	12
69	Unity UN 504	Everybody Needs Love/JUNIOR SMITH: Come Back Girl	7
69	Unity UN 508	For Once In My Life/Burning Desire	7
69	Unity UN 510	Zip A Dee Doo Dah/On Broadway	5
69	Unity UN 513	Let It Be Me/Love Makes Me Do Foolish Things (both with Paulette)	5
69	Unity UN 515	Somebody To Love/Confusion	7
69	Unity UN 520	Slip Away/Spanish Harlem	10
69	Unity UN 524	Sunny Side Of The Sea/A Place In The Sun	10
69	Unity UN 527	Blessed Are The Meek/Conversation	10
69	Unity UN 537	Keep That Light Shining On Me/Build My World Around You	7
69	Unity UN 539	Love Me Tender/This Feeling	7
69	Unity UN 542	Honey/There's A Light	7
69	Jackpot JP 703	If It Don't Work Out/Love Power	7
69	Gas GAS 132	The Vow (& Doreen Shaeffer)/JAMES NEPHEW: Why Don't You Say	5
70	Gas GAS 150	What Kind Of Life/MARTIN RILEY: It's All In The Game	7
70	Unity UN 570	Jenny/The Race	7
71	Supreme SUP 219	Stay/You're My Everything	7
71	Pama Supreme PS 334	Send Me Some Loving/I'm Lost	7
71	Camel CA 81	Spanish Harlem/Slip Away	8
71	Escort ERT 851	My Love Come True/This Feeling	6
71	Escort ERT 852	Life Keeps Turning/My Girl	6
71	Escort ERT 859	My Girl/RECO: Plus One	6
71	Jackpot JP 779	Keep Walking/Will You Still Love Me Tomorrow	7
72	Jackpot JP 786	I Need Your Loving/You've Got What It Takes	7
72	Jackpot JP 788	Take Me Back/Where Do I Turn	6
72	Jackpot JP 789	Rain From The Skies/You're No Good	8
72	Jackpot JP 798	Closer Together/Blinded By Love	6
72	Jackpot JP 799	Turning Point/Money Lover	6
72	Dynamic DYN 428	Just A Dream/Send Me Some Loving	6
72	Pama PM 850	The Time Has Come/RECO & HIS BAND: Version	6
72	Pama Supreme PS 373	A Place In The Sun/Stranger On The Shore	6
72	Camel CA 89	Take Me Back/Where Do I Turn	6
72	Explosion EX 2074	The Time Has Come/Blessed Is The Man	6
73	Explosion EX 2078	Stand Up And Fight/The Sunny Side Of The Sea	6
73	Green Door GD 4058	Let Me Love You/If It Don't Work Out	8
73	Bullet BU 523	A Place In The Sun/Burning Fire	6
69	Pama ECO 9	EVERYBODY NEEDS LOVE (LP)	40
72	Trojan TBL 186	JUST A DREAM (LP)	22
73	Trojan TBL 198	GREATEST HITS (LP)	20
70s	Lord Koos KLP 1	SLIM SMITH (LP)	22

(see also Wonder Boy, Pioneers, Uniques, Roy Shirley, Ron Sig, Dakota Jim, Dennis Alcapone, David Isaacs, John Holt, Heptones, Melodians, Count Ossie, Winston Williams)

SOMETHIN' SMITH & THE REDHEADS

58	Fontana H 112	I'm Gonna Wrap Up All My Heartaches/Ev'ry Night At Nine O'Clock (78)	6
58	Fontana H 154	I Don't Want To Set The World On Fire/You Made Me Love You	10
58	Fontana H 154	I Don't Want To Set The World On Fire/You Made Me Love You (78)	6
58	Fontana TFR 6005	PUT THE BLAME ON ME (10" LP)	22

STUART SMITH

68	Polydor 56271	She's A Woman Now/Where Did Holly Go	5
69	Polydor 56336	My Head Goes Around/Where You Are	5

TAB SMITH & HIS ORCHESTRA

53	Vogue V 2141	On The Sunny Side Of The Street/Milk Train (78)	7
53	Vogue V 2172	Ace High/Deejay Special (78)	10
54	Vogue V 2203	Down Beat/Boogie Joogie (78)	10
54	Vogue V 2282	Cuban Boogie/Red Hot And Blue (78)	10
55	Vogue V 2299	All My Life/Seven Up (78)	10
56	Vogue V 2410	Jump Time/Rock City	12
56	Vogue V 2410	Jump Time/Rock City (78)	8
56	Vogue V 2416	My Mother's Eyes/These Foolish Things (78)	8

MINT VALUE £

59	London HLM 8801	Smoke Gets In Your Eyes/My Happiness Cha-Cha	12
59	London HLM 8801	Smoke Gets In Your Eyes/My Happiness Cha-Cha (78)	15
60	Vogue V 2416	My Mother's Eyes/These Foolish Things	7
62	Vogue V 2299	All My Life/Seven Up	7

TERRY SMITH

69	Philips (S)BL 7871	FALL OUT (LP)	12
77	Lambert LAM 002	TERRY SMITH AND TONY LEE TRIO (LP)	22

(see also If)

TRIXIE SMITH

51	Tempo R 42	Black Bottom Stomp/He Likes It Slow (78)	25
52	Vocalion V 1006	Freight Train Blues/Trixie's Blues (78)	30
52	Vocalion V 1017	My Daddy Rocks Me (Parts 1 & 2) (78)	30
53	Jazz Collector L 102	The World's Jazz Crazy And So Am I/Railroad Blues (78)	12
50s	Poydras 101	TRIXIE SMITH (10" EP, 45 rpm)	12
50s	Ristic 12	TRIXIE SMITH (10" EP, 45 rpm)	12
50s	Audubon AAE	TRIXIE SMITH (10" LP)	30

TRIXIE SMITH/MA RAINEY

64	Jazz Collector JEL 22	FEMALE BLUES VOL. 3 (EP, 2 tracks each)	15

TRULY SMITH

66	Decca F 12373	My Smile Is Just A Frown Turned Upside Down/Love Is Me, Love Is You	22
66	Decca F 12415	I Love Him/Buttermilk Hill	6
66	Decca F 12489	You Are The Love Of My Life/The Merry Go Round Is Slowing	6
67	Decca F 12554	Windows And Doors/Take A Broken Heart	6
67	Decca F 12645	I Wanna Go Back There Again/Window Cleaner	25
67	Decca F 12700	The Boy From Chelsea/Little Man With A Stick	6
68	MGM MGM 1431	This Is The First Time/Taking Time Off	8

VERDELLE SMITH

66	Capitol CL 15234	In My Room/Like A Man	15
66	Capitol CL 15456	Tar And Cement/A Piece Of The Sky	12
66	Capitol CL 15481	I Don't Need Anything/If You Can't Say Anything Nice	15
67	Capitol CL 15516	There's So Much Love Around Me/Baby Baby	8

WARREN SMITH

60	London HL 7101	I Don't Believe I'll Fall In Love/Cave-In (export issue)	35
61	London HLG 7110	Odds And Ends/A Whole Lot Of Nothin' (export issue)	35
64	Liberty LIB 55699	Blue Smoke/Judge And Jury	15

WAYNE SMITH

85	Greensleeves GRED 169	Under Me Sleng Teng/MICHAEL BUCKLEY: Dance Gate (12", die-cut company sleeve)	10

WHISPERING SMITH

72	Blue Horizon 2431 015	OVER EASY (LP)	75

WHISTLING JACK SMITH

67	Deram DM 112	I Was Kaiser Bill's Batman/The British Grin And Bear	5
68	Decca F 12741	Havah Nagilah/RUDI BENNETT: I'm So Proud	5
67	Deram DML 1009	AROUND THE WORLD WITH WHISTLING JACK SMITH (LP)	15

(see also Rudi Bennett)

WILLIE 'THE LION' SMITH

72	Polydor 2460 156	PORK AND BEANS (LP)	12

SMITH & D'ABO

76	CBS 81583	SMITH & D'ABO (LP)	15

(see also Manfred Mann, Dave Clark Five, Band Of Angels, Mike Smith)

SMITH BROTHERS

51	London L 959	Castles In The Sand/Little Small Town Girl (78)	6
56	Decca F 10759	Smith (What A Name To Be Stuck With)/Bacon Barbecue	6

(see also Five Smith Brothers)

SMITH BROTHERS (U.S.)

78	Grapevine GRP 109	There Can Be A Better Way/Payback's A Drag	10

SMITHFIELD MARKET

73	Gloucester GLS 0435	LONDON IN 1665 (LP, private pressing, gatefold sleeve)	800
74	Globe/Gloucester GLS 0443	AFTER SHAKESPEARE (LP, private pressing, die-cut sleeve, with insert)	700

SMITH, PERKINS & SMITH

72	Island ILPS 9198	SMITH, PERKINS & SMITH (LP)	12

THE SMITHS

SINGLES

83	Rough Trade RT 131	Hand In Glove/Handsome Devil (p/s, original pressing with Manchester address on rear sleeve; later issue with London address)	18/12
83	Rough Trade RT 131	Hand In Glove/Handsome Devil (later pressing with misprinted blue/negative p/s)	400+
83	Rough Trade RT 136	Reel Around The Fountain/Jeane (unissued, white label test pressings only)	550
83	Rough Trade RT 136	This Charming Man/Jeane (with 'Smiths' credit; Rough Trade 'tower' or plain logo on p/s)	10
83	Rough Trade RT 136	This Charming Man/Jeane (without 'Smiths' credit & with either Rough Trade 'tower' or later plain logo on p/s)	10
83	Rough Trade RTT 136	This Charming Man (Manchester)/This Charming Man (London)/Accept Yourself/Wonderful Woman (12", with or without "Smiths" credit on p/s)	15
83	Rough Trade RTT 136NY	This Charming Man (New York Vocal)/This Charming Man (New York Instrumental) (12", p/s)	22
84	Rough Trade RT 146	What Difference Does It Make?/Back To The Old House ('Morrissey' or 'Terence Stamp' p/s)	8/10

			MINT VALUE £
84	Rough Trade RTT 146	What Difference Does It Make?/Back To The Old House/ These Things Take Time (12", Morrissey or Terence Stamp p/s)	12/15
84	Rough Trade RT 156	Heaven Knows I'm Miserable Now/Suffer Little Children (p/s)	5
84	Rough Trade RT 166	William, It Was Really Nothing/Please Please Please Let Me Get What I Want (original issue with 'man on bed' p/s)	8
84	Rough Trade RTT 166	William, It Was Really Nothing/How Soon Is Now?/Please Please Please Let Me Get What I Want (12", original with green 'man on bed' p/s)	8
85	Rough Trade RT 176	How Soon Is Now?/Well I Wonder	5
85	Rough Trade RTT 176	How Soon Is Now?/Well I Wonder/Oscillate Wildly (12", p/s)	8
85	Rough Trade RT 181	Shakespeare's Sister/What She Said (p/s)	5
85	Rough Trade RTT 181	Shakespeare's Sister/What She Said/Stretch Out And Wait (12", p/s & inner)	8
85	Rough Trade RT 186	MEAT IS MURDER (live EP, unissued, test pressings only)	1000+
85	Rough Trade RTT 186	MEAT IS MURDER (live 12" EP, unissued, test pressings only)	1000+
85	Rough Trade RT 186	That Joke Isn't Funny Anymore/Meat Is Murder (live) (p/s)	5
85	Rough Trade RTT 186	That Joke Isn't Funny Anymore/Nowhere Fast (live)/Stretch Out And Wait (live)/Shakespeare's Sister (live)/Meat Is Murder (live) (12", p/s)	8
85	Rough Trade RT 191	The Boy With The Thorn In His Side/Asleep (p/s)	5
86	Rough Trade RT 192	Bigmouth Strikes Again/Money Changes Everything (p/s)	5
86	Rough Trade RT 193	Panic/Vicar In A Tutu (p/s, with 'Hang The DJ' stickers)	10
86	Rough Trade RTT 193	Panic/Vicar In A Tutu/The Draize Train (12", p/s, with 'Hang The DJ' stickers)	15
86	Rough Trade RT 194C	Ask/Cemetry Gates/Golden Lights (cassette with picture inlay)	12
87	Rough Trade RTT 195	Shoplifters Of The World Unite/Half A Person/London (12", p/s, mispressing, A-side plays "You Just Haven't Earned It Yet Baby", some in carrier bag)	70/50
87	Rough Trade RTT 195	Shoplifters Of The World Unite/Half A Person/London (12", p/s, some in carrier bag)	30/20
87	Rough Trade RT 196	Sheila Take A Bow/Is It Really So Strange (p/s)	5
87	Rough Trade RT 197	Girlfriend In A Coma/Work Is A Four Letter Word (p/s)	5
87	Rough Trade RTT 197C	Girlfriend In A Coma/Work Is A Four Letter Word/I Keep Mine Hidden (cassette with picture inlay)	12
87	Rough Trade RT 198	I Started Something I Couldn't Finish/Pretty Girls Make Graves (Troy Tate demo) (p/s)	5
87	Rough Trade RTT 198C	I Started Something I Couldn't Finish/Pretty Girls Make Graves/ Some Girls Are Bigger Than Others/What's The World (live) (cassette)	12
87	Rough Trade RT 200	Last Night I Dreamt Somebody Loved Me/Rusholme Ruffians (John Peel version) (p/s)	5
87	Rough Trade RTT 200CD	Last Night I Dreamt Somebody Loved Me/Rusholme Ruffians (John Peel version)/ Nowhere Fast (John Peel version)/William, It Was Really Nothing (John Peel Version) (CD)	15
87	Rough Trade RT 166	William, It Was Really Nothing/Please Please Please Let Me Get What I Want (reissue, 'Billie Whitelaw' p/s)	15
87	Rough Trade RTT 166	William, It Was Really Nothing/How Soon Is Now?/Please Please Please Let Me Get What I Want (12", reissue, 'Billie Whitelaw' p/s)	25
88	Spiral Scratch SCRATCH 3	An Interview With The Smiths (with *Spiral Scratch* magazine, issue 3)	5
88	Rough Trade RT 136	This Charming Man/Jeane (reissue)	5

PROMOS

84	Rough Trade RT 61 DJ	Still Ill/You've Got Everything Now	25
86	no cat. No.	THE SMITHS (white label promo)	30
88	Rough Trade RTT 171	Barbarism Begins At Home (Edited Version)/ Barbarism Begins At Home (12", 1-sided, p/s)	35

CD SINGLES

88	Rough Trade RTT 146CD	What Difference Does It Make?/Back To The Old House/ These Things Take Time	15
88	Rough Trade RTT 156CD	Heaven Knows I'm Miserable Now/Girl Afraid/Suffer Little Children	12
88	Rough Trade RTT 166CD	William, It Was Really Nothing/How Soon Is Now?/ Please, Please, Please Let Me Get What I Want	18
88	Rough Trade RTT 171CD	Barbarism Begins At Home/Shakespeare's Sister/ Stretch Out And Wait	30
88	Rough Trade RTT 191CD	The Boy With The Thorn In His Side/Rubber Ring/Asleep	20
88	Rough Trade RTT 193CD	Panic/Vicar In A Tutu/The Draize Train	18
88	Rough Trade RTT 194CD	Ask/Cemetery Gates/Golden Lights	12
88	Rough Trade RTT 200CD	Last Night I Dreamt Somebody Loved Me/Rusholme Ruffians/ Nowhere Fast/William, It Was Really Nothing	15
88	Rough Trade RTT 215CD	The Headmaster Ritual/Nowhere Fast (live)/Stretch Out And Wait (live)/ Meat Is Murder (live)	25

ALBUMS

84	Rough Trade ROUGH 76	HATFUL OF HOLLOW (LP, original issue, gatefold sleeve & inner sleeve)	12
85	Rough Trade ROUGHCD 81	MEAT IS MURDER (CD, original issue)	22
86	Rough Trade ROUGHCD 61	THE SMITHS (CD, original issue)	20
86	Rough Trade ROUGHCD 96	THE QUEEN IS DEAD (CD, original issue)	20
87	Rough Trade ROUGH 101	THE WORLD WON'T LISTEN (LP, original issue, with inner)	12
87	R. Trade ROUGHCD 101	THE WORLD WON'T LISTEN (CD, original issue)	20
87	R. Trade ROUGHCD 106	STRANGEWAYS HERE WE COME (CD, original issue)	20
87	Rough Trade RT 225	LOUDER THAN BOMBS (2-LP, gatefold sleeve)	20
87	Rough Trade ROUGH CD 225	LOUDER THAN BOMBS (CD)	20
88	R. Trade ROUGH CD 76	HATFUL OF HOLLOW (CD, original sleeve)	18
88	R. Trade ROUGH 126	RANK (LP, gatefold sleeve, with inner, ltd. edition with poster)	15
88	R. Trade ROUGH 126D	RANK (DAT)	20

10" REISSUE ALBUMS

93	WEA SMITHS 1	THE SMITHS (2-LP)	12
93	WEA SMITHS 2	HATFUL OF HOLLOW (2-LP)	12
93	WEA SMITHS 3	MEAT IS MURDER (2-LP)	12

MINT VALUE £

93	WEA SMITHS 4	THE QUEEN IS DEAD (2-LP)	12
93	WEA SMITHS 5	THE WORLD WON'T LISTEN (2-LP)	12
93	WEA SMITHS 6	STRANGEWAYS HERE WE COME (2-LP)	12
93	WEA SMITHS 7	RANK (2-LP)	12

(see also Morrissey, Sandie Shaw, The The, Electronic)

SMITHY ALL STARS

71 Hillcrest HCT 3 — Witchfinder General/Deserted — 5

(see also Ian Smith & Inner Mind)

SALLY SMITT & HER MUSICIANS

80 Groovy STP 3 — SOUNDTRACK OF THE FILM HANGAHAIR (LP) — 12

SMOG

95 City Slang EFAD 49517 — A Hit/Wine Stained Lips (p/s, yellow vinyl) — 10

SMOKE

67	Columbia DB 8115	My Friend Jack/We Can Take It	30
67	Columbia DB 8252	If The Weather's Sunny/I Would If I Could, But I Can't	30
67	Island WIP 6023	It Could Be Wonderful/Have Some More Tea	50
68	Island WIP 6031	Utterly Simple/Sydney Gill (unreleased)	
70	Revolution Pop REVP 1002	Dreams Of Dreams/My Birth	20
71	Pageant SAM 101	Ride Ride Ride/Guy Fawkes	12
72	Regal Zonophone RZ 3071	Sugar Man/That's What I Want	25
74	Decca FR 13484	Shagalagalu/Gimme Good Loving	5
74	Decca FR 13514	My Lullaby/Looking High	5
70s	Gull	IT'S SMOKE TIME (LP, reissue of German-only LP)	25
88	M. Blue Town MBT 5001	MY FRIEND JACK (LP)	20

(see also Shots)

SMOKESTACK LIGHTNIN'

69	Bell BLL 1046	Light In My Window/Long Stemmed Eyes	5
69	Bell MBLL/SBLL 116	OFF THE WALL (LP)	25

SMOKEY BABE

62 '77' LA 12-12 — SMOKEY BABE AND HIS FRIENDS (LP) — 25

SMOKEY CIRCLES

70	Carnaby CNS 401	Long Long Long/Love Me While You Can	5
70	Carnaby CNLS 6006	THE SMOKEY CIRCLES ALBUM (LP)	30

SMOKIE & HIS SISTER

67 CBS 202605 — Creators Of Rain/In Dreams Of Silent Seas — 5

SMOKIN' ROADIE

83 Zone To Zone ZON 3 — Midnight/Ripp Off (p/s) — 35

SMOKEY SMOTHERS

69 Polydor 623 239 — THE DRIVING BLUES (LP) — 30

DES SMYTH & COLLEGEMEN

65	Pye 7N 15867	The Pillow That Whispers/Lonely Streets	7
65	Pye 7N 15996	Wedding Bells/All For The Love Of A Girl	7

GILLI SMYTH & MOTHER GONG

78 Charly CRL 5007 — MOTHER (LP, with insert) — 15

(see also Gong)

DONALD SMYTHE

71 Punch PH 83 — Where Love Goes/HURRICANES: You Can Run — 30

GLORIA SMYTHE

60 Vogue V 9159 — I'll Be Over After A While/Gee Baby Ain't I Good To You — 10

SNAFU

74	WWA WWS 007	Dixie Queen/Monday Morning	5
74	WWA WWA 003	SNAFU (LP, gatefold sleeve)	15
74	WWA WWA 013	SITUATION NORMAL (LP)	15

(see also Whitesnake, Freedom)

SNAKEBITE

83 Astor ASTOR 1 — Blow You Away/Thin Ice (no p/s) — 25

SNAKEFINGER

79	Virgin VS 312	Kill The Great Raven/What Wilbur (p/s)	5
79	Virgin V 2140	CHEWING HIDES THE SOUND (LP)	12

(see also Residents)

SNAPE

73 Transatlantic TRA 269 — ACCIDENTALLY BORN IN NEW ORLEANS (LP) — 20

(see also Alexis Korner)

SNAPPERS

59	Top Rank JAR 167	Big Bill/If There Were	15
59	Top Rank JAR 167	Big Bill/If There Were (78)	50

SNAPPERS

67 CBS 2719 — Upside Down Inside Out/Memories — 12

SNATCH

78	Lightning LIG 502	Stanley/I.R.T. (p/s)	10
78	Lightning LIG 505	All I Want/When I'm Bored ('foil' p/s)	10
80	Fetish FET 004	Shopping For Clothes/Joey/Red Army (12", die-cut p/s)	8

(see also Johnny Thunders, Judy Nylon)

SND

99 City Centre Offices BLOCK 4 — Medley Systems/(locked grooves) (1000 only) — 12

MINT VALUE £

SNEAKY PETES
60 Decca F 11199 — Savage (Parts 1 & 2) 12

SNEEKERS
64 Columbia DB 7385 — I Just Can't Get To Sleep/Bald Headed Woman 120

LEN SNIDER
63 London HLU 9790 — Everyone Knows/I'll Be Coming Home Tonight 7

SNIFF 'N' THE TEARS
79 Chiswick NS 40 — Driver's Seat (cancelled, test pressings only) 15

SNIVELLING SHITS
77 Ghetto Rockers PRE 2 — Terminal Stupid/I Can't Come (p/s) 10
89 Damaged Goods FNARR 4 — Isgodaman?/Terminal Stupid/I Can't Come (p/s) 20
89 Dam. Goods FNARR4B — Isgodaman?/Terminal Stupid/I Can't Come (box set with badge & inserts, pink vinyl in stamped plain white sleeve) 25
90 Dam. Goods FNARR LP 3 — I CAN'T COME (LP, brown vinyl) 12
(see also Doctor Dark)

SNOBS
64 Decca F 11867 — Buckle Shoe Stomp/Stand And Deliver 25

SNOOKY & MOODY
66 Blue Horizon 45-1003 — Snooky And Moody's Blues/Telephone Blues (99 copies only) 135

HANK SNOW (& RAINBOW RANCH BOYS)
52 HMV B 10203 — Down The Trail Of Achin' Hearts/PEE WEE KING: Slow Coach (78) 8
52 HMV B 10284 — My Two Timin' Woman/The Rhumba Boogie (78) 8
52 HMV B 10354 — Lady's Man/I Went To Your Wedding (78) 8
53 HMV JO 424 — The Alphabet/My Religion's Not Old Fashioned (But It's Real Genuine) (78, export issue) 7
54 HMV 7MC 7 — Why Do You Punish Me (For Loving You)/When Mexican Joe Meets Jole Blon (with Rainbow Ranch Boys) (export issue) 18
54 HMV 7MC 15 — Spanish Fire Ball/Between Fire And Water (with Rainbow Ranch Boys) (export issue) 18
54 HMV 7MC 24 — My Arabian Baby/I Don't Hurt Anymore (with Rainbow Ranch Boys) (export issue) 18
54 HMV 7MC 25 — My Religion's Not Old-Fashioned (But It's Real Genuine)/The Alphabet (with Rainbow Ranch Boys) (export issue) 18
54 HMV 7MC 31 — Yellow Roses/Would You Mind (with Rainbow Ranch Boys) (export issue) 18
59 RCA RCA 1151 — Old Shep/The Last Ride 10
59 RCA RCA 1151 — Old Shep/The Last Ride (78) 10
61 RCA RCA 1248 — Poor Little Jimmie/Beggar To A King 7
58 RCA RCX 116 — COUNTRY GUITAR NO. 4 (EP) 12
59 RCA RCX 142 — COUNTRY GUITAR NO. 7 (EP) 15
63 RCA RCX 7125 — WHEN TRAGEDY STRUCK (EP) 12
64 RCA RCX 7154 — THAT COUNTRY GENTLEMAN (EP) 15
59 RCA RD 27115 — WHEN TRAGEDY STRUCK (LP) 15
62 RCA Camden CDN 164 — SOUTHERN CANNONBALL (LP) 12
63 RCA Camden CDN 5102 — THE ONE AND ONLY HANK SNOW (LP) 12
63 RCA RD/SF 7579 — RAILROAD MAN (LP) 15
64 RCA RD/SF 7607 — I'VE BEEN EVERYWHERE (LP) 15
64 RCA Victor RD 7658 — SONGS OF TRAGEDY (LP) 15
65 RCA Camden CDN 5124 — THE OLD AND GREAT SONGS (LP) 12
66 RCA Victor RD 7741 — SINGS YOUR FAVOURITE COUNTRY HITS (LP) 15
67 RCA Victor RD 7831 — GOSPEL TRAIN (LP) 12
68 RCA RD/SF 7945 — HANK IN HAWAII (LP) 12
(see also Chet Atkins)

SNOWBOY
90s Acid Jazz AJTEN 1 — Theme From The New Avengers/(Mixes) (12") 15
90s Acid Jazz JAZIDLP 146 — THE MANY FACES OF SNOWBOY (2-LP) 25
90s Acid Jazz JAZIDCD146 — THE MANY FACES OF SNOWBOY (CD) 18

SNOWBOY & NOEL McKOY
90s Acid Jazz JAZID 42T — Lucky Fellow (12", p/s) 12

BILL SNYDER & HIS (MAGIC PIANO &) ORCHESTRA
51 London L 868 — Bewitched/Drifting Sands (B-side with Ralph Sterling) (78) 8
51 London L 870 — My Silent Love/Choppin' Up Chopin (78) 6
51 London L 971 — The Very Thought Of You/I Can't Believe That You're In Love (78) 8
53 Parlophone MSP 6005 — Bewitched/Drifting Sands (B-side with Ralph Sterling) 6
54 London REP 1011 — BEWITCHED (EP) 15
51 London H-APB 1004 — BEWITCHED (10" LP) 18
54 Brunswick LA 8667 — THE STARLIT HOUR (10" LP) 15
57 Brunswick LAT 8200 — CAFE RENDEZVOUS (LP) 12
58 Brunswick LAT 8254 — SWEET AND LOVELY (LP) 12

RON SNYDER
63 Parlophone R 4993 — Oh My Twisted Bach/Narcissus 6

ERROL SOBERS
70 Beacon BEA 159 — Sugar Shaker/You're In Love 10
(see also Bobby Bridger)

SOCIALITES
64 Warner Bros WB 148 — Jive Jimmy/You're Losing Your Touch 40

SOCIAL SECURITY
78 Heartbeat PULSE 1 — I Don't Want My Heart To Rule My Head/Stella's Got A Fella/Cider/Choc Ice (p/s). 15

SOCIETIE
67 Deram DM 162 — Bird Has Flown/Breaking Down 60

MINT VALUE £

SOCRATES

72	Deram DM 362	Eating Momma's Cookin'/Dearest Agnes	12

SODS

79	Tap TAP 1	Moby Grape/Negative Positive (p/s)	30
79	Stortbeat SB 5	No Pictures Of Us/Plaything (p/s)	30
79	Step Forward SFLP 3	MINUTES TO GO (LP)	20

SOFT BOYS

77	Raw RAW 5	GIVE IT TO THE SOFT BOYS (EP, acetate with withdrawn track, "Vyrna Knowl Is A Headbanger" in place of "Ventilator")	200
77	Raw RAW 5	GIVE IT TO THE SOFT BOYS (EP)	20
78	Radar ADA 8	(I Want To Be An) Anglepoise Lamp/Fat Man's Son (p/s)	8
79	Raw RAW 37	GIVE IT TO THE SOFT BOYS (EP, unreleased reissue)	
79	Raw RAW 41	Where Are The Prawns (unreleased)	
80	Armageddon AEP 002	NEAR THE SOFT BOYS (EP)	8
80	Armageddon AS 005	I Wanna Destroy You/I'm An Old Pervert (Disco) (p/s)	8
81	Armageddon AS 029	Only The Stones Remain/The Asking Tree (p/s)	8
82	Bucketfull Of Brains BOB 1	Love Poisoning/When I Was A Kid (p/s, with/without *Bucketfull Of Brains* magazine)	15/12
83	Midnight Music DING 4	He's A Reptile/Song No. 4 (p/s, 2 different designs)	8
87	Bucketfull Of Brains BOB 17	Deck Of Cards/ROBYN HITCHCOCK & PETER BUCK: Flesh No. 1 (flexidisc with *Bucketfull Of Brains* magazine, issue 23)	6/4
89	Overground OVER 4	The Face Of Death/The Yodelling Hoover (p/s, 600 yellow vinyl, 400 white vinyl, 15 gold test pressings)	6/6/15
85	Delorean SOFT 1P	WADING THROUGH A VENTILATOR (12" EP, picture disc)	10
79	Two Crabs CLAW 1001	A CAN OF BEES (LP, original issue, black & white labels)	20
80	Aura AUL 709	A CAN OF BEES (LP, reissue)	12
80	Armageddon ARM 1	UNDERWATER MOONLIGHT (LP)	12
82	Armageddon BYE 1	TWO HALVES FOR THE PRICE OF ONE (LP)	12
83	M. Music CHIME 0002	INVISIBLE HITS (LP)	12
84	Two Crabs CLAW 1001	A CAN OF BEES (LP, 2nd reissue, black & red labels)	12

(see also Robyn Hitchcock, Kimberley Rew)

SOFT CELL

80	Big Frock ABF 1	MUTANT MOMENTS (EP, plain p/s with postcard; beware of counterfeits without postcard & in wraparound p/s!)	75
81	Some Bizzare HARD 1	A Man Can Get Lost/Memorabilia (p/s, 10,000 only)	10
81	Some Bizzare HARD 12	Memorabilia (Extended)/Persuasion (Extended) (12", p/s)	10
81	Some Bizzare BZS 212	Tainted Love/Where Did Our Love Go/Tainted Dub/Memorabilia (12", p/s, limited edition with 4 tracks)	8
81	Some Bizzare No Cat. No.	Metro Mr. X/B-MOVIE: Remembrance Day (white label test pressing)	60
81	Lyntone LYN 10410	Metro Mr. X/B-MOVIE: Remembrance Day (red or green flexidisc, with/without *Flexipop* magazine, issue 12)	8/6
81	Some Bizzare BZS 612	Bedsitter/Facility Girls (12", p/s)	8
82	Some Bizzare BZS 912	Torch/Insecure Me (12", p/s)	8
82	Some Bizzare CELBX 1	THE 12" SINGLES (6 x 12" box set, with booklet)	50
83	Some Bizzare BZS 17	Numbers/Memorabilia (live) (foldout card p/s)	7
83	Some Bizzare BZS 2020	Soul Inside/You Only Live Twice//Loving You — Hating Me/ Her Imagination (double pack)	8
83	Lyntone (no cat. no.)	Say Hello, Wave Goodbye (live) (flexidisc, blue vinyl, fan club issue, 500 only)	18
84	Lyntone (no cat. no.)	Ghostrider (live '83) (flexidisc, blue, black or green vinyl, fan club issue)	15
84	Some Bizzare BZSR 2212	Down In The Subway (Remix)/Disease And Desire/Born To Lose (12", p/s)	18
91	Some Bizzare SOFCP 1	Say Hello, Wave Goodbye — '91/Numbers/Torch (Original Extended Version) (CD, picture disc)	8
91	Some Bizzare SOFCP 2	Tainted Love—Where Did Our Love Go/Loving You — Hating Me/ Where The Heart Is (CD, in different colours of leather pouch)	10
91	Some Bizzare (no cat. no.)	Megamix '91 (12", promo only, custom p/s)	12
01	no label	Tainted Love/Say Hello, Wave Goodbye (Mercury Almighty Mixes) (CD-R, title sleeve)	50
02	Cooking Vinyl COOK 245	CRUELTY WITHOUT BEAUTY (LP)	12

(see also Marc Almond, Marc & Mambas, Anne Hogan)

SOFTIES

77	Charly CYS 1036	Suicide Pilot/C.I. Angel (p/s)	5

(see also Captain Sensible)

MICK SOFTLEY

65	Immediate IM 014	I'm So Confused/She's My Girl	30
67	CBS 202469	Am I The Red One/That's Not My Kind Of Love	60
70	CBS 5130	Can You Hear Me Now/Time Machine	7
71	CBS 7337	Goin' Down The Road/Gypsy	7
72	CBS 8269	Lady Willow/From The Land Of The Crab	7
65	Columbia 33SX 1781	SONGS FOR SWINGIN' SURVIVORS (LP)	100
70	CBS 64098	SUNRISE (LP, gatefold sleeve)	30
71	CBS 64395	STREET SINGER (LP)	25
72	CBS 64841	ANY MOTHER DOESN'T GRUMBLE (LP)	25

SOFT MACHINE

67	Polydor 56151	Love Makes Sweet Music/Reelin' Feelin' Squeelin'	130
78	Harvest HAR 5155	Soft Space (Parts 1 & 2) (p/s)	8
69	Probe SPB 1002	THE SOFT MACHINE VOLUME TWO (LP)	25
70	CBS 66246	THIRD (2-LP)	20
71	CBS 64280	FOURTH (LP)	18
72	CBS 64806	FIFTH (LP)	18
73	CBS 68214	SIX (2-LP)	15
73	CBS 65799	SEVEN (LP, gatefold sleeve)	15
75	Harvest SHSP 404	BUNDLES (LP, with inner sleeve)	12
76	Harvest SHSP 4056	SOFTS (LP)	12

MINT VALUE £

77 Harvest SHTW 800 TRIPLE ECHO (3-LP, box set, with colour booklet) ... 40
78 Harvest SHSP 4083 ALIVE & WELL (LP) ... 12
(see also Robert Wyatt, Kevin Ayers, Hugh Hopper, Elton Dean, Daevid Allen, Matching Mole, 'Igginbottom, Lyn Dobson)

SOFT PEDALLING
70 Decca F 23034 It's So Nice/Rolling On Home ... 5

SOFT SHOE
78 Aardvark AARD 1 FOR THOSE ALONE (LP, with insert) ... 110

SOHEP
81 Merciful Release MR 3 So Much Fun/You Could Be So Nice Dear (p/s) ... 10

SOHO SKIFFLE GROUP
57 Melodisc 1403 Give Me A Big Fat Woman/The Midnight Special (78) ... 15
57 Melodisc 1421 Frankie And Johnny/Streamline Train (78) ... 15
57 Melodisc EMP 7 72 SOHO SKIFFLE GROUP (EP) ... 85

MARTIAL SOLAL
63 RCA Victor RD/SF 7614 AT NEWPORT '63 (LP) ... 12

SOLAR PLEXUS
73 Polydor 2383 222 SOLAR PLEXUS (LP) ... 20

SOLDIER
82 Heavy Metal HEAVY 12 Sheralee/Force (p/s, some with postcard) ... 35/25

SOLENT
73 Decca F 13375 My World Fell Down/The Sound Of Summer's Over ... 10

SOLID GOLD CADILLAC
73 RCA SF 8311 SOLID GOLD CADILLAC (LP) ... 20
73 RCA SF 8365 BRAIN DAMAGE (LP) ... 18
(see also Chris Spedding, Mike Westbrook)

SOLID ROCK BAND
78 Chapel Lane RWA 1 FOOTPRINTS ON THE WATER (LP, gatefold sleeve) ... 20

SOLID SENDERS
(see under Wilko Johnson)

SOL INVICTUS
90 Cerne 004 Abbatoirs Of Love/CURRENT 93: This Ain't The Summer Of Love (live in Japan, gig freebie, 93 only with insert & gig ticket [200 without insert]) ... 60/25
91 Shock SX 016 See The Dove Fall/Somewhere In Europe (numbered foldover p/s in poly bag, 1,000 only) ... 15
91 World Serpent WS7 002 Looking For Europe (1-sided, etched B-side, foldover sleeve in poly bag, 963 only) ... 15
00 Tursa 026 Eve (picture disc, 1,000 only) ... 20
01 Tursa 029 HILL OF CROSSES (LP, 1,000 only, signed) ... 20
02 Tursa 030 THRONES (LP, 1,000 only, signed) ... 12
02 Tursa 014 THE BLADE (LP, 1,000 only, signed) ... 12
89 SVL SVL 009 IN THE JAWS OF THE SERPENT (LP, with insert) ... 20
90 Tursa 001 TREES IN WINTER (LP) ... 30
90 Tursa 002 LEX TALIONIS (CD, special edit in leather wallet) ... 30
91 Tursa 003 KILLING TIDE (LP) ... 25
91 Tursa 003 KILLING TIDE (CD, special edit in felt bag) ... 20
(see also Current 93, Death In June, Nurse With Wound, Karl Blake, Shock Headed Peters)

SOLITAIRES
58 London HLM 8745 Walking Along/Please Kiss This Letter ... 125
58 London HLM 8745 Walking Along/Please Kiss This Letter (78) ... 55

BOBBY SOLO
64 Fontana TF 456 Una Lacrima Sul Viso/Ora Che Se I Già Una Donna (some in p/s) ... 10/6
65 Fontana TF 573 Se Piangi Se Ridi/Saro Un Illuso ... 6

SANDY SOLO
53 London L 1178 It Really Doesn't Matter/I'm Through With Love (78) ... 12
53 London L 1182 I D'Wanna Hear Sweet Music Tonight/Close Your Dreamy Eyes (78) ... 12

SOLSTICE
82 private pressing MORNING LIGHT (cassette EP) ... 10
83 Roke RO 001C New Life/Peace For The New Age (cassette) ... 6
84 Equinox EQRLP 001 SILENT DANCE (LP, gatefold sleeve) ... 25

SOLUTION
72 Decca SKL-R 5124 SOLUTION (LP) ... 12

SOME CHICKEN
77 Raw RAW 7 New Religion/Blood On The Wall (p/s) ... 20
78 Raw RAW 13 Arabian Daze/No. 7 (p/s) ... 15
78 Raw RAW 13 Arabian Daze/No. 7 (purple vinyl) ... 120
78 Raw RAWT 13 Arabian Daze/No. 7 (12") ... 8
78 Raw RAWT 17 Arabian Daze/No. 7 (12", reissue) ... 10

SOMEONE'S BAND
70 Deram DM 313 Story/Give It To You ... 12
70 Deram SML 1068 SOMEONE'S BAND (LP) ... 130

GORDON SOMERS & HIS GROUP
64 Top Ten TPSX 101 THE SOUND OF THE BEATLES (EP) ... 8

VIRGINIA SOMERS
54 Decca F 10301 Lovin' Spree/Cross Over The Bridge ... 10

MINT VALUE £

SOMETHING HAPPENS!

86	Prophet PRS 002	TWO CHANCES (EP, p/s)	8
86	Cooking Vinyl WILD 001	TWO CHANCES (EP, reissue, p/s with insert)	6

ELKE SOMMER

61	Columbia DB 4688	Be Not Notty/The Faithful Hussar	5

JOANIE SOMMERS

60	Warner Bros WB 23	Be My Love/Why Don't You Do Right?	6
61	Warner Bros WB 31	Ruby Duby Du/Bob White	6
61	Warner Bros WB 44	One Boy/I'll Never Be Free	6
62	Warner Bros WB 71	Johnny Get Angry/Summer Place	7
62	Warner Bros WB 78	Passing Strangers/When The Boys Get Together	7
63	Warner Bros WB 85	Goodbye Joey/Bobby's Hobbies	7
63	Warner Bros WB 105	Little Girl Bad/Wishing Well	8
65	Warner Bros WB 150	If You Love Him/I Think I'm Gonna Cry	15
60	Warner Bros WEP 6013	POSITIVELY THE MOST (EP, also stereo WSEP 2013)	15/20
61	Warner Bros WEP 6047	THE VOICE OF THE SIXTIES (EP, also stereo WSEP 2047)	15/20
64	Warner Bros W(S)EP 6121	JOHNNY GET ANGRY No. 1 (EP, mono/stereo)	15/20
64	Warner Bros W(S)EP 6123	JOHNNY GET ANGRY No. 2 (EP, mono/stereo)	15/20
61	Warner Bros WM 4045	THE VOICE OF THE 60s (LP, also stereo WS 8045)	20/25
62	Warner Bros WM 4062	FOR THOSE WHO THINK YOUNG (LP, also stereo WS 8062)	20/25
63	Warner Bros WM 8107	JOHNNY GET ANGRY (LP, also stereo WS 8107)	25/30
64	Warner Bros WM 8119	LET'S TALK ABOUT LOVE (LP, also stereo WS 8119)	18/20

(see also Ed Byrnes)

ROY SONE

59	Decca F 11159	Jenny/Why Do You Doubt Our Love	6
59	Decca F 11159	Jenny/Why Do You Doubt Our Love (78)	8

SONGSTERS

54	London HL 8100	Bahama Buggy Ride/It Isn't Right	25
54	London HL 8100	Bahama Buggy Ride/It Isn't Right (78)	10

SON HOUSE

60s	Saydisc Roots SL 504	THE VOCAL INTENSITY OF SON HOUSE (LP)	35
66	CBS (S)BPG 62604	THE LEGENDARY FATHER OF FOLK BLUES (LP)	35
70	Liberty LBS 83391	JOHN THE REVELATOR (LP)	45

SON HOUSE/J.D. SHORT

69	Xtra XTRA 1080	DELTA BLUES (LP)	30

SONIA

89	Chrysalis CHSR 123385	You'll Never Stop Me From Loving You (Sonia's Kiss Mix)/You'll Never Stop Me From Loving You (12", p/s)	10
89	Chrysalis CHSCD 3465	Listen To Your Heart/Better Than Ever/Listen To Your Heart (7" Mix) (CD)	20
90	Chrysalis CHSCD 3492	Counting Every Minute/Counting Every Minute (The Don Miguel Mix)/You'll Never Stop Me From Loving You (Sonia's Kiss Mix) (CD)	12
90	Chrysalis CHSCD 3557	End Of The World/Can't Help The Way That I Feel/Counting Every Minute (Tick Tock Remix) (CD)	18
90	Chrysalis CCD 1734	EVERYBODY KNOWS SONIA (CD)	25

SONIC ASSASSINS

81	Flicknife FLEP 101	SONIC ASSASSINS (12" EP, p/s)	8

(see also Hawkwind)

SONIC BOOM

90	Silvertone SONIC 1	Octaves/Tremeloes (10", orange vinyl PVC sleeve, mail-order only)	25
91	Silvertone SONIC 2	(I Love You) To The Moon And Back/Capo Waltz (live) (gig freebie in black die-cut sleeve, promo only, 33rpm, p/s later available separately)	12/8
90	Silvertone ORE ZLP 506	SPECTRUM (LP, gatefold rotatable plastic disc sleeve with inner)	20

(see also Spacemen 3, Spectrum)

SONIC YOUTH

86	Blast First BFFP 3	Flower/Halloween (12", p/s, some on yellow vinyl)	22/14
86	Blast First BFFP 3	Flower/Rewolf (12", p/s, censored version)	25
86	Blast First BFFP 3(B)	(Savage Pencil etch)/Halloween II (12", p/s, A-side engraved, 1st 100 signed)	40/20
86	Blast First BFFP 3X	Flower/Halloween/Satan Supermix (12", unreleased)	
86	Blast First BFFP 7	Starpower (edit)/Bubblegum (p/s, some with badge & poster)	12/4
88	Fierce FRIGHT 015/016	Stick Me Donna Magick Momma/Making The Nature Scene (live) (p/s, 2 x 1-sided 7" with etched B-sides)	25
88	Fierce FRIGHT 015/016	Stick Me Donna Magick Momma/Making The Nature Scene (live) (p/s, single disc reissue)	15
88	Catalogue CAT 064	Teenage Riot (square flexidisc sewn into 'The Catalogue' magazine)	15/8
89	Blast First BFFP 46	Touch Me I'm Sick/MUDHONEY: Halloween (12", p/s)	18
89	Blast First BFFP 48	Providence (stereo)/Providence (mono) (promo only)	5
90	Geffen GEF 81	KOOL THING EP: Kool Thing/That's All I Know (p/s)	8
92	Geffen DGCT 11	100% (10" EP, orange vinyl)	10
92	Geffen DGCT 11	100% (10" EP, black vinyl promo)	40
92	Geffen DGCT 11	100% (12" EP, promo only, white label)	50
92	Geffen DGCTD 11	100% (CD EP, digipak)	10
92	Geffen GFST 26	YOUTH AGAINST FASCISM: Purr/The Destroyed Room/YAF (12" EP)	12
92	Geffen GFSTD 26	YOUTH AGAINST FASCISM: Purr/The Destroyed Room/YAF (CD EP)	8
92	Geffen 7-19664 DJ	Personality Crisis/Dirty Boots (DJ promo only)	8
93	Blast First BFFP 26 T	MASTER DIK (12" EP, with inner)	8
94	Geffen GFSV 72	Bull In The Heather/Razor Blade/Doctor's Orders (10", silver vinyl, no'd p/s)	10
83	Neutral NEUTRAL 9	CONFUSION IS SEX (LP)	20
85	Blast First BFFP 1	BAD MOON RISING (LP, with lyric insert)	12
85	NOT NOT 1/BUT 2	WALLS HAVE EARS (2-LP, 2,000 copies only, numbered)	50

MINT VALUE £

87 Blast First CHAT 1 SISTER INTERVIEW DISC (LP). . . . 18
88 Blast First BFFP 34 DAYDREAM NATION (2-LP, 1st 1,000 with signed poster) 25
94 Geffen DGC 24632 EXPERIMENTAL JET SET, TRASH & NO STAR (LP, blue vinyl) 20
(see also Ciccone Youth, Mudhoney)

SONLIGHT ORCHESTRA
70s Myrrh MYR 1036 PLAYS LOVE & OTHER GREATS (LP) 18

SONNY
71 Ackee ACK 127 Love And Peace/LARRY & ALVIN: Throw Me Corn 10

SONNY (& SONNY'S GROUP)
65 Atlantic AT 4038 Laugh At Me/Tony (as Sonny & Sonny's Group). . . . 6
65 Atlantic AT 4060 The Revolution Kind/Georgia And John Quetzal (as Sonny & Sonny's Group). . . . 8
67 Atlantic 584 131 I Told My Love To Go Away/Misty Roses (solo). . . . 5
(see also Sonny & Cher)

SONNY (Burke) & YVONNE
64 Island WI 134 Life Without Fun/SONNY BURKE GROUP: Mount Vesuvius 30
(see also Sonny Burke)

SONNY & CHER
64 Reprise R 20309 Baby Don't Go/Walkin' The Quetzal 8
65 Atlantic AT 4035 I Got You Babe/It's Gonna Rain 5
65 Atlantic AT 4047 But You're Mine/Hello 5
65 Vocalion VL 9247 The Letter/Spring Fever (B-side by 'Sonny & Cher (Instrumental)'). . . . 8
66 Atlantic AT 4069 What Now My Love/I Look For You 6
66 Atlantic 584 018 Have I Stayed Too Long/Leave Me Be 5
66 Atlantic 584 040 Little Man/Monday 5
66 Atlantic 584 057 Living For You/Turn Around 5
67 Atlantic 584 078 The Beat Goes On/Love Don't Come 8
67 Atlantic 584 110 Podunk/Beautiful Story 6
67 Atlantic 584 129 It's The Little Things/Plastic Man 6
68 Atlantic 584 162 Good Combination/You And Me 6
68 Atlantic 584 168 Circus/SONNY BONO: I Would Marry You Today 6
68 Atlantic 584 215 You Gotta Have A Thing Of Your Own/I Got You Babe 6
70 Atco 2091 021 Get It Together/Hold You Tighter 5
71 MCA MU 1139 Real People/Somebody 5
72 MCA MU 1154 A Cowboy's Work Is Never Done/Somebody 5
72 MCA MU 1164 When You Say Love/Crystal Clear/Muddy Waters 5
73 MCA MUS 1211 The Greatest Show On Earth/You Know Darn Well 5
65 Reprise R 30056 CAESAR AND CLEO (EP, 2 tracks each by Sonny & Cher, Caesar & Cleo) 20
64 Atlantic ATL/STL 5036 LOOK AT US (LP, mono/stereo) 15/20
66 Atlantic 587 006 THE WONDROUS WORLD OF SONNY AND CHER (LP) 15
67 Atlantic 587/588 052 IN CASE YOU'RE IN LOVE (LP) 15
72 MCA MUPS 435 LIVE (LP) 12
72 MCA MUPS 452 ALL I EVER NEED IS YOU (LP) 12
(see also Caesar & Cleo, Cher, Sonny, Date With Soul)

SONNY & DAFFODILS
63 Ember EMB EP 4538 SONNY & DAFFODILS (EP) 65

SON OF A BITCH
96 Hengest SOABCDS 1 Treacherous Times/Victim You (CD, stickered jewel case) 10
(see also Saxon)

SONS & LOVERS
67 Camp 602 002 Matters/Peaceful Is The River 6
68 Beacon 3-101 Help Me (I'm On Top Of The World)/Feel Alright 5
68 Beacon 3-107 Happiness Is Love/Things You Do 5

SONS OF ALBATROSS
75 Decca FR 13605 Africa/Ha-ri-ah 35

SONS OF DEMENTED CHILDREN
87 Hatter MAD 003 Spoof Dealer/Busking (p/s, with insert). . . . 18

SONS OF FRED
65 Columbia DB 7605 Sweet Love/I'll Be There. . . . 100
65 Parlophone R 5391 I, I, I (Want Your Lovin')/She Only Wants A Friend. . . . 70
66 Parlophone R 5415 Baby What Do You Want Me To Do/You Told Me 140
(see also Odyssey)

SONS OF MAN
67 Oak RGJ 612 SONS OF MAN (EP, no p/s) . . . . 400+
(see also Aubrey Small)

SONS OF MOSES
75 MCA MCA 169 Soul Symphony/Fatback 8

SONS OF PILTDOWN MEN
63 Pye International 7N 25206 Mad Goose/Be A Party. . . . 18

SONS OF PIONEERS
54 HMV 7EG 8069 SONS OF THE PIONEERS (EP) 12
57 RCA RD 27016 FAVOURITE COWBOY SONGS (LP). . . . 15

SONS OF SOUL
66 Doctor Bird DB 1037 Yeah Yeah Baby/So Ashamed 18

SONSONG
76 Zebra ZM 5761 SONSONG (LP). . . . 30

SOPHOMORES
60s Seeco CELP 451 THE SOPHOMORES (LP) 30

MINT VALUE £

SOPWITH CAMEL

66 Kama Sutra KAS 205 Hello Hello/Treadin' . . . 5
74 Reprise K 44251 THE MIRACULOUS HUMP RETURNS FROM THE MOON (LP) . . . 15

SORROWS

65 Piccadilly 7N 35219 I Don't Wanna Be Free/Come With Me . . . 35
65 Piccadilly 7N 35230 Baby/Teenage Letter . . . 35
65 Piccadilly 7N 35260 Take A Heart/We Should Get Along Fine . . . 15
66 Piccadilly 7N 35277 You've Got What I Want/No, No, No, No (a few with export p/s) . . . 30/15
66 Piccadilly 7N 35309 Let The Live Live/Don't Sing No Sad Songs For Me . . . 35
66 Piccadilly 7N 35336 Let Me In/How Love Used To Be . . . 35
67 Piccadilly 7N 35385 Pink, Purple, Yellow And Red/My Gal . . . 70
66 Piccadilly N(S)PL 38023 TAKE A HEART (LP, mono/stereo) . . . 150/250
(see also Don Fardon)

SORT SOL

81 4AD AD 101 Marble Station/Misguided (p/s) . . . 10

S.O.U.L. (Sounds Of Unity & Love)

72 Pye Intl. NSPL 28162 CAN YOU FEEL IT (LP) . . . 35
70s Pye Intl. WHAT IS IT (LP) . . . 65

HORATIO SOUL

68 Island WI 3132 Ten White Horses/Angela (Sweet Sweet) . . . 12
69 Crystal CR 7006 Nobody's Gonna Sleep Tonight/Turn Around Baby . . . 6

JIMMY SOUL

62 Stateside SS 103 Twistin' Matilda/I Can't Hold Out Any Longer . . . 8
63 Stateside SS 178 If You Wanna Be Happy/Don't Release Me . . . 15
64 Stateside SS 274 I Hate You Baby/Change Partners . . . 10
64 Stateside SE 1010 IF YOU WANNA BE HAPPY (EP) . . . 30

JUNIOR SOUL (Murvin)

68 Doctor Bird DB 1112 Miss Cushie/LYNN TAITT & JETS: Dr. Paul . . . 25
68 Big Shot BI 503 Chattie Chattie/The Magic Touch . . . 12
69 Big Shot BI 527 The Hustler/The Magic Touch . . . 12
70 Gayfeet GS 205 Jennifer/Slipping . . . 12

SHARON SOUL

65 Stateside SS 411 How Can I Get To You/Don't Say Goodbye Love . . . 55

SOUL AGENTS

64 Pye 7N 15660 I Just Wanna Make Love To You/Mean Woman Blues . . . 35
64 Pye 7N 15707 Seventh Son/Let's Make It Pretty Baby . . . 60
65 Pye 7N 15768 Don't Break It Up/Gospel Train . . . 55
(see also Loot, Don Shinn, Hookfoot)

SOUL AGENTS (Jamaica)

67 Coxsone CS 7007 Get Ready It's Rocksteady/BOB & BELTONES: Smile Like An Angel (B-side actually by Bop & Beltones) . . . 20
67 Coxsone CS 7018 For Your Education/SUMMERTAIRES: Tell Me . . . 25
67 Coxsone CS 7027 Lecture/SOUL BOYS: Blood Pressure . . . 25

SOUL BOYS

66 Rio R120 Rudie Get Wise/JACKIE OPEL: I Don't Want Her . . . 30
67 Island WI 3052 Blood Pressure/RITA MARLEY: Come To Me . . . 30
(see also Soul Agents [Jamaica])

SOUL BROTHERS

65 Mercury MF 916 Gotta Get A Good Thing Going/Good Lovin' Never Hurt . . . 7
65 Decca F 12116 I Keep Ringing My Baby/I Can't Take It . . . 20
65 Parlophone R 5321 I Can't Believe It/You Don't Want To Know . . . 15

SOUL BROTHERS (Jamaica)

65 Ska Beat JB 226 Train To Skaville/WAILERS: I Made A Mistake . . . 45
66 Rio R 118 Crawfish/RITA MARLEY: You Lied . . . 30
66 Rio R 121 Mr T.N.T./MARCIA GRIFFITHS: Mr Everything . . . 18
66 Island WI 282 Green Moon/E Gal OK . . . 20
66 Island WI 294 Ska-Bostello/DON DRUMMOND: Looking Through The Window . . . 20
66 Island WI 296 Sound One/MARTINE: Grandfather's Clock (B-side actually by Emille Straker & Merrymen or Martinis) . . . 20
66 Island WI 3013 More & More/DELROY WILSON: Dancing Mood . . . 20
66 Island WI 3016 Mr Flint/Too Young To Love (B-side actually by Freddie McGregor) . . . 20
67 Island WI 3036 Sound Pressure/ETHIOPIANS: For You . . . 20
67 Island WI 3039 Hi-Life/DELROY WILSON: Close To Me . . . 20
67 Coxsone CS 7001 Take Ten/HUGH GODFREY: Deh Pon Dem . . . 20
67 Coxsone CS 7020 Hey Windell/KEN BOOTHE: Home Home Home . . . 20
67 Coxsone CS 7024 One Stop/TENNORS: Pressure And Slide . . . 20
67 Studio One SO 2006 Hot And Cold/TERMITES: Mercy Mr. Percy . . . 20
67 Studio One SO 2016 Honeypot/VICEROYS: Lose And Gain . . . 20
70 Pressure Beat PR 5506 Pussy Catch A Fire (actually by Soul Twins)/DESTROYERS: Follow This Beat (B-side actually "Secret Weapon" by Ansell Collins) . . . 12
67 Coxsone CSL 8001 HOT SHOT SKA (LP) . . . 85
67 Coxsone CSL 8002 CARIB SOUL (LP) . . . 90
(see also Earl Van Dyke & Soul Brothers, Soul Twins, Lee Perry, Tony Gregory, Ethiopians, Itals, Hortense & Delroy, Gaylads, Jennors, Derrick Morgan, Summertaires, Delroy Wilson)

SOUL BROTHERS SIX

67 Atlantic 584 118 Some Kind Of Wonderful/I'll Be Loving You . . . 40
69 Atlantic 584 256 Some Kind Of Wonderful/Somebody Else Is Loving My Baby . . . 8
72 Atlantic K 10204 Some Kind Of Wonderful/Check Yourself . . . 6
74 Atlantic K 10471 Thank You For Loving Me/Somebody Else Is Loving My Baby . . . 6

MINT VALUE £

SOUL CATS

69 Camel CA 23 — Keep It Moving/Your Sweet Love — 10
69 Gas GAS 109 — Choo Choo Train/The Load (actually "Swinging For Joy" by Count Ossie Band) — 10
71 Hillcrest HCT 2 — Reggay Got Soul (actually by Carl Bryan)/Land Of Love — 10
70s Junior JR 103 — Reggay Got Soul (actually by Carl Bryan)/Land Of Love (reissue) — 10

SOUL CHILDREN

69 Stax STAX 137 — The Sweeter He Is Parts 1 & 2 — 5
71 Stax 2025 050 — Give Me One Good Reason/Bring It Here — 5
72 Stax 2025 102 — Hearsay/Don't Take My Sunshine — 5
74 Stax STXS 2006 — Love Makes It Right/Love Makes It Right (mono) — 5
72 Stax 2325 076 — GENESIS (LP) — 12
74 Stax STX 1005 — FRICTION (LP) — 12

SOUL CITY

62 Cameo Parkway P 103 — Everybody Dance Now/Who Knows — 40

SOUL CITY EXECUTIVES

69 Soul City SC 109 — Happy Chatter/Falling In Love — 10

SOUL CLAN

68 Atlantic 584 202 — Soul Meeting/That's How It Feels (some in p/s) — 12/8
(see also Solomon Burke, Arthur Conley, Don Covay, Ben E. King, Joe Tex)

SOUL DEFENDERS

71 Banana BA 354 — Way Back Home/SOUL REBELS: Stand For Your Rights — 12
72 Ackee ACK 147 — Sound Almighty/COUNT OSSIE: Meditation — 12
(see also Eric Donaldson, Carey Johnson)

SOUL DIRECTIONS

70 Attack ATT 8011 — Su Su Su/Better Herring — 10

GEORGE SOULE

75 United Artists UP 35771 — Get Involved/Everybody's Got A Song To Sing — 8

SOULETTES

65 Ska Beat JB 204 — Opportunity/DIZZY JOHNNY & STUDIO 1 ORCHESTRA: Sudden Destruction — 25
70 Upsetter US 337 — Let It Be/UPSETTERS: Big Dog — 20
71 Jackpot JP 766 — My Desire/Bring It Up — 12
71 Jackpot JP 767 — All Of Your Loving/LLOYD CLARKE: Love Me — 12
73 Attack ATT 8044 — This World/Same Thing — 12
(see also Rita Marley, Ken Boothe, Roland Alphonso, Uniques)

SOUL EXPLOSION

69 Downtown DT 455 — Let's Try It Again/Gumpton Rock — 6
70 J-DAN JDN 4405 — My Mother's Eyes/Gum Pot — 7

SOUL FLAMES

68 Nu Beat NB 020 — Mini Really Fit Dem/Soul Train — 8

SOUL GENERATION

79 Grapevine GRP 131 — Hold On/The Lonely Sea — 15

SOULFUL STRINGS

67 Chess CRS 8068 — Burning Spear/Within You, Without You — 18
69 Chess CRS 8094 — I Wish It Would Rain/Listen Here — 12
69 Chess CRLS 4534 — GROOVIN' WITH THE SOULFUL STRINGS (LP) — 20

SOUL KINGS

69 Blue Cat BS 169 — The Magnificent Seven/RUPIE EDWARDS: Long Lost Love — 25

SOUL LEADERS

67 Rio R 134 — Pour On The Sauce/Beauty Is Only Skin Deep — 25

SOULMATES (Jamaica)

69 Amalgamated AMG 836 — Them A Laugh And A Ki Ki/The Hippys Are Here (B-side actually by Hippy Boys) — 20
69 Amalgamated AMG 842 — On The Move/Jump It Up (B-side actually by Viceroys) — 25
69 Camel CA 33 — Beware Of Bad Dogs/Short Cut (actually by Glen Adams) — 12
70 Unity UN 555 — Ten Cent/DOREEN SHAFFER: Stay With Me Forever — 10

SOULMATES (U.K.)

65 Parlophone R 5334 — Too Late To Say You're Sorry/Your Love — 10
66 Parlophone R 5407 — Bring Your Love Back Home (with Jet Set)/When Love Is Gone — 10
66 Parlophone R 5506 — Mood Melancholy/Sayin' Something — 8
67 Parlophone R 5601 — Is That You?/Time's Run Out — 7
(see also Liza Strike)

SOUL MERCHANTS

67 President PT 166 — Whole Lot Of Lovin'/Stormy Weather — 5

SOUL PARTNERS

69 Pama PM 766 — Walk On Judge/Lose The One You Love — 10

SOUL PEOPLE

68 Island WIP 6040 — Hummin'/Soul Drink — 12

SOUL PROPRIETORS

65 Concord CON STD 74 — All/Lonely Separation (private pressing) — 300

SOUL REBELS

72 Banana BA 374 — Listen And Observe/What's Love — 50
(see also Soul Defenders)

MINT VALUE £

SOUL RHYTHMS

69 Bullet BU 404 — Work Boy Work/CECIL THOMAS: Girl Lonesome Fever 12
69 High Note HS 013 — National Lottery/Round Seven.... 12
69 Gas GAS 113 — Soul Call/Musical Gate.... 12
(see also Hippy Boys, Max Romeo)

SOUL RUNNERS

67 Polydor 56732 — Grits 'n' Cornbread/Spreading Honey 10

SOUL SEARCHERS

74 Sussex SXX 2 — Blow Your Whistle (Parts 1 & 2).... 5
74 Sussex LPSX 4 — SALT OF THE EARTH (LP).... 20

SOUL SISTERS (U.S.)

64 Sue WI 312 — I Can't Stand It/Blueberry Hill 35
64 Sue WI 336 — Loop De Loop/Long Gone.... 35
65 London HLC 9970 — Foolish Dreamer/Good Time Tonight.... 40
72 United Artists UP 35388 — Good Time Tonight/Some Soul Food.... 7
64 Sue ILP 913 — THE SOUL SISTERS (LP).... 125

SOUL SISTERS (Jamaica)

69 Amalgamated AMG 839 — Wreck A Buddy/VERSATILES: Push It In.... 20
(see also Dennis Brown)

SOUL SOUNDS

67 Columbia S(C)X 6158 — SOUL SURVIVAL (LP).... 25
(see also Savages, Rebel Rousers)

SOUL STIRRERS

69 Duke DU 25 — Come See About Me/LLOYD CHARMERS: 5 To 5 10
(see also Sam Cooke)

SOUL SURVIVORS

67 Stateside SS 2057 — Expressway To Your Heart/Hey Gyp.... 20
68 Stateside SS 2094 — Explosion (In Your Soul)/Dathon's Theme 12
69 Atlantic 584 275 — Mama Soul/Tell Daddy 15

SOUL SYNDICATE

72 Green Door GD 4021 — Riot (actually by Johnny Moore & Soul Syndicate)/Smoke Without Fire (actually by Keith Hudson) 15
(see also Rockin' Horse)

SOUL TONES

70 Pama PM 790 — Dancing Time/BUNNY BARRETT: Love Locked Out 12

SOUL TWINS (Jamaica)

70 High Note HS 043 — Little Suzie/Cherrie.... 7
72 Clandisc CLA 238 — Don't Call Me Nigga/DYNAMITES: Joe Louis 6

SOUL TWINS (U.S.)

77 Grapevine GRP 101 — Quick Change Artist/Give The Man A Chance.... 15

SOUL VENDORS

67 Coxsone CS 7028 — You Troubled Me/BOP & BELTONES: Love 25
67 Coxsone CS 7029 — Fat Fish/MARCIA GRIFFITHS: Call To Me 50
67 Studio One SO 2018 — Rocking Sweet Pea/JOE HIGGS: Change Of Plans.... 45
67 Studio One SO 2022 — Cool Shade/RICHARD ACE: I Need You.... 25
67 Studio One SO 2028 — Just A Little Bit Of Soul/ALTON ELLIS: I Am Just A Guy 22
67 Studio One SO 2031 — Take Me/DELROY WILSON: I'm Not A King.... 25
67 Studio One SO 2032 — Pe Da Pa/ERNEST WILSON: Money Worries 25
67 Studio One SO 2034 — Hot Rod/GAYLADS: Africa (We Want To Go) 25
67 Studio One SO 2035 — Pupa Lick/ETHIOPIANS: Leave My Business Alone 25
68 Studio One SO 2038 — Psychedelic Rock/Gaylads: I'm Free.... 25
68 Studio One SO 2043 — Chinese Chicken/JACKIE MITTOO: Put It On 50
68 Studio One SO 2044 — Happy Ogan (actually titled "Happy Organ")/INVADERS: Soulful Music 25
68 Studio One SO 2048 — Evening Time/RIGHTEOUS FLAMES: Ease Up 25
68 Studio One SO 2058 — Frozen Soul/ERNEST WILSON: If I Were A Carpenter.... 25
68 Studio One SO 2066 — Soul Joint/Soul Limbo 25
68 Coxsone CS 7037 — Grooving Steady/ROY RICHARDS: Warm And Tender Ska 25
68 Coxsone CS 7038 — Whipping The Prince (actually by Ed Hangle & Alton Ellis)/ HEPTONES: If You Knew 18
68 Coxsone CS 7048 — Last Waltz/HAMLINS: Sentimental Reasons 25
68 Coxsone CS 7057 — Real Rock/AL CAMPBELL: Don't Run Away 25
68 Coxsone CS 7071 — West Of The Sun/ALTON ELLIS: A Fool.... 25
69 Coxsone CS 7084 — Sixth Figure/DENZIL LAING: Man Payaba 25
69 Studio One SO 2070 — Captain Cojoe/JACKIE MITTOO: Drum Song 25
67 Coxsone CSL 8010 — ON TOUR (LP).... 150
(see also Dobby Dobson)

SOUND

79 Tortch TOR 003 — PHYSICAL WORLD (EP).... 18
80 Korova KOW 10 — Heyday/Brute Force (p/s).... 6
81 Korova KOW 21 — Sense Of Purpose/Point Of No Return (p/s) 6
79 Tortch TOR 008 — THE SOUND (LP, possibly unissued)
80 Korova KODE 2 — JEOPARDY (LP, with inner) 15
85 Statik STAB 1 — SHOCK OF DAYLIGHT (mini-LP) 12
(see also Outsiders, Second Layer)

SOUND BARRIER

68 Beacon BEA 109 — She Always Comes Back To Me/Groovin' Slow.... 50

MINT VALUE £

SOUND CEREMONY

Year	Label / Cat. No.	Title	£
89	Celestial Sound SRT 8KF	You're Breaking My Heart (p/s)	10
79	Celestial Sound RWG 001	GUITAR STAR (LP)	20
79	Celestial Sound RWG 002	RON WARREN GANDERTON & SOUND CEREMONY (LP)	20
81	Celestial Sound RWG 003	PRECIOUS AS ENGLAND (LP)	20

SOUND DIMENSION

Year	Label / Cat. No.	Title	£
69	Coxsone CS 7083	Scorcia/CECIL & JACKIE: Breaking Up (B-side actually "Hold Me Baby" by Basil Daley)	22
69	Coxsone CS 7085	Soul Trombone (Suffering Stink)/LARRY & ALVIN: Your Cheating Heart	22
69	Coxsone CS 7090	Soulful Strut/Breaking Up	22
69	Coxsone CS 7093	More Scorcha/LENNIE HIBBERT: Village Soul	22
69	Coxsone CS 7097	Time Is Tight/BARRY LLEWELLYN: Sad Song	22
69	Bamboo BAM 5	Doctor Sappa Too/Soul Eruption (B-side actually by Roy Richards & Sound Dimension)	12
69	Bamboo BAM 7	Baby Face/GLADIATORS: Anywhere	12
69	Bamboo BAM 9	Jamaica Rag/C. MARSHALL: I Need Your Loving	12
69	Bamboo BAM 13	Whoopee/NORMA FRAZER: Working (B-side actually by Marcia Griffiths)	12
69	Bamboo BAM 14	Black Onion/Bitter Blood	12
70	Bamboo BAM 18	Poison Ivy/Botheration — Version	8
70	Bamboo BAM 50	Money Maker/BURNING SPEAR: Door Peeper	50
70	Banana BA 313	In The Summertime/In The Summertime — Version	8
70	Banana BA 338	My Sweet Lord (Instrumental)/DENNIS BROWN: Silky (B-side actually by Monty Alexander & Cyclones)	8
70	Supreme SUP 202	More Games/MR. FOUNDATION: Maga Dog (actually by Invaders)	8
72	Ackee ACK 149	Solas/GLADIATORS: Sonia	10

(see also Brentford Road Allstars, Jackie Mittoo, Bob Andy, Horace Andy, John Holt, Larry Marshall, Irving Brown, Heptones, Freedom Singers, Winston Francis, Jerry Jones, Ethiopians, Cables, Alton Ellis, Gladiators, Ken Boothe)

SOUNDGARDEN

Year	Label / Cat. No.	Title	£
90	A&M AMX 560	Hands All Over/Come Together/Heretic/Big Dumb Sex (10", foldout pack)	10
90	A&M AMY 574	Loud Love/Big Dumb Sex/Get On The Snake/Fresh Deadly Roses (12", etched, stickered p/s)	12
92	A&M AM 102	Outshined/I Can't Give You Anything (p/s, picture disc)	8
92	A&M AMY 102	Outshined/I Can't Give You Anything/Homicidal Suicidal (12", p/s, limited ed.)	18
92	A&M AMY 723	Rusty Cage/Touch Me/Show Me (12", poster p/s, 5000 only)	20
92	A&M AM 862	Jesus Christ Pose/Stray Cat Blues (picture disc, poly sleeve)	6
94	A&M 5805391	Spoonman/Cold Bitch/Fresh Tendrils/Exit Stonehenge (12", die-cut p/s, clear vinyl)	8
94	A&M 5805951	The Day I Tried To Live/Like Suicide/Kickstand (12", etched, p/s, with stencil)	8
94	A&M 5807532	Black Hole Sun/Birth Ritual/Beyond The Wheel/Fell On Black Days (CD, in box)	10
96	A&M 5818457	Burden In My Hand/Karaoke (p/s, white vinyl, numbered, 5000 only)	20

SOUND OF JIMMY NICOL

Year	Label / Cat. No.	Title	£
65	Decca F 12107	Clementine/Bim Bam	30

(see also Jimmy Nicol)

SOUND NETWORK

Year	Label / Cat. No.	Title	£
65	Mercury MF 944	Watching/How About Now	30

SOUNDS AROUND

Year	Label / Cat. No.	Title	£
66	Piccadilly 7N 35345	What Does She Do?/Sad Subject	20
67	Piccadilly 7N 35396	Red White And You/One Of Two	20

(see also Peter & Wolves, John Pantry, Norman Conquest, Factory)

SOUNDS COMBINE

Year	Label / Cat. No.	Title	£
71	Escort ERT 862	African Museum/African Museum — Version	6

SOUNDS GALACTIC

Year	Label / Cat. No.	Title	£
70	Phase 4 Stereo PFS 4208	AN ASTRONOMICAL ODYSSEY (LP)	15

SOUNDS INCORPORATED

Year	Label / Cat. No.	Title	£
61	Parlophone R 4815	Mogambo/Emily	15
62	Decca F 11540	Sounds Like Locomotion/Taboo	7
63	Decca F 11590	Stop/Go	8
63	Decca F 11723	Order Of The Keys/Keep Moving	25
64	Columbia DB 7239	The Spartans/Detroit	7
64	Columbia DB 7321	Spanish Harlem/Rinky Dink	7
64	Columbia DB 7404	William Tell/Bullets	7
65	Columbia DB 7545	Time For You/Hall Of The Mountain King	8
65	Columbia DB 7676	My Little Red Book/Justice Neddi	7
65	Columbia DB 7737	On The Brink/I'm Comin' Thru	30
67	Polydor 56209	How Do You Feel/Dead As You Go	8
69	Decca 22883	Warmth Of The Sun/Apollo (export)	5
64	Columbia SEG 8360	TOP GEAR (EP)	25
64	Columbia 33SX 1659	SOUNDS INCORPORATED (LP, also stereo SCX 3531)	25/30
65	EMI Regal SREG 1071	RINKY DINK (LP, export issue)	20
66	Studio Two TWO 144	SOUNDS INCORPORATED (LP)	15

(see also Tony Newman)

SOUND SIXTY-SIX

Year	Label / Cat. No.	Title	£
66	Decca F 12323	Flight 4864/The Bouncer	8

SOUNDS NICE

Year	Label / Cat. No.	Title	£
69	Parlophone R 5797	Love At First Sight/Love You Too ('featuring Tim Mycroft')	6
69	Parlophone R 5821	Sleepless Night/Continental Exchange ('featuring Tim Mycroft')	6
69	Parlophone PMC/PCS 7089	LOVE AT FIRST SIGHT (LP)	22

(see also Third Ear Band, Chris Spedding, Clem Cattini Ork)

SOUNDS OF JOHNNY HAWKSWORTH

Year	Label / Cat. No.	Title	£
66	Columbia DB 8059	Goal/"Goal — World Cup 1966" Theme	25

(see also Johnny Hawksworth)

MINT VALUE £

SOUNDS OF LES AND BARRY
65 Fontana TF 657 — Looie Girl/She Who Needs Me . . . 6

SOUNDS OF MODIFICATION
68 Stateside SL/SSL 10262 — SOUNDS OF MODIFICATION (LP) . . . 15

SOUNDS OF SALVATION
74 Reflection RL 310 — SOUNDS OF SALVATION (LP, with booklet) . . . 90
(see also Reflection)

SOUNDS OF ZION
60s Tabernacle TEP 1 — HOME TO GLORY (EP) . . . 8

SOUNDS ORCHESTRAL
66 Piccadilly 7N 35284 — Thunderball/Mr Kiss Kiss Bang Bang . . . 12
64 Piccadilly 7N 35206 — Cast Your Fate To The Wind/To Wendy With Love . . . 5
65 Piccadilly 7N 35248 — Moonglow/Scarlatti Potion No. 9 . . . 7
65 Pye NPL 38016 — THUNDERBALL — SOUNDS ORCHESTRAL MEET JAMES BOND (LP, some in gatefold sleeve) . . . 20/30

SOUNDS PROGRESSIVE
70 Eyemark EMCL 1009S — KID JENSEN INTRODUCES SOUNDS PROGRESSIVE (LP) . . . 25

SOUNDS SENSATIONAL
67 HMV POP 1584 — Love In The Open Air/Night Cry . . . 15

SOUND STAGE ORCHESTRA
76 BBC RESL 30 — Grandstand/Rugby Special . . . 6

SOUND SYSTEM
65 Island WI 258 — You Don't Know Like I Do/Take Me Serious . . . 25
(see also Owen Gray)

EPIC SOUNDTRACKS
81 Rough Trade RT 084 — Popular, Classical: Jelly Babies/A 3-Acre Floor/Pop In Packets (p/s) . . . 5
(see also Swell Maps, Thurston Moore Kim Gordon & Epic Soundtracks)

SOUND VISION
70s Key KL 007 — IN CONCERT (LP, featuring Judy MacKenzie) . . . 25

SOUP DRAGONS
86 Popshop 001/ Lyntone LYN 16674 — If You Were The Only Girl In The World/LEGEND: Talk Open (33rpm flexi with *Pure Popcorn* fanzine, later with *The Legend* fanzine) . . . 8/6/5
86 Subway Organisation SUBWAY 2 — THE SUN IS IN THE SKY (EP, unreleased, 1,000 only, foldaround p/s in poly bag) . . . 15
86 Subway Organisation SUBWAY 4 — Whole Wide World/I Know Everything (with insert in poly bag, orange or blue foldaround p/s) . . . 5
86 Raw TV Products RTV 1 — Hang Ten!/Slow Things Down (p/s, blue or red vinyl) . . . 5
86 Raw TV Products RTV 2 — Head Gone Astray/Girl In The World/So Sad I Feel (PVC sleeve, with poster) . . . 10
89 Raw TV Products — DEEP TRASH (cassette, withdrawn) . . . 15
90 Raw TV SOUPLP 2 — LOVEGOD (LP, with foiled sleeve & lyric sheet) . . . 12
(see also BMX Bandits, Future Pilot A.K.A.)

SOUP GREENS
65 Stateside SS 457 — That's Too Bad/Like A Rolling Stone . . . 45

SOUPHERBS
65 Oak RGJ 601 — SOUPHERBS (LP) . . . 220

HARRY SOUTH ORCHESTRA
75 EMI EMI 2252 — The Sweeney (TV Theme) (Parts 1 & 2) . . . 20
67 Mercury 20081 MCL — PRESENTING HARRY SOUTH (LP) . . . 22

JOE SOUTH
62 Oriole CB 1752 — Masquerade/I'm Sorry For You . . . 12
63 MGM MGM 1206 — Same Old Song/Standing Invitation . . . 8
65 MGM MGM 1267 — Concrete Jungle/Last One To Know . . . 8
65 HMV POP 1474 — I Want To Be Somebody/Deep Inside Me . . . 7
68 Capitol CL 15535 — Birds Of A Feather/It Got Away . . . 6
69 Capitol CL 15568 — Don't Throw Your Love To The Wind/Redneck . . . 6
69 Capitol CL 15579 — Games People Play/Mirror Of Your Mind . . . 6
69 Capitol CL 15594 — Leanin' On You/Don't Be Ashamed . . . 5
69 Capitol CL 15602 — Birds Of A Feather/These Are Not My People . . . 5
69 Capitol CL 15608 — Don't It Make You Want To Go Home/Heart's Desire . . . 8
70 Capitol CL 15625 — Walk A Mile In My Shoes/Shelter . . . 5
70 Capitol CL 15636 — The Clock Up On The Wall/What Makes Lovers Hurt One Another . . . 5
70 Capitol CL 15666 — Hush/Party People . . . 6
69 Capitol E-(S)T 108 — INTROSPECT (LP) . . . 18
70 Capitol ST 21548 — WALK A MILE IN MY SHOES (LP) . . . 15

SOUTH COAST SKA STARS
80 Safari SAFE 27 — South Coast Rumble/Head On (p/s) . . . 8
(see also Ray Fenwick)

JERI SOUTHERN
51 London L 1070 — I'm In Love Again/You're The Cause Of It All (78) . . . 20
54 Brunswick 05276 — That Old Devil Called Love/Autumn In My Heart (78) . . . 8
54 Brunswick 05343 — Remind Me/Little Boy Grown Tall . . . 15
55 Brunswick 05367 — The Man That Got Away/Speak Softly To Me . . . 15
55 Brunswick 05490 — An Occasional Man/It's D'Lovely . . . 15
56 Brunswick 05529 — Where Walks My True Love?/Don't Explain . . . 12
57 Brunswick 05665 — Fire Down Below/Smoke Gets In Your Eyes . . . 8
57 Brunswick 05665 — Fire Down Below/Smoke Gets In Your Eyes (78) . . . 10
57 Brunswick 05709 — Scarlet Ribbons (For Her Hair)/Would I . . . 7
57 Brunswick 05722 — Bells Are Ringing/Just In Time . . . 7

58 Brunswick 05737 I Waited So Long/The Mystery Of Love . . . 7
58 Brunswick 05737 I Waited So Long/The Mystery Of Love (78) . . . 10
59 Capitol CL 14993 Senor Blues/Take Me Back Again . . . 6
59 Capitol CL 15054 Run/Don't Look At Me That Way . . . 7
59 Brunswick OE 9438 CARESSES (EP) . . . 18
59 Columbia SEG 7935 RIDIN' HIGH (EP) . . . 18
55 Brunswick LA 8699 WARM (10" LP) . . . 35
56 Brunswick LAT 8100 THE SOUTHERN STYLE (LP) . . . 25
57 Brunswick LAT 8209 JERI GENTLY JUMPS (LP) . . . 25
58 Columbia 33SX 1110 SOUTHERN BREEZE (LP) . . . 20
58 Columbia 33SX 1134 COFFEE, CIGARETTES AND MEMORIES (LP) . . . 20
59 Columbia 33SX 1155 JERI SOUTHERN MEETS JOHNNY SMITH (LP) . . . 18
59 Capitol (S)T 1173 JERI SOUTHERN MEETS COLE PORTER (LP, mono/stereo) . . . 15/18
60 Capitol (S)T 1278 AT THE CRESCENDO (LP, mono/stereo) . . . 15/18

JOHNNY SOUTHERN & HIS WESTERN RHYTHM KINGS

57 Melodisc MEL 1413 We Will Make Love/Crazy Heart . . . 10
57 Melodisc MEL 1413 We Will Make Love/Crazy Heart (78) . . . 6
57 Melodisc MEL 1434 She's Long, She's Tall/Lonesome Whistle . . . 10
57 Melodisc MEL 1434 She's Long, She's Tall/Lonesome Whistle (78) . . . 6

SOUTHERN COMFORT

71 Harvest SHSP 4012 FROG CITY (LP) . . . 18
72 Harvest SHSP 799 SOUTHERN COMFORT (LP) . . . 18
72 Harvest SHSP 4021 STIR DON'T SHAKE (LP) . . . 15
(see also Matthews Southern Comfort)

SOUTHERN SOUND

66 Columbia DB 7982 Just The Same As You/I Don't Wanna Go . . . 350+

SOUTHERN TONES

58 Jazz Collector JEN 10 WAITING FOR THE LORD (EP) . . . 10

SOUTHLANDERS

55 Parlophone R 4025 The Crazy Otto Rag/Earth Angel (Will You Be Mine?) (78) . . . 6
55 Parlophone MSP 6182 Ain't That A Shame/Have You Ever Been Lonely . . . 22
55 Parlophone R 4069 Ain't That A Shame/Have You Ever Been Lonely (78) . . . 7
56 Parlophone MSP 6236 Hush-A-Bye Rock/The Wedding Of The Lucky Black Cat . . . 20
56 Parlophone R 4171 Hush-A-Bye Rock/The Wedding Of The Lucky Black Cat (78) . . . 7
57 Decca F 10946 Alone/Swedish Polka . . . 6
57 Decca F 10958 Peanuts/I Never Dreamed . . . 7
58 Decca F 10982 Put A Light In The Window/Penny Loafers And Bobby Socks . . . 10
58 Decca F 10982 Put A Light In The Window/Penny Loafers And Bobby Socks (78) . . . 12
58 Decca F 11014 Down Deep/Wishing For Your Love . . . 8
58 Decca F 11014 Down Deep/Wishing For Your Love (78) . . . 6
58 Decca F 11032 I Wanna Jive Tonight/Torero . . . 15
58 Decca F 11032 I Wanna Jive Tonight/Torero (78) . . . 7
58 Decca F 11067 The Mole In A Hole/Choo-Choo-Choo-Choo Cha-Cha-Cha (tri-centre, repressings have solid centre) . . . 12/5
58 Decca F 11067 The Mole In A Hole/Choo-Choo-Choo-Choo Cha-Cha-Cha (78) . . . 10
60 Top Rank JAR 403 Imitation Of Love/Charlie . . . 6
58 Decca DFE 6508 THE SOUTHLANDERS NUMBER ONE (EP) . . . 40

SOUTHSIDE JOHNNY & THE ASBURY DUKES

77 Epic EPC 5230 Little Girl So Fine/I Ain't Got The Fever (withdrawn) . . . 20

SOUTH SIDE MOVEMENT

73 Pye International 7N 25615 I Been Watchin' You/Have A Little Mercy . . . 5

SOUTHWEST F.O.B.

68 Stax STAX 107 Smell Of Incense/Green Skies . . . 20

SOUTHWIND

70 Harvest HAR 5019 Boogie Woogie Country Girl/Honky Tonkin' . . . 5

PHIL SOUTHWOOD

61 QRS 1-462 D's Dilemma/Sister Sadie (some in p/s) . . . 20/12

SOVEREIGNS

66 King KG 1050 Bring Me Home Love/That's The Way Love Is . . . 18

RED SOVINE

56 Brunswick 05513 Why Baby Why? (with Webb Pierce)/Sixteen Tons . . . 30
56 Brunswick 05513 Why Baby Why? (with Webb Pierce)/Sixteen Tons (78) . . . 15
62 Top Rank JKP 3015 COUNTRY MUSIC (EP) . . . 20
66 London HA-B 8288 GIDDY-UP GO (LP) . . . 15
67 London HA-R 8343 I DIDN'T JUMP THE FENCE (LP) . . . 15
69 London HA-B 8379 TELL MAUDE I SLIPPED (LP) . . . 15
(see also Webb Pierce)

BOB B. SOXX & THE BLUE JEANS

63 London HLU 9646 Zip-A-Dee-Doo-Dah/Flip And Nitty . . . 15
63 London HLU 9694 Why Do Lovers Break Each Other's Heart?/Dr Kaplan's Office . . . 20
63 London HLU 9754 Not Too Young To Get Married/Annette . . . 22
69 London HLU 10243 Zip-A-Dee-Doo-Dah/Why Do Lovers Break Each Other's Heart? . . . 6
63 London HA-U 8121 ZIP-A-DEE-DOO-DAH (LP) . . . 125
75 Phil Spector Intl. 2307 004 BOB B. SOXX & THE BLUE JEANS (LP) . . . 30ss
(see also Darlene Love, Bobby Sheen, Blossoms, Crystals, Phil Spector)

SPACE

79 Pye NSPH 28725 JUST BLUE (LP, picture disc) . . . 20
(see also Madeline Bell)

MINT VALUE £

SPACE

90	Space LP 1	SPACE (LP)	50
90	Space CD 1	SPACE (CD, beware of counterfeits)	40

(see also J.A.M.S., KLF, Timelords, Disco 2000)

SPACE

93	Hug HUG 1T	If It's Real/Lookin'/I'm Free (12", p/s with free 'fortune fish')	30
95	Home Recordings 12HOMEX 1	Money Remixes By Consolidated: Money (Lost In Space Remix)/(Still Lost In Space/Safe Bass Mix)/(Space Club Mix)/(Instrumental) (12", p/s, yellow vinyl)	8
95	Home Recordings CDHOME 1	Money (7" Radio Edit)/Kill Me (7" Radio Edit)/Money (Space Club Mix)/ Kill Me (Space Club Mix) (CD)	8
96	Gut CDGUT 1	Neighbourhood (Radio Edit)/Turn Me On To Spiders/Rejects/ Neighbourhood (Live It Club Mix) (CD)	10

SPACE ART

77	Arista AHAL 8001	SPACE ART (LP)	15

SPACEMEN

59	Top Rank JAR 228	The Clouds/The Lonely Jet Pilot	20

SPACEMEN 3

86	Glass GLAEP 105	Walkin' With Jesus (Sound Of Confusion)/Rollercoaster/Feel So Good (12" maxi-single, p/s, some with numbered insert)	75/60
87	Glass GLAEP 108	Transparent Radiation/Ecstasy Symphony/Transparent Radiation (Flashback)/Things'll Never Be The Same/Starship (12" maxi-single, p/s)	50
88	Glass GLASS 12054	Take Me To The Other Side/Soul 1/That's Just Fine (12", p/s)	35
88	Cheree CHEREE 5	Extract From An Evening Of Contemporary Sitar Music (flexi, p/s, with *Cheree* fanzine)	12
88	Fire BLAZE 29S	Revolution/Che (die-cut company sleeve)	10
88	Fire BLAZE 29T	Revolution/Che/May The Circle Be Unbroken (12")	10
88	Fire BLAZE 29CD	Revolution/Che/May The Circle Be Unbroken (3" CD)	8
89	Fire THREEBIE 3	Revolution/Suicide/Repeater/Love Intro Theme (Xtacy) (12", mail-order only, numbered p/s)	25
89	Sniffin' Rock SR 008	When Tomorrow Hits (some with *Sniffin' Rock* magazine)	15/10
89	Fire BLAZE 36S	Hypnotized/Just To See You Smile (Honey Pt 2) (die-cut company sleeve)	6
89	Fire BLAZE 36T	Hypnotized/Just To See You Smile (Honey Pt 2)/The World Is Dying (12", with poster)	15
89	Fire BLAZE 36CD	Hypnotized/Just To See You Smile (Honey Pt 2)/The World Is Dying (3" CD, with adaptor, 5" case)	10
91	Fire BLAZE 41	Big City (Edit)/Drive (p/s)	8
91	Fire BLAZE 41TR	Big City (Remix)/I Love You (Remix) (12", unissued, white label promo, 50 only)	50
91	Catalogue CAT 089	I Love You//Sometimes (2 x flexis, with *The Catalogue* magazine)	10
86	Glass GLALP 018	SOUND OF CONFUSION (LP)	25
87	Glass GLALP 026	THE PERFECT PRESCRIPTION (LP, gold/silver or bronze/silver sleeve)	25
88	Glass GLALP 030	PERFORMANCE (LP)	15
88	Glass GLACD 030	PERFORMANCE (CD)	18

(see also Sonic Boom, Spiritualized, Darkside, Spectrum)

SPACEPIMP

95	Clear CLR 415	The Pimp/Spacechace/K9 Law (12", p/s, some on clear vinyl)	25/20

SPAGHETTI HEAD

75	RCA RCA 2513	Big Noise From Winnetka/Funky Axe	5

(see also Clem Cattini Ork, Tornados)

SPAGHETTI JUNCTION

72	Columbia DB 8935	Work's Nice — If You Can Get It/Step Right Up	25

(see also Hank Marvin)

SPANIELS

60	Joy JOYS 197	THE SPANIELS (LP)	20

MUGGSY SPANIER & DIXIELAND/RAGTIME BAND

56	Tempo A 36	Tin Roof Blues/Muskrat Rumble	6
55	Tempo EXA 3	MUGGSY SPANIER'S DIXIELAND BAND (EP)	10
53	Vogue LDE 015	MUGGSY SPANIER BROADCASTS "THIS IS JAZZ" (10" LP)	18
54	London AL 3528	MUGGSY SPANIER AND THE BUCKTOWN FIVE (10" LP)	15
54	HMV DLP 1031	MUGGSY SPANIER AND HIS RAGTIME BAND (10" LP)	15
55	Brunswick LA 8722	MUGGSY SPANIER AND HIS BAND (10" LP)	15
57	Mercury MPL 6516	MUGGSY SPANIER AND HIS DIXIELAND BAND (LP)	12
63	MGM MGM-C 936	THE GEM OF THE OCEAN (LP)	12

(see also Sidney Bechet)

SPANISH BOYS

65	Blue Beat BB 331	I Am Alone/BUSTER'S ALL STARS: Vera Cruz	50

SPANISHTONIANS

67	Pyramid PYR 6005	Kisses/ROLAND ALPHONSO: Women Of The World	20
67	Pyramid PYR 6009	Suffer Me Not/ROLAND ALPHONSO: Guantanamera Ska	20
67	Pyramid PYR 6018	Rudie Gets Plenty/ROLAND ALPHONSO: Sock It To Me	20

SPANISHTOWN SKABEATS

65	Blue Beat BB 315	Oh My Baby (actually by Charmers)/Stop That Train	60
65	Blue Beat BB 320	King Solomon/BUSTER'S ALLSTARS: Devil's Daffodil	60

SPANKY & OUR GANG

67	Mercury MF 982	Sunday Will Never Be The Same/Distance	12
67	Mercury MF 999	Making Every Minute Count/If You Could Only Be Me	8
67	Mercury MF 1010	Lazy Day/It Ain't Necessarily Byrd Avenue	8
68	Mercury MF 1018	Sunday Mornin'/Echoes	5
68	Mercury MF 1023	Like To Get To Know You/Three Ways From Tomorrow	10
69	Mercury MF 1123	And She's Mine/Leopard Skin Phone	5
70s	Epic S EPC 3850	I Won't Brand You/When I Wanna	5

MINT VALUE £

67	Mercury 20114 (S)MCL	SPANKY AND OUR GANG (LP)	30
68	Mercury 20121 SCML	LIKE TO GET TO KNOW YOU (LP)	25
69	Mercury 20150 SCML	ANYTHING YOU CHOOSE/WITHOUT RHYME OR REASON (LP)	25

(see also Mama & Papas)

OTIS SPANN

64	Decca F 11972	Stirs Me Up/Keep Your Hand Out Of My Pocket	18
68	Blue Horizon 57-3142	Bloody Murder/Can't Do Me No Good	15
69	Blue Horizon 57-3155	Walkin'/Temperature Is Rising (with Fleetwood Mac)	25
64	Decca LK 4615	THE BLUES OF OTIS SPANN (LP)	80
64	Storyville SLP 157	GOOD MORNING MR. BLUES (LP)	35
64	Storyville SLP 168	PIANO BLUES (LP, with Memphis Slim)	35
65	Decca LK 4661	BLUES NOW (LP)	35
66	Stateside SL 10169	THE BLUES NEVER DIE (LP)	35
67	HMV CLP/CSD 3609	BLUES ARE WHERE IT'S AT (LP)	35
67	Storyville 670 157	PORTRAITS IN BLUES VOL. 3 (LP, reissue of SLP 157)	18
67	Polydor 545 030	NOBODY KNOWS MY TROUBLES (LP)	35
67	Bounty BY 6037	NOBODY KNOWS MY TROUBLES (LP)	22
68	Stateside (S)SL 10255	BOTTOM OF THE BLUES (LP)	35
69	Chess CRLS 4556	FATHERS AND SONS (LP)	22
69	Blue Horizon 7-63217	BIGGEST THING SINCE COLOSSUS (LP, with Fleetwood Mac)	65
69	Deram DML/SML 1036	CRACKED SPANNER HEAD (LP)	50
69	Python KM 4	RAISED IN MISSISSIPPI (LP, 99 copies only, with Robert Jnr. Lockwood)	60
70	Vanguard VSD 6514	CRYIN' TIME (LP)	15

(see also Fleetwood Mac, Memphis Slim, Johnny Shines, Lonnie Johnson)

SPANNER THRU MA BEATBOX

87	Earthly Delights EARTH 3	SPANNER THRU MA BEATBOX (LP)	15

SPARKERS

69	Blue Cat BS 155	Dig It Up/DELROY WILSON: This Life Makes Me Wonder	35

(see also Samuel Edwards)

LOU SPARKES

69	Gayfeet GS 203	By The Time I Get To Phoenix/Lover Boy	8
70	Gayfeet GS 208	We Will Make Love/ROLAND ALPHONSO: Sticker	8

(see also Eric Boswell)

KRISTINE SPARKLE

74	Decca F 13485	Hokey Cokey/Baby I Love You	6
74	Decca SKL 5192	IMAGE (LP)	12

SPARKLEHORSE

96	Parlophone CL 766	Someday I Will Treat You Good/London (p/s)	5
96	Parlophone CL 770	Hammering The Cramps/Spirit Ditch (p/s)	5
96	Parlophone CL 777	Rainmaker/I Almost Lost My Mind (p/s)	5
98	Parlophone CL 806	Painbirds/Maria's Little Elbows (p/s)	5
98	Parlophone CL 808	Sick Of Goodbyes/Good Morning Spider (BBC Radio 1 version) (p/s)	5

SPARKS

72	Bearsville K 15505	Wonder Girl/(No More) Mr. Nice Guy	12
74	Bearsville K 15516	Girl From Germany/Beaver O'Lindy (brown or white label)	10/7
74	Island WIP 6211	Never Turn Your Back On Mother Earth/Alabamy Right (p/s)	8
75	Island WIP 6221	Something For The Girl With Everything/Marry Me (title sleeve)	6
75	Island WIP 6236	Get In The Swing/Profile (title sleeve)	6
75	Island WIP 6239	Looks, Looks, Looks/Pineapple (title sleeve)	6
75	Island WIP 6249	Looks, Looks, Looks/Pineapple (DJ copy in promo p/s)	25
76	Island WIP 6282	I Want To Hold Your Hand/England (withdrawn after 1 day)	20
76	Island WIP 6357	I Like Girls/England	5
77	Island WIP 6282	I Want To Hold Your Hand/Under The Table With Her (promo only)	25
77	Island WIP 6193	This Town Ain't Big Enough For The Both Of Us/Barbecutie (reissue, orange sunset label)	25
79	Virgin VS 244	The No. 1 Song In Heaven/The No. 1 Song In Heaven (Version) (p/s, green vinyl)	8
79	Virgin VS 244-12	The No. 1 Song In Heaven/The No. 1 Song In Heaven (Long Version) (12", p/s, blue or red vinyl)	10
79	Virgin VS 270-12	Beat The Clock/Beat The Clock (Long Version) (12", black, blue, orange, yellow or pink vinyl, picture disc label, die-cut p/s)	each 10
79	Virgin VS 289-12	Tryouts For The Human Race/Tryouts For The Human Race (Long Version) (12", die-cut p/s, orange, yellow, blue or green vinyl, picture disc label)	each 10
79	Island WIP 6532	This Town Ain't Big Enough For The Both Of Us/Looks, Looks, Looks	7
80	Virgin VS 343-12	Young Girls (Disco Version)/Young Girls (Long Version)/ Just Because You Love Me (12", p/s)	10
81	Why Fi WHYT 1	Tips For Teens/Don't Shoot Me (12", p/s)	10
83	Atlantic A 9866	Cool Places/Sports (no p/s)	5
85	London LONX 69	Change/This Town Ain't Big Enough For Both Of Us (Acoustic Version) (12", p/s)	8
85	Epic A 6671	Armies Of The Night/EVELYN KING: Give It Up (p/s)	5
85	Epic TA 6671	Armies Of The Night/EVELYN KING: Give It Up (12", p/s)	12
86	Consolidated TOON T2	Music That You Can Dance To (UK Extended Club Version)/Fingertips (Extended Club Version) (12", p/s)	8
87	Consolidated TOON T4	Rosebud (Extended Club Mix)/Theme For Rosebud (Cinematic Mix)/Rosebud (FM Mix) (12", p/s)	8
88	Carrere CART 427	So Important (Extremely Important Mix)/(Incredibly Important Mix)/(Single Version) (12", p/s)	8
93	Finiflex FF 1004	National Crime Awareness Week (13 Minutes In Heaven)/National Crime Awareness Week (Perkins Playtime) (12", p/s)	15
93	Finiflex FFCD 1004	National Crime Awareness Week (Psycho Cut)/National Crime Awareness Week (Highly Strung Hoedown)/National Crime Awareness Week (Complete Psycho)/National Crime Awareness Week (13 Minutes In Heaven) (CD)	30
94	Logic 7432 134461	When Do I Get To Sing My Way/(mixes) (12", doublepack, p/s)	15

MINT VALUE £

94	Logic 74321 24302-2	Excerpts From Gratuitous Sax & Senseless Violins (CD, picture disc, gatefold card p/s, promo only)	50
97	Roadrunner RR 2262-6	The No. 1 Song In Heaven (Tin Tin Out Mix)/part 2/(Heavenly Dub) (with Jimmy Somerville) (12", die-cut sleeve)	10
99	Winney CD IFPI LAE 1	The Cute Candidate/This Town Ain't Big Enough For The Both Of Us (1920 Archival Recording)/The Winney Empire/The Cute Candidate On TV/The Race For President (CD, fan club only issue)	10
00	Recognition CDREC 14	The Calm Before The Storm (Radio Edit)/The Calm Before The Storm/It's Educational (CD, unreleased)	15
00	Recognition (no cat. no.)	The Calm Before The Storm (promo CD-R)	12
76	Bearsville K 85505	TWO ORIGINALS OF SPARKS (2-LP, gatefold sleeve with 12-page booklet)	18
79	Virgin V 2115	NO. 1 IN HEAVEN (LP, yellow vinyl with lyric inner sleeve)	12

(see also Les Rita Mitsouko, Noel, Adrian Musey, Trevor White)

L. SPARKS

72	Big Shot BI 601	You Don't Care/TONY'S ALL STARS: Must Care (Version)	6
72	Pama PM 833	You Don't Care/TONY'S ALL STARS: Must Care (Version)	6

(see also Lloyd Parks, Termites)

RANDY SPARKS

59	HMV POP 683	Birmingham Train/A Girl Like You	6
59	HMV 7EG 8531	RANDY SPARKS (EP)	8

CANDY SPARLING

62	Piccadilly 7N 35046	When's He Gonna Kiss Me?/Lonely For You	10
63	Piccadilly 7N 35096	Can You Keep A Secret/Charm Bracelet	10

SPARROW (Jamaica)

60	Kalypso XX 10	Carnival Boycott/Gloria (with Lord Melody)	5
60	Kalypso XX 17	The Sack/Round And Around	5
60s	Melodisc CAL 15	Leading Calypsonians/Love Is Everywhere	5
60s	Melodisc CAL 17	Clara Honey Bunch/Family Sized Cokes	5
60s	Melodisc CAL 18	Goaty/I Confess	5

(see also Mighty Sparrow, King Sparrow)

SPARROW (U.S.)

66	CBS 202342	Tomorrow's Ship/Isn't It Strange	45

(see also Steppenwolf)

JACK SPARROW

66	Doctor Bird DB 1005	Ice Water/ROLAND ALPHONSO: Ska-Culation	30
66	Doctor Bird DB 1027	More Ice Water/ROLAND ALPHONSO: Miss Ska-Culation	40

SPARTA

81	Suspect SUS 1	Fast Lane/Fighting To Be Free (some in p/s)	55/20
81	Suspect SUS 2	Angel Of Death/Tonight (wraparound p/s)	18

SPARTANS

62	Stateside SS 117	Can You Waddle? (Parts 1 & 2)	8

SPARTAN WARRIOR

83	Guardian GRC 2164	STEEL 'N' CHAINS (LP, textured sleeve)	12

SPAZZTIC BLUR

87	Earache MOSH 5	BEFO DA AWBUM (LP)	12

ROGER RUSKIN SPEAR

71	United Artists UP 35221	REBEL TROUSER: Trouser Freak/Trouser Press/Release Me/Drop Out (EP)	6
74	United Artists UP 35683	On Her Doorstep Last Night	5
74	United Artists UP 35745	I Love To Bumpity Bump/When Yuba Plays The Rumba	5
72	United Artists UAG 29381	ELECTRIC SHOCKS (LP)	18
74	United Artists UAS 29508	UNUSUAL (LP)	18

(see also Bonzo Dog [Doo Dah] Band)

SPEAR OF DESTINY

83	Epic SPEAR 13-1	Flying Scotsman (Extended)/Africa/The Man Who Tunes The Drums (12", p/s, with poster, some autographed)	10
83	Epic WA 3372	The Wheel/The Hop (picture disc)	5
83	Epic DA 3372	The Wheel/The Hop//Grapes Of Wrath (live)/The Preacher (live) (double pack)	6
84	Epic DA 4068	Prisoner Of Love/Rosie//Rainmaker (live)/Don't Turn Away (live) (double pack)	6
85	Epic DTA 6445	Come Back (Dub Mix)/Cole Younger//Young Men (Return Of)/ Come Back (WL Remix) (12", double pack)	7
86	Dale DALE 2	BOTTOM DRAWER (EP, p/s, white label, 500 only, numbered)	6

(see also Theatre Of Hate, Pack)

BRITNEY SPEARS

00	Jive BRITNEY no cat. no.	OOPS!... I DID IT AGAIN (CD, with promo-only 24pp book, "It's Britney")	40

SPECIAL DUTIES

81	Charnel H. SARCOPHAGI 2	Violent Society/Colchester Council (wraparound p/s)	8
82	Rondelet ROUND 15	VIOLENT SOCIETY (EP)	7
82	Rondelet ROUND 20	POLICE STATE (EP)	7
82	Rondelet ROUND 24	Bullshit Crass/You're Doing Yourself No Good (p/s)	7
83	Expulsion OUT 1	Punk Rocker/Too Much Talking (p/s)	7
82	Rondelet ABOUT 9	77 IN 82 (LP)	12

SPECIALS (THE SPECIAL A.K.A.)

79	2-Tone TT 1/TT 2	Gangsters (as The Special A.K.A.)/THE SELECTER: The Selecter (paper label, some in stamped plain white sleeve; matrix numbers TT1-3 & TT2-1)	20/15
79	2-Tone TT 1/TT 2	Gangsters (as The Special A.K.A.)/THE SELECTER: The Selecter (paper label, die-cut 2-Tone sleeve, 2nd issue with Chrysalis CHS TT 1/2 matrix no.)	8
79	2-Tone CHS TT 5	Message To You Rudy/Nite Klub (paper label, company sleeve, as The Specials featuring Rico)	8
80	2-Tone CHS TT 7	THE SPECIAL A.K.A. LIVE (EP, p/s, paper label)	8

80	2-Tone CHS TT 11	Rat Race/Rude Boys Outa Jail (company sleeve, paper label, as The Specials)	8
80	2-Tone CHS TT 13	Stereotype/International Jet Set (company sleeve, paper label, as The Specials)	8
80	2-Tone CHS TT 16	Do Nothing/Maggie's Farm (p/s, paper label, as The Specials)	8
81	2-Tone CHS TT 17	Ghost Town/Why/Friday Night Saturday Morning (company sleeve)	6
81	2-Tone CHS TT 1217	Ghost Town (6.02 Extended Version)/Why/Friday Night, Saturday Morning (12", p/s)	10
82	2-Tone CHS TT 1023	War Crimes (The Crime Is Still The Same)/War Crimes (The Crime Is Still The Same) (Version) (10", p/s, as The Special A.K.A.)	7
83	2-Tone CHS TPTT 23	Racist Friend/Bright Lights (picture disc, as The Special A.K.A.)	5
84	2-Tone CHS TT 26	Nelson Mandela/Break Down The Door (p/s)	5
84	2-Tone CHS TT 1226	Nelson Mandela/Break Down The Door (12", p/s)	8
84	2-Tone CHS TT 27	What I Like Most About You Is Your Girlfriend/Can't Get A Break//War Crimes (The Crime Is Still The Same)/(Version) (double pack, as The Special A.K.A.)	5
84	2-Tone CHS TPTT 27	What I Like Most About You Is Your Girlfriend/Can't Get A Break (picture disc)	6
84	2-Tone CHS TT 1227	What I Like Most About You Is Your Girlfriend/Can't Get A Break (12", poster p/s with free single)	10
87	Strange Fruit SFPSC 018	PEEL SESSION 23.5.79 (cassette EP)	5
79	2-Tone TT 5001	SPECIALS (LP)	15
80	2-Tone CDL TT 5001	MORE SPECIALS (LP, some with poster & bonus 7": Roddy Radiation & The Specials' "Braggin' And Tryin' Not To Lie"/Judge Roughneck's "Rude Buoys Outa Jail" [TT 999])	25/15

(see also Colourfield, Selecter, Rhoda, Rico)

SPECIMEN

83	London LON 24	Returning From A Journey/Kiss Kiss Bang Bang (bat-shaped disc)	10
80s	Trust TRUE T 001	Sharp Teeth (12", p/s)	12

SPECKLED RED

60s	Storyville SEP 384	STORYVILLE BLUES ANTHOLOGY VOL. 4 (EP)	15
63	Esquire 32-190	THE DIRTY DOZENS (LP)	35
66	Storyville DL 601	THE DIRTY DOZENS (LP, reissue)	12
71	VJM LC 11	OH RED (LP)	18

PHIL SPECTOR

63	London HA-U 8141	A CHRISTMAS GIFT FOR YOU (LP, various artists, Spector as producer; plum label, later black label)	60/25
72	Apple APCOR 24	PHIL SPECTOR'S CHRISTMAS ALBUM (LP, reissue of London HA-U 8141)	30
74	Warner Bros K 59010	PHIL SPECTOR'S CHRISTMAS ALBUM (LP, 2nd reissue, with poster)	18
76	Phil Spector Intl. 2307 008	RARE MASTERS VOL. 1 (LP, various artists, Spector as producer)	30
76	Phil Spector Intl. 2307 009	RARE MASTERS VOL. 2 (LP, various artists, Spector as producer)	30
80	Phil Spector Intl. 2307 015	PHIL SPECTOR '74/'79 (LP, various artists, Spector as producer)	22
81	Phil Spector Intl. WOS 001	WALL OF SOUND (9-LP box set, various artists, Spector as producer)	120

(see also Ronettes, Crystals, Darlene Love, Bob B. Soxx & Blue Jeans, Teddy Bears)

RONNIE SPECTOR

71	Apple APPLE 33	Try Some, Buy Some/Tandoori Chicken (initially with p/s)	35/12
77	Epic EPC 5185	Say Goodbye To Hollywood/Baby Please Don't Go (with E Street Band)	10
81	Red Shadow MS 488	Darlin'/Settin' The Woods On Fire (p/s)	5
81	Red Shadow LP 002	SIREN (LP)	18

(see also Ronettes)

SPECTRES

66	Piccadilly 7N 35339	I (Who Have Nothing)/Neighbour, Neighbour	350
66	Piccadilly 7N 35352	Hurdy Gurdy Man/Laticia	300
67	Piccadilly 7N 35368	We Ain't Got Nothin' Yet/I Want It (beware bootlegs)	275

(Demos are more common and worth £50 less than stock copies)
(see also Traffic Jam, Status Quo)

SPECTRES

80	Direct Hit DH 1	This Strange Effect/Getting Away With Murder (p/s)	7
81	Demon D 1002	Stories/Things (p/s)	5

(see also Rich Kids, Swingers)

SPECTRES (Ireland)

65	Lloyd Sound UED QU 1	The Facts Of Life/Whirlpool	280

SPECTRUM

65	Columbia DB 7742	Little Girl/Asking You	5
67	RCA RCA 1589	Samantha's Mine/Saturday's Child	5
67	RCA RCA 1619	Portobello Road/Comes The Dawn	8
67	RCA RCA 1651	Headin' For A Heatwave/I Wanna Be Happy With You	5
68	RCA RCA 1700	London Bridge Is Coming Down/Tables And Chairs	6
68	RCA RCA 1753	Little Red Boat By The River/Forget Me Not	5
68	RCA RCA 1775	Ob-La-Di, Ob-La-Da/Music Soothes The Savage Beast	5
69	RCA RCA 1853	Free/The Tale Of Wally Toft	5
69	RCA RCA 1883	Glory/Nodnol	5
70	RCA RCA 1976	Portobello Road/Comes The Dawn (reissue)	6
71	Parlophone R 5908	I'll Be Gone/Launching Place — Pt II	6
69	RCA Intl. INTS 118	THE LIGHT IS DARK ENOUGH (LP)	40

SPECTRUM

85	Phoenix Modernist 7-THE-1	All Or Nothing (Contemporary Version)/All Or Nothing (Traditional Version) (p/s)	5
85	Phoenix Modernist THE 1	All Or Nothing (Contemporary Version)/All Or Nothing (Traditional Version) (12", p/s; distributed by Stiff)	8
87	Phoenix Modernist THE 1	All Or Nothing (Contemporary Version)/All Or Nothing (Traditional Version) (12", p/s with 2 inserts & free 7", distributed by Nine Mile & Cartel)	8

(see also Steve Marriott, Chris Farlowe, P.P. Arnold, Creation)

MINT VALUE £

SPECTRUM

92	Beechwood TT 015e	Taste The Ozone/MOONSHAKE: Night Tripper	5
94	Silvertone	Soul Kiss Glide Divine/STEREOLAB: Tone Burst (demo)/Tempter (demo) (unrel., with colour photocopied wraparound p/s, 25 test pressings only)	150+

(see also Spacemen 3, Sonic Boom)

CHRIS SPEDDING

70	Harvest HAR 5013	Rock'n'Roll Band/BATTERED ORNAMENTS: Goodbye We Loved You (Madly)	12
75	Island WIP 6225	My Bucket's Got A Hole In It/I Can't Boogie	8
75	RAK RAK 210	Motor Bikin'/Working For The Union	5
76	RAK RAK 246	Pogo Dancing/Pose (p/s)	6
77	RAK RAK 261	Get Outa My Pagoda/Hey Miss Betty	5
70	Harvest SHSP 4004	BACKWOOD PROGRESSION (LP)	35
72	Harvest SHSP 4017	THE ONLY LICK I KNOW (LP)	22
70s	RAK SRAK 529	HURT (LP, with inner)	12

(see also Sharks, Nucleus, Sounds Nice, Panhandle, Solid Gold Cadillac, Matthew Ellis, Vibrators, Battered Ornaments, IOFR)

SPEED

78	It IT 1	Big City/All Day And All The Night (some in p/s)	40/15

(see also Cobra, Tearjerkers)

SPEED (Jamaica)

71	Bullet BU 477	There's A Train/Blue Moon	6

SPEEDBALL(S)

80	No Pap/Dirty Dick DD 1/2	No Survivors/Is Somebody There? (miscredited as 'Speedballs' on label, some in withdrawn printed die-cut sleeve)	18/25

SPEEDOMETERS

78	Mascot NICE 1	Disgrace/Work (p/s)	5
78	Mascot NICE 2	Liverpool Ladies (p/s)	5

SPEEDY J

94	Warp WAP 46	Pepper (The Hot Mix)/Beam Me Up (The Pegasus Mix) (12")	12
99	Nova Mute 12NOMU 069	Ieee Mitten Menu/(mix)/Fart Essen (12")	10
93	Warp WARP LP 14	GINGER (LP, ginger vinyl)	12

DAVEY SPEIRS

69	Beltona LBA/LBS 61	A MAN OF CONSTANT SORROW (LP)	15

SPELLBINDERS

66	CBS 202453	Help Me (Get Myself Back Together)/Danny Boy	20
67	CBS 202622	Chain Reaction/For You	25
67	CBS 2776	Since I Don't Have You/I Believe	10
69	Direction 58-3970	Help Me/Chain Reaction	7

BENNY SPELLMAN

62	London HLP 9570	Lipstick Traces/Fortune Teller	50

BARRINGTON SPENCE

75	Grounation GRO 2009	For The Rest Of My Life/Version	5

JOHNNY SPENCE

61	Parlophone R 4736	Wheels/First Romance	6
62	Parlophone R 4872	Dr. Kildare Theme/Midnight Theme	5
68	Verve (S)VLP 9222	WHY NOT? (LP, as Johnnie Spence Big Band)	18

DON SPENCER

62	HMV POP 1087	Fireball/I'm All Alone Again (blue or black labels)	15
63	HMV POP 1186	Busy Doing Nothing/The Joker	6
63	HMV POP 1205	Worried Mind/Give Give Give A Little	6
64	HMV POP 1306	Pride Is Such A Little Word/For Love (with Le Roys)	6
66	Page One POF 006	Why Don't They Understand/Marriage Is For Old Folks	5

(see also Le Roys)

DON SPENCER/XL5

63	HMV 7EG 8802	FIREBALL AND OTHER TITLES (EP, 2 tracks each)	45

JEREMY SPENCER (Band)

70	Reprise RS 27002	Linda/Teenage Darling	6
79	Atlantic K 11363	Travelling/Cool Breeze (as Jeremy Spencer Band)	5
70	Reprise RSLP 9002	JEREMY SPENCER (LP)	40
71	Reprise K 44105	JEREMY SPENCER (LP, reissue)	20
73	CBS 65387	JEREMY SPENCER AND THE CHILDREN OF GOD (LP)	12

(see also Fleetwood Mac)

JO SPENCER

71	Dynamic DYN 415	Bed Of Roses/Forgive Me	6

SONNY SPENCER

59	Parlophone R 4611	Oh Boy/Gilee	20

JON SPENCER BLUES EXPLOSION

94	Matador OLE 077	Afro/Relax Her (p/s)	6
95	Matador OLE 111	Bellbottoms/Miss Elaine (p/s, white vinyl)	5
95	Matador OLE 111.1	Bellbottoms/Flavor (12", p/s)	8
96	Mute MUTE 202.2	2 Kindsa Love/Let's Smerf (pink vinyl)	5
97	Mute MUTE 204	Wail/Judah Love Theme/Radio Spot (grey vinyl)	5
97	Mute MUTE 204	Wail/Flavor (green vinyl)	5
98	Mute MUTE 222	Magical Colors/Confused (red vinyl)	5
98	Mute MUTE 226	Talk About The Blues/Wait A Minute (orange vinyl)	5
91	Hut HUTLP 3	THE JON SPENCER BLUES EXPLOSION (LP)	15

(see also Pussy Galore)

MINT VALUE £

BRINDLEY D. SPENDER
68 Domain D 8 — The Company I Keep/On A Day Like Today ... 7

SPERMICIDE
79 No Wonder NOW 3 — Femme Prothèse/Belgique (p/s with lyrics) ... 20

SPHERES
78 Sphere — FESTIVAL AND SUNS (LP, with insert) ... 25
(see also Jimmy Winston)

SPHERICAL OBJECTS
78 Object Music OM 01 — The Kill/The Knot (p/s) ... 8
78 Object Music OM 04 — Seventies Romance/Sweet Tooth (p/s) ... 8
78 Object Music PBJ 001 — PAST & PARCEL (LP) ... 12
79 Object Music OBJ 004 — ELLIPTICAL OPTIMISM (LP) ... 12
80 Object Music OBJ 012 — FURTHER ELLIPSES (LP) ... 12
81 Object Music OBJ 016 — NO MAN'S LAND (LP) ... 12
(see also Alternomen Unlimited, Noyes Brothers)

SPHYNKTA
83 Sultanic SUL 666 — In The Shade Of The Gods/Jesus Bless My Upside-Down Cross (p/s, red vinyl, with 'devil' tattoo) ... 60
83 Sultanic SUL 999 — Death And Violence/Ritual Slaughter (Of Your Daughter) (p/s, red vinyl) ... 40
84 Sultanic SUL 000 — Spike Up My Sphynkta/No Pain No Gain (unissued) ... 100+

SPHYNX
78 Charisma CDS 4011 — XITINTODAY (LP, some with booklet) ... 15/25
(see also Inner City Unit, Gong, Radio Actors)

SPICE (Sweden)
68 Olga OLE 013 — Union Jack/Delicious ... 40

SPICE (U.K.)
68 United Artists UP 2246 — What About The Music?/In Love (demo only) ... 180
(see also Uriah Heep, Godz, Toe-Fat)

SPICE GIRLS
96 Virgin VSLH 1588 — Wannabe/Bumper To Bumper (jukebox issue, large centre hole) ... 7
96 Virgin VSTDJ 1588 — Wannabe/Wannabe (Vocal Slam)/Wannabe (Dub Slam)/ Wannabe (Instrumental Slam) (12" promo, stickered title p/s) ... 12
96 Virgin VSCXD 1588 — Wannabe (Radio Edit)/Wannabe (Dave Way Alternative Mix)/Wannabe (Dub Slam)/Wannabe (Instrumental) (CD, fold-out postcard inlay, stickered case) ... 25
96 Virgin VSLH 1601 — Say You'll Be There/Take Me Home (jukebox issue, large centre hole) ... 6
96 Virgin VSTDJ 1601 — Say You'll Be There (Junior's Main Pass)/Say You'll Be There (Junior's Dub Girls)/ Say You'll Be There (Junior's X-Beats Mix)/Say You'll Be There (Kurt's Dub) (12" promo, stickered title sleeve) ... 10
96 Virgin VSCDG 1601 — Say You'll Be There (Single Mix)/Say You'll Be There (Spice Of Life Mix)/ Say You'll Be There (Linslee's Extended Mix)/Say You'll Be There (Junior Vasquez's Dub Girls) (CD, digipak, with foldout poster in envelope) ... 15
96 Virgin VSLH 1607 — 2 Become 1/One Of These Girls (jukebox issue, large centre hole) ... 6
96 Virgin VSTDJ 1607 — 2 Become 1 (Dave Way Remix Edit)/Wannabe (Junior Vasquez Remix Edit)/ (Junior Vasquez Gomis Dub) (12" promo, stickered title p/s) ... 10
97 Virgin VSLH 1623 — Mama/Who Do You Think You Are (jukebox issue, large centre hole) ... 6
97 Virgin VSTDJ 1623 — Who Do You Think You Are (Morales Club Mix)/Who Do You Think You Are (Morales Dub Mix)/Who Do You Think You Are (Morales Bonus Mix) (12" promo, stickered title sleeve) ... 10
97 Virgin VSLH 1660 — Spice Up Your Life (Stent Radio Mix)/(Morales Radio Mix) (jukebox issue, large centre hole) ... 6
97 Virgin VSLH 1669 — Too Much (Radio Edit) (jukebox issue, large centre hole) ... 6
98 Virgin VSTDJ1679 — Stop (Morales Remix)/Stop (Stretch 'N' Vern's Rock & Roll Mix)/Stop (Morales Dub)/Stop (Stretch 'N' Vern's Dub) (12", doublepack, title stickered sleeve, promo only) ... 15
00 Virgin no cat. no. — HOLLER (CD-R EP, 7-track, paper title-sleeve) ... 40
96 Virgin CDVDJ 2812 — SPICE (CD, promo only, with intros by Andi Peters, card sleeve) ... 30
96 Virgin SGCDR 1 — FIVE GO MAD IN CYBERSPACE (CD ROM, promo only, card sl., Mac format) ... 50
00 Virgin CDVDJ 2928 — FOREVER (promo CD, card p/s in embroidered satin handbag, with postcard & Spice Girls lip balm) ... 35
(see also Geri Halliwell)

GEORGE SPICER
74 Topic 12T 235 — BLACKBERRY FOLD (LP) ... 20

SPIDELLS
66 Sue WI 4019 — Find Out What's Happening/That'll Make My Heart Break ... 30

SPIDER
66 Decca F 12430 — The Comedown Song/Blow Ya Mind ... 18

SPIDER
80 Alien ALIEN 14 — Children Of The Street/Down 'N' Out (some in p/s) ... 40/10
80 Alien ALIEN 16 — College Luv/Born To Be Wild (some in p/s) ... 40/8

SPIDER-MAN
73 Buddah 2318 075 — FROM BEYOND THE GRAVE (LP) ... 15

SPIDERS
66 Philips BF 1531 — Sad Sunset/Hey Boy ... 45

SPIDERS (U.S.)
54 London HL 8086 — I'm Slippin' In/I'm Searching (78) ... 60

MINT VALUE £

SPIDERS FROM MARS

75	Pye 7N 45549	White Man Black Man/National Poll	5
76	Pye 7N 45578	I Don't Wanna Limbo/Can't Be Fair	5
76	Pye NSPL 18479	SPIDERS FROM MARS (LP)	12

(see also David Bowie, Mick Ronson)

BERND SPIER

65	Oriole CB 1987	A Million And One Times/My Mistake	5

SPILL

92	Virgin VS 1141	Don't Wanna Know About Evil (7" Wireless Road Mix)/(Saspelofiska Dub Mix) (p/s)	10
92	Virgin VST 1141	Don't Wanna Know About Evil (Tumble Mix)/(Rumble Mix)/(Danny's Moto Mix)/(The Groovy Beats Mix) (12", p/s)	12
92	Virgin VSCDT 1141	Don't Wanna Know About Evil (Tumble Mix)/(Rumble Mix)/(7" Wireless Road Mix)/(Saspelofiska Dub Mix) (CD)	12

(see also Beth Orton)

ARTHUR SPINK BAND

68	Beltona BL 2766	Beatles Och Aye/Harry Lauder Medley	5

SPINNERS

59	Columbia DB 4243	This Old Man/Alive And Kicking (78)	6
59	Columbia DB 4267	The "I Had A Dream, Dear" Rock/Pedro The Fisherman (78)	8
60s	no label	FLOWERS OF MANCHESTER (EP)	30

(see also Liverpool Spinners, Shane Rimmer)

SPINNERS (U.S.)

61	Columbia DB 4693	That's What Girls Are Made For/Heebie Jeebies	160
65	Tamla Motown TMG 514	Sweet Thing/How Can I? (demos with 'Spinners' or 'Detroit Spinners' credit)	100/50
65	Tamla Motown TMG 514	Sweet Thing/How Can I? (stock copies credited to 'Spinners')	165

(see also Detroit Spinners)

SPINNING WHEEL

79	private pressing	JACOB'S FLEECE (LP)	25

(see also Dragonsfire)

SPIRALS

58	Capitol CL 14958	The Rockin' Cow/Everybody Knows	15

SPIRAL SKY

93	Acme AC 8002LP	SPIRAL SKY (LP, numbered & sealed with insert, 500 only)	15

(see also Sun Dial, Ohr Musik)

SPIRAL STAIRCASE

68	CBS 3507	Baby What I Mean/Makin' Your Mind Up	15
69	CBS 4187	More Today Than Yesterday/Broken Hearted Man	35
69	CBS 4524	No One For Me To Turn To/Sweet Little Thing	12

SPIRAL TRIBE

93	Butterfly BFL LP 6	TECNO TERRA (2-LP)	140

SPIRIT

68	CBS 3523	Uncle Jack/Mechanical World	6
69	CBS 3880	I Got A Line On You/She Smiles	6
69	CBS 4511	Dark Eyed Woman/Ice	5
69	CBS 4565	Dark Eyed Woman/New Dope In Town	5
70	CBS 4773	1984/Sweet Stella Baby	6
70	CBS 5149	Animal Zoo/Red Light Roll On	6
72	CBS 8083	Cadillac Cowboys/Darkness	5
73	Epic EPC 7082	Mr. Skin/Nature's Way	5
84	Mercury MER 1626	Fresh Garbage/Mr Skin (6", p/s)	5
78	Sound For Industry SFI 326	Midnight Train/Potatoland Theme (flexidisc free with *Dark Star* magazine)	8/5
68	CBS 63278	SPIRIT (LP, orange label)	18
68	CBS 63523	THE FAMILY THAT PLAYS TOGETHER (LP, orange label)	18
69	CBS 63729	CLEAR (LP, orange label)	20
71	Epic EPC 64191	THE TWELVE DREAMS OF DR. SARDONICUS (LP, g/fold sleeve, yellow label)	15
72	Epic EPC 64507	FEED-BACK (LP, yellow label)	12
81	Beggars Banquet BEGA 23	POTATOLAND (LP, with cartoon book)	15
88	Chord CHDAT 010	POTATOLAND (DAT)	15

(see also Kapt. Kopter & Fabulous Twirlybirds, Jo Jo Gunne)

SPIRIT OF JOHN MORGAN

69	Carnaby CNS 4005	Ride On/Along Came John	8
71	RCA RCA 2085	Floating Opera Show/Never Let Go	6
69	Carnaby CNLS 6002	THE SPIRIT OF JOHN MORGAN (LP)	55
70	Carnaby CNLS 6007	AGE MACHINE (LP)	55
71	Carnaby 6437 503	THE SPIRIT OF JOHN MORGAN (LP, reissue)	25

(see also John Morgan)

SPIRIT OF MEMPHIS QUARTET

58	Parlophone PMD 1070	NEGRO SPIRITUALS (10" LP)	25
65	Vogue LAE 1033	NEGRO SPIRITUALS (LP, reissue)	15

SPIRIT OF PLAY

88	Release KIDS 1988	Children In Need/Children In Need (Instrumental) (with Paul McCartney) (some in p/s)	50/10

SPIRITUALIZED

90	Dedicated ZB 43783	Anyway That You Want Me/Step Into The Breeze (p/s)	10
90	Dedicated ZT 43784	Anyway That You Want Me (Extended)/Step Into The Breeze 1 & 2 (12", p/s)	20
90	Dedicated ZT 43780	Anyway That You Want Me (Remix)/Step Into The Breeze 1 & 2 (12", p/s)	35
90	Dedicated ZD 43784	Anyway That You Want Me/Step Into The Breeze 1 & 2 (CD)	25
91	Fierce FRIGHT 053	Feel So Sad/I Want You (gig freebie, no p/s, stamped plain white sleeve with date & venue details)	30

MINT VALUE £

91	Dedicated SPIRT 001T	Feel So Sad (Rhapsodies)/(Glides And Chimes) (12", p/s)	10
91	Dedicated SPIRT 001CD	Feel So Sad (Rhapsodies)/(Glides And Chimes) (CD)	8
91	Dedicated SPIRT 002	Run/I Want You (p/s, some with luminous sleeve & clear luminous vinyl)	8/6
91	Dedicated SPIRT 002T	Run/Luminescence (Stay With Me)/I Want You/Effervescent (Chimes) (12", some with luminous sleeve)	15/10
91	Dedicated SPIRT 002CD/ ZD 44846	Run/Luminescence (Stay With Me)/I Want You/ Effervescent (Chimes) (CD)	15
91	Dedicated SPIRIT 003	Why Don't You Smile Now? (Edit)/Sway (clear vinyl, p/s)	6
91	Dedicated SPIRT 003 CD	Why Don't You Smile Now? (Edit)/Sway/Why Don't You Smile Now? (CD, front cover has "Smile/Sway")	8
91	Dedicated SPIRT 004	I Want You/You Know It's True (Instrumental)/100 Bars (Flashback) (p/s, mail-order with *NME* coupon only)	15
92	Dedicated SPIRT 004CD	I Want You/You Know It's True (Instrumental)/100 Bars (Flashback) (CD, no p/s, mail-order with *NME* coupon only)	15
92	Dedicated DEDCD 004	LAZER GUIDED MELODIES (CD EP, 4-track sampler of album)	12
92	Dedicated SPIRIT 005	Medication/Smiles (p/s, red vinyl, 3000 only)	6
92	Dedicated SPIRT 005T	Medication/Angel Sigh/Feel So Sad (12", p/s, with poster, 3000 only)	10
93	Dedicated SPIRT 006	Smiles (Live)/100 Bars (A Cappella) (7" flexidisc, fan-club only)	20
93	Greenpeace GR'NP'CE 001	Good Dope, Good Fun/MERCURY REV: 'Boys Peel Out (Live)' (gig 7", with booklet)	12
93	Dedicated SPIRT 007	ELECTRIC MAINLINE EP (Good Times/Lay Back In The Sun) (p/s, some on yellow vinyl)	5
93	Dedicated SPIRT 007CD	ELECTRIC MAINLINE EP (Good Times/Lay Back In The Sun/Electric Mainline) (CD)	8
94	Dedicated SPIRT 009	Let It Flow/Don't Go/Stay With Me/Don't Go/Stay With Me (The Individual) (10", p/s)	8
95	Dedicated 7432 13 11782	Lay Back In The Sun/The Slide Song/Spread Your Wings/ Lay Back In The Sun (CD)	15
96	Dedicated SPIRT 101T	Pure Phase Tones For DJs (12")	10
97	Dedicated SPIRT 011CD	Broken Heart (Instrumental) (CD, available via *NME*, 500 only)	35
98	Dedicated SPIRT 014T	I Think I'm In Love/(Chemical Brothers Vocal Mix)/(Chemical Brothers Inst.)	6
98	Dedicated SPIRT 014DJ	I Think I'm In Love/(Chemical Brothers Vocal Mix)/(Chemical Brothers Inst.) (12", DJ promo, 200 only)	30
98	Dedicated SPIRT 015DJ	Come Together (Death In Vegas Mix)/(Two Lone Swordsmen Mix) (12", p/s)	8
92	Dedicated DEDLP 004S	LAZER GUIDED MELODIES (LP, ltd. ed. with/without bonus 7" single 'Anyway That You Want Me'/'Why Don't You Smile Now?' [CWNN 7001])	25/20
93	Dedicated no cat. no.	SUMMER EUROPEAN 93 BOX (3-CD promo set, with ribbon and insert)	60
93	Dedicated DEDLP 008	FUCKED UP INSIDE (LP, mail-order only)	35
93	Dedicated DEDCD 008	FUCKED UP INSIDE (CD, mail-order only)	35
95	Dedicated DEDCD 017	PURE PHASE (CD, in luminous green case)	25
97	Dedicated DEDLP 034	LADIES AND GENTLEMEN WE ARE FLOATING IN SPACE (2-LP, limited issue)	25
97	Dedicated DEDCD 034S	LADIES AND GENTLEMEN WE ARE FLOATING IN SPACE (12 x 3" CDs, in blister packs in card box w/insert, 1000 only, 200 w/clear plastic backs)	80/120
97	Dedicated DEDCD 034P	LADIES AND GENTLEMEN WE ARE FLOATING IN SPACE (CD, 'Elvis version', given to Mercury Music Prize personnel, 50 copies only)	35
01	BMG/Arista OPM 001LP	LET IT COME DOWN (LP)	12

(see also Spacemen 3)

SPIROGYRA

72	Pegasus PGS 3	Dangerous Dave/Captain's Log	12
71	B&C CAS 1042	ST. RADIGUND'S (LP, with lyric inner)	70
72	Pegasus PEG 13	OLD BOOT WINE (LP)	70
73	Polydor 2310 246	BELLS, BOOTS AND SHAMBLES (LP)	200+

SPITFIRE (& BLACKFIRE BARMIES)

82	Carrere CAR 253	So You Want To Be A Rock'n'Roll Star/Spitfire Boogie	50

SPITFIRE BOYS

77	RK RK 1001	British Refugee/Mein Kampf (push-out centre)	100
77	RK RK 1001	British Refugee/Mein Kampf (reissue, solid centre, p/s)	90

(see also Frankie Goes To Hollywood)

SPITZBROOK

79	Ace SPIT 1	Stranger/Looking At You (p/s)	60

CHARLIE SPIVAK & HIS ORCHESTRA

54	Parlophone CMSP 14	Red Lilacs/Sentimental Trumpet (export issue)	8
50s	London BEP 6036	CHARLIE SPIVAK AND HIS ORCHESTRA (EP, export issue)	10

VICTORIA SPIVEY

60	Fontana TFE 17264	TREASURES OF NORTH AMERICAN NEGRO MUSIC NO. 5 (EP)	15
56	HMV 7EG 8190	VICTORIA SPIVEY (EP)	20
65	Xtra XTRA 1022	VICTORIA SPIVEY (LP)	25

SPIZZ (OIL/ENERGI)

79	Rough Trade RTSO 1	6000 Crazy/1989/Fibre (p/s)	5
79	Rough Trade RTSO 2	Cold City/Red And Black/Solarisation (Shun)/Platform 3 (as Spizz Oil) (p/s)	5
79	Rough Trade RTSO 3	Soldier Soldier/Virginia Plain (as Spizz Energi) (p/s)	5
79	Rough Trade RTSO 4	Where's Captain Kirk?/Amnesia (as Spizz Energi) (p/s)	5

S.P.K. (SEPPUKU/SURGICAL PENIS KLINIK)

80	Industrial IR 0011	MEAT PROCESSING SECTION (Mekano/Slogun) (p/s, labels list "Slogan"/ "Factory", with insert, as Surgical Penis Klinik)	18
83	Side Effekts SER 003	Dekompositiones (12", p/s, as Seppuku)	15
81	Side Effekts SER 01	INFORMATION OVERLOAD UNIT (LP, 1st 1,000 with booklet & poster)	30/20
83	Walter Ulbright WULP 002	AUTO-DA-FE (LP)	15
84	WEA WX 10	MACHINE AGE VOODOO (LP)	12
86	Sterile SRC 4	LIVE AT THE CRYPT (cassette)	12
80s	Side Effekts SER 002	LEICHENSCHREI (LP)	15

MINT VALUE £

SPLINTER

74	Dark Horse AMS 7135	Costafine Town/Elly May	6
75	Dark Horse AMS 5501	Drink All Day/Haven't Got Time (withdrawn)	15
75	Dark Horse AMS 5502	China Light/Drink All Day	10
75	Dark Horse AMS 5503	Which Way Will I Get Home/Green Bus Line	10
76	Dark Horse AMS 5506	Half Way There/What Is It (If You Never Ever Tried It Yourself)	10
77	Dark Horse K 17009	Round And Round/I'll Bend For You	8
77	Dark Horse K 17116	New York City (Who Am I)/Baby Love	8
78	Barn BARN 4	Danger Zone/Swear To God	10
76	Dark Horse DH 2	SPLINTER (LP, promo only, plain white sleeve)	150

(see also Elastic Oz Band)

SPLIT BEAVER

81	Heavy Metal HEAVY 7	Savage/Hound Of Hell (some with p/s)	18/5
82	Heavy Metal HMRLP 3	WHEN HELL WON'T HAVE YOU (LP, silver or red label)	15/12

SPLIT CROW

84	Guardian GRC 2167	ROCKSTORM (LP)	12

SPLIT ENZ

76	Chrysalis CHS 2120	Late Last Night/Walking Down The Road (p/s)	5
77	Chrysalis CHS 2131	Another Great Divide/Stranger Than Fiction (p/s)	5
77	Chrysalis CHS 2170	My Mistake/Crosswords (p/s)	5
77	Chrysalis CHS 2170-12	My Mistake/Crosswords/The Woman Who Loves You (12", p/s)	10
79	Illegal ILS 19	I See Red/Give It A Whirl/Hermit McDermitt (p/s)	7
80	A&M AMLH 64822	TRUE COLOURS (LP, some copies laser etched)	12/10

(see also Crowded House, Tim Finn)

SPLIT IMAGE

82	Heroes ER 01	Now That We've Parted	25

SPLIT KNEE LOONS

81	Avatar AAA 111	THE SPECIAL COLLECTORS EP (p/s, brown vinyl, some with badge)	10/8

(see also Gillan, Bernie Tormé, John McCoy,Colin Town[e]s)

SPLIT SCREENS

78	Rok ROK III/IV	Just Don't Try/JUST FRANK: You (die-cut company sleeve)	10

SPLODGENESSABOUNDS

80	Deram ROLF 1	Two Little Boys/Horse/Sox/Butterfly (p/s, some with 'Splodge' boomerang)	15/7
81	Deram BUM 3	COWPUNK MEDLUM (EP, p/s, with free flexi [BUMF 3])	10

SPOILERS

72	London HLU 10399	Turbo Rock/Sad Man's Land	10

SPOILT BRATZ

88	Spoilt Bratz SB 1	SPOILT BRATZ: (Not So) Hot/You Talk Too Much/I Could Die/She's A Drag (cassette, private issue, 200 only)	50
88	Spoilt Bratz SB 2	GASOLINE & SUICIDE: Sex Doll, Love Cramp/Going Down Again/ Stuck In A Rut/Crawling On Broken Glass (cassette, private issue, 200 only)	50
89	Spoilt Bratz BRAT 3	BE MY GUEST: Pain Reliever/Past Times/Ignorance (cassette, private issue)	50

(see also Terrorvision)

SPOKESMEN

65	Brunswick 05941	The Dawn Of Correction/For You Babe	10
65	Brunswick 05948	It Ain't Fair/Have Courage Be Careful	10
66	Brunswick 05950	Michelle/Better Days Are Yet To Come	8
66	Brunswick 05958	Today's The Day/Enchanté	8

SPONTANEOUS COMBUSTION

71	Harvest HAR 5046	Lonely Singer/200 Lives/Leaving	15
72	Harvest HAR 5060	Gay Time Night/Spaceship	10
73	Harvest HAR 5066	Sabre Dance/Part 2	8
72	Harvest SHVL 801	SPONTANEOUS COMBUSTION (LP)	50
72	Harvest SHVL 805	TRIAD (LP, with insert)	35

(see also Time)

SPONTANEOUS MUSIC ENSEMBLE

66	Eyemark EMP L1002	CHALLENGE (LP)	200
68	Island ILP 979	KARYOBIN ... ARE THE IMAGINARY BIRDS SAID TO LIVE IN PARADISE (LP, pink label)	100
69	Marmalade 608 008	SPONTANEOUS MUSIC ENSEMBLE (LP)	50
71	Tangent TNGS 107	SOURCE FROM AND TOWARDS (LP)	30
72	Marmalade 2384 009	SPONTANEOUS MUSIC ENSEMBLE (LP, reissue)	25
73	Emanem 303	FACE TO FACE (LP)	30
73	Tangent TNGS 118	SO WHAT DO YOU THINK (LP)	20
77	Incus INCUS 24	BIOSYSTEM (LP)	50

(see also Howard Riley Trio)

SPOOKY TOOTH

67	Island WIP 6022	Sunshine Help Me/Weird	12
68	Island WIP 6037	Love Really Changed Me/Luger's Grove	15
68	Island WIP 6046	The Weight/Do Right People	10
69	Island WIP 6048	Nobody There At All/ART: Room With A View (unissued, white labels only)	40
69	Island WIP 6060	Son Of Your Father/I've Got Enough Heartache	7
73	Island WIP 6168	All Sewn Up/As Long As The World Keeps Turning	6
68	Island ILP 980/ILPS 9080	IT'S ALL ABOUT (LP, pink or palm tree label)	50/20
69	Island ILPS 9098	SPOOKY TWO (LP, pink label)	40
69	Island ILPS 9107	CEREMONY (LP, with Pierre Henry, pink label, gatefold sleeve)	30
70	Island ILPS 9117	THE LAST PUFF (LP, pink label)	30

73 Island ILPS 9227 YOU BROKE MY HEART SO I BUSTED YOUR JAW (LP, pink rim label) 22
73 Island ILPS 9255 WITNESS (LP, pink rim label) 20
74 Good Ear EARL 2001 THE MIRROR (LP) 12
74 Island ILPS 9292 THE MIRROR (LP, export issue) 18
(see also Gary Wright, V.I.P.s, Art, Luther Grosvenor, Hellions, Revolution, State Of Mickey & Tommy, Mike Harrison, Foreigner)

SPORTS

78 Stiff LAST 5 WHO LISTENS TO THE RADIO EP: Who Listens To The Radio/Step By Step/So Obvious/Suspicious (originals have 'koala photo' p/s) 8
79 Sire SIR 6001 Who Listens To The Radio/Hit Single ('fireplace' p/s) 5
80 Sire SRUK 6001 WHO LISTENS TO THE RADIO (LP) 15

SPOTLIGHTERS

59 Vogue Pop V 9130 Please Be My Girlfriend/Whisper (with Bob Thompson & His Band) 500
59 Vogue Pop V 9130 Please Be My Girlfriend/Whisper (with Bob Thompson & His Band) (78) 120

SPOTLIGHTS

66 Philips BF 1485 Batman And Robin/Day Flower 10

SPOTNICKS

62 Oriole CB 1724 Orange Blossom Special/The Spotnicks Theme 7
62 Oriole CB 1755 Galloping Guitars/The Rocket Man 8
63 Oriole CB 1790 Hava Nagila/High Flyin' Scotsman 8
63 Oriole CB 1818 Just Listen To My Heart/Pony Express 8
63 Oriole CB 1844 Valentina/Save The Last Dance For Me/No Yaga Daga Blues 10
63 Oriole CB 1886 Anna/The Sailor's Hornpipe 12
64 Oriole CB 1953 Lovesick Blues/The Space Creatures 15
64 Oriole CB 1981 Donner Wetter/Shamus O'Toole 15
63 Oriole EP 7075 ON THE AIR (EP) 20
64 Oriole EP 7078 SPOTNICKS IN PARIS (EP) 20
64 Oriole EP 7079 SPOTNICKS AT THE OLYMPIA PARIS (EP) 22
63 Oriole PS 40036 OUT-A SPACE: THE SPOTNICKS IN LONDON (LP, also stereo SPS 40037) 30/40
64 Oriole PS 40054 THE SPOTNICKS IN SPAIN (LP) 25
65 Oriole PS 40064 THE SPOTNICKS IN BERLIN (LP) 35
81 Air CHM 1171 THE VERY BEST OF THE SPOTNICKS (LP) 12
(see also Bob Lander & Spotnicks, Shy Ones)

JACK SPRATT & LEROY SIBBLES & HEPTONES

69 Coxsone CS 7100 Give Me Your Love/LARRY & ALVIN: Magic Moments 30

SPREADEAGLE

72 Charisma CB 183 How Can We Be Lost/Nightmare 5
72 Charisma BCP 7 Nightingale Lane/Liar (p/s) 5
72 Charisma CAS 1055 THE PIECE OF PAPER (LP) 15

SPREDTHICK

78 An Actual ACT 003 SPREDTHICK (LP, with insert) 18

SPRIGUNS (OF TOLGUS)

76 Decca F 13676 Nothing Else To Do/Lord Lovell 8
77 Decca F 13739 White Witch/Time Will Pass 8
74 private pressing ROWDY DOWDY DAY (cassette, as Spriguns Of Tolgus) 50
75 Alida Star C'tage ASC7755 JACK WITH A FEATHER (LP, as Spriguns Of Tolgus) . . . . . 750+
76 Decca SKL 5262 REVEL WEIRD & WILD (LP, with lyric insert) 110
77 Decca SKL 5286 TIME WILL PASS (LP, with lyric insert) 110
92 Kissing Spell KSLP 002 ROWDY DOWDY DAY (LP, reissue) 15
(see also Mandy Morton Band, Terra Cotta)

SPRING

71 RCA Neon NE 6 SPRING (LP, foldout sleeve) 140

SPRINGBOARD

69 Polydor 545007 SPRINGBOARD (LP) 50

DUSTY SPRINGFIELD

SINGLES

63 Philips BF 1292 I Only Want To Be With You/Once Upon A Time 6
64 Philips BF 1313 Stay Awhile/Something Special 6
64 Philips BF 1348 I Just Don't Know What To Do With Myself/My Colouring Book 6
64 Philips BF 1369 Losing You/Summer Is Over 6
64 Philips BF 1381 Oh Holy Child/SPRINGFIELDS: Jingle Bells (some with p/s) 10/5
65 Philips BF 1396 Your Hurtin' Kinda Love/Don't Say It Baby 6
65 Philips BF 1418 In The Middle Of Nowhere/Baby Don't You Know 6
65 Philips BF 1430 Some Of Your Lovin'/I'll Love You For A While 6
66 Philips BF 1466 Little By Little/If It Hadn't Been For You 6
66 Philips BF 1482 You Don't Have To Say You Love Me/Every Ounce Of Strength 6
66 Philips BF 1502 Goin' Back/I'm Gonna Leave You 6
66 Philips BF 1510 All I See Is You/Go Ahead On (some with p/s) 10/8
67 Philips BF 1553 I'll Try Anything/The Corrupt Ones 10
67 Philips BF 1577 Give Me Time/The Look Of Love 6
67 Philips BF 1608 What's It Gonna Be/Small Town Girl 15
68 Philips BF 1682 I Close My Eyes And Count To Ten/No Stranger Am I 6
68 Philips BF 1706 I Will Come To You/The Colour Of Your Eyes 6
68 Philips BF 1730 Son Of A Preacher Man/Just A Little Lovin' 15
69 Philips BF 1811 Am I The Same Girl/Earthbound Gypsy 15
69 Philips BF 1826 Brand New Me/Bad Case Of The Blues 8
70 Philips BF 1835 Morning Please Don't Come (with Tom Springfield)/TOM SPRINGFIELD: Charley . 8
70 Philips 6006 045 How Can I Be Sure/Spooky 12
72 Philips 6006 214 Yesterday When I Was Young/I Start Counting 7
73 Philips 6006 295 Who Gets Your Love/Of All The Things 7

			MINT VALUE £
74	Philips 6006 325	Learn To Say Goodbye/Easy Evil	7
74	Philips 6006 350	What's It Gonna Be/Bring Him Back	8
75	Philips 6006 446	Yesterday When I Was Young/The Look Of Love	8
78	Mercury DUSTY 1	A Love Like Yours (Don't Come Knocking Every Day)/Hollywood Movie Girls	6
78	Mercury DUSTY 002	That's The Kind Of Love I've Got For You/Sandra	6
79	Mercury DUSTY 003	I'm Coming Home Again/Save Me Save Me	6
79	Mercury DUSTY 4	Baby Blue/Get Yourself To Love (p/s)	7
79	Mercury DUSTY 412	Baby Blue (Disco Version)/Baby Blue (7" Version) (12")	10
80	Mercury DUSTY 5	Your Love Still Brings Me To My Knees/ Let Me Love You Once Before You Go (withdrawn)	8
80	Mercury DUSTY 5	Your Love Still Brings Me To My Knees/I'm Your Child	5
84	Allegiance ALES 3	Private Number (with Spencer Davis)/SPENCER DAVIS: Don't Want You No More	6
85	Hippodrome HIPPO 103	Sometimes Like Butterflies/I Wanna Control You (p/s)	8
85	Hippodrome 12 HIPPO 103	Sometimes Like Butterflies (Extended Mix)/Sometimes Like Butterflies/ I Wanna Control You (12", p/s)	12
89	Parlophone RG 6207	Nothing Has Been Proved/Nothing Has Been Proved (Instrumental) (g/fold p/s)	5
89	Parlophone 12RG 6207	Nothing Has Been Proved (Dance Mix)/Nothing Has Been Proved/ Nothing Has Been Proved (Instrumental) (12", gatefold p/s)	8
89	Parlophone CDR 6207	Nothing Has Been Proved (Dance Mix)/Nothing Has Been Proved/ Nothing Has Been Proved (Instrumental) (CD, with Pet Shop Boys, card p/s)	15
89	Parlophone R 6234	In Private/In Private (Instrumental version) (p/s)	5
89	Parlophone 12RX 6234	In Private (Remix)/In Private (Dub)/In Private (Bonus Beats) (12", p/s)	8
89	Parlophone CDR 6234	In Private (12" Version)/(7" Version)/(Instrumental version) (CD)	10
90	Parlophone R 6253	Reputation/Rep U Dub 1 (p/s)	5
90	Parlophone 12R 6253	Reputation (Lots Of Fun 12" Mix)/Rep U Dub 1/Rep U Dub 2 (p/s)	8
90	Parlophone 12RX 6253	Reputation (The Alternative Mix)/Reputation (Lots Of Fun Single Mix)/ Getting It Right (12", p/s)	8
90	Parlophone CDR 6253	Reputation/Reputation (Lots Of Fun 12" Mix)/Rep U Dub 2 (CD)	8
90	Parlophone R 6266	Arrested By You/Arrested By You (Instrumental) (p/s)	5
90	Parlophone 12R 6266	Arrested By You (Extended Version)/Born This Way (12" Remix)/ Arrested By You (Instrumental) (12", p/s)	8
90	Parlophone CDR 6266	Arrested By You (7" Version)/Arrested By You (Extended Version)/ Born This Way (12" Version)/Getting It Right (CD)	8
93	Columbia 659856 7	Heart And Soul (with Cilla Black)/CILLA BLACK: A Dream Come True (p/s)	5
93	Columbia 659856 2	Heart And Soul (with Cilla Black) (7" Version)/A Capella Remix/Instrumental/ CILLA BLACK: A Dream Come True (CD)	8
94	Philips SPRCD 1	Goin' Back/Son Of A Preacher Man/Let Me Love You Once Before You Go/ What Are You Doing The Rest Of Your Life (CD)	8

EPs

64	Philips BE 12560	I ONLY WANT TO BE WITH YOU	20
64	Philips BE 12564	DUSTY	20
65	Philips BE 12572	DUSTY IN NEW YORK	20
65	Philips BE 12579	MADEMOISELLE DUSTY	30
68	Philips BE 12605	IF YOU GO AWAY	20
68	Philips 6850 751	STAR DUSTY (Audio Club Of Great Britain release)	12
68	Philips MCP 1004	THE HITS OF THE WALKER BROTHERS AND DUSTY SPRINGFIELD (cassette)	10
71	Philips MCP 100	THE HITS OF DUSTY SPRINGFIELD (cassette)	10
70s	Philips CUT 111	CLASSIC CUTS	12

LPs

64	Philips (S)BL 7594	A GIRL CALLED DUSTY (mono/stereo)	20/30
65	Philips (S)RBL 1002	EVERYTHING'S COMING UP DUSTY (gatefold sleeve with booklet, mono/stereo)	20/35
66	Philips (S)BL 7737	GOLDEN HITS	15
67	Philips (S)BL 7820	WHERE AM I GOING?	20
68	World Record Club ST 848	DUSTY SPRINGFIELD	15
68	Philips (S)BL 7864	DUSTY... DEFINITELY	20
69	Wing WL 1211	STAY AWHILE	15
69	Philips SBL 7889	DUSTY IN MEMPHIS	25
70	Philips SBL 7927	FROM DUSTY... WITH LOVE	20
71	Philips 6382 016	THIS IS DUSTY SPRINGFIELD	18
71	Audio Club/G.B. 6850 002	STAR DUSTY	15
71	Audio Club/G.B. 6856 020	SHEER MAGIC	40
72	Philips 6308 117	SEE ALL HER FACES	18
73	Philips 6382 063	THIS IS DUSTY SPRINGFIELD VOL. 2 — MAGIC GARDEN	18
73	Philips 6308 152	CAMEO	18
75	Philips 6382 105	SINGS BURT BACHARACH AND CAROLE KING	18
78	Mercury 9109 607	IT BEGINS AGAIN	15
79	Mercury 9109 617	LIVING WITHOUT YOUR LOVE	15

CDs

94	Philips 522 254-2	THE LEGEND OF DUSTY SPRINGFIELD (4-CD boxed set, 2,000 only)	75
96	DSB/Zone X001	WE WISH YOU A MERRY CHRISTMAS (with Springfields) (Bulletin charity issue)	15

(see also Lana Sisters, Springfields, Tom Springfield, Pet Shop Boys)

RICK SPRINGFIELD

72	Capitol EA-ST 80001	BEGINNINGS (LP)	10

TOM SPRINGFIELD (& HIS) ORCHESTRA

63	Philips BF 1294	The Moon Behind The Hill/The Londonderry Air	5
64	Philips BF 1331	Brazilian Shake/Brazilian Blues	5
65	Philips BF 1423	The Mogul Theme/Homage To Spewdley Parsons	5
69	Philips BF 1759	Theme From From The Troubleshooters/Homage To Spewdley Parsons (some with p/s)	8/5
69	Decca LK/SKL 5003	LOVE'S PHILOSOPHY BY... (LP, featuring Dusty Springfield)	30

(see also Springfields, Dusty Springfield)

MINT VALUE £

SPRINGFIELD PARK

68 CBS 3775 Never An Everyday Thing/I Can See The Sun Shine . . . 5

SPRINGFIELDS

61 Philips PB 1145 Dear John/I Done What They Told Me To . . . 7
61 Philips PB 1168 Breakaway/Good News . . . 6
61 Philips PB 1178 Bambino/Star Of Hope (some with p/s) . . . 12/6
62 Philips PB 1241 Silver Threads And Golden Needles/Aunt Rhody . . . 6
62 Philips 326 536 BF Swahili Papa/Gotta Travel On . . . 10
62 Philips 326 557 BF Island Of Dreams/The Johnson Boys . . . 5
63 Philips BF 1263 Come On Home/Pit A Pat . . . 5
63 Philips 326 577 BF Say I Won't Be There/Little Boat . . . 5
61 Philips BBE 12476 THE SPRINGFIELDS (EP, also stereo SBBE 9068) . . . 18/25
62 Lyntone P125E CHRISTMAS WITH THE SPRINGFIELDS (EP, mail-order via *Woman's Own*) . . . 10
62 Philips 433 622 BE KINDA FOLKSY (EP) . . . 18
63 Philips 433 623 BE KINDA FOLKSY No. 2 (EP) . . . 18
63 Philips 433 624 BE KINDA FOLKSY No. 3 (EP) . . . 18
63 Philips BBE 12538 HIT SOUNDS (EP) . . . 12
63 Philips 433 643 BE FOLK SONGS FROM THE HILLS (EP) . . . 12
62 Philips BBL 7551/SBBL 674 KINDA FOLKSY (LP, mono/stereo) . . . 18/25
63 Philips 632 304 BL FOLK SONGS FROM THE HILLS (LP) . . . 18
64 Philips BET 606 THE SPRINGFIELDS STORY (2-LP) . . . 25
69 Fontana SFL 13098 THE SPRINGFIELDS SING AGAIN (LP) . . . 18

(see also Dusty Springfield, Lana Sisters, Tom Springfield, Mike Hurst)

SPRINGFIELDS

88 Sarah SARAH 010 Sunflower/Clown/Are We Gonna Be Alright? (foldaround p/s with 14" x 10" poster in polyester bag; yellow p/s, later orange p/s) . . . 25/18
91 Sarah SARAH 040 Wonder (p/s, with insert) . . . 7

BRUCE SPRINGSTEEN

SINGLES

75 CBS A 3661 Born To Run/Meeting Across The River . . . 8
76 CBS A 3940 Tenth Avenue Freeze-Out/She's The One . . . 12
78 CBS A 6424 Prove It All Night/Factory . . . 15
78 CBS A 6532 Badlands/Something In The Night . . . 12
78 CBS A 6720 Promised Land/Streets Of Fire . . . 45
80 CBS A 9309 Hungry Heart/Held Up Without A Gun (p/s, blue or black lettering) . . . 40/30
80 CBS A 9568 Sherry Darling/Be True (p/s) . . . 25
81 CBS A 1179 The River/Independence Day (p/s) . . . 10
81 CBS A 13-1179 The River/Born To Run/Rosalita (12", p/s, some sleeves credit 'East Street Band') . . . 15/10
81 CBS A 1557 Cadillac Ranch/Wreck On The Highway (p/s) . . . 25
82 CBS A 2794 Atlantic City/Mansion On The Hill (p/s) . . . 40
82 CBS A 2969 Open All Night/The Big Pay Back (p/s) . . . 25
84 CBS A 4436 Dancing In The Dark/Pink Cadillac (p/s) . . . 7
84 CBS WA 4436 Dancing In The Dark/Pink Cadillac (Cadillac-shaped picture disc) . . . 30
84 CBS A 4662 Cover Me/Jersey Girl (live) (poster p/s) . . . 10
84 CBS WA 4662 Cover Me/Jersey Girl (live) (Bruce-shaped picture disc with plinth, withdrawn) . . 25
84 CBS DA 4662/A 4436 Cover Me/Jersey Girl (live)//Dancing In The Dark/Pink Cadillac (shrinkwrapped double pack, both 45s in p/s) . . . 12
84 CBS DA 4662/A 7077 Cover Me/Jersey Girl (live)//Born To Run/Meeting Across The River (shrinkwrapped double pack, no p/s on 2nd 45) . . . 12
84 CBS QTA 4662 Cover Me (Undercover Mix)/Cover Me (Dub)/Shut Out The Light/ Dancing In The Dark (Dub)/Jersey Girl (live) (12", p/s) . . . 8
84 CBS A 6561 I'm Going Down/Janey, Don't You Lose Heart (p/s) . . . 7
84 CBS A 6773 My Hometown/Santa Claus Is Comin' To Town (p/s) . . . 6
85 CBS A 7077 Born To Run/Meeting Across The River (reissue, blue p/s, withdrawn) . . . 25
85 CBS A 6342 I'm On Fire/Born In The U.S.A. (p/s, with competition postcard) . . . 10
85 CBS WA 6342 I'm On Fire/Born In The U.S.A. (p/s, flag-shaped picture disc) . . . 25
85 CBS TA 6342 I'm On Fire/Rosalita/Born In The U.S.A. (Freedom Mix)/Johnny Bye Bye (12", p/s) . . . 10
85 CBS QTA 6375 Glory Days/Stand On It/Sherry Darling/Racing In The Street (12", poster p/s) . . . 8
85 CBS BRUCE 1 BORN IN THE U.S.A. — THE 12" COLLECTION (4 x 12" & 7", box with poster) . . . 40
86 CBS 650 193-0 War (live)/Merry Xmas Baby (live)//My Home Town (live)/Santa Claus Is Coming To Town (live) (shrinkwrapped double pack, both 45s in p/s) . . . 12
86 CBS 650 193-7 War/Merry Xmas Baby (live) (p/s) . . . 5
86 CBS 650 193-6 War/Merry Xmas Baby (live)/Incident On 57th Street (live) (12", poster p/s) . . . 10
87 CBS 650 381-7 Fire (live)/For You (live) (p/s) . . . 6
87 CBS 650 381-6 Fire (live)/For You (live)/Born To Run (live)/No Surrender (live)/ 10th Avenue (live) Freeze-Out (live) (12", p/s) . . . 15
87 CBS BRUCE B2 Born To Run/Spirit In The Night//Johnny 99/Because The Night (double pack box set) . . . 10
87 CBS BRUCE BP 2 Born To Run (live)/Johnny 99 (live) (p/s, badge pack) . . . 5
87 CBS BRUCE C2 Born To Run (live)/Spirit In The Night (live)/Johnny 99 (live)/Seeds (live) (CD, card sleeve with gauze inner) . . . 10
87 CBS 651 141-0 Brilliant Disguise/Lucky Man (gatefold p/s, with discography) . . . 10
87 CBS 651 141-6 Brilliant Disguise/Lucky Man (12", p/s, with poster) . . . 12
87 CBS 651 295-7 Tunnel Of Love/Two For The Road (p/s) . . . 5
87 CBS 651 295-0 Tunnel Of Love/Two For The Road (postcard-shaped picture disc) . . . 15
87 CBS 651 295-8 Tunnel Of Love/Two For The Road/Santa Claus Is Coming To Town (12", p/s with poster) . . . 10
87 CBS 651 295-2 Tunnel Of Love/Santa Claus Is Coming To Town (live)/Two For The Road (CD, card sleeve) . . . 45
88 CBS BRUCE 3 Tougher Than The Rest/Tougher Than The Rest (live) (p/s, with patch) . . . 6
88 CBS BRUCE C3 Tougher Than The Rest/Roulette/Be True (Live)/Born To Run (New Live) (CD, card sleeve) . . . 10

MINT VALUE £

88 CBS BRUCE Q4 — Spare Parts/Cover Me (live)/Spare Parts (live)/I'm On Fire (live) (12", different p/s) 15
88 CBS BRUCE C4 — Spare Parts/Pink Cadillac/Spare Parts (live)/Chimes Of Freedom (live) (CD, card sleeve) 12
88 CBS BRUCE B4 — Spare Parts/Pink Cadillac/Spare Parts (live)/Chimes Of Freedom (live) (CD, BRUCE C4 disc in silver tin) 25
92 Sony 658 138-5 — 57 Channels (And Nothin' On)/Stand On It/Janey, Don't You Lose Heart (CD, picture disc, digipak) 25
92 Sony 658 369-2 — Leap Of Faith/Leap Of Faith (live)/30 Days Out (CD) 8
92 Columbia 657 890-8 — Better Days/Tougher Than The Rest/Part Man Part Monkey (12" picture disc) 10
94 Columbia 660 065-8 — Streets Of Philadelphia/If I Should Fall Behind/Growing Up/Big Muddy (12", picture disc) 12

LPs

73 CBS 65480 — GREETINGS FROM ASBURY PARK, N.J. (cutaway gatefold sleeve, orange label) 12
74 CBS 65780 — THE WILD, THE INNOCENT AND THE E STREET SHUFFLE (orange label, yellow lettering on sleeve; with "Ashbury" mis-spelling on label) 12
75 CBS 69170 — BORN TO RUN (with "*John* Landau" misprint on rear sleeve) 12
79 CBS 66353 — BRUCE SPRINGSTEEN (3-LP, box set) 22
84 CBS 11-86304 — BORN IN THE U.S.A. (picture disc) 30
87 CBS 460 270-0 — TUNNEL OF LOVE (picture disc) 15
87 CBS CDCBS 460 270-9 — TUNNEL OF LOVE (CD, picture disc) 20
92 Sony 471 423-0 — HUMAN TOUCH (picture disc) 15
92 Sony 471 424-0 — LUCKY TOWN (picture disc) 15

(see also Nils Lofgren, Roy Orbison)

SPRINGTIME

78 Sonet SON 2143 — Mrs Caroline Robinson/Honey Bye Bye (p/s) 6

SPROG & WIDGIT

72 Diddley Do DIDLP 02 — 32 ENGLISH FOLK SONGS IN THE SILLY TRADITION (2-LP, gatefold sleeve) 18

SPRONG & NYAH SHUFFLE

69 Grape GR 3001 — Moonwalk/Think 10

BILLY SPROUD & ROCK 'N' ROLL SIX

57 Columbia DB 3893 — Rock Mr. Piper/If You're So Smart (How Come You Ain't Rich) 45
57 Columbia DB 3893 — Rock Mr. Piper/If You're So Smart (How Come You Ain't Rich) (78) 12

SPROUTS

58 RCA RCA 1031 — Teen Billy Baby/Goodbye, She's Gone 60
58 RCA RCA 1031 — Teen Billy Baby/Goodbye, She's Gone (78) 25

SPUD

75 Philips 9108 002 — A SILK PURSE (LP) 20
75 Philips 9108 003 — A HAPPY HANDFUL (LP) 25
77 Sonet SNTF 742 — SMOKING IN THE BOG (LP, with lyric sheet) 15

SPUD AND THE FABS

80 Whitetower AMC 706 — Your Place Or Mine (p/s) 25

WILD JIMMY SPURRILL

60s XX MIN 717 — NOBLE 'THIN MAN' WATTS AND WILD JIMMY SPURRILL (EP) 18

(see also Noble 'Thin Man' Watts, Guitar Crusher)

SPURS

88 Outback OUT 1 — Soldier (p/s) 12

SPYROGYRA

79 Infinity (no cat. no.) — MORNING DANCE (LP, picture disc, in-house issue, top-flap poly sleeve, 50 copies) 75

SPYS

79 No Bad NB 3 — The Young Ones/Heavy Scene (p/s) 5

SQUAD

79 Squad SQS 1 — Red Alert/£8 A Week (some in die cut p/s) 40/20

SQUADRONAIRES

54 Decca F 10248 — Coach Call Boogie/Donegal Cradle Song 15
54 Decca F 10274 — Wolf On The Prowl/Mudhopper 15
57 Columbia DB 3882 — Rock And Roll Boogie/Right Now, Right Now 25
57 Columbia DB 3882 — Rock And Roll Boogie/Right Now, Right Now (78) 6
53 Decca LF 1141 — CONTRASTS IN JAZZ (10" LP) 20

LESTER SQUARE & THE SQUARE DEAL SURFS

84 Thin Sliced TSR 4T — The Plug (12", p/s) 10

(see also Monochrome Set)

SQUEEZE

77 BTM SBT 107 — Take Me I'm Yours/No, Disco Kid, No (unreleased)
77 Deptford Fun City DFC 01 — PACKET OF THREE (EP, red & blue photo p/s) 6
77 Deptford Fun City DFC 01 — PACKET OF THREE (12" EP, plain pink die-cut sleeve, 500 only) 10
78 A&M AMSP 7335 — Take Me I'm Yours/Night Nurse (12", p/s) 7
78 A&M AMS 7360 — Bang Bang/All Fed Up (p/s, green vinyl) 5
78 A&M AMS 7398 — Goodbye Girl/Saints Alive (3-D p/s) 5
79 A&M AMS 7426 — Cool For Cats/Model (p/s, brilliant pink vinyl, 5,000 only) 6
79 A&M AMS 7426 — Cool For Cats/Model (p/s, red vinyl, 1,000 only) 8
79 A&M AMSP 7426 — Cool For Cats/Model (12", p/s, pale pink vinyl) 10
79 A&M AMS 7495 — Christmas Day/Going Crazy (p/s, white vinyl) 5
79 A&M AMS 7507 — Another Nail In My Heart/Pretty Thing (p/s, clear vinyl) 5
80 Lyntone LYN 7010/1 — Wrong Way (green vinyl flexidisc, free with *Smash Hits*) 6/4
81 A&M AMS 8147 — Tempted/Yap Yap Yap (p/s, with free U.S. 5" single "Another Nail In My Heart"/"If I Didn't Love You", p/s, shrinkwrapped) 5
81 A&M AMS 8166 — Labelled With Love/Squabs On Forty Five (withdrawn p/s) 15

MINT VALUE £

SQUIBBY & REFLECTIONS

68	Direction 58-3453	Ragamuffin/For A Little While	5
68	Direction 58-3606	Loving You Has Made My Life Worthwhile/Better Off Without You	5
69	Direction 58-4073	You Got It/Come Back To Me	8

SQUIBS

81	Oily SLICK 1	On The Line (plain sleeve, with insert)	25
81	Oily SLICK 3	Parades/Out On The Town (p/s)	20

BILLY SQUIER

82	Capitol CL 231	Too Daze Gone/Whadda You Want From Me (p/s, coloured vinyl)	5
82	Capitol CL 261	Emotions In Motion/Catch 22 (p/s)	12
82	Capitol CL 261	Emotions In Motion/Catch 22 (picture disc)	15
84	Capitol SQD 1	Rock Me Tonite/Can't Get Next To You//She's A Runner/Listen To The Heart (double pack)	6
86	Capitol CL 433	Love Is The Hero/Learn How To Live (live) (p/s)	7
86	Capitol 12CL 433	Love Is The Hero (extended version with Freddie Mercury intro)/ Learn How To Live (live) (12", p/s)	65

(see also Freddie Mercury, Roger Taylor)

SQUIRE

79	Rok ROK I/II	Get Ready To Go/COMING SHORTLY: Doing The Flail (company sleeve)	30
79	I-Spy SEE 2	Walking Down The King's Road/It's A Mod Mod Mod Mod World (company sleeve)	7
79	I-Spy SEE 4	The Face Of Youth Today/I Know A Girl (keyhole company sleeve, paper or plastic labels)	4/6
80	Stage One STAGE 2	My Mind Goes Round In Circles/Does Stephanie Know? (p/s)	6
82	Hi-Lo HI 001	No Time Tomorrow/Don't Cry To Me (p/s)	5
82	Hi-Lo HI 002	Girl On A Train/Every Trick In The Book (p/s)	5
82	Hi-Lo HI 003	Every Trick In The Book/Every Trick In The Book (instrumental) (p/s)	5
83	Hi-Lo HIT 003	Every Trick In The Book/Every Trick In The Book (Elastic Mix) (12", p/s)	8
83	Hi-Lo HI 004	Jesamine/When I Try, I Lie (p/s)	10
84	Hi-Lo HI 005/SFC 2	The Young Idea/It's Getting Better (Squire Fan Club issue)	10
85	Hi-Lo LOX 1	Does Stephanie Know? (flexidisc)	12
94	Detour DR 020	The Place I Used To Live/Make Love To You/Over You (p/s, 900 only, 50 on white vinyl: 2nd pressing of 250 copies, white labels & purple print: 3rd pressing, 588 copies on clear splattered vinyl)	10/5/5/5
83	Hi-Lo LO 01	HITS FROM 3,000 YEARS AGO (LP)	18
83	Hi-Lo LO 02	GET SMART (LP, with poster)	15
85	Hi-Lo LO 03	THE SINGLES ALBUM (LP)	15

(see also Anthony Meynell)

CHRIS SQUIRE

75	Atlantic K 50203	FISH OUT OF WATER (LP, with inner sleeve & poster)	12

(see also Yes)

DOROTHY SQUIRES

53	Polygon P 1068	I'm Walking Behind You/Is There Any Room In Your Heart (78)	7
53	Polygon P 1076	From Your Lips To The Ears Of God/Sorrento & You (78)	7
57	Columbia DB 3985	Song Of The Valley/Our Song	7
58	Columbia DB 4070	Bewitched/A Secret That's Never Been Told	7
58	Pye 7N 15154	Torremelinos/This Is My Mother's Day	6
58	Pye 7N 15199	Sticks And Stones/Don't Search For Love	6
62	Columbia DB 4942	Are You/Moonlight And Roses	5
57	Pye NEP 24036	DOROTHY SQUIRES (EP)	15
58	Pye Nixa NPL 18015	SINGS BILLY REID (LP)	25
67	Ace Of Clubs SCL-R 1230	THIS IS MY LIFE (LP)	12
68	Marble Arch MAL(S) 1211	REFLECTIONS (LP, mono/stereo)	12/15
68	President PTL(S) 1023	SAY IT WITH FLOWERS (LP)	12
69	President PTL(S) 1032	SEASONS OF DOROTHY SQUIRES (LP)	12
70	President PTLS 1043/4	AT THE LONDON PALLADIUM (2-LP)	15
73	Pye NSPL 18425	CHEESE'N'WINE (LP, with Dennis Lotis)	12
73	EMI EMC 3004	LONDON PALLADIUM 1972 (LP)	15
74	Pye NSPD 501	LIVE AT THEATRE ROYAL, DRURY LANE (LP)	12

ROSEMARY SQUIRES

56	Decca F 10685	Band Of Gold/Where You Are	7
58	HMV POP 462	Happy Is The Bride/Give Me The Simple Life	6
58	HMV POP 541	There Goes My Lover/Please Be Kind	5
64	HMV POP 1288	Bluesette/Nothing's Changed	6
56	MGM MGM-EP 640	MY LOVE IS A WANDERER (EP)	18
60	HMV 7EG 8588	ROSEMARY (EP)	15
63	HMV CLP 1669	EVERYTHINGS COMING UP ROSY (LP, mono/stereo [CSD 1508])	25/30
65	HMV CLP 1832	SOMETHING TO REMEMBER ME BY (LP, mono/stereo [CSD 1586])	25/30

(see also Streamliners & Joanne)

S.R.C.

69	Capitol CL 15576	Black Sheep/Morning Mood	15
87	Bam Caruso OPRA 063	Black Sheep/BRAIN: Nightmares In Red (jukebox issue, die-cut company sleeve)	5
69	Capitol (S)T 2991	S.R.C. (LP)	40
69	Capitol E-(S)T 134	MILESTONES (LP)	40
70	Capitol E-(S)T 273	TRAVELLER'S TALE (LP)	40

STACCATOS

61	Parlophone R 4828	Main Line/Topaz	15

STACCATOS

68	Fontana TF 966	Butchers And Bakers/Imitations Of Love	25

MINT VALUE £

STACCATOS (U.S.)

66 Capitol CL 15478 Let's Run Away/Face To Face (With Love) 8
67 Capitol CL 15505 Half Past Midnight/Weatherman 8

CLARENCE STACEY

59 Pye International 7N 25025 Just Your Love/Lonely Guy 30
59 Pye International N 25025 Just Your Love/Lonely Guy (78) 15

GWEN STACEY

65 RCA RCX 7166 INTRODUCING GWEN STACEY (EP) 70

BOB STACKIE

68 Collins Downbeat CR 009 Grab It Hold It Feel It (with Sir Collins Band)/DAN SIMMONDS: Way Out Sound 40
(see also Sir Collins [Band], Owen Gray)

STACKRIDGE

71 MCA MKS 5065 Dora, The Female Explorer/Everyman 5
72 MCA MKS 5103 Anyone For Tennis?/Amazingly Agnes 5
71 MCA MDKS 8002 STACKRIDGE (LP, gatefold sleeve) 30
72 MCA MKPS 2025 FRIENDLINESS (LP) 15
74 MCA MCG 3501 THE MAN IN THE BOWLER HAT (LP, gatefold sleeve) 15
76 MCA MCF 2747 DO THE STANLEY (LP) 12
76 Rocket ROLL 3 MR. MICK (LP) 12

STACKWADDY

70 Dandelion S 5119 Roadrunner/Kentucky 12
72 Dandelion 2001 331 You Really Got Me/Willie The Pimp 10
71 Dandelion DAN 8003 STACKWADDY (LP, gatefold sleeve with inner sleeve; also listed as K 49003) 60
72 Dandelion 2310 231 BUGGER OFF! (LP) 65

STADIUM DOGS

77 Audiogenic A 17 Easy Beat/Android Rocker/Media Withdrawal (die-cut p/s) 10

JO STAFFORD

78s

58 Philips PB 812 Sweet Little Darlin'/Star Of Love 6
58 Philips PB 876 Hibiscus/How Can We Say Goodbye 6
59 Philips PB 935 Pine Top's Boogie Woogie/All Yours 6

45s

53 Columbia SCM 5011 Star Of Hope/Somebody 18
53 Columbia SCM 5012 It Is No Secret/He Bought My Soul At Calvary 20
53 Columbia SCM 5013 You Belong To Me/Jambalaya (On The Bayou) 40
53 Columbia SCM 5026 Keep It A Secret/Once To Every Heart 22
53 Columbia SCM 5046 Something To Remember You By/Blue Moon 15
53 Columbia SCM 5064 September In The Rain/JO STAFFORD & FRANKIE LAINE: Chow, Willy 30
57 Philips JK 1003 On London Bridge/Perfect Love (jukebox issue) 20
58 Philips PB 818 With A Little Bit Of Luck/Wouldn't It Be Loverly 8
58 Philips PB 876 Hibiscus/How Can We Say Goodbye 8
59 Philips PB 898 My Heart Is From Missouri/It Won't Be Easy 6
59 Philips PB 935 Pine Top's Boogie Woogie/All Yours 12
60 Philips PB 991 It Is No Secret/He Bought My Soul At Calvary (reissue) 7
60 Philips PB 1034 Candy/Indoor Sport 6
61 Capitol CL 15225 The Old Rugged Cross/In The Gloaming (with Gordon McRae) 5
62 Pye International 7N 25127 Adios My Love/Misty 5
62 Pye International 7N 25139 Symphony/If My Heart Had A Window 5

EPs

54 Columbia SEG 7516 WITH NELSON EDDY (plain sleeve) 10
54 Columbia SEG 7548 SHOW SONGS (plain sleeve) 10
55 Philips BBE 12014 JO STAFFORD No. 1 15
57 Philips BBE 12138 JO STAFFORD No. 2 15
57 Philips BBE 12141 JO STAFFORD WITH THE ART VAN DAMME QUINTET 12
57 Philips BBE 12147 JO STAFFORD SINGS SACRED SONGS 8
58 Philips BBE 12163 SINGS SONGS OF SCOTLAND 8
58 Philips BBE 12198 JO STAFFORD SINGS SACRED SONGS No. 2 8
58 Philips BBE 12214 T.V. SERIES 15
60 Philips BBE 12378 JO STAFFORD SINGS SACRED SONGS No. 3 8
60 Capitol EAP 20049 THE JO STAFFORD TOUCH 15
61 Capitol EAP 20154 SIMPLE MELODY 12
61 Philips BBE 12459 JO + JAZZ 12

LPs

50 Capitol LC 6500 AMERICAN FOLK SONGS (10") 30
51 Capitol LC 6515 KISS ME KATE (10", with Gordon MacRae) 18
53 Capitol LC 6575 CAPITOL PRESENTS JO STAFFORD (10") 35
53 Capitol LC 6611 SUNDAY EVENING SONGS (10", with Gordon MacRae) 20
54 Capitol LC 6635 CAPITOL PRESENTS JO STAFFORD, VOL. 2 (10") 30
54 Columbia 33S 1024 AS YOU DESIRE ME (10") 30
54 Philips BBR 8011 MY HEART'S IN THE HIGHLANDS (10") 20
56 Philips BBR 8076 THE VOICE OF YOUR CHOICE (10") 25
56 Philips BBL 7100 HAPPY HOLIDAY (soundtrack) 18
57 Philips BBL 7169 ONCE OVER LIGHTLY 15
57 Philips BBL 7187 SKI TRAILS 15
58 Philips BBL 7243 SWINGIN' DOWN BROADWAY 15
59 Philips BBL 7290 I'LL BE SEEING YOU 15
59 Philips BBL 7327 BALLAD OF THE BLUES 15
60 Philips BBL 7395 JO STAFFORD SHOWCASE 18
61 Philips BBL 7428 JO + JAZZ (also stereo SBBL 595) 15/18

MINT VALUE £

62 Capitol (S)T 1653 AMERICAN FOLK SONGS (reissue, mono/stereo) . . . 12/15
62 Capitol (S)T 1696 WHISPERING HOPE (with Gordon MacRae) . . . 12
63 Encore ENC 144 JO STAFFORD'S SMOKE DREAMS . . . 12
64 Capitol (S)T 1921 THE HITS OF JO STAFFORD . . . 12
(see also Jonathan & Darlene Edwards, Gordon MacRae, Tommy Dorsey)

JO STAFFORD & FRANKIE LAINE
53 Columbia SCM 5014 Settin' The Woods On Fire/Piece A-Puddin' . . . 30
55 Philips BBR 8075 FLOATIN' DOWN TO COTTON TOWN (10" LP) . . . 50
(see also Frankie Laine)

TERRY STAFFORD
63 Stateside SS 225 Heartache On The Way/You Left Me Here To Cry . . . 15
64 London HLU 9871 Suspicion/Judy . . . 10
64 London HLU 9902 Playing With Fire/I'll Touch A Star . . . 10
64 London HLU 9923 Follow The Rainbow/Are You A Fool Like Me . . . 10
64 London RE-U 1436 SUSPICION (EP) . . . 75
64 London HA-U 8200 SUSPICION (LP) . . . 75

STAGEFRIGHT
85 STN STN 1 Strangers In The Night/Heartless/Rock City (no p/s) . . . 150

STAIFFI & HIS MUSTAFAS
60 Pye International 7N 25057 Mustafa Cha Cha Cha/Zoubida . . . 6

STAINED GLASS
74 Sweet Folk & C. SFA 019 OPEN ROAD (LP) . . . 90

CHRIS STAINTON & GLEN TURNER
76 Decca SKL-R 5259 TUNDRA (LP) . . . 12
(see also Made In Sheffield, Joe Cocker, Grease Band)

STAIRS
92 Imaginary MIRAGE 029 Weed Bus (12", unissued, test pressings only, proof p/s) . . . 12

STAIRSTEPS
71 Buddah 2011 092 Stay Close To Me/I Made A Mistake . . . 10
75 Dark Horse AMS 5505 From Us To You/Time (some in USA p/s) . . . 20/10
76 Dark Horse AMS 5507 Pasado/Throwin' Stones Atcha . . . 10
71 Buddah 2359 021 STEP BY STEP BY STEP (LP) . . . 30
71 Buddah 2365 015 STAY CLOSE TO ME (LP) . . . 30
72 Buddah 2365 016 THE STAIRSTEPS (LP) . . . 30
76 Dark Horse AMLH 22004 2ND RESSURECTION (LP) . . . 35
(see also Five Stairsteps)

STAIRWAY
87 New World NWC 143 AQUAMARINE (cassette) . . . 12
88 New World NWCD 168 MOONSTONE (CD) . . . 18
88 New World NWC 168 MOONSTONE (cassette) . . . 12
89 New World NWC 179 CHAKRA DANCE (cassette) . . . 12
(see also Jane Relf, Yardbirds, Renaissance)

STAKKER
(see under Humanoid)

STAMFORD BRIDGE
70 Penny Farthing PEN 715 Peter Osgood/Stamford Bridge . . . 10

TERRY STAMP
75 A&M AMLH 68329 FAT STICKS (LP, with lyric insert) . . . 15
(see also Third World War)

STAMPEDE
82 Polydor POSP 507 Days Of Wine And Roses/Photographs (p/s) . . . 12
82 Polydor POSP 507 Photographs/Days Of Wine And Roses (A-side switched, no p/s) . . . 35
82 Polydor POSPX 507 Days Of Wine And Roses/Movin' On/Photographs/Missing You (12", p/s) . . . 30
83 Polydor POSP 592 The Other Side/The Runner (p/s) . . . 10
82 Polydor ROCK 1 OFFICIAL BOOTLEG (LP) . . . 20
83 Polydor POLS 1083 HURRICANE TOWN (LP) . . . 15

STAMPEDERS
72 Stateside SS 2202 Monday Morning Choo Choo/Then Came The White Man . . . 5
72 Regal Zonophone RZ 3069 Johnny Lightning/Today's The Beginning Of The Rest Of Your Life . . . 6
73 Regal Zonophone RZ 3079 Oh My Lady/No Destination . . . 6
72 Regal Zono. SLRZ 1032 THE STAMPEDERS (LP) . . . 18
74 Regal Zono. SLRZ 1039 FROM THE FIRE (LP) . . . 18

JOE STAMPLEY
73 Dot DOT 145 Soul Song/Not Too Long Ago . . . 8

JEAN STANBACK
69 Deep Soul DS 9101 I Still Love You/If I Ever Needed Love . . . 25

STANDELLS
64 Liberty LIB 55722 I'll Go Crazy/Help Yourself . . . 22
66 Capitol CL 15446 Dirty Water/Rari . . . 40
65 Liberty LBY 1243 THE STANDELLS IN PERSON AT P.J.'s (LP) . . . 55

JOHNNY STANDLEY
56 Capitol EAP 1020 IT'S IN THE BOOK (EP) . . . 10

STANDS
00s Echo ECS 142 When This River Rolls Over You/She Speaks Of These Things (autographed p/s, 1000 only) . . . 15
00s Echo ECSCD 142 When This River Rolls Over You/She Speaks Of These Things/So Many Ways (CD) . . . 8

MINT VALUE £

ARNOLD STANG

59 Fontana H 226 Where Ya' Calling From, Charlie/Ivy Will Cling . . . 7
59 Fontana H 226 Where Ya' Calling From, Charlie/Ivy Will Cling (78) . . . 8

IVAN STANG

97 XXX X-DAY 23 EMBRACE YOUR NORTH TIBETAN HERITAGE! (LP, 1-sided, with 'rant' insert) . . . 20

PAUL STANLEY

79 Casablanca CAN 140 Hold Me Touch Me/Goodbye (p/s) . . . 12
79 Casablanca CAN 140 Hold Me Touch Me/Goodbye (p/s, purple vinyl with mask & picture label, most with mispressed B-side: "Love In Chains") . . . 20
(see also Kiss)

PETE STANLEY & WIZZ JONES

65 Columbia DB 7776 The Ballad Of Hollis Brown/Riff Minor . . . 15
66 Columbia SX 6083 SIXTEEN TONS OF BLUEGRASS (LP) . . . 100
(see also Wizz Jones)

PETE STANLEY & ROGER KNOWLES

70s Xtra TRANS 1146 PICKING AND SINGING (LP) . . . 35

STANLEY BROTHERS

61 Melodisc MLP 12-118 MOUNTAIN SONG FAVOURITES (LP) . . . 12
61 Melodisc MLP 12-122 SACRED SONGS FROM THE HILLS (LP) . . . 12

ROY STANNARD ORCHESTRA

87 SS SS 100 The Peanut Vendor/'Swingin' ' The Blues . . . 5

STEVE STANNARD

60 Embassy WB 375 Reveille Rock/BOBBY BRITTON: Dance With Me . . . 5
60 Embassy WB 375 Reveille Rock/BOBBY BRITTON: Dance With Me (78) . . . 6
60 Embassy WB 385 Theme From A Summer's Place/RIKKI HENDERSON: What In The World . . . 5
60 Embassy WB 385 Theme From A Summer's Place/RIKKI HENDERSON: What In The World (78) . . . 6
60 Embassy WB 400 Down Yonder/RIKKI HENDERSON: Ain't Misbehavin' . . . 5
60 Embassy WB 400 Down Yonder/RIKKI HENDERSON: Ain't Misbehavin' (78) . . . 6
60 Embassy WB 415 Walk Don't Run/Never On Sunday . . . 5
60 Embassy WB 415 Walk Don't Run/Never On Sunday (78) . . . 8
(see also Bud Ashton, Matt Bryant & Linda Joyce, Bobby Britton, Rikki Henderson)

LISA STANSFIELD

81 Devil DEV 2 Your Alibis/Thought Police (p/s) . . . 6

VIV(IAN) STANSHALL

70 Liberty LBF 15309 Labio-Dental Fricative/Paper Round (with Sean Head Show Band featuring Eric Clapton) . . . 30
71 Fly BUG 4 Suspicion (with Gargantuan Chums)/Blind Date (with biG GRunt) . . . 12
74 Warner Bros K 16424 Lakonga/Baba Tunde . . . 7
76 Harvest HAR 5114 Young Ones/Are You Havin' Any Fun/Question . . . 20
80 Charisma CB 373 Terry Keeps His Clips On/King Cripple (p/s) . . . 6
81 Charisma CB 382 Calypso To Colapso/Smoke Signals At Night (p/s) . . . 5
74 Warner Bros K 56052 MEN OPENING UMBRELLAS AHEAD (LP, with inner) . . . 80
78 Charisma CAS 1139 SIR HENRY AT RAWLINSON END (LP, soundtrack, with insert) . . . 22
81 Charisma CAS 1153 TEDDY BOYS DON'T KNIT (LP) . . . 18
(see also Bonzo Dog [Doo Dah] Band, Grimms)

STAPLE SINGERS

64 Riverside 106902 RIF Hammer And Nails/Glory Land . . . 10
67 Columbia DB 8292 For What It's Worth/Are You Sure? . . . 25
69 Soul City SC 117 For What It's Worth/Are You Sure? (reissue) . . . 18
69 Stax STAX 118 I See It/The Ghetto . . . 5
71 Stax 2025 019 Heavy Makes You Happy/Love Is Plentiful . . . 5
72 Stax 2025 068 Respect Yourself/You're Gonna Make Me Cry . . . 5
72 Stax 2025 110 I'll Take You There/Just Another Soldier . . . 5
62 Riverside REP 3220 THE SAVIOUR IS BORN (EP) . . . 10
63 Stateside SL 10015 SWING LOW (LP) . . . 25
63 Riverside RLP 3501 HAMMER AND NAILS (LP) . . . 25
65 Fontana 688 515 ZL UNCLOUDY DAY (LP) . . . 20
66 Columbia SX 6023 FREEDOM HIGHWAY (LP) . . . 20
69 Stax (S)XATS 1004 SOUL FOLK IN ACTION (LP) . . . 15
69 Stax SXATS 1018 WE'LL GET OVER (LP) . . . 15
71 Stax 2362 005 THE STAPLE SINGERS (LP) . . . 12
71 Stax 2362 011 SOUL FOLK IN ACTION (LP, reissue) . . . 12
72 Stax STX 1001 CITY IN THE SKY (LP) . . . 12
72 Stax 2325 069 BEALTITUDE/RESPECT YOURSELF (LP) . . . 12

CYRIL STAPLETON & HIS ORCHESTRA

54 Decca F 10293 Long Distance Love/There'll Be No Teardrops Tonight . . . 8
55 Decca F 10456 Tango Mambo/Mexican Madness . . . 8
55 Decca F 10470 Fanfare Boogie/Time After Time . . . 10
55 Decca F 10488 Elephant Tango/Gabrielle . . . 15
55 Decca F 10559 Blue Star (The "Medic" Theme) (with Julie Dawn)/Honey Babe (with Gordon Langhorn) . . . 20
56 Decca F 10703 The Italian Theme/Come Next Spring . . . 12
56 Decca F 10735 The Happy Whistler (with Desmond Lane)/Tiger Tango . . . 8
56 Decca F 10793 Highway Patrol/Maids Of Madrid . . . 10
57 Decca F 10883 Rock, Fiddle, Rock/Chantez, Chantez . . . 7
57 Decca F 10912 Forgotten Dreams/It's Not For Me To Say . . . 6
58 Decca F 10979 Monday Blues (Parts 1 & 2) . . . 8
58 Decca F 11094 Nick Nack Paddy Whack/The Inn Of The Sixth Happiness . . . 5
59 Decca F 11180 North West Frontier/Third Man Theme . . . 5
66 Pye 7N 17040 The Theme From The Power Game/'Lil (some in p/s) . . . 8/5
67 Pye 7N 17397 No That's Me Over Here/The Flower Girls . . . 6

MINT VALUE £

68	Pye 7N 17629	The Forsyte Saga/The Lonely Sea And The Sky (some in p/s)	8/5
69	Pye 7N 17807	Department S (Theme)/W. Somerset Maugham TV Theme (some in p/s)	30/15
54	Decca DFE 6288	PRESENTING CYRIL STAPLETON (EP)	10
54	Decca DFE 6340	PRESENTING CYRIL STAPLETON NO. 2 (EP)	8
55	Decca DFE 6454	DANCING IN THE DARK NO. 1 (EP)	8
55	Decca DFE 6455	DANCING IN THE DARK NO. 2 (EP)	8
67	Pye NEP 24272	A COUNTESS FROM HONG KONG (EP)	10
62	Ace Of Clubs ACL 1114	COME TWISTIN' (LP)	20

(see also Gordon Langhorn, Desmond Lane)

STEVEN STAPLETON & DAVID TIBET

91	United Dairies UD 037	THE SADNESS OF THINGS/THE GRAVE AND BEAUTIFUL NAME OF SADNESS (LP, one side each)	35

(see also Current 93, Nurse With Wound, Tibet & Stapleton)

STA-PREST

80	Avatar AAA 103	Schooldays/Tomorrow (p/s)	75

BUDDY STARCHER

64	London RE-B 1424	BUDDY STARCHER AND HIS MOUNTAIN GUITAR VOL. 1 (EP)	20
64	London RE-B 1425	BUDDY STARCHER AND HIS MOUNTAIN GUITAR VOL. 2 (EP)	20
64	London RE-B 1426	BUDDY STARCHER AND HIS MOUNTAIN GUITAR VOL. 3 (EP)	20

STARFIGHTERS

80	Motor City MCR 105	I'm Falling/Heaven And Hell (some in p/s)	40/7
81	Jive JIV 003	Alley Cat Blues/Don't Touch Me (p/s)	7
81	Jive JIVET 003	Alley Cat Blues/Don't Touch Me (12", p/s)	15
81	Jive JIVET 6	Power Crazy/I Want You (p/s)	6
81	Jive JIVET 6	Power Crazy/I Want You/Get Out While You Can (12", p/s)	8
81	Jive HOP 200	STARFIGHTERS (LP, with inner)	22
82	Jive HOP 200	POWER CRAZY (LP)	10
82	Jive HOP 205	IN FLIGHT MOVIE (LP)	12

STARGAZERS

53	Beltona BL 2594	White Heather For Luck/Rothesay Bay (78)	7
53	Decca F 10047	Broken Wings/Make It Soon (78)	12
54	Decca F 10213	I See The Moon/Eh Cumpari	30
54	Decca F 10259	The Happy Wanderer/Till We Two Are One	20
54	Decca F 10379	365 Kisses/I Need You Now	10
54	Decca F 10412	Rose Of The Wildwood/Come The Morning	10
55	Decca F 10437	Somebody/(My Baby Don't Love Me) No More (& Sonny Farrar Banjo Band)	18
55	Decca F 10523	The Crazy Otto Rag/Hey, Mr. Banjo	15
55	Decca F 10569	At The Steamboat River Ball/I Love You A Mountain (with Sonny Farrar Banjo Band)	8
55	Decca F 10594	Close The Door/I've Got Four Big Brothers	18
55	Decca F 10626	Twenty Tiny Fingers/An Old Beer Bottle	18
55	Decca F 10668	(Love Is) The Tender Trap/When The Swallows Say Goodbye	8
56	Decca F 10696	Zambesi/When The Swallows Say Goodbye	12
56	Decca F 10731	Hot Diggity (Dog Ziggity Boom)/Rockin' And Rollin'	15
56	Decca F 10775	She Loves To Rock/John Jacob Jingleheimer Smith	15
57	Decca F 10867	You Won't Be Around/Mangos	7
57	Decca F 10898	Honky Tonk Song/Golly!	7
57	Decca F 10916	Who Is It? (It's The Milkman)/Sorry, You'll Have To Wait	6
57	Decca F 10969	The Skiffling Dogs/Out Of This World	6
57	Decca F 10969	The Skiffling Dogs/Out Of This World (78)	8
58	Decca F 11034	Big Man/Lonely For A Letter	5
58	Decca F 11034	Big Man/Lonely For A Letter (78)	8
59	Decca F 11105	My Blue Heaven/How Ja Lika	5
59	Decca F 11105	My Blue Heaven/How Ja Lika (78)	8
60	Palette PG 9003	Manhattan Spiritual/Three Beautiful Words	5
56	Decca DFE 6341	THE STARGAZERS (EP)	30
56	Decca DFE 6362	ROCKIN' AND ROLLIN' (EP)	25
54	Decca LF 1186	PRESENTING THE STARGAZERS (10" LP)	45
59	Decca LK 4309	SOUTH OF THE BORDER (LP)	35

(see also Roy Smith & Stargazers, Lita Roza, Dickie Valentine)

STARJETS

78	Epic S EPC 6902	Here She Comes Again/Watch Out	15
79	Epic S EPC 6968	It Really Doesn't Matter/Schooldays	12
79	Epic S EPC 7123	Run With The Pack/Watch Out	10
79	Epic S EPC 6968/7123	It Really Doesn't Matter/Schooldays//Run With The Pack/Watch Out (double pack, die-cut sleeves, promo only)	25
79	Epic S EPC 7417	Ten Years/One More Word (p/s)	10
79	Epic S EPC 7417	Ten Years/One More Word (Manchester gig issue, stamped white labels)	20
79	Epic S EPC 7770	War Stories/Do The Push (p/s)	15
79	Epic S EPC 7986	Schooldays/What A Life (p/s)	25
80	Epic S EPC 8276	Shiraleo/Standby 19 (p/s)	10
79	Epic EPC 83534	GOD BLESS STARJETS (LP)	25

STARLIGHTERS

50	Capitol CL 13263	Rag Mop/If Not Bad (78)	6

STARLINGS

80s	Ruffin A-M 029	NEW BLOOD (EP)	8

STARLITES

73	Downtown DT 502	You're A Wanted Man/G.G. ALL STARS: Back To Dubwise	6
74	Big Shot BI 629	Mama Dee Part One/Mama Dee Part Two	8
75	Bullet BU 554	Healing In The Barnyard/G.G. ALL STARS: Version	5

(see also Bellfield)

MINT VALUE £

CINDY STARR

68	C'mbia Blue Beat DB 107	Pain Of Love/Hippy Ska (as Cindy Starr & Rude Boys)	18
68	C'mbia Blue Beat DB 110	The Way I Do/Sad Movies (Make Me Cry) (as Cindy Starr & Mopeds)	15

(see also Mopeds, Teardrops)

EDWIN STARR

66	Polydor BM 56702	Stop Her On Sight (S.O.S.)/I Have Faith In You (demos £150)	20
66	Polydor BM 56717	Headline News/Harlem	18
67	Polydor BM 56726	It's My Turn Now/Girls Are Getting Prettier	20
68	Polydor BM 56753	Stop Her On Sight (S.O.S.)/Headline News (reissue)	10
67	Tamla Motown TMG 630	I Want My Baby Back/Gonna Keep On Tryin' Till I Win	20
68	Tamla Motown TMG 646	I Am The Man For You Baby/My Weakness Is You	30
68	Tamla Motown TMG 672	25 Miles/Mighty Good Lovin' (demos £30)	10
69	Tamla Motown TMG 692	Way Over There/If My Heart Could Tell The Story	10
69	Tamla Motown TMG 720	Oh How Happy/O, O, O, Baby (demos only, unissued, with Blinky)	150+
70	Tamla Motown TMG 725	Time/Running Back And Forth	8
70	Tamla Motown TMG 754	War/He Who Picks A Rose	6
71	Tamla Motown TMG 764	Stop The War Now!/Gonna Keep On Tryin' Till I Win	6
71	Tamla Motown TMG 790	Agent Double 0 Soul/Back Street	10
72	Tamla Motown TMG 810	Funky Music Sho' Nuff Turns Me On/Cloud Nine	5
73	Tamla Motown TMG 875	Love The Lonely People's Prayer/You've Got My Soul On Fire	5
73	Tamla Motown TMG 930	Ain't It Hell Up In Harlem/Who's Right Or Wrong	5
75	Bradleys BRAD 7520	Stay With Me/I'll Never Forget You	5
75	Bradleys BRAD 7531	Pain/Party	5
76	GTO GT 65	Accident/Eavesdropper	5
70s	Tamla Motown TMG 905	Stop Her On Sight/Headline News (reissue)	5
70s	Tamla Motown TMG 1028	Time/Running Back And Forth (reissue)	5
69	T. Motown (S)TML 11094	SOUL MASTER (LP)	35
69	T. Motown (S)TML 11115	25 MILES (LP)	30
70	T. Motown (S)TML 11131	JUST WE TWO (LP, as Edwin Starr & Blinky)	25
70	Tamla Motown STML 11171	WAR AND PEACE (LP)	15
72	Tamla Motown STML 11199	INVOLVED (LP)	15
72	Tamla Motown STML 11209	THE HITS OF EDWIN STARR (LP)	15
74	Tamla Motown STML 11260	HELL UP IN HARLEM (LP, soundtrack)	15

(see also Blinky & Edwin Starr, Holidays)

FRANK STARR

62	London HLU 9545	Little Bitty Feeling/Lost In A Dream	15

FREDDIE STARR & MIDNIGHTERS

63	Decca F 11663	Who Told You?/Peter Gunn Locomotion	30
63	Decca F 11786	It's Shaking Time/Baby Blue	35
64	Decca F 12009	Never Cry On Someone's Shoulder/Just Keep On Dreaming	40
71	A&M AMS 838	Naomi/Free To Carry On (solo)	5
78	PVK PVK 004	FREDDIE STARR (LP)	12

(see also Howie Casey & Seniors)

JIMMY STARR

58	London HL 8731	It's Only Make Believe/Ooh Crazy	30
58	London HL 8731	It's Only Make Believe/Ooh Crazy (78)	20

KAY STARR

78s

50	Capitol CL 13295	If I Could Be With You/Flow Gently Sweet Afton (with Red Nichols)	6
50	Capitol CL 13420	Oh Babe/The Texas Song	6
51	Vogue V 9009	Ain't Misbehavin'/Good For Nothin' Joe	7
51	Vogue V 9010	Them There Eyes/What Is This Thing Called Love?	7
58	RCA RCA 1065	Stroll Me/Rockin' Chair	6

45s

54	Capitol CL 14151	Am I A Toy Or A Treasure?/Fortune In Dreams	20
54	Capitol CL 14167	Fool, Fool, Fool/Allez-Vous En	20
55	HMV 7M 300	If Anyone Finds This, I Love You/Turn Right	15
55	HMV 7M 307	Foolishly Yours/For Better Or Worse	15
55	HMV 7M 315	Where, What Or When?/Good And Lonesome	15
56	HMV 7M 371	Rock And Roll Waltz/I've Changed My Mind 1,000 Times	20
56	HMV 7M 420	Second Fiddle/Love Ain't Right	15
57	HMV POP 345	A Little Loneliness/Touch And Go	10
57	HMV POP 357	Jamie Boy/The Things I Never Had	10
58	RCA RCA 1065	Stroll Me/Rockin' Chair	7
60	Capitol CL 15105	Riders In The Sky/Night Train	6
60	Capitol CL 15137	Wheel Of Fortune/If You Love Me (Really Love Me)	7
60	Capitol CL 15154	Just For A Thrill/Out In The Cold Again	5
61	Capitol CL 15194	Foolin' Around/Kay's Lament	6
61	Capitol CL 15213	Nobody/I'll Never Be Free	5
63	Capitol CL 15293	Swingin' At The Hungry O/Bossa Nova Cassanova	5
63	Capitol CL 15308	No Regrets/Cherche La Rose	5
64	Capitol CL 15354	It's Happening All Over Again/Dancing On My Tears	5

EPs

55	Vogue EPV 1014	KAY STARR	15
56	HMV 7EG 8165	WHAT A STAR IS KAY	12
56	HMV 7EG 8184	KAY STARR'S AGAIN	12
60	Top Rank JKP 2042	HEAVENLY KAY STARR	15
60	Capitol EAP1 1254	MOVING	12
60	Capitol EAP2 1254	MOVING PT. 2	12
60	Capitol EAP3 1254	MOVING PT. 3	15
61	Capitol EAP 1-20063	WHEEL OF FORTUNE	18
62	Capitol EAP 1-20210	WELL I ASK YOU	12

LPs

53	Capitol LC 6574	CAPITOL PRESENTS KAY STARR (10")	30
54	Capitol LC 6630	THE KAY STARR STYLE (10")	30
56	Capitol LC 6835	THE HITS OF KAY STARR (10")	30
57	Capitol T 580	IN A BLUE MOOD	20
57	London HA-U 2039	SWINGING WITH THE STARR	40
58	RCA RD 27056	BLUE STARR	20
60	Capitol (S)T 1254	MOVIN'!	15
60	Capitol (S)T 1303	LOSERS, WEEPERS	15
60	Capitol (S)T 1374	MOVIN' ON BROADWAY	15
61	Capitol T 1358	ONE MORE TIME	15
61	Capitol (S)T 1438	JAZZ SINGER	15
62	Capitol T 1468	ALL STARR HITS!	15
62	Capitol (S)T 1681	I CRY BY NIGHT	15
63	Capitol (S)T 1795	JUST PLAIN COUNTRY	15
64	Capitol (S)T 2106	THE FABULOUS FAVOURITES	15
60s	World Record Club T 100	WISH UPON A STARR	12

LUCILLE STARR

64	London HL 9900	The French Song/Sit Down And Write Me A Letter	7

LUCKY STARR

62	Parlophone R 4963	I've Been Everywhere/Wrong	7

MAXINE STARR

63	London HLU 9712	Wishing Star/Sailor Boy	10

RANDY STARR

57	London HL 8443	After School/Heaven High (Man So Low)	45
57	London HL 8443	After School/Heaven High (Man So Low) (78)	20
58	Felsted AF 106	Pink Lemonade/Count On Me	15
58	Felsted AF 106	Pink Lemonade/Count On Me (78)	10
60	Top Rank JAR 264	Workin' On The Santa Fe/You're Growing Up	7

RINGO STARR

71	Apple R 5898	It Don't Come Easy/Early 1970 (p/s, B-side with Ringo or George Harrison production credit)	6/5
72	Apple R 5944	Back Off Boogaloo/Blindman (p/s, blue label)	5
73	Apple R 5992	Photograph/Down And Out (p/s)	6
74	Apple R 5995	You're Sixteen/Devil Woman (p/s)	5
74	Apple R 6000	Only You/Call Me (p/s)	5
75	Apple R 6004	Snookeroo/Oo-wee	12
76	Apple R 6011	Oh My My/No No Song	20
76	Polydor 2001 694	A Dose Of Rock 'N' Roll/Cryin'	10
76	Polydor 2001 695	You Don't Know Me At All/Cryin' (unissued in U.K., Europe only)	
76	Polydor 2001 699	Hey Baby/Lady Gaye	10
77	Polydor 2001 734	Drowning In The Sea Of Love/Just A Dream	100
78	Polydor 2001 782	Lipstick Traces/Old Time Relovin' (unissued in U.K., Europe only)	
78	Polydor 2001 795	Tonight/Heart On My Sleeve	100
72	R.O.R. ROR 2001	Steel (1-sided promo-only interview disc for 'Ringo Or Robin' reception at Liberty's department store; available for 1 week only p/s)	900
74	Parlophone PSR 374	Interview By Bob Mercer With Ringo For The Salesmen And Uxbridge Road/Only You (promo only)	400
70s	Apple R 5944	Back Off Boogaloo/Blindman (green apple label)	250
70s	Parlophone R 5995	You're Sixteen/Devil Woman (p/s)	25
70	Apple PCS 7101	SENTIMENTAL JOURNEY (LP)	20
70	Apple TD-PCS 7101	SENTIMENTAL JOURNEY (reel-to-reel tape, jewel case)	25
70	Apple PAS 10002	BEAUCOUPS OF BLUES (LP, gatefold sleeve)	20
78	Polydor 2480 429	SCOUSE THE MOUSE (LP, with Adam Faith, Donald Pleasance etc.; some w/stickered sleeve & printed [not photocopied] competition insert)	110/50
78	Polydor 3194 429	SCOUSE THE MOUSE (cassette)	40
90	EMI EMS 1375	RINGO STARR & HIS ALL STARR BAND (LP)	30

(see also Beatles, Harry Nilsson, Billy Connolly & Chris Tummings, Traveling Wilburys)

STELLA STARR

67	Piccadilly 7N 35366	Bring Him Back/Say It	35

TONY STARR

64	Decca F 11847	I'll Take A Rocket To The Moon/Next Train Leaving	55

STARR BOUNDS

75	Horse HOSS 95	Heavenly (parts 1 & 2)	8

STARSAILOR

00s	Chrysalis CHS 5123	Fever/Coming Down/Love Is Here (gatefold p/s)	8
00s	Chrysalis CDCHSS 5123	Fever/Coming Down/Love Is Here (CD, digipak)	8
00s	Chrysalis CHS 5125	Good Souls/The Way Young Lovers Do (p/s, with fold-out picture insert)	6
00s	Chrysalis CHS 5130	Alcoholic/Let It Shine (p/s)	6
00s	Chrysalis CHSDJ 5136	Poor Misguided Fool (Soulsavers Remix)/(Single Version) (promo-only, die-cut sleeve)	10

STARS OF HEAVEN

85	Hotwire HWS 853	Clothes Of Pride/All About You (beige or black label, some with p/s)	8/6

STAR SPANGLES

02	Capitol R 6593	Which Of The Two Of Us Is Gonna Burn This House Down/Stain Glass Shoes (p/s)	10

STARTIME KIDS

59	Fontana H 182	The Railroad Song/I Don't Want To Walk Without You, Baby	6
59	Fontana H 182	The Railroad Song/I Don't Want To Walk Without You, Baby (78)	6

MINT VALUE £

STATE OF MICKEY & TOMMY

67	Mercury MF 996	With Love From One To Five/I Know What I Will Do	100
67	Mercury MF 1009	Frisco Bay/Nobody Knows Where You've Been	70

(see also Spooky Tooth, Nero & Gladiators, Foreigner)

STATESMEN

63	Studio Republic	FIVE PLUS ONE (LP, private pressing)	110

STATESMEN

63	Decca F 11687	Look Around/I'm Wondering	7
64	Fontana TF 432	I've Just Fallen In Love/It's All Happening	7

STATE STREET RAMBLERS

50	Tempo R 18	Weary Way Blues/Cootie Stomp (78)	6
60s	Collector JE 123	SMALL JAZZ BAND VOL. 1 (EP, shared with Lovey Austin Blue Serenaders)	8

STATE STREET SWINGERS/CHICAGO BLACK SWANS

73	Collectors Items 003	STATE STREET SWINGERS (LP)	12

STATE TROOPER

85	Neat 5212	SHE GOT THE LOOK (12" EP)	10

STATIC

67	Page One POF 039	When You Went Away/Let Me Tell You	10

STATIC

81	Eeyo EEYO 1	Voice On The Line/Stealin' (no p/s, 1,000 only)	10

(see also White Lightning)

STATIC

90s	City Centre Offices BLOCK 013	Headphones (plain sleeve with inserts, 1000 copies)	9
90s	City Centre Offices BLOCK 016	TURN ON SWITCH OFF (12" EP)	8
90s	City Centre Offices BLOCK 021	GHOST BOY (Feat. Ronald Lippok) (12" EP, custom sleeve)	8

STATION SKIFFLE GROUP

57	Esquire 10-503	Don't You Rock Me Daddy-O/Hugged My Honey (78)	12
57	Esquire 10-516	Steamboat Bill/Titanic (78)	22
58	Esquire EP 161	STATION SKIFFLE GROUP (EP)	65

(see also Jimmy Miller)

STATION 360

84	SRT STA 360	Optimist	30

STATLER BROTHERS

65	CBS 201796	Flowers On The Wall/Bill Christian	5
66	CBS BPG 62713	FLOWERS ON THE WALL (LP)	15

(see also Johnny Cash)

CANDI STATON

69	Capitol CL 15601	I'd Rather Be An Old Man's Sweetheart/For You	6
69	Capitol CL 15620	Heart On A String/I'm Just A Prisoner	5
70	Capitol CL 15646	Sweet Feeling/Evidence	5
70	Capitol CL 15658	Stand By Your Man/How Can I Put Out The Flame (When You Keep The Fire Burning)	5
75	United Artists UP 35823	Love Chain/I'm Gonna Hold On	6
70	Capitol ST 21631	I'M JUST A PRISONER (LP)	12

DAKOTA STATON

55	Capitol CL 14314	Don't Leave Me Now/A Little You	15
55	Capitol CL 14339	I Never Dreamt/Abracadabra	15
58	Capitol CL 14828	Trust In Me/The Late, Late Show	5
58	Capitol CL 14870	The Party's Over/Invitation	6
59	Capitol CL 14917	Confessin' The Blues/(I'm Left With The) Blues In My Heart (with George Shearing Quintet)	8
59	Capitol CL 14931	My Funny Valentine/A Foggy Day	6
59	Capitol EAP1 1054	THE DYNAMIC DAKOTA STATON (EP)	10
59	Capitol EAP2 1054	THE DYNAMIC DAKOTA STATON (EP)	10
59	Capitol EAP3 1054	THE DYNAMIC DAKOTA STATON (EP)	10
58	Capitol T 876	THE LATE, LATE SHOW (LP)	15
59	Capitol (S)T 1054	THE DYNAMIC DAKOTA STATON (LP)	15
59	Capitol T 1170	CRAZY HE CALLS ME (LP)	15
60	Capitol (S)T 1325	MORE THAN THE MOOD (LP)	15
60	Capitol (S)T 1387	BALLADS AND THE BLUES (LP)	15
61	Capitol (S)T 1241	TIME TO SWING (LP)	15
62	Capitol (S)T 1597	'ROUND MIDNIGHT (LP)	15
62	Capitol (S)T 1649	DAKOTA AT STORYVILLE (LP)	15

STATUES

60	London HLG 9192	Blue Velvet/Keep The Hall Burning	45

STATUS QUO

PYE SINGLES

68	Pye 7N 17449	Pictures Of Matchstick Men/Gentleman Joe's Sidewalk Café (some with '75c Minimum' on B-side label credit)	8
68	Pye 7N 17497	Black Veils Of Melancholy/To Be Free	20
68	Pye 7N 17581	Ice In The Sun/When My Mind Is Not Live	8
68	Pye 7N 17650	Technicolor Dreams/Paradise Flat (withdrawn, demos more common, £300)	1000
69	Pye 7N 17665	Make Me Stay A Bit Longer/Aunt Nellie	25
69	Pye 7N 17728	Are You Growing Tired Of My Love/So Ends Another Life	25
69	Pye 7N 17825	The Price Of Love/Little Miss Nothing	25

MINT VALUE £

70	Pye 7N 17907	Down The Dustpipe/Face Without A Soul (black, blue or reissue Precision labels)	5/5/5
70	Pye 7N 17998	In My Chair/Gerdundula (some with p/s)	75/8
71	Pye 7N 45077	Tune To The Music/Good Thinking	25
73	Pye 7N 45229	Mean Girl/Everything (blue labels)	5
73	Pye 7N 45253	Gerdundula/Lakky Lady (red label or PRT reissue)	8/7
77	Pye BD 103	Down The Dustpipe/Mean Girl/In My Chair/Gerdundula (12", generic sleeve, reissued on PRT)	8/10
78	Pye 7N 46095	Mean Girl/In My Chair	5
78	Pye 7N 46103	Pictures of Matchstick Men/Ice In The Sun (red labels, reissued on PRT)	each 5
79	Pye Flashbacks FBS 2	Pictures Of Matchstick Men/Down The Dustpipe (yellow vinyl, p/s)	8
79	Pye Flashbacks FBS 2	Pictures Of Matchstick Men/Down The Dustpipe (black vinyl, no p/s, reissued on PRT)	6
79	Pye 7P 103	In My Chair/Gerdundula (p/s)	8
79	Pye QUO 1/SFI 434	In My Chair (flexi, concert freebie, some with *Record Mirror* Quo special)	15/7

VERTIGO SINGLES

72	Vertigo 6059 071	Paper Plane/Softer Ride (swirl label, solid centre or large centre hole)	12/8
73	Vertigo 6059 085	Caroline/Joanne (with B-side miscredited to Lancaster)	6
74	Vertigo 6059 101	Break The Rules/Lonely Night (mispressed, B-side labels on both sides)	10
75	Vertigo QUO 13	STATUS QUO LIVE! (EP)	5
76	Vertigo 6059 153	Wild Side Of Life/All Through The Night (brown plastic labels)	6
77	Vertigo 6059 184	Rockin' All Over The World/Ring Of A Change (p/s, some with small poster)	25/15
78	Vertigo QUO 2	Accident Prone/Let Me Fly (p/s)	5
79	Vertigo 6059 242	Whatever You Want/Hard Ride (p/s)	5
79	Vertigo 6059 248	Living On An Island/Runaway (p/s)	5
80	Vertigo QUO 4	Lies/Don't Drive My Car (p/s, with B-side misspellings 'MyiCar' or 'Caf')	each 10
81	Vertigo QUO 5	Something 'Bout You Baby I Like/Enough Is Enough (red or blue p/s)	5
82	Vertigo QUO 8	She Don't Fool Me/Never Too Late (p/s)	5
82	Vertigo QUO 9	Jealousy/Calling The Shots (unreleased in U.K.; Irish promos only)	150+
82	Vertigo QUOP 10	Caroline (Live At The NEC)/Dirty Water (live) (picture disc)	8
82	Vertigo QUO 1012	Caroline (Live At The NEC)/Dirty Water (live)/Down Down (live) (12", p/s)	10
83	Vertigo QUO B-11	Ol' Rag Blues/Stay The Night (blue vinyl, different rear to p/s)	6
83	Vertigo QUO 1112	Ol' Rag Blues (Extended Remixed Edition)/Stay The Night/ Whatever You Want (live) (12", p/s)	12
83	Vertigo QUO 12	A Mess Of Blues/Big Man (reversed p/s with 'table' picture on rear)	12
83	Vertigo QUO 1212	A Mess Of Blues (Extended)/Big Man/Young Pretender (12", p/s)	15
83	Vertigo QUO 14	Marguerita Time/Resurrection (p/s, blue plastic or white paper label)	5/6
83	Vertigo QUOP 14	Marguerita Time/Resurrection (picture disc)	18
83	Vertigo QUO 1414	Marguerita Time/Resurrection//Caroline/Joanne (double pack, stickered gatefold p/s)	25
84	Vertigo QUO 15	Too Close To The Ground/I Wonder Why (release cancelled)	
84	Vertigo QUO 15	Going Down Tonight/Too Close To The Ground (p/s, some mispressed with A-side labels moulded onto both sides)	5/10
84	Vertigo QUO 16	The Wanderer/Can't Be Done (blue plastic labels)	6
84	Vertigo QUOP 16	The Wanderer/Can't Be Done (12" clear vinyl, picture labels)	20
85	Vertigo QUO 17	Naughty Girl (actually "Dreamin' ") (unreleased)	
86	Vertigo QUO 18	Rollin' Home/Lonely (p/s, blue or bronze plastic labels)	each 6
86	Vertigo QUOPD 18	Rollin' Home/Lonely ('Q'-shaped picture disc)	15
86	Vertigo QUOPD 18	Rollin' Home/Lonely (uncut picture disc)	175
86	Vertigo QUO 19	Red Sky/Don't Give It Up (p/s, blue plastic labels)	6
86	Vertigo QUODP 19	Red Sky/Don't Give It Up//Rockin' All Over The World/Whatever You Want (double pack, gatefold p/s)	10
86	Vertigo QUOPB 191	Red Sky/Don't Give It Up/The Milton Keynes Medley (12", 'Wembley Souvenir Pack', poster p/s)	20
86	Vertigo QUO 20	In The Army Now/Heartburn (stickered p/s, with sew-on patch, shrinkwrapped)	12
86	Vertigo QUOPD 20	In The Army Now/Heartburn (picture disc)	25
86	Vertigo QUODP 20	In The Army Now/Heartburn//Marguerita Time/ What You're Proposing (double pack, gatefold p/s)	10
86	Vertigo QUO 2012	In The Army Now (Military Mix)/Heartburn/Late Last Night (12", stickered p/s, with poster)	25
86	Vertigo QUOP 21	Dreamin'/Long-Legged Girls (p/s, with foldout poster/calendar)	15
88	Vertigo QUOH 22	Ain't Complaining/That's Alright ('History Pack' with family tree in envelope)	6
88	Vertigo QUOCD 22	Ain't Complaining (Extended)/That's Alright/Lean Machine/ In The Army Now (Remix) (CD, card sleeve)	15
88	Vertigo QUOH 23	Who Gets The Love?/Hallowe'en ('History Pack' with family tree part 2, in envelope p/s)	8
88	Vertigo QUOCD 23	Who Gets The Love? (Extended)/Hallowe'en/The Reason For Goodbye/ The Wanderer (Sharon The Nag Mix) (CD, card sleeve)	25
88	Vertigo QUACD 1	Running All Over The World (Extended)/Magic/Whatever You Want (CD, card sleeve)	20
88	Vertigo QUO 2512	Burning Bridges (On And Off And On Again) (Extended Version)/ Whatever You Want/Marguerita Time (12", mispressing also including 7" edit)	10
88	Vertigo QUOCD 25	Burning Bridges (On And Off And On Again) (Extended Version)/ Whatever You Want/Marguerita Time (CD)	15
89	Vertigo 080 322-2	Ain't Complaining (Extended)/That's Alright/Lean Machine/ In The Army Now (Remix)/Ain't Complaining (Video) (CD Video)	20
89	Vertigo 080 630-2	Burning Bridges (On And Off And On Again) (Extended Version)/ Whatever You Want (Extended Version)/Marguerita Time/ Who Gets The Love?/Burning Bridges (Video) (CD Video)	25
89	Vertigo QUOMC 26	Not At All/Gone Thru The Slips (cassette)	5
89	Vertigo QUOCD 26	Not At All/Everytime I Think Of You/Gone Thru The Slips (CD)	10
89	Vertigo QUOP 27	Little Dreamer/Rotten To The Bone (p/s, shrinkwrapped with sew-on patch)	6
89	Vertigo QUOX 2712	Little Dreamer/Rotten To The Bone/Doing It All For You (12", gatefold p/s)	8
89	Vertigo QUOMC 27	Little Dreamer/Rotten To The Bone (cassette)	5
89	Vertigo QUOCD 27	Little Dreamer/Rotten To The Bone/Doing It All For You (CD)	10

MINT VALUE £

90	Vertigo QUOG 28	The Anniversary Waltz - Part One/The Power Of Rock (p/s, silver vinyl, with booklet)	10
90	Vertigo QUO 2812	The Anniversary Waltz/The Power Of Rock/Perfect Remedy (12", p/s, mispress, B-side plays "Little Lady" (live) & exclusive "Paper Plane" re-recording)	45
90	Vertigo QUO 2812	The Anniversary Waltz/The Power Of Rock/Perfect Remedy (12", p/s, mispress, A-side plays "The Power Of Rock [Full Version]")	45
91	Vertigo QUO 31	Fakin' The Blues (Edit)/Heavy Daze (p/s, swirl label, release cancelled, approximately 25 copies only)	200
91	Vertigo QUO 3112	Fakin' The Blues (Edit)/Fakin' The Blues (Album Version)/Heavy Daze/Better Times (12", swirl label, p/s, cancelled, approx. 25 copies only)	200
91	Vertigo QUOCD 31	Fakin' The Blues (Edit)/Fakin' The Blues (Album Version)/Heavy Daze/Better Times (CD, unissued, 2,000 later sent out by fan club, no inlay)	30
92	Vertigo QUO 3212	Rock 'Til You Drop/Medley/Forty-Five Hundred Times (12", p/s, mispressing, omits "Forty-Five Hundred Times")	15
92	Vertigo QUOCD 32	Rock 'Til You Drop/Medley/Forty-Five Hundred Times (CD in no'd guitar-shaped case)	12

OTHER SINGLES

75	Lyntone LYN 3154/5	Down Down/Break The Rules (Smiths Crisps flexidisc, a few with 'Smiths' p/s)	15/6
80s	Lyntone QUO 1-4	Interview picture discs (4-single pack)	20
89	Old Gold OG 9567	Rockin' All Over The World/Paper Plane (reissue, 2 different designs of p/s)	6
92	Polydor QUODD 33	Roadhouse Medley (Anniversary Waltz Part 25) (Radio Edit)/(Extended)/ Don't Drive My Car (Live) (CD, numbered 4-fold digipak, 2nd CD card template)	10
94	Polydor QUO 34	I Didn't Mean It/Whatever You Want (p/s, blue vinyl)	5
94	Polydor QUODD 34	I Didn't Mean It (Acoustic Version)/(Hooligan Version)/Survival/She Knew Too Much (CD, numbered digipak, 2nd CD card template)	10
94	Polydor QUO 35	Sherri Don't Fail Me Now (Edit)/Beautiful (p/s, red vinyl)	5
94	Polydor QUODD 35	Sherri Don't Fail Me Now (Extended)/Tossin' And Turnin'/Down To You (CD, numbered digipak, 2nd CD card template)	10
94	Polydor QUO 36	Restless (Orchestral Version)/And I Do (p/s, clear vinyl)	5
94	Polydor QUODD 36	Restless (LP Version)/And I Do/Democracy (CD, no'd digipak, 2nd CD card template)	8
95	PolyGram TV 577 512-7	When You Walk In The Room/Tilting At The Mill (numbered picture disc)	5
95	PolyGram TV 576262 7	Fun Fun Fun (with The Beach Boys)/Mortified (numbered picture disc)	8
96	PolyGram TV 576634 7	Don't Stop/Temporary Friend (numbered picture disc)	5
96	PolyGram TV 5759447	All Around My Hat (with Maddy Prior)/I'll Never Get Over You (numbered picture disc)	6
99	From The Makers Of... FTMOCD1	FAKIN' THE BLUES (MILLENNIUM EDITION) (CD, fanclub mail order-only edition, hand-no'd exclusive p/s, contains unreleased Vertigo CD [QUOCD 31])	50
00	PolyGram PSPCD464	NIGHT & DAY (CD EP, 4-track sampler, mail order-only via tokens from *The Mail On Sunday*, insufficient pressed to meet demand)	25

PROMO-ONLY SINGLES

68	Pye 7N 17449	Pictures Of Matchstick Men/Gentleman Joe's Sidewalk Café (75c Minimum) ('A' label)	60
68	Pye 7N 17497	Black Veils Of Melancholy/To Be Free ('A' label)	70
68	Pye 7N 17581	Ice In The Sun/When My Mind Is Not Live ('A' label)	60
68	Pye 7N 17650	Technicolor Dreams/Paradise Flat('A' label)	400
69	Pye 7N 17665	Make Me Stay A Bit Longer/Aunt Nellie ('A' label)	70
69	Pye 7N 17728	Are You Growing Tired Of My Love/So Ends Another Life ('A' label)	70
69	Pye 7N 17825	The Price Of Love/Little Miss Nothing ('A' label)	70
70	Pye 7N 17907	Down The Dustpipe/Face Without A Soul ('A' label)	60
70	Pye 7N 17998	In My Chair/Gerdundula ('A' label)	60
71	Pye 7N 45077	Tune To The Music/Good Thinking ('A' label)	60
72	Phonogram DJ 005	Roadhouse Blues/BLACK SABBATH: Children Of The Grave (100 copies only)	375
72	Vertigo 6059 071	Paper Plane/Softer Ride ('A' label)	45
73	Pye 7N 45229	Mean Girl/Everything ('A' label)	50
73	Pye 7N 45253	Gerdundula/Lakky Lady ('A' label)	40
75	Lyntone LYN 3154	Down Down (Smiths Crisps 1-sided gold flexidisc test pressing, plays "Bye Bye Baby" by Bay City Rollers)	25
75	Lyntone LYN 3155	Break The Rules (Smiths Crisps 1-sided gold flexidisc test pressing, plays "Bye Bye Baby" by Bay City Rollers)	25
79	Pye 7P 103	In My Chair/Gerdundula ('A' label)	20
81	Vertigo QUO JB 6	Rock 'N' Roll/Hold You Back (jukebox issue, B-side at 33rpm)	10
86	Vertigo QUODJ 2112	Dreamin' (Wet Mix)/Long-Legged Girls/The Quo Xmas Cake Mix (12")	15
88	Vertigo QUOLP 99	Ain't Complaining (12" promo, 1-sided)	30
88	Vertigo QUODJ 2212	Ain't Complaining (Extended)/That's Alright/Lean Machine (12")	10
88	Vertigo QUODJ 25	Burning Bridges (On & Off & On Again)/Burning Bridges (On & Off & On Again)	12
90	Vertigo (no cat. no.)	The Power Of Rock (Album Version)/(Single Edit)/Perfect Remedy (12" white label)	100
90	Vertigo QUO DJ 28	Anniversary Waltz - Part 1/Part 2 (in stock Part 1 p/s)	20
90	Vertigo QUO DJ 28	Anniversary Waltz/The Power Of Rock/Perfect Remedy (12")	20
91	Vertigo QUO 30	Can't Give You More (Eau Eau Eau Eau)/Dead In The Water (black plastic labels)	5
91	Vertigo QUO DJ 30	Can't Give You More/Dead In The Water (swirl label)	12
91	Vertigo STATUS 30	Can't Give You More (Radio Edit)/Dead In The Water (in stk'd stock p/s)	30
91	Vertigo QUOCDJ 30	Can't Give You More (Radio Edit)/Dead In The Water/Mysteries From The Ball (CD)	25
94	Polydor QUO 34	I Didn't Mean It/Whatever You Want (black vinyl jukebox pressing)	6
94	Polydor QUOCD34DJ	I Didn't Mean It (CD, p/s)	12
94	Polydor QUOCD35 DJ	Sherri Don't Fail Me Now (Edit)/Beautiful/In The Army Now (live) (CD, promo p/s containing commercial CD [QUOCD 35])	10
96	PolyGram TV PTQUO4	All Around My Hat (featuring Maddy Prior) (CD, no p/s)	15
99	Eagle (no cat. no.)	The Way It Goes (CD-R, title insert in slimline jewel case)	30
99	Eagle EAGXS101	Little White Lies/I Knew The Bride/Pictures Of Matchstick Men (CD-R, title insert in slimline jewel case)	30
99	Eagle (no cat. no.)	Twenty Wild Horses (CD-R, title insert in slimline jewel case)	30

99	Eagle (no cat. no.)	Twenty Wild Horses/Analyse Time/Obstruction Day (CD-R, title insert in slimline jewel case)	35
00	Universal (no cat. no.)	Mony Mony (CD-R, title insert in slimline jewel case)	30
00	Universal (no cat. no.)	Old Time Rock 'N' Roll (CD-R, title insert in slimline jewel case)	30
02	Universal QUO01	Jam Side Down (CD, p/s)	8
02	Universal QUO02	Jam Side Down/Blues And Rhythm (CD, p/s, for export only)	20
02	Universal (no cat. no.)	Jam Side Down/The Madness/Down Down (TOTP2)/Rockin' All Over The World (TOTP2) (CD-R, title insert in PVC wallet)	25
02	Universal SQ02	All Stand Up (Single Edit)/Heavy Traffic (Single Edit) (CD, p/s)	12

LPs

68	Pye N(S)PL 18220	PICTURESQUE MATCHSTICKABLE MESSAGES (mono/stereo)	80/65
69	Pye N(S)PL 18301	SPARE PARTS (blue label, mono/stereo)	85/65
69	Marble Arch MAL(S) 1193	STATUS QUO-TATIONS (mono/stereo, most stereo copies exported)	30/50
70	Pye NSPL 18344	MA KELLY'S GREASY SPOON (very early copies with poster)	50/15
71	Pye NSPL 18371	DOG OF TWO HEAD (gatefold sleeve, blue labels, reissued with red, black or PRT "Piccadilly Circus" labels)	15/12/15/20
72	Vertigo 6360 082	PILEDRIVER (swirl label, gatefold sleeve)	18
73	Vertigo 6360 098	HELLO! (spaceship label, with inner sleeve & poster)	15
74	Vertigo 9102 001	QUO (with poster/lyric sheet; also Record Club issue [ACB 00217])	12/25
75	Vertigo 9102 002	ON THE LEVEL (gatefold sleeve, with inner sleeve)	12
76	Vertigo 9102 006	BLUE FOR YOU (gatefold sleeve, with inner sleeve)	12
77	Pye FILD 005	THE FILE SERIES (2-LP, single sleeve with inner sleeves; repressed on Precision)	20
79	Pye NPSL 18607	JUST FOR THE RECORD (red vinyl)	15
79	Pye FILD 005	THE FILE SERIES (2-LP, reissue with different sleeve, inners; repressed on PRT)	18
82	Phonogram PRO BX 1	FROM THE MAKERS OF... (3-LP, with inserts in round metal tin, some no'd)	20/18
82	Phonogram PRO BX 1	FROM THE MAKERS OF... (3-LP, with inserts in round metal tin, mispressing – record 3 plays side 5 twice)	25
82	Phonogram PRO BX 1	FROM THE MAKERS OF... (3-LP, with inserts in round metal tin, mispressing – record 1 side 2 plays Siouxsie & The Banshees' "Melt (12" Mix)")	25
82	Phonogram PRO LP 1	FROM THE MAKERS OF... (3-LP, with inserts in cardboard box)	15
83	PRT DOW 10	WORKS (10" mini-LP)	10
83	Vertigo VERH 10	BACK TO BACK (in-store promo copies with poster insert)	18
85	PRT Flashbacks FBLP 8082	NANANA	15
88	PRT PYX 4007	FROM THE BEGINNING (picture disc)	25
90	Essential! ESBLP 136	THE EARLY WORKS (5-LP box set with book)	30
91	Baktabak LINT 5003	INTROSPECTIVE (clear vinyl, 6 Pye-era tracks & interview)	20
92	Polydor 517 367-1	LIVE ALIVE QUO (with inner sleeve)	20
94	Polydor 523 607-1	THIRSTY WORK (with inner sleeve)	22
03	Earmark EAR 42046	PICTURESQUE MATCHSTICKABLE MESSAGES (180g reissue, stk'd PVC wallet)	15

CASSETTES

81	Vertigo 7215 038	THE MUSIC OF STATUS QUO VOLUME 1: 1972-1974 (cassette-only compilation)	25
82	Phonogram PRO MC 1	FROM THE MAKERS OF... (2 cassettes with inserts in 7" box)	15
98	Readers Digest RDC1831-4	THE COMPLETE STATUS QUO (4 cassettes & book, mail-order only)	35

CDs

83	Vertigo 800 035-2	1+9+8+2	40
83	Vertigo 800 053-2	NEVER TOO LATE	40
83	Vertigo 814 66-2	BACK TO BACK	30
85	PRT CDNSP 773	THE BEST OF STATUS QUO (THE EARLY YEARS)	18
86	PRT CDMP 8834	MA KELLY'S GREASY SPOON	18
86	PRT CDMP 8837	DOG OF TWO HEAD	18
89	Vertigo 842 098-2	PERFECT REMEDY (two different inlay designs)	each 30
91	Vertigo 848 087-2	WHATEVER YOU WANT & JUST SUPPOSIN'	50
91	Vertigo 848 090-2	IF YOU CAN'T STAND THE HEAT & 1+9+8+2	25
98	Readers Digest RDCD1831-4	THE COMPLETE STATUS QUO (4-CD, mail-order only)	60
01	From The Makers Of ... FTMOCD2	FTMO LIVE! NO.1 (fanclub mail-order only, soundchecks & interviews)	50
02	Time Life TL SQC 069 827-2	THE ULTIMATE COLLECTION (4-CD, mail-order only)	45
03	From The Makers Of... FTMO LIVE 2-1/2 [matrix]	FTMO LIVE! NO.2 (2-CD, fanclub mail-order only)	25

PROMO-ONLY ALBUMS & ALBUM SAMPLERS

82	Phonogram PRO BX 1	FROM THE MAKERS OF... (3-LP, 20 copies in bronze tin for in-house use)	300+
86	Vertigo MADDOX 18	IN THE ARMY NOW (LP, 4-track sampler, includes unreleased version of "Dreamin'")	75
88	Vertigo QUOLP 99	AIN'T COMPLAINING (LP, 4-track one-sided sampler)	25
88	Vertigo	AIN'T COMPLAINING (box set containing LP sampler [QUOLP 99], cassette, 1-track video, photo & press sheet)	100
88	Music & Media MM 1221	INTERVIEW (LP, uncut test pressing for unreleased saw-shaped picture disc)	50
89	Vertigo 842 077-9	LITTLE DREAMER (CD, card p/s, 4-track sampler for PERFECT REMEDY album)	50
90	Phonogram (no cat. no.)	ROCKING ALL OVER THE YEARS SNIPPETS (cassette, titles inlay)	20
90	Vertigo 846 797-2	ROCKING ALL OVER THE YEARS (CD, in Butlin's party pack containing "Kiss Me Quo" baseball cap, stick of Status Quo rock, and selection of party poppers, streamers, whistle, trumpet, silver Quo balloons & pack of condoms, all with "Anniversary Waltz" stickers in custom carrier bag)	75
94	Polydor WORK1CD	THIRSTY WORK (CD, 5-track sampler, p/s, slimline jewel case)	12
96	PolyGram TV SQRAD1	30TH ANNIVERSARY (CD, 4-track sampler for 'Don't Stop' album, no p/s)	10
97	PolyGram TV QUO 5	WHATEVER YOU WANT – THE VERY BEST OF STATUS QUO (CD, 5-track sampler, no p/s)	12
97	PolyGram TV QUO 5-2	WHATEVER YOU WANT – THE VERY BEST OF STATUS QUO (CD, 5-track sampler different to above, no p/s, withdrawn)	25
99	Eagle (no cat. no.)	UNDER THE INFLUENCE (CD-R, titles inlay in slimline jewel case)	40
00	Universal QUO 1	FAMOUS IN THE LAST CENTURY (CD, 5-track sampler, no p/s)	10
00	Universal QUO 2	FAMOUS IN THE LAST CENTURY (CD, 3-track sampler, no p/s)	15

MINT VALUE £

Year	Label / Cat. No.	Title	Value
01	Vertigo QUOBOX1	ROCKERS ROLLIN': QUO IN TIME 1972-2000 (CD, 10-track sampler, double card p/s)	20
01	Universal 5892162	ROCKERS ROLLIN': QUO IN TIME 1972-2000 (set of 4 CD-Rs with title inserts)	100
02	Universal (no cat. no.)	HEAVY TRAFFIC (CD-R, titles insert, 13- or 14-track version)	30/35
02	Universal (no cat. no.)	5 TRACKS TAKEN FROM THE FORTHCOMING ALBUM "HEAVY TRAFFIC" (CD-R, titles insert)	35
02	Sanctuary CMRCD 490	SWEDISH RADIO SESSIONS (CD-R, titles insert, commercial release cancelled)	50
03	Universal RIF1	RIFFS (CD, full album promo, p/s, slimline jewel case)	20
03	Universal RIF2	RIFFS (CD, 4-track sampler, p/s, slimline jewel case)	15

(see also Spectres, Traffic Jam, Rossi & Frost, Bob Young, Andy Bown, Alan Lancaster's Bombers, Partners In Crime, Party Boys, Rockers, John Du Cann, Manchester United Football Squad, Marietta, Stretch, Jimmy Sweep)

STAVELY MAKEPEACE

Year	Label / Cat. No.	Title	Value
69	Pyramid PYR 6072	(I Want To Love You Like A) Mad Dog/Greasy Haired Woman	6
70	Pyramid PYR 6082	Tarzan Harvey/Reggae Denny (unissued, test pressings exist)	10
70	Concord CON 008	Edna (Let Me Sing My Beautiful Song)/Tarzan Harvey ('fried egg' or multi-coloured label)	5
70	Concord CON 013	Smokey Mountain Rhythm Revue/Rampant On The Rage	5
71	Concord CON 018	Give Me That Pistol/The Sundance	5
72	Spark SRL 1066	Walking Through The Blue Grass/Swings And Roundabouts	5
72	Spark SRL 1081	Slippery Rock 70's/Don't Ride A Pillion Paula	5
73	Spark SRL 1085	Prima Donna/Swings And Roundabouts	5
73	Deram DM 386	Cajun Band/Memories Of Your Love	5
74	Deram DM 423	Runaround Sue/There's A Wall Between Us	5
77	Unigram U 6312	Baby Blue Eyes/Big Bad Baby Blondie	5
78	Barn 2014 118	No Regrets/You're Talking Out Of Your Head	5
79	Barn BARN 001	Coconut Shuffle/Napoleon Brandy	5
80	Hammer HS 304	Songs Of Yesterday/Storm	5

(see also Lieutenant Pigeon, Shel Naylor)

STAVERTON BRIDGE

Year	Label / Cat. No.	Title	Value
70s	Saydisc SDL 266	STAVERTON BRIDGE (LP, with lyrics)	35

MARY STAVIN & GEORGE BEST

Year	Label / Cat. No.	Title	Value
70s	Lifestyle LEG 22	IT TAKES TWO TO SHAPE UP (LP)	15

STEAM

Year	Label / Cat. No.	Title	Value
69	Fontana TF 1058	Na Na Hey Hey Kiss Him Goodbye/It's The Magic In You Girl	7

STEAMHAMMER

Year	Label / Cat. No.	Title	Value
69	CBS 4141	Junior's Wailing/Windmill	8
69	CBS 4496	Autumn Song/Blues For Passing People	7
71	Reflection HRS 9	Junior's Wailing/You'll Never Know	7
68	CBS (S) 63611	STEAMHAMMER (LP)	45
70	CBS (S) 63694	STEAMHAMMER MK. II (LP)	40
70	B&C CAS 1024	MOUNTAINS (LP)	30
70	Reflection REFL 1	STEAMHAMMER (LP, reissue, different sleeve)	25
71	Reflection REFL 12	STEAMHAMMER MK. II (LP, reissue)	20

(see also Armageddon)

STEAM-SHOVEL

Year	Label / Cat. No.	Title	Value
68	Trojan/Big Bear TR 635	Rudi, The Red Nosed Reindeer/White Christmas	7
68	Decca F 22863	Rudi, The Red Nosed Reindeer/White Christmas (export issue)	10

(see also Locomotive)

STEEL

Year	Label / Cat. No.	Title	Value
81	Neat NEAT 14	Rock Out/All Systems Go (p/s)	10

BETTE ANNE STEELE

Year	Label / Cat. No.	Title	Value
55	Capitol CL 14315	Barricade/Give Me A Little Kiss Will Ya, Huh?	8

DAVY STEELE

Year	Label / Cat. No.	Title	Value
83	Bracken BKN 1001	LONG TIME GETTING THERE (LP)	15

DORIS STEELE

Year	Label / Cat. No.	Title	Value
59	Oriole CB 1468	Why Must I?/Never Again	10
59	Oriole CB 1468	Why Must I?/Never Again (78)	10

JAN STEELE & JOHN CAGE

Year	Label / Cat. No.	Title	Value
76	Obscure OBS 5	VOICES AND INSTRUMENTS (LP)	12

SONDRA & JON STEELE

Year	Label / Cat. No.	Title	Value
55	Parlophone MSP 6166	I'm Crazy With Love/Fill My Heart With Happiness	8

TOMMY STEELE (& THE STEELMEN)

78s

Year	Label / Cat. No.	Title	Value
58	Decca F 11026	It's All Happening/What Do You Do	6
58	Decca F 11072	Come On Let's Go/Put A Ring On Her Finger	7
58	Weekend Mail (no cat. no.)	THE TRUTH ABOUT ME (6" in envelope, mail-order only)	20
59	Decca F 11117	Hiawatha/The Trial	6
59	Decca F 11152	Tallahassee Lassie/Give! Give! Give!	20
59	Decca F 11162	You Were Mine/Young Ideas	15
59	Decca F 11177	Little White Bull/Singing Time	25
60	Decca F 11245	What A Mouth (What A North And South)/Kookaburra	30

45s

Year	Label / Cat. No.	Title	Value
56	Decca F 10795	Rock With The Caveman/Rock Around The Town (with The Steelmen)	35
56	Decca F 10808	Doomsday Rock/Elevator Rock	30
56	Decca F 10819	Singing The Blues/Rebel Rock (with The Steelmen)	20
57	Decca F 10849	Knee Deep In The Blues/Teenage Party (with The Steelmen)	15
57	Decca F 10877	Butterfingers/Cannibal Pot	8
57	Decca F 10896	Shiralee/Grandad's Rock	12
57	Decca F 10923	Water Water/A Handful Of Songs	7

57	Decca F 10941	Hey You!/Plant A Kiss	8
58	Decca F 10976	Happy Guitar/Princess	6
58	Decca F 10991	Nairobi/Neon Sign	6
58	Decca F 11026	It's All Happening/What Do You Do	5
58	Decca F 11041	The Only Man On The Island/I Puts The Lightie On	6
58	Decca F 11072	Come On Let's Go/Put A Ring On Her Finger	10
58	Decca F 11089	A Lovely Night/Marriage Type Love	5
59	Decca F 11117	Hiawatha/The Trial	6
59	Decca F 11152	Tallahassee Lassie/Give! Give! Give!	8
59	Decca F 11162	You Were Mine/Young Ideas	5
59	Decca F 11177	Little White Bull/Singing Time (some in p/s)	10/5

(The above 45s were originally issued with triangular centres; later round-centre copies are worth two-thirds the values listed.)

60	Decca F 11245	What A Mouth (What A North And South)/Kookaburra	5
60	Decca F 11258	Drunken Guitar/Light Up The Sky (unreleased)	
60	Decca F 11275	Happy Go Lucky Blues/(The Girl With The) Long Black Hair	5
60	Decca F 11299	Must Be Santa/Boys And Girls	5
61	Decca F 11361	My Big Best Shoes/The Dit Dit Song	5
61	Decca F 11372	Writing On The Wall/Drunken Guitar	8
62	Decca F 11479	Hit Record/What A Little Darling	8
62	Decca F 11551	He's Got Love/Green Eyes	5
63	Decca F 11532	Where Have All The Flowers Gone/Butter Wouldn't Melt in Your Mouth	5
63	Decca F 11615	Flash, Bang, Wallop!/She's So Far Above Me	6
63	Columbia DB 7070	Egg And Chips/The Dream Maker (with John Barry)	8

EPs

56	Decca DFE 6388	YOUNG LOVE	25
56	Decca DFE 6389	SINGING THE BLUES	25
57	Decca DFE 6398	THE TOMMY STEELE STORY NO. 1	25
57	Decca DFE 6424	THE TOMMY STEELE STORY NO. 2	25
57	Decca F 10915	ALL STAR HIT PARADE NO. 2 (with other artists)	15

(The above EPs were originally issued with triangular centres; later round-centre reissues are worth two-thirds the values listed.)

58	Decca DFE 6472	THE DUKE WORE JEANS	15
58	Decca DFE 6551	C'MON LET'S GO	20
59	Decca DFE 6592	SWEET GEORGIA BROWN	20
59	Decca DFE 6607	TOMMY THE TOREADOR	12
60	Decca DFE 6660	WHAT A MOUTH	15

LPs

57	Decca LF 1287	THE TOMMY STEELE STAGE SHOW (10")	35
57	Decca LF 1288	THE TOMMY STEELE STORY (10")	30
58	Decca LF 1308	THE DUKE WORE JEANS (10", soundtrack)	22
60	Decca LK 4351	GET HAPPY WITH TOMMY	20
67	RCA Victor RB/SB 6735	HALF A SIXPENCE (soundtrack, gatefold sleeve)	12

STEELERS

70	Direction 58-4675	Get It From The Bottom/I'm Sorry	7

STEELEYE SPAN

71	B&C CB 164	Rave On/Reels/Female Drummer (p/s)	7
72	Pegasus PGS 6	JIGS AND REELS (maxi-single, some with p/s)	10/6
72	Chrysalis CHS 2005	John Barleycorn/Bride's Favourite/Tansey's Fancy	5
72	Chrysalis CHS 2007	Gaudete/The Holly And The Ivy (p/s)	6
74	Chysalis CHS 2026	Thomas The Rhymer/The Mooncoin Jig	5
75	Chysalis CHS 2061	New York Girls/Two Magicians	5
76	Mooncrest MOON 50	Rave On/False Knight On The Road	5
76	Chrysalis CHS 2085	Hard Times Of Old England/Cadgwith Anthem	6
76	Chrysalis CHS 2085	Hard Times Of Old England/Sum Waves (Tunes) (alternate B-side)	5
76	Chrysalis CHS 2107	London/Sligo Maid	5
76	Chrysalis CHS 2125	Fighting For Strangers/The Mooncoin Jig	5
77	Chrysalis CHS 2129	The Boar's Head Carol/Gaudete/Some Rival (p/s)	6
78	Chrysalis CHS 2233	Rag Doll/Saucy Sailor	5
80	Chrysalis CHS 2479	Sails Of Silver/Senior Service (p/s)	5
81	Chrysalis CHS 2503	Gone To America/Let Her Go Down (p/s)	5
82	Chrysalis CHS 2658	All Around My Hat/Fighting For Strangers/Gaudete/The Boar's Head Carol (p/s)	5
82	Chrysalis CHSDJ 2658	All Around My Hat/Gaudete (promo only)	5
89	Flutterby FLUT 3	Padstow/First House In Connaught/Sailor's Bonnet (Reel) (p/s, later pressed as Dover FLUT 3)	5/4
70	RCA SF 8113	HARK! THE VILLAGE WAIT (LP, with insert)	25
71	United Artists UAG 29160	HARK! THE VILLAGE WAIT (LP, reissue)	12
71	B&C CAS 1029	PLEASE TO SEE THE KING (LP, initially in 'hessian' textured sleeve)	18/12
72	Charisma CS 5	INDIVIDUALLY AND COLLECTIVELY (LP)	15
72	Pegasus PEG 9	TEN MAN MOP, OR MR. RESERVOIR BUTLER RIDES AGAIN (LP, gatefold sleeve, initially with 8-page booklet)	18/12
72	Chrysalis CHR 1008	BELOW THE SALT (LP, gatefold sleeve, green label)	12
73	Charisma CS 12	ALMANACK (LP)	12
73	Chrysalis CHR 1046	PARCEL OF ROGUES (LP, gatefold sleeve, with lyric insert)	12
74	Mooncrest CREST 8	PLEASE TO SEE THE KING (LP, reissue)	12
74	Chrysalis CHR 1053	NOW WE ARE SIX (LP, with lyric inner sleeve, green label)	12
74	Mooncrest CREST 9	TEN MAN MOP, OR MR. RESERVOIR BUTLER RIDES AGAIN (LP, initially in gatefold sleeve, later single)	15/12
75	Chrysalis CHR 1091	ALL AROUND MY HAT (LP, with lyric insert)	12
76	Chrysalis CHR 1123	ROCKET COTTAGE (LP, with lyric insert)	12
77	Chrysalis CHR 1151	STORM FORCE TEN (LP, with lyric insert)	12

(see also Maddy Prior, Tim Hart & Maddy Prior, Gay & Terry Woods, Ashley Hutchings, Fairport Convention, Martin Carthy, Silly Sisters, Bob Johnson & Pete Knight)

MINT VALUE £

STEEL MILL

71	Penny Farthing PEN 770	Green Eyed God/Zang Will	8
72	Penny Farthing PEN 783	Get On The Line/Summer's Child	8
75	Penny Farthing PEN 894	Green Eyed God/Zang Will (reissue)	6
71	Penny Farthing PELS 549	GREEN EYED GOD (LP)	150

STEEL PULSE

77	Anchor ANC 1046	Nyah Luv/Luv Nyah	5

STEELY DAN

72	Probe PRO 562	Dallas/Sail The Waterway	6
73	Probe PRO 577	Do It Again/Fire In The Hole	5
73	Probe PRO 587	Reelin' In The Years/Only A Fool	5
73	Probe PRO 602	Show Biz Kids/Razor Boy	5
73	Probe PRO 606	My Old School/Pearl Of The Quarter	5
74	Probe PRO 622	Rikki Don't Lose That Number/Any Major Dude Will Tell You	5
79	ABC ABC 4241	Rikki Don't Lose That Number/Any Major Dude Will Tell You (p/s, reissue, yellow vinyl)	5
73	Probe SPB 1062	CAN'T BUY A THRILL (LP, original)	12
73	Probe SPD 1079	COUNTDOWN TO ECSTASY (LP, original)	12
80s	MCA 203 16009	GAUCHO (LP, audiophile pressing)	12
82	MCA MCF 3165	GOLD (LP, with free EP [MSAMT 21])	12
80s	MCA 203 16016	GOLD (LP, audiophile pressing)	12

(see also Donald Fagen)

WOUT STEENHUIS

65	Columbia DB 7722	Desert Island/Teran Boelan	6
66	Columbia DB 8027	Nivram/Bay Of Paradise	6
65	Columbia SEG 8487	HAWAII (EP)	8
64	Columbia 33SX 1585	SURFIN' WITH STEENHUIS (LP)	12
65	Columbia 33SX 1695	HAWAIIAN SURF RIDE (LP)	12
66	Columbia SX 6024	PARADISE ISLAND (LP, mono)	12
66	Studio Two TWO 116	PARADISE ISLAND (LP, stereo)	12
74	Studio Two TWOX 1017	BEYOND THE REEF (LP)	12

STEEPLECHASE

71	Polydor 2489 001	LADY BRIGHT (LP)	12

STEERPIKE

68	(no label credit) ADM 417	STEERPIKE (LP, private pressing)	550

BILL STEGMEYER & HIS ORCHESTRA

54	London HL 8078	On The Waterfront (From The Film)/We Just Couldn't Say Good-Bye	35

LOU STEIN

57	London HLZ 8419	Almost Paradise/Soft Sands	22
58	Mercury 7MT 226	Who Slammed The Door/Got A Match?	8

JIM STEINMAN

81	Epic EPCA 1236	Rock And Roll Dreams Come Through/Love And Death And An American Guitar (p/s)	5
81	Epic EPCA 13-1236	Rock And Roll Dreams Come Through/Love And Death And An American Guitar/The Storm (12", p/s, blue vinyl)	8
81	Epic EPCA 1561	Lost Boys And Golden Girls/Left In The Dark (p/s)	5
81	Epic EPCA 1707	Dance In My Pants/Dance In My Pants (unissued, promo only)	6
84	MCA MCA 889	Tonight Is What It Means To Be Young/Hold That Snake (p/s)	5
84	MCA MCA T889	Tonight Is What It Means To Be Young/Hold That Snake (12", p/s)	12
81	Epic EPC 11-84361	BAD FOR GOOD (LP, picture disc)	15

(see also Meat Loaf)

STEINWAYS

85	Kent TOWN 106	You've Been Leading Me On/JOHNNY CASWELL: You Don't Love Me No More	8

STELLA

82	President PT 504	Si Tu Aimes Ma Musique/If You Do Like My Music (p/s)	7

STELLASTARR*

00s	2220 TWENTY-7 S001	Somewhere Across Forever/No Weather (p/s, 1000 only)	15
00s	2220 TWENTY-CDS 001	Somewhere Across Forever/No Weather/School Ya (CD, 1000 only)	15

STAN STENNETT

60s	Audio JDT 1	STYLE (EP)	8

MALCOLM STENT

70s	Starline SWL 2002	GO AND PLAY UP YOUR OWN END (LP)	15

STEP

80	Epic/Direction S DIR 8733	Love Letter/Land Of 1,000 Dances (p/s)	5
80	Epic/Direction S DIR 8944	Let Me Be The One/634 5789 (p/s)	5
80	Epic/Direction S DIR 9311	Tears That I Cry/Shake (p/s)	5
81	Epic EPC A 1291	Chain Gang/In The House (p/s)	5
81	Epic EPC A 1412	Model Soldiers/Hightime Havana (p/s)	5

STEPASIDE

80	Gale GALELP 01	SIT DOWN AND RELAPSE (LP)	20

EWAN STEPHENS

71	Decca F 13219	Queen Of The Good Times/We Can Give It A Try	5
72	Decca F 13299	Brother, Surely We Can Work It Out/Long, Long Summer	5

(see also Turquoise)

LEIGH STEPHENS

69	Philips SBL 7897	RED WEATHER (LP)	40
71	Charisma CAS 1040	AND A CAST OF THOUSANDS (LP)	30

(see also Blue Cheer)

STEPPENWOLF

68	RCA RCA 1679	Sookie Sookie/Take What You Need	10
68	RCA RCA 1735	Born To Be Wild/Everybody's Next One	10
68	Stateside-Dunhill SS 8003	Magic Carpet Ride/Sookie Sookie	8
69	Stateside-Dunhill SS 8013	Rock Me/Jupiter Child	6
69	Stateside-Dunhill SS 8017	Born To Be Wild/Everybody's Next One (reissue)	5
69	Stateside-Dunhill SS 8027	Magic Carpet Ride/Sookie Sookie (reissue)	5
70	Stateside-Dunhill SS 8035	Monster/Move Over	6
70	Stateside-Dunhill SS 8038	The Pusher/Your Wall's Too High	6
70	Stateside-Dunhill SS 8049	Hey Lawdy Mama/Twisted	6
70	Stateside-Dunhill SS 8056	Screaming Night Hog/Spiritual Fantasy	5
70	Probe PRO 510	Who Needs Ya/Earschplittenloudenboomer	5
71	Probe PRO 525	Snowblind Friend/Hippo Stomp	5
71	Probe PRO 534	Ride With Me/For Madmen Only	6
71	Probe PRO 544	For Ladies Only/Sparkle Eyes	5
68	RCA RD/SF 7974	STEPPENWOLF (LP, initially white sleeve, later silver sleeve)	35/25
68	Stateside (S)SL 5003	STEPPENWOLF THE SECOND (LP)	20
69	Stateside (S)SL 5011	AT YOUR BIRTHDAY PARTY (LP)	15
69	Stateside (S)SL 5015	EARLY STEPPENWOLF (LP)	15
69	Stateside (S)SL 10276	CANDY (LP, soundtrack, 2 tracks by Steppenwolf, 1 track by Byrds)	30
70	Stateside-Dunhill SSL 5020	STEPPENWOLF (reissue)	15
70	Stateside-Dunhill SSL 5021	MONSTER (LP, gatefold sleeve)	15
70	Stateside-Dunhill SSL 5029	STEPPENWOLF 'LIVE' (2-LP, gatefold sleeve)	15
70	Probe SPBA 6254	STEPPENWOLF 7 (LP)	15
71	Probe SPBA 6260	FOR LADIES ONLY (LP)	12
71	Probe SPBA 1033	GOLD (LP)	12
72	Probe SPBA 1059	REST IN PEACE (LP)	12

(see also Sparrow, John Kay)

STEPPES

79	South Circular SGS 108	The Beat Drill/FIFTY FANTASTICS: God's Got Religion (p/s, white label)	10

(see also Fifty Fantastics, Disco Zombies)

STEPPING TALK

79	Eustone/Rough Trade TO1	Alice In Sunderland/Health And Safety/Common Problems/ John Turtles (p/s, with stamped inner)	6

STEPS

97	Jive JIVECD 438	5,6,7,8 (Radio Edit)/5,6,7,8 (Extended Version)/Words Of Wisdom/5,6,7,8 (Instrumental) (CD)	12
98	Jive 052100-2	Last Thing On My Mind (Radio Edit)/5,6,7,8 (Radio Edit)/A Love To Last/Last Thing On My Mind (Instrumental) (CD, digipak, with poster)	12
98	Jive 0519102	One For Sorrow/One For Sorrow (W.I.P. Remix)/One For Sorrow (A Capella Mix) (CD, digipak, with poster)	10

STEPTOE & SON

(see under Wilfred Brambell & Harry H. Corbett)

STEREOLAB

SINGLES

91	Duophonic DS 45-01	SUPER 45: The Light That Will Cease To Fail/Au Grand Jour/Brittle/ Au Grand Jour! (10" EP, with insert, mail-order only, 40 with hand-painted p/s, 500 only in poly bag)	180/160
91	Too Pure PURE 4	SUPER ELECTRIC: Super-Electric/High Expectation/ The Way Will Be Opening/Contact (10" EP, with red on yellow sleeve, w/insert)	22
91	Duophonic DS 45-02	STUNNING DEBUT ALBUM: Doubt/Clanger (p/s, mail-order only, gatefold p/s with insert in poly bag; multicoloured vinyl export issue for France, withdrawn due to pressing fault/warping, 200 only)	200
91	Duophonic DS 45-02	STUNNING DEBUT ALBUM: Doubt/Clanger (p/s, mail-order only, gatefold p/s with insert in poly bag; 985 copies on clear vinyl)	60
92	Duophonic DS 45-04	Harmonium/Farfisa (p/s, mail-order only, 1,306 copies on transparent amber vinyl, with insert & fluorescent sticker)	40
93	Duophonic DS45-05/06	SHIMMIES IN SUPER 8 (2 x 7", green and white vinyl, foldout sleeve with inserts)	40
92	Too Pure PURE 14	Low Fi/Varoom!/Laissez-Faire/Elektro (He Held The World In His Iron Grip) (10", p/s, clear vinyl, 2,000 only)	25
93	Sub Pop SP107/283	Lo Boob Oscillator/Tempter (clear vinyl, p/s)	40
93	Spacewatch FLX 2107	Ronco Symphony (demo)/Seeming And The Meaning (demo)/ SUBMARINER: Lyricist Downer (clear vinyl flexi with paper strip insert)	25
93	Elektra 7-64615	Golden Ball/Jenny Ondioline (promo only, 3,200 on clear vinyl)	25
93	Duophonic D-UHF-D 01	Jenny Ondioline/Fruition/Golden Ball/French Disko (10", p/s)	15
93	Duophonic D-UHF-D 01	Jenny Ondioline (Part 1)/Golden Ball (Studio) (10", factory custom pressings; 5 copies on multicoloured vinyl; 36 on 'thin' clear vinyl, later endorsed & signed by band; no p/s)	100+/80
93	Duophonic D-UHF-CD 01	Jenny Ondioline/Fruition/Golden Ball/French Disko (CD)	15
93	Clawfist 20	CRUMB DUCK (10" EP, shared with Nurse With Wound, 1,450 only; 50 with handmade p/s)	80/50
93	Duophonic D-UHF-D 03	French Disko/Jenny Ondioline ('teaser' single, p/s, 1,500 only)	35
93	Duophonic D-UHF-D 01P	French Disko/Jenny Ondioline (CD, 1,000 only, hand-made p/s)	20
94	Duophonic D-UHF-D 04S	Ping Pong/Moogie Wonderland (p/s, 2,150 on pink vinyl, 3,322 on green, some on black)	15/10/10
94	Duophonic D-UHF-D 04T	Ping Pong/Moogie Wonderland (10", p/s)	10
94	Silvertone	Tone Burst (demo)/Tempter (demo)/SPECTRUM: Soul Kiss Glide Divine (unreleased, with colour photocopied wraparound p/s, 25 test pressings only)	150+
94	Duophonic D-UHF-07	Wow And Flutter/Heavy Denim (3,000 only with hand-painted p/s)	12
95	Wurlitzer Jukebox WJ 3	The Eclipse/Yes Sir! I Can Moogie/CAT'S MIAOW: Shoot The Moon (flexidisc, 1,000 only)	8

			MINT VALUE £
95	Duophonic Super 45s DS 45-10	Long Hair Of Death/YO LA TENGO: Evanescent Psychic Pez Drop (gig single, fluorescent yellow vinyl, plain white stickered card sleeve, 3,000 only)	20
95	Independent Project IP 060	Blue Milk/One Thousand Miles An Hour/Aluminum Tune (translucent vinyl, gatefold sleeve, with sheet of stamps)	10
95	Flying Nun STEREO 1	French Disko/Super Electric (CD, also listed as B 8595, promo only)	15
95	Duophonic STEREO 2	John Cage Bubblegum/Revox (CD, also listed as B 8895, promo only)	10
96	Duophonic D-UHF-D 10S	Cybele's Reverie/Brigitte (p/s, with insert)	5
96	Duophonic D-UHF-D 10	Cybele's Reverie/Les Yper Yper Sound/Brigitte/Young Lungs (10", p/s, 2,000 only)	18
96	Lissy's LISS 15	You Used To Call Me Sadness/FUXA: Skyhigh (p/s, 400 on white vinyl, 1,500 on black)	20/12
96	Die Stadt 011	Right Between Yr Eyes (p/s, Uberschall Festival single, with Faust and Foetus)	25
96	Duophonic D-UHF-D 12	Speedy Car/TORTOISE: Yaus (gig freebie, blue vinyl, p/s, 3,000 only)	22
96	Duophonic D-UHF-D 12	Speedy Car/TORTOISE: Yaus (orange vinyl export issue, p/s, 3,000 only)	20
96	Duophonic D-UHF-D 14S	Fluorescences/Pinball (p/s)	7
96	Duophonic D-UHF-D 14	Fluorescences/Pinball/You Used To Call Me Sadness/Soop Groove (12", p/s)	10
96	Duophonic D-UHF-D 15	Metronomic Underground (Wagon Christ Mix)/Percolations (12", plain red sleeve, 2,500 only)	12
97	Duophonic D-UHF-D 16S	Miss Modular/Allures (p/s)	5
97	Duophonic DS 4517	Splitting The Atom (Parts 1 & 2) (with Sonic Boom)/ Monkey Brain (p/s, 2,500 only)	10
97	Duophonic D-UHF-D 18	Iron Man/The Incredible He Woman (red vinyl, p/s, gig single, 1,000 only)	8
97	Duophonic Super 45s DS 3311	Simple Headphone Mind/NURSE WITH WOUND: Trippin' With The Birds (12", 5,000 copies, 1,000 copies on yellow vinyl, in sealed foil sleeve)	25/15
97	Duophonic Super 45s CD 3311	Simple Headphone Mind/NURSE WITH WOUND: Trippin' With The Birds (CD, sealed foil sleeve, 800 only, withdrawn)	40
98	Duophonic D-UHF-D 19	Refractions In The Plastic Pulse/Contronatura (12", die-cut stickered sleeve, yellow or black vinyl)	15/8
99	Duophonic D-UHF-D24	THE UNDERGROUND IS COMING: The Super-It/Monkey Jelly/Fried Monkey Eggs (Instrumental)/Fried Monkey Eggs (Vocal) (p/s)	20
ALBUMS			
90	Too Pure PURE 19	SPACE AGE BACHELOR PAD MUSIC (LP)	20
92	Too Pure PURELP 11	PENG! (LP)	20
92	Too Pure PUREL 78LP	SWITCHED ON (LP)	12
93	Duophonic D-UHF-D 02	TRANSIENT RANDOM NOISE-BURSTS WITH ANNOUNCEMENTS (2-LP, with inner sleeves, poor playing-quality gold vinyl, with stickered sleeve, 1,500 only)	35
95	Duophonic D-UHF-D 05X	MARS AUDIAC QUINTET (2-LP, gatefold sleeve, 1st 1,000 copies with bonus coloured vinyl single "Klang Tone"/"Ulan Bator" [D-UHF-06])	35
95	Duophonic D-UHF-CD 05	MARS AUDIAC QUINTET (CD, 1st 1,000 with bonus CD "Klang Tone"/"Ulan Bator" [D-UHF-CD 06])	30
95	Duophonic D-UHF-D 08	MUSIC FOR THE AMORPHOUS BODY STUDY CENTRE (10" LP, 3,000 only)	20
95	Duophonic D-UHF-CD 08	MUSIC FOR THE AMORPHOUS BODY STUDY CENTRE (CD, first issue with white cover & "1st edition" printed on disc available at Charles Long art exhibition; reissue has yellow sleeve)	40/25
96	United Dairies UD 059	CRUMB DUCK (LP, shared with Nurse With Wound, reissue of Clawfist EP, 50 copies on pink vinyl, 500 on fluorescent green vinyl)	60/40
96	Duophonic UHF D-UHF-D11	EMPEROR TOMATO KETCHUP (2-LP, yellow glitter vinyl, gatefold sleeve)	40

(see also McCarthy, Spectrum, Mouse On Mars, Clear Spot)

STEREOLAB & BRIGITTE FONTAINE

90s	Duophonic Super 45s DS 45-25	Caliméro/MONADE: Cache Cache (white vinyl, p/s)	8

STEREOPHONICS

96	V2 SPH 1	Looks Like Chaplin/More Life In A Tramp's Vest (p/s, 500 only)	70
96	V2 SPHD 1	Looks Like Chaplin/More Life In A Tramp's Vest/Raymond's Shops (CD)	40
96	V2 SPH 2	Local Boy In The Photograph/Too Many Sandwiches (p/s, 2,000 only)	15
97	V2 SPH 4	More Life In A Tramp's Vest/Raymond's Shop (p/s)	12
97	V2 VVR 500 0448	A Thousand Trees/Home To Me/Looks Like Chaplin/Summertime (CD, digipak)	15
99	V2 VVR 500 6777	Pick A Part That's New/Nice To Be Out (Demo) (p/s)	8
01	V2 VVR 501 6247	Have A Nice Day/Surprise (p/s)	6
01	V2 VVR 501 5937	Mr Writer/Maritime Belle Vue In Kiel (embossed p/s)	5
02	V2 VVR 501 9177	Vegas 2 Times/(Live Version) (p/s)	5
03	V2 VVR 502 1897	Maybe Tomorrow/Have Wheels, Will Travel (p/s)	5
99	V2 no catalogue number	PERFORMANCE AND COCKTAILS (7 x 10" box set, with booklet and CD, promo mail order only)	70
97	V2 VVR 1000 431	WORD GETS AROUND (LP, gatefold sleeve)	12
97	Banana VVR 1000431	WORD GETS AROUND (LP, with bonus 12")	30
01	V2 no cat. no.	THE SINGLES (10-track CD-R, paper p/s)	35

STEREOS

61	MGM MGM 1143	I Really Love You/Please Come Back To Me	45
61	MGM MGM 1149	The Big Knock/Sweet Water	30
66	MGM MGM 1328	Sweet Water/The Big Knock (reissue)	5

STEREOTYPES

79	Hinterland/SRT no cat. no.	THE STEREOTYPES EP (no p/s)	250

STEREOTYPES

80	Art Theft AT 001	Calling All The Shots/Lovers Of The Future (p/s)	8

DEAN STERLING & TEENBEATS

61	Pye 7N 15345	Send Me A Girl/Lost Love	10

MINT VALUE £

FITZROY STERLING

68	Gas GAS 102	Got To Play It Cool/Jezebel	10
70	Bullet BU 422	That's My Life/Queen Of Hearts	10
70	Bullet BU 438	Freedom Street/FITZROY ALL STARS: Freedom Street Version	10
71	Escort ERT 858	Girl Tell Me What To Do/Be Careful	10
71	Pama PM 820	My Sweet Lord/Darling That's Right	10

LESTER STERLING (& HIS GROUP)

63	Island WI 121	Clean The City/Long Walk Home (B-side actually by Charmers)	20
63	R&B JB 111	Air Raid Shelter/ROY & ANNETTE: I Mean It	15
63	R&B JB 115	Gravy Cool/WINSTON & BIBBY: Lover Lover Man	15
64	R&B JB 143	Peace And Love/HORACE SEATON: Hold On	15
64	R&B JB 150	Hot Cargo/MAYTALS: Marching On	18
64	R&B JB 155	Baskin' Hop (as Lester Sterling & His Group)/MAYTALS: Shining Light	18
64	R&B JB 172	Indian Summer (as Lester Sterling & His Group)/ STRANGER & PATSY: I'll Forgive You	18
66	Doctor Bird DB 1057	Inez (with Tommy McCook & Supersonics)/GLORIA CRAWFORD: Sad Movies	18
67	Doctor Bird DB 1107	Soul Voyage/ALVA LEWIS: Revelation	30
67	Collins Downbeat CR 001	Sir Collins Special/Lester Sterling '67	30
68	Coxsone CS 7080	Africkaan Beat/PARAGONS: My Satisfaction	22
68	Blue Cat BS 116	Zigaloo/Wiser Than Solomon	22
68	Unity UN 502	Bangarang (with Stranger Cole)/STRANGER COLE: If We Should Ever Meet	6
69	Unity UN 505	Reggae On Broadway/CLIQUE: Love Can Be Wonderful	6
69	Unity UN 509	Spoogy/TOMMY McCOOK: Monkey Fiddle	7
69	Unity UN 512	Regina/Bright As A Rose	7
69	Unity UN 517	1,000 Tons Of Megaton/KING CANNON: Five Card Stud	8
69	Unity UN 518	Man About Town/Man At The Door	6
69	Unity UN 531	Lonesome Feeling/Bright As A Rose	6
69	Big Shot BI 507	Forest Gate Rock/RAVING RAVERS: Rock Rock And Cry	8
69	Gas GAS 103	Reggae In The Wind/SOUL SET: Try Me One More Time (B-side actually by Stranger & Gladdy)	6
70	Unity UN 562	Slip Up/DAVE BARKER: On Broadway	8
71	Nu Beat NB 095	Iron Side Part 1/COXSON'S ALL STARS: Iron Side Part 2	8
71	Smash SMA 2321	Sir Collins Special/Version (actually "Heart Of The Knight" by Gaytones)	6
72	Ashanti ASH 409	Iron Side Part 1/COXSON'S ALL STARS: Iron Side Part 2	6
72	Ashanti ASH 410	War Is Not The Answer/COXSON'S ALL STARS: Version	6
69	Pama SECO 15	BANGARANG (LP)	50

(see also Mister Versatile, Bobby Aitken, Eric Morris, Sir Collins Band, Slickers, Uniques)

NINA STERN

65	Pye 7N 15823	Take It From Me/Please Come Back To Me	5

STEROID KIDDIES

70s	Steroid/Grundinga SK 001	THE KIDDIES EP	55

STEROID MAXIMUS

90s	Big Cat ABB 28	QUILOMBO (LP)	20

STEROIDS

78	Radar ADA 11	In The Colonies/Sha La La Loo Ley (p/s)	6

STEVE 'N' BONNIE

72	Young Blood YB 1033	Brief Encounter/Don't/Lady	6
72	Young Blood SSYB 16	BRIEF ENCOUNTER (LP)	18

STEVE & EYDIE

(see under Eydie Gorme & Steve Lawrence)

STEVE & STEVIE

68	Toast TLP 2	STEVE AND STEVIE (LP)	25

(see also Tin Tin, Fut)

APRIL STEVENS

53	Parlophone MSP 6060	C'est Si Bon/Soft Warm Lips	12
54	Parlophone MSP 6088	How Could Red Riding Hood (Have Been...)/You Said You'd Do It	12
67	MGM MGM 1366	Falling In Love Again/Wanting You	75
76	MGM 2006 586	Wanting You/Falling In Love Again (reissue)	5

(see also Nino Tempo & April Stevens)

BOBBY STEVENS

60	Embassy WB 390	Fall In Love With You/Wild One	5
60	Embassy WB 390	Fall In Love With You/Wild One (78)	6
60	Embassy WB 392	Stuck On You/Clementine	5
60	Embassy WB 392	Stuck On You/Clementine (78)	8
60	Embassy WB 397	Cradle Of Love/Heart Of A Teenage Girl	5
60	Embassy WB 397	Cradle Of Love/Heart Of A Teenage Girl (78)	6
60	Embassy WB 404	Shakin' All Over/Angela Jones	5
60	Embassy WB 404	Shakin' All Over/Angela Jones (78)	8
60	Embassy WB 412	A Mess Of Blues/Tie Me Kangaroo Down Sport	5
60	Embassy WB 412	A Mess Of Blues/Tie Me Kangaroo Down Sport (78)	8
60	Embassy WB 427	I Love You/Strawberry Fair (78)	7
60	Embassy WB 428	Lively/Lonely Pup (In A Christmas Shop) (78)	20

CAT STEVENS

66	Deram DM 102	I Love My Dog/Portobello Road	8
66	Deram DM 110	Matthew And Son/Granny	6
67	Deram DM 118	I'm Gonna Get Me A Gun/School Is Out	10
67	Deram DM 140	Bad Night/Laughing Apple	6
67	Deram DM 156	Kitty/Blackness Of The Night	10
68	Deram DM 178	Lovely City/Image Of Hell	6
68	Deram DM 211	Here Comes My Wife/It's A Supa (Dupa) Life	6
69	Deram DM 260	Where Are You/The View From The Top	6

MINT VALUE £

70	Island WIP 6086	Lady D'Arbanville/Time/Fill My Eyes (some in p/s)	8/5
67	Deram DML/SML 1004	MATTHEW AND SON (LP)	25
67	Deram DML/SML 1018	NEW MASTERS (LP)	22
67	Deram	CATS AND DOGS (LP, unreleased, test pressings only)	30
70	Island ILPS 9118	MONA BONE JAKON (LP, pink label)	75
70	Island ILPS 9135	TEA FOR THE TILLERMAN (LP, gatefold sleeve, pink label)	20
71	Island ILPS 9154	TEASER AND THE FIRECAT (LP, pink label)	20
75	Island ILPS 9310	GREATEST HITS (LP, with calendar & poster)	12

CHUCK STEVENS

57	Columbia DB 3883	Take A Walk/The Way I Do	8
57	Columbia DB 3938	My London/Couldn't Care More	7

CONNIE STEVENS

60	Warner Bros WB 3	Sixteen Reasons (with Don Ralke)/Little Sister (with Buddy Cole Trio)	10
60	Warner Bros WB 17	Too Young To Go Steady/A Little Kiss Is A Kiss, Is A Kiss	10
60	Warner Bros WB 25	Apollo/Why Do I Cry For Joey	10
61	Warner Bros WB 41	And This Is Mine/Make-Believe Lover	10
61	Warner Bros WB 47	The Greenwood Tree/If You Don't, Somebody Else Will	6
62	Warner Bros WB 63	Why'd You Wanna Make Me Cry/Just One Kiss	15
62	Warner Bros WB 73	Mr. Songwriter/I Couldn't Say No	10
64	Warner Bros WB 128	They're Jealous Of Me/A Girl Never Knows	10
60	Warner Bros WEP 6007	CONNIE STEVENS AS CRICKET (EP, also stereo WSEP 2007)	15/20
63	Warners WEP/WSE 6105	CONNIE STEVENS AS CRICKET NO. 2 (EP, mono/stereo)	15/20
63	Warners WEP/WSE 6112	CONNIE STEVENS AS CRICKET NO. 3 (EP, mono/stereo)	15/20
62	Warner Bros WM 4061	CONNIE (LP, also stereo WS 8061)	20/25
63	Warner Bros WM/WS 8111	THE HANK WILLIAMS SONG BOOK (LP)	18

(see also Edward Byrnes)

DODIE STEVENS

59	London HLD 8834	Pink Shoe Laces/Coming Of Age	20
59	London HLD 8834	Pink Shoe Laces/Coming Of Age (78)	20
60	London HLD 9174	No/A-Tisket A-Tasket	7
61	London HLD 9280	Yes, I'm Lonesome Tonight/Too Young	8
63	London HLP 9672	Don't Send Me Roses/Daddy Couldn't Get Me One Of Those	7
64	Liberty LIB 83	I Wore Out Our Record/You Don't Have To Prove A Thing	6

JOHNNY STEVENS & LES DAWSON SYNDICATE

62	Melodisc M 1586	Last Chicken In The Shop/Oh Yeah (some in p/s)	10

JOHNNY STEVENS & BLUE BEATS

64	Blue Beat BB 229	Shame/Ball And Chain	20

KIRK STEVENS

57	Decca F 10863	Once/This Silver Madonna	10

MEIC STEVENS

65	Decca F 12174	Did I Dream/I Saw A Field (as Mike Stevens)	15
70	Warner Bros WB 8007	Ballad Of Old Joe Blind/Blue Sleep	15
70	Warner Brothers WS 3005	OUTLANDER (LP, with insert)	150
79	Tic Toc no cat. no.	CANAEON CYNNAR (LP, private pressing)	220
97	Tenth Planet TP 028	GHOST TOWN (LP, gatefold sleeve, numbered, 1000 only)	12

(see also Gary Farr)

MICK STEVENS

71	Deroy (no cat. no.)	SEE THE MORNING (LP, private pressing)	250
75	Deroy (no cat. no.)	NO SAVAGE WORD (LP, private pressing)	250

MIKE STEVENS (& SHEVELLS)

65	Decca F 12174	Did I Dream/I Saw A Field (solo)	6
66	Pye 7N 17243	Cathy's Clown/Go-Go Train (as Mike Stevens & Shevells)	15
68	Polydor 56269	Guaranteed To Drive You Wild/Hog-Tied (as Mike Stevens & Shevells)	6

(see also Shevells)

MORT STEVENS & HIS ORCHESTRA

70	Capitol CL 15655	"Hawaii Five-O" Theme/McGarrett's Theme	6

RAY STEVENS

58	Capitol CL 14881	Chickie-Chickie Wah Wah/Crying Goodbye	15
61	Mercury AMT 1158	Jeremiah Peabody's Polyunsaturated Quick Dissolving Fast Acting Pleasant Tasting Green And Purple Pills/Teen Years	7
62	Mercury AMT 1184	Ahab The Arab/It's Been So Long	12
63	Mercury AMT 1207	Harry The Hairy Ape/Little Stone Statue	7
66	London HLU 10027	Devil May Care/Make A Few Memories	6
71	Mercury 6052 072	Bubble Gum The Bubble Dancer/Jeremiah Peabody's Polyunsaturated Quick Dissolving Fast Acting Pleasant Tasting Green And Purple Pills	6

RICKY STEVENS

61	Columbia DB 4739	I Cried For You/I Am	8
62	Columbia DB 4778	Forever/Now, It's All Over	7
63	Columbia DB 4981	My Mother's Eyes/I'll Get By	7
62	Columbia SEG 8172	I CRIED FOR YOU (EP)	60

ROY STEVENS

66	London HLU 10016	Party People/ABC	10

SHAKIN' STEVENS (& SUNSETS)

SINGLES

70	Parlophone R 5860	Spirit Of Woodstock/Down On The Farm	50
72	Polydor 2058 213	Sweet Little Rock'n'Roller/White Lightning	35
74	Emerald MD 1176	Honey Honey/Holey Moley 2001	30
76	Mooncrest MOON 51	Jungle Rock/Girl In Red	20

			MINT VALUE £
77	Track 2094 134	Never/You Always Hurt The One You Love	18
77	Track 2094 136	Somebody Touched Me/Way Down Yonder In New Orleans (some in p/s)	20/12
78	Track 2094 141	Justine/Wait And See	30
78	Epic SEPC 6567	Treat Her Right/I Don't Want No Other Baby	18
79	Epic SEPC 6845	Endless Sleep/Fire	18
79	Epic SEPC 7235	Spooky/I Don't Want No Other Baby	18
80	Epic SEPC 8090	Hot Dog/Apron Strings (p/s)	18
80	Epic SEPC 8573	Hey Mae/I Guess I Was A Fool (some in p/s)	15/6
80	Epic SEPC 8725	Marie Marie/Baby If We Touch (p/s)	5
80	Epic SEPC 8778	Solid As A Rock/Generation X (p/s)	6
80	Epic SEPC 9064	Shooting Gallery/Make It Right Tonight (p/s)	18
81	Epic SEPC 9555	This Ole House/Let Me Show You How (p/s)	5
81	Epic EPCA 1165	You Drive Me Crazy/Baby You're A Child (p/s)	5
81	Battle Of The Bands BOB 2	Jungle Rock/Girl In Red (p/s, reissue, as Shakin' Stevens & Sunsets)	8
81	Epic EPCA 1354	Green Door/Don't Turn Your Back (p/s)	5
81	Mint CHEW 51	No Other Baby/Manhattan Melodrama (p/s)	7
81	Epic A 1643	It's Raining/You And I Were Meant To Be (picture disc)	10
81	Solid Gold SGR 107	Shaky Sings Elvis (Parts 1 & 2) (medley) (p/s)	12
82	Epic EPCA 1742	Oh Julie/I'm Knocking (poster p/s)	6
82	Epic EPCA 40-2620	GREATEST ORIGINAL HITS (cassette EP)	7
82	Epic EPCA 2656	Give Me Your Heart Tonight/Thinkin' Of You (p/s, with poster)	6
82	Epic EPCA 2656	Give Me Your Heart Tonight/Thinkin' Of You (picture disc)	8
82	Everest/Premier RAY 1	Tiger/Give Me A Break (p/s)	7
82	Everest/Premier EV 1000	Tiger/Sweet Little Sixteen/Give Me A Break (picture disc)	8
83	Epic A 3565	It's Late/It's Good For You Baby (p/s)	5
83	Epic WA 3565	It's Late/It's Good For You Baby (feet-shaped picture disc)	12
83	Epic WA 3774	Cry Just A Little Bit/Love Me Tonight (picture disc)	8
83	Kelloggs KELL 1	Oh Julie/ABBA: I Have A Dream (free with Kelloggs' 'Rice Krispies')	8
84	Epic A 4291	A Love Waiting For You/As Long As I Have You (live) (poster p/s)	10
84	Epic QA 4677	A Letter To You/Come Back And Love Me (p/s, with free post bag game)	6
84	Epic DA 4882	Teardrops/You Shake Me Up//Shakin' Stevens Party Mix (Parts 1 & 2) (double pack)	10
85	Epic GA 6072	Breakin' Up My Heart/I'll Give You My Heart (gatefold pop-up p/s)	7
85	Epic GTA 6769	Merry Christmas Everyone/With My Heart (12", advent calendar p/s)	8
86	Epic QA 6819	Turning Away/Diddle (poster p/s)	5
86	Epic SHAKY 2	Because I Love You/Tell Me One More Time (2 picture sleeves, sealed together on edge with sticker, with autograph)	8
86	Epic SHAKY G2	Because I Love You/Tell Me One More Time (gatefold p/s)	7
86	Epic GA 6769	Merry Christmas Everyone/Blue Christmas (reissue, gatefold p/s)	6
87	Epic SHAKY C3	A Little Boogie Woogie (In The Back Of My Mind)/If You're Gonna Cry (cassette)	5
87	Epic SHAKY 5	What Do You Want To Make Those Eyes At Me For/You're Evil (p/s, with competition entry form)	5
87	Epic SHAKY P5	What Do You Want To Make Those Eyes At Me For/You're Evil (picture disc)	6
87	Epic SHAKY G5	What Do You Want To Make Those Eyes At Me For/You're Evil + 2 (g/fold p/s)	5
88	Epic SHAKY Q6	Feel The Need In Me/If I Can't Have You (poster p/s)	5
89	Epic SHAKY C10	Love Attack/Love Attack (Extended Version)/As Long As I Have You (live) (CD, card sleeve)	8
EPs			
81	Magnum Force MFEP 001	Memphis Earthquake/You Mostest Girl/Evil Hearted Ada/ My Bucket's Got A Hole In It (EP, p/s)	8
82	Magnum Force MFEP 007	Frantic/Ready Teddy/Tear It Up/Monkey's Uncle (EP, p/s)	8
83	Magnum Force MFEP 010	Justine/Jungle Rock/Story Of The Rockers/My Baby Died (EP, p/s)	8
83	Epic 40-2620	GREATEST ORIGINAL HITS (EP, cassette)	12
LPs			
70	Parlophone PCS 7112	A LEGEND (LP)	55
71	CBS 52901	I'M NO J.D. (LP)	45
72	Contour 2870 152	ROCKIN' AND SHAKIN' (LP)	20
73	Emerald GES 1121	SHAKIN' STEVENS AND THE SUNSETS (LP)	18
78	Track 2406 011	SHAKIN' STEVENS (LP)	15
80	Epic EPC 83978	TAKE ONE (LP)	12
80	Epic EPC 84547	MARIE MARIE (LP, withdrawn)	18
81	Epic EPC 10027	SHAKY (LP, feet-shaped picture disc)	12
83	Epic BX 86301	THE BOP WON'T STOP (LP & cassette, box set, with Shaky autograph book)	18
85	CJS CJS 1	MANHATTAN MELODRAMA (LP)	12

SHAKIN' STEVENS & BONNIE TYLER

83	Epic TA 4071	A Rockin' Good Way/Why Do You Treat Me This Way/The Bop Won't Stop (12", p/s)	8

TERRI STEVENS

59	Felsted AF 112	My Wish Tonight/All Alone	10
59	Felsted AF 112	My Wish Tonight/All Alone (78)	6
59	Felsted AF 126	Adonis/Vieni, Vieni	7
59	Felsted AF 126	Adonis/Vieni, Vieni (78)	10

VIKKI STEVENS

60	Embassy WB 410	As Long As He Needs Me/Where Is Love?	5
60	Embassy WB 410	As Long As He Needs Me/Where Is Love? (78, as Vicky Stevens)	8

VIRGINIA STEVENS

77	Mulligan LUN A 332	TIOCFAIDH AN SAMHRADH — TRADITIONAL SONGS FROM THE WEST OF IRELAND (LP, with booklet)	15

RICHARD STEVENSEN

70	Pye NSPL 18358	GATES OF ME (LP)	15

MICKEY STEVENSON

72	Ember EMBS 320	Here I Am/Joe Poor Loves Daphne Elizabeth Richard	5
72	Ember NR 5063	HERE I AM (LP)	12

MINT VALUE £

STEVIE'S BUZZ

96	Nice no cat. no.	Autumn Stone/P.P. & THE PRIMES: Understanding (promo only, large centre)	8

(see also P.P. Arnold, Buzzcocks, Primal Scream)

AL STEWART

66	Decca F 12467	The Elf/Turn To Earth	95
67	CBS 3034	Bedsitter Images/Swiss Cottage Manoeuvres	8
70	CBS 4843	Electric Los Angeles Sunset/My Enemies Have Sweet Voices	8
70	CBS 5351	The News From Spain/Elvaston Place	7
72	CBS 7763	You Don't Even Know Me/I'm Falling	6
72	CBS 7992	Amsterdam/Songs Out Of Clay	6
73	CBS SCBS 1971	Terminal Eyes/Last Day Of June 1934	6
76	RCA RCA 2771	Year Of The Cat/Broadway Hotel	5
67	CBS (S)BPG 63087	BEDSITTER IMAGES (LP)	80
69	CBS (S) 63460	LOVE CHRONICLES (LP, gatefold sleeve)	35
70	CBS 63848	ZERO SHE FLIES (LP, gatefold sleeve)	20
70	CBS 64023	FIRST ALBUM (BEDSITTER IMAGES) (LP, remixed reissue, different track listing)	20
72	CBS 64739	ORANGE (LP)	15
73	CBS 65726	PAST, PRESENT AND FUTURE (LP, gatefold sleeve)	12
75	CBS 80477	MODERN TIMES (LP)	12
80	Arista AL 9520	24 CARROTS (LP, with inner)	12

(see also Jimmy Page)

ANDY STEWART

60	Top Rank JAR 427	Donald, Where's Your Troosers?/Dancing In The Kyle	7
61	Top Rank JAR 565	The Battle's O'er/Tunes Of Glory	5
61	Top Rank JAR 594	Take Me Back/The Road And The Miles To Dundee	5
62	Top Rank JAR 616	Cowboy Jock From Skye/The Highland Twist	6
65	HMV POP 1454	Dr. Finlay/Oh! What A Ceilidh	6
61	Top Rank JKP 3009	ANDY SINGS (EP)	8

BILLY STEWART

62	Pye International 7N 25164	Reap What You Sow/Fat Boy	10
63	Pye International 7N 25222	Strange Feeling/Sugar And Spice	10
65	Chess CRS 8009	I Do Love You/Keep Loving	12
65	Chess CRS 8017	Sitting In The Park/Once Again	12
66	Chess CRS 8028	Because I Love You/Mountains Of Love	15
66	Chess CRS 8038	Love Me/Why Am I Lonely	15
66	Chess CRS 8040	Summertime/To Love To Love	12
66	Chess CRS 8045	Secret Love/Look Back And Smile	12
66	Chess CRS 8050	Ole Man River/Every Day I Have The Blues	15
67	Chess CRS 8067	Cross My Heart/Why (Do I Love You So)	7
69	Chess CRS 8092	Summertime/I Do Love You	8
72	Chess 6145 017	Sitting In The Park/Summertime	6
65	Chess CRE 6010	IN CROWD (EP, with Ramsey Lewis Trio, et al)	40
67	Chess CRE 6024	I DO LOVE YOU (EP)	25
66	Chess CRL 4523	UNBELIEVABLE (LP)	35
72	Chess 6310 125	GOLDEN DECADE (LP)	15

BOB STEWART

55	MGM SP 1114	It's A Woman's World/I Went Out Of My Way	6

BOB STEWART

75	Argo ZDA 207	THE UNIQUE SOUND OF THE PSALTERY (LP)	12

DAVID A. STEWART

92	Anxious ZT 43046	LILY WAS HERE (12", with 2 Orb mixes, featuring Candy Dulfer, p/s)	8

(see also Eurythmics, Longdancer, Stewart & Harrison)

DAVIE STEWART

78	Topic 12T 293	DAVIE STEWART (LP, with insert)	12

DELANO STEWART

68	Doctor Bird DB 1138	That's Life/Tell Me Baby	18
68	High Note HS 004	Let's Have Some Fun/Dance With Me	12
69	High Note HS 014	Rocking Sensation/GAYTONES: One Look	12
70	High Note HS 027	Got To Come Back/Don't Believe In Him	7
70	High Note HS 034	Hallelujah/I Wish It Could Last	6
70	High Hote HS 039	Wherever I Lay My Hat/Don't Believe Him (B-side actually by Gladstone Anderson & Gaytones)	10
70	High Note HS 041	Stay A Little Bit Longer/Stay A Little Bit Longer (Version II) (B-side actually by Gladstone Anderson & Gaytones)	12
70	Trojan TBL 138	STAY A LITTLE BIT LONGER (LP)	25

(see also Winston Stewart, Gaylads, Patsy Todd)

GRAHAM STEWART SEVEN

59	Tempo EXA 91	GRAHAM STEWART SEVEN (EP)	10

JAMES STEWART

65	Brunswick 05938	The Legend Of Shenandoah/CHARLES 'BUD' DANT CHORUS: We're Ridin' Out Tonight	12

JAMES STEWART & HENRY FONDA

70	Stateside SS 2179	Rolling Stone/Theme From Cheyenne Social Club	8

JOHN STEWART

69	Capitol CL 15589	July, You're A Woman/Shackles And Chains	5
69	Capitol E-(S)T 203	CALIFORNIA BLOODLINES (LP)	12
70	Capitol E-ST 540	WILLARD (LP)	12

(see also Kingston Trio, Cumberland Three)

MINT VALUE £

JOHNNY STEWART

58	HMV POP 480	Wishing For Your Love/Promise Me	7

PAUL STEWART (MOVEMENT)

66	Philips BF 1513	Queen Boadicea/Talkin'	7
67	Decca F 12577	Saturday Morning Man/Too Too Good (as Paul Stewart Movement)	12

(see also Hamilton & [Hamilton] Movement)

RAPHAEL STEWART & HOT TOPS

71	Punch PH 71	Put Your Sweet Lips/JUSTINS: Stand By Me	10

ROD STEWART

SINGLES

64	Decca F 11996	Good Morning Little Schoolgirl/I'm Gonna Move To The Outskirts Of Town	110
65	Columbia DB 7766	The Day Will Come/Why Does It Go On?	100
66	Columbia DB 7892	Shake/I Just Got Some	110
68	Immediate IM 060	Little Miss Understood/So Much To Say	90
70	Vertigo 6086 002	It's All Over Now/Jo's Lament	15
73	Mercury 6052 371	Oh No Not My Baby/Jodie (tartan sleeve)	6
76	Mercury 6160 006	Maggie May/You Wear It Well/Twistin' The Night Away (p/s)	5
77	Mercury 6160 007	Mandolin Wind/Girl From The North Country/Sweet Little Rock'N'Roller	5
76	Mercury 6167 327	It's All Over Now/Handbags And Gladrags	7
77	Riva RIVA 1	You're Insane/You're Insane (DJ copy, 500 only)	20
77	Riva RIVA 3	Tonight's The Night/The First Cut Is The Deepest (withdrawn B-side)	10
78	Riva RIVA 9	Sailing/Stone Cold Sober (p/s)	5
78	Riva RIVA 9	Sailing/Stone Cold Sober (HMS Ark Royal Commemorative issue, blue vinyl, p/s)	120
78	Riva RIVA 15	Ole Ola/Que Sera Sera — I'd Walk A Million Miles For One Of Your Goals (p/s)	5
80	Riva RIVA 23	If Lovin' You Is Wrong/Last Summer (p/s)	5
80	Virgin VS 366	Little Miss Understood/So Much To Say (p/s, reissue)	5
80	Riva W 7929TP	Excerpts From "Foolish Behaviour" (flexidisc free with *London Evening News*)	10/6
81	Riva RIVA 29M	Oh God I Wish I Was Home Tonight/Somebody Special (cassette)	5
82	Riva RIVA 35	How Long/Jealous (p/s, with free sticker)	5
82	Decca F 11996	Good Morning Little Schoolgirl/I'm Gonna Move To The Outskirts Of Town (reissue)	8
82	Immediate IM 060	Little Miss Understood/So Much To Say (reissue, p/s)	5
83	Warner Bros W 9440P	Sweet Surrender/Ghetto Blaster (picture disc)	7
83	Warner Bros W 96564T	Baby Jane/Ready Now/If Lovin' You Is Wrong (live) (12", p/s, with poster)	10
84	Warner Bros SAM 194	Infatuation (1-sided picture disc in wallet with interview cassette)	15
86	Warner Bros W 8668TP	Love Touch/Heart Is On The Line/Hard Lesson To Learn (12", picture disc)	10
86	Warner Bros W 8625TE	Every Beat Of My Heart (Tartan Mix)/Trouble/Some Guys Have All The Luck/ I Don't Want To Talk About It (live) (12", p/s with poster)	10
88	Warner Bros WX 152TP	Lost In You (Extended Remix)/Lost In You (Fade)/Almost Illegal (12", pic disc)	10
89	Warner Bros W 2686P	This Old Heart Of Mine/Ain't Love A Bitch/Tonight I'm Yours (Don't Hurt Me) (with Ronald Isley, shaped picture disc)	10
89	Warner Bros W 2647TG	Downtown Train/Stay With Me/Cindy Incidentally/To Love Somebody (12", gatefold p/s)	10
89	Warner Bros W 7729 TP	My Heart Can't Tell You No/The Wild Horse/Passion (12", p/s)	8
91	Warner Bros W 0030 TP	The Motown Song/Sweet Soul Music/Try A Little Tenderness (12", p/s)	10
91	Warner Bros W 0059 TE	Broken Arrow/The Killing Of Georgie Parts 1 & 2/I Was Only Joking (10", p/s)	8
70s	Mercury BRAUN 3	MAGGIE MAY (EP, freebie)	6

LPs

70	Vertigo VO 4	AN OLD RAINCOAT WON'T EVER LET YOU DOWN (gatefold sleeve, swirl label)	20
70	Vertigo 6360 500	GASOLINE ALLEY (gatefold sleeve, swirl label)	20
71	Mercury 6338 063	EVERY PICTURE TELLS A STORY (black label)	15
72	Mercury 6499 153	NEVER A DULL MOMENT (gatefold sleeve)	15
73	Mercury 6499 484	SING IT AGAIN, ROD	12
75	Riva RVLP 4	ATLANTIC CROSSING (gatefold sleeve, blue vinyl)	18
76	Mercury 6672 013	THE VINTAGE YEARS	12
76	Philips SON 001	RECORDED HIGHLIGHTS & ACTION REPLAYS	12
78	St. Michael 21020 102	REASON TO BELIEVE (only available in Marks & Spencer)	30
80	Phonogram IMP 117 2188/ 3014	MAGGIE MAY (only available in Marks & Spencer)	15
84	Warner Bros 9250 951	CAMOUFLAGE (with bonus 1-sided picture disc "Infatuation" in wallet with interview tape [SAM 194])	20

(see also Jeff Beck, Shotgun Express, Faces, Python Lee Jackson, Long John Baldry, Ted Wood)

ROMAN STEWART

72	Songbird SB 1075	Changing Times (with Dave)/CRYSTALITES: Changing Times Version	10
73	Downtown DT 518	Try Me/BIG YOUTH: Rhythm Style	12
73	Techniques TE 932	Tonight I'm Staying Here (& Tennors)/Lady Love (& Tennors)	8
75	Camel CA 2002	Wolverton Mountain/PITTERSON ALL STARS: Version	5

SANDY STEWART

58	London HLE 8683	A Certain Smile/Kiss Me Richard	15
58	London HLE 8683	A Certain Smile/Kiss Me Richard (78)	15
63	Pye International 7N 25176	My Colouring Book/I Heard You Cried Last Night	6

SONNY STEWART & HIS SKIFFLE KINGS

57	Philips PB 719	The Northern Line/Black Jack (78)	20
57	Philips PB 773	Let Me Lie/Mama Don't Allow It (78)	20

TINGA STEWART

71	Songbird SB 1048	Hear That Train/CRYSTALITES: Hear That Train — Version	6
72	Tropical AL 0018	A Brand New Me/BROWNS ALL STARS: Nice Version	6
74	Dragon DRA 1025	The Message/Dub	12

MINT VALUE £

WINSTON STEWART

64 R&B JB 147 But I Do/MAYTALS: Four Seasons ... 35
64 Port-O-Jam PJ 4002 All Of My Life/How Many Times ... 30
(see also Andy & Clyde, Gaylads, Delano Stewart, Winston & Tonettes)

WYNN STEWART

60 London HL 7087 Wishful Thinking/Uncle Tom Got Caught (export issue) ... 30

(Dave) STEWART & HARRISON

70 Multicord MULT SH 1 GIRL (EP) ... 15
(see also Longdancer, Eurythmics, David A. Stewart)

REX STEWART'S LONDON FIVE

55 Tempo EXA 8 REX STEWART'S LONDON FIVE (EP) ... 8

STICKERS

71 Bullet BU 492 One Night Of Sin/Sin (Version) (both sides actually by Jackie Brown) ... 6
(see also Jackie Brown)

STICK SHIFTS

80 Chiswick CHIS 118 Automobile/Parramatta Road (3 different p/s) ... 10

ARBEE STIDHAM

70s Mainstream MSL 1011 A TIME FOR BLUES (LP) ... 12

STIFF LITTLE FINGERS

78 Rigid Digits SRD-1 Suspect Device/Wasted Life (hand-made p/s, 500 only, red label with catalogue number on right-hand side) ... 75
78 Rigid Digits SRD-1 Suspect Device/Wasted Life (re-pressing, different machine-cut p/s, various colour labels/yellow labels) ... 15
78 Rough Trade RT 004 78 R.P.M./Alternative Ulster (p/s, A & B-sides reversed) ... 8
78 Rough Trade RT 004 Alternative Ulster/78 R.P.M. (p/s) ... 5
78 Rough Trade RT 006 Suspect Device/Wasted Life (reissue) ... 8
79 Rough Trade RT 015 Gotta Getaway/Bloody Sunday (p/s) ... 5
82 Chrysalis CHSDJ 2580 Listen/Two Guitars Clash (p/s, jukebox issue) ... 5
82 Chrysalis/Melody Maker [no cat. no.] Excerpts From "Now Then"/IGGY POP: Excerpts From "Zombie Birdhouse" (flexidisc, free with *Melody Maker*) ... 6/4
91 Essential ESSX 2007 Beirut Moon/Stand Up And Shout/Interview With Jake Burns (CD, limited edition) ... 70
02 EMI Gold 7243 5 38560 21 LIVE IN ABERDEEN (CD, withdrawn — available for only 1 day) ... 150
(see also Billy Karloff & Extremes)

STIFFS

79 Dork UR 1 Standard English/S.C. Rip/Brookside Riot Squad (die-cut sleeve) ... 25
79 Dork UR 2 Inside Out/Kids On the Street (die cut sleeve or later Zonophone Z3 p/s) ... 20
80 Zonophone Z 14 Volume Control/Nothing To Lose (p/s) ... 10
80 Stiff BUT 86 Goodbye My Love/Magic Roundabout (p/s) ... 10
85 Dork UR 7(12) The Young Guitars/Yer Under Attack (12", red or blue p/s) ... 10/8

STILETTOS

80 Ariola ARO 200 This Is The Way/Who Can It Be (p/s) ... 20

STILL LIFE

68 Columbia DB 8345 What Did We Miss/My Kingdom Cannot Lose ... 30
71 Vertigo 6360 026 STILL LIFE (LP, gatefold sleeve, swirl label) ... 110
(see also Jon, Titus Groan)

STEPHEN STILLS

71 Atlantic 2091 046 Love The One You're With/To A Flame ... 5
71 Atlantic 2091 069 Sit Yourself Down/We Are Not Helpless ... 5
71 Atlantic 2091 117 Change Partners/Relaxing Town ... 5
71 Atlantic 2091 141 Marianne/Nothing To Do But Today ... 5
70 Atlantic 2401 004 STEPHEN STILLS (LP) ... 15
71 Atlantic 2401 013 STEPHEN STILLS 2 (LP, gatefold sleeve) ... 12
73 Atlantic K 40440 DOWN THE ROAD (LP) ... 12
(see also Buffalo Springfield, Al Kooper Mike Bloomfield & Stephen Stills, Crosby Stills Nash & Young, Manassas, Stills-Young Band)

STILLWATER TRIO

70s Sharon 330 LIFE'S RAILROAD (LP) ... 18

STILLS-YOUNG BAND

76 Reprise K 14446 Long May You Run/12-8 Blues ... 5
76 Reprise K 14482 Like A Hurricane (edit)/Hold Back The Tears ... 5
76 Reprise K 54081 LONG MAY YOU RUN (LP) ... 12
(see also Stephen Stills, Manassas, Neil Young, Buffalo Springfield, Crosby Stills Nash & Young)

STING

87 A&M AMCD 410 We'll Be Together (Extended Mix 5.54)/(Previous Version 4.28)/ Conversation With A Dog/We'll Be Together (Instrumental Version) (3" CD, with adaptor in plastic tray in gatefold card sleeve) ... 10
87 A&M AMCD 431 Englishman In New York/Ghost In The Strand (Instrumental)/Bring On The Night-When The World Is Running Down (live) (CD) ... 10
88 A&M AMCD 439 Fragile/Fragile (Portuguese Version)/Fragilidad/Mariposa Libre (CD) ... 8
88 A&M AMCD 911 COMPACT HITS (CD EP) ... 8
88 A&M AMCD 458 They Dance Alone (Gueca Solo) (with Eric Clapton & Mark Knopfler)/ Ellas Damzon Solas (Gueca Solo)/St. Estamos Juntos (CD) ... 8
88 A&M AMCDR 580 Englishman In New York/Englishman In New York (Ben Liebrand Mix)/If You Love Somebody Set Them Free (Jellybean Dance Mix) (CD, picture disc) ... 8
85 A&M DREAMP 1 THE DREAM OF THE BLUE TURTLES (LP, picture disc, die-cut sl., with insert) .. 12
91 A&M 397 171-2 ACOUSTIC LIVE IN NEWCASTLE (CD, box set with book) ... 20
(see also Police, Last Exit, [Fast Breeder &] Radio Actors, Newcastle Big Band)

STINGERS

72	Upsetter US 395	Preacher Man/UPSETTERS: Version	15

STINGRAY (TV series)

(see under Century 21)

STING-RAYS

82	Rocket XPRES 78	Radiator Rock/Slap Bass Boogie (die-cut sleeve)	8
82	Big Beat SW 82	Dinosaurs/Math Of Trend/Another Cup Of Coffee/You're Gonna Miss Me (white label test pressing, 100 Club gig freebie, 80 only)	20
83	Big Beat SW 82	Dinosaurs/Math Of Trend/Another Cup Of Coffee/You're Gonna Miss Me (p/s)	6
84	Big Beat NS 95	Escalator/Loose Lip Synch Ship/Escalator (Instrumental) (p/s)	5
85	Big Beat NS 109	Don't Break Down/Don't Break Down (Version) (p/s)	5
85	Big Beat NST 109	Don't Break Down/Don't Break Down (Version) (12", p/s)	8
85	Media Burn MB 2/ Lyntone LYN 16436	Bonus Track/I Want My Woman/Flash On You (33 rpm, red vinyl flexidisc with *The Sting-Rays Story* magazine)	5
86	ABC ABCS 009T	June Rhyme/Militant Tendency/Wedding Ring (12", p/s)	8
86	Kaleidoscope Sound 702	Behind The Beyond (EP)	5
86	Kaleidoscope Sound 102	BEHIND THE BEYOND (12" EP)	8
83	Big beat WIKM 16	DINOSAURS (LP)	12
84	Media Burn MB 1	LIVE RETALIATION (LP, white or black vinyl)	15/12
87	K'scope Sound KSLP 1	CRYPTIC AND COFFEE TIME (LP)	12
88	Media Burn MB 18	GOODBYE TO ALL THAT — LIVE VOL. 2 (LP, red or black vinyl)	15/12

STINKY TOYS

77	Polydor 2056 630	Boozy Creed/Driver Blues (p/s)	15
77	Polydor 2393 174	STINKY TOYS (LP)	25

(PETER) LEE STIRLING (& BRUISERS)

63	Columbia DB 4992	My Heart Commands Me/Welcome Stranger (as Lee Stirling & Bruisers)	8
63	Parlophone R 5063	I Could If I Wanted To/Right From The Start (as Lee Stirling & Bruisers)	8
64	Parlophone R 5112	Now That I've Found You/I Believe (as Peter Lee Stirling & Bruisers)	8
64	Parlophone R 5158	Sad, Lonely And Blue/I'm Looking For Someone To Love (as Peter Lee Stirling & Bruisers)	8
64	Parlophone R 5198	Everything Will Be Alright/You'll Be Mine (as Peter Lee Stirling & Bruisers)	8
66	Decca F 12433	The Sweet And Tender Hold Of Your Love/Everybody Needs A Someone	7
66	Decca F 12535	Oh What A Fool/I'm Sportin' A New Baby	7
67	Decca F 12628	You Don't Live Twice/8.35 On The Dot	25
67	Decca F 12674	Goodbye Thimblemill Lane/Hey Conductor	7
69	MCA MU 1093	Big Sam/Mr. Average Man	7
70	MCA MK 5027	Goodbye Summer Girl/Judas In Blue	6

(see also Bruisers, Hungry Wolf)

GARY STITES

59	London HLL 8881	Lonely For You/Shine That Ring	25
59	London HLL 8881	Lonely For You/Shine That Ring (78)	20
59	London HLL 9003	Starry Eyed/Without Your Love	20
59	London HLL 9003	Starry Eyed/Without Your Love (78)	25
60	London HLL 9082	Lawdy, Miss Clawdy/Don't Wanna Say Goodbye	25

KING STITT

69	Clandisc CLA 200	Who Yea/DYNAMITES: Mr Midnight	8
69	Clandisc CLA 202	Vigerton Two/On The Street	8
69	Clandisc CLA 203	On The Street/CYNTHIA RICHARDS: Foolish Fool	10
69	Clandisc CLA 206	The Ugly One/CLANCY ECCLES: Dance Beat	8
70	Clandisc CLA 207	Herbsman Shuffle (with Andy [Capp])/HIGGS & WILSON: Don't Mind Me	8
70	Clandisc CLA 223	King Of Kings/DYNAMITES: Reggaedelic	8
71	Clandisc CLA 235	Merry Rhythm/CLANCY ECCLES: John Crow Skank	6
71	Banana BA 332	Back Out Version/VEGETABLES: Holly Rhythm	8
71	Banana BA 334	Rhyming Time/Reality	8

(see also Kurass)

SONNY STITT

53	Esquire 20-013	SONNY STITT-BUD POWELL QUARTET (10" LP)	18
58	Esquire 32-049	S.P.J. JAZZ (LP, with Bud Powell & J.J. Johnson)	15
58	Columbia Clef 33CX 10114	NEW YORK JAZZ (LP)	15
59	Esquire 32-078	STITT'S BITS (LP)	15
59	HMV CLP 1280	ONLY THE BLUES (LP)	12
60	HMV CLP 1363	PERSONAL APPEARANCE (LP)	12
60	HMV CLP 1384	SONNY STITT WITH THE OSCAR PETERSON TRIO (LP)	12
61	HMV CLP 1420/CSD 1341	BLOWS THE BLUES (LP, mono/stereo)	12/15
67	Marble Arch MAL 753	SONNY STITT (LP)	15

(see also Oscar Peterson, J.J. Johnson)

ALAN STIVELL

72	Philips 6009 208	Wind Of Keltia/Pop Plinn	5
72	Philips 6414 406	RENAISSANCE OF THE CELTIC HARP (LP)	12
73	Fontana 6399 005	A L'OLYMPIA (LP)	12
74	Fontana 6399 008	REFLECTIONS (LP)	12
74	Philips 6325 304	FROM CELTIC ROOTS (LP)	12
75	Fontana 9299 547	STIVELL (LP)	12

STOCK, AITKEN & WATERMAN

87	Breakout USAF 611	Roadblock/Roadblock (Horn Jammin' Dub) (12", p/s)	8
87	Breakout USAF 611§	Roadblack/ Roadblock (7" dub edit)	5
87	Breakout USAF 620	Packjammed (Writ Mix Extended Version)/Packjammed (12", p/s)	10
88	PWL PWLT 22R	SS Paparazzi (mixes) (12", p/s)	10

STOCKER, GREENWOOD & FRIENDS

79	Changes CR1400	BILLY + NINE (LP)	80

(see also Slack Alice)

MINT VALUE £

STOCKHOLM MONSTERS
81 Factory FAC 41 Fairytales/Death Is Slowly (p/s) . . . 15
82 Factory FAC 58 Happy Ever After/Soft Babies (p/s) . . . 15
84 Factory FAC 107 All At Once (p/s). . . 15

STOCKINGTOPS
68 Toast TT 500 You're Never Gonna Get My Lovin'/You Don't Know What Love Is All About . . . 12
68 CBS 3407 I Don't Ever Wanna Be Kicked By You/The World We Live In Is A Lonely Place . . . 7
(see also Sue & Sunny, Sue & Sunshine, Myrtelles)

STOCKTON'S WING
78 Tara 2004 STOCKTON'S WING (LP) . . . 12

STOICS
68 RCA RCA 1745 Earth, Fire, Air And Water/Search Of The Sea . . . 25

STOKES
65 London HLU 9955 Whipped Cream/Pie Crust . . . 12

SIMON STOKES & NIGHTHAWKS
70 Elektra EKSN 45082 Voodoo Woman/Can't Stop Now . . . 10

RHET STOLLER (& HIS ECHOES)
60 Decca F 11271 Walk Don't Run/All Rhet . . . 18
60 Decca F 11302 Chariot/Night Theme . . . 12
63 Decca F 11738 Countdown/Over The Steppes (as Rhet Stoller & His Echoes) . . . 12
64 Melodisc MEL 1595 Beat That/Treble Gold + One . . . 20
64 Windsor PS 118 Bandit/Tonight (unissued)
64 Windsor PS 119 Caravan/Short Cut . . . 20
64 Windsor PS 130 Ricochet/Knockout. . . 20
66 Columbia DB 8013 Uncrowned King/Surf Ride (unissued, demos only). . . 25
69 Mosaic MOSAIC 1 SUNSHINE ANYTIME (EP, as Rhet Stoller & Music) . . . 12
67 Coronet EC 101 THE INCREDIBLE RHET STOLLER (LP) . . . 30

JACKIE STOLLINGS (& NASHVILLE BOYS)
62 Starlite ST45 092 Footsteps Of A Fool/And Then I Knew (B-side with Nashville Boys). . . 6

MORRIS STOLOFF (& COLUMBIA PICTURES ORCHESTRA)
56 Brunswick 05553 Moonglow/Theme From "Picnic". . . 10
56 Brunswick 05597 Theme From "The Solid Gold Cadillac"/Sweet Sue Just You . . . 6
57 Brunswick 05618 Exactly Like You/Wanna Go Back To You. . . 5
57 Brunswick 05666 Theme From "Fire Down Below"/Theme From "Full Of Life" . . . 6

STOMPERS
62 Fontana H 385 Quarter To Four Stomp (Surf Stompin')/Foolish One . . . 25

ALEXANDER STONE
70 Gemini GMS 003 I Try To Make You Good/Man In A Suitcase . . . 5

CLIFFIE STONE & HIS ORCHESTRA
55 Capitol CL 14330 Barracuda/The Popcorn Song (with Billy Strange & Speedy West) . . . 110
55 Capitol CL 14330 Barracuda/The Popcorn Song (with Billy Strange & Speedy West) (78) . . . 25
56 Capitol CL 14666 Jingle Bells/Rudolph The Red Nosed Reindeer . . . 6
58 Capitol CL 14928 Near You/Nobody's Darlin' But Mine . . . 6
59 Capitol CL 14982 Maybe/I Don't Want To Walk Without You. . . 5
59 Capitol CL 14996 Blood On The Saddle/Cool Water . . . 6
59 Capitol T 1080 THE PARTY'S ON ME (LP). . . 15
(see also Jeanne Gayle, Billy Strange)

ELLA STONE & MOSS
70s Phoenix SNIX 128 The Prophet/Now Or Never . . . 6
(see also Helen Shapiro, Al Saxon)

GEORGE STONE
65 Stateside SS 479 Hole In The Wall/My Beat . . . 15

KIRBY STONE QUARTET/FOUR
56 Vogue Coral Q 72129 Honey Hush/Lassus Trombone . . . 15
56 Vogue Coral Q 72129 Honey Hush/Lassus Trombone (78). . . 10
59 Philips PB 903 That "I Had A Dream, Dear" Rock/Sweet Nothings . . . 5
59 Philips PB 903 That "I Had A Dream, Dear" Rock/Sweet Nothings (78) . . . 10
63 Warner Bros WB 102 The Great Escape (March)/Fancy Dan. . . 5
63 Warner Bros WB 118 Washington Guitar/Blue Guitar . . . 5
59 London HA-A 2164 MAN, I FLIPPED WHEN I HEARD THE KIRBY STONE FOUR (LP). . . 15

MARK STONE
58 London HLR 8543 Ever Since I Met Lucy/The Stroll . . . 80
58 London HLR 8543 Ever Since I Met Lucy/The Stroll (78) . . . 40

SLY (& FAMILY) STONE
68 Columbia DB 8369 Dance To The Music/Let Me Hear It From You . . . 100
68 Direction 58-3568 Dance To The Music/Let Me Hear It From You (reissue) . . . 5
68 Direction 58-3707 M'Lady/Life. . . 6
69 Direction 58-3938 Everyday People/Sing A Simple Song . . . 6
69 Direction 58-4279 Stand!/I Want To Take You Higher. . . 6
69 Direction 58-4471 Hot Fun In The Summertime/Fun. . . 6
70 Direction 58-4782 Thank You (Falettinme Be Mice Elf Agin)/Everybody Is A Star. . . 6
70 CBS 5054 I Want To Take You Higher/You Can Make It If You Try . . . 6
71 Epic EPC 7632 Family Affair/Luv n' Haight . . . 5
72 Epic EPC 7810 Running Away/Brave And Strong . . . 5
73 Epic EPC 1655 If You Want Me To Stay/Thankful & Thoughtful . . . 5
74 Epic EPC 2530 Time For Livin'/Small Talk (as Sly Stone) . . . 5
75 Epic EPC 2882 Loose Booty/Can't Strain My Brain (as Sly Stone). . . 5
70s CBS SEPC 3048 Dance To The Music/Stand/Ride The Rhythm/Colour Me True (promo-only) . . . 8

MINT VALUE £

68 Direction 8-63412 DANCE TO THE MUSIC (LP) 20
68 Direction 8-63461 M'LADY (LP) 20
69 Direction 8-63655 STAND! (LP, CBS sleeve with Direction label) 20
70 Epic EPC 69002 GREATEST HITS (LP, gatefold sleeve) 12
72 Epic EPC 64613 THERE'S A RIOT GOING ON (LP, gatefold sleeve, with free EP/newspaper) 15
73 CBS Q 69002 GREATEST HITS (LP, quadrophonic, gatefold sleeve) 15
73 Epic EPC 69039 FRESH (LP, gatefold sleeve) 12
74 Epic EPC 69070 SMALL TALK (LP) 12
75 Epic EPC 22004 HIGH ENERGY (2-LP, gatefold sleeve) 15
75 Epic EPC 69165 HIGH ON YOU (LP, as Sly Stone) 12
76 Epic EPC 81641 HEARD YA MISSED ME, WELL I'M BACK (LP) 12
(see also Rosie Banks)

STONE ANGEL
75 SSLP 04 STONE ANGEL (LP, private pressing) 220
94 Acme AC 8008 LP STONE ANGEL (LP, reissue, 500 only) 15
(see also Ken Saul)

STONED AID
80s Hit STONE 1 Are You Going To Stonehenge/Magical Carpet Ride (p/s) 5
(see also Cannibals)

STONEFIELD TRAMP
74 Acorn/Tramp CF 247 DREAMING 165
(see also Terry Friend, Rob Van Spyk)

STONE GRAPHICS
68 Parlophone R 5735 A Tale Of Long Ago/Travelling Man 12

STONEGROUND
71 Warner Bros K 16126 You Must Be One Of Us/It Takes A Lot To Laugh 5
71 Warner Bros K 46087 STONEGROUND (LP) 15
71 Warner Bros K 53999 FAMILY ALBUM (LP) 15

STONEGROUND BAND
70s Nut SUNSTRUCK!! (LP, stickered sleeve) 30

HARRY STONEHAM
70 Studio Two TWO 326 HIGH POWER HAMMOND (LP) 12
71 Contour 2870 112 HAMMOND MY WAY (LP) 12
71 Studio Two TWO 345 SOLID GOLD HAMMOND (LP) 12
72 Studio Two Q4TWO 375 HAMMOND HITS THE HIGHWAY (LP, quadrophonic) 12
73 Studio Two TWOX 1002 IT ALL HAPPENS ON SATURDAY (LP) 12
75 Studio Two TWOX 1046 HAMMOND HEATWAVE (LP) 12

HARRY STONEHAM & JOHNNY EYDEN
67 Tepee TPRLP 100 TWO GUYS TO FOLLOW (LP, mono [70s reissues credited soley to Harry Stoneham £15]) 25

STONEHENGE MEN
62 HMV POP 981 Big Feet/Pinto 45

STONEHOUSE
71 RCA SF 8197 STONEHOUSE CREEK (LP) 100

E.V. STONEMAN
63 London HA-B/SH-B 8089 E.V. STONEMAN AND THE STONEMAN FAMILY (LP) 12

STONEPILLOW
69 Phase 4 Stereo PFS 4163 ELEAZAR'S CIRCUS (LP) 10

STONE PONEYS
67 Capitol CL 15523 A Different Drum/I've Got To Know 10
(see also Linda Ronstadt)

STONE ROSES

SINGLES
85 Thin Line THIN 001 So Young/Tell Me (12", p/s, 1,200 only; beware of counterfeits!) 120
87 Black/Revolver 12 REV 36 Sally Cinnamon/Here It Comes/All Across The Sand (12", 'Printed In England' on rear p/s & no barcode, "All Across The Sands" listed on label; different mixes of 2 tracks to later reissue) 20
88 Silvertone ORE 1 Elephant Stone/The Hardest Thing In The World (catalogue number in black print on rear of p/s) 6
88 Silvertone ORE 1T Elephant Stone (4.48)/Elephant Stone (7" Version) (3.00)/Full Fathom Five/The Hardest Thing In The World (12", p/s, cat. no. in black print on rear of p/s) .. 10
89 Silvertone ORE 2 Made Of Stone/Going Down (p/s, cat. no. in black print on rear of p/s) 7
89 Silvertone ORE 2T Made Of Stone/Going Down/Guernica (12", p/s, catalogue number in black print on rear of p/s) 20
89 Silvertone ORE 6 She Bangs The Drums/Standing Here (p/s) 5
89 Silvertone OREX 6 She Bangs The Drums/Standing Here (p/s, with postcard, 3,000 only) 7
89 Silvertone OREZ 6 She Bangs The Drums/Mersey Paradise/Standing Here (12", p/s with colour print, 5,000 only) 12
89 Silvertone ORE 13 What The World Is Waiting For/Fools Gold 4.15 (paper label, with postcard stickered p/s credits "What The World Is Waiting For") 6
89 Silvertone ORE 13 Fools Gold 4.15/What The World Is Waiting For (repressing, p/s credits "Fools Gold") 5
89 Silvertone ORET 13 What The World Is Waiting For/Fools Gold 9.23 (12", stickered p/s credits "What The World Is Waiting For", with print) 10
89 Silvertone ORECD 13 Fools Gold 9.23/What The World Is Waiting For/Fools Gold 4.15 (CD, inlay credits "What The World Is Waiting For") 8
89 Black/Revolver REV 36 Sally Cinnamon/Here It Comes (p/s) 5
90 Silvertone ORE 1 Elephant Stone (7" Version)/The Hardest Thing In The World (catalogue number in red print on rear of p/s) 6

MINT VALUE £

90	Silvertone ORE 2	Made Of Stone/Going Down (p/s, cat. no. in blue print on rear of p/s)	5
90	Fierce FRIGHT 044	SPIKE ISLAND EP (fan interviews, P.A. announcements & fireworks, with cigarette, badge, bag of grass & banana sweet)	15
90	Silvertone ORE	One Love/Something's Burning (p/s, with postcard)	5
90	Silvertone ORET	One Love/Something's Burning (12", p/s, with print)	10
91	Silvertone ORE 31	I Wanna Be Adored (3.28)/Where Angels Play (p/s)	5
91	Silvertone OREZ 31	I Wanna Be Adored (4.52)/Where Angels Play/ Sally Cinnamon (live at the Hacienda) (12", stickered p/s with print)	40
92	Silvertone ORE 35	Waterfall (7" Version 3.31)/One Love (7" Version 3.40) (p/s)	5
92	Silvertone OREZT 35	Waterfall (12" Version 5.23)/One Love (Adrian Sherwood 12" Version 7.10) (12", p/s with print)	50
92	Silvertone ORE 40	I Am The Resurrection (Pan And Scan Radio Version)/I Am The Resurrection (Highly Resurrected Dub) (p/s)	5
92	Silvertone ORET 40	I Am The Resurrection (Extended 19:9 Ratio Club Mix)/(Original LP Version)/ Fools Gold (Bottom Won Mix) (12", some with print)	15/8
93	Silvertone ORECD 37	So Young/Tell Me (CD, from "CD Singles Collection")	12
92	Silvertone SRBX 2	12" SINGLES COLLECTION (10 x 12" singles box set, 1,000 only)	60
92	Silvertone SRBX 1	CD SINGLES COLLECTION (8 x CD singles box set, 1,000 only)	60
95	Geffen GFST 87	Ten Storey Love Song (12", p/s)	10
PROMOS			
90	Silvertone OREZ 13	Fools Gold (The Top Won Mix!)/(The Bottom Won Mix!) (12")	18
90	Silvertone OREZCD 13	Fools Gold (The Top Won Mix!)/(The Bottom Won Mix!) (gold CD)	12
90	Silvertone OREZ 17	One Love (Paul Schroeder Mix 7.08)/Something's Burning (12")	10
90	Silvertone STONE ONE	Fools Gold (A Guy Called Gerald Remix)/Elephant Stone (DJ Mix) (12", white label)	18
95	Silvertone OREDJ 71	Fools Gold (The Tall Paul Remix)/Fools Gold 9.23/ Fools Gold (Cricklewood Ballroom Mix) (12")	10
95	Geffen WGFSX 22060	Begging You (Album Version)/(Chic Mix)/(Stone Corporation Vox)/ (Young American Primitive Remix) (12", no p/s, some with press sheet)	15/10
95	Geffen WGFST 22060	Begging You (Album Version)/(Cox's Ultimatum Mix)/(Overworld Mix)/ (Lakota Mix) (12", no p/s)	10
95	Geffen WGFTD 22060	Begging You (Radio Edit)/(Chic Mix) (CD)	8
ALBUMS			
89	Silvertone ORE LP 502	THE STONE ROSES (LP, U.S. disc with "Elephant Stone", in U.K. embossed sleeve with gold lettering)	12
91	Silvertone ORE ZLP 502	THE STONE ROSES (2-LP, reissue, numbered gatefold sleeve with silver lettering)	15
95	Silvertone OREZCD 535	THE COMPLETE STONE ROSES (2-CD)	18

STONE'S MASONRY

66	Purdah 45-3504	Flapjacks/Hot Rock (99 copies only)	200

(see also Action, Mighty Baby, Savoy Brown)

STONE TEMPLE PILOTS

93	Atlantic A 5759 T	Sex Type Thing/Wicked Garden/Plush (12", p/s)	8
94	Atlantic A 7192 X	Interstate Love Song/Lounge Fly (purple vinyl)	6

STONE THE CROWS

70	Polydor 2066 060	Mad Dogs & Englishmen/Sad Mary	5
72	Polydor 2058 301	Good Time Girl/On The Highway	5
70	Polydor 2425 017	STONE THE CROWS (LP)	30
70	Polydor 2425 042	ODE TO JOHN LAW (LP)	20
71	Polydor 2425 701	TEENAGE LICKS (LP)	15
72	Polydor 2391 043	ONTINUOUS PERFORMANCE (LP)	15

(see also White Trash, Maggie Bell)

STONEY & MEAT LOAF

71	Rare Earth RES 103	What You See Is What You Get/The Way You Do The Things You Do	12
79	Prodigal PROD 10	What You See Is What You Get/The Way You Do The Things You Do (reissue)	8
72	Rare Earth SRE 3005	STONEY AND MEAT LOAF (LP)	25
79	Prodigal PDL 2010	MEAT LOAF (FEATURING STONEY & MEAT LOAF) (LP, revised reissue of "Stoney And Meat Loaf" with different tracks)	15
86	Motown ZL 72217	MEAT LOAF (FEATURING STONEY & MEAT LOAF) (LP, 2nd reissue)	12

(see also Meat Loaf)

STOOGES

89	Spiral Scratch SCRATCH 5	She Creatures Of Hollywood Hills/Untitled (as Iggy & Stooges, free with *Spiral Scratch* magazine, issue 5)	6/4
69	Elektra EKS 74051	THE STOOGES (LP, orange label)	70
70	Elektra EKS 74071	FUN HOUSE (LP, orange label)	70
70	Elektra 2410 009	FUN HOUSE (LP, reissue, red label)	20
73	CBS 65586	RAW POWER (LP, as Iggy & Stooges, plain orange label, with inner sleeve)	15
77	Elektra K 42032	THE STOOGES (LP, reissue, 'butterfly' label)	15
77	Elektra K 42051	FUN HOUSE (LP, reissue, 'butterfly' label)	15

(see also Iggy Pop)

STOP

80	Elite CAB 101	I Can Feel It/Iauwata (12")	12

STOPOUTS

78	Skeleton LYN 5912	Strange Thoughts/Just For You And Me (p/s)	15

STOREY SISTERS

58	London HLU 8571	Bad Motorcycle/Sweet Daddy	100
58	London HLU 8571	Bad Motorcycle/Sweet Daddy (78)	25

BILLY STORM

59	Philips PB 916	I've Come Of Age/This Is Always	15
59	Philips PB 916	I've Come Of Age/This Is Always (78)	10
60	London HLK 9236	Sure As You're Born/In The Chapel In The Moonlight	12

MINT VALUE £

DANNY STORM (& STROLLERS)

62	Piccadilly 7N 35025	Honest I Do/Sad But True (some in p/s)	15/10
62	Piccadilly 7N 35053	Just You/I Told You So	10
62	Piccadilly 7N 35091	I Just Can't Fool My Heart/Thinking Of You	12
63	Piccadilly 7N 35143	Say You Do/Let The Sunshine In (as Danny Storm & Strollers)	12

GALE STORM

56	London HLD 8222	I Hear You Knocking/Never Leave Me	45
56	London HLD 8222	I Hear You Knocking/Never Leave Me (78)	6
56	London HLD 8232	Memories Are Made Of This/A Teen-Age Prayer	40
56	London HLD 8283	Ivory Tower/I Ain't Gonna Worry	45
56	London HLD 8283	Ivory Tower/I Ain't Gonna Worry (78)	6
56	London HLD 8286	Why Do Fools Fall In Love/I Walk Alone	40
56	London HLD 8286	Why Do Fools Fall In Love/I Walk Alone (78)	6
56	London HL 7008	Why Do Fools Fall In Love/I Walk Alone (export issue)	20
56	London HLD 8311	Don't Be That Way (Please Listen To Me)/Tell Me Why	35
56	London HLD 8311	Don't Be That Way (Please Listen To Me)/Tell Me Why (78)	8
56	London HLD 8329	A Heart Without A Sweetheart/Now Is The Hour	22
56	London HLD 8329	A Heart Without A Sweetheart/Now Is The Hour (78)	10
57	London HLD 8393	Lucky Lips/On Treasure Island	35
57	London HLD 8393	Lucky Lips/On Treasure Island (78)	12
57	London HLD 8413	Orange Blossoms/My Heart Belongs To You	20
57	London HLD 8413	Orange Blossoms/My Heart Belongs To You (78)	10
57	London HLD 8424	Dark Moon/A Little Too Late	20
58	London HLD 8570	Love Theme From "Farewell To Arms"/I Get That Feeling	10
58	London HLD 8570	Love Theme From "Farewell To Arms"/I Get That Feeling (78)	15
58	London HLD 8632	You/Angry	15
58	London HLD 8632	You/Angry (78)	15
56	London HB-D 1056	PRESENTING GALE STORM (10" LP)	65
58	London HA-D 2104	SENTIMENTAL ME (LP)	50

RORY STORM & HURRICANES

63	Oriole CB 1858	Dr. Feelgood/I Can Tell	35
64	Parlophone R 5197	America/Since You Broke My Heart	20

(see also Keef Hartley, Paddy Klaus & Gibson)

STORM BUGS

80	Storm Bugs	STORM BUGS (EP, white label, foldout insert, plain white sleeve)	5

ROBB STORME (& WHISPERS)

60	Decca F 11282	1000, 900 And When/I Don't Need Your Love Anymore	15
61	Decca F 11313	Music/Five Minutes More (as Robb Storme & Whispers)	8
61	Decca F 11364	Near You/Lonely Town (as Robb Storme & Whispers)	8
61	Decca F 11388	Transistor Sister/Earth Angel	15
62	Decca F 11432	Pretty Hair And Angel Eyes/A Mile Of Broken Hearts	12
63	Pye 7N 15515	Sixteen Years Ago Tonight/Surprise Surprise	8
63	Piccadilly 7N 35133	Happens Ev'ryday/Surprise Surprise	7
63	Piccadilly 7N 35160	To Know Her Is To Love Her/Bu Bop A Lu Bop A Lie	7
65	Pye 7N 15819	Love Is Strange/Shy Guy	7
65	Columbia DB 7756	Where Is My Girl?/Double Oh Seven (as Robb Storme & Whispers)	10
66	Columbia DB 7993	Here Today/Don't Cry (as Robb Storme Group)	15
62	Decca DFE 6700	WHEELS (EP)	110

STORMER

78	Ring O' 2017 113	My Home Town/Shake It Baby (some in promo p/s)	70/40

STORMTROOPER

78	Solent SS 047	I'm A Mess/It's Not Me (some in stamped plain sleeve with insert)	30/12

STORMTROOPER

80	Heartbeat BEAT 1	Pride Before A Fall/Still Comin' Home (p/s)	25

STORYTELLER

71	CBS 7182	Remarkable/Laugh That Came Too Soon	5
70	Transatlantic TRA 220	STORYTELLER (LP)	25
71	Transatlantic TRA 232	MORE PAGES (LP)	30

(see also Johnny Neal & Starliners, Terry Durham, Other Two, Andy Bown)

STORYTELLER

85	Storyteller ZELSP 438	Mystery Girl (p/s)	50

WALLY STOTT

55	Philips BBE 12000	THE WALLY STOTT ORCHESTRA (EP)	8

(see also Scott Walker)

BABE STOVALL

76	Southern Sound SD 203	THE BABE STOVALL STORY (LP)	12

STOWAWAYS

79	Supermusic SUP 27	I Wanna Be Me/My Friends/You'll Tie Me Down (p/s)	25

STP 23

89	Wau! Mr. Modo WMS 001R	Let Jimi Take Over/Let Jimi Take Over (Remix By Youth) (12", p/s)	10

STRAFE FÜR REBELLION

80s	Touch TO 6	SANTA MARIA (LP, with inner)	15

MINT VALUE £

STRAIGHT EIGHT

78	Eel Pie EPS 003	Modern Times/Tell Me If You Wanna Bleed (p/s)	10
79	Warner Bros K 18049	Spread It Around/It Ain't Easy/Oh No (p/s)	5
80	Logo DEAL 1	I'm Sorry/Satisfied (p/s)	8
80	Logo DEAL 2	Tombstone/On The Rebound (p/s)	5
82	Logo GO 416	Tomorrow/Faded Stars/You Are What You Are (some with p/s)	10/8
79	Eel Pie EPRP 001	NO NOISE FROM HERE (LP)	12
80	Logo LOGO 1032	STRAIGHT TO THE HEART (LP)	12
80	Logo FLUSH 1	SHUFFLE'N'CUT (LP)	12

STRAIGHT UP

80	Rok XX/XIX	One Out All Out/JUSTIN CASE: T.V. (die-cut company sleeve)	10

EMILLE STRAKER & HIS MERRYMEN

(see under Merrymen)

PETER STRAKER

69	Polydor 56345	Breakfast In Bed/The Right To Cry	5
69	Polydor 56362	I Never Thought I'd Fall In Love/Birdie Told Me	5
70	Polydor 2058 039	Carousel/It's A New Day	5
77	EMI EMI 2700	Ragtime Piano Joe/Saddest Clown	10
78	EMI EMI 2758	Jackie/I've Been To Hell And Back	12
80	Rocket XPRES 35	Late Night Taxi Dancer/Real Natural Man (p/s)	5
77	EMI EMC 3204	THIS ONE'S ON ME (LP)	18

BILLY STRANGE (& CHALLENGERS)

61	London HLG 9321	Where Your Arms Used To Be/Sadness Done Come	10
64	Vocalion V-N 9228	The James Bond Theme/007 Theme	15
64	Vocalion V-N 9231	Goldfinger/"Munsters" Theme	22
66	Vocalion V-N 9257	Thunderball/"Ninth Man" Theme	15
66	Vocalion V-N 9259	Get Smart/Run Spy, Run	18
67	Vocalion V-N 9289	"A Few Dollars More" Theme/You Only Live Twice	12
63	Vocalion VA/SVN 8022	12-STRING GUITAR (LP)	18
64	Vocalion VAN 8026	MR GUITAR (LP)	20
64	Vocalion VAN/SAVN 8032	THE JAMES BOND THEME (LP)	25
65	Vocalion VAN/SAVN 8038	GOLDFINGER (LP)	25
65	Vocalion VAN/SAVN 8042	ENGLISH HITS OF '65 (LP)	15
65	Vocalion VAN/SAVN 8045	STRANGE PLAYS THE HITS (LP)	15
66	Vocalion VAN/SAVN 8050	FOLK-ROCK HITS (LP)	15
66	London HA-F/SH-F 8274	THE FUNKY 12 STRING GUITAR (LP, as Billy Strange & Transients)	12
66	Vocalion VAN/SAVN 8065	BILLY STRANGE & THE CHALLENGERS (LP)	15
70	London ZGL 104	GREAT WESTERN THEMES (LP)	15

(see also Cliffie Stone)

GILES STRANGE

66	Stateside SS 570	Watch The People Dance/You're Goin' Up To The Bottom	55

STEVE STRANGE

82	Palace PALACE 1	In The Year 2525/Strange Connexions (white label, unreleased)	60
82	Palace PALACE 1	In The Year 2525/Strange Connexions (p/s, available separately)	35

(see also Visage)

STRANGE CRUISE

86	EMI 12EMI 5549	Rebel Blue Rocker/Love Addiction (12", p/s)	10
86	EMI EMC 3513	STRANGE CRUISE (LP)	18

STRANGE DAYS

75	Retreat RTS 263	Monday Morning/Joe Soap	5
75	Retreat RTL 6005	NINE PARTS TO THE WIND (LP)	20

STRANGE FRUIT

71	Village Thing VTSX 1001	Cut Across Shorty/Shake That Thing	12

STRANGELOVE

92	Sermon SERT 001	Visionary/Front/Chances/Snakes (12", p/s, 1,000 only)	20
93	Sermon SERT 002	Hysteria/Unknown/My Dark Walls/Sea (12", some in p/s)	10/8
93	Sermon SERT 002CD	Hysteria/Unknown/My Dark Walls/Sea (CD)	15
93	R. T. Singles Club 45REV 18	Zoo'd Out/Circles (p/s)	12
94	Food 12FOOD 49	Time For The Rest Of Your Life/Motorpsycho Nitemare/It's So Easy (12", p/s)	8
94	Food CDFOOD 49	Time For The Rest Of Your Life/Motorpsycho Nitemare/It's So Easy (CD)	8
94	M. Tongue MOTHER 1F	All Because Of You/MY LIFE STORY: "Under The Ice" (flexidisc)	8
95	Food FOODDJ 62	World Outside (live)/Hysteria Unknown (live) (gig freebie, some with jukebox centre)	6
96	Food FOODLP 15	LOVE AND OTHER DEMONS (LP, with 12 page booklet)	12

STRANGELOVES

65	Stateside SS 446	I Want Candy/It's About My Baby	18
65	Immediate IM 007	Cara-Lin/Roll On Mississippi	18
66	London HLZ 10020	Night Time/Rhythm Of Love	25
66	London HLZ 10063	Hand Jive/I Gotta Dance	10
69	London HLZ 10238	Honey Do/I Wanna Do It	10

(see also Beach-Nuts)

STRANGE MOVEMENTS

79	Good Vibrations GOT 5	Dancing In The Ghetto/Amuse Yourself (foldout p/s)	25

STRANGER (Cole)

63	Blue Beat BB 165	Rough And Tough (with Duke Reid Band)/DUKE REID BAND: The Mood I Am In	25
63	Blue Beat BB 195	Miss Reamer/RICO & HIS BLUES BAND: Blues From The Hills	25

(see also Stranger Cole)

MINT VALUE £

STRANGER (Cole) & GLADY (Anderson)

67 Island WI 3128 Love Me Today/Over Again . . . 30
68 Amalgamated AMG 806 Seeing Is Knowing/ROY SHIRLEY: Music Is The Key . . . 25
71 Clandisc CLA 230 Tomorrow (as Stranger & Gladdy)/DYNAMITES: Tomorrow Version . . . 7
71 Supreme SUP 227 My Application (as Stranger & Gladdy)/TADDY & DIAMONDS: Oh No, My Baby . . . 7
73 Count Shelley CS 015 Don't Give Up The Fight (as Stranger & Gladdy)/TIDALS: Stand Firm . . . 5
73 Dragon DRA 1014 Conqueror/Conqueror (Instrumental Version) . . . 8
(see also Stranger Cole, Gladdy & Followers, Gladstone Anderson, Gladdy & Stranger, Charlie Kelly)

STRANGER (Cole) & HORTENSE (Ellis)

74 Count Shelley CS 049 Mocking Bird/Corra Bella Baby . . . 5

STRANGER (Cole) & KEN (Boothe)

63 R&B JB 120 Thick In Love/All Your Friends . . . 25
(see also Stranger Cole, Ken Boothe)

STRANGER (Cole) & PATSY (Todd)

63 Blue Beat BB 171 When I Call Your Name/Take My Heart (with Duke Reid All Stars) . . . 25
63 Island WI 113 Senor And Senorita/DON DRUMMOND: Snowboy . . . 30
64 Island WI 141 Oh Oh I Need You/DON DRUMMOND: J.F.K.'s Memory . . . 35
64 Island WI 144 Tom, Dick And Harry/We Two, Happy People . . . 25
64 Island WI 152 Yeah Yeah Baby/BABA BROOKS: Boat Ride . . . 30
64 Island WI 160 Miss B/Thing Come To Those Who Wait . . . 25
65 Black Swan WI 462 Hey Little Girl/CORNELL CAMBELL: Make Hay . . . 30
66 Rio R 81 Give Me One More Chance/Fire In Cornfield . . . 25
66 Doctor Bird DB 1050 Give Me The Right/Tonight . . . 25
67 Doctor Bird DB 1084 Tell It To Me/Your Photograph . . . 25
67 Doctor Bird DB 1087 Down The Trainlines/Sing And Pray . . . 25
69 Escort ES 807 My Love/SWEET CONFUSION: Windsor Castle . . . 12
69 Escort ES 811 Why Did You/Do You Remember . . . 10
(see also Stranger Cole, Patsy)

STRANGERS (with Mike Shannon)

64 Philips BF 1335 One And One Is Two/Time And The River (as Strangers with Mike Shannon) . . . 50
64 Philips BF 1378 Do You Or Don't You/What Can I Do . . . 8
(see also Shadows)

STRANGERS

67 Pye 7N 17240 Look Out (Here Comes Tomorrow)/Mary Mary . . . 18
67 Pye 7N 17351 You Didn't Have To Be So Nice/Daytime Turns To Night . . . 8
68 Pye 7N 17585 I'm On An Island/Step Inside . . . 7

STRANGE STONE

77 own label DER 1399 STRANGE STONE (LP, private pressing, numbered sleeve with insert, 255 only) . . . 500

STRANGER THAN FICTION

80s Ellie Jay EJSP 9301 Into The Void/Darkness (p/s) . . . 25

STRANGEWAYS

78 Real ARE 2 Show Her You Care/You're On Your Own (p/s) . . . 125
79 Real ARE 7 All The Sounds Of Fear/Wasting Time (p/s) . . . 125
(see also Ada Wilson)

STRANGLERS

SINGLES

77 United Artists UP 36211 (Get A) Grip (On Yourself)/London Lady (card/paper p/s) . . . 5/4
77 United Artists UP 36248 Peaches/Go Buddy Go ('group' p/s with 'blackmail' lettering, withdrawn) . . . 500
77 United Artists UP 36248 Peaches/Go Buddy Go ('peach' p/s) . . . 6
77 United Artists UP 36277 Something Better Change/Straighten Out (p/s) . . . 6
77 United Artists UP 36300 No More Heroes/In The Shadows (p/s, 'wreath' label) . . . 6
80 United Artists 12-BP 344 Bear Cage (Extended)/Shah Shah A Go Go (Extended) (12", p/s or company sleeve) . . . 12/8
81 Liberty BP 383 Thrown Away/Top Secret (p/s) . . . 5
81 Liberty BP 393 Just Like Nothing On Earth/Maninwhite (p/s) . . . 7
82 Epic EPCA A-2893 The European Female/Savage Breast (p/s, yellow vinyl) . . . 5
82 Epic EPCA 11-2893 The European Female/Savage Breast (picture disc) . . . 5
84 Epic A 4738 Skin Deep/Here And There ('skin-feel' p/s, with 'Skin Deep' tattoo, 10,000 only) . . . 6
84 Epic EPC GA 4921 No Mercy/In One Door//Hot Club (Riot Mix)/Head On The Line (double pack) . . . 8
84 Epic WA 4921 No Mercy/In One Door (ear-shaped picture disc) . . . 7
86 Epic 650 055-0 Nice In Nice/Since You Went Away (shaped picture disc) . . . 6
86 Epic SOLAR P1 Always The Sun/Norman Normal (shaped picture disc) . . . 5
86 Epic SOLAR D1 Always The Sun/Norman Normal//Nice In Nice/Since You Went Away (double pack, shrinkwrapped & stickered) . . . 6
86 Epic HUGE P1 Big In America/Dry Day (shaped picture disc) . . . 5
86 Epic HUGE D1 Big In America/Dry Day//Always The Sun/Norman Normal (double pack, shrinkwrapped & stickered) . . . 5
87 Epic SHEIK P1 Shakin' Like A Leaf/Hit Man (shaped picture disc) . . . 7
88 Epic VICE 1 All Day And All Of The Night/¡Viva Vlad! ('Monica Coughlan' p/s, withdrawn sold via fan club) . . . 6
88 Epic VICE P1 All Day And All Of The Night/¡Viva Vlad! (shaped picture disc) . . . 7
88 Epic CDVICE 1 All Day And All Of The Night (Jeff Remix)/¡Viva Vlad!/Who Wants The World (live)/Strange Little Girl (live) (CD, card sleeve, 5,000 only) . . . 10
89 Liberty EMR 84 Grip '89 — (Get A) Grip (On Yourself)/Waltzinblack (p/s, red vinyl with poster in gatefold PVC wallet, 5,000 only) . . . 5
89 Liberty CDEM 84 Grip '89 (Gripping Stuff 12" Mix)/Grip '89 (Single Mix)/Waltzinblack/ Tomorrow Was The Hereafter (CD) . . . 10
90 Epic TEARS Q1 96 Tears/Instead Of This (in embossed stickered tin) . . . 5
90 Epic TEARS P1 96 Tears/Instead Of This/Poisonality (CD, picture disc) . . . 8

MINT VALUE £

ALBUMS

77	United Artists UAG 30045	STRANGLERS IV — RATTUS NORVEGICUS (LP, 10,000 with 7" "Choosey Susie"/"Peasant In The Big Shitty" (Live At The Nashville, 12/76) [FREE 3, orange p/s,"What Do You Expect..." in run-off groove], some with sticker)	20/12
78	United Artists UAK 30222	BLACK AND WHITE (LP, 75,000 with white vinyl 7" "Walk On By"/"Tits"/ "Mean To Me" [FREE 9, black die-cut sleeve & card insert], some mispressed on blue or beige vinyl)	25/12
79	United Artists UAG 30262	THE RAVEN (LP, 20,000 with 3-D cover, cartoon on inner sleeve)	20
82	Liberty LBG 30353	THE COLLECTION '77-82 (LP, withdrawn plastic logo sleeve)	25
82	Liberty LBG 30353	THE COLLECTION '77-82 (LP, Stranglers' own concept sleeve, unissued)	
83	Epic EPC 25237	FELINE (LP, with bonus 1-sided 7" "Aural Sculpture" [XPS 167])	12
86	Epic EPC 26648	DREAMTIME (LP, picture disc)	12

FREEBIES, PROMOS & MISCELLANEA

75	Safari (no. cat no)	My Young Dreams/Wasted (existence unconfirmed)	150
77	United Artists FREE 4	Peaches (radio version)/Go Buddy Go (promo only, some with p/s)	500/100
77	United Artists UP 36262	Mony Mony/Mean To Me (p/s, as Celia And The Mutations)	7
77	United Artists UP 36277	Something Better Change/Straighten Out	25
77	United Artists FREE 8	No More Heroes (1-sided radio edit, promo only)	40
77	United Artists UP 36300	No More Heroes (1-sided, misprinted "No More Stheroes")	25
77	United Artists UP 36300	No More Heroes/In The Shadows (p/s, stamped, misprinted "No More Stheroes")	25
78	United Artists UP 36429	Walk On By (Promo Edit)/Old Codger/Tank	25
79	United Artists UA STR 1 DJ	Don't Bring Harry/HUGH CORNWELL: Wired (45rpm, promo only)	20
79	United Artists (no cat. no.)	Two Sunspots (unreleased)	30
80	Stranglers Info Service SIS 001	Tomorrow Was The Hereafter/Bring On The Nubiles (Cocktail Version) (numbered p/s, label has "Nublies")	8
82	SIS/Liberty FREE 3	Peasant In The Big Shitty (Live At The Nashville, 12/76)/Choosey Susie (fan club reissue, black p/s, with "Ello 'Elen" in run-off groove)	5
82	Epic EPC A2893	The European Female (In Celebration Of)/(Promo Edit)	10
82	Liberty BP 410	La Folie (Promo Edit)/Waltzinblack	10
82	SIS/Liberty UP 36350	5 Minutes/Rok It To The Moon (reissue)	5
82	SIS/Liberty UP 36429	Walk On By/Old Codger/Tank (reissue, 33rpm)	5
82	SIS/Liberty FREE 18	Mony Mony/Mean To Me (reissue, as Celia & the Mutations)	5
83	Epic/S.I.S. XPS 167	Aural Sculpture (reissue, 1-sided)	5
91	Stranglers Info S. SIS 004	New Day Today (flexidisc with *Strangled* fan magazine, issue 32)	5

MISPRESSINGS

78	United Artists UP 36248	Peaches/Go Buddy Go (p/s, mispressing, B-side plays Buzzcocks' "Oh Shit")	60
78	United Artists FREE 9	Walk On By/Mean To Me/Tits (EP [free with LP U.A. UAK 30222], mispressing, black die-cut sleeve & card insert, blue/clear or pink/clear vinyl)	30/15
78	United Artists UP 36379	Nice 'N' Sleazy/Shut Up (p/s, mispressing, B-side plays tracks by other artist)	30
81	Liberty BP 393	Just Like Nothing On Earth/Maninwhite (p/s, mispressing, plays A-side both sides)	20
82	United Artists BP 407	Golden Brown/Love 30 (B-side plays "Everybody Salsa")	20
79	United Artists UAG 30262	THE RAVEN (LP, mispressing, 2nd side plays country & western [B-side matrix: UAK 30263])	25

(see also Jean-Jacques Burnel [& Dave Greenfield], Celia & Mutations, A Marriage Of Convenience, Fools Dance)

STRAPPS

76	Harvest HAR 5108	In Your Ear/Rita B (p/s)	7
76	Harvest SHSP 4055	STRAPPS (LP)	12
77	Harvest SHSP 4064	SECRET DAMAGE (LP, with inner sleeve)	12

(see also Episode Six, Gillan, Quatermass)

STRAPS

80	Donut DONUT 1	Just Can't Take Anymore/New Age (p/s)	6
82	Donut DONUT 3	Brixton/No Liquor (p/s)	8
83	Cyclops CYC 2	THE STRAPS ALBUM (LP)	15

(see also Public Image Ltd.)

STRATEGY

82	Ebony EBON 7	Technical Overflow/Astral Planes (some in p/s)	60/50

STRATE JACKET

70s	Wessex	You're A Hit (stamped plain sleeve)	12

STRATUS

85	Steel Trax STEEL 31001	THROWING SHAPES (LP)	15

(see also Grand Prix, Uriah Heep, Iron Maiden, Praying Mantis)

SYD STRAW

89	Virgin America VUSCD 6	Future 40's (String Of Pearls) (with Michael Stipe)/ Taken/Learning The Game (3" CD, card sleeve)	8

STRAWBERRY ALARM CLOCK

67	Pye International 7N 25436	Incense And Peppermints/The Birdman Of Alkatrash	20
68	Pye International 7N 25446	Tomorrow/Birds In My Tree	15
68	Pye International 7N 25456	Sit With The Guru/Pretty Song From Psych-Out	15
69	MCA MU 1080	Good Morning Starshine/Me And The Township	8
68	Pye Intl. N(S)PL 28106	INCENSE AND PEPPERMINTS (LP)	50

STRAWBERRY CHILDREN

67	Liberty LBF 15012	Love Years Coming/One Stands Here	25

(see also Jim Webb)

STRAWBERRY JAM

69	Pye 7N 17711	Per-Son-Al-Ly/This Is To A Girl	10

STRAWBERRY PARK

82	Sonet 2245	Summer Is A Coming/Beach Party	5

MINT VALUE £

STRAWBERRY SWITCHBLADE

83	92 Happy Customers HAP 1	Trees And Flowers/Go Away (p/s)	10
83	92 Happy Cust. HAPT 1	Trees And Flowers/Go Away/Trees And Flowers (Just Music) (12", p/s)	10
85	Korova KOW 38TP	Since Yesterday/By The Sea/Sunday Mornings (12", picture disc)	8
85	Korova KOW 39	Let Her Go/Beautiful End (shaped picture disc)	7
85	Korova KOW 42	Jolene/Being Cold (strawberry-shaped picture disc)	8
85	Korova/Flexi FLX 388-1	Strawberry Switchblade LP sampler (clear vinyl square flexidisc sewn into gatefold booklet; cat. no. only visible in run-off groove)	6
85	Korova KODE 11	STRAWBERRY SWITCHBLADE (LP, with bonus 7" "Trees And Flowers", initially mispressed with some tracks playing twice & others out of order)	15/10

(see also Poems, Rose McDowall)

STRAWBS

68	A&M AMS 725	Oh How She Changed/Or Am I Dreaming	7
68	A&M AMS 738	The Man Who Called Himself Jesus/Poor Jimmy Wilson	8
70	A&M AMS 791	Forever/Another Day	8
71	A&M AMS 837	Witchwood/Keep The Devil Outside/We'll Meet Again Sometime (live) (withdrawn)	10
71	A&M AMS 874	Benedictus/Keep The Devil Outside	6
72	A&M AMS 7002	Here It Comes/Tomorrow	5
73	A&M AMS 7047	Part Of The Union/Will You Go (p/s)	5
76	Polydor 2066 751	So Close And Yet So Far Away/The Soldier's Tale	5
78	Arista ARIST 183	I Don't Want To Talk About It/Last Resort	5
80	L.O. LO 1	The King/Ringing Down The Years (with Maddy Prior, title sleeve)	10
91	Strawbs Fan Club	Might As Well Be On Mars/The King (fan club cassette)	5
69	private pressing	STRAWBERRY MUSIC SAMPLER NO. 1 (LP, publisher's sampler, 100 only)	500
69	A&M AMLS 936	STRAWBS (LP; disc inserted in middle or at edge of sleeve)	25/15
70	A&M AMLS 970	DRAGONFLY (LP, with lyric insert, mustard label)	20
70	A&M AMLS 994	JUST A COLLECTION OF ANTIQUES AND CURIOS (LP, gatefold sleeve, mustard label; 2 different rear sleeves)	20
71	A&M AMLH 64304	FROM THE WITCHWOOD (LP, gatefold sleeve)	15
72	A&M AMLH 68078	GRAVE NEW WORLD (LP, triple gatefold sleeve, with 12-page booklet)	15
73	A&M AMLH 68144	BURSTING AT THE SEAMS (LP, with inner sleeve)	12
73	Hallmark SHM 813	ALL OUR OWN WORK (LP, with Sandy Denny)	15
74	A&M AMLS 63607	HERO AND HEROINE (LP, with inner sleeve)	12
74	A&M AMLH 68259	BY CHOICE (LP, gatefold sleeve)	12
75	A&M AMLH 68277	GHOSTS (LP, with inner sleeve)	12
76	A&M AMLH 68331	NOMADNESS (LP, with lyric insert)	12
76	Oyster 2391 234	DEEP CUTS (LP, with lyric insert)	12
77	Oyster 2391 287	BURNING FOR YOU (LP, with inner sleeve)	12

(see also Dave Cousins, Sandy Denny, Fire, Foggy, Monks, Davey & Morris, Hudson-Ford)

STRAWHEAD

70s	Tradition TSR 032	FORTUNES OF WAR (LP)	12
84	Tradition TSR 045	GENTLEMEN OF FORTUNE: TALES OF ELIZABETHAN ADVENTURERS (LP)	12
85	Dragon DRGN 851	SEDGEMOOR: THE STORY OF MONMOUTH'S REBELLION IN THE WEST (LP)	12

STRAY

72	Big T BIG 141	Our Song/Mama's Coming Home	5
70	Transatlantic TRA 216	STRAY (LP, die-cut sleeve)	35
71	Transatlantic TRA 233	SUICIDE (LP)	30
72	Transatlantic TRA 248	SATURDAY MORNING PICTURES (LP, gatefold sleeve)	15
73	Transatlantic TRA 268	MUDANZAS (LP, gatefold sleeve)	15
74	Transatlantic TRA 281	MOVE IT (LP, die-cut sleeve with inner)	12
75	Transatlantic TRA 3066	TRACKS (LP)	12
75	Dawn DNLS 3066	STAND UP AND BE COUNTED (LP)	12
76	Pye NSPL 18482	HOUDINI (LP)	12
76	Pye NSPL 18512	HEARTS OF FIRE (LP)	12

STRAY CATS

81	Arista CSCAT 2	Rock This Town/Can't Hurry Love (cassette, flip-top case)	6
81	Arista SCAT 4	You Don't Believe Me/Cross That Bridge (p/s)	5
81	Arista SCAT 5	Little Miss Prissy/Sweet Love On My Mind (live)/Something Else (live) (p/s)	7
83	Arista SCAT 123	Stray Cat Strut/Built For Speed/Sweet Love On My Mind (live)/ Drink That Bottle Down (live) (12", p/s, reissue)	8
83	Arista SCAPD 6	(She's Sexy) And 17/Lookin' Better Every Beer (shaped picture disc)	10
83	Arista SCAT 126	(She's Sexy) And 17/Lookin' Better Every Beer/Cruisin'/Lucky Charm (12", p/s)	8
83	Arista SCAT 7	Rebels Rule/Lookin' Through My Back Door (p/s, with stickers)	6
83	Arista SCAT 127	Rebels Rule/Lookin' Through My Back Door/Look At That Cadillac (12", p/s)	8
89	EMI USA MT 62	Bring It Back Again/Runaway Boys (live) (p/s)	5
89	EMI USA MTS 62	Bring It Back Again/Runaway Boys (live) (p/s, with 3 postcards)	5
89	EMI USA CDMT 62	Bring It Back Again/Runaway Boys (live)/I Fought The Law (CD)	8
89	EMI USA 12MTP 67	Gina/Two Of A Kind (p/s)	5
89	EMI USA 12MTP 67	Gina/Two Of A Kind/Stray Cat Strut (Live Version) (12", poster p/s)	8
89	EMI USA CDMT 67	Gina/Two Of A Kind/Stray Cat Strut (Live Version) (CD)	8
92	Pump 907 047-0	Elvis On Velvet (Radio Edit)/Lust'n'Love (p/s)	5
92	Pump 907 047-2	Elvis On Velvet (Radio Edit)/Lust'n'Love/Elvis On Velvet (Album Version) (CD)	8

STRAY DOG

74	Manticore K 43506	STRAY DOG (LP)	12
74	Manticore K 53504	WHILE YOU'RE DOWN THERE (LP)	12

(see also Emerson Lake & Palmer)

STREAMLINERS & JOANNE

61	Columbia DB 4689	Frankfurter Sandwiches/Pachalafaka	8
62	Columbia DB 4808	Everybody's Doin' The Twist/Do Something	8

(see also Rosemary Squires)

STREET

69	London HLU 10275	Apollo... Amen/Why Concern Yourself	5

MINT VALUE £

DANNY STREET

63	Phillips BF 1250	Only Love Can Break A Heart/ Cold Cold Winter	6
65	Philips BF 1387	Don't Go To Him/As It's Meant To Be	5
60s	Domino DO 114	Melanie/Birds An' Bees An' Things	5
71	London HLU 10342	My Little Guy/You Blew It	6

GARY STREET & FAIRWAYS

68	Domain D 2	Flipperty Flop/Hold Me Closer	15

(see also Fairways)

HILLARD STREET

58	Capitol CL 14960	River Love/It Will Never Happen Again	6

JOHN STREET & INMATES OF NO. 12

67	Deram DM 147	Keep A Little Love/My Kind Of Luck	7

JUDY STREET

78	Grapevine GRP 106	What/You Turn Me On	12

STREETFIGHTER (U.K.)

81	Streetfighter 749	STREETFIGHTER (12" EP)	25

STREETFIGHTER

82	J.R. JR 7049S	CRAZY DREAM (EP)	35

STREET LEGAL

84	Weird Brothers SLW 1	Rollin' On/Mississippi Moonshine (p/s)	150

STREET PEOPLE

70	Stateside SS 2163	Jennifer Tomkins/All Night Long	7

STREETS

04	679 071	Fit But You Know It/FUTUREHEADS: Fit But You Know It (10", die-cut p/s, 150 only)	8

STREETWALKERS

74	Reprise K 54017	STREETWALKERS (LP, with lyric sheet)	12
75	Vertigo 6360 123	DOWNTOWN FLIER (LP)	12
77	Vertigo 9102 012	VICIOUS BUT FAIR (LP)	12
76	Vertigo 9102 010	RED CARD (LP, red vinyl with inner sleeve, numbered)	12

(see also Family)

BARBRA STREISAND

SINGLES

62	CBS AAG 130	My Colouring Book/Lover Come Back To Me	6
63	CBS AAG 179	Happy Days Are Here Again/Down With Love	6
64	CBS AAG 223	People/Draw Me A Circle	6
64	CBS AAG 233	Funny Girl/I Am A Woman	6
64	CBS 201543	People/I Am A Woman You Are Man (p/s)	12
65	CBS 201754	People/Funny Girl	6
65	CBS 202025	Second Hand Rose/He Touched Me	5
66	CBS 202417	Sleep In Heavenly Peace (Silent Night)/Gounod's "Ave Maria" (p/s)	7
70	CBS 5321	Stoney End/I'll Be Home	6
79	CBS 12 7714	The Main Event/Fight/Instrumental (12" picture label)	8
79	CBS 13 8000	No More Tears (with Donna Summer)/Wet (12", p/s)	7
81	CBS S CBS 9517	What Kind Of Fool/Make It Like A Memory (with Barry Gibb)	5
83	CBS A 3888	The Way He Makes Me Feel (Studio Version)/ The Way He Makes Me Feel (Film Version) (p/s)	5
83	CBS A 4125	No Matter What Happens (Studio Version)/ No Matter What Happens (Original Soundtrack Version) (p/s)	5
84	CBS TA 4754	Left In The Dark/Here We Are At LastWoman In Love/Guilty Memory (12", p/s, withdrawn)	50
85	CBS A 4994	Make No Mistake, He's Mine (with Kim Carnes)/Clear Sailing (p/s)	5
85	CBS A 4994	Make No Mistake, He's Mine (with Kim Carnes)/Clear Sailing// Memory/Evergreen (p/s, shrinkwrapped double pack)	8
86	CBS DA 6988	Send In The Clowns/Being Alive/Somewhere/Not While I'm Around (p/s, shrinkwrapped double pack)	10
88	CBS CD BARB 2	Till I Loved You (Love Theme From Goya) (Album Version) (with Don Johnson)/ Guilty (with Barry Gibb)/Left In The Dark/Two People (CD, card p/s)	8
89	CBS BARB 3	All I Ask Of You/On My Way To You (p/s)	5
89	CBS CD BARB 3	All I Ask Of You (from "The Phantom Of The Opera")/On My Way To You/ Life Story/Emotion (CD, card sleeve)	8
89	CBS CP BARB 3	All I Ask Of You (from "The Phantom Of The Opera")/Somewhere/ Memory/Send In The Clowns (CD, picture disc, 2,000 only)	20
89	CBS BARB QT 3	All I Ask Of You/On My Way To You/Make No Mistake, He's Mine (with Kim Carnes)/Since I Fell For You (12", p/s with poster, 3,000 only)	12
89	CBS BARBQT 4	We're Not Makin' Love Anymore/Wet/No More Tears (Enough Is Enough) (12", p/s)	8
89	CBS BARB 4	We're Not Makin' Love Anymore (7" Version)/Till I Loved You (with Don Johnson)/ Kiss Me In The Rain/The Places You Find Love (CD, card sleeve)	8
89	CBS BARB C4	We're Not Makin' Love Anymore/Wet/No More Tears (Enough Is Enough) (with Donna Summer) (CD, picture disc)	12
92	Columbia 657794 7	Places That Belong To You/For All We Know (p/s)	5
92	Columbia 657794 9	Places That Belong To You/Warm All Over/I Know Him So Well/ You'll Never Know (CD, picture disc)	15
93	Columbia 659342 7	With One Look/Memory (p/s)	5
94	Columbia 659738 2	The Music Of The Night/Children Will Listen/Move On (CD)	8
94	Columbia 660357 7	As If We Never Said Goodbye/Guilty (with Barry Gibb) (p/s)	5

EPs

63	CBS AGG 320042	LOVER COME BACK TO ME	15
63	CBS AGG 320054	BARBRA STREISAND	10

64 CBS EP 6048 EN FRANÇAIS . . . 12
65 CBS EP 6068 MY MAN . . . 12
66 CBS EP 6150 SECOND HAND ROSE . . . 10

LPs

64 Capitol (S)W 2059 FUNNY GIRL (original cast recording, mono/stereo) . . . 12
66 CBS (S)BPG 62784 HAROLD SINGS ARLEN (WITH FRIEND) (mono/stereo) . . . 12
71 CBS CQ 30378 STONEY END (quadrophonic) . . . 12
71 CBS CQ 30792 BARBRA JOAN STREISAND (quadrophonic) . . . 12
73 CBS SQ 30992 FUNNY GIRL (soundtrack, quadrophonic) . . . 12
73 CBS CQ 31760 LIVE CONCERT AT THE FORUM (quadrophonic) . . . 12
75 Arista ARTY 101 FUNNY LADY (soundtrack, gatefold sleeve) . . . 12
77 CBS 66349 BARBRA STREISAND DELUXE BOX SET ("Greatest Hits Volume 1"/"Stoney End"/"Streisand Superman") . . . 25
78 CBS 70163 EYES OF LAURA MARS (soundtrack) . . . 12
79 CBS 66349 BARBRA STREISAND: 3-RECORD BOX SET ("Greatest Hits Volume 1", "Volume 2" & "Wet") . . . 25
88 CBS 651379 6 NUTS (soundtrack) . . . 15
88 CBS 462943 1 TILL I LOVED YOU . . . 12
91 Columbia 468734 2 JUST FOR THE RECORD (4-CD box set with 92-page booklet) . . . 50
94 Columbia 4775 992 BARBRA — THE CONCERT (2-CD) . . . 20
94 Columbia XPCD 147 THE EVENT OF THE DECADE, A RETROSPECTIVE (2-CD, promo only) . . . 200

'TEXAS' BILL STRENGTH

55 Capitol CL 14357 Cry, Cry, Cry/The Yellow Rose Of Texas . . . 18
55 Capitol CL 14357 Cry, Cry, Cry/The Yellow Rose Of Texas (78) . . . 8

STRESS

85 Adventures In Reality ARR 14 THE BIG WHEEL (LP, with insert) . . . 40

STRETCH

75 Anchor ANCL 2014 ELASTIQUE (LP) . . . 15
76 Anchor ANCL 2016 YOU CAN'T BEAT YOUR BRAIN FOR ENTERTAINMENT (LP) . . . 12
77 Anchor ANCL 2023 LIFE BLOOD (LP) . . . 18
78 Hot Wax HW 1 FORGET THE PAST (LP) . . . 25

(see also Elmer Gantry, Kirby, Status Quo, Clifford Davis, Legs, Curved Air)

WILLIAM R. STRICKLAND

69 Deram DML/SML 1041 WILLIAM R. STRICKLAND IS ONLY THE NAME (LP) . . . 15

PETE STRIDE & JOHN PLAIN

80 Beggars Banquet BEGA 17 NEW GUITARS IN TOWN (LP, with inner sleeve) . . . 12

(see also Lurkers)

STRIDER

73 GM GMS 002 Higher And Higher/Ain't Got No Love . . . 5
74 GM GMS 023 Seems So Easy/Arthur Hydrogen . . . 5
73 GM GML 1002 EXPOSED (LP) . . . 18
74 GM GML 1012 MISUNDERSTANDING (LP) . . . 15

(see also Samson)

STRIFE

77 Outlaw OUT 1 School/Go/Feel So Good (p/s) . . . 10
75 Chrysalis 1063 RUSH (LP) . . . 12
78 Gull 1029 BACK TO THUNDER (LP, some on green vinyl) . . . 18/15

LIZA STRIKE

68 Parlophone R 5725 All's Quiet On West 23rd/Mr Daddy-Man . . . 7

(see also Liza & Jet Set, Soulmates, Vice Versa)

STRIKERS & CHILDREN OF SELSTON BAGTHORPE PRIMARY SCHOOL CHOIR

78 Eagle EGL 003 Good Old Charlie/Forest Fire . . . 8

STRING-A-LONGS

61 London HLU 9278 Wheels/Am I Asking Too Much . . . 5
61 London HLU 9354 Panic Button/Brass Buttons . . . 7
61 London HLU 9394 Should I/Take A Minute . . . 6
61 London HLU 9452 Scottie/Ming Bird . . . 10
62 London HLD 9535 Sunday/Twistwatch . . . 10
62 London HLD 9588 Spinning My Wheels/My Blue Heaven . . . 12
63 London HLD 9652 Mathilda/Replica . . . 12
61 London RE-U 1322 THE STRING-A-LONGS (EP) . . . 40
63 London RE-D 1350 THE STRING-A-LONGS (EP) . . . 40
63 London RE-D 1398 STRINGALONG WITH THE STRING-A-LONGS (EP) . . . 35
63 London HA-D/SH-D 8054 THE STRING-A-LONGS (LP, mono/stereo) . . . 50/60
69 London HAU/SHU 8371 WIDE WORLD HITS (LP) . . . 40

STRING CHEESE

72 RCA SF 8222 STRING CHEESE (LP) . . . 20

STRING DRIVEN THING

70 Concord CON 7 Another Night/Say What You Like . . . 15
72 Charisma CB 195 Eddie/Hooked On The Road . . . 5
70 Concord CON 1001 STRING DRIVEN THING (LP) . . . 135
72 Charisma CAS 1062 STRING DRIVEN THING (LP, pink label) . . . 20
73 Charisma CAS 1070 THE MACHINE THAT CRIED (LP, pink label, gatefold sleeve) . . . 15
74 Charisma CAS 1097 PLEASE MIND YOUR HEAD (LP, with lyric sheet) . . . 15
76 Charisma CAS 1112 KEEP YOUR 'AND ON IT (LP) . . . 15

STRIPES OF GLORY

62 Vogue V 9194 The Denial/O' Send The Fire . . . 18

MINT VALUE £

SYLVIA STRIPLIN
86 Music Of Love MOLS 8 — Give Me Your Love/Give Me Your Love (Version) (12") . . . 8

STROKES
01 Rough Trade RTRADES 010 — The Modern Age/Last Night (p/s, 2000 only) . . . 30
01 Rough Trade RTRADESCD 010 — The Modern Age/Last Night/Barely Legal (CD, card sleeve) . . . 10
01 Rough Trade RTRADES 023 — Hard To Explain/New York City Cops (p/s, 2000 only) . . . 8
01 Rough Trade RTRADESCD 0041 — Last Nite/When It Started (CD, withdrawn) . . . 8
02 Rough Trade RTRADES 063 — Someday/Alone Together/Is This It (p/s, yellow vinyl) . . . 12

STROLLERS
58 Vogue V 9113 — Jumping With Symphony Sid/Swinging Yellow Rose Of Texas . . . 35
58 Vogue V 9113 — Jumping With Symphony Sid/Swinging Yellow Rose Of Texas (78) . . . 20
58 Vogue V 9124 — Little Bitty Pretty One/Flute Cha-Lypso . . . 35
58 Vogue V 9124 — Little Bitty Pretty One/Flute Cha-Lypso (78) . . . 35

STROLLERS
61 London HLL 9336 — Come On Over/There's No One But You . . . 50

STROLLERS
65 Fontana TF 598 — Cuckoo/Rich And Rambling Boy . . . 5
(see also David & Toni Arthur)

BARRETT STRONG
60 London HLU 9088 — Money (That's What I Want)/Oh I Apologise . . . 165
76 Capitol CL 15864 — Man Up In The Sky/Gonna Make It Right . . . 6

CHAD STUART & JEREMY CLYDE
(see under Chad & Jeremy)

GLEN STUART
60s Honey Hit TB 126 — Make Me An Angel/Walking To Heaven (some with p/s) . . . 10/6
62 Melodisc MEL 1581 — Make Me An Angel/Walking To Heaven . . . 6

GLEN STUART & CLANSMEN
59 Pye 7N 15232 — Weepy Willow/Della Darling . . . 6
59 Pye N 15232 — Weepy Willow/Della Darling (78) . . . 6

KARL STUART & PROFILES
65 Mercury MF 870 — Love Of My Eyes/Not A Girl In A Million . . . 7
65 Mercury MF 875 — Haven't They Got Better Things To Do/The Touch Of Your Hand . . . 7
(see also Profile, Voice)

MIKE STUART SPAN
(see under 'M')

NAT STUCKEY
67 Pye International 7N 25403 — Sweet Thang/Paralyze My Mind . . . 6
69 RCA RCA 1833 — Loving You/Joe And Mabel's 12th Street Bar And Grill . . . 5
69 RCA RCA 1890 — Cut Across Shorty/Understand, Little Man . . . 5

STUD
70 Deram SML-R 1084 — STUD (LP) . . . 45
(see also Taste, Family, Blossom Toes, Eric Burdon & Animals)

STUDIO G's
70 LPSG 100 — BETA GROUP (LP, library edition) . . . 150
96 Tenth Planet TP 023 — BEAT GROUP (LP, 600 only) . . . 20

STUDIO ONE ALLSTARS
67 Island WI 3038 — Sherry (actually by Bumps Oakley)/Out Of My Mind (actually by Soul Junior) . . . 25

STUDIO SIX
66 Polydor 56131 — When I See My Baby/Don't Tell Lies . . . 10
67 Polydor 56162 — Bless My Soul (I've Been And Gone And Done It)/People Say . . . 10
67 Polydor 56189 — Times Were When/I Can't Sleep . . . 10
67 Polydor 56219 — Strawberry Window/Falling Leaves . . . 35
69 Polydor 56361 — Bless My Soul/People Say . . . 10

STUDIO 68
91 own label — Pop Stars Country Mansion/Lighthouse/Sign Of The Zodiac/Notting Hill Astrologer (12", p/s, 500 only) . . . 8

STUDIO SWEETHEARTS
79 DJM DJS 10915 — I Believe/It Isn't Me (p/s) . . . 20
(see also Cult, Slaughter & Dogs)

STUKAS
77 Sonet SON 2134 — I Like Sport/I'll Send You A Postcard/Dead Lazy (p/s) . . . 8
77 Chiswick NS 21 — Klean Living Kids/Oh Little Girl (p/s) . . . 15

STUMP
88 Ensign CHEN 9 — A FIERCE PANCAKE (LP, with inner lyric sleeve) . . . 12

STUPIDS
85 Children Of Rev. COR 3 — VIOLENT NUN (EP, some mispressed) . . . 6

STYLE COUNCIL
83 Polydor TSCX 2 — Money-Go-Round/ Money-Go-Round (Dance Mix) (12", white label, promo) . . . 8
85 Polydor TSDJ 8 — Walls Come Tumbling Down! (censored)/The Whole Point II/Blood Sports (12", no p/s, promo only) . . . 8
85 Polydor TSCG 9 — Come To Milton Keynes/(When You) Call Me (alternate gatefold p/s) . . . 5
85 Polydor TSC DP 10 — The Lodgers (re-recorded)/You're The Best Thing (live)/Big Boss Groove (live)// You're The Best Thing/Long Hot Summer (stickered, shrinkwrapped double pack) . . . 5

MINT VALUE £

86 Polydor CINE 1/CINEC 1 Have You Ever Had It Blue/Mr. Cool's Dream//Have You Ever Had It Blue/ Uncut Version/With Everything To Lose (live in London) (p/s, with free cassette & insert in printed PVC sleeve) . . . 6
87 Polydor TSCSX 14 Wanted/Cost Of Loving (Instrumental)/Cost Of Loving (Vocal) (12", p/s). . . 8
87 Polydor TSCCD 14 Wanted/Cost Of Loving (Instrumental)/Cost Of Loving (Vocal) (CD, card p/s). . . 10
87 Polydor TSCCD 101 CAFE BLUE (CD EP, card sleeve) . . . 10
87 Polydor TSCEP 2 THE BIRDS & THE B's (EP, p/s) . . . 5
87 Polydor TSCCD 102 THE BIRDS & THE B's (CD EP, card sleeve) . . . 10
87 Polydor TSCEP 3 MICK TALBOT IS AGENT '88 (EP, p/s) . . . 5
87 Polydor TSCCD 103 MICK TALBOT IS AGENT '88 (CD EP, card sleeve) . . . 8
88 Polydor TSCCD 15 Life At A Top People's Health Farm (7" Version)/Spank! (Life At A Top People's Health Club)/Sweet Loving Ways/Life At A Top People's Health Farm (Um & Argh Mix) (CD, card sleeve) . . . 10
88 Polydor TSCCD 16 1-2-3-4 EP: How She Threw It All Away/Love The First Time/ Long Hot Summer (Tom Mix)/I Do Like To Be B-Side The A-Side (CD) . . . 8
88 Polydor 080 400-2 1-2-3-4 EP: How She Threw It All Away/Love The First Time/ Long Hot Summer (Tom Mix)/How She Threw It All Away (Video) (CD Video). . . 12
88 Polydor 080 336-2 Have You Ever Had It Blue (Uncut Version)/Mr. Cool's Dream/With Everything To Lose (live in London)/Have You Ever Had It Blue (Video) (CD Video) . . . 12
88 Polydor 080 206-2 Long Hot Summer (Extended Version)/Party Chambers/The Paris Match/ Le Depart/Long Hot Summer (Video) (CD Video) . . . 12
88 Polydor 080 560-2 Life At A Top People's Health Farm (Extended Remix)/Spank! (Life At A Top People's Health Club)/Sweet Loving Ways/Life At A Top People's Health Farm (7" Version) (Video) (CD Video) . . . 12
89 Polydor TSCB 17 Promised Land (Juan Atkins Mix)/Can You Still Love Me (stickered box set, with numbered 7" & poster) . . . 5
89 Polydor TSC XS 17 Promised Land (Joe Smooth's Alternate Club Mix)/Can You Still Love Me (Club Vocal)/Can You Still Love Me (12 O'clock Dub) (12", orange p/s) . . . 8
89 Polydor TSCCD 17 The Promised Land (Longer Version Juan Atkins Mix)/(Pianopella)/ Can You Still Love Me? (Dub)/(Vocal) (CD) . . . 8
89 Polydor TSCD 17 The Promised Land (Radio Edit)/The Promised Land (Longer Version)/ Can You Still Love Me? (Vocal)/Can You Still Love Me? (Dub) (CD) . . . 10
89 Polydor LHSCD 1 Long Hot Summer '89 Mix/Everybody's On The Run (Version One)/ Everybody's On The Run (Version Two) (CD) . . . 10
84 Lyntone LYN 15344/45 It Just Came To Pieces In My Hands (Coventry)/Speak Like A Child (London) (33rpm fan club flexidisc) . . . 10
87 Polydor COST 2 Angel/Heaven's Above (12", promo only) . . . 10
87 Polydor TSCLP 4 THE COST OF LOVING (LP, single disc) . . . 12
87 Polydor 831 443-2 THE COST OF LOVING (CD) . . . 15
88 Polydor TSCIN 1 INTERVIEW WITH THE STYLE COUNCIL (LP, promo only) . . . 40
98 Polydor TSCLP 6 (/2) MODERNISM: A NEW DECADE (LP or 2 x 12", both in p/s, promo only) . . . each 90

(see also Council Collective, Paul Weller, Jam, Merton Parkas, King Truman)

STYLOS

64 Liberty LBS 10173 Head Over Heels/Bye Bye, Baby, Bye Bye . . . 120

POLY STYRENE

80 United Artists BP 370 Talk In Toytown/Sub Tropical (p/s) . . . 5
80 United Artists UAG 30320 TRANSLUCENCE (LP, with lyric inner) . . . 12

(see also X-Ray Spex, Mari Elliott)

STYX

75 RCA RCA 2518 Lady/Children Of The Land . . . 5
78 A&M AMS 7388 Blue Collar Man/Superstars (12", coloured vinyl) . . . 8
79 A&M AMS 7446 Renegade/Sing For The Day (p/s, red vinyl) . . . 5
81 A&M AMS 8102 The Best Of Times/Light (p/s, laser etched) . . . 5
81 A&M AMS 8118 Too Much Time On My Hands/Queen Of Spades (p/s, coloured vinyl) . . . 5
83 A&M AM 120 Don't Let It End/Rockin' The Paradise (shaped picture disc) . . . 6
78 A&M AMLH 64724 PIECES OF EIGHT (LP, translucent vinyl) . . . 12

SUBHUMANS

81 Spiderleg SDL 3 Religious Wars/Love Is.../Work Experience/It's Gonna Get Worse (p/s) . . . 8
82 Spiderleg SPIDL 5 Big City/Reason For Existence/Cancer/Peroxide (p/s) . . . 7

SUBMARINER

93 Spacewatch FLX 2107 Lyricist Downer/Seeming And The Meaning (demo)/STEREOLAB: Ronco Symphony (demo) (clear vinyl flexi with paper strip insert) . . . 25

SUBMARINES

87 Head HEAD 4 Grey Skies Blue/I Saw The Children (p/s) . . . 6

SUBS

78 Stiff OFF 1 Gimme Your Heart/Party Clothes (p/s) . . . 5

(see also Larry Wallis)

SUBSTITUTE

79 Ignition IR 2 The One/Look Sharp (some in p/s) . . . 35/20

(see also Vibrators)

SUB SUB

90s Ten Records Ltd. TENX 373 Space Face/Ecto-Jam-Sub (12", die-cut sleeve) . . . 45
90s Robs Records 12ROB 07 Coast/Inside Of This/Past/Inside Out (12", p/s) . . . 12
90s Robs Records 7ROB 9 Ain't No Love/Parkside Mix (p/s) . . . 8
90s Robs Records 12ROB 9 Ain't No Love (Original Mix)/(Parkside Mix)/(Parkside Raw Dub) (12", die-cut p/s) . 8
90s Robs Records 12ROB 09R Ain't No Love (On The Floor)/(On The House)/(On Yer Face) (12", die-cut p/s) . . . 8
90s Robs Records CDROB 9 Ain't No Love (Radio Edit)/(Original Mix)/(Parkside Mix)/ (On The House Mix) (CD) . . . 10
90s Robs Records 7ROB 19 Respect (Radio Edit)/(Dasliva-McCready Mix) . . . 8
90s Robs Records 12ROB 19 Respect (Original Mix)/(Dasliva-McCready Mix)/(Dasliva's Acid Dub) (12", p/s) . . . 8
90s Robs Records CDROB 19 Respect (Edit)/(Original Mix)/(Dasliva-McCready Mix)/(Dasliva's Acid Dub)/ (Primetime Mix) (CD) . . . 8

MINT VALUE £

90s	Robs Records 12ROB 29	Angel (Original Mix)/(Primetime Mix)/Senna/Southern Trees (Instrumental) (12", p/s)	8
90s	Robs Records 12ROB 29X	Angel (Primetime Dub)/(Deep Love Mix)/(Deep Love Instrumental)/(Pegasus Retro Mix) (12", p/s)	8
90s	Robs Records CDROB 29	Angel (Original Edit)/(Deep Love Mix)/(Primetime Mix)/Southern Trees (Inst.) (CD)	8
90s	Robs Records 12ROB 39	Southern Trees/Jaggernath/Northern Trees (12", p/s)	8
90s	Robs Records CDROB 39	Southern Trees (7" Edit)/(12" Mix)/Jaggernath/Northern Trees (CD)	10
90s	Robs Records 12ROB 51	Smoking Beagles/Crunch/(Instrumental Version) (12", custom stickered p/s)	8
90s	Robs Records 12ROB 53	This Time I'm Not Wrong/Heads Will Roll (Instrumental Demo)/Firesuite (12", p/s)	8
90s	Robs Records CDROB 53	This Time I'm Not Wrong (Edit)/This Time I'm Not Wrong/Heads Will Roll (Instrumental Demo)/Firesuite (CD)	8
90s	Robs Records CDROB 30	FULL FATHOM FIVE (CD)	18

(see also Doves)

SUBTERRANEANS

87	Mother MUM 6	Slum/Maxi Joy (p/s)	5
87	Mother 12MUM 6	Slum/Maxi Joy/Head For The Light (12", p/s)	8

SUBURBAN STUDS

77	Pogo POG 001/LYN 44845	No Faith/Questions (no p/s, 'with horns' version)	15
77	Pogo POG 001/LYN 44845	No Faith/Questions (p/s)	6
78	Pogo POG 002	I Hate School/Young Power (p/s)	6
78	Pogo POW 001	SLAM (LP)	20

SUBWAY SECT

78	Braik BRS 01	Nobody's Scared/Don't Split It (p/s)	12
79	Rough Trade RT 007	Ambition/A Different Story (initially in yellow text p/s, later orange text p/s)	7/6

(see also Vic Godard [& Subway Sect])

NIKKI SUDDEN

81	Rather GEAR 11	Back To The Start/Ringing On My Train (p/s)	5
82	Abstract ABS 009	Channel Steamer/Chelsea Embankment (p/s)	5
80s	Rather RATHER 10	BEAU GESTE (cassette, with insert)	12
85	Hotwire HWLP 8504	THE LAST BANDITS IN THE WORLD (LP)	12

(see also Swell Maps, Last Bandits, Jeremy Gluck)

(A) SUDDEN SWAY

80	Chant CHANT 1	Jane's Third Party/Don't Go (p/s, as A Sudden Sway)	15
80	own label	Jane's Third Party/Don't Go (cassette, as A Sudden Sway)	8
81	Chant CHANT 2/EJSP 9692	TO YOU, WITH REGARD (12" EP, with insert)	20
84	Chant CHANT 3	The Traffic Tax Scheme (12" with badge & inserts in folder)	12
86	WEA BYN 8B	Spacemate (2 x 12" box set with stickers, info sheets, 2 booklets & poster)	12
87	Strange Fruit SFPSC 005	PEEL SESSION 16.11.83 (EP, cassette)	5

SUE & MARY

62	Decca F 11517	Traitor In Disguise/I Love You	6

SUE & SUNNY

65	Columbia DB 7748	Every Ounce Of Strength/So Remember	8
67	Columbia DB 8099	You Can't By-Pass Love/I Like Your Style	15
68	CBS 3874	Little Black Book/The Show Must Go On	10
68	Island WIP 6043	Set Me Free/NIRVANA ORCHESTRA: City Of The South	10
69	CBS 4567	Let Us Break Bread/Stop Messing About With My Heart	7
70	CBS 4757	You Devil, Cotton-Eyed Joe/Night In The City	7
70	Deram DM 318	Ain't That Telling You People/Didn't I Blow Your Mind	10
71	Deram DM 328	Freedom/Break Up	10
71	Reflection HRS 10	Let Us Break Bread Together/Michael From Mountains	6
72	Deram DM 355	I'm Gonna Make You Love Me/High On The Thought Of You	8
70	CBS 63740	SUE AND SUNNY (LP)	25
70	Reflection REFL 4	SUE AND SUNNY (LP)	30

(see also Sue & Sunshine, Myrtelles, Stockingtops, Brotherhood Of Man)

SUE & SUNSHINE

64	Columbia DB 7409	A Little Love/If You See Me Crying	8
65	Columbia DB 7533	We're In Love/Don't Look Behind	7

(see also Sue & Sunny, Myrtelles, Stockingtops)

SUEDE

91	RML RML 001	Be My God/Art (12", unissued, 250+ white label copies only, no p/s; counterfeits have off-white labels)	80
92	Nude NUD 1 S	The Drowners (Radio Edit)/To The Birds (p/s, 1,000 copies only)	35
92	Nude NUD 1 CD	The Drowners (Radio Edit)/To The Birds/My Insatiable One (CD, promo only)	12
92	Nude NUD 3 T	Metal Mickey/Where Pigs Don't Fly/He's Dead (12", test pressing, plain sleeve)	40
93	Nude SUEDE 1	My Insatiable One (clear flexidisc, fan club/gig freebie)	18
93	Nude NUD 5 S	So Young/High Rising (p/s)	7
93	Nude NUD 5 T	So Young/High Rising/Dolly (12", p/s)	10
94	Nude NUD 10 S	We Are The Pigs/Killing Of A Flash Boy (numbered gatefold p/s)	8
94	Nude NUD 11 T	The Wild Ones/Eno's Introducing The Band/Asda Town (12", photo insert, p/s)	18
94	Nude NUD 11 CD 2	The Wild Ones/Eno's Introducing The Band/Asda Town (CD)	12
94	NME SUEDE 2	Dog Man Star sampler: The Wild Ones/Heroine/The Power/Still Life (flexi, p/s, includes spoken word excerpt from Brett, with/without NME)	8/6
94	Nude NUD 9 T	Stay Together/The Living Dead/My Dark Star (12", numbered gatefold p/s)	35
95	Nude NUD 12 CD 2	New Generation/Animal Nitrate (live)/The Wild Ones (live)/ Pantomime Horse (live) (CD, digipak)	25
96	Nude NUD 21S	Trash/Europe Is Our Playground (p/s, mail order only)	18
97	Nude SIS 1 CD	LIVE (CD EP, 6-track fan club-only issue)	20
97	Nude NUD 24 S	Saturday Night/Beautiful Ones (double pack, p/s, mail-order only)	15
97	Nude NUD 30 S	Film Star/(original version) (p/s)	5
97	Nude NUD 30 CD 2	Film Star (live)/Rent (live)/Saturday Night (live) (CD, featuring Neil Tennant)	12

MINT VALUE £

97 Nude PNUD 9 CD — SCI-FI LULLABIES (CD EP, promo only) 10
98 Nude SIS 2 CD — IMPLEMENT YEAH! (CD EP, fan club-only issue) 15
98 Nude SUEDE 1 CDF — ON FILM (CD EP, 6-track, promo only) 20
99 Nude NUD 667043 — ELECTRICITY EP (minidisc, withdrawn) 18
99 Nude FLOW RMX — Everything Will Flow (Rollo's Vocal)/(Rollo's Dub) (12", promo only) 15
99 Nude INT 1 CD — HEAD MUSING (CD, 2-track interview, promo only) 25
01 Nude PNUD 60 CD — SIMON (CD EP, promo only) 10
93 Nude NUDE 1LP — SUEDE (LP, with inner sleeve; some with carrier bag from Chain With No Name stores) 20/15
02 fan club — OBSESSIONS (2-CD, with DVD, fan club issue, in numbered box) 25
02 fan club — POSITIVITY (2-CD, with DVD, fan club issue, in numbered box) 25

(see also Elastica)

SUGAR (Simone) & DANDY (Livingstone)

63 Carnival CV 7006 — One Man Went To Mow/Cryin' 12
64 Carnival CV 7009 — Oh Dear What Can The Matter Be/Tra La La 12
64 Carnival CV 7015 — What A Life/Time And Tide 12
64 Carnival CV 7016 — I'm Not Crying Now/Blues Got A Hold On Me 12
65 Carnival CV 7023 — Let's Ska/Only Heaven Knows 12
65 Carnival CV 7024 — I'm Into Something Good/Crazy For You 12
65 Carnival CV 7027 — Think Of The Good Times/Girl Come See 12
65 Carnival CV 7029 — I Want To Be Your Lover/I Don't Know What I'm Going To Do Now 12
66 Blue Beat BB 367 — Meditation (as Jetliners)/GIRL SATCHMO & JET LINERS: Nature Of Love 20
67 Page One POF 044 — Let's Ska/Only Heaven Knows 12
64 Carnival CX 1000 — THE SKA'S THE LIMIT (LP) 60
67 Page One FOR 006 — THE SKA'S THE LIMIT (LP, reissue) 30

(see also Sugar Simone)

SUGAR & PEE WEE

58 Vogue Pop V 9112 — One, Two, Let's Rock/Just A Few Little Words 750
58 Vogue Pop V 9112 — One, Two, Let's Rock/Just A Few Little Words (78) 180

SUGAR & SPICE

69 London HLU 10259 — Cruel War/Not To Return 6

SUGAR BEARS

72 Philips 6073 812 — You Are The One/Someone Like You 5

SUGARBEATS

66 Polydor BM 56069 — I Just Stand Here/The Ballad Of Ole Betsy 15
66 Polydor BM 56120 — Alice Designs/Sunny Day Girl 12

(see also Tony Rivers & Castaways)

SUGARCUBES

87 One Little Indian 7z TP 7 — Birthday/Birthday (Icelandic) (p/s) 7
87 One Little Indian 12 TP 7 — Birthday/Birthday (Icelandic)/Cat (Icelandic) (12", p/s) 12
87 One Little Indian 7TP 7CD — Birthday/Motorcrash/Cat (Icelandic)/Birthday (Icelandic) (CD) 10
87 One Little Indian L12 TP 9 — Cold Sweat (Remix)/Birthday (Original Demo Version)/Dragon (Icelandic)/Traitor (Icelandic) (12", p/s, 5,000 only) 8
87 One Little Indian 7TP 9CD — Cold Sweat/Dragon (Icelandic)/Traitor (Icelandic)/Revolution (CD) 8
88 One Little Indian 10 TP 10 — Deus (Remix)/Luftgitar (Icelandic) (with Johnny Triumph)/Organic Prankster (10", p/s) 7
88 One Little Indian 7TP 10CD — Deus/Organic Prankster/Luftgitar (12" Version)/Night Of Steel (CD) 18
88 One Little Indian 12TP 11L — BIRTHDAY CHRISTMAS MIX (12" EP, double groove, with Jesus & Mary Chain) . 12
88 One L. Indian 12TP 11CDL — BIRTHDAY CHRISTMAS MIX (CD EP, with Jesus & Mary Chain) 8
89 House Of Dolls HOD 010 — Dark Disco/HOST: Homelands/MURRUMBRIDGE WHALERS: Giving Away To Trains/SHARK TABOO: Tinsel Town (live) (no p/s, with *House Of Dolls* mag) 6/4
90 One Little Indian TP BOX 2 — 7.8 (8 x 7" box set) 25
90 One Little Indian TP BOX 1 — 12.11 (11 x 12" box set) 40
90 One Little Indian TP BOX 3 — CD.6 (6 x CD box set) 45
88 One Little Indian DTPLP 5 — LIFE'S TOO GOOD (DAT) 20
89 One Little Indian TPLP 15SP — HERE TODAY, TOMORROW NEXT WEEK! (LP, silver vinyl, gatefold sleeve with sticker & inner) 20
89 One Little Indian TPLP 15L — SYKURMOLARNIR ILLUR ARFUR! (LP, as Sykurmolarnir, gatefold sleeve) 15

(see also Björk, Kukl, Ornamental)

SUGAR LOAF

70 RCA INTS 1113 — SOUL STURRING (LP) 40

SUGARLOAF

70 Liberty LBF 15401 — Green-Eyed Lady/West Of Tomorrow 5
71 Liberty LBS 83415 — SUGARLOAF (LP) 15
74 United Artists UAS 29165 — SPACESHIP EARTH (LP) 12
75 Polydor 2310 394 — DON'T CALL US, WE'LL CALL YOU (LP, with Jerry Corbetto) 15

SUGAR SHOPPE

68 Capitol CL 15555 — Skip-A-Long Sam/Let The Truth Come Out 20

SUGARPLUMS

70 Fab FAB 160 — Red River Reggae/Too Much 7

SUGGS

95 WEA YZ 975 — I'm Only Sleeping/Off On Holiday (unreleased)

(see also Madness)

SUICIDAL TENDENCIES

87 Virgin VS 967-12 — Possessed To Skate/Human Guinea Pig/Two Wrongs Don't Make A Right (12", picture disc) 10
88 Virgin VST 1039 — Institutionalised/War Inside My Head/Cyco (12", p/s) 15
88 Virgin V 2551 — HOW WILL I LAUGH TOMORROW WHEN I CAN'T EVEN SMILE TODAY? (LP) 15

SUICIDE

77	Sound For Industry SFI 323	Johnny/(Real Kids track) (flexidisc via *Circuit* magazine)	8
78	Red Star/Bronze BRO 57	Cheree/I Remember (p/s)	10
78	Red Star/Bronze 12 BRO 57	Cheree/I Remember (12", 'limited edition', p/s)	12
79	Island WIP 6543	Dream Baby Dream/Radiation (p/s)	6
79	Island 12 WIP 6543	Dream Baby Dream (Long Version)/Radiation (12", p/s)	10
86	Demon D 1046	Cheree/I Remember (promo only)	5
89	Chapter 22 12CHAP 36	Rain Of Ruin/Surrender (12")	10
89	Chapter 22 12CHAP 42	SUICIDE (12", unissued)	
77	Red Star/Bronze BRON 508	SUICIDE (LP)	12
78	Red Star FRANKIE 1	24 MINUTES OVER BRUSSELS (LP, official bootleg, 1,000 only, no p/s)	30
80	Ze/Island ILPS 7007	SUICIDE: ALAN VEGA/MARTIN REV (LP, with printed inner sleeve)	14
89	Contempo CONTE 148	HALF ALIVE (LP, clear vinyl, 1,000 only)	12
98	Blast First BFFP 133 1/2	SUICIDE (2-LP)	18
99	Blast First BFFP 162	FIRST REHEARSAL TAPES (2-LP)	15

(see also Alan Vega, Martin Rev)

SUICIDE TWINS

86	Lick LICLP 9	SILVER MISSILES AND NIGHTINGALES (LP)	12

(see also Hanoi Rocks)

BIG JIM SULLIVAN

61	Decca F 11387	You Don't Know What You've Got/Hot Hiss Of Steam (as Big Jim Sullivan Combo)	10
65	Mercury MF 928	She Walks Through The Fair/Don't Know What I'm Doing (as Jim Sullivan Sound)	22
73	MAM MAM 100	Out Of The Question/Alone Again	6
67	Mercury SML 30001	SITAR BEAT (LP)	40

(see also Maureeny Wishfull, Brian Bennett, Tiger)

MAXINE SULLIVAN

54	Parlophone MSP 6086	Boogie Woogie Maxine/Piper In The Glen (with Vic Ash)	15
54	Parlophone R 3833	Boogie Woogie Maxine/Piper In The Glen (78, with Vic Ash)	8

PHIL SULLIVAN with LONZO & OSCAR'S PEAPICKERS

59	Melodisc MEL 1512	Love Never Dies/Luckiest Man In Town	5

YMA SUMAC

52	Capitol CL 13746	Suray Surita/Zana (78)	10
52	Capitol CL 13766	Wimoweh/Babalu (78)	6
54	Capitol CL 14094	Ripui (Farewell)/Llulla Mak'ta (Andean Don Juan) (78)	10
50s	Parlophone DP 324	La Benita/A Ti Solita Tequiero (export 78)	8
50s	Parlophone DP 334	Amor Indo/Un Amor (export 78)	8
55	Capitol EAP1 564	YMA SUMAC MAMBO (EP)	20
55	Capitol EAP2 564	YMA SUMAC MAMBO (EP)	20
57	Capitol EAP1 770	LEGEND OF JIVARO PT. 1 (EP)	20
57	Capitol EAP2 770	LEGEND OF JIVARO PT. 2 (EP)	20
57	Capitol EAP3 770	LEGEND OF JIVARO PT. 3 (EP)	20
53	Capitol LC 6522	VOICE OF THE XTABAY (10" LP)	50
54	Capitol LC 6609	LEGEND OF THE SUN VIRGIN (10" LP)	40
59	Capitol T 1169	FUEGO DEL ANDE (LP)	40
64	Regal REG 2007	VOICE OF THE XTABAY (LP)	30
72	London HLU/SHU 8431	MIRACLES (LP)	40

HUBERT SUMLIN

65	Blue Horizon 45-1000	Across The Board/Sumlin Boogie (99 copies only)	110

(see also Howlin' Wolf)

DONNA SUMMER

74	People PEO 115	The Hostage/Let's Work Together Now	10
79	Casablanca SANL 151	Hot Stuff/Journey To The Centre Of Your Heart (12", red vinyl)	15
84	Casablanca FEEL 12	I Feel Love/I Feel Love (Version) (12")	12
87	WEA U 8237P	Dinner With Gershwin (Parts 1 & 2) (12", picture disc)	8
89	WEA U 7780P	This Time I Know It's For Real/Whatever Your Heart Desires (shaped pic disc)	5
89	WEA U 7780CD	This Time I Know It's For Real/Whatever Your Heart Desires/This Time I Know It's For Real (Extended Version) (3" CD)	15
89	WEA U 7567CD	I Don't Wanna Get Hurt/Dinner With Gershwin/I Don't Wanna Get Hurt (Instrumental) (3" CD)	15
89	WEA U 7494	Love's About To Change My Heart (Extended Remix)/Love's About To Change My Heart (Instrumental)/Jeremy (3" CD)	15
89	WEA U 7361	When Love Takes Over You (Extended Remix)/When Love Takes Over You (Instrumental)/Bad Reputation (3" CD)	15

(see also Donna Gaines, John Barry)

SUMMERHILL

69	Polydor 583 746	SUMMERHILL (LP)	30

ANDY SUMMERS & ROBERT FRIPP

82	A&M (no cat. no.)	Hardy Country/Stultified/Yellow Leader/I Advance Masked (clear flexidisc)	6

(see also Police, King Crimson)

BOB(BY) SUMMERS

59	Capitol CL 15063	Rattle Rhythm/Excitement (as Bob Summers)	15
60	Capitol CL 15130	Little Brown Jug/Twelfth Street Rag (as Bobby Summers)	8

SUMMER SET

66	Columbia DB 8004	Farmer's Daughter/Papa-Oom-Mow-Mow	30
66	Columbia DB 8004	Farmer's Daughter/What Are You Gonna Do (2nd issue with different B-side)	25
67	Columbia DB 8215	Overnight Changes/It's A Dream	60

(see also Candy Choir)

Year	Label / Cat. No.	Title	MINT VALUE £
SUMMERTAIRES			
66	Ska Beat JB 258	My Heart Cries Out/SOUL BROTHERS: James Bond Girl	30
(see also Jackie Mittoo, Soul Agents)			
SUMMER WINE			
72	Philips 6006 217	Why Do Fools Fall In Love/Ode To Steel Guitar	5
72	Philips 6006 238	Take A Load Off Your Feet/ Sound Of Summer's Over	5
73	Philips 6006 288	Living Right Next Door To An Angel/Sound Of Summer's Over	6
77	EMI EMI 2634	Why Do Fools Fall In Love/Sound Of Summer's Over	5
(see also Tony Rivers, John Perry)			
SUN			
78	Capitol EMC 3262	LIVE ON DREAM ON (LP)	12
SUN ALSO RISES			
70	Village Thing VTS 2	THE SUN ALSO RISES (LP)	20
SUN & MOON			
88	Geffen GEF 39	The Speed Of Life/Death Of Imagination (p/s)	5
88	Geffen GEF 39T	The Speed Of Life/Death Of Imagination/The Boy Who Sees Everything/ I Love You, You Bastard (12", p/s)	8
89	Midnight Music DONG 44CD	ALIVE; NOT DEAD (CD EP)	12
89	Geffen 9241 882	THE SUN AND THE MOON (CD)	15
(see also Chameleons)			
SUNDAE TIMES			
68	President PT 203	Baby Don't Cry/Aba-Aba	5
68	President PT 219	Jack Boy/I Don't Want Nobody	5
70	President PT 285	Live Today/Take Me Higher Baby	5
70	Joy JOYS 159	US COLOURED KIDS (LP)	20
SUNDANCE			
73	Decca F 13423	Coming Down/Eagles	5
73	Decca F 13461	Stand By/Willie The Gambler	5
74	Decca F 13494	Loving You/Can You Feel It	5
73	Decca TXS 111	RAIN STEAM SPEED (LP, with insert)	15
74	Decca SKL 5183	CHUFFER (LP)	15
SUNDAY AFTERNOONS			
70s	Longman	SUNDAY AFTERNOONS (LP)	90
SUNDAYS			
89	Rough Trade RTX 218	Can't Be Sure/I Kicked A Boy (export issue, brown p/s)	6
89	Rough Trade RTTX 218	Can't Be Sure/I Kicked A Boy/Don't Tell Your Mother (12", export issue, brown p/s)	10
89	Rough Trade RTT 218CD	Can't Be Sure/I Kicked A Boy/Don't Tell Your Mother (3" CD, card sleeve)	8
90	Catalogue CAT 076	I Won (square flexidisc with ***The Catalogue*** magazine)	10
97	Parlophone CDR 6475	Summertime/Nothing Sweet/Gone (CD)	8
90	Rough Trade ROUGH 148P	READING, WRITING AND ARITHMETIC (LP, picture disc, stickered sleeve)	20
SUNDAY SING TRIO			
70s	Sharon SHLP 1221	ONE OF THESE DAYS (LP)	15
SUN DIAL			
90	UFO 45 001T	Exploding In Your Mind/Otherside/Slow Motion (12", 1-sided, p/s)	10
91	Tangerine TANGERINE 111	Exploding In Your Mind (Colour Mix)/Otherside/Slow Motion (12", unreleased, 80 white label test pressings only)	30
91	UFO PF 2	Fireball/Only A Northern Song ('Pre-Flight' 7", promo only)	20
91	UFO UFO 45002 T	OVERSPILL EP (12", orange vinyl)	10
92	UFO UFO 45008 T	FAZER EP (12")	10
90	Tangerine MM 07	OTHER WAY OUT (LP, with insert, some signed in silver ink)	20/30
91	UFO UFO 1LP	OTHER WAY OUT (LP, reissue in gatefold sleeve)	12
92	UFO UFO 8	REFLECTER (LP, clear vinyl)	15
94	Acme AC 8001	RETURN JOURNEY (LP, official bootleg; 200 promos with inserts, 500 numbered commercial copies)	20/12
95	Acme AC 8011LP	ACID YANTRA (LP, gatefold sleeve)	12
(see also Modern Art, Spiral Sky, Quad)			
SUNDOWNERS			
63	Piccadilly 7N 35142	Baby Baby/House Of The Rising Sun	8
64	Piccadilly 7N 35162	Come On In/Shot Of Rhythm And Blues	8
65	Parlophone R 5243	Where Am I/Gonna Make The Future Bright	7
68	Columbia DB 8339	Dr. J. Wallace-Brown/Love Is In The Air	10
68	Spark SRL 1016	Gloria The Bosom Show/Don't Look Back	6
SUNDOWN PLAYBOYS			
72	Apple APPLE 44	Saturday Nite Special/Valse De Soleil Couche (some in p/s)	30/10
72	Apple APPLE 44	Saturday Nite Special/Valse De Soleil Couche (10", 78rpm, pink-patterned die-cut sleeve)	225
SUNDRAGON			
68	MGM MGM 1380	Green Tambourine/I Need All The Friends I Can Get	12
68	MGM MGM 1391	Blueberry Blue/Far Away Mountain	10
68	MGM MGM 1458	Five White Horses/Look At The Sun	7
68	MGM MGM-C(S) 8090	GREEN TAMBOURINE (LP)	70
(see also Sands, Others)			
SUNFIGHTER			
76	EMI EMI 2493	Drag Race Queen/Riding On Your Star	10
76	EMI EMI 2553	Such A Lovely Night/Don't Get Me Wrong	8
(see also Chris Rainbow)			
SUNFOREST			
70	Deram Nova (S)DN 7	SOUND OF SUNFOREST (LP, mono/stereo)	each 100

MINT VALUE £

SUNNY & HI-JUMPERS
65 Carnival CV 7022 Tarry Till You're Better/Dance Til You're Better 6
65 Carnival CV 7025 Going To Damascus/Sweet Potatoes 6

SUNNY & THE SUNGLOWS/SUNLINERS
63 London HL 9792 Talk To Me (as Sunny & the Sunglows)/Every Week, Every Month, Every Year (as Sunny & the Sunliners) 22

SUNNYLAND SLIM
65 '77' LA 12-23 CHICAGO BLUES SESSION (LP, with Little Brother Montgomery) 30
65 Storyville SLP 169 I DONE YOU WRONG (LP) 25
68 Storyville 670 169 PORTRAITS IN BLUES (LP, reissue of SLP 169) 20
69 Liberty LBS 83237 SLIM'S GOT THIS THING GOIN' ON (LP) 30
69 Blue Horizon 7-63213 MIDNIGHT JUMP (LP) 60
74 Sonet SNTF 671 THE LEGACY OF THE BLUES VOL. II (LP) 12

SUNNYSIDERS
55 London HL 8135 Hey! Mr. Banjo/Zoom, Zoom, Zoom 50
55 London HL 8160 Oh Me Oh My Oh/(Let's Gather Round) The Parlour Piano 30
55 London HLU 8180 Banjo Woogie/She Didn't Even Say Goodbye 30
55 London HLU 8202 I Love You Fair Dinkum/Stay On The Sunny Side 25
56 London HLU 8246 Doesn't He Love Me/Humdinger 30
56 London HLU 8246 Doesn't He Love Me/Humdinger (78) 6

SUN RA ARKESTRA
74 Decca F 13542 Don't Go/Can We Change 30
82 Y 1 RA NUCLEAR WAR (12" EP) 25
69 Fontana STL 5514 HELIOCENTRIC WORLDS VOL. 1 (LP) 40
69 Fontana STL 5499 HELIOCENTRIC WORLDS VOL. 2 (LP) 40
60s Sonet 23 SPL JAZZ BY SUN RA (LP) 30
71 Black Lion BLP 30103 PICTURES OF INFINITY — IN CONCERT (LP) 20
71 Byg 529 341 THE SOLAR MYTH APPROACH VOL. 2 (LP) 25
70s Polydor 2460 106 PICTURES OF INFINITY (LP) 25
78 Affinity AFF 10 S-M APPROACH (LP, with Solar-Myth Ark) 15
79 Cobra COB 37001 FATE IN A PLEASANT MOOD (LP) 18
70s Delmark DL 411 SUN SONG (LP) 20
70s Delmark DL 414 SOUND OF JOY (LP) 20
70s Y Y 19 STRANGE CELESTIAL ROAD (LP) 15
70s Recommended 11 RRA NIGHTS DE LA FONDATION MAEGHT VOL. 1 (LP, with insert) 15

SUN RA & MYTH SCIENCE ARKESTRA
90 Blast First BFFP 60 SUN RA & MYTH SCIENCE ARKESTRA (3 x 10", box set, with insert) 35

SUNRAYS
65 Capitol CL 15416 I Live For The Sun/Bye, Baby, Bye 10
66 Capitol CL 15433 Andrea/You Don't Phase Me 12

SUNRISE
76 Grapevine GRA 105 BEFORE MY EYES (LP) 30

SUNSET BOYS
79 Gimp GIM 1234 Wreck My Bed/Tutti Frutti/Copy Cat (Blues)/Wreck My Bed (Hippy Version) (p/s) 5
(see also Maxim's Trash)

SUN SET
67 Polydor BM 56193 East Baby/You Can Ride My Rainbow 10

SUNSETS
61 Ember EMB S 125 Cry Of The Wild Goose/Manhunt 15

SUNSHINE
72 Warner Brothers K 46169 SUNSHINE (LP) 12
(see also Pretty Things)

MONTY SUNSHINE
55 Tempo A 125 Wild Cat Blues/St. Philips St. Breakdown (78) 6
62 Pye Jazz 7NJ 2011 Hushabye/Whistling Rufus (with His Jazz Band) 5
62 London HLR 9629 Gonna Build A Mountain/Hushabye (with His Band) 6
63 London HLR 9822 Carnival — From "Black Orpheus"/Charmaine (with His Orchestra) 6
57 Pye Nixa NJE 1050 THE MONTY SUNSHINE SHOWCASE (EP) 8
61 Columbia SEG 8059 MONTY (EP) 10
61 Columbia SEG 8127 SUNSHINE (EP) 15
63 London RE-R 1368 GONNA BUILD A MOUNTAIN (EP, with His Band) 12
63 London HAR 8037 MONTY SUNSHINE AND HIS BAND (LP, also stereo [SHR 8037]) 20
64 London HAR 8158 BLACK MOONLIGHT & SUNSHINE (LP, also stereo [SHR 8158]) 20
69 Major Minor SMCP 5062 SHADES OF SUNSHINE (LP) 18
70s DJM DJB 26088 A TASTE OF SUNSHINE (LP) 15
(see also Lonnie Donegan)

MR. SUNSHINE
56 MGM SP 1160 Along The China Coast/MRS. SUNSHINE: Two Car Garage 7

SUNSHINE COMPANY
67 Liberty LBF 15008 Happy/Blue May 8
67 Liberty LBF 15034 Back On The Street Again/A Year Of Janie's Time 6
68 Liberty LBF 15060 Look Here Comes The Sun/It's Sunday 6
68 Liberty LBF 15149 On A Beautiful Day/To Put Up With You 7
68 Liberty LBL/LBS 83120 THE SUNSHINE COMPANY (LP) 25
69 Liberty LBL/LBS 83159 SUNSHINE AND SHADOWS (LP) 25

SUNSPOTS
63 Decca F 11672 Paella/Vancouver 7

MINT VALUE £

SUNSTROKE

78	Hot Stuff HS 004	SUNSTROKE (EP)	5

SUNTREADER

73	Island HELP 13	ZIN ZIN (LP)	12

(see also Stomu Yamashta)

SUPERBOYS

68	Giant GN 22	Ain't That A Shame/Do It Right Now	12
68	Giant GN 31	You're Hurtin' Me/Funky Soul	12

(see also Dandy & Superboys, Little Sal)

SUPERCHUNK

93	Domino RUG 9	Ribbon/Who Needs Light (p/s)	6

SUPER 8

95	García POUM 001	Billy The Kid/It Doesn't Matter/How Can I Understand The Flies? (p/s, 500 only, 37 sold, 35 returned for refund, the rest believed burned)	25

(see also Sheds)

SUPER FURRY ANIMALS

96	Creation CRE 222	Hometown Unicorn/Don't Be A Fool Billy (p/s)	12
96	Creation CRESCD 231	God! Show Me Magic/Death By Melody/Dim Bendith (CD, picture disc)	8
96	Creation CRESCD 235	Something For The Weekend/Waiting To Happen/Arnofio (Glow In The Dark) (CD)	8
96	Creation CRE 247	The Man Don't Give A Fuck (p/s, 1-sided, blue vinyl)	12
96	Creation CRE 247 T	The Man Don't Give A Fuck/(Howard Marks Mix)/(Wishmountain Mix)/ (Darren Price Mix) (12", p/s)	8
96	Creation CRESCD 247	The Man Don't Give A Fuck/(Howard Marks Mix)/(Wishmountain Mix) (CD, picture disc)	18
96	Debiel SS 01	(Nid) Hon Yw'r Gan Sy'n Mynd I Achub Yr Laith (1-sided gig freebie)	12
98	Creation CRE 288	Ice Hockey Hair/Smokin' (stickered p/s, limited edition)	8
03	Epic 6739067	Golden Retriever/Summer Snow/Blue Fruit (picture disc, limited edition, numbered, stickered poly sleeve)	12
95	Ankst ANKST 057	LLANFAIRPWLLGWYNGYLLGOGERYCHWYRNDROBWLLANTYSILIO-GOGOGOCHYNYGOFOD (IN SPACE) (EP)	15
95	Ankst ANKST 62	LLANFAIRPWLLGWYNGYLLGOGERYCHWYRNDROBWLLANTYSILIO-GOGOGOCHYNYGOFOD (IN SPACE) (EP, cassette)	5
95	Ankst ANKST 62	MOOG DROOG EP (EP, p/s)	8
95	Ankst ANKST 62	MOOG DROOG EP (CD)	10
96	Creation CRELP 190	FUZZY LOGIC (LP, with insert)	20
98	Creation CRECD 229 L	OUT SPACED (CD, rubber pack [black, green or blue])	18

SUPERGRASS

94	Backbeat (no cat. no.)	Caught By The Fuzz/Strange Ones (hand-stamped labels, 1,000 only, later re-pressed)	22
94	Backbeat (no cat. no.)	Mansize Rooster/Sitting Up Straight (luminous green vinyl, printed green cardboard or plain die-cut sleeve, 500 only)	25/15
94	Backbeat (no cat. no.)	Mansize Rooster/Sitting Up Straight (marbled green vinyl, plain sleeve)	8
94	Parlophone R 6396	Caught By The Fuzz/Strange Ones (p/s, reissue)	15
94	Parlophone 12R 6396DJ	Caught By The Fuzz/Strange Ones (12", p/s, promo only)	12
94	Parlophone CDR 6396	Caught By The Fuzz/Strange Ones/Caught By The Fuzz (Acoustic) (CD)	10
95	Parlophone R 6402	Mansize Rooster/Sitting Up Straight (p/s, red vinyl)	10
95	Parlophone CDR 6402	Mansize Rooster/Sitting Up Straight/Odd (CD)	8
95	Parlophone RS 6410	Lenny/Wait For The Sun (p/s, light blue vinyl)	7
95	Parlophone GRASS 2	Sofa (Of My Lethargy) (Radio Edit)/(Album Version) (CD, promo only, card p/s)	8
96	Parlophone R 6428	Going Out/Melanie Davis (p/s, burgundy vinyl)	7
97	Parlophone R 6461	Richard III/Nothing More's Gonna Get In My Way (p/s, yellow vinyl)	7
97	Parlophone R 6469	Sun Hits The Sky/Some Girls Are Bigger Than Others (numbered p/s, white vinyl)	7
97	Parlophone 12RDJ 6469	Sun Hits The Sky (Bentley Rhythm Ace Sun Hits The Sky Mix) (12", no p/s, promo only)	12
99	EMI CDIN 125	INTERVIEW (CD, tri-fold digipak, promo only)	15
99	Parlophone R 6531	Mary/(Live Version) (p/s, silver vinyl)	7
02	Parlophone R 6583	Never Done Nothing Like That Before (1-sided, stamped white label, die-cut black sleeve with barcode sticker, numbered, 1,500 only)	10
97	Parlophone GRASS 9497	THE SINGLES 1994-1997 (8 x 7" black vinyl, 'grass'-covered box set, with signed & numbered insert, promo only)	60
95	Parlophone PCSX 7373	I SHOULD COCO (LP, with inner & bonus single "Stone Free"/"Odd?" [PCSS 7373])	30

(see also Jennifers)

SUPERMATIX

81	MC 4	BAD TIMING EP (p/s)	6

SUPER$HIT666

00	Infernal INFERNAL003LP	SUPER$HIT666 (10" LP, with inner sleeve, purple or black vinyl)	15/12

(see also Backyard Babies, Hellacopters, Wildhearts)

SUPERSISTER

72	Polydor 2001 379	No Tree Will Grow/She Was Naked	5
71	Dandelion 2310 146	TO THE HIGHEST BIDDER (LP, gatefold sleeve)	25
71	Polydor 2419 030	SUPER STARSHINE 3 (LP)	15
72	Polydor 2419 061	PRESENT FROM NANCY (LP)	15
73	Polydor 2480 153	PUDDING & YESTERDAY (LP)	15
73	Polydor 2925 021	ISKANDER (LP, gatefold sleeve with lyric sheet)	12

SUPERSONICS

53	London L 1197	New Guitar Boogie Shuffle/The Sheik Of Araby (78)	15
54	London HL 8022	Cherokee/Linger Awhile (B-side with Arlene James) (78)	15

SUPERTONES

70	Banana BA 312	Freedom Blues/First Time I Met You	10

(see also Jackie Mittoo)

MINT VALUE £

SUPPORTERS

70 RCA 1972 Sing Your Own Team/On The Ball ... 30

(DIANA ROSS &) SUPREMES

SINGLES

64 Stateside SS 257 When The Lovelight Starts Shining Thru' His Eyes/ Standing At The Crossroads Of Love ... 45
64 Stateside SS 327 Where Did Our Love Go/He Means The World To Me ... 10
64 Stateside SS 350 Baby Love/Ask Any Girl ... 10
65 Stateside SS 376 Come See About Me/(You're Gone But) Always In My Heart ... 10
65 Tamla Motown TMG 501 Stop! In The Name Of Love/I'm In Love Again ... 8
65 Tamla Motown TMG 516 Back In My Arms Again/Whisper You Love Me Boy ... 15
65 Tamla Motown TMG 527 Nothing But Heartaches/He Holds His Own ... 18
65 Tamla Motown TMG 543 I Hear A Symphony/Who Could Ever Doubt My Love ... 8
66 Tamla Motown TMG 548 My World Is Empty Without You/Everything Is Good About You ... 12
66 Tamla Motown TMG 560 Love Is Like An Itching In My Heart/He's All I Got ... 30
66 Tamla Motown TMG 575 You Can't Hurry Love/Put Yourself In My Place ... 6
66 Tamla Motown TMG 585 You Keep Me Hangin' On/Remove This Doubt ... 6
67 Tamla Motown TMG 597 Love Is Here And Now You're Gone/There's No Stopping Us Now ... 6
67 Tamla Motown TMG 607 The Happening/All I Know About You ... 6
(The singles listed above are credited to Supremes.)
67 Tamla Motown TMG 616 Reflections/Going Down For The Third Time (push-out or solid centre) ... 7/6
67 Tamla Motown TMG 632 In And Out Of Love/I Guess I'll Always Love You ... 5
68 Tamla Motown TMG 650 Forever Came Today/Time Changes Things ... 5
68 Tamla Motown TMG 662 Some Things You Never Get Used To/You've Been So Wonderful To Me ... 5
68 Tamla Motown TMG 677 Love Child/Will This Be The Day? ... 5
69 Tamla Motown TMG 695 I'm Living In Shame/I'm So Glad I Got Somebody (Like You Around) ... 6
69 Tamla Motown TMG 704 No Matter What Sign You Are/The Young Folks ... 5
69 Tamla Motown TMG 721 Someday We'll Be Together/He's My Sunny Boy ... 5
(The singles listed above are credited to Diana Ross & Supremes.)
70 Tamla Motown TMG 735 Up The Ladder To The Roof/Bill, When Are You Coming Back ... 5
70 Tamla Motown TMG 747 Everybody's Got The Right To Love/But I Love You More ... 5
71 Tamla Motown TMG 760 Stoned Love/Shine On Me ... 5
71 Tamla Motown TMG 782 Nathan Jones/Happy (Is A Bumpy Road) ... 5
(The singles listed above are credited to Supremes and do not feature Diana Ross.)

EPs

65 Tamla Motown TME 2008 THE SUPREMES HITS (originally with flipback sleeve & push-out centre) ... 30/20
66 Tamla Motown TME 2011 SHAKE ... 65

LPs

64 Stateside SL 10109 MEET THE SUPREMES ... 35
65 Tamla Motown TML 11002 WITH LOVE — FROM US TO YOU ... 45
65 Tamla Motown TML 11012 WE REMEMBER SAM COOKE ... 50
65 Tamla Motown TML 11018 THE SUPREMES SING COUNTRY, WESTERN AND POP ... 50
65 Tamla Motown TML 11020 MORE HITS BY THE SUPREMES ... 20
66 T. Motown (S)TML 11026 THE SUPREMES AT THE COPA (mono/stereo) ... 18/22
66 T. Motown (S)TML 11028 I HEAR A SYMPHONY (mono/stereo) ... 18/22
66 T. Motown (S)TML 11039 SUPREMES A-GO GO (mono/stereo) ... 18/22
67 T. Motown (S)TML 11047 THE SUPREMES SING MOTOWN ... 20
67 T. Motown (S)TML 11054 THE SUPREMES SING RODGERS AND HART ... 20
(The LPs listed above are credited to Supremes.)
68 T. Motown (S)TML 11063 GREATEST HITS (original pressing with flipback laminated sleeve) ... 12
68 T. Motown (S)TML 11070 'LIVE' AT LONDON'S TALK OF THE TOWN ... 12
68 T. Motown (S)TML 11073 REFLECTIONS ... 15
69 T. Motown (S)TML 11088 SING & PERFORM FUNNY GIRL (mono/stereo) ... 18/15
69 T. Motown (S)TML 11095 LOVE CHILD (mono/stereo) ... 18/15
69 T. Motown (S)TML 11114 LET THE SUNSHINE IN (mono/stereo) ... 18/15
70 T. Motown (S)TML 11137 CREAM OF THE CROP (mono/stereo) ... 18/15
70 Tamla Motown STML 11157 RIGHT ON (as Supremes) ... 12
71 Tamla Motown STML 11189 TOUCH (LP, as Supremes) ... 12
73 T. Motown STML 11222 PRODUCED AND ARRANGED BY JIMMY WEBB (LP, as Supremes) ... 12
(The LPs listed above are credited to Diana Ross & Supremes unless otherwise stated.
All the albums listed above were originally issued with flipback sleeves; later pressings are worth two-thirds these values.)

SUPREMES & FOUR TOPS

71 Tamla Motown TMG 777 River Deep, Mountain High/It's Gotta Be A Miracle (This Thing Called Love) ... 5
71 Tamla Motown TMG 793 You Gotta Have Love In Your Heart/I'm Glad About It ... 5
71 T. Motown STML 11179 THE SUPREMES AND THE FOUR TOPS — MAGNIFICENT 7 (LP) ... 12

DIANA ROSS & THE SUPREMES & THE TEMPTATIONS

69 Tamla Motown TMG 685 I'm Gonna Make You Love Me/A Place In The Sun ... 5
69 Tamla Motown TMG 709 I Second That Emotion/The Way You Do The Things You Do ... 5
70 Tamla Motown TMG 730 Why (Must We Fall In Love)/Uptight (Everything Is Alright) ... 5
69 T. Motown (S)TML 11096 DIANA ROSS & THE SUPREMES JOIN THE TEMPTATIONS (LP) ... 12
69 T. Motown (S)TML 11110 THE ORIGINAL SOUNDTRACK FROM TCB (LP, gatefold laminated sleeve) ... 15
70 T. Motown STML 11122 TOGETHER (LP, flipback sleeve) ... 12
(see also Primettes, Diana Ross, Temptations, Four Tops, Florence Ballard)

ADAM SURF & PEBBLE BEACH BAND

76 Paladin PAL 3 Fun Fun Fun/Blue Surf ... 6

SURFARIS

63 London HLD 9751 Wipe Out/Surfer Joe ... 15
63 Brunswick 05894 Waikiki Run/Point Panic ... 15
64 Brunswick 05902 Scatter Shield/Bat Man ... 15
66 Dot DS 26756 Wipe Out/Surfer Joe (reissue) ... 6
73 Paramount PARA 3034 Wipe Out/Shake ... 5
63 London RE-D 1405 WIPE OUT (EP) ... 60

63	London HA-D 8110	WIPE OUT (LP)	50
63	Brunswick LAT/STA 8561	THE SURFARIS PLAY (LP, mono/stereo)	40/50
64	Brunswick LAT/STA 8567	HIT CITY '64 (LP, mono/stereo)	40/50
64	Brunswick LAT 8582	FUN CITY (LP)	45
65	Brunswick LAT 8605	HIT CITY '65 (LP)	45
65	Brunswick LAT 8631	IT AIN'T ME BABE (LP, also stereo STA 8631)	40/50
66	Dot DLP 3535	WIPE OUT (LP, reissue)	25
76	MCA MCF 2761	SURFERS RULE (LP)	18
77	MCA Coral CDL 8050	GONE WITH THE WAVE (LP)	18
87	MCA MCL 1842	WIPE OUT – THE SINGLES ALBUM 1963-1967 (LP, withdrawn)	30

SURFERS

59	Vogue V 9147	Mambo Jambo/ALAN KALANI: A Touch Of Pink	18

LES SURFS

64	RCA RCA 1432	Just For The Boy/Stop	10
65	RCA RCA 1461	Go Your Way/Chained To A Memory	7
67	Fontana TF 832	When I Tell You (That I Love You)/I Want To Be Free	6

SURGEONS

79	Surgery S-100	Sid Never Did It/Breaking Rocks On Ricker's Island	50

SURGICAL SUPPORTS

81	Industrious Youth CONSTRUCT 2	WITHDRAWN FOR DISPOSAL EP	30

JOHN SURMAN (Trio)

69	Deram DM 224	Obeah Wedding/Can't Stop The Carnival	40
68	Deram DML/SML 1030	JOHN SURMAN (LP)	65
69	Deram DML-R/SML-R 1045	HOW MANY CLOUDS CAN YOU SEE? (LP)	100
70	Futura GER 12	ALORS! (LP)	40
71	Dawn DNLS 3006	THE TRIO (LP)	60
71	Dawn DNLS 3018	WHERE FORTUNE SMILES (LP, with insert, with John McLaughlin, Karl Berger, Stu Martin & Dave Holland)	40
71	Dawn DNLS 3022	CONFLAGRATION (LP)	50
71	Deram SML 1094	TALES OF THE ALGONQUIN (LP, with John Warren)	100
72	Island HELP 10	WESTERING HOME (LP)	20
73	Island ILPS 9237	MORNING GLORY (LP)	20

(see also Morning Glory, Trio, Mike Westbook, John McLaughlin, Alan Skidmore/Mike Osborne/John Surman)

SURPLUS STOCK

79	Outatune OUT 7911	Spiv/Vips (p/s)	8

SURPRISES

79	Dead Dog DEAD 01	Jeremy Thorpe Is Innocent/Flying Attack/Little Sir Echo (p/s)	50

SURVIVORS

65	Rio R 55	Take Charge/Ska-Ology	10
65	Rio R 70	Rawhide Ska/OWEN GRAY: Girl I Want You	10

SUSIE

71	Decca F 13217	I Feel The Earth Move/We Are All The Same	8

SUSSED

80	Graduate GRAD 7	I've Got Me A Parka/Myself, Myself And I Repeated (p/s, paper labels; later reissued [1986] with silver labels)	6
81	Shoestring LACE 002	I Like You/Tango/The Perv (p/s)	10

(SCREAMING) LORD SUTCH (& THE SAVAGES)

61	HMV POP 953	Till The Following Night/Good Golly Miss Molly	20
63	Decca F 11598	Jack The Ripper/Don't You Just Know It	20
63	Decca F 11747	I'm A Hog For You/Monster In Black Tights	20
64	Oriole CB 1944	She's Fallen In Love With A Monster Man/Bye Bye Baby	50
64	Oriole CB 1962	Dracula's Daughter/Come Back Baby	50
65	CBS 201767	The Train Kept A-Rollin'/Honey Hush (as Lord Sutch)	50
66	CBS 202080	The Cheat/Black And Hairy	50
70	Atlantic 584 321	'Cause I Love You/Thumping Beat	12
70	Atlantic 2091 006	'Cause I Love You/Thumping Beat (reissue)	8
70	Atlantic 2091 017	Election Fever/Rock The Election	10
72	Atlantic K 10221	Gotta Keep A-Rockin'/Flashing Lights/Hands Of Jack The Ripper	10
76	SRT SRTS 76361	Monster Ball/Rang-Tang-A-Lang	6
76	SRT SRTS 76375	I Drink To Your Health Marie (Parts 1 & 2)	6
77	Decca F 13697	Jack The Ripper/I'm A Hog For You	5
81	Ridgemount RMR 45 010	LOONABILLY (EP, p/s, with bonus "Loon Party" single)	8
81	Ace SW 70	SCREAMING LORD SUTCH AND THE SAVAGES (EP)	8
94	Bareface 1	I'm Still Raving/Radio Edit/Loony Mix (12", no p/s)	8
70	Atlantic 2400 008	LORD SUTCH AND HIS HEAVY FRIENDS (LP)	30
72	Atlantic K 40313	HANDS OF JACK THE RIPPER (LP, as Lord Sutch & Heavy Friends)	30
81	Ace MAD 1	THE METEORS MEET SCREAMING LORD SUTCH (mini-LP, 1 side each, stickered cartoon print on plain grey card sleeve, 1,000 only)	125

(see also Savages, Meteors, Led Zeppelin, Cliff Bennett & Rebel Rousers, Circles, Nero & Gladiators, Neil Christian & Crusaders)

GLEN SUTTON

(see under Murray Kellum)

RALPH SUTTON

53	Lyragon LF 2	STRIDE PIANO (10" LP)	12

(see also Tony Parenti)

MINT VALUE £

SUZANNE

77 Ring O' 2017 108 — Born On Hallowe'en/Like No One Else (some in promo p/s) — 25/12
78 Ring O' 2017 111 — You Really Got A Hold On Me/You Could Be Right This Time — 10
78 Ring O' 2017 115 — single (unreleased)
78 Ring O' 2320 105 — SUZANNE (LP, unreleased)

SUZI & BIG DEE IRWIN

66 Polydor BM 65715 — Ain't That Lovin' You Baby/I Can't Get Over You — 15
(see also Big Dee Irwin)

PAT SUZUKI

58 RCA RCA 1069 — Daddy/Just One Of Those Things — 6
60 RCA RCA 1171 — I Enjoy Being A Girl/Sunday — 6

SUZY & THE RED STRIPES

77 A&M AMS 7461 — Seaside Woman/B-side To The Seaside (yellow vinyl, die-cut p/s) — 12
79 A&M AMSP 7461 — Seaside Woman/B-side To The Seaside (yellow vinyl, die-cut p/s, in box set with badge & 10 'saucy' mini-postcards) — 40
80 A&M AMS 7548 — Seaside Woman/B-side To The Seaside (reissue, cartoon p/s, as Linda McCartney alias Suzy & Red Stripes) — 10
80 A&M AMSP 7548 — Seaside Woman/B-side To The Seaside (12", as Linda McCartney alias Suzy & Red Stripes) — 12
86 EMI EMI 5572 — Seaside Woman/B-side To The Seaside (p/s) — 6
86 EMI 12EMI 5572 — Seaside Woman/B-side To The Seaside (12", p/s) — 10
(see also Paul McCartney [& Wings])

SVANTE

68 United Artists UP 2224 — Baby I Need Your Lovin'/Just One Word From You — 7

SVENSK

67 Page One POF 036 — Dream Magazine/Getting Old — 22
67 Page One POF 050 — You/All I Have To Do Is Dream — 18
(see also Jason Paul)

SWALLOWS

56 Vogue EPV 1113 — RHYTHM AND BLUES (EP, 2 tracks by Dominoes) — 300

SWALLOWS with SONNY THOMPSON

52 Vogue V 2136 — Roll, Roll Pretty Baby/It Ain't The Meat (78) — 40
(see also Sonny Thompson & His Rhythm & Blues Band)

SWAMP DOGG

74 Island USA 002 — Did I Come Back Too Soon/I Wouldn't Leave Here — 5
72 Mojo 2916 014 — TOTAL DESTRUCTION TO YOUR MIND (LP) — 15
(see also Jerry Williams, Brooks & Jerry)

BILLY SWAN

75 Monument MNT 80615 — I CAN HELP (LP) — 15
75 CBS 69162 — ROCK & ROLL MOON (LP) — 12
76 Monument MNT 81387 — BILLY SWAN (LP) — 12

SWAN ARCADE

73 Trailer LER 2032 — SWAN ARCADE (LP) — 20
84 Fellside FE 037 — TOGETHER FOREVER (LP) — 20

SWANEE RIVER BOYS

54 Parlophone CMSP 7 — Do You Believe/Gloryland Boogie (export issue) — 15
54 Parlophone DP 385 — Was He Quiet Or Did He Cry/I Have Desire (78, export issue) — 12
54 Parlophone DP 391 — When I Move/I've Got A Date To Meet An Angel (78, export issue) — 8
54 Parlophone DP 398 — Not Necessarily/He Lifted Me From Sin (78, export issue) — 8
56 Parlophone DP 509 — I Don't Worry/Fire's A Comin' (78, export issue) — 8
50s Parlophone DP 359 — What Am I Gonna Do/Wherever I Go (78, export issue) — 8
50s Parlophone DP 414 — Married Life/Because I Love You So (78, export issue) — 8

BETTYE SWANN

67 CBS 2942 — Make Me Yours/I Will Not Cry (demos in p/s) — 100
67 CBS 2942 — Make Me Yours/I Will Not Cry — 30
69 Capitol CL 15586 — Don't Touch Me/(My Heart Is) Closed For The Season — 20
72 Atlantic K 10174 — Victim Of A Foolish Heart/Cold Day In Hell — 10
72 Atlantic K 10273 — Today I Started Loving You Again/I'd Rather Go Blind — 8
73 Mojo 2092 059 — Make Me Yours/I Will Not Cry (reissue) — 6
75 Atlantic K 10622 — Doing It For The One I Love/All The Way In Or All The Way Out — 5
75 Contempo CS 9019 — Make Me Yours/I Will Not Cry (reissue) — 6
76 Atlantic K 10851 — Heading In The Right Direction/Be Strong Enough To Hold On — 10
(see also Sam Dees & Bettye Swann)

RUTH SWANN

75 Spark SRL 1124 — Tainted Love/Boy, You'd Better Move On — 20

SWANS

63 Stateside SS 224 — He's Mine/You Better Be A Good Girl Now — 30
64 Cameo Parkway C 302 — The Boy With The Beatle Hair/Please Hurry Home — 25

SWANS

86 K.422/Some Bizzare KDE 312 — A Screw (Holy Money)/Blackmail/A Screw (12", p/s) — 8
88 Product Inc. PROD 23 — Love Will Tear Us Apart/Trust Me (red vinyl, 750 only, p/s) — 12
88 Product Inc. 12PROD 23 — Love Will Tear Us Apart (Red Version)/Trust Me/Love Will Tear Us Apart (black Version)/Our Love Lies (12", black vinyl, p/s) — 20
80s Product Inc. 12PROD 16 — New Mind/Damn You To Hell/I'll Swallow You (12", p/s) — 8
84 K.422/Some Bizzare KCC 1 — COP (LP, with inner) — 30
85 Zensor NDO 3 — FILTH (LP) — 30
86 K. 422/Some Bizzare KCC 2 — GREED (LP, with inner) — 15
86 K. 422/Some Bizzare KCC 3 — HOLY MONEY (LP) — 15

86	no label BURN ONE	PUBLIC CASTRATION IS A GOOD IDEA (2-LP)	20
95	Young God YGLP 004	BODY TO BODY, JOB TO JOB (LP)	20
89	MCA MCG 6047	THE BURNING WORLD (LP, with insert)	12
95	Young God YGLP 005B	LOVE OF LIFE (LP, in box)	25

BENRICE SWANSON

65	Chess CRS 8008	Lying Awake/Baby I'm Yours	30

DAVE SWARBRICK

67	Bounty BYI 6030	RAGS, REELS AND AIRS (LP, with Martin Carthy & Diz Disley)	80
67	Polydor Special 236 514	RAGS, REELS AND AIRS (LP, reissue, with Martin Carthy & Diz Disley)	35
76	Transatlantic TRA 337	SWARBRICK (LP)	15
77	Transatlantic TRA 341	SWARBRICK 2 (LP)	15
78	Sonet SNTF 763	LIFT THE LID AND LISTEN (LP)	15
78	Sonet SNTF 764	THE CEILIDH ALBUM (LP, as Dave Swarbrick & Friends)	15
81	Logo LOGO 1029	SMIDDYBURN (LP)	15

(see also Martin Carthy & Dave Swarbrick, Fairport Convention, Young Tradition, Vashti Bunyan, Ian Campbell)

DAVE SWARBRICK & SIMON NICOL

81	White Bear WBR 001	LIVE AT THE WHITE BEAR (LP)	20
83	Woodworm WR 006	CLOSE TO THE WIND (LP)	15

(see also Dave Swarbrick, Fairport Convention, Young Tradition)

SWARBRIGG (PLUS TWO)

75	MCA MCA 179	That's What Friends Are For/Love Is	7
75	MCA MCA 202	Shuffle Into My Heart/Sing It Again	5
75	MCA MCA 214	Funny/To Love	5
77	EMI EMI 2606	It's Nice To Be In Love Again/Here We Are Again (as Swarbrigg Plus Two)	5

ROSALYN SWEAT & PARAGONS

73	Duke DU 160	Blackbird Singing/Always	10
74	Horse HRLP 703	BLACKBIRD SINGING (LP)	20

(see also Paragons)

SWE-DANES

60	Warner Bros WB 7	Scandinavian Shuffle/Hot Toddy	7
60	Warner Bros WB 22	Swe-Dane Shuffle/At A Georgia Camp Meeting	7
61	Warner Bros WEP 6017	THE SWE-DANES (EP; also stereo SWEP 2017)	18/25

(see also Alice Babbs)

SWEDEN THROUGH THE AGES

86	Snappy SW 001	IT HELPS TO CRY EP (12", p/s)	12

(see also Billy MacKenzie)

SWEDISH MODERN JAZZ GROUP

61	Tempo TAP 31	SAX APPEAL (LP)	220

SWEENEY'S MEN

67	Pye 7N 17312	Old Maid In The Garrett/Derby Ram	10
68	Pye 7N 17459	Waxies Dargle/Old Woman In Cotton	10
69	Transatlantic TRASP 19	Sullivan's John/Rattlin' Roarin' Willy	8
68	Transatlantic TRA 170	SWEENEY'S MEN (LP)	50
69	Transatlantic TRA 200	THE TRACKS OF SWEENEY (LP)	75
76	Transatlantic TRASAM 37	SWEENEY'S MEN (LP, reissue)	15
77	Transatlantic TRASAM 40	THE TRACKS OF SWEENEY (LP, reissue)	15

(see also Gay & Terry Woods, Dr. Strangely Strange)

JIM SWEENY

58	Philips PB 811	The Midnight Hour/Till The Right One Comes Along	15
58	Philips PB 811	The Midnight Hour/Till The Right One Comes Along (78)	8

JIMMY SWEEP

81	Tamarin TAM 3	London Town/Bridgetown Girls (written, produced by & feat. Alan Lancaster)	10
82	PRT 7P 233	London Town/Bridgetown Girls (reissue)	8

(see also Status Quo)

SWEET

SINGLES

68	Fontana TF 958	Slow Motion/It's Lonely Out There	500+
69	Parlophone R 5803	The Lollipop Man/Time	100
70	Parlophone R 5826	All You'll Ever Get From Me/The Juicer	40
70	Parlophone R 5848	Get On The Line/Mr. McGallagher	70
71	RCA RCA 2051	Funny Funny/You're Not Wrong For Loving Me	12
71	RCA RCA 2087	Co Co/Done Me Wrong, All Right	5
71	Parlophone R 5902	All You'll Ever Get From Me/The Juicer (reissue)	15
71	RCA RCA 2121	Alexander Graham Bell/Spotlight	5
73	RCA RCA 2403	Ballroom Blitz/Rock & Roll Disgrace (mispressed at wrong speed, 49rpm; matrix: 2403-A-1E)	15
74	RCA RCA 2480	Turn It Down/Someone Else Will	5
75	RCA RCA 2578	Action/Sweet FA	5
76	RCA RCA 2541	The Lies In Your Eyes/Cockroach	5
76	RCA RCA 2748	Lost Angels/Funk It Up	5
77	RCA PB 5011	Fever Of Love/A Distinct Lack Of Ancient	6
77	RCA PB 5046	Stairway To The Stars/Why Don't You Do It To Me	8
78	Polydor POSP 5	California Nights/Show Me The Way (unreleased)	
79	Polydor POSP 36	Call Me/Why Don't You	7
79	Polydor POSP 73	Big Apple Waltz/Why Don't You	35
80	RCA PE 5226	Fox On The Run/Hellraiser/Ballroom Blitz/Blockbuster (EP, p/s)	15
80	Polydor POSP 131	Give That Lady Some Respect/Tall Girls	7
80	Polydor POSP 160	Sixties Man/Tall Girls	5
80	Polydor POSP 160	Sixties Man/Oh Yeah	15
80	Polydor POSP 160	Sixties Man/Oh Yeah (mispressing, B-side plays "Tall Girls")	20

MINT VALUE £

81 RCA GOLD 524 Blockbuster/Hellraiser (pink 'Golden Groove' p/s) 8
81 RCA GOLD 551 Ballroom Blitz/Wig Wam Bam (pink 'Golden Groove' p/s) 8
84 Anagram ANA 27 The Sixteens/Action (p/s) 10
84 Anagram ANA 28 It's The Sweetest Mix/Fox On The Run (p/s) 5
84 Anagram 12 ANA 28 It's The Sweetest Mix/Fox On The Run (12" p/s; matrix no. 12 ANA 28 AI) 8
84 Anagram 12 ANA 28 It's The Sweetest Mix/Fox On The Run (12" p/s; matrix no. 12 ANA 28.A) 10
85 Anagram ANA 29 Sweet 2th — The Wig Wam-Willy Mix/The Teen Action Mix (p/s) 10
85 Anagram ANA 29 Sweet 2th — The Wig Wam-Willy Mix/The Teen Action Mix (12", p/s) 10
89 RCA PB 43337 Wig Wam Bam/Little Willy (p/s) 15
80s own label PR 001 THE LIVE EP (CD) 10

LPs

71 MFP MFP 5248 GIMME DAT DING (1 side each by Sweet & Pipkins) 12
71 RCA SF 8288 FUNNY HOW SWEET CO-CO CAN BE 25
74 RCA LPL 15039 SWEET FANNY ADAMS 12
76 RCA RS 1036 GIVE US A WINK 12
77 RCA PL 25072 OFF THE RECORD (with inner sleeve) 15
78 RCA Camden CDS 1168 THE SWEET 12
79 Polydor POLD 5022 CUT ABOVE THE REST (with inner sleeve) 15
70s RCA LPL 15080 DESOLATION BOULEVARD (LP, gatefold sleeve) 15
70s RCA SF 8316 THE SWEET'S BIGGEST HITS (LP) 12
80 Polydor POLS 1021 WATER'S EDGE 18
82 Polydor 2311 1179 IDENTITY CRISIS 22
84 Anagram GRAM 16 SWEET SIXTEEN (LP) 15
84 Anagram P GRAM 16 SWEET SIXTEEN (LP, picture disc) 30

(see also Brian Connolly, Mayfield's Mule, Elastic Band, Andy Scott)

SWEET AROMA

73 Rhino RNO 113 Happiness/Rock Reggae (demos or stock copies) 5

SWEET BLINDNESS

76 Quality QUPS 1 Cowboys To Girls/Give It To You Right Now 5

SWEET CHARIOT

69 MCA MK 5010 Heavenly Road/Wish I Were A Child 8
73 Columbia DB 8999 When I'm A Kid/Mozart '73 8
70s T.O.G. SCEP 001 Angelina/Young At Heart/America 8
72 De Wolfe DWLP 3230 SWEET CHARIOT & FRIENDS (LP, library issue only) 40

SWEET CHARLES

88 Urban URB 15 Yes It's You/LYN COLLINS: Rock Me Again And Again And Again (die-cut sleeve) 5
88 Urban URBX 15 Yes It's You/LYN COLLINS: Rock Me Again And Again And Again/ Think About It (12", die-cut sleeve) 10
88 Urban URBLP 9 FOR SWEET PEOPLE FROM SWEET CHARLES (LP) 15

SWEET CONFUSION

69 Escort ES 809 Elizabeth Serenade/Don At Rest 8
69 Escort ES 812 Hotter Scorcher/Conquer Lion 8

(see also Stranger & Patsy)

SWEET CORPORALS

59 Top Rank JAR 217 The Same Old Army/Warm And Willing 5

SWEET DREAMS

74 Bradleys BRADL 1008 WE'LL BE YOUR MUSIC (LP) 12

(see also Polly Brown, Jimmy Thomas)

SWEET DREAMS

83 Ariola AROPD 333 I'm Never Giving Up/Two Way Mirror (picture disc) 5

SWEET FEELING

67 Columbia DB 8195 All So Long Ago/Charles Brown 140

(see also Rupert's People)

SWEETHEARTS

65 Blue Beat BB 389 Sit Down And Cry (actually with Clinton & Rufus)/ PRINCE BUSTER: Ghost Dance 70

SWEET INSPIRATIONS

67 Atlantic 584 117 Why (Am I Treated So Bad)/I Don't Want To Go On Without You 6
67 Atlantic 584 132 Let It Be Me/When Something Is Wrong With My Baby 6
68 Atlantic 584 167 Sweet Inspiration/I'm Blue 8
68 Atlantic 584 233 What The World Needs Now Is Love/You Really Didn't Mean It 6
69 Atlantic 584 241 Sweet Inspiration/I'm Blue 5
69 Atlantic 584 279 Sweets For My Sweet/Get A Little Older 5
70 Atlantic 584 312 (Gotta Find) A Brand New Lover (Parts 1 & 2) 5
71 Atlantic 2091 073 Evidence/Change Me Not 5
68 Atlantic 587/588 090 THE SWEET INSPIRATIONS (LP) 15
69 Atlantic 587/588 137 WHAT THE WORLD NEEDS NOW IS LOVE (LP) 15
69 Atlantic 587/588 194 SWEETS FOR MY SWEET (LP) 15
70 Atlantic 2465 003 SWEET SWEET SOUL (LP) 15

(see also Cissy Houston)

SWEET JESUS

91 Chapter 22 CHAP 63 Cat Thing/Honey Loving Honey/Peach/Baby Blue (12" EP, unreleased, 25 test pressings only) 10

SWEET LITTLE BUNTY

75 Ackee ACK 540 I (Who Have Nothing)/Oh Me Oh My 5

SWEET PAIN

71 United Artists UP 35268 Timber Gibbs/Chain Up The Devil 5
69 Mercury 20146 SMCL SWEET PAIN (LP) 55

SWEET PLUM
69 Middle Earth MDS 103 — Lazy Day/Let No Man Steal Your Thyme ... 22
70 Middle Earth MDS 105 — Set The Wheels In Motion/Catch A Cloud ... 22

SWEET SAVAGE
81 Park PRK 1001 — Take No Prisoners/Killing TIme (p/s, red and yellow label) ... 200
80s Crashed CAR 48 — Straight Through The Heart/Teaser (no p/s) ... 150
80s private pressing — The Raid/Prosecutors Of Greed (possibly unreleased) ... 50+

SWEETSHOP
68 Parlophone R 5707 — Barefoot And Tiptoe/Lead The Way ... 20
(see also Mark Wirtz)

SWEET SLAG
71 President PTLS 1042 — TRACKING WITH CLOSE-UPS (LP) ... 150

SWEET THUNDER
78 Fantasy FTC 158 — Everybody's Singin' Love Songs/Joyful Noise ... 5

SWEET THURSDAY
69 Polydor 2310 051 — SWEET THURSDAY (LP) ... 20
(see also Nicky Hopkins, Mark-Almond)

SWEGAS
70 Trend 6099 001 — What You Gonna Do/There Is Nothing In It ... 8
71 Trend 6480 002 — CHILD OF LIGHT (LP, gatefold sleeve) ... 22

SWELL MAPS
78 Rather GEAR ONE — Read About Seymour/Ripped And Torn/Black Velvet (p/s) ... 15
79 Rough Trade RT 010/Rather GEAR ONE MK. 2 — Read About Seymour/Ripped And Torn/Black Velvet (p/s, reissue, different back sleeve) ... 7
79 R. Trade RT 012/GEAR 3 — Dresden Style/Mystery Track/Ammunition Train/Full Moon (Dub) (p/s) ... 7
79 R. Trade RT 021/GEAR 6 — Real Shocks/English Verse/Monlogues (p/s, 2 different colours) ... 8
79 R. Trade RT 036/GEAR 7 — Let's Build A Car/Big Maz In The Country/...Then Poland (p/s) ... 7
81 Rough Trade RT 012/Rather GEAR 3 — Dresden Style (new vocal)/Ammunition Train/Full Moon (Dub) (p/s, reissue, different back sleeve) ... 7
79 Rough Trade ROUGH 2/Rather TROY 1 — A TRIP TO MARINEVILLE (LP, with inner sleeve, some with bonus EP in die-cut sleeve [Rather GEAR FIVE]) ... 20/15
80 Rough Trade ROUGH 15 — SWELL MAPS IN 'JANE FROM OCCUPIED EUROPE' (LP) ... 12
81 Rough Trade ROUGH 21 — WHATEVER HAPPENS NEXT... (2-LP) ... 18
84 Rough Trade ROUGH 41 — SWELL MAPS IN 'COLLISION TIME' (LP) ... 12
(see also Cult Figures, Nikki Sudden, Steve Treatment, Phones Sportsman Band, Epic Soundtracks, Metrophase, Last Bandits)

ANTHONY SWETE
69 RCA RCA 1905 — Backfield in Motion/Soul Deep ... 6

JONATHAN SWIFT
70 MCA MU 1130 — Afraid Of Tomorrow/I Haven't Got Anything Better To Do ... 5
72 CBS 7931 — Corinna/Just This Morning ... 5
71 CBS 64412 — INTROVERT (LP, nude cover) ... 12
72 CBS 64751 — SONGS (LP, with lyric insert) ... 12

TUFTY SWIFT
77 Free Reed FRR 017 — HOW TO MAKE A BAKEWELL TART (LP, with booklet) ... 25
85 Shark SHARK 04 — YOU'LL NEVER DIE FOR LOVE (LP, private pressing) ... 15

ALAN SWIMMER & DEE DAVIDSON
70s Fab FAB 242 — Take Me Back To Jamaica/Thousands Of Children ... 5

SWINDLEFOLK
68 Deroy — A-ROVIN' (LP, private pressing) ... 150
69 Deroy — SWINDLED (LP, private pressing) ... 70

STEVE SWINDELLS
74 RCA LPL1 5057 — MESSAGES (LP, with insert) ... 15
(see also Hawkwind)

SWINGERS
60 Vogue V 9158 — Love Makes The World Go Round/Jackie ... 20

SWINGERS
81 Magnet MAG 202 — Be My Baby/Swinging ... 5
(see also Spectres, Rich Kids)

SWINGING BLUE JEANS
63 HMV POP 1170 — It's Too Late Now/Think Of Me ... 12
63 HMV POP 1206 — Do You Know/Angie ... 15
63 HMV POP 1242 — Hippy Hippy Shake/Now I Must Go ... 6
64 HMV POP 1273 — Good Golly Miss Molly/Shakin' Feelin' ... 6
64 HMV POP 1304 — You're No Good/Don't You Worry About Me ... 5
64 HMV POP 1327 — Promise You'll Tell Her/It's So Right ... 7
64 HMV POP 1375 — It Isn't There/One Of These Days ... 7
65 HMV POP 1409 — Make Me Know You're Mine/I've Got A Girl ... 7
65 HMV POP 1477 — Crazy 'Bout My Baby/Good Lovin' ... 10
66 HMV POP 1501 — Don't Make Me Over/What Can I Do Today ... 10
66 HMV POP 1533 — Sandy/I'm Gonna Have You ... 10
66 HMV POP 1564 — Rumours, Gossip, Words Untrue/Now The Summer's Gone ... 12
67 HMV POP 1596 — Tremblin'/Something's Coming Along ... 18
67 HMV POP 1605 — Don't Go Out Into The Rain/One Woman Man ... 12
64 HMV 7EG 8850 — SHAKE WITH THE SWINGING BLUE JEANS (EP) ... 55
64 HMV 7EG 8868 — YOU'RE NO GOOD MISS MOLLY (EP) ... 50
64 HMV CLP 1802 — BLUE JEANS A' SWINGING (LP, also stereo CSD 1570) ... 75/100

MINT VALUE £

64 Regal SREG 1073 TUTTI FRUTTI (LP, export issue) ... 55
67 MFP MFP 1163 SWINGING BLUE JEANS (LP, reissue of HMV CLP 1802) ... 15
74 Dart BULL 1001 BRAND NEW AND FADED (LP) ... 18
(see also Ray Ennis & Blue Jeans, Blue Jeans, Escorts, Terry Sylvester)

SWINGING CATS
80 Two Tone CHS TT 14 Mantovani/Away (p/s) ... 5

SWINGIN' MEDALLIONS
66 Philips BF 1500 Double Shot Of My Baby's Love/Here It Comes Again ... 6
66 Philips BF 1515 She Drives Me Out Of My Mind/You Gotta Have Faith ... 7

SWINGING SOUL MACHINE
69 Polydor 56760 Spooky's Day Off/Nobody Wants You ... 8
(see also Machine)

SWING OUT SISTER
88 Mercury 080 122-2 Breakout/Fooled By A Smile/Communion/Surrender (12" Version)/ Breakout (Video) (CD Video) ... 8
(see also Teresa Del Fuego)

SYBIL
87 Champion CHAMPR 1255 My Love Is Guaranteed (Red Ink Mix – Part 1)/My Love Is Guaranteed (Red Ink Mix – Part 2) (12") ... 10
87 Champion CHAMPZ 1255 My Love Is Guaranteed (Z Mix – Part 1)/My Love Is Guaranteed (Z Mix – Part 2) (12") ... 12
89 Champion CHAMPX 12-213 Don't Make Me Over (Remix)/Falling In Love (Remix)/My Love Is Guaranteed (Remix) (12") ... 10
89 Champion CHAMPCD 213 Don't Make Me Over (Remix)/Falling In Love/My Love Is Guaranteed (Z Mix) (CD) 12
90 Champion CHAMPX 12225 All Through The Night (Remix)/Walking In The Moonlight/Let Yourself Go (12") ... 10
90 Champion CHAMPCD 225 All Through The Night/Walking In The Moonlight/Let Yourself Go (CD) ... 12
90 PWL PWLT 48R Walk On By (PJD Remix)/Walk On By (Tony King Remix)/Here Comes My Love (12", p/s) ... 10
90 PWL PWCD 48 Walk On By/Walk On By/Walk On By (A Cappella Version) (CD) ... 12
90 PWL PWLT 65R Make It Easy On Me (The Remix Version)/Make It Easy On Me (The Drumming Remix)/Make It Easy On Me (The Morning Remix)/ Make It Easy On Me (Original Version) (12", p/s) ... 15
90 PWL PWCD 65 Make It Easy On Me (PWL Radio Mix)/Make It Easy On Me (UK Mix)/Living For The Moment (Vocal)/Living For The Moment (Instrumental) (CD) ... 12

SYD & JOE
72 Bullet BU 498 Three Combine/I'm The Nearest To Your Heart ... 5

SYDNEY (Crooks) ALL STARS
70 Bullet BU 436 The Return Of Batman/In Action ... 8
70 Bullet BU 437 Outer Space/Full Moon ... 8
(see also Pioneers, Junior English, Sammy Morgan)

ERIC SYKES & HATTIE JACQUES
62 Decca F 11512 Doctor Kildare/Bedtime Story ... 8
(see also Eric & Hattie, Goons)

JOHN SYKES
82 MCA MCA 792 Please Don't Leave Me/(Instrumental) (with Phil Lynott, some in p/s) ... 35/10
(see also Thin Lizzy, Phil Lynott, Tygers Of Pan Tang, Whitesnake)

ROOSEVELT SYKES
50 Jazz Collector L 40 Three, Six And Nine/We Can Sell That Thing (78) ... 12
56 Vogue V 2389 Fine And Brown/Too Hot To Hold ... 75
56 Vogue V 2389 Fine And Brown/Too Hot To Hold (78) ... 30
56 Vogue V 2393 Walkin' This Boogie/Security Blues ... 75
56 Vogue V 2393 Walkin' This Boogie/Security Blues (78) ... 30
66 Delmark DJB 2 BACK TO THE BLUES (EP) ... 30
59 Encore ENC 183 BIG MAN OF THE BLUES (LP) ... 18
61 Columbia 33SX 1343 FACE TO FACE WITH THE BLUES (LP) ... 30
62 Columbia 33SX 1422 THE HONEYDRIPPER (LP, with Alexis Korner) ... 65
65 Bluesville BVLP 1006 THE RETURN OF ROOSEVELT SYKES (LP) ... 30
67 '77' 77LEU 12-50 BLUES FROM BAR ROOMS (LP) ... 18
67 Riverside RLP 8819 MR SYKES' BLUES 1929-1932 (LP) ... 25
67 Ember EMB 3391 ROOSEVELT SYKES SINGS THE BLUES (LP) ... 18
71 Barclay 920 294 THE HONEYDRIPPERS' DUKE'S MIXTURE (LP) ... 12
70s Delmark DL 607 HARD DRIVIN' BLUES (LP, blue label) ... 12
(see also Robert Pete Williams)

SYKO & CARIBS
64 Blue Beat BB 213 Do The Dog/Jenny ... 25
64 Blue Beat BB 223 Big Boy/Sugar Baby ... 25

SYLTE SISTERS
63 London HLU 9753 Summer Magic/Well It's Summertime ... 12

SYLVAIN SYLVAIN
80 RCA PB 9500 Every Boy And Every Girl/Emily ... 5
(see also New York Dolls)

SYLVAN
65 Columbia DB 7674 We Don't Belong/Life's Colours Have Gone ... 18

FOSTER SYLVERS
73 MGM 2006 292 Misdemeanour/So Close ... 6

C. SYLVESTER & PLANETS
64 Blue Beat BB 206 Going South/LITTLE JOYCE: Oh Daddy ... 15

ROLAND SYLVESTER
64 Carnival CV 7018 Grandfather's Clock/SANDRA MURRAY: Nervous 6

TERRY SYLVESTER
74 Polydor 2383 394 I BELIEVE (LP, with insert). . . . 12
(see also Escorts, Swinging Blue Jeans, Hollies)

SYLVIA
67 Fontana TF 884 Make Me A Woman/Without Your Love 7
68 Fontana TF 932 Down Hill/A Few Sweet Moments Of Love 8

SYLVIA (U.S.)
68 Soul City SC 103 I Can't Help It/It's A Good Life 15
75 London HLU 10415 Pillow Talk/My Thing 7

DAVID SYLVIAN
84 Virgin VSY 633 Red Guitar/Forbidden Colours (Version) (picture disc) 5
84 Virgin VS 700 The Ink In The Well (Remix)/Weathered Wall (Instrumental) (poster p/s) 5
84 Virgin VS 700-12 The Ink In The Well/Weathered Wall (Instrumental) (12", poster p/s) 8
84 Virgin VS 717 Pulling Punches (7" Mix)/Backwaters (Remix) (p/s, with 3 postcards). . . . 5
84 Virgin VSY 717 Pulling Punches (7" Mix)/Backwaters (Remix) (picture disc). . . . 7
84 Virgin VS 717-12 Pulling Punches (Extended Mix)/Backwaters (Remix) (12", p/s, & 3 postcards) . . 10
85 Virgin VS 835-12 WORDS WITH THE SHAMAN (12" EP, p/s). . . . 10
86 Virgin VSS 815 Taking The Veil/Answered Prayers
(rectangular picture disc, stickered PVC sleeve) 7
86 Virgin VS 895 Silver Moon/Gone To Earth (p/s) 5
86 Virgin VSP 895 Silver Moon/Gone To Earth (gatefold p/s) 6
88 Virgin CDT 23 Words With The Shaman: Part 1 — Ancient Evening/Part 2 — Incantation/
Part 3 — Awakening (Songs From The Tree Tops) (3" CD, gatefold card p/s) 12
89 Virgin VSCD 1221 Pop Song/A Brief Conversation Ending In Divorce/
The Stigma Of Childhood (Kin) (3" CD, card sleeve) 25
89 Virgin VSCDX 1221 Pop Song/A Brief Conversation Ending In Divorce/
The Stigma Of Childhood (Kin) (CD, presentation card pack, with discography) . 50
85 Virgin SYL 1 ALCHEMY (Cassette) 12
89 Virgin DSCD 1 WEATHERBOX (5-CD box set, with poster & booklet) 150
98 Virgin CDIVDJ 2876 DEAD BEES ON A CAKE - PROMOTIONAL INTERVIEW CD (CD, card p/s,
promo only) 20
04 Townsend SOUNDLPSS 1 BLEMISH (LP, gatefold sleeve, featuring Derek Bailey, 2,000 only) 18
(See also Japan)

DAVID SYLVIAN & ROBERT FRIPP
93 Virgin VSC 1462 Jean The Birdman/Earthbound/Endgame (cassette, in slipcase). . . . 12
94 Virgin DAMAGE 1 DAMAGE (gold CD in silver-coloured box) 25

DAVID SYLVIAN & RYUICHI SAKAMOTO
82 Virgin VS 510 Bamboo Houses (7" Mix)/Bamboo Music (7" Mix) (some with gatefold p/s). . . . 5/4
83 Virgin VSY 601 Forbidden Colours/RYUICHI SAKAMOTO: The Seed And The Sower
88 Virgin CDT 18 Forbidden Colours/Bamboo Houses/Bamboo Music (3" CD, card sleeve) 15
92 Virgin VUSCD 57 Heartbeat (Tainal Kalki II)/Nuages (cassette, card slipcase). . . . 10
92 Virgin VUSDG 57 Heartbeat (Tainai Kaiki II)/Nuages/Forbidden Colours/Heartbeat I
(CD box set, with postcards) 12
(see also Japan, Yellow Magic Orchestra)

SYLVIN & GLENROY
70 Torpedo TOR 25 What You Gonna Do 'Bout It/KEN JONES: Sad Mood. . . . 6

SYMARIP
(see under Seven Letters/Symarip, see also Pyramids)

SYMBOLS
65 Columbia DB 7459 One Fine Girl/Don't Go. . . . 10
65 Columbia DB 7664 You're My Girl/Why Do Fools Fall In Love. . . . 10
66 President PT 104 See You In September/To Make You Smile Again 6
66 President PT 113 Canadian Sunset/The Gentle Art Of Loving 6
67 President PT 128 You'd Better Get Used To Missing Her/Hideaway 5
67 President PT 144 Bye Bye Baby/The Things You Do To Me. . . . 6
67 President PT 173 (The Best Part Of) Breaking Up/Again. . . . 7
68 President PT 190 Lovely Way To Say Goodnight/Pretty City. . . . 6
68 President PT 216 Do I Love You/Schoolgirl 15
75 Crystal CR 7021 Canadian Sunset (Instrumental)/Canadian Sunset (Vocal Recording). . . . 6
68 President PTL 1018 THE BEST PART OF THE SYMBOLS (LP) 30
(see also Johnny Milton & Condors)

SYMON & PI
68 Parlophone R 5662 Sha La La La Lee/Baby Baby. . . . 18
68 Parlophone R 5719 Got To See The Sunrise/Love Is Happening To Me 10

SYMPHONICS
73 Polydor 2058 341 Heaven Must Have Sent You/Using Me 8

SYMPHONIC SLAM
76 A&M AMLH 69023 SYMPHONIC SLAM (LP). . . . 80

PAT SYMS
64 Oriole CB 1971 It's Got To Be You Or No One/Lost. . . . 6

SYLVIA SYMS
58 Brunswick 05744 I Could Have Danced All Night/Be Good (To Me) 6
58 Brunswick 05771 The Night They Invented Champagne/The Nature Of Things 5

SYN
67 Deram DM 130 Created By Clive/Grounded. . . . 110
67 Deram DM 145 14-Hour Technicolour Dream/Flowerman 85
(see also Syndicats, Yes, Peter Banks)

MINT VALUE £

SYNCHROJAK
95 Ferox FER 014 — SYNCHROJAK (12" EP, plain sleeve) 8
95 Ferox FER 108 — PHAZE 11 (12" EP, plain sleeve) 8

SYNCHROMESH
80 Rok ROK XI/XII — October Friday/E.F. BAND: Another Day Gone (company die-cut sleeve) 40

SYNCOPATORS
61 Decca F 11359 — Everything Stops For Tea/If I Had A Talking Picture Of You 7

SYNDICATE
79 Stevenage/Rock Against Racism — One Way Or Another/I Want To Be Somebody/RESTRICTED HOURS: Getting Things Done/Still Living Out The Car Crash (white label, foldover p/s) 12
(see also Astronauts)

SYNDICATE OF SOUND
66 Stateside SS 523 — Little Girl/You 25
66 Stateside SS 538 — Rumours/The Upper Hand 15
66 Stateside S(S)L 10185 — LITTLE GIRL (LP) 55

SYNDICATS
64 Columbia DB 7238 — Maybellene/True To Me 200
65 Columbia DB 7441 — Howlin' For My Baby/What To Do 200
65 Columbia DB 7686 — On The Horizon/Crawdaddy Simone (demos more common, £420) .... 750+
(see also Peter Banks, Ray Fenwick, Syn, Tomorrow, Yes)

SYNANTHESIA
69 RCA SF 8058 — SYNANTHESIA (LP) 200

SYREETA
(see under Syreeta Wright)

SYRON VANES
84 Ebony EBON 23 — BRINGER OF EVIL (LP) 12
86 Ebony EBON 36 — REVENGE (LP) 12

SYRUP
70 Amity OTS 501 — Gentlemen Joe's Sidewalk Café/Love Is Love 5

SYSTEM
77 Tash — THE OTHER SIDE OF TIME (LP, 250 copies only) 110

SYZYGY
85 Taptag TAP 3 — LADY IN GREY (mini-LP) 20
(see also Blackthorn)

GABOR SZABO
86 Mercury 6167 780 — Keep Smilin' 5
66 HMV CLP 3614 — JAZZ RAGA (LP) 50
67 Impulse MILP 506 — THE SORCERER (LP, mono) 30

T. & UNKNOWN
80 Carrere CAR 142 — My Generation/Woodstock Rock (p/s) 15

ERROL T. & ROOSEVELT ALL STARS
72 Ashanti ASH 406 — Jamaica Born And Bred/Version 6

TABLE
77 Virgin VS 176 — Do The Standing Still/Magical Melon Of The Tropics (p/s) 8
78 Chiswick NS 28 — Sex Cells/The Road Of Lyfe (p/s) 7

TABLE TOPPERS
62 Starlite ST45 069 — Rocking Mountain Dew/My Wild Irish Rose Rock 20

CHARLIE TABOR
63 Island WI 061 — Blue Atlantic/Red Lion Madison 18

JUNE TABOR
86 Strange Fruit SFPS 015 — THE PEEL SESSIONS (12" EP) 15
76 Topic 12TS 298 — AIRS AND GRACES (LP) 15
77 Topic 12TS 360 — ASHES AND DIAMONDS (LP) 15
(see also Silly Sisters)

TAD & SMALL FRY
62 London HLU 9542 — Checkered Continental Pants/Pretty Blue Jean Baby 15

TADPOLES
69 High Note HS 032 — Rasta/Like Dirt 8

TAGES
66 Columbia DB 8019 — Crazy 'Bout My Baby/In My Dreams 12
66 HMV POP 1515 — So Many Girls/I'm Mad 50
67 Parlophone R 5640 — Treat Me Like A Lady/Wanting 12
68 Parlophone R 5702 — There's A Blind Man Playin' Fiddle In The Street/Like A Woman 12
68 MGM MGM 1443 — Halcyon Days/I Read You Like An Open Book 12
(see also Blond)

MINT VALUE £

BLIND JOE TAGGART

52	Tempo R 55	Religion Is Something Within You/Mother's Love (78)	20
55	Jazz Collector L 129	Religion Is Something Within You/Mother's Love (78, reissue)	15

TAGMEMICS

80	Index INDEX 003	Chimneys/(Do The) Big Baby/Take Your Brain Out For A Walk (p/s, with insert)	10

(see also Art Attacks)

JACQUELINE TAIEB

68	Fontana TF 952	Tonight I'm Going Home/7 A.M.	80

LYN(N) TAIT(T) (& THE JETS)

66	Doctor Bird DB 1006	Vilma's Jump Up (as Lyn Taitt & The Comets)/GLEN MILLER & HONEYBOY MARTIN: Dad Is Home	25
66	Doctor Bird DB 1047	Spanish Eyes (with Tommy McCook)/STRANGER & HORTENSE: Loving Wine	25
67	Island WI 3066	Something Stupid/Blue Tuesday (as Lyn Tait & the Jets)	22
67	Island WI 3075	I Don't Want To Make You Cry/Nice Time (as Lyn Tait & the Jets)	25
68	Island WI 3139	Napoleon Solo/Pressure And Slide (as Lyn Taitt & the Jets)	30
68	Amalgamated AMG 810	El Casino Royale/Dee's Special (as Lynn Taitt & the Jets)	20
68	Pama PM 723	Soul Food/Music Flames (as Lyn Tait & the Jets)	15
68	Island ILP 969	SOUNDS ROCK STEADY (LP, as Lyn Taitt & the Jets)	110
68	Big Shot BBTL 4002	GLAD SOUNDS (LP, as Lynn Taitt & the Jets)	60

(see also Justin Hines, Mike Thompson Jnr, ALton Ellis, Ken Boothe, Baba Brooks)

TAJ MAHAL

(see under 'M')

TAKE FIVE

60s	D.S.C.A (no cat. no.)	MY GIRL (EP, oversized p/s; Dundee Students Charity Appeal record)	40

TAKE IT

80s	Fresh Hold TRI	Man Made World/Taking Sides/How It Is (p/s)	40
80	Fresh Hold FHR 1	Twenty Lines/Armchairs/Friends And Relations (foldout p/s with insert)	20

'TAKERS

64	Pye 7N 15690	If You Don't Come Back/Think	20

(see also Undertakers, Jackie Lomax)

TAKE THAT

91	Dance U.K. DUK 2	Do What U Like/Waiting Around (p/s)	15
91	Dance U.K. CADUK 2	Do What U Like/Waiting Around (cassette)	10
91	Dance U.K. 12DUK 2	Do What U Like (Club Mix)/Do What U Like (Radio Mix)/Waiting Around (12", p/s; most with wrong tracks listed on sleeve)	25
91	RCA PB 45085	Promises/Do What U Like (p/s)	5
91	RCA PB 45085P	Promises/Do What U Like (poster p/s)	8
91	RCA PK 45085	Promises/Do What U Like (cassette)	5
91	RCA PT 45086	Promises (12" Mix)/Do What U Like (12" Mix) (12", p/s)	10
92	RCA PB 45257	Once You've Tasted Love/Guess Who Tasted Love (p/s)	5
92	RCA PB 45265	Once You've Tasted Love/Guess Who Tasted Love (spined p/s with pull-out hexagonal pop-up calendar)	15
92	RCA PK 45257	Once You've Tasted Love/Guess Who Tasted Love (cassette with stencil)	8
92	RCA PB 45258	Once You've Tasted Love (Aural Mix)/Guess Who Tasted Love (Guess Who Mix)/Once You've Tasted Love (Radio Version) (12" picture disc, with insert)	20
92	RCA 74321 10100 7	It Only Takes A Minute/Satisfied (p/s, with Mark & Robbie prints)	15
92	RCA 74321 10101 7	It Only Takes A Minute/It Only Takes A Minute (Royal Rave Mix) (different p/s, with Jason & Howard prints & paper frame)	8
92	RCA 74321 10814 7	I Found Heaven (7" Radio Mix)/(Mr. F's Garage Mix) (poster p/s)	10
92	RCA 74321 10813 7B	I Found Heaven (7" Radio Mix)/I'm Out (picture disc)	10
92	RCA 74321 11600 7	A Million Love Songs/A Million Love Songs (The Lovers Mix) (p/s, with tattoos)	10
92	RCA 74321 11630 7	THE LOVE SONGS (EP)	5
92	RCA 74321 112313 1	Could It Be Magic (Deep In Rapino's Club Mix)/Take That Club Megamix/ Could It Be Magic (Mr F Mix) (12", poster p/s)	10
93	RCA 74321 13311 7	Why Can't I Wake Up With You (Radio Edit)/Promises (live)/ Clap Your Hands (live) (EP)	5
95	RCA (no cat. no.)	Every Guy (CD, unreleased, 1-track promo only)	20
93	RCA 74321 16926-1	EVERYTHING CHANGES (LP, picture disc)	12

(see also Robbie Williams)

TALBOT BROTHERS

59	Melodisc MEL 1507	Bloodshot Eyes/She's Got Freckles	15
60s	Melodisc CAL 20	Bloodshot Eyes/She's Got Freckles (reissue)	6

ZIGGY TALENT

55	Brunswick 05506	Cheek To Cheek (Cha Cha)/Bozooki Blues	7

TALES OF JUSTINE

67	HMV POP 1614	Albert/Monday Morning (some in p/s)	140/50
97	Tenth Planet TP 034	PETALS FROM A SUNFLOWER (LP, gatefold sleeve, numbered, 1,000 only)	15

(see also Tim Rice)

TALION

89	Major WADES 1	KILLING THE WORLD (LP)	12

TALISKER

75	Caroline CA 1513	DREAMING OF GLENISLA (LP)	20

TALISMAN

73	Argo AFW 110	Stepping Stones/Dr Jazz	5
72	Argo ZFB 33	PRIMROSE DREAMS (LP)	15
73	Argo ZDA 161	STEPPING STONES (LP)	15

TALISMEN

65	Stateside SS 408	Masters Of War/Casting My Spell	50

MINT VALUE £

TALKING HEADS

Year	Label / Cat. No.	Title	£
77	Sire 6078 604	Love Goes To Building On Fire/New Feeling (p/s)	7
77	Sire SAM 87	Love Goes To Building On Fire/New Feeling (limited edition, some in p/s)	12/10
77	Sire 6078 610	Psycho Killer/I Wish You Wouldn't Say That (p/s)	8
77	Sire 6078 610	Psycho Killer/Psycho Killer (Acoustic)/I Wish You Wouldn't Say That (12", p/s)	10
78	Sire 6078 620	Pulled Up/Don't Worry About The Government (p/s)	7
79	Sire SIR 4004	Take Me To The River/Found A Job (p/s)	7
79	Sire SIR 4004/SAM 87	Take Me To The River/Found A Job//Love Goes To Building On Fire/ Psycho Killer (double pack, gatefold p/s)	15
79	Sire SIR 4027	Life During Wartime (live version)/Electric Guitar (p/s)	12
79	WEA SPC 9	Take Me To The River/Psycho Killer (cassette)	5
80	Sire SIR 4033	I Zimbra/Paper (p/s)	7
80	Sire SIR 4040	Cities/Cities (live) (p/s)	7
80	Sire SIR 4040T	Cities/Cities (live)/Artists Only (live) (12", p/s)	10
80	Sire SIR 4048	Once In A Lifetime/Seen And Not Seen (p/s)	5
80	Sire SIR 4050	Houses In Motion (Special Re-Mixed Version)/Air (p/s)	8
84	Sire W 9451T/SAM 176	This Must Be The Place (Full Version)/Moon Rocks//Slippery People (Remix)/ Making Flippy Floppy (Remix) (12", p/s, double pack)	15
84	EMI 12EMI 5504	Slippery People (live version)/This Must Be The Place (Naïve Melody) (12", p/s)	10
84	EMI 12EMI 5509	Girlfriend Is Better/Once In A Lifetime (12", p/s)	10
85	EMI 12EMI 5520	Lady Don't Mind (Extended Mix)/Give Me Back My Name (12", p/s)	10
85	EMI 12EMID 5520	Lady Don't Mind/Give Me Back My Name//Slippery People (live)/ This Must Be The Place (Naive Melody) (live) (12", p/s, double pack)	12
85	EMI EMIP 5530	Road To Nowhere/Television Man (picture disc)	6
85	EMI 12 EMID 5530/ 12 EMI 5504	Road To Nowhere/Television Man (Extended)//Slippery People (Long Live Version)/Naive Melody (live) (12", stickered double pack)	10
86	EMI 12EMI 5567	Wild Wild Life (Extended Mix)/People Like Us (12", p/s)	8
87	EMI EM 1	Radio Head (LP version)/Hey Now (p/s)	6
87	EMI EMD 1	Radio Head/Hey Now (Movie Version)//Radio Head (Movie Version)/ Radio Head (Extended Remix) (double pack, gatefold p/s)	8
88	EMI EM 68	Blind/Bill (p/s)	5
88	EMI CDEM 68	Blind (Vocal Mix)/Blind/Bill (CD)	15
88	EMI 10 EM 53	Nothing But Flowers/Mommy Daddy You And I/Ruby Dear (10", p/s)	10
88	EMI CDEM 53	Nothing But Flowers/Ruby Dear (Bush Mix)/Mommy Daddy You And I/Facts Of Life (CD)	12
92	EMI EM 250	Lifetime Piling Up/Love For Sale (p/s)	5
92	EMI CDEMS 250	Lifetime Piling Up/Road To Nowhere/Love For Sale/Lady Don't Mind (CD)	10
79	Sire K 56707	FEAR OF MUSIC (LP, with free single "Psycho Killer"/"New Feeling" [SAM 108])	15
83	EMI 9237711	SPEAKING IN TONGUES (LP, clear vinyl in special cover)	18

(see also David Byrne)

TALK TALK

Year	Label / Cat. No.	Title	£
82	EMI EMI 5265	Mirror Man/Strike Up The Band (p/s)	8
82	EMI 12EMI 5314	Today (Extended)/It's So Serious (12", p/s)	10
82	EMI EMI 5352	Talk Talk (Remix)/Mirror Man (p/s)	5
82	EMI EMIP 5352	Talk Talk (Remix)/Mirror Man (picture disc)	6
82	EMI EMIP 5352	Talk Talk (Extended)/Talk Talk (BBC Version) (12", p/s)	15
83	EMI 12EMI 5373	My Foolish Friend (Extended)/Call In The Nightboys/ My Foolish Friend (12", p/s)	8
84	EMI EMI 5433	Such A Shame/Again Again Again (p/s)	5
84	EMI 12EMI 5433	Such A Shame (Extended)/Such A Shame/Again, A Game... Again (12", p/s)	8
84	EMI EMID 5433	THE TALK TALK DEMOS (double pack, poster p/s [EMI 5433 & PSR 467])	12
84	EMI 12EMI 5443	It's My Life (Extended)/Does Caroline Know?/It's My Life (12", p/s)	15
84	EMI 12EMI 5480	Dum Dum Girl (Extended)/Such A Shame (Dub)/Without You (Extended)/ Dum Dum Girl (U.S. Mix) (12", p/s)	12
86	EMI EMI 5540	Life's What You Make it/It's Getting Late In The Evening (p/s)	5
86	EMI 12EMID 5540	Life's What You Make It (Extended)/It's Getting Late In The Evening// It's My Life/Does Caroline Know? (12", p/s, double pack)	20
86	EMI 12EMIX 5540	Life's What You Make It (Extended Dance Mix)/Life Is What You Make It (Early Mix)/It's Getting Late In The Evening (12", p/s)	8
86	EMI EMIP 5551	Living In Another World/For What It's Worth (shaped picture disc)	12
86	Parlophone 12R 6131	Give It Up/Pictures Of Bernadette (p/s)	5
88	Parlophone CDR 6189	I Believe In You/John Cope/Eden (Edited Version) (CD)	12
90	Parlophone R 6254	It's My Life/Rennee (live)	6
90	Parlophone CDR 6264	Life's What You Make it/(live)/Tomorrow Started (live) (CD)	8
91	Verve TALKD 1	After The Flood/Myrrhman (CD, picture disc in 3-CD box)	15
91	Verve TALKD 2	New Grass/Stump (CD, picture disc)	10
91	Verve TALKD 3	Ascension Day/5.09 (CD, picture disc)	10
91	Verve TALKD1/2/3	After The Flood/Myrrhman//New Grass/Stump//Ascension Day/5.09 (3-CD, in die-cut box)	40

(see also Reaction)

TOM TALL

Year	Label / Cat. No.	Title	£
55	London HL 8150	Are You Mine/Boom Boom Boomerang (as Ginny Wright & Tom Tall)	35
55	London HLU 8216	Give Me A Chance/Remembering You	50
55	London HLU 8216	Give Me A Chance/Remembering You (78)	12
56	London HLU 8231	Underway/Goldie Jo Malone	50
56	London HLU 8231	Underway/Goldie Jo Malone (78)	20
57	London HLU 8429	Don't You Know/If You Know What I Know (with Ruckus Taylor)	40
57	London HLU 8429	Don't You Know/If You Know What I Know (with Ruckus Taylor) (78)	25
55	London RE-U 1035	COUNTRY SONGS VOL. 2 (EP, as Tom Tall & Ginny Wright)	45

(see also Ginny Wright)

MINT VALUE £

TALL BOYS

82	Big Beat NS 79	Island Of Lost Souls/Another Half Hour Till Sunrise (p/s)	6
84	Big Beat NED 8	WEDNESDAY ADDAM'S BOYFRIEND (12" EP)	8
85	Big Beat NST 107	Final Kick/Interceptor/Dragster/Action Woman (12" EP)	8
86	Big Beat NST 114	Brand New Gun/Last House On The Left/Took A Long Time (12" EP)	8

(see also Meteors)

TALMY/STONE BAND

62	Decca F 11543	Madison Time/Madison Time (A-side with Alan Freeman)	6
62	Ace Of Clubs ACL 1134	ROSES ARE RED & OTHER HITS OF 1962 (LP)	18

TALULAH GOSH

86	53rd & 3rd AGARR 4	Beatnik Boy/My Best Friend (p/s)	8
86	53rd & 3rd AGARR 5	Steaming Train/Just A Dream (p/s)	6
86	53rd & 3rd AGARR 4/5T	Beatnik Boy/My Best Friend/Steaming Train/Just A Dream (12", p/s)	8
86	Sha La La 002/LYN 18147	WHO NEEDS THE BLOODY CARTEL ANYWAY (EP, p/s, flexidisc)	8
87	53rd & 3rd AGARR 8	Talulah Gosh/Don't Go Away (p/s)	6
87	53rd & 3rd AGARR 8T	Talulah Gosh/Don't Go Away (12", p/s)	8
88	53rd & 3rd AGARR 14	Bringing Up Baby/The Girl With The Strawberry Hair (p/s)	6
88	53rd & 3rd AGARR 14T	Bringing Up Baby/I Can't Get No Satisfaction, Thank God/The Girl With The Strawberry Hair/Do You Remember?/Sunny Inside (12", p/s)	8
88	53rd & 3rd AGARR 16	Testcard Girl (p/s)	6
87	53rd & 3rd AGAS 004	ROCK LEGENDS VOL. 69 (LP, clear vinyl)	15
91	Sarah 064	THEY'VE SCOFFED THE LOT (LP)	12

TAMANGOE'S

79	Grapevine GRP 122	I Really Love You/You've Been Gone So Long (withdrawn)	10

JAMES TAMLIN

65	Columbia DB 7438	Is There Time/Main Line Central Station	10
65	Columbia DB 7577	Yes I Have/Now There Are Two	7

TAMPA RED

50	Jazz Collector L 58	Easy Rider Blues/Come On Mama Do That Dance (78)	15
52	HMV JO 301	Pretty Baby Blues/Since Baby's Been Gone (78, export issue)	45
50s	Square M 2	Moot It Boy/She Rocks Me (With One Steady Roll) (78)	45
64	RCA RCX 7160	R & B VOL. 3 (EP)	25
60s	Memory TR 1	TAMPA RED (LP)	45

TAMPA RED/GEORGIA TOM

59	Jazz Collector JEL 3	THE MALE BLUES VOLUME 2 (EP)	20

TAMS

63	Stateside SS 146	Untie Me/Disillusioned	18
63	HMV POP 1254	What Kind Of Fool Do You Think I Am/Laugh It Off	18
64	HMV POP 1298	It's All Right, You're Just In Love/You Lied To Your Daddy	15
64	HMV POP 1331	Hey Girl Don't Bother Me/Take Away	70
65	HMV POP 1464	Concrete Jungle/Till The End Of Time	15
69	Stateside SS 2123	Be Young, Be Foolish, Be Happy/That Same Old Song	15
70	Capitol CL 15650	Too Much Foolin' Around/How Long Love	15
75	ABC ABC 4020	Hey Girl Don't Bother Me/Be Young, Be Foolish, Be Happy	5
68	Stateside (S)SL 10258	A LITTLE MORE SOUL (LP)	45
70	Stateside SSL 10304	BE YOUNG, BE FOOLISH, BE HAPPY (LP)	30
74	Probe SPB 1044	THE BEST OF THE TAMS (LP)	15
74	ABC ABCL 5118	THE BEST OF THE TAMS (LP, reissue)	12

JOCK TAMSON'S BAIRNS

(see under 'J')

TANAMO

63	Island WI 108	Come Down/I Am Holding On (actually by Lord Tanamo)	22

TANDOORI CASSETTE

83	IKA IKA 001	Angel Talk/Third World Brief Case (p/s, 5,000 only)	10

(see also Nazareth, Alex Harvey, Tear Gas)

SHARON TANDY

65	Mercury MF 898	Love Makes The World Go Round/By My Side	25
65	Pye 7N 15806	Now That You've Gone/Hurtin' Me	20
65	Pye 7N 15939	I've Found Love/Perhaps Not Forever	10
67	Atlantic 584 098	Toe Hold/I Can't Get Over It	18
67	Atlantic 584 124	Stay With Me/Hold On	35
67	Atlantic 584 137	Our Day Will Come/Look And Find	22
68	Atlantic 584 166	Fool On The Hill/For No One	22
68	Atlantic 584 181	Love Is Not A Simple Affair/Hurry Hurry Choo-Choo	20
68	Atlantic 584 194	You've Gotta Believe It/Border Town	20
68	Atlantic 584 214	The Way She Looks At You/He'll Hurt Me	20
68	Atlantic 584 219	Hold On/Daughter Of The Sun	80
69	Atlantic 584 242	Gotta Get Enough Time/Somebody Speaks Your Name	20

(see also Fleur-De-Lys, Tony & Tandy)

NORMA TANEGA

66	Stateside SS 496	Walkin' My Cat Named Dog/I'm In The Sky	10
66	Stateside SS 537	Bread/Waves	7
66	Stateside S(S)L 10182	WALKIN' MY CAT NAMED DOG (LP)	30

TANGERINE DREAM

74	Virgin PR 214	Phaedra (Edit)/Mysterious Semblance At The Strand Of Nightmares (promo)	30
76	Virgin VDJ 17	Stratosfear/The Big Sleep In Search Of Hades (promo only)	25
77	MCA PSR 413	Betrayal (Sorceror Theme)/Search (promo only)	25
77	Virgin VS 199	Encore/Hobo March	5
81	Virgin VS 444	Chronozon/Network 23 (p/s)	8
84	Jive Electro P 74	Warsaw In The Sun/Polish Dance (map-shaped picture disc)	20

MINT VALUE £

Year	Label / Cat. No.	Title	£
84	Jive Electro T 74	Warsaw In The Sun (Parts 1 & 2)/Polish Dance/Rare Bird (12", p/s)	15
85	Jive JIVE 101	Streethawk/Tear Garden (p/s)	15
85	Jive Electro T 101	STREETHAWK (12" EP)	20
87	Jive Electro 143	Tyger/21st Century Common Man II (p/s)	6
87	Jive Electro T 143	Tyger/Tyger (7" Version)/21st Century Common Man II (12", p/s)	10
89	Private 663 747	ORANGES DON'T DANCE (CD EP, promo only)	30
74	Polydor Super 2383 297	ATEM (LP)	15
75	Polydor Super 2383 314	ALPHA CENTAURI (LP)	15
79	Virgin V 2111	FORCE MAJEURE (LP, clear vinyl)	15
80	Virgin VBOX 2	TANGERINE DREAM '70-80 (4-LP box set)	25
80	Virgin TCVX 2	TANGERINE DREAM '70-80 (4-cassette box set)	25
81	Virgin V 2212	EXIT (LP, 1st 1,000 with poster)	12
84	MCA MCF 3233	FIRESTARTER (LP, soundtrack)	12
84	Jive HIP 22	POLAND — THE WARSAW CONCERT (2-LP, gatefold sleeve, with inners)	15
84	Jive Electro HIPX 22	POLAND — THE WARSAW CONCERT (2-LP, picture disc)	25
85	Heavy Metal HMI PD 29	FLASHPOINT (LP, soundtrack, picture disc)	15
85	Heavy Metal HMXD 29	FLASHPOINT (CD, soundtrack; playable CD [most copies faulty])	50
86	Jive Electro TANG 1	IN THE BEGINNING (6-LP box set, with booklet)	25
87	Jive HIP 26	LE PARC (LP)	12
87	Jive CHIP 26	LE PARC (CD, U.K. pressing [most copies pressed in Europe])	18
80s	Virgin V 2198	THIEF (LP)	12
80s	Jive HIP 47	TYGER (LP)	12
90	Virgin TD AK 11	TANGERINE DREAM (3-CD, 'Collector's Edition' box set)	25

(see also Edgar Froese, Klaus Schulze)

TANGERINE PEEL

Year	Label / Cat. No.	Title	£
67	United Artists UP 1193	Every Christian Lion-Hearted Man Will Show You/Trapped	22
68	CBS 3402	Solid Gold Mountain/Light Across The River	8
68	CBS 3676	Talking To No One/Wishing Tree	8
69	MGM MGM 1470	Never Say Never Again/A Thousand Miles Away	12
69	MGM MGM 1487	Play Me A Sad Song And I'll Dance/Wish You Could Be Here With Me	7
70	RCA RCA 1936	Move Into My World/In Between	6
70	RCA RCA 1990	Soft Delights/Thinking Of Me	6
70	RCA RCA 2036	What Am I To Do?/Don't Let Me Be Misunderstood	6
70	RCA LSA 3002	SOFT DELIGHTS (LP)	30

TANK

Year	Label / Cat. No.	Title	£
81	Kamaflage KAM 1	Don't Walk Away/Shellshock/Hammer On (p/s, some with cover mounted patch)	7/5
82	Kamaflage KAM 3	Turn Your Head Around/Steppin' On A Landmine (p/s)	15
82	Kamaflage KAM 7	Crazy Horses/Filth Bitch Boogie (p/s)	5
82	Kamaflage KAP 1	(He Fell In Love With A) Stormtrooper/Blood Guts And Beer (picture disc)	7
83	MFN KUT 101	ECHOES OF A DISTANT BATTLE (EP)	8
82	Kamaflage KAMLP 1	FILTH HOUNDS OF HADES (LP, 1st pressing, with black & yellow sleeve)	15
82	Kamaflage KAMLP 1	FILTH HOUNDS OF HADES (LP, 2nd pressing, with bonus p/s 7" "Don't Walk Away (live)"/"The Snake" [KAM F1])	12
83	Music For Nations MFN 3P	THIS MEANS WAR (LP, picture disc)	20
80s	Kamaflage KAMLP 3	POWER OF THE HUNTER (LP)	12

(see also Damned, UK)

TANNAHILL WEAVERS

Year	Label / Cat. No.	Title	£
76	Plant Life PLR 001	ARE YE SLEEPING MAGGIE? (LP, with lyric insert)	12
78	Plant Life PLR 010	THE OLD WOMAN'S DANCE (LP)	12

HOLLY TANNEN & PETE COOPER

Year	Label / Cat. No.	Title	£
79	Plant Life PLR 015	FROSTY MORNING (LP)	12

PHIL TANNER

Year	Label / Cat. No.	Title	£
68	EDF SSLP 1005	PHIL TANNER (LP, with lyric book)	25

TANTONES

Year	Label / Cat. No.	Title	£
57	Vogue V 9085	So Afraid/Tell Me	850
57	Vogue V 9085	So Afraid/Tell Me (78)	175

TANTRUM

Year	Label / Cat. No.	Title	£
80	Ovation OV 1247	RATHER BE ROCKIN' (LP)	12

TANZ DER YOUTH

Year	Label / Cat. No.	Title	£
78	Radar ADA 19	I'm Sorry, I'm Sorry/Delay (p/s)	5

(see also Brian James, Damned)

TAO JONES INDEX

Year	Label / Cat. No.	Title	£
97	RCA 512541	Pallas Athena (live)/V-2 Schneider (live) (12", p/s)	12

(see also David Bowie)

TAPESTRY

Year	Label / Cat. No.	Title	£
67	London HLZ 10138	Carnaby Street/Taming Of The Shrew	10
68	NEMS 56-3679	Like The Sun/Florence	6
69	NEMS 5639-64	Heart & Soul/Who Wants Happiness	30

DEMETRISS TAPP

Year	Label / Cat. No.	Title	£
64	Coral Q 72470	Lipstick Paint A Smile On Me/If You Find Love	7

TARANTULA

Year	Label / Cat. No.	Title	£
70	A&M AMLS 959	TARANTULA (LP)	15

JIMMY TARBUCK

Year	Label / Cat. No.	Title	£
65	Immediate IM 018	Someday/(We're) Wastin' Time	15
67	Philips	Stewball/When My Little Girl Is Smiling (p/s)	10

TARHEEL SLIM & LITTLE ANN

Year	Label / Cat. No.	Title	£
65	Sue WI 390	You Make Me Feel So Good/Got To Keep On Lovin' You	30

DAVE TARRIDA

99 Mosquito MSQ 013 — PLAYING THE GAME (12" EP) . . . 10

TARRIERS

56 London HLN 8340 — Cindy, Oh Cindy/Only If You Praise The Lord (gold or silver label lettering, as Vince Martin & Tarriers) . . . 35/20
56 London HLN 8340 — Cindy, Oh Cindy/Only If You Praise The Lord (as Vince Martin & Tarriers) (78) . . . 8
57 Columbia DB 3891 — The Banana Boat Song/No Hidin Place . . . 7
57 Columbia DB 3961 — Tom Dooley/Everybody Loves Saturday Night . . . 7
57 Columbia DB 4025 — Dunya/Quinto (My Little Pony) . . . 6
58 Columbia DB 4148 — I Know Where I'm Going/Acres Of Clams . . . 6
58 London HLU 8600 — Lonesome Traveller/East Virginia . . . 18
58 London HLU 8600 — Lonesome Traveller/East Virginia (78) . . . 10
60 London RET 1236 — HARD TRAVELIN' VOLUME 1 (EP) . . . 10
60 London RET 1237 — HARD TRAVELIN' VOLUME 2 (EP) . . . 10
57 Columbia 33S 1115 — THE TARRIERS (10" LP) . . . 25
(see also Vince Martin, Rooftop Singers)

TARTAN HORDE

75 United Artists UP 35891 — Bay City Rollers, We Love You/Rollers Theme . . . 12
(see also Nick Lowe, Rat Scabies, Roogalator)

TARTANS

67 Island WI 3058 — Dance All Night/What Can I Do . . . 20
68 Caltone TONE 115 — Awake The Town (with Lynn Taitt's Band)/LYNN TAITT & JETS: The Brush . . . 18
68 Caltone TONE 117 — Coming On Strong/It's Alright (with Tommy McCook's Band) . . . 18
71 Escort ERT 843 — A Day Will Come/ROBI'S All STARS: Version . . . 10
(see also Devon & Tartans, Kaddo Strings, Max Romeo, Derrick Morgan)

TASAVALLAN PRESIDENTTI

73 Sonet SNTF 636 — LAMBERTLAND (LP) . . . 40
74 Sonet SNTF 658 — MILKY WAY MOSES (LP, with insert) . . . 40

TASSELS

59 London HL 8885 — To A Soldier Boy/The Boy For Me . . . 100
59 London HL 8885 — To A Soldier Boy/The Boy For Me (78) . . . 40
59 Top Rank JAR 229 — To A Young Lover/My Guy And I . . . 30

TASTE

68 Major Minor MM 560 — Blister On The Moon/Born On The Wrong Side Of Time . . . 12
69 Polydor 56313 — Born On The Wrong Side Of Time/Same Old Story . . . 7
70 Major Minor MM 718 — Born On The Wrong Side Of Time/Blister On The Moon . . . 7
69 Polydor 583 042 — TASTE (LP) . . . 30
70 Polydor 583 083 — ON THE BOARDS (LP) . . . 30
71 Polydor 2310 082 — LIVE TASTE (LP) . . . 20
72 Polydor 2383 120 — TASTE — LIVE AT THE ISLE OF WIGHT (LP) . . . 15
(see also Rory Gallagher, Stud)

TASTE OF HONEY

69 Rim RIM 19 — 8.05/Charleston . . . 5

BUDDY TATE

58 Felsted FAJ 7004 — SWINGING LIKE TATE (LP) . . . 30

HOWARD TATE

66 Verve VS 541 — Ain't Nobody Home/How Come My Bulldog Won't Bark . . . 10
67 Verve VS 549 — Look At Granny Run Run/Half A Man . . . 10
67 Verve VS 552 — Get It While You Can/Glad I Knew Better . . . 10
67 Verve VS 555 — Baby I Love You/How Blue Can You Get . . . 10
67 Verve VS 556 — I Learned It All The Hard Way/Part Time Love . . . 7
68 Verve VS 565 — Stop/Shoot 'Em All Down . . . 10
68 Verve VS 571 — Night Owl/Every Day I Have The Blues . . . 10
70 Major Minor MM 696 — My Soul's Got A Hole In It/It's Too Late . . . 5
67 Verve (S)VLP 9179 — GET IT WHILE YOU CAN (LP) . . . 25

PHIL TATE ORCHESTRA

58 Oriole CB 1438 — Dream Lover/Zing, Went The Strings Of My Heart . . . 6
59 Oriole CB 1514 — Countdown (Jive)/Green Turtle . . . 6
60 Oriole CB 1539 — Falling In Love Again/Dancing On The Ceiling . . . 5
60 Oriole CB 1568 — Moulin Rouge Waltz/I Won't Dance (78) . . . 12
61 Oriole CB 1601 — Are You Lonesome Tonight/Whispering Tango . . . 7
61 Oriole CB 1601 — Are You Lonesome Tonight/Whispering Tango (78) . . . 15
63 Oriole CB 1832 — Hi-Lili, Hi-Lo/Theme From 'Dr. Kildare' . . . 6
63 Oriole CB 1878 — Devils Horn (Twist)/Hitch Hike (Twist) . . . 6
62 Oriole EP 7052 — PARTY DANCES (EP) . . . 8
62 Oriole EP 7060 — TUNES FOR TWISTERS (EP) . . . 10

TOMMY TATE

66 Columbia DB 8046 — Big Blue Diamonds/A Lover's Reward . . . 40

TATTY OLLITY

70s Tatty TR 101 — Punktuation . . . 10

ART TATUM

51 Melodisc MEL 1157 — Fine And Dandy/Ja Da (78) . . . 6
54 Vogue EPV 1008 — ART TATUM (EP) . . . 8
55 Columbia SEG 7540 — ART TATUM (EP) . . . 8
50s Melodisc EPM7 108 — ART TATUM TRIO (EP) . . . 8
55 Columbia Clef SEB 10003 — ART TATUM (EP) . . . 12
56 Columbia Clef SEB 10027 — TATUM-CARTER-BELLSON TRIO (EP, with Benny Carter & Louis Bellson) . . . 8
57 Columbia Clef SEB 10062 — TATUM-CARTER-BELLSON TRIO (EP, with Benny Carter & Louis Bellson) . . . 8
57 Philips BBE 12136 — UNFORGETTABLE ART (EP) . . . 8
57 Vogue EPV 1212 — ART TATUM (EP) . . . 8

MINT VALUE £

58	Columbia Clef SEB 10084	ART TATUM AT HOLLYWOOD BOWL (EP)	8
58	Columbia Clef SEB 10101	ART TATUM — BUDDY DE FRANCO QUARTET (EP)	8
59	Columbia Clef SEB 10116	DELICATE TOUCH OF ART TATUM (EP)	8
60	Fontana TFE 17235	ART TATUM NO. 1 (EP)	8
60	Fontana TFE 17236	ART TATUM NO. 2 (EP)	8
60	Fontana TFE 17237	ART TATUM NO. 3 (EP)	8
60	HMV 7EG 8604	THE GREATEST PIANO OF THEM ALL (EP)	8
60	HMV 7EG 8619	ART TATUM — BUDDY DE FRANCO QUARTET (EP)	8
61	HMV 7EG 8684	INCOMPARABLE MUSIC OF ART TATUM (EP)	8
62	Ember EMB 4502	MEMORIES OF ART TATUM (EP)	8
51	Capitol LC 6524	ART TATUM (10" LP)	18
53	Capitol LC 6625	OUT OF NOWHERE (10" LP)	40
54	Vogue LDE 081	ART TATUM "JUST JAZZ" (10" LP)	30
55	Vogue Coral LRA 10011	THE ART TATUM TRIO (10" LP)	15
55	Columbia Clef 33CX 10005	THE GENIUS OF ART TATUM (LP)	12
55	Capitol LC 6638	ART TATUM ENCORES (10" LP)	15
56	Columbia Clef 33CX 10053	THE GENIUS OF ART TATUM (NO. 2) (LP)	12
57	Columbia Clef 33C 9033	THE GENIUS OF ART TATUM (NO. 3) (10" LP)	15
57	Columbia Clef 33C 9039	PRESENTING THE ART TATUM TRIO (10" LP)	15
57	Vogue Coral LVA 9047	HERE'S ART TATUM (LP)	12
58	Columbia Clef 33CX 10115	ART TATUM (LP)	12
59	Columbia Clef 33CX 10137	ART TATUM-BEN WEBSTER QUARTET (LP)	40
60	Top Rank 35/067	ART TATUM DISCOVERIES (LP)	12
61	Brunswick LAT 8358	THE ART OF TATUM (LP)	12
61	Ember EMB 3314	MEMORIES OF ART TATUM (LP)	12
61	Ember EMB 3326	MEMORIES OF ART TATUM VOL. 2 (LP)	12
64	Xtra XTRA 1007	ART TATUM (LP)	12
67	Fontana FJL 904	ART (LP)	15

BERNIE TAUPIN

71	DJM DJLPS 415	TAUPIN (LP)	15

TAVARES

77	Capitol E-ST 11628	LOVE STORM (LP)	12

JOHN TAVENER

70	Apple SAPCOR 15	THE WHALE (LP, gatefold sleeve)	75
71	Apple SAPCOR 20	CELTIC REQUIEM (LP, gatefold sleeve, with insert & 'Apple' inner sleeve)	150
77	Ring O' 2320 104	THE WHALE (LP, reissue, different single sleeve)	50
92	Apple SAPCOR 15	THE WHALE (LP, 2nd reissue, gatefold sleeve with inner sleeve)	30
92	Apple SAPCOR 15	THE WHALE (CD)	30
93	Apple SAPCOR 20	CELTIC REQUIEM (LP, reissue, gatefold sleeve with inner sleeve)	30
93	Apple SAPCOR 20	CELTIC REQUIEM (CD)	50

TAVERNERS

69	Saga EROS 8146	SELDOM SOBER (LP)	20
73	Trailer LER 2080	BLOWING SANDS (LP, red label)	18
74	Folk Heritage FHR 062	TIMES OF OLD ENGLAND (LP)	25
78	Folk Heritage FHR 101	SAME OLD FRIENDS (LP, with insert)	12

TAW FOLK

75	Sentinel SENS 1030	DEVONSHIRE CREAM AND CIDER (LP)	12

CYRIL TAWNEY

69	Polydor 236 577	THE OUTLANDISH KNIGHT (LP)	25
70	Argo ZFB 4	SINGS CHILDREN'S SONGS FROM DEVON AND CORNWALL (LP)	25
70	Argo ZFB 9	A MAYFLOWER GARLAND (LP)	25
72	Argo ZFB 28	TAWNEY IN PORT (LP)	12
73	Argo ZFB 87	I WILL GIVE MY LOVE (LP)	12
76	Trailer LER 2095	DOWN AMONG THE BARLEY STRAW (LP)	12

ALLAN TAYLOR

71	Liberty LBF 15447	Sometimes/Song For Kathy	6
73	United Artists UP 35541	My Father's Room/Always You	6
71	Liberty LBS 83483	SOMETIMES (LP, gatefold sleeve)	22
72	United Artists UAS 29275	THE LADY (LP)	12
73	United Artists UAG 29468	THE AMERICAN ALBUM (LP, gatefold sleeve)	12

(see also Fairport Convention)

AUSTIN TAYLOR

60	Top Rank JAR 511	Push Push/A Heart That's True	12

BILLY TAYLOR (TRIO)

57	Esquire EP 115	BILLY TAYLOR (EP)	15
57	Esquire EP 169	BILLY TAYLOR TRIO (EP)	20
54	Felsted EDL 87009	JAZZ AT STORYVILLE (10" LP)	35
54	Esquire 20-053	AT THE TOWN HALL 1954 (LP)	30
54	Esquire 32-010	A TOUCH OF TAYLOR (LP)	30
57	HMV DLP 1181	MY FAIR LADY LOVES JAZZ (10" LP)	30
60	Vogue LAE 12192	TAYLOR MADE PIANO (LP)	30

BOBBY TAYLOR

64	Columbia DB 7282	Temptation/Mod Bod	10

BOBBY TAYLOR (& VANCOUVERS)

68	Tamla Motown TMG 654	Does Your Mama Know About Me/Fading Away (with Vancouvers)	50
73	Epic EPC 1720	I Can't Quit Your Love/Queen Of The Ghetto (solo)	8
69	T. Motown (S)TML 11093	BOBBY TAYLOR AND THE VANCOUVERS (LP)	70
70	T. Motown (S)TML 11125	TAYLOR MADE SOUL (LP, solo)	90

BRYAN TAYLOR

61	Piccadilly 7N 35018	The Donkey's Tale/Let It Snow On Christmas Day	40

MINT VALUE £

CECIL TAYLOR JAZZ UNIT
60s Fontana SFJL 926 NEFERTITI, THE BEAUTIFUL ONE HAS COME (LP) . . . 15

CECIL TAYLOR QUARTET
60 Contemporary LAC 12216 LOOKING AHEAD! (LP) . . . 15

CHIP TAYLOR
62 Warner Bros WB 82 Here I Am/I Love You But I Know . . . 7
73 Buddah 2011 151 Angel Of The Morning/Swear To God, Your Honor . . . 6
73 Buddah 2318 074 GASOLINE (LP) . . . 12
74 Warner Bros K 56032 CHIP TAYLOR'S LAST CHANCE (LP) . . . 12
(see also Wes Voigt)

DREW TAYLOR
60s One Up OU 2175 DREW'S BREW (LP) . . . 12

DUFFY TAYLOR BLUES
69 Page One POF 130 You Wrecked My Life/I'll Be There . . . 8

EDDIE TAYLOR
65 Big Bear BEAR 6 READY FOR EDDIE (LP) . . . 12

EDDIE TAYLOR & FLOYD JONES
60s XX MIN 712 EDDIE TAYLOR & FLOYD JONES (EP) . . . 20

EDDIE TAYLOR & JIMMY REED
60s XX MIN 704 EDDIE TAYLOR & JIMMY REED (EP) . . . 20
(see also Jimmy Reed)

ELIZABETH TAYLOR
63 Colpix PXL 459 IN LONDON (LP, TV soundtrack, music by John Barry, mono/stereo) . . . 40/50
(see also John Barry)

FELICE TAYLOR
67 President PT 120 It May Be Winter Outside/BOB KEENE ORCHESTRA: Winter Again . . . 8
67 President PT 133 I'm Under The Influence/BOB KEENE ORCHESTRA: Love Theme . . . 8
67 President PT 155 I Feel Love Comin' On/BOB KEENE ORCHESTRA: Comin' On Again . . . 10
68 President PT 193 Captured By Your Love/I Can Feel Your Love (Coming Down On Me) . . . 8
68 President PT 220 Suree-Surrender/All I Want To Do Is Love You . . . 8

GEOFF TAYLOR
55 Esquire EP 55 GEOFF TAYLOR SEXTET (EP) . . . 8
57 Esquire EP 105 GEOFF TAYLOR ALL STARS (EP) . . . 8

GLORIA TAYLOR
70 Polydor BM 56788 You Gotta Pay The Price/Loving You And Being Loved By You . . . 10

HOUND DOG TAYLOR
66 Outasite 45-504 Christine/Alley Music (99 copies only) . . . 80

JAMES TAYLOR
70 Apple APPLE 32 Carolina In My Mind/Something's Wrong . . . 12
68 Apple (S)APCOR 3 JAMES TAYLOR (LP, gatefold sleeve, black inner, orange cover lettering, mono/stereo) . . . 70/50
70 Apple SAPCOR 3 JAMES TAYLOR (LP, 2nd issue, gatefold sleeve, 'Apple' inner sleeve, black cover lettering) . . . 35
70 Warner Bros WS 1843 SWEET BABY JAMES (LP, orange label, later green label) . . . each 18
71 Warner Bros WS 2561 MUD SLIDE SLIM AND THE BLUE HORIZON (LP, g/fold sleeve, green label) . . . 18
72 Warner Bros K 46043 SWEET BABY JAMES (LP, reissue, green label) . . . 12
72 Warner Bros K 46085 MUD SLIDE SLIM AND THE BLUE HORIZON (LP, reissue, gatefold sleeve, green label) . . . 12
73 Warner Bros K 46185 ONE MAN DOG (LP, green label, with insert & stickered sleeve) . . . 12
91 Apple SAPCOR 3 JAMES TAYLOR (LP, reissue, gatefold sleeve) . . . 18
91 Apple SAPCOR 3 JAMES TAYLOR (CD) . . . 18

JAMES TAYLOR QUARTET
87 Re-Elect President FORD 1 Blow Up/One Mint Julep (p/s) . . . 8
88 Urban URB 24 Starsky And Hutch Theme/(Version) . . . 5
88 Urban URBX 24 Starsky And Hutch Theme/(Version) (12") . . . 8
92 Big Life JTQ 7 PROMO 1 Absolution (live) (gig freebie, plain black sleeve with postcard, 1 side etched) . . . 5
90s Big Life Hope And Pray (p/s) . . . 5
90s Acid Jazz JAZID 124S Whole Lotta Love (white label, withdrawn) . . . 100
90s Acid Jazz JAZID 124T Whole Lotta Love (12" EP, company sleeve) . . . 25
90s Acid Jazz JAZID 139 Creation (10", p/s, some mispressed with Hungarian porn music on A-side) . 75/15
90s Acid Jazz JTQ 1 Europa (Extended)/Redneck (12", company sleeve) . . . 40
87 Re-Elect Pres. REAGAN 2 MISSION: IMPOSSIBLE (mini-LP, 45rpm) . . . 12
87 Re-Elect Pres. KENNEDY 1 THE MONEY SPYDER (LP) . . . 12
90s Acid Jazz JAZID 110 EXTENDED PLAY (12" EP) . . . 10
95 Acid Jazz JAZIDLP 115L IN THE HANDS OF THE INEVITABLE (LP, with bonus 2-track 12") . . . 12
90s Acid Jazz AJXLP 117 THE PENTHOUSE SUITE (LP) . . . 12
(see also Prisoners, Daggermen, New Jersey Kings)

JEREMY TAYLOR
62 Decca F 11502 Ag. Pleeze Daddy/Jo'burg Talking Blues . . . 6
68 Fontana TF 962 Red Velvet Steering Wheel/Nasty Spider . . . 6
64 Decca DFE 8581 "WAIT A MINIM" SONGS (EP) . . . 8
66 Decca LK 4731 ALWAYS SOMETHING NEW (LP) . . . 50
68 Fontana (S)TL 5475 HIS SONGS (LP) . . . 18
69 Fontana (S)TL 5523 MORE OF HIS SONGS (LP) . . . 18
72 Galliard GAL 4018 PIECE OF GROUND (LP) . . . 35
73 Canon CPT 3982 JOBSWORTH (LP) . . . 12
75 Spark SRLP 115 COME TO BLACKPOOL (LP) . . . 12

MINT VALUE £

JOHN TAYLOR

71	Turtle TUR 301	PAUSE AND THINK AGAIN (LP)	40

JOHNNIE TAYLOR

67	Stax 601 003	Ain't That Lovin' You/Outside Love (dark blue label, later light blue)	30/20
68	Stax STAX 106	Who's Makin' Love/I'm Trying	7
69	Stax STAX 114	Take Care Of Your Homework/Hold On This Time	8
69	Stax STAX 122	(I Wanna) Testify/I Had To Fight With Love	7
69	Stax STAX 129	I Could Never Be President/It's Amazing	7
70	Stax STAX 141	Love Bones/Separation Line	7
70	Stax STAX 150	Steal Away/Friday Night	12
70	Stax STAX 156	I Am Somebody (Parts 1 & 2)	7
71	Stax 2025 021	Jody's Got Your Girl And Gone/A Fool Like Me	7
73	Stax 2025 083	Standing In For Jody/Shackin' Up	6
73	Stax 2025 194	I Believe In Love/Love Depression	6
75	Stax STXS 2021	It's September/Just One Moment	6
75	Stax STXS 2025	Friday Night/I Ain't Particular	8
76	CBS 4886	Disco Lady/Somebody's Gettin' It (blue vinyl)	6
67	Stax 589 008	WANTED, ONE SOUL SINGER (LP)	35
69	Stax (S)XATS 1006	WHO'S MAKING LOVE (LP)	30
69	Stax 228 008	LOOKING FOR JOHNNIE TAYLOR (LP)	25
69	Stax SXATS 1024	THE J.T. PHILOSOPHY CONTINUES (LP)	25
70	Soul City SCB 2	ROOTS OF JOHNNIE TAYLOR (LP)	45
71	Stax 2363 009	WHO'S MAKING LOVE (LP, reissue)	12
71	Stax 2362 015	GREATEST HITS (LP)	12
74	Stax STXH 5003	SUPER TAYLOR (LP)	15
75	Stax STS 3014	TAYLORED IN SILK (LP)	15
76	CBS 81201	EARGASM	12
78	CBS 82776	EVER READY (LP)	12

(LITTLE) JOHNNY TAYLOR

65	Vocalion V 9234	Part Time Love/Somewhere Down The Line	18
66	Vocalion VP 9264	One More Chance/Looking At The Future	18
72	Mojo 2092 033	Everybody Knows About My Good Thing (Parts 1 & 2)	7
72	Mojo 2092 044	It's My Fault Darling/There's Something On Your Mind	7
65	Vocalion VA-F 8031	LITTLE JOHNNY TAYLOR (LP)	85
72	Mojo 2916 015	EVERYBODY KNOWS ABOUT MY GOOD THING (LP)	35
73	Contempo COLP 1003	OPEN HOUSE AT MY HOUSE (LP)	15
74	Contempo CLP 502	SUPER TAYLORS (LP, with Ted Taylor)	15

JOSEPH TAYLOR

72	Leader LEA 4050	UNTO BRIGG FAIR (LP, gatefold sleeve with booklet)	20

KINGSIZE TAYLOR (& DOMINOS)

64	Polydor NH 66990	Memphis Tennessee/Money (reissue of Shakers single)	22
64	Polydor NH 66991	Hippy Hippy Shake/Dr. Feelgood (reissue of Shakers single)	22
64	Decca F 11874	Stupidity/Bad Boy	30
64	Decca F 11935	Somebody's Always Trying/Looking For My Baby (solo)	35
65	Polydor BM 56152	Thinkin'/Let Me Love You	30
63	Polydor EPH21 628	TWIST AND SHAKE (EP, manufactured in Germany)	110
64	Decca DFE 8569	TEENBEAT 2 — FROM THE STAR CLUB, HAMBURG (EP)	140

(see also Shakers, Paddy Klaus & Gibson)

KO KO TAYLOR

66	Chess CRS 8035	Wang Dang Doodle/Blues Heaven	18
72	Chess 6145 018	Violent Love/The Egg Or The Hen/Wang Dang Doodle	6

LIVINGSTON TAYLOR

70	Warner Bros WS 3006	LIVINGSTONE TAYLOR (LP)	12

MICK TAYLOR

65	CBS 201770	London Town/Hoboin'	18

MICK TAYLOR

79	CBS 82600	MICK TAYLOR (LP, with inner sleeve)	12
90	Maze 084 649	STRANGER IN THIS TOWN (LP)	12

(see also Rolling Stones, Gods, Institute Of Formal Research)

MIKE TAYLOR

65	Columbia SX 6042	PENDULUM (LP)	120
66	Columbia SX 6137	TRIO (LP)	120

(see also Jack Bruce)

MONTANA TAYLOR

52	Vocalion V 1011	Indiana Avenue Stomp/ROMEO NELSON: Head Rag Hop (78)	6

NEVILLE TAYLOR (& CUTTERS)

58	Parlophone R 4447	House Of Bamboo/Mercy, Mercy, Percy (solo)	40
58	Parlophone R 4447	House Of Bamboo/Mercy, Mercy, Percy (solo) (78)	18
58	Parlophone R 4476	Tears On My Pillow/I Don't Want To Set The World On Fire (solo)	20
58	Parlophone R 4476	Tears On My Pillow/I Don't Want To Set The World On Fire (solo) (78)	12
58	Parlophone R 4493	A Baby Lay Sleeping/The Miracle Of Christmas (solo)	12
58	Parlophone R 4493	A Baby Lay Sleeping/The Miracle Of Christmas (solo) (78)	7
59	Parlophone R 4524	Crazy Little Daisy/The First Words Of Love (solo)	30
59	Parlophone R 4524	Crazy Little Daisy/The First Words Of Love (solo) (78)	20
60	Oriole CB 1546	Dance With Dolly/Free Passes	30
60	Oriole CB 1546	Dance With Dolly/Free Passes (78)	10
60	Embassy WB 373	It Ain't Necessarily So/BOBBIE BRITTON: Woman Is A Sometime Love	6
60	Embassy WB 373	It Ain't Necessarily So/BOBBIE BRITTON: Woman Is A Sometime Love (78)	6
60s	Honey Hit TB 127	Joshua Fit The Battle Of Jericho/It's Me, It's Me, It's Me, My Love (some p/s)	12/6

(see also Hal Munro, Bobbie Britton)

MINT VALUE £

PEGGY TAYLOR

60 Top Rank JAR 421 (Won't You Come Home) Bill Bailey/So Similar . . . 7

R. DEAN TAYLOR

68 Tamla Motown TMG 656 Gotta See Jane/Don't Fool Around . . . 6
71 Tamla Motown TMG 763 Indiana Wants Me/Love's Your Name . . . 6
71 Tamla Motown TMG 786 Ain't It A Sad Thing/Backstreet (unissued)
71 Rare Earth RES 101 Ain't It A Sad Thing/Backstreet . . . 10
74 Tamla Motown TMG 896 There's A Ghost In My House/Let's Go Somewhere . . . 7
71 Tamla Motown STML 11185 INDIANA WANTS ME (LP) . . . 25

ROGER TAYLOR

77 EMI EMI 2679 I Wanna Testify/Turn On The TV (demo copies £60) . . . 50
81 EMI EMI 5157 Future Management/Laugh Or Cry (p/s) . . . 15
81 EMI EMI 5200 My Country (Edit)/Fun In Space (p/s) . . . 30
84 EMI EMI 5478 Man On Fire/Killing Time (p/s) . . . 12
84 EMI 12 EMI 5478 Man On Fire (Extended)/Killing Time (12", p/s) . . . 50
84 EMI EMI 5490 Strange Frontier/I Cry For You (Remix) (p/s) . . . 15
84 EMI 12 EMI 5490 Strange Frontier (Extended)/I Cry For You (Extended Remix)/ Two Sharp Pencils (Get Bad) (12", p/s) . . . 65
94 Parlophone R 6379 Nazis 1994/Nazis 1994 (Version) (red vinyl, numbered p/s) . . . 5
94 Parlophone 12RC 6379 Nazis 1994 (Single Version)/(Radio Mix)/(Makita Mix — Extended)/ (Big Science Mix) (12", clear vinyl, with numbered insert in PVC sleeve) . . . 8
94 Parlophone CDR 6379 Nazis 1994 (Single Version)/(Radio Mix)/(Kick Mix)/(Schindler's Mix — Extended)/(Makita Mix — Extended)/(Big Science Mix) (CD) . . . 8
94 Parlophone NAZIS 1 Nazis 1994 (Radio Mix)/Nazis 1944 (Kick Mix) (12", black vinyl, p/s, promo only) . 40
94 Parlophone NAZIS 3 Nazis 1994 (Radio Mix)/(Kick Mix)/(Big Science Mix)/(Makita Mix) (12", black vinyl, p/s, promo only) . . . 40
94 Parlophone NAZIS 4 Nazis 1994 (Schindler's Mix)/(Big Science Mix)/(Makita Mix — Extended) (12", black vinyl, p/s, promo only) . . . 40
94 Parlophone 12RDJ 6379 Nazis 1994 (Schindler's Mix)/(Big Science Mix)/(Makita Mix — Extended) (12", white label DJ promo) . . . 175
94 Parlophone R 6389 Foreign Sand (Single Version)/You Had To Be There (as Roger Taylor & Yoshiki) (blue vinyl, numbered p/s) . . . 6
94 Parlophone 12R 6389 Foreign Sand (Single Version)/(Album Version)/You Had To Be There/Final Destination (as Roger Taylor & Yoshiki) (12", picture disc, with no'd insert) . . . 8
94 Parlophone R 6399 Happiness/Ride The Wild Wind (live) (green vinyl, numbered p/s) . . . 6
94 Parlophone 12R 6399 Happiness/Dear Mr. Murdoch/Everybody Hurts Sometime (live)/ Old Friends (live) (12", picture disc, with numbered insert) . . . 8
94 Parlophone CDPCS 157 Happiness/Dear Mr. Murdoch/Everybody Hurts Sometime (live)/ Old Friends (live) (CD, numbered) . . . 25
81 EMI EMC 3369 FUN IN SPACE (LP) . . . 15
84 EMI RTA 1 STRANGE FRONTIER (LP) . . . 15
93 Parlophone PCSD 157 HAPPINESS? (LP, some numbered) . . . 40
(see also Queen, Cross, Hilary Hilary, Ian Hunter, Fox, Kansas, Camy Todorow, Mel Smith, Billy Squier)

ROSEMARY TAYLOR

75 JD 2009 TAYLORMAID (LP, private pressing with insert) . . . 200
(see also Great Saturday Night Swindle)

SAM ('THE MAN') TAYLOR

54 MGM SP 1106 Please Be Kind/This Can't Be Love (as Sam 'The Man' Taylor & Cat Men) . . . 30
56 MGM MGM-EP 531 SAM TAYLOR ORCHESTRA (EP) . . . 35
(see also Claude Cloud)

TED TAYLOR FOUR

58 Oriole CB 1464 Son Of Honky Tonk/Farrago . . . 15
58 Oriole CB 1464 Son Of Honky Tonk/Farrago (78) . . . 10
60 Oriole CB 1573 M.1./You Are My Sunshine . . . 15
61 Oriole CB 1574 Fried Onions/Yellow Rock Of Texas . . . 15
61 Oriole CB 1628 Cat's Eyes/Canyon . . . 10
61 Oriole CB 1630 Flyover/Haunted Pad . . . 18
62 Oriole CB 1713 Jericho/Everytime We Say Goodbye . . . 18
62 Oriole CB 1767 Surfrider/Talent Spot . . . 22

VERNON TAYLOR

59 London HLS 8905 Today Is A Blue Day/Breeze (unreleased)
60 London HLS 9025 Mystery Train/Sweet And Easy To Love . . . 90

VIC TAYLOR

67 Treasure Isle TI 7021 Heartaches/When It Comes To Loving You I'm Alright (B-side actually "Loving Pauper" by Dobby Dobson) . . . 18
71 Trojan TRLS 38 DOES IT HIS WAY (LP) . . . 22
(see also Tommy McCook)

VINCE TAYLOR (& HIS PLAYBOYS)

58 Parlophone R 4505 Right Behind You Baby/I Like Love (solo) . . . 60
58 Parlophone R 4505 Right Behind You Baby/I Like Love (solo) (78) . . . 45
59 Parlophone R 4539 Brand New Cadillac/Pledging My Love . . . 50
60 Palette PG 9001 I'll Be Your Hero/Jet Black Machine . . . 25
61 Palette PG 9020 Move Over Tiger/What'cha Gonna Do . . . 25
76 Chiswick (N)S 2 Brand New Cadillac/Pledging My Love (no p/s) . . . 5
97 Cruisin' 50 CASB 006 Brand New Cadillac/Right Behind You Baby (78, 300 only) . . . 10

WALTER TAYLOR

50s Poydras 2 Thirty-Eight And Plus/Diamond Ring Blues . . . 8

TAYLOR MAIDS

55 Capitol CL 14322 Po-Go Stick/Theme From "I Am A Camera" (Why Do I) . . . 12

MINT VALUE £

T-BONES

64 Columbia DB 7401 — How Many More Times/I'm A Lover Not A Fighter — 45
65 Columbia DB 7489 — Won't You Give Him (One More Chance)/Hamish's Express Relief — 40
(see also Gary Farr & T-Bones, Kevin Westlake)

T. CONNECTION

77 T.K. XC 9109 — Do What You Wanna Do/Got To See My Baby (12") — 8

TEA

74 Vertigo 6147 006 — Good Times/Judy — 5
75 Philips 6305 238 — TEA (LP) — 20
75 Philips 9118 001 — THE SHIP (LP) — 20

TEA & SYMPHONY

69 Harvest HAR 5005 — Boredom/Armchair Theatre — 10
69 Harvest SHVL 761 — AN ASYLUM FOR THE MUSICALLY INSANE (LP, gatefold sleeve) — 100
70 Harvest SHVL 785 — JO SAGO (LP) — 100

TEACHO & HIS STUDENTS

58 Felsted AF 104 — Rock-et/Stop — 60
58 Felsted AF 104 — Rock-et/Stop (78) — 60

TEA COMPANY

68 Mercury SMCL 20127 — COME AND HAVE SOME TEA WITH THE TEA COMPANY (LP) — 30

JACK TEAGARDEN

61 World Record Club TP 156 — TEAGARDEN PARTY (LP) — 12
63 Columbia 33SX 1553 — KING OF THE BLUES TROMBONE (LP) — 12

ANTHONY TEAGUE

62 Decca F 11548 — Like I Don't Love You/My Guardian Angel — 7

TEAM DOKUS

94 Tenth Planet TP 007 — TEAM DOKUS (LP, numbered, 500 only) — 15

TEA PARTY

94 Chrysalis CHR 6072 — SPLENDOR SOILS (LP) — 12
95 Chrysalis CHR 6108 — THE EDGES OF TWILIGHT (LP) — 12

TEARDROP EXPLODES

79 Zoo CAGE 003 — Sleeping Gas/Camera Camera/Kirkby Workers' Dream Fades (red or blue p/s) — 12/10
79 Zoo CAGE 005 — Bouncing Babies/All I Am Is Loving You (p/s) — 10
80 Zoo CAGE 008 — Treason (It's Just A Story)/Read It In Books (some in blue & green p/s) — 10/6
80 Mercury TEAR 1 — When I Dream/Kilimanjaro (p/s) — 5
80 Vertigo TEAR 2 — Reward/Strange House In The Snow (p/s) — 8
81 Mercury TEAR 312 — Treason (It's Just A Story) (Remix)/Traison (C'est Juste Une Histoire)/ Use Me (12", p/s) — 10
81 Mercury TEAR 4 — Ha Ha I'm Drowning/Poppies In The Field (some in withdrawn p/s) — 30/5
81 Mercury TEAR 44 — Ha Ha I'm Drowning/Poppies In The Field/Bouncing Babies/ Read It In Books (double pack, gatefold p/s) — 8
81 Mercury TEAR 44 — Ha Ha I'm Drowning/Poppies In The Field/Bouncing Babies/ Read It In Books (double pack, withdrawn gatefold p/s) — 20
81 Mercury TEAR 5 — Passionate Friend/Christ Versus Warhol (p/s) — 8
81 Mercury TEAR 512 — Passionate Friend/Christ Versus Warhol (12") — 8
81 Mercury TEAR 6 — Colours Fly Away/Window Shopping For A New Crown Of Thorns (p/s & insert) — 8
81 Mercury TEAR 612 — Colours Fly Away/East Of The Equator/Window Shopping (12", p/s) — 8
82 Mercury TEAR 7 — Tiny Children/Rachael Built A Steamboat (p/s) — 5
82 Mercury TEAR 7G — Tiny Children/Rachael Built A Steamboat (gatefold p/s) — 5
82 Mercury TEAR 712 — Tiny Children/Rachael Built A Steamboat/Sleeping Gas (live) (12", p/s) — 8
83 Mercury TEAR 88 — You Disappear From View/Suffocate//Ouch Monkey's/Soft Enough For You/ The In-Psychlopedia (double pack, gatefold p/s) — 8
89 Fontana DROP 112 — Serious Danger/Sleeping Gas/Seven Views Of Jerusalem (p/s) — 8
90 Fontana DROT 2 — Count To Ten And Run For Cover/Reward/Poppies/ Just Like Leila Khaled Said (12", p/s) — 8
90 Fontana DROCD 2 — Count To Ten And Run For Cover/Reward/Poppies/ Just Like Leila Khaled Said (CD) — 8
80 Mercury 6359 035 — KILIMANJARO (LP, original issue, 'group photo' on cover & inner sleeve) — 18
81 Mercury 6359056 — WILDER (LP) — 12
90 Mercury 8424391 — EVERYBODY WANTS TO SHAG THE TEARDROP EXPLODES (LP, with inner) — 15
(see also Julian Cope, Rabbi Joseph Gordan, Lori & Chameleons)

TEARDROPS (Jamaica)

71 Ackee ACK 126 — Let Me Be Free/CINDY STARR: Sentimental Girl — 7
71 Big Shot BI 582 — Two In One/LAURIE'S ALL STARS: Rock-A-Boogie — 7

TEARDROPS

78 Bent BIGB 3 — IN AND OUT OF FASHION (12" EP, foldout p/s in poly bag) — 18
79 TJM TJM 9 — Seeing Double/Teardrops And Heartaches (p/s) — 20
80s Illuminated JAMS 2 — FINAL VINYL (LP) — 15

TEAR GAS

70 Famous SFMA 5751 — PIGGY GO-GETTER (LP) — 50
71 Regal Zono. SLRZ 1021 — TEAR GAS (LP) — 100
(see also Alex Harvey, Tandoori Cassette)

TEARJERKERS

80 Back Door DOOR 1 — Murder Mystery/Heart On The Line (die cut p/s with insert) — 5
81 Good Vibrations GOT 9 — Love Affair/Bus Stop (p/s) — 5
(see also Speed)

MINT VALUE £

TEARS FOR FEARS

81	Mercury IDEA 1	Suffer The Children/Wino (p/s, original issue with light labels)	8
81	Mercury IDEA 12	Suffer The Children (Remix)/Wino/Suffer The Children (Instrumental) (12", p/s)	10
82	Mercury IDEA 212	Pale Shelter (You Don't Give Me Love) (Extended)/Pale Shelter/ The Prisoner (12", original p/s)	8
82	Mercury IDEA 33	Mad World/Mad World (World Remix) (p/s)	5
82	Mercury IDEA 33	Mad World/Mad World (World Remix)//Suffer The Children/ Ideas As Opiates (double pack)	10
82	Mercury IDEA 4	Change/The Conflict (poster p/s)	7
82	Mercury IDEA 4	Change/The Conflict (withdrawn 'fishing net' sleeve)	180
83	Mercury IDEA R/B 5	Pale Shelter/We Are Broken (p/s, red or blue vinyl)	each 5
83	Mercury IDEAG 5	Pale Shelter/We Are Broken (p/s, translucent green vinyl)	7
83	Mercury IDEAP 5	Pale Shelter/We Are Broken (picture disc)	12
83	Mercury IDEA 512	Pale Shelter/We Are Broken (12", p/s)	10
83	Mercury IDEA 6	(The) Way You Are/The Marauders (p/s, some with poster)	40/30
83	Mercury IDEAS 6	(The) Way You Are/The Marauders//Change (Live)/Start Of The Breakdown (live) (shrinkwrapped double pack)	8
84	Mercury IDEA 7	Mother's Talk/Empire Building (clear vinyl picture disc)	5
84	Mercury IDEA 7	Mother's Talk/Empire Building (green vinyl, p/s, with window sticker)	8
84	Mercury IDEA 12	Mother's Talk (Beat Of The Drum Mix)/Empire Building (12", p/s)	8
85	fan club ANTAR 4502	Mother's Talk/Interview	18
85	Mercury IDEC 8	Shout/The Big Chair (calendar pack with 6 cards)	7
85	Mercury IDEA 99	Everybody Wants To Rule The World/Pharaohs//Everybody Wants To Rule The World (Urban Mix)/Interview (double pack)	8
85	Mercury IDEA 910	Everybody Wants To Rule The World/Pharaohs (10", p/s)	7
85	Mercury RACE 112	Everybody Wants To Run The World/(Running Version) (12", p/s)	12
85	Mercury IDEAP 10	Head Over Heels (Remix)/When In Love With A Blind Man (poster p/s)	5
85	Mercury IDEP 10	Head Over Heels (Remix)/When In Love With A Blind Man (clover-shaped picture disc)	8
85	Mercury IDEA 11	I Believe/Sea Song (p/s, sealed with set of postcards, withdrawn)	8
85	Mercury IDEA 1111	I Believe (A Soulful Re-Recording)/Sea Song//I Believe (Original Version)/ Shout (Dub Version) (double pack, gatefold p/s)	5
85	Mercury IDEP 10	Head Over Heels/When In Love With A Blind Man (poster p/s)	8
89	Fontana IDCDL 12	Sowing The Seeds Of Love (Full Version)/Tears Roll Down/Shout (U.S. Remix) (3" CD, red/yellow plastic sunflower pack)	12
89	Fontana IDSUN 13	Woman In Chains/Always In The Past/My Life In The Suicide Ranks/ Woman In Chains (Instrumental) (3" CD, gold card 'sun' pack)	12
88	Mercury 080 032-2	Everybody Wants To Rule The World/The Marauders/When In Love With A Blind Man/Pharaohs/Everybody Wants To Rule The World (Video) (CD Video)	12
88	Mercury 080 064-2	Shout/Everybody Wants To Rule The World (Urban Mix)/Shout (U.S.A. Mix)/ Shout (Video) (CD Video)	12
88	Mercury 080 062-2	Head Over Heels/Sea Song/The Working Hour/Mother's Talk (U.S.A.)/ Head Over Heels (Video) (CD Video)	12
88	Mercury 080 068-2	I Believe (A Soulful Re-Recording)/Start Of The Breakdown/ Ideas As Opiates/Change/I Believe (Video) (CD Video)	12
89	Fontana IDPT 12	Sowing The Seeds Of Love/Tears Roll Down/Shout (US Remix) (12" picture disc, PVC sleeve)	12
89	Fontana 081 376-2	Sowing The Seeds Of Love (Full Version)/Tears Roll Down/ Shout (U.S. Remix)/Sowing The Seeds Of Love (Video) (CD Video)	12
89	Fontana IDEAB 13	Woman In Chains/Always In The Past (p/s, with badges)	6
89	Fontana IDSUN 13	Woman In Chains/(Instrumental Version)/Always In The Past (3" CD, in sun-shaped pack)	12
90	Fontana IDPOS 14	Advice For The Young At Heart/Johnny Panic And The Bible Of Dreams (poster p/s)	6
90	Fontana IDCDS 14	Advice For The Young At Heart/Johnny Panic And The Bible Of Dreams/Music For Tables (CD)	10
92	Fontana IDEAP 16	Woman In Chains/Always In The Past/Woman In Chains (Instrumental) (12" picture disc, numbered, with poster)	8
95	Mercury FFFCJ 1	Raoul And The Kings Of Spain/God's Mistake/Falling Down/Secrets (CD, sampler, promo only, card sleeve, withdrawn)	18
92	Mercury PROMO BOX	TEARS ROLL DOWN (box set, with CD, promo-only cassette & press release)	100
93	Mercury	THE ELEMENTAL INTERVIEW (CD, promo only)	18

(see also Graduate)

TEARS ON THE CONSOLE

75	Holyground HG 120	TEARS ON THE CONSOLE (LP, with booklet, 120 demo copies only)	125
90	Magic Mixture MM 3	TEARS ON THE CONSOLE (LP, reissue, 425 only, with insert)	12

(Band's name is actually Chick Shannon & Last Exit)

TEASER

89	LTW 9KS 2049	Here Tonight (p/s)	20

TEA SET

66	King KG 1048	Join The Tea Set/Ready Steady Go!	18

TEA SET

78	Waldo's Beat Series 003	CUPS AND SAUCERS (EP, with stapled lyric book sleeve)	8
79	Waldo's Beat PS 006	Parry Thomas/Tri-X Pan (gatefold p/s with poster 'mystery' envelope)	8
80	Demon D 1009	South Pacific/The Preacher (foldout p/s with inserts)	8

TECHNIQUES (Jamaica)

65	Island WI 231	Little Did You Know/DON DRUMMOND: Cool Smoke	22
67	Treasure Isle TI 7019	Queen Majesty/Fighting For The Right	25
67	Treasure Isle TI 7026	Love Is Not A Gamble/Bad-Minded People	22
68	Treasure Isle TI 7031	My Girl/Drink Wine (with Tommy McCook & Supersonics)	25
68	Treasure Isle TI 7038	Devoted/Bless You (with Tommy McCook & Supersonics)	22
68	Treasure Isle TI 7040	It's You I Love/Travelling Man (with Tommy McCook & Supersonics)	22
68	Duke DU 1	I Wish It Would Rain/There Comes A Time	18
69	Duke DU 6	A Man Of My Word/The Time Has Come	15

MINT VALUE £

69	Duke DU 22	What Am I To Do/You're My Everything	12
69	Duke DU 60	Where Were You/Just One Smile	12
69	Camel CA 10	Who You Gonna Run To/Hi There (B-side act. "Look Who's Back" by Carl Bryan)	10
69	Camel CA 19	Everywhere Everyone/Find Yourself Another Fool	10
67	Treasure Isle TI 7001	You Don't Care (with Tommy McCook & Supersonics Band)/ TOMMY McCOOK & SUPERSONICS BAND: Down On Bond Street	22
70	Treasure Isle TI 7054	He Who Keepeth His Mouth/One Day (act. by Johnny Osborne & Sensations)	12
70	Techniques TE 904	Lonely Man/I Feel Alive	10
70	Techniques TE 906	Feel A Little Better (actually by Techniques Allstars)/You'll Get Left	10
70	Big Shot BI 536	He Who Keepeth His Mouth/One Day (act. by Johnny Osborne & Sensations)	12
71	Banana BA 350	Since I Lost You/RILEY'S ALLSTARS: Version	12

(see also Techniques All Stars, Riots, Tommy McCook, Mighty Avengers, Gaylads, Rad Bryan)

TECHNIQUES (U.S.)

58	Columbia DB 4072	Hey! Little Girl/In A Round About Way	90
58	Columbia DB 4072	Hey! Little Girl/In A Round About Way (78)	25

TECHNIQUES ALL STARS

70	Big Shot BI 543	Come Back Darling/Move Over (actually by Johnny Osborne & Sensations)	8
70	Big Shot BI 545	Elfrego Bacca (actually by Dave Barker)/TECHNIQUES: Iron Joe (B-side actually by Techniques All Stars)	10
70	Techniques TE 900	Something Tender/CANNONBALL: Bewitch	6
70	Trojan TR 7728	El Dora/TECHNIQUES: If It's Not True (B-side actually by Techniques All Stars)	6

(see also Dennis Alcapone, Ansell Collins)

TEDDIE & THE TIGERS

67	Spin SP 2004	Hold On I'm Comin'/First Love Never Dies	22

TEDDY

71	Upsetter US 353	Elusion/UPSETTERS: Big John Wayne	15

TEDDY & THE CONQUERORS

71	High Note HS 053	Homebound/GAYTONES: Homebound Chapter 3	8

TEDDY & THE FRAT GIRLS

85	Alternative Tentacles VIRUS 19	I Wanna Be A Man/I Owe It All To The Girls/Clubnite/ Alophen Baby/The Eggman Don't Cometh (p/s)	5

TEDDY & PEARL

(see under Teddy Johnson & Pearl Carr)

TEDDY & THE TWILIGHTS

63	Stateside SS 167	I'm Just Your Clown/Bikini Bimbo	15

TEDDY BEARS

58	London HL 8733	To Know Him Is To Love Him/Don't You Worry, My Little Pet	12
58	London HL 8733	To Know Him Is To Love Him/Don't You Worry, My Little Pet (78)	15
59	London HLP 8836	I Don't Need You Anymore/Oh Why	25
59	London HLP 8836	I Don't Need You Anymore/Oh Why (78)	15
59	London HLP 8889	You Said Goodbye/If You Only Knew	35
59	London HLP 8889	You Said Goodbye/If You Only Knew (78)	20
59	London HA-P 2183	THE TEDDY BEARS SING! (LP)	250

(see also Phil Spector, Carol Connors)

WILLIE TEE

67	Atlantic 584 116	Thank You John/Walking Up A One-Way Street	25
71	Mojo 2092 025	Walking Up A One-Way Street/Thank You John/Teasin' You	10
78	Contempo CS 8002	Walking Up A One-Way Street/Thank You John (unissued)	

TEEGARDEN & VAN WINKLE

69	Atco 228028	BUT ANYHOW (LP)	15

TEENAGE FANCLUB

90	Paperhouse PAPER 003	Everything Flows/Primary Education/Speeeder (1,500 only, die-cut p/s)	18
90	Paperhouse PAPER 005	The Ballad Of John And Yoko (p/s, 1-sided, 5,000 only, 2nd side engraved)	12
90	Paperhouse PAPER 007T	God Knows It's True/Weedbreak/So Far Gone/Ghetto Blaster (12", p/s)	12
91	Creation CRESCD 105	Star Sign/(Demo Version)/Heavy Metal 6/Like A Virgin (CD, card sleeve)	12
91	Creation CRESCD 111	The Concept/What You Do To Me (Demo) (CD, card sleeve)	10
95	Creation CRESCD 216	HAVE LOST IT EP (CD, digipak)	8
97	Creation CRE 280	Start Again/How Many More Years (p/s)	6
03	Creation POOLS 5	Did I Say/The Cabbage (p/s, 500 only)	8
91	Creation CRELP 096	THE KING (LP, available for 1 week only, sprayed plain sleeve)	30
91	Creation CRECD 096	THE KING (CD, available for 1 week only, sprayed plain sleeve)	35

(see also Boy Hairdressers, BMX Bandits, Clouds, Eugenius)

TEENAGE FILMSTARS

79	Clockwork COR 002	(There's A) Cloud Over Liverpool/Sometimes Good Guys Don't Follow Trends (1st 150 with foldout p/s)	100/25
80	Wessex WEX 275	The Odd Man Out/I Apologise	25
80	Blueprint BLU 2013	The Odd Man Out/I Apologise (reissue, p/s)	20
80	Fab Listening FL 1	I Helped Patrick McGoohan Escape/We're Not Sorry (p/s)	15

(see also Television Personalities, Times, O Level)

TEENAGERS

57	RCA RCX 102	THE TEENAGERS (EP)	60

TEENAGERS featuring FRANKIE LYMON

(see under Frankie Lymon)

TEENBEATS

79	Safari SAFE 17	I Can't Control Myself/I Never Win (p/s)	15
79	Safari SAFE 19	Strength Of The Nation/I'm Gone Tomorrow (some with p/s)	20/8

TEEN BEATS (U.S.)

60 Top Rank JAR 342 — The Slop Beat/Califf Boogie (featuring Don Rivers & Califfs) ... 15

TEEN QUEENS

65 R&B MRB 5000 — Eddie My Love/Just Goofed ... 20

TEEN STARLETS

61 Top Rank JAR 583 — The Children's Picnic Song/Theme From 'Spinster' ... 6

TEE SET

70 Major Minor MM 666 — Ma Belle Amie/Angels Coming ... 7
70 Columbia DB 8375 — Mr Music Man/In My House ... 5
70s Waldo's 3 — CUPS AND SAUCERS EP (foldout sleeve) ... 8
70 Columbia SCX 6419 — MA BELLE AMIE (LP) ... 15

TEESIDE FETTLERS

74 Tradition TSR 016 — RING OF IRON (LP) ... 15
75 Tradition TSR 021 — TRAVELLING THE TEES (LP) ... 15

TEETH

79 Soho SH 8 — Say Hello To Suzy/Human Bondage (p/s) ... 5

JOHN TEJADA

98 Ferox 030 — SONIC LIFE EP (12", plain sleeve) ... 8

TELEGRAMS

78 Creole CR 163 — Oh Baby Please/Hey Baby ... 5
(See also Steve Allan, Alan Carvell, Carvells, Five Sapphires)

TELESCOPES

87 private cassette — THE TREE 'ATES EP (demo cassette) ... 10
88 Cheree CHEREE 1 — Forever Close Your Eyes/LOOP: Soundhead (33rpm flexi, p/s, 1,000 only) ... 6
89 Cheree CHEREE 2 — Kick The Wall/This Is The Last Of What's Coming Now (p/s, with insert, 1,000 only, light grey/blue p/s) ... 8
89 Cheree CHEREE 2 — Kick The Wall/This Is The Last Of What's Coming Now (numbered re-pressing, 500 only, red wraparound p/s) ... 15
89 Cheree CHEREET 4 — 7th Disaster/Nothing/This Planet/Cold (12", p/s) ... 10
80s What Goes On WHATGOES 15T — THE PERFECT NEEDLE EP (12", p/s) ... 10
80s What Goes On WHATGOES 18T — TO KILL A SLOW GIRL WALKING (12" EP) ... 8
90 Creation CRE 081T — Precious Little/Deep Hole Ends/Never Hurt You/I Sense (12", p/s) ... 10
90 Creation CRESCD 081 — Precious Little/Deep Hole Ends/Never Hurt You/I Sense (CD, card sleeve) ... 12
90 Creation CRE 092T — Everso/Never Learn Not To Love/Wish Of You (12", p/s) ... 10
90 Creation CRESCD 092 — Everso/Never Learn Not To Love/Wish Of You (CD, card sleeve) ... 12
91 Creation CRE 103T — Celeste/All A Dreams/Celestial (12", p/s) ... 10
91 Creation CRE 108T — Flying/Soul Full Of Tears/High On Fire/The Sleepwalk (12", p/s) ... 10
91 Creation CRESCD 108 — Flying/Soul Full Of Tears/High On Fire/The Sleepwalk (CD, card sleeve) ... 12
90 Fierce FRIGHT 039 — TRADE MARK OF QUALITY (LP) ... 12
92 Creation CRELP 079 — HIGH'R 'N' HIGHER (LP, with booklet) ... 12

TELEVISION

77 Elektra K 12252 — Marquee Moon Parts 1 & 2 ... 6
78 Elektra K 12287 — Foxhole/Careful (12", red vinyl) ... 8
79 Ork/WEA NYC 1T — Little Johnny Jewel Parts 1 & 2/Little Johnny Jewel (live) (12", p/s) ... 8
78 Elektra K 52072 — ADVENTURE (LP, red vinyl with lyric insert) ... 12
(see also Neon Boys)

TELEVISION PERSONALITIES

78 Teen '78 SRTS/CUS/77/089 — 14th Floor/Oxford Street W1 (p/s, various different sleeve designs) ... 35-50
78 Kings Road LYN 5976/7 — WHERE'S BILL GRUNDY NOW? (EP, hand-stamped label, 2,000 only) ... 25
78 Kings Road LYN 5976/7 — WHERE'S BILL GRUNDY NOW? (EP, white labels, various sleeves) ... 12
79 Rough Trade RT 033 — WHERE'S BILL GRUNDY NOW? (EP, reissue, different p/s, printed labels) ... 10
80 Rough Trade RT 051 — Smashing Time/King & Country (p/s) ... 15
81 Rough Trade RT 063 — I Know Where Syd Barrett Lives/Arthur The Gardener (p/s) ... 12
82 Whaam! WHAAM 4 — Three Wishes/Geoffrey Ingram/And Don't The Kids Just Love It (p/s, 2 different sleeve designs, 2,000 only) ... 15
82 Creation Artefact 002/ Lyntone LYN 13546 — Biff Bang Pow!/A Picture Of Dorian Gray (1-sided flexidisc, some with *Communication Blur* fanzine) ... 25/18
83 Rough Trade RT 109 — A Sense Of Belonging/Paradise Estate (p/s) ... 12
86 Dreamworld DREAM 4 — How I Learnt To Love The Bomb/Then God Snaps His Fingers/ Now You're Just Being Ridiculous (12", p/s, 3,700 only) ... 14
86 Dreamworld DREAM 10 — How I Learnt To Love The Bomb/Grocer's Daughter/ Girl Called Charity (7", reissue, p/s, 1,000 only) ... 15
87 Dreamworld DREAM 13(T) — Privilege/Me And My Desires (unreleased)
89 Overground OVER 03 — 14th Floor/Oxford Street W1 (numbered p/s, 600 yellow vinyl, 400 white vinyl; 1,000 black vinyl) ... 6/7/4
89 Caff CAFF 5 — I Still Believe In Magic/Respectable (p/s, some in poly bag, 500 only) ... 35/25
90 Overground OVER 13 — I Know Where Syd Barrett Lives/Arthur The Gardener (reissue, p/s, 2000 only) ... 6
90 Overground OVER 15 — Silly Girl (unissued, 100 test pressings only) ... 18
92 Seminal Twang TWANG 15 — We Will Be Your Gurus/Miro/An Exhibition By Jane/Love Is Better Than War (p/s) ... 7
81 Rough Trade ROUGH 24 — AND DON'T THE KIDS JUST LOVE IT (LP, 1st 1,000 with insert) ... 50/35
81 Whaam! WHAAM 3 — MUMMY YOU'RE NOT WATCHING ME (LP, 3,500 only, 1st 1,000 with insert) ... 50/35
82 Whaam! BIG 5 — THEY COULD HAVE BEEN BIGGER THAN THE BEATLES (LP, 2,500 only, hand-painted sleeve) ... 35
83 Whaam! BIG 10 — TURN ON ... TUNE IN (LP, unreleased)

MINT VALUE £

84 Dreamworld HWDS 001 I KNOW WHERE DAN TREACY LIVES (live at Forum 20/9/84) (cassette only, fan club issue) ... 35
85 Illuminated JAMS 37 THE PAINTED WORD (LP) ... 25
86 Dreamworld BIG DREAM 2 THEY COULD HAVE BEEN BIGGER THAN THE BEATLES (LP, reissue with insert) ... 20
86 Dreamworld BIG DREAM 4 MUMMY YOU'RE NOT WATCHING ME (LP, reissue with insert) ... 20
87 Dreamworld BIG DREAM 6 PRIVILEGE (LP, unreleased)
(see also Teenage Filmstars, Times, O Level, Missing Scientists, Reacta, Dry Rib, Slaughter, Gifted Children)

TELEX

78 Sire SIR 4006 Twist A Saint-Tropez/Le Fond De L'Air (p/s) ... 5
79 Sire SIR 4017 Moskow Diskow/Twist A Saint-Tropez (p/s) ... 6
79 Sire SIR 4017T Moskow Diskow (Disco Version)/Twist A Saint-Tropez (Disco Version) (12") ... 10
79 Sire SIR 4020 Rock Around The Clock/Moskow Diskow ... 5
79 Sire SIR 4020T Rock Around The Clock (Extended Version)/Moskow Diskow (Disco Version) (12") ... 8
80 Sire SIR 4039 Eurovision (English Version)/Eurovision (French Version) (p/s) ... 5
80 Sire SIR 4043 Getting Old (New Mix)/Tropical (p/s) ... 6
80 Sire SIR 4047 Soul Waves/Soul Waves (instrumental) (p/s) ... 6
80 Sire SIR 4047T Soul Waves (Extended)/Dance To The Music (Remix)/ Colonel Olrick (12") ... 12
82 Interdisc IN 2 L'amour Toujours/Cloche Et Sifflets (p/s) ... 5
79 Sire SRK 6072 LOOKING FOR ST. TROPEZ (LP, with lyric inner sleeve) ... 15
82 Interdisc INTO 1 BIRDS AND BEES (LP) ... 20

TELHAM TINKERS

84 Eron ERON 031 HOT IN ALICE SPRINGS (LP, with insert) ... 12

TELLERS

74 Pyramid PYR 7011 No Work, No Pay/Version ... 6
74 Dragon DRA 1031 Ta It Deh/Hit Dib ... 6

TELSTARS

62 Oriole CB 1754 I Went A' Walkin'/A Rose And A Thorn ... 15

TEMPERANCE SEVEN

61 Parlophone R 4757 You're Driving Me Crazy/Charley My Boy ... 6
61 Parlophone R 4781 Pasadena/Sugar ... 5
61 Parlophone R 4823 Hard Hearted Hannah/Chili Bom Bom ... 6
61 Parlophone R 4851 Charleston/Black Bottom ... 5
63 Parlophone R 5070 From Russia With Love/P.C.Q. (Please Charleston Quietly) ... 6
61 Argo EAF 14 THE TEMPERANCE SEVEN INCH RECORD (EP) ... 12
61 Argo RG 11 THE TEMPERANCE SEVEN PLUS ONE (LP) ... 20
61 Parlophone PMC 1152 THE TEMPERANCE SEVEN 1961 (LP, also stereo PCS 3021) ... 22
(see also Ted Wood)

TEMPEST

73 Bronze ILPS 9220 TEMPEST (LP, foldover cover with lyric inner sleeve) ... 50
74 Bronze ILPS 9267 LIVING IN FEAR (LP, die-cut cover with inner sleeve) ... 50
(see also Colosseum)

TEMPEST

85 Magnet PEST 1 Always The Same/Love In The Wintertime (p/s) ... 50
85 Magnet 10PEST 1 Always The Same/The Physical Act (10") ... 25
85 Magnet PEST 2 Bluebelle/I Want To Live (p/s) ... 50
85 Magnet 10PEST 2 Bluebelle/I Want To Live (10") ... 25
86 Magnet LAZY 1 Lazy Sunday/You've Always Got Something To Say (p/s) ... 15
86 Magnet PEST 3 Didn't We Have A Nice Time?/The Physical Act ... 50

BOBBY TEMPEST

59 Decca F 11125 Love Or Leave/Don't Leave Me ... 12
59 Decca F 11125 Love Or Leave/Don't Leave Me (78) ... 10

BOB TEMPLE

57 Parlophone R 4264 Come Back, Come Back/Vim Vam Vamoose ... 120
57 Parlophone R 4264 Come Back, Come Back/Vim Vam Vamoose (78) ... 10

GERRY TEMPLE

61 HMV POP 823 No More Tomorrows/So Nice To Walk You Home ... 40
61 HMV POP 939 Seventeen Come Sunday/Tell You What I'll Do ... 35
63 HMV POP 1114 Angel Face/Since You Went Away ... 40
68 RCA Victor RCA 1670 Lovin' Up A Storm/Everything I Do is Wrong ... 15

RICHARD TEMPLE

70 Jay Boy BOY 31 That Beatin' Rhythm/Could It Be ... 10

SHIRLEY TEMPLE

59 Top Rank JAR 139 On The Good Ship Lollipop/Animal Crackers In My Soup ... 8
59 Top Rank JAR 139 On The Good Ship Lollipop/Animal Crackers In My Soup (78) ... 25
59 Top Rank JKR 8003 I REMEMBER (EP) ... 20

TEMPLEAIRES

60s Vogue V 2421 He Spoke/What Will Heaven Have In Store For Me ... 18

TEMPLE OF THE DOG

92 A&M AM 0091 Hunger Strike/All Night Thing (picture disc) ... 15
92 A&M AMY 0091 Hunger Strike/Your Saviour/All Night Thing (12", p/s, with poster) ... 15
92 A&M AMCD 0091 Hunger Strike/Your Saviour/All Night Thing (CD, digipak) ... 20
(see also Pearl Jam)

TEMPLE ROW

72 Polydor 2058254 King & Queen/One Of A Million Faces ... 30

MINT VALUE £

NINO TEMPO

57	London HLU 8387	Tempo's Tempo/June's Blues (as Nino Tempo & His Band)	320
57	London HLU 8387	Tempo's Tempo/June's Blues (as Nino Tempo & His Band) (78)	80
75	A&M AMS 7190	Come See Me Round Midnight/High On Music (as Nino Tempo & 5th Avenue)	5
58	London HB-U 1075	ROCK 'N' ROLL BEACH PARTY (10" LP)	300

(see also Nino Tempo & April Stevens, April Stevens)

NINO TEMPO & APRIL STEVENS

62	London HLK 9580	Sweet And Lovely/TOP NOTES: Twist And Shout	15
63	London HLK 9782	Deep Purple/I've Been Carrying A Torch For You So Long That I Burned A Great Big Hole In My Heart	7
64	London HLK 9829	Whispering/Tweedle Dee	7
64	London HLK 9859	Stardust/1-45	8
64	London HLK 9890	Tea For Two/I'm Confessin' (That I Love You)	8
66	London HLU 10084	All Strung Out/I Can't Go On Living Baby Without You	12
67	Atlantic 584 048	Coldest Night Of The Year/Ooh La La (as April Stevens & Nino Tempo)	8
67	London HLU 10106	The Habit Of Lovin' You Baby/You'll Be Needing Me Baby	12
67	London HLU 10130	My Old Flame/Wings Of Love	7
68	Atlantic 584 151	Deep Purple/Sweet And Lovely	6
68	London HLU 10209	Ooh Poo Pah Doo/Let It Be Me	7
69	London HLU 10245	All Strung Out/My Old Flame	7
69	Bell BLL 1087	Sea Of Love/On The Dock Of The Bay/Twilight Time	6
73	A&M AMS 7075	Put It Where You Want It/I Can't Get Over You Baby	5
64	London RE-K 1412	DEEP PURPLE (EP)	22
64	London HA-K 8168	NINO TEMPO AND APRIL STEVENS — DEEP PURPLE (LP)	50
64	Atlantic (S)AL 5006	SING THE GREAT SONGS (LP, mono/stereo)	35/45
67	London HA-U/SH-U 8314	ALL STRUNG OUT (LP)	35

(see also Nino Tempo, April Stevens)

TEMPOS

59	Pye International 7N 25026	See You In September/Bless You My Love	80
59	Pye International N 25026	See You In September/Bless You My Love (78)	100

TEMPREES

72	Stax 2025 147	Explain To Her Mama/Dedicated To The One I Love	6
74	Stax STS 2027	At Last/I'll Live Her Life	6
72	Stax 2325 083	LOVE MEN (LP)	20
74	Stax STX 1040	THREE (LP)	22

TEMPTATIONS

60	Top Rank JAR 384	Barbara/Someday	40

TEMPTATIONS

SINGLES

64	Stateside SS 278	The Way You Do The Things You Do/Just Let Me Know	50
64	Stateside SS 319	I'll Be In Trouble/The Girl's Alright With Me	50
64	Stateside SS 348	Why You Wanna Make Me Blue/Baby Baby I Need You	60
65	Stateside SS 378	My Girl/(Talking 'Bout) Nobody But My Baby	45
65	Tamla Motown TMG 504	It's Growing/What Love Has Joined Together	40
65	Tamla Motown TMG 526	Since I Lost My Baby/You've Got To Earn It	35
65	Tamla Motown TMG 541	My Baby/Don't Look Back	35
66	Tamla Motown TMG 557	Get Ready/Fading Away	25
66	Tamla Motown TMG 565	Ain't Too Proud To Beg/You'll Lose A Precious Love	18
66	Tamla Motown TMG 578	Beauty Is Only Skin Deep/You're Not An Ordinary Girl	15
66	Tamla Motown TMG 587	(I Know) I'm Losing You/Little Miss Sweetness	12
67	Tamla Motown TMG 610	All I Need/Sorry Is A Sorry Word	18
67	Tamla Motown TMG 620	You're My Everything/I've Been Good To You	12
67	Tamla Motown TMG 633	(Loneliness Made Me Realise) It's You That I Need/I Want A Love I Can See	35
68	Tamla Motown TMG 641	I Wish It Would Rain/I Truly, Truly Believe	12
68	Tamla Motown TMG 658	I Could Never Love Another (After Loving You)/ Gonna Give Her All The Love I've Got	8
68	Tamla Motown TMG 671	Why Did You Leave Me Darling/How Can I Forget	10
69	Tamla Motown TMG 688	Get Ready/My Girl	6
69	Tamla Motown TMG 699	Ain't Too Proud To Beg/Fading Away	6
69	Tamla Motown TMG 707	Cloud Nine/Why Did She Have To Leave Me (Why Did She Have To Go)	7
69	Tamla Motown TMG 716	Runaway Child, Running Wild/I Need Your Lovin'	7
70	Tamla Motown TMG 722	I Can't Get Next To You/Running Away (Ain't Gonna Help You)	6
70	Tamla Motown TMG 741	Psychedelic Shack/That's The Way Love Is	5
70	Tamla Motown TMG 749	Ball Of Confusion (That's What The World Is Today)/It's Summer	5
71	Tamla Motown TMG 773	Just My Imagination (Running Away With Me)/You Make Your Own Heaven And Hell Right Here On Earth	5
71	Tamla Motown TMG 783	It's Summer/Unite The World (Ungena Za Ulimwengu)	5
72	Tamla Motown TMG 800	Superstar/Gonna Keep Tryin' Till I Win Your Love	5
72	Tamla Motown TMG 808	Take A Look Around/Smooth Sailing (From Now On)	5
72	Tamla Motown TMG 832	Smiling Faces Sometimes/Mother Nature	5
73	Tamla Motown TMG 839	Papa Was A Rolling Stone (Parts 1 & 2)	5

EPs

65	Tamla Motown TME 2004	THE TEMPTATIONS	45
66	Tamla Motown TME 2010	IT'S THE TEMPTATIONS	40

LPs

65	Tamla Motown TML 11009	MEET THE TEMPTATIONS	200
65	Tamla Motown TML 11016	SING SMOKEY	55
66	T. Motown (S)TML 11023	THE TEMPTIN' TEMPTATIONS (mono/stereo)	50/60
66	T. Motown (S)TML 11035	GETTIN' READY (mono/stereo)	45/55
67	T. Motown (S)TML 11042	GREATEST HITS	22
67	T. Motown (S)TML 11053	THE TEMPTATIONS LIVE!	25
67	T. Motown (S)TML 11057	WITH A LOT O'SOUL	30
68	T. Motown (S)TML 11068	IN A MELLOW MOOD	35

MINT VALUE £

68 T. Motown (S)TML 11079 THE TEMPTATIONS WISH IT COULD RAIN . . . 40
69 T. Motown (S)TML 11104 THE TEMPTATIONS LIVE AT THE COPA . . . 22
69 T. Motown (S)TML 11109 CLOUD NINE . . . 30
70 T. Motown (S)TML 11133 PUZZLE PEOPLE . . . 30
70 T. Motown (S)TML 11141 'LIVE' AT LONDON'S TALK OF THE TOWN . . . 20
70 Tamla Motown STML 11147 PSYCHEDELIC SHACK . . . 25
70 Tamla Motown STML 11170 GREATEST HITS Vol. 2 . . . 15
71 Tamla Motown STML 11184 THE SKY'S THE LIMIT . . . 18
72 Tamla Motown STML 11202 SOLID ROCK . . . 12
72 Tamla Motown STML 11218 ALL DIRECTIONS . . . 12
73 Tamla Motown STML 11229 MASTERPIECE . . . 12
(see also David Ruffin, Eddie Kendricks, Diana Ross)

TEMPUS FUGIT

69 Philips BF 1802 Come Alive/Emphasis On Love . . . 35
(see also Jensens)

TEN BENSON

98 Sweet SWEE 010 The Claw (p/s) . . . 5

10cc

72 UK UK 22 Johnny Don't Do It/4% Of Something . . . 6
74 UK UK 57 The Worst Band In The World/18 Carat Man Of Means . . . 6
73 UK UKAL 1005 10cc (LP) . . . 12
80s Mercury HS 9102 500 THE ORIGINAL SOUNDTRACK (LP, half-speed master) . . . 12
80s Mercury HS 9102 504 GREATEST HITS (LP, half-speed master) . . . 12
95 Avex AVEXLP MIRROR MIRROR (LP) . . . 12
(see also Godley & Creme, Graham Gouldman, Mindbenders, Mockingbirds, Hotlegs, Whirlwinds, Tristar Airbus, Yellow Bellow Room Boom, Peter Cowap, Nick Mason & Rick Fenn, Frabjoy & Runcible Spoon, Manchester Mob, Ramases)

TENDER SLIM

60s XX MIN 702 TENDER SLIM AND COUSIN LEROY (EP) . . . 20

TENDER TONES

69 Crab CRAB 38 Devil Woman/Nobody Cares . . . 8

TEN FEET

66 RCA RCA 1544 Got Everything But Love/Factory Worker . . . 28
67 CBS 3045 Shot On Sight/Losing Game . . . 40

TEN FEET FIVE

65 Fontana TF 578 Baby's Back In Town/Send Me No More Lovin' . . . 40
(see also Troggs)

TEN FOOT BONELESS

88 Fierce FRIGHT 027 Powerslide/Duane Peters Is God (12", yellow or white p/s, with inner) . . . 12
(see also Pooh Sticks)

TENNESSEE JAY BIRDS

51 London L 1007 Sticks And Stones/Trouble Trouble (78) . . . 10

TENNIS SHOES

78 Bonaparte BONE 3 (Do The) Medium Wave/Rolf Is Stranger Than Richard/So Large (p/s) . . . 8

TEN(N)ORS

68 Doctor Bird DB 1152 Massy Massa/CLIVE ALLSTARS: San Sebastian . . . 22
68 Doctor Bird DB 1175 Sufferer (Make It)/Little Things . . . 22
68 Island WI 3133 Ride Your Donkey/I've Got To Get You Off My Mind . . . 18
68 Island WI 3140 Copy Me Donkey (as Tenors)/The Stage (B-side actually by Ronnie Davis) . . . 20
68 Island WI 3156 Grampa/ROMEO STEWART: While I Was Walking . . . 22
68 Blue Cat BS 127 Khaki/LEYROY REID: Great Surprise (Pound Get A Blow) . . . 18
68 Big Shot BI 501 Reggae Girl/CLIVE ALLSTARS: Donkey Trot . . . 18
68 Fab FAB 41 Ride Your Donkey/I've Got To Get You Off My Mind . . . 12
68 Fab FAB 50 Let Go Yah Donkey/ROMEO STEWART: While I Was Walking . . . 12
69 Big Shot BI 514 You're No Good/Do The Reggae . . . 12
69 Big Shot BI 517 Another Scorcher/My Baby . . . 12
69 Duke Reid DR 2502 Hopeful Village/TOMMY McCOOK: The Village . . . 10
69 Bullet BU 406 Greatest Scorcher/Making Love . . . 6
69 Crab CRAB 26 Baff Boom/Feel Bad . . . 8
69 Crab CRAB 29 True Brothers/Sign Of The Time . . . 6
69 Crab CRAB 36 I Want Everything/Cherry . . . 6
73 Explosion EX 2079 Weather Report/Weather Report — Version . . . 6
73 Pyramid PYR 7000 Money Never Built A Mountain/My World . . . 5
(see also Jennors, Prince Buster, Soul Brothers)

TENPOLE TUDOR

80 Korova KOW 4 Real Fun/What's In A Word (p/s) . . . 5
(see also Sex Pistols)

10,000 MANIACS

84 Reflex RE 1 My Mother The War (Remix)/Planned Obsolescence/ National Education Week (12", p/s) . . . 20
84 Press P 2010 HUMAN CONFLICT 5 (12" EP, gatefold p/s) . . . 30
85 Lyntone LYN 15914 Grey Victory/SIMPLY RED: Something's Burning (33rpm 1-sided clear flexidisc free with ***Jamming!*** magazine, issue 29) . . . 12/8
85 Elektra EKR 11 Can't Ignore The Train/Daktari (p/s) . . . 7
85 Elektra EKR 11T Can't Ignore The Train/Daktari/Grey Victory/The Colonial Wing (12", p/s) . . . 18
85 Elektra EKR 19 Just As The Tide Was A-Flowin'/Among The Americans (p/s) . . . 10
86 Elektra EKR 28 Scorpio Rising/Arbor Day (no p/s) . . . 18
87 Elektra EKR 61 Peace Train/The Painted Desert (booklet p/s) . . . 6
87 Elektra EKR 64 Don't Talk/City Of Angels (7" with 12" p/s, with inserts) . . . 6

MINT VALUE £

88 Elektra EKR 77 — Like The Weather/A Campfire Song (p/s) . . . 6
88 Elektra EKR 71T — What's The Matter Here/Like The Weather (Live)/Gun Shy (Live)/Verdi Cries (12", p/s) . . . 15
88 Elektra EKR 71CD — What's The Matter Here/Like The Weather (Live)/Gun Shy (Live)/Verdi Cries (3" CD) . . . 12
89 Elektra EKR 93CD — Trouble Me (LP Version)/The Lion's Share (LP Version)/Party Of God (with Billy Bragg) (3" CD, gatefold card sleeve) . . . 8
89 Elektra EKR 93CDX — Trouble Me (LP Version)/The Lion's Share (LP Version)/Party Of God (with Billy Bragg) (3" CD, elephant-shaped card pack) . . . 15
89 Elektra EKR 100TE — Eat For Two/What's The Matter Here (Acoustic)/Eat For Two (Acoustic)/ From The Time You Say Goodbye (10", numbered p/s) . . . 7
89 Elektra EKR 100T — Eat For Two/Gun Shy (Acoustic)/Wildwood Flower/Hello — In There (12", p/s) . . . 8
89 Elektra EKR 100TW — Eat For Two/Gun Shy (Acoustic)/Wildwood Flower/Hello — In There (12", p/s, with limited edition print) . . . 10
89 Elektra EKR 100CD — Eat For Two/Gun Shy (Acoustic)/Wildwood Flower/ Hello — In There (3" CD, gatefold card sleeve) . . . 8
84 Press P 3001 LP — SECRETS OF THE I-CHING (LP, with insert; later re-pressed in different 'Chinese Chicken' sleeve, some with insert) . . . 40/30
87 Elektra EKT 41 — IN MY TRIBE (LP, with free 7" sampler: "What's The Matter Here?"/ X: "See How We Are"/CALL: "In The River" [SAM 390, gatefold p/s]) . . . 12

TEN WHEEL DRIVE (with GENYA RAVAN)

71 Polydor 2066 034 — Mornin' Much Better/Stay With Me . . . 6
69 Polydor 583 577 — CONSTRUCTION NO. 1 (LP) . . . 15
70 Polydor 2425 002 — BRIEF REPLIES (LP, with Genya Ravan) . . . 15
71 Polydor 2425 065 — PECULIAR FRIENDS (LP, with Genya Ravan) . . . 15

(see also Goldie [& Gingerbreads])

TEN YEARS AFTER

68 Deram DM 176 — Portable People/The Sounds . . . 10
68 Deram DM 221 — Hear Me Calling/I'm Going Home . . . 8
70 Deram DM 299 — Love Like A Man (studio)/Love Like A Man (live) (45/33rpm) . . . 10
70 Deram DM 310 — Love Like A Man (studio)/Love Like A Man (live) (reissue) . . . 6
71 Deram XDR 48532 — She Lies In The Morning/Sweet Little Sixteen (demo only) . . . 15
72 Chrysalis/Philips 6155 006 — One Of These Days/Baby Won't You Let Me Rock 'n' Roll You . . . 5
89 Chrysalis CHS 3477 — Highway Of Love/Rock 'n' Roll Music To The World (p/s) . . . 5
67 Deram DML/SML 1015 — TEN YEARS AFTER (LP, mono/stereo) . . . 55/40
68 Deram DML/SML 1023 — UNDEAD (LP, mono/stereo) . . . 45/35
69 Deram DML/SML 1029 — STONEDHENGE (LP, gatefold sleeve, mono/stereo) . . . 45/35
69 Deram DML/SML 1052 — SSSSH! (LP, gatefold sleeve, mono/stereo) . . . 35
70 Deram DML/SML 1065 — CRICKLEWOOD GREEN (LP, gatefold sleeve, initially with 'Alvin Lee' poster, mono/stereo) . . . 30/22
71 Deram SML 1078 — WATT (LP, gatefold sleeve) . . . 25
71 Chrysalis CHR 1001 — A SPACE IN TIME (LP) . . . 15
72 Deram SML 1096 — ALVIN LEE AND COMPANY (LP) . . . 15
72 Chysalis CHR 1009 — ROCK & ROLL MUSIC TO THE WORLD (gatefold sleeve) . . . 12
74 Chrysalis CHR 1060 — POSITIVE VIBRATIONS (LP) . . . 12

(see also Alvin Lee, Chick Churchill)

TERMINAL

80s Cargo CRS 0081 — Hold On (some in p/s) . . . 100/50

TERMITES

65 Oriole CB 1989 — Tell Me/I Found My Place . . . 30
65 CBS 201761 — Every Day Every Day/No-One In The Whole Wide World . . . 10

TERMITES (Jamaica)

67 Studio One SO 2006 — Mercy Mr. Percy/SOUL BROTHERS: Hot And Cold . . . 30
67 Studio One SO 2029 — It Takes Two To Make Love/Beach Boy . . . 25
67 Coxsone CS 7008 — Sign Up/DELROY WILSON: Troubled Man . . . 25
67 Coxsone CS 7025 — Do It Right Now/SUMMERTAIRES: Stay (B-side actually by Gaylads) . . . 25
68 Studio One SO 2040 — Mr D.J. (actually by Delroy Wilson)/Tripe Girl (actually by Heptones) . . . 30
68 Coxsone CS 7039 — Mama Didn't Know/I Made A Mistake . . . 25
68 Pama PM 729 — Push It Up/Two Of A Kind (B-side act. by Clancy Eccles & Cynthia Richards) . . . 12
68 Pama PM 738 — Show Me The Way/What Can I Do . . . 12
69 Nu Beat NB 017 — Push Push/Girls (actually by Hi Tones) . . . 12
67 Studio One SOL 9003 — DO THE ROCK STEADY (LP) . . . 120

(see also L. Sparks, Ken Boothe, Upsetters)

PETE TERRACE

67 Pye International 7N 25427 — At The Party/No! No! No! . . . 15
67 Pye International 7N 25440 — Shotgun Boo-Ga-Loo/I'm Gonna Make It . . . 20
67 Pye Intl. NPL 28102 — BOOGALOO (LP) . . . 30

TERRA COTTA

78 Terra Cotta TC 001 — To Be Near You (p/s, with insert) . . . 20

(see also Spriguns)

TERRAIN

83 Terrain Musak TS 001 — Who's To Blame?/Vacation (no p/s) . . . 150

TERRAPLANE

83 City NIK 8 — I Survive/Gimme The Money (p/s) . . . 15
83 City 12NIK 8 — I Survive/Gimme The Money (12", p/s) . . . 15
84 Epic GA 4936 — I Can't Live Without Your Love/Beginning Of The End (gatefold p/s) . . . 6
84 Epic TX 4936 — I Can't Live Without Your Love/Beginning Of The End/ Let The Wheels Go Round (12", p/s) . . . 10
85 Epic A 6110 — I Survive/All Night And Day (p/s) . . . 10
85 Epic TX 6110 — I Survive (You-C Factor Mix)/All Night And Day (12", p/s) . . . 10
85 Epic TX 6352 — WHEN YOU'RE HOT EP . . . 10
85 Epic A 6584 — Talking To Myself/Get Your Face Out Of My Dreams (p/s) . . . 6

MINT VALUE £

85	Epic TX 6584	Talking To Myself/Get Your Face Out Of My Dreams (12", p/s)	10
85	Flexi FLX 394/XPS 200	I'm The One (live)/When You're Hot (live) (p/s, flexidisc free with Meat Loaf's 'Bad Attitude' tour programme)	10/5
86	Epic TERRAD 1	If That's What It Takes/Living After Dark (p/s, with free single)	5
86	Epic TERRAP 1	If That's What It Takes/Living After Dark (car-shaped picture disc)	6
86	Epic TERRAP 1	If That's What It Takes (19th Nervous Breakdance Mix) (uncut picture disc)	50
87	Epic TERRA 2	Good Thing Going/A Night Of Madness (p/s)	7
87	Epic TERRAC 2	Good Thing Going/A Night Of Madness (cassette)	12
87	Epic TERRAG 3	Moving Target/When I Sleep Alone//I Survive (live)/ I Can't Live Without Your Love (double pack, gatefold p/s)	10
87	Epic TERRAG 3	Moving Target/When I Sleep Alone//I Survive (live)/ I Can't Live Without Your Love (12", gatefold p/s)	15
87	Epic TERRAQ 4	If That's What It Takes (19th Nervous Breakdance Mix) (12", reissue, w/poster)	15
85	Epic 26439	BLACK AND WHITE (LP)	25
85	Epic 40 26439	BLACK AND WHITE (cassette, with non-LP bonus tracks)	18
87	Epic 460157 1	MOVING TARGET (LP)	20
87	Epic 460157 4	MOVING TARGET (CD)	20

(see also Thunder, Nuthin' Fancy)

LLOYD TERRELL

68	Island WI 3158	My Argument (as Lloyd & Johnny Melody)/JOHNNY MELODY: Foey Man (B-side actually by George Dekker)	40
68	Pama PM 710	Bang Bang Lulu/MRS MILLER: I Never Knew	8
68	Pama PM 740	How Come (actually by Lee Perry)/MRS MILLER: Oh My Lover	10
69	Pama PM 752	Lulu Returns/MRS MILLER: I Feel The Music	10
69	Nu Beat NB 023	Mr Rhya/After Dark	12
70	Pama PM 792	Birth Control/VAL BENNET: Return To Peace	7
70	Bullet BU 434	Exposure/Baby Huey	7
71	Escort ERT 855	One Woman/CHARMERS: What Should I Do (act. by Dave Barker & Charmers)	7
73	Pama PM 863	Big Eight/JUNIOR BYLES: Auntie Lu Lu	7

(see also Charmers, Lloyd Charmers, Lloyd & Johnny, Lloyd & Ken, Lloydie & Lowbites)

TAMMI TERRELL

66	Tamla Motown TMG 561	Come On And See Me/Baby Don'tcha Worry	100
69	T. Motown (S)TML 11103	THE IRRESISTIBLE TAMMI TERRELL (LP)	85

(see also Marvin Gaye & Tammi Terrell)

TAMMI TERRELL/CHUCK JACKSON

69	Marble Arch MAL 1110	THE EARLY SHOW (LP)	20

(see also Chuck Jackson)

TERRI & TERRORS

79	Fresh FRESH 4	Laugh At Me/Laugh At Me (Again) (folded p/s)	5

TERRIS

90s	Rough Trade	TRIAL BY FIRE (EP, 500 only, with insert)	7

TERRORVISION

90	(own label)	TERRORVISION: Brand New Toy/Human Error/Pain Reliever/ The Pilgrims Rest (cassette, private issue)	40
91	(own label)	PUMP ACTION SUNSHINE: Urban Space Crime/My House/Jason (cassette, private issue)	40
91	(own label)	TERRORVISION: Blackbird/American TV/Pain Reliever/Human Being (cassette, private issue)	40
92	Total Vegas 12VEGAS 1	THRIVE EP (12" EP)	30
92	Total Vegas CDVEGAS 1	THRIVE EP (CD EP)	30
92	Total Vegas VEGAS 2	My House/Coming Up (green vinyl, p/s)	7
92	Total Vegas 12VEGAS 2	My House/Coming Up/Tea Dance (12", p/s)	15
92	Total Vegas CDVEGAS 2	My House/Coming Up/Tea Dance (CD)	20
93	Total Vegas 12ATVR 1	Problem Solved/Corpse Fly/We Are The Roadcrew/Sailing Home (12", p/s)	15
93	Total Vegas CDATVR 1	Problem Solved/Corpse Fly/We Are The Roadcrew/Sailing Home (CD)	25
93	Total Vegas 12VEGAS 3	American TV/Don't Shoot My Dog Again/Killing Time (12", p/s with poster)	12
93	Total Vegas CDPVEGAS 3	American TV/Psycho Killer/Hole For A Soul (CD)	15
93	Total Vegas VEGAS 4	New Policy One/Pain Reliever (live) (green vinyl, p/s)	7
93	Total Vegas 12VEGASSP 4	New Policy One/Ships That Sink (live)/Problem Solved (live) (12", p/s, with poster)	10
93	Total Vegas CDVEGASSP 4	New Policy One/Ships That Sink (live)/Problem Solved (live) (CD, 1st of 2-CD set)	10
93	Total Vegas CDVEGASSP 4	New Policy One/Psycho Killer/Tea Dance/My House (CD, 2nd of 2-CD set)	10
93	Total Vegas CDVEGAS 5	My House/Down Under/(Machete Mix) (CD, blue or purple picture disc)	12
93	Total Vegas CDVEGASS 6	Oblivion/The Model/Remember Zelda (CD, 1st of 2-CD set)	10
93	Total Vegas CDVEGASS 6	Oblivion/Problem Solved/What D'ya Do That For/Oblivion (CD, 2nd of 2-CD set)	10
94	Total Vegas 12VEGAS 7	Middleman/Surrender/The Passenger (12", copper vinyl, p/s, with poster)	10
94	Total Vegas NMD 1	Middleman (1-sided 12", etched brown vinyl, promo only)	50
96	Total Vegas 10VEGAS 14	Easy/Easy (Live)/Celebrity Hit List (Live)/Some People Say (Live) (10", clear vinyl)	8
96	Total Vegas VEGAS 11	Perserverance/Wake Up (blue vinyl, p/s, with insert)	6
92	Total Vegas ATVRLP 1	FORMALDEHYDE (LP, 14 tracks, green vinyl, 500 only, stickered sleeve)	90
92	Total Vegas ATVRCD 1	FORMALDEHYDE (CD, 14 tracks, 1,000 only)	75
93	Total Vegas VEGASLPS 1	FORMALDEHYDE (reissue LP, 12 tracks, 1,000 copies with 12-page booklet, stickered sleeve & lyric inner)	40
93	Total Vegas BOOT 1	LIVE AT THE DON VALLEY STADIUM (CD, picture disc, 250 promo copies only)	70
94	Total Vegas CDPRIMEDJ 1	PRIME TIME TERRORVISION (CD, picture disc, digipak, promo only)	22

(see also Spoilt Bratz)

TERRY

66	Fontana TF 751	Spilt Milk/The Way That I Remember Him	7

MINT VALUE £

CLARK TERRY (& BOB BROOKMEYER)

61 Riverside RLP 12-246 DUKE WITH A DIFFERENCE (LP) 12
65 Fontana TL 5265 TONIGHT (LP, with Bob Brookmeyer) 12
66 Fontana TL 5290 POWER OF POSITIVE SWINGING (LP, with Bob Brookmeyer) 12
66 Fontana TL 5373 MUMBLES (LP) 12
67 Fontana (S)TL 5394 GINGERBREAD MEN (LP, with Bob Brookmeyer) 12
68 Impulse MIPL/SIPL 507 IT'S WHAT'S HAPPENIN' (LP) 12
(see also Coleman Hawkins)

DEWEY TERRY

73 Tumbleweed TW 3502 CHIEF (LP) 15
(see also Don & Dewey, Don Harris, Harvey Mandel)

GORDON TERRY

57 London REA 1098 COUNTRY CLAMBAKE (EP) 45

PAT TERRY (GROUP)

70s Myrrh MYR 1031 PAT TERRY GROUP (LP) 18

SONNY TERRY (TRIO)

53 Parlophone MSP 6017 Hootin' Blues/TOMMY REILLY: Bop! Goes The Weasel 35
53 Parlophone R 3598 Hootin' Blues/TOMMY REILLY: Bop! Goes The Weasel (78) 8
55 Vogue V 2326 Fox Chase/John Henry (78) 6
56 Vogue EPV 1095 SONNY TERRY (EP) 50
55 Vogue LDE 137 FOLK BLUES (10" LP) 40
55 Vogue LDE 165 CITY BLUES (10" LP) 40
58 Melodisc MLP 516 WHOOPIN' THE BLUES (10" LP) 45
58 Topic 10T 30 HARMONICA BLUES (10" LP) 45
65 Topic 12T 30 HARMONICA BLUES (12" LP, reissue) 25
66 Xtra XTRA 5025 SONNY'S STORY (LP) 22
67 Capitol T 20906 WHOOPIN' THE BLUES (LP, reissue) 12
69 Ember CW 136 BLIND SONNY TERRY & WOODY GUTHRIE (LP) 15
69 Xtra XTRA 1064 SONNY TERRY (LP) 18
70 Xtra XTRA 1099 BLUES FROM EVERYWHERE (LP) 18
71 Xtra XTRA 1110 ON THE ROAD (LP, with J.C. Burris) 18
(see also Woody Guthrie)

SONNY TERRY & BROWNIE McGHEE

60 Columbia DB 4433 Talking Harmonica Blues/Rockin' And Whoopin' 30
64 Oriole CB 1946 Dissatisfied Woman/SONNY TERRY: Goin' Down Slow 18
50s Melodisc EPM7 83 ME AND SONNY (EP) 35
58 Pye Jazz NJE 1060 THE BLUEST (EP) 20
59 Pye Jazz NJE 1073 SONNY TERRY & BROWNIE McGHEE & CHRIS BARBER'S JAZZ BAND (EP) 20
59 Pye Jazz NJE 1074 TERRY AND McGHEE IN LONDON PT. 1 (EP) 25
59 Topic TOP 37 HOOTENANNY NEW YORK CITY (EP, with Pete Seeger) 25
61 Top Rank JKP 3007 WORK-PLAY-FAITH-FUN-SONGS (EP) 25
64 Ember EP 4562 SONNY TERRY AND BROWNIE McGHEE (EP) 30
64 Topic TOP 121 R AND B FROM S AND B (EP) 25
64 Realm REP 4002 PAWNSHOP BLUES (EP) 25
64 Vocalion EPV 1274 SONNY TERRY AND BROWNIE McGHEE (EP) 30
65 Vocalion EPV 1279 I SHALL NOT BE MOVED (EP) 30
58 Topic 12T 29 BROWNIE McGHEE AND SONNY TERRY (LP) 30
58 Pye Nixa Jazz NJT 515 SONNY, BROWNIE AND CHRIS (10" LP, with Chris Barber) 45
58 Pye Nixa Jazz NJL 18 SONNY TERRY AND BROWNIE McGHEE IN LONDON (LP) 30
58 London Jazz LTZ-C 15144 BACK COUNTRY BLUES (LP) 50
60 Columbia 33SX 1223 BLUES IS MY COMPANION (LP) 50
61 World Record Club 7379 SONNY TERRY AND BROWNIE McGHEE (LP) 20
61 Vogue LAE 12247 BLUES IS A STORY (LP, also stereo SEA 5014) 30/40
63 Vogue LAE 12266 DOWN SOUTH SUMMIT MEETIN' (LP) 25
63 CBS 52165 BACK COUNTRY BLUES (LP) 25
64 Xtra XTRA 1004 BIG BILL BROONZY/SONNY TERRY/BROWNIE McGHEE (LP) 30
64 Vogue LAE 552 BROWNIE McGHEE AND SONNY TERRY (LP) 30
64 Realm RM 165 BACK COUNTRY BLUES (LP) 18
64 Stateside SL 10076 BLUES HOOT (LP, some tracks by Lightnin' Hopkins) 40
64 Fontana 688 006ZL LIVIN' WITH THE BLUES (LP) 22
65 Society SOC 1015 BROWNIE & SONNY SING AND PLAY (LP) 12
66 Philips BL 7675 AT THE BUNK HOUSE (LP) 20
66 Verve (S)VLP 5010 GUITAR HIGHWAY (LP, mono/stereo) 20/25
66 Fontana TL 5289 HOMETOWN BLUES (LP) 20
67 Ace Of Hearts (Z)AHT 182 HOMETOWN BLUES (LP, reissue) 12
69 Capitol T 20906 WHOOPIN' THE BLUES (LP) 16
69 Stateside SSL 10291 LONG WAY FROM HOME (LP) 15
69 Marble Arch MAL 843 SONNY TERRY AND BROWNIE McGHEE IN LONDON (LP) 12
70 Fontana SFJL 979 WHERE THE BLUES BEGAN (LP) 15
73 Mainstream MSL 1019 HOMETOWN BLUES (LP, gatefold sleeve) 12
(see also Brownie McGhee, Chris Barber, Pete Seeger, Big Bill Broonzy, Lightnin' Hopkins, Big Joe Turner)

TERRY & JERRY

65 R&B MRB 5009 People Are Doing It Every Day/Mama Julie 22

TERRY, CARL & DERRICK

69 Grape GR 3012 True Love/ROY SMITH: Another Saturday Night 8

TERRY SISTERS

57 Parlophone R 4364 It's The Same Old Jazz/Broken Promises 12
57 Parlophone R 4364 It's The Same Old Jazz/Broken Promises (78) 6
58 Parlophone R 4509 Sweet Thing (Tell Me That You Love Me)/You Forgot To Remember 10
58 Parlophone R 4509 Sweet Thing (Tell Me That You Love Me)/You Forgot To Remember (78) 6

MINT VALUE £

TERRY-THOMAS ESQUIRE

56 Decca F 10804 A Sweet Old Fashioned Boy (with Rock 'N' Roll Rotters)/Lay Down Your Arms . . 18
56 Decca F 10804 A Sweet Old Fashioned Boy/Lay Down Your Arms (78) 6
61 Decca LK 4398 STRICTLY T-T (LP) 35

TESCO BOMBERS

82 Y Y14 Hernando's Hideaway/Break The Ice At Parties/Girl From Ipanema (p/s) 5
(see also Homosexuals)

TEST DEPARTMENT

83 Some Bizzare TEST 112 Compulsion/Pulsations (12", p/s) 10
87 Some Bizzare 12MOP 13 Victory (12", p/s). 10
80s Media City CMC 1 Gododdin (12", p/s, Welsh gig freebie with Brith Gof) 10
90 Mop MOP 5T Jihad/(Desert Mix)/(Oil Mix) (12", p/s) 12
93 Mop MOP 8T Bang On It/(Tao Systems Mix)/(TC Ruff House Remix) (12", die-cut p/s). 10
82 Test TEST ONE HISTORY (cassette, with booklet in plastic bag). 15
80s Pleasantly Surprised PS 5 ECSTASY UNDER DURESS (cassette, in bag with inserts, 2 editions) 20/15
84 Test TEST 33 BEATING THE RETREAT (LP, box set). 12
90s Mop MOP 3 A GOOD NIGHT OUT (LP) 12

JACK TETER TRIO

50 London L 501 Johnson Rag/ Back Of The Yards (78) 10
50 London L 689 Kansas City Kitty/Just A Little Nightcap (78) 6
51 London L 997 Here Comes My Ball And Chain/There's A Little White Horse (78). 8

ALAN TEW ORCHESTRA

76 Epic EPC 4676 The Sweeney/The Prowler 15
67 Decca Phase 4 PFS 4120 THIS IS MY SCENE (LP). 20
72 CBS 64665 LET'S FLY (LP) 15

JOE TEX

65 Atlantic AT 4015 Hold What You've Got/Fresh Out Of Tears 20
65 Atlantic AT 4021 You Better Get It/You Got What It Takes 18
65 Sue WI 370 Yum Yum Yum/You Little Baby Face Thing. 25
65 Atlantic AT 4027 A Woman Can Change A Man/Don't Let Your Left Hand Know. 12
65 Atlantic AT 4045 I Want To (Do Everything For You)/Funny Bone 15
65 Atlantic AT 4058 A Sweet Woman Like You/Close Your Door 15
66 Atlantic AT 4081 The Love You Save/If Sugar Was As Sweet As You. 12
66 Atlantic 584 016 S.Y.S.L.J.F.M. (Letter Song)/I'm A Man 8
66 Atlantic 584 035 You Better Believe It/I Believe I'm Gonna Make It. 8
67 Atlantic 584 068 Papa Was Too/The Truest Woman In The World 8
67 Atlantic 584 096 Hold What You've Got/A Sweet Woman Like You. 8
67 Atlantic 584 102 Show Me/Woman Sees A Hard Time (When Her Man Is Gone). 10
67 Atlantic 584 119 Woman Like That, Yeah/I'm Going And Get It 7
67 Atlantic 584 144 Skinny Legs And All/Watch The One (That Brings The Bad News) 7
68 Atlantic 584 171 Men Are Getting Scarce/You're Gonna Thank Me Woman 7
68 Atlantic 584 212 Go Home And Do It/Keep The One You Got 7
69 Atlantic 584 296 We Can't Sit Down Now/It Ain't Sanitary. 7
70 Atlantic 584 318 You're Alright Ray Charles/Everything Happens On Time 7
71 Mercury 6052 067 I Knew Him/Bad Feet 6
72 Mercury 6052 111 Give The Baby Anything/Takin' A Chance 6
72 Mercury 6052 129 I Got 'Cha/Mother Prayer 6
72 Mercury 6052 156 You Said A Bad Word/It Ain't Gonna Work Baby. 6
65 Atlantic ATL 5043 THE NEW BOSS (LP) 75
66 Atlantic ATL 587 009 THE LOVE YOU SAVE (LP). 40
67 Atlantic 587 053 I'VE GOT TO DO A LITTLE BETTER (LP). 30
67 Atlantic 587/588 059 THE NEW BOSS (LP, reissue) 22
67 London HA-U 8334 THE BEST OF JOE TEX (LP) 55
67 Atlantic 587/588 079 GREATEST HITS (LP). 20
68 Atlantic 587/588 104 LIVE AND LIVELY (LP) 30
68 Atlantic 587/588 118 SOUL COUNTRY (LP). 25
69 Atlantic 587/588 130 YOU BETTER GET IT (LP) 25
69 Atlantic 588 193 BUYING A BOOK (LP) 18
72 Atlantic K 40239 FROM THE ROOTS CAME THE RAPPER (LP) 12
72 Mercury 6338 093 I GOTCHA (LP) 12
(see also Soul Clan)

TEXANS

64 Columbia DB 7242 Being With You/Wondrous Look Of Love. 6

TEXAS

89 Mercury TEXCD 1 I Don't Want A Lover/Believe Me/In Vain (CD, slimline jewel case). 12
89 Mercury TEXP 212 Thrill Has Gone/Nowhere Left To Hide/Dimples (12", p/s, with poster) 12
89 Mercury TEXCD 2 Thrill Has Gone/Nowhere Left To Hide/Dimples (CD, slimline jewel case) 10
89 Mercury TEXCD 3 Everyday Now/Waiting For The Fall/Future Is Promises/Fool For Love
(CD, slimline jewel case) 10
89 Mercury TEXCD 4 Prayer For You/I Don't Want A Lover (Live)/Return/
Prayer For You (Acoustic Version) (CD, slimline jewel case) 10
91 Mercury TEXCD 5 Why Believe In You/Hold Me, Lord/How It Feels (CD, some in box) 12
91 Mercury TEX 612 In My Heart/Is What I Do Wrong/You Gave Me Love (12", fold-out sleeve). 10
91 Mercury TEXCB 7 Alone With You (Live)/Sweet Child O' Mine (CD, digipak) 10
92 Mercury TEXCD 8 Tired Of Being Alone/Thrill Has Gone/In My Heart (12")/
Prayer For You (Remixed by Kenny MacDonald) (CD, digipak). 10
92 Mercury TEXCB 8 Tired Of Being Alone/Why Believe In You (CD, card sleeve, with postcards). 15
93 Mercury TEXCX 9 So Called Friend/You're The One I Want It For/Mother's Heaven (French Remix)/
Tired Of Being Alone (CD, picture disc, in tin) 15
93 Mercury TEXCL10 You Owe It All To Me/I Don't Want A Lover/So Called Friend/Revolution
(CD, "Limited edition acoustic CD package", with 3 postcards, card outer pack) . 18
92 Mercury (no cat. no.) EXTRACTS FROM MOTHER HEAVEN (promo-only box set, with cassette & CD) . 40
99 Mercury NMR 2 THE HUSH (CD, 8" x 8" box with biography and 4 postcards, promo only). 25

MINT VALUE £

TEXAS RANGERS

57 HMV 7EG 8387 WAY OUT WEST (EP) 10

TEXTONES

87 Enigma 3268-1 CEDAR CREEK (LP) 15

TEXTOR SINGERS

54 Capitol CL 14211 Sobbin' Women/Remember Me 12

RUDY THACKER & STRINGBEANS

62 Starlite ST45 087 The Ballad Of Johnny Horton/Tomorrow Is My Last Day 20

JAKE THACKRAY

67 Columbia SCX 6178 LAST WILL AND TESTAMENT (LP) 18
69 Columbia SCX 6345 JAKE'S PROGRESS (LP) 12
71 Note NTS 105 LIVE PERFORMANCE (LP) 12
72 Columbia SCX 6506 BANTAM COCK (LP) 12

THAMESIDERS/DAVY GRAHAM

63 Decca DFE 8538 FROM A LONDON HOOTENANNY (EP, 2 tracks each) 40
(see also Davy Graham)

SISTER ROSETTA THARPE

52 Brunswick 04989 Cain't No Grave Hold My Body Down/Ain't No Room In Church For Liars (78) . . . 15
57 Mercury MT 126 When The Saints Go Marching In/Cain't No Grave Hold My Body Down (78) 10
57 Mercury MT 185 Up Above My Head There's Music In The Air/
Jericho (Joshua Fit The Battle Of Jericho) (78) 15
60 MGM MGM 1072 If I Can Help Somebody/Take My Hand, Precious Lord 8
58 Brunswick OE 9284 GOSPEL SONGS No. 2 (EP) 18
62 Mercury ZEP 10127 GOSPEL SINGER (EP, with Sally Jenkins Singers) 18
64 Mercury 10000MCE SISTER ROSETTA THARPE (EP) 18
62 MGM MGM-EP 746 SISTER ROSETTA THARPE (EP) 18
57 Mercury MPL 6529 GOSPEL TRAIN (LP) 35
59 Brunswick LAT 8290 GOSPEL TRAIN (LP) 22
61 Mercury MMC 14057 THE GOSPEL TRUTH (LP) 20
(see also Little Richard)

SISTER ROSETTA THARPE & SISTER MARIE KNIGHT

51 Brunswick 04851 Didn't It Rain/SISTER ROSETTA THARPE: Two Little Fishes And Five
Loaves Of Bread (78, with Sam Price Trio) 15
(see also Marie Knight, Rev. Kelsey, Sammy Price)

THAT PETROL EMOTION

85 Pink PINKY 4 Keen/A Great Depression On A Slum Night (p/s) 5
(see also Undertones)

T.H.C. ROLLER

94 Poor Person Prod. PPPR 4 CHAPTER IN THE LIFE OF T.H.C. ROLLER (LP, handmade sleeve
with insert & king-size rolling papers, numbered, 500 only) 20
94 Poor Person Prod. THIS MUST BE THE JOINT (LP, 500 only) 70

THEAUDIENCE

97 Mercury AUD 1 I Got The Wherewithal/Je Suis Content (red vinyl, limited edition) 18

THEATRE OF HATE

80 S.S. SS 3 Original Sin/Legion (p/s) 10
81 Burning Rome BRR 1 Rebel Without A Brain/My Own Invention (p/s, mispress with 2 B-side labels) 8
81 Burning Rome BRR 1 Rebel Without A Brain/My Own Invention (p/s) 6
82 Burning Rome BRRT 4 Eastworld/Assegai (12") 8
85 Bliss TOH 1EP The Wake/Love Is A Ghost/Poppies/Legion (EP, 33rpm,
with T-shirt in stickered pack, some sealed) 10/5
81 S.S. SSSSS 1P HE WHO DARES WINS — LIVE AT THE WAREHOUSE, LEEDS
(LP, white labels, some copies autographed) 12
81 Straight Music TOH 1 LIVE AT THE LYCEUM (cassette) 12
(see also Pack, Spear Of Destiny, Senate, Cult, Crisis)

THEE

65 Decca F 12163 Each And Every Day/There You Go! 40

THEE MIGHTY CAESARS

80s Swag SWG 001 She's Just Fifteen Years Old/The Swag (1-sided flexidisc) 6
88 Crypt LP 014 ENGLISH PUNK ROCK EXPLOSION (LP) 12
(see also Milkshakes, Prisoners, Billy Childish)

BOB THEIL

82 Private (no cat. no.) SO FAR (LP, private pressing) 180

THEM

64 Decca F 11973 Don't Start Crying Now/One Two Brown Eyes 55
64 Decca F 12018 Baby Please Don't Go/Gloria 10
65 Decca F 12094 Here Comes The Night/All For Myself 10
65 Decca F 12175 One More Time/How Long Baby? 10
65 Decca F 12215 (It Won't Hurt) Half As Much/I'm Gonna Dress In Black 10
65 Decca F 12281 Mystic Eyes/If You And I Could Be As Two 10
66 Decca F 12355 Call My Name/Bring 'Em On In 10
66 Decca F 12403 Richard Cory/Don't You Know? 10
67 Major Minor MM 509 Gloria/Friday's Child 18
67 Major Minor MM 513 The Story Of Them (Parts 1 & 2) 22
73 Deram DM 394 Gloria/Baby Please Don't Go (reissue) 7
65 Decca DFE 8612 THEM (EP) 120
65 Decca DFE 8612 THEM (EP, export-only 'band-on-ladder' p/s) 500
65 Decca LK 4700 (THE ANGRY YOUNG) THEM (LP, orig. label, some with flipback sleeve) 100/65
66 Decca LK 4751 THEM AGAIN (LP, original label, some with flipback sleeve) 100/65
70 Decca LK 4700 (THE ANGRY YOUNG) THEM (LP, re-pressing, red label, boxed Decca logo) 20

MINT VALUE £

Year	Label / Cat. No.	Title	Value
70	Decca LK 4751	THEM AGAIN (LP, re-pressing, red label, boxed Decca logo)	20
70	Decca (S)PA 86	THE WORLD OF THEM (LP, original issue)	20
78	Sonet SNTF 738	BELFAST GYPSIES (LP, features Them without Van Morrison)	25

(see also Van Morrison, Trader Horne, Taste, Sk'boo, Belfast Gypsies, Moses K. & Prophets, Light, Peter Barden, Jackie McCauley)

THEME MACHINE

81	BBC RESL 104	Themes Ain't What They Used To Be/Lost In A World Of Dreams	5

THERAPY

72	CBS 69017	ALMANAC (LP)	12
73	Indigo IRS 5124	ONE NIGHT STAND (LP, private pressing)	15

THERAPY?

89	demo cassette	THIRTY SECONDS OF SILENCE (cassette, 100 only)	15
90	demo cassette	MEAT ABSTRACT (cassette sold at gigs, 150 only)	15
90	Multifuckingnational MFN 1	Meat Abstract/Punishment Kisses (p/s, labels on wrong sides, 1,000 only)	15
92	A&M (no cat. no.)	TEETHGRINDER (12", double pack, white labels in presentation pack)	30
92	A&M THX 1	Have A Merry Fucking Christmas: Teenage Kicks/With Or Without You (Xmas gig freebie)	18
92	A&M AMY 0097	Teethgrinder/Summer Of Hate/Human Mechanism/Sky High McKave (12", p/s)	10
93	A&M 580305-2	FACE THE STRANGE EP: Turn/Speedball/Bloody Blue/Neckbrake (CD, digipak)	10
93	A&M 5803587	Opal Mantra/Innocent X/Potato Junkie/Nausea (blue or clear vinyl, with insert)	6/5
94	A&M 5805347	Trigger Inside/Nice 'N' Sleazy/Reuters/Tatty Seaside Town (yellow vinyl)	7
98	A&M 5826847	Lonely, Cryin', Only/Skyward (blue vinyl)	5
92	Wiiija WIJ 11	PLEASURE DEATH (mini-LP, 10 white labels)	75+
94	A&M 540196-1	TROUBLEGUM (LP, green vinyl, lyric inner)	20

THERMOMETERS

80	Fokker FEP 100	20th Century Girl/Newtown Refugees/Stole Your Drugs (some in oversized p/s)	20/15

THE THE

80	4AD AD 10	Controversial Subject/Black And White (p/s)	30
81	Some Bizzare BZS 4	Cold Spell Ahead/Hot Ice (p/s)	25
82	Epic EPC A 2787	Uncertain Smile/Three Orange Kisses From Kazan (p/s, some with insert)	8/7
82	Epic EPC A 13-2787	Uncertain Smile/Three Orange Kisses From Kazan/ Waitin' For The Upturn (12", p/s, some with photo insert)	18/10
82	Epic EPC A 13-2787	Uncertain Smile/Three Orange Kisses From Kazan/ Waitin' For The Upturn (12", yellow vinyl, p/s)	25
83	Epic TA 3588	Uncertain Smile/Soul Mining (12", p/s)	15
83	Epic EPC A 3119	Perfect/The Nature Of Virtue (p/s)	7
83	Epic EPC A 13-3119	Perfect/The Nature Of Virtue (12", p/s)	15
83	Epic A 3710	This Is The Day/Mental Healing Process (p/s)	5
83	Epic A 3710	This Is The Day/Mental Healing Process//Absolute Liberation/ Leap Into The Wind (double pack, gatefold p/s)	10
83	Epic TA 3710	This Is The Day/I've Been Waiting For Tomorrow (All Of My Life) (12", p/s)	12
83	Melody Maker [no cat. no.]	Dumb As Death's Head/SINES: Jonathon (flexidisc with *Melody Maker*)	7/5
86	Epic PS 215	Sweet Bird Of Truth (Radio Edit) (1-sided, promo only)	7
86	Epic TRUTH D2	Heartland/Born In The New S.A./Flesh And Bones//Perfect/ Fruit Of The Heart (12", p/s, double pack)	8
88	Epic TRUTHQ 2	Heartland/Sweet Bird Of Truth (12", p/s)	8
86	Epic TRUTH Q3	Infected/Infected (Energy Mix)/Disturbed (12", uncensored 'wank' p/s)	12
86	Epic TRUTH T3	Infected/Infected (Energy Mix)/Disturbed/Soul Mining (Remix)/ Sinking Feeling (12", p/s, double pack, with sticker)	10
87	Epic TENSE 1	Slow Train To Dawn/Harbour Lights (p/s, with 2 car stickers)	5
87	Epic CD THE 2	Sweet Bird Of Truth (12" Mix)/Harbour Lights/Sleeping Juice/ Soul Mining (12" Remix) (CD, card sleeve with gauze inner)	8
89	Epic CB EMU 8	The Beat(en) Generation/Angel/Soul Mining (The Previously Un-Released Mix) (3" CD, box set with folded card insert)	8
89	Epic CDEMU 10	ARMAGEDDON DAYS ARE HERE AGAIN (CD EP, card sleeve)	8
92	Epic 6584577	Dogs Of Lust/The Violence Of Truth (marbled pink vinyl, p/s)	5
92	Epic 6584576	Dogs Of Lust/The Violence Of Truth/Infected (Live) (12" picture disc, die-cut p/s)	12
82	private cassette	PORNOGRAPHY OF DESPAIR (LP, unreleased, cassettes exist)	
83	Epic EPC 25525	SOUL MINING (LP, with inner sleeve, initially with 12" single "Perfect"/"Soup Of Mixed Emotions"/"Fruit Of The Heart")	15
86	Epic EPC 26770	INFECTED (LP, with poster & inner, 1st 25,000 with 'torture' sleeve)	20/12
02	Sony 5079022	LONDON TOWN (5-CD box set)	30

(see also Matt Johnson, Gadgets)

LLANS THELWELL & HIS CELESTIALS

66	Island WI 262	Choo Choo Ska/Lonely Night (B-side vocal: Busty Brown)	20

THEY MUST BE RUSSIANS

80s	no label	UNTITLED EP (mail-order only, wraparound sleeve with insert)	10

(see also Joe 9T & Thunderbirds)

THICK PIGEON

80s	Factory FACT 85	TOO CRAZY COWBOYS (LP)	40

THIEVES

79	Arista ARIGV 226	400 Dragons/Headlights (green vinyl)	5

(see also Fairport Convention)

THIEVES LIKE US

80	Earlobe ELS 1	Mind Made/Strike Out (p/s)	8

THIGHPAULSANDRA

01	World Serpent ESKATON 27	Michel Publicity Window/Paralysed (p/s)	5

(see also Coil)

MINT VALUE £

THIN END OF THE WEDGE

81 Jungle JR 051S — Lights Are On Green/I'm Not Dead Yet (some in p/s) ... 30/6
(see also Damascus)

THINGS

80 Imperial IP 4301 — Pieces Of You/Lost Love (p/s) ... 10
88 Epitaph E 86402 — THINGS (LP) ... 12
(see also Buzzcocks)

THIN ICE

88 Blag It SJP 858 — Freedom Road (p/s) ... 40

THIN LIZZY

SINGLES

70 Parlophone DIP 513 — The Farmer/I Need You (Irish only, as Thin Lizzie) ... 1,000+
71 Decca F 13208 — NEW DAY (EP, 33rpm, some without p/s) ... 275/125
72 Decca F 13355 — Whiskey In The Jar/Black Boys On The Corner ... 8
72 Decca F 13355 — Whiskey In The Jar/Black Boys On The Corner (demos in p/s) ... 30
73 Decca F 13402 — Randolph's Tango/Broken Dreams (2 versions of A-side: matrices ZDR 53384 & ZCPDR 53312) ... each 15
73 Decca F 13467 — The Rocker/Here I Go Again (demos £25) ... 8
74 Decca F 13507 — Little Darlin'/Buffalo Gal ... 8
74 Vertigo 6059 111 — Philomena/Sha La La ... 8
75 Vertigo 6059 124 — Rosalie/Half Caste ... 6
75 Vertigo 6059 129 — Wild One/For Those Who Love To Die ... 8
76 Vertigo 6059 150 — Jailbreak/Running Back (p/s) ... 25
77 Vertigo 6059 177 — Dancing In The Moonlight/Bad Reputation (p/s) ... 10
78 Decca F 13748 — Whiskey In The Jar/Vagabond Of The Western World/Sitamoia (p/s) ... 6
79 Vertigo LIZZY 3 — Waiting For An Alibi/With Love (p/s, some with cartoon lyric sheet) ... 8/5
79 Vertigo LIZZY 4 — Do Anything You Want To/Just The Two Of Us (p/s) ... 5
79 Decca THIN 1 — Things Ain't Working Out Down At The Farm/The Rocker (10,000 with p/s) ... 8
79 Vertigo LIZZY 5 — Sarah/Got To Give Up (3 different p/s designs) ... each 7
70s Vertigo DJ 016 — It's Only Money/JANNE SCHAFFER: Dr Abraham (promo only, no p/s) ... 200
80 Vertigo LIZZY 6 — Chinatown/Sugar Blues (live) (silver lettered p/s) ... 5
80 Vertigo LIZZY 7 — Killer On The Loose/Don't Play Around (p/s) ... 6
80 Vertigo LIZZY 7 701 — Killer On The Loose/Don't Play Around//Got To Give It Up (live)/ Chinatown (live) (double pack) ... 10
81 Vertigo LIZZY 8 — LIVE KILLERS (EP) ... 5
81 Vertigo LIZZY 812 — LIVE KILLERS (12" EP, with extra track) ... 8
81 Lyntone LYN 10138/9 — Song For Jimmy/GRAHAM BONNET: Night Games/POLECATS: We Say Yeah/ WAY OF THE WEST: Monkey Love (orange vinyl flexidisc with/without *Flexipop*, issue 10) ... 12/6
81 Vertigo LIZZY 9 — Trouble Boys/Memory Pain (p/s) ... 5
82 Vertigo LIZZY 10 — Hollywood (Down On Your Luck)/Pressure Will Blow (p/s) ... 5
82 Vertigo LIZZY 10 — Hollywood (Down On Your Luck) (10", p/s, 1-sided, existence unconfirmed)
82 Vertigo LIZZY PD 10 — Hollywood (Down On Your Luck)/Pressure Will Blow (picture disc) ... 8
83 Vertigo LIZZY 1111/22 — Cold Sweat/Bad Habits//Angel Of Death (live)/Don't Believe A Word (live) (double pack) ... 10
83 Vertigo LIZZY 1112 — Cold Sweat/Bad Habits/Angel Of Death (live)/Don't Believe A Word (live) (12", p/s) ... 10
83 Vertigo LIZZY 12 — Thunder And Lightning/Still In Love With You (live) (p/s) ... 5
83 Vertigo LIZZY 1212 — Thunder And Lightning/Still In Love With You (live) (12", p/s, some with poster) ... 15/8
83 Vertigo LIZZY 13 — The Sun Goes Down/Baby Please Don't Go (p/s) ... 8
83 Vertigo LIZZY 1312 — The Sun Goes Down (Remix)/The Sun Goes Down/Baby Please Don't Go (12", p/s) ... 10

LPs

71 Decca SKL 5082 — THIN LIZZY (dark blue label, early copies laminated sleeve/later matt) ... 40/30
72 Decca TXS 108 — SHADES OF A BLUE ORPHANAGE (gatefold sleeve, dark blue label) ... 30
73 Decca SKL 5170 — VAGABONDS OF THE WESTERN WORLD (dark blue label, some with insert) ... 25/18
76 Decca SKL 5249 — REMEMBERING ... 15
83 Vertigo VERL 3 — THUNDER AND LIGHTNING (with free 12") ... 20
83 Vertigo — LIFE — LIVE (2-LP, gatefold sleeve, with inners) ... 15
(see also Phil Lynott, Wild Horses, Phenomena, Eric Bell Band, Funky Junction, Greedies, John Sykes, Gary Moore)

THIRD & FOURTH GENERATION

72 Punch PH 91 — Rudies Medley (actually by Peter Tosh & Soulmates)/Rude Boy — Version ... 15
(see also Peter Tosh)

THIRD DIMENSION

70 Unity UN 566 — Peace And Love/Peace And Love — Version ... 6

THIRD EAR BAND

69 Harvest SHVL 756 — ALCHEMY (LP) ... 35
70 Harvest SHSP 773 — THIRD EAR BAND: ELEMENTS (LP) ... 25
72 Harvest SHSP 4019 — MUSIC FROM MACBETH (LP) ... 18
76 Harvest SHSM 2007 — EXPERIENCES (LP) ... 12
(see also High Tide, Sounds Nice)

THIRD QUADRANT

82 Rock Cottage (no cat. no.) — SEEING YOURSELF AS YOU REALLY ARE (LP, private pressing, wraparound sleeve with handwritten insert, blank white label) ... 40
88 own label — LAYERED (private cassette, 500 only) ... 12

THIRD RAIL

67 Columbia DB 8274 — Run, Run, Run/No Return ... 25

MINT VALUE £

THIRD WORLD WAR

71 Fly BUG 7 — Ascension Day/Teddy Teeth Goes Sailing (p/s) ... 8
71 Fly BUG 11 — A Little Bit Of Urban Rock/Working Class Man ... 6
71 Fly FLY 4 — THIRD WORLD WAR (LP) ... 30
72 Track 2406 108 — THIRD WORLD WAR II (LP) ... 70
(see also Terry Stamp)

THIRTEEN SENSES

04 Vertigo 9816335 — Thru The Glass/No Other Life Is Attractive (p/s) ... 6

13TH FLOOR ELEVATORS

78 Radar/Sound For Industry SFI 347 — Reverberation/RED CRAYOLA: Hurricane Fighter Plane (flexidisc free with *Zig Zag* magazine, No. 88) ... 8/6
78 Radar ADA 13 — You're Gonna Miss Me/Tried To Hide (green vinyl) ... 6
78 Radar RAD 13 — THE PSYCHEDELIC SOUNDS OF ... (LP) ... 15
79 Radar RAD 15 — EASTER EVERYWHERE (LP) ... 15
(see also Roky Erickson, Red Crayola)

31ST OF FEBRUARY

69 Vanguard (S)VRL 19045 — THE 31ST OF FEBRUARY (LP) ... 20

35mm DREAMS

81 More Than This ASA 100 — More Than This/The Bearer (foldout p/s) ... 5
81 More Than This ASA 200 — Fasten Your Safety Belts/Corstorphine/Instamatic Dance (p/s) ... 5

39 LYON ST

(see under Associates)

32ND TURN-OFF

69 Jay Boy JSL 1 — 32ND TURN OFF (LP) ... 60
(see also Equals)

THIS DRIFTIN'S GOTTA STOP

70s private pressing — THIS DRIFTIN'S GOTTA STOP (LP) ... 15

THIS HEAT

80 Piano THIS 1201 — Health And Efficiency/Graphic/Varispeed (12", p/s with insert) ... 10
79 Piano THIS 1 — THIS HEAT (LP) ... 12
81 Rough Trade ROUGH 26 — DECEIT (LP, original) ... 12

THIS MORTAL COIL

83 4AD AD 310 — Song To The Siren/16 Days (Reprise) (p/s) ... 5
83 4AD BAD 310 — Song To The Siren/16 Days/Gathering Dust (12", p/s) ... 8
84 4AD AD 410 — Kangaroo/It'll End In Tears (p/s, 2 different designs & label colours, 2,500 of each) ... each 5
86 4AD BAD 608 — Come Here My Love/Drugs (10", p/s with inner sleeve) ... 10
91 4AD TMC 1CD — Extracts From "Blood": Late Night/You And Your Sister/I Come And Stand At Every Door/With Tomorrow (CD, card sleeve, promo only) ... 20
80s 4AD DAD 1005 — BLOOD (2-LP, with inners) ... 18
(see also Cocteau Twins, Modern English, Cindytalk)

THIS 'N' THAT

66 Mercury MF 938 — Someday/Loving You ... 18
67 Strike JH 310 — Get Down With It/I Care About You ... 8
(see also Cleo)

B.J. THOMAS

66 Hickory 45-1395 — Never Tell/Billy & Sue ... 10
66 Pye International 7N 25374 — Mama/Wendy ... 8
68 Pye International 7N 25467 — The Eyes Of A New York Woman/I May Never Get To Heaven ... 7
69 Pye International 7N 25487 — It's Only Love/You Don't Love Me Anymore (The Train Song) ... 6
69 Wand WN 1 — Raindrops Keep Falling On My Head/Never Had It So Good ... 5
70 Wand WN 5 — I Just Can't Help Believing/Send My Picture To Scranton, PA ... 6
72 Wand WN 24 — Rock And Roll Lullaby/Are We Losing Touch? ... 5

CARLA THOMAS

61 London HLK 9310 — Gee Whiz/For You ... 25
61 London HLK 9359 — A Love Of My Own/Promises ... 22
62 London HLK 9618 — I'll Bring It On Home To You/I Can't Take It ... 22
64 Atlantic AT 4005 — I've Got No Time To Lose/A Boy Named Tom ... 18
66 Atlantic AT 4074 — Comfort Me/I'm For You ... 15
66 Atlantic 584 011 — Let Me Be Good To You/Another Night Without My Man ... 8
66 Atlantic 584 042 — B-A-B-Y/What Have You Got To Offer Me ... 8
67 Stax 601 002 — Something Good (Is Going To Happen To You)/It's Starting To Grow (dark blue label, later light blue) ... 12/8
67 Stax 601 008 — When Tomorrow Comes/Unchanging Love (dark blue label, later light blue) ... 12/8
68 Stax 601 032 — Pick Up The Pieces/Separation ... 7
68 Stax STAX 103 — Where Do I Go/I've Fallen In Love ... 7
69 Stax STAX 112 — I Like What You're Doing To Me/Strung Out ... 7
69 Stax STAX 131 — Unyielding/I've Fallen In Love ... 6
72 Stax 2025 082 — Love Means/You've Got A Cushion To Fall On ... 5
91 Kent 6T 7 — I'll Never Stop Loving/Prophets Band/Peaches Baby ... 15
67 Stax 589 004 — CARLA THOMAS (LP) ... 35
67 Stax 589 012 — THE QUEEN ALONE (LP) ... 35
69 Stax SXATS 1019 — MEMPHIS QUEEN (LP) ... 30
71 Stax 2363 004 — MEMPHIS QUEEN (LP, reissue) ... 12
72 Stax 2362 023 — LOVE MEANS... (LP) ... 15
(see also Otis Redding & Carla Thomas)

CHARLIE THOMAS (& DRIFTERS)

74 EMI International INT 502 — Midsummer Night In Harlem/Lonely Drifter Don't Cry (with Drifters) ... 10
75 EMI International INT 506 — I'm Gonna Take You Home/Run, Run, Roadrunner ... 10

MINT VALUE £

CLAUDETTE THOMAS
68 Caltone TONE 116 — Roses Are Red My Love/YVONNE HARRISON: Near To You 15

CREEPY JOHN THOMAS
69 RCA RCA 1912 — Ride A Rainbow/Moon And Eyes Song 12
69 RCA SF 8061 — CREEPY JOHN THOMAS (LP) 75
(see also Paul Kossoff, Edgar Broughton Band)

DAVID THOMAS & THE PEDESTRIANS
83 Recommended REDT 7 — Didn't Have A (Very) Good Time (1-sided picture disc free with label's quarterly magazine) 8
84 Rough Trade ROUGH 30 — THE SOUND OF THE SAND (LP) 12
85 Rough Trade ROUGH 80 — MORE PLACES FOREVER (LP) 12
(see also Pere Ubu)

DON THOMAS
76 DJM DJS 10670 — Come On Train Parts 1 & 2 8

DYLAN THOMAS
60s Caedmon TCE 151 — A WINTER'S TALE (EP) 8
60s Caedmon TC 0997 — UNDER MILK WOOD VOL. 2 (LP) 15

GENE THOMAS
64 United Artists UP 1047 — Baby's Gone/Stand By Love 20

HERSAL THOMAS
50 Parlophone R 3261 — Suitcase Blues/Hersal Blues (78) 70

IRMA THOMAS
64 Liberty LIB 66013 — Breakaway/Wish Someone Would Care 25
64 Liberty LIB 66041 — Anyone Who Knows What Love Is (Will Understand)/Time Is On My Side 20
65 Liberty LIB 66080 — He's My Guy/True True Love 25
65 Liberty LIB 66095 — Some Things You Never Get Used To/You Don't Miss A Good Thing (Until It's Gone) 25
65 Sue WI 372 — Don't Mess With My Man/Set Me Free 35
65 Liberty LIB 66106 — I'm Gonna Cry Till My Tears Run Dry/Nobody Wants To Hear Nobody's Troubles 25
66 Liberty LIB 66137 — Take A Look/What Are You Trying To Do 25
66 Liberty LIB 66178 — It's A Man's-Woman's World 15
72 Atlantic K 10167 — Full Time Woman/She's Taking My Part 5
72 United Artists UP 35402 — Time Is On My Side/Anyone Who Knows What Love Is (Will Understand) (reissue) 5
65 Liberty LEP 4035 — TIME IS ON MY SIDE (EP) 75
68 Minit MLL/MLS 40004E — TAKE A LOOK (LP) 60
76 Island HELP 29 — LIVE (LP) 12

JAMO THOMAS & HIS PARTY BROTHERS ORCHESTRA
66 Polydor BM 56709 — I Spy (For The FBI)/Snake Hip Mama 10
69 Polydor 56755 — I Spy (For The FBI)/Snake Hip Mama (reissue) 6
69 Chess CRS 8098 — I'll Be Your Fool/Jamo Soul 12
71 Mojo 2092 013 — I Spy (For The FBI)/Snake Hip Mama (2nd reissue) 6

JIMMY THOMAS
69 Parlophone R 5773 — The Beautiful Night/Above A Whisper (withdrawn; demos more common, £70) . 120
69 Spark SRL 1035 — (We Ain't Looking For) No Trouble/Springtime 6
70 Spark SRL 1040 — White Dove/You Don't Have To Say Goodbye 6
72 Jay Boy BOY 67 — Where There's A Will/Just Tryin' To Please You 6
(see also Sweet Dreams)

KID THOMAS
70s JSP 4503 — Rockin' This Joint Tonight/Cozy Lounge Blues 5

KID THOMAS/EMANUEL BAND
64 '77' LA 12/26 — VICTORY WALK (LP, with Barry Martyn's Band) 30

LEON THOMAS
73 Philips 6369 417 — BLUES & SOULFUL TRUTH (LP) 15

NICKY THOMAS
70 Amalgamated AMG 863 — Danzella/JOE GIBBS ALLSTARS: Kingstonians Reggae 15
70 Trojan TR 7750 — Love Of The Common People/DESTROYERS: Compass 5
70 Trojan TR 7796 — God Bless The Children/Red Eye 5
71 Trojan TR 7807 — If I Had A Hammer/Lonely Feelin' 6
71 Trojan TR 7830 — Tell It Like It Is/B.B.C. 5
70 Trojan TBL 143 — LOVE OF THE COMMON PEOPLE (LP) 25
(see also Joe Gibbs)

PETER THOMAS SOUND ORCHESTRA
70 Polydor 2418 074 — CHARIOTS OF THE GODS (LP) 35

RAMBLIN' THOMAS
52 Tempo R 51 — Jug Head Blues/Hard Dallas Blues (78) 20
(see also Blind Blake, Blind Lemon Jefferson)

RUFUS THOMAS
63 London HLK 9799 — Walking The Dog/Fine And Mellow 25
64 London HLK 9850 — Can Your Monkey Do The Dog/I Want To Get Married 20
64 London HLK 9884 — Somebody Stole My Dog/I Want To Be Loved 20
64 Atlantic AT 4009 — Jump Back/All Night Worker 15
66 Atlantic 584 029 — Willy Nilly/Sho' Gonna Mess Him Up 10
67 Atlantic 584 089 — Jump Back/Walking The Dog 7
67 Stax 601 013 — Greasy Spoon/Sophisticated Sissy 8
68 Stax 601 028 — Down Ta My House/Steady Holding On 8
68 Stax 601 037 — The Memphis Train/I Think I Made A Boo-Boo 8

		MINT VALUE £
68 Stax STAX 105	Funky Mississippi/So Hard To Get Along With	6
71 Stax 2025 060	The Breakdown (Parts 1 & 2)	6
71 Stax 2025 080	Do The Funky Penguin (Parts 1 & 2)	6
64 Atlantic AET 6001	DO THE DOG (EP)	45
65 Atlantic AET 6011	JUMP BACK WITH RUFUS (EP)	50
64 London HA-K 8183	WALKING THE DOG (LP)	90
70 Stax SXATS 1033	FUNKY CHICKEN (LP)	30
71 Stax 2363 001	FUNKY CHICKEN (LP, reissue)	15
71 Stax 2362 010	DOING THE PUSH AND PULL LIVE AT P.J.'s (LP)	22
72 Stax 2362 028	DID YOU HEAR ME? (LP)	22
74 Stax STX 1004	CROWN PRINCE OF DANCE (LP)	20

TIMMY THOMAS

73 Mojo 2027 012	Why Can't We Live Together/Funky Me	7
77 T.K. XB 9052	The Magician/Don't Put It Down	5
73 Mojo 2956 002	WHY CAN'T WE LIVE TOGETHER (LP)	30

VAUGHAN THOMAS

70 Page One POF 167	Need You Girl/Come Together	6
70 Page One POF 178	Is This What I Get For Loving You/Since You've Been Mine	6
72 Jam JAL 101	VAUGHAN THOMAS (LP)	20

WAYNE THOMAS

67 Coral Q 72491	I've Never Known A Lady/My Life's Gonna Change	7

ANDREAS THOMOPOULOS

70 Mushroom 100 MR 1	SONGS OF THE STREET (LP)	45
71 Mushroom 150 MR 4	BORN OUT OF THE TEARS OF THE SUN (LP)	55

(see also Secondhand)

BARBARA THOMPSON

74 Explosion EX 2087	Single Girl/DANDY & COUNT PRINCE MILLER: Version	7

BOBBY THOMPSON

69 Columbia Blue Beat DB 113	That's How Strong My Love Is/Trouble In Town	10
69 Jolly JY 001	That's How Strong My Love Is/Trouble In The Town	6

(see also Dandy)

CHERYLE THOMPSON

64 Stateside SS 291	Teardrops/Black Night	12

CHRIS THOMPSON

73 Village Thing VTS 21	CHRIS THOMPSON (LP)	20

EDDIE THOMPSON

55 Jazz Today JTE 101	THE FABULOUS EDDIE THOMPSON (EP)	50
57 Nixa NJE 1030	PIANO MOODS VOLUME 6 (EP)	50
60 Ember EMB 3303	PIANO MOODS (LP)	100
60 Tempo TAP 24	HIS MASTER'S JAZZ (LP)	150
60s 77 LEU 12/39	BY MYSELF (LP)	40

ERIC THOMPSON

68 CBS EP 6398	THE MAGIC ROUNDABOUT NO. 1 (EP)	8
68 CBS EP 6399	THE MAGIC ROUNDABOUT NO. 2 (EP)	8

HANK THOMPSON (& BRAZOS VALLEY BOYS)

53 Capitol CL 13977	The Wild Side Of Life/Rub-A-Dub-Dub (78)	6
54 Capitol CL 14161	Honky-Tonk Girl/Wake-Up Irene (78)	6
56 Capitol CL 14517	Honey, Honey Bee Ball/Don't Take It Out On Me	15
56 Capitol CL 14517	Honey, Honey Bee Ball/Don't Take It Out On Me (78)	6
56 Capitol CL 14668	I'm Not Mad, Just Hurt/The Blackboard Of My Heart	15
58 Capitol CL 14869	Li'l Liza Jane/How Do You Hold A Memory	15
58 Capitol CL 14869	Li'l Liza Jane/How Do You Hold A Memory (78)	8
58 Capitol CL 14945	Gathering Flowers/Squaws Along The Yukon	8
58 Capitol CL 14961	I've Run Out Of Tomorrows/You're Going Back To Your Old Ways Again	7
59 Capitol CL 15014	Anybody's Girl/Total Strangers	6
59 Capitol CL 15074	I Guess I'm Getting Over You/I Didn't Mean To Fall In Love	6
60 Capitol CL 15114	A Six Pack To Go/What Made Her Change	25
60 Capitol CL 15156	She's Just A Whole Lot Like You/There My Future Goes (solo)	6
61 Capitol CL 15177	Will We Start It All Over Again/It Got To Be A Habit (solo)	6
62 Capitol CL 15247	The Wild Side Of Life (solo)/Give The World A Smile	6
76 Capitol CL 15877	Rockin' In The Congo/I Was The First One	5
56 Capitol EAP 1028	SONGS OF THE BRAZO VALLEY NO. 1 (EP)	18
57 Capitol EAP1-826	HANK (EP)	18
59 Capitol EAP1-1111	FAVOURITE WALTZES (EP)	15
57 Capitol T 729	HANK THOMPSON'S ALL-TIME HITS (LP)	25
58 Capitol T 975	DANCE RANCH (LP)	25
61 Capitol (S)T 1246	SONGS FOR ROUNDERS (LP)	20
61 Capitol (S)T 1469	THIS BROKEN HEART OF MINE (LP)	20
62 Capitol (S)T 1632	AT THE GOLDEN NUGGET (LP)	18
65 Capitol T 2089	GOLDEN COUNTRY HITS (LP)	18
66 Capitol T 2274	BREAKING IN ANOTHER HEART (LP)	15
68 Capitol T 2826	JUST AN OLD FLAME (LP)	15

JACKIE THOMPSON

69 Direction 58-4521	Bad Women A Dime A Dozen/Games People Play	6

JOHNNY THOMPSON & ONE-EYED JACKS

65 Ember EMB S 206	For Us There'll Be No Tomorrow/Soul Chant (some in p/s)	12/6

KAY THOMPSON

56 London HLA 8268	Eloise/Just One Of Those Things	40
56 London HLA 8268	Eloise/Just One Of Those Things (78)	10

MINT VALUE £

LINVAL THOMPSON
75 Faith FA 010 Girl You Got To Run/Run Come Feel . . . 10
75 Faith FA 018 Jah Redder Than Red/Version . . . 8

LUCKY THOMPSON
56 Vogue V 2388 But Not For Me/East Of The Sun . . . 12

MIKE THOMPSON Jnr.
67 Island WI 3090 Rocksteady Wedding/Flower Pot Bloomers (both with Lyn Taitt & Jets) . . . 25

MOLLIE THOMPSON
66 Asteroid JH 101 SONG NOTES SINGS FROM WORLDS AFAR (LP, private pressing) . . . 30

OWEN THOMPSON
72 Camel CA 103 Must I Be Blue/Version . . . 6

PETER THOMPSON & NTH DEGREE
65 Fontana TF 656 For Me It's All Over/The Way You Used To Do . . . 8

RICHARD THOMPSON
72 Island ILPS 9197 HENRY THE HUMAN FLY (LP, 'pink rim palm tree' label) . . . 12

RICHARD & LINDA THOMPSON
74 Island WIP 6186 I Want To See The Bright Lights Tonight/When I Get To The Border . . . 5
75 Island WIP 6220 Hokey Pokey/I'll Regret It All In The Morning . . . 5
73 Island ILPS 9266 I WANT TO SEE THE BRIGHT LIGHTS TONIGHT (LP) . . . 12
74 Island ILPS 9305 HOKEY POKEY (LP, 'palm tree' label with lyric insert) . . . 12
75 Island ILPS 9348 POUR DOWN LIKE SILVER (LP, 'palm tree' label with lyrics) . . . 12
75 Island OFFICIAL LIVE TOUR 1975 (LP, unreleased, test pressings may exist) . . . 100+
76 Island ICD 8 GUITAR/VOCAL (2-LP, gatefold sleeve) . . . 18
78 Chrysalis CHR 1177 FIRST LIGHT (LP) . . . 12
(see also Fairport Convention, Richard Thompson, Sandy Denny, Marc Ellington, Nick Drake, Bunch, Gary Farr, Paul McNeill & Linda Peters)

ROY THOMPSON
67 Columbia DB 8108 Sookie Sookie/Love You Say . . . 12

SIR CHARLES THOMPSON
53 Vogue LDE 032 SIR CHARLES THOMPSON'S ALL STARS WITH CHARLIE PARKER (10" LP) . . . 20
56 Vanguard PPT 12011 AND HIS BAND FEATURING COLEMAN HAWKINS (10" LP) . . . 18

SONNY THOMPSON & HIS RHYTHM & BLUES BAND
52 Vogue V 2143 Real, Real Fine (Parts 1 & 2) (78) . . . 45
53 Esquire 10-320 House Full Of Blues/Creepin' (78) . . . 45
53 Esquire 10-339 Screamin' Boogie/The Fish (78) . . . 50
60 Starlite ST45 008 Screamin' Boogie/The Fish . . . 250
56 Parlophone GEP 8562 SONNY THOMPSON INSTRUMENTALS (EP, as Sonny Thompson Orchestra) . . . 60
(see also Claude Cloud & Thunderclaps, Swallows)

SUE THOMPSON
54 Mercury MB 3133 I'm Not That Kind Of Girl/I Long To Tell You (78) . . . 8
61 Polydor NH 66967 Sad Movies/Throwing Kisses . . . 15
62 Polydor NH 66973 Norman/Never Love Again . . . 15
62 Polydor NH 66976 Two Of A Kind/It Has To Be Me . . . 8
62 Polydor NH 66979 Have A Good Time/If The Boy Only Knew . . . 8
63 Polydor NH 66987 What's Wrong Bill/I Need A Harbour . . . 8
62 Fontana 267 244TF James (Hold The Ladder Steady)/My Hero . . . 12
63 Fontana 267 262TF Willie Can/Too Much In Love . . . 10
64 Hickory 45-1240 Big Daddy/I'd Like To Know You Better . . . 7
64 Hickory 45-1255 Bad Boy/Toys . . . 10
65 Hickory 45-1284 Paper Tiger/Mama Don't Cry At My Wedding . . . 10
65 Hickory 45-1328 It's Break Up Time/Afraid . . . 10
65 Hickory 45-1340 Just Kiss Me/Sweet Hunk Of Misery . . . 8
65 Hickory 45-1359 I'm Looking For A World/Walkin' My Baby . . . 7
65 Hickory 45-1381 What Should I Do/After The Heartache . . . 10
67 London HLE 10142 Ferris Wheel/Don't Forget To Cry . . . 6
65 Hickory LPE 1507 INTRODUCING KRIS JENSEN AND SUE THOMPSON (EP, 2 tracks each) . . . 20
64 Hickory LPM 102 PAPER TIGER (LP) . . . 30
(see also Kris Jensen)

SUE THOMPSON & BOB LUMAN
63 Polydor NH 66989 I Like Your Kind Of Love/Too Hot To Dance . . . 15
63 Hickory 45-1221 I Like Your Kind Of Love/Too Hot To Dance (reissue) . . . 7
(see also Bob Luman)

THOMPSON TWINS
80 Dirty Discs RANK 1 Squares And Triangles/Could Be He... Could Be You (p/s, different colours) . . . 10
80 Latent LATE 1 She's In Love With Mystery/Fast Food/Food Style (p/s) . . . 8
81 T TEE 1 The Perfect Game/Politics (p/s) . . . 5
84 Arista TWISD 3 Doctor Doctor/Nurse Shark (square-shaped picture disc) . . . 5
84 Arista TWIJP 14/24/34 You Take Me Up/Passion Planet (3 different interlocking shaped pic discs). . each 5
84 Arista TWISD 4 You Take Me Up/Passion Planet (planet-shaped picture disc) . . . 5
84 Arista TWISD 5 Sister Of Mercy/Out Of The Gap (rocket-shaped picture disc) . . . 5
84 Arista TWISD 6 Lay Your Hands On Me/The Lewis Carol (diamond-shaped picture disc) . . . 5
85 Arista TWIN 8 Roll Over/Fools Paradise (p/s, unreleased) . . . 50
85 Arista TWINS 128 Roll Over/Fools Paradise/Roll Over Again (12", p/s, unreleased) . . . 100
85 Arista TWISD 9 Don't Mess With Doctor Dream/Big Business (baby-shaped picture disc) . . . 5
87 Arista TWINCD 13 Long Goodbye (Extended)/Dancing In Your Shoes (7" Version)/Hold Me Now (Dance Mix) (CD, gatefold card sleeve with gauze inner) . . . 8
82 T TELP 2 SET (LP, with free 7": "Squares And Triangles"/TOM BAILEY: "Weather Station"/BLANKETS: "Modern Plumbing" [T RANK 2]) . . . 12
86 fan club LIVE (LP, signed fan club freebie) . . . 20

MINT VALUE £

BILLY THORBURN & HIS STRICT TEMPO MUSIC

56 Parlophone MSP 6227 Jimmy Unknown/Ooh Bang Jiggilly Jang 8
57 Parlophone R 4276 True Love/Singing The Blues 8

GUNILLA THORN

63 HMV POP 1239 Merry-Go-Round/Go On Then 85

TRACEY THORN

82 Cherry Red CHERRY 53 Plain Sailing/Goodbye Joe (p/s) 5
(see also Marine Girls, Everything But The Girl, Grab Grab The Haddock)

DAVID THORNE

62 Stateside SS 141 The Alley Cat Song/The Moon Was Yellow 7
63 Stateside SS 190 One More Fool, One More Broken Heart/Don't Let It Get Away 8
64 Stateside SE 1020 WHAT WILL I TELL MY HEART (EP) 22
63 Stateside SL 10036 THE ALLEY CAT SONGSTER (LP) 35

KEN THORNE ORCHESTRA

63 HMV POP 1176 "The Legion's Last Patrol" Film Theme/Kisses In The Night 5
68 United Artists ULP 1201 INSPECTOR CLOUSEAU (LP, soundtrack) 30
69 Stateside S(S)L 10271 THE TOUCHABLES (LP, with Nirvana, Wynder K. Frog, et al.) 45

WOODY THORNE

62 Vogue Pop V 9202 Sadie Lou/Teenagers In Love 440

CLAUDE THORNHILL & HIS ORCHESTRA

54 London HL 8042 Pussy-Footin'/Adios 50
54 London HL 8042 Pussy-Footin'/Adios (78) 10
54 London RE-P 1009 CLAUDE THORNHILL GOES MODERN (EP) 20
54 London H-ABP 1019 CLAUDE THORNHILL GOES MODERN (10" LP) 25
54 London H-ABP 1021 DREAM MUSIC (10" LP) 25

EDDIE THORNTON OUTFIT

69 Instant IN 003 Baby Be My Gal/SONNY BURKE OUTFIT: All You 12

WILLIE MAE 'BIG MAMA' THORNTON

54 Vogue V 2284 Hound Dog/Mischievous Boogie (78) (as Willie Mae 'Big Mama' Thornton) 120
65 Sue WI 345 Tom Cat/Monkey In The Barn (as Willie Mae Thornton) 250
69 Mercury SMCL 20176 STRONGER THAN DIRT (LP) 40
78 Vanguard VPC 40001 MAMA'S PRIDE (LP) 22

GEORGE THOROGOOD & DESTROYERS

79 Sonet SON 2183 SO MUCH TROUBLE (EP) 5
77 Sonet SNTF 760 GEORGE THOROGOOD AND THE DESTROYERS (LP) 12

BILLY THORPE & AZTECS

65 Parlophone R 5381 Twilight Time/Over The Rainbow 7

THOR'S HAMMER

66 Parlophone DP 565 Once/A Memory (export issue) 140
66 Parlophone DP 567 If You Knew/Love Enough (export issue) 175
66 Parlophone CGEP 62 THOR'S HAMMER (EP, export issue, gatefold p/s, with bonus 45 "If You Knew"/"Love Enough" [CGEP 62]) 900

LINDA THORSON

68 Ember EMB S 257 Here I Am/Better Than Losing You (p/s) 45/30

THOSE HELICOPTERS

80 State Of The Art STATE 1 Shark/Eskimo (p/s) 25
81 Lavender LAVENDER 001 Dr. Janov/Technical Smack (p/s) 20

THOSE NAUGHTY LUMPS

79 Zoo CAGE 002 Iggy Pop's Jacket/Pure And Innocent (foldout p/s) 8
80 Open Eye OP-EP 1002 DOWN AT THE ZOO (EP) 8

THOUGHTS

66 Planet PLF 118 All Night Stand/Memory Of Your Love 80
(see also Tiffany [& Thoughts], Paul Dean & Soul Savages)

THOUGHTS & WORDS

69 Liberty LBF 15187 Morning Sky/Give Me A Reason 7
69 Liberty LBL 83224 THOUGHTS & WORDS (LP) 15

THOUGHTS OF DES COX

69 Morgan MR 4S Isn't It Nice/It's All Very Strange 6

THRASHER WONDERS

50s Melodisc MEL 1106 Charity/GOSPEL KEYS: Motherless Child (78) 6
50s Melodisc MEL 1190 Blind Old Barnabas/Jesus I Love You (78) 6

THREADBARE CONSORT

80s private pressing WEARING THIN (LP) 15

THREADS

86 Unicorn PHZ 2 Step Back/UNDERGROUND ARROWS: Backbeat Of Life (p/s) 10

THREADS OF LIFE

72 Alco ALC 530 THREADS OF LIFE (LP, actually by Alco) 400

THREATS

82 Rondelet ROUND 22 GO TO HELL (EP) 6
82 Rondelet ROUND 29 Politicians & Ministers/Writing's On The Wall/Deep End Depression (p/s) 5
82 Rondelet ROUND 1229 POLITICIANS & MINISTERS (12" EP) 8

THREE BARRY SISTERS

59 Decca F 11099 Little Boy Blue/My Sweetie's Coming To Call 10
59 Decca F 11099 Little Boy Blue/My Sweetie's Coming To Call (78) 6
59 Decca F 11118 Tall Paul/Till Then 15

59	Decca F 11118	Tall Paul/Till Then (78)	8
59	Decca F 11141	Jo Jo — The Dog Faced Boy/I-Aye Ove-Lay Oo-Yay	12
59	Decca F 11141	Jo Jo — The Dog Faced Boy/I-Aye Ove-Lay Oo-Yay (78)	8
60	Decca F 11201	Spoilsport/Bonnie Prince Charlie	8
60	Decca F 11201	Spoilsport/Bonnie Prince Charlie (78)	12

(see also Barry Sisters)

THREE BELLS

60	Pye 7N 15252	Steady Date/In Between (Wishing I Was Sweet Sixteen)	7
64	Columbia DB 7399	Softly In The Night/He Doesn't Love Me	10
65	Columbia DB 7570	Someone To Love/Over And Over Again	7
66	Columbia DB 7980	Cry No More/He Doesn't Want You	7

(see also Satin Bells)

THREE CAPS

66	Atlantic 584 043	I Got To Handle It/Zig-Zagging	10
69	Atlantic 584 251	Cool Jerk/Hello Stranger	10
71	Atlantic 2091 105	Cool Jerk/Hello Stranger (reissue)	6
66	Atlantic 587/588 019	DANCE THE COOL JERK (LP)	35

(see also Capitols)

THREE CHUCKLES

55	HMV 7M 292	Runaround/At Last You Understand	40
55	HMV B 10835	Runaround/At Last You Understand (78)	30
56	HMV 7M 333	Still Thinking Of You/Times Two I Love You	35
56	HMV POP 123	Still Thinking Of You/Times Two I Love You (78)	35
57	HMV POP 292	We're Gonna Rock Tonight/Want You Give Me A Chance	125
57	HMV POP 292	We're Gonna Rock Tonight/Want You Give Me A Chance (78)	50

(see also Teddy Randazzo)

THREE CITY FOUR

65	Decca LK 4705	THREE CITY FOUR (LP)	130
67	CBS 63039	SMOKE AND DUST WHERE THE HEART SHOULD HAVE BEEN (LP)	80

(see also Martin Carthy, Leon Rosselson)

THREE COINS

70	Sugar SU 106	Come And Do The Right Thing/It's So Long	6

3 COLOURS RED

96	Fierce Panda NING 17	This Is My Hollywood	6
99	Creation CRE 313	This Is My Time/Paranoid People (Demo) (numbered p/s, mail-order only)	6

THREE DEGREES

65	Stateside SS 413	Gee Baby I'm Sorry/Do What You're Supposed To Do	25
65	Stateside SS 459	Close Your Eyes/Gotta Draw The Line	50
71	Mojo 2092 001	Maybe/There's So Much Love Around Me	6
71	Mojo 2092 002	You're The One/Rose Garden	6
71	Mojo 2092 009	There's So Much Love Around Me/Maybe (reissue)	6
71	Mojo 2092 009	There's So Much Love Around Me/Yours (different B-side)	6
75	Pye International 7N 25671	Sugar On Sunday/Maybe	6
71	Mojo 2916 002	THE THREE DEGREES (LP)	30

THREE DOG NIGHT

69	Stateside-Dunhill SS 8008	Nobody/It's For You	6
70	Stateside-Dunhill SS 8052	Mama Told Me Not To Come/Rock And Roll Widow	7
69	Stateside-Dun. (S)SL 5006	THREE DOG NIGHT (LP)	18
69	Stateside-Dun. (S)SL 5013	SUITABLE FOR FRAMING (LP)	15
70	Stateside-Dunhill SSL 5023	CAPTURED LIVE AT THE FORUM (LP)	12
70	Probe SPBA 6251	IT AIN'T EASY (LP)	12

(see also Danny Hutton)

THREE DOLLS

57	MGM MGM 958	The Living End/The Octopus Song	10

THREE GOOD REASONS

65	Mercury MF 883	Build Your Love/Don't Leave Me Now	8
65	Mercury MF 899	Nowhere Man/Wire Wheels	12
65	Mercury MF 929	The Moment Of Truth/Funny Kind Of Loving	7

THREE JOHNS

82	CNT CNT 003	English White Boy Engineer/Secret Agent (p/s)	8
83	CNT CNT 011	Pink Headed Bug/Lucy In The Rain (p/s)	7
83	CNT CNT 013	Men Like Monkeys/Two Minute Ape!/Windolene/ Marx's Wife/Paris 1941 (12", p/s)	8

THREE KAYES (SISTERS)

56	HMV 7M 401	Ivory Tower/Mister Cuckoo (Sing Your Song)	35
56	HMV POP 251	Lay Down Your Arms/First Row Balcony (as Three Kaye Sisters)	25

(see also Kaye Sisters, Frankie Vaughan)

THREE MAN ARMY

72	Pegasus PGS 1	What's Your Name/Travellin'	6
74	Reprise K 14292	Polecat Woman/Take Me Down From The Mountain	5
71	Pegasus PEG 3	A THIRD OF A LIFETIME (LP)	35
73	Reprise K 44254	THREE MAN ARMY (LP)	25
74	Reprise K 54015	THREE MAN ARMY TWO (LP)	25

(see also Gun, Baker Gurvitz Army, Andy Newman)

THREE PEOPLE

66	Decca F 12473	Have You Ever Been There/Good Times	6
66	Decca F 12514	Suspicions/Easy Man To Find	6
67	Decca F 12581	Got To Find A Reason/Simple Thing Would Be For You To Start Loving Me	6

(see also John Bromley)

MINT VALUE £

THREE PIECES

75	Fantasy FTC 116	I Need You Girl/Short'nin' Bread	7

THREE PROFESSORS

56	Columbia DB 3845	Yew Stept Owt Offa Dreme/Vulgar Boatman Rock	7
56	Columbia DB 3845	Yew Stept Owt Offa Dreme/Vulgar Boatman Rock (78)	6

THREE QUARTERS

65	Columbia DB 7467	People Will Talk/Love Come A-Tricklin' Down	15
65	Columbia DB 7576	The Pleasure Girls/Little People	6

THREE'S A CROWD

66	Fontana TF 673	Look Around The Corner/Living In A Dream	15

(see also Embers, Writing On The Wall)

THREE SUNS

55	HMV 7M 297	Perdido/For You	7
55	HMV 7M 346	Cha Cha Joe/Arriverderci Darling (Arriverderci Roma)	7

THREE TOPS

67	Doctor Bird DB 1101	Miserable Friday/This World Has A Feeling	20
67	Studio One SO 2023	Moving To Progress/Love And Inspiration	22
67	Trojan TR 003	It's Raining/Sound Of Music	18
67	Treasure Isle TI 7008	Do It Right/You Should Have Known	20
68	Coxsone CS 7033	A Man Of Chances/HORTENSE ELLIS: A Groovy Kind Of Love	35
68	Coxsone CS 7051	Great Train In '68/You Should Have Known	20
73	Bullet BU 527	Take Time Out/Just Like A Log	10

(see also Dion Cameron & Three Tops, Sir Lord Comic, King Rocky)

THREE WISE MEN

83	Virgin VS 642	Thanks For Christmas/Countdown To Christmas Partytime (p/s)	10

(see also XTC)

THRILLERS

68	Blue Cat BS 128	The Last Dance/DELTA CATS: Unworthy Baby	15

(see also Phil Pratt)

PERCY 'THRILLS' THRILLINGTON

77	Regal Zono. EMI 2594	Uncle Albert — Admiral Halsey/Eat At Home	100
77	Regal Zono. EMC 3175	THRILLINGTON (LP, with inner sleeve)	150
77	Regal Zono. TC-EMC 3175	THRILLINGTON (cassette)	40

(see also Paul McCartney)

THRILLS

66	Capitol CL 15469	No One/What Can Go Wrong	50
79	Grapevine GRP 126	Show The World Where It's At/What Can Go Wrong	8

THRILLS

02	Virgin 5468857	Santa Cruz (You're Not That Fat)/Deckchairs And Cigarettes (p/s, white vinyl)	20
02	Virgin VSCDT 1842	Santa Cruz (You're Not That Fat)/Deckchairs And Cigarettes/Your Love is Like Las Vegas/Plans (CD)	25
03	Virgin VS 1862	Santa Cruz/Don't Play It Cool (p/s, purple vinyl)	5
00s	Virgin Virgin VS 1842	One Horse Town/Don't Play It Cool (yellow vinyl, p/s)	10
00s	Virgin VSCDT 1845	One Horse Town/Car Crash/Don't Play It Cool (CD)	8
00s	Virgin VS 1852	Big Sur/Your Love Is Like Las Vegas (blue vinyl, p/s)	8
00s	Virgin VSDJ 1855	Last Night I Dreamt That Somebody Loved Me (1-sided gig issue, p/s, 500 only)	45
00s	Virgin VS 1862	Santa Cruz/Don't Play It Cool (Original Version) (reissue, plum vinyl, p/s)	5
00s	Virgin VSCDX 1864	Don't Steal Our Sun/The One I Love (green vinyl, p/s)	5
03	Virgin V 2974	SO MUCH FOR THE CITY (LP)	12

THROBBING GRISTLE

78	Industrial IR 0003	United/Zyklon B Zombie (p/s)	10
78	Industrial IR 0003/U	United/Zyklon B Zombie (p/s, white or clear vinyl, 1,000 only of each)	20
80	Industrial IR 0003	United/Zyklon B Zombie (longer version) (p/s, reissue, 'Memorial Issue' scratched in matrix)	12
80	Industrial IR 0013	Subhuman/Something Came Over Me (in polythene camouflage bag)	15
80	Industrial IR 0015	Adrenalin/Distant Dreams (Part Two) (in polythene camouflage bag)	15
81	Fetish FET 006	Discipline (live, Berlin)/Discipline (live, Manchester) (12", p/s)	25
76	Industrial IR 0001	BEST OF VOLUME II (private cassette, 50 copies only)	50+
77	Industrial IR 0002	SECOND ANNUAL REPORT (LP, 785 only, white heavy duty sleeve, with questionnaire, xerox strip & 2 stickers)	90
78	Industrial IR 0004	D.O.A. THE THIRD AND FINAL REPORT (LP, 1st 1,000 with calendar & postcard)	30/15
78	Fetish FET 2001	SECOND ANNUAL REPORT (LP, 2,000 only, T.G. 'lightning flash' sleeve, with questionnaire & insert)	25
79	Fetish FET 2001	SECOND ANNUAL REPORT (LP, reissue, glossy sleeve with inserts)	15
79	Industrial IR 0004	D.O.A. THE THIRD AND FINAL REPORT (LP, re-pressing, 1,000 only, banded as 16 equal length tracks)	20
79	Industrial IR 0008	20 JAZZ FUNK GREATS (LP, 5,000 only, 1st 2,000 with b&w poster)	30/15
80	Industrial IR 0009	HEATHEN EARTH (LP, gatefold sleeve, 785 on blue vinyl)	80/18
81	Fetish FET 2001	SECOND ANNUAL REPORT (LP, backwards version, 1st 2,000 in T.G. 'flash' sleeve, later in black & white sleeve)	25/15
81	Fetish FX 1	A BOXED SET (5-LP box set with 28-page booklet & badge, 5,000 only)	125
82	Death 01	MUSIC FROM THE DEATH FACTORY, MAY '79 (LP, 50 only)	250+
82	Power Focus 001	ASSUME POWER FOCUS (LP, 500 only, numbered)	60
82	T.G. 33033	LIVE AT THE DEATH FACTORY, MAY '79 (LP, reissue picture disc, 1,355 only)	40
82	Walter Ulbricht 001	JOURNEY THROUGH THE BODY (LP, 1,000 only)	30
82	Karnage/Illuminated KILL 1	THEE PSYCHICK SACRIFICE (2-LP)	25
84	Illuminated JAMS 35	IN THE SHADOW OF THE SUN (LP, soundtrack)	18
84	Illuminated JAMS 39	THE INDUSTRIAL RECORDS STORY 1976-1981 (LP)	30

84 Casual Abandon CAS 1J — ONCE UPON A TIME (LP) . . . 25
84 Mental Decay 01-1 — SPECIAL TREATMENT (LP) . . . 25
80s Sprut 001 — VERY FRIENDLY — THE FIRST ANNUAL REPORT OF T.G. (LP) . . . 25
80s Industrial IRC 1-IRC 24 — 24 HOURS (box set of cassettes with total of 24 hours playing time; every set is unique) . . . 150-200
(see also Psychic TV, Coil, Sabres Of Paradise)

THROWING MUSES
89 4AD BADD 903 — Dizzy/Santa Claus/Mania (live)/Downtown (live) (10", gatefold p/s) . . . 10
93 4AD CADD 2013 — RED HEAVEN (LP, with free live Kristin Hersh LP) . . . 15
93 4AD CADD 2013CD — RED HEAVEN (CD, with free live Kristin Hersh CD) . . . 20
(see also Belly, Kristin Hersh)

THUNDER
89 EMI EMS 11 — She's So Fine/Girl's Going Out Of Her Head (p/s, some with free patch) . . . 8/5
89 EMI 12EMP 11 — She's So Fine/Girl's Going Out Of Her Head/Another Shot Of Love (12", p/s with poster) . . . 8
89 EMI CDEM 1 — She's So Fine/Girl's Going Out Of Her Head/Another Shot Of Love (CD) . . . 8
90 EMI EMG 126 — Dirty Love/Fired Up (gatefold booklet p/s) . . . 5
90 EMI EMPD 126 — Dirty Love/Fired Up (logo-shaped picture disc with insert in PVC sleeve) . . . 10
90 EMI EMPD 126 — Dirty Love/Fired Up (uncut picture disc with insert in PVC sleeve) . . . 35
90 EMI 12EM 126 — Dirty Love/Fired Up/She's So Fine (live) (12", p/s with poster) . . . 8
90 EMI CDEM 126 — Dirty Love/Fired Up/She's So Fine (live)/Brown Sugar (live) (CD) . . . 8
90 EMI EMS 137 — Back Street Symphony/No Way Out Of The Wilderness (box set with postcards, some also with badge) . . . 12/10
90 EMI 12 EMPD 137 — Back Street Symphony/No Way Out Of The Wilderness/An Englishman On Holiday (live) (12", picture disc with insert in PVC sleeve) . . . 8
90 EMI 10EM 148 — Gimme Some Lovin'/I Wanna Be Her Slave (10", red vinyl with gatefold booklet) . 12
90 EMI 10EM 158 — She's So Fine (Full Length Version)/Backstreet Symphony (Live At Donington '90)/I Can Still Hear The Music (10", blue vinyl, gatefold p/s) . . . 8
90 EMI 12EM 158 — She's So Fine/Don't Wait For Me (Live At Donington '90)/ I Can Still Hear The Music (12", p/s with poster) . . . 8
90 EMI CDEM 158 — She's So Fine/Don't Wait For Me (Live At Donington '90)/ I Can Still Hear The Music (CD) . . . 10
91 EMI 10EM 175 — Love Walked In/Flawed To Perfection (Demo)/World Problems: A Solution (10", p/s, white vinyl) . . . 7
91 EMI CDEMPD 175 — Love Walked In (LP Version)/Flawed To Perfection (Demo)/ Until My Dying Day (live) (CD picture disc) . . . 15
94 EMI EMPD 365 — Stand Up/Interview (picture disc, in 12" PVC sleeve with calendar poster) . . . 5
90s THUNDER 1 — She's So Fine/Until My Dying Day/Fired Up (flexidisc with *Raw* magazine) . . . 5
90s BENDER 1 — Fired Up (live) (flexidisc free with *Kerrang!* magazine) . . . 5
90 EMI PDEMC 3570 — BACK STREET SYMPHONY (LP, picture disc) . . . 15
(see also Terraplane, Nuthin' Fancy)

JOHNNY THUNDER
63 Stateside SS 149 — Loop De Loop/Don't Be Ashamed . . . 10
63 Stateside SS 168 — Rock-A-Bye My Darling/The Rosy Dance . . . 8
63 Stateside SS 200 — Jailer, Bring Me Water/Outlaw . . . 12
63 Stateside SS 229 — Hey Child/Everybody Likes To Dance With Johnny . . . 12
64 Stateside SS 337 — More, More, More Love, Love, Love/Shout It To The World . . . 10
65 Stateside SS 370 — Send Her To Me/Everybody Likes To Dance With Johnny . . . 8
65 Stateside SS 454 — Dear John I'm Going To Leave You/Suzie-Q . . . 10
65 Stateside SS 476 — Everybody Do The Sloopy/Beautiful . . . 10
66 Stateside SS 499 — My Prayer/A Broken Heart . . . 8
63 Stateside SL 10029 — LOOP DE LOOP (LP) . . . 75

JOHNNY THUNDER & RUBY WINTERS
67 Stateside SS 2005 — Make Love To Me/Teach Me Tonight . . . 15

MARGO THUNDER
75 Capitol CL 15808 — Expressway To Your Heart/Hush Up Your Mouth . . . 5

THUNDERBIRDS
66 Polydor 56710 — Your Ma Said You Cried (In Your Sleep Last Night)/Before It's Too Late . . . 55
(see also Chris Farlowe & Thunderbirds)

THUNDERBIRDS (Australia)
61 Oriole CB 1610 — Wild Weekend/Rat Race . . . 20
61 Oriole CB 1625 — New Orleans Beat/Delilah Jones . . . 20

THUNDERBIRDS (T.V.)
(see under Barry Gray)

THUNDERBIRDS (U.S.)
55 London HL 8146 — Ayuh, Ayuh/Blueberries . . . 100
55 London HL 8146 — Ayuh, Ayuh/Blueberries (78) . . . 25
(see also Bert Convy & Thunderbirds, Midnighters)

THUNDERBOLTS
62 Decca F 11522 — Fugitive/Feelin' In A Mood . . . 15

THUNDERBOYS
80 Recent EJSP 9339 — Fashion/Someone Like You (p/s) . . . 40

THUNDERCLAP NEWMAN
69 Track 604 031 — Something In The Air/Wilhelmina . . . 5
70 Track 2094 001 — Accidents/I See It All . . . 5
70 Track 2094 002 — Wild Country/Hollywood . . . 5
70 Track 2094 003 — The Reason/Stormy Petrel . . . 5
79 Track 2095 002 — Wild Country/Hollywood (reissue, p/s) . . . 8
70 Track 2406 003 — HOLLYWOOD DREAM (LP) . . . 25
(see also Stone The Crows, One In A Million, Paul McCartney & Wings, Speedy Keen, Andy Newman)

MINT VALUE £

THUNDER COMPANY

70 Columbia DB 8706 Ridin' On The Gravy Train (5.03)/Bubble Drum ... 35
70 Columbia DB 8706 Ridin' On The Gravy Train (2.35 Edit)/Bubble Drum (demo only) ... 45
(see also Brian Bennett, Shadows)

THUNDERMUG

73 London HLZ 10411 Africa/Will They Ever ... 6
72 Axe AXS 502 STRIKES (LP) ... 15

JOHNNY THUNDERS (& THE HEARTBREAKERS)

78 Real ARE 1 Dead Or Alive/Downtown (p/s) ... 15
78 Real ARE 3 You Can't Put Your Arms Around A Memory (Edit)/Hurtin' (p/s) ... 12
78 Real ARE 3T You Can't Put Your Arms Around A Memory/Hurtin' (12", p/s, blue or pink vinyl, die-cut company sleeve) ... 12
83 Jungle JUNG 5 VINTAGE '77 (12" EP) ... 12
84 Jungle JUNG 14P Get Off The Phone/All By Myself (picture disc) ... 10
84 Jungle JUNG 14T GET OFF THE PHONE EP (12") ... 8
85 Jungle JUNG 18T CHINESE ROCKS (12" EP) ... 8
85 Jungle JUNG 23P Crawfish/Tie Me Up (with Patti Palladin, picture disc) ... 8
87 Jungle JUNG 33T QUE SERA SERA (12" EP) ... 8
77 Real RAL 1 SO ALONE (LP, with inner sleeve) ... 12
(see also New York Dolls, Heartbreakers)

THUNDERSTICK

83 Thunderbolt THBE 1002 FEEL LIKE ROCK'N'ROLL (12" EP, p/s, some with patch) ... 12/8
83 Thunderbolt THBL 008 BEAUTY AND THE BEASTS (LP) ... 12
(see also Samson, Gillan)

THUNDERTHIGHS

74 Philips 6006 386 Central Park Arrest/Sally Wants A Dress (p/s) ... 10

THUNDERTRAIN

77 Jelly JPLP 1 TEENAGE SUICIDE (LP) ... 12

THURSDAY'S CHILDREN

66 Piccadilly 7N 35276 Just You/You Don't Believe Me ... 18
66 Piccadilly 7N 35306 Crawfish/Come Softly To Me ... 10
(see also Phil Cordell)

THYRDS

64 Oak RGJ 133 Hide 'N' Seek/I've Got My Mojo Working ... 245
64 Decca F 12010 Hide 'N' Seek/No Time Like The Present ... 55

TIARAS

63 Warner Bros WB 92 You Told Me/I'm Gonna Forget You ... 15

TIBET & STAPLETON

96 United Dairies UDOR 1 MUSICALISCHE KÜRBS HÜTTE (LP, clear vinyl, with insert) ... 25
(see also Current 93, Steven Stapleton & David Tibet)

TICH & QUACKERS

65 Oriole CB 1980 Santa Bring Me Ringo/Santa's Got Such A Terrible Cold ... 8

TICKAWINDA

75 Pennine PSS 153 ROSEMARY LANE (LP) ... 300

KATHRYN TICKELL

84 Saydisc SDL 343 ON KIELDER SIDE (LP) ... 12

TICKETS

79 Bridgehouse BHS 3 I'll Be Your Pin Up/Guess I Have To Sit Alone (p/s) ... 6
(see also Wasted Youth)

TICKLE

67 Regal Zonophone RZ 3004 Subway (Smokey Pokey World)/Good Evening ... 280
(see also Junior's Eyes, Outsider, Bunch Of Fives)

TICKLERS

52 Melodisc MEL 1214 Don't Fence Her In/Glamour Gal (78) ... 12
53 Motta's 13 Four Days Love/Healing In The Balm Yard (78) ... 7

TIDAL WAVE

69 Decca F 22973 With Tears In My Eyes/We Wanna Know ... 10
69 Storm PD 9616 Spider Spider/Crazy Horse ... 50

TIDBITS

71 Fly BUG 12 Jean Harlow/Vietnam/Six O'Clock Blues ... 6

PETER TIERNEY & NIGHTHAWKS

65 Fontana TF 547 Oh How I Need You/That's Too Bad ... 7

ROY TIERNEY

61 Philips BF 1159 Cupid/The Lonely One (some in p/s) ... 15/7
61 Philips BF 1194 Just Out Of Reach (Of My Two Empty Arms)/Casanova ... 8

TIERNEY'S FUGITIVES

65 Decca F 12247 Did You Want To Run Away?/Morning Mist ... 18

TIFFANIES

67 Chess CRS 8059 It's Got To Be A Great Song/He's Good For Me ... 55

TIFFANY (with THOUGHTS)

65 Parlophone R 5311 I Know/Am I Dreaming ... 12
66 Parlophone R 5439 Find Out What's Happening/Baby Don't Look Down (as Tiffany with Thoughts) ... 35
(see also Thoughts)

TIFFANY SHADE

68 Fontana (S)TL 5469 TIFFANY SHADE (LP) ... 50

MINT VALUE £

JIMMY & LOUISE TIG
69 Deep Soul DS 9105 — A Love That Never Grows Cold/Who Can I Turn To — 40

TIGER
75 United Artists UP 35848 — I Am An Animal/Stop That Machine — 5
76 Retreat RTL 6006 — TIGER (LP, with inner sleeve) — 12
(see also Hackensack, Samson, Brinsley Schwarz, Big Jim Sullivan)

TIGER (Jamaica)
70 New Beat NB 052 — Soul Of Africa/Dallas Texas — 6
70 New Beat NB 064 — Musical Scorcher/Three Dogs Night — 6
71 Camel CA 70 — Guilty/United We Stand — 7
71 New Beat NB 075 — African Beat/Black Man Land — 6
71 New Beat NB 088 — Have You Ever Been Hurt/Our Day Will Come — 6
(see also Clancy Eccles)

TIGER LILY
75 Gull GULS 12 — Monkey Jive/Ain't Misbehavin' — 8
77 Gull GULS 54 — Monkey Jive/Ain't Misbehavin' (reissue, p/s) — 15/5
80 Dead Good DEAD 11 — Monkey Jive/Ain't Misbehavin' (2nd reissue, different p/s) — 6
(see also Ultravox)

TIGERMOTH
84 Rogue FMSL 2006 — TIGERMOTH (LP) — 15

TIGERS
69 Polydor 56339 — Rain Falls On The Lonely/Smile For Me — 8

TIGERS
80s Strike KIK 1 — Kidding Stops/Big Expense, Small Income (p/s) — 8

TIGHT LIKE THAT
72 Village Thing VTS 12 — HOKUM (LP) — 22

TIGHTS
78 Cherry Red CHERRY 1 — Bad Hearts/It/Cracked (p/s) — 20
78 Cherry Red CHERRY 2 — Howard Hughes/China's Eternal (p/s) — 8
78 Ch. Red CSP-CHERRY 2 — Howard Hughes/China's Eternal (cassette) — 6

TIKKI, TAKI, SUZI, LIES
70 UPC UPC 102 — Welcome To My House/I Believe In Love — 5
70 UPC UPC 109 — Ba-Da-Da-Dum/Dream Stealer — 6

TILLER BOYS
79 New Hormones ORG 3 — Big Noise From The Jungle/Slaves And Pyramids/What Me Worry? (p/s) — 6
(see also Buzzcocks, Pete Shelley, Eric Random)

TILLERMEN
71 Duke DU 109 — Be Loving To Me/Judgement Rock — 7
(see also Greyhound)

MEL TILLIS
67 London HLR 10141 — Life Turned Her That Way/If I Could Only Start Over — 7
68 London HA-R 8345 — MR. MEL (LP) — 22

BERTHA TILLMAN
62 Oriole CB 1746 — Oh, My Angel/Lovin' Time — 60

JOHNNY TILLOTSON
59 London HLA 8930 — True True Happiness/Love Is Blind — 60
59 London HLA 8930 — True True Happiness/Love Is Blind (78) — 60
60 London HLA 9048 — Why Do I Love You So/Never Let Me Go — 40
60 London HLA 9101 — Earth Angel/Pledging My Love — 40
60 London HLA 9231 — Poetry In Motion/Princess, Princess — 7
61 London HLA 9275 — Jimmy's Girl/His True Love Said Goodbye — 8
61 London HLA 9412 — Without You/Cutie Pie — 15
62 London HLA 9514 — Dreamy Eyes/Much Beyond Compare — 7
62 London HLA 9550 — It Keeps Right On A-Hurtin'/She Gave Sweet Love To Me — 10
62 London HLA 9598 — Send Me The Pillow You Dream On/What'll I Do — 8
62 London HLA 9642 — I Can't Help It/I'm So Lonesome I Could Cry — 8
63 London HLA 9695 — Out Of My Mind/Judy, Judy, Judy — 10
63 London HLA 9811 — Funny How Time Slips Away/A Very Good Year For Girls — 7
63 MGM MGM 1214 — Talk Back Trembling Lips/Another You — 12
63 MGM MGM 1225 — Worried Guy/Please Don't Go Away — 7
63 MGM MGM 1235 — I'm Watching My Watch/I Rise, I Fall — 7
64 MGM MGM 1247 — Suffering From A Heartache/Worry — 7
64 MGM MGM 1252 — She Understands Me/Tomorrow — 10
64 MGM MGM 1266 — Angel/Little Boy — 8
65 MGM MGM 1275 — Then I'll Count Again/One's Yours, One's Mine — 7
65 MGM MGM 1281 — Heartaches By The Number/Your Memory Comes Along — 7
65 MGM MGM 1290 — Our World/My Gidget — 8
66 MGM MGM 1300 — Hello Enemy/I Never Loved You Anyway — 7
66 MGM MGM 1311 — Me Myself And I/Country Boy, Country Boy — 7
66 MGM MGM 1319 — No Love At All/What Am I Gonna Do — 7
68 MGM MGM 1393 — Cabaret/If I Were A Rich Man — 7
69 London HLU 10281 — Tears On My Pillow/Remember When — 6
62 London RE-A 1345 — JOHNNY TILLOTSON (EP) — 40
63 London RE-A 1388 — J.T. (EP) — 50
63 MGM MGM-EP 788 — JOHNNY TILLOTSON (EP) — 35
64 MGM MGM-EP 790 — JOHNNY TILLOTSON'S HIT PARADE (EP) — 35
61 London HA-A 2431 — JOHNNY TILLOTSON'S BEST (LP) — 100

MINT VALUE £

62 London HA-A 8019 IT KEEPS RIGHT ON A-HURTIN' (LP) . . . 70
64 MGM MGM-C 972 ALONE WITH YOU (LP) . . . 30
65 MGM C/CS 1002 SHE UNDERSTANDS ME (LP) . . . 30
65 MGM MGM-C(S) 8005 JOHNNY TILLOTSON SINGS OUR WORLD (LP) . . . 25
66 MGM MGM-C(S) 8025 NO LOVE AT ALL (LP) . . . 25

TILSLEY ORCHESTRA

66 Fontana TF 783 "Thunderbirds" Theme/Theme From "The Power Game" . . . 20
67 Polydor 56150 Mr. Aitch Theme/Cotton Reed . . . 8
67 Fontana (S)TL 5411 TOP T.V. THEMES (LP) . . . 25
69 Fontana SFL 13139 TOP T.V. THEMES (LP, reissue) . . . 12
(see also Electric Banana)

STEVE TILSTON

71 Village Thing VTS 5 AN ACOUSTIC CONFUSION (LP) . . . 22
72 Transatlantic TRA 252 COLLECTION (LP, gatefold sleeve) . . . 12
77 Cornucopia CR 1 SONGS FROM THE DRESS REHEARSAL (LP, with Rupert Hine/John Renbourn) . 20
83 TM PROP 4 IN FOR A PENNY IN FOR A POUND (LP, with Peter Bardens) . . . 12

TIMBER

71 Elektra K 12022 Bring America Home/Splinters From Timber . . . 6
72 Elektra K 12042 Outlaw/Song For Two Signs . . . 6
71 Elektra K 42093 BRING AMERICA HOME (LP) . . . 15

TIME

65 Pye 7N 17019 Take A Bit Of Notice/Every Now And Then . . . 50
66 Pye 7N 17146 The First Time I Saw The Sunshine/Annabel . . . 20

TIME

75 B.U.K. BULP 2005 TIME (LP) . . . 45
(see also Spontaneous Combustion)

T.I.M.E. (Trust In Men Everywhere)

69 Liberty LBF 15082 Take Me Along/Make It Alright . . . 10
69 Liberty LBL/LBS 83232 SMOOTH BALL (LP) . . . 80

TIMEBOX

67 Piccadilly 7N 35369 I'll Always Love You/Save Your Love . . . 40
67 Piccadilly 7N 35379 Soul Sauce/I Wish I Could Jerk Like My Uncle Cyril . . . 35
67 Deram DM 153 Walking Through The Streets Of My Mind/Don't Make Promises . . . 25
68 Deram DM 194 Beggin'/A Woman That's Waiting . . . 22
68 Deram DM 219 Girl Don't Make Me Wait/Gone Is The Sad Man . . . 25
69 Deram DM 246 Baked Jam Roll In Your Eye/Poor Little Heartbreaker . . . 20
69 Deram DM 271 Yellow Van/You've Got The Chance . . . 18
(see also Bo Street Runners, [Mike] Patto, V.I.Ps)

TIME CODE

86 Jive LOUT 1 Village House Stomp/Louie Louie (12") . . . 8

TIMELORDS

88 KLF 003GG Gary In The Tardis (Radio)/(Minimal) (white label promo, 500 only) . . . 15
88 KLF 003GG Gary In The Tardis (Radio)/(Minimal) (12", p/s) . . . 10
88 KLF 003P Doctorin' The Tardis (Radio)/(Minimal) (car-shaped picture disc) . . . 15
88 KLF 003R Doctorin' The Tardis (Radio)/Doctorin' The Tardis (Minimal)/
Gary Glitter Joins The JAMs (12", 4,000 only, most in stickered
black die-cut sleeve, some in full 'Gary Glitter' p/s) . . . 30/8
88 KLF TCD 003 Doctorin' The Tardis (12" mix)/What Time Is Love? (KLF original) (CD) . . . 10
88 KLF CD 003 Doctorin' The Tardis (Radio)/Doctorin' The Tardis (Minimal)/Doctorin'
The Tardis (Club Mix)/Doctorin' The Tardis (Video) (CD Video) . . . 30
(see also KLF, Disco 2000, JAMs, Bill Drummond, Orb, Space)

TIMES

65 EMI 7ES 24 Ooh Wee/Shepherd Blues/Suzie/Running And Hiding (EP, demo only) . . . 65
66 Columbia DB 7804 Think About The Times/Tomorrow Night . . . 25
66 Columbia DB 7904 (She Can't Replace) The Love We Knew/Reconciled . . . 35

TIMES

81 Whaam! WHAAM 2 Red With Purple Flashes/Biff! Bang! Pow! (p/s) . . . 35
82 Art Pop POP 50 Here Come The Holidays (Voici Les Vacances)/Three Cheers For The Sun
(A-side as Joni Dee & Times, p/s, some with 'Times' sticker) . . . 15/10
83 Art Pop POP 49 I Helped Patrick McGoohan Escape/The Theme From "Danger Man" (p/s) . . . 12
84 Art Pop POP 46 Boys Brigade/Power Is Forever (p/s) . . . 7
84 Art Pop POP 45 Blue Fire/Where The Blue Begins (p/s) . . . 6
85 Unicorn PHZ 1 London Boys/(Where To Go) When The Sun Goes Down (p/s) . . . 5
90 Caff CAFF 13 Extase/BIFF BANG POW!: Sleep (p/s, with insert) . . . 20
85 Art Pop 43DOZ BOYS ABOUT TOWN (EP) . . . 10
81 Whaam! BIG 1 POP GOES ART (LP, hand-sprayed sleeve) . . . 35
82 Art Pop ART 20 POP GOES ART! (LP, reissue, hand-sprayed sleeve, some with magazine
cuttings taped to plain white cover) . . . 25/20
83 Art Pop ART 19 THIS IS LONDON (LP, white label w/ blue print or black label w/ white print) . . 18/15
83 Art Pop No. 1 I HELPED PATRICK McGOOHAN ESCAPE (mini-LP) . . . 18
84 Art Pop ART 17 HELLO EUROPE (LP, purple or blue sleeve) . . . 12
85 Art Pop ARTPOP 2 BLUE PERIOD (mini-LP, grey or blue sleeve) . . . 12/10
86 Art Pop ART 16 UP AGAINST IT (LP) . . . 12
86 Art Pop ART 15 ENJOY! (LP, gatefold sleeve) . . . 12
90 Art Pop ART 20 POP GOES ART (LP, 'hand-painted' picture disc reissue, signed) . . . 15
93 Creation CRELP 137 ALTERNATIVE COMMERCIAL CROSSOVER (LP, with inner) . . . 12
(see also Television Personalities, Teenage Filmstars, O Level, Biff Bang Pow!, L'Orange Mechanik)

TIME UK

83 Red Bus TIM 123 The Cabaret/Remember Days (gatefold p/s) . . . 10
(see also the Jam)

TIME ZONE

88 Virgin CDT 29 — World Destruction (12" A)/(12" B)/(12" Instrumental Blast) (featuring John Lydon & Afrika Bambaataa) (3" CD, gatefold card p/s) . . . 8

(see also Public Image Ltd., Sex Pistols)

BOBBY TIMMONS

61 Riverside RLP 334 — SOUL TIME (LP, with Art Blakey, also stereo [RLP 9334]) . . . 15

SALLY TIMMS & DRIFTING COWGIRLS

87 T.I.M. 12 MOT 6 — This House Is A House Of Trouble! (Extended) (with Marc Almond)/ The Anchor Of Love/Heavenly Gates (12", p/s) . . . 10

(see also Marc Almond, Mekons)

TIMON

68 Pye 7N 17451 — Bitter Thoughts Of Little Jane/Ramblin' Boy . . . 60
70 Threshold TH 3 — And Now She Says She's Young/I'm Just A Travelling Man . . . 8

(see also Tymon Dogg)

TIMONEERS

76 WHM WHM 1919 — ROASTED LIVE (LP) . . . 20

AL TIMOTHY & HIS BAND

55 Decca F 10558 — Gruntin' Blues/You Mad Man! . . . 10

TIM TAM & TURN ONS

67 Island WIP 6007 — Wait A Minute/Ophelia . . . 35

TINA & MEXICANS

68 Pye 7N 17525 — One Love Two/Longing To Hold You . . . 6

TINDERSTICKS

92 Tippy Toe 1 — Patchwork/Milky Teeth (p/s, hand-coloured inner sleeve & insert; 1,000 only, numbered in positive or negative figures [from -500 to 500]) . . . 35
93 Tippy Toe/Ché TIPPY-CHE 2 — Marbles/Joe Stumble/For Those.../Benn (10", p/s, stickered PVC sleeve, innersleeve & insert, 2,000 only) . . . 20
93 Rough Trade 45rev16 — A Marriage Made In Heaven/A Marriage Made In Heaven (Instrumental) ('singles club' release, p/s, 5,000 only) . . . 30
93 Domino RUG 006 — UNWIRED EP: Feeling Relatively Good/Rotweilers And Mace/She/Kooks (EP, numbered p/s; 1 copy in 10 with 'Domino' stamp, 1,500 only) . . . 20
93 This Way Up WAY 1811 — City Sickness/Untitled/The Bullring (p/s, 1,500 only) . . . 8
93 This Way Up WAY 1899 — City Sickness/Untitled/The Bullring (CD) . . . 15
93 Clawfist XPIG 21 — We Have All The Time In The World/GALLON DRUNK: Known Not Wanted ('singles club' release, p/s, 1,400 only) . . . 25
93 Tippy Toe 003 — LIVE IN BERLIN: Raindrops/Tyed (in stamped brown paper bag, mail-order/tour release, 1,500 only) . . . 20
94 This Way Up WAY 2899 — Kathleen/Summat Moon/Sweet, Sweet Man/E Type Joe (CD) . . . 15
95 Sub Pop SP 297 — THE SMOOTH SOUND OF TINDERSTICKS: Here/Harry's Dilemma (p/s, 3,000 only) . . . 10
93 This Way Up — TINDERSTICKS (1st album) (LP) . . . 25
94 This Way Up — TINDERSTICKS (2nd album) (LP) . . . 25
94 This Way Up WAY 3288 — LIVE IN AMSTERDAM (10" LP, brown sleeve) . . . 20
94 This Way Up WAY 3299 — LIVE IN AMSTERDAM (CD, numbered brown paper sleeve) . . . 25
95 This Way Up — THE BLOOMSBURY THEATRE 12/3/95 (LP) . . . 50

PROMOS

93 This Way Up WAY 1755 — FIRST ALBUM SAMPLER (CD, card sleeve with 'dancer' postage stamp sticker, 1000 only) . . . 20
94 This Way Up WAY 3999 — TINDERSTICKS (CD, card sleeve, 300 in brown paper envelope hand-sealed with red wax) . . . 20
94 This Way Up WAY 4099 — SECOND ALBUM SAMPLER (CD, jewel case, 1,500 only) . . . 18
95 This Way Up WAY 4522 — Travelling Light/Waiting 'Round You/I've Been Loving You Too Long (10", unreleased, 25 white label test pressings only) . . . 30
96 This Way Up WAY 5655 — Petites Gouttes D'Eau/Ma Soeur (CD, sampler, 2,000 only) . . . 10
97 This Way Up WAY 6299 — CURTAINS (CD, card sleeve in stamped 5" box with booklet, biography, 1,800 only; 100 copies with 6 black & white photos) . . . 30/20
97 Chop 'Em Out (no cat. no.) — AN INTERVIEW WITH DAVE AND DICKON (CD-R, generic inlay, 20 copies only) . . . 25

(see also Asphalt Ribbons)

TINGA (Stewart) & ERNIE (Wilson)

69 Explosion EX 2009 — She's Gone/Old Old Song . . . 10

TINGHA & TUCKER

(see under Century 21)

TINKERBELL'S FAIRYDUST

67 Decca F 12705 — Lazy Day/In My Magic Garden . . . 30
68 Decca F 12778 — Twenty Ten/Walking My Baby . . . 30
69 Decca F 12865 — Sheila's Back In Town/Follow Me Follow . . . 35
69 Decca LK/SKL 5028 — TINKERBELL'S FAIRYDUST (LP, unreleased; finished copies or test pressings in sleeve) . . . 1,200/700

TINKERS

69 Fontana SFJL 935 — TIL THE WILD BIRDS (LP) . . . 18
72 Argo ZFB 35 — SPRING RAIN (LP) . . . 20

TIN MACHINE

89 EMI MT 68 — Under The God/Sacrifice Yourself (p/s) . . . 5
89 EMI USA 10MT 68 — Under The God/Sacrifice Yourself/The Interview (10", p/s) . . . 6
89 EMI USA CDMT 68 — Under The God/Sacrifice Yourself/The Interview (CD) . . . 8
89 EMI USA MTG 73 — Tin Machine/Maggie's Farm (live) (numbered gatefold p/s) . . . 7
89 EMI USA MTPD 73 — Tin Machine/Maggie's Farm (live) (shaped picture disc with card insert) . . . 10

MINT VALUE £

89	EMI USA 12MTP 73	Tin Machine/Maggie's Farm (live)/I Can't Read (live) (12", poster p/s)	8
89	EMI USA CDMT 73	Tin Machine/Maggie's Farm (live)/I Can't Read (live)/Bus Stop (live) (CD)	8
89	EMI USA MTS 76	Prisoner Of Love (Edit)/Baby Can Dance (live) (silver envelope with 4 cards)	7
89	EMI USA MTPD 76	Prisoner Of Love (Edit)/Baby Can Dance (live) (heart-shaped picture disc with printed PVC sleeve & insert)	12
89	EMI USA CDMT 76	Prisoner Of Love (Edit)/Baby Can Dance (live)/Crack City (live)/Prisoner (LP Version) (CD)	10
91	London LOCDT 305	You Belong In Rock'n'Roll/(Extended Mix)/(Album Version)/Amlapura (Indonesian Version)/Shakin' All Over (live) (CD, round pack with insert)	8
91	London LONX 310	Baby Universal/Big Hurt (Live)/Baby Universal (Live)/Stateside (Live)/If There Is Something (Live) (12", p/s)	8
91	London LOCDT 310	Baby Universal/Stateside/If There Is Something/Heaven's In Here (CD, in round tin)	10

(see also David Bowie)

BABS TINO

62	London HLR 9589	Forgive Me/If I Didn't Love You So Much	20
63	London RE-R 1377	FORGIVE ME (EP)	75

TIN PAN SKIFFLE GROUP

57	Nestles NR 06	Poor Howard (1-sided card flexi 78)	7

MICK TINSLEY

67	Decca F 12544	Let It Be Me/How're You Gonna Tell Me	6

(see also Hedgehoppers Anonymous)

TINTERN ABBEY

67	Deram DM 164	Beeside/Vacuum Cleaner	1000

TIN TIN

69	Polydor 56332	Only Ladies Play Croquet/He Wants To Be A Star	7
70	Polydor 2058 023	Toast And Marmalade For Tea/Manhattan Woman	10
70	Polydor 2058 076	Come On Over Again/Back To Winona	7
71	Polydor 2001 146	Shana/Rocky Mountain	5
71	Polydor 2058 114	Is That The Way/Swans On The Canal	6
72	Polydor 2058 232	Toast And Marmalade For Tea/Cavalry's Coming/Ships On The Starboard	5
72	Polydor 2058 238	Talking Turkey/Cavalry's Coming	5
69	Polydor 2384 011	TIN TIN (LP)	18
72	Polydor 2382 080	ASTRAL TAXI (LP)	15

(see also Steve & Stevie)

TINY ALICE

72	Kama Sutra 2013 043	Doctor Jazz/The Chocolate Dandies Of 1932/15¢ Hamburger Mama	5
72	Kama Sutra 2319 015	TINY ALICE (LP)	12

TINY TIM

68	Reprise RS 20760	Bring Back Those Rockabye Baby Days	7
68	Reprise RS 23258	Tiptoe Through The Tulips/I Got You Babe	6
68	Reprise RS 20769	Hello Hello/The Other Side	6
69	Reprise RS 20802	Great Balls Of Fire/As Time Goes By	6
69	Reprise RS 20845	Mickey The Monkey/Neighbourhood Children	6
71	Reprise RS 27004	There Will Always Be An England/Bless 'Em All/It's A Long Way To Tipperary/Have You Seen My Little Sue	5
71	Reprise RS 27004	There Will Always Be An England/Bless 'Em All/It's A Long Way To Tipperary/Have You Seen My Little Sue (78, union jack label or plain label)	12/7
72	Wand WN 33	Am I Just Another Pretty Face/Movies	5
74	Polydor 2058 485	Happy Wanderer/My Nose Always Gets In The Way	5
68	Reprise RSLP 6292	GOD BLESS TINY TIM (LP)	30
69	Reprise RSLP 6323	TINY TIM'S SECOND ALBUM (LP)	30
69	Reprise RSLP 6351	FOR ALL MY LITTLE FRIENDS (LP)	20

DIMITRI TIOMKIN

54	Vogue Coral Q 2016	The High And The Mighty/Dial M For Murder	15

TINY TOPSY (& CHARMS)

58	Parlophone R 4397	Come On, Come On, Come On/A Ring Around My Finger (with Charms)	120
58	Parlophone R 4397	Come On, Come On, Come On/A Ring Around My Finger (with Charms) (78)	30
58	Parlophone R 4427	You Shocked Me/Waterproof Eyes (solo)	80
58	Parlophone R 4427	You Shocked Me/Waterproof Eyes (solo) (78)	25
61	Pye International 7N 25104	After Marriage Blues/Working On Me Baby (solo)	30

KEITH TIPPETT

69	Polydor 2384 004	YOU ARE HERE, I AM THERE (LP)	70
71	Vertigo 6360 024	DEDICATED TO YOU BUT YOU WEREN'T LISTENING (LP, gatefold sleeve, swirl label)	65
72	RCA SF 8290	BLUEPRINT (LP)	45
76	Steam SJ 104	TNT (LP, with Stan Tracey)	15
77	Vinyl VS 101	WARM SPIRITS, COOL SPIRITS (LP)	12
78	Ogun OGD 003/4	FRAMES (2-LP)	22

(see also Centipede, Ovary Lodge, Nicra)

JULIE TIPPETTS

76	Utopia UTS 601	SUNSET GLOW (LP)	22

(see also Julie Driscoll, Brian Auger, Centipede, Keith Tippett, Elton Dean, Ninesense, Mark Charig)

TIPPIE & THE CLOVERS

63	Stateside SS 160	My Heart Said/Bossa Nova Baby	22

LESTER TIPTON

80	Grapevine GRP 138	This Won't Change/MASQUERADERS: How	15

TIP TOPS

63	Cameo Parkway P 868	He's Braggin'/Oo-Kook-A-Boo	35

MINT VALUE £

TÍR NA NOG
70 Chrysalis WIP 6090 I'm Happy To Be/Let My Love Grow . . . 5
72 Chrysalis CHS 2001 Lady I Love/Heidi . . . 5
73 Chrysalis CHS 2016 Strong In The Sun/The Mountain & I . . . 5
71 Chrysalis ILPS 9153 TÍR NA NOG (LP) . . . 20
72 Chrysalis CHR 1006 A TEAR AND A SMILE (LP) . . . 20
73 Chrysalis CHR 1047 STRONG IN THE SUN (LP) . . . 15

TITANIC
72 CBS 7278 Sante Fe/Half Breed . . . 5
72 CBS 8185 Rain 2,000/Blond . . . 5
73 CBS 1670 Richmond Express/Heia Valenga . . . 5
71 CBS 64104 TITANIC (LP) . . . 18
72 CBS 64791 SEA WOLF (LP) . . . 15
73 CBS 65661 EAGLE ROCK (LP) . . . 12

TITANS
58 London HLU 8609 Don't You Just Know It/Can It Be . . . 100
58 London HLU 8609 Don't You Just Know It/Can It Be (78) . . . 30

TITUS GROAN
70 Dawn DNX 2503 Open The Door Homer/Woman Of The World/Liverpool (p/s) . . . 18
70 Dawn DNLS 3012 TITUS GROAN (LP, gatefold sleeve) . . . 55

CAL TJADER
65 Verve VS 529 Soul Sauce/Naked City Theme . . . 25
58 Vocalion LAE 556 RITMO CALIENTE (LP, as Cal Tjader Quintet) . . . 25
62 HMV/Verve CLP 1587 IN A LATIN BAG (LP, as Cal Tjader Sextet, also stereo [CSD 1454]) . . . 15
65 Vocalion LAE-F 599 GREATEST HITS (LP) . . . 18
65 Verve (S)VLP 9136 SOUL BIRD: WHIFFENPOOF (LP) . . . 15
68 Verve (S)VLP 9192 THE BEST OF CAL TJADER (LP) . . . 15
68 Verve (S)VLP 9215 HIP VIBRATIONS (LP) . . . 15
69 Fontana STL 5527 SOLAR HEAT (LP) . . . 12

TNT
84 Neat NEAT 39 Back On The Road/Rockin' The Night (p/s) . . . 8

TOAD
72 RCA Victor SF 8241 TOAD (LP) . . . 50

TOAD THE WET SPROCKET
79 Sprockets BRS 004 Pete's Punk Song/Feel It (fold out p/s) . . . 40
80 Sprockets BRS 008 Reaching For The Sky/One Glass Of Whiskey (foldout stapled p/s) . . . 70

RUTH TOBI
69 Concord CON 002 Lazy/That's When I Cry . . . 5

TOBRUK
83 Neat NEAT 32 Wild On The Run/The Show Must Go On (p/s) . . . 7
85 Parlophone 12R 6093 Falling/Like Lightning/Under The Gun (12", p/s) . . . 8
85 Parlophone R 6101 On The Rebound/Poor Girl (p/s) . . . 10
88 FM WKFMLP 105 PLEASURE AND PAIN (LP) . . . 15

TOBY JUG
69 private pressing GREASY QUIFF (LP, with insert) . . . 275

TOBY JUG
71 Decca F 13173 Breakaway Man/Brotherhood . . . 5

TOBY TWIRL
68 Decca F 12728 Harry Faversham/Back In Time . . . 30
68 Decca F 12804 Toffee Apple Sunday/Romeo And Juliet 1968 . . . 70
69 Decca F 12867 Movin' In/Utopia Daydream . . . 20
(see also Shades Of Blue)

TODAY'S WITNESS
72 Emblem TDR 345 TODAY'S WITNESS (LP) . . . 35

ART & DOTTY TODD
52 HMV B 10399 Broken Wings/Heavenly — Heavenly (78) . . . 6
58 London HLB 8620 Chanson D'Amour (Song Of Love)/Along The Trail With You . . . 25
58 London HLB 8620 Chanson D'Amour (Song Of Love)/Along The Trail With You (78) . . . 8
59 London HLN 8838 Straight As An Arrow/Stand There, Mountain . . . 25
59 London HLN 8838 Straight As An Arrow/Stand There, Mountain (78) . . . 15

DIANE TODD
58 Decca F 10993 It's A Wonderful Thing To Be Loved/You Are My Favourite Dream . . . 8
58 Decca F 10993 It's A Wonderful Thing To Be Loved/You Are My Favourite Dream (78) . . . 8

EILEEN TODD
54 London HL 8010 Paradise/Ill Wind (78) . . . 6

GARY TODD & ROGER TURNER
79 Incus INCUS 79 SUNDAY BEST (LP) . . . 50

NICK TODD
57 London HLD 8500 Plaything/The Honey Song . . . 50
57 London HLD 8500 Plaything/The Honey Song (78) . . . 12
58 London HLD 8537 At The Hop/I Do . . . 18
58 London HLD 8537 At The Hop/I Do (78) . . . 7
59 London HLD 8902 Tiger/Twice As Nice . . . 35
59 London HLD 8902 Tiger/Twice As Nice (78) . . . 20

PATSY TODD
68 High Note HS 007 Fire In Your Wire/AL & VIBRATORS: Move Up Calypso . . . 6
69 High Note HS 012 We Were Lovers/Give Me A Chance (B-side with Delano Stewart) . . . 8
(see also Patsy, Stranger & Patsy, Derrick & Patsy)

MINT VALUE £

SHARKEY TODD & MONSTERS

59 Parlophone R 4536 Cool Gool/The Horror Show 22
59 Parlophone R 4536 Cool Gool/The Horror Show (78) 20
(see also Wally Whyton, Vipers [Skiffle Group])

WILF TODD COMBO

64 Blue Beat BB 240 He Took Her Away/Have You Ever Been Lonely 12

WILF TODD & HIS MUSIC

66 Oak WT 101 WILF TODD AND HIS MUSIC (LP) 15

CAMY TODOROW

85 Virgin VS 816 Bursting At The Seams/Don't Stop It, I Like It (with Roger Taylor) (p/s) 30
85 Virgin VS 816-12 Bursting At The Seams (Backroom Version)/Bursting At The Seams (Instrumental)/Don't Stop It, I Like It (12", p/s, with Roger Taylor) 50
(see also Roger Taylor)

TOE-FAT

70 Parlophone R 5829 Working Nights/Bad Side Of The Moon 20
72 Chapter One SCH 175 Brand New Band/Can't Live Without You 15
70 Parlophone PCS 7097 TOE-FAT (LP) 100
70 Regal Zono. SLRZ 1015 TOE-FAT TWO (LP) 85
(see also Cliff Bennett, Uriah Heep, Glass Menagerie)

TOGETHER

68 Columbia DB 8491 Henry's Coming Home/Love Mum And Dad 60
(see also Keith Relf)

TOGETHER

69 Aurora 4278 Memories Of Melinda/Good Morning World 8

TOGGERY FIVE

64 Parlophone R 5175 Bye Bye Bird/I'm Gonna Jump 45
65 Parlophone R 5249 I'd Much Rather Be With The Boys/It's So Easy 40

TOKENS

61 Parlophone R 4790 Tonight I Fell In Love/I Love My Baby 30
61 RCA RCA 1263 The Lion Sleeps Tonight/Tina 7
62 RCA RCA 1279 B'wa Nina (Pretty Girl)/Weeping River 8
62 RCA RCA 1313 I'll Do My Crying Tomorrow/Dream Angel Goodnight 12
62 RCA RCA 1322 Wishing/A Bird Flies Out Of Sight 7
64 Fontana TF 500 He's In Town/Oh Kathy 10
66 Fontana TF 683 I Hear Trumpets Blow/I Could See Me Dancing With You 7
67 Stateside SS 598 Green Plant/Saloogy 8
67 Warner Bros WB 5900 Portrait Of My Love/She Comes And Goes 6
67 Warner Bros WB 7056 It's A Happening World/How Nice? 6
68 Warner Bros WB 7169 Till/Poor Man 6
70 Buddah 2011 011 Don't Worry Baby/Some People Sleep 6
62 RCA RD 27256/SF 5128 THE LION SLEEPS TONIGHT (LP, mono/stereo) 50/70
62 RCA RD 7535 WE THE TOKENS SING FOLK (LP) 35
70 Buddah 2359 007 THE TOKENS (LP) 18
(see also U.S. Double Quartet, We Ugly Dogs)

TOKYO BLADE

83 Powerstation OHM 2 Powergame/Death On Main Street (p/s) 8
85 Powerstation LEG 1T THE CAVE SESSIONS (12" EP) 15
85 Tokyo Blade TBR 1 BLACKHEARTS AND JADED SPADES (LP, gatefold sleeve) 15

TOKYO OLYMPICS

83 Ritz 031 Shot By Love (Part 1)/(Part 2) (p/s) 5
83 Ritz 12 031 Shot By Love (Part 1)/(Part 2) (12", p/s) 8
83 Ritz 050 Radio (Turns Her On)/(Mix Version) (p/s) 5
83 Ritz 12 050 Radio (Turns Her On)/(Mix Version) (12", p/s) 8
83 Polydor 2078 143 One Step From Paradise/Paradise Disco Mix (p/s, Ireland-only) 5
82 Polydor 2908 046 RADIO (LP, Ireland-only, produced by Francis Rossi & Bernie Frost) 12
(see also Rossi & Frost)

TOKYO ROSE

83 Guardian GRC 270 Dry Your Eyes/This Is Tokyo Rose (p/s) 100

ISRAEL 'POPPER STOPPER' TOLBERT

70 Stax STAX 157 Big Leg Woman/I Got Love 6
71 Stax 2362 020 POPPER STOPPER (LP) 15

TOLL

86 Broken Flag BF V7 CHRIST KNOWS (LP, featuring Tim Gane) 20
(see also Ramleh, McCarthy)

GARY DALE TOLLETT & THE CRICKETS

01 Rollercoaster RRCT 1001 Go Boy Go/Gone (78, 250 only) 10

TOM & JERRIO

65 HMV POP 1435 Boo-Ga-Loo/Boomerang 20

TOM & JERRY (cartoon characters)

58 MGM MGM-EP 688 JOHANN MOUSE (EP) 15

TOM & JERRY

59 Gala GSP 806 Baby Talk/PAUL SHELDON: Thank You Pretty Baby (picture labels) 40
63 Pye International 7N 25202 I'm Lonesome/Looking At You 90
(see also Simon & Garfunkel)

TOM & MICK

69 Olga OLE 014 Somebody's Taken Maria Away/Pandemonium 8

MINT VALUE £

TOM CATS

61 Starlite ST45 054 — Tom Tom Cat/Big Brother . . . 25

TOMCATS

97 Essex ESSEX 1018LP — THE TOMCATS (LP, with bonus 7": "Seventh Son"/"Walking"/"You Gotta Help"/ "Looking For My Baby" by Second Thoughts [10187]) . . . 12

(see also July)

TOMITA

77 RCA Red Seal RL1 1919 — THE TOMITA PLANETS SUITE (LP, withdrawn after 1 day) . . . 20

LEE TOMLIN

66 CBS 202455 — Sweet Sweet Lovin'/Save Me . . . 6

ALBERT TOMLINSON

68 Giant GN 28 — Don't Wait For Me/LLOYD EVANS: Losing You . . . 75

ROY TOMLINSON

68 Coxsone CS 7056 — I Stand For I/MARTIN: I Second That Emotion (actually by Martin Riley) . . . 35

TOMMY (Cowan)

72 Dynamic DYN 433 — Geraldine/Reverend Leroy . . . 7

(see also Jamaicans)

TOMMY (McCook) & UPSETTERS

69 Trojan TR 7717 — Lock Jaw (actually by Dave Barker)/YARDBROOMS: My Desire . . . 15

(see also Tommy McCook, Upsetters)

TOMORROW

67 Parlophone R 5597 — My White Bicycle/Claramont Lake . . . 45
67 Parlophone R 5627 — Revolution/Three Jolly Little Dwarfs . . . 50
69 Parlophone R 5813 — My White Bicycle/Claramont Lake (reissue) . . . 35
68 Parlophone PMC/PCS 7042 — TOMORROW (LP, yellow/black label; mono/stereo) . . . 120/100
76 Harvest SHSP 2010 — TOMORROW (LP, reissue) . . . 15

(see also Keith West, Steve Howe, Twink, Four + One, In Crowd, Syndicats, Aquarian Age, Fairies, Bodast)

TOMORROW COME SOME DAY

69 SNB 97 — TOMORROW COME SOME DAY (LP) . . . 400

(see also Ithaca, Friends, Agincourt, Alice Through The Looking Glass, BBC Radiophonic Workshop/Peter Howell)

TOMORROW'S CHILDREN

70 Plexium PXM 17 — You're My Baby/Maybe Today . . . 5
71 Plexium PXM 25 — Sing A Song/Don't Believe . . . 5
71 Plexium PXM 26 — Keep A Little Love In Your Life/My Way Of Living . . . 5

TOMORROW'S CHILDREN (Jamaica)

67 Island WI 3073 — Bang Bang Rock Steady/Rain Rock Steady (some w/same label on both sides) . 18

TOMPALL & GLASER BROTHERS

68 MGM MGM-C 8082 — THROUGH THE EYES OF LOVE (LP) . . . 25

TONE DEAF & THE IDIOTS

80s Lyntone BLI 1/Angel BL 12 — Why Does Politics Turn Men Into Toads/Repatriate The National Front (flexi) . . . 10

(see also Idiots)

ELEANOR TONER

65 Decca F 12119 — All Cried Out/A Hundred Guitars . . . 7
65 Decca F 12192 — Will You Still Love Me Tomorrow/Between The Window And The Phone . . . 15
66 Decca F 12454 — Black Rose/Time To Spare Darling . . . 6

TONES ON TAIL

82 4AD BAD 203 — A Bigger Splash/Means Of Escape/Copper/Instrumental (12", p/s) . . . 10

(see also Bauhaus, Love & Rockets)

TONETTES

62 Island WI 064 — Love That Is Real/Pretty Baby . . . 22

(see also Marlene Webber, Lyrics, Don Drummond)

OSCAR TONEY JR.

67 Stateside SS 2033 — For Your Precious Love/Ain't That True Love . . . 20
67 Stateside SS 2046 — Turn On Your Love Light/Any Day Now . . . 15
67 Stateside SS 2061 — You Can Lead Your Woman To The Altar/Unlucky Guy . . . 15
68 Bell BLL 1003 — Without Love There Is Nothing/Love That Never Grows Cold . . . 8
68 Bell BLL 1011 — No Sad Songs/Never Get Enough Of Your Love . . . 10
69 Bell BLL 1057 — Down In Texas/Just For You . . . 8
72 Capricorn K 17505 — Thank You, Honey Chile/I Do What You Wish . . . 6
73 Contempo C 6 — Kentucky Bluebird/Everything I Own . . . 6
74 Contempo CS 2002 — Is It Because I'm Black/Make It Easy On Yourself . . . 6
75 Contempo CS 2043 — I've Been Loving You Too Long/For Your Precious Love . . . 6
67 Stateside (S)SL 10211 — FOR YOUR PRECIOUS LOVE (LP) . . . 60

TONGUE & GROOVE

69 Fontana STL 5528 — TONGUE & GROOVE (LP) . . . 35

(see also Charlatans)

TONIGHT

78 TDS 1 — Drummerman/Stroll On By (p/s) . . . 8
78 TDS 2 — Money, That's Your Problem/No Sympathy (p/s) . . . 5
78 TDS 4 — Wheels/I Can Play Faster Than You Can (p/s) . . . 5
78 TDS 5 — Jealousy Kills/Second Hand Man . . . 5

(see also Andy Arthurs, Celia & Mutations)

TERRY TONIK

80 Posh TOFF 1 — Just A Little Mod/Smashed And Blocked (some with die-cut p/s, a few also with promo A4 booklet) . . . 110/70/30

MINT VALUE £

TONTO

74 Polydor 2383 308 — IT'S ABOUT TIME (LP) . . . 12

(see also Tonto's Expanding Head Band)

TONTON (MACOUTE)

72 RCA 2190 — Summer Of Our Love/Greyhound Lady (as Tonton) . . . 12

71 RCA Neon NE 4 — TONTON MACOUTE (LP) . . . 55

TONTO'S EXPANDING HEAD BAND

71 Atlantic 2400 150 — ZERO TIME (LP, gatefold sleeve) . . . 25

(see also Tonto)

TONY & CHAMPIONS

70 Duke DU 90 — Eye For An Eye/CHAMPIONS: Broke My Heart — Version . . . 6

(see also Errol & Champions, Domino Johnson)

TONY & DENNIS

67 Trojan TR 002 — Folk Song/TOMMY McCOOK & SUPERSONICS: Starry Night . . . 35

TONY & GRADUATES

60s Hit HIT 13 — The Statue . . . 50

TONY & HIPPY BOYS

69 Gas GAS 121 — Janet/HARMONIANS: Believe Me . . . 7

TONY & HOWARD with DICTATORS

65 Oriole CB 307 — Just In Case/Walk Right Out Of The Blues . . . 20

TONY & HOWIE

72 Banana BA 371 — Fun It Up/Fun Version . . . 10

TONY & JOE

58 London HLN 8694 — The Freeze/Gonna Get A Little Kissin' Tonight . . . 45

58 London HLN 8694 — The Freeze/Gonna Get A Little Kissin' Tonight (78) . . . 20

TONY (Tomas) & LOUISE

62 Island WI 059 — Ups And Downs/TONY TOMAS: Brixton Lewisham . . . 20

(see also Tony Washington)

TONY & TANDY

69 Atlantic 584 262 — Two Can Make It Together/The Bitter And The Sweet (with Fleur De Lys) . . . 20

71 Atlantic 2091 075 — Two Can Make It Together/Look And Find. . . . 6

(see also Sharon Tandy, Fleur De Lys)

TONY & TYRONE

70 Ember EMBS 290 — Everyday Fun/Whip Your Loving On Me (p/s) . . . 5

TONY & VELVETS

63 Decca F 11637 — Sunday/One More Once . . . 7

TONY, CARO & JOHN

72 private pressing — ALL ON THE FIRST DAY (LP, with insert) . . . 300

TONY'S ALLSTARS

72 Green Door GD 4041 — Rub Up A Daughter/DENNIS ALCAPONE: Daughter Version . . . 6

72 Bullet BU 509 — Dub Up A Daughter (as Prince Tony's Allstars)/ DENNIS ALCAPONE: Daughter Version . . . 6

72 Big Shot BI 601 — Must Care/L. SPARKS: You Don't Care . . . 6

73 Downtown DT 508 — You Don't Say/DENNIS ALCAPONE: Version . . . 10

TONY'S DEFENDERS

66 Columbia DB 7850 — Yes I Do/It's Easy To Say Hello . . . 25

66 Columbia DB 7996 — Since I Lost You Baby/Waiting For A Call From You . . . 25

(see also Mike Stuart Span)

TOO FUNK

95 Ferox FER 008 — THE RETURN OF TOO FUNK (12" EP). . . . 15

95 Ferox FER 011 — STORM THE FUNK (12" EP, plain sleeve) . . . 8

96 Ferox FER 024 — HOTEL IBIS (12" EP) . . . 8

TOOLS

81 Oily SLICK 2 — Gotta Make Some Money Somehow/TV Eyes (p/s). . . . 8

STEVE TOOK

(see under Shagrat)

TOOMORROW

70 RCA RCA 1978 — You're My Baby Now/Goin' Back (in custom RCA sleeve) . . . 55

70 Decca F 13070 — I Could Never Live Without Your Love/Roll Like A River. . . . 55

70 RCA LSA 3008 — TOOMORROW (LP, soundtrack, with insert) . . . 120

(see also Olivia Newton-John)

TOO MUCH

78 Lightning GIL 513 — Who You Wanna Be/Another Time Another Place (some in p/s) . . . 25/8

78 Lightning GIL 552 — Lick Me One More Time//Be Mine/It's Only For Me (p/s) . . . 25

DAVID TOOP

75 Obscure OBS 48 — NEW AND REDISCOVERED MUSICAL INSTRUMENTS (LP, with Max Eastley & Brian Eno). . . . 25

70s Quartz — WOUNDS (LP, with Paul Burwell). . . . 25

(see also Brian Eno)

TOOTS

70 Upsetter US 327 — Do You Like It/UPSETTERS: Touch Of Fire . . . 10

(see also Maytals)

TOOTS & THE MAYTALS

(see under Maytals)

MINT VALUE £

TOP NOTES
(see under Nino Tempo & April Stevens)

TOPO D. BILL
70 Charisma CB 116 — Witchi Tai To/Jam (some in p/s) ... 10/7
(see also Bonzo Dog [Doo Dah] Band, Roger Ruskin Spear)

TOPO GIGIO
(see under Century 21)

TOPPERS
57 Brunswick 05678 — Stash Pandowski (She's Not Very Much Good For Pretty)/Pots And Pans ... 8

TOP SECRET
81 Cheapskate CHEAP 35 — She's So Ugly/I Love Me (no p/s) ... 5

TINY TOPSY
(see under Tiny)

TOP TOPHAM
69 Blue Horizon 57-3167 — Christmas Cracker/Cracking Up Over Christmas ... 22
70 Blue Horizon 7-63857 — ASCENSION HEIGHTS (LP) ... 120
(see also Fox, Yardbirds)

TORA TORA
80 Mancunian Metal TT 5000 — Red Sun Setting/Highway (Shooting Like A Bullet) (p/s) ... 15
80 Tora TT 5001 — Don't Want To Let You Go/Sorry I Broke Your Heart ... 40

SIDNEY TORCH ORCHESTRA
63 Decca F 11721 — The Trapeze Waltz/Soft Shoe Shuffler ... 6
58 Parlophone GEP 8716 — FIDDLIN' FOR FUN (EP) ... 8
58 Parlophone GEP 8723 — LATIN TINGE (EP) ... 8
53 Parlophone PMD 1008 — SIDNEY TORCH PROGRAMME (10" LP) ... 12

STEVE TORCH
70s Redball RR 005 — Live In Fear/Smoke Your Own (p/s) ... 5

(BERNIE) TORMÉ (BAND)
78 Jet JET 126 — I'm Not Ready/Free (p/s, as Bernie Tormé Band, orange or black vinyl) ... 8/6
79 Jet JET 137 — Weekend/Secret Service/All Night/Instant Impact (as Bernie Tormé Band, p/s) ... 6
70s Peter Collins PC 1 — The Hunter/Soul Sister ... 10
80 Island WIP 6586 — The Beat/I Want/Bony Maronie (p/s, pink vinyl, promos on black vinyl) ... 10
81 Fresh FRESH 7 — All Day And All Of The Night/What's Next (p/s, also listed as Parole PURL 5) ... 20
82 Kamaflage KAM 5 — America/Chelsea Girls (p/s) ... 5
82 Kamaflage KAM 8 — Shoorah Shoorah/Star//Search And Destroy (live)/Possession (live) (double pack, as Bernie Tormé & The Electric Gypsies) ... 6
84 Zebra RA 1 — I Can't Control Myself/Black Sunday (p/s) ... 5
84 Zebra RA 2 — My Baby Loves A Vampire/Lightning Strikes (p/s) ... 8
85 Zebra RA 5 — All Around The World/Come The Revolution (p/s) ... 5
82 Kamaflage KAMLP 2 — TURN OUT THE LIGHTS (LP, white vinyl) ... 12
85 Zebra ZEB 6 — BACK TO BABYLON (LP, red vinyl, as Tormé) ... 12
85 Raw Power RAWLP 010 — BACK WITH THE BOYS (LP) ... 12
87 Heavy Metal HMRLP 94 — DIE PRETTY DIE YOUNG (LP, with bonus 12" [12HM 95], stickered sleeve) ... 12
(see also Gillan, Split Knee Loons, Girl)

MEL TORME (& MEL-TONES)
SINGLES
56 Vogue Coral Q 72150 — Mountain Greenery/Jeepers Creepers ... 12
56 Vogue Coral Q 72159 — Blue Moon/That Old Black Magic ... 8
56 Vogue Coral Q 72185 — Love Is Here To Stay/Goody Goody ... 7
56 London HLN 8305 — Lulu's Back In Town/The Lady Is A Tramp ... 25
56 London HLN 8322 — Lullaby Of Birdland/I Love To Watch The Moonlight ... 25
56 Vogue Coral Q 72202 — All Of You/It Don't Mean A Thing ... 7
56 Decca F 10800 — Walkin' Shoes/The Cuckoo In The Clock (with Ted Heath & His Music) ... 6
56 Decca F 10809 — Waltz For Young Lovers/I Don't Want To Walk Without You ... 6
57 Vogue Coral Q 72217 — My Rosemarie/How (as Mel Torme & Mel-Tones) ... 7
60 Philips PB 1045 — The White Cliffs Of Dover/I've Got A Lovely Bunch Of Coconuts ... 5
61 HMV POP 859 — Blue Moon/The Moon Song ... 5
61 MGM MGM 1144 — The Christmas Song/Shine On Your Shoes ... 6
62 London HLK 9643 — Comin' Home Baby/Right Now ... 20
64 Verve VS 505 — Yes Indeed/Her Face ... 5
EPs
56 Decca DFE 6384 — WALKIN' SHOES ... 12
56 MGM MGM-EP 562 — VOICE IN VELVET ... 12
57 MGM MGM-EP 591 — VOICE IN VELVET NO. 2 ... 12
58 London Jazz EZ-N 19027 — MEL TORME SINGS FRED ASTAIRE PT. 1 ... 10
58 London Jazz EZ-N 19028 — MEL TORME SINGS FRED ASTAIRE PT. 2 ... 10
58 London Jazz EZ-N 19029 — MEL TORME SINGS FRED ASTAIRE PT. 3 ... 10
58 Philips BBE 12181 — TORME MEETS THE BRITISH ... 12
59 Coral FEP 2026 — MEL TORME SINGS AT THE CRESCENDO PT. 1 ... 12
59 Coral FEP 2027 — MEL TORME SINGS AT THE CRESCENDO PT. 2 ... 12
59 Coral FEP 2028 — MEL TORME SINGS AT THE CRESCENDO PT. 3 ... 12
59 Parlophone GEP 8790 — FOR SWINGERS ... 10
63 London REK 1372 — MAGIC OF MEL ... 15
LPs
55 Vogue Coral LVA 9004 — MEL TORME AT THE CRESCENDO ... 25
56 Vogue Coral LVA 9032 — MUSICAL SOUNDS ARE THE BEST SONGS ... 25
56 London Jazz LTZ-N 15009 — MEL TORME AND THE MARTY PAICH "DEK-TETTE" ... 20
56 London HA-N 2016 — IT'S A BLUE WORLD ... 20
57 London Jazz LTZ-N 15076 — MEL TORME SINGS FRED ASTAIRE ... 18
57 Philips BBL 7205 — TORME MEETS THE BRITISH ... 40

			MINT VALUE £
58	HMV CLP 1238	MEL TORME	15
59	Parlophone PMC 1096	GENE NORMAN PRESENTS MEL TORME AT THE CRESCENDO	18
60	Parlophone PMC 1114	SONGS FOR ANY TASTE	20
60	HMV CLP 1315	OLÉ TORMÉ (with Billy May)	15
60	HMV CLP 1382	BACK IN TOWN (with Mel-Tones)	18
60	HMV CLP 1405/CSD 1330	SWINGS SCHUBERT ALLEY (with Marty Paich Orch., mono/stereo)	18/20
61	HMV CLP 1449/CSD 1349	SWINGIN' ON THE MOON (mono/stereo)	18/20
62	HMV CLP 1584/CSD 1442	MY KIND OF MUSIC (mono/stereo)	18/20
63	London HA-K/SH-K 8021	MEL TORME AT THE RED HILL (with Jimmy Wisner Trio, mono/stereo)	18/20
63	London HA-K 8065	COMIN' HOME BABY	20
63	Verve (S)VLP 9027	I DIG THE DUKE, I DIG THE COUNT (mono/stereo)	12/15
64	Atlantic ATL/SAL 5005	SUNDAY IN NEW YORK (mono/stereo)	12/15
65	CBS (S) BPG 62250	THAT'S ALL	12
67	Atlantic Special 590 008	RIGHT NOW!	12
70	Capitol ST 21585	RAINDROPS KEEP FALLIN' ON MY HEAD (LP)	15

TORNADOS

62	Decca F 11449	Love And Fury/Popeye Twist	15
62	Decca F 11494	Telstar/Jungle Fever	5
63	Decca F 11562	Globetrotter/Locomotion With Me (some B-sides credit "Locomotion With You")	6
63	Decca F 11606	Robot/Life On Venus	7
63	Decca F 11662	The Ice Cream Man/Theme From "The Scales Of Justice"	7
63	Decca F 11745	Dragonfly/Hymn For Teenagers	10
64	Decca F 11838	Joystick/Hot Pot	10
64	Decca F 11889	Monte Carlo/Blue Blue Beat	15
64	Decca F 11946	Exodus/Blackpool Rock	15
65	Columbia DB 7455	Granada/Ragunboneman	20
65	Columbia DB 7589	Early Bird/Stompin' Through The Rye (as Tornados '65)	20
65	Columbia DB 7687	Stingray/Aqua Marina	40
66	Columbia DB 7856	Pop-Art Goes Mozart/Too Much In Love To Hear	30
66	Columbia DB 7984	Is That A Ship I Hear/Do You Come Here Often	40
62	Decca DFE 8510	THE SOUNDS OF THE TORNADOS (EP)	22
62	Decca DFE 8511	TELSTAR (EP)	22
63	Decca DFE 8521	MORE SOUNDS FROM THE TORNADOS (EP)	30
63	Decca DFE 8533	TORNADO ROCK (EP)	40
63	Decca LK 4552	AWAY FROM IT ALL (LP)	65
72	Decca SPA 253	THE WORLD OF THE TORNADOS (LP)	15
76	Decca REM 4	REMEMBERING...THE TORNADOS (LP)	12

(see also Heinz, Billy Fury, Clem Cattini Ork, Saints, Original Tornados, Roger LaVern & Microns, Saxons, George Bellamy, Gemini, Roger La Vern & Microns)

TO ROCOCO ROT

98	Fat Cat 12FAT 007	She Understands The Dynamics (12", custom sleeve)	8

MITCHELL TOROK

54	London HL 8004	Caribbean/Weep Away (with Louisiana Hayride Band) (tri or round centre)	60/40
54	London HL 8048	Hootchy Kootchy Henry (From Hawaii)/Gigolo	60
54	London HL 8048	Hootchy Kootchy Henry (From Hawaii)/Gigolo (78)	6
54	London HL 8083	The Haunting Waterfall/Dancerette (with Louisiana Hayride Band)	60
54	London HL 8083	The Haunting Waterfall/Dancerette (with Louisiana Hayride Band) (78)	6
55	Brunswick 05423	The World Keeps Turning Around/A Peasant's Guitar	20
55	Brunswick 05423	The World Keeps Turning Around/A Peasant's Guitar (78)	6
56	Brunswick 05586	When Mexico Gave Up The Rhumba/I Wish I Was A Little Bit Younger	20
56	Brunswick 05626	Red Light, Green Light (with Tulane Sisters)/Havana Huddle	20
56	Brunswick 05626	Red Light, Green Light (with Tulane Sisters)/Havana Huddle (78)	6
57	Brunswick 05642	Drink Up And Go Home/Take This Heart	15
57	Brunswick 05642	Drink Up And Go Home/Take This Heart (78)	6
57	Brunswick 05657	Pledge Of Love/What's Behind That Strange Door	15
57	Brunswick 05657	Pledge Of Love/What's Behind That Strange Door (78)	8
57	Brunswick 05718	Two Words (True Love)/You're Tempting Me (with Anita Kerr Quartet)	12
57	Brunswick 05718	Two Words (True Love)/You're Tempting Me (with Anita Kerr Quartet) (78)	9
60	London HLW 9130	Pink Chiffon/What You Don't Know (Won't Hurt You)	15
54	London RE-P 1014	LOUISIANA HAYRIDE (EP, with Louisiana Hayride Band)	60
60	London HA-W 2279	CARIBBEAN (LP)	90

TORPEDO (& THE CARIBBEANS)

55	Parlophone MP 143	Montego Bay/Lazy Jane (export 78)	12
56	Parlophone MP 148	Pretty Woman/War Man Power Man (export 78)	12

MICHELLE TORR

66	Fontana TF 676	Only Tears Are Left For Me/I Love That Man	15
77	Sonet SON 2104	I'm Just A Simple Country Girl From France/Une Petite Française (p/s)	5

GEORGE TORRENCE & NATURALS

68	London HLZ 10181	Lickin' Stick/So Long Goodbye	12
71	Jay Boy BOY 48	Lickin' Stick/So Long Goodbye (reissue)	6

EMILIANA TORRINI

01	Fat Cat 281 TP 7	E1 (Grain Remix)/(Process Remix) (p/s)	5
01	Fat Cat 282 TP 7	E2 (Mice Parade Remix)/(V/VM Remix)/(Mum Remix) (p/s)	7
01	Fat Cat 283 TP 7	E3 (Professor Ludlow & Dr Smith Remix)/(Stromba Remix) (p/s)	5
01	Fat Cat 284 TP 7	E4 (Antenna Farm Remix)/(Motion Remix) (p/s)	5
01	Fat Cat 285 TP 7	E5 (Lucky Kitchen Remix)/(Team Doyobi Remix) (p/s)	5
01	Fat Cat 286 TP 7	E6 (Foehn Remix)/(Chasm Remix) (p/s)	5
01	Fat Cat 287 TP 7	E7 (Immense Remix)/(Fonn Remix) (p/s)	5
01	Fat Cat 281 TP 7	E8 (Di Lacuna Remix)/(Transient Waves Remix) (p/s)	5

CLAIRE TORRY

67	Fontana TF 852	The Music Attracts Me/It Takes One To Make The Other Cry (as Claire Terry)	6
67	Fontana TF 878	Unsure Feelings/The End Of A Lifetime (as Claire Terry)	6
69	Decca F 12945	Love For Living/Love Tomorrow, Love Today (as Clare Torry)	6

TORTOISE

96 Duophonic D-UHF-D 12 — Yaus/STEREOLAB: Speedy Car (gig freebie, blue vinyl, p/s, 3,000 only) . . . 25
96 Duophonic D-UHF-D 12 — Yaus/STEREOLAB: Speedy Car (orange vinyl export issue, p/s, 3,000 only) . . . 25
96 City Slang EFA 04971 — RHYTHMS, RESOLUTIONS & CLUSTERS (LP, clear vinyl) . . . 25
Duophonic Super 45s DS 33 09 — Gamera/Cliff Dweller Society (12", 1500 on red vinyl, 1500 on clear vinyl, 1500 on black vinyl, 1000 on fluorescent yellow vinyl) . . . 25/25/25/30
(see also Sea & Cake)

TORTURE

81 Wildebeest WILD 1 — Last Post/Lucky/Finding My Way Home . . . 50

PETER TOSH

69 Unity UN 525 — The Return Of Al Capone/LENNEX BROWN: O Club (B-side actually by Lennon Brown) . . . 15
69 Unity UN 529 — Sun Valley (as Peter Touch)/HE(A)DLEY BENNETT: Drums Of Fu Manchu . . . 30
71 Bullet BU 486 — Maga Dog/THIRD & FOURTH GENERATION: Bull Dog . . . 18
72 Pressure Beat PR 5509 — Them A Fe Get A Beatin' (as Peter Touch)/ THIRD & FOURTH GENERATION: Version . . . 18
79 Rolling Stones RSR 103 — I'm The Toughest/Toughest Version (p/s) . . . 7
79 Rolling Stones RSR 104 — Buck In Hamm Palace/The Day The Dollar Die . . . 7
78 Rolling Stones COC 39109 — BUSH DOCTOR (LP, with inner sleeve and 'scratch & sniff' sticker) . . . 15
(see also Peter Touch, Bob Marley & Wailers, Cat & Nicky Campbell, Glen Adams)

TOTAL CHAOS

83 Volume VOL 1 — There Are No Russians In Afghanistan/Primitive Feeling/ Revolution Part 10 (p/s) . . . 6
83 Volume VOL 2 — Factory Man/Brixton Prison/She Don't Care/Die (p/s) . . . 7

TOTALLY OUTTA HAND BAND

78 Kilgaron KIL 1 — Teenage Revolution/Too Much Trouble By Far (p/s) . . . 8

TOTNAMITES

61 Oriole CB 1615 — Danny Boy/Tip Top Tottenham Hotspur . . . 10

TOTO

78 CBS S 11-6784 — Hold The Line/Takin' It Back (picture disc) . . . 6
82 CBS A 11-2079 — Rosanna/It's A Feeling (picture disc) . . . 6
82 CBS A 11-2510 — Africa/We Made It (Africa-shaped picture disc) . . . 10
83 CBS A 11-3392 — I Won't Hold You Back/Afraid Of Love (picture disc) . . . 6
88 CBS 651 411-2 — Stop Loving You/The Seventh One/I'll Be Over You (3" CD & adaptor, 5" case) . . . 8
88 CBS 651 607-2 — Pamela/Stay Away/Africa/Rosanna (CD, card sleeve) . . . 8
89 CBS 654 569-3 — SOLID GOLD (Pamela/Africa/Hold The Line) (3" CD EP, gatefold card sleeve) . . . 8
84 Polydor 422 8237-7 — DUNE (LP, soundtrack, 1 track by Brian Eno) . . . 15

TINA TOTT

69 Pye 7N 17823 — Take Away The Emptiness Too/Burning In The Background Of My Mind . . . 7

TOTTENHAM HOTSPUR F.C.

81 Towerbeu SHELF 1 — Ossie's Dream (Spurs Are On Their Way To Wembley)/Glory, Glory Tottenham Hotspur (12", blue vinyl) . . . 10
67 Columbia SEG 8532 — THE SPURS GO MARCHING ON: SINGALONG SPURS (EP) . . . 20
(see also Terry Venables)

TOUCH

69 Deram DM 243 — Miss Teach/We Feel Fine . . . 15
69 Deram DML/SML 1033 — THIS IS TOUCH (LP, some with poster) . . . 110/60

TOUCH

80 Ariola ARO 209 — When The Spirit Moves You/My Life Depends On You (p/s) . . . 5
80 Ariola ARO 243 — Don't You Know What Love Is/My Life Depends On You (some in p/s) . . . 20/6
80 Ariola ARO 250 — Love Don't Fail Me Now (p/s) . . . 6
80 Ariola ARL 5036 — TOUCH (LP) . . . 12

TOUCH

88 Touch T7:45 — Departing Platform 5/Touch Ritual (Radio Cut-Up) (p/s) . . . 5

PETER TOUCH

65 Island WI 211 — Hoot Nanny Hoot (actually by Peter Tosh & Wailers)/ BOB MARLEY: Do You Remember (actually Peter Tosh & Wailers) . . . 90
65 Island WI 215 — Shame And Scandal (with Wailers)/WAILERS: The Jerk . . . 90
67 Island WI 3042 — I Am The Toughest (actually by Peter Tosh & Wailers)/ MARCIA GRIFFITHS: No Faith . . . 90
69 Jackpot JP 706 — The Crimson Pirate/Moon Duck . . . 12
(see also Peter Tosh, Bop & The Beltone, Glen Adams)

TOURS

79 Tours T 1 — Language School/Foreign Girls (paper p/s) . . . 15
79 Tours T 1 — Language School/Foreign Girls (printed PVC sleeve) . . . 12
79 Virgin VS 307 — Tourist Information/You Knew (p/s) . . . 6

AL TOUSAN

61 London HLU 9291 — Naomi/Indinna (some copies miscredited to 'Al Pousan') . . . 15
(see also Allen Toussaint)

ALLEN TOUSSAINT

69 Soul City SC 119 — We The People/Tequila . . . 15
72 Reprise K 14200 — Soul Sister/She Once Belonged To Me . . . 5
72 Reprise K 44202 — LIFE, LOVE AND FAITH (LP) . . . 15
75 Reprise K 54021 — SOUTHERN NIGHTS (LP) . . . 12
(see also Al Tousan)

CALINE & OLIVER TOUSSAINT

78 Epic S EPC 6334 — The Gardens Of Monaco/Les Jardins De Monaco . . . 12

ROBERTA TOVEY

65 Polydor BM 56021 — Who's Who/Not So Old (some in p/s) . . . 45/25

MINT VALUE £

TOWER OF POWER

72 Reprise K 16190 Down To The Night Club/You Got To Funkifize . . . 5
73 Reprise K 16278 So Very Hard To Go/Clean Slate. . . 5
73 Reprise K 16211 You're Still A Young Man/Skating On Thin Ice . . . 5
74 Reprise K 16389 Don't Change Horses/Time Will Tell . . . 5
75 Reprise K 16543 It's Not The Crime/Only So Much Time On The Ground . . . 5
73 Reprise K 46223 TOWER OF POWER (LP) . . . 12
74 Reprise K 46282 BACK TO OAKLAND (LP). . . 12
75 Reprise K 56093 URBAN RENEWAL (LP) . . . 12

JOHNNY TOWERS

62 Philips 326554 BF The Lonely Man Theme/There's No Place Like Rome. . . 8
63 Philips 326570 BF This Kind Of Love/My First Romance . . . 7

COLIN TOWNS

78 Virgin VS 204 Full Circle (Main Theme)/Olivia (p/s) . . . 10
80 MCA MCA 643 Breakdown/Working Man (p/s, as Colin Towns) . . . 15
78 Virgin V 2093 FULL CIRCLE (LP, soundtrack, as Colin Towns). . . 12
(see also Gillan, Samson, Split Knee Loons)

TOWNSEL SISTERS

60 Polydor NH 66954 Will I Ever/I Know. . . 10

DEVIN TOWNSEND

98 USG/East West USG 1028-4 Christeen/Wild Colonial Boy/Night (CD, withdrawn). . . 12
(see also Wildhearts)

ED TOWNSEND

58 Capitol CL 14867 For Your Love/Over And Over Again . . . 10
58 Capitol CL 14927 When I Grow Too Old To Dream/You Are My Everything. . . 10
59 Capitol CL 14976 Richer Than I/Getting By Without You . . . 7
59 Capitol CL 15020 Don't Ever Leave Me/Lover Come Back To Me . . . 7
59 Capitol CL 15072 This Little Love Of Mine/Hold On . . . 7
60 Capitol CL 15141 Don't Get Around Much Anymore/Do Nothin' Till You Hear . . . 7
60 Warner Bros WB 21 Stay With Me (A Little While Longer)/I Love Everything About You . . . 12
59 Capitol EAP1 1091 ED TOWNSEND (EP). . . 18
59 Capitol T 1140 NEW IN TOWN (LP). . . 25

ED TOWNSEND

76 Curtom K 56180 NOW (LP) . . . 12

JOHN TOWNSEND

70s Sweet Folk All SFA 002 NO MUCKING ABOUT (LP) . . . 18

PETE TOWNSHEND

80 Atco K 11486 Let My Love Open The Door/Classified/Greyhound Girl (p/s, with sticker) . . . 5
82 Atco K 11751P Uniforms/Dance It All Away (picture disc) . . . 5
82 Atco K 11751PT Uniforms/Dance It All Away (12", picture disc). . . 8
82 Eva-Tone 623827XS My Generation/Pinball Wizard (U.S. square flexidisc sewn into U.K. copies of Richard Barnes' ***Maximum R&B*** book; with/without book) . . . 20/8
89 Virgin VSCD 1198 A Friend is A Friend (3.30)/Man Machines (Extended Mix)/Real World (Can You Really Dance?)/A Friend is A Friend (Album Version 4.45) (3" CD, card p/s). . . 10
89 Virgin VSCD 1209 I Won't Run Anymore/A Fool Says/Dig (Original Demo Version Recorded November 1987) (3" CD, card sleeve). . . 10
72 Track 2408 201 WHO CAME FIRST (LP, gatefold sleeve with poster) . . . 15
(see also The Who, Meher Baba, Billy Nicholls, Angie, Elton John)

PETE TOWNSHEND & RONNIE LANE

77 Polydor 2058 944 Street In The City/RONNIE LANE: Annie (limited issue). . . 15
77 Polydor 2058 944 Street In The City/RONNIE LANE: Annie (12", p/s) . . . 10
77 Polydor 2442 147 ROUGH MIX (LP, gatefold sleeve) . . . 12
(see also Who, Ronnie Lane)

TOY DOLLS

81 GBH SSM 005 Tommy Kowey's Car/She Goes To Finos (500 only) . . . 40
81 GRC GRC 104 Tommy Kowey's Car/She's A Working Ticket/Everybody Jitterbug/Teenager In Love/I've Got Asthma (yellow paper p/s, with insert). . . 30
82 Zonophone Z 31 Everybody Jitterbug/(She's A) Working Ticket (p/s) . . . 15
83 Volume VOL 3 Nellie The Elephant/Dig That Groove Baby (p/s). . . 12
83 Volume VOL 5 Cheerio And Toodle Pip/H.O. (p/s). . . 8
83 Volume VOL 7 Alfie From The Bronx/Hanky Panky (p/s) . . . 8
84 Volume VOL 10 We're Mad/Deirdre's A Slag (p/s). . . 6
84 Volume VOLT 10 We're Mad/Deirdre's A Slag/Rupert The Bear (12", p/s) . . . 10
84 Volume VOLP 1 DIG THAT GROOVE, BABY (LP). . . 15
85 Volume VOLP 2 A FAR OUT DISC (LP) . . . 12
(see also Showbiz Kids)

TOY DOLLS (U.S.)

63 London HLN 9647 Little Tin Soldier/Fly Away . . . 22

TOYS

79 SRT SRTS/79/CUS 345 My Mind Wanders/The Girl On My Wall/Toytime/I'd Do Anything For You (p/s) . . . 10
79 Toy TOYS 2 STILL DANCING (EP, hand-stamped white label, foldaround p/s) . . . 20

TOYS

80 Red Bus RBUS 54 Go To The Police/Breakdown . . . 50

TOYS (U.S.)

65 Stateside SS 460 A Lover's Concerto/This Night . . . 7
66 Stateside SS 483 Attack/See How They Run . . . 12
66 Stateside SS 502 May My Heart Be Cast Into Stone/On Backstreet . . . 18
66 Stateside SS 519 Silver Spoon/Can't Get Enough Of You Baby . . . 18
66 Stateside SS 539 Baby Toys/Happy Birthday Broken Heart . . . 12

67 Philips BF 1563 Ciao Baby/I Got Carried Away . . . 15
67 Philips BF 1581 My Love Sonata/I Close My Eyes . . . 10
69 Bell BLL 1053 A Lover's Concerto/Baby Toys . . . 6
66 Stateside (S)SL 10175 THE TOYS SING "A LOVER'S CONCERTO" AND "ATTACK" (LP, mono/stereo) . . . 35/45

TOYSHOP

69 Polydor 56317 Say Goodbye To Yesterday/Send My Love To Lucy . . . 6

TRACE

74 Vertigo 6360 852 TRACE (LP) . . . 20
75 Vertigo 6413 080 BIRDS (LP) . . . 20
(see also Curved Air)

AL TRACE & HIS LITTLE TRACERS

53 MGM MGM 693 Mocking Bird Boogie/You're Only A Part-Time Sweetheart (78) . . . 6

TRACE FAMILY TRIO

54 Parlophone DP 381 I'll Be No Stranger There/I've Got A Longing To Go (78, export issue) . . . 8

TRACER

83 Mouse Hole TRA 1 CHANNELLED AGGRESSION EP (p/s) . . . 125

MARK TRACEY

62 Parlophone R 4944 Caravan Of Lonely Men/Never Ending (with John Barry & His Orchestra) . . . 10

STAN TRACEY

58 Vogue LA 160130 STAN TRACEY SHOWCASE (LP) . . . 70
59 Vogue LA 160155 LITTLE KLUNK (LP, as Stan Tracey Trio) . . . 180
65 Columbia 33SX 1774 JAZZ SUITE (LP, as Stan Tracey Quartet, also stereo SCX 3589) . . . 75
66 Columbia S(C)X 6051 ALICE IN JAZZLAND (LP, as Stan Tracey Big Band) . . . 50
67 Columbia S(C)X 6124 STAN TRACEY... IN PERSON (LP) . . . 40
68 Columbia S(C)X 6205 WITH LOVE FROM JAZZ (LP) . . . 50
69 Ace Of Clubs ACL 1259 LITTLE KLUNK (LP, reissue) . . . 45
69 Columbia S(C)X 6320 WE LOVE YOU MADLY (LP, as Stan Tracey Big Brass) . . . 55
69 Columbia SCX 6358 THE LATIN AMERICAN CAPER (LP, with Big Brass & Woodwind) . . . 40
70 Columbia SCX 6385 FREE AN' ONE (LP, as Stan Tracey Quartet) . . . 70
70 Columbia SCX 6413 SEVEN AGES OF MAN (LP, as Stan Tracey Big Band) . . . 35
72 Columbia SCX 6485 PERSPECTIVES (LP as Stan Tracey Trio) . . . 40
(see also New Departures Quartet, Mike Osborne, Neil Ardley, Laurie Johnson)

ZEN TRACEY

62 Decca F 11492 Shamrocker (Phil The Fluter's Ball)/Two By Two . . . 6

TRACK

66 Columbia DB 7987 Why Do Fools Fall In Love?/Cry To Me . . . 18

TRACK 4

82 Track 4 TR4 001 Mr Charisma (p/s, with insert) . . . 100

TRACTOR

72 Dandelion 2001 282 Stone Glory/Marie/As You Say . . . 18
78 UK UK 93 Roll The Dice/Vicious Circle . . . 8
81 Cargo CRS 002 No More Rock & Roll/Northern City . . . 10
81 Roach RR 2 Average Man's Hero/Big Big Boy (p/s) . . . 5
72 Dandelion 2310 217 TRACTOR (LP) . . . 70
(see also Way We Live)

TRACY

66 Columbia DB 7802 Don't Hold It Against Me/These Four Walls . . . 12

TRACY

69 Columbia DB 8569 Life's Like That/Let Me Love You . . . 7
69 Columbia DB 8637 Follow Me/A City Called Soul . . . 12
71 Columbia DB 8750 Rock Me In The Cradle/Strange Love . . . 10

GRANT TRACY & SUNSETS

61 Ember EMB S 126 Say When/Please Baby Please . . . 20
61 Ember EMB S 130 Pretend/Love Me . . . 20
62 Ember EMB S 148 The Great Matchmaker/Tears Came Rolling Down . . . 20
62 Ember EMB S 155 Taming Tigers/The Painted Smile . . . 20
63 Decca F 11741 Everybody Shake/Turn The Lights Down, Jenny . . . 20
64 Ember EMB 3352 TEENBEAT (LP) . . . 75
(see also Pete Dello, Honeybus)

WENDALL TRACY

58 London HLM 8664 Who's To Know/Corrigidor Rock . . . 30
58 London HLM 8664 Who's To Know/Corrigidor Rock (78) . . . 10

TRADER HORNE

69 Pye 7N 17846 Morning Way/Sheena . . . 18
70 Dawn DNS 1003 Here Comes The Rain/Goodbye Mercy Kelly . . . 12
70 Dawn DNLS 3004 MORNING WAY (LP, with photo & insert) . . . 60
(see also Them, Fairport Convention, Jackie McAuley)

TRADEWINDS

59 RCA RCA 1141 Crossroads/Furry Murray . . . 20
59 RCA RCA 1141 Crossroads/Furry Murray (78) . . . 40

TRADE WINDS

65 Red Bird RB 10020 New York Is A Lonely Town/Club Seventeen . . . 20
66 Kama Sutra KAS 202 Mind Excursion/Little Susan's Dreaming . . . 20

TRAD GRADS

61 Decca F 11403 Runnin' Shoes/Rag-Day Jazz-Band Ball . . . 10
(see also Quarry Men)

MINT VALUE £

TRAFFIC

67	Island WIP 6002	Paper Sun/Giving To You (some in p/s)	18/7
67	Island WIP 6017	Hole In My Shoe/Smiling Phases (some in p/s)	15/7
67	Island WIP 6025	Here We Go Round The Mulberry Bush/Coloured Rain (1st 100,000 in p/s)	15/7
68	Island WIP 6030	No Face, No Name, No Number/Roamin' In The Gloamin' With 40,000 Headmen	8
68	Island WIP 6041	You Can All Join In/Withering Tree (unissued in U.K.)	
68	Island WIP 6041	Feelin' Alright/Withering Tree	10
68	Island WIP 6050	Medicated Goo/Shanghai Noodle Factory	7
74	Island WIP 6207	Walking In The Wind/Walking In The Wind (Instrumental)	7
78	Island IEP 7	HOLE IN MY SHOE (EP, picture disc)	10
67	Island ILP 961/ILPS 9061	MR FANTASY (LP, gatefold sleeve, 1st pressing pink label with black 'circle' logo, mono/stereo)	100/50
68	Island ILPS 9081T	TRAFFIC (LP, gatefold sleeve with stapled-in booklet; pink label with black 'circle' logo, or pink rim label with 'palm tree' logo)	35/18
69	Island ILP(S) 9097	LAST EXIT (LP, pink label with black 'circle' logo, or pink rim label with 'palm tree' logo)	45/20
69	Island ILP(S) 9112	THE BEST OF TRAFFIC (LP, 1st pressings have pink "I" label, subsequent pressings have pink rim label with 'palm tree' logo)	15/12
70	Island ILPS 9081	MR. FANTASY (LP, 2nd pressing, pink rim label with 'palm tree' logo)	15
70	Island ILPS 9116	JOHN BARLEYCORN MUST DIE (LP, gatefold sleeve, 1st pressings have pink "I" label)	22
71	Island ILPS 9142	LIVE — NOVEMBER '70 (LP, unreleased, may exist as test pressing)	75+

(see also Spencer Davis Group, Stevie Winwood, Revolution, Hellions, Dave Mason, Gordon Jackson)

TRAFFIC JAM

67	Piccadilly 7N 35386	Almost But Not Quite There/Wait Just A Minute	300

(Demos are more common and worth £50 less than stock copies)
(see also Status Quo, Spectres)

TRAGICIAN

79	Look LKSP 6411	The Wild The Scared And The Timid/Traces Of Impact (numbered gatefold p/s)	35

PHIL TRAINER

73	BASF 05 19573-5	Beautiful Jim/No No No (p/s)	5
73	BASF BAG 22 29107-3	PHIL TRAINER (LP)	20

(see also Trees)

TRAIN SET

80s	Play Hard DEC 11	She's Gone (12", p/s)	35
80s	Play Hard DEC 17	Hold On (12", p/s)	35

TRAITOR'S GATE

85	Bullet BOLT 12	DEVIL TAKES THE HIGH ROAD (EP)	8

TRAITS

67	Pye International 7N 25404	Harlem Shuffle/Strange Lips (Start Ole Memories)	18

(see also Roy Head)

ALAN TRAJAN

69	MCA MK 5002	Speak To Me, Clarissa/This Might Be My Last Number	15
69	MCA MKPS 2000	FIRM ROOTS (LP)	100

TRAMLINE

68	Island ILPS 9088	SOMEWHERE DOWN THE LINE (LP, pink label)	75
69	Island ILPS 9095	MOVES OF VEGETABLE CENTURIES (LP, pink label)	75

(see also Whitesnake)

BOBBY LEE TRAMMELL

64	Sue WI 326	New Dance In France/Carolyn	35

TRAMMY (Ron Wilson)

72	Techniques TE 920	Horns Of Paradise/TECHNIQUES ALL STARS: Grass Root	6

TRAMP

69	Young Blood SBY 4	Vietnam Rose/Each Day	12
74	Spark SRL 1107	Put A Record On/You've Gotta Move	8
69	Music Man SMLS 603	TRAMP (LP)	110
73	Spark Replay SRLM 2001	TRAMP (LP, reissue)	40
74	Spark SRLP 112	PUT A RECORD ON (LP)	45

(see also Dave Kelly, Jo-Ann Kelly, Brunning Hall Sunflower Blues Band, Fleetwood Mac)

TRAMP ATTACK

00s	Must Destroy DESTROYER 11	Eight Years Since School/Please Don't Come To My Wedding (hand-painted, autographed, numbered p/s, 40 only)	15
00s	Must Destroy DESTROYER 13	Oh When The Sun Comes Down/Holes In My Clothes (Demo) (p/s, in custom hand-numbered mailer, with badge, 40 only)	15
00s	Must Destroy DUSTY 013CD	Oh When The Sun Comes Down/Holes In My Clothes (Demo)/Supreme Being (CD, in custom hand-numbered mailer, with badge, 20 only)	18

TRAMWAY

80s	Sarah SRH 43	Maritime City/Boathouse/Star (p/s, with insert)	7

TRANSATLANTICS

65	Fontana TF 593	Many Things From Your Window/I Tried To Forget	30
65	Fontana TF 638	Stand Up And Fight Like A Man/But I Know	15
65	Mercury MF 948	Don't Fight It/Look Before You Leap	40
65	King KG 1033	Run For Your Life/It's All Over	15
66	King KG 1040	Louie Go Home/Find Yourself Another Guy	20

TRANSIENT WAVES

98	Fat Cat 12FAT 011	Born With A Body And Fucked In The Heads/(2 Lone Swordsmen Mix)/(Skye [Stasis] Mix) (12", custom embossed sleeve)	10

			MINT VALUE £

TRANSMITTERS

Year	Label	Title	Value
78	Ebony EYE 11	Party/0.5 Alive (p/s)	5
78	Ebony EYE 12	Nowhere Train/Uninvited Guest/Persons Unknown (die-cut p/s)	5
79	Step Forward SF 1212	The Ugly Man/The One That Won The War/Free Trade/Curious (12", p/s)	8
70s	Eccentric EX 2 C50	I JAX DUB (cassette)	12
78	Ebony EBY 1002	24 HOURS (LP)	15
81	Heartbeat MB 4	AND WE CALL THIS LEISURE TIME (LP)	12

TRANSPARENT ILLUSION

Year	Label	Title	Value
81	Vortex VEX 001/002	Vortex/Nuclear Release (p/s)	20
82	Vortex VEX 5	Guilty Rich Men (p/s)	10
81	Vortex VEX 3	STILL HUMAN (LP)	35
82	Vortex VEX 4	CHAGRIN RECEIVER (LP)	20

TRANSPORTER

Year	Label	Title	Value
70s	Mother Truck MT 1	Kids On The Run/Intoxicating	6

TRAPEZE

Year	Label	Title	Value
69	Threshold TH 2	Send Me No More Letters/Another Day	10
72	Threshold TH 11	Coast To Coast/Your Love Is Alright	10
75	Warner Bros K 16606	Sunny Side Of The Street/Monkey	10
79	Aura AUS 114	Don't Ask Me How I Know/Take Good Care (p/s)	15
80	Aura AUS 116	Running Away/Don't Break My Heart (p/s)	15
69	Threshold THS 2	TRAPEZE (LP)	30
70	Threshold THS 4	MEDUSA (LP)	30
73	Threshold THS 8	YOU ARE THE MUSIC ... WE'RE JUST THE BAND (LP)	15
74	Warner Bros K 56064	HOT WIRE (LP)	15
74	Threshold THS 11	THE FINAL SWING (LP)	12
79	Aura AUL 708	HOLD ON (LP)	15
81	Aura AUL 717	LIVE IN TEXAS ... DEAD ARMADILLOS (LP)	15

(see also Finders Keepers, Montanas, Deep Purple, Glenn Hughes, Judas Priest, Whitesnake)

TRASH

Year	Label	Title	Value
69	Apple APPLE 6	Road To Nowhere/Illusions (initial copies as White Trash, later Trash)	200/30
69	Apple APPLE 17	Golden Slumbers – Carry That Weight/Trash Can	18

(see also Poets, Pathfinders)

TRASHCAN SINATRAS

Year	Label	Title	Value
89	Go! Discs GODX 34	Obscurity Knocks/The Best Man's Fall/Drunken Chorus/Who's He? (12", p/s)	18
89	Go! Discs GODCD 34	Obscurity Knocks/The Best Man's Fall/Drunken Chorus/Who's He? (CD)	18
90	Go! Discs GOD 41	Only Tongue/Useless Begins With You/Tonight You Belong To Me (p/s)	8
90	Go! Discs GODX 41	Only Tongue/Useless Begins With You/Tonight You Belong To Me (12", p/s)	12
90	Go! Discs GODCD 41	Only Tongue/Useless Begins With You/Tonight You Belong To Me (CD, card sleeve)	20
90	Go! Discs GOD 46	Circling The Circumference/My Mistake (p/s)	10
90	Go! Discs GODX 46	Circling The Circumference/My Mistake/White Horses (12", p/s)	15
90	Go! Discs GODCD 46	Circling The Circumference/My Mistake/White Horses (CD)	15
93	Go! Discs GODX 98	Hayfever/Say/Kangaroo Court/Skin Diving (12", p/s)	10
93	Go! Discs GODCD 98	Hayfever/Say/Kangaroo Court/Skin Diving (CD, in box)	20
93	Go! Discs GOD 100	I've Seen Everything/Houseproud/I'm The One Who Fainted (p/s)	8
96	Go! Discs GOD 151	How Can I Apply?/Save Me (p/s)	8
96	Go! Discs GOD 157	To Sir With Love/Claw/A Boy And A Girl/You Only Live Twice (p/s)	5
90	Go! Discs 828 2011	CAKE (LP)	18
93	Go! Discs 828408-2	I'VE SEEN EVERYTHING (CD, digipak, with booklet & poster)	18

TRASHMEN

Year	Label	Title	Value
64	Stateside SS 255	Surfin' Bird/King Of The Surf	35
64	Stateside SS 276	Bird Dance Beat/A-Bone	35

TRAVELING WILBURYS

Year	Label	Title	Value
88	Warner Bros W 7732W	Handle With Care/Margarita (gatefold p/s with sticker, some sealed)	10/8
88	Warner Bros W 7732TE	Handle With Care (Extended)/Margarita (10", p/s)	10
88	Warner Bros W 7732T	Handle With Care (Extended)/Margarita (12", p/s)	10
88	Warner Bros W 7732CD	Handle With Care (LP Version)/Margarita/Handle With Care (Extended Version) (3" CD, with adaptor, 5" case)	12
89	Warner Bros W 7637TW	End Of The Line (Extended)/Congratulations (12", p/s, with/without sheet of stickers)	15/10
89	Warner Bros W 7637CD	End Of The Line (Extended Version)/Congratulations (3" CD, gatefold card p/s in PVC sleeve)	15
90	Warner Bros W 9773T	Nobody's Child/DAVE STEWART: Lumière/RINGO STARR: With A Little Help From My Friends (12", p/s)	12
90	Warner Bros W 9773CD	Nobody's Child/DAVE STEWART: Lumière/RINGO STARR: With A Little Help From My Friends (CD)	12
90	Warner Bros W 9523	She's My Baby/New Blue Moon (Instrumental Version) (p/s)	6
90	Warner Bros W 9523T	She's My Baby (LP Version)/New Blue Moon (Instrumental Version)/ Runaway (12", p/s)	12
90	Warner Bros W 9523CD	She's My Baby (LP Version)/New Blue Moon (Instrumental Version)/ Runaway (CD)	12
91	Warner Bros W 0019	Wilbury Twist/New Blue Moon (Instrumental) (p/s)	7
91	Warner Bros W 0018W	Wilbury Twist/New Blue Moon (Instrumental) (card p/s with 4 postcards)	12
91	Warner Bros W 0019T	Wilbury Twist/New Blue Moon (Instrumental)/Cool Dry Place (12", p/s)	12
91	Warner Bros W 0019CD	Wilbury Twist/New Blue Moon (Instrumental)/Cool Dry Place (CD, silver or black print)	12
88	Warner Bros WX 224W	VOLUME ONE (LP, some with stickered sleeve & sticker inserts)	45
88	Warner Bros WX 224CD	VOLUME ONE (CD)	75
90	Warner Bros WX 7799-2 324-2	VOLUME THREE (CD)	80

(see also George Harrison, Bob Dylan, Roy Orbison, Jeff Lynne, Tom Petty)

MINT VALUE £

TRAVELLING FOLK

70s Cuchulainn CCHS 1017 — TRAVELLING FOLK (LP) 15

PAT TRAVERS

76 Polydor SFI 221/2814 040 — Makes No Difference (1-sided flexidisc, promo only, black & white p/s) 15
77 Polydor Super 2383 436 — MAKIN' MAGIC (LP, with inner sleeve) 12
77 Polydor Super 2383 471 — PUTTING IT STRAIGHT (LP, with inner sleeve) 12
79 Polydor POLS 1011 — GO FOR WHAT YOU KNOW (LP, red vinyl) 12
(see also Nicko McBrain)

TRAVIS

73 A&M AMLS 68120 — SHINE ON ME (LP) 40
(see also Paul Travis)

TRAVIS

96 Red Telephone Box PHONE 001 — All I Want Do Is Rock/Line Is Fine/Funny Thing (10", numbered, stickered p/s, 750 only) 55
97 Independiente ISOM 1S — U16 Girls/Hazy Shades/Good Time Girls (p/s) 6
97 Independiente ISOM 3S — All I Want Do Is Rock/Blue On A Black Weekend (p/s) 12
97 Independiente ISOM 5S — Tied To The 90s/Me Beside You (p/s) 7
97 Independiente ISOM 5MS — Tied To The 90s/City In The Rain/Whenever She Comes Around/Standing On My Own (CD) 15
97 Independiente GOODT 1 — The Line Is Fine/All I Want To Do Is Rock/More Than Us/Tied To The 90s (12", promo only) 10
97 Independiente GOOD 1 — 5 GOOD FEELINGS: The Line Is Fine/All I Want To Do Is Rock/More Than Us/Funny Thing/Tied To The 90s (CD, promo only) 15
00 Independiente ISOM 45455 — Coming Around/Coming Around (Version) (juke box promo) 8
97 Independiente ISOM 1CD — GOOD FEELING (CD) 18
99 Independiente ISM 4946249 — THE MAN WHO (CD, with bonus CD [Driftwood/Slide Show/More Than Us]) 30

MERLE TRAVIS

53 Capitol CL45 13985 — Gamblers Guitar/Shut Up And Drink Your Beer 40
53 Capitol CL 13985 — Gamblers Guitar/Shut Up And Drink Your Beer (78) 6
54 Capitol CL 14051 — Green Cheese/Re-Enlistment Blues (78) 8
54 Capitol CL 14110 — Jolie Fille (Pretty Girl)/I Can't Afford The Coffee (78) 6
56 Capitol EAP1 032 — MERLE TRAVIS GUITAR (EP) 20
57 Capitol EAP2 650 — MERLE TRAVIS GUITAR NO. 2 (EP) 15
59 Capitol EAP1 891 — BACK HOME (EP) 15
63 Capitol EAP1 1391 — WALKIN' THE STRINGS (EP) 15
57 Capitol T 891 — BACK HOME (LP) 30
63 Capitol (S)T 1664 — TRAVIS! (LP) 20
65 Capitol T 2102 — MERLE TRAVIS & JOE MAPHIS (LP) 20
(see also Brown's Ferry Four)

PAUL TRAVIS

75 A&M AMLS 68290 — RETURN OF THE NATIVE (LP, with lyric inner) 20
(see also Travis)

TRAVIS & BOB

59 Pye International 7N 25018 — Tell Him No/We're Too Young 15
59 Pye International N 25018 — Tell Him No/We're Too Young (78) 10
61 Mercury AMT 1142 — Baby Stay Close To Me/Give Your Love To Me 7

TRAX FOUR

66 Ace Of Clubs S/ACL 1216 — WINGDING PARTY!!! (LP, mono/stereo) 30

JACK TRAYLOR & STEELWIND

73 Grunt FTR 0194 — CHILD OF NATURE (LP) 20

TREASURE BOY

67 Trojan TR 010 — Love Is A Treasure (actually by Freddie McKay)/TOMMY McCOOK: Zazuka 15

TREBLETONES

61 Butlin CP 2424 — Butlin Holiday/Butlin Holiday 8
63 Oriole CB 1838 — In Real Life/Dream Of A Lifetime 12

TREDEGAR

86 Aries CEP 0001 — Duma/The Jester (p/s) 75
86 Aries CEP LP 001 — TREDEGAR (LP, gatefold sleeve, embossed) 12
(see also Budgie)

HERBERT BEERBOHM TREE

65 OMY 69 — KEEP THOSE DOGS AWAY (EP) 25

TREEBOUND STORY

86 Fon ELM 1 — I REMEMBER EP (12", p/s) 8

TREES

70 CBS 5078 — Nothing Special/Epitaph 18
70 CBS 63837 — THE GARDEN OF JANE DELAWNEY (LP) 100
71 CBS 64168 — ON THE SHORE (LP) 100
87 Decal LIK 12 — ON THE SHORE (LP, reissue) 15
87 Decal LIK 15 — THE GARDEN OF JANE DELAWNEY (LP, reissue) 15
(see also Casablanca, Juliet Lawson, Trainer)

TREETOPS

67 Parlophone R 5628 — Don't Worry Baby/I Remember 12
68 Parlophone R 5669 — California My Way/Carry On Living 10
70 Columbia DB 8727 — Mississippi Valley/Man Is A Man 7
71 Columbia DB 8799 — Without The One You Love/So Here I Go Again 10

TREKKAS

65 Planet PLF 105 — Please Go/I Put A Spell On You 75

TREMBLING BLUE STARS

96 Shinkansen SHINKANSEN 1 Abba On The Jukebox/She's Always There (p/s, 1,000 only) . . . 8

TREMELOES

66 Decca F 12423 Blessed/The Right Time . . . 18
66 CBS 202242 Good Day Sunshine/What A State I'm In . . . 8
67 CBS 202519 Here Comes My Baby/Gentlemen Of Pleasure . . . 5
67 CBS 2723 Silence Is Golden/Let Your Hair Hang Down (p/s) . . . 6
67 CBS 2930 Even The Bad Times Are Good/Jenny's Alright (p/s) . . . 6
67 CBS 3043 Be Mine/Suddenly Winter . . . 5
68 CBS 3234 Suddenly You Love Me/As You Are . . . 5
68 CBS 2889 Helule Helule/Girl From Nowhere . . . 5
68 CBS 3680 My Little Lady/All The World To Me . . . 5
68 CBS 3873 I Shall Be Released/I Miss My Baby . . . 5
69 CBS 4065 Hello World/Up Down All Around . . . 5
69 CBS 4582 (Call Me) Number One/Instant Whip . . . 5
68 CBS Special Products WB 728 Here Comes My Baby/SIMON & GARFUNKEL: The 59th Street Bridge Song (p/s, mail-order only with Pepsi Cola tokens) . . . 6
73 Epic EPC 1399 Ride On/Hands Off . . . 5
73 CBS 1139 Here Comes My Baby/Silence Is Golden (p/s, 'Hall Of Fame Hits' series) . . . 5
84 Meteor MTS 002 Silence Is Golden (Acappella version)/The Last Word . . . 5
68 CBS EP 6402 MY LITTLE LADY (EP) . . . 18
67 CBS (S)BPG 63017 HERE COME THE TREMELOES (LP) . . . 20
68 CBS (S)BPG 63138 THE TREMELOES: CHIP, RICK, ALAN AND DAVE (LP) . . . 20
69 CBS 63547 THE TREMELOES 'LIVE' IN CABARET (LP) . . . 18
70 CBS 64242 MASTER (LP) . . . 15
(see also Brian Poole & Tremeloes, Trems, Chip Hawkes)

TREMORS

80s Redball RR 0002 Modern World/Smashed Reality (p/s) . . . 5

TREMS

73 Epic EPC 1660 Make It Break It/Movin' On . . . 5
(see also Tremeloes)

TREND

67 Page One POF 004 Boyfriends And Girlfriends/Shoot On Sight . . . 30

TREND

70 Trendy TREND 1 Teenage Crush/Cool Johnny (some with press sheet) . . . 50/40

TREND

80 MCA MCA 583 Polly And Wendy/Family Way (p/s) . . . 20
80 MCA MCA 629 This Dance Hall Must Have A Back Way Out/Fiction, Love & Romance (p/s) . . . 15

TRENDS

63 Piccadilly 7N 35171 All My Loving/Sweet Little Miss Love . . . 15
64 Pye 7N 15644 You're A Wonderful One/The Way You Do The Things You Do . . . 15
(see also Tammy St. John, Freddie Self, Freddie Ryder)

TRENDSETTERS

64 Silver Phoenix 1001 You Don't Care/My Heart Goes . . . 50

TRENDSETTERS

60s Oak RGJ 999 AT THE HOTEL DE FRANCE (EP) . . . 25

TRENDSETTERS LTD

64 Parlophone R 5118 In A Big Way/Lucky Date . . . 15
64 Parlophone R 5161 Hello Josephine/Move On Over . . . 18
64 Parlophone R 5191 Go Away/Lollipops And Roses . . . 12
65 Parlophone R 5324 You Sure Got A Funny Way Of Showing Your Love/I'm Coming Home . . . 10
(see also King Crimson, Giles Giles & Fripp, Brain)

CHARLES TRENET

58 Columbia SEG 7819 BOUM! (EP) . . . 8

TRENIERS

58 Coral Q 72319 Ooh-La-La/Pennies From Heaven . . . 45
58 Coral Q 72319 Ooh-La-La/Pennies From Heaven (78) . . . 12
58 Fontana H 137 Go! Go! Go!/Get Out Of The Car (featuring Don Hill, Alto Sax) . . . 150
58 Fontana H 137 Go! Go! Go!/Get Out Of The Car (featuring Don Hill, Alto Sax) (78) . . . 40
59 London HLD 8858 When Your Hair Has Turned To Silver/Never, Never . . . 45
59 London HLD 8858 When Your Hair Has Turned To Silver/Never, Never (78) . . . 50

JACKIE TRENT

61 Oriole CB 1711 Pick Up The Pieces/In Your Heart . . . 8
62 Oriole CB 1749 The One Who Really Loves You/Your Conscience Or Your Heart . . . 15
63 Piccadilly 7N 35121 Melancholy Me/So Did I . . . 8
64 Piccadilly 7N 35165 If You Love Me/Only One Such As You . . . 15
64 Pye 7N 15692 Somewhere In The World/I Heard Somebody Say . . . 6
64 Pye 7N 15742 Don't Stand In My Way/How Soon . . . 6
65 Pye 7N 15776 Where Are You Now (My Love)/On The Other Side Of The Tracks . . . 5
65 Pye 7N 15865 When Summertime Is Over/To Show I Love Him . . . 5
65 Pye 7N 15949 It's All In The Way You Look At Life/Time After Time . . . 6
66 Pye 7N 17047 You Baby/Send Her Away . . . 18
66 Pye 7N 17082 Love Is Me Love Is You/This Time . . . 6
66 Pye 7N 17158 If You Ever Leave Me/There Goes My Love, There Goes My Life . . . 6
67 Pye 7N 17249 Open Your Heart/Love Can Give . . . 6
67 Pye 7N 17323 Your Love Is Everywhere/It's Not Easy Loving You . . . 6
67 Pye 7N 17415 That's You/Stop Me And Buy One . . . 6
67 Pye 7N 17437 Bye Bye Love (German Version)/Alles Okay (Send Her Away) . . . 6
69 Pye 7N 17693 I'll Be There/Close To You . . . 5
78 Casino Classics CC 4 You Baby/Send Her Away/FAMILY AFFAIR: Love Hustle . . . 5

MINT VALUE £

65 Pye NEP 4225 WHERE ARE YOU NOW (EP) 20
65 Pye NPL 18125 THE MAGIC OF JACKIE TRENT (LP) 30
67 Pye NPL 18173 ONCE MORE WITH FEELING (LP) 22
67 Pye NPL 18201 STOP ME AND BUY ONE (LP) 25

TRESPASS
79 Trial CASE 1 One Of These Days/Bloody Moon (p/s) 20
80 Trial CASE 2 Jealousy/Live It Up! (p/s) 15
81 Trial CASE 3 Bright Lights/The Duel/Man And Machine (p/s) 15

TREVOR (Shield)
64 Blue Beat BB 228 Down In Virginia/Hey Little Schoolgirl (with Caribs) 15
68 Blue Cat BS 129 Tender Arms (with Joe White & Glen Brown)/DERMOTT LYNCH: Something Is Worrying Me 15
68 Blue Cat BS 130 Pretty Girl (with Joe White & Glen Brown)/DERMOTT LYNCH: You Went Away 12
69 Blue Cat BS 153 Everyday Is Like A Holiday/Have You Time (by Trevor & Maytones) 12

TREVOR & KEITH
70 Punch PH 41 The Ark/MINNA BOYS: False Reador (actually titled "Got To Move") 7
(see also Carl Bryan)

T. REX
(see under Marc Bolan /T. Rex; see also Tyrannosaurus Rex)

TRIARCHY
79 SRT/79/CUS 599 Save The Khan/Juliet's Tomb (some in p/s, 1,000 only) 80/30
79 Direct NEON 1 Save The Khan/Juliet's Tomb (reissue, p/s) 35
80 Direct NEON 2 Metal Messiah/Sweet Alcohol/Hell Hound On My Trail (some in p/s) 70/30

TRIBAN
69 Cambrian CSP 707 Leaving On A Jet Plane/Night In The City 6
71 Decca F 13115 Black Paper Roses/One Way Mirror 5
69 Cambrian MCT 592 TRIBAN (LP) 25
72 Cambrian RAINMAKER (LP) 20

TRIBE (U.K.)
66 Planet PLF 108 The Gamma Goochie/I'm Leavin' 70
67 RCA RCA 1592 Love Is A Beautiful Thing/Steel Guitar 20

TRIBE (U.S.)
66 Polydor 56510 Dancin' To The Beat Of My Heart/Woofin' 18

TRIBE
73 Probe PRO 597 Koke Parts 1 & 2 5

TONY TRIBE
69 Downtown DT 419 Red Red Wine/RECO & RUDIES: Blues 12
69 Downtown DT 439 Gonna Give You All The Love/HERBIE GREY: Why Wait 7

TRIBUTE
73 Jam JAM 48 Bobby Charlton/City Summer 12

TRICKY DISCO
91 Warp WAP 11 HOUSEFLY EP (12") 10

TRIDENT
84 SRT TRI 1 Destiny/Power Of The Trident 50
(see also Filthy Rich)

TRIFFIDS
65 Fontana TL 5231 THE TRIFFIDS ARE REALLY FOLK (LP) 15
75 DJM DJSL 051 STREETS OF LONDON (LP) 12

TRIFLE
69 United Artists UP 2270 All Together Now/Got My Thing 7
70 Dawn DNS 1008 Old-Fashioned Prayer Meeting/Dirty Old Town 6
71 Dawn DNLS 3017 FIRST MEETING (LP) 60
(see also George Bean)

PANDIT KANWAR SAIN TRIKHA
71 Mushroom 100 MR 7 THREE SITAR PIECES (LP) 45

TRILOGY
71 Mercury 6338 034 I'M BEGINNING TO FEEL IT (LP) 15

TOMMY TRINDER
59 Fontana H 204 La Plume De Ma Tante/On The Sunny Side Of The Street 10
59 Fontana H 204 La Plume De Ma Tante/On The Sunny Side Of The Street (78) 10

TRINIDAD ALL STARS
56 Parlophone DP 524 Trouble In Arima/Stone Cold Dead In De Market (78, export issue) 12

TRINIDAD STEEL BAND
51 Melodisc 1185 Caroline/Six String Calypso (78) 8
52 Vogue V 9017 Mango Walk/Take Me (78) 10
52 Vogue V 9018 Ramadin/Johnny (78) 10

TRINITY HOUSE
77 Profile GMOR 146 FLASHBACK THROUGH HISTORY (LP, private pressing, with insert) 40

TRIO
70 Dawn DNLS 3006 TRIO (2-LP, with poster) 40
71 Dawn DNLS 3022 CONFLAGRATION (LP, with poster) 55
76 Dawn DNLS 3072 LIVE AT WOODSTOCK TOWN HALL (LP, with Stu Martin) 18
(see also John Surnam)

TRIPLETS
69 President PT 245 When Lovers Say Goodbye/You Won't See Me Leaving 7

MINT VALUE £

TRIPPERS

66 Pye International 7N 25388 — Dance With Me/Keep A-Knockin' . . . 20

TRISHA

65 CBS 201800 — The Darkness Of My Night/Confusion . . . 7

TRISTAR AIRBUS

72 RCA RCA 2170 — Travellin' Man/Willie Morgan On The Wing . . . 10

(see also Wimple Winch, 10cc, Hotlegs)

TRIUMVIRAT

74 Harvest SHSP 4030 — ILLUSION ON A DOUBLE DIMPLE (LP) . . . 12
75 Harvest SHSP 4048 — SPARTACUS (LP) . . . 12

TRIXIE'S BIG RED MOTORBIKE

82 Chew CH 9271 — A Splash Of Red/Invisible Boyfriend (white label, stapled foldover p/s) . . . 15
83 Lobby Ludd (no cat. no.) — TRIXIE'S BIG RED MOTORBIKE (EP, plain sleeve with stapled strip) . . . 12
84 Lobby Ludd L 100001 — Norman And Narcissus/In Timbuktu (p/s) . . . 10
84 Lobby Ludd L 100002 — A Splash Of Red/Invisible Boyfriend (reissue, different p/s) . . . 10
84 Lobby Ludd L 100003 — TRIXIE'S BIG RED MOTORBIKE (EP, reissue, stapled p/s) . . . 10
84 Nathan NAT 001 — That's The End Of That/CLIVE PIG & LEE VALLEY: As Soon As She's Gone (33rpm flexi & sweet with *Wally's Dog* fanzine) . . . 6/4

TRIXONS

69 Major Minor MM 665 — Just Another Song/Sunny Side Sam . . . 7

MARCUS TRO

65 Ember EMB S 203 — Tell Me/What's The Matter Little Girl (some in p/s) . . . 12/7
65 Ember EMB 3365 — INTRODUCING MARCUS TRO (LP) . . . 35

TROGGS

SINGLES

66 CBS 202038 — Lost Girl/The Yella In Me . . . 40
66 Fontana TF 689 — Wild Thing/From Home . . . 8
66 Fontana TF 717 — With A Girl Like You/I Want You . . . 7
66 Page One POF 001 — I Can't Control Myself/Gonna Make You . . . 7
66 Page One POF 010 — Any Way That You Want Me/6-5-4-3-2-1 . . . 7
67 Page One POF 015 — Give It To Me/You're Lyin' . . . 7
67 Page One POF 022 — My Lady/Girl In Black (withdrawn) . . . 45
67 Page One POF 022 — Night Of The Long Grass/Girl In Black . . . 7
67 Page One POF 030 — Hi Hi Hazel/As I Ride By . . . 8
67 Page One POF 040 — Love Is All Around/When Will The Rain Come . . . 7
68 Page One POF 056 — Little Girl/Maybe The Madman? . . . 7
68 Page One POF 064 — Surprise Surprise/Marbles And Some Gum? . . . 8
68 Page One POF 082 — You Can Cry If You Want To/There's Something About You . . . 8
68 Page One POF 092 — Hip Hip Hooray/Say Darlin'! . . . 7
69 Page One POF 114 — Evil Woman/Sweet Madeline . . . 7
69 Page One POF 126 — Wild Thing/I Can't Control Myself . . . 7
70 Page One POF 164 — Easy Lovin'/Give Me Something . . . 7
70 Page One POF 171 — Lover/Come Now . . . 7
70 Page One POF 182 — The Raver/You . . . 7
71 DJM DJM 248 — Lazy Weekend/Let's Pull Together . . . 7
72 Jam JAM 25 — Wild Thing/With A Girl Like You/Love Is All Around . . . 5
72 Pye 7N 45147 — Everything's Funny/Feels Like A Woman . . . 7
73 Pye 7N 45244 — Listen To The Man/Queen Of Sorrow . . . 7
73 Pye 7N 45295 — Strange Movies/I'm On Fire . . . 8
75 Penny Farthing PEN 861 — Good Vibrations/Push It Up To Me . . . 6
75 Penny Farthing PEN 884 — Wild Thing (Reggae Version)/Jenny Come Down . . . 6
75 Penny Farthing PEN 889 — Summertime/Jenny Come Down . . . 6
75 Penny Farthing PEN 901 — (I Can't Get No) Satisfaction/Memphis, Tennessee . . . 6
76 Penny Farthing PEN 919 — I'll Buy You An Island/Supergirl . . . 5
77 Penny Farthing PEN 929 — Feeling For Love/Summertime . . . 5
78 Raw RAW 25 — Just A Little Too Much/The True Troggs Tapes (p/s) . . . 6
84 10 TENY 21 — Every Little Thing/Blackjack And Poker/With A Girl Like You (picture disc) . . . 5

EPs

67 Page One POE 001 — TROGGS TOPS (EP) . . . 22
67 Page One POE 002 — TROGGS TOPS VOLUME TWO (EP) . . . 40
67 Page One — TRACK A TROGG (EP, unreleased)
81 DJM DJS 6 — TROGGS TAPES (EP, double pack) . . . 10

LPs

66 Fontana (S)TL 5355 — FROM NOWHERE — THE TROGGS (LP, mono/stereo) . . . 35/45
66 Page One POL 001 — TROGGLODYNAMITE (LP) . . . 50
67 Page One FOR 001 — THE BEST OF THE TROGGS (LP) . . . 30
67 Page One POL(S) 003 — CELLOPHANE (LP, mono/stereo) . . . 50/65
68 Page One POL 1 — THE TROGGS ON TOUR (LP, export issue) . . . 150+
68 Page One FOR 007 — THE BEST OF THE TROGGS VOLUME TWO (LP) . . . 35
68 Page One POL(S) 012 — MIXED BAG (LP) . . . 110
69 Page One POS 602 — TROGGLOMANIA (LP) . . . 40
70 DJM Silverline DJML 009 — CONTRASTS (LP, original issue) . . . 25

(see also Reg Presley, Chris Britton, Ronnie Bond, Ten Feet Five)

CHUCK TROIS & AMAZING MAZE

68 Action ACT 4517 — Call On You/Woodsman . . . 15

TROJAN

88 GI GILP 444 — THE MARCH IS ON (LP) . . . 18

TROJANS

58 Decca F 11065 — Man I'm Gonna Be/Make It Up . . . 20
58 Decca F 11065 — Man I'm Gonna Be/Make It Up (78) . . . 15

MINT VALUE £

TROLL BROTHERS
73 SRT SRT 73316 You Turn Me On/Turn Out The Lights (p/s) 10

TROMBONES UNLIMITED
66 Liberty LIB 55874 Daydream/The Phoenix Love Theme (Senza Fine) 5
66 Liberty LBY 1350 YOU'RE GONNA HEAR FROM ME (LP) 12

TRONICS
61 Fontana H 348 Cantina/Pickin' & Stompin' 18

TRONICS
78 Tronics T 001 Suzie (actually "Suzie's Vibrator")/Favourite Girls (plain sleeve with inserts) 8
79 Tronics T 002 Time Off/Goodbye (p/s) 8
81 Alien ALIEN 18 Shark Fucks/Time Off (p/s, with insert) 6
81 Lyntone Love Backed By Force/(tracks by Dancing Did & Instant Automatons, flexidisc with *Chainsaw* fanzine, issue 12) 8
83 Red Rhino RED 3 Wild Cat Rock/Tonight (p/s) 5
82 Press PRESS 1 TRANZISTER SISTER (12" EP) 8
80 Tronics T 003 THE TRONICS (cassette) 12
81 Tronics T 004 WHAT'S THE HUBBUB BUBB (cassette) 12
81 Alien BALIEN 3 LOVE BACKED BY FORCE (LP) 12
(see also Les Zarjaz)

TROOPERS
57 Vogue V 9087 Get Out/My Resolution 800
57 Vogue V 9087 Get Out/My Resolution (78) 200

TROOPS OF TOMORROW
82 Troops TROOPS 1 TROOPS OF TOMORROW (12" EP) 8
(see also Vibrators, Fallen Angels)

TROPIC SHADOWS
72 Big Shot BI 603 Our Anniversary/Anniversary (Version) 6

ARCHIBALD TROTT
64 Black Swan WI 407 Get Together/Just Because 18
(see also Baba Brooks)

TROUBADORS/TROUBADOUR SINGERS
57 London HLR 8469 Fascination/Midnight In Athens 18
58 London HLR 8541 The Lights Of Paris/The Flaming Rose 15
58 London RE-R 1135 THE TROUBADORS (EP) 10
58 London HA-R 2095 THE TROUBADORS IN SPAIN (LP) 15
58 London HA-R 2106 THE TROUBADORS IN THE LAND OF THE GIPSIES (LP) 15
58 London HA-R 2114 THE TROUBADORS IN ROME (LP) 15
58 London HA-A 2121 THE TROUBADORS IN HAWAII (LP) 15
60 London HA-R 2249 THE TROUBADORS IN PARIS (LP) 15
66 London SH-F 8275 SING OUT BIG (LP, as Troubadour Singers, stereo) 15
(see also Jane Morgan)

BOBBY TROUP
55 Capitol CL 14219 Julie Is Her Name/Instead Of You 12
54 Capitol LC 6660 BOBBY TROUP (10" LP) 22

BOB TROW QUARTET
54 London HL 8082 Soft Squeeze Baby/I Went Along For The Ride 45
54 London HL 8082 Soft Squeeze Baby/I Went Along For The Ride (78) 10

ROBIN TROWER
78 Chrysalis CHS 2247 It's For You/My Love/In City Dreams (p/s, red vinyl) 5
81 Chrysalis CHS 2497 What It Is/Into Money (p/s, clear vinyl) 5
73 Chrysalis CHR 1039 TWICE REMOVED FROM YESTERDAY (LP) 12
74 Chrysalis CHR 1057 BRIDGE OF SIGHS (LP) 12
75 Chrysalis CHR 1073 FOR EARTH BELOW (LP) 12
(see also Paramounts, Procol Harum, Jack Bruce & Robin Trower)

TROY & T-BIRDS
61 London HL 9476 Twistle/Take Ten 18

DORIS TROY
63 London HLK 9749 Just One Look/Bossa Nova Blues 25
64 Atlantic AT 4011 What'cha Gonna Do About It/Tomorrow Is Another Day 18
65 Atlantic AT 4020 Please Little Angel/One More Chance 15
65 Atlantic AT 4032 Heartaches/You'd Better Stop 15
65 Cameo Parkway C 101 I'll Do Anything (He Wants Me To)/But I Love Him 70
68 Atlantic 584 148 Just One Look/What'cha Gonna Do About It 10
68 Toast TT 507 I'll Do Anything (Anything He Wants Me To)/Heartaches 12
70 Apple APPLE 24 Ain't That Cute/Vaya Con Dios (some with p/s) 22/10
70 Apple APPLE 28 Jacob's Ladder/Get Back 12
71 Mojo 2092 011 I'll Do Anything (He Wants Me To)/But I Love Him (reissue) 10
73 Mojo 2092 062 Baby I Love You/To My Father's House 6
74 People PEO 112 Stretchin' Out/Don't Tell Your Mama 6
65 Atlantic AET 6007 WATCHA GONNA DO ABOUT IT (EP) 70
70 Apple SAPCOR 13 DORIS TROY (LP) 45
73 Mojo 2956 001 THE RAINBOW TESTAMENT (LP, with Gospel Truth) 30
74 Polydor 2464 001 JUST ONE LOOK (LP) 18
74 People PLEO 12 STRETCHING OUT (LP) 18
92 Apple SAPCOR 13 DORIS TROY (LP, reissue, gatefold sleeve with bonus 12" [SAPCOR 132]) 12

WILLIAM TRUCKAWAY
69 Reprise RS 20842 Bluegreens On The Wing/Besides Yourself 10
71 Reprise K 44165 BREAKAWAY (LP, with lyric insert) 18

TRUFFLE

81	Chesnut NUT 6	Round Tower (p/s)	150

TRUTH

65	Pye 7N 15923	Baby Don't You Know/Come On Home	18
65	Pye 7N 15998	Who's Wrong/She's A Roller	25
66	Pye 7N 17035	Girl/Jailer Bring Me Water	12
66	Pye 7N 17095	I Go To Sleep/Baby You've Got It	40
66	Deram DM 105	Jingle Jangle/Hey Gyp (Dig The Slowness)	95
67	Decca F 12582	Walk Away Renee/Fly Away Bird	20
68	Decca F 22764	Seuno/Old Ma Brown	22

TRUTH

83	WEA TRUTH 1F	Confusion/Me And My Girl//Love A Go Go/From The Heart (p/s, doublepack)	8
84	IRS IRS 115	Exception Of Love/If You Ever Find Love (p/s)	5

TRUTH & BEAUTY

74	Rak RAK 181	Tuff Little Surfer Boy/Touch-a Touch-a Touch Me	12

TRUTH OF TRUTHS

71	Oak OR 1001	TRUTH OF TRUTHS (LP)	25

TRUX

82	Trux TRX 01	Bad Luck (no p/s)	200

TRYDAN

80	Sain SAIN 77S	Mods A Rocers/Di-Waith, Di-'Fynedd	5

TANIA TSANAKLIDOU

78	EMI EMI 2797	Charlie Chaplin (English)/Charlie Chaplin (Greek)	12

TSD

96	Avex AVEXCD 21	Heart & Soul (Hyper Go Go 7" Edit)/Heart & Soul (Strike 12")/Heart & Soul (Hyper Go Go 12")/Heart & Soul (Dyme Brothers 12")/Heart & Soul (Johnny Versace 12") (CD)	15
96	Avex AVEXT 34	Baby I Love You (Divine Bootleg Remix)/Baby I Love You (Daniele Davoli Remix)/Baby I Love You (Radio Edit) (12", p/s)	12
96	Avex AVEXCD 34	Baby I Love You (7" Edit)/Baby I Love You (Divine Bootleg)/Baby I Love You (Daniele Davoli Remix)/The Chris Rogers Interview (CD)	15

(see also STEPS)

T.S.O.L.

82	Alt. Tentacles VIRUS 10	WEATHERED STATUES (EP)	10

T2

70	Decca SKL 5050	IT'LL ALL WORK OUT IN BOOMLAND (LP)	60
97	Essex 1019LP	T2 (LP)	12

(see also Flies, Cross & Ross)

ERNEST TUBB (& HIS TEXAS TROUBADORS)

51	Brunswick 04783	Rose Of The Mountains/Kentucky Waltz (with Red Foley) (78)	8
52	Brunswick 04933	Walking The Floor Over You/Somebody's Stolen My Honey (78)	10
56	Brunswick 05527	Thirty Days/Answer The Phone (triangular centre)	50
56	Brunswick 05527	Thirty Days/Answer The Phone (78)	12
56	Brunswick 05587	So Doggone Lonesome/If I Never Have Anything Else	20
56	Brunswick 05587	So Doggone Lonesome/If I Never Have Anything Else (78)	10
50s	Decca BM 31214	What Am I Living For/Goodbye Sunshine, Hello Blues (export issue)	15
55	Brunswick OE 9148	COUNTRY DOUBLE DATE (EP)	22
58	Brunswick OE 9372	THE DADDY OF 'EM ALL PT. 1 (EP)	22
58	Brunswick OE 9373	THE DADDY OF 'EM ALL PT. 2 (EP)	22
58	Brunswick OE 9374	THE DADDY OF 'EM ALL PT. 3 (EP)	22
56	Brunswick LA 8736	JIMMIE RODGERS SONGS (10" LP)	50
57	Brunswick LAT 8161	FAVOURITES (LP)	20
58	Brunswick LAT 8260	THE DADDY OF 'EM ALL (LP)	20
59	Brunswick LAT 8292	THE IMPORTANCE OF BEING ERNEST (LP)	20
60	Brunswick LAT 8313	THE ERNEST TUBB STORY VOLUME ONE (LP)	15
60	Brunswick LAT 8314	THE ERNEST TUBB STORY VOLUME TWO (LP)	15
60	Brunswick LAT 8349	THE ERNEST TUBB RECORD SHOP (LP)	20
66	Brunswick LAT 8627	MY PICK OF THE HITS (LP)	20

(see also Red Foley & Ernest Tubb)

JUSTIN TUBB

54	Brunswick 05302	Somebody Ughed Over You/Something Called The Blues (78)	6
67	RCA Victor RCA 1585	But Wait There's More/The Second Thing I'm Gonna Do	6
64	RCA RCX 7133	JUSTIN TUBB (EP)	30
63	Ember CW 100	STAR OF THE GRAND OLE OPRY (LP, pink & grey labels)	12
64	Ember CW 110	THE MODERN COUNTRY MUSIC SOUND OF JUSTIN TUBB (LP, pink & grey labels)	12

TUBES

79	A&M AMS 7423	Prime Time (promo box of 7 different coloured vinyl editions & picture disc)	30

TUBEWAY ARMY

78	Beggars Banquet BEG 5	That's Too Bad/Oh! I Didn't Say (p/s)	8
78	Beggars Banquet BEG 8	Bombers/O.D. Receiver/Blue Eyes (p/s)	8
79	Beggars Banquet BEG 17T	Down In The Park/Do You Need The Service?/ I Nearly Married A Human 2 (12", p/s)	20
79	Banquet Banquet BEG 18P	Are "Friends" Electric?/We Are So Fragile (picture disc, with insert)	10
79	Banquet Banquet SPC 4	Are "Friends" Electric?/We Are So Fragile (cassette in cigarette-pack style box)	8
79	Beggars Banquet BACK 2	That's Too Bad/Oh! Didn't I Say/Bombers/Blue Eyes/O.D. Receiver (double pack, gatefold p/s)	5
79	Beggars Banquet BACK 2	That's Too Bad/Oh! Didn't I Say/Bombers/Blue Eyes/O.D. Receiver (double pack, gatefold p/s, mispressed 2nd disc omits "O.D. Receiver")	15

MINT VALUE £

Year	Label / Cat. No.	Title	Value
83	Beggars Banquet BEG 92E	TUBEWAY ARMY VOL. 1 (12" EP, with "That's Too Bad [Alternate Mix]", yellow vinyl)	10
85	Beggars Banquet BEG 123 E	1978-1979 VOL. 2 (12", blue vinyl, p/s)	10
85	Beggars Banquet BEG 124E	1978-1979 VOL. 3 (12", red vinyl, p/s)	10
78	Beggars Banquet BEGA 4	TUBEWAY ARMY (LP, blue vinyl, g/fold stickered sleeve, some w/ badge)	60/50
79	Beggars Banquet BEGA 7	REPLICAS (LP, with large black & white poster)	20
85	B. Banquet BEGC 7879	TUBEWAY ARMY 1978/1979 (cassette only)	12

(see also Gary Numan, Paul Gardiner)

BESSIE TUCKER
55 HMV 7EG 8085 — BLUES BY BESSIE (EP) 35

BILLY JOE TUCKER
61 London HLD 9455 — Boogie Woogie Bill/Mail Train 70

CY TUCKER
63 Fontana TF 424 — My Prayer/High School Dance (with Earl Preston & TTs) 8
64 Fontana TF 470 — I Apologise/Let Me Call You Sweetheart 10
65 Fontana TF 534 — My Friend/Hurt 10
(see also Earl Preston & TTs)

ORRIN TUCKER
50 London L 556 — I Need Lovin'/Everybody Loves My Baby (78) 6

SOPHIE TUCKER
54 Mercury MG 20035 — MY DREAM (LP) 18
54 Mercury MG 20046 — CABARET DAYS (LP) 18
54 Mercury MPL 6000 — LATEST AND GREATEST SPICY SAUCY SONGS (LP) 15
56 Mercury MPL 6503 — CABARET DAYS (LP, reissue) 12
57 Brunswick LAT 8144 — THE GREAT SOPHIE TUCKER (LP) 18
57 Mercury MPL 6513 — BIGGER AND BETTER THAN EVER (LP) 15

TOMMY TUCKER
64 Pye International 7N 25238 — Hi-Heel Sneakers/I Don't Want 'Cha 18
64 Pye International 7N 25246 — Long Tall Shorty/Mo' Shorty 18
64 London HLU 9932 — Oh! What A Feeling/Wine Bottles 40
69 Chess CRS 8086 — Hi-Heel Sneakers/I Don't Want 'Cha (reissue) 8
64 Pye Intl. NEP 44027 — HI HEEL SNEAKERS (EP) 45

WINSTON TUCKER
73 Explosion EX 2083 — I'm A Believer/You'll Be Mine 6
(see also Winston Groovy)

TUCKY BUZZARD
71 Capitol CL 15687 — She's A Striker/Heartbreaker 5
73 Purple PUR 113 — Gold Medallions/Fast Bluesy Woman 7
77 Purple PUR 134 — Gold Medallions/Superboy Rock 'N' Roller '73' 7
73 Purple TPSA 7510 — ALRIGHT ON THE NIGHT (LP) 22
73 Purple TPSA 7512 — BUZZARD (LP) 22
(see also End)

TUDOR LODGE
71 Vertigo 6059 044 — The Lady's Changing Home/Back To The Good Times We Had 18
71 Vertigo 6360 043 — TUDOR LODGE (LP, foldout textured sleeve, swirl label) 160

TUDOR MINSTRELS
66 Decca F 12536 — Love In The Open Air/A Theme From "The Family Way" 22

TUDORS
83 Stiff BUY 172 — Tied Up With Joe Cool/Cry Baby Cry (p/s) 7

TUESDAY'S CHILDREN
66 Columbia DB 7978 — When You Walk In The Sand/High And Drifting 18
66 Columbia DB 8018 — High On A Hill/Summer Leaves Me With A Sigh 16
67 King KG 1051 — A Strange Light From The East/That'll Be The Day 25
67 Pye 7N 17406 — Baby's Gone/Guess I'm Losin' You 15
68 Pye 7N 17474 — In The Valley Of The Shadow Of Love/Ain't You Got A Heart 10
68 Mercury MF 1063 — She/Bright-Eyed Apples 7
(see also Warm Sounds)

T.U.F.F.
80s SONO 001 — We've Got A Hot One (Speed Mix) (unreleased, white label promos only) 10
(see also Hard Corps)

TUFF GONG ALLSTARS
72 Punch PH 114 — You Should Have Known Better (actually by The Wailing Souls)/Known Better .. 12
(see also Wailing Souls)

TULIPS
74 Explosion EX 2091 — Mocking Bird/DES ALL STARS: Version 7

LEE TULLY
57 London HL 8363 — Around The World With Elwood Pretzel (Parts 1 & 2) (gold or silver print) 100/60
57 London HL 8363 — Around The World With Elwood Pretzel (Parts 1 & 2) (78) 20

TUNDRA
70s Greenwich Village GVR 208 — THE KENTISH SONGSTER (LP) 12
78 Sweet Folk & C. SFA 078 — A KENTISH GARLAND (LP, gatefold sleeve) 20

TUNE ROCKERS
58 London HLT 8717 — The Green Mosquito/Warm Up 35
58 London HLT 8717 — The Green Mosquito/Warm Up (78) 20

TUNEWEAVERS
57 London HL 8503 — Happy Happy Birthday Baby/PAUL GAYTEN: Yo, Yo, Walk 180
57 London HL 8503 — Happy Happy Birthday Baby/PAUL GAYTEN: Yo, Yo, Walk (78) 50
(see also Paul Gayten)

TUNJI with CHRIS McGREGOR
60s Jika 001 — Ko Gbele Oko/Lisabi Egba — 5

TUNNEL RUNNERS
80 Sonic International SI 4282 — Plastic Land/Drug (numbered p/s) — 80

PADDY TUNNEY
65 Topic 12T 139 — A WILD BEES NEST (LP, blue label, later reissued) — 15/10
66 Topic 12T 153 — IRELAND HER OWN (LP, with Arthur Kearney, Frank Kelly & Joe Tunney, blue label, later reissued) — 15/10
66 Topic 12T 165 — THE IRISH EDGE (LP, blue label, later reissued) — 15/10

TURBO
80 Cargo CRS 004 — STALLION (EP, p/s) — 100
82 Turbo CUS 1261 — Charged For Glory/Race For The Dawn — 8

TURGID TOOL
01 Stand STAND 11 — Terror In A Turgid Tool!/Stand Up For England (pop-up p/s) — 8

TURIN BRAKES
99 Anvil ANV 027 — THE DOOR EP (CD) — 25
99 Source SOURV 008 — THE STATE OF THINGS EP: Boss/Balham To Brooklyn/All Away/State Of Things (doublepack) — 12
99 Source SOUR 008 — THE STATE OF THINGS EP: Boss/Balham To Brooklyn/All Away/State Of Things (CD) — 12

BRUCE TURNER
54 Columbia SCMC 9 — Falling Leaves/I Wished On The Moon (export issue) — 6
60 Melodisc MEL 1551 — Nuages/My Guy's Come Back — 5
60s CRD 1000 — Jamaica Jump/Big Noise From Winetka — 5
62 Storyville SXP 2025 — BRUCE TURNER AND HIS JUMP BAND (EP) — 8
63 Philips 433 627 BE — JUMPING FOR JOY NO. 1 (EP) — 15
63 Philips 433 627 BE — JUMPING FOR JOY NO. 2 (EP) — 15
63 77 EP/EU 1 — LIVING JAZZ (EP) — 10
55 Jazz Today JTL 2 — BRUCE TURNER SHOWCASE (10" LP) — 18
61 77 LEU 12/2 — JUMPIN' AT THE N.F.T. (LP) — 12
64 Philips BL 7590 — GOING PLACES (LP) — 20

DENNIS TURNER
62 London HL 9537 — Lover Please/How Many Times — 25

GORDON TURNER
70 Charisma CAS 1009 — MEDITATION (LP) — 30

IKE TURNER
72 United Artists UP 35411 — Lawdy Miss Clawdy/Tacks In My Shoes/Soppin' Molasses (with Family Vibes) — 6
84 Fleetville FV 303 — New Breed Part 1/New Breed Part 2 — 5
60s Ember EMB 3395 — IKE TURNER ROCKS THE BLUES (LP) — 40
72 United Artists UAG 29362 — BLUES ROOTS (LP) — 15
75 DJM DJSLM 2010 — FUNKY MULE (LP) — 12
(see also Ike & Tina Turner)

IKE & TINA TURNER
SINGLES
60 London HLU 9226 — A Fool In Love/The Way You Love Me — 20
61 London HLU 9451 — It's Gonna Work Out Fine/Won't You Forgive Me — 22
64 Sue WI 306 — Gonna Work Out Fine/Won't You Forgive Me (reissue) — 25
64 Sue WI 322 — The Argument/Poor Fool — 25
64 Sue WI 350 — I Can't Believe What You Say/My Baby Now — 25
65 Warner Bros WB 153 — Finger Poppin'/Ooh Poo Pah Doo — 22
65 Sue WI 376 — Please, Please, Please/Am I A Fool In Love — 22
66 London HLU 10046 — River Deep — Mountain High/I'll Keep You Happy — 8
66 Warner Bros WB 5753 — Tell Her I'm Not Home/Finger Poppin' — 10
66 HMV POP 1544 — Anything You Wasn't Born With/Beauty Is Just Skin Deep — 25
66 London HLU 10083 — A Love Like Yours (Don't Come Knockin' Every Day)/Hold On Baby — 10
66 Stateside SS 551 — Goodbye, So Long/Hurt Is All You Gave Me — 12
66 Warner Bros WB 5766 — Somebody (Somewhere) Needs You/(I'll Do Anything) Just To Be With You — 30
67 HMV POP 1583 — I'm Hooked/Dust My Broom — 40
67 London HLU 10155 — I'll Never Need More Than This/Save The Last Dance For Me — 12
68 London HLU 10189 — So Fine/So Blue Over You — 10
68 London HLU 10217 — We Need An Understanding/It Sho' Ain't Me — 10
69 London HLU 10242 — River Deep — Mountain High/Save The Last Dance For Me — 5
69 Minit MLF 11016 — I'm Gonna Do All I Can/You've Got Too Many Ties That Bind — 10
69 London HLU 10267 — I'll Never Need More Than This/A Love Like Yours — 8
69 Liberty LBF 15223 — Crazy 'Bout You Baby/I've Been Lovin' You Too Long — 10
70 Liberty LBF 15303 — Come Together/Honky Tonky Women — 6
70 A&M AMS 783 — Make 'Em Wait/Everyday I Have To Cry — 12
70 Harvest HAR 5018 — The Hunter/Bold Soul Sister — 10
70 Liberty LBF 15367 — I Want To Take You Higher/Contact High — 5
71 Liberty LBF 15432 — Proud Mary/Funkier Than A Mosquito's Tweeter — 5
71 A&M AMS 829 — River Deep — Mountain High/Oh Baby — 7
71 United Artists UP 35245 — Ooh Poo Pah Doo/I Wanna Jump — 5
72 United Artists UP 35373 — Feel Good/Outrageous — 5

EPs
64 Sue IEP 706 — THE SOUL OF IKE AND TINA TURNER — 160
65 Warner Bros WEP 619 — THE IKE AND TINA TURNER SHOW — 50
66 Warner Bros WEP 620 — SOMEBODY NEEDS YOU — 50
83 Sue ENS 1 — SUE SESSIONS — 10

MINT VALUE £

LPs

65	Warner Bros WM 8170	THE IKE AND TINA TURNER SHOW	45
65	London HA-C 8248	THE GREATEST HITS OF IKE & TINA TURNER	60
66	Ember EMB 3368	THE IKE AND TINA TURNER REVUE	35
66	Warner Bros W 1579	THE IKE AND TINA TURNER SHOW	35
66	London HA-U/SH-U 8298	RIVER DEEP MOUNTAIN HIGH	50
67	Warner Bros WB 5904	THE IKE AND TINA TURNER SHOW VOL. 2	35
69	London HA-U/SH-U 8370	SO FINE (with Fontella Bass)	35
69	Liberty LBS 83241	OUTTA SEASON	22
69	Minit MLS 40014	IN PERSON	25
69	Warner Bros ES 1810	GREATEST HITS	18
70	Liberty LBS 83350	COME TOGETHER	18
70	Harvest SHSP 4001	THE HUNTER	45
71	Liberty LBS 83455	WORKIN' TOGETHER	18
71	Liberty LBS 83468/9	LIVE IN PARIS	15
71	Capitol E-ST 571	HER MAN...HIS WOMAN	15
71	United Artists UAD 60005/6	WHAT YOU HEAR IS WHAT YOU GET	15
72	United Artists UAG 29256	NUFF SAID	15
73	Mojo 2916 020	PEACHES (with tracks by Ikettes)	15

(see also Ike Turner, Tina Turner, Ikettes)

JESSE LEE TURNER

59	London HLL 8785	The Little Space Girl/Shake, Baby, Shake	55
59	London HLL 8785	The Little Space Girl/Shake, Baby, Shake (78)	30
60	London HLP 9108	I'm The Little Space Girl's Father/Valley Of Lost Soldiers	35
60	Top Rank JAR 303	That's My Girl/Teenage Misery	18
60	Top Rank JAR 516	Do I Worry (Yes I Do)/All Right, Be That Way	15
62	Vogue V 9201	The Voice Changing Song/All You Gotta Do Is Ask	15

(BIG) JOE TURNER

51	Parlophone DP 265	Roll 'Em Pete/Goin' Away Blues (with Pete Johnson) (78, export only)	60
56	London HLE 8301	Corrine Corrina/Morning, Noon And Night (triangular or round centre)	375/90
56	London HLE 8301	Corrine Corrina/Morning, Noon And Night (78)	40
56	London HLE 8332	Boogie Woogie Country Girl/The Chicken And The Hawk	750
56	London HLE 8332	Boogie Woogie Country Girl/The Chicken And The Hawk (78)	40
57	London HLE 8357	Lipstick, Powder And Paint/Rock A While (gold label print, later silver)	425/290
57	London HLE 8357	Lipstick, Powder And Paint/Rock A While (78)	40
60	London HLE 9055	Honey Hush/Tomorrow Night	55
60	London HLK 9119	My Little Honey Dripper/Chains Of Love	55
65	Atlantic AT 4026	Midnight Cannonball/Baby I Still Want You	20
56	London REE 1047	THE KING AND QUEEN OF R&B (EP, 2 tracks by Ruth Brown)	200
57	London REE 1111	PRESENTING JOE TURNER (EP, initially tri-centre, later round centre)	220/150
57	London Jazz LTZ-K 15053	BOSS OF THE BLUES (LP, also stereo SAH-K 6019)	80/100
59	London HA-E 2173	ROCKIN' THE BLUES (LP)	120
60	London Jazz LTZ-K 15205	BIG JOE RIDES AGAIN (LP, also stereo SAH-K 6123)	75/90
60	London HA-E 2231	BIG JOE IS HERE (LP)	80
64	Realm RM 207	JOE TURNER SINGS THE BLUES VOL. 1 (LP)	20
64	Realm RM 229	JOE TURNER SINGS THE BLUES VOL. 2 (LP)	20
65	CBS 52229	JOE TURNER SINGS THE BLUES VOL. 2 (LP, reissue)	15
65	Fontana 688 802 ZL	JUMPIN' THE BLUES (LP)	25
67	Atlantic Special 590 006	BOSS OF THE BLUES (LP)	18
68	Stateside (S)SL 10226	SINGING THE BLUES (LP)	22
70	Philips SBL 7911	THE REAL BOSS OF THE BLUES (LP)	15
74	Atlantic K 40525	HIS GREATEST RECORDINGS (LP)	12

(see also Pete Johnson, Meade Lux Lewis, Pete Johnson, Albert Ammons, Sonny Terry & Brownie McGhee)

JOE TURNER/RUTH BROWN

56	London REE 1047	KING AND QUEEN OF R&B (EP, 2 tracks each)	225

(see also Ruth Brown, Big Joe Turner)

JOE TURNER & PETE JOHNSON GROUP

56	Emarcy ERE 1500	JOE TURNER & PETE JOHNSON GROUP (EP)	45

(see also Pete Johnson, Big Joe Turner)

MEL TURNER (& Bandits)

61	Melodisc MEL 1580	Let Me Hold Your Hand/I'll Be With You In Apple Blossom Time (with Bandits)	22
62	Columbia DB 4791	Daddy Cool/Swing Low Sweet Chariot (with Bandits)	18
63	Columbia DB 4963	Don't Cry/I Need	8
63	Columbia DB 7076	I Can't Stand Up Alone/Doing The Ton (with Mohicans)	10
63	Carnival CV 7003	Mohican Crawl/White Christmas	10
66	Island WI 276	Welcome Home Little Darlin'/C'est L'Amour	15
70	United Artists UP 35121	Jungle Harlem/Runaway	7

NIK TURNER

(see under Inner City Unit, Sphynx, Hawkwind)

PRECIOUS CLARENCE TURNER

67	Saga SOC 1041	BOOGIE WOOGIE EXPLOSIONS (LP)	12

SAMMY TURNER

59	London HLX 8918	Lavender Blue (Dilly, Dilly)/Sweet Annie Laurie	18
59	London HLX 8918	Lavender Blue (Dilly, Dilly)/Sweet Annie Laurie (78)	10
59	London HLX 8963	Always/Symphony	12
59	London HLX 8963	Always/Symphony (78)	10
60	London HLX 9062	Paradise/I'd Be A Fool Again	12
62	London HLX 9488	Raincoat In The River/Falling	20
60	London HA-X 2246	LAVENDER BLUE MOODS (LP)	90

SIMON TURNER

73	UK UKAL 1003	SIMON TURNER (LP)	15

MINT VALUE £

SPYDER TURNER

67 MGM MGM 1332 — Stand By Me/You're Good Enough For Me 25
74 Kwanza K 19502 — Since I Don't Have You/Happy Days 7

TINA TURNER

78 United Artists UP 36513 — Sometimes When We Touch/Earthquakes And Hurricanes. . . . 5
82 Virgin VS 500 — Ball Of Confusion/Ball Of Confusion (Instrumental) (with B.E.F.) (p/s) 8
83 Capitol 12CLP 316 — Let's Stay Together/I Wrote A Letter (12", picture disc) 8
84 Capitol CLP 325 — Help/Rock'n'Roll Widow (picture disc) 7
84 Capitol CLP 338 — Better Be Good To Me/When I Was Young (picture disc) 7
84 Capitol CL 343 — Private Dancer/Nutbush City Limits (p/s) 5
85 Capitol CLP 364 — We Don't Need Another Hero/(Instrumental) (picture disc) 8
86 Capitol CLP 338 — Break Every Rule/Girls (picture disc) 7
86 Capitol CLX 430 — Two People/Havin' A Party (p/s, with poster) 6
87 Capitol CLD 439 — What You Get Is What You See/Tina Turner Montage (box set). . . . 6
87 Capitol 7CLD 439 — What You See Is What You Get/Take Me To The River// Tina Turner Montage Mix (Parts 1 & 2) (double pack). . . . 7
87 Capitol CLP 452 — Break Every Rule/Girls (picture disc) 7
87 Capitol CL 459 — Paradise Is Here/The Midnight Hour (p/s, with tour poster) 5
87 Capitol CLP 459 — Paradise Is Here/The Midnight Hour (picture disc). . . . 7
87 Capitol 12 CLP 459 — Paradise Is Here/The Midnight Hour (12", picture disc) 8
89 Capitol CLS 543 — The Best/Undercover Agent For The Blues (p/s, pack with 6 postcards). . . . 5
90 Capitol CLPD 593 — Be Tender With Me Baby/Be Tender With Me Baby (live) (picture disc) 5
91 10 FLX 2007-1 — A Change Is Gonna Come (Excerpt) (with B.E.F.) (flexidisc, p/s, from "Music Of Quality And Distinction Vol 2", promo only) 5
85 Capitol TINAP 1 — PRIVATE DANCER (LP, picture disc) 12
99 EMI CDIN 127 — INTERVIEW (CD, card sleeve with cues insert, promo only). . . . 25

(see also Ike & Tina Turner, Eric Clapton)

TITUS TURNER

60 London HLU 9024 — We Told You Not To Marry/Taking Care Of Business. . . . 25
61 Oriole CB 1611 — Pony Train/Bla Bla Cha Cha Cha 22
61 Parlophone R 4746 — Sound-Off/Me And My Lonely Telephone 25
61 Blue Beat BB 32 — Miss Rubberneck Jones/Way Down Yonder 18

ZEB TURNER

51 Vogue V 9002 — Chew Tobacco Rag/No More Nothin' (78) 20

TURNING SHRINES

86 Temple TOPY 7 — FACE OF ANOTHER (12" EP) 8

TURNSTYLE

68 Pye 7N 17653 — Riding A Wave/Trot. . . . 280

TURQUOISE

68 Decca F 12756 — 53 Summer Street/Tales Of Flossie Fillett. . . . 40
68 Decca F 12842 — Woodstock/Saynia 40

(see also Ewan Stephens)

STANLEY TURRENTINE

76 Fantasy FTC 131 — Have You Ever Seen The Rain/Tommy's Tune 5
78 Fantasy FTC 149 — Papa'T Parts 1 & 2 5
78 Fantasy FTC 162 — Disco Dancing/Heritage. . . . 5
66 Fontana TL 5300 — TIGER TAIL (LP) 15
72 Polydor 2383 111 — FLIPPED — FLIPPED OUT (LP). . . . 12
72 CTI CTL 2 — SUGAR (LP) 12
73 CTI CTL 8 — CHERRY (LP, with Milt Jackson) 12
77 Fantasy FT 535 — NIGHTWINGS (LP) 12
78 Fantasy FT 551 — WHAT ABOUT YOU (LP). . . . 12

(see also Milt Jackson & Stanley Turrentine)

TURTLES

65 Pye International 7N 25320 — It Ain't Me Babe/Almost There. . . . 12
66 Pye International 7N 25341 — Let Me Be/Your Ma Said You Cried (In Your Sleep Last Night) 12
66 Immediate IM 031 — You Baby/Wanderin' Kind. . . . 18
66 London HLU 10095 — Can I Get To Know You Better/Like The Seasons 10
67 London HLU 10115 — Happy Together/We'll Meet Again 7
67 Pye International 7N 25421 — Let Me Be/Almost There. . . . 8
67 London HLU 10135 — She'd Rather Be With Me/The Walking Song. . . . 7
67 London HLU 10153 — You Know What I Mean/Rugs Of Woods And Flowers 8
67 London HLU 10168 — She's My Girl/Chicken Little Was Right. . . . 10
68 London HLU 10184 — Sound Asleep/Umbassa The Dragon. . . . 10
68 London HLU 10207 — The Story Of Rock And Roll/Can't You Hear The Cows. . . . 10
68 London HLU 10223 — Elenore/Surfer Dan. . . . 7
69 London HLU 10251 — You Showed Me/Buzz-Saw. . . . 8
69 London HLU 10279 — You Don't Have To Walk In The Rain/Come Over. . . . 7
69 London HLU 10291 — Love In The City/Bachelor Mother 7
67 Pye Intl. NEP 44089 — IT AIN'T ME BABE (EP) 50
67 London HA-U 8330 — HAPPY TOGETHER (LP) 45
68 London HA-U/SH-U 8376 — THE TURTLES PRESENT THE BATTLE OF THE BANDS (LP) 45

(see also Flo & Eddie)

JANE TURZY

53 Brunswick 05186 — Call Me Up/I've Got A Letter (both with Grady Martin & Slewfoot Five) (78) 8

(see also Grady Martin)

RITA TUSHINGHAM & LYNN REDGRAVE

68 Stateside SS 2081 — Smashing Time/Waiting For My Friend 15

TUSKAN RAIDERS

95 Clear CLR 410(X) — Bantha Trax (12", p/s, some on clear vinyl) 40/25

(see also Mu-Ziq)

MINT VALUE £

TU-TONES

Year	Label/Cat. No.	Title	£
51	London L 1079	Oh You Million Dollar Doll/Don't Fence Me In (78, as Lee Monti's Tu-Tones)	8
59	London HLW 8904	Still In Love With You/Saccharin Sally	110
59	London HLW 8904	Still In Love With You/Saccharin Sally (78)	25

TUTTI'S TRUMPETS

(see under Camarata)

WESLEY & MARILYN TUTTLE

Year	Label/Cat. No.	Title	£
55	Capitol CL 14291	Jim, Johnny And Jonas/Say You Do	10

TUXEDOMOON

Year	Label/Cat. No.	Title	£
82	L. D. Du Crepuscule TWI 055	Ninotchka (12", p/s)	8
88	Cramboy CBOY 8080	Time To Lose (12", p/s)	8
80s	L. D. Du Crepuscule TWI 142	The Cage (12", p/s)	8

T.V. & TRIBESMEN

Year	Label/Cat. No.	Title	£
66	Pye International 7N 25375	Barefootin'/Fat Man	20

T.V. PERSONALITIES

(see under Television Personalities)

T.V. PRODUCT

Year	Label/Cat. No.	Title	£
79	Limited Edition TAKE 3	Nowhere's Safe/Jumping Off Walls/PRAMS: Me/Modern Man (folded p/s)	12

(see also Mission)

TV 21

Year	Label/Cat. No.	Title	£
80	Powbeat AAARGH! 1	Playing With Fire/Shattered By It All (foldout p/s)	12
80	Powbeat AAARGH! 2	Ambition/Ticking Away/This Is Zero (foldout p/s)	15
81	Demon D 1004	On The Run/End Of A Dream (p/s)	8
82	Decca	All Join Hands/A Journey Up The Zambezi (And Back) (p/s)	8

(see also DNV, Shake)

SHANIA TWAIN

Year	Label/Cat. No.	Title	£
95	Mercury MERCD 433	Any Man Of Mine/Raining On Our Love/God Ain't Gonna Getcha For That/Still Under The Weather (CD)	18
98	Mercury 568 493 2	You're Still The One (Radio Edit)/I'm Outta Here (Mutt Lange Remix)/You Win My Love (Mutt Lange Remix)/You're Still The One (Radio Edit with intro) (CD)	8
98	Mercury 566 119 2	When (Radio Edit)/You're Still The One (Soul Solution Edit)/ (Extended Club Mix)/Don't Be Stupid (You Know I Love You) (CD, some with poster)	10/8
99	Mercury 562 264 2	Man! I Feel Like A Woman (Original Version) (CD, digipak, with lyrics, withdrawn)	15
02	Mercury PRETTYCDP 1	She's Not Just A Pretty Face (CD, 1-track promo-only)	20
99	NMC PILOT 54	ON THE WAY (CD, withdrawn)	18

TWELFTH NIGHT

Year	Label/Cat. No.	Title	£
73	Acorn CF 239	TWELFTH NIGHT (EP)	8

TWELFTH NIGHT

Year	Label/Cat. No.	Title	£
80	Twelfth Night TN 001	THE FIRST 7" ALBUM ("The Cunning Man"/"Für Helene") (p/s)	30
80s	Revolution REV 009	Eleanor Rigby/East Of Eden (p/s)	25
86	Virgin/Charisma CB 424	Shame/Blue Powder Monkey (p/s)	5
86	Virgin/Charisma CBY 424	Shame/Blue Powder Monkey (picture disc)	8
86	Virgin/Charisma CB 424-12	Shame (Full Mix)/Shame (7")/Blue Powder Monkey (12", p/s)	8
86	Virgin/Charisma CBY 424-12	Shame (Full Mix)/Shame (7")/Blue Powder Monkey (12", picture disc)	10
86	Virgin/Charisma CB 425-12	Take A Look (Album Version)/Take A Look (Part 4)/ Blondon Fair (Extended) (12", p/s)	8
80	Twelfth Night TN 001	TWELFTH NIGHT (cassette)	15
81	Twelfth Night TN 002	LIVE AT THE TARGET (LP)	12
84	Music For Nations MFN 36	ART & ILLUSION (mini-LP)	10
86	Charisma CASG 1174	X (LP, fold-out cover)	15

20th CENTURY FOX ORCHESTRA

Year	Label/Cat. No.	Title	£
65	Stateside SS422	Those Magnificent Men In Their Flying Machines/Arizona	10

(see also Ron Goodwin)

25 RIFLES

Year	Label/Cat. No.	Title	£
79	25 Rifles TFR 1	World War 3/Revolution Blues/Hey Little/Dance 'Bout Now (12")	15

23 JEWELS

Year	Label/Cat. No.	Title	£
79	Temporary TEMP 1	You Don't Know Me/Playing Bogart (white labels, plain sleeve with photocopied insert)	10
80	Temporary TEMP 2	WELTSCHMERZ A GO-GO! (EP, white label)	8

23RD TURNOFF

Year	Label/Cat. No.	Title	£
67	Deram DM 150	Michael Angelo/Leave Me Here	50

(see also Kirkbys, Jimmy Campbell, Rockin' Horse)

23 SKIDOO

Year	Label/Cat. No.	Title	£
81	Pineapple PULP 23	Ethics/Another Baby's Face (p/s)	8
81	Fetish FE 10	Last Words/Version (promo only)	12
81	Fetish FE 11	The Gospel Comes To New Guinea/Last Words (12", p/s)	10
82	Fetish FP 20	Tearing Up The Plans/Just Like Everybody/Gregouka (12", p/s)	10
85	Illuminated ILL 2812	Coup/Version (In The Palace) (12", p/s)	8
82	Fetish FM 2008	SEVEN SONGS (mini-LP)	12

(see also Current 93)

22:20S

Year	Label/Cat. No.	Title	£
90s	own label 2201	Such A Fool/Baby, You're Not In Love (1,000 only, die-cut sleeve)	15

TWICE AS MUCH

Year	Label/Cat. No.	Title	£
66	Immediate IM 033	Sittin' On A Fence/Baby I Want You	12
66	Immediate IM 036	Step Out Of Line/Simplified	10
66	Immediate IM 039	True Story/You're So Good	15

Year	Label/Cat. No.	Title	MINT VALUE £
67	Immediate IM 042	Crystal Ball/Why Don't They All Go Away And Leave Me Alone	15
66	Immediate IMLP/IMSP 007	OWN UP (LP)	35
69	Immediate IMCP 013	THAT'S ALL (LP)	35

TWIGGY

Year	Label/Cat. No.	Title	MINT VALUE £
67	Ember EMB S 239	Beautiful Dreams/I Need Your Hand In Mine (some in p/s)	25/15
67	Ember EMB S 244	When I Think Of You/Over And Over (some in p/s)	25/15
71	Bell BLL 1158	Zoo Do Zoo Song/Little Pleasure Acre (as Twiggy & Friends)	5
72	Columbia DB 8853	A Room In Bloomsbury (with Chistopher Gable)/You Are My Lucky Star/ All I Do Is Dream	5
76	Mercury 6007 100	Here I Go Again/In Love Together (p/s)	5
78	Mercury 6007 175	Falling Angel/Virginia	5
72	Ember SE 8012	TWIGGY & THE GIRLFRIENDS (LP)	22
72	Columbia SCXA 9251	THE BOYFRIEND (LP, soundtrack, with Christopher Plummer)	15

TWIGGY & ANNIE

Year	Label/Cat. No.	Title	MINT VALUE £
66	Columbia DB 7799	Some Do, Some Don't/With Open Arms	8

TWILIGHTS (Australia)

Year	Label/Cat. No.	Title	MINT VALUE £
66	Columbia DB 8065	Needle In A Haystack/I Don't Know Where The Wind Will Blow Me	15
67	Columbia DB 8125	What's Wrong With The Way I Live/It's Dark	15
68	Columbia DB 8396	Cathy, Come Home/The Way They Play	18

TWILIGHTS (U.S.)

Year	Label/Cat. No.	Title	MINT VALUE £
65	London HLU 9992	Take What I Got/She's There	18

TWILIGHT ZONERZ

Year	Label/Cat. No.	Title	MINT VALUE £
79	ZIP/Dining Out ZERO ZERO 1	ZERO ZERO ONE (EP, various silk-screened in red & hand-coloured p/s, signed & numbered)	15
80	ZIP/Dining Out ZIP 002	Brighton Rock/Diversion (p/s)	6

(see also Occult Chemistry)

TWINK (& FAIRIES)

Year	Label/Cat. No.	Title	MINT VALUE £
78	Chiswick SWT 26	Do It '77/Psychedelic Punkeroo/Enter The Diamonds (12", p/s, with Fairies)	12
86	Twink TWK 2	SPACE LOVER (EP)	12
90	Twink 12TWK 5	PSYCHEDELIC PUNKEROO (12" EP)	8
70	Polydor 2343 032	THINK PINK (LP, with some insert)	120/80
70	Polydor 2343 032	THINK PINK (LP, red vinyl with insert)	300
90	Twink TWKLP 1	MR RAINBOW (LP)	12
91	Twink LP 2	ODDS & BEGINNINGS (LP, with insert, numbered & signed, some on red vinyl, 1,500 only)	10/15

(see also Pretty Things, Pink Fairies, Fairies, Tomorrow, Aquarian Age, Rings, Mick Farren, Magic Muscle)

TWINKLE (Ripley)

Year	Label/Cat. No.	Title	MINT VALUE £
64	Decca F 12013	Terry/The Boy Of My Dreams	6
65	Decca F 12076	Golden Lights/Ain't Nobody Home But Me	10
65	Decca F 12139	Tommy/So Sad	10
65	Decca F 12219	Poor Old Johnny/I Need Your Hand In Mine	10
65	Decca F 12305	The End Of The World/Take Me To The Dance	10
66	Decca F 12464	What Am I Doing Here With You?/Now I Have You	12
69	Instant IN 005	Micky/Darby And Joan	10
74	Bradleys BRAD 7418	Days/Caroline (as Twinkle Ripley)	7
82	EMI 5278	I'm A Believer/For Sale (p/s)	5
65	Decca DFE 8621	TWINKLE — A LONELY SINGING DOLL (EP)	55

(see also Bill & Coo, Silkie Davis)

TWINKLE & HOT ROD ALL STARS

Year	Label/Cat. No.	Title	MINT VALUE £
70	Torpedo TOR 3	Jook Jook/Graduate	7

TWINKLE BROTHERS

Year	Label/Cat. No.	Title	MINT VALUE £
70	Jackpot JP 731	Shu Be Du/All My Enemies Beware	12
70	Jackpot JP 740	Miss World/Take What You've Got	12
70	Jackpot JP 741	Sweet Young Thing/Grandma	12
71	Jackpot JP 768	Do Your Own Thing/BOY WONDER: They Talk About Love	22
71	Green Door GD 4007	Miss Labba Labba/The Best Is Yet To Come	10
71	Big Shot BI 593	You Took Me By Suprise/You Took Me By Surprise — Version (both sides actually by Tony Brevitt)	12
71	Big Shot BI 600	It's Not Who You Know/I Need Someone	8
71	Tropical AL 002	Love Sweet Love/HERON ATTAR: Poor Man's Life	8
72	Sioux SI 003	Happy Song/Little Caesar	7
73	Camel CA 106	Room Full All Full/Version	7
73	Magnet MG 033	Mother And Wife/Version	6
73	Pama PM 876	Push It Inna/Village Ram	7
75	Faith FA 007	Friends/No Big Thing	6
75	Faith FA 022	Mother And Wife/GENE RONDO: Impossible Dream	6
78	Front Line FCL 5001	LOVE (10" LP)	12

(see also Busty Brown, Sammy Jones)

TWINS

Year	Label/Cat. No.	Title	MINT VALUE £
73	Downtown DT 511	Rastafari Ruler/TYRONE TAYLOR: Yesterday	5

TWINSET

Year	Label/Cat. No.	Title	MINT VALUE £
67	Decca F 12629	Tremblin'/Sneakin' Up On You	12

TWIN-TONES

Year	Label/Cat. No.	Title	MINT VALUE £
58	RCA RCA 1040	Jo Ann/Before You Go	55
58	RCA RCA 1040	Jo Ann/Before You Go (78)	25

TWIN TUNES QUINTET

Year	Label/Cat. No.	Title	MINT VALUE £
58	RCA RCA 1046	The Love Nest/Baby Lover	18
58	RCA RCA 1046	The Love Nest/Baby Lover (78)	10

MINT VALUE £

TWIST

79 Polydor 2059 156 This Is Your Life/Life's A Commercial Break (p/s) . . . 10
79 Polydor POSP 84 Ads/Rebound . . . 10
79 Polydor 2383 552 THIS IS YOUR LIFE (LP) . . . 20

TWIST

91 East West YZ 586 The Fat Lady Sings/Heavy Duty (p/s) . . . 5

TWISTED ACE

81 Heavy Metal HEAVY 9 Firebird/I Won't Surrender (some in p/s) . . . 10/5

TWISTED SISTER

82 Secret SHH 137-12 RUFF CUTS (12" EP, p/s) . . . 12
83 Atlantic A 9827P The Kids Are Back/Shoot 'Em Down (shaped picture disc) . . . 8
86 Atlantic A 9478D Leader Of The Pack/I Wanna Rock (p/s, with free single) . . . 5
86 Atlantic A 9478P Leader Of The Pack/I Wanna Rock (shaped picture disc) . . . 6
85 Atlantic 781 275-1P COME OUT AND PLAY (LP, picture disc) . . . 12

TWISTERS

60 Capitol CL 15167 Turn The Page/Dancing Little Clown . . . 8
62 Aral/Windsor PSA 106 Peppermint Twist Time/Silly Chilli . . . 12

CONWAY TWITTY

78s

57 Mercury MT 173 Shake It Up/Maybe Baby . . . 50
58 MGM MGM 992 It's Only Make Believe/I'll Try . . . 6
59 MGM MGM 1003 The Story Of My Love/Make Me Know You're Mine . . . 15
59 MGM MGM 1016 Hey Little Lucy! (Don'tcha Put No Lipstick On)/When I'm Not With You . . . 25
59 MGM MGM 1029 Mona Lisa/Heavenly . . . 35
59 MGM MGM 1047 Rosaleena/Halfway To Heaven . . . 50

45s

58 MGM MGM 992 It's Only Make Believe/I'll Try . . . 10
59 MGM MGM 1003 The Story Of My Love/Make Me Know You're Mine . . . 10
59 MGM MGM 1016 Hey Little Lucy! (Don'tcha Put No Lipstick On)/ When I'm Not With You . . . 10
59 MGM MGM 1029 Mona Lisa/Heavenly . . . 7
59 MGM MGM 1047 Rosaleena/Halfway To Heaven . . . 10
60 MGM MGM 1056 Lonely Blue Boy/My One And Only You . . . 10
60 MGM MGM 1066 What Am I Living For/The Hurt In My Heart . . . 8
60 MGM MGM 1082 Is A Blue Bird Blue/She's Mine . . . 10
60 MGM MGM 1095 What A Dream/Tell Me One More Time . . . 8
60 MGM MGM 1108 Whole Lotta Shakin' Goin' On/The Flame . . . 12
61 MGM MGM 1118 C'est Si Bon/Don't You Dare Let Me Down . . . 8
61 MGM MGM 1129 The Next Kiss/Man Alone . . . 8
61 MGM MGM 1137 It's Drivin' Me Wild/Sweet Sorry . . . 10
62 MGM MGM 1152 Tower Of Tears/Portrait Of A Fool . . . 12
62 MGM MGM 1170 Comfy An' Cozy/Unchained Melody . . . 10
62 MGM MGM 1187 I Hope I Think I Wish/The Pick Up . . . 12
63 MGM MGM 1201 Handy Man/Little Piece Of My Heart . . . 12
63 MGM MGM 1209 She Ain't No Angel/Got My Mojo Workin' . . . 12
63 HMV POP 1258 Go On And Cry/She Loves Me . . . 8
68 MGM MGM 1404 It's Only Make Believe/Mona Lisa . . . 5
70 MCA MU 1120 That's When She Started To Stop Loving You/I'll Get Over Losing You . . . 5
70 MCA MU 1132 Hello Darlin'/Girl At The Bar . . . 5
72 MCA MMU 1149 Lead Me On/One's On The Way/You're Looking At Country (with Loretta Lynn) . . . 5
72 MCA MMU 1150 I Can't See Me Without You/I Wonder What She'll Think About Me Leaving/ After The Fire Is Gone . . . 5
72 MCA MU 1169 I Can't Stop Loving You/Since She's Not With The One She Loves . . . 5
73 MCA MU 1223 You've Never Been This Far Before/You Make It Hard . . . 5
75 MCA MCA 180 As Soon As I Hang Up The Phone/A Lifetime Before (with Loretta Lynn) . . . 5
75 MCA MCA 197 I See The Want-To In Your Eyes/The Girl From Tupelo . . . 5
75 MCA MCA 211 Don't Cry Joni/Touch The Hand . . . 5

EPs

58 MGM MGM-EP 684 IT'S ONLY MAKE BELIEVE . . . 65
59 MGM MGM-EP 698 HEY LITTLE LUCY . . . 65
60 MGM MGM-EP 719 SATURDAY NIGHT WITH CONWAY TWITTY . . . 65
60 Mercury ZEP 10069 I NEED YOUR LOVIN' . . . 190
60 MGM MGM-EP 738 IS A BLUEBIRD BLUE? . . . 65
61 MGM MGM-EP 752 THE ROCK 'N' ROLL STORY . . . 80

LPs

59 MGM MGM-C 781 CONWAY TWITTY SINGS . . . 90
60 MGM MGM-C 801 SATURDAY NIGHT WITH CONWAY TWITTY . . . 90
60 MGM MGM-C 829 LONELY BLUE BOY . . . 90
63 MGM MGM-C 950 R AND B '63 . . . 70
68 MCA MUP(S) 342 HERE'S CONWAY TWITTY (AND HIS LONELY BLUE BOYS) . . . 18
68 MGM C/CS 8100 THE ROCK AND ROLL STORY . . . 50
69 MCA MUPS 363 NEXT IN LINE . . . 18
69 MCA MUPS 386 DARLING, YOU KNOW I WOULDN'T LIE . . . 12
70 MCA MUP(S) 404 I LOVE YOU MORE TODAY . . . 12
70 MCA MUP(S) 412 TO SEE MY ANGEL CRY . . . 12
71 MCA MUPS 426 FIFTEEN YEARS AGO . . . 12
71 MCA MUPS 429 WE ONLY MAKE BELIEVE (with Loretta Lynn) . . . 12
72 MCA MUPS 443 I WONDER WHAT SHE'LL THINK ABOUT ME LEAVING . . . 12
74 MCA MCF 2547 LOUISANA WOMAN/MISSISSIPPI MAN (with Loretta Lynn) . . . 12
74 MCA MCF 2557 YOU'VE NEVER BEEN THIS FAR BEFORE . . . 12

(see also Loretta Lynn)

MINT VALUE £

TWO & A HALF

66 CBS 202248 Midnight Swim/Faith . . . 10
66 CBS 202404 Questions/In Harmony . . . 8
67 CBS 202526 The Walls Are High/Love You . . . 8
67 Decca F 22672 Suburban Early Morning Station/Just Couldn't Believe My Ears . . . 20
67 Decca F 22715 I Don't Need To Tell You/Christmas Will Be Round Again . . . 18

TWO FOR THE ROAD

70s Pastiche BJ 2929 TWO FOR THE ROAD (LP) . . . 20

TWO KINGS

65 Island WI 240 Rolling Stone/SUFFERER: Tomorrow Morning (B-side act. by Frank Cosmo) . . . 22
65 Island WI 249 Hit You Let You Feel It/Honey I Love You (both sides actually by Fugitives) . . . 20

TWO MAN SOUND

78 Miracle M12 Que Tal America/Brazil O Brazil (12") . . . 8

TWO MUCH

67 Fontana TF 858 Wonderland Of Love/Mister Money . . . 7
68 Fontana TF 900 It's A Hip Hip Hippy World/Stay In My World . . . 10

TWO-NINETEEN (2.19) SKIFFLE GROUP

57 Esquire 10-497 Freight Train Blues/Railroad Bill (78) . . . 15
57 Esquire 10-502 I'm A-Lookin' For A Home/When The Saints Go Marching In (78) . . . 15
57 Esquire 10-509 In The Valley/Tom Dooley (78) . . . 15
57 Esquire 10-512 Where Can I Go?/Roll The Union On (78) . . . 20
57 Esquire 10-515 This Little Light Of Mine/Union Maid (78) . . . 20
57 Esquire EP 126 TWO-NINETEEN SKIFFLE GROUP (EP) . . . 40
57 Esquire EP 146 TWO-NINETEEN SKIFFLE GROUP (EP) . . . 55
58 Esquire EP 176 TWO-NINETEEN SKIFFLE GROUP (EP) . . . 55
58 Esquire EP 196 TWO-NINETEEN SKIFFLE GROUP (EP) . . . 60

TWO OF CLUBS

64 Columbia DB 7371 The Angels Must Have Made You/True Love Is Here . . . 18

TWO OF EACH

67 Decca F 12626 Every Single Day/I'm Glad I Got You . . . 8
68 Pye 7N 17555 The Summer Of Our Love/Saturday Morning . . . 7

2.3

78 Fast Products FAST 2 Where To Now?/All Time Low (p/s) . . . 15

TWO PEOPLE

86 Polydor Mouth Of An Angel (p/s) . . . 20
80s Polydor This Is The Shirt (p/s) . . . 10

TWO SPARKS

72 Moodisc HM 113 Run Away Girl/When We Were Young . . . 6
(see also Carl Bryan, Winston Wright)

ARLYNE TYE

59 London HLL 8825 The Universe/Who Is The One . . . 25
59 London HLL 8825 The Universe/Who Is The One (78) . . . 20

TYGERS OF PAN TANG

79 Neat NEAT 03 Don't Touch Me There/Burning Up/Bad Times (p/s) . . . 12
80 MCA MCA 582 Don't Touch Me There/Burning Up/Bad Times (p/s, reissue) . . . 10
80 MCA MCA 612 Rock'n'Roll Man/All Right On The Night/Wild Man (p/s) . . . 5
80 MCA MCA 634 Suzie Smiled/Tush (p/s) . . . 5
80 MCA MCA 644 Euthanasia/Straight As A Die (p/s) . . . 5
81 MCA MCA 672 Hellbound/Bad Times//Bad Times/Don't Take Nothin'
('The Audition Tapes' double pack) . . . 6
81 MCA MCA 692 The Story So Far/Silver And Gold/All Or Nothing (p/s) . . . 5
81 MCA MCA 723 Don't Stop By/Slave To Freedom (p/s) . . . 5
81 MCA MCAT 723 Don't Stop By/Slave To Freedom (12", p/s) . . . 12
81 MCA MCA 755 Love Don't Stay/Paradise Drive (p/s) . . . 8
81 MCA MCA 759 Do It Good/Slip Away (no p/s) . . . 30
81 MCA MCA 769 Love Potion No. 9/The Stormlands (p/s) . . . 5
81 MCA MCAP 769 Love Potion No. 9/The Stormlands (picture disc) . . . 5
82 MCA MCA 777 Rendezvous/Life Of Crime (white vinyl, p/s) . . . 6
82 MCA MCA 777 Rendezvous/Life Of Crime (red or blue vinyl, p/s) . . . 5
82 MCA MCA 777 Rendezvous/Life Of Crime (p/s or poster p/s) . . . 4/5
82 MCA MCA 790 Paris By Air/Love's A Lie (poster p/s or standard p/s with earring) . . . 5/10
82 MCA MCA 798 Making Tracks/What You Saying (p/s) . . . 5
82 MCA MCAT 798 Making Tracks (Extended Remix)/What You Saying (12", p/s) . . . 10
80 MCA MCF 3075 WILD CAT (LP, with lyric insert) . . . 12
81 MCA MCF 3104 SPELLBOUND (LP, with poster) . . . 12
81 MCA MCF 3123 CRAZY NIGHTS (LP, stickered sleeve, with bonus 12" and insert) . . . 22
85 MFN MFN 50 THE WRECK AGE (LP, lyric sleeve) . . . 12
86 Neat 1037 FIRST KILL (LP, with inner) . . . 12
(see also John Sykes)

TYLA GANG

76 Stiff BUY 4 Styrofoam/Texas Chainsaw Massacre Boogie (die-cut printed sleeve) . . . 5
78 Beserkley BSERK 16 MOONPROOF (LP, yellow vinyl, with insert) . . . 12
(see also Ducks Deluxe)

BIG 'T' TYLER

57 Vogue V 9079 King Kong/Sadie Green . . . 200
57 Vogue V 9079 King Kong/Sadie Green (78) . . . 75

JIMMY TYLER & HIS ORCHESTRA

56 Parlophone MSP 6215 Fool 'Em Devil/Stardust . . . 18

MINT VALUE £

(Alvin) RED TYLER & GYROS

60 Top Rank JAR 306 — Junk Village/Happy Sax . . . 15

TERRY TYLER

61 Pye International 7N 25119 — A Thousand Feet Below/Answer Me . . . 8

TOBY TYLER

64 Emidisc no cat. no. — The Road I'm On (Gloria)/Blowin' In The Wind (acetate, 1 copy only) . . . 1,800
89 Archive Jive TOBY 1 — The Road I'm On (Gloria) (mail-order issue, numbered p/s, 1-sided, 1,500 only) . 10
93 Zinc Alloy ZAR CD 9006 — THE MAXIMUM SOUND SESSION (CD) . . . 20
(see also Marc Bolan)

T. TEXAS TYLER

59 Parlophone GEP 8788 — COUNTRY ROUND-UP (EP) . . . 30
67 London HA-B 8322 — MAN WITH A MILLION FRIENDS (LP) . . . 25

TYMES

63 Cameo Parkway P 871 — So Much In Love/Roscoe James McClain . . . 10
63 Cameo Parkway P 884 — Wonderful Wonderful/Come With Me To The Sea (some in p/s) . . . 25/12
64 Cameo Parkway P 891 — Somewhere/View From My Window . . . 12
64 Cameo Parkway P 908 — To Each His Own/Wonderland Of Love . . . 12
64 Cameo Parkway P 919 — The Magic Of Our Summer Love/With All My Heart . . . 12
64 Cameo Parkway P 924 — Here She Comes/Malibu . . . 65
64 Cameo Parkway P 933 — The Twelfth Of Never/Here She Comes (existence unconfirmed) . . . 75+
69 Direction 58-3903 — People/The Love of Ivy . . . 6
69 Direction 58-4450 — If You Love Me Baby/Find My Way . . . 6
71 CBS 7250 — Someone To Watch Over Me/She's Gone (featuring George Williams) . . . 6
63 Cameo Parkway P 7032 — SO MUCH IN LOVE (LP) . . . 65
69 Direction 8-63558 — PEOPLE (LP, mono or stereo) . . . 30
78 London HAU 8516 — CAMEO PARKWAY SESSIONS (LP) . . . 22

ROB TYNER & HOT RODS

77 Island WIP 6418 — 'Till The Night Is Gone (Let's Rock)/Flipside Rock (p/s) . . . 5
(see also MC 5, Eddie & Hot Rods)

TYPHOONS

63 Embassy WB 577 — Sweets For My Sweet/LES CARLE: You Can Never Stop Me Loving You . . . 5
63 Embassy WB 589 — Surf City/I Want To Stay Here . . . 10
63 Embassy WB 607 — Glad All Over/Money . . . 5
64 Embassy WB 642 — The House Of The Rising Sun/It's All Over Now . . . 5
64 Embassy WB 660 — One Way Love/Sha-La-La . . . 5
65 Embassy WB 677 — Tired Of Waiting For You/Baby Please Don't Go . . . 10
65 Embassy WT 1115 — Hard Day's Night/And I Love Her/I Should Have Known Better/Tell Me Why (EP) . 15
65 Embassy WT 2006 — Ticket To Ride/Here Comes The Night/I'll Be There/I Can't Explain (EP) . . . 20
(see also Bud Ashton, Ray Pilgrim, Mike Redway, Starlings)

TYPHOONS

81 Bohemian BO 1 — Telstar/In Fae A Brothin' (p/s) . . . 5
(see also Ruts)

TYRANNOSAURUS REX

68 Regal Zonophone RZ 3008 — Debora/Child Star (with promo only p/s, some with insert) . . . 350/400
68 Regal Zonophone RZ 3008 — Debora/Child Star . . . 30
68 Regal Zonophone RZ 3011 — One Inch Rock/Salamanda Palaganda (promo only p/s, some with insert) . . 350/400
68 Regal Zonophone RZ 3011 — One Inch Rock/Salamanda Palaganda . . . 45
69 Regal Zonophone RZ 3016 — Pewter Suitor/Warlord Of The Royal Crocodiles . . . 45
69 Regal Zonophone RZ 3022 — King Of The Rumbling Spires/Do You Remember (with promo only p/s) . . . 400
69 Regal Zonophone RZ 3022 — King Of The Rumbling Spires/Do You Remember . . . 45
70 Regal Zonophone RZ 3025 — By The Light Of A Magical Moon/Find A Little Wood . . . 45
72 Magni Fly ECHO 102 — Debora/One Inch Rock/The Woodland Bop/The Seal Of Seasons (p/s) . . . 5
82 Old Gold OG 9234 — Debora/One Inch Rock (1,000 mispressed with "Beltane Walk" on B-side) . . . 5
91 Tyrannosaurus Rex TYR 1 — Sleepy Maurice/1968 Radio Promos (Tyrannosaurus Rex Appreciation Society release, 2,000 only, p/s with card insert) . . . 8
68 Regal Zonophone LRZ 1003 — MY PEOPLE WERE FAIR AND HAD SKY IN THEIR HAIR BUT NOW THEY'RE CONTENT TO WEAR STARS ON THEIR BROWS (LP, mono, with lyric sheet & manuscript) . . . 80/40
68 Regal Zonophone SLRZ 1003 — MY PEOPLE WERE FAIR AND HAD SKY IN THEIR HAIR BUT NOW THEY'RE CONTENT TO WEAR STARS ON THEIR BROWS (LP, stereo, with lyric sheet & manuscript) . . . 40/20
68 Regal Zonophone TA-LRZ 1003 — MY PEOPLE WERE FAIR AND HAD SKY IN THEIR HAIR BUT NOW THEY'RE CONTENT TO WEAR STARS ON THEIR BROWS (reel-to-reel tape, mono) . . . 35
68 Regal Zonophone (S)LRZ 1005 — PROPHETS, SEERS AND SAGES, THE ANGELS OF THE AGES (LP, with lyric sheet, textured sleeve, mono/stereo) . . . 65/35
69 R. Zonophone (S)LRZ 1007 — UNICORN (LP, gatefold sleeve, original with blue label; mono/stereo) . . . 85/50
70 R. Zonophone (S)LRZ 1007 — UNICORN (LP, gatefold sleeve, later issue with red label; mono/stereo) . . . 60/30
70 R. Zonophone SLRZ 1013 — A BEARD OF STARS (LP, some with lyric sheet) . . . 60/30
(see also Marc Bolan/T. Rex, John's Children, Dib Cochran & Earwigs, Shagrat)

LLOYD TYRELL

(see under Lloyd Terrell)

TYSONDOG

83 Neat NEAT 33 — Eat The Rich/Dead Meat (p/s) . . . 7
85 Neat NEAT 46 — Shoot To Kill/Hammerhead (p/s) . . . 6
85 Neat NEAT 4612 — Shoot To Kill/Hammerhead/Changeling/Back To The Bullet (12", p/s) . . . 15
86 Neat NEAT 56 — School's Out/Don't Let The Bastards Grind You Down (p/s) . . . 8
86 Neat NEAT 1031 — CRIMES OF INSANITY (LP, with inner) . . . 15

TYTAN

82 Kamaflage KAM 6 — Blind Men And Fools/The Ballad Of Edward Case (p/s) . . . 18
82 Kamaflage KAMA 6 — Blind Men And Fools/The Ballad Of Edward Case (12", p/s) . . . 20
85 Metal Masters METALP 105 — ROUGH JUSTICE (LP) . . . 18

JUDIE TZUKE

78 Rocket ROKN 541 — For You/Sukarita 5
78 Rocket XPRES 2 — For You/Sukarita (reissue, p/s) 5
79 Rocket XPRES 17 — Stay With Me Till Dawn/New Friends Again (p/s) 7
85 Legacy LGY 22 — I'll Be The One/Falling (p/s, with postcards) 5

(see also Tzuke & Paxo, Zookie)

TZUKE & PAXO

76 Good Earth GD 12 — These Are The Laws/It's Only Fantasies 15

UBX

80 Crazy Plane SP 002 — Crazy Today/Mister Fix It (p/s) 150

U.F.O.

70 Beacon BEA 161 — Shake It About/Evil 25
70 Beacon BEA 165 — Come Away Melinda/Unidentified Flying Object 20
70 Beacon BEA 172 — Boogie For George/Treacle People (some with postcard) 18/25
71 Beacon BEA 181 — Prince Kajuku/The Coming Of Prince Kajuku 15
73 Chrysalis CHS 2024 — Give Her The Gun/Sweet Little Thing (unreleased in U.K.)
74 Chrysalis CHS 2040 — Doctor Doctor/Lipstick Traces 12
75 Chrysalis CHS 2072 — Shoot Shoot/Love Lost Love (unissued)
77 Chrysalis CHS 2146 — Alone Again Or/Electric Phase 10
77 Chrysalis CHS 2178 — Gettin' Ready/Lights Out (unissued)
78 Chrysalis CHS 2241 — Only You Can Rock Me/Cherry/Rock Bottom (p/s, some red vinyl, with frisbee offer) 6/8
79 Chrysalis CHS 2287 — Doctor Doctor (live)/On With The Action (live)/Try Me (p/s, clear or mauve vinyl) 6/10
79 Chrysalis CHS 2318 — Shoot Shoot (live)/Only You Can Rock Me (live)/I'm A Loser (live) (p/s, clear vinyl) 6
79 Chrysalis CHS 2321 — Shoot Shoot (Edit)/Only You Can Rock Me (Edit) (promo) 8
79 Chrysalis CHS 2399 — Young Blood/Lights Out (p/s, red vinyl) 6
80 Chrysalis CHS 2454 — Couldn't Get It Right/Hot 'n' Ready (live) (p/s, clear vinyl) 6
81 Chrysalis CHS 2482 — Lonely Heart/Long Gone (p/s, clear vinyl with patch) 5
81 Chrysalis CHS 2576 — Let It Rain/Heel Of A Stranger/You'll Get Love (p/s, clear vinyl) 5
81 Chrysalis CHS 12 2576 — Let It Rain/Heel Of A Stranger/You'll Get Love (12", p/s) 8
81 Chrysalis UFO DJ 1 — Call My Name (one-sided, promo only) 10
82 Chrysalis CHSP 2607 — Back Into My Life/The Writer (picture disc) 7
83 Lyntone LYN 12821 — Blinded By A Lie (edit)/Diesel In The Dust (edit)/When It's Time To Rock (edit) (flexidisc with/without *Metal Fury* magazine, issue 12) 15/10
83 Chrysalis CHS 2672 — When It's Time To Rock/Everybody Knows (p/s, with patch) 5
83 Chrysalis CHSP 2672 — When It's Time To Rock/Everybody Knows/Push It's Love (picture disc) 6
85 Chrysalis UFOP 1 — This Time/The Chase (shaped picture disc) 8
92 Essential ESS T 2009 — One Of Those Nights/Ain't Life Sweet/Long Gone (1991 Version) (12", p/s) 10
92 Essential ESS X 2009 — One Of Those Nights/She's The One/Long Gone (1991 Version) (CD) 12
70 Beacon BEAS 12 — U.F.O. 1 (LP) 30
72 Beacon BEAS 19 — U.F.O. 2 — FLYING (ONE HOUR SPACE ROCK) (LP, some with inner lyric sleeve) 22/30
74 Chrysalis CHS 1059 — PHENOMENON (LP, misprinted green label, matt sleeve, also on cassette) 18
75 Chrysalis CHR 1074 — FORCE IT (LP, green label, also on cassette) 14
76 Chrysalis CHR 1103 — NO HEAVY PETTING (LP, green label, also on cassette) 14
77 Chrysalis CHR 1127 — LIGHTS OUT (LP) 14
78 Chrysalis CDL 1182 — OBSESSION (LP, with poster) 18
80 Chrysalis CDL 1239 — NO PLACE TO RUN (LP, in six sleeve variations: green, blue, yellow, purple, turquoise, black) .... set 55
82 Chrysalis CHR 1360 — MECHANIX (LP, with poster) 12
82 AKA AKP 2 — LIVE IN JAPAN 1971 (LP, picture disc) 12
92 Essential ESS LP 178 — HIGH STAKES AND DANGEROUS MEN (LP) 12
97 Zoom Club ZCR CD 1 — ON WITH THE ACTION — THE ROUNDHOUSE LIVE, 1976 (CD, in tin with bonus track) 18

(see also Michael Schenker Group)

LESLIE UGGAMS

58 Columbia DB 4160 — The Ice Cream Man/I'm Old Enough 6
59 Philips PB 954 — One More Sunrise (Morgen)/The Eyes Of God 5
59 Philips PB 999 — The Carefree Years/Lullaby Of The Leaves 5
60 Philips PB 1063 — Inherit The Wind/Love Is Like A Violin 5
61 Philips PB 1124 — Sixteen Going On Seventeen/My Favourite Things 5
60 Philips BBL 7370 — THE EYES OF GOD (LP) 12

UGLY CUSTARD

70 Kaleidoscope KAL 100 — UGLY CUSTARD (LP) 75

(see also Hungry Wolf, Alan Parker, Rock Machine)

MINT VALUE £

UGLYS

65	Pye 7N 15858	Wake Up My Mind/Ugly Blues	50
65	Pye 7N 15968	It's Alright/A Friend	30
66	Pye 7N 17027	A Good Idea/A Quiet Explosion	50
66	Pye 7N 17178	End Of The Season/Can't Recall Her Name	50
67	CBS 2933	And The Squire Blew His Horn/Real Good Girl	75
69	MGM MGM 1465	I See The Light/Mary Cilento (6 demo copies only, pink/silver labels)	1500+

(see also Steve Gibbons, Balls, Lemon Tree, Move, Trevor Burton)

UK

88	Chain Reaction	UK (LP)	12

(see also Business, Tank)

U.K. BONDS

65	Polydor BM 56061	The World Is Watching Us/I Said Goodbye To The Blues	7
66	Polydor BM 56112	Anything You Do Is Alright/The Last Thing I Ever Do	15

U.K. DECAY

79	Plastic PLAS 001	U.K. Decay/Car Crash/PNEUMONIA: Exhibition/Coming Attack (folded p/s)	18
81	Plastic PLAS 002	BLACK EP (p/s, reissue has slightly different p/s)	6/5
81	Fresh FRESH 26	Unexpected Guest/Dresden (foldout p/s)	6
81	Fresh FRESH 33	Sexual/Twist In The Tale (poster p/s)	5
82	C. Christi CHRIST ITS 1	Rising From The Dread/Testament/Werewolf/Jerusalem Over (The White Cliffs Of Dover) (12", p/s with insert)	8

(see also Pneumonia)

U.K.s

64	HMV POP 1310	Ever Faithful, Ever True/Your Love Is All I Want	18
64	HMV POP 1357	I Will Never Let You Go/I Know	18

U.K. SUBS

78	City NIK 5	C.I.D./Live In A Car/B.I.C. (p/s, clear, red, blue, green or orange vinyl; also black vinyl)	7/5
79	Gem GEMS 5	Stranglehold/World War/Rockers (p/s, red vinyl)	5
79	Gem GEMS 10	Tomorrow's Girls/Scum Of The Earth/Telephone Numbers (p/s, blue vinyl)	6
79	Gem GEMS 14	She's Not There/Kicks/Victims/The Same Thing (p/s, green vinyl)	5
80	Gem GEMS 30	Teenage/Left For Dead/New York State Police (p/s, pink or orange vinyl)	4/5
82	Ramkup CAC 2	Party In Paris (1-sided fan club single, no p/s, 500 only)	25
83	Fall Out FALL 017	Another Typical City (p/s)	5
83	Fall Out FALL 12017	Another Typical City (12"p/s)	8
81	Gem GEMEP 45	KEEP RUNNIN' EP (Keep Runnin' [Till You Burn]/Ice Age/ Perfect Girl/Party In Paris [French Version])	8
82	Abstract ABS 012	SHAKE UP THE CITY (EP, red vinyl)	7
84	Gem FALL 12024	SPELL EP (12")	10
79	Gem GEMLP 100	ANOTHER KIND OF BLUES (LP, blue vinyl, with inner sleeve)	12
80	Gem GEMLP 106	BRAND NEW AGE (LP, clear vinyl, with insert)	12
80	Gem GEMLP 111	CRASH COURSE LIVE (LP, purple vinyl, 15,000 w/export 12" [GEMEP 1])	15/10
81	Gem GEMLP 112	DIMINISHED RESPONSIBILITY (LP, red vinyl with inner sleeve)	12
82	Abstract AABT 300	RECORDED '79-'81 (LP, blue vinyl with free stencil)	12
83	Scarlett FALLLP 018	FLOOD OF LIES (LP)	12

(see also Urban Dogs)

JAMES 'BLOOD' ULMER

81	Rough Trade RT 045	Are You Glad To Be In America?/T.V. Blues (p/s)	5

ULTERIOR MOTIVES

79	Motive Music MMR 1	Another Lover (p/s)	30

ULTIMATE SPINACH

68	MGM MGM-C(S) 8071	ULTIMATE SPINACH (LP)	50
68	MGM MGM-C(S) 8094	BEHOLD AND SEE (LP)	60

ULTRA HIGH FREQUENCY

74	Pye International 7N 25628	We're On The Right Track/We're On The Right Track (version)	6

ULTRAFUNK

74	Contempo CS 2001	Living In The City/Who Is He And What Is He To You	6
74	Contempo CS 2023	Freddy Mack/Kung Fu Man	6
75	Contempo CS 2020	Sweet F.A./Use Me	7
76	Contempo CX 14	Gotham City Boogie/Sunrise	7
76	Contempo CX 14	Gotham City Boogie/Sunrise (12")	8
77	Contempo CS 2071	Sting Your Jaws (Parts 1 & 2)	5
75	Contempo CLP 509	ULTRAFUNK (LP)	25

ULTRA VIOLENT

83	Riot City RIOT 25	CRIME FOR REVENGE (EP)	5

ULTRA VIVID SCENE

89	4AD BAD 906	Mercy Seat/Codeine/H Like In Heaven/Mercy Seat (LP Version) (12", uncut p/s [most copies die-cut])	22
89	4AD AD 908	Something To Eat/H Like In Heaven (freebie, 1,000 only)	10
90	4AD AD 0016	Special One/Kind Of Drag	7
90	4AD UVS 1	Staring At The Sun/Three Stars (12", promo only)	10
92	4AD UVS 2	Medicating Angels/Mirror To Mirror (12", promo only)	10

ULTRAVOX

77	Island WIP 6375	Dangerous Rhythm/My Sex (initially no p/s, later with p/s)	5/8
77	Island WIP 6392	Young Savage/Slip Away (p/s)	10
77	Island WIP 6404	Rockwrock/Hiroshima Mon Amour (p/s)	5
77	Island IEP 8	RETRO (EP, 33rpm)	6
78	Island WIP 6454	Slow Motion/Dislocation (p/s)	5
78	Island 12WIP 6454	Slow Motion/Dislocation (12", p/s, translucent vinyl)	8
78	Island WIP 6459	Quiet Men/Cross Fade (p/s)	7

MINT VALUE £

78 Island 12WIP 6459 Quiet Men/Cross Fade (12", p/s, white vinyl) 8
80 Chrysalis CHS 2441 Sleepwalk/Waiting (p/s, clear vinyl) 6
80 Chrysalis CHS 2481 Vienna/Passionate Reply (p/s, clear vinyl) 6
80 Chrysalis CHS 2457 Passing Strangers/Face To Face (p/s, clear vinyl) 5
80 Chrysalis CHS 12-2457 Passing Strangers/Face To Face/King's Lead Hat (12", p/s) 8
81 Fan Club The Voice (live) 5
86 Chrysalis UV 5 All Fall Down/Dreams (p/s, with free single) 5
77 Island ILPS 9449 ULTRAVOX (LP, gatefold sleeve) 12
77 Island ILPS 9505 HA! HA! HA! (LP, with 7" "Quirks"/"Modern Love" [WIP 6417] & inner sleeve) ... 12
82 Chrysalis PCDL 1394 QUARTET (LP, marbled picture disc) 12
86 Chrysalis CCD 1545 U-VOX (CD) 20
(see also Tiger Lily, John Foxx, Midge Ure, Helden)

MIYOSHI UMEKI

58 Mercury MT 188 The Mountains Beyond The Moon/Ooh What Good Company We Could Be (78, with Red Buttons) 8
58 Mercury 7MT 203 Sayonara/On And On 5
58 Mercury MT 203 Sayonara/On And On (78) 8

UMPS & DUMPS

80 Topic 12TS 416 THE MOON'S IN A FIT (LP) 15

UNANIMOUS DECISION

93 Kold Sweat KSMEP 301X It Ain't Clever (double pack EP) 7

UNCLE DOG

72 Signpost SG 4253 OLD HAT (LP) 30
(see also Carol Grimes)

UNCLE JOHN'S BAND

80 Ellie Jay EJSP 9422 DIFFERENT GAME (LP, private pressing) 12

UNCOMMUNITY

85 Black Dwarf BDBG 1 Brutality Of Fact/Wall Of Sleep (Soundtrack)/The Price Of Your Entry Is Sin (card sleeve, 525 only, numbered, hand-painted labels, with insert) 25
(see also McCarthy)

UNCOOL DANCEBAND

79 Polydor PB 30 Let Me Be Your Boyfriend/Heads I Win (no p/s) 100
81 Polydor POSP 253 Jacqueline/No. 17 (no p/s) 20

UNDEAD

82 Riot City RIOT 7 It's Corruption/Undead (p/s) 15
82 Riot City RIOT 15 VIOLENT VISIONS (EP) 10
84 City 006 KILLING OF REALITY (LP, lyric insert) 25

UNDERDOGS

83 Riot City RIOT 26 EAST OF DACHAU (EP) 10

UNDERGRADS

66 Decca F 12492 Looks Like It's Gonna Be My Year/Calling You 7

UNDERGROUND

69 Major Minor SMCP 5014 BEAT PARTY (LP) 25
(see also Madeline Bell)

UNDERGROUNDS

72 High Note HS 061 Skavito/Savito 12

UNDERGROUND SET

70 Pantonic PAN 6302 UNDERGROUND SET (LP) 35

UNDERGROUND SUNSHINE

69 Fontana TF 1049 Birthday/All I Want Is You 10

UNDERNEATH

86 él GPO 17 THE IMP OF THE PERVERSE (EP) 6
86 él GPO 17T THE IMP OF THE PERVERSE (12" EP) 8
86 él ACME 9 LUNATIC DAWN OF THE DISMANTLER (LP) 12
(see also Karl Blake, Shock Headed Peters, Lemon Kittens)

UNDERTAKERS

63 Pye 7N 15543 Everybody Loves A Lover/Mashed Potatoes 20
63 Pye 7N 15562 What About Us/Money 20
64 Pye 7N 15607 Just A Little Bit/Stupidity 20
(see also 'Takers, Jackie Lomax)

UNDER THE SUN

79 Redball RR 010 UNDER THE SUN (LP) 100

UNDERTONES

78 Good Vibrations GOT 4 TEENAGE KICKS (EP, pink poster p/s; later white) 12/10
78 Sire SIR 4007 TEENAGE KICKS (EP, reissue) 7
79 Sire SIR 4015 Jimmy Jimmy/Mars Bars (green vinyl, printed PVC sleeve & insert; also p/s) ... 5/4
79 Sire SIR 4022 Here Comes The Summer/One Way Love/Top Twenty (p/s) 5
79 Sire SIR 4024 You've Got My Number (Why Don't You Use It!)/Let's Talk About Girls (p/s) 5
79 no label CRACKS 90 MANAGEMENT EP: Teenage Kicks/Get Over You/Jimmy Jimmy/ Here Comes The Summer (promo-only, numbered with typed insert, 250 only) . 150
80 Sire SIR 4038 My Perfect Cousin/Hard Luck (Again) (p/s) 5
81 Ardeck 12 ARDS 6 My Perfect Cousin/Hard Luck (Again)/Don't Wanna See (You Again) (12", p/s) 8
81 Ardeck ARDS 9 Julie Ocean/Kiss In The Dark (p/s) 5
83 Ardeck ARDS 11 The Love Parade/Like That (p/s) 5
83 Ardeck 12 ARDS 11 The Love Parade/Like That/You're Welcome/Crises Of Mine/ Family Entertainment (12", p/s) 10
83 Ardeck ARDS 12 Got To Have You Back/Turning Blue (p/s) 8

MINT VALUE £

83	Ardeck ARDS 13	Chains Of Love/Window Shopping For New Clothes (p/s)	10
94	Dojo TONES 1	TEENAGE KICKS (EP, 2nd reissue, green vinyl, no'd poster p/s, 2,000 only)	6
79	Sire SRK 6071	UNDERTONES (LP, black & white cover, without "Teenage Kicks" & "Get Over You" & different version of "Here Comes The Summer" to reissue)	12
80	Sire SRK 6088	HYPNOTISED (LP, with cardboard mobile)	12
83	Ardeck ARD 104	THE SIN OF PRIDE (LP, mispressing with different tracks: "Bittersweet" & "Stand So Close")	40
94	Dojo DOJOLP 192	HYPNOTISED (10" LP, numbered, 500 only)	12
94	Dojo DOJOLP 193	POSITIVE TOUCH (10" LP, numbered, 500 only)	12
94	Dojo DOJOLP 194	THE SIN OF PRIDE (10" LP, numbered, 500 only)	12

(see also Feargal Sharkey, That Petrol Emotion)

UNDERWATER HAIRDRESSERS

79	Sassoon VIDAL 1	Swimmin' With The Wimmin/Underneath The Driers (p/s, with 'Henna' sachet)	475

(see also Dodo Resurrection)

UNDERWORLD

92	Tomato PLUM 2001	Mother Earth/Mother Earth (FM Mix)/The Hump/The Hump (Groove Without A Doubt Mix) (12", p/s)	50
93	Boys Own BOIX 13	Mmm... Skyscraper I Love You/Mmm... Skyscraper I Love You (Telegraph 6.11.92)/Mmm... Skyscraper I Love You (Jam Scraper) (12", p/s)	25
93	Boys Own BOIXCD 13	Mmm... Skyscraper I Love You/Mmm... Skyscraper I Love You (Telegraph 6.11.92)/Mmm... Skyscraper I Love You (Jam Scraper) (CD)	25
93	Boys Own Collect 002	Rez/Cowgirl (12", company sleeve)	10
93	Boys Own Collect 002P	Rez/Cowgirl (12", glossy pink sleeve, pink vinyl, white label)	30
94	Junior Boys Own JB 017	Spikee/Dogman Go Woof (12", p/s)	10

(see also Lemon Interrupt)

UNDISPUTED TRUTH

71	Tamla Motown TMG 776	Save My Love For A Rainy Day/Since I Lost You	10
71	Parlophone TMG 776	Save My Love For A Rainy Day/Since I Lost You (mispress on Parlophone)	20
71	Tamla Motown TMG 789	Smiling Faces Sometimes/You Got The Love I Need	10
72	Tamla Motown TMG 818	Superstar/Ain't No Sun Since You've Been Gone	8
74	Tamla Motown TMG 897	Help Yourself/What It Is	5
76	Warner Bros K 16804	You + Me = Love Parts 1 & 2	5
76	Warner Bros K 16804	You + Me = Love Parts 1 & 2 (12")	12
72	T. Motown STMA 8004	FACE TO FACE WITH THE TRUTH (LP)	18
72	T. Motown STML 11197	THE UNDISPUTED TRUTH (LP)	15
73	T. Motown STML 11240	THE LAW OF THE LAND (LP)	15
75	T. Motown STML 11277	DOWN TO EARTH (LP)	12
75	T. Motown STMA 8023	COSMIC TRUTH (LP)	12
75	T. Motown STML 12009	HIGHER THAN HIGH (LP)	12

UNEXPLORED BEATS

95	Unexplored Beats UXB 001	Skool Beats/Inner Life (12")	30

(see also Black Dog)

UNICORN

70	Hollick & Taylor HT 1258	Going Home/Another World	30

UNICORN

71	Transatlantic BIG 138	P.F. Sloan/Going Back Home	6
72	Transatlantic BIG 509	Cosmic Kid/All We Really Want To Do	6
71	Transatlantic TRA 238	UPHILL ALL THE WAY (LP)	18
74	Charisma CAS 1092	BLUE PINE TREES (LP)	12

UNIFICS

68	London HLR 10231	Court Of Love/Which One Should I Choose	12

UNION GAP

(see under Gary Puckett & Union Gap)

UNIQUES

80	Charly CTD 121	You Don't Miss Your Water/It's All Over Now/All These Things	5

UNIQUES (featuring Joe Stampley) (U.S)

65	Pye International 7N 25303	Not Too Long Ago/Fast Way Of Living	50
66	Pye Intl. NPL 28094	UNIQUELY YOURS (LP)	100

UNIQUES (Jamaica)

67	Collins Downbeat CR 002	Dry The Water/I'm A Fool For You	40
67	Island WI 3070	People Rock Steady/I'm Trying To Find A Home (credited to Roy Shirley)	30
67	Island WI 3084	Gypsy Woman/KEN ROSS: Wall Flower	22
67	Island WI 3086	Let Me Go Girl/SOULETTES: Dum Dum	22
68	Island WI 3087	Never Let Me Go/HENRY III: Won't Go Away	22
68	Island WI 3106	Speak No Evil/GLAN ADAMS: That New Girl	22
68	Island WI 3107	Lesson Of Love/DELROY WILSON: Til I Die	22
68	Island WI 3114	Build My World Around You/LLOYD CLARKE: I'll Never Change	25
68	Island WI 3117	Give Me Some More Of Your Loving/VAL BENNETT: Lovell's Special	22
68	Island WI 3122	My Conversation/SLIM SMITH: Love One Another	25
68	Island WI 3123	The Beatitude/KEITH BLAKE: Time On The River (actually "Time & The River")	22
68	Island WI 3145	Girl Of My Dreams/LESTER STERLING: Tribute To King Scratch	22
68	Trojan TR 619	Watch This Sound/Out Of Love	15
68	Trojan TR 645	A-Yuh/Just A Mirage	15
68	Blue Cat BS 126	Girls Like Dirt/GLEN ADAMS: She Is Leaving	20
69	Gas GAS 117	Too Proud To Beg/Love And Devotion	12
69	Nu Beat NB 034	Crimson And Clover/What A Situation	10
69	Nu Beat NB 037	I'll Make You Love Me/Lover's Prayer	10
69	Unity UN 527	The Beatitude/My Conversation	10
69	Trojan TRL 15	ABSOLUTELY THE UNIQUES (LP)	75

(see also Slim Smith, Melodians, Lloyd Charmers, Tommy McCook)

UNIQUES

72 Trojan TR 7852 — Mother And Child Reunion/Corner Hop . . . 6
72 Trojan TR 7866 — Lonely For Your Love/LIONS DEN: Chick-A-Bow . . . 6
(see also Pioneers)

UNITED SONS OF AMERICA

71 Mercury 6338 036 — GREETINGS FROM THE U.S. OF A. (LP) . . . 12

UNITED STATES DOUBLE QUARTET

67 Stateside SS 590 — Life Is Groovy/Split. . . . 12
67 BT Puppy BTS 45524 — Life Is Groovy/Split (reissue) . . . 10
(see also Tokens, Kirby Stone 4)

UNITED STATES OF AMERICA

68 CBS 3745 — Garden Of Earthly Delights/Love Song For The Dead Che . . . 15
68 CBS (S) 63340 — UNITED STATES OF AMERICA (LP, mono/stereo) . . . 35

UNITED STATES OF EXISTENCE

87 Bam Caruso OPRA 081 — Gone/PAUL ROLAND: Madam Guillotine (jukebox issue, company sleeve) . . . 5

UNIT 4 + 2

64 Decca F 11821 — The Green Fields/Swing Down Chariot . . . 15
64 Decca F 11994 — Sorrow And Pain/The Lonely Valley . . . 12
65 Decca F 12071 — Concrete And Clay/When I Fall In Love . . . 6
65 Decca F 12144 — (You've) Never Been In Love Like This Before/Tell Somebody You Know . . . 8
65 Decca F 12211 — Hark/Stop Wasting Your Time . . . 7
65 Decca F 12299 — You've Got To Be Cruel To Be Kind/I Won't Let You Down . . . 7
66 Decca F 12333 — Baby Never Say Goodbye/Rainy Day . . . 10
66 Decca F 12398 — For A Moment/Fables . . . 12
66 Decca F 12509 — I Was Only Playing Games/I've Seen The Light . . . 10
67 Fontana TF 834 — Too Fast, Too Slow/Booby Trap . . . 15
67 Fontana TF 840 — Butterfly/A Place To Go . . . 12
67 Fontana TF 891 — Loving Takes A Little Understanding/Would You Believe What I Say? (as Unit) . . . 8
68 Fontana TF 931 — You Ain't Goin' Nowhere/So You Want To Be A Blues Player . . . 12
69 Fontana TF 990 — I Will/3.30 . . . 30
65 Decca DFE 8619 — UNIT 4 + 2 (EP) . . . 60
65 Decca LK 4697 — UNIT 4 + 2 — FIRST ALBUM (LP) . . . 65
69 Fontana SFL 13123 — UNIT 4 + 2 (LP) . . . 60
(see also Roulettes, Tom Sawyer, Capability Brown, Argent)

UNIVERSAL INDICATOR

92 Rephlex TB-303 — 1-BLUE (12") . . . 25
92 Rephlex TR-606 — 2-RED (12") . . . 25
93 Rephlex MC-202 — 3-YELLOW (12") . . . 20
95 Rephlex SH-101 — 4-GREEN (7", 10" + 12" in bag, all green vinyl) . . . 30
(see also Kosmik Kommando)

UNIVERSALS

67 Page One POF 032 — I Can't Find You/Hey You . . . 100
67 Page One POF 049 — Green Veined Orchid/While The Cat's Away . . . 25
(see also Chris Lamb & Universals, Gidian, Lace, Gary Walker & Rain, Plastic Penny)

U.N.K.L.E.

97 Mo' Wax MW 069L — Berry Meditation (mixes) (12", clear etched vinyl promo, sealed/unsealed poly sleeve) . . . 40/25
99 Mo' Wax MW 108CD 1 — Be There/(Underdog Mixes) (CD, 1 of 2-CD set, card sleeve) . . . 10
99 Mo' Wax MW 108CD 2 — Be There/Knock/Rabbit In Your Headlights (CD, 2 of 2-CD set, card sleeve) . . . 10
95 Mo' Wax MW 028 — THE TIME HAS COME EP (2 x 12" EP, picture disc, later black vinyl) . . . 15/20
94 Mo' Wax MWCD 028 — THE TIME HAS COME EP (CD, picture disc, stickered card sleeve) . . . 8
98 Mo' Wax MW 085CDX — PSYENCE FICTION (CD, gatefold card sleeve) . . . 20
(see also DJ Shadow)

UNKNOWN ARTIST

57 Woodbine Cigarettes — Big Beat (78, same track on both sides) . . . 12
50s Capstan Cigarettes — Capstan Go (1-sided 78, promo) . . . 12
50s Capstan Cigarettes — Cha Cha (1-sided 78, promo) . . . 12
50s Strand Cigarettes — You're Never Alone With A Strand (78, p/s, same track on both sides) . . . 35
66 Major MAJ 1 — Roarin' 'N' Scorin'/The Toast Of Merseyside (p/s) . . . 25

UNKNOWNS

66 London HLU 10082 — Melody For An Unknown Girl/Peith's Song . . . 8

UNLIMITED TOUCH

83 Prelude PRL 25294 — YES, WE'RE READY (LP) . . . 12

UNTAMED

64 Decca F 12045 — So Long/Just Wait . . . 55
65 Parlophone R 5258 — Once Upon A Time/I'm Asking You . . . 105
65 Stateside SS 431 — I'll Go Crazy/My Baby Is Gone . . . 60
66 Planet PLF 103 — It's Not True/Gimme Gimme Some Shade . . . 70
(see also Lindsay Muir's Untamed)

UNTAMED YOUTH

79 Hardcore HAR 001 — Untamed Youth/Runnin' Wild (p/s, 1,000 only) . . . 15

UNTOUCHABLES

80 Fried Egg EGG 2 — Keep On Walking/Keep Your Distance (p/s) . . . 5

UNTOUCHABLES (Jamaica)

68 Blue Cat BS 137 — Prisoner In Love/EDWARD RAPHAEL: True Love . . . 25
68 Trojan TR 613 — Tighten Up/ROY SHIRLEY: Good Ambition . . . 12
70 Upsetter US 345 — Same Thing All Over/UPSETTERS: It's Over . . . 20
70 Upsetter US 350 — Knock On Wood/UPSETTERS: Tight Spot . . . 20

MINT VALUE £

71	Bullet BU 460	Can't Reach You/CARL DAWKINS: Natural Woman	10
73	Bread BR 1113	Pay For The Wicked/Pay For The Wicked – Version (actually titled "Pray For The Wicked')	10

(see also Inspirations, Dave Barker, Leroy Reid)

UNWANTED

77	Raw RAW 6	Withdrawal/1978/Bleak Outlook (p/s)	35
77	Raw RAWT 6	Withdrawal/1978/Bleak Outlook (12", reissue)	20
78	Raw RAW 15	Secret Police/These Boots Are Made For Walking (p/s)	20
78	Raw RAW 30	Memory Man/Guns Of Love (unissued)	

(see also Psychedelic Furs)

STANLEY UNWIN

61	Golden Guinea GGE 0088-4	FAIRY STORYS (EP)	10
61	Pye NPL 18062	ROTATEY DISKERS WITH UNWIN (LP)	20
68	Marble Arch MAL 837	ROTATEY DISKERS WITH UNWIN (LP, reissue)	12

UPBEATS

58	London HLU 8688	Just Like In The Movies/My Foolish Heart	25
58	London HLU 8688	Just Like In The Movies/My Foolish Heart (78)	12
59	Pye International 7N 25016	You're The One I Care For/Keep Cool Crazy Heart	12
59	Pye International N 25016	You're The One I Care For/Keep Cool Crazy Heart (78)	6
59	Pye International 7N 25028	Teenie Weenie Bikini/Satin Shoes	12
59	Pye International N 25028	Teenie Weenie Bikini/Satin Shoes (78)	15

PHIL UPCHURCH COMBO

61	HMV POP 899	You Can't Sit Down Parts 1 & 2	30
66	Sue WI 4005	You Can't Sit Down Parts 1 & 2 (reissue)	15
66	Sue WI 4017	Nothing But Soul/Evad	15
72	Blue Thumb ILPS 9219	DARKNESS, DARKNESS (LP)	20

ROBERT UPCHURCH

74	Phil. Intl. PIR 2652	The Devil Made Me Do It/Glad You're Mine	10
70s	Phil. Intl 82168 4ZP 2000	The Devil Made Me Do It/You're The Reason Why (12")	8

UPCOMING WILLOWS

65	Island WI 182	Jonestown Special/SHENLEY DUFFAS: La La La	30
65	Island WI 184	Red China/SHENLEY DUFFAS: You Are Mine	30

(see also Shenley Duffas)

UPP

75	Epic EPC 80625	UPP (LP)	12

(see also Clark-Hutchinson)

UPROAR

82	Beat The System RAW 1	Rebel Youth/No More War/Fallen Angel/Victims (p/s)	5
83	Lightbeat RAW 2	DIE FOR ME (EP)	5
83	Volume VOL 9	NOTHING CAN STOP YOU (EP)	5
80s	Beat The System BTSLP 1	AND THE LORD SAID LET THERE BE UPROAR (LP)	25

UPSETTERS

65	Island WI 223	Country Girl/Strange Country (both sides actually by Ossie & Upsetters)	35
65	Rio R 70	Walk Down The Aisle/So Bad	20
66	Doctor Bird DB 1034	Wildcat/I Love You So	20

(see also Ossie & Upsetters, Dave Barker)

UPSETTERS

69	Duke DU 11	Eight For Eight/Stand By Me (B-side actually by Inspirations)	25
69	Camel CA 13	Taste Of Killing/My Mob	18
69	Punch PH 18	Return Of The Ugly/I've Caught You	15
69	Punch PH 19	Dry Acid/REGGAE BOYS: Selassie	15
69	Punch PH 21	Clint Eastwood/Lennox Mood	15
69	Upsetter US 300	Eight For Eight/You Know What I Mean (B-side actually by Inspirations)	15
69	Upsetter US 301	Return Of Django/Dollar In The Teeth	8
69	Upsetter US 303	Ten To Twelve/LEE PERRY: People Funny Fi True	15
69	Upsetter US 307	Night Doctor/TERMITES: I'll Be Waiting	15
69	Upsetter US 309	Kiddyo/Endlessly (both sides actually by Silvertones)	15
69	Upsetter US 310	A Dangerous Man From MI5/WEST INDIANS: Oh Lord	15
69	Upsetter US 313	Live Injection/BLEECHERS: Everything For Fun	15
69	Upsetter US 315	Cold Sweat/Pound Get A Blow (B-side actually by Bleechers)	15
70	Upsetter US 317	Vampire/BLEECHERS: Check Him Out	15
70	Upsetter US 318	Soulful I/MILTON HENRY: Bread And Butter	15
70	Upsetter US 321	Drugs And Poison/Stranger On The Shore	15
70	Upsetter US 325	Kill Them All/Soul Walk	15
70	Upsetter US 326	Bronco/One More	15
70	Upsetter US 332	Na Na Hey Hey/Pick Folk Kinkyest	15
70	Upsetter US 333	Granny Show/Version	15
70	Upsetter US 334	Fire Fire/Jumper	15
70	Upsetter US 335	The Pillow/Grooving	15
70	Upsetter US 336	Self Control/The Pill	15
70	Upsetter US 338	Fresh Up/Toothaches	15
70	Upsetter US 342	Dreamland/BOB MARLEY: Version Of Cup	40
70	Upsetter US 343	Sipreano/Ferry Boat	15
70	Upsetter US 346	Bigger Joke/Return Of The Vampire	15
70	Upsetter US 349	Upsetting Station (actually plays "Did Your Grave" by Bob Marley & Wailers)/ UPSETTERS: Justice (Instrumental)	35
70	Upsetter US 352	Heart And Soul/Zig Zag	15
70	Spinning Wheel SW 100	Haunted House/Double Wheel	20
70	Spinning Wheel SW 101	The Miser/CHUCK JUNIOR: Do It Madly	20
70	Spinning Wheel SW 102	The Chokin' Kind/CHUCK JUNIOR: Penny Wise	20

70	Spinning Wheel SW 103	Land Of Kinks/O'NEIL HALL: This Man	20
70	Trojan TR 7748	Family Man/Mellow Mood	15
70	Trojan TR 7749	Capo/Mama Look	15
70	Punch PH 27	The Result/Feel The Spirit	15
71	Bullet BU 461	All Combine Parts 1 & 2	15
71	Bullet BU 499	Beat Down Babylon/JUNIOR BYLES: Version	15
71	Upsetter US 353	Illusion/Big John Wayne (as Upsetters & King Teddy)	15
71	Upsetter US 361	Capasetic (actually "Copasetic" by Lord Comic)/All Africans (actually "Don't Cross The Nation" by Little Roy)	15
71	Upsetter US 365	Earthquake/JUNIOR BYLES: Palace Called Africa	15
71	Upsetter US 370	Dark Moon/DAVID ISAACS: You'll Be Sorry	15
72	Upsetter US 385	French Connection/Version	15
72	Upsetter US 387	Festival Da Da/JUNIOR BYLES: Version	15
72	Upsetter US 393	Crummy People/BIG YOUTH: Moving — Version	15
72	Upsetter US 394	Water Pump Parts 1 & 2	15
72	Randy's RAN 523	Nebuchadnezzer/JUNIOR BYLES: King Of Babylon	15
72	Punch PH 109	Hail To Power/JUNIOR BYLES: Pharaoh Hiding	15
73	Upsetter US 396	Puss Sea Hole/WINSTON GROOVY: Want To Be Loved	15
73	Upsetter US 397	Jungle Lion/Freak Out Skank	15
73	Upsetter US 398	Cow Thief Skank (with Charlie Ace)/7 3/4 Skank	15
73	Downtown DT 499	Black Ipa/Ipa Skank	15
73	Downtown DT 506	Sunshine Showdown/Sunshine Version	15
73	Downtown DT 512	Tighten Up Skank/Mid-East Rock	15
73	Downtown DT 513	Sucky Skank/Yucky Skank	18
74	Count Shelly CS 052	San-San/OSBOURNE GRAHAM: Baby Don't Go	15
74	Dip DL 5031	Enter The Dragon/JOY WHITE: Lady Lady	15
74	Dip DL 5032	Rebels Train/Rebels Dub	15
75	Dip DL 5054	Cane River Rock/Riverside Rock	15
75	Dip DL 5056	I Man Free/King Burnett: Version	15
75	Dip DL 5073	Key Card/Domino Game	15
69	Pama Special PSP 1014	CLINT EASTWOOD (LP)	70
69	Trojan TTL 13	THE UPSETTER (LP)	40
69	Trojan TRL 19	THE RETURN OF DJANGO (LP)	40
70	Trojan TTL 28	SCRATCH THE UPSETTER AGAIN (LP)	40
70	Trojan TBL 119	THE GOOD, THE BAD AND THE UPSETTERS (LP)	50
70	Trojan TBL 125	EASTWOOD RIDES AGAIN (LP)	50
70	Pama SECO 24	THE MANY MOODS OF THE UPSETTERS (LP)	60
74	Trojan TRLS 70	DOUBLE SEVEN (LP)	35
75	DIP DLPD 6002	RETURN OF THE WAX (LP, white-label only, plain sleeve)	35
76	Island ILPS 9417	SUPER APE (LP)	22

(see also Lee Perry, Ossie & Upsetters, Hippy Boys, Bob Marley/Wailers, Family Man, Tommy McCook, Max Romeo, Melodians,
Lord Creator, Dennis Alcapone)

UPSETTING BROTHERS

71	Supreme SUP 229	Not You Baby/DREAD LOCK ALL-STARS: Baby (Version)	12

UPTOWNERS

64	London HLU 9877	If'n/Search Is Over	12

URBAN CLEARWAY

70	Torpedo TOR 21	Open Up Wide Parts 1 & 2	6

URBAN DISTURBANCE

79	Rok ROK V/VI	Wild Boys In Cortinas/V.I.P.s: Can't Let You Go (die-cut sleeve)	25

URBAN DOGS

82	Fallout FALL 008	New Barbarians/Speed Kills/Cocaine (p/s)	5
82	Fallout FALL 011	Limo Life/Warhead (p/s)	5
88	Fallout FALL LP 12	URBAN DOGS (LP)	12

(see Hanoi Rocks, U.K. Subs, Vibrators)

URCHIN

77	DJM DJS 10776	Black Leather Fantasy/Rock & Roll Woman (in promo p/s)	300
78	DJM DJS 10850	She's A Roller/Long Time No Woman (in promo p/s)	300

(see also A.S.A.P., Iron Maiden)

URCHINS

66	Polydor BM 56145	I Made Her That Way/Twas On A Night Like This	6

URIAH HEEP

70	Vertigo 6059 037	Lady In Black/Simon The Bullet Freak (unissued in U.K.)	
71	Bronze WIP 6111	Look At Yourself/Simon The Bullet Freak	7
72	Bronze WIP 6126	The Wizard/Gypsy	6
72	Bronze WIP 6140	Easy Livin'/Why	6
73	Bronze BRO 7	Stealin'/Sunshine	6
74	Bronze BRO 10	Something Or Nothing/What Can I Do	5
75	Bronze BRO 17	Prima Donna/Shout It Out	5
76	Bronze BRO 27	One Way Or Another/Misty Eyes	5
76	Bronze BRODJ 1	One Way Or Another/Misty Eyes (promo only p/s, 750 copies)	20
77	Bronze BRO 37	Wise Man/Crime Of Passion	5
77	Bronze BRO 47	Free Me/Masquerade (p/s)	6
78	Bronze BRO 62	Come Back To Me/Cheater	5
82	Bronze BRO 143	THE ABOMINOG JUNIOR (EP, p/s)	6
83	Bronze BROP 166	Lonely Nights/Weekend Warriors (picture disc)	8
83	Bronze BROG 168	Stay On Top/Playing For Time//Gypsy/Easy Livin'/Sweet Lorraine/ Stealin' (double pack, gatefold p/s)	7
85	Portrait WA 6103	Rockerama/Back Stage Girl (shaped picture disc)	10
88	Legacy LGYT 65	Easy Livin' (live)/Corina (live)/Gypsy (live) (12", red vinyl)	8
88	Castle Comms. CD3-16	URIAH HEEP (CD EP, 5,000 only)	10

MINT VALUE £

70 Vertigo 6360 006 VERY 'EAVY... VERY 'UMBLE (LP, gatefold sleeve, swirl label) . . . 40
71 Vertigo 6360 028 SALISBURY (LP, gatefold sleeve, swirl label) . . . 40
71 Bronze ILPS 9142 VERY 'EAVY... VERY 'UMBLE (LP, reissue) . . . 15
71 Bronze ILPS 9152 SALISBURY (LP, reissue) . . . 15
71 Bronze ILPS 9169 LOOK AT YOURSELF (LP, 'mirror' sleeve) . . . 15
89 Legacy LLP 120 RAGING SILENCE (LP, picture disc) . . . 12
(see also Gods, Head Machine, Natural Gas, Spice, King Crimson, John Lawton, Grand Prix)

URUSEI YATSURA

95 Modern Ind. MIR 001 Pampered Adolescent/BLISTERS: A Dull Thought In Itself (burgundy vinyl, p/s, 500 only) . . . 20
95 Ché CHÉ 38 Siamese/Lo-Fi (orange & grey vinyl, p/s) . . . 8
95 Love Train PUBE 08 Kernel/Teendream (p/s, 1,000 only) . . . 8

US

70s Jeff Wayne Music SD 015 You're OK With Us/Tomorrow (p/s, promo for Johnson Wax) . . . 10
(see also David Essex, Randells)

U.S. DOUBLE QUARTET

(see United States Double Quartet)

USELESS UNICORN

74 Horny HORN 11 RUBBER HORN (LP, gatefold sleeve, with pop-up horn) . . . 15

USERS

77 Raw RAW 1 Sick Of You/(I'm) In Love With Today (p/s, some numbered on rear) . . . 15/10
77 Raw RAWT 1 Sick Of You/(I'm) In Love With Today (12", no p/s) . . . 15
78 Warped WARP 1 Warped 45: Kicks In Style/Dead On Arrival (p/s, 5,000 only, numbered sleeve, some un-numbered) . . . 18

US FOLK

65 Eyemark EMS 1001 Funny Old World/Dives . . . 6

U.S. SKY

(see under Sky)

U.S. T-BONES

65 Liberty LIB 55836 No Matter What Shape/Feelin' Fine . . . 12
66 Liberty LIB 55867 Sippin'n'Chippin'/Moment Of Softness . . . 15
66 Liberty LIB 55951 The Proper Thing To Do/Tee-Hee-Hee . . . 15

PETER USTINOV

50 Parlophone R 3612 Mock Mozart (with Anthony Hopkins, Harpsichord)/Phoney Folk-Lore (78) . . . 10
53 Parlophone MSP 6012 Mock Mozart (with Anthony Hopkins, Harpsichord)/Phoney Folk-Lore . . . 10
(see also Peter Sellers)

UTOPIA (Germany)

73 United Artists UAG 29438 UTOPIA (LP) . . . 25
(see also Amon Düül II)

UTOPIA (U.S.)

77 Bearsville K 55514 RA (LP, with lyric inner & pyramid insert) . . . 12
82 Epic EPC 25207 UTOPIA (LP, with free 5-track EP) . . . 12
(see also Todd Rundgren)

U2

SINGLES: IRISH PRESSINGS

79 CBS 7951 U2: THREE (Out Of Control/Stories For The Boys/Boy-Girl) (p/s, black vinyl) . . . 35
80 CBS 7951 U2: THREE (Out Of Control/Stories For The Boys/Boy-Girl) (p/s, white vinyl) . . . 400
80 CBS 7951 U2: THREE (Out Of Control/Stories For The Boys/Boy-Girl) (p/s, orange vinyl) . . 125
80 CBS 7951 U2: THREE (Out Of Control/Stories For The Boys/Boy-Girl) (p/s, yellow vinyl) . . . 90
80 CBS 7951 U2: THREE (Out Of Control/Stories For The Boys/Boy-Girl) (p/s, brown vinyl mispressing, fewer than 50 copies exist) . . . 950
81 CBS 12-7951 U2: THREE (12" EP, with numbered sticker, orange CBS sleeve, 1,000 only) . . . 600
81 CBS 12-7951 U2: THREE (12" EP, reissue, die-cut CBS sleeve) . . . 40
81 CBS 12-7951 U2: THREE (12" EP, 2nd reissue, plain black sleeve, slightly different labels) . . . 40
85 CBS 40-7951 U2: THREE (cassette, reissue) . . . 40
80 CBS 8306 Another Day/Twilight (Demo Version) (p/s, yellow vinyl) . . . 150
80 CBS 8306 Another Day/Twilight (Demo Version) (p/s, orange vinyl) . . . 170
80 CBS 8306 Another Day/Twilight (Demo Version) (p/s, white vinyl) . . . 220
80 CBS 8306 Another Day/Twilight (Demo Version) (p/s, black vinyl, initially with postcard designed by Bono) . . . 350/60
80 CBS 8687 11 O'Clock Tick Tock/Touch (p/s, yellow vinyl) . . . 65
80 CBS 9065 I Will Follow/Boy-Girl (live) (p/s, yellow vinyl) . . . 60
80 CBS 9065 I Will Follow/Boy-Girl (live) (p/s, orange vinyl) . . . 125
80 CBS 9065 I Will Follow/Boy-Girl (live) (p/s, white vinyl) . . . 250
80 CBS 9065 I Will Follow/Boy-Girl (live) (p/s, brown vinyl, fewer than 50 copies) . . . 950
82 CBS PAC 1 4 U2 PLAY (4 x 7", each in p/s, black vinyl) . . . 150
82 CBS PAC 1 4 U2 PLAY (4 x 7", each in p/s, yellow vinyl) . . . 400
80s CBS PAC 2 PAC 2 (4 x 7" with p/s in plastic wallet) . . . 60
80s CBS PAC 3 PAC 3 (4 x 7" with p/s in plastic wallet) . . . 60

SINGLES: UK PRESSINGS

80 Island WIP 6601 11 O'Clock Tick Tock/Touch (p/s) . . . 35
80 Island WIP 6630 A Day Without Me/Things To Make And Do (p/s) . . . 30
80 Island WIP 6656 I Will Follow/Boy-Girl (live) (p/s) . . . 30
81 Island WIP 6679 Fire/J. Swallo (p/s) . . . 18
81 Island UWIP 6679 Fire/J. Swallo//11 O'Clock Tick Tock (live)/The Ocean (live)/Cry (live)/ The Electric Co. (live) (double pack, single p/s) . . . 22
81 Island WIP 6733 Gloria/I Will Follow (live) (p/s) . . . 18
82 Island WIP 6770 A Celebration/Trash, Trampoline And The Party Girl (p/s) . . . 40

			MINT VALUE £
83	Island WIP 6848	New Year's Day/Treasure (Whatever Happened To Pete The Chop) (p/s)	7
83	Island WIP 6848	New Year's Day/Treasure (Whatever Happened To Pete The Chop) (p/s, mispressing, B-side plays Martha Reeves, Motown label)	85
83	Island UWIP 6848	New Year's Day/Treasure (Whatever Happened To Pete The Chop)// Fire (live)/I Threw A Brick Through A Window (live)/A Day Without Me (live) (double pack, single p/s, black inners)	22
83	Island 12WIP 6848	New Year's Day/Treasure (Whatever Happened To Pete The Chop)/ Fire (live)/I Threw A Brick Through A Window/A Day Without Me (12", p/s)	15
83	Island IS 109	Two Hearts Beat As One/Endless Deep (p/s)	8
83	Island ISD 109	Two Hearts Beat As One/Endless Deep//New Year's Day (U.S.A. Remix)/ Two Hearts Beat As One (U.S.A. Remix) (p/s, double pack)	25
83	Island 12IS 109	Two Hearts Beat As One (Club Mix)/New Year's Day/ Two Hearts Beat As One (U.S Remix) (12", p/s)	18
84	Island IS 202	Pride (In The Name Of Love)/Boomerang 2 (Vocal) (p/s)	8
84	Island ISP 202	Pride (In The Name Of Love)/Boomerang 2 (Vocal) (picture disc)	40
84	Island ISD 202	Pride (In The Name Of Love)/4th Of July//Boomerang I (Instrumental)/ Boomerang 2 (Vocal) (double pack, gatefold p/s)	18
84	Island CIS 202	Pride (In The Name Of Love)/Boomerang I/4th Of July/Boomerang 2/ A Celebration (cassette)	25
84	Island 12IS 202	Pride (In The Name Of Love)/4th Of July/Boomerang 2 (12",white p/s)	12
84	Island 12ISX 202	Pride (In The Name Of Love)/Boomerang I/Boomerang 2/ 11 O'Clock Tick Tock/Touch (Full Length Version) (12", blue p/s)	30
85	Island ISD 220	The Unforgettable Fire/A Sort Of Homecoming (live)/Love Comes Tumbling/ Sixty Seconds In Kingdom Come/The Three Sunrises (double pack, gatefold p/s)	12
85	Island ISP 220	The Unforgettable Fire/A Sort Of Homecoming (live) (logo-shaped pic disc)	55
85	Island 12IS 220	The Three Sunrises/The Unforgettable Fire/A Sort Of Homecoming (live)/ Love Comes Tumbling/Bass Trap (12", p/s)	12
87	Island IS 319	With Or Without You/Walk To The Water/Luminous Times (Hold Onto Love) (p/s)	6
87	Island CIS 319	With Or Without You/Luminous Times (Hold Onto Love)/ Walk To The Water (cassette)	8
87	Island 12IS 319	With Or Without You/Luminous Times (Hold Onto Love)/ Walk To The Water (12", p/s)	12
87	Island CID 319	With Or Without You/Luminous Times (Hold Onto Love)/ Walk To The Water (CD, gatefold card p/s)	22
87	Island IS 328	I Still Haven't Found What I'm Looking For/Spanish Eyes/Deep In The Heart (p/s)	6
87	Island CIS 328	I Still Haven't Found What I'm Looking For/Spanish Eyes/ Deep In The Heart (cassette)	8
87	Island 12IS 328	I Still Haven't Found What I'm Looking For/Spanish Eyes/ Deep In The Heart (12", p/s)	12
87	Island IS 340	Where The Streets Have No Name/Silver And Gold/The Sweetest Thing (p/s, paper label)	8
87	Island CIS 340	Where The Streets Have No Name/Race Against Time/Silver And Gold/ The Sweetest Thing (cassette)	8
87	Island 12IS 340	Where The Streets Have No Name/Race Against Time/Silver And Gold/ The Sweetest Thing (12", p/s with "Silver And Gold" lyric insert)	30
87	Island CID 340	Where The Streets Have No Name (edit)/Race Against Time/Silver And Gold/ The Sweetest Thing (CD, gatefold p/s)	22
88	Island IS 400	Desire/Hallelujah Here She Comes (non-gatefold p/s)	6
88	Island ISG 400	Desire/Hallelujah Here She Comes (gatefold p/s)	5
88	Island CIDP 400	Desire/Hallelujah Here She Comes/Desire (Hollywood Remix) (CD, picture disc)	25
88	Island IS 402	Angel Of Harlem/A Room At The Heartbreak Hotel (p/s)	5
88	Island CIDP 402	Angel Of Harlem (Remix)/A Room At The Heartbreak Hotel/Love Rescue Me (Live At "Smile Jamaica" Concert London Oct '88) (CD, picture disc)	15
88	Island CIDX 402	Angel Of Harlem (Remix)/A Room At The Heartbreak Hotel/Love Rescue Me (live) (3" CD, long box, U.S. import with stickered U.K. matrix number)	25
88	Island U2 PK 1	THE JOSHUA TREE SINGLES (4 x 7"s in PVC wallet with 'obi' band)	40
89	Island IS 411	When Love Comes To Town/Dancing Barefoot (p/s)	5
89	Island CIDP 411	When Love Comes To Town/Dancing Barefoot/When Love Comes To Town (Live From The Kingdom Mix) (with BB King)/God Part II (The Hard Metal Dance Mix) (CD, picture disc)	15
89	Island CIDX 411	When Love Comes To Town/Dancing Barefoot/When Love Comes To Town (Live From The Kingdom Mix) (with Little Richard)/God Part II (The Hard Metal Dance Mix) (as U2 with B.B. King) (3" CD, long box, U.S. import with stickered U.K. matrix number)	25
89	Island 422	All I Want Is You/Unchained Melody (p/s)	5
89	Island ISB 422	All I Want Is You (Edit)/Unchained Melody (in numbered tin box)	25
89	Island CIS 422	All I Want Is You (Edit)/Unchained Melody (cassette)	7
89	Island 12IS 422	All I Want Is You (Full Version)/Unchained Melody/Everlasting Love (12", p/s)	10
89	Island 12 ISB 422	All I Want Is You (Full Version)/Unchained Melody/Everlasting Love (12", p/s, box set with 4 prints)	18
89	Island CIDP 422	All I Want Is You (4.14)/Unchained Melody/Everlasting Love/ All I Want Is You (Full Version) (CD, picture disc)	25
91	Island IS 500	The Fly/Alex Descends Into Hell For A Bottle Of Milk (p/s)	5
91	Island IS 509	Mysterious Ways/Mysterious Ways (Solar Plexus Club Mix) (p/s)	5
91	Island 12IS 509	Mysterious Ways (4.04)/(Solar Plexus Extended Club Mix 7.01)/ (Apollo 440 Magic Hour Remix)/(Tabla Motown Remix)/ (Solar Plexus Club Mix) (12", p/s, withdrawn)	18
92	Island IS 515	One/Satellite Of Love (p/s)	5
92	Island IS 525	Even Better Than The Real Thing/Salomé (p/s)	5
92	Island 12IS 525	Even Better Than The Real Thing/Salomé/Where Did It All Go Wrong/ Lady With The Spinning Head (UVI) (Extended Dance Mix) (12", with giant "Zoo TV" poster)	25
92	Island REAL U2	Even Better Than The Real Thing (Perfecto Mix)/(Trance Mix)/ (Sexy Dub Mix) (12", title sleeve)	10

MINT VALUE £

92	Island CREAL 2	Even Better Than The Real Thing (Perfecto Mix)/(Sexy Dub Mix)/ (Apollo 440 Stealth Sonic Remix)/(V16 Exit Wound Remix) (A440 Vs. U2 Instrumental Remix) (CD)	10
92	Island IS 550	Who's Gonna Ride Your Wild Horses (Temple Bar Edit)/Paint It Black (p/s)	5
92	Island CIDX 550	Who's Gonna Ride Your Wild Horses (Temple Bar Edit)/Paint It Black/Salomé (Zooromancer Remix)/Can't Help Falling In Love (Triple Peaks Remix) (CD, picture disc, tri-fold digipak with 4 prints, some sealed)	45/35
93	Island IS 578	Stay (Faraway, So Close!)/I've Got You Under My Skin (with Frank Sinatra)	6
93	Island CIDX 578	Stay (Faraway, So Close!)/Slow Dancing/Bullet The Blue Sky (live)/ Love Is Blindness (live) (CD, 'The Live Format', foldout digipak)	20
95	Atlantic A 7131	Hold Me, Thrill Me, Kiss Me, Kill Me/ELLIOTT GOLDENTHAL: Themes From Batman Forever (p/s, red vinyl)	7
95	Atlantic A 7131	Hold Me, Thrill Me, Kiss Me, Kill Me/ELLIOTT GOLDENTHAL: Themes From Batman Forever (p/s, red vinyl, B-side miscredited to U2)	20
93	Island CID 578	Stay (Faraway, So Close!)/I've Got You Under My Skin (as Frank Sinatra & Bono)/Lemon (Bad Yard Club)/Lemon (Perfecto Mix) (CD, 'The Swing Format')	18
97	Island 12IST 649	Discothèque (Howie B Hairy B Mix)/(Hexidecimal Mix)/(DM Deep Extended Club Mix)/(DM Deep Beats Mix) (12", barcoded p/s, poster)	18
97	Island ISD(X) 649 D(J)	Discothèque (Howie B Hairy B Mix)/Discothèque (Hexidecimal Mix)// Discothèque (DM Deep Extended Club Mix)/Discothèque (DM Deep Beats Mix)/ Discothèque (DM Tec Radio Mix)/Discothèque (DM Deep Instrumental Mix)// Discothèque (Single Version)/Discothèque (David Holmes Mix) (3 x 12" in silver title sleeve with pink, orange & blue inners; with barcode & front sticker)	18
97	Island CID 649	Discothèque/Holy Joe (Garage Mix)/Holy Joe (Guilty Mix) (CD, jewel case, withdrawn)	50
97	Island 12IS 684	Mofo (Mother's Mix)/Mofo (House Flavour Mix)/Mofo (Romin Mix)/Mofo (Phunk Force Mix)/Mofo (Black Hole Dub) (12", die-cut p/s, 2,000 only)	18
01	Island CIDX 780	Elevation (Tomb Raider Mix)/Last Night On Earth (Live)/Don't Take Your Guns To Town (CD, blue/silver poster pack, withdrawn)	55

DVD SINGLES

01	Island CIDV 780	Elevation (Tomb Raider Mix)/Elevation (Tomb Raider Mix [video])/ (excerpts from MTV's "Making Of The U2 Video")	12
01	Island CIDV 788	Walk On (Single Version)/(4 x 30 second clips from Elevation 2001 — U2 live from Boston)	10

PROMO-ONLY SINGLES

80	Island WIP 6601	11 O'Clock Tick Tock/Touch (p/s, 'A' label)	50
80	Island WIP 6630	A Day Without Me/Things To Make And Do (p/s, 'A' label)	50
80	Island WIP 6656 DJ	I Will Follow (Special Edited DJ Version) (1-sided, company sleeve)	75
81	WIP 6679	Fire (Radio Edit) (1-sided, p/s)	50
81	WIP 6733	Gloria (Radio Edit) (1-sided, p/s)	50
84	Island U2 2	Wire/Bad/The Unforgettable Fire (12", black die-cut sleeve)	65
87	Island ISJ 319	With Or Without You/Walk To The Water (jukebox issue, large centre hole)	15
87	Island ISJ 328	I Still Haven't Found What I'm Looking For/Spanish Eyes (jukebox issue, solid centre or large centre hole)	75/15
87	Island ISJB 340	Where The Streets Have No Name/Silver And Gold (jukebox issue, large centre hole)	15
88	Island 12ISX 400	Desire (9.23 Hollywood Remix) (12", 1-sided, custom black p/s, 800 only)	45
88	Island U2V 7	EXCERPTS FROM RATTLE AND HUM (In God's Country [live]/Hawkmoon 269/ Bad [live]/God Part II/With Or Without You [live]) (CD, card gatefold sleeve)	90
88	Island IS 319	With Or Without You/Luminous Times (Hold Onto Love)/Walk To The Water/ With Or Without You (Video) (CD Video, withdrawn, less than 100 copies)	750
89	Island 12 ISX 411	U2 3D DANCE MIXES: When Love Comes To Town (Live From The Kingdom Dance Mix)/God Part II (Hard Metal Dance Club Mix)/ Desire (Hollywood Remix 5.23) (12" EP, custom sleeve)	50
90	Island RHB 1	Night And Day (Twilight Remix)/Steel String Mix) (12", p/s, numbered, 4,000 copies only)	80
91	Island U2-3	OCTOBER 1991: I Will Follow/Pride (In The Name Of Love)/God Part II/ Where The Streets Have No Name) (CD EP, 250 only)	600
91	Island IS 500B	Alex Descends Into Hell (test pressings only, pink handwritten label, no p/s)	140
92	Island 12 IS 515B	Lady With The Spinning Head (UVI)/Satellite Of Love (12", test pressings only, with press release, white label)	150
92	Island 12IS 550DJ	Salomé (Zooromancer Remix 8.02)/Can't Help Falling In Love (Mystery Train Dub 8.20) (12", black die-cut sleeve, 1,000 only)	90
92	Island REAL 1	Even Better Than The Real Thing (The Perfecto Mix)/Even Better Than The Real Thing (Trance Mix)/Even Better Than The Real Thing (Sexy Dub Mix) (12", black die-cut sleeve with title sticker)	30
92	Island REAL 2DJ	Even Better Than The Real Thing (The Perfecto Mix-Radio Edit) (2-sided radio promo, some with p/s)	40/30
93	Island NUMJB 1	Numb (2-sided jukebox issue, large centre hole)	25
93	Island NUMCD 1	Numb (CD, 1-track, with lyric inner, 250 only)	100
93	Island 12LEM DJ 1	Lemon (Bad Yard Club)/(Momo Beats)/(Version Dub)/(Serious Def Dub)// (Perfecto Mix)/(Trance Mix) (12", double pack, p/s, 1,000 only, numbered with press sheets; discs sometimes sold individually - without outer sleeve - @ £25 each)	125
93	Island LEMCD 1	Lemon (Radio Edit) (CD, 1-track, with lyric inner)	45
95	Island 12 MELON 1	MELON (Salomé [Zooromancer Remix]/Lemon [Bad Yard Club Mix]/ Numb [The Soul Assassins Mix]/Numb [Gimme Some More Dignity Mix]) (12" EP, 800 only)	35
95	Atlantic A 7131	Hold Me, Thrill Me, Kiss Me, Kill Me/Themes From Batman Forever (black vinyl, jukebox issue, large centre hole)	18
95	Atlantic A 7131	Hold Me, Thrill Me, Kiss Me, Kill Me/Themes From Batman Forever (red vinyl, some with B-side miscredited to U2)	15/10
96	Island PRECD 1	U2 PREVIOUSLY: Lemon/Mysterious Ways/One/Desire/I Still Haven't Found What I'm Looking For (CD, card sleeve)	35
97	Island ISJB 649	Discothèque/Holy Joe (Garage Mix) (jukebox issue, large centre hole)	12

MINT VALUE £

97	Island ISD(X) 649 D(J)	Discothèque (Howie B Hairy B Mix)/Discothèque (Hexidecimal Mix)// Discothèque (DM Deep Extended Club Mix)/Discothèque (DM Deep Beats Mix)/ Discothèque (DM Tec Radio Mix)/Discothèque (DM Deep Instrumental Mix)// Discothèque (Single Version)/Discothèque (David Holmes Mix) (3 x 12" in silver title sleeve with pink, orange & blue inners; no barcode or front sticker)	45
97	Island DISCO 1	Discothèque (Radio Edit) (CD, 1-track, jewel case)	15
97	Island DISCO 2	Discothèque (Radio Edit)/Discothèque (Album Version) (CD, jewel case)	35
97	Island no cat. no.	Discothèque (Hexidecimal Remix — Radio Edit) (CD-R, 1-track, jewel case)	140
97	Island ISJB 658	Staring At The Sun/North And South Of The River (jukebox issue, large centre hole)	12
97	Island 12IS 658DJ	Staring At The Sun (Monster Truck Mix)/Staring At The Sun (Lab Rat Mix)/ Staring At The Sun (Sad Bastard's Mix) (12", p/s)	30
97	Island ISJB 664	Last Night On Earth (Single Mix)/Last Night On Earth (First Night In Hell Remix) (jukebox issue, large centre hole)	12
97	Island 12IS 664DJ	Last Night On Earth (First Night In Hell Remix)/Happiness Is A Warm Gun (The Gun Mix)/Pop Muzik (Pop Mart Mix)/Happiness Is A Warm Gun (The Danny Sabre Mix) (12", p/s)	35
97	Island MUZIK 1	Pop Muzik (Pop Mart Mix — Radio Edit) (CD, 1-track, picture disc, jewel case, 250 only)	65
97	Island ISJB 673	Please/Where The Streets Have No Name (live) (jukebox issue, large centre hole)	12
97	Island CIDDJ 673	Please/Please (Call Out Hook) (CD)	35
97	Island PLEASE CD 1	Please (Single Edit)/Please (Single Version) (CD, plain disc with handwritten title, jewel case, no inlay, less than 50 pressed)	125
97	Island PLEASE CD 1	Please (Single Edit)/Please (Single Version) (CD, 2-track, yellow graphics on disc, jewel case)	25
97	Island ISJB 684	If God Will Send His Angels (Single Vesion)/Sunday Bloody Sunday (live from Sarajevo) (jukebox issue, large centre hole)	12
97	Island 12MOFO 1	Mofo (Phunk Force Mix)/Mofo (Black Hole Dub)/Mofo (Romin Remix) (12", orange label, orange & silver die-cut title sleeve)	40
97	Island 12MOFO 2	Mofo (Mother's Mix)/Mofo (House Flavor Mix) (12", pink label, pink & silver die-cut title sleeve, 250 only)	55
97	Island 12MOFO 3	Mofo (Explicit Mix) (12", 1-sided, stamped white label, plain black die-cut sleeve, 200 only)	140
97	Island 12MOFO 3	Mofo (Explicit Mix)/Mofo (Explicit Mix) (12", 2-sided misspressing [same track both sides], stamped white label, plain black die-cut sleeve)	200
97	Island MOFOCD 1	Mofo (Album Version) (CD, 1-track, card sleeve, export issue [to Mexico])	150
97	Island MOFOCD 2	Mofo (Phunk Force Mix) (CD, 1-track, jewel case, export issue [to Mexico])	150
98	Island SWEET CD 1	Sweetest Thing (CD, 1-track)	15
98	Island SWEET CIDDJ 727	Sweetest Thing/Twilight (Live)/An Cat Dubh (Live)/Stories For Boys Out Of Control (Live) (CD, die-cut sleeve)	60
99	Columbia XPCD 1206	BONO & WYCLEF JEAN: New Day (Edit)/New Edit (Version) (CD, card sleeve)	15
00	Island GROUND CD 1	The Ground Beneath Her Feet/The Million Dollar Hotel Movie Trailer (CD-ROM, card sleeve, blue die-cut slipcase)	45
00	Island 12 BEAUT 1	Beautiful Day (Quincey & Sonance Mix) (1-sided 12", in black die-cut title sleeve)	40
01	Island STUCK CD 1	Stuck In A Moment You Can't Get Out Of (1-track CD, picture sleeve jewel case)	15
01	Island 12 ELE 1	Elevation (Escalation Mix)/Elevation (Influx Mix) (12", red custom p/s, 250 only)	30
01	Island ELE CD 2	Elevation (Tomb Raider Mix) (1-track CD, withdrawn)	45
01	Island 12 ELE 2	Elevation (Paul Vandyk Remix)/Elevation (The Vandit Club Mix) (12", blue custom p/s, 250 only, exclusive mixes)	40
01	Island ELE CD 2	Elevation (Tomb Raider Mix) (1-track CD, with withdrawn 'Lara Croft' sleeve or group sleeve)	50/15
01	Island WALKCD 1	Walk On (Single Version) (1-track CD, brown sleeve, jewel case, withdrawn)	35
01	Island WALKCD 2	Walk On (Single Version)/Walk On (Video Version) (CD, blue sleeve, jewel case)	15
02	Island STORM CD 1	Electrical Storm (William Orbit Mix)/Electrical Storm (Radio Edit) (CD)	15
02	Island CID 808	Electrical Storm (William Orbit Mix)/New York (Nice Mix)/New York (Nasty Mix)/ Bad (Live)/Where The Streets Have No Name (2-CD set in limited issue collectors' wallet, mail-order only from 'Propaganda' fan club)	50
03	Island HANDSCD 1	The Hands That Built America (promo only 1-track CD, card sleeve)	20
03	12 Sun U2	Staring At The Sun (Brothers In Rhythm Club Mix)/Staring At The Sun (Brothers In Rhythm Ambient Mix) (12", black die-cut custom sleeve)	25
02	Island 12REMIX U2 13	U2 REMIXES FROM THE 1990S (2 x 12" sampler, black inner sleeves, silver outer sleeve)	30
02	Island NEWCD U2 13	NEW SONGS AND MIXES FROM THE BEST OF 1990-2000 (CD sampler, black inner sleeve, silver outer sleeve)	50

ALBUMS

80	Island ICT 9646	BOY ('1+1' cassette)	35
81	Island ICT 9680	OCTOBER ('1+1' cassette, in plastic case or 'cigarette pack' card box)	35
83	Island PILPS 9733	WAR (LP, picture disc, beware of counterfeits with ILPS cat. no.)	75
83	Island ICT 9733	WAR ('1+1' cassette)	45
85	Island CID 112	WAR (LP, pink cover lettering)	125
85	Island CID 110	BOY (CD, with title rear sleeve; no bar code)	90
85	Island CID 111	OCTOBER (CD, with title rear sleeve; no bar code)	90
85	Island CID 113	UNDER A BLOOD RED SKY (CD, with picture rear sleeve; no bar code)	90
85	Island CID 102	THE UNFORGETTABLE FIRE (CD)	90
91	Island U2-8	ACHTUNG BABY (LP, with 10 art prints)	50
95	Island MELONCD 1	MELON (REMIXES FOR PROPAGANDA) (CD, 9-track compilation, card sleeve, fan club issue, 20,000 only; some sealed with *Propaganda* No. 21)	45/30
97	Island U2 10	POP (2-LP, gatefold sleeve)	20
98	Island U2 11	THE BEST OF 1980-1990 (2-LP, gatefold sleeve)	20

PROMO-ONLY ALBUMS

83	Island U2 1	UNDER A BLOOD RED SKY — A DIALOGUE WITH U2 LIVE (LP, custom sleeve, with cue sheet, numbered, 1,000 only)	75
87	Island U2-6	THE JOSHUA TREE (CD, LP & cassette in black/gold 'pizza' box set)	250

MINT VALUE £

87	Island U2 6-1 — U2 6-5	THE JOSHUA TREE COLLECTION Red Hill Mining Town/Where The Streets Have No Name//Trip Through Your Wires/Running To Stand Still//I Still Haven't Found What I'm Looking For/ One Tree Hill//Exit/Mothers Of The Disappeared//In God's Country/ Bullet The Blue Sky (5 x 7" set, in black box, 250 only)	600+
(The above singles sell for around £20-£25 individually, except for U2 6-2, £35)			
87	Island U2 6-1 — U2 6-5	THE JOSHUA TREE COLLECTION (5 x 7" black box set, with U2 6-1 mispressed with "Red Hill Mining Town" both sides, less than 50 copies)	1500
87	Island U2CLP 1	THE U2 TALKIE: A CONVERSATION WITH LARRY, BONO, ADAM & THE EDGE (LP, music & interview with Dave Fanning for "The Joshua Tree")	60
87	Island U2CC 1	THE U2 TALKIE (cassette)	30
87	Island BOU2 1	CASSETTE SAMPLER (cassette, 17-track instore 'best of' compilation)	45
88	Island U2-7	RATTLE AND HUM (CD, LP & cassette in flight case with leather tag, 250 only)	2000
89	Island U2 2D1	U2 2 DATE (LP, 8-track hits compilation)	35
91	Island U2-8	ACHTUNG BABY (CD, cassette in 'User's Kit', including map/poster, torch, key ring, spanner & screwdriver in printed green nylon kit bag)	900
91	Island CIDDJ U2-8	ACHTUNG (graphics CD, in jewel case marked "promo only — not for sale")	90
97	Island CID U2 10	POP (CD, in large cube-shaped picture box set, with prismatic pen & custom notepad)	300
97	Island POP 1	U2 TALK POP (CD, interview with Dave Fanning, card sleeve)	45
97	Island POP 2	U2 TALK POP (CD, interview with Dave Fanning, card sleeve, same tracks as POP 1)	45
97	Island POP 3	U2 TALK POP (CD, interview with Dave Fanning, card sleeve, same track as POP 1)	45
98	Island CIDDU211	THE BEST OF THE 'B' SIDES 1980-1990 (2-CD, discs marked 'A' and 'B', in card sleeves with gold slipcase)	65
98	Island BXU2 11	THE 'BEST OF' COLLECTION 1980-1990 (14 x 7" singles, 2-CDs, 16-page booklet, in gold box, 2,000 copies only)	500
00	Island MDH CD1	THE MILLION DOLLAR HOTEL (CD, card sleeve)	35
00	Island CID U212	ALL THAT YOU CAN'T LEAVE BEHIND (promo pack, with 1-track CD "Beautiful Day" [BEAUT CD 1] in blue picture slipcase, booklet, window sticker, video tape, "Playback" invitation, in laminated picture bag with rope handles; some with signed print)	500/175
00	no cat. no.	THE DAVE FANNING INTERVIEW (CD-R, dated 4.10.00, in white card sleeve, plastic outer sleeve)	80
00	no cat. no.	ALBUM INTERVIEW (CD-R, dated 25.10.00, in white card sleeve, plastic outer sl.)	75
01	no cat. no.	CD FREE WITH SUNDAY TIMES NEWSPAPER (5 tracks + 2 video tracks)	12/15
02	Island CIDDJ U2 13	THE BEST OF THE B-SIDES OF 1990-2000 (2-CD set card sleeves in card wallet)	50
02	Island BX U2 13	THE BEST OF COLLECTION 1990-2000 (15 x 7", with 2 CDs & 16-page booklet in silver fliptop card box)	350
02	Island REMIXCD U2 13	REMIXES FROM THE 90S (CD, 5-track album sampler in card sleeve, in silver card wallet)	40

(see also Bono & Gavin Friday, The Edge, Adam Clayton & Larry Mullen, Passengers)

UV POP

82	Pax PAX 9	Just A Game/No Song Tomorrow (individually screen-printed p/s, at least 2 different designs/colours)	each 10
85	Flowmotion FM 007	Anyone For Me/Hands To Me (p/s)	5
85	Flowmotion FM 007	Anyone For Me/Hands To Me (12", p/s, with 4 extra tracks)	10
85	Native NTV 4	Serious (12", p/s)	10

(see also Cabaret Voltaire)

U.V.X.

93	Magick Eye EYET 10	Elevator (12", purple vinyl)	10
96	Magick Eye EYET 20	Billy Whizz (12")	8

UZI

70	Beacon BEA 152	Morning Train/Where Were You Last Night	5

VACELS

65	Pye International 7N 25330	Can You Please Crawl Out Your Window/I'm Just A Poor Boy	20

VAGABONDS

63	Island ILP 916	PRESENTING THE FABULOUS VAGABONDS (LP)	100

(see also Jimmy James & Vagabonds, Jamaica's Own Vagabonds)

VAGINA DENTATA ORGAN

80s	WSNS 004	Cold Meat: Sex Star I/II (12", picture disc)	40
87	Temple TOPY 012	MUSIC FOR HASHASINS (LP)	50
80s	Cold Meat	EROS AND THANATOS (LP)	70

VAGRANTS

66	Fontana TF 703	I Can't Make A Friend/Young Blues	60

VALADIERS

63	Oriole CBA 1809	I Found A Girl/You'll Be Sorry Someday	630

MINT VALUE £

RICKY VALANCE

Year	Label / Cat. No.	Title	Value £
60	Columbia DB 4493	Tell Laura I Love Her/Once Upon A Time	10
60	Columbia DB 4543	Movin' Away/Lipstick On Your Lips	10
61	Columbia DB 4586	Jimmy's Girl/Only The Young	10
61	Columbia DB 4592	Why Can't We/Fisherboy	10
61	Columbia DB 4680	Bobby/I Want To Fall In Love	15
61	Columbia DB 4725	I Never Had A Chance/It's Not True	12
62	Columbia DB 4787	Try To Forget Her/At Times Like These	12
62	Columbia DB 4864	Don't Play No. 9/Till The Final Curtain Falls	12
65	Decca F 12129	Six Boys/Face The Crowd	15
76	Valley VLY 001	RICKY VALANCE (EP, no p/s)	25

(see also Jason Merryweather)

VAL & V's

Year	Label / Cat. No.	Title	Value £
67	CBS 2780	Do It Again A Little Bit Slower/For A Rainy Day	15
67	CBS 2956	I Like The Way/With This Theme	12
68	CBS 3316	This Little Girl/Dreamer	12

JERRY VALE

Year	Label / Cat. No.	Title	Value £
58	Philips PB 826	Goodbye Now/This Is The Place (with Mary Mayo)	5
59	Philips PB 963	The Moon Is My Pillow/The Flame	6

RITCHIE VALENS

Year	Label / Cat. No.	Title	Value £
58	Pye International 7N 25000	Come On Let's Go/Dooby Dooby Wah	200
58	Pye International N 25000	Come On Let's Go/Dooby Dooby Wah (78)	175
59	London HL 8803	Donna/La Bamba	25
59	London HL 8803	Donna/La Bamba (78)	110
59	London HL 7068	Donna/La Bamba (export issue)	30
59	London HL 8886	That's My Little Suzie/Bluebirds Over The Mountains (tri or round centre)	40/25
59	London HL 8886	That's My Little Suzie/Bluebirds Over The Mountains (78)	200
62	London HL 9494	La Bamba/Ooh, My Head	25
66	Sue WI 4011	Donna/La Bamba (reissue, unreleased)	
67	President PT 126	Donna/La Bamba (reissue)	7
59	London RE 1232	RITCHIE VALENS (EP, initially triangular centre, later round centre)	170/110
61	London HA 2390	RITCHIE (LP)	120
64	London HA 8196	HIS GREATEST HITS (LP)	70
67	President PTL 1001	I REMEMBER RITCHIE VALENS (LP)	25
79	London HA-R 8535	RITCHIE VALENS (LP)	15

CATERINA VALENTE

Year	Label / Cat. No.	Title	Value £
60	Polydor NH 66816	Malaguena/Secret Love	10
60	Polydor NH 66953	The Breeze And I (Andalucia)/Side By Side	8
60	Decca F 11306	Till/Amour	5
61	Decca F 11321	Canto De Ossanha/The Breeze And I (Andalucia)	5
63	Decca F 11621	La Malaguena/Together	5
69	Decca F 22881	Hare Krishna/Canto De Ossanha	5
62	London Globe GEB 7001	FRENESI (EP)	10
63	Polydor EPH 20 282	CATERINA VALENTE (EP)	8
63	Decca DFE 8544	MY HAHWAIIAN MELODY (EP)	7
60	Decca LK 4350	RENDEZVOUS WITH CATERINA (LP)	20
60	Polydor LPHM 46.065	COSMOPOLITAN LADY (LP)	20
61	Polydor LPHM 46.310	CATERINA CHERIE (LP)	20
61	RCA RD 27216/SF 5099	SUPERFONICS (LP)	18
62	Decca LK/SKL 4508	GREAT CONTINENTAL HITS (LP)	15
63	Decca LK/SKL 4537	VALENTE IN SWINGTIME (LP)	15
64	Decca LK 4604	VALENTE ON TV (LP)	15
64	Decca LK/SKL 4630	I HAPPEN TO LIKE NEW YORK (LP)	20
65	Decca LK/SKL 4646	VALENTE & VIOLINS (LP)	18

DINO VALENTI

Year	Label / Cat. No.	Title	Value £
68	CBS 65715	DINO (LP)	50

(see also Quicksilver Messenger Service)

BILLY VALENTINE

Year	Label / Cat. No.	Title	Value £
55	Capitol CL 14320	It's A Sin/Your Love Has Got Me (Reelin' And Rockin')	60
55	Capitol CL 14320	It's A Sin/Your Love Has Got Me (Reelin' And Rockin') (78)	8

DICKIE VALENTINE (& STARGAZERS)

78s

Year	Label / Cat. No.	Title	Value £
52	Melodisc P 210	Lorelei/Never (from 'Golden Girl')	7
59	Pye Nixa N 15192	Venus/Where? (In The Old Home Town)	10
59	Pye N 15202	A Teenager In Love/My Favourite Song	10
59	Pye N 15221	One More Sunrise (Morgen)/You Touch My Hand	6

45s

Year	Label / Cat. No.	Title	Value £
54	Decca F 10346	Endless/I Could Have Told You	40
54	Decca F 10394	The Finger Of Suspicion (with Stargazers)/ Who's Afraid (Not I, Not I, Not I)	35
54	Decca F 10415	Mister Sandman/Runaround	45
55	Decca F 10430	A Blossom Fell/I Want You All To Myself (Just You)	22
55	Decca F 10484	Ma Cherie Amie/Lucky Waltz	20
55	Decca F 10493	I Wonder/You Too Can Be A Dreamer	20
55	Decca F 10517	Hello Mrs. Jones (Is Mary There?)/Lazy Gondolier	18
55	Decca F 10549	No Such Luck/The Engagement Waltz	18
55	Decca F 10628	Christmas Alphabet/Where Are You Tonight?	35
55	Decca F 10645	The Old Pi-Anna Rag/First Love	20
55	Decca F 10667	Dreams Can Tell A Lie/Song Of The Trees	12
56	Decca F 10714	The Voice/The Best Way To Hold A Girl	12
56	Decca F 10753	My Impossible Castle/When You Came Along	10

MINT VALUE £

56	Decca F 10766	Day Dreams/Give Me A Carriage With Eight White Horses	10
56	Decca F 10798	Christmas Island/The Hand Of Friendship	12
56	Decca F 10820	Dickie Valentine's Rock 'N' Roll Party Medley (Parts 1 & 2)	12
57	Decca F 10874	Chapel Of The Roses/My Empty Arms	8
57	Decca F 10906	Puttin' On The Style/Three Sides To Every Story	10
57	Decca F 10949	Long Before I Knew You/Just In Time	8
57	Decca F 10950	Snowbound For Christmas/Convicted	10
58	Decca F 11005	Love Me Again/King Of Dixieland	10
58	Decca F 11020	In My Life/Come To My Arms	7
58	Decca F 11066	Take Me In Your Arms/An Old-Fashioned Song	7
59	Pye Nixa 7N 15192	Venus/Where? (In The Old Home Town)	8
59	Pye 7N 15202	A Teenager In Love/My Favourite Song	8
59	Pye 7N 15221	One More Sunrise (Morgen)/You Touch My Hand	6
60	Pye 7N 15255	Standing On The Corner/Roundabout	6
60	Pye 7N 15294	Once, Only Once/A Fool That I Am	6
61	Pye 7N 15336	How Unlucky Can You Be/Hold Me In Your Arms	6
61	Pye 7N 15366	Climb Ev'ry Mountain/Sometimes I'm Happy	5
61	Pye 7N 15381	Shalom/I'll Never Love Again	6
70	Polydor 56372	Fool Of A Man/Primrose Jill	6
EPs			
55	Decca DFE 6236	SWING ALONG WITH DICKIE VALENTINE	15
56	Decca DFE 6279	PRESENTING DICKIE VALENTINE	15
56	Decca DFE 6363	ONLY FOR YOU	15
57	Decca DFE 6427	DICKIE GOES DIXIE	15
57	Decca DFE 6429	STANDARDS	15
58	Decca DFE 6529	WITH VOCAL REFRAIN BY DICKIE VALENTINE	15
59	Decca DFE 6549	BELONGING TO SOMEONE	12
59	Pye NPL 24120	DICKIE VALENTINE HIT PARADE	12
LPs			
54	Decca LF 1163	PRESENTING DICKIE VALENTINE (10")	35
55	Decca LF 1211	HERE IS DICKIE VALENTINE (10")	30
56	Decca LF 1257	OVER MY SHOULDER (10")	30
58	Decca LK 4269	WITH VOCAL REFRAIN BY...	22
61	Ace Of Clubs ACL 1082	DICKIE	15
67	Philips BL 7831	AT THE TALK OF THE TOWN	20

JACK VALENTINE

55	MGM SPC 8	Dressing Up My Heart/Song Of The Bandit (export issue)	18

VALENTINES (Jamaica)

67	Doctor Bird DB 1065	Blam Blam Fever/BABA BROOKS: The Scratch	25

VALENTINES (U.S.)

60	Ember EMB S 123	Hey Ruby/That's How I Feel	80

VALENTINO

75	Gaiee GAE 101	I Was Born This Way/Liberation	7

ANNA VALENTINO

57	London HLD 8421	Calypso Joe/You're Mine	30
57	London HLD 8421	Calypso Joe/You're Mine (78)	20

DANNY VALENTINO

59	MGM MGM 1049	Stampede/(You Gotta Be A) Music Man	40
60	MGM MGM 1067	Biology/A Million Tears	20
60	MGM MGM 1109	Pictures/'Till The End Of Forever	15

MARK VALENTINO

63	Stateside SS 148	The Push And Kick/Walking Alone	12
63	Stateside SS 186	Do It/Hey You're Looking Good	12
63	Stateside SS 233	Jivin' At The Drive In/Part Time Job	22

VALENTINOS

68	Soul City SC 106	It's All Over Now/Tired Of Livin' In The Country	20
68	Stateside SS 2137	Tired Of Being Nobody/The Death Of Love	12
71	Polydor 2058 090	Don't Raise Up Your Hands In Anger/Stand Up And Be Counted	8
68	Soul City SCM 001	THE VALENTINOS/THE SIMS TWINS (LP, with Sims Twins)	40

(see also Bobby Womack)

VALERIE (The Rock 'N' Roll Youngster)

56	Columbia DB 3832	Tonight You Belong To Me/The Man Who Owns The Sunshine	20

DANA VALERY

64	Decca F 11881	This Is My Prayer/Would I Love You Again (Tien Va Pas)	5

JOE VALINO (& GOSPELAIRES)

57	HMV POP 283	The Garden Of Eden/Caravan	20
58	London HLT 8705	God's Little Acre/I'm Happy With What I've Got (with Gospelaires)	18
58	London HLT 8705	God's Little Acre/I'm Happy With What I've Got (78, with Gospelaires)	15
60	Columbia DB 4406	Hidden Persuasion/Back To Your Eyes	6

VALJEAN (At The Piano)

62	London HLL 9593	Till There Was You/The Eighteenth Variation	7
63	London HLL 9659	Mewsette (From "Gay Purr-Ee")/Mr Mozart's Mash	7
63	London RE-L 1366	MR MOZART'S MASH (EP)	15

VALKYRIES

64	Parlophone R 5123	Rip It Up/What's Your Name?	35

DIORIS VALLADARES ORCHESTRA

64	Island IEP 703	AUTHENTIC MERINGUE (EP)	12
64	Island ILP 910	LET'S GO LATIN (LP, withdrawn)	30+

MINT VALUE £

MARCOS VALLE

68 Verve SAMBA '68 (LP) . . . 18

RUDY VALLEE

53 HMV JO 394 Taps/The Whiffenpoof Song (78) . . . 7
54 HMV 7MC 8 The Whiffenpoof Song/Taps (export issue) . . . 12

VALLEY OF ACHOR

75 Dovetail DOVE 18 A DOOR OF HOPE (LP, gatefold sleeve) . . . 20
(see also Achor, Wine Of Lebanon)

VALLEY YOUTH CHORALE

63 London HLU 9818 The Little Bell/Do You Hear What I Hear . . . 7

FRANKIE VALLI

66 Philips BF 1467 (You're Gonna) Hurt Yourself/VALLI BOYS: Night Hawk . . . 15
66 Philips BF 1512 You're Ready Now/Cry For Me . . . 18
66 Philips BF 1529 The Proud One/Ivy . . . 7
67 Philips BF 1556 Beggin'/Dody . . . 7
67 Philips BF 1580 Can't Take My Eyes Off You/The Trouble With Me . . . 7
67 Philips BF 1603 I Make A Fool Of Myself/September Rain . . . 7
68 Philips BF 1634 To Give (The Reason I Live)/Watch Where You Walk . . . 7
69 Philips BF 1795 The Girl I'll Never Know/A Face Without A Name . . . 7
70 Philips 320 226 BF You're Ready Now/Cry For Me (reissue) . . . 6
74 Private Stock PVT 1 My Eyes Adored You/Watch You Walk . . . 6
67 Philips (S)BL 7814 SOLO (LP) . . . 22
69 Philips SBL 7856 TIMELESS (LP) . . . 20
75 Mowest MWS 7007 INSIDE YOU (LP) . . . 12
77 Private Stock PVLP 1029 LADY PUT THE LIGHT OUT (LP, withdrawn) . . . 25

FRANKIE VALLI & THE FOUR SEASONS

71 Warner Bros K 16107 Whatever You Say/Sleeping Man (only a few hundred pressed) . . . 30
72 Tamla Motown TMG 819 You're A Song/Sun Country . . . 5
72 Mowest MW 3002 The Night/When The Morning Comes . . . 10
73 Mowest MW 3003 Walk On, Don't Look Back/Touch The Rainchild . . . 8
75 Mowest MW 3024 The Night/When The Morning Comes (reissue) . . . 5
72 Mowest MWSA 5501 CHAMELEON (LP) . . . 18
(see also Four Seasons, Wonder Who)

JUNE VALLI

53 HMV B 10568 Crying In The Chapel/Love Every Moment You Live (78) . . . 8
53 HMV JO 324 Why Don't You Believe Me/A Shoulder To Weep On (78, export issue) . . . 8
54 HMV 7M 245 I Understand (Just How You Feel)/Old Shoes And A Bag Of Rice . . . 15
54 HMV 7M 259 Tell Me, Tell Me/Boy Wanted . . . 15
55 HMV 7M 284 Wrong, Wrong, Wrong/Ole Pappy Time . . . 12
56 HMV 7M 347 Por Favor (Please)/The Things They Say . . . 12
59 Mercury AMT 1034 The Answer To A Maiden's Prayer/In His Arms . . . 7
59 Mercury AMT 1048 An Anonymous Letter/Bygones . . . 7
60 Mercury AMT 1091 Apple Green/Oh! Why . . . 7
61 Mercury AMT 1130 I Guess Things Happen That Way/Tell Him For Me . . . 6

VALUES

66 Ember EMB S 211 Return To Me/That's The Way (some with p/s) . . . 80/50

VALVES

77 Zoom ZUM 1 Robot Love/For Adolfs Only (p/s) . . . 18
77 Zoom ZUM 3 Tarzan Of The Kings Road/Ain't No Surf In Portobello (p/s) . . . 15
79 Albion DEL 3 I Don't Mean Nothing At All/Linda Vindalco (p/s) . . . 8

VAMP

68 Atlantic 584 213 Floatin'/Thinkin' Too Much . . . 50
69 Atlantic 584 263 Green Pea/Wake Up And Tell Me (withdrawn) . . . 100+
(see also Sam Gopal, Viv Prince, Clark-Hutchinson)

VAMPIRES

59 Parlophone R 4599 Swinging Ghosts/Clap Trap . . . 12

VAMPIRES

68 Pye 7N 17553 Do You Wanna Dance/My Girl . . . 12

ILA VAN

74 Pye Intl. DDS 108 Can't Help Loving Dat Man/I've Got The Feeling . . . 10

PAUL VANCE

66 Pye International 7N 25387 Dommage, Dommage/Sexy . . . 7

TOMMY VANCE

66 Columbia DB 7999 You Must Be The One/Why Treat Me This Way . . . 6
66 Columbia DB 8062 Off The Hook/Summertime . . . 7

HARRY VANDA

69 Polydor 56357 I Love Marie/Gonna Make It . . . 7
(see also Easybeats)

VAN DER GRAAF GENERATOR

69 Polydor 56758 People You Were Going To/Firebrand . . . 220
70 Charisma CB 122 Refugees/The Boat Of Millions Of Years . . . 40
72 Charisma CB 175 Theme One/W (some with p/s) . . . 25/5
76 Charisma CB 297 Wondering/Meurglys III . . . 8
76 Charisma PRO 002 Wondering (Song)/Wondering (Heroics) (promo only) . . . 25
70 Charisma CAS 1007 THE LEAST WE CAN DO IS WAVE TO EACH OTHER (LP, pink label, original mix, matrices read: CAS 1007 A/B, gatefold sleeve, some with poster) . . . 60/35
70 Charisma CAS 1007 THE LEAST WE CAN DO IS WAVE TO EACH OTHER (LP, pink label, remix, matrices read: CAS 1007 A+G/B+G, gatefold sleeve; some with poster) . . . 45/20

MINT VALUE £

70	Charisma CAS 1027	H TO HE, WHO AM THE ONLY ONE (LP, pink label, gatefold sleeve)	18
71	Charisma CAS 1051	PAWN HEARTS (LP, gatefold sleeve, pink label, some with insert)	30/15
72	Charisma CS 2	1968-71 (LP, pink label)	12
75	Charisma CAS 1109	GODBLUFF (LP, with inner sleeve)	12
76	Charisma CAS 1116	STILL LIFE (LP)	12
76	Charisma CAS 1120	WORLD RECORD (LP)	12
80	Charisma BG 3	REPEAT PERFORMANCE (cassette, with extended "The Clot Thickens")	12

(see also Peter Hammill, Long Hello, Juicy Lucy, Misunderstood)

MAMIE VAN DOREN

58	Capitol CL 14850	Something To Dream About/I Fell In Love (promos in p/s)	25/20
58	Capitol CL 14850	Something To Dream About/I Fell In Love (78)	6

EARL VAN DYKE (& SOUL BROTHERS)

64	Stateside SS 357	Soul Stomp/Hot 'N' Tot	135
65	Tamla Motown TMG 506	All For You/Too Many Fish In The Sea (as Earl Van Dyke & Soul Brothers)	100
70	Tamla Motown TMG 759	Six By Six/All For You (matt black label, later shiny)	10/6
72	Tamla Motown TMG 814	I Can't Help Myself/How Sweet It Is (To Be Loved By You) (& Soul Brothers)	6
65	Tamla Motown TML 11014	THAT MOTOWN SOUND (LP)	150

GULLIVER VAN DYKE

69	Vogue VRS 7034	Set Me Free/The Day Has Gone	6

LEROY VAN DYKE

61	Mercury AMT 1166	Walk On By/My World Is Caving In	6
62	Mercury AMT 1173	Big Man In A Big House/Faded Love	6
62	Mercury AMT 1183	I Sat Back And Let It Happen/A Broken Promise	7
65	Warner Bros WB 5650	It's All Over Now Baby Blue/Just A State Of Mind	7
66	Warner Bros WB 5807	You Couldn't Get My Love Back/Fool Such As I	7
67	Warner Bros WB 5777	Almost Persuaded/Less Of Me	7
62	Mercury MMC 14101	WALK ON BY (LP)	50
63	Mercury MMC 14118	MOVIN' VAN DYKE (LP)	50

VANDYKE & BAMBIS

64	Piccadilly 7N 35180	Doin' The Mod/All I Want Is You	50

VAN DYKE PARKS

(see under 'P')

VAN DYKES

66	Stateside SS 504	No Man Is An Island/I Won't Hold It Against You	20
66	Stateside SS 530	I've Gotta Go On Without You/What Will I Do	25

LON & DERREK VAN EATON

73	Apple APPLE 46	Warm Woman/More Than Words (some in p/s)	55/22
75	A&M AMS 7157	Wildfire/Music Lover	5
75	A&M AMS 7178	Dancing In The Dark/All You're Hungry For Is Love	5
73	Apple SAPCOR 25	BROTHER (LP, gatefold sleeve, some with insert)	70/45

NICK VAN EEDE

78	Barn 201 4128	Rock'n'Roll Fool/Ounce Of Sense	6
79	Barn BARN 003	All Or Nothing/Hold On To Your Heart	7
79	Barn BARN 008	I Only Want/Dicing	7

(see also Drivers)

VANGELIS

75	BBC BBC 1	Heaven And Hell/Alpha (with or without BBC logo on p/s)	5
76	RCA RCA 2762	Pulstar/Alpha	8
78	RCA PB 5064	To The Unknown Man (Part 1)/To The Unknown Man (Part 2) (p/s)	6
79	RCA PC 5208	Pulstar/Dervish D/Spiral/Alpha (12", p/s)	8
79	Polydor POSP 57	The Long March (Part 1)/The Long March (Part 2)	5
80	Polydor 2059 251	Don't Be Foolish/Doesn't Matter (by Peter Marsh & Vangelis, no p/s)	6
81	RCA RCA 71	Heaven And Hell – 3rd Movement/Alpha	5
84	BBC RESL 144	Frame Of The Day: BBC Snooker Themes (To The Unknown Man) (p/s)	5
88	Arista 111 767	Will Of The Wind/Intergalactic Radio Station (p/s)	5
88	Arista 611 767	Will Of The Wind/Metallic Rain/Intergalactic Radio Station (12", p/s)	7
88	Arista 661 767	Will Of The Wind/Metallic Rain/Intergalactic Radio Station (CD)	10
75	RCA RS 1025	HEAVEN AND HELL (gatefold sleeve)	12
76	Polydor 2489 113	L'APOCALYPSE DES ANIMAUX (LP, TV soundtrack)	25
81	Polydor POLS 1026	CHARIOTS OF FIRE (LP, soundtrack, gatefold sleeve)	20
83	Polydor BOX 1	CHARIOTS OF FIRE (LP, soundtrack, box set)	20
89	Polydor VGPK 1	THEMES (LP, 'display pack')	15

(see also Aphrodite's Child, Forminx, Cosmic Baby, Jon & Vangelis)

VAN HALEN

78	Warner Bros K 17107	You Really Got Me/Atomic Punk	5
78	Warner Bros K 17162	Runnin' With The Devil/Eruption	5
79	Warner Bros K 17371	Dance The Night Away/Outta Love Again	7
79	Warner Bros K 17371P	Dance The Night Away/Outta Love Again (picture disc)	10
80	Warner Bros K 17645	And The Cradle Will Rock/Everybody Wants Some (p/s)	5
85	Warner Bros W 9199T	Hot For Teacher/Little Dreamer/Hear About It Later (12", p/s)	8
86	Warner Bros W 8740P	Why Can't This Be Love/Get Up (shaped picture disc with plinth, stickered PVC sleeve)	10
86	Warner Bros W 8642P	Dreams/Inside (car-shaped picture disc with stand, stickered PVC sleeve)	12
88	Warner Bros W 7816TW	When It's Love/Apolitical Blues (12", silver foldout p/s)	8
88	Warner Bros W 7816TP	When It's Love/Apolitical Blues (12", picture disc)	8
88	Warner Bros W 7816CD	When It's Love/Apolitical Blues/When It's Love (Edit)/ Why Can't This Be Love (3" CD, with adaptor, 5" case)	8
89	Warner Bros W 7565CD	Feels So Good (Remix/Edit)/Sucker In A 3-Piece/ Best Of Both Worlds (live) (3" CD, gatefold card sleeve)	8

(see also David Lee Roth, Sammy Hagar)

CHERRY VANILLA
77 RCA PB 5053 The Punk/Foxy Bitch (title sleeve) 8
78 RCA PL 25122 BAD GIRL (LP) 12
79 RCA PL 25217 VENUS DE VINYL (LP) 15

VANILLA FUDGE
67 Atlantic 584 123 You Keep Me Hanging On/Take Me For A Little While 6
67 Atlantic 584 139 (Illusions Of My Childhood) Eleanor Rigby (Parts 1 & 2) 7
68 Atlantic 584 179 Where Is My Mind?/The Look Of Love 7
69 Atlantic 584 257 Shotgun/Good Good Lovin' 6
69 Atlantic 584 276 Some Velvet Morning/Thoughts 5
67 Atlantic 587/588 086 VANILLA FUDGE (LP, red & plum label) 20
68 Atlantic 587/588 100 THE BEAT GOES ON (LP) 20
68 Atlantic 587/588 110 RENAISSANCE (LP) 20
69 Atco 228 020 NEAR THE BEGINNING (LP) 15
70 Atco 228 029 ROCK 'N' ROLL (LP) 15
(see also Beck Bogert & Appice, Cactus)

VANITY FARE
68 Page One POF 075 I Live For The Sun/On The Other Side Of Life 10
68 Page One POF 100 Summer Morning/Betty Carter 10
69 Page One POF 117 Highway Of Dreams/Waiting For The Downfall 10
69 Page One POF 142 Early In The Morning/You Made Me Love You 10
69 Page One POF 158 Hitchin' A Ride/Man Child 10
69 Page One POLS 010 THE SUN, THE WIND AND OTHER THINGS (LP) 35
(see also Avengers)

BILL VAN LOO
01 City Centre Offices BLOCK 12 Tones (For Sarah) (plain sleeve with inserts, 1000 only) 8

TEDDY VANN (ORCHESTRA)
60 London HLU 9097 Cindy/I'm Waiting 25
78 Capitol CL 16012 Theme From 'Coloured Man'/Intro To 'Coloured Man' (as Teddy Vann Orchestra) 6

ORNELLA VANONI
67 Decca F 22703 Only Two Can Play/Can I? 10

DAVE VAN RONK
65 Stateside SL 10153 INSIDE (LP) 15

ROB VAN SPYK
70s private pressing FOLLOW THE SUN (LP) 30
(see also Stonefield Tramp)

TOWNES VAN ZANDT
99 Exile EX 7013 Riding The Range/Dirty Old Town (p/s, 2000 only) 6
69 RCA SF 8040 OUR MOTHER THE MOUNTAIN (LP) 20
73 United Artists UAS 29442 THE LATE GREAT TOWNES VAN ZANDT (LP, gatefold sleeve) 30
87 Heartland HLD 003 AT MY WINDOW (LP) 15
01 Charly SNAB 903 CD TEXAS TROUBADOUR (4-CD, book-style box set) 35

VAPORS
79 United Artists BP 321 Prisoners/Sunstroke (p/s) 5

PETER VARDAS
59 Top Rank JAR 173 He Threw A Stone/Checkerboard Love 8
59 Top Rank JAR 173 He Threw A Stone/Checkerboard Love (78) 6

VARDI & HIS ORCHESTRA
62 London HLR 9518 Ballad Of A Soldier Theme/Exodus Theme 7

VARDIS
79 Redball RR 017 100 MPH (EP) 120
80 Castle C QUEL 2/100 MPH Out Of The Way/If I Were King (plain brown sleeve) 8
80 Logo VAR 1/FREE 1 Let's Go/Situation Negative//100 MPH/Out Of The Way (p/s, double pack) 5
80 Logo VAR 2 Too Many People/The Lion's Share/Blue Rock (I Miss You)/Dirty Money (p/s, single pack, with insert) 15
80 Logo VARFREE 2 Too Many People/The Lion's Share//Blue Rock (I Miss You)/Dirty Money (p/s, double pack, with insert) 6
81 Logo VAR 4 All You'll Ever Need/If I Were King/Jumping Jack Flash (p/s) 6
81 Logo GO 408 Gary Glitter pt. 1/To Be With You (p/s) 7
85 Big Beat NS 103 Standing In The Road/Freezing History (p/s) 7
85 Big Beat NST 103 Standing In The Road/Freezing History (12", p/s) 10
80 Logo MOGO 4012 100 MPH (LP, with poster) 12
81 Logo LOGO 1026 THE WORLD'S INSANE (LP, with insert) 12
82 Logo LOGO 1034 QUO VARDIS (LP, with free 45 "Situation Negative"/"Jeepster"/ "Too Many People"/"Steamin' " [VARFREE 1]) 12
83 Razor RAZ 3 THE LION'S SHARE (LP) 12

VARIATIONS
65 Immediate IM 019 The Man With All The Toys/She'll Know I'm Sorry 15
69 Major Minor MM 638 Crimson And Clover/She Couldn't Dance 10

VARIATIONS (U.S.)
75 UK USA 10 Sayin' It And Doin' It Pts I & II 5

VARICOSE VEINS
78 Warped WARP 1 INCREDIBLE (EP, mail-order only, 200 only, beware of counterfeits) 60
(see also Orange Disaster)

MINT VALUE £

PAUL VARNEY

Year	Label	Title	Value
91	PWL PWLT 201	If Only I Knew (On The Buses Piano Edit)/If Only I Knew (Hurley's House Mix)/ If Only I Knew (Silk's Answer)/If Only I Knew (Maurice's Underground Mix) (12", p/s)	15
91	PWL PWCD 201	If Only I Knew (7" Version)/If Only I Knew (12" Version)/ If Only I Knew (Dub)/If Only I Knew (On The Buses Piano Edit) (CD)	15

SYLVIE VARTAN

Year	Label	Title	Value
65	RCA Victor RCA 1490	One More Day/I Made My Choice	12
65	RCA Victor RCA 1495	Another Heart/Think About You	12
79	RCA PB 1578	I Don't Want The Night To End/Distant Shores (p/s, coloured vinyl)	6
65	RCA Victor RCX 7165	SYLVIE VARTAN (EP)	15

VARUKERS

Year	Label	Title	Value
81	Tempest/Inferno HELL 1	Protest And Survive/No Scapegoat (p/s)	6
83	Riot City RIOT 27	Die For Your Government/All Systems Fail (p/s)	7
83	Riot City RIOT 29	Led To The Slaughter/The End Is Nigh (p/s)	7
82	Tempest/Inferno HELL 4	DON'T WANNA BE A VICTIM (EP)	6
83	Riot City RIOT 31	ANOTHER RELIGION ANOTHER WAR (12" EP)	10
84	Rot ASS 16	MASSACRED MILLIONS (12" EP)	12
84	Attack ATTACK 001	PREPARE FOR THE ATTACK (LP)	15

VASELINES

Year	Label	Title	Value
87	53rd & 3rd AGARR 10	Son Of A Gun/Rory Rides Away/You Think You're A Man (12", die-cut sleeve)	20
88	53rd & 3rd AGARR 17	Dying For It/Molly's Lips (p/s)	10
88	53rd & 3rd AGARR 17T	Dying For It/Molly's Lips/Teenage Superstars/ Jesus Wants Me For A Sunbeam (12", p/s)	15
88	53rd & 3rd AGARR 17CD	Dying For It/Molly's Lips/Teenage Superstars/ Jesus Wants Me For A Sunbeam (CD)	15
90	53rd & 3rd AGAS 7	DUM DUM (LP)	15

(see also Pastels, BMX Bandits)

VASHTI

Year	Label	Title	Value
65	Decca F 12157	Some Things Just Stick In Your Mind/I Want To Be Alone	30
66	Columbia DB 7917	Train Song/Love Song	22

(see also Vashti Bunyan)

CLAUDE VASORI

Year	Label	Title	Value
99	Jazzman JM 010	Tic-Splash/VINCENT GEMINIANI: Ophis Le Serpentaire	5

RAY VASQUEZ

Year	Label	Title	Value
61	Starlite ST45-055	Nothing Ever Changes My Love For You/Easy To Love	6
61	Starlite STEP 17	IN THE STILL OF THE NIGHT (EP)	10

DENNY VAUGHAN

Year	Label	Title	Value
53	Parlophone R 3657	Forevermore/Take It Off (with Nancy Reed) (78)	6

(see also Nancy Reed)

FRANKIE VAUGHAN

78s

Year	Label	Title	Value
53	HMV B 10435	My Sweetie Went Away/Strange	6
53	HMV B 10498	Too Marvellous For Words/No Help Wanted	6
53	HMV B 10529	Look At That Girl/Send My Baby Back To Me	6
53	HMV B 10550	Bye Bye Baby/False-Hearted Lover	6
53	HMV B 10560	Hey Joe/So Nice In Your Arms	6
53	HMV B 10599	Istanbul (Not Constantinople)/Cloud Lucky Seven	6
54	HMV B 10635	The Cuff Of My Shirt/Heartless	6
54	HMV B 10655	She Took/From The Vine Came The Grape	6
54	HMV B 10712	Jilted/Do Do Do Do Do Do Do It Again (with Alma Cogan)	6
54	HMV B 10733	Out In The Middle Of The Night/Crazy 'Bout Ya Baby	6
54	HMV B 10766	My Son, My Son/Cinnamon Sinner (Selling Lollipop Lies)	6
54	HMV B 10783	Happy Days And Lonely Nights/Danger Signs	6
55	HMV B 10845	Too Many Heartaches/Unsuspecting Heart	6
55	Philips PB 423	Tweedlee-Dee/Give Me The Moonlight, Give Me The Girl	6
55	Philips PB 438	Wildfire/That's How A Love Song Was Born	6
55	Philips PB 482	Why Did The Chicken Cross The Road/Something's Gotta Give	6
55	Philips PB 511	Seventeen/Meet Me On The Corner	6
56	Philips PB 544	My Boy Flat Top/Stealin'	6
56	Philips PB 559	Rock Candy Baby/This Is The Night	6
57	Philips PB 775	Kisses Sweeter Than Wine/Rock-A-Chicka	6
58	Philips PB 793	We're Not Alone/Can't Get Along Without You	6
58	Philips PB 865	Am I Wasting My Time On You/So Happy In Love	6
59	Philips PB 895	That's My Doll/Love Is The Sweetest Thing	6
59	Philips PB 896	Honey Bunny Baby/The Lady Is A Square	6
59	Philips PB 913	Come Softly To Me/Say Something Sweet To Your Sweetheart (with Kaye Sisters)	10
59	Philips PB 930	The Heart Of A Man/Sometime Somewhere	8
59	Philips PB 931	Walkin' Tall/I Ain't Gonna Lead This Life	10
57	Rainbow/Weekend 14140	The Truth About Me (5", mail-order only, some with mailer)	10/15

45s

Year	Label	Title	Value
53	HMV 7M 167	Istanbul (Not Constantinople)/Cloud Lucky Seven	10
54	HMV 7M 182	The Cuff Of My Shirt/Heartless	10
54	HMV 7M 252	My Son, My Son/Cinnamon Sinner (Selling Lollipop Lies)	10
54	HMV 7M 270	Happy Days And Lonely Nights/Danger Signs	10
55	HMV 7M 298	Too Many Heartaches/Unsuspecting Heart	10
57	Philips JK 1002	Garden Of Eden/Priscilla (jukebox issue)	20
57	Philips JK 1014	What's Behind That Strange Door/Cold, Cold Shower (jukebox issue)	20
57	Philips JK 1022	These Dangerous Years/Isn't This A Lovely Evening (jukebox issue)	20
57	Philips JK 1030	Gotta Have Something In The Bank, Frank/Single (with Kaye Sisters, jukebox issue)	20

MINT VALUE £

57 Philips JK 1035 Kisses Sweeter Than Wine/Rock-A-Chicka (jukebox issue) . . . 30
57 Philips PB 775 Kisses Sweeter Than Wine/Rock-A-Chicka . . . 25
58 Philips PB 793 We're Not Alone/Can't Get Along Without You . . . 5
58 Philips PB 825 Kewpie Doll/So Many Women . . . 5
58 Philips PB 834 Wonderful Things/Judy . . . 5
58 Philips PB 865 Am I Wasting My Time On You/So Happy In Love . . . 5
59 Philips PB 423 Give Me The Moonlight, Give Me The Girl/Happy Go Lucky . . . 5
59 Philips PB 895 That's My Doll/Love Is The Sweetest Thing . . . 5
59 Philips PB 896 Honey Bunny Baby/The Lady Is A Square . . . 8
59 Philips PB 913 Come Softly To Me/Say Something Sweet To Your Sweetheart (& Kaye Sisters) . . . 5
59 Philips PB 930 The Heart Of A Man/Sometime Somewhere . . . 5
59 Philips PB 931 Walkin' Tall/I Ain't Gonna Lead This Life . . . 5
60 Philips PB 985 What More Do You Want/The Very Very Young . . . 5
60 Philips PB 1054 Kookie Little Paradise/Mary Lou . . . 6
60 Philips PB 1066 Milord/Do You Still Love Me? (some in p/s) . . . 5
61 Philips PB 1195 Tower Of Strength/Rachel . . . 5
61 Philips BF 1215 Don't Stop, Twist!/Red Red Roses . . . 5
62 Philips BF 1233 I'm Gonna Clip Your Wings/Travellin' Man . . . 5
62 Philips 326 542BF Hercules/Madeleine (Open The Door) . . . 5
63 Philips 326 566BF Loop De Loop/There'll Be No Teardrops Tonight . . . 5
63 Philips BF 1254 Hey Mama/Brand New Motor . . . 5
63 Philips BF 1280 You're The One For Me/I Told You So . . . 5
64 Philips BF 1310 Alley Alley Oh/Gonna Be A Good Boy Now . . . 5
64 Philips BF 1373 Susie Q/I'll Always Be In Love With You . . . 6
64 Philips BF 1339 Hello Dolly/Long Time No See . . . 5
65 Philips BF 1394 Someone Must Have Hurt You A Lot/Easter Time . . . 6
65 Philips BF 1460 Wait/There Goes The Forgotten Man . . . 7
67 Columbia DB 8248 There Must Be A Way/You're Nobody Until Somebody Loves You . . . 5
67 Columbia DB 8298 If I Didn't Care/So Tired . . . 5
68 Columbia DB 8354 Nevertheless/Girl Talk . . . 5

EPs

56 Philips BBE 12022 FRANKIE VAUGHAN . . . 15
57 HMV 7EG 8245 MISTER ELEGANT . . . 15
57 Woman's Own P 117 2E SWINGIN' . . . 10
57 Philips BBE 12111 FRANKIE VAUGHAN . . . 12
59 Philips BBE 12299 HEART OF A MAN . . . 12
61 Philips BBE 12484 LET ME SING AND I'M HAPPY (also in stereo SBBE 9071) . . . 15/20
61 Philips BBE 12485 LET ME SING AND I'M HAPPY NO. 2 (also in stereo SBBE 9072) . . . 15/20
61 Philips BBE 12486 LET ME SING AND I'M HAPPY NO. 3 (also in stereo SBBE 9073) . . . 15/20

LPs

57 Philips BBL 7198 HAPPY GO LUCKY . . . 25
58 Philips BBL 7233 THE FRANKIE VAUGHAN SHOWCASE . . . 25
59 Philips BBL 7330 AT THE LONDON PALLADIUM (also on stereo SBBL 511) . . . 18
61 Philips BBL 7482 LET ME SING — AND I'M HAPPY! (also stereo SBL 629) . . . 15/18
61 Philips BBL 7490 WARM FEELING (also stereo SBBL 645) . . . 15/18

(see also Kaye Sisters, Alma Cogan & Frankie Vaughan, Marilyn Monroe)

MALCOLM VAUGHAN

55 HMV 7M 317 More Than A Millionaire/Take Me Back Again . . . 5
55 HMV 7M 338 With Your Love/Small Talk . . . 5
56 HMV 7M 389 Only You (And You Alone)/I'll Be Near You . . . 5
56 HMV POP 250 St. Therese Of The Roses/Love Me As Though There Were Tomorrow . . . 5
57 HMV POP 303 The World Is Mine/Now . . . 5
57 HMV POP 325 Chapel Of The Roses/Guardian Angel . . . 5
57 HMV POP 381 What Is My Destiny/Oh! My Papa . . . 5
58 HMV POP 419 My Special Angel/The Heart Of A Child . . . 5
58 HMV POP 459 To Be Loved/My Loving Arms . . . 5
58 HMV POP 502 Ev'ry Hour, Ev'ry Day Of My Life/Miss You . . . 5
58 HMV POP 538 More Than Ever (Come Prima)/A Night To Remember . . . 5
59 HMV POP 590 Wait For Me/Willingly . . . 5
59 HMV POP 687 You'll Never Walk Alone/The Holy City . . . 5
59 HMV POP 687 You'll Never Walk Alone/The Holy City (78) . . . 8
60 HMV POP 700 Oh, So Wunderbar/For Everyone In Love . . . 5
60 HMV POP 700 Oh, So Wunderbar/For Everyone In Love (78) . . . 10

ROY VAUGHAN BOOGIE TRIO

50 Jazz Parade B 3 Oval Boogie/Rumble Boogie (78) . . . 10

SARAH VAUGHAN

78s

50 MGM MGM 331 Tenderly/I'll Wait And Pray . . . 6
51 MGM MGM 388 I'm Gonna Sit Right Down And Write Myself A Letter/I'm Thru With Love . . . 6
55 Mercury MB 3205 My Funny Valentine/How Important Can It Be . . . 6
55 Philips PB 455 Summertime/I Cried For You . . . 6
57 Mercury MT 151 Poor Butterfly/Whatever Lola Wants (Lola Gets) . . . 6
57 Mercury MT 176 Band Of Angels/Please Mr Brown . . . 6
58 Mercury MT 198 My Darling, My Darling/Bewitched . . . 6
58 Mercury MT 212 Padre/Spin Little Bottle . . . 6
58 Mercury MT 222 Too Much, Too Soon/What's So Bad About It . . . 8
59 Mercury AMT 1010 Everything I Do/I Ain't Hurtin' . . . 10
59 Mercury AMT 1029 Cool Baby/Are You Certain? . . . 10
59 Mercury AMT 1057 Broken-Hearted Melody/Misty . . . 18

SINGLES

58 Mercury 7MT 198 My Darling, My Darling/Bewitched . . . 10
58 Mercury 7MT 212 Padre/Spin Little Bottle . . . 10
58 Mercury 7MT 222 Too Much, Too Soon/What's So Bad About It . . . 10
59 Mercury AMT 1010 Everything I Do/I Ain't Hurtin' . . . 8

MINT VALUE £

59	Mercury AMT 1029	Cool Baby/Are You Certain?	10
59	Mercury AMT 1044	Careless/Separate Ways	7
59	Mercury AMT 1057	Broken-Hearted Melody/Misty	10
59	Mercury AMT 1080	You're My Baby/Eternally	6
59	Mercury AMT 1087	Don't Look At Me That Way/Sweet Affections	6
60	Columbia DB 4491	Ooh! What A Day/My Dear Little Sweetheart	10
60	Columbia DB 4511	If I Were A Bell/Teach Me Tonight (with Count Basie & Joe Williams)	6
60	Columbia DB 4542	Serenata/Let's	6
63	Columbia DB 4990	My Favourite Things/Great Day	6
69	Mercury AMT 1107	The Boy From Ipanema/The Fever (p/s)	6

EPs

56	London RE-U 1065	SARAH VAUGHAN SINGS (with John Kirby's Orchestra)	18
57	Emarcy YEP 9507	SARAH VAUGHAN	12
57	Mercury MEP 9511	SARAH VAUGHAN HIT PARADE	12
57	Mercury MEP 9519	SARAH VAUGHAN HIT PARADE NO. 2	12
59	Mercury ZEP 10011	SONGS FROM SARAH	12
59	Mercury ZEP 10030	AFTER HOURS AT THE LONDON HOUSE	12
59	Mercury ZEP 10041	SARAH WITH FEELING	12
59	Mercury ZEP 10101	NO COUNT SARAH	12
60	Mercury ZEP 10054	SMOOTH SARAH	12
60	Mercury ZEP 10087	LIVE FOR LOVE (also stereo SEZ 19006)	12/18
62	Mercury ZEP 10115	NO COUNT BLUES (also stereo SEZ 19023)	12/18

LPs

55	Oriole/Mercury MG 26005	IMAGES (10")	35
55	Mercury MG 25188	THE DIVINE SARAH	20
56	London HB-U 1049	SARAH VAUGHAN SINGS (10", with John Kirby & His Orchestra)	35
56	Emarcy EJL 100	IN THE LAND OF HI FI (10")	30
56	Philips BBL 7082	SARAH VAUGHAN	20
56	Mercury MPT 7503	MAKE YOURSELF COMFORTABLE (10")	35
57	Mercury MPT 7518	IMAGES (10", reissue)	22
57	Emarcy EJL 1258	SASSY	15
57	Mercury MPL 6522	SINGS GREAT SONGS FROM HIT SHOWS PART 1	18
57	Philips BBL 7165	LINGER AWHILE	18
57	Mercury MPL 6523	SINGS GREAT SONGS FROM HIT SHOWS PART 2	18
57	Mercury MPL 6525	SINGS GEORGE GERSHWIN VOL. 1	15
57	Mercury MPL 6527	SINGS GEORGE GERSHWIN VOL. 2	15
58	Mercury MPL 6532	WONDERFUL SARAH	18
58	Emarcy EJL 1273	SWINGIN' EASY	15
58	Mercury MPL 6540	IN ROMANTIC MOOD	18
58	Mercury MPL 6542	AT MISTER KELLY'S	18
59	Mercury CMS 18011	SINGS GEORGE GERSHWIN VOL. 1 (stereo reissue of MPL 6525)	18
59	Mercury CMS 18012	SINGS GEORGE GERSHWIN VOL. 2 (stereo reissue of MPL 6527)	18
59	Mercury MMC 14001	AFTER HOURS AT THE LONDON HOUSE	15
59	Mercury MMC 14011	VAUGHAN AND VIOLINS (also stereo CMS 18003)	15/18
60	Mercury MMC 14021	NO COUNT SARAH	15
60	Mercury MMC 14024	GREAT SONGS FROM HIT SHOWS PART 1 (reissue of MPT 6522)	12
60	Mercury CMS 18019	GREAT SONGS FROM HIT SHOWS PART 1 (stereo reissue of MPT 6522)	12
60	Mercury MMC 14026	GREAT SONGS FROM HIT SHOWS PART 2 (reissue of MPT 6523)	12
60	Mercury CMS 18023	GREAT SONGS FROM HIT SHOWS PART 2 (stereo reissue of MPT 6523)	12
60	Columbia 33SX 1252	DREAMY (also stereo SCX 3324)	15/18
61	Mercury MMC 14059	CLOSE TO YOU (also stereo CMS 18040)	15/18
62	Columbia 33SX 1340	THE DIVINE ONE (also stereo SCX 3390)	15/18
62	Columbia 33SX 1360	COUNT BASIE — SARAH VAUGHAN (also stereo SCX 3403)	15/18
64	Mercury 20011 (S)MCL	SASSY SWINGS THE TIVOLI (also stereo)	15
65	Mercury 20042 (S)MCL	MY HEART SINGS (also stereo)	15

SARAH VAUGHAN & BILLY ECKSTINE

57	Mercury MT 164	Passing Strangers/The Door Is Open (78)	8
59	Mercury AMT 1020	Alexander's Ragtime Band/No Limit	7
59	Mercury AMT 1020	Alexander's Ragtime Band/No Limit (78)	15
59	Mercury AMT 1071	Passing Strangers/SARAH VAUGHAN: Smooth Operator	8
56	MGM MGM-EP 561	DEDICATED TO YOU (EP)	10
59	MGM MGM-EP 690	BILLY ECKSTINE AND SARAH VAUGHAN (EP)	10
59	Mercury 10025 MCE	PASSING STRANGERS (EP)	10
60	Mercury 10027 MCE	TOGETHER AGAIN (EP)	10
61	Mercury ZEP 10108	BEST OF BERLIN VOL. 1 (EP, also stereo SEZ 19016)	10/15
58	Mercury MPL 6530	THE BEST OF IRVING BERLIN (LP)	20
60	Mercury MMC 14035	THE BEST OF IRVING BERLIN (LP, reissue)	12

(see also Billy Eckstine)

BILLY VAUGHN (& HIS ORCHESTRA)

78s

55	London HL 8112	Melody Of Love/Joy Ride	8
55	London HLD 8205	The Shifting Whispering Sands (Parts 1 & 2) (with Ken Nordine)	7
56	London HLD 8238	Theme From 'The Threepenny Opera'/I'd Give A Million Tomorrows	6
56	London HLD 8319	When The Lilac Blooms Again/Autumn Concerto	6
56	London HLD 8342	Petticoats From Portugal/La La Colette	8
57	London HLD 8417	The Ship That Never Sailed/Little Boy Blue	8
57	London HLD 8511	Johnny Tremain/Naughty Annetta	12
57	London HLD 8522	Raunchy/Sail Along Silvery Moon	6
58	London HLD 8612	Tumbling Tumbleweeds/Trying	12
58	London HLD 8680	Sail Along Silvery Moon/The Singing Hills	10
58	London HLD 8703	La Paloma/Here Is My Love	15
58	London HLD 8772	Cimarron (Roll On)/You're My Baby Doll	20
59	London HLD 8797	Blue Hawaii/Tico Tico	25
59	London HLD 8859	Your Cheatin' Heart/Lights Out	25

		MINT VALUE £
59 London HLD 8920	All Nite Long/Blues Stay Away From Me	30
59 London HLD 8952	Morgen (One More Sunrise)/Sweet Leilani	25
59 London HLD 8996	(It's No) Sin/After Hours	25
45s		
55 London HL 8112	Melody Of Love/Joy Ride (gold label print)	5
55 London HLD 8205	The Shifting Whispering Sands (Parts 1 & 2) (with Ken Nordine) (gold print)	5
56 London HLD 8238	Theme From 'The Threepenny Opera'/I'd Give A Million Tomorrows (gold label print, later with silver label print)	5
56 London HLD 8319	When The Lilac Blooms Again/Autumn Concerto (gold print, later silver)	5
56 London HLD 8342	Petticoats From Portugal/La La Colette (gold print, later silver)	5
57 London HLD 8417	The Ship That Never Sailed/Little Boy Blue (with Ken Nordine)	5
57 London HLD 8511	Johnny Tremain/Naughty Annetta (as Billy Vaughn's Orchestra & Chorus)	5
57 London HLD 8522	Raunchy/Sail Along Silvery Moon	5
58 London HLD 8612	Tumbling Tumbleweeds/Trying	5
58 London HLD 8680	Sail Along Silvery Moon/The Singing Hills	5
58 London HLD 8703	La Paloma/Here Is My Love	5
58 London HLD 8772	Cimarron (Roll On)/You're My Baby Doll	5
59 London HLD 8797	Blue Hawaii/Tico Tico	5
59 London HLD 8859	Your Cheatin' Heart/Lights Out	5
59 London HLD 8920	All Nite Long/Blues Stay Away From Me	5
59 London HLD 8952	Morgen (One More Sunrise)/Sweet Leilani	5
59 London HLD 8996	(It's No) Sin/After Hours	5
60 London HLD 9152	Look For A Star/He'll Have To Go	5
61 London HLD 9259	Theme From 'The Sundowners'/Old Cape Cod	5
61 London HLD 9279	Wheels/Orange Blossom Special	5
61 London HLD 9380	Blue Tomorrow/Red Wing	5
61 London HLD 9423	Berlin Melody/Theme From 'Come September'	5
62 London HLD 9507	Everybody's Twisting Down In Mexico/Melody In The Night	5
62 London HLD 9541	Chapel By The Sea/A Lover's Guitar	5
62 London HLD 9568	Continental Melody/Born To Be With You	5
62 London HLD 9578	A Swingin' Safari/Summertime	5
63 London HLD 9675	Meditation/Release Me	5
63 London HLD 9735	Happy Cowboy/Sukiyaki	5
64 London HLD 9865	Blue Tango/Boss	5
EXPORT SINGLES		
60 London HL 7093	Red Sails In The Sunset/Harbour Lights	5
60 London HL 7094	Brazil/Perfidia	5
60 London HLD 7107	La Paloma/Green Fields	5
EPs		
57 London RE-D 1083	THE GOLDEN INSTRUMENTALS NO. 1	10
57 London RE-D 1084	THE GOLDEN INSTRUMENTALS NO. 2	10
59 London RE-D 1189	SAIL ALONG SILVERY MOON	10
60 London RE-D 1248	THEMES FROM BILLY VAUGHN	8
61 London RE-D 1285	BILLY VAUGHN	8
62 London RE-D 1329	BILLY VAUGHN PLAYS THE HITS NO. 1	8
62 London RE-D 1330	BILLY VAUGHN PLAYS THE HITS NO. 2	8
63 London RE-D 1352	SWINGIN' SAFARI	10
63 London RE-D 1380	HAPPY COWBOY	8
63 London RE-D 1395	SIXTY-TWO'S GREATEST HITS	8
65 Dot DEP 20004	THE GREAT BILLY VAUGHN	8
LPs		
56 London HB-D 1048	MELODIES OF LOVE (10")	30
57 London HA-D 2025	THE GOLDEN INSTRUMENTALS (also stereo SAH-D 6018)	15/20
57 London HA-D 2045	SWEET MUSIC AND MEMORIES	12
58 London HA-D 2072	INSTRUMENTAL SOUVENIRS	12
58 London HA-D 2090	MELODIES IN GOLD	12
58 London HA-D 2120	SAIL ALONG SILVERY MOON (also stereo SAH-D 6037)	12/15
58 London HA-D 2129	PLAYS THE MILLION SELLERS (also stereo SAH-D 6003)	12/15
59 London HA-D 2151	LA PALOMA (also stereo SAH-D 6009)	12/15
59 London HA-D 2178	BILLY VAUGHN PLAYS	12
59 London HA-D 2195	CHRISTMAS CAROLS	12
59 London HA-D 2201	BLUE HAWAII	12
60 London HA-D 2209	GOLDEN HITS (also stereo SAH-D 6056)	12/15
60 London HA-D 2241	GOLDEN SAXOPHONES (also stereo SAH-D 6070)	12/15
60 London HA-D 2251	MUSIC FOR THE GOLDEN HOURS (also stereo SAH-D 6075)	12/15
60 London HA-D 2256	A SUMMER PLACE (also stereo SAH-D 6080)	12/15
60 London HA-D 2278	LINGER AWHILE (also stereo SAH-D 6096)	12/15
60 London HA-D 2292	LOOK FOR A STAR (also stereo SAH-D 6104)	12/15
61 London HA-D 2304	GREAT GOLDEN HITS (also stereo SAH-D 6114)	12/15
61 London HA-D 2324	HIT PARADE (also stereo SAH-D 6127)	12/15
62 London SAH-D 6228	GREATEST STRING BAND HITS (stereo)	15

(see also Hilltoppers, Ken Nordine)

MORRIS VAUGHN

69 Fontana TF 1031	My Love Keeps Growing/Make It Look Good	15

VAZZ

85 CRV 5401	Breath/Violent Silence (in folder & bag with postcards & inserts)	5

V.D.U.'s

79 Thin Sliced	Don't Cry For Me/Little White Lie/Holiday Romances (p/s)	6

(see also Boys Wonder)

CHUCK VEDDER

59 London HL 8951	Spanky Boy/Arriba	30
59 London HL 8951	Spanky Boy/Arriba (78)	20

MINT VALUE £

BOBBY VEE

SINGLES

60	London HLG 9179	Devil Or Angel/Since I Met You, Baby	25
61	London HLG 9255	Rubber Ball/Everyday	12
61	London HLG 9316	More Than I Can Say/Stayin' In	7
61	London HLG 9389	How Many Tears/Baby Face	8
61	London HLG 9438	Take Good Care Of My Baby/Bashful Bob	7
61	London HLG 7111	Take Good Care Of My Baby/Bashful Bob (export issue)	30
61	London HLG 9459	Love's Made A Fool Of You/Susie-Q	15
61	London HLG 9470	Run To Him/Walkin' With My Angel	7
62	Liberty LIB 55388	Run To Him/Walkin' With My Angel (reissue)	10
62	Liberty LIB 55419	Please Don't Ask About Barbara/I Can't Say Goodbye	8
62	Liberty LIB 55451	Sharing You/At A Time Like This	7
62	Liberty LIB 10046	A Forever Kind Of Love/Remember Me, Huh?	8
63	Liberty LIB 10069	The Night Has A Thousand Eyes/Tenderly Yours	7
63	Liberty LIB 55530	Bobby Tomorrow/Charms	7
63	Liberty LIB 10124	Stranger In Your Arms/Yesterday And You	7
64	Liberty LIB 10141	She's Sorry/Buddy's Song	12
64	Liberty LIB 55700	Hickory, Dick And Doc/I Wish You Were Mine Again	12
65	Liberty LIB 10197	Keep On Trying/Cross My Heart	10
65	Liberty LIB 10213	True Love Never Runs Smooth/Hey Little Girl	10
65	Liberty LIB 55828	Run Like The Devil/Take A Look Around Me	20
66	Liberty LIB 55877	Look At Me Girl/Save A Love	10
67	Liberty LIB 10272	Like You've Never Known Before/Growing Pains	10
67	Liberty LIB 15016	Come Back When You Grow Up/Let The Four Winds Blow	7
67	Liberty LIB 15042	Beautiful People/I May Be Gone	7
68	Liberty LBF 15058	Maybe Just Today/You're A Big Girl Now	7
68	Liberty LBF 15096	Medley, My Girl - Hey Girl/Take Good Care Of My Baby	7
68	Liberty LBF 15134	Do What You Gotta' Do/Thank You	7
69	Liberty LBF 15178	(I'm Into Looking For) Someone To Love Me/Sunrise Highway	7
69	Liberty LBF 15234	I'm Gonna Make It Up To You/Let's Call It A Day	10
69	Liberty LBF 15305	Electric Trains And You/In And Out Of Love	10
70	Liberty LBF 15370	Woman In My Life/No Obligations	6
70	Liberty LBF 15420	Sweet Sweetheart/Rock'n'Roll Music And You	6
73	United Artists UP 35516	Take Good Care Of My Baby/Every Opportunity (as Robert Thomas Velline)	6
76	Mint CHEW 4	(I'm) Lovin' You/Sayin' Goodbye	5
78	United Artists UP 36370	Well All Right/Something Has Come Between Us	5

EPs

61	London RE-G 1278	BOBBY VEE NO. 1	40
61	London RE-G 1299	BOBBY VEE NO. 2	40
61	London RE-G 1308	BOBBY VEE NO. 3	45
61	London RE-G 1323	BOBBY VEE NO. 4	50
61	London RE-G 1324	HITS OF THE ROCKIN' 50's	50
62	Liberty LEP 2053	SINCERELY	30
63	Liberty LEP 2084	JUST FOR FUN (2 tracks by Bobby Vee, 2 by Crickets)	30
63	Liberty LEP 2089	A FOREVER KIND OF LOVE	30
63	Liberty (S)LEP 2102	BOBBY VEE'S BIGGEST HITS (mono/stereo)	30/40
63	Liberty (S)LEP 2116	BOBBY VEE MEETS THE CRICKETS (mono/stereo)	35/45
64	Liberty LEP 2149	BOBBY VEE MEETS THE CRICKETS VOL. 2	35
64	Liberty LEP 2181	NEW SOUNDS	50
65	Liberty LEP 2212	BOBBY VEE MEETS THE VENTURES (with Ventures)	40

LPs

61	London HA-G 2320	BOBBY VEE SINGS YOUR FAVOURITES	100
61	London HA-G 2352	BOBBY VEE (also stereo SAH-G 6152)	75/100
61	London HA-G 2374	WITH STRINGS AND THINGS (also stereo SAH-G 6174)	75/100
61	London HA-G 2406	SINGS HITS OF THE ROCKIN' 50s (also stereo, SAH-G 6206)	75/10
61	London HA-G 2428	TAKE GOOD CARE OF MY BABY (also stereo, SAH-G 6224)	60/70
61	Liberty (S)LBY 1004	TAKE GOOD CARE OF MY BABY (reissue)	35/40
62	Liberty (S)LBY 1084	BOBBY VEE RECORDING SESSION (mono/stereo)	40/45
62	Liberty (S)LBY 1086	BOBBY VEE MEETS THE CRICKETS (mono/stereo)	25/35
62	Liberty (S)LBY 1112	BOBBY VEE'S GOLDEN GREATS (mono/stereo)	40/45
63	Liberty (S)LBY 1139	THE NIGHT HAS A THOUSAND EYES (mono/stereo)	40/45
63	Liberty (S)LBY 1147	BOBBY VEE MEETS THE VENTURES (with Ventures)	40/45
63	Liberty (S)LBY 1188	I REMEMBER BUDDY HOLLY (mono/stereo)	40/45
65	Liberty (S)LBY 1263	BOBBY VEE LIVE! ON TOUR (mono/stereo)	35/40
67	Liberty (S)LBY 1341	LOOK AT ME GIRL	25
68	Liberty LBL/LBS 83112E	JUST TODAY	22
68	Sunset SLS 50022	BOBBY VEE	12
69	Liberty LBL/LBS 83130E	DO WHAT YOU GOTTA DO	22
69	Sunset SLS 50050	A FOREVER KIND OF LOVE	12
73	United Artists UAS 29457	NOTHIN' LIKE A SUNNY DAY (as Robert Thomas Velline) (with inner lyric sleeve)	12

(see also Crickets, Ventures)

V8

85	Music Factory MF 104	Lonely Days	12

ALAN VEGA

81	Celluloid WIP 6744	Jukebox Babe/Lonely (p/s)	6
81	Celluloid 12WIP 6744	Jukebox Babe/Lonely (12", p/s)	12
88	Sniffin' Rock SR 009	WACKO WARRIOR/(track by African Headcharge) (with *Sniffin' Rock* fanzine No. 12)	8
81	Ze/Island ILPS 9692	COLLISION DRIVE (LP)	12

(see also Suicide, Future Pilot AKA Alan Vega)

SUZANNE VEGA

86 A&M CDQ 320 — Left Of Centre/Undertow/Cracking (live) (CD, foldout inlay) ... 10
87 A&M VEGCD 2 — Tom's Diner/Left Of Centre/Tom's Diner (live)/Luka (live) (CD, foldout inlay) ... 8
87 A&M VEGCD 3 — Solitude Standing/Ironbound-Fancy Poultry/Marlene On The Wall (live)/ Some Journey (live) (CD, foldout inlay) ... 8

JAKE VEGAS' NAKED KISS

93 Camden Town GNAR 004 — Jake's Flower Garden/Swamp Child ... 5

VEHICLE

71 Deram DM 342 — Mr. Organ Grinder/Cloudy Day ... 5

VEIN

(see under Intra Vein)

VEINS

80 Redball RR 3 — Complete Control Rock 'n' Roll/Champagne ... 25

VEJTABLES

65 Pye International 7N 25339 — I Still Love You/Anything ... 30

MARTHA VELEZ

69 London HLK 10266 — It Takes A Lot To Laugh/Come Here Sweet Man ... 12
69 London HLK 10280 — Tell Mama/Swamp Man ... 12
72 Blue Horizon 2096 010 — Boogie Kitchen/Two Bridges ... 18
69 London HA-K/SH-K 8395 — FIENDS AND ANGELS (LP) ... 30
70 Blue Horizon 7-63867 — FIENDS AND ANGELS AGAIN (LP) ... 60
76 Sire 9103 252 — ESCAPE FROM BABYLON (LP) ... 12

CAETANO VELOSO

71 Famous SFM 1002 — CAETANO VELOSO (LP) ... 12

VELOURS

77 MGM 2006 603 — I'm Gonna Change/Don't Pity Me ... 12
(see also Fantastics)

VELVELETTES

64 Stateside SS 361 — Needle In A Haystack/Should I Tell Them? ... 50
65 Stateside SS 387 — He Was Really Sayin' Something/Throw A Farewell Kiss ... 70
65 Tamla Motown TMG 521 — Lonely Lonely Girl Am I/I'm The Exception To The Rule ... 125
66 Tamla Motown TMG 580 — These Things Will Keep Me Loving You/Since You've Been Loving Me ... 30
65 Tamla Motown TMG 595 — He Was Really Sayin' Something/Needle In A Haystack (narrow label print) ... 22
67 Tamla Motown TMG 595 — He Was Really Sayin' Something/Needle In A Haystack (later pressing) ... 12
71 Tamla Motown TMG 780 — These Things Will Keep Me Loving You/Since You've Been Loving Me (reissue) .. 6
72 Tamla Motown TMG 806 — Needle In A Haystack/I'm The Exception To The Rule ... 6

VELVET HUSH

68 Oak RGJ 648 — Broken Heart/Lover Please ... 210
(see also Factory [Oak label])

VELVET LOVE

75 Alaska ALA 1010 — Symphony Of Dreams/Ridin' High ... 7

VELVET OPERA

69 CBS 4189 — Anna Dance Square/Don't You Realize ... 10
70 CBS 4802 — Black Jack Davy/Statesboro' Blues ... 10
70 Spark SRL 1045 — She Keeps Giving Me These Feelings/There's A Hole In My Pocket ... 7
69 CBS 63692 — RIDE A HUSTLER'S DREAM (LP) ... 55
(see also Elmer Gantry's Velvet Opera, Stretch, Hudson-Ford, Johnny Joyce)

VELVETS

61 London HLU 9328 — That Lucky Old Sun/Time And Time Again ... 25
61 London HLU 9372 — Tonight (Could Be The Night)/Spring Fever ... 30
61 London HLU 9444 — Laugh/Lana ... 30
61 London RE-U 1297 — VELVETS (EP) ... 165

VEL-VETS

74 Disco Demand DDS 109 — I Got To Find Me Somebody/What Now My Love ... 5

VELVETTES

64 Mercury MF 802 — He's The One I Want/That Little Boy Of Mine (some in p/s) ... 22/15

VELVETT FOGG

69 Pye 7N 17673 — Telstar '69/Owed To The Dip ... 12
69 Pye NSPL 18272 — VELVETT FOGG (LP, laminated sleeve; beware of non-laminated counterfeits) .. 85
(see also Ghost)

VELVET UNDERGROUND

71 Atlantic 2091 008 — Who Loves The Sun/Sweet Jane ... 18
73 MGM 2006 283 — I'm Waiting For The Man/Run Run Run/Candy Says (as Lou Reed & Velvet Underground) ... 8
73 Atlantic K 10339 — Sweet Jane/Rock And Roll (as Velvet Underground featuring Lou Reed) ... 8
82 Polydor POSPX 603 — Heroin/Venus In Furs/I'm Waiting For The Man/Run Run Run (12", p/s) ... 8
88 Old Gold OG 4049 — I'm Waiting For The Man/Heroin (12", no p/s) ... 8
88 Old Gold OG 4051 — Venus In Furs/All Tomorrow's Parties (12", no p/s) ... 8
67 Verve (S)VLP 9184 — THE VELVET UNDERGROUND AND NICO (LP, single sleeve, 'non-banana' cover, mono/stereo) ... 100/80
68 Verve 2315 056 — THE VELVET UNDERGROUND AND NICO (LP, UK pressing in stickered US peelable banana gatefold censored sleeve, stereo) ... 100
68 Verve (S)VLP 9201 — WHITE LIGHT WHITE HEAT (LP, 'skull' sleeve, mono/stereo) ... 100/70
69 MGM MGM-CS 8108 — THE VELVET UNDERGROUND (LP, 'Val Valentin mix', flapped sleeve, with horizontal split of Lou Reed picture on rear sleeve) ... 100
71 Atlantic 2400 111 — LOADED (LP) ... 18
71 MGM 2315 056 — THE VELVET UNDERGROUND AND NICO (LP, reissue, gatefold sleeve) ... 18
71 MGM Select 2353 022 — THE VELVET UNDERGROUND (LP, reissue, gatefold sleeve) ... 18

MINT VALUE £

71 MGM Select 2353 024 — WHITE LIGHT WHITE HEAT (LP, reissue) — 18
72 MGM Select 2683 006 — ANDY WARHOL'S VELVET UNDERGROUND (2-LP) — 22
72 Atlantic K 30022 — LIVE AT MAX'S KANSAS CITY (LP) — 12
73 Polydor 2383 180 — SQUEEZE (LP) — 12
84 Polydor SPELP 73 — WHITE LIGHT WHITE HEAT (LP, reissue, different sleeve) — 12
86 Polydor VUBOX 1 — THE VELVET UNDERGROUND BOX SET (5-LP box set, with booklet) — 40
87 Mercury 6641 900 — 1969 VOL. 1 (2-LP) — 15
88 HMV C88 1-15 — THE VELVET UNDERGROUND AND NICO (LP or CD box set, with booklet, 1500 only) — each 25

(see also Lou Reed, Nico, John Cale)

TERRY VENABLES

74 Decca F 13500 — What Do You Want To Make Those Eyes At Me For?/Lucy — 10

(see also Tottenham Hotspur F.C.)

VENDORS

64 Domino Studios (no cat. no.) — Don't Leave Me Now/Twilight Time/Take Your Time/Peace Pipe (acetate, private pressing, 12 copies only) — 500+

(see also 'N Betweens, Slade)

VENGERS

63 Oriole CB 1879 — Shake And Clap/Shakedown — 18

VENOM

81 Neat NEAT 08 — In League With Satan/Live Like An Angel, Die Like An Devil (p/s) — 15
82 Neat NEAT 13 — Bloodlust/In Nomine Satanas (p/s) — 15
82 Neat NEAT 13 — Bloodlust/In Nomine Satanas (purple vinyl) — 60
83 Neat NEAT 27 — Die Hard/Acid Queen (p/s, some with poster) — 15/10
83 Megaforce LOM 1/NEAT 27 — Die Hard/Acid Queen (picture disc, export issue, 1,000 only) — 20
84 Neat NEAT 38 — Warhead/Lady Lust (p/s) — 7
84 Neat NEATP 38 — Warhead/Lady Lust (p/s, mauve vinyl) — 18
84 Neat NEAT 3812 — Warhead/Lady Lust/Gates Of Hell (12", p/s) — 10
85 Neat NEATP 43 — Manitou/Woman (picture disc) — 12
85 Neat NEATSHAPE 43 — Manitou/Woman (shaped picture disc) — 15
85 Neat NEATC 43 — Manitou/Woman/Dead Of Night/Dutch Radio Interview (cassette) — 15
85 Neat NEAT 4312 — Manitou/Woman/Dead Of Night (12", p/s) — 15
85 Neat NEATS 47 — Nightmare/Satanarchist (shaped picture disc) — 20
85 Neat NEATSC 47 — Nightmare/Satanarchist/F.O.A.D./Radio Intro To Warhead/ Warhead (live)/Venoms (cassette) — 7
85 Neat NEAT 4712 — Nightmare/Satanarchist/F.O.A.D./Warhead (live) (12", 'face' p/s) — 15
85 Neat NEAT 4712 — Nightmare/Satanarchist/F.O.A.D./Warhead (live) (12", p/s, withdrawn) — 20
85 Neat NEATSP 4712 — Nightmare/Satanarchist/F.O.A.D./Warhead (live) (12", picture disc, withdrawn) — 35
85 Neat 5312 — HELL AT HAMMERSMITH EP (Witching Hour/Teacher's Pet/Poison) (12", 10,000 only) — 15
81 Neat 1002 — WELCOME TO HELL (LP, 1st issue, with poster and lyric insert) — 18
82 Neat 1005 — BLACK METAL (LP, 1st issue, textured sleeve, with poster, some on coloured vinyl) — 25/18
82 Neat NEAT 1005 — BLACK METAL (LP, green marbled vinyl) — 350
83 Neat NEATP 1002 — WELCOME TO HELL (LP, reissue, purple vinyl) — 45
84 Neat 1015 — AT WAR WITH SATAN (LP, textured sleeve, 1st 19,000 with poster) — 18/12
85 Neat NEATP 1005 — BLACK METAL (LP, reissue, picture disc) — 30
85 Neat NEATP 1015 — AT WAR WITH SATAN (LP, picture disc) — 30
85 Neat NEATP 1024 — POSSESSED (LP, picture disc) — 15
85 Neat NEAT 1024 — POSSESSED (LP, blue vinyl) — 15
86 Demon APKPD 12 — OBSCENE MATERIAL (LP, picture disc) — 15
86 Raw Power RAWLP 001 — FROM HELL TO THE UNKNOWN (2-LP) — 20
86 A.P. APK 12 — OFFICIAL BOOTLEG (LP, picture disc) — 12
89 Under One Flag FLAG 36P — PRIME EVIL (LP, numbered picture disc, stickered clear sleeve) — 18

CAROL VENTURA

65 Stateside SS 466 — Please Somebody Help Me/The Old Lady Of Threadneedle Street — 5
65 Stateside SL 10146 — CAROL! (LP) — 22
66 Stateside S(S)L 10180 — I LOVE TO SING (LP) — 22

CHARLIE VENTURA

54 Vogue Coral Q 2022 — I Love You/Intermezzo (unreleased)
55 Vogue Coral Q 72048 — I Love You/Intermezzo — 8

DAVE VENTURA

64 Mercury MF 805 — The Hurt Stays In The Heart/Is A Redbird Red? — 10
64 Mercury MF 827 — I Forgot What It Was Like/I'll Never Love Again — 8

DOLORES VENTURA (& Her Southernaires)

54 Decca F 10390 — Two Parrots/Ringin' The Rag — 8
56 Parlophone R 4160 — Georgian Rumba/Song Of The Andes — 7
56 Parlophone R 4243 — The Seven Hills Of Lisbon/When The Dog Sits On The Tucker Bo (as Dolores Ventura & Her Southernaires) — 7

TOBY VENTURA

63 Decca F 11581 — If My Heart Were A Storybook/Vagabond — 40

VENTURES

SINGLES

60 Top Rank JAR 417 — Walk Don't Run/Home — 10
60 London HLG 9232 — Perfidia/No Trespassing — 10
61 London HLG 9292 — Ram-Bunk-Shush/Lonely Heart — 10
61 London HLG 9344 — Lullaby Of The Leaves/Ginchy — 8
61 London HLG 9411 — Theme From 'Silver City'/Bluer Than Blue — 10
61 London HLG 9465 — Blue Moon/Wailin' — 15
61 London HLG 7113 — Lady Of Spain/Blue Moon (export issue) — 30

			MINT VALUE £
62	Liberty LIB 60	Lolita Ya-Ya/Lucille	8
62	Liberty LIB 67	The 2,000 Pound Bee Parts 1 & 2	12
63	Liberty LIB 68	El Cumbanchero/Skip To M'Limbo	8
63	Liberty LIB 78	The Ninth Wave/Damaged Goods	10
64	Liberty LIB 91	Journey To The Stars/Walkin' With Pluto	8
64	Liberty LIB 96	Walk Don't Run '64/The Cruel Sea	12
64	Liberty LIB 10142	Penetration/Solar Race	8
65	Liberty LIB 300	Slaughter On Tenth Avenue/Rap City	8
65	Liberty LIB 303	Diamond Head/Lonely Girl	10
65	Liberty LIB 306	The Swingin' Creeper/Pedal Pusher	8
65	Liberty LIB 308	The Stranger/Bird Rockers	8
65	Liberty LIB 10219	Sleigh Ride/White Christmas	8
66	Liberty LIB 316	Secret Agent Man/007-11	8
67	Liberty LIB 10266	Theme From The Wild Angels/High And Dry	8
67	Liberty LIB 55967	Strawberry Fields Forever/Endless Dream	8
68	Liberty LBF 15075	Flights Of Fantasy/Pandora's Box	15
70	Liberty LBF 15221	Hawaii Five-O — Theme/Higher Than Thou	15
71	United Artists UP 36316	Theme From 'Shaft'/Tight Fit	7
72	United Artists UP 35326	Joy/Cherries Jubilee	6
73	United Artists UP 35574	Skylab/Little People	8
75	United Artists UP 35951	Hawaii Five-O/Higher Than Thou (reissue)	5
75	United Artists UP 36009	Superstar Revue Parts 1 & 2	5
77	United Artists UP 36223	Starsky And Hutch/Charlie's Angels	6
EPs			
61	London REG 1279	THE VENTURES	25
61	London REG 1283	THE VENTURES (export issue)	35
61	London REG 1288	RAM-BUNK-SHUSH!	30
62	London REG 1326	ANOTHER SMASH	30
62	London REG 1328	COLOURFUL VENTURES	25
62	Liberty LEP 2058	TWIST WITH THE VENTURES	22
62	Liberty LEP 2131	SMASH HITS	22
63	Liberty LEP 2104	THE VENTURES PLAY TELSTAR AND LONELY BULL	25
64	Liberty LEP 2174	THE VENTURES PLAY COUNTRY GREATS	25
65	Liberty LEP 2212	BOBBY VEE MEETS THE VENTURES (with Bobby Vee)	40
66	Liberty LEP 2250	SECRET AGENT MEN	35
ORIGINAL LPs			
61	London HA-G 2340	THE VENTURES (also stereo SAH-G 6143)	40/55
61	London HA-G 2376	ANOTHER SMASH (also stereo SAH-G 6176)	30/45
61	London HA-G 2409	THE COLOURFUL VENTURES (also stereo SAH-G 6209)	30/45
62	Liberty LBY 1002	WALK DON'T RUN	25
62	London HA-G 2429	TWIST WITH THE VENTURES (also stereo SAH-G 6225)	30/45
62	Liberty LBY 1072	TWIST PARTY	25
63	Liberty (S)LBY 1110	GOING TO THE VENTURES DANCE PARTY! (mono/stereo)	25/35
63	Liberty (S)LBY 1147	BOBBY VEE MEETS THE VENTURES (with Bobby Vee)	35/45
63	Liberty (S)LBY 1150	SURFING (mono/stereo)	22/30
64	Liberty (S)LBY 1169	LET'S GO! (mono/stereo)	18/25
64	Liberty (S)LBY 1189	THE VENTURES IN SPACE (mono/stereo)	22/30
65	Liberty (S)LBY 1228	WALK DON'T RUN — VOL. 2 (mono/stereo)	22/30
65	Liberty (S)LBY 1252	KNOCK ME OUT (mono/stereo)	20/25
65	Liberty (S)LBY 1270	ON STAGE (mono/stereo)	20/25
66	Liberty (S)LBY 1274	VENTURES A-GO GO (mono/stereo)	18/25
66	Liberty (S)LBY 1285	THE VENTURES' CHRISTMAS ALBUM (mono/stereo)	22/30
66	Liberty (S)LBY 1297	WHERE THE ACTION IS! (mono/stereo)	18/22
66	Liberty (S)LBY 1323	GO WITH THE VENTURES (mono/stereo)	18/22
67	Liberty (S)LBY 1345	GUITAR FREAKOUT (mono/stereo)	18/22
67	Liberty (S)LBY 1372	SUPER PSYCHEDELICS (mono/stereo)	18/22
67	Liberty (S)LBY 1375	THE BEST OF THE VENTURES (mono/stereo)	18/22
68	Liberty LBL/LBS 83046E	GOLDEN GREATS (mono/stereo)	18/22
68	Liberty LBL/LBS 83085E	GREAT PERFORMANCES VOL. 1	18
68	Liberty LBL/LBS 83092E	$1,000,000 WEEKEND	18
68	Liberty LBL/LBS 83124E	LONELY BULL	15
68	Liberty LBX 2	VENTURES SAMPLER	15
68	Sunset SLS 50012E	GUITAR GENIUS	12
68	Sunset SLS 50045E	RUNNIN' STRONG	12
68	Liberty LBL/LBS 83138E	FLIGHTS OF FANTASY	15
69	Liberty LBL/LBS 83164E	THE HORSE	15
69	Liberty LBL/LBS 83193E	UNDERGROUND FIRE	15
70	Liberty LBL/LBS 83175	MORE GOLDEN GREATS (mono/stereo)	15/12
70	Liberty LBL/LBS 83279	SWAMP ROCK (mono/stereo)	15/12
71	United Artists UAS 29249	BEST OF POP SOUNDS (export issue)	15
72	United Artists UAS 29280	THEME FROM 'SHAFT'	12
72	United Artists UAS 29340	THE VENTURES PLAY THE CLASSICS — "JOY" (omits "One Fine Day", stickered sleeve)	12
76	Sunset SLS 50386	THE VERY BEST OF THE VENTURES	12
83	Valentine VAL 8054	THE VENTURES TODAY	12
90	See For Miles SEE 292	THE EP COLLECTION	12
REISSUE LPs			
68	Liberty LBL/LBS 83015E	ON STAGE (mono/stereo)	12/15
68	Liberty LBL/LBS 83033E	SUPER PSYCHEDELICS (mono/stereo)	15
68	Liberty LBL/LBS 83089E	GUITAR FREAKOUT (mono/stereo)	12/15
68	Liberty LBL/LBS 83116E	I LIKE IT LIKE THAT (reissue of "A-Go Go", different sleeve, mono/stereo)	12/15
68	Liberty LBL/LBS 83123E	WALK DON'T RUN (different sleeve, mono/stereo)	12/15
68	Liberty LBL/LBS 83125E	LET'S GO! (different sleeve, mono/stereo)	12/15
68	Liberty LBL/LBS 83126E	OUT OF LIMITS (reissue of "In Space", different sleeve, mono/stereo)	12/15
68	Liberty LBL/LBS 83127E	KNOCK ME OUT (different sleeve, mono/stereo)	12/15

(see also New Ventures, Bobby Vee)

MINT VALUE £

VENUS & RAZORBLADES

77 Spark SRL 1153	I Wanna Be Where The Boys Are/Dogfood (numbered p/s)	8
78 Spark SRL 1159	Workin' Girl/Midnight	8

BILLY VERA

68 Atlantic 584 196	With Pen In Hand/Good Morning Blues	7

BILLY VERA & JUDY CLAY

68 Atlantic 584 164	Storybook Children/Really Together	7
69 Atlantic 584 293	Reaching For The Moon/Tell It Like It Is	6
68 Atlantic 588 158	THE STORYBOOK CHILDREN (LP)	25

(see also Judy Clay)

JOHN VERITY BAND

74 Probe SPB 1087	JOHN VERITY BAND (LP)	12

(see also Argent)

TIM VERLANDER

72 Midas MR 007	TIM VERLANDER (LP, with booklet)	35

VERMILION

78 Illegal ILM 0010	Angry Young Women/Nymphomania/Wild Boys (p/s)	15
79 Illegal ILS 0015	I Like Motorcycles/The Letter (p/s)	8

(see also Menace)

VERN & ALVIN

69 Blue Cat BS 167	Everybody Reggae/Another Fool	12
69 Big Shot BI 525	Old Man Dead/G.G. RHYTHM SECTION: Reggae Me	10

(see also Maytones)

VERN & SON

71 G.G. GG 4523	Little Boy Blue/TYPHOON ALL STARS: Little Boy Blue — Version	6

(see also Maytones)

LARRY VERNE

60 London HLN 9194	Mr. Custer/Okeefenokee Two Step	10
61 London HLN 9263	Mr. Livingstone/Roller Coaster	10

LYN VERNON

60 Top Rank JAR 323	Woodchoppers Ball/Caravan	7

MIKE VERNON

72 Blue Horizon 2096 007	Let's Try It Again/Little Southern Country Girl	25
71 Blue Horizon 2931 003	BRING IT BACK HOME (LP, textured sleeve with insert)	110

VERNONS GIRLS

58 Parlophone R 4497	Lost And Found/White Bucks And Saddle Shoes	25
58 Parlophone R 4497	Lost And Found/White Bucks And Saddle Shoes (78)	6
59 Parlophone R 4532	Jealous Heart/Now Is The Month Of Maying	20
59 Parlophone R 4532	Jealous Heart/Now Is The Month Of Maying (78)	10
59 Parlophone R 4596	Don't Look Now But/Who Are They To Say?	20
60 Parlophone R 4624	We Like Boys/Boy Meets Girl	18
60 Parlophone R 4654	Madison Time (with Jimmy Saville)/The Oo-We	15
61 Parlophone R 4734	Ten Little Lonely Boys/Anniversary Song	12
61 Parlophone R 4832	Let's Get Together/No Message	12
62 Decca F 11450	Lover Please/You Know What I Mean	6
62 Decca F 11495	The Loco-motion/Don't Wanna Go	7
62 Decca F 11549	Funny All Over/See For Yourself	6
63 Decca F 11629	Do The Bird/I'm Gonna Let My Hair Down	7
63 Decca F 11685	He'll Never Come Back/Stay-At-Home	6
63 Decca F 11781	Tomorrow Is Another Day/Why Why Why	10
64 Decca F 11807	We Love The Beatles/Hey Lover Boy	15
64 Decca F 11887	Only You Can Do It/Stupid Little Girl	10
64 Decca F 12021	It's A Sin To Tell A Lie/Don't Say Goodbye	7
62 Decca DFE 8506	THE VERNONS GIRLS (EP)	45
58 Parlophone PMC 1052	THE VERNONS GIRLS (LP)	85

(see also Krimson Kake, Wilde Three, Jimmy Saville, Lee Francis, Samantha Jones, Breakaways)

LILI VERONA

54 HMV 7MC 13	Massa Johnny/Hoggin' In The Cocoa (export issue)	15
56 Melodisc MEL 1383	French Lesson/Pica Now (78, with Gulf Stream Calypso Boys)	12
59 HMV DLP 1202	JAMAICA SINGS (10" LP)	22

VERSATILE NEWTS

80 Shanghai No. 2	Newtrition/Blimp (p/s, stamped white label)	25

(see also Felt)

VERSATILES

68 Island WI 3142	Teardrops Falling/Someone To Love	20
68 Amalgamated AMG 802	Just Can't Win/LEADERS: Sometimes I Sit Down Down And Cry	20
68 Crab CRAB 1	Children Get Ready/Someone To Love	8
69 Big Shot BI 520	Worries A Yard/VAL BENNETT: Hound Dog Special	8
69 Crab CRAB 5	Spread Your Bed/Worries A Yard	8
69 Amalgamated AMG 854	Lu Lu Bell/Long Long Time	8
74 Dip DL 5039	Cutting Razor/UPSETTERS: Black Belt Jones	8

(see also Pioneers, Soul Sisters)

VERSATILES

70 New Beat NB 060	Pick My Pocket/FREEDOM SINGERS: Freedom	8
71 Nu Beat NB 076	Give To Me/TIGER: With Hot	7

VERUKAS

(see under Varukers)

VERVE

Year	Label	Title	Value
92	Hut HUT 12	All In The Mind/One Way To Go (p/s)	5
92	Hut HUTT 12	All In The Mind/Man Called Sun/One Way To Go (12" promo, white label)	25
92	Hut HUT 16	She's A Superstar (Edit)/Feel (p/s)	7
92	Hut HUTEN 21	GRAVITY GRAVE EP (Gravity Grave [Edit]/Endless Life/ She's A Superstar [Live at Clapham Grand]) (10", p/s)	10
92	Hut HUTT 16	She's A Superstar/Feel (12" promo, white label)	18
92	Strange Fruit SFPMA 214	HUT — THE PEEL SESSIONS (10", p/s)	7
92	Strange Fruit SFMCD 214	HUT — THE PEEL SESSIONS (CD)	8
93	Hut HUTUS 1/YARDCD 1	THE VERVE EP (Gravity Grave [Edit]/A Man Called Sun/She's A Superstar [Edit]/Endless Life/Feel) (CD, export issue to U.S., 3,000 issued in U.K.)	8
93	Hut HUTEN 29	Blue/Twilight/Where The Geese Go/No Come Down (10", p/s)	12
93	Hut HUTCD 29	Blue/Twilight/Where The Geese Go/No Come Down (CD)	8
93	Hut HUT 35	Slide Away/Make It 'Til Monday (pink vinyl, p/s)	6
93	(no label) FLEXI 1	Make It 'Til Monday (Glastonbury '93) (clear vinyl stickered flexi with magazine)	35
95	Hut HUT 54	This Is Music/Let The Damage Begin (purple vinyl, p/s)	8
95	Hut HUT 55	On Your Own/I See The Door (green vinyl, p/s)	8
95	Hut HUT 55	On Your Own/I See The Door (green vinyl, p/s, mispressing, B-side plays 'Friends' by Daryll-Ann)	15
97	Hut HUTTR 82	Bitter Sweet Symphony (James Lavelle Remix)/(James Lavelle Instrumental Remix) (12", stickered plain die-cut sleeve, promo only)	15
97	Hut HUTTP 82	Bitter Sweet Symphony (Extended Version)/(M.S.G. Mix)/(Instrumental) (12", plain die-cut sleeve, promo only)	8
97	Hut HUT 88	The Drugs Don't Work (Radio Edit)/(Demo Version)/Three Steps/The Crab (12", p/s, 5000 only)	8
97	Hut HUTLH 92	Lucky Man/Never Wanna See You Cry (jukebox issue)	7
97	Hut HUTT 92	Lucky Man/Never Wanna See You Cry/MSG/The Longest Day (12", p/s)	8
98	Hut HUTTX 100	Sonnet/Stamped/So Sister/Echo Bass (12", title sleeve)	12
97	Hut HUTLPX 45	URBAN HYMNS (2-LP)	18
97	Hut HUTLPX 45	URBAN HYMNS (2-LP, with inner sleeves, printed outer mailer, 5,000 only)	30
97	Hut CDPHUT 45	URBAN HYMNS (CD, ribbon-tied black gatefold sleeve, promo only)	40
93	Jolly Roger JOLLY ROGER 2	VOYAGER 1 (LP, official bootleg, blue vinyl, 1,000 only)	70

VETS

Year	Label	Title	Value
79	SRT SRTS 79	Flies/Contrix (no p/s)	120

V FOR VENDETTA

(see under David J.)

VHF

Year	Label	Title	Value
80	Lion PAW 1	Heart Of Stone	75

VIBES

Year	Label	Title	Value
84	Big Beat SW 99	Can You Feel.../The Underestimated Man/Double Decker Bus/ Mini Skirt Blues/Stranger In The House (p/s)	5

VIBRATIONS

Year	Label	Title	Value
61	Pye International 7N 25107	The Watusi/Wallflower	22
64	London HLK 9875	My Girl Sloopy/Daddy Woo Woo	20
66	Columbia DB 7895	Canadian Sunset/The Story Of A Starry Night	20
67	Columbia DB 8175	Pick Me/You Better Beware	22
67	Columbia DB 8318	Talkin' 'Bout Love/One Mint Julep	18
68	Direction 58-3511	Love In Them There Hills/Remember The Rain	15
67	Columbia SX 6106	NEW VIBRATIONS (LP)	60
69	Direction 8-63644	GREATEST HITS (LP)	35
72	RCA SF 8254	THE VIBRATIONS (LP)	20

(see also Jayhawks)

VIBRATORS

Year	Label	Title	Value
76	RAK RAK 245	We Vibrate/Whips And Furs	8
76	RAK RAK 246	Pogo Dancing/The Pose (as Vibrators with Chris Spedding)	8
77	RAK RAK 253	Bad Times/No Heart (unreleased, two acetates exist; £150)	
77	Epic EPC 5302	Baby Baby/Into The Future (p/s)	8
77	Epic EPC 5565	London Girls/Stiff Little Fingers (live) (p/s)	8
78	Epic EPC 6137	Automatic Lover/Destroy (p/s)	8
78	Epic EPC 6393	Judy Says (Knock You On The Head)/Pure Mania (p/s)	8
80	Rat Race RAT 2	Gimme Some Lovin'/Power Cry (live) (p/s, in slightly different colours)	5
80	Rat Race RAT 4	Disco In Mosco/Take A Chance (p/s, with various coloured writing)	6
77	Epic EPC 82097	PURE MANIA (LP)	12
78	Epic EPC 82495	V2 (LP, with inner lyric sleeve)	15

(see also Boyfriends, Chris Spedding, Nazis Against Fascism, Substitute, Troops Of Tomorrow, Urban Dogs)

VIBRATORS (Jamaica)

Year	Label	Title	Value
66	Doctor Bird DB 1036	Sloop John B/Amour	22

(see also Al & Vibrators, Wilbert Francis & Vibrators)

VICE CREEMS

Year	Label	Title	Value
78	Tiger GRRRR 1	Won't You Be My Girl?/01-01-212 (gatefold p/s)	30
79	Zig Zag ZZ22 001	Danger Love/Like A Tiger (p/s)	22

VICEROYS

Year	Label	Title	Value
67	Island WI 3095	Lip And Tongue/DAWN PENN: When Am I Gonna Be Free	40
67	Coxsone CS 7031	Magadown/RICHARD ACE: Don't Let The Sun Catch You Crying	35
67	Studio One SO 2016	Lose And Gain (as Voiceroys)/SOUL BROTHERS: Honey Pot	25
67	Studio One SO 2025	Shake Up/NORMA FRAZER: Telling Me Lies	25
68	Studio One SO 2064	Last Night/Ya Ho	25
68	Blue Cat BS 121	Fat Fish/OCTAVES: You're Gonna Lose	25
69	Studio One SO 2077	Things A-Come To Bump/LYRICS: Old Man Say	25
69	Punch PH 3	Jump In A Fire/Give To Get (as Voiceroys)	12
69	Crab CRAB 12	Work It/You Mean So Much To Me (B-side actually by Paragons)	12

MINT VALUE £

69 Crab CRAB 27 — Death A-Come (actually by Lloyd Robinson)/MATADOR ALLSTARS: The Sword . . 8
70 Bullet BU 441 — Chariot Coming/SYDNEY ALLSTARS: Stackata . . . 12
70 Bullet BU 444 — Power Control/SLICKERS: Dip Dip . . . 12
70 Bullet BU 450 — Come On Over/SYDNEY ALLSTARS: Version . . . 12
70 Bullet BU 453 — Fancy Clothes/BIGGIE: Jack And Jill . . . 15
71 Bullet BU 470 — Rebel Nyah/Feel The Spirit . . . 12
73 Harry J. HJ 6658 — Chucky (Parts 1 & 2) . . . 5
74 Harry J. HJ 6669 — Wheel & Jig (Parts 1 & 2) . . . 5
(see also Richard Ace, Interns [Jamaica], Derrick Morgan, Vincent Gordon, Hub)

VICE SQUAD

80 Riot City RIOT 1 — Last Rockers/Living On Dreams/Latex Love (p/s, with poster) . . . 8
81 Riot City RIOT 2 — Resurrection/Young Blood/Hurricane (p/s) . . . 6
82 Riot City RIOT 12 1/2 — SINGLES (12" EP) . . . 8
82 Zonophone Z 26 — Out Of Reach/Sterile/Out Of Reach (p/s) . . . 5
82 Zonophone Z 30 — Rock 'n' Roll Massacre/Stand Strong And Proud/Tomorrow . . . 5
80s Vice Squad Fan Club — EVIL (EP, flexidisc) . . . 12
(see also Sex Aids)

VICE VERSA

80 Neutron NT 001/PX 1092 — MUSIC 4 (EP, poster p/s) . . . 12
(see also Liza Strike)

VICIOUS PINK (PHENOMENA)

82 Mobile Suit Corp. CORP 1 — My Private Tokyo/Promises (p/s) . . . 5
82 Mobile Suit Corp. CORP 12 — My Private Tokyo (Long Version)/(Remix)/Promises (12", p/s) . . . 12
83 Warehouse WARE 1 — Je T'Aime (Moi Non Plus)/In The Swim (p/s) . . . 5
83 Warehouse WARE 1T — Je T'Aime (Moi Non Plus) (12" Disco Version)/In The Swim (12", p/s) . . . 10
(see also Soft Cell)

MIKE VICKERS (ORCHESTRA)

65 Columbia DB 7657 — On The Brink/The Puff Adder (as Mike Vickers & Orchestra) . . . 40
66 Columbia DB 7825 — Eleventy One/The Inkling . . . 12
66 Columbia DB 7906 — Morgan — A Suitable Case For Treatment/Gorilla Of My Dreams (as Mike Vickers Orchestra) . . . 15
67 Columbia DB 8171 — Air On A G-String/Proper Charles (as Mike Vickers Orchestra) . . . 8
67 Columbia DB 8281 — Captain Scarlet And The Mysterons/Kettle Of Fish . . . 22
90s Emidisc EMIDISC 101 — On The Brink/SAINT ETIENNE: Emidisc Theme (promo only) . . . 7
68 Columbia S(C)X 6180 — I WISH I WERE A GROUP AGAIN (LP) . . . 50
(see also Manfred Mann, Baker Street Philharmonic)

SUE VICKERS

72 Threshold TH 8 — Loving You The Way I Do/Take Me With You . . . 5

MACK VICKERY

60 Top Rank JAR 420 — Fantasy/Hawaiian Stroll . . . 12

VICKY

67 Philips BF 1565 — Colours Of Love (Love Is Blue)/Who Can Tell . . . 15
67 Philips BF 1599 — Sunshine Boy/Tell Me . . . 12
68 Philips BF 1631 — Dance With Me Until Tomorrow/Give Me Your Hand . . . 10
(see also Vicky Leandros)

VICKY & JERRY

60 HMV POP 715 — Don't Cry/A Year Ago Tonight . . . 20

VICTIM

78 Good Vibrations GOT 2 — Strange Things By Night/Mixed Up World (wraparound p/s) . . . 10
79 TJM TJM 13 — THE VICTIM (EP, unreleased)
79 TJM TJM 14 — Why Are Fire Engines Red/I Need You (p/s) . . . 25
80 TJM TJM 15 — The Teen Age/Junior Criminals/Hung On To Yourself (p/s) . . . 25
80 Illuminated ILL 1 — The Teen Age/Junior Criminals/Hung On To Yourself (p/s, reissue) . . . 15

VICTIMIZE

79 I.M.E. IME 1 — Baby Buyer/Hi Rising Failure (folded p/s) . . . 70
80 I.M.E. IME 2 — Wh?r? Did Th? Mon?y Go (p/s) . . . 80

VICTIMS OF CHANCE

70 Stable SLE 8004 — VICTIMS OF CHANCE (LP) . . . 50

VICTIMS OF CIRCUMSTANCE

80s Double Vision DV 1 — Very Little Glory/OPPOSITION: Wires (p/s) . . . 10

VICTIMS OF PLEASURE

80 P.A.M. VOP 1 — When You're Young/If I Was/Sporting Pastimes (p/s) . . . 10

VICTIMS OF VICTIMISATION

87 Death DEAD 2 — Kill Or Be Killed/As A Doornail (p/s) . . . 18

TONY VICTOR

62 Decca F 11459 — Dear One/There Was A Time . . . 25
63 Decca F 11626 — Thinking Of You/Hokey Cokey . . . 12
63 Decca F 11708 — In The Still Of The Night/Money . . . 12

VICTORIA

71 Atlantic 2091 084 — Tule's Blues/Helplessly Hoping . . . 6
71 Atlantic 2400 176 — VICTORIA (LP) . . . 30
71 Mojo 2466 008 — SECRET OF THE BLOOM (LP) . . . 45

VICTORIANS

64 Liberty LIB 55693 — Oh What A Night For Love/Happy Birthday Blue . . . 18

VICTORS

65 Oriole CB 1984 — Take This Old Hammer/Answer's No . . . 10

MINT VALUE £

VICTORS
69 High Note HS 019 Reggae Buddy/Easy Squeeze . . . 12
71 Escort ERT 846 Me A Tell Yuh/LLOYD'S ALL-STARS: More Echo . . . 8

VIDELS
60 London HLI 9153 Mister Lonely/I'll Forget You . . . 75

VIGILANTES
61 Pye International 7N 25082 Eclipse/Man In Space . . . 20

(PAUL) VIGRASS
68 RCA RCA 1755 New Man/Curly . . . 7
69 RCA RCA 1800 Suzie/Funky Piano Joe (as Vigrass) . . . 6
69 RCA RCA 1857 Free Lorry Ride/Flying . . . 6
70 RCA RCA 1911 Stop/Like It Never Was . . . 6

VIKINGS
63 Island WI 035 Maggie Don't Leave Me/Henchmen (both actually with Victor Wong) . . . 25
63 Island WI 065 Hallelujah/Helpin' Ages (actually by Maytals) . . . 25
63 Island WI 075 Six And Seven Books Of Moses/Zacions (actually by Maytals) . . . 18
63 Island WI 101 Never Grow Old/Irene (actually by Maytals) . . . 25
63 Island WI 107 Just Got To Be/You Make Me Do (actually by Maytals) . . . 25
63 Island WI 117 Fever/Cheer Up (actually by Maytals) . . . 18
64 Island WI 167 Daddy/It's You (actually by Maytals) . . . 40
64 Black Swan WI 423 Down By The Riverside/This Way . . . 25
64 Black Swan WI 428 Treat Me Bad/Sitting On Top . . . 40
64 Black Swan WI 430 Come Into My Parlour/I Am In Love . . . 25

(see also Maytals, Flames [Jamaica], Bonnie & Skitto)

VIKINGS
66 Alp 595 011 Bad News Feeling/What Can I Do . . . 22

VILENESS
90 Noisome STENCH 3 March Of The Vile/Sex Is Vile (12", vile-scented p/s) . . . 10

CLAUDIO VILLA
60s Centra SP 4024 Addio... Addio/Twist A Napoli (p/s) . . . 5

VILLAGE
69 Head HDS 4002 Man In The Moon/Long Time Coming . . . 45

(see also Peter Bardens, Quiver)

VILLAGE IDIOTS
66 Piccadilly 7N 35282 Laughing Policeman/I Know An Old Lady . . . 5

VILLAGERS/PARCEL OF ROGUES
73 Deroy (no cat. no.) PARCEL OF FOLK (LP, private pressing, with insert) . . . 200

VILLAGE SOUL CHOIR
70 Direction 58-4969 Catwalk/Country Walk . . . 7

VILLAGE STOMPERS
63 Columbia DB 7123 Washington Square/Turkish Delight . . . 8

CATERINA VILLALBA
60 Ember EMB S 104 Quando La Luna/Amore Fantastico (p/s) . . . 7

JOE VINA
59 Top Rank JAR 251 Marina/That's Alright . . . 5

RAE VINCE & VINCENTS
64 Piccadilly 7N 35211 One Fine Day/Little Girl, I'm Sad . . . 6

GENE VINCENT (& BLUE CAPS)

78s
56 Capitol CL 14599 Be-Bop-A-Lula/Woman Love . . . 12
56 Capitol CL 14628 Race With The Devil/Gonna Back Up, Baby . . . 30
56 Capitol CL 14637 Bluejean Bop/Who Slapped John? . . . 12
57 Capitol CL 14681 Jumps, Giggles And Shouts/Wedding Bells (Are Breaking Up That Old Gang Of Mine) . . . 35
57 Capitol CL 14693 Crazy Legs/Important Words . . . 35
57 Capitol CL 14722 Bi-I-Bickey-Bi, Bo-Bo-Go/Five Days, Five Days . . . 35
57 Capitol CL 14763 Lotta Lovin'/Wear My Ring . . . 30
57 Capitol CL 14808 Dance To The Bop/I Got It . . . 30
58 Capitol CL 14830 Walkin' Home From School/I Got A Baby . . . 45
59 Capitol CL 15053 Right Now/The Night Is So Lonely . . . 175

(The above 78s are credited to Gene Vincent & Blue Caps)

45s
56 Capitol CL 14599 Be-Bop-A-Lula/Woman Love . . . 40
56 Capitol CL 14628 Race With The Devil/Gonna Back Up, Baby . . . 100
56 Capitol CL 14637 Bluejean Bop/Who Slapped John? . . . 65
57 Capitol CL 14681 Jumps, Giggles And Shouts/Wedding Bells (Are Breaking Up That Old Gang Of Mine) (promo copy in p/s) . . . 150
57 Capitol CL 14681 Jumps, Giggles And Shouts/Wedding Bells (Are Breaking Up That Old Gang Of Mine) . . . 50
57 Capitol CL 14693 Crazy Legs/Important Words (promo copy in p/s) . . . 75
57 Capitol CL 14693 Crazy Legs/Important Words . . . 50
57 Capitol CL 14722 Bi-I-Bickey-Bi, Bo-Bo-Go/Five Days, Five Days (promo copy in p/s) . . . 150
57 Capitol CL 14722 Bi-I-Bickey-Bi, Bo-Bo-Go/Five Days, Five Days . . . 50
57 Capitol CL 14763 Lotta Lovin'/Wear My Ring . . . 45
57 Capitol CL 14808 Dance To The Bop/I Got It . . . 55
58 Capitol CL 14830 Walkin' Home From School/I Got A Baby (promo copy in p/s) . . . 70
58 Capitol CL 14830 Walkin' Home From School/I Got A Baby . . . 35
58 Capitol CL 14868 Baby Blue/True To You . . . 35

			MINT VALUE £
58	Capitol CL 14908	Rocky Road Blues/Yes I Love You, Baby	35
58	Capitol CL 14935	Git It/Little Lover	35
59	Capitol CL 14974	Say Mama/Be Bop Boogie Boy	30
59	Capitol CL 15000	Who's Pushin' Your Swing/Over The Rainbow	20
59	Capitol CL 15035	Summertime/Frankie And Johnnie	20
59	Capitol CL 15053	Right Now/The Night Is So Lonely	20
59	Capitol CL 15099	Wild Cat/Right Here On Earth	15
60	Capitol CL 15115	My Heart/I've Got To Get You Yet	15

(The above singles are credited to Gene Vincent & Blue Caps. Later 45s were solo, unless otherwise stated.)

60	Capitol CL 15136	Pistol Packin' Mama (as Gene Vincent & Beat Boys)/Weeping Willow	12
60	Capitol CL 15169	Anna-Annabelle/Ac-Cent-Tchu-Ate The Positive	15
61	Capitol CL 15179	Maybe/Jezebel	15
61	Capitol CL 15185	If You Want My Lovin'/Mister Loneliness	15
61	Capitol CL 15202	She She Little Sheila/Hot Dollar	15
61	Capitol CL 15215	I'm Going Home (To See My Baby)/Love Of A Man	12
61	Capitol CL 15231	Unchained Melody/Brand New Beat (with The Blue Caps)	15
62	Capitol CL 15243	Lucky Star/Baby Don't Believe Him (with Dave Burgess Band)	18
62	Capitol CL 15264	Be-Bop-A-Lula/The King Of Fools (with Charles Blackwell Orchestra)	18
63	Capitol CL 15290	Held For Questioning/You're Still In My Heart (with Charles Blackwell Orch.)	18
63	Capitol CL 15307	Rip It Up/High Blood Pressure (unissued, demo copies only)	275
63	Capitol CL 15307	Crazy Beat/High Blood Pressure	35
63	Columbia DB 7174	Temptation Baby/Where Have You Been All My Life	22
64	Columbia DB 7218	Humpity Dumpity/A Love 'Em And Leave 'Em Kinda Guy	22
64	Columbia DB 7293	La-Den-Da Den-Da-Da/The Beginning Of The End	22
64	Columbia DB 7343	Private Detective/You Are My Sunshine (as Gene Vincent & Shouts)	22
66	London HLH 10079	Bird Doggin'/Ain't That Too Much	40
66	London HLH 10099	Lonely Street/I've Got My Eyes On You	35
68	Capitol CL 15546	Be-Bop-A-Lula/Say Mama	15
69	Dandelion S 4596	Be-Bop-A-Lula '69/Ruby Baby	12
70	Dandelion S 4974	White Lightning/Scarlet Ribbons (For Her Hair)	15
71	Kama Sutra 2013 018	The Day The World Turned Blue/High On Life (some with large centre)	12
73	Spark SRL 1091	Story Of The Rockers/Pickin' Poppies (push-out or solid centre)	10
74	BBC BEEB 001	Roll Over Beethoven/Say Mama/Be-Bop-A-Lula '71 (push-out or solid centre)	8
77	Capitol CL 15906	Say Mama/Lotta Lovin'/Race With The Devil	6
81	Capitol CL 203	She She Little Sheila/Say Mama/Dance To The Bop (p/s)	5
87	Nighttracks SFNT 001	Nighttracks (Distant Drums/Be-Bop-A-Lula) (p/s, promo only with insert)	12

EPs

58	Capitol EAP 1-985	HOT ROD GANG	75
59	Capitol EAP 1-1059	A GENE VINCENT RECORD DATE	75
60	Capitol EAP 3-1059	A GENE VINCENT RECORD DATE PART 3	75
61	Capitol EAP 1-20173	IF YOU WANT MY LOVIN'	75
62	Capitol EAP 1-20354	RACE WITH THE DEVIL	75
63	Capitol EAP 1-20461	TRUE TO YOU	75
64	Capitol EAP 1-20453	THE CRAZY BEAT OF GENE VINCENT NO. 1	80
64	Capitol EAP 2-20453	THE CRAZY BEAT OF GENE VINCENT NO. 2	75
64	Capitol EAP 3-20453	THE CRAZY BEAT OF GENE VINCENT NO. 3	75
69	EMIdisc (no cat. no.)	LIVE & ROCKIN'! (fan club issue, mail-order, 99 only)	250
79	Rollin' Danny RD 1	RAINY DAY SUNSHINE (L.A. 1969 demos, 500 only)	15
81	Magnum Force MFEP 003	RAINY DAY SUNSHINE (reissue)	12

LPs

56	Capitol T 764	BLUEJEAN BOP! (originally with turquoise labels; later rainbow)	120/80
57	Capitol T 811	GENE VINCENT AND THE BLUECAPS (turquoise or rainbow labels)	120/80
58	Capitol T 970	GENE VINCENT ROCKS! & THE BLUECAPS ROLL (originally with turquoise labels, later rainbow labels)	120/80
59	Capitol T 1059	A GENE VINCENT RECORD DATE	80
59	Capitol T 1207	SOUNDS LIKE GENE VINCENT	80
60	Capitol (S)T 1342	CRAZY TIMES! (mono/stereo)	70/110
63	Capitol T 20453	THE CRAZY BEAT OF GENE VINCENT	70
64	Columbia 33SX 1646	SHAKIN' UP A STORM (as Gene Vincent & The Shouts)	80
65	Music F. Pleasure MFP 1053	CRAZY TIMES (reissue)	15
67	London HA-H 8333	GENE VINCENT	55

(The Capitol compilations listed above may exist with later label designs. These would be worth half the values listed.)

67	Capitol T 20957	THE BEST OF GENE VINCENT ('rainbow' label; reissue with pink label £12)	20
68	Capitol ST 21144	THE BEST OF GENE VINCENT VOL. 2 ('rainbow' label; reissue with pink label £12)	
22			
70	Dandelion 63754	I'M BACK AND I'M PROUD (gatefold sleeve)	35
71	Kama Sutra 2316 005	THE DAY THE WORLD TURNED BLUE	30
71	Kama Sutra 2316 009	IF YOU COULD ONLY SEE ME TODAY	30
72	Regal Starline SRS 5117	PIONEERS OF ROCK VOLUME 1	12
74	Regal Starline SRS 5177	THE KING OF FOOLS: PIONEERS OF ROCK VOLUME 4	12
74	Capitol ST 11287	THE BOP THAT JUST WON'T STOP	12
81	Capitol E-ST 26223	THE SINGLES ALBUM (with bonus "Vintage Vincent" EP [PSR 458])	12
87	Charly BOX 108	GENE VINCENT: THE CAPITOL YEARS '56-'63 (10-LP box set with 36-page booklet; later remastered and reissued with slimmer box, 1989)	70
90	EMI CDGV 1	THE GENE VINCENT BOX SET (Complete Capitol & Columbia Recordings, 1956-64) (6-CD set)	50

RORY VINCENT

73	Columbia SCXA 9254	SINGS THE MUSIC OF WLODEK GULGOWSKI (LP)	20

CAROLE VINCI

78	EMI EMI 2801	Vivre/Souffire Et Sourire	12

JOEY VINE

65	Immediate IM 017	Down And Out/The Out Of Towner	22

VINEGAR JOE

72	Island WIP 6125	Never Met A Dog/Speed Queen Of Ventura	5
72	Island WIP 6148	Rock'n'Roll Gypsies/So Long	5
73	Island WIP 6174	Black Smoke From The Calumet/Long Way Round	5
72	Island ILPS 9183	VINEGAR JOE (LP)	18
72	Island ILPS 9214	ROCK 'N ROLL GYPSIES (LP, gatefold sleeve)	12
73	Island ILPS 9262	SIX STAR GENERAL (LP, gatefold sleeve)	12

(see also Dada, Robert Palmer, Elkie Brooks)

VINES

01	RexRec REKD 195	Factory/Ain't No Room/Drown The Baptists (p/s, 500 only)	35
02	Heavenly HVN 112	Highly Evolved/Sun Child (p/s)	12
02	Heavenly HVN 113	Get Free/Blues Riff (p/s)	5
02	Heavenly HVN 120	Outtathaway!/Miss Jackson (p/s)	5
03	Heavenly NR 72435 5378477	Fuck The World/Fuck The World (white vinyl, title sleeve, 300 only)	20

EDDIE 'MR. CLEANHEAD' VINSON

51	Vogue V 2023	Queen Bee Blues/Jump And Grunt (78)	35
64	Riverside RLP 3302	BACK DOOR BLUES (LP)	40
72	Philips 6369 406	THE ORIGINAL CLEANHEAD (LP)	18

(see also Wynonie Harris)

V. VINSTRICK & J.J. ALLSTARS

68	Doctor Bird DB 1167	Love Is Not A Game/CINDERELLA: The Way I See You	20

BOBBY VINTON

61	Fontana H 307	Little Lonely One/Corrine Corrina	20
62	London HLU 9592	I Love You The Way You Are/CHUCK & JOHNNY: You Are My Girl	20
62	Columbia DB 4878	Roses Are Red/You And I	7
62	Columbia DB 4900	Rain Rain Go Away/Over Over	7
63	Columbia DB 4961	Trouble Is My Middle Name/Let's Kiss And Make Up	7
63	Columbia DB 7015	Over The Mountain/Faded Pictures	7
63	Columbia DB 7052	Blue On Blue/Those Little Things	7
63	Columbia DB 7110	Blue Velvet/Is There A Place	15
63	Columbia DB 7179	There! I've Said It Again/The Girl With The Bow In Her Hair	7
64	Columbia DB 7240	My Heart Belongs To Only You/Warm And Tender	7
64	Columbia DB 7303	Tell Me Why/Remembering	7
64	Columbia DB 7348	Clinging Vine/Imagination Is A Magic Dream	7
64	Columbia DB 7422	Mr Lonely/The Bell That Couldn't Jingle	15
65	Columbia DB 7514	Long Lonely Nights/Satin	7
65	Columbia DB 7628	Don't Go Away Mad/Lonely Girl	6
65	Columbia DB 7731	What Colour Is A Man/Love Of Infatuation	6
66	Columbia DB 7808	Satin Pillows/Careless	6
66	Columbia DB 7922	Dum De Da/The Exodus Song	6
67	Columbia DB 8114	Coming Home Soldier/Don't Let My Mary Go Around	6
67	Columbia DB 8319	Please Love Me Forever/Miss America	6
68	Columbia DB 8346	Just As Much As Ever/Another Memory	6
68	CBS 3636	Halfway To Paradise/(My Little) Christie	6
68	CBS 3897	I Love How You Love Me/Little Barefoot Boy	6
69	CBS 4451	Days Of Sand And Shovels/So Many Lonely Girls	6
69	CBS 4910	My Elusive Dreams/Over And Over	6
70	CBS 5106	No Arms Can Ever Hold You/I Love How You Love Me	6
62	Columbia SEG 8212	YOUNG IN HEART (EP)	25
64	Columbia SEG 8363	SONGS OF CHRISTMAS (EP)	25
63	Columbia 33SX 1517	SINGS THE BIG ONES (LP)	30
63	Columbia 33SX 1566	BLUE ON BLUE (LP)	30
63	Columbia 33SX 1611	MY HEART BELONGS TO ONLY YOU (LP)	25
65	Columbia 33SX 1649	TELL ME WHY (LP)	25

MATT VINYL

77	Housewife's Choice	Useless Tasks (p/s)	8

VIOLATORS

82	No Future OI 9	Gangland/Fugitive (p/s, with insert)	10
82	No Future OI 19	Summer Of '81/Live Fast Die Young (p/s)	8
83	Future FS 2	Life On The Red Line/Crossing The Sangsara (p/s)	6

VIOLENTS

63	HMV POP 1130	Alpen Ros/Ghia	18

VIOLENT THIMBLE

67	Polydor 56217	Gentle People Parts 1 & 2	10

VIPERS (SKIFFLE GROUP)

56	Parlophone R 4238	Ain't You Glad/Pick A Bale Of Cotton	22
57	Parlophone R 4261	Don't You Rock Me Daddy-O/10,000 Years Ago	22
57	Parlophone R 4286	Jim Dandy/Hi Liley, Liley Lo	20
57	Parlophone R 4289	The Cumberland Gap/Maggie May	20
57	Parlophone R 4308	Streamline Train/Railroad Steam Boat	18
57	Parlophone R 4351	Homing Bird/Pay Me My Money Down	18
57	Parlophone R 4371	Skiffle Party Medley Parts 1 & 2	18
58	Parlophone R 4393	Baby Why?/No Other Baby (as Vipers)	25
58	Parlophone R 4393	Baby Why?/No Other Baby (as Vipers) (78)	8
58	Parlophone R 4435	Make Ready For Love/Nothing Will Ever Change (My Love For You) (as Vipers)	15
58	Parlophone R 4435	Make Ready For Love/Nothing Will Ever Change (My Love For You) (78)	10
58	Parlophone R 4484	Summertime Blues/Liverpool Blues (as Vipers)	35
58	Parlophone R 4484	Summertime Blues/Liverpool Blues (as Vipers) (78)	25
57	Parlophone GEP 8615	SKIFFLE MUSIC VOL. 1 (EP)	20
57	Parlophone GEP 8626	SKIFFLE MUSIC VOL. 2 (EP)	25
57	Parlophone GEP 8655	SKIFFLING ALONG WITH THE VIPERS (EP)	30

MINT VALUE £

57	Parlophone PMD 1050	COFFEE BAR SESSION (10" LP)	60
86	Rollercoaster ROLL 2011	COFFEE BAR SESSION (LP)	12

(see also Jet Harris & Tony Meehan, Shadows, Wally Whyton, Sharkey Todd & Monsters)

VIPERS

78 Mulligan LUNS 718 — I've Got You/No Such Thing (p/s) 10

VIPPS

66 CBS 202031 — Wintertime/Anyone 60

(see also VIPS)

VIPS

64 RCA RCA 1427 — Don't Keep Shouting At Me/She's So Good 75
66 Island WI 3003 — I Wanna Be Free/Don't Let It Go 35
67 Island WIP 6005 — Straight Down To The Bottom/In A Dream 55

(see also Vipps, Art, Spooky Tooth, Felder's Orioles, Timebox, Patto, Baron & His Pounding Piano, Keith Emerson)

V.I.P.s

78 Bust SOL 3 — MUSIC FOR FUNSTERS (EP) 20
79 Rok ROK V/VI — Can't Let You Go/URBAN DISTURBANCE: Wild Boys In Cortinas 25
80 Gem GEMS 43 — I Need Somebody To Love (Could It Be You?)/One More Chance// Stuttgart Special/Who Knows/Janine (double pack, stickered p/s) 10

(see also Mood Six, Jed Dmochowski)

VIRGIL BROTHERS

69 Parlophone R 5787 — Temptation 'Bout To Get Me/Look Away 18
69 Parlophone R 5802 — Good Love/When You Walk Away 6

VIRGINIANS

63 Pye International 7N 25175 — Limbo Baby/Greenback Dollar 10

VIRGINIA TREE

75 Minstrel 0001 — FRESH OUT (LP) 30

(see also Shirley Kent, Ghost)

VIRGINIA WOLF

86 Atlantic A 9459 — Waiting For Your Love/Take A Chance (p/s) 10

VIRGINIA WOLVES

66 Stateside SS 563 — Stay/B.L.T. 30

VIRGIN PRUNES

81 Baby BABY 001 — TWENTY TENS (EP) 8
81 Rough Trade RT 072 — In The Greylight/War/Moments Of Mine (Despite Straight Lines) (1st issue in blue p/s with insert, later in black p/s without insert) 6/4
81 Rough Trade RT 090 — A New Form Of Beauty Part Two: Come To Daddy/Sweet Home Under White Clouds/Sad World (10", p/s, 33rpm) 7
81 Rough Trade RT 091T — A New Form Of Beauty Part Three: The Beast (Seven Bastard Suck)/ The Slow Children (Abbagal)/Brain Damage/No Birds To Fly (12", p/s) 8
81 Rough Trade RT 089-091 — A NEW FORM OF BEAUTY (7"/10"/12" box set) 22
82 Rough Trade RT 106 — Pagan Lovesong/Dave-id Is Dead (p/s) 5
82 Rough Trade 12 RT 106 — Pagan Lovesong (Vibe Akimbo)/Pagan Lovesong/Dave-id Is Dead (12", p/s) 8
87 Baby BABY 011 — HERESIE (10", double pack, gatefold p/s, 1st 1,000 on clear vinyl) 10/7

(see also Gavin Friday, Bono & Gavin Friday)

VIRGIN SLEEP

67 Deram DM 146 — Love/Halliford House 40
68 Deram DM 173 — Secret/Comes A Time 40

VIRTUE

85 Other OTH 1 — We Stand To Fight (p/s) 22

VIRTUES (Jamaica)

65 Island WI 196 — Your Wife And Mother/Amen (actually with Ambassadors) 22
68 Doctor Bird DB 1164 — High Tide/RUPIE EDWARDS & VIRTUES: Burning Love 22

(see also Lloyd & Devon)

VIRTUES (U.S.)

59 HMV POP 621 — Guitar Boogie Shuffle/Guitar In Orbit 25
59 HMV POP 637 — Flippin' In/Shufflin' Along 22
59 HMV POP 637 — Flippin' In/Shufflin' Along (78) 20

FRANK VIRTUOSO ROCKETS

56 Melodisc MEL 1386 — Rollin' And A-Rockin'/Rock — Good Bye Mambo (78) 25
56 Melodisc MEL 1393 — Toodle-Oo Kangaroo/Hop-Skip-Jump Mambo (78) 15
58 Melodisc MEL 1386 — Rollin' And A-Rockin'/Rock — Good Bye Mambo (red label, tri centre, export issue) 30
58 Melodisc MEL 1386 — Rollin' And Rockin'/Toodle-Oo Kangaroo (green label, round centre) 15

VISAGE

79 Radar ADA 48 — Tar/Frequency 7 (p/s) 10
81 Polydor POSPX 194 — Fade To Grey/The Steps (12", p/s) 15
81 Polydor POSPX 236 — Mind Of A Toy (Dance Mix)/We Move (Dance Mix)/Frequency 7 (Dance Mix) (12", p/s) 10
81 Polydor POSPX 293 — Visage (Dance Mix)/Second Steps (12", p/s) 15
82 Polydor POSPP 441 — Night Train/I'm Still Searching (picture disc) 5
82 Polydor POSPP 523 — Pleasure Boys/The Anvil (picture disc) 7
82 Polydor POSPX 523 — Pleasure Boys (Dance Mix)/The Anvil (Dance Mix) (12", 800 only) 12
82 Polydor POSPV 523 — Der Amboss (12", 1-sided, stickered plain black sleeve & labels, promo only) 12
88 Polydor 080 012-2 — Mind Of A Toy/We Move (Dance Mix)/Frequency 7 (Dance Mix)/ Mind Of A Toy (Video) (CD Video) 15
83 Polydor VIS 1 — FADE TO GREY (DANCE MIX PROMO) (LP, stamped white sleeve, promo only) 20

(see also Rich Kids, Steve Strange, Strange Cruise, Midge Ure, Ultravox)

TONY VISCONTI

79 Regal Zonophone RZ 3089 — I Remember Brooklyn/Sitting In A Field Of Heather 12

(see also Dib Cochran & Earwigs)

VISCOUNTS

60	Pye 7N 15249	That's All Right/Rockin' Little Angel	10
60	Pye 7N 15287	Shortnin' Bread/Fee-Fi-Fo-Fum	7
61	Pye 7N 15323	Money (Is The Root Of All Evil)/One Armed Bandit	7
61	Pye 7N 15344	Banned In Boston/Moonlight Promises	6
61	Pye 7N 15356	Joe Sweeney/Honey Come On And Dance With Me	6
61	Pye 7N 15379	Who Put The Bomp (In The Bomp, Bomp, Bomp)/What Am I Saying	7
62	Pye 7N 15414	Mama's Doin' The Twist/I'm Going But I'll Be Back	6
62	Pye 7N 15431	One Of The Guys/Dear Mary Brown	6
62	Pye 7N 15445	Everybody's Got A Ya Ya/Lot Of Livin' To Do	6
62	Pye 7N 15479	That Stranger Used To Be My Girl/Silent Night	6
63	Pye 7N 15510	Don't Let Me Cross Over/I'm Coming Home	6
63	Pye 7N 15536	It's You/I'll Never Get Over You	6
63	Columbia DB 7146	I Don't Care What People Say/Roll On Little Darlin'	6
64	Columbia DB 7253	Where Do You Belong/Kiss Me	6
64	Columbia DB 7436	Sally/On Broadway	6
60	Pye NEP 24132	VISCOUNTS' HIT PARADE (EP)	30

(see also Gordon Mills)

VISCOUNTS (U.S.)

59	Top Rank JAR 254	Harlem Nocturne/Dig	20
60	Top Rank JAR 388	The Touch (Le Grisbi)/Chug-A-Lug	20
60	Top Rank JAR 502	Night Train/Summertime	18
65	Stateside SS 468	Harlem Nocturne/Dig (reissue)	15
61	Top Rank JKP 3005	VISCOUNTS ROCK (EP)	90

VISIONS

69	Grape GR 3009	Captain Hook/The Girl	30

(see also King Horror)

VISITORS

78	NRG SRTS/NRG 002	Take It Or Leave It/No Compromise	30

VISITORS

79	Deep Heat DEEP ONE	Electric Heat/Moth/One Line (p/s)	8
80	Departure RAPTURE 1	Empty Rooms/The Orcadian Visitors (foldover p/s)	7
81	Rational RATE 2	Compatability/Poet's End (foldover p/s)	5

VISITORS

87	Sha La La BA BA BA BA BA 8	Goldmining/MAGIC SHOP: It's True (flexidisc, p/s, free with *Simply Thrilled* & other fanzines)	10/7

VITAL DISORDERS

85	Lowther International VD 3	Some People/Xmas Island Calypso (hand-screened p/s)	5

VITAL FORCE

87	Buce BUCE 1	Roll The Dice/Poor Little Rich Boy (no p/s)	25

AMOR VIVI

70	Big Shot BI 534	Dirty Dog/Round And Round The Moon	8

VIVIENNE

57	HMV 7EG 8290	VIVIENNE (EP)	8

VIXEN

88	EMI MTPD 48	Edge Of A Broken Heart/Charmed Life (shaped picture disc)	7
88	EMI MTL 1028	VIXEN (LP, early copies play extra track "Charmed Life", withdrawn)	12

VLADO & ISOLDA

84	Ariola 106 500	Ciao Amore (English)/Ciao Amore (Croatian)	10

VOGUES (U.K.)

66	Columbia DB 7985	Younger Girl/Lies	18

(see also Llan)

VOGUES (U.S.)

65	London HLU 9996	You're The One/Some Words	15
66	London HLU 10014	Five O'Clock World/Nothing To Offer You	15
66	King KG 1035	Magic Town/Humpty Dumpty	18
68	Reprise RS 20766	My Special Angel/I Keep It Hid	6
68	Reprise RS 20686	Turn Around Look At Me/Then	6
69	Reprise RS 20788	Till/I Will	6
69	London HLG 10247	Five O'Clock World/You're The One	15
69	Reprise RS 20820	Earth Angel/P.S. I Love You	6
69	Reprise RS 23366	No, Not Much/You Were Too Good To Me	6
69	Reprise RS 20844	Green Fields/Easy To Say	5
66	King KGL 4003	MEET THE VOGUES (LP)	40
66	King KGL 4006	FIVE O'CLOCK WORLD (LP)	35
69	Reprise RSLP 6314	TURN AROUND, LOOK AT ME (LP)	22
69	Reprise RSLP 6326	TILL (LP)	18

VOICE

66	Mercury MF 905	Train To Disaster/Truth	200

(see also Karl Stuart & Profile, Profile, Miller Anderson)

VOICEROYS

(see under Viceroys)

VOICES

56	Beltona BL 2667	Rock And Roll Hit Parade Medley (Parts 1 & 2)	25
56	Beltona BL 2667	Rock And Roll Hit Parade Medley (Parts 1 & 2) (78)	15

VOICES IN LATIN

68	Morgan MR 104P	VOICE IN LATIN (LP)	60

MINT VALUE £

VOICES OF EAST HARLEM
70 Elektra 2101 013 Right On Be Free/Gotta Be A Change — Oh Yeah . . . 7
70 Elektra 2101 018 No No No/Music In The Air. . . . 6
70 Elektra 2469 007 RIGHT ON BE FREE (LP) . . . 25

VOIDS
66 Polydor BM 56073 Come On Out/I'm In A Fix . . . 80

CRISTIAN VOGEL
94 Ferox FER 004 NARCO SYNTHESIS EP (12", plain sleeve) . . . 25
94 Mosquito MSQ 01 WE EQUATE MACHINES WITH FUNKINESS EP (12", custom sleeve) . . . 25
95 Mosquito MSQ 03 ARTISTS IN CHARGE OF EXPERT SYSTEMS EP (12", custom sleeve) . . . 20
99 Mosquito MSQ 014 BOOM BUSINE EP (12") . . . 12
(see also Blue Arsed Fly)

WES VOIGHT
59 Parlophone R 4586 I'm Movin' In/I'm Ready To Go Steady . . . 125
(see also Chip Taylor)

VOIZ
77 Pilgrim/Grapevine GRA 110 BOANERGES (LP, with insert) . . . 15

HOWARD VOKES COUNTRY BOYS
62 Starlite STEP 27 HOWARD VOKES COUNTRY BOYS (EP) . . . 20
63 Starlite STEP 37 MOUNTAIN GUITAR (EP) . . . 20
67 Starlite GRK 508 HOWARD VOKES COUNTRY BOYS
(EP; reissue, with sleeve sticker over original catalogue number) . . . 12

VOLCANOS
61 Philips PB 1098 Ruby Duby Du/Redhead . . . 20
61 Philips PB 1113 Tightrope/Great Imposter . . . 20
62 Philips PB 1246 Polaris/Scotch Mist . . . 18
60 Philips BBE 12432 THE VOLCANOS (EP) . . . 100

VOLTZ
82 Airship KNIGHT'S FALL (LP) . . . 100

VOLUMES
62 Fontana 270 109TF I Love You/Dreams . . . 120
63 London HL 9733 Sandra/Teenage Paradise . . . 70
68 Pama PM 755 I Just Can't Help Myself/One Way Lover (unreleased, test pressings only) . . . 300+

VOLUNTEERS
63 Parlophone R 5088 Farther Along/Little David . . . 10
(see also Karol Keyes)

VON BONDIES
03 Must Destroy DESTROYER 2 Tell Me What You See (p/s, 1-sided) . . . 15

VONTASTICS
66 Chess CRS 8043 Day Tripper/My Baby . . . 25
67 Stateside SS 2002 Lady Love/When My Baby Comes Back Home . . . 50

VON TRAP FAMILY
80 Woronzow W 001 Brand New Thrill/Dreaming/No Reflexes (p/s, 500 only) . . . 18
(see also Bevis Frond)

VOOMINS
65 Polydor 56001 If You Don't Come Back/March Of The Voomins . . . 18

VOXPOPPERS
58 Mercury 7MT 202 The Last Drag/Wishing For Your Love . . . 60
58 Mercury MT 202 The Last Drag/Wishing For Your Love (78) . . . 30
58 Mercury MEP 9533 VOXPOPPERS (EP) . . . 165

VOYAGER
85 Fighting Cock Run Away Heart/Don't Hold Back (p/s) . . . 15

V2
78 Bent SMALL BENT 1 Speed Freak/Nothing To Do/That's It (800 only, later reissued on red vinyl) . . . 15
79 TJM TJM 1 Man In The Box/When The World Isn't There (12", p/s) . . . 22
79 TJM TJM 6 Is Anybody Out There? (unissued)
70s Groove Gee Whiz It's You/Face In The Crowd (p/s, stamped white labels) . . . 30

VULCANS
73 Trojan TRLS 53 STAR TREK (LP) . . . 20

VULCAN'S HAMMER
73 Brown BVH 1 TRUE HEARTS AND SOUND BOTTOMS (LP, with insert) . . . 400+

VULTURES
79 Rubber Connection SP 522 Time Let's Go/Is This A Man (p/s, with insert & sticker) . . . 6

VULTURES
88 Narodnik NRK 006T Good Thing/You're Not Scared/What I Say/Jack The Ripper (12", p/s) . . . 8

V/VM
01 V/VM VVMT 147 SNOOKER LOOPY (SCREWED BACK BY V/VM) (8 x 7", unboxed set; red, yellow, green, brown, blue, pink, black, & white vinyl, poly inners with wraparound paper p/s; 147 sets only) . . . 40

V/VM & THIRD EYE FOUNDATION
97 Fat Cat 12FAT 006 Lumberjack WLTM/Female Pig Herder/Looks Unimportant Poss Romance/Will Travel North West/There's No End In Sight (12", custom 'bullet hole' sleeve) . . . 12

VYE
80 Dead Good DEAD 8 Five Hours 'Til Tonight/Right Girl, Wrong Time/Til Dawn (p/s, with insert) . . . 5

WACKERS
63 Oriole CB 1902 — I Wonder Why/Why Can't It Happen To Me . . . 18
64 Piccadilly 7N 35195 — Love Or Money/Hooka Tooka . . . 12
64 Piccadilly 7N 35210 — The Girl Who Wanted Fame/You're Forgetting . . . 12

ADAM WADE
60 Top Rank JAR 296 — Tell Her For Me/Don't Cry, My Love . . . 8
60 Top Rank JAR 370 — Ruby/Too Far . . . 8
60 HMV POP 764 — I Can't Help It/I Had The Craziest Dream . . . 6
60 HMV POP 787 — Speaking Of Her/Blackout The Moon . . . 6
60 HMV POP 807 — In Pursuit Of Happiness/For The Want Of Your Love . . . 7
61 HMV POP 843 — Take Good Care Of Her/Sleepy Time Gal . . . 6
61 HMV POP 896 — Point Of No Return/The Writing On The Wall . . . 6
61 HMV POP 913 — As If I Didn't Know/Playin' Around . . . 6
61 HMV POP 942 — Tonight I Won't Be There/Linda . . . 6
62 HMV POP 966 — Preview Of Paradise/Cold Cold Winter . . . 6
62 HMV POP 996 — Prisoner's Song/Them There Eyes . . . 6
62 Columbia DB 4891 — I'm Climbin'/They Didn't Believe Me . . . 5
63 Columbia DB 4962 — There'll Be No Teardrops Tonight/Here Comes The Pain . . . 5
63 Columbia DB 4986 — Don't Let Me Cross Over/Rain From The Skies . . . 5
63 Columbia DB 7045 — Why Do We Have To Wait So Long/They Say . . . 5
63 Columbia DB 7165 — Does Goodnight Mean Goodbye/Julie . . . 5
64 Columbia DB 7213 — Theme From 'Irma La Douce'/Charade . . . 5
60 HMV 7EG 8620 — AND THEN CAME ADAM (EP) . . . 18
64 Columbia SEG 8316 — FOUR FILM SONGS (EP) . . . 18
61 HMV CLP 1451 — ADAM AND EVENING (LP) . . . 30

CLIFF WADE
69 Morgan Bluetown BT 1S — You've Never Been To My House/Sister . . . 15

JOHNNY WADE
60 HMV POP 757 — Funny Thing/Shadow Love . . . 8

WELLINGTON WADE
63 Oriole CB 1857 — Let's Turkey Trot/It Ain't Necessarily So . . . 22
(see also Ian & Zodiacs)

ADRIAN WAGNER
74 Atlantic K 50082 — DISTANCES BETWEEN US (LP, with Robert Calvert) . . . 15
78 Charisma CAS 1135 — THE LAST INCA (LP, with booklet) . . . 12
(see also Robert Calvert)

ROBERT WAGNER
57 London HLU 8491 — Almost Eighteen/So Young . . . 22
57 London HLU 8491 — Almost Eighteen/So Young (78) . . . 10

CHUCK WAGON
79 A&M AMS 7450 — Rock 'n' Roll Won't Go Away/The Spy In My Face (p/s, black or purple vinyl) . 10/15
(see also Dickies)

PORTER WAGONER
67 RCA Victor RCA 1586 — The Cold Hard Facts Of Life/You Can't Make A Heel Toe The Mark . . . 6
64 RCA Victor RCX 7157 — A LITTLE SLICE OF LIFE (EP) . . . 15
64 RCA Victor RCX 7158 — Y'ALL COME (EP) . . . 15
64 RCA Victor RD 7693 — THE BLUE GRASS STORY (LP) . . . 20
65 RCA Camden CDN 5128 — AN OLD LOG CABIN FOR SALE (LP) . . . 12

WAH! (HEAT)
81 Inevitable INEV 001 — Better Scream/Joe (wraparound p/s in poly bag) . . . 5
81 Inevitable INEV 004 — Seven Minutes To Midnight/Don't Step On The Cracks (p/s, different colour sleeves) . . . 5
(see also Faction, Pete Wylie)

WAIKIKIS
61 Palette PG 9025 — Hawaii Tattoo/Waikiki Welcome . . . 6
65 Pye Intl. NPL 28060 — HAWAII BEACH PARTY (LP) . . . 12
65 Pye Intl. NPL 28063 — MERRY CHRISTMAS IN HAWAII (LP) . . . 12
65 Pye Intl. NPL 28072 — LOLLIPOPS AND ROSES (LP) . . . 12
66 Pye Intl. NPL 28081 — A TASTE OF HAWAII (LP) . . . 12

WAILERS (Jamaica)
(see under Bob Marley)

WAILERS (U.S.)
59 London HL 8958 — Tall Cool One/Road-Runner . . . 25
59 London HL 8958 — Tall Cool One/Road-Runner (78) . . . 15
59 London HL 8994 — Mau-Mau/Dirty Robber (tri centre, later round) . . . 150/75
59 London HL 8994 — Mau-Mau/Dirty Robber (78) . . . 120
64 London HL 9892 — Tall Cool One/Road-Runner (reissue) . . . 5

WAILING COCKS
78 Bird's Nest BN 116 — Rockin' Youth/Stand Up For Peace . . . 5
78 Bird's Nest BN 121 — Listen To The Wailing Cocks/Listen To The Wailing Cocks . . . 5

MINT VALUE £

WAILING SOULS

70	Banana BA 305	Row Fisherman Row/Thou Shalt Not Steal	18
70	Banana BA 307	Back Out/Pack Your Things	18
71	Banana BA 335	Walk Walk Walk/KING SPORTY: Love Me — Version (B-side actually by Denis Alcapone)	30
71	Green Door GD 4014	Harbour Shark/Harbour Shark — Version	25
72	Punch PH 106	Dungeon (as Wailing Soul)/NORA DEAN: Kiss Me Honey	45

(see also Denis Alcapone, Tuff Gong All Stars)

WAILING WAILERS

(see under Bob Marley & Wailers)

CHERRY WAINER

58	Pye 7N 15161	Itchy Twitchy Feeling/Cerveza	15
58	Pye N 15161	Itchy Twitchy Feeling/Cerveza (78)	6
58	Pye 7N 15170	Valencia/Blue Cha Cha	10
58	Pye N 15170	Valencia/Blue Cha Cha (78)	6
59	Pye 7N 15197	The Happy Organ/Spanish Marching Song	7
59	Pye N 15197	The Happy Organ/Spanish Marching Song (78)	6
59	Pye 7N 15217	The Song Of Lotus Lee/Iced Coffee	6
59	Pye N 15217	The Song Of Lotus Lee/Iced Coffee (78)	8
59	Top Rank JAR 253	I'll Walk The Line/Saturday Night In Tia Juana	8
60	Columbia DB 4528	Happy Like A Bell (Ding Dong)/Money (That's What I Want)	25
63	Honey Hit TB 128	Sleepwalk/Red River Rock (with Red Price Combo, some with p/s)	10/5
59	Pye NEP 24099	CHERRY WAINER (EP)	25
60	Top Rank BUY 042	WALTZES IN SPRINGTIME (LP)	18

(see also Red Price Combo)

PHIL WAINMAN

65	Columbia DB 7615	Hear Me A Drummer Man/Hear His Drums	12
68	Fontana TF 978	Going Going Gone/Hey Paradiddle	6

LOUDON WAINWRIGHT III

71	Atlantic 2400 103	ALBUM I (LP)	18
72	Atlantic K 40107	ALBUM I (LP, reissue)	12
72	Atlantic K 40272	ALBUM II (LP)	15

WAITING FOR THE SUN

78	Profile GMOR 167	WAITING FOR THE SUN (LP, private pressing)	75

(see also After The Fire)

TOM WAITS

79	Asylum K 12347	Somewhere/Red Shoes By The Drugstore	5
86	Island ISD 260	In The Neighbourhood/Singapore//Tango Till They're Sore/Rain Dogs (double pack, p/s)	5
73	Asylum SYM 9007	CLOSING TIME (LP, with insert)	22
74	Asylum SYM 9012	THE HEART OF SATURDAY NIGHT (LP)	18
75	Asylum SYSP 903	NIGHTHAWKS AT THE DINER (2-LP, gatefold sleeve)	20
76	Asylum K 53030	CLOSING TIME (LP, reissue)	12
76	Asylum K 53035	THE HEART OF SATURDAY NIGHT (LP, 'door' label)	12
77	Asylum K 53050	SMALL CHANGE (LP, 'sky' label)	12
77	Asylum K 53068	FOREIGN AFFAIRS (LP, with inner sleeve)	12
79	Asylum K 53088	BLUE VALENTINE (LP, gatefold sleeve)	12
80	Asylum K 52252	HEARTATTACK AND VINE (LP, with inner sleeve)	12
81	Elektra K 52316	BOUNCED CHEQUES (LP)	12
86	WEA 960 321-1	THE ASYLUM YEARS (2-LP, gatefold sleeve)	15
99	Epitaph 6457 251	MULE CONVERSATIONS (CD, p/s, jewel case, promo only)	20

(see also Roy Orbison)

WAKE

69	Pye 7N 17813	Angelina/So Happy	15
70	Carnaby CNS 4010	Live Today Little Girl/Days Of Emptiness	15
70	Carnaby CNS 4014	Boys In The Band/To Make You Happy	12
70	Carnaby CNS 4016	Noah/To Make You Happy	12
71	Carnaby 6151 001	Linda/Got My Eyes On You	12
70	Carnaby CNLS 6005	23.59 (LP)	90

WAKE

82	Scan SCN 01	On Our Honeymoon/Give Up (p/s in bag)	20
84	Scan 45/Factory FAC 88	Talk About The Past/Everybody Works So Hard (p/s)	7
84	Scan 45/Factory FAC 8812	Talk About The Past/Everybody Works So Hard (12", p/s)	12
87	Factory FAC12 178	Something No-one Else Can Bring/ Gruesome Castle	12
89	Sarah SARAH 21	Crush The Flowers/Carbrain (p/s)	7
90s	Sarah SARAH 48	Major John/Lousy Pop Group (p/s)	7
83	Factory FACT 60	HARMONY (LP)	25
91	Factory FACT 130	HERE COMES EVERYBODY (LP)	20
90s	Sarah SARAH 602	MAKE IT LOUD (LP)	15
90s	Sarah SARAH 618	TIDAL WAVE OF HYPE (LP)	15

JIMMY WAKELY

51	Capitol CL 13446	Telling My Troubles To My Old Guitar/My Heart Cries For You (78)	6
51	Capitol CL 13523	When You And I Were Young Maggie Blues/Fool's Paradise (78, with Margaret Whiting)	8
52	Capitol CL 13716	Missing In Action/Star Of Hope (with Margaret Whiting) (78)	6
52	Capitol CL 13787	A Four-Legged Friend/There's A Cloud In My Valley Of Sunshine (78, with Bob Hope)	8
52	Capitol CL 13812	I Went To Your Wedding/Pale Moon (78)	6
53	Capitol CL 13923	A Bushel And A Peck/Gomen-Nasai (Forgive Me) (78, with Margaret Whiting)	8
53	Capitol CL 14121	My Heart Knows/Tennessee Church Bells (78, with Margaret Whiting)	6
56	Vogue Coral Q 72125	Are You Mine? (with Ruth Ross)/Yellow Roses	15
56	Vogue Coral Q 72125	Are You Mine? (with Ruth Ross)/Yellow Roses (78)	8

			MINT VALUE £
56	Brunswick 05542	Are You Satisfied? (with Gloria Wood)/Mississippi Dreamboat	15
56	Brunswick 05542	Are You Satisfied? (with Gloria Wood)/Mississippi Dreamboat (78)	6
56	Brunswick 05563	Folsom Prison Blues/That's What The Lord Can Do	18
56	Brunswick 05563	Folsom Prison Blues/That's What The Lord Can Do (78)	10
57	Brunswick LAT 8179	SANTA FE TRAIL (LP)	22

(see also Karen Chandler, Bob Hope, Margaret Whiting)

RICK WAKEMAN (Band)

73	A&M AMS 7061	Catherine/Anne	5
75	A&M AMS 7206	Love's Dream/Orpheus' Song	6
75	A&M/Lyntone LYN 3176/7	Wagner's Dream/Love's Dream/Count Your Blessings (with 2 tracks by Roger Daltrey, flexidisc free with *19* magazine)	10/5
79	A&M AMS 7435	Birdman Of Alcatraz (Theme From 'My Son My Son')/Falcons De Neige (p/s)	5
79	A&M AMS 7436	Animal Showdown/Sea Horses (p/s)	5
79	A&M AMSP 7436	Animal Showdown/Sea Horses (picture disc, in PVC sleeve)	6
79	A&M AMS 7497	Swan Lager/Woolly Willy Tango	5
80	A&M AMS 7510	I'm So Straight I'm A Weirdo/Do You Believe In Fairies? (p/s)	5
80	WEA K 18354	The Spider/Danielle (some with p/s, 2,000 only)	8/4
71	Polydor 2460 135	PIANO VIBRATIONS (LP, with John Schroeder Orchestra)	15
74	A&M QU-84361	THE SIX WIVES OF HENRY VIII (LP, gatefold sleeve, quadrophonic mix)	18
75	A&M AMLH 64546	LISZTOMANIA (LP, soundtrack, with Roger Daltrey)	12
89	A&M RWCD 20	RICK WAKEMAN: 20TH ANNIVERSARY (4-CD box set, 1,000 only)	80

(see also Strawbs, Yes, Dib Cochran & Earwigs, Steve Howe, Jon Anderson)

ANTON WALBROOK

53	Parlophone MSP 6002	La Ronde De L'Amour/BERLIN 'SYMPHONIKER' ORCHESTRA: The Blue Waltz	10
54	Parlophone MSP 6099	Always Young/It Only Took A Minute	10
54	Parlophone MSP 6100	Strike Another Match/Man Is Man	10

JERRY WALD

60	London HLU 8909	Sheba/Moon Over Miami (unissued)	

HOWARD WALES

(see under Jerry Garcia)

WALHAM GREEN EAST WAPPING CARPET CLEANING RODENT & BOGGIT EXTERMINATING ASSOCIATION

68	Columbia DB 8426	Sorry Mr. Green/Death Of A Kind	55

ANNA WALKER & CROWNETTES

69	Pama PM 768	You Don't Know/Billy Joe	12

BILLY WALKER

64	Decca F 11917	My Heart Cries For You/Little On The Lonely Side	6
65	Columbia DB 7724	A Certain Girl/I Don't Wanna Fall In Love	7

BILLY WALKER (U.S.)

60	Philips PB 1001	Forever/Changed My Mind	8
66	London HLU 10060	Million And One/Close To Linda	8

BOOTS WALKER

69	London HLP 10265	No One Knows/Geraldine	7

CLINT WALKER

60	Warner Bros WEP 6006	INSPIRATION (EP, also stereo WSEP 2006)	12/18

DAVID WALKER

68	RCA RCA 1664	Ring The Changes/Keep A Little Love	40

(see also Paradox)

GARY WALKER (& RAIN)

66	CBS 202036	You Don't Love Me/Get It Right	20
66	CBS 202081	Twinkie-Lee/She Makes Me Feel Better	7
68	Polydor 56237	Spooky/I Can't Stand To Lose You (as Gary Walker & Rain)	15
69	Philips BF 1740	Come In You'll Get Pneumonia/Francis (as Gary Walker & Rain)	50
74	United Artists UP 35742	Hello How Are You/Fran	5
66	CBS EPS 5742	HERE'S GARY (EP)	35

(see also Walker Brothers, Paul & Ritchie & Cryin' Shames, Badfinger, Universals)

GRAHAM WALKER SOUND

69	Saga EROS 8126	FAMOUS TV THEMES (LP)	12

JACKIE WALKER

58	London HLP 8588	Oh Lonesome Me/Only Teenagers Allowed	270
58	London HLP 8588	Oh Lonesome Me/Only Teenagers Allowed (78)	60

JERRY JEFF WALKER

68	Atlantic 584 200	Mr Bojangles/Round And Round	6
68	Atco 228 006	MR BOJANGLES (LP)	15
71	Atlantic 2466 007	BEIN' FREE (LP)	15

JIMMY WALKER

53	Lyragon J 706	A Fine Romance/Hallelujah (78)	6

JOHN WALKER

67	Philips BF 1593	Anabella/You Don't Understand Me	10
67	Philips BF 1612	If I Promise/I See Love In You	6
68	Philips BF 1655	I'll Be Your Baby Tonight/Open The Door Homer	6
68	Philips BF 1676	Kentucky Woman/I Cried All The Way Home	6
68	Philips BF 1724	Woman/A Dream	5
69	Philips BF 1758	Yesterday's Sunshine/Little One	5
69	Carnaby CNS 4004	Everywhere Under The Sun/Traces Of Tomorrow	6
70	Carnaby CNS 4009	True Grit/Sun Comes Up	6
70	Carnaby CNS 4012	Cottonfields/Jamie	6

MINT VALUE £

70	Carnaby CNS 4017	Over And Over Again/Sun Comes Up	6
67	Philips (S)BL 7829	IF YOU GO AWAY (LP)	35
69	Carnaby CNLS 6001	THIS IS JOHN WALKER (LP)	35

(see also Walker Brothers, John & Scott Walker, Johnny & Judy)

JOHN & SCOTT WALKER

66	Philips BE 12597	SOLO JOHN — SOLO SCOTT (EP, 2 tracks each)	15

(see also Walker Brothers, Scott Walker, John Walker, Scott Engel)

JUNIOR WALKER & ALL STARS

65	Tamla Motown TMG 509	Shotgun/Hot'Cha	40
65	Tamla Motown TMG 520	Do The Boomerang/Tune Up	55
65	Tamla Motown TMG 529	Shake And Fingerpop/Cleo's Back	30
66	Tamla Motown TMG 550	Cleo's Mood/Baby You Know It Ain't Right	25
66	Tamla Motown TMG 559	Road Runner/Shoot Your Shot (original small label print, later large)	15/7
66	Tamla Motown TMG 571	How Sweet It Is (To Be Loved By You)/Nothing But Soul (small label print)	15
67	Tamla Motown TMG 571	How Sweet It Is (To Be Loved By You)/Nothing But Soul (later pressing)	7
66	Tamla Motown TMG 586	Money (That's What I Want) Parts 1& 2	18
67	Tamla Motown TMG 596	Pucker Up Buttercup/Any Way You Wanna	20
68	Tamla Motown TMG 637	Come See About Me/Sweet Soul	10
68	Tamla Motown TMG 667	Hip City Parts 1 & 2	15
69	Tamla Motown TMG 682	Home Cookin'/Mutiny	12
69	Tamla Motown TMG 691	Road Runner/Shotgun	6
69	Tamla Motown TMG 712	What Does It Take (To Win Your Love)/Brainwasher	5
70	Tamla Motown TMG 727	These Eyes/I've Got To Find A Way To Win Maria Back	8
70	Tamla Motown TMG 750	Do You See My Love (For You Growing)/Groove And Move	7
72	Tamla Motown TMG 824	Walk In The Night/Right On Brothers And Sisters/ Gotta Hold On To This Feeling (maxi-single)	5
73	Tamla Motown TMG 840	Take Me Girl, I'm Ready/I Don't Want To Do Wrong	5
73	Tamla Motown TMG 857	Way Back Home (Vocal)/Way Back Home (Instrumental)	8
73	Tamla Motown TMG 857	Way Back Home (Vocal)/Way Back Home (Instrumental)/Country Boy (reissue)	5
73	Tamla Motown TMG 872	Wholly Holy/Peace And Understanding Is Hard To Find	5
74	Tamla Motown TMG 889	Don't Blame The Children/Soul Clappin'	5
74	Tamla Motown TMG 894	Gotta Hold On To This Feeling/I Ain't Going Nowhere	5
76	Tamla Motown TMG 1027	I'm So Glad/Dancin' Like They Do On Soul Train (as Jr. Walker)	5
66	Tamla Motown TME 2013	SHAKE AND FINGERPOP (EP)	50
65	Tamla Motown TML 11017	SHOTGUN (LP)	65
66	T. Motown (S)TML 11029	SOUL SESSION (LP, mono/stereo)	45/60
66	T. Motown (S)TML 11038	ROAD RUNNER (LP, mono/stereo)	40/45
69	T. Motown (S)TML 11097	HOME COOKIN' (LP)	35
69	T. Motown (S)TML 11120	JUNIOR WALKER'S GREATEST HITS (LP, original with flipback sleeve)	20
70	T. Motown (S)TML 11140	THESE EYES (LP)	30
70	T. Motown STML 11152	LIVE (LP)	25
70	T. Motown STML 11167	A GASSSSSSSSSS! (LP)	25
72	T. Motown STML 11198	RAINBOW FUNK (LP)	18
72	T. Motown STML 11211	MOODY JR. (LP)	15
73	T. Motown STML 11234	PEACE AND UNDERSTANDING IS HARD TO FIND (LP)	12
75	T. Motown STML 11274	JR. WALKER AND THE ALL STARS (LP)	12
76	T. Motown STML 12018	HOT SHOT (by Jr. Walker)	15
76	T. Motown STML 12033	SAX APPEAL (by Jr. Walker)	15
76	Motown STML 12048	WHOPPER BOPPER SHOW STOPPER (by Jr. Walker)	12

KARL WALKER & ALLSTARS

66	Rymska RA 103	One Minute To Zero/Don't Come Back (both sides actually featuring Tommy McCook & Supersonics)	40

(see also Kent Walker, Ernel Braham)

KENT WALKER

68	Fab FAB 53	When You Going To Show Me How/Come Yah Come Yah	10

(see also Karl Walker, Ernel Braham)

ROB WALKER

71	Upsetter US 366	Run Up Your Mouth (actually by Stranger Cole)/UPSETTERS: Mouth Version	12
71	Jackpot JP 761	Hear My Heart/Puppet On A String	12

(see also Stranger Cole, Tommy McCook)

RONNIE WALKER

69	Stateside SS 2151	It's A Good Feeling/Precious	20
75	Polydor 2006 578	Magic's In The Air/They Can't Say Hello	6

SCOTT WALKER

67	Philips BF 1628	Jackie/The Plague	8
68	Philips BF 1662	Joanna/Always Coming Back To You	8
69	Philips BF 1793	Lights of Cincinnati/Two Weeks Since You've Gone	7
71	Philips 6006 168	I Still See You/My Way Home	7
73	Philips 6006 311	The Me I Never Knew/This Way Mary	6
73	CBS 1795	A Woman Left Lonely/Where Love Has Died	6
74	CBS 2521	Delta Dawn/We Had It All	6
84	Virgin VS 666	Track 3/Blanket Roll Blues (p/s)	5
67	Philips MCP 1006	GREAT SCOTT (cassette EP)	20
67	Philips (S)BL 7816	SCOTT (LP, mono/stereo)	18/22
68	Philips BL 7840	SCOTT 2 (LP, mono, originally with signed portrait)	25/15
68	Philips SBL 7840	SCOTT 2 (LP, stereo, originally with signed portrait)	35/20
68	Ember EMB LP 3393	LOOKING BACK WITH SCOTT WALKER (LP, mono or stereo)	25
69	Philips SBL 7882	SCOTT 3 (LP, gatefold sleeve)	35
69	Philips SBL 7900	SCOTT WALKER SINGS SONGS FROM HIS TV SERIES (LP)	18
69	Philips SBL 7910	THE BEST OF SCOTT WALKER VOL. 1 (LP)	18
69	Philips SBL 7913	SCOTT 4 (LP)	45
70	Philips 6308 035	'TIL THE BAND COMES IN (LP)	50

MINT VALUE £

72 Philips 6382 007 THIS IS... SCOTT WALKER (LP) 20
72 Philips 6308 127 THE MOVIEGOER (LP) 40
73 Philips 6308 148 ANY DAY NOW (LP) 40
73 CBS 65725 STRETCH (LP) 25
73 Philips 6850 013 THE ROMANTIC SCOTT WALKER (LP, Audio Club issue) 35
73 Philips 6856 022 TERRIFIC (LP, Audio Club issue, reissue of "Scott 2" with different tracks) 40
73 Philips 6382 052 THIS IS SCOTT WALKER VOL. 2 (LP) 12
74 CBS 80254 WE HAD IT ALL (LP) 20
76 Philips 6625 017 SPOTLIGHT ON SCOTT WALKER (2-LP) 18
81 Zoo ZOO 2 FIRE ESCAPE IN THE SKY — THE GODLIKE GENIUS OF SCOTT WALKER (LP) . 20
81 Philips 6359 090 SINGS JACQUES BREL (LP) 12
95 Fontana SWINT 1 TILT INTERVIEW CD (CD, promo only) 18
(see also Scott Engel, Scott Engel & John Stewart, John & Scott Walker, Walker Brothers, Routers)

STEWART WALKER

98 Mosquito MSQ 012 ARTIFICIAL MUSIC FOR ARTIFICIAL PEOPLE (12" EP) 15

T-BONE WALKER

54 London HL 8087 The Hustle Is On/Baby Broke My Heart (78) 30
65 Liberty LIB 12018 Party Girl/Here In The Dark 20
63 London REP 1404 TRAVELLIN' BLUES (EP) 100
54 Capitol LC 6681 CLASSICS IN JAZZ (10" LP) 80
63 Capitol T 1958 T-BONE WALKER (LP) 50
65 MFP MFP 1043 THE BLUES OF T-BONE WALKER (LP) 30
65 Liberty LBY 4047 SINGS THE BLUES (LP) 60
66 Liberty LBY 3057 SINGING THE BLUES (LP) 60
68 MCA MUPS 331 THE TRUTH (LP) 25
68 Stateside S(S)L 10223 STORMY MONDAY BLUES (LP) 40
69 Stateside S(S)L 10265 FUNKY TOWN (LP) 35
73 Reprise K 94001 VERY RARE (2-LP) 18
74 Atlantic K 40131 T-BONE BLUES (LP) 15

WENDY WALKER

63 Decca F 11573 Window Shopping/Ain't A Boy In The World 8
63 Decca F 11671 Boys Will Be Happy/Casanova 8

WALKER BROTHERS

65 Philips BF 1401 Pretty Girls Everywhere/Doin' The Jerk 12
65 Philips BF 1409 Love Her/The Seventh Dawn 8
65 Philips BF 1428 Make It Easy On Yourself/But I Do 6
65 Philips BF 1454 My Ship Is Coming In/You're All Around Me 6
66 Philips BF 1473 The Sun Ain't Gonna Shine Anymore/After The Lights Go Out 6
66 Philips BF 1497 (Baby) You Don't Have To Tell Me/My Love Is Growing 6
66 Philips BF 1514 Another Tear Falls/The Saddest Night In The World 7
66 Philips BF 1537 Deadlier Than The Male/Archangel 7
67 Philips BF 1548 Stay With Me Baby/Turn Out The Moon 7
67 Philips BF 1576 Walking In The Rain/Baby Make It The Last Time 7
76 GTO GT 42 No Regrets/Remember Me 5
76 GTO GT 67 Lines/First Day 6
77 GTO GT 78 We're All Alone/Have You Seen My Baby 6
78 GTO GT 230 The Electrician/Den Haague (p/s) 6
78 GTO GT 295 Shutout/The Electrician/Nite Flights/Fat Mama Kick 5
66 Philips BE 12596 I NEED YOU (EP) 15
67 Philips BE 12603 THE WALKER BROTHERS (EP, probably unreleased)
67 Philips MCP 1004 THE HITS OF THE WALKER BROTHERS & DUSTY SPRINGFIELD (cassette EP) . 12
65 Philips BL 7691 TAKE IT EASY WITH THE WALKER BROTHERS (LP) 18
66 Philips (S)BL 7732 PORTRAIT (LP, with photo insert, mono/stereo) 20/30
67 Philips (S)BL 7770 IMAGES (LP) 20
67 Philips DBL 002 THE WALKER BROTHERS STORY (2-LP) 20
68 Wing WL 1188 THE FABULOUS WALKER BROTHERS (LP) 15
(see also Scott Walker, Scott Engel, John Walker, John & Scott Walker, Gary Walker [& Rain], Routers)

WALKIE TALKIES

79 Sire SIR 4023 Rich And Nasty/Summer In Russia (p/s) 6
(see also Pauline Murray & Invisible Girls, Mission)

WALKING FLOORS

80s My Death Telephone TEL 1 No Next Time/Removal (foldover p/s) 8

FRED WALKING-STICK & ELECTRIC WIRELESS ORCHESTRA

61 Pye 7N 15390 Well I Ask Yew/Ain't She Sweet 5

DENNIS WALKS

68 Amalgamated AMG 816 Having A Party/GROOVERS: Day By Day 20
68 Blue Cat BS 144 Belly Lick/DRUMBAGO & BLENDERS: The Game Song 25
69 Bullet BU 402 Heart Don't Leap/CLARENDONIANS: I Am Sorry 12
69 Bullet BU 408 Love Of My Life/Under The Shady Tree 12
71 Moodisc HM 101 Time Will Tell/Under The Shady Tree 7
74 Magnet MG 062 Don't Play That Song/Version 6
(see also I Roy)

SHELTON WALKS

73 Bullet BU 550 No Money No Friend/BOB MAC ALL STARS: Money Dub 6
74 Dip DL 5026 One Of Us Will Weep/KING EDWARDS ALL STARS: Version 6

WALL

79 Small Wonder SMALL 13 New Way/Suckers/Uniforms (p/s) 5
80 Fresh FRESHLP 2 PERSONAL TROUBLES AND PUBLIC ISSUES (LP) 15
(see also Ski Patrol)

MINT VALUE £

MAX WALL

51	Polygon P 1028	Take It Easy/Me And My Tune (78)	6
73	York YR 203	The Fiddley Foodle Bird/Story Of The Fiddley Foodle Bird	6
75	DJM DJS 10352	Why Should I Care/Devil Bomb	5
77	Stiff BUY 12	England's Glory/Dream Tobacco (p/s)	5

REM WALL & HIS GREEN VALLEY BOYS

60	Top Rank JAR 324	Heartsick And Blue/One More Time	10

ERROL WALLACE

69	Escort ES 817	Bandit/ASTON BORROT: Family Man Mood (actually by Aston "Family Man" Barrett)	10

GIG WALLACE & HIS ORCHESTRA

60	Philips PB 981	Rockin' On The Railroad/Show Me The Way To Go Home	10
60	Philips PB 981	Rockin' On The Railroad/Show Me The Way To Go Home (78)	25

IAN WALLACE

61	Parlophone R 4726	I Can't Do My Bally Bottom Button Up/In Other Words	6

JERRY WALLACE

54	Polygon P 1133	Dixieanna/Runnin' After Love (78)	10
58	London HL 8719	With This Ring/How The Time Flies	30
58	London HL 8719	With This Ring/How The Time Flies (78)	15
58	London HL 7062	With This Ring/How The Time Flies (export issue)	15
59	London HLH 8943	Primrose Lane/By Your Side	12
59	London HLH 8943	Primrose Lane/By Your Side (78)	25
60	London HLH 9040	Little Coco Palm/Mission Bell Blues	12
60	London HLH 9110	You're Singing Our Love Song To Somebody Else/King Of The Mountain	12
60	London HLH 9177	Swingin' Down The Lane/Teardrop In The Rain	10
61	London HLH 9264	There She Goes/Angel On My Shoulder	10
61	London HLH 9363	Life's A Holiday/I Can See An Angel	10
62	London HLH 9630	Shutters And Boards/Am I That Easy To Forget	10
64	London HLH 9914	Even The Bad Times Are Good/In The Misty Moonlight	10
65	Mercury MF 853	Time/Rainbow	8

SIPPIE WALLACE

67	Storyville 671 198	SIPPIE WALLACE SINGS THE BLUES (LP)	25

WALLACE BROTHERS

64	Sue WI 334	Precious Words/You're Mine	30
65	Sue WI 355	Lover's Prayer/Love Me Like I Love You	35
67	Sue WI 4036	I'll Step Aside/Hold My Heart For A While	35
67	Sue ILP 950	SOUL CONNECTION (LP)	200

WALLACE COLLECTION

69	Parlophone R 5764	Daydream/Baby I Don't Mind	15
69	Parlophone R 5793	Fly Me To The Earth/Love	10
70	Parlophone R 5844	Serenade/Walk On Out	10
69	Parlophone PMC/PCS 7076	LAUGHING CAVALIER (LP)	25
70	Parlophone PCS 7099	WALLACE COLLECTION (LP)	22

'FATS' WALLER (& HIS RHYTHM)

SINGLES

50	London L 808	Laughin' Cryin' Blues/JAMES P. JOHNSON: Roumania (78)	6
51	HMV JO 205	It's A Sin To Tell A Lie/Come Down To Earth My Angel (78, export issue)	7
51	London L 1032	Cow Cow Boogie/TEDDY WEATHERFOOD: Sugar Foot Stomp (78)	7
52	HMV JO 291	I'm On A See-Saw/As Long As The World Goes 'Round (78, export issue)	6
53	HMV 7M 128	My Very Good Friend The Milkman/Shortnin' Bread	10
53	HMV 7M 157	A Good Man Is Hard To Find/The Girl I Left Behind Me	8
53	HMV 7M 142	Honey Hush/You've Been Reading My Mail	10
54	HMV 7M 208	You've Been Taking Lessons In Love/I've Got A New Lease Of Life	8
54	HMV 7M 244	By The Light Of The Silvery Moon/Romance A La Mode (with Deep River Boys)	10
54	HMV B 10748	By The Light Of The Silvery Moon/Romance A La Mode (78)	6
60	RCA RCA 1189	Dinah/When Somebody Thinks You're Wonderful	5

EPs

54	HMV 7EG 8022	FATS WALLER AND HIS RHYTHM	8
54	HMV 7EG 8042	FATS WALLER AND HIS RHYTHM	8
54	HMV 7EG 8054	FATS WALLER AND HIS RHYTHM	8
55	HMV 7EG 8078	FATS WALLER AND HIS RHYTHM	8
55	HMV 7EG 8098	FATS WALLER	8
56	HMV 7EG 8148	FATS WALLER AND HIS RHYTHM	8
56	HMV 7EG 8191	SWINGING AT THE ORGAN	8
57	HMV 7EG 8212	FATS WALLER	8
57	HMV 7EG 8242	FATS WALLER AND HIS RHYTHM	8
57	HMV 7EG 8255	FATS WALLER AND HIS RHYTHM	8
58	HMV 7EG 8304	FATS WALLER IN LONDON NO. 1	8
58	HMV 7EG 8341	FATS WALLER IN LONDON NO. 2	8
59	RCA RCX 1010	FATS WALLER	8
59	RCA RCX 1053	YOUR FEET'S TOO BIG	10
60	HMV 7EG 8602	FATS WALLER IN LONDON NO. 3	8

LPs

53	London AL 3507	REDISCOVERED FATS WALLER SOLOS (10")	25
53	HMV DLP 1008	FAVOURITES (10")	20
53	HMV DLP 1017	PLAYS AND SINGS (10")	20
54	HMV DLP 1056	RHYTHM AND ROMANCE WITH FATS WALLER (10")	15
54	London AL 3521	FATS AT THE ORGAN (10")	20
54	London AL 3522	JIVIN' WITH FATS (10")	20
55	HMV DLP 1082	FUN WITH FATS (10")	15

			MINT VALUE £
55	HMV CLP 1036	THOMAS "FATS" WALLER NO. 1	12
55	HMV CLP 1042	THOMAS "FATS" WALLER NO. 2	12
56	HMV DLP 1111	YOUNG FATS WALLER (10")	15
56	HMV DLP 1118	FAVOURITES NO. 2 (10")	15
57	HMV DLP 1138	SPREADIN' RHYTHM AROUND (10")	20
57	RCA RD 27047	FATS 1935-1937	15
58	RCA RC 24004	FATS 1938-1942 (10")	15
59	RCA Camden CDN 131	THE REAL FATS WALLER	12
60	RCA RD 27185	HANDFUL OF KEYS	12

(see also Louisiana Sugar Babies, Deep River Boys, James P. Johnson)

GORDON (WALLER)

68	Columbia DB 8337	Rosecrans Boulevard/Red, Cream And Velvet	12
68	Columbia DB 8440	Every Day/Because Of A Woman	10
68	Columbia DB 8518	Weeping Annaleah/The Seventh Hour	10
69	Bell BLL 1059	I Was A Boy When You Needed A Man/Lady In The Window	6
70	Bell BLL 1106	You're Gonna Hurt Yourself/Sunshine	6
72	Vertigo 6360 069	GORDON (LP, as Gordon, gatefold sleeve, swirl label)	90

(see also Peter & Gordon)

BOB WALLIS & HIS STORYVILLE JAZZMEN

60	Top Rank JAR 331	Bluebird/Captain Morgan	6
60	Top Rank JAR 365	Madison Time/Bonne Nuit, Ma Cherie	6
60	Pye Jazz 7NJ 2039	Jingle Bells/Chinatown, My Chinatown	5
61	Pye Jazz 7NJ 2043	I'm Shy Mary Ellen I'm Shy/Three Live Wires	6
61	Pye Jazz 7NJ 2048	Come Along Please/Bobbin' Along	6
57	77 EP 10	NEW ORLEANS JAM SESSION VOLUME 1 (EP)	25
60	Pye Jazz NJE 1079	BOB WALLIS STORYVILLE JAZZMEN (EP)	10
60	Pye Jazz NJE 1085	BOB WALLIS PLAYS (EP)	12
62	Storyville SEP 368	BOB WALLIS STORYVILLE JAZZMEN (EP)	10
59	77 Records 77LE 12/2	THE RAVING SOUNDS OF BOB WALLIS (LP)	50
60	Top Rank BUY 023	EVERYBODY LOVES SATURDAY NIGHT (LP)	30
61	Pye Jazz NJL 27	OLE MAN RIVER (LP)	40
61	Pye Jazz NJL 30	TRAVELLIN' BLUES (LP)	25
62	Pye Jazz NJL 41	THE WALLIS COLLECTION (LP)	20

BOB WALLIS & SANDY BROWN

62	Pye Jazz 7NJ 2060	Oh Didn't It Rain/In A Little Spanish Town	6

LARRY WALLIS

77	Stiff BUY 22	Police Car/On Parole (with p/s or die-cut company sleeve)	5/4

(see also Pink Fairies, Subs, Deviants, Shagrat, Peter Wyngarde)

SHANI WALLIS

60	Philips PB 1019	Sixteen Reasons (Why I Love You)/Forever, Forever	5
60	Philips PB 1076	Where's The Boy/And Now	5
63	Decca F 11632	My Heart Cries For You/All Over Again	5
67	London HLR 10125	Look Of Love/Let Your Love Come Through	5
68	London HLR 10225	As Long As He Needs Me/Where Is Love	5

(see also Kirchin Band)

WALL OF SLEEP

95	Woronzow WOO 24	WALL OF SLEEP (LP, with insert)	12

WALL OF VOODOO

82	Illegal ILS 31	On Interstate 15/There's Nothing On This Side	7
83	Illuminated ILS 0036	Mexican Radio/Call Of The West (p/s)	5

WALLY BROTHERS

74	Explosion EX 2090	The Man Who Sold The World/Version	5

WALRUS

70	Deram DM 308	Who Can I Trust?/Tomorrow Never Comes	18
71	Deram DM 323	Never Let My Body Touch Ground/Why?	15
71	Deram SML 1072	WALRUS (LP)	50

JAMES WALSH GYPSY BAND

79	RCA PB 1403	Cuz It's You Girl/Bring Yourself Together (withdrawn, demo-only)	20

SHEILA WALSH & CLIFF RICHARD

81	DJM DJS 10992	Star Song/Burn On (no p/s, as Sheila Walsh [Cliff Richard on backing vocals])	5
83	DJM SHEIL 1	Drifting/It's Lonely When The Lights Go Out (p/s)	5
83	DJM SHEIL 100	Drifting/It's Lonely When The Lights Go Out (picture disc)	10
83	DJM SHEILT 1	Drifting/It's Lonely When The Lights Go Out (12", p/s)	8
83	DJM SHEILT 100	Drifting/It's Lonely When The Lights Go Out (12", picture disc)	12
83	DJM DJF 20581	DRIFTING (LP, with inner sleeve, as Sheila Walsh)	12

(see also Cliff Richard)

BURT WALTERS

68	Trojan TR 636	Honey Love/KING CANNONBALL BRYAN: Thunderstorm	12

(see also Lee 'Scratch' Perry)

DAVE WALTON

66	CBS 202057	Love Ain't What It Used To Be/Tell Me A Lie	8
66	CBS 202098	Every Window In The City/I've Left The Troubled Ground	6
67	CBS 202508	After You There Can Be Nothing/Can I Get It From You	7

RON WALTON

76	Gull GULS40	Soul Disco/ Always Be The One	15

TRAVIS WAMMACK

65	Atlantic AT 4017	Scratchy/Fire Fly	30
72	United Artists UP 35412	Whatever Turns You On/Slip Away	5
73	United Artists UP 35468	So Good/Darling, You're All That I Need	5

MINT VALUE £

WANDERER

59	Top Rank JAR 183	The Happy Hobo/True True Happiness	7
59	Top Rank JAR 183	The Happy Hobo/True True Happiness (78)	12

WANDERERS

81	Polydor POSP 239	Ready To Snap/Beyond The Law	35
81	Polydor POSP 284	The Times They Are A'Changin'/Little Bit Frightening	8
81	Polydor POLS 1028	ONLY LOVERS LEFT (LP)	20

(see also Lords Of The New Church, Stiv Bators, Dead Boys)

WANDERERS (Jamaica)

69	Trojan TR 7721	Wiggle Waggle/Jaga Jaga War	7

WANDERERS (U.S.)

60	MGM MGM 1102	I Could Make You Mine/I Need You More	50
61	MGM MGM 1169	As Time Goes By/There Is No Greater Love	25
64	United Artists UP 1020	Run Run Senorita/After He Breaks Your Heart	30

(see also Ray Pollard)

WANGLERS

79	Matchbox Classics MC 5	KICKIN' OUT FOR THE COAST (EP, white label, yellow or red stickered foldover p/s)	25

DEXTER WANSEL

86	Streetwave SWAVE 9	Life On Mars (Parts 1 & 2) (12", p/s)	12
78	Phil. Intl. PIR 82786	VOYAGER (LP)	20

WAR

71	Liberty LBF 15443	Sun Oh Son/Lonely Feelin'	6
71	United Artists UP 35281	All Day Music/Get Down	6
72	United Artists UP 35327	Slippin' Into Darkness/Nappy Head	5
73	United Artists UP 35469	The World Is A Ghetto/Four Cornered Room	5
73	United Artists UP 35521	The Cisco Kid/Beetles In The Bag	5
73	United Artists UP 35576	Gypsy Man/Deliver The Word	5
74	United Artists UP 35623	Me And Baby Brother/In Your Eyes	5
75	United Artists UP 35836	Why Can't We Be Friends/In Mazatlan	5
76	Island WIP 6267	Low Rider/So	5
77	MCA MCA 339	Galaxy/Version (12")	5
71	Liberty LBG 83478	WAR (LP)	8
72	United Artists UAS 29269	ALL DAY MUSIC (LP)	15
73	United Artists UAS 29400	THE WORLD IS A GHETTO (LP)	15
73	United Artists UAG 29521	DELIVER THE WORD (LP)	12
75	United Artists UAG 29843	WHY CAN'T WE BE FRIENDS (LP)	12
76	Island ILPS 9413	GREATEST HITS (LP)	12
77	Island ILPS 9507	PLATINUM FUNK (LP)	12
78	MCA MCF 2822	GALAXY (LP)	12
79	MCA MCG 4001	THE MUSIC BAND (LP)	12
79	MCA MCF 2804	YOUNGBLOOD (LP, soundtrack)	12

(see also Eric Burdon & War)

BILLY WARD & HIS DOMINOES

53	Parlophone R 3789	Don't Thank Me/Rags To Riches (78)	55
54	Parlophone MSP 6112	Three Coins In The Fountain/Lonesome Road	175
54	Parlophone R 3882	Three Coins In The Fountain/Lonesome Road (78)	40
56	Brunswick 05599	St. Therese Of The Roses/Home Is Where You Hang Your Heart	55
56	Brunswick 05599	St. Therese Of The Roses/Home Is Where You Hang Your Heart (78)	6
57	Brunswick 05656	Evermore/Half A Love (Is Better Than None)	30
57	Brunswick 05656	Evermore/Half A Love (Is Better Than None) (78)	8
57	London HLU 8465	Stardust/Lucinda	25
57	London HLU 8465	Stardust/Lucinda (78)	6
57	London HLU 8502	Deep Purple/Do It Again	25
57	London HLU 8502	Deep Purple/Do It Again (78)	6
58	London HLU 8634	Jennie Lee/Music, Maestro, Please	35
58	London HLU 8634	Jennie Lee/Music, Maestro, Please (78)	25
59	London HLU 8883	Please Don't Say 'No'/Behave, Hula Girl	20
59	London HLU 8883	Please Don't Say 'No'/Behave, Hula Girl (78)	20
58	London REU 1114	BILLY WARD & HIS DOMINOES (EP)	190
58	Parlophone PMD 1061	BILLY WARD & HIS DOMINOES FEATURING CLYDE McPHATTER (10" LP)	700
58	London HA-U 2116	YOURS FOREVER (LP)	60

(see also Dominoes, Clyde McPhatter, Jackie Wilson)

CHRISTINE WARD

66	Decca F 12339	The Face Of Empty Me/Girl I Used To Know	18

CLARA WARD & HER SINGERS

65	Stateside SS 474	Gonna Build A Mountain/God Bless The Child	10

CLIFFORD T. WARD

72	Dandelion 2001 327	Carrie/Sidetrack	12
72	Dandelion 2001 382	Coathanger/Rayne	8
73	Charisma CB 212	Wherewithal/Thinking Of Something To Do	6
74	Charisma CB 233	Jayne/Maybe I'm Right	6
75	Charisma CB 248	Jigsaw Girl/Cellophane	6
75	Philips 6006 490	No More Rock'n'Roll/Gandalf	6
76	Philips 6006 542	Ocean Of Love/Tomorrow Night	6
77	Mercury 6007 132	Up In The World/Not Waving, Drowning (Revisited)	6
77	Mercury 6007 149	I Got Lost Tonight/Detriment (p/s)	7
77	Mercury LUV 1	Someone I Know/If I Had Known (gatefold p/s)	8
80	WEA K 18294	Convertible/Taking The Long Way Round	7
81	WEA K 18426	The Best Is Yet To Come/Lost Again	7
81	WEA K 18486	Contrary/Climate Of Her Favour	7

84 Philips 880 550 7 Messenger/Where Do Angels Really Come From (p/s) 8
86 Tembo TML 114 Cricket/Computer 10
86 Tembo TML 123 Sometime Next Year/Turbo (p/s) 8
72 Dandelion 2310 216 SINGER SONGWRITER (LP) 20
73 Charisma CAS 1006 HOME THOUGHTS (LP) 20
75 Charisma CAS 1098 ESCALATOR (LP) 18
75 Philips 9109 500 NO MORE ROCK'N'ROLL (LP) 15
75 Philips 9109 216 WAVES (LP) 15
77 Mercury 9109 605 NEW ENGLAND DAYS (LP, with insert) 12
84 Philips 814 777 BOTH OF US (LP, with insert) 15
86 Tembo TMB 111 SOMETIME NEXT YEAR (LP) 15
92 Ameless AME 101 LAUGH IT OFF (LP, first 100 with inserts) 15/12
(see also Secrets, Simon's Secrets, Martin Raynor & Secrets)

DALE WARD

64 London HLD 9835 Oh Julie/Letter From Sherry 18

HEDLEY WARD TRIO

50 HMV B 9911 Enjoy Yourself/Women (78) 6
50 HMV B 9951 Three Wheels On The Wagon/M-I-S-S-I-S-S-I-P-P-I (78) 8
55 Melodisc MEL 1344 Rock Around The Clock/Who Dat Up There (78) 12
56 Melodisc MEL 1352 Who's Sorry Now/Big Ears (78) 10
56 Melodisc MEL 1387 Steamboat Rock/My Baby's Got Such Lovin' Ways (78) 25

ROBIN WARD

63 London HLD 9821 Wonderful Summer/Dream Boy 18

TERRY WARD with BUMBLIES

65 Fontana TF 558 Gotta Tell/When I Come To You 8

SHEELAGH WARDE

59 Top Rank JAR 131 Let Mr. Maguire Sit Down/The Golden Jubilee 7
59 Top Rank JAR 131 Let Mr. Maguire Sit Down/The Golden Jubilee (78) 8

WARDENS

70s SNO PEAS TIC 001 Lust Like This/Do So Well (with insert) 20

WARD SINGERS

56 London Jazz EZ-C 19024 THE FAMOUS WARD SINGERS (EP) 22
56 London Jazz LZ-C 14013 THE FAMOUS WARD SINGERS (10" LP) 30

WARDS OF COURT

67 Deram DM 127 All Night Girl/How Could Say One Thing 40

LEON WARE

77 Motown STML 12050 MUSICAL MASSAGE (LP) 15

WARHORSE

71 Vertigo 6059 027 St. Louis/No Chance 18
70 Vertigo 6360 015 WARHORSE (LP, swirl label, gatefold sleeve) 40
72 Vertigo 6360 066 RED SEA (LP, swirl label, gatefold sleeve) 40
(see also Deep Purple, Nic Simper's Fandango)

FRED WARING & HIS PENNSYLVANIANS

59 Capitol CL 14981 Dry Bones/Way Back Home 5
55 Brunswick OE 9194 THE BALLAD OF DAVY CROCKETT (EP) 12
51 Brunswick LAT 8011 LISTENING TIME (LP) 15
53 Brunswick LA 8625 WALT DISNEY FILM SONGS (10" LP) 18
54 Brunswick LA 8651 A SONG OF EASTER (10" LP) 15
54 Brunswick LA 8678 SONGS OF INSPIRATION (10" LP) 15
54 Brunswick LA 8693 'TWAS THE NIGHT BEFORE CHRISTMAS (10" LP) 15
55 Brunswick LA 8704 HARMONIZIN' THE OLD SONGS (10" LP) 15
55 Brunswick LAT 8068 FOR LISTENING ONLY (LP) 12

RAY WARLEIGH

69 Philips (S)BL 7881 RAY WARLEIGH'S FIRST ALBUM (LP) 25
(see also John Mayall's Blues Breakers, Alexis Korner)

OZZIE WARLOCK & WIZARDS

59 HMV POP 635 Juke Box Fury/Wow! 18
(see also Tony Osbourne)

WARM

78 Warm 2001 It's The Kooler/Teenage Space Queen (p/s) 5
78 Warm SMS 001/2001/S THE DEMO TAPES (EP, double pack) 10
78 Warm WARM 2003 Floosie/Chewing Gum Sue/Bye Bye It's Blues/Sometimes (p/s) 5

JOHNNY WARMAN

78 Ring O' 2017 112 Head On Collision/London's Burning/Mind Games (some in p/s) 20/10

WARM DUST

71 Trend 6099 002 It's A Beautiful Day/Worm Dance 15
70 Trend TNLS 700 AND IT CAME TO PASS (2-LP) 50
71 Trend 6480 001 PEACE FOR OUR TIME (LP) 50

WARM EXPRESSION

70 Columbia DB 8672 Let No Man Put Asunder/The Holy City 5

WARM JETS

78 Bridgehouse BHS 1 Sticky Jack/Shell Shock (p/s, some with sides reversed & small extra labels) 8
79 RSO RSO 47 Big City Boys/Mr Natural (p/s) 5

WARM SENSATION

69 Columbia DB 8568 I'll Be Proud Of You/The Clown 8
(see also Ivy League)

MINT VALUE £

WARM SOUNDS
67 Immediate IM 058 Sticks And Stones/Angeline . . . 18
67 Deram DM 120 The Birds And Bees/Doo-Dah . . . 18
68 Deram DM 174 Nite Is A-Comin'/Smeta Mergaty . . . 35
(see also Denny Gerrard, Tuesday's Children, Open Road)

EDDIE WARNER
00 Jazzman JM 013 Devil's Anvil/Poppy Fiddles . . . 5

HERB & BETTY WARNER
59 Felsted AF 114 Slowly/'BUGS' BOWER GROUP: Slowly . . . 7
59 Felsted AF 114 Slowly/'BUGS' BOWER GROUP: Slowly (78) . . . 6

JACK WARNER
68 MFP MFP 1278 YER CAN'T 'ELP LAUGHIN' (LP) . . . 12
71 President PT 360 You Have Got The Gear/ Somebody Asked Me . . . 7

JACK WARNER with TOMMY REILLY
58 Oriole CB 1426 An Ordinary Copper/On The Way Up . . . 8
58 Oriole CB 1426 An Ordinary Copper/On The Way Up (78) . . . 6

FLORENCE WARNER
73 Epic EPC 1626 For No Good Reason/Remember . . . 6
75 Epic EPC 3817 Anyway I Love You/Dreamer . . . 6
73 Epic EPC 80077 FLORENCE WARNER (LP) . . . 18

GALE WARNING
56 Pye N 15061 Heartbreak Hotel/Met Rock (78) . . . 12
56 Oriole CB 1349 Rock Those Crazy Skins/I Need Your Love (78) . . . 12

WARP
70s Warped WPD 001 Do The Warp/(ECT: Here In Britain)/Fable/White (p/s) . . . 5

WARP NINE
75 Stax STXS 2030 Theme From 'Star Trek'/Para Song One . . . 5

ALMA WARREN
56 Parlophone MSP 6200 Stealin'/Now And Forever . . . 10

ELLIE WARREN
83 PRT 7P 263 Shattered Glass/Killer Touch . . . 5

FRAN WARREN
52 MGM MGM 548 What Is This Thing Called Love/One For The Wonder (78) . . . 5
59 MGM MGM 1008 Shame/As Long As You Believe Me . . . 10
59 MGM MGM 1008 Shame/As Long As You Believe Me (78) . . . 5

GUY WARREN OF GHANA
59 Brunswick 05791 Monkies And Butterflies/An African's Prayer (with Rod Saunders) . . . 6
59 Brunswick 05791 Monkies And Butterflies/An African's Prayer (78, with Rod Saunders) . . . 8
64 Columbia 33SX 1584 EMERGENT DRUMS (LP) . . . 90
69 Columbia SCX 6340 AFRO-JAZZ (LP, as Guy Warren Of Ghana) . . . 50
72 Regal Zono. SLRZ 1031 THE AFRICAN SOUNDS OF GUY WARREN OF GHANA (LP) . . . 35

SHORTY WARRENT & HIS WESTERN RANGE
52 London L 1125 I Thought She Was Local/You're Breaking The Only Heart (That Truly Loves You) (78) . . . 15

WARRIOR
72 Eden LP 27 INVASION! (LP, private pressing, plain white sleeve & label, some handwritten, 100 only) . . . 160

WARRIÖR
80 Rambert RAM ONE Don't Let It Show/The Lord's Prayer/Silver Lady (10", p/s) . . . 100
80 Goodwood GM 12326 TROUBLE MAKER (LP) . . . 150

WARRIOR
80 Rainbow RSL 132 LET BATTLE COMMENCE (LP, private pressing, 500 only) . . . 90

WARRIOR
82 Neat NEAT 20 Dead When It Comes To Love/Kansas City/Stab In The Back (some in die-cut p/s) . . . 15/10
84 Warrior WOO 2 Breakout/Dragon Slayer/Take Your Chance (paper sleeve) . . . 55
83 Warrior WOO 1 FOR EUROPE ONLY (mini-LP) . . . 20

WARRIORS
64 Decca F 11926 Don't Make Me Blue/You Came Along . . . 55
(see also Hans Christian, Jon Anderson)

WARSAW PAKT
78 Island PAKT 1 Safe And Warm/Sick And Tired (a few with p/s) . . . 30/18
77 Island ILPS 9515 NEEDLE TIME (LP, numbered stamped mailer p/s, with insert) . . . 50
79 Stuff Central SEE YOU IN COURT (cassette only) . . . 20

DEE DEE WARWICK
65 Mercury MF 860 Do It With All Your Heart/Happiness . . . 22
65 Mercury MF 867 We're Doin' Fine/You Don't Know . . . 22
65 Mercury MF 890 Gotta Get Hold Of Myself/Another Lonely Saturday . . . 20
66 Mercury MF 909 A Lover's Chant/Worth Every Tear I Cry . . . 45
65 Mercury MF 937 I Want To Be With You/Alfie . . . 15
65 Mercury MF 953 Yours Till Tomorrow/I'm Gonna Make You Love Me . . . 12
67 Mercury MF 974 When Love Slips Away/House Of Gold . . . 20
68 Mercury MF 1061 I'll Be Better Off (Without You)/Monday, Monday . . . 25
69 Mercury MF 1084 Foolish Heart/Thank God . . . 8
69 Mercury MF 1125 That's Not Love/It's Not Fair . . . 10
70 Atlantic 2091 011 She Didn't Know (She Kept On Talking)/Make Love To Me . . . 6

70 Atlantic 2091 037 — If This Was The Last Song/I'm Only Human — 6
71 Atlantic 2091 057 — Cold Night In Georgia/Searching — 6
71 Atlantic 2091 092 — Suspicious Minds/I'm Glad I'm A Woman — 6
75 Private Stock PVT 13 — Get Out Of My Life/Funny How Places Change — 6
66 Mercury 10036 MCE — WE'RE DOING FINE (EP) — 40
71 Atco — TURNIN' AROUND (LP) — 25

DIONNE WARWICK

SINGLES

63 Stateside SS 157 — Don't Make Me Over/I Smiled Yesterday — 18
63 Stateside SS 191 — This Empty Place/Wishin' And Hopin' — 18
63 Pye International 7N 25223 — Please Let Him Love Me/Make The Music Play (reissue) — 6
64 Pye International 7N 25234 — Anyone Who Had A Heart/The Love Of A Boy — 5
64 Pye International 7N 25241 — Walk On By/Anytime Of Day — 5
64 Pye International 7N 25256 — You'll Never Get To Heaven/A House Is Not A Home — 5
64 Pye International 7N 25265 — Reach Out For Me/How Many Days Of Sadness — 5
65 Pye International 7N 25290 — You Can Have Him/Don't Say I Didn't Tell You — 5
65 Pye International 7N 25302 — Who Can I Turn To/That's Not The Answer — 5
65 Pye International 7N 25310 — (Here I Go Again) Looking With My Eyes/Only The Strong, Only The Brave — 5
65 Pye International 7N 25316 — Here I Am/They Long To Be Close To You — 5
65 Pye International 7N 25338 — Are You There (With Another Girl)/If I Ever Make You Cry — 5
66 Pye International 7N 25357 — In Between The Heartaches/Long Day, Short Night — 5
66 Pye International 7N 25368 — A Message To Michael/Here Where There Is Love — 6
66 Pye International 7N 25378 — Trains And Boats And Planes/Don't Go Breaking My Heart — 5
66 Pye International 7N 25395 — Another Night/Go With Love — 5
67 Pye International 7N 25424 — Alfie/The Beginning Of Loneliness — 5
67 Pye International 7N 25428 — The Windows Of The World/Walk Little Dolly — 5
67 Pye International 7N 25435 — I Say A Little Prayer/Window Wishin' — 5
68 Pye International 7N 25445 — (Theme From) The Valley Of The Dolls/Zip-A-Dee-Doo-Dah — 5
68 Pye International 7N 25457 — Do You Know The Way To San Jose?/Let Me Be Lonely — 6
68 Pye International 7N 25474 — Who Is Gonna Love Me?/(There's) Always Something There To Remind Me — 5
75 Warner Bros WB 16530 — Take It From Me/Sure Thing — 6
75 Warner Bros K 16595 — Move Me No Mountain/We'll Burn Our Bridges Behind Us — 10
85 Arista ARIST 638 — That's What Friends Are For (as Dionne Warwick & Friends [Elton John, Gladys Knight & Stevie Wonder])/Two Ships Passing In The Night (p/s) — 5
85 Arista ARIST 12638 — That's What Friends Are For/That's What Friends Are For (Instrumental) (as Dionne Warwick & Friends [Elton John, Gladys Knight & Stevie Wonder])/ Two Ships Passing In The Night (12", p/s) — 10

EPs

64 Pye Intl. NEP 44024 — IT'S LOVE THAT REALLY COUNTS — 15
64 Pye Intl. NEP 44026 — DON'T MAKE ME OVER — 12
65 Pye Intl. NEP 44039 — WISHIN' AND HOPIN' — 12
65 Pye Intl. NEP 44044 — DIONNE — 12
65 Pye Intl. NEP 44046 — FOREVER MY LOVE — 12
65 Pye Intl. NEP 44049 — WHO CAN I TURN TO? — 12
66 Pye Intl. NEP 44051 — HERE I AM — 12
66 Pye Intl. NEP 44067 — MESSAGE TO MICHAEL — 15
66 Pye Intl. NEP 44073 — WINDOW WISHIN' — 15
66 Pye Intl. NEP 44077 — I JUST DON'T KNOW WHAT TO DO WITH MYSELF — 15
67 Pye Intl. NEP 44083 — I LOVE PARIS — 15
68 Pye Intl. NEP 44090 — DO YOU KNOW THE WAY TO SAN JOSE? — 15

LPs

64 Pye Intl. NPL 28037 — PRESENTING DIONNE WARWICK — 20
64 Pye Intl. NPL 28046 — MAKE WAY FOR DIONNE WARWICK — 18
65 Pye Intl. NPL 28055 — THE SENSITIVE SOUND OF DIONNE WARWICK — 18
66 Pye Intl. NPL 28071 — HERE I AM — 18
66 Pye Intl. NPL 28076 — DIONNE WARWICK IN PARIS — 18
67 Pye Intl. NPL 28096 — HERE WHERE THERE IS LOVE — 18
68 Pye Intl. N(S)PL 28114 — VALLEY OF THE DOLLS — 18
75 Warner Bros K 56178 — TRACK OF THE CAT — 12

WASHBOARD RHYTHM KINGS

56 HMV 7EG 8101 — WASHBOARD RHYTHM KINGS (EP) — 22

WASHBOARD SAM

72 RCA RD 8274 — FEELING LOWDOWN (LP, with Big Bill Broonzy & Memphis Slim) — 20

(see also Big Bill Broonzy, Memphis Slim)

ALBERT WASHINGTON & KINGS

67 President PT 137 — Doggin' Me Around/A Woman Is A Funny Thing — 8
68 President PT 182 — I'm The Man/These Arms Of Mine — 8
68 President PT 227 — Woman Love/Bring It On Up — 8
69 President PT 242 — Turn On The Bright Lights/Lonely Mountain — 8
73 President PT 391 — Rome, GA/Telling All Your Friends — 6

BABY WASHINGTON

64 Sue WI 302 — That's How Heartaches Are Made/Doodlin' — 50
64 Sue WI 321 — I Can't Wait Until I See My Baby/Who's Gonna Take Care Of Me — 50
65 London HLC 9987 — Only Those In Love/Ballad Of Bobby Dawn — 25
68 United Artists UP 2247 — Get A Hold Of Yourself/Hurt So Bad — 25
69 Atlantic 584 299 — I Don't Know/I Can't Afford To Lose Him — 15
70 Atlantic 584 316 — Breakfast In Bed/What Becomes Of A Broken Heart — 12
73 People PEO 105 — Just Can't Get You Out Of My Mind/You're Just A Dream — 6
74 People PEO 107 — I've Got To Break Away/Can't Get Over You — 6
66 London HA-C 8260 — THAT'S HOW HEARTACHES ARE MADE (LP) — 75
66 London HA-C 8292 — ONLY THOSE IN LOVE (LP) — 75
68 United Artists SULP 1217 — WITH YOU IN MIND (LP) — 55

(see also Baby Washington/Wilbert Harrison)

MINT VALUE £

BABY WASHINGTON & DON GARDNER

73 People PEO 101 Forever/Baby Let Me Get Close To You . . . 6
74 People PLEO 13 LAY A LITTLE LOVIN' ON ME (LP) . . . 15
(see also Don Gardner & Dee Dee Ford)

BABY WASHINGTON/WILBERT HARRISON

71 Joy JOYS 191 BATTLE OF THE GIANTS (LP) . . . 18

DINAH WASHINGTON

52 Oriole CB 1130 Mad About The Boy/I Can't Face The Music (78) . . . 20
54 Oriole CB 1266 My Man's An Undertaker/Since My Man Has Gone And Went (78) . . . 20
54 Oriole CB 1279 Fat Daddy/TV Is The Thing (78) . . . 20
54 Mercury MB 3132 Until Sunrise/Am I Blue (78) . . . 8
54 Mercury MB 3160 Dream/I Don't Hurt Anymore (78) . . . 10
55 Mercury MB 3188 Teach Me Tonight/Wishing Well (78) . . . 6
55 Mercury MB 3207 That's All I Want From You/You Stay On My Mind (78) . . . 6
56 Mercury MT 124 Cat On A Hot Tin Roof/The First Time (78) . . . 15
59 Mercury AMT 1051 What A Diff'rence A Day Made/Come On Home . . . 10
59 Mercury AMT 1069 Unforgettable/Nothing In The World . . . 7
60 Mercury AMT 1105 This Bitter Earth/I Understand . . . 7
60 Mercury AMT 1119 Love Walked In/I'm In Heaven Tonight . . . 7
61 Mercury AMT 1125 We Have Love/Looking Back . . . 7
61 Mercury AMT 1162 September In The Rain/Wake The Town And Tell The People . . . 8
62 Mercury AMT 1170 Tears And Laughter/If I Should Lose You . . . 6
62 Mercury AMT 1176 Dream/Such A Night . . . 10
63 Columbia DB 7049 Soulville/Let Me Be The First To Know . . . 20
56 Emarcy EJT 501 AFTER HOURS WITH MISS D. (10" LP) . . . 35
57 Emarcy EJL 1255 DINAH (LP) . . . 25
57 Mercury MPL 6519 SINGS THE BEST IN BLUES (LP) . . . 18
59 Top Rank RX 3006 THE BLUES (LP, with Betty Roche) . . . 15
60 Mercury MMC 14030 WHAT A DIFF'RENCE A DAY MADE (LP) . . . 18
60 Mercury MMC 14048 THE UNFORGETTABLE DINAH WASHINGTON (LP) . . . 18
61 Mercury MMC 14063 I CONCENTRATE ON YOU (LP, also stereo CMS 18043) . . . 15/18
61 Mercury MMC 14107 SEPTEMBER IN THE RAIN (LP) . . . 15
62 Mercury MMC 14085 FOR LONELY LOVERS (LP) . . . 15
62 Mercury MMC 14099 TEARS AND LAUGHTER (LP) . . . 15
65 Fontana FJL 125 DINAH! (LP) . . . 12
(see also Brook Benton & Dinah Washington)

ELLA WASHINGTON

69 Monument MON 1030 He Called Me Baby/You're Gonna Cry, Cry, Cry . . . 8

GENO WASHINGTON & RAM JAM BAND

66 Piccadilly 7N 35312 Water/Understanding . . . 8
66 Piccadilly 7N 35329 Hi! Hi! Hazel/Beach Bash . . . 7
66 Piccadilly 7N 35346 Que Sera Sera/All I Need . . . 7
66 Piccadilly 7N 35359 Michael/Hold On To My Love . . . 7
67 Piccadilly 7N 35392 She Shot A Hole In My Soul/I've Been Hurt By Love . . . 12
67 Piccadilly 7N 35403 Tell It Like It Is/Girl I Want To Marry . . . 8
67 Pye 7N 17425 Different Strokes/You Got Me Hummin' . . . 7
68 Pye 7N 17570 I Can't Quit Her/Put Out The Fire Baby . . . 7
68 Pye 7N 17649 I Can't Let You Go/Bring It To Me Baby . . . 10
69 Pye 7N 17745 My Little Chickadee/Seven Eleven . . . 7
71 Pye 7N 45019 Alison Please/Each And Every Part Me . . . 7
71 Pye 7N 45085 Feeling So Good/Would You Believe My Little Chickadee . . . 6
66 Piccadilly NEP 34054 HI (EP) . . . 25
68 Pye NEP 24293 DIFFERENT STROKES (EP) . . . 25
68 Pye NEP 24302 SMALL PACKAGE OF HIPSTERS (EP) . . . 30
66 Piccadilly NPL 38026 HAND CLAPPIN', FOOT STOMPIN', FUNKY-BUTT . . . LIVE! (LP) . . . 30
67 Piccadilly N(S)PL 38032 HIPSTERS, FLIPSTERS, FINGER-POPPIN' DADDIES! (LP) . . . 30
68 Piccadilly N(S)PL 38029 SHAKE A TAIL FEATHER! (LP) . . . 30
68 Pye N(S)PL 18219 LIVE! — RUNNING WILD (LP) . . . 22
(see also Ram Jam Band, Ram John Holder, Ram Holder Brothers, Dave Greenslade)

GEORGE E. WASHINGTON

64 Fontana TF 510 Spare A Thought For Me/Words Of Love . . . 5

GROVER WASHINGTON JR.

73 Kudu KUS 4001 Inner City Blues/Ain't No Sunshine . . . 5
75 Kudu KUDU 924 Mister Magic/Black Frost . . . 5
76 Kudu KUDU 930 Knucklehead Parts 1 & 2 . . . 5
72 Kudu KUL 1 INNER CITY BLUES (LP) . . . 15
72 Kudu KUL 5 ALL THE KING'S HORSES (LP, original issue) . . . 12
73 Kudu KULD 501 SOUL BOX (LP) . . . 12
75 Kudu KU 20 MISTER MAGIC (LP) . . . 15
75 Kudu KU 24 FEELS SO GOOD (LP) . . . 12
76 Kudu KU 32 A SECRET PLACE (LP) . . . 12

JERRY WASHINGTON

75 Contempo CS 2040 Right Here Is Where You Belong/In My Life I Haved Loved . . . 7
75 Contempo CLP 517 RIGHT HERE IS WHERE YOU BELONG (LP) . . . 18

KENNETH WASHINGTON (& CHRIS BARBER BAND)

67 CBS 202494 If I Had A Ticket/They Kicked Him Out Of Heaven (with Chris Barber & T-Bones) . 10
67 CBS 202592 Gimme That Old Time Religion (with Chris Barber Band)/
Just A Closer Walk With Thee . . . 5
(see also Chris Barber)

NORMAN T. WASHINGTON

68 Pama PM 730 Same Thing All Over/You've Been Cheating . . . 7
68 Pama PM 741 Tip Toe/Don't Hang Around . . . 8

69 Punch PH 11 — Oh Happy Day/Spinning. 8
70 Gas GAS 159 — It's Christmas Time Again/If I Could See You 8
70 Punch PH 26 — Sweeter Than Honey/1,000 Pearls 7
70 Punch PH 31 — Last Goodbye/Mother's Pride 7

SHERI WASHINGTON & BAND

57 Vogue V 9070 — I Got Plenty/Ain't I Talkin' To You Baby 550
57 Vogue V 9070 — I Got Plenty/Ain't I Talkin' To You Baby (78) 150

SISTER ERNESTINE B. WASHINGTON

50 Melodisc MEL 1101 — God's Amazing Grace/Where Could I Go But To The Lord (78) 10
55 Melodisc EPM 7-52 — SISTER ERNESTINE WASHINGTON (EP). 20

TONY WASHINGTON (& HIS D.C.s)

63 React EA 002 — Crying Man/Please Mr. DJ 20
63 Island WI 068 — Something Gotta Be Done/TONY & LOUISE: I Have Said. 20
64 Sue WI 327 — Show Me How (To Milk A Cow)/Boof Ska 25
64 Fontana TF 478 — Surely You Love Me/Man To Man 15
65 Black Swan WI 459 — But I Do/Night Train (as Tony Washington & His D.C.s) 25
65 Black Swan WI 460 — Dilly Dilly/Night Train (as Tony Washington & His D.C.s) 25
(see also Tony & Louise)

WASHINGTON D.C.s

64 Ember EMB S 190 — Kisses Sweeter Than Wine/Where Did You Go 18
66 CBS 202226 — 32nd Floor/Whole Lot More 18
67 CBS 202464 — Seek And Find/I Love Gerald Chevin The Great (some in p/s). 65/35
69 Domain D 9 — I've Done It All Wrong/Anytime 30
(see also Dave Clark Five, Freedom)

WASP

75 EMI EMI 2253 — Melissa/Little Miss Bristol 25
(see also Brian Bennett, Shadows)

W.A.S.P.

84 Music For Nations PKUT 109 — Animal (Fuck Like A Beast)/Show No Mercy (shaped picture disc, pig's head or codpiece designs). . . . . each 15
84 M. F. Nations 12KUT 109 — Animal (Fuck Like A Beast)/Show No Mercy (12", gold, white, clear or red vinyl, U.K. issue pressed in France) 35/15/20/10
84 Capitol CLP 336 — I Wanna Be Somebody/Tormentor (Ragewars) (p/s) 5
84 Capitol 12 CLP 336 — I Wanna Be Somebody/Tormentor (Ragewars) (12", picture disc) 10
84 Capitol CL 344 — Schooldaze/Paint It Black (poster p/s) 5
84 Capitol 12 CL 344 — Schooldaze/Paint It Black (12", p/s). 8
85 Capitol CLP 374 — Blind In Texas/Savage (shaped picture disc) 7
86 Capitol CLD 388 — Wild Child/Mississippi Queen//On Your Knees/Hellion (double pack) 5
86 Capitol 12CL 388 — Wild Child/Mississippi Queen (12", p/s) 8
86 Capitol CLP 432 — 9.5 N.A.S.T.Y./Easy Living (shaped picture disc) 6
87 Capitol CL 469 — I Don't Need No Doctor/Widowmaker (live) (p/s, blood pack) 5
87 Capitol CLB 469 — I Don't Need No Doctor/Widowmaker (live) (p/s, with backstage pass). 5
89 Capitol CLP 521 — Mean Man/Locomotive Breath (shaped picture disc). 5
89 Capitol CLPD 534 — The Real Me/The Lake Of Fools (shaped picture disc). 5
89 Capitol CLPD 546 — Forever Free (Eagle Edit)/L.O.V.E. Machine (Live '89) (die-cut pic. disc) 6

WASPS

77 4-Play FOUR 001 — Teenage Treats/She Made More Magic (p/s) 25
77 NEMS NES 115 — Can't Wait 'Til '78/MEAN STREET: Bunch Of Stiffs (p/s). 18
78 RCA PB 5137 — Rubber Cars/This Time (p/s) 12

WASTE

86 Morterhate MORT 21 — NOT JUST SOMETHING TO BE SUNG (EP, foldout p/s) 20

WASTED YOUTH

80 Bridge House BHS 5 — Jealousy/Baby (p/s, clear vinyl). 5
80s Bridge House BHFNEE 1 — (Do The) Caveman (1-sided, limited issue) 8

WASTELAND

79 Ellie Jay/Disaster EJSP 9261 — WANT NOT EP (p/s, 2,000 only). 50
80 Invicta INV 014 — Friends, Romans, Countrymen/Leave Me Alone (p/s, 1,000 only) 35

WATCH COMMITTEE

68 Philips BF 1695 — Throw Another Penny In The Well/Now I Think The Other Way. 5

WATERFALL

76 Bob FRR 001 — FLIGHT OF THE DAY (LP, private pressing). 50
79 Avada AVA 104 — THREE BIRDS (LP, with insert) 30
81 Gun Dog GUN 003LP — BENEATH THE STARS (LP, private pressing) 30

WATER FOR A THIRSTY LAND

74 MRA P 100 — WATER FOR A THIRSTY LAND (LP, with insert) 50

WATER INTO WINE BAND

73 Myrrh MYR 1004 — HILL CLIMBING FOR BEGINNERS (LP, brown or white cover, with insert) . . 180/150
76 CJT 002 — HARVEST TIME (LP, private pressing). 200

WATERLOO & ROBINSON

76 Cube BUG 67 — My Little World/Carry On 5

WATER PISTOLS

76 State STATE 38 — Gimme That Punk Junk/Soft Punk (p/s, with insert). 8

WATERPROOF CANDLE

68 RCA RCA 1717 — Electrically Heated Child/Saturday Morning Repentance. 15

ETHEL WATERS

66 World Record Club T 949 — ETHEL WATERS (LP) 12
(see also Ida Cox)

MINT VALUE £

MUDDY WATERS

53	Vogue V 2101	Walkin' Blues/Rollin' Stone Blues (78)	70
54	Vogue V 2273	Hello Little Girl/Long Distance Call (78)	70
55	Vogue V 2372	Honey Bee/Too Young To Know (78)	70
65	Chess CRS 8001	My John The Conquer Root/Short Dress Woman	20
65	Chess CRS 8019	I Got A Rich Man's Woman/My Dog Can't Bark	15
69	Chess CRS 8083	Let's Spend The Night Together/I'm A Man	12
69	Python PKM 04	Country Boy/All Night Long (99 copies only)	80
55	Vogue EPV 1046	MUDDY WATERS WITH LITTLE WALTER (EP)	175
56	London RU-E 1060	MISSISSIPPI BLUES (EP)	175
63	Pye Intl. NEP 44010	MUDDY WATERS (EP)	35
65	Chess CRE 6006	I'M READY (EP)	55
66	Chess CRE 6022	THE REAL FOLK BLUES VOL. 4 (EP)	45
59	London Jazz LJZ-M 15152	THE BEST OF MUDDY WATERS (LP)	75
61	Pye Jazz NJL 34	AT NEWPORT (LP)	50
64	Pye Intl. NPL 28038	MUDDY WATERS — FOLK SINGER (LP)	40
64	Pye Intl. NPL 28040	THE BEST OF MUDDY WATERS (LP)	100
64	Pye Intl. NPL 28048	MUDDY SINGS BIG BILL (LP)	40
65	Chess CRL 4513	AT NEWPORT (LP, reissue)	30
66	Chess CRL 4515	THE REAL FOLK BLUES (LP)	35
67	Chess CRL 4525	MUDDY, BRASS AND THE BLUES (LP)	35
67	Marble Arch MAL 661	AT NEWPORT (LP, 2nd reissue)	12
67	Chess CRL 4529	SUPER BLUES (LP, with Little Walter & Bo Diddley)	25
67	Marble Arch MAL 723	MUDDY SINGS BIG BILL (LP, reissue)	12
68	Chess CRL 4537	THE SUPER SUPER BLUES BAND (LP, with Howlin' Wolf & Bo Diddley)	50
68	Bounty BY 6031	DOWN ON STOVALL'S PLANTATION (LP)	30
69	Chess CRL 4542	ELECTRIC MUD (LP)	25
69	Chess CRL 4553	AFTER THE RAIN (LP)	30
69	Chess CRL 4556	FATHERS AND SONS (LP)	30
69	Polydor 236 574	BLUES MAN (LP)	18
69	Python PLP 12	MUDDY WATERS (LP, 99 copies only)	45
69	Python PLP 18	MUDDY WATERS VOLUME 2 (LP, 99 copies only)	45
69	Python PLP 19	MUDDY WATERS VOLUME 3 (LP, 99 copies only)	45
70	Syndicate Chapter SC 001/2	BACK IN THE EARLY DAYS (2-LP)	35
70	Syndicate Chapter SC 002	GOOD NEWS (LP)	30
70	Sunnyland KS 100	VINTAGE MUDDY WATERS (LP, gatefold sleeve with inserts, 99 copies only)	40
71	Chess 6671 001	McKINLEY MORGANFIELD AKA MUDDY WATERS (LP)	20
72	Black Bear LP 901	RARE LIVE RECORDINGS VOL. 1 (LP)	25
72	Black Bear LP 902	RARE LIVE RECORDINGS VOL. 2 (LP)	25
72	Black Bear LP 903	RARE LIVE RECORDINGS VOL. 3 (LP)	25
72	Chess 6310 121	THE LONDON SESSIONS (LP)	15
74	Chess 6310 129	CAN'T GET NO GRINDIN' (LP)	15
77	Blue Sky SKY 81853	HARD AGAIN (LP)	15

(see also Little Walter, Howlin' Wolf, Bo Diddley, Luther 'Georgia Boy Snake' Johnson)

ROGER WATERS

84	Harvest HAR 5228	5.01 AM (The Pros And Cons Of Hitch-Hiking)/ 4.30 AM (Apparently They Were Travelling Abroad) (p/s)	5
84	Harvest 12HAR 5228	5.01 AM (The Pros And Cons Of Hitch-Hiking)/4.30 AM (Apparently They Were Travelling Abroad)/4.33 AM (Running Shoes) (12", p/s)	8
84	Harvest HAR 5230	5.06 AM (Every Stranger's Eyes)/4.39 AM (For The First Time Today) (p/s)	15
87	EMI EM 6	Radio Waves/Going To Live In L.A. (Demo) (p/s)	6
87	EMI CDEM 6	Radio Waves (Remix)/Going To Live In L.A. (Demo)/ Radio Waves (7" Version) (CD)	10
87	EMI EM 20	Sunset Strip/Money (live) (unissued; Europe-only)	
87	EMI EM 37	The Tide Is Turning (After Live Aid)/Money ('live') (p/s)	6
87	EMI CDEM 37	The Tide Is Turning (After Live Aid)/Money ('live')/Get Back To Radio (Demo Recording) (CD)	10
90	Mercury 878 147-2	PIECES FROM THE WALL: Another Brick In The Wall Part 2 (Edit)/Young Lust (Edit)/Run Like Hell/In The Flesh? (CD, promo only)	20
92	Columbia 658 139 9	What God Wants Part I (Video Edit)/What God Wants Part I (Album Version)/ What God Wants Part III (CD, box set with prints)	12
92	Columbia 658 819 2	The Bravery Of Being Out Of Range/What God Wants Part I/ Perfect Sense Part I (CD)	8
70	Harvest SHSP 4008	MUSIC FROM THE FILM "THE BODY" (LP, with Ron Geesin, green labels, with Waters/Geesin photos)	18
70	Harvest SHSP 4008	MUSIC FROM THE FILM "THE BODY" (LP, with Ron Geesin, black labels)	12
87	EMI KAOS DJ 1	RADIO KAOS (LP, 'banded' radio promo, custom sleeve)	25
92	Columbia COL 4687610	AMUSED TO DEATH (2-LP, blue vinyl, with booklet)	18

(see also Pink Floyd, Ron Geesin)

LAL & MIKE WATERSON

73	Trailer LER 2076	BRIGHT PHOEBUS (LP, yellow label)	22

WATERSONS

65	Topic 12T 125	NEW VOICES (LP, blue label, with Harry Boardman & Maureen Craik)	18
65	Topic 12T 136	FROST AND FIRE (LP, blue label)	18
66	Topic 12T 142	WATERSONS (LP, blue label)	18
66	Topic 12T 167	A YORKSHIRE GARLAND (LP, blue label)	18
60s	Topic TS 346	THE WATERSONS SOUND (LP)	15

LOVELACE WATKINS

67	Fontana TF 879	I Apologise Baby/You Can't Stop Love	10
72	Uni UNLS 119	LOVE IS (LP)	15
72	York FYK 404	LOVE MAKES THE WORLD GO ROUND (LP)	15

DILYS WATLING
64 Philips BF 1305 — Don't Say You Love Me/Now's The Time 6
65 Philips BF 1393 — I'm Over You/Act Like A Lady 5
69 Pye 7N 17791 — Have Another Dream On Me/Sweet Darlin' 6

DOC WATSON
64 Fontana TFL 6045 — DOC WATSON (LP) 20
65 Fontana TFL 6055 — DOC WATSON & SON (LP) 20
72 Vanguard VSD 9/10 — ON STAGE (2-LP) 18

EARL WATSON
61 Ember EMB S 129 — Nightmare/That Old Black Magic 10

JOHN L. WATSON (& HUMMELFLUGS)
64 Pye 7N 15746 — Looking For Love/Dance With You 7
65 Piccadilly 7N 35233 — Standing By/I'll Make It Worth Your While 8
70 Deram DM-R 285 — A Mother's Love/Might As Well Be Gone (solo) 10
70 Deram SML 1061 — WHITE HOT BLUE BLACK (LP) 35
(see also Web)

JOHNNY WATSON & KAMPAI KINGS
60 Oriole CB 1532 — Moshi, Moshi, Anone!/ABDULLA & HIS LITTLE BAND: Fatima's Theme 5
60 Oriole CB 1532 — Moshi, Moshi, Anone!/ABDULLA & HIS LITTLE BAND: Fatima's Theme (78) 30

JOHNNY 'GUITAR' WATSON
76 Fantasy FTC 124 — I Don't Need A Lone Ranger/You Can Stay But The Noise Must Go 8
(see also Larry Williams & Johnny 'Guitar' Watson)

NEVILLE WATSON
73 Magnet MG 013 — Rasta Army/Version 5

ROGER WATSON
74 Tradition TSR 017 — THE PICK AND THE MALT SHOVEL (LP) 15

WAH WAH WATSON
76 CBS 4691 — Love Ain't Something You Get For Free/Bubbles 5
76 CBS 81582 — ELEMENTARY (LP) 12

BEN WATT
81 Cherry Red CHERRY 25 — Cant/Aubade/Tower Of Silence (p/s) 8
82 Cherry Red 12CHERRY 36 — SUMMER INTO WINTER (12" EP, with Robert Wyatt, p/s) 10
(see also Everything But The Girl)

LU WATTERS & AND HIS YERBA BUENA JAZZ BAND
52 Jazz Man 1 — Maple Leaf Rag/Black & White Rag (78) 7
52 Jazz Man 2 — Irish Black Bottom/Memphis Blues (78) 7
56 Vogue V 2125 — Muskrat Rumble/Frankie And Johnny 5
56 Vogue V 2315 — High Society/Aunt Hagar's Blues 5
55 Vogue EPV 1053 — LU WATTERS (EP) 8
56 Vogue EPV 1130 — LU WATTERS JAZZ BAND (EP) 8
56 Columbia CLEF SEB 10049 — LU WATTERS YERBA BUENA JAZZ BAND (EP) 8
57 Columbia CLEF SEB 10064 — LU WATTERS YERBA BUENA JAZZ BAND (EP) 8
52 Vogue LDE 009 — LU WATTERS AND HIS JAZZ BAND (10" LP) 15
55 Columbia Clef 33C 9004 — LU WATTERS AND HIS YERBA BUENA JAZZ BAND (10" LP) 15
56 London HB-U 1061 — LU WATTERS — 1947 (10" LP) 15
57 Columbia Clef 33C 9036 — DIXIELAND JAMBOREE (10" LP) 15

WATTS 103RD STREET RHYTHM BAND
(see under Charles Wright & Watts 103rd Street Rhythm Band)

CHARLIE WATTS
93 Continuum CDCTUM 103 — My Ship/You Got To Me Head (CD) 15
86 CBS 450 253-1 — LIVE AT FULHAM TOWN HALL (LP, as Charlie Watts & His Orchestra, with insert) 15
91 UFO UFO 2 LP — FROM ONE CHARLIE (10" LP, box set with book & Charlie Parker photo, some signed) 30/20
(see also Rolling Stones, People Band, Rocket 88)

NOBLE 'THIN MAN' WATTS (& HIS BAND)
57 London HLU 8627 — Hard Times (The Slop)/Midnight Flight (with His Rhythm Sparks) 75
57 London HLU 8627 — Hard Times (The Slop)/Midnight Flight (with His Rhythm Sparks) (78) 20
64 Sue WI 347 — Noble's Theme/JUNE BATEMAN: I Don't Wanna 60
60s XX MIN 717 — NOBLE 'THIN MAN' WATTS AND WILD JIMMY SPURRILL (EP) 30
79 Flybright 547 — BLAST OFF (LP, mono) 20
(see also Wild Jimmy Spurrill)

WATUSI WARRIORS
59 London HL 8866 — Wa-Chi-Bam-Ba/Kalahari 15
59 London HL 8866 — Wa-Chi-Bam-Ba/Kalahari (78) 5

NANCY WAYBURN
65 Warner Bros WB 5646 — The World Goes On Without Me/Listen To My Heart 8

WAYFARERS
61 Decca F 11370 — Whistle Down The Wind/Think Of A Stranger 8
70s MWM 1017 — SONGS & DANCE TUNES (LP) 15

WAYGOOD ELLIS
67 Polydor 56729 — I Like What I'm Trying To Do/Hey Lover 40
(see also Fleur-De-Lys)

ALVIS WAYNE
63 Starlite ST45 104 — Don't Mean Maybe, Baby/I'd Rather Be With You 650

MINT VALUE £

ARTIE WAYNE

52	London L 1164	Rachel/Tonight Or Never (78)	15

BOBBY WAYNE

51	London L 924	When The Wind Was Green/Buffalo Billy (78)	12
51	London L 968	Immaculate Mother/Mother At Your Feet Is Kneeling (78)	8
51	London L 972	Runnin' Around/Always You (78)	15
51	London L 973	Wild Card/Let Me In (78)	15
51	London L 1077	I Am Free/How Long Is Forever (78)	15
51	London L 1078	If You Turn Me Down/Let's Make Up Your Mind (78)	15
55	Mercury MB 3151	They Were Doin' The Mambo/A String Of Broken Hearts (78)	8

(see also Teresa Brewer)

BOBBY WAYNE

65	Pye International 7N 25315	Ballad Of A Teenage Queen/River Man	10

CARL WAYNE (& VIKINGS)

64	Pye 7N 15702	What's A Matter Baby/Your Loving Ways (as Carl Wayne & Vikings)	45
65	Pye 7N 15824	This Is Love/You Could Be Fun (as Carl Wayne & Vikings)	35
70	RCA RCA 2032	Maybe God's Got Something Up His Sleeve/Rosanna	6
72	RCA RCA 2177	Imagine/Sunday Kind Of Love	5
72	RCA RCA 2257	Take My Hands For A While/Sweet Seasons	5
73	Pye 7N 45290	You're A Star/Bluebird	6
72	RCA SF 8239	CARL WAYNE (LP)	18

(see also Move, Ace Kefford Stand, Cheetahs, Acid Gallery, Keith Powell [& Valets])

CHRIS WAYNE & ECHOES

60	Decca F 11231	Lonely/Counting Girls	15

JEFF WAYNE

69	Columbia S(C)X 6330	TWO CITIES (LP, soundtrack)	35

(see also Ran-Dells)

JERRY WAYNE

60	Vogue V 9169	Half-Hearted Love/Ten Thousand Miles	25

JOHN WAYNE

73	RCA PL 13484	AMERICA, WHY I LOVE HER (LP)	15

PAT WAYNE (& BEACHCOMBERS)

63	Columbia DB 7121	Go Back To Daddy/Jambalaya	20
63	Columbia DB 7182	Roll Over Beethoven/Is It Love?	20
64	Columbia DB 7262	Bye Bye Johnny/Strictly For The Birds	20
64	Columbia DB 7417	Brand New Man/Nobody's Child	18
65	Columbia DB 7603	Come Dance With Me/I Don't Want To Cry (solo)	10
65	Columbia DB 7739	My Friend/Tomorrow Mine (solo)	8
66	Columbia DB 7944	The Night Is Over/Hombre (solo)	10

RICK(Y) WAYNE (& OFF-BEATS)

60	Triumph RGM 1009	Chick A'Roo/Don't Pick On Me (with Fabulous Flee-Rakkers)	45
60	Top Rank JAR 432	Chick A'Roo/Don't Pick On Me (unreleased)	
60	Pye 7N 15289	Make Way Baby/Goodness Knows (as Ricky Wayne & Off-Beats)	40
65	Oriole CB 306	Say You're Gonna Be My Own/It's A Crying Shame (as Rick Wayne)	15
65	CBS 201764	In My Imagination/Don't Ever Share Your Love (as Rick Wayne)	10

(see also [Fabulous] Flee-Rekkers)

TERRY WAYNE

57	Columbia DB 4002	Matchbox/Your True Love	25
57	Columbia DB 4002	Matchbox/Your True Love (78)	6
57	Columbia DB 4035	Plaything/Slim Jim Tie	25
57	Columbia DB 4035	Plaything/Slim Jim Tie (78)	8
58	Columbia DB 4067	All Mama's Children/Forgive Me	25
58	Columbia DB 4067	All Mama's Children/Forgive Me (78)	8
58	Columbia DB 4112	Oh! Lonesome Me/There's Only One You	20
58	Columbia DB 4112	Oh! Lonesome Me/There's Only One You (78)	10
58	Columbia DB 4205	Little Brother/Where My Baby Goes	20
58	Columbia DB 4205	Little Brother/Where My Baby Goes (78)	15
59	Columbia DB 4312	Brooklyn Bridge/She's Mine	25
58	Columbia SEG 7758	TERRIFIC (EP)	100

THOMAS WAYNE

59	London HLU 8846	Tragedy/Saturday Date	35
59	London HLU 8846	Tragedy/Saturday Date (78)	20
59	London HL 7075	Tragedy/Saturday Date (export issue)	20

WAYS & MEANS

66	Columbia DB 7907	Little Deuce Coupe/The Little Old Lady From Pasadena	22
66	Pye 7N 17217	Sea Of Faces/Make The Radio A Little Louder	20
68	Trend TRE 1005	Breaking Up A Dream/She	50

WAY WE LIVE

71	Dandelion DAN 8004	A CANDLE FOR JUDITH (LP, gatefold sleeve, also listed as K 49004)	120

(see also Tractor, Beau)

WEAPON

80	Weapon WEAP 1	It's A Mad Mad World/Set The Stage Alight (p/s)	30
81	Virgin WEAPONE	It's A Mad Mad World/Set The Stage Alight (12", p/s, reissue)	40

(see also Headbangers, Wildfire)

WEASELSNOUT

72	Weaselsnout WUS 140	UNSUNG LIES (LP, private pressing)	165

MINT VALUE £

WEATHER
69 Philips BF 1734 — Look In My Eyes/Running Forward ... 5
69 Philips BF 1819 — Jamboree Special/Two Peculiar People ... 6

ALFIE WEATHERBY
58 Columbia DC 729 — 49 Juke Boxes/Why Am I Crying? (78, export issue) ... 25

WEATHER REPORT
71 CBS 64521 — WEATHER REPORT (LP) ... 15
72 CBS 64943 — I SING THE BODY ELECTRIC (LP) ... 15
73 CBS 65532 — SWEETNIGHTER (LP) ... 15
74 CBS 80027 — MYSTERIOUS TRAVELLER (LP) ... 15
(see also Joe Zawinul)

WEAVERS
59 Top Rank JAR 120 — Wild Goose Grasses/Meet The Johnson Boys ... 6
57 Vanguard PPL 11006 — AT THE CARNEGIE HALL (LP) ... 15
57 Vanguard PPL 11011 — ON TOUR (LP) ... 15
59 Top Rank RX 3008 — AT HOME (LP) ... 15
61 Brunswick LAT 8357 — BEST OF THE WEAVERS (LP) ... 12
62 Fontana TFL 6011 — WEAVERS' ALMANAC (LP) ... 12
(see also Pete Seeger)

JANE WEAVER v DOVES
98 Manchester MANC 9 — Seven Day Smile/ANDY VOTEL & JANE WEAVER: Gutter Girl (p/s) ... 8
98 Manchester MANCCD 9 — Seven Day Smile/ANDY VOTEL & JANE WEAVER: Gutter Girl/JANE WEAVER: You're Not The Only Person That I Used To Know (CD) ... 12
(see also Doves)

WEB
68 Deram DM 201 — Hatton Mill Morning/Conscience ... 30
68 Deram DM 217 — Baby Won't You Leave Me Alone/McVernon Street ... 30
69 Deram DM 253 — Monday To Friday/Harold Dubbleyew ... 30
68 Deram SML 1025 — FULLY INTERLOCKING (LP) ... 130
70 Deram SML 1058 — THERAPHOSA BLONDI (LP) ... 100
70 Polydor 2383 024 — I SPIDER (LP) ... 140
(see also John L. Watson [& Hummelflugs], Samurai, Greenslade)

WEB
96 Fat Cat 12FAT 001 — EVA EP (12", plain sleeve) ... 20

DEAN WEBB
59 Parlophone R 4549 — Warm Your Heart/Hey Miss Fannie ... 50
59 Parlophone R 4587 — The Rough And The Smooth/Streamline Baby ... 50

DON WEBB
60 Coral Q 72385 — Little Ditty Baby/I'll Be Back Home ... 100

GEORGE WEBB DIXIELANDERS
56 Decca DFE 6351 — AND HIS DIXIELANDERS (EP) ... 18
50s Melodisc EPM7 70 — THE GEORGE WEBB DIXIELANDERS (EP) ... 10

JANET WEBB
71 Polydor 2058-131 — I Cried For You/Mama (p/s) ... 10

JILLA WEBB
56 MGM SP 1180 — You Gotta Love Me Now/What Do You Think It Does To Me? ... 10

JIM(MY) WEBB
68 CBS 3672 — I Keep It Hid/I Need You (as Jim Webb) ... 15
71 Reprise RS 20978 — P.F. Sloan/Psalm One-Five-O ... 8
73 Reprise K 14279 — Campo De Encino/Once In The Morning ... 5
68 CBS (S) 63335 — JIM WEBB SINGS JIM WEBB (LP, as Jim Webb) ... 30
71 Reprise RSLP 6421 — WORDS AND MUSIC (LP, with insert) ... 22
71 Reprise K 44101 — WORDS AND MUSIC (LP, reissue) ... 15
72 Reprise K 44134 — AND SO ON (LP) ... 18
72 Reprise K 44173 — LETTERS (LP) ... 18
74 Asylum SYL 9014 — LAND'S END (LP, with inner sleeve) ... 18
77 Atlantic K 50370 — EL MIRAGE (LP, with inner sleeve) ... 15
(see also Strawberry Children, Glen Campbell)

JOHNNY WEBB
56 Columbia DB 3805 — Dig/Glendora ... 10
57 Columbia DB 3904 — The Song Of The Moonlight/Give Me More ... 8
60s Melodisc MEL 1617 — Travelin' Man/Hold Back The Town (some with p/s) ... 12/6
(see also June Laverick)

PETA WEBB
73 Topic 12TS 223 — I HAVE WANDERED IN EXILE (LP, blue label) ... 60
(see also Oak)

ROGER WEBB (& HIS TRIO)
71 Columbia DB 8803 — Strange Report/Summer Fancy ... 12
82 Chandos SBR 102 — The Gentle Touch/Arthur's Theme ... 6
84 Chips CH 104 — Hammer House Of Horror/Cover Theme (p/s) ... 12
64 Parlophone PMC 1233 — JOHN, PAUL AND ALL THAT JAZZ (LP) ... 12

SKEETER WEBB
55 Parlophone CMSP 32 — Was It A Bad Dream/Your Secret's Not A Secret Anymore (export issue) ... 15

SONNY WEBB & CASCADES
64 Oriole CB 1873 — You've Got Everything/Border Of The Blues ... 40
64 Polydor NH 52158 — You've Got Everything/Border Of The Blues (reissue) ... 12

MINT VALUE £

MARLENE WEBBER

70 Bamboo BAM 33 My Baby/BRENTFORD ALLSTARS: You Gonna Hold Me (Version) 10
71 Ackee ACK 120 Natengula/Natengula-Kera (as Merlin Webber) 7
71 Ackee ACK 122 Cumbaya/Hail-Hi Freedom (as Merlin Webber) 7
71 Smash SMA 2322 Hard Life/COLLINS ALL STARS: Version Life (as Merlene Webber) 7
71 Trojan TR 7815 Stand By Your Man/CLANCY ECCLES: Credit Squeeze 7
(see also Webber Sisters, Tonettes)

WEBBER SISTERS

67 Island WI 3109 My World/ALVA LEWIS: Lonely Still 70
(see also Delroy Wilson)

WEBS

68 London HLU 10188 This Thing Called Love/Tomorrow 10

WEBSPINNERS

73 Buddah 2011 150 Spider Man — Theme/Goin' 'Cross Town 6

BEN WEBSTER

55 Columbia CLEF 33CX 10014 MUSIC FOR LOVERS (LP) 25
65 Fontana FJL 126 INTIMATE! (LP) 50
66 Verve VLP 9100 BEN WEBSTER'S BIG SOUND (LP) 12
69 Ember CJS 822 BEN WEBSTER AT EASE (LP) 25
70 Fontana FJL 316 BIG BEN TIME (LP) 30
72 Philips 6308 101 WEBSTER'S DICTIONARY (LP) 50

CHASE WEBSTER

64 Hickory 45-1283 Life Can Have Meaning/Where Is Your Heart 6

DEENA WEBSTER

68 Parlophone R 5699 You're Losing/Wish You Were Here 10
68 Parlophone R 5721 Your Heart Is Free Just Like The Wind/Queen Merka And Me 8
68 Parlophone R 5738 Scarborough Fair/The Water Is Wide 7
69 Parlophone R 5798 Joey/It's Alright With Me 6
68 Parlophone PMC/PCS 7052 TUESDAY'S CHILD (LP) 35

WEDDING PRESENT

85 Reception REC 001 Go Out And Get 'Em Boy/(The Moment Before) Everything's Spoiled Again (p/s, 500 only, a few with poster & badge) 30/20
85 City Slang CSL 001 Go Out And Get 'Em Boy/(The Moment Before) Everything's Spoiled Again (reissue, different foldout p/s, 1,000 only) 10
86 Reception REC 002 Once More/At The Edge Of The Sea (p/s, 3,500 only) 8
86 Reception REC 002/12 DON'T TRY AND STOP ME MOTHER (12" EP, combines REC 001 & 002) 8
86 Reception REC 003 This Boy Can Wait/You Should Always Keep In Touch With Your Friends (p/s, matrix numbers: 003 A2 & 003 B1) 6
86 Reception REC 003 This Boy Can Wait/You Should Always Keep In Touch With Your Friends (p/s, mispress both sides play B-side, matrix numbers: 003 A1 & 003 A2) 5
86 Reception REC 003/12 This Boy Can Wait (Extended)/You Should Always Keep In Touch With Your Friends/Living And Learning (12", p/s) 8
87 Reception REC 005 My Favourite Dress/Every Mother's Son/Never Said (p/s, white vinyl, 3,000 only, 2,000 of which free with "George Best" LP) 6
87 Reception A Million Miles/What Did Your Last Servant Die Of? (DJ promo, 200 only) 8
87 Reception REC 006/C Anyone Can Make A Mistake/All About Eve/Getting Nowhere Fast (cassette, shrinkwrapped with badge) 5
88 Reception REC 010X Davni Chasy/Katrusya (promo only) 6
88 House Of Dolls HOD 004 Unfaithful (Peel Session)/TRUDY: Living On A Moon/HUNTERS CLUB: Little Sister/CLAYTOWN TROUPE: Real Life (free with *House Of Dolls* mag) 5
89 M'night Music DONG 39 CD Pourquoi Es Tu Devenue Si Raisonable? (CD, unreleased)
89 RCA Davni Chasy/Katrusya (promo only) 10
90 RCA PB 43403 Brassneck/Don't Talk, Just Kiss (custom hand-painted p/s, 3,000 only) 6
92 RCA PB 45185 Blue Eyes/Cattle And Cane (p/s) 8
92 RCA PB 45183 Go Go Dancer/Don't Cry No Tears (p/s) 5
92 RCA PB 45181 Three/Think That It Might (p/s) 5
92 RCA PB 45311 Silver Shorts/Falling (p/s) 5
92 RCA PB 45313 Come Play With Me/Pleasant Valley Sunday (p/s) 5
87 Reception LEEDS 1 GEORGE BEST (LP, 2,000 only with white vinyl 7": My Favourite Dress/ Every Mother's Son/Never Said [REC 005] & inner sleeve; later with bonus black vinyl 7" or 12" edition) 12/10
88 Reception LEEDS 2 TOMMY (LP, 1,000 signed by band, with poster & inner sleeve) 15
(see also Pop Guns)

WEDGEWOODS

64 Pye 7N 15642 September In The Rain/Gone Gone Away 10
65 Pye 7N 15846 Peace/Summer Love 8

BUDDY WEED & HIS ORCHESTRA

57 Vogue V 9075 The Kent Song/For Love 25
57 Vogue V 9075 The Kent Song/For Love (78) 8

BERT WEEDON

78s

56 Parlophone R 4178 The Boy With The Magic Guitar/Flannel-Foot 8
57 Parlophone R 4381 Play That Big Guitar/Quiet, Quiet, Ssh! 8
58 Parlophone R 4446 Big Note Blues/Rippling Tango 8
59 Top Rank JAR 117 Guitar Boogie Shuffle/Bert's Boogie 10
59 Top Rank JAR 121 Sing Little Birdie/The Lady Is A Tramp 6
59 Top Rank JAR 122 Petite Fleur/My Happiness 6
59 Top Rank JAR 123 Charmaine/It's Time To Say Goodnight 6
59 Top Rank JAR 136 Teenage Guitar/Blue Guitar 12
59 Top Rank JAR 210 Jealousy/Tango, Tango 8
59 Top Rank JAR 211 Stardust/Summertime 8
59 Top Rank JAR 221 Nashville Boogie/King Size Guitar 15

45s

56	Parlophone MSP 6242	The Boy With The Magic Guitar/Flannel-Foot	20
57	Parlophone R 4256	Theme From ITV's '$64,000 Question'/Twilight Time	18
57	Parlophone R 4315	The Jolly Gigolo/Soho Fair	18
57	Parlophone R 4381	Play That Big Guitar/Quiet, Quiet, Ssh!	12
58	Parlophone R 4446	Big Note Blues/Rippling Tango	12
59	Saga SAG 2906	Fifi/Cat On A Hot Tin Roof (as Bert Weedon & Rag Pickers)	18
59	Top Rank JAR 117	Guitar Boogie Shuffle/Bert's Boogie	7
59	Top Rank JAR 121	Sing Little Birdie/The Lady Is A Tramp	5
59	Top Rank JAR 122	Petite Fleur/My Happiness	5
59	Top Rank JAR 123	Charmaine/It's Time To Say Goodnight	5
59	Top Rank JAR 136	Teenage Guitar/Blue Guitar	6
59	Top Rank JAR 210	Jealousy/Tango, Tango	5
59	Top Rank JAR 211	Stardust/Summertime	5
59	Top Rank JAR 221	Nashville Boogie/King Size Guitar	6
60	Top Rank JAR 300	Big Beat Boogie/Theme From 'A Summer Place' (some with p/s)	8/5
60	Top Rank JAR 360	Twelfth Street Rag/Querida	5
60	Top Rank JAR 415	Apache/Lonely Guitar	6
60	Top Rank JAR 517	Sorry Robbie/Easy Beat	6
61	Top Rank JAR 537	Ginchy/Yearning	6
61	Top Rank JAR 559	Mr. Guitar/Eclipse	6
61	Top Rank JAR 582	Ghost Train/Fury	6
61	HMV POP 946	China Doll/Red Guitar	5
62	HMV POP 989	Twist A Napoli/Twist Me Pretty Baby	5
62	HMV POP 1043	Some Other Love/Tune For Two	5
62	HMV POP 1077	South Of The Border/Poinciana	5
63	HMV POP 1141	Night Cry/Charlie Boy	10
63	HMV POP 1216	Dark Eyes/Black Jackets	5
64	HMV POP 1248	It Happened In Monterey/Lonely Night	6
64	HMV POP 1302	Gin Mill Guitar/Can't Help Falling In Love	6
64	HMV POP 1355	Tokyo Melody/Theme From 'Limelight'	6
65	HMV POP 1387	Twelve String Shuffle/Colour Him Folksy	6
65	HMV POP 1485	High Steppin'/East Meets West	6
66	HMV POP 1535	Kick Off/McGregor's Leap	6
67	HMV POP 1592	Stranger Than Fiction/Malaguena	6
60s	Grosvenor GRS 1015	Watch Your Step/Safe And Sound (as Bert Weedon Quartet with Roy Edwards)	5

EPs

56	Esquire EP 56	WAXING THE WINNERS	25
59	Selmer Amplifiers	DEMONSTRATION RECORD WITH DAVID GELL	10
61	Top Rank JKP 3008	WEEDON WINNERS	15
64	HMV 7EG 8856	GUITAR MAN	15

LPs

60	Top Rank BUY 026	KINGSIZE GUITAR	35
61	Top Rank 35/101	HONKY TONK GUITAR	30
70	Fontana 6438 009	THE ROMANTIC GUITAR OF BERT WEEDON	12
70	Fontana 6438 031	ROCKIN' AT THE ROUNDHOUSE	12

(see also George Chisholm, Craig Douglas, Ragpickers)

WEEDS

86	In Tape IT 34	China Doll/Crazy Face (p/s)	12

WEE THREE

73	People PEO 104	Get On Board/Get On Board (Instrumental)	5

WEE WILLIE & WINNERS

74	Action ACT 4624	Get Some/A Plan For The Man	18
74	People PEO 116	I Don't Know What You Got But I Know What I Need (Parts 1 & 2)	5

WEEZER

94	Geffen GFS 85	Undone: The Sweater Song/Mykel And Carli/Susanne/Holiday (p/s)	15
94	Geffen GFSCD 85	Undone: The Sweater Song/Mykel And Carli/Susanne/Holiday (CD)	18
95	Geffen GFS 88	Buddy Holly/Jamie (p/s)	12
95	Geffen GFSV 95	Say It Ain't So (Remix)/No One Else (Live & Acoustic)/Jamie (10", p/s)	12
95	Geffen GEF 24629	WEEZER (LP)	18

WE FIVE

65	Pye International 7N 25314	You Were On My Mind/Small World	10
66	Pye International 7N 25346	Let's Get Together/Cast Your Fate To The Wind	15
66	Pye Intl. NEP 44056	LET'S GET TOGETHER (EP)	55
65	Pye Intl. NPL 28067	YOU WERE ON MY MIND (LP)	45

WE 4

67	HMV POP 1603	Pretty Flowers/I'll Make You A Miracle	5
69	Major Minor MM 593	Candy Floss Man/Perry Park	6

FRANN WEIGLE

50	London L 551	Rockin' Chair/My Diary Of Broken Dreams (78)	8

BRUCIE WEIL

53	London L 1203	Little Boy Blues/God Bless Us All (78)	8

BOB WEIR

72	Warner Bros WB 7611	One More Saturday Night/Cassidy	5
72	Warner Bros K 46165	ACE (LP)	15

(see also Grateful Dead, Kingfish, Bobby & Midnites)

FRANK WEIR & HIS ORCHESTRA

54	Decca F 10271	The Happy Wanderer/From Your Lips	8
54	Decca F 10291	The Bandit/By Candlelight	7
55	Decca F 10384	The Cuckoo Cries/Misty Islands Of The Horizons	7
55	Decca F 10435	Theme From 'Journey Into Space'/Serenade To An Empty Room	8

MINT VALUE £

55	Decca F 10646	I'm A Little Echo (with Eula Parker)/Castles In The Air	5
59	Oriole CB 1523	Swinging Ghosts/The Cool Spectre	5
60	Oriole CB 1559	Caribbean Honeymoon/Farewell My Love	7
63	Philips 326 560 BF	Manhunt/Chant Of The Jungle (as Frank Weir & Werewolves)	5
55	Decca LF 1208	PRESENTING FRANK WEIR AND HIS SAXOPHONE (10" LP)	18

(see also Bill Darnell, Vera Lynn, Janie Marden)

NORRIS WEIR (& JAMAICANS)

70	Duke DU 85	Hard On Me (with Jamaicans)/TOMMY COWAN & JAMAICANS: Please Stop The Wedding	10
74	Dragon DRA 1030	Reggay Revolution/Version	6
75	Horse HOSS 81	Dr. Honey/Honey Dub	6

(see also Jamaicans)

WEIRD STRINGS

80	Velvet Moon VM 1	Oscar Mobile/Ancient Square (foldover p/s)	10
80	Ace ACE 009	Criminal Cage/Mi££ionaire (p/s)	8

(see also Paul Roland, Midnight Rags)

FRANK WEISS

71	Stax 2362 011	WEISS TO MEMPHIS (LP)	12

BRUCE WELCH

74	EMI EMI 2141	Please Mr. Please/Song Of Yesterday	50

(see also Marvin, Welch & Farrar; Shadows, Cliff Richard)

ELIZABETH WELCH

80	Industrial IR 002	Stormy Weather/Ya're Blase (p/s)	10

HONEE WELCH

69	London HLU 10288	I'm Gonna Try/It's My Girl	7

KEN & MITZIE WELCH

62	London RE-R 1275	A PIANO, ICE BOX AND BED (EP)	12

LENNY WELCH

60	London HLA 9094	You Don't Know Me/I Need Someone	7
62	London HLA 9601	Taste Of Honey/Old Cathedral	8
63	London HLA 9810	Since I Fell For You/Are You Sincere	7
64	London HLA 9880	Ebb Tide/Congratulations Baby	7
64	London HLR 9910	If You See My Love/Father Sebastian	7
65	London HLR 9981	Darling Take Me Back/Time After Time	15
65	London HLR 9991	Two Different Worlds/I Was There	7
65	London HLR 10010	Run To My Lovin' Arms/Coronet Blue	15
66	London HLR 10031	Rags To Riches/I Want You To Worry	7
70	Major Minor MM 707	Breaking Up Is Hard To Do/Got To See If I Can Get My Mommy To Come Back Home	5
75	Mainstream MSS 307	When There's No Such Thing As Love/The Minx	5
66	London HA-R/SH-R 8267	TWO DIFFERENT WORLDS (LP)	25
66	London HA-R 8290	RAGS TO RICHES (LP)	25

TIM WELCH

60	Columbia DB 4529	Weak In The Knees/A Boy And A Girl In Love	7

WELD OF LIQUOR

95	Weld Record WELD 05	We Are The Weld/For Manze's Sake (vinegar-scented p/s)	10

WELFARE STATE

78	Look LKLP 6347	WELFARE STATE SONGS (LP, with insert)	60

LAWRENCE WELK ORCHESTRA

56	Vogue Coral Q 72140	Chain Gang/The Poor People Of Paris	7
56	Vogue Coral Q 72141	The 'Threepenny Opera' Theme/Rock And Roll Waltz	7
57	Vogue Coral Q 72233	Pizzicato Waltz/Whispering Heart	6
57	Vogue Coral Q 72256	Around The World In 80 Days/Ten Little Trees	7
61	London HLD 9261	Calcutta (Nicolette)/Melodie D'Amour	7
64	Dot DS 16697	The 'Addams Family' Theme/Apples And Bananas	20

PAUL WELLER (MOVEMENT)

SINGLES

91	Freedom High FHP 1	Into Tomorrow/Here's A New Thing (p/s, with or without 'Paul Weller Movement' on label)	8
91	Freedom High FHPC 1	Into Tomorrow/Here's A New Thing (cassette)	8
91	Freedom High FHPT 1	Into Tomorrow/Here's A New Thing/That Spiritual Feeling/ Into Tomorrow (8-Track Demo) (12", p/s)	30
91	Freedom High FHPCD 1	Into Tomorrow/Here's A New Thing/That Spiritual Feeling/ Into Tomorrow (8-Track Demo) (CD)	40
92	Go! Discs GOD 86	Uh Huh Oh Yeh/Fly On The Wall (paper or plastic labels, p/s)	8
92	Go! Discs GODX 86	Uh Huh Oh Yeh/Arrival Time/Fly On The Wall/Always There To Fool You (12", p/s)	12
92	Go! Discs GODCD 86	Uh Huh Oh Yeh/Fly On The Wall/Arrival Time/Always There To Fool You (CD, digipak)	14
92	Go! Discs GOD 91	Above The Clouds/Everything Has A Price To Pay (paper or plastic labels, p/s)	7
92	Go! Discs GODX 91	Above The Clouds/Everything Has A Price To Pay/All Year Round (live)/ Feeling Alright (12", p/s)	10
92	Go! Discs GODCD 91	Above The Clouds/Everything Has A Price To Pay/All Year Round (live)/ Feeling Alright (CD, digipak)	14
93	Go! Discs GOD 102	Sunflower/Bull-Rush — Magic Bus (p/s)	7
93	Go! Discs GODX 102	Sunflower/Kosmos SXDub 2,000/Bull-Rush — Magic Bus (live)/ That Spiritual Feeling (New Mix) (12", p/s)	10
93	Go! Discs GODCD 102	Sunflower/Kosmos SXDub 2,000/Bull-Rush — Magic Bus (live)/ That Spiritual Feeling (New Mix) (CD, digipak)	14

MINT VALUE £

93	Go! Discs GOD 104	Wild Wood/Ends Of The Earth (p/s)	6
93	Go! Discs GODT 104	Wild Wood/Ends Of The Earth (10", p/s, with poster)	12
93	Go! Discs GODCD 104	Wild Wood/Ends Of The Earth (CD, sealed with 5 postcards)	16
94	Go! Discs GOD 107	THE WEAVER EP (The Weaver/This Is No Time/Another New Day/Ohio [live]) (p/s)	6
94	Go! Discs GODT 107	THE WEAVER EP (10", numbered sticker on p/s)	12
94	Go! Discs GODCD 107	THE WEAVER EP (The Weaver/This Is No TIme/ Another New Day/Ohio [live]) (CD, digipak)	14
94	Go! Discs GOD 111	Hung Up/Foot Of The Mountain (live from Royal Albert Hall 23.11.93)/ The Loved/Kosmos (Lynch Mob Bonus Beats) (p/s)	6
94	Go! Discs GODX 111	Hung Up/Foot Of The Mountain (live from Royal Albert Hall 23.11.93)/ The Loved/Kosmos (Lynch Mob Bonus Beats) (12", p/s)	10
94	Go! Discs GODCD 111	Hung Up/Foot Of The Mountain (live from Royal Albert Hall 23.11.93)/ The Loved/Kosmos (Lynch Mob Bonus Beats) (CD, digipak)	12
94	Go! Discs GOD 121	Out Of The Sinking/Sunflower (Lynch Mob Dub)/Sexy Sadie (p/s)	6
94	Go! Discs GODCD 121	Out Of The Sinking/Sunflower (Lynch Mob Dub)/Sexy Sadie (CD)	10
95	Go! Discs GODCD 127	THE CHANGING MAN EP (CD, digipak)	12

ALBUMS

95	Go! Discs 850 070-7	STANLEY ROAD (LP, 6 x 7" in box set with booklet)	28
95	Go! Discs 828 620-2	STANLEY ROAD (CD, 12" box set with booklet)	22

PROMOS & FREEBIES

92	Go! Discs	Kosmos (12")	22
93	no label (WELLER+ F1)	The Loved (blank clear 1-sided flexi free with *The Big Issue* mag)	14/6
93	Go! Discs PWBCD 1	Wild Wood (The Sheared Wood Remix) (CD, no inlay)	16
94	Go! Discs PN PCD 2	Sexy Sadie (1-track CD, available via mail order with 1st 500 copies of "Highlights & Hang-Ups" video)	20
95	Go! Discs PW-G-CD 1	Into Tomorrow/Wild Wood/Out Of The Sinking (CD, free with *The Guardian Guide* magazine)	6
95	Go Discs SPLINT 1	Walk On Gilded Splinters (12", 1-sided white label)	65
95	Go Discs LYNCH 1	Whirlpools End (Lynch Mob Mix) (12", 1-sided white label, stamped 1-sided white label, 500 only)	65
97	Island ISJB 666	Brushed/Shoot The Dove (jukebox issue)	8
97	Island	Heavy Soul (1-sided)	55
99	Island 12 IS 734DJ	Wild Wood (Sheared Wood Remix) (12", 1 sided white label)	18
00	Island WELLERCD 1	HELIOCENTRIC SAMPLER (CD EP, with The Daily Telegraph, card sleeve)	10
00	Island SWEEPCD 1	Sweetpea, My Sweetpea (1-track CD, card sleeve)	10
89	EMI Mus. Pub. CDWELLER 3	THE SONGS OF PAUL WELLER 1982-1988 (CD, 10-track sampler)	110
95	Go! Discs (no cat. no.)	CD SAMPLER (CD, given away in queue for 100 Club secret gig, 200 only)	45
96	Go! Discs PWRT 1	PEACOCK SUIT (CD, 7-track picture disc)	28
97	Island PAUL-CD 1	WILD WOOD TO HEAVY SOUL (CD, 8-track sampler)	35
97	Southern Songs WELLER 1	PAUL WELLER (LP, white label, live at Hayward Gallery)	65
97	Island PW ICD 1	HEAVY SOUL (CD, promo-only interview, card sleeve or jewel case)	20/28
97	Island PW ICD 1	HEAVY SOUL (box set, including CD "Paul Weller Interview", EPK, 5 cards & insert)	45
97	Island KINGS 1	KINGS ROAD (CD sampler, 350 only)	45
98	Island CLASSICD 1	MODERN CLASSICS (CD, 5-track sampler, card sleeve, promo only)	28
99	Island INTCD 3	IN CONVERSATION (CD, interview, gatefold card p/s, promo only)	32
01	Independiente PROMO	DAYS OF SPEED SELECTIONS (3-CD, card sleeves, promo only)	45

(see also Jam, Style Council)

ORSON WELLES

59	Top Rank TR 5001	The Courtroom Scene From The Film 'Compulsion' (both sides) (some in p/s)	12/7

(see also Manowar)

NICK WELLINGS & SECTION

77	The Label TLR 011	You Better Move On/Punk Funk	6

BOBBY WELLINS

78	Vortex VS1	LIVE JUBILATION (LP)	40
78	Vortex VS2	DREAMS ARE FREE (LP)	40

BOBBY WELLS

68	Beacon 3-102	Let's Copp A Groove/Recipe For Love (yellow or green label)	12/8
79	Grapevine GRP 124	Be's That Way Sometimes/Recipe For Love	10

HOUSTON WELLS (& MARKSMEN)

62	Parlophone R 4955	This Song Is Just For You/Paradise	12
62	Parlophone R 4980	Shutters And Boards/North Wind	12
63	Parlophone R 5031	Only The Heartaches/Can't Stop Pretending	10
63	Parlophone R 5069	Blowing Wild (The Ballad Of Black Gold)/Crazy Dreams	12
64	Parlophone R 5099	Anna Marie/Moon Watch Over My Baby	12
64	Parlophone R 5141	Galway Bay/Livin' Alone (as Houston Wells & Outlaws)	12
65	Parlophone R 5226	Blue Of The Night/Coming Home (solo)	7
68	CBS 3572	Teach Me Little Children/Does My Ring Hurt Your Finger	6
63	Parlophone GEP 8878	JUST FOR YOU (EP)	50
64	Parlophone GEP 8914	RAMONA (EP)	70
64	Parlophone PMC 1215	WESTERN STYLE (LP)	50

(see also Marksmen, Outlaws)

JEAN WELLS

71	Mojo 2092 023	After Loving You/Puttin' The Best On The Outside	10
70	Sonet SNTF 606	WORLD! HERE COMES JEAN WELLS (LP)	30

JOHNNY WELLS

59	Columbia DB 4377	Lonely Moon/The One And Only One	15
67	Parlophone R 5559	Guess I'm Dumb/Wondering Why	12

MINT VALUE £

JUNIOR WELLS

66	Delmark DS 9612	Hoodoo Man Blues (blue label)	30
66	Delmark DS 628	Southside Blues Jam (blue label)	18
68	Mercury MF 1056	Girl You Lit My Fire/It's A Man Down There	8
66	Delmark DJB 1	BLUES WITH A BEAT (EP)	35
60s	XX MIN 715	JUNIOR WELLS (EP)	22
68	Fontana (S)TFL 6084	IT'S MY LIFE BABY (LP)	35
68	Vanguard SVRL 19011	COMING AT YOU (LP, also stereo, VSD 79262)	25/22
68	Vanguard SVRL 19028	IT'S MY LIFE BABY (LP, reissue)	15
68	Mercury SMCL 20130	YOU'RE TUFF ENOUGH (LP)	18
71	Delmark DS 628	SOUTHSIDE BLUES JAM (LP)	15
75	Delmark DS 635	JUNIOR WELLS ON TAP (LP)	15

(see also Buddy Guy)

KITTY WELLS

64	Brunswick 05920	I Gave My Wedding Dress Away/I've Thought Of Leaving You	7
55	Brunswick OE 9149	KITTY SINGS (EP)	22
61	Brunswick LAT 8361	KITTY'S CHOICE (LP)	25
64	Brunswick LAT 8575	QUEEN OF COUNTRY MUSIC (LP)	20
65	Brunswick LAT 8601	ESPECIALLY FOR YOU (LP)	20
65	Brunswick LAT 8621	LONESOME SAD AND BLUE (LP)	20
66	Brunswick LAT/STA 8646	SINGS SONGS MADE FAMOUS BY JIM REEVES (LP, mono/stereo)	18/22
66	Brunswick LAT 8659	COUNTRY ALL THE WAY (LP, mono/stereo)	18/22
67	Brunswick LAT 8683	LOVE MAKES THE WORLD GO ROUND (LP)	15

MARY WELLS

62	Oriole CBA 1762	You Beat Me To The Punch/Old Love	60
63	Oriole CBA 1796	Two Lovers/Operator	60
63	Oriole CBA 1829	Laughing Boy/Two Wrongs Don't Make A Right	60
63	Oriole CBA 1847	Your Old Standby/What Love Has Joined Together	60
63	Stateside SS 242	You Lost The Sweetest Boy/What's Easy For Two Is So Hard For One	30
64	Stateside SS 288	My Guy/Oh Little Boy	18
64	Stateside SS 316	Once Upon A Time (with Marvin Gaye)/What's The Matter With You, Baby	40
65	Stateside SS 372	Ain't It The Truth/Stop Takin' Me For Granted	25
65	Stateside SS 396	Use Your Head/Everlovin' Boy	18
65	Stateside SS 415	Never Never Leave Me/Why Don't You Let Yourself Go	18
65	Stateside SS 439	He's A Lover/I'm Learnin'	18
65	Stateside SS 463	Me Without You/I'm Sorry	18
68	Stateside SS 2111	The Doctor/Two Lovers' History	18
66	Atlantic AT 4067	Dear Lover/Can't You See (You're Losing Me)	25
66	Atlantic 584 054	Me And My Baby/Such A Sweet Thing	12
67	Atlantic 584 104	Hey You Set My Soul On Fire/Coming Home	8
70	Direction 58-4816	Dig The Way I Feel/Love Shooting Bandit	6
72	Atlantic K 10254	Dear Lover/Can't You See (You're Losing Me) (reissue)	5
65	Tamla Motown TME 2007	MARY WELLS (EP)	80
63	Oriole PS 40045	TWO LOVERS (LP)	125
63	Oriole PS 40051	BYE BYE BABY (LP)	150
64	Stateside SL 10095	SINGS MY GUY (LP)	50
65	Stateside SL 10133	MARY WELLS (LP)	50
65	Tamla Motown TML 11006	MY BABY JUST CARES FOR ME (LP)	55
66	Stateside S(S)L 10171	LOVE SONGS TO THE BEATLES (LP)	40
66	Tamla Motown TML 11032	GREATEST HITS (LP)	35
68	Stateside S(S)L 10266	SERVIN' UP SOME SOUL (LP)	35
68	Atlantic 587 049	THE TWO SIDES OF MARY WELLS (LP)	25
69	T. Motown (S)TML 11102	VINTAGE STOCK (LP, unissued)	
70	Regal Starline SRS 5040	MY GUY (LP)	12

(see also Marvin Gaye)

ALEX WELSH & DIXIELANDERS

55	Decca F 10538	I'll Build A Stairway To Paradise/Eccentric	5
55	Decca F 10557	Blues My Naughtie Sweetie Gives To Me/Shoe Shiner's Blues	5
55	Decca F 10607	As Long As I Live/New Orleans Stomp	10
55	Decca F 10651	Sugar/Smiles	5
55	Decca F 10652	What Can I Say After I Say I'm Sorry/Hard-Hearted Hannah	5
61	Columbia DB 4686	Tansy/Memphis March	6
55	Decca DFE 6254	DIXIELANDERS AT THE RFH (EP)	10
55	Decca DFE 6283	AND HIS DIXIELAND BAND (EP)	18
55	Decca DFE 6315	MUSIC FROM PETE KELLY (EP)	20
62	Columbia SEG 8143	WELSH WAILS (EP)	25
66	Strike JHE 201	ALEX WELSH ENTERTAINS (EP)	35
58	Nixa NJT 516	THE MELROSE FOLIO (LP)	15
59	Columbia 33SX 1219	MUSIC OF THE MAUVE DECADE (LP)	35
61	Columbia 33SX 1322	IT'S RIGHT HERE FOR YOU (LP)	35
62	Columbia 33SX 1429	ECHOES OF CHICAGO (LP)	35
66	Strike JHL 102	STRIKE ONE (LP)	25
68	Columbia SX 6213	AT HOME WITH... (LP)	18
69	Columbia SX 6333	AND HIS BAND '69 (LP)	35
70	Columbia SCX 6376	DIXIELAND PARTY (LP)	30
71	Polydor 2460-123	TRIBUTE TO LOUIS ARMSTRONG VOL. 1 (LP)	35
71	Polydor 2460-124	TRIBUTE TO LOUIS ARMSTRONG VOL. 2 (LP)	35
71	Polydor 2460-125	TRIBUTE TO LOUIS ARMSTRONG VOL. 3 (LP)	35
72	Black Lion BLP 12109	IF I HAD A TALKING PICTURE (LP)	15
72	Black Lion BLP 12112	AN EVENING WITH... VOL. 1 (LP)	25
72	Black Lion BLP 12113	AN EVENING WITH... VOL. 2 (LP)	25

72	Black Lion BLP 12115/6	IN CONCERT (2 LP)	15
75	Black Lion BLP 12120	BAND SHOWCASE VOL. 1 (LP)	20
76	Black Lion BLP 12121	BAND SHOWCASE VOL. 2 (LP)	22
76	Black Lion BLP 12131	DIXIELAND PARTY (LP)	30
76	Black Lion BLP 12161/2	SALUTE TO SATCHMO (2 LP)	30

DANNY WELTON

60	Coral Q 72409	Boogie Woogie/To Each His Own	8

WENDY & LEMMY

82	Bronze BRO 151	Stand By Your Man/No Class/Masterplan (p/s)	7

(see also Motörhead)

WE'RE TIRED

77	Deadline DEADS 8	My Life's On The Line/Against All Odds (p/s)	20
77	Deadline DEADS 11	Guide Me Through Hell/Time Is Against Me (p/s)	25
78	Deadline DEADS 15	Over The Edge/Anal Retentive (p/s, as We're Tired & We're Proud)	8
77	Deadline DEADLP 2	FIND THE PRICE IN TIME (LP)	50

WERLWINDS

61	Columbia DB 4650	Winding It Up/Dig Deep	20

HOWARD WERTH & MOONBEAMS

74	Charisma CB 225	Lucinda/Johan	5
75	Charisma CAS 11004	KING BRILLIANT (LP, with inner sleeve)	12

(see also Audience)

BRIAN WESKE

62	Oriole CB 1723	In The Midst Of The Crowd/All Mine Alone	10
62	Oriole CB 1776	24 Hours In A Day/Where Does The Clown Go	10

FRED WESLEY & J.B.s

73	Polydor 2066 322	Doing It To Death/Everybody Got Soul (with J.B.s)	10
74	Mojo 2093 025	J.B. Shout/Back Stabbers (with J.B.s)	8
80	RSO RSO 67	Houseparty/I Make Music (solo)	10
80	RSO RSO 67	Houseparty/I Make Music (12", solo)	18
74	Polydor 2391 125	DAMN RIGHT, I AM SOMEBODY (LP, with J.B.s)	50
74	Polydor 2391 161	BREAKIN' BREAD (LP, with J.B.s)	30

(see also James Brown, J.B.s)

WES MINSTER FIVE

64	Carnival CV 7017	Shakin' The Blues/Railroad Blues	12
65	Carnival CV 7019	Sticks And Stones/Mickey's Monkey	18

(see also Maynell Wilson, Dave Greenslade)

FRANK WESS

64	Fontana TL 5291	THE AWARD WINNER (LP)	12

ADAM 'BATMAN' WEST

76	Target TGT 111	Batman And Robin/The Story Of Batman	7

DODIE WEST

64	Decca F 12046	Goin' Out Of My Head/Is He Feeling Blue	12
65	Piccadilly 7N 35239	In The Deep Of The Night/Rovin' Boy (some in p/s)	15/8
65	Piccadilly 7N 35261	Thinking Of You/And Love Will Come	8
66	Piccadilly 7N 35287	Make The World Go Away/Who Does He Think He Is	8
68	Philips BF 1698	Living In Limbo/Birdie Told Me	7

KEITH WEST

67	Parlophone R 5623	Excerpt From "A Teenage Opera"/MARK WIRTZ ORCHESTRA: Theme From "A Teenage Opera"	6
67	Parlophone R 5651	Sam (From "A Teenage Opera')/MARK WIRTZ'S MOOD MOSAIC: Thimble Full Of Puzzles (promos in art sleeve)	20/8
68	Parlophone R 5713	On A Saturday/The Kid Was A Killer	50
72	Parlophone R 5957	Excerpt From "A Teenage Opera"/Sam (From "A Teenage Opera")	7
73	Deram DM 402	Riding For A Fall/Days About To Rain	7
74	Deram DM 410	Havin' Someone/Know There's No Livin' Without You	7
81	Video VID 02	Excerpt From "A Teenage Opera"/Count On Me (p/s)	5

(see also Tomorrow, Four + One, In Crowd, Mark Wirtz)

LESLIE WEST('S MOUNTAIN)

69	Bell BLL 1078	Dreams Of Milk And Honey/Wheels On Fire (as Leslie West's Mountain)	20
69	Bell SBLL 126	MOUNTAIN (LP, as Leslie West's Mountain)	20
75	RCA RS 1009	THE GREAT FATSBY (LP)	15
76	Phantom PHS 701	THE LESLIE WEST BAND (LP)	12

(see also Jolliver Arkansas, Mountain, West Bruce & Laing)

MAE WEST

67	Stateside SS 2021	Twist And Shout/Day Tripper	15
73	MGM 2006 203	Great Balls Of Fire/Men	12
56	Brunswick LAT 8082	THE FABULOUS MAE WEST (LP)	50
67	Stateside (S)SL 10197	WAY OUT WEST (LP)	30
73	Polydor 2315 207	GREAT BALLS OF FIRE (LP)	18

SPEEDY WEST & JIMMY BRYANT

55	Capitol EAP1 520	TWO GUITARS COUNTRY STYLE PT. 1 (EP)	30
55	Capitol EAP2 520	TWO GUITARS COUNTRY STYLE PT. 2 (EP)	30
53	Capitol LC 6619	CAPITOL PRESENTS SPEEDY WEST & JIMMY BRYANT (10" LP)	40
55	Capitol LC 6694	TWO GUITARS COUNTRY STYLE (10" LP)	40

TABBY WEST

58	Capitol CL 14861	All That I Want/If You Promise Not To Tell	8

			MINT VALUE £
WEST AFRICAN RHYTHM BOYS			
50s	Melodisc HI 1	Calar O/Y B Club	5
50s	Melodisc HI 2	Iwa D'arekere/Ero Ya Kowawo	5
58	Melodisc MEL 1505	Ominira/Gbonimawo	5
59	Melodisc MEL 1513	We Have It In Africa/Aye Wa Adara	5
60	Melodisc MEL 1567	Nigeria Odowoyin/Asikoloto	5
60	Melodisc MEL 1568	Nigeria Koniset/Jekafo Ju Agbawo	5
MIKE WESTBROOK (CONCERT BAND)			
69	Deram DM 234	A Life Of Its Own/Can't Get It Out Of My Mind	20
70	Deram DM 286	Requiem/Hooray	20
70	Deram DM 311	Magic Garden/Original Peter (with Norma Winstone)	30
67	Deram DML 1013	CELEBRATION (LP, as Mike Westbrook Concert Band)	120
68	Deram DML/SML 1031	RELEASE (LP)	70
69	Deram SML 1047	MARCHING SONG VOL. 1 (LP)	70
69	Deram SML 1048	MARCHING SONG VOL. 2 (LP)	70
70	Deram SML 1069	LOVE SONGS (LP, as Mike Westbrook Concert Band with Norma Winstone)	100
71	RCA SER 5612	TYGER: A CELEBRATION OF WILLIAM BLAKE (LP, with insert)	130
72	RCA Neon NE 10	MIKE WESTBROOK'S METROPOLIS (LP, gatefold sleeve)	70
72	Cadillac SGC 1001	LIVE (LP, private pressing)	30
75	RCA SF 8433	CITADEL/ROOM 315 (2-LP, with John Surman)	30
75	Transatlantic TRA 323	LOVE/DREAM & VARIATIONS (LP)	25
76	Transatlantic TRA 312	PLAYS FOR THE RECORD (LP)	20
78	Original ORA 001	GOOSE SAUCE (LP)	20
78	Original ORA 002	PIANO (LP)	20
79	RCA PL 25252	MAMA CHICAGO (LP)	20
80	Original ORA 203	WESTBROOK BLAKE (LP)	30
82	Original ORA 309	THE CORTEGE (LP)	30
83	Westbrook LWN 1	A LITTLE WESTBROOK MUSIC (LP)	35
88	Venture VEB 13	LONDON BRIDGE IS BROKEN DOWN (LP)	18
(see also Solid Gold Cadillac, John Surman, Norma Winstone)			
WEST, BRUCE & LAING			
73	RSO 2090 113	Dirty Shoes/Backfire	5
73	CBS 65314	WHY DONTCHA (LP)	15
73	RSO 2394 107	WHATEVER TURNS YOU ON (LP)	15
74	RSO 2394 128	LIVE 'N' KICKIN' (LP)	18
(see also Jack Bruce, Leslie West, Mountain)			
WEST COAST CONSORTIUM			
67	Pye 7N 17352	Some Other Someday/Looking Back	15
68	Pye 7N 17482	Colour Sergeant Lillywhite/Lady From Baltimore	35
(see also Consortium)			
WEST COAST DELEGATION			
67	Deram DM 113	Reach The Top/Mr. Personality Man	15
WEST COAST KNACK			
67	Capitol CL 15497	I'm Aware/Time Waits For No One	15
WEST COAST POP ART EXPERIMENTAL BAND			
68	Reprise RSLP 6298	A CHILD'S GUIDE TO GOOD AND EVIL (LP)	90
WEST END			
80s	Continental TIN 001	The Servant/Fiction (p/s)	5
JOHNNY WESTERN			
60	Philips PB 1030	The Ballad Of Paladin/The Guns Of Rio Muerto (B-side with Richard Boone)	7
WESTERNAIRES ORCHESTRA with CURLY WILLIAMS			
57	Brunswick 05692	Walking Alone In A Crowd/Sweet Talk (Won Her Loving Heart)	6
WEST FIVE			
65	HMV POP 1396	Congratulations/She Mine	35
65	HMV POP 1428	Someone Ain't Right/Just Like Romeo And Juliet	18
66	HMV POP 1513	If It Don't Work Out/Back To Square One	10
(see also Ferris Wheel)			
WEST INDIANS			
68	Doctor Bird DB 1121	Right On Time/Hokey Pokey	22
68	Doctor Bird DB 1127	Falling In Love/I Mean It	22
69	Camel CA 16	Strange Whisperings/CARL DAWKINS: Hard To Handle	15
71	Dynamic DYN 413	Never Gonna Give You Up/REBELLIOUS SUBJECTS: Never Give Up	10
(see also Prunes, Kilowatts, Upsetters)			
CLIVE WESTLAKE			
68	Fontana TF 940	199 Days/From The Beginning To The End	6
JILL WESTLAKE			
58	Columbia DB 4132	Sharin'/Over And Over Again	12
58	Columbia DB 4132	Sharin'/Over And Over Again (78)	10
KEVIN WESTLAKE & GARY FARR			
68	Marmalade 598 007	Everyday/Green	12
(see also Gary Farr & T-Bones, T-Bones, Blossom Toes, B.B. Blunder)			
WESTMORELITES			
70	Clandisc CLA 217	Zion/CLANCY ECCLES & DYNAMITES: Revival	8
(see also Minstrels)			
GLEN WESTON			
68	Columbia DB 8328	With This Ring/Liane	5

KIM WESTON

64 Stateside SS 359 — A Little More Love/Go Ahead And Laugh ... 65
65 Tamla Motown TMG 511 — I'm Still Loving You/Just Loving You ... 85
65 Tamla Motown TMG 538 — Take Me In Your Arms (Rock Me A Little While)/Don't Compare Me With Her ... 50
66 Tamla Motown TMG 554 — Helpless/A Love Like Yours ... 50
67 MGM MGM 1338 — I Got What You Need/Someone Like You ... 20
67 MGM MGM 1357 — That's Groovy/Land Of Tomorrow ... 25
68 MGM MGM 1382 — Nobody/You're Just The Kind Of Guy ... 25
69 Major Minor MM 619 — From Both Sides Now/We Try Harder ... 6
70 Major Minor MM 683 — Danger, Heartbreak Dead Ahead/I'll Be Thinking ... 10
75 Tamla Motown TMG 1000 — Do Like I Do/MARVELETTES: Finders Keepers, Losers Weepers ... 30
65 Tamla Motown TME 2005 — KIM WESTON (EP) ... 140
66 Tamla Motown TME 2015 — ROCK ME A LITTLE WHILE (EP) ... 300
67 MGM MGM-C(S) 8055 — FOR THE FIRST TIME (LP) ... 75
71 Stax 2362 021 — KIM KIM KIM (LP) ... 35

(see also Johnny Nash & Kim Weston, Marvin Gaye & Kim Weston)

PETE WESTON

70 Gas GAS 146 — Something Sweet/BIM & BAM: Love Letters ... 12
70 Punch PH 28 — In The Mood (& His Band)/Slide Mongoose (actually "Sly Mongoose") ... 12

(see also I Roy)

WEST ONE

88 Que Q 9 — California '69/Eurotrash (gig freebie, white label) ... 12
80s private cassette — WEST ONE (cassette) ... 12

WEST POINT SUPERNATURAL

67 Reaction 591 013 — Time Will Tell/Night Train ... 18

WESTSIDE

74 People PEO 111 — Running In And Out Of My Life/Highway Demon ... 5

WESTWIND

70 Penny Farthing PEN 737 — Love Is A Funny Sort Of Thing/Breakout ... 8
70 Penny Farthing PELS 505 — LOVE IS (LP) ... 120

WE THE PEOPLE

66 London HLH 10089 — He Doesn't Go About It Right/You Burn Me Up And Down ... 100

WE THREE TRIO

65 London HLA 9966 — Baby The Rain Must Fall/Shine For Me ... 7
67 Fontana TL 5308 — THE WE THREE TRIO (LP) ... 18

WET WET WET

86 Lyntone/Jamming! — I Can Give You Everything/FLOOR: Hold On (flexidisc free with *Jamming!* magazine) ... 12/7
87 Precious JWLD 3 — Wishing I Was Lucky (Remix)/Words Of Wisdom/Wishing I Was Lucky (Metal Mix)/I Still Can't Remember Your Name (12", double pack) ... 10
87 Precious JWLS 4 — Sweet Little Mystery/Don't Let Me Be Lonely Tonight (shaped picture disc) ... 10
87 Phonogram 870563-7 — Sweet Little Mystery/Don't Let Me Be Lonely Tonight//I Can Give You Everything/Heaven Help Us (double pack, gatefold p/s) ... 8
87 Precious JEWEL 412 — SWEET LITTLE MYSTERY EP: Sweet Little Mystery/Don't Let Me Be Lonely/Heaven Help Us All/May You Never (12", PVC 'wet cover') ... 12
87 Precious JEWEL 5 — I Remember/I Don't Believe (unreleased)
87 Precious JEWEL 512 — I Remember/I Don't Believe (12", unreleased)
87 Precious JEWEL 6 — Angel Eyes (Home And Away)/We Can Love (box set with calendar) ... 6
87 Precious JWLCD 6 — Angel Eyes (Home And Away — Full Length Version)/We Can Love/Home And Away (Original Demo — 7" Version) (CD) ... 10
88 Precious 080274-2 — Angel Eyes/I Don't Believe/Wishing I Was Lucky/Angel Eyes (video) (CD, some are golden) ... 25/20
88 Precious JEWEL 777 — Temptation/Bottled Emotions (Keen For Loving) (gatefold/booklet p/s) ... 5
88 Precious JWLCD 7 — Temptation (Extended)/Bottled Emotions/I Remember (Extended)/Heaven Helps Us All (CD) ... 10
88 Precious 080 476-2 — Temptation (Extended Version)/I Remember (Extended Version)/Bottled Emotions (Keen For Loving)/Heaven Help Us All (CD Video) ... 15
89 Precious JWPD 10 — Broke Away/You've Had It/Now For Something Completely Different (pic disc) ... 8
89 Phonogram JWLC 1012 — Broke Away/You've Had It/Now For Something Completely Different (12", box set with calendar) ... 8
89 Precious JWCD 10 — Broke Away (Original Version)/You've Had It (Club Mix)/Sweet Surrender (Club Mix) (CD, picture disc) ... 8
90 Precious JWLTP 11 — Hold Back The River/Keys To Your Heart (Original Demo)/With A Little Help From My Friends (Live) (12", p/s) ... 8

WE UGLY DOGS

67 BT Puppy BTS 45537 — First Spring Rain/Poor Man ... 7

(see also Tokens, U.S. Double Quartet)

W. GIMMICS

65 Polydor EPH 27 125 — HOT RODS (EP, manufactured in Europe) ... 60

WHALE FEATHERS

71 Blue Horizon 2431 009 — WHALE FEATHERS (LP) ... 70

WHALES

68 CBS 3766 — Come Down Little Bird/Beachcomber ... 10
69 CBS 4126 — Tell It To The Rain/Girl, Hey Girl ... 8

WHAM!

82 Innervision IVL A 2442 — Wham Rap! (Enjoy What You Do) (Special Club Remix)/(Special U.S. Mix) (p/s, 1st pressing, paper label, songwriting credit: "Panos/Ridgeley") ... 7
83 Innervision IVL A 2442 — Wham Rap! (Enjoy What You Do) (Special Club Remix)/(Special U.S. Mix) (reissue, red & blue title p/s) ... 5

MINT VALUE £

82	Innervision IVL A 13-2442	Wham Rap! (Enjoy What You Do) (Special Club Remix)/(Special U.S. Mix) (12", paper label, p/s, "Panos/Ridgeley" or "Michael/Ridgeley" songwriting credit)	12/7
82	Innervision IVL A 13-2442	Wham Rap! (Enjoy What You Do) (Social Mix)/(Unsocial Mix) (12", initially in p/s, later in plain black die-cut sleeve)	15/7
82	Innervision IVL A 2442	Wham Rap! (Enjoy What You Do) (Special Club Remix)/(Special U.S. Mix) (12", reissue, red & blue title p/s)	12
83	Innervision IVL A 13-2766	Young Guns (Go For It)/Going For It (12", p/s)	10
83	Innervision IVL A 3143	Bad Boys/Bad Boys (Instrumental) (poster p/s)	8
83	Innervision IVL WA 3143	Bad Boys/Bad Boys (Instrumental) (picture disc)	12
83	Innervision IVL WA 3613	Club Tropicana/Blue (Armed With Love) (picture disc)	15
84	Epic TA 4440	Wake Me Up Before You Go-Go/Wake Me Up (Instrumental)/ A Ray Of Sunshine (12", poster p/s)	15
84	Epic QA/WA 4743	Freedom/Freedom (Instrumental) (George Michael- or Andrew Ridgeley-shaped picture disc in wallet, PVC gatefold sleeve; each or as set)	18/30
85	Epic QTA 4949	Everything She Wants (U.S. Remix)/Last Christmas (The Pudding Mix) (12", reissue, A-sides reversed, some w/ stickered p/s & free calendar)	15/7
85	Epic WTA 6716	I'm Your Man (Extended Stimulation)/Do It Right (Instrumental)/ I'm Your Man (A Capella) (12", picture disc)	10
89	Epic 654 915-3	Wake Me Up Before You Go-Go/Freedom/The Edge Of Heaven (3" CD, 'Solid Gold Classics' series)	15
83	Epic (no cat. no.)	Bad Boys/(track by other artist) (no p/s, free with 'KP Crisps' offer)	7
84	Epic KELL 4	Club Tropicana/HERBIE HANCOCK: Rock It (no p/s, promo only, free with 'Rice Krispies' offer)	7
84	Epic (no cat. no.)	Merry Xmas From Wham (fan club Christmas single, no p/s)	10
86	Epic WHAM 2	THE FINAL (2-LP box, gold vinyl picture discs, with sealed T-shirt, calendar, pencil, note-pad and no'd certificate)	55
84	Innervision CDIVL 25328	FANTASTIC (CD)	45
84	Epic CDEPC 86311	MAKE IT BIG (CD)	45

(see also George Michael, Pepsi & Shirley)

PEETIE WHEATSTRAW

69	Matchbox SDR 191	THE DEVIL'S SON IN LAW (LP)	25
69	Matchbox SDR 192	THE HIGH SHERIFF FROM HELL (LP)	25

BILLY ED WHEELER

64	London HLR 9920	On The Outside (Lookin' In)/The Right Foot In His World	8
65	London HLR 9950	Ode To The Little Brown Shack Out Back/Sister Sara	8
65	London HAR/SHR 8221	MEMORIES OF AMERICA (LP)	18

KENNY WHEELER & JOHN DANKWORTH ORCHESTRA

68	Fontana STL 5494	WINDMILL TILTER (LP)	100
70s	Incus 10	SONG FOR SOMEONE (LP)	100

(see also Johnny Dankworth, Elton Dean)

WHEELS

65	Columbia DB 7682	Gloria/Don't You Know	135
66	Columbia DB 7827	Bad Little Woman/Road Block (mispressing, demos & a few issues play "Call My Name" on B-side)	135
66	Columbia DB 7827	Bad Little Woman/Road Block	350
66	Columbia DB 7981	Kicks/Call My Name	135

(see also James Brothers, Demick & Armstrong)

WHEELS OF TIME

67	Spin SP 62008	1984/So Long (some in company sleeves)	60/50

WHERE FORTUNE SMILES

(see under John Surman)

WHICHWHAT

69	Beacon BEA 127	Gimme Gimme Good Lovin'/Wonderland Of Love	25
69	Beacon BEA 131	Why Do Lovers Break Each Other's Heart/When I See Her Smile	6
69	Beacon BEA 133	In The Year 2525/Parting	6
69	Beacon BEA 144	I Wanna Be Free/It's All Over Again	6
70	Beacon BEA 169	Vietnam Rose/Shame And Solution	6
70	Beacon BEAS 14	WHICHWHAT'S FIRST (LP)	50

WHIPS

71	Mother MOT 6	Julie Ivory Towers/MUFF & BANKHOUSE ASSEMBLY: Funky Shoot Out	10

WHIRLWIND

78	Chiswick NS 25	Hang Loose/Together Forever (p/s)	10
78	Chiswick NS 42	I Only Wish (That I'd Been Told)/Ducktails (unissued)	
78	Chiswick CHIS 103	I Only Wish (That I'd Been Told)/Ducktails (p/s)	10
79	Chiswick CHIS 117	You Got Class/Losing To You (unissued in U.K.; France-only)	
80	Chiswick CHIS 122	Heaven Knows/Cruisin' Around (p/s)	10
80	Chiswick CHIS 127	Stayin' Out All Night/Running Wild (unissued; p/s only)	
80	Chiswick PSR 447	Midnight Blue/Honey Hush/Such A Fool/Stayin' Out All Night (promo only)	8
78	Chiswick CH 4	BLOWIN' UP A STORM (10" mini-LP)	12
78	Chiswick WIK 7	BLOWIN' UP A STORM (LP, with 2 extra tracks)	15
80	Chiswick CWK 3012	MIDNIGHT BLUE (LP)	15

WHIRLWINDS

64	HMV POP 1301	Look At Me/Baby Not Like You	55

(see also Mockingbirds, Graham Gouldman, 10cc)

NANCY WHISKEY (& HER SKIFFLERS)

57	Oriole CB 1394	He's Solid Gone/Ella Speed (as Nancy Whiskey & Her Skifflers)	22
57	Oriole CB 1394	He's Solid Gone/Ella Speed (as Nancy Whiskey & Her Skifflers) (78)	10
58	Oriole CB 1452	Hillside In Scotland/I Know Where I'm Goin'	18
58	Oriole CB 1452	Hillside In Scotland/I Know Where I'm Goin' (78)	10
59	Oriole CB 1485	The Old Grey Goose/Johnny Blue	15

59	Oriole CB 1485	The Old Grey Goose/Johnny Blue (78)	10
65	Fontana TF 612	Bowling Green/I'm Leaving Today	8
67	CBS 3090	Freight Train/The Game	8
57	Topic 7T 10	NANCY WHISKEY SINGS (7" LP)	35
57	Oriole MG 10018	THE INTOXICATING MISS WHISKEY (10" LP, with Chas McDevitt Skiffle Group)	30

(see also Chas McDevitt Skiffle Group)

WHISPERS

71	Mojo 2916 003	THE WHISPERS (LP)	35
74	Contempo CRM 106	THE WHISPERS (LP)	18
74	Janus 9104 400	WHISPERS GETTIN' LOUDER (LP)	18

WHISTLER

71	Deram SML 1083	HO-HUM (LP)	30

WHISTLING WILLIE

68	Duke DU 8	Penny Reel/Soul Tonic	10

(see also Neville, Neville Willoughby)

DAVE WHITAKER

65	CBS BPG 62532	MUSIC TO SPY BY (LP)	20

SHARON WHITCOMB & FRED

72	RA RALP 6011	SPICE OF LIFE (LP)	20

IAN WHITCOMB

65	Capitol CL 15382	This Sporting Life/Fizz	6
65	Capitol CL 15395	You Turn Me On/Poor But Honest	12
65	Capitol CL 15418	N-N-Nervous!/The End	6
66	Capitol CL 15431	Good Hard Rock/High Blood Pressure	7
66	Stateside SS 573	Where Did Robinson Crusoe Go With Friday/Poor Little Bird)	6
72	Ember EMBS 324	You Turn Me On/This Sporting Life (mono)	12
73	Ember NR 5065	YOU TURN ME ON (LP, with Jimmy Page & John Paul Jones)	50

BARRY WHITE

67	President PT 139	All In The Run Of A Day/Don't Take Your Love From Me	10

BRIAN WHITE & MAGNA JAZZ BAND

62	HMV CLP 1534	BRIAN WHITE AND THE MAGNA JAZZ BAND (LP)	125

(see also Magna Jazz Band)

BUKKA WHITE

66	Fontana 688 804 ZL	SKY SONGS (LP, with Big Willie)	35
66	CBS Realm 52629	BUKKA WHITE (LP)	55
69	Blue Horizon 7-63229	MEMPHIS HOT SHOTS (LP)	80
69	Sonet SNTF 609	THE LEGACY OF THE BLUES VOL. 1 (LP, with insert)	15

CHRIS WHITE

76	Charisma CB 272	Spanish Wine/She's Only Dancing	6
76	Charisma CB 282	Natural Rhythm/Another Little Miracle	6
76	Charisma CB 294	Don't Look Down/Summertime Summertime	6
77	Charisma CB 303	Don't Worry Baby/Child Of The Sun	10
76	Charisma CAS 1118	MOUTH MUSIC (LP)	18

(see also Joyce's Angels)

DANNY WHITE

67	Sue WI 4031	Keep My Woman Home/I'm Dedicating My Life	55
74	MCA MU 155	Cracked Up Over You/Taking Inventory	10

DUKE WHITE

63	Island WI 084	It's Over/Forever	25
64	Black Swan WI 442	Be Wise/BABA BROOKS: Musical Workshop	25
65	Black Swan WI 444	Sow Good Seeds/BABA BROOKS BAND: Bus Strike	25

ED WHITE

61	Pye 7N SR15320	Coral Reef/Tropical Blue (stereo only)	15

GEORGIA WHITE

54	Vocalion V 1038	Was I Drunk?/Moonshine Blues (78)	20

IAN WHITE

70	private pressing	IAN WHITE (LP)	20

JAY WHITE

56	London RE-F 1045	FAR-AWAY PLACES VOL. 1 (EP)	12

JEANETTE WHITE

69	A&M AMS 761	Music/No Sunshine	22

JOE WHITE

64	R&B JB 137	Sinners (as Joe White & Maytals)/ROLAND ALPHONSO: King Solomon	30
64	Ska Beat JB 180	Punch You Down (with Chuck)/TOMMY McCOOK: Cotton Tree	40
64	Island WI 145	When Are You Young/Wanna Go Home	30
64	Island WI 159	Hog In A Co Co/SKATALITES: Sandy Gully	30
64	Island WI 166	Downtown Girl/RICHARD BROS.: You Are My Sunshine (B-side is actually "Cool Smoke" by Don Drummond)	30
65	Island WI 201	Low-Minded People (as Chuck & Joe White)/Irene	30
66	Doctor Bird DB 1001	Every Night (with Chuck)/BABA BROOKS & HIS BAND: First Session	35
66	Doctor Bird DB 1024	My Love For You/SAMMY ISMAY & BABA BROOKS BAND: Cocktails For Two	30
66	Doctor Bird DB 1043	So Close (as Joe White & Della)/BABA BROOKS & HIS BAND: Eighth Games	30
67	Doctor Bird DB 1069	Rudies All Around/Bad Man	30
67	Doctor Bird DB 1080	Lonely Nights/I Need You	30
67	Doctor Bird DB 1090	I Need A Woman/Hot Hops	30
68	Blue Cat BS 108	Way Of Life (actually by Lyn Tait & Jets)/I'm So Proud	35

			MINT VALUE £
68	Blue Cat BS 119	Try A Little Tenderness/LYN TAITT & CARL BRYAN: Tender Arms	25
68	Blue Cat BS 130	Pretty Girl/DERMOTT LYNCH: You Went Away	25
69	Sugar ESS 102	My Guiding Star/If I Needed Someone	12
70	Sugar SU 103	Yesterday/I Am Free	12
70	Trojan TR 7742	So Much Love/Maybe Now	12
70	Trojan TR 7768	I'm Going To Get There/RUPIE EDWARDS ALLSTARS: Kinky Funky Reggae	12
70	Big BG 301	This Is The Time/The Other Day	12
71	Big BG 309	Baby I Care/Ain't Misbehavin'	12
72	Songbird SB 1072	Trinity/SCOTTY: Monkey Drop	12
72	Dynamic DYN 440	Kenyatta/RECORDING BAND: Version	12
73	Gayfeet GS 202	If It Don't Work Out/BABA BROOKS BAND: Ki Salaboca	12
73	Harry J. HJ 6648	Joe White (Mrs. Jones)/Joe White (Mrs. Jones) – Version (song actually titled "Me And Mrs Jones")	12
77	Ultra PFU 1002	Give And Take (On Both Sides)/Roots Dub	12
70s	Magnet MGT 006	SINCE THE OTHER DAY (LP)	25

(see also Chuck, Rue Lloyd)

JOSH WHITE

50	Jazz Parade B 10	I Want You And I Need You/One Meat Ball (78)	8
50	Jazz Parade B 11	The Blind Man Stood On The Road And Cried/St. James Infirmary (78)	8
50	Jazz Parade B 12	Got A Head Like A Rock/No. 12 Train (78)	10
50	London L 739	Take A Gal Like You/Wanderings (78)	6
50	London L 810	Like A Natural Man/The Foggy, Foggy Dew (78)	6
50	London L 828	I'm Gonna Move To The Outskirts Of Town/Hard Time Blues (78)	6
50	London L 907	T.B. Blues/Molly Malone (78)	8
50	Melodisc MEL 8008	Mean Mistreatin' Woman/Baby Baby (12" 78)	10
51	Melodisc MEL 1145	Fare Thee Well/Outskirts Of Town (78)	8
51	Melodisc MEL 1146	House I Live In/When I Lay Down (78)	6
51	Melodisc MEL 1155	Dupree/Miss Otis Regrets (78)	6
51	Vogue B 10	I Want You And I Need You/One Meat Ball (78)	6
51	London L 1028	On Top Of Old Smoky/Black Girl (with Bill Hill's Orchestra & Stargazers) (78)	6
51	London L 1138	Barbara Allen/The Lass With The Delicate Air (78)	6
52	London L 1142	Lonesome Road/He Never Said A Mumblin' Word (78)	8
52	London L 1143	Call Me Darling/I Want You, I Need You (78)	15
52	London L 1144	Waltzing Landing/Apples, Peaches And Cherries (78)	15
52	London L 1161	Free And Equal Blues (Parts 1 & 2) (78)	10
54	London L 907	T.B. Blues/Molly Malone (78, silver label reissue)	10
57	Pye NJE 1057	BLUES AND... PART 1 (EP)	12
57	Pye NJE 1058	BLUES AND... PART 2 (EP)	12
57	Pye NJE 1059	BLUES AND... PART 3 (EP)	12
57	HMV 7EG 8465	THE JOSH WHITE STORIES (EP)	15
58	Mercury YEP 9504	SOUTHERN BLUES (EP)	15
64	Storyville SEP 388	STORYVILLE BLUES ANTHOLOGY VOL. 8 (EP)	12
64	Mercury 10006 MCE	JOSH WHITE (EP)	15
51	London H-APB 1005	A JOSH WHITE PROGRAM (10" LP)	20
52	Brunswick LA 8562	BALLADS AND BLUES (10" LP)	18
54	Brunswick LA 8653	BALLADS AND BLUES VOL. 2 (10" LP)	18
54	London H-APB 1032	JOSH WHITE SINGS — VOL. 2 (10" LP)	18
54	Mercury MG 25014	SONGS BY JOSH WHITE (10" LP)	18
55	London H-APB 1038	JOSH COMES A-VISITIN' (10" LP)	18
56	Nixa Jazz Today NJL 2	BLUES AND... (LP)	18
58	HMV CLP 1159	JOSH WHITE STORIES VOLUME 1 (LP)	15
58	HMV CLP 1175	JOSH WHITE STORIES VOLUME 2 (LP)	15
62	Storyville SLP 123	JOHN HENRY, BALLADS, BLUES AND OTHER SONGS (LP)	15
62	Mercury MMC 14102	AT THE TOWN HALL (LP)	15
62	HMV CLP 1588	JOSH WHITE LIVE! (LP)	15
62	Golden Guinea GGL 0160	EMPTY BED BLUES (LP)	20
62	Golden Guinea GGL 0205	CHAIN GANG SONGS, SPIRITUALS AND BLUES (LP)	12
64	Mercury 20039 MCL	THE BEGINNING (LP)	18
64	Ace Of Hearts AH 65	JOSH WHITE (LP)	12
65	Mercury 20067 MCL	I'M ON MY OWN WAY (LP)	15
65	Saga SOC 988	JOSH WHITE AND CARL SANDBURG (LP)	12
67	MFP MFP 1139	GOOD MORNING BLUES (LP)	12
69	Decca SPA 44	THE WORLD OF JOSH WHITE (LP)	12
70	Marble Arch MAL 1208	IN MEMORIAM (LP)	12
60s	Storyville SLP 175	BLUES SINGER AND BALLADEER (LP)	12

(see also Teddy Moss/Josh White)

JOSH & BEVERLEY WHITE

64	Realm REP 4003	BEVERLEY & JOSH WHITE JNR (EP)	12

K.C. WHITE

72	Dynamic DYN 434	Man No Dead/Man No Dead — Version	8
73	Green Door GD 4056	First Cut Is The Deepest/No Good Girl	8
73	Technique TE 929	Anywhere But Nowhere/Bush In Session	8

KITTY WHITE

51	Brunswick 04726	Paradise/You're Tired Of Me (78)	8
51	Capitol CL 13549	I'm Playing With Fire/It Pays To Advertise (78)	8
54	London HL 8102	Jesse James/Scratch My Back (B-side with Dave Howard)	55
54	London HL 8102	Jesse James/Scratch My Back (78, B-side with Dave Howard)	20

LENNY WHITE

75	Atlantic K 50213	VENUSIAN SUMMER (LP)	12

LOUISA JANE WHITE

69	Philips BF 1810	When The Battle Is Over/Blue Ribbons	10
70	Philips BF 1834	How Does It Feel/Truth In My Tears	6

58	London HA-D 2109	GOIN' PLACES (LP)	30
61	HMV CLP 1418/CSD 1339	SINGS THE JEROME KERN SONGBOOK VOL. ONE (LP, mono/stereo)	15/18
61	HMV CLP 1419/CSD 1340	SINGS THE JEROME KERN SONGBOOK VOL. TWO (LP, mono/stereo)	15/18
61	London HA-D 2321	JUST A DREAM (LP)	25
67	London HA-U/SH-U 8317	THE WHEEL OF HURT (LP)	18
67	London HA-U 8332	MAGGIE ISN'T MARGARET ANYMORE (LP)	18

(see also Jimmy Wakely, Bob Hope, Dean Martin)

RAY WHITLEY

65	HMV POP 1473	I've Been Hurt/There Is One Boy	55

BOBBY WHITLOCK

72	CBS 65109	BOBBY WHITLOCK (LP)	12
73	CBS 65301	RAW VELVET (LP)	15

(see also Derek & Dominos)

SLIM WHITMAN

78s

53	London L 1186	How Can I Tell/Love Song Of The Waterfall (gold label print)	10
53	London L 1191	My Love Is Growing Stale/Bandera Waltz (gold label print)	15
53	London HL 1191	My Love Is Growing Stale/Bandera Waltz (re-pressing, silver label print)	20
53	London L 1194	Restless Heart/Song Of The Old Water Wheel (gold label print)	8
53	London L 1206	My Heart Is Broken In Three/Cold Empty Arms (gold label print)	12
54	London HL 1186	How Can I Tell/Love Song Of The Waterfall (re-pressing, silver label print)	12
54	London L 1226	North Wind/Darlin' Don't Cry (gold label print)	8
54	London HL 1226	North Wind/Darlin' Don't Cry (re-pressing, silver label print)	8
54	London HL 8018	Stairway To Heaven/Lord, Help Me To Be As Thou	15
54	London HL 8039	Secret Love/Why	10
54	London HL 8061	Rose Marie/We Stood At The Altar (gold label)	7
54	London HL 8080	Beautiful Dreamer/Ride Away	8
57	London HLP 8416	Curtain Of Tears/Smoke Signals	10
58	London HLP 8590	A Very Precious Love/Careless Hands	12
58	London HLP 8642	Candy Kisses/Tormented	10
58	London HLP 8708	Wherever You Are/At The End Of Nowhere	15
59	London HLP 8835	I Never See Maggie Alone/The Letter Edged In Black	25

SINGLES

54	London L 1149	Indian Love Call/China Doll	30
54	London HL 1149	Indian Love Call/China Doll (re-pressing with different prefix)	18
54	London L 1214	There's A Rainbow In Every Teardrop/Danny Boy	35
54	London HL 1214	There's A Rainbow In Every Teardrop/Danny Boy (re-pressing)	20
54	London L 1226	North Wind/Darlin' Don't Cry	40
54	London HL 1226	North Wind/Darlin' Don't Cry (re-pressing with different prefix)	25
54	London HL 8018	Stairway To Heaven/Lord, Help Me To Be As Thou	65
54	London HL 8039	Secret Love/Why	35
54	London HL 8061	Rose Marie/We Stood At The Altar	20
54	London HL 8080	Beautiful Dreamer/Ride Away	30
54	London HL 8091	The Singing Hills/I Hate To See You Cry	30
55	London HL 8125	When I Grow Too Old To Dream/Cattle Call	30
55	London HL 8141	Haunted Hungry Heart/Roll On, Silvery Moon	30
55	London HLU 8167	I'll Never Stop Loving You/I'll Never Take You Back Again	30
55	London HLU 8196	Song Of The Wild/You Have My Heart	30
56	London HLU 8230	Tumbling Tumbleweeds/Tell Me	25
56	London HLU 8252	I'm A Fool/My Heart Is Broken In Three	25
56	London HLU 8287	Serenade/I Talk To The Waves	25
56	London HLU 8327	Dear Mary/Whiffenpoof Song	25
56	London HLU 8350	I'm Casting My Lasso Towards The Sky/There's A Love Knot In My Lariat	30
57	London HLP 8403	I'll Take You Home Again Kathleen/Careless Love	20

(The above singles were originally issued with gold label print & tri-centres; later round-centre and/or silver label print copies are worth half these values.)

57	London HLP 8416	Curtain Of Tears/Smoke Signals (silver label print)	15
57	London HLP 8420	Gone/An Amateur In Love (gold label print)	30
57	London HLP 8434	Many Times/Warm, Warm Lips	15
57	London HLP 8459	Lovesick Blues/Forever	15
57	London HLP 8518	Unchain My Heart/Hush-A-Bye	15
58	London HLP 8590	A Very Precious Love/Careless Hands	15
58	London HLP 8642	Candy Kisses/Tormented	15
58	London HLP 8708	Wherever You Are/At The End Of Nowhere	12
59	London HLP 8835	I Never See Maggie Alone/The Letter Edged In Black	10
59	London HLP 8896	What Kind Of God (Do You Think You Are)/A Tree In The Meadow (unissued)	
60	London HLP 9103	Roll, River, Roll/Twilla Lee	7
61	London HLP 9302	Vaya Con Dios/Ramona	7
64	Liberty LIB 66040	I'll Hold You In My Heart/No Other Arms, No Other Lips	6
65	Liberty LIB 66103	Reminiscing/Mansion On The Hill	6
65	Liberty LIB 12013	Remember Me (I'm The One Who Loves You)/Virginia	6
65	Liberty LIB 12020	More Than Yesterday/Broken Down Merry-Go-Round	6
66	Liberty LIB 66181	A Travelin' Man/I Remember You	6
66	Liberty LIB 66212	One Dream/Jerry	6
67	Liberty LIB 66226	What's The World A-Comin' To/You Bring Out The Best In Me	6
68	Liberty LBF 15066	Cool Water/Down In The Valley	6
69	Liberty LBF 15198	My Happiness/Rose Marie	6
69	Liberty LBF 15220	Stranger On The Shore/Star Of Hope	6
70	Liberty LBF 15394	My Heart Has A Mind Of Its Own/How Could I Not Love You	6
70	Liberty LBF 15430	Snowbird/How Could I Not Love You	6
71	United Artists UP 35277	I Climbed The Mountain/Jerry	5
73	United Artists UP 35493	Got The All Overs For You (All Over Me)/I'll See You When	5
74	United Artists UP 35728	Happy Anniversary/What I Had With You	5
75	United Artists UP 35775	Honeymoon Feeling/Foolish Question	6
75	United Artists UP 36017	When You Were Sweet Sixteen/How Could I Not Love You	5

MINT VALUE £

SHEILA WHITE

66 CBS 202465 Misfit/Switch Off The Night . . . 7

STEVE WHITE & GARY WALLACE

90s Acid Jazz JAZID 20T Never Stop (12", company sleeve) . . . 35
(see also Style Council)

TAM WHITE

67 Decca F 12711 World Without You/Someone You Should Know (unreleased)
68 Decca F 12849 Waiting Till The Night Comes Around/Girl Watcher . . . 10
69 Deram DM 261 That Old Sweet Roll/Don't Make Promises . . . 25
70 Middle Earth MDS 104 Lewis Carroll/Future Thoughts . . . 50
70 Middle Earth MDLS 304 TAM WHITE (LP) . . . 50
(see also Buzz, Boston Dexters)

TERRY WHITE & TERRIERS

59 Decca F 11133 Rock Around The Mailbags/Blackout . . . 75
59 Decca F 11133 Rock Around The Mailbags/Blackout (78) . . . 40

TONY JOE WHITE

68 Monument MON 1024 Soul Francisco/Whompt Out On You . . . 6
69 Monument MON 1031 Polk Salad Annie/Aspen Colorado . . . 8
69 Monument MON 1036 Willie And Laura Mae Jones/Baby Scratch My Back . . . 5
68 Monument LMO/SMO 5027 BLACK AND WHITE (LP) . . . 20
70 Monument LMO/SMO 5035 TONY JOE WHITE CONTINUED (LP) . . . 20
70 Monument SMO 5043 TONY JOE (LP) . . . 20
71 Warner Bros WS 1900 TONY JOE WHITE (LP) . . . 15
71 Warner Bros K 46068 TONY JOE WHITE (LP, reissue) . . . 12
72 Warner Bros K 46147 THE TRAIN I'M ON (LP) . . . 15
73 Warner Bros K 46229 HOME-MADE ICE CREAM (LP) . . . 15
73 Warner Bros K 56149 THE BEST OF TONY JOE WHITE (LP) . . . 15

TREVOR WHITE

76 Island WIP 6291 Crazy Kids/Movin' In The Right Direction (some with p/s) . . . 10/5
(see also Sparks, Radio Stars)

WHITE DUCK

72 Uni UN 541 Billy Goat/Really . . . 8
73 Uni UN 555 Honey, You'll Be Alright/Carry Love . . . 8
72 Uni UNLS 123 WHITE DUCK (LP) . . . 20
73 Uni UNLS 129 IN SEASON (LP) . . . 20

WHITE ELEPHANT

70s White Elephant RIOCH 1 CITY WALLS (LP, with other artists) . . . 12

RICK WHITEFIELD

71 Horse HOSS 10 Hey Mama/Ride Baby Ride . . . 6

WHITEFIRE

78 Whitefire 98DB 001 SUZANNE (EP) . . . 40

WHITE HART

79 Tradition TSR 033 IN SEARCH OF REWARD (LP) . . . 60

WHITE HEAT

79 Valium VAL 01 Nervous Breakdown/Sammy Sez (gatefold p/s) . . . 35
80 Valium VAL 02 Finished With The Fashions/Ordinary Joe (p/s, with insert) . . . 22
81 Valium VAL 03 City Beat/It's No Use (Young Ones) (p/s) . . . 15
82 Valium VALP 101 IN THE ZERO HOUR (LP) . . . 20

WHITE HEAT

84 Rock Shop RSR 007 WHITE HEAT (LP) . . . 20

WHITEHOUSE

80 Come Org. WDC 881004 BIRTHDEATH EXPERIENCE (LP) . . . 100
80 Come Org. WDC 881005 TOTAL SEX (LP) . . . 100
80 Come Org. WDC 881007 ERECTOR (LP, different coloured vinyls) . . . 100
81 Come Org. WDC 881010 DEDICATED TO PETER KÜRTEN, SADIST AND MASS SLAYER (LP, some on coloured vinyl, some in custom sleeve) . . . 100
81 Come Org. WDC GREAT WHITE DEATH (LP) . . . 100
81 Come Org. WDC 881013 BÜCHENWALD (LP) . . . 100
81 Come Org. WDC 881017 NEW BRITAIN (LP, with insert) . . . 125
80s Come Org. WDC 881027 PSYCHOPATHIA SEXUALIS (LP, clear or black vinyl) . . . 100
80s Come Org. WDC 883033 RIGHT TO KILL — DEDICATED TO DENNIS ANDREW NEILSEN (LP, & inserts) . 100
80s Come Org. WDC 150 MURDEROUS PASSIONS (LP, with Nurse With Wound) . . . 75
80s United Dairies UD 009 150 MURDEROUS PASSIONS (LP, with Nurse With Wound, reissue) . . . 40
80s United Dairies UD 009 150 MURDEROUS PASSIONS (LP, with Nurse With Wound, export issue, sealed in black vinyl) . . . 125
(Many of the above LPs were issued in customised white card sleeves & were later available in a generic 'Peter Kürten' sleeve, originally used for the 2nd pressing of the 'Peter Kürten' LP. This latter design was also used for counterfeits. There may also be various coloured vinyl variations of the above LPs, worth around the same value.)
81 Come Org. WDC 881020 LIVE ACTION 1 (cassette) . . . 20
80s Come Org. WDC 881022 LIVE ACTION 2 (cassette) . . . 20
80s Come Org. WDC 883044 RADIO INTERVIEWS/LIVE ACTION USA VOL. 1 (cassette) . . . 12
80s Come Org. WDC 883046 LIVE ACTION 13 USA VOL. III (cassette) . . . 12
80s Come Org. WDC 883047 LIVE ACTION 14 USA VOL. IV (cassette) . . . 12
80s Come Org. WDC 883048 LIVE ACTION 15/LIVE ACTION 16 USA VOL. V (cassette) . . . 12
80s Come Org. WDC 883049 LIVE ACTION 20 USA VOL VI (cassette) . . . 12
80s Come Org. WDC 883050 LIVE ACTION 22/LIVE ACTION 23 (cassette) . . . 12
80s Come Org. WDC 883052 USA REHEARSAL (cassette) . . . 12
80s Come Org. WDC 883053 LIVE ACTION 24/LIVE ACTION 25 (cassette) . . . 12
80s Come Org. WDC 883055 LIVE ACTION 26 (cassette) . . . 12
80s Susan Lawley 1 CREAM OF THE SECOND COMING (2-LP) . . . 45

91 Susan Lawley SL 002 THANK YOUR LUCKY STARS (LP). . . . 30
92 Susan Lawley SL 003 TWICE IS NOT ENOUGH (LP). . . . 30
(see also Come, Nurse With Wound, New Order, Skullflower, Konstruktivits)

WHITE LIGHTNING

84 Wild Party PP 1000 This Poison Fountain/Hypocrite (no p/s, 1,000 only) 40
90 Workshop JOB LP 2 AS MIDNIGHT APPROACHES (LP, with inner). . . . 15
(see also Static)

WHITE NOISE

75 Virgin VDJ 2 An Extract From White Noise 2 (promo only) 5
69 Island ILPS 9099 AN ELECTRIC STORM (LP, pink label) 50
75 Virgin V 2032 WHITE NOISE 2 (LP) 20
(see also BBC Radiophonic Workshop)

WHITE ON BLACK

74 Saydisc SDL 251 WHITE ON BLACK (LP) 30

WHITE PLAINS

70 Deram DM 280 My Baby Loves Lovin'/Show Me Your Hand 6
70 Deram DM 291 Today I Killed A Man I Didn't Know/I've Got You On My Mind 6
70 Deram DM 315 Julie Do Ya Love Me/I Need Your Everlasting Love 6
71 Deram DM 325 Every Little Move She Makes/Carolina's Comin' Home 6
71 Deram DM 333 When You Are A King/The World Gets Better With Love. . . . 6
71 Deram DM 340 Gonna Miss Her Mississippi/I'll Go Blind 6
72 Deram DM 348 I Can't Stop/Julie Anne 6
72 Deram DM 365 Dad You Saved The World/Beachcomber. . . . 6
73 Deram DM 371 Step Into A Dream/Look To See. . . . 6
73 Deram DM 405 Sunny Honey Girl/Julie Anne. . . . 6
74 Deram DM 415 Ecstasy/A Simple Man 6
76 Bradley BRAD 7609 Summer Nights/Wildest Dreams 6
70 Deram SML 1067 WHITE PLAINS (LP) 35
71 Deram SML 1092 WHEN YOU ARE A KING (LP) 35
(see also Edison Lighthouse, David & Jonathan, Kestrels, Brotherhood Of Man, Peter's Faces, Carter-Lewis & Southerners, Ivy League)

WHITE RABBIT

69 NEMS 56-4165 Ain't That Something/I'll Do The Rest 5

WHITESNAKE

78 EMI International INEP 751 SNAKEBITE (EP, white vinyl, p/s; later black vinyl with no p/s). . . . each 10
78 EMI International INT 568 Lie Down/Don't Mess With Me 5
79 EMI International INT 578 The Time Is Right For Love/Come On (live) 5
80 United Artists BP 352 Fool For Your Loving/Mean Business/
Don't Mess With Me (some in luminous p/s) 8/5
82 Liberty BPP 416 Here I Go Again/Bloody Luxury (picture disc) 10
82 Liberty BP 418 Love An' Affection/Victim Of Love (withdrawn) 35
83 Liberty BPP 420 Guilty Of Love/Gambler (shaped picture disc) 10
84 Liberty BPP 423 Standing In The Shadows/All Or Nothing (US Mix) (picture disc) 6
87 EMI EMIW 5606 Still Of The Night/Here I Go Again (p/s, white vinyl with poster) 8
87 EMI 12 EMIP 5606 Still Of The Night/Here I Go Again/You're Gonna Break My Heart Again
(12", picture disc). . . . 10
87 EMI EMP 3 Is This Love/Standing In The Shadows '87/Need Your Love So Bad '87
(shaped picture disc, all mispressed with 2 tracks,
some with 3rd track on bonus white label 7") 10/6
87 EMI 12EMW 3 Is This Love/Standing In The Shadows '87/Need Your Love So Bad '87/
Still Of The Night (CD, card sleeve) 8
87 EMI CDEM 3 Is This Love/Standing In The Shadows '87/Need Your Love So Bad '87
(12", p/s, white vinyl) 8
87 EMI 10EMI 35 Here I Go Again '87 (US remix)/Guilty Of Love (10", p/s, white vinyl) 8
88 EMI 12EMP 23 Give Me All Your Love/Fool For Your Loving/Don't Break My Heart Again
(12", picture disc). . . . 8
90 EMI EMPD 128 The Deeper The Love/Judgement Day (picture disc, with insert). . . . 5
90 EMI EMPD 150 Now You're Gone (Remix)/Wings Of The Storm
(shaped picture disc with plinth). . . . 7
78 EMI Intl. INS 3022 TROUBLE (LP, grey or pink inner sleeve). . . . each 12
82 Liberty LBGP 30354 SAINTS AN' SINNERS (LP, picture disc) 15
84 Liberty LBGP 240 000 0 SLIDE IT IN (LP, picture disc, U.S. mixes) 15
87 EMI EMCP 3528 WHITESNAKE 1987 (LP, picture disc) 15
89 EMI EMCDJ 1013 SLIP OF THE TONGUE (LP, with track by track interview, promo only) 25
(see also David Coverdale, Deep Purple, Rainbow, Roger Glover, Bernie Marsden, Jon Lord, Phenomena, Cozy Powell, Young & Moody Band, Company, Snafu, Bogdon, Forcefield, Gogmagog, Tramline, National Health)

WHITE SPIRIT

80 Neat NEAT 05 Back To The Grind/Cheetah (p/s) 10
81 MCA MCA 638 Midnight Chaser/Suffragettes (p/s) 35
81 MCA MCA 652 High Upon High/No Reprieve/Arthur Guitar 15
80 MCA MCF 3079 WHITE SPIRIT (LP, with lyric insert) 18
(see also Gillan, Iron Maiden)

WHITE SS

78 White SS CIA 72 Mercy Killing/I'm Not One (live) (p/s). . . . 25

WHITE STRIPES

01 XL XLS 139 Hotel Yorba (Live At The Hotel Yorba)/Rated X (p/s, 4000 only) 10
01 XL XLS 139 CD Hotel Yorba/Rated X/Hotel Yorba — Live At Hotel Yorba (CD). . . . 15
02 XL XLS 142 Fell In Love With A Girl/I Just Don't Know What To Do With Myself
(p/s, 5000 only). . . . 8
02 XL XLS 142 CD/2 Fell In Love With A Girl/Let's Shake Hands/Lafayette Blues/Fell In Love With
A Girl (Live)/Lovesick (Live At The Forum)/I Just Don't Know What To Do With
Myself/Fell In Love With A Girl (Video) (2-CD). . . . 15

MINT VALUE £

Year	Label / Cat. No.	Title	MINT VALUE £
02	XL XLS 148	Dead Leaves And The Dirty Ground/Stop Breaking Down (Live) (p/s, 5000 only)	8
02	XL/MOJO no cat. no.	Red Death At 6:14 (1-sided, promo only, red vinyl, numbered label, 3000 only, mail order only via *Mojo* magazine, with letter)	40
02	XL XLS 162	Merry Christmas From The White Stripes: Candy Cane Children/The Reading Of The Story Of The Magi/The Singing Of Silent Night (1000 only, p/s)	30
03	XL XLS 166	I Just Don't Know What To Do With Myself/Who's To Say (p/s)	10
03	XL XLS 166 DVD	I Just Don't Know What To Do With Myself/Lafayette Blues (Live)/Black Math (Live) (CD)	15
02	XL no cat. no.	Fell In Love With A Girl/Let's Shake Hands/Lafayette Blues (printed CD-R, promo)	15
03	XL no cat. no.	I Just Don't Know What To Do With Myself/Who's To Say/Lafayette Blues (Live On Radio 1 Evening Session)/I'm Finding It Harder To Be A Gentleman (Live On The John Peel Show) (promo CD)	15
03	XL LP 162 DJ	Seven Nation Army — Elephant Sampler/In The Cold, Cold Night (p/s)	20
03	XL no cat. no.	Seven Nation Army (1-sided 12" promo, stamped white label, no p/s)	45
04	XL XLS 181	There's No Home For You Here/I Fought Piranhas/Let's Build A Home (p/s)	5
03	XL XLLP 162	ELEPHANT (2-LP, custom sleeve, 500 only)	125

WHITE TRASH

Year	Label / Cat. No.	Title	MINT VALUE £
69	Apple APPLE 6	Road To Nowhere/Illusions (early copies as White Trash, later Trash)	200/30

(see also Trash, Poets, Stone The Crows)

WHITE ZOMBIE

Year	Label / Cat. No.	Title	MINT VALUE £
89	Caroline CAROL 1457	God Of Thunder/Love Razor/Disaster Blaster 2 (12", withdrawn)	15

(see also Rob Zombie)

DAVID WHITFIELD

Year	Label / Cat. No.	Title	MINT VALUE £
54	Decca F 10242	The Book/Heartless (gold label, triangular centre)	5
54	Decca F 10327	Cara Mia/Love, Tears And Kisses (with Mantovani Orchestra)	5
54	Decca F 10355	Smile/How, When Or Where (B-side with Mantovani Orchestra)	5
54	Decca F 10399	Santo Natale/Adeste Fideles	5
55	Decca F 10458	Beyond The Stars/Open Up Your Heart (with Mantovani Orchestra)	5
55	Decca F 10515	Ev'rywhere/Mama	5
55	Decca F 10562	The Lady/Santa Rose Lea Rose	5
55	Decca F 10596	I'll Never Stop Loving You/Lady Of Madrid	5
55	Decca F 10627	When You Lose The One You Love/Angelus (with Mantovani Orchestra)	5
56	Decca F 10690	My September Love/The Rudder And The Rock	5
56	Decca F 10769	My Son John/My Unfinished Symphony	5
57	Decca F 10833	The Adoration Waltz/If I Lost You	5
57	Decca F 10864	I'll Find You/I'd Give You The World	5
57	Decca F 10890	Without Him/Dream Of Paradise	6
57	Decca F 10931	Ev'rything/Martinella	6
58	Decca F 10978	Cry My Heart/My One True Love (with Mantovani Orchestra)	6
58	Decca F 11018	On The Street Where You Live/Afraid	6
58	Decca F 11039	The Right To Love/That's When Your Heartaches Begin	6
58	Decca F 11079	This Is Lucia/Love Is A Stranger	6
59	Decca F 11101	Willingly/William Tell	6
60	Decca F 11289	I Believe/Hear My Song Violetta	6
61	Decca F 11336	Scottish Soldier/Scotland The Brave (withdrawn, export only)	10
62	HMV POP 1015	Impossible/As Long As You Love Me	5
63	HMV POP 1180	You Belong In Someone Else's Arms/This Heart Of Mine	5
77	Denman Discs DD 105	Land Of Hope And Glory/When You Lose The One You Love (p/s, fan club issue, with Carlton & District Male Voice Choir)	5

JUNE WHITFIELD

Year	Label / Cat. No.	Title	MINT VALUE £
53	Philips PB 137	Seven Lonely Days/Dancing With Someone (78)	5
53	Philips PB 195	Diamonds Are A Girl's Best Friend/Bye Bye Baby (78)	5

(see also Terry Scott)

WILBUR WHITFIELD

Year	Label / Cat. No.	Title	MINT VALUE £
57	Vogue V 9078	P.B. Baby/The One I Love	650
57	Vogue V 9078	P.B. Baby/The One I Love (78)	150

(see also Little Wilbur & Pleasers)

LEONARD WHITING

Year	Label / Cat. No.	Title	MINT VALUE £
65	Pye 7N 15943	Piper/That's What Mama Says	25

MARGARET WHITING

Year	Label / Cat. No.	Title	MINT VALUE £
55	Capitol CL 14213	My Own True Love (Tara's Theme)/Can This Be Love (triangular centre)	18
55	Capitol CL 14242	Heat Wave/Come Rain Or Shine (triangular centre)	18
55	Capitol CL 14307	Stowaway/All I Want Is All There Is And Then Some (triangular centre)	18
55	Capitol CL 14348	A Man/Mama's Pearls (triangular centre)	18
55	Capitol CL 14375	Lover, Lover/I Kiss You A Million Times (triangular centre)	18
56	Capitol CL 14527	I Love A Mystery/Bidin' My Time	10
56	Capitol CL 14591	Old Enough/Day In — Day Out	8
56	Capitol CL 14647	True Love/Haunting Love	8
57	Capitol CL 14685	The Money Tree/Maybe I Love Him	8
57	London HLD 8451	Kill Me With Kisses/Speak For Yourself, John	25
57	London HLD 8451	Kill Me With Kisses/Speak For Yourself, John (78)	15
58	London HLD 8562	I Can't Help (If I'm Still In Love With You)/That's Why I Was Born	20
58	London HLD 8562	I Can't Help (If I'm Still In Love With You)/That's Why I Was Born (78)	15
58	London HLD 8662	Hot Spell/I'm So Lonesome I Could Cry	20
58	London HLD 8662	Hot Spell/I'm So Lonesome I Could Cry (78)	20
66	London HLD 10078	Nothing Lasts Forever/The Wheel Of Hurt	8
67	London HLD 10114	Just Like A Man/The World Inside Your Arms	8
68	London HLU 10196	Faithfully/Am I Losing You	6
68	London HLU 10227	Maybe Just Once More/Can't Get You Out Of My Mind	6
53	Capitol LC 6585	CAPITOL PRESENTS MARGARET WHITING (10" LP)	30
56	Capitol LC 6811	MARGARET WHITING (10" LP)	30

MINT VALUE £

76 United Artists UP 36072 Everything Leads Back To You/Angel In An Apron . . . 5
76 United Artists UP 36110 Caramia/It's Your Day Today . . . 5
76 United Artists UP 36161 Mr Ting-A-Ling (Steel Guitar Man)/Silver Spurs . . . 6
77 United Artists UP 36220 Una Paloma Blanca/Somewhere My Love . . . 5
77 United Artists UP 36287 Home On The Range/I'm So Lonesome . . . 5
79 United Artists UP 36491 Ghost Riders In The Sky/Carolina Moon . . . 5
80 Liberty BP 377 That Silver Haired Daddy Of Mine/If I Could Dream (p/s) . . . 5
81 Liberty BP 394 When/Till We Meet Again (p/s) . . . 6
82 Liberty BP 408 Can't Help Falling In Love With You/Open Up Your Heart Again, Kathleen (p/s) . . . 6
84 Epic EPC A 4304 Blue Bayou/Blue Memories (p/s) . . . 5
84 Epic EPC A 4695 Four Walls/Trying To Outrun The Wind (p/s) . . . 5

EPs

54 London RE-P 1006 SLIM WHITMAN AND HIS SINGING GUITAR (at least 8 different colour sleeves, with matt or gloss finish & various label designs) . . . 12/18
55 London RE-P 1042 SONG OF THE WILD . . . 15
56 London RE-P 1064 SLIM WHITMAN VOL. 2 PT. 1 . . . 18
56 London RE-P 1070 SLIM WHITMAN VOL. 2 PT. 2 . . . 18
57 London RE-P 1100 SLIM WHITMAN VOL. 2 PT. 3 . . . 18
59 London RE-P 1199 SLIM WHITMAN SINGS (triangular silver-top centre, later round) . . . 18/12
60 London RE-P 1258 SLIM WHITMAN SINGS No. 2 . . . 18
63 London RE-P 1360 THE WAYWARD WIND . . . 18
64 Liberty LEP 4018 IRISH LOVE SONGS THE SLIM WHITMAN WAY . . . 15
65 Liberty LEP 4027 SLIM WHITMAN SINGS MORE IRISH SONGS . . . 15
66 Liberty LEP 4046 A SATISFIED MIND . . . 18

LPs

54 London H-APB 1015 SLIM WHITMAN & HIS SINGING GUITAR (10", gold or silver label print) . . . 55/35
56 London HA-U 2015 SLIM WHITMAN & HIS SINGING GUITAR VOL. 2 . . . 45
59 London HA-P 2139 SLIM WHITMAN SINGS . . . 30
59 London HA-P 2199 SLIM WHITMAN SINGS VOL. 2 . . . 30
60 London HA-P 2343 SLIM WHITMAN . . . 30
61 London HA-P 2392 JUST CALL ME LONESOME . . . 30
62 London HA-P 2443 SLIM WHITMAN SINGS VOL. 3 (also stereo SAH-P 6232) . . . 30/35
62 London HA-P 8013 SLIM WHITMAN SINGS VOL. 4 . . . 25
63 London HA-P 8059 HEART SONGS AND LOVE SONGS . . . 25
63 London HA-P 8093 I'M A LONELY WANDERER . . . 25
64 Liberty LBY 3032 YODELING . . . 15
65 Liberty LBY 3034 COUNTRY SONGS, CITY HITS . . . 15
65 Liberty LBY 3054 THE BEST OF SLIM WHITMAN VOL. 1 . . . 12
66 Liberty LBY 3060 THE BEST OF SLIM WHITMAN VOL. 2 . . . 15
66 Liberty LBY 3067 REMINISCING . . . 12
66 Liberty LBY 3003 IRISH SONGS . . . 12
67 Liberty (S)LBY 3079 A TRAVELIN' MAN . . . 12
67 Liberty (S)LBY 3086 A TIME FOR LOVE . . . 12
67 Liberty LBY 3092 THE BEST OF SLIM WHITMAN VOL. 3 . . . 20
67 Liberty LBL/LBS 83039 15TH ANNIVERSARY . . . 12
68 Liberty LBL/LBS 83064 GREAT PERFORMANCES . . . 12
68 Liberty LBL/LBS 83093 COUNTRY MEMORIES . . . 12
68 Liberty LBL/LBS 83109 COOL WATER . . . 12
68 Sunset SLS 50003 A LONESOME HEART . . . 12
68 Liberty LBL/LBS 83113 IN LOVE THE WHITMAN WAY . . . 12
68 Sunset SLS 50044 UNCHAIN YOUR HEART . . . 12
69 Liberty LBS 83182E HAPPY STREET . . . 12
69 Liberty LBS 83244 STRAIGHT FROM YOUR HEART . . . 12
70 Liberty LBS 83390 TOMORROW NEVER COMES . . . 12
70 Sunset SLS 50153 LOVE SONGS OF THE WATERFALL . . . 12
71 Sunset SLS 50219 GOD'S HAND IN MINE . . . 12
71 United Artists UAS 29151 SNOWBIRD . . . 12
71 Sunset SLS 50283 CHRISTMAS ALBUM . . . 12
71 United Artists UAS 29305 IT'S A SIN TO TELL A LIE . . . 12
73 United Artists UAS 29433 I'LL SEE YOU WHEN . . . 12
73 United Artists UAG 29488 25TH ANNIVERSARY CONCERT . . . 12
76 Sunset SLS 50384 I'LL WALK WITH GOD . . . 12

MARVA WHITNEY

70 Polydor 2001 036 This Girl's In Love With You/He's The One . . . 15
72 Mojo 2092 041 Daddy Don't Know About The Sugar Bear/We Need More . . . 8
69 Polydor 583 767 IT'S MY THING (LP) . . . 100+

(see also James Brown)

TIM WHITSETT

64 Sue WI 318 Macks By The Tracks/Shine . . . 30

TIM WHITSETT/STICKS HERMAN

60s Range JRE 7002 RHYTHM & BLUES (EP) . . . 30

PAUL WHITSUN JONES & WALLAS EATON & HOLLAND

65 Oriole CB 1991 Shake It Baby/Instant Marriage . . . 12

WHITSUNTIDE EASTER

77 Pilgrim/Grapevine GRA 109 NEXT TIME YOU PLAY A WRONG NOTE...MAKE IT A SHORT ONE (LP, gatefold sleeve) . . . 100

ROGER WHITTAKER (& COMPANIONS)

62 Fontana H 358 The Charge Of The Light Brigade/Keep It A Secret . . . 7
62 Fontana 267 217TF Steel Men/After The Laughter . . . 7
63 Fontana 267 258TF Butterfly/Times Is Tough . . . 7
63 Fontana TF 393 The Sinner/Settle Down (as Rog Whittaker & Companions) . . . 7
64 Fontana TF 437 Mud Puddle/Acre Of Wheat (as Rog Whittaker & His Companions) . . . 7

(see also Hank & Mellowmen)

MINT VALUE £

TOMMY WHITTLE (& HIS QUARTET)

54	Esquire 10-408	Martini/Yesterdays (78)	6
56	Esquire 10-468	How High The Moon/Lester Leaps In (78)	6
57	HMV POP 379	The Finisher/Cabin In The Sky (as Tommy Whittle & His Quartet)	5
55	Esquire EP 37	TOMMY WHITTLE QUINTET (EP)	15
56	Esquire EP 37	TOMMY WHITTLE QUINTET (EP)	20
58	HMV 7EG 8325	TOMMY WHITTLE QUARTET (EP)	40
54	Esquire 20-028	WAXING WITH WHITTLE (LP)	30
55	Esquire 20-048	TOMMY WHITTLE QUINTET (LP)	50
56	Esquire 20-061	SPOTLIGHTING TOMMY WHITTLE (LP)	75
56	Esquire 20-068	LULLABY & RHYTHM (LP)	125
60	Tempo TAP 27	NEW HORIZONS (LP)	100
60s	Ember EMB 3305	EASY LISTENING (LP)	75

WHIZZ KIDS

79	Dead Good DEAD SIX	P.A.Y.E./99% Proof/National Assistance/Cheek To Cheek (p/s, with insert)	20
80	Ovation OVS 1213	Suspect No. 1/Coma Life (ps)	10

THE WHO

SINGLES

65	Brunswick 05926	I Can't Explain/Bald Headed Woman	20
65	Brunswick 05935	Anyway Anyhow Anywhere/Daddy Rolling Stone	25
65	Brunswick 05944	My Generation/Shout And Shimmy	15
66	Brunswick 05951	Circles/Instant Party Mixture (unreleased)	
66	Reaction 591 001	Substitute/Circles (temporarily withdrawn)	35
66	Reaction 591 001	Substitute/Instant Party (temporarily withdrawn)	30
66	Brunswick 05956	The Kids Are Alright/The Ox (existence unconfirmed)	
66	Brunswick 05956	A Legal Matter/Instant Party	25
66	Reaction 591 001	Substitute/WHO ORCHESTRA: Waltz For A Pig (B-side actually by Graham Bond Organisation)	15
66	Brunswick 05965	The Kids Are Alright/The Ox	35
66	Brunswick 05968	La-La-La-Lies/The Good's Gone	30
66	Reaction 591 004	I'm A Boy/In The City	7
66	Reaction 591 010	Happy Jack/I've Been Away	7
67	Track 604 002	Pictures Of Lily/Doctor, Doctor	6
67	Track 604 006	The Last Time/Under My Thumb	45
67	Track 604 011	I Can See For Miles/Someone's Coming	7
68	Track 604 023	Dogs/Call Me Lightning	12
68	Track 604 024	Magic Bus/Dr. Jekyll And Mr Hyde	7
69	Track 604 027	Pinball Wizard/Dogs Part Two	6
70	Track 604 036	The Seeker/Here For More	6
70	Track 2094 002	Summertime Blues/Heaven And Hell	8
70	Track 2094 004	See Me, Feel Me/Overture From 'Tommy' (withdrawn)	18
71	Track 2094 009	Won't Get Fooled Again/Don't Know Myself (p/s)	18
73	Track 2094 115	5.15/Water	6
75	Polydor 2001 561	Overture/See Me Feel Me/Listening To You (from "Tommy" soundtrack, p/s)	5
76	Polydor 2058 803	Substitute/I'm A Boy/Pictures Of Lily (12", company sleeve)	8
79	Polydor WHO 2	Long Live Rock/I'm The Face/My Wife (withdrawn, blank run-off groove)	5
80	Polydor WHO 3	5.15/I'm One (p/s)	6
82	Polydor WHOP 6	Athena/A Man Is A Man (picture disc)	5
82	Polydor WHOPX 6	Athena/A Man Is A Man/Won't Get Fooled Again (12", picture disc)	8
82	Polydor WHOPX 6	Athena/A Man Is A Man/Won't Get Fooled Again (12", picture disc, mispressing, plays "Why Did I Fall For That")	15
89	Polydor POCD 907	My Generation/Substitute/Baba O'Riley/Behind Blue Eyes (CD, card sleeve)	10
89	Polydor POCD 917	Won't Get Fooled Again (Extended Version)/Bony Maronie/Dancing In The Street/Mary-Anne With The Shaky Hand (CD, card sleeve)	15

EXPORT SINGLES

66	Brunswick 05956	A Legal Matter/Instant Party (with Scandinavian p/s)	90
68	Decca AD 1001	My Generation/Shout And Shimmy (some in p/s)	135/90
68	Decca AD 1002	A Legal Matter/Instant Party	60
72	Track 2094 102	Join Together/Baby Don't You Do It (p/s, for Spain)	15

PROMO SINGLES

69	Track PRO 1	The Acid Queen/We're Not Gonna Take It (existence unconfirmed)	
69	Track PRO 2	Go To The Mirror!/Sally Simpson	60
69	Track PRO 3	I'm Free/1921	60
69	Track PRO 4	Christmas/Overture	60

EPs

66	Reaction 592 001	READY STEADY WHO	60
70	Track 2252 001	EXCERPTS FROM "TOMMY" (33rpm)	15
83	Reaction WHO 7	READY STEADY WHO (reissue)	15

LPs

65	Brunswick LAT 8616	MY GENERATION	160
66	Reaction 593 002	A QUICK ONE	75
67	Track 612 002	THE WHO SELL OUT (mono, 500 with stickered sleeve & poster)	300/40
67	Track 613 002	THE WHO SELL OUT (stereo, 500 with stickered sleeve & poster)	300/60
68	Track 612/613 006	DIRECT HITS (mono/stereo)	25/20
69	Track 613 013/014	TOMMY (2-LP, fold-out glossy gatefold sleeve, with numbered 12-page booklet)	100
70	Track 2406 001	LIVE AT LEEDS (foldout sleeve with 12 inserts including poster; blue or red print on sleeve)	25
70	Track 2407 008	BACKTRACK 8: A QUICK ONE (mono budget reissue)	18
70	Track 2407 009	BACKTRACK 9: SELL OUT (stereo budget reissue)	12
70	Track 2407 014	BACKTRACK 14: THE OX	20
70	Track 2856 001	WHO DID IT? (mail-order only, withdrawn)	400
71	Track 2408 102	WHO'S NEXT	15
71	Track 2406 006	MEATY, BEATY, BIG AND BOUNCY (gatefold sleeve)	12

MINT VALUE £

71	Track 2406 006	MEATY, BEATY, BIG AND BOUNCY (gatefold sleeve, mispressed, plays "The Seeker" instead of "Magic Bus")	25
72	Track 2406 007	TOMMY PART ONE	12
72	Track 2406 008	TOMMY PART TWO	12
73	Track 2657 013	QUADROPHENIA (2-LP, original with 22-page photo booklet, matt labels)	18
74	Track 2406 116	ODDS AND SODS (cut-away braille sleeve, with poster & lyric sheet)	12
75	Polydor 2490 129	THE WHO BY NUMBERS	12
80	Virgin V 2179	MY GENERATION (reissue)	15
81	Polydor 2675 216	PHASES (9-LP box set, stickered cover)	120

(see also High Numbers, Pete Townshend, Roger Daltrey, John Entwistle, Keith Moon, Kenney Jones, Graham Bond Organisation, Rigor Mortis, McEnroe & Cash)

WALLY WHYTON (& VIPERS)

59	Parlophone R 4585	Don't Tell Me Your Troubles/It's All Over You	8
60	Parlophone R 4630	All Over This World/Got Me A Girl	6
60	Parlophone (no mono no.)	WILLUM AND ME (EP, stereo/mono)	18/15
60	Pye 7N 15304	It's A Rat Race/Marriage Of Convenience/95% Of Me Loves You (with Sally Miles)/You're Going To Be Caught (as Wally Whyton & Vipers)	6
61	Piccadilly 7N 35089	Little Red Pony/Christmas Land	6
68	Fontana TF 960	Gentle On My Mind/Ballad Of The Bol Weevil	5
69	Fontana TF 994	Wichita Lineman/Leave Them A Flower	5
69	Fontana TF 1030	Jig Alone/Out On The Road	5
68	Fontana STL 5476	IT'S ME, MUM (LP)	12
70	Fontana STL 5535	LEAVE THEM A FLOWER (LP)	12

(see also Vipers, Sharkey Todd & Monsters)

INIA TE WIATA

57	HMV POP 301	Banana Boat Song/Call Of The Sea	5
59	HMV POP 572	The Twelth Of Never/Yellow Bird (78)	10

WICHITA FALL

69	Liberty LBS 83208	LIFE IS BUT A DREAM (LP)	12

WICHITA TRAIN WHISTLE

68	Dot DOT 111	Don't Cry Now/Tapioca Tundra (unissued)	
68	Dot (S)LPD 516	MICHAEL NESMITH PRESENTS THE WICHITA TRAIN WHISTLE SINGS (LP)	35

(see also Michael Nesmith)

WIDOWMAKER

76	Jet JET 766	On The Road/Pin A Rose On Me	7
76	Jet JET 767	When I Met You/Pin A Rose On Me	5
76	Jet JET 782	Pin A Rose On Me/On The Road	5
76	Jet 2310 432	WIDOWMAKER (LP)	18
77	United Artists UAG 30038	TOO LATE TO CRY (LP, gatefold sleeve)	12

(see also Luther Grosvenor, Steve Ellis, Huw Lloyd Langton)

WIGGANS

61	Blue Beat BB 29	Rock Baby/Let's Sing The Blues	20

PERCY WIGGINS

67	Atlantic 584 113	Book Of Memories/Can't Find Nobody	8

SPENCER WIGGINS

67	Stateside SS 2024	Uptight Good Woman/Anything You Do Is Alright	15
70	Pama PM 794	I'm A Poor Man's Son/That's How Much I Love You	15

WIKKYD VIKKER

83	Boogie FUR 0235	Black Of The Night/Release (no p/s)	120

WILBURN BROTHERS

59	Brunswick 05799	That Silver-Haired Daddy Of Mine/A Boy's Faithful Friend	10
59	Brunswick 05799	That Silver-Haired Daddy Of Mine/A Boy's Faithful Friend (78)	8
59	Brunswick LAT 8291	SIDE BY SIDE (LP)	20
61	Brunswick LAT 8501	CITY LIMITS (LP)	18
62	Brunswick LAT 8507	FOLK SONGS (LP)	15
67	Brunswick LAT 8686	COOL COUNTRY (LP)	15

WILD & WANDERING

86	Iguana VYK 14	2,000 LIGHT ALES FROM HOME (12" EP, with insert)	25

(see also Pop Will Eat Itself)

WILD ANGELS

68	Major Minor MM 569	Nervous Breakdown/Watch The Wheels Go Round	25
69	B&C CB 114	Buzz Buzz/Please Don't Touch	10
70	B&C CB 123	Sally-Ann/Wrong Number, Try Again	10
71	B&C CB 145	Three Nights A Week/Time To Kill	8
72	Decca F 13308	Jo-Jo Ann/My Way	7
72	Decca F 13356	Beauty School Dropout/Midnight Rider	7
73	Decca F 13374	Running Bear/Sussin'	6
73	Decca F 13412	Greased Lightning/Born To Hand-Jive/Beauty School Dropout	6
73	Decca F 13456	Clap Your Hands And Stamp Your Feet/Wild Angels Rock'n'Roll	5
70	B&C BCM 101	LIVE AT THE REVOLUTION (LP)	18
70	B&C BCM 102	RED HOT'N'ROCKIN' (LP)	18
72	Decca SKL 5134	OUT AT LAST (LP)	12

WILD BEASTS

79	Fried Egg EGG 2	Minimum Maximum/Another Noun (p/s)	5
80	Ring Piece CUS 886	Last One Of The Boys/We're Only Monsters (p/s)	5
81	Warped BEND 1	Life Is A Bum/Mary Lou/The Limit (p/s)	5

WILDCATS

59	London HLT 8787	Gazachstahagen/Billy's Cha Cha	22
59	London HLT 8787	Gazachstahagen/Billy's Cha Cha (78)	15
59	London HLT 8907	Dancing Elephants/King Size Guitar (unreleased)	

MINT VALUE £

JACK WILDE

69	Elektra EKSN 45068	Apple Pie Mother And The Flag/Ballad Of Baby Browning	6
70	Capitol ST 22545	THE JACK WILD ALBUM (LP)	12

KIM WILDE

83	Rak 12 RAK 365	Dancing In The Dark (Extended)/Dancing In The Dark (Instrumental) (12", p/s, with poster)	10
84	MCA KIMP 1	The Second Time/Lovers On A Beach (picture disc)	12
84	MCA KIMP 2	The Touch/Shangri-La (shaped picture disc)	10
85	MCA KIMP 3	Rage To Love/Putty In Your Hands (shaped picture disc)	10
88	MCA KIM X7	Hey Mister Heartache (Kilowatt Remix)/Hey Mister Heartache/ Tell Me Where You Are (12", p/s)	8
88	MCA DKIM 7	Hey Mister Heartache (Extended)/Tell Me Where You Are/ You Keep Me Hangin' On/Another Step (Closer To You) (Extended Version) (CD, 4th track w/Junior)	12
88	MCA KIMB 8	You Came/Stone (box set)	5
88	MCA DKIM 8	You Came (Extended)/You Came (7" Version)/Stone (5" CD, unreleased)	
88	MCA DIM 8	You Came (Extended)/You Came (7" Version)/Stone (3" CD)	12
88	MCA DKIM 9	Never Trust A Stranger (Extended Version)/You Came (Pettibone Mix)/ Wotcha Gonna Do? (CD)	12
88	MCA KIMB 10	Four Letter Word/She Hasn't Got Time For You ('88) (numbered box set)	5
89	MCA DKIMT 11	Love In The Natural Way (7" Version)/You'll Be The One Who'll Lose/ Love In The Natural Way (Extended Version) (CD, picture disc)	12

MARTY WILDE (& WILDCATS)

78s

57	Philips PB 750	Honeycomb/Wild Cat (as Marty Wilde & Wildcats)	15
58	Philips PB 781	Love Bug Crawl/Afraid Of Love	35
58	Philips PB 804	Sing, Boy, Sing/Oh-Oh, I'm Falling In Love Again (with Wildcats)	20
58	Philips PB 835	Endless Sleep/Her Hair Was Yellow (as Marty Wilde & Wildcats)	6
58	Philips PB 850	My Lucky Love/Misery's Child (as Marty Wilde & Wildcats)	12
58	Philips PB 875	No One Knows/The Fire Of Love	18
59	Philips PB 902	Donna/Love-a, Love-a, Love-a	25
59	Philips PB 926	A Teenager In Love/Danny	30
59	Philips PB 959	Sea Of Love/Teenage Tears	40
59	Philips PB 972	It's Been Nice/Bad Boy	55
60	Philips PB 1002	Johnny Rocco/My Heart And I	90

SINGLES

57	Philips JK 1028	Honeycomb/Wild Cat (as Marty Wilde & Wildcats) (jukebox issue)	55
58	Philips PB 804	Sing, Boy, Sing/Oh-Oh, I'm Falling In Love Again (with Wildcats)	40
58	Philips PB 835	Endless Sleep/Her Hair Was Yellow (as Marty Wilde & Wildcats)	12
58	Philips PB 850	My Lucky Love/Misery's Child (as Marty Wilde & Wildcats)	10
58	Philips PB 875	No One Knows/The Fire Of Love	12
59	Philips PB 902	Donna/Love-a, Love-a, Love-a	10
59	Philips PB 926	A Teenager In Love/Danny	10
59	Philips PB 959	Sea Of Love/Teenage Tears	10
59	Philips PB 972	It's Been Nice/Bad Boy	10
60	Philips PB 1002	Johnny Rocco/My Heart And I	10
60	Philips PB 1022	The Fight/Johnny At The Crossroads	12
60	Philips PB 1037	I Wanna Be Loved By You/Angry	12
60	Philips PB 1078	Little Girl/Your Seventeenth Spring	8
61	Philips PB 1101	Rubber Ball/Like Makin' Love	7
61	Philips PB 1121	When Does It Get To Be Love/Your Loving Touch	7
61	Philips PB 1161	Hide And Seek/Crazy Dream	7
61	Philips PB 1191	Tomorrow's Clown/The Hellions	7
61	Philips PB 1206	Come Running/Ev'ryone	7
62	Philips PB 1240	Jezebel/Don't Run Away	7
62	Philips 326 546BF	Ever Since You Said Goodbye/Send Me The Pillow You Dream On	8
63	Columbia DB 4980	Lonely Avenue/Brand New Love	7
63	Philips 326 579BF	No! Dance With Me/Little Miss Happiness	7
63	Columbia DB 7145	Save Your Love For Me/Bless My Broken Heart	7
64	Columbia DB 7198	When Day Is Done/I Can't Help The Way I Feel	7
64	Columbia DB 7285	Kiss Me/My, What A Woman	7
64	Decca F 11979	The Mexican Boy/Your Kind Of Love	7
66	Philips PB 1490	I've Got So Used To Loving You/The Beginning Of The End	8
68	Philips BF 1632	By The Time I Get To Phoenix/Shutters And Boards	7
68	Philips BF 1669	Abergavenny/Alice In Blue	7
69	Philips BF 1753	All The Love I Have/Any Day	6
69	Philips BF 1783	Endless Sleep/Donna	6
69	Philips BF 1815	Shelley/Jump On The Train (with Deke Leonard)	6
70	Philips BF 1839	No Trams To Lime Street/Prelude To Old Age	7
71	Philips 6006 126	Busker/It's So Real	6
72	Magnet MAG 15	I Love You/She's A Mover	6
82	Kaleidoscope KRLA 2003	In Dreams/Hard To Find, Easy To Love (p/s)	5

EPs

57	Philips BBE 12164	PRESENTING MARTY WILDE	65
58	Philips BBE 12200	MORE OF MARTY	50
59	Philips BBE 12327	SEA OF LOVE	50
60	Philips BBE 12385	VERSATILE MR. WILDE	55
60	Philips BBE 12422	MARTY WILDE FAVOURITES	50
62	Philips BBE 12517	COME RUNNING	45
63	Philips BE 433 638	MARTY	45

LPs

59	Philips BBL 7342	WILDE ABOUT MARTY	60
60	Philips BBL 7380	MARTY WILDE SHOWCASE	60
60	Philips BBL 7385	THE VERSATILE MR. WILDE (also stereo SBBL 570)	55/65

			MINT VALUE £
69	Philips SBL 7877	DIVERSIONS	18
70	Philips 6308 010	ROCK 'N' ROLL	15
74	Philips 6308 102	GOOD ROCKING — THEN AND NOW	12

(see also Wilde Three, Brian Bennett, Shadows, Keith Shields, Capricorn, Deke Leonard)

WILDER BROTHERS

57	HMV POP 365	I Want You/Teenage Angel	240
57	HMV POP 365	I Want You/Teenage Angel (78)	60

WILDERNESS ROAD

74	Dawn DNLS 3057	WILDERNESS ROAD (LP, unissued)	

WILDE THREE

65	Decca F 12131	Since You've Gone/Just As Long	60
65	Decca F 12232	I Cried/Well Who's That?	65

(see also Marty Wilde, Justin Hayward, Vernons Girls)

WILDFIRE

84	Mausoleum GUTS 8405	Jerusalem/Fight Fire With Fire (p/s)	5
83	Mausoleum SKUL 8307	BRUTE FORCE AND IGNORANCE (LP)	25
83	Mausoleum SKUL 8338	SUMMER LIGHTNING (LP, with insert)	15

(see also Weapon)

WILDHEARTS

SINGLES

92	East West YZ 669T	MONDO AKIMBO A-GO-GO (12" EP, with inner sleeve)	35
92	East West YZ 669TX	MONDO AKIMBO A-GO-GO (12" EP, white vinyl, with inner sleeve, advance copies with artwork postcard & press sheet)	60/50
92	East West YZ 669CD	MONDO AKIMBO A-GO-GO (CD EP)	40
93	East West YZ 773	Greetings From Shitsville/The Bullshit Goes On (p/s, brown vinyl, with insert)	12
93	East West YZ 784C	TV Tan/Show A Little Emotion (cassette)	5
93	East West YZ 784T	TV EP: TV Tan/Show A Little Emotion/Dangerlust/Down On London (12", p/s)	10
93	East West YZ 784CD	TV EP: TV Tan/Show A Little Emotion/Dangerlust/Down On London (CD)	8
94	East West YZ 794	Caffeine Bomb/Girlfriend Clothes (p/s, green vinyl, with insert)	8
94	East West YZ 794C	Caffeine Bomb/Girlfriend Clothes (cassette)	5
94	East West YZ 794T	Caffeine Bomb/Girlfriend Clothes/Shut Your Fucking Mouth And Use Your Fucking Brain/And The Bullshit Goes On (12", p/s)	15
94	East West YZ 794CD	Caffeine Bomb/Girlfriend Clothes/Shut Your Fucking Mouth And Use Your Fucking Brain/And The Bullshit Goes On (CD, digipak)	20
94	East West YZ 828TE	Suckerpunch/Beautiful Thing You/Two-Way Idiot Mirror/29 x The Pain (10", p/s, 1-sided, etched)	12
94	East West YZ 828C	Suckerpunch/Beautiful Thing You/Two-Way Idiot Mirror/29 x The Pain (cassette)	5
94	East West YZ 828CD	Suckerpunch/Beautiful Thing You/Two-Way Idiot Mirror/29 x The Pain (CD)	8
94	East West YZ 874TEX	If Life Is Like A Lovebank I Want An Overdraft/Geordie In Wonderland/ Hate The World Day/Fire Up (10", gatefold sleeve with banknote)	10
94	East West YZ 874CDX	If Life Is Like A Lovebank I Want An Overdraft/Geordie In Wonderland/ Hate The World Day/Fire Up (CD, 'wallet' pack with banknote)	8
95	East West YZ 923TEX	I Wanna Go Where The People Go/Shandy Bang/Can't Do Right For Doing Wrong/Give The Girl A Gun (10", p/s)	10
95	East West YZ 976TEX	Just In Lust/Mindslide/Friend For Five Minutes/S.I.N (In Sin) (10", p/s)	10
95	Round WILD1CDX	Sick Of Drugs/Underkill/Bad Time To Be Having A Bad Time/Skychaser High (CD, with grass-growing mat, title sticker, mispressing, plays Tony Christie)	15
97	Mushroom MUSH 6CD	Anthem/So Good To Be Back Home/Time To Let You Go (CD, mispressing, plays country music)	12
02	Round SMALP048	Vanilla Radio/Better Than Cable (picture disc, stickered PVC sleeve, 1500 only)	8

PROMO-ONLY SINGLES

92	East West WH-1	Turning American (1-sided 12", some with two Valentine's cards)	45/35
92	East West (no cat. no.)	MONDO AKIMBO A-GO-GO EP (cassette, unique "live" inlay)	30
92	East West SAM 1108	Splattermania/Something Weird (Going On In My Head)/Turning American/ Crying Over Nothing (12", picture labels)	40
93	East West (no cat. no.)	Suckerpunch/My Baby Is A Headfuck/Down On London (Demo) (cassette)	20
93	East West SAM 1212	Suckerpunch/My Baby Is A Headfuck (12", stickered plain sleeve)	25
93	East West SAM 1212CD	My Baby Is A Headfuck/Suckerpunch (CD-R, titles inlay & unissued black &	
§		white custom artwork, 5 copies only)	100
93	East West SAM 1262	Suckerpunch/CLAWFINGER: War Fair (Brixton Academy gig freebie)	35
93	East West YZ 773	Greetings From Shitsville/The Bullshit Goes On (clear vinyl w/l test press)	80
93	East West YZ 784	TV Tan/Show A Little Emotion (white vinyl test press for picture disc, no labels)	100
93	East West (no cat. no.)	TV Tan (9" custom pizza box containing commercial 7" picture disc & CD)	50
93	East West (no cat. no.)	TV EP (cassette, unique picture inlay)	10
94	East West (no cat. no.)	Caffeine Bomb/Girlfriend Clothes/Shut Your Fucking Mouth And Use Your Fucking Brain/And The Bullshit Goes On (cassette, unique luminous green pic inlay)	10
94	East West YZ 794 T	Caffeine Bomb/Girlfriend Clothes/Shut Your Fucking Mouth And Use Your Fucking Brain/And The Bullshit Goes On (12", generic p/s, with matrix: SAM 1298)	
15			
94	East West SAM 1385	Suckerpunch/Beautiful Thing You/Two-Way Idiot Mirror/29 x The Pain (12")	15
94	East West (no cat. no.)	Suckerpunch/Beautiful Thing You/Two-Way Idiot Mirror/29 x The Pain (cassette, unique picture inlay)	10
94	East West YZ828CDDJ	Suckerpunch/29 x The Pain (CD, radio edits, unique "live" p/s)	20
94	East West (no cat. no.)	Beautiful Thing You/Two-Way Idiot Mirror/29 x The Pain (Master)/29 x The Pain (Full Edit) (cassette, titles inlay)	20
94	East West (no cat. no.)	If Life Is Like A Lovebank I Want An Overdraft/Geordie In Wonderland/ Hate The World Day/Fire Up (cassette, unique banknote inlay, 100 copies only)	10
94	East West YZ 874CDDJ	If Life Is Like A Lovebank I Want An Overdraft/Geordie In Wonderland (CD, p/s)	10
94	East West (no cat. no.)	If Life Is Like A Lovebank I Want An Overdraft/Geordie In Wonderland/ Hate The World Day/Fire Up/Hate The World Day (Vox Up)/Fire Up (Vox Up)/ Geordie In Wonderland (No Shit Version) (CD-R with 3 unissued versions)	50

			MINT VALUE £
94	East West (no cat. no.)	Geordie In Wonderland (cassette, "Newcastle United strip" inlay, 20 copies only)	30
95	East West SAM 1555	Naivety Play (CD, "P.H.U.Q. Playback Party" freebie only)	40
95	East West YZ923CDDJ	I Wanna Go Where The People Go (Special Promo Version – Edit)/(Single Version)/Can't Do Right For Doing Wrong (CD, p/s)	12
95	East West (no cat. no.)	Just In Lust/Mindslide/Friend For Five Minutes/S.I.N (In Sin) (cassette, unique inlay, 50 copies with black spine & 50 copies with white spine)	10
95	East West YZ967CDDJ	Just In Lust (Special Promo Version)/(LP Version)/Mindslide (CD, p/s)	12
95	East West (no cat. no.)	Mindslide/Underkill/Friend For Five Minutes/S.I.N. [sic.]/Underkill (cassette, titles inlay, both versions of "Underkill" with unissued Sex Pistols sample)	25
96	Round (no cat. no.)	Sick Of Drugs/Underkill/Bad Time To Be Having A Bad Time/Skychaser High (cassette, unique picture inlay)	10
96	Round WILD1CDDJ	Sick Of Drugs (Edit)/Sick Of Drugs (CD, p/s)	10
96	Round (no cat. no.)	RED LIGHT – GREEN LIGHT EP (cassette, unique picture inlay)	10
96	Round (no cat. no.)	RED LIGHT – GREEN LIGHT EP (CD-R, unissued proof artwork inlay)	30
97	(no label) drop1	Pump It Up (CD, with bicycle pump attachment or football pump valve in jewel case spine, some with artist & title sticker)	20/25
97	Mushroom DROP 2	Anthem (Censored)/Anthem (CD, red jewel case, withdrawn)	15
97	Mushroom DROP 3	Heroin/Why You Lie (CD, red jewel case)	30
97	Mushroom DROP 4	Urge (CD, red jewel case)	12
97	Mushroom (no cat. no.)	Urge/Do The Fake/Kill Me To Death/Zomboid/Genius Penis/Lost Highway (cassette)	8
02	Round (no cat. no.)	Vanilla Radio/Stormy In The North, Karma In The South (CD-R, unique pic inlay)	25
03	Snapper (no cat. no.)	Stormy In The North – Karma In The South/Bang!/You Got To Get Through What You've Got To Go Through To Get What You Want, But You Got To Know What You Want To Get Through What You Got To Go Through (CD-R, pic inlay)	12
03	Gut (no cat. no.)	So Into You/Danny's Dancing/Lake Of Piss (CD-R [2 designs], trk 2 with original title)	10
03	Gut PRGUT49	So Into You (CD, p/s)	8
03	Gut (no cat. no.)	Top Of The World (Radio Edit) (CD-R [2 designs], pic inlay)	8
03	Gut (no cat. no.)	Top Of The World (Original Mix) (CD-R, pic inlay)	8
03	Gut (no cat. no.)	Top Of The World/6:30 Onwards/Eager To Leave 'Er/Cheers/L.T.D./Hit It On The Head (CD-R)	15
03	Gut (no cat. no.)	Cheers (Radio Edit) (CD-R, 3 different designs of custom label)	15

ALBUMS

92	East West 4509-91202-1	DON'T BE HAPPY... JUST WORRY (LP, as 2 x 12", with inner sleeves)	25
92	East West 4509-91202-2	DON'T BE HAPPY... JUST WORRY (2-CD, with bonus disc containing "Anti-Dance Mixes" of "Mondo Akimbo A-Go Go" tracks)	25
93	East West 4509-93287-1	EARTH VS THE WiLDHEARTS (LP, with exclusive uncredited track)	20
93	East West 4509-93201-2	EARTH VS THE WiLDHEARTS (CD, first issue with "93" rear artwork, without "Caffeine Bomb")	18
94	East West 4509-99039-2	FISHING FOR LUCKIES (CD, 6-track mini-album, fan club/mail-order only)	40
95	East West 0630-10404-1	P.H.U.Q. (LP, gatefold sleeve)	15
95	East West 0630-10437-2	P.H.U.Q. (CD, stickered felt case, unique inlay)	15
95	East West 0630-12850-1	FISHING FOR MORE LUCKIES (LP, reissue, with 3 extra tracks "Underkill", "Saddened" & "I Wanna Go Where The People Go [Early Version]", unreleased, most copies destroyed)	100
95	East West 0630-12850-4	FISHING FOR MORE LUCKIES (cassette, reissue, with 3 extra tracks, unreleased, most copies destroyed)	35

(CD copies of "Fishing For MORE Luckies" [0630-12850-2] were NOT destroyed and cut-outs were later made available at mid-price)

96	Round 0630-14888-1	FISHING FOR LUCKIES (2-LP, reissue, gatefold, Side 3 exclusive to vinyl)	18
97	Mushroom MUSH13LP	ENDLESS, NAMELESS (LP, inner sleeve)	15
98	Kuro Neko KNEKLP3	ANARCHIC AIRWAVES – THE WiLDHEARTS AT THE BBC (2-LP, 200 mail-order copies only — 1000 copies made but 800 destroyed)	25
98	Kuro Neko KNEK3L	ANARCHIC AIRWAVES – THE WiLDHEARTS AT THE BBC (CD in square stickered metal tin, no insert, 1000 copies only)	15
99	Kuro Neko KNEK3LTD	ANARCHIC AIRWAVES – THE WiLDHEARTS AT THE BBC (2-CD, with bonus disc "THE REST OF READING")	20
98	Kuro Neko KNEK4LB	LANDMINES & PANTOMIMES – THE LAST OF THE WiLDHEARTS...? (CD in square stickered metal tin in card box with insert, 1000 copies only)	30
03	Gut GUTLP25	THE WiLDHEARTS MUST BE DESTROYED (LP, gatefold sleeve)	12

PROMO-ONLY EPS

97	Mushroom DROP 5	ENDLESS, NAMELESS (CD, 4-track sampler, red jewel case)	15
03	Gut (no cat. no.)	THE WiLDHEARTS MUST BE DESTROYED (CD-R, 4-track sampler, 2 variations with different tracks, picture inlay)	each 15

PROMO-ONLY ALBUMS

92	East West (no cat. no.)	DESTROY ANAHEIM (cassette, "live" soundboard recording, titles inlay, unissued)	
92	East West (no cat. no.)	COMPILATION TAPE (cassette, whole of Side 2 contains unreleased versions)	50
93	East West (no cat. no.)	EARTH VS THE WiLDHEARTS (cassette, titles inlay, two extra tracks)	15
93	East West (no cat. no.)	EARTH VS THE WiLDHEARTS (cassette, unique picture inlay)	25
94	East West (no cat. no.)	DON'T BE HAPPY... JUST WORRY (cassette, unique picture inlay)	20
94	East West (no cat. no.)	FISHING FOR LUCKIES (cassette, unique picture inlay, only issued on CD)	20
95	East West (no cat. no.)	P.H.U.Q. 5 TRACK SAMPLER (cassette, unique picture inlay, with exclusive edit of "In Lilly's Garden")	20
95	East West (no cat. no.)	P.H.U.Q. (full album cassette, unique picture inlay)	18
95	East West SAM 1574	4-TRACK SAMPLER FOR THE FORTHCOMING ALBUM "P.H.U.Q." (CD, card p/s)	15
95	East West PROP21	P.H.U.Q. (CD, slim jewel case, titles inlay, withdrawn – misspelt "Wildhearts" & "PHUQ" & some song-titles inaccurate)	20
95	East West PROP21	P.H.U.Q. (CD, slim jewel case, corrected titles inlay & credited to "*The* Wildhearts")	18
95	East West SAM 1582	LIVING ON A LANDMINE: THE SINGLES 1993-95 (CD, 6-track sampler, card p/s)	25

MINT VALUE £

95	East West (no cat. no.)	GREETINGS FROM THE WiLDHEARTS – THE STORY SO FAR (unique compilation cassette, picture inlay)	20
95	East West (no cat. no.)	FISHING FOR MORE LUCKIES (cassette of unreleased album, unique inlay)	30
96	Round (no cat. no.)	FISHING FOR LUCKIES (cassette, unique picture inlay)	15
96	East West (no cat. no.)	THE BEST OF THE WiLDHEARTS (cassette, unique picture inlay)	18
03	Gut (no cat. no.)	THE WiLDHEARTS MUST BE DESTROYED (CD-R, picture inlay)	20
04	Gut PRGUTCD27	COUPLED WITH (CD, slim jewel case, p/s)	20

(see also Backyard Babies, Chasers, Energetic Krusher, Ginger, Honeycrack, Jellys, Quireboys, SilverGinger 5, Super$hit666, Devin Townsend, Yo-Yo's)

WILD HONEY

72	Mam MAM 97	He's My Sugar/People Of The Universe	8
72	Mam MAM 154	Baby Don't You Know Anymore/He's My Sugar (featuring Tina Charles)	8

(see also Tina Charles)

WILD HORSES

79	EMI International INTS 599	Criminal Tendencies/The Rapist (p/s)	5
80	EMI EMI 5047	Face Down/Dealer (p/s)	5
80	EMI EMI 5078	Fly Away/Blackmail (p/s, white vinyl; black vinyl demos £15)	6
80	EMI 12EMI 5078	Fly Away/Blackmail (12", p/s, white vinyl)	8
81	EMI EMI 5149	I'll Give You Love/Rocky Mountain Way (p/s)	5
81	EMI EMI 5149	I'll Give You Love/Rocky Mountain Way//The Kid/On A Saturday Night (double pack, gatefold p/s)	5
81	EMI EMI 5199	Everlasting Love/The Axe (no p/s)	5
80	EMI EMC 3326	WILD HORSES (LP, with inner sleeve)	12
81	EMI EMC 3368	STAND YOUR GROUND (LP, with inner sleeve)	15

(see also Thin Lizzy, Motörhead, Rainbow, Dio)

WILD INDIANS

84	Hullaballoo! HA! 001	Love Of My Life/The Biggest Man/Maybe (p/s)	5
80s	Having Fun IP 001	Stolen Courage/POP WALLPAPER: The Great Adventure (flexidisc, gatefold p/s)	5

WILD MAGNOLIAS

75	Barclay BAR 30	Smoke My Peace Pipe/Handa Wanda	5
75	Barclay BAR 34	They Call Us Wild/Jumalaka Boom Boom	6
75	Barclay 80 529	THE WILD MAGNOLIAS 1 (LP, gatefold sleeve)	18
75	Barclay 90 033	THEY CALL US WILD (LP, gatefold sleeve)	20

WILD OATS

63	Oak RGJ 117	WILD OATS (EP)	750+

WILD ONES

64	Fontana TF 468	Bowie Man/Purple Pill Eater	60
65	United Artsts ULP 1119	THE ARTHUR SOUND (LP)	40

WILD SILK

68	Polydor 56256	Poor Man/Stop Crying	6
69	Columbia DB 8534	(Visions In A) Plaster Sky/Toymaker	12
69	Columbia DB 8611	Help Me/Crimson And Gold	10

WILD SWANS

82	Zoo CAGE 009	The Revolutionary Spirit/God Forbid (unissued, stamped white label)	12
82	Zoo CAGE 009	The Revolutionary Spirit/God Forbid (12", p/s)	8
82	Zoo CAGE 009	The Revolutionary Spirit/God Forbid (12", p/s, with 'The Lament Of Icarus' painting in top right of front sleeve, withdrawn)	15

(see also Lotus Eaters, Care)

WILD THING

69	Elektra EKSN 45076	Old Lady/Next To Me	6
70	Elektra EKS 74059	PARTYIN' (LP)	18
71	Elektra 2410 003	PARTYIN' (LP, reissue)	12

WILD TURKEY

72	Chrysalis CHS 2004	Good Old Days/Life Is A Symphony	5
72	Chrysalis CHR 1002	BATTLE HYMN (LP, gatefold sleeve)	15
73	Chrysalis CHR 1010	TURKEY (LP)	15

(see also Babe Ruth, Jethro Tull, Man, Gary Pickford-Hopkins, Whitesnake)

WILD UNCERTAINTY

66	Planet PLF 120	Man With Money/Broken Truth	60

WILD WALLY

70	Concord CON 1003	I GO APE (LP)	18

WILDWEEDS

67	Chess CRS 8065	It Was Fun While It Lasted/Sorrow's Anthem	12

WILD WILL'S BLUE WASHBOARD BOYS

71	Flyright LP 4701	BABY YUM YUM (LP)	12

WILFRED & MILLICENT

65	Island WI 190	The Vow/I'll Never Believe In You	20

(see also Jackie [Edwards] & Millie [Small])

MIKE WILHELM

76	Zigzag/United Artists ZZ 1	MIKE WILHELM (LP, sold via *Zigzag* magazine)	45

(see also Charlatans, Flamin' Groovies)

ROBERT WILKINS

60s	Piedmont PLP 13162	REV ROBERT WILKINS (LP)	25

ROGER WILKINS

70	Spokane SPL 1002	BEFORE THE REVERENCE (LP)	40

MINT VALUE £

ARTHUR WILKINSON ORCHESTRA

65 HMV 7EG 8919 BEATLE CRACKER SUITE (EP) . . . 10

JESS WILLARD

51 Capitol CL 13443 If You've Got The Money I've Got The Time/RED MURREL: Ernest Tubb's Talking Blues (78) . . . 6

WILLETT FAMILY

62 Topic 12T 84 THE ROVING JOURNEYMAN (LP, blue label with booklet) . . . 20

AL WILLIAMS

80 Grapevine GRP 136 I Am Nothing/Brand New Love . . . 18

ANDY WILLIAMS

78s

56 London HLA 8284 Walk Hand In Hand/Not Any More . . . 10
57 London HLA 8487 Lips Of Wine/Straight From My Heart . . . 6
58 London HLA 8587 Are You Sincere/Be Mine Tonight . . . 6
58 London HLA 8710 Promise Me, Love/Your Hand, Your Heart, Your Love . . . 10
59 London HLA 8784 Hawaiian Wedding Song/House Of Bamboo . . . 6
59 London HLA 8957 Lonely Street/Summer Love . . . 10
59 London HLA 9018 The Village Of St. Bernadette/I'm So Lonesome I Could Cry . . . 20

SINGLES

56 London HLA 8284 Walk Hand In Hand/Not Any More . . . 35
56 London HLA 8315 Canadian Sunset/High Upon A Mountain (gold or silver label print) . . . 40/30
56 London HL 7013 Canadian Sunset/High Upon A Mountain (export issue) . . . 20
56 London HLA 8360 Baby Doll (From The Film)/Since I've Found My Baby (gold or silver print) . . . 45/25
57 London HLA 8399 Butterfly/It Doesn't Take Very Long . . . 25
57 London HLA 8437 I Like Your Kind Of Love/Stop Teasin' Me . . . 20
57 London HLA 8487 Lips Of Wine/Straight From My Heart . . . 20
58 London HLA 8587 Are You Sincere/Be Mine Tonight . . . 18
58 London HL 7034 Are You Sincere/Be Mine Tonight (export issue) . . . 12
58 London HLA 8710 Promise Me, Love/Your Hand, Your Heart, Your Love . . . 15
59 London HLA 8784 Hawaiian Wedding Song/House Of Bamboo . . . 10
59 London HLA 8957 Lonely Street/Summer Love . . . 8
59 London HLA 9018 The Village Of St. Bernadette/I'm So Lonesome I Could Cry . . . 7
60 London HLA 9099 Wake Me When It's Over/We Have A Date . . . 7
60 London HLA 9241 Don't Go To Strangers/You Don't Want My Love . . . 7
61 London HLA 9348 The Bilbao Song/How Wonderful To Know . . . 7
62 CBS AAG 103 Stranger On The Shore/I Want To Be Wanted . . . 5
63 CBS AAG 138 Can't Get Used To Losing You/The Days Of Wine And Roses . . . 5
64 CBS AAG 182 A Fool Never Learns/Charade . . . 5
67 CBS CBS 2675 Music To Watch Girls By/The Face I Love . . . 6
68 CBS 3298 Can't Take My Eyes Off You/You Are Where Everything Is . . . 5
72 CBS 8197 (Love Theme From) The Godfather/In The Summertime (p/s) . . . 5

EPs

57 London RE-A 1088 ANDY WILLIAMS' BIG HITS . . . 20
57 London RE-A 1102 ANDY WILLIAMS' BIG HITS No. 2. . . . 25
63 London RE-A 1394 ANDY WILLIAMS' BEST . . . 15

LPs

57 London HA-A 2054 ANDY WILLIAMS SINGS STEVE ALLEN . . . 40
58 London HA-A 2113 ANDY WILLIAMS SINGS RODGERS AND HAMMERSTEIN . . . 40
59 London HA-A 2203 TWO TIME WINNERS . . . 40
60 London HA-A 2238 LONELY STREET . . . 25
62 London HA-A 8005 ANDY WILLIAMS' BEST . . . 18
63 London HA-A 8090 UNDER PARIS SKIES . . . 25
73 CBS CQ 30797 YOU'VE GOT A FRIEND (quadrophonic) . . . 15
73 CBS CQ 31303/Q 64869 LOVE THEME FROM "THE GODFATHER" (quadrophonic) . . . 15
73 CBS CQ 31625 ALONE AGAIN (NATURALLY) (quadrophonic) . . . 12

AUDREY WILLIAMS

56 MGM SP 1179 Ain't Nothing Gonna Be All Right No How/Livin' It Up And Havin' A Ball . . . 25
56 MGM MGM 911 Ain't Nothing Gonna Be All Right No How/Livin' It Up And Havin' A Ball (78) . . . 10

(see also Hank Williams)

BIG JOE WILLIAMS

57 Jazz Collector JEN 3 A MAN SINGS THE BLUES (EP) . . . 15
57 Jazz Collector JEN 4 A MAN SINGS THE BLUES VOLUME 2 (EP) . . . 12
67 Delmark DJB 4 ON THE HIGHWAY (EP) . . . 12
60s XX MIN 700 BIG JOE WILLIAMS (EP) . . . 15
63 Esquire 32-191 BLUES ON HIGHWAY 51 (LP) . . . 40
63 '77' LA 12-19 PINEY WOODS BLUES (LP) . . . 30
64 CBS BPG 63813 CLASSIC DELTA BLUES (LP) . . . 15
64 Storyville SLP 158 PORTRAITS IN BLUES VOLUME 4 (LP) . . . 18
64 Storyville SLP 163 PORTRAITS IN BLUES VOLUME 7 (LP) . . . 18
65 Fontana 688 800 ZL TOUGH TIMES (LP) . . . 18
66 Xtra XTRA 1033 BIG JOE WILLIAMS (LP) . . . 25
66 Bounty BY 6018 BACK TO THE COUNTRY (LP) . . . 30
66 Society SOC 1020 BIG JOE, SONNY, BROWNIE, LIGHTNIN' (LP, with Lightnin' Hopkins, Sonny Terry & Brownie McGhee) . . . 12
69 Storyville 618 011 DON'T YOU LEAVE ME HERE (LP) . . . 18
69 Liberty LBL/LBS 83207 HAND ME DOWN MY OLD WALKING STICK (LP) . . . 20
69 Xtra XTRA 5059 LIVE AT FOLK CITY (LP) . . . 12
70 RCA Intl. INTS 1087 CRAWLIN' KING SNAKE (LP) . . . 18
72 Sonet SNTF 635 THE LEGACY OF THE BLUES VOL. 6 (LP, with insert) . . . 12
72 Delmark DS 627 NINE STRING GUITAR (LP) . . . 12

(see also Poor Joe Williams)

BILLY WILLIAMS (QUARTET)

78s

54 Vogue Coral Q 2012 Sh'Boom/Whenever Wherever . . . 18
54 Vogue Coral Q 2039 The Honeydripper/Love Me (as Billy Williams Quartet) . . . 20
56 Vogue Coral Q 72149 A Crazy Little Palace/Cry Baby (as Billy Williams Quartet) . . . 10
56 Vogue Coral Q 72180 Pray/You'll Reach Your Star . . . 10
57 Vogue Coral Q 72222 Follow Me/Shame, Shame, Shame (as Billy Williams Quartet) . . . 20
58 Coral Q 72303 Don't Let Go/Baby, Baby (as Billy Williams Quartet) . . . 8
58 Coral Q 72316 Steppin' Out Tonight/There I've Said It Again (as Billy Williams Quartet) . . . 10
58 Coral Q 72331 I'll Get By/It's Prayin' Time . . . 10
59 Coral Q 72359 Nola/Tied To The Strings Of Your Heart . . . 15
59 Coral Q 72369 Goodnight Irene/Red Hot Love . . . 25
59 Coral Q 72377 Telephone Conversation/Go To Sleep, Go To Sleep, Go To Sleep (with Barbara McNair) . . . 15

SINGLES

54 Vogue Coral Q 2039 The Honeydripper/Love Me (as Billy Williams Quartet) . . . 50
56 Vogue Coral Q 72149 A Crazy Little Palace/Cry Baby (as Billy Williams Quartet) . . . 50
56 Vogue Coral Q 72180 Pray/You'll Reach Your Star . . . 22
57 Vogue Coral Q 72222 Follow Me/Shame, Shame, Shame (as Billy Williams Quartet) . . . 35
57 Vogue Coral Q 72241 Butterfly/The Pied Piper . . . 35
57 Vogue Coral Q 72266 I'm Gonna Sit Right Down And Write A Letter/Date With The Blues . . . 18
57 Vogue Coral Q 72295 Got A Date With An Angel/The Lord Will Understand . . . 40
58 Coral Q 72303 Don't Let Go/Baby, Baby (as Billy Williams Quartet) . . . 40
58 Coral Q 72316 Steppin' Out Tonight/There I've Said It Again (as Billy Williams Quartet) . . . 55
58 Coral Q 72331 I'll Get By/It's Prayin' Time . . . 20
59 Coral Q 72359 Nola/Tied To The Strings Of Your Heart . . . 10
59 Coral Q 72369 Goodnight Irene/Red Hot Love . . . 30
59 Coral Q 72377 Telephone Conversation/Go To Sleep, Go To Sleep, Go To Sleep (with Barbara McNair) . . . 25
60 Coral Q 72402 I Cried For You/Lover Of All Lovers . . . 18
60 Coral Q 72414 Begin The Beguine/For You . . . 8

LPs

58 Coral LVA 9092 BILLY WILLIAMS . . . 100
60 Coral LVA 9120 HALF SWEET HALF BEAT . . . 40
61 Coral LVA 9139 THE BILLY WILLIAMS REVUE . . . 35
(see also Barbara McNair)

BOBBY WILLIAMS

68 Action ACT 4509 Baby I Need Your Love/Try It Again . . . 25
73 Contempo C 17 Let's Jam/You're My Baby . . . 8

CHRIS WILLIAMS & HIS MONSTERS

59 Columbia DB 4383 The Monster/The Eton Boating Song . . . 35
60 Triumph RGM 1003 Kicking Around/Midnight Rocker (unissued; white label demo copies only) . . 250+

CINDY WILLIAMS

67 Parlophone R 5648 They Talk About Us/Did He Call Today Mama . . . 8

CLARENCE WILLIAMS (& HIS WASHBOARD BAND)

54 Columbia SCM 5134 High Society/Left All Alone With The Blues . . . 15
54 Columbia DB 3513 High Society/Left All Alone With The Blues (78) . . . 6
58 Fontana TFE 17053 TREASURE OF NORTH AMERICAN MUSIC VOLUME 3 (EP) . . . 15
59 Parlophone GEP 8733 CLARENCE WILLIAMS' WASHBOARD BAND (EP) . . . 15
64 Jazz Collector JEL 18 JAZZ ORIGINATORS (EP) . . . 12
54 London AL 3526 CLARENCE WILLIAMS AND HIS ORCHESTRA (10" LP) . . . 20
55 Columbia 33S 1067 BACK ROOM SPECIAL (10" LP) . . . 20
57 London AL 3561 CLARENCE WILLIAMS AND HIS ORCHESTRA VOL. 2 (10" LP) . . . 20
60 Fontana TFL 5087 SIDNEY BECHET MEMORIAL (LP) . . . 15
62 Philips BBL 7521 CLARENCE WILLIAMS VOL. 1: 1927-1935 (LP) . . . 15

CLIVE WILLIAMS

70s Rock Steady Rev. REVR 6 Take Good Care Of My Baby/RICO: In Loving Memory Of Don Drummond . . . 12

COOTIE WILLIAMS

67 Transatlantic SOLID GOLD TRUMPET OF 67 (LP) . . . 10

DAN WILLIAMS & HIS ORCHESTRA

55 London CAY 110 Donkey City/SHAW PARK CALYPSO BAND: Take Her To Jamaica . . . 10
55 London CAY 110 Donkey City/SHAW PARK CALYPSO BAND: Take Her To Jamaica (78) . . . 6

DANNY WILLIAMS

59 HMV POP 624 Tall A Tree/I Look At You . . . 12
59 HMV POP 655 So High — So Low/My Own True Love . . . 12
59 HMV POP 703 Youthful Years/It Doesn't Matter . . . 12
60 HMV POP 803 A Million To One/Call Me A Dreamer . . . 10
61 HMV POP 839 We Will Never Be As Young As This Again/Passing Breeze . . . 8
61 HMV POP 885 The Miracle Of You/Lonely . . . 8
61 HMV POP 932 Moon River/A Weaver Of Dreams (repressings with black label, £5) . . . 8
62 HMV POP 968 Jeannie/It Might As Well Be Spring/Unchain My Heart . . . 6
62 HMV POP 1002 The Wonderful World Of The Young/A Kind Of Loving . . . 6
62 HMV POP 1035 Tears/Tiara Tahiti . . . 6
63 HMV POP 1112 My Own True Love/Who Can Say? . . . 6
63 HMV POP 1150 More/Rhapsody . . . 6
63 HMV POP 1172 The Wild Wind/Once Upon A Time . . . 6
63 HMV POP 1203 A Day Without You/Secret Love . . . 7
63 HMV POP 1236 How Do You Keep From Crying?/Now The Day Is Over . . . 7
63 HMV POP 1263 White On White/After You . . . 10
64 HMV POP 1305 Today/Lonely In A Crowd . . . 7
64 HMV POP 1325 The Seventh Dawn/The World Around Me . . . 7

			MINT VALUE £
64	HMV POP 1372	Forget Her, Forget Her/Lollipops And Roses	15
65	HMV POP 1388	The Roundabout Of Love/I Wanna Be Around	6
65	HMV POP 1410	Go Away/Masquerade	7
65	HMV POP 1455	Lovely Is She/Gone And Forgotten	6
65	HMV POP 1487	And So We Meet Again/Violets For Your Furs	6
66	HMV POP 1506	I've Got To Find That Girl Again/Throw A Little Lovin' My Way	10
66	HMV POP 1522	Don't Just Stand There/Now And Then	7
66	HMV POP 1560	Rain (Falling From The Skies)/I'm So Lost	7
67	Deram DM 149	Never My Love/Whose Little Girl Are You (with inverted matrix, later re-pressed with matrix correct way up)	12/6
68	Deram DM 199	Everybody Needs Somebody (I Need You)/They Will Never Understand	6
62	HMV 7EG 8748	HITS OF DANNY WILLIAMS (EP)	12
62	HMV 7EG 8763	DANNY WILLIAMS SWINGS WITH TONY OSBORNE (EP)	12
63	HMV 7EG 8800	"THE DAYS OF WINE AND ROSES" AND OTHER FILM FAVOURITES (EP)	12
61	HMV CLP 1458/CSD 1369	DANNY (LP, mono/stereo)	25/30
61	HMV CLP 1521	MOON RIVER AND OTHER TITLES (LP)	25
62	HMV CLP 1605/CSD 1471	SWINGING FOR YOU (LP, mono/stereo)	22/30
66	HMV CLP/CSD 3523	ONLY LOVE (LP)	30
66	Woman's Privilege AZ 3	ROMANCE WITH DANNY WILLIAMS (LP, mail-order via *Woman* magazine)	18
67	Deram DML 1017	DANNY WILLIAMS (LP)	20

DEL WILLIAMS

72	Grape GR 3027	Searching For Your Love/G.G. ALL STARS: Searching (Version)	6

DELROY WILLIAMS

71	Trojan TR 7813	Down In The Boondocks/Baby Make It	8

EDDIE WILLIAMS & LITTLE SONNY WILLIS

60s	XX MIN 707	GOING TO CALIFORNIA (EP)	22

GEORGE WILLIAMS

69	Bullet BU 405	No Business Of Yours/Mast It Up (actually titled "Mash It Up")	12

GEORGE WILLIAMS & HIS ORCHESTRA

55	Vogue Coral Q 72053	The Rompin' Stomper/Knock-Out Choo-Choo	8
56	HMV DLP 1140	RHYTHM WAS HIS BUSINESS (10" LP)	15
56	HMV DLP 1140	RHYTHM WAS HIS BUSINESS (LP)	15

GRANVILLE WILLIAMS ORCHESTRA

67	Island WI 3062	Hi-Life/More	18
67	Island ILP 971	HI-LIFE (LP)	75

(see also Silvertones)

HANK WILLIAMS (& HIS DRIFTING COWBOYS)

78s

50	MGM MGM 269	Lovesick Blues/Wedding Bells	8
51	MGM MGM 381	Moanin' The Blues/The Blues Come Around	8
51	MGM MGM 405	Dear John/Fly Trouble	8
51	MGM MGM 454	Hey, Good Lookin'/Howlin' At The Moon	8
51	MGM MGM 459	Cold, Cold Heart/I'm A Long Gone Daddy	8
52	MGM MGM 471	I Can't Help It (If I'm Still In Love With You)/Baby, We're Really In Love	8
52	MGM MGM 483	Why Don't You Love Me/I'd Still Want You	8
52	MGM MGM 505	Honky-Tonk Blues/I'm Sorry For You, My Friend	8
52	MGM MGM 527	Long Gone Lonesome Blues/Half As Much	8
52	MGM MGM 553	Nobody's Lonesome For Me/Mind Your Own Business	8
52	MGM MGM 566	Jambalaya (On The Bayou)/Settin' The Woods On Fire	8
53	MGM MGM 585	I'll Never Get Out Of This World Alive/I Could Never Be Ashamed Of You (as Hank Williams & His Drifting Cowboys)	8
53	MGM MGM 609	Kaw-Liga/Take These Chains From My Heart (& His Drifting Cowboys)	8
53	MGM MGM 630	I Saw The Light/ARTHUR 'GUITAR BOOGIE' SMITH: Recitation Sonny Smith: In Memory Of Hank Williams	8
53	MGM MGM 652	Ramblin' Man/I Won't Be Home No More	8
53	MGM MGM 666	My Bucket's Got A Hole In It/Let's Turn Back The Years	8
53	MGM MGM 678	Window Shopping/You Win Again	10
54	MGM MGM 704	Weary Blues (From Waitin')/I Can't Escape From You	10
54	MGM MGM 733	There'll Be No Teardrops Tonight/Crazy Heart	10
54	MGM MGM 768	I'm Satisfied With You/I Ain't Got Nothin' But Time	10
55	MGM MGM 799	I'm Gonna Sing/California Zephyr	12
56	MGM MGM 889	The First Fall Of Snow/Someday You'll Call My Name (withdrawn)	
56	MGM MGM 896	Your Cheatin' Heart/A Teardrop On A Rose	12
56	MGM MGM 921	There's No Room In My Heart (For The Blues)/I Wish I Had A Nickel	12
56	MGM MGM 931	Blue Love (In My Heart)/Singing Waterfall	15
57	MGM MGM 942	Low Down Blues/My Sweet Love Ain't Around	15
57	MGM MGM 957	Rootie Tootie/Lonesome Whistle	15
57	MGM MGM 966	Leave Me Alone With The Blues/With Tears In My Eyes	15

SINGLES

53	MGM SP 1016	I'll Never Get Out Of This World Alive/I Could Never Be Ashamed Of You (as Hank Williams & His Drifting Cowboys)	55
53	MGM SP 1034	Kaw-Liga/Take These Chains From My Heart (& His Drifting Cowboys)	50
53	MGM SP 1049	Ramblin' Man/I Won't Be Home No More	45
53	MGM SP 1048	My Bucket's Got A Hole In It/Let's Turn Back The Years	45
54	MGM SP 1067	Weary Blues (From Waitin')/I Can't Escape From You	45
54	MGM SP 1085	There'll Be No Teardrops Tonight/Crazy Heart	45
54	MGM SP 1102	I'm Satisfied With You/I Ain't Got Nothin' But Time	45
56	MGM SP 1163	The First Fall Of Snow/Someday You'll Call My Name (unreleased)	
56	MGM MGM 921	There's No Room In My Heart (For The Blues)/I Wish I Had A Nickel	35
56	MGM MGM 931	Blue Love (In My Heart)/Singing Waterfall	35
57	MGM MGM 942	Low Down Blues/My Sweet Love Ain't Around	35
57	MGM MGM 957	Rootie Tootie/Lonesome Whistle	35

57 MGM MGM 966 Leave Me Alone With The Blues/With Tears In My Eyes . . . 30
66 MGM MGM 1309 You Win Again/I'm So Lonesome I Could Cry . . . 15
66 MGM MGM 1322 Kaw-Liga/Let's Turn Back The Years . . . 10

EPs

54 MGM MGM-EP 512 HANK WILLIAMS AND HIS DRIFTING COWBOYS (company sleeve) . . . 25
54 MGM EPC 7 HANK WILLIAMS (export issue) . . . 30
55 MGM MGM-EP 551 JUST WAITIN' (as Luke The Drifter, company sleeve, later p/s) . . . 20/30
56 MGM MGM-EP 569 I SAW THE LIGHT (No. 1) (company sleeve, later p/s) . . . 15/20
57 MGM MGM-EP 582 HONKY TONKIN' . . . 22
57 MGM MGM-EP 608 I SAW THE LIGHT (No. 2) . . . 22
57 MGM MGM-EP 614 HONKY TONK BLUES . . . 22
58 MGM MGM-EP 639 SONGS FOR A BROKEN HEART (No. 1) . . . 22
58 MGM MGM-EP 649 SONGS FOR A BROKEN HEART (No. 2) . . . 22
58 MGM MGM-EP 675 HANK'S LAMENTS . . . 22
60 MGM MGM-EP 710 THE UNFORGETTABLE HANK WILLIAMS . . . 22
60 MGM MGM-EP 726 THE UNFORGETTABLE HANK WILLIAMS (No. 2) . . . 22
60 MGM MGM-EP 732 THE UNFORGETTABLE HANK WILLIAMS (No. 3) . . . 22
61 MGM MGM-EP 757 HANK WILLIAMS FAVOURITES . . . 22
63 MGM MGM-EP 770 THE AUTHENTIC SOUND OF THE COUNTRY HITS . . . 22

LPs

52 MGM MGM-D 105 HANK WILLIAMS SINGS (10, company sleeve, later p/s) . . . 40/55
53 MGM MGM-D 119 HANK WILLIAMS AS LUKE THE DRIFTER (10", company sleeve, later p/s) . . . 35/45
55 MGM MGM-D 137 HANK WILLIAMS MEMORIAL ALBUM (10") . . . 35
56 MGM MGM-D 144 MOANIN' THE BLUES (10") . . . 40
58 MGM MGM-D 150 SING ME A BLUE SONG (10") . . . 40
58 MGM MGM-D 154 THE IMMORTAL HANK WILLIAMS (10") . . . 40
59 MGM MGM-C 784 THE UNFORGETTABLE HANK WILLIAMS . . . 25
60 MGM MGM-C 811 THE LONESOME SOUND OF HANK WILLIAMS . . . 25
60 MGM MGM-C 834 WAIT FOR THE LIGHT TO SHINE . . . 22
62 MGM MGM-C 893 ON STAGE . . . 18
63 MGM MGM-C 956 THE SPIRIT OF HANK WILLIAMS . . . 20
66 MGM MGM-C 8019 MAY YOU NEVER BE ALONE . . . 18
66 MGM MGM-C 8020 IN MEMORY OF HANK WILLIAMS . . . 16
66 MGM MGM-C 8021 I'M BLUE INSIDE . . . 18
66 MGM MGM-C 8022 LUKE THE DRIFTER . . . 15
66 MGM MGM-C 8023 THE MANY MOODS OF HANK WILLIAMS . . . 16
67 MGM MGM-C(S) 8031 THE LEGEND LIVES ANEW . . . 12
67 MGM MGM-C(S) 8038 MORE HANK WILLIAMS AND STRINGS . . . 12
67 MGM MGM-C 8040 LOVE SONGS, COMEDY AND HYMNS . . . 18
68 MGM MGM-C(S) 8057 I WON'T BE HOME NO MORE . . . 12
68 MGM MGM-C(S) 8075 HANK WILLIAMS AND STRINGS VOL. 3 . . . 12
70 MGM MGM-CS 8114 THE ESSENTIAL HANK WILLIAMS . . . 12
74 MGM 2683 046 ON STAGE VOLUMES 1 & 2 (2-LP) . . . 15
76 MGM 2353 128 LIVE AT THE GRAND OL' OPRY . . . 12
79 World Records SM 551-556 THE LEGENDARY HANK WILLIAMS (6-LP box set) . . . 25

(see also Audrey Williams)

HANK WILLIAMS & HANK WILLIAMS Jr.

65 MGM MGM-C 1008 SINGING TOGETHER (LP) . . . 18

HANK WILLIAMS Jr.

63 MGM MGM 1223 Long Gone Lonesome Blues/Doesn't Anybody Know My Name . . . 7
63 MGM MGM 1242 Goin' Steady With The Blues/Guess What, That's Right, She's Gone . . . 6
64 MGM MGM 1254 Endless Sleep/My Bucket's Got A Hole In It . . . 6
65 MGM MGM 1276 Mule Skinner Blues/I Went To All That Trouble . . . 6
66 MGM MGM 1294 You're Ruinin' My Life/Pecos Jail . . . 5
66 MGM MGM 1299 Cold Cold Heart/Is It That Fun To Heart Someone . . . 5
66 MGM MGM 1316 Standing In The Shadows/It's Written All Over Your Face . . . 5
64 MGM MGM-C 996 YOUR CHEATIN' HEART (LP) . . . 12
67 MGM MGM-C(S) 8049 MY OWN WAY (LP) . . . 12
70 MGM MGM-CS 8116 LIVE AT COBO HALL, DETROIT (LP) . . . 12

(see also Connie Francis)

JABBO WILLIAMS

50 Jazz Collector L 51 Jab Blues/Pratt City (78) . . . 8

JEANETTE WILLIAMS

69 Action ACT 4534 Stuff/You Gotta Come Through . . . 15
70 Action ACT 4557 Hound Dog/I Can Feel A Heartbreak . . . 15

(LITTLE) JERRY WILLIAMS

65 Cameo Parkway C 100 Baby You're My Everything/Just What Do You Plan To Do About It . . . 75
74 Pye Disco Demand DDS 102 If You Ask Me/ Yvonne (as Jerry Williams) . . . 12

(see also Swamp Dogg, Brooks & Jerry)

JIMMY WILLIAMS

65 Atlantic AT 4042 Walking On Air/I'm So Lost . . . 15

JOE WILLIAMS

59 Columbia SCD 2116 Party Blues Parts 1 & 2 . . . 5
60 Columbia DB 4560 Somebody/One Is A Lonesome Number . . . 5
58 Columbia SEG 7810 JOE WILLIAMS WITH COUNT BASIE (EP) . . . 10
59 Columbia SEG 7984 BALLADS AND BLUES COLUMBIA (EP) . . . 10
59 Columbia/Clef SEB 10110 GROOVY JOE WILLIAMS (EP) . . . 10
60 Columbia SEG 8001 EVERYDAY I HAVE THE BLUES (EP) . . . 12
60 Columbia SEG 8016 JOE SINGS THE BLUES (EP) . . . 12
56 London HB-C 1065 JOE WILLIAMS SINGS (10" LP) . . . 25
57 HMV CLP 1109 THE GREATEST (LP) . . . 20
58 Columbia 33SX 1087 A MAN AIN'T SUPPOSED TO CRY (LP) . . . 20

MINT VALUE £

60	Columbia 33SX 1229	JOE WILLIAMS SINGS ABOUT YOU (LP, also stereo SCX 3308)	12/15
60	Columbia 33SX 1253	THAT KIND OF WOMAN (LP, also stereo SCX 3325)	12/15
61	Columbia SX 1392	TOGETHER (LP, with Harry "Sweets" Edison, also stereo SCX3421)	15

(see also Count Basie)

JOHN WILLIAMS

67	Columbia DB 8128	She's That Kind Of Woman/My Ways Are Set	15
67	Columbia DB 8251	Flowers In Your Hair/Can't Find Time For Anything Now	15
67	Columbia SX 6169	JOHN WILLIAMS (LP)	125

(see also Maureeny Wishfull)

JOHN WILLIAMS

84	Island IS 155	Paul McCartney's Theme From 'The Honorary Consul'/Clara's Theme (p/s)	12

JOHN WILLIAMS ORCHESTRA (U.S.)

76	MCA MCA 220	'Jaws' Theme (Parts 1 & 2)	5
78	Arista ARIST 177	'Close Encounters Of The Third Kind' (Parts 1 & 2) (p/s)	5
82	MCA MCA 800	Theme From 'E.T.'/Over The Moon (p/s)	5
66	Stateside S(S)L 10187	HOW TO STEAL A MILLION (LP, soundtrack)	45
83	MCA MCA 70000	E.T. — THE EXTRA TERRESTRIAL (LP, soundtrack, box set with booklet & poster)	75
83	MCA MCFP 3160	E.T. — THE EXTRA TERRESTRIAL (picture disc, soundtrack)	12
83	MCA CAC 70000	E.T. — THE EXTRA TERRESTRIAL (cassette, soundtrack box set with booklet & poster)	30

JOHNNY WILLIAMS

73	Epic S EPC 1007	Slow Motion/Shall We Gather By The Water	5
73	Epic S EPC 1547	Put It In Motion/It's So Wonderful	5
73	Contempo C 20	Just A Little Misunderstanding/Your Love Controls My Mind	7
74	Polydor 2001 596	You're Something Kinda Mellow/You Make Me Want To Last Forever	12

KENNETH WILLIAMS

63	Decca DFE 8548	EXTRACTS FROM PIECES OF EIGHT AND ONE OVER THE EIGHT (EP)	10
66	Decca DFE 8671	KENNETH WILLIAMS IN SEASON (EP)	12
67	Decca LK 4856	ON PLEASURE BENT (LP)	22
70	Regal Starline SRS 5034	THE BEST OF RAMBLING SYD RUMPO (LP)	12
70	Decca PA/SPA 64	THE WORLD OF KENNETH WILLIAMS (LP, mono/stereo)	15

(see also Rambling Syd Rumpo, Tony Hancock)

LARRY WILLIAMS

57	London HLN 8472	Short Fat Fannie/High School Dance	45
57	London HLN 8472	Short Fat Fannie/High School Dance (78)	8
58	London HLN 8532	Bony Moronie/You Bug Me Baby	30
58	London HLN 8532	Bony Moronie/You Bug Me Baby (78)	7
58	London HLU 8604	Dizzy Miss Lizzy/Slow Down	40
58	London HLU 8604	Dizzy Miss Lizzy/Slow Down (78)	25
59	London HLU 8844	She Said "Yeah"/Bad Boy	30
59	London HLU 8844	She Said "Yeah"/Bad Boy (78)	30
60	London HLU 8911	I Can't Stop Loving You/Steal A Little Kiss	30
60	London HLU 8911	I Can't Stop Loving You/Steal A Little Kiss (78)	50
60	London HLM 9053	Baby, Baby/Get Ready	30
65	Sue WI 371	Strange/Call On Me	30
65	Sue WI 381	Turn On Your Lovelight/Dizzy Miss Lizzy	22
68	MGM MGM 1447	Shake Your Body Girl/Love, I Can't Seem To Find It	12
59	London RE-U 1213	LARRY WILLIAMS (EP)	125
65	Sue ILP 922	LARRY WILLIAMS ON STAGE (LP)	80
70s	Specialty SNTF 5025	SLOW DOWN (LP)	18

LARRY WILLIAMS & JOHNNY 'GUITAR' WATSON

65	Decca F 12151	Sweet Little Baby/Slow Down	20
67	Columbia DB 8140	Mercy, Mercy, Mercy/A Quitter Never Wins	65
76	Epic EPC 4421	Too Late/Two For The Price Of One	12
65	Decca LK 4691	THE LARRY WILLIAMS SHOW (LP, with Stormsville Shakers)	75

(see also Johnny 'Guitar' Watson, Philip Goodhand-Tait [& Stormville Shakers])

LEONA WILLIAMS

74	Fountain FB 303	LEONA WILLIAMS AND HER DIXIE BAND (LP)	12

LEW WILLIAMS

50s	London (no cat. no.)	Cat Talk (1-sided, orange label demo-only)	50

LLOYD WILLIAMS

66	Doctor Bird DB 1051	Sad World/TOMMY McCOOK'S BAND: A Little Bit Of Heaven	25
68	Treasure Isle TI 7029	Funky Beat/Goodbye Baby	20
68	Doctor Bird DB 1135	Wonderful World (with Tommy McCook)/TOMMY McCOOK & SUPERSONICS: Mad Mad World	25
70	Bamboo BAM 41	I'm In Love With You/Little Girl	20

LORETTA WILLIAMS

66	Atlantic 584 032	Baby Cakes/I'm Missing You	30

LUCINDA WILLIAMS

89	Rough Trade 130	LUCINDA WILLIAMS (LP, with inner lyric bag)	12

LUTHER WILLIAMS ORCHESTRA

61	Limbo XL 101	Early In The Morning/Little Vilma	5
61	Melodisc MLP 12-125	TROPICAL RHYTHMS OF JAMAICA (LP)	15

MARY LOU WILLIAMS

53	London L 1174	Laughing Rag/Rag Of Rags (78)	6
54	Felsted ED 82011	Autumn In New York/En Ce Tempa-La (78)	6
64	Sue WI 311	Chuck-a-Lunk Jug (Parts 1 & 2)	30
55	Vogue EPV 1042	DON CARLOS MEETS MARY LOU WILLIAMS (EP)	12

			MINT VALUE £
56	Parlophone GEP 8567	AT THE PIANO (EP)	10
56	Columbia SEG 7608	MARY LOU WILLIAMS (EP)	10
55	Esquire EP 66	MARY LOU WILLIAMS QUARTET (EP)	12
53	Vogue LDE 022	PLAYS IN LONDON (10" LP)	25
54	Esquire 20-026	PIANO PANORAMA (10" LP)	25
55	Felsted EDL 87012	IN PARIS (10" LP)	20

MASON WILLIAMS

68	Warner Bros WB 7190	Classical Gas/Long Time Blues	7

MAURICE WILLIAMS (& ZODIACS)

60	Top Rank JAR 526	Stay/Do You Believe (as Maurice Williams & Zodiacs)	20
61	Top Rank JAR 550	I Remember/Always	15
61	Top Rank JAR 563	Come Along/Do I	30
61	Top Rank JKP 3006	STAY WITH MAURICE WILLIAMS & THE ZODIACS (EP)	175

(see also Gladiolas)

MIKE WILLIAMS

66	Atlantic 584 027	Lonely Soldier/If This Isn't Love	10

MOON WILLIAMS

73	DJM DJS1028	Forever Kind Of Love/ All For You (7")	150

OTIS WILLIAMS & HIS CHARMS

55	Parlophone CMSP 36	Ivory Tower/In Paradise (export issue)	325
56	Parlophone MSP 6239	Ivory Tower/In Paradise	500
56	Parlophone R 4175	Ivory Tower/In Paradise (78)	12
56	Parlophone R 4210	One Night Only/It's All Over	375
56	Parlophone R 4210	One Night Only/It's All Over (78)	25
57	Parlophone R 4293	Walkin' After Midnight/I'm Waiting Just For You	500
57	Parlophone R 4293	Walkin' After Midnight/I'm Waiting Just For You (78)	50
58	Parlophone R 4495	The Secret/Don't Wake Up The Kids	80
58	Parlophone R 4495	The Secret/Don't Wake Up The Kids (78)	70
62	Parlophone R 4860	The Secret/Two Hearts	65

(see also Charms)

PAT WILLIAMS ORCHESTRA

74	Capitol CL 15797	Police Story Theme/Magician Theme	7

PAUL WILLIAMS

73	Sonet SNTF 654	DELTA BLUES SINGER (LP)	15

PAUL WILLIAMS BIG ROLL BAND/SET

64	Columbia DB 7421	Gin House/Rockin' Chair (as Paul Williams Big Roll Band)	25
65	Columbia DB 7768	The Many Faces Of Love/Jumpback (as Paul Williams & Zoot Money Band)	25
68	Decca F 12844	My Sly Sadie/Stop The Wedding (as Paul Williams Set)	15

(see also Zoot Money's Big Roll Band, John Mayall's Bluesbreakers, Alan Price [Set], Juicy Lucy)

PAULINE WILLIAMS

73	Explosion EX 2084	My Island/My Island (Version)	5

POOR JOE WILLIAMS

60	Collector JEN 3	A MAN SINGS THE BLUES (EP)	18
60	Collector JEN 4	A MAN SINGS THE BLUES VOL. 2 (EP)	18

(see also Big Joe Williams)

RANNY/RONNY WILLIAMS

69	Bullet BU 426	Summer Place (with Hippy Boys)/Big Boy	10
69	Gas GAS 120	Throw Me Corn (as Ronny Williams)/HIPPY BOYS: Temptation	10
69	Unity UN 526	Ambitious Beggar/Pepper Seed	10
70	Punch PH 32	Smile/Musical I.D.	10

(see also Winston Reed)

RITA WILLIAMS

58	Oriole CB 1417	Looking For Someone To Love/Love Me Forever	12
58	Oriole CB 1417	Looking For Someone To Love/Love Me Forever (78)	8

ROBBIE WILLIAMS

98	Chrysalis CDCHSS 5080	Let Me Entertain You/Full Monty Medley: Make Me Smile (Come Up And See Me)/ You Can Leave Your Hat On/Land Of A 1000 Dances)/I Wouldn't Normally Do This Kind Of Thing)/I Am The Resurrection (CD)	8

PROMOS

96	RCA FREELX 1	Freedom '96 (Radio Edit)/Freedom '96 (Full Length Version) (jukebox issue)	8
96	RCA PROPERDJ 1	Freedom '96 (Radio Edit)/Freedom '96 (Full Length Version) (CD, test pressing, no text on disc)	20
97	Chrysalis CHSLH 5055	Old Before I Die/Making Plans For Nigel (jukebox issue)	8
97	Chrysalis CDCHSDJ 5055	Old Before I Die (CD, withdrawn, different sleeve)	15
97	Chrysalis CHSLH 5063	Lazy Days/Teenage Millionaire (jukebox issue)	8
97	Chrysalis CHSLH 5068	South Of The Border/Cheap Love Song (jukebox issue)	8
97	Chrysalis 12CHSDJ 5068	South Of The Border (remixes) (12", stickered black sleeve)	10
97	Chrysalis 12CHSDJS 5068	South Of The Border (remixes) (12", stickered white sleeve)	10
97	Chrysalis CDCHSDJ 5072	Angels (Edit) (CD)	10
97	Chrysalis CDCHSDJS 5072	Angels/Walk This Sleigh (CD)	10
98	Chrysalis 12CHSDJD 5080	Let Me Entertain You (remixes) (12", double-pack)	20
98	Chrysalis CDCHSDJ 5080	Let Me Entertain You (CD)	10
98	Chrysalis CHSCH 5099	Millennium/Angels (jukebox issue)	8
98	Chrysalis/HMV HMV 78	Millennium/ROYAL ALBERT HALL ORCHESTRA: Nimrod, Enigma Variations Op. 36 (78rpm, promo only, 1000 only, no'd p/s)	40
98	Chrysalis CDCHSDJ 5099	Millennium (CD, title sleeve)	10
99	Chrysalis CHSLH 5107	Strong/Antmusic (jukebox issue)	8
99	Chrysalis CDCHSLH 5112	It's Only Us/She's The One (jukebox issue)	8
99	Chrysalis CDCHSDJX 5122	It's Only Us/She's The One (CD, grey title sleeve)	10
00	Chrysalis CDCHSLH 5118	Rock DJ/She's The One (jukebox issue)	8

MINT VALUE £

00 EMI CDLIC 173 — United/United (Apollo 440 Remix)/CD-Rom Interview (CD, Pepsi freebie, card sleeve) 10
97 Chrysalis RWEPK 01 — THE EPK CD (interview and excerpts from "Life Thru A Lens") 30
98 Chrysalis CDPP 080 — I'VE BEEN EXPECTING YOU (metal case with album CD, interview disc in digipak, EPK video in p/s, gold press release and photos) 200
(see also Take That)

ROBERT PETE WILLIAMS

63 '77' LA 12-17 — THOSE PRISON BLUES (LP) 25
70s Blues Beacon 1932 101ST — SUGAR FARM (LP) 18
72 Saydisc AMS 2002 — ROBERT PETE WILLIAMS (LP) 15
73 Sonet SNTF 649 — LEGACY OF THE BLUES (LP) 12

ROBERT PETE WILLIAMS/ROOSEVELT SYKES

67 '77' LEU 12-50 — BLUES FROM THE BOTTOM (LP) 20
(see also Roosevelt Sykes)

ROBERT WILLIAMS

90 Blast First FU8 — CHROME, FIRE AND SMOKE (2-LP, picture disc, 1000 only) 35

ROGER WILLIAMS

55 London HLU 8214 — Autumn Leaves/Take Care 18
56 London HLU 8341 — Two Different Worlds (with Jane Morgan)/I'll Always Walk With You 22
56 London HLU 8341 — Two Different Worlds (with Jane Morgan)/I'll Always Walk With You (78) 8
57 London HLU 8379 — Anastasia/A Serenade For Joy 12
57 London HLR 8422 — Almost Paradise/For The First Time I've Fallen In Love 10
57 London HLR 8516 — Till/Big Town 10
58 London HLR 8572 — Arrivederci Roma/The Sentimental Touch 8
58 London HLR 8643 — Indiscreet/Young And Warm And Wonderful 7
58 London HLR 8690 — Near You/The Merry Widow Waltz 7
58 London HLR 8758 — The World Outside (Warsaw Concerto)/Piano Concerto No. 1 (Tchaikovsky) 6
59 London HLR 8820 — The Key To The Kingdom/Dearer Than Dear 6
59 London HLR 8820 — The Key To The Kingdom/Dearer Than Dear (78) 8
59 London HLR 8857 — Mockin' Bird Hill/Memories Are Made Of This 7
59 London HLR 8857 — Mockin' Bird Hill/Memories Are Made Of This (78) 10
59 London HLR 8986 — Mary's Boy Child/O Mio Babbino Caro (Oh! My Beloved Father) 6
59 London HLR 8986 — Mary's Boy Child/O Mio Babbino Caro (Oh! My Beloved Father) (78) 15
57 London RE-R 1090 — AT THE PIANO (EP) 8
57 London RE-R 1107 — AT THE PIANO — VOL. 2 (EP) 8
58 London RE-R 1131 — MUSIC OF THE MASTERS (EP) 8
57 London HA-R 2057 — SONGS OF THE FABULOUS FIFTIES VOL. 1 (LP) 15
57 London HA-R 2058 — SONGS OF THE FABULOUS FIFTIES VOL. 2 (LP) 15
58 London HA-R 2089 — THE BOY NEXT DOOR (LP) 12
58 London HA-R 2096 — SONGS OF THE FABULOUS FORTIES VOL. 1 (LP, stereo SAH-R 6035) 12
58 London HA-R 2097 — SONGS OF THE FABULOUS FORTIES VOL. 2 (LP, stereo SAH-R 6036) 12
(see also Jane Morgan)

SAM WILLIAMS

78 Grapevine GRP 116 — Love Slipped Thru' My Fingers/TOWANDA BARNES: You Don't Mean It 20

SMITTY WILLIAMS

62 MGM MGM 1167 — The Cure/Oh Seymour 8

SONNY WILLIAMS

59 London HLD 8931 — Bye Bye Baby Goodbye/Lucky Linda 40
59 London HLD 8931 — Bye Bye Baby Goodbye/Lucky Linda (78) 20

SPARKIE WILLIAMS (1958 Champion Talking Budgerigar)

58 Parlophone R 4475 — Sparkie Williams — Jailbird/Sparkie The Fiddle 5

SYLVIAN WILLIAMS

69 Big Shot BI 532 — Sweeter Than Honey/Son Of Reggae 10
69 Big Shot BI 533 — This Old Man/When Morning Comes 10

TEX WILLIAMS

50 Capitol CL 13312 — Birmingham Bounce/Artistry In Western Swing (78) 8
50 Capitol CL 13424 — Talking Boogie/Tamburitza Boogie (with His Western Caravan) (78) 8
51 Capitol CL 13217 — Ham 'N Eggs/Cowpuncher's Waltz (78) 8
54 Brunswick 05327 — River Of No Return/Dawn In The Meadow 15
54 Brunswick 05341 — This Ole House (with Rex Allen)/They Were Doin' The Mambo 15
55 Brunswick 05393 — Money/If You'd Believe Me 12
56 Brunswick 05516 — Be Sure You're Right (And Then Go Ahead)/Old Betsy 7
57 Brunswick 05684 — Talkin' To The Blues/Every Night (with Anita Kerr Singers) 12
60 Top Rank JAR 330 — The Keeper Of Boothill/Bummin' Around 10
55 Brunswick OE 9147 — ALL THE GREATS (EP) 15
61 Capitol (S)T 1463 — SMOKE, SMOKE, SMOKE! (LP) 18
(see also Roberta Lee, Rex Allen)

TONY WILLIAMS

61 Reprise RS 20019 — Sleepless Nights/Mandolino Mandolino 10
61 Reprise RS 20030 — My Prayer/Miracle 10
63 Philips BF 1282 — How Come/When I Had You 60
60 Mercury MMC 14027 — A GIRL IS A GIRL IS A GIRL (LP) 40
61 Reprise R 6001/ST R9 6006 — SINGS HIS GREATEST HITS (LP, mono/stereo) 20/30
(see also Platters, Linda Hayes)

TONY WILLIAMS' LIFETIME

69 Polydor 583 574 — EMERGENCY! (2-LP, gatefold sleeve) 45
70 Polydor 2425 019 — TURN IT OVER (LP) 20
71 Polydor 2425 065 — EGO (LP) 12
(see also Lifetime, John McLaughlin)

MINT VALUE £

WINSTON WILLIAMS

70 Jackpot JP 733 D.J.'s Choice/SLIM SMITH: Can't Do Without It (B-side actually titled "Lesson/Story Of Love" by Uniques) 12
70 Jackpot JP 743 The People's Choice/BOBBY JAMES: Let Me Go Girl 12
71 Jackpot JP 757 Love Version/SLIM SMITH: Ball Of Confusion 12

BOBBY WILLIAMSON

54 HMV 7MC 26 Sh-Boom/Love March (export issue) 20

CLAUDE WILLIAMSON

54 Capitol KC 65003 All God's Chillun Got Rhythm/Woody 'N' You 7

DUDLEY WILLIAMSON

67 Doctor Bird DB 1117 Coming On The Scene/Anything You Want 35
(see also Dudley & Attractions)

MARK WILLIAMSON

70s Myrrh MYR 1154 MISSING IN ACTION (LP) 15

ROBIN WILLIAMSON

72 Island HELP 2 MYRRH (LP) 15
78 Criminal STEAL 4 AMERICAN STONEHENGE (LP) 12
(see also Incredible String Band, Vashti Bunyan)

SONNY BOY WILLIAMSON (I)/BIG BILL BROONZY

65 RCA Victor RD 7685 BIG BILL BROONZY/SONNY BOY WILLIAMSON (LP) 60

SONNY BOY WILLIAMSON (I)

69 Matchbox SDR 169 SONNY BOY AND HIS PALS (LP) 25
70 RCA Intl. INTS 1088 BLUEBIRD BLUES (LP) 15

SONNY BOY WILLIAMSON (II)

63 Pye International 7N 25191 Help Me/Bye Bye Bird 20
64 Pye International 7N 25268 Lonesome Cabin/The Goat 18
65 Sue WI 365 No Nights By Myself/Boppin' With Sonny Boy 25
66 Chess CRS 8030 Bring It On Home/Down Child 15
66 Blue Horizon 45-1008 From The Bottom/Empty Bedroom 80
64 Pye Intl. NEP 44037 SONNY BOY WILLIAMSON (EP) 25
65 Chess CRE 6001 HELP ME (EP) 35
66 Chess CRE 6013 IN MEMORIAM (EP) 35
66 Chess CRE 6018 REAL FOLK BLUES VOL. 2 (EP) 30
64 Pye Intl. NPL 28036 DOWN AND OUT BLUES (LP) 50
64 Storyville SLP 158 PORTRAITS IN BLUES, VOL. 4 (LP) 35
65 Chess CRL 4510 IN MEMORIAM (LP) 40
66 Storyville SLP 170 THE BLUES OF SONNY BOY WILLIAMSON (LP) 30
66 Fontana 670 158 PORTRAITS IN BLUES, VOL. 4 (LP, reissue) 22
67 Storyville 671 170 THE BLUES OF SONNY BOY WILLIAMSON (LP, reissue) 22
67 Marble Arch MAL 662 DOWN AND OUT BLUES (LP, reissue) 12
68 Marmalade 607/608 004 DON'T SEND ME NO FLOWERS (LP, with Brian Auger & Jimmy Page) 60
74 Rarity RLP 1 THE LAST SESSIONS — 1963 (LP) 25
(see also Ottilie Patterson)

SONNY BOY WILLIAMSON (II) & YARDBIRDS

65 Fontana TL 5277 SONNY BOY WILLIAMSON & THE YARDBIRDS (LP) 150
68 Fontana SFJL 960 SONNY BOY WILLIAMSON & THE YARDBIRDS (LP, reissue, different sleeve) 30
71 Philips 6435 011 SONNY BOY WILLIAMSON & THE YARDBIRDS (LP, 2nd reissue) 15
(see also Yardbirds, Brian Auger)

STU WILLIAMSON

56 London Jazz LZ-N 14030 SAPPHIRE (10" LP) 20

WILLIE (Francis) & LLOYD (Lindsay)

71 Camel CA 80 Marcus Is Alive/GLADIATORS: Freedom Train 10
(see also Willie Francis)

WILLIE & WHEELS

77 ABC ABC 4184 Skateboard Craze/Do What You Did (p/s) 12
(see also P.F. Sloan)

FOY WILLING & RIDERS OF THE PURPLE SAGE

59 Columbia SEG 7834 COWBOY NUMBER 1 (EP) 10
59 Columbia SEG 7855 COWBOY NUMBER 2 (EP) 10

DORIS WILLINGHAM

69 Jay Boy BOY 1 You Can't Do That/Lost Again 10

CHUCK WILLIS

57 London HLE 8444 C.C. Rider/Ease The Pain 80
57 London HLE 8444 C.C. Rider/Ease The Pain (78) 35
57 London HLE 8489 That Train Has Gone/Love Me Cherry 70
57 London HLE 8489 That Train Has Gone/Love Me Cherry (78) 30
58 London HLE 8595 Betty And Dupree/My Crying Eyes 70
58 London HLE 8595 Betty And Dupree/My Crying Eyes (78) 30
58 London HLE 8635 What Am I Living For/Hang Up My Rock And Roll Shoes 50
58 London HLE 8635 What Am I Living For/Hang Up My Rock And Roll Shoes (78) 35
58 London HL 7039 What Am I Living For/Hang Up My Rock And Roll Shoes (export issue) 30
59 London HLE 8818 My Life/Thunder And Lightning 45
59 London HLE 8818 My Life/Thunder And Lightning (78) 45
59 Fontana TFE 17138 CHUCK WILLIS WAILS (EP) 250
65 Atlantic ATL 5003 I REMEMBER CHUCK WILLIS (LP) 80
69 Atlantic 588 145 I REMEMBER CHUCK WILLIS (LP, reissue) 20

DOUG WILLIS

97 Z Records ZEDD 12029 Get Your Own (12") 10

MINT VALUE £

HAL WILLIS

68	President PT 197	The Lumberjack/Klondike Mike	12

LLOYD WILLIS

70	Pressure Beat PR 5502	Mad Rooster (Parts 1 & 2)/As Far As I Can See (actually "The Wicked Must Survive" by Reggae Boys)	15
70	Unity UN 543	Ivan Hitler The Conqueror/The Splice	18

(see also Dynamic Gang, Urie Aldridge)

RALPH WILLIS

54	Esquire 10-370	Lazy Woman Blues/Goodbye Blues (78)	25
54	Esquire 10-380	Old Home Blues/Salty Dog (78)	25
61	Esquire EP 241	RALPH WILLIS (EP)	40
60s	XX MIN 703	RALPH WILLIS (EP)	15
60s	XX MIN 711	RALPH WILLIS (EP)	15

SLIM WILLIS

65	R&B MRB 5004	Running Around/No Feeling For You	25

TIMMY WILLIS

72	United Artists UP 35352	Mr. Soul Satisfaction/I'm Wondering	6
73	Epic EPC 1309	Give Me A Little Sign/Don't Want To Set Me Free	5

WILLIS BROTHERS

67	London HLB 10132	Bob/Show Her Lots Of Gold	8

NEVILLE WILLOUGHBY

72	Duke DU 140	Wheel And Tun Me/Hey Mama	6

(see also Neville, Whistling Willie)

WILLOWS

56	London HLU 8290	Church Bells May Ring/Baby Tell Me	750
56	London HLU 8290	Church Bells May Ring/Baby Tell Me (78)	130

(see also Tony Middleton)

BOB WILLS & HIS TEXAS PLAYBOYS

51	MGM MGM 455	'Tater Pie/Ida Red Likes The Boogie (78)	12
53	MGM MGM 613	Snatchin' And Grabbin'/I Want To Be Wanted (78)	12

BOB WILLS with TOMMY DUNCAN

60	London HL 7102	Heart To Heart Talk/What's The Matter With The Mill (export issue)	20

MICK WILLS

88	Woronzow WOO 9	FERN HILL (LP)	25
97	Acme AC 8013LP	THE MAGIC GARDEN (LP, foldover gatefold sleeve in poly bag)	20

VIOLA WILLS

68	President PT 108	Lost Without The Love Of My Guy/I Got Love	8
68	President PT 150	Together Forever/Don't Kiss Me Hello And Mean Goodbye	8
68	President PT 152	I've Got To Have All Of You/Night Scene	7
68	President PT 154	You're Out Of My Mind/Any Time	10
74	Goodear EAR 103	Run To The Nearest Exit/Day In The Life Of A Woman	8
74	Goodear EARLH 5002	SOFT CENTRES (LP)	12

WILMER & DUKES

68	Action ACT 4500	Give Me One More Chance/Get It	15

ADA WILSON

79	Ellie Jay EJSP 9288	In The Quiet Of My Room/I'm In Control Here (p/s)	12
80	Barn BARN 012	In The Quiet Of My Room/I'm In Control Here (reissue, no p/s)	6
80	Rockburgh ROCS 224	Head In The Clouds/It Doesn't Have To Be (p/s, with Keeping Dark)	5
85	Thin Sliced TSR 5	In The Quiet Of My Room (New Version)/In The Quiet Of My Room (p/s)	5

(see also Strangeways)

AL WILSON

68	Liberty LBF 15044	Do What You Gotta Do/Now I Know What Love Is	22
68	Liberty LBF 15121	The Snake/Who Could Be Lovin' You	22
69	Liberty LBF 15236	Shake Me Wake Me/I Stand Accused	8
69	Liberty LBF 15257	Lodi/By The Time I Get To Phoenix	8
75	Bell BLL 1436	The Snake/Willoughby Brook	8
69	Liberty LBS 83173	SEARCHING FOR THE DOLPHINS (LP)	25
74	Bell BELLS 247	LA LA PEACE SONG (LP)	15

BRIAN WILSON

66	Capitol CL 15438	Caroline, No/Summer Means New Love	25
88	Sire W 7814 CD	Love And Mercy (LP Version)/One For The Boys (LP Version)/ He Couldn't Get His Poor Old Body To Move (3" CD)	12
88	Sire W 7787 CD	Night Time (LP Version)/One For The Boys/Being With The One You Love (3" CD)	12
88	Sire W 7814 B	LOVE AND MERCY (7" box set, with interview and postcards, limited edition)	40
98	Giant/Mojo 74321 58760 2	INTERVIEW/IMAGINATION (promo CD, with Peter Buck)	30

(see also Beach Boys, Date With Soul, American Spring)

BRIAN WILSON & MIKE LOVE

67	Capitol CL 15513	Gettin' Hungry/Devoted To You (as Brian Wilson & Mike Love)	20

CARL WILSON

81	Caribou CRB 84840	CARL WILSON (LP, with lyric insert)	15
82	Caribou CRB 25225	YOUNGBLOOD (LP, with lyric Insert)	15

(see also Beach Boys)

CLIVE WILSON

64	R&B JB 144	Mango Tree/Midnight In Chicago	22

MINT VALUE £

DELROY WILSON

63	Island WI 097	Naughty People/I Shall Not Remove	25
63	Island WI 103	One, Two, Three/Back Biter	25
63	Island WI 116	You Bend My Love/Can't You See	25
63	R&B JB 108	Lion Of Judah/Joe Liges	25
63	R&B JB 128	Prince Pharoah/Don't Believe Him	25
63	R&B JB 132	Squeeze Your Toe/Sugar Pie	25
64	Black Swan WI 405	Spit In The Sky/Voodoo Man	25
64	Black Swan WI 420	Goodbye/Treat Me Good	25
64	R&B JB 148	Lover Mouth/Every Mouth Must Be Fed	25
64	R&B JB 168	Sammy Dead/CYNTHIA & ARCHIE: Every Beat	25
65	Island WI 205	Pick Up The Pieces/Oppression	25
66	Doctor Bird DB 1022	Give Me A Chance/(It's) Impossible	25
66	Island WI 3013	Dancing Mood/SOUL BROTHERS: More And More	25
67	Island WI 3033	Riding For A Fall/Got To Change Your Ways	25
67	Island WI 3037	Ungrateful Baby/ROY RICHARDS: Hopeful Village Ska	25
67	Island WI 3039	Close To Me/SOUL BROTHERS: Hi-Life	25
67	Island WI 3050	Get Ready/ROY RICHARDS: Port-O-Jam	45
67	Studio One SO 2009	Won't You Come Home Baby/PETER & HORTENSE: I've Been Lonely	25
67	Studio One SO 2014	Mother Word/HEPTONES: Fat Girl	25
67	Studio One SO 2019	Never Conquer/Run For Your Life	25
67	Studio One SO 2031	I'm Not A King/HEPTONES: Take Me (B-side actually by Soul Vendors)	25
68	Island WI 3099	This Old Heart Of Mine/GLEN ADAMS: Grab A Girl	40
68	Island WI 3127	Once Upon A Time/I Want To Love You (B-side actually with Stranger Cole)	25
68	Coxsone CS 7064	True Believer/MARSHALL WILLIAMS: College Girl	25
68	Studio One SO 2040	Mr. D.J./HEPTONES: Tripe Girl	25
68	Studio One SO 2046	Rain From The Skies/How Can I Love Someone	25
68	Studio One SO 2057	Feel Good All Over/I Like The Way You Walk	25
69	Studio One SO 2074	Easy Snappin'/WEBBER SISTERS: Come On	25
69	High Note HS 011	Put Yourself In My Place/It Hurts	12
69	High Note HS 015	I'm The One Who Loves You/AFROTONES: If I'm In A Corner	12
69	High Note HS 022	Your Number One/I've Tried My Best	12
69	High Note HS 028	Good To Me/What Do You Want Me To Do	12
69	Camel CA 15	Sad Mood (actually by Ken Parker)/STRANGER COLE: Give It To Me	12
70	Trojan TR 7740	Show Me The Way/BEVERLEY'S ALLSTARS: Version	10
70	Trojan TR 7769	Gave You My Love/BEVERLEY'S ALLSTARS: Version	10
70	Summit SUM 8503	Got To Get Away/BEVERLEY'S ALLSTARS: Version	8
70	Joe JRS 11	Don't Play That Song (with Reaction)/BOSS ALL STARS: Just One Look	8
70	Unity UN 559	Drink Wine, Everybody/Someone To Call My Own	6
71	Smash SMA 2317	I Am Trying/COLLINS ALLSTARS: Version	6
71	Smash SMA 2318	Satisfaction/Satisfaction Version (B-side with Alton Ellis)	7
71	Smash SMA 2323	What It Was/LLOYD CLARKE: Chicken Thief	7
71	Jackpot JP 763	Better Must Come/BUNNY LEE'S ALLSTARS: Better Must Come — Version	10
71	Jackpot JP 769	Cool Operator/I'm Yours	10
71	Jackpot JP 770	Try Again/AGGROVATORS: Try Again — Version	10
71	Jackpot JP 780	Keep Your Love Strong/Nice To Be Near	10
71	Jackpot JP 781	Peace And Love/JEFF BARNES: Who's Your Brother	10
71	Banana BA 333	Just Because Of You/I Love You Madly	10
72	Banana BA 367	You Keep On Running (& U Roy)/LARRY'S ALL STARS: Running Version	10
72	Bullet BU 520	Hear Come The Heartaches (actually "Here Come The Heartaches")/ You'll Be Sorry	6
72	Jackpot JP 792	Who Cares/HUGH ROY JUNIOR: Who Cares — Version	10
72	Jackpot JP 795	The Same Old Song/Stay By Me	10
72	Jackpot JP 804	Cheer Up/Loving You	10
72	Spur SP 2	Adis Ababa/KEITH HUDSON: Rudie Hot Stuff	40
73	Downtown DT 501	Pretty Girl/JOE GIBBS & PROFESSIONALS: Face Girl	10
73	Grape GR 3038	Can I Change My Mind/Just Because	6
73	Green Door GD 4060	Ain't That Peculiar/What Is Man	8
73	Smash SMA 2336	Trying To Wreck My Life/Live And Learn	15
74	Faith FA 006	Love Got Me Doing Things/PHIL PRATT ALL STARS: Version	5
74	Harry J. HJ 6667	What Will Happen To The Youth Of Today/Baby Don't Do It	5
75	Fab FAB 266	Dancing Mood/Version	8
64	R&B JBL 1112	I SHALL NOT REMOVE (LP)	175
68	Coxsone CSL 8016	GOOD ALL OVER (LP)	130
72	Trojan TRLS 44	BETTER MUST COME (LP)	30
73	Big Shot BILP 102	CAPTIVITY (LP)	30

(see also Hortense & Delroy, Joe Liges, Roy Richards, Soul Brothers, Dennis Alcapone, Stranger Cole, Uniques, Soul Vendors)

DENNIS WILSON (& RUMBO)

70	Stateside SS 2184	Sound Of Free/Lady (as Dennis Wilson & Rumbo)	50
77	Caribou CRB 5663	River Song/Farewell My Friend	10
77	Caribou CRB 81672	PACIFIC OCEAN BLUE (LP, gatefold sleeve, some on blue vinyl)	20/25

(see also Beach Boys)

DOYLE WILSON with JIMMY LACEY & BAND

58	Vogue Pop V 9117	Hey-Hey/You're The One For Me	600
58	Vogue Pop V 9117	Hey-Hey/You're The One For Me (78)	150

EDDIE WILSON

62	Oriole CB 1780	Dankeschoen-Bitteschoen-Wiederschoen/Rheinlaender Waltz	8

EDDIE WILSON

69	Action ACT 4536	Shing-A-Ling Stroll/Don't Kick The Teenager Around	20
70	Action ACT 4555	Get Out On The Street/Must Be Love	12

EDITH WILSON

60s	Fountain FB 302	1921-1922 WITH JOHNNY DUNN'S JAZZHOUNDS (LP)	15

MINT VALUE £

ERNEST ('SOUL') WILSON

67	Studio One SO 2032	Money Worries/SOUL VENDORS: Pe Da Pa	25
68	Studio One SO 2058	If I Were A Carpenter/SOUL VENDORS: Frozen Soul	40
68	Coxsone CS 7044	Storybook Children (as Ernest 'Soul' Wilson)/LITTLE FREDDIE: After Laughter (B-side actually by Freddie McGregor)	25
68	Coxsone CS 7059	Undying Love/SOUL VENDORS: Tropic Isle	25
69	Amalgamated AMG 837	Private Number/GLEN ADAMS: She's So Fine	15
69	Crab CRAB 9	Private Number/Another Chance	10
69	Crab CRAB 17	Freedom Train/STRANGER COLE: You Should Never Have To Come	10
69	Crab CRAB 21	Just Once In My Life (with Freddy)/GLEN ADAMS: Mighty Organ	10
76	Fab FAB 280	Storybook Children/SOUND DIMENSION: Version	10

(see also Tinga & Ernest)

ERNEST WILSON & FREDDY (McGregor)

70	Crab CRAB 45	Sentimental Man/It's A Lie	10
70	Unity UN 564	Love Makes The World Go Round/Love (Version Instrumental)	10
71	Gas GAS 168	What You Gonna Do About It/DOBBY DOBSON: Halfway To Paradise	10
71	Jackpot JP 765	Let Them Talk/The Truth Hurts	10

FRANK WILSON

79	Tamla Motown TMG 1170	Do I Love You (Indeed I Do)/Sweeter As The Days Go By (some promos in p/s)	30/20

FRANK WILSON & CAVALIERS

64	Fontana TF 505	Last Kiss/That's How Much I Love You	18

GADDY WILSON

60	Philips PB 980	Nothin' At Night/I'll Never Be Myself Again (78)	12

GARLAND WILSON

53	HMV 7M 122	Just You, Just Me/Sweet Georgia Brown	7

JACK WILSON QUARTET

64	London HA-K/SH-K 8170	THE JACK WILSON QUARTET (LP, featuring Roy Ayers)	30
66	Vocalion LAE-L 603	RAMBLIN' (LP)	35

(see also Roy Ayers)

JACKIE WILSON

78s

57	Vogue Coral Q 72290	Reet Petite/By The Light Of The Silvery Moon	8
57	Coral Q 72290	Reet Petite/By The Light Of The Silvery Moon (2nd pressing)	8
58	Coral Q 72306	To Be Loved/Come Back To Me	6
58	Coral Q 72332	I'm Wanderin'/As Long As I Live	15
58	Coral Q 72338	We Have Love/Singing A Song	15
58	Coral Q 72347	Lonely Teardrops/In The Blue Of The Evening	40
59	Coral Q 72366	That's Why/Love Is All	40
59	Coral Q 72372	I'll Be Satisfied/Ask	50
59	Coral Q 72380	You Better Know It/Never Go Away	75
59	Coral Q 72384	Talk That Talk/Only You, Only Me	80

45s

57	Vogue Coral Q 72290	Reet Petite/By The Light Of The Silvery Moon	25
57	Coral Q 72290	Reet Petite/By The Light Of The Silvery Moon (2nd pressing)	15
58	Coral Q 72306	To Be Loved/Come Back To Me	22
58	Coral Q 72332	I'm Wanderin'/As Long As I Live	22
58	Coral Q 72338	We Have Love/Singing A Song	22
58	Coral Q 72347	Lonely Teardrops/In The Blue Of The Evening	25
59	Coral Q 72366	That's Why/Love Is All	20
59	Coral Q 72366	That's Why/Love Is All (mispressing, B-side plays "You Better Know It")	18
59	Coral Q 72372	I'll Be Satisfied/Ask	18
59	Coral Q 72380	You Better Know It/Never Go Away	18
59	Coral Q 72384	Talk That Talk/Only You, Only Me	18
60	Coral Q 72393	Doggin' Around/The Magic Of Love	18
60	Coral Q 72407	A Woman, A Lover, A Friend/(You Were Made For) All My Love	15
60	Coral Q 72412	Alone At Last/Am I The Man	15
61	Coral Q 72421	The Tear Of The Year/My Empty Arms (withdrawn B-side, demos only)	65
61	Coral Q 72424	The Tear Of The Year/Your One And Only Love	15
61	Coral Q 72430	Please Tell Me Why/(So Many) Cute Little Girls	15
61	Coral Q 72434	I'm Comin' On Back To You/Lonely Life	15
61	Coral Q 72439	You Don't Know What It Means/Years From Now	15
61	Coral Q 72444	The Way I Am/My Heart Belongs To Only You	15
62	Coral Q 72450	The Greatest Hurt/There'll Be No Next Time	15
62	Coral Q 72453	Sing (And Tell The Blues So Long)/I Found Love (B-side with Linda Hopkins)	15
62	Coral Q 72454	I Just Can't Help It/My Tale Of Woe	15
63	Coral Q 72460	Baby Workout/What Good Am I Without You	15
63	Coral Q 72464	Shake A Hand/Say I Do (as Jackie Wilson & Linda Hopkins)	15
63	Coral Q 72465	Shake! Shake! Shake!/He's A Fool	15
63	Coral Q 72467	Baby Get It/The New Breed	15
64	Coral Q 72474	Big Boss Line/Be My Girl	15
64	Coral Q 72476	Squeeze Her — Tease Her (But Love Her)/Give Me Back My Heart	15
65	Coral Q 72480	Yes Indeed!/When The Saints Go Marching In (with Linda Hopkins)	15
65	Coral Q 72481	No Pity (In The Naked City)/I'm So Lonely	15
65	Coral Q 72482	I Believe I'll Love On/Lonely Teardrops	15
66	Coral Q 72484	To Make A Big Man Cry/Be My Love	15
66	Coral Q 72487	Whispers/The Fairest Of Them All	15
67	Coral Q 72493	(Your Love Keeps Lifting Me) Higher And Higher/I'm The One To Do It	15
67	Coral Q 72496	Since You Showed Me How To Be Happy/The Who-Who Song	15
68	MCA MU 1014	For Your Precious Love/Uptight (Everything's Alright) (with Count Basie)	6
68	Decca AD 1008	For Your Precious Love/Uptight (Everything's Alright) (export issue)	25
69	MCA Soul Bag BAG 2	(Your Love Keeps Lifting Me) Higher And Higher/Whispers (Gettin' Louder)	6

69	MCA Soul Bag BAG 7	Since You Showed Me How To Be Happy/Chain Gang	6
69	MCA MU 1104	Since You Showed Me How To Be Happy/The Who-Who Song (reissue)	6
69	MCA MU 1105	Helpless/Do It The Right Way	6
70	MCA MU 1131	(Your Love Keeps Lifting Me) Higher And Higher/Whispers (Gettin' Louder) (reissue)	5
72	MCA MU 1160	I Get The Sweetest Feeling/Soul Galore	6
73	Brunswick BR 3	Beautiful Day/What'cha Gonna Do About Love	6
75	Brunswick BR 18	I Get The Sweetest Feeling/(Your Love Keeps Lifting Me) Higher And Higher	5
75	Brunswick BR 23	Whispers (Gettin' Louder)/Reet Petite	5
75	Brunswick BR 28	Don't Burn No Bridges/Don't Burn No Bridges (Instrumental) (with Chi-Lites)	5
70s	Brunswick BR 43	It Only Happens When I Look At You/Just As Soon As The Feeling's Over	30

EPs

59	Coral FEP 2016	JACKIE WILSON (triangular or round centre)	90/65
60	Coral FEP 2043	THE DYNAMIC JACKIE WILSON (triangular or round centre)	90/65

LPs

58	Coral LVA 9087	HE'S SO FINE	150
59	Coral LVA 9108	LONELY TEARDROPS	150
60	Coral LVA 9121	SO MUCH	100
60	Coral LVA 9130	JACKIE SINGS THE BLUES	125
60	Coral LVA 9135	MY GOLDEN FAVOURITES	80
61	Coral LVA 9144	A WOMAN, A LOVER, A FRIEND	110
61	Coral LVA 9148	YOU AIN'T HEARD NOTHIN' YET	80
62	Coral LVA 9151	BY SPECIAL REQUEST (also stereo SVL 3018)	75/90
62	Coral LVA 9202	BODY AND SOUL	65
63	Coral LVA/SVL 9209	JACKIE (mono/stereo)	70/80
63	Coral LVA/SVL 9214	THE WORLD'S GREATEST MELODIES (mono/stereo)	55/65
66	Coral LVA 9231	SPOTLIGHT ON JACKIE WILSON	65
66	Coral LVA/SVL 9232	SOUL GALORE (mono/stereo)	70/80
67	Coral LVA 9235	WHISPERS	60
68	MCA MUP(S) 304	HIGHER AND HIGHER	15
68	MCA MUP(S) 333	TWO MUCH (with Count Basie & His Orchestra)	12
69	MCA MUPS 361	I GET THE SWEETEST FEELING	12
70	MCA MUPS 405	DO YOUR THING	20
73	Brunswick BRLS 3001	YOU GOT ME WALKIN'	12
73	Brunswick BRLS 3004	GREATEST HITS	12
75	Brunswick BRLS 3016	THE VERY BEST OF JACKIE WILSON	12

(see also Billy Ward & Dominoes, Clyde McPhatter, Count Basie, Chi-Lites, Linda Hopkins)

JACKIE WILSON/CLYDE McPHATTER

62	Ember JBS 705	Tenderly/CLYDE McPHATTER: Harbour Lights	250
62	Ember NR 5001	MEET BILLY WARD & THE DOMINOES (LP, 1 side each)	200

(see also Clyde McPhatter)

JOE WILSON

71	Pye International 7N 25550	Sweetness/When A Man Cries	6

LALA WILSON

(see under Alexander Jackson & Turnkeys)

MARTY WILSON & STRAT-O-LITES

58	Brunswick 05750	Hey! Eula/Hedge-Hopper	18
58	Brunswick 05750	Hey! Eula/Hedge-Hopper (78)	6

MAYNELL WILSON (actually Wilson Maynell) & WESTMINSTER FIVE

64	Carnival CV 7014	Hey Hey Johnny/Baby	8
67	CBM CBM 001	Motown Feeling/Mean Ole World	7

(see also Wes[t]minster Five)

MURRY WILSON

67	Capitol CL 15525	Plumber's Tune/Love Won't Wait	8
67	Capitol (S)T 2819	THE MANY MOODS OF MURRY WILSON (LP)	25

(see also Beach Boys)

NANCY WILSON

64	Capitol CL 15343	The Best Is Yet To Come/Never Let Me Go	5
64	Capitol CL 15352	(You Don't Know) How Glad I Am/Never Less Than Yesterday	5
65	Capitol CL 15378	Don't Come Running Back To Me/Love Has Many Faces	8
65	Capitol CL 15412	Where Does That Leave Me/Gentle Is My Love	15
66	Capitol CL 15443	Power Of Love/Rain Sometimes	12
66	Capitol CL 15466	You've Got Your Troubles/Uptight (Everything's Alright)	18
67	Capitol CL 15508	Don't Look Over Your Shoulder/Mercy, Mercy, Mercy	12
68	Capitol CL 15536	You Don't Know Me/Ode To Billie Joe	10
68	Capitol CL 15547	Face It Girl It's Over/The End Of Our Love	35
75	Capitol CL 15810	You're Right As Rain/There'll Always Be Forever	5
62	Capitol EAP1 20604	SECOND TIME AROUND (EP)	10
64	Capitol EAP4 2082	TODAY, TOMORROW, FOREVER (EP)	10
62	Capitol (S)T 1767	HELLO YOUNG LOVERS (LP, mono/stereo)	15/20
63	Capitol (S)T 1828	BROADWAY — MY LOVE (LP, mono/stereo)	15/20
63	Capitol (S)T 1934	HOLLYWOOD — MY WAY (LP, mono/stereo)	15/20
63	Capitol (S)T 2012	YESTERDAY'S LOVE SONGS (LP, mono/stereo)	15/20
64	Capitol (S)T 2082	TODAY, TOMORROW, FOREVER (LP)	18
65	Capitol (S)T 2136	THE NANCY WILSON SHOW (LP)	15
65	Capitol (S)T 2155	HOW GLAD I AM (LP)	18
65	Capitol (S)T 2321	TODAY— MY WAY (LP)	15
65	Capitol (S)T 2351	GENTLE IS MY LOVE (LP)	15
66	Capitol (S)T 2433	FROM BROADWAY WITH LOVE (LP)	15
66	Capitol (S)T 2495	A TOUCH OF TODAY (LP)	15
66	Capitol (S)T 2555	TENDER LOVING CARE (LP)	15
67	Capitol (S)T 2634	NANCY — NATURALLY (LP)	15

MINT VALUE £

67	Capitol (S)T 2757	LUSH LIFE (LP)	12
68	Capitol (S)T 2844	WELCOME TO MY LOVE (LP)	12
69	Capitol (S)T 2909	EASY (LP)	12
69	Capitol (S)T 2970	SOUND OF NANCY WILSON (LP)	12

NANCY WILSON & CANNONBALL ADDERLEY

63	Capitol EAP4 1657	NANCY WILSON & CANNONBALL ADDERLEY (EP)	8
62	Capitol (S)T 1657	NANCY WILSON & CANNONBALL ADDERLEY (LP, mono/stereo)	12/15

(see also Cannonball Adderley)

PEANUTS WILSON

58	Coral Q 72302	Cast Iron Arm/You've Got Love	500
58	Coral Q 72302	Cast Iron Arm/You've Got Love (78)	150
76	MCA MCA 240	Cast Iron Arm/DON WOODY: Barking Up The Wrong Tree	6

PHIL WILSON

87	Creation CRE 036D	Waiting For A Change/Even Now/Down In The Valley/Love In Vain (double pack)	5
89	Caff CAFF 3	Better Days/You Won't Speak (p/s, with insert, handwritten label)	12

(see also June Brides)

REUBEN WILSON

74	People PEO 109	I'll Take You There/Cisco Kid	6
76	Chess 6078 700	Got To Get Your Own Parts 1 & 2	12
72	Blue Note BST 84295	ON BROADWAY (LP)	15
72	Blue Note BST 84317	LOVE BUG (LP)	15
72	Blue Note BST 84343	BLUE MODE (LP)	15
73	People PLEO 01	CISCO KID (LP)	12
74	People PLEO 20	THE SWEET LIFE (LP)	12

RON WILSON

68	Island WI 3112	Dread Saras/DAVID BROWN: All My Life	25

(see also Winston Scotland, Douglas Brothers)

SHARK WILSON & BASEMENT HEATERS

71	Ashanti ASH 400	Make It Reggae/Version	20

SMILEY WILSON

60	London HLG 9066	Running Bear/Long As Little Birds Fly	40

TEDDY WILSON

55	Philips BBR 8065	PIANO MOODS (LP)	12

TONY WILSON

69	Bell BLL 1081	Baby, I Love, Love I Love You/Come Back To My Lonely World	6
77	Bearsville K 15530	Anything That Keeps You Satisfied/I Can't Leave It Alone	5
76	Bearsville K 55513	I LIKE YOUR STYLE (LP)	12

(see also Hot Chocolate)

TREVOR WILSON

65	Ska Beat JB 207	You Couldn't Believe/You Told Me You Care	25

GABY WILTON & CHARLIE ACE

72	Bullet BU 511	Babylon Falling/CHARLIE ACE: Make It Love	6

JOHNNY WILTSHIRE & HIS TREBLETONES

59	Oriole CB 1494	If The Shoe Fits/Cha Cha Choo Choo	40
59	Oriole CB 1494	If The Shoe Fits/Cha Cha Choo Choo (78)	30

TEACHO WILTSHIRE

57	Oriole CB 1376	Coffee Break/Shut-Eye (78)	12

(see also Annie Ross)

WIMPLE WINCH

66	Fontana TF 686	What's Been Done/I Really Love You	200
66	Fontana TF 718	Save My Soul/Everybody's Worried 'Bout Tomorrow	300
67	Fontana TF 781	Rumble On Mersey Square South/Typical British Workmanship	200
67	Fontana TF 781	Rumble On Mersey Square South/Typical British Workmanship (mispressing, B-side plays "Atmospheres")	400+

(see also Just Four Men, Four Just Men, Pacific Drift, Tristar Airbus)

LEM WINCHESTER & BENNY GOLSON

59	Esquire 32-142	WINCHESTER SPECIAL (LP)	25
61	Esquire 32-172	ANOTHER OPUS (LP)	12

KAI WINDING

50	Melodisc 1117	Sid's Bounce/A Night On Bop Mountain (78)	7
64	Verve VS 501	Baby Elephant Walk/Experiment In Terror	5
65	Verve VS 512	Comin' Home Baby/More	25
55	London LTZ-N 15003	K AND J.J. (LP, with J.J. Johnson Quintet)	15
61	Parlophone PMC 1138	SLIDE RULE (LP, with J.J. Johnson Quintet)	20

(see also Dizzy Gillespie, J.J. Johnson Quintet)

WIND IN THE WILLOWS

68	Capitol CL 15561	Moments Spent/Friendly Lion	18
68	Capitol ST 2956	WIND IN THE WILLOWS (LP)	25

(see also Debbie Harry, Blondie)

WINDMILL

69	MCA MU 1090	Big Bertha/Hey, Drummer Man	5
70	MCA MK 5024	Such Sweet Sorrow/I Can Fly	5
70	MCA MK 5045	Wilbur's Thing/Two's Company, Three's A Crowd	5

BARRY WINDOW

70	Baf BAF 7	I Thank You/End Of Our Road	5

MINT VALUE £

WINDOWS

78 Skeleton SKL 008 — Re-Arrange/Over Dub (p/s) 7
81 Skeleton SKULP 2 — UPPERS ON DOWNERS (LP, with inserts) 12
(see also Mutants)

BARBARA WINDSOR

62 HMV 45POP 1104 — It Had Better Be A Wonderful Life/ I'm Not That Sort Of Girl (with Harry Fowler & Kenny Lynch) 8
63 HMV POP 1128 — Sparrows Can't Sing/On Mother Kelly's Doorstep 8
67 Parlophone R 5629 — Don't Dig Twiggy/Swinging London 10
70 UPC UPC 101 — When I Was A Child/What A Right Carry On 6
72 Decca F 13323 — Grin And Bare It/Cheeky Sorta' Bird 6

WINDY & CARL

95 Enraptured RAPT 4501 — Emerald/Fragments Of Time And Space (500 in hand-painted p/s, 300 in tracing paper sleeve) 12/10
96 Enraptured RAPT 4509 — Christmas Song/GRIMBLE GRUMBLE: Odyssey And Oracle (no'd p/s, coloured vinyl, 350 only) 20

WINDY CORNER

73 Deroy DER 977 — THE HOUSE AT WINDY CORNER (LP, private pressing, 100 only) 400

WINE OF LEBANON

76 Dovetail DOVE 46 — WINE OF LEBANON (LP) 30
(see also Achor)

WINGS

(see under Paul McCartney & Wings)

WINGS OVER JORDAN

51 Vogue V 303 — Deep River/Old Ship Of Zion (78) 10

GODFREY WINN

67 Decca F12713 — Loveshade/ I Pass 5

PETE WINSLOW & KING SIZE BRASS

73 BBC 103S — GIRL ON THE TESTCARD (LP) 15

WINSTON

60s Holyground — WINSTON SINGS (EP) 10

WINSTON (Richards) & BIBBIE (Seaton)

63 R&B JB 115 — Lover Man/LESTER STIRLING: Gravy Cool 25

WINSTON (Francis) & CECIL (Locke)

70 Banana BA 306 — United We Stand/SOUND DIMENSION: Sweet Message 10

WINSTON & ERROL

71 Punch PH 74 — There Is A Land/Goodnight My Love 8

WINSTON & FAY

64 Blue Beat BB 272 — Fay Is Gone (Winston & Errol)/MONARCHS: Sauce And Tea 20

WINSTON & GEORGE

66 Pyramid PYR 6002 — Denham Town/Keep The Pressure On 15

WINSTON (Groovy) & PAT (Rhoden)

68 Trojan TR 605 — Pony Ride/Baby You Send Me 10
71 Bullet BU 475 — The Same Thing For Breakfast/Sweeter Than Honey 10
(see also Winston Tucker)

WINSTON & ROY

62 Blue Beat BB 80 — Babylon Gone/COUNT OSSIE ON AFRICAN DRUMS: First Gone 30

WINSTON & RUPERT

70 Bullet BU 425 — Come By Here/Somebody 10
70 Moodisc HM 106 — Musically Beat/Let Me Tell You Girl 10
(see also Eternals)

WINSTON (Richards) & TONETTES

65 Ska Beat JB 225 — You Make Me Cry/CHECKMATES: Invisible Ska 25

JIMMY WINSTON (& HIS REFLECTIONS)

66 Decca F 12410 — Sorry She's Mine/It's Not What You Do (But The Way That You Do It) 225
76 Nems NEMS 12 — Sun In The Morning/Just Wanna Smile (solo) 5
(see also Small Faces, Winston's Fumbs, Spheres)

ERIC WINSTONE (& HIS) ORCHESTRA

52 Nixa NY 7743 — I Don't Care/Slow Train Blues (78) 7
64 Pye 7N 15603 — "Dr. Who" Theme/Pony Express 18
73 Avenue AVINT 1005 — PLAYS 007 (LP) 20

NORMA WINSTONE

72 Argo ZDA 148 — EDGE OF TIME (LP) 100
(see also Mike Westbrook, Michael Garrick)

WINSTONS

69 Pye International 7N 25493 — Colour im Father/Amen, Brother 20
69 Pye International 7N 25500 — Love Of The Common People/Wheel Of Fortune 7

WINSTONS & M-SQUAD

71 Green Door GD 4003 — Carroll Street/Carroll Street — Version (B-side act. by Ansel Collins/ M-Squad) 6

WINSTON'S FUMBS

67 RCA RCA 1612 — Real Crazy Apartment/Snow White 300
(see also Small Faces, Jimmy Winston & His Reflections, Yes, Spheres, Federals)

MINT VALUE £

EDGAR WINTER (GROUP)

71 Epic EPC 7269 Where Would I Be/Good Morning Music (as Edgar Winter's White Trash) 5
72 Epic EPC 7550 Keep On Playin' That Rock'n'Roll/Dying To Live 5
70 CBS 64083 ENTRANCE (LP, as Edgar Winter) 15
71 CBS 64298 EDGAR WINTER'S WHITE TRASH (LP) 15
72 CBS 67244 ROAD WORK (2-LP) 15
73 CBS EQ 31584/Q 65074 THEY ONLY COME OUT AT NIGHT (LP, quadrophonic) 12

JOHNNY WINTER

69 CBS 4386 I'm Yours And I'm Hers/I'll Drown In My Tears. 6
69 Liberty LBF 15219 Rollin' And Tumblin'/Bad Luck And Trouble 7
70 CBS 4795 Johnny B. Goode/I'm Not Sure 6
70 CBS 5358 Rock 'N' Roll Hoochie Koo/21st Century Man 5
71 CBS 7227 Jumping Jack Flash/Good Morning Little School Girl 5
69 CBS 63619 JOHNNY WINTER (LP) 35
69 Liberty LBL/LBS 83240E THE PROGRESSIVE BLUES EXPERIMENT (LP) 20
70 CBS 66231 SECOND WINTER (2-LP, 3-sided). 22
70 Buddah 2359 011 FIRST WINTER (LP) 15
70 CBS 64117 JOHNNY WINTER AND... (LP) 15
71 CBS 64289 JOHNNY WINTER AND... LIVE (LP). 15
73 CBS 65484 STILL ALIVE AND WELL (LP) 12
74 CBS CQ 32188/Q 65484 STILL ALIVE AND WELL (LP, quadrophonic) 15
(see also Johnny & Jammers)

PAUL WINTER

69 A&M AMLS 942 WINTER CONSORT (LP) 12

HUGO WINTERHALTER ORCHESTRA

53 HMV 7M 120 Tic Tac Toe/Hesitation 7
54 HMV 7M 273 Land Of Dreams/Song Of The Barefoot Contessa 8
56 HMV POP 241 Canadian Sunset/This Is Real (with Eddie Haywood). 10
60 RCA RCA 1164 'Summer Place' Theme/Blue Strings (78) 12
68 Studio Two TWO 257 THE BIG THEMES (LP). 12

DON WINTERS

60 Brunswick 05827 Someday Baby/That's All I Need 15

LIZ WINTERS & BOB CORT SKIFFLE GROUP

57 Decca F 10878 Freight Train/Love Is Strange. 20
57 Decca F 10878 Freight Train/Love Is Strange (78) 12
57 Decca F 10899 Maggie May/Jessamine 18
57 Decca F 10899 Maggie May/Jessamine (78). 12
57 Decca DFE 6409 LIZ WINTERS AND BOB CORT (EP) 25
(see also Bob Cort Skiffle Group)

LOIS WINTERS

56 London HLD 8266 Japanese Farewell Song/JAN GARBER & HIS ORCHESTRA: My Dear 35
56 London HLD 8266 Japanese Farewell Song/JAN GARBER & HIS ORCHESTRA: My Dear (78). 10

MIKE & BERNIE WINTERS

57 Parlophone R 4384 How Do You Do?/Does My Baby? 10
57 Parlophone R 4384 How Do You Do?/Does My Baby? (78). 6
59 Parlophone R 4538 For Me and My Gal/Your Own Home Town 6
59 Parlophone R 4538 For Me and My Gal/Your Own Home Town (78). 8
66 CBS 202458 That Man Batman/Insky Spinsky Spider (some with p/s) 15/8
71 Decca F 13255 You're My Little Boy/How Do You Do. 5
72 Philips 6006 254 How I Love Them Old Songs/Everywhere There Is Love 5

RUBY WINTERS

68 Stateside SS 2090 I Want Action/Better 30
79 Creole CR 171 Baby Lay Down/Lovin' Me Is A Full Time Job 10
79 Creole CR 174 Back To Love/I've Been Waiting For You All My Life 10

WYOMA WINTERS

54 HMV 7M 222 Where Can I Go Without You?/Won't You Give A Repeat Performance 7
54 HMV 7M 260 Toy Balloon/Shish Kebab. 7

STEVIE WINWOOD

77 Island WIP 6394 Time Is Running Out/Penultimate Zone (12", pre-release sleeve) 10
80 Island IPR 2040 While You See A Chance/Vacant Chair (12", pre-release sleeve) 8
80 Island WIP 6655 While You See A Chance/Vacant Chair (p/s) 5
80 Island CWIP 6655 While You See A Chance/Vacant Chair (cassette, 5,000 only) 8
81 Island WIP 6747 There's A River/Two Way Stretch (p/s) 5
86 Island IS 294 Freedom Overspill/Spanish Dancer (p/s, with bonus cassette of LP highlights & interview [SW 2]). 6
86 Island 12 ISD 294 Freedom Overspill (Liberty Mix)/(LP Version)/Spanish Dancer (12", stickered g/fold p/s & t/p 7" "Low Spark Of High-Heeled Boys"/"Gimme Some Lovin' "). . . 10
88 Virgin VST 1085 Roll With It (12" Mix)/The Morning Side/Roll With It (7" Version) (12", g/fold p/s) . . 8
91 Virgin VSCDX 1317 I Will Be Here/Don't You Know What The Night Can Do (live)/In The Night Of Day (CD, velvet box with family tree and print). 8
86 Island SWCLP 1 A CONVERSATION WITH (LP, promo interview on "Back In The High Life" LP) . . 12
87 Island SWWLP 1 IN CONVERSATION (LP, promo interview on "Chronicles" LP) 12
87 Island SW 1/2/3 BACK IN THE HIGH LIFE (3 x 7" set, each in p/s, promo only). 20
87 Island CHRONICLES (5 x 7" box set, promo, 500 only) 30
(see also Winwood Kabaka Amoa, Anglos, Spencer Davis Group, Traffic, Blind Faith, Yamashta Winwood etc.)

WINWOOD/KABAKA/AMAO

73 Island HELP 14 AIYE-KETA THIRD WORLD (LP). 15
(see also Stevie WInwood)

WIPEOUT

82	M&L MNL 2/ACE 37	Baby Please Don't Go/Two-O-Five/Crawdaddy/Should A' Known Better (p/s)	15
83	Out OUT 1A/B1	NO SWEAT (LP)	15

WIPEOUT

90s	Deluxe DELUX 002	Snowflake/Confusion Bee (12")	10

WIPERS

84	Psycho PSYCHO 22	IS THIS REAL? (LP, with lyric insert)	12
84	Psycho PSYCHO 23	YOUTH OF AMERICA (LP)	12

WIRE

77	Harvest HAR 5144	Mannequin/Feeling Called Love/12XU (p/s)	12
78	Harvest HAR 5151	I Am The Fly/Ex-Lion Tamer (p/s)	12
78	Harvest HAR 5161	Dot Dash/Options R (p/s)	10
79	Harvest HAR 5172	Outdoor Miner/Practice Makes Perfect (p/s, some on white vinyl)	8/5
79	Harvest HAR 5187	A Question Of Degree/Former Airline (p/s)	7
79	Harvest HAR 5192	Map Ref 41° N 93° W/Go Ahead (p/s)	10
79	Harvest SPSLP 299	154 (12", p/s, white label sampler with insert & press release; beware of counterfeits)	30
81	Rough Trade RT 079	Our Swimmer/Midnight Bahnhof Cafe (p/s)	7
83	Rough Trade RTT 123	Crazy About Love/Second Length (Our Swimmer)/Catapult 30 (12", p/s, 2 different sleeve colours)	each 10
88	Mute MUTE 67	Kidney Bingos/Pieta (p/s)	6
89	Mute MUTE 87	Eardrum Buzz/The Offer (p/s, clear vinyl, withdrawn)	12
89	Mute CDMUTE 98	IN VIVO (CD EP)	8
77	Harvest SHSP 4076	PINK FLAG (LP, with lyric inner)	20
78	Harvest SHSP 4093	CHAIRS MISSING (LP, 1st 10,000 with lilac lyric inner sleeve)	20
79	Harvest SHSP 4105	154 (LP, with inner lyric sleeve & bonus 7" EP: "Song 2"/ "Get Down [Parts I & II]"/"Let's Panic"/"Later"/ "Small Electric Piece" [PSR 444, no p/s])	20
84	Rough Trade ROUGH 29	DOCUMENT AND EYEWITNESS (LP, with free 12" EP [ROUGH 2912])	20
84	Rough Trade COPY 004	DOCUMENT AND EYEWITNESS (cassette, in special box)	15
84	Rough Trade COPY 004	DOCUMENT AND EYEWITNESS (cassette with bonus 12" EP tracks)	12
86	Pink PINKY 7	PLAY POP (mini-LP)	10
87	Mute STUMM 42	THE IDEAL COPY (LP, with inner)	12
89	Mute STUMM 66	IBTABA (IT'S BEGINNING TO AND BACK AGAIN) (LP, with 4 postcards & signed print)	18

(see also Cupol, Colin Newman)

MARK WIRTZ (ORCHESTRA & CHORUS)

68	Parlophone R 5668	(He's Our Dear Old) Weatherman (From "A Teenage Opera")/Possum's Dance	22
68	Parlophone R 5683	Mrs. Raven/Knickerbocker Glory	12
69	CBS 4306	My Daddie Is A Baddie/I Love You Because	6
69	CBS 4539	Caroline/Goody, Goody, Goody	6
64	World Record Club T 452	TEN AGAIN (LP, by Belle Gonzalez & Russ Loader, Wirtz as producer)	35

(see also Mood Mosaic, Keith West, Sweet Shop, Philwit & Pegasus, Mark Rogers & Marksmen, Belle Gonzalez, Russ Loader, Zion De Gallier, Elmer Hockett's Hurdy Gurdy, Steve Flynn, Fickle Finger, Matchmaker)

WISDOM

76	Crystal CR 026	Nefertiti/What-Cha-Gonna-Du-About You	8

NORMAN WISDOM

56	Columbia SCM 5222	Two Rivers/Boy Meets Girl (with Ruby Murray)	5
57	Columbia DB 3864	Up In The World/Me And My Imagination	5
57	Columbia DB 3903	The Wisdom Of A Fool/Happy Ending	5
59	Top Rank JAR 246	Follow A Star/Give Me A Night In June	5
61	Columbia SCD 2160	Narcissus (The Laughing Record)/I Don't 'Arf Love You (with Joyce Grenfell)	5
69	CBS 4569	Where Do I Go From Here?/Just Like The Day	5
56	Columbia SEG 7612	NORMAN WISDOM (EP)	8
57	Columbia SEG 7687	NORMAN AND RUBY (EP, with Ruby Murray)	8
59	Top Rank JKP 2052	FOLLOW A STAR (EP)	8
58	Columbia 33SX 1085	NORMAN WISDOM IN "WHERE'S CHARLEY?" (LP)	15
67	Wing WL 1216	I WOULD LIKE TO PUT ON RECORD (LP)	12

(see also Ruby Murray)

WISE BLOOD

85	Wise 1-12	Motorslug/Death Rape 2000 (12", p/s)	12
86	Wise 2-12	Someone Drowned In My Pool/Stumbo (12", p/s)	12
91	Wise 003	DISHDIRT (LP, with sticker)	15
91	Big Cut 030X	PEDAL TO THE METAL (mini LP)	12

(see also Foetus)

WISE BOYS

60	Parlophone R 4693	Why, Why, Why/My Fortune	10

WISE GUYS

60	Top Rank JAR 271	(Little Girl) Big Noise/As Long As I Have You	12

MAC WISEMAN

55	London HLD 8174	The Kentuckian Song/Wabash Cannon Ball	65
55	London HLD 8174	The Kentuckian Song/Wabash Cannon Ball (78)	15
56	London HLD 8226	My Little Home In Tennessee/I Haven't Got The Right To Love You	65
56	London HLD 8226	My Little Home In Tennessee/I Haven't Got The Right To Love You (78)	20
56	London HLD 8259	Fireball Mail/When The Roses Bloom Again	65
56	London HLD 8259	Fireball Mail/When The Roses Bloom Again (78)	30
57	London HLD 8412	Step It Up And Go/Sundown	400
57	London HLD 8412	Step It Up And Go/Sundown (78)	50
59	London HL 7084	Jimmy Brown The Newsboy/I've Got No Use For Woman (export issue)	40
56	London RE-D 1056	SONGS FROM THE HILLS (EP)	35

MINT VALUE £

58	London RE-D 1147	SONGS FROM THE HILLS VOL. 2 (EP)	35
60	London RE-D 1242	SONGS FROM THE HILLS VOL. 3 (EP)	35
56	London HB-D 1052	SONGS FROM THE HILLS (10" LP)	65
60	London HA-D 2217	GREAT FOLK BALLADS (LP)	40

TREVOR WISHART

78	private pressing	RED BIRD: A POLITICAL PRISONER'S DREAM (LP, with insert)	20
79	private pressing	BEACH SINGULARITY AND MENAGERIE (LP, with insert)	20

WISHBONE ASH

70	MCA MK 5061	Blind Eye/Queen Of Torture	6
72	MCA MKS 5097	No Easy Road/Blowin' Free	6
73	MCA MUS 1210	So Many Things To Say/Rock'n'Roll Widow	5
74	MCA MCA 165	Hometown/Persephone	5
75	MCA MCA 176	Silver Shoes/Persephone	6
76	MCA/SFI 263	Outward Bound/Runaway/Mother Of Pearl/You Rescue Me (flexidisc, with/without "New England" tour programme)	12/5
77	MCA MCA 291	Phoenix/Blowin' Free/Jail Bait (p/s)	5
78	MCA MCA 392	You See Red/Bad Weather Blues (live) (p/s)	5
78	MCA 12MCA 392	You See Red/Bad Weather Blues (12", p/s)	7
79	MCA MCA 518	Come On/Fast Johnny (p/s)	5
80	MCA MCA 549	Living Proof/Jail Bait (live) (p/s)	5
80	MCA MCA 577	Helpless (live)/Blowin' Free (live) (p/s)	5
80	MCA MCAT 577	Helpless (live)/Blowin' Free (live) (12", p/s)	7
81	MCA MCA 695	Underground/My Mind Is Made Up (p/s)	5
81	MCA MCA 726	Get Ready/Kicks On The Street (p/s, some with patch)	8/5
81	MCA MCL 14	Get Ready/Kicks On The Street (p/s, alternate issue)	5
82	AVM WISH 1	Engine Overheat/Genevieve (p/s)	5
82	AVM 1002	No More Lonely Nights/Street Of Shame (no p/s)	5
88	I.R.S. IRM 164	In The Skin/Tangible Evidence (p/s)	5
89	I.R.S. EIRS 104	Cosmic Jazz/T-Bone Shuffle (p/s)	5
89	I.R.S. EIRS T104	Cosmic Jazz/T-Bone Shuffle/Bolan's Monument (12", p/s)	10
70	MCA MKPS 2014	WISHBONE ASH (LP, gatefold sleeve, black label)	20
71	MCA MDKS 8004	PILGRIMAGE (LP, gatefold sleeve, black label)	18
72	MCA MDKS 8006	ARGUS (LP, gatefold sleeve, black label)	18
73	MCA MDKS 8011	WISHBONE FOUR (LP, gatefold sleeve, black label, with poster & lyrics)	18

(Red/brown, red/yellow & red/pink label copies of the above LPs also exist, and are worth the same values.)

74	MCA MCSP 254	LIVE DATES (2-LP, gatefold sleeve)	15
74	MCA MCG 2585	THERE'S THE RUB (LP)	12
78	MCA MCG 3528	NO SMOKE WITHOUT FIRE (LP, with stickered sleeve & inner, with bonus live single "Come In From The Rain"/"Lorelei" [PSR 431])	12
80	MCA MCG 4012	LIVE DATES II (LP, gatefold sleeve, with live bonus LP)	15
82	AVM ASH 1	TWIN BARRELS BURNING (LP)	12
85	Neat NEAT 1027	RAW TO THE BONE (LP)	20
85	Neat NEATP 1027	RAW TO THE BONE (LP, picture disc, unissued)	

(see also Home)

WISHFUL THINKING

66	Decca F 12438	Turning Round/V.I.P.	12
66	Decca F 12499	Step By Step/Looking Around	7
67	Decca F 12598	Count To Ten/Hang Around Girl	8
67	Decca F 12627	Peanuts/Cherry Cherry	10
67	Decca F 22673	Meet The Sun/Easier Said Than Loving You	10
68	Decca F 22742	Alone/Vegetables (export issue)	10
68	Decca F 12760	It's So Easy/I Want You Girl	7
72	B&C CB 169	Lu La Le Lu/We're Gonna Change All This	7
72	B&C CB 184	Clear White Light/Hiroshima	7
67	Decca SKL 4900	LIVE VOL. 1 (LP)	45
71	Charisma CAS 1038	HIROSHIMA (LP)	25

WISHING STONES

86	Head HEAD 2	Beat Girl/Two Steps Take Me Back (p/s)	6
87	Head HEAD 6	New Ways/House Is Not A Home (p/s)	5
87	Head HEAD 612	New Ways/Wildwood/Hold Up/A House Is Not A Home (12", p/s)	8

(see also The Loft)

WITCHES BREW

80s	Pussy PU 016	Angeline (p/s)	20

WITCHFINDER GENERAL

81	Heavy Metal HEAVY 6	Burning A Sinner/Satan's Children (p/s)	30
82	Heavy Metal 12HM 17	Soviet Invasion/Rabies/R.I.P. (live) (12", p/s)	35
83	Heavy Metal HEAVY 21	Music/Last Chance (p/s)	12
83	Heavy Metal HMPD 21	Music/Last Chance (picture disc)	8
82	Heavy Metal HMRLP 8	DEATH PENALTY (LP, red, blue or clear vinyl, with inner)	25
82	Heavy Metal HMRPD 8	DEATH PENALTY (LP, picture disc)	18
83	Heavy Metal HMRLP 13	FRIENDS OF HELL (LP, red, silver or clear vinyl)	18
83	Heavy Metal HMRPD 13	FRIENDS OF HELL (LP, picture disc)	15

WITCHFYNDE

79	Rondelet ROUND 1	Give 'Em Hell/Getting' Heavy (p/s)	6
80	Rondelet ROUND 4	In The Stars/Wake Up Screaming (p/s)	5
83	Expulsion OUT 3	I'd Rather Go Wild/Cry Wolf (p/s)	20
80	Rondelet ABOUT 1	GIVE 'EM HELL (LP)	25
80	Rondelet ABOUT 2	STAGE FRIGHT (LP)	12
83	Expulsion EXIT 5	CLOAK AND DAGGER (LP)	12
83	Expulsion PEXIT 5	CLOAK AND DAGGER (LP, picture disc)	18
84	Mausoleum SKULL 8352	LORDS OF SIN (LP, gatefold sleeve, with bonus 12" [Cloak & Dagger/ I'd Rather Go Wild/Moon Magic/Give 'Em Hell])	12

BILL WITHERS

71	A&M AMS 845	Everybody's Talkin'/Harlem	6
71	A&M AMS 858	Ain't No Sunshine/Harlem	5
72	A&M AMS 7004	Lean On Me/Better Off Dead	5
72	A&M AMS 7038	Use Me/Let Me In Your Life	6
73	A&M AMS 7055	Kissing My Love/I Don't Know	5
73	A&M AMS 7068	Look What I Found/The Lady Is Waiting	6
73	A&M AMS 7080	Ain't No Sunshine/Harlem/Grandma's Hands	6
72	A&M AMLH 68107	STILL BILL (LP)	15
71	A&M AMLS 65002	JUST AS I AM (LP)	12
73	A&M AMLD 3001	LIVE AT CARNEGIE HALL (2-LP)	15
74	A&M AMLH 68230	'JUSTMENTS (LP)	12
75	Sussex LPSX 10	BEST OF BILL WITHERS (LP)	12

JIMMY WITHERSPOON

78s

54	Parlophone R 3914	It/Highway To Happiness	40
54	Parlophone R 3951	Oh Boy/I Done Told You	40
54	Vogue V 2261	Failing By Degrees/New Orleans Woman	40
54	Vogue V 2295	Who's Been Jivin' With You/Rain, Rain, Rain	40
56	Vogue V 2060	Big Fine Girl/No Rollin' Blues	40
56	Vogue V 2356	Jump, Children/Take Me Back Baby	40

SINGLES

54	Parlophone MSP 6125	It/Highway To Happiness	90
54	Parlophone MSP 6142	Oh Boy/I Done Told You	90
56	Vogue V 2060	Big Fine Girl/No Rollin' Blues	70
62	Vogue V 2420	When The Lights Go Out/All That's Good	70
64	Stateside SS 304	Evenin'/Money Is Getting Cheaper	15
64	Stateside SS 325	I Will Never Marry/I'm Coming Down With The Blues	15
64	Stateside SS 362	You're Next/Happy Blues	15
65	Stateside SS 429	Come Walk With Me/Oh How I Love You	15
65	Stateside SS 461	Love Me Right/Make My Heart Smile Again	15
66	Stateside SS 503	If There Wasn't Any You/I Never Thought I'd See The Day	15
66	Verve VS 538	It's All Over But The Crying/If I Could Have You Back Again	8
67	Verve VS 553	Past Forty Blues/My Baby's Quit Me	6
71	Probe PRO 526	Handbags And Gladrags/It's Time To Live	5
75	Capitol CL 15828	Fool's Paradise/Reflections	5

EPs

61	Vogue EPV 1269	JIMMY WITHERSPOON AT MONTEREY	35
61	Vogue EPV 1270	JIMMY WITHERSPOON AT MONTEREY No. 2	35
64	Vocalion EPVH 1278	JIMMY WITHERSPOON	25
65	Vocalion EPVH 1284	OUTSKIRTS OF TOWN	25
66	Vocalion VEH 170158	FEELING THE SPIRIT VOL. 1	25
66	Vocalion VEH 170159	FEELING THE SPIRIT VOL. 2	25

LPs

59	London Jazz LTZ-K 15150	NEW ORLEANS BLUES (with Wilbur de Paris)	40
60	Vogue LAE 12218	SINGIN' THE BLUES	40
61	Vogue LAE 12253	AT THE RENAISSANCE (with Gerry Mulligan)	35
64	Society SOC 968	SINGS THE BLUES	15
64	Stateside SL 10088	EVENIN' BLUES	40
65	Stateside SL 10105	BLUES AROUND THE CLOCK	45
65	Fontana 688 005 ZL	THERE'S GOOD ROCKIN' TONIGHT	35
65	Stateside SL 10114	SOME OF MY BEST FRIENDS ARE BLUES	45
65	Stateside SL 10139	BLUE SPOON	35
65	Vogue VRL 3005	JIMMY WITHERSPOON IN PERSON	35
66	Ember EMB 3369	JIMMY WITHERSPOON	30
67	Fontana (S)TL 5382	'SPOON SINGS AND SWINGS	40
67	Verve (S)VLP 9156	BLUE POINT OF VIEW	25
67	Transatlantic PR 7300	EVENIN' BLUES (reissue)	18
68	Transatlantic PR 7356	SOME OF MY BEST FRIENDS ARE THE BLUES (reissue)	18
68	Stateside (S)SL 10232	LIVE	30
68	Verve (S)VLP 9181	BLUES IS NOW (with Brother Jack McDuff)	22
68	Verve (S)VLP 9216	SPOONFUL OF SOUL	22
68	Transatlantic PR 7418	SPOON IN LONDON	25
68	Transatlantic PR 7475	BLUES FOR EASY LIVERS	18
69	Stateside SSL 10289	THE BLUES SINGER	22
69	Ember CJS 820	SINGS THE BLUES AT THE RENAISSANCE (reissue, with Gerry Mulligan)	12
69	Polydor Intl. 623 256	BACK DOOR BLUES	22
71	Probe SPB 1031	HANDBAGS AND GLADRAGS	15

(see also Eric Burdon & Jimmy Witherspoon, Brother Jack McDuff)

JIMMY WITHERSPOON/HELEN HUMES

60	Vogue EPV 1198	RHYTHM AND BLUES CONCERT (EP, 2 tracks each)	90

(see also Helen Humes)

BITTER WITHY

69	Nevis NEVIS R005	SAMPLER (LP)	20

WITNESSES

60s	Herald ELR 1076	THE WITNESSES (EP)	100

WIZARD'S CONVENTION

76	RCA RS 1085	WIZARD'S CONVENTION (LP, with insert)	15

(see also Deep Purple, Roger Glover, Jon Lord, David Coverdale, Ray Fenwick)

MINT VALUE £

WIZZARD

73	Warner Bros K 16336	I Wish It Could Be Christmas Every Day/Rob Roy's Nightmare (gatefold p/s, withdrawn)	10
73	Harvest HAR 5079	I Wish It Could Be Christmas Every Day/Rob Roy's Nightmare (reissue, gatefold p/s with Harvest sticker over Warner Bros. logo)	10
74	Warner Bros K 16357	Rock'n'Roll Winter/Dream Of Unwin (gatefold p/s)	5
74	Warner Bros K 16434	This Is The Story Of My Love (Baby)/Nixture	5
75	Jet JET 758	Rattlesnake Roll/Can't Help My Feelings	5
76	Jet JET 768	Indiana Rainbow/The Thing Is This (This Is The Thing) (as Roy Wood's Wizzard) (some in p/s)	10/5
73	Harvest SHSP 4025	WIZZARD BREW (LP, with lyric insert)	15
74	Warner Bros K 56029	INTRODUCING EDDY AND THE FALCONS (LP, gatefold sleeve with poster)	12

(see also Roy Wood, Balls, Idle Race, Grunt Futtock)

WKGB

79	Fetish FET 002	Non-Stop/Ultra Marine (p/s)	6

(DARRYL WAY'S) WOLF

73	Deram DM 378	Wolf/Spring Fever	8
73	Deram DM 395	A Bunch Of Fives/Five In The Morning	8
73	Deram DM 401	Two Sisters/Go Down	8
73	Deram SDL 14	CANIS LUPUS (LP, as Darryl Way's Wolf, gatefold sleeve)	25
73	Deram SML 1104	SATURATION POINT (LP, as Darryl Way's Wolf)	25
74	Deram SML 1116	NIGHT MUSIC (LP)	22
78	Island ILPS 9550	CONCERTO FOR ELECTRIC VIOLIN (LP)	12

(see also Curved Air, King Crimson, Marillion)

WOLF

81	Gremlin GREM 73	See Them Running/Creatures Of The Night (no p/s)	70

WOLF

82	Chrysalis CHS 2592	Head Contact/Rock'n'Roll (p/s, clear vinyl, some with sticker)	15/6
82	Chrysalis CHS 12 2592	Head Contact/Rock'n'Roll/Soul For The Devil (12", p/s)	8
84	Mausoleum 8323	EDGE OF THE WORLD (LP)	15

RICHARD WOLFE & HIS ORCHESTRA

60	London HLR 9143	Banjo Boy/Voila	8

WOLFETONES

65	Fontana STL 5244	THE FOGGY DEW (LP)	12

WOLFGANG PRESS

83	4AD (no cat. no.)	Kings Of Soul (Crowned Mix)/(De-Throned Mix)/(7" Mix) (12", same both sides, promo only, 50 copies pressed)	10
84	4AD BAD 409	SCARECROW: Desire/Respect/Ecstasy (12" EP)	8
94	4AD CADD 4016CD	FUNKY LITTLE DEMONS (CD, with free remix CD)	18

(see also Mass, Models)

WOLFRILLA

71	Concord CON 015	Song For Jimi/Come Tomorrow	7

WOOLLY WOLSTENHOLME

80	Polydor 2374 165	MAESTOSO (LP)	12

(see also Barclay James Harvest)

WOLVES

64	Pye 7N 15676	Journey Into Dreams/What Do You Mean	15
64	Pye 7N 15733	Now/This Year Next Year	25
65	Pye 7N 17013	At The Club/Distant Dreams	30
66	Parlophone R 5511	Lust For Life/My Baby Loves Them	60

BOBBY WOMACK

68	Minit MLF 11001	Broadway Walk/Somebody Special	12
68	Minit MLF 11005	What Is This?/What You Gonna Do	12
68	Minit MLF 11010	Fly Me To The Moon/Take Me	6
69	Minit MLF 11012	California Dreamin'/Baby You Oughta Think It Over	8
72	United Artists UP 35339	That's The Way I Feel About 'Cha/Come, L'Amore	7
72	United Artists UP 35375	Woman's Gotta Have It/If You Don't Want My Love	5
73	United Artists UP 35456	I Can Understand It/Harry Hippie (some in p/s)	10/5
73	United Artists UP 35512	Across 110th Street/Hang On In There (as Bobby Womack & Peace)	6
73	United Artists UP 35565	Nobody Wants You When You're Down And Out/ I'm Through Trying To Prove My Love For You	5
74	Jay Boy BOY 75	What Is This?/I Wonder	5
75	United Artists UP 35859	Check It Out/Interlude No. 2	5
76	United Artists UP 36042	Where There's A Will There's A Way/Everything's Gonna Be Alright	5
76	United Artists UP 36098	Daylight/Trust Me	5
79	Arista ARIST 284	How Could You Break My Heart/I Honestly Love You	5
82	Tamla Motown TMG1267	So Many Sides of You/ Just My Imagination (7", p/s)	30
87	Arista RIS 17	How Could You Break My Heart/Give It Up (p/s)	15
87	Arista RIST 17	How Could You Break My Heart/Give It Up/ Mr. D.J. Don't Stop The Music (12", p/s)	12
72	United Artists UAS 29365	UNDERSTANDING (LP)	12
73	United Artists UAS 29451	ACROSS 110TH STREET (LP, soundtrack, with J.J. Johnson)	25
73	United Artists UAS 29306	COMMUNICATION (LP)	12
73	United Artists UAG 29456	FACTS OF LIFE (LP)	12
74	United Artists UAS 29574	LOOKIN' FOR A LOVE AGAIN (LP)	12
75	United Artists UAG 29715	I CAN UNDERSTAND IT (LP)	12
75	United Artists UAG 29762	I DON'T KNOW WHAT THE WORLD IS COMING TO (LP)	12
79	Arista ARTY 165	ROADS OF LIFE (LP)	15

(see also Valentinos, Ted Wood)

WOMB
69 Dot DLP 25933 WOMB (LP) 25
70 Dot DLP 25959 OVERDUB (LP) 30

WOMENFOLK
64 RCA RCA 1439 Turn Around/One Man's Hand 6
65 RCA RCA 1480 My Heart Tells Me To Believe/The Way I Feel 6
66 RCA Victor RCA 1522 The Last Thing On My Mind/Meditation 6
65 RCA RD 7704 AT THE HUNGRY I (LP) 18

ALISON WONDER
70 Columbia DB 8667 Once More With Feeling/Black Paper Roses 10
(see also Cheryl St. Clair)

GIRL WONDER
66 Doctor Bird DB 1015 Mommy Out Of The Light/Cutting Wood 18

(LITTLE) STEVIE WONDER
SINGLES
63 Oriole CBA 1853 Fingertips (Parts 1 & 2) 30
63 Stateside SS 238 Workout, Stevie, Workout/Monkey Talk 45
64 Stateside SS 285 Castles In The Sand/Thank You (For Loving Me All The Way) 50
64 Stateside SS 323 Hey, Harmonica Man/This Little Girl 45
(The above singles were credited to Little Stevie Wonder.)
65 Tamla Motown TMG 505 Kiss Me Baby/Tears In Vain 55
65 Tamla Motown TMG 532 High-Heel Sneakers/Music Talk 45
66 Tamla Motown TMG 545 Uptight (Everything's Alright)/Purple Raindrops 15
66 Tamla Motown TMG 558 Nothing's Too Good For My Baby/With A Child's Heart 30
66 Tamla Motown TMG 570 Blowin' In The Wind/Ain't That Asking For Trouble 18
66 Tamla Motown TMG 588 A Place In The Sun/Sylvia 15
67 Tamla Motown TMG 602 Travelin' Man/Hey Love 8
67 Tamla Motown TMG 613 I Was Made To Love Her/Hold Me 7
67 Tamla Motown TMG 626 I'm Wondering/Every Time I See You I Go Wild 7
68 Tamla Motown TMG 653 Shoo-Be-Doo-Be-Doo-Da-Day/Why Don't You Lead Me To Love 6
68 Tamla Motown TMG 666 You Met Your Match/My Girl 8
68 Tamla Motown TMG 679 For Once In My Life/Angie Girl 5
69 Tamla Motown TMG 690 My Cherie Amour/I Don't Know Why I Love You 5
69 Tamla Motown TMG 717 Yester-Me, Yester-You, Yesterday/I'd Be A Fool Right Now 5
70 Tamla Motown TMG 731 Never Had A Dream Come True/Somebody Knows, Somebody Cares 5
70 Tamla Motown TMG 744 Signed, Sealed, Delivered, I'm Yours/I'm More Than Happy (I'm Satisfied) 5
70 Tamla Motown TMG 757 Heaven Help Us All/I Gotta Have A Song 5
71 Tamla Motown TMG 772 We Can Work It Out/Don't Wonder Why (some in p/s) 20/5
71 Tamla Motown TMG 779 Never Dreamed You'd Leave Me In Summer/If You Really Love Me 5
72 Tamla Motown TMG 798 If You Really Love Me/Think Of Me As Your Soldier 5
84 Tamla Motown TMGT 1368 Do I Do/I Ain't Gonna Stand For It (12", p/s) 8
EPs
64 Stateside SE 1014 I CALL IT PRETTY MUSIC BUT THE OLD PEOPLE CALL IT THE BLUES (EP) 150
65 Tamla Motown TME 2006 LITTLE STEVIE WONDER (EP) 100
LPs
63 Oriole PS 40049 TRIBUTE TO UNCLE RAY (LP) 220
63 Oriole PS 40050 THE TWELVE-YEAR-OLD GENIUS — LIVE (LP) 150
64 Stateside SL 10078 THE JAZZ SOUL OF LITTLE STEVIE WONDER (LP) 160
(The above EPs and LPs were credited to Little Stevie Wonder.)
65 Stateside SL 10108 HEY, HARMONICA MAN (LP) 175
66 T. Motown (S)TML 11036 UPTIGHT (EVERYTHING'S ALRIGHT) (LP, mono/stereo) 35/40
67 T. Motown (S)TML 11045 DOWN TO EARTH (LP, mono/stereo) 40/45
68 T. Motown (S)TML 11059 I WAS MADE TO LOVE HER (LP) 35
68 T. Motown (S)TML 11075 GREATEST HITS (LP) 18
68 T. Motown (S)TML 11085 SOMEDAY AT CHRISTMAS (LP) 40
69 T. Motown (S)TML 11098 FOR ONCE IN MY LIFE (LP) 25
69 T. Motown (S)TML 11128 MY CHERIE AMOUR (LP) 20
70 T. Motown STML 11150 STEVIE WONDER 'LIVE' (LP) 15
70 T. Motown STML 11164 'LIVE' AT THE TALK OF THE TOWN (LP) 15
70 T. Motown STML 11169 SIGNED, SEALED AND DELIVERED (LP) 15
71 T. Motown STML 11183 WHERE I'M COMING FROM (LP) 18
(The above albums originally came with flipback sleeves; see also Diana Ross, Dionne Warwick, Gary Byrd)

WONDER BOY
69 Jackpot JP 703 Sweeten My Coffee (actually by Slim Smith)/MISTER MILLER: Cherry Pink 10
69 Jackpot JP 705 Love Power (actually by Slim Smith)/PAT KELLY: Since You Are Gone 10
71 Jackpot JP 764 Just For A Day/He Ain't Heavy 10
71 Concord CON 015 Just For A Day/He Ain't Heavy 10
(see also Slim Smith, Pat Kelly)

WONDER BOY
75 Ackee ACK 546 Pressure Parts 1 & 2 5

WONDERLAND
68 Polydor 56539 Poochy/Moscow 12

ALICE WONDERLAND
63 London HLU 9783 He's Mine/Cha Linde 18

WONDER STUFF
87 Far Out GONE ONE It's Not True.../A Wonderful Day/Like A Merry-Go-Round/Down Here (EP, p/s) 30
87 Far Out GONE 002 Unbearable/Ten Trenches Deep (some with p/s) 10/5
87 Far Out GO BIG 002 Unbearable/Ten Trenches Deep/I Am A Monster/Frank (12", p/s) 8
88 Polydor GONE 3 Give Give Give Me More More More/A Song Without An End (p/s) 6
88 Polydor GONECD 3 Give Give Give Me More More More/A Song Without An End/ Meaner Than Mean/Sell The Free World (CD) 10

MINT VALUE £

88	Polydor 080 582-2	Give Give Give Me More More More (video)/A Song Without An End/ Meaner Than Mean/Sell The Free World (CD Video)	10
88	Polydor GONECD 4	A Wish Away/Jealousy/Happy-Sad/Goodbye Fatman (CD)	10
88	Polydor GONECD 5	It's Yer Money I'm After Baby/Astley In The Noose/Ooh, She Said/ Rave From The Grave (CD)	10
89	Polydor GONE 6	Who Wants To Be The Disco King?/(same) (promo only, with dayglo p/s)	12
89	Polydor GONECD 6	Who Wants To Be The Disco King? (Remix)/Unbearable (live)/No For The 13th Time (live)/Ten Trenches Deep (live) (CD)	8
89	House Of Dolls HOD 011	Who Wants To Be The Disco King? (King Of Disco Megamix)/PRUDES: Christmas/SANDKINGS: Colourblind/WORLD MUSIC: Stop Playing With My Heart (no p/s, free with *House Of Dolls* magazine)	6/4
89	Polydor GONECD 7	Don't Let Me Down Gently/It Was Me Don't Let Me Down Gently (Extended Version) (CD)	8
89	Polydor GONECD 8	Golden Green/Get Together/Gimme Some Truth (CD)	8
87	Far Out	A HANDFUL OF SONGS (private cassette)	20
87	Polydor	A HANDFUL OF SONGS (cassette, promo only, different to above)	15
88	Polydor GONECD 1	THE EIGHT-LEGGED GROOVE MACHINE (CD, mispressed with "Wish Away" printed on front cover)	30

(see also Vic Reeves)

WONDERWHEEL

(see under Gary Wright)

WONDER WHO

65	Philips BF 1440	Don't Think Twice, It's Alright/Sassy	10
66	Philips BF 1504	On The Good Ship Lollipop/You're Nobody Till Somebody Loves You	10
67	Philips BF 1600	Lonesome Road/FOUR SEASONS: Around And Around	10

(see also Four Seasons, Frankie Valli)

ROYCE WONG

65	Blue Beat BB 301	Everything's Gonna Be Alright/Hang Your Head And Cry	18

ANITA WOOD

62	London HLS 9585	I'll Wait Forever/I Can't Show You How I Feel	25
64	Sue WI 328	Dream Baby/This Happened Before	25

BOBBY WOOD

64	Pye International 7N 25264	I'm A Fool For Loving You/My Heart Went Boing! Boing! Boing!	12

BRENTON WOOD

67	Philips BF 1579	Oogum Boogum Song/I Like The Way You Love Me	8
67	Liberty LBF 15021	Gimme Little Sign/I Think You Got Your Fools Mixed Up	10
68	Liberty LBF 15065	Baby You Got It/Catch You On The Rebound	6
68	Liberty LBF 15103	Some Got It, Some Don't/Me And You	6
70	Pye International 7N 25522	Great Big Bundle Of Love/Can You Dig It	15
71	United Artists UP 35266	Gimme Little Sign/I Think You Got Your Fools Mixed Up (reissue)	6
73	Epic EPC 1383	Another Saturday Night/Attempted Love	6
67	Liberty LBL/LBS 83088E	GIMME A LITTLE SIGN (LP)	35

CHUCK WOOD

67	Big T BIG 104	Seven Days Too Long/Soul Shing-A-Ling	15
68	Big T BIG 107	I've Got My Lovelight Shining/Baby You Win	15
71	Mojo 2092 010	Seven Days Too Long/Soul Shing A Ling (reissue)	6

DEL WOOD

52	London L 1141	Ragtime Melody/Rainbow (78)	8
53	London L 1188	Twelfth Street Rag/Pickin' And Grinnin' (78)	6
54	London HL 8036	Ragtime Annie/Backroom Polka	50
54	London HL 8036	Ragtime Annie/Backroom Polka (78)	6
54	London RE-P 1007	RAGTIME PIANO (EP)	15
57	RCA RD 27011	DOWN YONDER (LP)	12

GLORIA WOOD

53	Capitol CL 13947	Hey, Bell Boy/Anybody Hurt? (78)	8

RONNIE WOOD

74	Warner Bros K 16463	I Can Feel The Fire/Breathe On Me	7
75	Warner Bros K 16618	If You Don't Want Me Love/I've Got A Feeling	7
76	Warner Bros K 16679	Big Bayou/Sweet Baby Mine	7
79	CBS 7785	Seven Days/Come To Realise	7
92	Continuum 12210-2	Show Me/Breathe On Me (CD, with Ronnie Wood print, signed & numbered, in black card case tied with ribbon, 600 only)	45
74	Warner Bros K 56065	I'VE GOT MY OWN ALBUM TO DO (LP, with insert)	15
75	Warner Bros K 56145	NOW LOOK (LP)	12
76	Atlantic K 50308	MAHONEY'S LAST STAND (LP, soundtrack, with Ronnie Lane)	15
79	CBS 83337	GIMME SOME NECK (LP, with inner sleeve)	12

(see also Faces, Rolling Stones, Jeff Beck, Ted Wood)

ROY WOOD

72	Harvest HAR 5048	When Gran'ma Plays The Banjo/Wake Up	7
75	Jet JET 754	Oh What A Shame/Bengal Jig (cartoon p/s)	5
75	Jet JET 761	Look Thru' The Eyes Of A Fool/Strider (some copies miscredited as "Looking Thru' The Eyes Of A Fool")	7/5
76	Jet JET 785	Any Old Time Will Do/The Rain Came Down On Everything	6
77	Warner Bros K 16961	The Stroll/Jubilee (p/s, by Wizzo Band)	6
77	Warner Bros K 17028	I Never Believed In Love/Inside My Life (as Roy Wood & Annie Haslam)	7
78	Warner Bros K 17094	Dancin' At The Rainbow's End/Waiting At This Door (p/s, as Wizzo Band)	5
79	Automatic K 17459P	(We're) On The Road Again/Saxmaniacs (picture disc)	7
80	Cheapskate CHEAP 6	Rock City/Givin' Your Heart Away (p/s, as Roy Wood's Helicopters)	5
80	Cheapskate CHEAP 12	Sing Out The Old (Bring In The New)/Watch This Space (some in p/s)	7/5
81	EMI EMI 5156	Green Glass Windows/The Driving Song (p/s, as Roy Wood's Helicopters)	6

81 EMI EMI 5203 Down To Zero/Olympic Flyer (p/s) ... 7
82 Speed SPEED 5 O.T.T./Mystery Song (B-side actually "California Man [live]" by Wizzo Band) ... 5
84 Harvest HAR 5173 I Wish It Could Be Christmas Every Day/WIZZARD: See My Baby Jive (g/f p/s) ... 5
85 Legacy LEGACY 32 Sing Out The Old... Bring In The New (Vocal)/(Instrumental) (p/s) ... 5
87 Jet JET 7048 One-Two-Three/Oh What A Shame (gatefold p/s) ... 5
76 Harvest SHDW 408 THE ROY WOOD STORY (2-LP) ... 15
82 Speed SPEED 1000 THE SINGLES (LP, initially without "I Wish It Could Be Christmas Everyday") ... 12
(see also Wizzard, Gerry Levine & Avengers, Mike Sheridan, Danny King['s Mayfair Set], Move, ELO, Renaissance [UK], Rockers, Birds)

TED WOOD
76 Penny Farthing PEN 891 Am I Blue/Shine (B-side features Rod Stewart, Ronnie Wood, Gary Glitter & Bobby Womack) ... 8
(see also Temperance Seven)

VICTORIA WOOD
70s EMI SCX 6716 LIVE (LP) ... 12

WOODEN HORSE
72 York SYK 526 Pick Up The Pieces/Wake Me In The Morning ... 20
73 York SYK 543 Wooden Horses/Typewriter And Guitar ... 20
72 York FYK 403 WOODEN HORSE (LP) ... 200
73 York FYK 413 WOODEN HORSE II (LP, withdrawn, some with sleeve) ... 800/500
(see also Fox)

WOODEN O & GUESTS
69 Middle Earth MDLS 301 A HANDFUL OF PLEASANT DELITES (LP) ... 95
(see also 'Middle Earth Sampler' in Various Artists section)

BARBARA WOODHOUSE
69 RCA International INT 1011 DOG TRAINING MY WAY (LP) ... 25

KEN WOODMAN & HIS PICCADILLY BRASS
66 Strike JLH 101 THAT'S NICE (LP) ... 35

WOODPECKERS
64 Decca F 11835 The Woodpecker/You Can't Sit Down ... 12
65 Oriole CB 311 Hey Little Girl/What's Your Name ... 20

STANLEY WOODRUFF & U.S. TRIO
77 Grapevine GP 102 What Took You So Long/Now Is Forever ... 10

CAROL WOODS
72 Ember EMB S 319 We'll Sing The Sunshine/I Wonder What Will Happen ... 5
72 Ember NR 5059 OUT OF THE WOODS (LP) ... 15

CHUCK WOODS
75 Pye Disco Demand DDS 111 Seven Days Too Long ... 5

CORA WOODS
56 Parlophone DP 505 Rocks In Your Head/I Don't Want To Cry (export 78) ... 10

DANNY WOODS
72 Invictus INV 532 Everybody's Tippin'/Roller Coaster ... 7

DONALD WOODS & EARL PALMER BAND
58 Vogue V 9107 Memories Of An Angel/That Much Of Your Love ... 600
58 Vogue V 9107 Memories Of An Angel/That Much Of Your Love (78) ... 150

GAY WOODS
84 Rewind REW 18 Something's Gotten Hold Of My Heart/Cellophane Rain (p/s) ... 5
(see also Gay & Terry Woods, Woods Band, Steeleye Span, Sweeney's Men)

GAY & TERRY WOODS
77 Polydor 2058 810 Save The Last Dance For Me/One More Time ... 6
78 Rockburgh ROCS 202 We Can Work This One Out/Piece Of Summer (p/s) ... 5
75 Polydor 2383 322 BACKWOODS (LP) ... 40
76 Polydor 2383 375 THE TIME IS RIGHT (LP, with lyric insert) ... 40
76 Polydor 2383 406 RENOWNED (LP, with lyric insert) ... 40
78 Rockburgh ROC 104 TENDER HOOKS (LP, with lyric insert) ... 20
(see also Woods Band, Gay Woods, Steeleye Span, Sweeney's Men)

NICK WOODS
62 London HLU 9621 Ballad Of Billy Budd/Don't Let Me Down ... 10

PHIL WOODS
55 Esquire 20-055 NEW JAZZ QUINTET (10" LP) ... 25

WOODS BAND
71 Greenwich GSLP 1004 THE WOODS BAND (LP, gatefold sleeve) ... 80
77 Rockburgh CREST 29 THE WOODS BAND (LP, reissue in different sleeve) ... 15
(see also Gay & Terry Woods)

EDWARD WOODWARD
69 Columbia DB 8547 Only A Fool/Independent Man ... 6
70 DJM DJS 211 Grains Of Sand/Thing Called Love ... 5
70 DJM DJS 218 This Man Alone/Today I Killed A Man ... 5
71 DJM DJS 232 The Way You Look Tonight/The Tide Will Turn For Rebecca ... 5
71 DJM DJS 249 It Had To Be You/Watch What Happens ... 5
70 DJM DJLPS 405 THIS MAN ALONE (LP) ... 12
71 DJM DJLPS 418 IT HAD TO BE YOU (LP) ... 12

MAGGIE WOODWARD
59 Vogue V 9148 Ali Bama/Zulu Warrior ... 18
59 Vogue V 9148 Ali Bama/Zulu Warrior (78) ... 25

MINT VALUE £

WOODY KERN

69	Pye 7N 17672	Biography/Tell You I'm Gone (demo)	110
69	Pye NSPL 18273	THE AWFUL DISCLOSURES OF MARIA MONK (LP)	30

BRIAN WOOLEY

58	Esquire EP 170	BRIAN WOOLEY'S JAZZMEN (EP)	10
58	Esquire EP 190	WILD 'N WOOLEY (EP)	12

SHEB WOOLEY

51	MGM MGM 439	Hoot Owl Boogie/Country Kisses (78)	18
54	MGM MGM 757	Panama Pete/Blue Guitar (78)	12
55	MGM SP 1130	38-24-35/I Flipped	25
55	MGM MGM 824	38-24-35/I Flipped (78)	12
55	MGM SPC 5	Hill Billy Mambo/I Go Outa My Mind (export issue)	30
58	MGM MGM 981	The Purple People Eater/I Can't Believe You're Mine	25
58	MGM MGM 981	The Purple People Eater/Recipe For Love (2nd pressing, different B-side)	15
58	MGM MGM 981	The Purple People Eater/I Can't Believe You're Mine (78)	8
58	MGM MGM 997	Santa And The Purple People Eater/Star Of Love	12
58	MGM MGM 997	Santa And The Purple People Eater/Star Of Love (78)	20
59	MGM MGM 1017	Sweet Chile/More	10
60	MGM MGM 1081	Luke The Spook/My Only Treasure	15
61	MGM MGM 1132	The Wayward Wind/Bars Across The Windows	10
61	MGM MGM 1147	That's My Pa/Meet Mr. Lonely	12
62	MGM MGM 1162	Laughing The Blues/Somebody Please	10
65	MGM MGM 1257	Hootenanny Hoot/Old Joe Rag	7
65	MGM MGM 1263	Blue Guitar/Natchez Landing	6
56	MGM MGM-EP 540	JEST PLAIN, WILD AND WOOLEY (EP)	40
61	MGM MGM-C 859	SONGS FROM THE DAYS OF RAWHIDE (LP)	25
62	MGM MGM-C 903	THAT'S MY MA AND THAT'S MY PA (LP)	25
63	MGM MGM-C 945	SPOOFING THE BIG ONES! (LP)	20
63	MGM MGM-C 955	TALES OF 'HOW THE WEST WAS WON' (LP)	20

(see also Ben Colder)

CHARLIE WOOLFE

68	NEMS 56-3675	Dance Dance Dance/Home	12

(see also At Last The 1958 Rock & Roll Show)

WOOLIES

67	RCA RCA 1602	Who Do You Love?/Hey Girl	40

WOOLLY

72	RCA RCA 2297	Golden Golden/Sugar Daddy Song	5
73	Mooncrest MOON 10	Sunshine Souvenirs/Living And Loving You	5

WOOLLY FISH

70	Plexium PXM 16	Way You Like It/Sound Of Thick	10

BRENDA WOOTTON

71	Sentinel SENS 1006	PASTIES & CREAM (LP, with John The Fish)	25
73	Sentinel SENS 1016	CROWDY CRAWN (LP, with Richard Gendall)	20
74	Sentinel SENS 1021	NO SONG TO SING? (LP, with Robert Bartlett, private pressing with lyric inner sleeve)	18
76	Sentinel SENS 1031	STARRY-GAZEY PIE (LP, with Robert Bartlett)	20

WORD

83	Word WORD 001	Colour It!/Recurring	5

WORDBUG

91	Boss Tuneage BOSSTAGE6	LOSING IT ALL (LP, also listed as Home 4, with insert)	18

WORK

81	Woof WOOF 2	I Hate America/Fingers & Toes/Duty (p/s, clear vinyl)	5
82	Recommended	SLOW CRIMES (LP, with insert)	12

(see also Art Bears)

JIMMY WORK

56	London HLD 8270	When She Said "You All"/There's Only One You	75
56	London HLD 8270	When She Said "You All"/There's Only One You (78)	20
56	London HLD 8308	You've Gotta Heart Like A Merry-Go-Round/Blind Heart	60
56	London HLD 8308	You've Gotta Heart Like A Merry-Go-Round/Blind Heart (78)	20
55	London RE-D 1039	COUNTRY SONGS — WORK STYLE (EP)	60

WORKFORCE

80s	WF WF 1	The Right To Work/Holy Moses (p/s)	8

WORKS

72	London HLU 10360	Orange Medley (Music Inspired By "A Clockwork Orange")/Sweet Charity	6

WORLD

70	Liberty LBF 15402	Angelina/Come Out Into The Open	7
70	Liberty LBG 83419	LUCKY PLANET (LP, gatefold sleeve)	22

(see also Neil Innes, Bonzo Dog [Doo-Dah] Band)

WORLD COLUMN

76	Capitol CL 15852	So Is The Sun/It's Not Right	10

WORLD OF OZ

68	Deram DM 187	The Muffin Man/Peter's Birthday (Black And White Rainbows)	15
68	Deram DM 205	King Croesus/Jack	12
69	Deram DM 233	Willow's Harp/Like A Tear	18
69	Deram DML/SML 1034	THE WORLD OF OZ (LP)	55

(see also David Kubinec)

WORLD OF TWIST

90 Circa YR 55 — The Storm/She's A Rainbow (p/s) 5
91 Circa YR 72 — Sweets/This Too Shall All Pass Away (p/s) 5
91 Circa YRCD 72 — Sweets/This Too Shall All Pass Away (CD, in denim sleeve) 8
92 Caff CAFF 16 — The Sausage/Skidding Into Love/Space Rockit (p/s, with insert) 10

BIMBI WORRICK

69 Polydor 56321 — Long Time Comin'/Tomorrow Is My Day 8

WORRYING KYNDE

67 Piccadilly 7N 35370 — Call Out The Name/Got The Blame 55

WORTH

70 CBS 5309 — Shoot 'Em Up Baby/Take The World In Your Hands 5

JOHNNY WORTH

57 Columbia DB 3962 — Let's Go/Just Because 8
57 Columbia DB 3962 — Let's Go/Just Because (78) 6
58 Embassy WB 312 — Tom Dooley/GORDON FRANKS: Hoots Mon 5
58 Embassy WB 312 — Tom Dooley/GORDON FRANKS: Hoots Mon (78) 6
59 Embassy WB 315 — It's Only Make Believe/Chantilly Lace 5
59 Embassy WB 315 — It's Only Make Believe/Chantilly Lace (78) 6
59 Embassy WB 317 — I Got Stung!/Baby Face 5
59 Embassy WB 317 — I Got Stung!/Baby Face (78) 6
59 Embassy WB 325 — (All Of A Sudden) My Hearts Sings/High School Confidential 5
59 Embassy WB 325 — (All Of A Sudden) My Hearts Sings/High School Confidential (78) 6
59 Embassy WB 329 — Donna/A Pub With No Beer 5
59 Embassy WB 329 — Donna/A Pub With No Beer (78) 6
59 Embassy WB 332 — It Doesn't Matter Anymore/By The Light Of The Silvery Moon (78) 6
59 Embassy WB 335 — A Fool Such As I/Idle On Parade 5
59 Embassy WB 335 — A Fool Such As I/Idle On Parade (78) 6
59 Embassy WB 338 — Mean Streak/Fort Worth Jail 5
59 Embassy WB 338 — Mean Streak/Fort Worth Jail (78) 6
59 Embassy WB 347 — Living Doll/Lonely Boy 5
59 Embassy WB 347 — Living Doll/Lonely Boy (78) 8
59 Embassy WB 354 — Sal's Got A Sugar Lip/Just A Little Too Much 5
59 Embassy WB 354 — Sal's Got A Sugar Lip/Just A Little Too Much (78) 8
59 Embassy WB 359 — Sea Of Love/BUD ASHTON: Sleep Walk 5
59 Embassy WB 359 — Sea Of Love/BUD ASHTON: Sleep Walk (78) 8
59 Embassy WB 369 — Oh Carol/What Do You Want? 5
59 Embassy WB 369 — Oh Carol/What Do You Want? (78) 8
59 Embassy WB 376 — Pretty Blue Eyes/Way Down Yonder In New Orleans 5
59 Embassy WB 376 — Pretty Blue Eyes/Way Down Yonder In New Orleans (78) 6
59 Embassy WB 379 — Poor Me/A Voice In The Wilderness 5
59 Embassy WB 379 — Poor Me/A Voice In The Wilderness (78) 8
60 Embassy WB 389 — Handy Man/GORDON FRANKS: Beatnik Fly 5
60 Embassy WB 389 — Handy Man/GORDON FRANKS: Beatnik Fly (78) 8
60 Embassy WB 393 — Someone Else's Baby/Footsteps 5
60 Embassy WB 393 — Someone Else's Baby/Footsteps (78) 15
60 Embassy WB 413 — How About That/Nine Times Out Of Ten 5
60 Embassy WB 413 — How About That/Nine Times Out Of Ten (78) 12
60 Oriole CB 1545 — Nightmare/Hold Me, Thrill Me, Kiss Me 7
60 Oriole CB 1545 — Nightmare/Hold Me, Thrill Me, Kiss Me (78) 15
62 Columbia DB 4811 — You Know What I Mean/All These Things 6
(see also Barry Kendall)

MARION WORTH

60 London HL 7089 — Are You Willing, Willie/This Heart Of Mine (export issue) 25
60 London HL 7097 — That's My Kind Of Love/I Lost Johnny (export issue) 25

STAN WORTH ORCHESTRA

63 London HLU 9703 — Roman Holiday/Wiggle Wobble Walkers 10

WRANGLERS

64 Parlophone R 5163 — Liza Jane/It Just Won't Work 60
(see also Kenny Bernard, Kenny & Wranglers)

LINK WRAY (& HIS RAY MEN)

58 London HLA 8623 — Rumble/The Swag (as Link Wray & His Ray Men) 40
58 London HLA 8623 — Rumble/The Swag (as Link Wray & His Ray Men) (78) 25
63 Stateside SS 217 — Jack The Ripper/The Black Widow 25
64 Stateside SS 256 — The Sweeper/Weekend 20
65 Stateside SS 397 — Good Rockin' Tonight/I'll Do Anything For You 22
71 Polydor 2066 120 — Fire And Brimstone/Jukebox Mama 6
73 Polydor 2066 320 — Lawdy Miss Clawdy/Shine The Light 6
73 Virgin VS 103 — I'm So Glad, I'm So Proud/Shawnee Tribe 6
76 Virgin VS 142 — I Know You're Leaving Me Now/Quicksand 6
78 Chiswick NS 32 — Batman Theme/Hidden Charms (unissued, demos probably exist) 15+
64 Stateside SE 1015 — MR. GUITAR (EP, sleeve credits *Link Ray*) 100
71 Polydor 2489 029 — LINK WRAY (LP) 20
71 Union Pacific UP 002 — THERE'S GOOD ROCKIN' TONIGHT (LP) 22
73 Virgin V 2006 — BEANS & FATBACK (LP) 15
73 Polydor 2391 063 — BE WHAT YOU WANT TO (LP) 12
74 Polydor 2391 128 — THE LINK WRAY RUMBLE (LP) 12
(see also Robert Gordon with Link Wray)

RAY WRAY QUARTET

62 Salvo SLO 1808 — When Your Lover Has Gone/A Song Is Born 22

WRECKERS

64 Granta GR 7EP 1010 — THE WRECKERS' SOUND (EP) 125

MINT VALUE £

JENNY WREN
66 Fontana TF 672 Chasing My Dreams All Over Town/A Thought Of You 90
66 Fontana TF 772 The Merry-Go-Round (Is Slowing You Down)/Take A Walk Bobby 15

JENNY WREN
79 RK RK 1017 I've Danced With A Man/Bring Down The Curtain 5

BIG JOHN WRENCHER
75 Big Bear BB 4 BIG JOHN'S BOOGIE (LP) 12

WRIGGLERS
68 Giant GN 26 The Cooler/You Cannot Know 20
68 Blue Cat BS 106 Get Right/If I Did Look 20
(see also Wrigglers)

BETTY WRIGHT
68 Atlantic 584 216 Girls Can't Do What The Guys Do/Sweet Lovin' Daddy 7
72 Atlantic K 10143 Clean Up Woman/I'll Love You Forever 6
72 Atlantic K 10190 Is It You Girl/Cryin' In My Sleep 5
75 RCA RCA 2548 Where Is The Love/My Baby Ain't My Baby Any More 5
72 Atlantic K 40364 I LOVE THE WAY YOU LOVE (LP) 15

BILLY WRIGHT
61 Parlophone 4852 SING-SONG JUST FOR KICKS (EP) 10

CHARLES WRIGHT & WATTS 103rd STREET RHYTHM BAND
69 Warner Bros WB 7250 Do Your Thing/A Dance, A Kiss And A Song 7
69 Warner Bros WB 7298 Till You Get Enough/Light My Fire 6
70 Warner Bros WB 7365 Love Land/Sorry Charlie 6
70 Warner Bros WB 7417 Express Yourself/Living On Borrowed Time 7
72 Jay Boy BOY 71 Spreadin' Honey/Charley (as Watts 103rd Street Rhythm Band) 10
70s Warner Bros EXPRESS YOURSELF (LP) 22

DALE WRIGHT
58 London HLD 8573 She's Neat/Say That You Care (as Dale Wright & Rock-Its) 220
58 London HLD 8573 She's Neat/Say That You Care (as Dale Wright & Rock-Its) (78) 65
59 Pye International 7N 25022 That's Show Biz/That's My Gal (as Dale Wright & Wright Guys) 100
59 Pye International N 25022 That's Show Biz/That's My Gal (as Dale Wright & Wright Guys) (78) 75

EARL WRIGHT
75 Capitol CL 15825 Thumb A Ride/Like A Rolling Stone 5

GARY WRIGHT('S WONDERWHEEL)
71 A&M AMS 812 Get On The Right Road/It Takes A Little Longer 5
71 A&M AMS 826 Get On The Right Road/Over You Now 5
71 A&M AMS 852 Stand For Our Rights/Can't See The Reason 5
72 A&M AMS 888 I Know It's Right 5
72 A&M AMS 7034 Ring Of Changes/Somebody (as Wonderwheel) 5
71 A&M AMLS 2004 EXTRACTIONS (LP) 15
72 A&M AMLS 64296 FOOTPRINT (LP) 15
72 A&M AMLH 64362 RING OF CHANGES (LP, as Wright's Wonderwheel; unissued, test pressings only) 50
(see also Spooky Tooth, Magic Christians, Thomas F. Browne)

GEORGE WRIGHT
54 Parlophone MSP 13 (The Gang That Sang) Heart Of My Heart/Whistling Blues (export issue) 6
50s Parlophone CGEP 4 GEORGE WRIGHT (EP, export) 8
50s Parlophone CGEP 11 GEORGE WRIGHT (EP, export) 8

GINNY WRIGHT (& TOM TALL)
55 London HL 8119 Indian Moon/Your Eyes Feasted Upon Her (solo) 55
55 London HL 8119 Indian Moon/Your Eyes Feasted Upon Her (solo) (78) 15
55 London HL 8150 Are You Mine?/Boom Boom Boomerang (with Tom Tall) 40
55 London RE-U 1035 COUNTRY SONGS VOL. 2 (EP, with Tom Tall) 45
(see also T. Tommy Cutrer & Ginny Wright, Tom Tall)

IAN WRIGHT
93 M&G MAGCD 45 Do The Right Thing (7" Version)/(Rollo — 2-1 Up Mix)/(Second To None Mix)/(Rollo Dub Mix)/(Air Max Mix)/(Rollo 1-0 Down Mix) (CD, slimline jewel case) 10
(see also Pet Shop Boys)

MILTON WRIGHT & TERRA SHIRMA STRINGS
77 Grapevine GRP 103 I Belong To You/The Gallop 10

NAT WRIGHT
59 HMV POP 629 Anything/For You My Love 65

OTIS WRIGHT
69 High Note HS 033 Man Of Galilee/Take Up The Cross 8
67 Doctor Bird DLM 5005 PEACE PERFECT PEACE (LP) 80
67 Doctor Bird DLM 5006 IT WILL SOON BE DONE (LP) 80
68 High Notes BSL5003 SACRED SONGS (LP) 30
60s Coxsone TLP 1001 OVER IN GLORYLAND (LP) 90
73 Tabernacle BSLP 5021 SOUL STIRRING GOSPEL SONGS (LP) 40

O.V. WRIGHT
65 Vocalion VP 9249 You're Gonna Make Me Cry/Monkey Dog 22
66 Vocalion VP 9255 Poor Boy/I'm In Your Corner 20
66 Vocalion VP 9272 Gone For Good/How Long Baby 18
67 London HLZ 10137 8 Men 4 Women/Fed Up With The Blues 15
68 Sue WI 4043 What About You/What Did You Tell This Girl Of Mine 35
68 Action ACT 4505 Oh Baby Mine/Working Your Game 20
69 Action ACT 4527 I Want Everyone To Know/I'm Gonna Forget About You 20
65 Vocalion VEP 170165 CAN'T FIND TRUE LOVE (EP) 100
68 Island ILP 975 8 MEN, 4 WOMEN (LP) 120

MINT VALUE £

OWEN WRIGHT
70 Banana BA 310 — Wala Wala (actually by Burning Spear)/JERRY & FREEDOM SINGERS: Got To Be Sure (B-side actually by Horace Andy) . . . 15

RICK WRIGHT
78 Harvest SHVL 818 — WET DREAM (LP, gatefold stickered sleeve). . . 12
(see also Pink Floyd, Zee)

RITA WRIGHT
68 Tamla Motown TMG 643 — I Can't Give Back The Love I Feel For You/Something On My Mind . . . 25
71 Tamla Motown TMG 791 — I Can't Give Back The Love I Feel For You/Something On My Mind (reissue) . . . 6

RITA WRIGHT
78 Jet UP 36382 — Love Is All You Need/Touch Me, Take Me. . . 45

RUBEN WRIGHT
66 Capitol CL 15460 — Hey Girl/I'm Walking Out On You . . . 35

RUBY WRIGHT
53 Parlophone MSP 6025 — Till I Waltz Again With You/When I Gave You My Love (with Charlie Gore). . . 35
54 Parlophone MSP 6073 — Bimbo/Boy, You Got Yourself A Gal . . . 35
54 Parlophone MSP 6133 — Santa's Little Sleigh Bells/Toodle-oo To You . . . 22
55 Parlophone MSP 6150 — What Have They Told You?/I Had The Funniest Feeling . . . 25
56 Parlophone MSP 6209 — I Fall In Love With You Ev'ry Day/Do You Believe? . . . 25
59 Parlophone R 4556 — Three Stars/I Only Have One Lifetime . . . 12
59 Parlophone R 4556 — Three Stars/I Only Have One Lifetime (78) . . . 30
59 Parlophone R 4589 — You're Just A Flower From An Old Bouquet/Sweet Night Of Love. . . 10
59 Parlophone GEP 8785 — THE THREE STARS GIRL (EP). . . 60

SAMUEL E. WRIGHT
73 Paramount PARA 3035 — There's Something Funny Going On/300 Pounds Of Hunger. . . 5

STEVE WRIGHT
59 London HLW 8991 — Wild, Wild, Woman/Love You . . . 250
59 London HLW 8991 — Wild, Wild, Woman/Love You (78). . . 125

SYREETA WRIGHT
72 Mowest MWS 7001 — SYREETA (LP) . . . 15

WINSTON WRIGHT
69 Doctor Bird DB 1308 — Five Miles High/CARL DAWKINS: Only Girl. . . 20
69 Camel CA 32 — Power Pack/TWO SPARKS: Throwing Stones . . . 12
69 Explosion EX 2003 — Barefoot Brigade/Slippery . . . 18
69 Trojan TR 7701 — Moonlight (Lover) Groover/SENSATIONS: Everyday Is Just A Holiday . . . 12
69 Trojan TR 7715 — Moon Invader (with Tommy McCook)/RADCLIFF RUFFIN: You Got To Love Me. . . 12
70 Trojan TR 7775 — Meshwire (with Tommy McCook)/BARONS: Darling Please Return . . . 15
70 Explosion EX 2011 — Flight 404/LLOYD & ROBIN: Gawling Come Down (B-side actually "Higher Than The Highest Mountain" by Monty Morris) . . . 15
70 Explosion EX 2015 — Funny Girl/Funny Girl Version II . . . 10
70 Duke DU 62 — Poppy Cock (with J.J. All Stars)/CARL DAWKINS: This World And Me (B-side actually "Satisfaction") . . . 10
70 Bamboo BAM 60 — Reggae Feet/DON DRUMMOND: Royal Flush (B-side act. titled "The Rocket"). . . 20
70 High Note HS 040 — Soul Pressure/Seed You Sow (with Gaytones) . . . 10
70 Moodisc MU 3501 — Musically Red (with Maudie's Allstars; actually also with Count Sticky)/RHYTHM RULERS: Bratah . . . 10
70 G.G. GG 4504 — It's Been A Long Time/PAULETTE & GEE: Feel It More And More . . . 10
70 Techniques TE 907 — Top Secret/Crazy Rhythm . . . 10
71 Upsetter US 378 — Example (with 3rd & 4th Generation)/UPSETTER: Version . . . 15
71 Duke DU 111 — Silhouettes/That Did It . . . 10
71 Camel CA 71 — Silhouettes/That Did It . . . 10
(see also Ethiopians, John Holt, J.J. Allstars, Slickers)

ZACHARIAH WRIGHT
70s Bamboo BAM 403 — Lumumba Limbo/Green, Red and Gold. . . 10

BERNARD WRIGLEY
74 Topic 12TS 241 — ROUGH AND WRIGLEY (LP) . . . 12
76 Transatlantic TRA 327 — SONGS, STORIES AND ELEPHANTS (LP). . . 12

WRIGLEYS
69 Page One POF 118 — A Little Bit/Come Down Little Bird. . . 10

WRIT
66 Decca F 12385 — Did You Ever Have To Make Up Your Mind/Solid Golden Teardrops . . . 10

WRITING ON THE WALL
69 Middle Earth MDS 101 — Child On A Crossing/Lucifer Corpus. . . 35
73 Pye 7N 45251 — Man Of Renown/Buffalo. . . 15
69 Middle Earth MDLS 303 — THE POWER OF THE PICTS (LP). . . 175
95 Pie & Mash PAM 003 — RARITIES FROM THE MIDDLE EARTH (LP, 500 copies only) . . . 12
95 Tenth Planet TP 017 — CRACKS IN THE ILLUSION OF LIFE (LP, gatefold sleeve) . . . 12
96 Tenth Planet TP 018 — BURGHLEY ROAD (LP, 1,000 copies only) . . . 12
(see also 'Middle Earth Sampler' in Various Artists; Three's A Crowd)

W12 SPOTS
70s Shepherds Bush SB 1 — Sid Never Did/COSMIC PUNKS: 99 Years . . . 12

WUGGERY
98 Wuggery WUG 1 — Wuggery Muggery/Wugwats Weekend (p/s) . . . 8

WURZEL
87 GWR GWR 4 — Bess/People Say I'm Crazy (p/s) . . . 8
87 GWR GWT 4 — Bess/People Say I'm Crazy/Midnight In London/E.S.P. (12", p/s) . . . 15
(see also Motörhead)

MINT VALUE £

WURZELS

77 EMI EMI 2686 One For The Bristol City/Cheddar Cheese (p/s) . . . 6

JOHNNY WYATT

68 President PT 109 This Thing Called Love/To Whom It May Concern. . . . 15

ROBERT WYATT

74 Virgin VS 114 I'm A Believer/Memories . . . 5
77 Virgin VS 115 Yesterday Man/Sonia . . . 6
82 Rough Trade RT 115 Shipbuilding/Memories Of You (reissue, foldout p/s) . . . 5
70 CBS 64189 THE END OF AN EAR (LP). . . . 30
74 Virgin V 2017 ROCK BOTTOM (LP) . . . 15
75 Virgin V 2034 RUTH IS STRANGER THAN RICHARD (LP). . . . 12
82 Rough Trade ROUGH 35 NOTHING CAN STOP US (LP, early pressing without "Shipbuilding") . . . 12
(see also Soft Machine, Matching Mole, Centipede, Ben Watt)

PETE WYLIE

86 Eternal MDM 712 Sinful/Sinful And Wicked (12", p/s) . . . 10
87 Siren SRN 54 Never Fall For A Whore/If I Love You (p/s). . . . 5
87 Siren SRN 59 Foureleventortyfour/The Marksman (p/s) . . . 5
88 Siren SRNCD 59 Foureleventortyfour/The Marksman/Sinful (Song Of The Sinful Angel) (CD). . . . 10
(see also Wah!)

RICHARD ('POPCORN') WYLIE

63 Columbia DB 7012 Brand New Man/So Much Love In My Heart (as Richard Wylie) . . . 40
77 Grapevine GRP 100 Rosemary What Happened (Parts 1 & 2) (as Richard 'Popcorn' Wylie) . . . 15

BILL WYMAN

74 Rolling Stones RS 19112 Monkey Grip Glue/What A Blow . . . 6
74 Rolling Stones RS 19115 White Lightning/Pussy. . . . 7
76 Rolling Stones RS 19119 A Quarter To Three/Soul Satisfying . . . 5
76 Rolling Stones RS 19120 Apache Woman/Soul Satisfying. . . . 8
81 Polydor POSP 259 Tenderness (Maria Muldaur)/Noche De Amor . . . 7
81 Polydor POSP 297 Green Ice Theme/Cloudhoppers (p/s) . . . 12
74 Rolling Stones COC 59102 MONKEY GRIP (LP) . . . 18
76 Rolling Stones COC 59105 STONE ALONE (LP) . . . 18
81 A&M AMLSP 68540 BILL WYMAN (LP, picture disc) . . . 15
81 Polydor POLS 11031 GREEN ICE (LP, soundtrack) . . . 15
83 Ripple (no cat. no.) DIGITAL DREAMS (LP, soundtrack, promo only). . . . 100
(see also Rolling Stones, End)

WYNDER K. FROG

66 Island WI 280 Turn On Your Lovelight/Zooming. . . . 30
66 Island WI 3011 Sunshine Superman/Blues For A Frog . . . 30
67 Island WIP 6006 Green Door/Dancing Frog . . . 30
67 Island WIP 6014 I Am A Man/Shook Shimmy & Shake . . . 40
68 Island WIP 6044 Jumping Jack Flash/Baldy. . . . 30
67 Island ILP 944/ILPS 9044 SUNSHINE SUPERFROG (LP, white label, mono/stereo) . . . 60/100
68 Island ILP 982/ILPS 9082 OUT OF THE FRYING PAN (LP, pink label) . . . 40
(see also Keef Hartley Band, Miller Anderson, Fair Weather, Grease Band)

MARTYN WYNDHAM-READ

70 Trailer LER 2009 NED KELLY AND THAT GANG (LP, white label, later 'highway' label) . . . 18/12
71 Trailer LER 2028 MARTYN WYNDHAM-READ (LP) . . . 15
73 Argo ZFB 82 HARRY THE HAWKER IS DEAD (LP). . . . 25
75 Trailer LER 2092 MAYPOLES TO MISTLETOE (LP) . . . 12
77 Broadside BRO 128 ENGLISH SPORTING BALLADS (LP, 1 side by High Level Ranters, 2000 only). . . 20
(see also A.L. Lloyd)

PETER WYNGARDE

70 RCA Victor RCA 1967 La Ronde De L'Amour/The Way I Cry Over You. . . . 30
70 RCA Victor PW 1 "Commits" Rape/The Way I Cry Over You (LP sampler, promo only) . . . 40
70 RCA Victor SF 8087 PETER WYNGARDE (LP, gatefold sleeve) . . . 80
(see also Larry Wallis, Tyrannosaurus Rex)

ALBERT WYNN CREOLE JAZZ

52 Vocalion V 1018 Down By The Levee/Parkway Stomp (78) . . . 6

SANDY WYNNS

65 Fontana TF 550 Touch Of Venus/Lovers' Quarrel . . . 200

MARK WYNTER

60 Decca F 11263 Image Of A Girl/Glory Of Love. . . . 8
60 Decca F 11279 Kickin' Up The Leaves/That's What I Thought . . . 8
61 Decca F 11323 Dream Girl/Two Little Girls . . . 8
61 Decca F 11354 Exclusively Yours/Warm And Willing . . . 8
61 Decca F 11380 Girl For Ev'ry Day/The Best Time For Love. . . . 10
62 Decca F 11434 Heaven's Plan/In Your Heart. . . . 12
62 Decca F 11467 Angel Talk/I Love Her Still . . . 15
62 Pye 7N 15466 Venus In Blue Jeans/Please Come Back To Me . . . 6
62 Pye 7N 15492 Go Away Little Girl/That Kinda Talk. . . . 5
63 Pye 7N 15511 Aladdin's Lamp/It Can Happen Any Day . . . 6
63 Pye 7N 15525 Shy Girl/Because Of You . . . 6
63 Pye 7N 15554 Running To You/Don't Cry . . . 8
63 Pye 7N 15577 It's Almost Tomorrow/Music To Midnight. . . . 5
64 Pye 7N 15595 The Boy You're Kissin'/I Learned A Lot From You. . . . 6
64 Pye 7N 15626 Only You/It's Love You Want. . . . 6
64 Pye 7N 15658 Answer Me/I Wish You Everything . . . 6
64 Pye 7N 15686 Love Hurts/Can't Help Forgiving You . . . 6
64 Pye 7N 15716 Forever And A Day/And I Love Her . . . 6
65 Pye 7N 15771 Can I Get To Know You Better/Am I Living A Dream. . . . 8
65 Pye 7N 15861 Someday You'll Want Me To Want You/Here Comes Summer . . . 6

MINT VALUE £

65	Pye 7N 15994	Babe I'm Gonna Leave You/The Very Thought Of You	6
66	Pye 7N 17051	Before Your Time/Something About You	6
66	Pye 7N 17122	We'll Sing In The Sunshine/Pencil And Paper	5
66	Pye 7N 17214	You Made Me What I Am/Oh Girl	6
68	Pye 7N 17438	Please Love Me Tender/The Best Thing In My Life	6
68	Pye 7N 17651	She's A Woman/Bless Your Little Heart	6
60	Decca DFE 6674	MARK TIME (EP)	45
63	Pye NEP 24176	IT'S MARK TIME (EP)	30
64	Pye NEP 24185	WYNTER TIME (EP)	30
61	Decca LK 4409	THE WARMTH OF WYNTER (LP)	50
64	Golden Guinea GGL 0250	MARK WYNTER (LP)	15
65	Ace Of Clubs ACL 1141	MARK WYNTER (LP)	30
67	Marble Arch MAL 647	MARK WYNTER (LP)	12

(see also Joe Brown & Mark Wynter)

GAIL WYNTERS

67	London HLE 10144	Snap Your Fingers/Find Myself A New Love	10

CARL WYNTON SOUND

75	Zella JHSPM 176	The Rams Song/The Supporter's Lament	5

JOHNNY X & THE SINGIN' SWINGIN' EIGHT

63	Fontana TF 408	Lemonade/Come Closer Melinda	15

X-CALIBURS

65	CBS 201805	We Will Love/Swing That Chariot	8
65	Mercury MF 941	You'll Find Out/That's What Happens (possibly as Xcalibres)	8

X-CELLS

81	Snotty Snail NEL COL 4	Freedom Man/SCHIZOID: Nowhere To Go (p/s)	12

X-CERTS

78	Zama	Feeling The Groove (p/s)	15
81	Recreational PLAY 1	Together/Untogether (p/s, with lyric insert)	6

X-DREAMYSTS

78	Good Vibrations GOT 5	Right Way Home/Dance Away Love (p/s)	18
79	Polydor 2059 129	Bad News/Money Talks (p/s)	10
80	Polydor 2059 235	I Don't Wanna Go/Silly Games (p/s)	10
80	Polydor 2059 252	Stay The Way You Are/Race Against Time (p/s)	10

X-E-CUTORS

80	Rok ROK 13/14	Too Far To Look Inside My Head/X-FILMS: After My Blood (die-cut co. sleeve)	10

XERO

83	Brickyard XERO 1	Oh Baby/Hold On (2-track issue, p/s)	22
83	Brickyard XERO 1	Oh Baby/Hold On/Lone Wolf (3-track limited issue, p/s)	15
83	Brickyard XERO 1T	Oh Baby/Hold On/Lone Wolf (12", plain card sleeve with sticker, withdrawn)	20
83	Brickyard XERO 1T	Oh Baby/Hold On/Killer Frog (12", reissue)	10

(see also Bruce Dickinson, Iron Maiden)

XILES

65	Xiles XIL 004	Our Love Will Never End/The Only People In This World	20

XIT

72	Rare Earth RES 107	I Was Raised/End	7
73	Rare Earth RES 111	Reservation Of Education/Young Warrior	7
72	Rare Earth SREA 4002	PLIGHT OF THE RED MAN (LP)	18

XL5

63	HMV POP 1148	XL5 (Zero G)/Caviare	22
63	HMV 7EG 8802	FIREBALL AND OTHER TITLES (EP, 2 tracks by Don Spencer)	50

XL5's

80	Fourplay FOUR 004	Fireball/Misirlou	8

X-MAL DEUTSCHLAND

83	4AD AD 311	Incubus Succubus II/Vito (p/s, some with "Vito" listed as A-side)	8/5

X-MEN

84	Creation CRE 006	Do The Ghost/Talk (foldaround p/s in bag, orange/blue or yellow/green p/s)	5
85	Creation CRE 013	Spiral Girl/Bad Girl (foldaround p/s in polyester bag)	5

X-O-DUS

79	Factory FAC 11	English Black Boys/See Them A-Come (12", dark-grey textured p/s, later light grey p/s)	12

XPOZEZ

80s	Fight FIGHT 1	SYSTEMS KILL (EP)	6
82	Red Rhino RED 15	1,000 Marching Feet/Terminal Case (p/s)	5
83	Sexual Phonograph SPH 2	(Be My) New York Doll/It's All Been Done Before (p/s)	5

MINT VALUE £

X-RAYS

59	London HLR 8805	Chinchilla/Out Of Control	40
59	London HLR 8805	Chinchilla/Out Of Control (78)	40

X-RAY SPEX

77	Virgin VS 189	Oh Bondage, Up Yours/I Am A Cliche (some in p/s)	18/5
77	Virgin VS 189-12	Oh Bondage, Up Yours/I Am A Cliche (12", company sleeve)	15
78	EMI International INT 553	The Day The World Turned Day-Glo/Lama Poseur (p/s, 15,000 orange vinyl)	8/5
78	EMI International INT 563	Identity/Let's Submerge (p/s, initially on pink vinyl)	8/5
78	EMI International INT 573	Germ Free Adolescents/Age (p/s)	7
79	EMI International INT 583	Highly Inflammable/Warrior In Woolworths (p/s, initially on red vinyl)	10/7
78	EMI Intl. INS 3023	GERM FREE ADOLESCENTS (LP, with lyric inner sleeve)	18
90s	EMI Intl. INS 3023	GERM FREE ADOLESCENTS (LP, orange vinyl reissue)	12

(see also Poly Styrene, Essential Logic)

XS DISCHARGE

80	G. Marxist COMMUNIQUE 3	Across The Border/Frustration (p/s)	15
80	Groucho Marxist WH 3	Life's A Wank (p/s)	20

XS ENERGY

78	World WRECK 1	Eighteen/Jenny's Alright/Horrorscope! (numbered foldover yellow or green p/s, stamped white labels)	12
79	Dead Good DEAD 1	Eighteen/Jenny's Alright/Horrorscope! (reissue, 'National Souvenir Issue', different foldover p/s, stamped white labels)	10
79	Dead Good DEAD 1	Eighteen/Jenny's Alright/Horrorscope! (stamped white sleeve & yellow printed labels)	8
79	Dead Good DEAD 3	Use You/Imaginary (p/s)	7

XTC

77	Virgin VS 188	Science Friction/She's So Square (unreleased, in picture sleeve)	800+
77	Virgin VS 188	Science Friction/She's So Square (unreleased, no picture sleeve)	60
77	Virgin VS 188-12	3D EP (12" version of the above, p/s)	8
78	Virgin VS 201	Statue Of Liberty/Hang On To The Night (p/s)	5
78	Virgin VS 209	This Is Pop?/Heatwave (p/s)	5
79	Virgin VS 259	Life Begins At The Hop/Homo Safari (30,000 clear vinyl, PVC sleeve & insert)	5
79	Virgin VS 282	Making Plans For Nigel/Bushman President (Homo Safari Series No. 2)/ Pulsing, Pulsing (initially with game-board p/s with playing pieces)	6/4
79	Smash Hits HIT 002	Ten Feet Tall/SKIDS: The Olympian (33rpm red flexidisc with Smash Hits)	6/5
80	Virgin VS 365	Generals And Majors/Don't Lose Your Temper//Smokeless Zone/ The Somnambulist (double pack)	5
81	Virgin VS 372	Towers Of London/Set Myself On Fire (live)//Battery Brides (live)/ Scissor Man (double pack)	5
81	RSO RSO 71	Take This Town/RUTS: Babylon's Burning (p/s)	5
81	Virgin VS 384	Sgt. Rock (Is Going To Help Me)/Living Through Another Cuba/Generals And Majors (1st 20,000 in poster p/s, with stickered PVC sleeve)	5/4
82	Lyntone LYN 11032	Looking For Footprints (flexidisc free with Flexipop magazine, issue 16; on red, blue, green or yellow vinyl)	7/5
82	Virgin VS 490	No Thugs In Our House/Chain Of Command/Limelight/ Over Rusty Water (9" die-cut gatefold p/s)	7
87	Virgin CDEP 3	Dear God/Homo Safari/Bushman President/Egyptian Solution/ Mantis On Parole/Frost Circus/Procession Toward Learning Land (CD, gatefold card sleeve)	8
88	Virgin CDT 9	Senses Working Overtime/Egyptian Solution (Homo Safari Series No. 3)/ Blame The Weather/Tissue Tigers (The Arguers) (3" CD, card sleeve)	8
89	Virgin VSCD 1158	Mayor Of Simpleton/Ella Guru/Living In A Haunted Heart/ The Good Things (3" CD, gatefold card sleeve)	10
89	Virgin VSCD 1177	King For A Day (7" Version)/King For A Day (12" Version)/ My Paint Heroes (Home Demo)/Skeletons (Home Demo) (3" CD, 'crown' pack)	10
92	Virgin VS 1426	Wrapped In Grey (p/s, withdrawn, 2,000 only)	50
92	Virgin VSCDT 1426	WRAPPED IN GREY (CD EP, withdrawn, 2,000 only)	40
78	Virgin V 2095	WHITE MUSIC (LP, with black inner sleeve)	12
78	Virgin V 2108	GO 2 (LP, with insert, 1st 15,000 with bonus 12" EP: "Go +")	15
79	Virgin V 2129	DRUMS AND WIRES (LP, with gatefold insert, 1st 15,000 with free 7": "Chain Of Command"/"Limelight" [VDJ 30])	12
80	Virgin V 2173	BLACK SEA (LP, with green paper outer sleeve & lyric insert)	12
84	Virgin V 2251	WAXWORKS (LP, with bonus LP, "Beeswax")	12
84	Virgin V 2325	THE BIG EXPRESS (LP, circular sleeve & lyric inner)	12
88	Virgin CDVT 2581	ORANGES AND LEMONS (LP, as 3-CD single box set)	12

(see also Mr Partridge, Barry Andrews, Three Wise Men, Dukes Of Stratosphere) Colonel, Spys)

XTRAVERTS

78	Spike SRTS SP 001	Blank Generation/A-Lad-In-Sane	120
78	Rising Sun RS 1	Police State/PLASTIC PEOPLE: Demolition (p/s, multi-coloured vinyl)	60
81	Xtraverts XTRA 001	Speed/1984 (white labels, 'photo' or 'no photo' foldout poster p/s)	35/40

YACHTS

77 Stiff BUY 19 — Suffice To Say/Freedom Is A Heavy Wine (p/s) 7
78 Radar ADA 23 — Look Back In Love (Not In Anger)/I Can't Stay Long (p/s, blue vinyl) 10
78 Radar ADA 25 — The Yachting Type/Hypnotising Lies (p/s) 6
79 Radar ADA 36 — Love You, Love You/Hazy People (p/s, orange vinyl) 6
79 Radar ADA 42 — Box 202/Permanent Damage (p/s) 6
77 Radar ADA 52 — There's A Ghost In My House/Revelry/The Yachting Type (p/s) 6
81 Demon D 1005 — Fool Like You/Dubmarine (p/s) 5
79 Radar RAD 19 — THE YACHTS (LP, with live 7" "Suffice To Say"/"On And On" [SAM 98, p/s]) 12

(see also Big In Japan)

YADS

92 Fairfields YAD 2 — Yippee For Shtonk/It's There, You Mong (p/s) 7

YA HO WA 13

83 Psycho PSYCHO 2 — GOLDEN SUNRISE (LP, 319 copies only, different coloured vinyls, some on black vinyl without sleeve) 60

(see also Seeds)

YAKS

65 Decca F 12115 — Yakety Yak/Back In '57 20

YAMASHTA/WINWOOD/SHRIEVE/SCHULZE/DIMEOLA

78 Island ILPS 9387 — GO (LP, with 7" booklet) 12

(see also Stevie Winwood, Suntreader)

YAMASUKIS

71 Dandelion DAN 7004 — Yamasuki/Aieaoa (p/s, also listed as K 19003) 5

YANA

56 HMV POP 252 — Climb Up The Wall/If You Don't Love Me 18
57 HMV POP 340 — Mr. Wonderful/Too Close For Comfort 15
58 HMV POP 481 — I Need You/I Miss You Mama 12
58 HMV POP 481 — I Need You/I Miss You Mama (78) 6
58 HMV POP 546 — Papa And Mama/In The Morning 12

YANCEY

79 Octane WS 302 — Standing Waiting/Woman (no p/s) 20
79 Hammer HS 302 — Standing Waiting/Woman (reissue) 8

JIMMY YANCEY

54 HMV 7EG 8062 — JIMMY YANCEY (EP) 20
55 HMV 7EG 8083 — JIMMY YANCEY (EP) 20
58 Vogue EPV 1203 — YANCEY'S PIANO (EP) 20
54 London AL 3525 — JIMMY YANCEY — A LOST RECORDING DATE (10" LP) 25
56 Vogue LDE 166 — JAZZ IMMORTALS VOLUME 2 (10" LP) 30
68 Atlantic 590 018 — LOWDOWN DIRTY BLUES (LP) 15
72 Gannet 5137 — JIMMY AND MAMA YANCEY (LP) 12

MAMA YANCEY/DON EWELL

57 Tempo LAP 7 — MAMA YANCEY-DON EWELL (10" LP) 30

(see also Don Ewell)

ZALMAN YANOVSKY

67 Kama Sutra KAS 209 — As Long As You're Here/Ereh Er'uoy Sa Gnol Sa (unreleased)
67 Pye International 7N 25438 — As Long As You're Here/Ereh Er'uoy Sa Gnol Sa 8
71 Kama Sutra 2316 003 — ALIVE AND WELL IN ARGENTINA (LP) 18

(see also Mugwumps, Lovin' Spoonful)

YARDBIRDS

64 Columbia DB 7283 — I Wish You Would/A Certain Girl 25
64 Columbia DB 7391 — Good Morning Little Schoolgirl/I Ain't Got You 25
65 Columbia DB 7499 — For Your Love/Got To Hurry 10
65 Columbia DB 7594 — Heart Full Of Soul/Steeled Blues 8
65 Columbia DB 7706 — Evil Hearted You/Still I'm Sad (some copies with A-side miscredited to "Samwell-Smith & McCartney") 5
66 Columbia DB 7848 — Shapes Of Things/You're A Better Man Than I 6
66 Columbia DB 7848 — Shapes Of Things/Still I'm Sad (mispressing) 45
66 Columbia DB 7928 — Over, Under, Sideways, Down/Jeff's Boogie 20
66 Columbia DB 8024 — Happenings Ten Years Time Ago/Psycho Daisies 30
67 Columbia DB 8165 — Little Games/Puzzles 30
68 Columbia DB 8368 — Goodnight Sweet Josephine/Think About It (unreleased; acetates only) .... 225+
64 Columbia SEG 8421 — FIVE YARDBIRDS (EP) 90
67 Columbia SEG 8521 — OVER UNDER SIDEWAYS DOWN (EP) 165
64 Columbia 33SX 1677 — FIVE LIVE YARDBIRDS (LP, 1st pressing, blue/black label, flipback sleeve) 120
69 Columbia 33SX 1677 — FIVE LIVE YARDBIRDS (LP, 2nd pressing, black/silver label, flipback sleeve) 22
60s Columbia TA SX 6063 — FIVE LIVE YARDBIRDS (reel-to-reel tape) 20
66 Columbia SCXC 28 — HAVING A RAVE UP WITH THE YARDBIRDS (LP, export issue) 120
66 Columbia S(C)X 6063 — THE YARDBIRDS (LP, 1st pressing, blue/black label, flipback sleeve, mono/stereo) 35/40

MINT VALUE £

69 Columbia S(C)X 6063 THE YARDBIRDS (LP, 2nd pressing, black/silver label, flipback sleeve) 18
70 Columbia S(C)X 6063 THE YARDBIRDS (LP, 3rd pressing, black/silver label, non-flipback sleeve; some sleeves misprinted without front cover illustration) 18/15
71 Regal Starline SRS 5069 REMEMBER... THE YARDBIRDS (LP) 12
84 Charly BOX 104 SHAPES OF THINGS (LP, box set) 30
(see also Eric Clapton, Jeff Beck, Jimmy Page, Keith Relf, Reign, Stairway, Sonny Boy Williamson & Yardbirds, Shoot)

PER YARROH
88 HMV PY 1 Laughing Inside/Laughing Inside (p/s, promo only; actually by Roy Harper) 7
(see also Roy Harper)

TOM YATES
67 CBS BPG 63094 SECOND CITY SPIRITUAL (LP, as Thomas Yates) 85
72 President PTLS 1053 LOVE COMES WELL ARMED (LP, with booklet) 40
77 Satril SATL 4007 SONG OF THE SHIMMERING WAY (LP, with insert) 35

Y BLEW
67 Qualiton QSP 7001 Maes 'B'/Beth Sy'n Dod Rhyngom Ni (p/s) 10

YEAH YEAH YEAHS
01 Wichita WEBB 029T YEAH YEAH YEAHS EP: Bang/Mystery Girl/Art Star/Miles Away/Our Time (12", p/s) 10

YEAR ONE
69 Major Minor MM 660 Eli's Comin'/Will You Be Staying After Sunday 10

YEH YEH
85 Berlin BRS 001 You Will Pay/7 Bells (1st pressing in grey p/s) 5

YELLO
81 Do It DUN 11 Bimbo/I.T. Splash (p/s) 10
82 Do It DUN 13 Bostich/She's Got A Gun (Instrumental) (p/s) 8
82 Do It DUNIT 13 Bostich/Downtown Samba/She's Got A Gun/Daily Disco (12", p/s) 8
82 Do It DUN 18 She's Got A Gun/Glue Head (p/s) 5
82 Do It DUNIT 18 She's Got A Gun/The Evening's Young/There Is No Reason (12", p/s) 8
82 Do It DUN 23 Pinball Cha Cha/Smile On You (p/s) 5
82 Do It DUNIT 23 Pinball Cha Cha/Smile On You (12", p/s) 10
83 Stiff PBUY 176 I Love You/Rubber West (3-D picture disc, some with glasses) 6/5
83 Stiff BUY 191 Lost Again/Base For Alec (p/s) 6
83 Stiff DBUY 191 Lost Again/Base For Alec//Let Me Cry/She's Got A Gun (double pack) 7
85 Elektra EKR 17T Desire/Oh Yeah (Indian Summer "Stella Suite Part 2"/Oh Yeah/ XS (First Ever Version) (12", double pack, some sealed) 15/12
86 Mercury MERDP 218 Goldrush/She's Got A Gun (live at Palladium N.Y.)//I Love You/ Desire (double pack, unreleased)
86 Mercury MERXD 218 Goldrush/Goldrush II/She's Got A Gun (live)//Pinball Cha-Cha/ Vicious Games (12", double pack) 10
87 Mercury MERXR 253 The Rhythm Divine (Version Two)/Dr. Van Steiner (Instrumental)/The Rhythm Divine (Original 7" Version) (12", p/s, as Yello featuring Billy MacKenzie) 30
87 Mercury YELCD 1 The Race (13.22)/La Habanera (CD, individually silk-screened card sleeve, various colours) 8
87 Mercury 080 528-2 The Race (Extended Version)/Another Race (Magician's Version)/ The Race (Video) (CD Video) 10
88 Mercury 080 644-2 Tied Up In Red (Video)/Wall St. Bongo/Third Of June (CD Video) 10
83 Stiff BUYIT 176 I Love You (Extended)/Swing/Bostich (12", p/s) 8
83 Stiff BUYIT 191 Lost Again/Base For Alec/No More Words/Pumping Velvet (12", p/s) 8
89 Mercury 080 832-2 Third Of June/Alhambra/Otto Di Cantania/Of Course I'm Lying (Video) (CD Video) 10
89 Mercury YELCD 4 Blazing Saddles (Latinohouse Remix)/I Love You (Emilio Pasquez Rubberband Mix)/The Rhythm Divine/Blue Nabou (CD, card sleeve with heat sensitive sticker) 8
83 Stiff SEEZ 48 YOU GOTTA SAY YES TO ANOTHER EXCESS (LP, with bonus white label 12": "I Love You"/"Lost Again"/"You Gotta Say Yes To Another Excess [remix]"/"Pumping Velvet") 15
87 Mercury MERH 100 ONE SECOND (LP, with bonus 12" in p/s: "Call It Love (Trego Snare Version) 2"/"Santiago [live at Roxy New York]") 20
88 Mercury 836 778-1 FLAG (LP, HMV competition issue, 100 only) 50
95 Urban 527 728-2 HANDS ON YELLO: THE UPDATES (2-CD, withdrawn) 30
(see also Associates)

YELLOTONE
03 Ai AI 004 GREEN MAYO EP (12", p/s) 8

YELLOW
70 CBS 4869 Roll It Down The Hill/Living A Lie 20

YELLOW BALLOON
67 Stateside SS 2008 Yellow Balloon/Noollab Wolley 18
68 Stateside SS 2124 Stained Glass Window/Can't Get Enough Of Your Love 15

YELLOW BELLOW ROOM BOOM
68 CBS 3205 Seeing Things Green/Easy Life 20
(see also 10cc, Frabjoy & Runcible Spoon)

YELLOW MAGIC ORCHESTRA
79 Alfa ALF 2145 Rydeen/Absolute Ego Dance (white vinyl, stickered sleeve) 7
79 A&M AMSP 7447 Tong Poo/Cosmic Surfin' (12", p/s, yellow vinyl) 10
80 A&M JAPAN 2 Nice Age/Rydeen (p/s, yellow vinyl) 7
80 A&M AMS 7502 Computer Game/Firecracker/Technopolis (yellow vinyl, PVC sleeve) 7
80 A&M AMS 7559 Behind The Mask/Yellow Magic (p/s, yellow vinyl) 7

80 A&M AMSX 7559 — Behind The Mask/Tong Poo/La Femme (12", p/s) 8
81 A&M AMSP 8104 — Tighten Up/Rydeen (12", p/s) 8
80 A&M LH 68516 — MULTIPLIES (LP, yellow vinyl) 12
(see also Ryuichi Sakamoto)

YELLOW PAGES
68 Page One POF 090 — Here Comes Jane/Ring-A-Ding 30
(see also Mirage)

YELLOW PAYGES
70 UNI UNS 516 — Follow The Bouncing Ball/Little Woman 8
71 UNI UNS 534 — Birds Of A Feather/Lady Friend 5

YELLOW 6
90s Enraptured RAPTLP 36 — OVERTONE (2-LP, clear vinyl, numbered, handprinted sleeve, 300 only) 20

YELLOWSTONE & VOICE
72 Parlophone R 5965 — The Flying Dutchman/Philosopher 5
72 Regal Zonophone RZ 3065 — Thinking About You And Me/Grandmother Says 5
73 Regal Zonophone RZ 3073 — Memories/Well Hello 5
72 Regal Zono. SRZA 8511 — YELLOWSTONE & VOICE (LP) 20

YEMM & YEMEN
66 Columbia DB 8022 — Black Is The Night/Do Blondes Really Have More Fun? 15

YES
69 Atlantic 584 280 — Sweetness/Something's Coming 40
69 Atlantic 584 298 — Looking Around/Everydays (unreleased; demos may exist) .... 150+
70 Atlantic 584 323 — Time And A Word/The Prophet 100
70 Atlantic 2091 004 — Sweet Dreams/Dear Father 35
71 Atlantic 2814 003 — I've Seen All Good People (a) Your Move/Starship Trooper (b) Life Seeker (promo only) 75
72 6-A1/-B1 — Siberian Khatru/And You And I (white label promo) 50
74 Atlantic K 10407 — Roundabout/And You And I 5
77 Atlantic K 10985 — Going For The One/Parallels (unreleased, copies may exist) .... 60+
77 Atlantic K 10985T — Going For The One (Extended)/Parallels (12", unreleased, copies may exist) .... 40+
77 Atlantic K 11047 — Going For The One/Awaken Part I (12", p/s) 8
78 Atlantic K 11184 — Don't Kill The Whale/Abiline (p/s) 5
83 Atco B 9817P — Owner Of A Lonely Heart/Our Song (blue, black or grey shaped picture disc) 8
83 Atco B 9817C — Owner Of A Lonely Heart/Our Song (cassette) 20
70s Lyntone LYN 2535 — Interview/Five Songs (flexidisc or vinyl, some with 80-page Yes songbook) 70/35
69 Atlantic 588 190 — YES (LP, red/plum label with lyric insert) 35
70 Atlantic 2400 006 — TIME AND A WORD (LP, red/plum label, with lyric insert) 25
71 Atlantic 2400 101 — THE YES ALBUM (LP, red/plum label, gatefold sleeve) 25
71 Atlantic 2401 019 — FRAGILE (LP, red/plum label, gatefold sleeve with booklet) 25
72 Atlantic K 50012 — CLOSE TO THE EDGE (LP, textured sleeve, with lyric insert) 25
77 Atlantic DSK 50379 — GOING FOR THE ONE (LP, as 3 x 12" singles, promo only) .... 100+
80 Atlantic K 50842 — CLASSIC YES (LP, with bonus 7" "Roundabout"/"Your Move" [SAM 141]) 15
80 Atlantic K 50842 — CLASSIC YES (LP, promo, with different sleeve) 50
(see also Jon Anderson, Hans Christian, Syn, Syndicats, Winston's Fumbs, Warriors, Federals, Peter Banks, Flash, Asia, Rick Wakeman, Steve Howe, Refugee, Chris Squire)

YETTIES
69 Acorn CF 203 — FIFTY STONE OF LOVELINESS (LP) 20

JOHN YLVISAKER
68 Avantgarde AV 107 — COOL LIVIN' (LP) 60

YOBS
77 NEMS NES 114 — Run Rudolph Run/The Worm Song (p/s) 5
78 Yob YOB 79 — Silent Night/Stille Nacht (p/s) 5
81 Safari YULE 1 — Rub-A-Dum-Dum/Another Christmas (p/s) 5
82 Fresh FRESH 41 — Yobs On 45/The Ballad Of Warrington (p/s) 5
80 Safari RUDE 1 — CHRISTMAS ALBUM (LP) 12
(see also Boys)

MAHARISHI MAHESH YOGI
67 Liberty LBS 83075E — MAHARISHI MAHESH YOGI (LP) 20

YOLANDA
60 Triumph RGM 1007 — With This Kiss/Don't Tell Me Not To Love You 35
(see also Kenny Graham & His Satellites)

YO LA TENGO
95 Duophonic Super 45s DS 45-10 — Evanescent Psychic Pez Drop/STEREOLAB: Long Hair Of Death (gig single, fluorescent yellow vinyl, plain white stickered card sleeve, 3,000 only) 20
96 Earworm WORM 4 — Blue — Green Arrow/Watching The Sun Set On Johnny Carson (2,000 only, 100 in handmade p/s) 12/8

YO-YO'S
98 Rebound BONG 1 — You Got Me Out Of My Mind/1000 Miles Away From Here (p/s) 6
99 Rebound BONG 2S — Rumble(d)/Too Lazy To Bleed (p/s) 5
(see also Chasers, Energetic Krusher, Wildhearts)

NOLA YORK
64 HMV POP 1326 — I Don't Understand/Here I Stand 6
66 Philips BF 1527 — A Whole Lotta Lovin'/You Just Didn't Wanna Know 7
67 Philips BF 1582 — Photographs/He's Looking At Her 6
67 Philips BF 1606 — There's So Much Love All Around Me/Sleeping Boutique 6
68 Philips BF 1714 — Ciao Baby/We'll Get To Heaven 8
(see also Bow Bells)

MINT VALUE £

PETE YORK PERCUSSION BAND

73	Decca TXS 109	PERCUSSION BAND (LP, with Ian Paice, gatefold sleeve)	30

(see also Spencer Davis Group, Hardin & York, Deep Purple)

RUSTY YORK

58	Parlophone R 4398	Peggy Sue/Shake 'Em Up Baby (unissued, demos only)	1,500

(see also Bonnie Lou & Rusty York)

STEVE YORK'S CAMELO PARDALIS

73	Virgin V 2003	MANOR LIVE (LP)	12

(see also Elkie Brooks, Boz Scaggs, Lol Coxhill, Graham Bond, Mike Patto)

YORK BROTHERS

54	Parlophone CMSP 5	Why Don't You Open The Door?/You're My Every Dream Come True (export issue)	22
54	Parlophone CMSP 22	Strange Town/Three O'Clock Blues (export issue)	22
54	Parlophone DP 392	Tight Wad/Kentucky (export 78)	8
55	Parlophone EP 417	I Get The Blues In The Springtime/Mister Midnight (export 78)	6
55	Parlophone DP 419	Deep Within My Heart/I'll Leave The Door Open (78, export issue)	10
55	Parlophone DP 421	That's All I Want From You/A Chip On Your Shoulder (78, export issue)	10
56	Parlophone DP 515	Don't Leave Me With The Yum Yum Blues/Why Did You Have To Go (78, export issue)	10
57	Parlophone DP 527	Lightning Struck My Heart/LESLIE YORK: I'll See It Happen To You (78, export issue)	10
58	Parlophone GEP 8736	COUNTRY AND WESTERN (EP)	40
58	Parlophone GEP 8753	COUNTRY AND WESTERN NO. 2 (EP)	40

YABBY YOU

77	Grove Music GMLP 001	DELIVER ME FROM MY ENEMIES (LP)	35
77	Grove Music GMLP 004	BEWARE (LP)	25
80	Island ILPS 9651	JAH JAH WAY (LP)	12

YOU & I

73	Grape GR 3055	Morning Has Broken/Don't Take Love For A Game	5

YOU KNOW WHO GROUP

65	London HLR 9947	Roses Are Red My Love/Playboy	18

CHRIS YOULDEN

73	Deram DM 377	Nowhere Road/Standing On The Corner	6
73	Deram SML 1099	NOWHERE ROAD (LP)	30
74	Deram SML 1112	CITY CHILD (LP)	30

(see also Savoy Brown)

BARRY YOUNG

65	Dot DS 16756	One Has My Name (The Other Has My Heart)/Show Me The Way	6

BILLY YOUNG

72	Atlantic K 10277	The Sloopy/Same Old Thing Again	8
72	Jay Boy BOY 55	I'm Available/Sweet Woman	5

BILLY YOUNG/LIZZIE MILES

56	HMV 7EG 8178	THE BLUES THEY SANG (EP, with Jelly Roll Morton)	30

BOB YOUNG

86	Making Waves SURF 115	Mean Girl/Living On An Island (p/s)	8
86	Making Waves SPRAY 104	IN QUO COUNTRY (LP)	15

(see also Status Quo, Young & Moody Band)

BRETT YOUNG (& GHOST SQUAD)

63	Pye 7N 15578	Guess What/It Just Happened	12
64	Pye 7N 15641	Never Again/You Can't Fool Me (as Brett Young & Ghost Squad)	12

COLIN YOUNG

71	Trend 6099 005	Anytime At All/You're No Good	8

DARREN YOUNG

63	Parlophone R 4919	My Tears Will Turn To Laughter/I've Just Fallen For Someone	25

(see also Johnny Gentle)

DESI YOUNG

70	Pressure Beat PB 5504	News Flash/JOE GIBBS & DESTROYERS: News Flash — Version	18

EVE YOUNG (& SNOOKY LANSON)

50	London L 659	But Me, I Love You/Comanchie Rose (78)	8
50	London L 751	Beloved, Be Faithful (with Snooky Lanson)/I'm In The Middle Of A Riddle (with Snooky Lanson) (78)	6
50	London L 774	Squeeze Me/Somewhere, Somehow, Someday (78)	6
50	London L 800	An Ordinary Broom (with Snooky Lanson)/Sometime (with Stuart Foster) (78)	6
51	London L 874	Sentimental Music/I Still Feel The Same About You (78)	8
51	London L 892	Just For Tonight/Would I Love You (78)	8

(see also Snooky Lanson)

FARON YOUNG

78s

55	Capitol CL 14336	Live Fast, Love Hard, Die Young/Forgive Me, Dear	8
56	Capitol CL 14574	If You Ain't Lovin' (You Ain't Livin')/All Right	8
56	Capitol CL 14655	I've Got 5 Dollars And It's Saturday Night/You're Still Mine	8
57	Capitol CL 14735	The Shrine Of St. Cecilia/He Was There	6
57	Capitol CL 14762	Love Has Finally Come My Way/Moonlight Mountain	6
57	Capitol CL 14793	Honey Stop! (And Think Of Me)/Vacation's Over	10
58	Capitol CL 14822	Snowball/The Locket	8

45s

55	Capitol CL 14336	Live Fast, Love Hard, Die Young/Forgive Me, Dear	35
56	Capitol CL 14574	If You Ain't Lovin' (You Ain't Livin')/All Right	25
56	Capitol CL 14655	I've Got 5 Dollars And It's Saturday Night/You're Still Mine	25
57	Capitol CL 14735	The Shrine Of St. Cecilia/He Was There	12
57	Capitol CL 14762	Love Has Finally Come My Way/Moonlight Mountain	10
57	Capitol CL 14793	Honey Stop! (And Think Of Me)/Vacation's Over	15
58	Capitol CL 14822	Snowball/The Locket	10
58	Capitol CL 14860	I Can't Dance/Rosalie (Is Gonna Get Married)	15
58	Capitol CL 14891	Every Time I'm Kissing You/Alone With You	10
58	Capitol CL 14930	I Hate Myself/That's The Way I Feel	7
59	Capitol CL 14975	Last Night At A Party/A Long Time Ago	15
59	Capitol CL 15004	That's The Way It's Gotta Be/We're Talking It Over	7
59	Capitol CL 15050	I Hear You Talkin'/Country Girl	25
59	Capitol CL 15093	Face To The Wall/Riverboat	6
60	Capitol CL 15133	I'll Be Alright (In The Morning)/Your Old Used To Be	6
60	Capitol CL 15151	Is She All You Thought She'd Be/There's Not Any Like You Left	6
60	Capitol CL 15173	Forget The Past/A World So Full Of Love	6
61	Capitol CL 15197	Hello Walls/Congratulations	6
62	Mercury AMT 1198	The Yellow Bandana/How Much I Must Have Loved You	6

EPs

57	Capitol EAP1 778	SWEETHEARTS OR STRANGERS PT. 1 (with Country Deputies)	20
57	Capitol EAP2 778	SWEETHEARTS OR STRANGERS PT. 2 (with Country Deputies)	20
58	Capitol EAP3 778	SWEETHEARTS OR STRANGERS PT. 3 (with Country Deputies)	20
63	Capitol EAP1 1549	HELLO WALLS	20

LPs

58	Capitol T 1004	OBJECTS OF MY AFFECTION	25
59	Capitol T 1096	THIS IS FARON YOUNG	25
64	Mercury 20026MCL	STORY SONGS FOR COUNTRY FOLK	20
64	Mercury 20025MCL	COUNTRY DANCE FAVOURITES	20
65	Capitol (S)T 2037	YOUNG'S MEMORY LANE	15
66	Capitol (S)T 1876	ALL-TIME GREAT HITS OF FARON YOUNG	12

GEORGIE YOUNG & ROCKIN' BOCS

58	London HLU 8748	Nine More Miles/The Sneak	15
58	London HLU 8748	Nine More Miles/The Sneak (78)	12

HARRY YOUNG

65	Dot DS 16756	Show Me The Way/One Has My Name	10

JIMMY YOUNG

54	Decca F 10232	A Baby Cried/Remember Me	25
54	Decca F 10406	Give Me Your Word/Lonely Nightingale	20
55	Decca F 10444	These Are The Things We'll Share/Don't Go To Strangers	15
55	Decca F 10483	If Anyone Finds This, I Love You/The Sand And The Sea	15
55	Decca F 10502	Unchained Melody/Help Me Forget	25
55	Decca F 10597	The Man From Laramie/No Arms Can Ever Hold You	25
55	Decca F 10640	Someone On Your Mind/I Look At You	18
56	Decca F 10694	Chain Gang/Capri In May	18
56	Decca F 10736	Rich Man, Poor Man/The Wayward Wind	15
56	Decca F 10774	More/I'm Gonna Steal You Away	15
57	Decca F 10842	Lovin' Baby/My Faith, My Hope, My Love	10
57	Decca F 10875	Round And Round/Walkin' After Midnight	10
57	Decca F 10925	Man On Fire/Love In The Afternoon	8
57	Decca F 10948	Deep Blue Sea/Harbour Of Desire	8
58	Columbia DB 4100	Love Me Again/A Very Precious Love	5
58	Columbia DB 4147	Her Hair Was Yellow/The State Of Happiness	5
58	Columbia DB 4176	Volare (Nel Blu Dipinto Di Blu)/Beats There A Heart So True?	5
58	Columbia DB 4211	There! I've Said It Again/I Could Be A Mountain	5
55	Pye NEP 24004	JIMMY YOUNG SINGS (EP)	20
56	Decca DFE 6277	PRESENTING JIMMY YOUNG (EP)	20
57	Decca DFE 6404	JIMMY YOUNG (EP)	20
55	Decca LF 1200	PRESENTING JIMMY YOUNG (10" LP)	45
57	Decca LK 4219	THE NIGHT IS YOUNG (LP)	30
58	Columbia 33SX 1102	YOU (LP)	15

JOE E. YOUNG & TONIKS

68	Toast TT 502	Life Time Of Lovin'/Flower In My Hand	10
69	Toast TT 514	Good Day Sunshine/Life Time Of Lovin'	10
68	Toast (S)TLP 1	SOUL BUSTER! (LP)	20

JOHNNY YOUNG

67	Decca F 22548	Step Back/Cara Lyn (as Johnny Young & Kompany)	8
67	Decca F 22636	Lady/Good Evening Girl	6
68	RCA RCA 1826	Always Thinking Of You/Dreaming Country (as Johnny Young Four)	6

JOHNNY YOUNG

70	Blue Horizon 7-63852	FAT MANDOLIN (LP)	90

KAREN YOUNG

65	Mercury MF 943	I'm Yours, You're Mine/Are You Kidding	8
65	Pye 7N 15956	We'll Start The Party Again/Wonderful Summer	8
68	Major Minor MM 584	Too Much Of A Good Thing/You Better Sit Down	15
69	M. Minor MMLP/SMLP 66	SINGS NOBODY'S CHILD AND 13 OTHER GREAT SONGS (LP)	25

KATHY YOUNG & INNOCENTS

61	Top Rank JAR 534	A Thousand Stars/Eddie My Darling	40
61	Top Rank JAR 554	Happy Birthday Blues/Someone To Love	30

(see also Innocents)

MINT VALUE £

LEON YOUNG STRINGS

64 Pye 7N 15646 This Boy/Glad All Over . . . 15

LESTER YOUNG (QUINTET)

56 Vogue V 2362 New Lester Leaps In/She's Funny That Way . . . 6
56 Vogue V 2384 You're Driving Me Crazy/East Of The Sun . . . 6
57 Columbia LB 16654 Encore/Too Marvellous For Words (with Buddy Rich) . . . 5
56 Vogue EPV 1127 LESTER YOUNG (EP) . . . 10
53 Mercury MG 25015 KANSAS CITY 7/THE LESTER YOUNG QUARTET (LP, 1 side each) . . . 15
55 Felsted EDL 87014 BATTLE OF THE SAXES (10" LP) . . . 15
55 Columbia Clef 33C 9001 LESTER YOUNG WITH THE OSCAR PETERSON TRIO (10" LP) . . . 15
56 Columbia Clef 33C 9015 LESTER YOUNG (10" LP) . . . 15
56 Columbia Clef 33CX 10031 THE PRESIDENT, LESTER YOUNG (LP) . . . 15
56 Columbia Clef 33CX 10054 THE JAZZ GIANTS '56 (LP) . . . 15
57 Columbia Clef 33CX 10070 PRES (LP) . . . 15
58 London Jazz LTZ-C 15132 BLUE LESTER (LP) . . . 15
59 HMV CLP 1302 PRES AND TEDDY (LP, with Teddy Wilson) . . . 12
59 Fontana TFL 5064 LESTER YOUNG MEMORIAL ALBUM VOL. 1 (LP, with Count Basie) . . . 15
60 Fontana TFL 5065 LESTER YOUNG MEMORIAL ALBUM VOL. 2 (LP, with Count Basie) . . . 15
62 Stateside SL 10002 LESTER YOUNG & KANSAS CITY 5 (LP) . . . 12
65 Fontana TL 5260 PREZ (LP) . . . 12
66 Fontana FJL 128 LESTER YOUNG LEAPS AGAIN (LP) . . . 12

(see also Count Basie, Coleman Hawkins & Lester Young, Oscar Peterson)

LESTER YOUNG & CHARLIE PARKER, ET AL.

50 Melodisc 8003 JAZZ AT THE PHILHARMONIC, VOL. 2: BLUES FOR NORMAN, PARTS 1 & 2 (12" 78) . . . 10

LLOYD YOUNG

72 Bullet BU 500 Bread And Butter/SHALIMAR ALLSTARS: Version . . . 12
72 Duke DU 135 Soup/J.J. ALLSTARS: Version . . . 25
72 Green Door GD 4037 Shalimar Special/G. MAHTANI ALLSTARS: Version . . . 7
72 Techniques TE 917 High Explosion/ANSELL COLLINS: Version . . . 7

(see also Carey & Lloyd)

MIGHTY JOE YOUNG

72 Sonet SNTF 633 THE LEGACY OF THE BLUES VOL. 4 (LP) . . . 15
72 Delmark DS 629 BLUES WITH A TOUCH OF SOUL (LP, blue label) . . . 18

NEIL YOUNG

69 Reprise RS 23405 The Loner/Everybody Knows This Is Nowhere . . . 20
70 Reprise RS 20861 Oh Lonesome Me (Long Version)/Sugar Mountain . . . 12
70 Reprise RS 23462 Down By The River (edit)/Cinnamon Girl (alternate mix) . . . 7
70 Reprise RS 20958 Only Love Can Break Your Heart/Birds . . . 6
71 Reprise RS 23488 When You Dance I Can Really Love/After The Goldrush . . . 6
72 Reprise K 14167 Old Man/The Needle And The Damage Done . . . 6
73 Reprise SAM 15 Don't Be Denied/Love In Mind/Last Dance (p/s, 1-sided, promo only sampler for "Time Fades Away" LP) . . . 20
74 Reprise K 14350 Southern Man/Till The Morning Comes/After The Goldrush/Heart Of Gold (special sleeve) . . . 5
76 Reprise K 14431 Don't Cry No Tears/Stupid Girl . . . 6
86 Geffen GEF 7T Weight Of The World (Extended Remix)/Pressure (12", p/s) . . . 8
90 Reprise W 2776CD Rockin' In The Free World (live)/Cocaine Eyes/Rockin' In The Free World (CD) . . . 8
93 Reprise PRO 808 The Needle And The Damage Done (from "Unplugged")/ Love Is A Rose (from "Decade") (CD, promo only) . . . 8
93 Columbia XPCD 308 My Back Pages/All Along The Watchtower/Knocking On Heaven's Door (CD, promo only) . . . 8
93 Geffen NYCD 1 LUCKY THIRTEEN ALBUM SAMPLER (Ain't It The Truth/Depression Blues/This Note's For You) (CD, promo only) . . . 15
94 Reprise WO 242CD Philadelphia/Such A Woman/Stringman (CD) . . . 8
69 Reprise RSLP 6317 NEIL YOUNG (LP, with/without name on front of sleeve) . . . 35/50
69 Reprise RSLP 6349 EVERYBODY KNOWS THIS IS NOWHERE (LP) . . . 20
70 Reprise RSLP 6383 AFTER THE GOLDRUSH (LP, gatefold sleeve with lyric insert) . . . 25
71 Reprise K 44059 NEIL YOUNG (LP, reissue) . . . 12
71 Reprise K 44073 EVERYBODY KNOWS THIS IS NOWHERE (LP, reissue) . . . 12
71 Reprise K 44088 AFTER THE GOLDRUSH (LP, reissue, gatefold sleeve with lyric insert) . . . 12
72 Reprise K 54005 HARVEST (LP, thick cardboard gatefold sleeve with insert) . . . 15
72 Reprise K 64015 JOURNEY THROUGH THE PAST (2-LP, soundtrack, fold-out sleeve & inners) . . . 20
73 Reprise K 54010 TIME FADES AWAY (LP, with lyric insert) . . . 15
74 Reprise K 54014 ON THE BEACH (LP, with inner sleeve) . . . 50
75 Reprise K 54040 TONIGHT'S THE NIGHT (LP, gatefold sleeve with inner sleeve & insert) . . . 15
75 Reprise K 54057 ZUMA (LP, with inner sleeve & lyric insert) . . . 15
77 Reprise K 54088 AMERICAN STARS AND BARS (LP, with inner sleeve) . . . 12
79 Reprise K 54105 RUST NEVER SLEEPS (LP, with inner sleeve & lyric insert) . . . 12
79 Reprise K 64041 LIVE RUST (2-LP, with inner sleeves) . . . 20
80 Reprise K 54109 HAWKS & DOVES (LP, with inner sleeve) . . . 15
85 Geffen GEF 26377 OLD WAYS (LP) . . . 15
94 Reprise SAM 1310 FOR THE TURNTABLES (CD, promo only) . . . 18

(see also Buffalo Springfield, Crosby Stills Nash & Young, Stills-Young Band, Crazy Horse)

RALPH YOUNG

55 Brunswick 05466 The Man From Laramie/The Bible Tells Me So . . . 18
55 Brunswick 05500 Bring Me A Bluebird/A Room In Paris . . . 12
56 Brunswick 05605 The Legend Of Wyatt Earp/Do You Know? . . . 12

(see also Jack Pleis)

ROGER YOUNG

66 Columbia DB 7869 Sweet, Sweet Morning/Whatcha Gonna Give Me? . . . 40
66 Columbia DB 8092 No Address/It's Been Nice . . . 200

ROY YOUNG (BAND)

59 Fontana H 200 Just Keep It Up/Big Fat Mama ... 22
59 Fontana H 200 Just Keep It Up/Big Fat Mama (78) ... 6
59 Fontana H 215 Hey Little Girl/Just Ask Your Heart ... 20
59 Fontana H 215 Hey Little Girl/Just Ask Your Heart (78) ... 10
60 Fontana H 237 I Hardly Know Me/Gilee ... 18
60 Fontana H 247 Taboo/I'm In Love ... 15
61 Fontana H 290 You Were Meant For Me/Plenty Of Love (as Roy Young & Hunters) ... 18
61 Ember EMB S 128 Four And Twenty Thousand Kisses/Late Last Evening ... 12
70 RCA RCA 2031 Granny's Got A Painted Leg/Revolution (as Roy Young Band) ... 5
72 MCA MKS 5080 Rag Mama Rag/Give It All To You ... 5
70 RCA SF 8161 ROY YOUNG BAND (LP) ... 18

SUSANNAH YOUNG

67 Philips BF 1559 Lazy Afternoon/Here's That Rainy Day ... 5
67 Philips BL 7728 SWEETEST SOUNDS (LP) ... 12

TERRY YOUNG

60 Pye 7N 15321 Partners/Maverick ... 6
61 Pye 7N 15353 Someone New/Now, Forever And A Day ... 6
62 Pye 7N 15416 They Took John Away/Joe's Been A-Gittin' There ... 6

TOMMIE YOUNG

73 Contempo C 12 Everybody's Got A Little Devil In Their Soul/Do You Still Feel The Same Way ... 5
73 Contempo C 23 She Don't Have To See You/That's All Part Of Loving Him ... 5
74 Contempo CLP 501 DO YOU STILL FEEL THE SAME WAY (LP) ... 15

VICKI YOUNG

54 Capitol CL 14144 Riot In Cell Block Number Nine/Honey Love (78) ... 6
55 Capitol CL 14228 Hearts Of Stone/Tweedlee Dee (triangular centre) ... 40
55 Capitol CL 14228 Hearts Of Stone/Tweedlee Dee (78) ... 8
55 Capitol CL 14281 Live Fast, Love Hard, Die Young/Zoom, Zoom, Zoom (triangular centre) ... 25
55 Capitol CL 14281 Live Fast, Love Hard, Die Young/Zoom, Zoom, Zoom (78) ... 8
56 Capitol CL 14528 Steel Guitar/Bye Bye For Just A While ... 12
56 Capitol CL 14528 Steel Guitar/Bye Bye For Just A While (78) ... 8
56 Capitol CL 14653 Spanish Main/Tell Me In Your Own Sweet Way (with Joe 'Fingers' Carr) ... 12
56 Capitol CL 14653 Spanish Main/Tell Me In Your Own Sweet Way (with Joe 'Fingers' Carr) (78) ... 6
56 Capitol EAP1 593 VICKI YOUNG (EP) ... 40

(see also Joe 'Fingers' Carr)

VICTOR YOUNG & HIS SINGING STRINGS

54 Brunswick 05320 The High And The Mighty/The Song From 'The Caine Mutiny' (I Can't Believe That You're In Love With Me) ... 6
54 Brunswick 05337 Lisa (The "Rear Window" Theme)/Smile (Theme From 'Modern Times') ... 6
54 Brunswick 05350 Moonlight And Roses/Magnificent Obsession ... 6
55 Brunswick 05386 You, My Love (From 'Young At Heart')/Passion Tango (From 'Passion') ... 6
55 Brunswick 05448 Cherry Pink And Apple Blossom White/The World Is Mine ... 7
55 Brunswick 05479 The Toy Tiger/Autumn Leaves ... 6
55 Brunswick 05498 Tall Men (adapted from 'Cindy')/Theme From 'The Left Hand Of God' ... 6
56 Brunswick 05579 Love Theme From 'The Proud And Profane' (To Love You)/East Of Eden – Theme ... 6
53 Brunswick LAT 8029 CINEMA RHAPSODIES (LP) ... 15

YOUNG AL CAPONE

71 Green Door GD 4012 Girl Called Clover/Girl Called Clover (Version) ... 15

YOUNG & MOODY (BAND)

77 Magnet MAG 87 Chicago Blue/Warm Winds ... 5
79 Fabulous JC 1 The Devil Went Down To Georgia/You Can't Catch Me ... 5
79 Fabulous JC 3 All The Good Friends/Playing Your Game (p/s) ... 6
81 Bronze BRO 120 These Eyes/I Won't Let Go (p/s) ... 6
81 Bronze BRO 130 Don't Do That/How Can I Help You Tonight (p/s, featuring Lemmy and Linda & Coleen Nolan) ... 6
77 Magnet MAG 5015 YOUNG AND MOODY (LP, with lyric insert, as Young & Moody) ... 12

(see also Bob Young, Whitesnake, Snafu, Cozy Powell, Motörhead, Nolan Sisters)

YOUNG BLOOD

68 Pye 7N 17495 Green Light/Don't Leave Me In The Dark ... 15
68 Pye 7N 17588 Just How Loud/Masquerade ... 15
68 Pye 7N 17627 Bang-Shang-A-Lang/I Can't Stop ... 15
69 Pye 7N 17696 The Continuing Story Of Bungalow Bill/I Will ... 15

(see also Cozy Powell, Ace Kefford Stand, Big Bertha)

YOUNG BLOOD

84 Landslide LAND 1 FIRST BLOOD (12" EP, p/s) ... 18

YOUNGBLOODS

69 RCA RCA 1821 Darkness, Darkness/On Sir Francis Drake ... 10
69 RCA RCA 1877 Get Together/Beautiful ... 10
70 RCA RCA 1955 Darkness Darkness/On Sir Francis Drake (reissue) ... 5
71 Warner Bros WB 7445 Hippie From Olena/Misty Roses ... 5
69 RCA SF 8026 ELEPHANT MOUNTAIN (LP) ... 22
70 Warner Bros WS 1878 ROCK FESTIVAL (LP) ... 18
70 RCA LSA 3012 THE BEST OF THE YOUNGBLOODS (LP) ... 12
71 Warner Bros K 46100 RIDE THE WIND (LP) ... 15
72 RCA Victor SF 8218 SUNLIGHT (LP) ... 15
87 Edsel ED 244 POINT REYES STATION (LP) ... 12

YOUNG BUCKS

77 Blueport BLU 1 Get Your Feet Back On The Ground/Cold, Cold Morning (p/s) ... 6

YOUNG DISCIPLES

90 Talkin' Loud TLKX 2 Get Yourself Together/Young Disciples Theme (12", p/s) ... 8

MINT VALUE £

YOUNGFOLK
68 President PT 136 — Lonely Girl/Joey ... 10

YOUNG FOLK
72 Midas MR 001 — RIBBLE VALLEY DREAM (LP) ... 30

YOUNG FREDDIE
70 Camel CA 38 — Drink And Gamble/LENNOX BROWN & HUE ROY: King Of The Road ... 10
(see also Freddie McGregor)

YOUNG GROWLER & CALYPSO RHYTHM KINGS
66 Columbia DB 7870 — Amy The Sunbather/Sweet Trinidad ... 7
66 Columbia DB 7958 — "V" For Victory/Be Nice To Women (some in 'Test Match' p/s) ... 12/7

YOUNG-HOLT TRIO
67 Coral Q 72489 — Wack Wack/This Little Light Of Mine ... 30

YOUNG-HOLT UNLIMITED
69 MCA MU 1053 — Soulful Strut/Country Slicker Joe ... 10
72 MCA MU 1159 — Just Ain't No Love/Love Makes A Woman ... 5
69 MCA MUP(S) 368 — SOULFUL STRUT (LP) ... 20
(see also Ramsey Lewis Trio)

YOUNG IDEA
66 Columbia DB 7961 — The World's Been Good To Me/It Can't Be ... 10
66 Columbia DB 8067 — Gotta Get Out Of The Mess I'm In/Games Men Play ... 8
67 Columbia DB 8132 — Peculiar Situation/Just Look At The Rain ... 8
67 Columbia DB 8205 — With A Little Help From My Friends/Colours Of Darkness ... 6
67 Columbia DB 8284 — Mister Lovin' Luggage Man/Room With A View ... 8
68 M. For Pleasure MFP 1225 — WITH A LITTLE HELP FROM MY FRIENDS (LP) ... 12

YOUNG JESSIE
58 London HLE 8544 — Shuffle In The Gravel/Make Believe ... 325
58 London HLE 8544 — Shuffle In The Gravel/Make Believe (78) ... 45

YOUNG MARBLE GIANTS
80 Rough Trade RT 043 — Final Day/Radio Silents/Cakewalking/(uncredited 4th track) (p/s) ... 8
81 Rough Trade RT 059 — TESTCARD (EP) ... 10
(see also Jah Scouse)

YOUNG MC
88 Delicious Vinyl BRW 120 — KNOW HOW (12", EP) ... 12

YOUNG ONES
63 Decca F 11705 — How Do I Tell You/Baby That's It ... 10

YOUNG ONES
78 Virgin VS 205 — Rock 'N' Roll Radio/Little Bit Of Loving (p/s) ... 8

YOUNG RASCALS
65 Atlantic AT 4059 — I Ain't Gonna Eat My Heart Out Anymore/Slow Down ... 12
66 Atlantic AT 4082 — Good Lovin'/Mustang Sally ... 10
66 Atlantic 584 024 — You Better Run/Love Is A Beautiful Thing ... 15
66 Atlantic 584 050 — Come On Up/What Is The Reason ... 15
66 Atlantic 584 067 — Too Many Fish In The Sea/No Love To Give ... 7
67 Atlantic 584 081 — I've Been Lonely Too Long/If You Knew ... 15
67 Atlantic 584 085 — I Ain't Gonna Eat My Heart Out Anymore/Good Lovin' ... 6
67 Atlantic 584 111 — Groovin'/Sueno ... 8
67 Atlantic 584 128 — A Girl Like You/It's Love ... 8
67 Atlantic 584 138 — How Can I Be Sure/I Don't Love You Anymore ... 6
68 Atlantic 584 161 — It's Wonderful/Of Course ... 10
66 Atlantic 587/588 012 — THE YOUNG RASCALS (LP) ... 30
67 Atlantic 587/588 060 — COLLECTIONS (LP) ... 22
67 Atlantic 587/588 074 — GROOVIN' (LP) ... 30
(see also Rascals, Joey Dee & Starlighters)

YOUNG SATCH
70 Black Swan BW 1401 — Bonga Bonga Bonga/HI-TALS: Ram Buck ... 15

YOUNG SISTERS
62 London HLU 9610 — Casanova Brown/My Guy ... 20

YOUNG SOULS
69 Amalgamated AMG 844 — Why Did You Leave/Main A Wail ... 18

YOUNG TIGER
53 Lyragon J 711 — He Like It, She Like It!/TONY JOHNSON: Donkey City (78) ... 7

YOUNG TRADITION
74 Argo AFW 115 — The Shepherd's Hymn/The Boar's Head Carol ... 6
68 Transatlantic TRAEP 164 — CHICKEN ON A RAFT (EP) ... 25
66 Transatlantic TRA 142 — THE YOUNG TRADITION (LP) ... 30
67 Transatlantic TRA 155 — SO CHEERFULLY ROUND (LP) ... 25
68 Transatlantic TRA 172 — GALLERIES (LP, with Dave Swarbrick) ... 25
68 Transatlantic TRASAM 13 — THE YOUNG TRADITION SAMPLER (LP) ... 18
73 Transatlantic TRASAM 30 — GALLERIES REVISITED (LP, reissue) ... 12
(see also Dave Swarbrick, Peter Bellamy)

YOUNG TURKS
66 CBS 202353 — Duel At Diablo/Our Lady From Maxim's ... 12

YOUNG WORLD SINGERS
64 Brunswick 05916 — Ringo For President/A Boy Like That ... 6

YOUR FAVOURITE HORSE
00s Endorphin ENDORLP 010 — EVERYDAY MAGIC (LP, orange vinyl) ... 12

MINT VALUE £

YOUTH
66 Polydor 56121 — As Long As There Is Your Love/Your One And Only Love — 15

YOUTH
69 Deram DM 226 — Meadow Of My Love/Love Me Or Leave Me — 15

JOHNNY YOUTH
69 Grape GR 3002 — Darling It Won't/HIP CITY BOYS: Moon Train — 10

YOUTH VALLEY CHORALE
63 London HLU 9818 — Do You Hear What I Hear/Little Bell — 6

YOU'VE GOT FOETUS ON YOUR BREATH
81 Self Immolation WOMB 07 — Wash It All Off/333 (p/s) — 20
80s Self Immolation — Tell Me, What Is The Bane Of Your Life? — 20
81 Self Imm. WOMB OYBL-1 — DEAF (LP) — 35
81 Self Imm. WOMB OYBL-2 — ACHE (LP) — 30
(see also Foetus etc., Philip & His Foetus Vibrations, Scraping Foetus Off The Wheel)

LES YPER SOUND
67 Fontana TF 880 — Too Fortiche/Psyche Rock — 35
69 Philips TFE 8004 — MASS FOR THE PRESENT TIME (LP) — 75

YR HWNTWS
82 Loco LOCO 1001 — YR HWNTWS (LP) — 80

Y TRWYNAU COCH
70s Record. Sqwar RSROC 1 — WASTOD AR Y TU FAS (BANANAS) (EP, around 1,000 only) — 50
78 Recordian Sqwar RSROC 002 — Merched Dan 15 (Girls Under 15)/Byw Ar Arian Fy Rhieni/ Mynd I'r Capel Mewn Levis/Ail Ddechre (around 1,000 only) — 50
80s Record. Coch OCHR 2198 — RHEDEG RHAG Y TORPIDOS (LP) — 30

JOHNNY YUKON
60 Top Rank JAR 347 — Made To Be Loved/Magnolia — 7

TIMI YURO
61 London HLG 9403 — Hurt/I Apologise — 15
62 London HLG 9484 — Smile/I Believe (B-side with Johnnie Ray) — 15
62 Liberty LIB 55410 — Satan Never Sleeps/Let Me Call You Sweetheart — 12
62 Liberty LIB 55469 — What's A-Matter Baby (Is It Hurting You)/Thirteenth Hour — 18
63 Liberty LIB 55519 — The Love Of A Boy/I Ain't Gonna Cry No More — 25
63 Liberty LIB 55587 — Make The World Go Away/Look Down — 12
63 Liberty LIB 55634 — Gotta Travel On/Down In The Valley — 7
64 Liberty LIB 10177 — Hurt/Be Anything (But Be Mine) — 10
64 Mercury MF 826 — If/I'm Afraid The Masquerade Is Over — 7
65 Mercury MF 848 — You Can Have Him/Could This Be Magic — 12
65 Mercury MF 859 — Get Out Of My Life/Can't Stop Running Away — 40
65 Mercury MF 903 — Once A Day/Pretend — 7
65 Mercury MF 949 — Turn The World Around The Other Way/Just A Ribbon — 7
66 Mercury MF 978 — Cuttin' In/Why Not Now — 8
68 Liberty LBF 15092 — Something Bad On My Mind/Wrong — 10
68 Liberty LIB 15142 — I Must Have Been Out Of My Mind/Interlude — 25
68 Liberty LIB 15182 — It'll Never Be Over For Me/As Long As There Is You — 300+
65 Liberty LEP 2214 — TIMI YURO: SOUL! (EP) — 30
66 Liberty LEP 2253 — MAKE THE WORLD GO AWAY (EP) — 25
62 London HA-G 2415 — TIMI YURO (LP) — 70
62 Liberty LBY 1042 — SOUL! (LP) — 30
63 Liberty (S)LBY 1154 — WHAT'S A-MATTER BABY (LP) — 25/30
64 Liberty LBY 1192 — MAKE THE WORLD GO AWAY (LP) — 25
64 Mercury 20032 MCL — THE AMAZING YURO (LP) — 22
65 Liberty LBY 1247 — HURT (LP) — 30
66 Liberty (S)LBY 1275 — LET ME CALL YOU SWEETHEART (LP) — 22/30
66 Liberty (S)LBY 1290 — THE BEST OF TIMI YURO (LP) — 18
68 Liberty LBL/LBS 83115 — GREAT PERFORMANCES (LP) — 15
68 Liberty LBL/LBS 83128 — TIMI IN THE BEGINNING (LP) — 18
69 Liberty LBS 83198E — SOMETHING BAD ON MY MIND (LP) — 35
69 Mercury SMWL 21010 — TALENTED TIMI (LP) — 18
(see also Johnnie Ray)

AFFIE YUSUF
93 Ferox FER 001 — ACID WAVES 1 (12" EP, plain sleeve) — 15
93 Ferox FER 003 — ACID WAVES 2 (12" EP, plain sleeve) — 15

(HELMUT) ZACHARIAS

57 Polydor BM 6058 — Rock 'N' Roll "Roll-Mops" Rock/Barock 'N' Roll Rock (with Hot Club) (78) ... 8
60 Polydor NH 66635 — Never On Sunday (Jamais Le Dimanche)/Theme From 'The Apartment' (as Zacharias And His Magic Violins) ... 5
64 Polydor NH 52341 — Tokyo Melody/Teatime In Tokyo ... 5
65 Polydor 236 809 — PLAYS THE HITS OF THE BEATLES (LP) ... 12

JOHN ZACHERLE

58 London HLU 8599 — Dinner With Drac Part 1/Dinner With Drac — Conclusion ... 40
58 London HLU 8599 — Dinner With Drac Part 1/Dinner With Drac — Conclusion (78) ... 25

(see also Dave Appell & Applejacks)

ZAFTIG MADEL

84 Shine SHTUP 3 — Dori Duz/Curvy 'N' Creamy (p/s) ... 6

ZAGER & EVANS

69 RCA 1860 — In The Year 2525 (Exordium & Terminus)/Little Kids ... 6
69 RCA SF 8056 — 2525 (LP) ... 25

ZAKARRIAS

71 Deram SML 1091 — ZAKARRIAS (LP) ... 300

ALEX ZANETIS

71 Moodisc HM 102 — Guilty/JOLLY BOYS: Do Fe Do ... 7

TOMMY ZANG

59 HMV POP 611 — Break The Chain/I'll Put A String On Your Finger ... 12
62 Polydor NH 66955 — I'm Gonna Slip You Offa My Mind/Every Hour, Every Day ... 10
62 Polydor NH 66957 — Hey, Good Lookin'/With Love (For You) ... 20
62 Polydor NH 66960 — Take These Chains From My Heart/Truly, Truly ... 10
62 Polydor NH 66977 — I Can't Hold Your Letters (In My Arms)/She's Getting Married ... 10
62 Polydor NH 66980 — Just Call My Name/I Love You Because ... 12

ZAPP

80 Warner K 17712 — More Bounce To The Ounce/Brand New Player ... 5
80 Warner K 17712T — More Bounce To The Ounce/Brand New Player (12") ... 8

FRANK ZAPPA/MOTHERS OF INVENTION

SINGLES

66 Verve VS 545 — It Can't Happen Here/How Could I Be Such A Fool (as Mothers Of Invention) ... 40
67 Verve VS 557 — Big Leg Emma/Why Don't You Do Me Right (as Mothers Of Invention) ... 40
71 Reprise K 14100 — Tears Began To Fall/Junier Mintz Boogie (as Mothers Of Invention) ... 35
71 United Artists UP 35319 — What Will This Evening Bring Me This Morning?/Daddy, Daddy, Daddy ... 35
74 Discreet K 19201 — Cosmic Debris/Uncle Remus ... 8
74 Discreet K 19202 — Don't Eat The Yellow Snow/Camarillo Brillo ... 8
79 CBS 7261 — Dancin' Fool/Baby Snakes ... 8
80 CBS 7950 — Joe's Garage/Catholic Girls ... 6
80 CBS 7950 — Joe's Garage/BOB DYLAN: When You Gonna Wake Up (mispressing) ... 30
80 CBS 8652 — I Don't Wanna Get Drafted/Ancient Armaments (p/s) ... 6
81 CBS A 1622 — You Are What You Is/Harder Than Your Husband (p/s) ... 6
81 CBS A 12-1622 — You Are What You Is/Pink Napkins/Harder Than Your Husband/Soup 'N Old Clothes (12", picture disc) ... 15
81 CBS XPS 147 — Shut Up 'N' Play Yer Guitar/Variation On The C. Santana Secret (p/s, issued free with "Ship Arriving Too Late To Save A Drowning Witch" LP) ... 6
82 CBS A 2412 — Valley Girl/Teenage Prostitute (p/s) ... 6
84 EMI EMI 5499 — Baby Take Your Teeth Out/Stevie's Spanking (p/s) ... 8
93 Zappa Records 12 FRANK 102 — Valley Girl/You Are What You Is (12", p/s) ... 8
91 Zappa Records 12 FRANK 101 — Stairway To Heaven/Bolero (12", p/s) ... 8

LPs: VERVE ORIGINALS

66 Verve (S)VLP 9154 — FREAK OUT! (as Mothers Of Invention, mono/stereo, single disc) ... 55/45
67 Verve (S)VLP 9174 — ABSOLUTELY FREE (as Mothers Of Invention, mono/stereo) ... 40/30
68 Verve (S)VLP 9199 — WE'RE ONLY IN IT FOR THE MONEY (as Mothers Of Invention, gatefold sleeve, mono/stereo) ... 45/30
68 Verve (S)VLP 9223 — LUMPY GRAVY (gatefold sleeve, mono/stereo) ... 45/35
69 Verve (S)VLP 9237 — CRUISING WITH RUBEN AND THE JETS (as Mothers Of Invention, mono/stereo) ... 40/30
69 Verve (S)VLP 9239 — MOTHERMANIA — THE BEST OF THE MOTHERS (as Mothers Of Invention, mono/stereo) ... 35/25

LPs: VERVE REISSUES

71 Verve/Polydor 2683 004 — FREAK OUT (2-LP) ... 30
72 Verve/Polydor 2317 034 — WE'RE ONLY IN IT FOR THE MONEY (gatefold sleeve) ... 25
72 Verve/Polydor 2317 035 — ABSOLUTELY FREE (gatefold sleeve) ... 25
72 Verve/Polydor 2317 046 — LUMPY GRAVY (gatefold sleeve) ... 25

			MINT VALUE £
72	Verve/Polydor 2317 047	MOTHERMANIA — THE BEST OF THE MOTHERS	30
73	Verve/Polydor 2352 017	MOTHERMANIA — THE BEST OF THE MOTHERS (2nd reissue)	30
73	Verve/Polydor 2317 069	CRUISIN' WITH RUBEN AND THE JETS (gatefold sleeve)	35
75	Verve/Polydor 2352 057	ROCK FLASHBACKS (LP)	15

LPs: ORIGINAL REPRISE/WARNERS/DISCREET ISSUES

70	Reprise RSLP 6356	HOT RATS (1st pressing, pink, gold & green 'riverboat' label, gatefold sleeve)	35
70	Reprise RSLP 6356	HOT RATS (2nd pressing, tan 'riverboat' label, gatefold sleeve)	22
70	Reprise RSLP 6370	BURNT WEENY SANDWICH (as Mothers Of Invention, 1st pressing, pink, gold & green 'riverboat' label, gatefold sleeve)	22
70	Reprise RSLP 2028	WEASELS RIPPED MY FLESH (as Mothers Of Invention, tan 'riverboat' label)	22
70	Reprise RSLP 2030	CHUNGA'S REVENGE (tan 'riverboat' label, green or red gatefold sleeve)	30/22
71	Reprise K 44150	FILLMORE EAST, JUNE 1971 (as Mothers Of Invention)	22
72	Reprise K 44179	JUST ANOTHER BAND FROM L.A. (as Mothers Of Invention, gatefold sleeve)	22
72	Reprise K 44203	WAKA/JAWAKA (HOT RATS)	18
72	Reprise K 44209	THE GRAND WAZOO (gatefold sleeve)	18
73	DiscReet K 41000	OVER-NITE SENSATION (as Mothers Of Invention, gatefold sleeve)	18
74	DiscReet K 69201	ROXY AND ELSEWHERE (2-LP, as Mothers Of Invention, gatefold sleeve)	20
74	DiscReet K 49201	APOSTROPHE (') (no lyric insert)	18
75	DiscReet K 59207	ONE SIZE FITS ALL (as Mothers Of Invention, gatefold sleeve)	18

(First pressings of the above LPs were issued without Warner Bros logo on label or sleeve; copies with Warners logos are post-1975 pressings worth £6-£8 each.)

76	Warner Bros K 56298	ZOOT ALLURES (LP)	12
77	DiscReet K 69204	ZAPPA IN NEW YORK (LIVE) (2-LP, with & without reference to "Punky's Whips")	25
77	DiscReet K 69204	ZAPPA IN NEW YORK (LIVE) (2-LP, "Punky's Whips" listed on sleeve but not on label or LP)	25
77	DiscReet K 69204	ZAPPA IN NEW YORK (LIVE) (2-LP, plays "Punky's Whips", listed on sleeve but not on label)	55
78	DiscReet K 59210	STUDIO TAN	12
78	DiscReet K 59211	SLEEP DIRT	12
78	DiscReet K 59212	ORCHESTRAL FAVORITES	12

LPs: REPRISE

71	Reprise K 44078	HOT RATS (tan 'riverboat' label, gatefold sleeve)	15
71	Reprise K 44083	BURNT WEENY SANDWICH (tan 'riverboat' label)	15
71	Reprise K 44019	WEASELS RIPPED MY FLESH (tan 'riverboat' label)	20
71	Reprise K 44020	CHUNGA'S REVENGE (tan 'riverboat' label, gatefold sleeve)	20

(The above LPs were issued without Warner Bros logo on label or sleeve; post-1975 pressings with logos are worth £6-£8 each.)

OTHER LPs

69	Transatlantic TRA 197	UNCLE MEAT (2-LP, as Mothers Of Invention)	30
71	United Artists UDF 50003	200 MOTELS (2-LP, with booklet & poster, as Frank Zappa & Mothers Of Invention)	50
79	CBS 88339	SHEIK YERBOUTI (2-LP, gatefold sleeve printed with lyrics)	18
79	CBS 86101	JOE'S GARAGE ACT 1 (gatefold sleeve, lyric insert)	12
79	CBS 88475	JOE'S GARAGE ACTS 2 & 3 (2-LP, gatefold sleeve, lyric insert)	18
81	CBS 88560	YOU ARE WHAT YOU IS (2-LP, gatefold sleeve, lyric insert)	18
81	CBS 88516	TINSELTOWN REBELLION (2-LP, gatefold sleeve with lyrics)	18
81	CBS 66368	SHUT UP 'N' PLAY YER GUITAR (3-LP box set, with inner sleeves)	30
82	CBS 85804	SHIP ARRIVING TOO LATE TO SAVE A DROWNING WITCH (with bonus 7" "Shut Up 'N' Play Yer Guitar"/"Variation On The C. Santana Secret" [XPS 147])	15
83	CBS 25251	THE MAN FROM UTOPIA	12
84	EMI EL 2701531	BOULEZ CONDUCTS ZAPPA: 'THE PERFECT STRANGER'	12
84	EMI no cat. no.	FRANCESCO ZAPPA (with inner sleeve)	15
84	EMI 2402943	THING-FISH (3-LP, box set, with libretto)	35
86	EMI EN 352	JAZZ FROM HELL	15
86	EMI EC 3507	FRANK ZAPPA MEETS THE MOTHERS OF PREVENTION (European version)	12
95	Simply Vinyl SLVP 0024	WEASELS RIPPED MY FLESH (180gm vinyl)	12
95	Simply Vinyl SLVP 0025	BURNT WEENY SANDWICH (gatefold sleeve, 180 gm vinyl)	12

LPs: EMI REISSUES

84	EMI EMC 3500	THE MAN FROM UTOPIA	12
84	EMI EMC 3501	SHIP ARRIVING TOO LATE TO SAVE A DROWNING WITCH (with inner sleeve)	15
84	EMI FZAP1	JOE'S GARAGE ACTS 1, 2 & 3 (3-LP, box set, inner sleeves only, with libretti)	30
84	EMI E5 0021	TINSELTOWN REBELLION (2-LP, gatefold sleeve, printed with lyrics)	18
84	EMI no cat. no.	SHEIK YERBOUTI (2-LP, gatefold sleeve, printed with lyrics)	18
84	EMI no cat. no.	SHUT UP 'N' PLAY YER GUITAR (3-LP box set, with inner sleeves)	30
84	EMI EN 2402343	THEM OR US (2-LP, gatefold sleeve, printed with lyrics)	18

LPs: ZAPPA

84	Zappa Records ZAPPA 1	FREAK OUT (2-LP, gatefold sleeve, some in single sleeve £35)	18
80s	Zappa Records ZAPPA 5	LONDON SYMPHONY ORCHESTRA VOLUME II	12
88	Zappa Records ZAPPA 6	GUITAR (2-LP, gatefold sleeve)	18
88	Zappa Records ZAPPA 7	YOU CAN'T DO THAT ON STAGE ANY MORE SAMPLER (2-LP, gatefold sleeve)	18
88	Zappa Records ZAPPA 14	BROADWAY THE HARD WAY (gatefold sleeve with inner sleeve)	15
90	Zappa Records ZAPPA 30	THEM OR US (2-LP, gatefold sleeve, printed with lyrics)	15
90	Zappa Records ZAPPA 20	JOE'S GARAGE ACTS 1, 2 & 3 (3-LP, box set, original sleeves, with libretti)	30
91	Zappa Records ZAPPA 28	SHEIK YERBOUTI (2-LP, gatefold sleeve without lyrics)	18
91	Zappa Records ZAPPA 35	BURNT WEENY SANDWICH (gatefold sleeve)	12
91	Zappa Records ZAPPA 37	ZAPPA IN NEW YORK (LIVE) (2-LP, plays "Punky's Whips", listed on label, but not on sleeve)	18
91	Zappa Records ZAPPA 42	SHIP ARRIVING TOO LATE TO SAVE A DROWNING WITCH	12
92	Zappa Records ZAPPA 39	ROXY AND ELSEWHERE (2-LP, as Mothers Of Invention, gatefold lyric sleeve)	18

(see also Flo & Eddie, Jeff Simmons, Wild Man Fischer, Captain Beefheart, John Lennon, Geronimo Black)

MINT VALUE £

ZAP POW
72 Harry J HJ 6650 Lottery Spin/Lottery Spin — Version . . . 6
73 Trojan TR 7886 Nice Nice Time/Version . . . 6
73 Trojan TR 7741 This Is Reggae Music/Break Down The Barriers . . . 5
73 Blue Mountain BM 1027 This Is Reggae Music/Break Down The Barriers . . . 5
74 Island WIP 6181 This Is Reggae Music/Break Down The Barriers . . . 5

LES ZARJAZ
85 Creation CRE 014 One Charming Nyte/My Baby Owns A Fallout Zone (foldover p/s, poly bag) . . . 8
86 Kaleid. Sound KS 104 INTER BLOCK ROCK (12" EP) . . . 7
(see also Tronics)

JOE ZAWINUL
71 Atlantic 2400 151 ZAWINUL (LP) . . . 12
(see also Weather Report)

PETE ZEAR
80 (no label) matrix: 22-1 Tomorrow's World/Fast Food (stamped white label, with insert, numbered) . . . 10
(see also Ruts, Rat Scabies)

ZED
79 Initial IRC 003 VISIONS OF DUNE (LP) . . . 12

ZEE
84 Harvest HAR 5277 Confusion/Eyes Of A Gypsy (p/s) . . . 8
84 Harvest HAR 125277 Confusion (Extended Mix)/Eyes Of A Gypsy (Dub) (12", p/s) . . . 10
84 Harvest SHSP 2401 018 IDENTITY (LP, with inner sleeve) . . . 15
84 Harvest SHSP 2401 018 IDENTITY (cassette, with extra track) . . . 15
(see also Rick Wright)

ZEITGEIST
80 Enchaine ENC 1 Shake-Rake/Sniper (p/s) . . . 6

ZENITH
86 ZENITH 5001 Heavy Heavy Heart (p/s) . . . 100

ZENITH SIX
56 Tempo A 145 Climax Rag/The Chant . . . 6
57 Tempo A 159 Mahogany Hall Stomp/Cannon Ball Blues . . . 6
56 Decca DFE 6255 THE ZENITH SIX AT THE ROYAL FESTIVAL HALL (EP) . . . 10
56 Tempo EXA 42 THE ZENITH SIX (EP) . . . 10
57 Tempo EXA 58 THE ZENITH SIX (EP) . . . 10

SI ZENTNER ORCHESTRA
62 Liberty LIB 55374 (Up A) Lazy River/Shufflin' Blues . . . 7
64 Liberty LIB 10169 The James Bond Theme/Bond's 007 Theme . . . 8
63 Liberty LBY 1164 RHYTHM PLUS BLUES (LP) . . . 25

ZEPHYR
70 Probe SPB 1006 ZEPHYR (LP) . . . 40
(see also Tommy Bolin)

ZEPHYRS
63 Decca F 11647 What's All That About/Oriental Dream . . . 35
64 Columbia DB 7199 I Can Tell/Sweet Little Baby . . . 30
64 Columbia DB 7324 A Little Bit Of Soap/No Message . . . 30
64 Columbia DB 7410 Wonder What I'm Gonna Do/Let Me Love You Baby . . . 30
65 Columbia DB 7481 She's Lost You/There's Something About You . . . 30
65 Columbia DB 7571 I Just Can't Take It/She Laughed . . . 30

ZERO
75 BEEB 014 Angels Theme/Truckin' . . . 5

ZERO FIVE
65 Columbia DB 7751 Dusty/Just Like A Girl . . . 8

ZEROS
77 Small Wonder SMALL 2 Hungry/Radio Fun . . . 20
79 Rok ROK XV/XVI What's Wrong With A Pop Group/ACTION REPLAY: Decisions (die-cut co. sleeve) . . . 20

021
81 UK UK 201 Pop Song (p/s) . . . 120

ZERO 7
00 Ultimate Dilemma UDR EP VOL. 1 (12") . . . 18
00 Ultimate Dilemma UDR 040 EP VOL. 2 (12") . . . 18

ZERO ZERO SEVEN
80s Scanlite BOND 1 Message From Bond/James Bond Theme (p/s) . . . 5

ZERO ZERO SEVEN BAND
65 Marble Arch MAL 590 JAMES BOND THRILLERS (LP) . . . 12

CATHERINE ZETA JONES
92 Columbia 6583547 For All Time/The Appian Way (p/s) . . . 6

MONICA ZETTERLUND
59 Columbia SEG 8015 SWEDISH SWEET (EP) . . . 60
58 Columbia 33CSX 20 SWEDISH SENSATION (LP, export only) . . . 65

Z'EV
82 Fetish FE 13 Wipeout!/Element L. (p/s) . . . 10

WARREN ZEVON
76 Atlantic K 13060 I'll Sleep When I'm Dead/Mohammed's Radio . . . 5
78 Atlantic K 13111 Werewolves Of London/Tenderness On The Block . . . 5

ZIMM & DEE DEE
71 Green Door GD 4006 You've Got A Friend (actually by Winston Francis & Donna Hinds)/GROOVERS: Cheep . . . 7
(see also Winston Francis)

MINT VALUE £

TUCKER ZIMMERMAN

69	Regal Zonophone RZ 3020	The Red Wind/Moondog	6
69	Regal Zono. (S)LRZ 1010	TEN SONGS BY TUCKER ZIMMERMAN (LP)	20
72	Village Thing VTS 13	TUCKER ZIMMERMANN (LP)	20

ZIOR

71	Nepentha 6129 002	Za Za Za Zilda/She's A Bad Bad Woman	18
71	Nepentha 6129 003	Cat's Eyes/I Really Do	18
71	Nepentha 6437 005	ZIOR (LP, gatefold sleeve)	60

(see also Monument, Cardboard Orchestra)

ZIPPERS

64	Hickory 45-1252	My Sailor Boy/Pretend You're Still Mine	8

ZIPZ

80	Voyage VOY 14	As I Pass You By/Tonight (p/s)	18

ZODIAC

68	Elektra EKL 4009	COSMIC SOUNDS (LP, also stereo EKS 74009)	30

ZODIAC MINDWARP AND THE LOVE REACTION

87	Mercury WARP 3	Prime Mover/Laughing In The Face Of Death/Hangover From Hell (12", limited issue, black vinyl sleeve)	8
87	Mercury ZODR 212A	Backseat Education/Whore Of Babylon/Lager Woman From Hell/Messin' With My Best Friend's Girl (12", rubber sleeve)	8

ZODIAC MOTEL

87	Swordfish SWF 004	Sunshine Miner/Crescendo (p/s)	8
87	Swordfish ZOMO 1	Sunshine Miner/Crescendo/Inside My Mind/Sugarblood (12", p/s)	8
87	Swordfish ZOMO 2	Crystal Injection/I Can Only Give You Everything/Destiny Ranch/ Stephanie Blue (12", p/s)	8
87	Swordfish SWFLP 001	THE STORY OF ROLAND FLAGG (LP)	12

ZODIACS

57	Oriole CB 1383	Why Don't They Understand/The Game Of Love (78)	12
58	Oriole CB 1432	The Yum-Yum Song/Secrets	6
58	Oriole CB 1432	The Yum-Yum Song/Secrets (78)	12

ZAC ZOLAR & ELECTRIC BANANA

84	Butt FUN 5	Take Me Home/James Marshall	5

(see also Pretty Things, Phil May, Fenmen, Electric Banana)

ROB ZOMBIE

98	Geffen GFS 22367	Dragular/Halloween (picture disc)	5
98	Geffen GFS 22367	Dragular/Dragular (remix) (picture disc)	5

(see also White Zombie)

ZOMBIES

64	Decca F 11940	She's Not There/You Make Me Feel Good	10
64	Decca F 12004	Leave Me Be/Woman	10
65	Decca F 12072	Tell Her No/What More Can I Do	10
65	Decca F 12125	She's Coming Home/I Must Move	12
65	Decca F 12225	Whenever You're Ready/I Love You	12
65	Decca F 12296	Is This The Dream/Don't Go Away	12
66	Decca F 12322	Remember You/Just Out Of Reach	15
66	Decca F 12426	Indication/How We Were Before	15
66	Decca F 12495	Gotta Get A Hold Of Myself/The Way I Feel Inside	15
67	Decca F 12584	Goin' Out Of My Head/She Does Everything For Me	15
68	Decca F 12798	I Love You/The Way I Feel Inside	15
67	CBS 2960	Friends Of Mine/Beechwood Park	35
67	CBS 3087	Care Of Cell 44/Maybe After He's Gone	35
68	CBS 3380	Time Of The Season/I'll Call You Mine	35
65	Decca DFE 8598	THE ZOMBIES (EP)	110
65	Decca LK 4679	BEGIN HERE (LP)	275
68	CBS (S)BPG 63280	ODESSEY AND ORACLE (LP, mono/stereo)	200/150
73	Epic EPC 65728	TIME OF THE ZOMBIES (2-LP)	30
65	RCA RD 7791	BUNNY LAKE IS MISSING (LP, soundtrack)	60

(see also Unit Four Plus Two, Argent, Neil MacArthur, Colin Blunstone)

ZONES

78	Zoom ZUM 4	Stuck With You/No Angels (p/s)	6
78	Arista ARTIST 205	Sign Of The Times/Away From It All	5
79	Arista SPART 1095	UNDER INFLUENCE (LP, with inner sleeve)	12

(see also PVC 2)

ZOO

70	Major Minor SMLP 74	ZOO (LP)	30
71	Barclay 521172	ZOO (LP)	30

ZOOKIE

77	DJM DJS 10796	Judie Judie Hold On/I Couldn't Be You	8
78	DJM DJS 10866	Bubbles/Don't Rock Me	8

(see also Judie Tzuke, Tzuke & Paxo)

ZOOT

(see under Zoot Simms)

ZORN

01	City Centre Offices BLOCK 11	Eckerman (plain sleeve with inserts, 1000 only)	10

ZORRO

79	Bridgehouse BHEP 1	'Arrods Don't Sell 'Em/Soldier Boy/Starflight (some with p/s)	60/25

ZORRO FIVE

70	Decca F 23042	Reggae Shhh!/Reggae Meadowlands	5

MINT VALUE £

ZOSKIA
84 All The Madmen MAD 8 — Rape/Thank You (p/s) 18
85 Temple TOPY 005 — Be Like Me (12", p/s, transparent vinyl) 20
86 All The Madmen MADT 8 — Rape/Black Action (12", p/s) 6

ZOSKIA MEETS SUGARDOG
84 Temple TOPYS 021 — J.G. /'That's Heavy Baby 10

ZOUNDS
81 Crass 4219844/3 — Can't Cheat Karma/War/Subvert (gatefold paper p/s, with poster) 8
81 Rough Trade RT 069 — Demystification/Great White Hunter (p/s) 8
82 Rough Trade RT 094 — Dancing/True Love (p/s) 8
82 Not So Brave NSB 001 — LA VACHE QUI RIT (EP, with poster) 8
82 Rough Trade RT 098 — More Trouble Coming Every Day/Knife (p/s) 10
80s Recommended RR 14.15 — Menáge (12.59) (1-sided, other side printed, foldout sleeve in PVC sleeve) 8
84 Rough Trade ROUGH 31 — THE CURSE OF ZOUNDS (LP) 12

ZOVIET-FRANCE
82 Red Rhino RED 12 — ZOVIET-FRANCE (12" EP, printed hessian sleeve) 60
83 Red Rhink RED 23 — NORSCHE (LP) 40
84 Red Rhink RED 40 — MOHNOMISCHE (LP) 40
84 Red Rhino REDLP 45 — ELSTRE (LP) 40

ZUIDERZEE
66 CBS 202062 — (You're My) Soul And Inspiration/Please Don't Call Me 6
66 CBS 202235 — Peace Of Mind/Provocative Child 8

TAPPA ZUKIE
76 KLIK 9022 — M.P.L.A. (LP) 18

ZUTONS
02 Deltasonic DKTCD 007 — Devil's Deal/Six Foot Man/Zutonkhamuun (CD) 20
03 Deltasonic DLT011 — Creepin' An A Crawlin'/Rumblin' Ramblin' (p/s, with sticker) 5

ZYGOAT
74 Polydor 2058 124 — Catching A Thief/Letitia's Song 5
74 Polydor 2383 270 — ELECTROPHON (LP) 15

ZZEBRA
74 Polydor 2058 446 — Zardoz/Amusofi 5
75 Polydor 2058 579 — Mr. J/Put The Light On Me 5
74 Polydor 2383 296 — ZZEBRA (LP) 12
75 Polydor 2383 326 — PANIC (LP) 12
(see also John McCoy, Gillan)

ZZ TOP
72 London HLU 10376 — Francene/Down Brownie 18
74 London HLU 10458 — Beer Drinkers And Hell Raisers/La Grange 12
75 London HLU 10475 — La Grange/Just Got Paid 18
75 London HLU 10495 — Tush/Blue Jean Blues 12
76 London HLU 10538 — It's Only Love/Asleep In The Desert 10
77 London HLU 10547 — Arrested For Driving While Blind/Neighbour, Neighbour 15
77 London HLU 10547 — Arrested For Driving While Blind/Neighbour, Neighbour (mispressing, B-side plays Ray Charles' "I Can See Clearly Now") 18
79 Warner Bros K 17647 — Cheap Sunglasses/Esther Be The One 8
80 Warner Bros K 17576 — I Thank You/A Fool For Your Stockings (p/s) 8
83 Warner Bros W 9693T — Gimme All Your Lovin'/If I Could Only Flag Her Down (car-shaped picture disc) 15
84 Warner Bros W 9334 — T.V. Dinners/Cheap Sunglasses (p/s) 5
84 Warner Bros W 9334T — T.V. Dinners (Full Length)/Cheap Sunglasses (12", p/s) 8
84 Warner Bros W 9334T — T.V. Dinners (Full Length)/Cheap Sunglasses//Legs (Metal Mix)/A Fool For Your Stockings (12" double pack) 10
84 Warner Bros W 9576 — Sharp Dressed Man/I Got The Fix (p/s) 5
84 Warner Bros W 9576T — Sharp Dressed Man/I Got The Fix/La Grange (12", p/s, some shrinkwrapped with sticker) 8
85 Warner Bros W 2001 — Sleeping Bag/Party On The Patio (p/s) 5
85 Warner Bros W 2001F — Sleeping Bag/Party On The Patio//Sharp Dressed Man/I Got The Fix (p/s, sealed, stickered double pack) 10
85 Warner Bros W 2001P — Sleeping Bag/Party On The Patio ('sphinx'-shaped picture disc) 10
85 Warner Bros W 2001P — Sleeping Bag/Party On The Patio (shaped pic-disc, part 1 of interlocking set) 25
85 Warner Bros W 2001DP — Sleeping Bag/Party On The Patio ('sleeping bag'-shaped picture disc) 10
85 Warner Bros W 2001T — Sleeping Bag/Party On The Patio/Blue Jean Blues (12", p/s) 10
86 Warner Bros W 2002 — Stages/Hi-Fi Mama (p/s) 5
86 Warner Bros W 2002BP — Stages/Hi-Fi Mama (shaped pic-disc, part 2 of interlocking set) 8
86 Warner Bros W 2002T — Stages (Extended Mix)/Stages/Hi-Fi Mama (12", p/s) 8
86 Warner Bros W 2003 — Rough Boy/Delirious (p/s) 5
86 Warner Bros W 2003FP — Rough Boy/Delirious (shaped pic-disc, part 3 of interlocking set, some shrinkwrapped with bonus 12") 30/20
86 Warner Bros W 2003T — Rough Boy/Delirious/Legs (12", p/s with poster) 8
86 Warner Bros W 8946 — SUMMER HOLIDAY EP: Beer Drinkers And Hell Raisers/I'm Bad, I'm Nationwide//Tush/Got Me Under Pressure (p/s) 5
72 London SH-U 8433 — RIO GRANDE MUD (LP, original issue) 20
73 London SH-U 8459 — TRES HOMBRES (LP, original issue) 20
75 London SH-U 8482 — FANDANGO! (LP, original issue) 15
76 London LDU 1 — TEJAS (LP, original foldout sleeve) 15
83 Warner Bros W 3774 — ELIMINATOR (LP, with bonus stickered p/s 12" "Legs [Metal Mix]") 18
85 Warner Bros W 3774P — ELIMINATOR (LP, picture disc) 12
87 Warner Bros 925 661-2 — ZZ TOP'S FIRST ALBUM/RIO GRANDE MUD/TRES HOMBRES/FANDANGO/TEJAS/EL LOCO (3-CD set of 1st 6 LPs, with booklet) 35

ZZY
91 Zebedee MAGICD 06 — Is This The Last Time?/Heading For The Light (Of The Soul) (CD) 15
93 Zebedee MAGICD 17 — Six Months From Freedom/Six Months From Freedom (You Think)/Six Months From Freedom (Don't Think, Act) (CD) 10

Various Artists

VARIOUS ARTISTS EPs 50s/60s (alphabetical by title)

A

56	Decca F 10752	ALL STAR HIT PARADE (Dickie Valentine/Joan Regan/Winifred Atwell/ Dave King/Lita Roza/David Whitfield)	12
57	Decca F 10915	ALL STAR HIT PARADE No. 2 (Johnston Bros/Bill Cotton/Jimmy Young/ Max Bygraves/Beverley Sisters/Tommy Steele)	12
63	Pye NEP 24168	ALL STAR HIT PARADE (Kenny Ball/Chris Barber Jazz Band/Joe Brown/ Lonnie Donegan Skiffle Group/Mary Wynter)	12
64	Pye NEP 24172	ALL STAR HIT PARADE VOL. 2 (Joe Brown/Petula Clark/Julie Grant/ Benny Hill/Mark Wynter)	12
64	Decca DFE 8571	AMERICAN COUNTRY JUBILEE NO. 1 (Ray Phillips/Audrey Inman/ Marvin McCullough/Billy Parker)	12

B

63	Concert Hall BPC 712	BEAT TIME (Timebeats/Charlie Young/Heartbeats)	18
57	Philips BBE 12148	THE BELLS ARE RINGING (Tony Bennett/Vic Damone/De John Sisters/ Jo Stafford)	10
60s	Melodisc EPM7 115	BEST OF BLUEGRASS (COUNTRY STRINGS) (Bill Browning/Buzz Busby/ Country Gentlemen/Williams Brothers)	10
58	Philips BBE 12225	BEST WISHES FOR CHRISTMAS (Beverley Sisters/David Hughes/ Wally Scott Orchestra)	8
59	Mercury ZEP 10024	THE BIG BAND SOUND (Quincy Jones/Ralph Marterie Orchestra)	8
63	Concert Hall BPC 717	THE BIG BEAT (Bob Miller & Millermen/Al Saxon/Roy Young/Duffy Power)	18
65	Embassy WT 2008	THE BIG FOUR (Jaybirds/Redd Wayne/Les Carle/Joan Baxter)	10
65	Embassy WT 2011	THE BIG FOUR (Jaybirds/Terry Brandon/Les Carle/Typhoons)	10
66	Fontana TF 17469	THE BIG FOUR (Dave Dee Dozy Beaky Mick & Tich/Spencer Davis Group/ Mindbenders/Pretty Things)	12
56	Philips BBE 12021	THE BIG FOUR (Roy Hamilton/Frankie Laine/Mitch Miller Orchestra/ Something Smith & Redheads)	15
56	Philips BBE 12040	THE BIG FOUR NO. 2 (Mindy Carson/Don Cherry/Frankie Laine/Jo Stafford)	15
56	Philips BBE 12088	THE BIG FOUR NO. 3 (Shirley Bassey/Ronnie Carroll/David Hughes/ Anne Shelton)	12
56	Philips BBE 12091	THE BIG FOUR NO. 4 (Rosemary Clooney/Doris Day/Four Lads/Frankie Laine)	15
57	Philips BBE 12114	THE BIG FOUR NO. 5 (Shirley Bassey/Ronnie Carroll/Anne Shelton/ Frankie Vaughan)	12
57	Philips BBE 12139	THE BIG FOUR NO. 6 (Shirley Bassey/Ronnie Carroll/Kaye Sisters/ Frankie Vaughan)	12
57	Philips BBE 12145	THE BIG FOUR NO. 7 (Tony Bennett/Doris Day/Guy Mitchell/Johnnie Ray)	15
57	Philips BBE 12158	THE BIG FOUR NO. 8 (Shirley Bassey/Robert Earl/Kaye Sisters/Steve Martin)	12
58	Philips BBE 12165	THE BIG FOUR NO. 9 (Robert Earl/Anne Shelton/Joyce Shock/ Frankie Vaughan & Kaye Sisters)	12
58	Philips BBE 12190	THE BIG FOUR NO. 10 (Jimmy Lloyd/Robert Earl/Kaye Sisters/Anne Shelton)	12
59	Philips BBE 12288	THE BIG FOUR NO. 11 (Shirley Bassey/Kaye Sisters/Frankie Vaughan/ Marty Wilde)	12
59	Philips BBE 12336	THE BIG FOUR NO. 12 (Frankie Laine/G. Mitchell/Johnnie Ray/Leslie Uggams)	15
66	Philips BBE 12593	THE BIG FOUR (Roger Miller/Four Seasons/Dusty Springfield/Walker Bros)	12
64	Fontana TFE 18010	BLOWIN' IN THE WIND (withdrawn; Bob Dylan/Joan Baez/Pete Seeger)	100
60s	Range JRE 7005	BLUEGRASS (Coney Carver/Freeman Ervin)	8
59	Fontana TFE 17081	THE BLUES (Danny Barker/Jimmy Giuffre/Jo Jones/Pee Wee Russell)	8
61	Pieces Of 8 PEP 605	THE BLUES (Big Bill Broonzy/Josh White)	12
64	Pye Intl. NEP 44029	THE BLUES VOL. 1 PT. 1 (John Lee Hooker/Muddy Waters/Sonny Boy Williamson/Jimmy Witherspoon)	30
64	Pye Intl. NEP 44035	THE BLUES VOL. 1 PT. 2 (Howling Wolf/Buddy Guy/Little Walter/ Muddy Waters)	30
66	Chess CRE 6011	THE BLUES VOL. 2 PT. 1 (Otis Rush/Chuck Berry/John Lee Hooker/ Little Walter)	30
64	Pye Intl. NEP 44038	BLUES FESTIVAL (Sugar Pie De Santo/Willie Dixon/Sonny Boy Williamson/ Howlin' Wolf)	30
63	Columbia SEG 8226	BLUES ON PARADE NO. 1 (Jimmy Cotton/Brownie McGhee/ Roosevelt Sykes/Sonny Terry)	25
56	HMV 7EG 8178	THE BLUES THEY SANG (Lizzie Miles/Billy Young & Jelly Roll Morton)	25
61	Pye NEP 24142	BYE BYE BIRDIE (Brook Brothers/Patti Brook/Joe Brown/Jimmy Justice/ Kids/Viscounts)	15
61	RCA RCX 205	BREAKFAST AT TIFFANY'S (Henry Mancini)	20
61	Philips BBE 12472	BYE BYE BIRDIE NO. 1 (original cast; Marty Wilde et al.; stereo SBBE 9064)	12/15
61	Philips BBE 12473	BYE BYE BIRDIE NO. 2 (original cast; Marty Wilde et al.; stereo SBBE 9065)	12/15
61	Philips BBE 12474	BYE BYE BIRDIE NO. 3 (original cast; Marty Wilde et al.; stereo SBBE 9066)	12/15
61	Philips BBE 12475	BYE BYE BIRDIE NO. 4 (original cast; Marty Wilde et al.; stereo SBBE 9067)	12/15

MINT VALUE £

C

Year	Label / Cat. No.	Title	Value £
63	Cameo Parkway CPE 552	CAMEO BIG FOUR (Bobby Rydell/Chubby Checker/Dovells/Orlons)	25
59	Mercury ZEP 10014	CHA CHA FOR NOW (Jan August/Sil Austin/Jerry Murad's Harmonicats)	8
62	Topic TOP 74	THE COLLIERS' RANT (Louis Killen/Johnny Handle/Colin Ross)	10
53	Columbia SCD 2008	COLUMBIA CAVALCADE (Marie Benson/Steve Conway/Beverley Sisters/ Teddy Johnson/Steve Race/Johnny Brandon/Ronnie Ronalde/Ensemble)	8
60s	Range JRE 7001	COUNTRY AND WESTERN (Jim Chriss/Bob Strack/Jimmy Strickland)	8
60s	Range JRE 7004	COUNTRY AND WESTERN (Gabe Dean/Jimmy Dry/Rex Dario)	8
60	Top Rank JKP 2055	COUNTRY AND WESTERN EXPRESS VOL. 1 (Bill Alex Dixie Drifters/ Jenny Herrill/Elmer Snodgrass/Musical Pioneers)	10
60	Top Rank JKP 2056	COUNTRY AND WESTERN EXPRESS VOL. 2 (Jack Chambers & Rainbow Boys/Ralph Hodge & Hodges Brothers Band)	10
60	Top Rank JKP 2063	COUNTRY AND WESTERN EXPRESS VOL. 4 (Claude Gray/Eddie Noack)	22
60	Top Rank JKP 2065	COUNTRY AND WESTERN EXPRESS VOL. 6 (Tony Douglas/James O'Gwynn)	22
63	CBS AGG 20033	COUNTRY AND WESTERN HITS VOL. 1 (Carl Butler/Lester Flatt & Earl Scruggs/Lefty Frizzell/Stonewall Jackson/Ray Price)	10
64	CBS AGG 20041	COUNTRY AND WESTERN HITS VOL. 2 (Johnny Cash/Lester Flatt & Earl Scruggs/Lefty Frizzell/Marty Robbins)	12
65	Hickory LPE 1505	COUNTRY AND WESTERN SHOWCASE VOL. 2 (Roy Acuff/Wilma Lee/ Stoney Cooper)	10
57	Philips BBE 12149	COUNTRY AND WESTERN SPECTACULAR (George Morgan/Ray Price/ Mel Tillis/Marty Robbins)	12
59	Mercury ZEP 10038	COUNTRY AND WESTERN TRAIL BLAZERS NO. 1 (Connie Hall/ James O'Gwynn/Jimmy Skinner/Charlie Walker)	12
60	Mercury ZEP 10052	COUNTRY AND WESTERN TRAIL BLAZERS NO. 2 (Bill Clifton & Dixie Mountain Boys/George Jones)	12
60	Mercury ZEP 10080	COUNTRY AND WESTERN TRAIL BLAZERS NO. 3 (James O'Gwynn/ Connie Hall)	12
60s	Heritage 105	THE COUNTRY BLUES (99 only)	60
58	RCA RCX 107	COUNTRY GUITAR VOL. 1 (Bonnie, Jim Edward & Maxine Brown/ Hank Locklin/Jim Reeves/Hank Snow)	12
58	RCA RCX 110	COUNTRY GUITAR VOL. 2 (Skeeter Davis/Don Gibson/Jim Reeves/Hank Snow)	15
59	RCA RCX 127	COUNTRY GUITAR VOL. 5 (Eddy Arnold/Browns/Skeeter Davis/ Johnny & Jack/Hank Snow/Porter Wagoner)	12
59	RCA RCX 141	COUNTRY GUITAR VOL. 6 (Hank Locklin/Eddy Arnold/Browns/Hank Snow/ Porter Wagoner/Johnny & Jack)	12
59	RCA RCX 147	COUNTRY GUITAR VOL. 8 (Browns/Don Gibson/Hawkshaw Hawkins/ Johnny & Jack/Jim Reeves)	12
59	RCA RCX 159	COUNTRY GUITAR VOL. 9 (Hank Locklin/Gail Davis/Skeeter Davis/Jimmy Driftwood/Jim Reeves)	15
59	RCA RCX 176	COUNTRY GUITAR VOL. 10 (Hank Locklin/Skeeter Davis/Hawkshaw Hawkins/Johnny & Jack/Sons Of The Pioneers/Hank Snow)	15
59	RCA RCX 177	COUNTRY GUITAR VOL. 11 (Browns/Eddy Arnold/Jack Clement/Hank Snow)	12
60	RCA RCX 185	COUNTRY GUITAR VOL. 12 (Eddy Arnold/Hawkshaw Hawkins/Jim Reeves/ Hank Snow/Porter Wagoner)	12
62	RCA RCX 7105	COUNTRY GUITAR VOL. 16 (Bill Monroe & Blue Grass Boys/Monroe Bros)	15
63	Decca DFE 8522	COUNTRY JUBILEE VOL. 1 (Sonny Miller/Ray Phillips/Ott Stephens/ Sonny Williams)	10
63	Decca DFE 8523	COUNTRY JUBILEE VOL. 2 (Kendall Hayes/Margie Laffery/ Lonesome Pine Fiddlers/Marvin McCullough)	10

D

Year	Label / Cat. No.	Title	Value £
56	Mercury MEP 9509	DAMN YANKEES (Rusty Draper/Vic Damone/Patti Page/Sarah Vaughan)	10
54	Capitol EAP1 518	DANCE CRAZE (Ray Anthony/Pee Wee Hunt/Stan Kenton)	10
60s	XX MIN 706	DARK MUDDY BOTTOM (Jimmy Slim/Good Jelly Bess/Lightning Leon/ Little Red Walters/Willie B.)	18
58	MGM MGM-EP 652	DEEP IN MY HEART Excerpts (Rosemary Clooney/Vic Damone/Tony Martin/ Jane Powell/Helen Traubel)	8
50s	Poydras 102	DEPRESSION BLUES	25
63	Decca DFE 8520	DISCS-A-GO GO (Karl Denver/Billy Fury/Jet Harris/Vernons Girls)	55
60s	Jan & Dil JR 450	DOWN HOME BLUES — SIXTIES STYLE (Lightning Leon/Jerry McCain/ Little Red Walters)	25
60s	XX MIN 709	DOWNHOME HARP (Kid Thomas/Eddie Hope/Jerry McCain)	15
59	Fontana TFE 17146	DRUMBEAT (Lana Sisters/Adam Faith/Bob Miller & Millermen/ Sylvia Sands/Roy Young)	40

E

Year	Label / Cat. No.	Title	Value £
65	Edinburgh S.C. ESC 02	EDINBURGH STUDENTS CHARITIES APPEAL (33rpm, die-cut paper p/s; Athenians/Avengers/Ray & Archie Fisher/Lynn & Kathy)	50
66	Edinburgh S.C. ESC 03	EDINBURGH STUDENTS CHARITIES APPEAL (33rpm, Athenians/Gear System/Old Bailey's Jazz Advocates)	60
60	Felsted ESD 3083	AN EVENING AT LA POUBELLE (Curly Hamner/Ben Dalida/Wackadous)	8
67	Philips P 160E	EXQUISITE FORM (freebie; Dave Dee, Dozy, Beaky, Mick & Tich/Herd/ Walker Brothers/Dusty Springfield)	18

F

Year	Label / Cat. No.	Title	Value £
59	Jazz Collector JEL 12	THE FEMALE BLUES VOL. 1 (Ida Cox/Ma Rainey)	18
60	Jazz Collector JEL 14	THE FEMALE BLUES VOL. 2 (Bertha Henderson/Rosa Henderson)	18
64	Jazz Collector JEL 22	THE FEMALE BLUES VOL. 3 (Ma Rainey/Trixie Smith)	18
64	Pye Intl. NEP 44030	FESTIVAL OF THE BLUES NO. 1 (Willie Dixon/Buddy Guy/Muddy Waters/ Sonny Boy Williamson)	22
58	Parlophone GEP 8694	FLUTE COCKTAIL (Bill Doggett/Johnny Pate Quartet)	10
66	HMV 7EG 8911	FOLKSOUND OF BRITAIN (Cyril Tawney/Lewis Johns/John Steele)	8
63	Ember EMB EP 4530	FOOL BRITANNIA (Peter Sellers/Dan Massey/Anthony Newley/Joan Collins/ Maureen Lipton)	12
57	Philips BBE 12140	FOUR GREAT MOVIE THEMES (Vic Damone/Hi-Lo's/Frankie Laine/Jerry Vale)	12

			MINT VALUE £
68	CBS WEP 1138	FOUR YOU (Gary Puckett, Johnny Mathis, Simon & Garfunkel, Tremeloes)	8
63	Decca DFE 8538	FROM A LONDON HOOTENANNY (Davy Graham/Thamesiders)	15

G

59	MGM MGM-EP 703	GIRLS AND MORE GIRLS (June Allyson/Ava Gardner/Judy Garland/ Kathryn Grayson)	10
67	Down with the Game 202	GOD DON'T LIKE IT	30
67	Down with the Game 203	GOD DON'T LIKE IT VOLUME 2	30
60s	XX MIN 707	GOING TO CALIFORNIA (Little Sonny Willis/Eddie Williams)	15
59	Philips BBE 12318	GREAT COUNTRY AND WESTERN HITS (Johnny Cash/Johnny Horton/ Stonewall Jackson/Carl Smith)	15
66	Pye Intl. NEP 45054	THE GREATEST ON STAGE (Maxine Brown/Chuck Jackson/Shirelles/ Dionne Warwick)	20
67	CBS WEP 1131	GREAT SCREEN THEMES (John Barry/Percy Faith & His Orchestra)	8
63	London RE-U 1393	GROUP OF GOODIES (Marcie Blane/Kokomo/Bill Black's Combo/ Ernie Maresca)	45
59	Mercury ZEP 10010	GROUPS GALORE (Del Vikings/Mark IV/Diamonds/Hi-Liters)	150
56	Philips BBE 12077	GUYS AND DOLLS (Frankie Laine/Rosemary Clooney/Jo Stafford/Jerry Vale)	12

H

64	Hickory LPE 1500	HICKORY SHOWCASE VOL. 1 (Roy Acuff/Wilma Lee/Stoney Cooper)	10
64	Hickory LPE 1501	HICKORY SHOWCASE VOL. 2 (Bobby Lord/Bob Luman)	20
64	Hickory LPE 1504	HICKORY SHOWCASE VOL. 3 (Bobby Lord/Bob Luman)	20
57	Capitol EAP1 852	HIT CALYPSOS (Andrews Sisters/Nat 'King' Cole/Stan Kenton/ Lord Flea Calypsonians)	10
55	MGM MGM-EP 525	HIT THE DECK — SOUNDTRACK EXCERPTS (Tony Martin/Jane Powell/ Debbie Reynolds)	8
55	MGM MGM-EP 526	HIT THE DECK — SOUNDTRACK EXCERPTS (Tony Martin/Jane Powell/ Anne Miller/Vic Damone)	8
65	Pye NEP 24213	THE HITMAKERS NO. 1 (Searchers/Kenny Ball Jazzmen/Dixie Cups/ Dionne Warwick)	15
65	Pye NEP 24214	THE HITMAKERS NO. 2 (Honeycombs/Tony Jackson/Kinks/Shangri-La's)	25
65	Pye NEP 24215	THE HITMAKERS NO. 3 (Chuck Berry/Julie Grant/Rockin' Berries/ Sandie Shaw)	18
66	Pye NEP 24241	THE HITMAKERS VOL. 1 (Ivy League/Tommy Quickly/Sandie Shaw/ Sounds Orchestral)	12
66	Pye NEP 24242	THE HITMAKERS VOL. 2 (Chuck Berry/Kinks/Sue Thompson/ Shangri-La's)	30
66	Pye NEP 24243	THE HITMAKERS VOL. 3 (Kinks/Lancastrians/Rockin' Berries/Searchers)	15
66	Piccadilly NEP 34100	THE HITMAKERS (Petula Clark/Kenny Ball/Anita Harris/Honeycombs)	10
66	Pye Intl. NEP 44065	HITMAKERS INTERNATIONAL (Fontella Bass/James Brown/Petula Clark/ Lovin' Spoonful)	25
56	Mercury MEP 9003	HIT PARADE VOL. 1 (Georgia Gibbs/Platters/Crew Cuts/Patti Page)	20
56	Mercury MEP 9510	HIT PARADE VOL. 2 (Sarah Vaughan/Ralph Marterie/Patti Page/Crew Cuts)	20
57	Brunswick OE 9340	HIT PARADE (Rex Allen/Peggy Lee/Jeri Southern/Victor Young Orchestra)	10
58	Brunswick OE 9450	HIT PARADE NO. 2 (Carmen Cavallaro/Four Aces/Grandpa Jones/ Jack Pleis & His Orchestra)	12
65	Decca DFE 8648	HITS VOL. 1 (Chris Andrews/Fortunes/Hedgehoppers Anonymous/ Jonathan King)	10
65	Decca DFE 8649	HITS VOL. 2 (Lulu/Chris Andrews/Marianne Faithfull/Fortunes)	12
65	Decca DFE 8653	HITS VOL. 3 (Pinkerton's Assorted Colours/St. Louis Union/Mexicans/ Paul & Barry Ryan)	15
66	Decca DFE 8662	HITS VOL. 4 (Dave Berry/Val Doonican/Joy Marshall/Crispian St. Peters)	12
66	Decca DFE 8663	HITS VOL. 5 (Animals/Los Bravos/Alan Price Set/Small Faces)	15
66	Decca DFE 8667	HITS VOL. 6 (Jonathan King/Lulu/Alan Price Set/Small Faces)	15
67	Decca DFE 8675	HITS VOL. 7 (Ronnie Aldrich/Val Doonican/Bachelors/Small Faces)	15
55	Capitol EAP1 482	HITS FROM CAN CAN (Les Baxter Orchestra/Nat 'King' Cole/Gordon MacRae/ Kay Starr)	8
62	Mercury ZEP 10133	HITSVILLE! (Brook Benton/Crew Cuts/Phil Philips/Diamonds)	30
59	Coral FEP 2034	HITSVILLE VOL. 1 (Buddy Holly/McGuire Sisters/Betty Madigan/ Billy Williams)	65
59	Coral FEP 2035	HITSVILLE VOL. 2 (Lennon Sisters/Art Lund/Teresa Brewer/ Jackie Wilson)	45
65	Tamla Motown TME 2001	HITSVILLE U.S.A. NO. 1 (Marvin Gaye/Brenda Holloway/Carolyn Crawford/ Eddie Holland)	125
66	Post War Blues 100	HOBOS AND DRIFTERS	40
58	Topic TOP 37	HOOTENANNY N.Y.C.	12

I

65	Chess CRE 6010	IN CROWD (Radiants/Ramsey Lewis Trio/Little Milton/Billy Stewart)	40
64	Concert Hall M 981	INTERNATIONAL FOLKLORE	8
56	Mercury MEP 9503	ITEMS FROM GUYS AND DOLLS (Richard Hayes/Kitty Kallen/Frankie Laine/ David Le Winter)	12
59	Mercury ZEP 10001	IT'S CHA CHA TIME (Jan August & Richard Hayman Orchestra/Jerry Murad's Harmonicats/Hi Liters/Ray Marterie Orchestra)	8
56	Columbia SEG 7639	IT'S GREAT TO BE YOUNG — FILM TUNES (Ruby Murray/Coronets/ Ray Martin Orchestra/Mr Dingle)	8
62	Pye Jazz NJE 1083	IT'S TRAD, DAD — FILM SOUNDTRACK (Bob Wallis/Kenny Ball & His Jazzmen)	15

J

67	Natchez NEP-701	THE JUG BANDS VOLUME 1	15
64	Columbia SEG 8337	JUST FOR YOU (Peter & Gordon/Freddie & Dreamers)	18

MINT VALUE £

K

63	Lyntone LYN 347/348	KEELE RAG RECORD (flexidisc; Rhythm Unlimited & Halettes/Keele Quintet)	18
64	Lyntone LYN 508/509	KEELE RAG RECORD NO. 2 (flexidisc; Escorts/Lance Harvey & Kingpins/ Keele Row; some in die-cut sleeve)	35/30
65	Lyntone LYN 765/766	KEELE RAG RECORD (flexidisc; Bob Wilson/Changing Times/ Lance Harvey & Kingpins/Incas)	45
56	London RE-E 1047	THE KING AND QUEEN OF R&B (Ruth Brown/Joe Turner)	200
61	RCA Victor RCX 203	KINGS OF THE BLUES VOL. 2 (Jazz Gillum/Big Maceo/Washboard Sam/ Sonny Boy Williamson)	18
61	RCA Victor RCX 204	KINGS OF THE BLUES VOL. 3 (Arthur Big Boy Crudup/Furry Lewis/ Poor Joe Williams)	20
59	Top Rank 45-TR 5004	KING SIZE (maxi-single; Craig Douglas/Sheila Buxton/Bert Weedon)	12
55	Mercury EP-1 3160	KISMET (Vic Damone/Georgia Gibbs/Ross Bagdasarian)	10
60	Warner Bros WEP 6010	KOOKIE STARS OF SEVENTY SEVEN SUNSET STRIP (Joannie Sommers/Eddie Byrne/Connie Stevens)	15

L

66	Holyground HG 111	THE LAST THING ON MY MIND (EP, 99 copies only)	80
59	Top Rank JKR 8008	LET'S GO NO. 1 (Jimmy Lee/Johnny Hines/Treetoppers)	25
59	Top Rank JKR 8012	LET'S GO NO. 2 (Johnny Hines/Billy Mack/Victors/Ted & Ray)	25
60	Philips BBE 12414/ SBBE 9031	LET'S MAKE LOVE — FILM SOUNDTRACK (Yves Montand/Marilyn Monroe/ Frankie Vaughan; mono/stereo)	60/75
57	London RE-D 1075	LONDON HIT PARADE NO. 1 (Tab Hunter/Hilltoppers/Pat Boone/ Fontane Sisters)	25
57	London RE-P 1096	LONDON HIT PARADE NO. 2 (Fats Domino/Slim Whitman/Ken Copeland/ Roy Brown)	90
58	London RE-D 1097	LONDON HIT PARADE NO. 3 (Pat Boone/Gale Storm/Tab Hunter/Jim Lowe)	25
58	London RE-D 1130	LONDON HIT PARADE NO. 4 (Pat Boone/Nick Todd/ Bonnie Guitar/Hilltoppers)	25
58	London RE-D 1136	LONDON TOPPERS NO. 2 (export issue; Pat Boone/Nick Todd/Tab Hunter/ Jim Lowe)	25
58	London RE-P 1137	LONDON TOPPERS NO. 3 (export issue; Slim Whitman/Fats Domino/ Ricky Nelson/Ernie Freeman)	80
58	London RE-D 1145	LONDON HIT PARADE NO. 5 (Pat Boone/Fontane Sisters/Frank De Rosa)	22

M

59	Jazz Collector JEL 2	THE MALE BLUES VOL. 1 (Georgia Slim/Walter Roland)	20
59	Jazz Collector JEL 4	THE MALE BLUES VOL. 3 (Blind Blake/Ramblin' Thomas)	20
59	Jazz Collector JEL 5	THE MALE BLUES VOL. 4 (Tall Tom/Pinewood Tom)	20
59	Jazz Collector JEL 8	THE MALE BLUES VOL. 5 (Blind Lemon Jefferson/Buddy Boy Hawkins)	20
60	Jazz Collector JEL 10	THE MALE BLUES VOL. 6 (Hound Head Henry/Frankie Jaxon)	20
60	Jazz Collector JEL 13	THE MALE BLUES VOL. 7 (Blind Lemon Jefferson/Ed Bell)	20
61	Jazz Collector JEL 24	THE MALE BLUES VOL. 8 (Blind Lemon Jefferson/Leadbelly)	20
67	Piccadilly NEP 34100	MAXWELL HOUSE PRESENTS HITMAKERS (Kenny Ball/Petula Clark/Honeycombs/Anita Harris)	10
57	Decca DFE 6408	MERRY CHRISTMAS (Dave King/Mantovani Orchestra/Dickie Valentine/ David Whitfield)	15
60	MGM MGM-EP 749	MGM EVERGREENS (Billy Eckstine/Tommy Edwards/Lennie Hayton/ Sam 'The Man' Taylor & Catmen)	15
69	Middle Earth MDE 201	MIDDLE EARTH SAMPLER (WRITING ON THE WALL: Aries/WOODEN O: Overture/ARCADIUM: Poor Lady) (promo only, 33rpm, no p/s)	100
64	RCA RCX 7159	MONTH'S BEST FROM THE COUNTRY AND WEST (Eddy Arnold/Bobby Bare/George Hamilton IV/Connie Smith)	10
64	RCA RCX 7162	MONTH'S BEST FROM THE COUNTRY AND WEST VOL. 2 (Skeeter Davis/Bobby Bare/Don Gibson/Jim Reeves/Hank Snow)	10
64	RCA RCX 7171	MONTH'S BEST FROM THE COUNTRY AND WEST VOL. 3 (Eddy Arnold/Archie Campbell/Porter Wagoner/Dottie West)	10
65	RCA RCX 7172	MONTH'S BEST FROM THE COUNTRY AND WEST VOL. 4 (Bobby Bare/Jim Edward Brown/Willie Nelson/Connie Smith)	10
65	RCA RCX 7178	MONTH'S BEST FROM THE COUNTRY AND WEST VOL. 5 (Bobby Bare/Norma Jean/Porter Wagoner/Connie Smith)	10
65	RCA RCX 7181	MONTH'S BEST FROM THE COUNTRY AND WEST VOL. 6 (Don Gibson/ Bobby Bare/Carl Belew/George Hamilton IV/Hank Locklin/Dottie West)	10
67	RCA RCX 7186	MONTH'S BEST FROM THE COUNTRY AND WEST VOL. 7 (Waylon Jennings/ Stu Phillips/Connie Smith/Dottie West)	10
60s	Jan & Dil TR 451	MORE DOWN HOME BLUES (Good Jelly Boss/Juke Boy Bonner/ Papa Lightfoot/Snooky Prior)	30
60	Philips BBE 12348	MOST HAPPY FELLA HITS (Doris Day/Four Lads/Frankie Laine/Jo Stafford)	12
64	Stateside SE 1021	MOVIE MUSIC (John Barry/Artie Butler/Eddie Heywood/Bill Ramal Combo)	20
60s	Mercury YARD 002	MUSIC FOR 5 AM (promo for Yardley; Hollies & others)	12

N

56	Vogue EPV 1106	NEGRO SPIRITUALS (Original Five Blind Boys/Sensational Nightingales)	18
64	Vocalion EPVP 1271	NEGRO SPIRITUALS (Dixie Hummingbirds/Sensational Nightingales)	18
64	Vocalion EPVP 1276	NEGRO SPIRITUALS (Five Blind Boys/Spirits Of Memphis)	18
66	Tamla Motown TME 2014	NEW FACES FROM HITSVILLE (Jimmy Ruffin/Chris Clark & Lewis Sisters/ Tammi Terrell/Monitors)	225
57	Pye NEP 24052	NIXA HIT PARADE NO. 1 (Gary Miller/Pet Clark/Lonnie Donegan/John Frazer)	15
58	Pye NEP 24064	NIXA HIT PARADE NO. 2 (Pearl Carr & Teddy Johnson/Petula Clark/ Lonnie Donegan Skiffle Group/Colin Hicks & Cabin Boys)	25
58	Pye NEP 24071	NIXA HIT PARADE NO. 3 (Marion Ryan/Gary Miller/Lonnie Donegan/ Edmund Hockridge)	15
58	Pye NEP 24078	NIXA HIT PARADE NO. 4 (Marion Ryan/Pet Clark/Joe Henderson/Gary Miller)	15

MINT VALUE £

58	Pye NEP 24082	NIXA HIT PARADE NO. 5 (Petula Clark/Lonnie Donegan Skiffle Group/ Marion Ryan/Bill Shepherd Orchestra)	15
58	Pye NEP 24090	NIXA HIT PARADE NO. 6 (Lita Roza/Petula Clark/Lonnie Donegan Skiffle Group/Joe Henderson)	15
59	Pye NEP 24100	NIXA HIT PARADE NO. 7 (Lita Roza/Petula Clark/Lonnie Donegan Skiffle Group/Edmund Hockridge)	15

O

65	Columbia SEG 8413	ON THE SCENE (Downliners Sect/Animals/Cherokees/Cheynes/ Georgie Fame/Yardbirds)	100
63	MGM MGM-EP 787	ORIGINAL HITS (Tommy Edwards/Johnny Ferguson/Jimmy Jones/ Conway Twitty)	45
63	London RE-K 1390	THE ORIGINAL HITS (Drifters/Ritchie Barrett/Coasters/Ben E. King)	60
65	Atlantic AET 6006	ORIGINAL HITS VOL. 2 (Barbara Lewis/Coasters/Solomon Burke/Drifters)	50
62	Ember EMB 4522	ORIGINAL RHYTHM AND BLUES HITS (Jesse Belvin/Ray Charles/ Linda Hayes/Jimmy McCracklin/Johnny Moore Blazers)	65
55	Pye Jazz NJE 1043	ORIGINS OF SKIFFLE (Isla Cameron/Guy Carawan/Peggy Seeger)	18
57	Columbia SEG 7669	OUR CHOICE (Eddie Calvert/Michael Holliday/Ruby Murray)	12
68	Apple (no cat. no.)	OUR FIRST FOUR (4 x 7" in presentation pack, including "Hey Jude" [R 5722] & "Those Were The Days" by Mary Hopkin [APPLE 2], "Sour Milk Sea" by Jackie Lomax [APPLE 3] & "Thingumybob" by Black Dyke Mills Band [APPLE 4]; each mounted in PVC pocket on printed dayglo card insert, in 10" x 12" card or plastic outer box)	750/1,000

P

55	London RE-A 1036	THE PAJAMA GAME (Archie Bleyer Orchestra/Stephen Douglas/ Douglas & Dorothy Evans/Arthur Malvin)	12
55	Decca DFE 6147	PARADE OF STARS (Joan Regan/Edmundo Ros & Stargazers/ Dickie Valentine/Stargazers)	12
58	Pye NSEP 85000	POPS GO STEREO (Marion Ryan/Tony Osborne Orch./Bill Shepherd Orch.)	12
68	CBS Spec. Prod. WEP 1135	POPSTER PACK (Georgie Fame/Anita Harris/Peddlers/Simon & Garfunkel)	7

R

67	Action ACT 002 EP	RAG GOES MAD AT THE MOJO (33rpm; Joe Cocker's Blues Band/ Tangerine Ayr Band/Pitiful Souls/Delroy Good Good Band; in conjunction with Sheffield University rag magazine *Twikker*)	85
56	Vogue EPV 1113	RHYTHM AND BLUES (Dominoes/Swallows)	275
60s	Range JRE 7002	RHYTHM AND BLUES (Sticks Herman/Tim Whitsett)	18
60s	Range JRE 7006	RHYTHM AND BLUES (Harry Lewis/Tommy Wills)	15
63	Stateside SE 1008	RHYTHM AND BLUES (Jimmy Reed/John Lee Hooker)	25
64	Stateside SE 1009	R&B CHARTMAKERS (Martha/Vandellas/Miracles/Marvin Gaye/ Marvelettes)	100
64	Stateside SE 1018	R&B CHARTMAKERS NO. 2 (Miracles/Kim Weston/Supremes/Marvelettes)	100
64	Stateside SE 1022	R&B CHARTMAKERS NO. 3 (Marvin Gaye/Darnells/Eddie Holland/ Martha & Vandellas)	100
64	Stateside SE 1025	R&B CHARTMAKERS NO. 4 (Supremes/Eddie Holland/Temptations/ Contours)	80
60	Vogue EPV 1198	RHYTHM AND BLUES CONCERT (Helen Humes/Jimmy Witherspoon)	90
64	Pye Intl. NEP 44021	RHYTHM AND BLUES SHOWCASE VOL. 1 (Don & Bob/Dale Hawkins/ Clarence Henry/Larry Williams)	30
64	Pye Intl. NEP 44022	RHYTHM AND BLUES SHOWCASE VOL. 2 (Jimmy McCracklin/ Muddy Waters/Little Walter/Howlin' Wolf)	30
57	Vogue VE 170111	ROCK AND ROLL (Mister Google Eyes August/Louis Jones Rock & Roll Band/Walter Price Rock & Roll Band/Clarence Gatemouth Brown)	160
62	Capitol EAP1 20197	ROUND-UP (Tommy Collins/Farmer Boys/Ferlin Husky/Texas Bill Strength)	15
60	Top Rank JKP 2060	RUSHING FOR PERCUSSION (Preston Epps/Sandy Nelson)	20

S

60s	S.A.U.C.C. PR 5462	ST. ANDREWS UNIVERSITY CHARITIES CAMPAIGN (20th Century Sounds/ Steve Hall & Roosters/Black Ring; no p/s)	50
63	Decca DFE 8541	SEA SHANTIES (FROM A LONDON HOOTENANNY) (Redd Sullivan/Lou Killen/Bob Davenport)	8
64	Lyntone LYN 738/739	SHEFFIELD UNIVERSITY RAG RECORD (flexidisc; Vantennas/Dave Allen Band/ Addy Street Five/Los Caribos; die-cut sleeve)	40
55	Columbia SEG 7528	SHOUT FOR JOY (Pete Johnson/Albert Ammons/Meade Lux Lewis)	30
63	London RE-P 1403	SINGING THE BLUES (Ernie K-Doe/Showmen/Jesse Hill/Chris Kenner)	90
58	MGM MGM-EP 671	SINGING IN THE RAIN (Debbie Reynolds/Gene Kelly/Donald O'Connor)	8
58	Decca DFE 6485	SIX FIVE SPECIAL (Jackie Dennis/Joan Regan/Diane Todd/ Dickie Valentine)	35
58	Pye NEP 24076	SIX HIT SONGS FROM MY FAIR LADY (Lita Roza/Petula Clark/Ray Ellington/ Gary Miller/Max Miller/Marion Ryan)	10
62	Pye NEP 24158	SOME PEOPLE (Eagles/Valerie Mountain)	10
66	Lyntone LYN 995	THE SOUND OF THE STARS (flexidisc with *Disc And Music Echo*; with/without mag & envelope/stamp)	20/10
65	Keele Rag/Lyntone LYN 951/952	SOUNDS OF SAVILE (flexidisc; Hipster Image/London Apprentices/ Tom & Brennie; some in die-cut title sleeve)	80/50
55	Decca DFE 6147	STAR PARADE (Stargazers/Edmundo Ros Orchestra/Joan Regan & Squadronaires/Dickie Valentine)	12
60s	208 Radio Luxembourg	STAR SOUVENIR GREETINGS (flexidisc)	15
60	Mercury ZEP 10088	SURPRISE PACKAGE (Ben Hewitt/Diamonds)	110
59	Top Rank JKR 8007	SWEET BEAT (Lee Allen Band/Fred Parris/Cindy Mann/Mellokings)	45
58	Capitol EAP1 1026	SWINGIN' DRUMS (Billy May & His Orchestra/Earl Palmer & His Orchestra)	10

MINT VALUE £

T

63	Oriole EP 7080	TAKE SIX (Mark Peters' Silhouettes/Ian & Zodiacs/Faron's Flamingos/Earl Preston & T.T.s/Rory Storm & Hurricanes/Sonny Wade & Cascades)	65
59	Mercury ZEP 10015	TEAR IT UP (Boyd Bennett Orchestra/Red Prysock/Hi-Liters)	150
57	Mercury MEP 9522	TEEN-AGE ROCK (Red Prysock/Rusty Draper/Chuck Miller/Crew Cuts)	120
58	RCA RCX 111	TEENAGE TOPS (Ray Peterson/Jimmy Dell/Marlin Greene/Barry De Vorzon)	40
64	Ember EMB 4540	TEEN SCENE '64 (Dave Clark Five/Ray Singer/Washington D. 99 copies only)	50
67	CBS Special Products WEP 1126	THEMES FROM JAMES BOND FILMS (John Barry Orchestra/Mertens Brothers Style/Percy Faith)	10
58	Brunswick OE 9425	THEY SOLD A MILLION NO. 9 (Bobby Helms/Four Aces/Jerry Lewis/ Kitty Kallen)	25
59	Brunswick OE 9426	THEY SOLD A MILLION NO. 10 (Andrews Sisters/Four Aces/Ink Spots/ Mills Brothers)	12
59	Brunswick OE 9427	THEY SOLD A MILLION NO. 11 (Ink Spots/Louis Jordan & His Tympany Five/ Mills Brothers/Weavers)	20
59	Brunswick OE 9431	THEY SOLD A MILLION NO. 15 (Four Aces/Bill Haley & His Comets)	25
60s	Argo EAF 66	THROUGH THE LOOKING GLASS (SCENES FROM) (soundtrack)	10
57	Decca DFE 6411	TOPS IN POPS NO. 1 (Beverley Sisters/Bob Cort Skiffle Group/Terry Dene/ Tommy Steele)	20
58	Decca DFE 6467	TOPS IN POPS NO. 3 (Jackie Dennis/D. King/Southlanders/David Whitfield)	18
59	Decca DFE 6583	TOPS IN POPS NO. 7 (Beverley Sisters/Ted Heath & His Music/ Lord Rockingham's XI/Tommy Steele)	15
63	Stateside SE 1004	TOP TEEN DANCES (Johnnie Morisette/Huey 'Piano' Smith & Clowns/ Al Brown's Tunetoppers/Spartans)	25
57	Parlophone R 4356	TOP TEN SPECIAL (Jim Dale/King Brothers/Vipers Skiffle Group)	15
67	Pye NEP 24276	TOP T.V. THEMES (Cyril Stapleton/Ron Grainer Orchestra/Barry Gray Orchestra/Eliminators/Johnny Keating & Z Men)	15
60	Fontana TFE 17265	TREASURES OF NORTH AMERICAN NEGRO MUSIC VOL. 6 (Reverend J.C. Burnett/Reverend J.M. Gates/Reverend W. Mosley)	15
65	Century 21 MA 105	T.V. CENTURY 21 THEMES (David Graham/Sylvia Anderson/Peter Dyneley/ Barry Gray Orchestra/Gary Miller/Eric Winstone Orchestra)	15
64	Decca DFE 8585	T.V. THEMES (Andrew Oldham Orchestra/Ted Heath Music/ Ron Grainer Music/Cyril Stapleton Orchestra)	40
66	Decca DFE 8661	T.V. THEMES (Magicians/Frank Chacksfield Orchestra/Larry Page Orchestra)	8
69	M.C.P.S. ATV 1	T.V. THEMES: A GIFT FROM PASCALL MURRAY (Laurie Johnson Orch. et al.; Pascal Fruits promo presented by Pete Murray)	10
66	Pye NEP 24244	T.V. THEMES 1966 (Laurie Johnson Orchestra/John Schroeder Orchestra/ Cyril Stapleton Orchestra)	12
62	Starlite STEP 31	TWIST OFF (Wayne Farmer/Medallions/Charles Perrywell/Piano Slim/ Teenbeats/Dellos)	200
62	Starlite STEP 29	TWIST ON (Mighty Trojans/Dee Dee Gaudet/Dixie Lee/ Percy & The Rocking Aces)	170

V

65	Vogue VRE 5002	VOGUE SURPRISE PARTIE (Petula Clark/Jean Jacques Debout/ Francoise Hardy/Michel Paje)	15

W

59	RCA RCX 128	WAGON TRAIN (Shorty Long/Prairie Chiefs/Sons Of The Pioneers)	8
69	Apple CT 1	WALLS ICE CREAM PRESENTS (Mary Hopkin/Iveys/Jackie Lomax/ James Taylor; with/without p/s)	35/10
65	Liberty LEP 4036	WE SING THE BLUES (Jesse Hill/Ernie K. Doe/Aaron Neville/Benny Spellman)	55
64	Fontana TFE 18009	WITH GOD ON OUR SIDE (withdrawn; Bob Dylan/Joan Baez/Pete Seeger)	100
66	Chess CRE 6009	WITH THE BLUES (Eddie Boyd Blues Combo/Buddy Guy)	35

Y

64	Fontana TFE 18011	YE PLAYBOYS AND PLAYGIRLS (withdrawn; Bob Dylan/Joan Baez/ Pete Seeger)	100
68	Chess CRE 6026	YOUR CHESS REQUESTS (Fontella Bass/Tony Clarke/Mitty Collier/ Billy Stewart)	55
57	Mercury MEP 9525	YOUR CHOICE (Hal Mooney Orchestra/Chuck Miller/Sarah Vaughan/ Florian Zabach)	20
58	Mercury MEP 9532	YOUR CHOICE NO. 2 (Ralph Marterie Orchestra/Patti Page/ Platters/Myoshi Umeki)	15

UNTITLED EPs

60s	Coxsone SCE 1	(no p/s, 33rpm; Gaylads/Hugh Godfrey/Glen & Dave/Roy Richards/ Cables/Richard Ace)	60
63	Embassy WEP 1086	(p/s; Mike Redway/Bud Ashton Group/Rory Pilgrim)	15
69	De Wolfe	(Lemon Dips, et al.)	30

MINT VALUE £

VARIOUS ARTISTS SINGLES & EPs 70s/80s/90s/00s (alphabetical by title)

A

90	Metro Music DWM-1	ABSLOM DAAK — DALEK KILLER (Mark Ayres/Dominic Glynn/ The Slaves Of Kane) (square flexi, with/without *Doctor Who Magazine*)	8/4
96	Sticky STICKY 19	ACOUSTICKY (Hood/Boyracer et al.)	10
97	Ferox FER 028	FURTHER ADVENTURES IN TECHNO SOUL (12" sampler; Dan Curtin/ The Invisibles et al.)	10
98	Twisted Nerve TN 003	ALL OAR NOTHING (10", p/s; Badly Drawn Boy/Mum & Dad/Dakota Oak/ Sirconical/Andy Votel)	35
56	Decca F 10752	ALL STAR HIT PARADE (EP, credited to the Lord's Taverners)	10
57	Decca F 10915	ALL STAR HIT PARADE NO. 2 (EP, credited to the Lord's Taverners)	8
85	Lyntone LYN 16705	ALTERNATIVE TOP OF THE POPS (flexidisc, spoken word)	8
84	Relegated	ARISTOCRAP (p/s; Pulex Irritans/Seventh Plague/Vendetta)	10
95	Sticky STICKY 16	AROUND THE WORLD WITH STICKY RECORDS (Rory Commodore [a.k.a. Tindersticks]/Boy Racer/Heck/Cornershop, picture disc, 700 only)	12

B

83	Secret SHH 138	BACK ON THE STREET (p/s; Skin Disease/Angela Rippon's Bum/Venom/ Strike/East End Badoes)	12
87	Other OTH 6	BATTLEAXE (p/s; Black Riders/Holosade/Kes/Teacher's Pet)	30
78	Good Vibrations GOT 7	BATTLE OF THE BANDS (double pack, no'd p/s; Idiots/Rudi/Outcasts/Spider)	18
95	Ka-boom KA-BOOM 1	BIG BOLLOCKED BONFIRE BLOW-UP (Hood, et al.)	12
80	Vinyl Drip DRIP 001	BLACKPOOL ROX (p/s; Membranes/Section 25/Syntax/Kenneth Turner Set)	8
79	Skeleton SKL 002	THE BLANK TAPES VOL. 1 (folded p/s; Attempted Moustache/Junk Act/ Geisha Girls/Zorkie Twins)	8
81	Secret SHH 126	BOLLOCKS TO CHRISTMAS (p/s; Business/4-Skins/Gonads/Max Splodge)	30
97	Fisheye FISH 2	BREAKING THE PLASTIC HYMEN: VINYL VIRGINS & LOW FI WHORES (2 x 7", Hood et al.)	7
80s	Secret	BRITANNIA WAIVES THE RULES (12", p/s; Exploited/Chron Gen/Infa Riot)	12
94	Fierce Panda NING 04	BUILT TO BLAST (double pack, p/s; Green Day/Flying Medallions/Fabric/ Understand/China Drum/Joeyfat)	6
80	Crass 421984/5	BULLSHIT DETECTOR (12", p/s; A.P.F. Brigade/Alternative/Amebix/ Clockwork Criminals/Counter Attack/Crass/Frenzy Battalion/Fuck The CIA/ Icon/Reputations In Jeopardy/Sceptics/Sinyx/Speakers/Andy T.)	20

C

95	Orange ORANGE 001	CARMIHOOD (Hood/Carmine)	8
98	Twisted Nerve TNXMS 1	CHRISTMAS STOCKING FILLER (Badly Drawn Boy/Dakota Oak/Sirconical/Mum & Dad/Elbow) (green vinyl in green wraparound sleeve or red vinyl in red sl.)	50
98	Twisted Nerve TNXM 025	CHRISTMAS STOCKING FILLER 2 (10", p/s; Andy Votel/D.O.T./Lost Children's Desk/Misty Dixon/Cherrystones)	10
95	Spangle SPANG 001	CLUB SPANGLE EP (p/s; Marion et al.)	6
97	SKAM 0161	COMPILATION (CD, Skam & V/VM artists)	18
80s	No Future	A COUNTRY FIT FOR HEROES (12", p/s)	12
80s	No Future	A COUNTRY FIT FOR HEROES VOL. 2 (12", p/s)	20
94	Fierce Panda NING 02	CRAZED AND CONFUSED (p/s; Supergrass/Ash et al.)	30
80	Clancrest FLX 135	CUP TRIUMPHS: EXCERPTS FROM FA CUP FINALS (gold flexi in card folder)	10

D

71	Dandelion DS 7001	DANDELION (die-cut sleeve; Principal Edwards Magic Theatre/Stackwaddy/ Siren/The Way We Live)	15
86	BBC ZRSL 193	DOCTOR WHO (cassette, holographic inlay; Dominic Glynn/Mankind/ BBC Radiophonic Workshop)	8
86	BBC 12RXL 193	DOCTOR WHO (12", holographic p/s; Dominic Glynn/Mankind/ BBC Radiophonic Workshop)	12
87	BBC RESL 193	DOCTOR WHO (p/s, reissue; Dominic Glynn/Mankind)	5

E

79	Fast Products FAST 9B	EARCOM 2 (12", p/s; Joy Division/Thursdays/Basczax)	12
79	Fast Products FAST 9C	EARCOM 3 (double pack, gatefold p/s with colour postcard insert; D.A.F./Middle Class/Noh Mercy/Stupid Babies)	5
97	Fat Cat 12FAT 003	8. 8.5, 9 (12", custom sleeve)	10
78	Stiff FREEBIE 2	EXCERPTS FROM STIFF'S GREATEST HITS (promo only sampler, 33rpm)	8
96	Mo' Wax MWEX 001-010	EXCURSIONS (10 x 12", box set; the Prunes/IO/Olde Scottish/David Caron/DJ Solo & DJ Aura/Midnight Funk Assoc./Stasis/Solo feat. JT/Twig Bud/ DJ Shadow)	40
99	AI AI 001	EXPERIMENTS IN COLOUR (12"; Normal/Cell/Fil)	20

F

78	Factory FAC 2	A FACTORY SAMPLE (double pack, p/s, in plastic bag, with 5 stickers; Joy Division/Cabaret Voltaire/Durutti Column/John Dowie; beware of counterfeits)	100/75
81	Pax PAX 1	5 MILES TO MIDNIGHT (12", p/s; Brothers/Doormen/I Scream/Mortuary In Wax)	8
95	555 5X555	5x555 (5x7" box set; Boyracer/Mike Nichols And His Excellency/Amy Linton & Stewart Anderson/Father/Hood)	30
91	Fontana FONT 1	THE FONTANA SINGLES BOX SET VOLUME 1 — HITS AND RARITIES (12-single box set, with 12 inserts)	30
91	Fontana FONT 2	THE FONTANA SINGLES BOX SET VOLUME 2 — HITS AND RARITIES (12-single box set, with 12 inserts)	30
95	Malpractice MAL 03	FORCED INDIGNATION (1000 only; Hood/Hem)	5
79	Heartbeat PULSE 4	4 ALTERNATIVES (p/s; 48 Hours/Joe Public/Numbers/X-Certs)	15

			MINT VALUE £
80	Con (no cat. no.)	THE FOUR EPs (cassette; Mark Perry et al.)	15
92	Kerrang! K/EMI 1	4 PLAY (with issue 397 of *Kerrang!*)	5
96	Ché CHE 059	4 TRACK 3 BAND TOUR EP (p/s, Mogwai/Urusei Yatsura/Backwater, 50 only)	25
94	Fierce Panda NING 05	FROM GREER TO ETERNITY (double pack, p/s; Lush/Ivy/Solar Race// Splendora/Jale/Fuzzy)	8
96	Mosquito MSQ 05	FRESH AS YOU FUCKIN' LIKE (12"; Paul Hannah/Russ Gabriel/Steve Patton/ Cristian Vogel/Si Begg)	25
		G	
72	Chess 6145 011	GENESIS — THE BEGINNINGS OF ROCK	10
83	Mouth MOUTH 1	G-FORCE (Shady Deal/Dead Loss/Blythe Rocket/Egypt)	20
70	Village Thing VTSX 1000	THE GREAT WHITE DAP (Wizz Jones/Sun Also Rises/Ian A. Anderson/ Pigsty Hill Light Orchestra)	20
		H	
80	Groucho Marxist COMMUNIQUE 2	HA! HA! FUNNY POLIS (PAISLEY ROCKS AGAINST RACISM) (p/s; Defiant Pose/Fegs/Urban Enemies/XS Discharge)	20
71	Abreaction ABR 001	HART ROCK (Brass Alley/Yellow/Trilogy/Lucas Tyson) (no p/s)	30
90s	Sub Pop	HELTER SHELTER (box set, 4 x 7", Elastica/Gene)	12
89	Hometown Atrocities 1	THE HOMETOWN ATROCITIES EP (wraparound p/s, either 'glossy', or 'kylie'; Headless Chickens/Jackson Penis/Beaver Patrol/Mad At The Sun)	150/200
88	House Of Dolls HOD 002	HOUSE OF DOLLS (no p/s; Cardiacs/Orange Cartest/In Two A Circle/ Decadent Few; free with *House Of Dolls* magazine)	7/5
88	House Of Dolls HOD 004	HOUSE OF DOLLS (no p/s; Wedding Present/Trudy/Hunters Club/ Claytown Troupe; free with *House Of Dolls* magazine)	7/5
89	House Of Dolls HOD 009	HOUSE OF DOLLS (no p/s; Pop Will Eat Itself/Wild Poppies/Blow Up/ Godspeed; free with *House Of Dolls* magazine)	7/5
89	House Of Dolls HOD 010	HOUSE OF DOLLS (no p/s; Sugarcubes/Host/Murrumbidgee Whalers/ Shark Taboo; free with *House Of Dolls* magazine)	7/5
89	House Of Dolls HOD 011	HOUSE OF DOLLS (no p/s; Wonder Stuff/Prudes/Sandkings/World Of Music; free with *House Of Dolls* magazine)	7/5
75	Solid Sender SEP 100	HOUSTON JUMP (James Widemouth Brown & His Orchestra/Henry Hayes Four Kings & Carl Campbell/Goree Carter & Hepcats)	10
		I	
97	B. Banquet Random 2.2	I DIE, YOU DIE (12", green vinyl promo, die-cut sleeve, 1200 only; Greenhaus/ Mike Dearborn/Dave Clarke)	10
78	Radar SAM 88	INTERNATIONAL ARTISTS (13th Floor Elevators/Red Crayola/ Lost & Found/Golden Dawn; Red Crayola Hope & Anchor gig freebie with *Howdy From Texas The Lone Star State* magazine)	12/8
83	Future FUTURE 1	THE INVISIBLE FRAME (p/s, Blitz/And Also The Trees & others)	7
		J	
93	Mo' Wax MW 010	JAZZ HIP JAP SAMPLER (12", stickered sleeve; Monday Michiru/Jeff Brown & 331/3; Magic Ware)	15
98	Fierce Panda NING 63	THE JOY OF PLECS (2 x 7"; Cay/Chicks/Max Tractor/The Monsoon Bassoon/ The Samurai Seven/Fantasmagroover) (wraparound p/s, with insert)	8
		L	
79	Decca FR 13864	THE LONDON BOYS (p/s; David Bowie/Small Faces/Birds/Dobie Gray)	7
73	Ronco MR EP 001	LONG LIVE ROCK (no p/s; Billy Fury/Eugene Wallace/Wishful Thinking)	15
87	Barracuda Blue 12UTA 9	LUNACY IS LEGEND (12", p/s; Times/Necessitarians/Nikki Sudden)	8
		M	
71	Track 2094 011	MAXI TRACK RECORD (John's Children/Crazy World Of Arthur Brown/ Thunderclap Newman/Jimi Hendrix; withdrawn blue sleeve crediting Pete Townshend as producer)	125
71	Track 2094 011	MAXI TRACK RECORD (John's Children/Crazy World Of Arthur Brown/ Thunderclap Newman/Jimi Hendrix; red & white sleeve with press pack, also maroon & gold sleeve without press pack)	60/10
86	MM Vinyl Conflict 1	MELODY MAKER EP (with magazine)	5
97	Begg. Banquet Random 2.1	METAL (12", red vinyl promo, die-cut sleeve, 1200 only; Robert Armani)	10
85	Davy Lamp DL 1	MINERS BENEFIT (numbered plain white sleeve; Newtown Neurotics/ Respect/Real By Real/Austin's Shirts)	6
97	V/VM VVMT4	MISSINGTOE & WHINE (EP, 500 only)	15
99	Twisted Nerve TN 009	MODERN MUSIC FOR MOTORCYCLES (10" EP, some on yellow vinyl; Dakota Oak/Alfie/Sirconical & Andy Votel/Mum & Dad/Badly Drawn Boy)	20/10
99	Twisted Nerve TNC 009	MODERN MUSIC FOR MOTORCYCLES (cassette; Dakota Oak/Alfie/Sirconical & Andy Votel/Mum & Dad/Badly Drawn Boy)	15
95	Fierce Panda NING 15	MORTAL WOMBAT (double pack, p/s; Super Furry Animals/Baby Bird/ Panda/Mexican Pets/Harvey's Rabbit/Spare Snare)	8
75	Happy Time HT12	MUSIC FROM THUNDERBIRDS AND DOCTOR WHO (p/s)	7
80	EMI 12EMI 5074	MUTHA'S PRIDE (12", p/s; Wildfire/Quartz/White Spirit/Baby Jane)	20
		N	
80	Neutron NT 003	1980! THE FIRST FIFTEEN MINUTES EP (gatefold p/s with inserts; Vice Versa/Clock DVA/I'm So Hollow/Stunt Kites)	15
87	NME	NME HAT TRICK (Sonic Youth/Sly & Robbie et al.)	7
		O	
95	Enraptured RAPT 4503	OMBRES (p/s; Amp/Third Eye Foundation/Saddar Bazaar)	6
82	Neat NEAT 25	ONE TAKE NO DUBS (12", p/s; Black Rose/Hellanbach/Alien/Avenger)	12
		P	
90s	Fierce Panda NING 12CD	PANDEMONIUM (Easyworld, et al.) (250 only)	10
80s	A&M A&M PARTY 1/2/3/4/5/6	THE PARTY PARTY PACK (6 x 7", with picture sleeves, in PVC outer sleeve; Sting/Pauline Black/Dave Edmunds/Midge Ure/Modern Romance/Bad Manners/ Chas & Dave/Bananarama/Elvis Costello/Bad Manners/Altered Images)	50

			MINT VALUE £
97	V/VM VVMT4	PRIVILEGED FRAMES FOR REFERENCE (12" EP, p/s, 450 only)	20
88	Bam Caruso BRAV 092	PSYCHE-OUT (Smoke) (flexi, given away with *Music Week*)	15
		R	
93	Raptor RAP 1	RAPTOR PRESENTS . . . (12", p/s, 500 only; Ash/Buttlip/Marrow Bone/Fat)	40
82	Recommended RR-8.9	RECOMMENDED RECORDS SAMPLER (Peter Blegvad/Homosexuals/Faust/ R. Stevie Moore; 1-sided, foldout p/s, clear vinyl, silk-screened PVC cover)	10
78	Virgin VR 08 10274/ SHOL 2550	RECORD MIRROR (no p/s; Tangerine Dream/XTC/Motors/U-Roy; with 2nd EP "The State Disco Party" & *Record Mirror* magazine)	7
91	Ptolemaic Terrascope POT 8	RED FLIPPER (no p/s, Nurse With Wound/The Underworlde/ Caravan Of Dreams)	15
91	Epic HOT 1	RED HOT & DANCE (4 x 12" promo box set with insert, sticker and condom)	18
94	Fierce Panda NING 03	RETURN TO SPLENDOUR (double pack in foldover p/s with insert in poly bag, 1,000 only; Bluetones et al.)	15
77	Rollercoaster RRCEP 00002	ROCKABILLY HOP (test pressings only)	15
83	Consett Music Project RD 1	ROCK AND DOLE (Obnoxious Tartus/Decade Waltz/Task Force/Hot Banana)	25
92	Melody Maker MMI	ROLLERCOASTER EP (CD, Blur/Jesus & Mary Chain/Dinosaur Jr./ My Bloody Valentine; 2,000 only)	10
80	Energy NRG 1	ROOM TO MOVE (p/s; Big Self/Outcasts/Shock Treatment/Vipers)	8
		S	
95	Atol ATOL 02	S4C MAKES ME WANT TO SMOKE CRACK VOL. 1 (500 only, Catatonia et al.)	25
81	Springtime RARA 1001	THE SECRET POLICEMAN'S OTHER BALL (Sting/Phil Collins/Bob Geldof) (10", promo only sampler)	15
94	Fierce Panda/ Damaged Goods NING 01	SHAGGING IN THE STREETS (double pack, wraparound p/s in poly bag, 1,000 only; S*M*A*S*H/Blessed Ethel/Mantaray/Done Lying Down/ These Animal Men/Action Painting!)	15
93	Duophonic DS 45-05/06	SHIMMIES IN SUPER 8 (double pack, 1 disc green vinyl, other white vinyl, numbered in poly bag, 800 with tri-foldout p/s, 400 also with sticker & 2 inserts; Stereolab/Huggy Bear/Darlin'/Colm)	each 35
95	Enraptured RAPT 4502	SILVER APPLES TRIBUTE (10", 12 in hand-drawn sleeve; Windy & Carl/Scaredycat/Third Eye Foundation/Flowchart/Sabine	25/10
80	Sleep 'N' Eat	SLEEP 'N' EAT (includes Originators)	6
80s	Smash Hits	SMASH HITS INTERVIEW PACK (4 flexidiscs in envelope sleeve; Duran Duran/Spandau Ballet/Boy George/Frankie Goes To Hollywood)	10
86	Broken Flag BF F1	THE SOFT VOLCANO ERUPTS (flexidisc; Controlled Bleeding/Kehamas Curse/ Uncommunity/Nails Of Christ/Cananes/Ramleh)	10
73	Sounds (SH 0999)	SOUNDS PRESENTS FROM POLYDOR'S 'THE GUITAR ALBUM' (flexidisc with *Sounds* magazine; Eric Clapton & others)	8/6
79	Groucho Marxist WH 1	SPECTACULAR COMMODITY (p/s; Mental Errors/Mod Cons/ Poems/Sneex/XS Discharge)	10
01	Simba SIM 014-2	SPLIT (Hundred Reasons/Garrison)	15
58	Decca F 11043	STAR BAND HIT PARADE (EP, credited to the Lord's Taverners)	6
70s	Stiff BUY 1-10	STIFF BOX SET NO. 1 (10 x 7" box set)	35
70s	Stiff BUY 11-20	STIFF BOX SET NO. 2 (10 x 7" box set)	35
88	Underground (no cat no)	STRUM + DRUM (Wedding Present & others) (cassette with *Underground* magazine, issue 13)	8/6
83	Sue ENS 3	SUE SOUL SISTERS	10
83	Sue ENS 4	SUE SOUL BROTHERS	10
83	Sue ENS 6	SUE INSTRUMENTALS	10
		T	
90s	Enraptured RAPT 4513	TERRASCOPE/TERRASTOCK (Bevis Frond/Damon & Naomi/Flying Saucer Attack/Silver Apples)	12
83	White Noise WN 3	THIS IS WHITE NOISE (p/s; Skrewdriver/Brutal Attack/Die Hards/A.B.H.)	35
02	Warner Bros 50466 13441	TOP-DECK SKA 45'S BOX (8 x 7"s, coloured vinyl in cardboard box)	25
82	Total Noise TOT 1	TOTAL NOISE # 1 (Business/Blitz/Dead Generation/Gonads)	15
95	Ankst CD 061	TRISKAIDEKAPHILIA (CD, Super Furry Animals/Catatonia et al.)	15
		U	
86	Underground 7	UNDERGROUND RHYTHM AND NOISE (cassette with *Underground* issue 7)	8/6
80s	Fierce FRIGHT/SFTRI 38	AN UNHOLY MONTAGE (200 only [100 U.K./100 U.S.], coloured vinyl with numbered insert)	25
98	Wurlitzer JUKEBOX 37	UNITED IN THE HATRED OF (676 only, 176 in embossed sleeve)	10/5
96	V/VM VVMT1	UPLINK DATA TRANSMISSIONS (12" EP, with 'data sheets', 250 only)	25
		W	
98	B.Banquet Random 2.3	WARRIORS (12", blue vinyl promo, die-cut sleeve, 1200 only; Dave Angel/ Liberator DJs/Steve Stoll)	8
98	B.Banquet Random 2.4	WE ARE GLASS (12", clear vinyl promo, die-cut sleeve, 1200 only; Claude Young/ Alex Hazzard/Peter Lazonby)	8
80	Fuck Off FEP 001	WEIRD NOISE (p/s, white labels; Danny & Dressmakers/The Door & The Window/Instant Automatons/012/Sell-Outs)	10
82	Bluurg FISH 1	WESSEX '82 (Subhumans/Pagans/Organized Chaos/The Heads)	6
75	Solid Sender SEP 101	WEST SIDE CHICAGO	10
77	MPL MPL 1	WE'VE MOVED! (Wings/Gene Vincent/Frank Sinatra et al., promo only excerpts sampler, some with press pack)	175/125
84	Rather/Seventeen GEAR 17	WHAT A NICE WAY TO TURN SEVENTEEN NO. 2 (p/s; Swell Maps & others; with magazine)	12
78	Spider SP 04 EP	WREXHAM IS THE NAME (Wrexham supporters/Arfon Griffiths et al.)	10
		Y	
80s	Wonderful World Of WOW 1	YOU ARE NOT ALONE (p/s, with insert; Oi Polloi/Hex/Stalag 17/Symbol Of Freedom)	8

MINT VALUE £

UNTITLED EPs & SINGLES

73	Buddah 2011 164	(Shangri-La's/Tradewinds/Ad Libs)	12
87	Metal Hammer METAL 1	(Paul Samson's Empire/Chariot/Heavy Pettin'/Strangeways; some with *Metal Hammer* magazine)	6/4
94	Kennel Club VTDOG 10	(Strangelove/Tindersticks/God Machine/Breed (10", numbered, 1,500 only, free with *Purr* magazine issue 2)	10/8
89	The Catalogue CAT 074	THE SHAMEN: Purple Haze/SLEEPING DOGS WAKE: This Little Piggy/SUGARCUBES: Cindy/KITCHENS OF DISTINCTION: Margaret's Injection/HAM: Voulez Vous (square flexidisc with *The Catalogue* magazine)	5/4
98	Fat Cat 12FAT 008	REMIXES (12", custom sleeve; remixes of Fat Cat 12FAT 003 by Autechre et al.)	12
94	Kennel Club VTDOG 10	TINDERSTICKS: Girl On Death Row/STRANGELOVE: Wolf's Story/GOD MACHINE: The Devil Song/BREED: Diamonds Are Forever (10", numbered p/s, free with *Purr* magazine, issue 2, 1,500 only)	10/8
96	SKAM MASK 1	UNTITLED (12", custom sleeve, 100 only; Freeform/Funkstorung/Boards Of Canada/Jega)	150
97	SKAM MASK 2	UNTITLED (12", custom sleeve, 350 only; Hellinterface/Funkstorung/Bola/Jega/Intron)	75
98	Mosquito MSQ 012.5	(10"; Si Begg/Blue Arsed Fly)	15

VARIOUS ARTISTS LPs & COMPILATIONS (alphabetical by title)

A

70	ATP 102	THE ABBEY TAVERN	20
88	Woronzow WOO 6	ACID JAM (with insert)	20
69	Action ACLP 6005	ACTION PACKED SOUL	50
70s	Jem JEM	A DEAL A DAY	25
96	Ferox FERLP 1	ADVENTURES IN TECHNO SOUL (2-LP; Too Funk/Paul Hannah/Carl Craig et al.)	20
85	United Dairies UD 012	AN AFFLICTED MAN'S MUSICA BOX (3 different editions, 1st in gatefold sleeve)	75/30/30
75	Leader LEE 4056	A FINE HUNTING DAY — SONGS OF THE HOLME VALLEY BEAGLES (with book)	15
70	Pama PMP 2004	AFRICAN MELODY	35
71	Trojan TBL 166	AFRICA'S BLOOD (Lee Perry, et al.) (orange/white label)	35
70s	Contempo 2870 311	AFRO ROCK FESTIVAL	15
70	Atlantic 2464 013	THE AGE OF ATLANTIC	15
66	Stateside SL 10172	AN ALBUM FULL OF SOUL	45
69	Key KL 002	ALIVE!	20
84	Creation CRELP 001	ALIVE IN THE LIVING ROOM	12
70	Talisman STAL 5013	ALL FOLK TOGETHER	20
84	Whaam! BIG 8	ALL FOR ART... AND ART FOR ALL	30
71	Utd. Artists UDX 201/202	ALL GOOD CLEAN FUN (2-LP)	20
83	Neat NEAT 102A/B	ALL HELL LET LOOSE	20
61	Blue Beat BBLP 801	ALL STARS — JAMAICAN BLUES	300
70	Speciality SPE 6609	ALL THE BLUES ALL THE TIME	20
62	Golden Guinea GGL 0162	ALL THE HITS BY ALL THE STARS	12
58	Pye Nixa NJT 509	ALL THE WINNERS (10")	15
76	Riva RVLP 2	ALL THIS AND WORLD WAR TWO (2-LP, box set with booklet)	15
58	Parlophone PMD 1064	ALL TIME COUNTRY AND WESTERN HITS (10")	30
68	Topic 12T 189	ALONG THE COALY TYNE (original sleeve)	12
90	Sound Of Spasm CLANG 4	ALVIN LIVES IN LEEDS	12
73	Polydor 2460 186	AMERICAN BLUES LEGENDS '73	12
63	Polydor LPHM 46 397	AMERICAN FOLK BLUES FESTIVAL (also stereo SLPHM 237 597)	18/22
70s	Rare Records 2	AMERICAN FOLK BLUES FESTIVAL 1962	18
64	Fontana TL 5204	AMERICAN FOLK BLUES FESTIVAL 1963	22
65	Fontana TL 5225	AMERICAN FOLK BLUES FESTIVAL 1964	22
66	Fontana TL 5286	AMERICAN FOLK BLUES FESTIVAL 1965	22
66	Fontana (S)TL 5389	AMERICAN FOLK BLUES FESTIVAL 1966 (mono/stereo)	22/35
70	CBS 63912	AMERICAN FOLK BLUES FESTIVAL 1969	15
70s	Lorimar/CBS 70172	AMERICATHON	12
70s	Skeleton SKLLP 1	AND THE DANCE GOES ON	12
80s	Pleasantly Surprised PS 2	THE ANGELS ARE COMING (2-cassette, with booklet)	25
83	No Future MPUNK 8	ANGELS WITH DIRTY FACES	12
60s	'77' 77LA 12/13	ANGOLA PRISON SPIRITUALS	15
80	Polydor EYETV 1	ANOTHER FEAST OF IRISH FOLK	12
69	Immediate IMAL 03/04	ANTHOLOGY OF BRITISH BLUES VOLUME 1 (2-LP, gatefold sleeve)	25
69	Immediate IMAL 05/06	ANTHOLOGY OF BRITISH BLUES VOLUME 2 (2-LP, gatefold sleeve)	25
64	London HA-K/SH-K 8174	APOLLO SATURDAY NIGHT (mono/stereo)	60/75
93	Art ART 2CD	APPLIED RHYMIC TECHNOLOGY (CD)	30
93	Art ART 4CD	APPLIED RHYMIC TECHNOLOGY (CD)	20
80s	Ram RAMLP 001	THE ART OF SOLVING PROBLEMS (with poster & insert)	18
74	Ashanti SHAN 106	ASHANTI SHOWCASE	15
69	Atco 228 021	ATCO BLOCKBUSTERS	15
69	Atlantic 587/588 180	ATLANTIC BLOCKBUSTERS	15
65	Atlantic ATL 5020	ATLANTIC DISCOTHEQUE	40
60s	Atlantic AP 2	ATLANTIC IS SOUL	18
60s	Atlantic AC 3	ATLANTICLASSICS	30
74	Horse HRLP 705	ATLANTIC ONE	12
67	Pye NPL 18198	AT LAST THE 1948 SHOW	15
90	Dover/PWL CCD 19	A TON OF HITS — THE HIT FACTORY VOL. 4 (2-CD)	30
64	Decca LK 4597	AT THE CAVERN	70
63	London HA-R 8133	AT THE HOOTENANNY — VOLUME 3	15

			MINT VALUE £
85	Sweatbox AMO 5	AUDIO VISUAL — ABSTRACT MAGAZINE NO. 5 (printed PVC sleeve)	15
85	Sweatbox SAM 006	AUDIO VISUAL — ABSTRACT MAGAZINE NO. 6 (embossed plastic wallet, with inner & magazine)	15
70	Beacon SBEAB 9	AUTHENTIC CHICAGO BLUES	22
72	Windmill WMD 124	AUTHENTIC CHICAGO BLUES	18
66	RCA RD 7776	AUTHENTIC COWBOYS & THEIR WESTERN FOLKSONGS	12
57	London WB 91034	AUTHENTIC CARIBBEAN CALYPSOS (10" LP)	30
64	Stateside SL 10107	AUTHENTIC SKA	60
64	Stateside SL 10068	AUTHENTIC R & B	40
79	Heartbeat HB 1	AVON CALLING — THE BRISTOL COMPILATION (with poster)	30
80	K-Tel NE 1100	AXE ATTACK (early copies with demo of Iron Maiden's "Running Free")	12
80s	Flaccid FLAC 1	AYLESBURY GOES FLACCID	25
74	Deroy DER 1052	AYRSHIRE FOLK (LP, private pressing)	80

B

70	Track 2407 001	BACKTRACK ONE	12
70	Track 2407 002	BACKTRACK TWO	12
70	Track 2407 006	BACKTRACK SIX	18
70	Track 2407 007	BACKTRACK SEVEN	12
54	London AL 3535	BACKWOODS BLUES (10")	60
73	Incus INCUS 11	BALANCE (Ian Brighton, et al.)	100
62	Fontana 688 200 ZL	BALLIN'	18
79	JSP 1005	BANDERA ROCKABILLIES	12
68	Pama PMLP 4	BANG BANG LULU	25
60	Melodisc 12-115	BANJO BREAKDOWN	15
63	Realm RM 182	BANJO JAMBOREE SPECTACULAR	12
64	Storyville 670 155	BARRELHOUSE BLUES AND BOOGIE-WOOGIE VOLUME 1	18
65	Storyville 670 183	BARRELHOUSE BLUES AND BOOGIE-WOOGIE VOLUME 2	18
65	Storyville SLP 213	BARRELHOUSE BLUES AND BOOGIE-WOOGIE VOL. 3	18
59	Fontana TFR 6018	BARRELHOUSE, BOOGIE WOOGIE AND BLUES (10")	25
58	Vogue Coral LRA 10022	BARRELHOUSE PIANO (10" LP)	25
59	Vogue Coral LRA 10023	BARRELHOUSE PIANO VOLUME 2 (10" LP)	25
83	London CAVE 1	THE BATCAVE — YOUNG LIMBS AND NUMB HYMNS	12
71	Trojan TBL 167	BATTLE AXE	25
52	Capitol LC 6510	BATTLE OF THE BANDS (10" LP)	12
71	B&C BCM 103	BATTLE OF THE BANDS VOL. 1	18
64	Melodisc MLP 12-192	BATTLE OF THE GIANTS	15
53	MGM MGM-D 115	A BATTLE OF JAZZ: HOT VERSUS COOL (10")	25
71	BBC REC 118	BBC's FOLK ON TWO PRESENTS NORTHUMBRIAN FOLK	18
69	Beacon BEAB 1	BEACON BRINGS IT TO YOU	18
71	Revival RVS 1004	BEALE STREET MESS AROUND	12
84	Well Suspect SUSS 1	THE BEAT GENERATION AND THE ANGRY YOUNG MEN	20
86	Mercury WILD 1	BEAT RUNS WILD (Wet Wet Wet et al.)	25
87	Pink PINKY 15	BEAUTY (McCarthy et al.)	12
80s	Porrit's Hill PHEW 2	BECKET HOUSE	12
77	Impulse IS/BED/123	BEDROCK — ALTOGETHER BEDROCK LP (private pressing)	12
68	Elektra EUK 262	BEGIN HERE (also stereo EUKS 7262)	20
78	Rip Off ROLP 1	BELFAST ROCKS	45
71	Delmark DS 622	BELL'S BLUES HARP	15
68	Bell MBLL 102	BELL'S CELLAR OF SOUL VOLUME 1	40
69	Bell MBLL 107	BELL'S CELLAR OF SOUL VOLUME 2	40
69	Bell MBLL 117	BELL'S CELLAR OF SOUL VOLUME 3	40
69	Bell MBLL/SBLL 111	THE BEST FROM BELL	18
69	Bell MBLL/SBLL 124	THE BEST FROM BELL VOLUME 2	18
78	Stiff ODD 2	BE STIFF (TOUR '78 OFFICIAL RELEASE) (promo only)	12
78	Stiff DEAL 1	BE STIFF ROUTE '78 (with 16-page booklet & biographies, etc.)	12
70s	Storyville 671 188	THE BEST OF THE BLUES	18
67	United Artists LAS 29021	THE BEST OF BOND (mono)	15
69	United Artists UAS 29021	THE BEST OF BOND (stereo)	15
65	Xtra XTRA 1031	THE BEST OF BRITISH FOLK	15
69	Pama SECO 18	THE BEST OF CAMEL	35
72	Paramount SPFL 286	BEST OF FILM MUSIC	15
76	Epic EPC 81224	THE BEST OF OKEH VOL. I	15
76	Epic EPC 81532	THE BEST OF OKEH VOL. II	15
69	President PTL 1016	THE BEST OF PRESIDENT VOLUME 1	15
69	President PTL 1036	THE BEST OF PRESIDENT VOLUME 2	15
67	Xtra XTRA 1053	BEST OF SCOTT!SH FOLK	12
83	Statik STATLP 14	THE BEST OF YOUR SECRET'S SAFE WITH US	15
87	Imaginary ILLUSION 001	BEYOND THE WILDWOOD — A TRIBUTE TO SYD BARRETT	12
73	Attack ATLP 1011	BIG BAMBOO	30
60	Fontana TFL 5080	THE BIG BEAT!	50
64	London HA-B 8199	THE BIG 'D' JAMBOREE	25
78	Giorno GPS	BIG EGO	20
69	Fontana SFXL 55	THE BIG FOLK	15
69	Minit MLL/MLS 40007E	THE BIG ONE	22
71	Wand WCS 1005	BIG SIXTEEN GOLDEN OLDIES	12
64	Capitol ST 2146	BIG SOUNDS OF THE DRAGS Vol 2	30
72	CBS 64844	THE BIG SUR FESTIVAL	15
70	Pama SECO 32	BIRTH CONTROL	25
70	Matchbox SDX 207/8	BLACK DIAMOND EXPRESS TO HELL (2-LP)	25
60	Columbia 33SX 1244	BLACKPOOL NIGHTS	30
58	HMV CLP 1167	BLACK SLACKS AND BOBBY SOCKS	225
70	Ember SE 8009	BLACK SOUL EXPLOSION	15
70	CBS 52796	BLACK WHITES AND BLUES	20
83	Quiet QLP 3	BLOOD ON THE ROQ! (withdrawn)	15
68	Coxsone CSP 1	BLUE BEAT SPECIAL	35

			MINT VALUE £
66	RCA Victor RD 7786	BLUEBIRD BLUES	25
63	Stateside SL 10021	THE BLUEGRASS HALL OF FAME	15
65	London HA-B 8227	BLUEGRASS HALL OF FAME VOL. 2	15
64	London HA-B 8118	BLUEGRASS SPECTACULAR	12
62	Columbia 33SX 1417	THE BLUES	50
68	Marble Arch MAL 804	THE BLUES	12
64	Pye Intl. NPL 28030	BLUES VOL. 1	20
64	Pye Intl. NPL 28035	BLUES VOL. 2	20
64	Pye Intl. NPL 28045	BLUES VOL. 3	20
64	Chess CRL 4003	BLUES VOL. 4	25
65	Chess CRL 4512	BLUES VOL. 5	25
67	Marble Arch MAL 664	BLUES & SOUL	12
68	Immediate IMLP 014	BLUES ANYTIME VOL. 1	22
68	Immediate IMCP 015	BLUES ANYTIME VOL. 2	22
68	Immediate IMLP 019	BLUES ANYTIME VOL. 3	22
70	Xtra XTRA 1105	THE BLUES ARE ALIVE AND WELL	12
65	Fontana TFL 6048	THE BLUES AT NEWPORT 1964 PART 1	25
69	Saga FID 2165	BLUES AT SUNRISE	22
66	London HA-S 8265	THE BLUES CAME DOWN FROM MEMPHIS	75
73	Flyright LP 504	BLUES CAME TO CHAPEL HILL	12
65	Storyville SLP 176	BLUESCENE USA: VOLUME 1 — CHICAGO	20
65	Storyville SLP 177	BLUESCENE USA: VOLUME 2 — LOUISIANA BLUES	20
65	Storyville SLP 181	BLUESCENE USA: VOLUME 3 — BLUES ALL AROUND MY BED	20
67	Storyville SLP 180	BLUESCENE USA: VOLUME 4 — MISSISSIPPI BLUES	20
71	Python PLP-KM 17	BLUES — CHICAGO STYLE (LP)	30
60	Philips BBL 7369	BLUES FELL THIS MORNING	50
73	Polydor 2383 257	BLUES FOR MR. CRUMP	25
72	Transatlantic TRASAM 25	BLUES FOR YOUR POCKET	15
69	Chess CRLS 4558	BLUES FROM BIG BILL'S COPACABANA	25
69	Python PLP 6	BLUES FROM CHICAGO (99 copies only)	40
70	Python PLP 9	BLUES FROM CHICAGO VOL. 2 (99 copies only)	40
71	Python PLP 15	BLUES FROM CHICAGO VOL. 3 (99 copies only)	40
60s	Heritage 1004	BLUES FROM MAXWELL STREET (99 copies only)	80
71	Pye Intl. NPL 28142	BLUES FROM THE BAYOU	22
72	Saydisc SDM 226	BLUES FROM THE DELTA	20
71	Python PLP 21	BLUES FROM THE WINDY CITY (99 copies only)	40
77	Flyright LP 4713	BLUES FROM THE WINDY CITY	12
80	Kicking Mule SNKF 159	BLUES GUITAR WORKSHOP	15
63	Stateside SL 10076	BLUES HOOT	25
57	Pye Nixa NJL 8	(ALAN LOMAX PRESENTS) BLUES IN THE MISSISSIPPI NIGHT	18
60s	Sunflower (no cat. no.)	BLUES IS MY COMPANION (99 copies only)	40
60s	Sunflower (no cat. no.)	BLUES KEEP FALLING (99 copies only)	40
64	Joy JOYS 177	BLUES JAM	12
69	Blue Horizon 7-66227	BLUES JAM AT CHESS (2-LP)	55
69	Immediate IMLP 024	BLUES LEFTOVERS	15
67	Saydisc Match. SDM 142	BLUES LIKE SHOWERS OF RAIN	80
68	Saydisc Match. SDM 167	BLUES LIKE SHOWERS OF RAIN VOLUME 2	80
65	Decca LK 4681	BLUES NOW	45
72	Blues Obscurities BOV 1	BLUES OBSCURITIES VOL. 1: SOUTHERN BLUES/DARK MUDDY BOTTOM (plain cover with photocopied inserts)	30
72	Blues Obscurities BOV 2	BLUES OBSCURITIES VOL. 2: LONESOME HARMONICA	30
72	Blues Obscurities BOV 3	BLUES OBSCURITIES VOL. 3: WEST COAST BLUES	30
72	Blues Obscurities BOV 4	BLUES OBSCURITIES VOL. 4: ONE RAINY MORNING	30
72	Blues Obscurities BOV 5	BLUES OBSCURITIES VOL. 5: SOMETHING'S GONE WRONG	30
72	Blues Obscurities BOV 6	BLUES OBSCURITIES VOL. 6: COMING BACK HOME	30
72	Blues Obscurities BOV 7	BLUES OBSCURITIES VOL. 7	30
72	Blues Obscurities BOV 8	BLUES OBSCURITIES VOL. 8	30
72	Blues Obscurities BOV 9	BLUES OBSCURITIES VOL. 9	30
72	Blues Obscurities BOV 10	BLUES OBSCURITIES VOL. 10	30
74	London HA-U 8454	BLUES OBSCURITIES VOL. 1: DARK MUDDY BOTTOM (reissue)	18
74	London HA-U 8455	BLUES OBSCURITIES VOL. 2: LONESOME HARMONICA (reissue)	18
74	London HA-U 8456	BLUES OBSCURITIES VOL. 3: STRETCHIN' OUT	18
69	Mercury SMXL 77	BLUES PACKAGE '69	18
69	Highway 51 H 102	BLUES PEOPLE	50
68	Matchbox SDR 146	BLUES PIANO	15
72	Atlantic K 40404	BLUES PIANO — CHICAGO PLUS	22
68	Kokomo K 1001	A BLUES POTPOURRI (99 copies only)	55
71	Rarities (Tony's Records)	BLUES RARITIES VOL. 1 (2-LP)	25
69	Atlantic Special 590 019	THE BLUES ROLL ON (reissue of "Southern Folk Heritage: The Blues Roll On")	12
69	Poppy PYM 11001	BLUES ROOTS VOLUME ONE	25
66	Decca LK 4748	BLUES SOUTHSIDE CHICAGO	55
71	Python PLP 16	BLUES TODAY — SOUTHERN STYLE (99 copies only)	40
71	Polydor 2675 007	BOMBERS	15
65	Topic 12T 128	BONNY LASS COME O'ER THE BURN	12
73	Storyville SLP 229	BOOGIE WOOGIE BOYS	15
70s	Milestone MLP 2009	BOOGIE WOOGIE RARITIES	15
60s	Storyville 670184	BOOGIE WOOGIE TRIO	15
55	London AL 3544	BOOGIE WOOGIE WITH THE BLUES (10")	45
69	Pama SECO 17	BOSS REGGAE	75
84	Frux FRLP 1	BORN OUT OF DREAMS	12
74	Eron 002	BOTH SIDES OF THE DOWNS (with insert)	25
80	Aardvark STEAL 2	BOUQUET OF STEEL (blue vinyl with 27-page booklet)	15
91	BBC CD 844	BRINGING IT ALL BACK HOME (2-CD, with booklet)	25
87	GWR GBS 1	BRISTOL CUSTOM BIKE SHOW 1986 (some with poster)	15/12
81	Bristol Recorder BR 002	THE BRISTOL RECORDER VOL. 2 (with magazine booklet)	15
82	Bristol Recorder BR 003	THE BRISTOL RECORDER VOL. 3 (with magazine booklet)	12

			MINT VALUE £
93	EMI CD 502046	BRITISH BEAT BEFORE THE BEATLES 1955/56 (CD)	18
93	EMI CD 502047	BRITISH BEAT BEFORE THE BEATLES 1957 (CD)	18
93	EMI CD 502048	BRITISH BEAT BEFORE THE BEATLES 1958 (CD)	18
93	EMI CD 502049	BRITISH BEAT BEFORE THE BEATLES 1959 (CD)	18
93	EMI CD 502050	BRITISH BEAT BEFORE THE BEATLES 1960 (CD)	18
93	EMI CD 502051	BRITISH BEAT BEFORE THE BEATLES 1961 (CD)	18
93	EMI CD 502052	BRITISH BEAT BEFORE THE BEATLES 1962 (CD)	18
68	Island ILP 966/ILPS 9066	BRITISH BLUE-EYED SOUL	70
67	Tamla Motown TML 11055	BRITISH MOTOWN CHARTBUSTERS (mono, flipback sleeve)	25
69	T. Motown STML 11055	BRITISH MOTOWN CHARTBUSTERS (stereo reissue, flipback sleeve)	18
68	T. Motown (S)TML 11082	BRITISH MOTOWN CHARTBUSTERS VOL. 2 (original, flipback sleeve)	18
93	Hammer (no catalogue no.)	BRITISH OI! — WORKING CLASS ANTHEMS	12
86	See For Miles SEE 66	THE BRITISH PSYCHEDELIC TRIP, 1966-69	12
86	See For Miles SEE 76	THE BRITISH PSYCHEDELIC TRIP, VOLUME TWO, 1966-69	12
87	See For Miles SEE 86	THE BRITISH PSYCHEDELIC TRIP, VOLUME THREE	12
87	See For Miles SEE 206	THE BRITISH PSYCHEDELIC TRIP, VOLUME FOUR	12
70	Trojan TBL 106	BRIXTON CAT	30
80	CBS 31845	BROADWAY MAGIC VOLUME 2: THE GREAT PERFORMERS	12
64	Decca LK 4598	BRUM BEAT	100
64	Dial DLP 1	BRUM BEAT	75
79	Big Bear BRUM 1	BRUM BEAT — LIVE AT THE BARREL ORGAN (2-LP, with inserts)	20
80	MCA MCF 3074	BRUTE FORCE	20
70	Buddah 2349 008	BUDDAH IN MIND	12
72	Flyright LP 106	BULL CITY BLUES	15
66	Decca LK 4734	BUMPER BUNDLE	25
77	Stiff SEEZ 2	A BUNCH OF STIFF RECORDS	12
79	Cherry Red ARED 2	BUSINESS UNUSUAL (with *Zig Zag* small labels catalogue)	15
81	Autumn AU 2	BUSTED AT OZ	20
84	Dambusters DAM 003	BUTTONS AND BOWS VOLUME 1 (2-LP)	30
84	Dambusters DAM 006	BUTTONS AND BOWS VOLUME 2 (2-LP)	30

C

56	Columbia 33S 1083	CABARET NIGHT IN PARIS (10" LP)	12
57	Columbia 33S 1099	CABARET NIGHT IN PARIS No. 4 (10" LP)	12
57	Columbia 33S 1105	CABARET NIGHT IN PARIS No. 5 (10" LP)	12
87	MCA MCLD 622	CALIFORNIA DREAMIN' (2-LP)	18
50s	Melodisc MLP 507	CALYPSO CARNIVAL (10" LP)	18
75	Sain SAIN 1031	CANEUON: RHWNG GWYL A GWAITH	15
72	Topic 12TS 219	CANNY NEWCASSEL (with booklet, blue label)	20
67	Bounty BY 6035	CAN'T KEEP FROM CRYING (TOPICAL BLUES ON THE DEATH OF PRESIDENT KENNEDY)	25
78	Capitol CAPS 1025	CAPITOL SOUL CASINO	12
50s	Parlophone CPMD 13	CARIBBEAN CALYPSO (10" LP)	25
71	Trojan TBL 171	CARIBBEAN DANCE FESTIVAL (wraparound paper sleeve)	15
73	Flyright LP 505	CAROLINA COUNTRY BLUES	15
81	Secret SEC 2	CARRY ON OI!	12
	City Centre Offices TOWERBLOCK 002LP	CASHIER ESCAPE ROUTE	18
73	Nottingham Festival FEST 2	CASTLE ROCK	125
65	Capitol T2340	CAT BALLOU AND OTHER MOTION PICTURE SONGS (Frankie De Vol/Nat 'King' Cole/Stubby Kaye)	15
78	Nice NICE 1	CATCH A WAVE (2 x 10", gatefold sleeve)	30
77	CBS 82401	CBS ROCKABILLY CLASSICS VOL. 1	12
78	CBS 82993	CBS ROCKABILLY CLASSICS VOL. 2	12
79	CBS 83911	CBS ROCKABILLY CLASSICS VOL. 3	12
86	NME 022	C-86 (LP, promo-only for cassette, 500 pressed)	12
90	Cerne CERNE 001/002/003	THE CERNE BOX SET (3-LP box set; Nurse With Wound/ Current 93/Sol Invictus; with 3 inserts)	125
80	Quality QP 32/80	CHAMPIONS AGAIN: HIGHLIGHTS OF 1979-80 SEASON	20
71	Chess 6671 102	CHARLIE PARKER MEMORIAL CONCERT	12
60s	Columbia	CHARTBUSTERS USA	40
73	Checker 6445 150	CHESS GOLDEN DECADE VOL. 1: THE EARLY 50s	12
73	Checker 6445 151	CHESS GOLDEN DECADE VOL. 2: 1956 TAKE IT EASY GREASY	12
73	Checker 6445 152	CHESS GOLDEN DECADE VOL. 3: 1957 DIMESTORE PONYTAIL	12
74	Chess 6445 153	CHESS GOLDEN DECADE VOL. 4: 1958-1959 BOOK OF LOVE	12
74	Chess 6445 154	CHESS GOLDEN DECADE VOL. 5: 1959-1961 GOOD MORNING LITTLE SCHOOLGIRL	12
74	Chess 6445 202	CHESS GOLDEN DECADE VOL. 6: 1961-1962 TALKIN' TRASH	12
74	Chess 6445 203	CHESS GOLDEN DECADE VOL. 7: 1963-1965 HIGH HEEL SNEAKERS (gatefold sleeve)	15
74	Chess 6445 204	CHESS GOLDEN DECADE VOL. 8: 1965-1966 THE IN CROWD	12
78	Chess 9124 213	CHESS ROCKABILLIES	12
64	Chess CRL 4004	CHESS STORY VOL. 1	50
65	Chess CRL 4516	CHESS STORY VOL. 2	50
72	Delmark DL 624	CHICAGO AIN'T NOTHING BUT A BLUES BAND	12
71	Vanguard VSD 79217	CHICAGO BLUES VOLUME 2	12
66	Fontana TFL 6068	CHICAGO/THE BLUES/TODAY	22
66	Fontana TFL 6069	CHICAGO/THE BLUES/TODAY VOLUME 2	22
66	Fontana TFL 6070	CHICAGO/THE BLUES/TODAY VOLUME 3	22
69	Vanguard SVRL 19020	CHICAGO/THE BLUES/TODAY VOLUME 1	25
69	Vanguard SVRL 19021	CHICAGO/THE BLUES/TODAY VOLUME 2	25
69	Vanguard SVRL 19022	CHICAGO/THE BLUES/TODAY VOLUME 3	20
68	Sunflower ET 1401	THE CHICAGO HOUSE BANDS (99 copies only)	40
70s	JSP 1004	CHICAGO JUMP	12
69	Kokomo K 1005	CHICAGO SESSIONS VOLUME 1 (99 copies only)	50
70	Flyright LP 4700	CHICKEN STUFF	15

			MINT VALUE £
80	Relics LSD 1	CHOCOLATE SOUP FOR DIABETICS VOL. 1	15
81	Relics ACID 1	CHOCOLATE SOUP FOR DIABETICS VOL. 2 (gatefold sleeve)	15
83	Relics CSFD 3	CHOCOLATE SOUP FOR DIABETICS VOL. 3	12
84	MCA CHUNK 1	CHUNKS OF FUNK	20
58	Philips BBR 8112	CHRISTMAS (10")	15
73	United Artists UDX 205/6	CHRISTMAS AT THE PATTI (2 x 10", gatefold sleeve)	18
68	Chess CRLS 4541	CHRISTMAS DEDICATION	22
81	Ze/Island ILPS 7017	A CHRISTMAS RECORD (LP, initially white vinyl, then black)	each 12
82	Ze/Island ILPS 7022	A CHRISTMAS RECORD (LP, 'improved 1982 edition', blue border on sleeve instead of black)	12
63	London HA-U 8141	A CHRISTMAS GIFT FOR YOU (plum label, later black label)	60/25
78	Incus INCUS 33	CIRCADIAN RHYTHM	50
72	Specialty SNTF 5015	CITY BLUES	12
80s	White Elephant RIOCH 1	CITY WALLS — A SOUTHAMPTON COMPILATION (with insert)	12
70	Charisma CAS 1008	CLASSICAL HEADS	12
55	London AL 3559	CLASSIC JAZZ PIANO (10")	25
52	Capitol LC 6559	CLASSICS IN JAZZ: PIANO ITEMS (10")	15
52	Capitol LC 6561	CLASSICS IN JAZZ: THE MODERN IDIOM (10")	15
52	Capitol LC 6562	CLASSICS IN JAZZ: DIXIELAND STYLE (10")	15
53	Capitol LC 6579	CLASSICS IN JAZZ: TRUMPET STYLISTS (10")	15
53	Capitol LC 6582	CLASSICS IN JAZZ: SAX STYLISTS (10")	15
53	Capitol LC 6598	CLASSICS IN JAZZ: COOL AND QUIET (10")	15
69	Atlantic 587 167	CLASSIC RHYTHM AND BLUES	12
89	Cavern FAB 1964	CLASS OF '64 (CD)	15
70s	Waldo's DS 005	CLEANING UP THE MUSIC BIZ	12
85	Pusmort 0012-02	CLEANSE THE BACTERIA	20
72	Pegasus PS 1	CLOGS (FOLK SAMPLER) (with insert)	12
90s	Distronics ITCD 3	THE CLOSING PARTY — IN THE CITY LIVE UNSIGNED (CD)	50
72	Pegasus PS 2	CLUB FOLK VOLUME ONE	18
72	Pegasus PS 3	CLUB FOLK VOLUME TWO	18
70	Trojan TBL 159	CLUB REGGAE VOLUME ONE	15
71	Trojan TBL 164	CLUB REGGAE VOLUME TWO	15
71	Trojan TBL 178	CLUB REGGAE VOLUME THREE	15
72	Trojan TBL 188	CLUB REGGAE VOLUME FOUR	15
70	Trojan TTL 54	CLUB ROCK STEADY	30
68	W.I.R.L. ILP 965	CLUB ROCK STEADY '68	60
67	W.I.R.L. ILP 948	CLUB SKA '67	55
67	W.I.R.L. ILP 956	CLUB SKA '67 VOL. 2	40
80	Island IRSP 4	CLUB SKA '67	12
70	Trojan TTL 48	CLUB SKA VOLUME ONE	20
70	Trojan TTL 51	CLUB SKA VOLUME TWO	30
68	Island ILP 964	CLUB SOUL	40
67	Elektra EUK 253	A COLD WIND BLOWS	15
65	Tamla Motown TML 11001	A COLLECTION OF 16 TAMLA MOTOWN HITS	50
67	Tamla Motown TML 11043	A COLLECTION OF 16 ORIGINAL BIG HITS VOL. 4	35
67	Tamla Motown TML 11050	A COLLECTION OF 16 ORIGINAL BIG HITS VOL. 5	30
68	T. Motown (S)TML 11074	A COLLECTION OF 16 ORIGINAL BIG HITS VOL. 6	25
69	T. Motown (S)TML 11092	A COLLECTION OF 16 ORIGINAL BIG HITS VOL. 7 — THE MOTOWN SOUND	25
70	T. Motown (S)TML 11130	A COLLECTION OF 16 ORIGINAL BIG HITS VOL. 8	18
75	Chicago 202	COLLECTORS BLUES SERIES VOL. 1	22
75	Chicago 205	COLLECTORS BLUES SERIES VOL. 2	22
75	Chicago 210	COLLECTORS BLUES SERIES VOL. 3	22
75	Chicago 212	COLLECTORS BLUES SERIES VOL. 4	22
75	Chicago 213	COLLECTORS BLUES SERIES VOL. 5	22
54	London AL 3514	COLLECTORS' ITEMS VOLUME ONE (10")	18
54	London AL 3533	COLLECTORS' ITEMS VOLUME TWO (10")	18
56	London AL 3550	COLLECTORS' ITEMS VOLUME THREE (10")	18
86	Color Disc COLORS 4	COLOR SUPPLEMENT (400 only)	15
93	2-Tone CHR TT 5013	THE COMPACT 2-TONE STORY (4-CD, box set with book)	35
76	Incus INCUS 21	COMPANY 1	50
77	Incus INCUS 29	COMPANY 6	50
77	Incus INCUS 30	COMPANY 7	50
72	Apple STCX 3385	THE CONCERT FOR BANGLA DESH (3-LP box set, with booklet)	22
70	Transatlantic TRASAM 14	THE CONTEMPORARY GUITAR SAMPLER	12
70	Transatlantic TRASAM 15	CONTEMPORARY GUITAR SAMPLER VOL. 2	12
64	Decca LK 4664	CONVERSATION WITH THE BLUES	70
57	Tempo TAP 10	COOL MUSIC FOR A HOT NIGHT – MOOD MUSIC IN THE MODERN MANNER	125
72	Wicksteed WCKLP 02	CORBY CATCHMENT AREA (private pressing)	350
78	ABC ABCL 5247	COTTON PICKIN' ROCK	12
80s	Third Mind TMLP 09	COULD YOU WALK ON THE WATER	15
64	London HA-B 8145	COUNTRY & WESTERN GOLDEN HIT PARADE VOL. 1	15
64	London HA-B 8146	COUNTRY & WESTERN GOLDEN HIT PARADE VOL. 2	15
60	Philips BBL 7410	COUNTRY AND WESTERN REQUESTS	12
62	Philips BBL 7552	COUNTRY AND WESTERN REQUESTS VOL. 2	12
63	Mercury 20015 MCL	COUNTRY AND WESTERN ROUND UP	12
60	Storyville SLP 129	THE COUNTRY BLUES	20
73	Specialty SNTF 5014	COUNTRY BLUES	15
60s	Saydisc Roots RL 334	COUNTRY BLUES OBSCURITIES VOLUME 1	20
66	Stateside SL 10170	COUNTRY COUSINS	15
56	Brunswick LA 8729	COUNTRY FAVOURITES VOL. ONE (10")	30
65	London HA-B 8243	COUNTRY GUITAR HALL OF FAME	15
64	London HA-B 8198	THE COUNTRY MUSIC FESTIVAL	12
66	London HA-B 8263	COUNTRY MUSIC FESTIVAL VOL. 2	12
66	London HA-B 8287	COUNTRY MUSIC FESTIVAL VOL. 3	12
63	Stateside SL 10017	THE COUNTRY MUSIC HALL OF FAME	15
63	London HA-B 8076	COUNTRY MUSIC HALL OF FAME VOL. 1	12

			MINT VALUE £
63	London HA-B 8077	COUNTRY MUSIC HALL OF FAME VOL. 2	15
64	London HA-B 8156	COUNTRY MUSIC HALL OF FAME VOL. 3	12
64	London HA-B 8157	COUNTRY MUSIC HALL OF FAME VOL. 4	12
65	London HA-B 8216	COUNTRY MUSIC HALL OF FAME VOL. 5	12
65	London HA-B 8217	COUNTRY MUSIC HALL OF FAME VOL. 6	12
66	London HA-B 8283	COUNTRY MUSIC HALL OF FAME VOL. 7	12
66	London HA-B 8284	COUNTRY MUSIC HALL OF FAME VOL. 8	12
67	London HA-B 8328	COUNTRY MUSIC HALL OF FAME VOL. 9	12
67	London HA-B 8329	COUNTRY MUSIC HALL OF FAME VOL. 10	12
68	London HA-B 8354	COUNTRY MUSIC HALL OF FAME VOL. 11	12
68	London HA-B 8355	COUNTRY MUSIC HALL OF FAME VOL. 12	12
65	London HA-B 8206	THE COUNTRY MUSIC MEMORIAL ALBUM	12
62	Stateside SL 10003	COUNTRY MUSIC SPECTACULAR	12
63	Starlite STLP 15	COUNTRY MUSIC U.S.A. (reissued as GRK 605)	15/12
64	London HA-B 8185	COUNTRY MUSIC U.S.A.	12
65	London HA-B 8224	COUNTRY MUSIC WHO'S WHO	12
59	Capitol T 1179	THE COUNTRY'S BEST	12
69	Pama ECO 2	CRAB — GREATEST HITS	35
80	Rabid/Absurd LAST 1	THE CRAP STOPS HERE	25
87	Supreme CDSU 1	THE CREAM OF SUPREME (CD)	25
60	Fontana TFL 5103	THE CREAM OF 'TAKE IT FROM HERE' (also stereo SFL 534)	12
60s	Saydisc Roots RL 332	CREAM OF THE CROP	12

D

68	H. Note/B. Shot BSLP 5002	DANCING DOWN ORANGE STREET	75
76	Dark Horse DH 1 (DHSAM 1)	DARK HORSE RECORDS '76 (promo only sampler, stickered sleeve & inner)	40
91	Liquid Noise LIQ 1	THE DARK SIDE OF THE POOL	12
86	EMI EQ 5003	DAVE CLARK'S TIME (2-LP, with brochure and lyric inner, some with hologram)	30/25
71	Dawn DNLB 3024	DAWN TAKEAWAY CONCERT	12
79	Dead Good DEAD 4	DEAD GOOD'S DEAD GOODS (unissued)	
78	Virgin VD 2508	DEAD ON ARRIVAL (2-LP, glow-in-the-dark vinyl with poster, gatefold sleeve)	30
66	Highway 51 H 100	DECADE OF THE BLUES — THE 1950's (99 copies only)	60
66	Highway 51 H 104	DECADE OF THE BLUES — THE 1950's VOLUME 2 (99 copies only)	50
54	Decca LF 1160	DECCA SHOWCASE VOL. 3 (10")	15
55	Decca LF 1265	DECCA SHOWCASE VOL. 5 (10")	18
65	London HA-B 8249	DECK OF CARDS	12
71	United Artists UAS 29153	DEEPER INTO THE VAULTS	12
69	Topic 12T 188	DEEP LANCASHIRE — SONGS & BALLADS OF THE INDUSTRIAL NORTH-WEST (blue label)	12
70	Polydor 2673 001	DEEP OVERGROUND POP	15
70	Stax SXATS 1037	THE DEEP SOUL OF STAX	20
71	Flyright LP 102	DEEP SOUTH COUNTRY BLUES	15
93	Beggars Banquet BBQLP399	DEAFENING DIVINITIES VOL. 2	12
93	Beggars Banquet	DEAFENING DIVINITIES WITH AURAL AFFINITIES	12
80	Deleted DEC 009	DELETED FUN TIME (cassette)	15
86	Decal LIK 9	DERAM DAYZE	15
68	Deram SML 1027	THE DERAM GOLDEN POPS SAMPLER	100
67	Island ILP 955	DERRICK HARRIOTT'S ROCK (SKA) STEADY PARTY	200
72	Trojan TTL 54	DERRICK HARRIOTT'S ROCKSTEADY PARTY (reissue)	50
85	Yangki 01	DEVASTATE TO LIBERATE	15
89	Blast First BFDJ 1	DEVIL'S JUKEBOX (10 x 7" in numbered box, with booklet, 3,000 only)	20
79	Topic 12TS 349	DEVON TRADITION — AN ANTHOLOGY FROM TRADITIONAL SINGERS	15
70	Mercury 6641 006	DIMENSION OF MIRACLES	15
80	DinDisc DONE 1	DINDISC 1980 (with free 20"x 20" game)	12
74	DIP DLP 5026	D.I.P. PRESENTS THE UPSETTER (Lee Perry et al.)	100
69	Minit MLL/MLS 40005	DIRT BLUES	30
70	BBC REC 65M	DISC A DAWN	25
57	RCA RC 2400	DISCTIONARY OF JAZZ (10")	12
67	Island ILP 943	DOCTOR SOUL	75
82	BBC 2-LP-22001	DOCTOR WHO COLLECTOR'S EDITION (2-LP, with poster)	30
80s	Pleasantly Surprised PS 12	DOCUMENT (cassette)	18
70	Python PLP	DOWNHOME BLUES (99 copies only)	40
70	Python PLP 14	DOWNHOME BLUES VOLUME 2 (99 copies only)	40
71	Python PLP 22	DOWNHOME BLUES VOLUME 3 (99 copies only)	40
73	Specialty SNTF 5024	DOWNHOME BLUES	12
71	Flyright LP 4703	DOWN IN HOGAN'S ALLEY	15
67	Down With The Game 200	DOWN WITH THE GAME VOLUME 1	45
67	Down With The Game 201	DOWN WITH THE GAME VOLUME 2	45
68	Down With The Game 203	DOWN WITH THE GAME VOLUME 3	45
68	Down With The Game 204	DOWN WITH THE GAME VOLUME 4	45
68	Down With The Game 205	DOWN WITH THE GAME VOLUME 5	45
68	Down With The Game 206	DOWN WITH THE GAME VOLUME 6	45
67	Island ILP 954	DR. KITCH	50
82	Beggars Banquet BEGA 35	DR. RHINO AND MR HYDE	12
85	Capitol EG 26 0573 1-4	DREAM BABIES	15
80s	Pleasantly Surprised PS 6	DREAMS AND DESIRES (cassette, in bag)	15
72	Ember EMB 3413	A DROP OF THE HARD STUFF	12
59	Parlophone PMC 1101	DRUMBEAT (Adam Faith et al.)	55
60	Columbia SCX 3359	DRUM NIGHT AT BIRDLAND	12
68	Island ILP 976	THE DUKE AND THE PEACOCK	70
69	Trojan TTL 8	DUKE REID'S GOLDEN HITS	40
67	Island ILP 958	DUKE REID'S ROCK STEADY	200
70	Trojan TTL 53	DUKE REID'S ROCK STEADY (reissue)	30
69	BBC REC 35S	DUNGEON FOLK	12
88	Big Beat WIK 74	DUNHILL FOLK ROCK VOL 1 – IS IT ANY WONDER	15
73	Dragon HELP 9	DYNAMIC SOUNDS OF JAMAICA VOL. 1	15

MINT VALUE £

E

70	Matchbox SDR 199	EARLY BLUES VOLUME 1: SKOODLE-UM-SKOO	18
70	Matchbox SDR 206	EARLY FOLK BLUES VOLUME 2: HOMETOWN SKIFFLE	18
70	Middle Earth MDLS 20	EARTHED	45
80	Dead Good GOOD 1	EAST (with inner & stickered sleeve)	25
73	Southern Sound SD 200	EAST VERNON BLUES	30
63	Decca LK 4546	EDINBURGH FOLK FESTIVAL VOLUME 1	25
63	Decca LK 4563	EDINBURGH FOLK FESTIVAL VOLUME 2	25
55	Philips BBR 8046	EIGHT EVERGREENS (10")	15
75	Island/Transatlantic FOLK 1001	ELECTRIC MUSE — THE STORY OF FOLK INTO ROCK (4-LP box set with booklet)	45
85	Push PUSH 001	ELEGANCE, CHARM AND DEADLY DANGER	25
80s	Master BBSLP 007	ELEMENTALS	20
83	Extract XX 001	THE ELEPHANT TABLE ALBUM (2-LP)	18
57	Philips BBR 8115	ELLA, LENA, BILLIE AND SARAH (10")	15
71	Island IDLP 1	EL PEA (2-LP, pink rim label)	20
57	Brunswick LAT 8166	ENCYCLOPAEDIA OF JAZZ ON RECORDS VOL. 1 — JAZZ OF THE TWENTIES	12
57	Brunswick LAT 8167	ENCYCLOPAEDIA OF JAZZ ON RECORDS VOL. 2 — JAZZ OF THE THIRTIES	12
57	Brunswick LAT 8168	ENCYCLOPAEDIA OF JAZZ ON RECORDS VOL. 3 — JAZZ OF THE FORTIES	12
57	Brunswick LAT 8169	ENCYCLOPAEDIA OF JAZZ ON RECORDS VOL. 4 — JAZZ OF THE FIFTIES	12
83	Psycho PSYCHO 1	ENDLESS JOURNEY VOL. 1 (numbered)	22
83	Psycho PSYCHO 3	ENDLESS JOURNEY VOL. 2 (numbered)	18
83	Psycho PSYCHO 19	ENDLESS JOURNEY VOL. 3 (numbered)	18
76	Topic 12T 296	ENGLISH COUNTRY MUSIC	15
88	MEK MEK 006	THE ENGLISH REBELS (with insert)	20
01	Ai AILP 002	ESTATE (CD, in stamped sleeve)	20
89	Gee Street GEE A 002	ETERNITY PROJECT ONE	20
89	Gee Street GEE ACD 002	ETERNITY PROJECT ONE (CD)	25
67	Speciality SPE 6601	EVERY DAY I HAVE THE BLUES	18
72	Blue Horizon 2683 007	THE EXCELLO STORY (2-LP)	80
68	Amal. AMGLP 2002	EXPLOSIVE ROCKSTEADY	65
66	Xtra XTRA 5004	EZZ-THETIC	12

F

72	Carnival 2941 201	FADED PICTURE BLUES	12
67	Elektra EUK 259	FANTASTIC FOLK	12
64	Topic 12T 110	FAREWELL NANCY (blue label)	15
76	Lightning LIP 2	FAREWELL TO THE ROXY (2-LP)	18
76	Polydor 2475 605	A FEAST OF IRISH FOLK	12
68	Zeus CF 201	FESTIVAL AT TOWERSEY	50
63	Pye Intl. NPL 28033	FESTIVAL OF THE BLUES	25
67	Marble Arch MAL 724	FESTIVAL OF THE BLUES (reissue)	12
61	Melodisc 12-116	FIDDLIN' COUNTRY STYLE	12
60s	Melodisc MS 4	15 OLDIES BUT GOODIES	18
65	Sue ILP 920	50 MINUTES & 24 SECONDS OF RECORDED DYNAMITE!	75
85	L.A.Y.L.A.H. LAY 10	THE FIGHT IS ON (Nurse With Wound, Organum, et al.)	30
72	Warner Bros K 66013	FILLMORE: THE LAST DAYS (3-LP box set with poster & booklet)	30
72	CBS 63816	FILLMORE WEST	12
65	London HA-B 8205	FINGERS ON FIRE	15
60	HMV CLP 1358/CSD 1298	FINGS AIN'T WOT THEY USED TO BE	30
64	London HA-B 8117	FIRE ON THE STRINGS	15
69	Music Man	FIREPOINT — A COLLECTION OF FOLK BLUES	100
73	Spark SRLM 2003	FIREPOINT — A COLLECTION OF FOLK BLUES (reissue)	40
71	CBS 66311	THE FIRST GREAT ROCK FESTIVALS OF THE 70s: ISLE OF WIGHT AND ATLANTA (3-LP)	35
58	Esquire 20-091	THE FIRST MODERNS (10")	15
57	Esquire 20-089	THE FIRST NATIONAL SKIFFLE CONTEST (10")	75
56	Mercury MPT 7512	FIRST ROCK 'N' ROLL PARTY (10")	125
89	Confection LC 7871	FLAIR: THE OTHER WORLD OF BRITISH FOOTBALL (2-LP)	20
75	Chrysalis CHR 1081	FLASH FEARLESS V THE ZORG WOMEN PARTS 5 & 6 (Alice Cooper, Elkie Brooks, et al.)	15
80s	Alt. Tentacles VIRUS 22	FLEX YOUR HEAD	15
64	Blue Beat BBLP 803	FLY FLYING SKA	300+
69	Atlantic 588 184	FLYING HIGH (record club edition)	15
76	Eron ERON 012	FOLK AT THE BLACK HORSE	12
76	Flams/Wounded WR 1068	FOLK AT THE CHEQUERS (private pressing)	15
64	Ember NR 5015	FOLK BLUES SONG FEST	20
66	Waverley ZLP 2067	FOLK FAVOURITES	12
69	World Rec. Club ST 890	FOLK FESTIVAL	20
76	Transatlantic TRA 324	FOLK FESTIVAL (2-LP)	20
60	Top Rank 35/070	FOLK FESTIVAL AT NEWPORT 1959 VOLUME 1	15
60	Top Rank 35/071	FOLK FESTIVAL AT NEWPORT 1959 VOLUME 2	15
60	Top Rank 35/072	FOLK FESTIVAL AT NEWPORT 1959 VOLUME 3	15
62	Fontana TFL 6000	FOLK FESTIVAL AT NEWPORT (VOL. 1)	15
62	Fontana TFL 6004	FOLK FESTIVAL AT NEWPORT (VOL. 2)	15
62	Fontana TFL 6009	FOLK FESTIVAL AT NEWPORT (VOL. 4)	15
63	Pye Intl. NPL 28033	FOLK FESTIVAL OF THE BLUES	20
73	Counterpoint CPT 3994	FOLK FROM McTAVISH'S KITCHENS	30
73	Windmill WMD	FOLK HERITAGE	30
82	Fuck Off (no cat. no.)	FOLK IN HELL (cassette)	15
73	Nottingham Festival FEST 1	FOLK NOTTINGHAM STYLE	250
65	Decca LK 4783	FOLK NOW	20
70	BBC REC 955	FOLK ON FRIDAY	18
71	Talisman STAL 5019	FOLK PHILOSOPHY	20
63	Golden Guinea GGL 0265	THE FOLK SCENE	15
66	Folkscene SSP 001	FOLK SCENE (LP, private pressing)	100

			MINT VALUE £
61	Topic 12T 157	THE FOLK SONGS OF BRITAIN — SONGS OF COURTSHIP	18
61	Topic 12T 158	THE FOLK SONGS OF BRITAIN VOL. 2 — SONGS OF SEDUCTION	18
61	Topic 12T 159	THE FOLK SONGS OF BRITAIN VOL. 3 — JACK OF ALL TRADES	18
61	Topic 12T 160	THE FOLK SONGS OF BRITAIN VOL. 4 — CHILD BALLADS 1	18
61	Topic 12T 161	THE FOLK SONGS OF BRITAIN VOL. 5 — CHILD BALLADS 2	18
61	Topic 12T 194	THE FOLK SONGS OF BRITAIN VOL. 6 — SAILORMEN AND SERVINGMAIDS	18
61	Topic 12T 195	THE FOLK SONGS OF BRITAIN VOL. 7 — FAIR GAME AND FOUL	18
61	Topic 12T 196	THE FOLK SONGS OF BRITAIN VOL. 8 — A SOLDIER'S LIFE FOR ME	18
61	Topic 12T 197	THE FOLK SONGS OF BRITAIN VOL. 9 — SONGS OF CEREMONY	18
61	Topic 12T 198	THE FOLK SONGS OF BRITAIN VOL. 10 — SONGS OF ANIMAL	18
(Each of the above 10 LPs came with blue labels and a booklet.)			
69	Topic	THE FOLK SONGS OF BRITAIN VOLS. 1-10 (10 x LP box set)	100
61	Topic TPS 201	TOPIC SAMPLER No. 6 — FOLK SONGS	12
57	HMV DLP 1143	FOLK SONG TODAY (SONGS AND BALLADS OF ENGLAND AND SCOTLAND) (10")	25
65	HMV CLP 1910	FOLKSOUND OF BRITAIN	18
71	Nicro K 220971	FOLK UPSTAIRS	80
63	Ember CEL 902	FOOL BRITANNIA	15
65	Decca LK 4695	FOURTEEN — THE LORD'S TAVERNERS' ALBUM	35
89	él	4-2-4 FOOTBALL CLASSICS	15
79	Pickwick PLD 8013	40 FOLK FAVOURITES (2-LP, limited edition)	18
70	Bamboo BLP 205	FREEDOM SOUNDS	60
81	Fresh FRESHLP 8	A FRESH SELECTION	12
72	Trojan TRL 51	FROM BAM BAM TO CHERRY OH BABY	15
80	Disques/Crepescule TWI 007	FROM BRUSSELS WITH LOVE (cassette, in pouch with booklet)	20
80s	Disques Du Crepuscule IPCD 72001	FROM BRUSSELS WITH LOVE (CD)	50
70	Liberty LBS 83321	FROM THE BAYOU	18
70	Liberty LBS 83278	FROM THE VAULTS	18
83	New European BADVC 666	FROM TORTURE TO CONSCIENCE (with insert)	80
71	Cutty Wren	FROST LANE	50
89	Sub Pop DAMP 104	FUCK ME, I'M RICH!	15
89	Unrest UNREST 14	FULL FORCE VOL. 3	15
70	Trojan TBL 137	FUNKY CHICKEN	35
87	Urban	(JAMES BROWN'S) FUNKY PEOPLE VOL. 1	12
87	Urban URBLP 14	(JAMES BROWN'S) FUNKY PEOPLE VOL. 2	12
70	Bamboo BLP 206	FUNKY REGGAE	70
82	Come Org. WDC 881021	FÜR ILSE KOCH (some on red vinyl; beware of bootlegs)	120/75
98	Ferox FER CD 4	FURTHER ADVENTURES IN TECHNO SOUL (CD)	18
70	Ember	FUTURE STAR EXPLOSION	12

G

69	Pama ECO 4	GAS — GREATEST HITS	45
66	Doctor Bird DLM 5001	GAYFEET	125
00	Ai AILP 001	GEMOTE (CD)	20
52	Brunswick LA 8544	GEMS OF JAZZ VOL. 1 (10")	15
52	Brunswick LA 8561	GEMS OF JAZZ VOL. 1 (10")	15
55	HMV DLP 1039	GENE NORMAN PRESENTS JUST JAZZ (10")	20
72	Chess 6641 047	GENESIS — THE BEGINNINGS OF ROCK (4-LP box set with booklet)	50
73	Chess 6641 125	GENESIS — MEMPHIS TO CHICAGO (4-LP box set with booklet)	50
75	Chess 6641 174	GENESIS — SWEET HOME CHICAGO (4-LP box set with booklet)	50
69	Kokomo K 1004	GEORGIA GUITARS 1927-1938 (99 copies only)	50
67	Coxsone CSL 8007	GET READY ROCK STEADY	135
60s	Riverside RLP 12-106	GIANTS OF BOOGIE WOOGIE	15
69	Pama SECO 20	A GIFT FROM PAMA	35
71	Wand WCS 1003	THE GIRLS WITH SOUL	12
80s	Sarah	GLASS ARCADE (The Field Mice/The Sea Urchins, et al.)	20
72	Revelation REV 1/2/3	GLASTONBURY FAYRE REVELATIONS — A MUSICAL ANTHOLOGY (3-LP, poster sleeve with booklets, pyramid & printed polythene bag)	100
66	Columbia SX 6062	GO!	85
80s	Touch & Go TG 11	GOD'S FAVOURITE DOG	20
95	Lissy's LISS 5	GODZ IS NOT A PUT ON (500 only, in hand-pressed sleeve; some with free 7")	30/20
72	Flyright LP 103	GOIN' AWAY WALKING	15
70	Python LP 1	GOIN' BACK TO CHICAGO (99 copies only)	40
70	Warner Bros WS 1874	GOING HOME	12
60s	Heritage 1003	GOING TO CALIFORNIA (99 copies only)	70
68	Decca LK 4931	GOIN' UP THE COUNTRY	15
69	Oliver & Boyd SBN 05 002118/9	THE GOLDEN BIRD (2-LP)	30
64	Columbia 33SX 1664	GOLDEN GOODIES VOL. 1	50
64	Columbia 33SX 1672	GOLDEN GOODIES VOL. 2	50
69	Roulette RCP 1000	GOLDEN GOODIES VOL. 1	20
69	Roulette RCP 1001	GOLDEN GOODIES VOL. 2	20
59	Philips BBL 7331	GOLDEN HITS	18
60	Philips BBL 7422	GOLDEN HITS VOL. 2	15
61	Philips BBL 7581	GOLDEN HITS VOL. 3	18
57	Capitol T 830	THE GOLD RECORD (blue label)	12
88	53rd & 3rd AGAS 3	GOOD FEELINGS	15
75	Eron 004	GOOD FOLK OF KENT (with insert)	40
65	Atlantic ATL 5004	GOOD OLD FIFTIES	50
68	Elek. EUK 260/EUKS 7260	GOOD TIME MUSIC (U.K. version of "What's Shakin' ", gold or red label)	40/30
72	CBS 67234	GOSPEL SOUND (2-LP)	20
59	Brunswick LAT 8290	GOSPEL TRAIN	20
64	London HA-B 8172	GRAND OLE OPRY SPECTACULAR VOL. 1	15

			MINT VALUE £
64	London HA-B 8173	GRAND OLE OPRY SPECTACULAR VOL. 2	15
86	BBC REB 609	GRANGE HILL — THE ALBUM	18
73	Greasy Truckers GT 4997	GREASY TRUCKERS — LIVE AT DINGWALLS DANCE HALL (2-LP with insert)	20
73	United Artists UDX 203/4	GREASY TRUCKERS PARTY (2-LP, gatefold sleeve)	25
72	Vanguard VSD 25/26	GREAT BLUESMEN (2-LP)	18
54	London AL 3530	THE GREAT BLUES SINGERS (10")	40
60s	Riverside RLP 12-121	THE GREAT BLUES SINGERS	25
75	D. Demand DDDDLP 5002	GREAT DISCO DEMANDS	12
55	HMV DLP 1025	GREAT ELLINGTON SOLOISTS (10")	25
70	Trojan TBL 111	GREATER JAMAICA	35
75	Brunswick BRLS 3006	GREATEST HITS	15
64	Stateside SL 10075	THE GREATEST GOSPEL SONGS OF OUR TIME	20
67	Doctor Bird DLM 5009	GREATEST JAMAICAN BEAT	125
66	Pye Intl. NPL 28052	THE GREATEST ON STAGE	12
65	RCA RD/SF 7755	GREAT MOMENTS IN JAZZ — NEWPORT JAZZ FESTIVAL 1964	12
70	Transatlantic TRASAM 17	GREAT SCOTS SAMPLER	20
70	Transatlantic TRASAM 21	GREAT SCOTS SAMPLER VOL. 2	20
54	HMV DLP 1054	GREAT TRUMPET SOLOISTS (10")	25
85	Crashed METALPS 107	GREEN METAL	30
60	Columbia 33SX 1296	GRETSCH DRUM NIGHT AT BIRDLAND (also stereo SCX 3359)	12
71	Bamboo BDLP 215	GROOVING WITH BAMBOO	65
69	Direction 8-63452	GROOVY BABY	25
63	Realm RM 149	GROUP BEAT '63	40
63	London HA-U 8086	GROUP OF GOODIES	50
64	World Record Club TP 444	GROUP '64	20
78	Virgin VCL 5001	GUILLOTINE (10" mini-LP, with inner sleeve)	18
60s	Storyville SLP 166	GUITAR BLUES	22
73	Transatlantic TRA 271	GUITAR WORKSHOP (2-LP)	20
71	Sunnyland KS 102	GULF COAST BLUES (99 copies only)	40
69	Trojan TTL 16	GUNS OF NAVARONE	22
69	Liberty LBX 3	GUTBUCKET	20
68	Island ILP 977	GUY STEVENS' TESTAMENT OF ROCK AND ROLL	40
71	Wand WCS 1002	THE GUYS WITH SOUL	20
68	Columbia S(C)X 6275	GYPSY SWING	12

H

58	Oriole MG 20033	HAIL VARIETY!	12
70	Probe PSS 1	HANDLE WITH CARE	12
88	HandMade (no cat. no.)	HANDMADE FILMS MUSIC — THE 10TH ANNIVERSARY (CD, promo only)	100
85	Anagram GRAM 23	HANG 11 (MUTANT SURF PUNKS)	18
68	Immediate IMLYIN 2	HAPPY TO BE PART OF THE INDUSTRY OF HUMAN HAPPINESS	15
77	VJM VLP 40	HARD LUCK BLUES	15
77	Revival RVS 1009	HARD TIMES BLUES	12
74	Decca DPA 3009/10	HARD UP HEROES 1963-68 (2-LP, gatefold sleeve)	25
57	London TKL 93119	HARLEM CONGREGATION	25
56	London AL 3553	HARLEM PIANO ROLL (10")	20
72	Carnival 2941 001	HARPIN' ON IT	12
71	Harvest SHSS 3	HARVEST BAG	12
69	Harvest SPSLP 118	HARVEST SAMPLER OF THE INITIAL FOUR JUNE RELEASES (promo only)	80
63	Reprise R 50001	HAVE YOURSELF A MERRY LITTLE CHRISTMAS	15
71	Sunnyland KS 101	HAVIN' A GOOD TIME — CHICAGO BLUES ANTHOLOGY (99 copies only)	40
66	Polydor 582 701	HEADLINE NEWS	15
71	Vertigo 6360 045	HEADS TOGETHER, FIRST ROUND (gatefold sleeve, swirl label)	20
94	Mo' Wax MWLP 026	HEADZ: A SOUNDTRACK OF EXPERIMENTAL BEATHEAD JAMS (3-LP)	25
96	Mo' Wax MW 061LP	HEADZ VOLUME 2A (4-LP)	25
90	Imaginary ILLUSION 016	HEAVEN AND HELL VOLUME 1: A TRIBUTE TO THE VELVET UNDERGROUND	70
81	Heavy Metal HMR LP 1	HEAVY METAL HEROES	30
82	Heavy Metal HMR LP 7	HEAVY METAL HEROES VOLUME 2	25
84	Heavy Metal HMR LP 24	HEAVY METAL RECORDS (blue vinyl, round sleeve)	15
68	Trojan TRL 6	HERE COMES THE DUKE	35
65	Pye NPL 18121	HERE COME THE GIRLS	15
85	Rock 'N' Dole RDR 2	HEROES (with poster)	18
80s	Temps Modernes LTMV:XI	HEURES SANS SOLEIL	25
69	Pama PSP 1002	HEY BOY HEY GIRL	35
58	Capitol T 926	HI-FI DRUMS	12
58	Melodisc MLP 518	HIGHLIFE: AUTHENTIC WEST AFRICAN MUSIC VOL. 1 (10")	12
58	Melodisc MLP 519	HIGHLIFE: AUTHENTIC WEST AFRICAN MUSIC VOL. 2 (10")	12
	BBC Radio Enterprises REC 29M	HIGHLIGHTS FROM 21 YEARS OF BBC'S SPORTS REPORT	12
59	Parlophone PMD 1085	HIGHWAY TO HEAVEN (10")	15
52	Capitol LC 6508	THE HISTORY OF JAZZ — THE SOLID SOUTH	30
52	Capitol LC 6520	THE HISTORY OF JAZZ — THEN CAME SWING	12
52	Capitol LC 6527	THE HISTORY OF JAZZ — THIS MODERN AGE	15
57	Capitol T 793	THE HISTORY OF JAZZ VOL. 1 — N'ORLEANS ORIGINS	12
57	Capitol T 794	THE HISTORY OF JAZZ VOL. 2 — THE TURBULENT TWENTIES	12
57	Capitol T 795	THE HISTORY OF JAZZ VOL. 3 — EVERYBODY SWINGS	12
57	Capitol T 796	THE HISTORY OF JAZZ VOL. 4 — ENTER THE COOL	12
68	Atlantic 587 094	HISTORY OF RHYTHM AND BLUES — VOL. 1, THE ROOTS 1947-52	15
68	Atlantic 587 095	HISTORY OF RHYTHM AND BLUES — VOL. 2, THE GOLDEN YEARS 1953-55	15
68	Atlantic 587 096	HISTORY OF RHYTHM AND BLUES — VOL. 3, ROCK 'N' ROLL 1956-57	15
68	Atlantic 587 097	HISTORY OF RHYTHM AND BLUES — VOL. 4, THE BIG BEAT 1958-60	15
68	Atlantic 587 140	HISTORY OF RHYTHM AND BLUES — VOL. 5	15
68	Atlantic 587 141	HISTORY OF RHYTHM AND BLUES — VOL. 6	15
69	Bamboo BDLP 203	HISTORY OF SKA VOLUME ONE	75
87	Stylus/PWL SMD 740	HIT FACTORY — THE BEST OF STOCK, AITKEN & WATERMAN VOL. 1 (CD)	30

			MINT VALUE £
87	Fanfare/PWL HFCD 4	HIT FACTORY — THE BEST OF STOCK, AITKEN & WATERMAN VOL. 2 (CD, with exclusive mix of Kylie Minogue's "I Should Be So Lucky", etc)	30
64	Pye NPL 18108	THE HITMAKERS	20
65	Pye NPL 18115	THE HITMAKERS VOL. 2	20
69	Marble Arch MAL 1259	THE HITMAKERS	12
57	Pye Nixa NPT 19015	HIT PARADE OF 1956 (10")	22
59	Pye Nixa NPT 19032	HIT PARADE OF 1958	15
66	Marble Arch MAL 650	HITS FROM THE IVY LEAGUE, THE ROCKIN' BERRIES & THE SORROWS	12
77	Stiff FIST 1	HITS — GREATEST STIFFS (with 7", Max Wall's "England's Glory" [BUY 12])	12
65	Tamla Motown TML 11019	HITSVILLE U.S.A.	100
67	Stax 589 005	HIT THE ROAD STAX	20
81	United Dairies UD 05	HOISTING THE BLACK FLAG	35
55	Philips BBR 8048	HOLLYWOOD DANCE DATE (10")	12
64	Ace Of Hearts AH 68	HOLLYWOOD SINGS: THE BOYS	12
64	Ace Of Hearts AH 69	HOLLYWOOD SINGS: THE BOYS AND THE GIRLS	12
56	London D 93076	HOMAGE TO DJANGO REINHARDT (10")	12
62	Golden Guinea GGL 0129	HONEY HIT PARADE	12
74	Melodisc 12-216	HONEYS	25
52	Capitol LC 6544	HONKY TONK PIANO (10")	15
60s	Riverside RLP 8806	HONKY TONK TRAIN (with booklet)	22
65	Summit ATL 4150	HOOTENANNY AT THE BARGE	15
64	Stateside SL 10079	HOOTENANNY AT THE TROUBADOUR	12
63	Decca LK 4544	HOOTENANNY IN LONDON	20
63	Fontana 688 009ZL	HOOTENANNY SATURDAY NIGHT	20
64	Waverley ZLP 2025	HOOT'NANNY SHOW VOLUME 1	20
64	Waverley ZLP 2032	HOOT'NANNY SHOW VOLUME 2	20
71	Pama PMP 2006	HOT NUMBERS	25
71	Pama PMP 2009	HOT NUMBERS VOLUME TWO	25
77	WEA M 100	HOT PLATTER CORDON BLEU (available via *Melody Maker*)	20
70	Trojan TBL 128	HOT SHOTS OF REGGAE	22
72	Hot Wax SHW 5008	HOT WAX GREATEST HITS	12
97	Virgin V 2831	HOUSE OF BAMBOO PRESENTS DANCE & MOOD MUSIC (2-LP, with inners, 3,000 only)	15
69	Track 613 016	THE HOUSE THAT TRACK BUILT (gatefold sleeve)	35
69	Blue Horizon PR 45/46	HOW BLUE CAN WE GET (2-LP, gatefold sleeve with insert)	35

I

69	Liberty LBL/LBS 83252	I ASKED FOR WATER ... AND SHE GAVE ME GASOLINE	60
80	TJM TJM 11	IDENTITY PARADE	12
88	Bam Caruso MARX 085	ILLUSIONS FROM THE CRACKLING VOID	15
90s	Dig The Fuzz DIG 013	ILLUSIONS OF ALICE IN WONDERLAND (650 only, with booklet)	20
69	Immediate IMLYIN 1	IMMEDIATE LETS YOU IN	15
86	Food BITE 4	IMMINENT VOL. 4	12
67	Parlophone PMC 7024	I'M SORRY, I'LL READ THAT AGAIN	18
70	Highway 51 H-104	I'M YOUR COUNTRY MAN (99 copies only)	40
77	United Artists UAS 30101	IMPERIAL ROCKABILLIES	12
79	United Artists UAS 30173	IMPERIAL ROCKABILLIES VOL. 2	12
80	United Artists UAS 30312	IMPERIAL ROCKABILLIES VOL. 3	12
66	CBS/Denson Shoes	THE IN CROWD (shoe offer compilation)	25
69	Trojan TTL 15	INDEPENDENT JAMAICA	30
67	Fontana TL 5426	INDIAN MUSIC	12
79	Object Music OBJ 002	INDISCRETE MUSIC — DUBIOUS COLLABORATION (500 only)	15
84	Illuminated JAMS 39	THE INDUSTRIAL RECORDS STORY 1976-1981	30
84	United Dairies UD 015	IN FRACTURED SILENCE	35
95	RCA 74321 315501	IN FROM THE STORM — THE MUSIC OF JIMI HENDRIX (LP, picture disc)	15
69	T. Motown (S)TML 11124	IN LOVING MEMORY (TRIBUTE TO MRS LOUCYE G. WAKEFIELD)	70
70	Blue Horizon PR 37	IN OUR OWN WAY (OLDIES BUT GOODIES)	35
70	Ember EMB 34111	IN REGGAE TIME	15
88	Secret Heart 1008	IN THE BEGINNING — TOMMY STEELE (with insert, 1,000 only)	12
66	Ember FA 2034	IRELAND'S GREATEST SOUNDS: FIVE TOP GROUPS FROM BELFAST'S MARITIME CLUB	75
64	Decca LK 4633	IRISH FOLK NIGHT	15
63	Topic 12T 86	THE IRON MUSE (blue label with lyric insert, later reissued)	15/10
79	Rationale RATE 8	IRRATIONALE (cassette, in bag with booklet)	20
61	Oriole MG 20046	IT'S ALL HAPPENING HERE	35
63	Pye Golden Guinea GGL 0249	IT'S DANCE TIME	18
88	Bam Caruso MARX 100	IT'S ONLY A PASSING PHASE	15
84	Sain 002	IT'S UNHEARD OF	150

J

69	Amalgamated CSP 3	JACKPOT OF HITS	35
77	Policy Wheel PW 4593	JACKSON BLUES BOYS	12
68	Blue Cat BCL 1	JAMAICAN MEMORIES	80
64	Atlantic 587 075	JAMAICA SKA (colour 'Dancers' sleeve)	60
67	Atlantic 587 075	JAMAICA SKA (reissue, orange sleeve)	35
68	Flyright LP 3502	JAMBALAYA ON THE BAYOU — VOLUME 1	20
69	Flyright LP 3503	JAMBALAYA ON THE BAYOU — VOLUME 2	20
72	Utd. Artists UAS 60027/8	THE JAMES BOND COLLECTION (2-LP, with booklet)	25
72	Rolling Stones COC 39100	JAMMING WITH EDWARD	15
55	Columbia Clef 33CX 10008	JAM SESSION	12
61	HMV/Utd Artists CSD 1381	JAZZ ALIVE — A NIGHT AT THE HALF NOTE	12
56	Tempo TAP 5	JAZZ AT THE FLAMINGO	75
55	Columbia 33CX 10078	JAZZ AT THE PHILHARMONIC, 1955 VOL. 1	12
55	Columbia 33CX 10079	JAZZ AT THE PHILHARMONIC, 1955 VOL. 2	12
68	Columbia SLJS 1	JAZZ EXPLOSION	12

			MINT VALUE £
72	Decca ECS 2114	JAZZ IN BRITAIN 1968-1969	25
62	Parlophone PMC 1195	JAZZ IN THE MAKING	12
84	Streetsounds MUSIC 1	JAZZ JUICE	30
85	Streetsounds SOUND 1	JAZZ JUICE (reissue)	25
86	Streetsounds SOUND 4	JAZZ JUICE 2	20
86	Streetsounds SOUND 5	JAZZ JUICE 3	20
86	Streetsounds SOUND 6	JAZZ JUICE 4	20
87	Streetsounds SOUND 8	JAZZ JUICE 5	18
87	Streetsounds SOUND 9	JAZZ JUICE 6	18
87	Streetsounds CDSND 9	JAZZ JUICE 6 (CD)	18
88	Streetsounds SOUND 10	JAZZ JUICE 7	18
88	Streetsounds CDSND 10	JAZZ JUICE 7 (CD)	18
88	Streetsounds SOUND 11	JAZZ JUICE 8	15
88	Streetsounds CDSND 11	JAZZ JUICE 8 (CD)	18
88	Streetsounds SOUND 12	JAZZ JUICE 9	15
88	Streetsounds CDSND 12	JAZZ JUICE 9 (CD)	18
57	London AL 3562	JAZZ OF THE ROARING TWENTIES VOL. 2 (10")	15
58	Philips BBL 7184	JAZZ OMNIBUS	12
63	VJM LC 6	JAZZ PANORAMA OF THE SIXTIES	12
58	Vogue LAE 12097	JAZZ PIANISTS GALORE	12
57	London AL 3565	JAZZ PIANO RARITIES (10")	20
55	Columbia Clef 33C 9007	JAZZ SCENE (10")	18
55	Columbia Clef 33C 9008	JAZZ SCENE VOL. 2 (10")	18
62	Parlophone PMC 1177	JAZZ SOUNDS OF THE 20s VOL. 4: BLUES SINGERS & ACCOMPANISTS	15
56	Vogue LAE 12038	JAZZ WEST COAST	12
57	Vogue LAE 12061	JAZZ WEST COAST VOLUME 2	12
58	Vogue LAE 12115	JAZZ WEST COAST VOLUME 3	12
61	Vogue LAE 12235	JAZZ WEST COAST VOLUME 5	12
77	Decca DPA 3035/3036	THE JOE MEEK STORY (2-LP)	35
60	Top Rank 35/064	JOHN HAMMOND'S SPIRITUALS TO SWING VOLUME 1	12
60	Top Rank 35/065	JOHN HAMMOND'S SPIRITUALS TO SWING VOLUME 2	12
72	Vanguard VRS 8523/4	JOHN HAMMOND'S SPIRITUALS TO SWING: LEGENDARY CARNEGIE HALL CONCERTS OF 1938/9 (2-LP)	18
69	BBC REC 52S	JOHN PEEL PRESENTS TOP GEAR	30
70	BBC REC 68M	JOHN PEEL'S ARCHIVE THINGS	20
60	HMV CLP 1327	A JUG OF PUNCH (also issued as XLP 50003)	35
67	Ace Of Hearts AH 163	JUGS AND WASHBOARDS	15
67	RCA Victor RD 7893	JUGS WASHBOARDS AND KAZOOS	15
70s	Eric's ERICS 008	JUKEBOX AT ERIC'S	12
76	RCA RS 1066	JUMPING AT THE GO GO	18
77	Policy Wheel PW 459-1	JUMPING ON THE HILL	12
64	R&B JBL 1111	JUMP JAMAICA WAY	250
69	RCA Intl. INT 1014	JUST A LITTLE BIT OF SOUL	20
79	Kick KK 1	JUST FOR KICKS	35

K

59	Capitol T 1057	K.C. IN THE 30's	20
72	Joy JOYS 223	KEEP THE FAITH VOL 1	12
72	Joy JOYS 224	KEEP THE FAITH VOL 2	12
72	Joy JOYS 225	KEEP THE FAITH VOL 3	12
56	Vogue LAE 12028	KENTON'S SIDEMEN (Don Rendell, et al.)	60
81	White Witch	KENT ROCKS (200 only)	180
54	HMV DLP 1048	KEYBOARD KINGS OF JAZZ (10")	25
72	Key	KEY COLLECTION (with insert)	15
70	Trojan TBL 140	KING SIZE REGGAE	30
77	Chrysalis CHR 1137	THE KING OF ELFLAND'S DAUGHTER	20
68	Polydor 623 273	KINGS OF RHYTHM AND BLUES	15
60s	Gryphon 13159	KINGS OF THE TWELVE STRING GUITAR	20
71	Flyright LP 101	KINGS OF THE TWELVE STRING GUITAR (reissue)	15
60s	Saydisc Roots RL 333	KINGS OF MEMPHIS TOWN 1927-1930	18
94	Mercury 522 476-1	KISS MY ASS (red, white or blue vinyl)	12
86	Ten DIX 28	KNIGHTS & EMERALDS	15
86	Ten XID 11	KNIGHTS & EMERALDS	15

L

79	The Label TRLP 002S	THE LABEL SOFA ('translumar defractor' 3D picture disc, stickered PVC sleeve)	35
79	Cherry Red ARED 4	LABELS UNLIMITED	12
83	Fetish FR 2011	THE LAST TESTAMENT (with inner, stickered sleeve)	18
87	Other OTH 10	LAST WARRIOR	18
68	Island ILP 986	LEAPING WITH MR LEE (by Bunny Lee All Stars)	175
80	Atra ATRA LP 1003	THE LEGENDS (Augustus Pablo et al.)	15
03	Ai AILP 004	LEISURE (100 copies only)	15
99	Jazzman 1	LE JAZZBEAT!	15
00	Jazzman 3	LE JAZZBEAT! 2	12
87	Ace CHD 215	LENNY COLEMAN & THE EBBTIDES SING 4 SEASONS AND 15 OTHERS	12
66	Blue Horizon LP 2	LET ME TELL YOU ABOUT THE BLUES	400
63	Polydor SLPHM 237 622	LET'S DO THE TWIST, HULLY GULLY, SLOP, SURF, LOCOMOTION, MONKEY	30
66	Neshoba N 11	LET'S GO DOWN SOUTH (99 copies only)	55
58	Brunswick LAT 8271	LET'S HAVE A PARTY	25
81	Alt. Tentacles VIRUS 4	LET THEM EAT JELLYBEANS (with lyric poster)	20
74	Sonet SNTX 1	LEGACY OF THE BLUES SAMPLER	12
80s	Third Mind/Abstract	LIFE AT THE TOP	25
81	WEA K 58412	LIFE IN THE EUROPEAN THEATRE	12
68	Transatlantic TRASAM 2	LISTEN HERE!	15
83	Polydor ROCK 2	A LITTLE BIT OF LIGHT RELIEF	12

			MINT VALUE £
81	NEMS NEL 6020	LIVE AND HEAVY	12
80	BUN 01	LIVE AT BUNJIES (gatefold sleeve with insert)	30
74	Key KL 021	LIVE AT SPREE	20
77	NEMS NEL 6013	LIVE AT THE VORTEX	15
65	Fontana TL 5240	LIVE AT THE WHISKEY A-GO-GO	35
68	Big Shot BBTL 4000	LIVE IT UP	75
64	Embassy WLP 6065	LIVERPOOL BEAT	15
65	Ember NR 5028	LIVERPOOL TODAY — LIVE AT THE CAVERN	35
64	CBS Realm RM 209	LIVIN' WITH THE BLUES	18
70	Trojan TBL 135	LOCH NESS MONSTER	100
87	4AD CAD 703D	LONELY IS AN EYESORE (cardboard pack with book)	30
87	4AD CADX 703	LONELY IS AN EYESORE (CD, LP & cassette, in wooden box with etching, screen print & video, 100 only)	250+
81	Plant Life PLR 032	LOVELY IN THE DANCES: SONGS OF SYDNEY CARTER	15
71	Count Shelly SSLP 03	LOOK BEFORE YOU LEAP	18
91	Holyground HG 121	LOOSE ROUTES (2-LP, gatefold foldover sleeve)	30
65	Storyville 616002	LOUISIANA PRISON BLUES	15
69	Pama PSP 1001	A LOVELY DOZEN	30

M

76	Cornish Legend CLM 1	MADE IN CORNWALL (with insert)	25
58	Pye Nixa Jazz NJL 13	(LEONARD FEATHER PRESENTS) MAD THAD	12
79	Object Music OBJ 003	A MANCHESTER COLLECTION	25
88	Bop BC V001	MANCHESTER, NORTH OF ENGLAND (white labels only)	12
70	Trojan TBL 129	MAN FROM CAROLINA	25
53	Brunswick LA 8567	MAN WITH A HORN (10" LP)	12
70	CBS 52798	MA RAINEY AND THE CLASSIC BLUES SINGERS	18
69	Marmalade 643 314	MARMALADE — 100% PROOF	18
72	Village Thing VTSAM 16	MATCHBOX DAYS	25
68	President PTL 1002	MAR-V-LUS SOUND OF R&B AND SOUL MUSIC	25
60s	Wudwink ISMF 107	MARY'S FOLK	200
78	CBS 82670	MAX'S KANSAS CITY	12
66	CBS Special Prod. WSR 853	McDONALDS ALL-STAR FAVOURITES	12
69	Liberty LBL/LBS 83190	ME AND THE DEVIL	50
78	Topic 12T 376	MELODEON GREATS — A COLLECTION OF MELODEON MASTERPIECES	15
69	Atco 228 023	MEMPHIS GOLD	15
64	London HA 8129	MEMORIES ARE MADE OF HITS VOL. 1	30
64	London HA 8130	MEMORIES ARE MADE OF HITS VOL. 2	30
64	London HA 8131	MEMORIES ARE MADE OF HITS VOL. 3	30
64	London HA 8138	MEMORIES ARE MADE OF HITS VOL. 4	30
64	London HA 8148	MEMORIES ARE MADE OF HITS VOL. 5	30
64	London HA 8171	MEMORIES ARE MADE OF HITS VOL. 6	30
64	London HA 8189	MEMORIES ARE MADE OF HITS VOL. 7	30
65	London HA 8213	MEMORIES ARE MADE OF HITS VOL. 8	30
54	Vogue Coral LVC 10008	MERRY CHRISTMAS (10")	20
69	T. Motown (S)TML 11126	MERRY CHRISTMAS FROM MOTOWN (mono/stereo)	25/22
67	Capitol T 9030	MERRY CHRISTMAS TO YOU	15
85	Neat NEAT 1014	METAL BATTLE	15
80	BBC REH 397	METAL EXPLOSION	30
82	Ebony EBON 1	METAL FATIGUE	15
80	EMI EMC 3318	METAL FOR MUTHAS	25
80	EMI EMC 3337	METAL FOR MUTHAS VOL. 2	15
82	Ebony EBON 8	METAL MANIAXE	15
87	Other OTH 9	METAL WARRIOR	50
60	RCA/Camden CDN 122	METRONOME ALL STARS	12
80	MGM 2315 394	THE MGM ROCKABILLY COLLECTION	12
56	Nixa Jazz Today NJL 3	MIDNIGHT AT NIXA	12
66	Atlantic 587 021	MIDNIGHT SOUL	20
69	Storyville 616 009	MIDNIGHT SPECIAL	15
62	Brunswick LAT 8401	MIDNIGHT JAMBOREE (also stereo STA 3061)	12
56	London AL 3554	MIDWESTERN JAZZ (10")	15
66	Xtra XTRA 1047	THE MIKE RAVEN BLUES SHOW	22
69	Transatlantic TRASAM 5	THE MIKE RAVEN BLUES SAMPLER	22
72	Polydor	MILL VALLEY JAM SESSION	12
60	Coral LVA 9126	MILLION-AIRS	18
80	Pipe PIPE 2	MINIATURES (with poster insert, 500 only)	15
80	Pipe PIPE 2	MINIATURES (cassette with mini-booklet insert, 100 only)	30
71	Trojan TBL 174	MISS LABBA LABBA REGGAE	22
60	Top Rank BUY 028	MR. BLUE	35
60s	Bounty BY 6025	MODERN CHICAGO BLUES	35
69	London HAB 8380	MODERN COUNTRY HITS OF TODAY VOL. 1	12
69	London HAB 8381	MODERN COUNTRY HITS OF TODAY VOL. 2	12
55	HMV DLP 1022	MODERN JAZZ PIANO (10")	22
56	Tempo TAP 2	MODERN JAZZ SCENE 1956	50
53	Esquire 20-011	MODERN MIXTURE VOLUME ONE (10")	20
79	Bridge House BHLP 003	MODS MAYDAY '79 (original issue)	20
80	Polydor 2488810	MONSTERS OF ROCK	15
73	Stax STX 1029	MONTREUX FESTIVAL 1973	12
70	Trojan TTL 31	MOONLIGHT GROOVER	25
80	Danceville	THE MOONLIGHT TAPES	12
70	Liberty LBS 83377	MORE FROM THE VAULTS	12
62	HMV CLP 1583	MORE OF YOUR FAVOURITE TV AND RADIO THEMES	15
68	Marble Arch MAL 813	MORE RHYTHM AND BLUES	12
65	private pressing	MORE SINGING AT THE COUNT HOUSE	30
72	Island HELP 5	MORRIS ON (black label with pink 'i')	18
81	cassette	MORROCCI KLUNG! (cassette, some in printed 5" x 9" mailing envelope)	20/12

			MINT VALUE £
80	Conventional CON 013	MOTHER OF A PUNK (cassette)	12
86	Iguana VYK LP 11	MOTOR CITY 9 (with booklet)	15
65	Tamla Motown TML 11007	THE MOTORTOWN REVUE LIVE	100
66	Tamla Motown TML 11027	THE MOTORTOWN REVUE IN PARIS	90
70	T. Motown (S)TML 11127	THE MOTORTOWN REVUE LIVE	15
69	T. Motown (S)TML 11121	MOTOWN CHARTBUSTERS VOL. 3 (original with flipback sleeve)	15
70	T. Motown STML 11162	MOTOWN CHARTBUSTERS VOL. 4 (original with flipback sleeve)	15
74	T. Motown STML 11270	MOTOWN CHARTBUSTERS VOL. 9 (green vinyl)	12
72	Tamla Motown STMA 8005	MOTOWN DISCO CLASSICS VOL. 2	12
66	Tamla Motown TML 11030	MOTOWN MAGIC	40
68	Tamla Motown TML 11064	MOTOWN MEMORIES (flipback sleeve)	50
68	Tamla Motown TML 11077	MOTOWN MEMORIES VOL. 2	50
70	T. Motown STML 11143	MOTOWN MEMORIES VOL. 3	50
72	Tamla Motown STML 11200	MOTOWN MEMORIES	15
80	Tamla Motown ZL 72032	MOTOWN MOD CLASSICS VOL. 1	15
80	Tamla Motown STML 12133	MOTOWN MOD CLASSICS VOL. 2	15
72	Tamla Motown TMSP 1130	THE MOTOWN STORY (5-LP box set)	25
83	Tamla Motown TMSP 6019	THE MOTOWN STORY — THE FIRST 25 YEARS (box set)	20
77	Mountain PSLP 200	MOUNTAIN ROCKS INTO '77 (Mountain label sampler, promo only)	20
53	London AL 3503	MUGGY, TESCH AND THE CHICAGOANS (10")	15
57	Pye NJL 11	MURDERER'S HOME	15
71	Mushroom 100 MR 16	THE MUSHROOM FOLK SAMPLER	35
57	Brunswick LAT 8201	MUSIC FOR THE BOYFRIEND — HE REALLY DIGS ROCK'N'ROLL	70
57	Brunswick LAT 8202	MUSIC FOR THE BOYFRIEND — HE REALLY DIGS JAZZ	15
57	Brunswick LAT 8205	MUSIC FOR THE BOYFRIEND — THE FEMININE TOUCH	15
67	Argo RG 533	MUSIC FROM THE FAR NORTH (with foldout inner)	15
73	Charisma CADS 101	MUSIC FROM FREE CREEK (2-LP)	20
71	Trojan TBL 170	MUSIC HOUSE	15
71	Trojan TBL 177	MUSIC HOUSE VOLUME TWO	15
54	Decca LF 1224	MUSIC OF AFRICA — BEST RECORDINGS OF 1953 (10")	12
54	Decca LF 1084	MUSIC OF AFRICA — TANGAKA (10")	12
54	Decca LF 1172	MUSIC OF AFRICA — CONGO SONGS & DANCES (10")	12
54	Decca LF 1173	MUSIC OF AFRICA — UGANDA PROTECTORATE (10")	12
70	Disques Vogue VRLS 3043	LA MUSIQUE PROGRESSIVE	12
81	Ze ISSP 4001	MUTANT DISCO (3 x 12" box set, numbered, 2,000 only)	12
77	EMI NUT 4	MY GENERATION	12

N

73	Enterprise ESAM 100	THE NAME OF THE GAME	15
71	Eden LP 43	NAPTON FOLK CLUB (private pressing, 100 only)	35
62	London HA-B 8003	NASHVILLE SATURDAY NIGHT	15
63	London HA-B 8028	NASHVILLE STEEL GUITAR	15
69	Bamboo BLP 201	NATURAL REGGAE VOLUME ONE	60
70	Bamboo BLP 204	NATURAL REGGAE VOLUME TWO	60
81	4AD CAD 117	NATURES MORTES — STILL LIVES (export issue)	60
85	Musique Brut BRV 002	NECROPOLIS, AMPHIBIANS AND REPTILES: THE MUSIC OF ADOLF WOLFLI	20
70s	Bounty BY 6012	NEGRO FOLKLORE FROM TEXAS STATE PRISON	22
57	Vogue LAE 12033	NEGRO SPIRITUALS	25
87	Broken Flag BF V8	NEVER SAY WHEN	40
72	Atlantic K 20024	THE NEW AGE OF ATLANTIC	15
80	Logo MOGO 4011	NEW ELECTRIC WARRIORS	20
53	London AL 3509	NEW ORLEANS HORNS (10")	15
56	London AL 3557	NEW ORLEANS HORNS VOLUME 2 (10")	15
67	Ace Of Hearts AH 140	NEW ORLEANS MEMORIES	12
74	Flyright LP 4708	NEW ORLEANS R&B VOLUME 1	15
74	Flyright LP 4709	NEW ORLEANS R&B VOLUME 2	15
60s	'77' 77LA 12/16	NEW ORLEANS TODAY	18
60s	'77' 77LA 12/29	NEW ORLEANS TODAY VOL. 2	18
65	Fontana TFL 6038	NEWPORT BROADSIDE — TOPICAL SONGS AT THE NEWPORT FOLK FESTIVAL 1963	25
65	Fontana TFL 6041	NEWPORT FOLK FESTIVAL EVENING CONCERT VOL. 1	25
65	Fontana TFL 6050	NEWPORT FOLK FESTIVAL VOL. 1	12
57	Philips BBL 7147	NEWPORT JAZZ FESTIVAL	12
57	Philips BBL 7152	NEWPORT JAZZ FESTIVAL	12
58	London Jazz LTZ C15155	NEWPORT SPIRITUAL STARS	22
03	Ai AILP 005	NEW TOWN (2-LP, 1500 copies only)	15
77	Vertigo 6300 902	NEW WAVE	15
72	Flyright LP 4706	NEW YORK CITY BLUES	15
55	London AL 3541	NEW YORK JAZZ OF THE ROARING TWENTIES (10")	15
72	Flyright LP 4707	NEW YORK RHYTHM AND BLUES	15
69	Island IWP(S) 6	NICE ENOUGH TO EAT (pink label)	12
57	Vanguard PPL 11004	A NIGHT AT THE APOLLO	15
69	Blue Horizon 7-63210	THE 1968 MEMPHIS COUNTRY BLUES FESTIVAL	50
83	DEL 306	19TH CAMBRIDGE FOLK FESTIVAL VOLUME 1	20
81	NMX	NMX: LIVE AT SHEFFIELD (cassette)	20
68	Spark SRLM 107	NO INTRODUCTION	20
82	ZG Music No. 5	NOISE FEST (cassette)	12
69	Trojan TTL 14	NO MORE HEARTACHES	25
70	Polydor 545 017	NON STOP SOUL	30
69	Regal Starline SRS 5013	NO ONE'S GONNA CHANGE OUR WORLD	18
64	Concert Hall AM 2339	NORTHUMBRIAN MINSTRELS	25
60	Fontana TFL 5123	NOTHIN' BUT THE BLUES (gatefold sleeve)	22
71	CBS 66278	NOTHING BUT THE BLUES (2-LP, Blue Horizon pressings may also exist)	35/50+
82	See For Miles CM 112	NOT JUST BEAT MUSIC, 1965-70	15
79	Giorno GPS	THE NOVA CONVENTION	20
70	Decca Nova SPA 72	NOVA SAMPLER	15

			MINT VALUE £
70s	Warm PFLP 201	NOVA-VAGA	15
79	A&M AMLE 68505	NO WAVE ('pizza' picture disc)	20
79	A&M AMLE 68505	NO WAVE (orange, mauve, white or blue vinyl)	each 18
69	Pama ECO 6	NU BEAT — GREATEST HITS	40
73	Elektra K 62012	NUGGETS (Original Artyfacts From The First Psychedelic Era 1965-1968) (2-LP, gatefold sleeve)	40
86	Numa NUMA 1004	NUMA RECORDS YEAR 1 (with bonus Italian 12" "My Dying Machine")	15
86	Numa NUMAC 1004	NUMA RECORDS YEAR 1 (cassette)	12
90s	NWOBHM CD 002	NWOBHM — VOLUME 2 (CD)	30
90s	NWOBHM CD 003	NWOBHM — VOLUME 3 (CD)	30

O

69	Liberty LBS 83234	OAKLAND BLUES	22
80	Object Music OBJ 006	OBJECTIVITY	15
79	Rok ROK LP 001	ODD BODS, MODS AND SODS	75
58	Parlophone PMC 1072	OH BOY!	60
78	Raw RAWLP 2	OH NO IT'S MORE FROM RAW (Users/Killjoys et al.)	20
72	Music F. Pleasure MFP 1416	OH! WHAT A CARRY ON	15
98	MPO IRL 01	OH YEAH (CD, 'Heineken Rock Awards' issued free with *Hot Press* magazine, with Neil Hannon/Ash et al.)	18
80	EMI ZIT 1	OI! — THE ALBUM (initially mail-order only from *Sounds* magazine)	30
87	Link LP 23	OI! GLORIOUS OI!	12
84	Syndicate SYNLP 4	OI! OF SEX	12
83	Secret SEC 5	OI! OI! THAT'S YER LOT	15
75	Super Beeb BELP 004	OLD GREY WHISTLE TEST	12
64	Stateside SL 10094	OLDIES R & B	55
69	Transatlantic XTRA 1076	O LIVERPOOL WE LOVE YOU (Stan Kelly/Bill Shankly/Jimmy Tarbuck et al.)	40
68	Big Shot BBTL 4001	ONCE MORE	75
69	Marmalade 643 314	100% PROOF	12
86	Stateside/EMI SSL 6002	ONE MINIT AT A TIME	12
73	Charisma CLASS 3	ONE MORE CHANCE	12
63	Columbia 33SX 1536	ONE NIGHT STAND	40
63	Stateside SL 10065	ON STAGE LIVE!	60
69	Atco 228 009/010	ON STAGE — LIVE (2-LP)	25
73	Xtra XTRA 1133	ON THE ROAD AGAIN	70
64	Columbia 33SX 1662	ON THE SCENE	100
84	Sane	ON THE STREETS	12
63	Stateside SL 10024	OPRY TIME IN TENNESSEE	15
65	Allegro ALL 778	ROY ORBISON SINGS (some tracks by Jerry Lee Lewis, Tommy Roe; black or blue label)	12
65	Ember FA 2005	ROY ORBISON AND OTHERS (with 4 tracks by Orbison)	12
67	Polydor 236 216	ORIGINAL AMERICAN FOLK BLUES FESTIVAL	15
64	Rio RLP 1	THE ORIGINAL COOL JAMAICAN SKA	135
70	Mercury SMCL 20182	ORIGINAL GOLDEN HITS OF THE GREAT BLUES SINGERS	15
73	Prince Buster PB 10	ORIGINAL GOLDEN OLDIES VOLUME 2	25
70	Mercury SMCL 20183	ORIGINAL GOLDEN RHYTHM AND BLUES HITS VOLUME 1	20
60	London HA-G 2308	THE ORIGINAL HITS	45
61	London HA-G 2339	THE ORIGINAL HITS VOL. 2	45
63	Golden Guinea GGL 0240	THE ORIGINAL HOOTENANNY	15
67	Ember SPE 6602	THE ORIGINAL SOUND OF DETROIT	18
68	United Artists ULP 1182	ORIGINAL SOUNDTRACKS OF HITS MUSIC	15
64	Vocalion VA 8017	ORIGINAL SURFIN' HITS	60
52	Vogue LDE 006	ORIGINATORS OF MODERN JAZZ (10")	15
75	Trailer LET SAM 2087	OUR FOLK MUSIC HERITAGE	12
62	London HA-U 2404	OUR SIGNIFICANT HITS	65
65	Ace Of Hearts AH 72	OUT CAME THE BLUES	18
67	Ace Of Hearts AH 158	OUT CAME THE BLUES VOLUME 2	18
71	Coral CP 58	OUT CAME THE BLUES (reissue)	12
76	ABC ABCL 5192	OUT ON THE STREETS AGAIN	12

P

64	Golden Guinea GGL 0268	PACKAGE TOUR	20
68	Topic 12T 176	PADDY IN THE SMOKE (original sleeve & blue label)	12
65	Blue Beat BBLP 804	PAIN IN MY BELLY	200
55	London HA-A 2001	THE PAJAMA GAME	15
67	Island ILP 945	PAKISTANI SOUL SESSION	60
61	Parlophone PMC 1134	PARADE OF THE POPS	15
57	HMV DLP 1076	PARIS TU N'A PAS CHANGÉ	12
85	LIL LP2	PARKSIDE STEELWORKS	60
68	Studio One SOL 9009	PARTY TIME IN JAMAICA	120
78	BFD BFD 5019	PEBBLES VOL. 2	12
66	Decca LK 4824	PENTHOUSE MAGAZINE PRESENTS THE BEDSIDE BOND	40
83	Psycho PSYCHO 6	THE PERFUMED GARDEN	20
84	Psycho PSYCHO 15	THE PERFUMED GARDEN II	20
81	Cherry Red BRED 15	PERSPECTIVES AND DISTORTION (gatefold sleeve)	15
76	RSO 2479 167	PETER AND THE WOLF	12
73	Phase 4 SPA 213	PHASE 4 WORLD OF SPY THRILLERS	12
86	Streetsounds PHST 1986	THE PHILADELPHIA YEARS (14-LP box set)	80
72	Apple APCOR 24	PHIL SPECTOR'S CHRISTMAS ALBUM (reissue of "A Christmas Gift For You")	30
75	Warner Bros K 59010	PHIL SPECTOR'S CHRISTMAS ALBUM (2nd reissue, some with poster)	18/12
80	Phil Spector Intl. 2307 015	PHIL SPECTOR '74/'79	20
67	Riverside RLP 8809	PIANO BLUES 1927-1933	20
70s	Storyville 671 187	PIANO BLUES	12
77	Magpie PY 4401	PIANO BLUES VOLUME 1: PARAMOUNT 1929-30	12
77	Magpie PY 4402	PIANO BLUES VOLUME 2: BRUNSWICK 1928-30	12
77	Magpie PY 4403	PIANO BLUES VOLUME 3: VOCALION 1928-30	12

			MINT VALUE £
77	Magpie PY 4404	PIANO BLUES VOLUME 4: THOMAS FAMILY 1925-1929	12
78	Magpie PY 4405	PIANO BLUES VOLUME 5: POSTSCRIPT 1927-1933	12
78	Magpie PY 4406	PIANO BLUES VOLUME 6: WALTER ROLAND 1933-1935	12
78	Magpie PY 4407	PIANO BLUES VOLUME 7: LEROY CARR 1930-1935	12
78	Magpie PY 4408	PIANO BLUES VOLUME 8: TEXAS SEAPORT 1934-1937	12
79	Magpie PY 4409	PIANO BLUES VOLUME 9: LOFTON/NOBLE 1935-36	12
79	Magpie PY 4410	PIANO BLUES VOLUME 10: TERRITORY BLUES 1934-41	12
80	Magpie PY 4411	PIANO BLUES VOLUME 11: TEXAS SANTA FE 1934-1937	12
80	Magpie PY 4412	PIANO BLUES VOLUME 12: THE BIG FOUR 1933-1941	12
80	Magpie PY 4413	PIANO BLUES VOLUME 13: CENTRAL HIGHWAY 1933-1941	12
80	Magpie PY 4414	PIANO BLUES VOLUME 14: THE ACCOMPANISTS 1933-41	12
81	Magpie PY 4415	PIANO BLUES VOLUME 15: DALLAS 1927-1929	12
81	Magpie PY 4416	PIANO BLUES VOLUME 16: CHARLIE SPAND 1929-1931	12
82	Magpie PY 4417	PIANO BLUES VOLUME 17: PARAMOUNT VOL. 2 1927-32	12
82	Magpie PY 4420	PIANO BLUES VOLUME 20: BARRELHOUSE YEARS 1928-33	12
82	Magpie PY 4421	PIANO BLUES VOLUME 21: UNISSUED BOOGIE 1938-1945	12
72	Delmark DL 626	PIANO BLUES ORGY	12
56	Vogue Coral LVA 9069	PIANO JAZZ — BARRELHOUSE AND BOOGIE WOOGIE	15
70s	Horse HRLP 704	PICK HITS	12
72	Flyright LP 104	PIEDMONT BLUES	15
82	Cherry Red PZRED 41	PILLOWS AND PRAYERS (picture disc in printed PVC sleeve)	12
60	HMV CLP 1362/XLP 50004	A PINCH OF SALT — BRITISH SEA SONGS OLD AND NEW	20
53	London AL 3506	PIONEERS OF BOOGIE WOOGIE (10")	40
54	London AL 3537	PIONEERS OF BOOGIE WOOGIE VOLUME TWO (10")	40
73	Trojan TBL 203	PIPELINE	18
80	Incus INCUS 37	PISA 1980: IMPROVISOR'S SYMPOSIUM	50
81	K-Tel NE 1134	THE PLATINUM ALBUM	12
70s	Flyright LP 4711	PLAY MY JUKEBOX	12
81	P. Surprised KLARK 002	PLEASANTLY SURPRISED — AN HOUR OF ELOQUENT SOUNDS (cassette)	20
71	Argo ZPR 264/5	POETRY AND JAZZ IN CONCERT 250	15
56	Mercury MPT	POP PARADE VOL. 1 (10")	18
56	Mercury MPT	POP PARADE VOL. 2 (10")	18
57	Mercury MPT 7519	POP PARADE VOL. 3 (10")	18
57	Mercury MPT 7523	POP PARADE VOL. 4 (10")	18
57	Mercury MPT 7525	POP PARADE VOL. 5 (10")	30
70	Polydor 2682 001	POP PARTY	12
68	Polydor 236 517/8/9	POP PARTY! (3-LP in box)	40
91	Shock SX 012	THE PORTABLE ALTAMONT (CD)	20
83	Fall Out FALL 032	POSH HITS VOL. 1	12
65	Post War Blues PWB 1	POST WAR BLUES: CHICAGO (99 copies only)	40
66	Post War Blues PWB 2	POST WAR BLUES: MEMPHIS ON DOWN (99 copies only)	40
67	Post War Blues PWB 3	POST WAR BLUES: EASTERN AND GULF COAST STATES (99 copies only)	40
68	Post War Blues PWB 4	POST WAR BLUES: TEXAS (99 copies only)	40
68	Post War Blues PWB 5	POST WAR BLUES: DETROIT (99 copies only)	40
60s	Post War Blues PWB 6	POST WAR BLUES: WEST COAST (99 copies only)	40
60s	Post War Blues PWB 7	POST WAR BLUES: THE DEEP SOUTH (99 copies only)	40
69	Python PWBC 1	POST WAR COLLECTOR SERIES VOL. 1 (99 copies only)	40
63	Stateside SL 10046	PREACHIN' THE BLUES	30
80	4AD BAD 11	PRESAGES (mini-LP, green/pink or brown sleeve)	15/20
79	Preseli PRE 001	PRESELI FOLK (private pressing with insert)	30
70	Kokomo K 1006	PRE-WAR TEXAS BLUES (99 copies only)	45
74	RSO SINGL 1	PRIME CUTS (10" mini-LP)	12
60s	Jazz Collector JGN 1001	PRIMITIVE PIANO	20
87	A&M AMA 3906	PRINCE'S TRUST 10TH ANNIVERSARY BIRTHDAY PARTY (2-LP, some stickered, with Paul McCartney 7": "Long Tall Sally"/"I Saw Her Standing There" [p/s, FREE 21])	40/25
63	London HA-B 8062	PRISONERS' SONGS	18
70	Lyntone LYN 2745	PRIVATE EYE'S GOLDEN YEARS OF SOUND 1964-70	20
02	Ai AILP 003	PRODUCE (300 only)	18
90	United Dairies UD 134	PSILOTRIPITAKA (3-LP [UD 01, 03 & 04], with bonus LP "Registered Nurse" [UD 00], 1,000 only, some possibly in leather bag)	400/125
90	United Dairies UD 134CD	PSILOTRIPITAKA (3-CD [UD 01, 03 & 04], with bonus CD "Registered Nurse" [UD 00CD], 1,000 only, 30 in 'leather bondage bag')	400/60
91	Delerium DELP 005	PSYCHEDELIC SAUNA (2-LP, 500 numbered on multi-coloured vinyl)	18
65	Sue ILP 919	PURE BLUES VOLUME ONE	60
83	Guardian GRC 2162	PURE OVERKILL	18
73	Purple TPSS 1	PURPLE PEOPLE	15
85	Color Disc COLORS 2	PURPLE TWILIGHT (400 only)	20
94	Blueye Dog PURR 2	PURR 2 (10", with *Purr* book)	12
68	Island ILP 978	PUT IT ON, IT'S ROCK STEADY	65
71	Pye PSA 6	PYE SALES SAMPLER (sampler for Pye & Dawn releases; 99 copies only, with release sheet)	20

Q

68	Stateside S(S)L 10209	A QUARTET OF SOUL	25
70	Trojan TBL 136	QUEEN OF THE WORLD	25
59	Vogue LAE 12031	THE QUINTET OF THE YEAR	15

R

69	Polydor 236 514	RAGS, REELS AND AIRS	12
54	London AL 3515	RAGTIME PIANO ROLL (10")	20
54	London AL 3523	RAGTIME PIANO ROLL VOLUME 2 (10")	20
55	London AL 3542	RAGTIME PIANO ROLL VOLUME 3 (10")	20
57	London AL 3563	RAGTIME PIANO ROLL VOLUME 4 (10")	20
81	Island ILPS 9705	RAIDERS OF THE LOST DUB (LP, withdrawn)	20
76	Phil Spector Intl. 2307 008	RARE MASTERS VOL. 1	25

			MINT VALUE £
76	Phil Spector Intl. 2307 009	RARE MASTERS VOL. 2	22
78	Polydor 2482 274	RARE TRACKS	12
69	United Artists (S)UX 1214	RAVE	25
74	Mooncrest CREST 17	RAVE ON	12
73	Attack ATLP 1012	RAVE ON BROTHER	15
67	Ace Of Clubs ACL 1220	RAW BLUES (also stereo SCL 1220)	18
77	Raw RAWLP 1	RAW DEAL (black & white sleeve & red/blue label)	15
79	Raw RAWLP 1	RAW DEAL (reissue, yellow/black sleeve & green/white label)	12
74	GM GML 1008	READING FESTIVAL '73	12
83	Mean MNLP 82	READING ROCK VOL. 1 (2-LP)	20
64	Decca LK 4577	READY, STEADY, GO!	40
68	Pama PMLP 3	READY STEADY GO ROCKSTEADY	45
64	Decca LK 4634	READY, STEADY, WIN	75
65	Stateside SL 10112	THE REAL R & B	40
80s	Recloose Org. LOOSE 12	R.O. (RECLOOSE ORGANISATION) (picture disc with insert)	20
82	Recommended 104	RECOMMENDED SAMPLER	15
79	Destiny DS 10001	THE RECORD COLLECTOR	20
81	Recorder BR 003	RECORDER THREE	20
70	CBS 52797	RECORDING THE BLUES	22
65	Red Bird RB 20-102	RED BIRD GOLDIES	60
81	WEA K 58344	RED HOT ROCKABILLIES (with inner sleeve)	12
69	Down Town TTL 11	RED, RED WINE	15
70	Trojan TBL 115	REGGAE FLIGHT 404	18
68	Big Shot BIL 3000	REGGAE GIRL	75
69	Pama ECO 3	REGGAE HITS '69 VOL. 1	25
69	Pama ECO 11	REGGAE HITS VOL. 2	25
69	Pama PTP 1001	REGGAE HIT THE TOWN	35
68	Studio One SOL 9007	REGGAE IN THE GRASS	110
71	Trojan TBL 181	REGGAE JAMAICA	15
71	Bamboo BDLP 208	REGGAEMATIC SOUNDS	70
70	Trojan TBL 144	REGGAE MOVEMENT	25
72	Trojan TBL 189	REGGAE POWER VOLUME TWO	18
70	Trojan TBL 130	REGGAE REGGAE REGGAE	18
71	Trojan TBL 176	REGGAE REGGAE REGGAE VOLUME TWO	18
70	London HA-J 8411	REGGAE REVOLUTION (unissued)	
70	London LGJ/ZGJ 101	REGGAE REVOLUTION	18
69	Coxsone CSP 2	REGGAE SPECIAL	40
70	Trojan TBL 151	REGGAE STEADY GO	18
68	Coxsone CSL 8017	REGGAE TIME	110
72	Ashanti ANB 201	REGGAE TIME	15
71	Pama PMP 2012	REGGAE TO REGGAE	30
69	Pama PSP 1004	REGGAE TO UK WITH LOVE	35
80s	Ré 0101	RE RECORDS QUARTERLY VOL. No. 1 (with book)	15
64	Decca LK 4616	RHYTHM AND BLUES	80
67	Marble Arch MAL 726	RHYTHM AND BLUES	12
64	Golden Guinea GGL 0280	RHYTHM AND BLUES VOL	20
64	Golden Guinea GGL 0351	RHYTHM AND BLUES VOL. 2	12
69	Liberty LBL 83216	RHYTHM AND BLUES VOLUME 1: END OF AN ERA	30
70	Liberty LBL 83328	RHYTHM AND BLUES VOLUME 2: SWEET 'N' GREASY	22
64	Golden Guinea GGL 0293	RHYTHM AND BLUES ALL STARS	12
69	Minit MLL/MLS 40008E	RHYTHM AND BLUES CLASSICS	25
69	Minit MLL/MLS 40009E	RHYTHM AND BLUES CLASSICS VOL. 2	22
63	CBS Realm RM 101	R&B GREATS VOLUME 1	22
64	CBS Realm RM 175	R&B GREATS VOLUME 2	22
64	Mercury MCL 20019	RHYTHM AND BLUES PARTY	60
76	Philips 6436 028	RHYTHM AND BLUES PARTY (reissue)	15
89	Performance PFP 1004	RHYTHM OF THE RAIN — 16 HITS OF THE 60s	12
73	Tamla Motown STML 11232	RIC TIC RELICS	18
68	Coxsone CSL 8015	RIDE ME DONKEY	130
69	Trojan TTL 18	RIDE YOUR DONKEY	25
86	SMP/Inferno SINLP 3	THE RIGHT TRACK	12
03	Dig The Fuzz DIG048	RIOT OF THE AMPHETAMINE GENERATION (400 copies only, with booklet)	40
55	Vogue Coral LRA 10023	RIVERBOAT JAZZ (10" LP)	15
71	London SHU 8245	RIVERTOWN BLUES	22
61	London HA-A 2338	ROCK-A-HITS	90
57	London HB-C 1067	ROCK 'N' ROLL (10")	100
59	London HA-E 2180	ROCK AND ROLL FOREVER	90
60	HMV DLP 1204	ROCKET ALONG — NEW BALLADS ON OLD LINES (10")	18
70s	Flynight FLY 662	ROCKIN' ACCORDION	12
58	Decca LF 1300	ROCKIN' AT THE '2 I'S' (10")	60
59	London HA-E 2167	ROCKIN' TOGETHER	80
63	Philips BL 7583	ROCKING GUITARS (LP)	30
69	Decca LK 5002	ROCK STEADY	18
69	Pama PMLP 7	ROCKSTEADY COOL	45
68	Coxsone CSL 8013	ROCKSTEADY COXSONE STYLE	125
80	Guardian GRC 80	ROKSNAX	50
80	Rapid Eye Movement	ROOM NOISE (cassette)	15
68	Atlantic Special 590 019	ROOTS OF THE BLUES	15
82	Guardian GRC 130	ROXCALIBUR	70
77	Harvest SHSP 4069	THE ROXY LONDON W.C.2 (JAN - APR 77) (with inner bag)	12
94	Mo' Wax MWLP 003	ROYALTIES OVERDUE (2-LP, coloured vinyl)	60
84	Bam Caruso KIRI 024	RUBBLE 1: THE PSYCHEDELIC SNARL (with 8-page insert; first 2,000 with inner sleeve and lightshow labels)	20/12
86	Bam Caruso KIRI 025	RUBBLE 2: POP-SIKE PIPE DREAMS (with inner sleeve)	20
86	Bam Caruso KIRI 026	RUBBLE 3: NIGHTMARES IN WONDERLAND (with inner sleeve)	20
88	Bam Caruso RUBBLE CD 2	RUBBLE 3: NIGHTMARES IN WONDERLAND (CD)	18

Year	Label	Title	MINT VALUE £
86	Bam Caruso KIRI 027	RUBBLE 4: THE 49 MINUTE TECHNICOLOUR DREAM (some with 4-page insert; first 2000 with inner sleeve and lightshow labels)	20/12
86	Bam Caruso KIRI 044	RUBBLE 5: THE ELECTRIC CRAYON SET (with inner sleeve)	15
86	Bam Caruso KIRI 049	RUBBLE 6: THE CLOUDS HAVE GROOVY FACES (with inner sleeve)	15
88	Bam Caruso KIRI 083	RUBBLE 7: PICTURES IN THE SKY (with inner sleeve)	15
91	Bam Caruso KIRI 051	RUBBLE 8: ALL THE COLOURS OF DARKNESS	15
85	Bam Caruso KIRI 065	RUBBLE 9: FROM THE HOUSE OF LORDS (1000 copies only)	18
91	Bam Caruso KIRI 079	RUBBLE 9: PLASTIC WILDERNESS	15
88	Bam Caruso KIRI 098	RUBBLE 10: PROFESSOR JORDAN'S MAGIC SOUND SHOW (with inner sleeve)	15
86	Bam Caruso KIRI 069	RUBBLE 11: ADVENTURES IN THE MIST (with inner sleeve)	20
86	Bam Caruso KIRI 070	RUBBLE 12: STAIRCASE TO NOWHERE (with inner sleeve)	20
89	Bam Caruso KIRI 102	RUBBLE 13: FREAK BEAT FANTOMS	20
88	Bam Caruso KIRI 106	RUBBLE 14: THE MAGIC ROCKING HORSE (with inner sleeve)	20
91	Bam Caruso KIRI 084	RUBBLE 15: 5000 SECONDS OVER TOYLAND	20
91	Bam Caruso KIRI 096	RUBBLE 16: GLASS ORCHID AFTERMATH	12
91	Bam Caruso KIRI 099	RUBBLE 17: A TRIP IN A PAINTED WORLD	20
92	Bam Caruso KIRI 101	RUBBLE 18: RAINBOW THYME WINDERS (unreleased, 25 test pressings only)	200
92	Bam Caruso KIRI 109	RUBBLE 19: EIDERDOWN MINDFOG (unreleased, 25 test pressings only)	200
90s	Bam Caruso KIRI 110	RUBBLE 20: THRICE UPON A TIME — NOTHING IS REAL (unreleased)	
92	Forty NME 40 LP	RUBY TRAX (3-LP, box set)	75
92	Forty NME 40 CD	RUBY TRAX (3-CD)	60
81	Naive NAIVE 2	RUPERT PREACHING AT A PICNIC (handmade sleeve)	25
69	Xtra XTRA 1035	RURAL BLUES (2-LP)	25
69	Liberty LBL 83213	RURAL BLUES VOLUME 1: GOIN' UP THE COUNTRY	25
69	Liberty LBL 83214	RURAL BLUES VOLUME 2: SATURDAY NIGHT FUNCTION	25
70	Liberty LBL 83329	RURAL BLUES VOLUME 3: DOWN HOME STOMP	25

S

Year	Label	Title	MINT VALUE £
70	Transworld SPLP 101	SAMANTHA PROMOTIONS (orange cover, private pressing, a few with poster)	500
70	Transworld SPLP 102	SAMANTHA PROMOTIONS (purple cover, private pressing, a few with poster)	500
60	Parlophone PMC 1130	SATURDAY CLUB	50
64	Decca LK 4583	SATURDAY CLUB	40
67	Atlantic Special 590 007	SATURDAY NIGHT AT THE APOLLO (reissue of "Apollo Saturday Night")	22
63	Brunswick LAT/STA 8520	SATURDAY NIGHT AT THE GRAND OLE OPRY	15
70	CBS 52799	SAVANNAH SYNCOPATORS	15
81	Suspect SU S3	SCENE OF THE CRIME	75
65	Columbia 33SX 1730	SCENE '65	150
74	Polydor 2383 282 A	SCOTLAND SCOTLAND (Scottish World Cup Squad/Rod Stewart/Dennis Law)	15
69	Bamboo BDLP 202	A SCORCHA FROM BAMBOO	65
80s	Barc. Towers SUPLP 2004	SCOTTISH KULTCHUR	12
79	Island ILPS 9583	SCRATCH ON THE WIRE (Lee Perry et al.)	18
68	CBS 63288	SCREENING THE BLUES	25
95	Blue Eyed Dog VTDOG 12	SEARCH AND DISOBEY (2-LP, 10")	25
81	Airship AP 342	SEASIDE ROCK (2-LP, with insert)	20
92	Imaginary ILLUSION 34	SECONDS OUT ROUND ONE — LIVE HIT THE NORTH SESSIONS (with bonus promo Boo Radleys/Scorpio Rising 12" [FREE 004])	12
81	Come Org. WDC 881008	THE SECOND COMING (various coloured vinyls)	30
84	Davies LP-D2 VOR 8	A SECRET LIVERPOOL (1-sided cardboard sleeve or 2-sided normal sleeve)	25/20
81	Island 12WIP 6598	THE SECRET POLICEMAN'S BALL (THE MUSIC) (mini-LP)	8
87	Cherry Red BRED 74	SEEDS I: POP (TV Personalities/Marine Girls, et al.)	30
87	Cherry Red BRED 76	SEEDS II: ART (Punishment Of Luxury/Nightingales, et al.)	15
68	Elektra EUK 261	SELECT ELEKTRA (also stereo EUKS 7261)	30
80	Kathedral KATH 1	SENT FROM COVENTRY (with booklet)	15
88	Sarah SARAH 587	SHADOW FACTORY (The Sea Urchins/14 Iced Bears, et al.)	18
68	Atlantic 587 109	SHAKE, RATTLE AND ROCK	25
74	Topic 12TS 234	SEA SHANTIES	15
78	GVR 201	THE SHANTY MEN	18
81	In Phaze	SHED SOUNDS SAMPLER (cassette)	15
74	Eron 003	SHEPWAY FOLK (with insert)	30
78	Virgin VCL 5003	SHORT CIRCUIT — LIVE AT THE ELECTRIC CIRCUS (10"; orange, yellow, blue or black vinyl)	70/40/12/7
78	Virgin VCL 5003	SHORT CIRCUIT — LIVE AT THE ELECTRIC CIRCUS (10"; black vinyl with free John Dowie EP [VED 1004])	12
90	Horaces HRH 101	SHRINE — THE RAREST SOUL LABEL	12
87	ABC NOSE 15	SICK SICK SICK	12
76	Topic 12TS 281	THE SILVER BOW — SHETLAND FOLK FIDDLING VOL. 1	15
66	Chess CRL 4519	SING A SONG OF SOUL	30
57	RCA Camden CDN 147	SINGIN' THE BLUES	12
79	Sire SMP 1	THE SIRE MACHINE TURNS YOU UP	12
57	Parlophone PMC 1047	SIX-FIVE SPECIAL	50
76	BBC REB 252	SIX-FIVE SPECIAL	12
71	Pama PMP 2015	16 DYNAMIC REGGAE HITS	20
72	Trojan TBL 191	16 DYNAMIC REGGAE HITS	20
66	Island ILP 930	SKA AT THE JAMAICA PLAYBOY CLUB (gatefold sleeve)	450
67	Coxsone CSL 8003	SKA-A-GO-GO	135
66	Doctor Bird DLM 5000	SKA-BOO-DA-BA	135
67	Studio One SOL 9000	SKA TO ROCKSTEADY	125
60s	Page One FOR 006	SKA'S THE LIMIT	30
68	Ace Of Clubs ACL 1250	SKIFFLE	35
80s	Kent KENT 052	SMART! 16 IMMACULATE CUTS TAILORED FOR STYLE	12
81	RSB 1	THE SNOOPIES ALBUM (THE LAST REMAINS OF A RICHMOND VENUE) (numbered, with booklet, 1,000 only)	20
67	Polydor 583 064	SOCK IT TO 'EM	18

			MINT VALUE £
60s	Solar	THE SOLAR BOX SET	40
70s	United Artists LBR 1007	SOLD ON SOUL	15
71	Bamboo BDLP 212	SOLID GOLD	70
66	Atlantic ATL 5048	SOLID GOLD SOUL	22
67	Atlantic 587 058	SOLID GOLD SOUL VOL. 2	22
75	Disco Demand DDLP 5002	SOLID SOUL SENSATIONS	18
81	Some Bizzare BZLP 1	THE SOME BIZZARE ALBUM	12
72	South. Preservation SPR 1	SOME COLD RAINY DAY	25
75	Flyright LP 114	SOME COLD RAINY DAY (reissue)	15
65	Lestar LLP 101	SOME FOLK IN LEICESTER (private pressing)	20
58	Decca LK 4292	SOMETHING NEW FROM AFRICA	18
70	Pama PMP 2003	SOMETHING SWEET FROM THE LADY	40
60	Topic 12001	SONGS AGAINST THE BOMB	12
72	Argo ZDA 147	SONGS AND MUSIC OF THE REDCOATS	15
77	Topic 12T 317	SONGS & SOUTHERN BREEZES — COUNTRY SINGERS FROM HAMPSHIRE & SUSSEX	15
77	private pressing	SONGS AT A SUSSEX FEAST	12
79	EMI NUT 18	SONGS LENNON AND McCARTNEY GAVE AWAY	12
67	Fontana STL 5436	SONGS OF GRIEF AND GLORY	12
69	Liberty LBX 4	SON OF GUTBUCKET	20
76	Harvest SHSM 2012	SON OF MORRIS ON	18
83	Syndicate SYNLP 3	SON OF OI!	12
72	Probe SPB 1061	SOUL BIBLE	15
69	Direction (S)PR 28	SOUL DIRECTION	20
69	Page One POS 608	SOULED AGAIN	20
69	Polydor 584 163	SOUL FEVER	20
60s	Minit MLL 40011E	SOUL FOOD	30
69	Soul City SCB 1	SOUL FROM THE CITY	35
70	Specialty SPE 6606	SOUL FROM THE VAULTS	15
74	Trojan TRL 65	SOULFUL REGGAE	18
70	Polydor 583 757	SOUL GOLD	18
72	Avco 6467 251	SOUL — IN THE BEGINNING	12
68	Trojan TRL 3	SOUL OF JAMAICA	45
68	Polydor Special 236 213	SOUL PARTY	18
69	Pama PMLP 8	SOUL SAUCE FROM PAMA	35
69	Polydor 236 554	SOUL SELLER	18
70s	United Artists UAL 229018	SOUL SENSATION	15
66	Stateside SL 10186	SOUL SIXTEEN	45
66	Sue ILP 934	SOUL '66	60
67	CBS BPG 62965	SOUL SOUNDS	20
67	HMV CLP 3617	SOUL SOUNDS OF THE 60s	35
67	Stateside SL 10203	SOUL SUPPLY	45
86	SMP/Inferno SIMLP 4	SOUL TIME	12
65	Pye Intl. NPL 28061	THE SOUND OF BACHARACH	20
95	EMI EMI 8322 801	THE SOUND GALLERY	20
58	Fontana TFL 5025	THE SOUND OF JAZZ	15
68	President PTL 1008	THE SOUND OF SOUL	22
72	United Artists UAS 29215	SOUND OF THE CITY	12
79	Grapevine GRAL 1001	SOUND OF THE GRAPEVINE	20
64	Stateside SL 10077	THE SOUND OF THE R&B HITS	60
69	Joy JOY 125	SOUNDS LIKE SKA	15
70	Sentinel SENS 1001	SOUNDS LIKE WEST CORNWALL	20
78	Sonet SNTF 806	SOUTHEND ROCK	12
69	London HAK 8405	SOUTHERN COMFORT	30
83	Spectrum ASPEC 001	SOUTHERN COMFORT	75
80s	Spectrum ASPEC 003	SOUTHERN COMFORT 3	50
60s	Saydisc Roots RL 328	SOUTHERN SANCTIFIED SINGERS	15
61	London Jazz LTZ-K 15209	SOUTHERN FOLK HERITAGE VOLUME 1: SOUNDS OF THE SOUTH	20
61	London Jazz LTZ-K 15210	SOUTHERN FOLK HERITAGE VOLUME 2: BLUE RIDGE MOUNTAIN MUSIC	20
61	London Jazz LTZ-K 15211	SOUTHERN FOLK HERITAGE VOLUME 3: ROOTS OF THE BLUES	20
61	London Jazz LTZ-K 15209	SOUTHERN FOLK HERITAGE VOLUME 7: THE BLUES ROLL ON	20
54	London AL 3529	SOUTHSIDE CHICAGO JAZZ (10")	18
71	Python PLP 10	SOUTHSIDE CHICAGO (99 copies only)	40
70	CBS Special Prod. WSR 932	SPARKLING COLOUR (multicoloured vinyl)	12
58	Tempo TAP 17	SPEAK LOW — MORE MUSIC IN THE MODERN MANNER	100
73	Tempo TMP 9001	SPIN A MAGIC TUNE	20
57	Pye Nixa NPT 19019	SPIN WITH THE STARS — SELECTION NO. 2 (10")	18
57	Pye Nixa NPT 19021	SPIN WITH THE STARS — SELECTION NO. 3 (10")	18
65	Fontana TL 5243	SPIRITUAL AND GOSPEL FESTIVAL	20
59	Top Rank 35/064	SPIRITUALS TO SWING VOLUME 1	20
59	Top Rank 35/065	SPIRITUALS TO SWING VOLUME 2	20
82	WEA K 58415	A SPLASH OF COLOUR	15
62	Liberty LBY 1001	THE STARS OF LIBERTY	30
57	Decca LF 1299	STARS OF THE 6.5 SPECIAL (10")	50
66	London HA-B 8269	STARS OF THE STEEL GUITAR	12
71	MFP MFP 5157	STARS SING LENNON AND McCARTNEY	12
84	Broken Flag BF V5	STATEMENT	40
84	Pleasantly Surprised PS 3	STATE OF AFFAIRS (cassette, in poly bag with foldout booklet & insert)	20
85	Statik POL 274	STATIK COMPILATION ONE (2-LP)	20
04	Ai AILP 006	STATION (2-LP, clear vinyl, 1000 copies only)	15
69	Stax XATS 1007	STAX SOUL EXPLOSION	18

			MINT VALUE £
70s	Stax STXH 5004	THE STAX STORY (VOL. 1)	15
70s	Stax STXH 5005	THE STAX STORY (VOL. 1)	15
67	Stax 589 010	THE STAX/VOLT SHOW VOL. 1	20
67	Stax 589 011	THE STAX/VOLT SHOW VOL. 2	20
78	Stiff GET 1	STIFFS LIVE STIFFS	12
60	Topic 10T 59	STILL I LOVE HIM	12
98	BMG BMGP 14	STOCK AITKEN & WATERMAN — DIAMONDS (2-CD, promo only)	40
84	ABC ABCLP 3	STOMPING AT THE KLUB FOOT VOL. 1	12
84	ABC ABCLP 4	STOMPING AT THE KLUB FOOT VOL. 2	12
69	CBS 66218	THE STORY OF THE BLUES (2-LP)	20
70	CBS 66232	THE STORY OF THE BLUES VOLUME 2 (2-LP)	20
94	Tenth Planet TP 010	THE STORY OF OAK RECORDS	25
94	Wooden Hill WHCD 007	THE STORY OF OAK RECORDS (CD)	18
70	Pama PMP 2002	STRAIGHTEN UP	25
71	Pama PMP 2007	STRAIGHTEN UP VOLUME TWO	25
71	Pama PMP 2014	STRAIGHTEN UP VOLUME THREE	25
72	Pama PMP 2017	STRAIGHTEN UP VOLUME FOUR	25
77	Beggars Banquet BEGA 1	STREETS	15
80s	Streetsounds	STREETSOUND ELECTRO (box set)	70
83	Streetsounds ELCST 1	STREETSOUND ELECTRO 1	18
83	Streetsounds ELCST 2	STREETSOUND ELECTRO 2	18
84	Streetsounds ELCST 3	STREETSOUND ELECTRO 3	18
84	Streetsounds ELCST 4	STREETSOUND ELECTRO 4	18
79	Open Eye OE LP 501	STREET TO STREET — A LIVERPOOL ALBUM	20
81	Open Eye OE LP 502	STREET TO STREET — A LIVERPOOL ALBUM VOL. 2	12
81	Decca SKIN 1	STRENGTH THROUGH OI!	50
85	Wonderful World WOWLP 3	STRENGTH THROUGH OI! (reissue)	20
80s	Private Pressing CFCEPI	STUFF THE NEIGHBOURS, PLAY IT LOUD (p/s, in poly bag, with fanzine)	12
86	Sub Pop SP 0010	SUB POP 100	20
81	Chick CHR 001	SUBWAY (clear vinyl)	15
80s	INST-4	SUCK	12
98	Sorted SRLP 04	SUCTION PRINTS (handpainted or wraparound sleeve)	35/15
65	Sue ILP 919	SUE SAMPLER RECORD FOR CLUBS (promo, no sleeve, typed labels with detail sheet)	120
65	London HA-C 8239	THE SUE STORY	50
65	Sue ILP 925	THE SUE STORY!	50
69	United Artists UAS 29028	THE SUE STORY (reissue)	18
66	Sue ILP 933	THE SUE STORY VOL. 2	50
66	Sue ILP 938	THE SUE STORY VOL. 3	50
76	Giorno GPS	SUGAR, ALCOHOL & MEAT	20
82	CBS 22139	SUMMER MEANS FUN (2-LP)	20
75	Island ISS 1	SUMMER '75 (promo-only sampler)	15
66	Reprise R 5031	THE SUMMIT	50
86	Sun/Charly BOX 105	SUN RECORDS: THE BLUES YEARS (9-LP box with booklet)	60
81	Sunset Gun	SUNSET GUN (cassette with *Sunset Gun* fanzine)	15
68	Ember NR 5038	SUNSTROKE	20
73	Philips 6369 416	SUPER BLACK BLUES	18
69	Blue Horizon (S)PR 31	SUPER DUPER BLUES	25
70	Polydor 2485 002	SUPERGROUPS	12
70	Polydor 2485 003	SUPERGROUPS VOL. 2	12
68	Pye Intl. NPL 28107	SUPER SOUL	25
74	People PLEO 24	SUPER SWEET SOUL	15
64	Vocalion VA 8018	SURF BATTLE	55
86	Capitol EMS 1180	SURF CITY/DRAG CITY	18
88	Decal LIK 39	SURFERS STOMP	18
71	Blue Horizon 7-66263	SWAMP BLUES (2-LP)	75
68	Stateside S(S)L 10243	SWEET SOUL SOUNDS	40
68	Coxsone CSL 8018	SWING EASY	120
68	Saga FID 2136	SWINGING SAGA	15
58	Tempo TAP 21	SWINGIN' THE BLUES	25
93	Tenth Planet TP 002	SYDE TRYPS ONE (numbered, 500 only, with insert)	25
93	Tenth Planet TP 004	SYDE TRYPS TWO … FROM THERE TO UNCERTAINTY (numbered, 500 only, with insert)	25
93	Tenth Planet TP 006	SYDE TRYPS THREE (numbered, 500 only, with insert)	25
94	Tenth Planet TP 008	SYDE TRYPS FOUR (numbered, 500 only, with insert)	25
96	Tenth Planet TP 024	SYDE TRYPS SIX (numbered, gatefold sleeve, 1,000 only)	18

T

72	Rubber RUB 001	TAKE OFF YOUR HEAD AND LISTEN	15
71	A&M Mayfair AMLB 51029	TAKE ONE	12
86	Subway Org. SUBORG 001	TAKE THE SUBWAY TO YOUR SUBURB (mini-LP, red or yellow sleeve)	10
78	Grapevine GRAL 1000	TALK OF THE GRAPEVINE	20
65	London HA-B 8250	THE TALL 12	12
67	London HA-B 8315	THE TALL 12 VOL. 2	12
80	Fuck Off (no cat. no.)	TAPEZINE 2 (cassette)	15
70s	REL RELP 466	TARTAN ALBUM (tartan picture disc)	12
58	Capitol T 1009	TEENAGE ROCK (turquoise or 'rainbow' label)	55/50
63	Stateside SL 10020	TENNESSEE GUITAR	18
56	Nixa Jazz Today NJL 4	TENORAMA	15
77	Talisman STAL 1051	10 YEARS ON — THE UNIVERSAL FOLK CENTRE (LP)	20
70s	Fountain FV 205	TEXAS BLUES	18
69	Highway 51 H 103	TEXAS-LOUISIANA BLUES (99 copies only)	60
62	Ace Of Clubs ACL 1108	THANK YOUR LUCKY STARS	25
63	Golden Guinea GGL 0190	THANK YOUR LUCKY STARS	15
63	Decca LK 4554	THANK YOUR LUCKY STARS VOLUME 2	35
72	Dandelion 2485 021	THERE IS SOME FUN GOING FORWARD (some with poster)	18/12

			MINT VALUE £
69	Action ACLP 6009	THESE KIND OF BLUES VOL. 1	45
82	MCA MCA 6111	THE THING	20
81	TTFTC 001	THE THING FROM THE CRYPT (I NEARLY DIED LAUGHING)	15
57	Tempo TAP 11	THIRD BRITISH FESTIVAL OF JAZZ	15
80s	Come Org. WDC 881021	33 FÜR ILSE KOCH (some on red vinyl)	60
68	Minit MLL/MLS 40002	THIRTY-THREE MINITS OF BLUES AND SOUL	25
83	2-Tone CHR TT 5007	THIS ARE 2-TONE (with free poster, green or pink sleeve)	15
64	Island ILP 910	THIS IS BLUE BEAT (unreleased, white labels may exist)	200+
69	Island IWP 5	THIS IS THE BLUES	25
69	Chess CRL 4540	THIS IS CHESS	20
72	Peg PS 2	THIS IS FOLK VOL. 1	12
72	Peg PS 3	THIS IS FOLK VOL. 2	12
76	Loma/Warners K 56265	THIS IS LOMA VOL. 1	15
76	Loma/Warners K 56266	THIS IS LOMA VOL. 2	12
76	Loma/Warners K 56267	THIS IS LOMA VOL. 3	12
76	Loma/Warners K 56268	THIS IS LOMA VOL. 4	12
76	Loma/Warners K 56269	THIS IS LOMA VOL. 5	12
76	Loma/Warners K 56270	THIS IS LOMA VOL. 6	12
63	Oriole PS 40047	THIS IS MERSEYBEAT VOL. 1	70
63	Oriole PS 40048	THIS IS MERSEYBEAT VOL. 2	70
80	Grapevine GRAL 1002	THIS IS NORTHERN SOUL	35
69	Pama PSP 1003	THIS IS REGGAE	35
73	Island ILPS 9251	THIS IS REGGAE MUSIC	12
71	Pama PMP 2005	THIS IS REGGAE VOLUME TWO	25
71	Pama PMP 2008	THIS IS REGGAE VOLUME THREE	25
72	Pama PMP 2016	THIS IS REGGAE VOLUME FOUR	25
60s	Island IWP 3	THIS IS SUE!	25
60	Philips BBL 7356	THIS WONDERFUL WORLD OF JAZZ	12
63	RCA RD/SF 7608	THE THREE GREAT GUYS (Paul Anka, Sam Cooke & Neil Sedaka)	30
70	Saydisc Matchbox SDR182	THOSE CAKEWALKIN' BABIES FROM HOME	22
66	Allegro ALL 807	THUNDERBALL AND OTHER SECRET AGENT THEMES	15
69	Trojan TTL 1	TIGHTEN UP (orange label)	18
69	Trojan TTL 7	TIGHTEN UP VOLUME TWO	15
69	Trojan TTL 7	TIGHTEN UP VOLUME TWO (pink Island label with different track listing & sleeve)	40+
69	Parlophone PMC 7072	THAT TODDLIN' TOWN — CHICAGO (1926-1928)	12
71	CBS SPR 52	TOGETHER!	12
92	Too Pure SFRLP 119	TOO PURE — THE PEEL SESSIONS (LP, limited issue, custom sleeve)	35
64	Ember FA 2018	TOP OF THE POPS	12
64	Golden Guinea GGL 0277	TOP 10 HITS, ORIGINAL ARTISTS	15
63	Golden Guinea GGL 0196	TOP TV THEMES	15
70	Marble Arch MALS 1359	TOP TV SOUNDTRACK THEMES	15
72	Studio 2 TWO 391	TOP TV THEMES AND COMMERCIALS	30
82	Zoo ZOO 4	TO THE SHORES OF LAKE PLACID (gatefold sleeve with 4-page booklet)	18
64	Topic TPS 114	TOPIC SAMPLER NO. 1 — FOLK SONGS (blue label)	20
66	Topic TPS 145	TOPIC SAMPLER NO. 2 — FOLK SONGS (blue label)	20
66	Topic TPS 166	TOPIC SAMPLER NO. 3 — MEN AT WORK (blue label)	20
66	Topic TPS 168	TOPIC SAMPLER NO. 4 — FROM ERIN'S GREEN SHORE (blue label)	20
66	Topic TPS 205	TOPIC SAMPLER No. 7 — SEA SONGS & SHANTIES (blue label)	20
72	Topic TPSS 221	TOPIC SAMPLER NO. 8 — ENGLISH GARLAND (blue label)	20
56	Tempo TAP 4	TOP TRUMPETS	12
90s	Acid Jazz JAZIDLP 13	TOTALLY WIRED	15
90s	Acid Jazz JAZIDLP 16	TOTALLY WIRED VOLUME TWO	15
90s	Acid Jazz JAZIDLP 22	TOTALLY WIRED VOLUME THREE	15
90s	Acid Jazz JAZIDLP 103	TOTALLY WIRED SWEDEN	15
55	Decca LK 4088	TRADITIONAL JAZZ AT THE ROYAL FESTIVAL HALL	20
55	Decca LK 4100	TRADITIONAL JAZZ AT THE ROYAL FESTIVAL HALL VOL. 2	15
56	Tempo LAP 8	TRADITIONAL JAZZ SCENE (10")	12
56	Tempo TAP 1	TRADITIONAL JAZZ SCENE 1956	12
77	Free Reed FRRD 021/022	THE TRANSPORTS (2-LP, with book)	60
76	Eron 006	TRAVELLING FOLK (with insert)	25
70	RCA Intl. INTS 1175	TRAVELLING THIS LONESOME ROAD	12
61	'77' LA 12-2	A TREASURY OF FIELD RECORDINGS VOLUME 1	25
61	'77' LA 12-3	A TREASURY OF FIELD RECORDINGS VOLUME 2	25
61	Embassy WLP 6041	TRIBUTE TO CLIFF	15
60	Embassy WLP 6034	TRIBUTE TO ELVIS	15
64	Columbia 33SX 1635	TRIBUTE TO MICHAEL HOLLIDAY	25
72	CBS 64861	A TRIBUTE TO WOODY GUTHRIE PART 1 (gatefold sleeve)	12
69	Key KL 003	A TRIBUTE TO YOUTH PRAISE	40
80	Skeleton SKL LP 1	A TRIP TO THE DENTIST (with insert)	15
61	Parlophone PMC 1139	TRIPLE TREAT	20
80	Skeleton SKLLP 1	A TRIP TO THE DENTIST (with insert)	30
71	Trojan TBL 172	TROJAN REGGAE PARTY	25
50s	Esquire 32-036	TROMBONE BY THREE	12
71	Revival RVS 1007	TROUBLE IN MIND... (GEORGIA BLUES)	15
67	Riverside RLP 8802	TUB JUG WASHBOARD BANDS	20
74	Melodisc 12-193	12 BIG HITS	20
74	Melodisc 12-217	12 CARAT GOLD	20
60s	Envoy VOY 9159	12 STRING STORY	12
66	London HA-F/SH-F 8285	THE TWELVE-STRING STORY — GUITAR SOLOS	18
79	Polydor POLS 1006	20 OF ANOTHER KIND	20
83	VCL VCLP 007	21ST ANNIVERSARY INSTRUMENTAL ALBUM	12
65	Ember EMB 3359	25 YEARS OF RHYTHM & BLUES HITS	40
89	WEA 241 690-1	TWIST & SHOUT – 12 ATLANTIC TRACKS PRODUCED BY PHIL SPECTOR (gatefold sleeve)	20
63	Philips BL 7578	TWIST AT THE STAR-CLUB, HAMBURG	70

MINT VALUE £

U - V

68	BBC REC 28M	ULSTER'S FLOWERY VALE	20
69	Island ILP 993/ILPS 9093	THE UNFOLDING OF THE BOOK OF LIFE VOL. 1	18
70s	Flyright FLY 577	UNISSUED CHICAGO BLUES	12
72	Nevis NEV R 007	UNITY CREATES STRENGTH	25
69	Pama ECO 7	UNITY'S GREATEST	35
90s	PWL SAWCD 1	UNPOLISHED DIAMONDS FROM THE SAW CATALOGUE (CD, promo only)	200
88	Unicorn PHZA 17	UNSUNG HEROES (red vinyl)	15
80	Safari UPP 1	UPPERS ON THE SOUTH DOWNS (original issue without Purple Hearts)	12
68	Atlantic 588 122	UPTOWN SOUL	18
88	Urban URBLP 15	URBAN ACID	15
77	Specialty SNTF 5023	URBAN BLUES	12
69	Liberty LBL 83215	URBAN BLUES VOLUME 1: BLUES UPTOWN	25
70	Liberty LBL 83327	URBAN BLUES VOLUME 2: NEW ORLEANS BOUNCE	22
80	Pungent PUN 1	URBAN DEVELOPMENT (cassette, with/without *Fumes* fanzine)	20/12
72	Village Thing VTSAM 15	US	12
50s	Audubon AAM	VAUDEVILLE (10")	20
70	VJM VLP 30	VAUDEVILLE BLUES	15
78	Attrix RB 03	VAULTAGE '78 (TWO SIDES OF BRIGHTON) (originally hand-screened sleeve, later with insert)	20/15
71	Trojan TBL 175	VERSION GALORE VERSION TWO	20
73	Trojan TBL 200	VERSION GALORE VERSION THREE	20
72	Trojan TBL 182	VERSION TO VERSION	15
73	Trojan TBL 206	VERSION TO VERSION VOLUME THREE	15
70	Vertigo 6499 407/8	VERTIGO ANNUAL 1970 (2-LP, set no.: 6657 001)	30
87	BB BBLP 02	VINYL FRONTIER	12
55	Philips BBR 8071	VISIT TO JAZZLAND (10")	12
55	Philips	VISIT TO JAZZLAND NO. 2 (10")	12
56	Philips BBR 8098	VISIT TO JAZZLAND NO. 3 (10")	12
83	Recommended RM 01	VOICES, NOTES AND NOISE (cassette)	15

W

70s	Object Music OBJ 007	WAITING ROOM	15
62	Columbia 33SX 1385	WAKEY WAKEY	25
85	Psycho PSYCHO 35	THE WAKING DREAM	15
64	Pye Intl. NPL 28041	WALKING BY MYSELF	40
64	Pye Intl. NPL 28044	WALKING THE BLUES	35
73	Flyright LP 503	THE WALKING VICTROLA	12
81	Phil Spector Intl. WOS 001	WALL OF SOUND (9-LP box set)	100
78	CBS WOW 100	THE WAR OF THE WORLDS (boxed 2-LP, book & poster)	18
63	Ace Of Hearts AH 55	WASHBOARD RHYTHM	15
70s	Polydor 218 006	WAY INTO THE 70'S	12
78	Bridgehouse BHLP 001	A WEEKEND AT THE BRIDGEHOUSE E16 (with bonus 12" EP)	30
57	Rainbow Records	WEEKEND FILM STAR RECORD ALBUM (5 x 8" flexi 78s, mail order from *Weekend* magazine)	75
85	Music For Nations MFN 49	WELCOME TO THE METAL ZONE (2-LP)	18
59	Coral LVA 9096	WE LIKE GIRLS	25
59	Coral LVA 9098	WE LIKE GUYS	25
71	Wand WCS 1004	WE'RE LEAVIN' IT UP TO YOU	12
63	London HA-P 8061	WE SING THE BLUES	80
65	Liberty LBY 3051	WE SING THE BLUES	60
65	Sue ILP 921	WE SING THE BLUES!	60
72	Syndicate Chapter SC 005	WE THREE KINGS	15
70	Trojan TTL 34	WHAT AM I TO DO	22
80s	Rather/17 RATHER 13	WHAT A NICE WAY TO TURN SEVENTEEN NO. 3 (with magazine)	12
80s	Seventeen SEVENTEEN 6	WHAT A NICE WAY TO TURN SEVENTEEN NO. 6 (with magazine)	12
68	Elektra EKS 7304	WHAT'S SHAKIN' (reissue of "Good Time Music")	15
80	S & T	WHERE THE HELL IS LEICESTER? (with bonus single & booklet)	25
86	Sunrise A40 111M	WHERE WOULD YOU RATHER BE TONIGHT?	25
83	Kamera KAM 14	THE WHIP (with insert)	20
79	London Bomp DHS-Z 3	WHO PUT THE BOMP? (2-LP, gatefold sleeve)	18
70	Trojan TBL 131	WHO YOU GONNA RUN TO	30
72	private pressing	WHOLLY GRAIL	70
74	Topic 12TS 227	WILD HILLS O'WANNIE — THE SMALL PIPES OF NORTHUMBRIA	12
61	Philips BBL 7430	WINNERS OF DOWNBEAT'S INTERNATIONAL CRITICS' POLL 1960	12
66	Dot DLP 3535	WIPE OUT	25
76	RCA RS 1085	WIZARD'S CONVENTION (with insert)	12
82	Womad WOMAD 001	WOMAD: RAINDROPS CLATTERING ON BANANA LEAVES	15
67	RCA Victor RD 7840	WOMEN OF THE BLUES	20
81	Stiff FREEB 3	WONDERFUL TIME OUT THERE (Xmas freebie)	12
81	Glass GLASS 010	THE WONDERFUL WORLD OF GLASS	15
87	Black Crow CRO 217 A	WOODY LIVES: A TRIBUTE TO WOODY GUTHRIE	15
96	Magna Carta MA 9010/2	WORKING MAN	15
63	London HA-P 8099	A WORLD OF BLUES	40
69	Decca (S)PA-R 14	THE WORLD OF BLUES POWER	12
70	Decca (S)PA 63	THE WORLD OF BLUES POWER VOL. 2	12
73	Decca SPA 263	THE WORLD OF BLUES POWER VOL. 3	18
69	Pama SECO 19	A WORLD OF BULLET	35
71	Decca SPA 156	WORLD OF CONTEMPORARY FOLK	12
71	Argo SPA-A 132	THE WORLD OF FOLK	20
73	Argo SPA-A 307	THE WORLD OF FOLK VOLUME 2	20
71	Decca SPA 124	THE WORLD OF SOUL POWER	12
72	Decca SPA 217	WORLD OF T.V. THEMES	12
70s	United Nations 88 888 DY	WORLD STAR FESTIVAL	12
78	Yuk NE 1023	THE WORLD'S WORST RECORD SHOW (multi-coloured vinyl)	20
69	Decca (S)PA 34	WOWIE ZOWIE! — THE WORLD OF PROGRESSIVE MUSIC	15

MINT VALUE £

Y-Z

70s	P. Spec. Intl. PSI 2307 007	YESTERDAY'S HITS TODAY	12
	Cathexis/Pleasantly Surprised PS 014	YOU BET WE'VE GOT SOMETHING AGAINST YOU	50
69	Island IWPS 2	YOU CAN ALL JOIN IN (pink label)	15
70	Trojan TBL 142	YOU CAN'T WINE	20
69	Trojan TTL 9	YOU LEFT ME STANDING	25
78	Stiff DEAL 1	YOU'RE EITHER ON THE TRAIN OR OFF THE TRAIN (promo only, with booklet)	12
62	HMV CLP 1565	YOUR FAVOURITE TV AND RADIO THEMES	15
63	HMV CLP 1676	YOUR FAVOURITE TV AND RADIO THEMES (VOL. 3)	15
63	HMV CLP 1762	YOUR FAVOURITE TV AND RADIO THEMES (VOL. 4)	15
66	HMV CLP 3521	YOUR FAVOURITE TV AND RADIO THEMES (VOL. 5)	15
71	Bamboo BDLP 211	YOUR JAMAICAN GIRL	70
82	Statik STATLP 7	YOUR SECRET'S SAFE WITH US (2-LP)	20
84	Zulu ZULU 6	THE ZULU COMPILATION	20
80s	Relentless R 101	!!?!... A TASTER	12

FILM & TV SOUNDTRACK LPs (alphabetical by title, composers/artists in brackets)

(N.B. Only the first issues of soundtracks by the Beatles and Elvis Presley are listed below: for later repressings see their individual entries.)

A

73	United Artists UAS 29451	ACROSS 110TH STREET (J.J. Johnson & Bobby Womack)	25
70	Paramount SPFL 260	THE ADVENTURERS (Antonio Carlos Jobim)	12
62	RCA RD 7512	ADVISE AND CONSENT (Jerry Fielding)	15
64	Parlophone PMC 1230	A HARD DAY'S NIGHT (Beatles) (1st pressing, with "The Parlophone Co. Ltd" label rim copy & "Sold In The UK..." text; mono, with mid-sized "mono" lettering on front cover)	60
64	Parlophone PCS 3058	A HARD DAY'S NIGHT (Beatles) (1st pressing, with "The Parlophone Co. Ltd" label rim copy & "Sold In The UK..." text; stereo, with mid-sized "stereo" lettering on front cover)	80
67	United Artists (S)ULP 1172	AFRICA ADDIO (Riz Ortolani/Jimmy Roselli)	20
66	United Artists (S)ULP 1151	AFTER THE FOX (Burt Bacharach/Hollies)	35
60	Philips BBL 7429	THE ALAMO (also stereo SBBL 599) (Dimitri Tiomkin)	12/15
56	Nixa NPT 19010	ALEXANDER THE GREAT (Mario Nascimbene) (10"; beware of counterfeits)	150
69	MGM CS 8112	ALFRED THE GREAT (Ray Leppard)	150
72	Warner Bros K 56009	ALICE'S ADVENTURES IN WONDERLAND (John Barry) (gatefold sleeve)	15
79	20th Century T 593	ALIEN (Jerry Goldsmith)	20
61	Fontana (S)TFL 591	ALL NIGHT LONG (mono/stereo, Dave Brubeck/Johnny Dankworth, et al.)	25/35
71	Buddah 2318 034	ALL THE RIGHT NOISES (Melanie)	15
65	Reprise R 6151	AMERICANIZATION OF EMILY (Johnny Mandel)	20
65	RCA RD 7732	THE AMOROUS ADVENTURES OF MOLL FLANDERS (John Addison)	35
57	Brunswick LAT 8175	ANASTASIA (Alfred Newman)	15
60	Philips SBBL 514	ANATOMY OF A MURDER (Duke Ellington)	15
76	BBC REB 236	ANGELS AND 15 OTHER BBC TV THEMES (Alan Parker, et al.)	15
72	Polydor 2383 109	ANTONY AND CLEOPATRA (John Scott) (foldout sleeve)	35
60	London HA-T 2287	THE APARTMENT (Adolph Deutsch)	15
79	Elektra K 62025	APOCALYPSE NOW (2-LP, music & dialogue)	20
69	CBS 70054	APRIL FOOLS (Marvin Hamlisch)	15
58	London HA-D 2078	APRIL LOVE (Pat Boone/Shirley Jones/Lionel Newman Orchestra)	15
66	RCA Victor RD 7817	ARABESQUE (Henry Mancini)	15
66	Fontana FJL 135	L'ASCENSEUR POUR L'ECHAFAUD/FEMME DISPARAISSANTE (Miles Davis/Art Blakey [1 side each])	50
54	HMV DLPC 1	AS LONG AS THEY'RE HAPPY (Jack Buchanan) (10")	50
87	Illegal ILP 017	ATHENS, GA. — INSIDE/OUT (R.E.M.)	12
67	Pye NPL 18198	AT LAST THE 1948 SHOW (TV soundtrack)	15
67	Marble Arch MAL 695	THE AVENGERS AND OTHER FAVOURITES (Laurie Johnson)	35

B

66	Fontana TL 5306	BABY, THE RAIN MUST FALL (Elmer Bernstein)	40
62	Pye Intl. NPL 28020	BARABBAS (Mario Nascimbene)	18
68	Stateside (S)SL 10260	BARBARELLA (Bob Crewe/Charles Fox)	140
67	London HA-D 8337	BAREFOOT IN THE PARK (Neal Hefti)	30
75	Warner Bros K 56189	BARRY LYNDON (Leonard Rosenman)	18
66	Stateside S(S)L 10179	BATMAN (Nelson Riddle) (TV show music)	60
89	W.B./Paisley Park WX 281P	BATMAN (Prince) (picture disc, die-cut sleeve)	20
89	W.B./Paisley Park 925 978-2	BATMAN (Prince) (CD, picture disc in 'Bat' tin with booklet)	18
69	United Artists UAS 29019	BATTLE OF BRITAIN (Ron Goodwin)	15
66	Warner Bros W 1617	BATTLE OF THE BULGE (Benjamin Frankel)	25
60	Columbia 33SX 1225	BEAT GIRL (John Barry/Adam Faith)	50
57	London HAP 2056	BEAU JAMES (Joseph Lilley)	30
64	RCA Victor RD 7679	BECKET (dialogue only)	15
68	Decca LK/SKL 4923	BEDAZZLED (Peter Cook/Dudley Moore)	200+
70	Island ILPS 9140	BE GLAD FOR THE SONG HAS NO ENDING (Incredible String Band)	15
60	Capitol W/SW 1435	BELLS ARE RINGING (André Previn) (mono/stereo)	15/18
73	Ronco RR 2006	THE BELSTONE FOX (Laurie Johnson) (gatefold sleeve)	15
60	MGM MGM-C(S) 802	BEN HUR (Miklos Rozsa) (box set with hardback book; mono/stereo)	15/20
70	Stateside SSL 10311	BEYOND THE VALLEY OF THE DOLLS (Stu Phillips/Strawberry Alarm Clock)	90
66	Stateside S(S)L 10188	THE BIBLE (Toshiro Mayuzumi)	15

			MINT VALUE £
59	London HA-T 2142	THE BIG COUNTRY (Jerome Moross) ('sun' cover)	18
61	HMV CSD 1408	THE BIG COUNTRY (Jerome Moross) ('cast' cover)	12
68	MGM MGM-C(S) 8066	BIGGEST BUNDLE OF THEM ALL (Riz Ortolani/Eric Burdon)	25
86	MCA MCF 3328	BIGGLES (Stanislas/Deep Purple/Motley Crue et al.)	18
69	United Artists (S)ULP 1228	THE BIG GUNDOWN (Ennio Morricone)	15
77	Warner Bros K 56375	BILITIS (gatefold sleeve) (Francis Lai)	15
67	United Artists (S)ULP 1183	BILLION DOLLAR BRAIN (Richard Rodney Bennett)	25
73	Polydor 2490 117	BLACK CAESAR (James Brown)	50
79	Pickwick SHM 3017	THE BLACK HOLE (John Barry)	12
62	Stateside SL 10026	BLACK NATIVITY (Alex Bradford)	20
72	Pye NSPL 18376	BLOOMFIELD	35
66	MGM MGM-C(S) 8039	BLOW-UP (Herbie Hancock/Yardbirds)	80
68	Dot (S)LPD 508	BLUE (Manos Hadjidakis)	30
61	RCA RD 27238/SF 5115	BLUE HAWAII (Elvis Presley) (black/silver label, mono/stereo)	25/40
66	RCA RD 7795	BOEING BOEING (Neal Hefti)	30
69	MCA MUPS 360	BOOM! (John Barry/Georgie Fame)	50
68	Warner Bros W 1742	BONNIE AND CLYDE (Charles Strouse)	20
66	MGM MGM-C(S) 8010	BORN FREE (John Barry/Matt Monro,1st pressing)	18
70	Paramount SPFL 263	BORSALINO (Claude Bolling)	15
58	RCA RD 27054	BOTH ENDS OF THE CANDLE (Gogi Grant)	15
72	Columbia SCXA 9251	THE BOYFRIEND (Twiggy/Christopher Plummer)	15
71	CBS 70078	THE BOY NAMED CHARLIE BROWN (Rod McKuen)	15
57	Brunswick LAT 8193	BOY ON A DOLPHIN (Hugo Friedhoffer)	40
79	A&M AMLH 64731	THE BOYS FROM BRAZIL (Jerry Goldsmith/Elaine Paige)	15
77	United Artists UAG 30097	A BRIDGE TOO FAR (John Addison) (gatefold sleeve)	12
80	MCA MCF 2013	BUCK ROGERS IN THE 25th CENTURY (Stu Phillips)	12
72	Bell BELLS 209	THE BURGLARS (Ennio Morricone)	15
66	RCA RD 7791	BUNNY LAKE IS MISSING (Paul Glass/Zombies)	60
65	Liberty LBY 1246	BURKE'S LAW (Herschel/Burke/Gilbert) (TV series music)	15
63	RCA Victor RD/SF 7580	BYE BYE BIRDIE (musical) (Charles Strouse; mono/stereo)	18/20

C

56	Philips BBR 8104	CALAMITY JANE (Doris Day/Howard Keel) (10")	20
66	RCA Victor RD/SF 7820	CALIFORNIA HOLIDAY (Elvis Presley) (black/red dot labels, mono/stereo)	25/40
69	Stateside (S)SL 10276	CANDY (Dave Grusin/Steppenwolf, et al.)	20
69	MCA MUPS 380	CAN HIERONYMUS MERKIN EVER FORGET MERCY HUMPPE AND FIND TRUE HAPPINESS? (Anthony Newley)	15
64	Philips SBL 7634	CAPTAIN FROM CASTILE (Robert Farnon)	12
60	Delyse DL 3057/DLS 6057	CAPTAIN HORATIO HORNBLOWER (Robert Farnon) (mono/stereo)	75/100
86	Virgin V 2401	CAPTIVE (The Edge et al.)	12
55	Brunswick LAT 8057	CARMEN JONES (Harry Belafonte, et al.)	20
64	MGM MGM-C 984	THE CARPETBAGGERS (Elmer Bernstein)	15
64	London HA-A/SH-A 8219	THE CARPETBAGGERS (Elmer Bernstein)	15
67	RCA Victor RD/SF 7874	CASINO ROYALE (Burt Bacharach/Herb Alpert/Dusty Springfield) (mono/stereo)	60/75
66	United Artists (S)ULP 1140	CAST A GIANT SHADOW (Elmer Bernstein/Vince Hill)	18
71	Polydor 2383 035	CATCH MY SOUL (P.J. Proby/P.P. Arnold, et al.)	15
65	Columbia SX 1756	CATCH US IF YOU CAN (Dave Clark Five)	45
62	Fontana TFL 5170/STFL 585	CHANNEL THRILL: THE T.V. THRILLER THEMES (Johnny Gregory)	12/15
62	Warner Bros WS 8177	THE CHAPMAN REPORT (Leonard Rosenman)	15
63	RCA SF 7620	CHARADE (Henry Mancini)	30
63	MGM MGM-C 969	THE CHARGE IS MURDER (John Green)	20
68	United Artists SULP 1189	THE CHARGE OF THE LIGHT BRIGADE (John Addison/Manfred Mann)	15
83	Polydor BOX 1	CHARIOTS OF FIRE (Vangelis) (box set)	20
66	CBS (S)BPG 62665	THE CHASE (John Barry) (mono/stereo)	30/40
69	Polydor 583 736	CHE! (Lalo Schifrin)	15
69	United Artists UAS 29049	CHICAGO, CHICAGO (Henry Mancini)	18
67	Fontana TL 5417	CHIMES AT MIDNIGHT (Angelo Lavagnino)	50
74	ABC ABCL 5068	CHINATOWN (Jerry Goldsmith)	22
68	United Artists (S)ULP 1200	CHITTY CHITTY BANG BANG (Sherman Brothers) (gatefold sleeve)	15
81	RCA BL 43606	CHRISTIANE F. WIR KINDER VOM BAHNOF ZOO (David Bowie)	12
50s	Columbia OL 5190	CINDERELLA (Oliver Wallace) (also stereo OS 2005)	12
50s	Columbia OL 6330	CINDERELLA (Oliver Wallace) (remake, also stereo OS 2730)	12
68	RCA Victor RD/SF 7917	CLAMBAKE (Elvis Presley) (black/red dot labels, mono/stereo)	20/30
01	Trunk SOUP 001LP	THE CLANGERS (Vernon Elliot) (TV soundtrack, with knitted sleeve, 26 only)	60
74	Buddah BDLP 4010	CLAUDINE (Curtis Mayfield/Gladys Knight)	15
63	Stateside S(S)SL 10044	CLEOPATRA (Alex North)	15
72	Warner Bros K 46127	A CLOCKWORK ORANGE (Walter Carlos)	12
73	Purple TPSM 2001	COLDITZ BREAKPOINT! (TV soundtrack)	12
65	Fontana (S)TL 5259	THE COLLECTOR (Maurice Jarre)	25
78	MGM 2315 398	COMA (Jerry Goldsmith)	15
67	MGM MGM-C(S) 8058	THE COMEDIANS (Laurence Rosenthal)	15
72	Pye NSPL 18389	CONCERTO FOR HARRY — SOMETHING TO HIDE (Roy Budd)	60
75	Polydor 2383 350	CONFESSIONS OF A POP PERFORMER (Three's A Crowd/Ed Welch)	12
71	Philips 6332 033	CONTINENTAL CIRCUS (Gong)	30
62	Parlophone PMC 1194	THE COOL MIKADO (John Barry Seven/Frankie Howerd, et al.)	80
67	Brunswick AXA 4544	COUNTESS FROM HONG KONG (Charles Chaplin) (with booklet)	15
70	Capitol E-ST 640	CROMWELL (Frank Cordell)	15
70	Word WST 5550	THE CROSS & THE SWITCHBLADE (Ralph Carmichael)	25
77	EMI EMA 782	CROSS OF IRON (Ernest Gold) (gatefold sleeve)	18
80	CBS 70182	CRUISING (John Hiatt/Willy DeVille/Germs)	12
73	Buddah 2318 091	CURTIS IN CHICAGO (Curtis Mayfield/Impressions/Jerry Butler, Gene Chandler, Leroy Hutson) (TV soundtrack, gatefold sleeve)	15
68	Stateside (S)SL 10222	CUSTER OF THE WEST (Bernardo Segall)	40

D

			MINT VALUE £
81	2-Tone CHR TT 5004	DANCE CRAZE (with poster)	20
62	Fontana TFL 5184	DANGEROUS FRIENDSHIPS (Art Blakey, et. al.)	18
70	RCA SF 8138	DARLIN' LILI (Henry Mancini) (gatefold sleeve)	15
63	MGM MGM-C 952	DAVID AND LISA (Mark Lawrence/Victor Feldman All Stars)	15
74	Phase 4 Stereo PFS 4339	THE DAY OF THE LOCUST (John Barry)	12
67	Stateside (S)SL 10217	THE DAY THE FISH CAME OUT (Mikis Theodorakis)	15
68	Stateside (S)SL 10263	DEADFALL (John Barry/Shirley Bassey)	35
73	Columbia SCX 6550	DEAF SMITH AND JOHNNY EARS (Daniele Patucchi)	40
74	CBS 80546	DEATH WISH (Herbie Hancock)	25
68	Stateside (S)SL 10259	DECLINE AND FALL... OF A BIRDWATCHER (Ron Goodwin)	100
55	MGM MGM-C 755	DEEP IN MY HEART (Howard Keel/Vic Damone, et al.)	12
73	Warner Bros K 46214	DELIVERANCE (Eric Weissberg)	15
58	London HA-D 2111	DESIRE UNDER THE ELMS (Elmer Bernstein)	25
63	Colpix PXL 440	DIAMOND HEAD (John Williams)	20
76	Pye Intl. NSPL 28219	DIAMOND MERCENARIES (Georges Garvarentz)	15
76	Bradley BRADS 8002	DIAMONDS (Roy Budd)	60
71	United Artists UAS 29216	DIAMONDS ARE FOREVER (John Barry/Shirley Bassey)	20
59	Top Rank RX 3016	THE DIARY OF ANNE FRANK (Alfred Newman)	30
83	Ripple (no cat. no.)	DIGITAL DREAMS (Bill Wyman) (promo only)	100
68	MGM MGM-C(S) 8048	DIRTY DOZEN (Frank de Vol) (yellow label)	18
67	Stateside S(S)L 10214	DOCTOR DOLITTLE (Lionel Newman) (foldout sleeve)	20
62	Columbia 33SX 1446	DON'T KNOCK THE TWIST (Chubby Checker/Gene Chandler, et al.)	25
67	RCA Victor RD/SF 7892	DOUBLE TROUBLE (Elvis Presley) (black/red dot labels, mono/stereo)	20/30
67	CBS S 63189	DR. FAUSTUS (Mario Nascimbene)	75
65	United Artists (S)ULP 1097	DOCTOR NO (Monty Norman) (mono/stereo)	30/35
69	Capitol EST 672	THE DOUBLE DECKERS (TV soundtrack)	25
87	Crammed MTM 14	DOWN BY LAW (John Lurie)	15
74	Studio Two TWO 500	DRACULA (HAMMER PRESENTS...) (Christopher Lee) (gatefold sleeve)	15
70	President PTLS 1068	DRAKE'S DREAM (Paul Jones)	20
59	Parlophone PMCL 1101	DRUMBEAT (Adam Faith/John Barry Seven, et al.)	60
60	HMV CLP 1352/CSD 1296	DRUM CRAZY (THE GENE KRUPA STORY) (Leith Stevens) (mono/stereo)	12/15
66	United Artists (S)ULP 1141	DUEL AT DIABLO (Neal Hefti)	20
58	Decca LF 1308	THE DUKE WORE JEANS (Tommy Steele) (10")	22
84	Polydor 422 8237-7	DUNE (Toto, 1 track by Brian Eno)	15

E

75	MCA MCF 2580	EARTHQUAKE (John Williams)	15
56	MGM D 140	EASTER PARADE/SINGIN' IN THE RAIN (Judy Garland/Gene Kelly) (10")	25
69	Stateside-Dunhill SSL 5018	EASY RIDER (Steppenwolf/Jimi Hendrix/Byrds, et al.)	15
58	HMV DLP 1088	EDDIE FOY AND THE SEVEN LITTLE FOYS (10", Bob Hope/James Cagney)	30
54	Brunswick LAT 8040	THE EGYPTIAN (Alfred Newman)	40
61	MGM MGM-C 876	EL CID (Miklos Rosza) (also stereo [CS 6048])	12/15
67	Columbia S(C)X 6155	EL DORADO (Nelson Riddle)	30
63	Colpix PXL 459	ELIZABETH TAYLOR IN LONDON (John Barry) (mono/stereo)	30/40
69	RCA Victor RD 8011	ELVIS ("TV Special", mono)	15
74	Warner Bros K 56084	EMMANUELLE (Pierre Bachelet)	15
76	Warner Bros K 56231	EMMANUELLE 2 (Francis Lai)	15
57	Vogue Coral LVA 9063	END AS A MAN (Kenyon Hopkins)	30
74	DJM DJLPS 431	ENGLAND MADE ME (John Scott)	12
74	Warner Bros K 46275	ENTER THE DRAGON (Lalo Schifrin)	35
84	Alt. Ten. VIRUS 30	ERASERHEAD (Fats Waller/Peter Ivers/et al.) (with insert)	20
76	EMI EMC 3148	ESCAPE FROM THE DARK (Ron Goodwin)	15
63	Parlophone PMC 1198	THE ESTABLISHMENT (Peter Cook, et al.)	15
82	MCA MCFP 3160	E.T. (THE EXTRA TERRESTRIAL) (John Williams) (picture disc)	15
83	MCA MCA 70000	E.T. — THE EXTRA TERRESTRIAL (John Williams) (box set, with booklet & poster)	40
83	MCA CAC 70000	E.T. — THE EXTRA TERRESTRIAL (John Williams) (cassette, box set, with booklet & poster)	20
67	Brunswick LAT 8678	AN EVENING WITH BORIS KARLOFF AND FRIENDS	60
60	RCA RD 27210	EXODUS (Ernest Gold) (also stereo SF 5093)	12
74	Warner Bros K 56071	THE EXORCIST (Jack Nitzsche, et al.)	20
71	Ember NR 5057	EXPERIENCE — THE ORIGINAL SOUNDTRACK (Jimi Hendrix) (g/fold sleeve)	12
72	Deram SML 1095	EXTREEMS (Tony Klinger & Michael Lyons)	25

F

57	Capitol LCT 6139	A FACE IN THE CROWD (Tom Glazer) (10")	20
64	CBS (S)BPG 62277	FALL OF THE ROMAN EMPIRE (Dimitri Tiomkin)	15
67	Decca LK/SKL 4847	THE FAMILY WAY (Paul McCartney/George Martin) (mono/stereo)	100
60	Top Rank 30/003/4/5	FANTASIA (various classical pieces) (3-LP, with book)	30
58	Capitol LCT 6162	A FAREWELL TO ARMS (Mario Nascimbene)	15
67	MGM MGM-C(S) 8053	FAR FROM THE MADDING CROWD (Richard Rodney Bennett)	20
68	London HA-U/SH-U 8358	THE FASTEST GUITAR ALIVE (Roy Orbison)	30
67	Stateside S(S)L 10213	FATHOM (Johnny Dankworth)	45
73	Pye NSPL 18398	FEAR IS THE KEY (Roy Budd)	120
70	United Artists UAS 29118	FELLINI-SATYRICON (Nino Rota)	20
65	Columbia 33SX 1693	FERRY CROSS THE MERSEY (Gerry & Pacemakers/Cilla Black/Fourmost) (also stereo SCX 3544)	30/40
63	CBS SBPG 62148	55 DAYS AT PEKING (Dimitri Tiomkin/Andy Williams)	18
66	Columbia S(C)X 6079	FINDERS KEEPERS (Cliff Richard) (with inner sleeve, mono/stereo)	15/20
68	Warner Bros WF(S) 2550	FINIAN'S RAINBOW (Fred Astaire/Petula Clark et al.)	25
57	Brunswick LAT 8194	FIRE DOWN BELOW (Arthur Benjamin)	40
84	MCA MCF 3233	FIRESTARTER (Tangerine Dream)	12
78	United Artists UAS 30181	F-I-S-T (Bill Conti)	15
67	RCA Victor RD/SF 7875	A FISTFUL OF DOLLARS (Ennio Morricone)	20

			MINT VALUE £
68	RCA Victor RD 7994	A FISTFUL OF DOLLARS/FOR A FEW DOLLARS MORE/ THE GOOD, THE BAD AND THE UGLY (Hugo Montenegro)	12
72	United Artists UAS 29345	A FISTFUL OF DYNAMITE (Ennio Morricone)	40
71	CBS 70091	FIVE EASY PIECES (Tammy Wynette, et al.)	12
59	London SH-U 6044	THE FIVE PENNIES (Danny Kaye, et al.) (gatefold sleeve)	12
65	RCA Victor RD 7723	FLAMING STAR AND SUMMER KISSES (Elvis Presley) (mono only, black labels, later orange)	100/350
85	Heavy Metal HMI PD 29	FLASHPOINT (Tangerine Dream) (picture disc)	20
85	Heavy Metal HMXD 29	FLASHPOINT (Tangerine Dream) (CD, playable [most copies faulty])	50
68	Stateside SSL 10253	A FLEA IN HER EAR (Bronislau Kaper)	12
71	Decca SKL 5093	FLIGHT OF THE DOVES (Roy Budd/Dana)	12
61	Golden Guinea GGL 0092	THE FLINTSTONES (TV soundtrack)	15
62	Brunswick LAT 8392	FLOWER DRUM SONG (Nancy Kwan, et al.) (also stereo STA 3054)	12/18
64	Ace Of Clubs ACL 1166	FLYING CLIPPER (Riz Ortolani)	15
63	MGM MGM-C/CS 6068	FOLLOW THE BOYS (Connie Francis) (mono/stereo)	15/20
62	MGM MGM-C 882	THE 4 HORSEMEN OF THE APOCALYPSE (André Previn)	12
59	RCA RB 16158	FOR THE FIRST TIME (Mario Lanza)	15
65	Ember NR 5029	FOUR IN THE MORNING (John Barry) (mono)	35
74	T. Motown STML 11269	FOXY BROWN (Willie Hutch)	15
66	RCA Victor RD/SF 7793	FRANKIE AND JOHNNY (Elvis Presley) (black/red dot labels, mono/stereo)	25/40
64	Fontana TL 5208	FREEDOM ROAD (Madeleine Bell, et al.) (TV production)	15
71	Paramount SPFL 269	FRIENDS (Elton John)	12
72	Fantasy FAN 9406	FRITZ THE CAT (Bo Diddley/Billie Holiday, et al.)	35
63	United Artists (S)ULP 1052	FROM RUSSIA WITH LOVE (John Barry/Matt Monroe) (mono/stereo)	25/35
60	London HA-T 2257	THE FUGITIVE KIND (Kenyon Hopkins)	15
67	RCA RD 7860	FUNERAL IN BERLIN (Konrad Elfers)	30
63	RCA Victor RD/SF 7609	FUN IN ACAPULCO (Elvis Presley) (black/silver label, mono/stereo)	20/45

G

65	Liberty (S)LBY 1261	GENGHIS KHAN (Dusan Radic) (mono/stereo)	20
56	Vogue Coral LVA 9003	GENTLEMEN MARRY BRUNETTES (Robert Farnon)	35
53	MGM MGM-D 116	GENTLEMEN PREFER BLONDES (Marilyn Monroe, et al.) (10")	100
65	Mercury 20061 MCL	GENTLE RAIN (Luis Bonfa & Deodato)	15
98	Stella STELP 2	GET CHISHOLM! (David Beaumont, et al.)	12
70	RCA SF 8137	GETTING STRAIGHT (Ronald Stein)	15
57	Capitol LCT 6122	GIANT (Dimitri Tiomkin)	15
60	RCA RD 27192/SF 5078	G.I. BLUES (Elvis Presley) (black/silver label, mono/stereo)	18/45
66	MGM MGM-C(S) 8034	GIRL FROM U.N.C.L.E. (Jerry Goldsmith & Teddy Randazzo)	50
65	RCA Victor RD/SF 7714	GIRL HAPPY (Elvis Presley) (black/red dot labels, mono/stereo)	18/40
68	Polydor 583 714	GIRL ON A MOTORCYCLE (Les Reed)	40
63	RCA Victor RD/SF 7534	GIRLS! GIRLS! GIRLS! (Elvis Presley) (black/silver labels, mono/stereo)	20/45
54	Brunswick LA 8647	THE GLENN MILLER STORY (10")	12
66	United Artists SULP 1120	THE GLORY GUYS (Riz Ortolani)	15
72	Paramount SPFA 7003	THE GODFATHER (Nino Rota) (gatefold sleeve)	20
75	ABC ABCL 5128	THE GODFATHER — PART 2 (Nino Rota) (gatefold sleeve)	20
58	London HA-T 2125	GOD'S LITTLE ACRE (Elmer Bernstein)	30
72	Mother MO 4001	GOLD (MC5/David McWilliams, et al.)	35
74	Philips 9299 225	GOLD (Elmer Bernstein)	15
73	United Artists UAS 29576	THE GOLDEN VOYAGE OF SINBAD (Miklos Rozsa)	18
64	United Artists (S)ULP 1076	GOLDFINGER (John Barry/Shirley Bassey) (mono/stereo)	22/25
64	Decca LK 4673	GONKS GO BEAT (Lulu/Nashville Teens/Graham Bond, et al.)	100
68	United Artists (S)ULP 1197	THE GOOD, THE BAD AND THE UGLY (Ennio Morricone)	18
61	HMV CSD 1386	GOODBYE AGAIN (Georges Auric)	12
65	Stateside SL 10126	GOODBYE CHARLIE (André Previn)	12
69	Warner Bros W(S) 1786	GOODBYE COLUMBUS (Charles Fox/Association)	20
70	DJM DJLPS 408	GOODBYE GEMINI (Christopher Gunning/Peddlers/Jackie Lee)	60
68	CBS (S) 70042	THE GRADUATE (Simon & Garfunkel) (original issue, blue label, laminated sleeve, mono/stereo)	18/15
66	MGM MGM-CS 8037	GRAND PRIX (Maurice Jarre)	15
53	HMV ALP 1071	THE GREAT CARUSO (Mario Lanza)	12
63	United Artists (S)ULP 1041	THE GREAT ESCAPE (Elmer Bernstein) (mono/stereo)	20
77	Arista SPARTY 1013	THE GREATEST (Michael Masser/George Benson)	12
65	United Artists SULP 1093	THE GREATEST STORY EVER TOLD (Alfred Newman)	15
65	RCA RD 7759	THE GREAT RACE (Henry Mancini)	30
71	Pye NSPL 18373	GREAT SONGS AND THEMES FROM GREAT FILMS (Roy Budd)	75
75	MCA MCF 2707	THE GREAT WALDO PEPPER (Henry Mancini)	15
68	United Artists SULP 1220	GREAT WESTERN FILM THEMES (Various Artists)	15
81	Polydor POLS 11031	GREEN ICE (Bill Wyman)	15
70	Polydor 2384 021	GROUPIE GIRL (Opal Butterfly/English Rose, et al.)	20
67	RCA RD/SF 7899	GUNN (Henry Mancini)	20
61	Philips BBL 7500	THE GUNS OF NAVARONE (Dimitri Tiomkin) (also stereo SBBL 646)	12/15
69	RCA SF 8025	THE GURU (Ustad Vilayet Khan)	18

H

67	RCA Victor RB/SB 6735	HALF A SIXPENCE (Tommy Steele, et al.) (gatefold sleeve)	12
65	United Artists SULP 1106	THE HALLELUJAH TRAIL (Elmer Bernstein)	15
75	Contour 2870 437	THE HANGED MAN (Bullet) (TV soundtrack)	60
68	United Artists SULP 1204	HANG 'EM HIGH (Dominic Frontiere)	15
69	United Artists SULP 1231	HANNIBAL BROOKS (Francis Lai)	15
70	United Artists UAS 29084	THE HAPPY ENDING (Michel Legrand)	20
56	Philips BBL 7100	HAPPY HOLIDAY (Jo Stafford)	15
65	RCA Victor RD/SF 7767	HAREM HOLIDAY (Elvis Presley) (black/red dot labels, mono/stereo)	20/30
65	Warner Bros W 1599	HARLOW (Neal Hefti)	30
66	United Artists (S)ULP 1154	HAWAII (Elmer Bernstein)	15
80s	PRT/Chips CHILP 1	HAWK THE SLAYER (Harry Robertson) (gatefold sleeve)	15
68	RCA RD/SF 8051	HEAD (Monkees) (mono/stereo)	80/55

			MINT VALUE £
73	Fantasy FT 516	HEAVY TRAFFIC (Chuck Berry/Sergio Mendes/et al.)	15
72	Reprise K 44168	THE HEIST (Quincy Jones/Little Richard)	35
74	Tamla Motown STML 11260	HELL UP IN HARLEM (Edwin Starr)	15
65	Parlophone PMC 1255	HELP! (Beatles) (1st pressing, with "The Gramophone Co. Ltd" & "Sold In The UK..." label text; mono, with "mono" in outline type on front cover)	40
65	Parlophone PCS 3071	HELP! (Beatles) (1st pressing, with "The Gramophone Co. Ltd" & "Sold In The UK..." label text; stereo, with "stereo" in outline type on front cover)	50
67	United Artists (S)ULP 1186	HERE WE GO ROUND THE MULBERRY BUSH (Spencer Davis/Traffic/Andy Ellison) (mono/stereo)	35/30
59	Capitol T 1160	HEY BOY! HEY GIRL! (Louis Prima/Keely Smith, et al.)	20
62	Columbia 33SX 1421	HEY, LET'S TWIST (Joey Dee, et al.)	20
83	A&R FILM 001	HIGH ROAD TO CHINA (John Barry)	18
70	Columbia SCX 6443	HIS LAND (Cliff Richard/Cliff Barrows)	25
67	United Artists ULP 1161	THE HONEY POT (John Addison)	15
59	London HA-T 2197	THE HORSE SOLDIERS (David Buttolph)	30
59	Philips BBL 7292	HOUSEBOAT (George Duning)	20
62	MGM MGM-C 915/CS 6061	HOW THE WEST WAS WON (Alfred Newman)	12
87	Silva Screen FILM 041	HOW TO GET AHEAD IN ADVERTISING/WITHNAIL & I	20
87	Silva Screen FILMCD 041	HOW TO GET AHEAD IN ADVERTISING/WITHNAIL & I (CD)	18
65	United Artists (S)ULP 1098	HOW TO MURDER YOUR WIFE (Neal Hefti)	25
68	CBS (S)BPG 63276	HOW TO SAVE A MARRIAGE AND RUIN YOUR LIFE (Michel Legrand/ Ray Conniff)	20
72	Atlantic K 40371	HOW TO STEAL A DIAMOND IN FOUR UNEASY LESSONS (Quincy Jones)	18
66	Stateside S(S)L 10187	HOW TO STEAL A MILLION (John Williams)	45
61	Golden Guinea GGL 0069	HUCKLEBERRY HOUND (TV soundtrack)	12
67	RCA Victor RD/SF 7877	HURRY SUNDOWN (Hugo Montenegro)	30

I

69	MGM MGM-C(S) 8101	ICE STATION ZEBRA (Michel Legrand)	15
70	United Artists UAS 29044	IF IT'S TUESDAY THIS MUST BE BELGIUM (Walter Scharf)	15
67	Brunswick LAT/STA 8689	I'LL NEVER FORGET WHAT'S 'ISNAME (Francis Lai)	30
65	United Artists ULP 1105	I'LL TAKE SWEDEN (Bob Hope/Frankie Avalon, et al.)	20
68	RCA Victor RD/SF 7931	IN COLD BLOOD (Quincy Jones)	45
65	RCA RD 7707	IN HARM'S WAY (Jerry Goldsmith)	18
67	Stateside S(S)L 10207	IN LIKE FLINT (Jerry Goldsmith)	50
63	Colpix PXL 459	IN LONDON (TV soundtrack) (Elizabeth Taylor/John Barry, mono/stereo)	40/50
68	United Artists ULP 1201	INSPECTOR CLOUSEAU (Ken Thorne)	20
69	RCA Victor RD/SF 7990	INTERLUDE (Georges Delarue/Timi Yuro)	25
62	Colpix PXL 427	THE INTERNS (Leith Stevens)	20
67	United Artists (S)ULP 1181	IN THE HEAT OF THE NIGHT (Quincy Jones/Ray Charles)	25
65	CBS BPG 62530	THE IPCRESS FILE (John Barry) (mono only)	50
84	Illuminated JAMS 35	IN THE SHADOW OF THE SUN (Throbbing Gristle)	18
63	United Artists SULP 1051	IRMA LA DOUCE (Andre Previn)	15
66	CBS (S)BPG 62843	IS PARIS BURNING? (Maurice Jarre)	25
69	Paramount SPFL 256	THE ITALIAN JOB (Quincy Jones/Matt Monro)	125
63	RCA Victor RD/SF 7565	IT HAPPENED AT THE WORLD'S FAIR (Elvis Presley) (black/silver label, mono/stereo)	20/45
63	Columbia 33SX 1533	IT'S ALL HAPPENING (Tommy Steele/Shane Fenton, et al.) (also stereo SCX 3486)	15/22
63	United Artists (S)ULP 1053	IT'S A MAD MAD MAD MAD WORLD (Ernest Gold)	20
62	Columbia 33SX 1412	IT'S TRAD, DAD! (Helen Shapiro/Gene Vincent, et al.)	25
65	Decca LK 4677	I'VE GOTTA HORSE (Billy Fury/Bachelors, et al.)	70
71	CBS 70083	I WALK THE LINE (Johnny Cash)	15
59	London LTZ-T 15160	I WANT TO LIVE (Johnny Mandel)	20

J

72	United Artists UAD 60027/8	THE JAMES BOND COLLECTION (John Barry) (2-LP, with booklet)	25
57	Capitol LCT 6140	THE JAMES DEAN STORY (Leith Stevens)	25
54	Brunswick LA 8671	JAZZ THEMES FROM "THE WILD ONE" (Leith Stevens) (10")	30
62	HMV CLP 1582	JESSICA (Mario Nascimbene)	15
77	Pye NSPH 28504	JESUS OF NAZARETH (Maurice Jarre) (gatefold sleeve)	15
73	Reprise K 64017	JIMI HENDRIX — SOUNDTRACK RECORDINGS FROM THE FILM (2-LP)	18
68	Stateside (S)SL 10264	JOANNA (Rod McKuen/Mike Sarne)	15
71	Mercury 6338 029	JOE (Bobby Scott/Jenny Butler)	20
64	United Artists ULP 1060	JOHNNY COOL (Billy May/Sammy Davis Jr.)	25
72	Reprise K 64015	JOURNEY THROUGH THE PAST (Neil Young) (2-LP, fold-out cover with inner sleeves)	20
77	Polydor/EG 2302 079	JUBILEE (Adam & Ants/Brian Eno, et al.)	12
61	HMV CLP 1545	JUDGMENT AT NUREMBURG (Ernest Gold)	20
66	RCA RD 7788	JUDITH (Sol Kaplan)	12
67	Fontana (S)TL 5317	JULIET OF THE SPIRITS (Nino Rota)	40
63	Decca LK 4524	JUST FOR FUN (Tornados/Karl Denver, et al.)	40
64	Decca LK 4620	JUST FOR YOU (Applejacks/Merseybeats, et al.)	40
70	Monument LMO/SMO 5031	JUSTINE (Jerry Goldsmith)	15

K

71	MGM 2315 019	KELLY'S HEROES (Lalo Schifrin/Mike Curb)	25
66	United Artists (S)ULP 1139	KHARTOUM (Frank Cordell)	40
72	Polydor 2383 102	KIDNAPPED (Roy Budd/Mary Hopkin)	25
58	RCA RD 27088	KING CREOLE (Elvis Presley) (black/silver labels)	50
76	Reprise K 54090	KING KONG (John Barry) (with poster)	15
61	MGM MGM-CS 6043	KING OF KINGS (Miklos Rozsa)	20
58	Capitol LCT 6165	KINGS GO FORTH (Elmer Bernstein)	15
66	Fontana (S)TL 5302	KING RAT (John Barry)	20
64	RCA Victor RD/SF 7645	KISSIN' COUSINS (Elvis Presley) (black/red dot labels, mono/stereo)	18/40
54	MGM MGM-C 753	KISS ME KATE (Howard Keel, et al.)	20

			MINT VALUE £
65	United Artists ULP 1104	THE KNACK (AND HOW TO GET IT) (John Barry)	30
54	Brunswick LA 8668	KNOCK ON WOOD (Danny Kaye) (10")	15
69	Stateside (S)SL 10277	KRAKATOA: EAST OF JAVA (Frank De Vol)	15
74	Warner Bros K 46271	KUNG FU (TV soundtrack) (with inner sleeve)	20

L

61	RCA RD 27202	LA DOLCE VITA (Nino Rota) (gatefold sleeve)	50
63	Ace Of Hearts AH 70	THE LADY AND THE TRAMP (Peggy Lee)	30
69	Stateside S(S)L 10267	LADY IN CEMENT (Hugo Montenegro)	45
73	Tamla Motown TMSP 1131	LADY SINGS THE BLUES (Diana Ross) (2-LP, with brown inner sleeves)	18
71	United Artists UAS 29120	THE LANDLORD (Al Kooper)	20
80	Charisma CDS 4020	LARK RISE TO CANDLEFORD (A COUNTRY TAPESTRY) (Keith Dewhurst & Albion Band)	12
72	MGM 2315 072	THE LAST RUN (Jerry Goldsmith/Steve Lawrence)	25
73	United Artists UAS 29440	LAST TANGO IN PARIS (Gato Barbieri)	20
71	Probe SPB 1027	THE LAST VALLEY (John Barry) (some with insert)	40/35
63	Pye Intl. NPL 28023	LAWRENCE OF ARABIA (Maurice Jarre)	12
85	United Artists 86002	LEGEND (Jerry Goldsmith)	25
71	M. F. Pleasure MFP 50034	THE LEGEND OF FRENCHIE KING (Francis Lai)	15
74	Warner Bros K 56085	THE LEGEND OF THE 7 GOLDEN VAMPIRES (James Bernard/Peter Cushing)	18
64	Stateside S(S)L 10058	THE LEOPARD (Nino Rota)	30
70	Apple PXS 1	LET IT BE (Beatles) (box set, 1st pressing, dark green label, red Apple logo on LP rear sleeve & white inner, with *Get Back* book housed in black card tray ['PXS 1' not listed on package])	300
70	Apple PCS 7096	LET IT BE (Beatles) (2nd pressing, green Apple logo on rear sleeve, plain white inner)	15
60	Philips BBL 7414/SBBL 592	LET'S MAKE LOVE (Marilyn Monroe/Yves Montand/Frankie Vaughan)	60/75
79	Warner Bros K 56751	LIFE OF BRIAN (Monty Python) (with inner sleeve)	12
59	Philips SBBL 565	LI'L ABNER (Nelson Riddle)	12
64	Columbia SX 1626	LILIES OF THE FIELD (Jerry Goldsmith)	20
69	CBS 70049	THE LION IN WINTER (John Barry)	20
66	MGM MGM-CS 8029	THE LIQUIDATOR (Lalo Schifrin/Shirley Bassey)	50
71	CBS 70087	LITTLE FAUSS AND BIG HALSY (Johnny Cash)	15
73	United Artists UAS 29475	LIVE AND LET DIE (George Martin/Wings) (gatefold sleeve)	25
87	Warner Bros 925 616-1	THE LIVING DAYLIGHTS (John Barry)	12
76	MGM 2315 376	LOGAN'S RUN (Jerry Goldsmith)	25
62	MGM MGM-C 896	LOLITA (Nelson Riddle)	25
67	Polydor 583 014	LONG DUEL (Patrick John Scott)	20
63	Stateside S(S)L 10045	THE LONGEST DAY (dialogue only)	20
83	CES CES 1001	THE LONG GOOD FRIDAY (Francis Monkman) (numbered sleeve with insert, black label print, 2,000 only)	50
83	CES CES 1001	THE LONG GOOD FRIDAY (Francis Monkman) (re-pressing, with insert, blue label print, 500 only)	70
84	CES CES 1001	THE LONG GOOD FRIDAY (Francis Monkman) (3rd pressing, with insert, blue label print, 5,000 only)	40
89	Silva Screen FILM 020	THE LONG GOOD FRIDAY (Francis Monkman) (reissue)	20
89	Silva Screen FILM 020	THE LONG GOOD FRIDAY (Francis Monkman) (CD)	25
65	MGM C/CS 6079	LOOKING FOR LOVE (Connie Francis)	18
70	CBS 70073	LOOT (Keith Mansfield/Steve Ellis)	60
65	Colpix PXL 521	LORD JIM (Bronislau Kaper)	20
69	Uni UNLS 103	LOST MAN (Quincy Jones)	25
70	CBS 70067	LOVE CIRCLE (Ennio Morricone)	60
57	RCA RC 24001	LOVING YOU (Elvis Presley) (10", silver spot label)	110
57	MGM MGM-D 141	LOVELY TO LOOK AT (Howard Keel, et al.) (10")	12

M

77	MCA MCF 2828	MACARTHUR (Jerry Goldsmith)	18
73	Tamla Motown STMA 8003	THE MACK (Willie Hutch)	15
69	RCA Victor SF 8017	MACKENNA'S GOLD (Quincy Jones/Jose Feliciano)	15
69	Warner Bros WS 1805	THE MADWOMAN OF CHAILLOT (Michael Lewis)	20
70	Pye Intl. NSPL 28133	THE MAGIC CHRISTIAN (Ken Thorne/Badfinger, et al.)	30
54	Brunswick LAT 8045	MAGNIFICENT OBSESSION (Frank Skinner)	30
65	MGM MGM-C 995	THE MAGNIFICENT SHOWMAN (Dimitri Tiomkin)	15
76	Atlantic K 50308	MAHONEY'S LAST STAND (Ronnie Lane & Ron Wood)	18
63	Ace Of Clubs ACL 1135	MAIGRET (Ron Grainer) (TV series music)	15
66	CBS SBPG 62525	MAJOR DUNDEE (Daniele Amfitheatrof)	15
67	United Artists SULP 1155	A MAN AND A WOMAN (Francis Lai)	18
66	Brunswick LAT/STA 8651	A MAN COULD GET KILLED (Bert Kaempfert)	20
67	RCA RB 6712/3	A MAN FOR ALL SEASONS (2-LP, dialogue only)	35
59	Top Rank 35/043	MAN FROM INTERPOL (Tony Crombie) (TV series music)	25
66	RCA Victor RD 7758	THE MAN FROM U.N.C.L.E. (Hugo Montenegro)	45
64	Stateside S(S)L 10087	MAN IN THE MIDDLE (Lionel Bart & John Barry)	30
56	Brunswick LAT 8101	THE MAN WITH THE GOLDEN ARM (Elmer Bernstein)	25
74	United Artists UAS 29671	THE MAN WITH THE GOLDEN GUN (John Barry/Lulu)	15
63	Stateside S(S)L 10048	MARILYN (Marilyn Monroe) (mono/stereo)	40/50
72	MCA MUPS 441	MARY QUEEN OF SCOTS (John Barry)	30
70	United Artists UAS 29122	MASTER OF THE ISLANDS (Henry Mancini)	18
69	Philips SBL 7876	MAYERLING (Francis Lai)	30
64	United Artists SULP 1059	McLINTOCK (Frank De Vol)	15
80	Polydor POLD 5034	McVICAR (Roger Daltrey) (some on clear vinyl)	20/15
71	Polydor 2383 043	MELODY (Bee Gees, Richard Hewson, et al.)	12
69	CBS 70061	ME, NATALIE (Henry Mancini/Rod McKuen)	18
57	London HA-P 2076	MEN IN WAR (Elmer Bernstein)	40
58	Capitol T 1016	MERRY ANDREW (Danny Kaye)	25
69	Bell BELL 6053	MERRY CHRISTMAS (David Frost/Billy Taylor)	40
76	EMI SCLW 1033	THE MESSAGE (Maurice Jarre) (gatefold sleeve)	12

			MINT VALUE £
65	MGM MGM-C(S) 8001	MICKEY ONE (Stan Getz & Eddie Sauter) (with booklet, mono/stereo)	20/25
69	United Artists UAS 29043	MIDNIGHT COWBOY (John Barry/Nilsson/Elephant's Memory) (orange/pink label)	15
66	Mercury 20072 (S)MCL	"MIRAGE" (LP)	30
61	HMV CLP 1481	THE MISFITS (Alex North)	25
68	Dot (S)LPD 503	MISSION: IMPOSSIBLE — MUSIC FROM THE TV SERIES (Lalo Schifrin)	40
54	Mercury 25181	MISS SADIE THOMPSON (George Duning) (10")	30
66	Fontana TL 5347	MODESTY BLAISE (Johnny Dankworth)	50
70	Paramount SPFL 259	THE MOLLY MAGUIRES (Henry Mancini)	12
80	BBC REB 384	MONKEY (Godiego) (TV soundtrack)	15
69	Paramount SPFL 255	MONTE CARLO OR BUST! (Ron Goodwin)	45
79	United Artists UAG 30247	MOONRAKER (John Barry/Shirley Bassey)	15
69	Columbia SCX 6346	MORE (Pink Floyd) (laminated flipback sleeve, 'couple facing west' photo on green-tinted rear sleeve)	35
70s	Columbia SCX 6346	MORE (Pink Floyd) (laminated non-flipback sleeve, 'couple facing west' photo on black-tinted rear sleeve)	25
70s	Columbia SCX 6346	MORE (Pink Floyd) (laminated non-flipback sleeve, 'couple facing east' photo on black-tinted rear sleeve)	35
72	Ember NR 5061	MORE EXPERIENCE (Jimi Hendrix)	12
69	Paramount SPFL 252	MORE 'MISSION: IMPOSSIBLE' (Lalo Schifrin)	40
60	MGM MGM-C(S) 857	MORE MUSIC FROM BEN-HUR (Miklos Rozsa)	15/20
66	RCA Victor RD 7832	MORE MUSIC FROM 'THE MAN FROM U.N.C.L.E.' (Hugo Montenegro)	45
62	MGM	MORE MUSIC FROM 'MUTINY ON THE BOUNTY' (Bronislau Kaper)	20
65	Columbia S(C)X 6303	MRS BROWN YOU'VE GOT A LOVELY DAUGHTER (Hermans Hermits, mono or stereo, some with manuscript)	25/30
77	Pye NSPH 19	MUPPET SHOW VOL. 1 (TV soundtrack) (gatefold sleeve)	12
78	Pye NSPH 21	MUPPET SHOW VOL. 2 (TV soundtrack)	12
62	MGM MGM-CS 6060	MUTINY ON THE BOUNTY (Bronislau Kaper)	20
67	RCA RD 7847	MURDERERS' ROW (Lalo Schifrin)	75
72	Harvest SHSP 4019	MUSIC FROM MACBETH (Third Ear Band)	15
80	Unicorn Kachana KPM 7009	MUSIC FROM THE AVENGERS, THE NEW AVENGERS AND THE PROFESSIONALS (Laurie Johnson/London Studio Orchestra) (gatefold sleeve)	20
70	Harvest SHSP 4008	MUSIC FROM THE BODY (Ron Geesin & Roger Waters) (black labels)	12
70	Harvest SHSP 4008	MUSIC FROM THE BODY (Ron Geesin & Roger Waters) (photos/green labels)	20
62	Warner Bros WS 8066	THE MUSIC MAN (Robert Preston, et al.)	12
85	Cloud Nine CN 4002	MYSTERIOUS ISLAND (Bernard Herrman)	25

N

70	United Artists UAS 29108	NED KELLY (Shel Silverstein/Mick Jagger/Waylon Jennings)	35
72	Bell BELLS 202	NICHOLAS AND ALEXANDRA (Richard Rodney Bennet)	15
67	RCA RD 7848	NIGHT OF THE GENERALS (Maurice Jarre)	20
65	MGM MGM-C 994	NIGHT OF THE IGUANA (Benjamin Frankel)	15
69	United Artists (S)ULP 1235	THE NIGHT THEY RAIDED MINSKY'S (Charles Strouse)	20
62	Decca LK 4527	NINE HOURS TO RAMA (Malcolm Arnold)	100
68	Dot (S)LPD 507	NO WAY TO TREAT A LADY (American Breed)	30
90	Mercury 846043-1	NUNS ON THE RUN	15
90	Mercury 846043-2	NUNS ON THE RUN (CD)	20

O

72	Harvest SHSP 4020	OBSCURED BY CLOUDS (Pink Floyd) (rounded sleeve)	18
76	Phase 4 Stereo PF5 4381	OBSESSION (Bernard Herrman)	15
83	A&M AMLX 64967	OCTOPUSSY (John Barry/Rita Coolidge)	12
83	A&M 394 967-2	OCTOPUSSY (John Barry) (CD, withdrawn)	75
68	Dot (S)LPD 514	THE ODD COUPLE (Neal Hefti)	30
60	London HA-T 2220	ODDS AGAINST TOMORROW (John Lewis)	12
75	MCA MCF 2591	ODESSA FILE (Andrew Lloyd Webber/Perry Como)	12
64	Stateside S(S)L 10056	OF LOVE AND DESIRE (Ronald Stein)	12
69	Paramount SPFL 251	OH! WHAT A LOVELY WAR (Alfred Ralston, et al.) (gatefold sleeve)	15
70	Starline SRS 5019	OLIVER IN THE OVERWORLD (Freddie Garrity)	20
73	Warner Bros K 46227	O LUCKY MAN! (Alan Price) (gatefold sleeve)	18
57	Brunswick LAT 8226	OMAR KHAYYAM/THE MOUNTAIN (Victor Young/Daniele Amfitheatrof)	30
75	Fantasy FTA 3004	ONE FLEW OVER THE CUCKOO'S NEST (Jack Nitzsche) (gatefold sleeve)	15
69	United Artists UAS 29020	ON HER MAJESTY'S SECRET SERVICE (John Barry) (foldout sleeve)	20
59	Columbia 33SX 1208	ON THE BEACH (Ernest Gold)	12
54	HMV DLP 1059	ORCHESTRA WIVES (Glenn Miller) (10")	12
70	Fontana SFJL 950	ORFEU NEGRO (BLACK ORPHEUS) (Luis Bonfa/Antonio Carlos Jobim)	15
69	RCA SF 8014	OTLEY (Stanley Myers/Don Partridge)	25
66	Stateside S(S)L 10174	OUR MAN FLINT (Jerry Goldsmith)	50
76	Warner Bros K 56286	THE OUTLAW JOSEY WALES (Jerry Fielding)	15

P

58	Philips BBL 7197	THE PAJAMA GAME (Doris Day, et al.)	12
63	Warner Bros WM 8141	PALM SPRINGS WEEKEND (Frank Perkins)	20
74	EMI EMC 3020	PAPILLON (Jerry Goldsmith)	15
66	RCA Victor RD/SF 7810	PARADISE, HAWAIIAN STYLE (Elvis Presley) (black/red dot labels, mono/stereo)	25/40
61	HMV CLP 1499	PARIS BLUES (Duke Ellington)	15
61	Warner Bros WS 8044	PARRISH (Max Steiner/George Creely)	20
73	CBS S 69042	PAT GARRETT & BILLY THE KID (Bob Dylan)	12
70	Stateside SSL 10302	PATTON (Jerry Goldsmith)	15
65	Mercury 20063 SML	THE PAWNBROKER (Quincy Jones)	25
66	Philips (S)BL 7782	THE PEKING MEDALLION (Georges Garvarentz/Dusty Springfield)	30
77	Atlantic K 50410	PELÉ (Sergio Mendes/Pelé)	15
67	Ember NR 5040	THE PENTHOUSE (John Hawksworth)	50

			MINT VALUE £
71	Pye NSPL 18365	PERCY (Kinks)	18
70	Warner Bros WS 2554	PERFORMANCE (Mick Jagger/Jack Nitzsche/Randy Newman, et al.)	30
71	CBS 64816	THE PERSUADERS (John Barry)	15
59	RCA RD 27123/SF 5033	PETER GUNN (Henry Mancini)	15
55	Philips BBL 7059	PETE KELLY'S BLUES (Sammy Cahn, Matty Matlock, et al.)	12
61	Ace Of Hearts AH 26	PETE KELLY'S BLUES (Peggy Lee, Ella Fitzgerald)	12
79	Gem GEM 102	PHANTASM (Fred Myrow & Malcolm Seagrave)	12
62	United Artists ULP 1016	PHAEDRA (Mikis Theodorakis)	12
56	Brunswick LAT 8120	PICNIC (George Duning)	25
76	United Artists UAS 30012	THE PINK PANTHER STRIKES AGAIN (Henry Mancini/Tom Jones)	18
68	Philips SBL 7858	PLAYTIME	35
70	Paramount SPFL 258	POOKIE (Fred Karlin/Sandpipers)	15
57	Capitol LCT 6141	THE PRIDE AND THE PASSION (Georges Antheil)	15
69	Stateside (S)SL 10278	THE PRIME OF MISS JEAN BRODIE (Rod McKuen/Mike Redway)	15
86	Bam Caruso WEBA 066	THE PRISONER (Ron Grainer, et al.) (fan club issue, gatefold sleeve with inner sleeve, booklet, membership form, map & poster)	35
66	HMV CLP/CSD 3623	PRIVILEGE (Paul Jones & Mike Leander)	18
69	RCA SF 8072	THE PRODUCERS (John Morris)	15
69	United Artists UAS 29005	A PROFESSIONAL GUN (Ennio Morricone)	30
67	RCA Victor RD/SF 7876	THE PROFESSIONALS (Maurice Jarre)	50
60	Contemporary LAC 12293	THE PROPER TIME (Shelly Manne)	15
68	Stateside S(S)L 10248	PRUDENCE AND THE PILL (Bernard Ebbinghouse)	25
75	Unicorn RHS 336	PSYCHO (Bernard Herrmann)	20

Q

71	Sonet SNTF 622	QUIET DAYS IN CLICHY (Country Joe McDonald)	12
66	CBS (S)BPG 62869	THE QUILLER MEMORANDUM (John Barry/Matt Monro) (mono/stereo)	20/30

R

88	Silva Screen FILM 033	THE RAGGEDY RAWNEY (Michael Kamen)	25
88	Silva Screen FILM 033	THE RAGGEDY RAWNEY (Michael Kamen) (CD)	20
71	Reprise K 44159	RAINBOW BRIDGE (Jimi Hendrix) (matt gatefold sleeve, 'steamboat' label)	12
75	Dart ARTS 65376	RANSOM (Jerry Goldsmith)	50
60	London HAD 2288	THE RAT RACE (Sam Butera & The Witnesses)	25
67	United Artists (S)ULP 1184	RED AND BLUE (Vanessa Redgrave)	40
72	Paramount SPFL 275	THE RED TENT (Ennio Morricone)	12
70	CBS 70068	THE REIVERS (John Williams)	12
76	United Artists UAS 30007	THE RETURN OF A MAN CALLED HORSE (Laurence Rosenthal)	12
75	RCA Red Seal RS 1010	THE RETURN OF THE PINK PANTHER (Henry Mancini)	18
67	United Artists (S)ULP 1156	RETURN OF THE SEVEN (Elmer Bernstein)	15
69	United Artists ULP 1226	REVOLUTION (Quicksilver Messenger Service/Steve Miller, et al.)	20
70	United Artists UAS 29137	RIDER IN THE RAIN (Francis Lai)	20
68	MGM MGM-C(S) 8079	THE RISE AND FALL OF THE THIRD REICH (Lalo Schifrin)	20
53	Brunswick LA 8578	ROAD TO BALI (Bob Hope, Bing Crosby) (10")	30
62	Decca LKR 4427	THE ROAD TO HONG KONG (Robert Farnon/Bob Hope & Bing Crosby)	12
67	Decca LK/SKL 4892	ROBBERY (Johnny Keating/Jackie Lee)	15
54	Brunswick LAT 8031	THE ROBE (Alfred Newman) (gold label)	20
64	Reprise R 2021	ROBIN AND THE SEVEN HOODS (Nelson Riddle)	30
61	RCA RD 27233	ROCCO AND HIS BROTHERS (Nino Rota)	18
57	Mercury MPT 7527	ROCK ALL NIGHT (Platters, Norah Hayes, et al.) (10")	175
67	Polydor 583 013	ROCKET TO THE MOON (John Scott)	150
57	Brunswick LAT 8162	ROCK, PRETTY BABY (Henry Mancini/Rod McKuen)	100
87	Ode RHBX 1	ROCKY HORROR BOX SET (Richard O'Brien) (4-LP box, with inserts, numbered, stickered, containing confetti)	30
87	Ode RHBXLP 1	ROCKY HORROR BOX SET (Richard O'Brien) (4-LP box, with different inserts to above)	25
75	Ode ODE 78332	THE ROCKY HORROR PICTURE SHOW (Richard O'Brien) (Original Soundtrack)	15
83	Ode OSVP 78332	THE ROCKY HORROR PICTURE SHOW ALBUM (picture disc)	20
86	Ode ODE 21653	THE ROCKY HORROR PICTURE SHOW ALBUM (reissue)	12
87	Ode OSVP 21653	THE ROCKY HORROR PICTURE SHOW ALBUM (reissue, picture disc)	20
90	Ode RHBXCD 1	THE ROCKY HORROR PICTURE SHOW — 15TH ANNIVERSARY (Richard O'Brien, et al.) (4-CD box)	45
75	United Artists UAS 29865	ROLLERBALL (Andre Previn)	15
77	MCA MCF 2813	ROLLERCOASTER (Lalo Schifrin/Sparks)	12
68	Dot (S)LPD 519	ROSEMARY'S BABY (Kryzstophe Komeda)	35
65	Parlophone PMC 1262	ROTTEN TO THE CORE (New Jazz Voices)	20
64	RCA Victor RD/SF 7678	ROUSTABOUT (Elvis Presley) (black/red dot labels, mono/stereo)	16/40
64	Capitol (S)T 1771	ROUTE 66 AND OTHER GREAT T.V. THEMES (Nelson Riddle) (TV show)	15
66	United Artists ULP 1147	THE RUSSIANS ARE COMING THE RUSSIANS ARE COMING (Johnny Mandel)	15
71	MGM 2315 028	RYAN'S DAUGHTER (Maurice Jarre) (gatefold sleeve)	12

S

72	RCA SF 8211	SACCO AND VANZETTI (Ennio Morricone/Joan Baez)	12
53	Brunswick LA 8604	SALOMÉ (George Duning) (10")	50
68	United Artists SULP 1202	SALT AND PEPPER (Johnny Dankworth/Sammy Davis Jr)	15
67	Stateside S(S)L 10198	THE SAND PEBBLES (Jerry Goldsmith)	15
65	Mercury MCL 20065	THE SANDPIPER (Johnny Mandel)	20
68	United Artists (S)ULP 1190	THE SCALPHUNTERS (Elmer Bernstein)	15
78	Polydor 2480 429	SCOUSE THE MOUSE (Ringo Starr/Adam Faith, et al.) (some w/stickered sleeve & printed [not photocopied] competition insert)	110/30
78	Polydor 3194 429	SCOUSE THE MOUSE (Ringo Starr/Adam Faith, et al.) (cassette)	40
70	CBS 70077	SCROOGE (Leslie Bricusse) (musical, gatefold sleeve)	12
80	EMI EMC 3340	THE SEA WOLVES (Roy Budd/Matt Monroe)	18
62	Reprise R 2013	SERGEANTS 3 (Billy May)	30
73	Paramount SPFL 296	SERPICO (Mikis Theodorakis)	25

			MINT VALUE £
64	United Artists ULP 1072	THE SEVENTH DAWN (Riz Ortolani)	15
74	United Artists UAS 29763	THE SEVENTH VOYAGE OF SINBAD (Bernard Hermann)	25
71	Stax 2659 007	SHAFT — ORIGINAL SOUNDTRACK (Isaac Hayes) (2-LP, gatefold sleeve)	22
73	Probe SPB 1077	SHAFT IN AFRICA (Johnny Pate/Four Tops)	35
74	ABC ABCL 5035	SHAFT IN AFRICA (Johnny Pate/Four Tops) (reissue)	35
72	MGM 2315 115	SHAFT'S BIG SCORE! (Gordon Parks/O.C. Smith/Isaac Hayes)	35
66	CBS BPG 62755	SHAKESPEARE WALLAH (Satyajit Ray)	15
68	Philips SBL 7867	SHALAKO (Robert Farnon)	15
80	Warner Bros K 56827	THE SHINING (Bela Bartok et al.)	25
69	MGM MGM-CS 8103	SHOES OF THE FISHERMAN (Alex North)	12
70	Stateside SSL 10307	THE SICILIAN CLAN (Ennio Morricone)	20
72	MCA MUPS 458	SILENT RUNNING (Pete Schikele/Joan Baez)	15
66	RCA RD 7792	THE SILENCERS (Elmer Bernstein/Vikki Carr)	45
58	MGM MGM-C 760	SILK STOCKINGS (Fred Astaire)	12
58	Capitol T 929	SING, BOY, SING (Tommy Sands)	75
56	MGM D 140	SINGIN' IN THE RAIN/EASTER PARADE (Gene Kelly/Judy Garland) (10")	25
66	MGM MGM-C(S) 8011	THE SINGING NUN (Debbie Reynolds)	15
78	Charisma CAS 1139	SIR HENRY AT RAWLINSON END (Vivian Stanshall) (with insert)	22
64	United Artists ULP 1071	633 SQUADRON (Ron Goodwin)	15
69	RCA SF 8010	SKIDOO (Nilsson)	20
74	Polydor 2442 126	SLADE IN FLAME (Slade)	12
73	Polydor 2391 084	SLAUGHTER'S BIG RIP-OFF (James Brown)	50
66	Mercury MCL 20080	THE SLENDER THREAD (Quincy Jones)	20
73	CBS 70127	SLEUTH (John Addison)	12
69	NEMS 6-70059	THE SMASHING BIRD I USED TO KNOW (Bobby Richards)	20
68	Stateside S(S)L 10224	SMASHING TIME (John Addison)	30
73	PRT FBLP 8085	SMIKE	15
56	Pye Disneyland DPL 39003	SNOW WHITE AND THE SEVEN DWARFS (Disney Orchestra)	50
61	Philips BBL 7504	SNOW WHITE AND THE THREE STOOGES	15
70	Pye NSPL 18348	SOLDIER BLUE AND OTHER THEMES (Roy Budd)	60
60	London HA-T 2221	SOLOMON AND SHEBA (Mario Nascimbene)	75
59	Capitol LCT 6180	SOME CAME RUNNING (Elmer Bernstein)	25
59	London HA-T 2176	SOME LIKE IT HOT (Marilyn Monroe) (also stereo SAH-T 6040)	90/110
83	Liberty UASP 30226	SOME LIKE IT HOT (Marilyn Monroe) (picture disc)	15
67	RCA RD 7845	SONGS FROM THE SWINGER (Marty Paich/Ann-Margret)	30
74	Rapple/RCA APL1-0220	SON OF DRACULA (Ringo Starr/Harry Nilsson, fold-out sleeve)	15
65	CBS (S)BPG 62558	THE SONS OF KATIE ELDER (Elmer Bernstein/Johnny Cash)	30/40
73	CBS 70123	SOUNDER (Taj Mahal)	12
69	RCA Victor SF 8024	THE SOUTHERN STAR (Matt Monro/Georges Garvarentz)	22
58	London HA-D 2079	SPANISH AFFAIR (Daniele Amfitheatrof)	50
76	Atlantic K 56248	SPARKLE (Curtis Mayfield/Aretha Franklin)	12
61	Brunswick LAT 8363	SPARTACUS (Alex North) (gatefold sleeve)	25
68	RCA Victor RD/SF 7957	SPEEDWAY (Elvis Presley/Nancy Sinatra) (black/red dot labels, mono/stereo)	25/30
53	Capitol CCL 7505	SPELLBOUND/THE RED HOUSE (Miklos Rosza) (10")	25
66	RCA RD 7787	THE SPY WHO CAME IN FROM THE COLD (Sol Kaplan)	20
77	United Artists UAG 30098	THE SPY WHO LOVED ME (Marvin Hamlisch) (gatefold sleeve)	12
68	CBS 62919	THE SPY WITH THE COLD NOSE (Riz Ortolani)	35
66	Fontana TL 5354	STAGECOACH (Jerry Goldsmith)	30
55	Philips BBL 7007	A STAR IS BORN (Judy Garland)	15
79	CBS 70174	STAR TREK — THE MOTION PICTURE (Jerry Goldsmith)	15
77	20th C. BTD 541	STAR WARS (John Williams) (2-LP, with insert)	18
62	London HA-D 2453	STATE FAIR (Pat Boone/Bobby Darin, et al.) (musical, also stereo SAH-D 6241)	12/15
69	CBS 70062	STILETTO (Sid Ramin)	30
52	Capitol LC 6542	A STREET CAR NAMED DESIRE (Alex North) (10")	50
59	RCA RB 16113	THE STUDENT PRINCE (Mario Lanza)	12
61	MGM MGM-C 864	THE SUBTERRANEANS (André Previn)	15
63	Columbia 33SX 1472	SUMMER HOLIDAY (Cliff Richard) (with inner sleeve, mono)	15
63	Columbia SCX 3462	SUMMER HOLIDAY (Cliff Richard) (stereo, with inner sleeve, initially with green labels, later with blue/black labels)	30/20
71	Warner Bros K 46098	SUMMER OF '42 (Michel Legrand)	12
57	London HA-R 2077	THE SUN ALSO RISES (Hugo Friedhofer)	25
70	Avco Embassy 6466 002	SUNFLOWER (Henry Mancini)	18
55	HMV DLP 1104	SUN VALLEY SERENADE (Glenn Miller)	15
62	Golden Guinea GGL 0106	SUPERCAR — FLIGHT OF FANCY (Barry Gray/Edwin Astley)	50
72	Buddah 2318 065	SUPERFLY (Curtis Mayfield) (gatefold sleeve)	20
73	Buddah 2318 087	SUPER FLY T.N.T. (Osibisa)	15
64	Stateside SL 10089	SURF PARTY (Astronauts, Routers, et al.)	50
79	EMI EMC 3222	SUSPIRIA (Goblin)	40
69	MCA MUCS 133	SWEET CHARITY (Shirley MacLaine, et al.)	25
57	Brunswick LAT 8195	SWEET SMELL OF SUCCESS (Elmer Bernstein)	25
68	Stateside S(S)L 10250	THE SWEET RIDE (Pete Rugolo/Dusty Springfield)	15
68	CBS 70043	THE SWIMMER (Marvin Hamlisch)	25
65	MGM MGM-C 8012	THE SWINGIN' SET (Dave Clark Five/Animals, et al.)	30
66	Mercury 20057 SMCL	SYLVIA (David Raksin)	15

T

70	Pye NSPL 18353	TAKE A GIRL LIKE YOU (Stanley Myers/Foundations)	20
73	EMI EMC 3016	TAKE ME HIGH (Cliff Richard) (some with poster)	25/15
67	RCA RB 6711	THE TAMING OF THE SHREW (dialogue only) (with insert)	15
57	Vogue Coral LVA 9070	TAMMY/INTERLUDE (Frank Skinner/Debbie Reynolds) (1 film per side)	40
63	United Artists ULP 1025	TARAS BULBA (Franz Waxman)	25
76	Arista ARTY 132	TAXI DRIVER (Bernard Herrman)	30
69	T. Motown (S)TML 11110	T.C.B. (Supremes/Temptations, et al.) (laminated gatefold sleeve)	15
58	London HA-D 2074-5	THE TEN COMMANDMENTS (Elmer Bernstein) (2-LP)	30
71	RCA Victor SF 8162	THAT'S THE WAY IT IS (Elvis Presley) (glossy or matt sleeve)	15/12

			MINT VALUE £
75	CBS 80575	THAT'S THE WAY OF THE WORLD (Earth, Wind & Fire)	12
79	Arista SPART 1088	THAT SUMMER (Boomtown Rats/Elvis Costello et al.) (yellow vinyl, g/fold sl.)	12
63	Parlophone PMC 1197	THAT WAS THE WEEK THAT WAS (Millicent Martin, et al.) (also stereo PCS 3040)	15
59	Coral LVA 9102	THEMES FROM HORROR MOVIES (Dick Jacobs)	25
70	United Artists UAS 29128	THEY CALL ME MISTER TIBBS (Quincy Jones)	60
69	Philips SBL 7898	THEY CAME TO ROB LAS VEGAS (Georges Gavarentz)	70
70	Stateside SSL 10305	THEY SHOOT HORSES, DON'T THEY? (John Green)	20
73	Elektra K 46239	THE THIEF WHO CAME TO DINNER (Henry Mancini)	18
82	MCA MCF 3148	THE THING (Ennio Morricone)	15
66	Verve VLP 9147	THIS PROPERTY IS CONDEMNED (Kenyon Hopkins)	15
68	United Artists SULP 1218	THE THOMAS CROWN AFFAIR (Michel Legrand/Noel Harrison)	35
68	Sunset SLS 50519	THE THOMAS CROWN AFFAIR (Michel Legrand, reissue)	12
65	Stateside SL 10136	THOSE MAGNIFICENT MEN IN THEIR FLYING MACHINES (Ron Goodwin)	30
54	Capitol LC 6665	THREE SAILORS AND A GIRL (Gordon MacRae, et al.) (10")	30
61	Golden Guinea GGL 0065	THREE WORLDS OF GULLIVER (Bernard Herrmann)	20
85	Cloud Nine CN 4003	THREE WORLDS OF GULLIVER (Bernard Herrmann) (reissue)	15
65	United Artists (S)ULP 1110	THUNDERBALL (John Barry) (mono/stereo)	18/20
67	United Artists (S)ULP 1159	THUNDERBIRDS ARE GO! (Barry Gray/Cliff Richard & Shadows) (mono/stereo)	110/130
69	Polydor 583 717	TILL DEATH DO US PART (Wilfred Burns)	15
72	RCA SF 8253	TIME FOR LOVING (Michel Legrand/Dusty Springfield, et al.)	12
63	MGM MGM-C 934	TO KILL A MOCKINGBIRD (Elmer Bernstein)	15
64	United Artists SULP 1062	TOM JONES (John Addison)	15
59	MGM MGM-C 772	TOM THUMB (Russ Tamblyn)	15
68	Instant INLP 002	TONITE LET'S ALL MAKE LOVE IN LONDON (Pink Floyd/Chris Farlowe, et al.)	100
70	RCA LSA 3008	TOOMORROW (with insert)	120
67	Fontana (S)TL 5446	TO SIR, WITH LOVE (Ron Grainer/ Lulu/Mindbenders)	30
69	Stateside S(S)L 10271	THE TOUCHABLES (Ken Thorne/Nirvana/Wynder K. Frog, et al.)	35
74	Stax STXH 5001	TOUGH GUYS (Isaac Hayes)	12
75	Warner Bros K 56102	THE TOWERING INFERNO (John Williams)	12
66	Polydor 582 004	THE TRAP (Ron Goodwin)	50
60	Pye Nonesuch PPLD 206	THE TRIAL OF LADY CHATTERLEY (drama/documentary)	12
67	United Artists ULP 1176	TRIPLE CROSS (Georges Garvarentz)	20
82	CBS 70223	TRON (Wendy Carlos/Journey)	15
73	T. Motown STML 11225	TROUBLE MAN (Marvin Gaye)	20
74	Stax STXD 4001/2	TRUCK TURNER (Isaac Hayes) (2-LP)	18
70	Capitol E-ST 263	TRUE GRIT (Elmer Bernstein/Glen Campbell)	18
61	Fontana TFL 5110	T.V. WESTERN THEMES (also stereo STFL 538) (Johnny Gregory)	10/12
69	Polydor 583 728	TWISTED NERVE/LES BICYCLETTES DE BELSIZE (Les Reed/Barry Mason, Bernard Herrman)	100
69	Columbia S(C)X 6330	TWO CITIES (Jeff Wayne)	35
67	RCA RD/SF 7891	TWO FOR THE ROAD (Henry Mancini)	20
63	United Artists ULP 1027	TWO FOR THE SEESAW (André Previn)	15
71	United Artists UDF 50003	200 MOTELS (Frank Zappa) (2-LP, with booklet & poster)	25
70	MCA MKPS 2013	TWO MULES FOR SISTER SARA (Ennio Morricone)	15
62	Columbia 33SX 1482	TWO TICKETS TO PARIS (Joey Dee)	20

U

67	RCA RB 6708	ULYSSES (Stanley Myers) (with insert)	15
60	London HA-T 2258	THE UNFORGIVEN (Dimitri Tiomkin)	18
68	Fontana (S)TL 5460	UP THE JUNCTION (Manfred Mann)	35
70	Fontana 6852 005	UP THE JUNCTION (Manfred Mann) (reissue)	12
69	Stax (S)XATS 1005	UPTIGHT (Booker T & MGs)	15

V

73	Philips 6303 075	THE VALACHI PAPERS (Riz Ortolani)	15
68	Stateside (S)SL 10228	VALLEY OF THE DOLLS (André Previn/John Williams)	30
71	London SH-U 8420	VANISHING POINT (Delaney & Bonnie/Sam & Dave, et al.)	35
82	MGM 2315 437	VICTOR, VICTORIA (Henry Mancini)	15
63	Colpix PXL 516	THE VICTORS (Sol Kaplan)	20
59	RCA SF 5092	VICTORY AT SEA (Richard Rogers)	12
85	Parlophone BOND 1	A VIEW TO A KILL (John Barry/Duran Duran)	12
58	London HAT 2118	THE VIKINGS (Mario Nascimbene)	50
68	Dot (S)LPD 515	VILLA RIDES (Maurice Jarre)	20
63	MGM MGM-C 951/CS 6074	THE VIPs (Miklos Rozsa)	20
66	United Artists (S)ULP 1126	VIVA MARIA! (Georges Delerue) (mono/stereo)	30/40
67	United Artists (S)ULP 1185	VIVRE POUR VIVRE (LIFE FOR LIFE) (Francis Lai)	18

W

60	Mercury MMC 14033	WAGON TRAIN (Stanley Wilson, et al.)	25
62	MGM MGM-C 891	WALK ON THE WILD SIDE (Elmer Bernstein)	20
66	Brunswick STA 8636	THE WAR LORD (Jerome Moross)	35
85	London YEAR 2	WATER	12
78	Satril SATL 4009	THE WATER MARGIN (Godiego) (TV soundtrack)	12
67	Virtuoso TPLS 13010	WELLES RAISES KANE (Bernard Herrman)	30
64	Piccadilly N(S)PL 38011	WHAT A CRAZY WORLD (Joe Brown/Susan Maughan/Marty Wilde; mono/stereo)	22/40
64	Golden Guinea GGL 0272	WHAT A CRAZY WORLD (Joe Brown/Susan Maughan/Marty Wilde) (reissue)	15
64	Stateside SL 10090	WHAT A WAY TO GO! (Nelson Riddle)	12
66	RCA SF 7818	WHAT DID YOU DO IN THE WAR, DADDY? (Henry Mancini)	20
65	United Artists ULP 1096	WHAT'S NEW PUSSYCAT? (Burt Bacharach/Tom Jones/Manfred Mann, et al.)	20
66	MGM MGM-C(S) 8006	WHEN THE BOYS MEET THE GIRLS (Connie Francis/Herman's Hermits) (mono/stereo)	15/18
69	MGM MGM-C(S) 8102	WHERE EAGLES DARE (Ron Goodwin)	12
69	Paramount SPFL 254	WHERE'S JACK? (Elmer Bernstein/Mary Hopkin)	12

			MINT VALUE £
66	United Artists (S)ULP 1166	WHIPLASH WILLIE (André Previn)	15
67	United Artists (S)ULP 1168	THE WHISPERERS (John Barry)	30
67	Warner Bros W 1656	WHO'S AFRAID OF VIRGINIA WOOLF? (Alex North)	25
98	Trunk BARKED 4	THE WICKER MAN (Giovanni) (with inserts, some red vinyl)	50/30
57	London HA-N 2023	WILD BILL HICKOCK AND JINGLES ON THE SANTA FE TRAIL (TV s/track)	18
69	Warner Bros WS 1814	THE WILD BUNCH (Jerry Fielding) (red label original)	50
71	Warner Bros K 46035	THE WILD BUNCH (Jerry Fielding) (reissue)	15
78	A&M AMLH 64730	THE WILD GEESE (Roy Budd/Joan Armatrading)	20
68	Capitol (S)T 5099	WILD IN THE STREETS (Les Baxter/Gurus) (original issue, black label, rainbow rim)	18
71	MGM 2315 062	WILD ROVERS (Jerry Goldsmith)	12
83	Chrysalis CHR 1453	WILD STYLE (various artists)	20
71	Paramount SPFL 274	WILLY WONKA AND THE CHOCOLATE FACTORY (Leslie Bricusse)	15
75	Arista ARTY 111	THE WIND AND THE LION (Jerry Goldsmith)	15
87	Filmtrax MOMENT 110	WITHNAIL AND I (David Dundas)	50
78	MCA MCSP 287	THE WIZ (Diana Ross/Michael Jackson, et al.) (gatefold sleeve with booklet & poster)	15
57	MGM MGM-C 757	THE WIZARD OF OZ (Judy Garland, et al.)	40
67	Capitol (S)T 2800	WOMAN TIMES SEVEN (Riz Ortolani)	20
64	Columbia SX 1628	WONDERFUL LIFE (Cliff Richard) (gatefold sleeve with inner, also stereo SCX 3515)	15/25
63	Elstree Extra Range	SUMMER HOLIDAY (2-LP, full soundtrack recording, 80 copies only)	350
64	Elstree Extra Range	WONDERFUL LIFE (2-LP, full soundtrack recording, 150 copies only)	350
68	Apple (S)APCOR 1	WONDERWALL MUSIC (George Harrison) (with insert & black inner sleeve, mono/stereo)	125/60
70	Atlantic 2663 001	WOODSTOCK (Jimi Hendrix/Who/Joe Cocker, et al.) (3-LP in foldout sleeve with inners)	20
60	RCA RD 27198	THE WORLD OF SUZIE WONG (George Duning)	15
57	Brunswick LAT 8174	WRITTEN ON THE WIND/FOUR GIRLS IN TOWN (Frank Skinner)	20
66	Fontana STL 5387	THE WRONG BOX (John Barry) (release cancelled)	

Y

65	MGM MGM-C 997	THE YELLOW ROLLS-ROYCE (Riz Ortolani)	15
69	Apple PMC 7070	YELLOW SUBMARINE (Beatles) (1st pressing, laminated flipback sleeve with red lines above & below rear liner note & black inner; with "Sold In The UK..." label text; mono)	250
69	Apple PCS 7070	YELLOW SUBMARINE (Beatles) (1st pressing, laminated flipback sleeve with red lines above & below rear liner note & black inner; with "Sold In The UK..." label text; stereo)	75
79	Warwick WW 5075	YESTERDAY'S HERO	20
61	Golden Guinea GGL 0081	YOGI BEAR TV SERIES (TV soundtrack)	12
69	CBS (S) 70045	YOU ARE WHAT YOU EAT (Tiny Tim/Electric Flag, et al.)	12
71	Ember NR 5055	YOU CAN'T HAVE EVERYTHING (Joe Parnello/Bobby Scott)	12
79	MCA MCF 2804	YOUNGBLOOD (War)	15
66	Philips (S)BL 7792	YOUNG GIRLS OF ROCHEFORT (Michel Legrand)	25
57	Brunswick LAT 8252	THE YOUNG LIONS (Hugo Friedhofer)	35
61	Columbia 33SX 1384	THE YOUNG ONES (Cliff Richard) (with inner sleeve, also stereo SCX 3397)	18/35
67	United Artists (S)ULP 1171	YOU ONLY LIVE TWICE (John Barry)	20
65	MGM MGM-CS 6081	YOUR CHEATIN' HEART (Hank Williams Jr.)	18
67	Kama Sutra KLP 402	YOU'RE A BIG BOY NOW (Lovin' Spoonful)	12

Z

70	MGM MGM CS 8120	ZABRISKIE POINT (Pink Floyd/Jerry Garcia/Kaleidoscope, et al.)	18
71	Probe SPB 1026	ZACHARIAH (Country Joe & Fish/James Gang, et al.)	12
64	Ember NR 5012	ZULU (John Barry) (yellow/orange label, flipback sleeve)	25

ORIGINAL STAGE SHOW & RADIO CAST RECORDING LPs (alphabetical by title)

A

64	Columbia SX 1676	ALADDIN AND HIS WONDERFUL LAMP (g/fold sleeve, also stereo SCX 3522)	18/22
70	Argo ZTA 501-2	ALICE IN WONDERLAND (2-LP)	20
71	RCA SER 5618	AMBASSADOR	20
82	Key LP 4	ANDY CAPP	15
70	CBS 70053	ANNE OF GREEN GABLES	15
50	Brunswick LAT 8002	ANNIE GET YOUR GUN	15
58	Capitol LCT 6150	ANNIE GET YOUR GUN	12
70	CBS 70052	ANN VERONICA	15
69	Studio Two TWO 233	ARCADIANS	15

B

66	Columbia S(C)X 6009	BABES IN THE WOOD (mono/stereo)	15/18
69	RCA Intl. INT 1037	BANDWAGON	12
59	Decca SKL 4136	BELLE — OR THE BALLAD OF DOCTOR CRIPPEN	15
58	Philips BBL 7201	BELLS ARE RINGING	12
64	Capitol (S)W 2191	BEN FRANKLIN IN PARIS	12
65	Parlophone PMC 1238	BEYOND OUR KEN	20
61	Parlophone PMC 1145	BEYOND THE FRINGE	15
74	CBS 70133	BILLY (gatefold sleeve, with lyric sheet)	15
66	Music F. Pleasure MFP 1091	BITTERSWEET	15
68	M. For Pleasure MFP 1263	BLESS THE BRIDE	12
62	HMV CLP 1569/CSD 1441	BLITZ! (mono/stereo)	18/15

			MINT VALUE £
54	HMV DLP 1078	THE BOYFRIEND (10")	15
63	Decca LK 4564	THE BOYS FROM SYRACUSE	15
63	Parlophone PMC 1190	BRIDGE ON THE RIVER WYE (also stereo PCS 3036)	15/20
61	Philips ABL 3383	BYE BYE BIRDIE — LONDON CAST (g/fold sleeve, also stereo SABL 205)	20/22

C

50s	Columbia KOS 3040	CABARET	15
69	CBS (S)BRG 70039	CABARET	15
64	Melodisc MLP 12-146	CALYPSO CARNIVAL	15
64	HMV CLP 1756/CSD 1559	CAMELOT	12
60s	CBS (S)BRG 70009	CAMELOT	12
60s	Encore	CAN CAN	40
64	Decca LK/SKL 4596	THE CANTERBURY TALES	12
65	Pye N(S)PL 18408	THE CARD	40
50	Brunswick LAT 8006	CAROUSEL	12
71	Polydor 2383 035	CATCH MY SOUL — THE ROCK-OTHELLO	15
66	CBS (S)BPG 62627	CHARLIE GIRL	15
58	Decca LK 4303	CINDERELLA	25
67	Columbia S(C)X 6103	CINDERELLA	35
64	Decca LK 4559	CINDY-ELLA	12
66	Decca LK/SKL 4810	COME SPY WITH ME	15
59	HMV CLP 1298	THE CROOKED MILE	15

D

75	Warner Bros K 56186	DAD'S ARMY	12
70	CBS 70063	DAMES AT SEA	20
57	HMV CLP 1108	DAMN YANKEES	12
65	Decca LK/SKL 4675	DIVORCE ME, DARLING	12
62	Decca LK 4413/SKL 4145	DO RE MI	12
61	RCA RD 27228/SF 5107	DO RE MI	15
82	Geffen GEF 85578	DREAMGIRLS (gatefold sleeve, with insert)	12

E

78	Astoria AST 1	ELVIS (P.J. Proby/Shakin' Stevens/Tim Whitnall) (sold at performances of "Elvis" show, laminated sleeve)	40
78	MCA MOG 3527	EVITA (silver sleeve)	12
58	Pye NPL 18016	EXPRESSO BONGO	18

F

60	MGM MGM-C 871	THE FANTASTICS	12
60	Decca SKL 4092	FINGS AIN'T WOT THEY USED TO BE	12
64	Reprise F(S) 2015	FINIAN'S RAINBOW — REPRISE REPERTORY THEATRE PRESENTS (mono/stereo)	15/18
59	Capitol SW 1321	FIORELLO!	12
60	HMV CSD 1305	FLOWER DRUM SONG	15
60	HMV CLP 1366	FOLLOW THAT GIRL	25
63	Ember CEL 902	FOOL BRITANNIA (radio show)	15
66	Parlophone PMC 7014	FOUR DEGREES OVER	12
57	Oriole MG 20016	FREE AS AIR	15
64	Parlophone PCS 3065	FUNNY GAME POLITICS	15
64	Capitol (S)W 2059	FUNNY GIRL (Original Broadway Cast) (mono/stereo)	12
60s	Ember NR 5039	A FUNNY THING HAPPENED ON THE WAY TO THE FORUM	15

G

72	Bell BELLS 203	GODSPELL	15
64	Capitol (S)W 2124	GOLDEN BOY	15
71	Columbia SCXA 9252	GONE WITH THE WIND (gatefold sleeve)	15
57	HMV CLP 1103	GRAB ME A GONDOLA	12
68	Instant INLP 003	GULLIVER'S TRAVELS (withdrawn)	50+
53	Brunswick LAT 8022	GUYS AND DOLLS	12
64	Reprise F(S) 2016	GUYS AND DOLLS — REPRISE REPERTORY THEATRE PRESENTS...	15/18
70s	RCA Red Seal SER 5686	GYPSY (gatefold sleeve)	15

H

68	RCA RD/SF 7959	HAIR (Broadway)	12
69	Polydor 583 043	HAIR (London)	12
63	Decca LK/SKL 4521	HALF-A-SIXPENCE	12
70s	Groovy STP 3	HANGAHAIR	12
57	Oriole MG 20014	HARMONY CLOSE	15
65	RCA Victor RD/SF 7768	HELLO, DOLLY! (with insert)	20
64	Pye NPL 18100/NSPL 83022	HIGH SPIRITS	30
60	Fontana TFL 5104	HITS FROM THE GANG SHOWS!	12
70	CBS BRG 70027	HOUDINI — MAN OF MAGIC	20
63	RCA RD/SF 7564	HOW TO SUCCEED IN BUSINESS WITHOUT REALLY TRYING	20

I

83	CBS Cameo 32265	I CAN GET IT FOR YOU WHOLESALE	12
68	RCA Victor RD/SF 7938	I DO! I DO!	18
64	Oriole PS 40062	INSTANT MARRIAGE	30
76	EMI EMC 3139	IRENE	12

MINT VALUE £

J

68	CBS 66207	JACQUES BREL IS ALIVE AND WELL AND LIVING IN PARIS (2-LP)	20
75	MCA MCF 2726	JEEVES	50
74	RSO 2394 141	JOHN, PAUL, GEORGE, RINGO AND BERT (with London cast)	30
66	HMV CLP/CSD 3591	JORROCKS	15
56	Philips	JOYCE GRENFELL REQUESTS THE PLEASURE	12

K

53	Brunswick LAT 8026	THE KING AND I	12
64	Reprise F(S) 2017	KISS ME KATE — REPRISE REPERTORY THEATRE PRESENTS	12/15

L

60	Capitol SW 1240	LITTLE MARY SUNSHINE	12
64	Pye NSPL 83023	LITTLE ME	12
59	Decca LK 4320	LOCK UP YOUR DAUGHTERS	12
73	Reflection RL 306	LONESOME STONE	22

M

64	Decca LK/SKL 4643	MAGGIE MAY (mono/stereo)	15/18
72	Columbia SCX 6504	MAID OF THE MOUNTAINS	12
60s	CBS (S) 70051	MAME	12
68	London HA-R/SH-R 8362	MAN OF LA MANCHA	12
59	HMV CLP 1275	MARIGOLD	12
61	Oriole MG 20054	MINE FAIR SADIE	20
60	HMV CLP 1365	THE MOST HAPPY FELLA!	20
68	CBS 70048	MR. & MRS.	18
57	Brunswick LAT 8184	MR. WONDERFUL	12
50s	Capitol W 990	THE MUSIC MAN	15

N

72	Ace Of Clubs ACL 1238	A NIGHT OF MUSIC HALL	25
63	Decca LK/SKL 4576	NO STRINGS	20

O

63	Decca LK/SKL 4542	OH! WHAT A LOVELY WAR	12
50	Brunswick LAT 8001	OKLAHOMA	12
60	Decca LK 4359	OLIVER! (also stereo SKL 4105)	15
60	World Record Club TP 151	OLIVER! (mono/stereo) (cast includes Steve Marriot)	20/25
61	HMV CLP 1459/CSD 1370	OLIVER! (mono/stereo)	40/55
60	London HA-T 2286	ONCE UPON A MATTRESS	12
80	Warner Bros K 56850	ONE MO' TIME	12
61	Decca LK 4393/SKL 4133	ONE OVER THE EIGHT (mono/stereo)	18/22
61	Decca LK 4395/SKL 4134	ON THE BRIGHTER SIDE	15
67	CBS	ON THE LEVEL	12
63	CBS 60005	ON THE TOWN	45
65	Parlophone PCS 3066	OUR MAN CRICHTON	12

P

65	CBS BPG 62598	PASSION FLOWER HOTEL (mono only)	30
65	Ace Of Clubs ACL 1112	PERCHANCE TO DREAM	15
63	Parlophone PMC 1198	PETER COOK PRESENTS THE ESTABLISHMENT	12
65	RCA RD 7722	PETER PAN	12
69	Philips SBL 7916	PHIL THE FLUTER	35
74	Fontana SFL 13190	PHIL THE FLUTER	12
67	Philips (S)AL 3431	PICKWICK (gatefold sleeve)	18
59	Decca LK 4337	PIECES OF EIGHT	12
59	Decca SKL 4084	PIECES OF EIGHT (stereo)	15
77	MCA MCF 2826	THE POINT	15
60	Melodisc MLP 12-117	PREACHIN', PRAYIN', SINGIN' AND SHOUTIN' GOSPEL	15
64	London HA-U/SH-U 8201	THE PRINCE AND THE PAUPER	12
78	EMI EMC 3233	PRIVATES ON PARADE	25
69	United Artists UAS 29075	PROMISES, PROMISES	15

R

65	HMV CLP 1820/CSD 1575	ROBERT AND ELIZABETH	15
75	UK UKAL 1015	THE ROCKY HORROR SHOW (London Cast)	15
74	Ode ODE 77026	THE ROCKY HORROR SHOW (U.S. Roxy Cast)	15

S

56	Oriole MG 20004	SALAD DAYS	12
70	Capitol E-ST 337	SALVATION	15
58	Pye NPL 18011	SHARE MY LETTUCE	30
59	Philips ABL 3370	THE SOUND OF MUSIC (gatefold sleeve)	12
61	HMV CLP 1453/CSD 1365	THE SOUND OF MUSIC	12
60s	Philips 632 303 BL	SPACE IS SO STARTLING	20
61	Decca LK 4408/SKL 4142	STOP THE WORLD I WANT TO GET OFF	12
67	Wing WL 1172	SUMMER SONG	20
67	CBS (S)BRG 70035	SWEET CHARITY	15

T

60	Fontana TFL 5103	TAKE IT FROM HERE (excerpts from radio show, also stereo STFL 534)	30/20
60	Capitol SW 1492	TENDERLOIN	12
63	Parlophone PMC 1197	THAT WAS THE WEEK THAT WAS (also stereo PCS 3040)	15

MINT VALUE £

67	World Record Club SH 849	THOROUGHLY MODERN MILLIE	15
72	Decca SKL 5137	TOM BROWNE'S SCHOOLDAYS	15
69	Columbia S(C)X 6330	TWO CITIES (Jeff Wayne)	25
66	United Artists (S)ULP 1116	TWANG! (Lionel Bart)	20

V

63	Decca LK/SKL 4536	VIRTUE IN DANGER	12

W

64	Decca LK/SKL 4610	WAIT A MINIM	15
65	HMV CLP 1834/CSD 1587	THE WAYWARD WAY	25
54	Parlophone PMD 1011	WEDDING IN PARIS (10")	25
61	HMV CLP 1467	WILDEST DREAMS	15
56	HMV DLP 1125	WILD GROWS THE HEATHER (10")	30

Y

68	RCA SB 6792	THE YOUNG VISITORS	20
67	MGM MGM-C(S) 8045	YOU'RE A GOOD MAN, CHARLIE BROWN	12

Z

69	Philips 600-287	ZITA	50

SPOKEN WORD RECORDINGS (LPs)

87	BBC Radio Derby	BACK TO THE TOP (cassette, limited edition)	20
77	Quality QP 23/77	BATTLE OF THE GIANTS: 1977 FA CUP FINAL — MANCHESTER UNITED V LIVERPOOL	15
78	Quality QP 26/78	BOBBY'S DAZZLERS: 1978 FA CUP FINAL — IPSWICH V ARSENAL	15
71	Quality QP 8/71	CHELSEA KINGS OF EUROPE: 1971 EUROPEAN CUP WINNERS CUP FINAL — CHELSEA V REAL MADRID	20
70	Quality QP 4/70	CHELSEA'S CUP: 1970 FA CUP FINAL — CHELSEA V LEEDS	20
85	BBC Radio Derby	THE DERBY COUNTY STORY (double cassette, in numbered foldout case)	20
73	Instant INLP 001	EUROPEAN CUP FINAL 1968 (round sleeve)	100
73	Quality QP 12/73	EUROPEAN CUP: THE MATCH 1968 — MANCHESTER UNITED V BENFICA	30
78	Quality QP 25/78	FABULOUS FOREST: 1978 LEAGUE CUP FINAL — FOREST V LIVERPOOL, WEMBLEY AND OLD TRAFFORD REPLAY	15
79	Quality QP 28/79	FOREST ARE MAGIC: 1979 LEAGUE CUP FINAL — FOREST V SOUTHAMPTON	15
80	Quality QP 33/80	FOREST'S EURO DOUBLE: 1979 EUROPEAN CUP FINAL V MALMÖ/1980 EUROPEAN CUP FINAL V HAMBURG	12
84	Quality HM 2	THE FRIENDLY FINAL: EVERTON V LIVERPOOL MILK CUP 1984	15
75	Quality QP 17/75	HAIL TO THE HAMMERS: 1975 FA CUP FINAL — WEST HAM V FULHAM	15
80	Quality QP 31/80	HAMMERS HEROES: 1980 FA CUP FINAL OFFICIAL SOUVENIR	15
81	Quality QP 34/81	LEAGUE CUP FINAL 1981: WEMBLEY HIGHLIGHTS AND THE REPLAY: LIVERPOOL V WEST HAM	15
76	Quality QP 18/76	LEAGUE CUP FINAL 1976: MANCHESTER CITY V NEWCASTLE UNITED	15
72	Quality QP 9/72	LEAGUE CUP FINAL 1972: CHELSEA V STOKE CITY	20
74	Quality QP 15/74	LIVERPOOL'S CUP: 1974 FA CUP FINAL — LIVERPOOL V NEWCASTLE	15
82	Quality QP 38/82	LIVERPOOL'S 1982 LEAGUE CUP DOUBLE: LIVERPOOL V SPURS	15
78	Quality QP 27/78	LIVERPOOL, THE LEGEND OF EUROPE: 1978 EUROPEAN CUP FINAL — LIVERPOOL V BRUGES	12
79	Quality QP 29/79	MATCH OF THE CENTURY: 1979 FA CUP FINAL — ARSENAL V MANCHESTER UNITED	15
71	Quality QP 7/71	1971 FA CUP FINAL: ARSENAL V LIVERPOOL	15
71	Quality QP 6/71	1971 LEAGUE CUP FINAL: SPURS V ASTON VILLA	20
72	BBC REC 122M	1972 FA CUP FINAL: LEEDS V ARSENAL	15
69	Quality QP 37/81	1969 FA CUP FINAL: MANCHESTER CITY V LEICESTER CITY	15
69	Quality QP 2/69	1969 HOME INTERNATIONAL TOURNAMENT: ENGLAND V SCOTLAND	15
73	Quality QP 15/74	SUNDERLAND'S CUP: 1973 FA CUP FINAL — SUNDERLAND V LEEDS	20
76	Quality QP 19/76	SUPER SAINTS: 1976 FA CUP FINAL — SOUTHAMPTON V MANCHESTER UNITED	15
81	Quality Products QP 36/81	VILLA THE CHAMPIONS: HIGHLIGHTS OF 1980-81 SEASON	12
77	Quality QP 22/77	VILLA'S HAT TRICK: ASTON VILLA V EVERTON 1977 LEAGUE CUP FINAL REPLAY	15
81	Quality QP 37/81	VIVA EL KOP: THE STORY OF LIVERPOOL'S 1981 EUROPEAN CUP VICTORY	12
75	Quality QP 16/75	VIVA THE VILLA: 1975 FOOTBALL LEAGUE CUP FINAL	15
76	Quality QP 21/76	WE'VE KOPPED THE CUP: 1976 UEFA CUP FINAL — LIVERPOOL V BRUGES	12
80	Quality QP 30/80	WOLVES CUP: 1980 FOOTBALL LEAGUE CUP (LP)	15
74	Quality QP 14/74	WONDERFUL WOLVES: 1974 LEAGUE CUP FINAL — WOLVERHAMPTON WANDERERS V MANCHESTER CITY	20
66	Centaur CPC 1234	WORLD CUP '66	40
81	Quality QP 35/81	YEAR OF THE COCKEREL: 1981 CENTENARY CUP FINAL	15

MUSIC LIBRARY LPs

81	Studio G LPSG 4004	ABSTRACTS	20
84	Bruton BRH 24	ACCENT ON RHYTHM	12
72	De Wolfe DW 3220	AFRO ROCK (Vecchio)	75
70s	Themes International TIM 1918	ALL AMERICAN POWERHOUSE (Alan Hawkshaw/Alan Parker/Alan Tew)	30
68	Sylvester SMC 515	AND SO ON (Paris Studio Group) (10" LP, 500 only)	18
71	KPM KPM 1088	BASS GUITAR & PERCUSSION (Herbie Flowers/Barry Morgan)	30
71	KPM KPM 1090	BASS GUITAR & PERCUSSION VOL. 3 (Chris Karan/Pete McGurk)	20
71	KPM KPM 1079	BEAT INDUSTRIAL (Alan Parker/Alan Hawkshaw/Johnny Hawksworth)	20
73	KPM KPM 1124	BIG BUSINESS/WIND OF CHANGE (David Snell/Keith Mansfield)	35

			MINT VALUE £
77	KPM KPM 1194	BIG CITY SUITE/JINGLE JANGLE JINGLES (Dave Gold)	20
72	KPM KPM 1100	THE BIG SCREEN (Johnny Pearson/Keith Mansfield)	20
70s	De Wolfe DW 3324	BITE HARD (Johnny Hawksworth)	40
71	Sylvester SMC 527	BLUE CYLINDER (Modern Jazz Group)	25
74	Chappell LP 1070	BRASS & RHYTHMS (Marc Duval & His Music)	35
72	KPM KPM 1111	BRASS PLUS MOOG (Mike Vickers)	25
74	Themes Int'l TIM 1013	BREATH OF DANGER (Alan Hawkshaw/Alan Parker)	25
76	KPM KPM 1178	CARICATURES (S. Gray/B. Bennett/D. Lamont/C. Hicks)	15
60	Chappell 672-677	CHAPPELL RECORDED MUSIC (library issue)	20
60	Chappell 678-682	CHAPPELL RECORDED MUSIC (library issue)	20
69	KPM KPM 1049	CHORUS & ORCHESTRA (Syd Dale/Keith Mansfield)	40
68	KPM KPM 1029	COLOURS IN RHYTHM (Johnny Pearson/Kenny Wheeler/Keith Mansfield)	40
70	KPM KPM 1063	CONTEMPORARY COLOUR (Syd Dale/Keith Mansfield/Alan Moorhouse)	20
75	KPM KPM 1168	DRAMA	20
78	Bruton BRJ 2	DRAMA MONTAGE (Brian Bennett)	25
70s	Themes International TIM 1008	DRAMATIC ACTION (Johnny Pearson/David Lindup)	25
68	KPM KPM 1037	FLAMBOYANT THEMES (Alan Hawkshaw/Keith Mansfield)	30
68	KPM KPM 1038	FLAMBOYANT THEMES VOL. 2 (Syd Dale/Keith Mansfield/Johnny Pearson)	30
68	Harmonic CBL 618	FONTEYN'S FOLK JAZZ (Sam Fonteyn) (mono, 500 only)	30
73	KPM KPM 1123	FRIENDLY FACES (Alan Hawkshaw/James Clarke)	25
70	KPM KPM 1059	GENTLE SOUNDS VOL. 3 (James Clarke/David Lindup/Stan Tracy)	20
70s	Standard Music ESL 117	GUITAR MUSIC/ORGAN & MUSIC (Tim Mycroft/John Gibson) (mono)	18
71	Bosworth BLP 120	HARD & FAST/MELLOW MOODS (Syd Dale) (mono, 300 only)	30
76	KPM KPM 1177	HOT WAX (Brian Bennett/Alan Hawkshaw)	20
76	KPM KPM 1171	IMPACT (Chris Gunning/Keith Mansfield)	20
70	KPM KPM 1061	IMPACT & ACTION VOL. 2 (Johnny Pearson/Kenny Wheeler/Keith Mansfield/ Syd Dale)	20
75	KPM KPM 1161	INDUSTRY VOL. 1 (S. Gray/Clive Hicks/Duncan Lamont/Brian Bennett)	25
75	KPM KPM 1165	A JAZZ INCLINATION (Tony Kinsey)	30
73	Bosworth BLP 130	KEYBOARD PLUS/MODERN MELODY (Anthony Mawer)	20
77	KPM KPM 1191	LANDSCAPES/THINGS TO COME/NEW INNOVATIONS SUITE (Johnny Pearson/ Dave Richmond)	20
74	Bosworth BLP 142	LET'S GO SOLO/ROCK BEAT/DRUMS & PERCUSSION (Gary Pacific Group/ Sperie Karas)	18
67	KPM KPM 1021	A LIGHT JAZZ FEELING (Johnny Pearson/Syd Dale/David Lindup)	30
73	Themes Int'l TIM 1003	LIGHT & ACTIVITY (Alan Tew/David Lindup)	25
70s	Studio G LPSG 2003	LIGHT MOVEMENT VOLUME 2	15
72	De Wolfe DW 3224	LITTLE BOSSA	25
73	KPM KPM 1119	LOOK ON THE BRIGHT SIDE	15
71	KPM KPM 1084	MEDITERRANEAN INTRIGUE/MARTENOT (Neil Ardley/John Leach)	40
76	KPM KPM 1183	MIDDLE EAST SUITE/INDIA (Clem Alford/Ali Isfahan/G. Behar)	25
72	Hudson HMC 506	MINDBENDER	20
70s	De Wolfe DWS 3323	MODERN GROUP SOUNDS (Sliced Orange)	20
73	Amphonic AMPSLP 1001	MOODSETTER/TRENDSETTER (James Clark Sounds)	40
69	Harmonic CBL 621	MORE BEAT (mono, 500 only)	20
72	Chappell LPC 1051	MUSIC BY (Les Mason & His Orchestra)	50
71	KPM KPM 1086	MUSIC FOR A YOUNG GENERATION (Alan Parker/Alan Hawkshaw) (mono)	60
66	Fountain Press KPM/ACW 1	MUSIC FOR YOUR MOVIES	12
73	Themes Int'l TIM 1002	NEW BLOOD (Alan Hawkshaw/Alan Parker)	30
75	KPM KPM 1167	OUTDOOR LIFE (Phillip Lane)	15
76	Themes Int'l TIM 1020	PAN-AMERICAN TRAVELOGUE (Alan Hawkshaw/Alan Parker)	20
75	KPM KPM 1166	PIANO VIBRATIONS (Francis Coppetiers)	25
73	Studio One SO 14	PIERRE LAVIN POP BAND	30
69	De Wolfe DW 3136	POP SOUNDS (The Cool)	75
76	Themes Int'l TIM 1023	PULSE OF EVENTS (Alan Hawkshaw/Alan Parker)	25
78	KPM KPM 1214	PULSE OF THE CITY (R. Morecombe/G. Castle)	15
74	Boosey & Hawkes SBH 3052	RECORDED MUSIC FOR FILM, RADIO & TELEVISION (Dennis Farnon)	15
74	Boosey & Hawkes SBH 3063	RECORDED MUSIC FOR FILM, RADIO & TELEVISION (John Scott/Trevor Bastow)	15
73	Bosworth BLP 135	RHYTHM AT RANDOM/MOVEMENT IN RHYTHM (Gary Pacific Group/Bernard Ebbinghouse)	50
76	De Wolfe DWS 3328	RYTHMES (Andre Ceccarelli)	60
74	Chappell LPC 1065	RHYTHM 'N' BRASS (Marc Duval Big Band)	50
77	KPM KPM 1192	THE ROAD FORWARD (Alan Hawkshaw)	20
76	Themes Int'l TIM 1017	ROCK COMEDY (Alan Parker)	20
77	KPM KPM 1196	ROCK ON (Danny Edmondson/Seamus Sell)	40
75	KPM KPM 1163	ROCK SPECTRUM (S. Gray/Dave Richmond)	20
69	KPM KPM 1046	SOUNDS IN PERCUSSION (Sam Fonteyn)	20
76	KPM KPM 1170	SOUNDS OF THE TIMES (Alan Hawkshaw)	20
80	Bruton BRI 9	SUSPENSION/GALAXY (James Cameron/Trevor Bastow)	12
75	Regency Line RL 1008	SYNTHESIZER SPOTS (Tony Turens)	15
71	KPM KPM 1087	TECHNICAL VIEWPOINT/SPICE OF LIFE (Peter Sander/Derrick Mason)	15
73	KPM KPM 1131	TRENDSETTERS (James Cameron/Keith Mansfield/James Clarke)	25
60s	Studio One SO 7	UNTITLED (500 only) (Maurice Pop Orchestra)	30
60s	Chappell LPC 672-677	UNTITLED (John Barry)	25
70	KPM KPMLP 35	UNTITLED (mono) (Johnny Pearson/Derrick Mason)	20
70	KPM KPMLP 37	UNTITLED (mono) (Syd Dale)	20
71	Chappell LPC 1040	UNTITLED (Ole Jensen & His Music)	15
72	Chappell LPC 1052	UNTITLED (Marc Duval & His Music)	35
76	KPM KPM 1172	VISUAL IMPACT (Johnny Pearson)	20
70s	De Wolfe	VOCAL SHADES & TONES (Barbara Moore Sound)	100

MINT VALUE £

Stop Press Additions

ACME ATTRACTIONS
80 A Trax KICK 007 Anyway (p/s) 100

ACTION PAINTING
90 Sarah SARAH 028 These Things Happen/Boy Meets World (wraparound p/s, with insert) 10

CANNONBALL ADDERLEY SEXTET
63 Riverside 10691R RIF Tengo Tango/Brother John Dix 15

ANTHONY ADVERSE
86 él GPO 13 Our Fairy Tale/Eine Symphonie Des Grauens (p/s) 10
87 él GPO 29 Imperial Violets/Fountain (p/s) 5

IBRAHAM ALFA
97 Mosquito MSQ 09 METHODS OF SIGNAL ANALYSIS (12") 10
98 Mosquito MSQ 011 PROCESSEN EP (12") 8
99 Mosquito MSQ 015 DECODE YOURSELF EP (12") 8

AUGUSTO ALGUERO & HIS ORCHESTRA
71 Polydor 2489 034 LAUGH! LAUGH! (LP) 20

ALONE AGAIN OR
84 All One ALG 1 Drum The Beat (In My Soul)/Smartie Edit (p/s) 10
(see also Shamen)

ALTHEA & DONNA
77 Lightning LIG 506 Uptown Top Ranking/Calico Suit 6
77 Lightning 12LIG 506 Uptown Top Ranking/Calico Suit (12") 8

UDELL T. ANDERSON
69 Direction 58-4459 Keep On Loving Me/Rainmaker 8

MARK ANSLEY
70 Mother MOT 2 909/Venus 10

APACHE INDIAN & TIM DOGG
94 Island 12IS586 Make Way For The Indian (12") 8

APHEX TWIN
93 Warp WAP 39R ON — REMIXES (12" EP) 20
93 Warp WAP 39 ON (12" EP) 15
93 Warp WAPCDR 39 ON — REMIXES (CD single) 12
93 Warp WAPCD 39 ON (CD single) 8
94 Warp WAP 60 VENTOLIN EP (2 x 12") 1594
94 Warp WAP 60R VENTOLIN EP — REMIXES (2 x 12") 20
94 Rephlex CATCD 019 ANALOGUE BUBBLEBATH 4 (CD single) 20
94 Warp WAPCDR 60 VENTOLIN EP REMIXES (CD single) 12
94 Warp WAPCD 60 VENTOLIN EP (CD single) 8
95 Warp WAP 63 Icct Hedral/Donkey Rhubarb (12") 15
95 Warp WAP 78 GIRL/BOY EP (12") 12
96 Warp WAP CD 78 GIRL/BOY EP (CD) 8
97 Warp WAP 94P Come To Daddy/Pappy Mix//Little Lord Fauntleroy Mix/Mummy Mix (2 x 12") 15
97 Warp WAP 94P Come To Daddy/Pappy & Fauntleroy Mix/Flim Mix/Bucephalus Mix (12") 10
97 Warp WAPCD 94 COME TO DADDY (CD single) 8
97 Warp WAPCDR 94 COME TO DADDY REMIXED (To Cure A Weakling/Contour Regard) (CD single) 10
99 Warp WAP 105 Window Licker/Nannou (12") 8
99 Warp WAPCD 105 Window Licker (CD) 5
01 no label 01 DRUKS Cock 10 (Delco Freedom Mix)/54 Cymru Beats (Argonaut Mix) 5
95 Warp WARPLP 30 I CARE BECAUSE YOU DO (2-LP) 20
96 Warp WARLP 43 RICHARD D. JAMES (LP) 15
01 Warp WARLP DRUKQS (4-LP) 25

APPALOOSA
94 Recoil RCL 003 UNPLUGGED EP (12", 3-track, die-cut sleeve) 15
(see also Global Communications)

APPOLINAIRES
80s Two Tone 20 TT Feelings Gone/Feelings Back (paper labels) 10

APRIL SHOWERS
84 Chrysalis CHS 122787 Abandon Ship/Everytime We Say Goodbye (12", p/s) 100

COLIN AREETY
72 Deram DM 360 To Give All Your Love Away/Poco Joe 5
72 Deram DM 370 Holy Cow/I Can't Do It For You 5

LOUIS ARMSTRONG
70 Philips 6369 401 FEATURING LEON THOMAS & HIS FRIENDS (LP) 20

AROVANE
99 City Centre Offices BLOCK 1 Occer (plain black sleeve, with inserts, 850 only) 20
00 City Centre Offices BLOCK 018 Minth (plain sleeve with inserts, 1000 only) 10
00 City Centre Offices TOWERBLOCK 001LP TIDES (LP) 18

MINT VALUE £

ARSENAL 1ST TEAM SQUAD

71	Pye 7N 46067	Good Old Arsenal/The Boys From Highbury (some in p/s)	15/5
78	Lightning LIG 544	Roll Out The Red Carpet/Kings Of London (p/s)	5
79	United Artists UP 36518	Super Arsenal FC/Sing With The Gunners (p/s)	5
89	Dover DE1N 1-2	We're Back Where We Belong/Spot The Ball (p/s)	5

ART OF NOISE

83	ZTT ZTIS 100	INTO BATTLE WITH THE ART OF NOISE (12" EP)	8
84	ZTT P ZTPS 01	Close (To The Edit)/A Time To Hear (Who's Listening) (picture disc)	5
84	ZTT 12 P ZTPS 01	Edited/A Time To Clear (It Up) (12", picture disc)	8
85	ZTT 12 ZTPS 1	CLOSE TO THE EDIT (12", stamped green label, unreleased)	8
85	ZTT P ZTPS 02	Moments In Love/Beatbox (tortoise-shaped picture disc)	6
91	China CHINX 23	Art Of Love/(Ambience Of Love Mix) (12", some in p/s)	15/8

ATTICA BLUES

95	Mo' Wax MW 038	BLUEPRINT (12" EP)	15

ALBERT AYLER

64	Transatlantic TRA 130	SPIRITS (LP)	40
64	Fontana Jazz SFJL 925	GHOSTS (LP)	40
64	Fontana Jazz STJL 927	MY NAME IS (LP)	40
65	Fontana 933 SFJL	SPIRITUAL UNITY (LP)	40
65	Fontana SFJL 925	GHOSTS (LP, reissue)	30
65	Fontana Jazz SFJL 927	MY NAME IS (LP, reissue)	30
67	Polydor 2383089	WITCHES & DEVILS (LP)	25
68	Impulse IMPL 8022	NEW GRASS (LP, gatefold sleeve)	25
69	Impulse SIPL 519	NEW GRASS (LP, reissue, single sleeve)	20
69	Sonet SNTF 604	FIRST RECORDINGS (LP)	15
70s	Freedom 40101 FLP	WITCHES & DEVILS (LP, reissue)	15
70s	Freedom 41000 FLP	VIBRATIONS (LP)	15

BABYSHAMBLES

04	(no cat. no.)	What Katie Did (Demo) (clear flexi, with *Annelise's Magazine*)	8
04	High Society	Babyshambles/At The Flophouse (p/s, 1000 only)	20

(see also Libertines)

BURT BACHARACH

65	London HLR 9958	24 Hours From Tulsa/Don't Go Breaking My Heart	8

BACKYARD BABIES

98	MVG SAM 3024	TOTAL 05 (CD sampler, card sleeve)	20
98	Coalition COLA 046	Look At You/Powderhead/Can't Find The Door/Wireless Mind (gatefold p/s)	8
98	Coalition COLA 051	Bombed (Out Of My Mind)/Rocker (featuring Michael Monroe) (yellow vinyl, fully-autographed numbered gatefold p/s, 2000 only)	20
99	Coalition COLA 073	Babylon (featuring "Wildhearted Ginger")/Stars (red vinyl, foldover p/s & insert in poly bag, 1000 copies sold at gigs only)	20
99	Coalition COLA073DDJ	Babylon (featuring "Wildhearted Ginger") (CD, pic-stickered PVC wallet, promo only)	15
99	Coalition COLA 073 TJ	Babylon (Infinite Mass Remix, feat. "Wildhearted Ginger") (12" w/label, promo only)	15

(see also Hanoi Rocks, Super$hit666, Wildhearts)

BANCO DE GAIA

95	Bark L 011 S	LAST TRAIN TO LHASA (4-LP, limited edition)	18

TIM BARKER & THE CARLISLE UNITED SINGERS

74	Keswick KES 001	Looking Good/We're Carlisle United/Going On	5

RIKKY BARON

63	Parlophone R 4754	Everybody/You're Breaking My Heart	10

MARK B & BLADE

00	Wordplay WORD005T	Ya Don't See The Signs (12")	8

(see also Blade)

BBC RADIOPHONIC WORKSHOP

73	BBC RED 93 S	FOURTH DIMENSION (LP)	15
70s	BBC REC 25 M	BBC RADIOPHONIC MUSIC — WORK BY DELIA DERBYSHIRE (LP)	20

BEAT

80	Go-Feet FEET 1217	Can't Get Used To Losing You (Remix Version)/Mirror In The Bathroom/Spar Wid Me (12", p/s)	8
80	Go-Feet BEAT 001	JUST CAN'T STOP IT (LP, with inner)	12

BILLY BEETHOVEN

75	DJM DJS 10377	Dreams (Out In The Forest)/We're Free	100

(see also Graham Bonnet)

SI BEGG

97	Mosquito MSQ 010	WORKING ON THE FRONT LINE EP (12")	20
00	Mosquito MSQ 016	BAD DOO DOO (mini-LP)	15

SI BEGG MEETS NEIL LANDSTRUMM

01	Mosquito MSQ 017	TOKYO ASSASSIN (12" EP)	10

DOMINIC BEHAN

68	Major Minor MM 575	Wormwood Scrubs/Rifles Of The IRA	8

CLIFF BENNETT

69	Parlophone R 5792	Memphis Streets/But I'm Wrong	8

MICHAEL BENTINE

62	Parlophone 4927	Football Results/The Astronauts	12

JUSTIN BERKOVI

97	Mosquito MSQ 07	CROUTON EP (12")	8

MINT VALUE £

KENNY BERNARD

70s Pye Disco Demand DDS 2004 What Love Brings/LEON YOUNG STRINGS: Glad All Over (company sleeve) . . . 8

SIR JOHN BETJEMAN

75 Charisma CAS 1096 LATE FLOWERING LOVE (LP, with Jim Parker) . . . 12

BITSTREAM

00s City Centre Offices BLOCK 015 Crab Nebula (plain sleeve with inserts, 1000 only) . . . 12

BJÖRK vs FUNKSTÖRUNG

98 Fat Cat 12FAT 022 All Is Full Of Love (FunkstÖrung Remix)/The Shit (12", custom stamped sleeve) . . . 12

BLACK COUNTRY THREE

66 W.F.C. WS 100 BLACK COUNTRY SONGS (EP) . . . 250

(see also Jon Raven)

BLACK RADICAL MKII

89 2 The Bone LYN2304 Monsoon/B Boys B Wisell (12") . . . 6

BLACK TWANG

95 Sound Of Money SNM005 Queen's Head (12") . . . 8

BLACK VELVET

71 Mams MAM 47 Make It Better/Tropicana . . . 15

BLADE

89 691 Influential BLADE1202 Lyrical Maniac (12") . . . 25
89 691 Influential BLADE1202 Mind Of An Ordinary Citizen/ Forward (12") . . . 15
91 691 Influential BLADE1202 Rough It Up/Watch Waiting For?/You Better Get Yours (12") . . . 12
92 691 Influential BLADE1202 Survival Of The Hardest Working (12" EP) . . . 8
93 691 Influential BLADE1202 Clear The Way (12") . . . 8
93 691 Influential BLADE1202 THE LION GOES FROM STRENGTH TO STRENGTH (LP) . . . 15

BLUE ARSED FLY

95 Ferox FER 012 IN THE BAG EP (12") . . . 15
96 Mosquito MSQ 04 BLUE ARSED FLY EP (12") . . . 20

(see also Christian Vogel, Neil Landstrumm)

BLUE BOYS OF IBROX

68 Hallmark HM 555 FOLLOW! FOLLOW! RANGERS: A TRIBUTE TO THE GREAT GLASGOW TEAM (LP) . . . 20

BLUR

95 Food LH 69 The Universal/Entertain Me (Live It! Remix) (DJ promo) . . . 5
02 no label no cat. no. (red label, bearing Arabic writing which translates as "Don't bomb when you are the bomb"; large centre hole; 1,000 were pressed, but many were blown up) . . . 50

ERIC BOGLE

81 Plant Life PLR 033 PLAIN AND SIMPLE (LP) . . . 15
83 Plant Life PLR 046 SCRAPS OF PAPER (LP) . . . 15
85 Topic 12TS 437 WHEN THE WIND BLOWS (LP) . . . 15
88 Plant Life PLR 042 NOW I'M EASY (LP) . . . 15

BOMB THE BASS

87 Misteron DOOD121 Beat Dis (12") . . . 8

ELI BONAPARTE

71 Decca F 13202 it's Your Love/Sometime You'll Find . . . 6

BONZO DOG (DOO-DAH) BAND

67 Sunset SLS 50160 GORILLA (LP) . . . 12
68 Sunset SLS 50210 THE DOUGHNUT IN GRANNY'S GREENHOUSE (LP, single sleeve) . . . 12
69 Sunset SLS 50375 KEYNSHAM (LP, single sleeve) . . . 12
69 Sunset SLS 50350 I'M THE URBAN SPACEMAN (LP) . . . 12

DAVID BOWIE

75 Decca F 13579 The London Boys/Love You Till Tuesday (Demo) . . . 200
88 PRT PYX 6001 I'm Not Losing Sleep/I Dig Everything/Can't Help Thinking/Do Anything You Say (picture disc) . . . 12
95 RCA OUT 1 The Heart's Filthy Lesson (12", 1-sided promo) . . . 10
96 BBC MMCD 0072 BBC SESSIONS 1969-1972 (CD, picture disc, promo-only, withdrawn) . . . 200
97 RCA 7432 1475841 Dead Man Walking/Hous/Vigor Mortis/Paradox (plain sleeve, stickered) . . . 8
83 RCA LIFETIMES 1 LIFETIMES (LP, promo, numbered, with insert) . . . 35

BREW

60s Oak LONDON Crossroads/Play Your Tune (acetate, unreleased, handwritten labels) . . . 150

(see also Camel)

MARK BROOM

95 Ferox FER 017 SHUFFLE THIS (12" EP) . . . 8

BROTHERHOOD

91 Bite It BITE1 Descendants Of The Holocaust . . . 8
92 Bite It BITE1 Way Of The Wise (12") . . . 8
93 Bite It BITE1 XXXIII (EP) . . . 10

(CRAZY WORLD OF) ARTHUR BROWN

88 Reckless 2 RECK STRANGELANDS (LP, unreleased)

MAXINE BROWN

90s Kent TOWN 110 It's Torture/I Got Love . . . 12

MINT VALUE £

BUCHANAN BROTHERS
69 Page One POF 139 — Medicine Man Part 1/Part 2 6

THE BUG
99 Fat Cat 12FAT 032 — LOWRIDER EP (12", custom sleeve) 9

BUG CENTRAL
00 BBP/Yellow Fever BBPV 5 — MONEY & RIOTS EP (with inserts) 8
99 Helen Of Troy HOO 48 — THE MEEK WILL INHERIT NOTHING (LP, with inserts) 15

SANDY BULL
69 Vanguard 19040 — E PLURIBUS UNUM (LP) 20

BULLY BOYS BAND
70 Stateside SSL 5032 — MOVIE SCENE — HEAVY SOUNDS FROM TODAY'S FILMS (LP) 15

SONNY BURKE OUTFIT
68 Instant IN 003 — Baby Be My Girl/All You 20
(see also Sonny Burke)

BILL CADDICK
79 Highway SHY 7006 — REASONS BRIEFLY SET DOWN (LP) 15

CAGLIOSTRO
86 él GPO 22 — Libera Me/Madmen And Lovers (p/s) 8

CALENNIG
80 Greenwich Village GVR 214 — SONGS AND TUNES FROM WALES (LP) 15

CANDY
69 Emerald MD 1119 — Little Bit Of Soul/Signs Of Love 12

MORGAN CANEY
00 City Centre Offices BLOCK 7 — Blanket/GEIOM: Four Forty Five (plain sleeve with inserts, 1000 only) 8

MORGAN CANEY & KAMAL JOORY
01 City Centre Offices BLOCK 014 — Darling (plain sleeve with inserts, 1000 only) 8

CARDIACS
88 Alphabet ALPH 009T — Susannah's Still Alive/Blind In Safety And Leafy In Love/All His Geese Are Swans (12", p/s) 8
89 Alphabet ALPH 011 — Baby Heart Dirt/I Hold My Love In My Arms (p/s) 5
88 Night Tracks SFNT 013 — RADIO ONE EVENING SESSION: R.E.S./ Buds And Spawn/In A City Lining/ Is This The Life/Cameras (12" EP) 10
88 Alphabet ALPHLP 010 — CARDIACS LIVE (LP) 15
88 Alphabet ALPH 012 — ON LAND AND IN THE SEA (LP) 15
91 Alphabet ALPHLP 014 — SONGS FOR SHIPS AND IRONS (LP) 12
92 Alphabet ALPHLP 017 — HEAVEN BORN AND EVER BRIGHT (LP) 12

(LITTLE) CARL CARLTON
90s Kent TOWN 105 — Competition Ain't Nothin'/HESITATIONS: I'm Not Built That Way 8

CARNABY
84 SOS SOS 004 — Jump & Dance/BOBBY PARIS: I Walked Away 12

CARPENTERS
70s MFP MFP 50431 — TICKET TO RIDE (LP) 12

CASINO
81 Ellie Jay EJSP 9609 — More Than Ever/Tonight (p/s) 10

CASINO VERSUS JAPAN
00 City Centre Offices TOWERBLOCK 003LP — GO HAWAII (2-LP) 15

CAVALIERS
86 él GPO 11 — It's A Beautiful Game/The I.T. Man (p/s) 12
86 él ACME 4 — A PERFECT ACTION (LP) 20

CAVEMAN
91 Profile PROFIT330DJ — I'm Ready/Pages & Pages/Back To Cause Mayhem (EP) 12

TERRY CAVENDISH ORCHESTRA
73 Pye NSPL 41023 — ALL IN AN AFTERNOON'S WORK (LP) 12

CELTIC F.C.
67 Thistle — Celtic Celtic (p/s) 12
73 Polydor 2058332 — Celtic Your Favourites In Green/Saturday 5

CEOLBEG
90 Ceolbeg Music CB 001 — NOT THE BUNNY HOP (LP) 20

CERTAIN LIONS & TIGERS
70 Polydor 2344 002 — SOUL CONDOR (LP) 40

CHAPTER FIVE
90s Goldmine/Soul Supply GS 009 — You Can't Mean It/One In A Million 8

RAY CHARLES
65 Summit ATL 4144 — THE INCOMPARABLE RAY CHARLES (LP, mono, some tracks by Memphis Slim) 12
60s WRC T 827 — C&W MEETS R&B (LP) 12
60s WRC T 566 — DEDICATED TO YOU (LP) 12

MINT VALUE £

CHARLIE BOY
71 Trojan TR 7823 — Funky Strip/UPSETTERS: Mellow Mood . . . 25
(see also Lee Perry/Upsetters)

CHARLY & THE BOURBON FAMILY
71 Decca F 23164 — Acapulco Gold/Boogachi . . . 8

CHASERS
01 Changes One ChangesCD-002 — ONWARDS & UPWARDS EP (CD EP, 1,060 copies only, many signed) . . . 18/10
(see also Energetic Krusher, Wildhearts, Yo-Yo's)

CHELSEA SQUAD
72 Penny Farthing PEN 782 — Blue Is The Colour/All Sing Together . . . 7
84 W&A YZ 23 — Back On The Ball/(Club Mix) (blue vinyl, p/s) . . . 5

ANTHONY CHILD/ANDREW READ
99 Fat Cat 12FAT 031 — Speedranch/Jansky Noise (12" EP, 'bullet hole' sleeve) . . . 12

CHUMBAWAMBA
88 Agit Prop PROP 3 — ENGLISH REBEL SONGS 1381-1914 (10" LP, with die-cut sleeve) . . . 15

CIM(M)AR(R)ONS
82 Safari/MPL SAFE 49 — Big Girls Don't Cry/How Can I Prove Myself To You? . . . 10
82 Safari/MPL SAFEL 49 — Big Girls Don't Cry/How Can I Prove Myself To You? (12") . . . 15
82 Safari/MPL SAFELX 49 — Big Girls Don't Cry/How Can I Prove Myself To You? (12", picture disc) . . . 20
83 MPL/Cimarons CIM 001 — Love And Affection . . . 18
83 MPL/Cimarons 12CIM 001 — Love And Affection (12", less than 1000 pressed) . . . 60
82 MPL/Pickwick SHM 3106 — REGGAEBILITY (LP) . . . 18

CLARO INTELECTO
02 Ai AI 003 — PEACE OF MIND (12", first pressings in blue p/s) . . . 15

COAST TO COAST
82 Polydor POSP 451 — The Bell/How Can I Be Sure . . . 8
(see also Status Quo)

COCKERAL CHORUS
72 Young Blood YB 1017 — Nice One Cyril/Cyril Marches On . . . 5
73 Young Blood YB 107 — NICE ONE CYRIL (LP) . . . 20

COLDCUT
88 Ahead Of Our Time AHED1201 — Beats & Pieces (12") . . . 60
88 Ahead Of Our Time AHED1201 — Beats & Pieces (Mo Bass Remix) (12") . . . 30
88 Urban URBX17DJ — Coldcut Meets The Godfather (12") . . . 10

COLDCUT Feat. QUEEN LATIFAH
89 Big Life CCUT8T — Find A Way/Ride The Pleasure (12") . . . 8

JOHNNY COLLINS
75 Tradition TSR 020 — JOHNNY'S PRIVATE ARMY (LP) . . . 18

JOHNNY COLLINS & FRIENDS
73 Tradition TSR 014 — THE TRAVELLER'S REST (LP) . . . 18

CONNARD
68 Spot JW 11 — Amadhan/Desdemona . . . 50

COOL SPOON (Jeff Dixon & Alton Ellis)
67 Coxsone CS 7031 — Yakety Yak/SOUL VENDORS: Drum Song . . . 25

COOL STICKY
68 Amalgamated AMG 825 — Train To Soulsville/ERIC MONTY MORRIS: Cinderella . . . 22

BOB & RON COPPER
63 EFDSS 1002 — BOB & RON COPPER (LP) . . . 35

COUNT HOUSE FOLK MUSIC CLUB
65 own label MSCH 2 — MORE SINGING AT THE COUNT HOUSE (LP, private pressing) . . . 250

GRAHAM COXON
04 EMI R 6632 — Freakin' Out/Feel Right (numbered p/s) . . . 7
01 Transcopic TRANLP 010 — CROW SIT ON BLOOD TREE (2-LP, with inners & print, some signed, 1,000 only) . . . 35/25

CRACKOUS ROCK 'N' ROLL
89 HTB BAR 6 — Back Home/Barrelhouse Cam In Vietnam (flexi, with *Hit The Bar* fanzine) . . . 5

JIMMY CRIKIT
70 MCA MK 5047 — Isabella/Love Is A See Saw . . . 10

GEOFF CRIPPS & LOUISA RUGG
85 Steam Pie SPR 1003S — ICARUS (LP) . . . 15

ANDREW CRONSHAW
77 Trailer LER 2104 — EARTHED IN CLOUD VALLEY (LP) . . . 15

DON CROWN & HIS BUSKING BUDGIES
71 President PT 340 — Mrs Wilson's Budgie/Flying Machines . . . 15

CURLEW
85 Topic 12TS 435 — FIDDLE MUSIC FROM SHETLAND AND BEYOND (LP) . . . 12

DAVID & MARIANNE DALMOUR
66 Columbia SCX 6005 — STRANGE ENCHANTMENT (LP) . . . 25

GLEN DALY
61 Piccadilly 7N 35017 — The Celtic Song/If Only We Had Old Ireland Over Here . . . 10

MINT VALUE £

ERROLL DANIEL

69 Paradox PAR 45902 — No Excuses/Go Back . . . 15

TROY DANTE (& INFERNOS)

69 MCA MK 5003 — It's About Time/Behold . . . 8

DARKNESS

02 Must Destroy DUSTY CD 001 — I Believe In A Thing Called Love (Single Version)/(Album Version) (CD) . . . 20
03 Must Destroy DUSTY 010 CD/DVD — Growing On Me/How Dare You Call This Love?/Bareback//Growing On Me/ Growing On Me (Video)/Out-takes (DVD/CD, double disc pack) . . . 10
03 Must Destroy DARK 01CD/ DVD — I Believe In A Thing Called Love/Makin' Out/Physical Sex//I Believe In A Thing Called Love/Out Of My Hands/I Believe In A Thing Called Love (Video)/Video Clips (DVD/CD, double disc pack, with poster) . . . 12
03 Must Destroy DARK 02 — Christmas Time (Don't Let The Bells End)/I Love You 5 Times (custom sleeve, with rub-on tattoo)
03 Must Destroy DARK 02 — Christmas Time (Don't Let The Bells End)/I Love You 5 Times (promo-only box set, in giftwrap, with card) . . . 60
03 Must Destroy DARK 02 CD/ DVD — Christmas Time (Don't Let The Bells End)/I Love You 5 Times//Christmas Time (Don't Let The Bells End) (Video)/I Believe In A Thing Called Love (Live At Knebworth 2003) (Video) (DVD/CD, double disc pack) . . . 10

DAVE & ANSELL COLLINS

73 Trojan TR 7891 — Bandwagon/Ton Up Kids . . . 6

RAY DAVIES (& BUTTONDOWN BRASS)

74 Philips 6382 103 — THEMES FROM THE EXORCIST, FRENCH CONNECTION AND OTHER GREAT FILMS (LP) . . . 15

SAMMY DAVIS (Jnr)

72 MGM 2006 095 — The Candy Man/I Want To Be Happy . . . 6

BRIAN DEE

75 Atlantic 2460 255 — HAMMOND EXCITEMENT (LP) . . . 12

SAM DEES

97 Goldmine/Soul Supply GS 0002 — Lonely For You Baby/SAM FLETCHER: I'd Think It Over (promos [GS 0002X] £12) . . . 10

DELLINGER

77 Carib Gems GG 004 — Melting Pot/Version . . . 7
(see also Dillinger)

ARIN DEMAIN

90s Goldmine/Soul Supply GS 028 — Silent Treatment/PARIS: Sleepless Nights . . . 8

DEMON BOYZ

88 Music Of Life NOTE 013 — Northside/Rougher Than An Animal . . . 6
88 Music Of Life NOTE 022 — Vibez (12") . . . 8
89 Music Of Life DEMON 1 — RECOGNITION (LP) . . . 8

DENZEL & HUHN

01 City Centre Offices BLOCK 8 — FILET (12" EP, p/s) . . . 8

DEPTH CHARGE

89 Vinyl Solution STORM 08 — Depth Charge (12") . . . 10
89 Vinyl Solution STORM 13 — Bounty Killers (12") . . . 12

DETROIT ESCALATOR CO.

96 Ferox FERLP 2 — SOUNDTRACK (313) (LP) . . . 20

JANINE DE WAYLENE & HER MARTENOT

60 Oriole CB 1576 — Faces In The Dark/Martenot Theme/Farewell Christina . . . 8

DIANE & THE NEW WORLDS

71 Stereo Gold Award MER 350 — TAMLA HITS (LP) . . . 12

DIGITAL PRINCESS

02 Mosquito MSQ 019 — LISTEN TO ME TENDER (12" EP) . . . 8

DIRECTIONS IN JAZZ UNIT

64 Philips BL 7625 — DIRECTIONS IN JAZZ (LP) . . . 120

DJ FOOD

95 Open 013 OPENT — Peace (Remixes)/Peace (Part 1 & 2)/Peace (Part 3) (12") . . . 8
95 Ninja Tune 1020 ZEN — A DUB PLATE OF FOOD (2 x 10") . . . 10
95 Ninja Tune 1229 — Freedom (Fila Brazilia Mix)/Cosmic Consciousness (Ashley Beadle Mix) (12") . . . 8
96 Ninja Tune 1221 ZEN — Peace/Dark Blood/Well Swung (12") . . . 6
96 Ninja Tune 212 ZEN — REFRIED FOOD PT 1 & 2 (2 x 12") . . . 10
96 Ninja Tune 1233 ZEN — REFRIED FOOD PT 2 (Journeymen Mix)/(Autechre Mix) . . . 8
96 Ninja Tune 1233 ZEN — REFRIED FOOD PART 2 (12") . . . 10
96 Ninja Tune 2113 ZEN — REFRIED FOOD PT 3 & 4 (2 x 12") . . . 8
96 Ninja Tune 2116 ZEN — REFRIED FOOD PT 5 & 6 (2 x 12") . . . 8
96 Ninja Tune 1 ZENKLON — Spiral/THE HERBALISER: Up For The Get Downs (12", 1-sided, some etched) . . . 10
90s Ninja Tune — FUNGLE JUNK (2 x 10") . . . 8
90s Ninja Tune 2 ZEN — JAZZ BRAKES VOLUME 1 (LP) . . . 15
90s Ninja Tune 3 ZEN — JAZZ BRAKES VOLUME 2 (LP) . . . 15
90s Ninja Tune 4 ZEN — JAZZ BRAKES VOLUME 3 (2-LP) . . . 15
90s Ninja Tune 106267 — REFRIED FOOD LUNCHBOX (3-LP) . . . 25

DJ MINK Feat. THE K.I.D & C

90 Warp WAR4 — Hey Hey Can U Relate (12") . . . 15

MINT VALUE £

DJ VADIM
94 Jazz Fudge JF001 — ABSTRACT HALLUCINATING GASSES EP (12") . . . 10

DOCTOR ROCKIT
96 Clear CLR 416 — D FOR DOKTOR EP (12", p/s) . . . 12

DODGE CITY
92 4th & Broadway 10BRW231DJ — The Clarity (10") . . . 7

DOONICANS
87 Probe Plus PP 23T — THE FISHERMAN'S WAY (12" EP) . . . 10

NICK DOW
79 Dingles DIN 306 — BURD MARGARET (LP) . . . 15

ROBIN & BARRY DRANSFIELD
70 Trailer LER 2011 — THE ROUT OF THE BLUES (LP, yellow label) . . . 30

DRIVER
80 Rods HOT 1 — YOU BETTER TAKE IT (LP, 300 only) . . . 110

EARTH & FIRE
70 Penny Farthing PEN 741 — Mechanical Lover/Ruby Is The One . . . 8

CLANCY ECCLES
67 Pama PMB 703 — Western Organ/Mother's Advice (actually by The Clancy Set) . . . 25

ALTON ELLIS
73 Spur SP 3 — All We Need Is Love/KEITH HUDSON: Better Love . . . 35

IAN ELMS
82 Squid Marks SMT 013 — GOOD NIGHT (LP, with insert) . . . 180

ENERGETIC KRUSHER
89 Vinyl Solution SOL 17 — PATH TO OBLIVION (LP, with insert, features Danny McCormack) . . . 20
(see also Chasers, Wildhearts, Yo-Yo's)

ENGLAND FOOTBALL SQUAD
70 Pye 7N 17920 — Back Home/Cinnamon Stick (some with 'footbal'l centre; some in p/s) . . . 7/15/25
70 Pye 7N 17920 — Back Home/Cinnamon Stick (in promo 'BOAC' sleeve) . . . 200
88 MCA GOAL 1 — All The Way (p/s, as 1988 England Squad with Stock, Aitken & Waterman) . . . 5
82 England ER 1 — This Time (We'll Get It Right)/England, We'll Fly The Flag (p/s) . . . 5
82 Ariola ER 1 — This Time (We'll Get It Right)/England, We'll Fly The Flag (Instrumental) (p/s) . . . 5
82 Original Sound ERP 1P — This Time (picture disc) . . . 20
86 EMI DB 9128 — We've Got The Whole World At Our Feet/When We Are Far From Home (p/s) . . . 5
86 EMI 12DBP 9128 — We've Got The Whole World At Our Feet/When We Are Far From Home (12" pic disc) . . . 8
70 Pye NSPL 18337 — THE WORLD BEATERS SING THE WORLD BEATERS (LP, round fold-out sleeve) 35
82 K-Tel NE 1169 — THIS TIME (LP, gatefold, with booklet) . . . 20
82 Event EV 002 — ENGLAND IN THE WORLD CUP 1982 (LP, gatefold sleeve) . . . 20

ENGLAND/NEW ORDER
90 Factory FAC 293-7 — World In Motion/The B-Side (p/s) . . . 5
(see also New Order)

ENGLISH COUNTRY BLUES BAND
83 Rogue FMSL 2004 — HOME AND DERANGED (LP) . . . 15

EPHEBE
96 Ferox FER 019 — ONE (12" EP) . . . 8
96 Ferox FER 022 — TWO (12" EP) . . . 8

ERASURE
89 Mute (no cat. no.) — WILD (CD, promo-only box set, with LP, 12", cassette, stickers, postcard, photo & info sheet) . . . 220
91 Mute CDSTUMM 95 — CHORUS (promo CD, with cassette and booklet) . . . 100
92 Mute (no cat. no.) — POP! THE FIRST 20 HITS (CD, promo-only box set, with T-shirt, info sheets, 2-LP, video tape, & cassette) . . . 220

ETERNAL
90 Sarah SARAH 031 — Sleep/Breathe/Take Me Down (p/s) . . . 8

EXPOSURE
80 Ahgular Music ACUTE 1 — Style & Fashion/Video Eyes (p/s) . . . 10

FACTION feat. PETE WYLIE
80s Inevitable INEV 006 — FACTION (LP, some in plastic bag) . . . 15/12

DON FARDON
69 Youngblood YB 1003 — I'm Alive/Keep On Loving Me . . . 40

VICTOR FELDMAN QUARTET
62 Fontana 267233 — A Taste Of Honey/Valerie . . . 10
80s Jasmine JASM 2002 — TRANSATLANTIC ALLIANCE (LP, reissue) . . . 12
80s Jasmine JASM 2023 — IN LONDON VOL. 1 (LP, reissue) . . . 12
80s Jasmine JASM — IN LONDON VOL. 2 (LP, reissue) . . . 12

JOSE FELICIANO
70 RCA RCA 1998 — Destiny/Susie-Q . . . 5
60s RCA LP 4370 — FIREWORKS (LP, embossed sleeve) . . . 12

FIELD MICE
80s Waaaaah BULL 40 — Burning Word (1-sided flexi) . . . 6
90 Sarah SARAH 024 — Autumn Store Pt. 1/If You Need Someone/World In Me (p/s) . . . 10
90 Sarah SARAH 025 — Autumn Store Pt. 2/Anyone Else Isn't You/Bleak (p/s) . . . 10

MINT VALUE £

FIFTH DIMENSION
68 Liberty LBF 15130 California Soul/It'll Never Be The Same . . . 12

JEM FINER
00s no cat. no. LONGPLAYER (LP, with book) . . . 15

ARCHIE FISHER, BARBARA DICKSON & JOHN MacKINNON
69 Trailer LER 3002 SONGS OF THE JACOBITE REBELLIONS (LP) . . . 25

CILLA FISHER & ARTIE TREZISE
79 Kettle KAC 1 FOR FOUL DAY AND FAIR (LP) . . . 15

FIRE ISLAND
94 Junior Boys Own JBO 18 There But For The Grace Of God (12") . . . 15
95 Junior Boys Own JBO 26 If You Should Need A Friend (12") . . . 15
97 Junior Boys Own JBO 51 White Powder Dreams/mixes (12") . . . 15
97 Junior Boys Own JNR 500 1576 Shout To The Top (12", featuring Loleatta Holloway) . . . 15

FITS OF GLOOM
92 Gem GEMX 002 Differences/mixes (12") . . . 12
94 MCA MCSTD 1981 Heaven/mixes (12") . . . 12
94 MCA MCST 2016 Power Of Love/mixes (12") . . . 12

PATRICK FITZGERALD
80s Final Solution FSEP 001 TONIGHT EP . . . 8

FIVE HAND REEL
78 RCA PL 25150 EARL O'MORAY (LP) . . . 15

FIZZARUM
99 City Centre Offices BLOCK 2 Phut Of Plex (clear vinyl, plain black sleeve, with inserts; 650 copies only) . . . 20

FLAMING LIPS
89 Glitterhouse EFA 40153 Drug Machine In Heaven/Strychnine/What's So Funny (About Peace, Love And Understanding) (p/s) . . . 15
91 City Slang 04063-05 Unconsciously Screamin'/Ma, I Didn't Notice/Let Me Be It/Lucifer Rising (clear vinyl, hologram sleeve) . . . 8
92 Warners PRO CD 5401 Everyone Wants To Live Forever (CD promo, title sleeve) . . . 20
92 Warners PRO S 5452 Ballrooms Of Mars/MR BUNGLE: Sudden Death (promo, grey vinyl, no p/s) . . . 15
92 Warners PRO CD 5628 Collector Scum Tantalizor (promo CD) . . . 20
94 Warners W 0246CDX She Don't Use Jelly/The Process/Moth In The Incubator (CD) . . . 8
94 Warners SAM 1431 She Don't Use Jelly/Translucent Egg/Turn It On (Bluegrass Version)/The Process (12" promo) . . . 15
95 Warners W 0322CD Bad Days (Edit)/She Don't Use Jelly (Primitive Demo)/Girl With Hair Like An Explosion/Giraffe (Demo Version) (CD) . . . 12
95 Warners W 0322CDX Bad Days (Edit)/Ice Drummer (Suicide Tribute Album Contribution)/When You Smiled (I Lost My Only Idea)/Put The Waterbug In The Policeman's Ear (Ghetto Blaster Recording At The Art School, Sept. '93) (CD, 'squidgy pack') . . . 15
95 Warners PRO S 7918 What's The New Mary Jane?/Under Pressure (promo, no p/s) . . . 15
96 Warners 9362-43672 This Here Giraffe/The Sun (Live Peel Session Version)/Hit Me Like You Did First Time (Live Peel Session Version) (star-shaped CD) . . . 10
96 Warners WO 370CD Brainville/Evil Will Prevail (Recorded On 'Brave New World', KCRW, Santa Monica)/Waterbug (Recorded On 'Brave New World', KCRW, Santa Monica) . . . 8
96 Warners WO 370 CDX Brainville/Brainville (Recorded On 'Brave New World', KCRW, Santa Monica)/ Raindrops (Written By Burt Bacharach) (Recorded On 'Brave New World', KCRW, Santa Monica) (CD, holographic sleeve) . . . 10
98 Warners PRO CD 9295 The Big Ol' Bug Is The New Baby Now (Stereo Mix) (enhanced CD-Rom, stickered cardboard sleeve) . . . 15
02 Warners (no cat. no.) Ego Tripping/It's Summertime (promo CD-R) . . . 20
00s Rykodisc/Restless PRCD RPRO 270 THE SHAMBOLIC BIRTH AND EARLY LIFE OF THE FLAMING LIPS CATALOG SAMPLER 1983-1991 (promo CD) . . . 25

RAY FLEMING
63 MGM MGM 1196 I'm Glad I Have You/Humpty Dumpty . . . 10

FLOWERS & FROLICS
77 Free Reed FRR 016 BEES ON HORSEBACK (LP, featuring June Tabor & Bob Davenport) . . . 35

FLUKE
89 Fluke FLUKE 001T Thumper!/Cool Hand Flute (12", stamped white label with stickered sleeve) . . . 10
90 Creation CRE 090T PHILLY (12") . . . 10

FLYING SQUAD
78 Epic S EPC 6375 Drive On/Baltimore Baby . . . 5
78 Epic S EPC 6542 Backroom Boys (Night After Night)/Tell Me What To Do . . . 5
78 Epic EPC 82875 FLYING SQUAD (LP) . . . 12
(see also Status Quo)

FONN
99 Fat Cat 12FAT 018 Untitled (2 x 12", embossed sleeve) . . . 10

FORMULA TWO
72 CBS SCBS 8285 Easy Times/Girl Who Lives Next Door . . . 6

KIM FOWLEY
80 Island WIP 278 The Trip/Beautiful People (p/s, reissue) . . . 10

BOB FOX & STU LUCKLEY
78 Rubber RUB 028 NOWT SO GOOD'LL PASS (LP) . . . 15

FRAN & ALAN
68 MGM MGM 1428 Such A Pity/Mrs Robinson . . . 8

MINT VALUE £

(KING) JOE FRANCIS
66 Rio R 94 — Days Are Lonely/My Baby 25

FREDDIE & THE DREAMERS
67 EMI Regal — See You Later Alligator (export issue) 35

FREED UNIT
99 Out-There OTT 06 — MASONIC YOUTH (9" EP, triangular clear vinyl, 100 only) 50
01 Out-There OTT 09 — SIX SIDED (9" EP, clear vinyl, 100 only) 25
98 Out-There OTTLP 04 — FIELD REPORTS FROM OUT-THERE (LP, clear vinyl) 18
98 Enraptured RAPTLP 19 — THINGS ARE LOOKING UP... (LP, orange vinyl) 15

FREEHOLD
68 Regent Sound — Lying Crying Dying (1-sided acetate, 1 copy only) 25
(see also Genesis)

FRENZY
86 ABC EYE T7 — I See Red/Whose Life (p/s) 8
86 I.D. NOSE 8 — CLOCKWORK TOY (LP) 15
87 I.D. NOSE 19 — SALLY'S PINK BEDROOM (LP) 15

CORNELIA FROBOESS
62 HMV HMV 1671 — GERMAN TEENAGERS (LP) 40

FRANK FROEBA
52 Brunswick LA 8547 — BACK ROOM PIANO (10" LP) 12
53 Brunswick LA 8611 — MOONLIGHT PLAYING TIME (10" LP) 12
53 Brunswick LA 8555 — PARLOR PIANO (10" LP) 12

BERNIE FROST
74 Vertigo 6059 108 — The House/What Do You Want To Hear Today 50
(see also Status Quo, Rossi & Frost, Boz Frost)

BOZ FROST
73 Vertigo 6059 083 — Foreign Lady/Big White Seagull 25
(see also Status Quo, Rossi & Frost, Bernie Frost)

FUSION
95 Ferox FER 015 — FREESTYLE EP (12") 8
96 Ferox FER 021 — GALAXY OF FUTURE VISIONS (12" EP) 10

FUTURE BEAT ALLIANCE
99 Ferox FER 035 — ABACO (12" EP) 10

RUSS GABRIEL
93 Ferox FER 002 — PEACE EP (12", plain sleeve) 20
94 Ferox FER 006 — DARWINIAN EP (12", plain sleeve) 20
(see also Fusion, Too Funk)

RUSS GABRIEL & AFFIE YUSUF
94 Ferox FER 005 — Sian's Tune/Deep Space (12") 20

KAY GARNER
60s Oriole CB 1951 — I Still Get Jealous/Squeeze Me 20

MARSHA GEE
80s Joker JK 001 — The Peanut Duck/ENCHANTMENTS: I'm In Love With Your Daughter/ H.B. BARNUM: It Hurts Too Much Too Cry 10

GEMINI
69 President PT 257 — Never Say Die/Something Special 6

GENTLE RESPITE
90 Sarah SARAH 026 — DARKEST BLUE EP: Summer In Me/Darkest Blue/If I Touch (wraparound p/s, with insert) 10

TERRY GIBBS SEXTET
56 Vogue Coral LVA 9013 — TERRY (LP) 20
56 Vogue Coral LVA 9009 — JAZZTIME USA (LP, as Terry Gibbs Quartet & Sextet) 20
(see also Terry Gibbs Big Band)

GINGER
01 Infernal/Round GINGERCD1 — I'm A Lover Not A Fighter/Don't Let Me Die Lonely/Thailand Uber Alles (CD) 30
01 Infernal/Round GINGERCD2 — Cars And Vaginas/You, Me And BT/Not Bitter, Just A Little Disappointed (CD) 25
02 Infernal/Round GINGERCD3 — And This Time I'm Serious/Re-Inventing The Wheel/Blinded By Absinthe (CD) 20
02 Infernal/Round GINGERCD4 — The Saga Of Me & You/Naked Innocence/Better Man (CD) 10
03 Infernal/Round GINGERCD5 — Virtual Love/Energetic O/Where Did Everyone Go? (CD) 8
(see also SilverGinger 5, Super$hit666, Wildhearts)

MARCELLO GIOMBINI
70 United Artists UP 35110 — Sabata — Main Title/Banjo Arrives 10

JIMMY GIUFFRE
58 London LTZ-K 15130 — JIMMY GIUFFRE 3 (LP) 15

GLASGOW RANGERS AFC BOYS CLUB
71 Hallmark SHM 759 — GLORY, GLORY GLASGOW RANGERS (LP) 20

GLORY LANDERS
69 IBA SECC 1203 — VOLUME 1 (LP) 15

DAVID GOLD
97 Fat Cat 10FAT 001 — Respect City Police (10") 40

GOLDIE LOOKIN' CHAIN
04 Must Destroy DESTROY12 001 — Half Man Half Machine/Self Suicide/Half Man Half Machine (Clean) (12", p/s, 1,000 only) 10
04 Gold Dust — THE MANIFESTO (CD, sold at gigs) 40

MINT VALUE £

GOL GAPPAS
86 él GPO 21 — West 14/Roman (p/s) 12

JOHN GOODLUCK
88 Sweet Folk & Country SFA 047 — SPEED THE PLOUGH: TRADITIONAL SONGS OF SUFFOLK (LP) 25
88 Big Ben FE 065 — THE MAN WHO PUT THE ENGINE IN THE CHIP SHOP: MORE RAILWAY SONGS OF DAVE GOULDER (LP) 15

VIN GORDON
70s Trojan TRO 9058 — Liquid Horns/JUNIOR: Liquidator 5

DAVE GOULDER
73 Big Ben BB 0004 — REQUIEM FOR STEAM: THE RAILWAY SONGS OF DAVE GOULDER (LP) 15

GRAIN
97 Fat Cat 12FAT 002 — Untitled 1 (12", plain sleeve) 8
99 Fat Cat 12FAT 015 — Untitled 2 (12", die-cut sleeve) 8
99 Fat Cat 12FAT 016 — Untitled 3 (12", die-cut sleeve) 8
02 Fat Cat 12FAT 041 — Untitled 4 (12", die-cut sleeve) 8

COLIN GRAINGER & THE FRANK CORDELL ORCHESTRA
58 HMV POP 484 — This I Know/Are You? 10
59 HMV POP 639 — Love Only Me/Plain And Simple Girl 10

ARTHUR GREENSLADE
72 Deram DM 349 — Flirt (Pour Un Flirt)/Rainy Day Love 5

GREGER
66 Polydor 249 1103 — IN THE NIGHT (LP) 25

GUTTERSNYPES
94 Liberty Grooves LIB 004 — Trials Of Life (Radio Edits) (12" EP) 12
94 Liberty Grooves LIB 005 — Trials Of Life (12" EP) 12

DARYL HALL & SOUNDS OF BLACKNESS
94 Mercury MERMC 404 — Gloryland/(mixes) (picture disc, in poster sleeve) 10

PAUL HANNAH
94 Ferox FER 007 — CONTROL EP (12", plain sleeve) 12
95 Ferox FER 010 — ADVENTURES IN TECHNO SOUL (12" EP) 8

HARDBACK
86 Streetwave 7 BOSS 3 — The Champ/Bust The Champ 6

MIKE HARDING
86 Moonraker M 003 — BOMBERS MOON (LP) 20

KURT HARRIS
90s Goldmine/Soul Supply GS 018 — Emperor Of My Baby's Heart/JIM McFARLAND: Lonely Lover 8

ALAN HAVEN
71 CBS S 63900 — ST. ELMO'S FIRE (LP) 12

COLEMAN HAWKINS GROUP
60s London LTZC 15048 — COLEMAN HAWKINS GROUP (LP) 20

(see also Coleman Hawkins)

HAYDEN HOUSE
69 NEMS 56-4499 — House Beside The Mine/Lady Wants More 25

TUBBY HAYES ORCHESTRA
81 Mole MOLE 2 — MEXICAN GREEN (LP, reissue) 20
81 Mole MOLE 4 — TUBBS' TOURS (LP, reissue) 15

TUBBY HAYES QUARTET
90 MMO 79 — 67 LIVE — FOR MEMBERS ONLY (LP) 20

TUBBY HAYES QUINTET
80s Jasmine JASM 2001 — TUBBY'S GROOVE (LP, reissue) 15
80s Jasmine JASM 2015 — AFTER LIGHTS OUT (LP, reissue) 15

HAYSTACKS BALBOA
70 Polydor 2489 002 — HAYSTACKS BALBOA (LP) 100

JIMMY HEATH
60 Riverside RLP 333 — REALLY BIG (LP) 15

HELLACOPTERS
99 Butcher's Hook HOOK 004 — A House Is Not A Motel/POWDER MONKEYS: Destination X (p/s) 5
01 Polar 158 801 2 — FLIGHT CASE (enhanced CD EP, box set with patch & insert) 12

(see also Super$hit666)

HERITAGE
82 Plant Life PLR 040 — LIVING BY THE AIR (LP) 15

WOODY HERMAN
66 CBS 202522 — Sidewinder/Playgirl 10

HERRMAN & KLEINE
99 City Centre Offices BLOCK 5 — TRANSALPIN EP (12", plain sleeve with inserts, 1050 only) 12

HIDDEN CAMERAS
04 Rough Trade RTRADST 117 — PLAY THE CBC SESSIONS EP (10", 2,000 only) 12

HIGHBURY MARCHERS
72 Columbia DB 8930 — The Official Arsenal March/Arsenal Boogie 5

MINT VALUE £

HIGH LEVEL RANTERS
69 Leader/Trailer LER 2007 — THE LADS OF NORTHUMBERLAND (LP) 15

HIGSONS
82 Two Tone 21 CHSTT — Tear The Whole Thing Down/Ylang Ylang (p/s, paper labels) 10
82 Two Tone 21 CHSTT — Tear The Whole Thing Down/Ylang Ylang (12", p/s) 15
83 Two Tone 24 CHSTT — Run Me Down/Put The Punk Back Into Funk (p/s, paper labels) 10
83 Two Tone 24 CHSTT — Run Me Down/Put The Punk Back Into Funk (12", p/s) 15
81 Waap 1 WAAP — Lost & The Lonely/It Goes Waap (p/s) 5
81 Waap 1 WAAPLP — ATTACK OF THE CANNIBAL ZOMBIE B MEN (LP) 15

HIJACK
88 Music Of Life NOTE016 — Style Wars (12") 15
88 Music Of Life NOTE021 — Hold No Hostage (12") 10
89 Music Of Life NOTE016R — Style Wars Revenge (12") 8
89 Rhyme Syndicate 7599-26386 — Badman is Robbin'/Hold No Hostage/Doomsday (12" EP) 15
91 Rhyme Syndicate 6555176 — HORNS OF JERICHO (LP) 20

AL HIRT
62 RCA Victor SF 7531 — HORN A-PLENTY (LP) 20

TREVOR HOCKEY
70s Beau Brummie TET 120ST — Happy 'Cos I'm Blue/THE BLUES PLAYERS: Keep Right On To The End Of The Road (p/s) 40

GLENN HODDLE ET AL.
80s Lyntone LYN 11782 — Mastermind Of Soccer (Parts 1 & 2) (coloured flexi, with *Match Weekly* magazine) 10/8
80s Flexi Ltd — Mastermind Of Soccer (Parts 1-3) (coloured flexi, with Peter Withe & Alan Kennedy, with *Match Weekly* magazine) 10/8

HOM BRU
82 Celtic Music CM 009 — OBADEEA: MUSIC FROM SHETLAND AND BEYOND (LP) 12

HOME SERVICE
84 Coda NAT 001 — THE MYSTERIES (LP) 15

HONEYCRACK
95 PPP1 — King Of Misery/5 Minutes (numbered p/s, 1500 only sold at gigs) 15
95 PPPCD1 — King Of Misery/5 Minutes (numbered card p/s, 1500 only sold at gigs) 20
96 Epic XPR 2062 — Animals (Martin Steib Industrial Remix)/Sitting At Home (Renegade Soundwave Mix) (12", title-stickered plain black sleeve, promo only) 15
96 EG EGO 52-P — Anyway (CD-R, info-stickered case, promo only) 12
96 Epic 484230 0 — PROZAIC (LP, with inner sleeve, white vinyl, 2000 only) 15
96 Epic 484230 1 — PROZAIC (LP, with inner sleeve, black vinyl) 15

(see also Jellys, Wildhearts)

HOT CITY
71 London HLU 10344 — Leaving/I Believe In Life 15

ROD HULL & EMU/BRISTOL ROVERS FOOTBALL TEAM
74 EMI EMI 2734 — I'd Do Anything/Bristol Rovers All The Way 5

HAMISH IMLACH
67 Xtra XTRA 1050 — LIVE! (LP) 12

I'M NOT A GUN
00s City Centre Offices BLOCK 018 — Make Sense And Loose/(mixes) (12" EP, custom sleeve) 8

INSIDE OF A ROUGH TRADE SHOP
98 For Us/Out-There FU 005/OV 003 — CARNAGE: LIVE EP (CD, 50 only, numbered, some with full-colour back tray art) 30/20

INSIDE OV A BUTCHER'S SHOP
98 Out-There OTT CD 2 — Banking On Death — Carnage (CD, 50 only, numbered hand-made sleeve with fake dollar bill) 30

INSIDE OV A COFFIN
98 Out-There OTT 1 — Banking On Death (7", existence unconfirmed)
98 Out-There OTT CD 1 — Banking On Death (CD, 50 only, in hand-made sleeve with fake dollar bill) 30

(see also Freed Unit)

INSYNC Vs MYSTERON
97 Fat Cat 12FAT 004 — TALES FROM THE CRYPT (12", custom sleeve) 15

INTIMATE STRANGERS
75 Alaska ALA 1005 — Love Sounds/The Track 50

IRON MAIDEN
98 EMI EM 507 — The Angel And The Gambler/Blood On The World's Hands (Live) (p/s) 5

JACKIE & BRIDIE
77 J & B CNN 5939 — COME DAY GO DAY (LP) 12
77 J & B CNN 5949 — HOW CAN YOU KEEP FROM SINGING WITH... (LP) 12

JACKSON SISTERS
00 Fab FAB 004 — Rocksteady/STOVELLS: Hang On In There 5

HANK JACOBS
83 Sue ENS 5 — SO FAR AWAY EP: So Far Away/Out Of Sight/Hank's Groove/Summertime 10

JASMIN T
69 Tangerine DP 13 — Some Other Guy/Evening (p/s) 150

MINT VALUE £

JAZZ COURIERS
50s (no cat. no.) Top Spot Blues/Monk Was Here/Last Minute Blues (square flexi) 100
80s Jasmine JASM 2004 THE JAZZ COURIERS (LP, reissue) 20
80s Jasmine JASM 2024 THE LAST WORD (LP, reissue) 15

JEGA
98 Planet Mu ZIQ 001 TYPE XERO EP (12") 50

JELLYS
98 Mission Impossible MIRVL1 WELCOME TO OUR WORLD (LP, with inner sleeve, mail-order only) 12
(see also Honeycrack, Wildhearts)

JIMBILIN
75 Ashanti ASH 421 Balaclava/Tacku 18

LAURIE JOHNSON
66 Pye NPL 18136 TWO CITIES SUITE (LP) 15
70 Columbia SCX 6412 SYNTHESIS (LP) 25

JONAH
85 MW MW 7853 Tough/This Is Love (no p/s) 280

ROBIN JONES & HIS QUINTET
71 Apollo Sound APPS 5012 DENGA (LP) 40
71 Apollo Sound EL MAJA (LP) 50

JOYFUL SOUND
73 SRT SRT 73278 IT WILL BE WORTH IT ALL (LP) 300

JSD BAND
72 Cube HFLY 11 JSD BAND (LP) 15

JUST BROTHERS
80s Soul City SC 127 Carlena/IVORIES: Please Stay (die-cut company sleeve) 8

JUSTIN & KARLSSON
67 Piccadilly 7N 35295 Somewhere They Can't Find Me/What More Do You Want 12

KIRI TE KANAWA
91 MPL/EMI KIRIS 1 The World You're Coming Into/Tres Conejos (p/s) 15
91 MPL/EMI KIRICD 1 The World You're Coming Into/Tres Conejos (CD) 25
91 MPL/EMI KIRIS 2 Save The Child/The Drinking Song (p/s) 15
91 MPL/EMI KIRICD 2 Save The Child/The Drinking Song (CD) 25
91 MPL/EMI CDKIRIS 2 Save The Child/The Drinking Song/The World You're Coming Into (CD) 150

KEANE
03 Fierce Panda NING 133 Everybody's Changing/Bedshaped/The Way You Want It (CD) 25
03 Fierce Panda NING 147 This Is The Last Time/Can't Stop Now/Allemande (CD, 4,000 only) 10

KEELE ROW & KEELE UNIVERSITY STUDENTS
64 Flexi STANLEY MATTHEWS (EP, flexi) 30

CALUM KENNEDY
62 Ember EMB 5167 The Celtic Chorus/Danny Boy 40

MIKE KENNEDY
72 Youngblood YB 1035 Louisiana/Look Up In The Sky 20

KICKS
80 Carrere CAR 138 Get Off The Telephone/Big Boys Don't Cry (p/s) 30

BOBBY KINGDOM
61 Bluebeat BB 44 Honey Please/BLUE BEATS: That's My Girl 25

KING HORROR
70 Reggae REG 3005 Slave Driver 20

KING OF LUXEMBOURG
86 él GPO 14 Valleri/Sketches Of Luxembourg (p/s) 12

KIRBY STONE FOUR
62 CBS BPG 62040 GUYS & DOLLS (LP, gatefold sleeve) 12

KLAXON 5
86 él GPO 20 Never Underestimate The Ignorance Of The Rich/
Great Railway Journeys (p/s) 10

MOE KOFFMAN
74 CBS S 73245 FOUR SEASONS IN ROCK (LP) 15

V. KONGS
63 Halagala HG 18 Tomorrow Will Soon Be Here/Pretty Little Girl 20

KOP CHOIR
72 Hallmark SHM 794 THE KOP CHOIR (LP) 30

ANNIE LENNOX
93 RCA 74321 12883-1 LITTLE BIRD EP (12", remixes by N-Joi et al.) 10

LEONARD FAMILY
72 Beacon BEA 186 Once You Understand/It Won't Happen Again 6

LITTLE ANN
99 Kent TOWN 112 Who Are You Trying To Fool/I Got To Have You 20

LOVECUT D.B.
92 Suburbs Of Hell SOH 011EP JOURNEY TO THE CENTRE OF LOVE EP (12") 10
(see also Sarah Cracknell, St. Etienne)

MINT VALUE £

LUCY SHOW
85 A&M AMY 261 — Ephemeral/White Space (12", p/s) 20

MARDEN HILL
86 él GPO 18 — Curtain/Let's Make Shane & MacKenzie (p/s) 10
87 él GPO 30 — Robe/Hangman (p/s) 8

McPEAKE FAMILY/FOLK GROUP
60s Topic TOP 92 — WILD MOUNTAIN THYME (EP) 12
60s Topic — IRISH TRADITIONAL FOLK SONGS AND MUSIC (LP, blue label) 30
60s Topic 12T 87 — THE McPEAKE FAMILY (LP) 20

MAX HEADROOM & THE CARPARKS
82 Bandwagon B001 — Soldier (no p/s) 30

MENACE
86 Razor RAZ 18 — GLC — RIP (LP) 25

MENACE
01 Plastica DPFT 004 — Reap What You Sow (12") 15

TONY MIDDLETON
80s Joker JK 0002 — Spanish Maiden/JIMMY MACK: My World Is On Fire/ METROS: Since I Found My Baby 8

MILLIONAIRES
67 Mercury 6052301 — Never For Me/If I Had You Babe 10

SEXTON MING
90s Hangman's Daughter HANG 018UP — 6 MORE MILES TO THE GRAVEYARD (LP) 12

MINTY
94 Candy CAN 1V — Useless Man (Version)/(King Rocker Mix)/(The Grid Extended Mix)/ (Dis-Cuss Mix)(12", p/s) 12
95 Sugar SUGA 6V — Plastic Bag/(Foil-Wrapped Mix)/(Partycrashers Mix)/ (French Movie Mix) (12", p/s) 8

BARBARA MOORE (SOUND)
01 Jazzman JM 018 — Hot Heels/Grey Sigh 5

GIORGIO MORODER
90s Cause-N-Effect — I Wanna Rock You (Thee Maddcat Mix)/(Thee DrumDrum Mix) (12", no p/s) 15
90s Cause-N-Effect — FROM HERE TO ETERNITY (LP) 20
00s Logic — THE CHASE (2-LP) 20

MOUSEFOLK
80s Tea Time SURFS UP 03 — Grannie's Cake Crisis/Mrs Marr's Daughter (foldaround p/s, with badge) 5

NINO NARDINI
01 Jazzman JM 019 — Tropicola/ANTHONY KING: Filigree Funk 5

NEGATIVES IN COLOUR
90s own label NEG 1 — Caught In Possession 15

NERVES
94 Inflammable Material BURN 2 — Bits/SUBSTANDARD: Rostock (p/s) 7

ART NEVILLE
58 Specialty SON 5008 — Cha-Dooky-Doo/Zing Zing 25

NEWS FROM BABEL
89 ReR 6116 RE 6116 — WORK RESUMED ON THE TOWER (LP) 18

PAUL NICHOLAS
71 Polydor 2058 086 — The World Is Beautiful/Lamplighter 30

999
79 Radar ADA 46 — Found Out Too Late/Lie, Lie, Lie 50

PARTISANS
82 No Future OI 2 — Police Story/Killing Machine (p/s) 12
82 No Future OI 12 — 17 Years Of Hell/The Power And The Greed/Bastards In Blue (p/s) 10
83 Cloak & Dagger PART 1 — Blind Ambition/Come Clean/Change (p/s) 12
83 No Future PUNK 4 — THE PARTISANS (LP) 18
84 Cloak & Dagger PARTLP 1 — THE TIME WAS RIGHT (LP, with lyric inner) 30

PET SHOP BOYS
88 Parlophone PCSX 7325 — INTROSPECTIVE (LP, 3 x black vinyl 12", with picture labels & wraparound paper obi strip) 15

PICARDY
68 Statside SIDE 8004 — Montage/How Sweet It Is 5

POOH STICKS
88 Fierce FRIGHT 023 — Heartbreak (1-sided, etched B-side, hand-coloured promo p/s, with insert) 40
80s Fierce FRIGHT 028 — HEROES AND VILLAINS (LP, with inner) 18

PRAMS
86 Classic Quotes CLASS 1 — Black Sheep/Classic Quotes (p/s) 5
80s Wabbit — WHAT'S THE TIME, MR WOLF? (LP) 20

ELVIS PRESLEY
04 BMG 82876 619211 — That's All Right/Blue Moon Of Kentucky (10", brown die-cut sleeve, with 'Sun' labels) 40

MINT VALUE £

PSYLONS

87	Iron Lung IL 001	All The Things We Need (12", p/s)	15
90	Unsigned UN 001	No Choice (p/s)	8
91	Unsigned UN 002	SAND MAN EP	8

PUSSY GALORE

87	Vinyl Drip SUK 001	GROOVY HATE FUCK (LP)	20
87	Product Inc. 33PROD 19	RIGHT NOW (LP)	18

QUATERMASS

97	Metropolitan MM 027	The Judgement (12", no p/s)	15

REDCELL

93	B12 008	INTERIM EP (12", no p/s)	18

RED CHAIR FADEAWAY

90s	Waterbomb SPLAT 002	Never Remember/FUDGE: unknown track (flexi, p/s)	12

RED LONDON

84	Razor RAZ 10	THIS IS ENGLAND (LP)	40

RIVAL SAVAGES

80	Savage VC 1968	Get Some (gatefold p/s)	25

JOHN SCOTT

68	Spark SRL 1008	Amsterdam Affair Theme/Kathleen	10

SEPTIC DEATH

88	Pusmort PUS 00703	Kichigai (p/s)	5

STEPPES

87	Help HELPF 101	History Hates No Man/BEVIS FROND: African Violets (flexi)	8

T.I.M.E. (Trust In Men Everywhere)

68	Liberty LBL/LBS 83144	T.I.M.E. (LP)	50

TIMES

89	Creation CRE 071 T	Manchester (12", p/s)	10

(see also Television Personalities, Teenage Filmstars, O Level, Biff Bang Pow!, L'Orange Mechanik)

T.S.O.L.

81	Frontier FLP 1004	DANCE WITH ME (LP)	18

DEXTER WANSEL

77	Phil. Intl ZS8 3616	Disco Lights/Ode Infinitum (no p/s)	18
78	Phil. Intl. PIR 6255	All Night Long/What The World Is Coming To	10
80s	CBS	LIFE ON MARS (LP)	25

PETA WEBB & PETE COOPER

86	Heart	HEART IS TRUE (LP)	15

LENNY WHITE

79	Elektra K 12328	Lady Madonna/12 Bars From Mars	5
81	Elektra K 12500	Kid Stuff/Slipaway	5
83	Elektra ED 4921	My Turn To Love You (Special Mix)/(Dub Version) (12")	12

PAUL WILLIAMS

74	A&M AMS 7125	That's What Friends Are For/Born To Fly	8
74	A&M AMLS 63653	PHANTOM OF THE PARADISE (LP, soundtrack)	20

PAUL WILLIAMS

70s	Parry Music Library PML 168	AQUARIUS (LP)	18

WONKY ALICE

92	Pomona POM 004	SIRIUS EP (12", p/s)	12

ROY WOOD

78	Warner Bros K 17248	Keep Your Hands On The Wheel/Giant Footsteps	6

WORDBUG

94	Boss Tunage BOSTAGE 021	Locked In (p/s)	8
94	Boss Tunage BOSTAGE 023	Died Waiting (p/s, blue vinyl, with insert)	7

YELLO

89	Phonogram YDJ 6	Metropolitan Mixdown Part 1 (12" promo, p/s)	10
89	Mercury YELLO 312	Of Course I'm Lying/Oh Yeah//Yello Metropolitan Mixdown (2x12" in gatefold sleeve, with inners)	10
92	Mercury MRXX 376	Jungle Bill (Andy Weatherall Mixes) (p/s)	5

ZEITGEIST

82	Jamming CREATE 4	Stop (p/s)	5

Z'EV

88	Coercion COERCIONLP 001	THE INVISIBLE MAN (LP)	30

VARIOUS ARTISTS

85	Steeltrax JCI 7102	AXE ATTACK (LP)	30

RECORD COLLECTOR BACK ISSUES

A COMPLETE INDEX TO ALL ARTISTS FEATURED IN PREVIOUS ISSUES

THE ARTISTS, SUBJECTS AND LABELS COVERED IN BACK ISSUES ARE LISTED IN ALPHABETICAL ORDER.

D – discography R – review I – interview F – feature

NOTE: Issues numbered 1 - 38, 146, 160, 170, 182, 183, 184, 240, 245, 249, 256, 283, 284, 285, 290, 291, 293, 294, 297, 298 are all OUT-OF-PRINT

Indexes to the UK SOUL, SPECIAL PRESSINGS and COLLECTABLE INDIE SINGLES series listings are printed at the end of the main listing. The issue in which artists/groups/labels appear is shown by the number in brackets after each entry. Issues up to and including No. 46 are A5 size and issues from No. 47 onwards are A4 size.

All the discographies are UK RELEASES ONLY unless stated otherwise. The values were current at the time each issue was published. (*) indicates the discography is unpriced.

For full details of how to obtain Back Issues, please see a current issue of **RECORD COLLECTOR** or email **janice.mayne@metropolis.co.uk** or phone **(+44) 0870 735 8080**

A

ABBA: Rarities (42); & D (144); D (158); R (184); R (212); F (217); F (6); D (265)
ABBEY ROAD: F & D (223)
ABC: I (263)
ABSURD LABEL: D (255)
ACE RECORDS: F (256)
AC/DC: D (91); I, D, F, (197); R & I (222)
ACID JAZZ: F (290)
ACID MOTHERS TEMPLE: F & D (261)
DAVID ACKLES: F & D (237)
A CERTAIN RATIO: I & D (188)
ACT: I (294)
THE ACTION: F & D (94)
ADAM & THE ANTS: F & D (114); D (256)
BRYAN ADAMS: F & D (148)
HASIL ADKINS: F (277)
THE ADVERTS: F & D (113)
AEROSMITH: F & D (119); R (173)
AEROVONS: F (282)
A-HA: F & D (80); F & D (116)
JAN AKKERMAN: F (219)
THE ALARM: F & D (84); R (253)
THE ALBION BAND: I & D (174)
ARTHUR ALEXANDER: F & D (66)
ALL ABOUT EVE: F & D (113)
THE ALLMAN BROTHERS: R (122)
ALL SAINTS: R & D (227)
ALL TOMORROW'S PARTIES: R (250)
MARC ALMOND/SOFT CELL: F & D (103); F & D (223); F & D (224); F & D(225); I (266). See also SOFT CELL.
ALTERED IMAGES: F & D (129)
ALTERNATIVE TV: F & D (211)
AMAZING BLONDEL: I & D (191)
AMBIENT MUSIC: F & D (178)
AMEN: I & D (266)
AMON DUUL II: F & D (167)
TORI AMOS: F & D (176); I & D (243)
GERRY ANDERSON: F & D (167); F & D (168); F & D (173)
IAN ANDERSON: F (264); I(293)
THE ANIMALS: D (76); I & D (183); F & D (184); F (256). See also ERIC BURDON.
PAUL ANKA: F & D (155)
ANTHRAX: F & D (101); I (247)
AOR: F (234)
APPLE LABEL: D (46); D & I (108); D(152)
ARAB STRAP: I & D (247)
JOAN ARMATRADING: F & D (158)
THE ART OF NOISE & ZTT: D (110); I (238)
PP ARNOLD: I (295)
THE ARTWOODS: I & D (153)
ASH: I & D (196)
ASIA: F & D (192); Geoff Downes: I. See also JOHN WETTON.
THE ASSOCIATES: F & R (252) See also BILLY MacKENZIE.
THE ASSOCIATION: F & D (118)
'AS TIME GOES BY': F (237); F (238); F (239); F (240)
RICK ASTLEY & D (115)
ATLANTIC JAZZ: D (270)
ATOMIC ROOSTER & D (104)
BRIAN AUGER: F (257)
AUCTIONS: F(218); F (221); F (230); F (239); F (291) See also BONHAM'S, CHRISTIE'S and SOTHEBY'S.
AUSTRALASIAN GARAGE ROCK: F (287)
AUTUMN RECORDS: D (210)
'THE AVENGERS' & D (171)
DAVID AXELROD & D (254); I (265)
KEVIN AYERS: I & D (154); I (229)
ROY AYERS: F (290)
AZTEC CAMERA: I & D (244)

B

BABES IN TOYLAND: I & D (190)
BABYBIRD: I (267)
BURT BACHARACH: R (196)
'BACKTRACK' LABEL & D (101)
BAD COMPANY: F (277)
BADFINGER & D (109); R (256)
BADLY DRAWN BOY: I & D (246)
DANNY BAKER: F (176)
LAVERN BAKER & D (61)
ED BALL: I & D (194)
HANK BALLARD: F (284)
BANANARAMA & D (38); D(101)
THE BAND & US/UK D (48); R (254) See also ROBBIE ROBERTSON.
THE BANGLES & D (91)
PETER BANKS: I & D (169)
BARCLAY JAMES HARVEST & D (111); R & D (240); F (276)
BASTA LABEL: F (230)
BBC RADIOPHONIC WORKSHOP: F (255)
BRIGITTE BARDOT: D (188)
SYD BARRETT & Pink Floyd: D (104); F (258); F (271) See also PINK FLOYD.
GARY BARLOW: R (205). See also TAKE THAT.
THE BARRON KNIGHTS & D (64)
JOHN BARRY: F & D 1957-64 (182); D (262)
SHIRLEY BASSEY: R (185); F & D (222)
BATH FESTIVAL R & F (259)
'BATMAN' & Related: D (217)
BAUHAUS & D (98); R (246)
BBC RADIO SESSIONS: I (113); I & R (149); I & R (169)
THE BEACH BOYS: D (40); D (65); D (80); I (133); D (141); R (201); F (224); R (229); F (248); I (259); R (262); F (270); F (300). See also MIKE LOVE, BRIAN WILSON.
THE BEASTIE BOYS & D (232); D (245)
THE BEATLES: D (38); F & D (41); F (44); D (45); F; I (50); D (62); D (70); D (83); R (92); F (94); R (94); F (98); I (108); D (112); D/R (115); D (122); F (128); R (132); D (140); D (146); D (151); F (158); F (166); D (170); D (175); D (176); I (177); D(178); D (181); D (182); D (183); R (184); F (187); I & D (193); F, R, F (195); I & D (196); R (197); R (200); F (206); R (207); R (208); F (211); F (212); F (215); R & I (219); I (227); D (230); F (233); F (235); F (236); F (241); F & I & R (242); R (243); F(250); R (253); F (254); R (256); F (267); F (268); F (270); F (278); F (283); F (284); R(292). See also GEORGE HARRISON, JOHN LENNON, PAUL McCARTNEY, RINGO STARR.

BEATS INTERNATIONAL & D (136)
See also THE HOUSEMARTINS.
THE BEAU BRUMMELS & UK/US D (75)
THE BEAUTIFUL SOUTH & D (136); I & D (240).
See also THE HOUSEMARTINS.
BE-BOP DELUXE & Bill Nelson: D (220)
BECK: I & D (224); I (280)
THE BEE GEES: F & D (85); F & D (100)
BELLE & SEBASTIAN & D (237)
ARIEL BENDER: I (207)
BOYD BENNETT: F (278)
CLIFF BENNETT & THE REBEL ROUSERS:
F & D (49); F & D (265)
CHUCK BERRY: D (53); R (124); R & D (150);
F (276)
DAVE BERRY & D (48)
RICHARD BERRY & D (173)
PETE BEST: I & D (193)
THE BETA BAND & D (239)
THE BETTERDAYS: I & D (143)
THE BEVIS FROND & D (116); I (174)
THE B-52s & D (132); I (228); D (271)
THE BIG BOPPER & D (116)
BIG BROTHER & THE HOLDING COMPANY
& Big Brother/Janis Joplin: D (88).
See also JANIS JOPLIN.
BIG COUNTRY & D (130); I (163); F (271); F (276)
THE BIG THREE & D (83)
THE BIRDS: F & D (239).
See also THE CREATION, QUIET MELON,
RONNIE WOOD.
JANE BIRKIN I (282)
THE BIRTHDAY PARTY & BOYS NEXT DOOR
& D (151); I (240).
See also NICK CAVE.
BJORK & Sugarcubes: D (175); D (234); I (276).
See also THE SUGARCUBES.
CILLA BLACK: I & D (51); I & D (217)
TONY BLACKBURN: I (280)
THE BLACK CROWES & D (169)
BLACK DOG: I (285)
BLACK FLAG: I & D (184).
See also HENRY ROLLINS.
RITCHIE BLACKMORE: I & D (228).
See also DEEP PURPLE.
CHARLES BLACKWELL: I & D (228)
OTIS BLACKWELL: F (277)
BLACK SABBATH & D (74); R (246).
See also TONY MARTIN, OZZY OSBOURNE.
BLAXPLOITATION: R (226); R (260)
BLIND FAITH & D (118).
See also ERIC CLAPTON.
'BLINDS & SHUTTERS': R (131)
BLONDIE: D (66); F & D (241); D (266)
BLODWYN PIG: I & D (200)
THE BLOW MONKEYS: I & D (183)
BLUE BEAT LABEL & D (192)
BLUE CHEER & D (197)
BLUE HORIZON LABEL: D (55); D (67)
BLUE OYSTER CULT: I (293)
BLUES: F & D (155); F (293)
THE BLUETONES: I & D (200)
COLIN BLUNSTONE: I & D (226).
See also THE ZOMBIES.
BLUR & D (179); I & R & D (211); F (224);
R & D (242)
CURT BOETTCHER & US: D (229)
MARC BOLAN/TYRANNOSAURUS REX/T.REX:
D (36); D (54); D (64); D (84); D (95); F & D (77);
F (127); F (128); F & D (144); R (179); F (190);
F & D (191); R (207); I (210); F & D (217);
F (257); I (277).
See also MICKEY FINN, JOHN'S CHILDREN.
GRAHAM BOND & D (38)
'JAMES BOND': F & D (158); CD Reissues (286)
BONHAM'S ROCK MEMORABILIA AUCTIONS: F (183)
BON JOVI & D (93); D (111)
BONNIE PRINCE BILLY: F & D & I (295)
BONZO DOG BAND & D (100); I (258)
BOOKER T. & THE MGs: R & D (231)
THE BOO RADLEYS: I & D (192)
BOOTLEGS: F (149); F (240); F (252); F (273)
BOSTON & D (234)
DAVID BOWIE: D(43); F (48); D (63); F (75); D (85);
F & D (90); F (109); F (97); F (103); F (116);
D (118); R (123); F (126); F & D (131);
F (137); F & D (141); F & D (147); F & D (153);
F (159); I & R (165); F & D (172); D (185);
R (190); R (197); F (207); D (208); R (215);
F (222); F (226); F (227); F (243); F & D (249);
F (251); F (254); F (259) F (278); R (283);
F (286); F (299).
See also TIN MACHINE.
JOE BOYD: I & D (122)
BOY GEORGE: I (240); I (277).
See also CULTURE CLUB.
BOYZONE & D (250)
KIRK BRANDON: I (191)
BRAZILIAN COLLECTABLES: F
BREAD: I & D (219)
THE BREEDERS: F & I (275)
BRITAIN'S RAREST RECORDS (232)
BRITISH COMEDY & D (236)
BRITISH INVASION & US D (114)
BRITISH ROCK'N'ROLL: I & D (161)
BRITPOP NOW (194)
BRITPOP THEN (195)
BRONSKI BEAT & D (72)
ELKIE BROOKS: I & D (177)
BROS & D (109)
ARTHUR BROWN: I & D (129); F (169)
JAMES BROWN & D (40); D (60); F & D (214);
F & D (215); F & D (216); D & F (217)
JOE BROWN & D (138)
PETE BROWN & D (114); I (270)
RUTH BROWN & D (65)
JACKSON BROWNE & D (102); I (220)
DENNY BRUCE: I (223)
BRUMBEAT F & D (180)
BUBBLEGUM MUSIC & D (74)
JEFF BUCKLEY & D (284)
TIM BUCKLEY & D (103)
BUFFALO SPRINGFIELD & D (142)
See also CS&N, CSN&Y, NEIL YOUNG.
ERIC BURDON & Animals: D (183); Solo: D (184);
I (209).
See also THE ANIMALS.
LEROY BURGESS: F (277)
SONNY BURGESS: I & D (153)
SOLOMON BURKE & D (69); I (276)
J.J. BURNEL: D & F (159).
See also THE STRANGLERS.
JOHNNY & DORSEY BURNETTE & D (146)
KEN BURNS: F (264)

JAMES BURTON: D162)
KATE BUSH: F & D (76); F (92); F & D (113); D (124); F (152); F (170); F & D (233); F (262).
THE BUTTERFIELD BLUES BAND & D (89)
THE BUTTHOLE SURFERS & D (114)
BUYING & SELLING BY POST (123)
BUZZCOCKS & D (113); I (167); F & I (213); F & D (249); F (272)
THE BYRDS: D (84); D (85); F (96); R (105); F & D (130); F & D (131); R (200); F (207); R (210); F (221); I (248); F (271); F (282). See also CHRIS HILLMAN.
BYG/ACTUEL Jazz reissue label (273)
DAVID BYRNE: I. See also TALKING HEADS.

C

CABARET VOLTAIRE & D (145); I (269)
TERRY CALLIER: D (222)
JOHN CALE: I & D (159); I (219); I (290). See also THE VELVET UNDERGROUND.
CAN & D (113); I (183); F (217); R (237)
CANNED HEAT & D (136); I (200)
FREDDY CANNON & D (142)
CANTERBURY SCENE: F (154)
CAPITAL RADIO HALL OF FAME (53)
CAPITOL RECORDS: F (255)
CAPTAIN BEEFHEART & D (90); F (217); F & I (224); R (243)
CAPTAIN SCARLET & D (173)
CARAVAN & D (83); I (176); R(260)
THE CARDIGANS: I & D (244)
BELINDA CARLISLE & Solo/Go-Go's: D (111)
MARY-CHAPIN CARPENTER: I (170)
THE CARPENTERS: I & D (125)
RONNIE CARROLL & D (209)
CARTER U.S.M. & D (151); I & F (222)
JOHNNY CASH & D (58); R (197); R (252); F (271); R (287)
CAST & D (217)
CATATONIA: I & D (236)
MALCOLM CATTO: I & F (266)
NICK CAVE AND THE BAD SEEDS: F (225); & D (226). See THE BIRTHDAY PARTY.
CAY: I & D (242)
CBGBs & Hilly Kristal: I (273)
CD ROM: Introduction (184)
CELEBRITY RECORDS: D (238)
GUY CHADWICK: I & D (222) See also THE HOUSE OF LOVE.
CHAS CHANDLER: F (205)
THE CHAMELEONS & D(137); I (265)
THE CHAMPS: D (84)
CHANGING FACE OF COLLECTING (122)
CHARISMA LABEL: R (172)
THE CHARLATANS: I & D (193); I (271)
RAY CHARLES & D (45); F (250); R (251); F (269); I (278)
CHARTS: F (159); F (279)
CHEAP TRICK & D (137); R (206)
CHELSEA: I & D (247)
THE CHEMICAL BROTHERS & D (242)
CHER & D (106)
CHERRY RED: F (286)
CHESS LABEL & D (127); D (273)
CHICAGO: R (178)
CHIFFONS & D (132)
CHILDREN'S RECORDS (208)
NICKY CHINN: I (233)
CHISWICK LABEL: I, D & R (196)
CHARLIE CHRISTIAN: F (281)
BILLY CHILDISH & I (291)
CHRISTIE'S ROCK MEMORABILIA AUCTIONS: F (72); F (76); F (78); F (86); F (98); F (110); F (118); F (122); F (131); F (139); F (143); F (159); F (165); F (170); F (180); F (183); F (192); F (234); F (286)
CHRISTMAS RECORDS 1995 & D (184); F (208); F (220); F (233); F (293)
THE CHURCH & D (138)
THE CLANGERS: F (266)
CLANNAD & D (202)
ERIC CLAPTON: D (40); F (52); D (94); R (106); R (152); R (200); F (238); I (282). See also BLIND FAITH, CREAM, THE YARDBIRDS.
THE DAVE CLARK FIVE: D (56); F & I (138); I & D (166)
PETULA CLARK & D (77); F & D (120); F & D (131); R (193); R (239)
THE CLASH & D (80); R (178); R (194); F (206); R (243); F (260). See also JOE STRUMMER
CLASS OF '96 (208); '97 (221); '98 (233)
MERRY CLAYTON: I (289)
CLEANING RECORDS (69)
CLINIC: I & D (252)
GEORGE CLINTON: I & D(162)
EDDIE COCHRAN: F & D (79); F (107); R (112); D (181); F & D (256)
JOE COCKER & D (46)
ALMA COGAN & D (81)
LEONARD COHEN & D (110)
NAT 'KING' COLE & D (66)
COLLECTING: F (240); F (242); F (245)
BOOTSY COLLINS & D (265)
EDWYN COLLINS: I (157); F & D (193); F & D (194)
GLENDA COLLINS: F & D (225)
PHIL COLLINS & D (87); F (257). See also GENESIS.
COLOSSEUM & D (164)
COME & D (163)

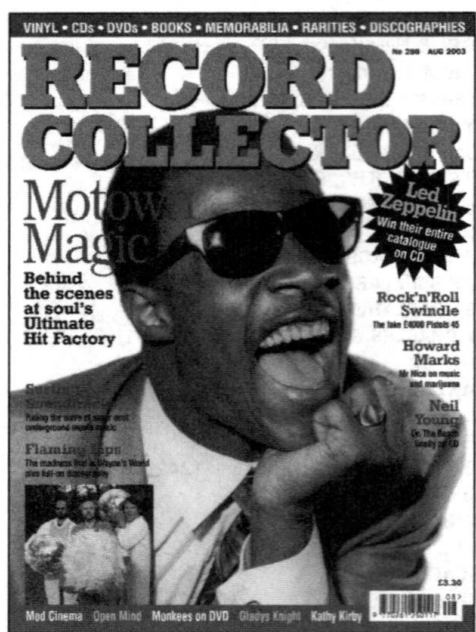

BRITISH COMEDY RECORDS: F (71)
THE COMMUNARDS & D (102)
COMPACT DISCS: F (93); F (87); F (88); F (89); F (90); F (94); D (104); F (105); F (106); F (107); F (108); D (109); D (110); F (152); F (223)
CONFLICT: F (270)
BRIAN CONNOLLY: F & D (212). See also THE SWEET.
CONVENTIONS: F (110)
RUSS CONWAY: R (195)
RY COODER & D (59)
SAM COOKE & D (44); D (243)
ALICE COOPER & D (97); R (238); I (267)
JULIAN COPE: I (267)
THE CORAL: I (283); F (290)
CORNERSHOP: I & D (225)
HUGH CORNWELL: I (168). See also THE STRANGLERS.
THE CORRS & D (239)
ELVIS COSTELLO: F (49); D (91); R (171); I & D (193); I & D (194)
COUGARS, BARONS, NERO & GLADIATORS & D (72)
COUNTRY JOE & FISH: F & D (83); R (204); I & D (227)
COUNTRY MUSIC: F(141); F (144); F (168)
COUNTRY ROCK SPECIAL: F & D (166)
JAYNE COUNTY: I & D (197)
COVER VERSIONS (209)
GRAHAM COXON: I (279)
KEVIN COYNE: I (275)
CRADLE OF FILTH: I & D (234)
CRAMPS & D (78)
CRASS: I (300)
RANDY CRAWFORD & D (54)
CREAM: F & D (101) R (217); I, F & D (218). See also ERIC CLAPTON.
THE CREATION: I, F & D (191); F & I (299). See also THE BIRDS.
THE CREATURES: I & D (240). See also SIOUXSIE & THE BANSHEES.
CREEDENCE CLEARWATER REVIVAL: F & D (98); F (269)
CRICKETS: F & D (128).
DAVID CROSBY: I (116); I (265). See also CS&N, CSN&Y.
CROSBY, STILLS & NASH & D (41). See also DAVID CROSBY.
CROSBY, STILLS, NASH & YOUNG & D (115); R (200). See also DAVID CROSBY, NEIL YOUNG.
SHERYL CROW & D (215)
CROWDED HOUSE & D (154). See also NEIL FINN.
GARY CROWLEY: I (294)
CRUSHED BUTLER: F (226)
THE CULT & D (94); I & D (182); I (264)
CULTURE CLUB & D (53); I & D (231). See also BOY GEORGE.
THE CURE & D (61); F (106); F & D (167); F & D (168); F & D (169); R (187); F (252); F (282); I (293)
CURVED AIR & D (102)

D

DAKOTAS, EAGLES, HUNTERS & D (67)
DICK DALE & D (203)
ROGER DALTREY: I (239). See also THE WHO.
THE DAMNED: F & D (81); F & D (82); I (198); I (265)
DANCE: F (239)
DANDELION LABEL & Listing (149)
TONY DANGERFIELD: I & D (241)
DANGER MAN/THE PRISONER: D (162)
TERENCE TRENT D'ARBY & D (106); F (282)
BOBBY DARIN & D (149); R (197)
DARK & D (172)
THE DARKNESS: I (290); F (295)
SHAUN DAVEY: I (182)
DAVE DAVIES: I (270)
BILLIE DAVIS: I & D (233)
MILES DAVIS: F (219); R & D (225); D (266); R (283)
THE SPENCER DAVIS GROUP: I & D (198)
DAWN OF THE REPLICANTS: I & D (237)
DANIELLE DAX & THE LEMON KITTENS: I & D (123)
DORIS DAY: F & D (148); R (192)
CHRIS DE BURGH & D (86); I (266)
DEACON BLUE & D (130);
RICKY ROSS: I (262)
DEAD OR ALIVE & D (150); I (180)
JAMES DEAN: F (270)
ROGER DEAN: F(267)
DEATH IN VEGAS: I & D (278)
DECCA LABEL: I (167)
DAVE DEE, DOZY, BEAKY, MICK, TICH & D (41)
DECAL LABEL: I (114)
DECEPTIVE LABEL: F (222)
KIKI DEE: I & D (197)
DEEP PURPLE: D (67); R (191); F (222); I (227); F (247); D (272). See also RITCHIE BLACKMORE, EPISODE SIX, GLENN HUGHES.
DEEP SOUL: F (252)
DEF JAM: R (251)
DEF LEPPARD: F & D (100); I (171)
DEL AMITRI: F & D (230)
DEL-FI LABEL: D (224)
DEMOS, PROMOS & ACETATES: F (148)

TERRY DENE & D (62)
DENIM: F (166)
SANDY DENNY & D (109)
DEPECHE MODE & D (117); F (129); F & D (230)
DERAM LABEL: F & D (112)
DETOUR RECORDS: D (177)
DEVIL DOLL: F & D (177)
DEXY'S MIDNIGHT RUNNERS: F & D (41); I (253); F & I (272)
NEIL DIAMOND: F & D (142); R (210)
BO DIDDLEY: F &D (46); I (203); F (279)
DIMENSION LABEL: I (239)
DINOSAUR JR: I & D (162)
CELINE DION: F & D (207)
DION & BELMONTS: F & D (57); I (258)
DIRE STRAITS & D (44); F & D (79); F (86); D (100); D (111); I & D (173).
See also MARK KNOPFLER.
THE DIVINE COMEDY: I & D (235)
DOC THOMAS GROUP: F (224)
COXSON(E) DODD: F (299)
DODO RESURRECTION: F & D (164)
DOGS D'AMOUR: F & D (127)
FATS DOMINO: D (111); R (172)
LONNIE DONEGAN: I (93); R (173); I & D (249)
TANYA DONELLY: I & D (219)
DONOVAN: F & D (44); F & D (113); I (207); F & I (299)
JASON DONOVAN & KYLIE MINOGUE & D (123)
THE DOORS: F & D (105); I & R (143); R (219); F (237); F (239); I (251); F (275)
DOO-WOP GROUPS: D (87); D (88); R & F (178); R (210); F (259)
LEE DORSEY & D (55)
THE DOWNLINERS SECT: F & D (151)
NICK DRAKE: F & D (150); F (245)
JUDGE DREAD: I & D (212)
DREAM SYNDICATE: I (266)
DREAM THEATER: F (253)
DR FEELGOOD: F & D (214); F (266)
DR HOOK: I & D (207)
THE DRIFTERS: F & D (39); I & D (183); R (202); F (289)
DR JOHN: I & D (226)
DR ROBERT: I & F (216).
See also THE BLOW MONKEYS.
DRUNKEN FISH LABEL & Listing (165)
DR WHO & D (209)
DUFFY POWER: F (270)
JOHNNY DUNCAN: F & D (81)
SIMON DUPREE & BIG SOUND: F & D (80)
DURAN DURAN: D (63); D (240)
DURUTTI COLUMN: F & D (144); I (269)
IAN DURY: F & I (249)
JACQUES DUTRONC & D (235)
DVD-A EXPLAINED (284)
BOB DYLAN: F (51); F & D (73); F & D (74); F (95); F & D (109); F (116); R (127); R (128); F & D (137); R (140); D (150); F & I (157); D (164); F (180); R (190); F & I (201); R (204); F (212); R (218); I (223); R (232); F (250); F (253); F & R (261); F (267); F (272); R (291); F (294)

E

EARACHE LABEL: R (249)
EARWORM LABEL: I & D (240)
EAST EUROPEAN LPs: D (124)
EAST 17 & D (187)
EASY LISTENING: Special (199)
ECHO & THE BUNNYMEN & D (59); Electrafixion I & D (189); F (190); I & F (264)
ECHOBOY: I & D (248)
DUANE EDDY: F (167); R (184); R (244)
DAVE EDMUNDS: F & D (74); F & D (75)
JACKIE EDWARDS: F & D (53)
808 STATE & D (164)
ELASTICA & D (186)
ELECTRIC EELS: F (259)
THE ELECTRIC PRUNES & D (85); F & D (214); F (278)
ELECTROCLASH: F (276)
ELEKTRA: F (268)
ELEKTRIC MUSIC: I (170)
MARC ELLINGTON: F (299)
STEVE ELLIS: I & D (224)
E.L.O. & D (38); D (182)
EMBER RECORDS: D (224)
EMBRACE & D (256)
EMERSON, LAKE & PALMER & D (192); I (265)
ENIGMA: I (269)
JOHN ENTWISTLE: F (287)
EMINEM: R (259)
THE END: F (222)
BRIAN ENO & D (101); R (171)
EPISODE SIX & D (126).
See also DEEP PURPLE.
ERASURE & D (107); D (125); F (153)
ROKY ERICKSON / THE 13TH FLOOR ELEVATORS & D (147)
DAVID ESSEX: F & D (138); I & D (214)
GLORIA ESTEFAN & THE MIAMI SOUND MACHINE: F & D (162)
EUROVISION SONG CONTEST SPECIAL: F & D (165)
EURYTHMICS & D (55); F & D (149)
THE EVERLY BROTHERS: D (49); D (63); D (175)
EVERYTHING BUT THE GIRL: I & D (198)
EXOTICA: F (174)
EXTREME & D (161)
EXTREME METAL: F (241)
THE EYES & D (144)

F

FACTORY: F & D (204)
FACTORY LABEL: F (83); F 270)
FAIRPORT CONVENTION & D (52); F (262)
FAITH NO MORE & D (133); R (284)
ADAM FAITH: F (285)
MARIANNE FAITHFULL: F & D (39)
THE FALL & D (79); I (271)
AGNETHA FALTSKOG: F (284)
GEORGIE FAME & D (45)
FAMILY & D (84)
FAN CLUB & NEW ROSE LABELS & D (116)
FANTASY & D (153)
THE FARM & D (138)
FATBOY SLIM: & D (257)
FAUST: I & D (255)
CHARLIE FEATHERS: F (280)
JULIE FELIX: I (284)
FELT: I & D (165)
RAY FENWICK: I (180)
BRYAN FERRY: D (72); I (244).
See also ROXY MUSIC.

FESTIVALS: F (120); F (170); R (176); F (215); F (216); F (220)
FIERCE PANDA: D & I (200); D & I (296)
50s BRITPOP: F (243)
FINE YOUNG CANNIBALS & D (122)
MICKEY FINN: I & D (189). See also MARC BOLAN.
NEIL FINN: I (246). See also CROWDED HOUSE.
FISH: I & D (159)
THE 5 AM EVENT & D (156)
FIVE STAR & D (98)
THE FLAMIN' GROOVIES & D (47)
THE FLAMING LIPS: I & D (172); I & D (288)
FLATT & SCRUGGS: R (199)
FLEETWOOD MAC: F & D (43); D (44); D (107); R, I & D (195); F & I (243); I (281). See also PETER GREEN.
FLY LABEL & Listing (88)
THE FLYING BURRITO BROTHERS: F & D (166); F & D (167). See also CHRIS HILLMAN, GRAM PARSONS.
FOCUS & D (141)
FOLK: F (175); R (223); F (235)
FONTANA LABEL: R & D (140)
WAYNE FONTANA & THE MINDBENDERS & D (53)
FOO FIGHTERS & D (246). See also NIRVANA (US).
FOOTBALL RECORDS (202); (299)
EMILE FORD & THE CHECKMATES: I & D (230)
FOREIGNER: I & D (184). See also IAN McDONALD.
THE FOUR PENNIES & D (63)
THE FOUR SEASONS: D & I (252)
THE FOUR TOPS & D (100)
JOHN FOXX: I (265)
RODDY FRAME: I & D (244)
PETER FRAMPTON: F & I (260)
CONNIE FRANCIS: F & D (151); F & D (152)
FRANKIE GOES TO HOLLYWOOD: F (64); D (111); F (172); I (255)
ARETHA FRANKLIN: D (96); F & D (258)
ERMA FRANKLIN & D (161)
FREAKBEAT & R&B: F (163)
FREE & D (54); R (250). See also PAUL RODGERS.
ALAN FREED & D (165)
FRENCH EPs: F (205)
FRENCH HOUSE: F (275)
FRENCH POP IN THE 1960s: F & D (230)
KINKY FRIEDMAN: I & D (169)
LEFTY FRIZZELL: R & D (154)
FRONT LINE: F (266)
THE FUGS: I & D (168)
BOBBY FULLER FOUR & D (92)
THE FUN BOY THREE & F.B.T: D (*) (38). See also TERRY HALL.
FUNK: D (119); F (187); F (272)
FUNKADELIC & D (163)
BILLY FURY & D (97); F (118); F (260)
PETER GABRIEL & D (106). See also GENESIS.
SERGE GAINSBOURG & D (229)

G

PETER GABRIEL: I (297)
GALAXIE 500: I & D (234)
RORY GALLAGHER: F & D (192); I (249); F (267)
GARAGE ROCK: F (248)
GARBAGE & D (209); I (225)
ART GARFUNKEL: I (283)
FREDDIE GARRITY: I (266)
GAY DAD: I & D (241)
MARVIN GAYE: D (78); R (190); F (256)
RON GEESIN & D (176)
BOB GELDOF: I (298)
GENE: I & D (199)
GENERATION X / BILLY IDOL: D (97) See also BILLY IDOL.
GENESIS: F & D (48); R & D (117); D (146); I & D (218); R & I (227); D (238); F/R (267); F (279). See also PHIL COLLINS, PETER GABRIEL, ANTHONY PHILLIPS.
GENTLE GIANT & D (137)
GHOST & D (119)
GILLAN & D (165); F (177)
DAVE GILMOUR & D (132); I (285). See also PINK FLOYD.
ALLEN GINSBERG: I & D (186)
GIRL GROUPS OF THE 50s/60s & D (246); D (263)
GLAM ROCK: F (81); F (269)
GARY GLITTER & D (65)
VIC GODARD & SUBWAY SECT & D (203); F (243)
GEOFF GODDARD: I & D (154)
GODSPEED YOU BLACK EMPEROR! & D (243)
THE GO-GO's: D (111)
GONG & D (175); I (189)
GOMEZ: I & D (250)
JACK GOOD: I (161)
GOODIES & BILL ODDIE: I (257)
LESLIE GORE & D (181)
CHARLIE GRACIE: I & D (195)
GRADING RECORDS (63)
DAVY GRAHAM: F (287)
GRANDADDY: I & D (261)
GRAND ROYAL: F (267)
GRAPEVINE LABEL (212)
THE GRATEFUL DEAD & D (64); R (117); R & F (194); D (195); D (196); D (197); R (246); R (268)
DAVID GRAY & D (271)
THE GREAT SOCIETY & D (125)
RICK GRECH & D (181)
GREEN DAY & D (270)
AL GREEN & D (51); F (268)
PETER GREEN: F & D (167); F & D (168). See also FLEETWOOD MAC.
GREEN ON RED & D (83); I & D (147)
SID GRIFFIN: I & D (212)
NANCI GRIFFITH & D (97); & Crickets: I (213)
THE GROUNDHOGS & D (107); I (167)
THE G.T.O.s/PAMELA DE BARRES: I & D (123)
GUIDED BY VOICES I (296)
GUNS N' ROSES & D (118); D (148); I (294)
ARLO GUTHRIE & D (107)

H

STEVE HACKETT: I (272)
MERLE HAGGARD & D, R (196)
LUKE HAINES: I (264)
NORMAN HAINES & D (169)
HAIRCUT 100: I & D (170)
BILL HALEY & D (38); R & D (139); I & D (176)
TERRY HALL: I & D (182). See also THE FUN BOY THREE.

HALL & OATES: I & D (170)
HAMBURG SCENE: R (240)
PETER HAMMILL / VAN DER GRAAF GENERATOR: D (83); I (166); I (261)
LIONEL HAMPTON: F (279)
HANOI ROCKS: F & D (141)
HAPPY MONDAYS: F & D (131)
HAPSHASH & THE COLOURED COAT: I (299)
HARDCORE: See under U.S. Hardcore.
HARD ROCK CAFE MEMORABILIA (178)
STEVE HARLEY & COCKNEY REBEL & D (136); I (155)
ROY HARPER & D (95); R (185)
EMMYLOU HARRIS: I & D (149); I (240)
JET HARRIS & TONY MEEHAN & D (74)
WEE WILLIE HARRIS: I & D (164)
GEORGE HARRISON: D (104); R (208); F (260); F (269).
See also THE BEATLES.
HARVEST LABEL: F (139); F & D (140); R (240)
ALEX HARVEY: F & D (107)
PJ HARVEY & D (188); D (229); D (257).
JULIANA HATFIELD: I & D (188)
RICHIE HAVENS: F (276)
RONNIE HAWKINS: I & D (89)
HAWKWIND & D (70); F & D (157); I & D (162); R (189); F (202); F (273)
ISAAC HAYES & I (264)
TUBBY HAYES: F (300)
JUSTIN HAYWARD: I (282)
LEE HAZLEWOOD: I & D (246)
JEFF HEALEY: I (255)
HEART & D (145)
HEAVY METAL: F & D (114); F (184); F (203); F (204); F (205)
HEFNER: I & D (245)
RICHARD HELL: I & D (215).
See also TELEVISION.
JIMI HENDRIX: D (50); F & D (85); D (86); D (121); R (124); F & D (133); F & D (134); D & R (140); I (153); D (162); I (166); D (171); R (176); F (179); F (188); R (196); F 1967 (209); I & R (214); R (215); R (219); F (228); F & D (248); F (255); R (263); F (295).
See also NOEL REDDING.
KEN HENSLEY & D (179)
HERE AND NOW TOURS & I (293)
HERMAN'S HERMITS & D (91)
NICK HEYWARD / HAIRCUT 100: I & D (170); I (270)
HI LABEL & Singles Listing (112)
HIGH LLAMAS & D (286)
CHRIS HILLMAN: I (230).
See also THE BYRDS, THE FLYING BURRITO BROTHERS.
HIP-HOP: F (246)
HOLE & D (191)
THE HOLLIES: D (71); I & D (109); I & D (110); I & D (111); F (260)
MARK HOLLIS: I (221).
See also TALK TALK.
BUDDY HOLLY: F (56); D (88); D (101); D (114); F (147); F (205); F (234); D (267)
HOLLYWOOD STARS: F (254)
THE HONEYBUS & D (111)
THE HONEYCOMBS & D (193)
HOOD & I (271)

MARY HOPKIN: I & D (108)
NICKY HOPKINS: F & D (183)
BRUCE HORNSBY: I (165)
HORSLIPS: I (255)
HOT CHOCOLATE & D (57)
HOT ROD: D (191)
THE HOUSE OF LOVE & D (127).
See also GUY CHADWICK.
THE HOUSEMARTINS & D (136).
See also BEATS INTERNATIONAL, THE BEAUTIFUL SOUTH.
WHITNEY HOUSTON & D (163)
HOWLIN' WOLF & D (78)
GLENN HUGHES: I (237).
See also DEEP PURPLE.
THE HUMAN LEAGUE: I & D (187); I (264)
IAN HUNTER: I & D (213); I (264).
See also MOTT THE HOOPLE.
HUSKER DU: I & D (158)
ASHLEY HUTCHINGS: I (267)
HMV: R (112)

I

IBIZA: F (242)
ICARUS (211)
THE IDLE RACE & D (181)
IDLEWILD: I & D (249); I & D (277)
BILLY IDOL & IDOL/GEN X: D (97); I (273)
See also GENERATION X.
IMMEDIATE LABEL: F (250)
THE INCREDIBLE STRING BAND & Solo: D (93); R (214)
THE IN CROWD: R (263)
INDEPENDENT LABELS: F (64); F (125); D (209); D (210).
See also BASTA, DECEPTIVE, DRUNKEN FISH, EARWORM, FACTORY, FIERCE PANDA, KOKOPOP, NEW ROSE/FAN CLUB, ROUGH TRADE, SKAM, SST, SUB POP, TJM, WURLITZER JUKEBOX, ZOOM & COLLECTABLE INDIE SINGLES series.
THE INDIGO GIRLS & D (193)
INDUSTRIAL MUSIC: F & D (185)
NEIL INNES: I & D (183)

INSPIRAL CARPETS: I & D (129)
INSTRUMENTALS: F & D (64)
INSTRUMENTAL GROUPS: F (67); F(72)
INSURING YOUR COLLECTION: F (166)
INTERNATIONAL ARTISTS LABEL: D (110)
INTERNET COLLECTING: F (246)
INVICTUS / HOT WAX LABELS: D (242)
INXS & D (114)
IQ & D (162)
IRON MAIDEN & D (98); D (135); I & D (206); R (257); R (272); I & D (289)
ISLAND LABEL: D (*) (60); F & D (Pt. 1) (201); D (Pt 2) (202); D (Pt 3), (203); D (Pt 4), D (204); D (205); D (206); D (207); D (208)
THE ISLEY BROTHERS: F & D (165)
IT BITES & D (129)

J

JANET JACKSON & D (189)
JAZZMAN RECORDS & Gerald Short: I (259)
JOE JACKSON & D (83)
MAHALIA JACKSON: D (268)
MICHAEL JACKSON: D (62); F & D (99); D (191); D (192); R (194); F (235)
TONY JACKSON & D(172)
CHRIS JAGGER: I & D (174)
JAH WOBBLE: I & D (228)
THE JAM & D (47); D (90); I (154); F (157); F (210).
See also THE STYLE COUNCIL, PAUL WELLER.
JAMAICAN SOUND SYSTEMS: I (289)
JAMES & D (137); F & I (224)
ELMORE JAMES: R & D (161); R (174)
ETTA JAMES & D (58); D(200)
THE J.A.M.s / THE KLF: I & D (140)
BERT JANSCH: F & D (171); F & D (173); F (235); F (251)
CHAS JANKEL: I (297)
JAPAN & D (36); I & D (298)
JAPANESE UNDERGROUND: F (250)
JEAN-MICHEL JARRE & D (134); F (220)
JASON & THE SCORCHERS: I & D (166)
JEFFERSON AIRPLANE/STARSHIP: F & D (91); F & D (92); R (159); F & D (211); I (234)
WAYLON JENNINGS: I & D (189)
THE JESUS & MARY CHAIN & D (116)
JESUS JONES & D (141)
JETHRO TULL & D (86); R (108); I & D (151); R (199); R (214); R (229); F (258)
JJ72: F & D & I (265)
BILLY JOEL & D (70)
JOHN'S CHILDREN & D (58).
See also MARC BOLAN.
JOHN THE POSTMAN: I & D (230)
ELTON JOHN: D (77); F (111); F (219); F & D (220); F & D (221); F & D (222); F (250); I (267).
BOB JOHNSTON F (296)
ROBERT JOHNSON & D (246)
BRIAN JONES: F (119).
See also THE ROLLING STONES.
HOWARD JONES & D (69); F (192)
JANIE JONES: I & D (166)
JOHN PAUL JONES: I (221); I (241).
See also LED ZEPPELIN.
TOM JONES: F (132); F & D (133); I (293)
WIZZ JONES: I (300)
JANIS JOPLIN & Big Brother/Joplin: D (88); R (175); F & I (213).
See also BIG BROTHER & THE HOLDING COMPANY.
THE JORDANAIRES: I & D (169)
JOURNEY & D (235)
JOY DIVISION: F (112); D & R (221); R & I (238).
See also NEW ORDER.
JUKEBOXES: F (186)
'JULIE AND THE CADILLACS': F (240)
JULY: I & D (190)

K

(UK) KALEIDOSCOPE & D (125); I (206)
(US) KALEIDOSCOPE & D (109)
EDEN KANE & D (102)
KATRINA AND THE WAVES & I (219)
NIGEL KENNEDY: I (205)
NIK KERSHAW: F (68)
CHAKA KHAN / RUFUS & D (68)
KID CREOLE: I (276)
KID KOALA: I (293)
JOHNNY KIDD & PIRATES & D (36); I & D (135); F & D (206)
KING BISCUIT FLOWER HOUR (225)
KING RECORDS: F & D (274)
ALBERT KING: F (274)
B.B. KING & D (52); R (265); F (274)
BEN E. KING: I & D (93)
CAROLE KING: F, D & I (239)
FREDDIE KING: F (274)
KING CRIMSON & D (101); I (148); R (264); F (274).
See also IAN McDONALD, JOHN WETTON.
THE KINGPINS (188)
THE KINKS: F (62); D (73); D (99); I & D (169); I (183); I (200); F & D + F & D (246); F (260)
KATHY KIRBY I & D (288)
KISS: F & D (146); F & D (147); I (204); I (252)
THE KLF: I & D (140)
GLADYS KNIGHT: I (288)
MARK KNOPFLER: I & D (173).
See also DIRE STRAITS.
KOKOPOP LABEL & Listing (163)

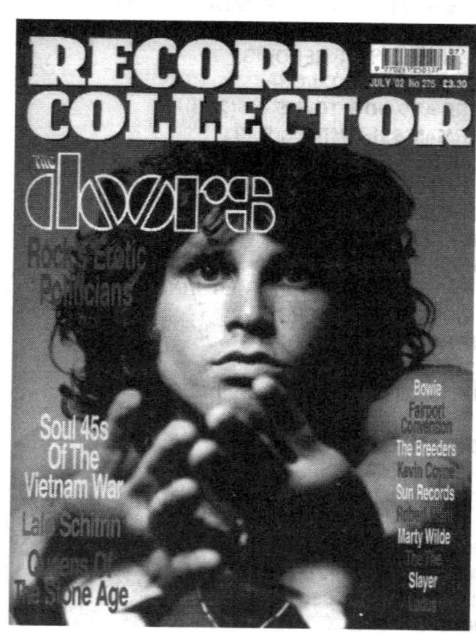

ALEXIS KORNER & D (58)
AL KOOPER: F (157); F & D (157); F & D (158)
KORN & D (248)
LEO KOTTKE & D (204)
KRAFTWERK & D (137); I (170); F (290)
BILLY J. KRAMER & D (73)
WAYNE KRAMER: I & D (205)
KRAUTROCK: F (205); F (254)
LENNY KRAVITZ: F & D (144)
KULA SHAKER: I & D (216)
FEMI KUTI: I (271)
SONJA KRISTINA: I (189)

L

DENNY LAINE: I & D (191)
STEVE LAMACQ: I (254)
LAMBCHOP: D & I (273)
RONNIE LANE: F & D (216)
K.D. LANG & D (165)
THE LA's: I & D (226)
BETTYE LAVETTE I (300)
LEAF HOUND: I & D (168)
THE LEAVES & D (89)
LED ZEPPELIN: D (39); F & D (97); F (105); R (131); D (145); F (170); F & D (177); I (184); R & D (191); F (196); F (213); D (218); R (219); F (220); F (229); R, D & I (233); D (244); F (251); R (270); F (284); F (286); F (298).
See also JOHN PAUL JONES, JIMMY PAGE, ROBERT PLANT.
ARTHUR LEE: I & D (155)
BRENDA LEE: I & D (157); R (198)
DAVE LEE: I (284)
THE LEFT BANKE & D (144)
TOM LEHRER: R (253)
LEIBER & STOLLER & D (*) (59); I (264)
THE LEMONHEADS & D (174)
THE LEMON KITTENS & DANIELLE DAX: I & D (123)
JOHN LENNON: F (42); F (59); D (81); D (88); F & D (110); F (118); F & D (119); F & D (134); I (190); F (215); D (235); F (244); F (256).
See also THE BEATLES.
LEVEL 42 & D (109); I & D (177)
THE LEVELLERS & D (173)
IAN LEVINE I (300)
HUEY LEWIS & THE NEWS & D (100); I & D (178)
JERRY LEE LEWIS: F & D (41); D (146); R (186); R (188); R (263); F (269)
LINDA GAIL LEWIS: I & D (146)
SMILEY LEWIS & D (177)
JOHN LEYTON & D (170); I (265)
LIEUTENANT PIGEON: I & D (206)
LIMP BIZKIT & D (263)
LINDISFARNE & D (198)
THE LIGHTNING SEEDS: I & D (205)
LITTLE ANGELS & D (143)
LITTLE FEAT & D (125); R (254)
LITTLE RICHARD & D (69); R (125); F (255)
NILS LOFGREN: I & D (204)
THE LOFT: F (242)
JULIE LONDON & D (45)
LONDON RECORDS: F (146)
THE LONG RYDERS & D(79)
JERRY LORDAN: F & D (196)
THE LOUDEST WHISPER & D (233)
LOVE & ARTHUR LEE I & D (155); F (262); I (277)
MARY LOVE: I & D (208)
MIKE LOVE: I(162); I (164).
See also THE BEACH BOYS.
THE LOVE AFFAIR: I & D (224).
See also STEVE ELLIS.
THE LOVIN' SPOONFUL & D & F (156)
LUDUS & I (275)
LULU & D (121)
LUSH & D (201)
LYDIA LUNCH & D (171)
LORETTA LYNN & Rarities (292)
FRANKIE LYMON & D (173)
LYNYRD SKYNYRD: R & D (152)

M

M: D (121)
KIRSTY MacCOLL: I & D (175)
BILLY MacKENZIE: F, I & D (218)
LONNIE MACK & D (81)
MAC MacLEOD & D (244)
STUART MACONIE: I (295)
MADNESS & D (155); I (244); I (280)
MADONNA & D (75); D (90); D (120); D (134); D (135); D (146); F (152); F (181); F & D (198); F & D (225); F (237); R (249); R (257); R (258); R (263); F (267)
MAGIC CARPET: I & D (164)
MAGNUM & D (130)
MAHAVISHNU ORCHESTRA (245)
MAIL ORDER: F (201)
MAJOR LANCE & D (59)
STEPHEN MALKMUS: I (284)
THE MAMAS & PAPAS: R (89); I & D (145)
MAN & D (142)
MANFRED MANN & D (137); I (195)
MANFRED MANN'S EARTH BAND & D (108); R (247)
MANIC STREET PREACHERS & D (156); R & D (213); F & D (260)
BARRY MANILOW & D (183)
GERED MANKOWITZ: I (191)
AIMEE MANN / 'TIL TUESDAY: I & D (170)
BARRY MANN / CYNTHIA WEIL: I (251)
MARILYN MANSON: I & D (231); D (246)
MANSUN: I & D (229)
MARILLION & D (82); I (155); I (262)
MARION: I & D (198)
HOWARD MARKS: I (288)
BOB MARLEY & THE WAILERS & D (38); D (141); R (231); F (246); F (261); F (265)
MARMALADE & D (186)
MARQUEE: F (278)
DEAN MARTIN & D (199)
GEORGE MARTIN: R (265)
TONY 'THE CAT' MARTIN: I (242).
See also BLACK SABBATH.
AL MARTINO: I & D (154)
JOHN MARTYN & D (140); I (298)
HANK MARVIN & BRUCE WELCH: I & D (171).
See also THE SHADOWS.
MARVIN, WELCH & FARRAR & D (80).
See also THE SHADOWS.
NICK MASON & Solo: D (132).
See also PINK FLOYD.
JOHNNY MATHIS & D (106)
JOHN MAYALL & D (65); F (203); I & D (213)
CURTIS MAYFIELD & D (95); R (200); F & D (247); F (248)
ELIOT MAZER: I (248)

DAVID McCALLUM: I (202)
PAUL McCARTNEY / WINGS: F (43); F (55); D (78); D (89); R (100); R (114); F & D (125); R & D (162); I (186); R & I (194); I & F (214); R & I (243); R (254); I (261); R (285).
See also THE BEATLES.
IAN McDONALD: I (241).
See also FOREIGNER, KING CRIMSON.
IAN McNABB: I & D (202)
CLYDE McPHATTER & D (281)
THE MC5 & D (138); I (248); I (285)
HENRY McCULLOUGH: I (179)
ALAN McGEE: I (254)
SHANE McGOWAN: I (293)
IAN McCLAGAN: I (298)
JOHN McLAUGHLIN: I & D (201)
CLYDE McPHATTER & D (76); R (102)
TONY McPHEE I (167).
See also THE GROUNDHOGS.
MEAT LOAF: I & D (173)
JOE MEEK: D (69); D (70); F & D (134); D (186); F & I (219); F (225)
MEGA CITY FOUR: I & D (155)
MEGADETH & D (121); I & D (216); I (242)
JOHN MELLENCAMP: I & D (207)
MELANIE: I & D (120)
MEMORABILIA: F (159)
MENTO: R (273)
MERCURY REV: I & D (272)
MERSEYBEAT: D (77); D (78); D (79); R (59); F (119)
MERSEYBEATS/MERSEYS & D (42); F (215)
METALLICA & D (112); & D (215); F (252); R (265); F (286)
METERS: F (263)
MEXICAN ELECTRONICA: F (290)
MIAMI SOUND MACHINE & GLORIA ESTEFAN & D (162)
GEORGE MICHAEL & D (112); D (221).
See also WHAM!
MIDDLE EARTH: D & I (200)
THE MIDKNIGHTS: I (207)
MIDSUMMER NUMBER ONES (202)
THE MIKE STUART SPAN: I & D (176)
JIMMY MILLER: I (171)
KYLIE MINOGUE & JASON DONOVAN & D (123)
THE MISSION & D (95); I (174)
GUY MITCHELL & D (53); F & D (244)
JONI MITCHELL & D (62)
MOBY & D (253); I (295)
THE MO-DETTES & D (124)
MOD: F & D (126); F & D (131); F (181); F & D (182); R (256); F (288)
MOGWAI: I & D (238)
THE MONKEES: D (57); & D (86); I (101); F (241); F (261).
See also MICHAEL NESMITH.
MATT MONRO & D (96)
BILL MONROE: F & D (207)
MONTEREY FESTIVAL: R (176)
MONTY PYTHON & D (193)
THE MOODY BLUES: D (81); D (82); R (185); I (207); R (215)
GARY MOORE & D (109); I (190); I (244); I (262); I (273).
See also THIN LIZZY.
SAM MOORE: I (269)
KEITH MOON: F (268)
ENNIO MORRICONE: R (270)
ALANIS MORISSETTE & D (208)
MORRISSEY & D (139); F (245).
See also THE SMITHS.
VAN MORRISON & D (57); F & D (178); F & D (179); F & D (180).
See also THEM.
MOTHER RECORDS & Listing (107)
THE MOTHERS OF INVENTION:
See under FRANK ZAPPA.
MOTLEY CRUE & D (123)
MOTOR CITY RECORDS: I & D (151)
MOTORHEAD & D (140); D (167); I (245)
MOTOWN LABEL: D (66); D (76); D (77); D (71); D (72); D (73); D (74); D (75); F (145); F (174); D (184); D (185); D (186); D (187); D (188); D (189); R (257); F (267); F (288)
MOTT THE HOOPLE & D (171).
See also IAN HUNTER.
BOB MOULD: I & D (158)
MOUSE LABEL: D & I (201)
THE MOVE & ROY WOOD: I & D (179); F (220); F (259).
See also ROY WOOD.
MO' WAX: I & D (245)
ALISON MOYET / YAZOO & D (67)
MP3: F (252)
MUDDY WATERS & D (68)
MOON MULLIGAN: F (278)
MOUNTAIN & LESLIE WEST: I (284)
MULL HISTORICAL SOCIETY: I (284)
MULTIMEDIA NETWORKING (188)
MUNGO JERRY & D (194)
MUSE: I & D (244)
MUSIC MACHINE & D (87); F (225)
MY BLOODY VALENTINE & D (128)
MY LIFE STORY: I & D (214)

N

THE NASHVILLE TEENS & D (52)
NAZARETH & D (179)
THE NAZZ & D (59)
RICK NELSON: F & D (78); F & D (264)
SANDY NELSON & D (55)
WILLIE NELSON & D (84); I (184); I (231)
NEO DOO-WOP: F (250)
NEO PROG: F (277)
MICHAEL NESMITH: I & D (147); I (216).
See also THE MONKEES.
MARK NEVIN: & I (275)
NEW KIDS ON THE BLOCK & D (128)
ANTHONY NEWLEY & D (238)
RANDY NEWMAN & D (76); I (237)
NEW MODEL ARMY & D (108)
NEW ORDER & D (105); D (135); D (136); I (264).
See also JOY DIVISION.
NEW ROMANTICS: F (199); F (298)
NEW ROSE & FAN CLUB LABELS: F (116)
OLIVIA NEWTON-JOHN & D (76)
NEW WAVE: F (178)
THE NEW YORK DOLLS & JOHNNY THUNDERS: D (143)
NEW YORK ROCK: F (236)
NEU! & I & D (262)
SCOUT NIBLETT: I (290)
NICK NICELY: I & D (210)
STEVIE NICKS: Solo & D (156)

NICO & D (98).
See also THE VELVET UNDERGROUND.
HARRY NILSSON: I & D (199); R (253)
999: I & D (235)
NINJA TUNE: D & I (255)
NIRVANA (UK) & D (96); I (172)
NIRVANA (US) & D (150); F (159); D (170); F (178); F (210); D (236); F (296)
See also FOO FIGHTERS.
JACK NITSZCHE: F(254)
THE NITTY GRITTY DIRT BAND & D (174)
THE NOLANS & D (139)
NORTHERN SOUL: F & D (145); D (206); F & I (222); F (240); F (297)
NORTON RECORDS: F (283)
NOW! COMPILATIONS: R (239)
TED NUGENT: I (269)
'NUGGETS' COMPILATIONS (84)
GARY NUMAN / TUBEWAY ARMY: D & I (76); F & D (133); F & D (134); I (200); F (218); I (259)
NURSE WITH WOUND: I (294)
NWOBHM F (296)
MICHAEL NYMAN: I (281)

O

OAK RECORDS & D (150)
OASIS & D (185); D (202); I (210); R & D (218); F (223); F (242); F & D (248)
OASIS: F (200)
OCEAN COLOUR SCENE: I & D (203)
PHIL OCHS: F & D (81)
SINEAD O'CONNOR & D (138)
OFFSPRING & D (262)
OI!: F & D (177)
OKEH: F & D (199)
MIKE OLDFIELD & D (128); F (206); F (226); R (252); I (264)
'THE OLD GREY WHISTLE TEST' ARCHIVES (177); I (265); F (290)
O.M.D. & D (143); I (230); I (263)
ONE HIT WONDERS: F & D (197)
THE ONLY ONES & D (117); I & F (186)
YOKO ONO: I & D (154)
THE OPEN MIND & D (288)
ORANGE JUICE: I (157); & D (193); R (225).
See also EDWYN COLLINS.
THE ORB: I & D (168)
ROY ORBISON & D (43); F & D (117); I (136); F (158); R (192); F & D (208); R (262)
GENESIS P-ORRIDGE: I & D (237).
See also THROBBING GRISTLE.
BETH ORTON: I & D (279)
OZZY OSBOURNE & D (115); I & D (240); R (263); I (280).
See also BLACK SABBATH.
OSCARS: F (283)
JIMMY OSMOND: I (261)
JOHN OTWAY: I & D (190)
THE OUTLAWS & D (36)
OVERGROUND LABEL: I & D (189)
OVERSEAS RELEASES: F (68)
OZRIC TENTACLES: R (175); I & D (260)

P

JIMMY PAGE: D & R (163); I (184); R & D (191); R & D (225).
See also LED ZEPPELIN.
ROBERT PALMER & D (102); I (279)
VANESSA PARADIS: F (300)
PARADISE GARAGE & F (252)
THE PARAMOUNTS:
See under PROCOL HARUM.
PARLIAMENT & D (163)
CHARLIE PARKER: R (258)
GRAHAM PARKER: F (266)
LARRY PARNES & D (122)
GRAM PARSONS & D (166); F (181)
DOLLY PARTON & D (66)
PATTO & D (132)
PAVEMENT: I & D (218)
PAVLOV'S DOG & D (262)
PEARL JAM & D (163)
JOHN PEEL: I (146); I (147); I (148); I (281)
PENETRATION: I & D (169)
THE PENGUINS & D (202)
DAN PENN & SPOONER OLDHAM: I (244)
PENTANGLE & D (173)
PERE UBU & D (119); I (206)
CARL PERKINS & D (73); F (76); F & D (223)
LEE 'SCRATCH' PERRY: F (249); R (268); I (289)
JEAN-JACQUES PERREY: I & D (214)
PETER & GORDON & D (107)
GILLES PETERSON: I (295)
PET SHOP BOYS: F & D (89); D (110); D (126); R (142); R (151); D (171); R (243); F (251); F (262); I (273)
PHILADELPHIA INTERNATIONAL: F (282)
ANTHONY PHILLIPS: D (156).
See also GENESIS.
SAM PHILLIPS: I (253)
PHILLIPS ROCK & POP MEMORABILIA AUCTIONS: F (91); F (98); F (106); F (110); F (118); F (122); F (131); F (134); F (143); F (159); F (164)
PIANO MAGIC & D (273)
WILSON PICKETT & D (48)
PICTURE DISCS (189)
PICTURE SLEEVES: F (151); F (188)
PiL & D (127)

PINK FAIRIES: F (300)
PINK FLOYD: D(59); & D (83); F & D (104); F & D (121); D (132); R (150); D (158); R (161); D (173); F (187); F (204); F (222); F (223); I & D (247); D (292). See also SYD BARRETT, DAVE GILMOUR, NICK MASON, ROGER WATERS, RICK WRIGHT.
GENE PITNEY: I & D (104); I (267)
THE PIXIES & D (146)
PLACEBO: I & D(254)
PLAGIARISM: F (284)
ROBERT PLANT & D (122); I (184); R (292). See also LED ZEPPELIN.
THE PLATTERS & D (49); F & D (140); R (178)
THE POETS & D (78)
THE POGUES & D (105)
POISON & D (125)
THE POLICE: D (52); D (72). See also STING.
BRIAN POOLE & THE TREMELOES & D (47); D (202)
POP: F (234)
IGGY POP & D (92); D (115); F & I (250)
THE POP GROUP & D (201)
POPOL VUH & D (190)
PORCUPINE TREE: F & D (207)
PORNOGRAPHY SPECIAL: F & I (223)
POP WILL EAT ITSELF & D (132)
POSTER ART: F (99)
COZY POWELL: I & D (203); R (238)
DUFFY POWER: I & D (187)
ELVIS PRESLEY: D (47); R (67); D 1950s (80); D (91); D (96); R (98); D (105); D (113); F (120); F & D (125); F & D (129); F (135); I & D (138); R (143); R (149); R (155); F (156); F (163); D (169); D (176); R (194); F (201); D (205); F & D (216); F (224); R, F & D (240); F (244); R (247); R (252); R (259); F (263); F (264); F (276); F (298)
THE PRETTY THINGS & D (69); R (193)
LLOYD PRICE & D (282)
RAY PRICE: R (198)
PRIMAL SCREAM & D (177)
THE PRIMITIVES & D (134)
PRINCE & D (84); D (103); D (122); F (130); D (147); R (156); F (180); R & F (224); F (269); F (274); F (298)
MADDY PRIOR: I (260)
'THE PRISONER / DANGER MAN' & D (161)
PRIVATE PRESSINGS & D (153)
P.J. PROBY & D (40); D (94); I & D (180)
PROCOL HARUM / THE PARAMOUNTS & D (39); I & D (185); R (247)
PRODIGY & D (204)
PROGRESSIVE ROCK: D (94); F & D (115); R (206); F & I (213); F (244); F (297)
PROPAGANDA & ZTT D (110); I (277)
PSYCHEDELIA: R (84); R (98); R (135); F (207); F (209); F (216); F (285)
PUBLIC ENEMY & D (158)
PULP: I & D (184); F (197)
PUNK: F & D (125); F & D (125); R (125); F (187); F, I & D (198); F (206); F (253); F (281)
POST-PUNK: F (176); F &D (177); F & D (178); F & D (179); F & D (180); F & D (181/182); F & D (183); F & D (184); F & D (185); R (268)
PSYCH: F (265); F (299)
PUSSY GALORE: I & D (170). See also THE JON SPENCER BLUES EXPLOSION.
PYE INTERNATIONAL R&B SERIES & Listing (166)

Q

THE QUARRY MEN (183); F (217)
SUZI QUATRO & D (62)
QUEEN: D (69); D (96); D (102); D (110); F & I (114); F & D (118); R (123); R (133); D (139); D (144); R & F (149); R (154); F (167); R (171); D (178); F (188); F (189); F (195); F (196); F (197); F (198); F (199); F (208); R (219); R & D (220); F (221); F (233); D (239); F (242); D (246); R (255); F (262); R (274); F (281).
QUEENS OF THE STONE AGE: I & D (275)
QUEENSRYCHE & D (185)
? & THE MYSTERIANS & D (235)
QUIET MELON: F (153). See also THE BIRDS.
QUOTES: F (200)

R

R&B & FREAKBEAT: F & D (163); F (251); F (251); F (294)
RABID LABEL & D (255)
RADIOHEAD: I & D (207); F (251); F & R (255); F (265); D (297)
RADIO ONE: F (218)
RADIO SHOWS: F (173)
RADIO STARS & D (246)
RAGE AGAINST THE MACHINE: F (248)
RAINBOW & D (81); I (251)
THE RAINCOATS & D (166)
BUCK RAM: F & D (140)
THE RAMONES & D (95); I (191); I (220); F (250); R (263)
ERNEST RANGLIN: I & D (220)
JOHNNIE RAY & D (266)
CHRIS REA & D (88); I (279)
MIKE READ: I & D (168)
'READY STEADY GO': R (60); F (209)
RECORD CARE: F (70)
RECORD COLLECTING: F (100); F (200); F (247)

RECORD COVERS OF THE 1950s (268)
RECORD FAIRS: F (269)
THE RED HOT CHILI PEPPERS & D (132); D (247)
NOEL REDDING: I (166).
See also JIMI HENDRIX.
OTIS REDDING & D (67); R (173); F & D (259)
DAVID REDFERN: I (294)
LOU REED & D (116); F & R (154); I (248).
See also THE VELVET UNDERGROUND.
JIM REEVES & D (179)
REGGAE: F (263); F (274)
TERRY REID: I & D (143)
R.E.M. & D (102); D (157); R (166); F & D (172); F & D (173); D (183); F & D (216); F & D (228); F (240); F (271)
THE REMAINS: I & D (151)
THE REPLACEMENTS: I (282)
THE RESIDENTS: D (121)
RESONANCE FM: F (282)
CHARLIE RICH & D (50); F & D (194); R (225)
RICH KIDS: I & D (227)
CLIFF RICHARD: F & D (39); R (54); D (68); D (83); D (98); I & D (119); D (120); D (121); D (122); D (183); F (214); F (225); R (231); R (265); F (284)
JONATHAN RICHMAN & D (210)
RIDE: I (267)
THE RIGHTEOUS BROTHERS & D (72)
MINNIE RIPPERTON: F (299)
JOHNNY RIVERS & D(203)
MARTY ROBBINS & D(220)
ROBBIE ROBERTSON & I (224).
See also THE BAND.
SMOKEY ROBINSON & THE MIRACLES & D (36); & D (266)
ROCKABILLY: F (139); D (239); D (262)
ROCKBITCH: I (240)
ROCK COMPILATIONS: F (61); D (98); D (99); R (84); R (98); R (125)
ROCK ON FILM: F & D (135); F & D (187); F (253)
ROCK ON TV: F (169); F (253)
ROCK'N'ROLL: F (102); R (110); F (146); F & D (161); D (174); F (176); F (187); F (252); F (252); F (253); D (192); D (193); F (201); D (210); F & D (235); F & D (236); F & D (237); F & D (238); F & D (239); F & D (240); F & D (241); R (242); D (245); F (248); F (250); F (267)
PAUL RODGERS: I (210). See also FREE.
KENNY ROGERS & D (75)
ROLLERCOASTER LABEL & Listing (198)
ROLLING STONE MAGAZINE: I & R (225)
THE ROLLING STONES: D (45); D (49); D (61); D (74); D (79); R (87); D (93); D (101); F (104); F (111); D (113); D (117); D (124); F (124); F (125); R (130); D (136); F & D (142); F & D (148); D (155); R & I (161); R/D (168); F & D (169); F & D (170); F & D (172); F & D (173); F & D (174); R (180); F & D (186); R (189); R (193); D (205); R (207); F (210); F (212); F (230); D (231) F (235); F (236); F, I & R (238); D (247) F (254); F (260); F (268); R (279); F (287); R (291).
See also BRIAN JONES, RONNIE WOOD, BILL WYMAN, CHARLIE WATTS.
HENRY ROLLINS: I & D (213).
See also BLACK FLAG.
MICK RONSON & D (167); R (185)
LINDA RONSTADT & D (182)
TIM ROSE: F (279)
EMPEROR ROSKO: & I (253)
DIANA ROSS & THE SUPREMES & D (170); F & D (172); F (255)
ROUGH TRADE LABEL: D (99); I (129); F (260)
THE ROULETTES & D (57)
ROXY MUSIC: F & D (72); I (190); I & D (244); I (264).
See also BRIAN FERRY
ROYAL VARIETY PERFORMANCE: F(274)
ROYALS ON RECORD (274)
'RUBBLE' COMPILATIONS (98)
THE RUBETTES & D (186)
THE RUNAWAYS & D (188)
TODD RUNDGREN/UTOPIA: D (60); I & D (186)
RUNRIG & D (172)
RUSH & D (136); I (257)
LEON RUSSELL: I (282)
THE RUTLES & D (148)
THE RUTS & D (192)
RYKODISC LABEL: I (153)

S

SADE: R (257)
SAGA & I (251)
DOUG SAHM: F & D (246)
SAINT ETIENNE: I & D (195); I (281)
BUFFY SAINTE-MARIE: I & D (152)
MIKE SAMMES: F (283)
SANTANA: R & D (112)
LEO SAYER & I (273)
THE SCAFFOLD & D (54)
MICHAEL SCHENKER: I & D (239)
LALO SCHIFRIN: F (263); I (275)
KLAUS SCHULZE: R (180)
THE SCORPIONS (GERMANY): I & D (242)
THE SCORPIONS (UK) & D (193)
JACK SCOTT & D (243)
SCOTTISH BEAT & D (126)
SEAFOOD: I & D (246)
THE SEARCHERS: I & D (223); F (261); F (272)
SEE FOR MILES LABEL: I (123)
THE SEEDS & D (86); I & D (292)
THE SEEKERS & D (115); I (177)
SENSELESS THINGS: I & D (153); F & D (174)
SEPULTURA & D (180)
THE SEX PISTOLS & D (87); I & D (104); F & D (174); F (204); F (208); I (212); R (239); R & I (241); F & I (249); F (256); F (267); F (274): D/F (288)
RON SEXSMITH: I (284)
THE SHADOWS: F & D (42); D (51); F & D (71); F & D (123); F & D (124); R (218) F (299).
See also HANK MARVIN & BRUCE WELCH; MARVIN, WELCH & FARRAR.
THE SHADOWS OF KNIGHT & D (139)
SHAGGS & D (185)
THE SHAMEN & D (147)
SHAM 69: F & I (297)
RAVI SHANKAR: I & D (229)
DEL SHANNON & D (129)
HELEN SHAPIRO & D (79); F (258)
FEARGAL SHARKEY / THE UNDERTONES & D (77)
SANDIE SHAW & D (57); I (184)
SHRED! F (295)

THE SHIRELLES & D (52)
SHRINE RECORDS & D (254)
JANE SIBERRY: I & D (211)
SIGUE SIGUE SPUTNIK & D (206);
THE RETURN! F (260)
SIMON & GARFUNKEL: F & D (36); F (204);
R (266).
See also PAUL SIMON.
PAUL SIMON: D (248).
See also SIMON & GARFUNKEL.
NINA SIMONE: F (286)
SIMPLE MINDS & D (60); F & D (83); F (96);
D (128); I & D (186); I (298)
SIMPLY RED & D (121); D (196)
FRANK SINATRA: D (51); D (90); R & D (137);
D (138); F (227); D (276)
SINGER VS SONG: D (257)
SINGLES: F (103)
SIOUXSIE & THE BANSHEES & D (65); D (108);
R (188).
See also THE CREATURES.
THE SISTERS OF MERCY & D (99)
SKA, ROCKSTEADY & REGGAE: F & D (182);
F (183)
RICKY SKAGGS: I & D (150)
SKAM LABEL & D (230)
SKIFFLE: R (234)
SLADE & D (58); I (212); I (242)
SLASH: I (258).
See also GUNS 'N ROSES
SLAYER & I (251)
PERCY SLEDGE & D (92)
EARL SLICK: I (294)
SLIPKNOT: F (248); F, I & D (258); I (266); R (272)
THE SLITS & D (139); I (217)
SLY & THE FAMILY STONE & D (164)
THE SMALL FACES & K. Jones: I & D (158); D (197);
R (214)
S*M*A*S*H & D (179)
THE SMASHING PUMPKINS & D (220)
CURT SMITH: I (225).
See also TEARS FOR FEARS
ELLIOTT SMITH: I (257)
PATTI SMITH & D (204)
THE SMITHS & D (73); D (96); D (104); I & D (159);
R (172); I (176); D (204); D (266); F (286).
See also MORRISSEY.
SMOG & D (251)
SOFT CELL & D (*) (43); D (103); I (278).
See also MARC ALMOND.
SOFT MACHINE: F (186).
See also ROBERT WYATT, KEVIN AYERS.
SOLESIDES RECORDS: I & D (257); R (258)
SONIC YOUTH & D (115)
SONNY & CHER & D (42); F & D (226)
SOTHEBY'S ROCK MEMORABILIA AUCTIONS:
F (42); F (62); F (74); F (73); F (86); F (97);
F (111); F (122); F (131); F (134); F (159);
F (170); F (183)
SOUL: F (105); F & D (145); F (249)
SOUL BROTHER: F (266)
SOUNDS INCORPORATED: F (288)
SOUNDTRACKS: F & D (188); F (226); F (273);
I (291).
See also ROCK ON FILM.
SOUND BURGER: F (279)
THE SOUND: I (271)
THE SOUP DRAGONS & D (133)
THE SOUTHLANDERS: F (261)
SPACE: I & D (223)
SPACEMEN 3: F (285)
SPANDAU BALLET & D (45)
SPARKLEHORSE & D (264)
SPARKS & D (61); I & D (183); I (254); I (287).
SPEAR OF DESTINY / THEATRE OF HATE: D (102).
See also KIRK BRANDON
BRITNEY SPEARS & D (252)
SPECIALTY LABEL: D (225)
PHIL SPECTOR & D (*) (61); D (*) (62); D (*) (63);
F & D (159)
RONNIE SPECTOR: I & D (234)
CHRIS SPEDDING: I & D (198)
SPEKTACLE MAGAZINE: I(265)
'SKIP' SPENCE: F (242)
THE JON SPENCER BLUES EXPLOSION:
I & D (248).
See also PUSSY GALORE.
THE SPICE GIRLS & D (213); R (217); F & D (226)
SPIRIT & D (127); F (211)
SPIRITUALIZED: I & D (268)
SPOCK'S BEARD: I (243)
SPOOKY TOOTH: D (82)
THE SPOTNICKS & D (66)
BUFFALO SPRINGFIELD: R (263)
DUSTY SPRINGFIELD & D (103); R (200); D (237);
R (254); F (279).
BRUCE SPRINGSTEEN: F (60); F & D (71);
D (82); R (89); F & D (99); F & D (106);
F & D (121); F (164); I (211); F & R (232);
I (234); F (283)
SQUEEZE & D (40); I & D (145); F (220); D (221);
I (263)
SST LABEL: F(164)
THE STANDELLS & D (141)
VIVIAN STANSHALL: I & D(189)
ALVIN STARDUST & D (60)
EDWIN STARR: F (286)
RINGO STARR & D (132); I (191); I (232); I (285).
See also THE BEATLES.
STARTING YOUR COLLECTION: F (146); F (147)
STATE OF THE MARKET: F (228); F (229)
STATIC CARAVAN: F (264)
STATUS QUO: F & D (89); F & D (90); F & D (175);
I & D (176); R & I (268); I (278)
STAX LABEL: F & D (72); F & D (73); R (174)
STEELEYE SPAN & D (225)
STEELY DAN & D (117); I & F (259)
STEPS & I (270)
STEREOLAB & D (174); F (259)
THE STEREOPHONICS & D (243)
SHAKIN' STEVENS & D (81)
AL STEWART: I & D (114); I (263)
ROD STEWART & D (116); I (280)
STIFF LITTLE FINGERS & D (152); I (293)
STING & D (166).
See also THE POLICE.
MIKE STOLLER: F (286)
THE STONE ROSES & D (126); I & D (222)
STONE THE CROWS: I (282)
THE STOOGES & D (115).
See also IGGY POP.
STORIES BEHIND THE SONGS (130)
RORY STORM & HURRICANES & D (99)
STORYTELLER: I & D (222)

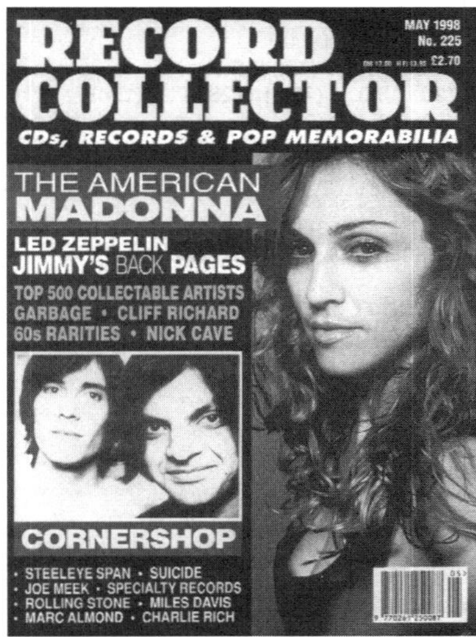

STRANGELOVE: I & D (218)
THE STRANGLERS & D (75); F (111); D (265); D (270).
See also J.J. BURNEL, HUGH CORNWELL.
THE STRAWBS & D (177)
BARBRA STREISAND & D (218)
STRONTIUM 90: F (218)
JOE STRUMMER: I (252).
See also CLASH
MARTY STUART: I & D (166)
STUDIO ONE LABEL: F (297)
THE STYLE COUNCIL & D (71); R (232).
See also THE JAM, PAUL WELLER.
SUB POP LABEL & D (159)
SUE: D (203); D (204)
SUEDE: F & D (164); I & D (206)
SUGAR: I & D (158)
THE SUGARCUBES & D (118); I (227).
See also BJORK.
SUGAR HILL RECORDS: F & D (244)
SUICIDE: I & D (225)
SUN LABEL: D (54); R (76); R (92); R (95); F (108); F, R & D (185); 7" reissues (271).
SUN RA: R (258)
SUNSHINE POP & D (217)
SUPER FURRY ANIMALS: I & D (238)
SUPERGRASS & D (191)
SUPERTRAMP: I (236)
THE SUPREMES:
See under DIANA ROSS & SUPREMES.
SURF: F & D (190); F & D (192); R (204); F (288)
SCREAMING LORD SUTCH & D (50); I & D (241)
STUART SUTCLIFFE: F (205)
BILLY SWAN: I & D (184)
THE SWEENEY: R (266)
THE SWEET & D (66).
See also BRIAN CONNOLLY.
SWELL MAPS: I & D (149)
THE SWINGING BLUE JEANS & D (40)
DAVID SYLVIAN: I & D (128); Pt 2 (129); F (260).
See also JAPAN.

T

TAKE THAT & D (168). See also GARY BARLOW & ROBBIE WILLIAMS
TALES OF JUSTINE: F (222)
TALKING HEADS & D (88).
See also DAVID BYRNE.
TALK TALK & D (148).
See also MARK HOLLIS.
SHEL TALMY: F (55); D (56)
TAMLA MOTOWN: See under MOTOWN.
SHARON TANDY: I (296)
TANGERINE DREAM & D (117); I (183)
HOWARD TATE: I (298)
JAMES TAYLOR: I (295)
JOHNNY TAYLOR: F (252)
THE TEARDROP EXPLODES & D (87)
TEARS FOR FEARS & D (70); D (124); I (262).
See also CURT SMITH
TEENAGE FANCLUB & D (167); I (282)
TELEVISION & D (148).
See also RICHARD HELL.
THE TELEVISION PERSONALITIES & TVP's: D (142)
THE TEMPTATIONS: I & D (150); I (260)
10CC: F & D 1964-72 (55); F & D (56); I & D (190)
10,000 MANIACS & D (159)
TEN YEARS AFTER: I & D (221)
TERRORVISION & D (190)
TEXAS & D (247)
THAMES TV RECORD SALE: F (162)
THE THE & D (120); I (168); I (275)
THEATRE OF HATE/SPEAR OF DESTINY: D (102).
See also KIRK BRANDON.
THEM: F & D (89); Van Morrison: D(149)
THERAPY? & D (181)
THIN LIZZY & D (99); F (268).
See also GARY MOORE.
THE THIRTEENTH FLOOR ELEVATORS / ROKY ERICKSON & D (147)
THIS HEAT & D (230)
RUFUS THOMAS: I & D (194)
RICHARD THOMPSON: I (283)
THE THOMPSON TWINS & D (58)
THRASH METAL: F (269)
THE THRILLS: I (289)
THROBBING GRISTLE & D (98); R (282).
See also GENESIS P-ORRIDGE.
THUNDER & D (142)
'THUNDERBIRDS' & D (167)
JOHNNY THUNDERS & THE NEW YORK DOLLS & D (143); F (183); F (261)
TANITA TIKARAM & D (127)
'TIL TUESDAY: I & D (170)
TIN MACHINE & D (131).
See also DAVID BOWIE.
TINDERSTICKS & D (175); I & D (231)
TINTERN ABBEY: F (284)
TINY TIM: F & D (210)
TJM RECORDS: D (126)
TOMORROW: I & D (187)
TOP 20 COLLECTABLE ARTISTS: F (158); F (245)
TOP 100 COLLECTABLE CDs (104)
TOP 100 UK AUCTION ITEMS (100)
TOP 100 UK EPs (101)
TOP 100 UK LPs (102)
TOP 100 UK SINGLES (100)
TOP 100 RAREST UK RECORDS (232)

TOP 200 ALBUMS OF THE 20TH CENTURY (245)
TOP 500 COLLECTABLE ARTISTS: 1996 (201); 1997 (213); 1998 (225); 1999 (237); 2000 (248)
TOP 1000 RARE RECORDS (77)
TOP OF THE POPS: F (173)
TOWERING INFERNO: I & D (194)
THE TORNADOS: I & D (211) Short Take (278). See also JOE MEEK.
TOTO & I (292)
ALLEN TOUSSAINT: F (256)
PETE TOWNSHEND: D (108); I & R (245). See also THE WHO.
T'PAU & D (104)
GRANT TRACY & SUNSETS: I & D (210)
STAN TRACY & I (272)
TRAFFIC & D (63); F (299)
TRANSVISION VAMP & D (119)
THE TRASHMEN: F, I & D (227)
TRAVIS & D (249)
THE TREMELOES & D (47)
T. REX: See under MARC BOLAN.
TRIUMPH LABEL: F (186)
THE TROGGS & D (46); R (273)
TROJAN RECORDS: F (251); F & D(287)
ROBIN TROWER: I & D(185); I (266)
TUBEWAY ARMY: See under GARY NUMAN.
MOE TUCKER: I & D (151). See also THE VELVET UNDERGROUND.
BIG JOE TURNER & D (241)
IKE & TINA TURNER & D (64)
SHANIA TWAIN & D (248)
2-TONE LABEL: D (122); D (123); R (171); F, I & D (300)
TWIGGY: I & D (219)
TWINKLE & D (178)
CONWAY TWITTY: R (82); F & D (168)
TYRANNOSAURUS REX: See under MARC BOLAN.

U

U2 & D (51); D (85); D (103); F & D (107); F & R (112); F & D (127); R (145); D (161); D (162); F (174); D (193); R & D (211); F (234); F & D (241); D (257)
UB40 & D (78)
UFO & D (259)
ULTRAVOX / JOHN FOXX: D (39)
THE UNDERTONES / FEARGAL SHARKEY: D (77); I (169); F (292)
UNIT FOUR PLUS TWO & D (71)
UNIVERSAL: F (268)
MIDGE URE: I (267)
URIAH HEEP & D (126); I (258)
U.S. HARDCORE: Overview Pt 1 (156); Overview Pt 2 & Top 100 7" Singles (157)

V

RICKY VALANCE & D (212)
RICHIE VALENS & D (76)
VAN DER GRAAF GENERATOR & PETER HAMMILL & D (83); F (255)
TOWNES VAN ZANDT & D (270)
VANGELIS & D (217)
THE VAPORS: F (210)
COLIN VEARNCOMBE: I (241)
THE VELVET UNDERGROUND & D (49); R (120); R (194); F (233); F (265). See also JOHN CALE, NICO, LOU REED, MOE TUCKER.
VENOM & I (250)
THE VENTURES & D (48)
MIKE VERNON & D (72); D (73)
VERTIGO LABEL: F (79); F (123); Pt 2 (124)
THE VERVE: F & D (219)
THE VIBRATORS & D (239)
VIDEO: I & F (144); F (150)
VIETNAM: F (275)
VILLAGE THING LABEL & D (169)
GENE VINCENT: F & D (70); R (103); I & D (213); D (247)
THE VIOLENT FEMMES: I & D (180)
TONY VISCONTI & D (78)
VOICE OF THE BEEHIVE & D (119)
VOLUME CD MAGAZINE: F (165)

W

TOM WAITS & D (236)
RICK WAKEMAN: I & D (196); I (292)
JUNIOR WALKER: F & D (198)
SCOTT WALKER & D (127)
THE WALKER BROTHERS & D (47)
WAR & D (196)
CLIFFORD T. WARD & D (246)
WARP RECORDS: F (244)
DIONNE WARWICK & D (41); I (281)
GENO WASHINGTON: I & D (253)
WAS (NOT WAS) & D (157); I (215)
W.A.S.P. & D (120)
THE WATERBOYS/MIKE SCOTT: D (142); I (226)
PETE WATERMAN: R (256)
ROGER WATERS & D (132). See also PINK FLOYD.
CHARLIE WATTS: D (253). See also ROLLING STONES.
ANDY WEATHERALL & D (257)
JIMMY WEBB: I & D (174)
THE WEDDING PRESENT & D (117); I & D (162); I (266)
BERT WEEDON & D (60); I (249)
PAUL WELLER: I (154); R (157); D (182); I (289). See also THE JAM, THE STYLE COUNCIL.
WET WET WET & D (108)
JOHN WETTON: I (244). See also ASIA, KING CRIMSON.
WHAM! & D (74); D (92); Short Take (220). See also GEORGE MICHAEL.
THE WHAT FOUR & D (239)
SNOWY WHITE: I (195)
THE WHITE STRIPES & D (291)
PETER WHITEHEAD: I (184)
WHITESNAKE & D (56); R (181)
SLIM WHITMAN & D (172)
THE WHO: F & D (53); D (66); D (76); R (79); D (84); R (126); F (164); F (165); R (179); I & D (181); I (192); R (203); F (211); F (215); F & D (228); F & D (229); F & D (230); F & D (241); R (246); R (255); R (263); F (268); F (277). See also ROGER DALTREY, PETE TOWNSHEND.
JANE WIEDLIN & SOLO / GO-GO's: D (111)
KIM WILDE & D (99); I & D (169)
MARTY WILDE & I (275)
THE WILDE FLOWERS (186)

THE WILDHEARTS: I & D (195)
WILD TURKEY: I & D (200)
THE WILD, WILD KLUBS: F (239)
ANDY WILLIAMS & I (251)
HANK WILLIAMS & D (125)
LARRY WILLIAMS & D (133)
ROBBIE WILLIAMS: D (245); R (256); F (262).
See also TAKE THAT.
BRIAN WILSON: I (185)
JACKIE WILSON & D (56)
WINGS: See under PAUL McCARTNEY.
STEVE WINWOOD & D (121); R (189).
See also BLIND FAITH, THE SPENCER DAVIS GROUP.
WIRE & D (100)
MARK WIRTZ & D (188)
WISHBONE ASH & D (186)
WIZZARD: See under ROY WOOD.
BOBBY WOMACK & D (77)
STEVIE WONDER: D (47); D (82)
THE WONDER STUFF & D (124); I (258)
'WONDERWALL': I (233)
RONNIE WOOD: F (228). See also THE BIRDS, THE CREATION, THE ROLLING STONES.
ROY WOOD / WIZZARD & D (80); I & F (179); I & D (180).
See also THE MOVE.
LINK WRAY & D (85); I (168)
RICK WRIGHT & SOLO: D (132); I & D (206).
See also PINK FLOYD.
WRITING ON THE WALL & D (201)
WURLITZER JUKEBOX LABEL & D (227)
ROBERT WYATT & D (80); I (154);
REISSUES DISCUSSED (264)
BILL WYMAN: I (231); I (261).
See also THE ROLLING STONES.
PETER WYNGARDE: I & D (206)

X

XOTIC MIND LABEL: F (196)
X-RAY SPEX & D (123); I (197)
XTC & D (135); I & D (209); F (261); I (272)

Y

THE YARDBIRDS: D & R (68); D (134); D (152); I & R (215).
See also ERIC CLAPTON.
YAZOO / ALISON MOYET & D (67)
YES & D (98); R (221); F & I (249); F (269).
See also PETER BANKS, TOMORROW.
NEIL YOUNG: F & D (143); F & D (144); F & D (145); F (176); F & D (192); R (200); I & D (203); F (253); F (272); I (278).
See also BUFFALO SPRINGFIELD, CSN&Y.
PAUL YOUNG & D (50)

Z

FRANK ZAPPA & THE MOTHERS OF INVENTION: F & D (61); D (93); F & D (118); D (165); D (171); D (177); D (191); R (199); R (205); F (251); R (266)
THE ZOMBIES & D (50).
See also COLIN BLUNSTONE.
ZOOM LABEL: D (74)
Z.T.T. LABEL: F & D (110); F & D (111); F & D (112)
ZZ TOP & D (103

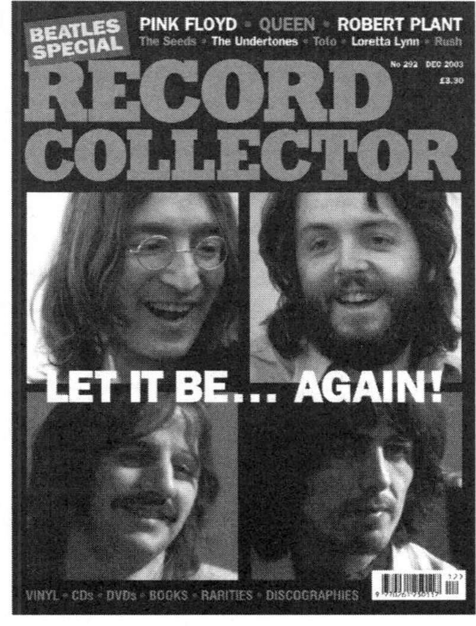

BRITISH PSYCHEDELIA GUIDE

This series of collectable British psychedelic records ran in alphabetical order:

231 Accent – Dantalian's Chariot
232 David – The Fut
233 Elmer Gantry's Velvet Opera – The Hush
234 Icarus – Junior's Eyes
235 Kaleidoscope – Lyons & Malone
236 Neil MacArthur – Mellow Candle
237 Mighty Baby – Motivation
238 The Move – Now
239 Octopus – Owl
240 Pandamonium – Pregnant Insomnia
241 The Pretty Things – The Rokes
242 The Rolling Stones
243 Rupert's People – The Searchers
244 Secondhand – Skip Bifferty
245 Sleepy – Soft Machine
246 Sons Of Man – The Sweet
247 Sweet Feeling – Tinkerbell's Fairydust
248 Tintern Abbey – Traffic
249 The Troggs – The 23rd Turnoff
250 Twink – Vamp
251 Van Der Graaf Generator
252 Velvet Hush – Walham Green
253 Gary Walker – White Trash
254 The Who
255 Wild Silk – Mark Wirtz
256 World Of Oz – Writing On The Wall
257 Yardbirds
258 Yes
259 The Zombies
260 "Chocolate Soup For Diabetics" compilations
261 "Perfumed Garden" compilations
262 "Rubble" & "Circus Days" compilations
263 "Rubble" compilations
264 Nuggets 2
265 Acid Drops, Space Dust, etc
266 Psych Comps A–E
267 See For Miles
268 Psych Comps E–H
269 Psych Comps H–M
270 Psych Comps Pa–Ps
271 Psych Comps Sa–We

NOTES

NOTES

NOTES

NOTES

NOTES

NOTES

NOTES

NOTES

RECORD COLLECTOR'S GRADING SYSTEM

In order to assist everyone who buys and sells rare discs, *Record Collector* magazine has originated a set of standards for the condition of second-hand records, cassettes and CDs. Anyone buying or selling records through the magazine must use our conditions to state what amount of wear and tear the disc, its sleeve and/or contents have been subject to. The seven standard condition categories, and a description of what each one means, are listed below:

MINT: The record itself is in brand new condition with no surface marks or deterioration in sound quality. The cover and any extra items such as the lyric sheet, booklet or poster are in perfect condition. Records advertised as Sealed or Unplayed should be Mint.

EXCELLENT: The record shows some signs of having been played, but there is very little lessening in sound quality. The cover and packaging might have slight wear and/or creasing.

VERY GOOD: The record has obviously been played many times, but displays no major deterioration in sound quality, despite noticeable surface marks and the occasional light scratch. Normal wear and tear on the cover or extra items, without any major defects, is acceptable.

GOOD: The record has been played so much that the sound quality has noticeably deteriorated, perhaps with some distortion and mild scratches. The cover and contents suffer from folding, scuffing of edges, spine splits, discoloration, etc.

FAIR: The record is still just playable but has not been cared for properly and displays considerable surface noise; it may even jump. The cover and contents will be torn, stained and/or defaced.

POOR: The record will not play properly due to scratches, bad surface noise, etc. The cover and contents will be badly damaged or partly missing.

BAD: The record is unplayable or might even be broken, and is only of use as a collection-filler.

CDs & CASSETTES: As a general rule, CDs and cassettes either play perfectly — in which case they are in Mint condition — or they don't, in which case their value is minimal. Cassette tape is liable to deteriorate with age, even if it remains unplayed, so care should be taken when buying old tapes. CDs are difficult to grade visually: they can look perfect but actually be faulty, while in other cases they may appear damaged but still play perfectly. Cassette and CD inlays and booklets should be graded in the same way as record covers and sleeves. In general, the plastic containers for cassettes and CDs can easily be replaced if they are broken or scratched, but card covers and digipaks are subject to the same wear as record sleeves.

RECORD COLLECTOR'S
GRADING READY RECKONER

This Ready Reckoner will help you work out the value of a record in any condition. For example, if you see a disc which is valued at £10 in Mint condition, but which you consider to be in only Very Good condition, then you can consult the Ready Reckoner and find out the appropriate price for the record — in this case, £5. As very few collectors are interested in records in Poor or Bad condition, we consider that any disc worth less than £10 in Mint condition is effectively worthless in Poor or Bad condition.

MINT	EX	VG	Good	Fair	Poor	Bad
1,000	800	500	300	150	80	25
500	400	250	150	75	40	12
300	240	150	90	45	25	8
250	200	125	75	38	20	6
200	160	100	60	30	15	5
150	120	75	45	25	13	4
125	100	60	38	18	12	3
100	80	50	30	15	8	2.50
75	60	35	22	10	6	2
50	40	25	15	8	4	1.50
40	32	20	12	6	3	1
30	25	15	9	4.50	2.50	—
25	20	12	7.50	3.50	2	—
22	18	11	6.50	3	1.75	—
20	16	10	6	2.50	1.50	—
15	12	8	4.50	2	1	—
12	10	6	3.50	1.75	0.75	—
10	8	5	3	1.50	—	—
8	6	4	2.50	1	—	—
7	5	3.50	2	0.75	—	—
6	4.50	3	1.75	—	—	—
5	4	2.50	1.50	—	—	—
4	3.25	2	1.25	—	—	—
3	2.50	1.50	1	—	—	—
2	1.75	1	—	—	—	—

ABBREVIATIONS
USED IN THIS GUIDE

act	actually
alt.	alternative
b&w	black and white
cass.	cassette
cat. no.	catalogue number
CD	compact disc
co.	company
d/pack	double pack
dble.	double
diff.	different
edn.	edition
EP	extended-play record
ext.	extended
flexi	flexidisc
g/f(old)	gatefold sleeve
inst	instrumental
intl.	international
LP	long-playing record
m/s	mono/stereo
mag.	magazine
no.	number
no'd	numbered
p/s	picture sleeve
pic disc.	picture disc
pt(s)	part(s)
sl.	sleeve
st.	stereo
stkr	sticker
t/p	test pressing
vers.	version
vol.	volume
w/	with
w/l	white label
2-CD	double CD
2-LP	double LP
2 x 45	two 45rpm singles
3-LP	triple LP
78	78rpm single

IMPORTANT RECORD COMPANY ABBREVIATIONS

Amalgam	Amalgamated
B. Banquet	Beggars Banquet
B'full/Brains	Bucketfull Of Brains
Col	Columbia
Elek	Elektra
Font	Fontana
L.T.T. Slaughter	Lambs To The Slaughter
M. For Nations	Music For Nations
MFP	Music For Pleasure
M. Minor.	Major Minor
Parl.	Parlophone
PSI	Phil Spector International
Pye Intl	Pye International
R. Digest	Readers Digest
Regal Zono	Regal Zonophone
R. Stones.	Rolling Stones
S'side.	Stateside
St. Tones	Street Tones
Sweet Folk & C.	Sweet Folk And Country
T. Motown	Tamla Motown
UA.	United Artists
W. Bros	Warner Brothers
WRC.	World Record Club